Webster's School Dictionary

A Merriam-Webster®

G. & C. MERRIAM COMPANY, *Publishers*
SPRINGFIELD, MASSACHUSETTS, U.S.A.

Library of Congress Cataloging in Publication Data

Main entry under title:

Webster's School dictionary.

"A Merriam-Webster."

SUMMARY: A student dictionary with approximately 77,000 entries and 900 illustrations

1. English language—Dictionaries, Juvenile.
[1. English language—Dictionaries] I. Title:
School dictionary.
PE1628.5.W4 1980 423 78-27467
ISBN 0-87779-280-1

Made in the United States of America

5 6 7 RRD 82

Contents

Preface

Webster's School Dictionary has been written especially for students at the high school level. The range of vocabulary covered is suited to the needs of older high school students, yet the definitions are written in everyday language that will be clear to young readers.

This dictionary has been produced by the oldest publisher of dictionaries in America, the company that publishes the unabridged *Webster's Third New International Dictionary,* used as the authority on the English language by schools, libraries, and publishers around the country, and *Webster's New Collegiate Dictionary,* the leading desk dictionary in the United States. *Webster's School Dictionary* has been edited by the permanent Merriam-Webster staff and has drawn on the millions of examples of word usage that were the foundation of the larger books. This dictionary makes use of information about the language used in books students read and the language used by today's teenager to ensure a comprehensive vocabulary of more than 77,000 entries ranging from the technical vocabulary of science to the everyday idiom of our modern culture.

In addition to information on spelling, pronunciation, and meaning, *Webster's School Dictionary* has all of the major special features of the larger Merriam-Webster dictionaries: there are etymologies that show the origin and development of words, explanatory paragraphs on synonyms to help you distinguish among similar and often confused words, guidance on proper usage, and separate sections in the back of the book for common abbreviations, biographical, biblical, and mythological names, geographical names, and a handbook of style to show you proper usage of punctuation, italics, and capitalization.

There is a wealth of information in this dictionary, and we urge you to explore the fascinating world of language contained in it. You will find, for example, that the word for the brief swimsuit known as the bikini is derived from the name of a tiny island in the South Pacific. You can discover what organisms cause red tide, and learn that a white elephant is not really an elephant at all. In *Webster's School Dictionary* you will find the symbol for sodium, the atomic weight of uranium, and the standard abbreviations for miles per hour, New Zealand, and British thermal unit. In addition, you can find out the names of the books of the Bible, learn how many ounces are in a liter, discover when George Washington was born and when he died, and find out the height of Mount Everest. In the more than 900 pictorial illustrations throughout the dictionary, you can find an example of Egyptian hieroglyphs, identify the different parts of a cell, and see the difference between an Asian and an African elephant.

Webster's School Dictionary is offered with pride and with the assurance that it will serve your needs well. But to be able to find and make use of all of the information in this book, you should read and become thoroughly familiar with the section "Using the Dictionary" that immediately follows this preface.

G. & C. Merriam Company

Using The Dictionary

Dictionary Entries

The dictionary is made up of many small paragraphs, each giving information about a particular word or phrase. These paragraphs are known as **dictionary entries,** and the word or phrase being explained is known as the **main entry** or **entry word.** Two features set off the main entry to make it easy to find: it is printed in **boldface type,** and it sticks out into the margin just a little to catch the eye.

The main entry may take any of several forms. It may be a single letter, like *a, b,* or *c*, or a combination of letters, like *TV* or *ESP*. Most main entries are single words, like *run, see, pretzel*, and *eugenics*, but many are combinations of words, like *hitchhike, nitty-gritty,* and *French horn*. There are also main entries that are only parts of words. These include prefixes like *anti-*, suffixes like *-ism*, and combining forms like *bio-* and *-ectomy* that are used only to form other words. Since it is possible to make any number of new words with prefixes, suffixes, and combining forms, you will be able to understand many new or unusual words not entered in *Webster's School Dictionary* by learning the meanings of these basic word elements.

Order of Entries

Everyone knows that entries in a dictionary are in alphabetical order, so it may seem unnecessary to say anything about the order of entries. But there are times when the principles of strict alphabetical order will not solve every problem of entering words, and it will help you to find the word quickly if you know just how we have arranged the entries.

Throughout the dictionary, words are alphabetized by first letter, then second letter, and so on, regardless of spaces, hyphens, or of meaning relationships. Thus, you will find the word *basenji* coming after *basement* and before *base on balls* and *houri* between *hourglass* and *hourly*.

Words spelled with a numeral or abbreviation (like *St.* or *Mc*) will be found in the place they would occupy if spelled out. *A-1* follows *A-OK* and comes before *aorta*, *4H* appears between *four-footed* and *four-hand*, and *McCoy* (entered as if spelled *MacCoy*) comes after *Maccabees* and before *mace*.

When main entries are spelled exactly alike but have different functions in the sentence or have different origins, they are called **homographs.** Each homograph is entered at its own place and distinguished from other homographs by a small raised numeral at the very beginning.

> [1]**American** . . . *n* . . .
> [2]**American** *adj* . . .

The order of homographs is historical. That is, the oldest word is entered first, and related homographs (all those having the same origin) are grouped together. Thus, [2]*bow* ("a bending of the head or body in respect, submission, agreement, or greeting"), which is related to [1]*bow* ("to bend the head, body, or knee in greeting, reverence, respect, or submission"), comes before [3]*bow* ("RAINBOW"). And [4]*bow* ("to bend into a curve") follows the related [3]*bow* and is ahead of [5]*bow* ("the forward part of a ship").

Main entries that are spelled with all of the same letters but differ in the appearance of a space or hyphen or in capitalization are *not* homographs. They are alphabetized according to the following rules.

- Full words are entered before word parts, and beginning word elements come ahead of final word elements.

> **ad** . . . *n* . . .
> **ad-** . . . *prefix* . . .
> **-ad** . . . *adv suffix* . . .

- Entries printed in small letters come before capitalized ones.

> [1]**box•er** . . . *n* . . .
> [2]**boxer** *n* . . .
> **Box•er** . . . *n* . . .

- Compounds that are written as one word are entered before hyphenated compounds, and hyphenated compounds are entered ahead of those made up of separate words.

> **lay•off** . . . *n* . . .
> **lay off** . . . *vb* . . .
>
> **lay–up** . . . *n* . . .
> **lay up** . . . *vt* . . .
>
> **low•down** . . . *n* . . .
> **low–down** . . . *adj* . . .

Guide Words

To aid you in finding the right word quickly, *Webster's School Dictionary* has a pair of **guide words** at the top of every page. The guide words are usually the alphabetically first and last boldface entries on the page. Any boldface term—a main entry, a variant spelling, an inflected form, a word run on undefined at the end of an entry, a phrase run on and defined at the end of an entry, or even a word in a list of undefined words—can be a guide word as long as it is alphabetically the first or last word on the page.

The first word of the pair is normally the first main entry on the page and the second is usually the last main entry. But this is not always the case. On page 172, for example, the last main entry is [2]*collapse,* but the last guide word for that page is *collapsible*, which is alphabetically later and which is run on undefined at [1]*collapse*.

The guide words themselves are always in alphabetical order. When the alphabetically last word on one page would follow the first guide word on the next page, it is not picked as a guide word. Thus, on page 164 the alphabetically last boldface term is *clue* (the variant at the main entry *clew*). But since *clue* would come after the first guide word on page 165 (which is *clew*), it cannot be used as the guide word on page 164.

Variant Entries

A number of main entries have a second or sometimes a third spelling shown in boldface type. These alternate spellings are called **variants.**

Variants separated by the word *or* are equal variants. That means each is current in standard English usage and either spelling is correct for you to use. When equal variants are used with about the same frequency, we list them in alphabetical order.

bobby socks *or* **bobby sox** . . .

But when the evidence indicates that one spelling is somewhat more common than another, the variants are listed in the order of relative frequency of use.

bo•gey *or* **bo•gy** *or* **bo•gie** . . .
skep•tic *or* **scep•tic** . . .

When the word *also* separates variants, it means that the following variant is considerably less common in standard English. Nevertheless, the *also* variant is a part of standard English usage and you may freely use it without being wrong, although many people prefer the more common spelling.

mor•tise *also* **mor•tice** . . .

Occasionally we use both *or* and *also* in separating a number of variants at a single entry.

ce•sar•e•an *or* **ce•sar•i•an** *also* **cae•sar•e•an** . . .
tick•tack•toe *also* **tic–tac–toe** . . . *or* **tit–tat–toe** . . .

In the first instance, the first two spellings are roughly equal in frequency and the last is of a secondary nature. In the second example, the last two variants are of relatively equal frequency with respect to each other, but they both are much less common than the first.

Whenever one variant form is more common with one meaning than with others, it is listed before the particular definition with some indication of how common or prominent it is.

[1]**clew** *or* **clue** . . . **2** *usually clue* . . .
[1]**nick•el** . . . **2 a** *also* **nick•le** . . .
[1]**la•bor** . . . **5** *usually* **La•bour** . . .

If the variant is shown in boldface at the beginning of the entry, it is shown in italic before the definition (as in the first example). When it is not shown at the beginning of the entry, it is given in boldface before the definition.

Centered Dots and Hyphenation

Printers, typists, and writers often have to divide a word at the end of a line if it is too long to fit on one line. The **centered dots** in the boldface entry words show you acceptable places to put a hyphen when the word is broken at the end of a line. For example, *mor·al·is·tic* may be divided at any of three places.

mor-
alistic or **moral-**
istic or **moralis-**
tic

We use centered dots in all boldface entries except as follows.

• Only the first of two or more homographs is divided if the pronunciation and division are the same for each.

[1]**mas•ter** . . . *n* . . .
[2]**master** *vt* . . .
[3]**master** *adj* . . .

• A word in a compound made up of two or more separate words is divided only if it is not entered as an individual entry. For example, we show no division for the entry *gamma radiation* because there are entries for *gam·ma* and *ra·di·a·tion.* The first word in the entry *Mol·o·tov cocktail* is divided but the second is not, because there is no separate entry for *Mol·o·tov* but there is for *cock·tail.* There are no entries for the individual elements of *pri·ma don·na,* thus both elements of the compound are divided.

It is customary to avoid breaking a word so as to leave a single letter at the end of one line or at the beginning of the next, so we do not show any division for single letters at the beginning or end of words, as in *idea* or *flighty.*

It is important to understand that the centered dots in the entry words *do not* necessarily separate the syllables of a word. Syllables are indicated *only* by the use of hyphens in the pronunciation, and the placement and number of centered dots is not always the same as the placement and number of hyphens in the pronunciation.

eter•ni•ty \i-ˈter-nət-ē\

When a boldface entry word is broken at the end of a line, a hyphen replaces the centered dots at that point. *Webster's School Dictionary* also uses a special **double hyphen** at the end of a line anytime the word that is divided is normally spelled with a hyphen. When you see the double hyphen, you will know to keep the hyphen even when you write the word all on one line.

self–mas•tery \ˈself-ˈmas-tə-rē, -trē\ *n* : SELF⸗
COMMAND, SELF-CONTROL

The double hyphen here indicates that *self-control* is always spelled with a hyphen.

Pronunciation

There are two major ways in which we use the English language: writing and speaking. The language used in both is the same language, but writing and speaking are themselves completely different. Writing is made up of marks on a surface such as paper. Speech is made up of a series of sounds. We cannot close our eyes and listen to writing, nor can we see the sounds of speech.

The spelling of written words is related to the sounds of spoken words. However, the relationship between spelling and sound in English is not always very close. It is often hard to tell from the spelling how to pronounce a word. On the one hand, different letters may be used to spell the same sound in different words. For example, the words *day*, *weigh*, *steak*, and *prey* all contain the same vowel sound. *Sight*, *site*, and *cite* are all pronounced alike. On the other hand, one letter or group of letters may be used to spell different sounds. For example, in *bat*, *late*, *any*, and *above* the letter *a* stands for a different sound in each word. In addition, there are many words that are pronounced in more than one way, although there may be only one accepted spelling.

In order to be able to indicate the sounds of words in a written form, we use a special alphabet of pronunciation symbols. Each pronunciation symbol stands for only one sound, and each sound is represented by only one symbol. There is a symbol for every important sound in English.

The pronunciation of most entry words is shown immediately following the boldface entry. To indicate that pronunciation symbols are being used and not regular letters, the symbols are always shown between slant lines \ \.

A complete list of pronunciation symbols used in this book appears on page 16a. After most of the symbols on the chart are words containing the sound of the symbol they follow. The boldface letters in these words are the letters which stand for the same sound as the symbol. If you say the sample words in your normal voice, you will be able to hear the sound meant by each symbol. In some cases the complete pronunciation of a sample word is given.

Hyphens are used with the pronunciation symbols to indicate the syllables of a word.

beast \'bēst\ (1 syllable)
be•cause \bi-'kȯz\ (2 syllables)
cast•away \'kas-tə-ˌwā\ (3 syllables)
des•po•tism \'des-pə-ˌtiz-əm\ (4 syllables)

Of course the syllables of words are not separated when we speak. One sound is connected to another without pause.

You will notice that in two of the above examples the number and position of the hyphens do not match the number and position of the centered dots in the headwords. The reason is that the centered dots do not separate syllables.

Some syllables of a word are spoken with greater force or emphasis than others. This relative emphasis is called **stress.** Three levels of stress are shown in *Webster's School Dictionary.* **Primary** (or strong) **stress** is indicated by a high vertical mark \'\ placed *before* the stressed syllable. **Secondary** (or medium) **stress** is indicated by a low vertical mark \ˌ\ placed *before* the stressed syllable. **Weak stress** is given to syllables which have no stress mark.

man•ner \'man-ər\ (primary \'man-\, weak \-ər\)
ob•vi•ate \'äb-vē-ˌāt\ (primary \'äb-\, weak \-vē-\, secondary \-ˌāt\)

Many words are pronounced in two, three, or even more different ways. **Variant** pronunciations are separated by commas and sometimes groups of variants are separated by semicolons. The order of variants does not mean that the first variant is any better than the following ones. All the variants shown in this book are perfectly acceptable and are used by large numbers of educated English speakers. When learning a new word, you should choose the pronunciation variant which sounds most natural to you.

In many entries the variants are shown in full

of•ten \'ȯ-fən, 'ȯf-tən\

but for words of two or more syllables, the variation may occur only in part of the word. For such words only the syllables that vary may be repeated.

hor•ri•ble \'hȯr-ə-bəl, 'här-\
pro•cess \'präs-ˌes, 'prōs-, -əs\

If all of these variant pronunciations were written out in full, they would take up much more space.

hor•ri•ble \'hȯr-ə-bəl, 'här-ə-bəl\
pro•cess \'präs-ˌes, 'prōs-ˌes, 'präs-əs, 'prōs-əs\

In some words there may be variation in the number of syllables pronounced. For instance, *celery* is pronounced both \'sel-rē\ and \'sel-ə-rē\, and *wiggler* is pronounced both \'wig-lər\ and \'wig-ə-lər\. To save space in the dictionary some of the syllables that do not change are not repeated.

cel•ery \'sel-rē, -ə-rē\
wig•gler \'wig-lər, -ə-lər\

A pronunciation variant following the word *also* is heard less frequently than the variants before it. A variant following *sometimes* is heard much less frequently than others. If a variant is used mostly in a particular region, the region may be identified.

help \'help, *South also* 'hep\
khaki \'kak-ē, 'käk-, *Canadian often* 'kärk-\

If an incomplete pronunciation is given for an entry word, the missing portions may be found at a preceding entry word.

rain•coat \'rān-ˌkōt\
rain•drop \-ˌdräp\

Thus, the full pronunciation of *raindrop* is \'rān-ˌdräp\. If the pronunciation and end-of-line divisions of homographs are the same, the pronunciation is given only for the first.

[1]**cheer** \'chiər\ *n* [2]**cheer** *vb*
[1]**her•ald** \'her-əld\ *n* [2]**herald** *vt*

Some run-on entries have no pronunciation shown. In these cases the pronunciation of the run-on is the pronunciation of the main entry plus the pronunciation of the suffix, which may be found at its own place in the dictionary.

re•spon•sive \ri-'spän-siv\ *adj* . . . — **re•spon•sive•ly** *adv* — **re•spon•sive•ness** *n*

This tells you that *responsively* is pronounced \ri-'spän-siv-lē\ and *responsiveness* is pronounced \ri-'spän-siv-nəs\.

The Function of Words

Words are used in many different ways in a sentence. A word may serve as the name of something being talked about or to indicate an action. It may be used to tell something about the thing or person being talked about or to describe the way something happens. The many different functions of words are known as **parts of speech.** *Webster's School Dictionary* identifies the function of most entry words with one of eight traditional part-of-speech labels, abbreviated and placed immediately after the boldface entry or after the pronunciation, when one is shown.

gui•tar . . . *n* (noun)
de•ploy . . . *vb* (verb)
snide . . . *adj* (adjective)
hap•pi•ly . . . *adv* (adverb)
you . . . *pron* (pronoun)
for . . . *prep* (preposition)
and . . . *conj* (conjunction)
ouch . . . *interj* (interjection)

When the main entry is a noun that is always used in the plural, the label *n pl* is used.

bin•oc•u•lars . . . *n pl* . . .

An entry word may be spelled as a plural and be considered a plural in some uses—such as being used with a plural verb—and yet be considered singular in other uses—such as being used with a singular verb.

ac•ro•bat•ics . . . *n sing or pl* . . .

(The word *acrobatics* may be singular in such uses as "acrobatics is a strenuous activity" or plural in "you make these acrobatics look easy.")

Some entries that are singular in most uses may have one or more specific plural uses.

fix•ing . . . *n* . . . **2** *pl* **:** TRIMMINGS

(In this sense the usage might be "a turkey dinner with all the fixings.")

Other entries will have one or more senses that are always spelled as plural but when used as the subject of a sentence will take a singular verb.

lanc•er . . . **2** *pl but sing in construction* . . .

(An example of this use might be "the lancers is an interesting dance.")

Pronouns, too, can sometimes be singular in form but take a plural or singular verb.

[3]all . . . *pron, pl in construction* . . .
[2]any *pron, sing or pl in construction* . . .

(A typical use in the first example might be "all of us are going," where the word *all* occurs only with a plural verb. In the second example, *any* may be used with a singular verb, as in "I want some pie. Is there any left?" or with a plural verb in "are any of you tired?")

When variant plural forms are shown for an entry but only one is used with a particular meaning, that plural is shown at the definition *following* the abbreviation *pl*.

[2]die . . . *n, pl* **dice** . . . *or* **dies**
1 *pl dice* **:** . . . **3** *pl dies* **:** . . .

(The plural form for the first meaning of *die*, the little cube with dots on it, is *dice*: "roll the dice." That for meaning 3, a tool to stamp an impression, is *dies*: "it takes two dies to stamp both sides of a coin.")

When a particular meaning is only plural and only one variant plural form is used for that meaning, the form is shown *ahead* of the abbreviation *pl*.

[1]folk . . . *n, pl* **folk** *or* **folks** . . .
3 *folks pl* **:** . . .

(In this meaning, the word is always plural and only the form *folks* is used: "I'm going home to see my folks.")

Webster's School Dictionary makes no distinction at *vb* entries between transitive verbs (those that take a direct object) and intransitive verbs. The label *vb* is used for verb entries that have both transitive and intransitive uses. Verb entries that are used only as transitive verbs or only as intransitive verbs are given a specific *vt* (transitive verb) or *vi* (intransitive verb) label.

an•nul . . . *vt* . . . **be•long** . . . *vi* . . .

In addition to the traditional part-of-speech labels, there are a number of other function labels that we use in this dictionary. *Prefix*, *suffix*, and *combining form* are relatively common and have already been introduced. The following identifying labels appear much less frequently.

may . . . *auxiliary verb* . . .
me•thinks . . . *vb impersonal*
gid•dap . . . *imperative verb*
an . . . *indefinite article*
the . . . *definite article*
Fris•bee . . . *trademark*
Air Express . . . *service mark*
Realtor . . . *collective mark*
-rd . . . *symbol*

Prefixes, suffixes, and combining forms are sometimes shown with a part-of-speech label when all compounds formed are of one part of speech.

-algia . . . *n combining form* . . .
-ana . . . *n pl suffix* . . .

In these examples, the compounds formed by either of these elements are always nouns, and in the second example the compounds are always plural nouns.

Sometimes an entry has more than one function label.

ago . . . *adj or adv* . . .
betwixt and between . . . *adv or prep* . . .

The *or* in these two examples indicates that the entry may at one time function as one part of speech and at another time as another part of speech without any significant difference in meaning.

We do not show part-of-speech labels or other function labels for idiomatic phrases defined at the end of a main entry or for main entry phrases that consist of two nouns joined by a preposition, like *act of God* and *man in the street*.

The Forms of Words

The plurals of nouns (and a few pronouns and adjectives), the past tense, past participle, and present participle forms of verbs, and the comparative and superlative forms of adjectives and adverbs are known as **inflected forms.** For most entries, these inflected forms are regular (that is, they are formed by the addition of *-s* or *-es* to nouns, *-ed* and *-ing* to verbs, and *-er* and *-est* to adjectives and adverbs), and these regular forms, since they normally present no problems in spelling, are not shown in *Webster's School Dictionary*.

We do show irregular inflected forms, such as those that involve a change in the spelling of the base word or a doubling of a final letter, and any that we feel you might have reasonable doubts about.

Plurals are shown in this book when there is no change made in the base word.

deer . . . *n, pl* **deer** . . .

when a final -y changes to *-i-* before the addition of *-es*,

ba•by . . . *n, pl* **babies** . . .

when the plural involves a change in the spelling of the base word,

ax•is . . . *n, pl* **ax•es** . . .
[1]that . . . *pron, pl* **those** . . .

and when the word has kept a foreign plural.

se•ta . . . *n, pl* **se•tae** . . .

Plurals are also shown for all nouns that end in *-o* or *-ey*,

ego . . . *n, pl* **egos** . . .
don•key . . . *n, pl* **donkeys** . . .

for those that pluralize in a way you may not expect,

[3]dry *n, pl* **drys** . . .
goose•foot . . . *n, pl* **goosefoots** . . .

and for any others we think you might have questions about.

[1]pi . . . *n, pl* **pis** . . .
ninth . . . *n, pl* **ninths** . . .

Most compounds pluralize the final element. These are considered regular plurals, and they are not shown when the final element is a recognizable word entered at its own place in the dictionary, such as *charwoman* or *thimbleberry*. We do show plurals for compounds that pluralize any element but the last,

moth•er-in-law . . . *n, pl* **moth•ers-in-law** . . .
postmaster general *n, pl* **postmasters general**

and for all entries that have variant plural forms.

bis•cuit . . . *n, pl* **biscuits** *also* **biscuit** . . .
[1]fish . . . *n, pl* **fish** *or* **fish•es** . . .

Plurals are not shown for nouns that do not regularly have a plural use, like *paleontology*.

Principal parts are usually not shown for regular verbs—those that simply add *-ed* and *-ing,* either directly to the base word or after dropping a final *-e*—but they are shown for verbs that inflect in other ways. In such cases the past tense and present participle forms are always shown. The past participle is shown only when it differs from the past tense, and when it is shown it comes between the past tense and the present participle.

Inflections are shown when one or more principal parts change the spelling of the base word,

[1]**know** . . . *vb* **knew** . . .; **known** . . .; **know•ing** . . .

when a final consonant is doubled before the addition of *-ed* or *-ing,*

[2]**crib** *vb* **cribbed**; **crib•bing** . . .

and when a final *-y* becomes *-i-* before *-ed.*

[1]**hur•ry** . . . *vb* **hur•ried**; **hur•ry•ing** . . .

Inflections are also shown for verbs when the final *-c* is changed to *-ck* before *-ed* and *-ing,*

[2]**picnic** *vi* **pic•nicked**; **pic•nick•ing**

when the base word ends in *-ee* or *-ey,*

agree . . . *vb* **agreed**; **agree•ing** . . .
[1]**sur•vey** . . . *vt* **sur•veyed**; **sur•vey•ing** . . .

when there are variant forms of the inflections,

[3]**bias** *vt* **bi•ased** *or* **bi•assed**; **bi•as•ing** *or* **bi•as•sing** . . .

and when we feel you might have reasonable doubts about the forms.

[2]**visa** *vt* **vi•saed** . . .; **vi•sa•ing**

In order to save space in showing inflections, we show only the last part of the inflected forms for long words—those of more than two syllables. The form is usually cut back to the point that corresponds to the last indicated end-of-line division in the main entry.

the•o•ry . . . *n, pl* **-ries** . . .
lot•tery . . . *n, pl* **-ter•ies**
lep•to•ceph•a•lus . . . *n, pl* **-li** . . .
mod•i•fy . . . *vb* **-fied**; **-fy•ing** . . .

The cutback form is also used for verbs that end in *-l* when there are space-consuming variant forms,

[3]**tinsel** *vt* **-seled** *or* **-selled**; **-sel•ing** *or* **-sel•ling** . . .

and for verb compounds when the second element is a recognizable verb with irregular inflections.

[1]**re•take** . . . *vt* **-took** . . .; **-tak•en** . . .; **-tak•ing** . . .

Most adjectives and adverbs form their comparatives and superlatives with *more* or *most* or with the addition of *-er* and *-est,* either directly to the base word or after dropping a final *-e*. These are considered regular formations and are not shown in *Webster's School Dictionary.* We do show all irregularly formed inflections of adjectives and adverbs, and many of these are cut back in the superlative to just *-est.*

Comparative and superlative forms are shown for entries that change the base word,

[1]**good** . . . *adj* **bet•ter** . . .; **best** . . .
[3]**well** *adv* **bet•ter** . . .; **best** . . .

for those that double the final consonant before *-er* or *-est,*

[1]**flat** . . . *adj* **flat•ter**; **flat•test** . . .

for those that change the final *-y* to an *-i-* before the suffixes,

handy . . . *adj* **hand•i•er**; **-est** . . .

for any adjectives or adverbs ending in *-ey,*

ca•gey . . . *adj* **ca•gi•er**; **-est** . . .

and for those with variant forms.

sly . . . *adj* **sli•er** *also* **sly•er** . . .; **sli•est** . . . *also* **sly•est** . . .

Whenever one inflected form but not another is in current use, we show only the current form in full with an appropriate label.

[2]**mere** *adj, superlative* **mer•est** . . .

Sometimes we write out in full regular inflections or inflections that might normally be cut back in order to show the pronunciation of one or more forms.

daz•zle . . . *vt* **daz•zled**; **daz•zling** \\'daz-ling, -ə-ling\\ . . .
[3]**model** *vb* **mod•eled** *or* **mod•elled**; **mod•el•ing** *or* **mod•el•ling** \\'mäd-ling, -l-ing\\ . . .
[1]**long** . . . *adj* **long•er** \\'lòng-gər\\; **long•est** \\'lòng-gəst\\ . .

The Meanings of Words

The **definition** is the core of the dictionary. It gives the meaning of the entry word. Every definition in *Webster's School Dictionary* is set off by a boldface colon whether or not there is a number before it.

blue jeans *n pl* **:** pants usually made of blue denim
blue law *n* **1 :** one of many strict laws regulating morals and conduct in colonial New England

Often an entry or numbered meaning has more than one definition set off by a colon.

[1]**glad** . . . **1 a :** experiencing pleasure, joy, or delight **:** made happy
[2]**glint** . . . **1 :** a small bright flash of light **:** SPARKLE

These different definitions, known as **substitutes,** are so close in meaning that either one can be substituted for the entry word in context without any change in meaning. Often the only difference between substitutes is in the point of view from which they are written.

When a main entry has a number of different **meanings** or **senses,** the meanings are arranged in historical order, with the oldest recorded meaning coming first, then the next oldest, and so on. The most recent meanings will normally be given last. With this method of ordering senses, you can follow the development of a word as the meanings have changed over the years. Here is an example that illustrates this historical development.

[4]**dock** *n* **1 :** an artificial basin to receive ships that has gates to keep the water in or out **2 :** a slip or waterway usually between two piers to receive ships **3 :** a wharf or platform for the loading or unloading of materials . . . **4 :** a place or scaffolding for the inspection and repair of aircraft

From the order of senses in this entry, the development of the various senses of *dock* can be seen at a glance. From the oldest meaning, that of a basin or surrounding structure for ships—often the dock was used for building and repairing ships—the word acquired a broader, though still nautical, meaning: an area partly surrounded by a structure at which a ship could tie up. The use gradually expanded to include the pier or platform itself to which the ship tied up for loading and eventually to include any loading platform—even for trucks. Finally, in the most recent use, the word has come to refer to a docking place for repairing aircraft—a meaning that recalls the original sense as it applied to ships.

The historical ordering of senses should not be taken to mean, however, that each sense necessarily developed directly from the earlier one. In many instances, each of the various successive senses may all have derived independently from the original meaning.

In addition to the division of definitions into numbered

senses, some entries have the meanings further broken down into **subsenses.** These subsenses, marked by letters (**a, b, c,** etc.) are used when related meanings are grouped together. The order of subsenses is historical insofar as the dates can be established, but subsenses may not be in strict historical order with respect to the broader numbered senses.

> [1]**bag** . . . *n* **1a :** a flexible usually closed container for holding, storing, or carrying something **b :** PURSE; *esp* **:** HANDBAG **c :** TRAVELING BAG, SUITCASE **2 :** something resembling a bag: as **a :** a pouched or pendulous bodily part or organ; *esp* **:** UDDER **b :** a puffed-out sag or bulge in cloth . . . **c :** a square white canvas container to mark a base in baseball **3 :** the amount contained in a bag **4 :** a quantity of game taken or permitted to be taken **5 :** a slovenly unattractive woman

In this example, the numbered senses of *bag* are all in historical order and the subsenses within a numbered sense grouping are also offered by date of first occurrence. But sense **lc**, meaning "a suitcase," properly belongs with the other senses that refer to a container—yet it actually came into use much later than sense number **4**. And the baseball sense, **2c**, also developed after sense **4**, but it is grouped with the other senses at **2** because it is related in the idea of "something resembling a bag."

When further subdivision of a sense is needed, we indicate it by numerals in parentheses.

> **food** . . . **1a :** . . . **b** (1) **:** inorganic substance absorbed by plants . . . (2) **:** organic material produced by green plants . . .

Sometimes senses are divided by one of two italic labels: We use the sense divider *esp* (especially) to introduce the most common meaning covered by the more general definition immediately before it (as in senses 1b and 2a of *bag*). We use *also* to introduce a closely related use obviously derived from the basic sense.

> **base•ball** . . . *n* **:** a game played with a bat and ball between two teams of nine players each on a field with four bases that mark the course a runner must take to score; *also* **:** the ball used in this game

Cross-references

Words printed in small capitals are **cross-references**. A cross-reference in a definition is called a **synonymous cross-reference**. It is another word that means the same thing as the main entry word, or a *synonym* of the word.

You may see a synonym appearing as a second substitute, as at the first sense of *glint* above, or standing in place of a definition.

> [3]**flip** *adj* **:** FLIPPANT

This tells you that the meaning of this homograph of *flip* and the meaning of *flippant* are the same and that the definition given at *flippant* also defines this use of *flip*.

Sometimes a synonymous cross-reference includes a sense number, meaning that only one sense of the synonym is the same as the entry word.

> **rile** . . . **1 :** ROIL 1
> **roil** . . . **1 :** to make cloudy or muddy by stirring up sediment

When we use a cross-reference, it is always to a word that is of the same part of speech as the entry word. For example, a cross-reference at a noun entry word is always to another noun. When the synonym has two homographs that are the same part of speech, we use a homograph number with the cross-reference.

> **fly ball** *n* **:** [2]FLY 5
> [2]**fly** *n, pl* **flies** . . . **5 :** a baseball hit high into the air

When a synonymous cross-reference is to a word with more than one sense and the cross-reference does not indicate a specific sense, you know that the words are synonymous in all senses.

> **cow•punch•er** . . . *n* **:** COWBOY
> **cow•boy** . . . *n* **1 :** one who tends or drives cattle; *esp* **:** a usually mounted cattle ranch hand **2 :** a participant in rodeos

Many entries or senses are defined only by two synonymous cross-references separated by a comma. You might think of these paired synonyms as two substitutes at a sense. When the first cross-reference is to an entry that has several senses, it usually includes a sense number,

> **cer•tain** . . . *adj* **1a :** FIXED 1C, SETTLED

unless both synonyms are common words that together help define the entry word and leave no doubt as to the intended meaning.

> . . . **3a:** DEPENDABLE, RELIABLE

In addition to the synonymous cross-references in the definitions, there are three other types of cross-references used in *Webster's School Dictionary*. Cross-references that follow a dash and the words *see* or *compare* (usually at the end of a definition) are called **directional cross-references**. They direct the reader to look at another entry for an explanation or related information.

> **digital computer** *n* **:** a computer that operates numbers in the form of digits — compare ANALOG COMPUTER
> **li•ter** *or* **li•tre** \'lēt-ər\ *n* **:** a metric unit of capacity equal to one cubic decimeter — see METRIC SYSTEM table

The "see" directional cross-reference may also be used in place of a definition.

> **Genesis** — see BIBLE table

Two other kinds of cross-references appear only in place of definitions. These are like the directional cross-references in that they direct the reader to other entries for information. The **cognate cross-reference** is used when a variant form of a word is entered at its own alphabetical place in the dictionary and the reader is directed to see the entry at the more common variant.

> **des•patch** \dis-'patch\ *variant of* DISPATCH
> **li•quo•rice** *chiefly British variant of* LICORICE

An **inflectional cross-reference** is used when an inflected form of an entry is entered at its own alphabetical place. It tells you to go to the base word.

> [1]**done** \'dən\ *past participle of* DO
> **was** *past 1st & 3d sing of* BE

The Usage of Words

New or unusual words, even when they have been defined, may sometimes seem like nothing more than abstractions to you until you understand how the words are actually used in writing or speaking. And there are times when an example of how a word is used can do more than a definition to convey meaning and proper usage. Sometimes too the meanings of individual senses are similar, but the way the senses are normally used in sentences is quite different. To help you better understand how the words are actually used, *Webster's School Dictionary* gives brief examples of the words in everyday language as illustrations of idiomatic usage for many of the entries and senses. These **verbal illustrations** follow the definitions and are enclosed in angle brackets, and the entry word, or an inflection of it, is printed in italics.

[1]**ar•rest** \ə-ˈrest\ *vt* **1 :** to stop the progress or movement of : CHECK, SLOW ⟨*arrest* a disease⟩ **2 :** to take or keep in custody by authority of law ⟨*arrested* on suspicion of robbery⟩ **3 :** to attract and hold the attention of ⟨colors that *arrest* the eye⟩

short•ly \ˈshȯrt-lē\ *adv* **1 a :** in a few words : BRIEFLY ⟨put it *shortly*⟩ **b :** in an abrupt manner : CURTLY **2 a :** in a short time : SOON ⟨will arrive *shortly*⟩ **b :** at a short interval ⟨*shortly* after⟩

Webster's School Dictionary also gives information about word usage in two other ways. The first is by means of italic labels immediately following the part-of-speech or function label or, when the information applies only to one sense, just after the sense number or letter. These labels indicate limited areas of use in the English-speaking world or special subject matter with which a word or sense is used. They also indicate when a word's use is restricted with respect to a standard usage and when you should capitalize the word.

A word or sense current chiefly in Great Britain or the British Commonwealth countries is labeled *British*, and there are labels for particular areas within the British Commonwealth.

an•o•rak . . . *n, chiefly British* : PARKA
foot•ball . . . **1** . . . **a** *British* : SOCCER
laird . . . *n, Scottish* : a landed proprietor

Many words or senses have use limited to a particular region of the United States.

grind•er . . . **3** *chiefly New England* : [2]SUBMARINE 2
pone . . . *n, South & Midland* : CORN PONE

And some words may be encountered only in dialect, but the use is over so wide an area that no specific regional label applies.

bit•ty . . . *adj, dialect* : very small

Italic labels are also used to indicate that various entries or individual senses are not current in English usage. We enter a few words in this dictionary because of their historical importance in literature, but the words have not been an active part of the language for many years. The label *obsolete* tells you a word or sense has not been used in more than 200 years.

[1]**tide** . . . **1a** *obsolete* : a space of time : PERIOD

Old words and meanings that have been used only occasionally or not at all during the 20th century or that may occur only in special uses (for example, in church liturgies) we label *archaic*.

for•fend . . . **1a** *archaic* : FORBID 1

Some of the entries in the dictionary, although commonly used, are still not a part of what is considered standard usage. To help the student recognize these words and meanings, most of which are not appropriate for formal writing, three additional labels are used: *substandard*, for words that have some currency in all areas of the United States but which are not normally used by educated writers and speakers; *nonstandard,* for words that are sometimes used by well-educated people but which nevertheless are not always considered appropriate for good usage; and *slang*, words and senses that convey a flavor of extreme informality, consist of colorful and sometimes unconventional coinages and figures of speech, and are used chiefly by a particular cultural group, such as students.

learn . . . **2** *substandard* : to cause to learn : TEACH
thoro . . . *nonstandard variant of* THOROUGH
[3]**flick** *n, slang* : MOVIE

Entry words are spelled without an initial capital letter if they usually occur in print without a capital or if most senses are not capitalized. The label *cap* shows that an entry may be capitalized in some uses and not in others,

an•gli•cize . . . *vt, often cap* . . .
ky•rie elei•son . . . *n, often cap K&E*

or in some senses and not in others.

am•a•zon . . . *n* **1** *cap* : a member of a race of women warriors . . . **2 :** a very tall strong woman
na•tion•al•ist . . . *n* **1 :** an advocate of nationalism **2** *cap* : a member of a political party . . .

Occasionally a word that is entered with an initial capital will have a particular sense used without a capital.

Ar•ab . . . *n* **1 a :** a member of the Semitic people of the Arabian peninsula . . . **2** *not cap* : STREET ARAB

The italic labels that appear before the definitions are one way we give information on how words are used. Another way is through **usage notes** that follow the definitions. A usage note is set off from the definition by a dash. These notes are normally used to give information on usage that is not a proper part of the definitions and that cannot be given adequately by labels.

One of the things usage notes give you is guidance on good usage.

bi- *prefix* . . . **2 b** . . . — often disapproved in this sense because of the likelihood of confusion with sense 1b; . . .

Usage notes usually show a limited range of application of the word

[2]**bias** . . . — used chiefly of fabrics and their cut
le•ga•to . . . *adv or adj* . . . — used as a direction in music
dick•ens . . . — used chiefly as a mild oath . . .

or give information about context.

[2]**knuckle** . . . **2** . . . — usually used with *under*
[1]**dint** . . . — used chiefly in the phrase *by dint of*

Sometimes when usage for a sense is mostly plural —but not enough to permit a *pl* label before the definition—we give you that information in a usage note.

[2]**narrow** . . . — usually used in pl.

There are times when we use usage notes in place of definitions if the word has a special use that cannot be easily explained in the definition.

[2]**please** *adv* **1** — used as function word to express politeness . . .
Ms. . . . *n* — used instead of Miss or Mrs. as a courtesy title for a woman whose marital status is unknown or irrelevant

The History of Words

Webster's School Dictionary shows when and how the various main-entry words originated and developed in the **etymology**, which is in square brackets following the definition.

The etymology traces the word as far back in English as possible, sometimes all the way to Old English, the earliest language of the English people—from about A.D. 600 to about 1100. In the etymology, the entry word's ancestors are given in italics and their meanings in quotation marks.

[3]**bit** *n* **1 :** a small piece or amount . . . ⟨a *bit* of luck⟩ . . . [Old English *bita* "piece bitten off"]

When the etymology gives a language from which the main-entry word derived but does not show the word form in that language, it means the form of the word in the earlier language was the same as that of the main entry. When there is no meaning given in the etymology, the meaning of the older word was the same as the *first* sense of the main entry.

¹arm . . . **1a :** a human upper limb; . . . [Old English *earm*]
¹blind . . . **1a :** SIGHTLESS . . . [Old English]

In the first example, the etymology shows that the modern English word *arm* can be traced back to the Old English word *earm* which had the same meaning as the first sense of *arm*. The second example tells us that the Old English word *blind*, meaning "without sight," was the ancestor of our modern English word *blind*.

When the etymology shows that an entry word has been traced back only into Middle English (from about 1100 to about 1500), it indicates that there is no evidence of it from Old English manuscripts and no indication that it was borrowed from another language.

¹bur•row . . . [Middle English *borow*]

The etymologies in *Webster's School Dictionary* trace the development of words in reverse order, giving the most recent ancestors first and moving backward to the oldest. Whenever a word form or a meaning is not shown at a particular stage in the etymology, it is the same as the form or meaning given before, or if none has been given before in the etymology, the same as that of the main entry.

pope . . . *n, often cap* **:** the head of the Roman Catholic Church [Old English *pāpa*, from Late Latin *papa*, from Greek *pappas*, title of bishops, literally, "papa"]

¹fi•nance . . . **1** *pl* **:** liquid resources (as money) . . . [Middle English, "payment, ransom", from Middle French, from *finer* "to end, pay", from *fin* "end", from Latin *finis*]

In the first example the modern English word *pope* is derived from Old English *pāpa*, meaning "pope," which in turn came from the Late Latin word *papa*, also meaning "pope." The Latin word came from the Greek *pappas*, which meant literally "papa" and had been used as a title of bishops. In the second example, the modern English word *finance* meaning "money resources" came from the Middle English word *finance*, which mean "payment" or "ransom." This Middle English word was derived from a Middle French word that had the same spelling and the same meaning as the Middle English word *finance*. This Middle French word came from an earlier Middle French word *finer*, which meant "payment" or "ransom." This Middle English word was derived from a Middle French word "end." And the early Middle French word *fin* was derived from the still earlier Latin word *finis*, which also meant "end."

Words borrowed directly into modern English show first the language from which the word was borrowed.

ro•deo . . . **1 :** ROUNDUP 1 . . . [Spanish, from *rodear* "to surround", from *rueda* "wheel", from Latin *rota* "wheel"]
te•pee . . . [of American Indian origin]
caf•tan *or* **kaf•tan** . . . [Russian *kaftan*, from Turkish, from Persian *qaftān*]
gin•seng . . . [Chinese (Pekingese dialect) *jen²-shen¹*]

The small numbers that appear at the end of words in languages—like Chinese—that distinguish similar sounds by voice tones are indications of the *tones* for the particular language and have nothing to do with meaning or homographs of English words.

Words that are formed in modern English from other English words do not normally have etymologies, since the origin is usually obvious. Thus, the entry *likable* does not have an etymology because the word is derived from English *like* by addition of an ordinary English suffix *-able*. However, etymologies are given for words that are made up of parts of other words.

aero•sol . . . [*aer-* + ³*sol*]
brunch . . . [*b*reakfast + *l*unch]
¹GI . . . [*g*alvanized *i*ron; from abbreviation used in listing such articles as garbage cans, but taken as an abbreviation for *government issue*]
ra•dar . . . [*ra*dio *d*etecting *a*nd *r*anging]

When a word comes from a person's name, we show that in the etymology,

der•by . . . **1 :** any of several horse races . . . [Edward Stanley, died 1834, 12th earl of *Derby*]

but we do not show the name of a person who first used a word—unless the word was coined, that is, created as an original word that did not exist before in English or any other language.

blurb . . . [coined by Gelett Burgess, died 1951, American humorist]

For a number of entries whose origins are particularly interesting, we give additional information in an **origin paragraph** beyond what is found in the etymology. In some cases the paragraph also contains information on how the meaning of the word has changed in English over the centuries.

Ori•ent \ˈōr-ē-ənt, ˈȯr-, -ē-ˌent\ *n* **:** EAST 2; *esp* **:** the countries of eastern Asia [Middle French, from Latin *oriens*, from *oriri* "to rise"]

△ **origin** The noun *orient* is derived from the Latin adjective *oriens*, which comes from the present participle of the verb *oriri*, "to rise or come forth". The earliest English sense of *orient* is "the place on the horizon where the sun rises when it is near one of the equinoxes", that is, the east. *Orient* has come to be used today to refer to the Asian countries to the east of Europe. With the spread of Christianity into Europe it became customary to build churches with their longitudinal axes pointing eastward toward Jerusalem. This practice gave rise to the use of *orient* as a verb meaning "to cause to face or point to the east". This sense became generalized to yield the sense "to set or arrange in any determinate position, especially in relation to the points of the compass".

Run-on Entries

At the end of many entries are additional boldface words and sometimes boldface phrases. These are known as **run-on entries.** These words and compounds are derived from the main-entry word in different ways. They may come about through a shift in function (as the verb *research* comes from the noun *research*) or they may be formed by the addition of suffixes (as the adverb *closely* and the noun *closeness* come from the adjective *close*). These derived words are run on without definitions when their meaning is obvious. But if the meaning of a derivative word is not obvious from the meaning of the base word and the meaning of any added suffix, we always enter it as a main entry with a definition.

Boldface phrases that are common idioms whose meanings are more than the sum of the meanings of the individual words, are run on with definitions as the last element of many entries. These phrases are generally entered under the first major element (for example, a noun or verb or sometimes an adjective or adverb, rather than a preposition or article).

For example, the phrases *on board, in any case,* and *to date* will appear at the entries *board*, *case*, and *date* respectively. But *break camp*, *cast lots*, *pull one's leg*, and *now and then* appear respectively under *break*, *cast*, *pull*, and *now*.

All run-ons, whether derivative words or idiomatic phrases, are introduced with a dash. Run-on derivatives always have a part-of-speech label, usually have centered dots to indicate end-of-line division, and often have a pronunciation. Run-on phrases have none of these.

Synonym Paragraphs

The synonyms that appear in small capitals in definitions are words that have essentially the same meaning as the main entry and can usually be substituted in most contexts. *Webster's School Dictionary* also treats a number of synonyms in individual synonym articles set off as separate paragraphs at the end of entries. These synonym paragraphs help the reader discriminate among a number of similar and often confused words. At the entry for every word that is discussed in a synonym paragraph, there is a cross-reference, indicated by "**syn** see . . . ," to the entry where the paragraph is located.

de•mol•ish . . . **syn** see DESTROY
de•stroy . . .
• **syn** DEMOLISH, ANNIHILATE: DESTROY implies any force that wrecks, kills, annihilates, or tears down or apart ⟨*destroy* a friendship by deceit⟩ DEMOLISH implies a pulling or smashing to pieces or a tearing down to the point of ruin ⟨*demolish* a building⟩ ANNIHILATE suggests destruction so complete as to make any restoration impossible ⟨*annihilate* a city by nuclear attack⟩

Lists of Undefined words

Lists of words without definitions appear at the following prefix entries in *Webster's School Dictionary:*

anti-	inter-	out-	super-
bi-	intra-	over-	trans-
co-	mal-	poly-	ultra-
counter-	mini-	post-	un-
equi-	mis-	pre-	vice-
extra-	mono-	quasi-	
hyper-	multi-	re-	
in-	non-	sub-	

The meanings of the compounds formed with these prefixes are readily understandable from the meaning of the prefix and the meaning of the base word, and these words are entered here to indicate to the reader that they are relatively common words and to show spelling. Compounds that are not readily understandable from the sum of the elements are given own-place entry with definitions.

Abbreviations Used in This Dictionary

A.D.	anno Domini
adj	adjective
adv	adverb
a.m.	ante meridiem
B.C.	before Christ
C	Celsius, centigrade
cap	capitalized
conj	conjunction
E	east, eastern
ENE	east-northeast
ESE	east-southeast
esp	especially
F	Fahrenheit
interj	interjection
n	noun
N	north, northern
NE	northeast, northeastern
NNE	north-northeast
NNW	north-northwest
n pl	noun plural
NW	northwest, northwestern
pl	plural
p.m.	post meridiem
prep	preposition
pron	pronoun
S	south, southern
SE	southeast, southeastern
sing	singular
SSE	south-southeast
SSW	south-southwest
SW	southwest, southwestern
syn	synonym
U.S.	United States
U.S.S.R.	Union of Soviet Socialist Republics
vb	verb
vi	verb intransitive
vt	verb transitive
W	west, western
WNW	west-northwest
WSW	west-southwest

Pronunciation Symbols

ə ..... (called *schwa* \ˈshwä\) banan**a**, c**o**llide, ab**u**t; in stressed syllables as in h**u**mdrum, m**o**ther, ab**u**t

ᵊ ..... used when needed to indicate that the following symbol stands for a syllabic consonant, as in shrapnel \ˈshrap-nᵊl\

ər .... f**ur**th**er**, m**er**g**er**

a ..... m**a**p, m**a**t, m**a**d, g**a**g, sn**a**p, p**a**tch

ā ..... d**ay**, f**a**de, m**a**te, dr**a**pe, c**a**pe, **a**orta

ä ..... b**o**ther, c**o**t and, with most American speakers, f**a**ther, c**a**rt

ȧ ..... f**a**ther as pronounced by those who do not rhyme it with *bother;* French p**a**tte

au̇ ... n**ow**, l**ou**d, **ou**t

b ..... **b**a**b**y, ri**b**

ch ... **ch**in, ma**tch**, na**t**ure \ˈnā-chər\; (actually, this sound is \t\ + \sh\)

d ..... **d**i**d**, a**dd**er

e ..... b**e**d, p**e**t

ē ..... b**ea**t, **ea**sy, carefr**ee**; in unstressed syllables as in eas**y**, dail**y**, cr**e**ation

f ..... **f**i**f**ty, cu**ff**

g ..... **g**o, bi**g**

h ..... **h**at, a**h**ead

hw ... **wh**ale as pronounced by those who do not pronounce *whale* and *wail* the same

i ..... b**i**d, t**i**p, act**i**ve, ban**i**sh

ī ..... s**i**te, s**i**de, b**uy**; (actually, this sound is \ä\ + \i\, or \ȧ\ + \i\)

j ..... **j**ob, **g**em, **j**u**dge**; (actually, this sound is \d\ + \zh\)

k ..... **k**in, **c**oo**k**, a**che**

k̲ ..... German i**ch**, Bu**ch**; one pronunciation of lo**ch**

l ..... **l**i**l**y, poo**l**, bui**l**d, co**l**d, batt**le**, hand**le**

m .... **m**ur**m**ur, di**m**, la**m**p, happ**en** \ˈhap-əm, ˈhap-m\

n..... **n**o, ow**n**, cott**on**, maid**en**

ⁿ ..... indicates that a preceding vowel or diphthong is pronounced with the nasal passages open, as in garçon \gär-ˈsōⁿ\

ng ... si**ng** \ˈsiŋ\, si**ng**er \ˈsiŋ-ər\, fi**ng**er \ˈfiŋ-gər\, i**n**k \ˈiŋk\, lock **and** key \ˈläk-ŋ-ˈkē\; (actually, this is a single sound, not two)

ō ..... b**o**ne, kn**ow**, s**oa**p

ȯ ..... s**aw**, **a**ll, t**au**t

œ .... French b**oeu**f, German H**ö**lle

œ̄ .... French f**eu**, German H**ö**hle

ȯi .... c**oi**n, destr**oy**

p ..... **p**e**pp**er, li**p**

r ..... **r**ed, **r**a**r**ity, **rh**yme, ca**r**

s ..... **s**our**c**e, le**ss**

sh ... **sh**y, mi**ssi**on, ma**ch**ine, spe**ci**al; (actually, this is a single sound, not two)

t ..... **t**ie, a**tt**ack, ho**t**, wa**t**er

th .... **th**in, e**th**er; (actually, this is a single sound, not two)

t̲h̲ .... **th**is, ei**th**er; (actually, this is a single sound, not two)

ü ..... r**u**le, y**ou**th, f**ew** \ˈfyü\, **u**nion \ˈyün-yən\

u̇ ..... p**u**ll, w**oo**d, f**oo**t, c**u**rable \ˈkyu̇r-ə-bəl\

ue .... German f**ü**llen, h**ü**bsch

ūe .... French r**ue**, German f**ü**hlen

v ..... **v**i**v**id, gi**v**e

w .... **w**e, a**w**ay

y ..... **y**ard, **y**oung, cue \ˈkyü\, union \ˈyün-yən\

ʸ ..... indicates that the sound represented by the preceding character is pronounced with the front of the tongue in the approximate position it has for the first sound of *yard,* as in French *digne* \dēnʸ\

yü ... **you**th, **u**nion, c**ue**, f**ew**, m**u**sic

yu̇ ... c**u**rable, f**u**ry

z ..... **z**one, rai**se**

zh.... vi**si**on, a**z**ure \ˈazh-ər\; (actually, this is a single sound, not two)

\ ..... slant line used in pairs to mark the beginning and end of a transcription

, ; .... a comma separates variant pronunciations; a semicolon separates groups of variants

ˈ ..... mark preceding a syllable with primary (strongest) stress: \ˈpen-mən\

ˌ ..... mark preceding a syllable with secondary (next-strongest) stress: \ˈpen-mən-ˌship\

- ..... a hyphen separates syllables in a transcription

A a—azygous

[1]a \ˈā\ *n, pl* **a's** or **as** \ˈāz\ *often cap* **1 :** the 1st letter of the English alphabet **2 :** the musical tone A **3 :** a grade rating a student's work as superior

[2]a \ə, ā, ˈā\ *indefinite article* **1 :** some one unspecified ⟨*a* person overboard⟩ ⟨*a* dozen⟩ **2 :** the same **:** ONE ⟨two of *a* kind⟩ ⟨birds of *a* feather⟩ **3 :** ANY ⟨*a* person who is sick can't work⟩ — used in all senses before words beginning with a consonant sound; compare [1]AN [Middle English *an, a,* from Old English *ān* "one"]

[3]a \ə\ *prep* **1** *chiefly dialect* **:** ON, IN, AT **2 :** in, to, or for each — used before words with an initial consonant sound ⟨twice *a* week⟩ ⟨dime *a* dozen⟩ [Old English *an, on, a-*]

[1]a- \ə\ *prefix* **1 :** on **:** in **:** at ⟨abed⟩ **2 :** in (such) a state or condition ⟨afire⟩ ⟨asleep⟩ **3 :** in (such) a manner ⟨aloud⟩ **4 :** in the act or process of ⟨gone *a*-hunting⟩ [Old English]

[2]a- \ā, ˈā, a, ˈa, ä, ˈä\ *or* **an-** \an, ˈan\ *prefix* **:** not **:** without ⟨asexual⟩ — *a-* before consonants other than *h* and sometimes even before *h, an-* before vowels and usually before *h* ⟨anastigmatic⟩ ⟨anhydrous⟩ [Greek]

aard•vark \ˈärd-ˌvärk\ *n* **:** a large burrowing African mammal with a long sticky tongue which it uses to feed on ants and termites [Afrikaans, literally, "earth pig"]

Aa•ron•ic \a-ˈrän-ik, e-\ *adj* **:** of or relating to the lower order of the Mormon priesthood [*Aaron,* brother of Moses]

ab- *prefix* **:** from **:** away **:** off ⟨abnormal⟩ [Latin *ab-, abs-, a-*]

ab•a•ca \ˌab-ə-ˈkä\ *n* **:** MANILA HEMP [Spanish *abacá,* from Tagalog *abaká*]

aback \ə-ˈbak\ *adv* **1** *archaic* **:** BACK, BACKWARD **2 :** by surprise **:** UNAWARES ⟨taken *aback* by the turn of events⟩

aba•cus \ˈab-ə-kəs, ə-ˈbak-əs\ *n, pl* **aba•ci** \ˈab-ə-ˌsī, -ˌkē; ə-ˈbak-ˌī\ *or* **aba•cus•es 1 :** a slab that forms the uppermost part of the capital of a column **2 :** an instrument for making calculations by sliding counters along rods or in grooves [Latin, from Greek *abax* "board, slab"]

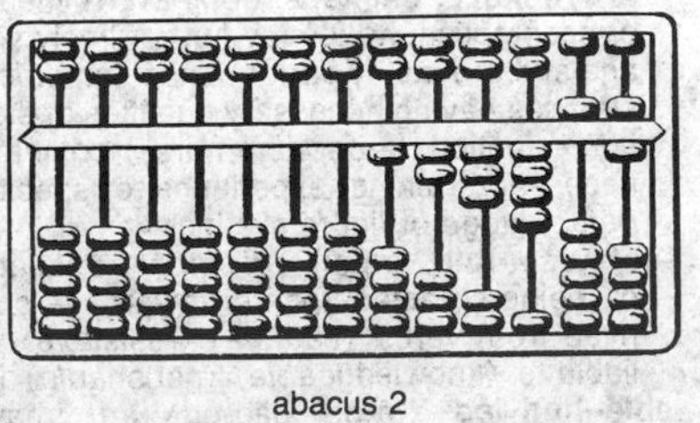

abacus 2

[1]abaft \ə-ˈbaft\ *adv* **:** toward or at the stern **:** AFT [[1]*a-* + obsolete *baft* "behind"]

[2]abaft *prep* **:** to the rear of; *esp* **:** toward the stern from

ab•a•lo•ne \ˌab-ə-ˈlō-nē\ *n* **:** any of several mollusks with flattened slightly spiral shells perforated along the edge and lined with mother-of-pearl [American Spanish *abulón*]

[1]aban•don \ə-ˈban-dən\ *vt* **1 :** to give up completely ⟨*abandon* a difficult task⟩ **2 :** to withdraw from often in the face of danger ⟨*abandon* ship⟩ **3 :** to withdraw protection, support, or help from **4 :** to give (oneself) over to a feeling or emotion without restraint [Middle French *abandoner,* from *a bandon* "in one's power"] — **aban•don•er** *n* — **aban•don•ment** \-dən-mənt\ *n*

• **syn** ABANDON, DESERT, FORSAKE mean to leave or go away from. ABANDON may stress withdrawing protection or care from ⟨*abandon* a property⟩ DESERT implies leaving in violation of a duty or promise ⟨*desert* a sentry post⟩ FORSAKE implies breaking ties with something familiar or cherished.

[2]abandon *n* **1 :** a complete yielding to natural impulses **2 :** carefree enthusiasm **:** EXUBERANCE

aban•doned \ə-ˈban-dənd\ *adj* **1 :** that has been deserted **:** FORSAKEN ⟨an *abandoned* house⟩ **2 :** wholly given up to wickedness or vice ⟨an *abandoned* criminal⟩

abase \ə-ˈbās\ *vt* **:** to lower in rank or position **:** HUMBLE, DEGRADE [Middle French *abaisser*] — **abase•ment** \-mənt\ *n*

abash \ə-ˈbash\ *vt* **:** to destroy the self-possession or self-confidence of **:** DISCONCERT [Middle French *esbaiss-,* stem of *esbair* "to be astonished", from *ex-* + *baer* "to yawn"] **syn** see EMBARRASS — **abash•ment** \-mənt\ *n*

abate \ə-ˈbāt\ *vb* **:** to reduce or decrease in degree, amount, or intensity **:** MODERATE [Old French *abattre* "to beat down"] — **abat•er** *n*

abate•ment \ə-ˈbāt-mənt\ *n* **1 :** the act or process of abating **:** the state of being abated **2 :** an amount abated; *esp* **:** a deduction from the full amount of a tax

ab•at•toir \ˈab-ə-ˌtwär\ *n* **:** SLAUGHTERHOUSE [French, from *abattre* "to beat down"]

ab•ba•cy \ˈab-ə-sē\ *n, pl* **-cies :** the office, term of office, position, or jurisdiction of an abbot

ab•ba•tial \ə-ˈbā-shəl, a-\ *adj* **:** of or relating to an abbot, abbess, or abbey

ab•bé \a-ˈbā, ˈab-ˌā\ *n* **:** a French cleric not in a religious order — used as a title [French, from Late Latin *abbas* "abbot"]

ab•bess \ˈab-əs\ *n* **:** the superior of a convent of nuns

ab•bey \ˈab-ē\ *n, pl* **abbeys 1 a :** a monastery governed by an abbot **b :** a convent governed by an abbess **2 :** a church that once belonged to an abbey ⟨Westminster *Abbey*⟩ [Old French *abaïe,* from Late Latin *abbatia,* from *abbas* "abbot"]

ab•bot \ˈab-ət\ *n* **:** the superior of a monastery [Old English *abbod,* from Late Latin *abbas,* from Late Greek, from Aramaic *abbā* "father"]

ab•bre•vi•ate \ə-ˈbrē-vē-ˌāt\ *vt* **:** to make briefer; *esp* **:** to reduce (as a word or phrase) to a shorter form intended to stand for the whole [Late Latin *abbreviare,* from Latin *ad-* + *brevis*

\ə\ **abut**	\au̇\ **out**	\i\ **tip**	\ȯ\ **saw**	\u̇\ **foot**
\ər\ **further**	\ch\ **chin**	\ī\ **life**	\ȯi\ **coin**	\y\ **yet**
\a\ **mat**	\e\ **pet**	\j\ **job**	\th\ **thin**	\yü\ **few**
\ā\ **take**	\ē\ **easy**	\ng\ **sing**	\th\ **this**	\yu̇\ **cure**
\ä\ **cot, cart**	\g\ **go**	\ō\ **bone**	\ü\ **food**	\zh\ **vision**

"short, brief"] **syn** see SHORTEN — **ab•bre•vi•a•tor** \-ˌāt-ər\ *n*

ab•bre•vi•a•tion \ə-ˌbrē-vē-ˈā-shən\ *n* **1 :** the act or result of abbreviating **:** ABRIDGMENT **2 :** a shortened form of a written word or phrase used in place of the whole

ABC \ˌā-ˌbē-ˈsē\ *n, pl* **ABC's** *or* **ABCs** \-ˈsēz\ **1 :** ALPHABET — usually used in pl. **2 a :** the rudiments of reading, writing, and spelling — usually used in pl. **b :** the rudiments of a subject

Ab•di•as \ab-ˈdī-əs\ *n* — see BIBLE table

ab•di•cate \ˈab-di-ˌkāt\ *vb* **:** to give up sovereign power, office, or responsibility usually formally **:** RENOUNCE [Latin *abdicare,* from *ab-* + *dicare* "to proclaim"] — **ab•di•ca•tion** \ˌab-di-ˈkā-shən\ *n* — **ab•di•ca•tor** \ˈab-di-ˌkāt-ər\ *n*

ab•do•men \ˈab-də-mən, ab-ˈdō-mən\ *n* **1 :** the part of the body between the chest and the pelvis; *also* **:** the body cavity containing the chief digestive organs **2 :** the hind portion of the body behind the thorax or cephalothorax in an arthropod [Latin] — **ab•dom•i•nal** \ab-ˈdäm-ən-l\ *adj* — **ab•dom•i•nal•ly** \-l-ē\ *adv*

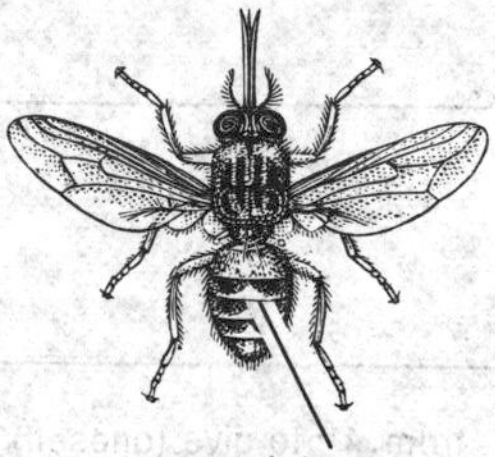

abdomen 2

ab•du•cens \ab-ˈdü-ˌsenz, -ˈdyü-\ *n* **:** either of the 6th pair of cranial nerves supplying muscles of the eyes — called also *abducens nerve* [Latin, "leading away"]

ab•duct \ab-ˈdəkt\ *vt* **1 :** to carry (a person) off by force **2 :** to draw (a part of the body) away from the median axis of the body; *also* **:** to move (similar parts) apart ⟨*abduct* adjoining fingers⟩ [Latin *abducere,* literally, "to lead away", from *ab-* + *ducere* "to lead"] — **ab•duc•tion** \-ˈdək-shən\ *n*

ab•duc•tor \-ˈdək-tər\ *n* **:** one that abducts; *esp* **:** a muscle that draws a body part away from the median axis — compare ADDUCTOR

abeam \ə-ˈbēm\ *adv or adj* **:** on a line at right angles to a ship's keel

abed \ə-ˈbed\ *adv or adj* **:** in bed

Ab•er•deen An•gus \ˌab-ər-ˌdē-ˈnang-gəs\ *n* **:** any of a breed of black hornless beef cattle originating in Scotland — called also *Angus* [*Aberdeen* and *Angus,* counties in Scotland]

ab•er•rant \a-ˈber-ənt\ *adj* **1 :** straying from the right or normal way **2 :** deviating from the usual or natural type **:** ATYPICAL [Latin *aberrare* "to go astray", from *ab-* + *errare* "to wander, err"] — **ab•er•rance** \-əns\ *n* — **ab•er•ran•cy** \-ən-sē\ *n* — **ab•er•rant•ly** *adv*

ab•er•ra•tion \ˌab-ə-ˈrā-shən\ *n* **1 :** the act of deviating especially from a moral standard or normal state **2 :** failure of a mirror or lens to produce exact correspondence between an object and its image **3 :** unsoundness or disorder of the mind **4 :** a small periodic change of apparent position in heavenly bodies due to the combined effect of the motion of light and the motion of the observer **5 :** an aberrant organ or individual **:** SPORT 5 — **ab•er•ra•tion•al** \-shnəl, -shən-l\ *adj*

abet \ə-ˈbet\ *vb* **abet•ted; abet•ting :** to encourage or aid especially in doing wrong [Middle French *abeter,* from *a-* "ad-" + *beter* "to bait"] **syn** see INCITE — **abet•ment** \-mənt\ *n* — **abet•tor**\-ˈbet-ər\ *n*

abey•ance \ə-ˈbā-əns\ *n* **:** a temporary suspension of activity ⟨plans held in *abeyance*⟩ [Middle French *abeance* "expectation", from *abaer* "to desire", from *a-* "ad-" + *baer* "to yawn, gape"] — **abey•ant** \-ənt\ *adj*

ab•hor \ab-ˈhȯr, əb-\ *vt* **ab•horred; ab•hor•ring 1 :** to feel extreme aversion for **:** LOATHE **2 :** to turn aside or keep away from in scorn or disgust **:** REJECT [Latin *abhorrēre,* from *ab-* + *horrēre* "to shudder"] **syn** see HATE — **ab•hor•rence** \-ˈhȯr-əns, -ˈhär-\ *n* — **ab•hor•rer** \-ˈhȯr-ər\ *n*

ab•hor•rent \-ˈhȯr-ənt, -ˈhär-*adj* **1 :** feeling or showing abhorrence **2 :** not agreeable ⟨a notion *abhorrent* to their philosophy⟩ **3 :** DETESTABLE **syn** see REPUGNANT — **ab•hor•rent•ly** *adv*

abid•ance \ə-ˈbīd-ns\ *n* **1 :** the act or state of abiding **2 :** COMPLIANCE ⟨*abidance* by the rules⟩

abide \ə-ˈbīd\ *vb* **abode** \-ˈbōd\ *or* **abid•ed; abid•ing 1** *archaic* **:** to wait for **:** AWAIT **2 a :** to endure without yielding **:** WITHSTAND **b :** to bear patiently **:** TOLERATE **3 :** to accept without objection ⟨*abide* the court's decision⟩ **4 :** to remain stable or fixed in a state **5 :** to reside or continue in a place **:** DWELL [Old English *ābīdan,* from *ā-,* prefix denoting completion + *bīdan* "to bide"] **syn** see STAY — **abid•er** *n* — **abide by :** to accept the terms of **:** be obedient to ⟨*abide by* the rules of the club⟩

abid•ing *adj* **:** LASTING, CONTINUING ⟨an *abiding* interest in nature⟩ — **abid•ing•ly** \-ing-lē\ *adv*

abil•i•ty \ə-ˈbil-ət-ē\ *n, pl* **-ties 1 a :** the quality or state of being able; *esp* **:** physical, mental, or legal power to do something **b :** competence in doing **:** SKILL **2 :** natural talent or acquired proficiency **:** APTITUDE

-abil•i•ty *also* **-ibil•i•ty** \ə-ˈbil-ət-ē\ *n suffix, pl* **-ties :** capacity, fitness, or tendency to act or be acted on in a (specified) way ⟨melt*ability*⟩ ⟨read*ability*⟩

abio•gen•e•sis \ˌā-ˌbī-ō-ˈjen-ə-səs\ *n, pl* **-e•ses** \-ˌsēz\ **:** SPONTANEOUS GENERATION

abi•ot•ic \ˌā-bī-ˈät-ik\ *adj* **:** not living or composed of living things ⟨soil acidity is an *abiotic* environmental factor⟩

ab•ject \ˈab-ˌjekt, ab-ˈ\ *adj* **1 :** sunk to a low condition **2 a :** having no pride or spirit **:** SPIRITLESS **b :** showing utter resignation **:** HOPELESS ⟨*abject* surrender⟩ **3 :** expressing or offered in a humble often ingratiating spirit ⟨an *abject* apology⟩ [Latin *abjectus,* from *abicere* "to cast off", from *ab-* + *jacere* "to throw"] — **ab•ject•ly** *adv* — **ab•ject•ness** *n*

ab•jure \ab-ˈju̇r\ *vt* **1 a :** to renounce upon oath ⟨*abjure* allegiance⟩ **b :** to reject solemnly **:** REPUDIATE ⟨*abjure* one's old beliefs⟩ **2 :** to abstain from **:** AVOID ⟨*abjure* extravagance⟩ [Latin *abjurare,* from *ab-* + *jurare* "to swear"] — **ab•ju•ra•tion** \ˌab-jə-ˈrā-shən\ *n* — **ab•jur•er** *n*

ab•late \a-ˈblāt\ *vb* **1 :** to remove by cutting, melting, evaporation, or vaporization **2 :** to undergo ablation

ab•la•tion \a-ˈblā-shən\ *n* **:** the process of ablating: as **a :** surgical removal **b :** removal of a part (as the outside of a nose cone) by melting or vaporization

ab•la•tive \ˈab-lət-iv\ *adj* **:** of, relating to, or constituting a grammatical case expressing typically the relations of separation and source and also frequently such relations as cause or instrument [Latin *ablat-,* stem of *auferre* "to carry away, remove", from *au-* "ab-" + *ferre* "to carry"] — **ablative** *n*

ablative absolute *n* **:** a construction in Latin that consists of a noun or pronoun and its modifier both in the ablative case and together forming an adverbial phrase expressing generally the time, cause, or an attendant circumstance of an action

ablaze \ə-ˈblāz\ *adj* **1 :** being on fire **2 :** radiant with light or bright color

able \ˈā-bəl\ *adj* **abler** \-bə-lər, -blər\; **ablest** \-bə-ləst, -bləst\ **1 a :** having enough power, skill, or resources to do something ⟨*able* to swim⟩ **b :** free from restrictions preventing an action ⟨*able* to vote⟩ **2 :** marked by intelligence, knowledge, skill, or competence ⟨an *able* news editor⟩ [Middle French, from Latin *habilis* "handy, apt", from *habēre* "to have, hold"] — **ably** \ˈā-blē\ *adv*

• **syn** ABLE, CAPABLE, COMPETENT mean having power to do or accomplish. ABLE may further imply skill that is above average and proved by performance ⟨an *able* trial lawyer⟩ CAPABLE stresses having necessary qualities or skill for a specified function or action ⟨a *capable* nurse⟩ COMPETENT suggests having necessary training, experience, or special knowledge ⟨a *competent* judge of figure skating⟩

-able *also* **-ible** \ə-bəl\ *adj suffix* **1 :** capable of, fit for, or worthy of (being so acted upon or toward) — chiefly in adjectives derived from verbs ⟨eat*able*⟩ ⟨resist*ible*⟩ **2 :** tending, given, or liable to ⟨knowledge*able*⟩ ⟨perish*able*⟩ [Latin *-abilis, -ibilis*]

able–bod•ied \ˌā-bəl-ˈbäd-ēd\ *adj* **:** having a sound strong body **:** physically fit

able seaman *n* **:** an experienced deckhand qualified to perform routine and emergency duties at sea — called also *able-bodied seaman*

abloom \ə-ˈblüm\ *adj* **:** being in bloom

ab•lu•tion \a-ˈblü-shən, ə-ˈblü-\ *n* **:** the washing of oneself especially as a religious rite [Latin *abluere* "to wash away", from *ab-* + *lavere* "to wash"]

ABM \ˌā-ˌbē-ˈem\ *n, pl* **ABM's** *or* **ABMs :** ANTIBALLISTIC MISSILE

ab•ne•gate \ˈab-ni-ˌgāt\ *vt* **1 :** to give up or surrender (as a right or privilege) **:** RELINQUISH **2 :** to deny to or reject for oneself **:** RENOUNCE ⟨*abnegate* outworn beliefs⟩ — **ab•ne•ga•tion**

\ˌab-ni-ˈgā-shən\ *n* — **ab•ne•ga•tor** \ˈab-ni-ˌgāt-ər\ *n*

ab•nor•mal \ab-ˈnȯr-məl, ˈab-ˈ\ *adj* **:** differing from the normal or average; *esp* **:** markedly irregular — **ab•nor•mal•ly** \-mə-lē\ *adv*

ab•nor•mal•i•ty \ˌab-nər-ˈmal-ət-ē, -nȯr-\ *n, pl* **-ties 1 :** the quality or state of being abnormal **2 :** something abnormal

[1]aboard \ə-ˈbōrd, -ˈbȯrd\ *adv* **1 :** on, onto, or within a car, ship, or airplane **2 :** ALONGSIDE

[2]aboard *prep* **:** on or into especially for passage ⟨go *aboard* ship⟩

abode \ə-ˈbōd\ *n* **:** a dwelling place **:** RESIDENCE [Middle English *abod,* from *abiden* "to abide"]

abol•ish \ə-ˈbäl-ish\ *vt* **:** to do away with wholly **:** put an end to [Middle French *aboliss-,* stem of *abolir,* from Latin *abolēre*] — **abol•ish•able** \-ə-bəl\ *adj* — **abol•ish•er** *n* — **abol•ish•ment** \-mənt\ *n*

ab•o•li•tion \ˌab-ə-ˈlish-ən\ *n* **:** the act of abolishing **:** the state of being abolished; *esp* **:** the abolishing of slavery — **ab•o•li•tion•ary** \-ˈlish-ə-ˌner-ē\ *adj*

ab•o•li•tion•ist \-ˈlish-nəst, -ə-nəst\ *n* **:** a person who is in favor of abolition especially of Negro slavery — **ab•o•li•tion•ism** \-ˈlish-ə-ˌniz-əm\ *n*

ab•oma•sum \ˌab-ō-ˈmā-səm\ *n, pl* **-sa** \-sə\ **:** the fourth or true digestive stomach of a ruminant (as a cow) [Latin *ab-* + *omasum* "tripe of a bullock"] — **ab•oma•sal** \-səl\ *adj*

A–bomb \ˈā-ˌbäm\ *n* **:** ATOM BOMB — **A–bomb** *vb*

abom•i•na•ble \ə-ˈbäm-nə-bəl, -ə-nə-\ *adj* **1 :** deserving or causing loathing or hatred **:** DETESTABLE ⟨*abominable* behavior⟩ **2 :** quite disagreeable ⟨*abominable* weather⟩ — **abom•i•na•bly** \-blē\ *adv*

abominable snow•man \-ˈsnō-mən, -ˌman\ *n, often cap A&S* **:** a creature thought to exist in the Himalayas and usually held to be a bear

abom•i•nate \ə-ˈbäm-ə-ˌnāt\ *vt* **:** to hate or loathe intensely **:** ABHOR [Latin *abominari,* literally, "to deprecate as an ill omen", from *ab-* + *omen* "omen"] — **abom•i•na•tor** \-ˌnāt-ər\ *n*

abom•i•na•tion \ə-ˌbäm-ə-ˈnā-shən\ *n* **1 :** something abominable **2 :** extreme disgust and hatred **:** LOATHING

ab•o•rig•i•nal \ˌab-ə-ˈrij-nəl, -ən-l\ *adj* **1 a :** INDIGENOUS, ORIGINAL **b :** PRIMITIVE 3a,b **2 :** of or relating to aborigines **syn** see NATIVE — **ab•o•rig•i•nal•ly** \-ē\ *adv*

ab•o•rig•i•ne \ˌab-ə-ˈrij-ə-ˌnē\ *n* **:** an indigenous inhabitant especially as contrasted with an invading or colonizing people [Latin *aborigines,* pl., from *ab origine* "from the beginning"]

aborn•ing \ə-ˈbȯr-ning\ *adv* **:** while being born or produced

abort \ə-ˈbȯrt\ *vb* **1 :** to bring forth or cause to bring forth premature offspring **2 :** to become checked in development ⟨pollen grains that *aborted*⟩ **3 :** to terminate prematurely ⟨*abort* a project⟩ [Latin *abortus,* past participle of *aboriri* "to miscarry", from *ab-* + *oriri* "to rise, be born"]

abor•tion \ə-ˈbȯr-shən\ *n* **1 :** a premature birth whether natural or induced artificially that occurs before the fetus can survive — compare MISCARRIAGE **2 :** failure of a project or action to reach full development; *also* **:** a result of such failure

abor•tion•ist \-shə-nəst, -shnəst\ *n* **:** a person who induces abortions especially illegally

abor•tive \ə-ˈbȯrt-iv\ *adj* **1 :** failing to achieve the desired end **:** UNSUCCESSFUL ⟨an *abortive* attempt⟩ **2 :** imperfectly formed or developed **:** RUDIMENTARY — **abor•tive•ly** *adv* — **abor•tive•ness** *n*

abound \ə-ˈbau̇nd\ *vi* **1 :** to be present in large numbers or in great quantity ⟨wildlife *abounds*⟩ **2 :** to be filled or abundantly supplied ⟨a stream *abounding* in fish⟩ [Middle French *abonder,* from Latin *abundare,* from *ab-* + *unda* "a wave"]

[1]about \ə-ˈbau̇t\ *adv* **1 :** on all sides **:** AROUND ⟨had neighbors living all *about*⟩ **2 a :** APPROXIMATELY ⟨*about* three years⟩ **b :** ALMOST ⟨*about* starved⟩ **3 :** here and there ⟨pace *about*⟩ **4 :** in the vicinity **:** NEAR ⟨people standing *about*⟩ **5 :** in succession **:** ALTERNATELY ⟨turn *about* is fair play⟩ **6 :** in the opposite direction ⟨face *about*⟩ [Old English *abūtan,* from [1]*a-* + *būtan* "outside", from *be* "by" + *ūtan* "outside", from *ūt* "out"]

[2]about *prep* **1 :** on every side of **:** AROUND **2 a :** in the immediate neighborhood of **:** NEAR ⟨fish are abundant *about* the reef⟩ **b :** on or near the person of ⟨carried a knife *about* him⟩ **c :** in the makeup of ⟨something strange *about* them⟩ **d :** at the command of ⟨keep your wits *about* you⟩ **3 a :** engaged in ⟨do it thoroughly while you're *about* it⟩ **b :** on the verge of ⟨*about* to join the army⟩ **4 :** with regard to **:** CONCERNING ⟨told me *about* it⟩ **5 :** over, through, or in different parts of ⟨traveled *about* the country⟩

about–face \ə-ˈbau̇t-ˈfās\ *n* **1 :** a reversal of direction **2 :** a reversal of attitude or point of view — **about–face** *vi*

[1]above \ə-ˈbəv\ *adv* **1 :** in or to a higher place **:** OVERHEAD **2 :** higher on the same page or on a preceding page **3 :** in or to a higher rank or number [Old English *abufan,* from [1]*a-* + *bufan* "above", from *be* "by" + *ufan* "above, over"]

[2]above *prep* **1 :** in or to a higher place than **:** OVER **2 a :** superior to (as in rank, quality, or degree) ⟨a captain is *above* a lieutenant⟩ **b :** out of reach of ⟨*above* criticism⟩ **c :** too proud or honorable to stoop to ⟨*above* such petty tricks⟩ **3 :** exceeding in number, quantity, or size ⟨*above* the average⟩

[3]above *n* **:** something that is above

[4]above *adj* **:** located or written higher on the same page or on a preceding page ⟨the *above* diagram⟩

above all *adv* **:** before every other consideration **:** ESPECIALLY

[1]above•board \ə-ˈbəv-ˌbōrd, -ˌbȯrd\ *adv* **:** in a straightforward manner **:** OPENLY

[2]aboveboard *adj* **:** free from concealment or deceit **:** STRAIGHTFORWARD

ab•ra•ca•dab•ra \ˌab-rə-kə-ˈdab-rə\ *n* **1 :** a magical charm or incantation against calamity **2 :** unintelligible language **:** JARGON [Late Latin]

abrade \ə-ˈbrād\ *vb* **1 :** to rub or wear away especially by friction **:** ERODE **2 :** to irritate or roughen by rubbing [Latin *abradere* "to scrape off", from *ab-* + *radere* "to scrape"] — **abrad•er** *n*

abra•sion \ə-ˈbrā-zhən\ *n* **1 :** a rubbing or wearing away ⟨protect the surface from *abrasion*⟩ **2 :** a place where the surface has been rubbed or scraped off ⟨had an *abrasion* on my knee⟩ [Medieval Latin *abrasio,* from Latin *abradere* "to abrade"]

[1]abra•sive \ə-ˈbrā-siv, -ziv\ *adj* **1 :** having the effect of abrading **2 :** causing annoyance ⟨an *abrasive* manner⟩

[2]abrasive *n* **:** a substance (as emery, pumice, fine sand) used for grinding, smoothing, or polishing

abreast \ə-ˈbrest\ *adv or adj* **1 :** side by side with bodies in line ⟨soldiers standing five *abreast*⟩ **2 :** up to a standard or level especially of knowledge ⟨keep *abreast* of the times⟩

abridge \ə-ˈbrij\ *vt* **1 a** *archaic* **:** DEPRIVE **b :** to reduce in scope **:** DIMINISH ⟨forbidden to *abridge* the rights of citizens⟩ **2 :** to shorten in duration or extent ⟨modern transportation that *abridges* distance⟩ **3 :** to shorten by omitting words without sacrificing the sense **:** CONDENSE [Middle French *abregier,* from Late Latin *abbreviare* "to abbreviate"] — **abridg•er** *n*

abridg•ment *or* **abridge•ment** \ə-ˈbrij-mənt\ *n* **1 :** the action of abridging **:** the state of being abridged **2 :** a shortened form of a work retaining the general sense and unity of the original

abroad \ə-ˈbrȯd\ *adv or adj* **1 :** over a wide area **:** WIDELY **2 :** away from one's home ⟨walk *abroad* after lunch⟩ **3 :** in or to foreign countries ⟨travel *abroad*⟩ **4 :** in wide circulation ⟨disturbing rumors were *abroad*⟩

ab•ro•gate \ˈab-rə-ˌgāt\ *vt* **1 :** to annul or repeal by authoritative action ⟨*abrogate* a law⟩ **2 :** to do away with [Latin *abrogare,* from *ab-* + *rogare* "to ask, propose"] — **ab•ro•ga•tion** \ˌab-rə-ˈgā-shən\ *n*

abrupt \ə-ˈbrəpt\ *adj* **1 :** broken off **2 a :** SUDDEN ⟨*abrupt* change in the weather⟩ **b :** impolitely curt ⟨*abrupt* manner⟩ **c :** marked by sudden changes in topic **:** DISCONNECTED ⟨an *abrupt* style of speaking⟩ **3 :** rising or dropping sharply **:** STEEP ⟨a high *abrupt* bank bounded the stream⟩ [Latin *abruptus,* from *abrumpere* "to break off", from *ab-* + *rumpere* "to break"] — **abrupt•ly** *adv* — **abrupt•ness** \ə-ˈbrəpt-nəs, -ˈbrəp-\ *n*

ab•scess \ˈab-ˌses\ *n* **:** a localized collection of pus surrounded by inflamed tissue [Latin *abscessus,* literally, "departure", from *abscedere* "to go away", from *ab-, abs-* + *cedere* "to go"] — **ab•scessed** \-ˌsest\ *adj*

ab•scis•sa \ab-ˈsis-ə\ *n, pl* **-scis•sas** *also* **-scis•sae** \-ˈsis-ē\ **:** the horizontal coordinate of a point in a plane Cartesian coordinate system obtained by measuring parallel to the x-axis — called also *x-coordinate;* compare ORDINATE [New Latin; from Latin *abscindere* "to cut off", from *ab-* + *scindere* "to cut"]

ab•scis•sion \ab-ˈsizh-ən\ *n* **:** the natural separation of flowers,

\ə\ abut	\au̇\ **out**	\i\ **tip**	\ȯ\ **saw**	\u̇\ **foot**
\ər\ **further**	\ch\ **chin**	\ī\ **life**	\ȯi\ **coin**	\y\ **yet**
\a\ mat	\e\ pet	\j\ **job**	\th\ **thin**	\yü\ **few**
\ā\ take	\ē\ **easy**	\ng\ **sing**	\t͟h\ **this**	\yu̇\ **cure**
\ä\ cot, cart	\g\ **go**	\ō\ bone	\ü\ **food**	\zh\ **vision**

fruit, or leaves from plants at a special separation layer

ab·scond \ab-ˈskänd\ *vi* : to depart secretly and hide oneself [Latin *abscondere* "to hide away", from *ab-, abs-* + *condere* "to store up, conceal", from *com-* + *-dere* "to put"] — **ab·scond·er** *n*

ab·sence \ˈab-səns\ *n* **1** : the state of being absent **2** : the time that one is absent **3** : WANT, LACK ⟨an *absence* of detail⟩ **4** : inattention to things present ⟨*absence* of mind⟩

[1]**ab·sent** \ˈab-sənt\ *adj* **1** : not present or attending : MISSING **2** : not existing : LACKING **3** : INATTENTIVE ⟨an *absent* mood⟩ [Latin *absens,* from *abesse* "to be away", from *ab-* + *esse* "to be"] — **ab·sent·ly** *adv*

[2]**ab·sent** \ab-ˈsent\ *vt* : to keep (oneself) away

ab·sen·tee \ˌab-sən-ˈtē\ *n* **1** : one that is absent **2** : a proprietor that lives elsewhere — **absentee** *adj*

absentee ballot *n* : a ballot submitted (as by mail) before an election by a voter who cannot be present at the polls

ab·sen·tee·ism \ˌab-sən-ˈtē-ˌiz-əm\ *n* **1** : protracted absence of an owner from his property **2** : chronic absence from duty

ab·sent·mind·ed \ˌab-sənt-ˈmīn-dəd\ *adj* : lost in thought and unaware of one's surroundings or actions — **ab·sent·mind·ed·ly** *adv* — **ab·sent·mind·ed·ness** *n*

ab·sinthe *or* **ab·sinth** \ˈab-ˌsinth\ *n* : a green liqueur flavored with aromatics (as wormwood and anise) [French *absinthe,* from Latin *absinthium* "wormwood", from Greek *apsinthion*]

ab·so·lute \ˈab-sə-ˌlüt, ˌab-sə-ˈ\ *adj* **1 a** : free from imperfection : PERFECT **b** : free or relatively free from mixture : PURE ⟨*absolute* alcohol⟩ **c** : OUTRIGHT ⟨an *absolute* lie⟩ **2** : completely free from constitutional or other restraint or limitation ⟨an *absolute* monarch⟩ **3 a** : lacking grammatical connection with any other word in a sentence ⟨the *absolute* construction *this being the case* in "this being the case, let us go"⟩ **b** : standing alone without a modified substantive ⟨the *absolute* adjective *blind* in "help the blind"⟩ ⟨the *absolute* possessive pronoun *ours* in "your work and ours"⟩ **c** : having no object in a particular construction though normally transitive ⟨*kill* in "if looks could kill" is an *absolute* verb⟩ **4** : having no restriction, exception, or qualification ⟨an *absolute* requirement⟩ ⟨*absolute* freedom⟩ **5** : free from doubt : CERTAIN, UNQUESTIONABLE ⟨*absolute* proof⟩ **6 a** : independent of standards of measurement : ACTUAL ⟨*absolute* brightness of a star⟩ ⟨*absolute* motion⟩ **b** : relating to or derived from the fundamental units of length, mass, and time ⟨*absolute* electric units⟩ **c** : relating to the absolute-temperature scale ⟨10° *absolute*⟩ **7** : perfectly embodying the nature of a thing ⟨*absolute* justice⟩ [Latin *absolutus,* from *absolvere* "to set free, absolve"] — **absolute** *n* — **ab·so·lute·ly** \ˈab-sə-ˌlüt-lē, ˌab-sə-ˈ\ *adv* — **ab·so·lute·ness** \-ˌlüt-nəs, -ˈlüt-\ *n*

absolute error *n* : the difference between the true value of a quantity and the experimental value

absolute pitch *n* **1** : the position of a tone in a standard scale independently determined by its rate of vibration **2** : the ability to sing a note asked for or name a note heard

absolute temperature *n* : temperature measured on a scale that has absolute zero as the zero point

absolute value *n* **1** : the numerical value of a real number without regard to its sign **2** : the positive square root of the sum of the squares of the real and imaginary parts of a complex number — called also *modulus*

absolute zero *n* : a hypothetical temperature characterized by complete absence of heat and equivalent to approximately −273.15°C or −459.67°F

ab·so·lu·tion \ˌab-sə-ˈlü-shən\ *n* : the act of absolving; *esp* : a forgiving of sins by a confessor in the sacrament of penance

ab·so·lut·ism \ˈab-sə-ˌlüt-ˌiz-əm\ *n* **1 a** : a political theory that absolute power should be vested in one or more rulers **b** : government by an absolute ruler or authority **2** : advocacy of absolute standards or principles — **ab·so·lut·ist** \-ˌlüt-əst\ *n or adj* — **ab·so·lu·tis·tic** \ˌab-sə-ˌlü-ˈtis-tik\ *adj*

ab·solve \əb-ˈzälv, -ˈsälv, -ˈzȯlv, -ˈsȯlv\ *vt* **1** : to set free from an obligation or from the consequences of guilt **2** : to forgive (a sin) by absolution [Latin *absolvere,* from *ab-* + *solvere* "to loosen"] — **ab·solv·er** *n*

ab·sorb \əb-ˈsȯrb, -ˈzȯrb\ *vt* **1** : to take in or swallow up : INCORPORATE ⟨the corporation *absorbed* three small companies⟩ **2** : to suck or take up or in ⟨a sponge *absorbs* water⟩ **3** : to engage or hold the interest of : ENGROSS ⟨*absorbed* in thought⟩ **4** : to receive without recoil or echo ⟨a sound-*absorbing* surface⟩ [Latin *absorbēre,* from *ab-* + *sorbēre* "to suck up"] — **ab·sorb·abil·i·ty** \əb-ˌsȯr-bə-ˈbil-ət-ē, -ˌzȯr-\ *n* — **ab·sorb·able** \əb-ˈsȯr-bə-bəl, -ˈzȯr-\ *adj* — **ab·sorb·er** *n*

• **syn** ABSORB, ASSIMILATE mean to take in. ABSORB may imply that matter or energy enters a body and is retained without essential change to itself or to the receiving body ⟨plant roots *absorb* moisture⟩ ASSIMILATE may apply to an active process of incorporating substance into the substance of the receiving body ⟨the body *assimilates* nourishment from milk⟩

ab·sorbed \-ˈsȯrbd, -ˈzȯrbd\ *adj* : wholly occupied or interested in a thought or activity : ENGROSSED — **ab·sorb·ed·ly** \-ˈsȯr-bəd-lē, -ˈzȯr-\ *adv*

ab·sorb·en·cy \əb-ˈsȯr-bən-sē, -ˈzȯr-\ *n, pl* **-cies** : the quality or state of being absorbent

ab·sorb·ent \-bənt\ *adj* : able to absorb ⟨*absorbent* cotton⟩ — **absorbent** *n*

ab·sorb·ing *adj* : fully taking one's attention : ENGROSSING — **ab·sorb·ing·ly** \-bing-lē\ *adv*

ab·sorp·tion \əb-ˈsȯrp-shən, -ˈzȯrp-\ *n* **1** : the process of absorbing or being absorbed: as **a** : the passing of digested food through the intestinal wall into the blood or lymph **b** : interception especially of light or sound waves **2** : complete occupation of the mind — **ab·sorp·tive** \-ˈsȯrp-tiv, -ˈzȯrp-\ *adj*

ab·stain \əb-ˈstān\ *vi* : to refrain voluntarily especially from an action ⟨*abstain* from voting⟩ [Middle French *abstenir,* from Latin *abstinēre,* from *ab-, abs-* + *tenēre* "to hold"] **syn** see REFRAIN — **ab·stain·er** *n*

ab·ste·mi·ous \ab-ˈstē-mē-əs\ *adj* : sparing especially in eating and drinking [Latin *abstemius,* from *ab-, abs-* + *temetum* "mead"] — **ab·ste·mi·ous·ly** *adv*

ab·sten·tion \əb-ˈsten-chən\ *n* : the act or practice of abstaining; *esp* : a usually formal refusal to vote ⟨3 ayes, 5 nays, and 2 *abstentions*⟩ [Late Latin *abstentio,* from Latin *abstinēre* "to abstain"] — **ab·sten·tious** \-chəs\ *adj*

ab·sti·nence \ˈab-stə-nəns\ *n* **1** : an abstaining especially from indulgence of appetite or from eating certain foods **2** : habitual abstaining from alcoholic liquors [Latin *abstinēre* "to abstain"] — **ab·sti·nent** \-nənt\ *adj* — **ab·sti·nent·ly** *adv*

[1]**ab·stract** \ab-ˈstrakt, ˈab-\ *adj* **1 a** : considered apart from a particular instance or object ⟨whiteness is an *abstract* quality⟩ ⟨*abstract* concept⟩ **b** : difficult to understand ⟨*abstract* problems⟩ **c** : IDEAL ⟨*abstract* justice⟩ **d** : insufficiently factual : purely formal ⟨possessed only an *abstract* right⟩ **2** : expressing a quality considered apart from an object ⟨the word *poem* is concrete; the word *poetry* is *abstract*⟩ **3 a** : dealing with a subject in purely abstract terms : THEORETICAL ⟨*abstract* algebra⟩ **b** : IMPERSONAL ⟨the *abstract* compassion of a surgeon⟩ **4** : having only generalized form with little or no attempt at precise representation ⟨*abstract* painting⟩ [Medieval Latin *abstractus,* from Latin *abstrahere* "to draw away", from *ab-, abs-* + *trahere* "to draw"] — **ab·stract·ly** \ab-ˈstrak-tlē, -lē, ˈab-ˌ\ *adv* — **ab·stract·ness** \ab-ˈstrakt-nəs, -ˈstrak-, ˈab-ˌ\ *n*

[2]**abstract** \ˈab-ˌstrakt, *in sense 2 also* ab-ˈ\ *n* **1** : a brief statement of the main points or facts : SYNOPSIS ⟨an *abstract* of a book⟩ **2** : an abstract thing or state **3** : ABSTRACTION 4

[3]**ab·stract** \ab-ˈstrakt, ˈab-ˌ, *in sense 3 usually* ˈab-ˌ\ *vt* **1** : REMOVE, SEPARATE ⟨add or *abstract* baser metal during minting⟩ **2** : to consider apart from application to a particular instance ⟨*abstract* the idea of roundness from a ball⟩ **3** : to make an abstract of : CONDENSE **4** : to draw away the attention of **5** : to take away secretly or dishonestly : STEAL — **ab·strac·tor** *or* **ab·stract·er** *n*

ab·stract·ed \ab-ˈstrak-təd, ˈab-ˌ\ *adj* : PREOCCUPIED, ABSENTMINDED ⟨the *abstracted* look of a professor⟩ — **ab·stract·ed·ly** *adv* — **ab·stract·ed·ness** *n*

ab·strac·tion \ab-ˈstrak-shən\ *n* **1 a** : the act or process of abstracting : the state of being abstracted **b** : an abstract idea or term ⟨a mind full of *abstractions*⟩ **2** : inattention to one's surroundings : ABSENTMINDEDNESS **3** : abstract quality or character **4** : an artistic composition or creation characterized by designs that do not precisely represent actual objects or figures — **ab·strac·tive** \-ˈstrak-tiv\ *adj*

ab·strac·tion·ism \ab-ˈstrak-shə-ˌniz-əm\ *n* **1** : the creation of abstractions in art **2** : the principles or ideals of abstract art — **ab·strac·tion·ist** \-shə-nəst, -shnəst\ *adj or n*

ab·struse \ab-ˈstrüs, əb-\ *adj* : hard to understand : DEEP [Latin *abstrusus,* from *abstrudere* "to conceal", from *ab-, abs-* + *trudere* "to push"] — **ab·struse·ly** *adv* — **ab·struse·ness** *n*

ab·surd \əb-ˈsərd, -ˈzərd\ *adj* : ridiculously unreasonable, unsound, or incongruous [Middle French *absurde,* from Latin *absurdus,* from *ab-* + *surdus* "deaf, stupid"] — **ab•surd•ly** *adv* — **ab•surd•ness** *n*

ab•sur•di•ty \əb-ˈsərd-ət-ē, -ˈzərd-\ *n, pl* **-ties 1 :** the state of being absurd **2 :** something that is absurd

abun•dance \ə-ˈbən-dəns\ *n* **1 :** an ample or overflowing quantity **:** PROFUSION **2 :** AFFLUENCE, WEALTH ⟨a life of *abundance*⟩ **3 :** relative quantity or amount **:** degree of plentifulness ⟨the *abundance* of various species⟩

abun•dant \-dənt\ *adj* **:** existing in or having abundance **:** ABOUNDING [Latin *abundare* "to abound"] **syn** see PLENTIFUL — **abun•dant•ly** *adv*

[1]**abuse** \ə-ˈbyüz\ *vt* **1 :** to attack in words **:** REVILE **2 :** to put to a wrong or improper use **:** MISUSE ⟨*abuse* a privilege⟩ **3 :** to use so as to injure or damage **:** MALTREAT ⟨*abused* the car⟩ ⟨*abused* the dog⟩ [Middle French *abuser,* from Latin *abuti* "to misuse", from *ab-* + *uti* "to use"] — **abus•er** *n*

[2]**abuse** \ə-ˈbyüs\ *n* **1 :** a corrupt practice or custom ⟨election *abuses*⟩ **2 :** improper use or treatment **:** MISUSE ⟨drug *abuse*⟩ **3 :** abusive language **4 :** physical maltreatment ⟨child *abuse*⟩ • **syn** ABUSE, INVECTIVE, VITUPERATION mean vigorous condemnation. ABUSE stresses the offensive character of the language used; INVECTIVE may add additional suggestion of logical effectiveness and serious purpose in directing abuse; VITUPERATION suggests an unrestrained torrent of abuse.

abu•sive \ə-ˈbyü-siv, -ziv\ *adj* **1 :** expressive of or characterized by disrespect or contempt ⟨an *abusive* manner⟩; *esp* **:** containing or using harsh insulting language **2 :** physically injurious — **abu•sive•ly** *adv* — **abu•sive•ness** *n*

abut \ə-ˈbət\ *vb* **abut•ted; abut•ting 1 :** to touch along a border or with a projecting part **:** BORDER ⟨the farm *abuts* on the road⟩ ⟨stores *abut* the sidewalk⟩ **2 a :** to terminate at a point of contact **b :** to lean for support [Old French *abouter,* from *a* "to" + *bout* "end"] — **abut•ter** *n*

abut•ment \ə-ˈbət-mənt\ *n* **1 :** the action or place of abutting **2 :** something against which another thing rests its weight or pushes with force ⟨*abutments* that support a bridge⟩

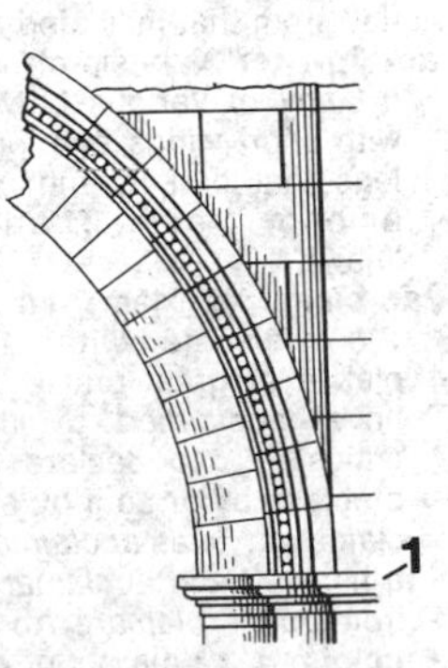

1 abutment of an arch

abut•tals \ə-ˈbət-lz\ *n pl* **:** the boundaries of lands with respect to adjacent lands

abysm \ə-ˈbiz-əm\ *n* **:** ABYSS [Old French *abisme,* from Late Latin *abyssus*]

abys•mal \ə-ˈbiz-məl\ *adj* **1 :** resembling an abyss **:** immeasurably deep **2 :** ABYSSAL 2 — **abys•mal•ly** \-mə-lē\ *adv* • **syn** ABYSMAL, ABYSSAL mean unfathomable by ordinary means. ABYSMAL applies chiefly to figurative depths that seem to be without a lower limit ⟨*abysmal* ignorance⟩ ⟨*abysmal* poverty⟩ ABYSSAL refers to the ocean bottom at great depths ⟨fauna of the *abyssal* zone⟩ ⟨*abyssal* sediments⟩.

abyss \ə-ˈbis\ *n* **1 :** the bottomless gulf, pit, or chaos in old accounts of the origins of the universe **2 :** an immeasurably deep gulf or great space [Late Latin *abyssus,* from Greek *abyssos,* from *abyssos* "bottomless", from *a-* + *byssos* "depth"]

abys•sal \ə-ˈbis-əl\ *adj* **1 :** UNFATHOMABLE **2 :** of or relating to the bottom waters of the ocean depths **syn** see ABYSMAL

Ab•ys•sin•i•an cat \ˌab-ə-ˌsin-ē-ən-, -ˌsin-yən-\ *n* **:** any of a breed of small slender cats of African origin with short brownish hair ticked with darker color

ac- — see AD-

-ac \ˌak, *in a few words* ik *or* ək\ *n suffix* **:** one affected with ⟨insomniac⟩ [Greek *-akos* "of or relating to"]

aca•cia \ə-ˈkā-shə\ *n* **1 :** any of numerous woody plants of the legume family with ball-shaped white or yellow flower clusters and often pinnate leaves **2 :** GUM ARABIC [Latin]

ac•a•deme \ˈak-ə-ˌdēm\ *n* **1 a :** a place of instruction **:** SCHOOL **b :** the academic environment **2 :** PEDANT 2

ac•a•dem•ic \ˌak-ə-ˈdem-ik\ *adj* **1 :** of or relating to school or college ⟨*academic* costume⟩ **2 :** literary or general rather than technical or vocational ⟨took the *academic* course⟩ **3 :** conforming to the traditions or rules of a school (as of literature or art) or an official academy **:** CONVENTIONAL ⟨*academic* verse⟩ **4 :** having no practical significance **:** THEORETICAL ⟨an *academic* question⟩ — **ac•a•dem•i•cal•ly** \-ˈdem-i-kə-lē, -klē\ *adv*

academic freedom *n* **:** freedom to teach or to learn without interference (as by government officials)

ac•a•de•mi•cian \ˌak-əd-ə-ˈmish-ən, ə-ˌkad-ə-\ *n* **:** a member of an academy for promoting science, art, or literature

ac•a•dem•i•cism \ˌak-ə-ˈdem-ə-ˌsiz-əm\ *also* **acad•e•mism** \ə-ˈkad-ə-ˌmiz-əm\ *n* **:** academic manner, style, or content **:** FORMALISM

acad•e•my \ə-ˈkad-ə-mē\ *n, pl* **-mies 1** *cap* **:** the school of philosophy founded by Plato **2 a :** a school usually above the elementary level; *esp* **:** a private high school **b :** an institution for training in special subjects or skills **3 :** a society of learned persons united to advance art, science, or literature [Greek *Akadēmeia,* gymnasium in the suburbs of Athens where Plato established his school]

Aca•di•an \ə-ˈkād-ē-ən\ *n* **1 :** a native or inhabitant of Acadia **2 a :** a Louisianian descended from French-speaking immigrants from Acadia **b :** a dialect of French spoken by Acadians

acan•thus \ə-ˈkan-thəs, -ˈkant-\ *n, pl* **acan•thus•es** *also* **acan•thi** \-ˈkan-ˌthī\ **1 :** any of a genus of prickly herbs of the Mediterranean region **2 :** an ornamentation representing the leaves of the acanthus [Greek *akanthos,* a kind of acanthus]

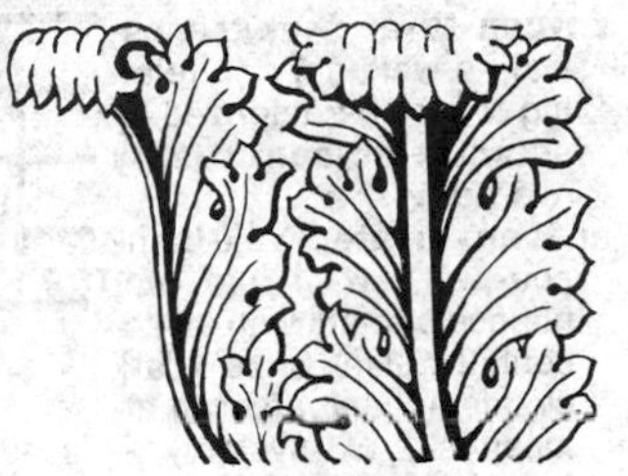
acanthus 2

a cap•pel•la *also* **a ca•pel•la** \ˌäk-ə-ˈpel-ə\ *adv or adj* **:** without instrumental accompaniment [Italian *a cappella* "in chapel style"]

ac•cede \ak-ˈsēd\ *vi* **1 a :** to become a party (as to an agreement) ⟨were invited to *accede* to the treaty⟩ **b :** to give consent **:** AGREE ⟨*accede* to a proposed plan⟩ **2 :** to enter upon an office or dignity ⟨*acceded* to the throne in 1838⟩ [Latin *accedere* "to go to", from *ad-* + *cedere* "to go"] **syn** see ASSENT

ac•ce•le•ran•do \ä-ˌchel-ə-ˈrän-dō\ *adv or adj* **:** gradually faster — used as a direction in music [Italian]

ac•cel•er•ate \ik-ˈsel-ə-ˌrāt, ak-\ *vb* **1 :** to bring about at an earlier time ⟨*accelerated* their departure⟩ **2 a :** to hasten the ordinary progress or development of **b :** to speed up (a course of study) **3 a :** to add to the speed of **b :** to cause to undergo acceleration; *esp* **:** to increase the velocity of **4 :** to move or progress faster [Latin *accelerare,* from *ad-* + *celer* "swift"] — **ac•cel•er•a•tive** \-ˌrāt-iv\ *adj*

ac•cel•er•a•tion \ik-ˌsel-ə-ˈrā-shən, ak-\ *n* **1 :** the act or process of accelerating **:** the state of being accelerated **2 :** change of velocity or the time rate of such change

acceleration of gravity : the acceleration of a freely falling body under the influence of gravity expressed as the rate of increase of velocity per unit of time with the value being about 980.616 centimeters per second per second

ac•cel•er•a•tor \ik-ˈsel-ə-ˌrāt-ər, ak-\ *n* **:** one that acclerates: as **a :** a pedal in a motor vehicle used for varying the supply of fuel-air mixture to the combustion chamber and so controlling the speed of the motor **b :** an apparatus for imparting high velocities to charged particles (as electrons and protons)

accelerator nerve *n* **:** a nerve which functions to increase the rate of the heartbeat

ac•cel•er•om•e•ter \ik-ˌsel-ə-ˈräm-ət-ər, ak-\ *n* **:** an instrument for measuring acceleration or vibrations

[1]**ac•cent** \ˈak-ˌsent\ *n* **1 :** a peculiar or characteristic manner of speech ⟨foreign *accent*⟩ ⟨southern *accent*⟩ **2 :** special prominence given to one syllable of a word or group of words in speaking especially by increase of stress or change of pitch ⟨*before* has the *accent* on the last syllable⟩ **3 :** rhythmically significant stress on the syllables of a verse usually at regular intervals **4** *archaic* **:** UTTERANCE **5 a :** a mark (as ˊ, ˋ, ˆ) used chiefly to indicate a specific sound value, stress, or pitch —

compare ACUTE, CIRCUMFLEX, GRAVE **b** : a mark (as ˈ or ˌ) identifying a syllable that is accented in speaking **6 a** : greater stress given to one musical tone than to its neighbors; *also* : a mark indicating this **b** : the principle of regularly recurring stresses which serve to distribute a succession of pulses into measures **7 a** : EMPHASIS 2 **b** : a small detail in sharp contrast with its surroundings **8** : a mark placed to the right of a letter or number and usually slightly above it: **a** (1) : a double prime (2) : PRIME 6 **b** : a mark used singly and doubly with numbers to denote respectively minutes and seconds of time or of an angle or arc or to denote respectively feet and inches **[**Middle French, from Latin *accentus,* from *ad-* + *cantus* "song, chant"**]**

²accent \ak-ˈsent, ˈak-ˌ\ *vt* **1 a** : to utter with accent : STRESS ⟨*accent* the first syllable of *after*⟩ **b** : to mark with a written or printed accent **2** : to give prominence to or increase the prominence of

accent mark *n* **1** : ACCENT 5 **2** : one of several symbols used to indicate musical accent

accent mark 2

ac•cen•tu•al \ak-ˈsench-wəl, -ə-wəl\ *adj* : of, relating to, or characterized by accent — **ac•cen•tu•al•ly** \-ē\ *adv*

ac•cen•tu•ate \ak-ˈsen-chə-ˌwāt\ *vt* **1** : to pronounce or mark with an accent **2** : EMPHASIZE ⟨dark clouds *accentuated* an atmosphere of mystery⟩ — **ac•cen•tu•a•tion** \ak-ˌsen-chə-ˈwā-shən\ *n*

ac•cept \ik-ˈsept, ak-\ *vb* **1** : to receive with consent or approval ⟨*accept* a gift⟩ ⟨was *accepted* as a member⟩ **2 a** : to receive as true **b** : to regard as proper, normal, or inevitable **c** : to take without protest : TOLERATE **3 a** : to make an affirmative or favorable response to ⟨*accept* an offer⟩ **b** : to undertake the responsibility of **4** : to assume an obligation to pay ⟨*accept* a bill of exchange⟩ **5** : to receive officially ⟨the Senate *accepted* the report⟩ **[**Middle French *accepter,* from Latin *acceptare,* from *accipere* "to receive", from *ad-* + *capere* "to take"**]** **syn** see RECEIVE — **ac•cept•er** *or* **ac•cep•tor** \-ˈsep-tər\ *n*

ac•cept•able \ik-ˈsep-tə-bəl, ak-\ *adj* **1** : capable or worthy of being accepted : SATISFACTORY ⟨an *acceptable* excuse⟩ **2** : barely adequate ⟨plays an *acceptable* game⟩ **3** : capable of being endured : TOLERABLE ⟨the maximum *acceptable* damage from nuclear attack⟩ — **ac•cept•abil•i•ty** \-ˌsep-tə-ˈbil-ət-ē\ *n* — **ac•cept•able•ness** \-ˈsep-tə-bəl-nəs\ *n* — **ac•cept•ably** \-blē\ *adv*

ac•cept•ance \ik-ˈsep-təns, ak-\ *n* **1 a** : the act of accepting **b** : favorable reception : APPROVAL **2** : the quality or state of being accepted or acceptable

ac•cep•ta•tion \ˌak-ˌsep-ˈtā-shən\ *n* **1** : ACCEPTANCE; *esp* : favorable reception **2** : the generally accepted meaning of a word or expression

ac•cess \ˈak-ˌses\ *n* **1** : a sudden outburst of intense feeling **2 a** : permission, liberty, or ability to enter, approach, communicate with, pass to and from, or make use of ⟨*access* to the president⟩ **b** : a way or means of approach ⟨a nation's *access* to the sea⟩ **3** : an increase by addition ⟨a sudden *access* of wealth⟩ **[**Latin *accessus* "approach", from *accedere* "to go to", from *ad-* + *cedere* "to go"**]**

ac•ces•si•ble \ak-ˈses-ə-bəl, ik-\ *adj* **1** : easy to reach ⟨*accessible* by train or car⟩ **2** : open to influence ⟨a mind *accessible* to reason⟩ **3** : OBTAINABLE ⟨*accessible* information⟩ — **ac•ces•si•bil•i•ty** \ˌak-ˌses-ə-ˈbil-ət-ē, ik-\ *n* — **ac•ces•si•ble•ness** \ak-ˈses-ə-bəl-nəs, ik-\ *n* — **ac•ces•si•bly** \-blē\ *adv*

ac•ces•sion \ak-ˈsesh-ən, ik-\ *n* **1** : something added : ACQUISITION ⟨new *accessions* to the museum⟩ **2** : ADHERENCE ⟨*accession* to a treaty⟩ **3 a** : increase by something added **b** : acquisition of additional property (as by growth or increase) **4** : the act of assenting or agreeing ⟨*accession* to a proposal⟩ **5** : the act of coming to high office or a position of honor or power ⟨the *accession* of a king⟩ **6** : ACCESS 1 — **ac•ces•sion•al** \-ˈsesh-nəl, -ən-l\ *adj*

¹ac•ces•so•ry *also* **ac•ces•sa•ry** \ak-ˈses-rē, ik-, -ə-rē\ *n, pl* **-ries** **1 a** : a thing of secondary or subordinate importance : ADJUNCT **b** : an object or device not essential in itself but adding to the beauty, convenience, or effectiveness of something else ⟨automobile *accessories*⟩ **2** : a person who aids or encourages another in the commission of a crime or an attempt to escape justice

²accessory *adj* : aiding or contributing in a secondary way : SUPPLEMENTARY

accessory fruit *n* : a fruit (as the apple or the strawberry) of which a conspicuous part consists of tissue other than that of the ripened ovary

ac•ci•dence \ˈak-səd-əns, -sə-ˌdens\ *n* : the part of grammar that deals with inflections

ac•ci•dent \ˈak-səd-ənt, -sə-ˌdent\ *n* **1 a** : an event occurring by chance or from unknown causes **b** : lack of intention or necessity : CHANCE ⟨we met by *accident*⟩ **2** : an unintended and usually sudden and unexpected happening and especially one resulting in loss or injury ⟨an automobile *accident*⟩ **3 a** : a nonessential property : ATTRIBUTE **b** : a chance circumstance ⟨the *accident* of noble birth⟩ **[**Middle French, from Latin *accidens* "nonessential quality, chance", from *accidere* "to happen, befall", from *ad-* + *cadere* "to fall"**]**

¹ac•ci•den•tal \ˌak-sə-ˈdent-l\ *adj* **1** : arising from secondary causes : NONESSENTIAL **2 a** : occurring unexpectedly or by chance ⟨an *accidental* discovery of oil⟩ **b** : happening without intent or from carelessness often with unfortunate results ⟨an *accidental* shooting⟩ — **ac•ci•den•tal•ly** \-ˈdent-lē, -ˈdent-l-ē\ *adv* — **ac•ci•den•tal•ness** \-ˈdent-l-nəs\ *n*

• **syn** ACCIDENTAL, CASUAL, FORTUITOUS mean happening by chance. ACCIDENTAL implies an absence of immediate intention ⟨an *accidental* discovery⟩ or reasonably foreseeable probability ⟨*accidental* death⟩ CASUAL stresses absence of prearrangement or premeditation ⟨*casual* encounters with friends⟩ FORTUITOUS stresses chance so strongly that it often connotes entire absence of cause ⟨*fortuitous* presence of a witness⟩

²accidental *n* : a note whose pitch is altered (as by a sharp or flat) from that indicated by the key signature

ac•cip•i•ter \ak-ˈsip-ət-ər\ *n* : any of various hawks with short wings and long legs that dart in and out among trees **[**Latin, "hawk"**]**

accipiter

¹ac•claim \ə-ˈklām\ *vb* **1** : to welcome with applause or great praise ⟨a novel *acclaimed* by the critics⟩ **2** : to declare or proclaim by or as if by acclamation ⟨was *acclaimed* a hero⟩ **[**Latin *acclamare,* from *ad-* + *clamare* "to shout"**]** — **ac•claim•er** *n*

²acclaim *n* **1** : the act of acclaiming **2** : APPLAUSE, PRAISE ⟨the symphony received worldwide *acclaim*⟩

ac•cla•ma•tion \ˌak-lə-ˈmā-shən\ *n* **1** : a loud eager expression of approval, praise, or assent **2** : an overwhelming affirmative vote by voice rather than by ballot ⟨elected by *acclamation*⟩

ac•cli•mate \ə-ˈklī-mət, ˈak-lə-ˌmāt\ *vt* : ACCLIMATIZE — **ac•cli•ma•tion** \ˌak-ˌlī-ˈmā-shən, -lə-\ *n*

ac•cli•ma•tize \ə-ˈklī-mə-ˌtīz\ *vb* : to adapt to a new temperature, altitude, climate, environment, or situation — **ac•cli•ma•ti•za•tion** \ə-ˌklī-mət-ə-ˈzā-shən\ *n*

ac•cliv•i•ty \ə-ˈkliv-ət-ē, a-\ *n, pl* **-ties** : a slope that ascends **[**Latin *acclivitas,* from *ad-* + *clivus* "slope"**]**

ac•co•lade \ˈak-ə-ˌlād\ *n* **1** : a ceremonial embrace **2** : a formal salute (as a tap on the shoulder with the blade of a sword) that marks the conferring of knighthood **3 a** : a mark of recognition of merit : COMMENDATION **b** : AWARD 1 **[**French, from *accoler* "to embrace", derived from Latin *ad-* + *collum* "neck"**]**

ac•com•mo•date \ə-ˈkäm-ə-ˌdāt\ *vb* **1 a** : to make fit or suitable : ADAPT **b** : to adapt oneself; *esp* : to undergo accommodation **2** : to furnish with something desired: as **a** : to provide with lodgings **b** : to have or make room for **[**Latin *accommodare,* derived from *ad-* + *commodus* "convenient, suitable"**]** **syn** see ADAPT, CONTAIN — **ac•com•mo•da•tive** \-ˌdāt-iv\ *adj* — **ac•com•mo•da•tive•ness** *n*

ac•com•mo•dat•ing *adj* : inclined to be helpful or obliging — **ac•com•mo•dat•ing•ly** \-ˌdāt-ing-lē\ *adv*

ac•com•mo•da•tion \ə-ˌkäm-ə-ˈdā-shən\ *n* **1 a** : something supplied for convenience or to satisfy a need **b** *pl* : lodging, food, and services or seat, berth, or other space occupied together with services available ⟨overnight *accommodations*⟩ **2** : the act of accommodating : the state of being accommodated: as **a** : the provision of what is needed or desired for convenience ⟨tables for the *accommodation* of picnickers⟩ **b** : an adjustment of differences : SETTLEMENT **c** : the automatic adjustment of the eye for seeing at different distances

ac•com•pa•ni•ment \ə-'kəmp-nē-mənt, -ə-nē-\ *n* **1** : music to support or complement a principal voice or instrument **2** : an accompanying object, situation, or event

ac•com•pa•nist \ə-'kəmp-nəst, -ə-nəst\ *n* : one (as a pianist) that plays an accompaniment

ac•com•pa•ny \ə-'kəmp-nē, -ə-nē\ *vb* **-nied**; **-ny•ing 1** : to go with or attend as an associate or companion **2** : to perform an accompaniment to or for **3** : to occur at the same time as or along with ⟨a thunderstorm *accompanied* by high winds⟩

ac•com•plice \ə-'käm-pləs, -'kəm-\ *n* : one associated with another in wrongdoing [archaic *complice* (in the phrase *a complice*), derived from Latin *com-* + *plicare* "to fold"]

ac•com•plish \ə-'käm-plish, -'kəm-\ *vt* : to bring to a successful finish : PERFORM [Middle French *acompliss-*, stem of *acomplir,* from Latin *ad-* + *complēre* "to fill up, complete"] — **ac•com•plish•able** \-ə-bəl\ *adj*

ac•com•plished *adj* **1** : ESTABLISHED ⟨an *accomplished* fact⟩ **2 a** : complete in skills or acquirements as the result of practice or training : EXPERT ⟨an *accomplished* pianist⟩ **b** : proficient in social graces : POLISHED ⟨an *accomplished* hostess⟩

ac•com•plish•ment \ə-'käm-plish-mənt, -'kəm-\ *n* **1** : the act of accomplishing : COMPLETION **2** : something accomplished : ACHIEVEMENT **3** : an ability, a social quality, or a special skill acquired by training or practice

[1]**ac•cord** \ə-'kȯrd\ *vb* **1** : to grant as suitable or proper ⟨*accords* the right of appeal⟩ **2** : to be in harmony : AGREE ⟨the decision *accords* with our sense of justice⟩ [Old French *acorder,* from Latin *ad-* + *cord-*, *cor* "heart"]

[2]**accord** *n* **1 a** : AGREEMENT, HARMONY ⟨were in *accord* with the company's policy⟩ **b** : an agreement between parties ⟨the disputants reached an *accord*⟩ **2** : voluntary or spontaneous impulse to act

ac•cor•dance \ə-'kȯrd-ns\ *n* **1** : AGREEMENT, CONFORMITY ⟨in *accordance* with a rule⟩ **2** : the act of according

ac•cor•dant \-'kȯrd-nt\ *adj* **1** : CONSONANT 1, AGREEING **2** : HARMONIOUS ⟨*accordant* tones⟩ — **ac•cor•dant•ly** *adv*

ac•cord•ing as *conj* **1** : in accord with the way in which **2 a** : depending on how **b** : depending on whether : IF

ac•cord•ing•ly \ə-'kȯrd-ing-lē\ *adv* **1** : in accordance : CORRESPONDINGLY ⟨believed they had won, and acted *accordingly*⟩ **2** : CONSEQUENTLY, so ⟨unable to find jobs, many graduates *accordingly* returned to school⟩

according to *prep* **1** : in agreement or conformity with ⟨lined up *according to* height⟩ **2** : as stated by ⟨*according to* our teacher⟩ **3** : depending on ⟨will succeed or fail *according to* circumstances⟩

[1]**ac•cor•di•on** \ə-'kȯrd-ē-ən\ *n* : a portable keyboard wind instrument in which the wind is forced past metallic reeds by means of a hand-operated bellows [German *akkordion*] — **ac•cor•di•on•ist** \-ē-ə-nəst\ *n*

[1]accordion

[2]**accordion** *adj* : folding or creased or hinged to fold like an accordion ⟨*accordion* doors⟩

ac•cost \ə-'kȯst\ *vt* : to approach and speak first to often in a challenging or aggressive way [Middle French *accoster,* derived from Latin *ad-* + *costa* "rib, side"]

[1]**ac•count** \ə-'kaůnt\ *n* **1** : a chronological record of debits and credits covering transactions involving a particular item, person, or concern **2** : a collection of items to be balanced **3** : an explanation of one's conduct **4 a** : a list of charged purchases and credits presented periodically **b** : the transactions between a business and an individual customer **5 a** : VALUE, IMPORTANCE ⟨a person of little *account*⟩ **b** : ESTEEM ⟨held in high *account*⟩ **6** : PROFIT, ADVANTAGE ⟨used our knowledge to good *account*⟩ **7 a** : a statement of reasons, causes, or motives **b** : a reason giving rise to an action or other result ⟨on that *account* we refused the offer⟩ **c** : careful thought : CONSIDERATION ⟨take *account* of the unexpected⟩ **8** : a statement of facts or events ⟨newspaper *accounts* of the trial⟩ **9** : HEARSAY, REPORT — usually used in pl. ⟨by all *accounts* a dedicated artist⟩ **10** : a sum of money deposited in a bank and subject to withdrawal by the depositor — **on account** : on credit — **on account of** : for the sake of : by reason of : because of — **on no account** : under no circumstances — **on one's account** : for one's benefit or sake ⟨don't do it just *on my account*⟩

[2]**account** *vb* **1** : to think of as ⟨*account* oneself lucky⟩ **2** : to furnish a detailed analysis or a justifying explanation ⟨*account* for your expenditures⟩ **3 a** : to be the reason ⟨poor diet *accounts* for many illnesses⟩ **b** : to bring about the capture or destruction of something ⟨*accounted* for two rabbits⟩ [Middle French *acompter,* from *a-* "ad-" + *compter* "to count"]

ac•count•able \ə-'kaůnt-ə-bəl\ *adj* **1** : responsible for giving an account (as of one's acts) : ANSWERABLE ⟨*accountable* to one's superiors⟩ **2** : capable of being accounted for : EXPLAINABLE — **ac•count•abil•i•ty** \-,kaůnt-ə-'bil-ət-ē\ *n* — **ac•count•able•ness** \-'kaůnt-ə-bəl-nəs\ *n* — **ac•count•ably** \-blē\ *adv*

ac•coun•tan•cy \ə-'kaůnt-n-sē\ *n* : the profession or practice of accounting

ac•coun•tant \ə-'kaůnt-nt\ *n* : a person professionally trained in the practice of accounting **syn** see BOOKKEEPER

ac•count•ing \ə-'kaůnt-ing\ *n* **1** : the system or practice of recording and analyzing money transactions of a person or business **2** : the action of giving an account ⟨management is required to make an *accounting* to the stockholders⟩

ac•cou•tre *or* **ac•cou•ter** \ə-'küt-ər\ *vt* **-cou•tred** *or* **-cou•tered**; **-cou•tring** *or* **-cou•ter•ing** \-'küt-ə-ring, -'kü-tring\ : to provide with equipment or furnishings : OUTFIT [French *accoutrer*]

ac•cou•tre•ment *or* **ac•cou•ter•ment** \ə-'kü-trə-mənt, -'küt-ər-mənt\ *n* **1** : the act of accoutring : the state of being accoutred **2** : EQUIPMENT; *esp* : a soldier's outfit other than clothes and weapons — usually used in pl.

ac•cred•it \ə-'kred-ət\ *vt* **1 a** : to send with credentials and authority to act as an official representative ⟨*accredit* an ambassador to France⟩ **b** : to vouch for as in conformity with a standard **c** : to recognize (an educational institution) as maintaining standards that qualify the graduates for admission to higher or more specialized institutions or for professional practice **2** : CREDIT 3 — **ac•cred•i•ta•tion** \ə-,kred-ə-'tā-shən\ *n*

ac•cre•tion \ə-'krē-shən\ *n* **1** : the process of growth or enlargement; *esp* : increase by external addition or accumulation **2** : a product or result of accretion [Latin *accretio,* from *accrescere* "to increase", from *ad-* + *crescere* "to grow"] — **ac•cre•tion•ary** \-shə-,ner-ē\ *adj*

ac•cru•al \ə-'krü-əl\ *n* **1** : the action or process of accruing **2** : something that accrues or has accrued

ac•crue \ə-'krü\ *vb* **1** : to come by way of increase or addition ⟨benefits *accrue* to society from education⟩ **2** : to accumulate over a period of time ⟨*accrued* interest⟩ [Middle French *acreue* "increase", from *acreistre* "to increase", from Latin *accrescere*] — **ac•crue•ment** \-mənt\ *n*

ac•cul•tur•a•tion \ə-,kəl-chə-'rā-shən\ *n* : modification of the culture of one or more peoples or of an individual through continuous and prolonged contact with an alien people — **ac•cul•tur•ate** \-'kəl-chə-,rāt\ *vb*

ac•cu•mu•late \ə-'kyü-myə-,lāt\ *vb* **1** : to pile up : AMASS ⟨*accumulated* old newspapers⟩ **2** : COLLECT, GATHER ⟨*accumulates* friends easily⟩ **3** : to increase in quantity, number, or amount ⟨rubbish *accumulates* quickly⟩ [Latin *accumulare,* derived from *ad-* + *cumulus* "heap, pile"] — **ac•cu•mu•la•tor** \-,lāt-ər\ *n*

• **syn** ACCUMULATE, AMASS mean to collect so as to form a large quantity. ACCUMULATE implies building up by successive small increases ⟨knickknacks *accumulate* dust⟩ AMASS suggests a more vigorous action during a limited time and applies

especially to a putting together of something valuable ⟨*amass* a fortune⟩
ac•cu•mu•la•tion \ə-ˌkyü-myə-ˈlā-shən\ *n* **1** : a collecting together : AMASSING **2** : increase or growth by addition especially when continuous or repeated ⟨*accumulation* of interest⟩ **3** : something that has accumulated or has been accumulated
ac•cu•mu•la•tive \ə-ˈkyü-myə-ˌlāt-iv, -lət-\ *adj* : CUMULATIVE — **ac•cu•mu•la•tive•ly** *adv* — **ac•cu•mu•la•tive•ness** *n*
ac•cu•ra•cy \ˈak-yə-rə-sē\ *n, pl* **-cies** **1** : freedom from mistake or error : CORRECTNESS **2 a** : conformity to a standard : EXACTNESS **b** : degree of conformity of a measure to a standard or a true value
ac•cu•rate \ˈak-yə-rət\ *adj* **1** : free from mistakes especially as the result of care **2** : conforming exactly to truth or to a standard : EXACT ⟨*accurate* instruments⟩ [Latin *accuratus,* from *accurare* "to take care of", from *ad-* + *cura* "care"] **syn** see CORRECT — **ac•cu•rate•ly** \-yə-rət-lē, -yərt-\ *adv* — **ac•cu•rate•ness** \-nəs\ *n*
ac•cursed \ə-ˈkərst, -ˈkər-səd\ *or* **ac•curst** \ə-ˈkərst\ *adj* **1** : being under a curse **2** : DETESTABLE, DAMNABLE — **ac•curs•ed•ly** \-ˈkər-səd-lē\ *adv* — **ac•curs•ed•ness** \-ˈkər-səd-nəs\ *n*
ac•cus•al \ə-ˈkyü-zəl\ *n* : ACCUSATION
ac•cu•sa•tion \ˌak-yə-ˈzā-shən\ *n* **1** : the act of accusing : the state or fact of being accused **2** : a charge of wrongdoing
ac•cu•sa•tive \ə-ˈkyü-zət-iv\ *adj* **1** : of, relating to, or constituting the grammatical case that marks the direct object of a verb or the object of any of several prepositions — compare OBJECTIVE **2** : ACCUSATORY — **accusative** *n*
ac•cu•sa•to•ry \ə-ˈkyü-zə-ˌtōr-ē, -ˌtȯr-\ *adj* : expressing accusation
ac•cuse \ə-ˈkyüz\ *vb* : to charge with a fault or wrong or especially with a criminal offense [Old French *acuser,* from Latin *accusare* "to call to account", from *ad-* + *causa* "lawsuit, cause"] — **ac•cus•er** *n* — **ac•cus•ing•ly** \-ˈkyü-zing-lē\ *adv*
ac•cused \ə-ˈkyüzd\ *n, pl* **accused** : one charged with an offense; *esp* : the defendant in a criminal case
ac•cus•tom \ə-ˈkəs-təm\ *vt* : to make familiar through use or experience : HABITUATE
ac•cus•tomed \-təmd\ *adj* **1** : familiar through use or long experience **2** : being in the habit or custom ⟨*accustomed* to making decisions⟩ **syn** see USUAL
[1]**ace** \ˈās\ *n* **1 a** : a die face or domino end marked with one spot **b** : a playing card bearing in its center one large pip **2** : a very small amount or degree ⟨came within an *ace* of winning⟩ **3** : a point scored on a stroke (as in tennis) that an opponent fails to touch **4** : a golf hole made in one stroke **5** : a combat pilot who has brought down at least five enemy airplanes **6** : one that excels at something [Old French *as,* from Latin, "unit, a copper coin"]
[2]**ace** *vt* **1** : to score an ace against (as a tennis opponent) **2** : to earn a grade of A on (an examination)
[3]**ace** *adj* : of first or high rank or quality ⟨an *ace* reporter⟩
acel•lu•lar \ˈā-ˈsel-yə-lər\ *adj* : not made up of cells
-a•ceous \ˈā-shəs\ *adj suffix* **1** : characterized by : consisting of : having the nature or form of ⟨carbon*aceous*⟩ ⟨sapon*aceous*⟩ **2** : of or relating to a group of animals characterized by (such) a form or (such) a feature ⟨cet*aceous*⟩ ⟨test*aceous*⟩ [Latin *-aceus*]
acerb \ə-ˈsərb, a-\ *adj* : ACID 2 [Latin *acerbus,* from *acer* "sharp"]
acer•bic\ə-ˈsər-bik\ *adj* : ACERB — **acer•bi•cal•ly** \-bi-kə-lē, -klē\ *adv*
acer•bi•ty\ə-ˈsər-bət-ē\ *n, pl* **-ties** : sharpness of temper, manner, or tone
acet- *or* **aceto-** *combining form* : acetic acid : acetic ⟨*acetyl*⟩ [Latin *acetum* "vinegar"]
ac•e•tab•u•lum \ˌas-ə-ˈtab-yə-ləm\ *n, pl* **-lums** *or* **-la**\-lə\ : a cup-shaped socket (as in the hipbone) [Latin, literally, "vinegar cup"]
ac•et•al•de•hyde \ˌas-ə-ˈtal-də-ˌhīd\ *n* : a colorless volatile water-soluble liquid compound C_2H_4O used chiefly in making organic chemicals
ac•et•amin•o•phen \ˌas-ət-ə-ˈmin-ə-fən\ *n* : a crystalline compound $C_8H_9NO_2$ used in chemical synthesis and in medicine to relieve pain and fever
ac•et•an•i•lide *or* **ac•et•an•i•lid** \ˌas-ə-ˈtan-l-ˌīd, -l-əd\ *n* : a white crystalline compound C_8H_9NO made from aniline and acetic acid and used especially to check pain or fever
ac•e•tate \ˈas-ə-ˌtāt\ *n* **1** : a salt or ester of acetic acid **2** : cellulose acetate or one of its products **3** : a phonograph recording disc made of an acetate or coated with cellulose acetate
ace•tic \ə-ˈsēt-ik\ *adj* : of, relating to, or producing acetic acid or vinegar [Latin *acetum* "vinegar", from *acēre* "to be sour", from *acer* "sharp"]
acetic acid *n* : a colorless pungent liquid acid $C_2H_4O_2$ that is the chief acid of vinegar and that is used especially in synthesis (as of plastics)
ac•e•tone \ˈas-ə-ˌtōn\ *n* : a volatile fragrant colorless flammable liquid compound C_3H_6O used chiefly as a solvent and in organic synthesis
ace•tyl \ə-ˈsēt-l\ *n* : the radical CH_3CO of acetic acid
ace•tyl•cho•line \ə-ˌsēt-l-ˈkō-ˌlēn\ *n* : a compound $C_7H_{17}NO_3$ released at autonomic nerve endings that functions in the transmission of nerve impulses
ace•tyl•cho•lin•es•ter•ase \-ˌkō-lə-ˈnes-tə-ˌrās, -ˌrāz\ *n* : an enzyme that promotes the hydrolysis of acetylcholine
ace•tyl-coA \ə-ˌsēt-l-ˌkō-ˈā\ *n* : ACETYL COENZYME A
acetyl coenzyme A *n* : a compound $C_{25}H_{38}N_7O_{17}P_3S$ formed as an intermediate in metabolism and active as a coenzyme in biological reactions involving addition of an acetyl radical
acet•y•lene \ə-ˈset-l-ən, -l-ˌēn\ *n* : a colorless gaseous hydrocarbon C_2H_2 made especially by the action of water on calcium carbide and used chiefly as a fuel in welding and soldering and in organic synthesis
ace•tyl•sal•i•cyl•ic acid \ə-ˈsēt-l-ˌsal-ə-ˌsil-ik-\ *n* : ASPIRIN 1
[1]**Achae•an** \ə-ˈkē-ən, -ˈkā-\ *adj* : of or relating to a group of city-states in the southern part of ancient Greece forming a political confederation about 280 B.C.
[2]**Achaean** *n* **1** : one of a Greek people dominant on the Greek mainland from 1600 to 1100 B.C. **2** : a Greek of the Homeric period
[1]**ache** \ˈāk\ *vi* **1** : to suffer a usually dull persistent pain **2** : to long earnestly : YEARN [Old English *acan*]
[2]**ache** *n* : a usually dull persistent pain — **achy** \ˈā-kē\ *adj*
achene \ə-ˈkēn\ *n* : a small dry one-seeded fruit (as of the buttercup) that ripens without bursting its sheath [[2]*a-* + Greek *chainein* "to yawn"]
achieve \ə-ˈchēv\ *vb* **1** : to bring to a successful conclusion : ACCOMPLISH ⟨*achieved* our purpose⟩ **2** : to get by effort : WIN ⟨*achieve* greatness⟩ [Middle French *achever,* from *a-* "ad-" + *chief* "head"] — **achiev•able** \-ˈchē-və-bəl\ *adj* — **achiev•er** *n*
achieve•ment \-mənt\ *n* **1** : the act of achieving **2** : something achieved especially by great effort or persistence ⟨heroic *achievements* of the early settlers⟩ **syn** see FEAT
Achil•les' heel \ə-ˌkil-ēz-ˈhēl\ *n* : a vulnerable point [from the legend that Achilles was vulnerable only in the heel]
Achilles tendon *n* : the strong tendon joining the muscles in the calf of the leg to the bone of the heel
achon•dro•pla•sia \ˌā-ˌkän-drə-ˈplā-zhē-ə, -zhə\ *n* : failure of normal development of cartilage resulting in dwarfism [[2]*a-* + Greek *chondros* "grain, cartilage"] — **achon•dro•plas•tic** \-ˈplas-tik\ *adj*
ach•ro•mat•ic \ˌak-rə-ˈmat-ik\ *adj* **1** : giving an image practically free from colors not in the object ⟨*achromatic* lens⟩ **2** : being black, gray, or white : COLORLESS
[1]**ac•id** \ˈas-əd\ *adj* **1** : sour, sharp, or biting to the taste : resembling vinegar in taste **2** : sour in temper : CROSS ⟨*acid* remarks⟩ **3** : of, relating to, or having the characteristics of an acid [Latin *acidus,* from *acēre* "to be sour", from *acer* "sharp"] **syn** see SOUR — **ac•id•ly** *adv* — **ac•id•ness** *n*
[2]**acid** *n* **1** : a sour substance **2** : any of various typically water-soluble and sour compounds that are capable of reacting with a base to form a salt, that redden litmus, that are hydrogen-containing molecules or ions able to give up a proton to a base, or that are substances able to accept an unshared pair of electrons from a base **3** : LSD
ac•id-fast \ˈas-əd-ˌfast\ *adj* : not easily decolorized by acids
acid•ic \ə-ˈsid-ik\ *adj* **1** : acid-forming **2** : ACID
acid•i•fy \ə-ˈsid-ə-ˌfī\ *vb* **-fied**; **-fy•ing** **1** : to make or become acid **2** : to change into an acid — **acid•i•fi•ca•tion** \ə-ˌsid-ə-fə-ˈkā-shən\ *n*
acid•i•ty \ə-ˈsid-ət-ē\ *n, pl* **-ties** **1** : the quality, state, or degree of being acid : TARTNESS **2** : the quality or state of being abnormally or excessively acid : HYPERACIDITY

ac·i·do·sis \ˌas-ə-ˈdō-səs\ *n* : an abnormal state of reduced alkalinity of the blood and of the body tissues — **ac·i·dot·ic** \-ˈdät-ik\ *adj*

acid test *n* : a severe or crucial test

acid·u·late \ə-ˈsij-ə-ˌlāt\ *vt* : to make acid or slightly acid — **acid·u·la·tion** \ə-ˌsij-ə-ˈlā-shən\ *n*

acid·u·lous \ə-ˈsij-ə-ləs\ *adj* : acid in taste or manner : HARSH ⟨an *acidulous* remark⟩

ack–ack \ˈak-ˌak\ *n* : an antiaircraft gun; *also* : antiaircraft fire [British signalmen's pronunciation of *AA*, abbreviation of *antiaircraft*]

ac·knowl·edge \ik-ˈnäl-ij, ak-\ *vt* **1** : to admit the truth or existence of ⟨*acknowledged* our mistake⟩ **2** : to recognize the rights, authority, or status of **3** : to make known that something has been received or noticed ⟨*acknowledge* a letter⟩ [*ac-* (as in *accord*) + *knowledge*] — **ac·knowl·edge·able** \-ij-ə-bəl\ *adj*

• **syn** ACKNOWLEDGE, ADMIT, CONFESS mean to disclose against one's will or inclination. ACKNOWLEDGE implies disclosing what has been or might be denied or concealed; ADMIT implies some degree of reluctance in disclosing or conceding; CONFESS implies admitting a weakness, failure, or guilt usually under compulsion.

ac·knowl·edged \-ijd\ *adj* : generally recognized or accepted ⟨the *acknowledged* leader of the group⟩ — **ac·knowl·edged·ly** \-ij-dlē, -ij-əd-\ *adv*

ac·knowl·edg·ment *or* **ac·knowl·edge·ment** \ik-ˈnäl-ij-mənt, ak-\ *n* **1 a** : the act of acknowledging **b** : recognition or favorable notice of an act or achievement **2** : a thing done or given in recognition of something received

ac·me \ˈak-mē\ *n* : the highest point : PEAK ⟨the *acme* of a scientist's ambition⟩ [Greek *akmē*]

ac·ne \ˈak-nē\ *n* : a skin disorder caused by inflammation of skin glands and hair follicles and characterized by pimples especially on the face [Greek *aknē* "eruption on the face", from *akmē*, literally, "point"]

ac·o·lyte \ˈak-ə-ˌlīt\ *n* **1** : a person who assists the clergyman in a service **2** : one that attends or assists : FOLLOWER [Medieval Latin *acoluthus*, from Greek *akolouthos* "following", from *a-*, *ha-* "same" + *keleuthos* "path"]

ac·o·nite \ˈak-ə-ˌnīt\ *n* **1** : any of a genus of poisonous usually blue-flowered or purple-flowered plants related to the buttercups — compare MONKSHOOD **2** : a drug obtained from the common Old World monkshood [Greek *akoniton*]

acorn \ˈā-ˌkȯrn, -kərn\ *n* : the nut of an oak tree [Old English *æcern*]

acorn squash *n* : an acorn-shaped dark green winter squash with a ridged surface and sweet yellow to orange flesh

acorn worm *n* : any of a group of burrowing marine animals resembling worms that have an acorn-shaped proboscis and are usually classed with the chordates

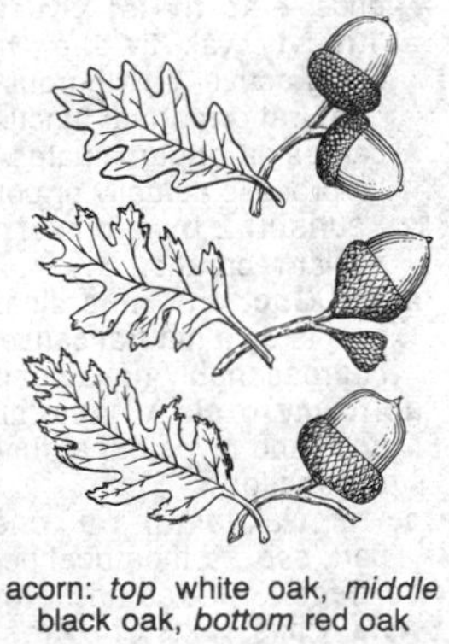

acorn: *top* white oak, *middle* black oak, *bottom* red oak

acous·tic \ə-ˈkü-stik\ *adj* **1** : of or relating to the sense or organs of hearing, to sound, or to the science of sounds: as **a** : deadening or absorbing sound ⟨*acoustic* tile⟩ **b** : operated by or utilizing sound waves **2** : of, relating to, or being a musical instrument whose sound is not electronically modified ⟨an *acoustic* guitar⟩ [Greek *akoustikos* "of hearing", from *akouein* "to hear"] — **acous·ti·cal** \-sti-kel\ *adj* — **acous·ti·cal·ly** \-sti-kə-lē, -klē\ *adv*

ac·ous·ti·cian \ˌak-ü-ˈstish-ən, ə-ˌkü-\ *n* : a specialist in acoustics

acous·tics \ə-ˈkü-stiks\ *n sing or pl* **1** : the science dealing with sound **2** *also* **acous·tic** \-stik\ : the qualities in a room or hall that make it easy or hard for a person in it to hear distinctly

ac·quaint \ə-ˈkwānt\ *vt* **1** : to cause to know socially ⟨became *acquainted* through mutual friends⟩ **2** : to make familiar ⟨*acquainted* us with our duties⟩ [Old French *acointier*, derived from Late Latin *accognoscere* "to know perfectly", from Latin *ad-* + *cognoscere* "to know"]

ac·quain·tance \ə-ˈkwānt-ns\ *n* **1** : knowledge gained by personal observation, contact, or experience ⟨had some *acquaintance* with the subject⟩ **2** : a person one knows but not intimately — **ac·quain·tance·ship** \-ˌship\ *n*

ac·qui·esce \ˌak-wē-ˈes\ *vi* : to accept, agree, or comply silently or passively [French *acquiescer*, from Latin *acquiescere*, from *ad-* + *quiescere* "to be quiet"] — **ac·qui·es·cence** \-ˈes-ns\ *n*

ac·qui·es·cent \-ˈes-nt\ *adj* : acquiescing or disposed to acquiesce — **ac·qui·es·cent·ly** *adv*

ac·quire \ə-ˈkwīr\ *vt* **1** : to come into possession of especially by one's own efforts : GAIN ⟨*acquired* great wealth⟩ **2 a** : to come to have as a characteristic, trait, or ability often by sustained effort ⟨*acquired* good study skills⟩ **b** : to develop after birth usually as a result of environmental forces ⟨an *acquired* disease⟩ **3** : to locate and hold (a desired object) in a detector ⟨*acquire* a target by radar⟩ [Middle French *aquerre*, from Latin *acquirere*, from *ad-* + *quaerere* "to seek"] — **ac·quir·able** \-ˈkwī-rə-bəl\ *adj*

ac·quire·ment \-ˈkwīr-mənt\ *n* **1** : the act of acquiring **2** : an attainment of mind or body usually resulting from continued effort ⟨the *acquirements* expected of a high-school graduate⟩

ac·qui·si·tion \ˌak-wə-ˈzish-ən\ *n* **1** : the act of acquiring ⟨the *acquisition* of property⟩ **2** : something acquired or gained ⟨the book was a recent *acquisition*⟩ [Latin *acquisitio*, from *acquirere* "to acquire"]

ac·quis·i·tive \ə-ˈkwiz-ət-iv\ *adj* : strongly desirous of acquiring — **ac·quis·i·tive·ly** *adv* — **ac·quis·i·tive·ness** *n*

ac·quit \ə-ˈkwit\ *vt* **ac·quit·ted**; **ac·quit·ting** **1** : to set free or discharge completely (as from an obligation or accusation) ⟨the court *acquitted* the prisoner⟩ **2** : to conduct (oneself) usually satisfactorily ⟨the recruits *acquitted* themselves like veterans⟩ [Old French *aquiter*, from *a-* "ad-" + *quite* "free, quit"] — **ac·quit·ter** *n*

ac·quit·tal \ə-ˈkwit-l\ *n* : the setting free of a person from the charge of an offense by verdict, sentence, or other legal process

ac·quit·tance \-ns\ *n* : a document (as a receipt) showing a release from an obligation

acr- *or* **acro-** *combining form* **1** : beginning : end ⟨*acro*nym⟩ **2 a** : peak : height ⟨*acro*phobia⟩ **b** : extremity of the body ⟨*acro*megaly⟩ [Greek *akros* "topmost, extreme"]

acre \ˈā-kər\ *n* **1** *pl* : LANDS, ESTATE **2** : a unit of area equal to 43,560 square feet (about 4047 square meters) — see MEASURE table **3** : a broad expanse or great quantity [Old English *æcer*]

acre·age \ˈā-kə-rij, -krij\ *n* : area in acres : ACRES

acre–foot \ˈā-kər-ˈfu̇t\ *n* : the volume (as of irrigation water) that would cover one acre to a depth of one foot and that is equal to 43,560 cubic feet (about 1233 cubic meters)

ac·rid \ˈak-rəd\ *adj* **1** : sharp and harsh or unpleasantly pungent in taste or odor : BITTER **2** : bitterly irritating to the feelings ⟨an *acrid* remark⟩ [Latin *acr-*, *acer* "sharp"] — **acrid·i·ty** \a-ˈkrid-ət-ē, ə-\ *n* — **ac·rid·ly** \ˈak-rəd-lē\ *adv* — **ac·rid·ness** *n*

ac·ri·mo·ni·ous \ˌak-rə-ˈmō-nē-əs\ *adj* : marked by acrimony : BITTER, RANCOROUS ⟨an *acrimonious* dispute⟩ — **ac·ri·mo·ni·ous·ly** *adv* — **ac·ri·mo·ni·ous·ness** *n*

ac·ri·mo·ny \ˈak-rə-ˌmō-nē\ *n*, *pl* **-nies** : harsh or biting sharpness especially of words, manner, or disposition [Latin *acrimonia*, from *acr-*, *acer* "sharp"]

ac·ro·bat \ˈak-rə-ˌbat\ *n* **1** : one that performs feats requiring agility and balance **2** : one adept at swiftly changing position or viewpoint [Greek *akrobatēs*, from *akros* "topmost" + *bainein* "to step, go"] — **ac·ro·bat·ic** \ˌak-rə-ˈbat-ik\ *adj* — **ac·ro·bat·i·cal·ly** \-ˈbat-i-kə-lē, -klē\ *adv*

ac·ro·bat·ics \ˌak-rə-ˈbat-iks\ *n sing or pl* **1** : the art or performance of an acrobat **2** : a striking performance involving great agility or maneuverability ⟨the soprano's vocal *acrobatics*⟩

ac·ro·meg·a·ly \ˌak-rō-ˈmeg-ə-lē\ *n* : a disorder caused by excessive secretion of the pituitary gland and marked by progressive enlargement of hands, feet, and face [*acr-* + Greek *megal-*, *megas* "large"] — **ac·ro·me·gal·ic** \-mə-ˈgal-ik\ *adj*

ac•ro•nym \'ak-rə-ˌnim\ *n* : a word (as *radar*) formed from the initial letter or letters of each of the successive parts or major parts of a compound term [*acr-* + *-onym* (as in *homonym*)]

ac•ro•pho•bia \ˌak-rə-'fō-bē-ə\ *n* : abnormal dread of being at a great height

acrop•o•lis \ə-'kräp-ə-ləs\ *n* : the upper fortified part of an ancient Greek city [Greek *akropolis*, from *akros* "topmost" + *polis* "city"]

¹across \ə-'kròs\ *adv* **1** : so as to reach or pass from one side to the other ⟨boards sawed directly *across*⟩ **2** : to or on the opposite side ⟨got *across* in a boat⟩ **3** : so as to be understandable, acceptable, or successful ⟨put a point *across*⟩ [Anglo-French *an crois-*, from *an* "in" + *crois* "cross", from Latin *crux*]

²across *prep* **1** : to or on the opposite side of ⟨*across* the street⟩ **2** : so as to intersect or pass at an angle ⟨lay one stick *across* another⟩ **3** : into an accidental meeting or contact with ⟨ran *across* an old friend⟩

across–the–board *adj* **1** : placed in combination to win, place, or show ⟨an *across-the-board* bet⟩ **2** : including or affecting all classes or categories ⟨an *across-the-board* wage increase⟩

acros•tic \ə-'kròs-tik, -'kräs-\ *n* : a composition usually in verse in which sets of letters (as the initial or final letters of the lines) taken in order form a word or phrase or a regular sequence of letters of the alphabet [Greek *akrostichis*, from *akros* "extreme" + *stichos* "line"] — **acrostic** *adj* — **acros•ti•cal•ly** \-ti-kə-lē, -klē\ *adv*

¹acryl•ic \ə-'kril-ik\ *adj* : of or relating to acrylic acid or its derivatives ⟨*acrylic* polymers⟩ [derived from Latin *acr-*, *acer* "sharp"]

²acrylic *n* **1 a** : ACRYLIC RESIN **b** : a paint in which the vehicle is acrylic resin **2** : ACRYLIC FIBER

acrylic acid *n* : an unsaturated liquid acid $C_3H_4O_2$ that polymerizes readily to form useful products (as a constituent of paint)

acrylic fiber *n* : a quick-drying synthetic textile fiber made by the polymerization of acrylonitrile

acrylic resin *n* : a glassy synthetic organic plastic used for cast and molded parts or as coatings and adhesives

ac•ry•lo•ni•trile \ˌak-rə-lō-'nī-trəl, -ˌtrēl\ *n* : a colorless flammable liquid C_3H_3N used chiefly in polymerization

¹act \'akt\ *n* **1** : something that is done : DEED ⟨an *act* of kindness⟩ **2** : the doing of something ⟨caught in the *act* of murder⟩ **3** : a law made by a governing body (as a legislature) ⟨an *act* of Congress⟩ **4 a** : one of the main divisions of a play or opera **b** : one of the successive parts of a variety show or circus **5** : a display of insincere behavior : PRETENSE [Latin *actus* "action" and *actum* "thing done", both derived from *agere* "to do"]

²act *vb* **1** : to represent or perform especially on the stage **2** : to play the part of ⟨*act* the villain⟩ **3 a** : to behave in a manner suitable to ⟨*act* your age⟩ **b** : to conduct oneself ⟨*act* like a fool⟩ **4** : PRETEND 2 **5** : to take action : MOVE ⟨think before you *act*⟩ **6 a** : to perform a specified function : SERVE ⟨trees *acting* as a windbreak⟩ **b** : to produce an effect : WORK ⟨wait for a medicine to *act*⟩ **7** : to make a decision ⟨*act* on a proposal⟩ — **act•abil•i•ty** \ˌak-tə-'bil-ət-ē\ *n* — **act•able** \'ak-tə-bəl\ *adj*

ACTH \ˌā-ˌsē-ˌtē-'āch\ *n* : a protein hormone of the anterior lobe of the pituitary gland that stimulates the cortex of the adrenal gland [adrenocorticotrophic hormone]

ac•tin \'ak-tən\ *n* : a protein of muscle that is active in muscular contraction [Latin *actus* "action"]

¹act•ing \'ak-ting\ *adj* : serving temporarily or in place of another ⟨*acting* president⟩

²acting *n* **1** : the art or practice of representing a character on a stage or before cameras **2** : affected behavior

ac•ti•nide \'ak-tə-ˌnīd\ *n* : a heavy radioactive metallic element in the series of increasing atomic numbers beginning with actinium or thorium and ending with lawrencium

ac•ti•nism \'ak-tə-ˌniz-əm\ *n* : the property of radiant energy by which chemical changes are produced — **ac•tin•ic** \ak-'tin-ik\ *adj*

ac•tin•i•um \ak-'tin-ē-əm\ *n* : a radioactive metallic element found especially in pitchblende [Greek *aktin-*, *aktis* "ray"] — see ELEMENT table

ac•ti•no•my•cete \ˌak-tə-nō-'mī-ˌsēt, -mī-'sēt\ *n* : any of an order (Actinomycetales) of filamentous or rod-shaped bacteria including soil saprophytes and disease producers [Greek *aktis* "ray" + *mykēs* "fungus"]

ac•ti•no•my•co•sis \ˌak-tə-nō-mī-'kō-səs\ *n* : infection with or disease caused by actinomycetes — **ac•ti•no•my•cot•ic** \-'kät-ik\ *adj*

ac•tion \'ak-shən\ *n* **1** : a proceeding in a court of justice by which one demands or enforces one's right or the redress or punishment of a wrong **2** : the working of one thing on another so as to produce a change ⟨the *action* of acids on metals⟩ **3** : the doing of something usually in stages or with the possibility of continuation ⟨the *action* of singing⟩ **4 a** : a thing done : DEED **b** *pl* : BEHAVIOR, CONDUCT **c** : readiness to engage in daring activity : INITIATIVE ⟨a person of *action*⟩ **5** : combat in war **6** : the unfolding of the events of a drama or work of fiction : PLOT **7** : an operating mechanism ⟨the *action* of a firearm⟩ **8** : an area or state of vigorous activity ⟨where the *action* is⟩

ac•tion•able \'ak-shə-nə-bəl, -shnə-\ *adj* : subject to or giving ground for a legal action or lawsuit ⟨*actionable* negligence⟩ — **ac•tion•ably** \-blē\ *adv*

ac•ti•vate \'ak-tə-ˌvāt\ *vt* : to make active or more active: as **a** : to make (as molecules) reactive **b** : to make (a substance) radioactive **c** : to treat (as carbon or alumina) so as to improve adsorptive properties **d** : to aerate (sewage) so as to favor the growth of organisms that cause decomposition **e** : to place on active duty ⟨*activate* the reserves⟩ — **ac•ti•va•tion** \ˌak-tə-'vā-shən\ *n* — **ac•ti•va•tor** \'ak-tə-vāt-ər\ *n*

ac•tive \'ak-tiv\ *adj* **1** : characterized by action rather than contemplation **2** : producing, requiring, or involving action or movement ⟨an *active* sport⟩ **3** : of, relating to, or constituting a verb form or voice indicating that the person or thing represented by the grammatical subject performs the action represented by the verb ⟨*hit* in "they hit the ball" is *active*⟩ **4** : quick in physical movement : LIVELY **5 a** : disposed to action : ENERGETIC ⟨*active* interest⟩ **b** : engaged in an action or activity : PARTICIPATING ⟨an *active* club member⟩ **c** : marked by vigorous activity : BUSY ⟨an *active* mind⟩ **6** : involving full-time service especially in the armed forces ⟨*active* duty⟩ **7** : marked by present action, operation, movement, or use ⟨an *active* account⟩ ⟨a student's *active* vocabulary⟩ **8 a** : capable of acting or reacting **b** : tending to progress or increase ⟨*active* tuberculosis⟩ — **ac•tive•ly** *adv* — **ac•tive•ness** *n*

active immunity *n* : immunity produced by the individual when exposed to an antigen — compare PASSIVE IMMUNITY

active transport *n* : movement of a substance by expenditure of energy through a gradient (as across a cell membrane) in concentration or electrical potential opposite to the direction of normal diffusion

ac•tiv•ism \'ak-ti-ˌviz-əm\ *n* : a doctrine or practice that emphasizes vigorous action (as a mass demonstration) for political ends — **ac•tiv•ist** \-vəst\ *n or adj*

ac•tiv•i•ty \ak-'tiv-ət-ē\ *n, pl* **-ties** **1** : the quality or state of being active **2** : vigorous or energetic action : LIVELINESS **3 a** : natural or normal function **b** (1) : a process that an organism carries on or participates in by virtue of being alive (2) : a similar process actually or potentially involving mental function **4 a** : PURSUIT 2 **b** : a form of organized, supervised, often extracurricular recreation

act of God: an extraordinary interruption of the usual course of events by a natural cause (as a flood or earthquake) that could not reasonably have been foreseen or prevented

ac•to•my•o•sin \ˌak-tə-'mī-ə-sən\ *n* : a contractile complex of actin and myosin that functions together with ATP in muscular contraction

ac•tor \'ak-tər\ *n* **1 a** : one that acts : DOER **b** : one that acts a part; *esp* : a theatrical performer **2** : PARTICIPANT

ac•tress \'ak-trəs\ *n* : a woman who is an actor

Acts \'aks, 'akts\ *or* **Acts of the Apostles** *n* — see BIBLE table

ac•tu•al \'ak-chə-wəl, -chəl; 'aksh-wəl\ *adj* **1 a** : existing in fact : EXISTENT ⟨our *actual* intentions⟩ **b** : really acted on or carried out ⟨in *actual* life⟩ ⟨the *actual* conditions⟩ **2** : not false : GENUINE **3** : present or active at the time [Middle French *actuel*, derived from Latin *actus* "act"] **syn** see REAL

ac•tu•al•i•ty \ˌak-chə-'wal-ət-ē\ *n, pl* **-ties** **1** : the quality or state of being actual **2** : something that is actual ⟨face the *actualities* of the situation⟩

ac•tu•al•ize \'ak-chə-wə-ˌlīz, -chə-ˌlīz, 'aksh-wə-\ *vb* : to make or become actual — **ac•tu•al•iza•tion** \ˌak-chə-wə-lə-'zā-shən, -chə-lə-, ˌaksh-wə-\ *n*

ac•tu•al•ly \'ak-chə-wə-lē, -chə-lē, 'aksh-wə-, 'aksh-lē\ *adv* : in fact : in truth : REALLY ⟨can *actually* read Latin⟩ ⟨*actually*, I haven't done it yet⟩

ac•tu•ary \'ak-chə-ˌwer-ē\ *n, pl* **-ar•ies :** one that calculates insurance and annuity premiums, reserves, and dividends [Latin *actuarius* "one who keeps accounts", from *actum* "thing done, record"] — **ac•tu•ar•i•al** \ˌak-chə-'wer-ē-əl\ *adj* — **ac•tu•ar•i•al•ly** \-ē-ə-lē\ *adv*

ac•tu•ate \'ak-chə-ˌwāt\ *vt* **1 :** to put into action ⟨the windmill *actuates* the pump⟩ **2 :** to move to action **:** arouse to activity ⟨the students were *actuated* by the hope of winning prizes⟩ [Medieval Latin *actuare,* from Latin *actus* "act"] **syn** see MOVE — **ac•tu•a•tion** \ˌak-chə-'wā-shən\ *n*

act up *vi* **:** to act or function in an unruly, abnormal, or annoying way

acu•ity \ə-'kyü-ət-ē\ *n* **:** keenness of perception **:** SHARPNESS ⟨visual *acuity*⟩ [Middle French *acuité,* derived from Latin *acutus* "sharp"]

acu•men \ə-'kyü-mən\ *n* **:** keenness of insight especially in practical matters **:** SHREWDNESS [Latin, literally, "point", from *acuere* "to make sharp"]

acu•punc•ture \'ak-yü-ˌpəng-chər, -ˌpəngk-\ *n* **:** an originally Chinese practice of puncturing the body (as with needles) to cure disease or relieve pain [Latin *acus* "needle" + English *puncture*]

acute \ə-'kyüt\ *adj* **1 a :** measuring less than a right angle ⟨*acute* angle⟩ **b :** composed of acute angles ⟨*acute* triangle⟩ **2 a :** marked by keen discernment or intellectual perception especially of subtle distinctions **:** PENETRATING **b :** responsive to slight impressions or influences ⟨*acute* observer⟩ **3 :** marked by sharpness or severity ⟨an *acute* pain⟩ **4 :** HIGH, SHRILL ⟨an *acute* sound⟩ **5 a :** having a sudden onset and short duration ⟨*acute* disease⟩ **b :** being at or near a turning point **:** URGENT, CRITICAL ⟨an *acute* situation that may lead to war⟩ **6 :** of, marked by, or being an accent mark having the form ´ [Latin *acutus* "sharp", from *acuere* "to sharpen", from *acus* "needle"] **syn** see SHARP — **acute•ly** *adv* — **acute•ness** *n*

ad \'ad\ *n* **:** ADVERTISEMENT 2

ad- *or* **ac-** *or* **af-** *or* **ag-** *or* **al-** *or* **ap-** *or* **as-** *or* **at-** *prefix* **1 :** to **:** toward — usually *ac-* before *c, k,* or *q* ⟨*ac*culturation⟩ and *af-* before *f* and *ag-* before *g* and *al-* before *l* ⟨*al*literation⟩ and *ap-* before *p* and *as-* before *s* and *at-* before *t* ⟨*at*tune⟩ and *ad-* before other sounds but sometimes *ad-* even before one of the listed consonants ⟨*ad*sorb⟩ **2 :** near **:** adjacent to — in this sense always *ad-* ⟨*ad*renal⟩ [Latin, from *ad* "to"]

-ad \ˌad, əd\ *adv suffix* **:** in the direction of **:** toward ⟨caud*ad*⟩ [Latin *ad* "to"]

ad•age \'ad-ij\ *n* **:** a saying often in metaphorical form that embodies a common observation [Middle French, from Latin *adagium*]

[1]**ada•gio** \ə-'däj-ō, -'däj-ē-ˌō, -'däzh-\ *adv or adj* **:** in an easy graceful manner **:** SLOWLY — used chiefly as a direction in music [Italian, from *ad* "to" + *agio* "ease"]

[2]**adagio** *n, pl* **-gi•os 1 :** a musical composition or movement in adagio tempo **2 :** a ballet duet by a man and woman or a trio of dancers displaying difficult feats of balance, lifting, or spinning

Adam *adj* **:** of or relating to an 18th century style of furniture characterized by straight lines, surface decoration, and conventional designs (as festooned garlands and medallions) [Robert *Adam,* died 1792, and James *Adam,* died 1794, Scottish designers]

[1]**ad•a•mant** \'ad-ə-mənt *also* -ˌmant\ *n* **1 :** a stone believed to be of impenetrable hardness **2 :** an extremely hard substance [Old French, from Latin *adamas* "hardest metal, diamond", from Greek]

[2]**adamant** *adj* **:** unshakable or immovable especially in opposition **:** UNYIELDING — **ad•a•man•cy** \-mən-sē\ *n* — **ad•a•mant•ly** *adv*

ad•a•man•tine \ˌad-ə-'man-ˌtēn, -ˌtīn\ *adj* **1 :** made of or having the quality of adamant **2 :** rigidly firm **:** UNYIELDING **3 :** resembling the diamond in hardness or luster

Ad•am's apple \ˌad-əmz-\ *n* **:** the projection in the front of the neck formed by the largest cartilage of the larynx

adapt \ə-'dapt\ *vb* **:** to make or become suitable; *esp* **:** to change so as to fit a new or specific use or situation ⟨*adapt* to life in a new school⟩ ⟨*adapt* the novel for children⟩ [Latin *adaptare,* derived from *ad-* + *aptus* "apt, fit"] — **adapt•abil•i•ty** \-ˌdap-tə-'bil-ət-ē\ *n* — **adapt•able** \-'dap-tə-bəl\ *adj*

• syn ADAPT, ADJUST, ACCOMMODATE, CONFORM mean to bring one into correspondence with another. ADAPT implies suiting or fitting by modification and may suggest pliability or readiness; ADJUST implies bringing into close or exact correspondence; ACCOMMODATE implies adapting or adjusting to by yielding or compromising; CONFORM implies bringing or coming into accord with a pattern or principle.

ad•ap•ta•tion \ˌad-ˌap-'tā-shən, -əp-\ *n* **1 :** the act or process of adapting **:** the state of being adapted **2 :** adjustment to environmental conditions: as **a :** adjustment of a sense organ to the intensity or quality of stimulation **b :** inherited modification of an organism that increases its chances for survival in its environment; *also* **:** a change or structure resulting from such modification **3 :** something that is adapted; *esp* **:** a composition rewritten into a new form ⟨the movie is an *adaptation* of the book⟩ — **ad•ap•ta•tion•al** \-shnəl, -shən-l\ *adj* — **ad•ap•ta•tion•al•ly** \-ē\ *adv*

adapt•ed \ə-'dap-təd\ *adj* **:** SUITABLE 1

adapt•er *also* **adap•tor** \ə-'dap-tər\ *n* **1 :** one that adapts **2 a :** a device for connecting two parts (as of different diameters) of an apparatus **b :** an attachment for adapting apparatus for uses not originally intended

adap•tive \ə-'dap-tiv\ *adj* **:** showing or having a capacity for or tendency toward adaptation — **adap•tive•ly** *adv*

ad•ax•i•al \'a-'dak-sē-əl\ *adj* **:** situated on the same side as or facing the axis especially of a plant

add \'ad\ *vb* **1 :** to join or unite to a thing so as to enlarge or improve it ⟨*add* a wing to the house⟩ **2 :** to introduce as an addition ⟨*add* sugar to tea⟩ ⟨let me *add* a word⟩ **3 :** to combine numbers into a single sum [Latin *addere,* from *ad-* + *-dere* "to put"] — **add•able** *or* **add•ible** \'ad-ə-bəl\ *adj*

ad•dax \'ad-ˌaks\ *n, pl* **ad•dax•es :** a large light-colored antelope of North Africa, Arabia, and Syria [Latin]

addax

ad•dend \'ad-ˌend, ə-'dend\ *n* **:** a number that is to be added to another number [short for *addendum*]

ad•den•dum \ə-'den-dəm\ *n, pl* **-den•da** \-'den-də\ **:** a thing added **:** ADDITION [Latin, from *addere* "to add"]

[1]**ad•der** \'ad-ər\ *n* **1 :** a poisonous European viper; *also* **:** any of several related snakes **2 :** any of several harmless North American snakes (as a hognose snake) [Middle English *nadder* (the phrase *a nadder* being understood as *an adder*), from Old English *nædre*]

[2]**add•er** \'ad-ər\ *n* **:** one that adds

ad•der's–tongue \'ad-ərz-ˌtəng\ *n* **1 :** a fern whose fruiting spike resembles a snake's tongue **2 :** DOGTOOTH VIOLET

[1]**ad•dict** \ə-'dikt\ *vt* **1 :** to devote or surrender (oneself) to something habitually or obsessively ⟨*addicted* to gambling⟩ **2 :** to cause (a person) to become physically dependent upon a drug [Latin *addicere* "to favor", from *ad-* + *dicere* "to say"]

[2]**ad•dict** \'ad-ikt, -ˌikt\ *n* **1 :** one who is addicted (as to a drug) **2 :** DEVOTEE 2 ⟨a detective novel *addict*⟩

ad•dic•tion \ə-'dik-shən\ *n* **1 :** the quality or state of being addicted ⟨*addiction* to reading⟩ **2 :** compulsive physical need for a habit-forming drug (as heroin)

ad•dic•tive \ə-'dik-tiv\ *adj* **:** causing or characterized by addiction ⟨an *addictive* drug⟩

Ad•di•son's disease \'ad-ə-sənz-\ *n* **:** a destructive disease marked by deficient secretion of the adrenal cortical hormone [Thomas *Addison,* died 1860, English physician]

ad•di•tion \ə-'dish-ən\ *n* **1 :** the result of adding **:** INCREASE **2 :** the act or process of adding **3 :** the operation of adding numbers to obtain their sum **4 :** a part added (as to a building) **5 :** direct chemical combination of substances into a single product — **in addition :** [1]BESIDES — **in addition to :** over and above

ad•di•tion•al \-'dish-nəl, -'dish-ən-l\ *adj* **:** being an addition **:** ADDED ⟨an *additional* charge⟩ — **ad•di•tion•al•ly** \-ē\ *adv*

[1]**ad•di•tive** \'ad-ət-iv\ *adj* **:** relating to, characterized by, or pro-

\ə\ **abut**	\aù\ **out**	\i\ **tip**	\ȯ\ **saw**	\ù\ **foot**
\ər\ **further**	\ch\ **chin**	\ī\ **life**	\ȯi\ **coin**	\y\ **yet**
\a\ **mat**	\e\ **pet**	\j\ **job**	\th\ **thin**	\yü\ **few**
\ā\ **take**	\ē\ **easy**	\ng\ **sing**	\t͟h\ **this**	\yù\ **cure**
\ä\ **cot, cart**	\g\ **go**	\ō\ **bone**	\ü\ **food**	\zh\ **vision**

duced by addition — **ad•di•tive•ly** *adv*

[2]additive *n* : a substance added to another in relatively small amounts to impart or improve desirable properties or suppress undesirable properties ⟨a gasoline *additive* intended to improve engine performance⟩ ⟨food *additives*⟩

additive identity *n* : an element (as zero in the set of real numbers) of a mathematical set that leaves every element of the set unchanged when added to it

additive inverse *n* : a number of opposite sign with respect to a given number so that addition of the two numbers gives zero ⟨the *additive inverse* of 4 is −4⟩

ad•dle \ˈad-l\ *vb* **ad•dled**; **ad•dling** \ˈad-ling, -l-ing\ **1** : to make or become confused **2** : to become rotten : SPOIL ⟨*addled* eggs⟩ **[**from earlier *addle* "rotten, empty", from Old English *adela***]**

[1]ad•dress \ə-ˈdres\ *vt* **1 a** : to direct the attention of (oneself) ⟨*addressed* myself to my work⟩ **b** : to deal with : TREAT ⟨failed to *address* the issues⟩ **2 a** : to communicate directly to a person or group ⟨*address* a petition to the governor⟩ **b** : to deliver a formal speech to ⟨*address* the convention⟩ **3** : to mark directions for delivery on ⟨*address* a letter⟩ **4** : to greet by a prescribed form **[**Middle French *adresser,* from *a-* "ad-" + *dresser* "to arrange, dress"**]** — **ad•dress•er** *n*

[2]ad•dress \ə-ˈdres, *for 4, 5, & 7 also* ˈad-ˌres\ *n* **1** : dutiful attention especially in courtship — usually used in pl. **2** : readiness and capability for dealing (as with a person or problem) skillfully **3 a** : BEARING, DEPORTMENT ⟨a person of rude *address*⟩ **b** : the manner of speaking or singing : DELIVERY **4** : a formal communication; *esp* : a prepared speech **5 a** : a place where a person or organization may be communicated with **b** : directions for delivery on the outside of an object (as a letter or package) **c** : the designation of place of delivery above the salutation on a business letter **6** : a location (as in the memory of a computer) where particular information is stored; *also* : the digits that identify it

ad•dress•ee \ˌad-ˌres-ˈē, ə-ˌdres-ˈē\ *n* : one to whom something is addressed

ad•duce \ə-ˈdüs, -dyüs\ *vt* : to offer as example, reason, or proof in discussion or analysis **[**Latin *adducere,* literally, "to lead to", from *ad-* + *ducere* "to lead"**]** — **ad•duc•er** *n*

ad•duct \ə-ˈdəkt\ *vt* : to draw (a part of the body) toward or past the median axis of the body; *also* : to bring (similar parts) together **[**Latin *adductus,* past participle of *adducere* "to lead to, adduce"**]** — **ad•duc•tive** \-ˈdək-tiv\ *adj*

ad•duc•tion \ə-ˈdək-shən\ *n* **1** : the action of adducting : the state of being adducted **2** : the act or action of adducing or bringing forward

ad•duc•tor \ə-ˈdək-tər\ *n* : a muscle that draws a body part toward the median axis — compare ABDUCTOR

-ade \ˈād\ *n suffix* **1** : act : action ⟨block*ade*⟩ **2** : product; *esp* : sweet drink ⟨lime*ade*⟩ **[**derived from Latin *-ata,* feminine of *-atus* "-ate"**]**

ad•e•nine \ˈad-n-ˌēn\ *n* : a purine base $C_5H_5N_5$ that is a constituent of ATP and that codes hereditary information in the polynucleotide chain of DNA and RNA — compare CYTOSINE, GUANINE, THYMINE, URACIL **[**Greek *adēn* "gland"; from its presence in glandular tissue**]**

[1]ad•e•noid \ˈad-n-ˌȯid, ˈad-ˌnȯid\ *or* **ad•e•noi•dal** \ˌad-n-ˈȯid-l\ *adj* **1** : of, relating to, or resembling glands or glandular or lymphoid tissue **2** : of or relating to adenoids or adenoid disorder **[**Greek *adenoeidēs* "glandular", from *adēn* "gland"**]**

[2]adenoid *n* : an enlarged mass of lymphoid tissue at the back of the pharynx characteristically obstructing breathing — usually used in pl.

aden•o•sine \ə-ˈden-ə-ˌsēn\ *n* : a compound $C_{10}H_{13}N_5O_4$ that is a constituent of RNA and ATP and that is composed of adenine and ribose **[**blend of *adenine* and *ribose***]**

adenosine di•phos•phate \-dī-ˈfäs-ˌfāt\ *n* : ADP

adenosine mo•no•phos•phate \-ˌmän-ə-ˈfäs-ˌfāt, -ˌmō-nə-\ *n* : AMP

adenosine tri•phos•phate \-trī-ˈfäs-ˌfāt\ *n* : ATP

[1]ad•ept \ˈad-ˌept\ *n* : a highly skilled or well-trained individual : EXPERT **[**New Latin *adeptus* "alchemist who has attained the knowledge of how to change base metals to gold", from Latin *adipisci* "to attain", from *ad-* + *apisci* "to reach"**]**

[2]adept \ə-ˈdept\ *adj* : thoroughly proficient : EXPERT **syn** see PROFICIENT — **adept•ly** *adv* — **adept•ness** \-ˈdep-nəs, -ˈdept-\ *n*

ad•e•quate \ˈad-i-kwət\ *adj* **1** : suitable or fully sufficient for a specific requirement **2** : barely sufficient or satisfactory ⟨their performance was *adequate* but not really good⟩ **[**Latin *adaequare* "to make equal", from *ad-* + *aequus* "equal"**]** **syn** see SUFFICIENT — **ad•e•qua•cy** \-kwə-sē\ *n* — **ad•e•quate•ly** \-kwət-lē\ *adv* — **ad•e•quate•ness** *n*

ad•here \ad-ˈhiər, əd-\ *vi* **1** : to give support or maintain loyalty (as to a cause or belief) **2** : to hold fast or stick by or as if by gluing **3** : to agree to observe ⟨*adhere* to a treaty⟩ **[**Latin *adhaerēre* "to stick to", from *ad-* + *haerēre* "to stick"**]** **syn** see STICK

ad•her•ence \-ˈhir-əns\ *n* **1** : the action or quality of adhering **2** : steady or faithful attachment : FIDELITY ⟨*adherence* to a cause⟩

[1]ad•her•ent \-ˈhir-ənt\ *adj* **1** : able or tending to adhere **2** : connected or associated with something ⟨nations *adherent* to the world organization⟩ — **ad•her•ent•ly** *adv*

[2]adherent *n* : one that adheres: as **a** : a follower of a leader or party **b** : a believer in or advocate of something (as an idea or church)

ad•he•sion \ad-ˈhē-zhən, əd-\ *n* **1** : steady or firm attachment : ADHERENCE **2** : the action or state of adhering **3** : the abnormal union of tissues by fibrous tissue following inflammation (as after surgery) **4** : the molecular attraction exerted between the surfaces of bodies in contact **[**Latin *adhaesio,* from *adhaerēre* "to adhere"**]** — **ad•he•sion•al** \-ˈhēzh-nəl, -ˈhē-zhən-l\ *adj*

[1]ad•he•sive \ad-ˈhē-siv, əd-, -ziv\ *adj* **1** : tending to remain in association or memory **2** : tending to adhere **3** : prepared for adhering : STICKY — **ad•he•sive•ly** *adv* — **ad•he•sive•ness** *n*

[2]adhesive *n* : an adhesive substance (as glue or cement)

adhesive tape *n* : tape coated on one side with an adhesive and used especially for fixing bandages or supporting injuries

ad hoc \ad-ˈhäk, ˈad-, -ˈhōk\ *adv or adj* : for the particular purpose or case at hand ⟨a decision made *ad hoc*⟩ ⟨an *ad hoc* committee⟩ **[**Latin, "for this"**]**

ad ho•mi•nem \ad-ˈhäm-ə-ˌnem, ˈad-\ *adj* : appealing to feelings or prejudices rather than intellect especially through attack on an opponent's character rather than response to the opponent's arguments ⟨an *ad hominem* argument⟩ **[**New Latin, literally, "to the man"**]**

adi•a•bat•ic \ˌad-ē-ə-ˈbat-ik, ˌā-ˌdī-ə-\ *adj* : occurring without loss or gain of heat ⟨*adiabatic* expansion of a body of air⟩ **[**Greek *adiabatos* "impassable", from *a-* + *dia-* + *bainein* "to go"**]** — **adi•a•bat•i•cal•ly** \-ˈbat-i-kə-lē, -klē\ *adv*

adieu \ə-ˈdü, -ˈdyü\ *n, pl* **adieus** *or* **adieux** \-ˈdüz, -ˈdyüz\ : FAREWELL 1 — often used interjectionally **[**Middle French, from *a* "to" + *Dieu* "God"**]**

ad in•fi•ni•tum \ˌad-ˌin-fə-ˈnīt-əm\ *adv or adj* : without end or limit **[**Latin**]**

ad in•ter•im \ad-ˈin-tə-rəm, ˈad-, -ˌrim\ *adv or adj* : for the intervening time ⟨serving *ad interim*⟩ ⟨an *ad interim* appointment⟩ **[**Latin**]**

ad•i•pose \ˈad-ə-ˌpōs\ *adj* : of or relating to animal fat : FATTY **[**Latin *adip-, adeps* "fat"**]** — **ad•i•pos•i•ty** \ˌad-ə-ˈpäs-ət-ē\ *n*

adipose tissue *n* : tissue in which fat is stored and which has the cells swollen by droplets of fat

ad•ja•cent \ə-ˈjās-nt\ *adj* **1 a** : not distant ⟨the city and *adjacent* suburbs⟩ **b** : having a common border ⟨a field *adjacent* to the road⟩ **2** : having a vertex or a vertex and side in common ⟨*adjacent* angles⟩ ⟨*adjacent* sides of a rectangle⟩ **[**Latin *adjacēre* "to lie near", from *ad-* + *jacēre* "to lie"**]** — **ad•ja•cen•cy** \-n-sē\ *n* — **ad•ja•cent•ly** *adv*

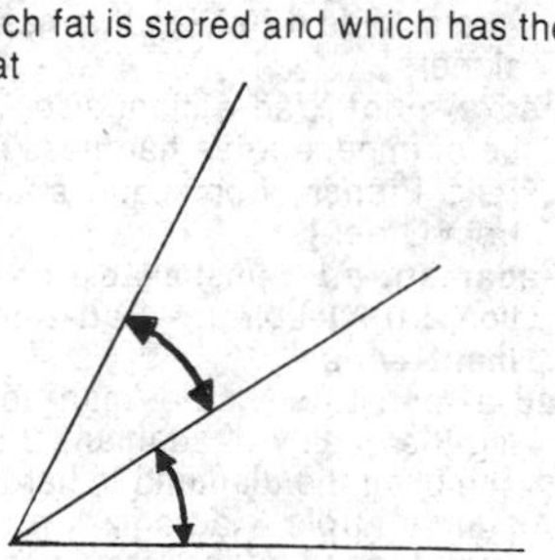

adjacent 2

ad•jec•ti•val \ˌaj-ik-ˈtī-vəl\ *adj* : ADJECTIVE — **ad•jec•ti•val•ly** \-və-lē\ *adv*

[1]ad•jec•tive \ˈaj-ik-tiv\ *adj* : of, relating to, or functioning as an adjective ⟨*adjective* clause⟩ **[**Late Latin *adjectivus,* from Latin *adjicere* "to throw to, add to", from *ad-* + *jacere* "to throw"**]** — **ad•jec•tive•ly** *adv*

[2]adjective *n* : a word typically serving as a modifier of a noun to denote a quality of the thing named, to indicate its quantity or extent, or to specify a thing as distinct from something else

ad·join \ə-ˈjȯin\ *vt* **1** : to add or attach by joining **2** : to lie next to or in contact with

ad·join·ing *adj* : touching or bounding at a point or line ⟨*adjoining* lots⟩

ad·journ \ə-ˈjərn\ *vb* **1** : to suspend further proceedings or business for an indefinite or stated period of time ⟨Congress *adjourned*⟩ ⟨*adjourn* a meeting⟩ **2** : to move to another place ⟨*adjourn* to the study after dinner⟩ [Middle French *ajourner,* from *a-* "ad-" + *jour* "day"] — **ad·journ·ment** \-mənt\ *n*

ad·judge \ə-ˈjəj\ *vt* **1** : to decide or rule upon as a judge : ADJUDICATE **2** : to hold or pronounce to be : DEEM ⟨*adjudged* the book to be a success⟩

ad·ju·di·cate \ə-ˈjüd-i-ˌkāt\ *vt* : to settle judicially ⟨*adjudicate* a claim⟩ [Latin *adjudicare,* from *ad-* + *judicare* "to judge"] — **ad·ju·di·ca·tive** \-ˌkāt-iv\ *adj* — **ad·ju·di·ca·tor** \-ˌkāt-ər\ *n*

ad·ju·di·ca·tion \-ˌjüd-i-ˈkā-shən\ *n* **1** : the act or process of adjudicating **2** : a judicial decision — **ad·ju·di·ca·to·ry** \-ˈjüd-i-kə-ˌtōr-ē, -ˌtȯr-\ *adj*

1**ad·junct** \ˈaj-ˌəngt, -ˌəngkt\ *n* **1** : something joined or added to another thing but not an essential part of it **2** : a word or word group that qualifies or completes the meaning of another word or other words and is not a major structural element in its sentence ⟨in the sentence "most children eat heartily", *most* is an *adjunct* to the subject *children* and *heartily* is an *adjunct* to the verb *eat*⟩ **3** : a person associated with or assisting another [Latin *adjunctum,* from *adjungere* "to adjoin", from *ad-* + *jungere* "to join"] — **ad·junc·tive** \a-ˈjəng-tiv, -ˈjəngk-\ *adj*

2**adjunct** *adj* **1** : added or joined as an accompanying object or circumstance **2** : attached in a subordinate or temporary capacity to a staff ⟨an *adjunct* psychiatrist⟩

ad·jure \ə-ˈju̇r\ *vt* **1** : to charge or command solemnly under or as if under oath **2** : to entreat or advise earnestly [Latin *adjurare,* from *ad-* + *jurare* "to swear"] — **ad·ju·ra·tion** \ˌaj-ə-ˈrā-shən\ *n* — **ad·jur·a·to·ry** \ə-ˈju̇r-ə-ˌtōr-ē, -ˌtȯr-\ *adj*

ad·just \ə-ˈjəst\ *vb* **1** : to bring to a more satisfactory state: **a** : SETTLE, RESOLVE ⟨*adjust* conflicts⟩ **b** : RECTIFY ⟨*adjust* an error⟩ **c** : to make correspondent or conformable : ADAPT **2** : to move the parts of an instrument or a piece of machinery until they fit together in the best working order ⟨*adjust* a watch⟩ ⟨*adjust* the brakes on a car⟩ **3** : to determine the amount of an insurance claim **4** : to adapt oneself to external conditions ⟨had to *adjust* to city living⟩ [French *ajuster,* from *a-* "ad-" + *juste* "exact, just"] **syn** see ADAPT — **ad·just·able** \-ˈjəs-tə-bəl\ *adj* — **ad·just·er** *also* **ad·jus·tor** \-ˈjəs-tər\ *n*

ad·just·ment \ə-ˈjəst-mənt, -ˈjəs-\ *n* **1** : the act or process of adjusting **2** : a settlement of a claim or debt **3** : the state of being adjusted **4** : a means of adjusting one part (as in a machine) to another ⟨an *adjustment* for focusing a microscope⟩ **5** : a correction or modification to reflect actual conditions — **ad·just·ment·al** \ə-ˌjəst-ˈment-l, -ˌjəs-\ *adj*

ad·ju·tan·cy \ˈaj-ət-ən-sē\ *n* : the office or rank of an adjutant

ad·ju·tant \ˈaj-ət-ənt\ *n* **1** : a staff officer (as in the army) assisting the commanding officer and responsible especially for correspondence **2** : one who helps : ASSISTANT [Latin *adjutare* "to aid"]

adjutant general *n, pl* **adjutants general** : the chief administrative officer of an army or of one of its major units (as a division or corps)

ad·ju·vant \ˈaj-ə-vənt\ *n* : something (as a drug or procedure) that enhances the effectiveness of medical treatment [Latin *adjuvare* "to aid"]

1**ad–lib** \ad-ˈlib, ˈad-\ *adj* : spoken, composed, or performed without preparation

2**ad–lib** *vb* **ad–libbed; ad–lib·bing 1** : to deliver spontaneously **2** : to improvise lines or a speech

ad lib *adv* : without restraint or limit [New Latin *ad libitum* "in accordance with desire"]

ad li·bi·tum \ad-ˈlib-ət-əm, ˈad-\ *adj* : omissible according to a performer's wishes — used as a direction in music [New Latin]

ad·man \ˈad-ˌman\ *n* : one who writes, solicits, or places advertisements

ad·min·is·ter \əd-ˈmin-ə-stər\ *vb* **ad·min·is·tered; ad·min·is·ter·ing** \-stə-ring, -string\ **1** : to manage or supervise the execution, use, or conduct of ⟨*administer* a trust fund⟩ **2 a** : to mete out : DISPENSE ⟨*administer* justice⟩ **b** : to give ritually ⟨*administer* last rites⟩ **c** : to give as a remedy ⟨*administer* a drug⟩ **3** : to furnish aid or relief ⟨*administer* to an ailing friend⟩ — **ad·min·is·tra·ble** \-strə-bəl\ *adj* — **ad·min·is·trant** \-strənt\ *n*

ad·min·is·tra·tion \əd-ˌmin-ə-ˈstrā-shən, ˌad-\ *n* **1** : the act or process of administering **2** : performance of executive duties : MANAGEMENT **3** : the execution of public affairs as distinguished from policy making **4 a** : a body of persons who administer **b** *cap* : the people who make up the political executive in a presidential government **c** : a governmental agency or board **5** : the term of office of an administrative officer or body

ad·min·is·tra·tive \əd-ˌmin-ə-ˌstrāt-iv, -strət-\ *adj* : of or relating to administration ⟨an *administrative* position⟩ **ad·min·is·tra·tive·ly** *adv*

ad·min·is·tra·tor \əd-ˈmin-ə-ˌstrāt-ər\ *n* **1** : one that is legally appointed to administer an estate **2 a** : one that administers especially business, school, or governmental affairs **b** : a priest appointed to administer temporarily a diocese or parish

ad·min·is·tra·trix \-ˌmin-ə-ˈstrā-triks\ *n, pl* **-is·tra·tri·ces** \-ˈstrā-trə-ˌsēz\ : a woman who administers an estate

ad·mi·ra·ble \ˈad-mə-rə-bəl, -mrə-bəl\ *adj* : deserving the highest esteem : EXCELLENT — **ad·mi·ra·ble·ness** *n* — **ad·mi·ra·bly** \-blē\ *adv*

ad·mi·ral \ˈad-mə-rəl, -mrəl\ *n* **1 a** : a naval officer of flag rank **b** : an officer rank in the Navy and Coast Guard above vice admiral **2** : any of several brightly colored butterflies [Medieval Latin *admirallus,* from Arabic *amīr-al-bahr* "commander of the sea"]

△ **origin** *Admiral,* in spite of its appearance, is not related to *admire.* It is a descendant of Arabic *amīr-al-baḥr* "commander of the sea". (*Amīr* means "commander"; *baḥr* means "sea"; *al* is the definite article.) When *amīr-al-* was borrowed into Latin in the Middle Ages, the insertion of a *d* into the word was probably influenced by the similar Latin word *admirari* "to admire". The two words are not otherwise connected. A relative of *admiral* is *emir,* also derived from Arabic *amīr.*

1**ad·mi·ral·ty** \ˈad-mə-rəl-tē, -mrəl-\ *n* **1** *cap* : a body of officials formerly having general authority over the British navy **2** : a court having jurisdiction of maritime questions

2**admiralty** *adj* : of, relating to, or having jurisdiction over maritime affairs ⟨*admiralty* law⟩

ad·mi·ra·tion \ˌad-mə-ˈrā-shən\ *n* **1** : an object of admiring esteem **2** : a feeling of delighted approval

ad·mire \əd-ˈmīr\ *vt* **1** *archaic* : to marvel at **2** : to look at with a feeling of pleasure ⟨*admire* the view⟩ **3** : to think highly of ⟨*admired* their capacity for work⟩ [Middle French *admirer,* from Latin *admirari,* from *ad-* + *mirari* "to wonder"] **syn** see REGARD — **ad·mir·er** \-ˈmīr-ər\ *n*

ad·mis·si·ble \əd-ˈmis-ə-bəl\ *adj* : that can be or is worthy to be admitted or allowed : ALLOWABLE ⟨*admissible* evidence⟩ — **ad·mis·si·bil·i·ty** \-ˌmis-ə-ˈbil-ət-ē\ *n*

ad·mis·sion \əd-ˈmish-ən\ *n* **1** : a granting of something that has not been fully proved ⟨an *admission* of guilt⟩ **2** : the act of admitting **3** : the right or permission to enter ⟨standards of *admission* to a school⟩ **4** : the price of entrance to a place [Latin *admissus,* past participle of *admittere* "to admit"] **syn** see ADMITTANCE — **ad·mis·sive** \-ˈmis-iv\ *adj*

ad·mit \əd-ˈmit\ *vb* **ad·mit·ted; ad·mit·ting 1** : to allow scope : PERMIT ⟨a question that *admits* of two answers⟩ **2** : to allow entry : let in ⟨*admit* a state to the Union⟩ **3** : to concede as true or valid ⟨reluctantly *admitted* failure⟩ [Latin *admittere* "to allow entry, permit", from *ad-* + *mittere* "to send, let go"] **syn** see ACKNOWLEDGE — **ad·mit·ted·ly** \-ˈmit-əd-lē\ *adv*

ad·mit·tance \əd-ˈmit-ns\ *n* : permission to enter a place : ENTRANCE

• **syn** ADMITTANCE, ADMISSION mean permitted entrance. ADMITTANCE applies usually to mere physical entrance into a building or locality; ADMISSION implies formal acceptance that carries with it rights, privileges, or membership.

ad·mix \ad-ˈmiks\ *vt* : MINGLE, MIX ⟨*admix* soil and gravel⟩ [back-formation from obsolete *admixt* "mingled (with)", from Latin *admixtus*]

ad·mix·ture \ad-ˈmiks-chər\ *n* **1 a** : the act of mixing ⟨made by *admixture* of chemicals⟩ **b :** the fact of being mixed **2 a :** something added by mixing **b :** a product of mixing : MIXTURE

ad•mon•ish \ad-'män-ish\ *vt* **1 :** to reprove gently but seriously : warn of a fault **2 :** to give friendly advice or encouragement to [Middle French *admonester,* from Latin *admonēre* "to warn", from *ad-* + *monēre* "to save, remind"] — **ad•mon•ish•er** *n* — **ad•mon•ish•ing•ly** \-'män-i-shing-lē\ *adv* — **ad•mon•ish•ment** \-'män-ish-mənt\ *n*

ad•mo•ni•tion \,ad-mə-'nish-ən\ *n* : a gentle or friendly reproof or warning [Middle French, from Latin *admonitio,* from *admonēre* "to admonish"]

ad•mon•i•to•ry \ad-'män-ə-,tōr-ē, -,tȯr-\ *adj* : expressing admonition : WARNING

ad nau•se•am \ad-'nȯ-zē-əm\ *adv* : to a sickening degree [Latin]

ado \ə-'dü\ *n* : FUSS, TROUBLE ⟨much *ado* about nothing⟩

ado•be \ə-'dō-bē\ *n* **1 :** a brick made of clayey mud dried in the sun **2 :** a building made of adobe bricks [Spanish, from Arabic *aṭ-ṭub* "the brick"]

adobe 2

ad•o•les•cence \,ad-l-'es-ns\ *n* : the state or process of growing up; *also* : the period of life from puberty to maturity

[1]ad•o•les•cent \-nt\ *n* : one that is in the state of adolescence : a person not fully mature [Latin *adolescere* "to grow up"]

[2]adolescent *adj* : of, relating to, or being in adolescence

adopt \ə-'däpt\ *vt* **1 :** to take legally as one's own child ⟨*adopt* an orphan⟩ **2 :** to take up and practice as one's own **3 :** to accept formally and put into effect ⟨the assembly *adopted* a constitution⟩ **4 :** to choose (a textbook) for required study in a course [Middle French *adopter,* from Latin *adoptare,* from *ad-* + *optare* "to choose"] — **adopt•abil•i•ty** \ə-,däp-tə-'bil-ət-ē\ *n* — **adopt•able** \ə-'däp-tə-bəl\ *adj* — **adopt•er** *n* — **adop•tion** \ə-'däp-shən\ *n*

adop•tive \ə-'däp-tiv\ *adj* : made by or associated with adoption ⟨*adoptive* parents⟩ — **adop•tive•ly** *adv*

ador•able \ə'dōr-ə-bəl, -'dȯr-\ *adj* **1 :** deserving to be adored **2 :** extremely charming ⟨an *adorable* child⟩ — **ador•abil•i•ty** \ə-,dōr-ə-'bil-ət-ē, -,dȯr-\ *n* — **ador•able•ness** *n* — **adorably** \ə-'dōr-ə-blē, -'dȯr-\ *adv*

adore \ə-'dōr, -'dȯr\ *vt* **1 :** WORSHIP ⟨*adore* God⟩ **2 :** to be extremely fond of [Middle French *adorer,* from Latin *adorare,* from *ad-* + *orare* "to speak, pray"] — **ad•o•ra•tion** \,ad-ə-'rā-shən\ *n* — **ador•er** \ə-'dōr-ər, -'dȯr-\ *n*

adorn \ə-'dȯrn\ *vt* : to decorate with ornaments : BEAUTIFY [Middle French *adorner,* from Latin *adornare,* from *ad-* + *ornare* "to furnish, ornament"]

• **syn** DECORATE, EMBELLISH: ADORN implies enhancing appearance by adding something beautiful in itself ⟨*adorned* with jewels⟩ DECORATE suggests relieving plainness or monotony by adding color or design ⟨*decorate* a birthday cake with colored icing⟩ EMBELLISH often stresses the adding of superfluous ornament ⟨*embellish* a page with floral borders⟩

adorn•ment \-mənt\ *n* **1 :** the action of adorning : the state of being adorned **2 :** something that adorns

ADP \,ā-,dē-'pē, ā-'dē-,pē\ *n* : a derivative of adenosine that is formed in living cells and is reversibly converted to ATP by the addition of a phosphate group [adenosine *di*phosphate]

[1]ad•re•nal \ə-'drēn-l\ *adj* **1 :** adjacent to the kidneys **2 :** of, relating to, or derived from adrenal glands or secretion

[2]adrenal *n* : ADRENAL GLAND

adrenal cor•ti•co•tro•phic hormone \-,kȯrt-i-kō-'trō-fik-\ *n* : ACTH

adrenal gland *n* : either of a pair of complex endocrine organs occurring one near each kidney and consisting of an outer cortex that produces steroid hormones and an inner medulla that produces adrenaline

Adren•a•lin \ə-'dren-l-ən\ *trademark* — used for a preparation of adrenaline

adren•a•line \-l-ən\ *n* : EPINEPHRINE

ad•ren•er•gic \,ad-rə-'nər-jik\ *adj* : liberating or activated by adrenaline or a substance like adrenaline ⟨an *adrenergic* nerve⟩ [Greek *ergon* "work"]

adre•nin \ə-'drēn-ən, -'dren-\ *n* : ADRENALINE

ad•re•no•cor•ti•cal \ə-,drē-nō-'kȯrt-i-kəl\ *adj* : of, relating to, or derived from the cortex of the adrenal glands

ad•re•no•cor•ti•co•tro•phic hormone \ə-,drē-nō-,kȯrt-i-kō-,trō-fik-\ *or* **ad•re•no•cor•ti•co•trop•ic hormone** \-,träp-ik-\ *n* : ACTH

adrift \ə-'drift\ *adv or adj* **1 :** without motive power, anchor, or mooring ⟨a damaged ship *adrift* in the storm⟩ **2 :** without guidance or purpose

adroit \ə-'drȯit\ *adj* **1 :** skillful in the use of the hands **2 :** showing shrewdness or resourcefulness in coping with difficulty or danger [French, from *à droit* "properly", from à "to, at" + *droit* "right"] **syn** see DEXTEROUS — **adroit•ly** *adv* — **adroit•ness** *n*

ad•sorb \ad-'sȯrb, -'zȯrb\ *vt* : to take up and hold by adsorption [*ad-* + *-sorb* (as in *absorb*)] — **ad•sor•bent** \-'sȯr-bənt, -'zȯr-\ *adj or n*

ad•sorp•tion \-'sȯrp-shən, -'zȯrp-\ *n* : the adhesion in an extremely thin layer of molecules (as of gases, solutes, or liquids) to the surfaces of solid bodies or liquids with which they are in contact — compare ABSORPTION — **ad•sorp•tive** \-'sȯrp-tiv, -'zȯrp-\ *adj*

ad•u•late \'aj-ə-,lāt\ *vt* : to flatter or admire excessively or slavishly [derived from Latin *adulari* "to flatter"] — **ad•u•la•tion** \,aj-ə-'lā-shən\ *n* — **ad•u•la•tor** \'aj-ə-,lāt-ər\ *n* — **ad•u•la•to•ry** \'aj-ə-lə-,tōr-ē, -,tȯr-\ *adj*

[1]adult \ə-'dəlt, 'ad-,əlt\ *adj* **1 :** fully developed and mature : GROWN-UP **2 :** of, relating to, or characteristic of adults [Latin *adultus,* past participle of *adolescere* "to grow up"] — **adulthood** \ə-'dəlt-,hu̇d\ *n* — **adult•ness** \ə-'dəlt-nəs, 'ad-,əlt-\ *n*

[2]adult *n* **1 :** a fully grown person, animal, or plant **2 :** a person having attained legal majority

adul•ter•ant \ə-'dəl-tə-rənt\ *n* : something used to adulterate another thing

adul•ter•ate \ə-'dəl-tə-,rāt\ *vt* : to weaken or make impure by adding a foreign or inferior substance; *esp* : to prepare for sale by replacing more valuable with less valuable ingredients [Latin *adulterare,* from *ad-* + *alter* "other"] — **adul•ter•a•tion** \ə-,dəl-tə-'rā-shən\ *n* — **adul•ter•a•tor** \-,rāt-ər\ *n*

adul•tery \ə-'dəl-tə-rē, -trē\ *n, pl* **-ter•ies** : voluntary sexual intercourse by a married person with anyone other than his or her spouse — compare FORNICATION [Latin *adulterium,* from *adulterare* "to adulterate"] — **adul•ter•er** \-tər-ər\ *n* — **adul•ter•ess** \-tə-rəs, -trəs\ *n* — **adul•ter•ous** \-tə-rəs, -trəs\ *adj* — **adul•ter•ous•ly** *adv*

ad•um•brate \'ad-əm-,brāt, ə-'dəm-\ *vt* **1 :** to foreshadow vaguely : INTIMATE **2 :** to suggest or disclose partially [Latin *adumbrare,* from *ad-* + *umbra* "shadow"] — **ad•um•bra•tion** \,ad-,əm-'brā-shən\ *n* — **ad•um•bra•tive** \ə-'dəm-brət-iv\ *adj* — **ad•um•bra•tive•ly** *adv*

ad va•lo•rem \,ad-və-'lōr-əm, -'lȯr-\ *adj* : based on a percentage of the monetary value of the goods ⟨an *ad valorem* tariff⟩ [Latin, "according to the value"]

[1]ad•vance \əd-'vans\ *vb* **1 :** to move forward ⟨*advance* a few yards⟩ **2 :** to further the progress of ⟨*advance* the cause of freedom⟩ **3 :** to raise to a higher rank : PROMOTE ⟨was *advanced* from clerk to assistant manager⟩ **4 :** to supply in expectation of repayment ⟨*advance* a loan⟩ **5 :** to bring forward : PROPOSE ⟨*advance* a new plan⟩ **6 :** to raise or rise in rate or price ⟨gasoline *advanced* another two cents⟩ [Old French *avancier,* from Latin *abante* "before", from *ab* "from" + *ante* "before"] — **ad•vanc•er** *n*

[2]advance *n* **1 :** a forward movement **2 :** progress in development : IMPROVEMENT **3 :** a rise in price, value, or amount **4 :** a first approach : OFFER **5 a :** a provision of something (as money or goods) before a return is received ⟨never ask for an *advance* on your salary⟩ **b :** the money or goods supplied — **in advance** : BEFORE, BEFOREHAND ⟨knew of the change two weeks *in advance*⟩ — **in advance of** : ahead of

[3]advance *adj* **1 :** made, sent, or furnished ahead of time ⟨an *advance* payment⟩ **2 :** going or situated before

ad•vanced \əd-'vanst\ *adj* **1 :** far on in time or course ⟨an *advanced* case of tuberculosis⟩ **2 a :** being beyond the elementary or introductory ⟨*advanced* mathematics⟩ **b :** being far along in progress or development ⟨an *advanced* civilization⟩

ad•vance•ment \əd-'vans-mənt\ *n* : the action of advancing : the state of being advanced: **a :** promotion to a higher rank **b :** progression to a higher stage of development

ad·van·tage \əd-ˈvant-ij\ *n* **1** : superiority of position or condition ⟨high ground gave the enemy the *advantage*⟩ **2** : BENEFIT, GAIN; *esp* : benefit resulting from a course of action ⟨changing jobs will be of *advantage* to you⟩ **3** : something that benefits its possessor ⟨speed is an *advantage* in sports⟩ **4** : the 1st point won in tennis after deuce [Middle French *avantage*, from *avant* "before", from Latin *abante*] — **to advantage** : so as to produce a favorable impression or effect

ad·van·ta·geous \ˌad-ˌvan-ˈtā-jəs, -vən-\ *adj* : giving an advantage : HELPFUL, FAVORABLE **syn** see BENEFICIAL — **ad·van·ta·geous·ly** *adv* — **ad·van·ta·geous·ness** *n*

ad·vec·tion \ad-ˈvek-shən\ *n* : the horizontal movement of a mass of air causing weather changes (as a drop in temperature) [Latin *advectio* "act of bringing", from *advehere* "to carry to", from *ad-* + *vehere* "to carry"] — **ad·vec·tive** \-ˈvek-tiv\ *adj*

Ad·vent \ˈad-ˌvent\ *n* **1** : a penitential season beginning four Sundays before Christmas **2** : the coming of Christ at the Incarnation or as judge on the last day **3** *not cap* : first or new appearance ⟨the *advent* of spring⟩ [Medieval Latin *adventus*, from Latin, "arrival", from *advenire* "to arrive, happen", from *ad-* + *venire* "to come"]

Ad·vent·ist \əd-ˈvent-əst, ad-ˈ, ˈad-ˌ\ *n* **1** : one who believes Christ's second coming near at hand **2** : SEVENTH DAY ADVENTIST — **Ad·vent·ism** \ˈad-ˌvent-ˌiz-əm\ *n* — **Adventist** *adj*

ad·ven·ti·tious \ˌad-vən-ˈtish-əs\ *adj* **1** : not inherent or fundamental ⟨*adventitious* additions to a plan⟩ **2** : appearing out of the usual or normal place ⟨*adventitious* buds⟩ [Latin *adventicius* "coming from outside", from *advenire* "to arrive"] — **ad·ven·ti·tious·ly** *adv* — **ad·ven·ti·tious·ness** *n*

Advent Sunday *n* : the first Sunday in Advent

[1]**ad·ven·ture** \əd-ˈven-chər\ *n* **1** : an undertaking involving unknown dangers and risks **2** : the encountering of risks **3** : an unusual experience [Old French *aventure*, from Latin *advenire* "to arrive, happen", from *ad-* + *venire* "to come"]

[2]**adventure** *vb* **-ven·tured**; **-ven·tur·ing** \-ˈvench-ring, -ə-ring\ **1** : RISK 1, VENTURE ⟨*adventure* their capital in foreign trade⟩ **2** : to proceed despite danger or risk

ad·ven·tur·er \-ˈvench-rər, -ə-rər\ *n* **1** : one that adventures: as **a** : SOLDIER OF FORTUNE **b** : one that engages in risky commercial enterprises for profit **2** : a person who lives by his wits : a smooth operator

ad·ven·ture·some \-ˈven-chər-səm\ *adj* : inclined to take risks : DARING

ad·ven·tur·ess \-ˈvench-rəs, -ə-rəs\ *n* : a woman adventurer; *esp* : one who lives by her wits

ad·ven·tur·ous \əd-ˈvench-rəs, -ə-rəs\ *adj* **1** : ready to seek adventure or to cope with the new and unknown **2** : characterized by unknown dangers and risks — **ad·ven·tur·ous·ly** *adv* — **ad·ven·tur·ous·ness** *n*

• **syn** VENTURESOME, DARING: ADVENTUROUS stresses a willingness to try the unknown regardless of possible or probable danger; VENTURESOME may stress the tendency to take chances; DARING heightens the implication of fearlessness in accepting risks that could be avoided.

ad·verb \ˈad-ˌvərb\ *n* : a word used to modify a verb, an adjective, another adverb, a preposition, a phrase, a clause, or a sentence and often used to show degree, manner, place, or time [Middle French *adverbe*, from Latin *adverbium*, from *ad-* + *verbum* "word, verb"] — **adverb** *adj*

ad·ver·bi·al \ad-ˈvər-bē-əl\ *adj* : of, relating to, or having the function of an adverb ⟨*adverbial* phrase⟩ — **adverbial** *n* — **ad·ver·bi·al·ly** \-bē-ə-lē\ *adv*

ad·ver·sary \ˈad-vər-ˌser-ē, -və-\ *n, pl* **-sar·ies** : one that contends with, opposes, or resists **syn** see OPPONENT

ad·ver·sa·tive \əd-ˈvər-sət-iv\ *adj* : expressing opposition or adverse circumstance ⟨the *adversative* conjunction *but*⟩ — **ad·ver·sa·tive·ly** *adv*

ad·verse \ad-ˈvərs, ˈad-ˌ\ *adj* **1** : acting in a contrary direction ⟨*adverse* winds⟩ **2** : actively opposed : ANTAGONISTIC ⟨a mind *adverse* to compromise⟩ **3** : having an unfavorable or harmful effect ⟨*adverse* criticism⟩ ⟨the *adverse* effects of a drug⟩ [Middle French *advers*, from Latin *adversus*, from *advertere* "to turn toward", from *ad-* + *vertere* "to turn"] — **ad·verse·ly** *adv* — **ad·verse·ness** *n*

ad·ver·si·ty \ad-ˈvər-sət-ē\ *n, pl* **-ties** : a condition or experience of serious or continued misfortune

ad·vert \ad-ˈvərt\ *vb* : to direct attention : REFER ⟨*advert* to a previous remark⟩ [Middle French *advertir*]

ad·ver·tise \ˈad-vər-ˌtīz\ *vb* **1** : to announce publicly especially by a printed notice or a broadcast ⟨*advertise* a sale⟩ **2** : to call public attention to especially by emphasizing desirable qualities so as to arouse a desire to buy or patronize ⟨*advertise* a breakfast food⟩ **3** : to issue or sponsor advertising ⟨*advertise* for a secretary⟩ [Middle French *advertiss-*, stem of *advertir* "to inform", from Latin *advertere* "to turn toward"] — **ad·ver·tis·er** *n*

ad·ver·tise·ment \ˌad-vər-ˈtīz-mənt, əd-ˈvərt-əz-\ *n* **1** : the act or process of advertising **2** : a public notice; *esp* : one published or broadcast

ad·ver·tis·ing \ˈad-vər-ˌtī-zing\ *n* **1** : the action of calling something to the attention of the public especially by paid announcements **2** : ADVERTISEMENTS **3** : the business of preparing advertisements for publication or broadcast

ad·vice \əd-ˈvīs\ *n* **1** : recommendation regarding a decision or course of conduct : COUNSEL **2** : information or notice given : NEWS — usually used in pl. [Old French *avis* "opinion"]

ad·vis·able \əd-ˈvī-zə-bəl\ *adj* : reasonable or proper under the circumstances : WISE, PRUDENT ⟨it is *advisable* to stay fit⟩ **syn** see EXPEDIENT — **ad·vis·abil·i·ty** \əd-ˌvī-zə-ˈbil-ət-ē\ *n* — **ad·vis·ably** \əd-ˈvī-zə-blē\ *adv*

ad·vise \əd-ˈvīz\ *vb* **1 a** : to give advice to : COUNSEL **b** : RECOMMEND ⟨they *advised* caution⟩ **2** : to give information or notice to : INFORM **3** : to take counsel : CONSULT ⟨they *advised* with their lawyer⟩ — **ad·vis·er** *or* **ad·vi·sor** \-ˈvī-zər\ *n*

ad·vis·ed·ly \-ˈvī-zəd-lē\ *adv* : with or after consideration : DELIBERATELY

ad·vise·ment \əd-ˈvīz-mənt\ *n* : careful consideration ⟨take a matter under *advisement*⟩

ad·vi·so·ry \əd-ˈvīz-rē, -ə-rē\ *adj* **1** : having the power or right to advise ⟨an *advisory* committee⟩ **2** : giving or containing advice ⟨an *advisory* opinion⟩ — **advisory** *n*

ad·vo·ca·cy \ˈad-və-kə-sē\ *n* : the act of advocating : public support ⟨*advocacy* of a proposal⟩

[1]**ad·vo·cate** \ˈad-və-kət, -ˌkāt\ *n* **1** : one that pleads the cause of another especially before a court **2** : one that argues for, recommends, or supports a cause or policy [Middle French *advocat*, from Latin *advocatus*, from *advocare* "to summon", from *ad-* + *vocare* "to call"]

[2]**ad·vo·cate** \-ˌkāt\ *vt* : to support or recommend openly ⟨*advocate* a new plan⟩

adz *or* **adze** \ˈadz\ *n* : a cutting tool that has a thin arched blade set at right angles to the handle and is used for shaping wood [Old English *adesa*]

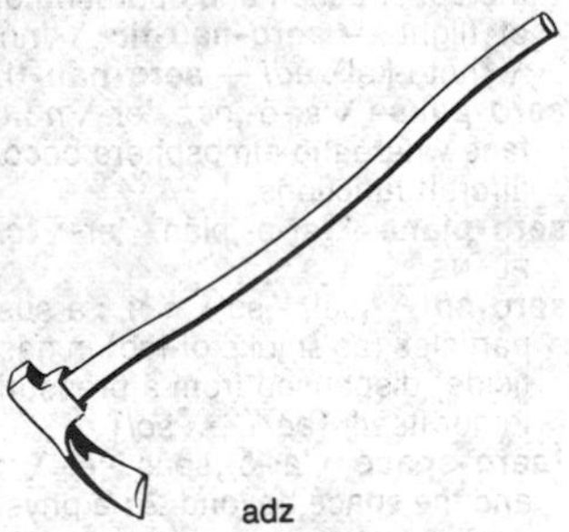

adz

ae \ˈā\ *adj, chiefly Scottish* : ONE [Middle English *a*]

ae·cio·spore \ˈē-sē-ə-ˌspōr, -ˌspȯr\ *n* : a spore formed in an aecium

ae·ci·um \ˈē-shē-əm, -sē-\ *n, pl* **-cia** \-shē-ə, -sē-ə\ : a fruiting body of a rust fungus in which the first binucleate spores are formed [Greek *aikia* "assault"] — **ae·cial** \ˈē-shē-əl, -shəl, -sē-əl\ *adj*

aë·des \ā-ˈēd-ēz\ *n, pl* **aëdes** : any of a genus of mosquitoes including carriers of disease (as yellow fever) [Greek *aēdēs* "unpleasant", from *a-* + *ēdos* "pleasure"]

ae·dile \ˈē-ˌdīl\ *n* : an official in ancient Rome in charge of public works and games, police, and the grain supply [Latin *aedilis*, from *aedes* "temple"]

ae·gis \ˈē-jəs\ *n* **1** : PROTECTION 1, DEFENSE **2** : PATRONAGE 1, SPONSORSHIP [Greek *aigis* "shield made of goatskin"]

-aemia — see -EMIA

ae·o·lian \ē-ˈō-lē-ən, -ˈōl-yən\ *variant of* EOLIAN

Aeolian *n* : one of a group of ancient Greeks colonizing Lesbos and the adjacent coast of Asia Minor

aeolian harp *n* : a box-shaped musical instrument that produces musical sounds when air currents pass over stretched strings

\ə\ **abut**	\au̇\ **out**	\i\ **tip**	\ȯ\ **saw**	\u̇\ **foot**
\ər\ **further**	\ch\ **chin**	\ī\ **life**	\ȯi\ **coin**	\y\ **yet**
\a\ **mat**	\e\ **pet**	\j\ **job**	\th\ **thin**	\yü\ **few**
\ā\ **take**	\ē\ **easy**	\ng\ **sing**	\t͟h\ **this**	\yu̇\ **cure**
\ä\ **cot, cart**	\g\ **go**	\ō\ **bone**	\ü\ **food**	\zh\ **vision**

ae•on *or* **eon** \'ē-ən, 'ē-,än\ *n* **1** : an immeasurably or indefinitely long period of time : AGE **2** : a unit of geologic time equal to one billion years [Latin, from Greek *aiōn*]
aer- *or* **aero-** *combining form* **1** : air : atmosphere ⟨*aer*ate⟩ **2** : gas ⟨*aero*sol⟩ **3** : aviation ⟨*aero*drome⟩ [Greek *aēr*]
aer•ate \'ar-,āt, 'er-\ *vt* **1** : to supply (blood) with oxygen by respiration **2** : to supply or impregnate with air **3** : to combine or charge with gas — **aer•a•tion** \,ar-'ā-shən, ,er-\ *n* — **aer•a•tor** \'ar-,āt-ər, 'er-\ *n*
1ae•ri•al \'ar-ē-əl, 'er-; ā-'ir-ē-əl\ *adj* **1 a** : of, relating to, or occurring in the air or atmosphere **b** : living or growing in the air rather than on the ground or in water **c** : operating or operated overhead on elevated cables or rails **2 a** : lacking substance : THIN **b** : IMAGINARY, IDEAL **3 a** : of or relating to aircraft **b** : designed for use in, taken from, or operating from or against aircraft — **ae•ri•al•ly** \-ē-ə-lē\ *adv*
2aer•i•al \'ar-ē-əl, 'er-\ *n* **1** : ANTENNA **2** : FORWARD PASS
ae•ri•al•ist \'ar-ē-ə-ləst, 'er-, ā-'ir-\ *n* : a performer of feats above the ground especially on a flying trapeze
aerial root *n* : a root (as for clinging to a wall) that does not enter the soil and usually arises adventitiously
ae•rie \'aər-ē, 'eər-, 'iər-\ *or* **ey•rie** \'īər-ē, *or like* AERIE\ *n* **1** : the nest of a bird on a cliff or a mountaintop **2** : a dwelling or room placed high up [Medieval Latin *aerea,* from Old French *aire,* from Latin *area* "area, barnyard"]
aer•o•bat•ics \,ar-ə-'bat-iks, ,er-\ *n sing or pl* : performance of stunts in an airplane or glider [*aer-* + *-batics* (as in *acrobatics*)]
aer•o•bic \,a-'rō-bik, ,e-\ *adj* **1** : living or active only in the presence of oxygen **2** : of, relating to, or caused by aerobic organisms — **aer•obe** \'ar-,ōb, 'er-\ *n* — **aer•o•bi•cal•ly** \,a-'rō-bi-kə-lē, ,e-, -klē\ *adv*
aero•drome \'ar-ə-,drōm, 'er-\ *n, British* : AIRFIELD, AIRPORT
aero•dy•nam•ics \,ar-ō-dī-'nam-iks, ,er-\ *n* : a branch of dynamics that deals with the motion of gaseous fluids (as air) and with the forces acting on bodies in motion relative to such fluids — **aero•dy•nam•ic** \-ik\ *adj* — **aero•dy•nam•i•cal•ly** \-i-kə-lē, -klē\ *adv*
aero•naut \'ar-ə-,nȯt, 'er-, -,nät\ *n* : one that operates or travels in an airship or balloon [French *aéronaute,* from *aér-* "aer-" + Greek *nautēs* "sailor"]
aero•nau•tics \,ar-ə-'nȯt-iks, ,er-\ *n* **1** : a science dealing with the construction and operation of aircraft **2** : the art or science of flight — **aero•nau•tic** \-'nȯt-ik\ *adj* — **aero•nau•ti•cal** \-'nȯt-i-kəl\ *adj* — **aero•nau•ti•cal•ly** \-i-kə-lē, -klē\ *adv*
aero•pause \'ar-ō-,pȯz, 'er-\ *n* : the level above the earth's surface where the atmosphere becomes ineffective for human and aircraft functions
aero•plane \'ar-ə-,plān, 'er-\ *chiefly British variant of* AIRPLANE
aero•sol \-,säl, -,sȯl\ *n* **1** : a suspension of fine solid or liquid particles (as smoke or fog) in gas **2** : a substance (as an insecticide) dispensed from a pressurized container; *also* : the container itself [*aer-* + 3*sol*]
1aero•space \'ar-ō-,spās, 'er-\ *n* **1** : the earth's atmosphere and the space beyond **2** : a physical science dealing with aerospace
2aerospace *adj* : of or relating to aerospace, to the manufacture or use of vehicles used in aerospace, or to travel in aerospace
aery \'aər-ē, 'eər-\ *adj* **aer•i•er**; **-est** : having an aerial quality : ETHEREAL
Ae•so•pi•an \ē-'sō-pē-ən\ *adj* : conveying an innocent meaning to an outsider but a concealed meaning to an informed member of a conspiracy or underground movement ⟨*Aesopian* language⟩
aes•thete *also* **es•thete** \'es-,thēt\ *n* : one having or pretending sensitivity to the beautiful especially in art
aes•thet•ic *or* **es•thet•ic** \es-'thet-ik, is-\ *adj* **1** : having to do with beauty or with what is beautiful especially as distinguished from what is useful ⟨an *aesthetic* interest in antique furniture⟩ **2** : appreciative of or responsive to what is beautiful ⟨an *aesthetic* person⟩ [derived from Greek *aisthanesthai* "to perceive"] **syn** see ARTISTIC — **aes•thet•i•cal•ly** \-'thet-i-kə-lē, -klē\ *adv*
aes•thet•i•cism \es-'thet-ə-,siz-əm, is-\ *n* : devotion to or emphasis on beauty or the cultivation of the arts
aes•thet•ics *also* **es•thet•ics** \es-'thet-iks, is-\ *n sing or pl* **1** : a branch of philosophy that studies and explains the principles and forms of beauty especially in art and literature **2** : description and explanation of artistic effects and aesthetic experience by means of other sciences (as psychology, sociology, or history)
aes•ti•vate *or* **es•ti•vate** \'es-tə-,vāt\ *vi* : to pass the summer in a state of torpor [Latin *aestivare* "to spend the summer", from *aestivus* "of summer", from *aestas* "summer"] — **aes•ti•va•tion** \,es-tə-'vā-shən\ *n*
af- — see AD-
afar \ə-'fär\ *adv* : from, to, or at a great distance
afeard *or* **afeared** \ə-'fiərd\ *adj, dialect* : AFRAID
af•fa•ble \'af-ə-bəl\ *adj* **1** : being pleasant and at ease in talking to others **2** : characterized by ease and friendliness ⟨an *affable* manner⟩ [Middle French, from Latin *affabilis,* from *affari* "to speak to", from *ad-* + *fari* "to speak"] — **af•fa•bil•i•ty** \,af-ə-'bil-ət-ē\ *n* — **af•fa•bly** \'af-ə-blē\ *adv*
af•fair \ə-'faər, -'feər\ *n* **1 a** *pl* : personal, commercial, professional, or public business ⟨government *affairs*⟩ **b** : MATTER, CONCERN ⟨not your *affair* at all⟩ **2 a** : EVENT, ACTIVITY ⟨attended a social *affair*⟩ **b** : PRODUCT, THING ⟨a flimsy *affair* of ropes bridging the river⟩ **3 a** *also* **af•faire** : a typically brief romantic or passionate relationship **b** : a matter causing public anxiety, controversy, or scandal [Middle French *affaire,* from *a faire* "to do"]
1af•fect \ə-'fekt, a-\ *vt* **1** : to be given to : FANCY ⟨*affect* flashy clothes⟩ **2** : to make a display of liking or using ⟨*affect* a worldly manner⟩ **3** : to put on a pretense of : FEIGN ⟨*affect* indifference, though deeply hurt⟩ [Middle French *affecter,* from Latin *affectare* "to aim at", from *afficere* "to act on, influence"]
2affect *vt* : to produce an effect upon: as **a** : to produce a usually harmful physical effect upon or change in ⟨lungs *affected* by cancer⟩ **b** : to produce a material change in **c** : to act upon so as to bring about a response ⟨constant criticism *affected* their efforts⟩
• **syn** AFFECT, EFFECT are often confused because both verbs take the same word *effect* as the corresponding noun. AFFECT applies to the action of an agency in causing a change in or alteration of something ⟨moisture *affects* steel⟩ ⟨the climate *affected* their health⟩ EFFECT applies to the producing of a result by an intelligent agent ⟨asked how the prisoner *effected* the escape⟩ **syn** see in addition INFLUENCE
af•fec•ta•tion \,af-,ek-'tā-shən\ *n* **1** : an assuming or displaying of an attitude or kind of behavior not natural or not genuine **2** : artificial quality in speech or behavior
• **syn** MANNERISM, POSE: AFFECTATION applies to a specific trick of speech or behavior that impresses others as being deliberately assumed and insincere; MANNERISM designates a peculiarity or eccentricity in behavior that is not deliberately assumed but results from unconscious, accidentally acquired habit; POSE implies an attitude deliberately assumed in order to impress others.
af•fect•ed *adj* : not natural or genuine ⟨an *affected* interest in music⟩ ⟨*affected* manners⟩ — **af•fect•ed•ly** *adv* — **af•fect•ed•ness** *n*
af•fect•ing *adj* : arousing pity, sympathy, or sorrow ⟨an *affecting* story⟩ — **af•fect•ing•ly** \ə-'fek-ting-lē, a-\ *adv*
1af•fec•tion \ə-'fek-shən\ *n* **1** : a tender feeling of attachment : FONDNESS **2** : PROPENSITY, BENT
2affection *n* : DISEASE, DISORDER ⟨an *affection* of the brain⟩
af•fec•tion•ate \ə-'fek-shə-nət, -shnət\ *adj* : feeling or showing a great liking for a person or thing : TENDER — **af•fec•tion•ate•ly** *adv*
af•fec•tive \a-'fek-tiv\ *adj* : relating to, arising from, or influencing feelings or emotions : EMOTIONAL
af•fer•ent \'af-ə-rənt, 'af-,er-ənt\ *adj* : bearing or conducting inward; *esp* : conveying impulses toward a nerve center — compare EFFERENT [Latin *afferre* "to bring to", from *ad-* + *ferre* "to carry"]
af•fi•ance \ə-'fī-əns\ *vt* : to solemnly promise (oneself or another) in marriage : BETROTH ⟨the *affianced* couple⟩
af•fi•da•vit \,af-ə-'dā-vət\ *n* : a sworn written statement; *esp* : one made under oath before an authorized official [Medieval Latin, "he has made an oath", from *affidare* "to give surety", derived from Latin *ad-* + *fides* "faith"]
1af•fil•i•ate \ə-'fil-ē-,āt\ *vb* : to connect closely often as a member, branch, or associate ⟨*affiliated* themselves with a political party⟩ ⟨a school *affiliated* with the university⟩ [Medieval Latin *affiliare* "to adopt as a son", from Latin *ad-* + *filius* "son"] —

af·fil·i·a·tion \ə-ˌfil-ē-ˈā-shən\ *n*

[2]af·fil·i·ate \ə-ˈfil-ē-ət\ *n* : an affiliated person or organization

af·fin·i·ty \ə-ˈfin-ət-ē\ *n, pl* **-ties 1** : relationship by marriage **2 a** : sympathy marked by community of interest : KINSHIP ⟨they felt a strange *affinity* with each other⟩ **b** : an attraction to or liking for ⟨developed an *affinity* for politics⟩ **c** : an attractive force between substances or particles that causes them to enter into and remain in chemical combination **3** : a relation between biological groups indicating community of origin [Latin *affinitas,* from *affinis* "bordering on, related by marriage", from *ad-* + *finis* "end, border"]

af·firm \ə-ˈfərm\ *vb* **1 a** : CONFIRM, RATIFY ⟨*affirm* a contract⟩ **b** : to state positively or with confidence : declare to be true **2** : to make a solemn and formal declaration or assertion in place of an oath [Middle French *afermer,* from Latin *affirmare,* from *ad-* + *firmus* "firm"]

[1]af·firm·a·tive \ə-ˈfər-mət-iv\ *adj* **1** : asserting that the fact is so **2** : capable of being applied in a constructive way ⟨an *affirmative* approach to the problem⟩ **3** : favoring or supporting a proposition or motion — **af·firm·a·tive·ly** *adv*

[2]affirmative *n* **1** : an expression (as the word *yes*) of affirmation or agreement **2** : the affirmative side in a debate or vote

affirmative action *n* : the establishment of policies and practices intended to discourage discrimination (as in employment) on the basis of race or sex

[1]af·fix \ə-ˈfiks\ *vt* **1** : to attach physically : FASTEN ⟨*affix* a stamp to a letter⟩ **2** : to attach in any way : connect with : ADD ⟨*affix* one's signature to a letter⟩ — **af·fix·a·tion** \ˌaf-ˌik-ˈsā-shən\ *n*

[2]af·fix \ˈaf-ˌiks\ *n* : one or more sounds or letters attached to the beginning or end of a word and serving to produce a derivative word or an inflectional form — **af·fix·al** \-ˌik-səl\ *or* **af·fix·i·al** \a-ˈfik-sē-əl\ *adj*

af·fla·tus \ə-ˈflāt-əs\ *n* : a divine imparting of knowledge or power : INSPIRATION [Latin, "act of blowing or breathing on", from *afflare* "to blow on"]

af·flict \ə-ˈflikt\ *vt* **1** : to distress so severely as to cause continued suffering ⟨people *afflicted* by famine⟩ **2** : to have a harmful effect on ⟨political theories *afflicted* with confused thinking⟩ [Latin *affligere* "to cast down", from *ad-* + *fligere* "to strike"] • **syn** TORMENT, TORTURE, RACK: AFFLICT is general and applies to the causing of pain, annoyance, or distress; TORMENT suggests persecution or the repeated inflicting of suffering or annoyance; TORTURE adds the implication of causing to writhe with unbearable pain; RACK stresses straining or wrenching.

af·flic·tion \ə-ˈflik-shən\ *n* **1** : the state of being afflicted **2** : a cause of continued pain or distress

af·flic·tive \ə-ˈflik-tiv\ *adj* : causing affliction : DISTRESSING — **af·flic·tive·ly** *adv*

af·flu·ence \ˈaf-ˌlü-əns *also* a-ˈflü- *or* ə-ˈflü-\ *n* **1** : an abundant flow or supply **2** : abundance of wealth or property

[1]af·flu·ent \-ənt\ *adj* **1** : flowing in abundance : COPIOUS **2** : having an abundance of material possessions : WEALTHY, RICH [Middle French, from Latin *affluere* "to flow to", from *ad-* + *fluere* "to flow"] — **af·flu·ent·ly** *adv*

[2]affluent *n* : a tributary stream

af·ford \ə-ˈfōrd, -ˈfȯrd\ *vt* **1** : to manage to do, give, or bear without serious harm ⟨you can't *afford* to waste your strength⟩ **2** : to manage to pay for ⟨unable to *afford* a new car⟩ **3** : PROVIDE 4, FURNISH ⟨playing tennis *affords* healthful exercise⟩ [Old English *geforthian* "to carry out"] — **af·ford·able** \-ə-bəl\ *adj*

af·for·es·ta·tion \ˌa-ˌfȯr-ə-ˈstā-shən, -ˌfär-\ *n* : the act or process of establishing a forest especially on land not previously forested

af·fray \ə-ˈfrā\ *n* : a noisy quarrel or fight : BRAWL [Middle French, from *affreer* "to startle"]

af·fri·cate \ˈaf-ri-kət\ *n* : a stop immediately followed by a related fricative (as the \d\ and \zh\ that make up the \j\ sounds of *judge*)

[1]af·fright \ə-ˈfrīt\ *vt* : FRIGHTEN 1, ALARM

[2]affright *n* : sudden and great fear : TERROR

[1]af·front \ə-ˈfrənt\ *vt* **1** : to insult especially to the face by language or behavior : OFFEND **2** : to face in defiance : CONFRONT [Middle French *afronter* "to defy", derived from Latin *ad-* + *frons* "forehead"] **syn** see OFFEND

[2]affront *n* : a deliberately offensive act or utterance • **syn** INSULT, INDIGNITY: AFFRONT implies an open, deliberate act of disrespect; INSULT implies an attack intended to humiliate and degrade; INDIGNITY suggests an outrageous offense to one's personal dignity.

Af·ghan \ˈaf-ˌgan *also* -gən\ *n* **1** : a native or inhabitant of Afghanistan **2** : PASHTO **3** *not cap* : a blanket or shawl of colored wool knitted or crocheted in strips or squares — **Afghan** *adj*

Afghan hound *n* : a tall slim swift hunting dog native to the Near East with a coat of silky thick hair and a long silky topknot

Afghan hound

afi·cio·na·do \ə-ˌfish-ē-ə-ˈnäd-ō, -ˌfis-ē-\ *n, pl* **-dos** : DEVOTEE 2, FAN [Spanish]

afield \ə-ˈfēld\ *adv* **1** : to, in, or on the field **2** : away from home **3** : out of a regular, planned, or proper course : ASTRAY ⟨a rambling speech that wandered far *afield*⟩

afire \ə-ˈfīr\ *adj or adv* : on fire : BLAZING

aflame \ə-ˈflām\ *adj or adv* : AFIRE

afloat \ə-ˈflōt\ *adv or adj* **1 a** : borne on or as if on the water **b** : at sea **2** : free of difficulties : SELF-SUFFICIENT ⟨enough money to keep the business *afloat*⟩ **3** : circulating about : RUMORED **4** : flooded with or submerged under water : AWASH

aflut·ter \ə-ˈflət-ər\ *adj* **1** : moving with brisk irregularity **2** : nervously excited

afoot \ə-ˈfu̇t\ *adv or adj* **1** : on foot ⟨they traveled *afoot*⟩ **2** : in the process of development : under way ⟨a plan was *afoot* to seize power⟩

afore \ə-ˈfōr, -ˈfȯr\ *adv or conj or prep, chiefly dialect* : BEFORE

afore·men·tioned \-ˌmen-chənd\ *adj* : mentioned previously

afore·said \-ˌsed\ *adj* : said or named previously

afore·thought \-ˌthȯt\ *adj* : previously in mind : DELIBERATE ⟨with malice *aforethought*⟩

a for·ti·o·ri \ˌä-ˌfȯrt-ē-ˈōr-ē, ˌā-fȯrt-ē-ˈōr-ˌī, -ˈȯr-\ *adv* : with greater reason or more convincing force — used in drawing a conclusion that is inferred to be even more certain than another [New Latin, literally, "from the stronger (argument)"]

afoul of \ə-ˈfau̇l-əv\ *prep* **1** : in or into collision or entanglement with ⟨one ship ran *afoul of* the other⟩ **2** : in or into conflict with ⟨they fell *afoul of* the law⟩

Afr- *or* **Afro-** *combining form* **1** : African ⟨*Afro*-American⟩ **2** : African and ⟨*Afro*-Asiatic⟩

afraid \ə-ˈfrād, *South also* -ˈfreəd *or* -ˈfred\ *adj* **1** : filled with fear or apprehension ⟨*afraid* of snakes⟩ **2** : filled with concern or regret over a possibly unfavorable occurrence ⟨*afraid* that they might be late⟩ **3** : UNWILLING, AVERSE ⟨*afraid* to work hard⟩ [Middle English *affraied,* from past participle of *affraien* "to frighten"]

afresh \ə-ˈfresh\ *adv* : from a new start : AGAIN

Af·ri·can \ˈaf-ri-kən\ *n* **1** : a native or inhabitant of Africa **2** : a person of African and especially black ancestry — **African** *adj*

African sleeping sickness *n* : SLEEPING SICKNESS 1

African violet *n* : a tropical African plant related to the gloxinias and widely grown as a house plant for its velvety fleshy leaves and showy purple, pink, or white flowers

Af·ri·kaans \ˌaf-ri-ˈkäns, -ˈkänz\ *n* : a language developed from 17th century Dutch that is one of the official languages of the Republic of South Africa [Afrikaans, from *afrikaans* "African"]

Af·ri·ka·ner \-ˈkän-ər\ *n* : a native South African of European descent; *esp* : an Afrikaans-speaking descendant of the 17th century Dutch settlers [Afrikaans]

[1]Af·ro \ˈaf-ˌrō\ *adj* : having the hair shaped into a round bushy mass [probably from *Afro-American*]

[2]Afro *n, pl* **Afros** : an Afro hairstyle

Af·ro-Amer·i·can \ˌaf-rō-ə-ˈmer-ə-kən\ *adj* : of or relating to Americans of African and especially of black ancestry ⟨*Afro*=

\ə\ abut	\au̇\ **out**	\i\ **tip**	\ȯ\ **saw**	\u̇\ **foot**
\ər\ **further**	\ch\ **chin**	\ī\ **life**	\ȯi\ **coin**	\y\ **yet**
\a\ **mat**	\e\ **pet**	\j\ **job**	\th\ **thin**	\yü\ **few**
\ā\ **take**	\ē\ **easy**	\ng\ **sing**	\t͟h\ **this**	\yu̇\ **cure**
\ä\ **cot, cart**	\g\ **go**	\ō\ **bone**	\ü\ **food**	\zh\ **vision**

American history⟩ — **Afro–American** *n*

Af•ro–Asi•at•ic languages \ˌaf-rō-ˌā-zhē-ˌat-ik-, -zē-\ *n pl* : a family of languages widely distributed over southwestern Asia and northern Africa comprising the Semitic, Egyptian, Berber, Cushitic, and Chad subfamilies

aft \ˈaft\ *adv* : near, toward, or in the stern of a ship or the tail of an aircraft [Old English *æftan* "from behind, behind"]

¹af•ter \ˈaf-tər\ *adv* : following in time or place : AFTERWARD, BEHIND ⟨returned 20 years *after*⟩ [Old English *æfter*]

²after *prep* **1 a** : behind in place ⟨following *after* them⟩ **b** : following in time or order ⟨*after* dinner⟩ **c** : subsequent to and in view of ⟨*after* all our advice⟩ **2** — used as a function word to indicate an object or goal ⟨go *after* gold⟩ ⟨ask *after* a friend⟩ **3 a** : in accordance with ⟨*after* an old custom⟩ **b** : with the name of or a name derived from that of ⟨named Pennsylvania *after* William Penn⟩ **c** : in imitation or resemblance of ⟨patterned *after* a Gothic cathedral⟩

³after *conj* : later than the time when

⁴after *adj* **1** : later in time : SUBSEQUENT ⟨in *after* years⟩ **2** : located toward the stern of a ship or tail of an aircraft

after all *adv* : NEVERTHELESS ⟨decided to take the train *after all*⟩

af•ter•birth \ˈaf-tər-ˌbərth\ *n* : the placenta and fetal membranes that are expelled from the uterus after delivery

af•ter•burn•er \-ˌbər-nər\ *n* **1** : an auxiliary burner attached to the tail pipe of a turbojet engine for injecting fuel into the hot exhaust gases and burning it to provide extra thrust **2** : a device for removing unburned carbon compounds from exhaust gases (as of a car)

af•ter•care \-ˌkeər, -ˌkaər\ *n* : the care, nursing, or treatment of a convalescent patient

af•ter•deck \-ˌdek\ *n* : the rear half of the deck of a ship

af•ter•ef•fect \-ə-ˌfekt\ *n* : an effect that follows its cause after some time has passed or after a first effect has subsided ⟨the *aftereffects* of surgery⟩

af•ter•glow \-ˌglō\ *n* **1** : a glow remaining (as in the sky after sunset) where a light has disappeared **2** : a reflection of past splendor, success, or emotion

af•ter•im•age \-ˌim-ij\ *n* : a usually visual sensation continuing after the stimulus causing it has ended

af•ter•life \-ˌlīf\ *n* **1** : an existence after death **2** : a later period in one's life

af•ter•math \ˈaf-tər-ˌmath\ *n* **1** : a second-growth crop especially of hay **2** : EFFECT 1, RESULT ⟨felt guilty as an *aftermath* of the accident⟩ **3** : the period immediately following a usually ruinous event ⟨in the *aftermath* of the war⟩ [Old English *mæth* "mowing", from *māwan* "to mow"]

af•ter•noon \ˌaf-tər-ˈnün\ *n* : the part of day between noon and sunset — **afternoon** *adj*

af•ter•noons \-ˈnünz\ *adv* : in the afternoon repeatedly ⟨*afternoons* we take a nap⟩

af•ter•taste \ˈaf-tər-ˌtāst\ *n* : a sensation (as of flavor) continuing after the stimulus causing it has ended

af•ter•thought \-ˌthȯt\ *n* **1** : an idea occurring later **2** : a part, feature, or device added to an earlier whole ⟨the porch was added as an *afterthought*⟩

af•ter•ward \ˈaf-tər-wərd, -tə-\ *or* **af•ter•wards** \-wərdz\ *adv* : at a later time

af•ter•world \ˈaf-tər-ˌwərld\ *n* : a future world : a world after death

ag- — see AD-

again \ə-ˈgen, -ˈgin, -ˈgān\ *adv* **1** : in return ⟨give them the message and bring us word *again*⟩ **2** : another time : ANEW ⟨come see us *again*⟩ **3** : in addition ⟨half as much *again*⟩ **4** : on the other hand ⟨we may, and *again* we may not⟩ **5** : FURTHER, MOREOVER ⟨*again,* there is another matter to consider⟩ [Middle English, "opposite, again", from Old English *ongēan* "opposite, back", from *on* + *gēan* "still, again"]

against \ə-ˈgenst, -ˈginst, -ˈgānst\ *prep* **1** : directly opposite : FACING ⟨over *against* the park⟩ **2 a** : in opposition or hostility to ⟨campaign *against* the enemy⟩ **b** : as a protection from ⟨a shield *against* aggression⟩ **3** : in preparation for ⟨storing food *against* the winter⟩ **4 a** : in the direction of and into contact with ⟨ran *against* a tree⟩ **b** : in contact with ⟨leaning *against* the wall⟩ **5** : in a direction opposite to ⟨walk *against* the wind⟩ **6** : before the background of ⟨green trees *against* the blue sky⟩ **7** : as a basis for disapproval of ⟨I have nothing *against* them⟩ **8** : in exchange for ⟨lend money *against* a promissory note⟩ [Middle English, from *again*]

¹agape \ə-ˈgāp *also* ə-ˈgap\ *adj* : having the mouth open (as in wonder or surprise)

²aga•pe \ä-ˈgä-ˌpā, ˈäg-ə-ˌpā\ *n* **1** : LOVE 3a **2** : LOVE FEAST 1 [Greek *agapē,* literally, "love"]

agar \ˈäg-ˌär\ *or* **agar–agar** \ˌäg-ˌär-ˈäg-ˌär\ *n* **1** : a jellylike extract of a red alga used especially in culture media or as a stabilizing agent in foods **2** : a culture medium containing agar [Malay *agar-agar*]

aga•ric \ˈag-ə-rik, ə-ˈgar-ik\ *n* **1** : any of several corky fungi used especially in the preparation of punk **2** : any of a family of gill fungi including the common brown-spored edible meadow mushroom [Greek *agarikon,* a kind of fungus]

ag•ate \ˈag-ət\ *n* **1** : a fine-grained variegated quartz having its colors arranged in stripes, blended in clouds, or showing mosslike forms **2** : a child's playing marble of agate or of glass resembling agate **3** : a small size of type approximately 5½ point [Middle French, from Latin *achates,* from Greek *achatēs*]

ag•ate•ware \-ˌwaər, -ˌweər\ *n* : pottery veined and mottled to resemble agate

aga•ve \ə-ˈgäv-ē\ *n* : any of a genus of plants of the amaryllis family which have spiny-edged leaves and flowers in tall branched clusters and some of which are cultivated for fiber or for ornament [Greek *Agauē,* a daughter of Cadmus]

¹age \ˈāj\ *n* **1 a** : the time from birth to a specified date ⟨a child six years of *age*⟩ **b** (1) : the time of life when a person attains some right or capacity ⟨voting *age*⟩ (2) : MAJORITY **c** : the later part of life **d** : normal lifetime **2** : a period of time in history or in the development of human beings or in the history of the earth; *esp* : one characterized by some distinguishing feature ⟨machine *age*⟩ ⟨*Age* of Discovery⟩ ⟨*Age* of Reptiles⟩ **3** : a long period of time ⟨it happened *ages* ago⟩ [Old French *aage,* from Latin *aetas*] **syn** see PERIOD — **of age** : having reached a time of maturity and especially of legal majority

²age *vb* **aged; ag•ing** *or* **age•ing 1** : to become old : show the effects of increasing age **2** : to become or cause to become mellow or mature : RIPEN **3** : to cause to seem old especially prematurely (as by strain or suffering)

-age \ij\ *n suffix* **1** : aggregate : collection ⟨track*age*⟩ **2 a** : action : process ⟨haul*age*⟩ **b** : cumulative result of ⟨break*age*⟩ **c** : rate of ⟨dos*age*⟩ **3** : house or place of ⟨orphan*age*⟩ **4** : state : rank ⟨vassal*age*⟩ **5** : fee : charge ⟨post*age*⟩ [Old French, from Latin *-aticum*]

aged \ˈā-jəd, *in senses 1b and 2b* ˈājd\ *adj* **1** : grown old: as **a** : of an advanced age **b** : having reached a specified age ⟨a person *aged* 40 years⟩ **2 a** : typical of old age **b** : having gained a desirable quality with age ⟨*aged* whiskey⟩ — **aged•ness** *n*

age•ism *also* **ag•ism** \ˈā-ˌjiz-əm\ *n* : prejudice or discrimination against people of a particular age and especially against the elderly — **age•ist** \-jist\ *adj*

age•less \ˈāj-ləs\ *adj* **1** : not growing old or showing the effects of age **2** : TIMELESS, ETERNAL ⟨an *ageless* story⟩ — **age•less•ly** *adv* — **age•less•ness** *n*

age•long \ˈāj-ˌlȯng\ *adj* : lasting for a long time : EVERLASTING

agen•cy \ˈā-jən-sē\ *n, pl* **-cies 1** : the capacity, condition, or state of acting or of exerting power : OPERATION **2** : a person or thing through which power is exerted or an end is achieved ⟨registered my complaint through the *agency* of my lawyer⟩ **3 a** : the office or function of an agent **b** : the relationship between a principal and his or her agent **4** : an establishment engaged in doing business for another ⟨advertising *agency*⟩ **5** : an administrative division (as of a government) ⟨Central Intelligence *Agency*⟩

agen•da \ə-ˈjen-də\ *n* : a list of things to be considered (as at a meeting) or done [Latin, "things to be done", from *agere* "to do"]

agent \ˈā-jənt\ *n* **1 a** : something that produces or is capable of producing an effect ⟨a cleansing *agent*⟩ **b** : a chemically, physically, or biologically active principle **2** : one that acts or exerts power **3** : one who acts for or in the place of another and by the other's authority ⟨government *agents*⟩ ⟨a real estate *agent*⟩ [Medieval Latin *agens,* from Latin *agere* "to drive, lead, act, do"]

agent pro•vo•ca•teur \ˌäzh-ˌäⁿ-prō-ˌväk-ə-ˈtər, ˈā-jənt-\ *n, pl* **agents provocateurs** \ˌäzh-ˌäⁿ-prō-ˌväk-ə-ˈtər, ˈājəns-prō-\ : a person paid to associate with members of a suspected group and to pretend sympathy with their aims so as to incite them to a legally punishable act [French, literally, "provoking agent"]

Age of Fishes : DEVONIAN 1
Age of Mammals : CENOZOIC 1
Age of Reptiles : MESOZOIC 1
age–old \'ā-'jōld\ *adj* : having existed for ages : ANCIENT
ag•er•a•tum \ˌaj-ə-'rāt-əm\ *n* : any of a large genus of tropical American composite herbs often cultivated for their small showy heads of blue, white, or pink flowers [Greek *agēratos* "ageless", from *a-* + *gēras* "old age"]
Ag•ge•us \a-'gē-əs\ *n* — see BIBLE table
ag•gie \'ag-ē\ *n* : an agate playing marble
[1]**ag•glom•er•ate** \ə-'gläm-ə-ˌrāt\ *vb* : to gather into a ball, mass, or cluster [Latin *agglomerare* "to heap up", from *ad-* + *glomus* "ball"]
[2]**ag•glom•er•ate** \-rət\ *n* **1** : a jumbled mass or collection **2** : a rock composed of volcanic fragments of various sizes
ag•glom•er•a•tion \ə-ˌgläm-ə-'rā-shən\ *n* **1** : the action or process of collecting in a mass **2** : a heap or cluster of dissimilar elements — **ag•glom•er•a•tive** \ə-'gläm-ə-ˌrāt-iv\ *adj*
ag•glu•ti•nate \ə-'glüt-n-ˌāt\ *vb* **1** : to cause to adhere : FASTEN **2** : to cause to clump **3** : to unite into a group or gather into a mass **4** : to form words by agglutination [Latin *agglutinare,* from *ad-* + *gluten* "glue"]
ag•glu•ti•na•tion \ə-ˌglüt-n-'ā-shən\ *n* **1** : the action or process of agglutinating **2** : a mass or group formed by the union of separate elements **3** : the formation of derivative or compound words by putting together constituents of which each expresses a single definite meaning **4** : a reaction in which particles (as red blood cells or bacteria) suspended in a liquid collect into clumps usually as a response to a specific antibody — **ag•glu•ti•na•tive** \ə-'glüt-n-ˌāt-iv\ *adj*
ag•glu•ti•nin \ə-'glüt-n-ən\ *n* : an antibody causing agglutination
ag•glu•tin•o•gen \ˌag-lü-'tin-ə-jən\ *n* : an antigen whose presence results in the formation of an agglutinin
ag•gran•dize \ə-'gran-ˌdīz, 'ag-rən-\ *vt* : to make great or greater (as in power or resources) [French *agrandiss-,* stem of *agrandir,* from *a-* "ad-" + *grandir* "to increase"] — **ag•gran•dize•ment** \ə-'gran-dəz-mənt, -ˌdīz-; ˌag-rən-'dīz-mənt\ *n* — **ag•gran•diz•er** *n*
ag•gra•vate \'ag-rə-ˌvāt\ *vt* **1** : to make worse, more serious, or more severe ⟨problems *aggravated* by neglect⟩ **2** : to rouse to displeasure or anger by usually persistent often petty goading [Latin *aggravare* "to make heavier", from *ad-* + *gravis* "heavy, grave"] **syn** see INTENSIFY, IRRITATE
ag•gra•va•tion \ˌag-rə-'vā-shən\ *n* **1** : the act of making something worse or more severe : an increase in severity ⟨the treatment caused an *aggravation* of the pain⟩ **2** : something that aggravates ⟨the cold winter was an *aggravation* of their misery⟩ **3** : the act of irritating or annoying
[1]**ag•gre•gate** \'ag-ri-gət\ *adj* **1** : formed by the collection of units or particles into a whole ⟨*aggregate* expenses⟩ **2** : clustered in a dense mass or head ⟨an *aggregate* flower⟩ [Latin *aggregare* "to add to", from *ad-* + *greg-, grex* "flock"] — **ag•gre•gate•ly** *adv* — **ag•gre•gate•ness** *n*
[2]**ag•gre•gate** \-ˌgāt\ *vt* **1** : to collect or gather into a mass or whole **2** : to amount to altogether : TOTAL 2
[3]**ag•gre•gate** \-gət\ *n* **1** : a collection or sum of units or parts somewhat loosely associated **2** : the whole sum or amount : SUM TOTAL **3 a** : any of several hard inert materials used for mixing with a cementing material to form concrete, mortar, or plaster **b** : a clustered mass of individual soil particles considered the basic structural unit of soil **syn** see SUM
aggregate fruit *n* : a compound fruit (as a raspberry) made up of the several separate ripened ovaries of a single flower
ag•gre•ga•tion \ˌag-ri-'gā-shən\ *n* **1** : the collecting of units or parts into a mass or whole **2** : a group, body, or mass composed of many distinct parts : ASSEMBLAGE
ag•gres•sion \ə-'gresh-ən\ *n* **1** : a forceful action or procedure; *esp* : an unprovoked attack **2** : the practice of making attacks or encroachments; *esp* : unprovoked violation by one country of the territorial integrity of another **3** : hostile, injurious, or destructive behavior or outlook especially when caused by frustration [Latin *aggressus,* past participle of *aggredi* "to attack", from *ad-* + *gradi* "to step, go"]
ag•gres•sive \ə-'gres-iv\ *adj* **1 a** : tending toward or practicing aggression ⟨an *aggressive* nation⟩ **b** : showing readiness to fight or attack ⟨an *aggressive* dog⟩ **2 a** : marked by initiative and vigor ⟨an *aggressive* fund-raising campaign⟩ **b** : obtrusively self-assertive ⟨annoyed by an *aggressive* salesperson⟩ — **ag•gres•sive•ly** *adv* — **ag•gres•sive•ness** *n*
ag•gres•sor \ə-'gres-ər\ *n* : one that commits or practices aggression
ag•grieved \ə-'grēvd\ *adj* **1** : troubled or distressed in spirit **2** : having a grievance; *esp* : suffering from injury or loss
aghast \ə-'gast\ *adj* : struck with terror, amazement, or horror : SHOCKED [Middle English *agast,* from *agasten* "to frighten", from *gast, gost* "ghost"]
ag•ile \'aj-əl\ *adj* **1** : able to move quickly and easily : NIMBLE **2** : mentally quick ⟨an *agile* thinker⟩ [Middle French, from Latin *agilis,* from *agere* "to act, do"] — **ag•ile•ly** \-əl-lē, -ə-lē\ *adv*
agil•i•ty \ə-'jil-ət-ē\ *n, pl* **-ties** : the quality or state of being agile ⟨the grace and *agility* of a gymnast⟩
aging *present participle of* AGE
agism, agist *variant of* AGEISM, AGEIST
ag•i•tate \'aj-ə-ˌtāt\ *vb* **1** : to shake jerkily : set in violent irregular motion ⟨water *agitated* by wind⟩ **2** : to stir up : EXCITE, DISTURB ⟨*agitated* by bad news⟩ **3** : to attempt to arouse or influence public interest in something especially by discussion or appeals ⟨*agitate* for better schools⟩ [Latin *agitare,* from *agere* "to drive, act, do"] **syn** see SHAKE — **ag•i•tat•ed•ly** \-ˌtāt-əd-lē\ *adv* — **ag•i•ta•tion** \ˌaj-ə-'tā-shən\ *n*
agi•ta•to \ˌaj-ə-'tät-ō\ *adv or adj* : in a restless and agitated manner — used as a direction in music [Italian]
ag•i•ta•tor \'aj-ə-ˌtāt-ər\ *n* : one that agitates: as **a** : one who stirs up public feeling on controversial issues **b** : a device for stirring or shaking
agleam \ə-'glēm\ *adj* : BRIGHT, SHINING ⟨eyes *agleam* with tears⟩
agley \ə-'glā, -'glē, -'glī\ *adv, chiefly Scottish* : AWRY 2, WRONG [Scots, from [1]*a-* + *gley* "to squint"]
aglit•ter \ə-'glit-ər\ *adj* : GLITTERY, SPARKLING
aglow \ə-'glō\ *adj* : radiating (as heat, light, or emotion) strongly
ag•nos•tic \ag-'näs-tik, əg-\ *n* : a person who holds that whether God exists is not known and probably cannot be known [Greek *agnōstos* "unknown, unknowable", from *a-* + *gnōstos* "known", from *gignōskein* "to know"] **syn** see ATHEIST — **agnostic** *adj* — **ag•nos•ti•cism** \-'näs-tə-ˌsiz-əm\ *n*
Ag•nus Dei \ˌäg-ˌnu̇s-'dā-ˌē, ˌän-ˌyüs-, -'dā; ˌag-nəs-'dē-ˌī\ *n* **1** : a liturgical prayer said or sung to Christ as Savior **2** : an image of a lamb often with a halo and a banner and cross as a symbol of Christ [Late Latin, "lamb of God"; from its opening words]
ago \ə-'gō\ *adj or adv* : earlier than the present time ⟨a week *ago*⟩ [Middle English *agon, ago,* from *agon* "to pass away", from Old English *āgān,* from *ā-,* prefix denoting completion + *gān* "to go"]
agog \ə-'gäg\ *adj* : full of intense interest or excitement : EAGER [Middle French *en gogues* "in mirth"]
a–go–go \ä-'gō-ˌgō\ *n* : a usually small nightclub for dancing to live music [*Whisky à Gogo,* cafe and nightclub in Paris, France, from French *à gogo* "galore"]
ag•o•nal \'ag-ən-l\ *adj* : of, relating to, or associated with agony and especially the death agony
ag•o•nize \'ag-ə-ˌnīz\ *vb* **1** : to suffer or cause to suffer extreme physical or mental pain or anguish **2** : to strive desperately : STRUGGLE — **ag•o•niz•ing•ly** \-ˌnī-zing-lē\ *adv*
ag•o•ny \'ag-ə-nē\ *n, pl* **-nies 1 a** : intense physical or mental pain : ANGUISH, TORTURE **b** : the throes of death **2** : a strong sudden display of emotion ⟨an *agony* of delight⟩ [Greek *agōnia* "struggle, anguish", from *agōn* "gathering, contest for a prize"] **syn** see DISTRESS

△ **origin** In ancient Greece *agōn* was a public assembly or gathering, especially one for games and athletic contests. *Agōnia* was the struggle for the prize in such contests. From the meaning "a struggle for victory in the games", *agōnia* came to be used first for any physical struggle, then for any activity involving difficulty or pain, and finally for mental anguish as well. Our English word *agony* is a descendant of this Greek *agōnia.*

ag•o•ra \'ag-ə-rə\ *n, pl* **-ras** *or* **-rae** \-ˌrē, -ˌrī\ : the marketplace or place of assembly in an ancient Greek city [Greek]

ag•o•ra•pho•bia \ˌag-ə-rə-ˈfō-bē-ə\ *n* : abnormal fear of crossing or of being in open spaces — **ag•o•ra•pho•bic** \-ˈfō-bik, -ˈfäb-ik\ *adj*

agou•ti \ə-ˈgüt-ē\ *n* **1** : a tropical American rodent about the size of a rabbit **2** : a grizzled color of fur resulting from the barring of each hair in several alternate dark and light bands [French, from Spanish *agutí,* of American Indian origin]

agouti 1

[1]**agrar•i•an** \ə-ˈgrer-ē-ən, -ˈgrar-\ *adj* **1** : of or relating to the land or its ownership ⟨*agrarian* reforms⟩ **2** : of, relating to, or concerned with farmers or farming interests ⟨an *agrarian* political party⟩ **3** : AGRICULTURAL 2 ⟨an *agrarian* country⟩ [Latin *agr-, ager* "field"]

[2]**agrarian** *n* : a member of an agrarian party or movement

agrar•i•an•ism \-ē-ə-ˌniz-əm\ *n* : a social or political movement designed chiefly to improve the economic status of the farmer

agree \ə-ˈgrē\ *vb* **agreed; agree•ing 1** : to give one's approval : CONSENT ⟨*agree* to a plan⟩ **2** : ADMIT, CONCEDE ⟨*agreed* it was a good idea⟩ **3** : to be alike : CORRESPOND ⟨both copies *agree*⟩ **4** : to get on well together **5** : to come to terms ⟨*agree* on a price⟩ **6** : to be fitting or healthful : SUIT ⟨the climate *agrees* with them⟩ **7** : to correspond grammatically in gender, number, case, or person [Middle French *agreer,* from *a-* "ad-" + *gre* "pleasure", from Latin *gratus* "pleasant, agreeable"]

agree•able \ə-ˈgrē-ə-bəl\ *adj* **1** : pleasing to the mind or senses ⟨an *agreeable* climate⟩ ⟨an *agreeable* fragrance⟩ **2** : ready or willing to agree **3** : being in harmony : CONSONANT — **agree•able•ness** *n* — **agree•ably** \-blē\ *adv*

agreed \ə-ˈgrēd\ *adj* : settled by agreement ⟨a previously *agreed* price⟩

agree•ment \ə-ˈgrē-mənt\ *n* **1 a** : the act of agreeing **b** : harmony of opinion, action, or character : CONCORD **2** : a mutual arrangement or understanding as to a course of action; *also* : a written record of such an agreement **3** : the fact of agreeing grammatically

ag•ri•cul•tur•al \ˌag-ri-ˈkəlch-rəl, -ə-rəl\ *adj* **1** : of, relating to, or used in agriculture **2** : engaged in or concerned with agriculture ⟨an *agricultural* society⟩ — **ag•ri•cul•tur•al•ly** \-ē\ *adv*

ag•ri•cul•ture \ˈag-ri-ˌkəl-chər\ *n* : the science, art, or occupation of cultivating the soil, producing crops, and raising livestock : FARMING [French, from Latin *agricultura,* from *ager* "field" + *cultura* "cultivation"] — **ag•ri•cul•tur•ist** \ˌag-ri-ˈkəlch-rəst, -ə-rəst\ *n*

ag•ri•mo•ny \ˈag-rə-ˌmō-nē\ *n, pl* **-nies** : a common yellow-flowered herb of the rose family having toothed leaves and fruits like burs [Latin *agrimonia*]

agron•o•my \ə-ˈgrän-ə-mē\ *n* : a branch of agriculture that deals with the raising of crops and the care of the soil [Greek *agros* "field" + *nomos* "law"] — **ag•ro•nom•ic** \ˌag-rə-ˈnäm-ik\ *adj* — **ag•ro•nom•i•cal•ly** \-ˈnäm-i-kə-lē, -klē\ *adv* — **agron•o•mist** \ə-ˈgrän-ə-məst\ *n*

aground \ə-ˈgrau̇nd\ *adv or adj* **1** : on or onto the shore or the bottom of a body of water ⟨a ship run *aground*⟩ **2** : on the ground ⟨planes aloft and *aground*⟩

ague \ˈā-gyü\ *n* **1** : a fever (as malaria) marked by outbreaks of chills, fever, and sweating that recur at regular intervals **2** : a fit of shivering : CHILL [Middle French *agüe,* from Medieval Latin *febris acuta,* literally, "sharp fever"] — **agu•ish** \ˈā-ˌgyü-ish\ *adj* — **agu•ish•ly** *adv*

ah \ˈä\ *interj* — used to express delight, relief, regret, or contempt [Middle English]

aha \ä-ˈhä\ *interj* — used to express surprise, triumph, or derision [Middle English]

ahead \ə-ˈhed\ *adv or adj* **1 a** : in a forward direction or position : FORWARD ⟨go *ahead*⟩ **b** : in front ⟨the car *ahead*⟩ **2** : in, into, or for the future ⟨think *ahead*⟩ **3** : in or toward a more advantageous position ⟨trying to get *ahead*⟩ **4** : in advance ⟨make payments *ahead*⟩

ahead of *prep* **1** : in front or advance of **2** : in excess of : ABOVE

ahem *a throat-clearing sound; often read as* ə-ˈhem\ *interj* — used especially to attract attention [imitative]

A–ho•ri•zon \ˈā-hə-ˌrīz-n\ *n* : the outermost dark-colored layer of a soil profile consisting of topsoil containing partly disintegrated organic debris

ahoy \ə-ˈhȯi\ *interj* — used in hailing ⟨ship *ahoy*⟩ [*a-* (as in *aha*) + Middle English *hoy,* interjection]

[1]**aid** \ˈād\ *vb* **1** : to provide with what is useful or necessary in achieving an end **2** : to give assistance [Middle French *aider,* from Latin *adjutare,* from *adjutus,* past participle of *adjuvare,* from *ad-* + *juvare* "to help"]

[2]**aid** *n* **1 a** : the act of helping **b** : help given : ASSISTANCE **2 a** : an assisting person or group **b** : something (as a device) by which assistance is given ⟨an *aid* to understanding⟩ ⟨a visual *aid*⟩

aide \ˈād\ *n* : one that acts as an assistant; *esp* : a military officer acting as assistant to a superior [short for *aide-de-camp*]

aide–de–camp \ˌād-di-ˈkamp, -ˈkä^n\ *n, pl* **aides–de–camp** \ˌādz-di-\ : a military aide [French *aide de camp,* literally, "camp assistant"]

ai•grette \ā-ˈgret, ˈā-ˌ\ *n* : a plume or decorative tuft for the head [French]

ai•ki•do \ˌī-ki-ˈdō\ *n* : a Japanese art of self-defense that consists of not actively resisting an attack but moving in such a way that the attacker's own momentum works against him [Japanese *aikidō,* from *ai-* "together" + *ki* "spirit" + *dō* "art"]

ail \ˈāl\ *vb* **1** : to be the matter with : TROUBLE ⟨what *ails* you?⟩ **2** : to have something the matter; *esp* : to suffer ill health [Old English *eglan*]

ai•lan•thus \ā-ˈlan-thəs, -ˈlant-\ *n* : a widely grown quick-growing Asian tree with pinnate leaves and terminal clusters of ill-scented greenish flowers — called also *tree of heaven* [Amboinese (the language of Ambon, an Indonesian island) *ai lanto,* literally, "tree of heaven"]

ai•le•ron \ˈā-lə-ˌrän\ *n* : a movable portion of an airplane wing or a movable airfoil external to the wing for imparting a rolling motion [French, from *aile* "wing", from Latin *ala*]

ail•ment \ˈāl-mənt\ *n* : a bodily disorder : SICKNESS

[1]**aim** \ˈām\ *vb* **1 a** : to direct a course ⟨a goal to *aim* for⟩ **b** : to point a weapon at an object **2** : to direct one's efforts : ASPIRE ⟨*aim* high⟩ **3** : to have as a purpose : INTEND ⟨*aims* to win⟩ **4** : POINT 5a ⟨telescopes *aimed* toward Mars⟩ [Middle French *aesmer* "to aim, estimate", from Latin *aestimare* "to estimate"]

[2]**aim** *n* **1 a** : the pointing of a weapon or a missile at a mark **b** : the ability to hit a target ⟨your *aim* is deadly⟩ **2** : GOAL 2, PURPOSE **syn** see INTENTION

aim•less \ˈām-ləs\ *adj* : lacking aim or purpose ⟨*aimless* wandering⟩ — **aim•less•ly** *adv* — **aim•less•ness** *n*

ain't \ˈānt\ **1 a** : are not **b** : is not **c** : am not — though disapproved by many and more common in less educated speech, used orally in most parts of the United States by many educated speakers especially in the phrase *ain't I* **2** *substandard* **a** : have not **b** : has not [probably contraction of *are not*]

Ai•nu \ˈī-nü\ *n* **1** : a member of an indigenous Caucasoid people of Japan living chiefly in the northern islands **2** : the language of the Ainu people [Ainu, literally, "man"]

[1]**air** \ˈaər, ˈeər\ *n* **1 a** : the invisible mixture of odorless tasteless gases (as nitrogen and oxygen) that surrounds the earth **b** : a light breeze **2** : COMPRESSED AIR ⟨*air* sprayer⟩ **3 a** : a field of operation for aircraft ⟨transport by *air*⟩ **b** : AIRCRAFT ⟨*air* attack⟩ ⟨*air* mechanic⟩ ⟨*air* patrol⟩ **c** : AVIATION ⟨*air* safety⟩ ⟨*air* rights⟩ **d** : AIR FORCE ⟨*air* headquarters⟩ **e** (1) : the medium of transmission of radio waves (2) : RADIO, TELEVISION ⟨went on the *air*⟩ **4 a** : outward appearance : apparent nature ⟨an *air* of dignity⟩ **b** *pl* : an artificial or affected manner : HAUGHTINESS ⟨put on *airs*⟩ **c** : a surrounding or pervading influence : ATMOSPHERE ⟨an *air* of mystery⟩ **5** : TUNE 1, MELODY [Old French, from Latin *aer,* from Greek *aēr*]

[2]**air** *vt* **1** : to place in the air for cooling, refreshing, or cleansing ⟨*air* blankets⟩ **2** : to make known in public ⟨*air* one's complaints⟩

air bladder *n* : a sac in a fish containing gas and especially air and serving as a float regulating buoyancy or assisting respiration — called also *swim bladder*

air•borne \-ˌbōrn, -ˌbȯrn\ *adj* : supported or transported by air

air brake *n* **1** : a brake operated by a piston driven by compressed air **2** : a surface that may be projected into the air for lowering the speed of an airplane

air•brush \-ˌbrəsh\ *n* : an atomizer for applying by compressed air a fine spray (as of paint) — **airbrush** *vt*

airbrush

air–con•di•tion \ˌaər-kən-ˈdish-ən, ˌeər-\ *vt* **:** to equip with an apparatus for cleaning air and controlling its humidity and temperature — **air con•di•tion•er** \-ˈdish-nər, -ə-nər\ *n*

air–cool \ˈaər-ˈkül, ˈeər-\ *vt* **:** to cool the cylinders of (an internal-combustion engine) solely by the use of air

air•craft \ˈaər-ˌkraft, ˈeər-\ *n, pl* **aircraft :** a machine (as an airplane, blimp, or helicopter) for navigation of the air that is supported either by its own buoyancy or by the action of the air against its surfaces

aircraft carrier *n* **:** a warship with a deck on which airplanes can be launched and landed

air•crew \ˈaər-ˌkrü, ˈeər-\ *n* **:** the crew manning an airplane

air•drome \-ˌdrōm\ *n* **:** AIRPORT

air•drop \-ˌdräp\ *n* **:** delivery of cargo or personnel by parachute from an airplane in flight — **air–drop**\-ˌdräp\ *vt*

Aire•dale \ˈaər-ˌdāl, ˈeər-\ *n* **:** any of a breed of large terriers with a hard wiry coat that is dark on the back and sides and tan elsewhere [*Airedale,* valley of the Aire river, England]

Air Express *service mark* — used for package transport by air

air•field \ˈaər-ˌfēld, ˈeər-\ *n* **1 :** the landing field of an airport **2 :** AIRPORT

air•foil \-ˌfȯil\ *n* **:** an airplane surface (as a wing or rudder) designed to produce reaction (as lift or drag) from the air through which it moves

air force *n* **:** the military organization of a nation for air warfare

air•frame \-ˌfrām\ *n* **:** the structure of an airplane or rocket without the power plant

air gun *n* **:** any of various hand tools that work by compressed air; *esp* **:** AIRBRUSH

air hole *n* **1 :** a hole to admit or discharge air **2 :** AIR POCKET

air lane *n* **:** an airway that is customarily followed by airplanes

air letter *n* **1 :** a letter sent by airmail **2 :** a sheet of airmail stationery that can be folded and sealed with the message inside and the address outside

air•lift \ˈaər-ˌlift, ˈeər-\ *n* **:** a supply line operated by aircraft — **airlift** *vt*

air•line \-ˌlīn\ *n* **:** an air transportation system including equipment, routes, and personnel

air line *n* **:** BEELINE

air•lin•er \-ˌlī-nər\ *n* **:** an airplane operated by an airline

air lock *n* **:** an air space with two airtight doors for permitting movement between two spaces with different pressures or different atmospheres

air•mail \ˈaər-ˈmāl, ˈeər-, -ˌmāl\ *n* **:** the system of transporting mail by airplanes; *also* **:** the mail transported — **airmail** *vt*

air•man \-mən\ *n* **1 :** an enlisted rank in the Air Force above airman basic and below airman first class **2 :** a civilian or military pilot or aviator

airman basic *n* **:** the lowest enlisted rank in the Air Force

airman first class *n* **:** an enlisted rank in the Air Force above airman and below sergeant

air mass *n* **:** a body of air extending hundreds or thousands of miles horizontally and sometimes as high as the stratosphere and maintaining as it travels nearly uniform conditions of temperature and humidity at any given level

air mattress *n* **:** MATTRESS 2

air–mind•ed \ˈaər-ˈmīn-dəd, ˈeər-\ *adj* **:** interested in aviation or in air travel — **air–mind•ed•ness** *n*

air piracy *n* **:** the hijacking of a flying airplane

air•plane \-ˌplān\ *n* **:** a fixed-wing aircraft heavier than air that is driven by a propeller or by a rearward jet and supported by the reaction of the air against its wings [alteration of *aeroplane,* from Greek *aēr* "air" + *planos* "wandering", from *planasthai* "to wander"]

air plant *n* **1 :** EPIPHYTE **2 :** BRYOPHYLLUM

air pocket *n* **:** a condition of the atmosphere (as a down current) that causes an airplane to drop suddenly

air police *n* **:** the military police of an air force

air•port \ˈaər-ˌpōrt, ˈeər-, -ˌpȯrt\ *n* **:** a tract of land or water that is maintained for the landing and takeoff of airplanes and for receiving and discharging passengers and cargo and that usually has facilities for the shelter, supply, and repair of planes

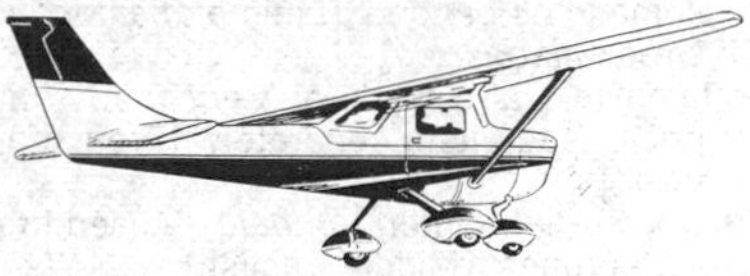

airplane

air pump *n* **:** a pump for exhausting air from a closed space or for compressing air or forcing it through other apparatus

air raid *n* **:** an attack by armed aircraft on a surface target

air rifle *n* **:** a rifle that shoots BBs or pellets by compressed air

air sac *n* **1 :** one of the air-filled spaces connected with the lungs of a bird **2 :** one of the thin-walled microscopic pouches in which gases are exchanged in the lungs — called also *alveolus*

air•ship \ˈaər-ˌship, ˈeər-\ *n* **:** a lighter-than-air aircraft having propulsion and steering systems

air•sick \-ˌsik\ *adj* **:** affected with motion sickness associated with flying — **air•sick•ness** *n*

air•space \-ˌspās\ *n* **:** the space lying above a nation and coming under its jurisdiction

air•speed \-ˌspēd\ *n* **:** the speed of an airplane relative to the air as opposed to its speed relative to the earth

air•strip \-ˌstrip\ *n* **:** a runway without normal airport facilities

air•tight \-ˈtīt\ *adj* **1 :** so tightly sealed that no air can get in or out **2 :** leaving no opening for attack ⟨*airtight* defenses⟩ ⟨an *airtight* argument⟩ — **air•tight•ness** *n*

air•wave\-ˌwāv\ *n* **:** the medium of radio and television transmission — usually used in pl.

air•way \-ˌwā\ *n* **1 :** a passage for a current of air **2 :** a regular route for airplanes from airport to airport; *esp* **:** such a route equipped with navigational aids **3 :** AIRLINE

air•wor•thy \-ˌwər-t͟hē\ *adj* **:** fit or safe for operation in the air ⟨a very *airworthy* plane⟩ — **air•wor•thi•ness** *n*

airy \ˈaər-ē, ˈeər-\ *adj* **air•i•er; -est 1 a :** of or relating to air **:** ATMOSPHERIC **b :** high in the air **:** LOFTY ⟨*airy* perches⟩ **2 :** consisting of air **3 :** performed in the air **:** AERIAL ⟨*airy* leaps⟩ **4 :** lacking a sound or solid basis ⟨*airy* romance⟩ **5 :** resembling air in lightness **:** ETHEREAL **6 :** open to the air **:** BREEZY ⟨an *airy* room⟩ — **air•i•ly** \ˈar-ə-lē, ˈer-\ *adv* — **air•i•ness** \ˈar-ē-nəs, ˈer-\ *n*

aisle \ˈīl\ *n* **1 :** the side of a church separated by piers from the nave **2 a :** a passage (as in a theater) between sections of seats **b :** a passage (as in a store) for inside traffic [Middle French *aile* "wing", from Latin *ala*]

ajar \ə-ˈjär\ *adj or adv* **:** slightly open ⟨a door *ajar*⟩ [earlier *on char,* from *on* + *char* "turn", from Old English *cierr*]

akim•bo \ə-ˈkim-bō\ *adj or adv* **1 :** having the hand on the hip and the elbow turned outward **2 :** set in a bent position ⟨legs *akimbo*⟩ [Middle English *in kenebowe*]

akin \ə-ˈkin\ *adj* **1 :** related by blood **:** descended from a common ancestor or prototype **2 :** essentially similar or related **:** ALIKE

Ak•ka•di•an \ə-ˈkād-ē-ən\ *n* **1 :** one of a Semitic people invading and settling central Mesopotamia north of the Sumerians (3000–1900 B.C.) **2 :** an ancient Semitic language of Mesopotamia used from about the 28th to the 1st century B.C. — **Akkadian** *adj*

al- — see AD-

¹-al \əl, ᵊl\ *adj suffix* **:** of, relating to, or characterized by ⟨direc*tional*⟩ ⟨fic*tional*⟩ [Latin *-alis*]

²-al *n suffix* **:** action **:** process ⟨rehears*al*⟩ [Old French *-aille,* from Latin *-alia,* neuter plural of *-alis*]

ala \ˈā-lə\ *n, pl* **alae** \-ˌlē\ **:** a wing-shaped anatomic process or part **:** WING [Latin] — **alar** \ˈā-lər\ *adj* — **ala•ry**\-lə-rē\ *adj*

a la *or* **à la** \ˌal-ə, ˌäl-ə, ˌäl-, ˌä\ *prep* **:** in the manner of [French *à la*]

al•a•bas•ter \ˈal-ə-ˌbas-tər\ *n* **1 :** a compact fine-textured usually white and translucent gypsum that is carved into objects (as vases) **2 :** a hard compact calcite that is translucent and sometimes banded [Latin *alabaster* "vase of alabaster", from Greek *alabastros*]

a la carte \ˌal-ə-ˈkärt, ˌäl-\ *adj or adv* **:** according to a menu that prices each item separately [French *à la carte* "by the bill of fare"]

alack \ə-ˈlak\ *interj, archaic* — used to express sorrow, regret, or reproach [Middle English]

alac•ri•ty \ə-ˈlak-rət-ē\ *n* **:** promptness in response **:** a cheerful readiness to do something [Latin *alacritas,* from *alacer* "lively, eager"] **syn** see CELERITY — **alac•ri•tous** \-rət-əs\ *adj*

a la mode \ˌal-ə-ˈmōd, ˌäl-\ *adj* **1 :** FASHIONABLE, STYLISH **2 :** topped with ice cream [French *à la mode* "according to the fashion"]

al•a•nine \ˈal-ə-ˌnēn\ *n* **:** amino acid $C_3H_7NO_2$ formed especially by the hydrolysis of proteins [German *alanin,* derived from *aldehyd* "aldehyde"]

[1]**alarm** \ə-ˈlärm\ *also* **alar•um** \ə-ˈlär-əm, -ˈlar-\ *n* **1** *usually* *alarum, obsolete* **:** a call to arms **2 a :** a signal (as a loud noise or flashing light) that warns or alerts **b :** a device that warns or signals **3 :** fear caused by a sudden sense of danger [Middle French *alarme,* from Italian *all'arme* "to arms"]

[2]**alarm** *also* **alarum** *vt* **1 :** to notify of danger **:** put on the alert **2 :** to strike with fear **:** FRIGHTEN — **alarm•ing•ly** \-ˈlär-ming-lē\ *adv*

alarm clock *n* **:** a clock that can be set to sound an alarm at a desired time

alarm•ist \ə-ˈlär-məst\ *n* **:** one inclined to alarm others especially needlessly — **alarm•ism** \-ˌmiz-əm\ *n*

alas \ə-ˈlas\ *interj* — used to express unhappiness, pity, or concern [Old French, from *a* "ah" + *las* "weary", from Latin *lassus*]

Alas•kan malamute \ə-ˌlas-kən-\ *n* **:** any of a breed of powerful heavy-coated deep-chested dogs of Alaskan origin with erect ears, heavily cushioned feet, and plumy tail

Alas•ka time \ə-ˈlas-kə-\ *n* **:** the time of the 10th time zone west of Greenwich that includes central Alaska

alate \ˈā-ˌlāt\ *adj* **:** having wings or a winglike part [Latin *alatus,* from *ala* "wing"]

alb \ˈalb\ *n* **:** a full-length white linen vestment with long sleeves worn by a priest at Mass [Medieval Latin *alba,* from Latin *albus* "white"]

al•ba•core \ˈal-bə-ˌkōr, -ˌkȯr\ *n, pl* **-core** *or* **-cores :** a large pelagic tuna with long pectoral fins that is the source of most canned tuna; *also* **:** any of several tunas [Portuguese *albacor,* from Arabic *al-bakūrah* "the albacore"]

Al•ba•nian \al-ˈbā-nē-ən, -nyən\ *n* **1 :** a native or inhabitant of Albania **2 :** the Indo-European language of the Albanian people — **Albanian** *adj*

al•ba•tross \ˈal-bə-ˌtrȯs, -ˌträs\ *n, pl* **-tross** *or* **-tross•es :** any of various large web-footed seabirds that are related to the petrels and include the birds of the sea with the greatest wingspread [probably alteration of *alcatras* "water bird", from Portuguese or Spanish *alcatraz* "pelican"]

albatross

al•be•do \al-ˈbēd-ō\ *n* **:** the fraction of incident radiant energy reflected from a surface (as of the earth) [Late Latin, "whiteness", from Latin *albus* "white"]

al•be•it \ȯl-ˈbē-ət, al-\ *conj* **:** even though **:** ALTHOUGH [Middle English, literally, "all though it be"]

al•bi•no \al-ˈbī-nō\ *n, pl* **-nos :** an organism deficient in coloring matter; *esp* **:** a human being or lower animal that is congenitally deficient in pigment and usually has a milky or translucent skin, white or colorless hair, and eyes with pink or blue iris and deep red pupil [Portuguese, from Spanish, from *albo* "white", from Latin *albus*] — **al•bi•nism** \ˈal-bə-ˌniz-əm, al-ˈbī-\ *n* — **al•bi•nis•tic** \ˌal-bə-ˈnis-tik\ *adj* — **albino** *adj* — **al•bi•not•ic** \ˌal-bə-ˈnät-ik, -ˌbī-\ *adj*

al•bite \ˈal-ˌbīt\ *n* **:** a usually white feldspar containing sodium [Swedish *albit,* from Latin *albus* "white"]

al•bum \ˈal-bəm\ *n* **1 a :** a book with blank pages used for a collection (as of photographs) **b :** a container for a phonograph record **c :** one or more phonograph records or tape recordings produced as a single unit **2 :** a collection usually in book form of literary selections, musical compositions, or pictures **:** ANTHOLOGY [Latin, "white tablet", from *albus* "white"]

al•bu•men \al-ˈbyü-mən\ *n* **1 :** the white of an egg **2 :** ALBUMIN [Latin, from *albus* "white"]

al•bu•min \al-ˈbyü-mən\ *n* **:** any of numerous heat-coagulable water-soluble proteins found especially in blood, the whites of eggs, and various animal and plant tissues [Latin *albumen* "white of an egg"]

al•bu•min•ous \al-ˈbyü-mə-nəs\ *adj* **:** relating to, containing, or having the properties of albumen or albumin

al•ca•zar \al-ˈkäz-ər, -ˈkaz-\ *n* **:** a Spanish fortress or palace [Spanish *alcázar,* from Arabic *al-qaṣr* "the castle"]

al•che•my \ˈal-kə-mē\ *n* **1 :** a medieval chemical science and philosophy aiming to achieve the conversion of base metals into gold, the discovery of a universal cure for disease, and the discovery of a means of indefinitely prolonging life **2 :** a power or process of transforming something common into something precious [Medieval Latin *alchymia,* from Arabic *al-kīmiyā'* "the alchemy", from Late Greek *chēmeia* "alchemy"] — **al•chem•i•cal** \al-ˈkem-i-kəl\ *adj* — **al•chem•i•cal•ly** \-kə-lē, -klē\ *adv* — **al•che•mist** \ˈal-kə-məst\ *n*

al•co•hol \ˈal-kə-ˌhȯl\ *n* **1 a :** a colorless volatile flammable liquid C_2H_5OH that is the intoxicating agent in fermented and distilled liquors (as beer, wine, whiskey) — called also *ethyl alcohol* **b :** any of various carbon compounds that are similar to ethyl alcohol in having at least one hydroxyl group **2 :** a beverage (as beer, wine, or whiskey) containing alcohol; *also* **:** LIQUORS [Medieval Latin, "powdered antimony", from Spanish, from Arabic *al-kuḥul* "the powdered antimony"]

[1]**al•co•hol•ic** \ˌal-kə-ˈhȯl-ik, -ˈhäl-\ *adj* **1 :** of, relating to, caused by, or containing alcohol **2 :** affected with alcoholism — **al•co•hol•i•cal•ly** \-i-kə-lē, -klē\ *adv*

[2]**alcoholic** *n* **:** one affected with alcoholism

al•co•hol•ism \ˈal-kə-ˌhȯ-ˌliz-əm\ *n* **:** continued excessive and usually uncontrollable use of alcoholic drinks; *also* **:** the abnormal state associated with such use

al•cove \ˈal-ˌkōv\ *n* **1 :** a small recessed section of a room **:** NOOK **2 :** an arched opening (as in a wall) **:** NICHE [French *alcôve,* from Spanish *alcoba,* from Arabic *al-qubbah* "the arch"]

Al•deb•a•ran \al-ˈdeb-ə-rən\ *n* **:** a red star that is seen in the eye of Taurus and is the brightest star in the Hyades [Arabic *al-dabarān,* literally, "the follower"]

al•de•hyde \ˈal-də-ˌhīd\ *n* **1 :** ACETALDEHYDE **2 :** any of various highly reactive organic compounds typified by acetaldehyde and characterized by the group — CHO [German *aldehyd,* from New Latin *al. dehyd.,* abbreviation of *alcohol dehydrogenatum* "dehydrogenated alcohol"]

al•der \ˈȯl-dər\ *n* **:** any of a genus of toothed-leaved trees or shrubs related to the birches and found especially in moist ground [Old English *alor*]

al•der•fly \-ˌflī\ *n* **:** any of several winged insects closely related to the dobsonflies

al•der•man \ˈȯl-dər-mən\ *n* **1 :** a high Anglo-Saxon government official **2 :** a member of a governing or legislative body of some counties, cities, towns, or boroughs [Old English *ealdorman,* from *ealdor* "elder, parent"] — **al•der•man•ic** \ˌȯl-dər-ˈman-ik\ *adj*

al•der•wom•an \-ˌwu̇m-ən\ *n* **:** a woman with the rank and office of an alderman

al•dol•ase \ˈal-də-ˌlās, -ˌlāz\ *n* **:** an enzyme of living systems that catalyzes reversibly the cleavage of a fructose ester into sugars with three carbon atoms [derived from *aldehyde*]

al•do•ste•rone \al-ˈdäs-tə-ˌrōn, ˌal-dō-stə-ˈrōn\ *n* **:** a steroid hormone of the adrenal cortex that functions in the regulation of the salt and water balance of the body [derived from *aldehyde*]

al•drin \ˈȯl-drən, ˈal-\ *n* **:** a long-acting insecticide that is a chlorinated derivative of naphthalene [Kurt *Alder,* died 1958, German chemist]

ale \ˈāl\ *n* **1 :** an alcoholic beverage brewed from malt and hops that is usually heavier bodied and more bitter than beer **2 :** an English country festival at which ale is the chief beverage [Old English *ealu*]

alee \ə-ˈlē\ *adv* **:** on or toward the lee

ale•house \'āl-,hau̇s\ *n* : a place where ale is sold to be drunk on the premises

alem•bic \ə-'lem-bik\ *n* : an apparatus formerly used in distillation [Medieval Latin *alembicum,* from Arabic *al-anbīq* "the still", derived from Greek *ambix* "cap of a still"]

aleph–null \'äl-,ef-'nəl, -əf-\ *n* : a number that is the smallest infinite cardinal number and that is equal to the number of elements in any set that can be put into a one-to-one correspondence with the positive integers [from *aleph,* the first letter of the Hebrew alphabet]

[1]alert \ə-'lərt\ *adj* **1 a :** watchful and prompt to meet danger **b :** quick to perceive and act **2 :** briskly active : LIVELY ⟨an *alert* movement⟩ [Italian *all'erta,* literally, "on the ascent"] **syn** see CLEVER, WATCHFUL — **alert•ly** *adv* — **alert•ness** *n*

[2]alert *n* **1 :** a signal of danger **2 a :** the state of readiness of those warned by an alert **b :** the period during which an alert is in effect — **on the alert :** on the lookout for danger

[3]alert *vt* : to call to a state of readiness : WARN

al•eu•rone \'al-yə-,rōn\ *n* : granular protein matter in the endosperm of a seed [Greek *aleuron* "flour"]

Aleut \ə-'lüt\ *n* **1 :** a member of a people of the Aleutian and Shumagin islands and the western part of Alaska peninsula **2 :** the language of the Aleuts [Russian]

ale•wife \'āl-,wīf\ *n* : an anadromous food fish of the herring family abundant along the Atlantic coast

Al•ex•an•dri•an \,al-ig-'zan-drē-ən, ,el-\ *adj* : HELLENISTIC [from the prominence of Alexandria, Egypt, in the intellectual and cultural life of the Hellenistic period]

al•ex•an•drine \-'zan-drən\ *n, often cap* : a line of poetry consisting of six iambic feet [Middle French *vers alexandrin,* literally, "verse of Alexander"; from its use in a poem on Alexander the Great]

al•fal•fa \al-'fal-fə\ *n* : a deep-rooted European leguminous plant with purple flowers and leaves like clover that is widely grown for hay and forage [Spanish, from Arabic dialect *al-faṣfaṣah* "the alfalfa"]

al•fres•co \al-'fres-kō\ *adv or adj* : in the open air ⟨an *alfresco* lunch⟩ [Italian]

al•ga \'al-gə\ *n, pl* **al•gae** \'al-jē\ : any plant of a group (Algae) that forms the lowest division of the plant kingdom and includes seaweeds and related forms mostly growing in water, lacking a vascular system, and having chlorophyll often masked by brown or red coloring matter [Latin, "seaweed"] — **al•gal** \'al-gəl\ *adj*

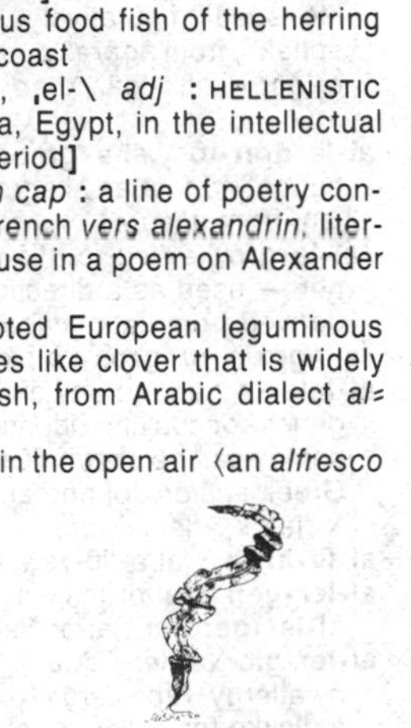

alga: *top* laminaria, *middle* ulva, *bottom* kelp

al•ge•bra \'al-jə-brə\ *n* : a branch of mathematics in which symbols (as letters and numerals) representing various entities (as numbers or functions) are combined according to special rules of operation [Medieval Latin, from Arabic *al-jabr,* literally, "the reduction"] — **al•ge•bra•ist** \-,brā-əst\ *n*

al•ge•bra•ic \,al-jə-'brā-ik\ *adj* **1 :** of or relating to algebra ⟨*algebraic* expression⟩ **2 :** involving only a finite number of repetitions of addition, subtraction, multiplication, division, extraction of roots, and raising to powers — **al•ge•bra•i•cal•ly** \-'brā-ə-kə-lē, -klē\ *adv*

-al•gia \'al-jē-ə, -jə\ *n combining form* : pain ⟨neuralgia⟩ [Greek *algos*]

al•gin \'al-jən\ *n* : any of various colloidal substances from brown algae including some used especially as stabilizers or emulsifiers

Al•gol \'al-,gäl, -,gȯl\ *n* : a binary star in the constellation Perseus whose larger component revolves about and eclipses the smaller brighter star causing periodic variation in brightness [Arabic *al-ghūl,* literally, "the ghoul"]

AL•GOL \'al-,gäl, -,gȯl\ *n* : a language for programming a computer especially to work scientific problems [*algo*rithmic *l*anguage]

Al•gon•qui•an \al-'gän-kwē-ən, -'gäŋ-\ *n* **1 :** an Indian people of the Ottawa river valley **2 :** a stock of Indian languages spoken from Labrador to the Carolinas and westward to the Great Plains **3 :** a member of the Indian peoples speaking Algonquian languages — **Algonquian** *adj*

al•go•rithm \'al-gə-,rith-əm\ *n* : a rule of procedure for solving a mathematical problem (as of finding the greatest common divisor of two numbers) in a finite number of steps that frequently involves repetition of an operation [Medieval Latin *algorismus,* from Arabic *al-khuwārizmi,* from *al-Khuwarizmi,* flourished 825 A.D., Arab mathematician] — **al•go•rith•mic** \,al-gə-'rith-mik\ *adj*

[1]alias \'ā-lē-əs, 'āl-yəs\ *adv* : otherwise called : otherwise known as [Latin, "otherwise", from *alius* "other"]

[2]alias *n* : an assumed name

[1]al•i•bi \'al-ə-,bī\ *n* **1 :** a plea made by an accused person that he was elsewhere when the incident occurred; *also* : the fact or state of having been elsewhere at the time **2 :** a plausible excuse (as for failure) [Latin, "elsewhere", from *alius* "other"]

[2]alibi *vb* **-bied; -bi•ing 1 :** to offer an excuse **2 :** to make an excuse for

[1]alien \'ā-lē-ən, 'āl-yən\ *adj* **1 :** belonging or relating to another person or place : STRANGE **2 :** relating, belonging, or owing allegiance to another country : FOREIGN ⟨*alien* residents⟩ **3 :** wholly different in nature or character ⟨an effect *alien* from the one intended⟩ **4 :** not properly belonging to something ⟨a detail *alien* to the argument⟩ **5 :** repugnant in nature ⟨an *alien* idea⟩ [Old French, from Latin *alienus,* from *alius* "other"]

[2]alien *n* **1 :** a person of another family, race, or nation **2 :** a foreign-born resident who has not been naturalized and is still a subject or citizen of a foreign country

alien•able \'āl-yə-nə-bəl, 'ā-lē-ə-nə-\ *adj* : transferable to the ownership of another ⟨*alienable* property⟩ — **alien•abil•i•ty** \,āl-yə-nə-'bil-ət-ē, ,ā-lē-ə-nə-\ *n*

alien•ate \'ā-lē-ə-,nāt, 'āl-yə-,nāt\ *vt* **1 :** to transfer (as a title, property, or right) to another **2 :** to cause to lose feelings of love, loyalty, or attachment ⟨*alienated* by their constant complaints⟩ **3 :** to cause to be withdrawn or diverted ⟨*alienate* funds from a project⟩ — **alien•ation** \,ā-lē-ə-'nā-shən, ,āl-yə-'nā-\ *n* — **alien•ator** \'ā-lē-ə-,nāt-ər, 'āl-yə-,nāt-\ *n*

alien•ist \'ā-lē-ə-nəst, 'āl-yə-nəst\ *n* : PSYCHIATRIST; *esp* : one who testifies in a legal proceeding

[1]alight \ə-'līt\ *vi* **alight•ed** \-'līt-əd\ *also* **alit** \ə-'lit\; **alight•ing 1 :** to come down from something : DISMOUNT **2 :** to descend from the air and settle : LAND

[2]alight *adj* : lighted up : ILLUMINATED

align *also* **aline** \ə-'līn\ *vb* **1 :** to bring or come into line or alignment **2 :** to cause to support or to disapprove something (as a cause or party) [French *aligner,* from Old French, from *ligne* "line", from Latin *linea*] — **align•er** *n*

align•ment *also* **aline•ment** \ə-'līn-mənt\ *n* **1 a :** the act of aligning : the state of being aligned **b :** the proper positioning or state of adjustment of parts (as of a mechanical or electronic device) in relation to each other **2 :** an arrangement of groups or forces ⟨a new political *alignment*⟩

[1]alike \ə-'līk\ *adj* : LIKE 1a — **alike•ness** *n*

[2]alike *adv* : in the same manner, form, or degree

al•i•ment \'al-ə-mənt\ *n* : NUTRIMENT; *also* : food for the mind or spirit [Latin *alimentum,* from *alere* "to nourish"] — **al•i•men•tal** \,al-ə-'ment-l\ *adj* — **al•i•men•tal•ly** \-l-ē\ *adv*

al•i•men•ta•ry \,al-ə-'ment-ə-rē, -'men-trē\ *adj* : of or relating to nourishment or nutrition

alimentary canal *n* : the tube that extends from mouth to anus and functions in digestion and absorption of food and in elimination of residual waste

al•i•mo•ny \'al-ə-,mō-nē\ *n, pl* **-nies :** an allowance of money made to one spouse by the other for support pending or after legal separation or divorce [Latin *alimonia* "support", from *alere* "to nourish"]

al•i•phat•ic \,al-ə-'fat-ik\ *adj* : belonging to a group of organic compounds whose structure is in the form of a chain whose ends are not joined [Greek *aleiphar* "oil"]

al•i•quot \'al-ə-,kwät, -kwət\ *adj* : contained an exact number of times in another ⟨5 is an *aliquot* part of 15⟩ [Medieval Latin *aliquotus,* from Latin *aliquot* "some, several"]

alive \ə-'līv\ *adj* **1 :** having life : LIVING ⟨the proudest person alive⟩ **2** : still in existence, force, or operation : ACTIVE ⟨keep hope *alive*⟩ **3** : knowingly aware or conscious : SENSITIVE ⟨we were *alive* to the danger⟩ **4** : marked by much life, animation, or activity : SWARMING ⟨blossoms *alive* with bees⟩ — **alive•ness** *n*

aliz•a•rin \ə-ˈliz-ə-rən\ *n* : an orange or red crystalline compound $C_{14}H_8O_4$ made synthetically and used as a red dye and in making red pigments [probably from French *alizarine*]

al•ka•li \ˈal-kə-ˌlī\ *n, pl* **-lies** *or* **-lis** **1** : a substance (as a hydroxide or carbonate of an alkali metal) having marked basic properties **2** : ALKALI METAL **3** : a soluble salt or a mixture of soluble salts present in some soils of arid regions [Medieval Latin, from Arabic *al-qili* "the soda ash"]

alkali metal *n* : any of the univalent mostly basic metals of the group lithium, sodium, potassium, rubidium, cesium, and francium

al•ka•line \ˈal-kə-ˌlīn, -lən\ *adj* : of, relating to, or having the properties of an alkali; *esp* : having a pH of more than 7 — **al•ka•lin•i•ty** \ˌal-kə-ˈlin-ət-ē\ *n*

alkaline earth *n* **1** : an oxide of any of several strongly basic metals comprising calcium, strontium, and barium and sometimes also magnesium, radium, or less often beryllium **2** : ALKALINE-EARTH METAL

alkaline-earth metal *n* : any of the metals whose oxides are the alkaline earths

al•ka•loid \ˈal-kə-ˌlȯid\ *n* : any of numerous usually colorless, complex, and bitter organic bases (as morphine or codeine) that contain nitrogen and usually oxygen and occur especially in seed plants — **al•ka•loi•dal** \ˌal-kə-ˈlȯid-l\ *adj*

al•kyd \ˈal-kəd\ *n* : any of numerous thermoplastic synthetic resins made by heating alcohols with acids or their anhydrides and used especially for protective coatings [probably derived from German *alkohol* "alcohol"]

[1]**all** \ˈȯl\ *adj* **1 a** : the whole of ⟨sat up *all* night⟩ **b** : the greatest possible ⟨told in *all* seriousness⟩ **2** : every member or individual part of ⟨*all* students will go⟩ **3** : the whole number or sum of ⟨*all* the angles of a triangle are equal to two right angles⟩ **4** : EVERY ⟨*all* manner of hardship⟩ **5** : any whatever ⟨beyond *all* doubt⟩ **6 a** : completely taken up with or absorbed by ⟨became *all* attention⟩ **b** : having or seeming to have a prominent physical feature ⟨*all* thumbs⟩ **c** : paying full attention with ⟨*all* ears⟩ **7** : being more than one person or thing ⟨who *all* was there⟩ [Old English *eall*]

[2]**all** *adv* **1** : WHOLLY, ALTOGETHER ⟨sat *all* alone⟩ ⟨*all* across the country⟩ **2** *obsolete* : ONLY 1b, SOLELY **3** *archaic* : quite as indicated : JUST **4** : so much ⟨*all* the better for it⟩ **5** : for each side : APIECE ⟨the score is two *all*⟩

[3]**all** *pron, pl in construction* **1** : the whole number, quantity, or amount ⟨*all* that I have⟩ ⟨*all* of us⟩ **2** : EVERYBODY, EVERYTHING ⟨sacrificed *all* for love⟩ ⟨known to *all*⟩ — **all in all** : on the whole ⟨*all in all,* it could be worse⟩ — **at all** : in any way ⟨no good *at all*⟩

all- *or* **allo-** *combining form* : other : different : atypical ⟨*allo*tropy⟩ [Greek *allos* "other"]

[1]**al•la breve** \ˌal-ə-ˈbrev, ˌäl-ə-ˈbrev-ˌā\ *adv or adj* : in duple or quadruple time with the beat represented by the half note [Italian, literally, "according to the breve"]

[2]**alla breve** *n* : the sign ₵ marking a piece or passage to be played alla breve; *also* : a passage so marked

Al•lah \ˈal-ə, ˈäl-ə, ˈäl-ˌä\ *n* : the Supreme Being of Islam [Arabic *Allāh*]

all-Amer•i•can \ˌȯl-ə-ˈmer-ə-kən\ *adj* **1** : representative of American ideals ⟨an *all-American* city⟩ **2** : selected as the best in the United States ⟨the *all-American* team⟩ — **all-American** *n*

al•lan•to•is \ə-ˈlant-ə-wəs\ *n, pl* **al•lan•to•ides** \ˌal-ən-ˈtō-ə-ˌdēz\ : a fetal membrane of higher vertebrates that is covered with blood vessels and is associated with the chorion in formation of the placenta in mammals [New Latin, derived from Greek *allas* "sausage"] — **al•lan•to•ic** \ˌal-ən-ˈtō-ik\ *adj*

al•lar•gan•do \ˌäl-ˌär-ˈgän-dō\ *adv or adj* : gradually slower with the same or greater volume — used as a direction in music [Italian, literally, "widening"]

all-around \ˌȯ-lə-ˈraủnd\ *adj* : competent in many fields

al•lay \ə-ˈlā\ *vt* **-layed**; **-lay•ing** **1** : to make less severe : RELIEVE ⟨*allay* pain⟩ **2** : to make quiet : CALM ⟨*allay* anxiety⟩ [Old English *ālecgan,* from *ā-,* prefix denoting completion + *lecgan* "to lay"]

all but *adv* : very nearly : ALMOST ⟨*all but* disappeared from public notice⟩ ⟨makes travel *all but* impossible⟩

all clear *n* : a signal that a danger has passed

al•le•ga•tion \ˌal-i-ˈgā-shən\ *n* **1** : the act of alleging **2** : something alleged; *esp* : an assertion unsupported by proof or evidence

al•lege \ə-ˈlej\ *vt* **1** : to state positively but without offering proof ⟨the newspaper *alleged* the mayor's guilt⟩ **2** : to offer as a reason or an excuse ⟨*allege* illness to avoid work⟩ [Old French *alleguer,* from Latin *allegare* "to dispatch, cite", from *ad-* + *legare* "to depute"]

al•leged \ə-ˈlejd, -ˈlej-əd\ *adj* : asserted or believed to be so without proof ⟨the *alleged* criminal⟩ — **al•leg•ed•ly** \ə-ˈlej-əd-lē\ *adv*

al•le•giance \ə-ˈlē-jəns\ *n* **1** : loyalty and obedience owed to one's country or government **2** : devotion or loyalty to a person, group, or cause [Middle English *allegeaunce,* from Old French *ligeance,* from *lige* "liege"] **syn** see FIDELITY

al•le•go•rize \ˈal-ə-ˌgōr-ˌīz, -ˌgȯr-, -gər-\ *vt* **1** : to make into allegory **2** : to treat or explain as allegory — **al•le•go•ri•za•tion** \ˌal-ə-ˌgōr-ə-ˈzā-shən, -ˌgȯr-\ *n* — **al•le•go•riz•er** *n*

al•le•go•ry \ˈal-ə-ˌgōr-ē, -ˌgȯr-\ *n, pl* **-ries** : a story in which the characters and events are symbols expressing truths about human life [Latin *allegoria,* from Greek *allēgoria,* from *allēgorein* "to speak figuratively", from *allos* "other" + *-agorein* "to speak", from *agora* "public assembly"] — **al•le•gor•i•cal** \ˌal-ə-ˈgȯr-i-kəl, -ˈgär-\ *adj* — **al•le•gor•i•cal•ly** \-kə-lē, -klē\ *adv*

al•le•gret•to \ˌal-ə-ˈgret-ō, äl-\ *adv or adj* : faster than andante but not so fast as allegro — used as a direction in music [Italian, from *allegro*]

[1]**al•le•gro** \ə-ˈleg-rō, -ˈlā-grō\ *adv or adj* : in a brisk lively manner — used as a direction in music [Italian, literally, "merry", derived from Latin *alacer* "lively"]

[2]**allegro** *n, pl* **-gros** : a piece or movement in allegro tempo

al•lele \ə-ˈlēl\ *n* : any of the group of genes from which a pair of genes occupying identical places on homologous chromosomes can be drawn [German *allel,* short for *allelomorph,* from Greek *allēlōn* "of one another" + *morphē* "form"] — **al•le•lic** \-ˈlē-lik, -ˈlel-ik\ *adj*

al•le•lu•ia \ˌal-ə-ˈlü-yə\ *interj* : HALLELUJAH

al•ler•gen \ˈal-ər-jən\ *n* : a substance that induces allergy — **al•ler•gen•ic** \ˌal-ər-ˈjen-ik\ *adj*

al•ler•gic \ə-ˈlər-jik\ *adj* **1** : of, relating to, inducing, or affected by allergy ⟨an *allergic* reaction⟩ ⟨*allergic* to cat fur⟩ **2** : having a dislike for ⟨*allergic* to hard work⟩

al•ler•gist \ˈal-ər-jəst\ *n* : a specialist in allergy

al•ler•gy \ˈal-ər-jē\ *n, pl* **-gies** **1** : exaggerated or abnormal reaction (as by sneezing, itching, or rashes) to substances, situations, or physical states that do not have such a strong effect on most people **2** : a feeling of dislike [German *allergie,* from Greek *allos* "other" + *ergon* "work"]

al•le•vi•ate \ə-ˈlē-vē-ˌāt\ *vt* **1** : to make more bearable : RELIEVE ⟨*alleviate* pain⟩ **2** : to remove or correct in part ⟨*alleviate* a labor shortage⟩ [Late Latin *alleviare,* from *ad-* + *levis* "light"] **syn** see RELIEVE — **al•le•vi•a•tion** \ə-ˌlē-vē-ˈā-shən\ *n* — **al•le•vi•a•tive** \ə-ˈlē-vē-ˌāt-iv\ *adj*

[1]**al•ley** \ˈal-ē\ *n, pl* **al•leys** **1** : a garden or park walk bordered by trees or bushes **2** : a place for bowling or skittles; *esp* : a hardwood lane for bowling **3** : a narrow street or passageway between buildings; *esp* : one giving access to the rear of buildings [Old French *alee,* from *aler* "to go", from Latin *ambulare* "to walk"]

[2]**alley** *n, pl* **alleys** : a superior playing marble [from *alabaster*]

al•ley•way \ˈal-ē-ˌwā\ *n* **1** : a narrow passageway **2** : ALLEY 3

All Fools' Day *n* : APRIL FOOLS' DAY

all fours *n pl* : all four legs of a four-legged animal or the two legs and two arms of a person

all get-out \ˌȯl-ˈget-ˌaủt; -get-ˈaủt, -git-\ *n* : the highest degree ⟨talented as *all get-out*⟩

all hail *interj* — used to express greeting, welcome, or acclamation

All•hal•lows \ȯl-ˈhal-ōz, -əz\ *n* : ALL SAINTS' DAY

al•li•ance \ə-ˈlī-əns\ *n* **1 a** : the state of being allied **b** : a bond or connection between families, parties, or individuals **2 a** : an association (as by treaty) of two or more nations to further their common interests **b** : a treaty of alliance

al•lied \ə-ˈlīd, ˈal-ˌīd\ *adj* **1** : joined together ⟨two families *allied* by marriage⟩ **2 a** : joined in alliance especially by treaty ⟨*allied* nations⟩ **b** *cap* : of or relating to the nations united against the Central European powers in World War I or those united against the Axis powers in World War II **3 :** related especially by common properties, characteristics, or ancestry ⟨chemistry and *allied* subjects⟩

al•li•ga•tor \ˈal-ə-ˌgāt-ər\ *n* **1 :** either of two large short-legged reptiles resembling crocodiles but having a shorter and broader snout **2 :** leather made from alligator's hide [Spanish *el lagarto* "the lizard"]

alligator 1

alligator pear *n* **:** AVOCADO

all–im•por•tant \ˌȯ-lim-ˈpȯrt-nt, -ənt\ *adj* **:** of very great importance

al•lit•er•ate \ə-ˈlit-ə-ˌrāt\ *vb* **1 :** to form an alliteration **2 :** to arrange so as to make alliteration

al•lit•er•a•tion \ə-ˌlit-ə-ˈrā-shən\ *n* **:** the repetition of a sound at the beginning of two or more neighboring words (as in *wild and woolly* or *a babbling brook*) [*ad-* + Latin *littera* "letter"] — **al•lit•er•a•tive** \ə-ˈlit-ə-ˌrāt-iv, -rət-\ *adj* — **al•lit•er•a•tive•ly** *adv*

allo- — see ALL-

al•lo•cate \ˈal-ə-ˌkāt\ *vt* **1 :** to divide and distribute for a specific purpose or among particular persons or things ⟨*allocate* funds among charities⟩ **2 :** to set aside for a particular purpose ⟨*allocate* materials for a project⟩ **syn** see ALLOT — **al•lo•ca•tion** \ˌal-ə-ˈkā-shən\ *n*

al•lo•phone \ˈal-ə-ˌfōn\ *n* **:** one of two or more variants of the same phoneme ⟨the \t\ of *tip* and the \t\ of *pit* are *allophones* of the phoneme \t\⟩ — **al•lo•phon•ic** \ˌal-ə-ˈfän-ik\ *adj*

all–or–none \ˌȯ-lər-ˈnən\ *adj* **:** marked either by entire or complete operation or effect or by none at all

al•lot \ə-ˈlät\ *vt* **al•lot•ted; al•lot•ting :** to assign as a share or portion **:** ALLOCATE ⟨*allot* 10 minutes for each speech⟩ [Middle French *aloter,* from *a-* "ad-" + *lot* "lot", of Germanic origin] **• syn** APPORTION, ASSIGN, ALLOCATE: ALLOT may imply haphazard or arbitrary distribution; ASSIGN may stress an authoritative and fixed allotting without implying an even division; APPORTION implies a dividing according to some regular principle; ALLOCATE implies a fixed appropriation for a particular use.

al•lot•ment \ə-ˈlät-mənt\ *n* **1 :** the act of allotting **2 :** something that is allotted

al•lot•ro•py \ə-ˈlä-trə-pē\ *n* **:** the existence of a chemical element in two or more different forms in the same phase that show different chemical or physical properties ⟨diamond and graphite show the *allotropy* of carbon⟩ [Greek *tropos* "turn, manner"] — **al•lo•trope** \ˈal-ə-ˌtrōp\ *n* — **al•lo•trop•ic** \ˌal-ə-ˈträp-ik\ *adj*

all–out \ˈȯ-ˈlau̇t\ *adj* **:** made with maximum effort ⟨an *all-out* effort to win⟩

all out *adv* **:** with maximum effort ⟨go *all out*⟩

all•over \ˈȯ-ˌlō-vər\ *adj* **:** covering the whole extent or surface

all over *adv* **:** EVERYWHERE

al•low \ə-ˈlau̇\ *vb* **1 a :** to assign as a share or suitable amount (as of time or money) **b :** to allot as a deduction or an addition ⟨*allow* a gallon for leakage⟩ **2 :** ADMIT 3, CONCEDE ⟨*allowed* that the situation was serious⟩ **3 a :** PERMIT ⟨gaps *allow* passage⟩ ⟨refused to *allow* smoking⟩ **b :** to fail to restrain or prevent **:** LET ⟨*allow* the roast to burn⟩ **4 :** to make allowance ⟨*allow* for growth⟩ [Middle French *alouer* "to assign, allocate" (from Medieval Latin *allocare*) and *allouer* "to approve", from Latin *allaudare,* from *ad-* + *laudare* "to praise"] **syn** see LET — **al•low•able** \-ə-bəl\ *adj*

al•low•ance \ə-ˈlau̇-əns\ *n* **1 a :** a share or portion allotted or granted **b :** a sum granted ⟨a weekly *allowance*⟩ ⟨*allowance* for expenses⟩ **c :** a reduction from a list price or stated price ⟨a trade-in *allowance*⟩ **2 :** an allowed dimensional difference between mating parts of a machine **3 :** the act of allowing **:** PERMISSION **4 :** the taking into account of things that may partly excuse an offense or mistake ⟨make *allowances* for inexperience⟩

[1]al•loy \ˈal-ˌȯi, ə-ˈlȯi\ *n* **:** a substance composed of two or more metals or of a metal and a nonmetal united usually by being melted together [Middle French *aloi,* from *aloier* "to ally, combine", from Latin *alligare* "to bind"]

[2]al•loy \ə-ˈlȯi, ˈal-ˌȯi\ *vt* **1 :** to reduce the purity of by mixing with a less valuable metal **2 :** to mix so as to form an alloy **3 :** to debase by admixture

all–pur•pose \ˈȯl-ˈpər-pəs\ *adj* **:** suitable for many uses ⟨*all-purpose* flour⟩

[1]all right *adv* **1 :** reasonably well ⟨does *all right* in school⟩ **2 :** very well **:** YES ⟨*all right,* I'll be there⟩ **3 :** beyond doubt **:** CERTAINLY ⟨that's fast, *all right*⟩

[2]all right *adj* **1 :** SATISFACTORY, CORRECT **2 :** SAFE, WELL

all–round \ˈȯl-ˈrau̇nd\ *adj* **:** ALL-AROUND

All Saints' Day *n* **:** November 1 observed as a church festival in honor of the saints

All Souls' Day *n* **:** November 2 observed in some churches as a day of prayer for the souls of the faithful departed

all•spice \ˈȯl-ˌspīs\ *n* **:** the berry of a West Indian tree of the myrtle family; *also* **:** a mildly pungent and aromatic spice prepared from it

all–star \ˌȯl-ˌstär\ *adj* **:** made up chiefly or entirely of stars ⟨an *all-star* cast⟩ ⟨an *all-star* team⟩ — **all–star** \ˈȯl-ˌstär\ *n*

all told *adv* **:** with everything counted **:** in all

al•lude \ə-ˈlüd\ *vi* **:** to make indirect reference ⟨*alluding* to a recent scandal⟩ [Latin *alludere,* literally, "to play with", from *ad-* + *ludere* "to play"] **syn** see REFER

[1]al•lure \ə-ˈlu̇r\ *vt* **:** to attract by something tempting or fascinating — **al•lure•ment** \-mənt\ *n*

[2]allure *n* **:** power of attraction **:** CHARM

al•lu•sion \ə-ˈlü-zhən\ *n* **1 :** the act of alluding or hinting **2 :** an implied or indirect reference [Latin *allusus,* past participle of *alludere* "to play with"] — **al•lu•sive** \ə-ˈlü-siv, -ziv\ *adj* — **al•lu•sive•ly** *adv* — **al•lu•sive•ness** *n*

al•lu•vi•al \ə-ˈlü-vē-əl\ *adj* **:** relating to, composed of, or found in alluvium

al•lu•vi•um \-vē-əm\ *n, pl* **-vi•ums** *or* **-via** \-vē-ə\ **:** soil material (as clay, silt, sand, or gravel) deposited by running water [Late Latin, from Latin *alluere* "to wash against", from *ad-* + *lavere* "to wash"]

[1]al•ly \ə-ˈlī, ˈal-ˌī\ *vb* **al•lied; al•ly•ing 1 :** to form (as by marriage or treaty) a connection between **:** join in an alliance **:** UNITE **2 :** to form (as by likeness or compatibility) a relation between [Old French *alier,* from Latin *alligare* "to bind to", from *ad-* + *ligare* "to bind"]

[2]al•ly \ˈal-ˌī, ə-ˈlī\ *n, pl* **al•lies 1 :** a plant or animal linked to another by genetic or evolutionary relationship ⟨ferns and their *allies*⟩ **2 a :** one associated or united with another for a common purpose **b** *pl, cap* **:** the Allied nations in World War I or World War II

-al•ly \ə-lē, lē\ *adv suffix* **:** [2]-LY ⟨terrific*ally*⟩ — in adverbs formed from adjectives in *-ic* with no alternative form in *-ical* [[1]*-al* + *-ly*]

al•ma ma•ter \ˌal-mə-ˈmät-ər\ *n* **:** a school, college, or university that one has attended [Latin, "fostering mother"]

al•ma•nac \ˈȯl-mə-ˌnak, ˈal-\ *n* **1 :** a publication containing astronomical and meteorological data arranged according to the days, weeks, and months of the year and often including various other information **2 :** an annual publication containing statistical and general information [Medieval Latin *almanach,* probably from Arabic *al-manākh* "the almanac"]

al•man•dine \ˈal-mən-ˌdēn\ *n* **:** ALMANDITE

al•man•dite \-ˌdīt\ *n* **:** a deep red garnet containing iron and aluminum [derived from Medieval Latin *alabandina,* from *Alabanda,* ancient city in Asia Minor]

al•mighty \ȯl-ˈmīt-ē\ *adj, often cap* **:** having absolute power over all ⟨*Almighty* God⟩

Almighty *n* **:** GOD 1 — used with *the*

al•mond \ˈäm-ənd, ˈam-; ˈal-mənd\ *n* **:** a small tree of the rose family having flowers like those of a peach tree; *also* **:** the edible kernel of its fruit used as a nut [Old French *almande,* from Late Latin *amandula,* from Latin *amygdala,* from Greek *amygdalē*]

\ə\ **abut**	\au̇\ **out**	\i\ **tip**	\ȯ\ **saw**	\u̇\ **foot**
\ər\ **further**	\ch\ **chin**	\ī\ **life**	\ȯi\ **coin**	\y\ **yet**
\a\ **mat**	\e\ **pet**	\j\ **job**	\th\ **thin**	\yü\ **few**
\ā\ **take**	\ē\ **easy**	\ng\ **sing**	\th\ **this**	\yu̇\ **cure**
\ä\ **cot, cart**	\g\ **go**	\ō\ **bone**	\ü\ **food**	\zh\ **vision**

almond eye *n* : a somewhat triangular obliquely set eye — **almond–eyed** \-ˈīd\ *adj*
al•mo•ner \ˈal-mə-nər, ˈäm-ə-\ *n* : a person who distributes alms [Old French *almosnier,* from *almosne* "alms", from Late Latin *eleemosyna*]
al•most \ˈȯl-ˌmōst, ȯl-ˈ\ *adv* : only a little less than : NEARLY
alms \ˈämz, ˈälmz\ *n, pl* **alms** : something (as money) given to help the poor [Old English *ælmesse,* from Late Latin *eleemosyna,* from Greek *eleēmosynē* "pity, alms"] — **alms•giv•er** \-ˌgiv-ər\ *n* — **alms•giv•ing** \-ˌgiv-ing\ *n*
al•ni•co \ˈal-ni-ˌkō\ *n* : a powerful permanent-magnet alloy containing iron, nickel, aluminum, and one or more of the elements cobalt, copper, and titanium [*al*uminum + *ni*ckel + *co*balt]
al•oe \ˈal-ō\ *n* **1** : any of a large genus of succulent chiefly southern African plants of the lily family with spikes of often showy flowers **2** *usually pl* : the dried bitter juice of the leaves of an aloe used as a purgative and tonic [Late Latin, from Latin, "dried juice of aloe leaves", from Greek *aloē*]
aloft \ə-ˈlȯft\ *adv or adj* **1** : at or to a great height **2** : in the air; *esp* : in flight **3** : at, on, or to the masthead or the higher rigging of a ship [Old Norse *ā lopt,* from ā "in" + *lopt* "air"]
alo•ha \ə-ˈlō-ə, ä-, -ˌhä\ *interj* — used to express greeting or farewell [Hawaiian *aloha* "love"]
¹**alone** \ə-ˈlōn\ *adj* **1** : separated from others : ISOLATED ⟨*alone* in my room⟩ **2** : exclusive of anyone or anything else ⟨I *alone* know the secret⟩ [Middle English, from *al* "all" + *one* "one"] • **syn** LONELY, LONESOME: ALONE stresses the objective fact of being entirely by oneself; LONELY adds the suggestion of longing for companionship; LONESOME may add an impression of being deserted or desolate.
²**alone** *adv* **1** : without any other : SOLELY, EXCLUSIVELY ⟨the proof rests on that statement *alone*⟩ **2** : without company, aid, or support ⟨I'd rather do it *alone*⟩
¹**along** \ə-ˈlȯng\ *prep* **1** : lengthwise of : parallel with the length or direction of ⟨walk *along* the beach⟩ **2** : in accordance with ⟨research *along* several lines⟩ [Old English *andlang,* from *and-* "against" + *lang* "long"]
²**along** *adv* **1** : progressively onward ⟨hurry *along* toward home⟩ **2** : as a companion or associate ⟨brought the child *along*⟩ ⟨work *along* with colleagues⟩ **3 a** : at or to an advanced point ⟨plans are far *along*⟩ **b** : throughout the time ⟨knew the truth all *along*⟩ **4** : at or on hand ⟨had their guns *along*⟩
along•shore \-ˌshōr, -ˌshȯr\ *adv or adj* : along the shore or coast
¹**along•side** \-ˌsīd\ *adv* : along or close at the side : in parallel position
²**alongside** *prep* : side by side with; *esp* : parallel to
¹**aloof** \ə-ˈlüf\ *adv* : at a distance : out of involvement ⟨stood *aloof* from their quarrels⟩ [obsolete *aloof* "to windward"]
²**aloof** *adj* : removed or distant in interest or feeling : RESERVED ⟨a shy, *aloof* manner⟩ — **aloof•ly** *adv* — **aloof•ness** *n*
aloud \ə-ˈlau̇d\ *adv* **1** *archaic* : LOUDLY **2** : so as to be clearly heard
alp \ˈalp\ *n* **1** : a high rugged mountain **2** : a mountain pasture [from *Alps,* mountain system of Europe]
al•paca \al-ˈpak-ə\ *n* **1** : a mammal with fine long woolly hair domesticated in Peru and related to the llama **2** : wool of the alpaca or a thin cloth made of it; *also* : a rayon or cotton imitation of this cloth [Spanish, of American Indian origin]

alpaca 1

al•pha \ˈal-fə\ *n* **1** : the 1st letter of the Greek alphabet — Α or α **2** : something that is first : BEGINNING **3** : the chief or brightest star of a constellation
al•pha•bet \ˈal-fə-ˌbet, -bət\ *n* **1** : the characters (as letters) of a written language arranged in their customary order **2** : a system of signs or signals that serve as equivalents for letters [Greek *alphabētos,* from *alpha* + *bēta* "beta"]
al•pha•bet•i•cal \ˌal-fə-ˈbet-i-kəl\ *or* **al•pha•bet•ic** \-ˈbet-ik\ *adj* **1** : of, relating to, or employing an alphabet **2** : arranged in the order of the letters of the alphabet — **al•pha•bet•i•cal•ly** \-i-k(ə-)lē\ *adv*
al•pha•bet•ize \ˈal-fə-bə-ˌtīz\ *vt* : to arrange in alphabetical order — **al•pha•bet•i•za•tion** \ˌal-fə-ˌbet-ə-ˈzā-shən\ *n* — **al•pha•bet•iz•er** \ˈal-fə-bə-ˌtī-zər\ *n*
alpha helix *n* : the coiled structural arrangement of many proteins consisting of a single amino-acid chain that is stabilized by hydrogen bonds
al•pha•nu•mer•ic \ˌal-fə-nü-ˈmer-ik, -nyü-\ *adj* : consisting of both letters and numbers
alpha particle *n* : a positively charged particle that is identical with the nucleus of a helium atom, consists of 2 protons and 2 neutrons, and is ejected at high speed in various radioactive transformations
alpha ray *n* **1** : an alpha particle moving at high speed **2** : a stream of alpha particles — called also *alpha radiation*
alpha rhythm *or* **alpha wave** *n* : electrical activity of the brain that can be recorded by an electroencephalograph and is often associated with a state of wakeful relaxation
al•pine \ˈal-ˌpīn\ *n* : a plant native to alpine or boreal regions
Alpine *adj* **1** *often not cap* **a** : relating to or resembling the Alps or any mountains **b** : of, relating to, or growing on upland slopes above timberline **2** : of or relating to a central and southeastern European human Caucasoid stock marked by broad heads, stocky build, medium height, and brown hair and eyes
al•ready \ȯl-ˈred-ē\ *adv* **1** : before a stated or implied time : PREVIOUSLY ⟨we had *already* been there⟩ **2** : so soon ⟨surprised to find it done *already*⟩
al•right \ȯl-ˈrīt, ˈäl-; ˈȯl-ˌ\ *adv or adj* : all right
Al•sa•tian \al-ˈsā-shən\ *n* : GERMAN SHEPHERD [*Alsace*]
al•sike clover \ˌal-ˌsak-, -ˌsīk-\ *n* : a European perennial clover widely grown as a forage plant [*Alsike,* Sweden]
al•so \ˈȯl-sō\ *adv* **1** : LIKEWISE 1 **2** : in addition : TOO
al•so–ran \-ˌran\ *n* **1** : a horse or dog that finishes out of the money in a race **2** : a contestant that does not win
Al•ta•ic \al-ˈtā-ik\ *n* : a language family including the Turkic, Tungusic, and Mongolic subfamilies [*Altai* mountains, Asia] — **Altaic** *adj*
Al•tair \al-ˈtīr, -ˈtaər, -ˈteər\ *n* : the first-magnitude star in Aquila [Arabic *al-ṭā'ir,* literally, "the flier"]
al•tar \ˈȯl-tər\ *n* **1** : a usually raised structure or place on which sacrifices are offered or incense is burned in worship **2** : a table used in consecrating the eucharistic elements or as a center of worship or ritual [Old English, from Latin *altare*]
altar boy *n* : ACOLYTE 1
altar call *n* : an appeal by an evangelist to worshipers to come forward and commit their lives to Christ
al•tar•piece \ˈȯl-tər-ˌpēs\ *n* : a work of art to decorate the space above and behind the altar
al•ter \ˈȯl-tər\ *vb* **1** : to change partly but usually not completely ⟨*alter* a dress⟩ ⟨my opinion has never *altered*⟩ **2** : CASTRATE, SPAY [Middle French *alterer,* from Medieval Latin *alterare,* from *alter* "other (of two)"] **syn** see CHANGE — **al•ter•abil•i•ty** \ˌȯl-tə-rə-ˈbil-ət-ē, -trə-ˈ\ *n* — **al•ter•able** \ˈȯl-tə-rə-bəl, -trə-bəl\ *adj* — **al•ter•ably** \-blē\ *adv*
al•ter•ation \ˌȯl-tə-ˈrā-shən\ *n* **1** : the act or process of altering **2** : the result of altering : MODIFICATION
al•ter•ca•tion \ˌȯl-tər-ˈkā-shən\ *n* : a noisy or angry dispute : WRANGLE [Latin *altercari* "to wrangle", from *alter* "other"]
al•ter ego \ˌȯl-tər-ˈē-gō *also* -ˈeg-ō\ *n* **1** : a trusted friend or personal representative **2** : oneself in a changed form [Latin, literally, "second I"]
¹**al•ter•nate** \ˈȯl-tər-nət *also* ˈal-\ *adj* **1** : occurring or succeeding by turns ⟨a day of *alternate* sunshine and rain⟩ **2 a** : occurring first on one side and then on the other at different levels along an axis ⟨leaves *alternate*⟩ — compare OPPOSITE **b** : arranged one above or alongside another ⟨*alternate* layers of cake and filling⟩ **3** : every other : every second ⟨works on *alternate* days⟩ **4** : being an alternative ⟨took the *alternate* route⟩ [Latin *alternare* "to alternate", from *alternus* "alternate", from *alter* "other"] — **al•ter•nate•ly** *adv*
²**al•ter•nate** \-ˌnāt\ *vb* **1** : to do, occur, or act by turns **2** : to cause to alternate
³**al•ter•nate** \-nət\ *n* **1** : ALTERNATIVE **2** : a person named to take the place of another whenever necessary
alternate angle *n* : either of a pair of angles that are on opposite sides of a transversal at its intersection with two other lines: **a** : one of a pair of angles inside the two intersected lines —

called also *alternate interior angle* **b** : one of a pair of angles outside the two intersected lines — called also *alternate exterior angle*

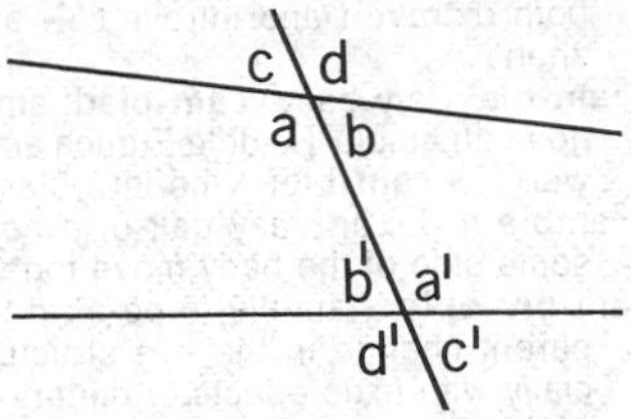

alternate angles: a, a¹; b, b¹; c, c¹; d, d¹

alternating current *n* : an electric current that reverses its direction at regular intervals — abbreviation *AC*

al·ter·na·tion \ˌȯl-tər-ˈnā-shən *also* ˌal-\ *n* **1** : the act or process of alternating **2** : alternate position or occurrence : SUCCESSION

alternation of generations : the successive occurrence of two or more different forms in the life cycle of a plant or animal; *esp* : the alternation of a sexual generation with an asexual one

[1]**al·ter·na·tive** \ȯl-ˈtər-nət-iv *also* al-\ *adj* : offering or expressing a choice ⟨*alternative* sources of energy⟩ — **al·ter·na·tive·ly** *adv* — **al·ter·na·tive·ness** *n*

[2]**alternative** *n* **1** : a chance to choose between two things ⟨the *alternative* of going by train or by air⟩ **2** : one of two or more things among which a choice is to be made **syn** see CHOICE

al·ter·na·tor \ˈȯl-tər-ˌnāt-ər *also* ˈal-\ *n* : an electric generator for producing alternating current

alt·horn \ˈalt-ˌhȯrn\ *n* : the alto member of the saxhorn family used chiefly in bands where it often replaces the French horn [German, from *alt* "alto" + *horn* "horn"]

al·though *also* **al·tho** \ȯl-ˈthō\ *conj* : in spite of the fact that : THOUGH

al·tim·e·ter \al-ˈtim-ət-ər, ˈal-tə-ˌmēt-ər\ *n* : an instrument for measuring altitude; *esp* : an aneroid barometer that registers changes in atmospheric pressure accompanying changes in altitude

al·ti·tude \ˈal-tə-ˌtüd, -ˌtyüd\ **1 a** : the angular height of a celestial object above the horizon **b** : the vertical distance of an object above sea level **c** : a perpendicular line segment from a vertex of a geometric figure (as a triangle or a pyramid) to the opposite side or the opposite side extended or from a side or face to a parallel side or face or the side or face extended **d** : the length of an altitude **2 a** : vertical distance or extent **b** : position at a height **c** : an elevated region — usually used in pl. [Latin *altitudo* "height, depth", from *altus* "high, deep"] **syn** see HEIGHT — **al·ti·tu·di·nal** \ˌal-tə-ˈt(y)üd-nəl, -n-əl\ *adj*

al·to \ˈal-tō\ *n, pl* **altos 1 a** : COUNTERTENOR **b** : CONTRALTO **c** : the second highest voice part in a 4-part chorus — compare BASS, SOPRANO, TENOR **2** : the second highest member of a family of musical instruments; *esp* : ALTHORN [Italian, literally, "high", from Latin *altus*]

al·to·cu·mu·lus \ˌal-tō-ˈkyü-myə-ləs\ *n* : a fleecy cloud formation consisting of large whitish globular cloudlets with shaded portions

[1]**al·to·geth·er** \ˌȯl-tə-ˈgeth-ər\ *adv* **1** : WHOLLY, THOROUGHLY ⟨the tool was *altogether* useless⟩ **2** : in all : all told ⟨the bill comes to $14 *altogether*⟩ **3** : on the whole ⟨*altogether* it compares favorably⟩

[2]**altogether** *n* : NUDE 2 ⟨posed in the *altogether*⟩

al·to·stra·tus \ˌal-tō-ˈstrāt-əs, -ˈstrat-\ *n* : a cloud formation similar to cirrostratus but darker and at a lower level

al·tri·cial \al-ˈtrish-əl\ *adj* : having the young hatched in a very immature and helpless condition so as to require care for some time — compare PRECOCIAL [Latin *altrix* "nurse", from *alere* "to nourish"]

al·tru·ism \ˈal-trü-ˌiz-əm\ *n* : unselfish interest in or care for the welfare of others [French *altruisme*, from *autrui* "other people", derived from Latin *alter* "other"] — **al·tru·ist** \-trü-əst\ *n* — **al·tru·is·tic** \ˌal-trü-ˈis-tik\ *adj* — **al·tru·is·ti·cal·ly** \-ˈis-ti-kə-lē, -klē\ *adv*

al·um \ˈal-əm\ *n* **1** : either of two colorless crystalline compounds containing aluminum $KAl(SO_4)_2 \cdot 12H_2O$ or $NH_4Al(SO_4)_2 \cdot 12H_2O$ that have a sweetish-sourish taste and a puckering effect on the mouth and are used in medicine (as to check local sweating or to stop bleeding) **2** : an aluminum compound $Al_2(SO_4)_3$ made from bauxite and used in paper manufacture, dyeing, and sewage treatment [Middle French, from Latin *alumen*]

alu·mi·na \ə-ˈlü-mə-nə\ *n* : the oxide of aluminum Al_2O_3 that occurs native as corundum and in bauxite and is used as a source of aluminum, as an abrasive, and as an absorbent

al·u·min·i·um \ˌal yə ˈmin ē əm\ *n, chiefly British* : ALUMINUM

alu·mi·nize \ə-ˈlü-mə-ˌnīz\ *vt* : to treat or coat with aluminum

alu·mi·num \ə-ˈlü-mə-nəm\ *n* : a silver-white malleable ductile light metallic element with good electrical and thermal conductivity and resistance to oxidation that is the most abundant metal in the earth's crust — see ELEMENT table [Latin *alumen* "alum"]

aluminum oxide *n* : ALUMINA

alum·na \ə-ˈləm-nə\ *n, pl* **-nae** \-ˌnē\ : a girl or woman who has attended or has graduated from a particular school, college, or university [Latin, feminine of *alumnus*]

alum·nus \ə-ˈləm-nəs\ *n, pl* **-ni** \-ˌnī\ : one and especially a man or boy that has attended or graduated from a particular school, college, or university [Latin, "foster son, pupil", from *alere* "to nourish"]

al·ve·o·lar \al-ˈvē-ə-lər\ *adj* **1** : of, relating to, resembling, or having alveoli **2** : pronounced with the tip of the tongue touching or near the teethridge — **al·ve·o·lar·ly** *adv*

al·ve·o·lus \al-ˈvē-ə-ləs\ *n, pl* **-li** \-ˌlī, -ˌlē\ **1** : a small cavity or pit: as **a** : a socket for a tooth **b** : AIR SAC 2 **2** : TEETHRIDGE [Latin, from *alveus* "cavity, hollow", from *alvus* "belly"]

al·way \ˈȯl-ˌwā\ *adv, archaic* : ALWAYS

al·ways \ˈȯl-wēz, -wəz, -ˌwāz\ *adv* **1** : at all times : INVARIABLY ⟨you're *always* right⟩ **2** : through all time : FOREVER ⟨remember me *always*⟩

alys·sum \ə-ˈlis-əm\ *n* **1** : any of a genus of Old World herbs of the mustard family with small usually yellow flowers **2** : SWEET ALYSSUM [Greek *alysson*, a plant believed to cure rabies, from *a-* + *lyssa* "rabies"]

am *present 1st sing of* BE [Old English *eom*]

amah \ˈäm-ə, ˈam-ˌä\ *n* : an Oriental woman employed as a servant; *esp* : a Chinese nurse [Portuguese *ama* "wet nurse", from Medieval Latin *amma*]

amain \ə-ˈmān\ *adv* **1** : with all one's might **2 a** : at full speed **b** : in great haste

amal·gam \ə-ˈmal-gəm\ *n* **1** : an alloy of mercury with some other metal or metals that is used for tooth filling **2** : a combination or mixture of different ingredients [Middle French *amalgame*, from Medieval Latin *amalgama*]

amal·gam·ate \ə-ˈmal-gə-ˌmāt\ *vb* **1** : to unite in an amalgam **2** : to combine into a single body — **amal·gam·ator** \-ˌmāt-ər\ *n*

amal·gam·ation \ə-ˌmal-gə-ˈmā-shən\ *n* **1 a** : the act or process of amalgamating ⟨the *amalgamation* of mercury with silver⟩ **b** : the state of being amalgamated **2** : the result of amalgamating; *esp* : a combination of different elements (as business corporations) into a single body — **amal·gam·ative** \-ˈmal-gə-ˌmāt-iv\ *adj*

am·a·ni·ta \ˌam-ə-ˈnīt-ə, -ˈnēt-\ *n* : any of various mostly poisonous white-spored fungi with a bulbous sac about the base of the stem [Greek *amanitai*, a kind of fungus]

aman·u·en·sis \ə-ˌman-yə-ˈwen-səs\ *n, pl* **-en·ses** \-ˌsēz\ : a person employed to write from dictation or to copy manuscript : SECRETARY [Latin, from *servus a manu* "slave with secretarial duties"]

am·a·ranth \ˈam-ə-ˌranth\ *n* **1** : an imaginary flower that never fades **2** : any of a large genus of coarse herbs including pigweeds and various forms cultivated for their showy flowers or for color [Latin *amarantus*, a kind of flower, from Greek *amaranton*, from *a-* + *marainein* "to wither, fade"]

am·a·ran·thine \ˌam-ə-ˈran-thən, -ˈran-ˌthīn\ *adj* : relating to or resembling an amaranth : UNFADING, UNDYING

am·a·ryl·lis \ˌam-ə-ˈril-əs\ *n* : any of various plants of a family related to the lily family; *esp* : any of several African bulbous herbs grown for their umbels of large showy flowers [probably from the name of a shepherdess in Vergil's *Eclogues*]

amass \ə-ˈmas\ *vt* **1** : to collect for oneself : ACCUMULATE ⟨*amass* a fortune⟩ **2** : to pile up into a mass : GATHER ⟨*amass* statistics from many sources⟩ **syn** see ACCUMULATE — **amass·er** *n*

am·a·teur \ˈam-ə-ˌtər, -ət-ər, -ə-ˌtu̇r, -ə-ˌtyu̇r\ *n* **1** : a person who takes part in an activity (as a study or sport) for pleasure and not for pay **2 :** a person who engages in something without experience or competence [French, literally, "lover", from Latin *amator,* from *amare* "to love"] — **amateur** *adj* — **am•a•teur•ish** \ˌam-ə-ˈtər-ish, -ˈtu̇r-, -ˈtyu̇r-\ *adj* — **am•a•teur•ish•ly** adv — **am•a•teur•ish•ness** n — **am•a•teur•ism** \ˈam-ə-ˌtər-ˌiz-əm, -ət-ər-, -ə-ˌtu̇r-, -ə-ˌtyu̇r-\ *n*

am•a•to•ry \ˈam-ə-ˌtōr-ē, -ˌtȯr-\ *adj* **:** of, relating to, or expressing sexual love

amaze \ə-ˈmāz\ *vt* **:** to surprise or astonish greatly **:** fill with wonder **:** ASTOUND [Old English *āmasian*]

amaze•ment \ə-ˈmāz-mənt\ *n* **:** great surprise or astonishment

amaz•ing *adj* **:** causing amazement or wonder — **amaz•ing•ly** \-ˈmā-zing-lē\ *adv*

am•a•zon \ˈam-ə-ˌzän, -ə-zən\ *n* **1** *cap* **:** a member of a race of women warriors repeatedly warring with the Greeks in classical mythology **2 :** a tall very strong woman

Am•a•zo•nian \ˌam-ə-ˈzō-nē-ən, -ˈzō-nyən\ *adj* **1 :** of, relating to, or resembling an Amazon **2 :** of or relating to the Amazon river or its valley

am•bas•sa•dor \am-ˈbas-əd-ər, əm-\ *n* **1 :** an official envoy; *esp* **:** a diplomatic agent of the highest rank who is the resident representative of his or her own government or appointed for a special temporary assignment **2 :** an authorized representative or messenger [Middle French *ambassadeur,* of Germanic origin] — **am•bas•sa•do•ri•al** \am-ˌbas-ə-ˈdōr-ē-əl, -ˈdȯr-\ *adj* — **am•bas•sa•dor•ship** \am-ˈbas-əd-ər-ˌship\ *n*

am•ber \ˈam-bər\ *n* **1 :** a hard yellowish to brownish translucent fossil resin that takes a fine polish and is used mostly for jewelry **2 :** a dark orange yellow [Middle French *ambre,* from Medieval Latin *ambra,* from Arabic *ʽanbar* "ambergris"] — **amber** *adj*

am•ber•gris \ˈam-bər-ˌgris, -ˌgrēs\ *n* **:** a waxy substance from the sperm whale that is used in the manufacture of perfumes [Middle French *ambre gris,* literally, "gray amber"]

ambi- *prefix* **:** both ⟨*ambi*valent⟩ [Latin, "both, around"]

am•bi•dex•trous \ˌam-bi-ˈdek-strəs\ *adj* **:** using both hands with equal ease [Latin *ambi-* + *dextera* "right hand"] — **am•bi•dex•trous•ly** *adv*

am•bi•ence *or* **am•bi•ance** \ˈam-bē-əns, äⁿ-byäⁿs\ *n* **:** a feeling or mood associated with a particular place, person, or thing **:** ATMOSPHERE [French *ambiance,* from *ambiant* "ambient"]

am•bi•ent \ˈam-bē-ənt\ *adj* **:** surrounding on all sides **:** ENCOMPASSING [Latin *ambiens,* present participle of *ambire* "to go around"]

am•bi•gu•i•ty \ˌam-bə-ˈgyü-ət-ē\ *n, pl* **-ties 1 :** the quality or state of being ambiguous in meaning **2 :** an ambiguous word or passage

am•big•u•ous \am-ˈbig-yə-wəs\ *adj* **1 :** doubtful or uncertain especially from being obscure or indistinct ⟨eyes of an *ambiguous* color⟩ **2 :** not clear in meaning because of being able to be understood in more than one way [Latin *ambiguus,* from *ambigere* "to wander about", from *ambi-* "around" + *agere* "to lead, drive"]

am•bi•tion \am-ˈbish-ən\ *n* **1 a :** a strong desire for status, fame, or power **b :** desire to achieve a particular end **:** ASPIRATION **2 :** the object of ambition ⟨attain your life's *ambition*⟩ **3 :** desire to work or be active ⟨I have no *ambition* today⟩ [Latin *ambitio* "canvass for votes", literally, "going around", from *ambire* "to go around", from *ambi-* "around" + *ire* "to go"]

△ **origin** The literal meaning of Latin *ambitio,* a derivative of *ambire* "to go around", was "going around". The word also meant "soliciting of votes", because candidates for public office in ancient Rome were in the habit of going about the city for that purpose. From this political sense *ambitio* was extended a bit further, to mean "desire for honor or power". This is the meaning of English *ambition,* derived from Latin *ambitio.*

• **syn** ASPIRATION: AMBITION implies a strong desire for personal advancement and may apply either to a praiseworthy or an inordinate and ruthless desire; ASPIRATION implies a striving after something higher than oneself which may be admirable and ennobling or merely presumptuous.

am•bi•tious \am-ˈbish-əs\ *adj* **1 a :** having or driven by ambition ⟨an *ambitious* politician⟩ **b :** having a particular ambition ⟨*ambitious* to be captain of the team⟩ **2 :** showing ambition ⟨an *ambitious* plan⟩ — **am•bi•tious•ly** *adv*

am•biv•a•lence \am-ˈbiv-ə-ləns\ *n* **:** simultaneous attraction toward and repulsion from something or someone — **am•biv•a•lent** \-lənt\ *adj* — **am•biv•a•lent•ly** *adv*

am•bi•vert \ˈam-bi-ˌvərt\ *n* **:** a person having characteristics of both extravert and introvert — **am•bi•ver•sion** \ˌam-bi-ˈvər-zhən\ *n*

¹am•ble \ˈam-bəl\ *vi* **am•bled; am•bling** \-bə-ling, -bling\ **:** to go at an amble [Middle French *ambler,* from Latin *ambulare* "to walk"] — **am•bler** \-bə-lər, -blər\ *n*

²amble *n* **1 :** an easy gait of a horse in which the legs on the same side of the body move together **2 :** a gentle easy pace

am•bly•opia \ˌam-blē-ˈō-pē-ə\ *n* **:** dimness of sight without apparent change in the eye structures that is associated especially with toxic effects or dietary deficiencies [Greek *amblyōpia,* from *amblys* "dull" + *-ōpia* "vision"]

am•bro•sia \am-ˈbrō-zhē-ə, -zhə\ *n* **1 :** the food of the Greek and Roman gods **2 :** something extremely pleasing to taste or smell [Latin, from Greek, literally, "immortality", from *ambrotos* "immortal"] — **am•bro•sial** \-zhē-əl, -zhəl\ *adj* — **am•bro•sial•ly** \-ē\ *adv*

am•bu•lance \ˈam-byə-ləns\ *n* **:** a vehicle equipped for transporting the injured or the sick [French, "field hospital", from *ambulant* "itinerant", from Latin *ambulare* "to walk"]

am•bu•lant \ˈam-byə-lənt\ *adj* **:** moving about; *esp* **:** AMBULATORY

am•bu•late \-ˌlāt\ *vi* **:** to move or walk from place to place

¹am•bu•la•to•ry \ˈam-byə-lə-ˌtōr-ē, -ˌtȯr-\ *adj* **1 :** of, relating to, or adapted to walking **2 :** able to walk about ⟨*ambulatory* patients in a hospital⟩ [Latin *ambulare* "to walk"]

²ambulatory *n, pl* **-ries :** a sheltered place (as a cloister) for walking

am•bus•cade \ˈam-bə-ˌskād\ *n* **:** AMBUSH [Middle French *embuscade*] — **ambuscade** *vb* — **am•bus•cad•er** *n*

¹am•bush \ˈam-ˌbu̇sh\ *vt* **1 :** to station (as troops) in ambush **2 :** to attack from an ambush **:** WAYLAY [Old French *embuschier,* from *en* "in" + *busche* "firewood"]

²ambush *n* **:** a trap in which concealed persons lie in wait to attack by surprise; *also* **:** the persons so concealed or their position

am•bys•to•ma \am-ˈbis-tə-mə\ *n* **:** TIGER SALAMANDER [derived from Greek *amblys* "dull, blunt" + *stoma* "mouth"]

ame•ba, ame•ban, ame•bic, ame•boid *variant of* AMOEBA, AMOEBAN, AMOEBIC, AMOEBOID

am•e•bi•a•sis \ˌam-i-ˈbī-ə-səs\ *n, pl* **-a•ses** \-ə-ˌsēz\ **:** infection with or disease caused by amoebas

amebic dysentery *n* **:** acute intestinal amebiasis of humans marked by dysentery, griping pain, and injury to the intestinal wall

ame•lio•rate \ə-ˈmēl-yə-ˌrāt\ *vb* **:** to make or grow better or more tolerable **:** IMPROVE [alteration of *meliorate*] — **ame•lio•ra•tion** \-ˌmēl-yə-ˈrā-shən\ *n* — **ame•lio•ra•tive** \-ˈmēl-yə-ˌrāt-iv\ *adj* — **ame•lio•ra•tor** \-ˌrāt-ər\ *n* — **ame•lio•ra•to•ry** \-rə-ˌtōr-ē, -ˌtȯr-\ *adj*

amen \ˈā-ˈmen, ˈā-; ˈä- *when sung*\ *interj* — used to express solemn agreement or hearty approval [Hebrew *āmēn*]

ame•na•ble \ə-ˈmē-nə-bəl, -ˈmen-ə-\ *adj* **1 :** liable to be called to account ⟨*amenable* to the law⟩ **2 :** easily influenced or managed **:** RESPONSIVE ⟨*amenable* to discipline⟩ [Middle French *amener* "to lead to" from *a-* "ad-" + *mener* "to lead", from Latin *minare* "to drive"] — **ame•na•bil•i•ty** \-ˌmē-nə-ˈbil-ət-ē, -ˌmen-ə-\ *n* — **ame•na•bly** \-ˈmē-nə-blē, -ˈmen-ə-\ *adv*

amend \ə-ˈmend\ *vb* **1 :** to change for the better **:** IMPROVE **2 :** ALTER 1; *esp* **:** to alter formally by modification, deletion, or addition ⟨*amend* the constitution⟩ [Old French *amender,* from Latin *emendare* "to emend"] **syn** see CORRECT — **amend•able** \-ˈmen-də-bəl\ *adj* — **amen•da•to•ry** \-ˈmen-də-ˌtōr-ē, -ˌtȯr-\ *adj* — **amend•er** *n*

amend•ment \ə-ˈmend-mənt, -ˈmen-\ *n* **1 :** the act or process of amending especially for the better **2 :** a modification, addition, or deletion (as to a law, bill, or motion) made or proposed ⟨an *amendment* to the constitution⟩

amends \ə-ˈmenz\ *n sing or pl* **:** something done or given to make up for a loss or injury one has caused ⟨make *amends*⟩

ame•ni•ty \ə-ˈmen-ət-ē, -ˈmē-nət-\ *n, pl* **-ties 1 :** the quality of being pleasant or agreeable **2 :** something that makes life easier or more pleasant — usually used in pl. [Latin *amoenitas,* from *amoenus* "pleasant"]

ament \ˈam-ənt, ˈā-mənt\ *n* **:** a flower cluster in which flowers all of one sex and without petals grow in close circular rows on a slender stalk (as in the alder, willow, birch, and poplar) **:** CATKIN [Latin *amentum* "thong, strap"]

¹Amer•i•can \ə-ˈmer-ə-kən\ *n* **:** a native or inhabitant of North

America or South America; *esp* : a citizen of the United States

[2]**American** *adj* **1** : of or relating to America or its inhabitants ⟨the *American* coastline⟩ **2** : of or relating to the United States or its inhabitants

Amer•i•ca•na \ə-ˌmer-ə-ˈkan-ə, -ˈkän-ə, -ˈkā-nə\ *n pl* : materials about America, its civilization, or its culture; *also* : a collection of such materials

American bison *or* **American buffalo** *n* : BUFFALO 2a

American chameleon *n* : a long-tailed lizard of the southeastern United States that can change its color

American cheese *n* : a mild process cheese made from American cheddar cheese

American egret *n* : a large North American heron with a yellow bill, snow white plumage, and black legs and feet

American Indian *n* : INDIAN 2a

Amer•i•can•ism \ə-ˈmer-ə-kə-ˌniz-əm\ *n* **1** : a characteristic feature of English as used in the United States **2** : attachment or loyalty to the traditions, interests, or ideals of the United States **3** : a custom or trait peculiar to the United States or to Americans

amer•i•can•ize \-kə-ˌnīz\ *vb, often cap* : to make or become American — **amer•i•can•iza•tion** \ə-ˌmer-ə-kə-nə-ˈzā-shən\ *n, often cap*

American lobster *n* : the common lobster of the northeastern coast of North America

American plan *n* : a hotel plan whereby the daily rate covers the cost of both room and meals — compare EUROPEAN PLAN

American robin *n* : ROBIN 2

am•er•i•ci•um \ˌam-ə-ˈrish-ē-əm, -ˈris-\ *n* : a radioactive metallic chemical element produced by bombardment of plutonium with high-energy neutrons — see ELEMENT table [New Latin, from *America*]

Am•er•in•di•an \ˌam-ə-ˈrin-dē-ən\ *n* : a member of any of the native peoples of the western hemisphere constituting one of the divisions of the Mongoloid stock — **Am•er•ind** \ˈam-ə-ˌrind\ *n* — **Amerindian** *adj* — **Am•er•in•dic** \ˌam-ə-ˈrin-dik\ *adj*

am•e•thyst \ˈam-ə-thəst\ *n* **1** : a clear purple or bluish violet variety of crystallized quartz used as a gem **2** : a moderate purple [Greek *amethystos,* from *a-* + *methyein* "to be drunk"; from its supposed usefulness as a remedy for drunkenness]

△ **origin** Gemstones were once believed to have magical and medicinal properties. An amethyst, for example, was supposed to have the power to prevent or cure drunkenness in its wearer. For this reason the Greeks gave it a name, *amethystos,* derived from the prefix *a-,* meaning "not", and *methyein* "to be drunk", from *methy* "wine".

ami•a•ble \ˈā-mē-ə-bəl\ *adj* : generally agreeable; *esp* : having a friendly and sociable disposition [Middle French, from Late Latin *amicabilis* "friendly", from Latin *amicus* "friend"] — **ami•a•bil•i•ty** \ˌā-mē-ə-ˈbil-ət-ē\ *n* — **ami•a•ble•ness** \ˈā-mē-ə-bəl-nəs\ *n* — **ami•a•bly** \-blē\ *adv*

am•i•ca•ble \ˈam-i-kə-bəl\ *adj* : characterized by friendly goodwill : PEACEABLE ⟨an *amicable* settlement of differences⟩ — **am•i•ca•bil•i•ty** \ˌam-i-kə-ˈbil-ət-ē\ *n* — **am•i•ca•ble•ness** *n* — **am•i•ca•bly** \ˌam-i-kə-blē\ *adv*

am•ice \ˈam-əs\ *n* : a white linen cloth worn about the neck and shoulders under other vestments by a priest at Mass [probably derived from Latin *amictus* "cloak"]

amid \ə-ˈmid\ *or* **amidst** \-ˈmidst, -ˈmitst\ *prep* : in or into the middle of : AMONG

am•ide \ˈam-ˌīd, -əd\ *n* : a compound resulting from replacement of an atom of hydrogen in ammonia by a metal or radical or of one or more atoms of hydrogen in ammonia by univalent acid radicals [*ammonia* + *-ide*]

amid•ships \ə-ˈmid-ˌships\ *adv* : in or near the middle of a ship

amine \ə-ˈmēn, ˈam-ˌēn\ *n* : any of various compounds derived from ammonia by replacement of hydrogen by one or more univalent hydrocarbon radicals

ami•no \ə-ˈmē-nō\ *adj* : relating to or containing the group NH_2 united to a radical

amino acid *n* : any of numerous organic acids that contain the amino group NH_2 and include some which can combine in chains to form proteins and are synthesized by living cells or are obtained as essential components of the diet

amir \ə-miər, ä-\ *variant of* EMIR

Amish \ˈäm-ish, ˈam-, ˈā-\ *adj* : of or relating to a strict Mennonite sect that settled in America [Jacob *Amman* or *Amen,* flourished 1693, Swiss Mennonite bishop] — **Amish** *n* — **Amishman** \-ish-mən\ *n*

[1]**amiss** \ə-ˈmis\ *adv* **1** : in a mistaken way : WRONGLY **2** : off the right path

[2]**amiss** *adj* : not satisfactory : WRONG, FAULTY ⟨something is *amiss* here⟩

ami•to•sis \ˌā-mī-ˈtō-səs\ *n, pl* **-to•ses** \-ˈtō-ˌsēz\ : cell division in which simple cleavage of the nucleus is followed by the division of the cytoplasm without the appearance of chromosomes or a spindle [[2]*a-* + *mitosis*] — **ami•tot•ic** \-ˈtät-ik\ *adj*

am•i•ty \ˈam-ət-ē\ *n, pl* **-ties** : friendly relations especially between nations [Middle French *amité,* from Medieval Latin *amicitas,* from Latin *amicus* "friend"]

am•me•ter \ˈam-ˌēt-ər\ *n* : an instrument for measuring electric current in amperes

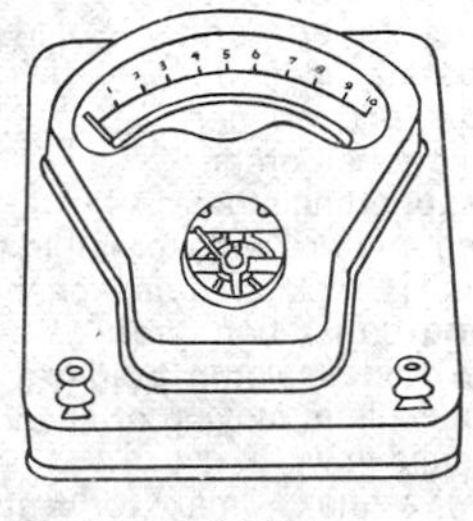

ammeter

am•mo \ˈam-ō\ *n, pl* **am•mos** : AMMUNITION

am•mo•nia \ə-ˈmō-nyə\ *n* **1** : a colorless gas NH_3 that is a compound of nitrogen and hydrogen, has a sharp smell and taste, is very soluble in water, can be easily liquefied by cold and pressure, is used in the manufacture of fertilizers and explosives, and is the chief nitrogenous waste product of many aquatic organisms **2** : a solution of ammonia in water — called also *ammonia water* [Latin *sal ammoniacus* "sal ammoniac", literally, "salt of Ammon"; from its discovery near a temple of the Egyptian god Ammon (Amon)] — **am•mo•ni•a•cal** \ˌam-ə-ˈnī-ə-kəl\ *adj*

am•mo•ni•fi•ca•tion \ə-ˌmän-ə-fə-ˈkā-shən, -ˌmō-nə-\ *n* : decomposition with production of ammonia or ammonium compounds especially by the action of bacteria on nitrogenous organic matter — **am•mo•ni•fy** \-ˌfī\ *vb*

am•mo•nite \ˈam-ə-ˌnīt\ *n* : any of numerous flat spiral fossil shells of mollusks especially abundant in the Mesozoic [Latin *cornu Ammonis,* literally, "horn of Ammon (Amon)"]

Am•mon•ite \ˈam-ə-ˌnīt\ *n* : a member of a Semitic people living in Old Testament times east of the Jordan river [*Ammon,* son of Lot] — **Ammonite** *adj*

am•mo•ni•um \ə-ˈmō-nē-əm\ *n* : an ion $NH_4{}^+$ or radical NH_4 derived from ammonia by combination with a hydrogen ion or atom and known in compounds (as ammonium chloride)

ammonium chloride *n* : a white crystalline volatile salt NH_4Cl used in dry cells and as an expectorant — called also *sal ammoniac*

ammonium hydroxide *n* : a compound NH_5O that is formed when ammonia dissolves in water and that exists only in solution

ammonium nitrate *n* : a colorless crystalline salt $N_2H_4O_3$ used in explosives and fertilizers

ammonium sulfate *n* : a colorless crystalline salt $N_2H_8SO_4$ used chiefly as a fertilizer

am•mu•ni•tion \ˌam-yə-ˈnish-ən\ *n* **1** : something that can be hurled at a target; *esp* : something (as a bullet, shell, grenade, or bomb) propelled by or containing explosives **2** : material that may be used (as in a controversy) in attack or defense [obsolete French *amunition,* alteration of *munition*]

am•ne•sia \am-ˈnē-zhə\ *n* : loss of memory due usually to brain injury, shock, fatigue, repression, or illness [Greek *amnēsia* "forgetfulness"] — **am•ne•si•ac** \-zhē-ˌak, -zē-\ *or* **am•ne•sic** \-zik, -sik\ *adj or n*

am•nes•ty \ˈam-nə-stē\ *n, pl* **-ties** : a general pardon granted by a ruler or government to a large group of persons guilty of a political offense (as treason or rebellion) [Greek *amnēstia* "forgetfulness", from *a-* + *mnasthai* "to remember"]

am•nio•cen•te•sis \ˌam-nē-ō-ˌsen-ˈtē-səs\ *n, pl* **-te•ses** \-ˈtē-ˌsēz\ : the surgical insertion of a hollow needle through the ab-

\ə\ **a**but	\au̇\ **ou**t	\i\ t**i**p	\ȯ\ s**aw**	\u̇\ f**oo**t
\ər\ f**ur**th**er**	\ch\ **ch**in	\ī\ l**i**fe	\ȯi\ c**oi**n	\y\ **y**et
\a\ m**a**t	\e\ p**e**t	\j\ **j**ob	\th\ **th**in	\yü\ f**ew**
\ā\ t**a**ke	\ē\ **ea**sy	\ng\ si**ng**	\t͟h\ **th**is	\yu̇\ c**u**re
\ä\ c**o**t, c**a**rt	\g\ **g**o	\ō\ b**o**ne	\ü\ f**oo**d	\zh\ vi**si**on

dominal wall and uterus of a pregnant female into the amnion especially to obtain amniotic fluid for the determination of sex or of chromosomal abnormality in the fetus [*amnion* + Greek *kentesis* "puncture", from *kentein* "to prick"]

am•ni•on \'am-nē-,än, -ən\ *n, pl* **-nions** *or* **-nia** \-nē-ə\ : a thin membrane forming a closed sac about the embryo of a reptile, bird, or mammal and containing a serous fluid in which the embryo is immersed [Greek, "caul"] — **am•ni•ot•ic** \,am-nē-'ät-ik\ *adj*

amoe•ba *also* **ame•ba** \ə-'mē-bə\ *n, pl* **-bas** *or* **-bae** \-,bē\ : any of numerous naked protozoans (group Rhizopoda) that have lobed and separate pseudopodia and no permanent cell organs or supporting structures and are widespread in fresh and salt water and in moist soils [Greek *amoibē* "change"] — **amoe•bic** \-bik\ *also* **amoe•ban** \-bən\ *adj*

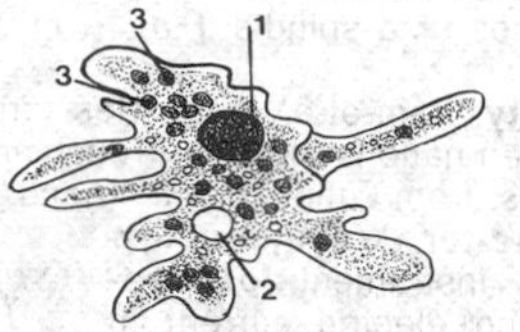

amoeba; *1* nucleus, *2* contractile vacuole, *3* food vacuoles

amoe•boid *also* **ame•boid** \-,bȯid\ *adj* : resembling an amoeba especially in moving or changing in shape by means of protoplasmic flow

amok \ə-'mək, -'mäk\ *or* **amuck** \-'mək\ *adv* : in a violently frenzied state ⟨run *amok*⟩ [Malay]

among \ə-'məng\ *also* **amongst** \-'məngst, 'məngkst\ *prep* **1** : in or through the midst of ⟨*among* the crowd⟩ **2** : in company with ⟨living *among* artists⟩ **3** : through all or most of ⟨discontent *among* the poor⟩ **4** : in the number or class of ⟨wittiest *among* poets⟩ **5** : in shares to each of ⟨divided *among* the heirs⟩ **6** : through the joint action of ⟨made a fortune *among* themselves⟩ [Old English *on gemonge* "in the crowd"] **syn** see BETWEEN

amon•til•la•do \ə-,män-tə-'läd-ō\ *n, pl* **-dos** : a pale dry sherry [Spanish, from *a* "to" + *montilla,* a wine from Montilla, Spain]

amor•al \ā-'mȯr-əl, a-, 'ā-, 'a-, -'mär-\ *adj* : neither moral nor immoral; *esp* : outside the sphere to which moral judgments apply — **amor•al•ly** \-ə-lē\ *adv*

Am•o•rite \'am-ə-,rīt\ *n* : a member of one of various Semitic peoples living in Mesopotamia, Syria, and Palestine during the 3d and 2d millenniums B.C.; *esp* : one of the group founding the first Babylonian empire [Hebrew *Ĕmōrī*] — **Amorite** *adj*

am•o•rous \'am-rəs, -ə-rəs\ *adj* **1** : inclined to love : easily falling in love ⟨an *amorous* nature⟩ **2** : of, relating to, or caused by love ⟨an *amorous* glance⟩ [Middle French, from Latin *amor* "love", from *amare* "to love"] — **am•o•rous•ly** *adv* — **am•o•rous•ness** *n*

amor•phous \ə-'mȯr-fəs\ *adj* **1** : having no determinate form : SHAPELESS **2** : having no crystalline form [Greek *amorphos,* from *a-* + *morphē* "form"] — **amor•phous•ly** *adv* — **amor•phous•ness** *n*

am•or•tize \'am-ər-,tīz *also* ə-'mȯr-,tīz\ *vt* : to pay off (an obligation) gradually usually by periodic payments on the principal [Middle French *amortir* "to deaden", from Latin *ad-* + *mors* "death"] — **am•or•ti•za•tion** \,am-ərt-ə-'zā-shən *also* ə-,mȯrt-ə-\ *n*

Amos \'ā-məs\ *n* — see BIBLE table

[1]**amount** \ə-'maůnt\ *vi* **1** : to add up ⟨the bill *amounted* to 10 dollars⟩ **2** : to be equivalent ⟨acts that *amount* to treason⟩ [Old French *amonter,* from *amont* "upward", from *a-* "ad-" + *mont* "mountain"]

[2]**amount** *n* **1** : the total number or quantity : AGGREGATE **2** : the whole effect, significance, or import **3** : a principal sum and the interest on it **syn** see SUM

amour \ə-'mu̇r, a-, ä-\ *n* : a love affair; *esp* : a secret love affair [Old French, "love", from Latin *amor*]

amour pro•pre \,am-,u̇r-'prōpr, ,äm-\ *n* : SELF-ESTEEM [French *amour-propre,* literally, "love of oneself"]

AMP \,ā-,em-'pē\ *n* : a compound of adenine that is reversibly convertible to ADP and ATP in metabolic reactions [adenosine monophosphate]

am•per•age \'am-pə-rij, -prij, -,piər-ij\ *n* : the strength of a current of electricity expressed in amperes

am•pere \'am-,piər, -peər\ *n* : a unit of electric current equal to a constant current which when maintained in two straight parallel conductors of infinite length and negligible cross section one meter apart in a vacuum produces between the conductors a force equal to 2×10^{-7} newton per meter of length [André M. *Ampère,* died 1836, French physicist]

am•per•sand \'am-pər-,sand\ *n* : a character & standing for the word *and* [*and* (&) *per se and,* literally, "(the character) & by itself (is the word) *and*"]

am•phet•amine \am-'fet-ə-,mēn, -mən\ *n* : a compound $C_9H_{13}N$ or one of its derivatives used especially as a stimulant of the central nervous system and formerly for relief of nasal congestion [*a*lpha + *m*ethyl + *phe*n- + e*t*hyl + *amine*]

amphi- *or* **amph-** *prefix* : on both sides : of both kinds : both ⟨*amphi*oxus⟩ [Greek *amphi* "around, on both sides"]

am•phib•ia \am-'fib-ē-ə\ *n pl* : AMPHIBIANS

am•phib•i•an \-ē-ən\ *n* **1** : an amphibious organism; *esp* : any of a class (Amphibia) of cold-blooded vertebrate animals (as frogs and newts) that are intermediate in many respects between fishes and reptiles and have gilled aquatic larvae and air-breathing adults **2** : an airplane designed to take off from and land on either land or water **3** : a flat-bottomed vehicle that moves on tracks having finlike extensions by means of which it is propelled on land or water — **amphibian** *adj*

am•phib•i•ous \-ē-əs\ *adj* **1** : able to live both on land and in water ⟨*amphibious* plants⟩ **2 a** : relating to or adapted for both land and water ⟨*amphibious* vehicles⟩ **b** : trained or organized for invasion from the sea; *also* : executed by amphibious forces ⟨an *amphibious* assault⟩ [Greek *amphi* + *bios* "life, mode of life"] — **am•phib•i•ous•ly** *adv* — **am•phib•i•ous•ness** *n*

am•phi•bole \'am-fə-,bōl, 'amp-\ *n* : any of a group of white, gray, green, or black rock-forming minerals that are complex hydrous silicates and contain calcium, magnesium, iron, aluminum, and sodium [French, derived from Greek *amphibolos* "ambiguous"]

am•phi•ox•us \,am-fē-'äk-səs, ,amp-\ *n, pl* **-oxi** \-'äk-,sī\ *or* **-oxus•es** : any of various small translucent marine animals related to the vertebrates — called also *lancelet* [*amphi-* + Greek *oxys* "sharp"]

am•phi•pod \'am-fi-,päd, 'amp-\ *n* : any of a large group (Amphipoda) of crustaceans comprising the beach fleas and related forms — **amphipod** *adj*

am•phi•the•ater \'am-fə-,thē-ət-ər, 'amp-\ *n* **1** : a round or oval building with seats rising in curved rows around an open space on which games and plays take place **2** : something resembling an amphitheater (as a piece of level ground surrounded by hills) [derived from Greek *amphitheatron,* from *amphi* "around" + *theatron* "theater"]

am•pho•ra \'am-fə-rə, 'amp-\ *n, pl* **-pho•rae** \-,rē, -,rī\ *or* **-pho•ras** : an ancient Greek or Roman jar with two handles that rise almost to the level of the mouth [Latin, from Greek *amphoreus,* from *amphi* + *pherein* "to carry"]

amphora

am•pho•ter•ic \,am-fə-'ter-ik, ,amp-\ *adj* : capable of reacting chemically either as an acid or as a base [Greek *amphoteros* "each of two", from *amphō* "both"]

am•pi•cil•lin \,am-pə-'sil-ən\ *n* : an antibiotic of the penicillin group that is effective against many bacteria [*am*ine + *penicillin*]

am•ple \'am-pəl\ *adj* **am•pler** \-pə-lər, -plər\; **am•plest** \-pə-ləst, -pləst\ **1** : generous in size, scope, or capacity : COPIOUS **2** : enough to satisfy : ABUNDANT [Middle French, from Latin *amplus*] **syn** see PLENTIFUL — **am•ple•ness** *n* — **am•ply** \-plē\ *adv*

am•pli•fi•ca•tion \,am-plə-fə-'kā-shən\ *n* **1** : an act, example, or product of amplifying **2 a** : matter by which a statement is expanded **b** : an expanded statement

am•pli•fi•er \'am-plə-,fīr\ *n* : one that amplifies; *esp* : an electronic device used to obtain amplification of voltage, current, or power

am•pli•fy \'am-plə-,fī\ *vt* **-fied**; **-fy•ing** **1** : to make larger; *esp*

: to expand with clarifying details or illustration ⟨*amplify* a statement⟩ **2** : to increase (voltage, current, or power) in magnitude or strength **3** : to make louder ⟨*amplify* the voice by using a megaphone⟩

am•pli•tude \ˈam-plə-ˌtüd, -ˌtyüd\ *n* **1** : the quality or state of being ample **2** : the extent or range of something: as **a** : the extent of a vibratory movement (as of a pendulum) measured from the mean position to an extreme **b** : the height or depth of a periodic wave (as an alternating current) compared to its average value **3** : the angle that determines the final position of the radius vector in polar coordinates

amplitude modulation *n* : modulation of the amplitude of a radio carrier wave in accordance with the strength of the audio or other signal; *also* : a broadcasting system using such modulation — abbreviation *AM*

am•pul *or* **am•pule** *or* **am•poule** \ˈam-ˌpyül, -ˌpül\ *n* : a small sealed bulbous glass vessel used to hold a solution for hypodermic injection [derived from Latin *ampulla* "flask"]

am•pul•la \am-ˈpu̇l-ə, -ˈpəl-\ *n, pl* **-lae** \-ˌē, -ˌī\ **1** : a glass or earthenware flask with a globular body and two handles **2** : an anatomic sac or pouch [Latin] — **am•pul•lar** \-ər\ *adj*

am•pu•tate \ˈam-pyə-ˌtāt\ *vt* : to cut or lop off; *esp* : to cut (as a limb) from the body [Latin *amputare,* from *am-, amb-* "around" + *putare* "to cut, prune"] — **am•pu•ta•tion** \ˌam-pyə-ˈtā-shən\ *n* — **am•pu•ta•tor** \ˈam-pyə-ˌtāt-ər\ *n*

am•pu•tee \ˌam-pyə-ˈtē\ *n* : one that has had a limb amputated

amuck *variant of* AMOK

am•u•let \ˈam-yə-lət\ *n* : a small object worn as a charm against evil [Latin *amuletum*]

amuse \ə-ˈmyüz\ *vt* **1** : to entertain or occupy with something pleasant ⟨*amuse* a child with a toy⟩ **2** : to appeal to the sense of humor of ⟨the story *amused* everyone⟩ [Middle French *amuser,* from *a-* "ad-" + *muser* "to muse"] — **amus•ing•ly** \-ˈmyü-zing-lē\ *adv*

• **syn** ENTERTAIN, DIVERT: AMUSE implies engaging the attention so as to keep one interested usually lightly or frivolously; ENTERTAIN suggests supplying amusement by specially prepared activity or performance; DIVERT stresses distracting the attention from worry or routine concern especially with something causing laughter or gaiety.

amuse•ment \ə-ˈmyüz-mənt\ *n* **1** : the condition of being amused **2** : pleasant diversion **3** : something that amuses

amusement park *n* : a commercially operated park with various devices (as a merry-go-round or roller coaster) for entertainment

am•yl \ˈam-əl\ *n* : a univalent hydrocarbon radical C_5H_{11} occurring in various isomeric forms [derived from Greek *amylon* "starch"]

amyl alcohol *n* : any of eight isomeric alcohols $C_5H_{12}O$ used especially as solvents

am•y•lase \ˈam-ə-ˌlās, -ˌlāz\ *n* : an enzyme that accelerates the hydrolysis of starch or glycogen

am•y•lop•sin \ˌam-ə-ˈläp-sən\ *n* : the amylase of the pancreatic juice

¹an \ən, an, ˈan\ *indefinite article* : ²A — used (1) usually in speech and writing before words beginning with a vowel sound ⟨*an* oak⟩ ⟨*an* hour⟩ ⟨*an* X ray⟩; (2) usually in speech and less often in writing before *h*-initial words with an unstressed first syllable in which \h\ is often lost after *an* ⟨*an* historian⟩; (3) sometimes especially in England before words whose initial letter is a vowel and whose initial sound is a consonant ⟨*an* unique occurrence⟩ ⟨such *an* one⟩; compare ²A [Old English *ān* "one"]

²an \ən, an\ *prep* : ³A 2 — used before words with an initial vowel sound ⟨once *an* afternoon⟩ ⟨fifty cents *an* hour⟩ [Old English *an, on, a-* "on, in"]

³an *or* **an'** *conj* **1** *see* AND\ : AND **2** \(ˈ)an\ *archaic* : IF 1

an- — see A-

¹-an *or* **-ian** *also* **-ean** *n suffix* **1** : one that belongs to ⟨American⟩ ⟨Bostonian⟩ ⟨crustacean⟩ **2** : one skilled in or specializing in ⟨phonetician⟩ [Latin *-anus, -ianus,* adjective and noun suffix]

²-an *or* **-ian** *also* **-ean** *adj suffix* **1** : of or belonging to ⟨American⟩ ⟨Floridian⟩ **2** : characteristic of : resembling ⟨Mozartean⟩

³-an *n suffix* **1** : unsaturated carbon compound **2** : anhydride of a carbohydrate [alteration of *-ane*]

ana- *or* **an-** *prefix* : up : upward ⟨anabolism⟩ [Greek, "up, back, again"]

-ana \ˈan-ə, ˈän-ə, ˈā-nə\ *or* **-i•ana** \ē-ˈ\ *n pl suffix* : collected items of information especially anecdotal or bibliographical concerning ⟨Americana⟩ ⟨Johnsoniana⟩ [Latin, neuter plural of *-anus, -ianus* "-an"]

an•a•bae•na \ˌan-ə-ˈbē-nə\ *n* : a common filamentous freshwater blue-green alga [Greek *anabainein* "to go up, shoot up"]

Ana•bap•tist \ˌan-ə-ˈbap-təst\ *n* : a Protestant of one of several 16th century sects rejecting infant baptism [Late Greek *anabaptizein* "to rebaptize"] — **Anabaptist** *adj*

anab•o•lism \ə-ˈnab-ə-ˌliz-əm\ *n* : metabolism concerned with building up the substance of plants and animals — compare CATABOLISM [*ana-* + *-bolism* (as in *metabolism*)] — **an•a•bol•ic** \ˌan-ə-ˈbäl-ik\ *adj*

anach•ro•nism \ə-ˈnak-rə-ˌniz-əm\ *n* **1** : the placing of persons, events, objects, or customs in times to which they do not belong **2** : a person or thing especially from a former age that is out of place in the present [Late Greek *anachronizein* "to be late", from Greek *ana-* + *chronos* "time"] — **anach•ro•nis•tic** \ə-ˌnak-rə-ˈnis-tik\ *adj* — **anach•ro•nis•ti•cal•ly** \-ti-kə-lē, -klē\ *adv*

an•a•co•lu•thon \ˌan-ə-kə-ˈlü-ˌthän\ *n, pl* **-tha** \-thə\ *or* **-thons** : lack of connection between the parts of one continuous stretch of speech or writing especially as the result of a shift from one construction to another in the middle of a sentence (as in "you really ought — well, do it your own way") [Greek *a-* + *akolouthos* "following"]

an•a•con•da \ˌan-ə-ˈkän-də\ *n* : a large South American snake of the boa family that kills or quiets its prey by squeezing in its coils [probably from Sinhalese *henakandayā,* a kind of snake]

anaconda

an•a•dem \ˈan-ə-ˌdem\ *n, archaic* : a wreath for the head [Latin *anadema,* from Greek *anadēma,* from *anadein* "to wreathe"]

anad•ro•mous \ə-ˈnad-rə-məs\ *adj* : ascending rivers from the sea for breeding ⟨shad and some salmon are *anadromous*⟩ — compare CATADROMOUS [Greek *anadromos* "running upward"]

anae•mia *variant of* ANEMIA

an•aer•obe \ˈan-ə-ˌrōb; an-ˈar-ˌōb, -ˈer-\ *n* : an anaerobic organism

an•aer•o•bic \ˌan-ə-ˈrō-bik; ˌan-ˌa-ˈrō-, -ˌe-ˈrō-\ *adj* : living, active, or occurring in the absence of free oxygen — **an•aer•o•bi•cal•ly** *adv*

anaerobic respiration *n* : FERMENTATION 1

an•aes•the•sia, an•aes•thet•ic, anaes•the•tist, anaes•the•tize *variant of* ANESTHESIA, ANESTHETIC, ANESTHETIST, ANESTHETIZE

ana•gram \ˈan-ə-ˌgram\ *n* : a word or phrase made out of another by changing the order of the letters ⟨*rebate* is an *anagram* of *beater*⟩ [derived from Greek *anagrammatizein* "to transpose letters", from *ana-* + *gramma* "letter"]

anal \ˈān-l\ *adj* : of, relating to, or situated near the anus — **anal•ly** \-l-ē\ *adv*

anal fin *n* : an unpaired median fin located behind the vent of a fish

an•al•ge•sia \ˌan-l-ˈjē-zhə, -zhē-ə, -zē-ə\ *n* : insensibility to pain without loss of consciousness [Greek *analgēsia,* from *a-* + *algos* "pain"] — **an•al•ge•sic** \-ˈjē-zik, -sik\ *adj or n* — **an•al•get•ic** \-ˈjet-ik\ *adj or n*

analog computer *n* : a computer that operates with numbers represented by directly measurable physical quantities — compare DIGITAL COMPUTER

an•a•log•i•cal \ˌan-l-ˈäj-i-kəl\ *adj* **1** : of, relating to, or based on analogy **2** : expressing or implying analogy — **an•a•log•i•cal•ly** \-kə-lē, -klē\ *adv*

anal•o•gous \ə-ˈnal-ə-gəs\ *adj* **1** : showing an analogy or a

\ə\ **abut**	\au̇\ **out**	\i\ **tip**	\ȯ\ **saw**	\u̇\ **foot**
\ər\ **further**	\ch\ **chin**	\ī\ **life**	\ȯi\ **coin**	\y\ **yet**
\a\ **mat**	\e\ **pet**	\j\ **job**	\th\ **thin**	\yü\ **few**
\ā\ **take**	\ē\ **easy**	\ng\ **sing**	\t͟h\ **this**	\yu̇\ **cure**
\ä\ **cot, cart**	\g\ **go**	\ō\ **bone**	\ü\ **food**	\zh\ **vision**

likeness permitting one to draw an analogy **2 :** similar in biological function but different in structure and origin ⟨the wing of a bird is *analogous* to the wing of a butterfly⟩ **[**Latin *analogus,* from Greek *analogos,* literally, "proportionate", from *ana* "up, in accordance with" + *logos* "reason, ratio"**] syn** see SIMILAR — **anal•o•gous•ly** *adv* — **anal•o•gous•ness** *n*

an•a•logue *or* **an•a•log** \'an-l-,óg, -,äg\ *n* **:** something that is analogous or similar to something else

anal•o•gy \ə-'nal-ə-jē\ *n, pl* **-gies 1 :** an inference that if two or more things agree with one another in some respects they will probably agree in others **2 :** resemblance in some particulars between things otherwise unlike **:** SIMILARITY **3 :** correspondence in function between anatomical parts of different structure and origin — compare HOMOLOGY

an•a•lyse *chiefly British variant of* ANALYZE

anal•y•sis \ə-'nal-ə-səs\ *n, pl* **anal•y•ses** \-'nal-ə-,sēz\ **1 :** separation of a whole into its parts **2 a :** an examination of a whole to discover its elements and their relations **b :** a statement of such an analysis **c :** an examination and interpretation of the nature and significance of something (as a news event) **3 :** the identification or separation of ingredients of a substance **4 :** proof of a proposition by assuming the result and deducing a valid statement by a series of reversible steps **5 :** PSYCHOANALYSIS **[**Greek, from *analyein* "to break up", from *ana-* + *lyein* "to loosen"**]**

an•a•lyst \'an-l-əst\ *n* **1 :** a person who analyzes or who is skilled in analysis ⟨a news *analyst*⟩ **2 :** a specialist in psychoanalysis **:** PSYCHOANALYST

an•a•lyt•ic \,an-l-'it-ik\ *adj* **1 a :** of or relating to analysis; *esp* **:** separating something into its parts or elements **b :** skilled in or using analysis **2 :** involving or applying the methods of algebra and calculus rather than geometry ⟨*analytic* trigonometry⟩ — **an•a•lyti•cal** \-i-kəl\ *adj* — **an•a•lyt•i•cal•ly** \-kə-lē, -klē\ *adv*

analytic geometry *n* **:** the study of geometric properties by means of algebraic symbols representing parts or relations of figures in a coordinate system — called also *coordinate geometry*

an•a•lyze \'an-l-,īz\ *vt* **:** to make an analysis of; *esp* **:** to study or determine the nature and relationship of the parts of by analysis ⟨*analyze* a traffic pattern⟩ — **an•a•lyz•a•ble** \-,ī-zə-bəl\ *adj* — **an•a•lyz•er** \-,ī-zər *n*

an•a•pest \'an-ə-,pest\ *n* **:** a metrical foot consisting of two unaccented syllables followed by one accented syllable (as in *the accused*) **[**Latin *anapaestus* "foot of two short syllables followed by one long", from Greek *anapaistos,* literally, "struck back", from *ana-* + *paiein* "to strike"; from its being a dactyl reversed**]** — **an•a•pes•tic** \,an-ə-'pes-tik\ *adj*

ana•phase \'an-ə-,fāz\ *n* **:** the stage of mitosis and meiosis in which the chromosomes move toward the opposite poles of the spindle

ana•phy•lax•is \,an-ə-fə-'lak-səs\ *n* **:** hypersensitivity (as to a drug) resulting from sensitization during an earlier exposure to the causative agent **[***ana-* + *-phylaxis* (as in *prophylaxis*)**]** — **ana•phy•lac•tic** \-'lak-tik\ *adj*

an•ar•chic \a-'när-kik, ə-\ *adj* **:** of, relating to, or tending toward anarchy **:** LAWLESS — **an•ar•chi•cal** \-ki-kəl\ *adj* — **an•ar•chi•cal•ly** \-ki-kə-lē, -klē\ *adv*

an•ar•chism \'an-ər-,kiz-əm, -,är-\ *n* **1 :** a political theory that holds all governmental authority to be unnecessary and undesirable and advocates a society based on the voluntary cooperation of individuals and groups **2 :** the support or practice of anarchistic principles

an•ar•chist \'an-ər-kəst, -,är-\ *n* **1 :** one who rebels against any authority, established order, or ruling power **2 :** one who believes in, supports, or promotes anarchism; *esp* **:** one who uses violent means to overthrow the established order — **anarchist** *or* **an•ar•chis•tic** \,an-ər-'kis-tik, -,är-\ *adj*

an•ar•chy \'an-ər-kē, -,är-\ *n* **1 :** the condition of a society without a government **2 :** a state of lawlessness, confusion, or disorder **3 :** an ideal society made up of individuals who have no government and enjoy complete freedom **[**Greek *anarchia,* from *a-* + *archein* "to rule"**]**

• syn ANARCHY, CHAOS mean absence, suspension, or breakdown of government, law, and order. ANARCHY stresses the absence of government; CHAOS implies the utter absence of order.

an•astig•mat•ic \,an-ə-stig-'mat-ik, ,an-,as-tig-\ *adj* **:** not astigmatic — used especially of lenses that are able to form approximately point images of object points — **an•as•tig•mat** \a-'nas-tig-,mat, ,an-ə-'stig-\ *n*

anas•to•mose \ə-'nas-tə-,mōz, -,mōs\ *vb* **:** to connect or communicate by anastomosis

anas•to•mo•sis \ə-,nas-tə-'mō-səs\ *n, pl* **-mo•ses** \-,sēz\ **:** the union of parts or branches (as of streams or blood vessels) so as to intercommunicate; *also* **:** NETWORK, MESH **[**Greek *anastomōsis,* from *ana-* + *stoma* "mouth, opening"**]**

anath•e•ma \ə-'nath-ə-mə\ *n* **1 a :** a curse solemnly pronounced by church authority and accompanied by excommunication **b :** a vigorous denunciation **:** CURSE **2 :** one that is cursed or intensely disliked **[**Greek**]**

anath•e•ma•tize \-,tīz\ *vt* **:** to pronounce an anathema upon **:** DAMN

anat•o•mist \ə-'nat-ə-məst\ *n* **:** a specialist in anatomy

anat•o•mize \-,mīz\ *vt* **1 :** to dissect so as to show or to examine the structure and use of the parts **2 :** ANALYZE

anat•o•my \ə-'nat-ə-mē\ *n, pl* **-mies 1 :** a branch of knowledge that deals with the structure of organisms; *also* **:** a writing on bodily structure **2 :** structural makeup especially of an organism or any of its parts **3 :** separation into parts for examination **:** ANALYSIS **[**derived from Greek *anatemnein* "to dissect", from *ana-* + *temnein* "to cut"**]** — **an•a•tom•ic** \,an-ə-'täm-ik\ *or* **an•a•tom•i•cal** \-'täm-i-kəl\ *adj* — **an•a•tom•i•cal•ly** \-kə-lē, -klē\ *adv*

-ance \əns, ^{ə}ns\ *n suffix* **1 :** action or process ⟨further*ance*⟩ **:** instance of an action or process ⟨perform*ance*⟩ **2 :** quality or state **:** instance of a quality or state ⟨protuber*ance*⟩ **3 :** amount or degree ⟨conduct*ance*⟩ **[**Latin *-antia,* from *-ans* "-ant"**]**

an•ces•tor \'an-,ses-tər\ *n* **1 :** one from whom an individual, group, or species is descended **2 :** FORERUNNER 2, PROTOTYPE **[**Old French *ancestre,* from Latin *antecessor* "one that goes before", from *antecedere* "to go before"**]**

an•ces•tral \an-'ses-trəl\ *adj* **:** of, relating to, or derived from an ancestor ⟨an *ancestral* home⟩ — **an•ces•tral•ly** \-trə-lē\ *adv*

an•ces•tress \'an-,ses-trəs\ *n* **:** a female ancestor

an•ces•try \'an-,ses-trē\ *n* **1 :** line of descent **:** LINEAGE **2 :** individuals making up a line of descent **:** ANCESTORS

[1]an•chor \'ang-kər\ *n* **1 :** a heavy iron or steel device attached to a boat or ship by a cable and so made that when thrown overboard it digs into the bottom and holds the boat or ship in place **2 :** something that secures or steadies or that gives a feeling of stability **3 a :** ANCHORMAN 1 **b :** ANCHORPERSON **[**Latin *anchora,* from Greek *ankyra*]

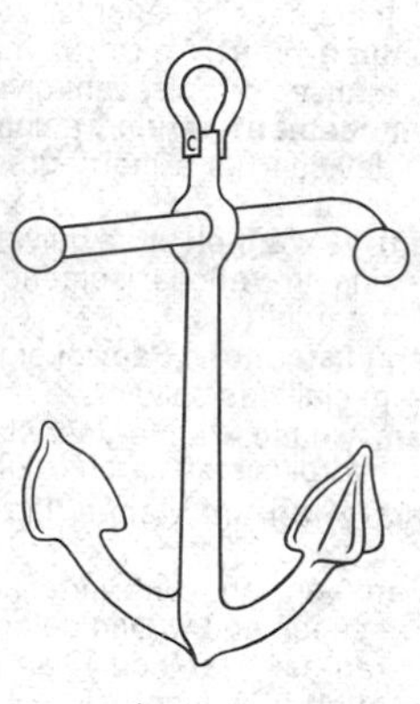

[1]anchor 1

[2]anchor *vb* **an•chored; an•chor•ing** \-kə-ring, -kring\ **1 :** to hold in place by means of an anchor ⟨*anchor* a ship⟩ **2 :** to secure firmly ⟨*anchor* the cables of a bridge⟩ **3 :** to drop anchor **:** become anchored ⟨the boat *anchored* in the harbor⟩ **4 :** to act as an anchorperson

an•chor•age \'ang-kə-rij, -krij\ *n* **1 :** a place where boats may be anchored **2 :** a secure hold to resist a strong pull **3 :** a means of security **:** REFUGE

an•cho•rite \'ang-kə-,rīt\ *n* **:** a person who gives up worldly things and lives in solitude usually for religious reasons **[**Medieval Latin *anchorita,* from Late Greek *anachōrētēs,* from Greek *anachorein* "to withdraw"**]**

an•chor•man \'ang-kər-,man\ *n* **1 :** one who competes or is placed last ⟨the *anchorman* on a relay team⟩ **2 :** ANCHORPERSON

an•chor•per•son \-,pərs-n\ *n* **:** a news broadcaster who coordinates the activities of other broadcasters

an•cho•vy \'an-,chō-vē, an-'\ *n, pl* **-vies** *or* **-vy :** any of numerous small fishes resembling herrings; *esp* **:** a common Mediterranean fish used especially for sauces and relishes **[**Spanish *anchova***]**

an•cien ré•gime \ä^{n}s-ya^{n}-rā-zhēm\ *n* **1 :** the political and social system of France before the Revolution of 1789 against the monarchy and aristocracy **2 :** a system or mode no longer prevailing [French, literally, "old regime"]

1an•cient \'ān-shənt, -chənt; 'āng-shənt, 'āngk-\ *adj* **1** : having existed for many years : very old ⟨*ancient* customs⟩ **2** : of or relating to a period of time long past or to those living in such a period; *esp* : of or relating to the historical period from the earliest civilizations to the fall of the western Roman Empire A.D. 476 **3** : having the qualities of age or long existence [Middle French *ancien,* from Latin *ante* "before"] **syn** see OLD — **an•cient•ness** *n*

2ancient *n* **1** : an aged person **2** *pl* : the civilized peoples of ancient times and especially of Greece and Rome

an•cient•ly \-lē\ *adv* : in ancient times

an•cil•lary \'an-sə-,ler-ē, an-'sil-ə-rē\ *adj* **1** : SUBSIDIARY 1b **2** : serving to aid or assist : SUPPLEMENTARY [Latin *ancilla* "female servant"]

-an•cy \ən-sē, ən-sē\ *n suffix, pl* **-ancies** : quality or state ⟨piquancy⟩ [Latin *-antia* "-ance"]

and \ənd, ən, and, an, 'and, *usually* ənd *or* ən *after* t, d, s, z, *often* əm *after* p *or* b, *sometimes* əng *after* k *or* g\ *conj* **1** : added to ⟨2 *and* 2 make 4⟩ **2** : as well as ⟨you *and* I⟩ — used as a function word to join words or word groups of the same grammatical rank or function (as two nouns that are subjects of the same verb) [Old English]

1an•dan•te \än-'dän-,tā, an-'dant-ē\ *adv or adj* : moderately slow — used as a direction in music [Italian, literally, "going"]

2andante *n* : a musical piece or movement in andante tempo

an•dan•ti•no \,än-,dän-'tē-nō\ *adv or adj* : somewhat quicker in tempo than andante — used as a direction in music [Italian, from *andante*]

an•des•ite \'an-di-,zīt\ *n* : an extrusive usually dark grayish rock consisting essentially of feldspar [*Andes* mountains] — **an•des•it•ic** \,an-di-'zit-ik\ *adj*

and•iron \'an-,dīrn, -,dī-ərn\ *n* : either of a pair of metal supports for firewood in a fireplace [Old French *andier*]

and/or \'and-'ór\ *conj* — used as a function word to indicate that either *and* or *or* may apply ⟨cats *and/or* dogs means cats *and* dogs or cats *or* dogs⟩

an•dra•dite \an-'dräd-,īt, 'an-drə-,dīt\ *n* : a garnet ranging from yellow and green to brown and black and containing calcium and iron [José B. de *Andrada* e Silva, died 1838, Brazilian geologist]

an•dro•gen \'an-drə-jən\ *n* : a male sex hormone [Greek *andr-, anēr* "male"] — **an•dro•gen•ic** \,an-drə-'jen-ik\ *adj*

an•drog•y•nous \an-'dräj-ə-nəs\ *adj* **1** : having both male and female characteristics **2** : bearing both staminate and pistillate flowers in the same cluster [Greek *andr-, anēr* "man, male" + *gynē* ["woman"]

An•drom•e•da \an-'dräm-əd-ə\ *n* : a northern constellation directly south of Cassiopeia between Pegasus and Perseus

-ane \,ān\ *n suffix* : saturated or completely hydrogenated carbon compound (as a hydrocarbon) ⟨meth*ane*⟩ [alteration of *-ene, -ine*]

an•ec•dote \'an-ik-,dōt\ *n* : a short narrative of an interesting, amusing, or biographical incident [French, derived from Greek *anekdotos* "unpublished", from *a-* + *ekdidonai* "to publish", from *ex-* "out" + *didonai* "to give"] — **an•ec•dot•al** \,an-ik-'dōt-l\ *adj* — **an•ec•dot•al•ly** \-l-ē\ *adv*

ane•mia *also* **anae•mia** \ə-'nē-mē-ə\ *n* **1** : a condition in which the blood is deficient in red blood cells, in hemoglobin, or in total volume and which is usually marked by pale skin, shortness of breath, and irregular heart action **2** : lack of vitality [Greek *anaimia* "bloodlessness", from *a-* + *haima* "blood"] — **ane•mic** \-mik\ *adj* — **ane•mi•cal•ly** \-mi-kə-lē, -klē\ *adv*

an•e•mom•e•ter \,an-ə-'mäm-ət-ər\ *n* : an instrument for measuring the speed of the wind [Greek *anemos* "wind"]

anem•o•ne \ə-'nem-ə-nē\ *n* **1** : any of a large genus of herbs related to the buttercups that have showy flowers without petals but with conspicuous often colored sepals — called also *windflower* **2** : SEA ANEMONE [Latin, from Greek *anemōnē*]

anent \ə-'nent\ *prep* : ABOUT 4, CONCERNING [Old English *on efen* "together, alongside", from *on* + *efen* "even"]

an•er•oid barometer \,an-ə-,róid-\ *n* : a barometer in which a change in atmospheric pressure is made to move a pointer [French *anéroïde* "without liquid", from *a-* + Late Greek *nēron* "water"]

an•es•the•sia *also* **an•aes•the•sia** \,an-əs-'thē-zhə\ *n* : loss of bodily sensation with or without loss of consciousness [Greek *anaisthēsia* "insensibility", from *a-* + *aisthanesthai* "to perceive"]

an•es•the•si•ol•o•gist \-,thē-zē-'äl-ə-jəst\ *n* : ANESTHETIST; *esp* : a physician specializing in anesthesia and the administration of anesthetics — **an•es•the•si•ol•o•gy** \-jē\ *n*

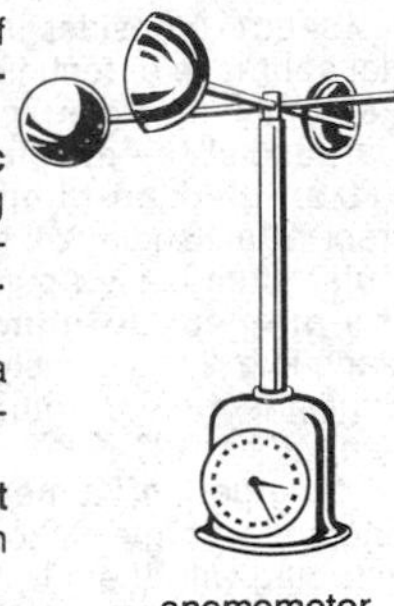
anemometer

1an•es•thet•ic *also* **an•aes•thet•ic** \,an-əs-'thet-ik\ *adj* : of, relating to, or capable of producing anesthesia — **an•es•thet•i•cal•ly** \-'thet-i-kə-lē, -klē\ *adv*

2anesthetic *also* **anaesthetic** *n* : a substance that produces either local or general anesthesia

anes•the•tist *also* **anaes•the•tist** \ə-'nes-thət-əst\ *n*: a person who administers anesthetics

anes•the•tize *also* **anaes•the•tize** \ə-'nes-thə-,tīz\ *vt* : to make insensible to pain especially by the use of an anesthetic

an•eu•rysm *also* **an•eu•rism** \'an-yə-,riz-əm\ *n* : a permanent abnormal expansion of a blood vessel containing fluid or clotted blood and resulting from disease of the vessel wall [Greek *aneurysma,* from *aneurynein* "to dilate", from *ana-* + *eurys* "wide"]

anew \ə-'nü, -'nyü\ *adv* : over again : AFRESH ⟨begin *anew*⟩

an•gel \'ān-jəl\ *n* **1 a** : a spiritual being serving God especially as a messenger or as a guardian of people **b** : a robed winged figure of human form in fine art **2** : an attendant spirit or guardian **3** : a person felt to resemble (as in virtue, innocence, or beauty) an angel **4** : a financial backer (as of a theatrical venture) [Old French *angele,* from Late Latin *angelus,* from Greek *angelos,* literally, "messenger"] — **an•gel•ic** \an-'jel-ik\ *or* **an•gel•i•cal** \-i-kəl\ *adj* — **an•gel•i•cal•ly** \-i-kə-lē, -klē\ *adv*

an•gel•fish \'ān-jəl-,fish\ *n* **1** : any of several compressed bright-colored bony fishes of warm seas **2** : SCALARE

an•gel•i•ca \an-'jel-i-kə\ *n* : a biennial herb of the carrot family whose roots and fruits furnish a flavoring oil

An•ge•lus \'an-jə-ləs\ *n* **1** : a Roman Catholic devotion that commemorates the Incarnation and is said morning, noon, and evening **2** : a bell announcing the time for the Angelus [Medieval Latin, "angel"; from the first word of the opening versicle]

1an•ger \'ang-gər\ *n* : a strong feeling of displeasure and usually of antagonism ⟨easily aroused to *anger*⟩ [Middle English, "affliction, anger", from Old Norse *angr* "grief"]

• **syn** RAGE, WRATH, FURY: ANGER is the general term for an emotional reaction of displeasure in any degree of intensity; RAGE implies loss of self-control from violence of emotion; WRATH implies usually righteous rage with a desire to avenge or punish; FURY suggests a violence of emotion amounting to temporary madness.

2anger *vt* **an•gered**; **an•ger•ing** \-gə-ring, -gring\ : to make angry

An•ge•vin \'an-jə-vən\ *adj* : of, relating to, or characteristic of Anjou or the Plantagenets [French, derived from Medieval Latin *Andegavia* "Anjou"] — **Angevin** *n*

an•gi•na \an-'jī-nə, 'an-jə-\ *n* : a disorder marked by spasmodic attacks of intense pain: as **a** : a severe inflammatory condition of the mouth or throat **b** : ANGINA PECTORIS [Latin, "quinsy", from *angere* "to choke"] — **an•gi•nal** \an-'jīn-l, 'an-jən-\ *adj*

angina pec•to•ris \-'pek-tə-rəs, -trəs\ *n* : a heart disorder marked by brief recurrent attacks of intense chest pain caused by insufficient supply of oxygen to the heart muscles by the blood [New Latin, literally, "angina of the chest"]

an•gio•sperm \'an-jē-ə-,spərm\ *n* : FLOWERING PLANT [Greek *angeion* "vessel" + *sperma* "seed"] — **an•gio•sper•mous** \,an-jē-ə-'sper-məs\ *adj*

1an•gle \'ang-gəl\ *n* **1** : the figure formed by two lines extend-

\ə\ abut	\aú\ out	\i\ tip	\ó\ saw	\ú\ foot
\ər\ further	\ch\ chin	\ī\ life	\ói\ coin	\y\ yet
\a\ mat	\e\ pet	\j\ job	\th\ thin	\yü\ few
\ā\ take	\ē\ easy	\ng\ sing	\th\ this	\yú\ cure
\ä\ cot, cart	\g\ go	\ō\ bone	\ü\ food	\zh\ vision

ing from the same point or by two plane surfaces diverging from the same line **2 :** a measure of the amount of turning that would be required to cause one line of an angle to coincide with the other at all points **3 :** a sharp projecting corner **4 a :** POINT OF VIEW, ASPECT ⟨consider the problem from a new *angle*⟩ **b :** a special approach or technique for accomplishing an objective **5 :** an abruptly diverging course or direction **[**Latin *angulus* "corner, angle"**]** — **an•gled** \-gəld\ *adj*

[2]angle *vb* **an•gled**; **an•gling** \-gə-ling, -gling\ **1 :** to turn, move, or direct at an angle **2 :** to present (as a news story) from a particular often biased point of view **:** SLANT

[3]angle *vi* **an•gled**; **an•gling** \-gə-ling, -gling\ **1 :** to fish with hook and line **2 :** to use sly means to get what one wants **[**Middle English *angelen,* from *angel* "fishhook", from Old English, from *anga* "hook"**]**

An•gle \'ang-gəl\ *n* **:** a member of a Germanic people conquering England with the Saxons and Jutes in the 5th century A. D. and merging with them to form the Anglo-Saxon people **[**Latin *Angli* "Angles", of Germanic origin**]**

angle bracket *n* **:** BRACKET 3b

angle of depression : an angle formed by the horizontal plane at the level of the eye and the line of sight to an object below this plane

angle of elevation : an angle formed by the horizontal plane at the level of the eye and the line of sight to an object above this plane

angle of incidence : the angle that a line (as a ray of light) falling on a surface makes with a perpendicular to the surface at the point of incidence

angle of reflection : the angle between a reflected ray and the perpendicular to a reflecting surface drawn at the point of incidence

an•gler \'ang-glər\ *n* **1 :** FISHERMAN; *esp* **:** a person who fishes for sport **2 :** a sea fish having a large flat head with projections that attract other fish within reach of its broad mouth

an•gler•fish \-ˌfish\ *n* **:** ANGLER 2

an•gle•worm \'ang-gəl-ˌwərm\ *n* **:** EARTHWORM **[**[3]*angle***]**

An•gli•can \'ang-gli-kən\ *n* **:** a member of the established Church of England or of one of the related churches in communion with it **[**Medieval Latin *anglicus* "English", from Latin *Angli* "Angles"**]** — **Anglican** *adj* — **An•gli•can•ism** \-kə-ˌniz-əm\ *n*

an•gli•cism \'ang-glə-ˌsiz-əm\ *n, often cap* **1 :** a characteristic feature of English occurring in another language **2 :** adherence or attachment to English customs or ideas

an•gli•cize \'ang-glə-ˌsīz\ *vt, often cap* **1 :** to make English (as in habits, speech, character, or outlook) **2 :** to borrow (a foreign word or phrase) into English without changing form or spelling and sometimes without changing pronunciation — **an•gli•ci•za•tion** \ˌang-glə-sə-'zā-shən\ *n, often cap*

an•gling \'ang-gling\ *n* **:** the act or sport of fishing with hook and line

An•glo- *combining form* **1** \'ang-ˌglō, -glə\ **:** English ⟨*Anglo*-Norman⟩ **2** \-ˌglō\ **:** English and ⟨*Anglo*-Japanese⟩ **[**Late Latin *Angli* "English people", from Latin, "Angles"**]**

An•glo–French \ˌang-glō-'french\ *n* **:** the French language used in medieval England

An•glo–Nor•man \-'nȯr-mən\ *n* **1 :** one of the Normans living in England after the Norman conquest **2 :** the form of Anglo-French used by Anglo-Normans

an•glo•phile \'ang-glə-ˌfīl\ *n, often cap* **:** a person who greatly admires England and English things

an•glo•phobe \-ˌfōb\ *n, often cap* **:** a person who strongly dislikes England and English things

An•glo–Sax•on \ˌang-glō-'sak-sən\ *n* **1 :** a member of the Germanic people conquering England in the 5th century A.D. and forming the ruling class until the Norman conquest — compare ANGLE, JUTE, SAXON **2 :** a native or inhabitant of England **3 :** a person of English ancestry **4 a :** OLD ENGLISH 1 **b :** direct plain English — **Anglo–Saxon** *adj*

an•go•ra \ang-'gōr-ə, an-, -'gȯr-\ *n* **1 :** yarn or cloth made from the hair of the Angora goat or the Angora rabbit **2** *cap* **a :** ANGORA CAT **b :** ANGORA GOAT **c :** ANGORA RABBIT

Angora cat *n* **:** a long-haired domestic cat **[***Angora* (Ankara), Turkey**]**

Angora goat *n* **:** any of a breed or variety of the domestic goat raised for its long silky hair which is the true mohair

Angora rabbit *n* **:** a usually white rabbit raised for its long fine soft hair

Angora goat

an•gry \'ang-grē\ *adj* **an•gri•er**; **-est** **1 a :** stirred by anger **:** ENRAGED ⟨became *angry* at the insult⟩ **b :** showing or arising from anger ⟨angry words⟩ **c :** threatening as if in anger ⟨an *angry* sky⟩ **2 :** painfully inflamed ⟨an *angry* rash⟩ — **an•gri•ly** \-grə-lē\ *adv* — **an•gri•ness** \-grē-nəs\ *n*

angst \'ängst, 'angst\ *n* **:** a feeling of anxiety **:** DREAD **[**German**]**

ang•strom \'ang-strəm\ *n* **:** a unit of length used especially of wavelengths (as of light) and equal to one ten-billionth of a meter — abbreviation Å **[**Anders J. *Ångström,* died 1874, Swedish physicist**]**

an•guish \'ang-gwish\ *n* **:** extreme pain or distress of body or mind **[**Old French *angoisse,* from Latin *angustiae* "straits, distress", from *angustus* "narrow"**]** **syn** see SORROW

an•guished \'ang-gwisht\ *adj* **:** full of anguish **:** TORMENTED ⟨an *anguished* call for help⟩

an•gu•lar \'ang-gyə-lər\ *adj* **1 a :** having one or more angles **b :** forming an angle **:** sharp-cornered **:** POINTED ⟨an *angular* mountain peak⟩ **2 :** measured by an angle ⟨*angular* distance⟩ **3 :** being lean and bony ⟨an *angular* figure⟩ — **an•gu•lar•i•ty** \ˌang-gyə-'lar-ət-ē\ *n* — **an•gu•lar•ly** *adv*

angular velocity *n* **:** the time rate of change of angular position

An•gus \'ang-gəs\ *n* **:** ABERDEEN ANGUS

an•hy•dride \an-'hī-ˌdrīd, 'an-\ *n* **:** a compound derived from another (as an acid) by removing a molecule of water

an•hy•drite \-'hī-ˌdrīt\ *n* **:** a mineral $CaSO_4$ consisting of an anhydrous calcium sulfate

an•hy•drous \-'hī-drəs\ *adj* **:** free from water and especially water of crystallization

an•i•line \'an-l-ən\ *n* **:** an oily liquid poisonous amine C_6H_7N made especially from nitrobenzene and used chiefly in organic synthesis (as of dyes) **[**German *anilin,* from *anil* "indigo", derived from Arabic *an-nīl* "the indigo plant", from Sanskrit *nīlī,* from *nīla* "dark blue"**]**

an•i•mad•ver•sion \ˌan-ə-ˌmad-'vər-zhən, -məd-, -shən\ *n* **1 :** a critical remark or comment **2 :** unfriendly criticism

an•i•mad•vert \-'vərt\ *vi* **:** to make a critical remark **:** comment unfavorably ⟨*animadvert* on a display of bad manners⟩ **[**Latin *animadvertere* "to pay attention to, censure", from *animum advertere* "to turn the mind to"**]**

[1]an•i•mal \'an-ə-məl\ *n* **1 :** any of a kingdom (Animalia) of living beings typically differing from plants in capacity for active movement, in rapid response to stimulation, and in lack of cellulose cell walls **2 a :** one of the lower animals as distinguished from humans **b :** MAMMAL **[**Latin, from *animalis* "animate", from *anima* "breath, soul"**]**

[2]animal *adj* **1 :** of, relating to, or derived from animals **2 :** of or relating to the physical nature of a person as contrasted with the intellectual; *esp* **:** SENSUOUS ⟨the *animal* appetites that plague humanity⟩

an•i•mal•cule \ˌan-ə-'mal-kyül\ *n* **:** a very small animal that is invisible or nearly invisible to the naked eye **[**New Latin *animalculum,* from Latin *animal***]**

animal heat *n* **:** heat produced in the body of a living animal by its chemical and physical activity

animal husbandry *n* **:** a branch of agriculture concerned with the production and care of domestic animals

an•i•mal•ism \'an-ə-mə-ˌliz-əm\ *n* **1 :** qualities typical of animals **2 :** total concern with the satisfaction of physical needs or wants — **an•i•mal•ist** \-mə-ləst\ *n* — **an•i•mal•is•tic** \ˌan-ə-mə-'lis-tik\ *adj*

animal kingdom *n* **:** the one of the three basic groups of natural objects that includes all living and extinct animals — compare MINERAL KINGDOM, PLANT KINGDOM

animal starch *n* **:** GLYCOGEN

[1]an•i•mate \'an-ə-mət\ *adj* **1 :** having life **:** ALIVE **2 :** ANIMATED 1b, c, LIVELY **[**Latin *animare* "to give life to", from *anima* "breath, soul"**]** — **an•i•mate•ly** *adv* — **an•i•mate•ness** *n*

[2]an•i•mate \'an-ə-ˌmāt\ *vt* **1 :** to give life to **:** make alive ⟨belief that the soul *animates* the body⟩ **2 :** to give spirit and vigor to

: ENLIVEN **3** : to make appear to move ⟨*animate* a cartoon⟩

an·i·mat·ed \-ˌmāt-əd\ *adj* **1 a** : ALIVE 1, LIVING **b** : full of movement and activity **c** : full of vigor and spirit : VIVACIOUS **2** : having the appearance or movement of something alive **syn** see LIVELY — **an·i·mat·ed·ly** *adv*

animated cartoon *n* : a motion picture made from a series of drawings simulating motion by means of slight progressive changes

an·i·ma·tion \ˌan-ə-ˈmā-shən\ *n* **1** : SPIRIT 4, LIVELINESS ⟨discussed their plans with *animation*⟩ **2 a** : ANIMATED CARTOON **b** : the preparation of animated cartoons

an·i·ma·to \ˌan-ə-ˈmät-ō\ *adv or adj* : with animation — used as a direction in music **[**Italian**]**

an·i·ma·tor \ˈan-ə-ˌmāt-ər\ *n* : one that contributes to the making of an animated cartoon

an·i·mism \ˈan-ə-ˌmiz-əm\ *n* : attribution of conscious life to nature as a whole or to inanimate objects — **an·i·mist** \-məst\ *n* — **an·i·mis·tic** \ˌan-ə-ˈmis-tik\ *adj*

an·i·mos·i·ty \ˌan-ə-ˈmäs-ət-ē\ *n, pl* **-ties** : ill will or resentment tending toward active hostility **[**Late Latin *animositas,* derived from Latin *animus* "spirit, mind, courage, anger"**]** **syn** see ENMITY

an·i·mus \ˈan-ə-məs\ *n* **1** : basic attitude : INTENTION **2** : deep-seated hostility : ANTAGONISM **[**Latin, "mind, spirit, anger"**]**

an·ion \ˈan-ˌī-ən\ *n* : a negatively charged ion **[**Greek, from *anienai* "to go up", from *ana-* + *ienai* "to go"**]** — **an·ion·ic** \ˌan-ī-ˈän-ik\ *adj*

an·ise \ˈan-əs\ *n* : an herb of the carrot family with aromatic seeds; *also* : ANISEED **[**derived from Greek *anison***]**

ani·seed \ˈan-ə-ˌsēd, -əs-\ *n* : the seed of anise often used as a flavoring in cordials and in cooking

an·isog·a·mous \ˌan-ī-ˈsäg-ə-məs\ *adj* : involving unlike gametes ⟨*anisogamous* reproduction⟩ — **an·isog·a·my** \-ī-ˈsäg-ə-mē\ *n*

ankh \ˈängk\ *n* : a cross having a loop for its upper vertical arm and serving especially in ancient Egypt as an emblem of life **[**Egyptian *ʿnḥ***]**

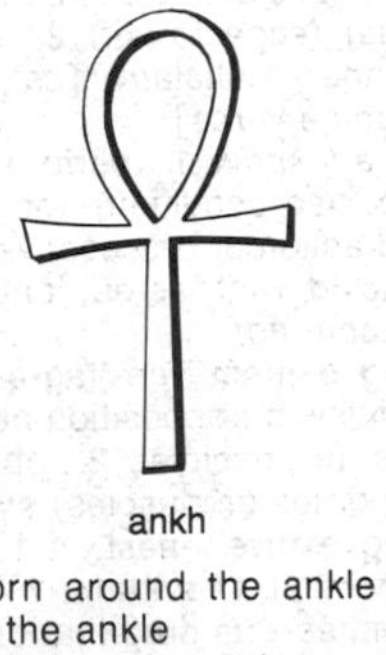
ankh

an·kle \ˈang-kəl\ *n* : the joint between the foot and the leg; *also* : the region of this joint **[**Old English *ancleōw***]**

an·kle·bone \-ˈbōn, -ˌbōn\ *n* : TALUS 1

an·klet \ˈang-klət\ *n* **1** : something (as an ornament) worn around the ankle **2** : a short sock reaching slightly above the ankle

an·ky·lo·sis \ˌang-ki-ˈlō-səs\ *n, pl* **-lo·ses** \-ˌsēz\ : a growing together of parts (as bones) into a rigid whole; *also* : stiffness of a joint resulting from such growth **[**derived from Greek *ankylos* "crooked"**]** — **an·ky·lose** \ˈang-ki-ˌlōs, -ˌlōz\ *vb*

an·na \ˈän-ə\ *n* **1** : a former monetary unit of Burma, India, and Pakistan equal to 1/16 rupee **2** : a coin representing one anna **[**Hindi *ānā***]**

an·nal·ist \ˈan-l-əst\ *n* : a writer of annals : HISTORIAN — **an·nal·is·tic** \ˌan-l-ˈis-tik\ *adj*

an·nals \ˈan-lz\ *n pl* **1** : a record of events arranged in yearly sequence **2** : historical records : CHRONICLES **3** : records of the activities of an organization **[**Latin *annales,* from *annalis* "yearly", from *annus* "year"**]**

An·nam·ese \ˌan-ə-ˈmēz, -ˈmēs\ *n, pl* **Annamese 1 a** : a Mongolian people of Vietnam **b** *or* **An·nam·ite** \ˈan-ə-ˌmīt\ : a member of this people **2** : the language of the Annamese people : VIETNAMESE **[***Annam,* region of Vietnam**]** — **Annamese** *adj*

an·neal \ə-ˈnēl\ *vt* **1** : to heat and then cool (as steel or glass) for softening and making less brittle **2** : STRENGTHEN, TOUGHEN ⟨*annealed* by hardship⟩ **[**Old English *onǣlan* "to set on fire", from *on* + *ǣlan* "to burn"**]**

an·ne·lid \ˈan-l-əd\ *n* : any of a phylum (Annelida) of long segmented invertebrate animals (as an earthworm or a leech) having a body cavity **[**Latin *annellus* "little ring", from *annulus* "ring"**]** — **annelid** *adj*

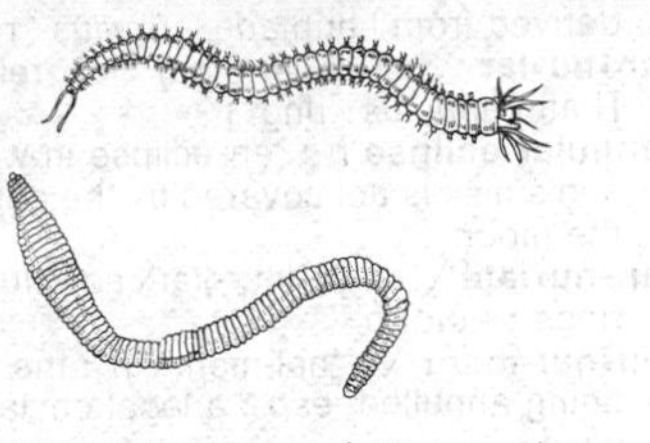
annelid: *top* clam worm, *bottom* earthworm

1an·nex \ə-ˈneks; ˈan-ˌeks\ *vt* **1** : to add as an additional part : APPEND ⟨a protocol *annexed* to the treaty⟩ **2** : to incorporate (a territory) within one's own domain ⟨the United States *annexed* Texas in 1845⟩ **[**Middle French *annexer,* from Latin *annectere* "to bind to", from *ad-* + *nectere* "to bind"**]** — **an·nex·a·tion** \ˌan-ˌek-ˈsā-shən\ *n* — **an·nex·a·tion·al** \-shnəl, -shən-l\ *adj* — **an·nex·a·tion·ist** \-shə-nəst, -shnəst\ *n*

2an·nex \ˈan-ˌeks, -iks\ *n* : something annexed or appended; *esp* : a part (as a wing) added to a building

an·ni·hi·late \ə-ˈnī-ə-ˌlāt\ *vt* : to destroy completely ⟨*annihilate* an entire army⟩ **[**Latin *annihilare* "to reduce to nothing", from *ad-* + *nihil* "nothing"**]** **syn** see DESTROY — **an·ni·hi·la·tion** \-ˌnī-ə-ˈlā-shən\ *n* — **an·ni·hi·la·tor** \-ˈnī-ə-ˌlāt-ər\ *n*

an·ni·ver·sa·ry \ˌan-ə-ˈvers-rē, -ə-rē\ *n, pl* **-ries 1** : the annual recurrence of a date marking a notable event **2** : the celebration of an anniversary **[**Latin *anniversarius* "returning annually", from *annus* "year" + *vertere* "to turn"**]**

an·no Do·mi·ni \ˌan-ō-ˈdäm-ə-nē, -ˈdō-mə-, -ˌnī\ *adv, often cap A* — used to indicate that a time division falls within the Christian era; abbreviation A.D. **[**Medieval Latin, "in the year of the Lord"**]**

an·no·tate \ˈan-ə-ˌtāt \ *vb* : to make or furnish with critical or explanatory notes or comment — **an·no·ta·tor** \-ˌtāt-ər\ *n*

an·no·ta·tion \ˌan-ə-ˈtā-shən\ *n* **1** : the act of annotating **2** : a note of comment or explanation

an·nounce \ə-ˈnau̇ns\ *vb* **1** : to make known publicly : PROCLAIM **2 a** : to give notice of the arrival, presence, or readiness of **b** : to indicate beforehand : FORETELL **3** : to serve as an announcer **[**Middle French *annoncer,* from Latin *annuntiare,* from *ad-* + *nuntiare* "to report", from *nuntius* "messenger"**]** **syn** see DECLARE

an·nounce·ment \ə-ˈnau̇ns-mənt\ *n* **1** : the act of announcing **2** : a public notice announcing something

an·nounc·er \ə-ˈnau̇n-sər\ *n* : one that announces; *esp* : a person who introduces television or radio programs, makes announcements, and gives the news and station identification

an·noy \ə-ˈnȯi\ *vb* : to disturb or irritate especially by repeated disagreeable acts : VEX **[**Old French *enuier,* from Late Latin *inodiare* "to make hateful", from Latin *in* "in" + *odium* "hatred"**]** — **an·noy·er** *n* — **an·noy·ing·ly** \-ing-lē\ *adv*

• **syn** ANNOY, WORRY, HARASS mean to disturb or irritate by persistent acts. ANNOY implies disturbing one's composure or peace of mind by intrusion, interference, or petty attacks; WORRY suggests incessant attacks intending to drive one to desperation or defeat; HARASS implies petty persecutions or burdensome demands that exhaust one's nervous or mental power.

an·noy·ance \ə-ˈnȯi-əns\ *n* **1 a** : the act of annoying or of being annoyed **b** : the state or feeling of being annoyed : VEXATION **2** : a source of irritation : NUISANCE

1an·nu·al \ˈan-yə-wəl, ˈan-yəl\ *adj* **1** : covering the period of a year **2** : occurring or performed once a year : YEARLY **3** : completing the life cycle in one growing season **[**Late Latin *annualis,* from Latin *annus* "year"**]** — **an·nu·al·ly** \-ē\ *adv*

2annual *n* **1** : a publication appearing yearly **2** : an event that occurs yearly **3** : an annual plant

annual ring *n* : the layer of wood produced by a single year's growth of a woody plant

an·nu·itant \ə-ˈnü-ət-ənt, -ˈnyü-\ *n* : a beneficiary of an annuity

an·nu·ity \ə-ˈnü-ət-ē, -ˈnyü-\ *n, pl* **-ties 1** : a sum of money paid at regular intervals (as every year) **2** : a contract providing for the payment of an annuity **[**Middle French *annuité,* derived from Latin *annuus* "yearly", from *annus* "year"**]**

an·nul \ə-ˈnəl\ *vt* **an·nulled**; **an·nul·ling 1** : to make ineffective or inoperative ⟨*annul* a drug's effect⟩ **2** : to declare or make legally void ⟨*annul* a marriage⟩ **[**Middle French *annuller,*

\ə\ **abut**	\au̇\ **out**	\i\ **tip**	\ȯ\ **saw**	\u̇\ **foot**
\ər\ **further**	\ch\ **chin**	\ī\ **life**	\ȯi\ **coin**	\y\ **yet**
\a\ **mat**	\e\ **pet**	\j\ **job**	\th\ **thin**	\yü\ **few**
\ā\ **take**	\ē\ **easy**	\ng\ **sing**	\t͟h\ **this**	\yu̇\ **cure**
\ä\ **cot, cart**	\g\ **go**	\ō\ **bone**	\ü\ **food**	\zh\ **vision**

derived from Latin *ad-* + *nullus* "not any"] **syn** see NULLIFY

an•nu•lar \'an-yə-lər\ *adj* **:** of, relating to, or forming a ring [Latin *annulus* "ring"]

annular eclipse *n* **:** an eclipse in which a thin outer ring of the sun's disk is not covered by the apparently smaller dark disk of the moon

an•nu•late \'an-yə-lət, -ˌlāt\ *adj* **:** furnished with or composed of rings **:** RINGED

an•nul•ment \ə-'nəl-mənt\ *n* **:** the act of annulling or state of being annulled; *esp* **:** a legal declaration that a marriage is invalid

an•nu•lus \'an-yə-ləs\ *n, pl* **-li** \-ˌlī, -ˌlē\ *also* **-lus•es :** RING; *esp* **:** a part, structure, or marking resembling a ring ⟨*annuli* of the earthworm⟩ [Latin]

an•nun•ci•ate \ə-'nən-sē-ˌāt\ *vt* **:** ANNOUNCE — **an•nun•ci•a•tor** \-ˌāt-ər\ *n* — **an•nun•ci•a•to•ry** \-sē-ə-ˌtōr-ē, -ˌtȯr-\ *adj*

an•nun•ci•a•tion \ə-ˌnən-sē-'ā-shən\ *n* **:** the act of announcing **:** ANNOUNCEMENT

Annunciation *n* **:** March 25 observed as a church festival in commemoration of the announcement of the Incarnation to the Virgin Mary

an•ode \'an-ˌōd\ *n* **1 :** the positive electrode of an electrolytic cell to which the negative ions are attracted — compare CATHODE **2 :** the negative terminal of a primary cell or of a storage battery that is delivering current **3 :** the electron-collecting electrode of an electron tube [Greek *anodos* "way up", from *ana-* + *hodos* "way"] — **an•od•ic** \a-'näd-ik\ *adj*

an•od•ize \'an-ə-ˌdīz\ *vt* **:** to subject (a metal) to electrolytic action as the anode of a cell in order to coat with a protective or decorative film

[1]**an•o•dyne** \'an-ə-ˌdīn\ *adj* **:** serving to relieve pain **:** SOOTHING [Greek *anōdynos,* from *a-* + *odynē* "pain"]

[2]**anodyne** *n* **:** an anodyne drug or agent

anoint \ə-'nȯint\ *vt* **1 :** to rub over with oil or an oily substance **2 a :** to apply oil to as a sacred rite **b :** to consecrate with or as if with oil [Middle French *enoindre,* from Latin *inunguere,* from *in-* + *unguere* "to smear"] — **anoint•er** *n* — **anoint•ment** \-mənt\ *n*

anointing of the sick : a sacrament that consists of anointing a usually critically ill person and praying for his or her recovery and salvation

anom•a•lous \ə-'näm-ə-ləs\ *adj* **1 :** deviating from a general rule or method or from accepted notions of fitness or order **2 :** being not what would naturally be expected [Late Latin *anomalus,* from Greek *anōmalos,* literally, "uneven", from *a-* + *homalos* "even", from *homos* "same"] — **anom•a•lous•ly** *adv* — **anom•a•lous•ness** *n*

anom•a•ly \ə-'näm-ə-lē\ *n, pl* **-lies 1 :** deviation from what is usual or expected **2 :** something anomalous

anon \ə-'nän\ *adv* **1** *obsolete* **:** at once **:** IMMEDIATELY **2** *archaic* **:** SHORTLY 2a, SOON **3 :** after a while **:** LATER [Old English *on ān,* from *on* "in" + *ān* "one"]

an•o•nym•i•ty \ˌan-ə-'nim-ət-ē\ *n, pl* **-ties 1 :** the quality or state of being anonymous **2 :** one that is anonymous

anon•y•mous \ə-'nän-ə-məs\ *adj* **1 :** having or giving no name ⟨an *anonymous* author⟩ **2 :** of unknown or unnamed source or origin ⟨*anonymous* gifts⟩ ⟨an *anonymous* letter⟩ **3 :** lacking individuality or personality [Late Latin *anonymus,* from Greek *anōnymos,* from *a-* + *onyma* "name"] — **anon•y•mous•ly** *adv* — **anon•y•mous•ness** *n*

anoph•e•les \ə-'näf-ə-ˌlēz\ *n* **:** any of a genus of mosquitoes that includes all mosquitoes which transmit malaria to humans [Greek *anōphelēs* "useless"] — **anoph•e•line** \-ˌlīn\ *adj or n*

an•o•rak \'an-ə-ˌrak\ *n, chiefly British* **:** PARKA [Greenland Eskimo *ánorâq*]

an•or•thite \ə-'nȯr-ˌthīt\ *n* **:** a white, grayish, or reddish calcium-containing feldspar [French, from Greek *a-* + *orthos* "straight"]

an•or•tho•site \ə-'nȯr-thə-ˌsīt\ *n* **:** a granular plutonic igneous rock composed chiefly of a plagioclase feldspar (as labradorite) [French *anorthose,* from Greek *a-* + *orthos* "straight"]

[1]**an•oth•er** \ə-'nəth-ər\ *adj* **1 :** different or distinct from the one considered ⟨from *another* angle⟩ **2 :** some other **:** LATER ⟨at *another* time⟩ **3 :** being one more in addition ⟨bring *another* cup⟩

[2]**another** *pron* **1 :** an additional one **2 :** one that is different from the first or present one **3 :** one of an indefinite or unspecified group ⟨for one reason or *another*⟩

an•ox•ia \a-'näk-sē-ə\ *n* **:** a condition (as at high altitudes) in which insufficient oxygen reaches the tissues — **an•ox•ic** \-sik\ *adj*

[1]**an•swer** \'an-sər\ *n* **1 a :** something spoken or written in reply especially to a question **b :** a correct response **2 :** a reply to a charge or accusation **:** DEFENSE **3 :** an act done in response **4 :** a solution to a problem [Old English *andswaru*]

[2]**answer** *vb* **an•swered; an•swer•ing** \'ans-ring, -ə-ring\ **1 :** to speak or write in reply or in reply to **2 a :** to be or make oneself responsible or accountable ⟨*answered* for the children's safety⟩ **b :** to make amends **:** ATONE ⟨must *answer* for their negligence⟩ **3 :** CONFORM, CORRESPOND ⟨*answered* to the description⟩ **4 :** to act in response ⟨the ship *answers* to the helm⟩ **5 :** to be adequate **:** SERVE ⟨*answer* the purpose⟩ **6 :** to offer or find a solution for — **an•swer•er** \'an-sər-ər\ *n*

an•swer•able \'ans-rə-bəl, -ə-rə-\ *adj* **1 :** subject to be called to account **:** RESPONSIBLE ⟨*answerable* for a debt⟩ **2 :** capable of being answered ⟨an *answerable* argument⟩

ant \'ant\ *n* **:** any of a family of colonial insects that are related to the wasps and bees and have a complex social organization with various castes performing special duties [Middle English *ante, emete,* from Old English *æmette*]

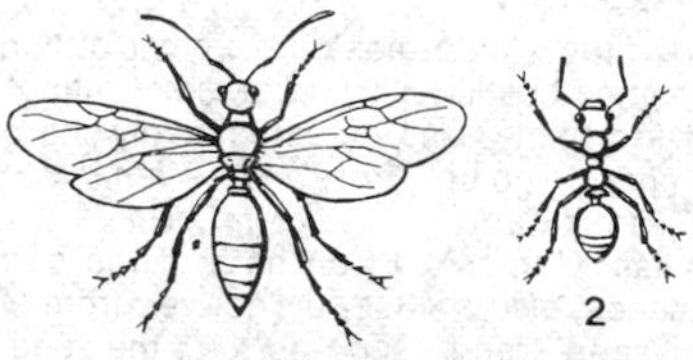

ant: *1* winged male, *2* worker

ant- — see ANTI-

[1]**-ant** \ənt, ᵊnt\ *n suffix* **1 a :** one that performs (a specified action) ⟨cool*ant*⟩ **b :** one that promotes (a specified action or process) ⟨expector*ant*⟩ **2 :** one that is acted upon (in a specified manner) ⟨inhal*ant*⟩ [Latin *-ant-, -ans,* present participle suffix of some verbs]

[2]**-ant** *adj suffix* **1 :** performing (a specified action) or being (in a specified condition) ⟨somnambul*ant*⟩ **2 :** promoting (a specified action or process) ⟨expector*ant*⟩

ant•ac•id \ant-'as-əd, 'ant-\ *n* **:** a remedy for stomach acidity — **antacid** *adj*

an•tag•o•nism \an-'tag-ə-ˌniz-əm\ *n* **1 a :** active opposition or hostility **b :** opposition between two conflicting forces, tendencies, or principles **2 :** opposition in physiological action (as of two drugs or muscles) **syn** see ENMITY

an•tag•o•nist \-nəst\ *n* **1 :** one that opposes another especially in combat **:** ADVERSARY **2 :** an agent of physiological antagonism; *esp* **:** a drug that opposes the action of another **syn** see OPPONENT

an•tag•o•nis•tic \an-ˌtag-ə-'nis-tik\ *adj* **:** characterized by or resulting from antagonism — **an•tag•o•nis•ti•cal•ly** \-ti-kə-lē, -klē\ *adv*

an•tag•o•nize \an-'tag-ə-ˌnīz\ *vt* **1 :** to act in opposition to **:** COUNTERACT **2 :** to incur or provoke the hostility of [Greek *antagōnizesthai,* from *anti-* + *agōn* "contest"]

ant•arc•tic \ant-'ärk-tik, 'ant-, -'ärt-ik\ *adj, often cap* **:** of or relating to the south pole or to the region near it [Latin *antarcticus,* from Greek *antarktikos,* from *anti-* + *arktikos* "arctic"]

antarctic circle *n, often cap A&C* **:** the parallel of latitude that is approximately 66½ degrees south of the equator

An•tar•es \an-'taər-ˌēz, -'teər-\ *n* **:** a giant red star of very low density that is the brightest star in Scorpio [Greek *Antarēs*]

ant bear *n* **:** a large South American anteater with shaggy gray fur, a black band across the breast, and a white shoulder stripe

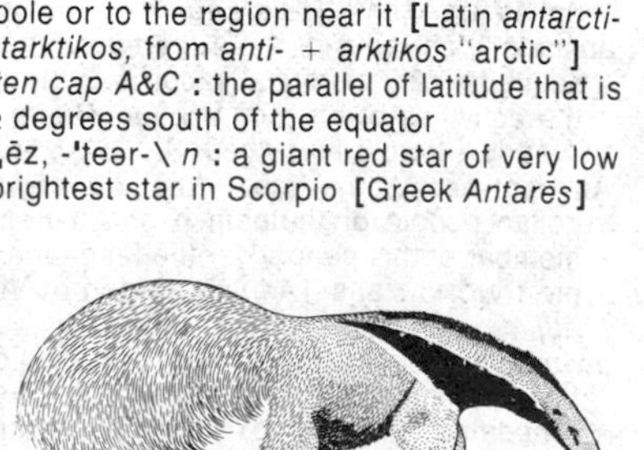
ant bear

ant cow *n* **:** an aphid from which ants obtain honeydew

[1]**an•te** \'ant-ē\ *n* **:** a poker stake usually put up before the deal to build the pot [*ante-*]

[2]**ante** *vt* **an•ted; an•te•ing :** to put up (an ante); *also* **:** PAY 1 — often used with *up*

ante- *prefix* **1 :** prior to **:** earlier ⟨*ante*date⟩ **2 :** anterior **:** in front of ⟨*ante*room⟩ [Latin *ante* "before, in front of"]

ant•eat•er \'ant-,ēt-ər\ *n* **:** any of several mammals (as an echidna or aardvark) that feed largely or entirely on ants; *esp* **:** an edentate with a long narrow snout and very long extensible tongue

an•te•bel•lum \,ant-i-'bel-əm\ *adj* **:** existing before a war; *esp* **:** existing before the Civil War [Latin *ante bellum* "before the war"]

¹an•te•ce•dent \,ant-ə-'sēd-nt\ *n* **1 :** a noun, pronoun, phrase, or clause referred to by a personal or relative pronoun ⟨in "the house that Jack built", *house* is the *antecedent* of *that*⟩ **2 :** the first term of a mathematical ratio **3 :** a preceding event, condition, or cause **4 a :** a predecessor in a series; *esp* **:** a model or stimulus for later developments **b** *pl* **:** ANCESTORS, PARENTS [Latin *antecedens* "one that goes before", from *antecedere* "to go before", from *ante-* + *cedere* "to go"]

²antecedent *adj* **:** coming earlier in time or order **syn** see PRECEDING — **an•te•ce•dent•ly** *adv*

an•te•cham•ber \'ant-i-,chām-bər\ *n* **:** ANTEROOM

an•te•date \'ant-i-,dāt\ *vt* **1 :** to date (as a check) with a date prior to that of actual writing **2 :** to precede in time ⟨automobiles *antedate* airplanes⟩

an•te•di•lu•vi•an \,ant-i-də-'lü-vē-ən, -dī-\ *adj* **1 :** of or relating to the period before the Flood described in the Bible **2 :** very old or old-fashioned **:** ANTIQUATED [*ante-* + Latin *diluvium* "flood"] — **antediluvian** *n*

an•te•lope \'ant-l-,ōp\ *n, pl* **-lope** *or* **-lopes 1 a :** any of various Old World ruminant mammals that are related to the goats and oxen but differ from the true oxen especially in lighter racier build and horns directed upward and backward **b :** PRONGHORN **2 :** leather from antelope hide [Middle English, a fabulous heraldic beast, probably from Middle French *antelop,* a savage animal with sawlike horns, derived from Late Greek *antholops*]

antelope 1a: *top* hartebeest, *bottom* kudu

an•te me•ri•di•em \,ant-i-mə-rid-ē-əm, -ē-,em\ *adj* **:** being before noon — abbreviation *a.m.* [Latin]

an•ten•na \an-'ten-ə\ *n, pl* **-ten•nae** \-'ten-,ē\ *or* **-tennas 1 :** any of one or two pairs of long slender segmented sensory organs on the head of an arthropod (as an insect or a crab) **2** *pl usually antennas* **:** a usually metallic device (as a rod or wire) for sending or receiving radio waves [Latin, "sail yard"]

△ **origin** Latin *antenna* meant "sail yard" — a sail yard is a long spar that supports and spreads the sail on a sailing vessel. The Greek word for a sail yard was *keraia,* but "sail yard" was only the secondary meaning of this word. The primary meaning was "horn". The philosopher Aristotle used *keraiai* for the feelers of insects, probably because of their resemblance to the horns of some larger animals. In a Latin translation of Aristotle's work made during the Renaissance, the word *antennae* was used for Greek *keraiai.* In English we still use *antennae* for insects' feelers. And now we also use *antenna* with a regular English plural ending *-s* for the metal rods which pick up radio waves and seem to feel the air like the antennae of an insect.

an•ten•nule \an-'ten-yül\ *n* **:** a small antenna (as of a crayfish)

an•te•pen•di•um \,ant-i-'pen-dē-əm\ *n, pl* **-di•ums** *or* **-dia** \-dē-ə\ **:** a hanging for the front of an altar, pulpit, or lectern [Medieval Latin, from Latin *ante-* + *pendēre* "to hang"]

an•te•pe•nult \,ant-i-'pē-,nəlt\ *n* **:** the 3d syllable of a word counting from the end ⟨*-cu-* is the *antepenult* in *accumulate*⟩ — **an•te•pen•ul•ti•mate** \-'pi-'nəl-tə-mət\ *adj or n*

an•te•ri•or \an-'tir-ē-ər\ *adj* **1 a :** situated before or toward the front **b :** situated near or toward the head or the part most nearly corresponding to a head **2 :** coming before in time **:** ANTECEDENT [Latin, comparative of *ante* "before"] — **an•te•ri•or•ly** *adv*

an•te•room \'ant-i-,rüm, -,rum\ *n* **:** a room used as an entrance to another room or as a waiting room

anth- — **syn** see ANTI-

an•them \'an-thəm, 'ant-\ *n* **1 :** a sacred vocal composition with words usually from the Scriptures **2 :** a song or hymn of praise or gladness [Old English *antefn* "antiphon", from Late Latin *antiphona*]

an•ther \'an-thər, 'ant-\ *n* **:** the part of a stamen that produces and contains pollen and is usually borne on a stalk [Latin *anthera* "medicine made of flowers", from Greek *anthēra,* from *anthos* "flower"] — **an•ther•al** \-thə-rəl\ *adj*

an•ther•id•i•um \,an-thə-'rid-ē-əm, ,ant-\ *n, pl* **-ia** \-ē-ə\ **:** the male reproductive organ of a cryptogamic plant (as a moss or club moss) — **an•ther•id•i•al** \-ē-əl\ *adj*

ant•hill \'ant-,hil\ *n* **:** a mound thrown up by ants or termites in digging their nest

an•tho•cy•a•nin \,an-thə-'sī-ə-nən, ,ant-\ *n* **:** any of various soluble pigments producing blue to red coloring in flowers and plants [Greek *anthos* "flower" + *kyanos* "dark blue"]

an•thol•o•gize \an-'thäl-ə-,jīz\ *vt* **:** to compile or publish in an anthology ⟨the story has often been *anthologized*⟩ — **an•thol•o•gist** \-jəst\ *n*

an•thol•o•gy \an-'thäl-ə-jē\ *n, pl* **-gies 1 :** a collection of selected literary pieces or passages **2 :** a collection of selected pieces in any art form (as songs, recordings, or paintings) [Greek *anthologia* "gathering of flowers", from *anthos* "flower" + *legein* "to gather"]

an•tho•zo•an \,an-thə-'zō-ən, ,ant-\ *n* **:** any of a class (Anthozoa) of marine coelenterates (as the corals and sea anemones) having polyps with radial partitions [Greek *anthos* "flower" + *zōion* "animal"] — **anthozoan** *adj*

an•thra•cene \'an-thrə-,sēn, 'ant-\ *n* **:** a crystalline hydrocarbon $C_{14}H_{10}$ obtained from coal-tar distillation

an•thra•cite \'an-thrə-,sīt, 'ant-\ *n* **:** a hard glossy coal that burns without much smoke or flame [Greek *anthrakitis,* from *anthrax* "coal, carbuncle"] — **an•thra•cit•ic** \,an-thrə-'sit-ik, ,ant-\ *adj*

an•thrax \'an-,thraks\ *n* **:** an infectious and usually fatal bacterial disease of warm-blooded animals (as cattle and sheep) that is transmissible to humans [Latin *anthrax* "carbuncle", from Greek, "coal, carbuncle"]

anthrop- *or* **anthropo-** *combining form* **:** human being ⟨*anthropo*centric⟩ [Greek *anthrōpos*]

an•thro•po•cen•tric \,an-thrə-pə-'sen-trik, ,ant-\ *adj* **:** interpreting or regarding the world in terms of human values and experiences

¹an•thro•poid \'an-thrə-,pȯid, 'ant-\ *adj* **1 :** resembling a human being **2 :** resembling an ape ⟨*anthropoid* mobsters⟩

²anthropoid *n* **:** any of a family of large tailless upright apes including the gibbons, chimpanzee, orangutan, and gorilla

an•thro•pol•o•gy \,an-thrə-'päl-ə-jē, ,ant-\ *n* **:** a science that deals with human beings and especially with their physical characteristics, origin and distribution into races, environmental and social relations, and culture — **an•thro•po•log•i•cal** \-pə-'läj-i-kəl\ *adj* — **an•thro•po•log•i•cal•ly** \-'läj-i-kə-lē, -klē\ *adv* — **an•thro•pol•o•gist** \-'päl-ə-jəst\ *n*

an•thro•pom•e•try \,an-thrə-'päm-ə-trē, ,ant-\ *n* **:** the study of human body measurements — **an•thro•po•met•ric** \-pə-'me-trik\ *adj*

an•thro•po•mor•phic \,an-thrə-pə-'mȯr-fik, ,ant-\ *adj* **1 :** described or thought of as having a human form or human attributes ⟨*anthropomorphic* deities⟩ **2 :** ascribing human characteristics to nonhuman things ⟨*anthropomorphic* interpretations of animal behavior⟩ — **an•thro•po•mor•phi•cal•ly** \-fi-kə-lē, -klē\ *adv* — **an•thro•po•mor•phism** \-,fiz-əm\ *n*

an•thro•po•mor•phize \-'mȯr-,fīz\ *vt* **:** to attribute human form or personality to

an•thro•poph•a•gous \,an-thrə-'päf-ə-gəs, ,ant-\ *adj* **:** feeding on human flesh — **an•thro•poph•a•gy** \-'päf-ə-jē\ *n*

¹an•ti \'an-,tī, 'ant-ē\ *n* **:** one that is opposed [*anti-*]

²anti *prep* **:** opposed to **:** AGAINST

anti- *or* **ant-** *or* **anth-** *prefix* **1 :** opposite in kind, position, or action ⟨*anti*climax⟩ ⟨*anti*clockwise⟩ ⟨*anti*matter⟩ **2 a :** hostile toward ⟨*anti*clerical⟩ ⟨*anti*-Semite⟩ **b :** opposing in effect or activity : counteracting ⟨*ant*acid⟩ ⟨*anti*coagulant⟩ **3 :** serving to prevent or cure ⟨*anti*malarial⟩ **4 :** combating or defending against ⟨*anti*aircraft⟩ ⟨*anti*ballistic missile⟩ [Greek *anti* "against"]

See *anti-* and 2d element

antiabortion
antiabortionist
antiabrasion
antiacademic
antiadministration
antiaggression
antiaggressive
antiaging
antialien
anti-American
anti-Americanism
antianarchic
antianarchist
antiannexation
antiannexationist
antiapartheid
anti-Arab
antiaristocrat
antiaristocratic
antiarsonist
antiart
antiarthritic
antiarthritis
antiasthma
antiasthmatic
antiatheism
antiatheist
antiauthoritarian
antiauthoritarianism
antibank
antibias
antibigotry
antibillboard
antiblack
anti-Bolshevik
anti-Bolshevism
anti-Bolshevist
antibourgeois
antiboxing
antiboycott
anti-British
antibureaucratic
antiburglar
antiburglary
antibusiness
anticapitalism
anticapitalist
anticapitalistic
anticar
anticarcinogen
anticarcinogenic
anticaries
anti-Catholic
anticensorship
anti-Chinese
anti-cholera
anticholesterol
anti-Christian
anti-Christianity
antichurch
anticigarette
anticlassical
anticlotting
anticollision
anticolonial
anticolonialism
anticolonialist
anticommercialism
anticommunism
anticommunist
anticonformist
anticonservation
anticonservationist
anticonsumer
anticonsumerism
anticonventional
anticorrosion
anticorrosive
anticorruption
anticrime
anticruelty
anticultural
antidandruff
anti-Darwinian
anti-Darwinism
antidemocratic
antidiabetic
antidiarrheal
antidiphtheria
antidiscrimination
antidogmatic
antidrug
antidumping
antieavesdropping
antiecclesiastic
antiecclesiastical
antieconomic
antiemetic
anti-English
antiepilepsy
antiepileptic
antierotic
antiestablishment
anti-ethnic
antievangelical
antievolution
antievolutionary
antievolutionism
antievolutionist
antifanatic
anti-fascism
anti-fascist
antifatigue
antifemale
antifeminine
antifeminism
antifeminist
antiflu
antiforeclosure
antiforeign
antiforeigner
antifraud
anti-French
antifundamentalist
antifungus
antigambling
anti-German
antiglare
antigonococcal
antigonorrheal
antigovernment
antigraft
antiguerrilla
antigun
antihijack
antihomosexual
antihuman
antihumanism
antihumanistic
antihumanity
antihunting
antihygienic
antihysteric
anti-icing
anti-imperialism
anti-imperialist
anti-infective
anti-inflammatory
anti-inflation
anti-inflationary
anti-institutional
anti-integration
anti-intellectual
anti-intellectualism
anti-intellectualist
anti-Irish
anti-Italian
antijamming
anti-Japanese
anti-Jewish
antilabor
antileprosy
antileukemic
antiliberal
antiliberalism
antilitter
antilittering
antiloitering
antilottery
antilynching
antimalaria
antimale
antimanagement
antimaterialism
antimaterialist
antimaterialistic
anti-Mexican
antimilitarism
antimilitarist
antimilitaristic
antimilitary
antimiscegenation
antimonarchist
antimonopolist
antimonopoly
antimosquito
antinausea
antinepotism
antinoise
antiobesity
antiobscenity
antiorganization
antipapal
antipesticide
antiplague
antipleasure
antipolice
antipolio
antipoliomyelitis
anti-Polish
antipornographic
antipornography
antipoverty
antiproductive
antiprofiteering
antiprogressive
antiprostitution
antirabic
antirabies
antiracing
antiracketeering
antiradical
antirape
antirealism
antirealistic
antirecession
antireform
antirejection
antireligious
antirepublican
antirevolutionary
antirevolutionist
antirheumatic
antiriot
antirobbery
antiromantic
antiromanticism
anti-Russian
antirust
antisecrecy
antisegregation
antisegregationist
antisentimental
antisex
antisexist
antisexual
antisexuality
antishock
antishoplifting
antiskyjacking
antislavery
antisleep
antislip
antismoking
antismuggling
antismut
anti-Soviet
anti-Spanish
antispeculative
antispending
antistatic
antisterility
antistimulant
antistrike
antistudent
antisubmarine
antisubversion
antisubversive
antisuicide
antisyphilis
antisyphilitic
anti-tarnish
antitax
antitechnological
antitechnology
antiterrorism
antiterrorist
antitetanus
antitheft
antitheological
antitheoretical
antitobacco
antitotalitarian
antitraditional
antitubercular
antituberculosis
antitumor
antityphoid
antiulcer
anti-unemployment
antiunion
antiuniversity
antiurban
antivandalism
antivenereal
antiviolence
antiviral
antivivisection
antivivisectionist
antiwar
antiwear
antiweed
anti-West
anti-Western
antiwhite
antiwiretapping
antiwoman
antiwrinkle

an•ti•air•craft \\,ant-ē-'aər-,kraft, -'eər-\\ *adj* **:** designed or used for defense against aircraft — **antiaircraft** *n*

an•ti•bac•te•ri•al \\,ant-i-bak-'tir-ē-əl, ,an-,tī-\\ *adj* **:** directed or effective against bacteria

an•ti•bal•lis•tic missile \\,ant-i-bə-,lis-tik-, ,an-,tī-\\ *n* **:** a missile for intercepting and destroying ballistic missiles

an•ti•bi•o•sis \\-bī-'ō-səs, -bē-\\ *n* **:** antagonistic association between organisms to the detriment of one of them or between one organism and a metabolic product of another

an•ti•bi•ot•ic \\-bī-'ät-ik, -bē-\\ *n* **:** a substance produced by a microorganism (as a fungus or bacterium) that in dilute solution inhibits or kills another microorganism — **antibiotic** *adj* — **an•ti•bi•ot•i•cal•ly** \\-'ät-i-kə-lē, -klē\\ *adv*

an•ti•body \\'ant-i-,bäd-ē\\ *n* **:** any of several globulins in the blood that react with specific antigens (as a toxin), bacteria, or cells to render them harmless to the organism

an•ti•bus•ing \\,ant-i-'bəs-ing, ,an-,tī-\\ *adj* **:** opposed to the busing of children as a means of racially balancing pupil population in the schools

[1]an•tic \\'ant-ik\\ *n* **1 :** a silly, playful, or ludicrous act or action **:** CAPER ⟨carnival *antics*⟩ **2** *archaic* **:** CLOWN, BUFFOON [Italian *antico,* adj., "ancient", from Latin *antiquus*]

△ **origin** In the ruins of ancient Roman buildings Renaissance Italians found fantastic mural paintings. In Renaissance England any similarly fantastic painting of more modern date that showed strange combinations of human, animal, and floral forms was called *antike* or *anticke,* from the Italian word for "ancient", *antico.* And any odd gesture or strange behavior reminiscent of the ancient Roman paintings became in English an *antic.*

[2]antic *adj* **1** *archaic* **:** GROTESQUE, BIZARRE **2 :** whimsically grotesque or extravagant ⟨an *antic* comedy⟩

an•ti•can•cer \\,ant-i-'kan-sər, ,an-,tī-\\ *also* **an•ti•can•cer•ous** \\-'kans-rəs, -ə-rəs\\ *adj* **:** used or effective against cancer ⟨*anticancer* drugs⟩

An•ti•christ \\'ant-i-,krīst\\ *n* **1 :** one who denies or opposes Christ; *esp* **:** a great antagonist expected to fill the world with wickedness but to be conquered forever by Christ at the second coming **2 :** a false Christ

an•tic•i•pate \\an-'tis-ə-,pāt\\ *vb* **1 a :** to take into consideration in advance ⟨*anticipate* the result of an action⟩ ⟨*anticipate* a plan⟩ **b :** to deal with before the expected or proper time ⟨*anticipate* a bill⟩ **2 a :** to deal with before another can act or interfere ⟨an idea *anticipated* by an earlier inventor⟩ **b :** to act before (another) often so as to check or counter **3 :** to use in advance of actual possession ⟨*anticipate* one's income⟩ **4 :** to look forward to **:** EXPECT ⟨*anticipate* a holiday⟩ [Latin *anticipare,* from *ante-* + *capere* "to take"] **syn** see FORESEE — **an•tic•i•pa•tor** \\-,pāt-ər\\ *n*

an•tic•i•pa•tion \\,an-,tis-ə-'pā-shən\\ *n* **1 a :** a prior action that takes into account or forestalls a later action **b :** the act of looking forward; *esp* : pleasurable expectation **2** : a picturing beforehand of a future event or state — **an•tic•i•pa•to•ry** \an-'tis-ə-pə-,tōr-ē, -,tȯr-\ *adj*

an•ti•cler•i•cal \,ant-i-'kler-i-kəl, ,an-,tī-\ *adj* : opposed to the influence of the clergy in secular affairs — **anticlerical** *n* — **an•ti•cler•i•cal•ism** \-'kler-i-kə-,liz-əm\ *n*

an•ti•cli•max \,ant-i-'klī-,maks\ *n* **1** : the usually sudden change in writing or speaking from a significant idea to a trivial or ludicrous idea; *also* : an instance of such change **2** : an event especially closing a series that is strikingly less important than what has preceded it — **an•ti•cli•mac•tic** \-klī-'mak-tik\ *adj* — **an•ti•cli•mac•ti•cal•ly** \-ti-kə-lē, -klē\ *adv*

an•ti•cline \'ant-i-,klīn\ *n* : an arch of stratified rock in which the layers bend downward in opposite directions from the crest — compare SYNCLINE [Greek *klinein* "to lean"]

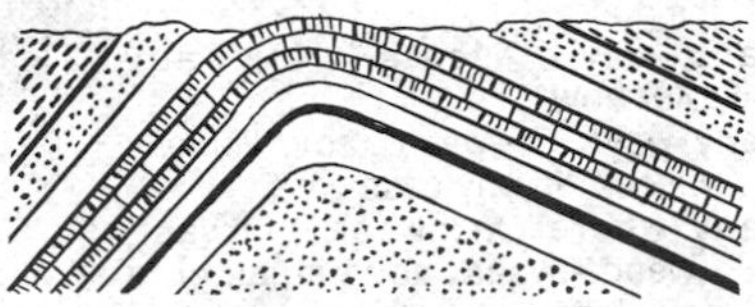

anticline

an•ti•clock•wise \,ant-i-'kläk,wīz, ,an-,tī-\ *adj or adv* : COUNTERCLOCKWISE

an•ti•co•ag•u•lant \-kō-'ag-yə-lənt\ *n* : a substance that hinders clotting of blood — **anticoagulant** *adj*

an•ti•com•pet•i•tive \-kəm-'pet-ət-iv\ *adj* : tending to restrict free competition

an•ti•cy•clone \,ant-i-'sī-,klōn\ *n* : a system of winds that rotates about a center of high atmospheric pressure clockwise in the northern hemisphere and counterclockwise in the southern, that usually advances at 30 to 40 kilometers per hour, and that usually has a diameter of 2500 to 4000 kilometers — **an•ti•cy•clon•ic** \-sī-'klän-ik\ *adj*

an•ti•de•pres•sant \,ant-i-di-'pres-nt, ,an-,tī-\ *or* **an•ti•de•pres•sive** \-di-'pres-iv\ *adj* : used or tending to relieve psychic depression — **antidepressant** *n*

an•ti•dote \'ant-i-,dōt\ *n* **1** : a remedy to counteract the effects of poison **2** : something that relieves, prevents, or counteracts [Latin *antidotum,* from Greek *antidotos,* derived from *anti-* + *didonai* "to give"]

an•ti•elec•tron \,ant-ē-ə-'lek-,trän, ,an-,tī-\ *n* : POSITRON

an•ti–fed•er•al•ist \,ant-i-'fed-rə-ləst, ,an-,tī-, -ə-rə-\ *n, often cap A&F* : a member of the group that opposed in 1787–88 the adoption of the United States Constitution

an•ti•fer•til•i•ty \-fər-'til-ət-ē\ *adj* : intended to control excess or unwanted fertility : CONTRACEPTIVE

an•ti•freeze \'ant-i-,frēz\ *n* : a substance (as ethylene glycol) added to a liquid (as the water in an automobile radiator) to prevent its freezing

an•ti•gen \'ant-i-jən\ *n* : a substance (as a toxin or enzyme) that when introduced into the body stimulates the production of an antibody — **an•ti•gen•ic** \,ant-i-'jen-ik\ *adj* — **an•ti•gen•i•cal•ly** \-'jen-i-kə-lē, -klē\ *adv* — **an•ti•ge•nic•i•ty** \-jə-'nis-ət-ē\ *n*

an•ti•he•mo•phil•ic \,ant-i-,hē-mə-'fil-ik, ,an-,tī-\ *adj* : counteracting the bleeding tendency in hemophilia

an•ti•hero \'ant-i-,hē-,rō, 'an-,tī-, -,hiər-,ō\ *n* : a principal character (as in a story or play) completely lacking in heroic qualities — **an•ti•he•ro•ic** \,ant-i-hi-'rō-ik, ,an-,tī-\ *adj*

an•ti•his•ta•mine \,ant-i-'his-tə-,mēn, ,an-,tī-, -mən\ *n* : any of various drugs that counteract histamine in the body and are used for treating allergic reactions and cold symptoms

an•ti•knock \,ant-i-'näk\ *n* : a substance that when added to the fuel of an internal-combustion engine helps to prevent knocking

an•ti•log•a•rithm \,ant-i-'lȯg-ə-,rith-əm, ,an-,tī-, -'läg-\ *n* : the number corresponding to a given logarithm

an•ti•ma•cas•sar \,ant-i-mə-'kas-ər\ *n* : a covering to protect the back or arms of furniture [*anti-* + *Macassar oil,* a hair dressing]

an•ti•ma•lar•i•al \,ant-i-mə-'ler-ē-əl, ,an-,tī-\ *adj* : serving to prevent, check, or cure malaria — **antimalarial** *n*

an•ti•mat•ter \'ant-i-,mat-ər\ *n* : matter composed of antiparticles

an•ti•mi•cro•bi•al \,ant-i-mī-'krō-bē-əl\ *adj* : inhibiting or destructive to microbes — **antimicrobial** *n*

an•ti•mo•ny \'ant-ə-,mō-nē\ *n* : a metallic silvery white crystalline and brittle element that is used especially as a constituent of alloys and in medicine — see ELEMENT table [Medieval Latin *antimonium*] — **an•ti•mo•ni•al** \,ant-ə-'mō-nē-əl\ *adj*

an•ti•neu•tri•no \,ant-i-nü-'trē-,nō, ,an-,tī-, -nyü-\ *n* : the antiparticle of the neutrino

an•ti•neu•tron \-'nü-,trän, -'nyü-\ *n* : the antiparticle of the neutron

an•ti•ox•i•dant \,ant-ē-'äk-səd-ənt, ,an-,tī-\ *n* : a substance that opposes oxidation or inhibits reactions promoted by oxygen — **antioxidant** *adj*

an•ti•par•ti•cle \'ant-i-,pärt-i-kəl, 'an-,tī-\ *n* : an elementary particle identical to another in mass but opposite to it in electric or magnetic properties that when brought together with its counterpart produces mutual annihilation

an•ti•pas•to \,ant-i-'pas-tō, ,änt-i-'päs-\ *n, pl* **-pas•ti** \-tē\ : any of various typically Italian hors d'oeuvres; *also* : a number of these served especially as the first course of a meal [Italian, from *anti-* "before" (from Latin *ante-*) + *pasto* "food", from Latin *pastus*]

an•tip•a•thy \an-'tip-ə-thē\ *n, pl* **-thies** **1** : strong feeling against someone or something : AVERSION **2** : a person or thing that arouses strong dislike — **an•ti•pa•thet•ic** \,ant-i-pə-'thet-ik\ *adj* — **an•ti•pa•thet•i•cal•ly** \-i-kə-lē, -klē\ *adv*

an•ti•per•son•nel \,ant-i-,pərs-n-'el, ,an-,tī-\ *adj* : designed for use against military personnel

an•ti•per•spi•rant \-'pər-spə-rənt, -sprənt\ *n* : a cosmetic preparation used to check excessive perspiration

an•ti•phon \'ant-ə-fən, -,fän\ *n* **1** : a psalm, anthem, or verse sung alternately by divisions of a choir or congregation **2** : a verse usually from Scripture said or sung before and after a canticle, psalm, or psalm verse [Late Latin *antiphona,* from Late Greek *antiphōna,* from Greek *antiphōnos* "responsive", from *anti-* + *phōnē* "sound"]

an•tiph•o•nal \an-'tif-ən-l\ *adj* : performed by two alternating groups ⟨*antiphonal* singing⟩ — **an•tiph•o•nal•ly** \-l-ē\ *adv*

an•tip•o•dal \an-'tip-əd-l\ *adj* **1** : of or relating to the antipodes; *esp* : situated at the opposite side of the earth **2** : diametrically opposite **3** : differing greatly

an•ti•pode \'ant-ə-,pōd\ *n, pl* **an•tip•o•des** \an-'tip-ə-,dēz\ **1** : the parts of the earth diametrically opposite — usually used in pl. **2** : the exact opposite or contrary [Latin *antipodes* "persons living at opposite points on the globe", from Greek, from *antipous* "with feet opposite", from *anti-* + *pous* "foot"] — **an•tip•o•de•an** \,an-,tip-ə-'dē-ən\ *adj*

an•ti•pol•lu•tion \,ant-i-pə-'lü-shən, ,an-,tī-\ *adj* : intended to prevent, reduce, or eliminate pollution ⟨*antipollution* devices on automobiles⟩

an•ti•pope \'ant-i-,pōp\ *n* : one elected or claiming to be pope in opposition to the pope canonically chosen

an•ti•pro•ton \,ant-i-'prō-,tän, ,an-,tī-\ *n* : the antiparticle of the proton

an•ti•py•ret•ic \-pī-'ret-ik\ *n* : an agent that reduces fever [Greek *pyretos* "fever", from *pyr* "fire"] — **antipyretic** *adj*

[1]**an•ti•quar•i•an** \,ant-ə-'kwer-ē-ən\ *n* : ANTIQUARY

[2]**antiquarian** *adj* : of or relating to antiquaries or antiquities

an•ti•quary \'ant-ə-,kwer-ē\ *n, pl* **-quar•ies** : a person who collects or studies antiquities

an•ti•quate \'ant-ə-,kwāt\ *vt* : to make old or obsolete

an•ti•quat•ed *adj* **1** : OLD-FASHIONED, OUTMODED **2** : of long standing or great age ⟨*antiquated* prejudices⟩

[1]**an•tique** \an-'tēk\ *adj* **1** : belonging to antiquity **2** : belonging to an earlier period ⟨*antique* furniture⟩ **3** : belonging to or resembling a former style or fashion : OLD-FASHIONED ⟨silver of an *antique* design⟩ [Middle French, from Latin *antiquus,* from *ante* "before"] **syn** see OLD — **an•tique•ly** *adv* — **an•tique•ness** *n*

[2]**antique** *n* : an object of an earlier period; *esp* : a work of art, piece of furniture, or decorative object made at an earlier period

an•tiq•ui•ty \an-'tik-wət-ē\ *n, pl* **-ties** **1** : ancient times; *esp* : those before the Middle Ages **2** : the quality of being ancient **3** *pl* **a** : relics or monuments of ancient times **b** : matters relating to the life or culture of ancient times

\ə\ **abut**	\au̇\ **out**	\i\ **tip**	\ȯ\ **saw**	\u̇\ **foot**
\ər\ **further**	\ch\ **chin**	\ī\ **life**	\ȯi\ **coin**	\y\ **yet**
\a\ **mat**	\e\ **pet**	\j\ **job**	\th\ **thin**	\yü\ **few**
\ā\ **take**	\ē\ **easy**	\ng\ **sing**	\t͟h\ **this**	\yu̇\ **cure**
\ä\ **cot, cart**	\g\ **go**	\ō\ **bone**	\ü\ **food**	\zh\ **vision**

an•ti•scor•bu•tic \ˌant-i-skȯr-ˈbyüt-ik, ˌan-ˌtī-\ *adj* **:** tending to prevent or relieve scurvy

an•ti–Sem•ite \-ˈsem-ˌīt\ *n* **:** a person who is hostile to or discriminates against Jews — **anti–Se•mit•ic** \-sə-ˈmit-ik\ *adj* — **an•ti–Sem•i•tism** \-ˈsem-ə-ˌtiz-əm\ *n*

an•ti•sepsis \ˌant-ə-ˈsep-səs\ *n* **:** the inhibiting of the growth and multiplication of microorganisms by antiseptic means

an•ti•sep•tic \ˌant-ə-ˈsep-tik\ *adj* **1 :** preventing or stopping the growth of germs that cause disease or decay ⟨*antiseptic* agents⟩ **2 :** relating to or characterized by the use of antiseptics ⟨*antiseptic* treatments⟩ **3 a :** protecting or protected from what is undesirable ⟨lives in *antiseptic* seclusion⟩ **b :** marked by cleanliness, orderliness, and neatness; *esp* **:** neat to the point of being bare or uninteresting **c :** free from living microorganisms **:** ASEPTIC ⟨*antiseptic* wounds⟩ **d :** coldly impersonal ⟨an *antiseptic* greeting⟩ [*anti-* + Greek *sēptikos* "putrefying, septic"] — **antiseptic** *n* — **an•ti•sep•ti•cal•ly** \-ti-kə-lē, -klē\ *adv*

an•ti•se•rum \ˈant-i-ˌsir-əm, ˈan-ˌtī-, -ˌser-\ *n* **:** a serum containing antibodies

an•ti•so•cial \ˌant-i-ˈsō-shəl, ˌan-ˌtī-\ *adj* **1 :** contrary or hostile to the well-being of society ⟨crime is *antisocial*⟩ **2 :** disliking or avoiding the company of others **:** UNSOCIABLE

an•ti•tank \-ˈtangk\ *adj* **:** designed to destroy or check tanks

an•tith•e•sis \an-ˈtith-ə-səs\ *n, pl* **-e•ses** \-ə-ˌsēz\ **1 :** the rhetorical contrast of ideas by means of parallel arrangements of words, clauses, or sentences **2 a :** a direct or striking contrast **b :** the second of two contrasted things **3 :** the direct opposite ⟨dictatorship is the *antithesis* of democracy⟩ [Late Latin, from Greek, literally, "opposition", from *antitithenai* "to place opposite, oppose", from *anti-* + *tithenai* "to put"] — **an•ti•thet•ic** \ˌant-ə-ˈthet-ik\ *adj* — **an•ti•thet•i•cal** \-ˈthet-i-kəl\ *adj* — **an•ti•thet•i•cal•ly** \-i-kə-lē, -klē\ *adv*

an•ti•tox•in \ˌant-i-ˈtäk-sən\ *n* **:** an antibody that is capable of neutralizing a particular toxin, is formed in response to the introduction of toxin into the body, and is produced commercially in lower animals for use in treating human diseases (as diphtheria) in which such a toxin is present; *also* **:** a serum containing antitoxins — **an•ti•tox•ic** \-sik\ *adj*

an•ti•trust \ˌant-i-ˈtrəst, ˌan-ˌtī-\ *adj* **:** opposing or designed to restrict the power of trusts and similar business combinations ⟨*antitrust* laws⟩

an•ti•ven•in \ˌant-i-ˈven-ən, ˌan-ˌtī-\ *n* **:** a serum containing an antitoxin to a venom (as of a snake)

ant•ler \ˈant-lər\ *n* **:** the solid deciduous horn of an animal of the deer family or a branch of such horn [Middle French *antoillier,* derived from Latin *ante-* + *oculus* "eye"] — **ant•lered** \-lərd\ *adj*

ant lion *n* **:** any of various 4-winged insects (order Neuroptera) with a long-jawed larva that digs a conical pit in which it lies in wait to catch insects (as ants) on which it feeds

an•to•nym \ˈant-ə-ˌnim\ *n* **:** a word of opposite meaning ⟨*hot* and *cold* are *antonyms*⟩ [*anti-* + Greek *onyma, onoma* "name"] — **an•ton•y•mous** \an-ˈtän-ə-məs\ *adj*

an•uran \ə-ˈnu̇r-ən, a-, -ˈnyu̇r-\ *adj or n* **:** SALIENTIAN [[2]*a-* + Greek *oura* "tail"]

anus \ˈā-nəs\ *n* **:** the posterior opening of the alimentary canal [Latin]

an•vil \ˈan-vəl\ *n* **1 :** a heavy usually steel-faced iron block on which metal is shaped **2 :** INCUS [Old English *anfilt*]

anx•i•ety \ang-ˈzī-ət-ē\ *n, pl* **-eties 1 a :** painful or fearful uneasiness of mind usually over an impending or anticipated event **b :** a cause of such uneasiness **2 :** a strong concern or desire mixed with doubt and fear ⟨*anxiety* to succeed⟩ [Latin *anxietas,* from *anxius* "anxious"]

anx•ious \ˈang-shəs, ˈangk-\ *adj* **1 :** fearful of what may happen **:** WORRIED ⟨*anxious* about their son's health⟩ **2 :** desiring earnestly ⟨*anxious* to make good⟩ [Latin *anxius*] **syn** see EAGER — **anx•ious•ly** *adv* — **anx•ious•ness** *n*

[1]**any** \ˈen-ē\ *adj* **1 a :** one taken at random ⟨*any* person you meet⟩ **b :** EVERY — used to indicate one selected without restriction ⟨*any* child would know that⟩ **2 :** one, some, or all indiscriminately of whatever quantity ⟨have you *any* money⟩ ⟨need *any* help they can get⟩ **3 :** unmeasured or unlimited in amount, number, or extent ⟨*any* quantity you desire⟩ [Old English *ǣnig*]

[2]**any** *pron, sing or pl in construction* **1 :** any person or persons **2 a :** any thing or things **b :** any part, quantity, or number

[3]**any** *adv* **:** to any extent or degree **:** at all ⟨can't go *any* farther⟩ ⟨you're not helping *any*⟩

any•body \ˈen-ē-ˌbäd-ē, -bəd-\ *pron* **:** ANYONE

any•how \-ˌhau̇\ *adv* **1 :** in any way, manner, or order **2 :** at any rate **:** in any case

any•more \ˌen-ē-ˈmōr, -ˈmȯr\ *adv* **:** at the present time **:** NOWADAYS ⟨we never see them *anymore*⟩

any•one \ˈen-ē-ˌwən, -wən\ *pron* **:** any person at all

any•place \-ˌplās\ *adv* **:** in any place **:** ANYWHERE

any•thing \-ˌthing\ *pron* **:** any thing at all

any•way \ˈen-ē-ˌwā\ *adv* **:** ANYHOW

any•ways \-ˌwāz\ *adv, chiefly dialect* **:** in any case

aoudad

any•where \-ˌhweər, -ˌhwaər, -ˌweər, -ˌwaər\ *adv* **:** in, at, or to any place

any•wise \-ˌwīz\ *adv* **:** in any way whatever **:** at all

A–OK \ˌā-ˌō-ˈkā\ *adj* **:** working or going well **:** FINE

A1 \ˈā-ˈwən\ *adj* **:** of the finest quality **:** FIRST-RATE

aor•ta \ā-ˈȯrt-ə\ *n, pl* **aortas** *or* **aor•tae** \-ˈȯrt-ē\ **:** the main artery of the circulatory system that carries blood from the heart to be distributed by branch arteries through the body [Greek *aortē,* from *aeirein* "to lift"] — **aor•tic** \-ˈȯrt-ik\ *adj*

aou•dad \ˈau̇-ˌdad, ˈä-u̇-\ *n* **:** a wild sheep of North Africa [French, from Berber *audad*]

[1]**ap-** — see AD-

[2]**ap-** *or* **apo-** *prefix* **:** away from **:** off ⟨*aphelion*⟩ [Greek *apo* "away, off"]

apace \ə-ˈpās\ *adv* **:** at a quick pace **:** SWIFTLY

apache \ə-ˈpach-ē, *in sense 2* ə-ˈpash\ *n, pl* **apache** *or* **apaches** \-ˈpach-ēz, -ˈpash-əz\ **1** *cap* **:** a member of an Indian people of the American Southwest **2 a :** a member of a gang of criminals especially in Paris **b :** RUFFIAN [sense 1 from Spanish; sense 2 from French, from *Apache* "Apache Indian"]

[1]**apart** \ə-ˈpärt\ *adv* **1 :** at a distance in space or time ⟨two towns five miles *apart*⟩ **2 :** as a separate unit **:** INDEPENDENTLY ⟨considered *apart* from other points⟩ **3 :** ASIDE ⟨joking *apart,* that's probably true⟩ **4 :** into pieces ⟨tear a book *apart*⟩

[2]**apart** *adj* **1 :** different or separated from others ⟨a breed *apart*⟩ ⟨a place *apart*⟩ **2 :** holding different opinions **:** DIVIDED — **apartness** *n*

apart from *prep* **:** other than **:** BESIDES

apart•heid \ə-ˈpär-ˌtāt, -ˌtīt\ *n* **:** a policy of racial segregation practiced in the Republic of South Africa [Afrikaans, literally, "separateness"]

apart•ment \ə-ˈpärt-mənt\ *n* **1 :** a room or set of rooms used as a dwelling **2 :** ROOM 2a **3 :** APARTMENT BUILDING

apartment building *n* **:** a building divided into individual dwelling units — called also *apartment house*

ap•a•thet•ic \ˌap-ə-ˈthet-ik\ *adj* **1 :** having or showing little or no feeling or emotion **:** SPIRITLESS **2 :** having little or no interest or concern **:** INDIFFERENT **syn** see IMPASSIVE — **ap•a•thet•i•cal•ly** \-ˈthet-i-kə-lē, -klē\ *adv*

ap•a•thy \ˈap-ə-thē\ *n* **1 :** lack of feeling or emotion **2 :** lack of interest or concern **:** INDIFFERENCE

ap•a•tite \ˈap-ə-ˌtīt\ *n* **:** any of a group of minerals of variable color that are phosphates of calcium usually with some fluorine and that are used as a source of phosphorus and its compounds [German *apatit,* from Greek *apatē* "deceit"]

[1]**ape** \ˈāp\ *n* **1 a :** MONKEY; *esp* **:** one of the larger tailless or short-tailed forms **b :** any of a family of large semierect primates (as the chimpanzee or gorilla) **2 a :** MIMIC **b :** a large uncouth person [Old English *apa*] — **ape•like** \ˈā-ˌplīk\ *adj*

[2]**ape** *vt* **:** to follow as a pattern or model **syn** see IMITATE — **ap•er** *n*

ape–man \ˈāp-ˈman, -ˌman\ *n* **:** a primate (as pithecanthropus) intermediate in character between true humans and the higher apes

ape•ri•ent \ə-ˈpir-ē-ənt\ *n* **:** LAXATIVE [Latin *aperire* "to open"] — **aperient** *adj*

aper•i•tif \ˌäp-ˌer-ə-ˈtēf, ə-ˈper-ə-\ *n* **:** an alcoholic drink taken (as a cocktail) before a meal as an appetizer [French *apéritif,* derived from Latin *aperire* "to open"]

ap•er•ture \'ap-ər-,chůr, 'ap-ə-, -chər\ *n* **1 :** an opening or open space : HOLE **2 :** the opening in a lens that admits light; *also* **:** the diameter of this opening [Latin *apertura,* from *aperire* "to open"]

apex \'ā-,peks\ *n, pl* **apex•es** *or* **api•ces** \'ā-pə-,sēz, 'ap-ə-\ **1 a :** the uppermost point : TOP **b :** the narrowed or pointed end : TIP ⟨*apex* of a leaf⟩ **2 :** the highest or culminating point ⟨*apex* of a career⟩ [Latin] **syn** see SUMMIT

apha•sia \ə-'fā-zhē-ə, -zhə\ *n* **:** loss or impairment of the power to use and understand words [Greek, from *a-* + *phasia* "speech", from *phanai* "to say"] — **apha•sic** \-zik\ *n or adj*

aph•elion \a-'fēl-yən\ *n, pl* **aph•elia** \-yə\ **:** the point of a planet's or comet's orbit most distant from the sun — compare PERIHELION [*apo-* + Greek *hēlios* "sun"]

aphid \'ā-fəd, 'af-əd\ *n* **:** any of numerous small sluggish insects that suck the juices of plants

aphis \'ā-fəs, 'af-əs\ *n, pl* **aphi•des** \'ā-fə-,dēz, 'af-ə-\ **:** APHID [New Latin *Aphid-, Aphis,* genus name]

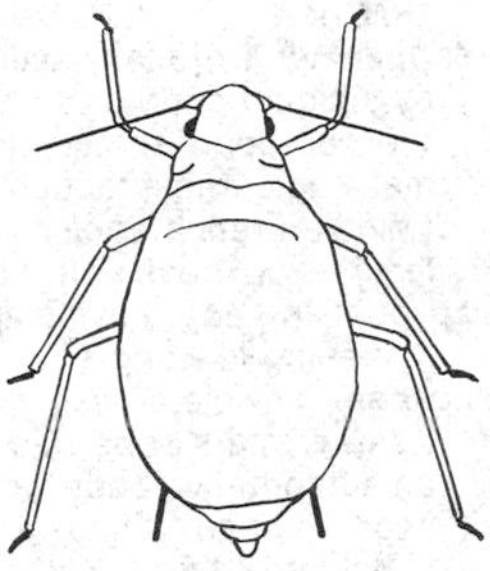

aphid

aph•o•rism \'af-ə-,riz-əm\ *n* **:** a short sentence stating a general truth or practical observation [Middle French *aphorisme,* derived from Greek *aphorizein* "to define", from *apo-* + *horizein* "to bound"] — **aph•o•rist** \-rəst\ *n* — **aph•o•ris•tic** \,af-ə-'ris-tik\ *adj* — **aph•o•ris•ti•cal•ly** \-ti-kə-lē, -klē\ *adv*

aph•ro•dis•i•ac \,af-rə-'dē-zē-,ak, -'diz-ē-\ *adj* **:** exciting sexual desire [Greek *aphrodisiakos* "sexual", derived from *Aphroditē* "Aphrodite"] — **aphrodisiac** *n* — **aph•ro•di•si•a•cal** \,af-rəd-ə-'zī-ə-kəl, -'sī-\ *adj*

api•ary \'ā-pē-,er-ē\ *n, pl* **-ar•ies :** a place where bees are kept; *esp* **:** a collection of hives of bees [Latin *apiarium,* from *apis* "bee"]

ap•i•cal \'ā-pi-kəl *also* 'ap-i-\ *adj* **:** of, relating to, or situated at an apex [Latin *apic-, apex* "apex"] — **ap•i•cal•ly** \-kə-lē, -klē\ *adv*

apiece \ə-'pēs\ *adv* **:** for each one : INDIVIDUALLY ⟨selling for ten cents *apiece*⟩

ap•ish \'ā-pish\ *adj* **1 :** given to slavish imitation **2 :** extremely silly or affected — **ap•ish•ly** *adv* — **ap•ish•ness** *n*

aplomb \ə-'pläm, -'pləm\ *n* **:** complete composure or self-assurance : POISE [French, literally, "perpendicularity", from *à plomb* "according to the plumb bob"]

apo- — see ²AP-

apoc•a•lypse \ə-'päk-ə-,lips\ *n* **1 a :** a Jewish or early Christian symbolic writing about a final cataclysm destroying the powers of evil and ushering in the kingdom of God **b** *cap* **:** the biblical book of Revelation **2 :** a prophetic revelation [Late Latin *apocalypsis,* from Greek *apokalypsis,* literally, "uncovering", from *apo-* + *kalyptein* "to cover"] — **apoc•a•lyp•tic** \ə-,päk-ə-'lip-tik\ *adj* — **apoc•a•lyp•ti•cal•ly** \-'lip-ti-kə-lē, -klē\ *adv*

apoc•o•pe \ə-'päk-ə-,pē\ *n* **:** the loss of one or more sounds or letters at the end of a word (as in *sing* from Old English *singan*) [Late Latin, from Greek *apokopē,* literally, "cutting off"]

apoc•ry•pha \ə-'päk-rə-fə\ *n sing or pl* **1 :** writings or statements of dubious authenticity **2** *cap* **a :** books included in the Septuagint and Vulgate but excluded from the Jewish and Protestant canons of the Old Testament — see BIBLE table **b :** early Christian writings not included in the New Testament [Medieval Latin, from Late Latin *apocryphus* "not canonical", from Greek *apokryphos* "obscure", from *apokryptein* "to hide away", from *apo-* + *kryptein* "to hide"]

apoc•ry•phal \-fəl\ *adj* **1** *often cap* **:** of or resembling the Apocrypha **2 :** of doubtful authenticity : SPURIOUS — **apoc•ry•phal•ly** \-fə-lē\ *adv* — **apoc•ry•phal•ness** *n*

apo•gee \'ap-ə-,jē\ *n* **1 :** the point farthest from the center of a celestial body (as the earth or moon) reached by an object (as a satellite) orbiting it — compare PERIGEE **2 :** the farthest or highest point : CULMINATION [French *apogée,* derived from Greek *apo-* + *gē* "earth"]

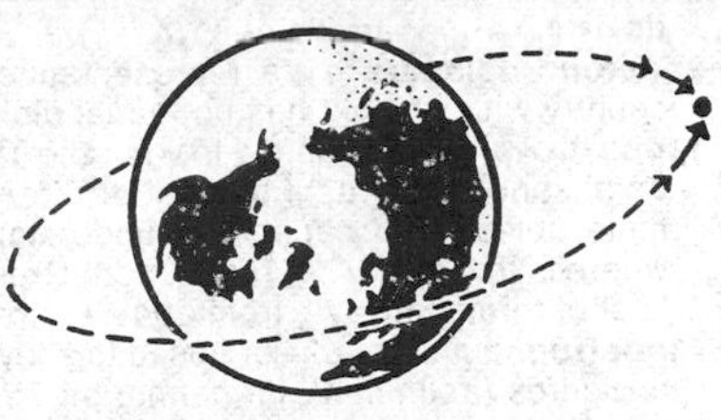

apogee 1

apol•o•get•ic \ə-,päl-ə-'jet-ik\ *adj* **1 :** offered in defense or by way of excuse or apology **2 :** expressing or seeming to express apology ⟨an *apologetic* face⟩ — **apol•o•get•i•cal•ly** \-'jet-i-kə-lē, -klē\ *adv*

apol•o•get•ics \-'jet-iks\ *n* **:** systematic argument in defense especially of the divine origin and authority of Christianity; *also* **:** a branch of theology devoted to the defense of a religious faith

apo•lo•gia \,ap-ə-'lō-jē-ə, -jə\ *n* **:** a defense especially of one's opinions, actions, or position [Late Latin]

apol•o•gist \ə-'päl-ə-jəst\ *n* **:** one who speaks or writes in defense of a faith, a cause, a person, or an institution

apol•o•gize \ə-'päl-ə-,jīz\ *vi* **:** to make an apology : express regret for something one has done — **apol•o•giz•er** *n*

apol•o•gy \-jē\ *n, pl* **-gies 1 :** a formal justification or defense **2 :** an admission of error or discourtesy accompanied by an expression of regret **3 :** a poor substitute [Middle French *apologie,* from Late Latin *apologia,* from Greek, from *apo-* + *logos* "speech"]

• **syn** EXCUSE: APOLOGY implies that one has been actually or apparently in the wrong; it may offer an explanation or it may simply acknowledge error and express regret; EXCUSE implies an intent to remove blame or censure for a wrong, mistake, or failure.

apo•mix•is \,ap-ə-'mik-səs\ *n, pl* **-mix•es** \-,sēz\ **:** reproduction (as parthenogenesis) involving specialized generative tissues but not dependent on fertilization [*apo-* + Greek *mixis* "act of mixing"]

ap•o•plec•tic \,ap-ə-'plek-tik\ *adj* **1 :** of, relating to, or caused by apoplexy ⟨*apoplectic* symptoms⟩ **2 a :** affected with or inclined to apoplexy ⟨*apoplectic* patients⟩ **b :** highly excited or excitable — **ap•o•plec•ti•cal•ly** \-ti-kə-lē, -klē\ *adv*

ap•o•plexy \'ap-ə-,plek-sē\ *n, pl* **-plex•ies :** STROKE 5 [Late Latin *apoplexia,* derived from Greek *apoplēssein* "to cripple by a stroke", from *apo-* + *plēssein* "to strike"]

apos•ta•sy \ə-'päs-tə-sē\ *n, pl* **-sies 1 :** renunciation of a religious faith **2 :** abandonment of a previous loyalty : DEFECTION [Late Latin *apostasia,* from Greek, literally, "revolt", from *aphistasthai* "to revolt", from *apo-* + *histasthai* "to stand"]

apos•tate \ə-'päs-,tāt, -tət\ *n* **:** one who commits apostasy — **apostate** *adj*

apos•ta•tize \ə-'päs-tə-,tīz\ *vi* **:** to commit apostasy

a pos•te•ri•o•ri \,ä-pä-,stir-ē-'ōr-ē, -pō-, -,ster-, -'ór-\ *adj* **:** relating to or derived by reasoning from known or observed facts to a conclusion [Latin, literally, "from the latter"] — **a posteriori** *adv*

apos•tle \ə-'päs-əl\ *n* **1 :** one sent on a religious mission: as **a** *often cap* **:** one of an authoritative New Testament group made up especially of Christ's twelve original disciples and Paul **b :** the first Christian missionary to a region **2 a :** one that first advocates a cause or movement **b :** an ardent advocate or supporter [Late Latin *apostolus,* from Greek *apostolos,* literally, "one sent forth", from *apo-* + *stellein* "to send"] — **apos•tle•ship** \-əl-,ship\ *n*

Apostles' Creed *n* **:** a Christian creed ascribed to the Twelve Apostles that begins "I believe in God the Father Almighty"

apos•to•late \ə-'päs-tə-,lāt, -lət\ *n* **1 :** the office or mission of an apostle **2 :** a group dedicated to the spreading of a religion or a doctrine

ap•os•tol•ic \,ap-ə-'stäl-ik\ *adj* **1 a :** of or relating to an apostle **b :** of or relating to the New Testament apostles or their times or teachings **2 a :** of or forming a succession of spiritual authority from the apostles held in Catholic tradition to be perpetuated by successive ordinations of bishops and to be necessary for the validity of sacraments and orders **b :** PAPAL — **apos•to-**

lic•i•ty \ə-ˌpäs-tə-ˈlis-ət-ē\ *n*
apostolic delegate *n* : a representative of the Holy See in a country with which it has no formal diplomatic relations
[1]**apos•tro•phe** \ə-ˈpäs-trə-fē\ *n* : the rhetorical addressing of an absent person as if present or of an abstract idea or inanimate object as if capable of understanding (as in "O grave, where is thy victory?") [Latin, from Greek *apostrophē,* literally, "act of turning away", from *apo-* + *strephein* "to turn"]
[2]**apostrophe** *n* : a mark ' or ' used to show the omission of letters or figures (as in *can't* for *cannot* or *'76* for *1776*), the possessive case (as in *Chicago's*), or the plural of letters or figures (as in *cross your t's, six 7's*)
apos•tro•phize \ə-ˈpäs-trə-ˌfīz\ *vb* **1** : to address by or in apostrophe **2** : to make use of apostrophe
apothecaries' weight *n* : a system of weights used chiefly by pharmacists — see MEASURE table
apoth•e•cary \ə-ˈpäth-ə-ˌker-ē\ *n, pl* **-car•ies 1** : DRUGGIST, PHARMACIST **2** : PHARMACY 2 [Late Latin *apothecarius* "shopkeeper", from Latin *apotheca* "storehouse", from Greek *apothēkē,* from *apotithenai* "to put away"]
apo•thegm \ˈap-ə-ˌthem\ *n* : a concise instructive saying or formulation : APHORISM [Greek *apophthegma,* from *apo-* + *phthengesthai* "to utter"]
apo•them \ˈap-ə-ˌthem\ *n* : the perpendicular from the center to one of the sides of a regular polygon [*apo-* + Greek *thema* "something laid down, theme"]

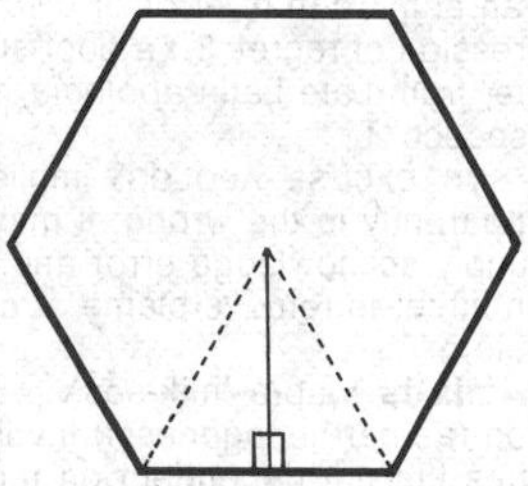
apothem

apo•the•o•sis \ə-ˌpäth-ē-ˈō-səs, ˌap-ə-ˈthē-ə-səs\ *n, pl* **-o•ses** \-ˈō-ˌsēz, -ə-ˌsēz\ **1** : elevation to divine status : DEIFICATION **2** : a perfect example [Late Latin, from Greek *apotheōsis,* from *apotheoun* "to deify", from *apo-* + *theos* "god"] — **ap•o•the•o•size** \ˌap-ə-ˈthē-ə-ˌsīz, ə-ˈpäth-ē-ə-\ *vt*
ap•pall \ə-ˈpȯl\ *vt* : to overcome with fear or dread : HORRIFY, SHOCK [Middle French *apalir* "to make pale", from *a-* "ad-" + *palir* "to grow pale"]
ap•pall•ing *adj* : inspiring horror or dismay : SHOCKING ⟨living under *appalling* conditions⟩ — **ap•pall•ing•ly** \-ˈpȯ-ling-lē\ *adv*
Ap•pa•loo•sa \ˌap-ə-ˈlü-sə\ *n* : a rugged American saddle horse that has a mottled skin and a dark-blotched patch of white hair over the rump and loins [probably from *Palouse,* an Indian people of Washington and Idaho]

Appaloosa

ap•pa•nage \ˈap-ə-nij\ *n* **1** : a grant (as of land or revenue) made by a sovereign or a legislative body to a member of the royal family or a person of noble rank **2** : a customary or rightful possession or privilege [French *apanage,* from Provençal *apanar* "to support", derived from Latin *ad-* + *panis* "bread"]
ap•pa•rat \ˈap-ə-ˌrat, ˌäp-ə-ˈrät\ *n* : APPARATUS 2 [Russian]
ap•pa•ra•tchik \ˌäp-ə-ˈräch-ik\ *n, pl* **-ratchiks** *or* **-ra•tchi•ki** \-ˈräch-ə-ˌkē\ : a member of a Communist apparatus [Russian, from *apparat*]
ap•pa•ra•tus \ˌap-ə-ˈrat-əs, -ˈrāt-\ *n, pl* **-tus•es** *or* **-tus 1 a** : the equipment used to do a particular kind of work **b** : an instrument or appliance for a specific operation **2** : the system of persons and agencies through which an organization functions; *esp* : the administrative machinery of a Communist party [Latin, from *apparare* "to prepare", from *ad-* + *parare* "to prepare"]
[1]**ap•par•el** \ə-ˈpar-əl\ *vt* **-eled** *or* **-elled**; **-el•ing** *or* **-el•ling 1** : CLOTHE, DRESS **2** : ADORN, EMBELLISH [Old French *apareiller* "to prepare", from Latin *apparare*]
[2]**apparel** *n* : personal attire : CLOTHING
ap•par•ent \ə-ˈpar-ənt, -ˈper-\ *adj* **1** : open to view : VISIBLE ⟨the flaw in the material was *apparent*⟩ **2** : clear to the understanding ⟨it was *apparent* that the road was little used⟩ **3** : seemingly real or true ⟨an *apparent* contradiction⟩ [Old French *aparent,* from Latin *apparēre* "to appear"] — **ap•par•ent•ly** *adv* — **ap•par•ent•ness** *n*
• **syn** APPARENT, EVIDENT mean readily perceived or grasped. APPARENT implies having outward signs that may prove on deeper analysis to be misleading ⟨the *apparent* cause of the accident⟩ EVIDENT suggests an appearance unmistakably corresponding with reality ⟨our *evident* delight at your gift⟩
ap•pa•ri•tion \ˌap-ə-ˈrish-ən\ *n* **1** : an unusual or unexpected sight : PHENOMENON **2** : GHOST 2 [Late Latin *apparitio* "appearance", from Latin *apparēre* "to appear"] — **ap•pa•ri•tion•al** \-ˈrish-nəl, -ən-l\ *adj*
[1]**ap•peal** \ə-ˈpēl\ *n* **1 a** : a legal proceeding by which a case is brought from a lower to a higher court for a reexamination **b** : a request for such a proceeding **2 a** : a request made to an authority for a confirmation or decision ⟨an *appeal* to the referee⟩ **b** : an earnest request : PLEA ⟨an *appeal* for financial support⟩ **3** : the power of arousing a sympathetic response : ATTRACTION
[2]**appeal** *vb* **1** : to take action to have a case or decision reviewed by a higher court or authority ⟨*appeal* to the supreme court⟩ **2** : to call upon another for corroboration or vindication **3** : to make an earnest request **4** : to arouse a sympathetic response [Middle French *apeler* "to accuse, appeal", from Latin *appellare*] — **ap•peal•able** \ə-ˈpē-lə-bəl\ *adj*
ap•peal•ing *adj* : having appeal : ATTRACTIVE — **ap•peal•ing•ly** \-ˈpē-ling-lē\ *adv*
ap•pear \ə-ˈpiər\ *vi* **1** : to come into sight : become evident : SHOW ⟨stars *appeared* in the sky⟩ **2** : to come formally before an authoritative body ⟨*appear* in court⟩ **3** : to have an outward aspect : SEEM ⟨things are not always as they *appear*⟩ ⟨*appear* to be tired⟩ **4 a** : to come out in printed form ⟨a book scheduled to *appear* next month⟩ **b** : to come before the public on stage or screen ⟨*appears* on television⟩ [Old French *aparoir,* from Latin *apparēre,* from *ad-* + *parēre* "to show oneself"]
ap•pear•ance \ə-ˈpir-əns\ *n* **1** : the act, action, or process of appearing **2 a** : outward aspect : LOOK **b** : external show : SEMBLANCE **c** *pl* : outward indications or show ⟨guilty to all *appearances*⟩ ⟨keep up *appearances*⟩ **3 a** : something that appears : PHENOMENON **b** : an instance of appearing ⟨a personal *appearance*⟩
ap•pease \ə-ˈpēz\ *vt* **1** : to make calm or quiet : ALLAY **2** : to make concessions to (a potential aggressor) usually at the sacrifice of principles : CONCILIATE [Old French *apaisier,* from *a-* "ad-" + *pais* "peace"] **syn** see PACIFY — **ap•pease•ment** \-mənt\ *n* — **ap•peas•er** *n*
ap•pel•lant \ə-ˈpel-ənt\ *n* : one that appeals; *esp* : one that appeals from a judicial decision or decree
ap•pel•late \ə-ˈpel-ət\ *adj* : of or relating to appeals ⟨*appellate* jurisdiction⟩; *esp* : having the power to review the decisions of a lower court ⟨an *appellate* court⟩
ap•pel•la•tion \ˌap-ə-ˈlā-shən\ *n* : an identifying or descriptive name or title : DESIGNATION
ap•pel•lee \ˌap-ə-ˈlē\ *n* : one against whom an appeal is taken
ap•pend \ə-ˈpend\ *vt* : to add as a supplement ⟨*append* a postscript to a letter⟩ [French *appendre,* from Latin *appendere* "to weigh", from *ad-* + *pendere* "to weigh"]
ap•pend•age \ə-ˈpen-dij\ *n* **1** : something attached to a larger or more important thing **2** : a subordinate or derivative body part; *esp* : a limb or an analogous part
ap•pen•dec•to•my \ˌap-ən-ˈdek-tə-mē\ *n, pl* **-mies** : surgical removal of the human appendix
ap•pen•di•ci•tis \ə-ˌpen-də-ˈsīt-əs\ *n* : inflammation of the appendix
ap•pen•dic•u•lar \ˌap-ən-ˈdik-yə-lər\ *adj* : of or relating to an appendage and especially a limb ⟨the *appendicular* skeleton⟩
ap•pen•dix \ə-ˈpen-diks\ *n, pl* **-dix•es** *or* **-di•ces** \-də-ˌsēz\ **1** : supplementary material usually attached at the end of a piece of writing **2 a** : a small tubular outgrowth from the cecum of the intestine — called also *vermiform appendix* **b** : a bodily outgrowth or process other than the appendix of the intestine [Latin, "addition", from *appendere* "to append"]
ap•per•ceive \ˌap-ər-ˈsēv\ *vt* : to understand (something perceived) in terms of previous experience
ap•per•cep•tion \ˌap-ər-ˈsep-shən\ *n* : the process of apperceiving — **ap•per•cep•tive** \-ˈsep-tiv\ *adj*

ap•per•tain \ˌap-ər-ˈtān\ *vi* : to belong or be connected as a possession, part, or right : PERTAIN ⟨duties that *appertain* to the office of governor⟩ [Middle French *apartenir,* derived from Latin *ad-* + *pertinēre* "to belong"]
ap•pe•tite \ˈap-ə-ˌtīt\ *n* **1** : one of the instinctive desires necessary to keep up organic life; *esp* : the desire to eat **2 a** : an inherent craving **b** : TASTE 5, PREFERENCE [Middle French *apetit,* from Latin *appetitus,* from *appetere* "to strive after", from *ad-* + *petere* "to go to"]
ap•pe•tiz•er \-ˌtī-zər\ *n* : a food or drink that stimulates the appetite and is usually served before a meal
ap•pe•tiz•ing \-ˌtī-zing\ *adj* : appealing to the appetite — **ap•pe•tiz•ing•ly** \-zing-lē\ *adv*
ap•plaud \ə-ˈplȯd\ *vb* **1** : PRAISE, APPROVE ⟨*applaud* their efforts⟩ **2** : to show approval especially by clapping the hands [Latin *applaudere,* from *ad-* + *plaudere* "to clap"] — **ap•plaud•able** \-ə-bəl\ *adj* — **ap•plaud•ably** \-blē\ *adv* — **ap•plaud•er** *n*
ap•plause \ə-ˈplȯz\ *n* : approval publicly expressed (as by clapping the hands) : ACCLAIM [Medieval Latin *applausus,* from Latin *applaudere* "to applaud"]
ap•ple \ˈap-əl\ *n* : a rounded fruit with a red, yellow, or green skin, firm white flesh, a seedy core, and usually a tart taste; *also* : the tree of the rose family that bears this fruit [Old English *æppel*]
ap•ple•cart \-ˌkärt\ *n* : PLAN, SCHEME ⟨upset the *applecart*⟩
ap•ple•jack \-ˌjak\ *n* : brandy distilled from cider
apple–pie \ˌap-əl-ˌpī\ *adj* **1** : EXCELLENT, PERFECT ⟨in *apple–pie* order⟩ **2** : of or relating to traditional American values ⟨*apple-pie* wholesomeness⟩
ap•pli•ance \ə-ˈplī-əns\ *n* **1** : a piece of equipment for adapting a tool or machine to a special purpose : ATTACHMENT **2** : an instrument or device designed for a particular use; *esp* : a piece of household equipment that is operated by gas or electricity
ap•pli•ca•ble \ˈap-li-kə-bəl, ə-ˈplik-ə-\ *adj* : capable of being or suitable to be applied : APPROPRIATE — **ap•pli•ca•bil•i•ty** \ˌap-li-kə-ˈbil-ət-ē, ə-ˌplik-ə-\ *n*
ap•pli•cant \ˈap-li-kənt\ *n* : a person who applies for something ⟨an *applicant* for work⟩ ⟨*applicants* for admission⟩
ap•pli•ca•tion \ˌap-lə-ˈkā-shən\ *n* **1** : the act or an instance of applying ⟨*application* of paint to a house⟩ **2** : something put or spread on a surface ⟨hot *applications* on a sprained ankle⟩ **3** : ability to fix one's attention on a task **4 a** : PETITION ⟨an *application* for aid⟩ **b** : a request made personally or in writing ⟨an *application* for a job⟩; *also* : a form used in making such a request **5** : capacity for practical use
ap•pli•ca•tor \ˈap-lə-ˌkāt-ər\ *n* : one that applies; *esp* : a device for applying a substance (as medicine or polish)
ap•plied \ə-ˈplīd\ *adj* : put to practical use; *esp* : applying general principles to solve definite problems ⟨*applied* sciences⟩
[1]**ap•pli•qué** \ˌap-lə-ˈkā\ *n* : a cutout decoration fastened to a larger piece of material [French, past participle of *appliquer* "to put on", from Latin *applicare*]
[2]**appliqué** *vt* **-quéd**; **-qué•ing** : to apply (an appliqué) to a larger surface
ap•ply \ə-ˈplī\ *vb* **ap•plied**; **ap•ply•ing** **1 a** : to put to use especially for some practical or specific purpose ⟨*apply* knowledge⟩ **b** : to bring into action ⟨*apply* the brakes⟩ **c** : to lay or spread on ⟨*apply* paint with a brush⟩ **d** : to place in contact ⟨*apply* heat⟩ **e** : to put into operation or effect ⟨*apply* a law⟩ **2** : to employ diligently or with close attention ⟨*apply* yourself to your work⟩ **3** : to have relevance ⟨this law *applies* to everyone⟩ **4** : to make an appeal or request especially in the form of a written application ⟨*apply* for a job⟩ [Middle French *aplier,* from Latin *applicare,* from *ad-* + *plicare* "to fold"] — **ap•pli•er** \-ˈplī-ər\ *n*
ap•pog•gia•tu•ra \ə-ˌpäj-ə-ˈtu̇r-ə\ *n* : an embellishing note or tone preceding an essential melodic note or tone and usually written as a note of smaller size [Italian, literally, "support"]
ap•point \ə-ˈpȯint\ *vt* **1** : to fix or set officially ⟨*appoint* a day for a meeting⟩ **2** : to name officially especially to an office or position ⟨the president *appoints* the members of the cabinet⟩ [Middle French *apointier,* from *a-* "ad-" + *point* "point"]
ap•point•ed *adj* : FURNISHED, EQUIPPED ⟨a well-*appointed* house⟩
ap•poin•tee \ə-ˌpȯin-ˈtē, ˌa-ˌpȯin-\ *n* : a person appointed to a position or an office
ap•point•ive \ə-ˈpȯint-iv\ *adj* : of, relating to, or filled by appointment ⟨an *appointive* office⟩

appoggiatura

ap•point•ment \ə-ˈpȯint-mənt\ *n* **1** : the act or an instance of appointing : DESIGNATION ⟨holds office by *appointment*⟩ **2** : a position or office to which a person is named but not elected ⟨received an *appointment* from the president⟩ **3** : an agreement to meet at a fixed time ⟨an *appointment* with the dentist⟩ **4** : EQUIPMENT, FURNISHINGS — usually used in pl. ⟨a house with modern *appointments*⟩
ap•por•tion \ə-ˈpōr-shən, -ˈpȯr-\ *vt* **-tioned**; **-tion•ing** \-shə-ning, -shning\ : to divide and distribute proportionately ⟨time carefully *apportioned* among various projects⟩ **syn** see ALLOT
ap•por•tion•ment \-shən-mənt\ *n* : the act or result of apportioning; *esp* : the apportioning of representatives or taxes among states or districts according to population
ap•pose \a-ˈpōz\ *vt* : to place near or in close relationship [Middle French *aposer,* from *a-* "ad-" + *poser* "to place, pose"]
ap•po•site \ˈap-ə-zət\ *adj* : highly pertinent or appropriate : APT [Latin *appositus,* from *apponere* "to place near", from *ad-* + *ponere* "to put"] — **ap•po•site•ly** *adv* — **ap•po•site•ness** *n*
ap•po•si•tion \ˌap-ə-ˈzish-ən\ *n* **1 a** : a grammatical construction in which a noun or noun equivalent is followed by another that explains it (as *the poet* and *Burns* in "a biography of the poet Burns") **b** : the relation of one of such a pair of nouns or noun equivalents to the other **2 a** : the deposition of new layers (as in cell walls) upon those already present **b** : the state of being in close relationship — **ap•po•si•tion•al** \-ˈzish-nəl, -ən-l\ *adj*
[1]**ap•pos•i•tive** \ə-ˈpäz-ət-iv\ *adj* : of, relating to, or standing in grammatical apposition — **ap•pos•i•tive•ly** *adv*
[2]**appositive** *n* : the second of a pair of nouns or noun equivalents in apposition
ap•prais•al \ə-ˈprā-zəl\ *n* **1** : an act or instance of appraising **2** : a determination of the value of property by an appraiser; *also* : the value so determined
ap•praise \ə-ˈprāz\ *vt* **1** : to set a value on; *esp* : to give an expert judgment of the money value of ⟨a house *appraised* at $39,000⟩ **2** : to estimate the significance or status of ⟨*appraise* the situation⟩ [Middle French *aprisier,* from *a-* "ad-" + *prisier* "to value, prize"] **syn** see ESTIMATE — **ap•praise•ment** \-mənt\ *n*
ap•prais•er \ə-ˈprā-zər\ *n* : one that appraises; *esp* : an official who appraises real estate and personal property for purposes of taxation
ap•pre•cia•ble \ə-ˈprē-shə-bəl *also* -ˈprish-ə-\ *adj* : large enough to be recognized and measured or to be felt ⟨an *appreciable* difference in temperature⟩ — **ap•pre•cia•bly** \-blē\ *adv*
ap•pre•ci•ate \ə-ˈprē-shē-ˌāt *also* -ˈprish-ē-ˌāt\ *vb* **1 a** : to grasp with full knowledge and understanding ⟨*appreciate* the difference between right and wrong⟩ **b** : to admire greatly **c** : to appraise perceptively : be fully aware of ⟨had to see it to *appreciate* it⟩ **d** : to recognize with gratitude ⟨I *appreciate* your help⟩ **2** : to increase in number or value [Late Latin *appretiare,* from Latin *ad-* + *pretium* "price"] — **ap•pre•ci•a•tor** \-ˌāt-ər\ *n*
ap•pre•ci•a•tion \ə-ˌprē-shē-ˈā-shən *also* -ˌprē-sē- *or* -ˌprish-ē-\ *n* **1** : the action or an instance of appreciating **2 a** : awareness or grasp of worth or value **b** : expression of appreciation ⟨this commendation in *appreciation* of your work⟩ **3** : a gain in value
ap•pre•cia•tive \ə-ˈprē-shət-iv, -shē-ˌāt-iv *also* -ˈprish-ət-, -ˈprish-ē-\ *adj* : having or showing appreciation ⟨an *appreciative* audience⟩ — **ap•pre•cia•tive•ly** *adv* — **ap•pre•cia•tive•ness** *n*

\ə\ **abut**	\au̇\ **out**	\i\ **tip**	\ȯ\ **saw**	\u̇\ **foot**
\ər\ **further**	\ch\ **chin**	\ī\ **life**	\ȯi\ **coin**	\y\ **yet**
\a\ **mat**	\e\ **pet**	\j\ **job**	\th\ **thin**	\yü\ **few**
\ā\ **take**	\ē\ **easy**	\ng\ **sing**	\t͟h\ **this**	\yu̇\ **cure**
\ä\ **cot, cart**	\g\ **go**	\ō\ **bone**	\ü\ **food**	\zh\ **vision**

ap•pre•hend \ˌap-ri-ˈhend\ *vb* **1 :** ARREST, SEIZE ⟨*apprehend* a suspect⟩ **2 a :** to become aware of **:** PERCEIVE **b :** to anticipate especially with anxiety, dread, or fear **3 :** to grasp with the understanding **:** UNDERSTAND [Latin *apprehendere,* literally, "to seize", from *ad-* + *prehendere* "to seize, grasp"] — **ap•pre•hen•si•ble** \-ˈhen-sə-bəl\ *adj* — **ap•pre•hen•si•bly** \-blē\ *adv*

ap•pre•hen•sion \ˌap-ri-ˈhen-chən\ *n* **1 :** CAPTURE, ARREST ⟨*apprehension* of a burglar⟩ **2 :** COMPREHENSION 2, UNDERSTANDING **3 :** fear of what may be coming **:** dread of the future [Late Latin *apprehensio,* from Latin *apprehendere* "to seize"]

ap•pre•hen•sive \ˌap-ri-ˈhen-siv\ *adj* **:** feeling apprehension **:** fearful of what may be coming — **ap•pre•hen•sive•ly** *adv*

[1]**ap•pren•tice** \ə-ˈprent-əs\ *n* **1 :** a person legally bound to serve a master for a specified period to receive instruction in an art or trade **2 :** one who is learning a trade, art, or calling by practical experience under skilled workers [Middle French *aprentis,* from *aprendre* "to learn", from Latin *apprehendere* "to apprehend"] — **ap•pren•tice•ship** \-ə-ˌship, -əsh-ˌship, -əs-ˌship\ *n*

[2]**apprentice** *vt* **:** to bind or set at work as an apprentice

ap•prise \ə-ˈprīz\ *vt* **:** to give notice to **:** INFORM [French *appris,* past participle of *apprendre* "to learn, teach", from Latin *apprehendere* "to apprehend"]

[1]**ap•proach** \ə-ˈprōch\ *vb* **1 a :** to draw close **:** come near or nearer **b :** APPROXIMATE 2 **2 :** to take preliminary steps toward [Old French *aprochier,* from Late Latin *appropiare,* from Latin *ad-* + *prope* "near"]

[2]**approach** *n* **1 a :** an act or instance of approaching ⟨the *approach* of winter⟩ **b :** APPROXIMATION **2 a :** a preliminary step toward an end **b :** way of dealing with something (as a problem) ⟨try a new *approach*⟩ **3 a :** a means of access **:** AVENUE **b :** the descent of an aircraft as it nears an airport and prepares to land

ap•proach•able \ə-ˈprō-chə-bəl\ *adj* **1 :** capable of being approached **:** ACCESSIBLE **2 :** easy to meet or deal with ⟨a very *approachable* person⟩ — **ap•proach•abil•i•ty** \-ˌprō-chə-ˈbil-ət-ē\ *n*

ap•pro•ba•tion \ˌap-rə-ˈbā-shən\ *n* **1 :** the act of approving formally or officially **2 :** COMMENDATION, PRAISE [Latin *approbare* "to approve"]

[1]**ap•pro•pri•ate** \ə-ˈprō-prē-ˌāt\ *vt* **1 :** to take exclusive possession of **2 :** to set apart for a particular purpose or use ⟨Congress *appropriated* funds for naval research⟩ **3 :** to take without permission **:** STEAL [Late Latin *appropriare,* from Latin *ad-* + *proprius* "one's own"] — **ap•pro•pri•a•tor** \-ˌāt-ər\ *n*

[2]**ap•pro•pri•ate** \-prē-ət\ *adj* **:** especially suitable or fitting **:** PROPER **syn** see FIT — **ap•pro•pri•ate•ly** *adv* — **ap•pro•pri•ate•ness** *n*

ap•pro•pri•a•tion \ə-ˌprō-prē-ˈā-shən\ *n* **1 :** an act or instance of appropriating **2 :** something that has been appropriated; *esp* **:** a sum of money formally set aside for a specific use

ap•prov•al \ə-ˈprü-vəl\ *n* **1 :** an act or instance of approving **:** APPROBATION **2** *pl* **:** postage stamps for collectors sent on approval to prospective purchasers — **on approval :** subject to a prospective buyer's acceptance or refusal ⟨goods sent *on approval*⟩

ap•prove \ə-ˈprüv\ *vb* **1 :** to have or express a favorable judgment **:** take a favorable view **2 a :** to accept as satisfactory **b :** to give formal or official sanction to ⟨the council *approved* the plans for the new school⟩ [Old French *aprover,* from Latin *approbare,* from *ad-* + *probare* "to prove"] — **ap•prov•ing•ly** \-ˈprü-ving-lē\ *adv*

• **syn** APPROVE, ENDORSE, SANCTION mean to have or express a favorable opinion of. APPROVE may imply no more than this or it may suggest some degree of admiration; ENDORSE adds the implication of backing with an explicit statement; SANCTION implies both approving and authorizing.

[1]**ap•prox•i•mate** \ə-ˈpräk-sə-mət\ *adj* **:** nearly correct or exact ⟨the *approximate* cost⟩ [Late Latin *approximare* "to come near", from Latin *ad-* + *proximus* "nearest, next"] — **ap•prox•i•mate•ly** *adv*

[2]**ap•prox•i•mate** \-ˌmāt\ *vb* **1 :** to bring or come close together ⟨*approximate* two boards⟩ **2 :** to find the approximate value of ⟨*approximate* a cost⟩

ap•prox•i•ma•tion \ə-ˌpräk-sə-ˈmā-shən\ *n* **1 :** the act or process of approximating **2 :** the quality or state of being close especially in value **3 :** something that is approximate; *esp* **:** a nearly exact estimate of a value or cost

ap•pur•te•nance \ə-ˈpərt-nəns, -n-əns\ *n* **:** something (as a right or fixture) that belongs to or goes along with another usually larger and more important thing ⟨a house for sale with its furniture and all other *appurtenances*⟩ [Anglo-French *apurtenance,* from Old French *apartenir* "to appertain"] — **ap•pur•te•nant** \-ˈpərt-nənt, -n-ənt\ *adj*

ap•ri•cot \ˈap-rə-ˌkät, ˈā-prə-\ *n* **:** an oval orange-colored fruit resembling the related peach and plum in flavor; *also* **:** a tree that bears apricots [derived from Arabic *al-birqūq* "the apricot"]

April \ˈā-prəl\ *n* **:** the 4th month of the year [Latin *Aprilis*]

April fool *n* **:** a person who is tricked on April Fools' Day

April Fools' Day *n* **:** April 1 characteristically marked by the playing of practical jokes

a pri•o•ri \ˌä-prē-ˈōr-ē, -ˈȯr-\ *adj* **1 :** of or relating to reasoning from self-evident propositions **2 :** estimated from available facts without close examination **:** PRESUMPTIVE [Latin, "from the former"] — **a priori** *adv*

apron \ˈā-prən, -pərn\ *n* **1 :** a garment worn on the front of the body to protect the clothing **2 :** the part of the stage in front of the proscenium arch **3 :** a shield (as of concrete, planking, or brushwood) along the bank of a river to prevent erosion **4 :** the extensive paved part of an airport immediately adjacent to the terminal area or hangars [Middle English *napron* (the phrase *a napron* being understood as *an apron*), from Middle French *naperon,* from *nape* "cloth", from Latin *mappa* "napkin"]

[1]**ap•ro•pos** \ˌap-rə-ˈpō, ˈap-rə-ˌ\ *adv* **1 :** at the right time **:** SEASONABLY **2 :** by the way **:** INCIDENTALLY [French *à propos,* literally, "to the purpose"]

[2]**apropos** *adj* **:** being to the point **:** PERTINENT

apropos of *prep* **:** with regard to **:** CONCERNING

apse \ˈaps\ *n* **:** a usually semicircular projection on the end of a building (as a church) [Medieval Latin *apsis,* from Latin, "arch, orbit", from Greek *hapsis,* from *haptein* "to fasten"] — **ap•si•dal** \ˈap-səd-l\ *adj*

apt \ˈapt\ *adj* **1 :** FITTING, SUITABLE ⟨an *apt* quotation⟩ **2 a :** having a tendency **:** LIKELY **b :** ordinarily disposed ⟨*apt* to worry⟩ **3 :** keenly alert **:** quick to learn ⟨an *apt* pupil⟩ [Latin *aptus,* literally, "fastened", from *apere* "to fasten, fit"] — **apt•ly** *adv* — **apt•ness** \ˈap-nəs, ˈapt-\ *n*

• **syn** LIKELY, LIABLE: APT implies an inherent or habitual tendency and may apply to the past or present as well as the future ⟨children are *apt* to imitate their parents⟩ LIKELY stresses probability and is used in predictions ⟨it is *likely* to rain tomorrow⟩ LIABLE implies exposure to a risk or danger and suggests chance rather than probability ⟨cars are *liable* to skid on wet roads⟩

ap•ti•tude \ˈap-tə-ˌtüd, -ˌtyüd\ *n* **1 :** capacity for learning **2 :** a natural inclination or ability **:** TALENT, BENT ⟨an *aptitude* for mathematics⟩

aqua•cade \ˈak-wə-ˌkād, ˈäk-\ *n* **:** an elaborate water spectacle consisting of exhibitions of swimming, diving, and acrobatics accompanied by music [*Aquacade,* a water spectacle originally at Cleveland, Ohio (1937), from Latin *aqua* "water" + English *-cade* (as in *cavalcade*)]

aqua•cul•ture *also* **aqui•cul•ture** \ˈak-wə-ˌkəl-chər, ˈäk-\ **:** the cultivation of the natural produce of water; *esp* **:** the raising of fish in enclosed ponds [Latin *aqua* "water" + English *-culture* (as in *agriculture*)] — **aqua•cul•tur•al** \-ˌkəlch-rəl, -ə-rəl\ *adj*

aqua•for•tis \ˌak-wə-ˈfȯrt-əs, ˌäk-\ *n* **:** NITRIC ACID [New Latin *aqua fortis,* literally, "strong water"]

aqua•ma•rine \ˌak-wə-mə-ˈrēn, ˌäk-\ *n* **1 :** a transparent semiprecious bluish or greenish stone that is a variety of beryl **2 :** a pale blue to light greenish blue [Latin *aqua marina* "sea water"]

aqua•naut \ˈak-wə-ˌnȯt, ˈäk-, -ˌnät\ *n* **:** one that lives for an extended period in an underwater shelter which serves as a base for research [Latin *aqua* + English *-naut* (as in *aeronaut*)]

aqua•plane \ˈak-wə-ˌplān, ˈäk-\ *n* **:** a board towed behind a speeding motorboat and ridden by a person standing on it — **aquaplane** *vi* — **aqua•plan•er** *n*

aqua re•gia \ˌak-wə-ˈrē-jē-ə, ˌäk-, -jə\ *n* **:** a mixture of nitric and hydrochloric acids that dissolves gold or platinum [New Latin, literally, "royal water"]

aquar•ist \ə-ˈkwar-əst, -ˈkwer-\ *n* **:** one who keeps an aquarium

aquar•i•um \ə-ˈkwar-ē-əm, -ˈkwer-\ *n, pl* **-i•ums** *or* **-ia** \-ē-ə\ **:** a container (as a glass tank) in which living water animals or plants are kept; *also* **:** an establishment where such aquatic collections are kept and shown [Latin, "watering place for cattle", from *aqua* "water"]

Aquar•i•us \ə-'kwar-ē-əs, -'kwer-\ *n* **1 :** a zodiacal constellation south of Pegasus **2 :** the 11th sign of the zodiac; *also* **:** one born under this sign [Latin, literally, "water carrier"]

[1]**aquat•ic** \ə-'kwät-ik, -'kwat-\ *adj* **1 :** growing or living in or frequenting water **2 :** performed in or on water ⟨*aquatic* sports⟩ — **aquat•i•cal•ly** \-i-kə-lē, -klē\ *adv*

[2]**aquatic** *n* **1 :** an aquatic animal or plant **2** *pl* **:** water sports

aq•ua•tint \'ak-wə-,tint, 'äk-\ *n* **:** an etching in which the printing plate is treated to produce an effect resembling a drawing in watercolors or india ink — **aquatint** *vt*

aq•ue•duct \'ak-wə-,dəkt\ *n* **1 :** an artificial channel for carrying flowing water **2 :** a structure that carries the water of a canal over a river or hollow [Latin *aquaeductus,* from *aqua* "water" + *ductus* "act of leading"]

aqueduct 2

aque•ous \'ā-kwē-əs, 'ak-wē-\ *adj* **1 :** of, relating to, or resembling water **2 :** made of, by, or with water ⟨an *aqueous* solution⟩

aqueous humor *n* **:** a clear fluid between the lens and the cornea of the eye

aq•ui•fer \'ak-wə-fər, 'äk-\ *n* **:** a water-bearing stratum of permeable rock, sand, or gravel — **aquif•er•ous** \a-'kwif-ə-rəs, ä-\ *adj*

Aq•ui•la \'ak-wə-lə\ *n* **:** a northern constellation in the Milky Way south of Lyra and Cygnus [Latin, literally, "eagle"]

aq•ui•le•gia \,ak-wə-'lē-jē-ə, -jə\ *n* **:** COLUMBINE [New Latin, genus name]

aq•ui•line \'ak-wə-,līn, -lən\ *adj* **1 :** of, relating to, or resembling an eagle **2 :** curving like an eagle's beak ⟨an *aquiline* nose⟩ [Latin *aquilinus,* from *aquila* "eagle"]

-ar \ər *also* ,är\ *adj suffix* **:** of or relating to **:** being **:** resembling ⟨molecul*ar*⟩ ⟨oracul*ar*⟩ ⟨spectacul*ar*⟩ [Latin *-aris,* alteration of *-alis* "-al"]

Ar•ab \'ar-əb, *in sense 2 often* 'ā-,rab\ *n* **1 a :** a member of the Semitic people of the Arabian peninsula **b :** a member of an Arabic-speaking people **2** *not cap* **:** STREET ARAB **3 :** a horse of the stock used by the natives of Arabia and adjacent regions; *esp* **:** one of a breed noted for graceful build, speed, intelligence, and spirit — **Arab** *adj*

ar•a•besque \,ar-ə-'besk\ *n* **:** an ornament or a style of decoration consisting of interlacing lines and figures usually of flowers, foliage, or fruit [French from Italian *arabesco* "Arabian in style"] — **arabesque** *adj*

[1]**Ara•bi•an** \ə-'rā-bē-ən\ *adj* **:** of or relating to Arabia or the Arabs

[2]**Arabian** *n* **:** a native or inhabitant of Arabia **:** ARAB

Arabian horse *n* **:** ARAB 3

[1]**Ar•a•bic** \'ar-ə-bik\ *adj* **1 :** ARABIAN, ARAB **2 :** expressed in or utilizing Arabic numerals ⟨21 is an *Arabic* number⟩ ⟨*Arabic* notation⟩

[2]**Arabic** *n* **:** a Semitic language of Arabia spoken also in Jordan, Lebanon, Syria, Iraq, Egypt, and parts of northern Africa

Arabic numeral *n* **:** one of the number symbols 1, 2, 3, 4, 5, 6, 7, 8, 9, and 0 — see NUMBER table

ar•a•ble \'ar-ə-bəl\ *adj* **:** fit for or cultivated by plowing or tillage **:** suitable for producing crops [Latin *arabilis,* from *arare* "to plow"] — **ar•a•bil•i•ty** \,ar-ə-'bil-ət-ē\ *n* — **arable** *n*

arach•nid \ə-'rak-nəd, -,nid\ *n* **:** any of a class (Arachnida) of arthropods including the spiders, scorpions, mites, and ticks and having a segmented body divided into two regions of which the front part bears four pairs of legs but no antennae [derived from Greek *arachnē* "spider"] — **arachnid** *adj*

arach•noid \-,nȯid\ *n* **:** a thin membrane of the brain and spinal cord that lies between the dura mater and the pia mater [derived from Greek *arachnē* "spider, spider web"] — **arachnoid** *adj*

ara•go•nite \ə-'rag-ə-,nīt, 'ar-ə-gə-\ *n* **:** a mineral that is chemically the same as calcite but is denser and has different crystalline form [German *aragonit,* from *Aragon,* Spain]

Ar•a•mae•an \,ar-ə-'mē-ən\ *n* **1 :** a member of a Semitic people of the 2d millennium B.C. in Syria and Upper Mesopotamia **2 :** ARAMAIC [Latin *Aramaeus,* derived from Hebrew *'Arām,* ancient name for Syria] — **Aramaean** *adj*

Ar•a•ma•ic \,ar-ə-'mā-ik\ *n* **:** a Semitic language of the Aramaeans later used extensively in southwest Asia (as by the Jews after the Babylonian exile) — **Aramaic** *adj*

Arap•a•ho *or* **Arap•a•hoe** \ə-'rap-ə-,hō\ *n, pl* **-ho** *or* **-hos** *or* **-hoe** *or* **-hoes :** a member of an Algonquian people of the central western plains

Arau•ca•ni•an \ə-,rau̇-'kän-ē-ən\ *n* **:** a member of a group of Indian peoples of Chile and Argentina [Spanish *araucano,* from *Arauco,* province in Chile] — **Araucanian** *adj*

Ar•a•wak \'ar-ə-,wäk\ *n, pl* **-wak** *or* **-waks :** a member of an Indian people chiefly of Guyana

ar•bi•ter \'är-bət-ər\ *n* **1 :** ARBITRATOR, UMPIRE **2 :** a person having absolute authority to judge and decide what is right or proper ⟨an *arbiter* of taste⟩ [Latin]

ar•bit•ra•ment \är-'bi-trə-mənt\ *n* **1 :** the settling of a dispute by an arbiter **:** ARBITRATION **2 :** a decision or award made by an arbiter

ar•bi•trary \'är-bə-,trer-ē\ *adj* **1 :** depending on choice or discretion rather than defined by law ⟨an *arbitrary* settlement of a dispute⟩ **2 :** based on opinion, preference, or whim ⟨made an *arbitrary* choice⟩ **3 :** not controlled or restrained by law **:** DESPOTIC ⟨*arbitrary* use of power by government officials⟩ — **ar•bi•trar•i•ly** \,är-bə-'trer-ə-lē\ *adv* — **ar•bi•trar•i•ness** \'är-bə-,trer-ē-nəs\ *n*

ar•bi•trate \'är-bə-,trāt\ *vb* **1 :** to settle a dispute after hearing and considering the arguments of both sides **:** hear and decide as an arbiter ⟨a committee appointed to *arbitrate* between the company and the union⟩ **2 :** to submit to arbitration ⟨agreed to *arbitrate* their differences⟩ [Latin *arbitrari* "to render judgment", from *arbiter* "judge"] — **ar•bi•tra•ble** \-bə-trə-bəl\ *adj* — **ar•bi•tra•tive** \-,trāt-iv\ *adj*

ar•bi•tra•tion \,är-bə-'trā-shən\ *n* **:** the act of arbitrating; *esp* **:** the settling of a dispute in which both parties agree beforehand to abide by the decision of an arbitrator or body of arbitrators — **ar•bi•tra•tion•al** \-shnəl, -shən-l\ *adj*

ar•bi•tra•tor \'är-bə-,trāt-ər\ *n* **:** a person chosen to settle differences between two parties in controversy

[1]**ar•bor** \'är-bər\ *n* **:** a bower of vines or branches or of latticework covered with climbing shrubs or vines [Old French *herbier* "plot of grass", from *herbe* "herb, grass"]

[2]**arbor** *n* **:** a shaft on which a revolving cutting tool is mounted or on which the work is mounted for turning [Latin, "tree, shaft"]

Arbor Day *n* **:** a day set aside for planting trees

ar•bo•re•al \är-'bōr-ē-əl, -'bȯr-\ *adj* **1 :** of, relating to, or resembling a tree **2 :** living in or frequenting trees [Latin *arboreus,* from *arbor* "tree"] — **ar•bo•re•al•ly** \-ē-ə-lē\ *adv*

ar•bo•res•cent \,är-bə-'res-nt\ *adj* **:** resembling a tree in growth, structure, or appearance; *esp* **:** branching repeatedly like a tree — **ar•bo•res•cence** \-ns\ *n* — **ar•bo•res•cent•ly** *adv*

ar•bo•re•tum \,är-bə-'rēt-əm\ *n, pl* **-re•tums** *or* **-re•ta** \-'rēt-ə\ **:** a place where trees, shrubs, and herbaceous plants are grown for scientific and educational purposes [Latin, "place grown with trees", from *arbor* "tree"]

ar•bor•ist \'är-bə-rəst\ *n* **:** a specialist in the care and maintenance of trees

ar•bor•vi•tae \,är-bər-'vīt-ē\ *n* **:** any of various evergreen trees of the pine family that have leaves closely overlapping like scales and are often grown for ornament and in hedges [New Latin *arbor vitae,* literally, "tree of life"]

ar•bu•tus \är-'byüt-əs\ *n* **1 :** any of a genus of shrubs and trees of the heath family with white or pink flowers and scarlet berries **2 :** a trailing plant of the heath family that has fragrant pinkish flowers borne in early spring and is found in eastern North America — called also *mayflower, trailing arbutus* [Latin, a kind of tree of the heath family]

[1]**arc** \'ärk\ *n* **1 :** something arched or curved; *esp* **:** a sustained luminous discharge of electricity across a gap in a circuit or

between electrodes **2** : a continuous portion (as part of the circumference of a circle) of a curved line [Middle French, "bow", from Latin *arcus* "bow, arch, arc"]

[2]**arc** *vi* **arced** \'ärkt\; **arc•ing 1** : to form an electric arc **2** : to follow an arc-shaped course

ar•cade \är-'kād\ *n* **1** : a row of arches with the columns that support them **2** : an arched or covered passageway; *esp* : one lined with shops [French, from Italian *arcata,* from *arco* "arch"] — **ar•cad•ed** \-'kād-əd\ *adj*

ar•ca•dia \är-'kād-ē-ə\ *n, often cap* : a region or scene of simple pleasure and quiet [*Arcadia,* region of ancient Greece often chosen as a setting for pastoral poetry] — **ar•ca•di•an** \-ē-ən\ *adj or n, often cap*

ar•cane \är-'kān\ *adj* : SECRET 1a, MYSTERIOUS [Latin *arcanus,* from *arca* "chest for valuables"]

ar•ca•num \är-'kā-nəm\ *n, pl* **-na** \-nə\ : mysterious knowledge known only to the initiate [Latin, from *arcanus* "secret"]

[1]**arch** \'ärch\ *n* **1** : a usually curved structural member spanning an opening and serving as a support (as for the wall above the opening) **2** : something resembling an arch in form or function; *esp* : either of two vaulted portions of the bony structure of the foot that impart elasticity to it and cushion it against shock (as in running and walking) **3** : ARCHWAY [Old French *arche,* from Latin *arcus* "bow, arch"]

[1]arch 1: *1* round, *2* lancet, *3* trefoil, *4* ogee

[2]**arch** *vb* **1** : to cover or provide with an arch **2** : to form or bend into an arch **3** : to move in an arch : ARC

[3]**arch** *adj* **1** : PRINCIPAL, CHIEF ⟨their *arch* foe⟩ **2** : playfully saucy : ROGUISH, MISCHIEVOUS ⟨an *arch* smile⟩ [*arch-*] — **arch•ly** *adv* — **arch•ness** *n*

arch- *prefix* **1** : chief : principal **2** : extreme [Greek *arch-, archi-,* from *archein* "to begin, rule"]

archae- *or* **archaeo-** *also* **archeo-** *combining form* : ancient : primitive ⟨*Archeo*zoic⟩ [Greek *archaios* "ancient", from *archē* "beginning"]

ar•chae•ol•o•gy *or* **ar•che•ol•o•gy** \,är-kē-'äl-ə-jē\ *n* : the science that deals with past human life and activities as shown by fossil relics and by the monuments and artifacts left by ancient peoples — **ar•chae•o•log•i•cal** \-kē-ə-'läj-i-kəl\ *adj* — **archae•ol•o•gist** \-kē-'äl-ə-jəst\ *n*

ar•chae•op•ter•yx \,är-kē-'äp-tə-riks\ *n* : a primitive extinct Mesozoic European bird with reptilian characteristics as well as wings and feathers [Greek *pteryx* "wing"]

ar•cha•ic \är-'kā-ik\ *adj* **1** : of, relating to, or characteristic of an earlier or more primitive time : ANTIQUATED **2** : having the characteristics of the language of the past and surviving chiefly in specialized uses ⟨the *archaic* words *methinks* and *saith*⟩ **3** : surviving from an earlier period ⟨an *archaic* plant⟩ [Greek *archaïkos,* from *archē* "beginning"] **syn** see OLD

ar•cha•ism \'är-kē-,iz-əm, -kā-\ *n* **1** : the use of archaic words **2** : an archaic word or expression

arch•an•gel \'ärk-,ān-jəl\ *n* : an angel of high rank — **archan•gel•ic** \,ärk-,an-'jel-ik\ *adj*

arch•bish•op \'ärch-'bish-əp\ *n* : the bishop of highest rank in a group of dioceses — **arch•bish•op•ric** \-'bish-ə-prik\ *n*

arch•dea•con \'ärch-'dē-kən\ *n* : an ecclesiastical dignitary usually ranking below a bishop — **arch•dea•con•ate** \-kə-nət\ *n* — **arch•dea•con•ry** \-kən-rē\ *n*

arch•di•o•cese \'ärch-'dī-ə-səs, -,sēz, -,sēs\ *n* : the diocese of an archbishop — **arch•di•oc•e•san** \,ärch-dī-'äs-ə-sən\ *adj*

arch•du•cal \'ärch-'dü-kəl, -'dyü-\ *adj* : of or relating to an archduke or archduchy

arch•duch•ess \'ärch-'dəch-əs\ *n* **1** : the wife or widow of an archduke **2** : a woman having in her own right the rank of archduke

arch•duchy \-'dəch-ē\ *n* : the territory of an archduke or archduchess

arch•duke \-'dük, -'dyük\ *n* : a sovereign prince; *esp* : a prince of the imperial family of Austria — **arch•duke•dom** \-dəm\ *n*

ar•che•go•ni•um \,är-ki-'gō-nē-əm\ *n, pl* **-nia** \-nē-ə\ : a flask-shaped female sex organ found especially in mosses and ferns [Greek *archegonos* "originator", from *archein* "to begin" + *gonos* "procreation"] — **ar•che•go•ni•al** \-nē-əl\ *adj*

arch•en•e•my \'ärch-'en-ə-mē\ *n* : a principal enemy

arch•en•ter•on \är-'kent-ə-,rän, -rən\ *n* : the cavity of the gastrula of an embryo

Ar•cheo•zo•ic \,är-kē-ə-'zō-ik\ *n* : the earliest of the five eras of geological history; *also* : the corresponding system of rocks — see GEOLOGIC TIME table — **Archeozoic** *adj*

ar•cher \'är-chər\ *n* : a person who uses a bow and arrow [Old French, derived from Latin *arcus* "bow"]

ar•chery \'ärch-rē, -ə-rē\ *n* **1** : the art, practice, or skill of shooting with bow and arrow **2** : a body of archers

ar•che•type \'är-ki-,tīp\ *n* : the original pattern or model of a work or the model from which others are copied : PROTOTYPE [Latin *archetypum,* from Greek *archetypon,* from *archein* "to begin" + *typos* "type"] — **ar•che•typ•al** \,är-ki-'tī-pəl\ *or* **ar•che•typ•i•cal** \-'tip-i-kəl\ *adj*

arch•fiend \'ärch-'fēnd\ *n* : a chief fiend; *esp* : DEVIL 1

ar•chi•epis•co•pal \,är-kē-ə-'pis-kə-pəl\ *adj* : of or relating to an archbishop [Late Latin *archiepiscopus* "archbishop", from Late Greek *archiepiskopos,* from *archi-* "arch-" + *episkopos* "bishop"]

ar•chi•pel•a•go \,är-kə-'pel-ə-,gō, ,är-chə-\ *n, pl* **-goes** *or* **-gos 1** : an expanse of water with many scattered islands **2** : a group of islands [*Archipelago* "Aegean sea", from Italian *Arcipelago,* literally, "chief sea", from *arci-* "arch-" + Greek *pelagos* "sea"] — **ar•chi•pe•lag•ic** \-pə-'laj-ik-\ *adj*

ar•chi•tect \'är-kə-,tekt\ *n* : a person who designs buildings and oversees their construction [derived from Greek *architektōn* "master builder", from *archi-* "arch-" + *tektōn* "builder, carpenter"]

ar•chi•tec•ton•ic \,är-kə-,tek-'tän-ik\ *adj* : of, relating to, or according with the principles of architecture : ARCHITECTURAL — **ar•chi•tec•ton•i•cal•ly** \-'tän-i-kə-lē, -klē\ *adv*

ar•chi•tec•ton•ics \-'tän-iks\ *n sing or pl* : structural design : STRUCTURE, ORDER, PLAN

ar•chi•tec•tur•al \,är-kə-'tek-chə-rəl, -'tek-shrəl\ *adj* : of, relating to, or conforming to the rules of architecture — **ar•chi•tec•tur•al•ly** \-ē\ *adv*

ar•chi•tec•ture \'är-kə-,tek-chər\ *n* **1** : the art or science of designing and building habitable structures **2** : the style of building that architects produce or imitate ⟨a church of modern *architecture*⟩ **3** : architectural work : BUILDINGS

ar•chi•trave \'är-kə-,trāv\ *n* : the lowest division of an entablature resting immediately on the capital of the column in an ancient Greek or Roman building [Middle French, from Italian, from *archi-* "arch-" + *trave* "beam", from Latin *trabs*]

ar•chive \'är-,kīv\ *n* : a place in which public records or historical documents are preserved; *also* : the material preserved — usually used in pl. [Latin *archivum,* from Greek *archeia* "government documents", from *archē* "beginning, rule, government"] — **ar•chi•val** \är-'kī-vəl\ *adj*

ar•chi•vist \'är-kə-vəst, -,kī-\ *n* : a person in charge of archives

ar•chon \'är-,kän, -kən\ *n* : one of the chief magistrates in ancient Athens [Latin, from Greek *archōn,* from *archein* "to rule"]

arch•way \'ärch-,wā\ *n* : a way or passage under an arch; *also* : an arch over a passage

-ar•chy \,är-kē, *in a few words also* ər-kē\ *n combining form, pl* **-ar•chies** : rule : government ⟨squire*archy*⟩ [Greek *-archia,* from *archein* "to rule"]

arc lamp *n* : a lamp whose light is produced when an electric current passes between two hot electrodes surrounded by gas — called also *arc light*

[1]**arc•tic** \'ärk-tik, 'ärt-ik\ *adj* **1** *often cap* : of or relating to the north pole or the region around it **2** : very cold : FRIGID [Latin *arcticus,* from Greek *arktikos,* from *arktos* "bear, Ursa Major, north"]

[2]**arc•tic** \'ärt-ik, 'ärk-tik\ *n* : a rubber overshoe reaching to the ankle or above

arctic circle *n, often cap A&C* : the parallel of latitude that is approximately 66½ degrees north of the equator

arctic fox *n* : a small fox of arctic regions that is blue-gray or brownish in summer and white in winter

Arc•tu•rus \ärk-'tür-əs, -'tyür-\ *n* : a large bright fixed star in Boötes [Latin, from Greek *Arktouros,* literally, "bear watcher"]

-ard \-ərd\ *also* **-art** \ərt\ *n suffix* : one that is characterized by performing some action, possessing some quality, or being associated with some thing especially conspicuously or excessively ⟨bragg*art*⟩ ⟨dull*ard*⟩ [Old French, of Germanic origin]

arctic fox

ar•dent \ˈärd-nt\ *adj* **1 a** : characterized by warmth of feeling : PASSIONATE ⟨an *ardent* admirer⟩ **b** : ZEALOUS, DEVOTED ⟨an *ardent* champion of justice⟩ **2** : extremely hot : FIERY ⟨the *ardent* sun⟩ [Middle French, from Latin *ardēre* "to burn"] — **ar•den•cy** \-n-sē\ *n* — **ar•dent•ly** *adv*

ar•dor \ˈärd-ər\ *n* **1** : a warmth of feeling or sentiment **2** : ZEAL, EAGERNESS [Latin, from *ardēre* "to burn"] **syn** see PASSION

ar•du•ous \ˈärj-wəs, -ə-wəs\ *adj* : extremely difficult : LABORIOUS, STRENUOUS ⟨an *arduous* climb⟩ [Latin *arduus* "steep, high, difficult"] — **ar•du•ous•ly** *adv* — **ar•du•ous•ness** *n*

[1]**are** *present 2d sing or present pl of* BE [Old English *earun*, present plural]

[2]**are** \ˈaər, ˈeər, ˈär\ *n* — see METRIC SYSTEM table [French, from Latin *area* "level space"]

ar•ea \ˈar-ē-ə, ˈer-\ *n* **1** : a particular piece of ground often set aside for special use ⟨a picnic *area*⟩ **2** : the amount of surface included within a closed figure; *also* : the number of unit squares equal in measure to the surface **3 a** : REGION ⟨a farming *area*⟩ **b** : a field of activity ⟨*area* of knowledge⟩ **4** : a part of the cerebral cortex having a particular function [Latin, "piece of level ground, threshing floor", from *arēre* "to be dry, burn"] — **ar•e•al** \-ē-əl\ *adj* — **ar•e•al•ly** \-ē-ə-lē\ *adv*

area code *n* : a 3-digit number that identifies a particular telephone service area in the United States or Canada

area•way \-ē-ə-ˌwā\ *n* : a sunken space affording access, air, and light to a basement

are•na \ə-ˈrē-nə\ *n* **1** : an area in a Roman amphitheater for gladiatorial combats **2 a** : an enclosed area used for public entertainment **b** : a building containing an arena **3** : a sphere of interest or activity ⟨political *arena*⟩ [Latin, "sand, sandy place"]

arena theater *n* : a theater having the stage in the center of the auditorium with the audience seated on all sides

aren't \ärnt, ˈärnt, ˈär-ənt\ : are not

are•o•la \ə-ˈrē-ə-lə\ *n, pl* **-lae** \-ˌlē\ *or* **-las** : a colored ring (as about the nipple) [Latin, "small open space", from *area*] — **are•o•lar** \-lər\ *adj*

arête \ə-ˈrāt\ *n* : a sharp-crested ridge in rugged mountains [French, literally, "fish bone", from Latin *arista* "beard of grain"]

[1]**ar•gent** \ˈär-jənt\ *n* : the heraldic color silver or white [Latin *argentum* "silver"]

[2]**argent** *adj* : resembling silver : SILVERY, SHINING

ar•gen•tite \ˈär-jən-ˌtīt\ *n* : a dark gray mineral Ag_2S that is a silver sulfide and constitutes an ore of silver

ar•gil•la•ceous \ˌär-jə-ˈlā-shəs\ *adj* : of, relating to, or containing clay or the minerals of clay [Latin *argilla* "clay"]

ar•gi•nine \ˈär-jə-ˌnēn\ *n* : an amino acid $C_6H_{14}O_2N_4$ found in various proteins and essential to the diet of rats [German *arginin*]

Ar•give \ˈär-ˌjīv, -ˌgīv\ *adj* : of or relating to the Greeks or Greece and especially to the Achaean city of Argos or the surrounding territory of Argolis — **Argive** *n*

ar•gon \ˈär-ˌgän\ *n* : a colorless odorless inert gaseous chemical element found in the air and in volcanic gases and used especially as a filler for electric bulbs — see ELEMENT table [Greek, neuter of *argos* "idle, lazy", from *a-* + *ergon* "work"]

argonaut *n* **1** *cap* : one of a band of heroes sailing with Jason in quest of the Golden Fleece **2** : PAPER NAUTILUS [Greek *Argonautēs*, from *Argō*, name of Jason's ship + *nautēs* "sailor"]

ar•go•sy \ˈär-gə-sē\ *n, pl* **-sies** : a large ship; *esp* : a large merchant ship [Italian *ragusea* "vessel of Ragusa", from *Ragusa*, Dalmatia (now Dubrovnik, Yugoslavia)]

ar•got \ˈär-gət, -gō\ *n* : a more or less secret vocabulary used by a particular class or group — compare DIALECT [French]

ar•gu•able \ˈär-gyə-wə-bəl\ *adj* : open to argument, dispute, or question — **ar•gu•ably** \-blē\ *adv*

ar•gue \ˈär-ˌgyü\ *vb* **1** : to give reasons for or against ⟨*argue* in favor of lowering taxes⟩ **2** : to debate or discuss some matter : DISPUTE ⟨*argue* about politics⟩ **3** : to persuade by giving reasons ⟨tried to *argue* their parents into getting a new car⟩ **4** : INDICATE ⟨your manner *argues* your guilt⟩ [Latin *arguere* "to make clear, accuse" and Middle French *arguer* "to accuse, reason", from Latin *argutare* "to orate", from *arguere* "to make clear"] **syn** see DISCUSS — **ar•gu•er** *n*

ar•gu•ment \ˈär-gyə-mənt\ *n* **1 a** : a reason for or against something **b** : a discussion in which arguments are presented : DISPUTE, DEBATE **2** : a heated dispute : QUARREL

ar•gu•men•ta•tion \ˌär-gyə-mən-ˈtā-shən, -ˌmen-\ *n* **1** : the act or process of forming reasons and of drawing conclusions and applying them to a case under discussion **2** : DEBATE, DISCUSSION

ar•gu•men•ta•tive \ˌär-gyə-ˈment-ət-iv\ *adj* : marked by or given to argument : DISPUTATIOUS — **ar•gu•men•ta•tive•ly** *adv*

Ar•gus–eyed \ˌär-gə-ˈsīd\ *adj* : vigilantly observant

ar•gyle \ˈär-ˌgīl, är-ˈ\ *n* : a geometric knitting pattern of variously colored diamonds on a single background color; *also* : a sock knit in this pattern [*Argyle*, branch of the Scottish clan of Campbell, from whose tartan the design was adapted]

Ar•gy•rol \ˈär-jə-ˌrȯl, -ˌrōl\ *trademark* — used for a silver-protein compound whose aqueous solution is used as an antiseptic

aria \ˈär-ē-ə\ *n* : MELODY, TUNE; *esp* : an accompanied elaborate melody sung (as in an opera) by a single voice [Italian, literally, "atmospheric air", from Latin *aer*, from Greek *aēr*]

-ar•i•an \ˈer-ē-ən, ˈar-\ *n suffix* **1** : believer ⟨Unit*arian*⟩ : advocate ⟨latitudin*arian*⟩ **2** : producer ⟨disciplin*arian*⟩ [Latin *-arius* "-ary" + English *-an*]

ar•id \ˈar-əd\ *adj* **1** : very dry; *esp* : having too little rainfall to support agriculture **2** : lacking in interest : DULL [Latin *aridus*] — **arid•i•ty** \ə-ˈrid-ət-ē, a-\ *n*

Ar•ies \ˈer-ˌēz, ˈer-ē-ˌēz, ˈar-\ **1** : a zodiacal constellation between Pisces and Taurus **2** : the 1st sign of the zodiac; *also* : one born under this sign [Latin, literally, "ram"]

ar•il \ˈar-əl\ *n* : an outer covering or appendage of some seeds that develops after fertilization [probably from Medieval Latin *arillus* "raisin, grape seed"]

arise \ə-ˈrīz\ *vi* **arose** \-ˈrōz\; **aris•en** \-ˈriz-n\; **aris•ing** \-ˈrī-zing\ **1** : to move upward : ASCEND **2** : to get up from sleep or after lying down **3** : to come into existence : spring up ⟨a dispute *arose* between the leaders⟩ [Old English *ārisan*, from *ā-*, prefix denoting completion + *rīsan* "to rise"]

ar•is•toc•ra•cy \ˌar-ə-ˈstäk-rə-sē\ *n, pl* **-cies** **1** : government by the best individuals or by a small privileged class **2 a** : a government in which power is exercised by a minority especially of those felt to be best qualified **b** : a state with such a government **3 a** : a governing body or upper class usually made up of an hereditary nobility **b** : a group felt to be superior in birth, wealth, culture, or intelligence [derived from Greek *aristokratia*, from *aristos* "best" + *-kratia* "-cracy"]

aris•to•crat \ə-ˈris-tə-ˌkrat, a-; ˈar-ə-stə-\ *n* **1** : a member of an aristocracy; *esp* : NOBLE **2** : one with habits and viewpoints typical of the aristocracy — **aris•to•crat•ic** \ə-ˌris-tə-ˈkrat-ik, a-ˌris-tə-, ˌar-ə-stə-\ *adj* — **aris•to•crat•i•cal•ly** \-i-kə-lē, -i-klē\ *adv*

Ar•is•to•te•lian *or* **Ar•is•to•te•lean** \ˌar-ə-stə-ˈtēl-yən\ *adj* : of, relating to, or characteristic of Aristotle or his philosophy — **Ar•is•to•te•lian•ism** \-yə-ˌniz-əm\ *n*

arith•me•tic \ə-ˈrith-mə-ˌtik\ *n* **1** : a branch of mathematics that deals with real numbers and computations with them **2** : an act or method of computing : CALCULATION ⟨a mistake in *arithmetic*⟩ [Old French *arismetique*, from Latin *arithmetica*, from Greek *arithmētikē*, from *arithmein* "to count", from *arithmos* "number"] — **ar•ith•met•ic** \ˌar-ith-ˈmet-ik\ *or* **ar•ith•met•i•cal** \-ˈmet-i-kəl\ *adj* — **ar•ith•met•i•cal•ly** \-kə-lē, -klē\ *adv*

arith•me•ti•cian \ə-ˌrith-mə-ˈtish-ən\ *n* : a person skilled in arithmetic

arithmetic mean \ˌar-ith-ˌmet-ik-\ *n* **1** : a value computed by

\ə\ abut	\au̇\ out	\i\ tip	\ȯ\ saw	\u̇\ foot
\ər\ further	\ch\ chin	\ī\ life	\ȯi\ coin	\y\ yet
\a\ mat	\e\ pet	\j\ job	\th\ thin	\yü\ few
\ā\ take	\ē\ easy	\ng\ sing	\t͟h\ this	\yu̇\ cure
\ä\ cot, cart	\g\ go	\ō\ bone	\ü\ food	\zh\ vision

dividing the sum of a set of terms by the number of terms ⟨the *arithmetic mean* of 6, 5, and 4 is 5⟩ **2 :** one of the terms in an arithmetic progression between two given terms ⟨in 3, 5, 7, and 9 . . . , the terms 5 and 7 are *arithmetic means* between 3 and 9⟩

arithmetic progression \ˌar-ith-ˌmet-ik-\ *n* **:** a sequence of numbers (as 3, 5, 7, 9, . . .) in which the difference between any two successive terms is the same

-ar•i•um \ˈar-ē-əm, ˈer-\ *n suffix, pl* **-ar•i•ums** *or* **-ar•ia** \-ē-ə\ **:** thing or place relating to ⟨planet*arium*⟩ [Latin, from neuter of *-arius* "-ary"]

ark \ˈärk\ *n* **1 a :** the ship in which Noah and his family were preserved from the Flood **b :** a clumsy boat or ship **2 a :** a sacred chest in which the ancient Hebrews kept the two tablets of the Law **b :** a place of deposit in or against the wall of a synagogue for the scrolls of the Torah [Old English *arc,* from Latin *arca* "chest"]

¹arm \ˈärm\ *n* **1 a :** a human upper limb; *esp* **:** the part between the shoulder and wrist **b :** a corresponding limb of a lower vertebrate **2 :** something resembling an arm: as **a :** a lateral branch of a tree **b :** an inlet of water (as from the sea) **c :** a slender usually functional projecting part (as of a machine) **3 :** POWER, MIGHT ⟨the *arm* of the law⟩ **4 :** a support (as on a chair) for the elbow and forearm **5 :** SLEEVE 1 **6 :** a division of an organization [Old English *earm*] — **armed** \ˈärmd\ *adj* — **arm•less** \ˈärm-ləs\ *adj*

²arm *vb* **1 :** to provide with weapons ⟨*arm* a new regiment⟩ **2 :** to provide with a means of defense ⟨*arm* oneself with facts⟩ **3 :** to provide oneself with arms and armament ⟨the country *armed* for war⟩ **4 :** to equip or ready for action or operation ⟨*arm* a bomb⟩ [Old French *armer,* from Latin *armare,* from *arma* "weapons, tools"]

³arm *n* **1 a :** a means of offense or defense **:** WEAPON; *esp* **:** FIREARM **b :** a branch of an army (as the infantry or artillery) that actually fights **c :** a branch of the military forces (as the navy) **2** *pl* **:** the heraldic devices of a family or a government **3 a** *pl* **:** active hostilities **:** WARFARE **b** *pl* **:** military service — **armed** \ˈärmd\ *adj*

ar•ma•da \är-ˈmäd-ə, -ˈmad-, -ˈmād-\ *n* **1 :** a large fleet of warships **2** *cap* **:** the fleet sent by Spain against England in 1588 **3 :** a large number of moving objects (as vehicles) [Spanish, from Medieval Latin *armata* "army, fleet", from Latin *armare* "to arm"]

ar•ma•dil•lo \ˌär-mə-ˈdil-ō\ *n, pl* **-los :** any of several small burrowing chiefly nocturnal mammals of warm parts of the Americas having body and head encased in small bony plates [Spanish, from *armado* "armed one", from Latin *armare* "to arm"]

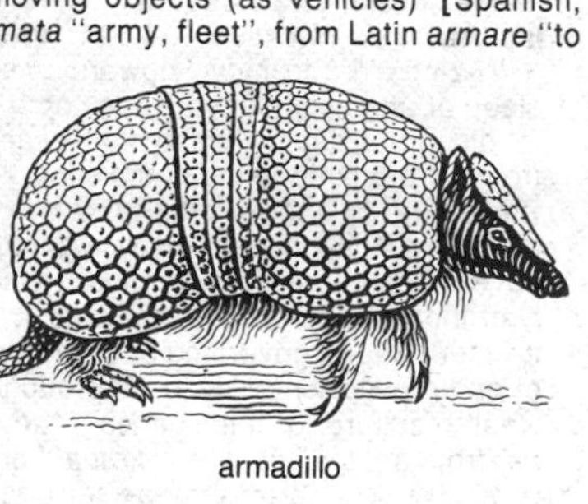
armadillo

Ar•ma•ged•don \ˌär-mə-ˈged-n\ *n* **1 a :** a final and conclusive battle between the forces of good and evil **b :** the site or time of Armageddon **2 :** a vast decisive conflict [Greek *Armageddōn,* scene of the battle foretold in Revelation 16:14–16]

ar•ma•ment \ˈär-mə-mənt\ *n* **1 :** the whole military strength and equipment of a nation **2 :** the total supply of war materials (as of a military unit or system of defense) **3 :** means of protection or defense **:** ARMOR **4 :** the process of preparing for war

ar•ma•ture \ˈär-mə-chər, -ˌchu̇r\ *n* **1 :** a protective or defensive mechanism or covering (as the spines of a cactus) **2 :** the part of an electric generator that consists of coils of wire around an iron core and that induces an electric current when it is rotated in a magnetic field **3 :** the part of an electric motor that consists of coils of wire around an iron core and that is caused to rotate in a magnetic field when an electric current is passed through the coils **4 :** the movable part of an electromagnetic device (as an electric bell) **5 :** a framework used by a sculptor to support a figure being modeled (as in clay) [Latin *armatura* "armor, equipment", from *armare* "to arm"]

¹arm•chair \ˈärm-ˌcheər, -ˌchaər, ˈärm-ˈ\ *n* **:** a chair with arms

²armchair *adj* **1 :** remote from direct dealing with problems ⟨*armchair* strategist⟩ **2 :** sharing vicariously in another's experiences ⟨*armchair* traveler⟩

armed forces *n pl* **:** the combined military, naval, and air forces of a nation

Ar•me•ni•an \är-ˈmē-nē-ən, -nyən\ *n* **1 :** a member of a people dwelling chiefly in Armenia **2 :** the Indo-European language of the Armenians — **Armenian** *adj*

arm•ful \ˈärm-ˌfu̇l\ *n, pl* **arm•fuls** \-ˌfu̇lz\ *or* **arms•ful** \ˈärmz-ˌfu̇l\ **:** as much as a person's arm can hold ⟨carrying an *armful* of books⟩

arm•hole \ˈärm-ˌhōl\ *n* **:** an opening for the arm in a garment

ar•mi•stice \ˈär-mə-stəs\ *n* **:** a pause in fighting brought about by agreement between the two sides **:** TRUCE [New Latin *armistitium,* from Latin *arma* "arms" + *-stitium* (as in *solstitium* "solstice")]

Armistice Day *n* **:** VETERANS DAY [from the armistice which ended World War I on November 11, 1918]

arm•let \ˈärm-lət\ *n* **:** a bracelet or band for the upper arm

ar•mor \ˈär-mər\ *n* **1 :** defensive covering for the body; *esp* **:** covering (as of metal) used in combat **2 :** something that affords protection ⟨safe in the *armor* of wealth⟩ **3 :** a protective covering (as the steel plates of a battleship or a sheathing for wire) **4:** armored forces and vehicles (as tanks) [Old French *armure,* from Latin *armatura,* from *armare* "to arm"]

armor 1

ar•mored \-mərd\ *adj* **1 :** protected by armor ⟨an *armored* car⟩ ⟨*armored* reptiles⟩ **2 :** supplied with armored equipment ⟨an *armored* force⟩

ar•mor•er \ˈär-mər-ər\ *n* **1 :** one that makes armor or arms **2 :** one that repairs, assembles, and tests firearms or that services and loads aircraft armament including bombs

ar•mo•ri•al \är-ˈmōr-ē-əl, -ˈmȯr-\ *adj* **:** of, relating to, or bearing heraldic arms

ar•mo•ry \ˈärm-rē, -ə-rē\ *n, pl* **-ries 1 :** a supply of arms **2 :** a place where arms are stored; *esp* **:** one used for training military reserve personnel **3 :** a place where arms are manufactured

ar•mour \ˈär-mər\ *chiefly British variant of* ARMOR

arm•pit \ˈärm-ˌpit\ *n* **:** the hollow beneath the junction of the arm and shoulder

arm•rest \-ˌrest\ *n* **:** a support for the arm

arm wrestling *n* **:** a contest of strength in which individuals face each other and place usually their right elbows on a surface, grasp hands, and seek to force the other person's arm down

ar•my \ˈär-mē\ *n, pl* **ar•mies 1 a :** a large body of persons organized and armed for land warfare **b :** a military unit capable of independent action and consisting usually of a headquarters, two or more corps, and auxiliary troops **c** *often cap* **:** the complete military organization of a nation for land warfare **2 :** a great multitude ⟨an *army* of insects⟩ **3 :** a body of persons organized to advance a cause [Middle French *armee,* from Medieval Latin *armata* "army, fleet", from Latin *armare* "to arm"]

army ant *n* **:** any of various nomadic social ants

ar•my•worm \-ˌwərm\ *n* **:** any of numerous moth larvae that are often abundant and destructive on crops (as grasses or grain); *also* **:** any other stage of this insect

ar•ni•ca \ˈär-ni-kə\ *n* **:** dried flower heads of a mountain herb related to the daisies that are used especially in the form of a tincture as a liniment; *also* **:** this tincture [New Latin, genus name]

aro•ma \ə-ˈrō-mə\ *n* **1 :** a distinctive and usually pleasing smell ⟨the *aroma* of fresh coffee⟩ — compare FRAGRANCE **2 :** a distinctive quality or atmosphere **:** FLAVOR ⟨the *aroma* of suspense⟩ [Old French *aromat* "spice", from Latin *aroma,* from Greek *arōma*] **syn** see SMELL

ar•o•mat•ic \ˌar-ə-ˈmat-ik\ *adj* **1 :** of, relating to, or having aroma **2 :** of, relating to, or characterized by the presence of at least one benzene ring — used of hydrocarbons and their derivatives — **aromatic** *n*

arose *past of* ARISE

¹around \ə-ˈrau̇nd\ *adv* **1 a :** in circumference ⟨a tree five feet *around*⟩ **b** : in, along, or through a curving or roundabout course ⟨the road goes *around* by the lake⟩ **2 a** : on all or various sides ⟨papers lying *around*⟩ **b** : NEARBY ⟨stick *around*⟩ **3 a** : here and there in various places ⟨traveled *around* from state to state⟩ **b** : to a particular place ⟨come *around* for dinner⟩ **4 a** : in rotation or succession ⟨pass the candy *around*⟩ **b** : from beginning to end ⟨mild the year *around*⟩ **c** : to a customary or improved condition ⟨the medicine brought the patient *around*⟩ **5** : in or to an opposite direction or position ⟨turned *around* and waved goodbye⟩ **6** : APPROXIMATELY ⟨a price of *around* $20⟩

[2]around *prep* **1 a** : on all or various sides of ⟨yard with a fence *around* it⟩ ⟨fields *around* the village⟩ **b** : so as to encircle or enclose ⟨seated *around* the table⟩ **c** : on or to another side of ⟨voyage *around* Cape Horn⟩ **d** : in the neighborhood of : NEAR ⟨somewhere *around* here⟩ **2** : here and there in or throughout ⟨traveling *around* the country⟩

arous•al \ə-ˈrau̇-zəl\ *n* : the act of arousing or the state of being aroused

arouse \ə-ˈrau̇z\ *vb* **1** : to awaken from sleep **2** : to rouse to action : EXCITE [*a-* (as in *arise*) + *rouse*]

ar•peg•gio \är-ˈpej-ō, -ˈpej-ē-ˌō\ *n, pl* **-gi•os** : production of the tones of a chord in succession and not simultaneously; *also* : a chord so played [Italian, from *arpeggiare* "to play on the harp", from *arpa* "harp", of Germanic origin]

ar•que•bus \ˈär-kwi-bəs, -ˌbəs\ *variant of* HARQUEBUS

ar•raign \ə-ˈrān\ *vt* **1** : to call before a court to answer to an indictment : CHARGE **2** : to accuse of wrong, inadequacy, or imperfection [Middle French *araisnier* "to speak to, arraign", from *a-* "ad-" + *raisnier* "to speak", from Latin *ratio* "reason"] — **ar•raign•ment** \-mənt\ *n*

ar•range \ə-ˈrānj\ *vb* **1** : to put in order; *esp* : to put in a particular order ⟨*arrange* books on shelves⟩ **2** : to make plans for ⟨*arrange* a meeting⟩ **3** : ADJUST, SETTLE ⟨*arrange* one's affairs to have the weekend free⟩ **4** : to make a musical arrangement of [Middle French *arangier*, from Old French *a-* "ad-" + *reng* "row, rank"] — **ar•rang•er** *n*

ar•range•ment \ə-ˈrānj-mənt\ *n* **1** : a putting in order : the order in which things are put ⟨the *arrangement* of furniture in a room⟩ **2** : a preliminary measure : PREPARATION ⟨travel *arrangements*⟩ **3** : something made by arranging ⟨a flower *arrangement*⟩ **4** : an adaptation of a musical composition to voices or instruments other than those originally intended

ar•rant \ˈar-ənt\ *adj* **1** : THOROUGHGOING, EXTREME ⟨an *arrant* individualist⟩ **2** : being utterly or notoriously such ⟨*arrant* cowardice⟩ [alteration of *errant*] — **ar•rant•ly** *adv*

[1]ar•ray \ə-ˈrā\ *vt* **1** : to set in order : draw up : MARSHAL **2** : to dress or decorate especially splendidly or impressively : ADORN [Old French *arayer*, of Germanic origin] — **ar•ray•er** *n*

[2]array *n* **1** : regular order or arrangement; *also* : military order ⟨troops in *array*⟩ **2** : rich or beautiful apparel : FINERY **3** : an imposing group : large number ⟨an *array* of problems⟩ **4** : a group of mathematical elements (as numbers or letters) arranged in rows and columns

ar•rears \ə-ˈriərz\ *n pl* **1** : the state of being behind in paying debts owed ⟨two months in *arrears* on their rent⟩ **2** : an unpaid and overdue debt [Middle French *arrere* "behind, backward", from Latin *ad* "to" + *retro* "backward"]

[1]ar•rest \ə-ˈrest\ *vt* **1** : to stop the progress or movement of : CHECK, SLOW ⟨*arrest* a disease⟩ **2** : to take or keep in custody by authority of law ⟨*arrested* on suspicion of robbery⟩ **3** : to attract and hold the attention of ⟨colors that *arrest* the eye⟩ [Middle French *arester* "to rest, arrest", from Latin *ad-* + *restare* "to remain, rest"]

[2]arrest *n* **1 a** : the act of stopping : CHECK **b** : the state of being stopped **2** : the act of taking or holding in custody by authority of law

ar•rest•ing *adj* : catching the attention : STRIKING

ar•riv•al \ə-ˈrī-vəl\ *n* **1** : the act of arriving ⟨await the *arrival* of guests⟩ **2** : a person or thing that has arrived ⟨late *arrivals* at a concert⟩

ar•rive \ə-ˈrīv\ *vi* **1** : to reach a destination ⟨*arrive* home at six o'clock⟩ **2** : to gain an end or object ⟨*arrive* at a decision⟩ **3** : COME 4a ⟨the moment has *arrived*⟩ **4** : to be successful [Old French *ariver*, from Latin *ad* "to" + *ripa* "shore"]

ar•ro•gance \ˈar-ə-gəns\ *n* : a sense of one's own superiority that shows itself in an offensively proud manner : HAUGHTINESS

ar•ro•gant \-gənt\ *adj* **1** : exaggerating one's own worth or importance in an overbearing manner **2** : marked by arrogance ⟨*arrogant* remarks⟩ [Latin *arrogare* "to claim", from *ad-* + *rogare* "to ask"] — **ar•ro•gant•ly** *adv*

ar•ro•gate \ˈar-ə-ˌgāt\ *vt* **1** : to take or claim for one's own without justification ⟨the dictator *arrogated* the powers of parliament⟩ **2** : to attribute to another especially without good reason — **ar•ro•ga•tion** \ˌar-ə-ˈgā-shən\ *n*

ar•ron•disse•ment \ə-ˈrän-dəs-mənt, ˈar-ˌōⁿ-dē-ˈsmäⁿ\ *n* **1** : the largest division of a French governmental department **2** : an administrative district of some large French cities [French]

ar•row \ˈar-ō\ *n* **1** : a missile that is intended to be shot from a bow and that usually has a slender shaft, a pointed head, and feathers at the butt **2** : a mark (as on a map or signboard) to indicate direction [Old English *arwe*]

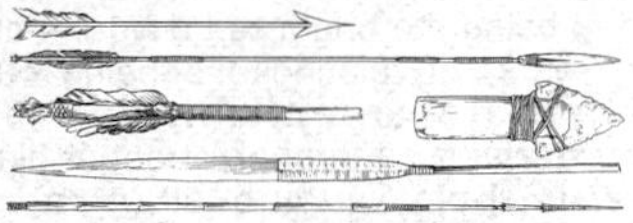

arrow 1

ar•row•head \-ˌhed\ *n* **1** : the usually wedge-shaped piercing tip fixed to the front of an arrow **2** : something (as a wedge-shaped mark) resembling an arrowhead **3** : any of a genus of aquatic plants with leaves shaped like arrowheads

ar•row•root \-ˌrüt, -ˌru̇t\ *n* : any of several tropical American plants with starchy tuberous roots; *also* : an edible starch from these roots

ar•row•worm \-ˌwərm\ *n* : any of a small phylum (Chaetognatha) of marine worms with movable bristles on either side of the mouth

ar•royo \ə-ˈrȯi-ə, -ˈrȯi-ō\ *n, pl* **-roy•os** **1** : a watercourse (as a creek or stream) in a dry region **2** : an often dry gully or channel carved by water [Spanish]

ar•se•nal \ˈärs-nəl, -n-əl\ *n* **1 a** : a place where arms are manufactured or stored **b** : a collection of weapons **2** : STORE 2, SUPPLY [Italian *arsenale*, from Arabic *dār sināʻah* "house of manufacture"]

ar•se•nic \ˈärs-nik, -n-ik\ *n* **1** : a solid poisonous chemical element commonly metallic steel-gray, crystalline, and brittle — see ELEMENT table **2** : a white poisonous trioxide As_2O_3 or As_4O_6 of arsenic used especially as an insecticide or weed killer — called also *arsenic trioxide* [Latin *arsenicum*, from Greek *arsenikon* "yellow orpiment"]

ar•sen•i•cal \är-ˈsen-i-kəl\ *adj* : of, relating to, or containing arsenic ⟨an *arsenical* drug⟩ — **arsenical** *n*

ar•se•no•py•rite \ˌärs-n-ō-ˈpī-ˌrīt\ *n* : a hard tin-white mineral FeAsS consisting of iron, arsenic, and sulfur

ar•sine \är-ˈsēn, ˈär-ˌ\ *n* : a colorless flammable extremely poisonous gas AsH_3 with an odor like garlic

ar•son \ˈärs-n\ *n* : the malicious burning of property (as a building) [Old French, derived from Latin *ardēre* "to burn"] — **ar•son•ist** \ˈärs-nəst, -n-əst\ *n*

ars•phen•a•mine \ärs-ˈfen-ə-ˌmēn, -mən\ *n* : an arsenic-containing substance formerly used in the treatment of spirochetal diseases [*arsenic* + *phen-* + *amine*]

[1]art \ärt, ˈärt, ərt\ *archaic present 2d sing of* BE [Old English *eart*]

[2]art \ˈärt\ *n* **1** : skill in performance acquired by experience, study, or observation : KNACK ⟨the *art* of making friends⟩ **2** : an occupation that requires a natural skill in addition to training and practice ⟨the *art* of cooking⟩ **3** : the rules or ideas that a person must know in order to follow a profession or craft ⟨the *art* of medicine⟩ ⟨the theater *arts*⟩ **4** : a branch of learning; *esp* : one of the nonscientific branches of learning (as history or literature) — usually used in pl. ⟨College of *Arts* and Sciences⟩ **5** : the study of drawing, painting, and sculpture **6** : the works produced by artists (as painters, sculptors, or writers) [Old French, from Latin *ars*]

• **syn** SKILL, CRAFT: ART may be distinct from the other two in implying personal, unanalyzable creative or imaginative power and resource; SKILL stresses technical knowledge and proficiency gained through practice and experience; CRAFT implies expertness in workmanship.

-art — see -ARD

art de•co \ˌär-dā-ˈkō, ˌärt-; är-ˈdā-ˌ, ärt-\ *n, often cap A&D* : a decorative style of the 1920s and 1930s characterized by bold outlines, streamlined forms, and the use of new materials (as plastic) [French *Art Déco,* from *Exposition Internationale des Arts Décoratifs,* an exposition of decorative arts held in Paris, France in 1925]

artefact *variant of* ARTIFACT

arteri- *or* **arterio-** *combining form* : artery : arterial and ⟨*arteriovenous*⟩

1**ar•te•ri•al** \är-ˈtir-ē-əl\ *adj* **1 a** : of or relating to an artery **b** : being the bright red oxygen-rich blood present in most arteries **2** : of, relating to, or being routes for through traffic ⟨*arterial* roads⟩ — **ar•te•ri•al•ly** \-ē-ə-lē\ *adv*

2**arterial** *n* : a through street or highway

ar•te•ri•ole \är-ˈtir-ē-ˌōl\ *n* : a very small artery connecting a larger artery with capillaries — **ar•te•ri•o•lar** \-ˌtir-ē-ˈō-ˌlär, -lər\ *adj*

ar•te•rio•scle•ro•sis \är-ˌtir-ē-ō-sklə-ˈrō-səs\ *n* : a chronic disease in which the arterial walls are abnormally thickened and hardened — **ar•te•rio•scle•rot•ic** \-ˈrät-ik\ *adj or n*

ar•te•rio•ve•nous \är-ˌtir-ē-ō-ˈvē-nəs\ *adj* : of, relating to, or connecting the arteries and veins

ar•tery \ˈärt-ə-rē\ *n, pl* **-ter•ies** **1** : one of the tubular branching muscular-walled and elastic-walled vessels that carry blood from the heart through the body **2** : a channel (as a river or highway) of transportation or communication [Latin *arteria,* from Greek *artēria*]

ar•te•sian well \är-ˌtē-zhən-\ *n* **1** : a bored well from which water flows up like a fountain **2** : a deep-bored well [French *artésien,* literally, "of Artois", from *Artois,* region of France where such wells were common]

art•ful \ˈärt-fəl\ *adj* **1** : performed with or showing art or skill ⟨an *artful* violin performance⟩ **2** : produced by art : ARTIFICIAL **3 a** : using or characterized by art and skill : DEXTEROUS ⟨an *artful* writing style⟩ **b** : skillful or ingenious in gaining an end : WILY ⟨an *artful* cross-examiner⟩ **syn** see SLY — **art•ful•ly** \-fə-lē\ *adv* — **art•ful•ness** *n*

ar•thri•tis \är-ˈthrīt-əs\ *n* : inflammation of the joints [Latin, from Greek, from *arthron* "joint"] — **ar•thrit•ic** \-ˈthrit-ik\ *adj or n* — **ar•thrit•i•cal•ly** \-ˈthrit-i-kə-lē, -klē\ *adv*

ar•thro•pod \ˈär-thrə-ˌpäd\ *n* : any of a phylum (Arthropoda) of invertebrate animals (as insects, arachnids, and crustaceans) with body and limbs segmented [Greek *arthron* "joint" + *pod-, pous* "foot"] — **arthropod** *adj* — **ar•throp•o•dan** \är-ˈthräp-əd-ən\ *adj*

ar•ti•choke \ˈärt-ə-ˌchōk\ *n* : a tall herb resembling the thistle; *also* : its edible flower head which is cooked as a vegetable [Italian dialect *articiocco,* from Arabic *al-khurshūf* "the artichoke"]

artichoke

1**ar•ti•cle** \ˈärt-i-kəl\ *n* **1** : a distinct part of a document (as a contract or treaty) dealing with a single subject **2** : a nonfictional prose composition forming an independent part of a publication and usually dealing with a single topic ⟨an *article* on winter sports⟩ **3** : a word (as *a, an,* or *the*) used with nouns to limit or give definiteness to their application **4** : a member of a class of things; *esp* : COMMODITY b ⟨*articles* of value⟩ [Old French, from Latin *articulus* "joint, division", from *artus* "joint"]

2**article** *vt* **-cled**; **-cling** \-kə-ling, -kling\ : to bind by the articles of a contract ⟨an *articled* apprentice⟩

ar•tic•u•lar \är-ˈtik-yə-lər\ *adj* : of or relating to a joint

1**ar•tic•u•late** \är-ˈtik-yə-lət\ *adj* **1 a** : divided clearly into words and syllables : INTELLIGIBLE **b** : able to speak; *esp* : able to express oneself clearly or effectively **2** : consisting of segments united by joints : JOINTED ⟨*articulate* animals⟩ [Latin *articulus* "joint"] — **ar•tic•u•late•ly** *adv* — **ar•tic•u•late•ness** *n*

2**ar•tic•u•late** \-ˌlāt\ *vb* **1 a** : to speak in distinct syllables or words **b** : to express clearly and distinctly ⟨*articulate* every shade of meaning⟩ **2** : to unite or become united or connected by or as if by a joint

ar•tic•u•la•tion \är-ˌtik-yə-ˈlā-shən\ *n* **1** : the action or manner of articulating : the state of being articulated **2** : the making of articulate sounds (as in pronunciation) **3 a** : a joint between rigid parts of an animal; *esp* : one between bones or cartilages **b** : a joint between plant parts; *also* : a node or internode of a stem — **ar•tic•u•la•to•ry** \är-ˈtik-yə-lə-ˌtōr-ē, -ˌtòr-\ *adj*

ar•tic•u•la•tor \är-ˈtik-yə-ˌlāt-ər\ *n* : a movable vocal organ (as a lip or the tongue)

ar•ti•fact *or* **ar•te•fact** \ˈärt-ə-ˌfakt\ *n* : a usually simple object (as a tool or ornament) showing human work or alteration [Latin *arte factum* "made by art"] — **ar•ti•fac•tu•al** \ˌärt-ə-ˈfak-chə-wəl, -chəl\ *adj*

ar•ti•fice \ˈärt-ə-fəs\ *n* **1 a** : a wily or artful stratagem : TRICK **b** : false or insincere behavior ⟨social *artifices*⟩ **2** : clever or artful skill : INGENUITY [Middle French, from Latin *artificium,* from *artifex* "artificer", from *art-, ars* "art" + *facere* "to make"]

ar•tif•i•cer \är-ˈtif-ə-sər, ˈärt-ə-fə-sər\ *n* : a skilled or artistic worker

ar•ti•fi•cial \ˌärt-ə-ˈfish-əl\ *adj* **1** : built or produced by humans ⟨an *artificial* lake⟩ **2** : lacking in natural quality : AFFECTED ⟨an *artificial* smile⟩ **3** : made or changed to resemble something natural : IMITATION ⟨*artificial* flowers⟩ — **ar•ti•fi•ci•al•i•ty** \-ˌfish-ē-ˈal-ət-ē\ *n* — **ar•ti•fi•cial•ly** \-ˈfish-lē, -ə-lē\ *adv* — **ar•ti•fi•cial•ness** \-ˈfish-əl-nəs\ *n*

• **syn** SYNTHETIC, ERSATZ: ARTIFICIAL may apply to anything that is not the result of natural process or conditions ⟨the state is an *artificial* society⟩ but especially to something that has a natural counterpart ⟨*artificial* teeth⟩ SYNTHETIC applies especially to a manufactured substance or to a natural substance that is treated to resemble and substitute for another; ERSATZ often implies the use of an inferior substitute for a natural product.

artificial insemination *n* : introduction of semen into the uterus or oviduct by artificial means

artificial respiration *n* : the rhythmic forcing of air into and out of the lungs of one whose breathing has stopped

artificial selection *n* : the process of modifying organisms by selection in breeding controlled by the breeder

ar•til•lery \är-ˈtil-rē, -ə-rē\ *n* **1** : large-caliber crew-operated mounted firearms (as guns, howitzers, or rockets) **2** : a branch of an army armed with artillery [Middle French *artillerie*]

ar•tio•dac•tyl \ˌärt-ē-ō-ˈdak-tl\ *n* : any of an order (Artiodactyla) of hoofed mammals (as the camel or ox) with an even number of functional toes on each foot [Greek *artios* "fitting, even-numbered" + *daktylos* "finger, toe"]

ar•ti•san \ˈärt-ə-zən\ *n* : a person (as a carpenter) who works at a trade requiring skill with the hands [Middle French, from Italian *artigiano,* from *arte* "art", from Latin *ars*]

art•ist \ˈärt-əst\ *n* **1** : a person skilled in one of the arts (as painting, sculpture, music, or writing); *esp* : PAINTER **2** : a person showing unusual ability in an occupation requiring skill ⟨a makeup *artist*⟩

ar•tiste \är-ˈtēst\ *n* : a skilled adept performer; *esp* : a musical or theatrical entertainer [French]

ar•tis•tic \är-ˈtis-tik\ *adj* **1** : relating to or characteristic of art or artists **2** : showing imaginative skill in arrangement or execution — **ar•tis•ti•cal•ly** \-ˈtis-ti-kə-lē, -klē\ *adv*

• **syn** AESTHETIC: ARTISTIC implies the point of view of one who produces art and thinks in terms of creating beautiful forms; AESTHETIC stresses the point of view of one who analyzes and reflects upon the effect a work of art has; either term may suggest a contrast with the practical, the functional, or the moral aspects of anything.

art•ist•ry \ˈärt-ə-strē\ *n* **1** : artistic quality of effect or workmanship **2** : artistic ability

art•less \ˈärt-ləs\ *adj* **1** : lacking art, knowledge, or skill : UNCULTURED **2 a** : made without skill : CRUDE **b** : being simple and natural ⟨*artless* grace⟩ **3** : free from guile or deceit — **art•less•ly** *adv* — **art•less•ness** *n*

art nou•veau \ˌär-nü-ˈvō, ˌärt-\ *n, often cap A&N* : a decorative style of late 19th century origin characterized by curving lines and leaflike forms [French, literally, "new art"]

arty \ˈärt-ē\ *adj* **art•i•er**; **-est** : showily or pretentiously artistic — **art•i•ly** \'ärt-l-ē\ *adv* — **art•i•ness** \'ärt-ē-nəs\ *n*

ar•um \'ar-əm, 'er-\ *n* : any of a family of plants (as the jack-in-the-pulpit or the skunk cabbage) having heart-shaped or sword-shaped leaves and flowers in a fleshy spike enclosed in a leafy sheath [Latin, from Greek *aron*]

[1]**-ary** *usually* ˌer-ē *after an unstressed syllable,* ə-rē *or* rē *after a stressed syllable, in Britain usually* ə-rē *or* rē *in all cases*\ *n suffix, pl* **-aries** : thing or person belonging to or connected with ⟨syllab*ary*⟩ ⟨function*ary*⟩ [Latin *-arius, -aria, -arium,* from *-arius,* adjective suffix]

[2]**-ary** *adj suffix* : of, relating to, or connected with ⟨budget*ary*⟩ [Latin *-arius*]

[1]**Ary•an** \'ar-ē-ən, 'er-, 'är-yən\ *adj* **1** : INDO-EUROPEAN **2** : of or relating to the Aryans **3** : of or relating to a hypothetical ethnic type represented by early speakers of Indo-European languages

[2]**Aryan** *n* **1** : a member of the Indo-European-speaking people occupying the Iranian plateau and later entering India and conquering the non-Indo-European inhabitants **2 a** : a member of the people speaking the language from which the Indo-European languages are derived **b** : a member of any of the peoples speaking an Indo-European language **c** : NORDIC 2 **d** : GENTILE 1 [Sanskrit *ārya* "noble, Aryan"]

[1]**as** \əz, az, ˌaz\ *adv* **1** : to the same degree or extent ⟨*as* light as a feather⟩ **2** : for instance ⟨various trees, *as* oak or pine⟩ [Old English *eallswā* "likewise, just a", from *eall* "all" + *swā* "so"]

[2]**as** *conj* **1** : as if ⟨felt *as* I were dead⟩ **2** : in or to the same degree that ⟨bright *as* day⟩ **3** : in the way or manner that ⟨do *as* I do⟩ **4** : WHILE, WHEN ⟨spilled the milk *as* I got up⟩ **5** : regardless of the degree to which : THOUGH ⟨strange *as* it seems, it's true⟩ **6** : for the reason that ⟨stayed home *as* they had no car⟩ **7** : that the result is — used after *so* or *such* ⟨so clearly guilty *as* to leave no doubt⟩

[3]**as** *pron* **1** : THAT, WHO, WHICH — used after *same* or *such* ⟨the same school *as* the mayor attended⟩ **2** : a fact that ⟨is a foreigner, *as* is evident from the accent⟩

[4]**as** *prep* **1** : LIKE 2 ⟨all rose *as* one person⟩ **2** : in the character or position of ⟨working *as* an editor⟩

[5]**as** \'as\ *n, pl* **as•ses** \'as-ˌēz, 'as-əz\ **1** : an ancient Roman unit of value **2** : a bronze coin representing one as [Latin]

[5]as 2

as- — see AD-

as•a•fet•i•da *or* **as•a•foe•ti•da** \ˌas-ə-'fit-əd-ē, -'fet-əd-ə\ *n* : a gum resin that comes from several oriental plants of the carrot family, has an unpleasant smell and taste, and was formerly used in medicine [Medieval Latin *asafoetida,* from Persian *azā* "mastic" + Latin *foetidus* "fetid"]

as•bes•tos \as-'bes-təs, az-\ *n* : a mineral (as chrysotile) that readily separates into long flexible fibers suitable for use as a fireproof, nonconducting, and chemically resistant material [derived from Greek *asbestos* "quicklime", from *asbestos* "inextinguishable"]

as•ca•rid \'as-kə-rəd\ *n* : any of a family of roundworms that includes the common large roundworm parasitic in the human intestine [derived from Greek *askaris* "intestinal worm"]

as•ca•ris \'as-kə-rəs\ *n, pl* **as•car•i•des** \ə-'skar-ə-ˌdēz\ : ASCARID

as•cend \ə-'send\ *vb* **1** : to go up or upward : CLIMB, RISE ⟨*ascend* a hill⟩ ⟨smoke *ascends*⟩ **2** : to succeed to : OCCUPY ⟨*ascended* the throne in 1918⟩ [Latin *ascendere,* from *ad-* + *scandere* "to climb"] — **as•cend•able** \-'sen-də-bəl\ *adj*

• **syn** ASCEND, MOUNT, CLIMB, SCALE mean to move upward or toward the top. ASCEND implies no more than this; MOUNT implies reaching the top ⟨*mount* a ladder⟩ CLIMB suggests effort and often the use of hands and feet; SCALE implies the use of a ladder or rope in climbing vertically.

as•cen•dan•cy \ə-'sen-dən-sē\ *n* : governing or controlling influence : DOMINATION **syn** see SUPREMACY

[1]**as•cen•dant** \ə-'sen-dənt\ *n* **1** : the sign of the zodiac on the eastern horizon **2** : a state or position of dominant power or importance

[2]**ascendant** *adj* **1** : moving or directed upward : RISING **2** : increasingly superior in position or power

as•cen•sion \ə-'sen-chən\ *n* : the act or process of ascending

Ascension Day *n* : the Thursday 40 days after Easter observed in some churches in commemoration of Christ's ascension into heaven

as•cent \ə-'sent\ *n* **1** : the act of rising or moving upward : CLIMB **2** : an upward slope : RISE

as•cer•tain \ˌas-ər-'tān\ *vt* : to learn with certainty : find out ⟨*ascertain* the date of the concert⟩ [Middle French *acertainer,* from *a-* "ad-" + *certain*] — **as•cer•tain•able** \-'tā-nə-bəl\ *adj* — **as•cer•tain•ment** \-'tān-mənt\ *n*

as•cet•ic \ə-'set-ik\ *adj* **1** : practicing strict self-denial especially for religious discipline ⟨*ascetic* in their way of life⟩ **2** : harshly simple or restrained : AUSTERE ⟨*ascetic* surroundings⟩ [Greek *askētikos,* literally, "laborious", from *askein* "to work, exercise"] — **ascetic** *n* — **as•cet•i•cism** \ə-'set-ə-ˌsiz-əm\ *n*

as•cid•i•an \ə-'sid-ē-ən\ *n* : any of various simple or compound tunicates [derived from Greek *askidion* "little wineskin", from *askos* "wineskin, bladder"]

as•co•carp \'as-kə-ˌkärp\ *n* : the fruiting body of an ascomycetous fungus

as•co•my•cete \ˌas-kō-'mī-ˌsēt, -mī-'sēt\ *n* : any of a class (Ascomycetes) of higher fungi (as yeasts, molds) with septate hyphae and spores formed in asci [Greek *askos* "wineskin, bladder" + *mykēs* "fungus"] — **as•co•my•ce•tous** \-mī-'sēt-əs\ *adj*

ascor•bic acid \ə-ˌskȯr-bik-\ *n* : VITAMIN C [[2]*a-* + New Latin *scorbutus* "scurvy"]

as•co•spore \'as-kə-ˌspōr, -ˌspȯr\ *n* : a spore produced in an ascus

as•cot \'as-kət, -ˌkät\ *n* : a broad scarf with one end passed over the other under the chin and often pinned [*Ascot* Heath, English racetrack]

ascot

as•cribe \ə-'skrīb\ *vt* : to refer to a supposed cause, source, or author : ATTRIBUTE [Middle French *ascrivre,* from Latin *ascribere,* from *ad-* + *scribere* "to write"] — **as•crib•able** \-'skrī-bə-bəl\ *adj*

• **syn** ASCRIBE, ATTRIBUTE, IMPUTE, CREDIT mean to lay something to the account of a person or thing. ASCRIBE suggests inferring or conjecturing the cause, source, or author of something; ATTRIBUTE implies more definiteness or stronger evidence for ascribing; IMPUTE suggests ascribing something that brings discredit by way of accusation or blame; CREDIT implies ascribing a thing to a person or other thing as its agent, source, or explanation.

as•crip•tion \ə-'skrip-shən\ *n* : the act of ascribing : ATTRIBUTION

as•cus \'as-kəs\ *n, pl* **as•ci** \'as-ˌī, -ˌkī, -ˌkē\ : a membranous oval or tubular spore sac of an ascomycete usually bearing eight spores [Greek *askos* "wineskin, bladder"]

-ase \ˌās, ˌāz\ *n suffix* : enzyme ⟨malt*ase*⟩ [French, from *diastase* "diastase, enzyme"]

asep•sis \ā-'sep-səs, ə-\ *n* : the condition of being aseptic; *also* : the methods of making or keeping aseptic

asep•tic \-'sep-tik\ *adj* **1** : preventing infection; *also* : free or freed from disease-causing microorganisms **2 a** : lacking life, emotion, or warmth ⟨*aseptic* essays⟩ **b** : being emotionally detached : OBJECTIVE ⟨an *aseptic* view of life⟩ — **asep•ti•cal•ly** \-ti-kə-lē, -klē\ *adv*

asex•u•al \ā-'sek-shə-wəl, 'ā-, -shəl\ *adj* **1** : lacking sex ⟨*asexual* organisms⟩ **2** : occurring or formed without sexual action ⟨*asexual* reproduction⟩ ⟨*asexual* spores⟩ — **asex•u•al•ly** \-ē\ *adv*

as for *prep* : with regard to : CONCERNING ⟨*as for* me⟩

\ə\ **abut**	\au̇\ **out**	\i\ **tip**	\ȯ\ **saw**	\u̇\ **foot**
\ər\ **further**	\ch\ **chin**	\ī\ **life**	\ȯi\ **coin**	\y\ **yet**
\a\ **mat**	\e\ **pet**	\j\ **job**	\th\ **thin**	\yü\ **few**
\ā\ **take**	\ē\ **easy**	\ng\ **sing**	\t͟h\ **this**	\yu̇\ **cure**
\ä\ **cot, cart**	\g\ **go**	\ō\ **bone**	\ü\ **food**	\zh\ **vision**

as good as *adv* : in effect : PRACTICALLY ⟨*as good as* new⟩
1ash \'ash\ *n* **1** : any of a genus of trees of the olive family with thin furrowed bark and winged seeds **2** : the tough elastic wood of an ash [Old English *æsc*]
2ash *n* **1 a** : the solid residue left when material is thoroughly burned or is oxidized by chemical means **b** : fine particles of mineral matter from a volcanic vent **2** *pl* **a** : a collection of ash left after something has been burned **b** : the last traces of something : RUINS **c** : the remains of a dead human body especially after cremation **3** *pl* : something that symbolizes grief, repentance, or humiliation **4** *pl* : deathly pallor [Old English *asce*]
ashamed \ə-'shāmd\ *adj* **1** : feeling shame, guilt, or disgrace ⟨*ashamed* of your behavior⟩ **2** : kept back by pride ⟨*ashamed* to beg⟩ — **asham•ed•ly** \-'shā-məd-lē\ *adv*
1ash•en \'ash-ən\ *adj* : of, relating to, or made from the wood of the ash tree
2ashen *adj* **1** : of the color of ashes **2** : deadly pale : BLANCHED ⟨*ashen* with fear⟩
Ash•ke•nazi \ˌash-kə-'naz-ē\ *n, pl* **-naz•im** \-'naz-əm\ : a member of one of the two great divisions of Jews comprising the eastern European Yiddish-speaking Jews — compare SEPHARDI [Hebrew *Ashkĕnāzī*] — **Ash•ke•naz•ic** \-'naz-ik\ *adj*
ash•lar \'ash-lər\ *n* **1** : dressed or squared stone; *also* : masonry of such stone **2** : a thin squared and dressed stone used for facing [Middle French *aisselier* "traverse beam", derived from Latin *assis* "board"]
ashore \ə-'shōr, -'shȯr\ *adv* : on or to the shore
ash•tray \'ash-ˌtrā\ *n* : a container for tobacco ashes and cigarette and cigar butts
Ash Wednesday *n* : the first day of Lent
ashy \'ash-ē\ *adj* **ash•i•er**; **-est** **1** : of, relating to, or resembling ashes **2** : 2ASHEN 2
Asian \'ā-zhən, 'ā-shən\ *n* **1** : a native or inhabitant of Asia **2** : a person of Asian descent — **Asian** *adj*
Asian influenza *or* **Asian flu** *n* : influenza caused by a mutant strain of the influenza virus discovered in China in 1957
Asi•at•ic cholera \ˌā-zhē-ˌat-ik-, -zē-\ *n* : a destructive bacterial disease of humans especially in Asia marked by violent vomiting and purging
1aside \ə-'sīd\ *adv* **1** : to or toward the side ⟨stepped *aside*⟩ **2** : out of the way : AWAY ⟨took them *aside*⟩ **3** : out of one's thoughts ⟨all kidding *aside*⟩
2aside *n* **1** : words meant to be inaudible to someone; *esp* : an actor's words supposedly not heard by others on the stage **2** : a straying from the theme : DIGRESSION
aside from *prep* **1** : in addition to : BESIDES **2** : except for
as if *conj* **1** : as it would be if ⟨it was *as if* you had lost your last friend⟩ **2** : as one would do if ⟨they ran *as if* ghosts were chasing them⟩ **3** : THAT ⟨it seemed *as if* the day would never end⟩
as•i•nine \'as-n-ˌīn\ *adj* **1** : OBSTINATE 1 **2** : marked by inexcusable failure to use intelligence or good judgment ⟨an *asinine* statement⟩ [Latin *asininus*, from *asinus* "ass"] — **as•i•nine•ly** *adv* — **as•i•nin•i•ty** \ˌas-n-'in-ət-ē\ *n*
ask \'ask\ *vb* **1** : to seek information : INQUIRE **2** : to make a request ⟨*ask* for help⟩ **3** : to set as a price ⟨*ask* $20 for a bicycle⟩ **4** : INVITE ⟨*ask* friends to a party⟩ **5** : to seek or look for punishment or retaliation ⟨*asking* for trouble⟩ [Old English *āscian*] — **ask•er** *n*
• **syn** ASK, REQUEST mean to try to obtain by making known one's wants. ASK implies simply the statement of the desire; REQUEST suggests some formality or courtesy in asking and implies an expectation of an affirmative response.
askance \ə-'skans\ *adv* **1** : with a side glance : OBLIQUELY **2** : with disapproval or distrust [origin unknown]
askew \ə-'skyü\ *adv or adj* : out of line : AWRY ⟨the picture hung *askew*⟩ **syn** see CROOKED
1aslant \ə-'slant\ *adv or adj* : in a slanting direction : OBLIQUELY
2aslant *prep* : over or across in a slanting direction
1asleep \ə-'slēp\ *adj* **1** : being in a state of sleep **2** : lacking sensation : NUMB ⟨my arm is *asleep*⟩ **3** : not alert : SLUGGISH
2asleep *adv* : into a state of sleep
as long as *conj* **1** : provided that ⟨the team can get away with murder *as long as* they win⟩ **2** : inasmuch as : SINCE ⟨*as long as* you're going, I'll go too⟩
aso•cial \ā-'sō-shəl\ *adj* **1** : inconsiderate of others : SELFISH **2** : withdrawn from social activity — compare ANTISOCIAL 2
as of *prep* : ON, AT, FROM ⟨takes effect *as of* July 1⟩
asp \'asp\ *n* : a small venomous snake of Egypt [Latin *aspis*, from Greek]
as•par•a•gine \ə-'spar-ə-ˌjēn\ *n* : an amino acid $C_4H_8N_2O_3$ that is found in many plants [French, from Latin *asparagus*]
as•par•a•gus \ə-'spar-ə-gəs\ *n* : a tall branching perennial herb of the lily family widely grown for its thick edible young shoots [Latin, from Greek *asparagos*]

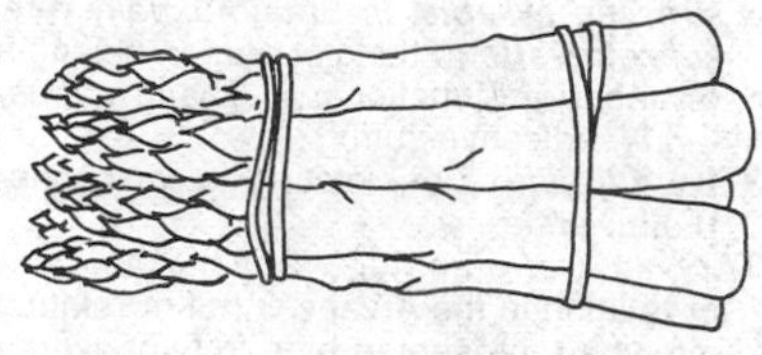
asparagus

as•par•tic acid \ə-ˌspärt-ik-\ *n* : a crystalline amino acid $C_4H_7NO_4$ found especially in plants [derived from Latin *asparagus*]
as•pect \'as-ˌpekt\ *n* **1 a** : the position of planets or stars with respect to one another held by astrologers to influence human affairs **b** : a position facing a particular direction : EXPOSURE ⟨the house has a southern *aspect*⟩ **2** : a particular way in which something appears or may be regarded ⟨studied every *aspect* of the question⟩ [Latin *aspectus*, from *aspicere* "to look at", from *ad-* + *specere* "to look"] — **as•pec•tu•al** \a-'spek-chə-wəl, -chəl\ *adj*
as•pen \'as-pən\ *n* : any of several poplars with leaves that flutter in the lightest breeze [Old English *æspe*]
as•per•i•ty \a-'sper-ət-ē, ə-'sper-\ *n, pl* **-ties** **1** : RIGOR 3, SEVERITY ⟨the *asperities* of winter weather⟩ **2** : roughness of surface (as of a leaf) : UNEVENNESS **3** : harshness of temper, manner, or tone ⟨argued with *asperity*⟩ [Old French *aspreté*, from *aspre* "rough", from Latin *asper*]
as•perse \ə-'spərs, a-\ *vt* : to make aspersions against : SLANDER ⟨*asperse* someone's character⟩ [Latin *aspergere*, literally, "to sprinkle", from *ad-* + *spargere* "to scatter"]
as•per•sion \ə-'spər-zhən\ *n* : an injurious or offensive charge or implication ⟨cast *aspersions* on a person⟩
1as•phalt \'as-ˌfȯlt\ *or* **as•phal•tum** \as-'fȯl-təm\ *n* **1** : a brown to black substance that is found in natural beds or obtained as a residue in petroleum refining and that consists chiefly of hydrocarbons **2** : any of various compositions of asphalt having diverse uses (as for pavement or for waterproof cement or paint) [Late Latin *aspaltus*, from Greek *asphaltos*] — **as•phal•tic** \as'fȯl-tik\ *adj*
2asphalt *vt* : to cover or impregnate with asphalt
as•pho•del \'as-fə-ˌdel\ *n* : any of several herbs of the lily family with white or yellow flowers in long erect spikes [Latin *asphodelus*, from Greek *asphodelos*]
as•phyx•ia \as-'fik-sē-ə\ *n* : a lack of oxygen or excess of carbon dioxide in the body that is usually caused by interruption of breathing and results in unconsciousness [Greek, "stopping of the pulse", from *a-* + *sphyzein* "to throb"]
as•phyx•i•ate \as-'fik-sē-ˌāt\ *vt* : to cause asphyxia in; *also* : to kill or make unconscious by interference with the normal oxygen intake — **as•phyx•i•a•tion** \ˌas-ˌfik-sē-'ā-shən\ *n* — **as•phyx•i•a•tor** \as-'fik-sē-ˌāt-ər\ *n*
as•pic \'as-pik\ *n* : a jelly (as of fish or meat stock) used cold especially to mold meat, fish, or vegetables [French, literally, "asp"]
as•pi•dis•tra \ˌas-pə-'dis-trə\ *n* : an Asian plant of the lily family with large basal leaves that is often grown as a houseplant [derived from Greek *aspis* "shield"]
as•pi•rant \'as-pə-rənt, -prənt, ə-'spī-rənt\ *n* : one that aspires
1as•pi•rate \'as-pə-ˌrāt\ *vt* **1** : to pronounce with an initial \h\ sound ⟨we do not *aspirate* the word *hour*⟩ **2** : to draw or remove by suction ⟨blood *aspirated* from a vein by a syringe⟩ [Latin *aspirare* "to breathe on, aspire"]
2as•pi•rate \'as-pə-rət, -prət\ *n* **1** : an independent sound \h\ or a character (as the letter *h*) representing it **2** : a consonant having as its final element an \h\-like sound in the same syllable (\t\ in English *toe* is an *aspirate*)
as•pi•ra•tion \ˌas-pə-'rā-shən\ *n* **1 a** (1) : pronunciation with an aspirate ⟨*aspiration* of the word *herb*⟩ (2) : pronunciation as an aspirate ⟨occasional *aspiration* of the final \t\ in *hot*⟩ **b** : an independent sound \h\ or its symbol **2** : a drawing of something in, out, up, or through by or as if by suction **3 a** : a strong

desire to achieve something high or great **b** : an object of such desire **syn** see AMBITION

as·pi·ra·tor \'as-pə-,rāt-ər\ *n* : an apparatus for producing suction or moving or collecting materials by suction

as·pire \ə-'spīr\ *vb* : to seek to attain something high or great ⟨*aspired* to the presidency⟩ [Latin *aspirare* "to breathe on, favor, aspire", from *ad-* + *spirare* "to breathe"] — **as·pir·er** *n*

as·pi·rin \'as-pə-rən, -prən\ *n* **1** : a white crystalline drug $C_9H_8O_4$ used as a remedy for pain and fever — called also *acetylsalicylic acid* **2** : a tablet of aspirin [acetyl + *spir*aeic acid (former name of salicylic acid), from New Latin *Spiraea*, genus of shrubs]

as regards *or* **as respects** *prep* : in regard to : with respect to

ass \'as\ *n* **1** : an animal resembling but smaller than the related horse and having a shorter mane, shorter hair on the tail, and longer ears : DONKEY **2** : a dull stupid person [Old English *assa*]

as·sail \ə-'sāl\ *vt* : to attack violently with blows or words [Old French *asaillir*, from Latin *assilire* "to leap upon", from *ad-* + *salire* "to leap"] **syn** see ATTACK — **as·sail·able** \-'sā-lə-bəl\ *adj* — **as·sail·ant** \-'sā-lənt\ *n*

as·sas·sin \ə-'sas-n\ *n* : a person who kills another by surprise attack; *esp* : a murderer of a prominent person either for hire or from fanatical motives [Medieval Latin *assassinus*, from Arabic *ḥashshāshīn*, plural of *ḥashshāsh* "one who chews or smokes hashish"]

△ origin During the time of the Crusades the members of a certain secret Muslim sect terrorized their enemies by performing murders as a religious duty. Because these acts were carried out under the influence of hashish, the killers became known as *ḥashshāshīn*, "eaters or smokers of hashish". This Arabic term was brought back to the West by the Crusaders, passing into Medieval Latin and thence into other European languages. English *assassin* was eventually extended to mean any murderer, though it is used especially for one who murders a politically important person either for hire or from fanatical motives.

as·sas·si·nate \ə-'sas-n-,āt\ *vt* **1** : to murder by a surprise attack especially for pay **2** : to injure or destroy unexpectedly and treacherously ⟨*assassinate* a person's character⟩ **syn** see KILL — **as·sas·si·na·tion** \ə-,sas-n-'ā-shən\ *n*

[1]as·sault \ə-'sȯlt\ *n* **1** : a violent physical or verbal attack : ONSLAUGHT **2** : an apparent attempt or a threat to do harm to another — compare BATTERY 1b [Old French *assaut*, from Latin *ad-* + *saltus* "leap", from *salire* "to leap"]

[2]assault *vt* : to make an assault upon **syn** see ATTACK

[1]as·say \'as-,ā, a-'sā\ *n* **1** *archaic* : TRIAL, ATTEMPT **2** : analysis (as of an ore, a metal, or a drug) to determine the presence, absence, or quantity of one or more substances [Old French *essai, assai* "test, essay, effort"]

[2]as·say \a-'sā, 'as-,ā\ *vb* **1** : TRY, ATTEMPT ⟨*assayed* to explain their position⟩ **2 a** : to analyze (as an ore) for one or more valuable substances **b** : to judge the worth of : ESTIMATE ⟨*assayed* the value of the book⟩ — **as·say·er** *n*

as·se·gai *or* **as·sa·gai** \'as-i-,gī\ *n* : a slender hardwood usually iron-tipped spear used in southern Africa [derived from Arabic *az-zaghāya* "the assegai"]

as·sem·blage \ə-'sem-blij\ *n* **1** : a collection of persons or things : GATHERING **2** : the act of assembling : the state of being assembled

as·sem·ble \ə-'sem-bəl\ *vb* **-bled**; **-bling** \-bə-ling, -bling\ **1** : to collect into one place or group ⟨*assembled* the crew⟩ **2** : to fit together the parts of ⟨*assemble* a bicycle⟩ **3** : to meet together : CONVENE ⟨the right to *assemble* peacefully⟩ [Old French *assembler*, from Latin *ad-* + *simul* "together"] **syn** see GATHER — **as·sem·bler** \-bə-lər, -blər\ *n*

as·sem·bly \ə-'sem-blē\ *n, pl* **-blies 1** : a body of persons gathered together (as for deliberation, worship, or entertainment) **2** *cap* : a legislative body; *esp* : the lower house of a legislature **3** : the act or state of coming together : ASSEMBLAGE **4** : a signal for troops to assemble **5** : a collection of parts that go to make up a complete unit ⟨the tail *assembly* of an airplane⟩

assembly line *n* : an arrangement of machines, equipment, and workers in which work passes from operation to operation in direct line until the product is assembled

as·sem·bly·man \ə-'sem-blē-mən\ *n* : a member of a legislative assembly

as·sem·bly·wom·an \-,wu̇m-ən\ *n* : a woman who is a member of a legislative assembly

[1]as·sent \ə-'sent\ *vi* : to agree to something especially after thoughtful consideration : CONCUR [Old French *assenter*, from Latin *assentire*, from *ad-* + *sentire* "to feel"]

• **syn** ASSENT, CONSENT, ACCEDE mean to agree with what has been proposed. ASSENT implies the action of the understanding or judgment toward propositions or opinions; CONSENT involves the will or the feelings and indicates acceptance or approval of or compliance with what is desired or requested; ACCEDE suggests a yielding, often under pressure, of assent or consent.

[2]assent *n* : an act of assenting : ACQUIESCENCE, AGREEMENT

as·sert \ə-'sərt\ *vt* **1** : to state clearly and strongly : declare positively ⟨*assert* an opinion in a loud voice⟩ **2** : to defend forcefully ⟨*assert* your rights⟩ [Latin *asserere*, from *ad-* + *serere* "to join"]

• **syn** DECLARE, AFFIRM, AVOW: ASSERT implies stating confidently without need for proof or evidence; DECLARE often adds to ASSERT an implication of open or public statement; AFFIRM implies conviction of truth and willingness to stand by one's statement; AVOW implies open and emphatic declaration and personal responsibility for a statement. **syn** see in addition MAINTAIN

— **assert oneself** : to insist that others recognize one's rights

as·ser·tion \ə-'sər-shən\ *n* : the act of asserting; *also* : something asserted : DECLARATION

as·sert·ive \ə-'sərt-iv\ *adj* : characterized by self-confidence and boldness in expressing opinions — **as·sert·ive·ly** *adv* — **as·sert·ive·ness** *n*

asses *pl of* AS *or of* ASS

as·sess \ə-'ses\ *vt* **1** : to fix the rate or amount of ⟨*assessed* damages of $5000⟩ **2** : to set a value on (as property) for tax purposes ⟨a house *assessed* at $40,000⟩ **3** : to lay a tax or charge on ⟨the city *assessed* all car owners $5.00⟩ **4** : to determine the importance, size, or value of ⟨*assess* your chances of winning⟩ [probably from Medieval Latin *assessus*, past participle of *assidēre* "to assess", from Latin, "to sit beside, assist in giving judgment", from *ad-* + *sedēre* "to sit"] **syn** see ESTIMATE — **as·sess·able** \ə-'ses-ə-bəl\ *adj*

as·sess·ment \ə-'ses-mənt\ *n* **1** : the act of assessing : APPRAISAL **2** : the amount or value assessed ⟨a special *assessment* for new sewers⟩

as·ses·sor \ə-'ses-ər\ *n* : an official who assesses property for taxation

as·set \'as-,et\ *n* **1** *pl* : all the property (as cash, securities, real estate, or goods) of a person, corporation, or estate that may be used in payment of debts **2** : ADVANTAGE, RESOURCE ⟨your wit is your chief *asset*⟩ [back-formation from obsolete *assets*, singular, "sufficient property to pay debts and legacies", from Old French *assez* "enough", from Latin *ad* "to" + *satis* "enough"]

as·sev·er·ate \ə-'sev-ə-,rāt\ *vt* : to state firmly or earnestly : AVER [Latin *asseverare*, from *ad-* + *severus* "severe"] — **as·sev·er·a·tion** \ə-,sev-ə-'rā-shən\ *n*

as·si·du·i·ty \,as-ə-'dü-ət-ē, -'dyü-\ *n* : the quality or state of being assiduous : DILIGENCE

as·sid·u·ous \ə-'sij-wəs, -ə-wəs\ *adj* : steadily attentive : DILIGENT [Latin *assiduus*, from *assidēre* "to sit beside", from *ad-* + *sedēre* "to sit"] — **as·sid·u·ous·ly** *adv* — **as·sid·u·ous·ness** *n*

as·sign \ə-'sīn\ *vt* **1** : to transfer to another ⟨*assign* a patent to the heirs⟩ **2 a** : to appoint to a post or duty **b** : PRESCRIBE ⟨*assign* the lesson⟩ **3** : to fix authoritatively ⟨*assign* a limit⟩ **4** : to attribute as a motive or reason ⟨ill health was *assigned* as the cause of the suicide⟩ [Old French *assigner*, from Latin *assignare*, from *ad-* + *signare* "to mark", from *signum* "mark, sign"] **syn** see ALLOT — **as·sign·able** \ə-'sī-nə-bəl\ *adj* — **as·sign·er** \ə-'sī-nər\ *n*

as·sig·na·tion \,as-ig-'nā-shən\ *n* **1** : ASSIGNMENT **2** : TRYST 1

as·sign·ee \ə-,sī-'nē, ,as-,ī-; ,as-ə-'nē\ *n* : a person to whom something is assigned

as·sign·ment \ə-'sīn-mənt\ *n* **1** : the act of assigning ⟨*assign-*

\ə\ **abut**	\au̇\ **out**	\i\ **tip**	\ȯ\ **saw**	\u̇\ **foot**
\ər\ **further**	\ch\ **chin**	\ī\ **life**	\ȯi\ **coin**	\y\ **yet**
\a\ **mat**	\e\ **pet**	\j\ **job**	\th\ **thin**	\yü\ **few**
\ā\ **take**	\ē\ **easy**	\ng\ **sing**	\th\ **this**	\yu̇\ **cure**
\ä\ **cot, cart**	\g\ **go**	\ō\ **bone**	\ü\ **food**	\zh\ **vision**

ment of seats⟩ **2 :** something assigned **:** an assigned task ⟨an *assignment* in arithmetic⟩ **syn** see TASK

as•sim•i•late \ə-ˈsim-ə-ˌlāt\ *vb* **1 a :** to take something in and make it part of and like the thing it has joined ⟨*assimilate* nutrients into the body⟩ ⟨the nation *assimilated* millions of immigrants⟩ **b :** to comprehend thoroughly **:** ABSORB **2 a :** to make similar **b :** to alter by assimilation **[**Medieval Latin *assimilare,* from Latin *assimulare* "to make similar", from *ad-* + *simulare* "to make similar, simulate"**]** **syn** see ABSORB — **as•sim•i•la•bil•i•ty** \-ˌsim-ə-lə-ˈbil-ət-ē\ *n* — **as•sim•i•la•ble** \-ˈsim-ə-lə-bəl\ *adj* — **as•sim•i•la•tor** \-ˈsim-ə-ˌlāt-ər\ *n*

as•sim•i•la•tion \ə-ˌsim-ə-ˈlā-shən\ *n* **1 :** the act or process of assimilating; *esp* **:** the conversion of nutrients (as digested food) into protoplasm **2 :** change of a sound in speech so that it becomes identical with or similar to a neighboring sound ⟨in the word *impractical* the \n\ of the prefix *in-* has undergone *assimilation*⟩ — **as•sim•i•la•tive** \-ˈsim-ə-ˌlāt-iv, -lət-\ *adj*

[1]**as•sist** \ə-ˈsist\ *vb* **:** to give support or aid **:** HELP **[**Latin *assistere* "to help, stand by", from *ad-* + *sistere* "to stand"**]**

[2]**assist** *n* **1 :** an act of assistance **:** AID **2 :** the action of a player who by passing a ball or puck enables a teammate to make a putout or score a goal

as•sis•tance \ə-ˈsis-təns\ *n* **:** the act of assisting or the aid supplied **:** SUPPORT

as•sis•tant \ə-ˈsis-tənt\ *n* **:** one that assists **:** HELPER; *also* **:** one that serves in a subordinate capacity — **assistant** *adj*

as•size \ə-ˈsīz\ *n* **:** a session of an English superior court formerly held periodically for the trial of civil and criminal cases in most counties by judges traveling on circuit — usually used in pl. **[**Old French *assise* "session, settlement", from *asseoir* "to seat", from Latin *assidēre* "to sit beside"**]**

[1]**as•so•ci•ate** \ə-ˈsō-shē-ˌāt, -sē-ˌāt\ **1 :** to join or come together as partners, friends, or companions **2 :** to connect or bring (as ideas) together or into a relationship **3 :** to combine or join with other parts **:** UNITE **[**Latin *associare* "to unite", from *ad-* + *sociare* "to join", from *socius* "companion"**]**

[2]**as•so•ci•ate** \ə-ˈsō-shət; ə-ˈsō-shē-ət, -ˈsō-sē-, -ˌāt\ *n* **1 :** a fellow worker **:** COLLEAGUE **2 :** COMPANION 1, COMRADE **3** *often cap* **:** a degree conferred especially by a junior college ⟨*associate* in arts⟩ — **associate** *adj*

as•so•ci•a•tion \ə-ˌsō-sē-ˈā-shən, -ˌsō-shē-\ *n* **1 :** the act of associating **:** the state of being associated **2 :** an organization of persons having a common interest **:** SOCIETY **3 :** a feeling, memory, or thought connected with a person, place, or thing ⟨pleasant *associations* with the beach⟩ **4 :** the formation of polymers by linkage through hydrogen bonds **5 :** a major ecological unit characterized by essential uniformity — **as•so•ci•a•tion•al** \-shnəl, -shən-l\ *adj*

association football *n* **:** SOCCER

as•so•ci•a•tive \ə-ˈsō-shē-ˌāt-iv, -ˈsō-sē-, -ˈsō-shət-iv\ *adj* **1 :** of, relating to, or involved in association and especially mental association ⟨*associative* powers of the mind⟩ **2 :** dependent on or acquired by association or learning **3 :** combining or concerning the combination of mathematical elements in such a manner that when the order remains the same the result is independent of the grouping — **as•so•ci•a•tive•ly** *adv* — **as•so•cia•tiv•i•ty** \ə-ˌsō-shē-ə-ˈtiv-ət-ē, -ˌsō-sē-ə-, -ˌsō-shə-ˈtiv-\ *n*

associative neuron *n* **:** a neuron that transmits impulses along the path from a sensory neuron to a motor neuron

as•so•nance \ˈas-ə-nəns\ *n* **1 :** resemblance of sound in words or syllables **2 :** repetition of vowels without repetition of consonants (as in *story* and *holy*) used as an alternative to rhyme in verse **[**French, from Latin *assonare* "to answer with the same sound", from *ad-* + *sonare* "to sound"**]** — **as•so•nant** \-nənt\ *adj or n*

as soon as *conj* **:** immediately at or just after the time that ⟨left *as soon as* the meeting was over⟩

as•sort \ə-ˈsȯrt\ *vb* **1 :** to distribute into groups of a like kind **:** CLASSIFY **2 :** to agree in kind **:** HARMONIZE ⟨the outfit *assorts* well with your complexion⟩ **[**Middle French *assortir,* from *a-* "ad-" + *sorte* "sort"**]** — **as•sort•a•tive** \ə-ˈsȯrt-ət-iv\ *adj* — **as•sort•er** *n*

as•sort•ed \ə-ˈsȯrt-əd\ *adj* **1 :** consisting of various kinds **2 :** suited by nature, character, or design ⟨an ill-*assorted* pair⟩

as•sort•ment \ə-ˈsȯrt-mənt\ *n* **1 a :** arrangement in classes **b :** VARIETY **2 :** a collection of assorted things or persons

as•suage \ə-ˈswāj\ *vt* **1 :** to lessen the intensity of (as pain) **:** EASE **2 :** SLAKE 2, QUENCH ⟨*assuage* thirst with cool water⟩ **[**Old French *assouagier,* from Latin *ad-* + *suavis* "sweet, pleasant"**]** — **as•suage•ment** \-mənt\ *n*

as•sume \ə-ˈsüm\ *vb* **1 :** to take up or in or on **:** RECEIVE ⟨what values may *x assume*⟩ **2 a :** to take to or upon oneself ⟨*assume* a responsibility⟩ **b :** to put on (clothing) **:** DON **3 :** to take as one's right or possession **:** SEIZE **4 :** to put on in appearance only **:** FEIGN **5 :** to take for granted **:** SUPPOSE **[**Latin *assumere,* from *ad-* + *sumere* "to take up, take", from *sub-* "up" + *emere* "to take, buy"**]**

• **syn** ASSUME, PRESUME mean to suppose to be true or real. ASSUME may imply either reasonable grounds for supposing or a deliberate purpose in taking as definite something not actually settled or determined; PRESUME implies greater confidence in supposing without proof or justification.

as•sumed \ə-ˈsümd\ *adj* **1 a :** PRETENDED ⟨an *assumed* role⟩ **b :** FALSE ⟨an *assumed* name⟩ **2 :** taken for granted ⟨the *assumed* reason for absence⟩

as•sum•ing *adj* **:** ARROGANT 1, PRESUMPTUOUS

as•sump•tion \ə-ˈsəm-shən, -ˈsəmp-\ **1** *cap* **:** August 15 observed as a church festival in commemoration of the taking up of the Virgin Mary into heaven **2 :** a taking to or upon oneself **3 :** the act of laying claim to or taking possession of **4 a :** the supposition that something is true **b :** a fact or statement taken for granted **[**Latin *assumptio* "taking up", from *assumere* "to take up, assume"**]**

as•sur•ance \ə-ˈshu̇r-əns\ *n* **1 :** the act of assuring **:** PLEDGE **2 :** the state of being sure or certain **3 :** SAFETY 1 **4** *chiefly British* **:** INSURANCE 2 **5 :** SELF-RELIANCE **6 :** extreme self-confidence **:** PRESUMPTION

as•sure \ə-ˈshu̇r\ *vt* **1 :** INSURE 1 **2 :** REASSURE 2 ⟨tried to *assure* the worried neighbors⟩ **3 :** to make sure or certain **4 :** to inform positively ⟨can *assure* you of their dependability⟩ **[**Middle French *assurer,* from Medieval Latin *assecurare,* from Latin *ad-* + *securus* "secure"**]**

[1]**as•sured** \ə-ˈshu̇rd\ *adj* **1 :** characterized by certainty or security **:** GUARANTEED ⟨an *assured* market⟩ **2 a :** SELF-CONFIDENT ⟨an *assured* dancer⟩ **b :** SELF-SATISFIED **3 :** satisfied as to the certainty or truth of a matter **:** CONVINCED — **as•sur•ed•ly** \-ˈshu̇r-əd-lē\ *adv* — **as•sur•ed•ness** \-əd-nəs\ *n*

[2]**assured** *n* **:** a person whose life or property is insured

As•syr•i•an \ə-ˈsir-ē-ən\ *n* **1 :** a member of an ancient Semitic race forming the Assyrian nation **2 :** the Semitic language of the Assyrians — **Assyrian** *adj*

as•ta•tine \ˈas-tə-ˌtēn\ *n* **:** a radioactive chemical element discovered by bombarding bismuth with helium nuclei — see ELEMENT table **[**Greek *astatos* "unsteady", from *a-* + *statos* "standing", from *histanai* "to cause to stand"**]**

as•ter \ˈas-tər\ *n* **1 :** any of various mostly fall-blooming leafy-stemmed composite herbs usually with showy white, pink, purple, or yellow flower heads **2 :** a system of radiating fibers about a centrosome of a cell occurring especially during mitosis and meiosis **[**Latin, from Greek *astēr,* literally, "star"**]**

as•ter•isk \ˈas-tə-ˌrisk\ *n* **:** a character * used as a reference mark or to show the omission of letters or words **[**Late Latin *asteriscus,* from Greek *asteriskos,* literally, "little star", from *astēr* "star"**]** — **asterisk** *vt*

as•ter•ism \ˈas-tə-ˌriz-əm\ *n* **:** a star-shaped figure of light exhibited by some crystals and caused by reflection from internal imperfections

astern \ə-ˈstərn\ *adv* **1 :** behind a ship or airplane **:** in the rear **2 :** at or toward the stern of a ship or aircraft **3 :** BACKWARD

as•ter•oid \ˈas-tə-ˌrȯid\ *n* **:** one of thousands of small planets chiefly between Mars and Jupiter with diameters from a fraction of a kilometer to nearly 800 kilometers **[**Greek *asteroeidēs* "starlike", from *astēr* "star"**]**

as•the•nia \as-ˈthē-nē-ə\ *n* **:** lack or loss of strength **:** DEBILITY **[**Greek *asthenia,* from *asthenēs* "weak", from *a-* + *sthenos* "strength"**]**

as•then•ic \-ˈthen-ik\ *adj* **1 :** of, relating to, or exhibiting asthenia **:** WEAK **2 :** characterized by slender build and slight muscular development **:** ECTOMORPHIC

as•theno•sphere \as-ˈthen-ə-ˌsfiər\ *n* **:** a zone of the earth which lies beneath the lithosphere and within which material yields readily to persistent stresses **[**Greek *asthenēs* "weak" + English *sphere***]**

asth•ma \ˈaz-mə\ *n* **:** a condition often of allergic origin that is marked by labored breathing with wheezing, a feeling of tightness in the chest, and coughing **[**Medieval Latin *asma,* from Greek *asthma***]** — **asth•mat•ic** \az-ˈmat-ik\ *adj or n* — **asth-**

mat•i•cal•ly \-'mat-i-kə-lē, -klē\ *adv*
as though *conj* : as if
astig•ma•tism \ə-'stig-mə-ˌtiz-əm\ *n* : a defect of an optical system (as of the eye) that prevents light from focusing accurately and results in a blurred image or indistinct vision [2*a-* + Greek *stigma* "mark"] — **as•tig•mat•ic** \ˌas-tig-'mat-ik\ *adj* — **as•tig•mat•i•cal•ly** \-'mat-i-kə-lē, -klē\ *adj*
astir \ə-'stər\ *adj* **1** : being in a state of activity **2** : being out of bed : UP
as to *prep* **1** : with regard or reference to : as for : ABOUT ⟨at a loss *as to* how to explain the mistake⟩ **2** : according to : BY ⟨graded *as to* size and color⟩
as•ton•ish \ə-'stän-ish\ *vt* : to strike with sudden wonder : surprise greatly : AMAZE [probably from earlier *astony,* from Old French *estoner,* from Latin *ex-* + *tonare* "to thunder"] **syn** see SURPRISE
as•ton•ish•ing *adj* : causing astonishment : AMAZING — **as•ton•ish•ing•ly** \-'stän-i-shing-lē\ *adv*
as•ton•ish•ment \ə-'stän-ish-mənt\ *n* **1** : the state of being astonished **2** : a cause of amazement or wonder
as•tound \ə-'staund\ *vb* : to fill with bewilderment and wonder [Middle English *astoned,* past participle of *astonen* "to astonish", from Old French *estoner*] **syn** see SURPRISE
astrad•dle \ə-'strad-l\ *adv or prep* : ASTRIDE
as•trag•a•lus \ə-'strag-ə-ləs\ *n, pl* **-li** \-ˌlī, -ˌlē\ : a proximal bone of the tarsus [New Latin, from Greek *astragalos*]
as•tra•khan *or* **as•tra•chan** \'as-trə-kən, -ˌkan\ *n, often cap* **1** : karakul of Russian origin **2** : a cloth with a usually wool, curled, and looped pile resembling karakul [*Astrakhan,* Soviet Union]
as•tral \'as-trəl\ *adj* **1** : of or relating to the stars : STARRY **2** : of or relating to a cell aster **3 a** : VISIONARY **b** : elevated in station or position [Latin *astrum* "star", from Greek *astron*] — **as•tral•ly** *adv*
astray \ə-'strā\ *adv or adj* **1** : off the right path or route : STRAYING **2** : into error : MISTAKEN
1astride \ə-'strīd\ *adv* : with one leg on each side
2astride *prep* : on or above and with one leg on each side of
1as•trin•gent \ə-'strin-jənt\ *adj* **1** : able or tending to shrink body tissues ⟨*astringent* lotions⟩ ⟨an *astringent* fruit⟩ **2** : AUSTERE 1a ⟨an *astringent* manner⟩ [derived from Latin *astringere* "to bind fast, contract", from *ad-* + *stringere* "to bind tight"] — **as•trin•gen•cy** \-jən-sē\ *n* — **as•trin•gent•ly** *adv*
2astringent *n* : an astringent agent or substance
astro- *combining form* : star : heavens : astronomical ⟨*astro*physics⟩ [Greek *astron* "star"]
as•tro•labe \'as-trə-ˌlāb\ *n* : a compact instrument used to observe the positions of celestial bodies before the invention of the sextant [Medieval Latin *astrolabium,* derived from Greek *astrolabos,* from *astron* "star" + *lambanein* "to take"]
as•trol•o•ger \ə-'sträl-ə-jər\ *n* : one who practices astrology
as•trol•o•gy \-jē\ *n* : study of or divination based on the effect that the stars and their aspects and positions are held to have on human affairs — **as•tro•log•i•cal** \ˌas-trə-'läj-i-kəl\ *adj* — **as•tro•log•i•cal•ly** \-'läj-i-kə-lē, -klē\ *adv*
as•tro•naut \'as-trə-ˌnȯt, -ˌnät\ *n* : a traveler in a spacecraft; *also* : a trainee for spaceflight [*astro-* + *-naut* (as in *aeronaut*)] — **as•tro•nau•ti•cal** \ˌas-trə-'nȯt-i-kəl\ *adj* — **as•tro•nau•ti•cal•ly** \-i-kə-lē, -klē\ *adv*
as•tro•nau•tics \-'nȯt-iks\ *n* : the science of the construction and operation of spacecraft
as•tron•o•mer \ə-'strän-ə-mər\ *n* : one who is skilled in astronomy or who observes celestial phenomena
as•tro•nom•i•cal \ˌas-trə-'näm-i-kəl\ *or* **as•tro•nom•ic** \-'näm-ik\ *adj* **1** : of or relating to astronomy **2** : extremely or unimaginably large ⟨an *astronomical* amount of money⟩ — **as•tro•nom•i•cal•ly** \-'näm-i-kə-lē, -klē\ *adv*
astronomical unit *n* : a unit of length used in astronomy equal to the mean distance of the earth from the sun or about 150 million kilometers
as•tron•o•my \ə-'strän-ə-mē\ *n* : the science of the celestial bodies and of their physical characteristics, relative motions, composition, and history [Old French *astronomie,* from Latin *astronomia,* from Greek, from *astron* "star" + *nomos* "law"]
as•tro•phys•ics \ˌas-trə-'fiz-iks\ *n* : a branch of astronomy dealing with the physical and chemical makeup of the celestial bodies — **as•tro•phys•i•cal** \-'fiz-i-kəl\ *adj* — **as•tro•phys•i•cist** \-'fiz-ə-səst\ *n*
as•tute \ə-'stüt, a-, -'styüt\ *adj* : CLEVER ⟨an *astute* business person⟩; *also* : SLY 1 [Latin *astutus,* from *astus* "craft"] **syn** see SHREWD — **as•tute•ly** *adv* — **as•tute•ness** *n*
asun•der \ə-'sən-dər\ *adv or adj* **1** : into parts ⟨torn *asunder*⟩ **2** : apart from each other (as in position or nature)
1as well as *prep* : in addition to : BESIDES ⟨the coach, *as well as* the team, is ready for the game⟩
2as well as *adv* : and in addition : and moreover ⟨brave *as well as* loyal⟩
as yet *adv* : up to the present time : YET
asy•lum \ə-'sī-ləm\ *n* **1** : a place of refuge and protection giving shelter to criminals and debtors **2** : a place of retreat and security : SHELTER **3** : protection afforded by or as if by an asylum : REFUGE ⟨a political refugee given *asylum* in the embassy⟩ **4** : an institution for the relief or care of the destitute or afflicted and especially the insane [Latin, from Greek *asylon,* from *asylos* "inviolable", from *a-* + *sylon* "right of seizure"]
asym•met•ric \ˌā-sə-'me-trik\ *adj* : not symmetrical — **asym•met•ri•cal** \-tri-kəl\ *adj* — **asym•met•ri•cal•ly** \-tri-kə-lē, -klē\ *adv* — **asym•me•try** \'ā-'sim-ə-trē\ *n*
as•ymp•tote \'as-əm-ˌtōt, -əmp-\ *n* : a straight line that is approached more and more closely by a curve that never coincides with it no matter how far the curve is extended [Greek *asymptōtos* "not meeting", from *a-* + *sympiptein* "to meet", from *syn-* + *piptein* "to fall"] — **as•ymp•tot•ic** \ˌas-əm-'tät-ik, -əmp-\ *adj*

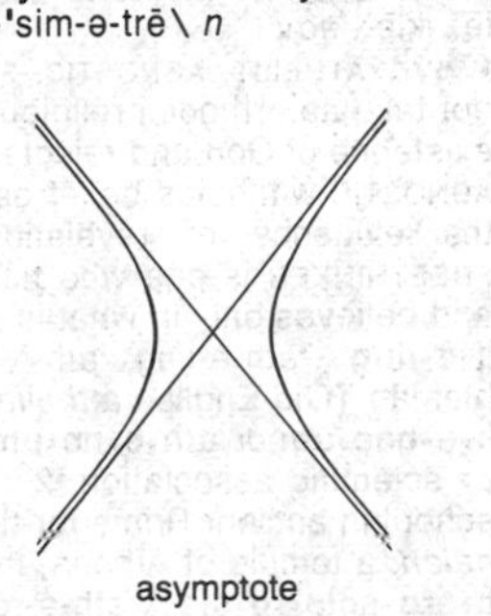

asymptote

asyn•de•ton \ə-'sin-də-ˌtän\ *n, pl* **-de•tons** *or* **-de•ta** \-dət-ə\ : omission of the connectives ordinarily expected (as in *I came, I saw, I conquered*) [Late Latin, from Greek, from *asyndetos* "unconnected", from *a-* + *syndein* "to bind together", from *syn-* + *dein* "to bind"] — **as•yn•det•ic** \ˌas-n-'det-ik\ *adj* — **as•yn•det•i•cal•ly** \-'det-i-kə-lē, -klē\ *adv*
at \ət, at, 'at\ *prep* — used as a function word to indicate (1) location in space or time ⟨staying *at* a hotel⟩ ⟨be here *at* six⟩ ⟨sick *at* heart⟩, (2) a goal ⟨aim *at* a target⟩ ⟨laugh *at* them⟩, (3) a condition ⟨*at* work⟩ ⟨*at* liberty⟩ ⟨*at* ease⟩, (4) a means, cause, or source ⟨sold *at* auction⟩ ⟨angry *at* this answer⟩ ⟨suffered *at* their hands⟩, or (5) a rate, degree, or position in a scale or series ⟨drove *at* 40 kilometers an hour⟩ ⟨retire *at* 65⟩ [Old English *æt*]
at- — see AD-
at all \ət-'ȯl, ə-'tȯl, at-'ȯl\ *adv* : in any way or respect : to the least extent or degree : under any circumstances ⟨not *at all* likely⟩ ⟨doesn't smoke *at all*⟩
at•a•rac•tic \ˌat-ə-'rak-tik\ *or* **at•a•rax•ic** \-'rak-sik\ *n* : a tranquilizer drug [Greek *ataraktos* "calm", from *a-* + *tarassein* "to disturb"] — **ataractic** *adj*
at•a•vism \'at-ə-ˌviz-əm\ *n* **1** : recurrence in an organism of a character typical of ancestors more remote than the parents usually due to recombination of ancestral genes **2** : an individual or character manifesting atavism [French *atavisme,* from Latin *atavus* "ancestor"] — **at•a•vis•tic** \ˌat-ə-'vis-tik\ *adj*
atax•ia \ə-'tak-sē-ə, ā-\ *n* : inability to coordinate voluntary muscular movements [Greek, "confusion", from *a-* + *tassein* "to put in order"] — **atax•ic** \-sik\ *adj*
ate *past of* EAT
1-ate \ət, ˌāt\ *n suffix* **1** : one acted upon (in a specified way) ⟨distill*ate*⟩ **2** : chemical compound derived from a (specified) compound or element; *esp* : salt or ester of an acid with a name ending in *-ic* ⟨bor*ate*⟩ [Latin *-atus, -atum,* masculine and neuter of *-atus,* past participle ending]
2-ate *n suffix* **1** : office : function : rank : group of persons holding a (specified) office or rank ⟨professor*ate*⟩ **2** : state : dominion : jurisdiction ⟨emir*ate*⟩ ⟨khan*ate*⟩ [Latin *-atus*]
3-ate *adj suffix* : marked by having ⟨chord*ate*⟩ [Latin *-atus,* past participle ending]

\ə\ **abut**	\au̇\ **out**	\i\ **tip**	\ȯ\ **saw**	\u̇\ **foot**
\ər\ **further**	\ch\ **chin**	\ī\ **life**	\ȯi\ **coin**	\y\ **yet**
\a\ **mat**	\e\ **pet**	\j\ **job**	\th\ **thin**	\yü\ **few**
\ā\ **take**	\ē\ **easy**	\ng\ **sing**	\t͟h\ **this**	\yu̇\ **cure**
\ä\ **cot, cart**	\g\ **go**	\ō\ **bone**	\ü\ **food**	\zh\ **vision**

4-ate \ˌāt\ *vb suffix* **1 :** cause to be modified or affected by ⟨camphor*ate*⟩ **2 :** cause to become ⟨activ*ate*⟩ **3 :** furnish with ⟨aer*ate*⟩ [Middle English *-aten,* from Latin *-atus,* past participle ending]

ate•lier \ˌat-l-ˈyā\ *n* **1 :** an artist's or designer's studio **2 :** WORKSHOP [French]

a tem•po \ä-ˈtem-pō\ *adv or adj* **:** in time — used as a direction in music to return to the original rate of speed [Italian]

Ath•a•na•sian Creed \ˌath-ə-ˌnā-zhən-, -ˌnā-shən-\ *n* **:** a Christian creed originating in Europe about A.D. 400 and relating especially to the Trinity and Incarnation [*Athanasius,* died 373, bishop of Alexandria]

athe•ism \ˈā-thē-ˌiz-əm\ *n* **:** the belief that there is no God **:** denial of the existence of a supreme being [Middle French *athéisme,* from Greek *atheos* "godless", from *a-* + *theos* "god"]

athe•ist \-thē-əst\ *n* **:** a person who believes there is no God — **athe•is•tic** \ˌā-thē-ˈis-tik\ *adj* — **athe•is•ti•cal•ly** \-ˈis-ti-kə-lē, -klē\ *adv*

• **syn** ATHEIST, AGNOSTIC, FREETHINKER mean one who does not take an orthodox religious position. An ATHEIST denies the existence of God and rejects all religious faith and practice; an AGNOSTIC withholds belief because of unwillingness to accept the evidence of revelation and spiritual experience; a FREETHINKER is one who has lost or rejected traditional faith and believes only in what is rational and credible.

ath•e•ling \ˈath-ə-ling, ˈath-\ *n* **:** an Anglo-Saxon prince or nobleman [Old English *ætheling,* from *æthelu* "nobility"]

ath•e•nae•um *or* **ath•e•ne•um** \ˌath-ə-ˈnē-əm\ *n* **1 :** a literary or scientific association **2 :** LIBRARY 1 [Latin *Athenaeum,* a school in ancient Rome for the study of arts, from Greek *Athēnaion,* a temple of Athena, from *Athēnē* "Athena"]

ath•ero•scle•ro•sis \ˌath-ə-rō-sklə-ˈrō-səs\ *n* **:** an arteriosclerosis in which fatty substances are deposited in the inner layer of the arteries [Latin *atheroma* "tumor containing matter resembling gruel", from Greek *athērōma,* from *athēra* "gruel"] — **ath•ero•scle•rot•ic** \-sklə-ˈrät-ik\ *adj*

athirst \ə-ˈthərst\ *adj* **1** *archaic* **:** THIRSTY **2 :** having a strong desire **:** EAGER [Old English *ofthyrst,* past participle of *ofthyrstan* "to suffer from thirst", from *of* "off, from" + *thyrstan* "to thirst"]

ath•lete \ˈath-ˌlēt\ *n* **:** a person who is trained in or good at games and exercises that require physical skill, endurance, and strength [Latin *athleta,* from Greek *athlētēs,* from *athlein* "to contend for a prize", from *athlon* "prize, contest"]

athlete's foot *n* **:** ringworm of the feet

ath•let•ic \ath-ˈlet-ik\ *adj* **1 :** of, relating to, or characteristic of athletes or athletics **2 :** VIGOROUS 1, ACTIVE **3 :** characterized by heavy frame, large chest, and powerful muscular development **4 :** used by athletes — **ath•let•i•cal•ly** \-ˈlet-i-kə-lē, -klē\ *adv*

ath•let•ics \ath-ˈlet-iks\ *n sing or pl* **:** games, sports, and exercises requiring strength and skill

athletic supporter *n* **:** a supporter for the genitals worn by men participating in sports or other strenuous activities

-athon \ə-ˌthän\ *n combining form* **:** contest of endurance [*marathon*]

1athwart \ə-ˈthwȯrt, *nautical often* -ˈthȯrt\ *adv* **:** across especially in an oblique direction

2athwart *prep* **1 :** ACROSS **2 :** in opposition to

atilt \ə-ˈtilt\ *adj or adv* **:** in a tilted position

-a•tion \ˈā-shən\ *n suffix* **:** action or process **:** something connected with an action or process ⟨discolor*ation*⟩ ⟨flirt*ation*⟩ [Latin *-ation-, -atio,* from *-atus* "-ate" + *-ion-, -io* "-ion"]

-a•tive \ˌāt-iv, ət-\ *adj suffix* **1 :** of, relating to, or connected with ⟨authorit*ative*⟩ **2 :** tending to ⟨talk*ative*⟩ [Latin *-ativus,* from *-atus* "-ate" + *-ivus* "-ive"]

At•lan•tic salmon \ət-ˈlant-ik-\ *n* **:** SALMON 1a

Atlantic time *n* **:** the time of the 4th time zone west of Greenwich that includes the Canadian Maritime provinces

at•las \ˈat-ləs\ *n* **1 a :** a book of maps often including descriptive text **b :** a book of tables, charts, or illustrations ⟨an *atlas* of anatomy⟩ **2 :** the first vertebra of the neck [*Atlas,* a Titan of Greek mythology]

△ **origin** Atlas was one of the Titans or giants of Greek mythology, whose rule of the world in an early age was overthrown by Zeus in a mighty battle. Atlas was believed to be responsible for holding up the sky, a task which he tried unsuccessfully to have Hercules assume. In his published collection of maps, the 16th century Flemish cartographer Gerhardus Mercator included on the title page a picture of Atlas supporting the heavens, and he gave the book the title *Atlas.* Other early collections of maps subsequently included similar pictures of Atlas, and such books came to be called *atlases.*

at•mo•sphere \ˈat-mə-ˌsfiər\ *n* **1 a :** the whole mass of air surrounding the earth **b :** a gaseous mass surrounding a celestial body (as a planet) **2 :** the air in a particular place ⟨the stuffy *atmosphere* of this room⟩ **3 :** a surrounding influence or environment ⟨the home *atmosphere*⟩ **4 :** a unit of pressure equal to the pressure of the air at sea level or about 14.7 pounds per square inch (about 10 newtons per square centimeter) [Greek *atmos* "vapor" + Latin *sphaera* "sphere"] — **at•mo•spher•ic** \ˌat-mə-ˈsfiər-ik, -ˈsfer-\ *adj* — **at•mo•spher•i•cal•ly** \-i-kə-lē, -klē\ *adv*

at•mo•spher•ics \ˌat-mə-ˈsfiər-iks, -ˈsfer-\ *n pl* **:** static produced by atmospheric electrical phenomena (as lightning); *also* **:** the electrical phenomena causing such disturbances

atoll \ˈa-ˌtȯl, -ˌtäl, -ˌtōl, ˈā-\ *n* **:** a ring-shaped coral island or string of islands consisting of a coral reef surrounding a lagoon [*atolu,* native name in the Maldive islands]

at•om \ˈat-əm\ *n* **1 :** a tiny particle **:** BIT **2 a :** the smallest particle of an element that can exist either alone or in combination ⟨an *atom* of hydrogen⟩ **b :** ATOMIC ENERGY [Latin *atomus* "indivisible particle", from Greek *atomos,* from *atomos* "indivisible", from *a-* + *temnein* "to cut"]

△ **origin** Some ancient philosophers believed that matter is infinitely divisible, that any particle, no matter how small, can always be divided into smaller particles. Others believed that there must be a limit, that everything in the universe must be made up of tiny indivisible particles. Such a hypothetical particle was called in Greek *atomos,* which means "indivisible". According to modern atomic theory, all matter is made up of tiny particles called *atoms* after the ancient Greek *atomos,* and the atoms of any one chemical element are identical. Although the atom is the smallest particle of an element that has the characteristics of that element, it has turned out that atoms are not indivisible after all. Indeed, the splitting of atoms has been used, as in the explosion of atom bombs, to produce vast amounts of energy.

atom bomb *n* **:** a bomb whose violent explosive power is due to the sudden release of atomic energy; *esp* **:** a bomb whose energy results from the splitting of nuclei of a heavy chemical element (as plutonium or uranium) by neutrons in a very rapid chain reaction — called also *fission bomb* — **at•om-bomb** \ˌat-əm-ˈbäm\ *vt*

atom•ic \ə-ˈtäm-ik\ *adj* **1 :** of, relating to, or concerned with atoms, atomic energy, or atom bombs **2 :** extremely small **:** MINUTE **3 :** existing in the state of separate atoms ⟨*atomic* hydrogen⟩ — **atom•i•cal•ly** \-i-kə-lē, -klē\ *adv*

atomic age *n* **:** the period of history characterized by the use of atomic energy

atomic bomb *n* **:** ATOM BOMB

atomic clock *n* **:** a precision clock that depends for its operation on an electrical oscillator regulated by the natural vibration frequencies of an atomic system (as a cesium atom)

atomic energy *n* **:** energy that can be liberated by changes in the nucleus of an atom (as by fission of a heavy nucleus or fusion of light nuclei into heavier ones with accompanying loss of mass)

atomic mass *n* **:** the mass of any species of atom usually expressed in atomic mass units

atomic mass unit *n* **:** a unit of mass for expressing masses of atoms, molecules, or nuclear particles equal to 1/12 of the atomic mass of the most abundant isotope of carbon

atomic number *n* **:** a number that is characteristic of a chemical element and represents the number of protons in the nucleus

atomic pile *n* **:** REACTOR 2b

atom•ics \ə-ˈtäm-iks\ *n pl* **:** the science of atoms especially when involving atomic energy

atomic theory *n* **1 :** a theory of the nature of matter: all material substances are composed of minute particles or atoms of a comparatively small number of kinds and all the atoms of the same kind are uniform in size, weight, and other properties **2 :** any of several theories of the structure of the atom; *esp* **:** one holding that the atom is composed essentially of a small positively charged comparatively heavy nucleus surrounded by a comparatively large arrangement of electrons

atomic weight *n* **:** the relative weight of an atom of a chemical element in comparison with that of an oxygen atom assigned a relative weight of 16 or a carbon atom assigned a relative weight of 12 taken as a standard

at·om·ize \'at-ə-ˌmīz\ *vt* **1** : to reduce to minute particles or to a fine spray **2** : to treat as made up of many discrete units **3** : to subject to atom-bombing — **at·om·iza·tion** \ˌat-ə-mə-'zā-shən\ *n*

at·om·iz·er \'at-ə-ˌmī-zər\ *n* : a device for atomizing a liquid (as a perfume or disinfectant)

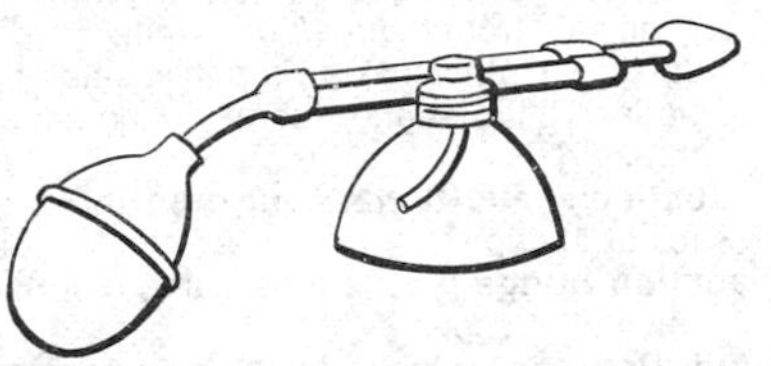
atomizer

atom smasher *n* : ACCELERATOR b

aton·al \'ā-'tōn-l, 'a-\ *adj* : characterized by avoidance of traditional musical tonality — **ato·nal·i·ty** \ˌā-tō-'nal-ət-ē\ *n* — **aton·al·ly** \'ā-'tōn-l-ē, 'a-\ *adv*

atone \ə-'tōn\ *vb* : to do something to make up for a wrong done : make amends [Middle English *atonen* "to become reconciled", from *at on* "in harmony", from *at* + *on* "one"]

atone·ment \-mənt\ *n* **1** : the reconciliation of God and humanity held by Christians to have come through the death of Jesus Christ **2** : reparation for an offense or injury : SATISFACTION

[1]**atop** \ə-'täp\ *prep* : on top of

[2]**atop** *adv* : on, to, or at the top

ATP \ˌā-ˌtē-'pē, ā-'tē-ˌpē\ *n* : a nucleotide that is a derivative of adenosine and supplies energy for many processes of living cells by undergoing conversion to ADP and surrendering a phosphate group [adenosine *tri*phosphate]

atri·al \'ā-trē-əl\ *adj* : of or relating to an atrium

atrio·ven·tric·u·lar \ˌā-trē-ō-ven-'trik-yə-lər, -vən-\ *adj* : of, relating to, or located between an atrium and ventricle of the heart

atri·um \'ā-trē-əm\ *n, pl* **atria** \-trē-ə\ *also* **atri·ums** **1** : the central hall of a Roman house **2** : an anatomical cavity or passage; *esp* : the chamber or either of the chambers of the heart that receives blood from the veins [Latin]

atro·cious \ə-'trō-shəs\ *adj* **1** : extremely wicked, brutal, or cruel **2** : APPALLING ⟨the *atrocious* weapons of modern war⟩ **3 a** : utterly revolting ⟨*atrocious* working conditions⟩ **b** : of very bad quality ⟨*atrocious* handwriting⟩ [Latin *atroc-, atrox* "gloomy, atrocious", from *ater* "black"] **syn** see OUTRAGEOUS — **atro·cious·ly** *adv* — **atro·cious·ness** *n*

atroc·i·ty \ə-'träs-ət-ē\ *n, pl* **-ties** **1** : the quality or state of being atrocious **2** : an atrocious act, object, or situation

[1]**at·ro·phy** \'a-trə-fē\ *n, pl* **-phies** : decrease in size or wasting away of a body part or tissue [Late Latin *atrophia,* from Greek, from *atrophos* "ill fed", from *a-* + *trephein* "to nourish"] — **atroph·ic** \ā-'trō-fik, 'ā-'\ *adj*

[2]**at·ro·phy** \'a-trə-fē, -ˌfī\ *vi* **-phied; -phy·ing** : to undergo atrophy

at·ro·pine \'a-trə-ˌpēn\ *n* : a poisonous white crystalline compound $C_{17}H_{23}NO_3$ from belladonna and related plants used especially to relieve spasms and to dilate the pupil of the eye [New Latin *Atropa,* genus name of belladonna, from Greek *Atropos,* one of the Fates]

at·tach \ə-'tach\ *vb* **1** : to take money or property by legal authority especially to secure payment of a debt ⟨*attach* one's salary⟩ **2** : to tie or bind by feelings of affection ⟨they were *attached* to their dog⟩ **3** : to fasten to something (as by tying or gluing) ⟨*attach* a label to a package⟩ **4** : to think of as belonging to something : ATTRIBUTE ⟨*attach* no importance to a remark⟩ **5** : to be associated or connected ⟨the interest that naturally *attaches* to a statement by the president⟩ [Middle French *attacher,* from Old French *estachier,* from *estache* "stake", of Germanic origin] — **at·tach·able** \-ə-bəl\ *adj*

at·ta·ché \ˌat-ə-'shā, ˌa-ˌta-, ə-ˌta-\ *n* **1** : a technical expert on the diplomatic staff of a country at a foreign capital ⟨a military *attaché*⟩ **2** : ATTACHÉ CASE [French, past participle of *attacher*]

at·ta·ché case \ə-'tash-ˌā-; ˌat-ə-'shā-, ˌa-ˌta-\ *n* : a small suitcase used especially for carrying papers and documents

at·tach·ment \ə-'tach-mənt\ *n* **1** : a seizure by legal process or the writ commanding such seizure **2** : the state of being personally attached : FIDELITY, FONDNESS **3** : a device that can be attached to a machine or implement ⟨*attachments* for a vacuum cleaner⟩ **4** : the physical connection by which one thing is attached to another **5** : the process of physically attaching

[1]**at·tack** \ə-'tak\ *vb* **1** : to set upon forcefully **2** : to threaten (a piece in chess) with immediate capture **3** : to use unfriendly or bitter words against **4** : to begin to affect or to act upon injuriously ⟨*attacked* by fever⟩ **5** : to set to work on ⟨*attack* a problem⟩ [Middle French *attaquer,* from Italian *attaccare* "to attach, attack", of Germanic origin] — **at·tack·er** *n*

• **syn** ASSAIL, ASSAULT, STORM: ATTACK implies taking the initiative in a struggle; ASSAIL implies trying to break down resistance by repeated blows or shots; ASSAULT suggests a direct attempt to overpower by suddenness and violence; STORM implies trying to overrun or capture a defended position by the irresistible weight of rapidly advancing numbers.

[2]**attack** *n* **1** : the act of attacking : ASSAULT **2** : the beginning of destructive action (as by a chemical agent) **3** : a setting to work : START **4** : a fit of sickness; *esp* : an active episode of a chronic or recurrent disease **5 a** : an offensive or scoring action in a game **b** : offensive players on a team

at·tain \ə-'tān\ *vb* **1** : GAIN 1, ACHIEVE **2** : to come into possession of : OBTAIN **3** : to arrive or arrive at ⟨*attain* the top of the mountain⟩ ⟨*attain* to maturity⟩ [Old French *ataindre,* from Latin *attingere,* from *ad-* + *tangere* "to touch"] — **at·tain·abil·i·ty** \ə-ˌtā-nə-'bil-ət-ē\ *n* — **at·tain·able** \-'tā-nə-bəl\ *adj* — **at·tain·able·ness** *n*

at·tain·der \ə-'tān-dər\ *n* : the taking away of a person's civil rights when the person has been declared an outlaw or sentenced to death [Middle French *ataindre* "to attain, accuse"]

at·tain·ment \ə-'tān-mənt\ *n* **1** : the act of attaining : the state of being attained **2** : something attained : ACCOMPLISHMENT

at·tar \'at-ər, 'a-ˌtär\ *n* : a fragrant essential oil (as from rose petals) [Persian *'atir* "perfumed", from Arabic, from *'itr* "perfume"]

[1]**at·tempt** \ə-'tempt\ *vt* : to make an effort to do, accomplish, or solve ⟨*attempt* to swim the river⟩ [Latin *attemptare,* from *ad-* + *temptare* "to touch, try"] **syn** see TRY

[2]**attempt** *n* : the act or an instance of attempting; *esp* : an unsuccessful effort

at·tend \ə-'tend\ *vb* **1** : to look after : take charge of ⟨*attend* to your own work⟩ **2** : to go or stay with as a servant, nurse, or companion ⟨royalty *attended* by a court⟩ **3** : to be present at ⟨*attend* a party⟩ **4** : to be present with : ACCOMPANY ⟨illness *attended* by fever⟩ **5** : to pay attention : HEED [Old French *atendre,* from Latin *attendere,* from *ad-* + *tendere* "to stretch"]

at·ten·dance \ə-'ten-dənts\ *n* **1** : the act of attending ⟨a doctor in *attendance*⟩ **2 a** : the persons or number of persons attending **b** : the number of times a person attends

[1]**at·ten·dant** \ə-'ten-dənt\ *adj* : accompanying or following as a consequence

[2]**attendant** *n* : one that attends another to perform a service; *esp* : an employee who waits on customers ⟨a parking-lot *attendant*⟩

at·ten·tion \ə-'ten-chən\ *n* **1** : the act or the power of fixing one's mind upon something : careful listening or watching **2** : careful consideration of something with a view to taking action on it ⟨a matter requiring *attention*⟩ **3** : an act of kindness, care, or courtesy **4** : a position taken by a soldier with heels together, body erect, arms at the side, and eyes to the front — often used as a command [Latin *attentio,* from *attendere* "to attend"] — **at·ten·tion·al** \ə-'tench-nəl, -'ten-chən-l\ *adj*

at·ten·tive \ə-'tent-iv\ *adj* **1** : paying attention : OBSERVANT **2** : heedful of the comfort of others : COURTEOUS — **at·ten·tive·ly** *adv* — **at·ten·tive·ness** *n*

at·ten·u·ate \ə-'ten-yə-ˌwāt\ *vb* : to make or become thin or less (as in density, force, value, or vitality) ⟨*attenuate* a virus⟩ ⟨*attenuate* oil by heating⟩ ⟨sorrows *attenuate* with time⟩ [Latin *attenuare,* from *ad-* + *tenuis* "thin"] — **at·ten·u·a·tion** \ə-ˌten-yə-'wā-shən\ *n*

at·test \ə-'test\ *vb* **1** : to indicate to be true or genuine especially by signing as a witness ⟨*attest* a will⟩ **2** : to be proof of : SHOW ⟨my conduct *attests* my innocence⟩ **3** : TESTIFY ⟨*attest* to the truth of the statement⟩ [Middle French *attester,* from Latin *attestari,* from *ad-* + *testis* "witness"] — **at·tes·ta·tion** \ˌa-ˌtes-ˈtā-shən\ *n* — **at·test·er** \ə-ˈtes-tər\ *n*

at·tic \ˈat-ik\ *n* **1 :** a low story or wall at the top of a classical facade **2 :** a room or a space immediately below the roof of a building [French *attique,* from *attique* "of Attica", from Latin *Atticus*]

△ **origin** The ancient Greek city-state of Athens included the whole of the Attic peninsula, the region called Attica. Typical of the Athenian or Attic style of architecture is the use of rectangular columns projecting from, but attached to, the wall. These take the place of the freestanding and usually rounded pillars common in other architectural styles. Occasionally the large columns at the front of a building are topped by a similar but smaller decorative structure, usually in the Attic style. The French named this structure *attique.* The English borrowed the name, respelling it according to a common pattern. From its originally specialized sense, *attic* was extended to cover the top story, just under the roof, of any building.

At·tic \ˈat-ik\ *adj* **1 :** of or relating to Athens **2 :** marked by simplicity, purity, and refinement [Latin *Atticus* "of Attica, Athenian", from Greek *Attikos,* from *Attikē* "Attica, Greece"]

[1]at·tire \ə-ˈtīr\ *vt* **:** to put garments on **:** DRESS; *esp* **:** to clothe in rich garments [Old French *atirier,* from *a-* "ad-" + *tire* "order, rank", of Germanic origin]

[2]attire *n* **:** DRESS, CLOTHES; *esp* **:** fine clothing

at·ti·tude \ˈat-ə-ˌtüd, -tyüd\ *n* **1 :** the arrangement of the body or figure **:** POSTURE **2 :** a mental position or feeling regarding a fact or state **3 :** the position of something (as an aircraft or spacecraft) in relation to a reference point (as the horizon or a star) [French, from Italian *attitudine,* literally, "aptitude", from Late Latin *aptitudo*]

at·ti·tu·di·nize \ˌat-ə-ˈtüd-n-ˌīz, -ˈtyüd-\ *vi* **:** to assume an affected mental attitude **:** POSE

at·to- \ˈat-ō\ *combining form* **:** one quintillionth (10^{-18}) part of [Danish or Norwegian *atten* "eighteen"]

at·tor·ney \ə-ˈtər-nē\ *n, pl* **-neys :** one who is legally appointed by another to transact business for him; *esp* **:** LAWYER [Middle French *atorné,* past participle of *atorner* "to transfer homage or service", from *a-* "ad-" + *torner* "to turn"]

attorney general *n, pl* **attorneys general** *or* **attorney generals :** the chief law officer of a nation or state who represents the government in legal matters and serves as its principal legal advisor

at·tract \ə-ˈtrakt\ *vb* **:** to cause to approach or adhere: as **a :** to pull to or toward oneself or itself ⟨a magnet *attracts* iron⟩ **b :** to draw by appealing to interest or feeling ⟨*attract* attention⟩ [Latin *attrahere,* from *ad-* + *trahere* "to draw"]

at·trac·tant \ə-ˈtrak-tənt\ *n* **:** something that attracts; *esp* **:** a substance (as a pheromone) that attracts animals (as insects)

at·trac·tion \ə-ˈtrak-shən\ *n* **1 a :** the act, process, or power of attracting **b :** a feature that attracts; *esp* **:** personal charm or beauty **2 :** a force acting mutually between particles of matter, tending to draw them together, and resisting their separation

at·trac·tive \ə-ˈtrak-tiv\ *adj* **:** having the power or quality of attracting; *esp* **:** CHARMING, PLEASING ⟨an *attractive* smile⟩ — **at·trac·tive·ly** *adv* — **at·trac·tive·ness** *n*

[1]at·tri·bute \ˈa-trə-ˌbyüt\ *n* **1 :** an inherent characteristic or quality **2 :** an object closely associated with a specific person, thing, or office ⟨crown and scepter are *attributes* of royalty⟩ **3 :** a word ascribing a quality; *esp* **:** ADJECTIVE [Latin *attributus,* past participle of *attribuere* "to attribute", from *ad-* + *tribuere* "to bestow"] **syn** see QUALITY

[2]at·trib·ute \ə-ˈtrib-yət\ *vt* **1 :** to explain by way of cause ⟨*attribute* their success to hard work⟩ **2 a :** to regard as characteristic of a person or thing ⟨*attributed* the worst motives to them⟩ **b :** to consider to have originated in an indicated fashion **syn** see ASCRIBE — **at·trib·ut·able** \-yət-ə-bəl\ *adj* — **at·trib·ut·er** *n*

at·tri·bu·tion \ˌa-trə-ˈbyü-shən\ *n* **:** the act of attributing; *also* **:** an ascribed quality, character, or right

at·trib·u·tive \ə-ˈtrib-yət-iv\ *adj* **:** relating to or of the nature of an attribute; *esp* **:** joined directly to a modified noun without a linking verb ⟨*red* in *red hair* is an *attributive* adjective⟩ — compare PREDICATE — **attributive** *n* — **at·trib·u·tive·ly** *adv*

at·tri·tion \ə-ˈtrish-ən\ *n* **1 :** the act of wearing or grinding down by friction **2 :** the act of weakening or exhausting by constant harassment or abuse **3 :** gradual reduction of personnel as a result of resignation, retirement, or death [Latin *attritio,* from *atterere* "to rub against", from *ad-* + *terere* "to rub"] — **at·tri·tion·al** \-ˈtrish-nəl, -ən-l\ *adj*

at·tune \ə-ˈtün, -ˈtyün\ *vt* **:** to bring into harmony **:** TUNE — **at·tune·ment** \-mənt\ *n*

atyp·i·cal \ā-ˈtip-i-kəl, ˈā-ˈ\ *adj* **:** not typical **:** IRREGULAR — **atyp·i·cal·ly** \-kə-lē, -klē\ *adv*

au·burn \ˈȯ-bərn\ *adj* **:** of a reddish brown color ⟨*auburn* hair⟩ [Middle French *auborne* "blond", from Medieval Latin *alburnus* "whitish", from Latin *albus* "white"]

[1]auc·tion \ˈȯk-shən\ *n* **:** a public sale of property to the highest bidder [Latin *auctio,* literally, "increase", from *augēre* "to increase"]

[2]auction *vt* **auc·tioned; auc·tion·ing** \-shə-ning, -shning\ **:** to sell at auction

auction bridge *n* **:** a bridge game differing from contract bridge only in the scoring

auc·tion·eer \ˌȯk-shə-ˈniər\ *n* **:** a person who conducts an auction — **auctioneer** *vt*

auc·to·ri·al \ȯk-ˈtōr-ē-əl, -ˈtȯr-\ *adj* **:** of or relating to an author

au·da·cious \ȯ-ˈdā-shəs\ *adj* **1 a :** FEARLESS, DARING, ADVENTUROUS **b :** recklessly bold **:** RASH **2 :** INSOLENT, IMPUDENT [Middle French *audacieux,* from *audace* "boldness", derived from Latin *audax* "bold", from *audēre* "to dare", from *avidus* "eager, avid"] — **au·da·cious·ly** *adv* — **au·da·cious·ness** *n*

au·dac·i·ty \ȯ-ˈdas-ət-ē\ *n, pl* **-ties 1 :** DARING, BOLDNESS **2 :** a disrespectful or insolent attitude **syn** see TEMERITY

au·di·ble \ˈȯd-ə-bəl\ *adj* **:** loud enough to be heard [Latin *audire* "to hear"] — **au·di·bil·i·ty** \ˌȯd-ə-ˈbil-ət-ē\ *n* — **au·di·bly** \ˈȯd-ə-blē\ *adv*

au·di·ence \ˈȯd-ē-əns\ *n* **1 :** an assembled group that listens or watches (as at a play) **2 :** an opportunity of being heard; *esp* **:** a formal interview with a person of high rank **3 :** those of the general public who give attention to something said, done, or written ⟨the radio *audience*⟩ ⟨the *audience* for a new novel⟩ [Middle French, from Latin *audientia,* from *audire* "to hear"]

[1]au·dio \ˈȯd-ē-ˌō\ *adj* **1 :** of or relating to electrical or other vibrational frequencies corresponding to normally audible sound waves which are of frequencies approximately from 15 to 20,000 hertz **2 a :** of or relating to sound or its reproduction and especially high-fidelity reproduction **b :** relating to or used in the transmission or reception of sound — compare VIDEO

[2]audio *n* **1 :** the transmission, reception, or reproduction of sound **2 :** the section of television equipment that deals with sound

audio- *combining form* **1 :** hearing ⟨*audio*meter⟩ **2 :** sound ⟨*audio*phile⟩ **3 :** auditory and ⟨*audio*visual⟩ [Latin *audire* "to hear"]

au·di·om·e·ter \ˌȯd-ē-ˈäm-ət-ər\ *n* **:** an instrument used in measuring acuteness of hearing — **au·dio·met·ric** \ˌȯd-ē-ə-ˈme-trik\ *adj* — **au·di·om·e·try** \ˌȯd-ē-ˈäm-ə-trē\ *n*

au·dio·phile \ˈȯd-ē-ō-ˌfīl\ *n* **:** one who is enthusiastic about high-fidelity sound reproduction

au·dio·vi·su·al \ˌȯd-ē-ō-ˈvizh-wəl, -ˈvizh-ə-wəl, -ˈvizh-əl\ *adj* **:** of, relating to, or making use of both hearing and sight ⟨*audiovisual* teaching aids⟩

au·dio·vi·su·als \-wəlz, -əlz\ *n pl* **:** audiovisual instructional materials

[1]aud·it \ˈȯd-ət\ *n* **:** a thorough examination and verification of accounts and account books especially of a business or society; *also* **:** the final report of such an examination [Latin *auditus* "act of hearing", from *audire* "to hear"]

[2]audit *vt* **:** to make an audit of ⟨*audit* accounts⟩

[1]au·di·tion \ȯ-ˈdish-ən\ *n* **1 :** the power or sense of hearing **2 :** a critical hearing; *esp* **:** a trial performance to appraise an entertainer's merits

[2]audition *vb* **-di·tioned; -di·tion·ing** \-ˈdish-ning, -ə-ning\ **1 :** to test in an audition ⟨*audition* a new trumpeter⟩ **2 :** to give a trial performance ⟨the singers *auditioned* for the choir⟩

au·di·tor \ˈȯd-ət-ər\ *n* **1 :** one that hears or listens **2 :** a person authorized to audit accounts

au·di·to·ri·um \ˌȯd-ə-ˈtōr-ē-əm, -ˈtȯr-\ *n* **1 :** the part of a public building where an audience sits **2 :** a room, hall, or building used for public gatherings

au·di·to·ry \ˈȯd-ə-ˌtōr-ē, -ˌtȯr-\ *adj* **:** of or relating to hearing or to the sense or organs of hearing ⟨*auditory* canal⟩ ⟨*auditory* sensation⟩

auditory nerve *n* **:** either of the 8th pair of cranial nerves that connect the inner ear with the brain and transmit impulses concerned with hearing and balance

Au·ge·an \ȯ-ˈjē-ən\ *adj* **:** extremely difficult and sometimes distasteful [from *Augeas,* king of Elis; from the legend that his stable, left neglected for 30 years, was finally cleaned by Hercules]

Augean stable *n* **:** a condition or place marked by great accumulation of filth or corruption — usually used in pl.

au·ger \ˈȯ-gər\ *n* **1 :** a tool for boring holes in wood **2 :** any of various instruments made like an auger and used for boring (as in soil) [Middle English *nauger* (the phrase *a nauger* being understood as *an auger*), from Old English *nafogār,* from *nafu* "nave" + *gār* "spear"; from its use for boring holes in the naves of wheels]

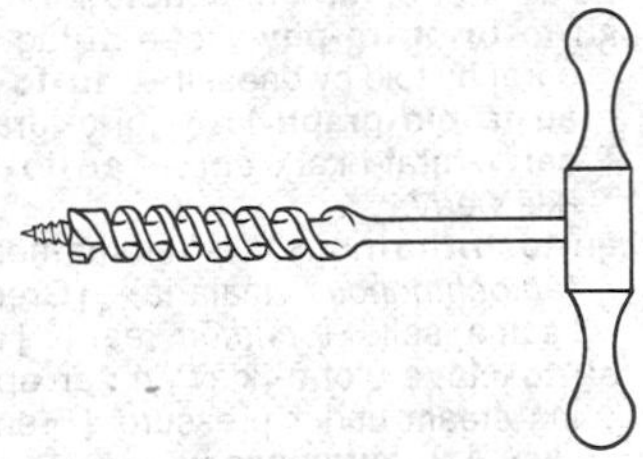

auger 1

△ **origin** Old English *nafela,* "navel", is closely related to Old English *nafu,* "nave". The nave is the central part of a wheel. From it the spokes radiate, and through it a hole is pierced for the axle. (This is not the same word as the *nave* of a church.) The navel is the depression more or less in the center of a person's abdomen. In Old English a compound was formed from *nafu* and *gār,* "spear". *Nafogār* was the "nave spear", the tool used to pierce the hole in the nave of a wheel. The form of the word became *nauger* in Middle English, and in the 15th century *a nauger* began to be divided as *an auger.* Thus we have the modern name of a tool used for boring holes.

¹aught \ˈȯt, ˈät\ *pron* **1** *archaic* **:** ANYTHING **2 :** ALL ⟨for *aught* I care, you can stay home⟩ [Old English *āwiht,* from *ā* "ever" + *wiht* "creature, thing"]

²aught *n* **:** ZERO 1, CIPHER [*naught,* the phrase *a naught* being understood as *an aught*]

au·gite \ˈȯ-ˌjīt\ *n* **:** a black to dark green variety of pyroxene [Latin *augites,* a kind of precious stone, from Greek *augitēs*]

aug·ment \ȯg-ˈment\ *vb* **:** to enlarge or increase especially in size, amount, or degree [Middle French *augmenter,* from Late Latin *augmentare,* from *augmentum* "increase", from Latin *augēre* "to increase"] — **aug·ment·able** \-ə-bəl\ *adj* — **aug·ment·er** *n*

aug·men·ta·tion \ˌȯg-mən-ˈtā-shən, -ˌmen-\ *n* **1 :** the act of augmenting **2 :** something that augments **:** INCREASE, ENLARGEMENT

aug·men·ta·tive \ȯg-ˈment-ət-iv\ *adj* **:** capable of augmenting or serving to augment

au gra·tin \ō-ˈgrät-n, ȯ-, -ˈgrat-\ *adj* **:** covered with bread crumbs, butter, and cheese and browned [French]

¹au·gur \ˈȯ-gər\ *n* **:** SOOTHSAYER, DIVINER [Latin]

²augur *vb* **1 :** to predict especially from signs or omens **2 :** to serve as a sign **:** INDICATE ⟨the report *augurs* well for our success⟩

au·gu·ry \ˈȯ-gyə-rē, -gə-\ *n, pl* **-ries 1 :** divination from omens or portents or from chance events (as the fall of lots) **2 :** an indication of the future **:** OMEN

au·gust \ȯ-ˈgəst\ *adj* **:** marked by majestic dignity or grandeur [Latin *augustus*] — **au·gust·ly** *adv* — **au·gust·ness** *n*

Au·gust \ˈȯ-gəst\ *n* **:** the 8th month of the year [Latin *Augustus,* from *Augustus* Caesar]

Au·gus·tan \ȯ-ˈgəs-tən\ *adj* **:** of, relating to, or characteristic of Augustus Caesar or his time — **Augustan** *n*

¹Au·gus·tin·i·an \ˌȯ-gə-ˈstin-ē-ən\ *adj* **1 :** of or relating to Saint Augustine or his doctrines **2 :** of or relating to any of several religious orders under a rule ascribed to Saint Augustine — **Au·gus·tin·i·an·ism** \-ē-ə-ˌniz-əm\ *n*

²Augustinian *n* **1 :** a follower of Saint Augustine **2 :** a member of an Augustinian order; *esp* **:** a friar of the Hermits of Saint Augustine founded in 1256 and devoted to educational, missionary, and parish work

auk \ˈȯk\ *n* **:** any of several thickset black-and-white short-necked diving seabirds that breed in colder parts of the northern hemisphere [Old Norse *ālka*]

auld \ˈȯl, ˈōld, ˈäl, ˈäld\ *adj, chiefly Scottish* **:** OLD

auld lang syne \ˌōl-ˌang-ˈzīn, -ˌdang-, -ˌlang-, -ˌdlang-, ˌȯl-\ *n* **:** the good old times [Scottish, literally, "old long ago"]

auk

aunt \ˈant, ˈȧnt\ *n* **1 :** the sister of one's father or mother **2 :** the wife of one's uncle [Old French *ante,* from Latin *amita*]

au·ra \ˈȯr-ə\ *n* **1 :** a distinctive atmosphere or impression surrounding a person or thing ⟨an *aura* of respectability⟩ **2 :** a luminous radiation **:** NIMBUS [Latin, "air, breeze", from Greek]

au·ral \ˈȯr-əl\ *adj* **:** of or relating to the ear or sense of hearing [Latin *auris* "ear"] — **au·ral·ly** \-ə-lē\ *adv*

au·re·ate \ˈȯr-ē-ət\ *adj* **1 :** of a golden color or brilliance **2 :** GRANDILOQUENT, ORNATE ⟨*aureate* rhetoric⟩ [Medieval Latin *aureatus* "adorned with gold", from Latin *aureus* "golden", from *aurum* "gold"]

au·re·lia \ȯ-ˈrēl-yə\ *n* **:** any of a genus of large jellyfishes [probably from Latin *aurum* "gold"]

au·re·ole \ˈȯr-ē-ˌōl\ *or* **au·re·o·la** \ȯ-ˈrē-ə-lə\ *n* **1 :** a radiant light around the head or body of a representation of a sacred person **2 :** a bright area surrounding a bright light (as the sun) when seen through thin cloud or mist [Medieval Latin *aureola,* from Latin *aureolus* "golden", from *aurum* "gold"]

au·ric \ˈȯr-ik\ *adj* **:** of, relating to, or derived from gold especially when trivalent [Latin *aurum* "gold"]

au·ri·cle \ˈȯr-i-kəl\ *n* **1 :** PINNA 2 **2 :** an atrium of a heart [Latin *auricula,* from *auris* "ear"]

au·ric·u·lar \ȯ-ˈrik-yə-lər\ *adj* **1 :** of or relating to the ear or the sense of hearing **2 :** told privately ⟨an *auricular* confession⟩ **3 :** known by the sense of hearing **4 :** of or relating to an auricle [Latin *auricula* "little ear", from *auris* "ear"]

au·ric·u·lo·ven·tric·u·lar \ȯ-ˌrik-yə-ˌlō-ven-ˈtrik-yə-lər\ *adj* **:** ATRIOVENTRICULAR

au·rif·er·ous \ȯ-ˈrif-rəs, -ə-rəs\ *adj* **:** gold-bearing [Latin *aurum* "gold"]

Au·ri·ga \ȯ-ˈrī-gə\ *n* **:** a constellation between Perseus and Gemini [Latin, literally, "charioteer"]

Au·ri·gna·cian \ˌȯr-ēn-ˈyā-shən\ *adj* **:** of or relating to an Upper Paleolithic culture with finely made stone and bone tools, paintings, and engravings [*Aurignac,* France]

au·rochs \ˈau̇r-ˌäks, ˈȯr-\ *n, pl* **aurochs** *also* **au·rochs·es 1 :** URUS **2 :** WISENT [German]

au·ro·ra \ə-ˈrōr-ə, ȯ-ˈrōr-, -ˈrȯr-\ *n, pl* **auroras** *or* **au·ro·rae** \-ˌē\ **1 :** DAWN 1 **2 :** AURORA BOREALIS **3 :** AURORA AUSTRALIS [Latin] — **au·ro·ral** \-əl\ *adj*

aurora aus·tra·lis \-ȯ-ˈstrā-ləs, -ä-ˈstrā-\ *n* **:** a display of light in the southern hemisphere corresponding to the aurora borealis [New Latin, literally, "southern aurora"]

aurora bo·re·al·is \-ˌbōr-ē-ˈal-əs, -ˌbȯr-\ *n* **:** streamers or arches of light in the sky at night of geomagnetic and electrical origin that appear to best advantage in the arctic regions [New Latin, literally, "northern aurora"]

au·rous \ˈȯr-əs\ *adj* **:** of, relating to, or containing gold especially when univalent [Latin *aurum* "gold"]

aus·cul·ta·tion \ˌȯ-skəl-ˈtā-shən\ *n* **:** the act of listening to sounds arising within organs (as the lungs) as an aid to diagnosis and treatment [Latin *auscultatio* "act of listening", from *auscultare* "to listen"] — **aus·cul·tate** \ˈȯ-skəl-ˌtāt\ *vt*

aus·pice \ˈȯ-spəs\ *n, pl* **aus·pic·es** \-spə-səz, -ˌsēz\ **1 :** observation especially of the flight and feeding of birds to discover omens **2 :** OMEN; *esp* **:** a favorable omen **3** *pl* **:** kindly patronage and guidance **:** PROTECTION ⟨a concert given under the *auspices* of the school⟩ [Latin *auspicium,* from *auspex* "diviner by birds", from *avis* "bird" + *specere* "to look at"]

aus·pi·cious \ȯ-ˈspish-əs\ *adj* **1 :** promising success **:** FAVORABLE ⟨an *auspicious* beginning⟩ **2 :** blessed with good auspices **:** HAPPY, FORTUNATE ⟨on this *auspicious* occasion⟩ — **aus·pi·cious·ly** *adv* — **aus·pi·cious·ness** *n*

aus•tere \ȯ-ˈstiər\ *adj* **1 a :** stern and cold in appearance or manner ⟨*austere* Puritans⟩ **b :** SOMBER, GRAVE ⟨an *austere* critic⟩ **2 :** morally strict **:** ASCETIC **3 :** plainly simple and unadorned ⟨an *austere* office⟩ ⟨an *austere* style of writing⟩ ⟨wore *austere* black⟩ **4 :** giving little or no scope for pleasure ⟨an *austere* budget⟩ ⟨*austere* diets⟩ [Middle French, from Latin *austerus,* from Greek *austēros* "harsh, severe"] **syn** see SEVERE — **aus•tere•ly** *adv* — **aus•tere•ness** *n*

aus•ter•i•ty \ȯ-ˈster-ət-ē\ *n, pl* **-ties 1 :** the quality or state of being austere **2 :** something that is austere **3 :** enforced or extreme economy

¹Austr- *or* **Austro-** *combining form* **1 :** south **:** southern **2 :** Australian and ⟨*Austro*-Malayan⟩ [Latin *Austr-, Auster* "south wind"]

²Austr- *or* **Austro-** *combining form* **:** Austrian and ⟨*Austro*-Hungarian⟩

aus•tral \ˈȯs-trəl, ˈäs-\ *adj* **:** SOUTHERN

Aus•tra•lian ballot \ȯ-ˌstrāl-yən-, ä-\ *n* **:** an official ballot printed at public expense containing the names of all candidates and all proposals, distributed only at the polling place, and marked in secret

Aus•tra•loid \ˈȯs-trə-ˌlȯid, ˈäs-\ *adj* **:** of or relating to an ethnic group including the Australian aborigines and related peoples — **Australoid** *n*

aus•tra•lo•pith•e•cine \ȯ-ˌstrā-lō-ˈpith-ə-ˌsīn, ä-ˌstrā-\ *adj* **:** of or relating to a group of extinct southern African apes with near-human dentition [Latin *australis* "southern" + Greek *pithēkos* "ape"] — **australopithecine** *n*

aut- *or* **auto-** *combining form* **1 :** self **:** same one ⟨*auto*biography⟩ **2 :** automatic **:** self-acting **:** self-regulating [Greek *autos* "same, self"]

aut•ecol•o•gy \ˌȯt-i-ˈkäl-ə-jē\ *n* **:** ecology dealing with individual organisms or individual kinds of organisms

au•then•tic \ə-ˈthent-ik, ȯ-\ *adj* **1 :** being really what it seems to be **:** GENUINE ⟨an *authentic* signature of George Washington⟩ **2 :** true to life or to the facts ⟨an *authentic* copy of an antique table⟩ [Middle French *autentique,* derived from Greek *authentikos,* from *authentēs* "perpetrator, author"] — **au•then•ti•cal•ly** \-ˈthent-i-kə-lē, -klē\ *adv* — **au•then•tic•i•ty** \ˌȯ-ˌthen-ˈtis-ət-ē, -thən-\ *n*

• **syn** GENUINE, BONA FIDE: AUTHENTIC implies being fully trustworthy as according with fact or actuality ⟨an *authentic* record of the campaign⟩ GENUINE implies accordance with an original or an accepted type without counterfeiting, admixture, or adulteration ⟨*genuine* maple syrup⟩ BONA FIDE often applies when good faith or sincerity is in question ⟨a *bona fide* proposal⟩

au•then•ti•cate \ȯ-ˈthent-i-ˌkāt, ə-\ *vt* **:** to prove, establish, or attest to be authentic **syn** see CONFIRM — **au•then•ti•ca•tion** \ə-ˌthent-i-ˈkā-shən, ȯ-\ *n* — **au•then•ti•ca•tor** \ə-ˈthent-i-ˌkāt-ər, ȯ-\ *n*

au•thor \ˈȯ-thər\ *n* **1 :** a person who writes or composes a literary work (as a book) **2 :** one that originates or makes **:** CREATOR [Old North French *auctour,* from Latin *auctor* "promoter, originator, author", from *augēre* "to increase"] — **author** *vt* — **au•tho•ri•al** \ȯ-ˈthōr-ē-əl, -ˈthȯr-\ *adj*

au•thor•ess \ˈȯ-thə-rəs, -thrəs\ *n* **:** a woman who is an author

au•thor•i•tar•i•an \ə-ˌthȯr-ə-ˈter-ē-ən, ȯ-, -ˌthär-\ *adj* **:** relating to or demanding total submission to authority especially as concentrated in a powerful leader ⟨an *authoritarian* government⟩ — **authoritarian** *n* — **au•thor•i•tar•i•an•ism** \-ē-ə-ˌniz-əm\ *n*

au•thor•i•ta•tive \ə-ˈthȯr-ə-ˌtāt-iv, ȯ-, -ˈthär-\ *adj* **1 :** having authority **:** coming from or based on authority ⟨*authoritative* teachings⟩ **2 :** entitled to obedience or acceptance ⟨an *authoritative* order⟩ **3 :** having an air of authority **:** POSITIVE ⟨an *authoritative* manner⟩ ⟨*authoritative* tones⟩ — **au•thor•i•ta•tive•ly** *adv* — **au•thor•i•ta•tive•ness** *n*

au•thor•i•ty \ə-ˈthȯr-ət-ē, ȯ-, -ˈthär-\ *n, pl* **-ties 1 a :** a person, text, or prior decision used to support a position **b :** a person appealed to as an expert **2 :** the right to give commands or to carry out or enforce others' commands **3 :** a person or persons having powers of government ⟨local *authorities*⟩ [Old French *auctorité,* from Latin *auctoritas* "opinion, decision, power", from *auctor* "author"]

au•tho•rize \ˈȯ-thə-ˌrīz\ *vt* **1 :** to give authority to **:** EMPOWER **2 :** to give legal or official approval to ⟨*authorize* a loan⟩ ⟨an *authorized* abridgment⟩ **3 :** to establish by or as if by authority **:** SANCTION ⟨customs *authorized* by time⟩ — **au•tho•ri•za•tion** \ˌȯ-thə-rə-ˈzā-shən, -thrə-ˈzā-\ *n* — **au•tho•riz•er** \ˈȯ-thə-ˌrī-zər\ *n*

au•thor•ship \ˈȯ-thər-ˌship\ *n* **1 :** the profession of writing **2 :** the origin of a literary production ⟨a novel of unknown *authorship*⟩

au•tism \ˈȯ-ˌtiz-əm\ *n* **:** absorption in self-centered mental activity (as daydreams, fantasies, delusions, and hallucinations) especially when accompanied by marked withdrawal from reality — **au•tis•tic** \ȯ-ˈtis-tik\ *adj*

au•to \ˈȯt-ō, ˈät-\ *n, pl* **autos :** AUTOMOBILE

au•to•bi•og•ra•phy \ˌȯt-ə-bī-ˈäg-rə-fē, -bē-\ *n* **:** one's own biography told by oneself — **au•to•bi•og•ra•pher** \-rə-fər\ *n* — **au•to•bio•graph•ic** \-ˌbī-ə-ˈgraf-ik\ *or* **au•to•bio•graph•i•cal** \-ˈgraf-i-kəl\ *adj* — **au•to•bio•graph•i•cal•ly** \-i-kə-lē, -klē\ *adv*

au•toch•tho•nous \ȯ-ˈtäk-thə-nəs\ *adj* **:** INDIGENOUS, NATIVE ⟨*autochthonous* malaria⟩ [Greek *autochthōn,* from *autos* "same, self" + *chthōn* "earth"]

au•to•clave \ˈȯt-ō-ˌklāv\ *n* **:** an apparatus (as for sterilizing) using steam under pressure [French, from *aut-* + Latin *clavis* "key"] — **autoclave** *vt*

au•toc•ra•cy \ȯ-ˈtäk-rə-sē\ *n, pl* **-cies 1 :** government in which one person possesses unlimited power **2 :** a community or state governed by autocracy

au•to•crat \ˈȯt-ə-ˌkrat\ *n* **:** a person having or acting as if having unlimited power

au•to•crat•ic \ˌȯt-ə-ˈkrat-ik\ *adj* **:** of, relating to, characteristic of, or resembling autocracy or an autocrat ⟨*autocratic* rule⟩ — **au•to•crat•i•cal•ly** \-ˈkrat-i-kə-lē, -klē\ *adv*

au•to•cross \ˈȯt-ō-ˌkrȯs, ˈät-\ *n* **:** an automobile contest that tests driving skill

au•to•erot•i•cism \ˌȯt-ō-i-ˈrät-ə-ˌsiz-əm\ *n* **:** sexual gratification without the participation of someone else — **au•to•erot•ic** \-ˈrät-ik\ *adj* — **au•to•erot•i•cal•ly** \-ˈrät-i-kə-lē, -klē\ *adv*

au•tog•e•nous \ȯ-ˈtäj-ə-nəs\ *or* **au•to•gen•ic** \ˌȯt-ə-ˈjen-ik\ *adj* **:** originating within or derived from the same individual ⟨an *autogenous* graft⟩ — **au•tog•e•nous•ly** *adv*

¹au•to•graph \ˈȯt-ə-ˌgraf\ *n* **:** something written with one's own hand; *esp* **:** a person's handwritten signature

²autograph *vt* **:** to write one's signature in or on

au•to•im•mune \ˌȯt-ō-im-ˈyün\ *adj* **:** of, relating to, or caused by antibodies produced by an organism against constituents of its own tissues ⟨*autoimmune* diseases⟩

au•to•in•tox•i•ca•tion \ˌȯt-ō-in-ˌtäk-sə-ˈkā-shən\ *n* **:** a state of being poisoned by substances produced within the body

Au•to•mat \ˈȯt-ə-ˌmat\ *service mark* — used for a cafeteria in which food is obtained especially from coin-operated compartments

au•to•mate \ˈȯt-ə-ˌmāt\ *vt* **1 :** to operate by automation **2 :** to convert to automatic operation

¹au•to•mat•ic \ˌȯt-ə-ˈmat-ik\ *adj* **1 a :** largely or wholly involuntary; *esp* **:** REFLEX 2 **b :** acting or done spontaneously or unconsciously **c :** resembling an automaton **:** MECHANICAL **2 :** having a self-acting or self-regulating mechanism ⟨*automatic* washer⟩ [Greek *automatos* "self-acting"] **syn** see SPONTANEOUS — **au•to•mat•i•cal•ly** \-ˈmat-i-kə-lē, -klē\ *adv*

²automatic *n* **:** an automatic machine or apparatus; *esp* **:** an automatic firearm

au•to•ma•tion \ˌȯt-ə-ˈmā-shən\ *n* **1 :** the method of making an apparatus, a process, or a system operate automatically **2 :** the state of being operated automatically **3 :** automatic operation of an apparatus, process, or system by mechanical or electronic devices that take the place of human operators

au•tom•a•tize \ȯ-ˈtäm-ə-ˌtīz\ *vt* **:** to make automatic — **au•tom•a•ti•za•tion** \ȯ-ˌtäm-ət-ə-ˈzā-shən\ *n*

au•tom•a•ton \ȯ-ˈtäm-ət-ən, -ˈtäm-ə-ˌtän\ *n, pl* **-atons** *or* **-a•ta** \-ət-ə\ **1 :** a mechanism that is relatively self-acting; *esp* **:** ROBOT **2 :** a person who acts in a mechanical fashion

¹au•to•mo•bile \ˌȯt-ə-mō-ˈbēl, -ˈmō-ˌbēl\ *adj* **:** AUTOMOTIVE

²automobile *n* **:** a usually four-wheeled motor vehicle designed for passenger transportation on streets and roadways and commonly propelled by an internal-combustion engine — **automobile** *vi* — **au•to•mo•bil•ist** \-mo-ˈbē-ləst\ *n*

au•to•mo•tive \ˌȯt-ə-ˈmōt-iv\ *adj* **1 :** SELF-PROPELLED **2 :** of, relating to, or concerned with automotive vehicles and especially automobiles and motorcycles

au•to•nom•ic \ˌȯt-ə-ˈnäm-ik\ *adj* **:** of, relating to, controlled by, or being the autonomic nervous system — **au•to•nom•i•cal•ly** \-ˈnäm-i-kə-lē, -klē\ *adv*

autonomic nervous system *n* : a part of the vertebrate nervous system that regulates activity (as of glands, cardiac muscle, or smooth muscle) not under voluntary control and that consists of two parts — compare PARASYMPATHETIC NERVOUS SYSTEM, SYMPATHETIC NERVOUS SYSTEM

au•ton•o•mous \ȯ-ˈtän-ə-məs\ *adj* **1** : possessing autonomy : SELF-GOVERNING **2** : existing, responding, reacting, or developing independently of the whole ⟨an *autonomous* growth⟩ [Greek *autonomos* "independent", from *autos* "self" + *nomos* "law"] — **au•ton•o•mous•ly** *adv*

au•ton•o•my \-mē\ *n, pl* **-mies** : the power or right of self-government

au•top•sy \ˈȯ-ˌtäp-sē, ˈȯt-əp-\ *n, pl* **-sies** : POSTMORTEM EXAMINATION [Greek *autopsia* "act of seeing with one's own eyes", from *autos* "self" + *opsis* "sight"] — **autopsy** *vt*

au•to•ra•dio•graph \ˌȯt-ō-ˈrād-ē-ə-ˌgraf\ *or* **au•to•ra•dio•gram** \-ˌgram\ *n* : an image produced on a photographic film or plate by the radiations from a radioactive substance in an object — **au•to•ra•dio•graph•ic** \-ˌrād-ē-ə-ˈgraf-ik\ *adj* — **au•to•ra•di•og•ra•phy** \-ˌrād-ē-ˈäg-rə-fē\ *n*

au•to•some \ˈȯt-ə-ˌsōm\ *n* : a chromosome other than a sex chromosome — **au•to•so•mal** \ˌȯt-ə-ˈsō-məl\ *adj*

au•to•sug•ges•tion \ˌȯt-ō-səg-ˈjes-chən, -sə-ˈjes-, -ˈjesh-\ *n* : an influencing of one's own attitudes, behavior, or physical condition by mental processes other than conscious thought

au•tot•o•my \ȯ-ˈtät-ə-mē\ *n, pl* **-mies** : reflex separation of a part from the body : division of the body into two or more pieces

au•to•troph \ˈȯt-ə-ˌtrōf, -ˌträf\ *n* : an organism that is able to live and grow on carbon from carbon dioxide or carbonates and on nitrogen from a simple inorganic compound [German, from Greek *autotrophos* "supplying one's own food", from *autos* "self" + *trephein* "to nourish"] — **au•to•tro•phic** \ˌȯt-ə-ˈtrōf-ik\ *adj* — **au•to•tro•phi•cal•ly** \ˌȯt-ə-ˈträf-i-kə-lē, -klē\ *adv* — **au•to•tro•phy** \ȯ-ˈtä-trə-fē\ *n*

au•tumn \ˈȯt-əm\ *n* **1** : the season between summer and winter comprising in the northern hemisphere usually the months of September, October, and November or, as determined astronomically, extending from the September equinox to the December solstice — called also *fall* **2** : a time of full maturity or beginning decline ⟨in the *autumn* of our lives⟩ [Latin *autumnus*] — **au•tum•nal** \ȯ-ˈtəm-nəl\ *adj*

autumn crocus *n* : MEADOW SAFFRON

[1]**aux•il•ia•ry** \ȯg-ˈzil-yə-rē; -ˈzil-rē, -ə-rē\ *adj* **1** : offering or providing help : SUPPLEMENTARY ⟨an *auxiliary* engine⟩ **2** : being a verb that accompanies another verb and typically expresses such things as person, number, mood, or tense [Latin *auxiliaris*, from *auxilium* "help"]

[2]**auxiliary** *n, pl* **-ries** **1** : an auxiliary person, group, or device **2** : an auxiliary verb

aux•in \ˈȯk-sən\ *n* : a plant hormone (as indoleacetic acid) that stimulates shoot elongation and plays a role in water metabolism in the plant; *also* : PLANT HORMONE [Greek *auxein* "to increase"]

[1]**avail** \ə-ˈvāl\ *vb* : to be of use or advantage : HELP ⟨all our effort *availed* nothing⟩ [Middle English *vailen, availen*, from Old French *valoir* "to be of worth", from Latin *valēre* "to be strong"] — **avail oneself of** : to make use of : take advantage of ⟨we must *avail ourselves of* the facilities we now have⟩

[2]**avail** *n* : help or benefit toward reaching a goal : USE ⟨the effort was of little *avail*⟩

avail•able \ə-ˈvā-lə-bəl\ *adj* **1** : present or ready for use : at hand ⟨will use any *available* excuse to stay home⟩ **2** : ACCESSIBLE, OBTAINABLE ⟨the book is *available* at your library⟩ — **avail•abil•i•ty** \ə-ˌvā-lə-ˈbil-ət-ē\ *n* — **avail•able•ness** \ə-ˈvā-lə-bəl-nəs\ *n* — **avail•ably** \-blē\ *adv*

av•a•lanche \ˈav-ə-ˌlanch\ *n* **1** : a large mass of snow, ice, earth, or rock sliding down a mountainside or over a steep cliff **2** : a sudden overwhelming rush of something seeming to come down like an avalanche ⟨an *avalanche* of words⟩ [French]

avant-garde \ˌäv-ˌän-ˈgärd, ˌäv-ˌänt-, ˌav-, ˌäv-; ə-ˈvänt-\ *n* : people (as artists) who create or use new or experimental ideas [French, "vanguard"] — **avant-garde** *adj*

av•a•rice \ˈav-rəs, -ə-rəs\ *n* : too strong a desire for wealth or gain : GREED [Old French, from Latin *avaritia*, from *avarus* "greedy", from *avēre* "to covet"]

av•a•ri•cious \ˌav-ə-ˈrish-əs\ *adj* : greedy especially for money **syn** see COVETOUS — **av•a•ri•cious•ly** *adv* — **av•a•ri•cious•ness** *n*

avast \ə-ˈvast\ *imperative verb* — used as a nautical command to stop or cease [perhaps from Dutch *houd vast* "hold fast"]

av•a•tar \ˈav-ə-ˌtär\ *n* : an embodiment (as of a concept, philosophy, or tradition) usually in human form [Sanskrit *avatāra* "descent, incarnation of a deity"]

avaunt \ə-ˈvȯnt, ə-ˈvänt\ *adv, archaic* : AWAY, HENCE — used as an interjection [Middle French *avant*, from Latin *abante* "forward, before", from *ab* "from" + *ante* "before"]

Ave Ma•ria \ˌäv-ˌā-mə-ˈrē-ə\ *n* : HAIL MARY [Medieval Latin, "hail, Mary"]

avenge \ə-ˈvenj\ *vt* : to take vengeance for or on behalf of ⟨*avenge* an insult⟩ [Middle English *vengen, avengen*, from Old French *vengier*, from Latin *vindicare*] — **aveng•er** *n*

• **syn** REVENGE: AVENGE implies inflicting deserved punishment especially on one who has injured someone other than oneself; REVENGE implies getting even or paying back in kind or degree.

av•e•nue \ˈav-ə-ˌnü, -ˌnyü\ *n* **1** : a way or passage by which a place may be approached or left **2** : a way or means to an end **3** : a street especially when broad and attractive [Middle French, from *avenir* "to come to", from Latin *advenire*, from *ad-* + *venire* "to come"]

aver \ə-ˈvər\ *vt* **averred**; **aver•ring** : to declare positively : ASSERT [Middle French *averer* "to verify", derived from Latin *ad-* + *verus* "true"]

[1]**av•er•age** \ˈav-rij, -ə-rij\ *n* **1** : a single value representative of a set of other values; *esp* : ARITHMETIC MEAN **2** : something typical of a group, class, or series ⟨their work is above the *average*⟩ **3** : a ratio of successful tries to total tries ⟨batting *average*⟩ [earlier *average* "distribution of costs of damage to ship or cargo", from Middle French *avarie* "damage to ship or cargo", from Italian *avaria*, from Arabic *'awārīyah* "damaged merchandise"]

△ **origin** *Average* came into English from Middle French *avarie*, a derivative (by way of Italian) of Arabic *'awārīyah*, "damaged merchandise". French *avarie* originally meant damage sustained by a ship or its cargo. It came, by transference, to mean the expenses of such damage and later included other maritime expenses. When the English borrowed the French word, they altered it to conform to the pattern of such English words as *pilotage* and *towage*. When a ship or its cargo was damaged at sea, the owners or insurers of both ship and cargo had to share the expense or average. An average-adjuster determined a fair division of costs among those held accountable. An *average* then became any equal distribution or division, like the determination of an arithmetic mean. Soon the arithmetic mean itself was called an *average*. Now the word may be applied to any mean or middle value or level.

• **syn** AVERAGE, MEAN, MEDIAN apply to a value that represents in some way a middle point between extremes. AVERAGE is the result obtained by dividing the sum total of a set of figures by the number of figures; MEAN may be the average or it may be the value midway between two extremes ⟨a high of 70° and a low of 50° give a *mean* of 60°⟩ MEDIAN applies to the value that represents the point at which there are as many instances above as there are below ⟨the *average* of a group of persons earning 3, 4, 5, 8, and 10 dollars an hour is 6 dollars an hour, but the *median* is 5 dollars⟩

[2]**average** *adj* **1** : equaling or approximating an arithmetic mean **2 a** : being about midway between extremes **b** : being not out of the ordinary : COMMON ⟨the *average* person⟩ — **av•er•age•ly** *adv* — **av•er•age•ness** *n*

[3]**average** *vb* **1** : to do, get, or have on the average ⟨we *average* six calls a day⟩ **2** : to amount to on the average : be usually ⟨those children *average* four feet in height⟩ **3** : to find the average of **4** : to divide among a number proportionally

averse \ə-ˈvərs\ *adj* : having an active feeling of repugnance or distaste ⟨*averse* to strenuous exercise⟩ [Latin *aversus*, past participle of *avertere* "to turn away, avert"] — **averse•ly** *adv* — **averse•ness** *n*

aver•sion \ə-ˈvər-zhən\ *n* **1** : a strong feeling of dislike ⟨an *aversion* to spiders⟩ **2** : something disliked ⟨carrots are my *aversion*⟩

\ə\ abut	\au̇\ **out**	\i\ **tip**	\ȯ\ **saw**	\u̇\ **foot**
\ər\ **further**	\ch\ **chin**	\ī\ **life**	\ȯi\ **coin**	\y\ **yet**
\a\ mat	\e\ pet	\j\ **job**	\th\ **thin**	\yü\ **few**
\ā\ take	\ē\ **easy**	\ng\ **sing**	\t͟h\ **this**	\yu̇\ **cure**
\ä\ cot, cart	\g\ **go**	\ō\ **bone**	\ü\ **food**	\zh\ **vision**

avert \ə-'vərt\ *vt* **1** : to turn away ⟨*avert* one's eyes⟩ **2** : to prevent from happening ⟨narrowly *averted* an accident⟩ [Middle French *avertir,* from Latin *avertere,* from *ab-* + *vertere* "to turn"] **syn** see PREVENT

avi•an \'ā-vē-ən\ *adj* : of, relating to, or derived from birds [Latin *avis* "bird"]

avi•ary \'ā-vē-ˌer-ē\ *n, pl* **-ar•ies** : a place (as a large cage or a building) where many live birds are kept usually for exhibition — **avi•a•rist** \-vē-ə-rəst\ *n*

avi•a•tion \ˌā-vē-'ā-shən, ˌav-ē-\ *n* **1** : the operation of heavier-than-air aircraft **2** : military aircraft **3** : aircraft manufacture, development, and design [French, from Latin *avis* "bird"] — **aviation** *adj*

aviation cadet *n* : a student officer in the air force

avi•a•tor \'ā-vē-ˌāt-ər, 'av-ē-\ *n* : the pilot of a heavier-than-air aircraft — **avi•a•tress** \-ˌā-trəs\ *n* — **avi•a•trix** \ˌā-vē-'ā-triks, ˌav-ē-\ *n*

av•id \'av-əd\ *adj* **1** : desirous to the point of being greedy : craving very much ⟨*avid* for praise⟩ **2** : marked by eagerness and enthusiasm ⟨*avid* readers⟩ [Latin *avidus,* from *avēre* "to covet"] — **avid•i•ty** \ə-'vid-ət-ē, a-\ *n* — **av•id•ly** \'av-əd-lē\ *adv* — **av•id•ness** n

avi•on•ics \ˌā-vē-'än-iks, ˌav-ē-\ *n* : the development and production of electrical and electronic devices for use in aviation, missilery, and astronautics [*avi*ation electr*onics*] — **avi•on•ic** \-ik\ *adj*

avi•ta•min•osis \ˌā-ˌvīt-ə-mə-'nō-səs\ *n, pl* **-min•oses** \-'nō-ˌsēz\ : disease resulting from a deficiency of one or more vitamins — **avi•ta•min•ot•ic** \-mə-'nät-ik\ *adj*

av•o•ca•do \ˌav-ə-'käd-ō, ˌäv-\ *n, pl* **-dos** : the usually green pulpy pear-shaped or egg-shaped oily edible fruit of a tropical American tree; *also* : the tree that bears this fruit — called also *alligator pear* [Spanish *aguacate,* from Nahuatl *ahuacatl*]

av•o•ca•tion \ˌav-ə-'kā-shən, 'av-ə-ˌ\ *n* : an occupation or interest pursued especially for enjoyment : HOBBY [Latin *avocatio,* from *avocare* "to call away", from *ab-* + *vocare* "to call"] **syn** see VOCATION — **av•o•ca•tion•al** \-shnəl, -shən-l\ *adj*

av•o•cet \'av-ə-ˌset\ *n* : any of several rather large long-legged shorebirds with webbed feet and a slender upward-curving bill [French *avocette,* from Italian *avocetta*]

avoid \ə-'vȯid\ *vt* **1** : to make legally void : ANNUL ⟨*avoid* a contract⟩ **2 a** : to keep away from : SHUN ⟨*avoid* quarrelsome neighbors⟩ **b** : to keep from happening ⟨*avoid* accidents⟩ [Middle English *avoiden* "to empty out", from Old French *esvuidier,* from *es-* "ex-" + *vuide* "empty, void"] — **avoid•able** \-ə-bəl\ *adj* — **avoid•ably** \-blē\ *adv*

avoid•ance \ə-'vȯid-ns\ *n* **1** : the act of annulling **2** : the act of keeping away from or clear of

avocado: *1* flowering branch, *2* fruit

av•oir•du•pois \ˌav-ərd-ə-'pȯiz\ *n* **1** : AVOIRDUPOIS WEIGHT **2** : HEAVINESS, WEIGHT [Middle English *avoir de pois* "goods sold by weight", from Old French, literally, "goods of weight"]

avoirdupois weight *n* : the series of units of weight based on the pound of 16 ounces and the ounce of 16 drams — see MEASURE table

avouch \ə-'vau̇ch\ *vt* **1** : to declare positively : AFFIRM **2** : to vouch for : GUARANTEE [Middle English *avouchen* "to cite as authority", from Middle French *avochier* "to summon", from Latin *advocare,* from *ad-* + *vocare* "to call"] — **avouch•ment** \-mənt\ *n*

avow \ə-'vau̇\ *vt* : to declare or acknowledge openly and frankly [Old French *avouer* "to appeal to", from Latin *advocare* "to summon", from *ad-* + *vocare* "to call"] **syn** see ASSERT

avow•al \ə-'vau̇-əl, -'vau̇l\ *n* : an open declaration or acknowledgment

avowed \ə-'vau̇d\ *adj* : openly acknowledged or declared : ADMITTED — **avowed•ly** \-'vau̇-əd-lē, -'vau̇d-lē\ *adv*

avun•cu•lar \ə-'vəng-kyə-lər\ *adj* : of, relating to, or characteristic of an uncle [Latin *avunculus* "maternal uncle"]

aw \'ȯ\ *interj* — used to express mild sympathy, entreaty, disbelief, or disgust

await \ə-'wāt\ *vb* **1** : to wait for : stay for : EXPECT ⟨*await* a train⟩ **2** : to be ready or waiting for ⟨a reward *awaits* them⟩

[1]awake \ə-'wāk\ *vb* **awoke** \-'wōk\ *or* **awaked** \-'wākt\; **awak•ing 1** : to cease sleeping **2** : to become aware of something ⟨*awoke* to their danger⟩ **3** : AROUSE 1 **4** : to make or become active : STIR ⟨*awoke* old memories⟩

[2]awake *adj* : roused from sleep : ALERT

awak•en \ə-'wā-kən\ *vb* **awak•ened**; **awak•en•ing** \-'wāk-ning, -ə-ning\ : AWAKE — **awak•en•er** \-'wāk-nər, -ə-nər\ *n*

[1]award \ə-'wȯrd\ *vt* **1** : to give by judicial decision (as after a lawsuit) ⟨*award* damages⟩ **2** : to give or grant as a reward ⟨*award* a prize⟩ [Old North French *eswarder* "to examine, decide", from *es-* "ex-" + *warder* "to watch, guard", of Germanic origin] — **award•able** \-ə-bəl\ *adj* — **award•er** *n*

[2]award *n* : something that is conferred or bestowed : PRIZE

aware \ə-'waər, -'weər\ *adj* : having or showing realization, perception, or knowledge : CONSCIOUS [Old English *gewær,* derived from *wær* "wary"] — **aware•ness** *n*

awash \ə-'wȯsh, -'wäsh\ *adj* **1** : washed by waves or tide **2** : floating in water : AFLOAT **3** : overflowed by water

[1]away \ə-'wā\ *adv* **1** : on the way : ALONG ⟨get *away* early⟩ **2** : from this or that place : HENCE, THENCE ⟨go *away*⟩ **3 a** : in another place ⟨stayed *away*⟩ **b** : in another direction ⟨turn *away*⟩ **4** : out of existence : to an end ⟨echoes dying *away*⟩ **5** : from one's possession ⟨gave *away* a fortune⟩ **6 a** : without stopping : CONTINUOUSLY ⟨clocks ticking *away*⟩ **b** : without hesitation or delay ⟨talk *away*⟩ **7** : by a long distance or interval : FAR ⟨*away* back in 1910⟩

[2]away *adj* **1** : absent from a place : GONE ⟨be *away* from home⟩ **2** : DISTANT ⟨a lake 10 kilometers *away*⟩

[1]awe \'ȯ\ *n* **1** : a profoundly humble and reverential attitude in the presence of deity or something sacred or sublime **2** : abashed fear inspired by authority or power [Middle English, "terror, awe", from Old Norse *agi* "terror"]

[2]awe *vt* : to inspire with awe

aweigh \ə-'wā\ *adj* : raised just clear of the bottom — used of an anchor

awe•some \'ȯ-səm\ *adj* **1** : expressive of awe ⟨an *awesome* silence⟩ **2** : inspiring awe ⟨an *awesome* responsibility⟩ — **awe•some•ly** *adv* — **awe•some•ness** *n*

awe•strick•en \'ȯ-ˌstrik-ən\ *or* **awe•struck** \-ˌstrək\ *adj* : filled with awe

[1]aw•ful \'ȯ-fəl\ *adj* **1** : inspiring awe **2** : very disagreeable or objectionable **3** : very great ⟨took an *awful* chance⟩ — **aw•ful•ness** *n*

[2]awful *adv* : VERY 1, EXTREMELY

aw•ful•ly *usually* 'ȯ-fə-lē *in sense* 1, 'ȯ-flē *in senses* 2 & 3\ *adv* **1** : in a manner to inspire awe **2** : in a disagreeable or objectionable manner **3** : VERY 1, ⟨an *awfully* cold day⟩

awhile \ə-'hwīl, -'wīl\ *adv* : for a while : for a short time

awhirl \ə-'hwərl, -'wərl\ *adv or adj* : in a whirl

awk•ward \'ȯ-kwərd\ *adj* **1** : lacking dexterity or skill especially in the use of the hands or of instruments : CLUMSY **2 a** : lacking ease or grace of movement or expression **b** : large and badly proportioned **3** : causing embarrassment **4** : poorly adapted for use or handling [Middle English *awke* "turned the wrong way", from Old Norse *öfugr*] — **awk•ward•ly** *adv* — **awk•ward•ness** *n*

• **syn** CLUMSY, GAUCHE, INEPT: AWKWARD is widely applicable and may suggest unhandiness or inconvenience of things, lack of muscular coordination or grace of movement, lack of tact, or embarrassment of circumstances or situation; CLUMSY implies stiffness and heaviness and so connotes unwieldiness or lack of ordinary skill; GAUCHE implies the effects of shyness or inexperience; INEPT is likely to imply a general inadequacy.

awl \'ȯl\ *n* : a pointed tool for marking surfaces or making small holes (as in leather or wood) [Old Norse *alr*]

awn \'ȯn\ *n* : one of the slender bristles that terminate the glumes in some cereal and other grasses [Old Norse *ögn*] — **awned** \'ȯnd\ *adj* — **awn•less** \'ȯn-ləs\ *adj*

aw•ning \'ȯn-ing, 'än-\ *n* : a rooflike cover extending over or in front of something to provide shade or shelter [origin unknown]

awoke *past of* AWAKE

AWOL \'ā-ˌwȯl, ˌā-ˌdəb-əl-yü-ˌō-'el\ *n* : a person (as a soldier or sailor) who is absent without permission [*a*bsent *w*ithout *l*eave] — **AWOL** *adv or adj*

awry \ə-'rī\ *adv or adj* **1** : turned or twisted toward one side : ASKEW **2** : out of the right course : AMISS **syn** see CROOKED

ax *or* **axe** \'aks\ *n* **1** : a cutting tool that consists of a heavy edged head fixed to a handle and is used for chopping and splitting wood **2** : abrupt discharge or removal (as from a job or a budget) ⟨get the *ax*⟩ [Old English *æcx*] — **ax** *or* **axe** *vt* — **ax to grind** : a usually selfish reason for wanting something done

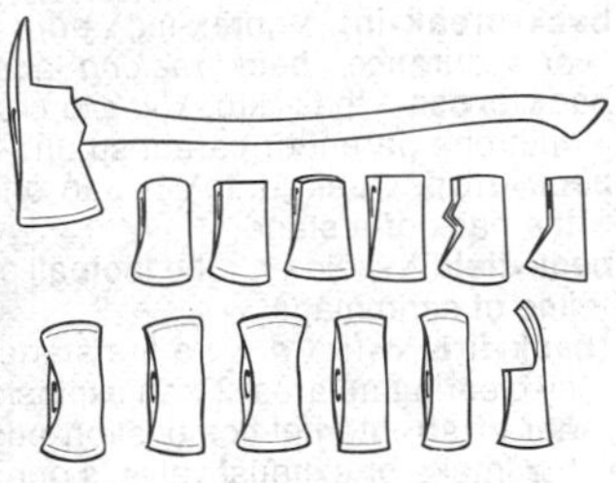

ax 1

ax•i•al \'ak-sē-əl\ *or* **ax•al** \-səl\ *adj* **1** : of, relating to, or functioning as an axis **2** : situated around, in the direction of, on, or along an axis — **ax•i•al•ly** \-sē-ə-lē\ *adv*

axial skeleton *n* : the skeleton of the trunk and head

ax•il \'ak-səl, -ˌsil\ *n* : the angle between a branch or leaf and the stem from which it arises [Latin *axilla* "armpit"]

ax•il•la \ag-'zil-ə, ak-'sil-\ *n, pl* **-lae** \-ē, -ˌī\ *or* **-las** : ARMPIT [Latin]

ax•il•lary \'ak-sə-ˌler-ē\ *adj* **1** : of, relating to, or located near the axilla **2** : found in or growing from an axil — **axillary** *n*

ax•i•om \'ak-sē-əm\ *n* **1** : a maxim widely accepted as obvious **2 a** : a proposition regarded as a self-evident truth **b** : POSTULATE 1 [Latin *axioma,* from Greek *axiōma,* literally, "honor", from *axioun* "to think worthy", from *axios* "worthy"]

ax•i•om•at•ic \ˌak-sē-ə-'mat-ik\ *adj* : of, relating to, or having the nature of an axiom : SELF-EVIDENT — **ax•i•om•at•i•cal•ly** \-'mat-i-kə-lē, -klē\ *adv*

ax•is \'ak-səs\ *n, pl* **ax•es** \'ak-ˌsēz\ **1 a** : a straight line about which a body or a geometric figure rotates or may be supposed to rotate **b** : AXIS OF SYMMETRY **c** : one of the reference lines of a coordinate system **2 a** : the second vertebra of the neck on which the head turns as on a pivot **b** : an anatomical structure that is an axis of symmetry ⟨the cerebrospinal *axis*⟩; *esp* : the main stem of a plant from which leaves and branches arise **3** : a main line of direction, motion, growth, or extension **4** : ALLIANCE 2a [Latin, "axis, axle"]

Axis *adj* : of or relating to the three powers Germany, Italy, and Japan engaged against the Allies in World War II

axis of symmetry : a straight line with respect to which a body, figure, or curve is symmetrical ⟨a circle has an infinite number of *axes of symmetry* but a parabola only one⟩

ax•le \'ak-səl\ *n* **1** : a pin or shaft on or with which a wheel or pair of wheels revolves **2** : AXLETREE [derived from Old Norse *öxull* "axle"]

axle•tree \-ˌtrē\ *n* : a fixed bar with bearings at its ends on which wheels (as of a cart) revolve

ax•o•lotl \'ak-sə-ˌlät-l\ *n* : any of several salamanders of mountain lakes of Mexico and the western United States that ordinarily live and breed without metamorphosing [Nahuatl, literally, "water doll"]

ax•on \'ak-ˌsän\ *also* **ax•one** \-ˌsōn\ *n* : a usually long and single nerve-cell process that as a rule conducts impulses away from the cell body [Greek *axōn*]

ayah \'ī-ə; 'ä-yə, -ˌyä\ *n* : a native nurse or maid in India [Hindi *āyā*, from Portuguese *aia,* from Latin *avia* "grandmother"]

1**aye** *also* **ay** \'ā\ *adv* : FOREVER 1, ALWAYS [Old Norse *ei*]

2**aye** *also* **ay** \'ī\ *adv* : YES [perhaps from Middle English *ye*]

3**aye** *also* **ay** \'ī\ *n, pl* **ayes** : an affirmative vote or voter

aye–aye \'ī-ˌī\ *n* : a nocturnal lemur of Madagascar [French, from Malagasy *aiay*]

Ayr•shire \'aər-ˌshiər, 'eər-, -shər\ *n* : any of a breed of hardy dairy cattle that vary in color from white to red or brown

aza•lea \ə-'zāl-yə\ *n* : any of numerous shrubs with funnel-shaped flowers that are related to the true rhododendrons but usually have deciduous leaves [Greek *azaleos* "dry"]

az•i•muth \'az-məth, -ə-məth\ *n* : an arc of the horizon measured between a fixed point (as true north) and the vertical circle passing through the center of an object [Arabic *as-sumūt* "the azimuth", plural of *as-samt* "the way"]

azo \'az-ō\ *adj* : relating to or containing the group of nitrogen atoms —N═N— united at both ends to carbon ⟨an *azo* dye⟩ [French *azote* "nitrogen", from Greek *a-* + *zōē* "life"]

azon•al \'ā-'zōn-l\ *adj* : of, relating to, or being a soil or a major soil group lacking well-developed horizons — compare INTRAZONAL

Az•tec \'az-ˌtek\ *n* **1** : a member of a Nahuatl people that founded the Mexican empire and were conquered by Cortes in 1519 **2** : the language of the Aztec people [Spanish *azteca* from Nahuatl, plural of *aztecatl*] — **Az•tec•an** \-ən\ *adj*

azure \'azh-ər\ *n* : the blue color of the clear sky [Old French *azur,* derived from Arabic *lāzaward*] — **azure** *adj*

azur•ite \'azh-ə-ˌrīt\ *n* : a blue mineral $Cu_3(OH)_2(CO_3)_2$ consisting of carbonate of copper, occurring in crystals, in mass, and in earthy form, and constituting an ore of copper

B b—Byzantine

b \'bē\ *n, pl* **b's** *or* **bs** \'bēz\ *often cap* **1** : the 2d letter of the English alphabet **2** : the musical tone B **3** : a grade rating a student's work as good

baa *or* **ba** \'ba, 'bä\ *n* : the bleat of a sheep [imitative] — **baa** *vi*

Baal \'bāl, 'bā-əl\ *n, pl* **Baals** *or* **Baa•lim** \'bā-ləm, -ə-ləm\ : one of the local fertility gods of ancient Canaan [Hebrew *ba'al* "lord"]

Bab•bitt \'bab-ət\ *n* : a business or professional person who accepts without thought prevailing middle-class standards [George F. *Babbitt,* character in the novel *Babbitt* (1922) by Sinclair Lewis] — **Bab•bitt•ry** \'bab-ə-trē\ *n*

babbitt metal *n* : an alloy used for bearings; *esp* : one containing tin, copper, and antimony [Isaac *Babbitt,* died 1862, American inventor]

bab•ble \'bab-əl\ *vb* **bab•bled; bab•bling** \'bab-ling, -ə-ling\ **1 a** : to make meaningless sounds **b** : to talk foolishly or excessively : CHATTER **2** : to sound as though babbling ⟨a *babbling* brook⟩ **3** : to reveal by too free talk ⟨*babble* a secret⟩ [Middle English *babelen*] — **babble** *n* — **bab•bler** \'bab-lər, -ə-lər\ *n*

babe \'bāb\ *n* : INFANT, BABY

ba•bel \'bā-bəl, 'bab-əl\ *n, often cap* **1** : a confusion of sounds or voices **2** : a scene of noise or confusion [Hebrew *Bābhel,* a city where the building of a tower is said in the Book of Genesis to have been interrupted by the confusion of tongues]

ba•boon \ba-'bün\ *n* : any of several large African and Asian apes having a doglike muzzle and usually a short tail [Middle French *babouin,* from *baboue* "grimace"] — **ba•boon•ish** \-'bü-nish\ *adj*

ba•bush•ka \bə-'büsh-kə, -'bu̇sh-\ *n* : a kerchief for the head usually folded triangularly [Russian, "grandmother"]

1**ba•by** \'bā-bē\ *n, pl* **babies 1 a** : a very young child or animal **b** : the youngest of a group **2** : a childish person [Middle English] — **ba•by•hood** \-ˌhu̇d\ *n* — **ba•by•ish** \-ish\ *adj*

2**baby** *vt* **ba•bied; ba•by•ing 1** : to treat as a baby : FONDLE, PET **2** : to treat or operate with care

Bab•y•lon \'bab-ə-lən, -ˌlän\ *n* : a city noted for its wealth, luxury, and vice [*Babylon,* ancient capital of Babylonia]

baby's breath *n* : a tall much-branched perennial gypsophila having clusters of small white or pink flowers

ba•by-sit \'bā-bē-ˌsit\ *vi* **-sat** \-ˌsat\; **-sit•ting** : to care for children usually during a short absence of the parents [back-formation from *baby-sitter*] — **ba•by-sit•ter** *n*

\ə\ **abut**	\au̇\ **out**	\i\ **tip**	\ȯ\ **saw**	\u̇\ **foot**
\ər\ **further**	\ch\ **chin**	\ī\ **life**	\ȯi\ **coin**	\y\ **yet**
\a\ **mat**	\e\ **pet**	\j\ **job**	\th\ **thin**	\yü\ **few**
\ā\ **take**	\ē\ **easy**	\ng\ **sing**	\t͟h\ **this**	\yu̇\ **cure**
\ä\ **cot, cart**	\g\ **go**	\ō\ **bone**	\ü\ **food**	\zh\ **vision**

bac·ca·lau·re·ate \ˌbak-ə-ˈlȯr-ē-ət, -ˈlär-\ *n* **1** : the degree of bachelor conferred by universities and colleges **2** : a sermon to a graduating class or the service at which such a sermon is delivered [Medieval Latin *baccalaureatus,* from *baccalaureus* "bachelor"]

bac·ca·rat \ˌbäk-ə-ˈrä, ˌbak-\ *n* : a card game played in casinos [French *baccara*]

Bac·chae \ˈbak-ˌē, -ˌī\ *n pl* : the women attendants or priestesses of Bacchus [Greek *Bakchai,* from *Bakchos* "Bacchus"]

[1]**bac·cha·nal** \ˈbak-ən-l\ *adj* : BACCHANALIAN

[2]**bac·cha·nal** \ˈbak-ən-l; ˌbak-ə-ˈnal, -ˈnäl\ *n* **1 a** : a devotee of Bacchus; *esp* : one who celebrates the Bacchanalia **b** : CAROUSER **2** : BACCHANALIA

bac·cha·na·lia \ˌbak-ə-ˈnāl-yə\ *n, pl* **bacchanalia 1** *pl, cap* : a Roman festival of Bacchus celebrated with dancing, song, and revelry **2** : a drunken feast : ORGY [Latin] — **bac·cha·na·lian** \-ˈnāl-yən\ *adj or n*

bac·chant \bə-ˈkant, -ˈkänt; ˈbak-ənt\ *n, pl* **bacchants** *or* **bacchantes** \bə-ˈkants, -ˈkänts, -ˈkant-ēz, -ˈkänt-ēz\ : BACCHANAL 1 — **bacchant** *adj* — **bac·chan·tic** \bə-ˈkant-ik, -ˈkänt-\ *adj*

bac·chante \bə-ˈkant, -ˈkänt, -ˈkant-ē, -ˈkänt-ē\ *n* : a priestess or woman follower of Bacchus

bac·chic \ˈbak-ik\ *adj* **1** : of or relating to Bacchus **2** : BACCHANALIAN

bach·e·lor \ˈbach-lər, -ə-lər\ *n* **1** : a young knight who fights under the banner of another **2** : a person who has received what is usually the lowest degree conferred by a four-year college, university, or professional school ⟨*bachelor* of arts⟩ **3 a** : an unmarried man **b** : an unmated male animal [Old French *bacheler,* from Medieval Latin *baccalarius, baccalaureus* "tenant farmer, advanced student", of Celtic origin] — **bach·e·lor·hood** \-ˌhu̇d\ *n*

bachelor's button *n* : a European plant of the aster family that has blue, pink, or white flower heads and is often cultivated in North America — called also *cornflower*

bac·il·la·ry \ˈbas-ə-ˌler-ē, bə-ˈsil-ə-rē\ *or* **ba·cil·lar** \bə-ˈsil-ər, ˈbas-ə-lər\ *adj* **1** : shaped like a rod; *also* : consisting of small rods **2** : of, relating to, or produced by bacilli

ba·cil·lus \bə-ˈsil-əs\ *n, pl* **-cil·li** \-ˈsil-ˌī, *also* -ē\ : any of numerous straight aerobic rod-shaped bacteria usually producing endospores; *also* : a disease-producing bacterium [Medieval Latin, "small staff, rod", from Latin *baculus* "staff, rod"]

[1]**back** \ˈbak\ *n* **1 a** (1) : the rear part of the human body especially from the neck to the end of the spine (2) : the corresponding part of a quadruped or other lower animal **b** (1) : SPINAL COLUMN ⟨break one's *back*⟩ (2) : the muscles and ligaments near the spinal column ⟨strain one's *back*⟩ **2 a** : the hinder part : REAR; *also* : the farther or reverse side **b** : something at or on the back for support ⟨the *back* of a chair⟩ **3** : a position in some games behind the front line of players; *also* : a player in this position [Old English *bæc*] — **backed** \ˈbakt\ *adj* — **backless** \ˈbak-ləs\ *adj*

[2]**back** *adv* **1 a** : to, toward, or at the rear **b** : in or into the past : AGO **c** : in or into a reclining position **d** : under restraint ⟨held *back*⟩ **2 a** : to, toward, or in a former place, state, or time ⟨go *back*⟩ **b** : in return or reply ⟨write *back*⟩

[3]**back** *adj* **1 a** : being at or in the back ⟨*back* door⟩ **b** : distant from a central or main area or route : REMOTE ⟨*back* roads⟩ **c** : pronounced with closure or narrowing at or toward the back of the oral passage ⟨the *back* vowels \ä\ and \ü\⟩ **2** : being in arrears : OVERDUE ⟨*back* rent⟩ **3** : moving or operating backward **4** : not current ⟨*back* numbers of a magazine⟩

[4]**back** *vb* **1 a** : to give aid or support to : ASSIST ⟨*backed* the new enterprise by investing in it⟩ **b** : SUBSTANTIATE 1 **2** : to move or cause to move back, backward, or in reverse ⟨*back* a car⟩ **3 a** : to furnish with a back **b** : to be at the back of **c** : to form a back for — **back·er** *n*

back·ache \ˈbak-ˌāk\ *n* : pain in the back; *esp* : dull persistent pain in the lower back

back–bench·er \-ˈben-chər\ *n* : a rank-and-file member of a British legislature

back·bite \-ˌbīt\ *vb* **-bit** \-ˌbit\; **-bit·ten** \-ˌbit-n\; **-bit·ing** \-ˌbīt-ing\ : to say mean or spiteful things about someone who is absent : SLANDER — **back·bit·er** *n*

back·board \-ˌbōrd, -ˌbȯrd\ *n* : a board or construction placed at the back or serving as a back; *esp* : one behind the basket on a basketball court

back·bone \-ˈbōn, -ˌbōn\ *n* **1** : SPINAL COLUMN **2** : the foundation or sturdiest part of something **3** : firm and resolute character — **back·boned** \-ˈbōnd, -ˌbōnd\ *adj*

back·break·ing \-ˌbrāk-ing\ *adj* : demanding all one's strength or endurance ⟨*backbreaking* labor⟩

back·cross \ˈbak-ˌkrȯs\ *vt* : to cross (a first-generation hybrid) with one parent or parent strain — **backcross** *n*

back·drop \ˈbak-ˌdräp\ *n* : an often scenic cloth hung across the back of a stage

back·field \-ˌfēld\ *n* : the football players who line up behind the line of scrimmage

[1]**back·fire** \-ˌfīr\ *n* **1** : a fire started to check an advancing fire by clearing an area **2** : an explosion of fuel mixture in the cylinder of an internal-combustion engine that occurs while either the intake or exhaust valve is open and results in a loud detonation

[2]**backfire** *vi* **1** : to make or undergo a backfire **2** : to have an effect opposite to the one desired or expected

back–formation *n* **1** : a word formed by dropping a real or supposed affix from an already existing longer word (as *pea* from *pease*) **2** : the creation of a back-formation

back·gam·mon \ˈbak-ˌgam-ən, bak-ˈ\ *n* : a game played by two persons on a double board with 12 spaces on each side in which each player has 15 pieces whose movements are determined by throwing dice [perhaps from *back* + Middle English *gamen, game* "game"]

back·ground \-ˌgrau̇nd\ *n* **1** : the scenery, ground, or surface behind an object seen or represented (as in a painting) **2** : an inconspicuous position ⟨keeps in the *background*⟩ **3 a** : the setting within which something takes place **b** (1) : the circumstances or events leading up to a situation or development (2) : information essential to understanding a problem or situation **c** : the total of a person's experience, knowledge, and education **4** : sound that interferes with received or recorded electronic signals

[1]**back·hand** \ˈbak-ˌhand\ *n* **1 a** : a stroke made with the back of the hand turned in the direction of movement **b** : a catch made with the arm across the body and the palm turned away from the body **2** : handwriting whose strokes slant downward from left to right

[1]backhand 1a

[2]**backhand** *adj* : using or made with a backhand

[3]**backhand** *vt* : to do, hit, or catch with a backhand

[4]**backhand** *or* **back·hand·ed** \-ˌhan-dəd\ *adv* : with a backhand

back·hand·ed \-ˌhan-dəd\ *adj* **1** : BACKHAND **2 a** : not direct or straightforward **b** : SARCASTIC ⟨a *backhanded* compliment⟩ **3** : written in backhand

back·ing \-ing\ *n* **1** : something forming a back **2 a** : SUPPORT, AID **b** : APPROVAL 1, ENDORSEMENT **3** : those who support a person or enterprise ⟨a candidate with a wide *backing*⟩

back·lash \ˈbak-ˌlash\ *n* **1** : a sudden violent backward movement or reaction **2** : a strong adverse reaction (as to a recent social or political development)

back·log \-ˌlȯg, -ˌläg\ *n* **1** : a large log at the back of a hearth fire **2** : a reserve especially of unfilled orders **3** : an accumulation of work not done

back of *prep* : BEHIND

[1]**back·pack** \-ˌpak\ *n* : a camping pack worn on the back

[2]**backpack** *vb* **1** : to carry (supplies) in a backpack **2** : to hike with a backpack — **back·pack·er** *n*

back·rest \ˈbak-ˌrest\ *n* : something to support the back

back·side \ˈbak-ˈsīd\ *n* : BUTTOCK 2

back·slap \-ˌslap\ *vb* : to be excessively cordial — **back·slap·per** *n* — **back·slap·ping** *n*

back·slide \-ˌslīd\ *vi* **-slid** \-ˌslid\; **-slid** *or* **-slid·den** \-ˌslid-n\; **-slid·ing** \-ˌslīd-ing\ : to slip back into bad moral or religious practices — **back·slid·er** \-ˌslīd-ər\ *n*

back·spin \-ˌspin\ *n* : a backward rotary motion (as of a ball)

[1]**back·stage** \ˈbak-ˈstāj\ *adv* **1** : in or to a backstage area **2** : in

secret or private ⟨worked *backstage* to gain support⟩
[2]backstage *adj* **1 :** of, relating to, or occurring in the backstage **2 :** SECRET, HIDDEN, COVERT ⟨*backstage* negotiations⟩
[3]backstage *n* **:** the part of a theater behind the curtain and especially behind the stage
back•stay \-ˌstā\ *n* **1 :** a stay extending from the mastheads to the side of a ship and slanting aft **2 :** a strengthening or supporting device at the back
[1]back•stop \-ˌstäp\ *n* **:** something serving as a stop behind something else; *esp* **:** a screen or fence used in baseball or other games to keep a ball from leaving the field of play
[2]backstop *vt* **:** to back up **:** SUPPORT ⟨found funds to *backstop* the program⟩ — **back•stop•per** *n*
back•stretch \-ˌstrech, -ˈstrech\ *n* **:** the side opposite the homestretch on a racecourse
back•stroke \-ˌstrōk\ *n* **:** a swimming stroke executed by a swimmer lying on his back
back•swept \-ˌswept\ *adj* **:** swept or slanting backward
back swimmer *n* **:** a water bug that swims on its back
back'talk *n* **:** an insolent or argumentative reply
back•track \ˈbak-ˌtrak\ *vi* **1 :** to retrace one's course **2 :** to reverse a position or stand
[1]back•ward \-wərd\ *or* **back•wards** \-wərdz\ *adv* **1 a :** toward the back ⟨look *backward*⟩ **b :** with the back foremost ⟨ride *backward*⟩ **2 a :** in a reverse or opposite direction or way ⟨count *backward*⟩ **b :** toward the past **c :** toward a worse state
[2]backward *adj* **1 a :** directed or turned backward ⟨a *backward* glance⟩ **b :** done or executed backward **2 :** DIFFIDENT, SHY **3 :** relatively undeveloped ⟨*backward* nations⟩ — **back•ward•ly** *adv* — **back•ward•ness** *n*
back•wash \-ˌwȯsh, -ˌwäsh\ *n* **1 :** backward movement (as of water or air) produced by a propelling force (as the motion of oars) **2 :** a consequence or by-product of an event **:** AFTERMATH
back•wa•ter \ˈbak-ˌwȯt-ər, -ˌwät-\ *n* **1 :** a body of relatively stagnant water formed by the back flow or overflow of a river or sea **2 :** a backward stagnant place or condition
back•woods \-ˈwu̇dz, -ˌwu̇dz\ *n pl* **1 :** wooded or partly cleared areas on a frontier **2 :** a remote and culturally backward area — **back•woods•man** \-mən\ *n*
back•yard \-ˈyärd\ *n* **1 :** an often enclosed area behind a dwelling **2 :** an accessible place or situation ⟨we must clean up our own *backyard* before criticizing others⟩
ba•con \ˈbā-kən\ *n* **:** salted and smoked meat from the sides and sometimes the back of a pig [Middle French, of Germanic origin]
Ba•co•ni•an \bā-ˈkō-nē-ən\ *adj* **:** of, relating to, or characteristic of Francis Bacon or his doctrines
bacteria *pl of* BACTERIUM
bac•te•ri•cid•al \bak-ˌtir-ə-ˈsīd-l\ *adj* **:** destroying bacteria — **bac•te•ri•cide** \-ˈtir-ə-ˌsīd\ *n*
bac•te•rio•chlo•ro•phyll \bak-ˌtir-ē-ō-ˈklōr-ə-ˌfil, -ˈklȯr-\ *n* **:** a substance in photosynthetic bacteria related to the chlorophyll of higher plants
bac•te•ri•ol•o•gy \bak-ˌtir-ē-ˈäl-ə-jē\ *n* **1 :** a science that deals with bacteria and their relations to medicine, industry, and agriculture **2 :** bacterial life and phenomena — **bac•te•ri•o•log•ic** \-ē-ə-ˈläj-ik\ *or* **bac•te•ri•o•log•i•cal** \-ˈläj-i-kəl\ *adj* — **bac•te•ri•o•log•i•cal•ly** \-ˈläj-i-kə-lē, -klē\ *adv* — **bac•te•ri•ol•o•gist** \-ē-ˈäl-ə-jəst\ *n*
bac•te•rio•phage \bak-ˈtir-ē-ə-ˌfāj, -ˌfäzh\ *n* **:** any of various viruses that attack bacteria
bac•te•rio•stat•ic \bak-ˌtir-ē-ō-ˈstat-ik\ *adj* **:** tending to inhibit growth of bacteria without causing their destruction
bac•te•ri•um \bak-ˈtir-ē-əm\ *n, pl* **-ria** \-ē-ə\ **:** any of a class of microscopic plants that live in soil, water, organic matter, or the bodies of plants and animals and are important to man because of their chemical effects and as causers of disease [New Latin, from Greek *baktērion* "small staff"] — **bac•te•ri•al** \-ē-əl\ *adj*
Bac•tri•an camel \ˌbak-trē-ən-\ *n* **:** CAMEL 1b
[1]bad \ˈbad\ *adj* **worse** \ˈwərs\; **worst** \ˈwərst\ **1 a :** below standard **:** POOR ⟨in *bad* repair⟩ **b :** UNFAVORABLE ⟨made a *bad* impression⟩ **c :** ROTTEN 1 **2 a :** morally evil **b :** NAUGHTY, DISOBEDIENT **3 :** INADEQUATE ⟨*bad* lighting⟩ **4 :** of a kind to pain or distress ⟨*bad* news⟩ **5 a :** INJURIOUS, HARMFUL **b :** SEVERE ⟨had a *bad* cold⟩ **6 :** INCORRECT, FAULTY ⟨*bad* spelling⟩ **7 :** ILL, SICK ⟨feel *bad*⟩ **8 :** REGRETFUL, SORRY ⟨felt *bad* about the fire⟩ **9 :** INVALID, VOID ⟨a *bad* check⟩ [Middle English] — **bad** *adv* — **bad•ly** *adv* — **bad•ness** *n*
[2]bad *n* **1 :** something that is bad **2 :** an evil or unhappy state ⟨go to the *bad*⟩
bad blood *n* **:** ill feeling **:** BITTERNESS ⟨*bad blood* existed between the two branches of the family⟩
bade *past of* BID
badge \ˈbaj\ *n* **1:** something (as an emblem or device) worn to show that a person belongs to a certain group, class, or rank ⟨a police officer's *badge*⟩ **2 :** an outward sign **3 :** an emblem awarded for some achievement ⟨a scout's merit *badge*⟩ [Middle English *bage, bagge*]
[1]bad•ger \ˈbaj-ər\ *n* **:** any of several sturdy burrowing mammals widely distributed in the northern hemisphere; *also* **:** the pelt or fur of a badger [probably from *badge;* from the white mark on its forehead]

[1]badger

[2]badger *vt* **bad•gered**; **bad•ger•ing** \ˈbaj-ring, -ə-ring\ **:** to harass or annoy persistently [from the practice of baiting badgers]
bad•i•nage \ˌbad-n-ˈäzh\ *n* **:** playful talk back and forth **:** BANTER [French]
bad•land \ˈbad-ˌland\ *n* **:** a region where erosion has formed the soft rocks into sharp and intricate shapes and where plant life is scarce — often used in pl. ⟨the *badlands* of South Dakota⟩
bad•min•ton \ˈbad-ˌmint-n\ *n* **:** a court game played with a light racket and a shuttlecock volleyed over a net [*Badminton,* residence of the Duke of Beaufort, England]
[1]baf•fle \ˈbaf-əl\ *vt* **baf•fled**; **baf•fling** \ˈbaf-ling, -ə-ling\ **1 :** to defeat or check by confusing **2 a :** to check or turn the flow of by or as if by a baffle **b :** to prevent (sound waves) from interfering with each other (as by a baffle) [probably from Middle English *bawchillen* "to discredit publicly"] **syn** see FRUSTRATE — **baf•fle•ment** \-əl-mənt\ *n* — **baf•fler** \ˈbaf-lər, -ə-lər\ *n*
[2]baffle *n* **:** a device (as a plate, wall, or screen) to deflect, check, or regulate flow (as of a fluid or of light or sound)
[1]bag \ˈbag\ *n* **1 a :** a flexible usually closed container for holding, storing, or carrying something **b :** PURSE; *esp* **:** HANDBAG **c :** TRAVELING BAG, SUITCASE **2 :** something resembling a bag: as **a :** a pouched or pendulous bodily part or organ; *esp* **:** UDDER **b :** a puffed-out sag or bulge in cloth ⟨had *bags* in the knees of new trousers⟩ **c :** a square white canvas container to mark a base in baseball **3 :** the amount contained in a bag **4 :** a quantity of game taken or permitted to be taken **5 :** a slovenly unattractive woman [Old Norse *baggi*] — **bag•like** \-ˌlīk\ *adj* — **in the bag :** SURE, CERTAIN
[2]bag *vb* **bagged**; **bag•ging** **1 a :** to swell out **:** BULGE **b :** to hang loosely **2 :** to put into a bag **3 a :** to take (animals) as game **b :** CAPTURE, SEIZE; *also* **:** to shoot down **:** DESTROY ⟨*bag* an enemy plane⟩
ba•gasse \bə-ˈgas\ *n* **:** plant residue (as of sugarcane) left after a product (as juice) has been extracted [French]
bag•a•telle \ˌbag-ə-ˈtel\ *n* **1 :** TRIFLE 1 **2 :** a game played with a cue and balls on an oblong table having cups or cups and arches at one end [French, from Italian *bagattella*]
ba•gel \ˈbā-gəl\ *n* **:** a hard glazed doughnut-shaped roll [Yiddish *beygel,* from Old High German *boug* "ring"]
bag•gage \ˈbag-ij\ *n* **1 :** the traveling bags and personal belongings of a traveler **:** LUGGAGE **2 :** the equipment carried with a military force **3 :** unnecessary or unwanted things or circumstances or ideas **4 :** a worthless saucy woman or girl [Middle French *bagage,* from *bague* "bundle"]
bag•ging \ˈbag-ing\ *n* **:** material (as cloth) for bags
bag•gy \ˈbag-ē\ *adj* **bag•gi•er**; **-est :** loose, puffed out, or hanging like a bag ⟨*baggy* pants⟩ — **bag•gi•ly** \ˈbag-ə-lē\

\ə\ **abut**	\au̇\ **out**	\i\ **tip**	\ȯ\ **saw**	\u̇\ **foot**
\ər\ **further**	\ch\ **chin**	\ī\ **life**	\ȯi\ **coin**	\y\ **yet**
\a\ **mat**	\e\ **pet**	\j\ **job**	\th\ **thin**	\yü\ **few**
\ā\ **take**	\ē\ **easy**	\ng\ **sing**	\t͟h\ **this**	\yu̇\ **cure**
\ä\ **cot, cart**	\g\ **go**	\ō\ **bone**	\ü\ **food**	\zh\ **vision**

adv — **bag•gi•ness** \'bag-ē-nəs\ *n*

ba•gnio \'ban-yō\ *n, pl* **bagnios** : BROTHEL [obsolete English *bagnio* "prison", from Italian *bagno* "public bath, prison"]

bag•pipe \'bag-,pīp\ *n* : a wind instrument consisting of a leather bag, a valve-stopped tube, and three or four pipes — often used in pl. — **bag•pip•er** \-,pī-pər\ *n*

bagpipe

ba•guette \ba-'get\ *n* : a gem having the shape of a long narrow rectangle [French, literally, "rod"]

bag•worm \'bag-,wərm\ *n* : a moth whose larva lives in a silk case covered with plant debris and is often destructive to the foliage of trees and shrubs

bah \'bä, 'ba\ *interj* — used to express disdain or contempt

1**bail** \'bāl\ *n* **1** : security that guarantees the appearance of a prisoner in court when legally required and that is given in order to obtain his or her release from prison until that time **2** : the temporary release of a prisoner upon security **3** : one who provides bail [Middle French, "custody", from *baillier* "to have in charge", from Latin *bajulare* "to carry a burden", from *bajulus* "porter"]

2**bail** *vt* **1** : to entrust (personal property) to another for a specific purpose and a limited time **2 a** : to release under bail **b** : to gain the release of by giving bail — **bail•able** \'bā-lə-bəl\ *adj*

3**bail** *n* : a container used to remove water from a boat [Middle French *baille* "bucket", from Medieval Latin *bajula* "water vessel", from Latin *bajulus* "porter"]

4**bail** *vt* : to remove (water) from a boat by dipping and throwing over the side; *also* : to clear (a boat) of water in this way

5**bail** *n* **1 a** : a supporting half hoop **b** : a hinged bar for holding paper against the platen of a typewriter **2** : the arched handle of a kettle or pail [Middle English *beil, baile*]

bail•ee \bā-'lē\ *n* : the person to whom property is bailed

bai•ley \'bā-lē\ *n* : an outer wall of a castle or the space within it [Old French *baille, balie*]

bai•liff \'bā-ləf\ *n* **1 a** : an official employed by a British sheriff to serve writs and processes and make arrests **b** : a minor officer of some United States courts usually serving as a messenger or doorkeeper **2** *chiefly British* : one who manages an estate or farm [Old French *baillif*, from *bail* "custody"] — **bailiff•ship** \-,ship\ *n*

bai•li•wick \'bā-li-,wik\ *n* **1** : the office or jurisdiction of a bailiff **2** : one's area of special interest, competence, or authority [Middle English *baillif* "bailiff" + *wik* "dwelling place, village"]

bail•or \bā-'lȯr, 'bā-lər\ *or* **bail•er** \'bā-lər\ *n* : one that entrusts personal property to another

bail out *vb* **1** : to jump with a parachute from an airplane in flight **2** : to escape or help to escape a difficult situation — **bail•out** \'bāl-,au̇t\ *n*

bails•man \'bālz-mən\ *n* : one who gives bail for another

bairn \'baərn, 'beərn\ *n, chiefly Scottish* : CHILD [Middle English *bern, barn*, from Old English *bearn* and Old Norse *barn*]

1**bait** \'bāt\ *vt* **1 a** : to torment by repeated and usually unfair verbal attacks **b** : to nag at : GOAD **2 a** : to abuse (an animal) by setting on dogs **b** : to attack by biting and tearing **3 a** : to furnish (as a hook) with bait **b** : ENTICE, LURE **4** : to give food and drink to (an animal) especially on the road [Old Norse *beita*] — **bait•er** *n*

2**bait** *n* **1** : something used in luring especially to a hook or trap; *also* : a poisonous material distributed in food to kill pests **2** : an often treacherous lure

baize \'bāz\ *n* : a coarse woolen or cotton fabric finished to imitate felt [Middle French *baies*, from *bai* "bay-colored"]

1**bake** \'bāk\ *vb* **1** : to cook or be cooked in a dry heat especially in an oven **2** : to dry or harden by heat ⟨*bake* bricks⟩ **3** : to prepare baked foods ⟨mother *bakes* on Thursday⟩ [Old English *bacan*] — **bak•er** *n*

2**bake** *n* : the act or process of baking ⟨this cake needs a long slow *bake*⟩

Ba•ke•lite \'bā-kə-,līt, -,klīt\ *trademark* — used for any of various synthetic resins and plastics

baker's dozen *n* : THIRTEEN

baker's yeast *n* : a yeast used or suitable for use as leaven — compare BREWER'S YEAST

bak•ery \'bā-kə-rē, -krē\ *n, pl* **-er•ies** : a place where bread, cakes, and pastry are made or sold

bake•shop \'bāk-,shäp\ *n* : BAKERY

baking powder *n* : a powder that consists of a carbonate, an acid, and a starch and that makes the dough (as of cake) rise and become light

baking soda *n* : SODIUM BICARBONATE

bak•sheesh \'bak-,shēsh, bak-'\ *n, pl* **baksheesh** : money paid for service especially in the Near East [Persian *bakhshīsh*]

bal•a•lai•ka \,bal-ə-'lī-kə\ *n* : a triangular wooden instrument related to the guitar and used especially in the Soviet Union [Russian]

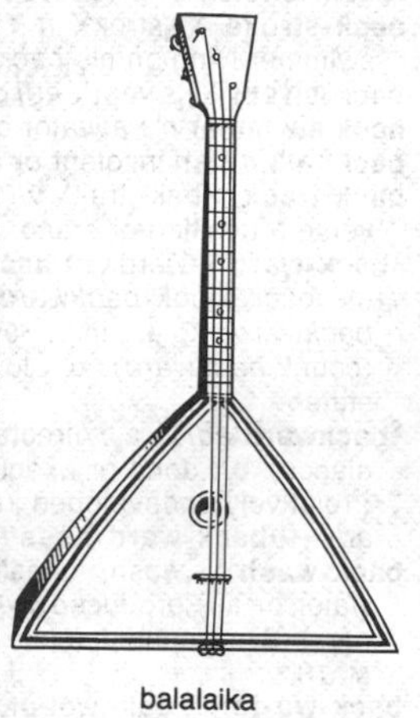
balalaika

1**bal•ance** \'bal-əns\ *n* **1** : an instrument for weighing; *esp* : a beam that is supported freely in the center and has two pans of equal weight suspended from its ends **2** : a counterbalancing weight, force, or influence **3** : a vibrating wheel operating with a hairspring to regulate the movement of a timepiece **4 a** : equilibrium between contrasting or interacting elements ⟨reaching a sane *balance* between right and need⟩ ⟨the *balance* of nature⟩ **b** : equality between the totals of the two sides of an account **5** : an aesthetically pleasing integration of elements : HARMONY **6** : something left over : REMAINDER; *esp* : the amount by which one side of an account is greater than the other ⟨a *balance* of $10 on the credit side⟩ **7** : mental and emotional steadiness [Old French, derived from Latin *bi-* "two" + *lanx* "plate"]

• **syn** BALANCE, REMAINDER, REST mean that which is left after subtraction or removal of a part. BALANCE strictly involves a comparison of two amounts, where one falls short of the other and must be equalized ⟨a bank *balance* is the amount left in an account after withdrawals and other deductions⟩ REMAINDER refers to what remains after a major or significant part of a group or mass has been taken away or accounted for ⟨a few went ahead, but the *remainder* of the party turned back⟩ REST and REMAINDER are interchangeable although REST often suggests a less precisely measured REMAINDER ⟨the United States and the *rest* of the free world⟩

2**balance** *vb* **1 a** (1) : to compute the difference between the debits and credits of an account (2) : to pay the amount due on : SETTLE **b** : to make two parts exactly equal ⟨*balance* equations⟩ **c** : to complete (a chemical equation) so that the same number of atoms of each kind appears on each side **2 a** : to make up for : OFFSET **b** : to equal or equalize in weight, number, or proportion **3** : to compare the weight of in or as if in a balance **4 a** : to bring or come to a state or position of equilibrium **b** : to poise in or as if in balance **c** : to bring into harmony or proportion; *also* : to so plan and prepare that all needed elements will be present ⟨*balance* a diet⟩ ⟨a *balanced* aquarium⟩ **5** : to move with a swaying or swinging motion **syn** see COMPENSATE — **bal•anc•er** *n*

balance beam *n* : a narrow wooden beam supported in a horizontal position above the floor and used for balancing feats in gymnastics

balance of power **1** : an equilibrium of power between states or groups of states such as to prevent any one state or group from becoming strong enough to dominate another **2** : the power or influence of a third group or force sufficient when exerted to decide a conflict in favor of one of two equally powerful opponents

balance of trade : the difference in value over a period of time between a country's imports and exports

balance sheet *n* : a statement of the financial condition of an enterprise at a given date

balance wheel *n* : a wheel that regulates or stabilizes the motion of a mechanism (as in a timepiece or a sewing machine)

ba•la•ta \bə-'lät-ə\ *n* : a substance like gutta-percha that is the dried juice of tropical American trees related to the sapodilla and is used especially in belting and golf balls; *also* : a tree yielding balata [Spanish, of American Indian origin]

bal•boa \bal-'bō-ə\ *n* **1** : the basic monetary unit of Panama **2** : a coin representing one balboa [Spanish, from Vasco Núñez de *Balboa,* died 1517, Spanish explorer]

bal•brig•gan \bal-'brig-ən\ *n* : a knitted cotton fabric used especially for underwear or hosiery [*Balbriggan,* Ireland]

bal•co•ny \'bal-kə-nē\ *n, pl* **-nies** **1** : a platform enclosed by a low wall or a railing and built out from the side of a building **2** : a gallery inside a building (as a theater or auditorium) [Italian *balcone,* of Germanic origin]

bald \'bȯld\ *adj* **1** : lacking a natural or usual covering (as of hair) **2** : free from frills : PLAIN ⟨told the *bald* truth⟩ [Middle English *balled*] — **bald•ly** *adv* — **bald•ness** \'bȯld-nəs, 'bȯl-\ *n*

bal•da•chin \'bȯl-də-kən, 'bal-\ *or* **bal•da•chi•no** \ˌbal-də-'kē-nō, ˌbäl-\ *n, pl* **-chins** *or* **-chi•nos** : an ornamental canopy fixed or carried over a dignitary or sacred object as a mark of honor [Italian *baldacchino,* from *Baldacco* "Baghdad"]

bald cypress *n* : either of two large swamp trees of the southern United States; *also* : the hard red wood of bald cypress

bald eagle *n* : an eagle of North America that is wholly dark when young but has white feathers covering the head and neck when mature

bal•der•dash \'bȯl-dər-ˌdash\ *n* : NONSENSE 1 [origin unknown]

bald•pate \'bȯld-ˌpāt, 'bȯl-\ *n* **1** : a bald-headed person **2** : a white-crowned North American widgeon

bal•dric \'bȯl-drik\ *n* : an often ornamented belt worn over one shoulder to support a sword or bugle [Middle English *baudrik*]

[1]bale \'bāl\ *n* **1** : great evil **2** : mental suffering : WOE [Old English *bealu*]

[2]bale *n* **1** : a large bundle of goods; *esp* : one closely pressed, bound together, and often wrapped ⟨a *bale* of hay⟩ **2** : a large amount ⟨we've *bales* of new ideas⟩ [Old French, of Germanic origin]

[3]bale *vt* : to make up into a bale — **bal•er** *n*

ba•leen \bə-'lēn\ *n* : WHALEBONE [Latin *ballaena* "whale", from Greek *phallaina*]

baleen whale *n* : WHALEBONE WHALE

bale•ful \'bāl-fəl\ *adj* **1** : having a deadly or harmful influence **2** : portending evil — **bale•ful•ly** \-fə-lē\ *adv* — **bale•ful•ness** *n*

[1]balk \'bȯk\ *n* **1** : a ridge of land left unplowed or missed in plowing **2** : BEAM, RAFTER **3** : something that hinders **4** : failure of a player to complete a motion begun; *esp* : an illegal motion of a baseball pitcher while in position [Old English *balca*]

[2]balk *vb* **1** *archaic* : to pass over : fail to grasp **2** : to check or stop by or as if by an obstacle : BLOCK **3** : to stop short and refuse to continue or act ⟨they *balked* at the extra work⟩ **4** : to commit a balk in sports — **balk•er** *n*

bal•kan•ize \'bȯl-kə-ˌnīz\ *vt, often cap* : to break up (as a region) into smaller and often hostile units [*Balkan* peninsula] — **bal•kan•iza•tion** \ˌbȯl-kə-nə-'zā-shən\ *n, often cap*

balky \'bȯ-kē\ *adj* **balk•i•er; -est** : likely to balk — **balk•i•ness** *n*

[1]ball \'bȯl\ *n* **1** : a round or roundish body or mass: as **a** : a usually spherical body used in a game or sport **b** : EARTH, GLOBE **c** : a usually round solid shot for a firearm **d** (1) : the rounded bulge at the base of the thumb (2) : the rounded broad part of the sole of the human foot between the toes and the arch **2** : a game in which a ball is thrown, kicked, or struck; *esp* : BASEBALL **3** : a pitched baseball not struck at by the batter that fails to pass through the strike zone [Old Norse *böllr*]

[2]ball *vb* : to form or gather into a ball

[3]ball *n* : a large formal gathering for social dancing [French *bal,* derived from Late Latin *ballare* "to dance", from Greek *ballizein*]

bal•lad \'bal-əd\ *n* **1** : a simple song : AIR **2** : a narrative poem usually in stanzas of two or four lines and suitable for singing; *esp* : one of unknown authorship handed down orally from generation to generation **3** : a popular song; *esp* : a slow romantic or sentimental dance song [Middle French *balade,* from Provençal *balada* "dance, dancing song", from Late Latin *ballare* "to dance"] — **bal•lad•ry** \-ə-drē\ *n*

ball-and-socket joint *n* : a joint (as in the hip) in which a rounded part moves within a socket so as to allow movements in many directions

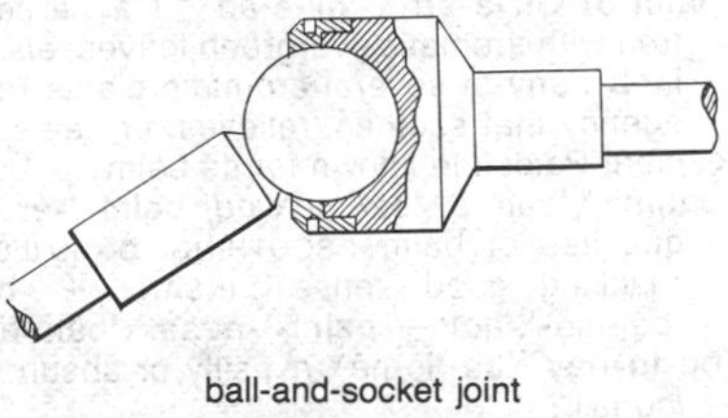

ball-and-socket joint

[1]bal•last \'bal-əst\ *n* **1** : heavy material used to improve the stability and control the draft of a ship or the ascent of a balloon **2** : gravel, cinders, or crushed stone used in making a roadbed (as of a railroad) or in making concrete [probably from Low German, of Scandinavian origin]

[2]ballast *vt* : to provide with ballast

ball bearing *n* **1** : a bearing in which the revolving part turns on steel balls that roll easily in a groove **2** : one of the balls in a ball bearing

ball boy *n* : a boy who retrieves balls for the players in a tennis tournament

ball•car•ri•er \'bȯl-ˌkar-ē-ər\ *n* : the football player carrying the ball in an offensive play

bal•le•ri•na \ˌbal-ə-'rē-nə\ *n* : a woman ballet dancer [Italian]

bal•let \'ba-ˌlā, ba-'\ *n* **1 a** : dancing in which conventional poses and steps are combined with light flowing figures and movements **b** : a theatrical art form using ballet dancing to convey a story, theme, or atmosphere **2** : music for a ballet **3** : a group that performs ballets [French, from Italian *balletto,* derived from Late Latin *ballare* "to dance"]

bal•let•o•mane \ba-'let-ə-ˌmān\ *n* : a person who loves ballet [*ballet* + *-o-* + *-mane,* from *mania*]

ball girl *n* : a girl who retrieves balls for the players in a tennis tournament

bal•lis•ta \bə-'lis-tə\ *n* : an ancient military weapon used for hurling large missiles [Latin, derived from Greek *ballein* "to throw"]

bal•lis•tic \bə-'lis-tik\ *adj* : of or relating to ballistics or to a body in motion according to the laws of ballistics

ballistic missile *n* : a self-propelled missile guided in the ascent of a high-arch path and freely falling in the descent

bal•lis•tics \bə-'lis-tiks\ *n sing or pl* **1 a** : the science of the motion of projectiles in flight **b** : the flight characteristics of a projectile **2** : the firing characteristics of a firearm or cartridge

ball lightning *n* : a rare form of lightning consisting of a luminous ball that may move along solid objects or float in the air

[1]bal•loon \bə-'lün\ *n* **1** : a nonporous bag filled with heated air or with a gas lighter than air so as to rise and float above the ground **2** : a toy consisting of a rubber bag that can be inflated with air or gas [French *ballon,* from Italian dialect *ballone,* from *balla* "ball", of Germanic origin] — **bal•loon•ist** \-'lü-nəst\ *n*

[2]balloon *vb* **1** : to ascend or travel in a balloon **2** : to swell or puff out **3** : to increase rapidly ⟨costs *ballooned*⟩

[1]bal•lot \'bal-ət\ *n* **1 a** : a small ball used in secret voting **b** : a sheet of paper used to cast a vote **2 a** : the action or a system of secret voting **b** : the right to vote **3** : the number of votes cast [Italian *ballotta,* from *balla* "ball"]

[2]ballot *vi* : to vote or decide by ballot — **bal•lot•er** *n*

ball park *n* : a park in which ball and especially baseball is played — **in the ball park** : reasonably accurate or acceptable

ball-point pen *n* : a pen having as the writing point a small rotating steel ball that inks itself by contact with an inner ink supply

ball•room \'bȯl-ˌrüm, -ˌrům\ *n* : a large room for dances

bal•ly•hoo \'bal-ē-ˌhü\ *n, pl* **-hoos** **1** : a noisy attention-getting demonstration or talk **2** : sensational or exaggerated advertising or propaganda [origin unknown] — **ballyhoo** *vt*

balm \'bäm, 'bälm\ *n* **1** : a resin from small tropical evergreen trees **2** : a fragrant healing or soothing preparation (as an ointment) **3** : something that comforts or refreshes ⟨sleep is *balm* to a tired body⟩ **4** : any of several spicy fragrant herbs (as

\ə\ **abut**	\au̇\ **out**	\i\ **tip**	\ȯ\ **saw**	\u̇\ **foot**
\ər\ **further**	\ch\ **chin**	\ī\ **life**	\ȯi\ **coin**	\y\ **yet**
\a\ **mat**	\e\ **pet**	\j\ **job**	\th\ **thin**	\yü\ **few**
\ā\ **take**	\ē\ **easy**	\ng\ **sing**	\t͟h\ **this**	\yu̇\ **cure**
\ä\ **cot, cart**	\g\ **go**	\ō\ **bone**	\ü\ **food**	\zh\ **vision**

lemon balm) **5** : a spicy aromatic odor [Old French *baume,* from Latin *balsamum* "balsam"]

balm of Gil•e•ad \-'gil-ē-əd\ **1 a** : a small African and Asian tree with aromatic evergreen leaves; *also* : its fragrant oleoresin **b** : any of several aromatic plants (as a balsam fir) **2** : an agency that soothes, relieves, or heals [*Gilead,* region of ancient Palestine known for its balm]

balmy \'bäm-ē, 'bäl-mē\ *adj* **balm•i•er**; **-est 1 a** : having the qualities of balm : SOOTHING **b** : MILD ⟨*balmy* weather⟩ **2** : lacking good sense : INSANE — **balm•i•ly** \'bäm-ə-lē, 'bäl-mə-\ *adv* — **balm•i•ness** \'bäm-ē-nəs, 'bäl-mē-\ *n*

ba•lo•ney \bə-'lō-nē\ *n* : silly or absurd talk : NONSENSE [*bologna*]

bal•sa \'bȯl-sə\ *n* **1** : a tropical American tree with extremely light strong wood used especially for floats; *also* : its wood **2** : a raft made of bundles of grass or reeds lashed together **3** : a life raft made of two cylinders of metal or wood joined by a framework and often used for reaching the shore through surf [Spanish]

bal•sam \'bȯl-səm\ *n* **1 a** : an aromatic and usually oily and resinous substance flowing from various plants **b** : a preparation containing or smelling like balsam **2 a** : a tree that yields balsam **b** : IMPATIENS; *esp* : one grown as an ornamental **3** : BALM 2 [Latin *balsamum,* from Greek *balsamon*] — **bal•sam•ic** \bȯl-'sam-ik\ *adj*

balsam fir *n* : a resinous American evergreen tree of the pine family widely used for pulpwood and as a Christmas tree

balsam of Pe•ru \-pə-'rü\ : a balsam from a tropical American leguminous tree used in perfumery and medicine

balsam poplar *n* : a North American poplar with resin-coated buds that is often cultivated as a shade tree — called also *hackmatack, tacamahac*

Bal•tic \'bȯl-tik\ *adj* **1** : of or relating to the Baltic sea or to the states of Lithuania, Latvia, and Estonia **2** : of or relating to a branch of the Indo-European languages containing Latvian and Lithuanian

Bal•ti•more oriole \,bȯl-tə-,mōr-, -,mȯr-, -mər-\ *n* : a common American oriole of which the male is brightly colored with orange, black, and white and the female is largely brown and greenish yellow [George Calvert, Lord *Baltimore*]

bal•us•ter \'bal-ə-stər\ *n* : an upright rounded, square, or vase-shaped support of a rail (as in the railing of a staircase or balcony) [French *balustre,* from Italian *balaustro,* from *balaustra* "pomegranate flower"]

bal•us•trade \'bal-ə-,strād\ *n* : a row of balusters topped by a rail; *also* : a low parapet or barrier

bam•bi•no \bam-'bē-nō\ *n, pl* **bambinos** *or* **bam•bi•ni** \-'bē-nē\ **1** : CHILD 2a; *esp* : BABY 1 **2** *pl usually bambini* : a representation of the infant Christ [Italian]

bam•boo \bam-'bü\ *n, pl* **bamboos 1** : any of various chiefly tropical tall woody grasses including some with strong hollow stems used for building, furniture, or utensils **2** : the tough woody stem or tissue of a bamboo [Malay *bambu*] — **bamboo** *adj*

bamboo 1

bamboo curtain *n* : an iron curtain isolating areas under Chinese Communist control

bam•boo•zle \bam-'bü-zəl\ *vt* **-boo•zled**; **-boo•zling** \-'büz-ling, -ə-ling\ : to deceive by trickery : HOODWINK [origin unknown] — **bam•boo•zle•ment** \-'bü-zəl-mənt\ *n*

[1]**ban** \'ban\ *vb* **banned**; **ban•ning 1** *archaic* : CURSE 1 **2** : to prohibit especially by legal means or social pressure [Old English *bannan* "to summon"] **syn** see FORBID

[2]**ban** *n* **1** : ANATHEMA 1a **2** : MALEDICTION, CURSE **3** : an official prohibition **4** : censure or condemnation especially through public opinion

ba•nal \bə-'nal, ba-, -'näl; bā-'nal; 'bān-l\ *adj* : lacking originality, freshness, or novelty : TRITE, COMMONPLACE [French, from Middle French, "of feudal service, commonplace", from *ban* "summons to feudal service", of Germanic origin] **syn** see INSIPID — **ba•nal•i•ty** \bā-'nal-ət-ē, bə-\ *n* — **ba•nal•ly** \bə-'nal-lē, -'näl-; bān-l-lē, -ē\ *adv*

ba•nana \bə-'nan-ə\ *n* : a treelike tropical plant with large leaves and with flower clusters that develop into a bunch of finger-shaped fruit which are yellow or red when ripe; *also* : its fruit [of African origin]

banana

banana oil *n* : a colorless liquid acetate that has a pleasant fruity odor and is used as a solvent

[1]**band** \'band\ *n* **1** *archaic* : something (as a fetter or shackle) that confines or constricts **2** : something that binds or restrains legally, morally, or spiritually ⟨we must break the *bands* of prejudice⟩ **3** : a strip serving to join or hold things together **4** : a thin encircling strip that confines, supports, or protects ⟨protect the baby's navel with a soft *band*⟩ **5 a** : a strip with a distinctive characteristic (as color, texture, or composition) ⟨a *band* of nerve fibers⟩ **b** : a range of wavelengths or frequencies between two specified limits **c** : a narrow strip serving chiefly as decoration **d** *pl* : a pair of strips hanging at the front of the neck as part of a clerical, legal, or academic dress **e** : a strip of grooves on a phonographic record containing a single piece or a section of a long piece [partly from Old Norse, "something that constricts" and partly from Middle French *bende, bande* "strip", of Germanic origin] — **band•ed** \'ban-dəd\ *adj*

[2]**band** *vb* **1** : to put a band on or fasten with a band **2** : to finish with a band **3 a** : to attach (oneself) to a group **b** : to gather together or summon for a purpose **c** : to unite in a company or confederacy or for a common purpose — **band•er** *n*

[3]**band** *n* : a group of persons, animals, or things; *esp* : a group of musicians organized for playing together [Middle French *bande* "troop"]

ban•dage \'ban-dij\ *n* : a strip of fabric used especially to dress and bind up wounds — **bandage** *vt*

Band-Aid \'ban-'dād\ *trademark* — used for a small adhesive strip with a gauze pad for covering minor wounds

ban•dan•na *or* **ban•dana** \ban-'dan-ə\ *n* : a large figured handkerchief with usually a red or blue background [Hindi *bā̃dhnū,* cloth dyed by knotting portions so as to leave them undyed, derived from Sanskrit *badhnāti* "he ties"]

band•box \'band-,bäks, 'ban-\ *n* : a usually cylindrical box for holding light articles of clothing

ban•deau \ban-'dō\ *n, pl* **ban•deaux** \-'dōz\ **1** : a band especially for the hair **2** : BRASSIERE [French]

ban•de•role *or* **ban•de•rol** \'ban-də-,rōl\ *n* : a long narrow forked flag or streamer [French *banderole,* from Italian *banderuola,* from *bandiera* "banner", of Germanic origin]

ban•di•coot \'ban-di-,küt\ *n* : any of various small insect-eating and plant-eating marsupial mammals especially of Australia [Telugu (a Dravidian language of India) *pandikokku*]

bandicoot

ban•dit \'ban-dət\ *n, pl* **ban•dits 1** *pl also* **ban•dit•ti** \ban-'dit-ē\ : BRIGAND **2** : an unethical or criminal person (as a profiteer or gangster) [Italian *bandito,* from *bandire* "to banish", of Germanic origin] — **ban•dit•ry** \'ban-də-trē\ *n*

band•mas•ter \'band-,mas-tər, 'ban-\ *n* : a conductor of a musical band

ban•dog \'ban-,dȯg\ *n* : a fierce dog formerly kept tied as a watchdog [Middle English *band* + *dogge* "dog"]

ban•do•lier *or* **ban•do•leer** \,ban-də-'liər\ *n* : a belt worn over the shoulder and across the breast to carry something (as cartridges) or as part of an official or ceremonial dress [Middle

French *bandouliere*, derived from Spanish *bando* band]

band saw *n* : a saw in the form of an endless steel belt running over pulleys

band shell *n* : a bandstand backed by a sounding board shaped like a huge concave seashell

bands·man \'banz-mən, 'bandz-\ *n* : a member of a musical band

band·stand \'ban-ˌstand, 'band-\ *n* : a usually roofed outdoor platform on which a band or orchestra performs

band·wag·on \-ˌwag-ən\ *n* **1** : a wagon carrying musicians in a parade **2** : a candidate, side, or movement that attracts increasing support or approval because it seems to be winning or gaining popularity — used in phrases like *climb on the bandwagon*

[1]**ban·dy** \'ban-dē\ *vb.* **ban·died**; **ban·dy·ing** **1** : to treat in a careless or high-handed manner **2 a** : EXCHANGE; *esp* : to exchange in argument ⟨*bandy* sharp words⟩ **b** : to discuss lightly or glibly or as a subject of gossip **3** *archaic* : to band together [probably from Middle French *bander* "to bat a tennis ball back and forth"]

[2]**bandy** *adj* : curved especially outward : BOWED ⟨*bandy* legs⟩ [probably from *bandy* "hockey stick"]

ban·dy–legged \ˌban-dē-'legd, -'leg-əd\ *adj* : having bandy legs : BOWLEGGED

bane \'bān\ *n* **1** : something that destroys life; *esp* : deadly poison **2** : a source of injury, harm, ruin, or woe : a destructive influence [Old English *bana* "murderer"]

bane·ful \'bān-fəl\ *adj* **1** *archaic* : having poisonous qualities : NOXIOUS **2** : causing destruction or woe : RUINOUS — **bane·ful·ly** \-fə-lē\ *adv*

[1]**bang** \'bang\ *vb* **1** : to strike against : BUMP **2** : to strike with a sharp noise **3** : to produce a sharp often explosive noise or series of noises [probably of Scandinavian origin]

[2]**bang** *n* **1** : a resounding blow **2** : a sudden loud noise **3 a** : a sudden striking effect **b** : a quick burst of energy **c** : an emotional thrill

[3]**bang** *adv* : EXACTLY, DIRECTLY ⟨*bang* in the middle⟩

[4]**bang** *n* : a fringe of banged hair — usually used in pl. [probably from *bangtail* "short tail"]

[5]**bang** *vt* : to cut (as front hair) short and squarely across

ban·gle \'bang-gəl\ *n* **1** : an ornamental circlet worn as a bracelet or anklet **2** : a small ornament hanging (as from a bracelet) loosely [Hindi *baṅglī*]

bang·tail \'bang-ˌtāl\ *n* **1** : RACEHORSE **2** : a wild horse

bang–up \'bang-ˌəp\ *adj* : of the best quality : FIRST-RATE ⟨had a *bang-up* time⟩

ban·ish \'ban-ish\ *vt* **1** : to compel by authority to leave a country ⟨the king *banished* the traitors⟩ **2** : to drive out from or as if from a home : EXPEL ⟨*banish* fears⟩ [Middle French *baniss-*, stem of *banir*, of Germanic origin] — **ban·ish·er** *n* — **ban·ish·ment** \-ish-mənt\ *n*

ban·is·ter *also* **ban·nis·ter** \'ban-ə-stər\ *n* **1** : one of the upright supports of a handrail alongside a staircase **2** : a handrail with its supporting posts **3** : HANDRAIL [alteration of *baluster*]

ban·jo \'ban-ˌjō\ *n, pl* **banjos** *also* **banjoes** : a musical instrument related to the guitar with a long narrow fretted neck and small drum-shaped body [probably of African origin] — **ban·jo·ist** \-ˌjō-əst\ *n*

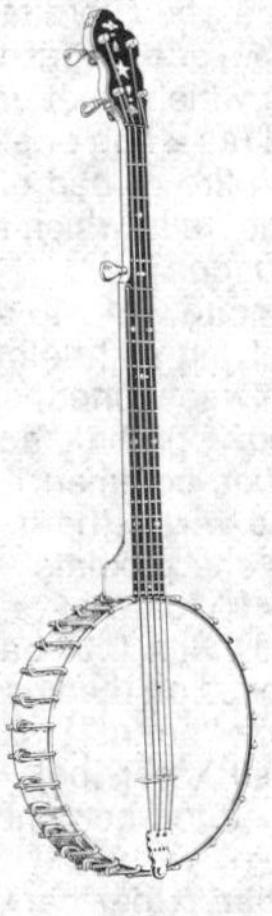

banjo

[1]**bank** \'bangk\ *n* **1** : a mound, pile, or ridge (as of earth) **2** : a piled up mass of cloud or fog **3** : an undersea elevation rising especially from the continental shelf : SHOAL **4** : rising ground bordering a lake, river, or sea or forming the edge of a hollow (as a cut) **5** : a steep slope (as of a hill) **6** : the inward tilt of a surface along a curve or of a vehicle (as an airplane) when taking a curve [probably of Scandinavian origin]

[2]**bank** *vb* **1** : to raise a bank about **2** : to heap or pile in a bank **3** : to rise in or form a bank **4** : to cover (a fire) with fresh fuel so as to reduce the speed of burning **5** : to build (a curve) with the roadbed or track inclined laterally upward from the inside edge **6** : to incline an airplane laterally when turning **7** : to form or group in a tier

[3]**bank** *n* **1** : a bench for the rowers of a galley **2** : a group or series of objects (as oars or typewriter keys) arranged close together in a row or a tier [Old French *banc* "bench", of Germanic origin]

[4]**bank** *n* **1** : a place of business that receives, lends, issues, exchanges, and takes care of money, extends credit, and provides ways of sending funds quickly from place to place **2** : a small container in which coins or bills are saved **3 a** : a supply of something held in reserve **b** (1) : the fund of the banker or dealer in a card or board game (2) : a fund of pieces belonging to a game (as dominoes) from which the players draw **4** : a storage place for a reserve supply ⟨eye *bank*⟩ [Italian *banca*, literally, "bench", of Germanic origin]

△ **origin** The literal meaning of Italian *banca* was "bench", but the word was also used for the benchlike counter at which an early money changer transacted business and later for the money changer's shop itself, the bank. When the banking trade spread from Italy to France, and so to England, the Italian word went with it and became our English *bank*.

Although they come from different languages, the English homographs of *bank* are all related and are related to the English word *bench* as well. The original meaning of the words in this group was probably something like "shelf".

[5]**bank** *vb* **1** : to act as a banker **2** : to have an account in a bank **3** : to deposit in a bank ⟨*banks* $10 every week⟩ — **bank on** *or* **bank upon** : to depend upon

bank·book \'bangk-ˌbu̇k\ *n* : a depositor's book in which a bank records each deposit and withdrawal — called also *passbook*

bank discount *n* : the interest discounted in advance on a note and computed on the face value of the note — compare TRUE DISCOUNT

bank·er \'bang-kər\ *n* **1** : one that engages in the business of banking **2** : the player who keeps the bank in a card or board game

bank holiday *n, British* : LEGAL HOLIDAY

bank·ing *n* : the business of a bank or a banker

bank note *n* : a promissory note issued by a bank, payable to bearer on demand without interest, and acceptable as money

bank·roll \'bangk-ˌrōl\ *n* : supply of money : FUNDS

[1]**bank·rupt** \'bang-ˌkrəpt\ *n* **1** : a person who becomes unable to pay his debts; *esp* : one whose property is turned over by court order to a trustee to be administered for the benefit of his creditors **2** : one that lacks completely a specified quality or thing ⟨a moral *bankrupt*⟩ [Italian *bancarotta* "bankruptcy", literally, "broken bank"]

[2]**bankrupt** *vt* : to make bankrupt

[3]**bankrupt** *adj* **1 a** : fallen into a state of financial ruin : IMPOVERISHED **b** : legally declared a bankrupt **2** : DEPLETED, DESTITUTE **1** — used with *of* or *in*

bank·rupt·cy \'bang-ˌkrəp-sē, -ˌkrəp-\ *n, pl* **-cies** : the condition of being bankrupt

[1]**ban·ner** \'ban-ər\ *n* **1 a** : a piece of cloth attached by one edge to a staff and used as a standard **b** : [4]FLAG **1** **c** : an ensign displaying a distinctive or symbolic device or inscription **2** : a headline in large type running across a newspaper page **3** : a strip of cloth on which a sign is painted **4** : a name, slogan, or goal associated with a particular group or point of view ⟨crusading under the *banner* of progress⟩ [Old French *banere*, of Germanic origin]

[2]**banner** *adj* : much better than usual ⟨a *banner* year for apple growers⟩

ban·nock \'ban-ək\ *n* : an often unleavened bread of oat or barley flour baked in flat loaves [Middle English *bannok*]

banns \'banz\ *n pl* : public announcement especially in church of a proposed marriage [Middle English *bane, ban* "proclamation, ban"]

[1]**ban·quet** \'bang-kwət, 'ban-, -ˌkwet\ *n* : an elaborate often ceremonious meal for many people frequently in celebration of a special occasion [Middle French, from Italian *banchetto*, from *banca* "bench, bank"]

[2]**banquet** *vb* **1** : to entertain with a banquet : FEAST **2** : to par-

\ə\ **abut**	\au̇\ **out**	\i\ **tip**	\ȯ\ **saw**	\u̇\ **foot**
\ər\ **further**	\ch\ **chin**	\ī\ **life**	\ȯi\ **coin**	\y\ **yet**
\a\ **mat**	\e\ **pet**	\j\ **job**	\th\ **thin**	\yü\ **few**
\ā\ **take**	\ē\ **easy**	\ng\ **sing**	\t͟h\ **this**	\yu̇\ **cure**
\ä\ **cot, cart**	\g\ **go**	\ō\ **bone**	\ü\ **food**	\zh\ **vision**

take of a banquet — **ban·quet·er** *n*

ban·quette \bang-ˈket, ban-\ *n* **:** a long upholstered seat especially along a wall

ban·shee \ˈban-ˌshē, ban-ˈ\ *n* **:** a female spirit in Gaelic folklore whose appearance or wailing warns of approaching death [Scottish Gaelic *bean-sīth*]

1ban·tam \ˈbant-əm\ *n* **1 :** any of numerous small domestic fowls that are often miniatures of members of the standard breeds **2 :** a small and often quarrelsome person [*Bantam,* former territorial unit in Java]

2bantam *adj* **1 :** SMALL 1, DIMINUTIVE **2 :** pertly quarrelsome **:** SAUCY

ban·tam·weight \-ˌwāt\ *n* **:** a boxer in a weight division having the approximate range of 51 to 54 kilograms

1ban·ter \ˈbant-ər\ *vb* **1 :** to speak to in a witty and teasing manner **:** RALLY **2 :** to talk or act playfully or wittily [origin unknown] — **ban·ter·er** \-ər-ər\ *n* — **ban·ter·ing·ly** \ˈbant-ə-ring-lē\ *adv*

2banter *n* **:** good-natured and witty teasing or joking

bant·ling \ˈbant-ling\ *n* **:** a very young child [perhaps from German *bänkling* "bastard"]

Ban·tu \ˈban-ˌtü, ˈbän-\ *n* **1 :** a member of a family of negroid peoples occupying equatorial and southern Africa **2 :** a group of African languages spoken generally south of a line from Cameroons to Kenya — **Bantu** *adj*

Ban·tu·stan \ˌban-tü-ˈstan, ˌbän-tü-ˈstän\ *n* **:** an all-black unit of territory in the Republic of South Africa with a limited degree of self-government [*Bantu* + *-stan* "land" (as in *Hindustan*)]

ban·yan \ˈban-yən\ *n* **:** a large East Indian tree related to the fig from whose branches aerial roots grow downward into the ground and form new supporting trunks [*banyan* "Hindu merchant", from Hindi *baniyā;* from a merchant's pagoda built under such a tree in Iran]

ban·zai \bän-ˈzī, ˈbän-\ *n* **:** a Japanese cheer or cry of triumph — usually used interjectionally [Japanese]

bao·bab \ˈbau̇-ˌbab, ˈbā-ə-ˌbab\ *n* **:** an Old World tropical tree with a broad trunk, an edible acid fruit resembling a gourd, and bark used in making paper, cloth, and rope [probably native name in Africa]

bap·tism \ˈbap-ˌtiz-əm\ *n* **1 :** a Christian sacrament signifying spiritual rebirth and admitting the recipient to the Christian community through the ritual use of water **2 :** a non-Christian ceremony using water for ritual purification **3 :** an act, experience, or ordeal by which one is named, purified, or initiated into a new life ⟨a soldier's *baptism* of fire⟩ — **bap·tis·mal** \bap-ˈtiz-məl\ *adj* — **bap·tis·mal·ly** \-mə-lē\ *adv*

Bap·tist \ˈbap-təst\ *n* **:** a Protestant of an evangelical denomination practicing congregational government and baptism by immersion for believers — **Baptist** *adj*

bap·tis·tery *or* **bap·tis·try** \ˈbap-tə-strē\ *n, pl* **-ter·ies** *or* **-tries :** a part of a church or formerly a separate building used for baptism

bap·tize \bap-ˈtīz, ˈbap-ˌ\ *vt* **1 :** to administer baptism to **2 a :** to purify spiritually especially by a cleansing experience or ordeal **b :** INITIATE 1 **3 :** to give a name to (as at baptism) **:** CHRISTEN [Greek *baptizein* "to dip, baptize"] — **bap·tiz·er** *n*

1bar \ˈbär\ *n* **1 a :** a rigid piece (as of wood or metal) that is longer than it is wide and has various uses (as for a lever, barrier, or fastening) **b :** a usually rectangular solid piece or block of material longer than it is wide ⟨*bar* of soap⟩ ⟨candy *bar*⟩ **2 :** something that obstructs or prevents passage, progress, or action **:** IMPEDIMENT: as **a :** any intangible or nonphysical impediment **b :** a submerged or partly submerged bank along a shore or in a river **3 a :** the railing in a courtroom that encloses the place where the business of the court is transacted **b :** a court or system of courts **c :** an authority or tribunal that renders judgment ⟨before the *bar* of public opinion⟩ **d :** the body of lawyers qualified to practice in a jurisdiction ⟨the New York *bar*⟩; *also* **:** the profession of lawyer **4 :** a straight stripe, band, or line much longer than it is wide **5 a :** a counter for serving food or especially alcoholic beverages **b :** BARROOM **6 a :** a vertical line across the musical staff before the initial measure accent **b :** MEASURE 4c [Old French *barre*]

1bar 6a

2bar *vt* **barred; bar·ring 1 a :** to fasten with a bar **b :** to place bars across to prevent passage **2 :** to mark with bars **:** STRIPE **3 :** to block off **:** OBSTRUCT ⟨*bar* the road to traffic⟩ **4 a :** to keep out **:** EXCLUDE ⟨*bar* reporters from the meeting⟩ **b :** PREVENT, FORBID ⟨the order *bars* discrimination in hiring⟩

3bar *prep* **:** with the exception of ⟨*bar* none⟩

1barb \ˈbärb\ *n* **1 a :** a sharp projection extending backward (as from the point of an arrow or fishhook) and preventing easy removal **b :** any of various natural objects (as a hooked plant hair or a lateral filament of a feather) resembling a barb **2 :** a biting or pointedly critical remark or comment [Middle French *barbe,* literally, "beard", from Latin *barba*]

2barb *vt* **:** to furnish with a barb

3barb *n* **:** a horse of a breed related to the Arab and introduced into Spain by the Moors [French *barbe,* from Italian *barbero,* from *barbero* "of Barbary"]

bar·bar·i·an \bär-ˈber-ē-ən, bär-ˈbar-\ *adj* **1 :** of, relating to, or being a land, culture, or people alien to and usually felt to be inferior to one's own **2 :** lacking refinement, learning, or artistic or literary culture [Latin *barbarus,* from Greek *barbaros* "foreign, ignorant"] — **barbarian** *n* — **bar·bar·i·an·ism** \-ē-ə-ˌniz-əm\ *n*

• **syn** BARBARIAN, BARBAROUS, BARBARIC, SAVAGE mean characteristic of an uncivilized person. BARBARIAN often implies a state somewhere between tribal savagery and full civilization; BARBAROUS tends to stress the harsher or more brutal side of uncivilized life; BARBARIC suggests crudeness of taste and fondness for gorgeous and unrestrained display; SAVAGE suggests more primitive culture than BARBARIAN and greater harshness or fierceness than BARBAROUS.

bar·bar·ic \bär-ˈbar-ik\ *adj* **1 :** of, relating to, or characteristic of barbarians **2 a :** marked by a lack of restraint **b :** having a bizarre, primitive, or unsophisticated quality ⟨*barbaric* splendor⟩ **syn** see BARBARIAN

bar·ba·rism \ˈbär-bə-ˌriz-əm\ *n* **1 :** an idea, act, word, or expression that offends against contemporary standards of good taste or acceptability **2 a :** a barbarian state of social or intellectual development **b :** the practice or display of barbarian acts, attitudes, or ideas

bar·bar·i·ty \bär-ˈbar-ət-ē\ *n, pl* **-ties 1 :** BARBARISM **2 a :** barbarous cruelty **b :** an act or instance of barbarous cruelty

bar·ba·rize \ˈbär-bə-ˌrīz\ *vb* **:** to make or become barbarian or barbarous — **bar·ba·ri·za·tion** \ˌbär-bə-rə-ˈzā-shən, -brə-\ *n*

bar·ba·rous \ˈbär-bə-rəs, -brəs\ *adj* **1 :** characterized by the use of barbarisms in speech or writing **2 a :** of or relating to a backward land or people **b :** lacking culture or refinement **3 :** mercilessly harsh or cruel **syn** see BARBARIAN — **bar·ba·rous·ly** *adv* — **bar·ba·rous·ness** *n*

Bar·ba·ry ape \ˌbär-bə-rē-, -brē-\ *n* **:** a tailless monkey of North Africa and Gibraltar

1bar·be·cue \ˈbär-bi-ˌkyü\ *n* **1 :** an often portable fireplace over which meat and fish are roasted or broiled **2 :** a large animal (as a hog or steer) roasted or broiled whole or split over an open fire or bed of hot coals **3 :** a social gathering especially outdoors at which barbecued food is eaten [American Spanish *barbacoa*]

2barbecue *vt* **1 :** to roast or broil on a rack over hot coals or on a revolving spit before or over a source of heat **2 :** to cook in a highly seasoned vinegar sauce

barbed \ˈbärbd\ *adj* **1 :** having a barb **2 :** bitingly critical ⟨a *barbed* comment⟩

barbed wire \ˈbärb-ˈdwīr, ˈbäb-, -ˈwīr\ *n* **:** twisted wires armed with sharp points — called also *barbwire*

bar·bel \ˈbär-bəl\ *n* **1 :** a European freshwater fish of the carp family with four barbels on its upper jaw **2 :** a slender tactile process on the lips of a fish [Middle French, derived from Latin *barba* "beard"]

bar·bell \ˈbär-ˌbel\ *n* **:** a bar with adjustable weighted disks attached to each end that is used for exercise and in weight lifting

1bar·ber \ˈbär-bər\ *n* **:** one whose business is cutting and dressing hair, shaving and trimming beards, and performing related services [Middle French *barbeor,* from *barbe* "beard", from Latin *barba*]

[2]**barber** *vb* **bar•bered**; **bar•ber•ing** \-bə-riŋ, -briŋ\ : to perform the services of a barber

bar•ber•ry \'bär-ˌber-ē\ *n* : any of a genus of spiny yellow-flowered shrubs with bright red oblong berries often grown for hedges or ornament [Arabic *barbārīs*]

[1]**bar•ber•shop** \'bär-bər-ˌshäp\ *n* : a barber's place of business

[2]**barbershop** *adj* : having a style of unaccompanied vocal harmonizing of popular songs especially by a quartet

barber's itch *n* : ringworm of the face and neck

bar•bette \bär-'bet\ *n* : a cylinder of armor protecting a gun turret on a warship

bar•bi•can \'bär-bi-kən\ *n* : an outer defensive work; *esp* : a tower at a gate or bridge [Medieval Latin *barbacana*]

bar•bi•tal \'bär-bə-ˌtȯl\ *n* : a white habit-forming drug used especially to induce sleep

bar•bi•tu•rate \bär-'bich-ə-rət, -ˌrāt\ *n* : any of various derivatives of barbituric acid used especially as sedatives or hypnotics

bar•bi•tu•ric acid \ˌbär-bə-ˌtyu̇r-ik-, -ˌtu̇r-\ *n* : a crystalline acid $C_4H_4N_2O_3$ used in making plastics and drugs [German *barbitursäure*, derived from the name *Barbara* + New Latin *urea* + German *säure* "acid"]

bar•bule \'bär-ˌbyül\ *n* : a minute barb; *esp* : one of the processes that fringe the barbs of a feather

bar•ca•role *or* **bar•ca•rolle** \'bär-kə-ˌrōl\ *n* **1** : a Venetian boat song characterized by a beat suggesting a rowing rhythm **2** : a piece of music imitating a barcarole [French *barcarolle*, from Italian *barcarola*, from *barca* "bark"]

bar chart *n* : BAR GRAPH

bard \'bärd\ *n* **1** : a tribal poet-singer gifted in composing and reciting verses on heroes and their deeds **2** : POET [Irish and Scottish Gaelic] — **bard•ic** \'bärd-ik\ *adj*

[1]**bare** \'baər, 'beər\ *adj* **1 a** : lacking a natural, usual, or appropriate covering ⟨trees *bare* of leaves⟩ **b** : lacking clothing **2** : open to view : EXPOSED ⟨their guilt was laid *bare*⟩ **3 a** : completely unfurnished or only scantily supplied **b** : DESTITUTE ⟨*bare* of all safeguards⟩ **4 a** : having nothing left over or added : MERE ⟨a *bare* majority⟩ **b** : not adorned or expanded : PLAIN ⟨the *bare* facts⟩ [Old English *bær*] — **bare•ness** *n*

[2]**bare** *vt* : to make or lay bare : UNCOVER, REVEAL

[3]**bare** *archaic past of* BEAR

bare•back \-ˌbak\ *or* **bare•backed** \-'bakt\ *adv or adj* : on the bare back of a horse : without a saddle ⟨learned to ride *bareback*⟩ ⟨a *bareback* rider in the circus⟩

bare•faced \-'fāst\ *adj* **1** : having the face uncovered **2** : SHAMELESS, BOLD ⟨a *barefaced* lie⟩ — **bare•faced•ly** \-'fā-səd-lē, -'fāst-lē\ *adv* — **bare•faced•ness** \-'fā-səd-nəs; -'fāst-nəs\ *n*

bare•foot \-ˌfu̇t\ *or* **bare•foot•ed** \-'fu̇t-əd\ *adv or adj* : with the feet bare : UNSHOD ⟨went *barefoot* in summer⟩

bare•hand•ed \-'han-dəd\ *adv or adj* **1** : with the hands bare : without gloves or mittens **2** : without tools or weapons ⟨fight an animal *barehanded*⟩

bare•head•ed \-'hed-əd\ *adv or adj* : with the head bare : without a hat

bare•ly *adv* **1** : SCARCELY, HARDLY ⟨*barely* enough money to live on⟩ **2** : in a scanty manner ⟨a *barely* furnished room⟩

barf \'bärf\ *vi* : VOMIT 1 [origin unknown]

[1]**bar•gain** \'bär-gən\ *n* **1** : an agreement between parties settling what each is to give or receive in a transaction **2** : something gained by or as if by bargaining; *esp* : an advantageous purchase ⟨at 35 percent off, the suit was a real *bargain*⟩ **3** : a situation or event with important good or bad results ⟨got the worst of a bad *bargain*⟩ [Middle French *bargaigne*, from *bargaigner* "to bargain", of Germanic origin]

[2]**bargain** *vb* **1** : to talk over the terms of a purchase, agreement, or contract; *esp* : to try to win advantageous terms from the other party to a proposed bargain **2** : to sell or dispose of by bargaining — **bar•gain•er** *n* — **bargain for** : to count on in advance : EXPECT ⟨more trouble than we *bargained for*⟩

[1]**barge** \'bärj\ *n* **1** : a broad flat-bottomed boat used chiefly for the transport of goods on inland waterways **2** : a ship's boat for the use of a naval officer ranking above a captain [Old French, "boat, small ship", from Late Latin *barca*]

[2]**barge** *vb* **1** : to carry by barge **2** : to move or thrust oneself clumsily or rudely ⟨they *barged* right in without being invited⟩

barge•man \-mən\ *n* : the master or a deckhand of a barge

bar graph *n* : a graphic means of comparing numbers by rectangles whose lengths are proportional to the numbers represented — called also *bar chart*

bar•ite \'baər-ˌīt, 'beər-\ *n* : barium sulfate $BaSO_4$ occurring as a mineral

[1]**bari•tone** *also* **bary•tone** \'bar-ə-ˌtōn\ *n* **1 a** : a male singing voice of medium range between bass and tenor **b** : a man having such a voice **2** : the saxhorn intermediate in size between althorn and tuba — called also *baritone horn* [derived from Greek *barys* "heavy" + *tonos* "tone"] — **bari•tonal** \ˌbar-ə-'tōn-l\ *adj*

[2]**baritone** *also* **barytone** *adj* : relating to or having the range or part of a baritone

bar•i•um \'bar-ē-əm, 'ber-\ *n* : a silver-white malleable toxic bivalent metallic chemical element that occurs only in combination — see ELEMENT table [New Latin, from Greek *barys* "heavy"]

barium sulfate *n* : a colorless crystalline insoluble compound $BaSO_4$ that is used as a pigment, as a filler, and as a substance opaque to X rays in medical photography of the alimentary canal

[1]**bark** \'bärk\ *vb* **1** : to utter a bark or similar sound **2** : to speak or utter in a curt loud usually angry tone ⟨*bark* out an order⟩ **3** : to advertise by persistent outcry ⟨vendors *barked* their wares⟩ [Old English *beorcan*] — **bark up the wrong tree** : to speak or act on the basis of a misunderstanding

[2]**bark** *n* : the characteristic short loud cry of a dog

[3]**bark** *n* : the tough largely corky exterior covering of a woody root or stem [Old Norse *börkr*]

[4]**bark** *vt* **1** : to strip the bark from **2** : to rub off or abrade the skin of

[5]**bark** *or* **barque** *n* **1 a** : a small sailing ship **b** : a 3-masted sailing vessel with foremast and mainmast square-rigged and mizzenmast fore-and-aft rigged **2** : a craft propelled by sails or oars [Middle French *barque*, from Provençal *barca*, from Late Latin]

bar•keep•er \'bär-ˌkē-pər\ *or* **bar•keep** \-ˌkēp\ *n* : one that owns, operates, or tends a bar for the sale of alcoholic beverages

bar•ken•tine *also* **bar•quen•tine** \'bär-kən-ˌtēn\ *n* : a 3-masted sailing vessel having the foremast square-rigged and the mainmast and mizzenmast fore-and-aft rigged [[5]*bark* + *-entine*, alteration of *-antine* (as in *brigantine*)]

bark•er \'bär-kər\ *n* : a person who stands at the entrance to a show and tries to attract customers to it with loud fluent talk ⟨a sideshow *barker*⟩

barky \'bär-kē\ *adj* **bark•i•er**; **-est** : covered with or resembling bark

bar•ley \'bär-lē\ *n* : a cereal grass with flowers in dense spikes with three spikelets at each joint; *also* : its seed used in malt beverages and as food or stock feed [Old English *bærlic* "of barley"]

bar•ley•corn \-ˌkȯrn\ *n* : a grain of barley

barm \'bärm\ *n* : yeast formed on fermenting malt liquors [Old English *beorma*]

bar•maid \'bär-ˌmād\ *n* : a woman who works as a bartender

bar•man \-mən\ *n* : a man who works as a bartender

Bar•me•cid•al \ˌbär-mə-'sīd-l\ *or* **Bar•me•cide** \'bär-mə-ˌsīd\ *adj* : providing only an apparent abundance ⟨a *Barmecidal* feast⟩ [*Barmecide*, a wealthy Persian, who, in a tale of *The Arabian Nights*, invited a beggar to a feast of imaginary food]

[1]**bar mitz•vah** \bär-'mits-və\ *n*, *often cap B&M* **1** : a Jewish boy who reaches his 13th birthday and attains the age of religious duty and responsibility **2** : the ceremony recognizing a boy as a bar mitzvah [Hebrew *bar miṣwāh*, literally, "son of the law"]

[2]**bar mitzvah** *vt* **bar mitz•vahed**; **bar mitz•vah•ing** : to administer the ceremony of bar mitzvah to

barn \'bärn\ *n* : a building used chiefly for storing grain and hay and for housing farm animals (as cows and horses) [Old English *bereærn*, from *bere* "barley" + *ærn* "place"]

bar•na•cle \'bär-ni-kəl\ *n* : any of numerous marine crustaceans (order Cirripedia) that are free-swimming as larvae but fixed (as to rocks or pilings) as adults [Middle English *bernake*,

\ə\ **abut**	\au̇\ **out**	\i\ **tip**	\ȯ\ **saw**	\u̇\ **foot**
\ər\ **further**	\ch\ **chin**	\ī\ **life**	\ȯi\ **coin**	\y\ **yet**
\a\ **mat**	\e\ **pet**	\j\ **job**	\th\ **thin**	\yü\ **few**
\ā\ **take**	\ē\ **easy**	\ŋ\ **sing**	\t͟h\ **this**	\yu̇\ **cure**
\ä\ **cot, cart**	\g\ **go**	\ō\ **bone**	\ü\ **food**	\zh\ **vision**

a goose once believed to grow from barnacles, of Celtic origin] — **bar·na·cled** \-kəld\ *adj*

barn dance *n* : an American social dance originally held in a barn and featuring square dances, round dances, and traditional music and calls

barn·storm \ˈbärn-ˌstȯrm\ *vi* **1** : to tour through rural districts staging theatrical performances usually in one-night stands **2** : to travel from place to place making brief stops (as in political campaigning) **3** : to pilot an airplane in sight-seeing flights with passengers or in exhibition stunts in an unscheduled course especially in rural districts — **barn·storm·er** *n*

barn swallow *n* : a common swallow of both the Old World and the New World that usually attaches its nest to beams and rafters of barns

barn·yard \-ˌyärd\ *n* : a usually fenced area adjoining a barn

baro- *combining form* : weight : pressure ⟨*baro*meter⟩ [Greek *baros* "weight"]

baro·graph \ˈbar-ə-ˌgraf\ *n* : a self-registering barometer

ba·rom·e·ter \bə-ˈräm-ət-ər\ *n* **1** : an instrument for determining the pressure of the atmosphere that is used to forecast weather and to determine altitude **2** : something that registers changes (as in public opinion) — **bar·o·met·ric** \ˌbar-ə-ˈme-trik\ *adj*

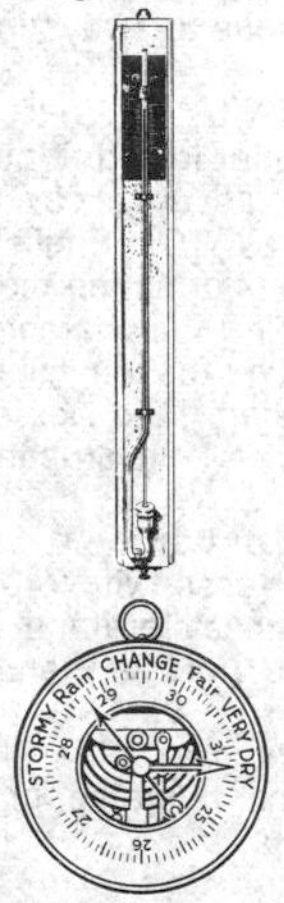

barometer 1: *top* mercury, *bottom* aneroid

bar·on \ˈbar-ən\ *n* **1 a** : a tenant holding rights and title usually by military service directly from a feudal superior (as a king) **b** : a member of the nobility : PEER **2** : a member of the lowest grade of the British peerage **3** : a person of great or excessive power or influence in some field ⟨cattle *baron*⟩ [Old French, of Germanic origin]

bar·on·age \-ə-nij\ *n* : the whole body of barons or peers

bar·on·ess \-ə-nəs\ *n* **1** : the wife or widow of a baron **2** : a woman who holds a baronial title in her own right

bar·on·et \ˈbar-ə-nət\ *n* : a person holding a rank of honor below a baron but above a knight

ba·ro·ni·al \bə-ˈrō-nē-əl\ *adj* : of, relating to, or suitable for a baron or the baronage ⟨lives in *baronial* splendor⟩

bar·ony \ˈbar-ə-nē\ *n, pl* **bar·on·ies** : the domain, rank, or dignity of a baron

ba·roque \bə-ˈrōk, ba-, -ˈräk\ *adj* : of or relating to a style of artistic expression especially of the 17th century marked by elaborate and sometimes grotesque ornamentation and the use of curved and exaggerated figures in art and architecture, by improvisation, contrast, and tension in music, and by complex form and bizarre, ingenious, and often ambiguous imagery in literature [French, from Italian *barocco*] — **baroque** *n*

ba·rouche \bə-ˈrüsh\ *n* : a four-wheeled carriage with a driver's seat high in front, two double seats inside facing each other, and a folding top [German *barutsche*, from Italian *biroccio*, derived from Latin *bi-* "two" + *rota* "wheel"]

barque \ˈbärk\ *variant of* BARK

barquentine *variant of* BARKENTINE

bar·rack \ˈbar-ək, -ik\ *n* **1** : a building or group of buildings in which soldiers are quartered — usually used in pl. **2** : a plain large building — usually used in pl. [French *baraque* "hut", from Catalan *barraca*]

bar·ra·cu·da \ˌbar-ə-ˈküd-ə\ *n, pl* **-da** *or* **-das** : any of several large predatory marine fishes of warm seas related to the gray mullets [American Spanish]

[1]**bar·rage** \ˈbär-ij\ *n* : an artificial dam placed in a watercourse to increase the depth of water or to divert it into a channel for navigation or irrigation [French, from *barrer* "to bar"]

[2]**bar·rage** \bə-ˈräzh, -ˈräj\ *n* **1** : a barrier of continuous artillery or machine-gun fire directed upon a narrow strip of ground close to friendly troops to screen and protect them **2** : a rapid or concentrated delivery or outpouring (as of speech or writing) — **barrage** *vt*

bar·ra·try \ˈbar-ə-trē\ *n, pl* **-tries** **1** : the purchase or sale of offices of honor or profit in church or state **2** : a fraudulent breach of duty by the master or crew of a ship intended to harm the owner or cargo **3** : the practice of inciting lawsuits or quarrels [Middle French *baraterie* "deception", from *barater* "to deceive, exchange"]

barred \ˈbärd\ *adj* : having alternate bands of different color

[1]**bar·rel** \ˈbar-əl\ *n* **1** : a round bulging container that is longer than it is wide and has flat ends **2 a** : the amount held by a barrel; *esp* : the amount (as 159 liters of petroleum) fixed for a product and used as a unit of measure **b** : a great quantity ⟨a *barrel* of fun⟩ **3** : a cylindrical or tubular part ⟨gun *barrel*⟩ **4** : the body proper of a four-footed animal [Middle French *baril*] — **bar·reled** \-əld\ *adj*

[2]**barrel** *vb* **-reled** *or* **-relled**; **-rel·ing** *or* **-rel·ling** **1** : to put or pack in a barrel **2** : to travel at a high speed

bar·rel·ful \ˈbar-əl-ˌfu̇l\ *n, pl* **bar·rel·fuls** \-əl-ˌfu̇lz\ *or* **bar·rels·ful** \-əlz-ˌfu̇l\ : as much or as many as a barrel will hold

barrel organ *n* : a musical instrument consisting of a revolving cylinder studded with pegs that open a series of valves to admit air from a bellows to a set of pipes

[1]**bar·ren** \ˈbar-ən\ *adj* **1 a** : incapable of producing offspring **b** : habitually failing to bear fruit ⟨*barren* apple trees⟩ **2 a** : producing little or no vegetation : DESOLATE ⟨*barren* deserts⟩ **b** : producing inferior crops ⟨*barren* soil⟩ **c** : unproductive of results or gain : FRUITLESS ⟨a *barren* scheme⟩ **3** : lacking interest, information, or charm [Old French *barain*] — **bar·ren·ly** *adv* — **bar·ren·ness** \-ən-nəs\ *n*

[2]**barren** *n* **1** : a tract of barren land **2** *pl* : a wide usually level tract with stunted or scrub trees or little vegetation

bar·rette \bä-ˈret, bə-\ *n* : a clip or bar for holding the hair in place [French]

[1]**bar·ri·cade** \ˈbar-ə-ˌkād, ˌbar-ə-ˈ\ *vt* **1** : to block off or stop up with a barricade **2** : to prevent access to by means of a barricade

[2]**barricade** *n* : a hastily made barrier for protecting against attack or for blocking the way [French, derived from Middle French *barrique* "barrel"]

bar·ri·er \ˈbar-ē-ər\ *n* **1** : a material object or set of objects that separates or marks off or serves as a barricade **2** : something immaterial that separates ⟨language *barriers* between peoples⟩ **3** : a factor (as a canyon or lack of food) that keeps organisms from interbreeding or spreading into new territory [Middle French *barriere*, from *barre* "bar"]

barrier reef *n* : a coral reef roughly parallel to a shore and separated from it by a lagoon

bar·ring \ˈbär-ing\ *prep* **1** : with the exception of ⟨*barring* none⟩ **2** : apart from the possibility of ⟨we will be there on time, *barring* accidents⟩

bar·rio \ˈbär-ē-ˌō, ˈbar-\ *n, pl* **-ri·os** **1** : a district of a city or town in Spanish-speaking countries **2** : a Spanish-speaking section of a city or town in the United States [Spanish, from Arabic *barrī* "of the open country"]

bar·ris·ter \ˈbar-ə-stər\ *n* : a British lawyer who is permitted to plead cases in court — compare SOLICITOR [derived from [1]*bar*]

bar·room \ˈbär-ˌrüm, -ˌru̇m\ *n* : a room or establishment whose main feature is a bar for the sale of liquor

[1]**bar·row** \ˈbar-ō\ *n* : a large burial mound of earth or stones [Old English *beorg* "mountain, mound"]

[2]**barrow** *n* : a male hog castrated before sexual maturity [Old English *bearg*]

[3]**barrow** *n* **1 a** : HANDBARROW **b** : WHEELBARROW **2** : a cart with a shallow box body, two wheels, and shafts for pushing it : PUSHCART [Old English *bearwe*]

bar·tend·er \ˈbär-ˌten-dər\ *n* : one that serves alcoholic beverages at a bar

[1]**bar·ter** \ˈbärt-ər\ *vb* : to trade one commodity directly for another without the use of money ⟨*bartered* for furs with tobacco and rum⟩ [Middle French *barater*] — **bar·ter·er** \ˈbärt-ər-ər\ *n*

[2]**barter** *n* : the exchange of goods without the use of money; *also* : something given in such an exchange

Bar·tho·lin's gland \ˌbärt-l-ənz-, ˌbär-thə-lənz-\ *n* : either of two oval racemose glands lying one to each side of the lower part of the vagina and secreting a lubricating mucus [Kaspar *Bartholin*, died 1738, Danish physician]

bar·ti·zan \ˈbärt-ə-zən\ *n* : a small overhanging or projecting structure (as a turret) for lookout or defense [Middle English *bretasing*]

Ba·ruch \bə-ˈrük, ˈbär-ˌük\ *n* — see BIBLE table

bary•on \'bar-ē-ˌän\ *n* : any of a group of elementary particles that have a mass equal to or greater than that of the proton [Greek *barys* "heavy"]

bary•tone \'bar-ə-ˌtōn\ *variant of* BARITONE

bas•al \'bā-səl, -zəl\ *adj* **1** : relating to, situated at, or forming the base **2** : of, relating to, or forming a foundation or basis : FUNDAMENTAL — **bas•al•ly** \-ē\ *adv*

basal body *n* : a minute distinctively staining cell organelle found at the base of a flagellum or cilium and resembling a centriole in structure

basal metabolic rate *n* : the rate at which heat is given off by an organism at complete rest

basal metabolism *n* : the metabolic activities of a fasting and resting organism in which energy is being used solely to maintain vital cellular activity, respiration, and circulation

ba•salt \bə-'sȯlt, 'bā-ˌ\ *n* : a dark fine-grained igneous rock [Latin *basaltes*] — **ba•sal•tic** \bə-'sȯl-tik\ *adj*

bas•cule \'bas-ˌkyül\ *n* : an apparatus or structure (as a bridge) in which one end is counterbalanced by the other on the principle of the seesaw or by weights [French, "seesaw"]

1**base** \'bās\ *n, pl* **bas•es** \'bā-səz\ **1 a** : the bottom of something that serves as its support : FOUNDATION **b** : a side or face of a geometrical figure usually from which an altitude can be constructed; *esp* : one on which the figure stands **c** : the length of a base **2 a** : a main ingredient **b** : an inert ingredient that carries the main ingredient (as of a medicine) **3** : the fundamental part of something : GROUNDWORK **4 a** : the point or line from which a start is made in an action or undertaking **b** : the locality or installations from which a military force operates **c** : a number (as 5 in $5^{6.44}$ or 5^7) that is raised to a power; *esp* : the number that when raised to a power equal to the logarithm of a number yields the number itself ⟨the logarithm of 100 to the *base* 10 is 2 since $10^2 = 100$⟩ **d** : a number equal to the number of units in a given digit's place that for a given system of writing numbers is required to give the numeral 1 in the next higher place ⟨the decimal system uses a *base* of 10⟩; *also* : such a system of writing numbers using an indicated base ⟨convert from *base* 10 to *base* 2⟩ **e** : ROOT 5 **5 a** : the starting place or goal in various games **b** : any of the four stations a runner in baseball must touch in order to score **6** : any of various compounds that are capable of reacting with an acid to form a salt, that when dissolved in water have a strong somewhat salty taste, turn litmus blue, and yield hydroxyl ions, that have a molecule or ion which can take up a proton from an acid, or that are substances able to give up to an acid an unshared pair of electrons [Latin *basis,* from Greek, from *bainein* "to go"] — **based** \'bāst\ *adj* — **off base 1** : seriously or absurdly mistaken **2** : by surprise : UNAWARES

2**base** *vt* **1** : to make, form, or serve as a base for **2** : to use as a base or basis for : ESTABLISH **3** : STATION

3**base** *adj* : constituting or serving as a base

4**base** *adj* **1** *archaic* : of humble birth : LOWLY **2 a** : being of comparatively low value and having inferior properties (as resistance to corrosion) ⟨a *base* metal such as iron⟩ **b** : made of or alloyed with a base metal **3** : morally low : MEAN, CONTEMPTIBLE ⟨*base* conduct⟩ [Middle French *bas* "low", from Medieval Latin *bassus*] — **base•ly** *adv* — **base•ness** *n*

base angle *n* : either of the angles of a triangle that have one side in common with the base

base•ball \'bās-ˌbȯl\ *n* : a game played with a bat and ball between two teams of nine players each on a field with four bases that mark the course a runner must take to score; *also* : the ball used in this game

base•board \-ˌbōrd, -ˌbȯrd\ *n* : a line of boards or molding covering the joint of a wall and a floor

base•born \-'bȯrn\ *adj* **1** : of humble birth : LOWLY **2** : of illegitimate birth : BASTARD

base exchange *n* : a post exchange at a naval or air force base

base hit *n* : a hit in baseball enabling the batter to reach base safely with no error made and no base runner forced out

base•less \'bās-ləs\ *adj* : having no cause or reason : GROUNDLESS ⟨a *baseless* accusation⟩

base line *n* **1** : a line that forms or represents a base **2** : the area within which a baseball player must keep when running between bases

base•ment \'bās-mənt\ *n* **1** : the part of a building that is wholly or partly below ground level **2** : BASE 1a

ba•sen•ji \bə-'sen-jē, -'zen-\ *n* : any of an African breed of small compact curly-tailed dogs that have a chestnut-brown coat and that rarely bark [of Bantu origin]

base on balls : an advance to first base given to a baseball player who receives four balls during a turn at bat

base path *n* : the area between the bases of a baseball field used by a base runner

base runner *n* : a baseball player of the team at bat who is on base or is attempting to reach a base — **base•run•ning** \'bās-ˌrən-ing\ *n*

1**bash** \'bash\ *vb* **1** : to strike violently : BEAT **2** : to smash by a blow **3** : CRASH 1a [origin unknown]

2**bash** *n* **1** : a forceful blow **2** : a festive social gathering : PARTY **3** : TRY, ATTEMPT

bash•ful \'bash-fəl\ *adj* **1** : inclined to shrink from public attention : SHY, DIFFIDENT **2** : characterized by or resulting from extreme sensitiveness or self-consciousness [Middle English *basshen* "to be abashed"] **syn** see SHY — **bash•ful•ly** \-fə-lē\ *adv* — **bash•ful•ness** *n*

1**ba•sic** \'bā-sik, -zik\ *adj* **1** : of, relating to, or forming the base or foundation : FUNDAMENTAL ⟨*basic* industries⟩ ⟨the *basic* facts⟩ **2** : constituting or serving as a basis or starting point ⟨*basic* course in French⟩ **3 a** : of, relating to, containing, or having the character of a base **b** : having an alkaline reaction **4** : containing relatively little silica ⟨*basic* rocks⟩ — **ba•si•cal•ly** \-si-klē, -kə-lē\ *adv* — **ba•sic•i•ty** \bā-'sis-ət-ē\ *n*

2**basic** *n* : something that is basic : FUNDAMENTAL ⟨the *basics* of education⟩

BA•SIC \'bā-sik, -zik\ *n* : a relatively easy language for programming and interacting with a computer [*B*eginner's *A*ll-purpose *S*ymbolic *I*nstruction *C*ode]

ba•sid•io•my•cete \bə-ˌsid-ē-ō-'mī-ˌsēt, -ˌmī-'sēt\ *n* : any of a large class (Basidiomycetes) of fungi (as rusts, smuts, or puffballs) having septate hyphae and spores borne on a basidium [*basidium* + Greek *mykēt-, mykēs* "fungus"] — **ba•sid•io•my•ce•tous** \-ō-mī-'sēt-əs\ *adj*

ba•sid•io•spore \bə-'sid-ē-ə-ˌspōr, -ˌspȯr\ *n* : a spore produced by a basidium

ba•sid•i•um \bə-'sid-ē-əm\ *n, pl* **-ia** \-ē-ə\ : a specialized cell of a basidiomycete bearing usually four basidiospores [New Latin, from Latin *basis*]

bas•il \'baz-əl, 'bāz-, 'bas-, 'bās-\ *n* : any of several plants of the mint family; *esp* : either of two plants with aromatic leaves used in cookery [Greek *basilikon,* from *basilikos* "royal"]

bas•i•lar \'baz-ə-lər, 'bas-\ *adj* : of, relating to, or situated at a base

ba•sil•i•ca \bə-'sil-i-kə, -'zil-\ *n* **1** : an oblong public building of ancient Rome ending in an apse **2** : an early Christian church building consisting of nave and aisles with clerestory and apse **3** : a Roman Catholic church with certain ceremonial privileges [Latin, from Greek *basilikē,* literally, "royal (hall)", from *basileus* "king"] — **ba•sil•i•can** \-kən\ *adj*

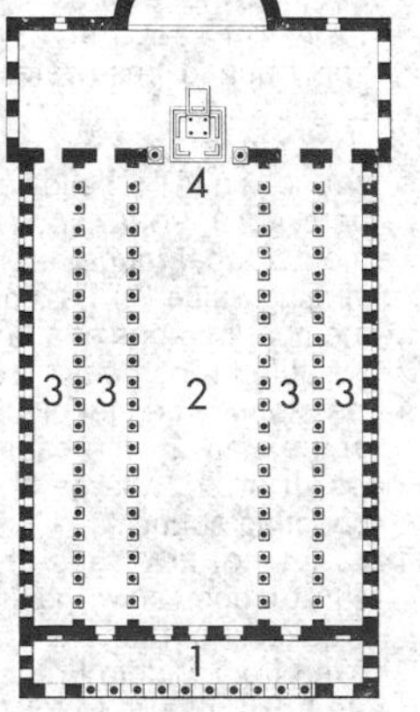

basilica 2: *1* narthex, *2* nave, *3* aisle, *4* altar

bas•i•lisk \'bas-ə-ˌlisk, 'baz-\ *n* **1** : a legendary reptile with fatal breath and glance **2** : any of several crested tropical American lizards related to the iguanas

ba•sin \'bās-n\ *n* **1 a** : a wide shallow usually round dish or bowl with sloping or curving sides for holding liquid **b** : the amount that a basin holds **2** : a natural or artificial hollow or enclosure usually containing water; *esp* : a partly enclosed water area for anchoring ships **3** : the land drained by a river and its branches [Old French *bacin,* from Late Latin *bacchinon*]

ba•sis \'bā-səs\ *n, pl* **ba•ses** \'bā-ˌsēz\ **1** : the base, foundation, or chief supporting part **2** : the principal component of something **3** : something on which something else is con-

\ə\ **abut**	\au̇\ **out**	\i\ **tip**	\ȯ\ **saw**	\u̇\ **foot**
\ər\ **further**	\ch\ **chin**	\ī\ **life**	\ȯi\ **coin**	\y\ **yet**
\a\ **mat**	\e\ **pet**	\j\ **job**	\th\ **thin**	\yü\ **few**
\ā\ **take**	\ē\ **easy**	\ng\ **sing**	\t͟h\ **this**	\yu̇\ **cure**
\ä\ **cot, cart**	\g\ **go**	\ō\ **bone**	\ü\ **food**	\zh\ **vision**

structed or established **4 :** the basic principle [Latin]

bask \'bask\ *vi* **:** to lie in or expose oneself to a pleasant warmth or atmosphere ⟨*basked* in the sun⟩ ⟨*basking* in their recent fame⟩ [Old Norse *bathask* "to bathe oneself"]

bas•ket \'bas-kət\ *n* **1 a :** a woven container (as of cane or strips of wood) **b :** the contents of a basket **2 :** something that resembles a basket in shape or use **3 a :** a net open at the bottom and suspended from a metal ring that forms the goal in basketball **b :** a field goal in basketball [Middle English] — **bas•ket•work** \-ˌwərk\ *n*

bas•ket•ball \-ˌbȯl\ *n* **:** a court game in which each of two teams of five players each tries to toss an inflated ball through a raised goal; *also* **:** the ball used in this game

basket–of–gold *n* **:** a European perennial herb widely cultivated for its grayish foliage and yellow flowers

basket case *n* **1 :** a person who has had all four limbs amputated **2 :** one that is totally disabled or inoperative

bas•ket•ry \'bas-kə-trē\ *n* **1 :** the art or craft of making baskets or objects woven like baskets **2 :** objects produced by basketry

basket weave *n* **:** a textile weave resembling the checkered pattern of a plaited basket

bas mitz•vah \bä-'smits-və\ *n, often cap B&M* **1 :** a Jewish girl who at about 13 years of age assumes religious responsibilities **2 :** the ceremony recognizing a girl as a bas mitzvah [Hebrew *bath miṣwāh,* literally, "daughter of the law"]

ba•so•phil \'bā-sə-ˌfil, -zə-\ *or* **ba•so•phile** \-ˌfīl\ *n* **:** a basophilic substance or structure; *esp* **:** a white blood cell with basophilic granules

ba•so•phil•ic \ˌbā-sə-'fil-ik, -zə-\ *adj* **:** staining readily with basic dyes

Basque \'bask\ *n* **1 :** a member of a people inhabiting a region bordering on the Bay of Biscay in northern Spain and southwestern France **2 :** the language of the Basque people [French, from Latin *Vasco*] — **Basque** *adj*

bas–re•lief \ˌbä-ri-'lēf\ *n* **:** a sculpture in relief in which the design is raised very slightly from the background [French, from *bas* "low" + *relief* "raised work"]

bas-relief

1bass \'bas\ *n, pl* **bass** *or* **bass•es** **:** any of several spiny-finned freshwater or marine sport and food fishes [Old English *bærs*]

2bass \'bās\ *n* **1 :** a deep or low-pitched tone **:** a low-pitched sound **2 a** (1) **:** the lowest voice part in a 4-part chorus — compare ALTO, SOPRANO, TENOR (2) **:** the lower half of the instrumental tonal range — compare TREBLE **b** (1) **:** the lowest male singing voice (2) **:** a singer having such a voice **c :** the lowest member in range of a family of instruments; *esp* **:** DOUBLE BASS [Middle French *bas* "low, base"] — **bass** *adj*

bass clef *n* **1 :** a clef placing the F below middle C on the 4th line of the staff **2 :** the bass staff

bass drum *n* **:** a large drum having two heads and giving a low booming sound

bas•set hound \'bas-ət-\ *n* **:** any of an old French breed of short-legged slow-moving hunting dogs with very long ears and crooked front legs — called also *basset* [French *basset,* derived from Middle French *bas* "low"]

bass horn *n* **:** TUBA

bas•si•net \ˌbas-ə-'net\ *n* **:** an infant's bed often with a hood over one end [probably from French *barcelonnette,* from *berceau* "cradle"]

bas•so \'bas-ō, 'bäs-\ *n, pl* **bassos :** a bass singer; *esp* **:** an operatic bass [Italian, from Medieval Latin *bassus* "low"]

bas•soon \bə-'sün, ba-\ *n* **:** a tenor or bass woodwind instrument having a long doubled conical wooden body connected to the mouthpiece by a thin metal tube [French *basson,* from Italian *bassone,* from *basso*] — **bas•soon•ist** \-'sü-nəst\ *n*

bass viol *n* **:** DOUBLE BASS

bass•wood \'bas-ˌwu̇d\ *n* **1 :** any of several linden trees of North America **2 :** the pale straight-grained wood of a basswood [*bass* "bast", alteration of *bast*]

bast \'bast\ *n* **1 :** PHLOEM **2 :** a strong woody fiber obtained chiefly from the phloem of plants and used especially in cordage and matting [Old English *bæst*]

bassoon

1bas•tard \'bas-tərd\ *n* **1 :** an illegitimate child **2 :** something that is spurious, irregular, inferior, or of questionable origin [Old French] — **bas•tard•ly** *adj*

2bastard *adj* **1 :** ILLEGITIMATE **2 :** of an inferior or irregular kind, stock, or form **3 :** not genuine or authoritative — **bas•tardy** \-ē\ *n*

1baste \'bāst\ *vt* **:** to sew with long loose temporary stitches [Middle French *bastir,* of Germanic origin] — **bast•er** *n*

2baste \'bāst\ *vt* **:** to moisten (as roasting meat) with a sauce or fat [origin unknown] — **bast•er** *n*

Bastille Day *n* **:** July 14 observed in France as a national holiday in commemoration of the fall of the Bastille in 1789

bas•ti•na•do \ˌbas-tə-'nād-ō, -'näd-\ *n, pl* **-does :** a punishment consisting of beating the soles of the feet with a stick [Spanish *bastonada,* from *bastón* "stick", from Late Latin *bastum*] — **bastinado** *vt*

bast•ing \'bā-sting\ *n* **:** the thread used in loose stitching or the stitching made by this thread

bas•tion \'bas-chən\ *n* **1 :** a projecting part of a fortification **2 :** a fortified area or position **3 :** a firmly established place or position [Middle French, from *bastille* "fort", from Provençal *bastida,* from *bastir* "to build", of Germanic origin]

1bat \'bat\ *n* **1 :** a stout solid stick **:** CLUB **2 :** a sharp blow **3 a :** a wooden implement used for hitting the ball in various games **b :** a paddle used in various games (as table tennis) **4 :** a turn at batting **5** *or* **batt :** BATTING 2 — usually used in pl. **6 :** BINGE [Old English *batt*] — **at bat :** serving as the batter in baseball — **off the bat :** IMMEDIATELY

2bat *vb* **bat•ted; bat•ting 1 :** to strike or hit with or as if with a bat **2 a :** to advance (a base runner) by batting **b :** to have a batting average of **3 :** to take one's turn at bat in baseball

3bat *n* **:** any of an order (Chiroptera) of nocturnal flying mammals with the forelimbs modified to function as wings [alteration of Middle English *bakke*]

4bat *vt* **bat•ted; bat•ting :** to wink especially in surprise or emotion ⟨never *batted* an eye⟩

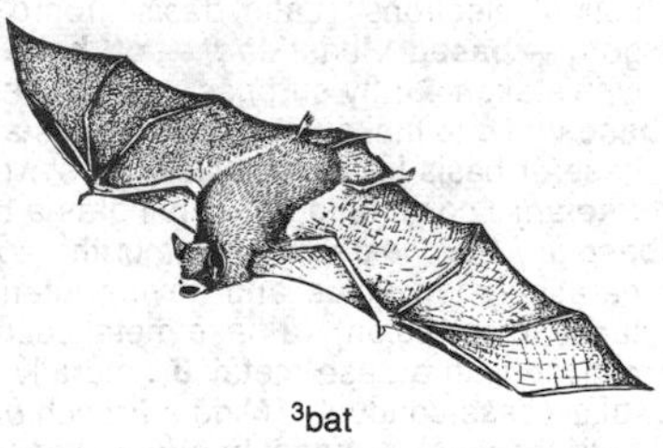
3bat

bat•boy \'bat-ˌbȯi\ *n* **:** a boy who looks after the equipment (as bats) for a baseball team

batch \'bach\ *n* **1 :** a quantity baked at one time ⟨the first *batch* of cookies⟩ **2 :** a quantity of any material for use at one time or produced at one operation ⟨a *batch* of cement⟩ **3 :** a group of persons or things **:** LOT ⟨a *batch* of letters⟩ [Middle English *bache*]

bate \'bāt\ *vt* **1 :** to reduce the force or intensity of ⟨listen with *bated* breath⟩ **2 :** to take away **:** DEDUCT ⟨refuse to *bate* a jot of their claim⟩ [Middle English *baten,* from *abaten* "to abate"]

ba•teau *also* **bat•teau** \ba-'tō\ *n, pl* **ba•teaux** \-'tō, -'tōz\ **:** any of various small craft; *esp* **:** a flat-bottomed boat with slanted bow and stern and flaring sides [French *bateau,* from Old English *bāt* "boat"]

bath \'bath, 'bȧth\ *n, pl* **baths** \'ba*th*z, 'baths, 'bȧ*th*z, 'bȧths\ **1 :** a washing or soaking (as in water) of all or part of the body **2 a :** water used for bathing ⟨drew a *bath*⟩ **b :** a liquid in which objects are placed so that it can act upon them ⟨a dyeing *bath*⟩; *also* **:** the container holding such a liquid **c :** a contained medium for regulating the temperature of something ⟨a hot water *bath*⟩ **3 a :** BATHROOM ⟨a house with two *baths*⟩ **b :** a building containing rooms designed for bathing **c :** SPA — usually used in pl. [Old English *bæth*]

bathe \'bā*th*\ *vb* **1 :** to take a bath **2 :** to go swimming **3 a :** to wash in a liquid (as water) **b** : MOISTEN, WET **4** : to apply water or a liquid medicament to **5** : to flow along the edge of : LAVE **6** : to surround or cover as a liquid does ⟨trees *bathed* in moonlight⟩ — **bath·er** \ˈbā-thər\ *n* — **bath·ing** \-thing\ *n*

ba·thet·ic \bə-ˈthet-ik\ *adj* : characterized by bathos — **ba·thet·i·cal·ly** \-i-kə-lē, -klē\ *adv*

bath·house \ˈbath-ˌhau̇s, ˈbȧth-\ *n* **1** : a building equipped for bathing **2** : a building containing dressing rooms for bathers

bathing suit *n* : SWIMSUIT

batho·lith \ˈbath-ə-ˌlith\ *n* : a great mass of intrusive plutonic rock of unknown depth

ba·thos \ˈbā-ˌthäs\ *n* **1 a** : the sudden appearance of the commonplace in otherwise elevated matter or style **b** : ANTICLIMAX **2** : FLATNESS, TRITENESS **3** : insincere or overdone pathos [Greek, literally, "depth"]

bath·robe \ˈbath-ˌrōb, ˈbȧth-\ *n* : a loose usually absorbent robe worn before and after bathing or as a dressing gown

bath·room \ˈbath-ˌrüm, ˈbȧth-, -ˌru̇m\ *n* : a room containing a bathtub or shower and usually a washbowl and toilet

bath·tub \ˈbath-ˌtəb, ˈbȧth-\ *n* : a usually fixed tub for bathing

bathy·al \ˈbath-ē-əl\ *adj* : DEEP-SEA

bathy·scaphe \ˈbath-i-ˌskaf, -ˌskāf\ *also* **bathy·scaph** \-ˌskaf\ *n* : a navigable submersible ship for deep-sea exploration having a spherical watertight cabin attached to its underside [Greek *bathys* "deep" + *skaphē* "light boat"]

bathy·sphere \ˈbath-i-ˌsfiər\ *n* : a strongly built sphere-shaped diving apparatus for deep-sea observation

ba·tik \bə-ˈtēk, ˈbat-ik\ *n* **1 a** : an Indonesian method of hand-printing textiles by coating the parts not to be dyed with wax **b** : a design so executed **2** : a fabric printed by batik [Malay]

ba·tiste \bə-ˈtēst, ba-\ *n* : a fine soft sheer fabric of plain weave [French]

bat·man \ˈbat-mən\ *n* : an orderly of a British military officer [derived from Greek *bastazein* "to carry"]

ba·ton \bə-ˈtän, ba-, -ˈtōⁿ\ *n* **1** : a staff borne as a symbol of office **2** : a stick or wand with which a leader directs a band or orchestra **3** : a hollow cylinder carried by each member of a relay team and passed to the succeeding runner **4** : a smooth staff with a ball usually at one end carried by a drum major or baton twirler [French *bâton* "stick", derived from Late Latin *bastum*]

ba·tra·chi·an \bə-ˈtrā-kē-ən\ *n* : FROG 1a, TOAD, SALIENTIAN [Greek *batrachos* "frog"] — **batrachian** *adj*

bats·man \ˈbat-smən\ *n* : a batter especially in cricket

batt *variant of* BAT

bat·tal·ion \bə-ˈtal-yən\ *n* **1** : a large organized body of troops : ARMY **2** : a military unit made up of a headquarters and two or more companies, batteries, or subunits **3** : a large body of persons organized to act together ⟨labor *battalions*⟩ [derived from Late Latin *battalia* "combat"]

[1]**bat·ten** \ˈbat-n\ *vb* **bat·tened**; **bat·ten·ing** \ˈbat-ning, -n-ing\ **1 a** : to grow or make fat : FATTEN **b** : to feed gluttonously **2** : to grow prosperous : THRIVE [probably from Old Norse *batna* "to improve"]

[2]**batten** *n* **1** : a thin narrow strip of lumber used especially to seal or reinforce a joint **2** : a strip, bar, or support like or used like a batten [French *bâton* "stick"]

[3]**batten** *vt* : to furnish or fasten with battens ⟨*batten* down the hatches⟩

[1]**bat·ter** \ˈbat-ər\ *vb* **1** : to beat with successive violent, heavy, or shattering blows ⟨*batter* down the door⟩ **2** : to wear or damage by blows or hard usage ⟨a hat *battered* by long use⟩ [Middle English *bateren*, probably from *batten* "to bat"]

[2]**batter** *n* : a mixture that consists chiefly of flour and liquid and is thin enough to pour or drop from a spoon

[3]**batter** *n* : one that bats; *esp* : the baseball player who is batting

battering ram *n* **1** : a military siege engine used in ancient times to beat down the walls of a besieged place **2** : a heavy metal bar with handles used to batter down doors and walls

bat·tery \ˈbat-ə-rē, ˈba-trē\ *n, pl* **-ter·ies** **1 a** : the act of battering or beating **b** : the unlawful beating or use of force upon a person — compare ASSAULT 2 **2 a** : a tactical grouping of artillery pieces **b** : the guns of a warship **3** : an artillery unit in the army equivalent to a company **4** : a group of two or more electric cells connected together for furnishing electric current; *also* : a single electric cell ⟨a flashlight *battery*⟩ **5 a** : a number of machines or devices grouped together or forming a unit ⟨a *battery* of lights or of cameras⟩ **b** : a group of persons working together **6** : the pitcher and catcher of a baseball team

battery jar *n* : a round, square, or rectangular glass container with straight sides and an open top

bat·ting \ˈbat-ing\ *n* **1 a** : the action of one who bats **b** : use of or ability with a bat **2** : layers or sheets of raw cotton or wool used for lining quilts or for stuffing or packaging

batting average *n* : a ratio of base hits to official times at bat for a baseball player or team

[1]**bat·tle** \ˈbat-l\ *n* **1** : a general encounter between armies, ships of war, or airplanes **2** : a combat between two persons ⟨trial by *battle*⟩ **3** : an extended contest, struggle, or controversy ⟨a *battle* of wits⟩ [Old French *bataille*, from Late Latin *battalia* "combat", derived from Latin *battuere* "to beat", of Celtic origin]

[2]**battle** *vb* **bat·tled**; **bat·tling** \ˈbat-ling, -l-ing\ **1** : to engage in battle : FIGHT ⟨armies *battling* for a city⟩ **2** : to struggle using all possible resources (as strength or craft) ⟨*battle* for a cause⟩ **3** : to fight against ⟨*battle* a forest fire⟩ — **bat·tler** \-lər, -l-ər\ *n*

bat·tle–ax *or* **bat·tle–axe** \ˈbat-l-ˌaks\ *n* : a broadax formerly used as a weapon of war

battle cruiser *n* : a large heavily armed warship that is lighter, faster, and more maneuverable than a battleship

battle cry *n* : WAR CRY

bat·tle·field \-ˌfēld\ *n* : a place where a battle is fought — called also *battleground*

battle group *n* : a military unit normally made up of five companies

bat·tle·ment \ˈbat-l-mənt\ *n* : a parapet placed at the top of a wall for ornament or defense — **bat·tle·ment·ed** \-ˌment-əd\ *adj*

battlement

battle royal *n, pl* **bat·tles royal** *or* **battle royals** **1 a** : a fight involving more than two combatants; *esp* : such a contest in which the last one in the ring or standing is declared the winner **b** : a violent struggle **2** : a heated dispute

bat·tle·ship \ˈbat-l-ˌship\ *n* : a warship of the largest and most heavily armed and armored class [short for *line-of-battle ship*]

bat·tle·wag·on \-ˌwag-ən\ *n* : BATTLESHIP

bat·ty \ˈbat-ē\ *adj* **bat·ti·er**; **-est** : mentally unstable : CRAZY [[3]*bat*]

bau·ble \ˈbȯ-bəl, ˈbäb-əl\ *n* **1** : TRINKET 1 **2** : a jester's scepter **3** : TRIFLE 1 [Middle French *babel*]

baux·ite \ˈbȯk-ˌsīt, ˈbäk-\ *n* : an impure mixture of earthy hydrous aluminum oxides and hydroxides that is the principal ore of aluminum [French, from *Les Baux*, near Arles, France]

baw·bee *or* **bau·bee** \ˈbȯ-bē, -ˌbē\ *n* **1** : HALFPENNY **2** : TRIFLE 1 [probably from Alexander Orrok, laird of Sille*bawbe*, flourished 1538, Scottish master of the mint]

bawd \ˈbȯd\ *n* : one that keeps a house of prostitution; *also* : PROSTITUTE [Middle English *bawde*]

bawd·ry \ˈbȯ-drē\ *n, pl* **bawdries** : offensively suggestive or dirty language : BAWDINESS

bawdy \ˈbȯd-ē\ *adj* **bawd·i·er**; **-est** : OBSCENE 2, LEWD — **bawd·i·ly** \ˈbȯd-l-ē\ *adv* — **bawd·i·ness** \ˈbȯd-ē-nəs\ *n*

bawdy house *n* : BROTHEL

[1]**bawl** \ˈbȯl\ *vb* **1** : to cry out loudly and without restraint : YELL **2** : WEEP 1, WAIL [Middle English *baulen*] — **bawl·er** *n*

[2]**bawl** *n* : a loud prolonged cry : OUTCRY

bawl out *vb* : to scold severely

[1]**bay** \ˈbā\ *adj* : of the color bay [Middle French *bai*, from Latin *badius*]

[2]**bay** *n* **1** : a horse with a bay-colored body and black mane, tail, and points — compare CHESTNUT 3 **2** : a reddish brown

[3]**bay** *n* **1 a** : LAUREL 1 **b** : any of several shrubs or trees resem-

bling the laurel **2 :** a wreath especially of laurel given as a token of honor for victory or excellence — usually used in pl. [Middle French *baie* "berry", from Latin *baca*]

4bay *n* **1 :** a section of a building set off from other parts (as by pillars or beams) **2 :** a compartment in a barn for storing fodder (as hay) **3 :** BAY WINDOW 1 **4 a :** the forward part of a ship on each side between decks that is often used as a ship's hospital **b :** any of several compartments in the fuselage of an airplane **5 :** a vertical support for electronic equipment [Old French *baee* "opening", from *baer* "to gape"]

5bay *vb* **1 :** to utter a bay or similar sound **2 a :** to bark at ⟨wolves *baying* the moon⟩ **b :** to utter in long deep tones ⟨*bay* a welcome⟩ **3 :** to bring (as an animal) to bay [Old French *abaüer*]

6bay *n* **1 :** the position of one unable to retreat and forced to face danger ⟨the stag at *bay* turned on its pursuers⟩ **2 :** the position of one checked ⟨kept the hounds at *bay*⟩ **3 :** a deep prolonged bark

7bay *n* **:** an indentation into the land formed by a body of water and usually larger than an inlet and smaller than a gulf [Middle French *baie*] **syn** see GULF

bay•ber•ry \ˈbā-ˌber-ē\ *n* **1 :** a West Indian tree of the myrtle family yielding a yellow aromatic oil **2 a :** a hardy shrub of coastal eastern North America related to the wax myrtles and bearing dense clusters of small globular nuts covered with grayish white wax **b :** the fruit of a bayberry

bay leaf *n* **:** the dried leaf of the European laurel used in cooking

1bay•o•net \ˈbā-ə-nət, -ˌnet, ˌbā-ə-ˈnet\ *n* **:** a steel blade made to be attached at the muzzle end of a rifle and used in hand-to-hand combat [French *baïonette,* from *Bayonne,* France]

2bayonet *vt* **-net•ed** *also* **-net•ted; -net•ing** *also* **net•ting :** to stab with a bayonet

bay•ou \ˈbī-ō, ˈbī-ü\ *n* **:** a usually marshy or sluggish body of water (as a stream on a delta or an offshoot of a river) [Louisiana French, from Choctaw *bayuk*]

bay rum *n* **:** a fragrant cosmetic and medicinal liquid

bay window *n* **1 :** a window or a set of windows in a compartment that projects outward from the wall of a building **2 :** POTBELLY 1

ba•zaar \bə-ˈzär\ *n* **1 :** an Oriental market that consists of rows of shops or stalls selling miscellaneous goods **2 a :** a place for the sale of goods **b :** DEPARTMENT STORE **3 :** a fair for the sale of articles especially for charitable purposes [Persian *bāzār*]

ba•zoo•ka \bə-ˈzü-kə\ *n* **:** a light portable shoulder weapon that consists of a tube open at both ends and shoots an explosive rocket able to pierce armor [*bazooka,* a crude musical instrument made of pipes and a funnel]

BB \ˈbē-ˌbē\ *n* **:** a small round shot pellet

B complex *n* **:** VITAMIN B COMPLEX

be \bē, ˈbē\ *vb, past 1st and 3d sing* **was** \wəz, ˈwəz, ˈwäz\; *2d sing* **were** \wər, ˈwər\; *pl* **were**; *past subjunctive* **were**; *past part* **been** \bin, ˈbin, *chiefly British* bēn *or* ˈbēn\; *pres part* **be•ing** \ˈbē-iŋ\; *pres 1st sing* **am** \əm, m, am, ˈam\; *2d sing* **are** \ər, är, ˈär\; *3d sing* **is** \iz, ˈiz, əz, z\; *pl* **are**; *pres subjunctive* **be 1 a :** to have the same meaning as **:** serve as a sign for ⟨January *is* the first month⟩ ⟨let *x be* 10⟩ **b :** to have identity with ⟨the first person I met *was* my best friend⟩ **c :** to constitute the same class as **d :** to have the quality or character of ⟨the leaves *are* green⟩ **e :** to belong to the class of ⟨the fish *is* a trout⟩ ⟨apes *are* mammals⟩ **2 a :** to have reality **:** EXIST, LIVE ⟨I think, therefore I *am*⟩ ⟨once there *was* a knight⟩ **b :** to have, keep, or occupy a place, situation, or position ⟨the book *is* on the table⟩ **c :** to remain unmolested, undisturbed, or uninterrupted — used only in infinitive form ⟨let it *be*⟩ **d :** to take place **:** OCCUR ⟨the concert *was* last night⟩ **3** — used with the past participle of transitive verbs as a passive-voice auxiliary ⟨the money *was* found⟩ ⟨the house has *been* built⟩ **4** — used as the auxiliary of the present participle in progressive tenses expressing continuous action ⟨I have *been* sleeping⟩ **5** — used with the past participle of some intransitive verbs as an auxiliary forming archaic perfect tenses **6** — used with the infinitive with *to* to express futurity, arrangement in advance, or obligation ⟨I *am* to interview them today⟩ ⟨they *were* to become famous⟩ [Old English *bēon*]

be- *prefix* **1 :** on **:** around **:** over ⟨*be*daub⟩ ⟨*be*smear⟩ **2 :** to a great or greater degree **:** thoroughly ⟨*be*fuddle⟩ ⟨*be*rate⟩ **3 :** excessively **:** ostentatiously ⟨*be*deck⟩ **4 :** about **:** to **:** upon ⟨*be*speak⟩ ⟨*be*stride⟩ **5 :** make **:** cause to be ⟨*be*fool⟩ ⟨*be*little⟩ **6 :** affect, provide, or cover with especially excessively ⟨*be*fog⟩ [Old English *bi-*, *be-*]

1beach \ˈbēch\ *n* **:** a shore of an ocean, sea, or lake or the bank of a river covered by sand, gravel, or larger rock fragments **:** STRAND [origin unknown]

2beach *vt* **:** to run or drive ashore ⟨*beach* a boat⟩

beach•comb•er \ˈbēch-ˌkō-mər\ *n* **1 :** a drifter, loafer, or casual worker along the seacoast **2 :** one that searches along a shore for useful or salable debris and refuse

beach flea *n* **:** any of numerous small leaping crustaceans common on seabeaches

beach•head \ˈbēch-ˌhed\ *n* **1 :** an area of an enemy-held shore occupied by an advance attacking force to protect the later landing of troops or supplies **2 :** FOOTHOLD 2

beach plum *n* **:** a shrubby plum with showy white flowers that grows along the Atlantic shores of the northern United States and Canada; *also* **:** its dark purple fruit often used in preserves

beach wagon *n* **:** STATION WAGON

1bea•con \ˈbē-kən\ *n* **1 :** a signal fire commonly on a hill, tower, or pole **2 a :** a signal (as a lighthouse) for guidance **b :** a radio transmitter sending out signals for guidance of aircraft [Old English *bēacen* "sign"]

2beacon *vb* **1 :** to furnish or light up with a beacon **2 :** to shine as a beacon

1bead \ˈbēd\ *n* **1** *pl* **:** a series of prayers said with a rosary **2 :** a small piece of material pierced for threading on a string or wire **3 :** a small ball-shaped body: as **a :** a drop of sweat or blood **b :** a bubble formed in or on a beverage **c :** a small metal knob on a firearm used as a front sight **4 :** a projecting rim, band, or molding [Middle English *bede* "prayer, prayer bead", from Old English *bed* "prayer"]

△ **origin** Middle English *bede* originally meant "a prayer". The word is related to modern English *bid.* The number and order of a series of prayers are often kept track of with the aid of a string of small round balls. Because each of these balls stands for a prayer, the word *bede,* now *bead* in modern English, was transferred to the balls themselves. Today *bead* is used to refer to any small piece of material pierced for threading on a string or wire. The sense is also extended to refer to any small, round object, such as a drop of sweat.

2bead *vb* **1 :** to adorn or cover with beads or beading **2 :** to string together like beads **3 :** to form into a bead

bead•ing \ˈbēd-iŋ\ *n* **1 :** material or a part or piece consisting of beads **2 :** an openwork trimming **3 :** BEADWORK

bea•dle \ˈbēd-l\ *n* **:** a minor parish official whose duties include ushering and keeping order in church and sometimes at civic functions [Old English *bydel*]

bead•roll \ˈbēd-ˌrōl\ *n* **1 :** a list of names **:** CATALOG **2 :** ROSARY [from the reading in church of a list of names of persons for whom prayers are to be said]

beads•man \ˈbēdz-mən\ *n, archaic* **:** a person who prays for another

bead•work \ˈbēd-ˌwərk\ *n* **:** ornamental work of or with beads

beady \ˈbēd-ē\ *adj* **bead•i•er; -est :** resembling beads; *esp* **:** small, round, and shiny with interest or greed ⟨*beady* eyes⟩

bea•gle \ˈbē-gəl\ *n* **:** a small short-legged smooth-coated hound [Middle English *begle*]

beak \ˈbēk\ *n* **1 a :** the bill of a bird; *esp* **:** the bill of a bird of prey adapted for striking and tearing **b :** any of various rigid projecting mouth structures (as of a turtle); *also* **:** the long sucking mouth of some insects **c :** the human nose **2 :** a pointed structure or formation: **a :** a pointed beam projecting from the bow of an ancient galley for piercing an enemy ship **b :** the spout of a vessel [Old French *bec,* from Latin *beccus,* of Gaulish origin] **syn** see BILL — **beaked** \ˈbēkt\ *adj*

bea•ker \ˈbē-kər\ *n* **1 :** a large widemouthed drinking cup **2 :** a deep widemouthed vessel that often has a projecting lip and is used especially by chemists and pharmacists [Old Norse *bikarr*]

1beam \ˈbēm\ *n* **1 a :** a long heavy piece of timber or metal used especially as a main horizontal support of a building or a ship **b :** a wood or metal cylinder in a loom on which the warp is wound **2 :** the bar of a balance from which the scales hang **3 :** the width of a ship at its widest part **4 a :** a ray or shaft of light **b :** a collection of nearly parallel rays (as X rays) or particles (as electrons) **5 :** a constant directional radio signal sent out for the guidance of pilots along a particular course; *also* **:** the course indicated by this signal [Old English *bēam* "tree, beam"] — **off the beam 1** : on a wrong course **2** : INCORRECT, MISTAKEN — **on the beam 1** : on a true course **2** : exactly correct

beaker 2

[2]beam *vb* **1** : to send out in beams or as a beam **2 a** : to aim (a broadcast) by directional antennas **b** : to direct to a particular audience **3** : to send out beams of light **4** : to smile with joy

bean \ˈbēn\ *n* **1 a** : BROAD BEAN **b** : the seed or pod of any of various erect or climbing leguminous plants **c** : a plant bearing beans **2 a** : a valueless item **b** *pl* : the slightest amount ⟨doesn't know *beans* about it⟩ **3** : a seed or fruit like a bean ⟨coffee *beans*⟩ **4** : HEAD, BRAIN [Old English *bēan*]

bean•bag \ˈbēn-ˌbag\ *n* **1** : a small cloth bag partly filled with beans and used (as for tossing or passing) in many games **2** : a game played with one or more beanbags

bean•ie \ˈbē-nē\ *n* : a small round tight-fitting skullcap

[1]bear \ˈbaər, ˈbeər\ *n, pl* **bears 1** *or pl* **bear** : any of a family (order Carnivora) of large heavy mammals having long shaggy hair and rudimentary tail, walking on the soles of its feet, and feeding largely on fruit and insects as well as on flesh **2** : a surly, uncouth, or clumsy person **3** : one who sells securities or commodities in expectation of a price decline — compare [1]BULL 2 [Old English *bera*] — **bear•able** \ˈbar-ə-bəl, ˈber-\ *adj*

[2]bear *vb* **bore** \ˈbōr, ˈbȯr\; **borne** \ˈbōrn, ˈbȯrn\ *also* **born** \ˈbȯrn\; **bear•ing 1 a** : to move while holding up : CARRY ⟨arrived *bearing* gifts⟩ **b** : to be equipped with ⟨entitled to *bear* arms⟩ **c** : to have as a feature or characteristic ⟨*bears* a good reputation⟩ ⟨*bore* a resemblance to a cousin⟩ **d** : to hold in the mind : HARBOR ⟨has *borne* a grudge for years⟩ **e** : to pass on to others ⟨constantly *bearing* tales⟩ **f** : to bring foward in testifying ⟨*bear* false witness⟩ **g** : BEHAVE 1, CONDUCT ⟨*bore* themselves proudly⟩ **2 a** : to give birth to ⟨has *borne* many children⟩ **b** : PRODUCE 2, YIELD **3 a** : to support the weight of : hold up : SUSTAIN ⟨a colonnade *bore* the roof⟩ **b** : to support a burden or strain ⟨*bears* up well in times of grief⟩ **c** : ENDURE 2 **d** : ASSUME 2a, ACCEPT ⟨*bore* all the costs⟩ ⟨had to *bear* the blame⟩ **e** : to be able to withstand : ALLOW ⟨can hardly *bear* scrutiny⟩ **4** : THRUST 1, PRESS ⟨*borne* along by the crowd⟩ **5 a** : to move, extend, or incline in an indicated direction ⟨*bear* right at the next fork⟩ **b** : to become directed or aimed ⟨brought the guns to *bear* on the target⟩ **6 a** : APPLY 3, PERTAIN ⟨facts *bearing* on the question⟩ **b** : to exert influence or force ⟨brings pressure to *bear* to win votes⟩ [Old English *beran*]

bear•ber•ry \ˈbaər-ˌber-ē, ˈbeər-\ *n* : a trailing evergreen plant of the heath family with glossy red berries; *also* : any of several related plants (as a cranberry)

[1]beard \ˈbiərd\ *n* **1** : the hair that grows on a man's face and neck; *also* : a growth of beard in a particular style often not including a mustache **2** : a hairy or bristly growth or tuft (as on the chin of a goat or on a head of rye) [Old English] — **beard•ed** \-əd\ *adj* — **beard•less** \-ləs\ *adj*

[2]beard *vt* : to confront and oppose daringly : DEFY

bear down *vb* **1** : OVERWHELM, OVERCOME **2** : to press or weigh down **3** : to make an all-out effort — **bear down on 1** : to weigh heavily on : BURDEN **2** : to approach rapidly ⟨the storm *bore down on* them⟩

bear•er \ˈbar-ər, ˈber-\ *n* : one that bears: as **a** : PORTER **b** : a plant yielding fruit **c** : a person holding a check, draft, or order for payment **d** : PALLBEARER

bear hug *n* : a vigorous tight embrace

bear•ing \ˈbaər-ing, ˈbeər-\ *n* **1** : the manner in which one bears or comports oneself : CARRIAGE, BEHAVIOR **2 a** : the act, power, or time of bringing forth offspring or fruit **b** : a product of bearing : CROP **3 a** : PRESSURE 2, THRUST **b** : ENDURANCE 2 **4 a** : an object, surface, or point that supports something **b** : a machine part in which one part (as a journal or pin) turns or slides **5** : a figure in a coat of arms ⟨armorial *bearings*⟩ **6 a** : the position or direction of one point with respect to another or to the compass **b** : a determination of position ⟨to take a *bearing*⟩ **c** *pl* : comprehension of one's position, environment, or situation ⟨lose one's *bearings*⟩ **d** : CONNECTION 2 ⟨the cost had no *bearing* at all on the decision⟩

bear•ish \-ish\ *adj* **1** : resembling a bear in roughness, gruffness, or surliness **2** : marked by or expecting a decline in stock prices — **bear•ish•ly** *adv* — **bear•ish•ness** *n*

bear out *vt* : to attest to the truth of : CONFIRM ⟨research *bore out* the theory⟩

bear•skin \ˈbaər-ˌskin, ˈbeər-\ *n* **1** : the skin of a bear **2** : an article (as a rug or military hat) made of the skin of a bear

beast \ˈbēst\ *n* **1 a** : ANIMAL 1; *esp* : a lower mammal as distinguished on the one hand from humans and on the other from lower vertebrate and invertebrate animals **b** : a domesticated mammal ⟨the care of a farmer for his or her *beasts*⟩; *esp* : a draft animal **2** : a vicious or brutal person [Old French *beste*, from Latin *bestia*]

[1]beast•ly \ˈbēst-lē\ *adj* **beast•li•er**; **-est 1** : of, relating to, or resembling a beast : BESTIAL **2** : ABOMINABLE 2, NASTY ⟨*beastly* weather⟩ — **beast•li•ness** *n*

[2]beastly *adv* : VERY ⟨a *beastly* cold day⟩

beast of burden : an animal (as a mule or an ox) used for carrying or pulling heavy loads

[1]beat \ˈbēt\ *vb* **beat**; **beat•en** \ˈbēt-n\ *or* **beat**; **beat•ing 1** : to strike repeatedly: **a** : to hit repeatedly so as to inflict pain **b** : to dash against ⟨rain *beating* on the roof⟩ **c** : to range over to stir up or drive out game **d** : to mix by stirring : WHIP **e** : to strike repeatedly to produce music or a signal ⟨*beat* a drum⟩ **2 a** : to drive or force by blows ⟨*beat* off the intruder⟩ **b** : to make by repeated treading or driving over ⟨a *beaten* path⟩ **c** : to shape by repeated blows ⟨*beat* swords into plowshares⟩; *esp* : to flatten thin by blows **d** : to sound or express especially by a drumbeat **3** : to cause to strike or flap repeatedly **4 a** : OVERCOME 1, DEFEAT; *also* : SURPASS 1 **b** : to prevail despite ⟨*beat* the odds⟩ **c** : BEWILDER 2, BAFFLE **d** : EXHAUST 2b, DISPIRIT **e** : CHEAT **5 a** (1) : to act ahead of usually so as to forestall (2) : to report a news item in advance of **b** : to come or arrive before **c** : to evade or offset the effects of : CIRCUMVENT ⟨*beat* the system⟩ **6** : to indicate by beats ⟨*beat* the tempo⟩ **7 a** : DASH 1 **b** : to glare or strike with oppressive intensity **8 a** : PULSATE **b** : TICK 1 **c** : to sound upon being struck **9 a** : to sail with much tacking **b** : to progress with difficulty [Old English *bēatan*] — **beat about the bush** *or* **beat around the bush** : to approach a matter in a roundabout manner — **beat it** : to leave immediately : SCRAM — **beat the bushes** : to search thoroughly through all possible areas

[2]beat *n* **1 a** : a single stroke or blow especially in a series; *also* : PULSATION, TICK **b** : a sound produced by or as if by beating ⟨the *beat* of waves against the rock⟩ **c** : a driving impact or force **2** : each of the pulsations of amplitude produced by the union of sound or radio waves or electric currents having different frequencies **3 a** : a metrical or rhythmic stress in poetry or music or the rhythmic effect or pattern produced by such stresses **b** : musical tempo as indicated by the conductor's baton or hand **4** : a regularly traversed round ⟨a police officer's *beat*⟩ **5 a** : something that excels **b** : the reporting of a news story ahead of competitors **6** : DEADBEAT

[3]beat *adj* **1** : very tired **2** : sapped of resolution or morale

beat•er \ˈbēt-ər\ *n* **1** : one that beats **2** : a person who flushes game for hunters

be•a•tif•ic \ˌbē-ə-ˈtif-ik\ *adj* : giving or expressing great joy or blessedness : BLISSFUL ⟨a *beatific* experience⟩ ⟨a *beatific* smile⟩ — **be•a•tif•i•cal•ly** \-ˈtif-i-kə-lē, -klē\ *adv*

beatific vision *n* : the direct knowledge of God held to be enjoyed by the blessed in heaven

be•at•i•fy \bē-ˈat-ə-ˌfī\ *vt* **-fied**; **-fy•ing 1** : to make supremely happy **2** : to declare to have attained the blessedness of heaven and authorize the title "Blessed" and limited public religious honor for [Late Latin *beatificare*, from Latin *beatus* "blessed, happy"] — **be•at•i•fi•ca•tion** \-ˌat-ə-fə-ˈkā-shən\ *n*

be•at•i•tude \bē-ˈat-ə-ˌtüd, -ˌtyüd\ *n* **1** : supreme bliss **2** : a declaration made in the Sermon on the Mount (Matthew 5:3–12) beginning "Blessed are"

beat•nik \ˈbēt-nik\ *n* : a person who expresses dissatisfaction with established values and mores by withdrawing from society and dressing and behaving unconventionally

\ə\ **abut**	\au̇\ **out**	\i\ **tip**	\ȯ\ **saw**	\u̇\ **foot**
\ər\ **further**	\ch\ **chin**	\ī\ **life**	\ȯi\ **coin**	\y\ **yet**
\a\ **mat**	\e\ **pet**	\j\ **job**	\th\ **thin**	\yü\ **few**
\ā\ **take**	\ē\ **easy**	\ng\ **sing**	\t͟h\ **this**	\yu̇\ **cure**
\ä\ **cot, cart**	\g\ **go**	\ō\ **bone**	\ü\ **food**	\zh\ **vision**

beau \ˈbō\ *n, pl* **beaux** \ˈbōz\ *or* **beaus** \ˈbōz\ **1 :** a man who dresses very carefully in the latest fashion **:** DANDY **2 a :** a man who is courting **:** LOVER, ADMIRER **b :** ESCORT 1b [French, from *beau* "beautiful", from Latin *bellus* "pretty"]

Beau Brum•mell \bō-ˈbrəm-əl\ *n* **:** BEAU 1 [nickname of George B. Brummell, died 1840, English dandy]

Beau•fort scale \ˌbō-fərt-\ *n* **:** a scale in which the force of the wind is indicated by numbers from 0 for velocities less than 1.6 kilometers per hour to 12 for velocities greater than 117.5 kilometers per hour [Sir Francis *Beaufort*, died 1857, British admiral]

beau geste \bō-ˈzhest\ *n, pl* **beaux gestes** *or* **beau gestes** \bō-ˈzhest\ **:** a gracious or generous act; *esp* **:** one made to please or impress someone else [French, "beautiful gesture"]

beau ide•al \ˌbō-ˌī-ˈdē-əl, -ˈdēl\ *n, pl* **beau ideals :** the perfect type or model [French *beau idéal* "ideal beauty"]

beau monde \bō-ˈmänd\ *n, pl* **beau mondes** *or* **beaux mondes** \bō-ˈmänz\ **:** the world of high society and fashion [French, literally, "beautiful world"]

beau•te•ous \ˈbyüt-ē-əs\ *adj* **:** BEAUTIFUL 1 — **beau•te•ous•ly** *adv* — **beau•te•ous•ness** *n*

beau•ti•cian \byü-ˈtish-ən\ *n* **:** COSMETOLOGIST

beau•ti•ful \ˈbyüt-i-fəl\ *adj* **1 :** having beauty **:** pleasing to the mind, spirit, or senses ⟨a *beautiful* picture⟩ **2 :** generally agreeable **:** FINE ⟨*beautiful* weather⟩ ⟨a *beautiful* dinner⟩ — **beau•ti•ful•ly** \-fə-lē, -flē\ *adv* — **beau•ti•ful•ness** \-fəl-nəs\ *n*
• **syn** LOVELY, FAIR, PRETTY: BEAUTIFUL applies to whatever excites the keenest pleasure in the mind and senses and stirs emotion by its suggestion of perfection or the ideal ⟨a *beautiful* scene⟩ LOVELY is close to BEAUTIFUL but applies to a narrower range of emotional excitation in suggesting the graceful, delicate, or exquisite ⟨a *lovely* melody⟩ FAIR suggests beauty because of purity, flawlessness, or freshness ⟨a *fair* face⟩ PRETTY often implies an immediate but superficial or insubstantial impression of attractiveness.

beau•ti•fy \ˈbyüt-ə-ˌfī\ *vt* **-fied; -fy•ing :** to make beautiful or more beautiful — **beau•ti•fi•ca•tion** \ˌbyüt-ə-fə-ˈkā-shən\ *n* — **beau•ti•fi•er** \ˈbyüt-ə-ˌfīr\ *n*

beau•ty \ˈbyüt-ē\ *n, pl* **beauties 1 :** the qualities of a person or a thing that give pleasure to the senses **:** LOVELINESS **2 :** a lovely person or thing **3 :** someone or something outstanding ⟨that's a *beauty* of a black eye⟩ [Old French *biauté*, from *biau* "beautiful", from Latin *ballus* "pretty"]

beauty shop *n* **:** an establishment or department where hairdressing, facials, and manicures are done — called also *beauty parlor, beauty salon*

beaux arts \bō-ˈzär\ *n pl* **:** FINE ARTS [French]

[1]bea•ver \ˈbē-vər\ *n, pl* **beaver** *or* **beavers 1 :** a large fur-bearing mammal with webbed hind feet and a broad flat tail that builds dams and underwater houses of mud and branches; *also* **:** its fur **2 :** a hat made of beaver fur or of a fabric imitating it [Old English *beofor*]

[1]beaver 1

[2]beaver *n* **1 :** a piece of armor protecting the lower part of the face **2 :** a helmet visor [Middle French *baviere*]

be•calm \bi-ˈkäm, -ˈkälm\ *vt* **1 :** to bring to a stop or keep motionless by lack of wind **2 :** to make calm **:** SOOTHE

be•cause \bi-ˈkȯz, -ˈkəz, -kəz\ *conj* **:** for the reason that

because of *prep* **:** by reason of **:** on account of

be•chance \bi-ˈchans\ *vb, archaic* **:** BEFALL

bêche-de-mer \ˌbāsh-də-ˈmeər\ *n, pl* **bêche-de-mer** *or* **bêches-de-mer** \ˌbāsh-də-, ˌbāsh-əz-də-\ **:** TREPANG [French]

beck \ˈbek\ *n* **1 :** a beckoning gesture **2 :** SUMMONS 3, COMMAND ⟨servants at their *beck* and call⟩

beck•et \ˈbek-ət\ *n* **:** a device for holding something in place; *esp* **:** a loop of rope with a knot at one end [origin unknown]

beck•on \ˈbek-ən\ *vb* **beck•oned; beck•on•ing** \ˈbek-ning, -ə-ning\ **1 :** to summon or signal to a person with a gesture (as a wave or nod) **2 :** to appear inviting **:** ATTRACT [Old English *bīecnan*, from *bēacen* "sign"]

be•cloud \bi-ˈklau̇d\ *vt* **:** to obscure with or as if with a cloud

be•come \bi-ˈkəm\ *vb* **-came** \-ˈkām\; **-come; -com•ing 1 :** to grow to be ⟨a tadpole *becomes* a frog⟩ ⟨the days *become* shorter as summer ends⟩ **2 :** to look well on **:** be suitable to **:** SUIT — **become of :** to happen to **:** be the state of ⟨whatever *became* of them⟩

be•com•ing \bi-ˈkəm-ing\ *adj* **:** SUITABLE; *esp* **:** attractively suitable ⟨a *becoming* outfit⟩ — **be•com•ing•ly** \-ing-lē\ *adv*

[1]bed \ˈbed\ *n* **1 a :** a piece of furniture on or in which one may lie and sleep **b :** a place or time for sleeping **2 :** a flat or level surface: as **a :** a plot of ground prepared for plants **b :** the bottom of a body of water **3 :** a supporting surface or structure **:** FOUNDATION **4 :** LAYER 2, STRATUM [Old English *bedd*]

[2]bed *vb* **bed•ded; bed•ding 1 a :** to furnish with a bed or bedding **b :** to put or go to bed ⟨*bedded* down for the night⟩ **2 a :** to fix in a foundation **:** EMBED ⟨*bedded* on rock⟩ **b :** to plant or arrange in beds **3 :** to lay flat or in a layer ⟨*bed* bricks in mortar⟩ **4 :** to form a layer

be•daub \bi-ˈdȯb, -ˈdäb\ *vt* **:** to daub over with something dirty or sticky

be•daz•zle \bi-ˈdaz-əl\ *vt* **:** DAZZLE — **be•daz•zle•ment** \-əl-mənt\ *n*

bed•bug \ˈbed-ˌbəg\ *n* **:** a wingless bloodsucking bug sometimes infesting houses and especially beds

bed•clothes \ˈbed-ˌklōz, -ˌklōthz\ *n pl* **:** the covering (as sheets and blankets) used on a bed

bed•ding \ˈbed-ing\ *n* **1 :** BEDCLOTHES **2 :** a bottom layer **:** FOUNDATION **3 :** material to provide a bed for livestock **4 :** the arrangement of rock in layers

be•deck \bi-ˈdek\ *vt* **:** to adorn with showy things ⟨*bedecked* with furs and jewels⟩

be•dev•il \bi-ˈdev-əl\ *vt* **:** to drive frantic **:** HARASS, TORMENT — **be•dev•il•ment** \-mənt\ *n*

be•dew \bi-ˈdyü, -ˈdü\ *vt* **:** to wet with or as if with dew

bed•fast \ˈbed-ˌfast\ *adj* **:** BEDRIDDEN

bed•fel•low \ˈbed-ˌfel-ō\ *n* **1 :** one who shares a bed with another **2 :** a close associate **:** ALLY ⟨politics makes strange *bedfellows*⟩

be•dight \bi-ˈdīt\ *adj, archaic* **:** ADORNED, DECORATED [Middle English *dighten* "to adorn", from Old English *dihtan* "to arrange, compose", derived from Latin *dictare* "to dictate, compose"]

be•dim \bi-ˈdim\ *vt* **:** to make dim or obscure

be•di•zen \bi-ˈdīz-n, -ˈdiz-\ *vt* **:** to dress or adorn in a gaudy way [*disen* "to dress a distaff with flax", from Dutch] — **be•di•zen•ment** \-mənt\ *n*

bed•lam \ˈbed-ləm\ *n* **:** a place or scene of uproar and confusion [*Bedlam*, popular name for the Hospital of Saint Mary of Bethlehem, London, an insane asylum, from Middle English *Bedlem* "Bethlehem"]

bed•lam•ite \ˈbed-lə-ˌmīt\ *n* **:** a crazy person

Bed•ling•ton terrier \ˌbed-ling-tən-\ *n* **:** a swift rough-coated terrier of light build usually groomed to resemble a lamb [*Bedlington*, England]

bed•ou•in \ˈbed-wən, -ə-wən\ *n, pl* **bedouin** *or* **bedouins** *often cap* **:** a nomadic Arab of the Arabian, Syrian, or North African deserts [French *bédouin*, from Arabic *bidwān*, pl. of *badawi* "desert dweller"]

bed•pan \ˈbed-ˌpan\ *n* **:** a shallow pan for use as a toilet by a person confined to bed

bed•post \-ˌpōst\ *n* **:** a usually turned or carved post of a bed

be•drag•gled \bi-ˈdrag-əld\ *adj* **1 :** limp, soggy, or dirty from or as if from rain or mud ⟨a wet and *bedraggled* cat⟩ **2 :** showing the effect of much use or lack of care **:** SHABBY, DILAPIDATED ⟨*bedraggled* buildings⟩

bed•rid•den \ˈbed-ˌrid-n\ *adj* **:** confined to bed by illness or weakness [Old English *bedreda* "one confined to bed", literally, "bed rider"]

bed•rock \ˈbed-ˈräk, -ˌräk\ *n* **1 :** the solid rock underlying surface materials (as soil) **2 :** a solid foundation

bed•roll \ˈbed-ˌrōl\ *n* **:** bedding rolled up for carrying

bed•room \-ˌrüm, -ˌru̇m\ *n* **:** a room used for sleeping

bed•side \ˈbed-ˌsīd\ *n* **:** the side of a bed or the place beside a bed especially of a sick or dying person

bedside manner *n* **:** the often solicitous and sympathetic manner that a physician assumes toward a patient

bed•sore \ˈbed-ˌsōr, -ˌsȯr\ *n* **:** a sore caused by constant pressure against a bed (as in a long illness)

bed•spread \-ˌspred\ *n* **:** a decorative cloth cover for a bed

bed•spring \-ˌspriŋ\ *n* : a spring supporting a mattress
bed•stead \-ˌsted\ *n* : the framework of a bed usually including head, foot, and side rails
bed•straw \-ˌstrȯ\ *n* : an herb of the madder family with angled stems, opposite or whorled leaves, and small flowers **[**from its former use for mattresses**]**
bed•time \ˈbed-ˌtīm\ *n* : time to go to bed
bedtime story *n* : a simple story for children at bedtime
bee \ˈbē\ *n* **1** : a social colonial 4-winged insect often kept in hives for the honey that it produces; *also* : any of numerous related insects that differ from the wasps especially in the heavier hairier body and in having sucking as well as chewing mouthparts **2** : an eccentric notion : FANCY ⟨a *bee* in one's bonnet⟩ **3** : a gathering of people for a specific purpose ⟨quilting *bee*⟩ **[**Old English *bēo***]**
bee balm *n* : any of several plants (as Oswego tea) of the mint family attractive to bees
bee•bread \ˈbē-ˌbred\ *n* : a bitter yellowish brown pollen mixture stored in honeycomb cells and used with honey by bees as food
beech \ˈbēch\ *n, pl* **beech•es** *or* **beech** : any of a genus of hardwood trees with smooth gray bark and small edible nuts; *also* : the wood of a beech **[**Old English *bēce***]** — **beech•en** \ˈbē-chən\ *adj* — **beech•wood** \ˈbēch-ˌwu̇d\ *n*
beech•nut \ˈbēch-ˌnət\ *n* : the edible nut of a beech
[1]**beef** \ˈbēf\ *n, pl* **beefs** \ˈbēfs\ *or* **beeves** \ˈbēvz\ **1** : the flesh of a steer, cow, or bull; *also* : the dressed carcass of a beef animal **2** : a steer, cow, or bull especially when fattened for food **3** : muscular flesh : BRAWN **4** *pl beefs* : COMPLAINT **[**Old French *buef* "ox, beef", from Latin *bov-, bos* "head of cattle"**]**
[2]**beef** *vb* **1** : to add weight, strength, or power to — usually used with *up* ⟨*beef* up the staff⟩ **2** : COMPLAIN ⟨*beefing* about homework assignments⟩
beef cattle *n pl* : cattle developed primarily for the efficient production of meat and marked by capacity for rapid growth, heavy well-fleshed body, and stocky build
beef•eat•er \ˈbē-ˌfēt-ər\ *n* : a yeoman of the guard of an English king or queen
beef•steak \ˈbēf-ˌstāk\ *n* : a slice of beef suitable for broiling or frying
beefy \ˈbē-fē\ *adj* **beef•i•er**; **-est** : THICKSET, BRAWNY ⟨a *beefy* bodyguard⟩
[1]**bee•hive** \ˈbē-ˌhīv\ *n* **1** : a hive for bees **2** : something resembling a hive for bees; *esp* : a scene of crowded activity
[2]**beehive** *adj* : resembling a dome-shaped or conical beehive
bee•keep•er \-ˌkē-pər\ *n* : one that raises bees — **bee•keep•ing** *n*
bee•line \ˈbē-ˌlīn\ *n* : a straight direct course **[**from the belief that nectar-laden bees return to their hives in a direct line**]**
been *past part of* BE
beer \ˈbiər\ *n* **1** : an alcoholic drink made from malt and flavored with hops **2** : a nonalcoholic drink made from roots or other parts of plants ⟨ginger *beer*⟩ **[**Old English *bēor***]** — **beery** \ˈbiər-ē\ *adj*
bees•wax \ˈbēz-ˌwaks\ *n* : WAX 1
beet \ˈbēt\ *n* : a biennial garden plant of the goosefoot family with thick long-stalked edible leaves and a swollen root used as a vegetable, as a source of sugar, or for forage; *also* : this root **[**Old English *bēte,* from Latin *beta***]**
[1]**bee•tle** \ˈbēt-l\ *n* **1** : any of an order (Coleoptera) of insects having four wings of which the outer pair are modified into stiff cases that protect the inner membranous pair when at rest **2** : any of various insects resembling a beetle **[**Old English *bitula,* from *bītan* "to bite"**]**

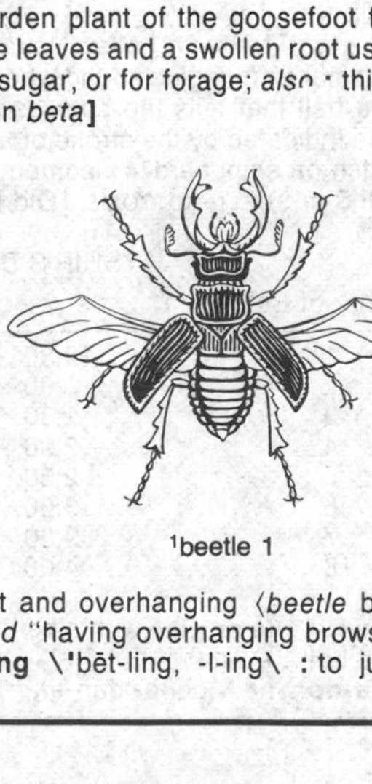

[1]beetle 1

[2]**beetle** *n* : a heavy tool usually with a wooden head for hammering **[**Old English *bīetel***]**
[3]**beetle** *adj* : being prominent and overhanging ⟨*beetle* brows⟩ **[**Middle English *bitel-browed* "having overhanging brows"**]**
[4]**beetle** *vi* **bee•tled**; **bee•tling** \ˈbēt-liŋ, -l-iŋ\ : to jut out : OVERHANG

be•fall \bi-ˈfȯl\ *vb* **-fell** \-ˈfel\; **-fall•en** \-ˈfȯ-lən\; **-fall•ing** **1** : to come to pass : HAPPEN **2** : to happen to
be•fit \bi-ˈfit\ *vt* : to be suitable to or proper for ⟨words that *befit* the occasion⟩
be•fit•ting \bi-ˈfit-iŋ\ *adj* : SUITABLE 1, 2 — **be•fit•ting•ly** *adv*
be•fog \bi-ˈfȯg, -ˈfäg\ *vt* **1** : to make foggy : OBSCURE **2** : CONFUSE 2a
be•fool \bi-ˈfül\ *vt* : DECEIVE 1
[1]**be•fore** \bi-ˈfōr, -ˈfȯr\ *adv* **1** : in advance : AHEAD ⟨go on *before*⟩ **2** : at an earlier time : PREVIOUSLY ⟨has been here *before*⟩ ⟨tomorrow and not *before*⟩ **[**Old English *beforan,* from *be-* + *foran* "before"**]**
[2]**before** *prep* **1 a** (1) : in front of ⟨sat *before* the fire⟩ (2) : in the presence of ⟨speaking *before* the whole class⟩ **b** : under the consideration of ⟨the case *before* the court⟩ **c** : in store for ⟨many years of life still *before* them⟩ **2** : earlier than : previously to ⟨come *before* six o'clock⟩ **3** : in a higher or more important position than ⟨put quantity *before* quality⟩
[3]**before** *conj* **1** : earlier than the time when ⟨think *before* you speak⟩ **2** : more willingly than ⟨I will starve *before* I will steal⟩
be•fore•hand \-ˌhand\ *adv* : in advance : ahead of time ⟨think out *beforehand* what you are going to say⟩
be•foul \bi-ˈfau̇l\ *vt* : to make dirty : SOIL
be•friend \bi-ˈfrend\ *vt* : to act as a friend to
be•fud•dle \bi-ˈfəd-l\ *vt* **1** : to dull the senses of : STUPEFY ⟨the drugs had *befuddled* them⟩ **2** : to confuse the understanding of : PERPLEX ⟨a problem that has *befuddled* the experts⟩ — **be•fud•dle•ment** \-l-mənt\ *n*
beg \ˈbeg\ *vb* **begged**; **beg•ging** **1** : to ask for money, food, or help as a charity ⟨*beg* in the streets⟩ **2** : to ask earnestly or politely ⟨*beg* a favor⟩ **[**Middle English *beggen***]**
• **syn** BEG, BESEECH, IMPLORE, ENTREAT mean to ask urgently: BEG suggests earnestness or insistence especially in asking for a favor; BESEECH implies great eagerness or anxiety; IMPLORE adds a suggestion of greater urgency or anguished appeal; ENTREAT implies an attempt to persuade or to overcome resistance.
—**beg the question** **1** : to assume as true or take for granted the thing that is the subject of the argument **2** : to dodge the issue
be•gat \bi-ˈgat\ *archaic past of* BEGET
be•get \bi-ˈget\ *vt* **-got** \-ˈgät\; **-got•ten** \-ˈgät-n\ *or* **-got**; **-get•ting** **1** : to become the father of : SIRE **2** : CAUSE 1 — **be•get•ter** *n*
[1]**beg•gar** \ˈbeg-ər\ *n* **1** : one that begs; *esp* : one that lives by asking for gifts **2** : PAUPER **3** : FELLOW 4b
[2]**beggar** *vt* **1** : to reduce to beggary **2** : to exceed the resources or capacity of ⟨the lavish costumes *beggar* description⟩
beg•gar•ly \ˈbeg-ər-lē\ *adj* **1** : befitting or resembling a beggar **2** : contemptibly small, poor, or mean — **beg•gar•li•ness** *n*
beg•gar's-lice \ˈbeg-ərz-ˌlīs\ *or* **beg•gar-lice** \-ər-ˌlīs\ *n sing or pl* : any of several plants with prickly or adhesive fruits; *also* : one of these fruits
beg•gar-ticks *or* **beg•gar's-ticks** \-ˌtiks\ *n sing or pl* **1** : BUR MARIGOLD; *also* : its prickly fruits **2** : BEGGARS-LICE
beg•gary \ˈbeg-ə-rē\ *n* : extreme poverty
be•gin \bi-ˈgin\ *vb* **be•gan** \-ˈgan\; **be•gun** \-ˈgən\; **be•gin•ning** **1 a** : to do the first part of an action ⟨please *begin*⟩ **b** : to undertake or undergo initial steps : COMMENCE ⟨*began* the program with a song⟩ **2 a** : to come into existence : ARISE ⟨how the Civil War *began*⟩ **b** : to have a starting point ⟨the road *begins* there⟩ **3** : to do or succeed in the least degree ⟨does not *begin* to fill our needs⟩ **4** : to bring into existence : FOUND ⟨*begin* a dynasty⟩ **5** : to come first in ⟨the letter *A begins* the alphabet⟩ **[**Old English *beginnan***]**
be•gin•ner \bi-ˈgin-ər\ *n* : one that is beginning something or doing something for the first time
be•gin•ning \bi-ˈgin-iŋ\ *n* **1** : the point at which something begins **2** : the first part **3** : primary source or cause : ORIGIN **4** : a first stage or early period
be•gone \bi-ˈgȯn, -ˈgän\ *vi* : to go away : DEPART — usually used in the imperative ⟨*begone* from my sight!⟩
be•go•nia \bi-ˈgō-nyə\ *n* : any of a large genus of tropical herbs

often grown for their shining leaves and bright waxy flowers [Michel *Bégon,* died 1710, French governor of Santo Domingo]

be•grime \bi-ˈgrīm\ *vt* **:** to make dirty with grime

be•grudge \bi-ˈgrəj\ *vt* **1 :** to give, do, or allow reluctantly ⟨*begrudge* a person a favor⟩ **2 :** to envy a person's possession or enjoyment of ⟨I don't *begrudge* them their success⟩ — **be•grudg•ing•ly** \-ing-lē\ *adv*

be•guile \bi-ˈgīl\ *vt* **1 :** to deceive by cunning means ⟨was *beguiled* by vague promises⟩ **2 :** to draw notice or interest by wiles or charm ⟨the view *beguiled* them⟩ **3 :** to cause (as time) to pass pleasantly **:** while away ⟨*beguile* the wait by telling stories⟩ **syn** see DECEIVE — **be•guile•ment** \-mənt\ *n* — **be•guil•er** *n*

be•guine \bi-ˈgēn\ *n* **:** a vigorous popular dance of the islands of Saint Lucia and Martinique [American French *béguine,* from French *béguin* "flirtation"]

be•gum \ˈbē-gəm\ *n* **:** a Muslim woman of high rank [Hindi *begam*]

be•half \bi-ˈhaf, -ˈhȧf\ *n* **:** useful aid **:** HELP, SUPPORT ⟨spoke in my *behalf*⟩ [Middle English, from *by* + *half* "half, side"] — **in behalf of** *or* **on behalf of 1 :** in the interest of **:** for the benefit of ⟨worked *in behalf of* the government⟩ **2 :** as a representative of ⟨accepting the award *on behalf of* the whole class⟩

be•have \bi-ˈhāv\ *vb* **1 :** to conduct oneself in a particular way ⟨*behaved* badly⟩ **2 :** to conduct oneself in a proper manner ⟨please *behave*⟩ **3 :** to act, function, or react in a particular way **:** exhibit reaction (as to an environment) [Middle English *be-* + *haven* "to have, hold"]

be•hav•ior \bi-ˈhā-vyər\ *n* **:** the way in which a person or thing behaves — **be•hav•ior•al** \-vyə-rəl\ *adj* — **be•hav•ior•al•ly** \-rə-lē\ *adv*

be•head \bi-ˈhed\ *vt* **:** to cut off the head of

be•he•moth \bi-ˈhē-məth, ˈbē-ə-ˌmäth\ *n* **1** *often cap* **:** an animal described in the Bible that is probably the hippopotamus **2 :** something of monstrous size or power [Hebrew *bĕhēmōth*]

be•hest \bi-ˈhest\ *n* **:** ORDER 5c, COMMAND [Old English *behǣs* "promise"]

¹be•hind \bi-ˈhīnd\ *adv* **1 a :** in a place, situation, or time that is being or has been departed from ⟨stay *behind*⟩ ⟨leaving years of poverty *behind*⟩ **b :** at, to, or toward the back ⟨look *behind*⟩ **2 a :** in a secondary or inferior position ⟨lag *behind* in competition⟩ **b :** in a state of failing to keep up to schedule ⟨*behind* in the car payments⟩

²behind *prep* **1 a :** at, to, or toward the back of ⟨look *behind* you⟩ ⟨a garden *behind* the house⟩ **b :** beyond in past time ⟨good fortune has put their worries *behind* them⟩ **2 :** inferior to ⟨sales *behind* those of last year⟩ **3 :** retarded in relation to ⟨*behind* the rest of the class⟩ **4 a :** in the background of ⟨the conditions *behind* the strike⟩ **b :** in support of ⟨solidly *behind* their candidate⟩

³behind *n* **:** BUTTOCKS

be•hind•hand \bi-ˈhīnd-ˌhand\ *adv or adj* **:** not keeping up **:** LATE ⟨*behindhand* with the rent⟩

be•hold \bi-ˈhōld\ *vb* **1 :** SEE 1a **2 :** to gaze upon **:** OBSERVE — **be•hold•er** *n*

be•hold•en \bi-ˈhōl-dən\ *adj* **:** being under obligation for a favor or gift **:** INDEBTED

be•hoof \bi-ˈhüf\ *n* **:** BENEFIT 1a [Old English *behōf*]

be•hoove \bi-ˈhüv\ *or* **be•hove** \-ˈhōv\ *vt* **:** to be necessary, fitting, or proper for ⟨it *behooves* a soldier to obey orders⟩ ⟨such behavior ill *behooves* you⟩

beige \ˈbāzh\ *n* **:** a light grayish yellowish brown [French] — **beige** *adj*

be•ing \ˈbē-ing\ *n* **1 a :** EXISTENCE 1 **b :** LIFE 1 **2 :** the totality of existing things **3 :** a living thing; *esp* **:** PERSON

bel \ˈbel\ *n* **:** ten decibels [Alexander Graham *Bell*]

be•la•bor \bi-ˈlā-bər\ *vt* **1 :** to work on or at to absurd lengths ⟨*belabor* the obvious⟩ **2 :** ASSAIL, ATTACK

be•lat•ed \bi-ˈlāt-əd\ *adj* **:** delayed beyond the usual time — **be•lat•ed•ly** *adv* — **be•lat•ed•ness** *n*

be•lay \bi-ˈlā\ *vb* **1 :** to make fast (as a rope) by turns around a cleat or pin **2 :** CEASE, STOP [Old English *belecgan* "to beset", from *be-* + *lecgan* "to lay"]

belch \ˈbelch\ *vb* **1 :** to expel gas suddenly from the stomach through the mouth **2 :** to give off or issue forth violently ⟨smoke *belched* from the chimney⟩ [Old English *bealcian*] — **belch** *n*

bel•dam *or* **bel•dame** \ˈbel-dəm\ *n* **:** an old woman [Middle English *beldam* "grandmother", from Middle French *bel* "beautiful" + Middle English *dam*]

be•lea•guer \bi-ˈlē-gər\ *vt* **-guered; -guer•ing** \-gə-ring, -gring\ **1 :** to surround with an army so as to prevent escape **:** BESIEGE **2 :** to subject to troublesome forces **:** HARASS ⟨the pests that *beleaguer* farmers⟩ [Dutch *belegeren,* from *be-* "be-" + *leger* "camp"]

bel•em•nite \ˈbel-əm-ˌnīt\ *n* **:** a conical fossil shell of an extinct cephalopod [Greek *belemnon* "dart"] — **bel•em•noid** \ˈbel-əm-ˌnȯid\ *adj or n*

belfry

bel•fry \ˈbel-frē\ *n, pl* **belfries :** a tower or a room in a tower for a bell or set of bells [Middle French *berfrei*]

Bel•gae \ˈbel-ˌgī, -ˌjē\ *n pl* **:** a people occupying northern France and Belgium in Julius Caesar's time [Latin] — **Bel•gic** \-jik\ *adj*

Bel•gian hare \ˈbel-jən-\ *n* **:** any of a breed of slender dark red domestic rabbits

Belgian sheepdog *n* **:** any of a breed of hardy black or gray dogs developed in Belgium especially for herding sheep

be•lie \bi-ˈlī\ *vt* **-lied; -ly•ing 1 :** to give a false impression of ⟨a vigor that *belied* their years⟩ **2 :** to be false or unfaithful to ⟨*belie* their principles⟩ **3 :** to show to be false ⟨your actions *belie* your promise⟩ — **be•li•er** *n*

be•lief \bə-ˈlēf\ *n* **1 :** mental acceptance of something as real or true ⟨a *belief* in miracles⟩ ⟨a *belief* in your own ability⟩ **2 :** religious faith; *esp* **:** CREED 1 **3 :** the thing that is believed **:** CONVICTION, OPINION ⟨political *beliefs*⟩ [Middle English *beleave*]

• **syn** BELIEF, FAITH, CREDENCE mean the assent to the truth of something offered for acceptance. BELIEF may or may not imply certitude in the believer, whereas FAITH always does and implies trust and confidence even when there is no evidence or proof; CREDENCE implies intellectual acceptance but offers nothing about the soundness of the grounds for acceptance. **syn** see in addition OPINION

be•lieve \bə-ˈlēv\ *vb* **1 :** to have a firm religious faith **2 :** to have a firm conviction as to the reality or goodness of something ⟨*believe* in fair play⟩ ⟨*believe* in magic⟩ **3 :** to accept as true or honest ⟨*believe* the reports⟩ **4 :** to hold as an opinion **:** THINK, SUPPOSE [Old English *belēfan,* from *be-* + *lēfan* "to allow, believe"] — **be•liev•a•ble** \-ˈlē-və-bəl\ *adj* — **be•liev•a•bly** \-və-blē\ *adv* — **be•liev•er** *n*

be•like \bi-ˈlīk\ *adv, archaic* **:** most likely **:** PROBABLY

be•lit•tle \bi-ˈlit-l\ *vt* **-lit•tled; -lit•tling** \-ˈlit-ling, -ˈlit-l-ing\ **:** to speak of in a slighting way **:** DISPARAGE ⟨*belittle* the success of a rival⟩ — **be•lit•tle•ment** \-l-mənt\ *n* — **be•lit•tler** \-ˈlit-lər, -l-ər\ *n*

¹bell \ˈbel\ *n* **1 :** a hollow usually cup-shaped metallic device that makes a ringing sound when struck **2 :** the stroke or sound of a bell that tells the hour especially on shipboard **3 a :** the time indicated by the stroke of a bell **b :** a half hour period of a watch on shipboard **4 :** something (as a flower) shaped like a bell **5** *pl* **:** BELL-BOTTOMS [Old English *belle*]

SHIP'S BELLS

Number of Bells	Hour (A.M. or P.M.)		
1	12:30	4:30	8:30
2	1:00	5:00	9:00
3	1:30	5:30	9:30
4	2:00	6:00	10:00
5	2:30	6:30	10:30
6	3:00	7:00	11:00
7	3:30	7:30	11:30
8	4:00	8:00	12:00

²bell *vb* **1 :** to provide with a bell ⟨*bell* a cat⟩ **2 :** to take the form of a bell **:** FLARE

bel•la•don•na \ˌbel-ə-ˈdän-ə\ *n* **1 :** a European poisonous herb of the potato family with reddish bell-shaped flowers, shining black berries, and root and leaves that yield atropine **2 :** a drug or extract from the belladonna plant [Italian, literally, "beautiful lady"]

bell•bird \ˈbel-ˌbərd\ *n* **:** any of several birds whose notes are likened to the sound of a bell

bell–bot•toms \-ˈbät-əmz\ *n pl* **:** pants with legs that flare at the bottom — **bell–bottom** *or* **bell–bot•tomed** \-ˈbät-əmd\ *adj*

bell•boy \-ˌbȯi\ *n* **:** BELLHOP

belle \ˈbel\ *n* **:** a popular attractive girl or woman [French, from the feminine of *beau* "beautiful"]

belles let•tres \bel-letrᵊ\ *n pl* **:** literature of primarily artistic interest and not simply practical or informative [French, literally, "fine letters"] — **bel•le•tris•tic** \ˌbel-ə-ˈtris-tik\ *adj*

bell•flow•er \ˈbel-ˌflau̇-ər, -ˌflau̇r\ *n* **:** CAMPANULA

bell•hop \ˈbel-ˌhäp\ *n* **:** a hotel or club employee who escorts guests to rooms, carries luggage, and runs errands [short for *bell-hopper*]

bel•li•cose \ˈbel-ə-ˌkōs\ *adj* **:** showing a readiness to quarrel or fight [Latin *bellicosus*, from *bellum* "war"] — **bel•li•cos•i•ty** \ˌbel-ə-ˈkäs-ət-ē\ *n*

bel•lig•er•ence \bə-ˈlij-rəns, -ə-rəns\ *n* **:** a belligerent attitude or disposition

bel•lig•er•en•cy \-rən-sē\ *n* **1 :** the status of a nation that is at war **2 :** BELLIGERENCE

bel•lig•er•ent \bə-ˈlij-rənt, -ə-rənt\ *adj* **1 :** waging war; *esp* **:** belonging to or recognized as a power at war and protected by and subject to the laws of war ⟨*belligerent* nations⟩ **2 :** showing a readiness to fight [Latin *belligerare* "to wage war", from *bellum* "war" + *gerare* "to wage"] — **belligerent** *n* — **bel•lig•er•ent•ly** *adv*

bell jar *n* **:** a bell-shaped usually glass vessel designed to cover objects or to contain gases or a vacuum

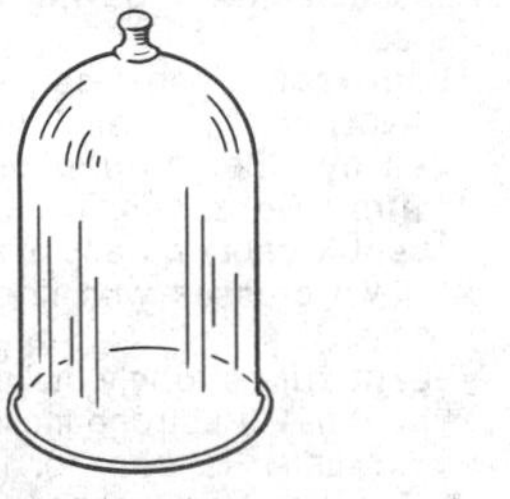

bell jar

bell•man \ˈbel-mən\ *n* **1 :** one (as a town crier) who rings a bell **2 :** BELLHOP

bel•low \ˈbel-ō\ *vb* **1 :** to make the loud deep hollow sound characteristic of a bull **2 :** to shout in a deep voice **:** BAWL [Old English *bylgian*] — **bellow** *n*

bel•lows \ˈbel-ōz, -əz\ *n sing or pl* **1 :** a device (as for blowing fires or operating an organ) that by alternate expansion and contraction draws in air through a valve and expels it forcibly through a tube; *also* **:** any of various blowers or enclosures of variable volume **2 :** the pleated expandable part of some cameras [Middle English *bely, below* "belly, bellows"]

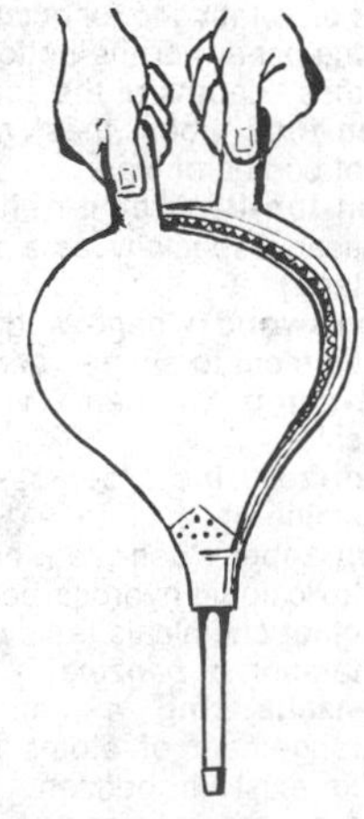

bellows 1

bell pepper *n* **:** SWEET PEPPER

bell•pull \ˈbel-ˌpu̇l\ *n* **:** a cord or wire with a handle by which one rings a bell

bell•weth•er \ˈbel-ˈweth-ər\ *n* **1 :** a belled usually wether sheep that runs with and identifies the location of a flock **2 :** one that takes the lead or initiative

¹bel•ly \ˈbel-ē\ *n, pl* **bellies 1 a :** ABDOMEN 1 **b :** the underside of an animal's body; *also* **:** hide from this part **c :** UTERUS **d :** STOMACH 1a **2 :** an internal cavity **:** INTERIOR **3 :** a surface or object curved or rounded like a human belly ⟨the *belly* of an airplane⟩ **4 a :** the part of a sail that swells out when filled with wind **b :** the enlarged fleshy body of a muscle [Middle English *bely* "bellows, belly", from Old English *belg* "bag"]

²belly *vb* **bel•lied**; **bel•ly•ing :** to swell or bulge out

¹bel•ly•ache \ˈbel-ē-ˌāk\ *n* **:** pain in the abdomen and especially in the bowels

²bellyache *vi* **:** to complain in a whining or peevish way

bel•ly•band \ˈbel-ē-ˌband\ *n* **:** a band around or across the belly: as **a :** GIRTH 1 **b :** BAND 4

belly button *n* **:** NAVEL 1

belly flop *or* **belly flop•per** *n* **:** a dive in which the front of the body lands flat against a surface (as of water or the top of a coasting sled)

bel•ly•ful \ˈbel-ē-ˌfu̇l\ *n* **:** an excessive amount

belly laugh *n* **:** a deep hearty laugh

be•long \bə-ˈlȯŋ\ *vi* **1 :** to be suitable or appropriate **:** have a proper place ⟨a dictionary *belongs* in every home⟩ ⟨this *belongs* on the table⟩ **2 a :** to be the property of a person or thing ⟨this book *belongs* to me⟩ **b :** to become attached or bound; *esp* **:** to be a member of an organization **3 :** to be an attribute, part, adjunct, or function of a person or thing ⟨parts *belonging* to a watch⟩ **4 :** to be properly classified ⟨whales *belong* among the mammals⟩ [Middle English *be-* + *longen* "to be suitable"]

be•long•ings \bə-ˈlȯŋ-iŋz\ *n pl* **:** the things that belong to a person **:** POSSESSIONS

be•loved \bi-ˈləvd, -ˈləv-əd\ *adj* **:** dearly loved — **beloved** *n*

¹be•low \bə-ˈlō\ *adv* **1 :** in or to a lower place **2 a :** on earth **b :** in or to Hades or hell **3 :** on or to a lower floor or deck **4 :** lower on the same page or on a following page

²below *prep* **:** lower than in place, rank, or value ⟨*below* sea level⟩ ⟨*below* average⟩

• syn UNDER, BENEATH: BELOW is opposed to *above* and implies only that one thing is on a lower level than another ⟨ten degrees *below* zero⟩ UNDER is opposed to *over* and implies a relation between two things such as contact, support, subjection, inferiority ⟨my legs doubled *under* me⟩ ⟨held the cup *under* the spout⟩ ⟨troops *under* their command⟩ BENEATH is chiefly poetical for UNDER or BELOW except when expressing moral or social inferiority ⟨actions *beneath* contempt⟩ ⟨thought manual labor was *beneath* them⟩

¹belt \ˈbelt\ *n* **1 :** a strip of flexible material (as leather or cloth) worn around a person's body for holding in or supporting clothing or weapons or for ornament **2 :** something resembling a belt **:** BAND, CIRCLE ⟨a *belt* of trees⟩ **3 a :** a flexible endless band running around wheels or pulleys and used for moving or carrying something ⟨a fan *belt* on a car⟩ **b :** a band of strong reinforcing material laid beneath the tread of a tire **4 :** a natural area marked by some distinctive feature, product, or activity ⟨the corn *belt*⟩ [Old English, derived from Latin *balteus*] — **belt•ed** \ˈbel-təd\ *adj* — **below the belt :** not fair **:** in an unfair manner — **under one's belt 1 :** in one's stomach ⟨a couple of drinks *under my belt*⟩ **2 :** as part of one's experience ⟨100 hours of flying time *under my belt*⟩

²belt *vt* **1 :** to put a belt on or around **2 a :** to beat with or as if with a belt **b :** to hit or strike powerfully ⟨*belted* a home run⟩ **3 :** to mark with a band **4 :** to sing in a forceful manner ⟨*belt* out a song⟩

³belt *n* **1 :** a jarring blow **2 :** DRINK 2 ⟨a *belt* of whiskey⟩

belt•ing \ˈbel-tiŋ\ *n* **:** material for belts

belt•way \ˈbelt-ˌwā\ *n* **:** a highway going around an urban area — called also *belt highway*

be•lu•ga \bə-ˈlü-gə\ *n* **1 :** a sturgeon especially of the Black and Caspian seas **2 :** a mammal of the dolphin family becoming about 3 meters long and white when adult [sense 1 from Russian *beluga*, from *belyĭ* "white"; sense 2 from Russian *belukha*, from *belyĭ*]

bel•ve•dere \ˈbel-və-ˌdiər\ *n* **:** GAZEBO [Italian, literally, "beautiful view"]

be•mire \bi-ˈmīr\ *vt* **1 :** to cover or soil with mire **2 :** to sink in mire

be•moan \bi-ˈmōn\ *vt* **1 :** to express grief over **:** LAMENT **2 :** to look upon with regret or displeasure

be•muse \bi-ˈmyüz\ *vt* **:** to make confused **:** BEWILDER

¹bench \ˈbench\ *n* **1 :** a long seat for two or more persons **2 :** a long table for holding work and tools ⟨a carpenter's *bench*⟩ **3 a :** the seat where a judge sits in a court of law **b :** the position or rank of a judge **c :** a person or persons sitting as judge **4 :** a seat where the members of a team wait for an opportunity to play **5 :** TERRACE 2, SHELF [Old English *benc*] — **bench•like** \-ˌlīk\ *adj*

\ə\ **abut**	\au̇\ **out**	\i\ **tip**	\ȯ\ **saw**	\u̇\ **foot**
\ər\ **further**	\ch\ **chin**	\ī\ **life**	\ȯi\ **coin**	\y\ **yet**
\a\ **mat**	\e\ **pet**	\j\ **job**	\th\ **thin**	\yü\ **few**
\ā\ **take**	\ē\ **easy**	\ŋ\ **sing**	\t͟h\ **this**	\yu̇\ **cure**
\ä\ **cot, cart**	\g\ **go**	\ō\ **bone**	\ü\ **food**	\zh\ **vision**

[2]**bench** *vt* **1 :** to seat on a bench **2 :** to remove from or keep out of a game

bench mark *n* **1 :** a mark on a permanent object indicating elevation and serving as a reference in geological surveys **2** *usually* **benchmark :** something that serves as a standard by which others may be measured

[1]**bend** \'bend\ *n* **1 :** a diagonal band in heraldry **2 :** a knot by which one rope is fastened to another or to some object **[**sense 1 from Middle French *bende, bande* "strip, band"; sense 2 from Old English *bend* "fetter"**]**

[2]**bend** *vb* **bent** \'bent\; **bend•ing 1 :** to pull taut or tense ⟨*bend* a bow⟩ **2 :** to curve or cause a change of shape ⟨*bend* a wire into a circle⟩ **3 :** to turn in a certain direction ⟨*bent* their steps toward town⟩ **4 :** to force to yield ⟨*bent* the family to our will⟩ **5 :** to apply or apply oneself closely ⟨*bend* your energy to the task⟩ **6 :** to curve out of line ⟨the road *bends* to the left⟩ **7 :** to curve downward **:** STOOP ⟨backs *bent* by age⟩ **8 :** YIELD, SUBMIT **[**Old English *bendan***]**

[3]**bend** *n* **1 :** the act or process of bending **:** the state of being bent **2 :** something that is bent; *esp* **:** a curved part of a stream **3** *pl* **:** CAISSON DISEASE

bend•er \'ben-dər\ *n* **1 :** one that bends **2 :** SPREE

[1]**be•neath** \bi-'nēth\ *adv* **1 :** in or to a lower position **2 :** directly under **[**Old English *beneothan,* from *be-* + *neothan* "below"**]**

[2]**beneath** *prep* **1 a :** in or to a lower position than **b :** directly under ⟨the ground *beneath* one's feet⟩ **2 :** unworthy of ⟨*beneath* our dignity⟩ **syn** see BELOW

Ben•e•dic•tine \ˌben-ə-'dik-tən, -ˌtēn\ *n* **:** a monk or a nun of a religious order following the rule of Saint Benedict and devoted especially to scholarship and liturgical worship — **Benedictine** *adj*

bene•dic•tion \ˌben-ə-'dik-shən\ *n* **:** the invocation of a blessing; *esp* **:** a short blessing at the end of a religious service **[**Late Latin *benedicere* "to bless", from Latin, "to speak well of", from *bene* "well" + *dicere* "to say"**]** — **bene•dic•to•ry** \-'dik-tə-rē, -trē\ *adj*

Ben•e•dict's solution \'ben-ə-ˌdiks-, -ˌdikts-\ *n* **:** a blue solution that yields a red, yellow, or orange precipitate upon warming with a sugar (as glucose or maltose) capable of reducing a mild oxidizing agent **[**Stanley R. *Benedict,* died 1936, American chemist**]**

Bene•dic•tus \ˌben-ə-'dik-təs\ *n* **1 :** a canticle from Matthew 21:9 beginning "Blessed is he that cometh in the name of the Lord" **2 :** a canticle from Luke 1:68 beginning "Blessed be the Lord God of Israel" **[**Late Latin, "blessed"**]**

bene•fac•tion \'ben-ə-ˌfak-shən, ˌben-ə-'\ *n* **1 :** the action of benefiting **2 :** a benefit given; *esp* **:** a charitable donation **[**Late Latin *benefactio,* derived from Latin *bene facere* "to do good"**]**

bene•fac•tor \'ben-ə-ˌfak-tər\ *n* **:** one that gives help; *esp* **:** one that gives or bequeaths financial aid

bene•fac•tress \-ˌfak-trəs\ *n* **:** a woman who is a benefactor

ben•e•fice \'ben-ə-fəs\ *n* **:** a post held by a member of the clergy that gives the right to use certain property and to receive income from stated sources **[**Medieval Latin *beneficium,* from Latin, "benefit, favor, promotion"**]** — **benefice** *vt*

be•nef•i•cence \bə-'nef-ə-səns\ *n* **1 :** the quality or state of being beneficent **2 :** BENEFACTION

be•nef•i•cent \-sənt\ *adj* **:** doing or producing good; *esp* **:** performing acts of kindness and charity — **be•nef•i•cent•ly** *adv*

ben•e•fi•cial \ˌben-ə-'fish-əl\ *adj* **:** producing good effects **:** HELPFUL, ADVANTAGEOUS **[**Latin *beneficium* "kindness, benefit", from *beneficus* "conferring benefits", from *bene* "well" + *facere* "to do"**]** — **ben•e•fi•cial•ly** \-'fish-ə-lē\ *adv* — **ben•e•fi•cial•ness** *n*

• syn BENEFICIAL, ADVANTAGEOUS, PROFITABLE mean bringing good or gain. BENEFICIAL implies promoting health or well-being; ADVANTAGEOUS stresses a choice or preference that brings superiority or greater success in attaining an end; PROFITABLE implies the yielding of useful or lucrative returns.

ben•e•fi•ci•ary \-'fish-ē-ˌer-ē; -'fish-rē, -ə-rē\ *n, pl* **-ar•ies :** a person who benefits or is expected to benefit from something ⟨the *beneficiary* of a life insurance policy⟩

[1]**ben•e•fit** \'ben-ə-ˌfit\ *n* **1 a :** something that promotes well-being **:** ADVANTAGE **b :** useful aid **:** HELP **2 :** money paid (as by an insurance company or a public agency) at death or when one is sick, retired, or unemployed **3 :** an entertainment or social event to raise funds for a person or cause **[**Anglo-French *benfet* "good deed", from Latin *bene factum,* literally, "thing well done"**]**

[2]**benefit** *vb* **-fit•ed** *or* **-fit•ted**; **-fit•ing** *or* **-fit•ting 1 :** to be useful or profitable to **2 :** to receive benefit

be•nev•o•lence \bə-'nev-ləns, -ə-ləns\ *n* **1 :** disposition to do good **2 a :** an act of kindness **b :** a generous gift

be•nev•o•lent \-lənt\ *adj* **1 :** having or showing goodwill **:** KINDLY **2 :** freely or generously giving to charity **3 :** existing or operated to help others and not for profit ⟨*benevolent* institutions⟩ **[**Latin *benevolens,* from *bene* "well" + *velle* "to wish"**]** — **be•nev•o•lent•ly** *adv* — **be•nev•o•lent•ness** *n*

Ben•gali \ben-'gò-lē, beng-\ *n* **1 :** a native or inhabitant of Bengal **2 :** the modern Indic language of Bengal — **Bengali** *adj*

ben•ga•line \'beng-gə-ˌlēn\ *n* **:** fabric with a crosswise rib **[**French, from *Bengal***]**

be•night•ed \bi-'nīt-əd\ *adj* **1 :** overtaken by night or darkness **2 :** IGNORANT 1a, 2

be•nign \bi-'nīn\ *adj* **1 :** of a gentle disposition **:** GRACIOUS **2 a :** showing kindness and gentleness ⟨a *benign* face⟩ **b :** FAVORABLE 2 ⟨a *benign* climate⟩ **3 :** of a mild character; *esp* **:** not malignant ⟨a *benign* tumor⟩ **[**Latin *benignus* "good-natured", from *bene* "well" + *gigni* "to be born"**]** — **be•nig•ni•ty** \-'nig-nət-ē\ *n* — **be•nign•ly** \-'nīn-lē\ *adv*

• syn BENIGN, BENIGNANT both mean kindly or favorable in appearance, but BENIGN suggests actual effect given by action or appearance ⟨the weather remained *benign*⟩ ⟨a frown on a usually *benign* face⟩ BENIGNANT tends to suggest conscious feeling or intention of kindliness ⟨giving out candy with a *benignant* smile for each child⟩

be•nig•nant \bi-'nig-nənt\ *adj* **1 :** showing kindly feelings or intentions ⟨a *benignant* smile⟩ **2 :** FAVORABLE 2, BENEFICIAL **syn** see BENIGN — **be•nig•nan•cy** \-nən-sē\ *n* — **be•nig•nant•ly** *adv*

ben•i•son \'ben-ə-sən, -zən\ *n* **:** BLESSING 1, 2, 3; *also* **:** BENEDICTION **[**Old French *beneiçon,* from Late Latin *benedictio***]**

ben•ny \'ben-ē\ *n, pl* **bennies** *slang* **:** a tablet of amphetamine **[**from *Benzadrine***]**

[1]**bent** \'bent\ *n* **:** any of a genus of mostly perennial pasture and lawn grasses with fine velvety or wiry herbage **[**Middle English**]**

[2]**bent** *adj* **:** strongly inclined **:** DETERMINED ⟨*bent* on winning⟩

[3]**bent** *n* **1 a :** strong inclination or interest **b :** a natural capacity **:** TALENT ⟨a *bent* for languages⟩ **2 :** capacity for endurance **[**derived from [2]*bend***]**

ben•thic \'ben-thik, 'bent-\ *or* **ben•thon•ic** \ben-'thän-ik\ *adj* **:** of, relating to, or occurring in the depths of a body of water (as the ocean) or the bottom underlying these depths **[**Greek *benthos* "depths of the sea"**]**

ben•thos \'ben-ˌthäs\ *n* **:** organisms that live on or in the bottom of bodies of water

ben•ton•ite \'bent-n-ˌīt\ *n* **:** an absorptive and colloidal clay used especially as a filler (as in paper) **[**Fort *Benton,* Montana**]**

bent•wood \'bent-ˌwu̇d\ *adj* **:** made of wood that is bent rather than cut to shape ⟨*bentwood* furniture⟩

be•numb \bi-'nəm\ *vt* **:** to make numb ⟨*benumbed* by the cold⟩

Ben•ze•drine \'ben-zə-ˌdrēn\ *trademark* — used for amphetamine

ben•zene \'ben-ˌzēn, ben-'\ *n* **:** a colorless volatile flammable toxic liquid hydrocarbon C_6H_6 used as a solvent and in making other chemicals (as dyes and drugs) — called also *benzol* **[**alteration of *benzine***]**

benzene ring *n* **:** an arrangement of atoms held to exist in benzene and other aromatic compounds that is marked by six carbon atoms linked by alternate single and double bonds in a hexagon

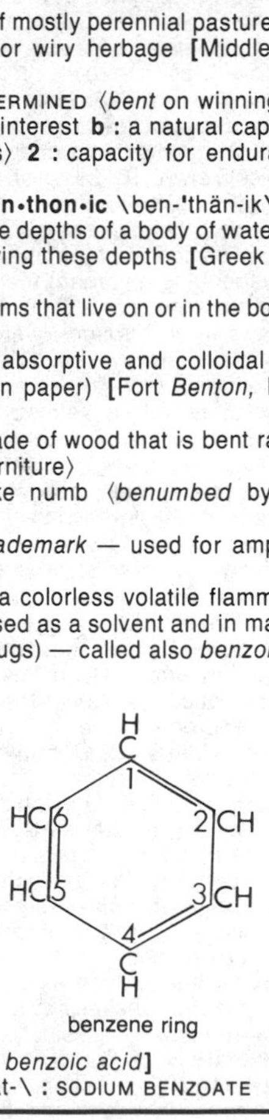

benzene ring

ben•zine \'ben-ˌzēn, ben-'\ *n* **1 :** BENZENE **2 :** any of various volatile flammable petroleum distillates used especially as solvents for fatty substances or as motor fuels **[**from *benzoic acid***]**

ben•zo•ate of soda \ˌben-zə-ˌwāt-\ **:** SODIUM BENZOATE

ben•zo•ic acid \ben-ˌzō-ik-\ *n* : a white crystalline acid $C_7H_6O_2$ found naturally (as in cranberries) or made synthetically and used especially as a preservative and as an antiseptic [*benzoin*]

ben•zo•in \ˈben-zə-wən, -ˌwēn; -ˌzȯin\ *n* : a hard fragrant yellowish resin from trees of southeastern Asia used especially in medicine, as a fixative in perfumes, and as incense [Middle French *benjoin*, from Catalan *benjuí*, from Arabic *lubān jāwi*, literally, "frankincense of Java"]

ben•zol \ˈben-ˌzȯl, -ˌzōl\ *n* : BENZENE; *also* : a mixture of benzene and other aromatic hydrocarbons

be•queath \bi-ˈkwēth, -ˈkwēth\ *vt* **1** : to give or leave (personal property) by will **2** : to hand down ⟨ideas *bequeathed* by our ancestors⟩ [Old English *becwethan*, from *be-* + *cwethan* "to say"] — **be•queath•al** \-əl\ *n*

be•quest \bi-ˈkwest\ *n* **1** : the act of bequeathing **2** : something bequeathed : LEGACY

be•rate \bi-ˈrāt\ *vt* : to scold forcefully

Ber•ber \ˈbər-bər\ *n* **1** : a member of a people of northwestern Africa **2** : any of a group of languages spoken in northwestern Africa [Arabic *Barbar*] — **Berber** *adj*

be•reave \bi-ˈrēv\ *vt* **-reaved** \-ˈrēvd\ *or* **-reft** \-ˈreft\; **-reav•ing** *archaic* : to deprive of something [Old English *berēafian*, from *be-* + *rēafian* "to rob"]

[1]**be•reaved** \bi-ˈrēvd\ *adj* : suffering the death of a loved one ⟨*bereaved* parents⟩

[2]**bereaved** *n, pl* **bereaved** : one who is bereaved

be•reave•ment \bi-ˈrēv-mənt\ *n* : the state or fact of being bereaved

be•reft \bi-ˈreft\ *adj* **1** : not having something needed, wanted, or expected **2** : BEREAVED

be•ret \bə-ˈrā\ *n* : a soft flat wool cap without a visor [French *béret*, from Provençal *berret*]

beret

berg \ˈbərg\ *n* : ICEBERG

ber•ga•mot \ˈbər-gə-ˌmät\ *n* **1** : a pear-shaped orange whose rind yields an oil used in perfumery; *also* : the tree or oil **2** : any of several mints (as Oswego tea) [French *bergamote*]

beri•beri \ˌber-ē-ˈber-ē\ *n* : a deficiency disease marked by weakness, wasting, and damage to nerves and caused by a dietary lack of or inability to assimilate thiamine [Sinhalese *bæribæri*]

Be•ring time \ˈbiər-ing-, ˈbeər-\ *n* : the time of the 11th time zone west of Greenwich that includes western Alaska and the Aleutian islands

berke•li•um \ˈbər-klē-əm; bər-ˈkē-lē-əm, ˌbər-\ *n* : a radioactive chemical element produced by bombarding americium with helium ions — see ELEMENT table [New Latin, from *Berkeley*, California]

Berk•shire \ˈbərk-ˌshiər, -shər\ *n* : any of a breed of medium-sized swine that are black with white markings [*Berkshire*, England]

berm *or* **berme** \ˈbərm\ *n* : a narrow shelf, path, or ledge typically at the top or bottom of a slope [French *berme*, from Dutch *berm* "strip of ground along a dike"]

Ber•mu•da grass \bər-ˈmyüd-ə-\ *n* : a trailing southern European grass widely grown in tropical and subtropical regions especially as a turf grass

Bermuda shorts *n pl* : knee-length walking shorts

[1]**ber•ry** \ˈber-ē\ *n, pl* **berries** **1 a** : a small pulpy and usually edible fruit (as a strawberry or raspberry) **b** : a fruit (as a currant, grape, tomato, or banana) that develops from a single ovary and has the wall of the ripened ovary pulpy or fleshy **c** : the dry seed of some plants (as coffee) **2** : an egg of a fish or lobster [Old English *berie*] — **ber•ried** \ˈber-ēd\ *adj*

[2]**berry** *vi* **ber•ried**; **ber•ry•ing** **1** : to bear or produce berries ⟨*berrying* wheat⟩ **2** : to gather or seek berries ⟨go *berrying* every summer⟩

[1]**ber•serk** \bər-ˈsərk, bə-, -ˈzərk, ˈbər-ˌ\ *or* **ber•serk•er** \-ər\ *n* : an ancient Scandinavian warrior frenzied in battle and held to be invulnerable [Old Norse *berserkr*, from *björn* "bear" + *serkr* "shirt"]

[2]**berserk** *adj* : FRENZIED, CRAZED — **berserk** *adv*

[1]**berth** \ˈbərth\ *n* **1** : distance sufficient to maneuver a ship **2** : a place where a ship lies at anchor or at a wharf **3** : a place to sit or sleep on a ship or vehicle **4** : a job especially on a ship [probably from [2]*bear* + *-th*]

[2]**berth** *vb* **1** : to bring or come into a berth **2** : to allot a berth to

ber•tha \ˈbər-thə\ *n* : a wide round collar covering the shoulders [French *berthe*, from *Berthe* (Bertha), died 783, queen of the Franks]

ber•yl \ˈber-əl\ *n* : a mineral $Be_3Al_2Si_6O_{18}$ consisting of a silicate of beryllium and aluminum of great hardness and occurring in green, bluish green, yellow, pink, or white prisms [Greek *bēryllos*, of Indic origin]

be•ryl•li•um \bə-ˈril-ē-əm\ *n* : a steel-gray light strong brittle metallic element — see ELEMENT table

be•seech \bi-ˈsēch\ *vb* **be•sought** \-ˈsȯt\ *or* **be•seeched**; **be•seech•ing** : to ask for earnestly : IMPLORE [Middle English *besechen*, from *be-* + *sechen* "to seek"] **syn** see BEG

be•seem \bi-ˈsēm\ *vb, archaic* : to be fitting or becoming : BEFIT

be•set \bi-ˈset\ *vt* **-set**; **-set•ting** **1** : to place at intervals in or on : STUD ⟨a pin *beset* with gems⟩ **2** : to trouble with problems : HARASS **3 a** : to set upon : ASSAIL **b** : to hem in : SURROUND

be•set•ting *adj* : constantly present or attacking ⟨a *besetting* sin⟩

be•shrew \bi-ˈshrü\ *vt, archaic* : CURSE

[1]**be•side** \bi-ˈsīd\ *adv, archaic* : BESIDES

[2]**beside** *prep* **1 a** : by the side of ⟨walk *beside* me⟩ **b** : in comparison with ⟨the kitten looks like a midget *beside* the big dog⟩ **2** : BESIDES **3** : not relevant to ⟨*beside* the point⟩ — **beside oneself** : out of one's wits

[1]**be•sides** \bi-ˈsīdz\ *adv* : in addition : ALSO ⟨the play is excellent, and *besides* the tickets cost very little⟩

[2]**besides** *prep* : in addition to : other than ⟨no news *besides* what I told you⟩

be•siege \bi-ˈsēj\ *vt* **1** : to surround with or as if with armed forces : lay siege to **2** : to press especially with questions or requests — **be•sieg•er** *n*

be•smear \bi-ˈsmiər\ *vt* : SMEAR

be•smirch \bi-ˈsmərch\ *vt* : to reduce the quality or purity of : SULLY

be•som \ˈbē-zəm\ *n* : a broom made of twigs [Old English *besma*]

be•sot \bi-ˈsät\ *vt* **be•sot•ted**; **be•sot•ting** : to make dull or stupid : STUPEFY; *esp* : to muddle with drink

be•spat•ter \bi-ˈspat-ər\ *vt* : SPATTER

be•speak \bi-ˈspēk\ *vt* **-spoke** \-ˈspōk\; **-spo•ken** \-ˈspō-kən\; **-speak•ing** **1 a** : to hire or arrange for beforehand **b** : REQUEST **2 a** : to give evidence of **b** : FORETELL

Bes•se•mer converter \ˌbes-ə-mər-\ *n* : the furnace used in the Bessemer process [Sir Henry *Bessemer*]

Bessemer process *n* : a process of making steel from pig iron by burning out impurities (as carbon) by means of a blast of air forced through the molten metal

[1]**best** \ˈbest\ *adj* **1** : good or useful in the highest degree : most excellent **2** : MOST, LARGEST ⟨the *best* part of a week⟩ [Old English *betst*]

[2]**best** *adv* **1** : in the best way **2** : to the highest degree : MOST ⟨*best* able to do the work⟩

[3]**best** *n* **1** : the best state or part **2** : one that is best ⟨trying to be the *best*⟩ **3** : one's maximum effort ⟨do your *best*⟩ **4** : best clothes ⟨wear your Sunday *best*⟩ — **at best** **1** : under the most favorable conditions **2** : at most

[4]**best** *vt* : to get the better of : OUTDO

bes•tial \ˈbes-chəl, ˈbēs-\ *adj* **1 a** : of or relating to beasts **b** : resembling a beast **2 a** : lacking intelligence or reason **b** : VICIOUS, BRUTAL [Latin *bestia* "beast"] — **bes•tial•ly** \-chə-lē\ *adv*

bes•ti•al•i•ty \ˌbes-chē-ˈal-ət-ē, ˌbēs-\ *n* **1** : the condition or status of a lower animal **2** : display or indulgence of bestial traits or desires

bes•ti•ary \ˈbes-chē-ˌer-ē, ˈbēs-\ *n, pl* **-ar•ies** : a medieval al-

\ə\ **abut**	\au̇\ **out**	\i\ **tip**	\ȯ\ **saw**	\u̇\ **foot**
\ər\ **further**	\ch\ **chin**	\ī\ **life**	\ȯi\ **coin**	\y\ **yet**
\a\ **mat**	\e\ **pet**	\j\ **job**	\th\ **thin**	\yü\ **few**
\ā\ **take**	\ē\ **easy**	\ng\ **sing**	\th\ **this**	\yu̇\ **cure**
\ä\ **cot, cart**	\g\ **go**	\ō\ **bone**	\ü\ **food**	\zh\ **vision**

legorical or moralizing work on the appearance and habits of animals

be•stir \bi-'stər\ *vt* : to stir up : rouse to action

best man *n* : a male friend who stands with the bridegroom at a wedding

be•stow \bi-'stō\ *vt* **1** : APPLY 1, USE **2** : QUARTER 2, LODGE **3** : to present as a gift : CONFER — **be•stow•al** \-'stō-əl\ *n*

be•stride \bi-'strīd\ *vt* **-strode** \-'strōd\; **-strid•den** \-'strid-ⁿn\; **-strid•ing** **1** : to ride, sit, or stand astride : STRADDLE **2** : to tower over : DOMINATE

best seller *n* : an article (as a book) whose sales are among the highest of its class

[1]bet \'bet\ *n* **1 a** : an agreement based on the result of a contest or the outcome of an event requiring the person whose guess proves wrong to give something to a person whose guess proves right **b** : the making of such an agreement : WAGER **2** : the money or thing risked ⟨a *bet* of 10 cents⟩ [origin unknown]

[2]bet *vb* **bet** *or* **bet•ted**; **bet•ting** **1** : to risk in a bet **2** : to make a bet with **3** : to lay a bet

be•ta \'bāt-ə\ *n* **1** : the 2d letter of the Greek alphabet — Β or β **2** : the second brightest star of a constellation

be•take \bi-'tāk\ *vt* **-took** \-'tu̇k\; **-tak•en** \-'tā-kən\; **-tak•ing** \-'tā-king\ : to cause (oneself) to go

beta particle *n* : an electron or positron ejected from the nucleus of an atom during radioactive decay; *also* : a high-speed electron or positron

beta ray *n* **1** : BETA PARTICLE **2** : a stream of beta particles

be•ta•tron \'bāt-ə-,trän\ *n* : a device that accelerates electrons by the inductive action of a rapidly varying magnetic field

be•tel \'bēt-l\ *n* : a climbing pepper whose dried leaves are chewed with betel nut and lime [Portuguese, from Tamil *verrilai*]

Be•tel•geuse \'bet-l-,jüz, 'bēt-, -,jüz, -,jərz\ *n* : a variable red giant star near one shoulder of Orion [French *Bételgeuse*, from Arabic *bayt al-jawzā'* "Gemini", literally, "the house of the twins"]

betel nut *n* : the astringent seed of an Asian palm that is chewed with betel and lime as a stimulant especially by southeastern Asians

bête noire \,bet-nə-'wär, ,bāt-\ *n, pl* **bêtes noires** \,bet-nə-'wär, ,bāt-, -wärz\ : a person or thing strongly detested or avoided : BUGBEAR [French, literally, "black beast"]

beth•el \'beth-əl\ *n* : a place of worship especially for sailors [Hebrew *bēth'ēl* "house of God"]

be•think \bi-'thingk\ *vt* **-thought** \-'tho̊t\; **-think•ing** **1 a** : REMEMBER, RECALL **b** : to cause (oneself) to be reminded **2** : to cause (oneself) to consider

be•tide \bi-'tīd\ *vb* : to happen or happen to : BEFALL

be•to•ken \bi-'tō-kən\ *vt* : to be a sign of : INDICATE

be•tray \bi-'trā\ *vt* **1** : to give over to an enemy by treachery or fraud **2** : to be unfaithful or treacherous to : FAIL ⟨*betray* a trust⟩ **3** : to reveal unintentionally ⟨*betray* one's ignorance⟩ **4** : to tell in violation of a trust [Middle English *betrayen*, from *be-* + *trayen* "to betray", from Old French *traïr*, from Latin *tradere* "to hand over, betray"] — **be•tray•al** \-'trā-əl, -'trāl\ *n* — **be•tray•er** \-'trā-ər\ *n*

be•troth \bi-'träth, -'tro̊th, -'trōth, *or with* th\ *vt* : to promise to marry or give in marriage

be•troth•al \-'trōth-əl, -'tro̊th-, -'trōth-\ *n* **1** : an engagement to be married **2** : the act or ceremony of becoming engaged to be married

be•trothed *n* : the person to whom one is betrothed

bet•ta \'bet-ə\ *n* : any of a genus of small brilliantly colored long-finned freshwater fishes of southeastern Asia [genus name]

[1]bet•ter \'bet-ər\ *adj* **1** : more than half ⟨the *better* part of a week⟩ **2** : improved in health **3** : of higher quality [Old English *betera*]

[2]better *adv* **1** : in a more excellent manner **2 a** : to a higher or greater degree **b** : MORE ⟨published *better* than 50 years ago⟩

[3]better *n* **1 a** : something better **b** : a superior especially in merit or rank **2** : ADVANTAGE, VICTORY ⟨got the *better* of me⟩

[4]better *vt* **1** : to make better **2** : to surpass in excellence : EXCEL

bet•ter•ment \'bet-ər-mənt\ *n* : IMPROVEMENT

bet•tor *or* **bet•ter** \'bet-ər\ *n* : one that bets

[1]be•tween \bi-'twēn\ *prep* **1 a** : by the common action of ⟨shared the work *between* the two of them⟩ **b** : with shares to each of : AMONG ⟨divided the fortune *between* the two heirs⟩ **2** : in the time, space, or interval that separates ⟨*between* nine and ten o'clock⟩ ⟨*between* the desk and the wall⟩ **3** : DISTINGUISHING ⟨the difference *between* soccer and football⟩ **4** : by comparison of ⟨choose *between* the two coats⟩ **5** : from one to the other or another of ⟨the bond *between* friends⟩ [Old English *betwēonum*, from *be-* + *-twēonum* "two"]

• **syn** AMONG: BETWEEN indicates a relation of two objects in position, distribution, participation, or communication ⟨*between* two fires⟩ ⟨lost it *between* school and home⟩ but may be used of more than two if it brings them individually into the expressed relation ⟨the four children had only seven dollars *between* them⟩ ⟨a treaty *between* three countries⟩ AMONG always implies more than two objects which it brings less definitely or individually into the relationship ⟨scattered the corn *among* the chickens⟩ ⟨it was whispered *among* their friends that they were bankrupt⟩

[2]between *adv* : in an intermediate space or interval

be•tween•ness \-nəs\ *n* : the quality or state of an element that is between two others in an ordered set

be•twixt \bi-'twikst\ *adv or prep* : BETWEEN [Old English *betwux*]

betwixt and between *adv or adj* : in an intermediate position or state

[1]bev•el \'bev-əl\ *adj* : OBLIQUE 1, BEVELED [derived from Old French *baïf* "with open mouth", from *baer* "to yawn"]

[2]bevel *n* **1 a** : the angle that one surface or line makes with another when they are not at right angles **b** : the slant or inclination of such a surface or line **2** : an instrument consisting of two rules or arms jointed together and opening to any angle for drawing angles or adjusting surfaces to be given a bevel

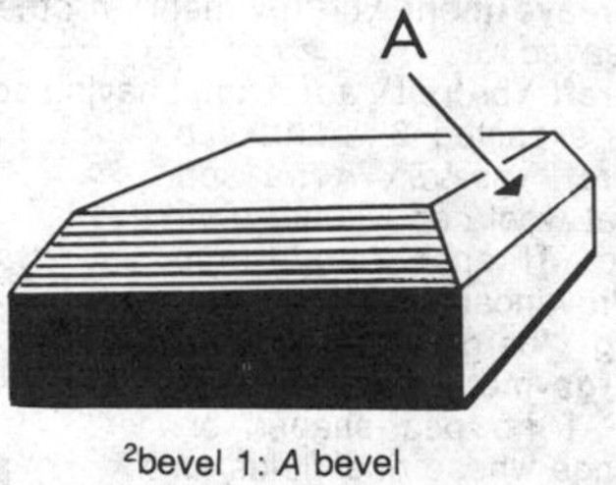

[2]bevel 1: *A* bevel

[3]bevel *vb* **bev•eled** *or* **bev•elled**; **bev•el•ing** *or* **bev•el•ling** \'bev-ling, -ə-ling\ **1** : to cut or shape (as an edge or surface) to a bevel **2** : INCLINE 3, SLANT

bev•er•age \'bev-rij, -ə-rij\ *n* : a liquid for drinking; *esp* : one other than water [Middle French *bevrage*, from *beivre* "to drink", from Latin *bibere*]

bevy \'bev-ē\ *n, pl* **bev•ies** : CLUSTER 1, GROUP, COLLECTION ⟨a *bevy* of quail⟩ [Middle English *bevey*]

be•wail \bi-'wāl\ *vt* **1** : to wail over **2** : to express deep regret for

be•ware \bi-'waər, -'weər\ *vb* : to be wary or wary of [Middle English *been war*, from *been* "to be" + *war* "wary"]

be•wil•der \bi-'wil-dər\ *vt* **-dered**; **-der•ing** \-də-ring, -dring\ **1** : to cause to lose one's bearings **2** : to perplex or confuse especially by a complex variety or large number of objects or possibilities — **be•wil•der•ing•ly** \-də-ring-lē, -dring-lē\ *adv* — **be•wil•der•ment** \-dər-mənt\ *n*

be•witch \bi-'wich\ *vt* **1** : to gain an influence over by means of magic or witchcraft : put under a spell **2** : FASCINATE, CHARM — **be•witch•ery** \-ə-rē\ *n* — **be•witch•ment** \-mənt\ *n*

be•wray \bi-'rā\ *vt, archaic* : DIVULGE, BETRAY, REVEAL [Middle English *bewreyen*, from *be-* + *wreyen* "to accuse", from Old English *wrēgan*]

bey \'bā\ *n* **1** : a provincial governor in the Ottoman Empire **2** : the former native ruler of Tunis [Turkish, "gentleman, chief"]

[1]be•yond \bē-'änd\ *adv* : on or to the farther side ⟨extending to the river and *beyond*⟩

[2]beyond *prep* **1 a** : on or to the farther side of ⟨*beyond* that tree⟩ **b** : later than ⟨*beyond* closing time⟩ **2** : out of the reach or sphere of ⟨*beyond* help⟩ **3** : out of the comprehension of ⟨these ideas are *beyond* me⟩

[3]beyond *n* : HEREAFTER

be•zel \'bē-zəl, 'bez-əl\ *n* **1** : a sloping edge or face especially on a cutting tool **2** : the top part of a ring setting that holds a stone or ornament; *also* : the top including the stone **3** : the grooved rim that holds the crystal on a watch; *also* : a rim that holds a covering (as on a clock dial or headlight) [probably derived from French *biseau* "bevel, bezel"]

be•zoar \'bē-ˌzōr, -ˌzȯr\ *n* : a hard mass of ingested material (as hair) that forms and lodges in the stomach or intestine of a ruminant (as a cow) and was formerly believed to possess magical properties [Spanish, from Arabic *bāzahr*]

bhang \'baŋ, 'bäŋ\ *n* : the leaves and flowering tips of hemp; *also* : a narcotic and intoxicant product from this — compare CANNABIS, HASHISH, MARIJUANA [Hindi *bhā̃g*]

B–horizon *n* : a soil layer immediately beneath the A-horizon from which it obtains material by leaching and from which it is usually distinguished by less weathering

bi- *prefix* **1 a** : two ⟨*bi*racial⟩ **b** : coming or occurring every two ⟨*bi*monthly⟩ ⟨*bi*weekly⟩ **c** : into two parts ⟨*bi*sect⟩ **2 a** : twice : doubly : on both sides ⟨*bi*convex⟩ **b** : coming or occurring two times ⟨*bi*monthly⟩ ⟨*bi*weekly⟩ — often disapproved in this sense because of the likelihood of confusion with sense 1b; compare SEMI- [Latin]

See *bi-* and 2d element

bicolor	**biethnic**	**binuclear**
bicolored	**biethnically**	**biparental**
biconcave	**bifunctional**	**biracial**
biconvex	**bilabiate**	**biracially**
bicultural	**binational**	**bitonal**
bidirectional	**binationalism**	**bitonality**

bi•an•nu•al \bī-'an-yə-wəl, 'bī-, -'an-yəl\ *adj* : occurring twice a year — compare BIENNIAL — **bi•an•nu•al•ly** \-ē\ *adv*

¹bi•as \'bī-əs\ *n* **1** : a line diagonal to the grain of a fabric often utilized in the cutting of garments for smoother fit **2** : an inclination of temperament or outlook; *esp* : such an inclination marked by strong prejudice **3** : the tendency of a bowl in lawn bowling to swerve on the green; *also* : the uneven shape of the bowl causing this tendency **4** : a voltage applied to a device (as the grid of an electron tube) to establish a reference level for operation [Middle French *biais*] **syn** see PREJUDICE

²bias *adj* : DIAGONAL, SLANTING — used chiefly of fabrics and their cut

³bias *vt* **bi•ased** *or* **bi•assed**; **bi•as•ing** *or* **bi•as•sing** : to give a bias to : PREJUDICE

bi•ath•lon \bī-'ath-lən, -ˌlän\ : a contest consisting of cross-country skiing and rifle target shooting [*bi-* + Greek *athlon* "contest"]

bib \'bib\ *n* **1** : a cloth, paper, or plastic shield tied under the chin (as of a child at mealtime) to protect the clothes **2** : the part of an apron or of overalls extending above the waist in front [Middle English *bibben* "to drink"]

bib and tucker *n* : an outfit of clothing

bib•ber \'bib-ər\ *n* : TIPPLER — **bib•bery** \-ə-rē\ *n*

bi•be•lot \'bē-bə-ˌlō\ *n* : a small household ornament or decorative object [French]

Bi•ble \'bī-bəl\ *n* **1** : a book made up of the writings accepted by Christians as inspired by God and comprising the Old Testament and the New Testament **2** : a book containing the sacred writings of another religion (as Judaism) **3** *not cap* : a publication that is outstandingly authoritative [Medieval Latin *biblia*, from Greek, from *biblion* "book", from *byblos* "papyrus, book", from *Byblos*, ancient Phoenician city from which papyrus was exported]

BOOKS OF THE OLD TESTAMENT

ROMAN CATHOLIC CANON	PROTESTANT CANON	ROMAN CATHOLIC CANON	PROTESTANT CANON
Genesis	Genesis	Wisdom	
Exodus	Exodus	Ecclesiasticus	
Leviticus	Leviticus	Isaias	Isaiah
Numbers	Numbers	Jeremias	Jeremiah
Deuteronomy	Deuteronomy	Lamentations	Lamentations
Josue	Joshua	Baruch	
Judges	Judges	Ezechiel	Ezekiel
Ruth	Ruth	Daniel	Daniel
1 & 2 Kings	1 & 2 Samuel	Osee	Hosea
3 & 4 Kings	1 & 2 Kings	Joel	Joel
1 & 2 Paralipomenon	1 & 2 Chronicles	Amos	Amos
		Abdias	Obadiah
1 Esdras	Ezra	Jonas	Jonah
2 Esdras	Nehemiah	Micheas	Micah
Tobias		Nahum	Nahum
Judith		Habacuc	Habakkuk
Esther	Esther	Sophonias	Zephaniah
Job	Job	Aggeus	Haggai
Psalms	Psalms	Zacharias	Zechariah
Proverbs	Proverbs	Malachias	Malachi
Ecclesiastes	Ecclesiastes	1 & 2 Machabees	
Canticle of Canticles	Song of Solomon		

JEWISH SCRIPTURE

Law	1 & 2 Kings	Nahum	Song of Songs
Genesis	Isaiah	Habakkuk	Ruth
Exodus	Jeremiah	Zephaniah	Lamentations
Leviticus	Ezekiel	Haggai	Ecclesiastes
Numbers	Hosea	Zechariah	Esther
Deuteronomy	Joel	Malachi	Daniel
Prophets	Amos	*Hagiographa*	Ezra
Joshua	Obadiah	Psalms	Nehemiah
Judges	Jonah	Proverbs	1 & 2 Chronicles
1 & 2 Samuel	Micah	Job	

PROTESTANT APOCRYPHA

1 & 2 Esdras	Wisdom of Solomon	Baruch	Susanna
Tobit	Ecclesiasticus or the Wisdom of Jesus Son of Sirach	Prayer of Azariah and the Song of the Three Holy Children	Bel and the Dragon
Judith			The Prayer of Manasses
Additions to Esther			1 & 2 Maccabees

BOOKS OF THE NEW TESTAMENT

Matthew	Romans	1 & 2 Thessalonians	1 & 2 Peter
Mark	1 & 2 Corinthians	1 & 2 Timothy	1, 2, 3 John
Luke	Galatians	Titus	Jude
John	Ephesians	Philemon	Revelation (Roman Catholic canon: Apocalypse)
Acts of the Apostles	Philippians	Hebrews	
	Colossians	James	

bib•li•cal \'bib-li-kəl\ *adj* **1** : of, relating to, or in accord with the Bible **2** : suggestive of the Bible or Bible times — **bib•li•cal•ly** \-kə-lē, -klē\ *adv*

biblio- *combining form* : book [Greek *biblion*]

bib•li•og•ra•pher \ˌbib-lē-'äg-rə-fər\ *n* **1** : an expert in bibliography **2** : a compiler of bibliographies

bib•li•og•ra•phy \ˌbib-lē-'äg-rə-fē\ *n, pl* **-phies 1** : the history, identification, or description of writings or publications **2** : a list often with descriptive or critical notes of writings relating to a particular subject, period, or author; *also* : a list of works written by an author or printed by a publishing house **3** : a list of the works referred to in a text or consulted by the author in its production — **bib•li•o•graph•ic** \ˌbib-lē-ə-'graf-ik\ *or* **bib•lio•graph•i•cal** \-'graf-i-kəl\ *adj* — **bib•li•o•graph•i•cal•ly** \-kə-lē, -klē\ *adv*

bib•lio•phile \'bib-lē-ə-ˌfīl\ *n* : a lover of books; *also* : a book collector

bib•u•lous \'bib-yə-ləs\ *adj* **1** : highly absorbent **2 a** : inclined to drink **b** : of or relating to drink or drinking [Latin *bibulus*, from *bibere* "to drink"] — **bib•u•lous•ly** *adv* — **bib•u•lous•ness** *n*

bi•cam•er•al \bī-'kam-rəl, 'bī-, -ə-rəl\ *adj* : having, consisting of, or based on two legislative chambers ⟨*bicameral* legislatures⟩ [Latin *camera* "room, chamber"] — **bi•cam•er•al•ism** \-rə-ˌliz-əm\ *n*

bi•car•bon•ate \bī-'kär-bə-ˌnāt, 'bī-, -nət\ *n* : an acid carbonate

bicarbonate of soda : SODIUM BICARBONATE

bi•cen•te•na•ry \ˌbī-sen-'ten-ə-rē, -'tē-nə-; bī-'sent-n-ˌer-ē\ *n* : BICENTENNIAL — **bicentenary** *adj*

bi•cen•ten•ni•al \ˌbī-sen-'ten-ē-əl\ *n* : a 200th anniversary or its celebration — **bicentennial** *adj*

\ə\ **abut**	\au̇\ **out**	\i\ **tip**	\ȯ\ **saw**	\u̇\ **foot**
\ər\ **further**	\ch\ **chin**	\ī\ **life**	\ȯi\ **coin**	\y\ **yet**
\a\ **mat**	\e\ **pet**	\j\ **job**	\th\ **thin**	\yü\ **few**
\ā\ **take**	\ē\ **easy**	\ŋ\ **sing**	\t͟h\ **this**	\yu̇\ **cure**
\ä\ **cot, cart**	\g\ **go**	\ō\ **bone**	\ü\ **food**	\zh\ **vision**

bi·ceps \'bī-ˌseps\ *n* : a muscle having two heads; *esp* : a large flexor muscle of the front of the upper arm [Latin *biceps* "two-headed", from *bi-* + *caput* "head"]

bi·chlo·ride \bī-'klōr-ˌīd, 'bī-, -'klȯr-\ *n* **1** : DICHLORIDE **2** *or* **bichloride of mercury** : MERCURIC CHLORIDE

bi·chro·mate \bī-'krō-ˌmāt, 'bī-\ *n* : DICHROMATE

bick·er \'bik-ər\ *vi* **bick·ered**; **bick·er·ing** \'bik-ring, -ə-ring\ : to engage in an angry and often petty quarrel : WRANGLE [Middle English *bikeren*] — **bicker** *n*

bi·con·di·tion·al \ˌbī-kən-'dish-nəl, -ən-l\ *n* : a logical relationship between two propositions such that the truth of the first implies the second and the truth of the second implies the first; *also* : a statement of this kind ⟨the statement "*q* if and only if *p*" is a *biconditional*⟩

[1]**bi·cus·pid** \bī-'kəs-pəd, 'bī-\ *adj* : having or ending in two points [Latin *cuspis* "point, cusp"]

[2]**bicuspid** *n* : PREMOLAR

bicuspid valve *n* : a heart valve guarding the opening between the left auricle and ventricle and consisting of two triangular flaps — called also *mitral valve*

[1]**bi·cy·cle** \'bī-ˌsik-əl\ *n* : a vehicle with two wheels one behind the other, a tubular metal frame, a steering handle, a saddle seat, and pedals by which it is propelled [Greek *kyklos* "wheel"] — **bi·cy·clist** \-ˌsik-ləst, -ə-ləst\ *n*

[2]**bicycle** *vi* **bi·cy·cled**; **bi·cy·cling** \-ˌsik-ling, -ə-ling\ : to ride a bicycle — **bi·cy·cler** \-ˌsik-lər, -ə-lər\ *n*

[1]**bid** \'bid\ *vb* **bade** \'bad, 'bād\ *or* **bid**; **bid·den** \'bid-n\ *or* **bid** *also* **bade**; **bid·ding** **1 a** : to issue an order to : TELL ⟨did as I was *bidden*⟩ **b** : to request to come : INVITE **2** : to give expression to ⟨*bade* me farewell⟩ **3** *past* **bid a** : to offer (a price) for something (as at an auction) **b** : to make a bid of in a card game [partly from Old English *biddan* "to ask, pray"; partly from Old English *bēodan* "to offer, command"] — **bid·der** *n* — **bid fair** : to seem likely

[2]**bid** *n* **1** : an offer to pay a stated sum for something or to do something at a stated fee; *also* : the price or fee offered **2** : an opportunity or turn to bid **3** : INVITATION **4 a** : an announcement of what a card player will attempt to win **b** : the amount of such a bid **5** : an attempt or effort to win, achieve, or attract

bid·da·ble \'bid-ə-bəl\ *adj* **1** : OBEDIENT, DOCILE **2** : capable of being bid (as in a card game) — **bid·da·bly** \-blē\ *adv*

bide \'bīd\ *vb* **bode** \'bōd\ *or* **bid·ed**; **bided**; **bid·ing** : to continue in a state or condition; *also* : WAIT ⟨*bide* a while⟩ [Old English *bīdan*] — **bid·er** *n* — **bide one's time** : to wait for an appropriate moment before acting

bi·en·ni·al \bī-'en-ē-əl, 'bī-\ *adj* **1** : occurring every two years — compare BIANNUAL **2 a** : continuing or lasting for two years **b** : growing vegetatively during the first year and fruiting and dying during the second — **biennial** *n* — **bi·en·ni·al·ly** \-ē-ə-lē\ *adv*

bi·en·ni·um \bī-'en-ē-əm\ *n, pl* **-ni·ums** *or* **-nia** \-ē-ə\ : a period of two years [Latin, from *bi-* + *annus* "year"]

bier \'biər\ *n* : a stand on which a corpse or coffin is placed; *also* : a coffin together with its stand [Old English *bǣr*]

bi·fid \'bī-ˌfid, -fəd\ *adj* : divided into two equal lobes or parts by a median cleft ⟨a *bifid* leaf⟩ [Latin *bifidus*, from *bi-* + *findere* "to split"]

[1]**bi·fo·cal** \bī-'fō-kəl, 'bī-\ *adj* : having two focal lengths

[2]**bifocal** *n* **1** : a bifocal glass or lens **2** *pl* : eyeglasses with bifocal lenses

bi·fur·cate \'bī-fər-ˌkāt, bī-'fər-\ *vb* : to divide into two branches or parts [Latin *furca* "fork"] — **bi·fur·cate** \bī-'fər-kət, 'bī-, -ˌkāt; 'bī-fər-ˌkāt\ *adj* — **bi·fur·ca·tion** \ˌbī-fər-'kā-shən, -ˌfər-\ *n*

[1]**big** \'big\ *adj* **big·ger**; **big·gest** **1** : of great force ⟨a *big* storm⟩ **2 a** : large in size, bulk, or extent ⟨a *big* house⟩ **b** : conducted on a large scale ⟨*big* government⟩ **3 a** : PREGNANT ⟨*big* with child⟩ **b** : full to overflowing : BRIMMING ⟨eyes *big* with tears⟩ **c** : being full and resonant ⟨a *big* voice⟩ **4 a** : of great importance or significance; *esp* : CHIEF, PREDOMINANT ⟨the *big* issue of the campaign⟩ **b** : IMPOSING, PRETENTIOUS; *also* : BOASTFUL ⟨*big* talk⟩ **c** : MAGNANIMOUS [Middle English] **syn** see LARGE — **big·ness** *n*

[2]**big** *adv* **1** : to a large amount or extent **2 a** : in an outstanding manner ⟨made it *big* in television⟩ **b** : POMPOUSLY, PRETENTIOUSLY ⟨talk *big*⟩

big·a·mist \'big-ə-məst\ *n* : a person who commits bigamy

big·a·my \'big-ə-mē\ *n* : the statutory offense of marrying one person while still legally married to another — **big·a·mous** \-məs\ *adj* — **big·a·mous·ly** *adv*

big bang theory *n* : a theory in astronomy: the universe originated billions of years ago from the explosion of a single mass of material so that the pieces are still flying apart — compare STEADY STATE THEORY

Big Dipper *n* : DIPPER 2a

big·eye \'big-ˌī\ *n* : either of two small widely distributed marine reddish to silvery food fishes related to the perches

big·gish \'big-ish\ *adj* : somewhat big : comparatively big

big·horn \'big-ˌhȯrn\ *n, pl* **bighorn** *or* **bighorns** : a usually grayish brown wild sheep of mountainous western North America

bighorn

bight \'bīt\ *n* **1 a** : the slack middle part of a rope when it is fastened at both ends **b** : a loop or double part of a bent rope **2** : a bend or curve especially in a river **3** : a bend in a coast or the bay it forms [Old English *byht* "bend"]

big·ot \'big-ət\ *n* : a person obstinately or intolerantly devoted to his or her own group, beliefs, or opinions [Middle French]

big·ot·ed \'big-ət-əd\ *adj* : obstinately attached to a belief, opinion, or practice and intolerant of the ideas and opinions of others

big·ot·ry \'big-ə-trē\ *n, pl* **-ries** : the state of mind of a bigot; *also* : behavior or beliefs arising from such a state of mind

big shot *n* : an important person

big stick *n* : coercive use or threat of military or political intervention [from Theodore Roosevelt's belief that "we must speak softly but carry a big stick"]

big time *n* : the top rank (as of a profession) where income and prestige are greatest

big toe *n* : the innermost and largest digit of the foot

big top *n* **1** : the main tent of a circus **2** : CIRCUS 2

big tree *n* : a California evergreen of the pine family that often exceeds 90 meters in height — called also *giant sequoia, sequoia;* compare REDWOOD

big·wig \'big-ˌwig\ *n* : an important person

bike \'bīk\ *n or vi* : BICYCLE, MOTORCYCLE — **bik·er** *n*

bi·ki·ni \bə-'kē-nē\ *n* : a woman's scanty two-piece bathing suit [French, from *Bikini,* atoll of the Marshall islands]

bi·la·bi·al \bī-'lā-bē-əl, 'bī-\ *adj* : of, relating to, or produced with both lips ⟨a *bilabial* consonant⟩

bi·lat·er·al \bī-'lat-ə-rəl, 'bī-, -'la-trəl\ *adj* **1** : having or involving two sides; *esp* : affecting reciprocally two sides or parties ⟨a *bilateral* treaty⟩ **2** : characterized by bilateral symmetry — **bi·lat·er·al·ism** \-ˌiz-əm\ *n* — **bi·lat·er·al·ly** \-ē\ *adv*

bilateral symmetry *n* : a pattern of animal symmetry in which similar parts are arranged on opposite sides of a median axis so that one and only one plane can divide the individual into essentially identical halves — compare RADIAL SYMMETRY

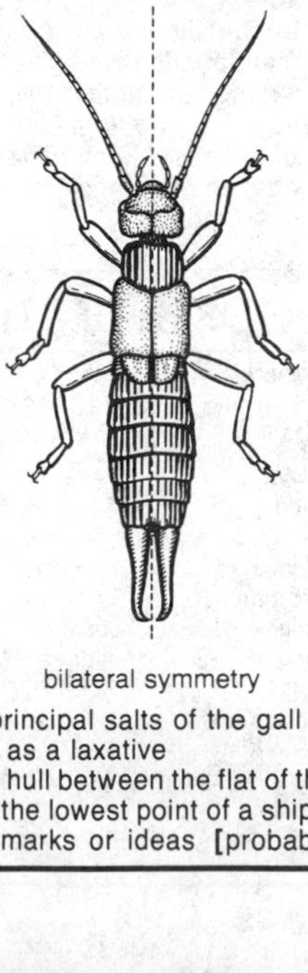
bilateral symmetry

bil·ber·ry \'bil-ˌber-ē\ *n* : any of several blueberries with flowers and fruit borne in leaf axils; *also* : the sweet edible bluish fruit [probably of Scandinavian origin]

bile \'bīl\ *n* **1** : a thick bitter yellow or greenish fluid secreted by the liver and functioning in the duodenum in the digestion and absorption of fats **2** : tendency toward anger : ILL WILL [French, from Latin *bilis*]

bile duct *n* : a canal by which bile passes from the liver or gall bladder to the duodenum

bile salts *n pl* : a dry mixture of the principal salts of the gall of the ox used as a liver stimulant and as a laxative

bilge \'bilj\ *n* **1 a** : the part of a ship's hull between the flat of the bottom and the vertical topsides **b** : the lowest point of a ship's inner hull **2** : stale or worthless remarks or ideas [probably

from Middle French *boulge, bouge* "leather bag, curved part"]
bilge water *n* : water that collects in the bilge of a ship
bil•i•ary \'bil-ē-,er-ē\ *adj* : of, relating to, or conveying bile
bi•lin•gual \'bī-'ling-gwəl, 'bī-, -gyə-wəl\ *adj* **1** : of, containing, expressed in, or involving the use of two languages ⟨a *bilingual* dictionary⟩ ⟨*bilingual* education⟩ **2** : able to use two languages especially with fluency [Latin *lingua* "tongue, language"] — **bilingual** *n* — **bi•lin•gual•ism** \-,iz-əm\ n
bil•ious \'bil-yəs\ *adj* **1 a** : of or relating to bile **b** : marked by or suffering from disordered liver function **2** : of an irritable ill-natured disposition : PEEVISH — **bil•ious•ly** *adv* — **bil•ious•ness** *n*
bil•i•ru•bin \,bil-ə-'rü-bən, 'bil-ə-,\ *n* : a reddish yellow pigment occurring in bile, blood, urine, and gallstones [Latin *ruber* "red"]
bil•i•ver•din \-'vərd-n, -,vərd-\ *n* : a green pigment occurring in bile [obsolete French *verd* "green"]
bilk \'bilk\ *vt* : to cheat out of what is due : SWINDLE [perhaps alteration of [2]*balk*]
[1]**bill** \'bil\ *n* **1** : the jaws of a bird together with their horny covering **2** : a beak (as of a turtle) or a mouth structure resembling a bird's bill **3** : a projection of land like a beak **4** : the visor of a cap [Old English *bile*] — **billed** \'bild\ *adj*
• **syn** BILL, BEAK mean the horny two-parted projection that serves a bird for jaws. In popular usage BEAK is applied especially to the strong triangular pointed or hooked shape associated with striking, tearing, or crushing ⟨an eagle's *beak*⟩ while BILL applies to the structure in any bird ⟨a duck's *bill*⟩
[2]**bill** *vi* **1** : to touch bill to bill **2** : to caress and kiss affectionately ⟨lovers *billing* and cooing⟩
[3]**bill** *n* : a weapon used up to the 18th century that consists of a long staff with a hook-shaped blade at one end [Old English]
[4]**bill** *n* **1** : a draft of a law presented to a legislature for enactment **2** : a written statement of a wrong one person has suffered from another or of a breach of law by some person ⟨a *bill* of complaint⟩ **3** : an itemized list : a detailed statement of items **4** : an itemized account of the cost of goods sold or work done : INVOICE **5 a** : an advertisement posted or distributed to announce an event (as a theatrical entertainment) **b** : an entertainment program or the entertainment presented on it **6** : NOTE 3a; *esp* : a piece of paper money [Medieval Latin *billa* "formal document", from *bulla* "seal, sealed document", from Latin, "bubble"]
[5]**bill** *vt* **1 a** : to make a bill of ⟨*bill* the goods to my account⟩ **b** : to submit a bill of charges to ⟨*bill* a customer⟩ **2 a** : to advertise especially by posters or placards **b** : to arrange for the presentation of (as a play) — **bill•er** *n*
bill•board \'bil-,bōrd, -,bȯrd\ *n* : a flat surface on which bills are posted; *esp* : a large vertical panel designed to carry outdoor advertising
bill•bug \-,bəg\ *n* : a usually small dark weevil with larvae that eat the roots of grasses
[1]**bil•let** \'bil-ət\ *n* **1** : an official order directing that a soldier be lodged (as in a private home) **2** : quarters assigned (as to a soldier) [Middle French *billette* "note, letter", derived from Medieval Latin *bulla* "document"]
[2]**billet** *vb* **1** : to assign lodging to by a billet : QUARTER **2** : to have quarters : LODGE
[3]**billet** *n* **1** : a short thick piece of wood (as for firewood) **2** : a bar of metal; *esp* : one of iron or steel [Middle French *billette*, from *bille* "log", of Celtic origin]
bil•let-doux \,bil-ā-'dü\ *n, pl* **bil•lets-doux** \-ā-'dü, -ā-'düz\ : a love letter [French *billet doux*, literally, "sweet note"]
bill•fold \'bil-,fōld\ *n* : a usually leather container for paper money and identification and credit cards that may have compartments for photographs and loose change and that can be folded and carried in a pocket or handbag

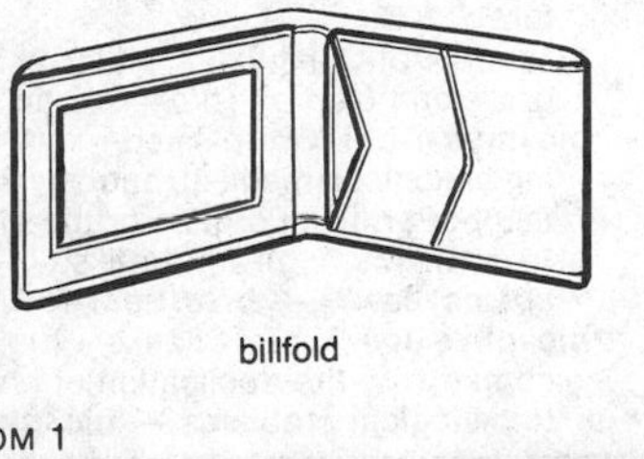
billfold

bill•head \-,hed\ *n* : a printed form usually headed with a business address and used for billing charges
bil•liard \'bil-yərd\ *n* : CAROM 1
bil•liards \-yərdz\ *n* : any of several games played on an oblong table by driving small balls against one another or into pockets with a cue; *esp* : a game in which one scores by causing a cue ball to hit in succession two object balls [Middle French *billard* "billiard cue, billiards", from *bille* "log"]
bil•lings•gate \'bil-ingz-,gāt\ *n* : coarsely abusive language [*Billingsgate*, a fish market in London, England]
bil•lion \'bil-yən\ *n* **1** — see NUMBER table **2** : a very large or indefinitely large number ⟨*billions* of dollars⟩ [French, from *bi-* "two" + *-llion* (as in *million*)] — **billion** *adj* — **bil•lionth** \-yənth, -yəntth\ *adj or n*
bil•lion•aire \,bil-yə-'naər, -'neər, 'bil-yə-,\ *n* : one whose wealth is a billion or more
bill of exchange : a written order from one individual to another to pay a specified sum of money to a designated third : DRAFT 11a
bill of fare : MENU
bill of health : a certificate given to a ship's master on leaving port that indicates the state of health of the ship's company and of the port with regard to infectious diseases
bill of lad•ing \-'lād-ing\ : a receipt listing goods shipped that is signed by the agent of the owner of a ship or issued by a common carrier
bill of rights *often cap B&R* : a statement of fundamental rights and privileges guaranteed to a people against violation by the state; *esp* : the first 10 amendments to the United States Constitution
bill of sale : a formal document showing transfer of ownership of personal property
[1]**bil•low** \'bil-ō\ *n* **1** : WAVE; *esp* : a great wave or surge of water **2** : a rolling mass (as of flame or smoke) like a high wave [probably from Old Norse *bylgja*] — **bil•lowy** \'bil-ə-wē\ *adj*
[2]**billow** *vb* **1** : to rise or roll in waves or surges ⟨the *billowing* ocean⟩ **2** : to bulge or swell out (as through action of the wind) ⟨sails *billowing* in the breeze⟩
bil•ly \'bil-ē\ *n, pl* **billies** : CLUB 1a; *esp* : a police officer's club — called also *billy club*
bil•ly goat \'bil-ē-\ *n* : a male goat
bi•lobed \'bī-'lōbd\ *adj* : divided into two lobes
bi•met•al \'bī-,met-l\ *adj* : BIMETALLIC
bi•me•tal•lic \,bī-mə-'tal-ik\ *adj* **1** : of or relating to bimetallism **2** : composed of two different metals — often used of devices having a part in which two metals that expand differently are bonded together — **bimetallic** *n*
bi•met•al•lism \bī-'met-l-,iz-əm, 'bī-\ *n* : the use of two metals (as gold and silver) jointly as a monetary standard — **bi•met•al•list** \-l-əst\ *n* — **bi•met•al•list•ic** \,bī-,met-l-'is-tik\ *adj*
[1]**bi•month•ly** \bī-'mənth-lē, 'bī-, -'məntth-\ *adj* **1** : occurring every two months **2** : occurring twice a month : SEMIMONTHLY
[2]**bimonthly** *n* : a bimonthly publication
[3]**bimonthly** *adv* **1** : once every two months **2** : twice a month
bin \'bin\ *n* : an enclosed place (as a box or crib) used for storage [Old English *binn*]
[1]**bi•na•ry** \'bī-nə-rē\ *adj* **1** : compounded or consisting of or characterized by two often similar things or parts **2** : relating to, being, or belonging to a system of numbers having two as its base **3** : relating two logical or mathematical elements ⟨addition and multiplication are *binary* operations⟩ [Latin *bini* "two each"]
[2]**binary** *n, pl* **-ries** : something constituted of two things or parts
binary fission *n* : reproduction of a cell by division into two approximately equal parts
binary notation *n* : expression of a number with a base of 2 using only the digits 0 and 1 with each digital place representing a power of 2 instead of a power of 10 as in decimal notation
binary star *n* : a system of two stars that revolve around each other under their mutual gravitation
bin•au•ral \bī-'nȯr-əl, 'bī-\ *adj* **1** : of, relating to, or used with two or both ears **2 a** : of, relating to, or constituting a three-dimensional effect of reproduced sound involving the use of two separate recording paths **b** : STEREOPHONIC [Latin *bini* "two each" + *auris* "ear"] — **bin•au•ral•ly** \-ə-lē\ *adv*

[1]**bind** \'bīnd\ *vb* **bound** \'bau̇nd\; **bind•ing 1 a :** to tie together or tie securely **b :** to confine, restrain, restrict, or attach by force, obligation, or strong feeling ⟨*bound* by friendship⟩ **c :** to hamper free movement of ⟨the tight jacket *bound* the hiker⟩ **2 a :** to wrap around with something so as to enclose, encircle, or cover ⟨a sash *bound* the child's waist⟩ **b :** BANDAGE ⟨*bound* up the wound⟩ **3 a :** to stick together **b :** to form a cohesive mass **c :** to take up and hold by chemical forces **4 :** CONSTIPATE **5 :** to make firm : ESTABLISH ⟨a deposit *binds* the sale⟩ **6 a :** to protect, strengthen, or decorate by a band or binding **b :** to apply the cover to (a book) **7 :** INDENTURE, APPRENTICE [Old English *bindan*]

[2]**bind** *n* **:** something that binds — **in a bind :** in a difficult situation

bind•er \'bīn-dər\ *n* **1 :** one that binds something (as books) **2 a :** something used in binding **b :** a detachable cover or device for holding together sheets of paper or similar material **c :** a harvesting machine that cuts grain and ties it in bundles **3 :** something (as tar or cement) that produces or promotes cohesion in loosely assembled substances

bind•ery \'bīn-də-rē, -drē\ *n, pl* **-er•ies :** a place where books are bound

bind•ing \'bīn-diŋ\ *n* **1 :** the action of one that binds **2 :** a material or device used to bind: as **a :** the cover and fastenings of a book **b :** a narrow fabric used to finish raw edges **c :** a device for securing a boot to a ski

binding energy *n* **:** the energy required to break up a molecule, atom, or atomic nucleus into its constituent particles

bind over *vt* **:** to put (a person) under a legal obligation to appear in court or to perform or refrain from some specific action

bind•weed \'bīnd-ˌwēd\ *n* **:** any of various twining plants especially of the morning-glory family that grow matted or interlaced with other plants

bine \'bīn\ *n* **:** a twining stem or flexible shoot (as of the hop) [alteration of [2]*bind*]

binge \'binj\ *n* **:** a period of unrestrained indulgence ⟨went on a *binge* and got drunk⟩ ⟨a buying *binge*⟩ [English dialect *binge* "to drink heavily"]

bin•go \'biŋ-gō, -ˌgō\ *n* **:** a game of chance played with cards having numbered squares corresponding to numbered balls drawn at random and won by the player first covering five squares in a row [earlier *bingo*, interjection used to announce an unexpected event]

bin•na•cle \'bin-i-kəl\ *n* **:** a case, box, or stand containing a ship's compass and a lamp [Middle English *bitakille*, derived from Latin *habitaculum* "habitation"]

bin•oc•u•lar \bī-'näk-yə-lər, bə-\ *adj* **:** of, relating to, using, or adapted to the use of both eyes ⟨*binocular* vision⟩ [Latin *bini* "two each" + *oculus* "eye"] — **bin•oc•u•lar•ly** *adv*

bin•oc•u•lars \bə-'näk-yə-lərz, bī-\ *n pl* **:** a hand-held magnifying optical instrument similar to field glasses but having a set of prisms which increase the focal length and magnifying ability without increasing the size of the instrument — often used with *pair; also* **:** FIELD GLASSES

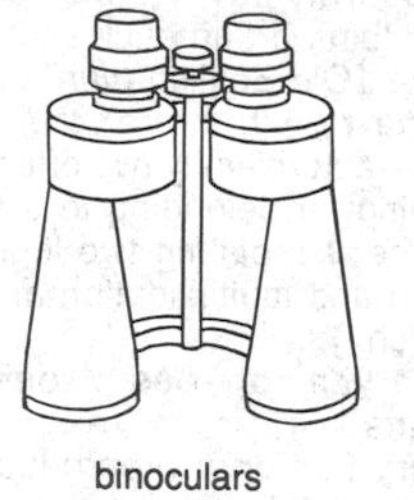
binoculars

bi•no•mi•al \bī-'nō-mē-əl\ *n* **1 :** a mathematical expression consisting of two terms connected by a plus sign or minus sign **2 :** a biological species name consisting of two terms [Latin *bi-* + *nomen* "name, term"] — **binomial** *adj* — **bi•no•mi•al•ly** \-mē-ə-lē\ *adv*

binomial coefficient *n* **:** one of the coefficients obtained when the binomial $(x + y)^n$ is expanded according to the binomial theorem

binomial nomenclature *n* **:** a system of nomenclature in which each species of animal or plant receives a binomial name of which the first term identifies the genus to which it belongs and the second the species itself

binomial theorem *n* **:** a theorem that specifies the expansion of a binomial of the form $(x + y)^n$ in $n + 1$ terms of which the general term is of the form

$$\frac{n!}{k!(n-k)!}x^k y^{(n-k)}$$

bi•nu•cle•ate \bī-'nyü-klē-ət, 'bī-, -'nü-\ *adj* **:** having two nuclei

bio- *combining form* **1 :** life ⟨*bio*sphere⟩ **2 :** living organisms or tissue ⟨*bio*luminescence⟩ [Greek *bios* "life, mode of life"]

bio•as•say \ˌbī-ō-'as-ˌā, -a-'sā\ *n* **:** determination of relative strength (as of a drug) by comparison of effect on a test organism with that of a standard preparation — **bio•as•say** \-a-'sā, -'as-ˌā\ *vt*

bio•chem•is•try \-'kem-ə-strē\ *n* **:** chemistry that deals with the chemical compounds and processes occurring in living things — **bio•chem•i•cal** \ˌbī-ō-'kem-i-kəl\ *adj* — **bio•chem•i•cal•ly** \-kə-lē, -klē\ *adv* — **bio•chem•ist** \-'kem-əst\ *n*

bio•de•grad•able \-di-'grād-ə-bəl\ *adj* **:** capable of being broken down especially into relatively harmless products by the action of living beings (as microorganisms) — **bio•de•grad•abil•i•ty** \-ˌgrād-ə-'bil-ət-ē\ *n* — **bio•de•grade** \-di-'grād\ *vt*

bio•en•er•get•ics \-ˌen-ər-'jet-iks\ *n* **:** the biology of energy transformations and energy exchanges (as in photosynthesis) within and between living things and their environments — **bio•en•er•get•ic** \-ik\ *adj*

bio•feed•back \-'fēd-ˌbak\ *n* **:** the technique of making unconscious or involuntary bodily processes (as heartbeat or brain waves) perceptible to the senses (as by the use of an oscilloscope) in order to manipulate them by conscious mental control

bio•gen•e•sis \ˌbī-ō-'jen-ə-səs\ *n* **:** the development of life from preexisting life — **bio•gen•e•sist** \-ə-səst\ *n* — **bio•ge•net•ic** \-jə-'net-ik\ *adj*

biogenetic law *n* **:** a theory in biology: an organism passes through successive stages in development resembling the series of evolutionary ancestors from which it is descended

bio•ge•og•ra•phy \ˌbī-ō-jē-'äg-rə-fē\ *n* **:** a branch of biology that deals with the geographical distribution of animals and plants — **bio•ge•og•ra•pher** \-jē-'äg-rə-fər\ *n* — **bio•geo•graph•ic** \-ˌjē-ə-'graf-ik\ *or* **bio•geo•graph•i•cal** \-'graf-i-kəl\ *adj*

bi•og•ra•pher \bī-'äg-rə-fər, bē-\ *n* **:** a writer of a biography

bio•graph•i•cal \ˌbī-ə-'graf-i-kəl\ *or* **bio•graph•ic** \-'graf-ik\ *adj* **1 :** of, relating to, or constituting biography ⟨a *biographical* sketch⟩ **2 :** consisting of biographies ⟨a *biographical* dictionary⟩ — **bio•graph•i•cal•ly** \-'graf-i-kə-lē, -klē\ *adv*

bi•og•ra•phy \bī-'äg-rə-fē, bē-\ *n, pl* **-phies 1 :** a usually written history of a person's life **2 :** biographical writings in general **3 :** a life history ⟨the *biography* of a building⟩

[1]**bi•o•log•i•cal** \ˌbī-ə-'läj-i-kəl\ *or* **bi•o•log•ic** \-'läj-ik\ *adj* **:** of or relating to biology or to life and living processes ⟨*biological* supplies⟩ ⟨*biological* forces⟩ — **bi•o•log•i•cal•ly** \-'läj-i-kə-lē, -klē\ *adv*

[2]**biological** *or* **biologic** *n* **:** a medicinal product of biological origin

biological clock *n* **:** an inherent timing mechanism in a living being responsible for various cyclical physiological and behavioral responses

biological control *n* **:** elimination or reduction in numbers of pest organisms by interference with their ecological adjustment (as by the introduction of parasites or disease)

biological warfare *n* **:** warfare in which living organisms (as disease germs) are used to harm the enemy or his livestock and crops

bi•ol•o•gy \bī-'äl-ə-jē\ *n* **1 :** a branch of knowledge that deals with living organisms and life processes **2 :** the life processes of an organism or a group ⟨the *biology* of insects⟩ — **bi•ol•o•gist** \-jəst\ *n*

bio•lu•mi•nes•cence \ˌbī-ō-ˌlü-mə-'nes-nts\ *n* **:** the emission of light by living organisms — **bio•lu•mi•nes•cent** \-nt\ *adj*

bio•mass \'bī-ō-ˌmas\ *n* **:** the amount of living matter (as in a unit area of a natural habitat or in a unit volume of a liquid culture)

bi•ome \'bī-ˌōm\ *n* **:** a major ecological community type ⟨the grassland *biome*⟩ [*bio-* + Latin *-oma* "group, mass"]

bio•med•i•cal \ˌbī-ō-'med-i-kəl\ *adj* **:** of, relating to, or involving biological, medical, and physical science (as in the development of artificial organs or the alteration of human genes)

bi•o•nom•ics \ˌbī-ə-'näm-iks\ *n sing or pl* **:** ECOLOGY [Greek *nomos* "law"] — **bi•o•nom•ic** \-ik\ *adj*

bio•phys•ics \ˌbī-ō-'fiz-iks\ *n* **:** a branch of knowledge concerned with the application of physical principles and methods to biological problems — **bio•phys•i•cal** \ˌbī-ō-'fiz-i-kəl\ *adj*

— **bio•phys•i•cist** \-'fiz-ə-səst\ *n*

bi•op•sy \'bī-,äp-sē\ *n, pl* **-sies** : the removal and examination of tissue, cells, or fluids from the living body [*bio-* + Greek *opsis* "appearance"]

bio•sphere \'bī-ə-,sfiər\ *n* : the part of the world in which life can exist

bio•syn•the•sis \,bī-ō-'sin-thə-səs, -'sint-\ *n* : the production of a chemical compound by a living organism — **bio•syn•thet•ic** \-sin-'thet-ik\ *adj*

bi•o•ta \bī-'ōt-ə\ *n* : the flora and fauna of a region [New Latin, from Greek *biotē* "life"]

bi•ot•ic \bī-'ät-ik\ *adj* : of or relating to life; *esp* : composed of or caused by living things ⟨a *biotic* community⟩ [Greek *biōtikos*, from *bioun* "to live", from *bios* "life"]

biotic potential *n* : the inherent capacity of an organism or species to reproduce and survive

bi•o•tin \'bī-ə-tən\ *n* : a colorless crystalline growth vitamin of the vitamin B complex found especially in yeast, liver, and egg yolk [Greek *biotos* "life, sustenance"]

bi•o•tite \'bī-ə-,tīt\ *n* : a generally black or dark green mica containing iron, magnesium, potassium, and aluminum [Jean B. *Biot*, died 1862, French mathematician]

bi•par•ti•san \bī-'pärt-ə-zən, 'bī-\ *adj* : of, relating to, or involving members of two parties ⟨a *bipartisan* foreign policy⟩ — **bi•par•ti•san•ism** \-zə-,niz-əm\ *n* — **bi•par•ti•san•ship** \-zən-,ship\ *n*

bi•par•tite \bī-'pär-,tīt, 'bī-\ *adj* **1** : being in two parts **2** : shared by two ⟨a *bipartite* treaty⟩ — **bi•par•tite•ly** *adv* — **bi•par•ti•tion** \,bī-,pär-'tish-ən\ *n*

bi•ped \'bī-,ped\ *n* : a 2-footed animal [Latin *ped-, pes* "foot"] — **bi•ped•al** \bī-'ped-l, 'bī-\ *adj*

bi•pin•nate \bī-'pin-,āt, 'bī-\ *adj* : twice pinnate ⟨*bipinnate* leaves⟩ — **bi•pin•nate•ly** *adv*

bi•plane \'bī-,plān\ *n* : an airplane with two sets of wings usually placed one above the other

bi•po•lar \bī-'pō-lər, 'bī-\ *adj* **1** : having or involving two poles **2** : having or marked by two mutually repellent forces or wholly opposed natures or views — **bi•po•lar•i•ty** \,bī-pō-'lar-ət-ē\ *n*

bi•ra•mous \bī-'rā-məs, 'bī-\ *adj* : having two branches [*bi-* + *ramous* "having branches", from Latin *ramosus*, from *ramus* "branch"]

[1]**birch** \'bərch\ *n* **1** : any of a genus of deciduous trees or shrubs having simple leaves with petioles and typically a membranous outer bark that occurs in layers and peels readily; *also* : its hard pale close-grained wood **2** : a birch rod or bundle of twigs for whipping [Old English *beorc*] — **birch** *adj*

[2]**birch** *vt* : to beat with or as if with a birch : WHIP

[1]**bird** \'bərd\ *n* **1** : any of a class (Aves) of warm-blooded egg-laying vertebrate animals with the body covered with feathers and the forelimbs modified as wings **2** : FELLOW 4a; *esp* : a peculiar person **3** : SHUTTLECOCK [Old English *bridd*] — **bird•like** \-,līk\ *adj* — **for the birds** : being worthless or ridiculous

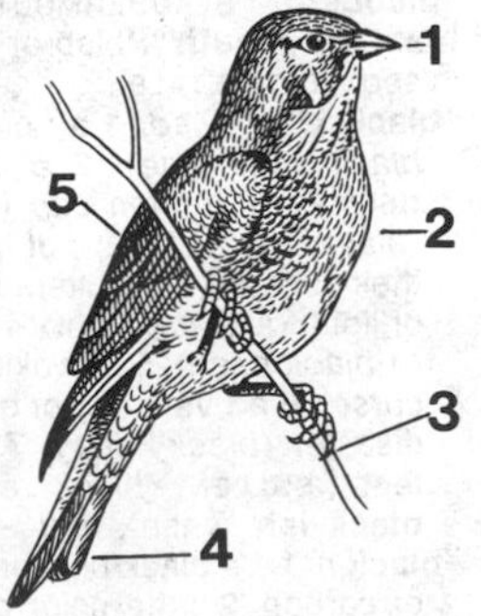

[1]bird 1: *1* bill, *2* breast, *3* claw, *4* tail, *5* wing

[2]**bird** *vi* : to observe or identify wild birds in their natural environment — **bird•er** *n*

bird•bath \'bərd-,bath, -,bȧth\ *n* : a basin set up for birds to bathe in

bird•brain \-,brān\ *n* : a flighty thoughtless person : SCATTERBRAIN

bird dog *n* : a dog trained to hunt or retrieve birds

bird•house \'bərd-,haùs\ *n* : an artificial nesting place for birds; *also* : AVIARY

[1]**bird•ie** \'bərd-ē\ *n* : a golf score of one stroke less than par on a hole

[2]**birdie** *vt* **bird•ied; bird•ie•ing** : to shoot (a hole in golf) in one stroke under par

bird•lime \'bərd-,līm\ *n* : a sticky substance smeared on twigs to catch and hold small birds

bird•man \'bərd-mən *also* -,man\ *n* **1** : one who deals with birds: as **a** : FOWLER **b** : ORNITHOLOGIST **2** : AVIATOR

bird of paradise : any of numerous brilliantly colored plumed birds related to the crows and found in the New Guinea area

bird of passage : a migratory bird

bird of prey : a carnivorous bird (as a hawk or owl) that feeds wholly or chiefly on meat taken by hunting

bird•seed \'bərd-,sēd\ *n* : a mixture of seeds (as of sunflowers or millet) used for feeding birds

bird's–eye \'bərd-,zī\ *adj* **1** : seen from above as if by a flying bird ⟨a *bird's-eye* view⟩ **2** : marked with spots resembling birds' eyes ⟨*bird's-eye* maple⟩; *also* : made of a bird's-eye wood

bird's–foot trefoil \,bərdz-,fůt-\ *n* : a European legume with claw-shaped pods that is widely used as a forage and fodder plant

bi•rec•tan•gu•lar \,bī-,rek-'tang-gyə-lər\ *adj* : having two right angles ⟨a *birectangular* spherical triangle⟩

bi•reme \'bī-,rēm\ *n* : a galley with two banks of oars [Latin *remus* "oar"]

bi•ret•ta \bə-'ret-ə\ *n* : a square cap with three upright ridges on top worn especially by the Roman Catholic clergy [Italian *berretta*, from Provençal *berret* "cap"]

biretta

birth \'bərth\ *n* **1 a** : the emergence of a new individual from the body of its parent **b** : the act or process of bringing forth young from the womb **2** : a person's descent : LINEAGE ⟨one of noble *birth*⟩ **3** : a coming into existence : BEGINNING ⟨the *birth* of an idea⟩ [Old Norse *byrth*]

birth control *n* : control of the number of children born especially by preventing or lessening the frequency of conception

birth•day \'bərth-,dā\ *n* **1** : the day of a person's birth **2** : a day of origin or beginning **3** : an anniversary of a birth ⟨our nation's 200th *birthday*⟩

birth•mark \-,märk\ *n* : an unusual mark or blemish on the skin at birth — **birthmark** *vt*

birth•place \-,plās\ *n* : the place where a person was born or something began

birth•rate \-,rāt\ *n* : the number of births for every hundred or every thousand persons in a given area or group during a given time

birth•right \-,rīt\ *n* : a right, privilege, or possession to which a person is entitled by birth

birth•stone \-,stōn\ *n* : a jewel associated symbolically with the month of one's birth

bis•cuit \'bis-kət\ *n, pl* **biscuits** *also* **biscuit** **1** : a crisp flat cake; *esp, British* : CRACKER 2 **2** : earthenware or porcelain after the first firing and before glazing **3** : a small quick bread made from dough that has been rolled and cut or dropped from a spoon [Middle French *bescuit*, from *pain bescuit* "twice-cooked bread"]

△ **origin** In earlier ages the preservation of food was often a great problem, especially on long journeys. One expedient was to preserve flat cakes of bread by baking them a second time in order to dry them out. In Middle French, this bread was called *pain bescuit* "twice-cooked bread". The second element of the phrase was borrowed into English, and, the notion of cooking twice having been lost, *biscuit* came to be used for any of various hard or crisp, dry baked products, more often called *crackers* in the United States. A small quick bread of similar size and shape is also called *biscuit*.

bi•sect \'bī-,sekt, bī-'\ *vb* **1** : to divide into two usually equal parts ⟨the river *bisects* the town⟩ ⟨*bisect* an angle⟩ **2** : INTERSECT 2 [Latin *sect-, secare* "to cut"] — **bi•sec•tion** \'bī-sek-shən, bī-'\ *n*

bi•sec•tor \'bī-,sek-tər, bī-'\ *n* : one that bisects; *esp* : a straight line that bisects an angle or a line segment

\ə\ **abut**	\aù\ **out**	\i\ **tip**	\ȯ\ **saw**	\ù\ **foot**
\ər\ **further**	\ch\ **chin**	\ī\ **life**	\ȯi\ **coin**	\y\ **yet**
\a\ **mat**	\e\ **pet**	\j\ **job**	\th\ **thin**	\yü\ **few**
\ā\ **take**	\ē\ **easy**	\ng\ **sing**	\th\ **this**	\yù\ **cure**
\ä\ **cot, cart**	\g\ **go**	\ō\ **bone**	\ü\ **food**	\zh\ **vision**

bi•sex•u•al \bī-'sek-shə-wəl, 'bī-, -shəl\ *adj* **1 :** possessing characters of or sexually oriented toward both sexes **2 :** of, relating to, or involving two sexes — **bisexual** *n* — **bi•sex•u•al•i•ty** \ˌbī-ˌsek-shə-'wal-ət-ē\ *n* — **bi•sex•u•al•ly** \-ē\ *adv*
bish•op \'bish-əp\ *n* **1 a :** a high-ranking member of the clergy typically governing a diocese **b :** a member of the clergy who oversees a church district **2 :** a chess piece that can move diagonally across any number of unoccupied squares [Old English *bisceop,* from Late Latin *episcopus,* from Greek *episkopos,* literally, "overseer", from *epi-* "upon" + *skeptesthai* "to look at"]
bish•op•ric \'bish-ə-prik\ *n* **1 :** DIOCESE **2 :** the office of bishop [Old English *bisceop* + *rīce* "realm"]
bis•muth \'biz-məth\ *n* **:** a heavy brittle grayish white metallic element that is chemically like arsenic and antimony and is used in alloys and medicine — see ELEMENT table [German *wismut, bismut*]
bi•son \'bīs-n, 'bīz-\ *n, pl* **bison :** any of several large shaggy-maned usually gregarious recent or extinct mammals of the ox family with a large head, short horns, and heavy forequarters surmounted by a large fleshy hump: as **a :** WISENT **b :** BUFFALO 2a [Latin, of Germanic origin] — **bi•son•tine** \-n-ˌtīn\ *adj*
bisque \'bisk\ *n* **1 :** a thick cream soup made of shellfish, meat, or vegetables **2 :** ice cream containing powdered nuts or macaroons [French]
bis•ter *or* **bis•tre** \'bis-tər\ *n* **:** a grayish to yellowish brown [French *bistre*]
bis•tro \'bēs-ˌtrō, 'bis-\ *n, pl* **bistros 1 :** a small European wineshop or restaurant **2 a :** a small bar or tavern **b :** NIGHTCLUB [French]
bi•sul•fate \bī-'səl-ˌfāt, 'bī-\ *n* **:** an acid sulfate
bi•sul•fide \-ˌfīd\ *n* **:** DISULFIDE
bi•sul•fite \-ˌfīt\ *n* **:** an acid sulfite
¹bit \'bit\ *n* **1 :** the part of a bridle inserted in the mouth of a horse **2 :** the biting or cutting edge or part of a tool; *also* **:** a replaceable part of a compound tool that actually performs the function (as drilling or boring) for which the whole tool is designed **3 :** something that curbs or restrains [Middle English *bitt,* from Old English *bite* "act of biting"]
²bit *vt* **bit•ted; bit•ting 1 :** to put a bit in the mouth of (a horse) **2 :** to control as if with a bit **:** CURB
³bit *n* **1 :** a small piece or amount ⟨a *bit* of cheese⟩ ⟨a little *bit* of luck⟩ **2 :** a short time **:** WHILE ⟨rest a *bit*⟩ **3 :** one having a quality or nature to some extent ⟨a *bit* of a fool⟩ [Old English *bita* "piece bitten off"]
⁴bit *n* **1 :** a unit of computer information equivalent to the result of a choice between two alternatives (as *yes* or *no, on* or *off*) **2 :** the physical representation of a bit (as a hole on a card or a magnetized spot on a tape) whose presence or absence stands for data [*bi*nary digi*t*]
bitch \'bich\ *n* **:** a female dog [Old English *bicce*]
¹bite \'bīt\ *vb* **bit** \'bit\; **bit•ten** \'bit-n\; **bit•ing** \'bīt-ing\ **1 :** to seize, grip, or cut into with or as if with teeth ⟨*bite* an apple⟩ ⟨a steam shovel *bites* into the earth⟩ **2 :** to wound or pierce with or as if with fangs ⟨*bitten* by a snake⟩ **3 :** to make a gash or cut ⟨the sword *bit* into the soldier's arm⟩ **4 :** to cause to smart **:** STING ⟨pepper *bites* the mouth⟩ **5 :** to eat into **:** CORRODE **6 :** to respond to a lure **:** take a bait ⟨the fish are really *biting*⟩ [Old English *bītan*] — **bit•er** *n* — **bite the dust :** to fall dead especially in battle
²bite *n* **1 :** a seizing of something with the teeth or the mouth **2 a :** the amount of food taken at a bite **b :** a light informal meal **:** SNACK **3 :** a wound made by biting **4 :** a sharp penetrating quality or effect
bit•ing \'bīt-ing\ *adj* **:** causing bodily or mental distress **:** CUTTING ⟨*biting* remarks⟩ ⟨a *biting* wind⟩ **syn** see INCISIVE — **bit•ing•ly** *adv*
bitt \'bit\ *n* **:** a post or pair of posts on the deck of a ship for securing mooring lines [perhaps from Old Norse *biti* "beam"]
¹bit•ter \'bit-ər\ *adj* **1 :** being or inducing the one of the four basic taste sensations characterized by a disagreeable acrid taste ⟨*bitter* as quinine⟩ **2 a :** hard to bear **:** PAINFUL ⟨*bitter* disappointment⟩ **b :** being relentlessly determined **:** VEHEMENT ⟨*bitter* partisans⟩ **c :** sharp and resentful ⟨a *bitter* answer⟩ **d :** unpleasantly cold or raw ⟨a *bitter* wind⟩ **3 :** expressing severe pain, grief, or regret ⟨*bitter* tears⟩ [Old English *biter*] — **bit•ter•ish** \'bit-ə-rish\ *adj* — **bit•ter•ly** \'bit-ər-lē\ *adv* — **bit•ter•ness** *n*
²bitter *adv* **:** BITTERLY ⟨it's *bitter* cold⟩
³bitter *n* **1 :** bitter sensation or quality **2** *pl* **:** a usually alcoholic solution of bitter and often aromatic plant products used in mixing drinks and as a mild tonic
bit•tern \'bit-ərn\ *n* **:** any of various small or medium-sized nocturnal herons that have a characteristic booming cry [Middle French *butor*]
¹bit•ter•sweet \'bit-ər-ˌswēt\ *n* **1 :** something that is bittersweet **2 a :** a sprawling poisonous weedy nightshade with purple flowers and oval reddish orange berries **b :** a North American woody climbing plant with yellow capsules that open when ripe and disclose the scarlet seed covers
²bittersweet *adj* **1 :** being both bitter and sweet; *esp* **:** pleasant but marked by elements of suffering or regret ⟨*bittersweet* memories⟩ **2 :** of or relating to a prepared chocolate containing little sugar
bit•ty *or* **bit•tie** \'bit-ē\ *adj, dialect* **:** very small ⟨a little *bitty* dog⟩
bi•tu•men \bə-'tyü-mən, bī-, -'tü-\ *n* **:** any of various dark or black mixtures of hydrocarbons (as asphalt, crude petroleum, or tar) [Latin, "asphalt"]
bi•tu•mi•nous \-mə-nəs\ *adj* **:** resembling, containing, or impregnated with bitumen
bituminous coal *n* **:** a coal that when heated yields considerable volatile bituminous matter — called also *soft coal*
bi•va•lent \bī-'vā-lənt, 'bī-\ *adj* **:** having a valence of two
¹bi•valve \'bī-ˌvalv\ *also* **bi•valved** \-ˌvalvd\ *adj* **1 :** having a shell composed of two movable valves **2 :** having or consisting of two corresponding movable pieces
²bivalve *n* **:** an animal (as a clam) with a bivalve shell
¹biv•ouac \'biv-ˌwak, -ə-ˌwak\ *n* **1 :** a usually temporary encampment offering little or no shelter **2 :** a camping out for a night [French, from Low German *biwake,* from *bi* "by, at" + *wake* "guard"]
²bivouac *vi* **biv•ouacked; biv•ouack•ing :** to encamp with little or no shelter
¹bi•week•ly \bī-'wē-klē, 'bī-\ *adj* **1 :** occurring or produced every two weeks **:** FORTNIGHTLY **2 :** occurring or produced twice a week — **biweekly** *adv*
²biweekly *n* **:** a biweekly publication
bi•year•ly \bī-'yiər-lē, 'bī-\ *adj* **1 :** BIENNIAL 1 **2 :** BIANNUAL
bi•zarre \bə-'zär\ *adj* **:** strikingly unusual or odd; *esp* **:** having sensational contrasts or incongruities ⟨*bizarre* costumes⟩ [French, from Italian *bizarro*] **syn** see FANTASTIC — **bi•zarre•ly** *adv* — **bi•zarre•ness** *n*
¹blab \'blab\ *n* **1 :** TATTLETALE **2 :** idle or excessive talk **:** CHATTER [Middle English *blabbe*] — **blab•by** \'blab-ē\ *adj*
²blab *vb* **blabbed; blab•bing 1 :** to reveal (secrets) by careless talking **:** TATTLE **2 :** BABBLE 1b
¹blab•ber \'blab-ər\ *vb* **blab•bered; blab•ber•ing** \'blab-ring, -ə-ring\ **:** BABBLE 1b [Middle English *blaberen*]
²blabber *n* **:** idle talk **:** BABBLE
³blabber *n* **:** BLABBERMOUTH
blab•ber•mouth \'blab-ər-ˌmau̇th\ *n* **:** one that talks too much; *esp* **:** TATTLETALE
¹black \'blak\ *adj* **1 a :** of the color black **b :** very dark ⟨a face *black* with rage⟩ **2 a :** having dark skin, hair, and eyes **:** SWARTHY **b** *often cap* (1) **:** of or relating to the Negro race ⟨*black* Africans⟩ (2) **:** of or relating to black Afro-Americans or their culture ⟨*black* literature⟩ **3 :** characterized by the absence of light ⟨a *black* night⟩ **4 :** thoroughly sinister or evil **:** WICKED ⟨a *black* deed⟩ **5 :** invoking evil supernatural powers ⟨a *black* curse⟩ **6 a :** very sad or gloomy ⟨*black* despair⟩ **b :** marked by disaster ⟨*black* Friday⟩ **7 :** characterized by hostility or discontent **:** SULLEN ⟨*black* resentment⟩ [Old English *blæc*] — **black•ish** \-ish\ *adj* — **black•ly** *adv* — **black•ness** *n*
²black *n* **1 :** a black pigment or dye; *esp* **:** one consisting largely of carbon **2 :** the color of soot or coal **3 :** something that is black; *esp* **:** black clothing **4** *often cap* **:** a person belonging to a dark-skinned race or one stemming in part from such a race; *esp* **:** NEGRO **5 :** absence of light **:** DARKNESS ⟨the *black* of night⟩ **6 :** the dark-colored pieces of a two-handed board game (as chess) **7 :** the condition of making a profit ⟨in the *black*⟩
³black *vb* **:** BLACKEN
black-and-blue \ˌblak-ən-'blü\ *adj* **:** darkly discolored (as from a bruise)
Black and Tan *n* **:** one recruited in England in 1920-21 into the Royal Irish Constabulary to suppress the Irish revolution [from the color of the uniform]
¹black•ball \'blak-ˌbȯl\ *n* **1 :** a small black ball used to cast a

negative vote **2 :** an adverse vote especially against admitting someone to membership in an organization
[2]**blackball** *vt* **:** to vote against; *esp* **:** to exclude from membership by casting a negative vote
black bass *n* **:** any of several freshwater sunfishes native to eastern and central North America
black bear *n* **:** the common usually largely black-furred bear of North America
black belt *n* **1 :** an area characterized by rich black soil **2** *often cap both Bs* **:** an area inhabited by large numbers of blacks
black•ber•ry \'blak-,ber-ē\ *n* **1 :** the usually black or dark purple juicy but seedy edible fruit of various brambles **2 :** a plant that bears blackberries
black•bird \'blak-,bərd\ *n* **:** any of various birds of which the males are largely or entirely black: as **a :** a common and familiar British thrush **b :** any of several American birds (as the red-winged blackbird) related to the bobolink
black•board \'blak-,bōrd, -,bȯrd\ *n* **:** a hard smooth usually dark surface used for writing or drawing on with chalk
black•body \'blak-'bäd-ē\ *n* **:** a body or surface that completely absorbs all radiant energy falling upon it
black book *n* **:** a book containing a blacklist
black box *n* **1 :** an electronic module (as for a spacecraft) **2 :** a usually electronic device whose components are hidden from or mysterious to the user
black•cap \'blak-,kap\ *n* **1 :** any of several black-crowned birds (as the chickadee) **2 :** BLACK RASPBERRY
black•cock \-,käk\ *n* **:** BLACK GROUSE; *esp* **:** the male black grouse
black crappie *n* **:** a silvery black-mottled sunfish of the central and eastern United States
black death *n* **:** a form of plague epidemic in Europe and Asia in the 14th century [from the black patches on the skin of its victims]
black•en \'blak-ən\ *vb* **black•ened; black•en•ing** \'blak-ning, -ə-ning\ **1 :** to make or become black **2 :** to injure the reputation of — **black•en•er** \-nər, -ə-nər\ *n*
black eye *n* **:** a puffy darkening of the area about an eye caused by bruising (as from a blow)
black-eyed pea \,blak-,īd-\ *n* **:** COWPEA
black-eyed Su•san \-'süz-n\ *n* **:** an American daisy with deep yellow or orange petals and a dark center
black•face \'blak-,fās\ *n* **:** makeup for a Negro role especially in a minstrel show
black•fish \-,fish\ *n* **1 :** any of numerous dark-colored fishes: as **a :** TAUTOG **b :** a small food fish of Alaska and Siberia that is especially resistant to cold **2 :** any of several small toothed whales related to the dolphins
black flag *n* **:** JOLLY ROGER
black•fly \'blak-,flī\ *n* **:** any of several small dark-colored insects; *esp* **:** a two-winged biting fly whose larvae live in flowing streams
Black•foot \-,fu̇t\ *n, pl* **Black•feet** \-,fēt\ *or* **Blackfoot :** a member of a people belonging to an Indian confederacy of Montana, Alberta, and Saskatchewan
black grouse *n* **:** a large grouse of Europe and western Asia of which the male is black with white wing patches and the female is barred and mottled
[1]**black•guard** \'blag-ərd, -,ärd; 'blak-,gärd\ *n* **:** a rude or unscrupulous person — **black•guard•ly** \-lē\ *adj or adv*
[2]**blackguard** *vt* **:** to abuse with bad language **:** REVILE
black gum *n* **:** an important timber tree of the southeastern United States with light and soft but tough wood
black hand *n, often cap B&H* **:** a lawless secret society engaged in crime [*Black Hand,* a Sicilian and Italian-American society of the late 19th and 20th centuries] — **black-hand•er** *n*
black•head \'blak-,hed\ *n* **:** a small oily plug blocking the duct of a sebaceous gland
black hole *n* **:** a hypothetical celestial body with a small diameter and an intense gravitational field that is held to be a collapsed star
black•ing \'blak-ing\ *n* **:** a substance that makes things black; *esp* **:** a paste or liquid used in shining black shoes
black•jack \'blak-,jak\ *n* **1 :** a small leather-covered club with a flexible handle **2 :** a common often scrubby oak of the southern United States with black bark **3 :** a card game the object of which is to be dealt cards having a higher count than those of the dealer up to but not exceeding 21 — called also *twenty-one*
black lead \-'led\ *n* **:** GRAPHITE
black•leg \'blak-,leg\ *n* **:** a usually fatal toxemia especially of young cattle
black light *n* **:** invisible ultraviolet or infrared light
black•list \-,list\ *n* **:** a list of persons who are disapproved of and are to be punished (as by refusal of jobs or a boycott) — **blacklist** *vt*
black lung *n* **:** a disease of the lungs caused by habitual inhalation of coal dust
black•mail \-,māl\ *n* **:** the forcing of someone to pay money by threatening to reveal a secret that will bring trouble and disgrace; *also* **:** the money paid under threat of blackmail [Scots *mail* "payment", from Old English *māl* "agreement, pay", from Old Norse, "agreement"] — **blackmail** *vt* — **black•mail•er** *n*
Black Ma•ria \,blak-mə-'rī-ə\ *n* **:** PATROL WAGON
black market *n* **:** illicit trade in violation of official regulations; *also* **:** a place where such trade is carried on — **black-market** *vb* — **black mar•ke•teer** \-,mär-kə-'tiər\ *n*
black oak *n* **:** any of several American oaks having dark bark or foliage; *esp* **:** a large timber tree of the eastern and central United States having a yellow inner bark used for tanning
black•out \'blak-,au̇t\ *n* **1 :** a period of darkness resulting from absence of artificial light; *esp* **:** one due to power failure **2 :** a transient dulling or loss of vision or consciousness **3 :** a blotting out by or as if by censorship ⟨a news *blackout*⟩
black out \blak-'au̇t, 'blak-\ *vb* **1 :** to be affected by a blackout ⟨*black out* from exhaustion⟩ **2 :** to cause a blackout of ⟨an ice storm *blacked* the city *out*⟩ ⟨*black out* the news⟩
black pepper *n* **:** a pungent seasoning that consists of the fruit of the East Indian pepper ground with the black husk still on
black power *n* **:** the political and economic power of black Americans especially when used to further racial equality
black racer *n* **:** an American blacksnake common in the eastern United States
black raspberry *n* **:** a raspberry with a purplish black fruit that is native to eastern North America
black sheep *n* **:** a disreputable member of an otherwise respectable group ⟨the *black sheep* of the family⟩
Black•shirt \'blak-,shərt\ *n* **:** a member of a fascist group having a black shirt as a distinctive part of its uniform; *esp* **:** a member of the Italian Fascist party
black•smith \'blak-,smith\ *n* **:** a worker who shapes iron by heating and then hammering it [from the blacksmith's working with iron, which was known as "black metal" to distinguish it from tin, or "white metal"] — **black•smith•ing** *n*
black•snake \-,snāk\ *n* **1 :** any of several snakes largely black or dark in color; *esp* **:** a black racer or a related harmless snake **2 :** a long tapering braided whip
black studies *n pl* **:** studies (as history and literature) relating to the culture of black Americans
black•thorn \'blak-,thȯrn\ *n* **1 :** a European spiny plum with hard wood and small white flowers **2 :** any of several American hawthorns
black tie *n* **:** semiformal evening dress for men — **black-tie** \blak-'tī, 'blak-\ *adj*
black•top \'blak-,täp\ *n* **:** a bituminous material used especially for surfacing roads; *also* **:** a surface paved with blacktop — **blacktop** *vt*
black walnut *n* **:** a walnut of eastern North America with hard strong heavy dark brown wood and oily edible nuts; *also* **:** its wood or nut
black widow *n* **:** a poisonous New World spider having the female black with an hourglass-shaped red mark on the underside of the abdomen

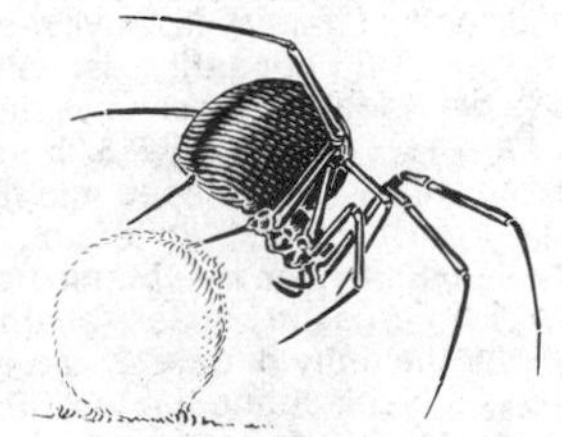
black widow

blad•der \'blad-ər\ *n* **1 :** a membranous sac in an ani-

\ə\ abut	\au̇\ out	\i\ tip	\ȯ\ saw	\u̇\ foot
\ər\ further	\ch\ chin	\ī\ life	\ȯi\ coin	\y\ yet
\a\ mat	\e\ pet	\j\ job	\th\ thin	\yü\ few
\ā\ take	\ē\ easy	\ng\ sing	\th\ this	\yu̇\ cure
\ä\ cot, cart	\g\ go	\ō\ bone	\ü\ food	\zh\ vision

mal in which a liquid or gas is stored; *esp* **:** one in a vertebrate into which urine passes from the kidneys **2 :** something resembling a bladder; *esp* **:** an inflatable bag or container [Old English *blǣdre*] — **blad•der•like** \-ˌlīk\ *adj*
bladder worm *n* **:** a bladderlike larval tapeworm
blad•der•wort \'blad-ər-ˌwərt, -ˌwȯrt\ *n* **:** any of several slender plants growing in water or on wet shores and having insect-catching bladders on the stem, scalelike leaves, and irregular yellow or purple flowers
blade \'blād\ *n* **1 a :** a leaf of a plant and especially of a grass **b :** the broad flat part of a leaf as distinguished from its stalk **2 :** something resembling the blade of a leaf: as **a :** the broad flattened part of a paddle **b :** an arm of a propeller, electric fan, or steam turbine **c :** the upper flat part of the tongue immediately behind the tip **3 a :** the cutting part of an implement **b** (1) **:** SWORD 1 (2) **:** SWORDSMAN (3) **:** a dashing lively fellow **c :** the runner of an ice skate [Old English *blæd*] — **blad•ed** \'blād-əd\ *adj*
blah \'blä\ *adj* **:** lacking interest or excitement ⟨a *blah* winter day⟩ [imitative]
blahs \'bläz\ *n pl* **:** a feeling of boredom, discomfort, or general dissatisfaction ⟨the post-vacation *blahs*⟩
blain \'blān\ *n* **:** an inflammatory swelling or sore [Old English *blegen*]
[1]**blame** \'blām\ *vt* **1 :** to find fault with **:** CENSURE **2 a :** to hold responsible ⟨*blame* them for the failure⟩ **b :** to place responsibility for ⟨*blamed* the error on me⟩ [Old French *blamer,* from Late Latin *blasphemare* "to blaspheme"] — **blam•able** \'blā-mə-bəl\ *adj* — **blam•ably** \-ə-blē\ *adv* — **blam•er** *n*
• syn BLAME, CENSURE, CONDEMN, CRITICIZE mean to find fault with openly. BLAME may imply simply the opposite of *praise* but often suggests an accusation or the placing of responsibility for something bad or unfortunate; CENSURE carries a stronger suggestion of authority and reprimanding than BLAME; CONDEMN usually suggests an unqualified and final unfavorable judgment; CRITICIZE implies finding fault especially with methods or policies or intentions.
[2]**blame** *n* **1 :** expression of disapproval **2 :** responsibility for something felt to deserve censure
blame•less \'blām-ləs\ *adj* **:** free from blame or fault — **blame•less•ly** *adv* — **blame•less•ness** *n*
blame•wor•thy \'blām-ˌwər-thē\ *adj* **:** deserving blame — **blame•wor•thi•ness** *n*
blanch \'blanch\ *vb* **1 :** to take the color out of: **a :** to bleach by excluding light ⟨*blanch* celery⟩ **b :** to scald in order to remove the skin from or whiten ⟨*blanch* almonds⟩ **2 :** to become white or pale [Middle French *blanchir,* from *blanc* "white"] **syn** see WHITEN — **blanch•er** *n*
blanc•mange \blə-'mänj, -'mänzh\ *n* **:** a dessert made from gelatin or a starchy substance and milk usually sweetened and flavored [Middle French *blanc manger,* literally, "white food"]
bland \'bland\ *adj* **1 :** smooth and soothing in manner **:** GENTLE ⟨a *bland* smile⟩ **2 :** having soft and soothing qualities **:** not irritating ⟨a *bland* diet⟩ [Latin *blandus*] **syn** see SUAVE — **bland•ly** *adv* — **bland•ness** \'bland-nəs, 'blan-\ *n*
blan•dish \'blan-dish\ *vt* **:** to coax with flattery **:** CAJOLE [Middle French *blandiss-,* stem of *blandir,* from Latin *blandiri,* from *blandus* "bland"] — **blan•dish•er** *n* — **blan•dish•ment** \-mənt\ *n*
[1]**blank** \'blangk\ *adj* **1 :** free from writing, printing, or marks ⟨*blank* sheets of paper⟩ **2 :** having empty spaces to be filled in ⟨a *blank* form⟩ **3 :** appearing dazed or confused **:** EXPRESSIONLESS ⟨a *blank* look⟩ **4 :** lacking variety, change, or accomplishment **:** EMPTY ⟨a *blank* day⟩ **5 :** ABSOLUTE 4, UNQUALIFIED ⟨a *blank* refusal⟩ **6 :** not shaped into finished form ⟨a *blank* key⟩ [Middle French *blanc* "white", of Germanic origin] **syn** see EMPTY — **blank•ly** *adv* — **blank•ness** *n*
[2]**blank** *n* **1 a :** an empty space (as on a paper) **b :** a paper with spaces for the entry of data **2 :** an empty space or period ⟨my mind was a *blank* during the test⟩ **3 :** the bull's-eye of a target **4 a :** a piece of material prepared to be made into something (as a key) by a further operation **b :** a cartridge loaded with powder but no bullet **5 :** VOID 4
[3]**blank** *vt* **1 a :** to make obscure **:** OBLITERATE ⟨*blank* out a line⟩ **b :** to stop up **:** SEAL ⟨*blank* off a tunnel⟩ **2 :** to keep from scoring ⟨*blanked* for eight innings⟩
blank check *n* **1 :** a signed check with the amount unspecified **2 :** complete freedom of action
[1]**blan•ket** \'blang-kət\ *n* **1 :** a usually heavy woven covering for a bed **2 :** a covering layer ⟨a *blanket* of snow⟩ [Old French *blankete,* from *blanc* "white"]
[2]**blanket** *vt* **:** to cover with or as if with a blanket
[3]**blanket** *adj* **:** covering all members of a group ⟨a *blanket* wage increase⟩ ⟨*blanket* rules⟩
blank verse *n* **:** unrhymed verse; *esp* **:** unrhymed iambic pentameter verse
[1]**blare** \'blaər, 'bleər\ *vb* **1 :** to sound loud and harsh **2 :** to utter in a harsh noisy way ⟨radios *blaring* advertisements⟩ [Middle English *bleren*]
[2]**blare** *n* **:** a harsh loud noise ⟨the *blare* of radios⟩
blar•ney \'blär-nē\ *n* **:** skillful flattery [*Blarney stone,* a stone in Blarney Castle near Cork, Ireland, held to make those who kiss it skilled in flattery] — **blarney** *vb*
bla•sé \blä-'zā\ *adj* **:** indifferent to pleasure or excitement as a result of excessive indulgence; *also* **:** SOPHISTICATED 2b [French]
blas•pheme \blas-'fēm, 'blas-ˌ\ *vb* **1 a :** to speak of or address with irreverence **b :** to utter blasphemy **2 :** ABUSE 1, REVILE [Late Latin *blasphemare,* from Greek *blasphēmein*] — **blas•phem•er** *n*
blas•phe•my \'blas-fə-mē\ *n, pl* **-mies :** great disrespect shown to God or to sacred persons or things — **blas•phe•mous** \-məs\ *adj* — **blas•phe•mous•ly** *adv* — **blas•phe•mous•ness** *n*
• syn PROFANITY: BLASPHEMY applies in strict use to an intentional utterance defying or offering indignity to God; PROFANITY includes all irreverent reference to holy persons or things; it is particularly applicable when the name of God is used lightly or irreverently
[1]**blast** \'blast\ *n* **1 :** a strong gust of wind **2 :** a current of air or gas forced through an opening (as in an organ or furnace) **3 :** the blowing that a charge of ore or metal receives in a blast furnace **4 :** the sound made by a wind instrument (as a horn) or by a whistle **5 a :** EXPLOSION; *esp* **:** an explosion (as of dynamite) for shattering rock **b :** an explosive charge for this purpose **c :** the sudden air pressure produced in the vicinity of an explosion that has the effect of a violent wind **6 :** a sudden harmful effect from or as if from a hot wind; *esp* **:** a withering blight of plants [Old English *blǣst*]
[2]**blast** *vb* **1 :** to produce a loud harsh sound **2 a :** to use an explosive **b :** to fire a gun **3 :** to injure by or as if by the action of wind **:** BLIGHT **4 a :** to shatter by or as if by an explosive **:** DEMOLISH **b :** to strike with explosive force — **blast•er** *n*
blast- *or* **blasto-** *combining form* **:** bud **:** germ **:** embryo in its early stages ⟨*blasto*coel⟩ [Greek *blastos* "bud, shoot, embryo"]
blast furnace *n* **:** a furnace in which combustion is forced by a current of air under pressure; *esp* **:** one for the reduction of iron ore

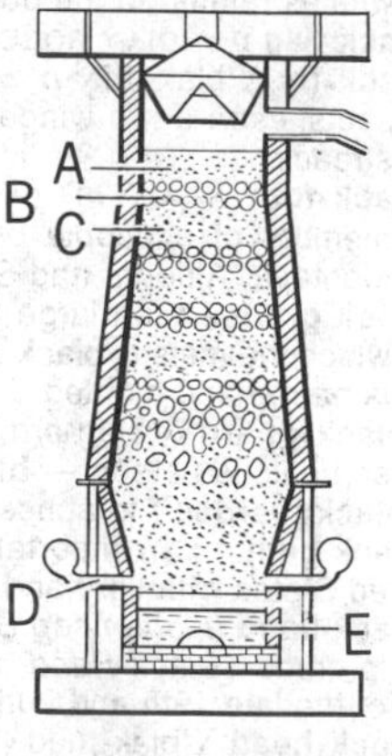

blast furnace: *A* coke, *B* ore, *C* limestone, *D* hot blast, *E* molten iron

blas•to•coel *or* **blas•to•coele** \'blas-tə-ˌsēl\ *n* **:** the cavity of a blastula — **blas•to•coe•lic** \ˌblas-tə-'sē-lik\ *adj*
blas•to•cyst \'blas-tə-ˌsist\ *n* **:** the modified blastula of a placental mammal
blas•to•derm \-tə-ˌdərm\ *n* **:** a discoidal blastula formed especially in an egg with much yolk — **blas•to•der•mic** \-'dər-mik\ *adj*
blast off \blas-'tȯf, 'blas-\ *vi* **:** to take off — used of rocket-propelled missiles and vehicles — **blast-off** \'blas-ˌtȯf\ *n*
blas•to•mere \'blas-tə-ˌmiər\ *n* **:** a cell produced during cleavage of an egg — **blas•to•mer•ic** \ˌblas-tə-'miər-ik, -'mer-\ *adj*
blas•to•pore \'blas-tə-ˌpōr, -ˌpȯr\ *n* **:** the opening of the cavity of the gastrula
blas•tu•la \'blas-chə-lə\ *n, pl* **-las** *or* **-lae** \-ˌlē, -ˌlī\ **:** an early metazoan embryo typically having the form of a hollow fluid-filled rounded cavity bounded by a single layer of cells — compare GASTRULA, MORULA [New Latin, from Greek *blastos* "bud, embryo"] — **blas•tu•lar** \-lər\ *adj*
blat \'blat\ *vi* **blat•ted; blat•ting :** BLEAT 1 [imitative] — **blat** *n*
bla•tant \'blāt-nt\ *adj* **1 :** noisy especially in a vulgar or offen-

sive way : CLAMOROUS **2 :** completely obvious or conspicuous especially in an offensive way [perhaps from Latin *blatire* "to chatter"] — **bla•tan•cy** \-n-sē\ *n* — **bla•tant•ly** *adv*

blath•er \'blath-ər\ *vi* **blath•ered**; **blath•er•ing** \-ring, -ə-ring\ **:** to talk foolishly [Old Norse *blathra*] — **blather** *n* — **blath•er•er** \-ər-ər\ *n*

blath•er•skite \'blath-ər-,skīt\ *n* **:** a blustering talkative person [*blather* + Scots dialect *skate* "contemptible person"]

1**blaze** \'blāz\ *n* **1 a :** an intensely burning fire **b :** intense direct light often accompanied by heat ⟨the *blaze* of the sun⟩ **c :** a sudden outburst of flame **2 a :** a dazzling display ⟨a *blaze* of color⟩ **b :** a sudden outburst (as of anger) [Old English *blæse* "torch"]

2**blaze** *vi* **1 a :** to burn brightly **b :** to flare up : FLAME ⟨suddenly *blazed* with anger⟩ **2 :** to be conspicuously brilliant ⟨fields *blazing* with flowers⟩ **3 :** to shoot rapidly and repeatedly ⟨*blaze* away at a target⟩

3**blaze** *vt* **:** to make public : PROCLAIM ⟨*blaze* the news abroad⟩ [Dutch *blāsen* "to blow"]

4**blaze** *n* **1 :** a white mark usually running lengthwise on the face of an animal **2 :** a mark made on a tree by chipping off a piece of the bark usually to leave a trail [German *blas*]

5**blaze** *vt* **:** to mark (as a trail) with blazes

blaz•er \'blā-zər\ *n* **:** a sports jacket often with notched collar and patch pockets [2*blaze*]

blazing star *n* **:** any of several plants having conspicuous flower clusters; *esp* **:** any of a genus of composite American herbs with slender grassy leaves and spikes of rose-purple or white flower heads

1**bla•zon** \'blāz-n\ *n* **1 a :** COAT OF ARMS **b :** the proper description of a coat of arms **2 :** ostentatious display : SHOW [Middle French *blason*]

2**blazon** *vt* **bla•zoned**; **bla•zon•ing** \'blāz-ning, -n-ing\ **1 a :** to describe (heraldic or armorial bearings) in technical terms **b :** to represent (armorial bearings) in a drawing or engraving **2 :** to depict in colors **3 :** to cover as if with blazons ⟨*blazoned* the building with posters — **bla•zon•er** \'blāz-nər, -n-ər\ *n*

bla•zon•ry \'blāz-n-rē\ *n, pl* **-ries 1 a :** BLAZON 1b **b :** COAT OF ARMS **2 :** a dazzling display

1**bleach** \'blēch\ *vb* **1 :** to remove color or stains from **2 :** to make or become whiter or lighter [Old English *blǣcean*] **syn** see WHITEN

2**bleach** *n* **1 :** the act or process of bleaching **2 :** a preparation used in bleaching

bleach•er \'blē-chər\ *n* **1 :** one that bleaches or is used in bleaching **2 :** a usually uncovered stand of tiered planks providing seats for spectators — usually used in pl.

bleaching powder *n* **:** a mixture of calcium hydroxide, chloride, and hypochlorite used as a bleach, disinfectant, or deodorant

bleak \'blēk\ *adj* **1 :** exposed to wind or weather ⟨a *bleak* coast⟩ **2 :** lacking warmth or kindliness ⟨a *bleak* personality⟩ **3 :** COLD 1, RAW ⟨a *bleak* day⟩ **4 :** severely simple : AUSTERE [Middle English *bleke* "pale"] — **bleak•ly** *adv* — **bleak•ness** *n*

1**blear** \'bliər\ *vt* **1 :** to make (the eyes) sore or watery **2 :** DIM 1, BLUR ⟨*bleared* sight⟩ [Middle English *bleren*]

2**blear** *adj* **:** dim with water or tears — used of the eyes — **blear–eyed** \-'īd\ *adj*

bleary \'bliər-ē\ *adj* **1 :** dull or dimmed especially from fatigue or sleep ⟨*bleary* eyes⟩ **2 :** poorly outlined or defined : DIM — **blear•i•ly** \'blir-ə-lē\ *adv* — **blear•i•ness** \'blir-ē-nəs\ *n*

1**bleat** \'blēt\ *vb* **1 :** to utter a bleat or similar sound **2 :** to utter in a bleating manner [Old English *blǣtan*]

2**bleat** *n* **:** the characteristic cry of a sheep or goat

bleb \'bleb\ *n* **:** a small blister [perhaps alteration of *blob*] — **bleb•by** \-ē\ *adj*

bleed \'blēd\ *vb* **bled** \'bled\; **bleed•ing 1 :** to lose blood ⟨a cut finger *bleeds*⟩ **2 :** to be wounded ⟨fought and *bled* for their country⟩ **3 :** to feel pain or deep sympathy ⟨my heart *bleeds* for them⟩ **4 :** to flow from or as if from a wounded surface ⟨pitch *bleeding* from the broken bark⟩ **5 :** to draw fluid (as blood or sap) from ⟨*bleed* a patient⟩ ⟨*bleed* a tire⟩ **6 :** to extort money from [Old English *blēdan*, from *blōd* "blood"]

bleed•er \'blēd-ər\ *n* **:** one that bleeds; *esp* : HEMOPHILIAC

bleeding heart *n* **1 :** a garden plant of the poppy family with drooping spikes of deep pink heart-shaped flowers **2 :** a person extravagantly sympathetic toward one felt to be abused

1**blem•ish** \'blem-ish\ *vt* **:** to spoil by a flaw [Middle French *blesmiss-*, stem of *blesmir* "to make pale, wound", of Germanic origin]

2**blemish** *n* **:** something (as a mark) that impairs appearance or quality : FLAW

• **syn** BLEMISH, DEFECT, FLAW mean an imperfection that mars or damages. BLEMISH suggests something, as a spot or stain, that mars the surface or appearance; DEFECT implies a lack, often hidden, of something essential to completeness ⟨a *defect* in the organs of vision⟩ FLAW suggests a defect in continuity or cohesion, as a crack, break, or fissure.

1**blench** \'blench\ *vi* **:** to shrink back out of fear : FLINCH [Old English *blencan* "to deceive"]

2**blench** *vb* **:** to grow or make pale : BLANCH [alteration of *blanch*]

1**blend** \'blend\ *vb* **1 :** to mix so thoroughly that the separate things mixed cannot be distinguished **2 :** to shade into each other : MERGE, HARMONIZE ⟨furniture that *blends* with the draperies⟩ [Old Norse *blanda*] **syn** see MIX — **blend•er** *n*

2**blend** *n* **1 :** a thorough mixture **2 :** a product (as coffee) prepared by blending **3 :** a word produced by combining parts of other words (as *motel* from *motor* and *hotel*)

blend•ing inheritance *n* **:** inheritance involving expression in the offspring of characters intermediate between those of the parents due especially to incomplete genetic dominance

blen•ny \'blen-ē\ *n, pl* **blennies :** any of numerous usually small and elongated and often scaleless fishes living about rocky seashores [Latin *blennius*, a sea fish, from Greek *blennos*]

bless \'bles\ *vt* **blessed** \'blest\ *also* **blest** \'blest\; **bless•ing 1 :** to consecrate by religious rite or word ⟨*bless* an altar⟩ **2 :** to make the sign of the cross upon or over **3 :** to ask divine care or protection for **4 :** PRAISE 2, GLORIFY **5 :** ENDOW 2 ⟨*blessed* with good health⟩ [Old English *blētsian*, from *blōd* "blood"; from the use of blood in consecration]

bless•ed \'bles-əd, 'blest\ *also* **blest** \'blest\ *adj* **1 :** honored in worship ⟨the *blessed* Trinity⟩ **2 a :** bringing or enjoying happiness ⟨a *blessed* relief from pain⟩ **b :** enjoying the bliss of heaven — used as a title for a beatified person — **bless•ed•ly** \'bles-əd-lē\ *adv* — **bless•ed•ness** \'bles-əd-nəs\ *n*

Bless•ed Sacrament \,bles-əd-\ *n* **1 :** EUCHARIST **2 :** the consecrated Host

bless•ing *n* **1 a :** the act of one that blesses **b :** APPROVAL ⟨give one's *blessing* to a plan⟩ **2 :** something conducive to happiness or welfare **3 :** grace said at a meal

blew *past of* BLOW

1**blight** \'blīt\ *n* **1 a :** a disease or disorder of plants resulting in withering and death without rotting **b :** an organism that causes blight **2 a :** something that impairs or destroys ⟨the *blight* of totalitarianism⟩ **b :** an impaired or decayed condition ⟨urban *blight*⟩ [origin unknown]

2**blight** *vb* **1 :** to affect with blight **2 :** to cause to deteriorate **3 :** to suffer from or become affected with blight

blimp \'blimp\ *n* **:** a nonrigid airship [imitative; from the sound made by striking the gas bag with the thumb]

1**blind** \'blīnd\ *adj* **1 a :** SIGHTLESS **b :** having less than 1/10 normal vision in the best eye even with the aid of glasses **2 :** lacking in judgment or understanding **3 a :** closed at one end ⟨a *blind* street⟩ **b :** having no opening ⟨a *blind* wall⟩ **4 :** made or done without the aid of sight; *esp* **:** performed solely by the aid of instruments within an airplane ⟨a *blind* landing⟩ [Old English] — **blind•ly** *adv* — **blind•ness** \'blīnd-nəs, 'blīn-\ *n*

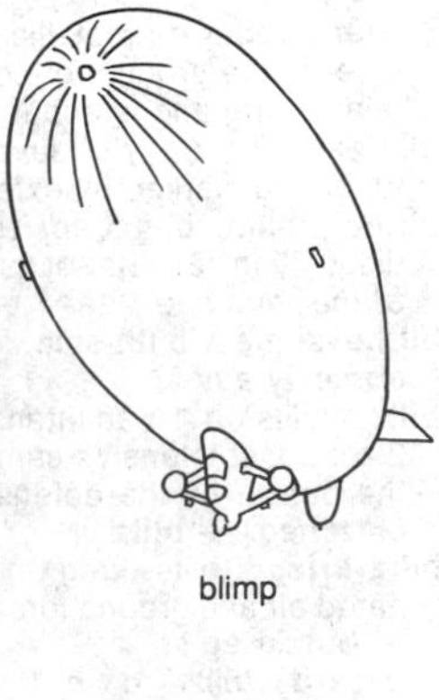
blimp

2**blind** *vt* **1 a :** to make blind **b :** to make temporarily blind : DAZZLE ⟨*blinded* by oncoming headlights⟩ **2 :** to deprive of judgment or understanding ⟨love may *blind* parents to a child's faults⟩ **3 :** to make dim by comparison **:** OUTSHINE

[3]blind *n* **1 :** a device to hinder sight or keep out light ⟨window *blinds*⟩ **2 :** a place of concealment especially for hunters

[4]blind *adv* **1 :** BLINDLY; *esp* **:** to the point of insensibility ⟨*blind* drunk⟩ **2 :** without seeing outside of an airplane ⟨fly *blind* with the aid of instruments⟩

blind date *n* **1 :** a date between two persons who have not previously met **2 :** either participant in a blind date

blind·er \ˈblīn-dər\ *n* **:** either of two flaps on a horse's bridle to prevent sight of objects at its sides

[1]blind·fold \ˈblīnd-ˌfōld, ˈblīn-\ *vt* **:** to cover the eyes of with or as if with a piece of material [Middle English *blindfellen,* literally, "to strike blind", from *blind* + *fellen* "to fell"] — **blindfold** *adj*

[2]blindfold *n* **:** a covering for the eyes

blind·man's buff \ˌblīnd-ˌmanz-ˈbəf, ˌblīn-\ *also* **blindman's bluff** \-ˈbləf\ *n* **:** a group game in which a blindfolded player tries to catch and identify another player

blind spot *n* **1 :** a point in the retina through which the optic nerve enters and which is insensitive to light **2 :** an area of weakness (as in judgment) **3 :** a locality in which radio reception is poor

blind·worm \ˈblīnd-ˌwərm\ *n* **:** a small burrowing limbless lizard with minute eyes

[1]blink \ˈblingk\ *vb* **1 a :** to look with half-shut winking eyes **b :** to close and open the eyes involuntarily **2 :** to wink repeatedly or rapidly ⟨*blink* back tears⟩ **3 :** to shine dimly or intermittently **4 a :** to shut one's eyes to **:** IGNORE ⟨*blink* the facts⟩ **b :** to look with surprise or dismay [Middle English *blinken* "to open one's eyes"] **syn** see WINK

[2]blink *n* **1 :** GLIMMER, SPARKLE **2 :** a usually involuntary shutting and opening of the eye — **on the blink :** not functioning properly **:** DISABLED

blink·er \ˈbling-kər\ *n* **:** one that blinks; *esp* **:** a light that flashes on and off (as for signaling)

blin·tze \ˈblin-sə, ˈblint-\ *or* **blintz** \ˈblins\ *n* **:** a thin rolled pancake with a filling usually of cheese [Yiddish *blintse,* from Russian *blinets,* from *blin* "pancake"]

blip \ˈblip\ *n* **:** an image on a radar screen [earlier *blip* "a short sound", of imitative origin]

bliss \ˈblis\ *n* **:** complete happiness and joy [Old English] — **bliss·ful** \-fəl\ *adj* — **bliss·ful·ly** \-fə-lē\ *adv* — **bliss·ful·ness** *n*

[1]blis·ter \ˈblis-tər\ *n* **1 :** a raised area of the outer skin containing watery liquid **2 :** a raised spot (as in paint) resembling a blister **3 :** any of various structures that bulge out (as a gunner's compartment on an airplane) [Dutch *bluyster*] — **blis·tery** \-tə-rē, -trē\ *adj*

[2]blister *vb* **blis·tered; blis·ter·ing** \-tə-ring, -tring\ **1 :** to develop a blister **:** rise in blisters **2 :** to raise a blister on

blister beetle *n* **:** any of a family of soft-bodied beetles including some whose dried bodies are used medicinally to blister the skin

blister copper *n* **:** metallic copper that has a black blistered surface, is the product of converting a crude smelted sulfur-containing ore, and is about 98.5 to 99.5 percent pure

blister rust *n* **:** any of several diseases of pines caused by rust fungi and marked by external blisters

blithe \ˈblīth, ˈblī͟th\ *adj* **1 :** of a happy lighthearted character or disposition **2 :** HEEDLESS ⟨*blithe* unconcern⟩ [Old English *blīthe*] **syn** see MERRY — **blithe·ly** *adv*

blithe·some \ˈblīth-səm, ˈblī͟th-\ *adj* **:** GAY 1, MERRY — **blithe·some·ly** *adv*

blitz \ˈblits\ *n* **1 :** an intensive series of air raids; *also* **:** AIR RAID **2 a :** a fast intensive campaign ⟨a publicity *blitz*⟩ **b :** a rush of the passer by the defensive linebackers in football [short for *blitzkrieg*] — **blitz** *vt*

blitz·krieg \ˈblits-ˌkrēg\ *n* **:** a swift surprise offensive by coordinated air and ground forces [German, literally, "lightning war"] — **blitzkrieg** *vt*

bliz·zard \ˈbliz-ərd\ *n* **1 :** a long severe snowstorm **2 :** an intensely strong cold wind filled with fine snow **3 :** an overwhelming rush or deluge ⟨a *blizzard* of fan mail⟩ [origin unknown]

[1]bloat \ˈblōt\ *vb* **:** to swell by or as if by filling with water or air **:** puff up [Middle English *blout* "bloated"]

[2]bloat *n* **:** a disorder of cattle marked by abdominal bloating

bloat·er \ˈblōt-ər\ *n* **:** a large fat herring or mackerel lightly salted and briefly smoked [obsolete *bloat* "to cure"]

blob \ˈbläb\ *n* **:** a small lump or drop of something thick ⟨a *blob* of paste⟩ [Middle English]

bloc \ˈbläk\ *n* **1 :** a group of legislators who act together on some issues regardless of party lines ⟨the farm *bloc* in Congress⟩ **2 :** a combination of persons, groups, or nations united by treaty, agreement, or common interest ⟨the Soviet *bloc*⟩ [French, literally, "block"]

[1]block \ˈbläk\ *n* **1 a :** a solid piece of material (as stone or wood) usually with one or more flat sides ⟨building *blocks*⟩; *also* **:** a hollow rectangular building unit **b :** a piece of wood on which condemned persons are beheaded **c :** a stand for something to be sold at auction **d :** a mold or form on which something is shaped ⟨a hat *block*⟩ **2 a :** OBSTACLE **b :** an obstruction of an opponent's play in sports **c :** interruption of normal function of body or mind ⟨heart *block*⟩ ⟨a mental *block*⟩ **3 :** a wooden or metal case enclosing one or more pulleys **4 :** a quantity, number, or section of things thought of as forming a group or unit ⟨a *block* of seats⟩ **5 a :** a large building divided into separate houses or shops **:** a number of houses or shops joined ⟨an apartment *block*⟩ **b :** a space enclosed by streets **c :** the length of one of the sides of such a block ⟨three *blocks* south⟩ **6 :** a section of railroad track controlled by block signals **7 :** a piece of material having a hand-cut design on its surface from which impressions are to be printed [Middle French *bloc,* from Dutch *blok*]

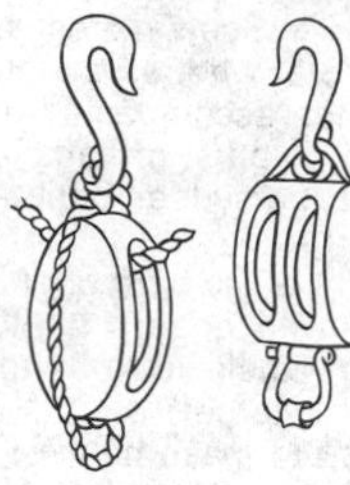

[1]block 3

[2]block *vt* **1 a :** to stop up or close off **:** OBSTRUCT **b :** to hinder the progress or advance of; *esp* **:** to interfere with an opponent (as in football) **c :** to prevent normal functioning of ⟨*block* a nerve with an anesthetic⟩ **2 :** to mark the chief lines of ⟨*block* out a sketch⟩ **3 :** to shape on, with, or as if with a block **4 :** to make (lines of writing or type) flush at the left or at both left and right **5 :** to secure, support, or provide with a block — **block·er** *n*

block·ade \blä-ˈkād\ *n* **:** the isolation of an area by means of troops or warships to prevent passage of persons or supplies in or out — **blockade** *vt* — **block·ad·er** *n*

block·ade-run·ner \-ˌrən-ər\ *n* **:** a ship or person that attempts to sail through a blockade — **block·ade-run·ning** \-ˌrən-ing\ *n*

block·age \ˈbläk-ij\ *n* **:** an act or instance of obstructing **:** the state of being blocked ⟨*blockage* of blood flow in an artery⟩

block and tackle *n* **:** pulley blocks with associated rope or cable for hoisting or hauling

block·bust·er \ˈbläk-ˌbəs-tər\ *n* **1 :** a very large high-explosive demolition bomb **2 :** an enormously successful product or entertainment

block·head \ˈbläk-ˌhed\ *n* **:** a stupid person

block·house \-ˌhau̇s\ *n* **1 :** a building of heavy timbers or of concrete built with holes in its sides through which persons inside may fire out at an enemy **2 :** a building serving as an observation point for an operation likely to be accompanied by heat, blast, or radiation hazard

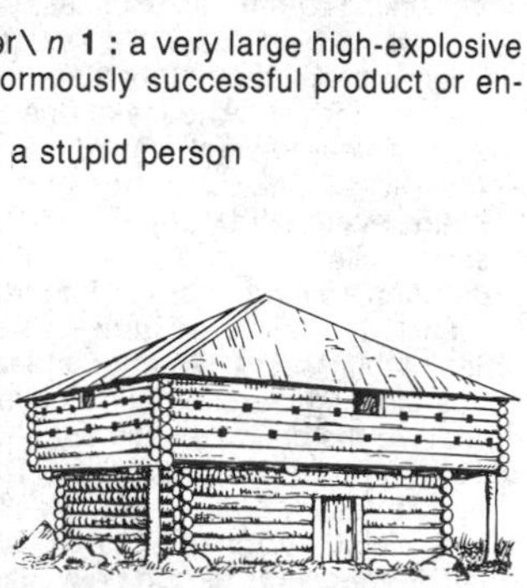

blockhouse 1

block·ish \ˈbläk-ish\ *adj* **:** lacking intelligence **:** STUPID — **block·ish·ly** *adv*

block letter *n* **:** a bold simple capital letter composed of strokes of uniform thickness

block printing *n* **:** printing from carved wooden or linoleum blocks

block signal *n* **:** a fixed signal at the entrance of a section of railroad track to govern trains entering and using it

blocky \ˈbläk-ē\ *adj* **block·i·er; -est :** resembling a block **:** solidly built ⟨a *blocky* physique⟩

bloke \ˈblōk\ *n, chiefly British* **:** MAN 1a [origin unknown]

¹blond *also* **blonde** \'bländ\ *adj* **1 a :** of a pale yellowish brown color ⟨*blond* hair⟩ **b :** of a pale white or rosy white color ⟨*blond* skin⟩ **2 a :** of a light color **b :** of the color blond [French] — **blond•ness** \'bländ-nəs, 'blän-\ *n*

²blond *or* **blonde** *n* **1 :** a blond person **2 :** a light yellowish brown to dark grayish yellow

¹blood \'bləd\ *n* **1 :** the red fluid that circulates in the heart, arteries, capillaries, and veins of a vertebrate animal carrying nourishment and oxygen to and bringing away waste products from all parts of the body; *also* **:** a fluid resembling this **2 a :** LINEAGE 2, DESCENT; *esp* **:** royal lineage ⟨a prince or princess of the *blood*⟩ **b :** relationship by descent from a common ancestor **:** KINSHIP **c :** descent from parents of superior status or breeding **3 :** ANGER [Old English *blōd*]

²blood *vt* **:** to give experience to ⟨troops *blooded* in battle⟩

blood bank *n* **:** a reserve supply of blood or plasma or the place where it is stored

blood•bath \-ˌbath, -ˌbȧth\ *n* **:** a great slaughter **:** MASSACRE

blood brother *n* **1 :** a brother by birth **2 :** one that is bound in ceremonial blood brotherhood

blood brotherhood *n* **:** a solemn friendship established between usually unrelated men by a ceremonial use of each other's blood

blood cell *n* **:** a cell normally present in blood

blood count *n* **:** the determination of the number of blood cells in a definite volume of blood; *also* **:** the number of cells so determined

blood•cur•dling \'bləd-ˌkərd-liŋ\ *adj* **:** arousing fear or horror **:** TERRIFYING, HORRIBLE ⟨*bloodcurdling* screams⟩

blood•ed \'bləd-əd\ *adj* **1 :** entirely or largely of pure blood or stock ⟨*blooded* horses⟩ **2 :** having blood of a specified kind ⟨warm-*blooded*⟩

blood feud *n* **:** a feud between different clans or families

blood fluke *n* **:** a flatworm (as a schistosome) parasitic in blood vessels

blood group *n* **:** one of the classes into which human beings can be separated on the basis of the presence or absence in their blood of specific antigens — called also *blood type* — **blood grouping** *n*

blood•guilt \'bləd-ˌgilt\ *n* **:** guilt resulting from bloodshed — **blood•guilt•i•ness** \-ˌgil-tē-nəs\ *n* — **blood•guilty** \-tē\ *adj*

blood•hound \'bləd-ˌhau̇nd\ *n* **:** a large powerful hound of a breed of European origin with a keen sense of smell

blood•less \'bləd-ləs\ *adj* **1 :** deficient in blood **2 :** not accompanied by loss of blood or by bloodshed ⟨a *bloodless* revolution⟩ **3 :** lacking in spirit or feeling — **blood•less•ly** *adv* — **blood•less•ness** *n*

blood•let•ting \-ˌlet-iŋ\ *n* **1 :** the opening of a vein for removing or releasing blood **2 :** BLOODSHED

blood•line \-ˌlīn\ *n* **:** a sequence of direct ancestors especially in a pedigree; *also* **:** FAMILY

blood•mo•bile \bləd-mō-ˌbēl\ *n* **:** an automobile staffed and equipped for collecting blood from donors [*blood* + *automobile*]

blood money *n* **1 :** money obtained at the cost of another's life **2 :** money paid to the next of kin of a slain person by the slayer or his relatives

blood plasma *n* **:** the fluid part of whole blood — compare BLOOD SERUM

blood platelet *n* **:** one of the minute protoplasmic disks of vertebrate blood that assist in blood clotting

blood poisoning *n* **:** invasion of the bloodstream by virulent microorganisms from a local seat of infection accompanied especially by chills, fever, and prostration — called also *septicemia;* compare SEPSIS

blood pressure *n* **:** pressure of the blood on the walls of blood vessels and especially arteries that varies with physical condition and age

blood•red \'bləd-'red\ *adj* **:** having the color of blood

blood•root \-ˌrüt, -ˌru̇t\ *n* **:** a plant of the poppy family having a red root and sap and bearing a single lobed leaf and white flower in early spring

blood serum *n* **:** blood plasma from which the fibrin has been removed (as by clotting)

blood•shed \'bləd-ˌshed\ *n* **1 :** the shedding of blood **2 :** the taking of life **:** SLAUGHTER

blood•shot \-ˌshät\ *adj* **:** inflamed to redness ⟨*bloodshot* eyes⟩

blood•stain \-ˌstān\ *n* **:** a discoloration caused by blood — **blood•stained** \-ˌstānd\ *adj*

blood•stone \-ˌstōn\ *n* **:** a green quartz speckled with red jasper

blood•stream \-ˌstrēm\ *n* **:** the flowing blood in a circulatory system

blood•suck•er \-ˌsək-ər\ *n* **1 :** an animal that sucks blood; *esp* **:** LEECH **2 :** a person who sponges or preys on another — **blood•suck•ing** \-ˌsək-iŋ\ *adj*

blood sugar *n* **:** the glucose in the blood; *also* **:** its concentration (as in milligrams per 100 milliliters)

blood test *n* **:** a test of the blood; *esp* **:** a serologic test for syphilis

blood•thirsty \'bləd-ˌthər-stē\ *adj* **:** eager for or marked by the shedding of blood — **blood•thirst•i•ly** \-stə-lē\ *adv* — **blood•thirst•i•ness** \-stē-nəs\ *n*

blood type *n* **:** BLOOD GROUP — **blood-type** *vt*

blood vessel *n* **:** a vessel (as an artery, vein, or capillary) in which blood circulates during life

blood•worm \'bləd-ˌwərm\ *n* **:** any of various reddish annelid worms often used as bait

bloody \'bləd-ē\ *adj* **blood•i•er; -est 1 :** smeared or stained with blood ⟨a *bloody* handkerchief⟩; *also* **:** BLEEDING ⟨a *bloody* nose⟩ **2 :** causing or accompanied by bloodshed ⟨a *bloody* battle⟩ **3 :** BLOODTHIRSTY, MURDEROUS ⟨a *bloody* band of pirates⟩ — **blood•i•ly** \'bləd-l-ē\ *adv* — **blood•i•ness** \'bləd-ē-nəs\ *n* — **bloody** *vt*

¹bloom \'blüm\ *n* **1 :** a mass of wrought iron from a forge or puddling furnace **2 :** a bar of iron or steel hammered or rolled from an ingot [Old English *blōma*]

²bloom *n* **1 a :** FLOWER ⟨a large yellow *bloom*⟩ **b :** flowers or amount of flowers ⟨the apple trees had a very light *bloom* this spring⟩ **c :** the flowering state ⟨the roses are in *bloom*⟩ **d :** a period of flowering ⟨the spring *bloom*⟩ **e :** an excessive growth of plankton **2 :** a state or time of beauty, freshness, and vigor **3 :** a surface coating or appearance: as **a :** a delicate powdery coating on some fruits and leaves **b :** a rosy appearance of the cheeks; *also* **:** an outward evidence of freshness or healthy vigor **4 :** the bouquet of a wine [Old Norse *blōm*] — **bloomy** \'blü-mē\ *adj*

³bloom *vi* **1 :** to produce or yield flowers **2 a :** to be in a state of youthful beauty or freshness **:** FLOURISH **b :** SHINE, GLOW **3 :** to appear unexpectedly in large quantities — **bloom•er** *n*

bloo•mers \'blü-mərz\ *n pl* **:** full loose trousers gathered at the knee formerly worn by women (as for athletics); *also* **:** underpants of similar design worn chiefly by girls [Amelia *Bloomer,* died 1894, American pioneer in feminism]

bloop•er \'blü-pər\ *n* **:** an embarrassing blunder made in public [*bloop* "an unpleasing sound"]

¹blos•som \'bläs-əm\ *n* **1 a :** the flower of a seed plant ⟨apple *blossoms*⟩ **b :** the state of flowering ⟨apple trees in *blossom*⟩ **2 :** a peak period of stage of development suggesting the unfolding of a flower [Old English *blōstm*] — **blos•somy** \-ə-mē\ *adj*

²blossom *vi* **1 :** BLOOM 1 **2 :** to unfold like a blossom: as **a :** to flourish and prosper markedly **b :** DEVELOP 5a, EXPAND **c :** to come into being

¹blot \'blät\ *n* **1 :** SPOT, STAIN **2 :** a flaw in morals or reputation [Middle English]

²blot *vb* **blot•ted; blot•ting 1 :** to spot, stain, or spatter with a discoloring substance **2 :** to make obscure **:** DIM **3 :** to bring shame to **:** DISGRACE **4 :** to dry or remove with or as if with blotting paper **5 :** to become marked with a blot

blotch \'bläch\ *n* **1 :** FLAW, BLEMISH **2 :** a spot or mark (as of color or ink) especially when large or irregular [probably alteration of *botch*] — **blotch** *vt* — **blotched** \'blächt\ *adj* — **blotchy** \'bläch-ē\ *adj*

blot out *vt* **1 a :** to make unimportant or trivial **b :** to make obscure ⟨clouds *blotted out* the sun⟩ **2 :** DESTROY 1, KILL

blot•ter \'blät-ər\ *n* **1 :** a piece of blotting paper **2 :** a book in which entries are made temporarily ⟨a police *blotter*⟩

blotting paper *n* **:** a soft spongy paper used to absorb wet ink

blouse \'blau̇s *also* 'blau̇z\ *n, pl* **blous•es** \'blau̇-səz, -zəz\ **1**

: a loose overgarment like a shirt or smock varying from hip-length to calf-length **2 :** the upper outer garment of a uniform **3 :** a usually loose-fitting garment covering the body from the neck to the waist **[**French**]**

¹blow \'blō\ *vb* **blew** \'blü\; **blown** \'blōn\; **blow•ing 1 :** to move or become moved especially with speed or with power ⟨wind *blowing* from the north⟩ **2 :** to send forth a strong current of air ⟨*blow* on one's hands⟩ **3 :** to drive or become driven by a current of air ⟨a tree *blown* down in a storm⟩ **4 :** to make a sound or cause to sound by blowing ⟨*blow* a horn⟩ ⟨*blew* a tune⟩ **5 :** to breathe hard or rapidly **:** PANT **6 a :** to melt when overloaded ⟨the fuse *blew*⟩ **b :** to cause (a fuse) to blow **7 a :** to release suddenly the contained air through a rupture ⟨the tire *blew* out⟩ **b :** to rupture by too much pressure ⟨*blew a gasket*⟩ **8 :** to clear of contents by forcing air through **9 :** to produce or shape by the action of blown or injected air ⟨*blow* glass⟩ **10 :** to shatter or destroy by explosion **11 a :** to put out of breath with exertion **b :** to let (as a horse) pause to catch the breath **12 :** to spend recklessly ⟨*blew* all my money⟩ **[**Old English *blāwan***]**

²blow *n* **1 :** a blowing of wind especially when violent **:** GALE **2 :** a forcing of air from the mouth or nose or through some instrument

³blow *vi* **blew** \'blü\; **blown** \'blōn\; **blow•ing :** FLOWER 1, BLOOM **[**Old English *blōwan***]**

⁴blow *n* **1 :** a display of flowers **2 :** ²BLOOM 1c ⟨lilacs in full *blow*⟩

⁵blow *n* **1 :** a forcible stroke delivered with a part of the body or with an instrument **2 :** a hostile act **:** COMBAT ⟨come to *blows*⟩ **3 :** a forcible or sudden act or effort **:** ASSAULT **4 :** a severe and sudden calamity ⟨a heavy *blow* to the nation⟩ **[**Middle English *blaw***]**

• syn STROKE: BLOW implies violence or force; STROKE suggests suddenness or definiteness or precision.

blow–by–blow \-bī-, -bə-\ *adj* **:** minutely detailed ⟨a *blow-by-blow* account⟩

blow•er \'blō-ər, 'blōr\ *n* **1 :** one that blows **2 :** a device for producing a current of air or gas

blow•fly \'blō-ˌflī\ *n* **:** any of various two-winged flies (as a bluebottle) that deposit their eggs or maggots on meat or in wounds

blow•gun \-ˌgən\ *n* **:** a tube from which an arrow or a dart may be shot by the force of the breath

blow•hard \-ˌhärd\ *n* **:** BRAGGART

blow•hole \-ˌhōl\ *n* **1 :** a nostril in the top of the head of a whale or related animal **2 :** a hole in the ice to which aquatic mammals (as seals) come to breathe

blown \'blōn\ *adj* **1 :** SWOLLEN; *esp* **:** afflicted with bloat **2 :** FLYBLOWN 1 **3 :** being out of breath

blow•out \'blō-ˌau̇t\ *n* **1 :** a big social affair **2 :** a bursting of a container (as a tire) by pressure of the contents on a weak spot; *also* **:** a hole made in a container by such bursting

blow out \blō-'au̇t, 'blō-\ *vb* **1 :** to extinguish or become extinguished by a gust **2 :** to dissipate (itself) by blowing — used of a storm

blow•pipe \'blō-ˌpīp\ *n* **1 :** a small round tube for blowing a jet of gas (as air) into a flame so as to concentrate and increase the heat **2 :** BLOWGUN

blow•sy *also* **blow•zy** \'blau̇-zē\ *adj* **:** DISHEVELED, SLOVENLY; *also* **:** COARSE 3 **[**English dialect *blowse* "wench"**]**

blow•torch \'blō-ˌtȯrch\ *n* **:** a small portable burner that intensifies combustion by means of a blast of air or oxygen and that usually includes a fuel tank pressurized by a hand pump

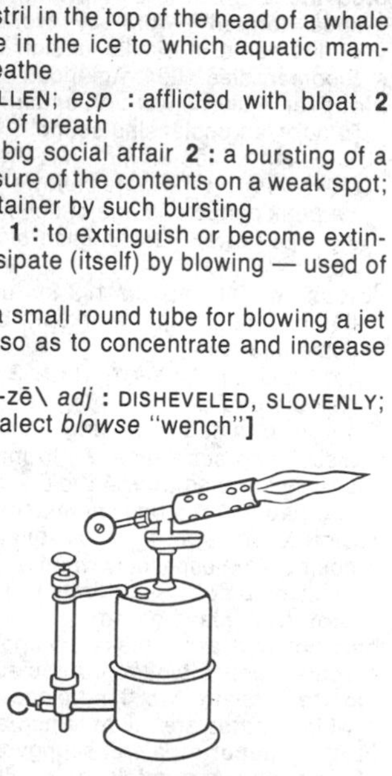
blowtorch

blow•up \'blō-ˌəp\ *n* **1 :** EXPLOSION **2 :** an outburst of temper **3 :** a photographic enlargement

blow up *vb* **1 a :** to destroy or become destroyed by explosion **b :** to become violently angry **2 :** to build up, expand, or become expanded to unreasonable proportions **3 :** to fill up with a gas ⟨*blow up* a balloon⟩ **4 :** to make a photographic enlargement of

blowy \'blō-ē\ *adj* **blow•i•er; -est :** WINDY 1

¹blub•ber \'bləb-ər\ *n* **1 a :** the fat of large sea mammals (as whales) **b :** excessive fat on the body **2 :** the action of blubbering **[**Middle English *bluber* "bubble, foam"**]**

²blubber *vb* **blub•bered; blub•ber•ing** \'bləb-ring, -ə-ring\ **1 :** to weep noisily **2 :** to utter while weeping **[**Middle English *blubren* "to make a bubbling sound", from *bluber***]**

³blub•ber \-ər\ *or* **blub•bery** \'bləb-rē, -ə-rē\ *adj* **:** puffed out **:** THICK ⟨*blubber* lips⟩

bludg•eon \'bləj-ən\ *n* **:** a short club with one end thicker and heavier than the other **[**origin unknown**]** — **bludgeon** *vt*

¹blue \'blü\ *adj* **1 :** of the color blue **2 a :** BLUISH **b :** LIVID 1, 2 **c :** bluish gray **3 a :** low in spirits **:** MELANCHOLY **b :** tending to lower the spirits **4 :** PURITANICAL **[**Old French *blou,* of Germanic origin**]** — **blue•ly** *adv* — **blue•ness** *n*

²blue *n* **1 :** the color of the clear daytime sky **:** a color lying between green and violet in the spectrum **2 :** blue clothing or cloth **3 a :** SKY 1 **b :** the far distance **c :** SEA 1a — **out of the blue :** UNEXPECTEDLY

³blue *vt* **blued; blue•ing** *or* **blu•ing 1 :** to make blue **2 :** to add bluing to so as to make white ⟨*blue* the sheets⟩

blue baby *n* **:** an infant with a bluish tint because of insufficient oxygenation of the blood due to a congenital defect of the heart

blue•beard \'blü-ˌbiərd\ *n* **:** a man who marries and kills one woman after another **[***Bluebeard,* a fairy-tale character**]**

blue•bell \-ˌbel\ *n* **:** any of various plants (as a grape hyacinth) with blue bell-shaped flowers; *esp* **:** HAREBELL

blue•ber•ry \'blü-ˌber-ē, -bə-rē, -brē\ *n* **:** the edible blue or blackish small-seeded berry of any of several plants of the heath family; *also* **:** a low or tall shrub producing these berries — compare HUCKLEBERRY

blue•bird \-ˌbərd\ *n* **:** any of several small North American songbirds related to the robin but with blue above especially in the male

blue blood *n* **1** \'blü-'bləd\ **:** aristocracy by birth **2** \-ˌbləd\ **:** a member of a noble or socially prominent family — **blue–blood•ed** \-'bləd-əd\ *adj*

blue•bon•net \'blü-ˌbän-ət\ *n* **:** a low-growing annual lupine of Texas with silky foliage and blue flowers

blue•bot•tle \-ˌbät-l\ *n* **:** any of several blowflies with the abdomen or the whole body iridescent blue in color

blue cheese *n* **:** cheese ripened by and marked with greenish blue mold

blue chip *n* **:** a stock issue that commands a high price because of public faith in its worth and stability **[**from the high value of blue chips in games of chance**]**

blue–col•lar \'blü-'käl-ər\ *adj* **:** of, relating to, or constituting the wage-earning class

blue crab *n* **:** a largely blue edible crab of the Atlantic and Gulf coasts

blue•fin \'blü-ˌfin\ *n* **:** a very large tuna with short pectoral fins that is dark blue above and lighter colored below

blue•fish \-ˌfish\ *n* **:** an active saltwater food and sport fish that is related to the pompanos and is bluish above and silvery below; *also* **:** any of several bluish food fishes

blue flag *n* **:** a blue-flowered iris; *esp* **:** a common iris of the eastern United States with a root formerly used medicinally

blue•gill \'blü-ˌgil\ *n* **:** a common food and sport sunfish of the eastern and central United States

blue•grass \-ˌgras\ *n* **1 :** a widely used pasture and lawn grass with bluish green stems **2 :** country music played on unamplified stringed instruments (as banjos, fiddles, guitars, and mandolins) **[**sense 2 from the *Blue Grass Boys,* performing group, from *Bluegrass state,* nickname of Kentucky**]**

blue–green alga \ˌblü-ˌgrēn-\ *n* **:** any of a major group (Cyanophyta) of algae having the chlorophyll masked by bluish green pigments

blue jay \-ˌjā\ *n* **:** any of several largely blue and usually crested American jays

blue jeans *n pl* **:** pants usually made of blue denim

blue law *n* **1 :** one of many strict laws regulating morals and conduct in colonial New England **2 :** a statute limiting work, commerce, and amusements on Sundays or holidays

blue line *n* **:** either of two wide blue lines that cross an ice hockey rink and divide it approximately into thirds

blue mold *n* **:** a fungus and especially a penicillium that produces blue or blue-green surface growths

blue moon *n* **:** a very long period of time ⟨once in a *blue moon*⟩

blue•nose \'blü-ˌnōz\ *n* **:** one who advocates a strict moral code

blue plate \-ˌplāt\ *n* **:** a main course (as of meat and vegetables) served as a single menu item
blue•point \-ˌpȯint\ *n* **:** a small oyster typically from the south shore of Long Island [*Blue Point,* Long Island]
[1]**blue•print** \-ˌprint\ *n* **1 :** a photographic print in white on a blue ground used especially for copying mechanical drawings and architects' plans **2 :** a detailed plan or program of action
[2]**blueprint** *vt* **:** to make a blueprint of or for
blue racer *n* **:** a blacksnake of a bluish green subspecies occurring from Ohio to Texas
blue ribbon *n* **1 :** a blue ribbon awarded the first-place winner in a competition **2 :** an honor or award gained for outstanding performance
blues \'blüz\ *n pl* **1 :** low spirits **:** MELANCHOLY **2 :** a song expressing melancholy and composed in a style originating among the American Negroes **3 :** a blue uniform
blue–sky law \'blü-'skī-\ *n* **:** a law providing for the regulation of the sale of securities [*blue-sky stock* "worthless stock"; from the emptiness of the sky]
blue spruce *n* **:** COLORADO BLUE SPRUCE
blue•stem \'blü-ˌstem\ *n* **:** either of two important hay and forage grasses of the western United States with smooth bluish leaf sheaths
blue•stock•ing \-ˌstäk-ing\ *n* **:** a woman having intellectual or literary interests [*Bluestocking* society, 18th century literary clubs]
blue streak *n* **1 :** something that moves very fast **2 :** a constant stream of words ⟨talked a *blue streak*⟩
blu•et \'blü-ət\ *n* **:** a small American herb with solitary bluish flowers and stems arranged in tufts
blue vitriol *n* **:** a hydrated copper sulfate $CuSO_4 \cdot 5H_2O$
blue whale *n* **:** a whale that may reach a weight of 90 metric tons and a length of 30 meters and is generally considered the largest living animal

blue whale

[1]**bluff** \'bləf\ *adj* **1 :** rising steeply with a broad front (as from a plain or shore) ⟨a *bluff* coastline⟩ **2 :** blunt and outspoken in a good-natured manner [Dutch *blaf* "flat"] — **bluff•ly** *adv* — **bluff•ness** *n*
[2]**bluff** *n* **:** a high steep bank **:** CLIFF
[3]**bluff** *vb* **:** to deceive or frighten by pretending to have strength or confidence that one does not really have [probably from Dutch *bluffen* "to boast"] — **bluff•er** *n*
[4]**bluff** *n* **1 a :** an act or instance of bluffing **b :** the practice of bluffing **2 :** one who bluffs
blu•ing *or* **blue•ing** \'blü-ing\ *n* **:** a preparation of blue or violet dyes used in washing clothes to prevent yellowing of white fabrics
blu•ish *or* **blue•ish** \'blü-ish\ *adj* **:** somewhat blue
[1]**blun•der** \'blən-dər\ *vb* **blun•dered; blun•der•ing** \-də-ring, -dring\ **1 :** to move unsteadily or blindly **:** STUMBLE **2 :** to make a mistake (as through stupidity or carelessness) **3 :** to say stupidly or thoughtlessly **:** BLURT [Middle English *blundren*] — **blun•der•er** \-dər-ər\ *n*
[2]**blunder** *n* **:** a mistake resulting especially from stupidity or carelessness **syn** see ERROR
blun•der•buss \'blən-dər-ˌbəs\ *n* **1 :** a short firearm usually with a flaring muzzle that was formerly used for firing at close range without taking precise aim **2 :** a blundering person [obsolete Dutch *donderbus,* literally, "thunder gun"]

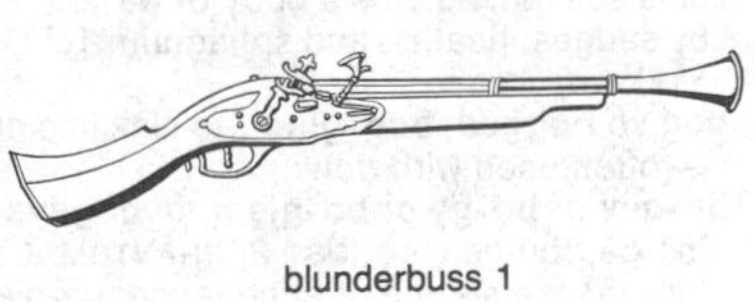
blunderbuss 1

[1]**blunt** \'blənt\ *adj* **1 a :** lacking in feeling **:** INSENSITIVE **b :** slow in understanding or in making distinctions **:** DULL **2 :** having an edge or point that is not sharp **3 :** abrupt in speech or manner [Middle English] — **blunt•ly** *adv* — **blunt•ness** *n*
• **syn** DULL, OBTUSE: BLUNT suggests an innate or inherent lack of sharpness or quickness of feeling or perception ⟨a *blunt* refusal⟩ DULL suggests lack or loss of keenness, zest, or pungency ⟨a *dull* report⟩ OBTUSE implies bluntness or insensitivity in perception or imagination ⟨an *obtuse* audience⟩
[2]**blunt** *vb* **:** to make or become blunt
[1]**blur** \'blər\ *n* **1 :** a smear or stain that dims but does not completely cover **2 :** something vague or lacking definite outline ⟨saw only a *blur* of words through the tears⟩ [perhaps related to *blear*] — **blur•ry** \-ē\ *adj*
[2]**blur** *vb* **blurred; blur•ring 1 :** to make indistinct by or as if by smearing ⟨damp fingers *blurred* the manuscript⟩ **2 :** to make (as the senses) dim or confused **3 :** to become vague, indistinct, or indefinite
blurb \'blərb\ *n* **:** a brief notice (as in advertising) praising a product extravagantly [coined by Gelett Burgess, died 1951, American humorist]
blurt \'blərt\ *vt* **:** to utter suddenly and thoughtlessly ⟨*blurt* out a secret⟩ [probably imitative]
[1]**blush** \'bləsh\ *vi* **1 :** to become red in the face especially from shame, modesty, or confusion **2 :** to feel shame or embarrassment **3 :** to have a rosy or fresh color **:** BLOOM [Old English *blyscan* "to redden", from *blysa* "flame"] — **blush•er** *n*
[2]**blush** *n* **1 :** outward appearance **:** VIEW ⟨at first *blush*⟩ **2 :** a reddening of the face especially from shame, modesty, or confusion **3 :** a red or rosy tint — **blush•ful** \-fəl\ *adj*
[1]**blus•ter** \'bləs-tər\ *vi* **blus•tered; blus•ter•ing** \-tə-ring, -tring\ **1 :** to blow violently and noisily **2 :** to talk or act in a noisy boastful way [Middle English *blustren*] — **blus•ter•er** \-tər-ər\ *n*
[2]**bluster** *n* **1 :** a violent noisy blowing **2 :** noisy boisterous activity **3 :** loudly boastful or threatening speech — **blus•tery** \-tə-rē, -trē\ *adj*
boa \'bō-ə\ *n* **1 :** a large snake (as the boa constrictor or python) that crushes its prey **2 :** a long fluffy scarf of fur, feathers, or delicate fabric [Latin, a kind of water snake]
boa con•stric•tor \-kən-'strik-tər\ *n* **:** a mottled brown tropical American boa
boar \'bōr, 'bȯr\ *n* **1 :** a male swine; *also* **:** the male of any of several mammals **2 :** WILD BOAR [Old English *bār*] — **boar•ish** \-ish\ *adj*
[1]**board** \'bōrd, 'bȯrd\ *n* **1 :** the side of a ship — often used in combination ⟨star*board*⟩ ⟨over*board*⟩ **2 a :** a thin flat relatively long piece of lumber **b** *pl* **:** STAGE 2a ⟨trod the *boards* for 40 years⟩ **3 a :** a dining table **b :** regular meals especially when furnished for pay ⟨room and *board*⟩ **c :** a group of persons who manage, direct, or investigate ⟨*board* of directors⟩ ⟨school *board*⟩ ⟨*board* of examiners⟩ **4 a :** a flat usually rectangular piece of material designed for a special purpose ⟨cutting *board*⟩: as (1) **:** a flat surface specially marked for the positioning and advancing of men or markers in certain games (2) **:** BACKBOARD (3) **:** SURFBOARD **b :** a surface, frame, or device for posting notices or listing market quotations **5 a :** a flat rectangular sheet formed of wood pulp or composition materials **:** PAPERBOARD **b :** a piece of stiff cardboard for the side of a book cover [Old English *bord*] — **by the board 1 :** over the side of a ship **2 :** into a state of discard, neglect, or ruin ⟨all our plans went *by the board*⟩ — **on board :** ABOARD
[2]**board** *vb* **1 :** to go aboard **:** get on ⟨*boarded* the plane in New York⟩ **2 :** to cover with boards ⟨*boarded* up a window⟩ **3 :** to provide or be provided with regular meals and often lodging usually for pay
board•er \'bōrd-ər, 'bȯrd-\ *n* **:** one that boards; *esp* **:** one who receives regular meals and sometimes lodging at another's house for pay
board foot *n* **:** a unit of quantity for lumber equal to the volume of a board 12 × 12 × 1 inches (about 30.5 × 30.5 × 2.5 centimeters)
board game *n* **:** a game of strategy (as chess, checkers, or backgammon) played by moving pieces on a board
board•ing•house \'bōrd-ing-ˌhau̇s, 'bȯrd-\ *n* **:** a house at which persons are boarded

boarding school *n* : a school in which pupils are boarded and lodged as well as taught

board measure *n* : measurement in board feet

board of trade : an organization of business people to promote and protect business interests — compare CHAMBER OF COMMERCE

board•walk \ˈbōrd-ˌwȯk, ˈbȯrd-\ *n* **1** : a walk constructed of planking **2** : a walk constructed along a beach

¹**boast** \ˈbōst\ *n* **1** : the act of boasting : BRAG **2** : a cause for pride [Middle English *boost*] — **boast•ful** \ˈbōst-fəl\ *adj* — **boast•ful•ly** \-fə-lē\ *adv* — **boast•ful•ness** *n*

²**boast** *vb* **1** : to praise oneself ⟨*boasting* of your ability⟩ **2** : to tell with extreme pride : BRAG ⟨*boasting* about their money⟩ **3** : to possess or display proudly ⟨our band *boasted* new uniforms⟩ — **boast•er** *n*

¹**boat** \ˈbōt\ *n* **1** : a small vessel propelled by oars or paddles or by sail or power **2** : SHIP **3** : a boat-shaped utensil or device ⟨gravy *boat*⟩ [Old English *bāt*] — **in the same boat** : in the same situation

²**boat** *vb* **1** : to place in or bring into a boat ⟨*boated* a large halibut⟩ **2** : to travel by boat — **boat•er** *n*

boat hook *n* : a hook with a point on the back fixed to a pole and used especially to pull or push a boat into place

boat•house \ˈbōt-ˌhau̇s\ *n* : a building to house and protect boats

boat•load \-ˌlōd\ *n* : a boat's full load or a quantity equal to such a load ⟨a *boatload* of passengers⟩

boat•man \ˈbōt-mən\ *n* : a person who manages, works on, or deals in boats — **boat•man•ship** \-ˌship\ *n*

boat•swain *also* **bo•s'n** *or* **bo•sun** \ˈbōs-n\ *n* : a warrant officer on a warship or a petty officer on a merchant ship in charge of the hull and all related equipment [Middle English *boot* "boat" + *swein* "boy, servant"]

¹**bob** \ˈbäb\ *vb* **bobbed**; **bob•bing 1 a** : to move or cause to move up and down in a short quick movement ⟨a cork *bobbing* in the water⟩ **b** : to emerge or appear suddenly or unexpectedly ⟨this question *bobs* up often⟩ **2** : to grasp or make a grab with the teeth ⟨*bob* for apples⟩ [Middle English *boben*]

²**bob** *n* : a short jerky motion ⟨a *bob* of the head⟩

³**bob** *n* **1** : a woman's or child's short haircut **2** : a ball or weight hanging from a rod or line **3** : a device (as a cork) for buoying up the baited end of a fishing line [Middle English *bobbe* "bunch, cluster"]

⁴**bob** *vt* **bobbed**; **bob•bing 1** : to cut shorter : CROP **2** : to cut (hair) in the style of a bob

⁵**bob** *n, pl* **bob** *British* : SHILLING [perhaps from the name *Bob*]

⁶**bob** *n* : BOBSLED

bob•ber \ˈbäb-ər\ *n* : one that bobs

bob•bin \ˈbäb-ən\ *n* **1** : a cylinder or spindle on which yarn or thread is wound (as in a sewing machine) **2** : a coil of insulated wire or the reel it is wound on [origin unknown]

bob•ble \ˈbäb-əl\ *vb* **bob•bled**; **bob•bling** \ˈbäb-ling, -ə-ling\ **1** : ¹BOB 1a **2** : FUMBLE 2 [from ¹*bob*] — **bobble** *n*

bob•by \ˈbäb-ē\ *n, pl* **bobbies** *British* : POLICEMAN [*Bobby*, nickname for *Robert*, from Sir *Robert* Peel, died 1850, organizer of the London police force]

bob•by pin \ˈbäb-ē-\ *n* : a flat wire hairpin with prongs that press close together [³*bob*]

bobby socks *or* **bobby sox** *n pl* : girls' socks reaching above the ankle [from the name *Bobby*]

bob•by–sox•er \ˈbäb-ē-ˌsäk-sər\ *or* **bob•by–sock•er** \-ˌsäk-ər\ *n* : an adolescent girl

bob•cat \ˈbäb-ˌkat\ *n* : a common usually rusty-colored North American lynx [³*bob*; from the stubby tail]

bob•o•link \ˈbäb-ə-ˌlingk\ *n* : an American migratory songbird related to the blackbirds [imitative]

bob•sled \ˈbäb-ˌsled\ *n* **1** : a short sled usually used as one of a joined pair **2** : a racing sled with two sets of runners in tandem, a seat for two or four riders, a steering device, and a brake — **bobsled** *vi* — **bob•sled•der** *n*

bob•stay \ˈbäb-ˌstā\ *n* : a stay used to hold a ship's bowsprit down

bob•tail \ˈbäb-ˌtāl\ *n* **1 a** : a bobbed tail **b** : a horse or dog with a bobbed tail **2** : something shortened or abbreviated — **bobtail** \-ˌtāl\ *or* **bob•tailed** \-ˌtāld\ *adj*

bob•white \bäb-ˈhwīt, ˈbäb-, -ˈwīt\ *n* : any of several American quails; *esp* : a gray, white, and reddish game bird of the eastern and central United States — called also *partridge* [imitative]

boc•cie *or* **boc•ci** *or* **boc•ce** \ˈbäch-ē\ *n* : a game similar to lawn bowling played on a long narrow usually dirt court [Italian *bocce* "balls"]

bock \ˈbäk\ *n* : a heavy dark rich beer usually sold in the early spring [German]

¹**bode** \ˈbōd\ *vb* **1** : to indicate by signs **2** : to give promise of something : PRESAGE [Old English *bodian*] — **bode•ment** \-mənt\ *n*

bobwhite

²**bode** *past of* BIDE

bod•ice \ˈbäd-əs\ *n* : the part of a woman's dress that covers the body from neck to waist

△ **origin** *Bodice* is derived from *body*. One sense of the word *body* is "the part of a garment covering the body or trunk". In the 17th and 18th centuries a woman's corset was often called a "pair of bodies". The plural *bodies*, or *bodice*, was eventually interpreted as a singular. *Bodice* is now most often used to refer to the upper part of a woman's dress.

bod•ied \ˈbäd-ēd\ *adj* : having a body or such a body ⟨long=*bodied*⟩

bod•i•less \ˈbäd-i-ləs, ˈbäd-l-əs\ *adj* : having no body or substance ⟨*bodiless* ghosts⟩ ⟨a *bodiless* rumor⟩

¹**bod•i•ly** \ˈbäd-l-ē\ *adj* **1** : having a body **2** : of or relating to the body ⟨*bodily* organs⟩ ⟨*bodily* comfort⟩

²**bodily** *adv* **1** : in the flesh **2** : as a whole : ALTOGETHER

bod•ing \ˈbōd-ing\ *n* : FOREBODING

bod•kin \ˈbäd-kən\ *n* **1 a** : DAGGER 1 **b** : a sharp slender instrument for making holes in cloth **2** : a blunt needle with a large eye for drawing tape or ribbon through a loop or hem [Middle English]

body \ˈbäd-ē\ *n, pl* **bod•ies 1 a** : the physical whole of a living or dead organism **b** : the trunk or main part of a plant or animal body as distinguished from the head, appendages, or branches **c** : HUMAN BEING, PERSON **2** : the main or central part: as **a** : the box of a vehicle on or in which the load is placed **b** : the main part of a document **3** : the part of a garment covering the body or trunk **4** : a mass or portion of matter distinct from other masses ⟨a *body* of water⟩ ⟨a *body* of cold air⟩ **5 a** : a group of individuals united for some purpose ⟨a legislative *body*⟩ **b** : a unit formed of a number of persons or things : a collective whole ⟨a *body* of laws⟩ **6 a** : VISCOSITY ⟨paint with a good *body*⟩ **b** : richness of flavor (as of wine) [Old English *bodig*]

body cavity *n* : a cavity within an animal body; *esp* : COELOM

body English *n* : the instinctive attempt of a person to influence the movement of a propelled object (as a ball) by moving the body in the desired direction

body•guard \ˈbäd-ē-ˌgärd\ *n* : a person or group of persons whose duty it is to protect someone

body louse *n* : a sucking louse that lives in the clothing and feeds on the human body

body politic *n* : a group of persons politically organized under a single government

body snatcher *n* : one that steals corpses from graves usually for dissection

body•surf \ˈbäd-ē-ˌsərf\ *vi* : to ride a wave on the chest and stomach without a surfboard — **body•surf•er** *n*

Boer \ˈbōr, ˈbȯr, ˈbu̇r\ *n* : a South African of Dutch or Huguenot descent [Dutch, literally, "farmer"]

¹**bog** \ˈbäg, ˈbȯg\ *n* : wet spongy ground; *esp* : poorly drained acid soil that adjoins a body of water and is usually grown over by sedges, heaths, and sphagnum [of Celtic origin] — **bog•gy** \-ē\ *adj*

²**bog** *vb* **bogged**; **bog•ging** : to sink into or as if into a bog : MIRE — often used with *down*

¹**bo•gey** *or* **bo•gy** *or* **bo•gie** *n, pl* **bogeys** *or* **bogies 1** \ˈbu̇g-ē, ˈbō-gē, ˈbü-gē\ : GHOST 2, PHANTOM **2** \ˈbō-gē *also* ˈbu̇g-ē *or* ˈbü-gē\ : a source of annoyance, perplexity, or harassment **3** \ˈbō-gē\ : one golf stroke over par on a hole [probably from English dialect *bogle* "terrifying apparition"]

²**bo•gey** \ˈbō-gē\ *vt* **bo•geyed**; **bo•gey•ing** : to shoot (a hole in golf) in one over par

bo•gey•man \ˈbu̇g-ē-ˌman, ˈbō-gē-, ˈbü-gē-, ˈbu̇g-ər-\ *n* : a terrifying person or thing : MENACE; *esp* : a monstrous imaginary figure used especially in threatening children

bog•gle \'bäg-əl\ *vb* **bog•gled**; **bog•gling** \'bäg-liŋ, -ə-liŋ\ **1 :** to start with fright or amazement **2 :** to hesitate because of doubt, fear, or scruples **3 :** to overwhelm with wonder or confusion [perhaps from English dialect *bogle* "terrifying apparition"] — **boggle** *n*

bo•gie *also* **bo•gey** *or* **bo•gy** \'bō-gē\ *n, pl* **bogies** *also* **bogeys 1 :** a low strong cart **2 :** the driving-wheel assembly of a 6-wheel automotive truck consisting of the rear four wheels [origin unknown]

bo•gus \'bō-gəs\ *adj* **:** not genuine **:** SPURIOUS, SHAM [*bogus*, a machine for making counterfeit money]

bo•he•mia \bō-'hē-mē-ə\ *n, often cap* **:** a community of bohemians **:** the world of bohemians

Bo•he•mi•an \bō-'hē-mē-ən\ *n* **1 a :** a native or inhabitant of Bohemia **b :** the group of Czech dialects used in Bohemia **2** *often not cap* **a :** one who wanders from place to place; *esp* **:** GYPSY **b :** a writer or artist living an unconventional life — **bohemian** *adj, often cap* — **bo•he•mi•an•ism** \-mē-ə-ˌniz-əm\ *n, often cap*

[1]**boil** \'bȯil\ *n* **:** a painful swollen inflamed area in the skin resulting from infection and usually ending with the discharge of pus and a hardened core — compare CARBUNCLE [Old English *bȳl*]

[2]**boil** *vb* **1 a :** to produce bubbles of vapor when heated ⟨the water is *boiling*⟩ **b :** to come or bring to the boiling point **2 :** to become agitated like boiling water **:** SEETHE ⟨*boiling* flood waters⟩ **3 :** to be excited or stirred up ⟨*boiling* with anger⟩ **4 :** to subject to the action of a boiling liquid ⟨*boil* eggs⟩ [Old French *boillir*, derived from Latin *bulla* "bubble"]

[3]**boil** *n* **:** the act or state of boiling

boil•er \'bȯi-lər\ *n* **1 :** a container in which something is boiled **2 :** a tank holding hot water **3 :** a strong metal container used in making steam for heating buildings or for driving engines

boil•er•mak•er \-ˌmā-kər\ *n* **:** a workman who makes, assembles, or repairs boilers

boiling point *n* **:** the temperature at which a liquid boils

bois•ter•ous \'bȯi-stə-rəs, -strəs\ *adj* **1 a :** noisily rough **:** ROWDY ⟨a *boisterous* crowd⟩ **b :** marked by exuberance and high spirits ⟨*boisterous* laughter⟩ **2 :** vigorously active **:** VIOLENT ⟨*boisterous* winds⟩ — [Middle English *boistous* "rough"] — **bois•ter•ous•ly** *adv* — **bois•ter•ous•ness** *n*

bo•la \'bō-lə\ *or* **bo•las** \-ləs\ *n, pl* **bo•las** \-ləz\ **:** a weapon consisting of two or more stone or iron balls attached to the ends of a cord for hurling at and entangling an animal [American Spanish *bolas*, from Spanish *bola* "ball"]

bold \'bōld\ *adj* **1 a :** fearless in meeting danger **:** INTREPID **b :** showing a courageous daring spirit ⟨a *bold* plan⟩ **2 :** IMPUDENT, PRESUMPTUOUS **3 :** very steep **:** SHEER ⟨*bold* cliffs⟩ **4 :** standing out prominently **:** CONSPICUOUS ⟨a dress with *bold* stripes⟩ [Old English *beald*] — **bold•ly** *adv* — **bold•ness** \'bōld-nəs, 'bōl-\ *n*

bold•face \'bōld-ˌfās, 'bōl-\ *n* **:** a typeface having thick dark lines

bold–faced \-'fāst\ *adj* **1 :** bold in manner or conduct **:** FORWARD **2 :** set in boldface

bole \'bōl\ *n* **:** the trunk of a tree [Old Norse *bolr*]

bo•le•ro \bə-'leər-ō\ *n, pl* **-ros 1 :** a Spanish dance in 3/4 time; *also* **:** the music for it **2 :** a loose waist-length jacket open at the front [Spanish]

bo•li•var \bə-'lē-ˌvär, 'bäl-ə-vər\ *n, pl* **bo•li•vars** *or* **bo•li•va•res** \ˌbäl-ə-'vär-ˌās, ˌbō-li-\ **1 :** the basic monetary unit of Venezuela **2 :** a coin representing one bolivar [Simón *Bolívar*]

bo•li•vi•a•no \bə-ˌliv-ē-'än-ō\ *n, pl* **-nos 1 :** a former monetary unit of Bolivia **2 :** a coin or note representing one boliviano [Spanish]

boll \'bōl\ *n* **:** a seedpod or capsule of a plant (as cotton) [Middle English]

bol•lard \'bäl-ərd\ *n* **1 :** a post on a wharf around which to fasten mooring lines **2 :** BITT [perhaps from *bole*]

boll weevil *n* **:** a small grayish weevil whose larva lives in and feeds on the buds and bolls of the cotton plant

boll•worm \'bōl-wərm\ *n* **:** CORN EARWORM; *also* **:** any of several other moths or the immature stages of moths that feed on cotton bolls as larvae

bo•lo \'bō-lō\ *n, pl* **bolos :** a long heavy single-edged knife used in the Philippines [Spanish]

bo•lo•gna \bə-'lō-nē *also* -nyə *or* -nə\ *n* **:** a large smoked sausage of beef, veal, and pork [*Bologna*, Italy]

bo•lom•e•ter \bə-'läm-ət-ər\ *n* **:** a very sensitive thermometer based on varying electrical resistance and used to measure feeble thermal radiation [Greek *bolē* "stroke, beam of light"]

bolero 2

Bol•she•vik \'bōl-shə-ˌvik\ *n, pl* **Bolsheviks** *or* **Bol•she•vi•ki** \ˌbōl-shə-'vik-ē\ **1 :** a member of the radical wing of the Russian Social Democratic party that favored the overthrow of capitalism by force and seized power in Russia by the revolution of November 1917 **2 :** COMMUNIST [Russian *bol'shevik*, from *bol'she* "larger"] — **Bolshevik** *adj*

Bol•she•vism \'bōl-shə-ˌviz-əm\ *n* **:** the theories and practices of Bolsheviks — **Bol•she•vist** \-vəst\ *n or adj* — **Bol•she•vis•tic** \ˌbōl-shə-'vis-tik\ *adj*

[1]**bol•ster** \'bōl-stər\ *n* **1 :** a long pillow or cushion extending the full width of a bed **2 :** a structural part designed to eliminate friction or provide support [Old English]

[2]**bolster** *vt* **bol•stered**; **bol•ster•ing** \-stə-riŋ, -striŋ\ **:** to support with or as if with a bolster; *also* **:** REINFORCE — **bol•ster•er** \-stər-ər\ *n*

[1]**bolt** \'bōlt\ *n* **1 a :** a shaft or missile for a crossbow or catapult **b :** a lightning stroke **:** THUNDERBOLT **2 :** a sliding bar used to fasten a door **3 :** the part of a lock worked by a key **4 :** a metal pin or rod usually with a head at one end and a screw thread at the other that is used to hold something in place **5 :** a roll of cloth or wallpaper of a specified length **6 :** the breech closure of a breech-loading firearm [Old English]

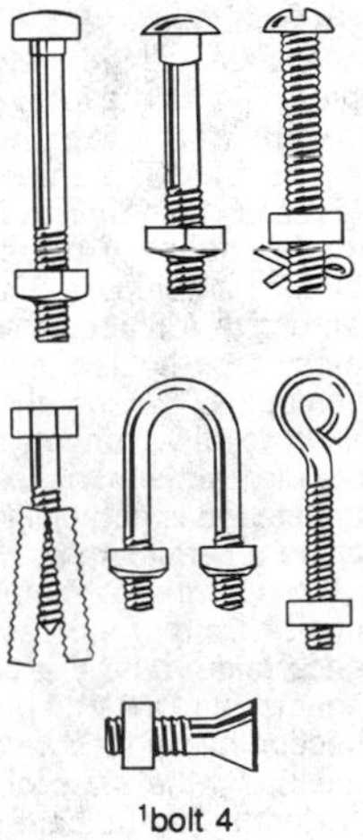

[1]bolt 4

[2]**bolt** *vb* **1 :** to move suddenly or nervously **2 :** to move rapidly **:** DASH ⟨reporters *bolted* for the door⟩ **3 :** to run away ⟨the horse shied and *bolted*⟩ **4 :** to break away from or oppose (as one's political party) **5 :** to say impulsively **:** BLURT **6 :** to fasten with a bolt **7 :** to swallow hastily or without chewing ⟨*bolted* down our dinner and rushed out⟩ — **bolt•er** *n*

[3]**bolt** *n* **:** an act of bolting

[4]**bolt** *vt* **:** to sift (as flour) usually through fine-meshed cloth [Old French *buleter*, of Germanic origin] — **bolt•er** *n*

bo•lus \'bō-ləs\ *n* **:** a rounded mass: as **a :** a large pill **b :** a soft mass of chewed food [Greek *bōlos* "lump"]

[1]**bomb** \'bäm\ *n* **1 :** an explosive device fused to detonate under planned conditions **2 :** a container in which a substance (as an insecticide) is stored under pressure and from which it is released in the form of a fine spray **3 :** a rounded mass of lava exploded from a volcano [French *bombe*, from Italian *bomba*]

[2]**bomb** *vb* **:** to attack with bombs

[1]**bom•bard** \'bäm-ˌbärd\ *n* **:** a cannon used in late medieval times chiefly to hurl large stones [Middle French *bombarde*]

[2]**bom•bard** \bäm-'bärd, bəm-\ *vt* **1 :** to attack with artillery **2 :** to attack vigorously or persistently (as with questions) **3 :** to subject to the impact of rapidly moving particles (as electrons or alpha rays) — **bom•bard•ment** \-mənt\ *n*

bom•bar•dier \ˌbäm-bə-'diər, -bər-\ *n* **:** a member of a bomber

\ə\ **abut**	\au̇\ **out**	\i\ **tip**	\ȯ\ **saw**	\u̇\ **foot**
\ər\ **further**	\ch\ **chin**	\ī\ **life**	\ȯi\ **coin**	\y\ **yet**
\a\ **mat**	\e\ **pet**	\j\ **job**	\th\ **thin**	\yü\ **few**
\ā\ **take**	\ē\ **easy**	\ŋ\ **sing**	\th\ **this**	\yu̇\ **cure**
\ä\ **cot, cart**	\g\ **go**	\ō\ **bone**	\ü\ **food**	\zh\ **vision**

crew whose duty is to release the bombs
bom•bast \'bäm-ˌbast\ *n* : pompous speech or writing [obsolete *bombast* "padding", from Middle French *bombace* "cotton", derived from Latin *bombyx* "silkworm, silk", from Greek] — **bom•bas•tic** \bäm-'bas-tik\ *adj* — **bom•bas•ti•cal•ly** \-ti-kə-lē, -klē\ *adv*
bom•ba•zine \ˌbäm-bə-'zēn\ *n* : a twilled and usually silk fabric used especially for mourning wear [Middle French *bombasin*, derived from Latin *bombyx* "silk"]
bomb bay *n* : a bomb-carrying compartment in the underside of a combat airplane
bomb•er \'bäm-ər\ *n* : one that bombs; *esp* : an airplane designed for dropping bombs
bom•bi•nate \'bäm-bə-ˌnāt\ *vi* : DRONE, BUZZ [derived from Latin *bombus* "deep hollow sound"] — **bom•bi•na•tion** \ˌbäm-bə-'nā-shən\ *n*
bomb•proof \'bäm-'prüf\ *adj* : safe against the explosive force of bombs
bomb•shell \'bäm-ˌshel\ *n* **1** : BOMB 1 **2** : a stunning or upsetting surprise
bomb•sight \-ˌsīt\ *n* : a sighting device on an airplane for aiming bombs
bo•na fide \'bō-nə-ˌfīd, 'bän-ə-; ˌbō-nə-'fīd-ē, -'fīd-ə\ **1 a** : made or carried out in good faith without fraud or deceit ⟨a *bona fide* offer⟩ **b** : acting in good faith without fraud or deceit ⟨*bona fide* purchasers⟩ **2** : GENUINE 1 ⟨a *bona fide* cowboy⟩ [Latin, "in good faith"] **syn** see AUTHENTIC
bo•nan•za \bə-'nan-zə\ *n* **1** : a rich mass of ore in a mine **2** : something that brings a rich return [Spanish, literally, "fair weather", from Medieval Latin *bonacia*, alteration of Latin *malacia* "calm at sea", from Greek *malakia*, literally, "softness", from *malakos* "soft"]
Bo•na•part•ism \'bō-nə-ˌpärt-ˌiz-əm\ *n* : a political movement associated chiefly with authoritarian rule [Napoleon *Bonaparte*] — **Bo•na•part•ist** \-ˌpärt-əst\ *n*
bon•bon \'bän-ˌbän\ *n* : a candy with chocolate or fondant coating and a soft center with fruits and nuts sometimes added [French, from *bon* "good"]
¹bond \'bänd\ *n* **1** : something that restrains : FETTER **2** : a binding agreement **3 a** : material or a device for binding **b** : an attractive force that acts between atoms, ions, or groups of atoms and holds them together in a molecule or crystal **c** : a cementing material that combines, unites, or strengthens **4** : a tie of loyalty, sentiment, or friendship **5 a** : a pledge to do an act or pay a sum on or before a stated day or to forfeit a sum if the pledge is not fulfilled **b** : one that gives bail or acts as surety **c** : a certificate bearing interest and promising payment of a certain sum on or before a stated day and issued by a government or corporation as an evidence of indebtedness **d** : insurance taken out by a party (as a contractor) to insure another against his failure to perform an obligation **6** : a binding or connection made by overlapping parts of a structure (as in laying brick) **7** : the state of goods manufactured, stored, or transported under the care of bonded agencies until taxes on them are paid [Old Norse *band*]
²bond *vb* **1** : to protect or secure by or operate under a bond ⟨*bonded* locksmiths⟩; *esp* : to secure payment of taxes on (goods) by giving a bond **2 a** : to cause to adhere firmly **b** : to embed in a cementing material **c** : to hold together or make solid by or as if by means of a bond or binder — **bond•able** \'bän-də-bəl\ *adj* — **bond•er** *n*
bond•age \'bän-dij\ *n* : involuntary personal servitude (as serfdom or slavery) [Middle English *bonde* "peasant, serf", from Old English *bōnda* "householder", from Old Norse *bōndi*]
bond•hold•er \'bänd-ˌhōl-dər\ *n* : the owner of a government or corporation bond
bond•man \'bänd-mən, 'bän-\ *n* : SERF, SLAVE
bond paper *n* : a strong durable paper used especially for documents
bond servant *n* : a person bound to service without wages; *also* : SLAVE
¹bonds•man \'bänz-mən\ *n* : BONDMAN
²bondsman *n* : SURETY 3
bond•wom•an \'bän-ˌdwu̇m-ən\ *n* : a woman who is a slave or serf
¹bone \'bōn\ *n* **1 a** : the hard largely calcareous connective tissue of which the skeleton of most vertebrate animals is formed; *also* : one of the hard pieces in which this tissue occurs ⟨break a *bone*⟩ **b** : a similar hard animal substance (as whalebone or ivory) **2 a** *pl* : something (as dice) usually or originally made from bone **b** : STAY 1b **3** *pl* : an end man in a minstrel show [Old English *bān*] — **bone•less** \-ləs\ *adj* — **bone to pick** : a matter to argue or complain about
²bone *vb* **1** : to remove the bones from ⟨*bone* a fish⟩ **2** : to provide (a garment) with stays **3** : to study hard ⟨*bone* up on math⟩
bone black *n* : the black chiefly carbon residue of bones heated in a closed vessel that is used especially as a pigment or a decolorizing material — called also *bone char*
bone–dry \'bōn-'drī\ *adj* : very dry
bone•fish \'bōn-ˌfish\ *n* **1** : a slender silvery small-scaled fish that is a sport and food fish of warm seas **2** : LADYFISH
bone•head \-ˌhed\ *n* : a stupid person : NUMSKULL — **bone•head•ed** \-'hed-əd\ *adj*
bone meal *n* : fertilizer or feed made of crushed or ground bone
bon•er \'bō-nər\ *n* **1** : one that bones **2** : a stupid or ridiculous mistake
bon•fire \'bän-ˌfīr\ *n* : a large fire built in the open air [Middle English *bonefire* "fire of bones"]
bong \'bäng, 'bȯng\ *n* : a deep resonant sound (as of a bell) [imitative] — **bong** *vb*
bon•go \'bäng-gō\ *n, pl* **bongos** *also* **bongoes** : one of a pair of small tuned drums played with the hands [American Spanish *bongó*]
bon•ho•mie *also* **bon•hom•mie** \ˌbän-ə-'mē, ˌbō-nə-\ *n* : good-natured easy friendliness : GENIALITY [French *bonhomie*, from *bonhomme* "good-natured man", from *bon* "good" + *homme* "man"]
bon•i•face \'bän-ə-fəs, -ˌfās\ *n* : the proprietor of a hotel, nightclub, or restaurant [*Boniface*, innkeeper in *The Beaux' Stratagem* (1707), play by George Farquhar]
bo•ni•to \bə-'nēt-ō, -'nēt-ə\ *n, pl* **bonitos** *or* **bonito** : any of various medium-sized tunas [Spanish, from *bonito* "pretty", from Latin *bonus* "good"]
bon mot \bōⁿ-'mō\ *n, pl* **bons mots** \bōⁿ-'mō, -'mōz\ *or* **bon mots** \-'mō, -'mōz\ : a clever remark : WITTICISM [French, literally, "good word"]
bon•net \'bän-ət\ *n* **1** : a head covering often tied under the chin by ribbons or strings and now worn mostly by small children **2** : a soft woolen cap worn by men in Scotland **3** : the headdress of an American Indian **4** *British* : an automobile hood [Middle French *bonet*]
bon•ny *also* **bon•nie** \'bän-ē\ *adj, chiefly British* : having a pleasing look or quality [Old French *bon* "good", from Latin *bonus*] — **bon•ni•ly** \'bän-l-ē\ *adv*
bon•sai \bōn-'sī, 'bōn-ˌ\ *n, pl* **bonsai** : a potted plant (as a tree) dwarfed by special methods of culture [Japanese]
bon•spiel \'bän-ˌspēl\ *n* : a match or tournament between curling clubs [perhaps from Dutch *bond* "league" + *spel* "game"]
bon ton \bän-'tän, 'bän-ˌ\ *n* **1** : fashionable manner or style **2** : the fashionable or proper thing [French, literally, "good tone"]
bo•nus \'bō-nəs\ *n* : something given in addition to what is usual or strictly due; *esp* : money given in addition to salary or wages [Latin, "good"]
bon vi•vant \ˌbän-vē-'vänt, ˌbōⁿ-vē-'väⁿ\ *n, pl* **bons vivants** \ˌbän-vē-'vänts; ˌbōⁿ-vē-'väⁿ, -'väⁿz\ *or* **bon vivants** *same*\ : a person having cultivated or refined tastes especially in food and drink [French, literally, "good liver"]
bon voy•age \ˌbōⁿ-ˌvwī-'äzh, -ˌwä-'yäzh; ˌbōⁿ-ˌvȯi-'äzh, ˌbän-\ *n* : FAREWELL 1 — often used interjectionally [French, literally, "good trip"]
bony \'bō-nē\ *adj* **bon•i•er**; **-est 1** : of or relating to bone ⟨the *bony* structure of the body⟩ **2** : full of bones **3** : resembling bone especially in hardness ⟨a *bony* substance⟩ **4** : having large or prominent bones ⟨a rugged *bony* face⟩ **5** : SCRAWNY, SKINNY ⟨*bony* underfed children⟩
bony fish *n* : any of a class (Teleostomi) comprising higher fishes with usually well-developed bony skeletons
¹boo \'bü\ *interj* — used to express contempt or disapproval or to startle or frighten [Middle English *bo*]
²boo *n* : a shout of disapproval or contempt — **boo** *vb*
boob \'büb\ *n* **1** : SIMPLETON **2** : BOOR 2b [short for *booby*]
boo-boo \'bü-ˌbü\ *n* **1** : a usually small bruise or scratch especially on a child **2** : a foolish mistake [probably alteration of *boohoo*, imitative of the sound of weeping]
boo•by \'bü-bē\ *n, pl* **boobies 1** : a foolish person : DOPE **2**

: any of several small tropical gannets [Spanish *bobo,* from Latin *balbus* "stammering"]

booby prize *n* : an award for the poorest performance in a game or competition

booby trap *n* : a trap for a careless or unwary person; *esp* : a concealed explosive device set to go off when some harmless-looking object is touched — **boo•by–trap** \ˈbü-bē-ˌtrap\ *vt*

boo•dle \ˈbüd-ᵊl\ *n* **1** : a large group of people : CROWD **2** : bribe money [Dutch *boedel* "estate, lot"]

boo•gie–woo•gie \ˌbu̇g-ē-ˈwu̇g-ē, ˌbüg-ē-ˈwüg-ē\ *n* : a percussive style of playing blues on the piano characterized by a steady rhythmic bass and a simple often improvised melody — called also *boogie* [origin unknown]

[1]**book** \ˈbu̇k\ *n* **1 a** : a set of written, printed, or blank sheets of paper bound together into a volume **b** : a long written or printed literary composition **c** : a major division of a literary work **d** : a volume of business records (as a ledger) **2** *cap* : BIBLE 1 **3** : something regarded as a source of enlightenment or instruction **4 a** : all the knowledge available about a task or problem ⟨tried every trick in the *book* to win⟩ **b** : the standards or authority relevant in a situation ⟨follow the *book* and you'll be all right⟩ **5** : all the charges that can be made against an accused person ⟨threw the *book* at them⟩ **6 a** : LIBRETTO **b** : the script of a play **7** : a packet of commodities bound together ⟨a *book* of matches⟩ **8** : the bets registered by a bookmaker **9** : the tricks a cardplayer must win before scoring [Old English *bōc*]

△ **origin** The word *book* is related to the word *beech.* Early Germanic peoples often carved runic characters on tablets made of beech wood. It was probably this practice that gave the book its name. — **in one's book** : in one's opinion — **in one's good books** : in favor with one — **one for the book** : an act or occurrence worth noting

[2]**book** *vb* **1 a** : to engage transportation or reserve lodgings **b** : to schedule engagements for ⟨*book* an entertainer⟩ **2** : to enter charges against in a police register — **book•er** *n*

[3]**book** *adj* **1** : derived from books ⟨*book* learning⟩ **2** : shown by books of account ⟨*book* value⟩

book•bind•ing \ˈbu̇k-ˌbīn-diŋ\ *n* **1** : the binding of a book **2** : the art or trade of binding books — **book•bind•er** *n* — **book•bind•ery** \-də-rē, -drē\ *n*

book•case \ˈbu̇k-ˌkās\ *n* : a piece of furniture consisting of shelves to hold books

book•end \ˈbu̇k-ˌend\ *n* : a support placed at the end of a row of books to hold them up

book•ie \ˈbu̇k-ē\ *n* : BOOKMAKER

book•ish \ˈbu̇k-ish\ *adj* **1** : fond of books and reading **2** : inclined to rely on knowledge from books rather than practical experience **3** : resembling or derived from the language of books : FORMAL ⟨many English words derived from Latin have a *bookish* tone⟩ — **book•ish•ly** *adv* — **book•ish•ness** *n*

book•keep•er \ˈbu̇k-ˌkē-pər\ *n* : a person who keeps accounts (as of a business) — **book•keep•ing** \-piŋ\ *n*

• **syn** ACCOUNTANT: a BOOKKEEPER keeps regular, concise, accurate records of business transactions by entering them in account books; an ACCOUNTANT is an expert bookkeeper who may be employed to organize or set up a system of records or to investigate or report upon the financial condition of an organization.

book•let \ˈbu̇k-lət\ *n* : a little book *esp* : PAMPHLET

book louse *n* : any of several tiny wingless insects (order Corrodentia) injurious especially to books

book lung *n* : a specialized breathing organ of spiders and related animals containing numerous thin folds of membrane arranged like the leaves of a book

book•mak•er \ˈbu̇k-ˌmā-kər\ *n* : one who determines odds and receives and pays off bets — **book•mak•ing** \-kiŋ\ *n*

book•mark \ˈbu̇k-ˌmärk\ *or* **book•mark•er** \-ˌmär-kər\ *n* : a marker for keeping one's place in a book

book•mo•bile \ˈbu̇k-mō-ˌbēl\ *n* : a vehicle that serves as a traveling library [*book* + auto*mobile*]

Book of Common Prayer : the service book of the Anglican Communion

book•plate \ˈbu̇k-ˌplāt\ *n* : a label placed in a book showing who owns it

book review *n* : a critical estimate of a book

book•sell•er \ˈbu̇k-ˌsel-ər\ : the proprietor of a bookstore

book•stall \-ˌstȯl\ *n* **1** : a stall where books are sold **2** *chiefly British* : NEWSSTAND

book•store \-ˌstōr, -ˌstȯr\ *n* : a retail store where books are the main item for sale — called also *bookshop*

book•worm \-ˌwərm\ *n* **1** : any of various insect larvae that feed on the binding and paste of books **2** : a person unusually devoted to reading and study

Bool•ean algebra \ˌbü-lē-ən-\ *n* : a mathematical set together with two commutative operations (as the taking of unions and intersections of subsets) whose rules of combination can be described by any of various equivalent systems of postulates [George *Boole,* died 1864, English mathematician]

[1]**boom** \ˈbüm\ *n* **1** : a long pole; *esp* : one for stretching the bottom of a sail **2 a** : a long beam projecting from the mast of a derrick to support or guide the thing that is being lifted **b** : a long movable arm used to manipulate a microphone **3** : a line of connected floating timbers to hold logs together in a river [Dutch, "tree, beam, boom"]

[2]**boom** *vb* **1** : to make a deep hollow sound **2 a** : to increase in esteem or importance **b** : to experience a boom (as in growth) **3** : to cause to resound — often used with *out* ⟨their voices *boomed* out the song⟩ [imitative]

[3]**boom** *n* **1** : a booming sound or cry **2** : a rapid expansion or increase: as **a** : a general movement in support of a candidate for office **b** : rapid settlement and development of a town or district **c** : a rapid widespread expansion of business activity

boo•mer•ang \ˈbü-mə-ˌraŋ\ *n* **1** : a curved club or stick usually somewhat flat that can be thrown so as to return near the starting point **2** : an act or utterance that backfires on its originator [native name in Australia] — **boomerang** *vi*

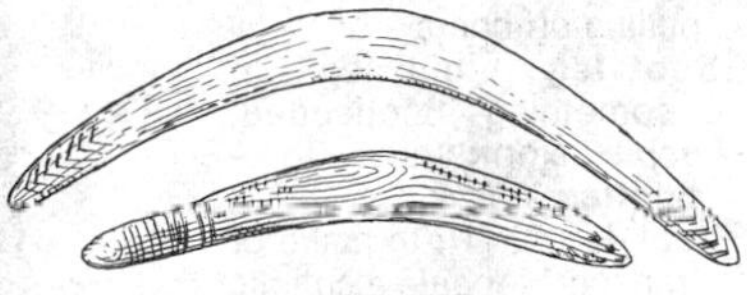
boomerang 1

boom•town \ˈbüm-ˌtau̇n\ *n* : a town undergoing a sudden growth in business activity and population

[1]**boon** \ˈbün\ *n* : FAVOR 2, KINDNESS: as **a** : one given in answer to a request **b** : a timely benefit : BLESSING [Old Norse *bōn* "petition"]

[2]**boon** *adj* **1** : having a kindly nature **2** : CONVIVIAL, MERRY ⟨a *boon* companion⟩ [Middle French *bon* "good", from Latin *bonus*]

boon•docks \ˈbün-ˌdäks\ *n pl* **1** : rough country filled with dense brush **2** : a rural area : STICKS [Tagalog *bundok* "mountain"]

boon•dog•gle \ˈbün-ˌdäg-əl, -ˌdȯg-\ *n* : a trivial, useless, or wasteful activity [coined by Robert H. Link, died 1957, American scoutmaster] — **boondoggle** *vi* — **boon•dog•gler** \-lər, -ə-lər\ *n*

boor \ˈbu̇r\ *n* **1** : PEASANT 1 **2 a** : a rough clownish rustic : BUMPKIN **b** : a rude or insensitive person [Dutch *boer*]

boor•ish \ˈbu̇r-ish\ *adj* : resembling a boor : RUDE — **boor•ish•ly** *adv* — **boor•ish•ness** *n*

[1]**boost** \ˈbüst\ *vt* **1** : to push or shove up from below **2** : to make greater especially in amount ⟨*boost* prices⟩ ⟨*boost* morale⟩ **3** : to promote enthusiastically the cause or interests of [origin unknown] **syn** see LIFT

[2]**boost** *n* **1** : a push upward **2** : an increase in amount **3** : an act that brings help or encouragement

boost•er \ˈbü-stər\ *n* : one that boosts: as **a** : an enthusiastic supporter **b** : a device for strengthening radio or television signals in areas where reception is weak **c** : a supplementary dose of an immunizing agent given to maintain or revive a previously established immunity **d** : the first stage of a multistage rocket providing thrust for the launching and the initial part of the flight

[1]**boot** \ˈbüt\ *n, chiefly dialect* : something to equalize a trade [Old English *bōt* "advantage, remedy"] — **to boot** : 1 : [1]BESIDES

[2]**boot** *vb, archaic* : to be of use : HELP, PROFIT

[3]**boot** *n* **1** : a covering (as of leather or rubber) for the foot and

leg **2 :** a protective sheath or casing **3 :** a patch for the inside of a tire casing **4** *British* **:** an automobile trunk **5 :** a blow delivered by the foot **:** KICK; *also* **:** a rude discharge or dismissal **6 :** a navy or marine recruit undergoing basic training [Middle French *bote*]

4boot *vt* **1 :** to put boots on **2 a :** KICK **b :** to eject or discharge rudely — often used with *out* ⟨was *booted* out of the office⟩

boot•black \'büt-ˌblak\ *n* **:** a person who shines boots and shoes

boot camp *n* **:** a camp for the basic training of navy or marine recruits

boot•ee *or* **boot•ie** \'büt-ē\ *n* **:** an infant's knitted or crocheted sock

Bo•ö•tes \bō-'ōt-ēz\ *n* **:** a northern constellation containing the bright star Arcturus [Greek *Boōtēs,* literally, "plowman", from *bous* "head of cattle"]

booth \'büth\ *n, pl* **booths** \'bü*th*z, 'büths\ **1 :** a temporary shelter **2 a :** a stall or stand (as at a fair) for the sale or exhibition of goods **b** (1) **:** a small enclosure affording privacy for one person at a time ⟨voting *booth*⟩ ⟨telephone *booth*⟩ (2) **:** a small enclosure that separates its occupant from customers or patrons ⟨a ticket *booth*⟩ **c :** a restaurant accommodation consisting of a table between two backed benches [Middle English *bothe,* of Scandinavian origin]

boot•jack \'büt-ˌjak\ *n* **:** a V-shaped device used in pulling off boots

bootjack

1boot•leg \'büt-ˌleg\ *n* **:** something bootlegged; *esp* **:** MOONSHINE 3 — **bootleg** *adj*

2boot•leg *vb* **1 :** to make or transport for sale alcoholic liquor contrary to law **2 a :** to produce or sell illicitly **b :** SMUGGLE 1 [from the carrying of illicit liquor concealed in the leg of a boot] — **boot•leg•ger** \-ˌleg-ər\ *n*

boot•less \'büt-ləs\ *adj* **:** FRUITLESS 2 — **boot•less•ly** *adv* — **boot•less•ness** *n*

boot•lick \-ˌlik\ *vb* **:** to fawn on **:** curry favor **:** FAWN — **boot•lick•er** *n*

boo•ty \'büt-ē\ *n* **1 :** SPOIL 1b; *esp* **:** goods seized from the enemy in war **2 :** a rich gain or prize [Middle French *butin*]

1booze \'büz\ *vi* **:** to drink intoxicating liquor to excess [Dutch *būsen*] — **booz•er** \'bü-zər\ *n*

2booze *n* **:** intoxicating liquor — **booz•i•ly** \'bü-zə-lē\ *adv* — **boozy** \'bü-zē\ *adj*

bor•age \'bȯr-ij, 'bär-\ *n* **:** a hairy blue-flowered European herb used medicinally and in salads [Middle French *bourage*]

bo•rate \'bōr-ˌāt, 'bȯr-\ *n* **:** a salt or ester of a boric acid

bo•rax \'bōr-ˌaks, 'bȯr-\ *n* **:** a crystalline slightly alkaline compound $Na_2B_4O_7 \cdot 10H_2O$ that is a borate of sodium, occurs as a mineral, and is used as a flux, cleansing agent, and antiseptic [Medieval Latin, from Arabic *būraq,* from Persian *būrah*]

Bo•ra•zon \'bōr-ə-ˌzän, 'bȯr-\ *trademark* — used for a boron nitride abrasive

bor•deaux mixture \bȯr-'dō-\ *n, often cap B* **:** a fungicide made by reaction of copper sulfate, lime, and water

1bor•der \'bȯrd-ər\ *n* **1 :** an outer part or edge **2 :** FRONTIER 1, BOUNDARY **3 :** a narrow bed of planted ground along the edge of a garden or walk **4 :** an ornamental design at the edge of a fabric or rug [Middle French *bordure,* from *border* "to border", from *bort* "border", of Germanic origin] — **bor•dered** \-ərd\ *adj*

• **syn** BORDER, EDGE, MARGIN mean a line or narrow space marking the limit or outermost bound of something. A BORDER is that part of a surface lying along its boundary line; EDGE denotes specifically the terminating line made by two converging surfaces as of a blade or a box; MARGIN suggests a border of definite width or distinctive character ⟨the sandy *margin* of the sea⟩

2border *vb* **bor•dered; bor•der•ing** \'bȯrd-ring, -ə-ring\ **1 :** to put a border on **2 :** to touch at the edge or boundary **:** BOUND **3 :** to lie on the border of something ⟨the town *borders* on the sea⟩ **4 :** to approach the nature of a specified thing **:** VERGE ⟨*border* on the ridiculous⟩ — **bor•der•er** \-ər-ər\ *n*

bor•der•land \'bȯrd-ər-ˌland\ *n* **1 :** territory at or near a border **:** FRONTIER **2 :** a vague intermediate state or region ⟨the *borderland* between fantasy and reality⟩

bor•der•line \-ˌlīn\ *adj* **1 :** situated at or near a border or boundary **2 a :** situated between two points or states **:** INTERMEDIATE **b :** not quite average, normal, or acceptable ⟨*borderline* intelligence⟩ ⟨a *borderline* joke⟩

1bore \'bōr, 'bȯr\ *vb* **1 :** to pierce with or as if with a rotary tool ⟨*bore* a piece of wood⟩ **2 :** to make by piercing or drilling ⟨*bore* a hole⟩ ⟨*bore* a well⟩ **3 :** to make a hole by boring [Old English *borian*]

2bore *n* **1 :** a hole made by or as if by boring **2 :** an interior lengthwise cylindrical cavity; *esp* **:** the interior cavity of a gun **3 a :** the diameter of a hole or tube; *esp* **:** the interior diameter of a gun barrel **b :** the diameter of an engine cylinder

3bore *past of* BEAR

4bore *n* **:** a tidal flood with a high abrupt front [Old Norse *bāra* "wave"]

5bore *n* **:** one that causes boredom [origin unknown]

6bore *vt* **:** to weary by being dull or monotonous

bo•re•al \'bōr-ē-əl, 'bȯr-\ *adj* **:** of, relating to, or located or growing in northern or mountainous regions ⟨*boreal* coniferous forests⟩ [Greek *Boreas* "north wind, north"]

bore•dom \'bōrd-əm, 'bȯrd-\ *n* **:** the state of being bored

bor•er \'bōr-ər, 'bȯr-\ *n* **:** one that bores: as **a :** a tool used for boring **b** (1) **:** SHIPWORM (2) **:** an insect that as a larva or an adult bores in the woody parts of plants

bo•ric acid \ˌbōr-ik-, ˌbȯr-\ *n* **:** a white crystalline weak acid H_3BO_3 easily obtained from its salts and used especially as a mild antiseptic

bor•ing \'bōr-ing, 'bȯr-\ *adj* **:** causing boredom **:** TIRESOME

born \'bȯrn\ *adj* **1 a :** brought into life by birth **b :** NATIVE 2 ⟨American-*born*⟩ **2 :** having from birth special natural abilities or character ⟨a *born* leader⟩ **3 :** destined from or as if from birth ⟨*born* to succeed⟩ [Old English *boren,* past participle of *beran* "to bear"]

borne *past participle of* BEAR

born•ite \'bȯr-ˌnīt\ *n* **:** a brittle metallic-looking mineral Cu_5FeS_4 consisting of a sulfide of copper and iron and constituting a valuable ore of copper [Ignaz von *Born,* died 1791, Austrian mineralogist]

bo•ron \'bōr-ˌän, 'bȯr-\ *n* **:** a metalloid element found in nature only in combination (as in borax) — see ELEMENT table [*bor*ax + *-on* (as in *carbon*)]

bor•ough \'bər-ō\ *n* **1 a :** a town or urban constituency in Great Britain that sends a member to Parliament **b :** a self-governing incorporated urban area in Great Britain **2 a :** a municipal corporation in some states corresponding to the incorporated town or village of the other states **b :** one of the five constituent political divisions of New York City **3 :** a civil division of the state of Alaska corresponding to a county in most other states [Old English *burg* "fortified town"]

bor•row \'bär-ō\ *vb* **1 :** to take or receive something with the promise or intention of returning it **2 :** to take for one's own use ⟨*borrow* a phrase⟩ **3 :** to take 1 from a digit of the minuend in subtraction and add it as 10 to the digit holding the next lower place [Old English *borgian*] — **bor•row•er** \'bär-ə-wər\ *n*

borscht *also* **borsch** \'bȯrsht, 'bȯrsh\ *n* **:** a soup made largely of beets and served hot or cold often with sour cream [Russian *borshch*]

bor•zoi \'bȯr-ˌzȯi\ *n* **:** any of a breed of large long-haired dogs of the greyhound type developed in Russia especially for pursuing wolves [Russian *borzoĭ,* from *borzoĭ* "swift"]

bos•cage *also* **bos•kage** \'bäs-kij\ *n* **:** a growth of shrubs or trees **:** THICKET [Middle French *boscage,* from *bois, bosc* "forest"]

bosh \'bäsh\ *n* **:** foolish talk **:** NONSENSE [Turkish *boş* "empty"]

bosky \'bäs-kē\ *adj* **:** covered with trees or shrubs [Middle English *bush, bosk* "bush"]

bo•s'n *or* **bo•sun** *variant of* BOATSWAIN

1bos•om \'bu̇z-əm\ *n* **1 :** the front of the human chest; *esp* **:** the female breasts **2 a :** the center of secret thoughts and feelings **b :** intimate association ⟨something only whispered in the *bosom* of the family⟩ **3 :** the part of a garment covering the breast [Old English *bōsm*] — **bos•omed** \-əmd\ *adj*

2bosom *adj* **:** CLOSE, INTIMATE ⟨*bosom* friends⟩

1boss \'bäs, 'bȯs\ *n* **:** a projecting and typically rounded part; *also* **:** a raised or projecting ornament (as on a shield or a ceiling) [Old French *boce*]

[2]**boss** *vt* : to ornament with bosses : EMBOSS
[3]**boss** \ˈbȯs\ *n* **1** : one who has control or authority; *esp* : one who directs or supervises workers **2 a** : a politician who controls votes or dictates appointments or legislative measures **b** : an official having dictatorial authority over an organization [Dutch *baas* "master"] — **boss** *adj* — **boss•ism** \-ˌiz-əm\ *n*
[4]**boss** \ˈbȯs\ *vt* **1** : to exercise control of : DIRECT **2** : ORDER ⟨refused to be *bossed* around⟩
bos•sa no•va \ˌbäs-ə-ˈnō-və\ *n* **1** : a Brazilian dance characterized by the step pattern of the samba and a subtle bounce **2** : music influenced by jazz and rhythmically similar to the samba [Portuguese, literally, "new trend"]
[1]**bossy** \ˈbō-sē\ *n, pl* **boss•ies** : cow 2 [English dialect *buss, boss* "young calf"]
[2]**bossy** *adj* **boss•i•er**; **-est** : inclined to act like a boss — **boss•i•ness** *n*
Bos•ton cream pie \ˌbȯ-stən-\ *n* : a rich cake that is usually split, filled with custard or cream, and often topped with icing [*Boston,* Massachusetts]
Boston fern *n* : a fern widely grown for its often drooping much-divided fronds
Boston ivy *n* : a woody Asian vine of the grape family with 3-lobed leaves that is often grown over walls
Boston terrier *n* : any of a breed of small smooth-coated brindle or black terriers with white markings — called also *Boston bull*
bot \ˈbät\ *n* : the larva of a botfly [perhaps from Scottish Gaelic *boiteag* "maggot"]
[1]**bo•tan•i•cal** \bə-ˈtan-i-kəl\ *also* **bo•tan•ic** \-ik\ *adj* : of or relating to plants or botany — **bo•tan•i•cal•ly** \-i-kə-lē, -klē\ *adv*
[2]**botanical** *n* : a vegetable drug especially in the crude state
bot•a•nize \ˈbät-n-ˌīz\ *vi* : to collect and study plants
bot•a•ny \ˈbät-n-ē, ˈbät-nē\ *n* **1** : a branch of biology dealing with plant life **2 a** : plant life ⟨the *botany* of a region⟩ **b** : the biology of a plant or plant group [Greek *botanē* "pasture, herb", from *boskein* "to graze"] — **bot•a•nist** \ˈbät-n-əst, ˈbät-nəst\ *n*
[1]**botch** \ˈbäch\ *vt* **1** : to repair or patch poorly **2** : BUNGLE [Middle English *bocchen*]
[2]**botch** *n* : a botched job : BUNGLE, MESS — **botchy** \-ē\ *adj*
bot•fly \ˈbät-ˌflī\ *n* : any of various stout two-winged flies whose larvae are parasitic in cavities or tissues of various mammals
[1]**both** \ˈbōth\ *adj* : being the two : involving the one and the other ⟨*both* feet⟩ [Old Norse *bāthir*]
[2]**both** *pron, pl in construction* : the one as well as the other ⟨*both* of us⟩ ⟨we are *both* well⟩
[3]**both** *conj* — used as a function word to indicate and stress the inclusion of each of two or more things specified by coordinated words, phrases, or clauses ⟨*both* New York and London⟩
[1]**both•er** \ˈbäth-ər\ *vb* **both•ered**; **both•er•ing** \ˈbäth-ring, -ə-ring\ **1 a** : to upset with often minor annoyances : TRY **b** : to intrude upon : INTERRUPT **2 a** : to cause to be anxious or concerned : TROUBLE **b** : to feel concern or anxiety **3** : to take pains : make an effort ⟨don't *bother* to knock⟩ [perhaps from Irish Gaelic *bodhar* "bothered"]
[2]**bother** *n* **1 a** : a state of petty annoyance **b** : something that causes such a state **2** : FUSS 2, DISTURBANCE
both•er•some \ˈbäth-ər-səm\ *adjcausing bother*
[1]**bot•tle** \ˈbät-l\ *n* **1 a** : a container typically of glass or plastic with a narrow neck and mouth and usually no handle **b** : a bag made of skin **c** : the quantity held by a bottle **2 a** : intoxicating drink ⟨hit the *bottle*⟩ **b** : bottled milk used in place of mother's milk [Middle French *bouteille,* derived from Late Latin *buttis* "cask"] — **bot•tle•ful** \-ˌfu̇l\ *n*
[2]**bottle** *vt* **bot•tled**; **bot•tling** \ˈbät-ling, -l-ing\ **1** : to put into a bottle **2** : to confine or hold back as if in a bottle — usually used with *up* — **bot•tler** \ˈbät-lər, -l-ər\ *n*
bottled gas *n* : gas under pressure in portable cylinders
bot•tle•neck \ˈbät-l-ˌnek\ *n* **1** : a narrow passageway **2** : a place, condition, or point where progress is held up ⟨a *bottleneck* for traffic⟩ **3** : a style of guitar playing using an object (as a metal bar) pressed against the strings
bot•tle-nosed dolphin \ˌbät-l-ˌnōz-\ *n* : any of various moderately large stout-bodied toothed whales with a prominent beak and sickle-shaped dorsal fin — called also *bottle-nosed porpoise*
[1]**bot•tom** \ˈbät-əm\ *n* **1 a** : the under surface of something **b** : a supporting surface or part : BASE **c** : BUTTOCK 2 **2** : the bed of a body of water **3 a** : the part of a ship's hull lying below the water **b** : BOAT, SHIP **4** : the lowest part, place, or point ⟨the *bottom* of the page⟩ **5** : low land along a river ⟨the Mississippi river *bottoms*⟩ **6** *pl* : the trousers of pajamas **7** : the main plowing mechanism of a plow [Old English *botm*] — **bot•tomed** \-əmd\ *adj* — **at bottom** : BASICALLY, REALLY
[2]**bottom** *vb* : to rest on, bring to, or reach the bottom
bot•tom•land \ˈbät-əm-ˌland\ *n* : BOTTOM 5
bot•tom•less \-ləs\ *adj* **1** : having no bottom **2** : very deep ⟨a *bottomless* pond⟩ — **bot•tom•less•ly** *adv* — **bot•tom•less•ness** *n*
bot•u•lism \ˈbäch-ə-ˌliz-əm\ *n* : an acute food poisoning caused by bacterial toxin formed by clostridia in food [from *Clostridium botulinum,* a species of bacterium]
bou•clé *or* **bou•cle** \bü-ˈklā\ *n* **1** : a yarn made of three plies one of which is looped at intervals **2** : a fabric made from bouclé yarn [French *bouclé* "curly"]
bou•doir \ˈbüd-ˌwär, ˈbu̇d-\ *n* : a dressing room, bedroom, or private sitting room [French, from *bouder* "to pout"]
bouf•fant \bü-ˈfänt, ˈbü-ˌ\ *adj* : puffed out ⟨*bouffant* hairdos⟩ [French, from Middle French *bouffer* "to puff"]
bough \ˈbau̇\ *n* : a branch of a tree; *esp* : a main branch [Old English *bōg* "shoulder, bough"] — **boughed** \ˈbau̇d\ *adj*
bought *past of* BUY
bouil•la•baisse \ˌbü-yə-ˈbās\ *n* : a highly seasoned fish stew made of at least two kinds of fish [French]
bouil•lon \ˈbu̇l-ˌyän, -yən; ˈbü-ˌyän, ˈbu̇-\ *n* : a clear seasoned soup made usually from lean beef or chicken [French, from *bouillir* "to boil"]
boul•der *also* **bowl•der** \ˈbōl-dər\ *n* : a large detached and rounded or much-worn mass of rock [of Scandinavian origin] — **boul•dery** \-də-rē, -drē\ *adj*
bou•le•vard \ˈbu̇l-ə-ˌvärd, ˈbül-\ *n* : a broad often landscaped thoroughfare [French, from Dutch *bolwerc* "bulwark"]
[1]**bounce** \ˈbau̇ns\ *vb* **1** : to rebound or cause to rebound **2 a** : DISMISS 2, FIRE **b** : to throw out from a place by force **3** : to recover quickly from a blow or defeat — usually used with *back* **4** : to be returned by a bank as no good ⟨the check *bounced*⟩ **5** : to leap suddenly : BOUND [Middle English *bounsen*]
[2]**bounce** *n* **1 a** : a sudden leap or bound **b** : a bouncing back : REBOUND **2** : ENERGY 1, LIVELINESS
bounc•er \ˈbau̇n-sər\ *n* : one that bounces; *esp* : a person employed in a public place to remove disorderly patrons
bounc•ing \-sing\ *adj* : enjoying good health : ROBUST ⟨a *bouncing* baby⟩ — **bounc•ing•ly** \-sing-lē\ *adv*
bouncing bet \ˌbau̇n-sing-ˈbet\ *n, often cap 2d B* : a European perennial herb of the pink family that is widely naturalized in the United States and has pink and white flowers and leaves which yield a detergent when bruised — called also *soapwort* [*Bet,* nickname for Elizabeth]
[1]**bound** \ˈbau̇nd\ *adj* : going or intending to go ⟨*bound* for home⟩ [Middle English *boun,* from Old Norse *būinn* "ready", from *būa* "to dwell, prepare"]
[2]**bound** *n* **1** : a boundary line (as of a piece of property) **2** : a point or a line beyond which one cannot go : LIMIT ⟨out of *bounds*⟩ ⟨beyond the *bounds* of reason⟩ **3** : the land within specific bounds — usually used in pl. [Old French *bodne,* from Medieval Latin *bodina*]
[3]**bound** *vt* **1** : to set limits to : CONFINE **2** : to form a bound or boundary of : ENCLOSE; *also* : ADJOIN 2 **3** : to name the boundaries of ⟨*bound* the state of Ohio⟩
[4]**bound** *adj* **1 a** : fastened by or as if by a band : CONFINED ⟨desk-*bound*⟩ **b** : CERTAIN, SURE ⟨*bound* to rain soon⟩ **2 a** : OBLIGED ⟨duty-*bound*⟩ **b** : RESOLVED, DETERMINED ⟨*bound* to have your own way⟩ **3** : always occurring in combination with another linguistic form (as *un-* in *unknown, -er* in *speaker*) — compare FREE 14 [from past participle of *bind*]
[5]**bound** *n* **1** : LEAP 1a, JUMP **2** : BOUNCE 1b, REBOUND [Middle French *bond,* from *bondir* "to leap"]
[6]**bound** *vi* **1** : to move by leaping **2** : REBOUND 1, BOUNCE
bound•a•ry \ˈbau̇n-də-rē, -drē\ *n, pl* **-ries** : a line or strip that marks or shows a limit or end (as of a region or a piece of land)

: a line that bounds, divides, or separates
bound•en \'baün-dən\ *adj* : OBLIGATORY, BINDING ⟨our *bounden* duty⟩
bound•er \'baün-dər\ *n* **1** : one that bounds **2** *chiefly British* : a person of objectionable social behavior : CAD, BOOR
bound•less \'baünd-ləs\ *adj* : having no boundaries or limits : VAST — **bound•less•ly** *adv* — **bound•less•ness** *n*
boun•te•ous \'baünt-ē-əs\ *adj* **1** BOUNTIFUL 1 **2** : liberally provided or bestowed : AMPLE — **boun•te•ous•ly** *adv* — **boun•te•ous•ness** *n*
boun•ti•ful \'baünt-i-fəl\ *adj* **1** : giving liberally : GENEROUS ⟨a *bountiful* contributor⟩ **2** : PLENTIFUL, ABUNDANT ⟨a *bountiful* supply⟩ **syn** see GENEROUS — **boun•ti•ful•ly** \-fə-lē, -flē\ *adv* — **boun•ti•ful•ness** \-fəl-nəs\ *n*
boun•ty \'baünt-ē\ *n, pl* **bounties** **1 a** : GENEROSITY 1a **b** : something given generously **2** : money given as a reward or inducement (as for the killing of vermin) [Old French *bonté* "goodness", from Latin *bonitas,* from *bonus* "good"]
bou•quet \bō-'kā, bü-\ *n* **1** : a bunch of flowers **2** : FRAGRANCE ⟨the *bouquet* of good wine⟩ [French, from Middle French, "thicket", derived from Old French *bosc* "forest"]
bour•bon \'bür-bən, *usually* 'bər- *in sense 3*\ n **1** *cap* : a member of a French family to which belong many kings of France, Spain, Naples, and the kingdom of the Two Sicilies **2** *often cap* : a person who clings firmly to outmoded social and political ideas **3** : a whiskey distilled from corn mash; *esp* : one distilled from a mash of corn, malt, and rye [from *Bourbon,* seigniory in France; sense 3 from *Bourbon* county, Kentucky] — **bour•bon•ism** \-bə-,niz-əm\ *n, often cap*
[1]**bour•geois** \'bürzh-,wä, bürzh-'\ *n, pl* **bour•geois** \-,wä, -,wäz, -'wä, -'wäz\ **1 a** : an inhabitant of a borough or a town **b** : a middle-class person **2** : a person whose social behavior and political views are held to be influenced by interest in private property; *esp* : CAPITALIST **3** *pl* : BOURGEOISIE [Middle French, derived from Old French *borc* "town", from Late Latin *burgus* "fortified place", of Germanic origin]
[2]**bourgeois** *adj* **1** : of, relating to, or characteristic of town dwellers or of the middle class **2** : marked by a concern for material interests and respectability and a leaning toward mediocrity **3** : controlled by commercial and industrial interests : CAPITALISTIC
bour•geoi•sie \,bürzh-,wä-'zē\ *n* **1** : the middle class of society **2** : a social order controlled by bourgeois [French, from *bourgeois*]
[1]**bourn** *or* **bourne** \'bōrn, 'börn, 'bürn\ *n* : STREAM 1, BROOK [Middle English *burn, bourne*]
[2]**bourn** *or* **bourne** *n* **1** *archaic* : BOUNDARY, LIMIT **2** *archaic* : GOAL 2, DESTINATION [Middle French *bourne,* alteration of Old French *bodne*]
bour•rée \bü-'rā\ *n* : a lively 17th century French dance [French]
bourse \'bürs\ *n* : EXCHANGE 5a; *esp* : a European stock exchange [French, literally, "purse", from Medieval Latin *bursa*]
bout \'baüt\ *n* : a spell of activity: as **a** : an athletic match (as of boxing) **b** : OUTBREAK, ATTACK ⟨a *bout* of measles⟩ **c** : SESSION 5 ⟨a drinking *bout*⟩ [English dialect, "a trip going and returning in plowing", from Middle English *bought* "bend"]
bou•tique \bü-'tēk\ *n* : a small fashionable specialty shop; *also* : a small shop within a large department store [French, "shop"]
bou•ton•niere \,büt-n-'iər, ,bü-tən-'yeər\ *n* : a flower or bouquet worn in a buttonhole [French *boutonnière* "buttonhole", from *bouton* "button"]
[1]**bo•vine** \'bō-,vīn, -,vēn\ *adj* **1** : of, relating to, or resembling the ox or cow **2** : both sluggish and patient ⟨a *bovine* disposition⟩ [Latin *bov-, bos* "ox, cow"]
[2]**bovine** *n* : a bovine animal
[1]**bow** \'baü\ *vb* **1** : to bend the head, body, or knee in greeting, reverence, respect, or submission **2** : SUBMIT, YIELD ⟨*bow* to authority⟩ **3** : BEND ⟨*bowed* with age⟩ **4** : to express by bowing ⟨*bow* one's thanks⟩ [Old English *būgan* "to bend, bow"]
[2]**bow** *n* : a bending of the head or body in respect, submission, agreement, or greeting
[3]**bow** \'bō\ *n* **1** : RAINBOW 1 **2** : a weapon for shooting arrows that is made of a strip of elastic material (as wood) bent by a cord connecting the two ends **3** : something shaped in a curve like a bow : BEND **4** : a wooden rod with horsehairs stretched from end to end used for playing a violin or similar instrument **5** : a knot formed by doubling a ribbon or string into loops [Old English *boga*]
[4]**bow** \'bō\ *vb* **1** : to bend into a curve **2** : to play a stringed instrument with a bow
[5]**bow** \'baü\ *n* : the forward part of a ship [probably from Danish *bov* "shoulder, bow"]
bowd•ler•ize \'bōd-lə-,rīz, 'baüd-\ *vt* : to clean up (as a book) by removing or altering parts considered objectionable [Thomas *Bowdler,* died 1825, English editor of Shakespeare] — **bowd•ler•i•za•tion** \,bōd-lə-rə-'zā-shən, ,baüd-\ *n*
bow•el \'baü-əl, 'baül\ *n* **1 a** : INTESTINE, GUT — usually used in pl. **b** : a division of the intestine **2** *archaic* : the seat of pity or tenderness — usually used in pl. **3** *pl* : the interior parts ⟨the *bowels* of the earth⟩ [Old French *boel,* derived from Latin *botulus* "sausage"]
bow•er \'baü-ər, 'baür\ *n* **1** : a place for rest : RETREAT **2** : a shelter (as in a garden) made with tree boughs or vines twined together : ARBOR [Old English *būr* "dwelling"] — **bow•ery** \-ē\ *adj*
bow•er•bird \-,bərd\ *n* : any of various birds especially of Australia and New Guinea that build chambers or passages arched over with twigs and grasses
bow•fin \'bō-,fin\ *n* : a predaceous dull green iridescent American freshwater fish related to the sturgeons
bow•ie knife \'bü-ē-, 'bō-ē-\ *n* : a stout straight single-edged hunting knife [James *Bowie,* died 1836, American soldier]
bow•knot \'bō-,nät, -'nät\ *n* : a knot with decorative loops
[1]**bowl** \'bōl\ *n* **1** : a rounded hollow dish **2** : the contents of a bowl **3** : the bowl-shaped part of something (as a spoon or a tobacco pipe) **4** : a bowl-shaped amphitheater; *esp* : STADIUM 2b [Old English *bolla*] — **bowled** \'bōld\ *adj*
[2]**bowl** *n* **1 a** : a ball shaped so as to curve to one side when rolled **b** *pl* : the game of lawn bowling **2** : a delivery of the ball in bowling or bowls [Middle French *boule* "ball", from Latin *bulla* "bubble"]
[3]**bowl** *vb* **1** : to roll a ball or participate in bowling or lawn bowling **2** : to travel smoothly and rapidly **3 a** : to strike with a swiftly moving object **b** : to stun with surprise ⟨the news *bowled* us over⟩
bowlder *variant of* BOULDER
bow•leg \'bō-,leg, -'leg\ *n* : a leg bowed outward at or below the knee — **bow•legged** \'bō-'leg-əd, -'legd\ *adj*
[1]**bowl•er** \'bō-lər\ *n* : one that bowls
[2]**bow•ler** \'bō-lər\ *n* : DERBY 3 [*Bowler,* 19th century family of English hatters]
bowl game *n* : a football game played after the regular season between specially invited teams
bow•line \'bō-lən, -,līn\ *n* **1** : a rope used to keep the windward edge of a square sail pulled forward **2** : a knot used for making a loop that will not slip [Middle English *bouline*]
bowl•ing \'bō-ling\ *n* **1** : a game played by rolling balls so as to knock down wooden pins set up at the far end of an alley : ninepins or tenpins **2** : LAWN BOWLING
bow•man \'bō-mən\ *n* : ARCHER
Bow•man's capsule \,bō-mənz-\ *n* : a thin membranous double-walled structure enclosing each glomerulus of a vertebrate kidney [Sir William *Bowman,* died 1892, English surgeon]
bow•sprit \'baü-,sprit, 'bō-\ *n* : a large spar projecting forward from the bow of a ship [Middle English *bouspret*]
bow•string \'bō-,string\ *n* : the cord connecting the two ends of a bow
bow tie \'bō-\ *n* : a short necktie tied in a bowknot
bow window \'bō-\ *n* : a curved bay window
bow•yer \'bō-yər\ *n* : one that makes shooting bows
[1]**box** \'bäks\ *n, pl* **box** *or* **box•es** : an evergreen shrub or small tree used especially for hedges [Old English, from Latin *buxus,* from Greek *pyxos*]
[2]**box** *n* **1 a** : a usually 4-sided receptacle with a bottom and often a cover **b** : the amount held by a box **2** : a small compartment for a group of spectators in a theater **3** : BOX STALL **4** : the driver's seat on a carriage **5** : a shed that protects ⟨sentry *box*⟩ **6** : a boxlike housing (as for a bearing) **7** : printed matter enclosed by rules or white space **8** : any of the spaces on a baseball diamond where a batter, coach, pitcher, or catcher stands [Old English, from Late Latin *buxis,* from Greek *pyxis,* from *pyxos* "box tree, boxwood"]
[3]**box** *vt* : to enclose in or as if in a box — **box the compass 1** : to name the 32 points of the compass in their order **2** : to make a complete reversal

[4]**box** *n* **:** a punch or slap especially on the ear [Middle English]
[5]**box** *vb* **1 :** to strike with the hand **2 :** to engage in boxing **:** fight with the fists
box•car \'bäk-,skär\ *n* **:** a railroad freight car with a roof and usually with sliding doors in the sides
box elder *n* **:** a North American maple with compound leaves
[1]**box•er** \'bäk-sər\ *n* **:** one that engages in the sport of boxing
[2]**boxer** *n* **:** a compact medium-sized short-haired usually fawn or brindle dog of a breed originating in Germany
Box•er \'bäk-sər\ *n* **:** a member of a Chinese secret society that in 1900 attempted by violence to drive foreigners out of China and to force native converts to abandon Christianity [translation of Chinese (Pekingese) *i*[4] *ho*[2] *ch'üan*[2], literally, "righteous harmonious fist"]
△ **origin** In the late 19th century, a group of Chinese who were opposed to the spread of Western customs in their country formed a secret society. Among the rituals they practiced were boxing and calisthenics, from which they believed they would gain supernatural strength. They named their society *I ho ch'üan*, which means "righteous harmonious fist". English-speaking foreigners simplified the name in translating it and called the group *Boxers*. The rebellion which the Boxers led was unsuccessful, and Western influence remained important in China.
box•ing *n* **:** the art of attack and defense with the fists practiced as a sport
Box•ing Day \'bäk-sing-\ *n* **:** the first weekday after Christmas observed as a legal holiday in parts of the British Commonwealth [from the giving of Christmas boxes on this day to service workers (as postmen)]
boxing glove *n* **:** one of a pair of padded leather mittens worn in boxing
box kite *n* **:** a tailless kite consisting of two or more open-ended connected boxes
box•like \'bäk-,slīk\ *adj* **:** resembling a box especially in shape
box office *n* **1 :** an office in a public place (as a theater) where tickets of admission are sold **2 :** the financial results of an entertainment enterprise; *also* **:** something affecting these results ⟨westerns are good *box office*⟩
box pleat *n* **:** a pleat made by forming two folded edges one facing right and the other left
box score *n* **:** a printed summary of a game usually in the form of a table giving essential details of play
box seat *n* **:** an advantageous position for viewing something
box spring *n* **:** a bedspring that consists of spiral springs attached to a foundation and enclosed in a cloth-covered frame
box stall *n* **:** an individual enclosure for an animal
box turtle *n* **:** any of several North American land tortoises able to withdraw completely into the shell
box•wood \'bäk-,swu̇d\ *n* **:** the close-grained tough hard wood of the box; *also* **:** [1]BOX

box turtle

boy \'bȯi\ *n* **1 :** a male child from birth to young manhood **2 :** SON 1 **3 :** a male servant [Middle English] — **boy•hood** \-,hu̇d\ *n* — **boy•ish** \-ish\ *adj* — **boy•ish•ly** *adv* — **boy•ish•ness** *n*
bo•yar \bō-'yär\ *n* **:** a member of a Russian aristocratic order next in rank below the ruling princes until its abolition by Peter the Great [Russian *boyarin*]
[1]**boy•cott** \'bȯi-,kät\ *vt* **:** to jointly refuse to deal with (as a person or country) or use (as a product) usually to express disapproval or force concessions [Charles C. *Boycott*, died 1897, English land agent in Ireland who was ostracized for refusing to reduce rents]
[2]**boycott** *n* **:** the process or an instance of boycotting
boy•friend \'bȯi-,frend\ *n* **:** a male friend or companion especially of a girl or woman
boy scout *n* **:** a member of the Boy Scouts of America
boy•sen•ber•ry \'bȯiz-n-,ber-ē, 'bȯis-\ *n* **:** the large edible fruit of a trailing hybrid bramble; *also* **:** this bramble [Rudolph *Boysen*, died 1950, American horticulturist]

bra \'brä\ *n* **:** BRASSIERE
[1]**brace** \'brās\ *n, pl* **brac•es** *or* **brace 1 :** two of a kind ⟨several *brace* of quail⟩ **2 :** something (as a clasp) that connects or fastens **3 :** a crank-shaped instrument for turning a wood-boring bit **4 a :** something that transmits, directs, resists, or supports weight or pressure; *esp* **:** an inclined timber used as a support **b** *pl* **:** SUSPENDERS **c :** a device for supporting a body part (as the shoulders) **d :** a dental appliance worn on the teeth to correct irregularities of growth and position **5 a :** a mark { or } used to connect words or items to be considered together **b :** this mark connecting two or more musical staffs the parts on which are to be performed simultaneously; *also* **:** the group of staffs so connected [Middle English, "pair, clasp", from Middle French, "two arms", from Latin *bracchia*, plural of *bracchium* "arm"]
[2]**brace** *vb* **1 a :** to make firm or taut ⟨*brace* a drum⟩ **b :** to get ready or set **:** STEEL ⟨*braced* themselves for the test⟩ **c :** INVIGORATE, FRESHEN **2 a :** to furnish or support with a brace **b :** to make stronger **:** REINFORCE **3 :** to plant firmly ⟨*bracing* my feet⟩ **4 :** to take heart ⟨*brace* up, all is not lost⟩
brace•let \'brā-slət\ *n* **1 :** an ornamental band or chain worn around the wrist **2 :** something (as handcuffs) resembling a bracelet [Middle French, from *bras* "arm", from Latin *bracchium*]
bra•cer \'brā-sər\ *n* **:** an arm or wrist protector
brace root *n* **:** PROP ROOT
bra•chi•al \'brā-kē-əl\ *adj* **:** of or relating to the arm or a comparable structure [Latin *bracchium, brachium* "arm"]
brachial plexus *n* **:** a network of nerves lying mostly in the armpit and supplying nerves to the chest, shoulder, and arm
bra•chi•ate \'brā-kē-,āt\ *vi* **:** to progress by swinging from one hold to another by the arms ⟨a *brachiating* gibbon⟩ — **bra•chi•a•tion** \,brā-kē-'ā-shən\ *n*
bra•chio•pod \'brā-kē-ə-,päd\ *n* **:** any of a phylum (Brachiopoda) of marine invertebrate animals with bivalve shells and a pair of arms bearing tentacles — called also *lampshell* [Latin *bracchium* "arm" + Greek *pod-, pous* "foot"] — **brachiopod** *adj*
brachy- *combining form* **:** short ⟨*brachy*cephalic⟩ [Greek *brachys*]
brachy•ce•phal•ic \,brak-i-sə-'fal-ik\ *adj* **:** having a head that is relatively short from front to back or relatively wide from side to side — **brachy•ceph•a•ly** \-i-'sef-ə-lē\ *n*
brac•ing \'brā-sing\ *adj* **:** giving strength or freshness ⟨a *bracing* wind⟩
brack•en \'brak-ən\ *n* **:** a large coarse branching fern; *also* **:** a growth of such ferns [Middle English *braken*]
[1]**brack•et** \'brak-ət\ *n* **1 :** an overhanging member or fixture that projects from a structure (as a wall) and is usually intended to support a vertical load or to strengthen an angle **2 :** a short wall shelf **3 a :** one of a pair of marks [ ] used to enclose matter or in mathematics used as signs indicating that two or more terms are treated as one quantity — called also *square bracket* **b :** one of a pair of marks ⟨ ⟩ used to enclose matter — called also *angle bracket* **4 :** a section of a continuously numbered or graded series; *esp* **:** one of a series of groups graded by income ⟨the $20,000 *bracket*⟩ [Middle French *braguette* "projecting part on breeches", from *brague* "breeches", derived from Latin *braca*, from Gaulish *brāca*, of Germanic origin]
[2]**bracket** *vt* **1 :** to place within or as if within brackets **2 :** to furnish with brackets **3 :** to put into the same category **:** ASSOCIATE **4 :** to get the range on (a target) by firing over and short
bracket fungus *n* **:** a basidiomycete that forms shelflike fruiting bodies
brack•ish \'brak-ish\ *adj* **:** somewhat salty ⟨*brackish* water⟩ [Dutch *brac* "salty"]
bract \'brakt\ *n* **1 :** a leaf from the axil of which a flower or flower cluster arises **2 :** a leaf that grows on a flower-bearing stem [Latin *bractea* "thin metal plate"] — **bract•ed** \'brak-təd\ *adj*
brad \'brad\ *n* **:** a slender nail with a small often indented head [Old Norse *broddr* "spike"]

\ə\ **abut**	\au̇\ **out**	\i\ **tip**	\ȯ\ **saw**	\u̇\ **foot**
\ər\ **further**	\ch\ **chin**	\ī\ **life**	\ȯi\ **coin**	\y\ **yet**
\a\ **mat**	\e\ **pet**	\j\ **job**	\th\ **thin**	\yü\ **few**
\ā\ **take**	\ē\ **easy**	\ng\ **sing**	\t͟h\ **this**	\yu̇\ **cure**
\ä\ **cot, cart**	\g\ **go**	\ō\ **bone**	\ü\ **food**	\zh\ **vision**

brae \'brā\ *n, chiefly Scottish* : a hillside especially along a river [Old Norse *brā* "eyelash"]

[1]**brag** \'brag\ *n* **1** : a pompous or boastful statement **2** : arrogant talk or manner : COCKINESS **3** : BRAGGART [Middle English]

[2]**brag** *vb* **bragged**; **brag•ging** : to talk or assert boastfully — **brag•ger** \'brag-ər\ *n*

brag•ga•do•cio \ˌbrag-ə-'dō-shē-ˌō, -shē-ō, -shō\ *n, pl* **-cios 1** : BRAGGART, BOASTER **2 a** : empty boasting **b** : COCKINESS [*Braggadochio,* personification of boasting in *Faerie Queene* by Edmund Spenser]

brag•gart \'brag-ərt\ *n* : a loud arrogant boaster — **braggart** *adj*

Brah•ma \'bräm-ə\ *n* : the ultimate ground of all being in Hinduism [Sanskrit *brahman*]

Brah•man *or* **Brah•min** \'bräm-ən; *2 is* 'brām-, 'bräm-, 'bram-\ **1 a** : a Hindu of the highest and traditionally the priestly caste **b** : BRAHMA **2** : ZEBU; *esp* : a large vigorous heat-resistant tick-resistant usually silvery gray animal developed in the southern United States by interbreeding Indian cattle [Sanskrit *brāhmana,* from *brahman* "prayer, sacred lore"] — **Brahman** *or* **Brah•man•ic** \brä-'man-ik\ *adj*

Brah•man•ism \'bräm-ə-ˌniz-əm\ *n* : orthodox Hinduism that follows the Vedas in accepting the forces and laws of the universe as divine and in practicing ancient rites and ceremonies

Brah•min \'bräm-ən\ *n* : an aloof intellectually and socially cultivated person; *esp* : such a person from one of the older New England families — **Brah•min•i•cal** \brä-'min-i-kəl\ *adj* — **Brah•min•ism** \'bräm-ə-ˌniz-əm\ *n*

[1]**braid** \'brād\ *vt* **1** : to form (three or more strands) into a braid **2** : to ornament especially with ribbon or braid [Old English *bregdan* "to move suddenly"] — **braid•er** *n*

[2]**braid** *n* **1** : a cord or ribbon with usually three or more strands forming a regular diagonal pattern down its length; *esp* : a narrow fabric of intertwined threads used especially for trimming **2** : a length of braided hair

braid•ing \'brād-ing\ *n* : something made of braided material

brail \'brāl\ *n* : a rope fastened to the leech of a sail for hauling the sail up or in [Old French *braiel* "strap"] — **brail** *vt*

braille \'brāl\ *n, often cap* : a system of writing for the blind that uses characters made up of raised dots [Louis *Braille*]

[1]**brain** \'brān\ *n* **1 a** : the portion of the vertebrate central nervous system that is the organ of thought and nervous coordination, is made up of neurons and supporting and nutritive structures, is enclosed within the skull, and is continuous with the spinal cord **b** : a major nervous center in an invertebrate animal **2 a** (1) : INTELLECT ⟨has a clever *brain*⟩ (2) : INTELLIGENCE — often used in pl. **b** (1) : a very intelligent or intellectual person (2) : the chief planner of an enterprise — usually used in pl. [Old English *brægen*]

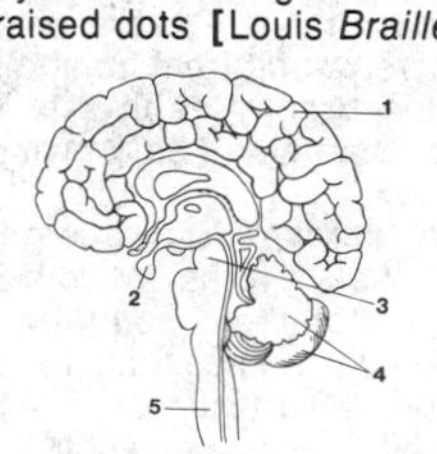

[1]brain 1a: *1* cerebrum, *2* pituitary gland, *3* midbrain, *4* cerebellum, *5* spinal cord

[2]**brain** *vt* **1** : to kill by smashing the skull **2** : to hit on the head

brain•case \-ˌkās\ *n* : the cranium enclosing the brain

brain•child \-ˌchīld\ *n* : a product of one's creative imagination

brain•less \'brān-ləs\ *adj* : UNINTELLIGENT, SILLY — **brain•less•ly** *adv* — **brain•less•ness** *n*

brain stem *n* : the posterior and lower part of the brain including the midbrain, pons, and medulla oblongata

brain•storm \'brān-ˌstȯrm\ *n* **1** : a temporary but violent mental upset or disturbance **2** : a sudden inspiration

brain trust *n* : a group of expert advisers dealing especially with planning and strategy and often lacking official status — **brain trust•er** \-ˌtrəs-tər\ *n*

brain•wash•ing \'brān-ˌwȯsh-ing, -ˌwäsh-\ *n* : a forcible attempt by indoctrination to induce someone to give up basic political, social, or religious beliefs and attitudes and to accept contrasting regimented ideas — **brain•wash** *vb*

brain wave *n* : rhythmic fluctuations of voltage between parts of the brain resulting in the flow of an electric current

brainy \'brā-nē\ *adj* **brain•i•er**; **-est** : INTELLIGENT — **brain•i•ness** *n*

braise \'brāz\ *vt* : to cook slowly in fat and then in a little liquid in a closed pot [French *braiser*]

[1]**brake** \'brāk\ *archaic past of* BREAK

[2]**brake** *n* : a coarse fern often growing up to a meter high : BRACKEN [Middle English]

[3]**brake** *n* **1** : a toothed instrument or machine for separating out the fiber of flax or hemp **2** : a machine for bending sheet metal [Low German]

[4]**brake** *n* : a device for slowing or stopping motion (as of a wheel, vehicle, or engine) especially by friction [Middle English]

[5]**brake** *vb* **1** : to slow or stop by or as if by a brake **2** : to operate a brake especially on a vehicle

[6]**brake** *n* : rough or marshy land thickly overgrown usually with one kind of plant [Middle English *-brake*] — **braky** \'brā-kē\ *adj*

brake•man \'brāk-mən\ *n* : a freight or passenger train crew member who inspects the train and assists the conductor

bram•ble \'bram-bəl\ *n* : any of a large genus of usually prickly shrubs of the rose family including the raspberries and blackberries [Old English *brēmel*] — **bram•bly** \-bə-lē, -blē\ *adj*

bran \'bran\ *n* : the broken coat of the seed of cereal grain separated from the flour or meal by sifting or bolting [Old French]

[1]**branch** \'branch\ *n* **1** : a natural subdivision (as a bough arising from a trunk or a twig from a bough) of a plant stem **2** : something (as a tributary of a river or a secondary road) forming a part of a larger whole in a manner suggesting the relation of a branch to a tree ⟨a *branch* of an antler⟩ ⟨the *branches* of an artery⟩: as **a** : a division of a family descending from a particular ancestor **b** : a division of an organization ⟨executive *branch* of the government⟩ **c** : a subordinate office or part of a central system ⟨a *branch* of a bank⟩ **d** : a part of a mathematical curve separated from others [Old French *branche,* from Late Latin *branca* "paw"] — **branched** \'brancht\ *adj* — **branch•less** \'branch-ləs\ *adj* — **branchy** \'bran-chē\ *adj*

[2]**branch** *vi* **1** : to develop branches : spread or separate into branches ⟨a great elm *branches* over the yard⟩ **2** : to spring out (as from a main stem) : DIVERGE ⟨streets *branching* off the highway⟩ **3** : to extend activities ⟨the business is *branching* out all over the state⟩

bran•chi•al \'brang-kē-əl\ *adj* : of, relating to, or situated near the gills [Latin *branchia* "gill", from Greek *branchion*]

[1]**brand** \'brand\ *n* **1** : a charred or burning piece of wood **2** : SWORD **3 a** : a mark made by burning (as on cattle) to show ownership or origin **b** : a mark made (as on freight) with a stamp or stencil for similar purposes **c** : a mark put on criminals with a hot iron **d** : a mark of disgrace : STIGMA **4 a** : a class of goods identified by name as the product of a single firm or manufacturer **b** : a characteristic or distinctive kind : VARIETY [Old English, "torch, sword"]

[2]**brand** *vt* **1** : to mark with or as if with a brand **2** : to mark with disapproval : STIGMATIZE — **brand•er** *n*

bran•dish \'bran-dish\ *vt* **1** : to shake or wave (as a weapon) threateningly **2** : to display in a showy or aggressive manner ⟨*brandishing* their intelligence⟩ [Middle French *brandiss-,* stem of *brandir,* from *brand* "sword", of Germanic origin] — **brandish** *n*

brand–new \'bran-'nü, -'nyü\ *adj* : conspicuously new and unused

[1]**bran•dy** \'bran-dē\ *n, pl* **-dies** : an alcoholic liquor distilled from wine or fermented fruit juice (as of apples) [short for *brandywine,* from Dutch *brandewijn,* from *brant* "distilled" + *wijn* "wine"]

△ **origin** An earlier English form of the word *brandy* is *brandywine,* which was borrowed from Dutch *brandewijn.* The second element of this compound is Dutch for "wine". The first means "burnt". The name "burnt wine" refers to wine that has been distilled over a fire.

[2]**brandy** *vt* **bran•died**; **bran•dy•ing** : to flavor, blend, or preserve with brandy ⟨*brandied* cherries⟩

brant \'brant\ *n, pl* **brant** *or* **brants** : a wild goose; *esp* : any of several small dark geese that breed in the Arctic [origin unknown]

brash \'brash\ *adj* **1** : IMPETUOUS, RASH ⟨a *brash* attack⟩ **2** : aggressively self-assertive : IMPUDENT ⟨a person *brash* to the point of arrogance⟩ **3** : piercingly sharp : HARSH ⟨a *brash* squeal of brakes⟩ [origin unknown] — **brash•ly** *adv* — **brash•ness** *n*

brass \'bras\ *n* **1** : an alloy consisting essentially of copper and zinc; *also* : the reddish yellow color of this alloy **2 a** : brass musical instruments — often used in pl. **b** : a usually brass memorial tablet **c** : bright metal fittings or utensils **3** : brazen self-assurance : GALL **4** : BRASS HATS [Old English *bræs*] — **brass** *adj*

brass band *n* : a band consisting chiefly or solely of brass and percussion instruments

brass·bound \ˈbras-ˌbau̇nd, -ˈbau̇nd\ *adj* **1** : having trim made of brass ⟨a *brassbound* trunk⟩ **2** : strictly bound by tradition : INFLEXIBLE

brass hat *n* : a person (as a military officer) in a high-ranking position

bras·siere \brə-ˈziər *also* ˌbras-ē-ˈeər\ *n* : a woman's close-fitting undergarment with cups for bust support [obsolete French *brassière* "bodice", from Old French *braciere* "arm protector", from *bras* "arm"]

brass knuckles *n pl* : KNUCKLE 3

brass tacks *n pl* : details of immediate practical importance — usually used in the phrase *get down to brass tacks*

brassy \ˈbras-ē\ *adj* **brass·i·er**; **-est** **1 a** : shamelessly bold **b** : UNRULY **2** : resembling brass especially in color **3** : resembling the sound of a brass instrument — **brass·i·ly** \ˈbras-ə-lē\ *adv* — **brass·i·ness** \ˈbras-ē-nəs\ *n*

brat \ˈbrat\ *n* : CHILD; *esp* : an ill-mannered annoying child [perhaps from English dialect *brat* "ragamuffin"] — **brat·tish** \ˈbrat-ish\ *adj* — **brat·ty** \ˈbrat-ē\ *adj*

bra·va·do \brə-ˈväd-ō\ *n, pl* **-does** *or* **-dos** **1** : blustering swaggering conduct **2** : a pretense of bravery [Middle French *bravade*, from Italian *bravata*, from *bravo* "courageous"]

[1]**brave** \ˈbrāv\ *adj* **1** : COURAGEOUS **2** : making a fine show : COLORFUL ⟨*brave* banners flying in the wind⟩ **3** : SPLENDID ⟨the business collapsed despite a *brave* start⟩ [Middle French, from Italian and Spanish *bravo* "wild, courageous", from Latin *barbarus* "barbarous"] — **brave·ly** *adv*

[2]**brave** *vt* : to face or endure with courage ⟨*braved* the taunts of the mob⟩

[3]**brave** *n* : one who is brave; *esp* : an American Indian warrior

brav·ery \ˈbrāv-rē, -ə-rē\ *n, pl* **-er·ies** **1 a** : fine clothes **b** : showy display **2** : the quality or state of being brave : FEARLESSNESS **syn** see COURAGE

[1]**bra·vo** \ˈbräv-ō\ *n, pl* **bravos** *or* **bravoes** : VILLAIN, DESPERADO; *esp* : a hired assassin [Italian, from *bravo* "wild, courageous"]

[2]**bra·vo** \ˈbräv-ō, brä-ˈvō\ *n, pl* **bravos** : a shout of approval — often used interjectionally in applauding a performance

[3]**bra·vo** \ˈbräv-ō, brä-ˈvō\ *vt* **bra·voed**; **bra·vo·ing** : to applaud by shouts of *bravo*

bra·vu·ra \brə-ˈvyu̇r-ə, -ˈvu̇r-\ *n* **1** : a florid brilliant musical style **2** : a musical passage requiring agility and skill to perform **3** : a show of daring or brilliance [Italian, literally, "bravery"]

braw \ˈbrȯ\ *adj, chiefly Scottish* : GOOD, FINE; *also* : well dressed [Middle French *brave*]

[1]**brawl** \ˈbrȯl\ *vi* **1** : to quarrel or fight noisily **2** : to make a loud confused noise ⟨the river *brawling* by⟩ [Middle English *brawlen*] — **brawl·er** *n*

[2]**brawl** *n* : a noisy quarrel or fight

brawn \ˈbrȯn\ *n* **1** : full strong muscles especially of the arm or leg **2** : muscular strength [Middle French *braon* "muscle", of Germanic origin]

brawny \ˈbrȯ-nē\ *adj* **brawn·i·er**; **-est** : having large strong muscles — **brawn·i·ness** *n*

[1]**bray** \ˈbrā\ *vb* **1** : to utter a bray or similar sound **2** : to utter or play loudly, harshly, or discordantly [Old French *braire* "to cry"]

[2]**bray** *n* : the characteristic loud harsh cry of a donkey

bray·er \ˈbrā-ər\ *n* : a hand roller for inking something (as a block) to be printed [Middle English *brayen* "to crush to powder", from Middle French *broiier*]

braze \ˈbrāz\ *vb* : to solder with a nonferrous alloy having a relatively high melting point [probably from French *braser*, derived from Old French *brese* "live coals"]

[1]**bra·zen** \ˈbrāz-n\ *adj* **1** : made of brass **2 a** : sounding harsh and loud like struck brass **b** : of the color of polished brass **3** : IMPUDENT, SHAMELESS ⟨a *brazen* violation of the rules⟩ [Old English *bræsen*, from *bræs* "brass"] — **bra·zen·ly** *adv* — **bra·zen·ness** \ˈbrāz-n-nəs, -əs\ *n*

[2]**brazen** *vt* **bra·zened**; **bra·zen·ing** \ˈbrāz-ning, -n-ing\ : to face with defiance or impudence ⟨would the prisoner *brazen* it out or break down and confess⟩

bra·zen–faced \ˌbrāz-n-ˈfāst\ *adj* : showing insolence and bold disrespect ⟨a *brazen-faced* liar⟩

[1]**bra·zier** \ˈbrā-zhər\ *n* : one that works in brass [Middle English *brasier*, from *bras* "brass"]

[2]**brazier** *n* **1** : a pan for holding burning coals **2** : a utensil on which food is exposed to heat (as from burning charcoal) through a grill [French *brasier*, derived from Old French *brese* "hot coals"]

Bra·zil nut \brə-ˈzil-\ *n* : one of the 3-sided oily edible nuts that occur packed inside the round fruit of a large Brazilian tree

[1]**breach** \ˈbrēch\ *n* **1** : violation of a law, duty, or tie ⟨a *breach* of trust⟩ **2 a** : a broken, ruptured, or torn condition or area **b** : a gap (as in a wall) made by battering **3 a** : a break in accustomed friendly relations **b** : a temporary gap in continuity : HIATUS [Old English *bryce*]

[2]**breach** *vb* **1** : to make a breach in ⟨*breach* the city walls⟩ **2** : BREAK, VIOLATE ⟨*breach* an agreement⟩ **3** : to leap out of water ⟨an otter *breaching*⟩

breach of promise : violation of a promise especially to marry

[1]**bread** \ˈbred\ *n* **1** : a baked food made of a mixture whose basic constituent is flour or meal **2** : FOOD, SUSTENANCE ⟨our daily *bread*⟩ **3 a** : LIVELIHOOD ⟨earn one's *bread* as a laborer⟩ **b** *slang* : MONEY [Old English *brēad*]

[2]**bread** *vt* : to cover with bread crumbs ⟨*breaded* veal cutlet⟩

bread–and–but·ter \ˌbred-n-ˈbət-ər\ *adj* **1 a** : of, relating to, or affecting a means of livelihood ⟨unions concerned with *bread-and-butter* issues⟩ **b** : DEPENDABLE ⟨*bread-and-butter* products that always sell⟩; *also* : COMMONPLACE, EVERYDAY ⟨*bread-and-butter* language⟩ **2** : sent or given as thanks for hospitality ⟨a *bread-and-butter* letter⟩

bread and butter *n* : a means of livelihood

bread·bas·ket \ˈbred-ˌbas-kət\ *n* **1** *slang* : STOMACH **2** : a major cereal-producing region

bread·board \-ˌbōrd, -ˌbȯrd\ *n* **1** : a board on which dough is kneaded or bread cut **2** : a board on which electric or electronic circuits may be laid out

bread·fruit \-ˌfrüt\ *n* : a round usually seedless fruit that resembles bread in color and texture when baked; *also* : a tall tropical tree of the mulberry family that bears this fruit

breadfruit

bread mold *n* : any of several molds (as a rhizopus) that are found especially on bread

bread·stuff \-ˌstəf\ *n* **1** : a cereal product (as grain or flour) **2** : BREAD

breadth \ˈbredth, ˈbreth, ˈbretth\ *n* **1** : distance from side to side : WIDTH **2 a** : something of full width **b** : a wide expanse **3** : COMPREHENSIVENESS, SCOPE ⟨the remarkable *breadth* of a scholar's learning⟩ [Old English *brǣdu*, from *brād* "broad"]

bread·win·ner \ˈbred-ˌwin-ər\ *n* : a member of a family whose wages supply its livelihood

[1]**break** \ˈbrāk\ *vb* **broke** \ˈbrōk\; **bro·ken** \ˈbrō-kən\; **break·ing** **1 a** : to separate suddenly or violently into parts : SHATTER ⟨*break* a dish⟩ **b** : FRACTURE **c** : MAIM **d** : RUPTURE **e** : to curl over and fall apart ⟨waves *breaking* against the shore⟩ **2** : VIOLATE, TRANSGRESS ⟨*broke* the law⟩ **3 a** : to force a way into, out of, or through ⟨burglars *broke* into the house⟩ **b** : to escape with sudden effort ⟨*broke* away from our captors⟩ **c** : to develop, appear, or burst forth with suddenness or force ⟨day *breaks* in the east⟩ ⟨*broke* into laughter⟩ **d** : to become fair ⟨waited for the weather to *break*⟩ **e** : to make a sudden dash ⟨*break* for cover⟩ **f** : to make or effect by cutting, forcing, or pressing ⟨*break* open a package⟩ **g** : PENETRATE, PIERCE **4** : LOOSEN, SUNDER ⟨*break* a hold⟩ **5** : to cut into and turn over the surface of : PLOW ⟨*break* ground for a new school⟩ **6 a** : to

disrupt the order or uniformity of ⟨*break* ranks⟩ **b :** to end by or as if by dispersing ⟨police *broke* up the mob⟩ **c :** to give way in disorderly retreat ⟨the soldiers *broke* under fire⟩ **d :** to decline suddenly and sharply in price or value **e :** to end a relationship or accord — usually used with *with* **7 a :** to subdue completely **:** CRUSH ⟨*broke* the revolt⟩ **b :** to lose or cause to lose health, strength, or spirit ⟨*broke* under the strain⟩ **c :** to become inoperative because of damage, wear, or strain ⟨the TV set is *broken*⟩ **d :** to ruin financially **e :** to reduce in rank **f :** to force (a strike) to end by measures outside bargaining practices **g :** to ruin the prospects of ⟨could make or *break* my career⟩ **8 a :** to bring to an end suddenly ⟨*break* a deadlock⟩ ⟨*broke* the silence⟩ **b :** INTERRUPT, SUSPEND ⟨*broke* in with a comment⟩ ⟨*broke* their tour for a rest⟩ **9 a :** to make (an animal) fit for use (as by training) **b :** to accustom to an activity or occurrence ⟨*break* in a new worker⟩ **10 :** to make known ⟨*break* the news to them⟩ **11 :** to check the force or intensity of ⟨the bushes *broke* my fall⟩ **12 :** EXCEED, SURPASS ⟨*broke* all records⟩ **13 :** OPEN ⟨*break* an electric circuit⟩ **14 :** to split the surface of ⟨fish *breaking* water⟩ **15 :** to cause to discontinue a habit ⟨*broke* the child of thumb-sucking⟩ **16 :** SOLVE ⟨*broke* the enemy code⟩ **17 a :** to alter course sharply ⟨*broke* to the left⟩ **b :** to curve, drop, or rise sharply ⟨the pitch *broke* over the plate for a strike⟩ **c :** to alter sharply in tone, pitch, or intensity ⟨a voice *breaking* with emotion⟩ **d :** to shift abruptly from one register to another **18 :** HAPPEN, DEVELOP ⟨everything *broke* right for us⟩ [Old English *brecan*] — **break•able** \'brā-kə-bəl\ *adj* — **break camp :** to pack up gear and leave a camp — **break cover :** to start from a covert or lair ⟨the hunted fox *broke cover*⟩ — **break one's heart :** to crush emotionally with sorrow — **break the back :** to subdue the main force ⟨*break the back* of inflation⟩ — **break the ice 1 :** to make a beginning **2 :** to get through the first difficulties in starting a conversation — **break wind :** to expel gas from the intestine

[2]break *n* **1 a :** an act or action of breaking **b :** the opening shot in a game of pool or billiards **2 a :** a condition produced by breaking ⟨a *break* in the clouds⟩ **b :** a gap in an electric circuit interrupting the flow of current **3 :** an interruption in continuity: as **a :** a respite from work or duty **b :** a planned interruption in a radio or television program ⟨a commercial *break*⟩ **c :** a noticeable change (as in a surface, course, movement, or direction) **d :** a notable variation of pitch, intensity, or tone in the voice **e :** an abrupt run **:** DASH **f :** the act of separating after a boxing or wrestling clinch **4 :** a rupture in previously friendly relations ⟨a *break* between the two countries⟩ **5 :** a place or situation at which a break occurs: as **a :** the point where one musical register changes to another **b :** the place at which a word is divided **c :** CAESURA **6 :** social blunder; *esp* **:** an indiscreet remark that causes embarrassment **7 :** a stroke of luck ⟨a bad *break*⟩; *esp* **:** a stroke of good luck ⟨got all the *breaks*⟩

break•age \'brā-kij\ *n* **1 a :** the action of breaking **b :** a quantity broken ⟨a *breakage* of 10 percent⟩ **2 :** loss due to or a charge for things broken

break•down \'brāk-ˌdau̇n\ *n* **1 a :** a failure to function properly **b :** a physical, mental, or nervous collapse **2 :** DECOMPOSITION **3 :** division into categories **:** CLASSIFICATION

break down \brāk-'dau̇n, 'brāk-\ *vb* **1 a :** to cause to fall or collapse by breaking or shattering **b :** to make ineffective **2 a :** to separate (as a protein) into simpler substances **:** DECOMPOSE **b :** to undergo decomposition **3 :** to become subdivided or separated by analysis

break•er \'brā-kər\ *n* **1 :** one that breaks **2 :** a wave breaking into foam against the shore

break even *vi* **:** to end up with neither gain nor loss ⟨gamblers who barely *break even*⟩

break•fast \'brek-fəst\ *n* **:** the first meal of the day especially when taken in the morning — **breakfast** *vb*

break•neck \'brāk-ˌnek\ *adj* **:** very fast or dangerous ⟨*breakneck* speed⟩

break•out \'brāk-ˌau̇t\ *n* **:** a violent or forceful break from restraint

break out \brāk-'au̇t, 'brāk-\ *vb* **:** to be affected with a skin eruption

break•through \'brāk-ˌthrü\ *n* **1 :** an act or point of breaking through an obstruction or defensive line **2 :** an important advance in knowledge or technique

break•wa•ter \'brāk-ˌwȯt-ər, -ˌwät-\ *n* **:** an offshore structure (as a wall) to protect a harbor or beach from the force of waves

bream \'brim, 'brēm\ *n, pl* **bream** *or* **breams :** any of various mostly freshwater spiny-finned fishes; *esp* **:** any of several sunfishes (as a bluegill) [Middle French *breme,* of Germanic origin]

[1]breast \'brest\ *n* **1 :** either of two protuberant milk-producing glandular organs situated on the front of the chest in the human female and some other mammals; *also* **:** any mammary gland **2 :** the front or ventral part of the body between the neck and the abdomen **3 :** the center of emotion and thought **:** BOSOM **4 :** something resembling a breast [Old English *brēost*] — **breast•ed** \'bres-təd\ *adj*

[2]breast *vt* **:** to face or oppose boldly **:** BRAVE ⟨ships *breasting* the waves⟩

breast•bone \'brest-'bōn, 'bres-, -ˌbōn\ *n* **:** STERNUM

breast–feed \'brest-ˌfēd\ *vt* **-fed** \-ˌfed\; **-feed•ing :** to feed (a baby) from a mother's breast rather than from a bottle

breast•plate \'brest-ˌplāt, 'bres-\ *n* **:** a metal plate worn as defensive armor for the chest

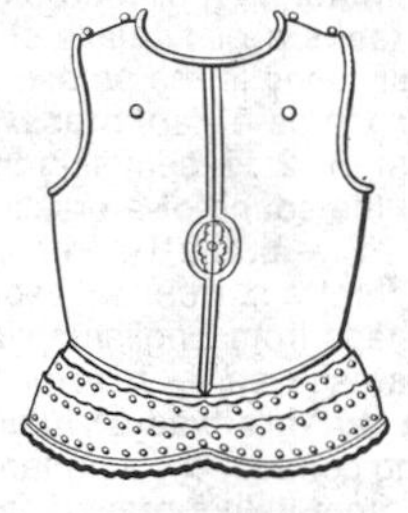

breastplate

breast•stroke \'brest-ˌstrōk, 'bres-\ *n* **:** a swimming stroke performed by extending the arms in front of the head while drawing the knees forward and outward and then sweeping the arms back with palms out while kicking outward and backward

breast•work \'bres-ˌtwərk\ *n* **:** an improvised or temporary fortification

breath \'breth\ *n* **1 :** a slight indication **:** SUGGESTION **2 a :** the power of breathing **b :** an act of breathing **c :** RESPITE 2, BREATHER **3 :** a slight breeze **4 a :** air inhaled and exhaled in breathing **b :** something (as moisture on a cold surface) produced by breathing **5 :** a spoken sound **:** UTTERANCE **6 :** expiration of air with the glottis wide open in the formation of speech sounds [Old English *brǣth*] — **out of breath :** breathing very rapidly (as from strenuous exercise)

breathe \'brēth\ *vb* **1 :** to draw air into and expel it from the lungs **:** RESPIRE **2 :** LIVE 1 **3 :** to pause and rest before continuing **4 a :** to send out by exhaling **b :** to instill by or as if by breathing ⟨*breathe* new life into the movement⟩ **5 :** to tell to someone ⟨don't *breathe* a word of it⟩ **6 :** to allow to rest after exertion ⟨*breathe* a horse⟩ **7 :** to take in in breathing — **breath•able** \'brē-thə-bəl\ *adj*

breathed \'bretht\ *adj* **:** VOICELESS 2

breath•er \'brē-thər\ *n* **1 :** one that breathes **2 :** a break in activity for rest

breath•ing \'brē-thing\ *n* **:** either of the marks ʽ and ʼ used in writing Greek to indicate an intial *h*-sound or its absence

breath•less \'breth-ləs\ *adj* **1 a :** not breathing **b :** DEAD **2 :** gasping for breath **:** PANTING **b :** leaving one breathless ⟨*breathless* excitement⟩ — **breath•less•ly** *adv* — **breath•less•ness** *n*

breath•tak•ing \'breth-ˌtā-king\ *adj* **1 :** making one out of breath ⟨a *breathtaking* climb⟩ **2 :** of a kind to excite or thrill ⟨*breathtaking* beauty⟩ — **breath•tak•ing•ly** \-king-lē\ *adv*

brec•cia \'brech-ə, -ē-ə\ *n* **:** a rock consisting of sharp fragments embedded in a fine-grained material [Italian]

breech \'brēch; *"breeches" (garment) is usually* 'brich-əz\ *n* **1** *pl* **a :** short trousers fitting snugly at or just below the knee **b :** PANTS 1 **2 :** BUTTOCK 2 **3 :** the part of a firearm at the rear of the bore [Old English *brēc* "breeches", plural of *brōc* "leg covering"]

breech•es buoy \'brē-chəz- *also* 'brich-əz-\ *n* **:** a canvas sling in the form of a pair of short-legged breeches hung from a life buoy running along a rope that is used to take persons off a ship especially in rescue operations

breech•load•er \'brēch-ˌlōd-ər\ *n* **:** a firearm that receives its ammunition at the breech

[1]breed \'brēd\ *vb* **bred** \'bred\; **breed•ing 1 a :** BEGET 1 **b :** to be the source of ⟨wars *breed* depressions⟩ **2 :** to propagate (plants or animals) sexually and usually under controlled conditions **3 a :** to bring up **:** NURTURE **b :** to instill by training **4 :** to mate with **5 :** to produce offspring sexually [Old English *brēdan*] — **breed•er** *n*

[2]breed *n* **1 :** a group of presumably related animals or plants visibly similar in most characters; *esp* : one differentiated from the wild type under the influence of humans **2** : CLASS 3a, KIND

breed•ing *n* **1** : ANCESTRY **2** : training or education especially in manners **3** : the sexual propagation of plants or animals

[1]**breeze** \'brēz\ *n* **1 a** : a gentle wind **b** : a wind of from 1.6 to 13.8 meters per second **2** : something easily done : CINCH [Middle English *brise*]

[2]**breeze** *vi* : to proceed quickly and easily ⟨*breezed* through the report⟩

breeze•way \'brēz-ˌwā\ *n* : a roofed open passage connecting two buildings (as a house and garage) or parts of a building

breezy \'brē-zē\ *adj* **breez•i•er**; **-est 1** : swept by breezes **2** : both lively and informal ⟨a *breezy* manner⟩ — **breez•i•ly** \-zə-lē\ *adv* — **breez•i•ness** \-zē-nəs\ *n*

breth•ren \'bret͟h-rən, -ərn, -ə-rən\ *pl of* BROTHER — used chiefly in formal or solemn address

Bret•on \'bret-n\ *n* **1** : a native or inhabitant of Brittany **2** : the Celtic language of the Bretons — **Breton** *adj*

breve \'brēv, 'brev\ *n* **1** : a mark ˘ placed over a vowel to show that the vowel is short **2** : a note equivalent to four half notes [Latin, neuter of *brevis* "brief"]

bre•via•ry \'brē-vyə-rē, -və-; -vē-ˌer-ē\ *n, pl* **-ries** : a book containing the prayers, hymns, and readings prescribed especially for priests for each day of the year [Latin *breviarium,* from *brevis* "brief"]

brev•i•ty \'brev-ət-ē\ *n* **1** : shortness of duration **2** : expression in few words : CONCISENESS

[1]**brew** \'brü\ *vb* **1** : to prepare (as beer or ale) by steeping, boiling, and fermentation **2** : to form a plot or plan : CONTRIVE **3** : to prepare (as tea) by steeping in hot water **4** : to be forming ⟨a storm is *brewing*⟩ [Old English *brēowan*] — **brew•er** \'brü-ər, 'brů-ər, 'brůr\ *n*

[2]**brew** *n* **1** : a brewed beverage **2** : a product of brewing

brewer's yeast *n* : a yeast used or suitable for use in brewing; *also* : the dried pulverized cells of such a yeast used as a source of B-complex vitamins — compare BAKER'S YEAST

brew•ery \'brü-ə-rē, 'brů-ər-ē, 'brůr-ē\ *n, pl* **-er•ies** : a plant where malt liquors are manufactured

bri•ar *variant of* BRIER

[1]**bribe** \'brīb\ *n* : money or favor given or promised to influence improperly the judgment or conduct of a person in a position of trust **2** : something that serves to induce or influence [Middle English, "something stolen", from Middle French, "bread given to a beggar"]

[2]**bribe** *vb* : to influence by or as if by giving bribes — **brib•able** \'brī-bə-bəl\ *adj* — **brib•er** *n*

brib•ery \'brī-bə-rē, -brē\ *n, pl* **-er•ies** : the act or practice of giving bribes

bric-a-brac \'brik-ə-ˌbrak\ *n* : small ornamental articles : KNICKKNACKS [French *bric-à-brac*]

[1]**brick** \'brik\ *n* **1 a** : a building or paving material made from clay molded into blocks and hardened in the sun or baked **b** : a rectangular block made of brick **2** : a brick-shaped mass ⟨a *brick* of ice cream⟩ [Middle French *brique,* from Dutch *bricke*]

[2]**brick** *vt* : to stop up, face, or pave with bricks

brick•bat \'brik-ˌbat\ *n* **1** : a piece of a broken brick; *esp* : one thrown as a missile **2** : an uncomplimentary remark

brick•lay•er \'brik-ˌlā-ər, -ˌle-ər -ˌler\ *n* : a person who builds or paves with bricks — **brick•lay•ing** \-ˌlā-ing\ *n*

brick•work \'brik-ˌwərk\ *n* : work of or with brick

brick•yard \-ˌyärd\ *n* : a place where bricks are made

[1]**brid•al** \'brīd-l\ *n* : a marriage ceremony : WEDDING [Old English *brȳdealu,* from *brȳd* "bride" + *ealu* "ale, festival"]

[2]**bridal** *adj* : of or relating to a bride or a wedding : NUPTIAL

bridal wreath *n* : a spirea widely grown for its slender drooping branches and clusters of small white flowers borne in spring

bride \'brīd\ *n* : a woman newly married or about to be married [Old English *brȳd*]

bride•groom \-ˌgrüm, -ˌgrům\ *n* : a man newly married or about to be married [Old English *brȳdguma,* from *brȳd* "bride" + *guma* "man"]

brides•maid \'brīdz-ˌmād\ *n* : a woman who attends a bride at her wedding

[1]**bridge** \'brij\ *n* **1** : a structure built over a depression or an obstacle (as a river or a railroad) to allow passage **2** : a platform above and across the deck of a ship for the captain or officer in charge **3** : something resembling a bridge in form or function: as **a** : the upper bony part of the nose **b** : an arch serving to raise the strings of a musical instrument **4** : something (as a partial denture anchored to adjacent teeth) that fills a gap [Old English *brycg*]

[2]**bridge** *vt* : to make a bridge over or across ⟨*bridge* a gap⟩ — **bridge•able** \-ə-bəl\ *adj*

[3]**bridge** *n* : any of various card games for four players developed from whist; *esp* : CONTRACT BRIDGE [earlier *biritch,* of unknown origin]

bridge•head \-ˌhed\ *n* **1** : a fortified position protecting a bridge **2** : a position seized in enemy territory as a foothold for further advance

bridge•work \-ˌwərk\ *n* : the dental bridges in a mouth

[1]**bri•dle** \'brīd-l\ *n* **1** : the headgear with which a horse is controlled consisting of a headstall, a bit, and reins **2** : CURB 2, RESTRAINT [Old English *brīdel*]

[2]**bridle** *vb* **bri•dled**; **bri•dling** \'brīd-ling, -l-ing\ **1** : to put a bridle upon **2** : to restrain with or as if with a bridle **3** : to show hostility or resentment especially by drawing back the head and chin

bridle path *n* : a trail suitable for horseback riding

[1]**brief** \'brēf\ *adj* **1** : short in duration or extent ⟨a *brief* visit⟩ **2 a** : expressed in few words : CONCISE **b** : CURT, ABRUPT [Middle French, from Latin *brevis*] — **brief•ly** *adv* — **brief•ness** *n*

[2]**brief** *n* **1 a** : a brief summary of an argument, set of facts, or document **b** : a concise statement of the case a lawyer will present in court **2** *pl* : short snug underpants

[3]**brief** *vt* **1** : to make a summary of **2 a** : to give final instructions to ⟨*brief* a bombing crew⟩ **b** : to give essential information to ⟨*brief* reporters⟩

brief•case \-ˌkās\ *n* : an often flat flexible case (as of leather) for carrying papers

[1]**bri•er** *or* **bri•ar** \'brī-ər, 'brīr\ *n* : a plant (as the blackberry or the wild rose) with a thorny or prickly woody stem [Old English *brēr*] — **bri•ery** \'brī-ər-ē, 'brīr-ē\ *adj*

[2]**brier** *or* **briar** *n* : a heath of southern Europe the root of which is used for making tobacco pipes [French *bruyère*]

[1]**brig** \'brig\ *n* : a 2-masted square-rigged sailing vessel [short for *brigantine*]

[2]**brig** *n* : a place (as on a ship) for temporary confinement of offenders in the United States Navy

[1]brig

bri•gade \brig-'ād\ *n* **1** : a military unit composed of one or more units of infantry or armor with supporting units **2** : a group of people organized for special activity ⟨fire *brigade*⟩ [French, from Italian *brigata,* from *briga* "strife"]

brig•a•dier \ˌbrig-ə-'diər\ *n* : BRIGADIER GENERAL

brigadier general *n* : an officer rank in the Army, Marine Corps, and Air Force above colonel and below major general

brig•and \'brig-ənd\ *n* : a person who lives by plunder usually as a member of a band : BANDIT [Middle French, from Italian *brigante,* from *briga* "strife", of Celtic origin] — **brig•and•age** \-ən-dij\ *n* — **brig•and•ism** \-ˌdiz-əm\ *n*

brig•an•tine \'brig-ən-ˌtēn\ *n* : a 2-masted square-rigged sailing vessel differing from a brig in not carrying a square mainsail [Middle French *brigantin,* from Italian *brigantino,* from *brigante* "brigand"]

bright \'brīt\ *adj* **1** : shedding much light : SHINING, GLOWING ⟨a *bright* fire⟩ **2** : very clear or vivid in color ⟨a *bright* red⟩ **3** : quick in learning : INTELLIGENT **4** : full of life : CHEERFUL **5** : promising success ⟨a *bright* future⟩ [Old English *beorht*] — **bright** *adv* — **bright•ly** *adv* — **bright•ness** *n*

bright•en \'brīt-n\ *vb* **bright•ened**; **bright•en•ing** \'brīt-ning, -n-ing\ : to make or become bright or brighter

Bright's disease \'brīts-\ *n* : kidney disease in which albumin appears in the urine [Richard *Bright,* died 1858, English physician]

\ə\ **abut**	\au̇\ **out**	\i\ **tip**	\ȯ\ **saw**	\u̇\ **foot**
\ər\ **further**	\ch\ **chin**	\ī\ **life**	\ȯi\ **coin**	\y\ **yet**
\a\ **mat**	\e\ **pet**	\j\ **job**	\th\ **thin**	\yü\ **few**
\ā\ **take**	\ē\ **easy**	\ng\ **sing**	\t͟h\ **this**	\yu̇\ **cure**
\ä\ **cot, cart**	\g\ **go**	\ō\ **bone**	\ü\ **food**	\zh\ **vision**

brill \'bril\ *n, pl* **brill** : a European flatfish related to the turbot [perhaps from Cornish *brȳthel* "mackerel"]

[1]**bril•liant** \'bril-yənt\ *adj* **1** : very bright : GLITTERING ⟨*brilliant* jewels⟩ **2 a** : outstandingly successful : DISTINGUISHED **b** : unusually keen or alert in mind [French *brillant,* from *briller* "to shine", derived from Latin *beryllus* "beryl"] — **bril•liance** \-yəns\ *or* **bril•lian•cy** \-yən-sē\ *n* — **bril•liant•ly** *adv* — **bril•liant•ness** *n*

[2]**brilliant** *n* : a gem (as a diamond) cut with numerous facets so as to have particular brilliance

bril•lian•tine \'bril-yən-ˌtēn\ *n* **1** : a preparation for making hair glossy **2** : a light lustrous fabric similar to alpaca

[1]**brim** \'brim\ *n* **1** : the rim especially of a cup, bowl, or depression ⟨the *brim* of the crater⟩ **2** : the projecting rim of a hat [Middle English *brimme*] **syn** see RIM — **brim•ful** \-'fu̇l\ *adj* — **brim•less** \-ləs\ *adj*

[2]**brim** *vb* **brimmed**; **brim•ming** **1** : to fill or become filled to overflowing **2** : to reach or overflow a brim

brim•stone \'brim-ˌstōn\ *n* : SULFUR [Middle English *brinston,* probably from *brinnen* "to burn" + *ston* "stone"]

brin•dle \'brin-dl\ *n* : a brindled color or animal

brin•dled \-dld\ *or* **brin•dle** \-dl\ *adj* : having faint dark streaks or flecks on a gray or tawny ground [Middle English *brended*]

brine \'brīn\ *n* **1** : water containing a great deal of salt **2 a** : OCEAN **b** : the water of an ocean, sea, or salt lake [Old English *brȳne*]

brine shrimp *n* : any of a genus of crustaceans found in salt lakes and the brine of saltworks

bring \'bring\ *vt* **brought** \'brȯt\; **bring•ing** \'bring-ing\ **1** : to cause to come with one by carrying or leading ⟨*bring* a lunch⟩ ⟨*bring* a friend⟩ **2** : to cause to be, act, or move in a special way ⟨their screams *brought* the neighbors⟩ **3** : to cause to come into a particular state or condition ⟨*bring* water to a boil⟩ **4** : to cause to exist or occur ⟨winter will *bring* snow⟩ **5** : to sell for ⟨apples will *bring* a good price⟩ [Old English *bringan*] — **bring•er** \'bring-ər\ *n*

• **syn** BRING, TAKE may denote identical action performed in opposite directions in relation to the speaker. BRING implies carrying, leading, transporting *toward* a point where the speaker is or will be; TAKE implies the same action *away* from the speaker ⟨*take* this message to the superintendent and *bring* back an answer⟩

— **bring up the rear** : to come last or behind

bring about *vt* : to cause to take place : EFFECT

bring around *vt* **1** : to cause (someone) to adopt an opinion or a course of action : PERSUADE **2** : to restore to consciousness : REVIVE

bring forth *vt* : to bear or give birth to : PRODUCE

bring in *vt* **1** : to produce as profit or return **2** : INCLUDE 2, INTRODUCE ⟨*bring in* a new topic⟩ **3** : EARN 2 ⟨*brings in* a good salary⟩

bring off *vt* : to carry to a successful conclusion : ACHIEVE

bring out *vt* : to present to the public ⟨*bring out* a new book⟩

bring to *vt* : to restore to consciousness

bring up *vb* **1** : EDUCATE 2, REAR **2** : to stop suddenly **3** : to bring to attention : INTRODUCE

brink \'bringk\ *n* **1** : EDGE; *esp* : the edge at the top of a steep place **2** : the point of onset : VERGE ⟨at the *brink* of war⟩ [Middle English]

brink•man•ship \-mən-ˌship\ *also* **brinksmanship** *n* : the practice of pushing a dangerous situation to the limit of safety before stopping

briny \'brī-nē\ *adj* **brin•i•er**; **-est** : of or resembling brine : SALTY — **brin•i•ness** *n*

brio \'brē-ō\ *n* : VIVACITY, SPIRIT [Italian]

bri•quette *or* **bri•quet** \brik-'et\ *n* : a compacted often brick-shaped mass of usually fine material ⟨charcoal *briquette*⟩ [French *briquette,* from *brique* "brick"]

[1]**brisk** \'brisk\ *adj* **1** : very active or alert : LIVELY **2** : REFRESHING ⟨*brisk* autumn weather⟩ **3** : full of energy : QUICK ⟨a *brisk* pace⟩ [probably from Middle French *brusque*] — **brisk•ly** *adv* — **brisk•ness** *n*

[2]**brisk** *vb* : to make or become brisk

bris•ket \'bris-kət\ *n* : the breast or lower chest of a quadruped animal [Middle English *brusket*]

bris•ling *or* **bris•tling** \'briz-ling, 'bris-\ *n* : a small herring that resembles and is processed like a sardine [Norwegian *brisling*]

[1]**bris•tle** \'bris-əl\ *n* : a short stiff coarse hair or filament [Old English *byrst*] — **bris•tled** \-əld\ *adj* — **bris•tly** \'bris-lē, -ə-lē\ *adj*

[2]**bristle** *vi* **bris•tled**; **bris•tling** \'bris-ling, -ə-ling\ **1** : to rise and stand stiffly erect ⟨quills *bristling* in all directions⟩ **2** : to show signs of anger or defiance ⟨people who *bristle* at criticism⟩ **3** : to appear as if covered with bristles ⟨a harbor *bristling* with the masts of ships⟩

bris•tle•cone pine \ˌbris-əl-ˌkōn-\ *n* : a pine of the western United States of which some specimens are held to be nearly 5000 years old

bristlecone pine

bris•tle•tail \'bris-əl-ˌtāl\ *n* : any of various wingless insects (orders Thysanura and Entotrophi) with two projecting tail bristles

bris•tol \'bris-tl\ *n* : cardboard with a smooth surface suitable for writing or printing — called also *bristol board* [*Bristol,* England]

brit *or* **britt** \'brit\ *n* : tiny sea animals important as fish food [Cornish *brȳthel* "mackerel"]

Bri•tan•nia metal \bri-ˌtan-yə-\ *n* : a silver-white alloy similar to pewter composed largely of tin, antimony, and copper [Latin *Britannia* "Great Britain"]

britch•es \'brich-əz\ *n pl* : BREECHES

Brit•i•cism \'brit-ə-ˌsiz-əm\ *n* : a characteristic feature of British English [*Brit*ish + *-icism* (as in *gallicism*)]

[1]**Brit•ish** \'brit-ish\ *n* **1** *pl in construction* : the people of Great Britain or their descendants **2** : British English

[2]**British** *adj* **1** : of, relating to, or characteristic of the original inhabitants of Britain **2 a** : of, relating to, or characteristic of Great Britain or the British **b** : ENGLISH

Brit•ish•er \'brit-i-shər\ *n* : BRITON 2

British thermal unit *n* : the quantity of heat required to raise the temperature of one pound of water one degree Fahrenheit at or near 60°F — abbreviation *Btu*

Brit•on \'brit-n\ *n* **1** : a member of one of the peoples inhabiting Britain previous to the Anglo-Saxon invasions **2** : a native or subject of Great Britain

Brit•ta•ny spaniel \ˌbrit-n-ē-\ *n* : a large active spaniel of a French breed developed by interbreeding pointers with spaniels of Brittany

Brittany spaniel

brit•tle \'brit-l\ *adj* **1 a** : easily broken, cracked, or snapped ⟨*brittle* clay⟩ ⟨*brittle* glass⟩ **b** : not firm or substantial : FRAIL ⟨a *brittle* promise⟩ **2** : lacking warmth, depth, or generosity of spirit : COLD ⟨a hard *brittle* disposition⟩ [Middle English *britil*] — **brit•tle•ness** *n*

• **syn** BRITTLE, CRISP, FRIABLE, FRAGILE mean tending to break easily. BRITTLE implies hardness without toughness or elasticity and susceptibility to snapping or fracture; CRISP suggests the light firmness and brittleness desirable in some foods as opposed to limpness or sogginess ⟨*crisp* lettuce⟩ ⟨*crisp* crackers⟩ FRIABLE is applied to substances that are readily crumbled or pulverized ⟨*friable* soil⟩ FRAGILE is applicable to anything that must be handled with care and implies delicacy of material or structure.

brittle star *n* : any of a group (Ophiuroidea) of sea animals similar to the related starfishes but having slender flexible arms

[1]**broach** \'brōch\ *n* **1** : any of various pointed or tapered tools, implements, or parts: as **a** : a spit for roasting meat **b** : a tool for tapping casks **c** : a cutting tool with a series of teeth in a straight line used especially for shaping a hole already bored **2** : BROOCH [Middle French *broche,* derived from Latin *broccus* "projecting"]

[2]**broach** *vb* **1** : to pierce (as a cask) in order to draw the contents : TAP **2** : to shape or enlarge (a hole) with a broach **3** : to introduce or make known for the first time ⟨*broach* a subject for

discussion⟩ **4 :** to break the surface from below ⟨saw a whale *broaching*⟩ — **broach•er** *n*

broad \ˈbrȯd\ *adj* **1 :** not narrow **:** WIDE ⟨a *broad* highway⟩ **2 :** extending far and wide **:** SPACIOUS ⟨*broad* prairies⟩ **3 :** being such to a full degree ⟨*broad* daylight⟩ **4 :** UNMISTAKABLE ⟨a *broad* hint⟩ **5 :** COARSE 3, INDELICATE **6 :** liberal in thought ⟨*broad* religious views⟩ **7 :** not limited **:** extended in range or amount ⟨a *broad* choice of topics⟩ ⟨education in its *broadest* sense⟩ **8 :** being main and essential ⟨*broad* outlines of a problem⟩ **9 :** ³LOW 12 — used specifically of *a* pronounced as in *father* [Old English *brād*] — **broad•ly** *adv* — **broad•ness** *n*

• **syn** BROAD, WIDE mean having horizontal extent; they apply to a surface measured or viewed from side to side. BROAD is preferred when full horizontal extent is considered ⟨*broad* shoulders⟩ WIDE is commonly used with units of measure ⟨rugs eight feet *wide*⟩ or is applied when the distance between limits or the extent of an opening is in mind ⟨a *wide* view⟩ ⟨*wide* doorways⟩

broad•ax *or* **broad•axe** \ˈbrȯ-ˌdaks\ *n* **:** a broad-bladed ax

broad bean *n* **:** the large flat edible seed of an Old World upright vetch; *also* **:** this plant widely grown for its seeds and as fodder

¹broad•cast \ˈbrȯd-ˌkast\ *adj* **1 :** cast or scattered in all directions **2 :** made public by means of radio or television — **broadcast** *adv*

²broadcast *n* **1 :** the action of transmitting sound or images by radio or television **2 :** a single radio or television program

³broadcast *vb* **-cast** *also* **-cast•ed; -cast•ing 1 :** to scatter or sow (as seed) broadcast **2 :** to make widely known **3 a :** to send out a broadcast from a radio or television transmitting station **b :** to speak or perform on a broadcast program — **broadcast•er** *n*

broad•cloth \ˈbrȯd-ˌklȯth\ *n* **1 :** a fine woolen cloth made compact and glossy in finishing **2 :** a fine cloth (as of cotton or silk) with plain or ribbed weave

broad•en \ˈbrȯd-n\ *vb* **broad•ened; broad•en•ing** \ˈbrȯd-ning, -n-ing\ **:** to make or become broad or broader

broad jump *n* **:** LONG JUMP — **broad jumper** *n*

broad•leaf \ˈbrȯd-ˌlēf\ *adj* **:** BROAD-LEAVED

broad–leaved \-ˈlēvd\ *or* **broad–leafed** \-ˈlēft\ *adj* **:** having broad leaves; *esp* **:** having leaves that are not needles ⟨*broad-leaved* evergreens⟩

broad•loom \-ˌlüm\ *adj* **:** woven on a wide loom ⟨*broadloom* carpets⟩ — **broadloom** *n*

broad–mind•ed \-ˈmīn-dəd\ *adj* **1 :** tolerant of differing views **2 :** inclined to tolerate minor departures from conventional behavior — **broad–mind•ed•ly** *adv* — **broad–mind•ed•ness** *n*

¹broad•side \ˈbrȯd-ˌsīd\ *n* **1 :** the part of a ship's side above the waterline **2 a :** all the guns that can be fired from the same side of a ship **b :** a discharge of all these guns together **3 :** a storm of abuse **:** a strongly worded attack **4 :** a sheet of paper printed on one or both sides; *also* **:** something (as a ballad or an advertisement) printed on a broadside

²broadside *adv* **1 :** with the broad side toward a given object or point ⟨struck the car *broadside*⟩ **2 :** in one volley — **broadside** *adj*

broad–spectrum *adj* **:** effective against various microorganisms ⟨*broad-spectrum* antibiotics⟩

broad•sword \ˈbrȯd-ˌsōrd, -ˌsȯrd\ *n* **:** a broad-bladed sword for cutting rather than thrusting

broad•tail \-ˌtāl\ *n* **:** the fur or skin of a very young or premature karakul lamb characterized by a flat and wavy appearance resembling moiré silk — compare PERSIAN LAMB

Brob•ding•nag•ian \ˌbräb-ding-ˈnag-ē-ən, -dig-\ *adj* **:** very large **:** TREMENDOUS [*Brobdingnag,* country inhabited by giants in *Gulliver's Travels* by Jonathan Swift]

bro•cade \brō-ˈkād\ *n* **:** a heavy fabric (as of silk) with raised interwoven patterns [Spanish *brocado,* from Italian *broccato,* derived from *brocco* "small nail", from Latin *broccus* "projecting"] — **bro•cad•ed** \-ˈkād-əd\ *adj*

broc•co•li \ˈbräk-lē, -ə-lē\ *n* **:** a garden plant that is usually considered a form of cauliflower but differs from cauliflower in producing open branching green flower shoots used as a vegetable [Italian, from *brocco* "small nail, sprout"]

bro•chette \brō-ˈshet\ *n* **:** a small spit **:** SKEWER [French, derived from Old French *broche* "pointed tool"]

bro•chure \brō-ˈshu̇r\ *n* **:** PAMPHLET [French, from *brocher* "to sew", derived from Old French *broche* "pointed tool"]

brock \ˈbräk\ *n* **:** BADGER [Old English *broc,* of Celtic origin]

bro•gan \ˈbrō-gən, brō-ˈgan\ *n* **:** a heavy shoe; *esp* **:** a work shoe reaching to the ankle [Irish Gaelic *brōgan*]

¹brogue \ˈbrōg\ *n* **1 :** a heavy shoe often with a hobnailed sole **:** BROGAN **2 :** a sturdy oxford often with an ornamental toe cap [Irish and Scottish Gaelic *brōg,* derived from Old Norse *brōk* "leg covering"]

²brogue *n* **:** a marked dialect or regional pronunciation; *esp* **:** an Irish accent [perhaps from Irish Gaelic *barrōg* "wrestling hold"]

broi•der \ˈbrȯid-ər\ *vt* **:** EMBROIDER — **broi•dery** \ˈbrȯid-rē, -ə-rē\ *n*

¹broil \ˈbrȯil\ *vb* **:** to cook or become cooked by direct exposure to a source of heat (as fire or flame) [Middle French *bruler* "to burn"]

²broil *vi* **:** BRAWL 1 [Middle French *brouiller* "to mix, confuse"]

³broil *n* **:** a confused or noisy disturbance; *esp* **:** a loud quarrel

broil•er \ˈbrȯi-lər\ *n* **1 :** a rack and pan or an oven equipped with a rack and pan for broiling meats **2 :** a young chicken suitable for broiling

¹broke *past of* BREAK

²broke \ˈbrōk\ *adj* **:** having no money **:** PENNILESS [Middle English, from *broken*]

bro•ken \ˈbrō-kən\ *adj* **1 :** shattered into pieces ⟨*broken* glass⟩ **2 a :** RUGGED 1, ROUGH ⟨*broken* country⟩ **b :** having gaps or breaks ⟨a *broken* line⟩ **3 :** not kept ⟨a *broken* promise⟩ **4 :** SUBDUED, CRUSHED ⟨a *broken* spirit⟩ **5 a :** lacking continuity **:** FRAGMENTARY **b :** imperfectly spoken ⟨*broken* English⟩ **6 :** FRACTURED ⟨a *broken* leg⟩ [Old English *brocen,* past participle of *brecan* "to break"] — **bro•ken•ly** *adv* — **bro•ken•ness** \-kən-nəs\ *n*

bro•ken•heart•ed \ˌbrō-kən-ˈhärt-əd\ *adj* **:** crushed by grief or despair

bro•ker \ˈbrō-kər\ *n* **:** a person who acts as an agent for others in the purchase and sale of property [Middle English, "negotiator"]

bro•ker•age \ˈbrō-kə-rij, -krij\ *n* **1 :** the business of a broker **2 :** the fee or commission charged by a broker

bro•me•li•ad \brō-ˈmē-lē-ˌad\ *n* **:** any of a family of chiefly tropical American plants (as the pineapple and Spanish moss) that often grow on the surface of other plants [Olaf *Bromelius,* died 1705, Swedish botanist]

bro•mide \ˈbrō-ˌmīd\ *n* **1 :** any of various compounds of bromine with another element or a radical including some (as potassium bromide) used as sedatives **2 :** a commonplace or trite expression or idea

△ **origin** The word *bromide* is derived from *bromine.* Several compounds of bromine, especially potassium bromide, are used as sedatives. They can calm a nervous, restless person and help that person to get to sleep. *Bromide* has come to be used too for a boring or tiresome talker, who can often put listeners to sleep as effectively as any drug.

bro•mid•ic \brō-ˈmid-ik\ *adj* **:** DULL, TRITE ⟨*bromidic* remarks⟩

bro•mine \ˈbrō-ˌmēn\ *n* **:** a chemical element that is a deep red corrosive toxic liquid giving off an irritating reddish brown vapor of disagreeable odor — see ELEMENT table [Greek *brōmos* "bad smell"]

bro•mo•thy•mol blue \ˌbrō-mō-ˌthī-ˌmȯl-, -ˌmōl-\ *or* **brom•thy•mol blue** \ˌbrōm-ˌthī-ˌmȯl-, -ˌmōl-\ *n* **:** a dye derived from thymol that is an acid-base indicator

bronc \ˈbrängk\ *n* **:** BRONCO

bron•chi•al \ˈbräng-kē-əl\ *adj* **:** of, relating to, or involving the bronchi or their branches

bronchial tube *n* **:** a primary bronchus or any of its branches

bron•chi•ole \ˈbräng-kē-ˌōl\ *n* **:** a tiny thin-walled branch of a bronchial tube

bron•chi•tis \brän-ˈkīt-əs, bräng-\ *n* **:** acute or chronic inflammation of the bronchial tubes or a disease marked by this — **bron•chit•ic** \-ˈkit-ik\ *adj*

bron•cho•pneu•mo•nia \ˌbräng-kō-nu̇-ˈmō-nyə, -nü-, ˌbrän-\ *n* **:** pneumonia involving many relatively small areas of lung tissue — called also *bronchial pneumonia*

bron•chus \ˈbräng-kəs\ *n, pl* **bron•chi** \ˈbrän-ˌkī, ˈbräng-, -ˌkē\ **:** either of the main divisions of the trachea each leading

to a lung [Greek *bronchos* "windpipe"]
bron•co \ˈbräng-kō, ˈbrän-\ *n, pl* **broncos** : an unbroken or partly broken range horse of western North America; *also* : MUSTANG [Mexican Spanish, from Spanish, "rough, wild"]
bron•co•bust•er \-ˌbəs-tər\ *n* : a person who breaks wild horses to the saddle
bron•to•sau•rus \ˌbränt-ə-ˈsȯr-əs\ *also* **bron•to•saur** \ˈbränt-ə-ˌsȯr\ *n* : any of several very large four-footed and probably herbivorous dinosaurs — called also *thunder lizard* [Greek *brontē* "thunder" + *sauros* "lizard"]
Bronx cheer \ˈbrängks-\ *n* : RASPBERRY 2
[1]**bronze** \ˈbränz\ *vt* : to give the appearance of bronze to
[2]**bronze** *n* **1** : an alloy of copper and tin and sometimes other elements (as zinc) **2** : a work of art (as a statue, bust, or medallion) made of bronze **3** : a moderate yellowish brown [French, from Italian *bronzo*] — **bronzy** \ˈbrän-zē\ *adj*
Bronze Age *n* : a period of human culture characterized by the use of bronze tools and held to begin in Europe about 3500 B.C. and in western Asia and Egypt somewhat earlier
brooch \ˈbrōch, ˈbrüch\ *n* : an ornamental clasp or pin ⟨wore a diamond *brooch* on the lapel⟩ [Middle English *broche* "pointed tool, brooch"]
[1]**brood** \ˈbrüd\ *n* **1** : a family of young animals or children; *esp* : the young (as of a bird) hatched or cared for at one time **2** : a group resembling (as in similarity of form or nature) a brood of young [Old English *brōd*]
[2]**brood** *vb* **1** : to sit on eggs in order to hatch them **2** : to cover young with the wings **3** : to think anxiously or moodily upon a subject : PONDER **4** : to hover over : LOOM ⟨*brooding* clouds⟩ — **brood•ing•ly** \-ing-lē\ *adv*
[3]**brood** *adj* : kept for breeding ⟨*brood* mare⟩ ⟨*brood* flock⟩
brood•er \ˈbrüd-ər\ **1** : one that broods **2** : a heated structure used for raising young fowl
broody \ˈbrüd-ē\ *adj* **1** : physiologically ready to brood **2** : inclined to brood : MOODY — **brood•i•ness** *n*
[1]**brook** \ˈbru̇k\ *vt* : to put up with : BEAR, TOLERATE ⟨*brooks* no interference⟩ [Old English *brūcan* "to use, enjoy"]
[2]**brook** *n* : CREEK 2 [Old English *brōc*]
brook•let \ˈbru̇k-lət\ *n* : a small brook
brook trout *n* : a common speckled cold-water char of eastern North America
broom \ˈbrüm, ˈbru̇m\ *n* **1** : a plant of the pea family with long slender branches along which grow many drooping yellow flowers **2** : a usually long-handled brush used for sweeping and originally made from twigs of broom [Old English *brōm*]
broom•corn \-ˌkȯrn\ *n* : a tall cultivated sorghum whose stiff branched flower cluster is used in brooms and brushes
broom•stick \-ˌstik\ *n* : the handle of a broom
broth \ˈbrȯth\ *n, pl* **broths** \ˈbrȯths, ˈbrȯthz\ : liquid in which food has been cooked : STOCK [Old English]
broth•el \ˈbräth-əl, ˈbrȯth-\ *n* : an establishment in which prostitutes are available [Middle English, "worthless fellow, prostitute", derived from Old English *brēothan* "to waste away"]
broth•er \ˈbrəth-ər\ *n, pl* **brothers** *or* **breth•ren** \ˈbreth-rən, -ərn, -ə-rən\ **1** : a male who has one or both parents in common with another **2** : KINSMAN **3** : a fellow member — used as a title for ministers in some evangelical denominations ⟨*Brother* Smith⟩ **4** : one related to another by common ties (as of race or interests) **5** *often cap* : a man who is a religious but not a priest ⟨a lay *brother*⟩ — often used as a title ⟨*Brother* John, S.J.⟩ [Old English *brōthor*]
broth•er•hood \ˈbrəth-ər-ˌhu̇d\ *n* **1** : the state of being brothers or a brother **2** : an association (as a labor union) for a particular purpose **3** : the whole body of persons engaged in a business or profession : FRATERNITY
broth•er–in–law \ˈbrəth-rən-ˌlȯ, -ə-rən-, ˈbrəth-ərn-ˌlȯ\ *n, pl* **broth•ers–in–law** \ˈbrəth-ər-zən-\ **1** : the brother of one's spouse **2** : the husband of one's sister
broth•er•ly \ˈbrəth-ər-lē\ *adj* **1** : of or relating to brothers **2** : natural or becoming to brothers ⟨*brotherly* love⟩ ⟨*brotherly* rivalry⟩ — **broth•er•li•ness** *n*
brougham \ˈbrü-əm, ˈbrüm, ˈbrō-əm\ *n* **1** : a light closed horse-drawn carriage with seats inside for two or four **2** : a 2-door sedan or coupe [Henry Peter *Brougham*, Baron Brougham and Vaux, died 1868, Scottish jurist]
brought *past of* BRING
brou•ha•ha \ˈbrü-ˌhä-ˌhä, ˌbrü-ˌhä-ˈhä, brü-ˈhä-ˌhä\ *n* : FUROR 2, HUBBUB [French]
brow \ˈbrau̇\ *n* **1 a** : EYEBROW **b** : the ridge on which the eyebrow grows **c** : FOREHEAD **2** : the edge or projecting upper part of a steep slope ⟨on the *brow* of a hill⟩ [Old English *brū*]

brougham 1

brow•beat \ˈbrau̇-ˌbēt\ *vt* **-beat**; **-beat•en** \-ˌbēt-n\; **-beat•ing** : to frighten by a stern manner or threatening speech
[1]**brown** \ˈbrau̇n\ *adj* : of the color brown; *also* : of dark or tanned complexion [Old English *brūn*]
[2]**brown** *n* : any of a group of dull colors between red and yellow in hue — **brown•ish** \ˈbrau̇-nish\ *adj*
[3]**brown** *vb* : to make or become brown
brown alga *n* : any of a division (Phaeophyta) of mostly marine algae with chlorophyll masked by brown pigment
brown coal *n* : LIGNITE
Brown•i•an movement \ˌbrau̇-nē-ən-\ *n* : a random movement of microscopic particles suspended in liquids or gases that results from the impact of molecules of the fluid on the particles — called also *Brownian motion* [Robert *Brown*, died 1858, Scottish botanist]
brown•ie \ˈbrau̇-nē\ *n* **1** : a good-natured sprite who performs helpful services at night **2** : a member of the Girl Scouts of the United States of America program for girls of the age range 7–9 **3** : a small square or rectangle of rich usually chocolate cake containing nuts
brown•stone \ˈbrau̇n-ˌstōn\ *n* **1** : a reddish brown sandstone used for building **2** : a dwelling faced with brownstone
brown study *n* : a state of deep absorption in thought or musing
brown sugar *n* : soft sugar whose crystals are covered by a film of refined dark syrup
brown–tail moth *n* : a tussock moth whose larva feeds on foliage and has hairs irritating to the skin
brown trout *n* : a speckled European trout widely introduced as a game fish
[1]**browse** \ˈbrau̇z\ *n* **1** : tender shoots, twigs, and leaves of trees and shrubs fit for food for cattle **2** : an act or instance of browsing [probably from Middle French *brouts* "sprouts"]
[2]**browse** *vb* **1** : to nibble or feed on leaves and shoots **2 a** : to skim a book reading random passages **b** : to look over a number of things casually in search of something of interest **syn** see GRAZE — **brows•er** *n*
bru•cel•lo•sis \ˌbrü-sə-ˈlō-səs\ *n, pl* **-lo•ses** \-ˌsēz\ : UNDULANT FEVER [*Brucella*, genus of bacteria]
bru•in \ˈbrü-ən\ *n* : BEAR 1 [Dutch, name of the bear in the beast epic *Reynard the Fox*]
[1]**bruise** \ˈbrüz\ *vb* **1** : to inflict or cause a bruise on **2** : to break down (as leaves or berries) by rubbing or pounding : CRUSH **3** : to wound or hurt the feelings of **4** : to become bruised or show bruises ⟨a baby *bruises* easily⟩ [partly from Middle French *bruisier* "to break", of Celtic origin; partly from Old English *brӯsan* "to bruise"]
[2]**bruise** *n* : an injury (as from a blow) in which the skin is not broken but is discolored from the breaking of small underlying blood vessels : CONTUSION
bruis•er \ˈbrü-zər\ *n* : a big husky person
[1]**bruit** \ˈbrüt\ *n archaic* : REPORT, RUMOR [Old French, "noise"]
[2]**bruit** *vt* : to noise abroad : RUMOR
[1]**brum•ma•gem** \ˈbrəm-i-jəm\ *adj* : being showy and cheap [alteration of *Birmingham*, England, the source in the 17th century of counterfeit groats]
[2]**brummagem** *n* : something showy but shoddy
brunch \ˈbrənch\ *n* : a late breakfast, an early lunch, or a combination of the two [*breakfast* + *lunch*]
bru•net *or* **bru•nette** \brü-ˈnet\ *adj* : of dark or relatively dark complexion; *esp* : having brown or black hair and eyes [French, from *brun* "brown", of Germanic origin]
brunt \ˈbrənt\ *n* : the main force of a blow or an attack : the heaviest shock, stress, or strain ⟨coastal towns bore the *brunt* of the storm⟩ [Middle English]
[1]**brush** \ˈbrəsh\ *n* **1** : BRUSHWOOD **2** : scrubby vegetation; *also* : land covered with this [Middle French *broce* "brushwood"]

[2]brush *n* **1 :** a device composed of bristles set into a handle and used especially for sweeping, scrubbing, or painting **2 :** a bushy tail (as of a fox or squirrel) **3 :** an electrical conductor that makes sliding contact between a moving and a nonmoving part of an electric motor or generator **4 a :** an act of brushing **b :** a quick light touch or momentary contact [Middle French *broisse,* from *broce* "brushwood"]

[3]brush *vb* **1 a :** to apply a brush to **b :** to apply with a brush **2 a :** to remove with or as if with a brush **b :** to dispose of in an offhand way **:** DISMISS ⟨*brushed* my protest aside⟩ **3 :** to pass lightly across **:** touch gently in passing **4 :** to move so as to graze something gently ⟨*brushed* past the receptionist⟩ — **brush•er** *n*

[4]brush *n* **:** a brief encounter or skirmish [Middle French *brosser* "to dash through underbrush", from *broce* "brushwood"]

brush–off \'brəsh-ˌȯf\ *n* **:** an abrupt or offhand dismissal

brush up *vb* **:** to refresh one's memory of **:** renew one's skill or knowledge

brush•wood \'brəsh-ˌwu̇d\ *n* **1 :** small branches cut from trees or shrubs **2 :** a thicket of shrubs and small trees

[1]brushy \'brəsh-ē\ *adj* **brush•i•er; -est :** SHAGGY 1, ROUGH

[2]brushy *adj* **brush•i•er; -est :** covered with or abounding in brush or brushwood

brusque \'brəsk\ *adj* **:** unpleasantly curt in manner or speech ⟨a *brusque* answer⟩ [French, from Italian *brusco,* from Medieval Latin *bruscus,* a kind of plant with stiff branches] — **brusque•ly** *adv* — **brusque•ness** *n*

brus•sels sprout \ˌbrəs-əlz-\ *n, often cap B* **:** one of the edible small green heads borne on the stem of a plant related to the cabbage; *also* **:** this plant [*Brussels,* Belgium]

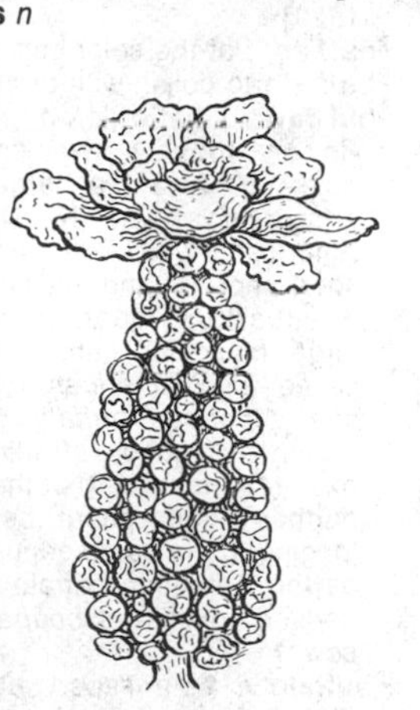

brussels sprout

bru•tal \'brüt-l\ *adj* **:** befitting a brute: as **a :** lacking all mercy **b :** causing injury or misery **c :** HARSH 3, SEVERE — **bru•tal•ly** \-l-ē\ *adv*

• syn BRUTE, BRUTISH: BRUTAL applies only to human behavior, stresses lack of humanity, and always implies moral condemnation; BRUTE stresses crude force or strength in contrast with skill or intelligence; BRUTISH stresses lack of refinement and sensitivity and often suggests stupidity rather than cruelty.

bru•tal•i•ty \brü-'tal-ət-ē\ *n, pl* **-ties 1 :** the quality or state of being brutal **2 :** a brutal act or course of action

bru•tal•ize \'brüt-l-ˌīz\ *vt* **1 :** to make brutal, unfeeling, or inhuman **2 :** to treat brutally — **bru•tal•iza•tion** \ˌbrüt-l-ə-'zā-shən\ *n*

[1]brute \'brüt\ *adj* **1 :** of, relating to, or typical of lower animals as distinguished from humans **2 :** resembling an animal in quality, action, or instinct: as **a :** irrationally cruel **:** SAVAGE **b :** grossly sensual **c :** UNREASONING **d :** wholly physical ⟨moved the rock by *brute* strength⟩ [Middle French *brut,* from Latin *brutus* "stupid"] **syn** see BRUTAL

[2]brute *n* **1 :** BEAST 1 **2 :** a brutal person

brut•ish \'brüt-ish\ *adj* **1 :** of or resembling a beast **2 a :** grossly sensual **:** INSENSITIVE **b :** UNREASONING, IRRATIONAL **syn** see BRUTAL — **brut•ish•ly** *adv* — **brut•ish•ness** *n*

bry•ol•o•gy \brī-'äl-ə-jē\ *n* **:** a branch of botany that deals with mosses and liverworts [Greek *bryon* "moss"]

bry•o•ny \'brī-ə-nē\ *n, pl* **-nies :** any of a genus of tendril-bearing vines of the gourd family with large leaves, red or black fruit, and a cathartic root [Greek *bryōnia*]

bry•o•phyl•lum \ˌbrī-ə-'fil-əm\ *n* **:** a kalanchoe often grown as a foliage plant especially from leaf cuttings — called also *air plant, life plant*

bry•o•phyte \'brī-ə-ˌfīt\ *n* **:** any of a division (Bryophyta) of nonflowering green plants comprising the mosses and liverworts [Greek *bryon* "moss" + *phyton* "plant"] — **bry•o•phyt•ic** \ˌbrī-ə-'fit-ik\ *adj*

bry•o•zo•an \ˌbrī-ə-'zō-ən\ *n* **:** any of a phylum or class (Bryozoa) of aquatic invertebrate animals that usually form branching, flat, or mosslike colonies and reproduce by budding — **bryozoan** *adj* [Greek *bryon* "moss" + *zoion* "animal"]

[1]bub•ble \'bəb-əl\ *vb* **bub•bled; bub•bling** \'bəb-ling, -ə-ling\ **1 :** to form bubbles **2 :** to flow out with a gurgling sound **3 a :** to utter as though giving off bubbles ⟨*bubbling* praise of the new teacher⟩ **b :** to be or become lively **:** EFFERVESCE ⟨*bubbling* with joy⟩ **4 a :** to cause to bubble **b :** BURP 2 [Middle English *bublen*]

[2]bubble *n* **1 :** a small typically hollow and light globule: as **a :** a small body of gas within a liquid **b :** a thin film of liquid inflated with air or gas ⟨a soap *bubble*⟩ **c :** a globule in a transparent solid **2 a :** something that lacks firmness, solidity, or reality **b :** a delusive scheme **3 :** a sound like that of bubbling

bubble chamber *n* **:** a chamber of heated liquid in which the path of an ionizing particle is made visible by a string of vapor bubbles

bubble gum *n* **:** a chewing gum that can be blown into large bubbles

bub•bler \'bəb-lər, -ə-lər\ *n* **:** a drinking fountain from which a stream of water bubbles upward

bub•bly \'bəb-lē, -ə-lē\ *adj* **bub•bli•er; -est 1 :** full of bubbles **:** EFFERVESCENT **2 :** resembling a bubble

bu•bo \'bü-bō, 'byü-\ *n, pl* **buboes :** an inflammatory swelling of a lymph node especially in the groin [Medieval Latin, from Greek *boubōn*] — **bu•bon•ic** \bü-'bän-ik, byü-\ *adj*

bubonic plague *n* **:** plague in which the formation of buboes is a prominent feature

buc•cal \'bək-əl\ *adj* **:** of, relating to, near, or being the surface of a tooth next to the cheek [Latin *bucca* "cheek"] — **buc•cal•ly** \-ē\ *adv*

buc•ca•neer \ˌbək-ə-'niər\ *n* **:** PIRATE [French *boucanier*] — **buccaneer** *vi*

[1]buck \'bək\ *n, pl* **buck** *or* **bucks 1 :** a male animal; *esp* **:** a male deer or antelope **2 a :** a male human being **:** MAN **b :** DANDY 1 **3 a :** BUCKSKIN; *also* **:** an article made of buckskin **b** *slang* **:** DOLLAR 3b **4 a :** a supporting rack or frame **b :** a short thick leather-covered block for gymnastic vaulting [Old English *bucca* "stag, he-goat"]

[2]buck *vb* **1 a :** to spring with a quick plunging leap ⟨a *bucking* horse⟩ **b :** to throw (as a rider) by bucking **2 a :** to move or act forcefully in opposition to ⟨snowplows *bucking* the drifts⟩ **b :** to stand firm in opposition to **:** RESIST ⟨determined to *buck* city hall⟩ **3 :** to start, move, or react jerkily **4 :** to strive for advancement or promotion ⟨*bucking* for sergeant⟩ — **buck•er** *n*

[3]buck *adj* **:** of the lowest grade within a military category ⟨*buck* private⟩

buck•a•roo *or* **buck•er•oo** \ˌbək-ə-'rü\ *n, pl* **-aroos** *or* **-eroos :** COWBOY [Spanish *vaquero,* from *vaca* "cow", from Latin *vacca*]

buck•board \'bək-ˌbōrd, -ˌbȯrd\ *n* **:** a four-wheeled horse-drawn vehicle with a springy platform carrying the seat [obsolete English *buck* "body of a wagon"]

[1]buck•et \'bək-ət\ *n* **1 :** a typically round vessel for catching, holding, or carrying liquids or solids **2 :** an object resembling a bucket in collecting, scooping, or carrying something: as **a :** the scoop of an excavating machine **b :** one of the vanes of a turbine rotor **3 a :** BUCKETFUL **b :** a large quantity ⟨it rained *buckets*⟩ [Anglo-French *buket,* from Old English *būc* "pitcher"]

[2]bucket *vb* **1 :** to draw or lift in or as if in buckets **2 :** HUSTLE 2, HURRY **3 a :** to go about haphazardly or irresponsibly **b :** to move roughly or jerkily

bucket brigade *n* **:** a chain of persons acting to put out a fire by passing buckets of water from hand to hand

buck•et•ful \'bək-ət-ˌfu̇l\ *n, pl* **buck•et•fuls** \-ət-ˌfu̇lz\ *or* **buck•ets•ful** \-əts-ˌfu̇l\ **:** the amount held by a bucket

bucket seat *n* **:** a low individual seat used chiefly in automobiles and airplanes

bucket shop *n* **:** a dishonest brokerage house [earlier, a saloon in which liquor was sold in buckets or pitchers]

buck•eye \'bək-ˌī\ *n* **:** a shrub or tree of the horse-chestnut family; *also* **:** its large nutlike seed

buck fever *n* **1 :** nervous excitement of an inexperienced hunter at the sight of game **2 :** tension or nervousness accompanying exposure to a new or unexpected responsibility

[1]buck•le \ˈbək-əl\ *n* **1 :** a fastening for two loose ends that is attached to one and holds the other by a catch **2 :** an ornamental device that suggests a buckle ⟨silver shoe *buckles*⟩ **[**Middle French *boucle* "boss of a shield, buckle", derived from Latin *bucca* "cheek"**]**

△ **origin** The literal meaning of Latin *buccula* was "little cheek", but *buccula* was also the name for the part of a helmet that protects the cheek. Its Middle French descendant, *boucle,* was the word for the boss of a shield, which looks a little like a small cheek on the face of the shield. The use of the word was later extended to belt fasteners. In this sense, the word was borrowed into English.

[2]buckle *vb* **buck•led; buck•ling** \ˈbək-ling, -ə-ling\ **1 :** to fasten with a buckle **2 :** to apply oneself with vigor ⟨*buckle* down to a job⟩ **3 :** to bend, warp, or kink usually under the influence of some external agency ⟨the pavement *buckled* in the heat⟩ ⟨knees *buckling* from fatigue⟩ **4 :** to give way **:** YIELD

[3]buckle *n* **:** a product of buckling **:** BEND

buck•ler \ˈbək-lər\ *n* **1 :** SHIELD 1; *esp* **:** a small round shield used to parry blows **2 :** one that shields and protects

buck passer *n* **:** a person who habitually evades responsibility — **buck–pass•ing** \ˈbək-ˌpas-ing\ *n*

buck•ram \ˈbək-rəm\ *n* **:** a stiff-finished heavily sized fabric of cotton or linen used in garments, millinery, and bookbindings **[**Old French *boquerant,* from Provençal *bocaran,* from *Bokhara,* city in central Asia**]** — **buckram** *adj*

buck•saw \ˈbək-ˌsȯ\ *n* **:** a saw set in a usually H-shaped frame and used for sawing wood on a sawhorse

buck•shot \-ˌshät\ *n* **:** a coarse lead shot used in shotgun shells

buck•skin \-ˌskin\ *n* **1 a :** the skin of a buck **b :** a soft pliable usually suede-finished leather **2** *pl* **:** buckskin breeches **3 :** a horse of a light yellowish dun color usually with dark mane and tail

buck•thorn \-ˌthȯrn\ *n* **:** any of a genus of often thorny trees or shrubs some of which yield purgatives or pigments

buck•tooth \-ˈtüth\ *n* **:** a large projecting front tooth — **buck–toothed** \-ˈtütht\ *adj*

buck up *vb* **:** to become or cause to become encouraged **:** cheer up

buck•wheat \ˈbək-ˌhwēt\ *n* **:** any of several herbs with pinkish white flowers and triangular seeds; *also* **:** the seeds used as a cereal grain

[1]bu•col•ic \byü-ˈkäl-ik\ *adj* **1 :** of or relating to shepherds or herdsmen **:** PASTORAL **2 :** RUSTIC 1 **[**Latin *bucolicus,* from Greek *boukolikos,* from *boukolos* "cowherd", from *bous* "cow" + *-kolos* "herd"**]** — **bu•col•i•cal•ly** \-i-kə-lē, -klē\ *adv*

[2]bucolic *n* **:** a pastoral poem **:** ECLOGUE

[1]bud \ˈbəd\ *n* **1 :** a small growth at the tip or on the side of a plant stem that later develops into a flower, leaf, or new shoot **2 :** a flower that has not fully opened **3 :** a part that grows out from the body of an organism and develops into a new organism **:** GEMMA **4 :** a stage of development in which something is not yet fully developed **:** an early stage or condition ⟨trees in *bud*⟩ ⟨a plan still in the *bud*⟩ **[**Middle English *budde***]**

[2]bud *vb* **bud•ded; bud•ding 1 a :** to set or put forth buds **b :** to reproduce asexually by forming and developing buds **2 :** to be or develop like a bud (as in freshness and promise of growth) ⟨a *budding* diplomat⟩ **3 :** to insert a bud from one plant into an opening cut in the bark of (another plant) in order to propagate a desired variety — **bud•der** *n*

Bud•dha \ˈbüd-ə, ˈbu̇d-\ *n* **1 :** a person who has attained the perfect spiritual fulfillment sought in Buddhism **2 :** a representation of Gautama Buddha ⟨a little bronze *Buddha*⟩ **[**Sanskrit, "enlightened"**]**

Bud•dhism \ˈbü-ˌdiz-əm, ˈbu̇d-ˌiz-\ *n* **:** a religion chiefly of eastern and central Asia growing out of the teaching of Gautama Buddha that suffering is inherent in life and that one can be liberated from it by mental and moral self-purification — **Buddhist** \ˈbüd-əst, ˈbu̇d-\ *n or adj* — **Bud•dhis•tic** \bü-ˈdis-tik, bu̇-\ *adj*

bud•dy \ˈbəd-ē\ *n, pl* **buddies :** COMPANION 1, PARTNER, PAL **[**probably baby talk for *brother***]**

buddy system *n* **:** an arrangement in which two individuals are paired for safety (as in swimming)

budge \ˈbəj\ *vb* **:** to start to move; *esp* **:** to give or cause to give way **[**Middle French *bouger,* derived from Latin *bullire* "to boil"**]**

bud•ger•i•gar \ˈbəj-rē-ˌgär, -ə-rē-\ *n* **:** a small Australian parrot usually light green with black and yellow markings in the wild but bred under domestication in many colors **[**native name in Australia**]**

[1]bud•get \ˈbəj-ət\ *n* **1 :** a supply available or at hand **2 a :** a statement of estimated expenditures (as of a nation) during a period and of proposals to finance them **b :** a plan for using resources to finance expenditures **c :** the amount of money available for or assigned to some purpose ⟨a low-*budget* operation⟩ **[**Middle French *bougette,* from *bouge* "leather bag", from Latin *bulga,* of Gaulish origin**]**

[2]budget *vb* **1 :** to put in or on a budget ⟨*budget* money for food⟩ ⟨*budget* yourself carefully⟩ **2 :** to provide funds for in a budget ⟨*budget* a new car⟩ **3 :** to plan or provide for the use of ⟨*budget* your time wisely⟩

bud•get•ary \ˈbəj-ə-ˌter-ē\ *adj* **:** of or relating to a budget

bud•gie \ˈbəj-ē\ *n* **:** BUDGERIGAR

bud scale *n* **:** one of the leaves resembling scales that form the sheath of a plant bud

[1]buff \ˈbəf\ *n* **1 :** a garment made of buff leather **2 :** the bare skin **3 a :** a light yellowish brown **b :** a light to moderate yellow **4 :** a device (as a stick or wheel) with a soft absorbent surface for applying polishing material **5 :** FAN, ENTHUSIAST **[**Middle French *buffle* "wild ox", from Italian *bufalo;* sense 5 from earlier *buff* "one enthusiastic about going to fires", from the buff overcoats worn by volunteer firemen in New York City about 1820**]**

[2]buff *adj* **:** of the color buff

[3]buff *vt* **:** to polish with or as if with a buff

[1]buf•fa•lo \ˈbəf-ə-ˌlō\ *n, pl* **-lo** *or* **-loes 1 :** WATER BUFFALO **2 a :** a large shaggy-maned North American wild ox with short horns and heavy forequarters bearing a large muscular hump — called also *American bison, American buffalo* **b :** any of a genus of wild oxen (as the wisent) of the northern hemisphere belonging to the same genus as the American buffalo **[**Italian *bufalo* and Spanish *búfalo,* derived from Greek *boubalos* "African gazelle", from *bous* "ox, cow"**]**

[1]buffalo 2a

[2]buffalo *vt* **1 :** BAFFLE 1, BEWILDER **2 :** OVERAWE, INTIMIDATE

buffalo bug *n* **:** CARPET BEETLE

buffalo grass *n* **:** a low-growing native fodder grass of the American plains and prairies

[1]buff•er \ˈbəf-ər\ *n* **:** one that buffs

[2]buffer *n* **1 :** a device or material for reducing shock due to contact **2 a :** BUFFER STATE **b :** a person who shields another especially from annoying routine matters **3 :** a substance capable in solution of neutralizing both acids and bases and thereby maintaining approximately the original pH of the solution **4 :** a temporary storage unit (as for a computer) that can receive data at one rate and transmit it at a different rate **[***buff* "to act like a soft body when struck"**]**

[3]buffer *vt* **:** to treat or prepare (a solution) with a buffer

buffer state *n* **:** a small neutral state lying between two larger potentially rival powers

[1]buf•fet \ˈbəf-ət\ *n* **:** a blow especially with the hand **[**Middle French**]**

[2]buffet *vb* **1 :** STRIKE 2a: as **a :** CUFF, SLAP **b :** to pound repeatedly ⟨*buffeted* by the crowd⟩ ⟨waves *buffeted* the cliff⟩ **2 a :** to contend against **:** STRUGGLE ⟨*buffeting* the wind⟩ **b :** to make one's way by fighting or struggling ⟨*buffeted* on through the storm⟩

[3]buf•fet \bə-ˈfā, bü-, ˈbü-ˌ\ *n* **1 :** SIDEBOARD **2 :** a cupboard or set of shelves for the display of tableware **3 a :** a counter for refreshments **b** *chiefly British* **:** a restaurant operated as a public convenience (as in a railway station) **c :** a meal set out on a buffet or table for guests to serve themselves **[**French**]**

buff leather *n* **:** a strong supple oil-tanned leather produced chiefly from cattle hides

buf•fle•head \ˈbəf-əl-ˌhed\ *n* **:** a small North American diving duck **[**archaic English *buffle* "buffalo"**]**

buf•foon \bə-ˈfün, ˌbə-\ *n* **1 :** a person who amuses others by tricks, jokes, and antics : CLOWN **2** : a coarse crude person [Middle French *bouffon,* from Italian *buffone,* derived from Latin *bufo* "toad"] — **buf•foon•ish** \-'fü-nish\ *adj*

buf•foon•ery \-'fün-rē, -ə-rē\ *n, pl* **-er•ies** : the art or the conduct of a buffoon; *esp* : coarse crude behavior

¹bug \'bəg\ *n* **1 a** : an insect or other creeping or crawling invertebrate; *esp* : an obnoxious insect (as a bedbug or head louse) **b** : any of an order (Hemiptera) of insects with sucking mouthparts and incomplete metamorphosis that includes many destructive plant pests — called also *true bug* **2** : an unexpected defect, fault, flaw, or imperfection **3** : a disease-producing germ or a disease caused by it **4 a** : FAD, ENTHUSIASM **b** : ENTHUSIAST **5** : a concealed listening device [Middle English *bugge* "scarecrow"]

△ **origin** In Middle English *bugge* meant "scarecrow" or "hobgoblin". In the 17th century, the word *bug* came to be used for insects, especially the bedbug. The specific use of *bug* to mean "bedbug" led to the word's becoming a name for any of the hemipterans, members of the bedbug's order. Entomologists insist that no insect outside of this order is a true bug, though popular usage persists in applying the word even to such creatures as spiders.

²bug *vt* **bugged**; **bug•ging 1** : ANNOY, BOTHER **2** : to plant a concealed microphone in

bug•a•boo \'bəg-ə-ˌbü\ *n, pl* **-boos** : BUGBEAR, BOGEY [origin unknown]

bug•bear \'bəg-ˌbaər, -ˌbeər\ *n* **1** : an imaginary goblin or specter used to cause fear **2** : an object or source of dread

¹bug•gy \'bəg-ē\ *adj* **bug•gi•er**; **-est 1** : infested with bugs **2** *slang* : CRAZY 2, SILLY

²buggy *n, pl* **buggies** : a light single-seated carriage usually drawn by one horse [origin unknown]

¹bug•house \'bəg-ˌhau̇s\ *n, slang* : an insane asylum

²bughouse *adj, slang* : mentally deranged : CRAZY

¹bu•gle \'byü-gəl\ *n* : a European annual mint with spikes of blue flowers that is naturalized in the United States [Old French, from Late Latin *bugula*]

²bugle *n* : a brass musical instrument that resembles the trumpet but usually has no valves [Old French, "buffalo, instrument made from a buffalo horn, bugle", from Latin *buculus,* from *bos* "head of cattle"]

³bugle *vb* **bu•gled**; **bu•gling** \-gə-ling, -gling\ : to sound or summon by or as if by a bugle — **bu•gler** \-glər\ *n*

bu•gloss \'byü-ˌgläs, -ˌglȯs\ *n* : any of a genus of coarse hairy herbs of the borage family [Middle French *buglosse,* derived from Greek *bous* "head of cattle" + *glōssa* "tongue"]

buhr•stone \'bər-ˌstōn\ *n* : a siliceous rock used for millstones; *also* : a millstone of this rock [probably from *burr*]

¹build \'bild\ *vb* **built** \'bilt\; **build•ing 1** : to make by putting together parts or materials : CONSTRUCT ⟨*build* a bridge⟩ **2** : to produce or create gradually especially by effort ⟨*build* a winning team⟩ **3** : to cause to be constructed ⟨the city *built* a new station⟩ **4** : to engage in building **5** : to become greater ⟨costs are *building* rapidly⟩ **6** : to progress toward a peak ⟨tension *building* up⟩ [Old English *byldan*]

²build *n* : form or style of structure; *esp* : PHYSIQUE

build•ed \'bil-dəd\ *archaic past of* BUILD

build•er \'bil-dər\ *n* : one that builds; *esp* : a person whose business is the construction of buildings

build in *vt* : to construct as an integral part of something ⟨*build in* a bookcase⟩

build•ing \'bil-ding\ *n* **1** : a usually roofed and walled structure built for permanent use (as for a dwelling) **2** : the art, work, or business of assembling materials into a structure ⟨bridge *building*⟩

build•up \'bil-ˌdəp\ *n* **1** : an often gradual increase (as in amount or numbers) ⟨a *buildup* of resentment⟩ **2** : something (as publicity) intended to attract favorable attention (as to a politician)

built–in \'bil-'tin\ *adj* **1** : forming an integral part of a structure; *esp* : constructed as or in a recess in a wall ⟨*built-in* bookcases⟩ **2** : INHERENT

bulb \'bəlb\ *n* **1 a** : a plant underground resting stage consisting of a short stem base bearing one or more buds enclosed in thickened storage leaves — compare CORM, TUBER **b** : a fleshy structure (as a tuber or corm) resembling a bulb in appearance or function **c** : a plant having or developing from a bulb **2 a** : an incandescent electric lamp **b** : a rounded or swollen anatomical structure [Latin *bulbus,* from Greek *bolbos* "bulbous plant"] — **bulbed** \'bəlbd\ *adj*

bul•bar \'bəl-bər\ *adj* : of or relating to a bulb; *also* : involving the medulla oblongata

bul•bil \'bəl-bəl, -ˌbil\ *n* : a small or secondary plant bulb; *esp* : one produced in a leaf axil or replacing the flowers [French *bulbille,* from *bulbe* "bulb"]

bul•bous \'bəl-bəs\ *adj* **1** : having a bulb : growing from or bearing bulbs **2** : resembling a bulb : ROUNDED, SWOLLEN — **bul•bous•ly** *adv*

bul•bul \'bu̇l-ˌbu̇l\ *n* **1** : a Persian songbird that is probably a nightingale **2** : any of various social songbirds of Asia and Africa [Persian, from Arabic]

Bul•gar \'bəl-ˌgär, 'bu̇l-\ *n* : BULGARIAN

Bul•gar•i•an \ˌbəl-'gar-ē-ən, bu̇l-, -'ger-\ *n* **1** : a native or inhabitant of Bulgaria **2** : the Slavic language of the Bulgarians — **Bulgarian** *adj*

¹bulge \'bəlj\ *n* : a swelling or distended part; *also* : a part with an outward bend ⟨a *bulge* in a line⟩ [Middle French *boulge* "leather bag", from Latin *bulga*] — **bulgy** *adj*

²bulge *vb* : to become or cause to become bent or swollen outward

¹bulk \'bəlk\ *n* **1** : greatness of size or extent : MAGNITUDE, VOLUME **2** : a large body or mass **3** : the main or greater part [Old Norse *bulki* "cargo"]

• **syn** BULK, MASS, VOLUME mean the whole that makes up a body or unit with reference to its size or amount. BULK implies a whole that is large, heavy, or unwieldy; MASS suggests a whole made by piling together things of the same kind; VOLUME applies to a whole without shape or outline and capable of flowing or fluctuating ⟨a large *volume* of water⟩ ⟨the *volume* of traffic⟩ — **in bulk** : in a mass : not divided into parts or packaged in separate units

²bulk *vb* **1** : to swell or bulge or cause to swell or bulge **2** : to have a bulky appearance : LOOM ⟨storm clouds *bulking* on the horizon⟩

bulk•head \'bəlk-ˌhed, 'bəl-ˌked\ *n* **1** : an upright partition separating compartments on a ship **2** : a structure or partition to resist pressure or to shut off water, fire, or gas **3** : a framework projecting from the outside of a building that has a sloping door giving access to a cellar stairway

bulky \'bəl-kē\ *adj* **bulk•i•er**; **-est** : having bulk: as **a** : large of its kind; *esp* : both large and unwieldy **b** : having great volume in proportion to weight — **bulk•i•ly** \-kə-lē\ *adv* — **bulk•i•ness** \-kē-nəs\ *n*

¹bull \'bu̇l\ *n* **1 a** : an adult male bovine animal; *also* : a usually adult male of various large animals **b** : ELEPHANT **2** : one who buys commodities or securities in expectation of a price rise — compare BEAR 3 **3** : one that resembles a bull **4** : BULLDOG **5** *slang* : POLICE OFFICER, DETECTIVE [Old English *bula*]

²bull *adj* **1 a** : MALE **b** : of, relating to, or resembling a bull **2** : large of its kind

³bull *vb* : to act or act on with the violence of a bull : FORCE ⟨*bulling* their way ahead⟩

⁴bull *n* : a papal pronouncement of the most formal and important kind [Medieval Latin *bulla* "papal seal, papal bull", from Latin, "bubble, amulet"]

⁵bull *n* **1** : a grotesque blunder in language **2** *slang* **a** : empty boastful talk **b** : NONSENSE

¹bull•dog \'bu̇l-ˌdȯg\ *n* : a compact muscular short-haired dog of English origin with forelegs set widely apart and an undershot lower jaw

²bulldog *adj* : felt to resemble a bulldog especially in firmness of purpose ⟨*bulldog* courage⟩

³bulldog *vt* : to throw (a steer) by seizing the horns and twisting the neck

bull•doze \'bu̇l-ˌdōz\ *vt* **1** : BULLY, INTIMIDATE **2** : to move, clear, gouge out, or level off with a bulldozer **3** : to force as if by using a bulldozer ⟨*bulldoze* one's way through brush⟩ [perhaps from ¹*bull* + alteration of *dose*]

bull•doz•er \-ˌdō-zər\ *n* **1** : one that bulldozes **2** : a tractor-driven machine having a broad horizontal blade or ram for pushing (as in clearing land or road building)

bul•let \'bu̇l-ət\ *n* **1** : a shaped piece of metal made to be shot

from a firearm **2 :** something suggesting a bullet (as in form or vigor of action) [Middle French *boulet,* from *boule* "ball"]
bul•le•tin \'bul-ət-n\ *n* **1 :** a brief public notice usually from an authoritative source ⟨a weather *bulletin*⟩ **2 :** a periodical publication; *esp* **:** one issued by an institution or association [French, from Italian *bullettino,* from *bulla* "papal bull"]
bulletin board *n* **:** a board for posting notices
bul•let•proof \,bul-ət-'prüf\ *adj* **:** so made as to prevent the passing through of bullets ⟨*bulletproof* glass⟩
bull fiddle *n* **:** DOUBLE BASS — **bull fiddler** *n*
bull•fight \'bul-,fīt\ *n* **:** a spectacle in which persons ceremonially excite, fight with, and usually kill bulls in an arena for public entertainment — **bull•fight•er** *n* — **bull•fight•ing** \-ing\ *n*
bull•finch \-,finch\ *n* **:** a thick-billed red-breasted European songbird often kept as a cage bird
bull•frog \-,frög, -,fräg\ *n* **:** FROG; *esp* **:** a large heavy frog that makes a booming or bellowing sound
bull•head \-,hed\ *n* **:** any of various large-headed fishes; *esp* **:** any of several common freshwater catfishes of the United States
bull•head•ed \'bul-'hed-əd\ *adj* **:** stupidly stubborn **:** HEADSTRONG — **bull•head•ed•ly** *adv* — **bull•head•ed•ness** *n*
bul•lion \'bul-yən\ *n* **:** gold or silver metal; *esp* **:** gold or silver in bars or ingots [Anglo-French, "mint"]
bull•ish \'bul-ish\ *adj* **1 :** suggestive of a bull **2 a :** marked by, tending to cause, or hopeful of rising prices (as in a stock market) **b :** OPTIMISTIC — **bull•ish•ly** *adv* — **bull•ish•ness** *n*
bull mastiff *n* **:** a large powerful dog of a breed developed by crossing bulldogs with mastiffs
Bull Moose \'bul-'müs\ *n* **:** a follower of Theodore Roosevelt in the United States presidential campaign of 1912 [*bull moose,* emblem of the Progressive party of 1912]
bull neck *n* **:** a thick short powerful neck — **bull•necked** \'bul-'nekt\ *adj*
bull•ock \'bul-ək\ *n* **1 :** a young bull **2 :** a castrated bull **:** STEER — **bull•ocky** \-ə-kē\ *adj*
bull•pen \'bul-,pen\ *n* **1 :** a large cell where prisoners are held until brought into court **2 a :** a place on a baseball field where relief pitchers warm up during a game **b :** the relief pitchers of a team
bull•ring \'bul-,ring\ *n* **:** an arena for bullfights
bull session *n* **:** an informal rambling group discussion
bull's–eye \'bul-,zī\ *n* **1 :** a small thick disk of glass inserted (as in a deck) to let in light **2 :** a very hard globular candy **3 a :** the center of a target; *also* **:** something central or critical **b :** a shot that hits a bull's-eye; *also* **:** a complete success **4 :** a simple lens for concentrating rays of light
bull snake *n* **:** any of several large harmless North American snakes feeding chiefly on rodents
bull•ter•ri•er \'bul-'ter-ē-ər\ *n* **:** a short-haired terrier of a breed originated in England by crossing the bulldog with terriers
bull•whip \'bul-,hwip, -,wip\ *n* **:** a rawhide whip with a braided lash 4 to 7 meters long
[1]**bul•ly** \'bul-ē\ *n, pl* **bullies :** a rough browbeating person; *esp* **:** one habitually cruel to others who are weaker [probably from Dutch *boel* "lover"]
△ **origin** The earliest meaning of English *bully* was "sweetheart". The word was probably borrowed from Dutch *boel* "lover". Later *bully* was used for anyone who seemed a good fellow, then for a blustering daredevil. Today, a bully is usually one whose claims to strength and courage are based on the intimidation of those who are weaker.
[2]**bully** *adj* **:** EXCELLENT, FIRST-RATE — often used interjectionally ⟨*bully* for you⟩
[3]**bully** *vb* **bul•lied; bul•ly•ing :** to play the bully toward **:** act like a bully
bul•ly•rag \'bul-ē-,rag\ *vt* **1 :** to make timid or fearful by bullying **2 :** to annoy by teasing **:** BADGER [origin unknown]
bul•rush \'bul-,rəsh\ *n* **:** any of several large sedges growing in wet land or water [Middle English *bulrysche*]
[1]**bul•wark** \'bul-wərk, -,wərk, -,work; 'bəl-wərk, -,wərk\ *n* **1 a :** a solid wall built for defense **b :** BREAKWATER, SEAWALL **2 :** a strong support or protection **3 :** the side of a ship above the upper deck — usually used in pl. [Dutch *bolwerc,* from Middle High German, literally, "plank work"]
[2]**bulwark** *vt* **:** to strengthen or safeguard with a bulwark **:** PROTECT
[1]**bum** \'bəm\ *vb* **bummed; bum•ming 1 :** to go around in the manner of a bum: **a :** LOAF 1 **b :** to wander like a tramp **2 :** to obtain by begging [probably derived from German *bummler* "loafer"]
[2]**bum** *n* **1 :** a person who avoids work and tries to live off others **2 :** TRAMP 1
[3]**bum** *adj* **1 :** of poor quality **:** INFERIOR ⟨*bum* advice⟩ **2 :** physically disabled ⟨a *bum* knee⟩
bum•ble•bee \'bəm-bəl-,bē\ *n* **:** any of numerous large robust hairy social bees [Middle English *bomblen* "to boom"]
bum•boat \'bəm-,bōt\ *n* **:** a boat that brings provisions and commodities for sale to ships in port or offshore [probably from Low German *bumboot,* from *bum* "tree' + *boot* "boat"]
[1]**bump** \'bəmp\ *vb* **1 :** to strike or knock against something with force **2 :** to collide with **3 :** to proceed in a series of bumps **:** JOLT [imitative] — **bump into :** to meet especially by chance
[2]**bump** *n* **1 :** a sudden forceful blow or jolt **2 a :** a rounded projection or bulge; *esp* **:** a swelling of tissue (as from a blow or sting) **b :** an irregularity in a road surface likely to cause a jolt
[1]**bump•er** \'bəm-pər\ *n* **:** a cup or glass filled to the brim [probably from *bump* "to bulge"]
[2]**bumper** *adj* **:** unusually large or fine ⟨a *bumper* crop⟩
[3]**bumper** *n* **:** a device for absorbing shock or preventing damage (as in collision); *esp* **:** a metal bar at either end of an automobile
bump•kin \'bəm-kən, 'bəmp-\ *n* **:** an awkward and crude rustic [perhaps from Flemish *bommekijn* "small cask"]
bump•tious \'bəm-shəs, 'bəmp-\ *adj* **:** stupidly and often noisily self-assertive **:** PRESUMPTUOUS [[1]*bump* + *-tious* (as in *fractious*)] — **bump•tious•ly** *adv* — **bump•tious•ness** *n*
bumpy \'bəm-pē\ *adj* **bump•i•er; -est :** causing, having, or covered with bumps ⟨a *bumpy* ride⟩ ⟨a *bumpy* surface⟩ — **bump•i•ly** \-pə-lē\ *adv* — **bump•i•ness** \-pē-nəs\ *n*
bun \'bən\ *n* **1 :** a sweet or plain small bread; *esp* **:** a round roll **2 :** a knot of hair shaped like a bun [Middle English *bunne*]
[1]**bunch** \'bənch\ *n* **1 :** BULGE, SWELLING **2 a :** a number of things of the same kind **:** CLUSTER ⟨a *bunch* of grapes⟩ **b :** GROUP 2 ⟨a *bunch* of friends⟩ [Middle English *bunche*] — **bunch•i•ly** \'bən-chə-lē\ *adv* — **bunchy** \-chē\ *adj*
[2]**bunch** *vb* **:** to form in or gather into a group or cluster
bunch•ber•ry \'bənch-,ber-ē\ *n* **:** a creeping perennial herb related to the dogwood with whorled leaves and white floral bracts followed by clusters of red berries
bunch•grass \-,gras\ *n* **:** any of several grasses chiefly of the western United States that grow in tufts
bun•co *or* **bun•ko** \'bəng-kō\ *n, pl* **buncos** *or* **bunkos :** a swindling game or scheme [perhaps from Spanish *banca* "bench, bank"] — **bunco** *vt*
bund \'bund, 'bənd\ *n, often cap* **:** a political association; *esp* **:** a pro-Nazi German-American organization of the 1930s [German, "league"] — **bund•ist** \-əst\ *n, often cap*
[1]**bun•dle** \'bən-dl\ *n* **1 a :** a group of things tied together **b :** PARCEL 4 **c :** a large sum of money **2 a :** a small band of mostly parallel fibers (as of nerve) **b :** VASCULAR BUNDLE [Dutch *bundel*]
[2]**bundle** *vb* **bun•dled; bun•dling** \'bən-dling, -dl-ing\ **1 :** to make into a bundle **:** WRAP **2 :** to hurry or send away unceremoniously ⟨*bundled* the children off to school⟩ **3 :** to take part in bundling — **bun•dler** \-dlər, -dl-ər\ *n*
bundle up *vb* **:** to dress warmly
bun•dling \'bən-dling, -dl-ing\ *n* **:** a former custom in which a couple during courtship would occupy the same bed without undressing
[1]**bung** \'bəng\ *n* **1 :** the stopper in the bunghole of a cask; *also* **:** BUNGHOLE **2 :** the cecum or anus especially of a slaughtered animal [Dutch *bonghe,* from Late Latin *puncta* "puncture", from Latin *pungere* "to prick"]
[2]**bung** *vt* **:** to plug with or as if with a bung
bun•ga•low \'bəng-gə-,lō\ *n* **:** a usually one-stored house with a low-pitched roof [Hindi *baṅglā,* literally, (house) "in the Bengal style"]
bung•hole \'bəng-,hōl\ *n* **:** a hole for emptying or filling a cask
bun•gle \'bəng-gəl\ *vb* **bun•gled; bun•gling** \-gə-ling, -gling\ **:** to act, do, make, or work in a clumsy manner [perhaps of Scandinavian origin] — **bungle** *n* — **bun•gler** \-gə-lər, -glər\ *n*
bung up *vt* **:** BATTER, BRUISE
bun•ion \'bən-yən\ *n* **:** an inflamed swelling on the first joint of the big toe [probably from *bunny* "swelling"]
[1]**bunk** \'bəngk\ *n* **1 :** a built-in bed (as on a ship) that is often

one of a tier **2 :** a sleeping place [probably short for *bunker*]
[2]bunk *vb* **1 :** to occupy a bunk **2 :** to provide with a bunk
[3]bunk *n* **:** NONSENSE 1 [short for *bunkum*]
bun•ker \'bəng-kər\ *n* **1 :** a bin or compartment for storage (as for coal or oil on a ship) **2 a :** a protective dugout; *esp* **:** a fortified chamber mostly below ground **b :** a sand trap on a golf course [Scots *bonker* "chest, box"]
bunk•house \'bəngk-,haůs\ *n* **:** a rough simple building providing sleeping quarters (as for construction workers)
bun•kum *or* **bun•combe** \'bəng-kəm\ *n* **:** NONSENSE 1 [*Buncombe* County, North Carolina; from the statement by its congressional representative in defending a seemingly irrelevant speech that he was speaking to Buncombe]
bun•ny \'bən-ē\ *n, pl* **bunnies :** RABBIT [English dialect *bun* "rabbit"]
Bun•sen burner \,bən-sən-\ *n* **:** a gas burner consisting typically of a tube with small holes at the bottom where air enters and mixes with the gas to produce a very hot blue flame [Robert W. *Bunsen,* died 1899, German chemist]

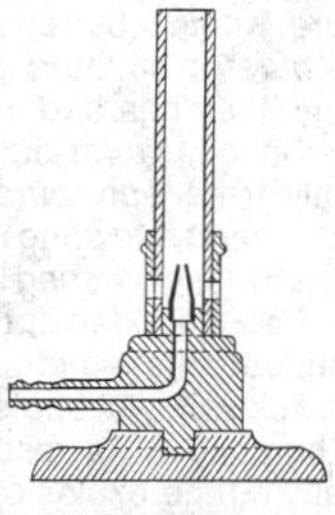
Bunsen burner

[1]bunt \'bənt\ *n* **:** the middle part of a square sail [perhaps from Low German, "bundle"]
[2]bunt *n* **:** a destructive smut of wheat in which the grains are replaced by greasy masses of dark ill-smelling spores [origin unknown]
[3]bunt *vb* **1 :** to strike or push with or as if with the head **:** BUTT **2 :** to push or tap a baseball lightly without swinging the bat [alteration of [1]*butt*] — **bunt•er** *n*
[4]bunt *n* **1 :** an act or instance of bunting **2 :** a bunted ball
[1]bun•ting \'bənt-ing\ *n* **:** any of various stout-billed finches of the size and habits of a sparrow [Middle English]
[2]bunting *n* **1 :** a thin cloth used chiefly for making flags and decorations **2 :** flags or decorations made of bunting [perhaps from English dialect *bunt* "to sift"]
bunt•line \'bənt-,līn, -lən\ *n* **:** one of the ropes attached to the foot of a square sail to haul the sail up to the yard for furling
[1]buoy \'bü-ē, 'bȯi\ *n* **1 :** a floating marker anchored in a body of water to point out a channel or warn of danger **2 :** LIFE BUOY [Middle English *boye*]
[2]buoy *vt* **1 :** to mark by or as if by a buoy **2 a :** to keep afloat **b :** to raise the spirits of **:** SUSTAIN ⟨*buoyed* up by the news⟩
buoy•an•cy \'bȯi-ən-sē, 'bü-yən-\ *n* **1 a :** the tendency of a body to float or to rise when submerged in a fluid ⟨the *buoyancy* of a cork in water⟩ **b :** the power of a fluid to exert an upward force on a body placed in it ⟨the *buoyancy* of seawater⟩ **2 :** natural lightness of spirit **:** LIGHTHEARTEDNESS
buoy•ant \'bȯi-ənt, 'bü-yənt\ *adj* **1 :** able to rise and float in the air or on the surface of a liquid **2 :** able to keep a body afloat ⟨hawks gliding in *buoyant* currents of air⟩ **3 :** LIGHTHEARTED **syn** see ELASTIC — **buoy•ant•ly** *adv*
bur *variant of* BURR
bur•ble \'bər-bəl\ *vi* **bur•bled; bur•bling** \'bər-bə-ling, -bling\ **1 :** to make a bubbling sound **:** GURGLE **2 :** to talk constantly and enthusiastically **:** BABBLE [Middle English *burblen*] — **burble** *n* — **bur•bler** \-bə-lər, -blər\ *n* — **bur•bly** \-bə-lē, -blē\ *adj*
bur•bot \'bər-bət\ *n, pl* **burbot** *also* **burbots :** a northern freshwater fish related to the cod but somewhat resembling an eel [Middle French *bourbotte,* from *bourbe* "mud"]
[1]bur•den \'bərd-n\ *n* **1 a :** something that is carried **:** LOAD **b :** something borne as a duty or responsibility often with labor or difficulty ⟨tax *burdens*⟩ **c :** the duty of doing or providing something ⟨*burden* of proof⟩ **2 :** something hard to bear **:** ENCUMBRANCE **3 a :** the bearing of a load ⟨beasts of *burden*⟩ **b :** capacity for carrying cargo ⟨a ship of 100 tons *burden*⟩ [Old English *byrthen*]
[2]burden *vt* **bur•dened; bur•den•ing** \'bərd-ning, -n-ing\ **:** to put a burden on **:** LOAD, OPPRESS
[3]burden *n* **1 :** the refrain or chorus of a song **2 :** a main theme or central idea **:** GIST [Middle English *burdoun* "bass part", from Middle French *bourdon* "bass horn"]
bur•den•some \'bərd-n-səm\ *adj* **:** difficult to bear **:** OPPRESSIVE — **bur•den•some•ly** *adv* — **bur•den•some•ness** *n*
bur•dock \'bər-,däk\ *n* **:** any of a genus of coarse herbs related to the daisy that have globular flower heads with prickly bracts
bu•reau \'byůr-ō\ *n, pl* **bu•reaus** *also* **bu•reaux** \-ōz\ **1 a** *British* **:** a writing desk; *esp* **:** one with drawers and a slant top **b :** a low chest of drawers with a mirror for use in a bedroom **2 a :** a subdivision of a governmental department performing a particular function ⟨Federal *Bureau* of Investigation⟩ **b :** a commercial agency providing services for the public or for other businesses ⟨a travel *bureau*⟩ [French, "desk, cloth covering for desks", derived from Late Latin *burra* "shaggy cloth"]
bu•reau•cra•cy \byů-'räk-rə-sē\ *n, pl* **-cies 1 :** a body of appointed or hired government officials **2 a :** a system of administration characterized by specialization of functions, adherence to fixed rules, and a hierarchy of authority **b :** a system of administration marked by constant strivings for power and by ever increasing inefficiency and red tape
bu•reau•crat \'byůr-ə-,krat\ *n* **:** a member of a bureaucracy; *esp* **:** one that carries out duties in a narrow routine way
bu•reau•crat•ic \,byůr-ə-'krat-ik\ *adj* **:** of, relating to, or having the characteristics of a bureaucracy or a bureaucrat ⟨*bureaucratic* government⟩ — **bu•reau•crat•i•cal•ly** \-'krat-i-kə-lē, -klē\ *adv*
bu•rette *or* **bu•ret** \byů-'ret\ *n* **:** a graduated glass tube usually with a small opening at the bottom and a stopcock for delivering measured quantities of liquid or for measuring the liquid or gas received or discharged [French *burette,* from Middle French *buire* "pitcher", of Germanic origin]
burg \'bərg\ *n* **1 :** a medieval fortress or walled town **2 :** CITY, TOWN [Old English]
bur•gee \,bər-'jē\ *n* **:** a swallow-tailed flag used especially by ships for signals or identification [perhaps from French dialect *bourgeais* "shipowner"]
bur•geon \'bər-jən\ *vi* **1 a :** to put forth new growth (as buds) **b :** to burst into bloom **:** BLOSSOM **2 :** to expand rapidly and widely [Middle English *burjon* "bud", from Old French, derived from Late Latin *burra* "shaggy cloth"]
bur•gess \'bər-jəs\ *n* **1 :** a citizen of a British borough **2 :** a representative in the lower house of the legislature of colonial Virginia [Middle English *burgeis* "burgher", from Old French *borjois*]
burgh \'bər-ō, 'bə-rō\ *n* **:** BOROUGH; *esp* **:** a Scottish town with certain local lawmaking rights [Old English *burg* "fortified town"]
bur•gher \'bər-gər\ *n* **:** an inhabitant of a borough or a town
bur•glar \'bər-glər\ *n* **:** a person who commits burglary **:** THIEF [Anglo-French *burgler,* from Medieval Latin *burglator,* probably derived from Latin *burgus* "fortified place"]
bur•glar•ize \'bər-glə-,rīz\ *vt* **:** to break into and steal from
bur•glary \'bər-glə-rē\ *n, pl* **-glar•ies :** the act of breaking into a building (as a house) especially at night and for the purpose of committing a crime (as stealing)
bur•go•mas•ter \'bər-gə-,mas-tər\ *n* **:** the chief magistrate of a town in some European countries [Dutch *burgemeester,* from *burg* "town" + *meester* "master"]
Bur•gun•dy \'bər-gən-dē\ *n* **:** a red or white table wine from parts of Burgundy; *also* **:** a similar wine made elsewhere
buri•al \'ber-ē-əl\ *n* **:** the act of burying
bu•rin \'byůr-ən, 'bər-\ *n* **1 :** a pointed steel cutting tool used by engravers **2 :** a prehistoric flint tool with a point like that of a chisel [French]
[1]burl \'bərl\ *n* **1 :** a knot or lump in thread or cloth **2 :** a gnarled woody outgrowth on a tree; *also* **:** veneer cut from this [Middle English *burle,* derived from Late Latin *burra* "shaggy cloth"]
[2]burl *vt* **:** to finish (cloth) especially by repairing burls — **burl•er** *n*
bur•lap \'bər-,lap\ *n* **:** a coarse fabric made usually from jute or hemp and used principally for bags and wrappings [earlier *borelapp*]
[1]bur•lesque \bər-'lesk, ,bər-\ *n* **1 a :** a witty or derisive literary or dramatic imitation **b :** mockery usually by caricature **2 :** theatrical entertainment consisting especially of low comedy

\ə\ **abut**	\aů\ **out**	\i\ **tip**	\ȯ\ **saw**	\ů\ **foot**
\ər\ **further**	\ch\ **chin**	\ī\ **life**	\ȯi\ **coin**	\y\ **yet**
\a\ **mat**	\e\ **pet**	\j\ **job**	\th\ **thin**	\yü\ **few**
\ā\ **take**	\ē\ **easy**	\ng\ **sing**	\t͟h\ **this**	\yů\ **cure**
\ä\ **cot, cart**	\g\ **go**	\ō\ **bone**	\ü\ **food**	\zh\ **vision**

skits and dance routines involving displays of partial nudity [French, "comical", from Italian *burlesco,* from *burla* "joke", from Spanish] **syn** see CARICATURE — **burlesque** *adj*

²burlesque *vt* **:** to imitate in such a way as to make ridiculous — **bur•lesqu•er** *n*

bur•ly \'bər-lē\ *adj* **bur•li•er; -est :** strongly and heavily built **:** HUSKY [Middle English] — **bur•li•ness** *n*

bur marigold *n* **:** any of a genus of coarse herbs related to the daisies with burs that adhere to clothing

Bur•mese \,bər-'mēz, -'mēs\ *n, pl* **Burmese 1 :** a native or inhabitant of Burma **2 :** the language of the Burmese people — **Burmese** *adj*

¹burn \'bərn\ *n, British* **:** CREEK 2 [Old English]

²burn *vb* **burned** \'bərnd, 'bərnt\ *or* **burnt** \'bərnt\; **burn•ing 1 a :** BLAZE ⟨the fire *burned* brightly⟩ **b :** to undergo combustion; *also* **:** to undergo nuclear fission or fusion **2 a :** to feel hot ⟨the *burning* sand⟩ **b :** to become affected by or as if by the action of fire or heat; *esp* **:** SCORCH **c :** to give off light **:** GLOW ⟨left the lights *burning*⟩ **d :** to set on fire; *esp* **:** to destroy by fire ⟨*burn* trash⟩ **e :** to use as fuel ⟨this furnace *burns* gas⟩ **3 :** to produce by the action of fire or heat ⟨*burned* a hole in my shirt⟩ **4 :** to injure or alter by or as if by fire or heat ⟨*burned* the roast⟩ ⟨*burn* out a bearing⟩ [Old English *byrnan* and *baernan*] — **burn•able** \'bər-nə-bəl\ *adj* — **burn•ing•ly** \-ning-lē\ *adv* — **burn one's bridges :** to cut off all means of retreat — **burn the candle at both ends :** to be very wasteful of one's energy or resources

³burn *n* **:** injury, damage, or effect produced by or as if by burning

burn•er \'bər-nər\ *n* **:** one that burns; *esp* **:** the part of a fuel-burning device (as a stove or furnace) where the flame or heat is produced

¹bur•nish \'bər-nish\ *vt* **:** to make shiny or lustrous especially by rubbing **:** POLISH [Middle French *bruniss-,* stem of *brunir,* literally, "to make brown", from *brun* "brown"] — **bur•nish•er** *n*
• syn BURNISH, POLISH mean to smooth or brighten by rubbing. BURNISH applies chiefly to metals that are rubbed until they become lustrous; POLISH implies friction and usually the application of a substance (as wax) that gives a smooth and glossy surface.

²burnish *n* **:** LUSTER 1

bur•noose *or* **bur•nous** \bər-'nüs, ,bər-\ *n* **:** a hooded cloak worn by Arabs and Moors [French *burnous,* from Arabic *burnus*]

burn•out \'bər-,naůt\ *n* **:** the stoppage of a jet or rocket engine; *also* **:** the point at which burnout occurs

burn•sides \'bərn-,sīdz\ *n pl* **:** a beard consisting of side-whiskers and a mustache [Ambrose E. *Burnside*]

¹burp \'bərp\ *n* **:** the act or an instance of expelling stomach gas through the mouth **:** BELCH [imitative]

²burp *vb* **1 :** BELCH 1 **2 :** to help (a baby) expel gas from the stomach especially by patting or rubbing the back

burp gun *n* **:** SUBMACHINE GUN

¹burr \'bər\ *n* **1** *usually* **bur a :** a rough or prickly envelope of a fruit **b :** a plant that bears burs **2 :** BURL 2 **3 :** a roughness left by a tool in cutting or shaping metal **4 a :** a trilled uvular \r\ as used by some speakers of English especially in northern England and in Scotland **b :** a tongue-point trill that is the usual Scottish \r\ **5 a :** a small rotary cutting tool **b** *usually* **bur :** a bit used on a dental drill **6 :** a rough humming sound **:** WHIR [Middle English *burre*] — **burred** \'bərd\ *adj*

²burr *vb* **1 :** to speak or pronounce with a burr **2 :** to make a whirring sound **3 a :** to form into a rough edge **b :** to remove burrs from (as a sharp edge) — **burr•er** \'bər-ər\ *n*

bur reed *n* **:** any of a genus of plants with globe-shaped fruits resembling burs

bur•ro \'bər-ō, 'bůr-; 'bə-rō\ *n, pl* **burros :** DONKEY; *esp* **:** a small one used as a pack animal [Spanish, from Late Latin *burricus* "small horse"]

¹bur•row \'bər-ō, 'bə-rō\ *n* **:** a hole in the ground made by an animal (as a rabbit) for shelter and habitation [Middle English *borow*]

²burrow *vb* **1 :** to construct by tunneling ⟨*burrow* a passage through the hill⟩ **2 :** to conceal oneself in or as if in a burrow **3 a :** to make a burrow **b :** TUNNEL ⟨they *burrowed* under the wall⟩ **4 :** to make a thorough search **:** DELVE ⟨*burrowed* through the files⟩ **5 :** to make a motion suggestive of burrowing **:** NESTLE — **bur•row•er** *n*

bur•ry \'bər-ē\ *adj* **:** containing burs

bur•sa \'bər-sə\ *n, pl* **bur•sas** *or* **bur•sae** \-,sē, -,sī\ **:** a bodily pouch or sac; *esp* **:** a small serous sac between a tendon and a bone [Medieval Latin, "bag, purse", from Greek *byrsa* "animal skin"] — **bur•sal** \-səl\ *adj*

bur•sar \'bər-sər, -,sär\ *n* **:** a treasurer especially of a college or monastery [Medieval Latin *bursarius,* from *bursa* "bag, purse"]

bur•sa•ry \'bərs-rē, -ə-rē\ *n, pl* **-ries :** the treasury of a college or monastery

burse \'bərs\ *n* **:** a square cloth case for carrying the corporal in a Communion service [Medieval Latin *bursa* "bag, purse"]

bur•si•tis \bər-'sīt-əs\ *n* **:** inflammation of a bursa especially of the shoulder or elbow

¹burst \'bərst\ *vb* **burst; burst•ing 1 a :** to break open, apart, or into pieces from or as if from impact or from or as if from pressure within ⟨buds ready to *burst* open⟩ **b :** to cause to burst ⟨*burst* a balloon⟩ **2 a :** to give way from an excess of emotion ⟨their hearts *burst* with grief⟩ **b :** to give vent suddenly to an emotion ⟨*burst* out laughing⟩ **3 a :** to emerge or spring suddenly ⟨the sun *burst* through the clouds⟩ **b :** LAUNCH, PLUNGE ⟨*burst* into song⟩ **4 :** to be filled to the point of breaking or overflowing ⟨*bursting* with pride⟩ [Old English *berstan*]

²burst *n* **1 a :** a sudden outbreak or outburst ⟨a *burst* of laughter⟩ **b :** a sudden intense effort or exertion ⟨a *burst* of speed⟩ **c :** a short quick volley of shots ⟨fire a machine gun in *bursts*⟩ **2 :** an act of bursting **3 :** a result of bursting; *esp* **:** a visible puff accompanying the explosion of a shell

bur•then \'bər-t͟hən\ *archaic variant of* BURDEN

bur•weed \'bər-,wēd\ *n* **:** any of various plants with the fruit enclosed in a bur

bury \'ber-ē\ *vt* **bur•ied; bury•ing 1 :** to deposit (a dead body) in the earth, in a tomb, or in the sea especially with funeral ceremonies **2 :** to place in the ground and cover over ⟨*bury* treasure⟩ **3 :** CONCEAL, HIDE ⟨*bury* one's face in one's hands⟩ **4 :** to remove from the world of action ⟨*bury* oneself in a book⟩ [Old English *byrgan*] — **bur•i•er** *n* — **bury the hatchet :** to settle a disagreement **:** become reconciled

¹bus \'bəs\ *n, pl* **bus•es** *or* **bus•ses 1 a :** a large motor vehicle for carrying passengers especially on an established route according to a schedule **b** *slang* **:** AUTOMOBILE **2 :** a conductor for collecting electric currents and distributing them to outgoing feeders — called also *bus bar* [short for *omnibus*]

△ **origin** Latin *omnibus,* the dative plural of *omnis* "all", means "for all". In English, *omnibus* has several meanings. An omnibus may be a public vehicle which carries all or a waiter's assistant who does all odd jobs. The shortening of *omnibus* has given us *bus,* the usual word for the vehicle.

²bus *vb* **bused** *or* **bussed; bus•ing** *or* **bus•sing :** to travel or transport by bus

bus•boy \'bəs-,bȯi\ *n* **:** a person employed in a restaurant to remove dirty dishes and reset tables after use [*omnibus* "busboy"]

bus•by \'bəz-bē\ *n, pl* **busbies 1 :** a military full-dress fur hat with a bag hanging down on one side **2 :** the bearskin worn by British guardsmen [probably from the name *Busby*]

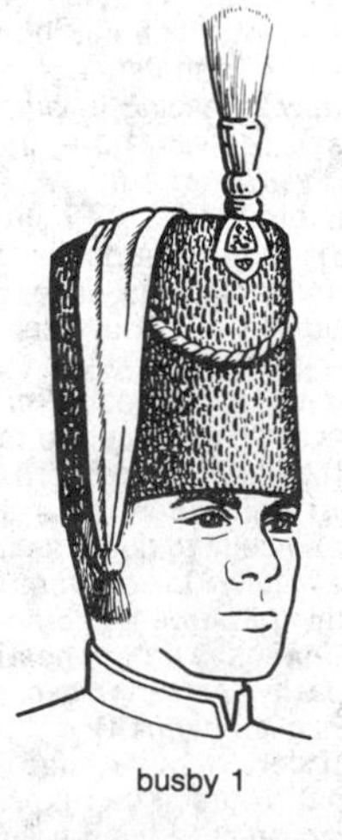
busby 1

bus girl *n* **:** a woman or girl employed as a busboy

bush \'bůsh\ *n* **1 :** SHRUB; *esp* **:** a low densely branched shrub **2 :** a large uncleared or sparsely settled area (as in Australia) **3 :** a bushy tuft or mass; *esp* **:** BRUSH 2 [Middle English]

bush baby *n* **:** any of several small African lemurs

bushed \'bůsht\ *adj* **:** worn out with fatigue **:** EXHAUSTED

bush•el \'bush-əl\ *n* **1 :** any of various units of dry capacity — see MEASURE table **2 :** a container holding a bushel **3 :** a large quantity **:** LOTS [Old French *boissel,* of Celtic origin]

Bu•shi•do \'bůsh-i-,dō, 'büsh-\ *n* **:** a Japanese code of feudal chivalry emphasizing loyalty and valuing honor above life [Japanese *bushidō*]

bush•ing \'bu̇sh-iŋ\ *n* **1 :** a usually removable cylindrical lining in an opening of a mechanical part to limit the size of the opening, resist wear (as in a bearing for an axle), or serve as a guide **2 :** an electrically insulating lining for a hole to protect a conductor [Dutch *bus* "bushing, box", from Late Latin *buxis* "box"]

Bush•man \'bu̇sh-mən\ *n* **:** a member of a nomadic hunting people of southern Africa

bush•mas•ter \-,mas-tər\ *n* **:** a tropical American pit viper that is the largest New World venomous snake

bush pilot *n* **:** a pilot who flies a small plane over uncleared or sparsely settled country especially away from regular commercial air routes

bush•whack \'bu̇sh-,hwak, -,wak\ *vb* **1 :** to clear a path through woods by cutting bushes and low branches **2 :** to live or hide out in the woods **3 :** to attack from a place of hiding **:** AMBUSH — **bush•whack•er** *n* — **bush•whack•ing** *n*

bushy \'bu̇sh-ē\ *adj* **bush•i•er; -est 1 :** full of or overgrown with bushes **2 :** resembling a bush especially in thick spreading form or growth ⟨*bushy* eyebrows⟩ — **bush•i•ness** *n*

busi•ness \'biz-nəs, -nəz\ *n* **1 a :** an activity that takes a major part of the time, attention, or effort of a person or group **b :** a commercial or mercantile activity engaged in as a means of livelihood **2 :** an immediate task or objective **:** MISSION ⟨get down to *business*⟩ **3 a :** a commercial or industrial enterprise **b :** the area of economic activity that usually includes trade, commerce, finance, and industry **c :** transactions of any sort; *esp* **:** PATRONAGE ⟨took their *business* elsewhere⟩ **4 :** AFFAIR, MATTER ⟨a strange *business*⟩ **5 :** personal concern ⟨none of your *business*⟩ [Middle English *bisinesse,* from *bisy* "busy"]
• syn BUSINESS, COMMERCE, TRADE, INDUSTRY mean activity in supplying commodities. BUSINESS may be an inclusive term but specifically applies to the activities of all engaged in the sale and purchase of commodities or in related financial transactions; COMMERCE and TRADE apply to the exchange and transportation of commodities; INDUSTRY applies to the producing of commodities, especially by manufacturing or processing.

busi•ness•like \'biz-nəs-,līk, -nəz-\ *adj* **1 :** having or showing qualities desirable in business **2 :** SERIOUS, PURPOSEFUL

busi•ness•man \'biz-nə-,sman\ *n* **:** a man engaged in a business enterprise especially on an executive level

busi•ness•wom•an \-,swu̇m-ən\ *n* **:** a woman engaged in a business enterprise especially on an executive level

bus•kin \'bəs-kən\ *n* **1 :** a boot reaching halfway to the knee **2 :** TRAGEDY 1; *esp* **:** tragedy resembling ancient Greek drama [perhaps from Spanish *borceguí*]

bus•man's holiday \,bəs-mənz-\ *n* **:** a holiday spent in doing something similar to one's usual occupation

buss \'bəs\ *n* **:** KISS 1 [probably imitative] — **buss** *vt*

¹bust \'bəst\ *n* **1 :** a piece of sculpture representing the upper part of the human figure including the head and neck **2 :** the upper portion of the human torso between neck and waist; *esp* **:** the breasts of a woman [French *buste,* from Italian *busto,* from Latin *bustum* "tomb"]

²bust *vb* **bust•ed** *also* **bust; bust•ing 1 :** HIT, PUNCH **2 a :** to break up or apart ⟨*bust* trusts⟩; *also* **:** FRACTURE **b :** to ruin financially **3 :** to demote especially in military rank **4 :** BURST ⟨laughing fit to *bust*⟩ **5** *slang* **:** ARREST 2 [alteration of *burst*] — **bust•er** *n*

³bust *n* **1 :** ²PUNCH 2 **2 :** a complete failure **3 :** SPREE **4** *slang* **:** ARREST 2

bus•tard \'bəs-tərd\ *n* **:** any of various Old World and Australian game birds [Middle French *bistarde,* from Italian *bistarda,* from Latin *aves tarda,* literally, "slow bird"]

¹bus•tle \'bəs-əl\ *vi* **bus•tled; bus•tling** \'bəs-liŋ, -ə-liŋ\ **1 :** to move about busily and noisily ⟨*bustling* about the house⟩ **2 :** to be busily astir **:** SEETHE ⟨the wharf *bustled* with activity⟩ [probably derived from *busk* "to prepare"]

²bustle *n* **:** noisy or energetic activity

³bustle *n* **:** a pad or a light frame formerly worn by women just below the back waistline to give fullness to the skirt [origin unknown]

¹busy \'biz-ē\ *adj* **bus•i•er; -est 1 a :** engaged in action **:** OCCUPIED ⟨too *busy* to eat⟩ **b :** being in use ⟨a *busy* telephone⟩ **2 :** full of activity **:** BUSTLING ⟨a *busy* street⟩ **3 :** OFFICIOUS, MEDDLING **4 :** full of distracting detail ⟨a *busy* design⟩ [Old English *bisig*] — **bus•i•ly** \'biz-ə-lē\ *adv*

²busy *vb* **bus•ied; busy•ing :** to make or keep busy **:** OCCUPY

busy•body \'biz-ē-,bäd-ē\ *n* **:** a person who meddles in the affairs of others

busy•ness \'biz-ē-nəs\ *n* **:** the quality or state of being busy

¹but \bət, 'bət\ *conj* **1 a :** except that **:** UNLESS ⟨it never rains *but* it pours⟩ **b :** that . . . not ⟨not so stupid *but* you could learn⟩ **c :** THAT — used after a negative ⟨there is no doubt *but* we won⟩ **2 a** (1) **:** on the contrary ⟨not peace *but* a sword⟩ ⟨was called *but* did not answer⟩ (2) **:** despite that fact **:** YET ⟨was poor *but* honest⟩ ⟨we tried *but* we failed⟩ **b :** with this exception, namely ⟨no one *but* you may enter⟩ [Old English *būtan* "outside, except, except that"]

²but *prep* **1 :** with the exception of ⟨no one came *but* us⟩ **2 :** other than ⟨this letter is nothing *but* an insult⟩

³but *adv* **1 :** no more than **:** ONLY ⟨we are *but* children⟩ **2 :** otherwise than ⟨who knows *but* that we may succeed⟩

bu•ta•di•ene \,byüt-ə-'dī-,ēn, -,dī-'\ *n* **:** a flammable gaseous hydrocarbon C_4H_6 used in making synthetic rubbers [*but*ane + *di-* + *-ene*]

bu•tane \'byü-,tān\ *n* **:** either of two flammable gaseous hydrocarbons C_4H_{10} obtained usually from petroleum or natural gas [*but*yric + *-ane*]

¹butch•er \'bu̇ch-ər\ *n* **1 a :** a person who slaughters animals or dresses their flesh **b :** a dealer in meat **2 :** one that kills ruthlessly or brutally **3 :** a vendor especially on a train or at a circus [Old French *bouchier,* from *bouc* "he-goat"]

²butcher *vt* **butch•ered; butch•er•ing** \'bu̇ch-riŋ, -ə-riŋ\ **1 :** to slaughter and dress for meat ⟨*butchered* hogs last week⟩ **2 :** to kill in a barbarous manner **3 :** to make a mess of **:** BOTCH — **butch•er•er** \-ər-ər\ *n*

butch•er•bird \'bu̇ch-ər-,bərd\ *n* **:** any of various shrikes that impale their prey upon thorns

butch•ery \'bu̇ch-rē, -ə-rē\ *n, pl* **-er•ies 1** *chiefly British* **:** SLAUGHTERHOUSE **2 :** the business of a butcher **3 :** brutal murder **:** great slaughter

bu•teo \'byüt-ē-,ō\ *n, pl* **-te•os :** any of various hawks with broad rounded wings and soaring flight [Latin, a kind of hawk]

but•ler \'bət-lər\ *n* **:** the chief male servant of a household [Old French *bouteillier* "servant in charge of wine", from *bouteille* "bottle"]

butler's pantry *n* **:** a service room between kitchen and dining room

¹butt \'bət\ *vb* **:** to strike with the head or horns [Old French *boter,* of Germanic origin]

²butt *n* **:** a blow or thrust usually with the head or horns

³butt *n* **1 a :** a mound, bank, or structure for stopping missiles shot at a target **b :** TARGET 1a **c** *pl* **:** RANGE 5b **2 :** a target of abuse or ridicule ⟨the *butt* of a joke⟩ [Middle French *but* "target", of Germanic origin]

⁴butt *vb* **1 :** ABUT 1 **2 :** to place end to end without overlapping

⁵butt *n* **1 :** BUTTOCK 2 **2 :** the large or thicker end of something; *esp* **:** the thicker or handle end of a tool or weapon **3 :** an unused remainder ⟨a cigarette *butt*⟩ [Middle English]

⁶butt *n* **1 :** a large cask especially for wine, beer, or water **2 :** any of various units of liquid capacity; *esp* **:** a measure equal to 108 imperial gallons (about 491 liters) [Middle French *botte,* derived from Late Latin *buttis*]

butte \'byüt\ *n* **:** an isolated hill with steep sides usually having a smaller summit area than a mesa [French]

¹but•ter \'bət-ər\ *n* **1 :** a solid yellow emulsion of fat, air, and water made by churning milk or cream and used as food **2 :** a substance resembling butter in appearance, texture, or use ⟨apple *butter*⟩ [Old English *butere,* from Latin *butyrum,* from Greek *boutyron,* from *bous* "cow" + *tyros* "cheese"]

²butter *vt* **:** to spread with or as if with butter

but•ter–and–eggs \,bət-ə-rə-'negz, -'nāgz\ *n sing or pl* **:** a common European herb of the snapdragon family that has showy yellow and orange flowers and is a naturalized weed in much of North America — called also *toadflax*

butter bean *n* **1 :** WAX BEAN **2 :** LIMA BEAN **3 :** a green shell bean especially as opposed to a snap bean

but•ter•cup \'bət-ər-,kəp\ *n* **:** any of a genus of yellow-flowered herbs with usually five petals and five sepals, usually lobed leaves, and fruits that are achenes

but·ter·fat \-,fat\ *n* : the natural fat of milk and chief constituent of butter

but·ter·fin·gered \'bət-ər-,fing-gərd\ *adj* : likely to let things fall or slip through the fingers

but·ter·fish \-,fish\ *n* : any of numerous fishes with a slippery coating of mucus

but·ter·fly \'bət-ər-,flī\ *n* **1** : any of numerous slender-bodied day-flying insects (order Lepidoptera) often with large broad usually brightly colored wings — compare MOTH **2** : a person who dresses gaudily or who is chiefly occupied in the pursuit of pleasure **3** : a swimming stroke performed by moving both arms together in a circular motion while kicking the legs up and down **4** *pl* : a queasy feeling caused by nervousness or anxiety

butterfly fish *n* : any of various fishes having variegated colors, broad expanded fins, or both

butterfly weed *n* : a showy orange-flowered milkweed of eastern North America

but·ter·milk \'bət-ər-,milk\ *n* **1** : the liquid left after the butterfat has been churned from milk or cream **2** : cultured milk made by the addition of certain organisms to sweet milk

but·ter·nut \-,nət\ *n* **1** : the edible oily nut of an American tree of the walnut family **2** : a butternut tree

butternut squash *n* : a smooth buff to yellow winter squash

but·ter·scotch \-,skäch\ *n* : a candy made from sugar, corn syrup, and water; *also* : the flavor of such candy — **butterscotch** *adj*

[1]but·tery \'bət-ə-rē, 'bə-trē\ *n, pl* **-ter·ies** *chiefly dialect* : PANTRY [Middle French *boterie* "storeroom for liquors", from *botte* "cask, butt"]

[2]but·tery \'bət-ə-rē\ *adj* **1** : having the qualities, consistency, or appearance of butter **2** : spread with butter **3** : FLATTERING ⟨*buttery* praise⟩

butt hinge *n* : a hinge usually set flush into the edge of a door

butt in *vi* : to meddle in the affairs of others

butt joint *n* : a joint made by fastening the parts together end-to-end without overlap and often with reinforcement

but·tock \'bət-ək\ *n* **1** : the back of the hip which forms one of the fleshy parts on which a person sits **2** *pl* : the seat of the human body [Middle English *buttok*]

[1]but·ton \'bət-n\ *n* **1** : a small knob or disk (as of shell, leather, or plastic) used for holding parts of a garment together or as an ornament **2** : something (as an immature mushroom) that resembles a button [Middle French *boton,* from *boter* "to thrust, butt"]

[2]button *vb* **but·toned**; **but·ton·ing** \'bət-ning, -n-ing\ : to close or fasten with buttons — **but·ton·er** \'bət-nər, -n-ər\ *n*

[1]but·ton·hole \'bət-n-,hōl\ *n* : a slit or loop for fastening a button

[2]buttonhole *vt* **1** : to furnish with buttonholes **2** : to work with buttonhole stitch

[3]buttonhole *vt* : to hold in conversation by or as if by clutching the clothes — **but·ton·hol·er** *n*

buttonhole stitch *n* : a closely worked loop stitch used to make a firm edge (as on a buttonhole)

but·ton·hook \'bət-n-,hu̇k\ *n* : a hook for drawing small buttons through buttonholes

but·ton·wood \'bət-n-,wu̇d\ *n* : PLANE TREE

[1]but·tress \'bə-trəs\ *n* **1** : a projecting structure (as of masonry) that supports or stabilizes a wall or building **2** : something that supports, props, or strengthens [Middle French *bouterez* from *bouter* "to thrust"]

[2]buttress *vt* : to support with or as if with a buttress : PROP, STRENGTHEN ⟨*buttress* an argument with facts⟩

bu·tyl alcohol \,byüt-l-\ *n* : any of four flammable alcohols C_4H_9OH derived from butanes and used in organic synthesis and as solvents [*butyric* + *-yl*]

bu·tyr·ic acid \byü-,tir-ik-\ *n* : an acid $C_4H_8O_2$ of unpleasant odor found in rancid butter and perspiration [Latin *butyrum* "butter"]

bux·om \'bək-səm\ *adj* : vigorously or healthily plump; *also* : having a large bosom [Middle English *buxsum* "obedient, tractable", from Old English *būgan* "to bend"] — **bux·om·ly** *adv* — **bux·om·ness** *n*

[1]buy \'bī\ *vt* **bought** \'bȯt\; **buy·ing 1** : to become owner of by giving money in exchange **2** : to obtain by sacrificing something ⟨*buy* peace at the cost of freedom⟩ **3** : to secure decisive control over by bribery ⟨*buy* votes⟩ **4** : to be sufficient to purchase ⟨$5000 will *buy* this land⟩ **5** : BELIEVE 3, ACCEPT [Old English *bycgan*]

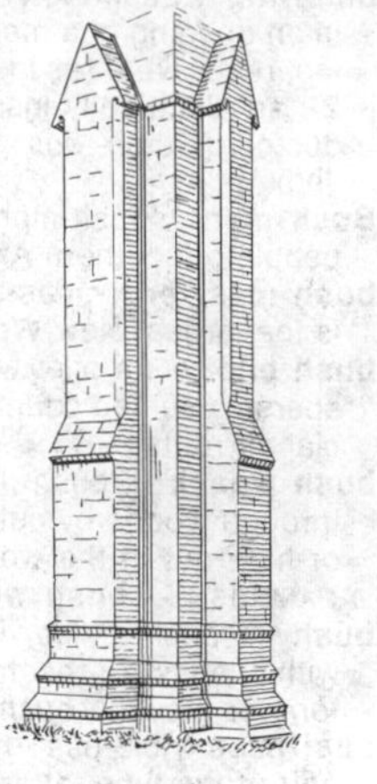
[1]buttress 1

[2]buy *n* **1** : an act of buying : PURCHASE **2** : something sold or for sale at a price favorable to a buyer : BARGAIN

buy·er \'bī-ər, 'bīr\ *n* : one that buys; *esp* : a person who purchases goods to be sold in a retail store

buyer's market *n* : a market with many goods at relatively low prices — compare SELLER'S MARKET

buy up *vt* : to buy all of the available supply of

[1]buzz \'bəz\ *vb* **1** : to make a low continuous humming sound like that of a bee **2** : to be filled with a confused murmur ⟨the room *buzzed* with excitement⟩ **3** : to summon or signal with a buzzer **4** : to fly low and fast over ⟨planes *buzzed* the crowd⟩ [Middle English *bussen*]

[2]buzz *n* **1** : a persistent sound produced by or as if by rapid vibrations **2** : a confused murmur or flurry of activity **3 a** : a signal conveyed by buzzer **b** : a call on the telephone

buz·zard \'bəz-ərd\ *n* **1** *chiefly British* : BUTEO **2** : any of several vultures; *esp* : TURKEY BUZZARD [Old French *busard,* derived from Latin *buteo,* a kind of hawk]

buzz·er \'bəz-ər\ *n* : an electric signaling device that makes a buzzing sound

buzz saw *n* : CIRCULAR SAW

[1]by \bī, 'bī, *especially before consonants* bə\ *prep* **1** : close to : NEAR ⟨*by* the sea⟩ **2 a** : ALONG, THROUGH ⟨*by* a different route⟩ ⟨enter *by* the door⟩ **b** : PAST ⟨went right *by* us⟩ **3 a** : during the course of ⟨studied *by* night⟩ **b** : not later than ⟨be there *by* 2 p.m.⟩ **4** : through the agency or instrumentality of ⟨painted *by* a master⟩ ⟨a town taken *by* force⟩ **5** : with the witness or sanction of ⟨swear *by* all that is holy⟩ **6 a** : in conformity with ⟨*by* the rules⟩ **b** : in terms of ⟨sold *by* the pound⟩ **7** : with respect to ⟨a doctor *by* profession⟩ **8** : in or to the amount or extent of ⟨win *by* a nose⟩ **9** — used as a function word to indicate a succession of units or groups ⟨walk two *by* two⟩ **10 a** — used as a function word in multiplication, in division, and in measurements ⟨divide 12 *by* 4⟩ ⟨a room 4 meters *by* 6 meters⟩ **b** : plus one point toward ⟨north *by* northeast⟩ [Old English *be, bī*]

• **syn** BY, THROUGH, WITH are used in explaining or accounting for an action or effect. BY names the immediate agent or causative agency ⟨a novel *by* Dickens⟩ ⟨destroyed *by* fire⟩ THROUGH implies intermediateness and names a means or medium ⟨express feelings *through* music⟩ ⟨money lost *through* carelessness⟩ WITH names an instrument or instrumentality used in or accompanying an action ⟨wrote *with* a pen⟩ ⟨amused them *with* a story⟩

[2]by \'bī\ *adv* **1 a** : close at hand : NEAR ⟨standing *by*⟩ **b** : at or to another's home ⟨stop *by* for a chat⟩ **2** : PAST ⟨saw the parade go *by*⟩ **3** : in reserve for future using ⟨putting some money *by*⟩

[3]by *or* **bye** \'bī\ *n, pl* **byes** \'bīz\ : something of secondary importance — **by the by** : by the way : INCIDENTALLY

by-and-by \,bī-ən-'bī\ *n* : a future time or occasion

by and by \,bī-ən-'bī\ *adv* : before long : SOON

by and large \,bī-ən-'lärj\ *adv* : on the whole : in general

bye-bye *or* **by-by** \'bī-,bī, bī-'bī\ *interj* — used to express farewell [from *goodbye*]

by-elec·tion \'bī-ə-,lek-shən\ *n* : a special election held between regular elections in order to fill a vacancy

by·gone \'bī-,gȯn *also* -,gän\ *adj* : gone by : PAST ⟨a *bygone* era⟩ — **bygone** *n*

by·law \'bī-,lȯ\ *n* : a rule adopted by an organization (as a club or municipality) for the regulation of its affairs [Middle English *bilawe,* probably from Old Norse *bȳr* "town" + *lōg* "law"]

by-line \'bī-,līn\ *n* : a line at the head of a newspaper or magazine article giving the writer's name

[1]by·pass \'bī-,pas\ *n* **1** : a passage to one side or around a congested area **2** : a channel through which a fluid passes back to the main stream

[2]**bypass** *vt* : to make a detour or circuit around ⟨*bypass* a city⟩

by•path \'bī-ˌpath, -ˌpȧth\ *n* : BYWAY 1

by•play \-ˌplā\ *n* : action occurring on the side while the main action proceeds (as in a play)

by–prod•uct \'bī-ˌpräd-əkt, -ˌəkt\ *n* **1** : something produced (as in manufacturing) in addition to the principal product **2** : a secondary and often unexpected or unintended result

byre \'bīr\ *n, chiefly British* : a cow barn [Old English *bȳre*]

by•road \'bī-ˌrōd\ *n* : BYWAY 1

By•ron•ic \bī-'rän-ik\ *adj* : of, relating to, or having the characteristics of the poet Byron or his writings — **By•ron•i•cal•ly** \-'rän-i-kə-lē, -klē\ *adv* — **By•ron•ism** \'bī-rə-ˌniz-əm\ *n*

bys•sus \'bis-əs\ *n* : a tuft of long tough filaments by which some mollusks (as mussels) attach themselves (as to rocks) [Greek *byssos* "flax", of Semitic origin]

by•stand•er \'bī-ˌstan-dər\ *n* : a person present or standing near but taking no part in something going on

by•street \'bī-ˌstrēt\ *n* : a street off a main thoroughfare : a side street

by the way *adv* : in passing : INCIDENTALLY

by•way \'bī-ˌwā\ *n* **1** : a little-traveled side road **2** : a secondary or little known aspect or field

by•word \'bī-ˌwərd\ *n* **1** : a proverbial saying **2 a** : a person or thing typical especially of some bad class or quality **b** : an object of scorn or contempt

[1]**Byz•an•tine** \'biz-n-ˌtēn *also* -ˌtīn\ *n* : a native or inhabitant of Byzantium or of the Byzantine Empire

[2]**Byzantine** *adj* **1** : of, relating to, or characteristic of the ancient city of Byzantium or the Eastern Roman Empire **2** : of or relating to a style of architecture developed in the Byzantine Empire especially in the 5th and 6th centuries characterized by a central dome over a square space and by much use of mosaics **3** : of or relating to the Eastern Orthodox Church **4** : intricately involved and often devious ⟨*Byzantine* political maneuvering⟩

C

c — Czechish

c \'sē\ *n, pl* **c's** *or* **cs** \'sēz\ *often cap* **1** : the 3d letter of the English alphabet **2** : one hundred in Roman numerals **3** : the musical tone C **4** : a grade rating a student's work as fair or mediocre

cab \'kab\ *n* **1 a** : a light closed horse-drawn carriage (as a hansom) **b** : a carriage for hire **2** : TAXICAB **3 a** : the part of a locomotive that houses the engineer and operating controls **b** : a comparable shelter on a truck, tractor, or crane [short for *cabriolet*]

ca•bal \kə-'bal, -'bäl\ *n* : a small group of persons working together to promote their own plans or interests especially by intrigue [French *cabale,* from Medieval Latin *cabbala* "cabala", from Hebrew *qabbālāh,* literally, "received (lore)"]

ca•ba•la *or* **cab•ba•la** *or* **cab•ba•lah** *or* **kab•ba•la** *or* **kab•ba•lah** *or* **ka•ba•la** \'kab-ə-lə, kə-'bäl-ə\ *n, often cap* **1** : a system of Jewish mysticism and magic using a cipher method of interpreting Scripture **2** : a strange and abstruse doctrine or mysterious art [Medieval Latin *cabbala*] — **cab•a•lism** \'kab-ə-ˌliz-əm\ *n* — **ca•ba•list** \'kab-ə-ləst, kə-'bäl-əst\ *adj* — **cab•a•lis•tic** \ˌkab-ə-'lis-tik\ *adj*

ca•bal•le•ro \ˌkab-ə-'leər-ō, -əl-'yeər-, -ə-'yeər-\ *n, pl* **-ros** *chiefly Southwest* : HORSEMAN [Spanish, derived from Latin *caballus* "horse"]

ca•bana \kə-'ban-yə, -'ban-ə\ *n* : a shelter resembling a cabin usually with an open side facing a beach or swimming pool [Spanish *cabaña,* literally "hut", from Medieval Latin *capanna*]

cab•a•ret \ˌkab-ə-'rā\ *n* : a restaurant serving liquor and providing entertainment (as by singers or dancers) [French]

cab•bage \'kab-ij\ *n* : a garden plant related to the turnip but lacking a swollen root and producing a dense globular head of leaves used as a vegetable [Old North French *caboche* "head"]

cab•by *or* **cab•bie** \'kab-ē\ *n, pl* **cabbies** : a driver of a cab

cab•driv•er \'kab-ˌdrī-vər\ *n* : a driver of a cab

cab•in \'kab-ən\ *n* **1 a** : a private room on a ship for one or a few persons **b** : a compartment below deck on a small boat for passengers or crew **c** : an airplane or airship compartment for cargo, crew, or passengers **2** : a small one-story dwelling usually of simple construction [Middle French *cabane,* from Provençal *cabana* "hut", from Medieval Latin *capanna*]

cabin boy *n* : a boy working as servant on a ship

cabin class *n* : a class of accommodations on a passenger ship superior to tourist class and inferior to first class

cabin cruiser *n* : CRUISER 3

cab•i•net \'kab-ə-nət, 'kab-nət\ *n* **1 a** : a case or cupboard usually having doors and shelves **b** : an upright case housing a radio, television, or phonograph : CONSOLE **2 a** : a group of ministers acting as advisers to a monarch or chief of state but constituting the real political executive in a cabinet government ⟨the British *cabinet*⟩ **b** : a body of advisers to the president of the United States consisting chiefly of the heads of the executive departments [Middle French, "small room", from Old North French *cabine* "gambling house"]

cabinet government *n* : a government in which the real executive and policy-making power is held by a cabinet of ministers who are responsible to the legislature

cab•i•net•mak•er \-ˌmā-kər\ *n* : a skilled woodworker who makes fine furniture — **cab•i•net•mak•ing** \-king\ *n*

cab•i•net•work \-ˌwərk\ *n* : the finished work of a cabinetmaker

[1]**ca•ble** \'kā-bəl\ *n* **1 a** : a strong rope especially of 25 or more centimeters in circumference **b** : a wire rope or metal chain of great strength **c** : a wire or wire rope by which force is exerted to operate a mechanism **2** : CABLE LENGTH **3 a** : a bundle of electrical conductors insulated from each other but held together usually by being twisted around a central core **b** : CABLEGRAM [Old North French, from Medieval Latin *capulum* "lasso", from Latin *capere* "to take"]

[2]**cable** *vb* **ca•bled**; **ca•bling** \'kā-bling, -bə-ling\ **1** : to fasten or provide with a cable **2** : to telegraph by submarine cable

cable car *n* : a car moved on a railway by an endless cable or along an overhead cableway

ca•ble•gram \'kā-bəl-ˌgram\ *n* : a message sent by submarine cable

cable length *n* : a maritime unit of length variously reckoned as 100 fathoms, 120 fathoms, or 608 feet (about 183, 220, or 185 meters)

cable railway *n* : a railway on which the cars grip and are moved by an endless cable that is driven by a stationary engine

cable TV *n* : a system of television reception in which signals are picked up by a single antenna and sent by cable to the receivers of paying subscribers — called also *cable television*

ca•ble•way \'kā-bəl-ˌwā\ *n* : a suspended cable used as a track along which carriers can be pulled

cab•o•chon \'kab-ə-ˌshän\ *n* : a gem or bead cut in convex form and highly polished but not faceted [Middle French, from Old North French *caboche* "head"] — **cabochon** *adv*

ca•boose \kə-'büs\ *n* : a freight-train car attached usually to the rear mainly for the use of the train crew and railroad workers [probably from Dutch *kabuis* "ship's galley"]

cab•ri•o•let \ˌkab-rē-ə-'lā\ *n* **1** : a light 2-wheeled one-horse carriage with a folding leather top and upward-curving shafts **2** : a convertible coupe [French, from *cabriole* "caper", from Middle French *capriole*]

cab•stand \'kab-ˌstand\ *n* : a place for cabs to park while waiting for passengers

ca•cao \kə-'kau̇, kə-'kā-ō\ *n, pl* **cacaos** **1** : a South American tree with small yellowish flowers followed by fleshy yellow pods with many seeds **2** : the dried partly fermented fatty seeds of the cacao from which cocoa and chocolate are made — called also *cacao bean, cocoa bean* [Spanish, from Nahuatl *cacahuatl* "cacao beans"]

¹cache \ˈkash\ *n* **1** : a place for hiding, storing, or safeguarding treasure or food and supplies **2** : the material hidden or stored in a cache [French, from *cacher* "to hide"]

²cache *vt* : to place, hide, or store in a cache

ca•chet \ka-ˈshā\ *n* **1** : a seal especially of official approval **2** : a characteristic feature or quality conferring prestige **3** : a design on an envelope commemorating an event important to stamp collectors ⟨a *cachet* on a first day cover⟩ [Middle French, from *cacher* "to press, hide"]

ca•chex•ia \kə-ˈkek-sē-ə, ka-\ *n* : general physical wasting and malnutrition usually associated with chronic disease [Late Latin, from Greek *kachexia* "bad condition", from *kakos* "bad" + *hexis* "condition"] — **ca•chec•tic** \-ˈkek-tik\ *adj*

ca•cique \kə-ˈsēk\ *n* : an Indian chief in Latin America [Spanish, of American Indian origin]

cack•le \ˈkak-əl\ *vi* **cack•led**; **cack•ling** \ˈkak-ling, -ə-ling\ **1** : to make the sharp broken noise or cry characteristic of a hen especially after laying **2** : to laugh or chatter noisily [Middle English *cakelen,* of imitative origin] — **cackle** *n* — **cack•ler** \ˈkak-lər, -ə-lər\ *n*

ca•coph•o•ny \kə-ˈkäf-ə-nē, ka-\ *n, pl* **-nies** : harsh or discordant sound : DISSONANCE [Greek *kakophōnia,* from *kakos* "bad" + *phōnē* "sound"] **ca•coph•o•nous** \-nəs\ *adj*

cac•tus \ˈkak-təs\ *n, pl* **cac•tus•es** *or* **cac•ti** \-ˌtī, -ˌtē, -tē\ : any of a large family of flowering plants able to live in dry regions and having fleshy stems and branches that bear scales or prickles instead of leaves [Latin, "cardoon", from Greek *kaktos*]

cad \ˈkad\ *n* : a person who behaves in a usually deliberately callous way [English dialect, "unskilled assistant", from Scottish *caddie*]

ca•dav•er \kə-ˈdav-ər\ *n* : a dead body especially of a human being : CORPSE [Latin, from *cadere* "to fall"] — **ca•dav•er•ic** \-ˈdav-rik, -ə-rik\ *adj*

ca•dav•er•ous \kə-ˈdav-rəs, -ə-rəs\ *adj* : of, relating to, or resembling a cadaver: as **a** : GHASTLY 2, PALE **b** : THIN 3, HAGGARD — **ca•dav•er•ous•ly** *adv*

¹cad•die *or* **cad•dy** \ˈkad-ē\ *n, pl* **caddies** : a person who carries a golfer's clubs [Scottish *caddie* "one who does odd jobs", from French *cadet* "military cadet"]

²caddie *or* **caddy** *vi* **-died**; **-dy•ing** : to work as a caddie

cad•dis fly \ˈkad-əs-\ *n* : any of an order (Trichoptera) of 4-winged insects with aquatic larvae — compare CADDISWORM

cad•dish \ˈkad-ish\ *adj* : resembling a cad or the behavior of a cad — **cad•dish•ly** *adv* — **cad•dish•ness** *n*

cad•dis•worm \ˈkad-əs-ˌwərm\ *n* : a caddis-fly larva that lives in and carries around a silken case covered with bits of debris [probably from obsolete *codworm,* from Middle English *cod* "bag"]

cad•dy \ˈkad-ē\ *n, pl* **caddies** : a small box, can, or chest; *esp* : one to keep tea in [Malay *kati,* a unit of weight]

ca•dence \ˈkād-ns\ *n* **1 a** : rhythmic flow of sounds in language **b** : the beat, time, or measure of rhythmical motion or activity **2** : the close of a musical strain; *esp* : a musical chord sequence moving to a harmonic close or point of rest [Italian *cadenza,* from *cadere* "to fall", from Latin] — **ca•denced** \-nst\ *adj*

ca•den•za \kə-ˈden-zə\ *n* **1** : an added flourish in a solo piece (as an aria) commonly just before the end **2** : a technically brilliant sometimes improvised solo passage toward the close of a movement of a concerto [Italian, "cadence, cadenza"]

ca•det \kə-ˈdet\ *n* **1 a** : a younger brother or son **b** : a younger branch of a family or a member of it **2** : one in training for a military commission; *esp* : a student in a service academy **3** : a student at a military school **4** : a boy or girl in any of various organizations usually associated with an adult group organized on military lines [French, from French dialect *capdet* "chief", from Late Latin *capitellum,* from *caput* "head"] — **ca•det•ship** \-ˌship\ *n*

cadge \ˈkaj\ *vb* : BEG 1, SPONGE [back-formation from Scottish *cadger* "peddler", from Middle English *caggen* "to tie"] — **cadg•er** *n*

cad•mi•um \ˈkad-mē-əm\ *n* : a bluish white malleable ductile metallic element used especially in protective platings and in bearing metals — see ELEMENT table [Latin *cadmia* "calamine"; from the occurrence of its ores together with calamine]

cad•re \ˈkad-rē, ˈkäd-, -ˌrā\ *n* **1** : a nucleus of trained personnel capable of assuming leadership and control and of training others **2** : a member of a cadre [French, "frame, framework", from Italian *quadro,* from Latin *quadrum* "square"]

ca•du•ceus \kə-ˈdü-sē-əs, -ˈdyü-, -shəs\ *n, pl* **-cei** \-sē-ˌī\ **1 a** : the symbolic staff of a herald **b** : a representation of a staff with two entwined snakes and two wings at the top **2** : an insignia bearing a caduceus and symbolizing a physician [Latin, from Greek *karykeion,* from *karyx, kēryx* "herald"] — **ca•du•cean** \-sē-ən, -shən\ *adj*

cae•cal, cae•cum *variant of* CECAL, CECUM

cae•ci•lian \si-ˈsil-yən, -ˈsēl-\ *n* : any of an order (Gymnophiona) of chiefly tropical burrowing amphibians resembling worms [Latin *caecilia,* a kind of lizard, from *caecus* "blind"] — **caecilian** *adj*

Cae•sar \ˈsē-zər\ *n* **1** : any of the Roman emperors succeeding Augustus Caesar — used as a title **2 a** *often not cap* : a powerful ruler: (1) : EMPEROR (2) : DICTATOR 1b, AUTOCRAT **b** : the civil power : a temporal ruler [from Gaius Julius *Caesar;* sense 2b from the reference in Matthew 22:21] — **Cae•sar•e•an** *or* **Cae•sar•i•an** \si-ˈzar-ē-ən, -ˈzer-\ *adj*

cae•sar•e•an *variant of* CESAREAN

cae•si•um *variant of* CESIUM

cae•su•ra *also* **ce•su•ra** \si-ˈzůr-ə, -ˈzhůr-\ *n, pl* **-su•ras** *or* **-su•rae** \-ˈzůr-ē, -ˈzhůr-\ : a break in the flow of sound usually in the middle of a line of verse [Latin, "act of cutting", from *caedere* "to cut"] — **cae•su•ral** \-ˈzůr-əl, -ˈzhůr-\ *adj*

ca•fé *also* **ca•fe** \ka-ˈfā, kə-\ *n* **1** : COFFEEHOUSE **2** : BARROOM, SALOON **3** : RESTAURANT; *also* : NIGHTCLUB [French *café* "coffee, café", from Turkish *kahve*]

ca•fé au lait \ka-ˌfā-ō-ˈlā\ *n* : coffee with usually hot milk in about equal parts [French, "coffee with milk"]

caf•e•te•ria \ˌkaf-ə-ˈtir-ē-ə\ *n* : a restaurant in which the customers serve themselves or are served at a counter but take the food to tables to eat [American Spanish *cafetería* "coffee store", from Spanish *café* "coffee", from French]

caf•feine \ˈka-ˌfēn, ka-ˈfēn\ *n* : a bitter stimulating compound $C_8H_{10}N_4O_2$ found especially in coffee, tea, and kola nuts [German *kaffein,* from *kaffee* "coffee", from French *café*]

caf•tan *or* **kaf•tan** \kaf-ˈtan, ˈkaf-ˌ\ *n* : an ankle-length garment with long sleeves that is worn in the Levant; *also* : a comparable garment widely used as a housecoat [Russian *kaftan,* from Turkish, from Persian *qaftān*]

¹cage \ˈkāj\ *n* **1** : a largely openwork enclosure for confining or carrying an animal (as a bird) **2** : an enclosure like a cage in form or purpose **3** : a goal structure consisting of posts or a frame with a net attached (as in ice hockey) **4** : a large building with unobstructed interior for practicing outdoor sports [Old French, from Latin *cavea* "cavity, cage", from *cavus* "hollow" — see JAIL *origin*]

²cage *vt* : to confine or keep in or as if in a cage

cage•ling \ˈkāj-ling\ *n* : a caged bird

ca•gey *also* **ca•gy** \ˈkā-jē\ *adj* **ca•gi•er**; **-est** : wary of being trapped or deceived : SHREWD, CAUTIOUS [origin unknown] — **ca•gi•ly** \-jə-lē\ *adv* — **ca•gi•ness** \-jē-nəs\ *n*

ca•hoot \kə-ˈhüt\ *n* : PARTNERSHIP 1, LEAGUE — usually used in pl. ⟨in *cahoots* with the devil⟩ [perhaps from French *cahute* "cabin, hut"]

cai•man *or* **cay•man** \ˈkā-mən; kā-ˈman, kī-\ *n* : any of several Central and South American reptiles basically similar to alligators but often superficially resembling crocodiles [Spanish *caimán,* probably from Carib *caymán*]

ca•ïque \kä-ˈēk\ *n* **1** : a light skiff used on the Bosporus **2** : a Greek sailing vessel usually equipped with an auxiliary engine [Turkish *kayık*]

cairn \ˈkaərn, ˈkeərn\ *n* : a heap of stones piled up as a landmark or as a memorial [Scottish Gaelic *carn*]

cairn terrier *n* : a small compactly built terrier of Scottish origin with a weather resistant coat of harsh texture [from its use in hunting among cairns]

cais•son \ˈkā-ˌsän, ˈkās-n\ *n* **1 a** : a chest for ammunition **b** : a 2-wheeled vehicle for artillery ammunition **2 a** : a watertight chamber used in construction work under water or as a foundation **b** : a float for raising a sunken vessel [French, from *caisse* "box", derived from Latin *capsa* "chest, case"]

caisson disease *n* : a severe disorder marked by pain (as in joints and limbs), distress in breathing, and often collapse and caused by release of gas bubbles in the tissues upon too rapid decrease in air pressure after a stay in a compressed atmosphere — called also *bends*

cai•tiff \'kāt-əf\ *adj* : being base, cowardly, or contemptible [Old North French *caitif* "captive, vile", from Latin *captivus* "captive"] — **caitiff** *n*

ca•jole \kə-'jōl\ *vt* : to coax or persuade especially by flattery or false promises : WHEEDLE [French *cajoler* "to chatter like a jay in a cage, cajole", from Middle French *gaioler,* from Old North French *gaiole* "bird cage", from Latin *caveola,* from *cavea* "cage"] — **ca•jol•ery** \-'jōl-rē, -ə-rē\ *n*

Ca•jun \'kā-jən\ *n* : a Louisianian descended from French-speaking immigrants from Acadia [alteration of *Acadian*]

^{1}**cake** \'kāk\ *n* **1** : a small mass of food (as dough, meat, or fish) baked or fried **2** : a baked food made from a mixture chiefly of flour, sugar, eggs, liquid, and flavoring **3** : a substance hardened or molded into a solid mass ⟨a *cake* of soap⟩ [Old Norse *kaka*]

^{2}**cake** *vb* **1** : ENCRUST **2** : to form or harden into a mass

cal•a•bash \'kal-ə-,bash\ *n* **1** : GOURD; *esp* : one whose hard shell is used for a utensil (as a bottle) **2** : a tropical American tree related to the trumpet creeper; *also* : its hard round fruit **3** : a utensil made from the shell of a calabash [Spanish *calabaza*]

cal•a•boose \'kal-ə-,büs\ *n, dialect* : JAIL [Spanish *calabozo* "dungeon"]

ca•la•di•um \kə-'lād-ē-əm\ *n* : any of a genus of tropical American herbs related to the arums and often grown for their showy brightly colored leaves [Malay *kĕladi,* a plant of the arum family]

cal•a•mine \'kal-ə-,mīn, -mən\ *n* : a mixture of zinc oxide and a small amount of ferric oxide used in lotions, liniments, and ointments in skin treatment [French, "zinc ore", from Medieval Latin *calamina,* from Latin *cadmia,* from Greek *kadmeia,* literally, "Theban (earth)", from *kadmeios* "Theban", from *Kadmos* "Cadmus", founder of Thebes]

cal•a•mite \'kal-ə-,mīt\ *n* : a Paleozoic fossil plant resembling a giant equisetum [Latin *calamus* "reed"]

ca•lam•i•ty \kə-'lam-ət-ē\ *n, pl* **-ties** **1** : a state of deep distress or misery caused by major misfortune or loss **2** : an extraordinarily grave event marked by great loss and lasting distress and affliction [Middle French *calamité,* from Latin *calamitas*] **syn** see DISASTER — **ca•lam•i•tous** \-ət-əs\ *adj* — **ca•lam•i•tous•ly** *adv* — **ca•lam•i•tous•ness** *n*

cal•a•mus \'kal-ə-məs\ *n, pl* **-mi** \-,mī, -,mē\ **1** : the sweet flag or its aromatic root **2** : QUILL 2a [Latin, "reed, reed pen", from Greek *kalamos*]

ca•lash \kə-'lash\ *n* **1** : a light small-wheeled 4-passenger carriage with a folding top **2** : a large hood on a hoop frame worn by women in the 18th century [French *calèche,* from German *kalesche,* from Czech *kolesa* "wheels, carriage"]

calc- *or* **calci-** *or* **calco-** *combining form* : calcium : calcium salt ⟨*calci*fy⟩

cal•ca•ne•us \kal-'kā-nē-əs\ *n, pl* **-nei** \-nē-,ī\ : a tarsal bone that in humans is the great bone of the heel [Late Latin, "heel", from Latin *calcaneum,* from *calx* "heel"]

cal•car•e•ous \kal-'kar-ē-əs, -'ker-\ *adj* **1** : resembling calcite or calcium carbonate especially in hardness **2** : consisting of or containing calcium carbonate; *also* : containing calcium — **cal•car•e•ous•ly** *adv* — **cal•car•e•ous•ness** *n*

cal•ce•o•lar•ia \,kal-sē-ə-'lar-ē-ə, -'ler-\ *n* : any of a genus of tropical American plants of the snapdragon family widely grown for their showy pouch-shaped flowers [Latin *calceolus* "small shoe", from *calceus* "shoe", from *calx* "heel"]

cal•ces *pl of* CALX

cal•cif•er•ol \kal-'sif-ə-,ròl, -,rōl\ *n* : a vitamin D prepared by irradiation of ergosterol

cal•cif•er•ous \kal-'sif-rəs, -ə-rəs\ *adj* : producing or containing calcium carbonate

cal•ci•fi•ca•tion \,kal-sə-fə-'kā-shən\ *n* **1** : the process of calcifying; *esp* : deposition of insoluble lime salts (as in tissue) ⟨bone formation by *calcification* of cartilage⟩ **2** : a calcified structure

cal•ci•fy \'kal-sə-,fī\ *vb* **-fied**; **-fy•ing** **1** : to make calcareous by deposit of calcium salts **2** : to become calcareous

cal•ci•mine *or* **kal•so•mine** \'kal-sə-,mīn\ *n* : a white or tinted wash of glue, whiting or zinc white, and water used especially on plastered surfaces [*calcimine* alteration of *kalsomine,* of unknown origin] — **calcimine** *vt*

cal•cine \kal-'sīn, 'kal-,\ *vt* : to heat to a high temperature but without fusing in order to drive off volatile matter (as carbon dioxide from limestone) [Middle French *calciner,* from Latin *calx* "lime"] — **cal•ci•na•tion** \,kal-sə-'nā-shən\ *n*

cal•cite \'kal-,sīt\ *n* : a crystalline mineral $CaCO_3$ composed of calcium carbonate and found in numerous forms including limestone, chalk, and marble — **cal•cit•ic** \kal-'sit-ik\ *adj*

cal•ci•to•nin \,kal-sə-'tō-nən\ *n* : THYROCALCITONIN [*calc-* + ^{1}*tonic* + *-in*]

cal•ci•um \'kal-sē-əm\ *n* : a silver-white bivalent soft metallic chemical element that is found only in combination with other chemical elements (as in limestone) and that is one of the essential parts of the bodies of most plants and animals — see ELEMENT table [New Latin, from Latin *calx* "lime"]

calcium carbide *n* : a usually dark gray crystalline compound CaC_2 used for the generation of acetylene

calcium carbonate *n* : a solid substance $CaCO_3$ found in nature as limestone and marble and in plant ashes, bones, and shells

calcium chloride *n* : a salt $CaCl_2$ that absorbs moisture from the air and that is used as a drying agent and in a hydrated state to control dust and melt ice on roads

calcium phosphate *n* : any of various phosphates of calcium: as **a** : the phosphate $Ca_3(PO_4)_2$ used as a fertilizer **b** : a naturally occurring phosphate containing other elements (as fluorine) and occurring as the chief constituent of phosphate rock, bones, and teeth

cal•cu•late \'kal-kyə-,lāt\ *vb* **1 a** : to determine by mathematical processes **b** : to reckon by an informed guess : ESTIMATE **2** : to make a calculation **3** : to plan by careful thought ⟨a program *calculated* to succeed⟩ **4** : RELY, DEPEND [Latin *calculare,* from *calculus* "pebble (used in reckoning)", from *calx* "stone used in gaming, lime"] — **cal•cu•la•ble** \-kyə-lə-bəl\ *adj* — **cal•cu•la•bly** \-blē\ *adv*

cal•cu•lat•ed \-,lāt-əd\ *adj* : undertaken after estimating the probability of success or failure ⟨a *calculated* risk⟩ — **cal•cu•lat•ed•ly** *adv*

cal•cu•lat•ing \-,lāt-ing\ *adj* **1** : designed to make calculations ⟨*calculating* machine⟩ **2** : marked by shrewd analysis of one's own self-interest : SCHEMING — **cal•cu•lat•ing•ly** \-ing-lē\ *adv*

cal•cu•la•tion \,kal-kyə-'lā-shən\ *n* **1 a** : the process or an act of calculating **b** : the result of an act of calculating **2** : studied care in analyzing or planning : CAUTION — **cal•cu•la•tive** \'kal-kyə-,lāt-iv\ *adj*

cal•cu•la•tor \'kal-kyə-,lāt-ər\ *n* : one that calculates; *esp* : a machine for performing mathematical operations mechanically or electronically

cal•cu•lus \'kal-kyə-ləs\ *n, pl* **-li** \-,lī, -,lē\ *also* **-lus•es** **1** : a mass usually of mineral salts deposited in or around organic material in a hollow organ or bodily duct **2 a** : a method of computation or calculation in a special symbolic notation **b** : the mathematical methods comprising differential and integral calculus [Latin, "pebble, stone"]

cal•de•ra \kal-'der-ə, kòl-, -'dir-\ *n* : a large crater formed by the collapse or explosion of a volcanic cone [Spanish, literally, "caldron", from Late Latin *caldaria*]

cal•dron *also* **caul•dron** \'kòl-drən\ *n* : a large kettle or boiler [Old North French *cauderon,* from Late Latin *caldaria,* from Latin, "warm bath", from *calidus* "warm"]

^{1}**cal•en•dar** \'kal-ən-dər\ *n* **1 a** : an arrangement of time into days, weeks, months, and years **b** : a record of such an arrangement for a certain period and usually for a year **2** : an orderly list: as **a** : a list of cases to be tried in court **b** : a list of bills to be considered by a legislative assembly **c** : a schedule of coming events [Medieval Latin *kalendarium,* from Latin *kalendae* "calends"]

^{2}**calendar** *vt* **-dared**; **-dar•ing** \-də-ring, -dring\ : to enter in a calendar

^{1}**cal•en•der** \'kal-ən-dər\ *vt* **-dered**; **-der•ing** \-də-ring, -dring\ : to press (as cloth or paper) between rollers or plates in order to smooth and glaze or thin into sheets [Middle French *calendrer,* from *calandre* "calender", from Greek *kylindros* "cylinder"] — **cal•en•der•er** *n*

2calender *n* : a machine for calendering cloth or paper

cal•ends *or* **kal•ends** \ˈkal-ənz\ *n pl* : the first day of the ancient Roman month [Latin *kalendae*]

ca•len•du•la \kə-ˈlen-jə-lə\ *n* : any of a small genus of yellow-rayed herbs related to the daisies — compare POT MARIGOLD [derived from Latin *kalendae* "calends"]

1calf \ˈkaf, ˈkȧf\ *n, pl* **calves** \ˈkavz, ˈkȧvz\ **1 a** : the young of the domestic cow **b** : the young of various large animals (as the elephant or whale) **2** *pl* **calfs** : CALFSKIN **3** : a boy or youth held to be awkward or silly [Old English *cealf*]

2calf *n, pl* **calves** : the fleshy back part of the leg below the knee [Old Norse *kālfi*]

calf•skin \ˈkaf-ˌskin, ˈkȧf-\ *n* : leather made of the skin of a calf

cal•i•ber *or* **cal•i•bre** \ˈkal-ə-bər\ *n* **1** : the diameter of a bullet or other projectile **2** : the diameter of the bore of a gun — usually expressed in hundredths or thousandths of an inch and as a decimal fraction ⟨.32 *caliber*⟩ **3 a** : mental ability or moral quality **b** : degree of excellence : QUALITY [Middle French *calibre,* from Italian *calibro,* from Arabic *qālib* "shoemaker's last"]

cal•i•brate \ˈkal-ə-ˌbrāt\ *vt* **1** : to measure the caliber of **2** : to determine, correct, or put the measuring marks on (as a thermometer tube) — **cal•i•bra•tion** \ˌkal-ə-ˈbrā-shən\ *n* — **cal•i•bra•tor** \ˈkal-ə-ˌbrāt-ər\ *n*

cal•i•co \ˈkal-i-ˌkō\ *n, pl* **-coes** *or* **-cos** **1** : cotton cloth; *esp* : cotton cloth with a colored pattern printed on one side **2** : a blotched or spotted animal (as a piebald horse) [*Calicut,* city in India] — **calico** *adj*

Cal•i•for•nia condor \ˌkal-ə-ˌfȯr-nyə-\ *n* : a large nearly extinct vulture of mountainous southern California that is related to the condor of South America — called also *condor*

California condor

California poppy *n* : any of a genus of herbs of the poppy family including one widely grown for its pale yellow to red flowers

cal•i•for•ni•um \ˌkal-ə-ˈfȯr-nē-əm\ *n* : an artificially prepared radioactive chemical element — see ELEMENT table [New Latin, from *California,* United States]

cal•i•per *or* **cal•li•per** \ˈkal-ə-pər\ *n* : a measuring instrument with two legs or jaws that can be adjusted to determine thickness, diameter, and distance between surfaces — usually used in pl. ⟨a pair of *calipers*⟩ [alteration of *caliber*]

ca•liph *or* **ca•lif** \ˈkā-ləf, ˈkal-əf\ *n* : a successor of Muhammad as temporal and spiritual head of Islam — used as a title [Middle French *calife,* from Arabic *khalīfah* "successor"] — **ca•liph•ate** \-ˌāt\ *n*

cal•is•then•ics \ˌkal-əs-ˈthen-iks\ *n sing or pl* **1** : systematic rhythmic bodily exercises performed usually without apparatus **2** : the art or practice of calisthenics [Greek *kalos* "beautiful" + *sthenos* "strength"] — **cal•is•then•ic** \-ik\ *adj*

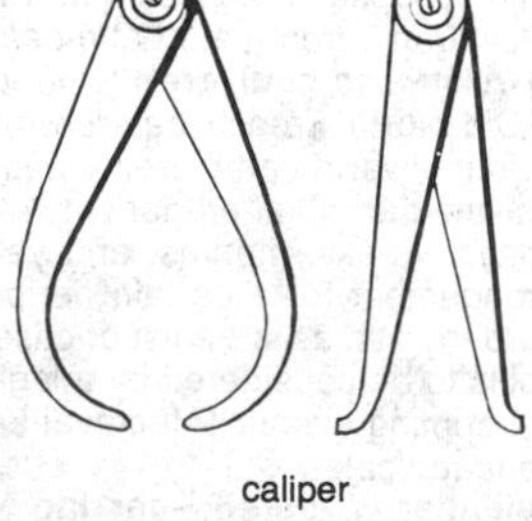

caliper

1calk \ˈkȯk\ *variant of* CAULK

2calk *or* **caulk** *n* : a tapered piece projecting downward from a shoe (as of a horse) to prevent slipping [probably derived from Old North French *calcain* "heel", from Latin *calcaneum,* from *calx* "heel"]

3calk *or* **caulk** *vt* **1** : to furnish with calks **2** : to wound with a calk

1call \ˈkȯl\ *vb* **1** : to speak in a loud distinct voice so as to be heard at a distance : SHOUT **2** : to utter in a loud clear voice ⟨*call* out a command⟩ **3** : to announce with authority : PROCLAIM **4 a** : to summon with or as if with a shout ⟨*call* the children to dinner⟩ **b** : to cause to come ⟨*call* to mind an old saying⟩ **5** : to bring into action or discussion ⟨*call* a case into court⟩ **6** : to make an appeal, request, or demand ⟨*call* on a person's sense of decency⟩ **7** : to get in touch with by telephone : make a telephone call **8** : SUMMON ⟨*call* a meeting⟩ **9** : to make a brief visit **10** : to give a name to : address by name **11** : to regard as being of a certain kind : CONSIDER **12** : to estimate as being ⟨*call* it an even dollar⟩ **13 a** : to utter a characteristic note or cry — used of an animal **b** : to attract (as game) by imitating the characteristic cry **14** : to make a demand in card games (as for a particular card or for a show of hands) **15** : to halt (as a baseball game) because of unsuitable conditions **16** : SUSPEND ⟨time was *called* while the field was cleared⟩ [probably from Old Norse *kalla*] — **call•able** \ˈkȯ-lə-bəl\ *adj* — **call•er** *n* — **call in question** : to challenge the accuracy or truth of — **call it a day** : to stop at least for the present whatever one has been doing — **call the tune** : to be in charge or control — **call to account** : to hold responsible

2call *n* **1 a** : an act of calling with the voice; *also* : SHOUT **b** : a cry of an animal (as a bird); *also* : an imitation of this or a device used (as in calling game) to make such an imitation **2 a** : a request or command to assemble **b** : a signal on a drum or bugle **c** : an invitation to become the minister of a church or to accept a professional appointment **d** : a divine or inner prompting to a course of action **e** : the attraction or appeal of a particular activity, condition, or place ⟨the *call* of the wild⟩ **3 a** : DEMAND, CLAIM ⟨my family has first *call* on my time⟩ **b** : NEED, JUSTIFICATION ⟨no *call* to apologize⟩ **c** : REQUEST ⟨many *calls* for Christmas stories⟩ **4** : a short visit **5** : a name or thing called ⟨the *call* was heads⟩ **6** : the act of calling in a card game **7** : the act of calling on the telephone **8** : a direction or set of directions for a square dance rhythmically called to the dancers **9** : a decision or ruling made by an official of a sports contest

cal•la \ˈkal-ə\ *n* : a plant of the arum family often grown for its white showy spathe surrounding a fleshy spike of yellow florets — called also *calla lily* [Greek *kallaia* "rooster's wattles"]

call–board \ˈkȯl-ˌbōrd, -ˌbȯrd\ *n* : BULLETIN BOARD

call•boy \ˈkȯl-ˌbȯi\ *n* **1** : BELLHOP, PAGE **2** : a boy who summons actors to go on stage

call down *vt* : REPRIMAND

cal•lig•ra•phy \kə-ˈlig-rə-fē\ *n* **1** : beautiful or elegant handwriting; *also* : the art of producing such writing **2** : PENMANSHIP 2 [Greek *kalligraphia,* from *kallos* "beauty" + *-graphia* "-graphy"] — **cal•lig•ra•pher** \-fər\ *n* — **cal•li•graph•ic** \ˌkal-ə-ˈgraf-ik\ *adj* — **cal•li•graph•i•cal•ly** \-ˈgraf-i-kə-lē, -klē\ *adv*

call•ing \ˈkȯ-ling\ *n* **1** : a strong inner impulse; *esp* : one toward the ministry or priesthood **2** : one's customary profession

cal•li•o•pe \kə-ˈlī-ə-ˌpē, ˈkal-ē-ˌōp\ *n* : a keyboard musical instrument resembling an organ and consisting of a series of whistles sounded by steam or compressed air [*Calliope,* a Greek muse]

cal•li•op•sis \ˌkal-ē-ˈäp-səs\ *n* : COREOPSIS — used especially of annual forms [Greek *kallos* "beauty" + *opsis* "appearance"]

call letters *n pl* : CALL SIGN

call loan *n* : a loan payable on demand of either party

call number *n* : a combination of characters assigned to a library book to indicate its place on a shelf

call off *vt* **1** : to draw away : DIVERT ⟨*call off* your dog⟩ **2** : CANCEL ⟨*call off* a meeting⟩

cal•los•i•ty \ka-ˈläs-ət-ē, kə-\ *n, pl* **-ties** **1** : the quality or state of being callous **2** : CALLUS 1

1cal•lous \ˈkal-əs\ *adj* **1** : so thickened and usually hardened as to form callus or a callus **2** : lacking in emotional response : UNFEELING ⟨a *callous* disregard for human rights⟩ [Middle French *calleux,* from Latin *callosus,* from *callus* "callous skin"] — **cal•lous•ly** *adv* — **cal•lous•ness** *n*

2callous *vt* : to make callous

cal•low \ˈkal-ō\ *adj* : lacking adult sophistication : IMMATURE [Old English *calu* "bald"] — **cal•low•ness** *n*

call sign *n* : the combination of identifying letters assigned to a radio or television station

call–up \ˈkȯl-ˌəp\ *n* : an order to report for military service

1cal•lus \ˈkal-əs\ *n* **1** : a thickening of or a hard thickened area on skin or bark **2** : a mass of exudate and connective tissue that surrounds a break in a bone and is converted into bone in the healing of the break **3** : tissue that forms over an injured plant surface [Latin]

2callus *vi* : to form callus or a callus

1calm \ˈkäm, ˈkälm\ *n* **1** : a period or condition of freedom from

storm, wind, or rough activity of water **2 :** a state of repose and freedom from turmoil or agitation **:** QUIET [Middle French *calme,* from Italian *calma,* derived from Greek *kauma* "heat"]
[2]**calm** *adj* **1 :** marked by calm **:** STILL ⟨a *calm* sea⟩ **2 :** free from agitation, excitement or disturbance ⟨a *calm* manner⟩ — **calm•ly** *adv* — **calm•ness** *n*
• syn CALM, TRANQUIL, SERENE, PLACID mean quiet and free from whatever disturbs or hurts. CALM implies a contrast with a foregoing or nearby state of agitation or violence; TRANQUIL suggests a very deep quietude or composure; SERENE stresses an unclouded and lofty tranquillity; PLACID suggests an undisturbed appearance and often implies a degree of complacency.
[3]**calm** *vb* **1 :** to become calm **2 :** to make calm
cal•o•mel \ˈkal-ə-məl, -ˌmel\ *n* **:** a white tasteless substance Hg_2Cl_2 that occurs as a mineral or is made chemically and that is used as a purgative, fungicide, and insecticide — called also *mercurous chloride* [Greek *kalos* "beautiful" + *melas* "black"]
[1]**ca•lor•ic** \kə-ˈlȯr-ik, -ˈlōr, ˈ-lär; ˈkal-ə-rik\ *n* **:** a supposed form of matter formerly held responsible for the phenomena of heat and combustion
[2]**caloric** *adj* **1 :** of or relating to heat **2 :** of or relating to calories — **ca•lor•i•cal•ly** \-i-kə-lē, -i-klē\ *adv*
cal•o•rie *also* **cal•o•ry** \ˈkal-rē, -ə-rē\ *n, pl* **-ries 1 :** a unit of heat: **a :** the heat required to raise the temperature of one gram of water one degree Celsius — called also *small calorie;* abbreviation *cal* **b :** 1000 small calories — used especially to indicate the heat-producing or energy-producing value of foods; called also *large calorie;* abbreviation *Cal* **2 :** the amount of food producing one large calorie [French *calorie,* from Latin *calor* "heat", from *calēre* "to be warm"]
cal•o•rif•ic \ˌkal-ə-ˈrif-ik\ *adj* **:** CALORIC
cal•o•rim•e•ter \ˌkal-ə-ˈrim-ət-ər\ *n* **:** an apparatus for measuring quantities of absorbed or evolved heat or for determining specific heats — **cal•o•ri•met•ric** \ˌkal-ə-rə-ˈme-trik\ *adj* — **cal•o•ri•met•ri•cal•ly** \-ˈme-tri-kə-lē, -klē\ *adv* — **cal•o•rim•e•try** \-ˈrim-ə-trē\ *n*
cal•u•met \ˈkal-yə-ˌmet, -mət\ *n* **:** an ornamented shaft of reed or wood used as a peace pipe or ceremonial object by American Indians [American French, from French dialect, "straw", derived from Latin *calamus* "reed"]

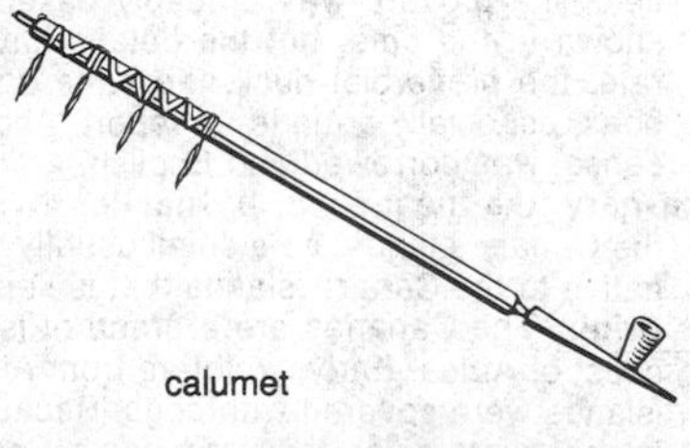
calumet

ca•lum•ni•ate \kə-ˈləm-nē-ˌāt\ *vt* **:** to speak falsely and maliciously about **:** SLANDER — **ca•lum•ni•a•tion** \-ˌləm-nē-ˈā-shən\ *n* — **ca•lum•ni•a•tor** \-ˈləm-nē-ˌāt-er\ *n*
cal•um•ny \ˈkal-əm-nē\ *n, pl* **-nies :** a false charge made to injure another person's reputation; *also* **:** the uttering of such charges [Latin *calumnia,* from *calvi* "to deceive"] — **ca•lum•ni•ous** \kə-ˈləm-nē-əs\ *adj* — **ca•lum•ni•ous•ly** *adv*
calve \ˈkav, ˈkȧv\ *vi* **:** to give birth to a calf; *also* **:** to produce offspring
calves *pl of* CALF
Cal•vin•ism \ˈkal-və-ˌniz-əm\ *n* **:** the theological system of John Calvin and his followers emphasizing the absolute power of God and especially the doctrine of predestination to eternal life — **Cal•vin•ist** \-və-nəst\ *n or adj* — **Cal•vin•is•tic** \ˌkal-və-ˈnis-tik\ *adj*
calx \ˈkalks\ *n, pl* **calx•es** *or* **cal•ces** \ˈkal-ˌsēz\ **:** the crumbly residue left when a metal or mineral has been subjected to calcination or combustion [Latin, "lime"]
ca•lyp•so \kə-ˈlip-sō\ *n, pl* **-sos :** a ballad of West Indian origin having usually improvised lyrics set to an African rhythm [probably from *Calypso,* a sea nymph in Homer's *Odyssey*] — **ca•lyp•so•ni•an** \kə-ˌlip-ˈsō-nē-ən, ˌkal-ip-\ *adj or n*
ca•lyp•tra \kə-ˈlip-trə\ *n* **:** a covering of a plant reproductive structure suggestive of a cap or hood [Greek *kalyptra* "veil", from *kalyptein* "to cover"]
ca•lyx \ˈkā-liks *also* ˈkal-iks\ *n, pl* **ca•lyx•es** *or* **ca•ly•ces** \ˈkā-lə-ˌsēz *also* ˈkal-ə-\ **1 :** the external usually green or leafy part of a flower consisting of sepals **2 :** an animal structure shaped like a cup [Latin, from Greek *kalyx*]
cam \ˈkam\ *n* **:** a device that consists of a plate or cylinder on a revolving shaft and that transmits motion by means of its edge or a groove to another mechanical part (as a rod or lever) so that circular motion may be transformed into intermittent or back-and-forth motion [perhaps from French *came,* from German *kamm,* literally, "comb"]
ca•ma•ra•de•rie \ˌkäm-ˈräd-ə-rē, -ə-ˈräd-, ˌkam-, -ˈrad-\ *n* **:** good feeling existing between comrades [French, from *camarade* "comrade"]
cam•as *or* **cam•ass** \ˈkam-əs\ *n* **:** any of a genus of plants of the lily family of the western United States with edible bulbs — compare DEATH CAMAS [of American Indian origin]
[1]**cam•ber** \ˈkam-bər\ *vb* **cam•bered; cam•ber•ing** \-bə-ring, -bring\ **:** to curve upward in the middle **:** arch slightly [French *cambrer,* derived from Latin *camur* "curved"]
[2]**camber** *n* **1 :** a slight convexity, arching, or curvature (as of a beam, deck, or road) **2 :** a setting of the wheels of an automotive vehicle closer together at the bottom than at the top
cam•bi•um \ˈkam-bē-əm\ *n, pl* **-bi•ums** *or* **-bia** \-bē-ə\ **:** a thin cell layer between the xylem and phloem of most vascular plants from which new cells (as of wood and bark) develop [Medieval Latin, "exchange", from Latin *cambiare* "to exchange"] — **cam•bi•al** \-bē-əl\ *adj*
Cam•bri•an \ˈkam-brē-ən\ *n* **:** the earliest period of the Paleozoic era marked by fossils of every great animal type except the vertebrate and by scarcely recognizable plant fossils; *also* **:** the corresponding system of rocks — see GEOLOGIC TIME table [Medieval Latin *Cambria* "Wales", from Welsh *Cymry* "Welshmen"] — **Cambrian** *adj*
cam•bric \ˈkām-brik\ *n* **1 :** a fine thin white linen fabric **2 :** a cotton fabric that resembles cambric [obsolete Flemish *Kameryk* "Cambrai", city in France]
came *past of* COME
cam•el \ˈkam-əl\ *n* **1 :** either of two large cud-chewing mammals used as draft and saddle animals in desert regions especially of Africa and Asia: **a :** DROMEDARY 2 **b :** a 2-humped camel of central Asian origin — called also *Bactrian camel* **2 :** a light brown color [Latin *camelus,* from Greek *kamēlos,* of Semitic origin]

camel 1b

cam•el•back \-ˌbak\ *n* **:** an uncured compound chiefly of reclaimed or synthetic rubber used for retreading or recapping pneumatic tires
cam•el•eer \ˌkam-ə-ˈliər\ *n* **:** a camel driver
ca•mel•lia *also* **ca•me•lia** \kə-ˈmēl-yə\ *n* **:** any of several shrubs or trees of the tea family; *esp* **:** a greenhouse shrub with glossy evergreen leaves and showy roselike flowers [*Camellus* (Georg Josef Kamel), died 1706, Moravian Jesuit missionary]
Cam•e•lot \ˈkam-ə-ˌlät\ *n* **1 :** the site of King Arthur's palace and court in Arthurian legend **2 :** a time or place of idyllic happiness
camel's hair *n* **:** a fabric made of the hair of camels or of a mixture of this hair with wool
Cam•em•bert \ˈkam-əm-ˌbeər\ *n* **:** a soft cheese with a thin grayish white rind and a yellow interior [*Camembert,* Normandy, France]
cam•eo \ˈkam-ē-ˌō\ *n, pl* **-e•os :** a carved gem in which the design is higher than its background [Italian]
cam•era \ˈkam-rə, -ə-rə\ *n* **:** a judge's private office ⟨hearings held in *camera*⟩ **2 :** a lightproof box fitted with a lens through the opening of which the image of an object is recorded on a material that is sensitive to light **3 :** the part of a television transmitting apparatus in which the image to be televised is formed for change into electrical impulses [Late Latin, "room, chamber"; sense 2 from New Latin *camera obscura,* literally, "dark chamber"]

cam•era•man \-ˌman, -mən\ *n* : the operator of a camera
cam•era•wom•an \-ˌwu̇m-ən\ *n* : a woman who operates a camera
cam•i•sole \ˈkam-ə-ˌsōl\ *n* : a short sleeveless undergarment for women [French]
cam•o•mile *variant of* CHAMOMILE
cam•ou•flage \ˈkam-ə-ˌfläzh, -ˌfläj\ *n* **1** : the disguising especially of military equipment or installations with paint, nets, or foliage; *also* : the disguise so applied **2 a** : concealment by means of disguise **b** : behavior or a trick intended to deceive or hide [French, from *camoufler* "to disguise", from Italian *camuffare*] — **camouflage** *vt*
[1]**camp** \ˈkamp\ *n* **1 a** : ground on which tents or buildings for temporary residence are erected **b** : a group of buildings or tents erected on such ground **c** : a temporary shelter (as a cabin or tent) **d** : an open-air location where persons camp **e** : a new lumbering or mining town **2 a** : a body of persons encamped **b** (1) : a group of persons promoting a theory or doctrine ⟨liberal and conservative *camps*⟩ (2) : an ideological position **3** : military service or life [Middle French, derived from Latin *campus* "plain, field"]
[2]**camp** *vi* **1** : to make camp or occupy a camp **2** : to live temporarily in a camp or outdoors ⟨*camp* out overnight⟩
cam•paign \kam-ˈpān\ *n* **1** : a series of military operations forming a distinct phase of a war **2** : a series of operations designed to bring about a particular result ⟨an election *campaign*⟩ [French *campagne,* derived from Late Latin *campania* "level country"] — **campaign** *vi* — **cam•paign•er** *n*
cam•pa•nile \ˌkam-pə-ˈnē-lē, *of United States structures also* -ˈnēl\ *n, pl* **-niles** *or* **-ni•li** \-ˈnē-lē\ : a usually freestanding bell tower [Italian, from *campana* "bell", from Late Latin]
cam•pan•u•la \kam-ˈpan-yə-lə\ *n* : any of a large genus of herbs with regular bell-shaped flowers including several grown as ornamentals [Late Latin *campana* "bell"]
camp•er \ˈkam-pər\ *n* **1** : one that camps **2** : a portable dwelling (as a specially equipped automotive vehicle) for use during casual travel and camping
cam•pes•tral \kam-ˈpes-trəl\ *adj* : of or relating to fields or open country : RURAL [Latin *campester,* from *campus* "field"]
camp fire girl *n* : a member of a national organization for girls from 7 to 18 [*Camp Fire Girls,* Incorporated]
cam•phor \ˈkam-fər, ˈkamp-\ *n* : a tough gummy volatile fragrant crystalline compound $C_{10}H_{16}O$ obtained especially from the wood and bark of the camphor tree and used as a stimulant, as a plasticizer, and as an insect repellent [Medieval Latin *camphora,* from Arabic *kāfūr,* from Malay *kāpūr*]
cam•phor•ate \-fə-ˌrāt\ *vt* : to impregnate with camphor ⟨*camphorated* oil⟩
camphor tree *n* : a large evergreen tree of the laurel family
cam•pi•on \ˈkam-pē-ən\ *n* : any of various plants of the pink family [probably from obsolete *campion* "champion"]
camp meeting *n* : a series of evangelistic meetings usually held outdoors or in a tent and attended by families who often camp nearby
camp•o•ree \ˌkam-pə-ˈrē\ *n* : a gathering of boy scouts or girl scouts from a given area [*camp* + jamboree]
camp•stool \ˈkamp-ˌstül\ *n* : a folding stool
cam•pus \ˈkam-pəs\ *n* : the grounds and buildings of a school (as a college) [Latin, "field, plain"]
cam•shaft \ˈkam-ˌshaft\ *n* : a shaft to which a cam is fastened
[1]**can** \kən, kan, ˈkan\ *auxiliary verb, past* **could** \kəd, ku̇d, ˈku̇d\; *present sing & pl* **can 1 a** : know how to ⟨you *can* read⟩ **b** : be physically or mentally able to ⟨I *can* lift 100 kilograms⟩ **c** : be permitted by conscience or feeling ⟨you *can* hardly blame them⟩ **d** : be inherently able or designed to ⟨everything that money *can* buy⟩ **e** : be enabled by law, agreement, or custom to **2** : have permission to — used interchangeably with *may* ⟨you *can* go now if you like⟩ [Old English, "know, knows, am able, is able"]
• **syn** MAY: CAN primarily implies physical or mental ability ⟨I *can* run very fast⟩ or circumstantial possibility ⟨we *can* take an earlier train⟩ MAY expresses primarily permission or sanction, not capability ⟨you *may* leave when you wish⟩ but CAN is frequently used in asking permission ⟨*can* I help you⟩ and normally used in denying it ⟨you *cannot* smoke here⟩
[2]**can** \ˈkan\ *n* **1** : a usually cylindrical container: **a** : a vessel for holding liquids; *esp* : a drinking vessel **b** : a container (as for milk, oil, or garbage) usually with an open top and often with a cover **c** : a container (as of tinplate) in which a perishable product (as food) is hermetically sealed **d** : a jar for packing or preserving fruit or vegetables **2** : the contents of a can [Old English *canne*]
[3]**can** \ˈkan\ *vt* **canned**; **can•ning 1** : to put in a can; *esp* : to preserve by sealing in an airtight can or jar **2** *slang* : to discharge from a job — **can•ner** *n*
Can•a•da balsam \ˌkan-əd-ə-\ *n* : a viscid yellowish to greenish resin exuded by the balsam fir that solidifies to a transparent mass and is used as a transparent cement especially in microscopy
Canada goose *n* : a common wild goose of North America that is mostly gray and brownish in color with black head and neck
Ca•na•di•an lynx \kə-ˌnād-ē-ən-\ *n* : LYNX C
ca•naille \kə-ˈnī, -ˈnāl\ *n* : RABBLE 2, RIFFRAFF [French, from Italian *canaglia,* from *cane* "dog", from Latin *canis*]
ca•nal \kə-ˈnal\ *n* **1** : a tubular anatomical passage or channel : DUCT **2** : an artificial waterway for navigation or for draining or irrigating land [Latin *canalis* "pipe, channel", from *canna* "reed, cane"]
ca•nal•boat \-ˌbōt\ *n* : a boat for use on a canal
can•a•lic•u•lus \ˌkan-l-ˈik-yə-ləs\ *n, pl* **-u•li** \-yə-ˌlī, -ˌlē\ : a minute bodily canal (as in bone) [Latin, from *canalis* "canal"]
can•a•li•za•tion \ˌkan-l-ə-ˈzā-shən\ *n* **1** : an act or instance of canalizing **2** : a system of channels
can•a•lize \ˌkan-l-ˌīz\ *vt* **1** : to provide with a canal **2** : to make into or like a canal
can•a•pé \ˈkan-ə-pē, -ˌpā\ *n* : an appetizer consisting of a piece of bread or toast or a cracker topped with a spread (as of fish or cheese) [French, literally, "sofa"]
ca•nard \kə-ˈnärd\ *n* : a false or unfounded report or story; *esp* : one deliberately made up [French, literally, "duck", from Middle French *vendre des canards à moitié* "to cheat", literally, "to half-sell ducks"]
△ **origin** In 16th century France "vendre des canards à moitié" was a colorful way of saying "to cheat". The French phrase means, literally, "to half-sell ducks". Unfortunately, no one now knows just what was meant by "to half-sell" — "vendre à moitié". The proverb was probably based on some story widely known at the time, but the details have not survived. At any rate, the proverbial duck, the *canard,* came to stand for any hoax, especially a made-up report. And French *canard,* in this sense, was borrowed into English.
ca•nary \kə-ˈnear-ē\ *n, pl* **-nar•ies 1** : a sweet wine made in the Canary islands **2** : a small usually yellow or greenish finch native to the Canary islands that is kept as a cage bird
△ **origin** The Canaries are a group of islands off the northwest coast of Africa. Early explorers from Africa reported that these islands were covered with dogs. Because of these reports the islands were given the Latin name *Canariae insulae,* "dog islands". In fact, the dogs that gave the islands their name had probably not always been there but had been brought by still earlier invaders from Africa. Native to the islands, however, were small greenish brown birds. Some of these were taken to Europe in the 16th century and were called *canary birds* in England. The yellow domestic canary is a descendant of the wild greenish birds of the dog islands.
canary yellow *n* : a light to a moderate yellow
ca•nas•ta \kə-ˈnas-tə\ *n* **1** : rummy using two decks plus four jokers **2** : a combination of seven cards of the same rank in canasta [Spanish, literally, "basket"]
can•can \ˈkan-ˌkan\ *n* : a woman's dance of French origin characterized by high kicking [French]
[1]**can•cel** \ˈkan-səl\ *vb* **-celed** *or* **-celled**; **-cel•ing** *or* **-cel•ling** \-sə-ling, -sling\ *vb* **1 a** : to mark or strike out for deletion **b** : DELETE, OMIT **2 a** : to destroy the force, effectiveness, or validity of : ANNUL ⟨*cancel* a magazine subscription⟩ **b** : to match in force or effect : OFFSET — often used with *out* **c** : to call off usually without expecting to reschedule ⟨*cancel* a party because of bad weather⟩ **3 a** : to remove (a common divisor) from numerator and denominator **b** : to remove (equivalents) on opposite sides of an equation or account **4** : to mark (a postage stamp or check) so as to prevent reuse [Middle French *canceller,* from Late Latin *cancellare,* from Latin, "to make like a lattice", from *cancelli* "latticework, grating"] **syn** see ERASE — **can•cel•er** *or* **can•cel•ler** \-sə-lər, -slər\ *n*
△ **origin** The original meaning of *cancel* is "to mark out or cross out". The cross-hatchings which sometimes cover a canceled document resemble a lattice. This resemblance was reflected

in the formation of the Latin verb *cancellare* from the noun *cancelli* "lattice". *Cancelli* is a diminutive form of *cancer.* This *cancer* is not related to its homonym *cancer,* "crab, disease". Rather it is the word for the type of latticed barrier used to restrain a prisoner. It is an altered form of Latin *carcer,* "prison", the word which has also given us *incarcerate.*

[2]cancel *n* : CANCELLATION

can•cel•la•tion *also* **can•cel•ation** \ˌkan-sə-ˈlā-shən\ *n* **1 :** an act of canceling ⟨*cancellation* of a game because of bad weather⟩ **2 :** a mark made to cancel something ⟨a *cancellation* on a postage stamp⟩

can•cel•lous \ˈkan-sə-ləs\ *adj* **:** having a porous structure ⟨*cancellous* bone⟩ **[**Latin *cancelli* "lattice"**]**

can•cer \ˈkan-sər\ *n* **1** *cap* **a :** a northern zodiacal constellation between Gemini and Leo **b :** the 4th sign of the zodiac; *also* **:** one born under this sign **2 :** a malignant tumor that tends to spread locally and to other parts of the body; *also* **:** an abnormal state marked by such tumors **3 :** a source of evil or anguish ⟨the *cancer* of hatred⟩ **[**Latin, "crab, Cancer, cancer"**]** — **can•cer•ous** \ˈkans-rəs, -ə-rəs\ *adj*

can•de•la \kan-ˈdē-lə, -ˈdel-ə\ *n* **:** CANDLE 2 **[**Latin, "candle"**]**

can•de•la•bra \ˌkan-də-ˈläb-rə, -ˈlab-, -ˈlāb-\ *n* **:** CANDELABRUM

can•de•la•brum \-rəm\ *n, pl* **-bra** \-rə\ *also* **-brums :** a candlestick or lamp with branches holding sockets for lights **[**Latin, from *candela* "candle"**]**

candelabrum

can•des•cent \kan-ˈdes-ⁿt\ *adj* **:** glowing or dazzling especially from great heat **[**Latin *candescere* "to grow light or bright", from *candēre* "to shine"**]** — **can•des•cence** \-ⁿs\ *n*

can•did \ˈkan-dəd\ *adj* **1 :** free from prejudice **:** FAIR **2 a :** marked by honest sincere expression **b :** showing sincere honesty and absence of deception **3 :** relating to photography of subjects acting naturally or spontaneously without being posed ⟨a *candid* snapshot⟩ **[**French *candide,* from Latin *candidus* "shining, white", from *candēre* "to shine"**] syn** see FRANK — **can•did•ly** *adv* — **can•did•ness** *n*

can•di•da•cy \ˈkan-dəd-ə-sē\ *n, pl* **-cies :** the state of being a candidate ⟨announce one's *candidacy* for office⟩

can•di•date \ˈkan-də-ˌdāt, -ə-, -dət\ *n* **:** one who offers oneself or is proposed by others for an office, membership, right, or honor ⟨the party's *candidate* for mayor⟩ **[**Latin *candidatus,* literally, "one clothed in white", from *candidus* "white"; from the white toga worn by candidates for office in ancient Rome**]**

can•died \ˈkan-dēd\ *adj* **1 :** encrusted or coated with sugar **2 :** baked with sugar or syrup until translucent

[1]can•dle \ˈkan-dl\ *n* **1 :** a usually cylindrical mass of tallow or wax containing a loosely twisted linen or cotton wick that is burned to give light **2 :** a unit of luminous intensity equal to one sixtieth of the luminous intensity of one square centimeter of a blackbody surface at the solidification temperature of platinum — called also *candela* **[**Latin *candela,* from *candēre* "to shine"**]**

[2]candle *vt* **can•dled; can•dling** \ˈkan-dling, -dl-ing\ **:** to examine (an egg) by holding between the eye and a light — **can•dler** \-dlər, -dl-ər\ *n*

can•dle•light \ˈkan-dl-ˌlīt, -ˌīt\ *n* **1 a :** the light of a candle **b :** a soft artificial light **2 :** the time when candles are lit **:** TWILIGHT

Can•dle•mas \ˈkan-dl-məs\ *n* **:** February 2 observed as a church festival in commemoration of the presentation of Christ in the temple and the purification of the Virgin Mary **[**Old English *candelmæsse,* from *candel* "candle" + *mæsse* "mass, feast"; from the candles blessed and carried in celebration of the feast**]**

can•dle•pin \ˈkan-dl-ˌpin\ *n* **1 :** a slender bowling pin tapering toward top and bottom **2** *pl* **:** a bowling game using candlepins and a smaller ball than that used in tenpins

can•dle•pow•er \-ˌpaủ-ər, -ˌpaủr\ *n* **:** luminous intensity (as of a light bulb) expressed in candles

can•dle•stick \-ˌstik\ *n* **:** a holder with a socket for a candle

can•dor \ˈkan-dər\ *n* **1 :** freedom from prejudice **2 :** unreserved, honest, or sincere expression **:** FRANKNESS **[**Latin, literally, "whiteness", from *candēre* "to shine"**]**

[1]can•dy \ˈkan-dē\ *n, pl* **-dies 1 :** crystallized sugar formed by boiling down sugar syrup **2 a :** a rich food made largely of sugar often with flavoring and filling **b :** a piece of such food **[**Middle French *sucre candi,* from Italian *zucchero candi,* from *zucchero* "sugar" + Arabic *qandī* "candied", from *qand* "cane sugar"**]**

[2]candy *vb* **can•died; can•dy•ing 1 :** to coat or become coated with sugar often by cooking **2 :** to make seem attractive **:** SWEETEN **3 :** to crystallize into sugar

can•dy•tuft \ˈkan-dē-ˌtəft\ *n* **:** any of a genus of plants related to the mustards and grown for their white, pink, or purple flowers **[***Candy* (now *Candia*) "Crete", Greek island + English *tuft***]**

[1]cane \ˈkān\ *n* **1 a :** a hollow or pithy and usually slender, flexible, and jointed stem (as of a reed or bramble) **b :** any of various tall woody grasses or reeds; *esp* **:** SUGARCANE **2 a :** WALKING STICK 1; *esp* **:** a cane walking stick **b :** a rod for flogging **c :** RATTAN 1b; *esp* **:** split rattan for wickerwork or basketry **[**Middle French, derived from Latin *canna,* from Greek *kanna,* of Semitic origin**]**

[2]cane *vt* **1 :** to beat with a cane **2 :** to make or repair with cane ⟨*cane* the seat of a chair⟩

cane•brake \-ˌbrāk\ *n* **:** a thicket of cane

cane sugar *n* **:** sugar from sugarcane commonly used at the dining table and in cooking **:** SUCROSE

[1]ca•nine \ˈkā-ˌnīn\ *adj* **1 :** of or relating to dogs or to the family that includes the dogs, wolves, jackals, and foxes **2 :** resembling a dog **[**Latin *caninus,* from *canis* "dog"**]**

[2]canine *n* **:** a conical pointed tooth situated between the outer incisor and the first premolar — called also *cuspid*

Ca•nis Ma•jor \ˌkā-nəs-ˈma-jər, ˌkan-əs-\ *n* **:** a constellation to the southeast of Orion containing Sirius **[**Latin, literally, "greater dog"**]**

Canis Mi•nor \-ˈmī-nər\ *n* **:** a constellation to the east of Orion containing Procyon **[**Latin, literally, "lesser dog"**]**

can•is•ter \ˈkan-ə-stər\ *n* **1 :** a small box or can for holding a dry product (as tea) **2 :** a shell for close-range artillery fire consisting of a number of bullets enclosed in a lightweight case that is burst by the firing charge **3 :** a perforated box for gas masks that contains material to adsorb, filter, or make harmless a poisonous or irritating substance in the air **[**Latin *canistrum* "basket", from Greek *kanastron,* from *kanna* "reed"**]**

[1]can•ker \ˈkang-kər\ *n* **1 a :** a spreading sore that eats into the tissue **b :** an area of necrosis in a plant **c :** any of various disorders of animals marked by chronic inflammatory changes **2 :** a source of corruption or destruction **[**Old North French *cancre,* from Latin *cancer* "crab, cancer"**]** — **can•ker•ous** \ˈkang-kə-rəs, -krəs\ *adj*

[2]canker *vb* **can•kered; can•ker•ing** \ˈkang-kə-ring, -kring\ **1 :** to become affected by canker **2 :** to become or cause to become malignant ⟨a mind *cankered* by hate⟩

canker sore *n* **:** a small painful ulcer especially of the mouth

can•ker•worm \ˈkang-kər-ˌwərm\ *n* **:** a moth larva that injures plants especially by feeding on buds and foliage

can•na \ˈkan-ə\ *n* **:** a tall tropical herb with large leaves and an unbranched stem bearing bright-colored flowers at the end **[**Latin, "reed"**]**

can•na•bis \ˈkan-ə-bəs\ *n* **:** the dried flowering spikes of the pistillate plants of the hemp — compare BHANG, HASHISH, MARIJUANA **[**Latin, "hemp", from Greek *kannabis***]**

canned \ˈkand\ *adj* **1 :** preserved in a sealed can or jar **2 :** recorded for radio or television use ⟨*canned* laughter⟩

can•nel coal \ˌkan-l-\ *n* **:** a bituminous coal containing much volatile matter that burns brightly **[**probably from English dialect *cannel* "candle"**]**

can•nery \ˈkan-rē, -ə-rē\ *n, pl* **-ner•ies :** a factory for the canning of food

can•ni•bal \ˈkan-ə-bəl\ *n* **1 :** a human being who eats human flesh **2 :** an animal that eats its own kind **[**Spanish *Canibal* "Carib", of American Indian origin**]** — **cannibal** *adj* — **can•ni•bal•ism** \-bə-ˌliz-əm\ *n* — **can•ni•bal•is•tic** \ˌkan-ə-bə-ˈlis-tik\ *adj*

can•ni•bal•ize \ˈkan-ə-bə-ˌlīz\ *vt* **:** to dismantle (a machine) for parts to be used as replacements in other machines

can•non \ˈkan-ən\ *n, pl* **cannons** *or* **cannon** **1 :** a heavy gun mounted on a carriage and fired from that position **:** a piece of artillery **2 :** a heavy-caliber automatic gun on an airplane [Middle French *canon,* from Italian *cannone,* literally, "large tube", from *canna* "reed, tube", from Latin, "reed, cane"]

[1]**can•non•ade** \ˌkan-ə-ˈnād\ *n* **:** a heavy firing of artillery

[2]**cannonade** *vb* **:** to attack with artillery

can•non•ball \ˈkan-ən-ˌbȯl\ *n* **:** a round solid missile made for firing from a cannon

cannon bone *n* **:** a bone in hoofed mammals that supports the leg from the hock joint to the fetlock

can•non•eer \ˌkan-ə-ˈniər\ *n* **:** a person who tends and fires cannon **:** GUNNER

can•not \ˈkan-ät, -ˌät; kə-ˈnät, ka-ˈ\ **:** can not — **cannot but :** to be bound to **:** MUST

can•ny \ˈkan-ē\ *adj* **can•ni•er; -est :** being cautious and shrewd **:** watchful of one's own interests ⟨very *canny* with money⟩ [[1]*can*] — **can•ni•ly** \ˈkan-l-ē\ *adv* — **can•ni•ness** \ˈkan-ē-nəs\ *n*

[1]**ca•noe** \kə-ˈnü\ *n* **:** a long light narrow boat with sharp ends and curved sides that is usually paddled by hand [French, from Spanish *canoa,* of American Indian origin]

[2]**canoe** *vb* **ca•noed; ca•noe•ing :** to travel or transport in a canoe — **ca•noe•ist** *n*

[1]**can•on** \ˈkan-ən\ *n* **1 :** a church law or decree **2 :** the fundamental and unvarying part of the Mass including the consecration of the bread and wine **3 :** an official or authoritative list (as of the saints or of the books of the Bible) **4 :** an accepted principle or rule ⟨the *canons* of good taste⟩ **5 :** a musical composition in two or more voice parts in which the melody is imitated exactly and completely by the successive voices [Latin, "ruler, rule, model, standard", from Greek *kanōn*]

[2]**canon** *n* **1 :** a member of the clergy who is on the staff of a cathedral **2 :** CANON REGULAR

[3]**ca•ñon** \ˈkan-yən\ *variant of* CANYON

ca•non•i•cal \kə-ˈnän-i-kəl\ *adj* **1 :** of, relating to, or complying with church law **2 :** accepted as authoritative — **ca•non•i•cal•ly** \-kə-lē; -klē\ *adv*

canonical hour *n* **1 :** a time of day canonically appointed for an office of devotion **2 :** one of the daily offices in the breviary including matins with lauds, prime, terce, sext, none, vespers, and compline

ca•non•i•cals \kə-ˈnän-i-kəlz\ *n pl* **:** the vestments prescribed by church law for an officiating member of the clergy

can•on•ic•i•ty \ˌkan-ə-ˈnis-ət-ē\ *n* **:** the quality or state of being canonical

can•on•ize \ˈkan-ə-ˌnīz\ *vt* **:** to declare to be a saint and worthy of public veneration [Late Latin *canon* "catalog of saints", from Latin, "standard"] — **can•on•i•za•tion** \ˌkan-ə-nə-ˈzā-shən\ *n*

canon law *n* **:** the body of laws governing a church

canon regular *n, pl* **canons regular :** a member of one of several Roman Catholic religious institutes of regular priests living in community

Ca•no•pus \kə-ˈnō-pəs\ *n* **:** a star of the first magnitude not visible north of 37° latitude [Latin, from Greek *Kanōpos*]

[1]**can•o•py** \ˈkan-ə-pē\ *n, pl* **-pies 1 a :** a covering suspended over a bed, throne, or shrine or carried on poles over a person of high rank or over some sacred object **b :** an overhanging shade or shelter ⟨a *canopy* of chestnut trees⟩ **c :** the uppermost spreading branchy layer of a forest **2 a :** the transparent covering over an airplane cockpit **b :** the lifting or supporting surface of a parachute [Medieval Latin *canopeum* "mosquito net", from Latin *conopeum,* from Greek *kōnōpion,* from *kōnōps* "mosquito"] — **can•o•py•like** \-ˌlīk\ *adj*

[2]**canopy** *vt* **-pied; -py•ing :** to cover with or as if with a canopy

canst \kənst, kanst, ˈkanst\ *archaic present 2d sing of* CAN

[1]**cant** \ˈkant\ *n* **:** a slanting surface or its slope [probably from Old North French, "edge, corner", from Latin *canthus, cantus* "iron tire"]

[2]**cant** *vt* **:** to give a slant to

[3]**cant** *vi* **:** to talk hypocritically [probably from Old North French *canter* "to tell", literally, "to sing", from Latin *cantare*]

[4]**cant** *n* **1 a :** ARGOT **b :** JARGON **2 :** insincere speech; *esp* **:** insincerely pious words or statements

can't \ˈkant, ˈkȧnt, *especially South* ˈkānt\ **:** can not

can•ta•bi•le \kän-ˈtäb-ə-ˌlā, kan-ˈtab-ə-lē\ *adv or adj* **:** in a singing smoothly flowing manner — used as a direction in music [Italian, from Latin *cantare* "to sing"]

Can•ta•bri•gian \ˌkant-ə-ˈbrij-ən, -ē-ən\ *n* **:** a student or graduate of Cambridge University **2 :** a native or resident of Cambridge [Medieval Latin *Cantabrigia* "Cambridge"] — **Cantabrigian** *adj*

can•ta•loupe \ˈkant-l-ˌōp\ *n* **:** MUSKMELON; *esp* **:** a muskmelon with a hard ridged or warty rind and reddish orange flesh [*Cantalupo,* former papal villa near Rome, Italy]

can•tan•ker•ous \kan-ˈtang-kə-rəs, kən-, -krəs\ *adj* **:** ILL-NATURED, QUARRELSOME [perhaps from obsolete *contack* "contention"] — **can•tan•ker•ous•ly** *adv* — **can•tan•ker•ous•ness** *n*

can•ta•ta \kən-ˈtät-ə\ *n* **:** a poem or narrative set to music to be sung by a chorus and soloists [Italian, from Latin, "sung mass", from *cantare* "to sing"]

can•teen \kan-ˈtēn\ *n* **1 :** a store (as in a camp or a factory) in which food, drinks, and small supplies are sold **2 :** a place of recreation and entertainment for military service people **3 :** a small container used for carrying liquid (as drinking water) [French *cantine* "bottle case, sutler's shop", from Italian *cantina* "wine cellar", from *canto* "corner", from Latin *canthus* "iron tire"]

[1]**can•ter** \ˈkant-ər\ *vb* **:** to move or cause to move at or as if at a canter [from *Canterbury,* England; from the supposed gait of pilgrims to Canterbury]

[2]**canter** *n* **:** a 3-beat gait (as of a horse) resembling but smoother and slower than the gallop

Can•ter•bury bell \ˌkant-ər-ˌber-ē-, -ə-ˌber-ē-\ *n* **:** a cultivated campanula

cant hook *n* **:** a stout wooden lever used especially in handling logs that has a blunt usually metal-clad end and a movable metal arm with a sharp spike [[1]*cant*]

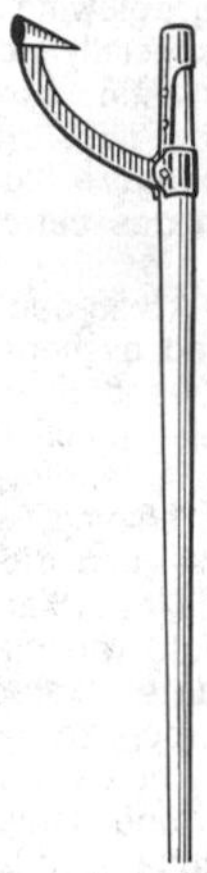

cant hook

can•ti•cle \ˈkant-i-kəl\ *n* **1 :** SONG **2 :** any of several liturgical songs taken from the Bible [Latin *canticulum* "little song", from *canticum* "song", from *canere* "to sing"]

Canticle of Canticles — see BIBLE table

can•ti•le•ver \ˈkant-l-ˌē-vər *also* -ˌev-ər\ *n* **1 :** a projecting beam or similar structure fastened (as by being built into a wall or pier) only at one end **2 :** either of two beams or structures that project from piers toward each other and when joined form a span in a bridge [perhaps from [1]*cant* + *-i-* + *lever*]

can•tle \ˈkant-l\ *n* **:** the upwardly projecting rear part of a saddle [Old North French *cantel* "little corner, part cut off", from *cant* "edge, corner"]

can•to \ˈkan-ˌtō\ *n, pl* **cantos :** one of the major divisions of a long poem [Italian, from Latin *cantus* "song", from *canere* "to sing"]

[1]**can•ton** \ˈkant-n, ˈkan-ˌtän\ *n* **1 :** a small division of a country; *esp* **:** one of the states of the Swiss confederation **2 :** the top inner quarter of a flag [Middle French, from Italian *cantone,* from *canto* "corner", from Latin *canthur* "iron tire"] — **can•ton•al** \ˈkant-n-əl, kan-ˈtän-l\ *adj*

[2]**can•ton** \ˈkant-n, ˈkan-ˌtän, *in sense 2 usually* kan-ˈtōn *or* -ˈtän\ *vt* **1 :** to divide into parts; *esp* **:** to divide into cantons **2 :** to allot quarters to (troops)

Can•ton•ese \ˌkant-n-ˈēz, -ˈēs\ *n, pl* **Cantonese 1 :** a native or inhabitant of Canton, China **2 :** the dialect of Chinese spoken in and around Canton — **Cantonese** *adj*

can•ton flannel \ˌkan-ˌtän-\ *n, often cap C* **:** FLANNEL 1b [*Canton,* China]

can•ton•ment \kan-ˈtōn-mənt, -ˈtän-\ *n* **:** a group of temporary structures for housing troops

can•tor \ˈkant-ər\ *n* **1 :** a choir leader **2 :** a synagogue official who sings or chants the liturgy and leads the congregation in prayer [Latin, "singer", from *canere* "to sing"]

Ca•nuck \kə-ˈnək\ *n* **1 :** CANADIAN **2** *chiefly Canadian* **:** FRENCH CANADIAN [perhaps alteration of *Canadian*]

can•vas \ˈkan-vəs\ *n* **1 :** a strong cloth of hemp, flax, or cotton that is used for making tents and sails and as a material on which oil paintings are made **2 a :** something made of canvas or on canvas **b :** OIL PAINTING **3 :** the floor of a boxing ring [Old North French *canevas,* from Latin *cannabis* "hemp"]

can•vas•back \-ˌbak\ *n* **:** a North American wild duck with reddish head and grayish back

can•vass \ˈkan-vəs\ *vb* **1 a :** to examine in detail; *esp* **:** to investigate officially ⟨*canvass* election returns⟩ **b :** DISCUSS, DEBATE ⟨*canvass* a question⟩ **2 a :** to go through (an area) soliciting something (as information, contributions, or votes) **b :** to ask for information, money, or votes ⟨*canvass* faculty members for opinions⟩ [obsolete *canvass* "to toss in a canvas sheet, beat thoroughly"] — **canvass** *n* — **can•vass•er** *n*

can•yon *also* **ca•ñon** \ˈkan-yən\ *n* **:** a deep valley with high steep slopes and often with a stream flowing through it [American Spanish *cañón*]

caou•tchouc \ˈkau̇-ˌchu̇k, -ˌchük, -ˌchü\ *n* **:** RUBBER 2a [French, from obsolete Spanish *cauchuc,* from Quechua]

[1]cap \ˈkap\ *n* **1 :** a head covering; *esp* **:** one that has a visor and no brim **2 :** something like a cap in appearance, position, or function ⟨a bottle *cap*⟩ ⟨the *cap* of a fountain pen⟩ **3 :** a natural cover or top: as **a :** the umbrella-shaped part that bears the spores of a mushroom — called also *pileus* **b :** the top of a bird's head **4 :** a paper or metal container holding an explosive charge (as for a toy pistol) **5 :** the symbol ∩ indicating the intersection of two sets — compare CUP 6 [Late Latin *cappa* "head covering, cloak"]

[2]cap *vt* **capped; cap•ping 1 :** to provide with a cap **2 :** to match with something better ⟨*cap* one story with another⟩

ca•pa•bil•i•ty \ˌkā-pə-ˈbil-ət-ē\ *n, pl* **-ties 1 :** the quality or state of being capable **2 :** a feature or faculty that can be developed **:** POTENTIALITY

ca•pa•ble \ˈkā-pə-bəl\ *adj* **1 :** having the ability, capacity, or power to do something ⟨a room *capable* of holding 50 people⟩ **2 :** of such a nature as to permit **:** SUSCEPTIBLE ⟨a remark *capable* of being misunderstood⟩ **3 :** having general ability [Late Latin *capabilis,* from Latin *capere* "to take"] **syn** see ABLE — **ca•pa•bly** \-blē\ *adv*

ca•pa•cious \kə-ˈpā-shəs\ *adj* **:** able to contain a great deal **:** not narrow ⟨*capacious* pockets⟩ ⟨students with *capacious* minds⟩ [Latin *capax* "capacious, capable", from *capere* "to take"] — **ca•pa•cious•ly** *adv* — **ca•pa•cious•ness** *n*

ca•pac•i•tance \kə-ˈpas-ət-əns\ *n* **:** the property of a system of conductors and dielectrics that permits the storage of electrical energy; *also* **:** a measure of this property — **ca•pac•i•tive** \-ət-iv\ *adj*

ca•pac•i•tor \kə-ˈpas-ət-ər\ *n* **:** a device giving capacitance and usually consisting of conducting plates separated by layers of dielectric with the plates on opposite sides of the dielectric layers oppositely charged by a source of voltage — called also *condenser*

ca•pac•i•ty \kə-ˈpas-ət-ē, -ˈpas-tē\ *n, pl* **-ties 1 a :** the ability to hold or accommodate ⟨the seating *capacity* of a room⟩ **b :** a measure of content **:** VOLUME ⟨a jug with a *capacity* of one gallon⟩ **c :** productive ability or potential ⟨a plant with a *capacity* of 50 metric tons a month⟩ **2 :** ABILITY, CALIBER ⟨an individual of unknown *capacity*⟩ **3 :** a position or character assigned or assumed ⟨in one's *capacity* as a judge⟩ [Middle French *capacité,* from Latin *capacitas,* from *capax* "capacious"]

ca•par•i•son \kə-ˈpar-ə-sən\ *n* **1 a :** an ornamental covering for a horse **b :** decorative trappings and harness **2 :** rich clothing **:** ADORNMENT [Middle French *caparaçon,* from Spanish *caparazón*] — **caparison** *vt*

[1]cape \ˈkāp\ *n* **:** a point or extension of land jutting out into water either as a peninsula or as a projecting point [Middle French *cap,* from Provençal, from Latin *caput* "head"]

[2]cape *n* **:** a sleeveless outer garment or part of a garment that fits closely at the neck and hangs loosely from the shoulders [probably from Spanish *capa,* from Late Latin *cappa* "head covering, cloak"]

cap•e•lin \ˈkap-lən, -ə-lən\ *n* **:** a small northern sea fish related to the smelts and often used as cod bait [French *capelan* "codfish", derived from Medieval Latin *cappellanus* "chaplain"]

Ca•pel•la \kə-ˈpel-ə\ *n* **:** a bright star in Auriga [Latin, literally, "she-goat", from *caper* "he-goat"]

[1]ca•per \ˈkā-pər\ *n* **1 :** any of a genus of low prickly shrubs of the Mediterranean region; *esp* **:** one cultivated for its buds **2 :** one of the flower buds or young berries of the caper pickled for use as a relish [Latin *capparis,* from Greek *kapparis*]

[2]caper *vi* **ca•pered; ca•per•ing** \-pə-ring, -pring\ **:** to leap about playfully or wildly [probably from *capriole*]

[3]caper *n* **1 :** an unrestrained bounding leap **2 :** PRANK, ANTIC

cap•er•cail•lie \ˌkap-ər-ˈkāl-yē, -ē\ *or* **cap•er•cail•zie** \-yē, -zē\ *n* **:** the largest Old World grouse [Scottish Gaelic *capalcoille,* literally, "horse of the woods"]

cape•skin \ˈkāp-ˌskin\ *n* **:** a leather made from sheepskins with the natural grain retained [*Cape* of Good Hope]

Ca•pe•tian \kə-ˈpē-shən\ *adj* **:** of or relating to the French dynasty founded by Hugh Capet — **Capetian** *n*

cap•il•lar•i•ty \ˌkap-ə-ˈlar-ət-ē\ *n* **:** the action by which the surface of a liquid where (as in a slender tube) it is in contact with a solid is raised or lowered depending upon the relative attraction of the molecules of the liquid for each other and for those of the solid

[1]cap•il•lary \ˈkap-ə-ˌler-ē\ *adj* **1 :** resembling a hair in having a slender elongated form; *esp* **:** having a very small bore ⟨a *capillary* tube⟩ **2 :** involving, held by, or resulting from surface tension ⟨*capillary* water in the soil⟩ **3 :** of or relating to capillaries or capillarity [Latin *capillaris,* from *capillus* "hair"]

[2]capillary *n, pl* **-lar•ies :** a capillary tube; *esp* **:** any of the tiny blood vessels connecting arterioles with venules and forming networks throughout the body

[1]cap•i•tal \ˈkap-ət-l, ˈkap-tl\ *adj* **1 a :** punishable by death ⟨a *capital* crime⟩ **b :** resulting in death ⟨*capital* punishment⟩ **2 :** being a letter that belongs to or conforms to the series A, B, C, etc. rather than a, b, c, etc. **3 :** being the seat of government ⟨the *capital* city⟩ **4 :** of or relating to capital ⟨*capital* costs⟩ **5 :** EXCELLENT ⟨a *capital* performance⟩ [Latin *capitalis,* from *caput* "head"]

[2]capital *n* **1 a :** accumulated goods on hand at a specified time in contrast to income received over a specified period; *also* **:** the value of such goods **b :** the excess of assets over liabilities **2 a :** capital goods and invested savings used in the process of production **b :** possessions (as money) used to bring in income **c :** persons owning or investing capital **d :** CAPITAL STOCK **3 :** ADVANTAGE, GAIN ⟨make *capital* out of another's weakness⟩ **4 :** a capital letter ⟨begin each sentence with a *capital*⟩ **5 :** a capital city ⟨the *capital* of Vermont⟩ [Italian *capitale,* from *capitale,* adjective, "chief, principal", from Latin *capitalis* "capital"]

[3]capital *n* **:** the top part or piece of an architectural column [Old North French *capitel,* from Late Latin *capitellum* "small head, top of column", from Latin *caput* "head"]

[3]capital: *1* Doric, *2* Ionic, *3* Corinthian

capital goods *n pl* **:** machinery, tools, factories, and commodities used in the production of goods

cap•i•tal•ism \ˈkap-ət-l-ˌiz-əm\ *n* **:** an economic system in which natural resources and means of production are privately owned, investments are determined by private decision rather than by state control, and prices, production, and the distribution of goods are determined mainly by competition in a free market — **cap•i•tal•ist** \-l-əst\ *or* **cap•i•tal•is•tic** \ˌkap-ət-l-ˈis-tik\ *adj* — **cap•i•tal•is•ti•cal•ly** \-ti-kə-lē, -klē\ *adv*

cap•i•tal•ist \ˈkap-ət-l-əst, ˈkap-tl-\ *n* **1 :** a person who has capital; *esp* **:** one who has or controls a great amount of business capital **2 :** a person who favors capitalism

cap•i•tal•i•za•tion \ˌkap-ət-l-ə-ˈzā-shən, ˌkap-tl-\ *n* **1 :** the act or process of capitalizing **2 :** the amount of money used as capital in a business

cap•i•tal•ize \ˈkap-ət-l-ˌīz, ˈkap-tl-\ *vb* **1 :** to write or print with an initial capital or in capitals **2 a :** to charge (an expenditure) to a capital account **b** (1) **:** to supply capital for ⟨*capitalize* an enterprise at $50,000⟩ (2) **:** to use as capital ⟨*capitalize* reserve funds⟩ **3 :** to use to help oneself ⟨*capitalize* on an opponent's mistake⟩

\ə\ **abut**	\au̇\ **out**	\i\ **tip**	\ȯ\ **saw**	\u̇\ **foot**
\ər\ **further**	\ch\ **chin**	\ī\ **life**	\ȯi\ **coin**	\y\ **yet**
\a\ **mat**	\e\ **pet**	\j\ **job**	\th\ **thin**	\yü\ **few**
\ā\ **take**	\ē\ **easy**	\ng\ **sing**	\t͟h\ **this**	\yu̇\ **cure**
\ä\ **cot, cart**	\g\ **go**	\ō\ **bone**	\ü\ **food**	\zh\ **vision**

cap·i·tal·ly \ˈkap-ət-l-ē, -tl-ē\ *adv* : in a capital manner : EXCELLENTLY ⟨got along *capitally* in school⟩

capital ship *n* : a warship (as a battleship or aircraft carrier) of the greatest size or offensive power

capital stock *n* : the amount invested by stockholders in a corporation as holders of its shares; *also* : the shares of stock held by these stockholders

cap·i·ta·tion \ˌkap-ə-ˈtā-shən\ *n* : a direct uniform tax imposed upon each person [Late Latin *capitatio,* from Latin *caput* "head"]

cap·i·tol \ˈkap-ət-l, ˈkap-tl\ *n* **1** : a building in which a state legislative body meets **2** *cap* : the building in which the United States Congress meets in Washington [Latin *Capitolium,* a temple of Jupiter in Rome on the Capitoline hill]

Cap·i·to·line \ˈkap-ət-l-ˌīn\ *adj* : of or relating to the smallest of the seven hills of ancient Rome, the temple on it, or the gods worshiped there [Latin *capitolinus,* from *Capitolium,* a temple of Jupiter]

ca·pit·u·late \kə-ˈpich-ə-ˌlāt\ *vi* : to surrender usually on terms agreed upon in advance [Medieval Latin *capitulare* "to draw up under chapters, negotiate", from Late Latin *capitulum* "chapter", from Latin *caput* "head"]

ca·pit·u·la·tion \kə-ˌpich-ə-ˈlā-shən\ *n* **1** : a set of terms or articles constituting an agreement between governments **2** : an act of capitulating : a surrender on agreed terms

ca·pit·u·lum \kə-ˈpich-ə-ləm\ *n, pl* **-la** \-lə\ **1** : a rounded knob (as on a bone) **2** : HEAD 7a [Latin, "small head", from *caput* "head"]

ca·pon \ˈkā-ˌpän, -pən\ *n* : a castrated male chicken [Old English *capūn*]

ca·pric·cio \kə-ˈprē-chō, -chē-ˌō\ *n, pl* **-cios** : an instrumental piece in fanciful irregular form usually lively in tempo [Italian, "whim, capriccio"]

ca·price \kə-ˈprēs\ *n* **1** : a sudden unpredictable turn or change; *esp* : WHIM **2** : an inclination to change one's mind impulsively **3** : CAPRICCIO [French, from Italian *capriccio* "whim, shudder", literally, "head with hair standing on end", from *capo* "head" + *riccio* "hedgehog"]

• **syn** CAPRICE, WHIM, VAGARY, CROTCHET mean an irrational or unpredictable idea or desire. CAPRICE stresses lack of apparent motivation and suggests a degree of willfulness; WHIM implies a fantastic, capricious turn or inclination; VAGARY stresses the erratic, irresponsible character of the notion or desire; CROTCHET implies an eccentric opinion or preference.

ca·pri·cious \kə-ˈprish-əs, -ˈprē-shəs\ *adj* : moved or controlled by caprice : apt to change suddenly : FICKLE, CHANGEABLE ⟨a *capricious* child⟩ ⟨*capricious* weather⟩ — **ca·pri·cious·ly** *adv* — **ca·pri·cious·ness** *n*

Cap·ri·corn \ˈkap-rə-ˌkȯrn\ *also* **Cap·ri·cor·nus** \ˌkap-rə-ˈkȯr-nəs\ *n* **1** : a southern zodiacal constellation between Sagittarius and Aquarius **2** : the 10th sign of the zodiac; *also* : one born under this sign [Latin *Capricornus,* from *caper* "goat" + *cornu* "horn"]

cap·ri·ole \ˈkap-rē-ˌōl\ *n* : an upward leap of a horse with a backward kick of the hind legs at the height of the leap [Italian *capriola* "caper", from *capriolo* "roebuck", from Latin *capreolus* "goat, roebuck", from *caper* "he-goat"]

cap·si·cum \ˈkap-si-kəm\ *n* : any of a genus of tropical herbs and shrubs of the potato family widely cultivated for their many-seeded usually fleshy-walled fruits — called also *pepper* [New Latin, genus name]

cap·size \ˈkap-ˌsīz, kap-ˈ\ *vb* : to turn over : UPSET ⟨canoes *capsize* easily⟩ [origin unknown]

cap·stan \ˈkap-stən\ *n* : a mechanical device that consists of an upright drum to which a rope is fastened, is used on ships for moving or raising weights and for exerting pulling force, and is rotated manually or by steam or electric power [Middle English]

capstan

cap·su·lar \ˈkap-sə-lər\ *adj* : of, relating to, or resembling a capsule

cap·su·lat·ed \-ˌlāt-əd\ *adj* : enclosed in a capsule

[1]**cap·sule** \ˈkap-səl, -ˌsül\ *n* **1** : a membrane or sac enclosing a body part ⟨the *capsule* of a joint⟩ **2** : a closed receptacle containing spores or seeds: as **a** : a dry dehiscent usually many-seeded fruit composed of two or more carpels **b** : the spore sac of a moss **3** : an edible shell (as of gelatin) enclosing medicine **4** : an often polysaccharide envelope surrounding a microorganism ⟨some bacteria are encased in a slimy *capsule*⟩ **5** : an extremely brief condensation **6** : a small pressurized compartment for an aviator or astronaut for flight or emergency escape [French, from Latin *capsula* "small box", from *capsa* "box, case"]

[2]**capsule** *adj* **1** : extremely brief ⟨a *capsule* review of the news⟩ **2** : being small and very compact

[1]**cap·tain** \ˈkap-tən\ *n* **1** : a leader of a group ⟨the *captain* of a team⟩ **2 a** : an officer rank in the Navy and Coast Guard above commander and below rear admiral **b** : an officer rank in the Army, Marine Corps, and Air Force above first lieutenant and below major **3** : the commanding officer of a ship **4** : a fire or police department officer usually ranking between a chief and a lieutenant [Middle French *capitain,* from Late Latin *capitaneus* "chief", from Latin *caput* "head"] — **cap·tain·ship** \-ˌship\ *n*

[2]**captain** *vt* : to be captain of : LEAD

cap·tain·cy \ˈkap-tən-sē\ *n, pl* **-cies** : a captain's rank or position

[1]**cap·tion** \ˈkap-shən\ *n* **1** : the heading especially of an article or document **2** : the explanation accompanying a pictorial illustration **3** : a motion-picture subtitle [Latin *captio* "act of taking", from *capere* "to take"]

[2]**caption** *vt* : to furnish with a caption

cap·tious \ˈkap-shəs\ *adj* : quick to find fault especially over trifles [Latin *captiosus* "designed to entrap", from *captio* "act of taking, deception"] — **cap·tious·ly** *adv* — **cap·tious·ness** *n*

cap·ti·vate \ˈkap-tə-ˌvāt\ *vt* : to attract and win over : CHARM, FASCINATE ⟨music that *captivated* everybody who heard it⟩ — **cap·ti·va·tion** \ˌkap-tə-ˈvā-shən\ *n* — **cap·ti·va·tor** \ˈkap-tə-ˌvāt-ər\ *n*

cap·tive \ˈkap-tiv\ *adj* **1 a** : taken and held prisoner especially in war **b** : held or confined so as to prevent escape **c** : owned or controlled by a business to meet its own needs rather than to produce for the market ⟨a *captive* mine⟩ **2** : of or relating to captivity [Latin *captivus,* from *capere* "to take, capture"] — **captive** *n*

cap·tiv·i·ty \kap-ˈtiv-ət-ē\ *n, pl* **-ties** : the state of being captive

cap·tor \ˈkap-tər\ *n* : one that has captured a person or thing

[1]**cap·ture** \ˈkap-chər\ *n* **1** : the act of catching or gaining control by force or trickery **2** : one that has been taken captive [Middle French, from Latin *captura,* from *capere* "to take"]

[2]**capture** *vt* **cap·tured**; **cap·tur·ing** \ˈkap-chə-ring, ˈkap-shring\ **1 a** : to make captive : TAKE ⟨*capture* a city⟩ **b** : to preserve in a relatively permanent form ⟨*capture* a smile on film⟩ **c** : to captivate and hold the interest of ⟨*captured* their imagination⟩ **2** : to take according to rules of a game (as chess) **syn** see CATCH

ca·pu·chin \ˈkap-yə-shən, -ə-, *sense 2 also* kə-ˈpü-shən, -ˈpyü-\ *n* **1** *cap* : a member of an austere branch of the first order of Saint Francis of Assisi engaged in missionary work and preaching **2** : a South American monkey with the forehead bare and bordered by a fringe of dark hair [Middle French, from Italian *cappuccino,* from *cappuccio* "hood, cowl", from *cappa* "cloak", from Late Latin; from the cowl worn by members of this order]

cap·y·bara \ˌkap-i-ˈbar-ə, -ˈbär-\ *n* : a tailless largely aquatic South American rodent often exceeding a meter in length [Portuguese *capibara,* from Tupi]

car \ˈkär\ *n* **1** : a vehicle (as a railroad coach or an automobile) that moves on wheels **2** : the compartment of an elevator **3** : the part of a balloon or an airship in which passengers or equipment are carried [Anglo-French *carre,* from Latin *carrus,* of Celtic origin]

ca·ra·bao \ˌkar-ə-ˈbau̇, ˌkär-\ *n, pl* **-bao** *or* **-baos** : WATER BUFFALO [Philippine Spanish, from Eastern Bisayan (a language of the Visayan islands, Philippines) *karabáw*]

car·a·bi·neer *or* **car·a·bi·nier** \ˌkar-ə-bə-ˈniər\ *n* : a soldier armed with a carbine [French *carabinier,* from *carabine* "carbine"]

ca·ra·ca·ra \ˌkar-ə-ˈkar-ə, -ə-kə-ˈrä\ *n* : any of various large long-legged mostly South American hawks resembling vultures in habits [Spanish, from Tupi *caracará*]

car•a•cole \ˈkar-ə-ˌkōl\ *n* : a half turn to right or left performed by a mounted horse [French, from Spanish *caracol* "snail, spiral stair, caracole"] — **caracole** *vb*

car•a•cul \ˈkar-ə-kəl\ *n* : the pelt of a karakul lamb after the curl begins to loosen [alteration of *karakul*]

ca•rafe \kə-ˈraf, -ˈräf\ *n* : a bottle with a wide base and flaring lip used to hold water or beverages [French, from Italian *caraffa, from* Arabic *gharrāfah*]

car•a•mel \ˈkär-məl; ˈkar-ə-mel, -ˌmel\ *n* **1** : a brittle brown and somewhat bitter substance obtained by heating sugar and used as a coloring and flavoring agent **2** : a firm chewy candy [French, from Spanish *caramelo,* from Portuguese, "icicle, caramel", from Late Latin *calamellus* "small reed", from *calamus* "reed"]

car•a•mel•ize \-mə-ˌlīz\ *vb* : to turn into caramel — **car•a•mel•i•za•tion** \ˌkär-mə-lə-ˈzā-shən, ˌkar-ə-mə-\ *n*

car•a•pace \ˈkar-ə-ˌpās\ *n* : a bony or chitinous case or shield covering all or part of the back of an animal (as a turtle or crayfish) [French, from Spanish *carapacho*]

[1]carat *variant of* KARAT

[2]car•at \ˈkar-ət\ *n* : a unit of weight for precious stones (as diamonds) equal to 200 milligrams [probably from Medieval Latin *carratus,* from Arabic *qīrāt* "bean pod, a small weight", from Greek *keration,* from *keras* "horn"]

car•a•van \ˈkar-ə-ˌvan\ *n* **1 a** : a company of travelers on a journey through desert or hostile regions **b** : a train of pack animals or of vehicles traveling together **2** : a covered vehicle: as **a** : one equipped as traveling living quarters **b** *British* : TRAILER 2b [Italian *caravana,* from Persian *kārwān*]

car•a•van•sa•ry \ˌkar-ə-ˈvan-sə-rē\ *or* **car•a•van•se•rai** \-sə-ˌrī\ *n, pl* **-ries** *or* **-rais 1** : a lodging place in eastern countries for caravans **2** : HOTEL, INN [Persian *kārwānsarāī,* from *kārwān* "caravan" + *sarāī* "palace, inn"]

car•a•vel \ˈkar-ə-ˌvel, -vəl\ *n* : a small 15th and 16th century ship with broad bows, high narrow poop, and lateen sails [Middle French *caravelle,* from Portuguese *caravela*]

car•a•way \ˈkar-ə-ˌwā\ *n* **1** : a usually white-flowered aromatic herb of the carrot family **2** : the aromatic pungent fruit of the caraway used in seasoning and medicine — called also *caraway seed* [probably from Medieval Latin *carvi,* from Arabic *karawyā,* from Greek *karon*]

carb- *or* **carbo-** *combining form* : carbon : carbonic : carbonyl : carboxyl ⟨*carb*ide⟩ ⟨*carbo*hydrate⟩

car•bide \ˈkär-ˌbīd\ *n* : a compound of carbon with another element; *esp* : CALCIUM CARBIDE

car•bine \ˈkär-ˌbēn, -ˌbīn\ *n* : a short light rifle [French *carabine*]

car•bo•hy•drase \ˌkär-bō-ˈhī-ˌdrās, -ˌdrāz\ *n* : an enzyme (as amylase) that promotes decomposition or synthesis of carbohydrate

car•bo•hy•drate \-ˌdrāt\ *n* : any of various neutral compounds of carbon, hydrogen, and oxygen (as sugars, starches, or celluloses) most of which are formed by green plants and which constitute a major class of animal foods

car•bol•ic acid \ˌkär-ˌbäl-ik-\ *n* : PHENOL 1 [*carb-* + Latin *oleum* "oil"]

car•bon \ˈkär-bən\ *n* **1** : a nonmetallic chiefly tetravalent chemical element found native (as in the diamond and graphite) or as a constituent of coal, petroleum, and asphalt, of limestone and other carbonates, and of organic compounds or obtained artificially — see ELEMENT table **2 a** : a sheet of carbon paper **b** : CARBON COPY 1 **3** : a carbon rod used in an arc lamp [French *carbone,* from Latin *carbo* "ember, charcoal"]

car•bo•na•ceous \ˌkär-bə-ˈnā-shəs\ *adj* : relating to, containing, or composed of carbon

car•bo•na•do \ˌkär-bə-ˈnād-ō, -ˈnäd-\ *n, pl* **-nados** : an impure opaque dark-colored fine-grained aggregate of diamond particles valuable for its superior toughness [Portuguese, literally, "carbonated"]

[1]car•bon•ate \ˈkär-bə-ˌnāt, -nət\ *n* : a salt or ester of carbonic acid

[2]car•bon•ate \-ˌnāt\ *vt* **1** : to convert into a carbonate **2** : to impregnate with carbon dioxide ⟨a *carbonated* beverage⟩ — **car•bon•ation** \ˌkär-bə-ˈnā-shən\ *n*

carbon black *n* : any of various colloidal black substances consisting wholly or principally of carbon obtained as soot and used especially as pigments

carbon copy *n* **1** : a copy made by carbon paper **2** : DUPLICATE 1

carbon cycle *n* : the cycle of carbon in living beings in which carbon dioxide fixed by photosynthesis to form organic nutrients is ultimately restored to the inorganic state by respiration and decay

carbon dating *n* : the determination of age (as of an archaeological find) by means of the content of carbon 14

carbon dioxide *n* : a heavy colorless gas CO_2 that does not support combustion, dissolves in water to form carbonic acid, is formed especially by the combustion and decomposition of organic substances (as in animal respiration), is absorbed from the air by plants in photosynthesis, and is used in the carbonation of beverages

carbon disulfide *n* : a colorless flammable poisonous liquid CS_2 used as a solvent for rubber — called also *carbon bisulfide*

carbon 14 *n* : a heavy radioactive form of carbon that has mass number 14, is formed especially by the action of cosmic rays on nitrogen in the atmosphere, and is used as a tracer or for determining the age of very old specimens of formerly living materials (as bones or charcoal)

car•bon•ic \kär-ˈbän-ik\ *adj* : of, relating to, or derived from carbon, carbonic acid, or carbon dioxide

carbonic acid *n* : a weak acid H_2CO_3 that decomposes readily into water and carbon dioxide

carbonic an•hy•drase \-an-ˈhī-ˌdrās, -ˌdrāz\ *n* : a zinc-containing enzyme that occurs in living tissues (as red blood cells) and aids carbon-dioxide transport from the tissues and its release from the blood in the lungs by catalyzing the reversible hydration of carbon dioxide to carbonic acid

car•bon•if•er•ous \ˌkär-bə-ˈnif-rəs, -ə-rəs\ *adj* **1** : producing or containing carbon or coal **2** *cap* : of, relating to, or being the Carboniferous

Carboniferous *n* : the period of the Paleozoic era between the Devonian and the Permian during which reptiles first appeared in the fossil record and tremendous deposits of coal were formed; *also* : the corresponding system of rocks

car•bon•ize \ˈkär-bə-ˌnīz\ *vb* : to convert or become converted into carbon — **car•bon•i•za•tion** \ˌkär-bə-nə-ˈzā-shən\ *n*

carbon monoxide *n* : a colorless odorless very poisonous gas CO formed by the incomplete burning of carbon

carbon paper *n* : a thin paper faced with a transferable waxy pigmented coating so that when placed between two sheets of paper the pressure of writing or typing on the top sheet causes reproduction of the graphic material on the bottom sheet

carbon tetrachloride *n* : a colorless nonflammable poisonous liquid CCl_4 that has an odor resembling that of chloroform and is used as a solvent especially of grease and as a refrigerant

car•bon•yl \ˈkär-bə-ˌnil, -ˌnēl\ *n* : a bivalent radical CO occurring in aldehydes, ketones, esters, and amides

Car•bo•run•dum \ˌkär-bə-ˈrən-dəm\ *trademark* — used for various abrasives

car•box•yl \kär-ˈbäk-səl\ *n* : a univalent radical — COOH typical of organic acids — **car•box•yl•ic** \ˌkär-bäk-ˈsil-ik\ *adj*

car•box•yl•ase \kär-ˈbäk-sə-ˌlās, -ˌlāz\ *n* : an enzyme that catalyzes the addition or removal of carboxyl or carbon dioxide

car•boy \ˈkär-ˌbȯi\ *n* : a large bottle cushioned in a special container [Persian *qarāba,* from Arabic *qarrābah* "demijohn"]

car•bun•cle \ˈkär-ˌbəng-kəl\ *n* **1** : a cut cabochon garnet **2** : a painful inflammation of the skin and deeper tissues that discharges pus from several openings — compare BOIL [Middle French, from Latin *carbunculus* "small coal, carbuncle", from *carbo* "charcoal, ember"] — **car•bun•cled** \-kəld\ *adj* — **car•bun•cu•lar** \kär-ˈbəng-kyə-lər\ *adj*

car•bu•re•tor \ˈkär-bə-ˌrāt-ər, -byə-\ *n* : an apparatus for supplying an internal-combustion engine with vaporized fuel mixed with air in an explosive mixture [*carburet* "to combine with carbon", from obsolete *carburet* "carbide"]

car•case \ˈkär-kəs\ *British variant of* CARCASS

car•cass \ˈkär-kəs\ *n* **1** : a dead body; *esp* : the dressed body of a meat animal **2** : the living body **3** : the foundation structure of something (as a tire) [Middle French *carcasse*]

car•cin•o•gen \kär-ˈsin-ə-jən, ˈkärs-n-ə-ˌjen\ *n* : a substance or agent producing or inciting cancer [Greek *karkinos* "crab, cancer"] — **car•ci•no•gen•ic** \ˌkärs-n-ō-ˈjen-ik\ *adj* — **car•ci•no•ge•nic•i•ty** \-jə-ˈnis-ət-ē\ *n*

car•ci•no•ma \ˌkärs-n-ˈō-mə\ *n, pl* **-mas** *or* **-ma•ta** \-mət-ə\ : a malignant tumor originating in epithelium — **car•ci•no•ma•tous** \ˌkärs-n-ˈō-mət-əs\ *adj*

[1]**card** \ˈkärd\ *vt* : to clean and untangle (fibers) by combing with a card before spinning — **card•er** *n*

[2]**card** *n* : an instrument usually having bent wire teeth and used for combing fibers (as wool or cotton) [Middle French *carde,* from Latin *carduus* "thistle"]

[3]**card** *n* **1** : PLAYING CARD **2** *pl* **a** : a game played with cards **b** : card playing **3** : an amusing person : WAG **4 a** : a flat stiff usually small and rectangular piece of paper or thin paperboard (as a postcard) **b** : a sports program ⟨a racing *card*⟩ **c** (1) : a wine list (2) : MENU 1 [Middle French *carte,* derived from Latin *charta* "leaf of papyrus", from Greek *chartēs*] — see CARTEL origin

car•da•mom \ˈkärd-ə-məm, -ˌmäm\ *n* : the aromatic capsular fruit of an East Indian herb of the ginger family with seeds used as a condiment and in medicine; *also* : this plant [Latin *cardamomum,* from Greek *kardamōmon*]

card•board \ˈkärd-ˌbōrd, -ˌbȯrd\ *n* : a paperboard usually made from wood pulp

cardi- *or* **cardio-** *combining form* : heart ⟨*cardiogram*⟩ [Greek *kardia*]

[1]**car•di•ac** \ˈkärd-ē-ˌak\ *adj* **1** : of, relating to, situated near, or acting on the heart **2** : of, relating to, or being the part of the stomach into which the esophagus opens [Latin *cardiacus,* from Greek *kardiakos,* from *kardia* "heart"]

[2]**cardiac** *n* : a person with heart disease

cardiac muscle *n* : striated muscle tissue that is found in the heart, is made up of contractile cells whose protoplasm is continuous from one cell to another, and is not under voluntary control — compare SMOOTH MUSCLE

car•di•gan \ˈkärd-i-gən\ *n* : a usually collarless sweater opening the full length of the front [James Thomas Brudenell, 7th earl of *Cardigan,* died 1868, English soldier]

Cardigan *n* : a Welsh corgi with rounded ears, slightly bowed forelegs, and long tail — called also *Cardigan Welsh Corgi* [*Cardigan* county, Wales]

[1]**car•di•nal** \ˈkärd-nəl, -n-əl\ *adj* : of basic importance : MAIN, CHIEF, PRIMARY [Old French, from Late Latin *cardinalis,* from Latin *cardo* "hinge"] — **car•di•nal•ly** \-ē\ *adv*

[2]**cardinal** *n* **1** : one of the high officials of the Roman Catholic Church who rank next below the pope and who form his advisory and administrative council and elect his successor **2** : CARDINAL NUMBER — usually used in pl. **3** : any of several American finches of which the male is bright red with a black face and pointed crest [sense 3 from its color, resembling that of a cardinal's robes]

car•di•nal•ate \-ət, -ˌāt\ *n* : the office, rank, or dignity of a cardinal

cardinal flower *n* : the brilliant red flower of a North American lobelia; *also* : this plant

car•di•nal•i•ty \ˌkärd-n-ˈal-ət-ē\ *n, pl* **-ties** : the numbers of elements in a given mathematical set

cardinal number *n* : a number (as 1, 5, 15) that is used in simple counting and that indicates how many elements there are in a set but not the order in which they are arranged — compare ORDINAL NUMBER; see NUMBER table

cardinal point *n* : one of the four principal points of the compass: north, south, east, or west

car•dio•gram \ˈkärd-ē-ə-ˌgram\ *n* : the curve or tracing made by a cardiograph

car•dio•graph \-ˌgraf\ *n* : an instrument that records graphically the duration and character of the heart movements — **car•dio•graph•ic** \ˌkärd-ē-ə-ˈgraf-ik\ *adj*

car•di•ol•o•gy \ˌkärd-ē-ˈäl-ə-jē\ *n* : the study of the heart and its action and diseases — **car•di•ol•o•gist** \-jəst\ *n*

car•dio•vas•cu•lar \-ˈvas-kyə-lər\ *adj* : of, relating to, or involving the heart and blood vessels

car•doon \kär-ˈdün\ *n* : a large perennial plant related to the artichoke and sometimes grown for its edible root and leafstalks [French *cardon,* from Late Latin *cardo* "thistle", from Latin *carduus*]

card•play•er \ˈkärd-ˌplā-ər\ *n* : one that plays cards

card•sharp \-ˌshärp\ *or* **card•sharp•er** \-ˌshär-pər\ *n* : a skilled cheater at cards

[1]**care** \ˈkeər, ˈkaər\ *n* **1** : a heavy sense of responsibility : WORRY, ANXIETY, CONCERN **2** : painstaking or watchful attention : HEED ⟨take *care* in crossing streets⟩ **3** : SUPERVISION ⟨under a doctor's *care*⟩ **4** : an object of one's watchful attention [Old English *caru*]

[2]**care** *vb* **1 a** : to feel trouble or anxiety **b** : to feel interest or concern ⟨*care* about freedom⟩ **2** : to give care ⟨*care* for the sick⟩ **3 a** : to have a liking, fondness, or taste ⟨don't *care* for sweets⟩ **b** : to have an inclination ⟨would you *care* for some pie⟩ — **car•er** *n*

ca•reen \kə-ˈrēn\ *vb* **1** : to cause a boat to lean or tilt over on one side for cleaning, caulking, or repairing **2** : to sway from side to side : LURCH [Middle French *carène* "keel", derived from Latin *carina* "keel", literally, "nutshell"]

[1]**ca•reer** \kə-ˈriər\ *n* **1 a** : COURSE 1a **b** : speed in a course ⟨ran at full *career*⟩ **2** : a course of continued progress or activity **3** : a profession for which one trains and which is undertaken as a permanent calling [Middle French *carrière,* from Provençal *carriera* "street", from Medieval Latin *carraria* "road for vehicles", from Latin *carrus* "car"]

[2]**career** *vi* : to go at top speed especially in a headlong manner ⟨a car *careering* down the road⟩

care•free \ˈkeər-ˌfrē, ˈkaər-\ *adj* : free from care

care•ful \-fəl\ *adj* **1** : using or taking care : WATCHFUL, HEEDFUL ⟨a *careful* driver⟩ **2** : made, done, or said with care ⟨*careful* examination⟩ — **care•ful•ly** \-fə-lē, -flē\ *adv* — **care•ful•ness** \-fəl-nəs\ *n*

• **syn** METICULOUS, SCRUPULOUS, PUNCTILIOUS: CAREFUL implies attentiveness and cautiousness in avoiding mistakes ⟨a *careful* worker⟩ ⟨*careful* nursing⟩ METICULOUS may imply either commendable extreme carefulness or a hampering finicky caution over small points; SCRUPULOUS applies to what is proper or fitting or ethical ⟨*scrupulous* honesty⟩ PUNCTILIOUS implies minute, even excessive attention to fine points.

care•less \ˈkeər-ləs, ˈkaər-\ *adj* **1** : CAREFREE **2** : not taking proper care : HEEDLESS ⟨*careless* of danger⟩ **3** : done, made, or said without due care ⟨a *careless* mistake⟩ — **care•less•ly** *adv* — **care•less•ness** *n*

[1]**ca•ress** \kə-ˈres\ *n* : a tender or loving touch or embrace [French *caresse,* from Italian *carezza,* from *caro* "dear", from Latin *carus*] — **ca•res•sive** \-ˈres-iv\ *adj* — **ca•res•sive•ly** *adv*

[1]**caress** *vt* : to touch or stroke lightly in a loving manner — **ca•ress•er** *n*

car•et \ˈkar-ət\ *n* : a mark ∧ used to show where something is to be inserted in written or printed matter [Latin, "there is lacking", from *carēre* "to lack"]

care•tak•er \ˈkeər-ˌtā-kər, ˈkaər-\ *n* : one that takes care of buildings or land often for an absent owner

care•worn \-ˌwōrn, -ˌwȯrn\ *adj* : showing the effect of grief or anxiety

car•fare \ˈkär-ˌfaər, -ˌfeər\ *n* : the fare charged a passenger (as on a bus or streetcar)

car•go \ˈkär-ˌgō\ *n, pl* **cargoes** *or* **cargos** : the goods or merchandise carried in a ship, airplane, or vehicle : FREIGHT [Spanish, "load, charge", from *cargar* "to load, charge", from Late Latin *carricare*]

car•hop \ˈkär-ˌhäp\ *n* : one who serves customers at a drive-in restaurant [*car* + *-hop* (as in *bellhop*)]

Car•ib \ˈkar-əb\ *n* **1** : a member of an Indian people of northern South America and the Lesser Antilles **2** : the language of the Caribs [Spanish *Caribe,* of American Indian origin]

ca•ri•be \kə-ˈrē-bē\ *n* : PIRANHA [American Spanish, from Spanish, "Carib, cannibal"]

car•i•bou \ˈkar-ə-ˌbü\ *n, pl* **-bou** *or* **-bous** : any of several large deer of northern North America closely related to the reindeer [Canadian French, of American Indian origin]

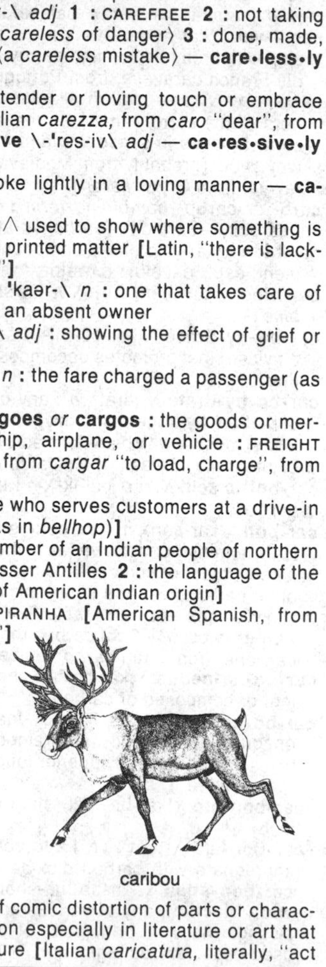
caribou

car•i•ca•ture \ˈkar-i-kə-ˌchu̇r\ *n* **1** : exaggeration by means of comic distortion of parts or characteristics **2** : a representation especially in literature or art that has the qualities of caricature [Italian *caricatura,* literally, "act of loading", from *caricare* "to load", from Late Latin *carricare*] — **caricature** *vt* — **car•i•ca•tur•ist** \-əst\ *n*

• **syn** CARICATURE, BURLESQUE, PARODY, TRAVESTY mean a comic or grotesque imitation. CARICATURE implies ludicrous exaggeration of the characteristic features of a subject; BURLESQUE implies the ridiculous effect resulting either from treating a trivial subject in a mock-heroic style or from giving a serious or lofty subject a frivolous treatment; PARODY applies to treatment of a trivial or ludicrous subject in the exactly imitated style of a particular author or work; TRAVESTY implies that the subject remains unaltered but that the style and effect is extravagant or absurd.

car•ies \'kaər-ēz, 'keər-\ *n, pl* **caries** : a progressive destruction of bone or tooth; *esp* : tooth decay [Latin, "decay"] — **car•i•ous** \'kar-ē-əs, 'ker-\ *adj*

car•il•lon \'kar-ə-ˌlän, -lən\ *n* **1** : a set of bells sounded by hammers controlled by a keyboard **2** : a tune for the carillon [French, from Old French *quarregnon,* from Late Latin *quaternio* "set of four"]

car•il•lon•neur \ˌkar-ə-lə-'nər, ˌkar-ē-ə-'nər\ *n* : a carillon player [French, from *carillon*]

ca•ri•na \kə-'rī-nə, -'rē-\ *n, pl* **-rinas** *or* **-ri•nae** \-'rī-ˌnē, -'rē-ˌnī\ : a keel-shaped anatomical part, ridge, or process [Latin, "keel"]

car•i•ole \'kar-ē-ˌōl\ *n* : a dog-drawn toboggan [French *carriole* "light carriage", derived from Latin *carrus* "car"]

car•load \'kär-'lōd\ *n* : a load that fills a car

Car•mel•ite \'kär-mə-ˌlīt\ *n* : a friar or nun of the Roman Catholic Order of Our Lady of Mount Carmel founded in the 12th century — **Carmelite** *adj*

car•mi•na•tive \kär-'min-ət-iv, 'kär-mə-ˌnāt-iv\ *adj* : helping to expel gas from the alimentary canal [French *carminatif,* from Latin *carminare* "to card, comb out knots in"] — **carminative** *n*

car•mine \'kär-mən, -ˌmīn\ *n* **1** : a rich crimson or scarlet coloring matter made from cochineal **2** : a vivid red [French *carmin,* from Medieval Latin *carminium,* from Arabic *qirmiz* "kermes" + Latin *minium* "red lead"]

car•nage \'kär-nij\ *n* : great and bloody slaughter (as in battle) [Middle French, from Medieval Latin *carnaticum* "tribute of animals or meat", from Latin *caro* "flesh"]

car•nal \'kärn-l\ *adj* **1** : of or relating to the body : CORPORAL **2** : marked by sexuality : SENSUAL **3** : characterized by physical rather than spiritual orientation [Late Latin *carnalis,* from Latin *carn-, caro* "flesh"] — **car•nal•i•ty** \kär-'nal-ət-ē\ *n* — **car•nal•ly** \'kärn-l-ē\ *adv*

car•nas•si•al \kär-'nas-ē-əl\ *adj* : of, relating to, or being teeth of a carnivore adapted for cutting rather than tearing [French *carnassier* "carnivorous", derived from Latin *caro* "flesh"] — **carnassial** *n*

car•na•tion \kär-'nā-shən\ *n* **1** : a moderate red **2** : any of the numerous cultivated usually double-flowered pinks derived from the common gillyflower [Middle French, "color of human flesh", derived from Latin *caro* "flesh"]

car•nau•ba \kär-'nò-bə, -'naù; ˌkär-nə-'ü-bə\ *n* **1** : a Brazilian palm that yields a brittle yellowish wax used especially in polishes — called also *carnauba palm* **2** : the wax produced by the carnauba — called also *carnauba wax* [Portuguese]

car•ne•lian \kär-'nēl-yən\ *n* : a hard tough reddish quartz used as a gem [Middle French *corneline*]

car•ni•val \'kär-nə-vəl\ *n* **1** : a season or festival of merrymaking before Lent **2** : a merrymaking, feasting, or masquerading **3 a** : a traveling enterprise offering amusements **b** : an organized program of entertainment ⟨a winter *carnival*⟩ [Italian *carnevale,* alteration of earlier *carnelevare,* literally, "removal of meat"]

car•niv•o•ra \kär-'niv-rə, -ə-rə\ *n pl* : carnivorous mammals [New Latin]

car•ni•vore \'kär-nə-ˌvōr, -ˌvòr\ *n* : a flesh-eating animal; *esp* : any of an order (Carnivora) of flesh-eating mammals

car•niv•o•rous \kär-'niv-rəs, -ə-rəs\ *adj* **1** : subsisting or feeding on animal tissues **2** : of or relating to the carnivores [Latin *carnivorus,* from *carn-, caro* "flesh" + *vorare* "to devour"] — **car•niv•o•rous•ly** *adv* — **car•niv•o•rous•ness** *n*

car•no•tite \'kär-nə-ˌtīt\ *n* : a mineral consisting of a radioactive compound of potassium, uranium, vanadium, and oxygen [M. A. *Carnot,* died 1920, French inspector general of mines]

car•ob \'kar-əb\ *n* : one of the long pods of a Mediterranean tree of the pea family; *also* : its sweet pulp [Middle French *carobe,* from Medieval Latin *carrubium,* from Arabic *kharrūbah*]

[1]**car•ol** \'kar-əl\ *n* **1** : an old round dance with singing **2** : a song of joy or mirth **3** : a popular song of religious joy ⟨Christmas *carol*⟩ [Old French *carole,* from Late Latin *choraula* "choral song", from Latin, "choral accompanist", from Greek *choraulēs,* from *choros* "chorus" + *aulein* "to play a reed instrument", from *aulos,* a kind of reed instrument]

[2]**carol** *vb* **-oled** *or* **-olled**; **-ol•ing** *or* **-ol•ling** **1** : to sing especially in a joyful way **2** : to sing carols — **car•ol•er** *or* **car•ol•ler** *n*

Car•o•line \'kar-ə-ˌlin, -lən\ *adj* : of or relating to Charles I or Charles II of England [Medieval Latin *Carolus* "Charles"]

Car•o•lin•gian \ˌkar-ə-'lin-jē-ən, -jən\ *adj* : of or relating to a Frankish dynasty dating from about A.D. 613 and ruling France from 751 to 987, Germany from 752 to 911, and Italy from 774 to 961 [French *carolingien,* from Medieval Latin *karolingi* "French people", probably derived from Old High German *Karl* "Charles"] — **Carolingian** *n*

[1]**car•om** \'kar-əm\ *n* **1** : a shot in billiards in which the cue ball strikes each of two object balls **2** : a rebounding especially at an angle [Spanish *carambola*]

[2]**carom** *vi* **1** : to make a carom **2** : to strike and rebound at an angle : GLANCE

car•o•tene \'kar-ə-ˌtēn\ *n* : any of several orange or red hydrocarbon pigments (as $C_{40}H_{56}$) that occur in plants and in the fatty tissues of plant-eating animals and are convertible to vitamin A [Late Latin *carota* "carrot"]

ca•rot•enoid \kə-'rät-n-ˌòid\ *n* : any of various usually yellow to red pigments (as carotenes) found widely in plants and animals and characterized chemically by a long chain of carbon atoms — **carotenoid** *adj*

ca•rot•id \kə-'rät-əd\ *n* : the chief artery or one of the pair of arteries that pass up each side of the neck and supply the head — called also *carotid artery* [Greek *karōtides* "carotid arteries"] — **carotid** *adj*

ca•rous•al \kə-'raù-zəl\ *n* : CAROUSE

[1]**ca•rouse** \kə-'raùz\ *n* : a drunken revel [Middle French *carousse,* from *boire carous* "to empty the cup", from *boire* "to drink" + German *garaus* "all out"]

[2]**carouse** *vi* : to drink liquor freely — **ca•rous•er** *n*

car•ou•sel *or* **car•rou•sel** \ˌkar-ə-'sel *also* -'zel\ *n* : MERRY-GO-ROUND 1 [French *carrousel,* from Italian *carosello*]

[1]**carp** \'kärp\ *vi* : to find fault : complain fretfully [of Scandinavian origin] — **carp•er** *n*

[2]**carp** *n, pl* **carp** *or* **carps** : a large variable Old World soft-finned freshwater fish noted for its longevity and often raised for food; *also* : any of various related or similar fishes [Middle French *carpe,* from Late Latin *carpa*]

-carp \ˌkärp\ *n combining form* **1** : part of a fruit ⟨meso*carp*⟩ **2** : fruit ⟨schizo*carp*⟩ [Greek *karpos* "fruit"]

[1]**car•pal** \'kär-pəl\ *adj* : relating to the carpus

[2]**carpal** *n* : a carpal bone or cartilage

car•pel \'kär-pəl\ *n* : one of the structures of the innermost whorl of a flower that together form the ovary of a seed plant [New Latin *carpellum,* from Greek *karpos* "fruit"]

carpel: *1* petal, *2* stamen, *3* carpel, *4* sepal

car•pen•ter \'kär-pən-tər, 'kärp-m-tər\ *n* : a worker who builds or repairs wooden structures [Old North French *carpentier,* from Latin *carpentarius* "carriage maker", from *carpentum* "carriage", of Celtic origin] — **carpenter** *vb* — **car•pen•try** \-trē\ *n*

car•pet \'kär-pət\ *n* **1 a** : a heavy woven or felted fabric used as a floor covering **b** : a floor covering made of this fabric **2** : a surface resembling a carpet ⟨a *carpet* of leaves⟩ [Middle French *carpite,* from Italian *carpita,* from *carpire* "to pluck", from Latin *carpere*] — **carpet** *vt*

\ə\ **abut**	\aù\ **out**	\i\ **tip**	\ò\ **saw**	\ù\ **foot**
\ər\ **further**	\ch\ **chin**	\ī\ **life**	\òi\ **coin**	\y\ **yet**
\a\ **mat**	\e\ **pet**	\j\ **job**	\th\ **thin**	\yü\ **few**
\ā\ **take**	\ē\ **easy**	\ng\ **sing**	\th\ **this**	\yù\ **cure**
\ä\ **cot, cart**	\g\ **go**	\ō\ **bone**	\ü\ **food**	\zh\ **vision**

[1]**car•pet•bag** \-ˌbag\ *n* : a traveling bag made of carpeting common in the 19th century
[2]**carpetbag** *adj* : of, relating to, or characteristic of carpetbaggers
car•pet•bag•ger \-ˌbag-ər\ *n* : a Northerner in the South during the reconstruction period seeking private gain by taking advantage of unsettled conditions and political corruption [from their carrying their belongings in carpetbags] — **car•pet•bag•gery** \-ˌbag-rē, -ə-rē\ *n*
carpet beetle *n* : a small beetle whose larva damages woolen goods
car•pet•ing \ˈkär-pət-ing\ *n* : material for carpets; *also* : CARPET 1b
carp•ing *adj* : tending to carp — **carp•ing•ly** \ˈkär-ping-lē\ *adv*
car•po•go•ni•um \ˌkär-pə-ˈgō-nē-əm\ *n, pl* **-nia** \-nē-ə\ : the flask-shaped egg-bearing organ of some thallophytes [Greek *karpos* "fruit" + *gonos* "procreation, seed"] — **car•po•go•ni•al** \-nē-əl\ *adj*
car•port \ˈkär-ˌpōrt, -ˌpȯrt\ *n* : an open-sided automobile shelter usually formed by extension of a roof from the side of a building
car•pus \ˈkär-pəs\ *n, pl* **car•pi** \-ˌpī, -ˌpē\ : the wrist or its bones [New Latin, from Greek *karpos* "wrist"]
car•rack \ˈkar-ək\ *n* : a large armed merchant ship chiefly of the 16th and 17th centuries [Middle French *caraque,* from Spanish *carraca,* from Arabic *qarāqīr,* plural of *qurqūr* "merchant ship"]
car•rel \ˈkar-əl\ *n* : a table that is often partitioned or enclosed for individual study in a library [Middle English *carole* "round dance, carol, ring", from Old French]
car•riage \ˈkar-ij\ *n* **1 a** : the act of carrying **b** : manner of bearing the body : POSTURE **2** : the cost of carrying **3 a** : a wheeled vehicle; *esp* : a horse-drawn vehicle for carrying persons **b** *British* : a railway passenger coach **4** : a wheeled support carrying a load ⟨a gun *carriage*⟩ **5** : a movable part of a machine for supporting or carrying some other movable object or part
carriage trade *n* : trade especially from well-to-do people
car•ri•er \ˈkar-ē-ər\ *n* **1** : one that carries **2 a** : a person or firm engaged in transporting passengers or goods **b** : a postal employee who delivers or collects mail **c** : one that delivers newspapers **3 a** : a bearer and transmitter of disease germs; *esp* : one that carries in his system germs of a disease (as typhoid fever) to which he is immune **b** : one having a specified gene and capable of transmitting it to his offspring but not exhibiting its typical expression **4** : a substance (as a catalyst) by means of which energy, a charged particle, or an ion is transferred from one source to another ⟨ATP is an energy *carrier*⟩ **5** : AIRCRAFT CARRIER **6** : an electric wave or alternating current whose modulations are used as signals in radio, telephonic, or telegraphic transmission
car•ri•on \ˈkar-ē-ən\ *n* : dead and decaying flesh [Anglo-French *caroine,* derived from Latin *caro* "flesh"]
car•rot \ˈkar-ət\ *n* : a biennial herb with a usually orange spindle-shaped edible root; *also* : its root [Middle French *carotte,* from Late Latin *carota,* from Greek *karōton*]
car•roty \-ət-ē\ *adj* : resembling carrots in color
[1]**car•ry** \ˈkar-ē\ *vb* **car•ried; car•ry•ing 1 a** : to support and take from one place to another : TRANSPORT, CONVEY ⟨*carry* a package⟩ **b** : to act as a bearer — often used in the phrase *fetch and carry* **2** : to influence by mental or emotional appeal ⟨the speaker *carried* the audience⟩ **3** : to get possession or control of : CAPTURE ⟨*carry* off a prize⟩ **4** : to transfer from one place to another; *esp* : to transfer (a number) in adding columns of figures from the sum obtained in adding a single column to the next column on the left **5** : to contain and direct the course of : CONDUCT ⟨a pipe *carries* water⟩ **6 a** : to wear or have on one's person ⟨*carries* a gun⟩ **b** : to bear upon or within one ⟨*carries* a scar⟩ ⟨*carry* an unborn child⟩ **c** : to include as a necessary or natural effect ⟨the crime *carries* a penalty⟩ **7** : to conduct oneself in a specified way **8** : to bear the weight of ⟨pillars *carry* an arch⟩ **9** : to sing in correct pitch ⟨*carry* a tune⟩ **10** : to keep in stock for sale ⟨*carries* three brands of tires⟩ **11** : to provide sustenance for ⟨land *carrying* 10 head of cattle⟩ **12** : to maintain on a list or record ⟨*carry* them on the payroll⟩ **13** : to prolong in space, time, or degree ⟨*carried* the argument too far⟩ **14 a** : to gain victory for; *esp* : to win adoption or the adoption of ⟨*carry* a bill⟩ **b** : to win a majority of votes in ⟨*carry* a state⟩ **15** : PUBLISH 2a ⟨the paper *carries* weather reports⟩ **16 a** : to bear the charges of holding (as merchandise) **b** : to keep on one's books as a debtor ⟨a merchant *carries* a customer⟩ **17** : to penetrate to a distance ⟨a voice that *carries* well⟩ [Old North French *carier* "to transport in a vehicle", from *car* "vehicle", from Latin *carrus*]
[2]**carry** *n, pl* **carries 1** : the range of a gun or projectile or of a struck or thrown ball **2 a** : the act or method of carrying ⟨one-hand *carry*⟩ **b** : PORTAGE 2
car•ry•all \ˈkar-ē-ˌȯl\ *n* **1** : a light covered carriage for four or more persons **2** : a passenger automobile similar to a station wagon but with a higher body often on a truck chassis **3** : a capacious bag or case [by folk etymology from French *carriole,* derived from Latin *carrus* "car"]
carry away *vt* : to arouse to a high and often excessive degree of emotion or enthusiasm
carrying capacity *n* : the population (as of deer) that an area will support without undergoing ecological deterioration
carrying charge *n* : a charge added to the price of merchandise sold on the installment plan
carry on *vb* **1** : to oversee and make decisions about : CONDUCT ⟨*carries on* a dry cleaning business⟩ **2** : to behave in a foolish, excited, or improper manner ⟨embarrassed at the way they *carried on*⟩ **3** : to continue in spite of hindrance or discouragement
car•ry•out \ˈkar-ē-ˌau̇t\ *n* : a food product prepared to be eaten away from its place of sale
carry out *vt* **1** : to put into execution ⟨*carry out* a plan⟩ **2** : to bring to a successful conclusion
car•sick \ˈkär-ˌsik\ *adj* : affected with motion sickness especially in an automobile — **car sickness** *n*
[1]**cart** \ˈkärt\ *n* **1** : a heavy usually horse-drawn 2-wheeled vehicle **2** : a light usually 2-wheeled vehicle drawn by a horse, pony, or dog **3** : a small wheeled vehicle ⟨a garden *cart*⟩ [Middle English]
[2]**cart** *vt* : to convey in or as if in a cart — **cart•er** *n*
cart•age \ˈkärt-ij\ *n* : the act of or rate charged for carting
carte blanche \ˈkärt-ˈbläⁿsh, -ˈblänch\ *n, pl* **cartes blanches** *same*\ : full discretionary power [French, literally, "blank document"]
car•tel \kär-ˈtel\ *n* : a combination of independent commercial enterprises designed to limit competition [Middle French, "letter of defiance", from Italian *cartello,* literally, "placard", from *carta* "leaf of paper"] **syn** see MONOPOLY
△ **origin** The literal meaning of Italian *cartello,* a derivative of *carta,* "leaf of paper", is "placard". The word is also used for a letter of defiance or a challenge. In this sense the Italian word was borrowed into Middle French as *cartel,* and the French word was borrowed into English. In English, a *cartel* was originally a letter of defiance. Later the word came to be used for a written agreement between warring nations to regulate such matters as the treatment and exchange of prisoners. Another type of agreement, a combination of commercial enterprises, is now called a *cartel. Cartel* is ultimately derived from Greek *chartēs* "leaf of papyrus" and is thus a relative of *card* and *chart.*
Car•te•sian \kär-ˈtē-zhən\ *adj* : of or relating to René Descartes, his philosophy, or his mathematical methods [New Latin *Cartesius* "Descartes"]
Cartesian coordinate *n* : either of two coordinates that locate a point on a plane and measure its distance from one of two usually perpendicular axes along a line parallel to the other axis
Cartesian coordinate system *n* : a coordinate system based on Cartesian coordinates
Cartesian plane *n* : a plane whose points are labeled with Cartesian coordinates
Cartesian product *n* : a set that is constructed from two given sets and comprises all pairs of elements such that one element of the pair is from the first set and the other element is from the second set
Car•thu•sian \kär-ˈthü-zhən, -ˈthyü-\ *n* : a member of a religious order founded in 1084 and devoted to prayer and meditation [Medieval Latin *cartusiensis,* from Old French *Chartrouse,* motherhouse of the Carthusian order, near Grenoble, France]
car•ti•lage \ˈkärt-l-ij\ *n* **1** : a translucent elastic tissue that composes most of the skeleton of embryonic and very young vertebrates and becomes for the most part converted into bone in the higher vertebrates **2** : a part or structure composed of cartilage [Latin *cartilago*]

car·ti·lag·i·nous \ˌkärt-l-ˈaj-ə-nəs\ *adj* **1 :** of, relating to, or resembling cartilage **2 :** having a skeleton mostly of cartilage

car·tog·ra·phy \kär-ˈtäg-rə-fē\ *n* **:** the making of maps [French *cartographie,* from *carte* "card, map"] — **car·tog·ra·pher** \-fər\ *n* — **car·to·graph·ic** \ˌkärt-ə-ˈgraf-ik\ *adj*

car·ton \ˈkärt-n\ *n* **:** a paperboard box or container [French, from Italian *cartone* "pasteboard"]

car·toon \kär-ˈtün\ *n* **1 :** a preparatory design, drawing, or painting **2 a :** a satirical drawing commenting on public and usually political matters **b :** COMIC STRIP **3 :** ANIMATED CARTOON [Italian *cartone* "pasteboard, cartoon", from *carta* "leaf of paper", from Latin *charta* "piece of papyrus"] — **cartoon** *vb* — **car·toon·ist** \-ˈtü-nəst\ *n*

car·tridge \ˈkär-trij\ *n* **1 a :** a tube of metal or paper containing a charge and a bullet or shot for a firearm **b :** a case containing an explosive charge for blasting **2 :** an often cylindrical container of material for insertion into a larger mechanism or apparatus **3 a :** a phonograph pickup that translates stylus motion into electrical voltage **b :** a case containing a reel and endless loop of film or magnetic tape for use without threading [Middle French *cartouche* "scroll, cartridge", from Italian *cartoccio,* from *carta* "paper", from Latin *charta* "piece of papyrus"]

cart·wheel \ˈkärt-ˌhwēl, -ˌwēl\ *n* **1 :** a large coin (as a silver dollar) **2 :** a handspring performed to one side with arms and legs extended

car·un·cle \ˈkar-ˌəng-kəl, kə-ˈrəng-\ *n* **:** a fleshy outgrowth (as on a seed) [obsolete French *caruncule,* from Latin *caruncula* "little piece of flesh", from *caro* "flesh"]

carve \ˈkärv\ *vb* **1 :** to cut with care or precision especially artistically ⟨*carve* a statuette from wood⟩ **2 :** to make or get by cutting — often used with *out* ⟨*carve* out a fortune⟩ **3 :** to cut into pieces or slices **4 :** to cut up and serve meat [Old English *ceorfan*] — **car·ver** *n*

carv·en \ˈkär-vən\ *adj* **:** made by carving

carv·ing \ˈkär-ving\ *n* **1 :** the act or art of one who carves **2 :** a carved object, design, or figure

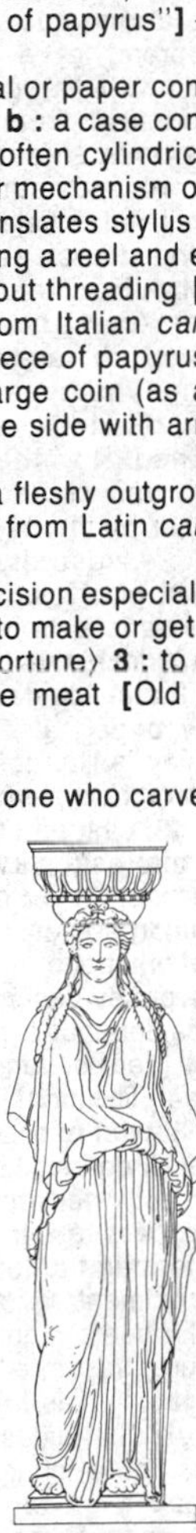

caryatid

cary·at·id \ˌkar-ē-ˈat-əd\ *n, pl* **-at·ids** *or* **-at·i·des** \-ˈat-ə-ˌdēz\ **:** a statue of a woman in flowing robes used as an architectural column [Latin *caryatides,* plural, from Greek *karyatides* "priestesses of Artemis at Caryae in Laconia, caryatids", from *Karyai* "Caryae"]

cary·op·sis \ˌkar-ē-ˈäp-səs\ *n, pl* **-op·ses** \-ˈäp-ˌsēz\ *or* **-op·sides** \-ˈäp-sə-ˌdēz\ **:** a small one-seeded dry indehiscent fruit in which the fruit and seed fuse in a single grain [Greek *karyon* "nut, kernel" + *opsis* "appearance"]

ca·sa·ba *or* **cas·sa·ba** \kə-ˈsäb-ə\ *n* **:** any of several winter melons with yellow rind and sweet flesh — called also *casaba melon, cassaba melon* [*Kasaba* (now Turgutlu), Turkey]

[1]**cas·cade** \kas-ˈkād\ *n* **1 :** a steep usually small fall of water; *esp* **:** one of a series **2 :** something arranged in a series or in a succession of stages so that each stage derives from or acts upon the product of the preceding ⟨a *cascade* amplifier⟩ **3 :** something falling or rushing forth in quantity ⟨a *cascade* of sound⟩ [French, from Italian *cascata,* from *cascare* "to fall"]

[2]**cascade** *vi* **:** to fall in a cascade

cas·cara \kas-ˈkar-ə\ *n* **:** the dried laxative bark of a buckthorn tree that grows along the Pacific coast of the United States [Spanish *cáscara* "bark"]

[1]**case** \ˈkās\ *n* **1 :** a special set of circumstances or conditions **2 a :** a situation requiring investigation or action ⟨a *case* for the police⟩ **b :** an object of investigation or consideration **3 a :** a form of a noun, pronoun, or adjective indicating its grammatical relation to other words ⟨the word *child's* in "the child's shirt" is in the possessive *case*⟩ **b :** such a relation whether indicated by inflection or not ⟨the subject of a verb is in the nominative *case*⟩ **4 :** what actually exists or happens **:** FACT ⟨if that's the *case*⟩ **5 a :** a legal suit or action **b (1) :** the evidence supporting a conclusion or judgment **(2) :** ARGUMENT; *esp* **:** a convincing argument **6 a :** an instance of disease or injury; *also* **:** PATIENT **b :** an instance that calls attention to or exemplifies a situation **:** EXAMPLE ⟨a clear *case* of negligence⟩ [Old French *cas,* from Latin *casus* "fall, chance", from *cadere* "to fall"] **syn** see INSTANCE — **in any case :** without regard to or in spite of other considerations — **in case 1 :** IF 1 **2 :** as a precaution **3 :** as a precaution against the event that

[2]**case** *n* **1 a :** a box or receptacle to contain something **b :** a box with its contents **c :** a set of like or related things; *esp* **:** PAIR ⟨a *case* of pistols⟩ **2 :** an outer covering, sheath, or housing ⟨spore *cases*⟩ **3 :** a shallow divided tray for printing type **4 :** the frame of a door or window **:** CASING [Old North French *casse,* from Latin *capsa* "chest, case", from *capere* "to take"]

[3]**case** *vt* **:** to enclose in or cover with a case

case hard·en \ˈkās-ˌhärd-n\ *vt* **:** to treat (an iron alloy) so that the outside is harder than the interior — **case–hard·ened** *adj*

case history *n* **:** a record of history, environment, and relevant details (as of individual behavior or condition) especially for use in analysis or illustration

ca·sein \kā-ˈsēn, ˈkā-sē-ən\ *n* **1 :** a phosphorus-containing protein that is precipitated from milk by heating with an acid or by lactic acid in souring and that is used in making paints and adhesives **2 :** a phosphorus-containing protein that is produced when milk is curdled by rennet, that is one of the chief constituents of cheese, and that is used in making plastics [derived from Latin *caseus* "cheese"]

case knife *n* **1 :** SHEATH KNIFE **2 :** a table knife

case·mate \ˈkās-ˌmāt\ *n* **:** a fortified position or enclosure from which guns are fired through openings [Middle French, from Italian *casamatta*]

case·ment \ˈkās-mənt\ *n* **:** a window sash opening on hinges like a door; *also* **:** a window with such a sash [Middle English, "hollow molding", probably from Old North French *encassement* "frame", from *en-* "in" + *casse* "case"]

case·work \ˈkās-ˌwərk\ *n* **:** social work involving direct consideration of the individual case including study of and treatment for its needs and problems — **case·work·er** *n*

[1]**cash** \ˈkash\ *n* **:** ready money [Italian *cassa* "money box", from Latin *capsa* "case, chest"]

[2]**cash** *vt* **:** to pay or obtain cash for ⟨*cash* a check⟩

[3]**cash** *n, pl* **cash :** any of various coins of small value in China and India; *esp* **:** a Chinese coin with a square hole in the center [Portuguese *caixa,* from Tamil *kācu,* a small copper coin]

cash–and–carry \ˌkash-ən-ˈkar-ē\ *n* **:** the policy of selling for cash and without delivery service

cash·book \ˈkash-ˌbu̇k\ *n* **:** a book in which records are kept of all cash received and paid out

cash·ew \ˈkash-ü, kə-ˈshü\ *n* **:** a tropical American tree of the sumac family grown for its edible kidney-shaped nut and receptacle and for the gum it yields; *also* **:** its nut [Portuguese *acajú, cajú,* of American Indian origin]

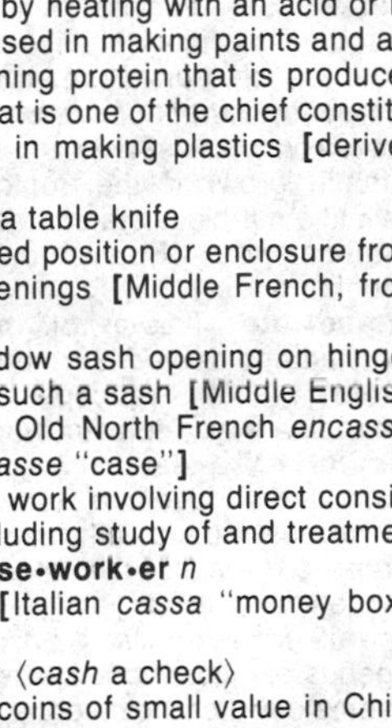

cashew

[1]**ca·shier** \ka-ˈshiər, kə-\ *vt* **:** to discharge in disgrace from a position of responsibility or trust [Dutch *casseren,* from Middle French *casser* "to discharge, annul", from Latin *cassus* "void"]

[2]**cash·ier** \ka-ˈshiər\ *n* **1 :** a high officer of a bank responsible for all money received and paid out **2 :** one who receives and records payments ⟨a *cashier* in a supermarket⟩ [Middle French *cassier,* from *casse* "money box", from Italian *cassa*]

cashier's check *n* **:** a check drawn by a bank on its own funds and signed by its cashier

cash·mere \ˈkazh-ˌmiər, ˈkash-\ *n* **1 :** fine wool from the undercoat of Kashmir goats; *also* **:** a yarn of this wool **2 :** a soft twilled fabric made originally from cashmere wool [*Cashmere* "Kashmir"]

cash register *n* : a business machine that usually has a money drawer, records money received, and shows the amount of each sale

cas•ing \ˈkā-sing\ *n* : something that encases : material for encasing: as **a** : an enclosing frame especially around a door or window opening **b** : TIRE 2b **c** : a membranous case for processed meat (as bologna)

ca•si•no \kə-ˈsē-nō\ *n, pl* **-nos 1** : a building or room used for social amusements; *esp* : one used for gambling **2** *or* **cas•si•no** : a card game in which players try to match cards in their hands with exposed cards on the table [Italian, from *casa* "house", from Latin, "cabin"]

cask \ˈkask\ *n* : a barrel-shaped container usually for liquids; *also* : the quantity contained in a cask [Middle French *casque* "helmet", from Spanish *casco* "potsherd, skull, helmet", from *cascar* "to break"]

cas•ket \ˈkas-kət\ *n* **1** : a small chest or box (as for jewels) **2** : a usually fancy coffin [Middle French *cassette,* from Old North French *casse* "case"]

casque \ˈkask\ *n* : a piece of armor for the head : HELMET [Middle French, from Spanish *casco*]

cas•sa•ba *variant of* CASABA

cas•sa•va \kə-ˈsäv-ə\ *n* : any of several plants of the spurge family grown in the tropics for their fleshy rootstocks which yield a nutritious starch; *also* : the rhizome or its starch — compare TAPIOCA [Spanish *cazabe* "cassava bread", of American Indian origin]

cas•se•role \ˈkas-ə-ˌrōl\ *n* **1** : a dish in which food can be baked and served **2** : the food cooked and served in a casserole [French, "saucepan", from Middle French *casse* "ladle, dripping pan", derived from Greek *kyathos* "ladle"]

cas•sette \kə-ˈset\ *n* **1** : a lightproof container for holding film or plates for use in a camera **2** : a small plastic box containing two reels wound with magnetic tape in which the tape on one reel passes to the other during recording and playback [French, "casket"]

cas•sia \ˈkash-ə\ *n* **1** : a coarse cinnamon bark **2** : any of a genus of leguminous herbs, shrubs, and trees of warm regions some of which yield senna [Latin, from Greek *kassia,* of Semitic origin]

cas•si•mere \ˈkaz-ə-ˌmiər, ˈkas-\ *n* : a smooth twilled usually wool fabric [obsolete *Cassimere* "Kashmir"]

cas•si•no *variant of* CASINO

Cas•si•o•pe•ia \ˌkas-ē-ə-ˈpēə, -ˈpē-yə\ *n* : a northern constellation between Andromeda and Cepheus [*Cassiopeia,* mythical queen of Ethiopia and mother of Andromeda]

Cassiopeia's Chair *n* : a group of stars in the constellation Cassiopeia

cas•sit•er•ite \kə-ˈsit-ə-ˌrīt\ *n* : a brown or black mineral SnO_2 that consists of tin dioxide and is the chief source of tin [Greek *kassiteros* "tin"]

cas•sock \ˈkas-ək\ *n* : an ankle-length gown worn especially in Roman Catholic and Anglican churches by the clergy and by lay people assisting at services [Middle French *casaque,* from Persian *kazhāghand* "padded jacket", from *kazh* "raw silk" + *āghand* "stuffed"]

cas•so•wary \ˈkas-ə-ˌwer-ē\ *n, pl* **-war•ies** : any of several tall swift-running birds of New Guinea and Australia closely related to the emu [Malay *kĕsuari*]

cassowary

[1]**cast** \ˈkast\ *vb* **cast**; **cast•ing 1 a** (1) : THROW 2 ⟨*cast* a stone⟩ (2) : to throw out a lure or line with a fishing rod **b** : to point or project in a specified direction : DIRECT ⟨*cast* a glance⟩ **c** : to place as if by throwing ⟨*cast* doubt on their integrity⟩ **d** : to deposit (a ballot) formally **e** : to throw off, out, or away ⟨the horse *cast* a shoe⟩ : as (1) : to get rid of : DISCARD ⟨*cast* aside all restraint⟩ (2) : SHED, MOLT ⟨a snake *casts* its skin⟩ **2 a** : COMPUTE, FIGURE **b** : to calculate by astrology ⟨*cast* a horoscope⟩ **3 a** : to assign the parts of to actors ⟨*cast* a play⟩ **b** : to assign (an actor) to a part **4 a** : to give shape to (a substance) by pouring in liquid or plastic form into a mold or form and letting harden without pressure ⟨*cast* steel⟩ **b** : to form by this process ⟨*cast* machine parts⟩ [Old Norse *kasta*] — **cast lots** : to draw lots to determine a matter by chance

[2]**cast** *n* **1 a** : an act or instance of casting **b** : something that happens as a result of chance **2 a** : the form in which a thing is constructed **b** : the characters or the actors in a narrative or play **3** : the distance to which a thing can be thrown **4** : a turning of the eye in a particular direction; *also* : EXPRESSION **5** : something thrown or the quantity thrown **6 a** : something formed by casting in a mold or form : CASTING ⟨a bronze *cast* of a statue⟩ **b** : a rigid dressing of gauze impregnated with plaster of paris for immobilizing a diseased or broken part **7** : a forecast about future events or conditions ⟨to make a long *cast* ahead⟩ **8** : an overspread of a color : SHADE ⟨gray with a greenish *cast*⟩ **9** : physical form or character : APPEARANCE ⟨features of delicate *cast*⟩ **10** : something thrown out or off, shed, or ejected; *esp* : the excrement of an earthworm

cast about *vi* : to look around : SEEK ⟨*cast about* for a seat⟩

cas•ta•net \ˌkas-tə-ˈnet\ *n* : a rhythm instrument that consists of two small ivory, wood, or plastic shells fastened to the thumb and clicked together by the fingers — usually used in pl. [Spanish *castañeta,* from *castaña* "chestnut", from Latin *castanea*]

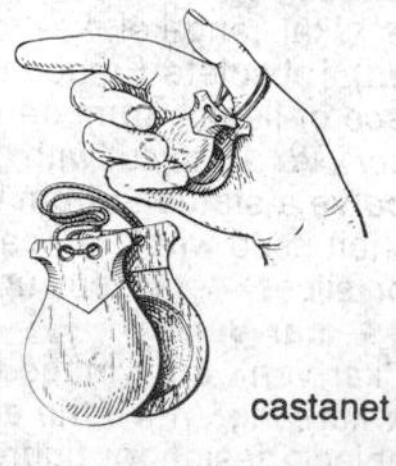

castanet

cast•away \ˈkas-tə-ˌwā\ *adj* **1** : thrown away **2** : cast adrift or ashore as a survivor of a shipwreck — **castaway** *n*

caste \ˈkast\ *n* **1** : one of the hereditary classes formerly dividing Hindu society **2 a** : a division of society based on differences of wealth, inherited rank, or occupation **b** : the position conferred by caste standing : PRESTIGE **3** : a specialized form that carries out a particular function in the colony of a social insect (as the honeybee) [Portuguese *casta,* literally, "race, lineage", from *casto* "pure, chaste", from Latin *castus*]

cas•tel•lat•ed \ˈkas-tə-ˌlāt-əd\ *adj* : having battlements like a castle [Medieval Latin *castellare* "to fortify", from Latin *castellum* "castle, fortress"]

cast•er \ˈkas-tər\ *n* **1** : one that casts **2** : a small container with a perforated top for sprinkling food seasoning **3** : a small tray for condiment containers **4** *or* **cas•tor** \ˈkas-tər\ : a wheel or set of wheels mounted in a swivel frame used for supporting furniture, trucks, and portable machines

cas•ti•gate \ˈkas-tə-ˌgāt\ *vt* : to punish, reprove, or criticize severely [Latin *castigare* "to correct, chasten, castigate", from *castus* "pure, chaste"] — **cas•ti•ga•tion** \ˌkas-tə-ˈgā-shən\ *n* — **cas•ti•ga•tor** \ˈkas-tə-ˌgāt-ər\ *n*

cas•tile soap \ˌkas-ˌtēl-\ *n, often cap C* : a hard bland soap made from olive oil and sodium hydroxide [*Castile,* region of Spain]

Cas•til•ian \ka-ˈstil-yən\ *n* **1 a** : a native or inhabitant of Castile **b** : SPANIARD **2** : the official and literary language of Spain based on the dialect of Castile — **Castilian** *adj*

cast•ing *n* **1** : the act of one that casts **2** : something cast in a mold ⟨a bronze *casting*⟩ **3** : something (as skin or excrement) that is cast out or off

casting vote *n* : a deciding vote cast by a presiding officer in case of a tied vote

cast iron *n* : a hard brittle alloy of iron, carbon, and silicon that is cast in a mold

[1]**cas•tle** \ˈkas-əl\ *n* **1 a** : a large fortified building or set of buildings **b** : a massive or imposing house **2** : [3]ROOK [Old North French *castel,* from Latin *castellum* "fortress, castle", from *castrum* "fortified place"]

[2]**castle** *vb* **cas•tled**; **cas•tling** \ˈkas-ling, -ə-ling\ **1** : to establish in a castle **2** : to move a chess king two squares toward a rook and the rook to the square next past the king on a single move

castle in the air : an impracticable project : DAYDREAM — called also *castle in Spain*

cast–off \'kas-,tóf\ *adj* : thrown away or aside — **castoff** *n*
cast off \'kas-'tof\ *vi* : to unfasten or untie a boat or a line securing a boat
cas•tor \'kas-tər\ *n* **1** : a bitter strong-smelling orange-brown substance obtained from the beaver and used by perfumers **2** : a beaver hat [Latin, "beaver", from Greek *kastōr*]
Cas•tor \'kas-tər\ *n* : the more northern of the two bright stars in Gemini
castor bean *n* : the very poisonous seed of the castor-oil plant; *also* : this plant
castor oil *n* : a thick yellowish oil extracted from castor beans and used as a lubricant, in soap, and as a cathartic [probably from its former use as a substitute for castor in medicine]
castor–oil plant *n* : a tropical Old World herb widely grown as an ornamental or for its oil-rich castor beans
1cas•trate \'kas-,trāt\ *vt* : to deprive of the testes or ovaries [Latin *castrare*] — **cas•tra•tion** \ka-'strā-shən\ *n*
2castrate *n* : a castrated individual
ca•su•al \'kazh-wəl, -ə-wəl; 'kazh-əl\ *adj* **1** : subject to or occurring by chance **2** : occurring without regularity : OCCASIONAL **3 a** : feeling or showing little concern : NONCHALANT **b** : INFORMAL 1, 2 [Late Latin *casualis*, from Latin *casus* "fall, chance", from *cadere* "to fall"] **syn** see ACCIDENTAL, RANDOM — **ca•su•al•ly** \-ē\ *adv* — **ca•su•al•ness** *n*
ca•su•al•ty \'kazh-əl-tē; 'kazh-wəl-, -ə-wəl-\ *n, pl* **-ties 1** : serious or fatal accident : DISASTER **2 a** : a military person lost (as by death or capture) during warfare **b** : a person or thing injured, lost, or destroyed **3** : injury or death from accident
ca•su•ist•ry \'kazh-wə-strē, -ə-wə-\ *n, pl* **-ries 1** : the study or resolution of questions of right and wrong in conduct **2** : false reasoning or application of principles especially with regard to morals or law [probably from Spanish *casuista* "casuist", from Latin *casus* "fall, chance", from *cadere* "to fall"] — **ca•su•ist** \'kazh-wəst, -ə-wəst\ *n* — **ca•su•is•tic** \,kazh-ə-'wis-tik\ *adj*
cat \'kat\ *n* **1 a** : a small flesh-eating mammal long domesticated and kept by humans as a pet or for catching rats and mice **b** : an animal (as a lion, tiger, leopard, jaguar, cougar, wildcat, lynx, or cheetah) of the same family as the domestic cat **2** : CAT-O'-NINE-TAILS **3** : CATFISH [Old English *catt*]
ca•tab•o•lism \kə-'tab-ə-,liz-əm\ *n* : the part of metabolism concerned with the destruction of the substance of plants and animals involving the breakdown of complex materials and the release of energy — compare ANABOLISM [Greek *katabolē* "throwing down", from *kataballein* "to throw down", from *kata* "down" + *ballein* "to throw"] — **cat•a•bol•ic** \,kat-ə-'bäl-ik\ *adj*
cat•a•clysm \'kat-ə-,kliz-əm\ *n* **1** : a great flood : DELUGE **2** : a violent and destructive natural event (as an earthquake) **3** : a violent social or political upheaval [French *cataclysme*, from Latin *cataclysmos*, from Greek *kataklysmos*, from *kataklyzein* "to inundate", from *kata* "down" + *klyzein* "to wash"] **syn** see DISASTER — **cat•a•clys•mal** \,kat-ə-'kliz-məl\ *adj* — **cat•a•clys•mic** \-'kliz-mik\ *adj*
cat•a•comb \'kat-ə-,kōm\ *n* : an underground burying place; *esp* : one that has passages with hollowed places in the sides for tombs — usually used in pl. [Middle French *catacombe*, derived from Late Latin *catacumbae* "catacombs"]
ca•tad•ro•mous \kə-'tad-rə-məs\ *adj* : living in fresh water and going to the sea to spawn ⟨the freshwater eel is *catadromous*⟩ — compare ANADROMOUS [Greek *kata* "down" + *dramein* "to run"]
cat•a•falque \'kat-ə-,falk, -,fólk, -,fȯk\ *n* : a structure sometimes used in funerals to support the coffin [Italian *catafalco*]
Cat•a•lan \'kat-l-ən, -,an\ *n* **1** : a native or inhabitant of Catalonia **2** : the Romance language of Catalonia, Valencia, Andorra, and the Balearic islands — **Catalan** *adj*
cat•a•lase \'kat-l-,ās, -,āz\ *n* : an enzyme that catalyzes the decomposition of hydrogen peroxide into water and oxygen and the oxidation by hydrogen peroxide of alcohols to aldehydes
cat•a•lep•sy \'kat-l-,ep-sē\ *n, pl* **-sies** : a condition of suspended animation and loss of voluntary motion in which the limbs hold any position they are placed in [Medieval Latin *catalepsia*, from Greek *katalēpsis*, literally, "act of seizing", from *katalambanein* "to seize", from *kata* "down" + *lambanein* "to take"] — **cat•a•lep•tic** \,kat-l-'ep-tik\ *adj or n*
1cat•a•log *or* **cat•a•logue** \'kat-l-,ȯg\ *n* **1** : a list of names, titles, or articles arranged according to a system **2 a** : a book or a file containing a catalog **b** : the items listed in such a book or file [Middle French *catalogue*, from Late Latin *catalogus*, from Greek *katalogos*, from *katalegein* "to list", from *kata* "down" + *legein* "to gather, speak"]
2catalog *or* **catalogue** *vt* **1** : to make a catalog of **2** : to enter in a catalog; *esp* : to classify (books or information) descriptively — **cat•a•log•er** *or* **cat•a•logu•er** *n*
ca•tal•pa \kə-'tal-pə, -'tól-\ *n* : a small tree of America and Asia with broad oval leaves, flowers brightly striped inside and spotted outside, and long narrow pods [Creek *kutuhlpa*, literally, "head with wings"]
ca•tal•y•sis \kə-'tal-ə-səs\ *n* : the change and especially increase in the rate of a chemical reaction brought about by a catalyst [Greek *katalysis* "dissolution", from *katalyein* "to dissolve", from *kata* "down" + *lyein* "to loosen, dissolve"] — **cat•a•lyt•ic** \,kat-l-'it-ik\ *adj* — **cat•a•lyt•i•cal•ly** \-'it-i-kə-lē, -klē\ *adv*
cat•a•lyst \'kat-l-əst\ *n* : a substance that changes the rate of a chemical reaction but is itself unchanged at the end of the process; *esp* : such a substance that speeds up a reaction or enables it to proceed under milder conditions than otherwise possible
catalytic converter *n* : a pollution-control device attached to the exhaust system of an automotive vehicle that contains a chemical catalyst which converts pollutants (as carbon monoxide and unburned hydrocarbons) to other products (as carbon dioxide and water)
cat•a•lyze \'kat-l-,īz\ *vt* : to bring about or produce by chemical catalysis — **cat•a•lyz•er** *n*
cat•a•ma•ran \,kat-ə-mə-'ran, 'kat-ə-mə-,ran\ *n* **1** : a raft propelled by paddles or sails **2** : a boat with twin hulls side by side [Tamil *kaṭṭumaram*, from *kaṭṭu* "to tie" + *maram* "tree"]

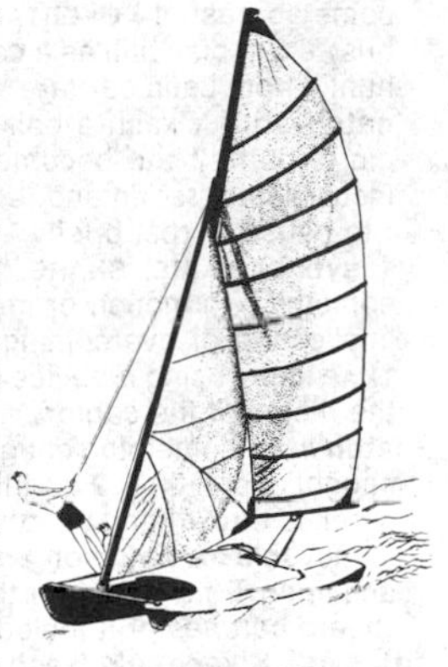
catamaran 2

cat•a•mount \'kat-ə-,maůnt\ *n* : any of various wild cats: as **a** : COUGAR **b** : LYNX [Middle English *cat of the mountain*]
1cat•a•pult \'kat-ə-,pəlt, -,půlt\ *n* **1** : an ancient military device for hurling missiles **2** : a device for launching an airplane at flying speed (as from the deck of an aircraft carrier) [Latin *catapulta*, from Greek *katapaltēs*, from *kata* "down" + *pallein* "to hurl"]

1catapult 1

2catapult *vb* **1** : to throw or launch by or as if by a catapult **2** : to become catapulted
cat•a•ract \'kat-ə-,rakt\ *n* **1** : a clouding of the lens of the eye or of its capsule obstructing the passage of light **2 a** : WATERFALL; *esp* : a large one over a precipice **b** : steep rapids in a river **c** : FLOOD 3 ⟨a *cataract* of words⟩ [Latin *cataracta* "waterfall, portcullis", from Greek *kataraktēs*, from *katarassein* "to dash down", from *kata* "down" + *arassein* "to strike, dash"]
ca•tarrh \kə-'tär\ *n* : inflammation of a mucous membrane; *esp* : one chronically affecting the human nose and air passages [Late Latin *catarrhus*, from Greek *katarrhous*, from *katarrhein* "to flow down", from *kata* "down" + *rhein* "to flow"] — **ca•tarrh•al** \-'tär-əl\ *adj*
ca•tas•tro•phe \kə-'tas-trə-fē\ *n* **1** : the final event of the dramatic action especially of a tragedy **2** : a momentous tragic event : DISASTER **3** : a violent and sudden change in a feature of the earth **4** : utter failure or ruin : FIASCO [Greek *katas-*

\ə\ **abut**	\aů\ **out**	\i\ **tip**	\ȯ\ **saw**	\ů\ **foot**
\ər\ **further**	\ch\ **chin**	\ī\ **life**	\ȯi\ **coin**	\y\ **yet**
\a\ **mat**	\e\ **pet**	\j\ **job**	\th\ **thin**	\yü\ **few**
\ā\ **take**	\ē\ **easy**	\ng\ **sing**	\t͟h\ **this**	\yů\ **cure**
\ä\ **cot, cart**	\g\ **go**	\ō\ **bone**	\ü\ **food**	\zh\ **vision**

trophē, from *katastrephein* "to overturn", from *kata* "down" + *strephein* "to turn, twist"] **syn** see DISASTER — **cat•a•stroph•ic** \ˌkat-ə-ˈsträf-ik\ *adj* — **cat•a•stroph•i•cal•ly** \-ˈsträf-i-kə-lē, -klē\ *adv*

cat•bird \ˈkat-ˌbərd\ *n* **:** a dark gray American songbird with black cap and reddish under tail coverts

cat•boat \-ˌbōt\ *n* **:** a sailboat with a single mast set far forward and a single large sail extended by a long boom

cat•call \-ˌkȯl\ *n* **:** a loud or raucous cry made to express disapproval (as at a sports event) — **catcall** *vb*

[1]**catch** \ˈkach, ˈkech\ *vb* **caught** \ˈkȯt\; **catch•ing 1 a :** to capture or seize in flight or motion ⟨*catch* a thief⟩ ⟨*catch* a ball⟩ **b :** TRAP 1a ⟨*caught* in a lie⟩ **c :** DECEIVE 1, MISLEAD **2 a :** to discover unexpectedly ⟨was *caught* in the act⟩ **b :** to check suddenly ⟨*catch* oneself before giving away a secret⟩ **3 a :** to take in and retain ⟨a barrel to *catch* rainwater⟩ **b :** to take in with the mind or senses ⟨*catch* an explanation⟩ ⟨barely *caught* the whisper⟩ **4 a :** to get entangled ⟨*catch* a sleeve on a nail⟩ **b :** to engage firmly ⟨this lock will not *catch*⟩ **c :** to fasten in position **5 :** to become affected by ⟨*catch* a cold⟩ **6 :** to take or get momentarily or quickly ⟨*catch* a glimpse of a friend⟩ **7 a :** to come abreast of **:** OVERTAKE **b :** to get aboard in time ⟨*catch* a bus⟩ **8 :** to play ball as a catcher [Old North French *cachier* "to hunt", from Latin *captare* "to chase", from *capere* "to take"] — **catch•able** \ˈkach-ə-bəl, ˈkech-\ *adj* — **catch fire 1 :** to begin to burn **2 :** to become excited or exciting — **catch it :** to incur blame, reprimand, or punishment — **catch one's breath :** to pause or rest briefly

• syn CAPTURE, SNARE, TRAP: CATCH implies the seizing of something in motion or in flight or in hiding; CAPTURE adds an implication of overcoming resistance or difficulty; SNARE and TRAP imply using a device that catches by surprise and holds at the mercy of the captor.

[2]**catch** *n* **1 :** something caught; *esp* **:** the total quantity (as of fish) caught at one time **2 a :** the act of catching **b :** a game in which a ball is thrown and caught **3 :** something that checks or holds immovable ⟨a *catch* on a safety pin⟩ **4 :** one worth catching or acquiring **5 :** a round for three or more voices **6 :** FRAGMENT 1 ⟨heard *catches* of a melody⟩ **7 :** a concealed difficulty

catch•all \ˈkach-ˌȯl, ˈkech-\ *n* **:** something to hold odds and ends

catch•er \ˈkach-ər, ˈkech-\ *n* **:** one that catches; *esp* **:** a baseball player stationed behind home plate

catch•ing *adj* **1 :** INFECTIOUS, CONTAGIOUS **2 :** CATCHY 1

catch•ment \ˈkach-mənt, ˈkech-\ *n* **1 :** the action of catching water **2 :** something that catches water

catch on *vi* **1 :** to understand the nature of something ⟨*caught on* to the plot⟩ **2 :** to become popular ⟨a tune that really *caught on*⟩

catch•pen•ny \ˈkach-ˌpen-ē, ˈkech-\ *adj* **:** intended to appeal to the ignorant or unwary especially by cheap or sensational quality **:** GIMCRACK

catch•up \ˈkech-əp, ˈkach-; ˈkat-səp\ *variant of* CATSUP

catch•word \ˈkach-ˌwərd, ˈkech-\ *n* **1 :** GUIDE WORD **2 :** a word or expression repeated until it becomes associated with a party, school, or viewpoint

catchy \ˈkach-ē, ˈkech-ē\ *adj* **catch•i•er**; **-est 1 :** likely to attract ⟨a *catchy* tune⟩ **2 :** apt to entangle one **:** TRICKY ⟨a *catchy* question⟩

cat•e•chism \ˈkat-ə-ˌkiz-əm\ *n* **1 :** a summary of religious doctrine often in the form of questions and answers **2 :** a set of formal questions put as a test — **cat•e•chet•i•cal** \ˌkat-ə-ˈket-i-kəl\ *adj* — **cat•e•chis•mal** \-ˈkiz-məl\ *adj* — **cat•e•chis•tic** \-ˈkis-tik\ *adj*

cat•e•chist \ˈkat-ə-ˌkist, -i-kəst\ *n* **:** one that catechizes

cat•e•chize \ˈkat-ə-ˌkīz\ *vt* **1 :** to instruct systematically especially by questions, answers, and explanations and corrections; *esp* **:** to give religious instruction in this manner **2 :** to question systematically or closely [Late Latin *catechizare,* from Greek *katēchein* "to teach", literally, "to din into", from *kata* "down" + *ēchein* "to resound", from *ēchē* "sound"] — **cat•e•chiz•er** *n*

cat•e•chu•men \ˌkat-ə-ˈkyü-mən\ *n* **1 :** a convert to Christianity receiving training in doctrine and discipline before baptism **2 :** one receiving instruction in the basic doctrines of Christianity before being admitted as a member of a church [derived from Greek *katēchoumenos,* from *katēchein* "to teach, catechize"]

cat•e•gor•i•cal \ˌkat-ə-ˈgȯr-i-kəl, -ˈgär-\ *also* **cat•e•gor•ic** \-ik\ *adj* **1 :** involving neither qualification nor reservation **:** ABSOLUTE ⟨a *categorical* denial⟩ **2 :** of, relating to, or being a category [Late Latin *categoricus,* from Greek *katēgorikos,* from *katēgoria* "affirmation, category"] — **cat•e•gor•i•cal•ly** \-i-kə-lē, -klē\ *adv*

cat•e•go•rize \ˈkat-i-gə-ˌrīz\ *vt* **:** to put into a category **:** CLASSIFY — **cat•e•go•ri•za•tion** \ˌkat-i-gə-rə-ˈzā-shən\ *n*

cat•e•go•ry \ˈkat-ə-ˌgōr-ē, -ˌgȯr-\ *n, pl* **-ries 1 :** a division in a system of classification ⟨courses in the liberal arts *category*⟩ **2 :** a unit of a larger whole made up of members sharing one or more characteristics **:** CLASS ⟨a new *category* of computers⟩ [Late Latin *categoria,* from Greek *katēgoria* "predication, category", from *katēgorein* "to accuse, affirm, predicate", from *kata* "down" + *agora* "public assembly"]

cat•e•nate \ˈkat-ə-ˌnāt\ *vt* **:** to connect in a series **:** LINK [Latin *catenare,* from *catena* "chain"] — **cat•e•na•tion** \ˌkat-ə-ˈnā-shən\ *n*

ca•ter \ˈkāt-ər\ *vi* **1 :** to provide a supply of food **2 :** to supply what is required or desired ⟨*catered* to their whims⟩ [Anglo-French *acatour* "buyer of provisions", from Old North French *acater* "to buy"]

cat•er•cor•ner \ˌkat-ē-ˈkȯr-nər, ˌkat-ə-, ˌkit-ē-\ *or* **cat•er-cor•nered** \-nərd\ *or* **cat•ty-cor•ner** *or* **kit•ty-cor•ner** \-nər\ *or* **cat•ty-cor•nered** *or* **kit•ty-cor•nered** \-nərd\ *adv or adj* **:** in a diagonal or oblique position **:** on a diagonal or oblique line [obsolete *cater* "four in cards or dice"]

ca•ter•er \ˈkāt-ər-ər\ *n* **:** one that caters; *esp* **:** one that provides food and service for a social affair

cat•er•pil•lar \ˈkat-ə-ˌpil-ər, ˈkat-ər-ˌ\ *n* **:** the wormlike larva of a butterfly or moth; *also* **:** any of various similar insect larvae (as of a sawfly) [Old North French *catepelose,* literally, "hairy cat"]

caterpillar

Caterpillar *trademark* — used for a tractor that travels on two endless belts for use on rough or soft ground

cat•er•waul \ˈkat-ər-ˌwȯl\ *vi* **:** to utter the characteristic harsh cry of a rutting cat or a similar sound [Middle English *caterwawen*] — **caterwaul** *n*

cat•fish \ˈkat-ˌfish\ *n* **:** any of numerous usually stout-bodied large-headed fishes (order Ostariophysi) with long sensory barbels

cat•gut \-ˌgət\ *n* **:** a tough cord made usually from sheep intestines and used for strings of musical instruments and rackets and for sewing in surgery

ca•thar•sis \kə-ˈthär-səs\ *n, pl* **-thar•ses** \-ˈthär-ˌsēz\ **1 :** a purification that brings about spiritual renewal or release from tension ⟨the *catharsis* of tears⟩ **2 :** release from an emotional problem through expression of its unconscious basis [Greek *katharsis,* from Greek *kathairein* "to purge", from *katharos* "pure"]

[1]**ca•thar•tic** \-ˈthärt-ik\ *adj* **:** of or relating to catharsis or to a cathartic

[2]**cathartic** *n* **:** PURGATIVE, LAXATIVE

ca•the•dra \kə-ˈthē-drə\ *n* **:** a bishop's official throne [Latin, "chair", from Greek *kathedra,* from *kata* "down" + *hedra* "seat"]

[1]**ca•the•dral** \kə-ˈthē-drəl\ *adj* **1 :** of, relating to, or containing a bishop's throne **2 :** of or relating to a cathedral

[2]**cathedral** *n* **:** a church that contains a bishop's throne and is the principal church of a diocese

ca•thep•sin \kə-ˈthep-sən\ *n* **:** a proteinase that functions inside the body cells [Greek *kathepsein* "to digest", from *kata* "down" + *hepsein* "to boil"]

cath•e•ter \ˈkath-ət-ər\ *n* **:** a slender tube for insertion (as for medication or removal of contents) into a bodily passage or cavity [Late Latin, from Greek *kathetēr,* from *kathienai* "to send down", from *kata* "down" + *hienai* "to send"]

cath•ode \ˈkath-ˌōd\ *n* **1 :** the negative electrode of an electrolytic cell to which the positive ions are attracted — compare ANODE **2 :** the positive terminal of a primary cell or of a storage battery that is delivering current **3 :** the electron-emitting electrode of an electron tube [Greek *kathodos* "way down", from *kata* "down" + *hodos* "way"] — **ca•thod•ic** \ka-ˈthäd-ik\ *adj*

cathode ray *n* **1 :** one of the high-speed electrons projected in a stream from the heated cathode of a vacuum tube under the propulsion of a strong electric field **2 :** a stream of cathode-ray electrons

cathode-ray tube *n* **:** a vacuum tube in which cathode rays usually in the form of a slender beam are projected upon a fluorescent screen and produce a luminous spot

cath•o•lic \ˈkath-lik, -ə-lik\ *adj* **1 :** COMPREHENSIVE 1, UNIVERSAL; *esp* **:** broad in sympathies, tastes, or interests **2** *cap* **a :** of, relating to, or forming the church universal **b :** of or relating to the church of which the pope is head **:** Roman Catholic [Late Latin *catholicus,* from Greek *katholikos* "universal, general", from *katholou* "in general", from *kata* "by" + *holos* "whole"] — **ca•thol•i•cal•ly** \kə-ˈthäl-i-kə-lē, -klē\ *adv* — **Ca•thol•i•cism** \kə-ˈthäl-ə-ˌsiz-əm\ *n* — **ca•thol•i•cize** \kə-ˈthäl-ə-ˌsīz\ *vb*

Catholic *n* **1 :** a person who belongs to the universal Christian church **2 :** a member of a Catholic church; *esp* **:** ROMAN CATHOLIC

cath•o•lic•i•ty \ˌkath-ə-ˈlis-ət-ē\ *n* **1** *cap* **:** the character of being in conformity with a Catholic church **2 a :** liberality of sentiments or views **b :** comprehensive range

cat•ion \ˈkat-ˌī-ən\ *n* **:** the ion in an electrolyzed solution that migrates to the cathode; *also* **:** a positively charged ion [Greek *kation,* from *katienai* "to go down", from *kata* "down" + *ienai* "to go"]

cat•kin \ˈkat-kən\ *n* **:** a flower cluster that is a usually long ament densely crowded with bracts [from its resemblance to a cat's tail]

cat•like \ˈkat-ˌlīk\ *adj* **:** resembling a cat; *esp* **:** STEALTHY

cat•nap \-ˌnap\ *n* **:** a very short light nap — **catnap** *vi*

cat•nip \-ˌnip\ *n* **:** a common strong-scented mint of which cats are especially fond [*cat* + obsolete *nep* "catnip", from Old English *nepte,* from Latin *nepeta*]

cat-o'-nine-tails \ˌkat-ə-ˈnīn-ˌtālz\ *n, pl* **cat-o'-nine-tails :** a whip used in flogging and made of nine knotted cords fastened to a handle

cat's cradle *n* **:** a game in which a string looped on the fingers in such a way as to resemble a small cradle is transferred to the hands of another person

cat's-eye \ˈkats-ˌī\ *n* **1 :** any of various gems (as a chrysoberyl or a chalcedony) exhibiting opalescent reflections from within **2 :** a glass playing marble with a colored area that resembles the eye of a cat

cat's-paw \ˈkats-ˌpȯ\ *n* **1 :** a light breeze that ruffles the surface of the water in patches **2 :** a person used by another person for his or her own ends

cat•sup *or* **ketch•up** *or* **catch•up** \ˈkech-əp, ˈkach-; ˈkat-səp\ *n* **:** a thick seasoned sauce usually with a tomato base [Malay *kĕchap* "spiced fish sauce"]

cat•tail \ˈkat-ˌtāl\ *n* **:** a tall reedy marsh plant with brown furry spikes of very tiny flowers

cat•tle \ˈkat-l\ *n, pl* **cattle 1 :** domesticated mammals held as property or raised for use; *esp* **:** bovine animals kept on a farm or ranch **2 :** people held to be or treated as if of little importance or worth [Old North French *catel* "personal property", from Medieval Latin *capitale,* from Latin *capitalis* "of the head, capital"]

cattle egret *n* **:** a small white buff-backed egret that is native to the Old World but is now found in parts of the eastern United States

cattle guard *n* **:** a device that consists of a shallow ditch across which ties or rails are laid far enough apart to prevent livestock from crossing and that is often used instead of a gate at a fence opening

cat•tle•man \-mən, -ˌman\ *n* **:** a person who tends or raises cattle

cat•ty \ˈkat-ē\ *adj* **cat•ti•er; -est :** resembling or held to resemble a cat; *esp* **:** slyly spiteful — **cat•ti•ly** \ˈkat-l-ē\ *adv* — **cat•ti•ness** \ˈkat-ē-nəs\ *n*

cat•ty-cor•ner *or* **cat•ty-cor•nered** *variant of* CATERCORNER

cat•walk \ˈkat-ˌwȯk\ *n* **:** a narrow walk or way (as along a bridge or over some structure)

Cau•ca•sian \kȯ-ˈkā-zhən, -ˈkazh-ən\ *adj* **1 :** of or relating to the Caucasus or its inhabitants **2 a :** of, relating to, or designating the white race of humankind as classified according to physical features **b :** of, relating to, or designating the white race as defined by law (as in South Africa) as composed of persons of European, North African, or southwest Asian ancestry — **Caucasian** *n* — **Cau•ca•soid** \ˈkȯ-kə-ˌsȯid\ *adj or n*

cau•cus \ˈkȯ-kəs\ *n* **:** a closed meeting of members of the same political party or faction usually to select candidates or decide policy [probably of American Indian origin] — **caucus** *vi*

cau•dad \ˈkȯ-ˌdad\ *adv* **:** toward the tail or posterior end [Latin *cauda* "tail" + English *-ad*]

cau•dal \ˈkȯd-l\ *adj* **1 :** of, relating to, or being a tail **2 :** situated in or directed toward the hind part of the body [Latin *cauda* "tail"] — **cau•dal•ly** \-l-ē\ *adv*

caudal fin *n* **:** the unpaired fin at the posterior end of the body of a fish

cau•di•llo \kau̇-ˈthē-yō, -ˈthēl-yō\ *n, pl* **-di•llos :** a Spanish or Latin-American military dictator [Spanish, from Late Latin *capitellum* "small head", from Latin *caput* "head"]

cau•dle \ˈkȯd-l\ *n* **:** a drink usually of warm ale or wine mixed with bread or gruel, eggs, sugar, and spices [Old North French *caudel,* from *caut* "warm", from Latin *calidus*]

caught *past of* CATCH

caul \ˈkȯl\ *n* **1 :** the large fatty omentum covering the intestines **2 :** the amnion especially when covering the head at birth [Middle French *cale*]

caul•dron *variant of* CALDRON

cau•li•flow•er \ˈkȯ-li-ˌflau̇-ər, -ˌflau̇r\ *n* **:** a garden plant closely related to the cabbage and grown for its compact edible head of usually white undeveloped flowers; *also* **:** the flower head used as a vegetable [Italian *cavolfiore,* from *cavolo* "cabbage" (from Latin *caulis* "stem, cabbage") + *fiore* "flower", from Latin *flor-, flos*]

caulifower ear *n* **:** an ear deformed from injury and excessive growth of scar tissue

[1]**caulk** *or* **calk** \ˈkȯk\ *vt* **1 :** to waterproof the seams of by filling with a watertight substance **2 :** to make tight against leakage [Old North French *cauquer* "to trample", from Latin *calcare,* from *calx* "heel"] — **caulk•er** *n*

[2]**caulk** *variant of* CALK

caus•al \ˈkȯ-zəl\ *adj* **1 :** expressing or indicating cause **2 :** of, relating to, or being a cause **3 :** involving causation or a cause **4 :** having a cause — **caus•al•ly** \-zə-lē\ *adv*

cau•sal•i•ty \kȯ-ˈzal-ət-ē\ *n, pl* **-ties 1 :** a causal quality or agency **2 :** the relation between a cause and its effect or between regularly related events or facts

cau•sa•tion \kȯ-ˈzā-shən\ *n* **1 a :** the act or process of causing **b :** the act or agency by which an effect is produced **2 :** CAUSALITY

caus•ative \ˈkȯ-zət-iv\ *adj* **1 :** functioning as a cause or agent **2 :** expressing causation — **caus•ative•ly** *adv*

[1]**cause** \ˈkȯz\ *n* **1 :** something or someone that brings about a result **:** one that is the source of an action or state **2 :** a good reason ⟨a *cause* for anxiety⟩ **3 a :** a ground of legal action **b :** CASE 5a **c :** a matter or question to be decided (as by a court) **4 :** a principle or movement strongly defended or supported [Old French, from Latin *causa*] — **cause•less** \-ləs\ *adj*

• **syn** CAUSE, REASON, OCCASION mean something that produces an effect. CAUSE applies to any event, circumstance, or condition that brings about or helps bring about a result ⟨an icy road was the *cause* of the accident⟩ REASON applies to a traceable or explainable cause of a known effect or action ⟨the *reason* I was late was that my car would not start⟩ OCCASION applies to a particular time or situation at which underlying causes become effective ⟨the assassination was the *occasion* of the war⟩

[2]**cause** *vt* **1 :** to serve as cause of ⟨fire *caused* the damage⟩ **2 :** to bring about by command, authority, or force ⟨*caused* all offenders to appear⟩ — **caus•er** *n*

cause cé•lè•bre \ˌkōz-sā-ˈlebr, ˌkȯz-\ *n, pl* **causes cé•lè•bres** *same*\ **:** something (as a scandalous affair or a controversial legal case) that attracts great interest [French, literally, "celebrated case"]

cau•se•rie \ˌkōz-ˈrē, -ə-rē\ *n* **1 :** light informal talk **2 :** a short informal composition [French, from *causer* "to chat", from Latin *causari* "to plead, discuss", from *causa* "cause"]

cause•way \ˈkȯz-ˌwā\ *n* **:** a raised way especially across wet ground or water [Middle English *cauciwey,* from *cauci* "cause-

way" (from Old North French *caucie,* from Medieval Latin *calciata* "paved highway", from *calciatus* "paved with limestone", from Latin *calx* "limestone") + *wey* "way"]
caus•tic \ˈkȯ-stik\ *adj* **1 :** capable of eating away by chemical action : CORROSIVE **2 :** CUTTING 3, INCISIVE ⟨*caustic* wit⟩ [Latin *causticus,* from Greek *kaustikos,* from *kaiein* "to burn"] — **caustic** *n* — **caus•ti•cal•ly** \-sti-kə-lē, -klē\ *adv*
caustic lime *n* : LIME 2a
caustic potash *n* : POTASSIUM HYDROXIDE
caustic soda *n* : SODIUM HYDROXIDE
cau•ter•ize \ˈkȯt-ə-ˌrīz\ *vb* : to burn with a hot iron or a caustic substance usually to destroy infected tissue ⟨*cauterize* a wound⟩ [derived from Greek *kaiein* "to burn"] — **cau•ter•iza•tion** \ˌkȯt-ə-rə-ˈzā-shən\ *n*
¹cau•tion \ˈkȯ-shən\ *n* **1 :** ADMONITION, WARNING **2 :** careful avoidance of unnecessary risk [Latin *cautio* "precaution", from *cavēre* "to be on one's guard"]
²caution *vt* **cau•tioned; cau•tion•ing** \ˈkȯ-shə-ning, ˈkȯsh-ning\ : to advise caution to **syn** see WARN
cau•tion•ary \ˈkȯ-shə-ˌner-ē\ *adj* : serving as or offering a warning ⟨a *cautionary* tale⟩
cau•tious \ˈkȯ-shəs\ *adj* : marked by or given to caution ⟨a *cautious* reply⟩ ⟨a *cautious* driver⟩ — **cau•tious•ly** *adv* — **cau•tious•ness** *n*
cav•al•cade \ˌkav-əl-ˈkād, ˈkav-əl-ˌ\ *n* **1 a :** a procession of riders or carriages **b :** a procession of vehicles or ships **2 :** a sequence of dramatic scenes : PAGEANT ⟨a *cavalcade* of American history⟩ [Middle French, "horseback ride", from Italian *cavalcata,* from *cavalcare* "to go on horseback", from Latin *caballus* "horse"]
¹cav•a•lier \ˌkav-ə-ˈliər\ *n* **1 :** a gentleman trained in arms and horsemanship **2 :** a mounted soldier : KNIGHT **3** *cap* **:** an adherent of Charles I of England **4 :** GALLANT 2a [Middle French, from Italian *cavaliere,* derived from Latin *caballus* "horse"]
²cavalier *adj* **1 :** DEBONAIR **2 :** treating important matters or the interests of other people with contemptuous disregard **3 a** *cap* **:** of or relating to the party of Charles I of England in his struggles with the Puritans and Parliament **b :** ARISTOCRATIC — **cav•a•lier•ly** *adv* — **cav•a•lier•ness** *n*
cav•al•ry \ˈkav-əl-rē\ *n, pl* **-ries :** a highly mobile army component mounted on horseback or moving in motor vehicles [Italian *cavalleria* "cavalry, chivalry", from *cavaliere* "cavalier"] — **cav•al•ry•man** \-rē-mən, -ˌman\ *n*
¹cave \ˈkāv\ *n* : a hollowed-out place in the earth and especially in the side of a hill or cliff; *esp* **:** a cavern that opens to the surface of the ground [Old French, from Latin *cava,* from *cavus* "hollow"]
²cave *vb* **1 :** to fall or cause to fall in or down especially from being undermined : COLLAPSE ⟨the wall *caved* in⟩ **2 :** to cease to resist : SUBMIT ⟨the defenders *caved* in and surrendered⟩
ca•ve•at \ˈkā-vē-ˌat, ˈkav-ē-; ˈkäv-ē-ˌät\ *n* : WARNING 2 [Latin, "let him or her beware", from *cavēre* "to be on one's guard"]
caveat emp•tor \-ˈem-tər, -ˈemp-, -ˌtȯr\ *n* : a warning that without a warranty the buyer of goods takes the risk of their quality upon himself [New Latin, "let the buyer beware"]
cave dweller *n* : one (as a prehistoric human) that lives in a cave
cave–in \ˈkā-ˌvin\ *n* **1 :** the action of caving in **2 :** a place where earth has caved in
cave•man \ˈkāv-ˌman\ *n* **1 :** a cave dweller especially of the Stone Age **2 :** a man who acts with rough or violent directness especially toward women
cav•ern \ˈkav-ərn\ *n* : a usually natural underground chamber often of large or indefinite extent [Middle French *caverne,* from Latin *caverna,* from *cavus* "hollow"]
cav•ern•ous \-ər-nəs\ *adj* **1 :** having caverns or cavities **2 :** constituting or suggesting a cavern **3 :** composed largely of vascular spaces and capable of filling with blood to bring about the enlargement of a body part — **cav•ern•ous•ly** *adv*
cav•i•ar *or* **cav•i•are** \ˈkav-ē-ˌär *also* ˈkäv-\ *n* : processed salted roe of a large fish (as the sturgeon) prepared as an appetizer [obsolete Italian *caviaro,* from Turkish *havyar*]
cav•il \ˈkav-əl\ *vb* **cav•iled** *or* **cav•illed; cav•il•ing** *or* **cav•il•ling** \ˈkav-ling, -ə-ling\ : to raise trivial and frivolous objections : QUIBBLE [Latin *cavillari* "to jest, cavil", from *cavilla* "raillery"] — **cavil** *n* — **cav•il•er** *or* **cav•il•ler** \-lər, -ə-lər\ *n*
cav•ing \ˈkā-ving\ *n* : the sport of exploring caves : SPELUNKING
cav•i•ta•tion \ˌkav-ə-ˈtā-shən\ *n* : the formation of partial vacuums in a liquid by a swiftly moving body (as a propeller) or by high-frequency sound waves [*cavity* + *-ation*]
cav•i•ty \ˈkav-ət-ē\ *n, pl* **-ties :** an unfilled space within a mass : a hollow place : HOLE ⟨a *cavity* in a tooth⟩ [Middle French *cavité,* derived from Latin *cavus* "hollow"]
ca•vort \kə-ˈvȯrt\ *vi* : to bound or frisk about : CAPER [perhaps alteration of *curvet*]
ca•vy \ˈkā-vē\ *n, pl* **cavies :** any of several short-tailed rough-haired South American rodents; *esp* **:** GUINEA PIG [obsolete Portuguese *çavía* (now *savía*), from Tupi *sawiya* "rat"]
caw \ˈkȯ\ *vi* : to utter the characteristic harsh raucous cry of a crow or a similar sound [imitative] — **caw** *n*
cay \ˈkē, ˈkā\ *n* : a small low island or emergent reef of sand or coral : ISLET, KEY [Spanish *cayo*]
cay•enne pepper \ˌkī-ˌen-, ˌkā-\ *n* : a pungent condiment consisting of the ground dried fruits or seeds of hot peppers; *also* **:** a plant bearing such fruits [Tupi *kyinha*]
cay•man *variant of* CAIMAN
Ca•yu•ga \kē-ˈü-gə, kā-ˈyü-, kī-\ *n* : a member of an Iroquoian people of what is now western New York
cay•use \ˈkī-ˌüs, -ˌyüs; kī-ˈ\ *n* **1** *cap* **:** a member of an Indian people of what is now northeastern Oregon **2 :** a native range horse of the western United States
C clef *n* : a movable clef indicating middle C by its placement on one of the lines of the staff
¹cease \ˈsēs\ *vb* : to come or bring to an end ⟨ordered the soldiers to *cease* firing⟩ [Old French *cesser,* from Latin *cessare* "to delay", from *cessus,* past participle of *cedere* "to withdraw, cede"] **syn** see STOP
²cease *n* : CESSATION — usually used with *without*
cease–fire \ˈsēs-ˈfīr\ *n* **1 :** a military order to cease firing **2 :** a suspension of active hostilities
cease•less \ˈsē-sləs\ *adj* : continuing without end — **cease•less•ly** *adv* — **cease•less•ness** *n*
ce•cro•pia moth \si-ˌkrō-pē-ə-\ *n* : a large silkworm moth that is the largest moth of the eastern United States [Latin *Cecropius* "Athenian", from Greek *Kekropios,* from *Kekrops* "Cecrops", legendary first king of Athens]
ce•cum *or* **cae•cum** \ˈsē-kəm\ *n, pl* **ce•ca** *or* **cae•ca** \-kə\ : a cavity open at one end; *esp* **:** the blind pouch in which the large intestine begins and into which the ileum opens from one side [Latin *intestinum caecum,* literally, "blind intestine"] — **ce•cal** \-kəl\ *adj*
ce•dar \ˈsēd-ər\ *n* **1 a :** any of a genus of usually tall trees of the pine family noted for their fragrant durable wood **b :** any of numerous coniferous trees (as some junipers or arborvitaes) resembling the true cedars especially in the fragrance and durability of their wood **2 :** the wood of a cedar [Old French *cedre,* from Latin *cedrus,* from Greek *kedros*]
ce•dar•bird \ˈsēd-ər-ˌbərd\ *n* : CEDAR WAXWING
cedar waxwing *n* : a long-crested brown waxwing of temperate North America with a yellow band on the tip of the tail
cede \ˈsēd\ *vt* **1 :** to give up or grant usually by treaty **2 :** ASSIGN 1 ⟨*ceded* the farm to their children⟩ [Latin *cedere* "to go, withdraw, yield"] — **ced•er** *n*
ce•dil•la \si-ˈdil-ə\ *n* : a mark placed under the letter *c* (as ç) to show that the *c* is to be pronounced like *s* [Spanish, "the obsolete letter ç (actually a medieval form of the letter *z*), cedilla", from *ceda, zeda* "the letter z", from Late Latin *zeta* "zeta", from Greek *zēta*]
cei•ba \ˈsā-bə\ *n* : a massive tropical tree related to the silk-cotton tree that bears large pods containing a silky floss which yields the fiber kapok [Spanish]
ceil•ing \ˈsē-ling\ *n* **1 :** the overhead inside surface of a room **2 :** something that overhangs like a shelter **3 a :** the greatest height at which an airplane can maintain level flight or operate efficiently **b :** the height above the ground of the base of the lowest layer of clouds when over half of the sky is obscured **4 :** an upper usually prescribed limit ⟨a price *ceiling*⟩ [Middle English *celen* "to furnish with a ceiling", probably from Latin *caelare* "to carve", from *caelum* "chisel", from *caedere* "to cut"]
cel•an•dine \ˈsel-ən-ˌdīn, -ˌdēn\ *n* **1 :** a yellow-flowered biennial herb related to the poppy **2 :** a perennial tuber-forming buttercup — called also *lesser celandine* [Middle French *celidoine,* from Latin *chelidonia,* derived from Greek *chelidōn* "swallow"]
cel•e•brant \ˈsel-ə-brənt\ *n* : one who celebrates; *esp* **:** the priest who is celebrating a mass
cel•e•brate \ˈsel-ə-ˌbrāt\ *vb* **1 :** to perform publicly and accord-

ing to rule or form : officiate at ⟨*celebrate* a mass⟩ **2** : to honor or honor something (as a holiday or event) with special activities or festivities ⟨*celebrate* one's birthday with a party⟩ **3** : to praise or make known publicly [Latin *celebrare* "to frequent, celebrate", from *celeber* "much frequented, famous"] **syn** see KEEP — **cel•e•bra•tion** \ˌsel-ə-ˈbrā-shən\ *n* — **cel•e•bra•tor** \ˈsel-ə-ˌbrāt-ər\ *n*

cel•e•brat•ed *adj* : widely known and often referred to : RENOWNED **syn** see FAMOUS — **cel•e•brat•ed•ness** *n*

ce•leb•ri•ty \sə-ˈleb-rət-ē\ *n, pl* **-ties** **1** : the state of being celebrated **2** : a celebrated person ⟨television *celebrities*⟩

ce•le•ri•ac \sə-ˈler-ē-ˌak, -ˈlir-\ *n* : a celery grown for its thickened edible root [derived from *celery*]

ce•ler•i•ty \sə-ˈler-ət-ē\ *n, pl* **-ties** : rapidity of motion or action : SWIFTNESS [Middle French *célérité,* from Latin *celeritas,* from *celer* "swift"]

• **syn** CELERITY, ALACRITY mean quickness of movement or action. CELERITY stresses speed in moving especially so as to accomplish work ⟨got dinner ready with remarkable *celerity*⟩ ALACRITY stresses promptness in responding and often suggests readiness or eagerness ⟨the students volunteered with surprising *alacrity*⟩

cel•ery \ˈsel-rē, -ə-rē\ *n* : a European herb of the carrot family widely grown for its thick edible leafstalks; *also* : leafstalks of celery used for food [probably from Italian dialect *selero,* from Late Latin *selinon,* from Greek]

ce•les•ta \sə-ˈles-tə\ *n* : a keyboard instrument with hammers that strike steel plates producing a tone similar to that of a glockenspiel [French *célesta,* from *céleste,* literally, "heavenly", from Latin *caelestis*]

ce•les•tial \sə-ˈles-chəl\ *adj* **1** : of, relating to, or suggesting the spiritual heaven : HEAVENLY ⟨*celestial* beings⟩ **2** : of or relating to the sky or heavens ⟨a star is a *celestial* body⟩ [Middle French, from Latin *caelestis,* from *caelum* "sky, heaven"] — **ce•les•tial•ly** \-chə-lē\ *adv*

celestial equator *n* : the great circle on the celestial sphere midway between the celestial poles

celestial navigation *n* : navigation by observation of the positions of celestial bodies

celestial pole *n* : one of the two points on the celestial sphere around which the diurnal rotation of the stars appears to take place

celestial sphere *n* : an imaginary sphere of infinite radius against which the celestial bodies appear to be projected

ce•li•ac \ˈsē-lē-ˌak\ *adj* : of or relating to the abdominal cavity [Latin *coeliacus,* from Greek *koiliakos,* from *koilia* "cavity", from *koilos* "hollow"]

celiac disease *n* : a chronic nutritional disorder in young children in which fats are not digested and used in a normal way

cel•i•ba•cy \ˈsel-ə-bə-sē\ *n* : the state of not being married; *esp* : the state of one bound by vow not to marry

cel•i•bate \ˈsel-ə-bət\ *n* : one who lives in celibacy [Latin *caelibatus,* from *caelebs* "unmarried"] — **celibate** *adj*

cell \ˈsel\ *n* **1 a** : a one-room dwelling occupied by a solitary person (as a hermit) **b** : a single room (as in a convent or prison) usually for one person **2** : a small compartment (as in a honeycomb), receptacle (as for a polyp), cavity (as in a plant ovary), or bounded space (as in an insect wing) **3** : a tiny mass of protoplasm that includes a nucleus and is enclosed by a semipermeable membrane and that is the fundamental unit of living matter and the basic structural element of plants and animals **4 a** : a receptacle (as a jar) containing electrodes and an electrolyte either for generating electricity by chemical action or for use in electrolysis **b** : a single unit in a device for converting radiant energy into electrical energy or for varying the intensity of an electric current in accordance with radiation **5** : the basic and usually smallest unit of an organization or movement; *esp* : the primary unit of a Communist organization [derived from Latin *cella* "small room"] — **celled** \ˈseld\ *adj*

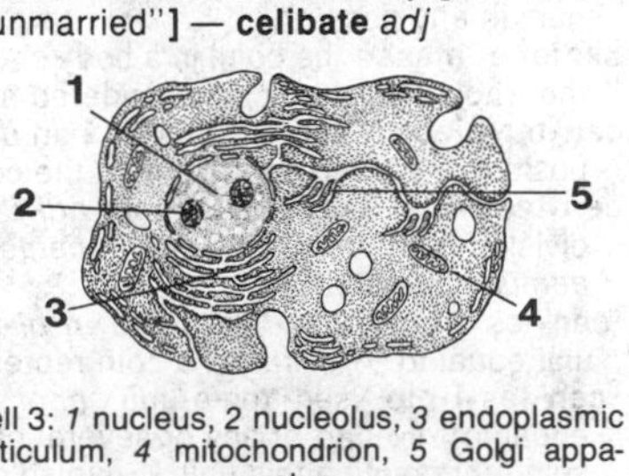

cell 3: *1* nucleus, *2* nucleolus, *3* endoplasmic reticulum, *4* mitochondrion, *5* Golgi apparatus

cel•lar \ˈsel-ər\ *n* **1** : BASEMENT 1 **2** : a stock of wines [Anglo-French *celer,* from Latin *cellarium* "storeroom", from *cella* "small room"]

cel•lar•age \ˈsel-ə-rij\ *n* **1** : a cellar especially for storage **2** : charge for storage in a cellar

cell body *n* : the nucleus-containining central part of a neuron exclusive of its axons and dendrites

cell division *n* : the process by which cells multiply involving both nuclear and cytoplasmic divisions — compare MEIOSIS, MITOSIS

cel•list \ˈchel-əst\ *n* : one that plays the cello

cell membrane *n* **1** : PLASMA MEMBRANE **2** : CELL WALL

cel•lo \ˈchel-ō\ *n, pl* **cellos** : the member of the violin family tuned an octave below the viola [short for *violoncello*]

cel•lo•phane \ˈsel-ə-ˌfān\ *n* : a thin transparent usually waterproof material made from cellulose and used especially as a wrapping [French, from *cellulose* + *-phane* (as in *diaphane* "diaphanous")]

cell plate *n* : the rudiment of a new cell wall that forms between dividing plant cells

cell sap *n* : the liquid consisting of a watery solution of nutrients and wastes that fills the vacuole of most plant cells

cell theory *n* : a generally accepted theory in biology that the cell is the fundamental structural and functional unit of living matter and that all cells come from preexisting cells

cel•lu•lar \ˈsel-yə-lər\ *adj* **1** : of, relating to, or consisting of cells **2** : containing cavities : having a porous texture — **cel•lu•lar•i•ty** \ˌsel-yə-ˈlar-ət-ē\ *n*

cellular respiration *n* : the metabolic oxidative processes of the cell (as the Krebs cycle) by means of which organic molecules (as glucose, fatty acids, and proteins) are broken down to provide energy which is stored in ATP

cel•lu•lase \ˈsel-yə-ˌlās, -ˌlāz\ *n* : an enzyme that hydrolyzes cellulose

cel•lu•loid \ˈsel-yə-ˌlȯid, -ə-\ *n* **1** : a tough flammable thermoplastic composed essentially of cellulose nitrate and camphor **2** : a motion-picture film

cel•lu•lose \ˈsel-yə-ˌlōs\ *n* : a complex carbohydrate constituting the chief part of the cell walls of plants, yielding many fibrous products, and being commonly obtained from vegetable matter (as wood or cotton) as a white fibrous substance that is used in making various products (as rayon and cellophane) [French, from *cellule* "living cell", from New Latin *cellula,* from Latin *cella* "small room"]

cellulose acetate *n* : any of several compounds formed especially by the action of acetic acid, anhydride of acetic acid, and sulfuric acid on cellulose and used for making textile fibers, packaging sheets, photographic films, and varnishes

cellulose nitrate *n* : a compound formed by the action of nitric acid on cellulose in the presence of sulfuric acid and used for making explosives, plastics, rayon, and varnishes

cel•lu•los•ic \ˌsel-yə-ˈlō-sik, -zik\ *adj* : of, relating to, or made from cellulose ⟨*cellulosic* fibers⟩ — **cellulosic** *n*

cell wall *n* : the firm nonliving and usually chiefly cellulose wall that encloses and supports most plant cells

Cel•sius \ˈsel-sē-əs, ˈsel-shəs\ *adj* : relating to, conforming to, or having a thermometer scale on which the interval between the freezing point and the boiling point of water is divided into 100 degrees with 0° representing the freezing point and 100° the boiling point ⟨10° *Celsius*⟩ — abbreviation *C* [Anders *Celsius,* died 1744, Swedish astronomer]

Celt \ˈkelt, ˈselt\ *also* **Kelt** \ˈkelt\ *n* **1** : a member of a division of the early Indo-European peoples distributed from the British Isles and Spain to Asia Minor **2** : a modern Gael, Highland Scot, Irishman, Welshman, Cornishman, or Breton [French *Celte,* from Latin *Celtae* "Celts"]

¹Celt•ic \ˈkel-tik, ˈsel-\ *or* **Kelt•ic** \ˈkel-\ *adj* : of, relating to, or characteristic of the Celts or their languages

²Celtic *or* **Keltic** *n* : a branch of the Indo-European language family containing Irish Gaelic, Scottish Gaelic, Manx, Welsh, Breton, and Cornish

cel•tuce \ˈsel-təs\ *n* : a vegetable related to lettuce but grown for its leafstalks that combine the flavor of celery and lettuce [*cel*ery + let*tuce*]

\ə\ **abut**	\au̇\ **out**	\i\ **tip**	\ȯ\ **saw**	\u̇\ **foot**
\ər\ **further**	\ch\ **chin**	\ī\ **life**	\ȯi\ **coin**	\y\ **yet**
\a\ **mat**	\e\ **pet**	\j\ **job**	\th\ **thin**	\yü\ **few**
\ā\ **take**	\ē\ **easy**	\ng\ **sing**	\t͟h\ **this**	\yu̇\ **cure**
\ä\ **cot, cart**	\g\ **go**	\ō\ **bone**	\ü\ **food**	\zh\ **vision**

cem•ba•lo \'chem-bə-,lō\ *n, pl* **-los** *or* **-li** \-,lē\ : HARPSICHORD [Italian]

[1]**ce•ment** \si-'ment\ *n* **1 a :** a powder of alumina, silica, lime, iron oxide, and magnesia burned together in a kiln and finely pulverized and used as an ingredient of mortar and concrete **b** (1) : CONCRETE (2) : MORTAR **2 :** a binding element or agency: as **a :** a substance to make objects adhere to each other **b :** a notion or feeling serving to unite firmly **3 :** CEMENTUM [Old French *ciment,* from Latin *caementum* "stone chips used in making mortar", from *caedere* "to cut"]

[2]**cement** *vb* **1 :** to unite by or as if by cement **2 :** to overlay with concrete — **ce•ment•er** *n*

ce•men•ta•tion \,sē-,men-'tā-shən\ *n* : the act or process of cementing

ce•ment•ite \si-'ment-,īt\ *n* : a hard brittle carbide of iron Fe_3C in steel, cast iron, and iron-carbon alloys

ce•men•tum \si-'ment-əm\ *n* : a specialized external bony layer of the part of a tooth normally within the gum

cem•e•tery \'sem-ə-,ter-ē\ *n, pl* **-ter•ies** : a burial ground [Middle French *cimitere,* from Late Latin *coemeterium,* from Greek *koimētērion* "sleeping chamber, burial place", from *koiman* "to put to sleep"]

cen- *or* **ceno-** *combining form* : new : recent ⟨*Cenozoic*⟩ [Greek *kainos*]

-cene \,sēn\ *adj combining form* : Cenozoic ⟨Eo*cene*⟩

cen•o•bite \'sen-ə-,bīt\ *or* **coe•no•bite** \'sē-nə-\ *n* : a member of a religious group living together [Late Latin *coenobita,* from *coenobium* "monastery", from Late Greek *koinobion,* from Greek *koinos* "common" + *bios* "life"] — **cen•o•bit•ic** \,sen-ə-'bit-ik\ *or* **cen•o•bit•i•cal** \-'bit-i-kəl\ *adj*

cen•o•taph \'sen-ə-,taf\ *n* : a tomb or a monument erected in honor of a person whose body is elsewhere [French *cénotaphe,* from Latin *cenotaphium,* from Greek *kenotaphion,* from *kenos* "empty" + *taphos* "tomb"]

Ce•no•zo•ic \,sē-nə-'zō-ik, ,sen-ə-\ *n* **1 :** the most recent of the five eras of geological history that extends to the present time and is marked by a rapid evolution of mammals and birds and of grasses, shrubs, and various flowering plants — called also *Age of Mammals;* see GEOLOGIC TIME table **2 :** the system of rocks corresponding to the Cenozoic — **Cenozoic** *adj*

cen•ser \'sen-sər\ *n* : a vessel for burning incense; *esp* : a covered incense burner swung on chains in a religious ritual [Middle English *censen* "to burn incense"]

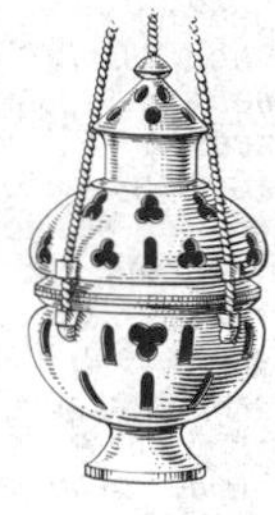

censer

[1]**cen•sor** \'sen-sər\ *n* **1 :** one of two magistrates of ancient Rome acting as census takers, assessors, and inspectors of morals and conduct **2 :** an official who examines publications or communications for objectionable matter [Latin, from *censēre* "to assess, tax"] — **cen•so•ri•al** \sen-'sōr-ē-əl, -'sȯr-\ *adj*

[2]**censor** *vt* **cen•sored; cen•sor•ing** \'sens-ring, -ə-ring\ : to examine in order to suppress or delete anything thought to be harmful or dangerous

• **syn** CENSOR, CENSURE are not actually synonymous but are easily confused. CENSOR denotes examining officially in order to suppress or alter anything thought morally or politically objectionable; CENSURE denotes criticizing adversely and usually publicly or officially.

cen•so•ri•ous \sen-'sōr-ē-əs, -'sȯr-\ *adj* : marked by or given to censure : sternly critical — **cen•so•ri•ous•ly** *adv* — **cen•so•ri•ous•ness** *n*

cen•sor•ship \'sen-sər-,ship\ *n* : the institution, system, or practice of censoring or of censors

[1]**cen•sure** \'sen-chər\ *n* **1 :** the act of blaming or condemning sternly **2 :** an official reprimand [Latin *censura,* from *censēre* "to assess, tax"]

[2]**censure** *vt* **cen•sured; cen•sur•ing** \'sench-ring, -ə-ring\ : to find fault with : criticize as blameworthy **syn** see BLAME, CENSOR — **cen•sur•able** \'sench-rə-bəl, -ə-rə-\ *adj* — **cen•sur•er** \'sen-chər-ər\ *n*

cen•sus \'sen-səs\ *n* **1 :** a periodic governmental counting of population and usually gathering of related statistics **2 :** COUNT 1, TALLY [Latin, from *censēre* "to assess, tax"]

cent \'sent\ *n* **1 :** a unit of value equal to 1/100 part of a basic monetary unit (as of a dollar) **2 :** a coin, token, or note representing one cent [Middle French, "hundred", from Latin *centum*]

cent•are \'sen-,taər, -,teər, -,tär\ *or* **cen•ti•are** \'sent-ē-,aər, -,eər, -,är\ *n* — *see* METRIC SYSTEM table [French *centiare*]

cen•taur \'sen-,tȯr\ *n* : one of a race in Greek mythology who are half man and half horse [Latin *Centaurus,* from Greek *Kentauros*]

cen•ta•vo \sen-'täv-ō\ *n, pl* **-vos 1 :** a unit of value equal to 1/100 part of any of several basic monetary units (as the peso or cruzeiro) **2 :** a coin representing one centavo [Spanish, literally, "hundredth", from Latin *centum* "hundred"]

cen•te•nar•i•an \,sent-n-'er-ē-ən\ *n* : a person who is 100 years old or older — **centenarian** *adj*

cen•ten•a•ry \sen-'ten-ə-rē, 'sent-n-,er-ē\ *n, pl* **-ries** : CENTENNIAL [Latin *centenarius* "of a hundred", from *centeni* "a hundred each", from *centum* "hundred"] — **centenary** *adj*

cen•ten•ni•al \sen-'ten-ē-əl\ *n* : a 100th anniversary or its celebration [Latin *centum* "hundred" + English *-ennial* (as in *biennial*)] — **centennial** *adj* — **cen•ten•ni•al•ly** \-ē-ə-lē\ *adv*

[1]**cen•ter** \'sent-ər\ *n* **1 :** the point in the plane of a circle equidistant from all points on its circumference; *also* : the point within a sphere equidistant from all points on its surface **2 a :** a point, area, person, or thing that is most important in relation to an indicated activity, interest, or condition ⟨*center* of the controversy⟩ **b :** a group of nerve cells having a common function ⟨respiratory *center*⟩ **c :** a region of concentrated population **3 a :** a middle part (as of an army or stage) **b** *often cap* (1) : individuals holding moderate political views especially between those of conservatives and liberals (2) : the views of such individuals **4 :** a player occupying a middle position on a team [Middle French *centre,* from Latin *centrum,* from Greek *kentron* "sharp point, center of a circle", from *kentein* "to prick"]

[2]**center** *vb* **cen•tered; cen•ter•ing** \'sent-ə-ring, 'sen-tring\ **1 :** to place or fix at or around a center or central area or position ⟨*center* a title on the page⟩ **2 :** to gather to a center : CONCENTRATE ⟨*centered* their attention on finances⟩ **3 :** to adjust (as lenses) so that the axes coincide **4 :** to have a center ⟨the search *centered* on one building⟩ **5 a :** to pass (a ball or puck) from either side to or toward the middle of a playing area **b :** to snap (the ball) in football

cen•ter•board \'sent-ər-,bōrd, -,bȯrd\ *n* : a retractable keel used especially in sailboats

center field *n* **1 :** the part of the baseball outfield between right and left field **2 :** the position of the player defending center field — **center fielder** *n*

center of gravity 1 : CENTER OF MASS **2 :** the point at which the entire weight of a body may be considered as concentrated so that if supported at this point the body would remain in equilibrium in any position

center of mass : the point in a body or system of bodies at which the whole mass may be considered as concentrated

cen•ter•piece \'sent-ər-,pēs\ *n* : an object occupying a central position; *esp* : an adornment in the center of a table

cen•tes•i•mal \sen-'tes-ə-məl\ *adj* : marked by or relating to division into hundredths [Latin *centesimus* "hundredth", from *centum* "hundred"]

[1]**cen•tes•i•mo** \chen-'tez-ə-,mō\ *n, pl* **-mi** \-,mē\ **1 :** a monetary unit equal to 1/100 lira **2 :** a coin representing this unit [Italian]

[2]**cen•tes•i•mo** \sen-'tes-ə-,mō\ *n, pl* **-mos 1 :** a monetary unit equal to 1/100 part of any of several basic monetary units **2 :** a coin representing this unit [Spanish *centésimo*]

centi- *combining form* : hundredth part ⟨*centi*meter⟩ [French, from Latin *centum* "hundred"]

cen•ti•grade \'sent-ə-,grād, 'sänt-\ *adj* : CELSIUS — abbreviation *C* [French, from Latin *centum* "hundred" + *gradus* "step, degree"]

cen•ti•gram \-,gram\ *n* — *see* METRIC SYSTEM table

cen•ti•li•ter \-,lēt-ər\ *n* — *see* METRIC SYSTEM table

cen•time \'sän-,tēm, 'sen-\ *n* **1 :** a unit of value equal to 1/100 franc **2 :** a coin representing one centime [French, from *cent* "hundred", from Latin *centum*]

cen•ti•me•ter \'sent-ə-,mēt-ər, 'sänt-\ *n* — *see* METRIC SYSTEM table

centimeter-gram-second *adj* : of, relating to, or being a system of units based upon the centimeter as the unit of length, the gram as the unit of mass, and the second as the unit of time — abbreviation *cgs*

cen•ti•mo \'sent-ə-,mō\ *n, pl* **-mos 1** : a unit of value equal to 1/100 part of any of several basic monetary units (as the peseta) **2** : a coin representing one centimo [Spanish *céntimo*]

cen•ti•pede \'sent-ə-,pēd\ *n* : any of a class (Chilopoda) of long flattened many-segmented arthropods with each segment bearing one pair of legs of which the foremost pair is modified into poison fangs — compare MILLIPEDE [Latin *centipeda,* from *centum* "hundred" + *ped-, pes* "foot"]

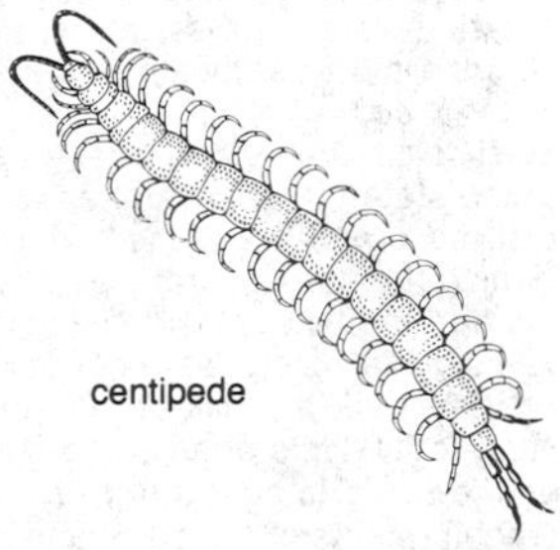
centipede

centr- *or* **centri-** *or* **centro-** *combining form* : center ⟨centroid⟩ [Greek *kentron*]

[1]**cen•tral** \'sen-trəl\ *adj* **1** : containing or constituting a center **2** : ESSENTIAL 3, PRINCIPAL **3** : situated at, in, or near the center **4** : controlling or directing local or branch activities **5** : holding to a middle between extremes : MODERATE **6** : of, relating to, or comprising the brain and spinal cord; *also* : originating within the central nervous system ⟨*central* deafness⟩ — **cen•tral•i•ty** \sen-'tral-ət-ē\ *n* — **cen•tral•ly** \'sen-trə-lē\ *adv*

[2]**central** *n* : a telephone exchange or operator

central angle *n* : an angle with its vertex at the center of a circle and with sides that are radii of the circle

central committee *n* : a large central executive body of a Communist party that is elected to function between party congresses and that elects in turn from its own membership a powerful executive presidium

cen•tral•ism \'sen-trə-,liz-əm\ *n* : the concentration of power and control in the central authority especially of a nation — compare FEDERALISM — **cen•tral•ist** \-ləst\ *n or adj* — **cen•tral•is•tic** \,sen-trə-'lis-tik\ *adj*

cen•tral•ize \'sen-trə-,līz\ *vt* : to concentrate (as authority) in a center or central organization — **cen•tral•i•za•tion** \,sen-trə-lə-'zā-shən\ *n* — **cen•tral•iz•er** \'sen-trə-,lī-zər\ *n*

central nervous system *n* : the part of the nervous system which in vertebrates consists of the brain and spinal cord, to which sensory impulses are transmitted and from which motor impulses pass out, and which supervises and coordinates the activity of the entire nervous system

Central Powers *n* : a coalition of nations in World War I consisting of Germany and Austria-Hungary and their allies Bulgaria and Turkey

Central time *n* : the time of the 6th time zone west of Greenwich that includes the central United States

cen•tre \'sent-ər\ *chiefly British variant of* CENTER

cen•tric \'sen-trik\ *adj* : concentrated about or directed to a center — **cen•tri•cal•ly** \-tri-kə-lē, -klē\ *adv* — **cen•tric•i•ty** \sen-'tris-ət-ē\ *n*

-cen•tric \'sen-trik\ *adj combining form* : having (such) a center or (such or so many) centers : having (something specified) as its center ⟨helio*centric*⟩

cen•trif•u•gal \sen-'trif-yə-gəl, -'trif-i-gəl\ *adj* **1** : proceeding or acting in a direction away from a center or axis **2** : using or acting by centrifugal force ⟨a *centrifugal* pump⟩ [Latin *centrum* "center" + *fugere* "to flee"] — **cen•trif•u•gal•ly** \-gə-lē\ *adv*

centrifugal force *n* : the force that tends to impel a thing or parts of a thing outward from a center of rotation

[1]**cen•tri•fuge** \'sen-trə-,fyüj, 'sän-\ *n* : a machine using centrifugal force for separating substances of different densities, for removing moisture, or for simulating gravitational effects — compare SEPARATOR

[2]**centrifuge** *vt* : to subject to centrifugal action especially in a centrifuge — **cen•trif•u•ga•tion** \,sen-,trif-yə-'gā-shən, -,trif-ə-, ,sän-\ *n*

cen•tri•ole \'sen-trē-,ōl\ *n* : one of a pair of cellular organelles that are adjacent to the nucleus, function in the formation of the mitotic apparatus, and consist of a cylinder with nine tiny tubules arranged peripherally in a circle [German *zentriol,* from *zentrum* "center"]

cen•trip•e•tal \sen-'trip-ət-l\ *adj* : proceeding or acting in a direction toward a center or axis [Latin *centrum* "center" + *petere* "to seek"] — **cen•trip•e•tal•ly** \-l-ē\ *adv*

centripetal force *n* : the force that tends to impel a thing or parts of a thing inward toward a center of rotation

cen•troid \'sen-,trȯid\ *n* : the point of intersection of the medians of a triangle

cen•tro•mere \'sen-trə-,miər\ *n* : the point on a chromosome by which it appears to attach to the spindle in mitosis — **cen•tro•mer•ic** \,sen-trə-'mer-ik, -'miər-\ *adj*

cen•tro•some \'sen-trə-,sōm\ *n* **1** : the centriole-containing region of clear cytoplasm adjacent to the cell nucleus **2** : CENTRIOLE

cen•trum \'sen-trəm\ *n, pl* **centrums** *or* **cen•tra** \-trə\ : the body of a vertebra [Latin, "center"]

cen•tu•ri•on \sen-'tu̇r-ē-ən, -'tyu̇r-\ *n* : an officer commanding a century in a Roman legion [Latin, from *centuria* "century"]

cen•tu•ry \'sench-rē, -ə-rē\ *n, pl* **-ries 1** : a subdivision of the Roman legion **2** : a group, sequence, or series of 100 like things **3** : a Roman voting unit based on property qualifications **4** : a period of 100 years; *esp* : one of the 100-year divisions of the Christian era or of the preceding period [Latin *centuria,* from *centum* "hundred"]

century plant *n* : a commonly cultivated Mexican agave maturing and flowering only once in many years and then dying

cephal- *or* **cephalo-** *combining form* : head ⟨*cephalo*thorax⟩ [Greek *kephalē*]

ce•phal•ic \sə-'fal-ik\ *adj* **1** : of or relating to the head **2** : directed toward or situated on or in or near the head — **ce•phal•i•cal•ly** \-i-kə-lē, -klē\ *adv*

ceph•a•lo•pod \'sef-ə-lə-,päd\ *n* : any of a class (Cephalopoda) of mollusks including the squids, cuttlefishes, and octopuses and having a tubular siphon under the head, a group of muscular sucker-bearing arms, highly developed eyes, and usually a bag of inky fluid which they can eject — **cephalopod** *adj* — **ceph•a•lop•o•dan** \,sef-ə-'läp-əd-ən\ *adj or n*

ceph•a•lo•tho•rax \,sef-ə-lō-'thōr-,aks, -'thȯr-\ *n* : a united head and thorax (as of a spider or crustacean) — **ceph•a•lo•tho•rac•ic** \-thə-'ras-ik\ *adj*

Ce•phe•id \'sē-fē-əd\ *n* : one of a class of pulsating stars whose light variations are very regular

Ce•pheus \'sē-,fyüs, -fē-əs\ *n* : a constellation between Cygnus and the north pole [Latin, from Greek *Kēpheus*]

ce•ra•mal \sə-'ram-əl, 'ser-ə-,mal\ *n* : CERMET [*ceram*ic *al*loy]

[1]**ce•ram•ic** \sə-'ram-ik\ *adj* : of or relating to a product (as earthenware, porecelain, or brick) made essentially from a nonmetallic mineral by firing at high temperatures [Greek *keramikos,* from *keramos* "pottery"]

[2]**ceramic** *n* **1** *pl* : the art of making ceramic articles **2** : a product of ceramic manufacture

ce•ram•ist \sə-'ram-əst\ *or* **ce•ram•i•cist** \-'ram-ə-səst\ *n* : one that engages in ceramics

cer•car•ia \sər-'kar-ē-ə, -'ker-\ *n, pl* **-i•ae** \-ē-,ē\ *also* **-i•as** : a usually tadpole-shaped larval trematode worm produced in a molluscan host by a redia [Greek *kerkos* "tail"] — **cer•car•i•al** \-ē-əl\ *adj*

cer•cus \'sər-kəs\ *n, pl* **cer•ci** \'sər-,sī\ : a many-jointed posterior appendage of an insect [Greek *kerkos* "tail"]

[1]**ce•re•al** \'sir-ē-əl\ *adj* : relating to grain or to the plants that produce it; *also* : made of grain [Latin *cerealis,* literally, "of Ceres"]

[2]**cereal** *n* **1** : a plant (as a grass) yielding starchy grain suitable for food; *also* : its grain **2** : a prepared foodstuff of grain

cer•e•bel•lum \,ser-ə-'bel-əm\ *n, pl* **-bel•lums** *or* **-bel•la** \-'bel-ə\ : a large part of the brain especially concerned with the coordination of muscles and the maintenance of bodily equilibrium and situated in front of and above the medulla which it partly overlaps [Medieval Latin, from Latin *cerebrum* "brain"] — **cer•e•bel•lar** \-'bel-ər\ *adj*

cerebr- *or* **cerebro-** *combining form* **1** : brain : cerebrum ⟨*cerebration*⟩ **2** : cerebral and ⟨*cerebro*spinal⟩ [Latin *cerebrum* "brain"]

ce•re•bral \sə-'rē-brəl, 'ser-ə-\ *adj* **1 a** : of or relating to the brain or the intellect **b** : of, relating to, or being the cerebrum **2** : appealing to the intellect — **ce•re•bral•ly** \-brə-lē\ *adv*

\ə\ abut	\au̇\ **out**	\i\ **tip**	\ȯ\ **saw**	\u̇\ **foot**
\ər\ **further**	\ch\ **chin**	\ī\ **life**	\ȯi\ **coin**	\y\ **yet**
\a\ **mat**	\e\ **pet**	\j\ **job**	\th\ **thin**	\yü\ **few**
\ā\ **take**	\ē\ **easy**	\ng\ **sing**	\th\ **this**	\yu̇\ **cure**
\ä\ **cot, cart**	\g\ **go**	\ō\ **bone**	\ü\ **food**	\zh\ **vision**

cerebral cortex *n* : the surface layer of gray matter of each cerebral hemisphere that functions chiefly in the coordination of higher nervous activity
cerebral hemisphere *n* : either of the two hollow convoluted lateral halves of the cerebrum
cerebral palsy *n* : a disability resulting from damage to the brain usually before or during birth and outwardly manifested by muscular incoordination and speech disturbances
cer•e•brate \'ser-ə-ˌbrāt\ *vi* : to use the mind : THINK — **cer•e•bra•tion** \ˌser-ə-'brā-shən\ *n*
ce•re•bro•spi•nal \sə-ˌrē-brō-'spīn-l, ˌser-ə-brō-\ *adj* : of or relating to the brain and spinal cord or to these together with the cranial and spinal nerves that innervate voluntary muscles
cerebrospinal fluid *n* : a liquid comparable to serum that occupies the cavities of the brain and spinal cord and the space between these and the meninges
ce•re•brum \sə-'rē-brəm, 'ser-ə-brəm\ *n, pl* **-brums** *or* **-bra** \-brə\ **1** : BRAIN 1a **2** : an enlarged anterior or upper part of the brain; *esp* : the expanded anterior portion of the brain that consists of cerebral hemispheres and connecting structures and is held to be the seat of conscious mental processes [Latin]
cere•cloth \'siər-ˌklȯth\ *n* : cloth treated with melted wax or gummy matter and formerly used especially for wrapping a dead body [derived from Latin *cera* "wax"]
cer•e•ment \'ser-ə-mənt, 'siər-mənt\ *n* : a shroud for the dead; *esp* : CERECLOTH — usually used in pl.
[1]**cer•e•mo•ni•al** \ˌser-ə-'mō-nē-əl\ *adj* : of, relating to, or forming a ceremony — **cer•e•mo•ni•al•ism** \-nē-ə-ˌliz-əm\ *n* — **cer•e•mo•ni•al•ist** \-ləst\ *n* — **cer•e•mo•ni•al•ly** \-nē-ə-lē\ *adj* — **cer•e•mo•ni•al•ness** n
• **syn** CEREMONIOUS: CEREMONIAL applies to things that are themselves ceremonies or an essential part of them ⟨*ceremonial* offerings⟩ ⟨a *ceremonial* gown⟩ CEREMONIOUS applies to a person overly careful to observe formalities or to acts performed elaborately or pompously ⟨the *ceremonious* courtier entered with a flourish⟩ ⟨took *ceremonious* leave⟩
[2]**ceremonial** *n* : a ceremonial act, action, or system
cer•e•mo•ni•ous \ˌser-ə-'mō-nē-əs\ *adj* **1** : CEREMONIAL **2** : careful to observe forms and ceremony : FORMAL **3** : according to formal usage or prescribed procedures **syn** see CEREMONIAL — **cer•e•mo•ni•ous•ly** *adv* — **cer•e•mo•ni•ous•ness** *n*
cer•e•mo•ny \'ser-ə-ˌmō-nē\ *n, pl* **-nies** **1** : a formal act or series of acts prescribed by ritual or custom ⟨graduation *ceremonies*⟩ **2** : a conventional act of politeness or etiquette ⟨went through the *ceremony* of introductions⟩ **3** : the social behavior required by strict etiquette : FORMALITY ⟨dined without *ceremony*⟩ [Middle French *cérémonie,* from Latin *caerimonia*]
Ce•res \'siər-ˌēz\ *n* : the largest asteroid and the one first discovered
ce•re•us \'sir-ē-əs\ *n* : any of various cacti of the western United States and tropical America often with showy flowers [Latin, "wax candle", from *cera* "wax"]
ce•rise \sə-'rēs, -'rēz\ *n* : a moderate red [French, literally, "cherry"]
ce•ri•um \'sir-ē-əm\ *n* : a gray malleable ductile metallic element used especially in alloys — see ELEMENT table [*Ceres,* an asteroid]
cer•met \'sər-ˌmet\ *n* : a strong alloy of a heat-resistant compound (as carbide of titanium) and a metal (as nickel) used especially for turbine blades — called also *ceramal* [*ceramic metal*]
cer•tain \'sərt-n\ *adj* **1 a** : FIXED 1c, SETTLED **b** : proved to be true **2** : implied as being specific but not named : PARTICULAR ⟨a *certain* town in Maine⟩ **3 a** : DEPENDABLE, RELIABLE **b** : INDISPUTABLE **4 a** : INEVITABLE **b** : incapable of failing : DESTINED **5** : assured in mind or action [Old French, from Latin *certus,* from *cernere* "to sift, decide"] **syn** see SURE — **certain•ly** *adv*
cer•tain•ty \-tē\ *n, pl* **-ties** **1** : something that is certain **2** : the quality or state of being certain
• **syn** CERTAINTY, CERTITUDE, CONVICTION mean a state of being free from doubt. CERTAINTY and CERTITUDE are frequently interchangeable but CERTAINTY may stress objective proof or evidence supporting a belief ⟨scientific *certainty*⟩ CERTITUDE stresses rather the strength of inner belief in something not needing or not capable of proof; CONVICTION applies especially to a strong individual belief concerned with moral or spiritual rather than merely factual matters.
[1]**cer•tif•i•cate** \sər-'tif-i-kət\ *n* **1** : a document containing a certified statement especially as to the truth of something; *esp* : one certifying that a person has fulfilled the requirements of a school or profession ⟨a teaching *certificate*⟩ **2** : a document evidencing ownership or debt ⟨stock *certificates*⟩
[2]**cer•tif•i•cate** \-'tif-ə-ˌkāt\ *vt* : to testify to, furnish with, or authorize by a certificate — **cer•tif•i•ca•to•ry** \-'tif-i-kə-ˌtōr-ē, -ˌtȯr-\ *adj*
cer•ti•fi•ca•tion \ˌsərt-ə-fə-'kā-shən\ *n* **1** : the act of certifying : the state of being certified **2** : a certified statement
certified check *n* : a check drawn on a depositor's account for which the bank guarantees payment
certified mail *n* : uninsured first class mail for which the addressee signs a receipt as proof of delivery
certified milk *n* : milk of high quality produced under the rules and regulations of an authorized medical milk commission
certified public accountant *n* : an accountant who has met the requirements of state law and has been granted a state certificate
cer•ti•fy \'sərt-ə-ˌfī\ *vt* **-fied**; **-fy•ing** **1 a** : to attest formally or authoritatively **b** : to guarantee to be true or valid or as represented or meeting a standard **2** : GUARANTEE 1 **3** : to provide with a usually professional certificate or license ⟨*certify* a teacher⟩ [Middle French *certifier,* from Late Latin *certificare,* from Latin *certus* "certain"] — **cer•ti•fi•able** \-ˌfī-ə-bəl\ *adj* — **cer•ti•fi•er** \-ˌfī-ər, -ˌfīr\ *n*
cer•ti•tude \'sərt-ə-ˌtüd, -ˌtyüd\ *n* **1** : the state of being or feeling certain : CONFIDENCE **2** : an end, event, or concept that is certain and unfailing ⟨moral *certitudes*⟩ **syn** see CERTAINTY — **cer•ti•tu•di•nous** \ˌsərt-ə-'tüd-n-əs, -'tyüd-\ *adj*
ce•ru•le•an \sə-'rü-lē-ən\ *adj* : resembling the blue of the sky : AZURE [Latin *caeruleus* "dark blue"]
ce•ru•men \sə-'rü-mən\ *n* : EARWAX [derived from Latin *cera* "wax"] — **ce•ru•mi•nous** \-mə-nəs\ *adj*
cer•vi•cal \'sər-vi-kəl\ *adj* : of or relating to a neck or cervix
cer•vine \'sər-ˌvīn\ *adj* : of, relating to, or resembling deer [Latin *cervus* "stag, deer"]
cer•vix \'sər-viks\ *n, pl* **cer•vi•ces** \'sər-və-ˌsēz\ *or* **cer•vix•es** : a constricted portion of an organ or part; *esp* : the narrow outer end of the uterus [Latin, "neck"]
ce•sar•e•an *or* **ce•sar•i•an** *also* **cae•sar•e•an** \si-'zar-ē-ən, -'zer-\ *n* : surgical incision of the walls of the abdomen and uterus for delivery of offspring [from the belief that Julius Caesar was born this way] — **cesarean** *or* **cesarian** *also* **caesarean** adj
ce•si•um *also* **cae•si•um** \'sē-zē-əm\ *n* : a silver-white soft ductile element used as a getter in electron tubes and in photoelectric cells — see ELEMENT table [Latin *caesius* "bluish gray"]
ces•sa•tion \se-'sā-shən\ *n* : a temporary or final ceasing (as of action) : STOP [Middle French, from Latin *cessatio* "delay, idleness", from *cessare* "to delay, be idle"]
ces•sion \'sesh-ən\ *n* : a giving up (as of territory or rights) to another [Middle French, from Latin *cessio,* from *cedere* "to withdraw, cede"]
cess•pool \'ses-ˌpül\ *n* : an underground pit or tank for liquid waste (as household sewage) [by folk etymology from Middle English *suspiral* "vent, cesspool", from Middle French *souspirail* "ventilator", from *soupirer* "to sigh, breathe", from Latin *suspirare*]
ces•ta \'ses-tə\ *n* : a narrow curved wicker basket used in jai alai [Spanish, literally, "basket", from Latin *cista* "box, basket"]

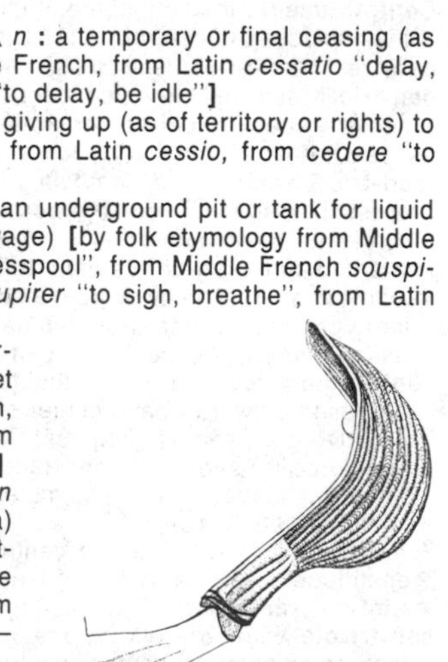
cesta

ces•tode \'ses-ˌtōd\ *n* : any of a group (Cestoda) of internally parasitic flatworms comprising the tapeworms [derived from Greek *kestos* "girdle"] — **cestode** *adj*
cesura *variant of* CAESURA
ce•ta•cean \si-'tā-shən\ *n* : any of an order (Cetacea) of aquatic mammals including the whales, dolphins, porpoises, and related forms [Latin *cetus* "whale", from Greek *kētos*] — **cetacean** *adj* — **ce•ta•ceous** \-shəs\ *adj*

Ce•tus \ˈsēt-əs\ *n* : an equatorial constellation south of Pisces and Aries [Latin, literally, "whale"]

cgs system \ˌsē-ˌjē-ˈes-\ *n* : a system of metric measure based on the centimeter, gram, and second as fundamental units

Chad \ˈchad\ *n* : a branch of the Afro-Asiatic language family comprising numerous languages of northern Nigeria and Cameroons

chae•tog•nath \ˈkēt-ˌäg-ˌnath, -əg-, -ə-\ *n* : any of a class (Chaetognatha) of small free-swimming marine worms with movable curved bristles on each side of the mouth [Greek *chaitē* "long" + *gnathos* "jaw"] — **chaetognath** *adj* — **chae•tog•na•than** \kē-ˈtäg-nə-thən\ *adj or n*

¹chafe \ˈchāf\ *vb* **1 a** : IRRITATE 1, VEX **b** : to feel irritation or discontent : FRET **2** : to warm by rubbing **3 a** : to rub so as to wear away : ABRADE **b** : to make sore by or as if by rubbing ⟨a tight collar *chafed* the dog's neck⟩ [Middle French *chaufer* "to warm", from Latin *calefacere*, from *calēre* "to be warm" + *facere* "to make"]

²chafe *n* **1** : a state of vexation : RAGE **2** : injury or wear caused by friction; *also* : FRICTION

cha•fer \ˈchā-fər\ *n* : any of various large beetles [Old English *ceafor*]

¹chaff \ˈchaf\ *n* **1** : the debris (as seed coverings) separated from the seed in threshing grain **2** : something trivial or worthless [Old English *ceaf*] — **chaffy** \-ē\ *adj*

²chaff *n* : light jesting talk : BANTER

³chaff *vb* : to tease good-naturedly : BANTER

chaf•fer \ˈchaf-ər\ *vb* : HAGGLE 2, BARGAIN [Middle English *chaffare* "a dispute about price", from *chep* "trade" + *fare* "journey"] — **chaf•fer•er** *n*

chaf•finch \ˈchaf-ˌinch, -inch\ *n* : a European finch of which the male has reddish breast plumage and a cheerful song

chaf•ing dish \ˈchā-fing-\ *n* : a utensil for cooking or warming food at the table [Middle English *chafen* "to warm, chafe"]

¹cha•grin \shə-ˈgrin\ *n* : a feeling of annoyance caused by failure or disappointment [French, from *chagrin* "sad"]

²chagrin *vt* **cha•grined** \-ˈgrind\; **cha•grin•ing** \-ˈgrin-ing\ : to cause to feel chagrin

¹chain \ˈchān\ *n* **1 a** : a series of connected usually metal links or rings **b** (1): a measuring instrument of 100 links (about 20 meters) used in surveying (2) : a unit of length equal to 66 feet (about 20 meters) **2** : something that confines or restrains **3 a** : series of things linked, connected, or associated together **b** : a number of atoms or chemical groups united like links in a chain ⟨a polypeptide *chain*⟩ [Old French *chaeine*, from Latin *catena*]

²chain *vt* : to fasten, bind, or connect with or as if with a chain

chain gang *n* : a group of convicts chained together

chain mail *n* : flexible armor of interlinked metal rings — called also *chain armor*

chain reaction *n* **1** : a series of events so related to each other that each one initiates the succeeding one **2** : a chemical or nuclear reaction yielding energy or products that cause further reactions of the same kind — **chain-re•act** \ˌchān-rē-ˈakt\ *vt*

chain saw *n* : a portable power saw that has teeth linked together to form an endless chain

chain-smoke \ˈchān-ˈsmōk\ *vb* : to smoke cigarettes one right after another — **chain-smok•er** *n*

chain stitch *n* : an ornamental stitch like the links of a chain

chain store *n* : one of numerous usually retail stores under the same ownership and general management and selling the same lines of goods

chair \ˈcheər, ˈchaər\ *n* **1** : a seat with legs and a back for use by one person **2 a** : an official seat or a seat of authority or dignity **b** : an office or position of authority or dignity **c** : the presiding officer of a meeting or an organization or committee **3** : any of various supporting devices [Old French *chaiere*, from Latin *cathedra*, from Greek *kathedra*, from *kata* "down" + *hedra* "seat"]

chair lift *n* : a motor-driven conveyor for skiers consisting of a series of seats suspended from an overhead cable

chair•man \-mən\ *n* : CHAIR 2c — **chair•man•ship** \-ˌship\ *n*

chair•per•son \-ˌpərs-n\ *n* : CHAIR 2c

chair•wom•an \-ˌwu̇m-ən\ *n* : a woman who is the presiding officer of a meeting, organization, or committee

chaise \ˈshāz\ *n* **1** : a 2-wheeled carriage with a folding top **2** : a light carriage or pleasure cart [French, "chair, chaise", alteration of Old French *chaiere* "chair"]

chaise longue \ˈshāz-ˈlȯŋ\ *n, pl* **chaise longues** *also* **chaises longues** \ˈshāz-ˈlȯŋ, -ˈlȯŋz\ : a long chair for reclining [French, literally, "long chair"]

chaise lounge \ˈshāz-ˈlau̇nj, ˈchās-\ *n* : CHAISE LONGUE [by folk etymology from *chaise longue*]

chal•ce•do•ny \kal-ˈsed-n-ē, ˈchal-sə-ˌdän-ē\ *n, pl* **-nies** : a translucent quartz commonly pale blue or gray with nearly waxy luster [Late Latin *chalcedonius*, a precious stone, from Greek *Chalkēdōn* "Chalcedon, former city in Turkey"]

chal•cid \ˈkal-səd\ *n* : any of a large group of mostly tiny insects related to the bees and ants and parasitic in the larval state on the larvae or pupae of other insects [derived from Greek *chalkos* "copper"] — **chalcid** *adj*

chal•co•cite \ˈkal-kə-ˌsīt\ *n* : a black or gray mineral Cu_2S of metallic luster that is an important ore of copper [derived from Greek *chalkos* "copper"]

chal•co•py•rite \ˌkal-kə-ˈpīr-ˌīt\ *n* : a yellow mineral $CuFeS_2$ consisting of copper-iron sulfide and constituting an important ore of copper

Chal•de•an \kal-ˈdē-ən\ *n* **1** : one of an ancient Semitic people founding the second Babylonian Empire in the 7th century B.C. **2** : the Semitic language of the Chaldeans [*Chaldea*, region of ancient Babylonia] — **Chal•da•ic** \kal-ˈdā-ik\ *adj or n* — **Chaldean** *adj*

Chal•dee \ˈkal-ˌdē\ *n* : CHALDEAN

cha•let \sha-ˈlā, ˈshal-ˌā\ *n* **1** : a remote herdsman's hut in the Alps **2 a** : a Swiss dwelling with a wide roof overhang **b** : a cottage in chalet style [French]

chal•ice \ˈchal-əs\ *n* **1** : a drinking cup : GOBLET; *esp* : the liturgical vessel in which wine is consecrated **2** : a flower cup [Anglo-French, from Latin *calix*]

¹chalk \ˈchȯk\ *n* **1** : a soft white, gray, or buff limestone chiefly composed of the shells of foraminifers **2** : chalk or a chalky material especially when used in the form of a crayon [Old English *cealc*, from Latin *calx* "lime", from Greek *chalix* "pebble"] — **chalky** \ˈchȯ-ke\ *adj*

²chalk *vt* **1** : to rub, mark, write, or draw with chalk **2 a** : to make a rough sketch of **b** : to record or add up with or as if with chalk

chalk•board \-ˌbōrd, -ˌbȯrd\ *n* : BLACKBOARD

chalk up *vt* **1** : ASCRIBE, CREDIT ⟨*chalk* success *up* to hard work⟩ **2** : ATTAIN 1, ACHIEVE ⟨*chalk up* a victory⟩

¹chal•lenge \ˈchal-ənj\ *vb* **1** : to claim as due or deserved ⟨an act that *challenged* everyone's admiration⟩ **2** : to halt and demand the countersign from **3 a** : to take exception to : object to ⟨*challenge* a juror⟩ **b** : to question the legality or legal qualifications of ⟨*challenge* a vote⟩ **4 a** : to call out to duel or combat **b** : to invite into competition **5** : STIMULATE 1, EXCITE [Old French *chalengier* "to accuse", from Latin *calumniari* "to accuse falsely", from *calumnia* "calumny"] — **chal•leng•er** *n*

²challenge *n* **1** : an objection raised to something or someone **2** : a sentry's command to halt and prove identity **3** : an often threatening or provocative summons or invitation to compete; *esp* : a summons to a duel **4** : a test of immunity by exposure to virulent infective material after specific immunization

chal•lis \ˈshal-ē\ *n, pl* **chal•lises** \ˈshal-ēz\ : a lightweight soft clothing fabric especially of cotton or wool [probably from the name *Challis*]

¹cham•ber \ˈchām-bər\ *n* **1** : ROOM; *esp* : BEDROOM **2** : an enclosed space or compartment **3 a** : a meeting hall of a deliberative, legislative, or judicial body **b** : a room where a judge transacts business out of court **c** : the reception room of a person of rank or authority **4 a** : a legislative or judicial body; *esp* : either of the houses of a bicameral legislature **b** : a voluntary board or council (as of businessmen) **5 a** : the part of the bore of a gun that holds the cartridge **b** : a compartment in the cartridge cylinder of a revolver [Old French *chambre*, from Late Latin *camera*, from Latin, "vault", from Greek *kamara*] — **cham•bered** \-bərd\ *adj*

²chamber *vt* : to place or hold in or as if in a chamber

³chamber *adj* : intended for performance by a few musicians for a small audience ⟨*chamber* music⟩

chambered nautilus *n* : NAUTILUS 1

cham•ber•lain \ˈchām-bər-lən\ *n* **1** : a chief officer in the

household of a sovereign or noble **2** : TREASURER [Old French *chamberlayn,* derived from Late Latin *camera* "chamber"]
cham•ber•maid \'chām-bər-,mād\ *n* : a maid who makes beds and does general cleaning of bedrooms (as in a hotel)
chamber of commerce : an association of business people to promote commercial and industrial interests
chamber pot *n* : a handled and often lidded bowl for urination and defecation
cham•bray \'sham-,brā, -brē\ *n* : a lightweight clothing fabric with colored and white yarns [*Cambrai,* France]
cha•me•leon \kə-'mēl-yən\ *n* : a lizard that has the ability to vary the color of its skin [derived from Greek *chamaileōn,* from *chamai* "on the ground" + *leōn* "lion"]
[1]**cham•fer** \'cham-fər, 'champ-\ *n* : a beveled edge [Middle French *chanfraindre* "to bevel", from *chant* "edge" (from Latin *canthus* "iron tire") + *fraindre* "to break", from Latin *frangere*]
[2]**chamfer** *vt* **1** : to cut a furrow in (as a column) : GROOVE **2** : to make a chamfer on : BEVEL
cham•ois \'sham-ē\ *n, pl* **cham•ois** *also* **cham•oix** \'sham-ēz\ **1** : a small goatlike mountain antelope of Europe and the Caucasus **2** *also* **cham•my** *or* **sham•my** \'sham-ē\ : a soft pliant leather prepared from the skin of the chamois or from sheepskin [Middle French, from Late Latin *camox*]

chamois 1

cham•o•mile *or* **cam•o•mile** \'kam-ə-,mīl, -,mēl\ *n* : any of a genus of strong-scented herbs related to the daisies with flower heads that contain a bitter medicinal principle [Medieval Latin *camomilla,* derived from Greek *chamaimēlon,* from *chamai* "on the ground" + *mēlon* "apple"]
[1]**champ** \'champ\ *vb* **1** : to bite and chew noisily ⟨a horse *champing* its bit⟩ **2** : to show impatience [perhaps imitative]
[2]**champ** *n* : CHAMPION 3
cham•pagne \sham-'pān\ *n* : a white sparkling wine made in Champagne, France; *also* : a similar wine made elsewhere
cham•paign \sham-'pān\ *n* : an expanse of level open country : PLAIN [Middle French *champagne,* from Late Latin *campania,* from Latin *campus* "field, plain"]
[1]**cham•pi•on** \'cham-pē-ən\ *n* **1** : a militant advocate or defender **2** : one that fights for another's rights or honor **3 a** : a person formally acknowledged as better than all others in a sport or in a game of skill **b** : the winner of first place in a competition [Old French, "warrior", from Medieval Latin *campio,* of Germanic origin]
[2]**champion** *vt* : to protect or fight for as a champion
cham•pi•on•ship \-,ship\ *n* **1** : the act of defending as a champion ⟨known for their *championship* of states' rights⟩ **2 a** : the position or title of champion **b** : a contest held to determine a champion
[1]**chance** \'chans\ *n* **1** : the way in which things happen without apparent cause or intent ⟨meet by *chance*⟩ ⟨the outcome depends on *chance*⟩ **2** : OPPORTUNITY ⟨had a *chance* to travel⟩ **3** : RISK, GAMBLE ⟨take *chances*⟩ **4 a** : the possibility of an indicated outcome in an uncertain situation ⟨a good *chance* of failure⟩ ⟨a 50–50 *chance*⟩ **b** : at least a slight possibility of a favorable outcome ⟨does stand a *chance* of winning⟩ **c** : the more likely of possible outcomes ⟨*chances* are they've already left⟩ **5** : a ticket in a raffle [Old French, derived from Latin *cadere* "to fall"] — **chance** *adj*
[2]**chance** *vb* **1 a** : to take place or come about by chance : HAPPEN **b** : to be found by chance **c** : to have good or bad luck ⟨*chanced* to miss the train⟩ **2** : to come casually and unexpectedly — used with *on* or *upon* **3** : to accept the hazard of : RISK **syn** see HAPPEN
chan•cel \'chan-səl\ *n* : the part of a church containing the altar and seats for the clergy and choir [Middle French, from Latin *cancelli* "lattice"; from the latticework enclosing it]
chan•cel•lery *or* **chan•cel•lory** \'chan-sə-lə-rē, -slə-rē\ *n, pl* **-ler•ies** *or* **-lor•ies 1 a** : the position or department of a chancellor **b** : the building or room where a chancellor's office is located **2** : the office or staff of an embassy or consulate
chan•cel•lor \'chan-sə-lər, -slər\ *n* **1** : the head of a university **2** : a judge in a court of chancery or equity **3** : the chief minister of state in some European countries [Old French *chancelier,* from Late Latin *cancellarius* "doorkeeper, secretary", from Latin *cancelli* "lattice"] — **chan•cel•lor•ship** \-,ship\ *n*
chancellor of the exchequer : a member of the British cabinet in charge of the public income and expenditure
chan•cery \'chans-rē, -ə-rē\ *n, pl* **-cer•ies 1** : a court of equity **2** : a record office for public archives **3** : CHANCELLERY [Middle English *chancerie,* alteration of *chancellerie* "chancellery"]
chan•cre \'shang-kər\ *n* : a primary sore or ulcer at the site of entry of an infective agent (as of syphilis) [French, from Latin *cancer*] — **chan•crous** \-kə-rəs, -krəs\ *adj*
chancy \'chan-sē\ *adj* **chanc•i•er; -est** : uncertain in outcome or prospect : RISKY
chan•de•lier \,shan-də-'liər\ *n* : a branched often ornate lighting fixture usually suspended from a ceiling [French, from Latin *candelabrum* "candlestick"]
chan•dler \'chan-dlər\ *n* **1** : a maker or seller of candles **2** : a dealer in supplies or equipment especially for ships [Middle French *chandelier,* from Old French *chandelle* "candle", from Latin *candela*] — **chan•dlery** \-dlə-rē\ *n*
[1]**change** \'chānj\ *vb* **1** : to make or become different : MODIFY **2 a** : to give a different position, course, or direction to **b** : REVERSE ⟨*change* one's vote⟩ **3** : to replace with another : SWITCH **4** : to put fresh clothes or covering on ⟨*change* a bed⟩ **5** : to shift one's means of transportation : TRANSFER **6** : to undergo transformation, transition, or substitution **7** : to give up one thing for something else in return : EXCHANGE ⟨*change* places⟩ [Old French *changier,* from Latin *cambiare* "to exchange", of Celtic origin] — **chang•er** *n*
• **syn** ALTER, MODIFY, VARY : CHANGE implies making either an essential difference amounting to loss of original identity or a substitution of one thing for another; ALTER implies a difference in some respect without loss of identity; MODIFY suggests a difference that limits, restricts, or adapts to a new purpose; VARY stresses a breaking away from exact repetition.
— **change hands** : to pass from the possession of one person to that of another
[2]**change** *n* **1** : the act, process, or result of changing: as **a** : ALTERATION ⟨a *change* in routine⟩ **b** : TRANSFORMATION ⟨a *change* of seasons⟩ **c** : SUBSTITUTION ⟨a *change* of jobs⟩ **2** : a fresh set of clothes **3 a** : money in small denominations received in exchange for an equivalent sum in larger denominations **b** : money returned when a payment exceeds the amount due **c** : COINS ⟨a pocketful of *change*⟩
change•able \'chān-jə-bəl\ *adj* **1** : capable of or given to change : VARIABLE ⟨*changeable* weather⟩ **2** : appearing different (as in color) from different points of view — **change•abil•i•ty** \,chān-jə-'bil-ət-ē\ *n* — **change•able•ness** *n* — **change•ably** \'chān-jə-blē\ *adv*
change•ful \'chānj-fəl\ *adj* : full of or given to change : UNCERTAIN — **change•ful•ly** \-fə-lē\ *adv* — **change•ful•ness** *n*
change•less \'chānj-ləs\ *adj* : marked by the absence of change : CONSTANT — **change•less•ly** *adv* — **change•less•ness** *n*
change•ling \'chānj-ling\ *n* : a child secretly exchanged for another in infancy
change of life : MENOPAUSE; *also* : a corresponding period in the male
change ringing *n* : the art or practice of ringing a set of tuned bells in continually varying order
[1]**chan•nel** \'chan-l\ *n* **1 a** : the bed of a stream **b** : the deeper part of a river, harbor, or strait **c** : a strait or narrow sea between two close landmasses ⟨the English *Channel*⟩ **2 a** : a means aiding communication or exchange ⟨trade *channels*⟩ **b** : a way or course of thought or action ⟨turn one's thoughts into new *channels*⟩ **3** : a long gutter, groove, or furrow **4** : a range of frequencies of sufficient width for a single radio or television transmission [Old French *chanel,* from Latin *canalis* "pipe, channel, canal"]
[2]**channel** *vt* **-neled** *or* **-nelled; -nel•ing** *or* **-nel•ling 1 a** : to form, cut, or wear a channel in **b** : GROOVE ⟨*channel* a chair leg⟩ **2** : to direct into or through a channel
chan•nel•ize \'chan-l-,īz\ *vt* : CHANNEL — **chan•nel•iza•tion** \,chan-l-ə-'zā-shən\ *n*
chan•son \shä^{n}-sō^{n}\ *n, pl* **chan•sons** \-sō^{n}, -sō^{n}z\ : SONG; *esp* : a French song [French]

[1]**chant** \'chant\ *vb* **1 :** SING; *esp* **:** to sing a chant **2 :** to recite in a monotonous repetitive tone [Middle French *chanter,* from Latin *cantare,* from *canere* "to sing"]

[2]**chant** *n* **1 :** a melody in which several words or syllables are sung on one tone **2 :** a rhythmic monotonous utterance

chan•te•relle \,shant-ə-'rel, ,shänt-\ *n* **:** an edible mushroom of rich yellow color and pleasant aroma [French]

chan•teuse \shä^{n}-'tüz, -'tərz, shan-'tüz\ *n* **:** a woman concert or nightclub singer [French, from *chanter* "to sing"]

chan•tey *or* **chan•ty** \'shant-ē, 'chant-\ *n, pl* **chanteys** or **chanties :** a song sung by sailors in rhythm with their work [French *chanter* "to sing, chant"]

chan•ti•cleer \,chant-ə-'kliər, ,shant-\ *n* **:** [1]COCK 1 [Old French *Chantecler,* rooster in the beast epic *Reynard the Fox*]

cha•os \'kā-,äs\ *n* **:** a state of utter confusion ⟨the citywide blackout caused *chaos*⟩ [Latin, from Greek] **syn** see ANARCHY — **cha•ot•ic** \kā-'ät-ik\ *adj* — **cha•ot•i•cal•ly** \-i-kə-lē, -klē\ *adv*

[1]**chap** \'chap\ *n* **:** FELLOW 4a [short for *chapman*]

[2]**chap** *vb* **chapped; chap•ping :** to open in slits **:** CRACK ⟨*chapped* lips⟩ [Middle English *chappen*]

[3]**chap** *n* **:** a crack in or a sore roughening of the skin from exposure

[4]**chap** \'chäp, 'chap\ *n* **:** JAW **:** the fleshy covering of a jaw; *also* **:** the forepart of the face — usually used in pl. [[2]*chap*]

chap•ar•ral \,shap-ə-'ral, -'rel\ *n* **:** a thicket of dwarf evergreen oaks; *also* **:** a dense impenetrable thicket [Spanish, from *chaparro* "dwarf evergreen oak," from Basque *txapar*]

chap•book \'chap-,bu̇k\ *n* **:** a small book containing ballads, tales, or tracts [*chapman* + *book*]

cha•peau \sha-'pō\ *n, pl* **cha•peaus** \-'pōz\ *or* **cha•peaux** \-'pō, -'pōz\ **:** HAT [Middle French, derived from Medieval Latin *cappellus* "head covering", from Late Latin *cappa*]

chap•el \'chap-əl\ *n* **1 :** a place of worship in a residence or institution **2 :** a building or a room or recess for prayer or special religious services **3 :** a service of worship in a school or college **4 :** a place of worship used by British Nonconformists [Old French *chapele,* from Medieval Latin *cappella,* from Late Latin *cappa* "cloak"; from the preservation of the cloak of Saint Martin of Tours in a chapel built for that purpose]

[1]**chap•er•on** *or* **chap•er•one** \'shap-ə-,rōn\ *n* **:** a person who accompanies and is responsible for (as at a dance) a young woman or a group of young people [French *chaperon,* literally, "hood", derived from Late Latin *cappa* "head covering, cloak"]

[2]**chaperon** *or* **chaperone** *vb* **:** to act as a chaperon **:** ESCORT — **chap•er•on•age** \-,rō-nij\ *n*

chap•fall•en \'chap-,fō-lən, 'chäp-\ *or* **chop•fall•en** \'chäp-\ *adj* **:** cast down in spirits **:** DEPRESSED

chap•lain \'chap-lən\ *n* **1 :** a member of the clergy appointed to serve a dignitary, institution, or military force **2 :** a person chosen to conduct religious exercises for an organization [Old French *chapelain* "clergyman in charge of a chapel", from Medieval Latin *cappellanus,* from *cappella* "chapel"] — **chap•lain•cy** \-sē\ *n* — **chap•lain•ship** \-,ship\ *n*

chap•let \'chap-lət\ *n* **1 :** a wreath worn on the head **2 a :** a string of beads **b :** a part of a rosary comprising five decades [Middle French *chapelet,* derived from Late Latin *cappa* "head covering, cloak"]

chap•man \'chap-mən\ *n, British* **:** a traveling merchant [Old English *cēapman,* from *cēap* "trade" + *man*]

chaps \'shaps, 'chaps\ *n pl* **:** leather leggings resembling trousers without a seat that are worn especially by western ranch hands [Mexican Spanish *chaparreras*]

chap•ter \'chap-tər\ *n* **1 :** a main division of a book or of a law code **2 :** a local branch of a society or fraternity [Old French *chapitre,* from Late Latin *capitulum,* from Latin *caput* "head"]

[1]**char** \'chär\ *n, pl* **char** or **chars :** any of a genus of small-scaled trouts including the common brook trout [origin unknown]

[2]**char** *vb* **charred; char•ring 1 :** to change to charcoal by burning **2 :** to burn slightly **:** SCORCH **3 :** to burn to a cinder [back-formation from *charcoal*]

[3]**char** *n* **:** a charred substance

[4]**char** *vi* **charred; char•ring :** to work as a charwoman

char•a•banc \'shar-ə-,bang\ *n, British* **:** a sight-seeing bus [French *char à bancs,* literally, "wagon with benches"]

char•a•cin \'kar-ə-sən\ *n* **:** any of a family of usually small brightly colored tropical fishes [derived from Greek *charax* "pointed stake, a kind of fish"] — **characin** *adj*

char•ac•ter \'kar-ik-tər\ *n* **1 a :** a conventional marking indicating origin or ownership **b :** a mark or symbol (as a hieroglyph or a letter of an alphabet) used in writing or printing **2 a** (1) **:** a distinguishing feature **:** CHARACTERISTIC (2) **:** the sum total of the distinguishing qualities of a person, group, or thing **:** NATURE **b :** the detectable result of the action of a gene or group of genes **3 :** POSITION, STATUS ⟨in their *character* of children⟩ **4 :** a person having notable traits or characteristics; *esp* **:** an odd or peculiar person **5 :** a person in a story, novel, or play **6 :** REPUTATION 1 **7 :** moral excellence and strength [Middle French *caractère,* from Latin *character* "mark, distinctive quality", from Greek *charaktēr,* from *charassein* "to scratch, engrave"] — **char•ac•ter•less** \-ləs\ *adj*

chaps

[1]**char•ac•ter•is•tic** \,kar-ik-tə-'ris-tik\ *adj* **:** serving to mark the distinctive character of an individual, group, or class — **char•ac•ter•is•ti•cal•ly** \-ti-kə-lē, -klē\ *adv*
• syn CHARACTERISTIC, INDIVIDUAL, DISTINCTIVE, PECULIAR mean indicating a special quality or identity. CHARACTERISTIC applies to something that marks a person or thing or class; INDIVIDUAL stresses qualities that distinguish one from all other members of the same kind or class; DISTINCTIVE indicates qualities that are distinguishing and uncommon and often superior or praiseworthy; PECULIAR applies to qualities possessed only by a particular individual or class.

[2]**characteristic** *n* **1 :** a distinguishing trait, quality, or property **2 :** the integral part of a common logarithm

char•ac•ter•iza•tion \,kar-ik-tə-rə-'zā-shən\ *n* **1 :** the act of characterizing **:** description by a statement of characteristics **2 :** the creation of characters in fiction or drama **:** the artistic representation of fictitious persons

char•ac•ter•ize \'kar-ik-tə-,rīz\ *vt* **1 :** to indicate the character or characteristics of **:** DESCRIBE **2 :** to be characteristic of

character sketch *n* **:** a usually short piece of writing dealing with a character of strongly marked individuality

char•ac•tery \'kar-ik-tə-rē, -trē\ *n* **:** characters or symbols used to express ideas

cha•rades \shə-'rādz\ *n pl* **:** a game in which each syllable of a word to be guessed is acted out by some of the persons playing the game while the others try to guess the word [French]

cha•ras \'chär-əs\ *n* **:** HASHISH [Hindi *caras*]

char•coal \'chär-,kōl\ *n* **1 :** a dark or black porous carbon prepared from vegetable or animal substances (as from wood by charring in a kiln from which air is excluded) **2 a :** a piece or pencil of fine charcoal used in drawing **b :** a charcoal drawing [Middle English *charcole*]

chard \'chärd\ *n* **:** a beet that lacks a swollen root and forms large leaves and succulent stalks often cooked as a vegetable — called also *Swiss chard* [French *carde,* from Provençal *cardo* "cardoon", from Latin *carduus* "thistle, artichoke"]

[1]**charge** \'chärj\ *vb* **1 a :** to place a charge (as of powder) in ⟨*charge* the magazine with three rounds⟩ **b :** to load or fill to capacity **c** (1) **:** to impart an electric charge to (2) **:** to restore the active materials in (a storage battery) by the passage of a direct current through in the opposite direction to that of discharge **2 a :** to impose a task or responsibility on **b :** to command, instruct, or exhort with right or authority ⟨*charge* a jury⟩ **3 :** ACCUSE, BLAME ⟨*charged* them with murder⟩ **4 :** to rush against or bear down upon a place **:** ASSAULT, ATTACK **5 a :** to impose a monetary charge upon a person ⟨*charged* me $50⟩ **b :** to fix or ask as fee or payment ⟨*charge* $2.50 for a ticket⟩ **c :** to ask or set a price ⟨*charges* too much⟩ [Old French *char-*

gier "to load", from Late Latin *carricare,* from Latin *carrus* "car, wheeled vehicle"] — **charge•able** \'chär-jə-bəl\ *adj* — **charge•able•ness** *n*

[2]**charge** *n* **1 :** a figure borne on a heraldic field **2 a :** the quantity of material that an apparatus (as a gun, furnace, or the clyinder of an internal-combustion engine) is intended to receive at one time **b :** a store or accumulation of force **c :** a definite quantity of electricity; *esp* **:** an excess or deficiency of electrons **3 a :** OBLIGATION 2, REQUIREMENT **b :** MANAGEMENT 1, SUPERVISION **c :** a person or thing committed to the care of another **4 :** INSTRUCTION, COMMAND ⟨a *charge* to a jury⟩ **5 a :** EXPENSE 1, COST **b :** the price of something **c :** a debit to an account **6 a :** an often formal accusation of a wrong or offense **b :** an expression of hostile criticism ⟨made a *charge* of widespread insensitivity toward minorities⟩ **7 :** a rush to attack an enemy **:** ASSAULT

charge account *n* **:** a customer's account with a creditor (as a merchant) to which the purchase of goods is charged

char•gé d'af•faires \'shär-ˌzhād-ə-'faər, -feər\ *n, pl* **char•gés d'af•faires** \-ˌzhād-ə-, -ˌzhāz-də-\ **1 :** a diplomat who substitutes for an absent ambassador or minister **2 :** a diplomat of inferior rank [French, literally, "one charged with affairs"]

[1]**char•ger** \'chär-jər\ *n, archaic* **:** a large flat platter for carrying meat

[2]**charg•er** \'chär-jər\ *n* **1 :** a cavalry horse **2 :** a device for charging storage batteries

char•i•ot \'char-ē-ət\ *n* **:** a 2-wheeled horse-drawn battle car of ancient times used also in processions and races [Middle French, from *char* "car", from Latin *carrus*]

chariot

char•i•o•teer \ˌchar-ē-ə-'tiər\ *n* **1 :** a driver of a chariot **2** *cap* **:** the constellation Auriga

cha•ris•ma \kə-'riz-mə\ *n, pl* **-ma•ta** \-mət-ə\ **1 :** an extraordinary power (as of healing) given a Christian by the Holy Spirit for the good of the church **2 a :** a personal magic of leadership arousing popular loyalty or enthusiasm for a public figure **b :** a special magnetic charm or appeal [Greek, "favor, gift", from *charis* "grace"] — **char•is•mat•ic** \ˌkar-əz-'mat-ik\ *adj*

char•i•ta•ble \'char-ət-ə-bəl\ *adj* **1 :** liberal with money or help for poor and needy persons **:** GENEROUS **2 :** given for or serving the needy ⟨*charitable* funds⟩ **3 :** generous and kindly in judging other people — **char•i•ta•bly** \-blē\ *adv*

char•i•ty \'char-ət-ē\ *n, pl* **-ties 1 :** love for one's fellow human beings **2 :** kindliness in judging others **3 a :** the giving of aid to the poor and suffering **b :** public aid for the poor **c :** an institution or fund for aiding the needy [Old French *charité,* from Latin *caritas* "dearness", from *carus* "dear"]

char•la•tan \'shär-lə-tən\ *n* **:** a person who pretends to have a particular knowledge or ability **:** QUACK [Italian *ciarlatano,* alteration of *cerretano,* literally, "inhabitant of Cerreto, village in Italy"] — **char•la•tan•ism** \-tə-ˌniz-əm\ *n* — **char•la•tan•ry** \-tən-rē\ *n*

△ **origin** In the early 16th century quacks wandered through Italy, peddling medicines and treatments of doubtful value. Because the village of Cerreto seemed to produce so many of these unskilled practitioners of medicine, the name *Cerretano,* "inhabitant of Cerreto", came to mean "quack". Such quacks always have a ready line of glib talk to help them sell their wares. Thus, under the influence of *ciarlare,* "to chatter", *Cerretano* was altered to *ciarlatano,* from which we get our English *charlatan.*

Charles•ton \'chärl-stən\ *n* **:** a dance in which the knees are twisted in and out and the heels are swung sharply outward on each step [*Charleston,* South Carolina]

char•ley horse \'chär-lē-ˌhȯrs\ *n* **:** pain and stiffness from muscular strain especially in a leg [*Charley,* nickname for *Charles*]

char•lotte russe \ˌshär-lət-'rüs\ *n* **:** a dessert made with sponge cake or ladyfingers and a whipped-cream or custard-gelatin filling [French, from *charlotte,* a kind of dessert + *russe* "Russian"]

[1]**charm** \'chärm\ *n* **1 :** a word, action, or thing believed to have magic powers **2 :** something worn or carried to keep away evil and bring good luck **3 :** a small decorative object worn on a chain or bracelet **4 a :** a quality that attracts and pleases **b :** physical grace or attractiveness [Old French *charme,* from Latin *carmen* "song, charm", from *canere* "to sing"]

[2]**charm** *vt* **1 :** to affect or influence by or as if by magic **:** COMPEL **2 :** to protect by or as if by a charm ⟨a *charmed* life⟩ **3 :** to control (an animal) by charms (as the playing of music) ⟨*charm* a snake⟩ **4 :** to attract by grace or beauty — **charm•er** *n*

charm•ing \'chär-ming\ *adj* **:** pleasant and attractive especially in manner ⟨a very *charming* person⟩

char•nel \'chärn-l\ *n* **:** a building or chamber in which dead bodies or bones are deposited [Middle French, from Medieval Latin *carnale,* from Late Latin *carnalis* "of the flesh", from Latin *caro* "flesh"] — **charnel** *adj*

charr *variant of* CHAR

[1]**chart** \'chärt\ *n* **1 :** MAP: as **a :** an outline map exhibiting something (as climatic or magnetic variations) in its geographical aspects **b :** a map with specific information for use by navigators **2 :** a sheet giving information in the form of a table or of lists or by means of diagrams or graphs; *also* **:** GRAPH **3 :** a sheet of paper ruled and graduated for use in a recording instrument [Middle French *charte,* from Latin *charta* "piece of papyrus, document", from Greek *chartēs* "piece of papyrus"] — see CARTEL *origin*

[2]**chart** *vt* **1 :** to make a chart of ⟨set out to *chart* the coast⟩ **2 :** to lay out a plan for ⟨*charting* campaign strategy⟩

[1]**char•ter** \'chärt-ər\ *n* **1 a :** an official document granting, guaranteeing, or defining the rights and duties of the body (as a municipality, corporation, or a local society) to which it is issued **b :** CONSTITUTION ⟨the United Nations *Charter*⟩ **2 :** a special privilege or immunity **3 :** a contract by which the owners of a ship lease it to others — called also *charter party* [Old French *chartre,* from Medieval Latin *chartula,* from Latin *charta* "document"]

[2]**charter** *vt* **1 :** to grant a charter to **2 :** to hire (as a ship or a bus) for one's own use — **char•ter•er** \'chärt-ər-ər\ *n*

Char•tism \'chärt-ˌiz-əm\ *n* **:** the principles and practices of a body of 19th century English political reformers advocating better social and industrial conditions for the working classes [Medieval Latin *charta* "charter", from Latin, "document"] — **Char•tist** \'chärt-əst\ *adj or n*

char•treuse \shär-'trüz, -'trüs\ *n* **:** a brilliant yellow green [*Chartreuse,* trademark used for a green or yellow liqueur]

char•wom•an \'chär-ˌwu̇m-ən\ *n* **1** *British* **:** a woman hired to do household work **2 :** a cleaning woman usually in a large building [Middle English *char* "turn, piece of work", from Old English *cierr*]

chary \'chaər-ē, 'cheər-\ *adj* **char•i•er; -est 1 :** cautiously sparing or frugal ⟨*chary* of giving praise⟩ **2 :** cautiously watchful especially in preserving something ⟨*chary* of one's reputation⟩ [Old English *cearig* "sorrowful", from *caru* "sorrow, care"] — **char•i•ly** \'char-ə-lē, 'cher-\ *adv* — **char•i•ness** \'char-ē-nəs, 'cher-\ *n*

[1]**chase** \'chās\ *vb* **1 a :** to follow rapidly **:** PURSUE **b :** HUNT 1 **2 :** to seek out **3 :** to drive away or out ⟨*chase* a dog off the lawn⟩ [Middle French *chasser,* from Latin *captare,* from *capere* "to take"]

• **syn** PURSUE, FOLLOW, TRAIL: CHASE implies going swiftly after and trying to overtake something running or fleeing usually in full view ⟨a dog *chasing* a cat⟩ PURSUE may add the suggestion of a continuing effort to overtake ⟨*pursue* a fox⟩ FOLLOW puts less emphasis upon speed and may not imply intent to overtake ⟨a stray dog *followed* me home⟩ TRAIL applies to a following of tracks or traces rather than a visible object ⟨*trail* a deer through the snow⟩

[2]**chase** *n* **1 a :** the act of chasing **:** PURSUIT **b :** HUNTING — used with *the* **2 :** something pursued **3 :** a tract of unenclosed land used as a game preserve

[3]**chase** *vt* **:** to ornament (metal) by embossing or engraving ⟨*chased* bronze⟩ [Middle French *enchasser* "to set"]

[4]**chase** *n* **:** a channel (as in a wall) for something to lie in or pass through [French *chas* "eye of a needle", from Late Latin *capsus* "enclosed space", from Latin *capsa* "box"]

[5]**chase** *n* **:** a rectangular steel or iron frame into which letterpress matter is locked for printing or plating [probably from French *châsse* "frame", from Latin *capsa* "box"]

chas•er \'chā-sər\ *n* **1 :** one that chases **2 :** a mild drink (as water or beer) taken after hard liquor

Cha•sid *or* **Chas•sid** \'has-əd, 'ḵäs-\ *n, pl* **Cha•si•dim** *or* **Chas•si•dim** \'has-əd-əm, ḵä-'sēd-\ *variant of* HASID

chasm \'kaz-əm\ *n* **1** : a deep cleft in the earth : GORGE **2** : a marked division, separation, or difference [Latin *chasma,* from Greek]

chas•seur \sha-'sər\ *n* : one of a body of light cavalry or infantry trained for rapid maneuvering [French, from Middle French *chasser* "to chase"]

chas•sis \'shas-ē, 'chas-ē\ *n, pl* **chas•sis** \-ēz\ : a supporting framework (as that bearing the body of an automobile or airplane or the parts of a radio or television receiving set) [French *châssis,* derived from Latin *capsa* "box"]

chaste \'chāst\ *adj* **1 a** : innocent of unlawful sexual intercourse **b** : CELIBATE **2** : pure in thought and act : MODEST **3** : pure or severe in design and expression [Old French, from Latin *castus* "pure, chaste"] — **chaste•ly** *adv* — **chaste•ness** \'chās-nəs, 'chāst-\ *n*

• **syn** CHASTE, PURE, MODEST mean free from all taint of what is lewd or salacious. CHASTE implies a refraining from acts, thoughts, or desires that are not virginal or not sanctioned in marriage; it may suggest avoidance of anything that cheapens or debases; PURE implies innocence and absence of temptation; MODEST applies especially to behavior and dress as outward signs of chastity or purity.

chas•ten \'chās-n\ *vt* **chas•tened; chas•ten•ing** \'chās-ning, -n-ing\ **1** : to correct by punishment or suffering : DISCIPLINE **2** : to purify of excess, pretense, or falsity : REFINE [Old French *chastier,* from Latin *castigare,* from *castus* "pure, chaste"] — **chas•ten•er** \'chās-nər, -n-ər\ *n*

chas•tise \chas-'tīz\ *vt* **1** : to inflict punishment on (as by whipping) **2** : to censure severely : CASTIGATE [Middle English *chastisen,* alteration of *chasten*] **syn** see PUNISH — **chas•tise•ment** \chas-'tīz-mənt, 'chas-təz-\ *n* — **chas•tis•er** \chas-'tī-zər\ *n*

chas•ti•ty \'chas-tət-ē\ *n* : the quality or state of being chaste; *esp* : personal purity and modesty

cha•su•ble \'chazh-ə-bəl, 'chaz-ə-, 'chas-ə-\ *n* : a sleeveless outer vestment worn by the officiating priest at mass [French, from Late Latin *casubla* "hooded garment"]

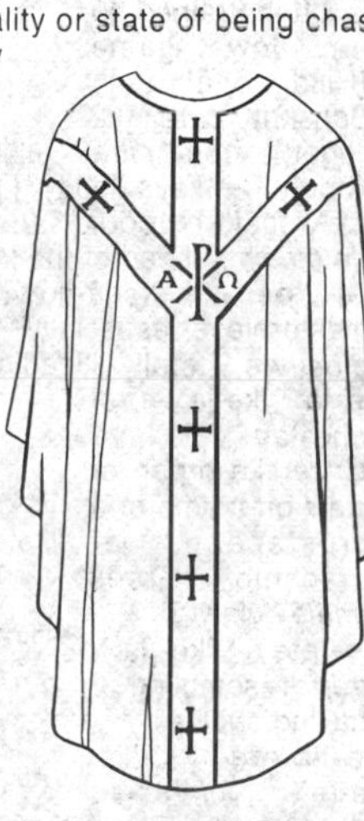

chasuble

[1]**chat** \'chat\ *vi* **chat•ted; chat•ting 1** : CHATTER 2 **2** : to talk in a light, informal, or familiar manner

[2]**chat** *n* **1 a** : light familiar talk **b** : an informal conversation **2** : any of several songbirds with a chattering call

châ•teau \sha-'tō\ *n, pl* **châ•teaus** \-'tōz\ *or* **châ•teaux** \-'tō, -'tōz\ **1** : a feudal castle in France **2** : a large country house **3** : a French vineyard estate [French, from Latin *castellum* "castle"]

chat•e•laine \'shat-l-,ān\ *n* **1** : the mistress of a château or a household **2** : an ornamental clasp or hook for a watch, purse, or bunch of keys [French]

chat•tel \'chat-l\ *n* **1** : SLAVE 1, BONDMAN **2** : an item of property (as animals, furniture, money, or goods) other than real estate [Old French *chatel* "property", from Medieval Latin *capitale,* from Latin *capitalis* "of the head, capital"]

chat•ter \'chat-ər\ *vb* **1** : to utter rapidly succeeding sounds suggesting speech but lacking meaning ⟨squirrels *chattered* angrily⟩ **2** : to speak idly, continuously, or rapidly : JABBER **3 a** : to click repeatedly or uncontrollably ⟨*chattering* teeth⟩ **b** : to vibrate rapidly in cutting ⟨a *chattering* tool⟩ [Middle English *chatteren*] — **chatter** *n* — **chat•ter•er** \'chat-ər-ər\ *n*

chat•ter•box \'chat-ər-,bäks\ *n* : a person who talks continuously : a constant chatterer

chat•ty \'chat-ē\ *adj* **chat•ti•er; -est 1** : fond of chatting : TALKATIVE **2** : having the style and manner of light informal conversation ⟨a *chatty* letter⟩ — **chat•ti•ly** \'chat-l-ē\ *adv* — **chat•ti•ness** \'chat-ē-nəs\ *n*

[1]**chauf•feur** \'shō-fər, shō-'\ *n* : a person employed to drive an automobile for the transportation of persons or property [French, literally, "stoker", from *chauffer* "to heat", from Latin *calefacere,* from *calēre* "to be warm" + *facere* "to make"]

△ **origin** The French verb *chauffer* means "to heat", so the literal meaning of the noun *chauffeur* is "heater, one that heats". *Chauffeur* is the French name for the stoker who heats a steam engine and keeps it going. In the early days of the automobile, the French gave the nickname *chauffeur* to motorists. As automobiles became more common, *chauffeur* came to be used especially for people hired to drive for others. This is the sense of English *chauffeur,* borrowed from the French.

[2]**chauffeur** *vb* **1** : to do the work of a chauffeur **2** : to drive or transport as or as if a chauffeur ⟨*chauffeur* children to school⟩

chau•tau•qua \shə-'tò-kwə\ *n* : an institution of the late 19th and early 20th centuries offering educational entertainment (as lectures) in circuit performances often in a tent [*Chautauqua* lake, New York]

chau•vin•ism \'shō-və-,niz-əm\ *n* : excessive or blind patriotism or devotion to a group to which one belongs ⟨male *chauvinism*⟩ [French *chauvinisme,* from Nicolas *Chauvin,* 19th century French soldier excessively devoted to Napoleon and his regime] — **chau•vin•ist** \-və-nəst\ *n* — **chau•vin•is•tic** \,shō-və-'nis-tik\ *adj* — **chau•vin•is•ti•cal•ly** \-ti-kə-lē, -klē\ *adv*

cheap \'chēp\ *adj* **1** : of low cost or price ⟨a *cheap* watch⟩ **2** : worth little : of inferior quality ⟨*cheap* material wears out quickly⟩ **3 a** : gained with little effort **b** : not worth gaining ⟨*cheap* applause⟩ **4** : lowered in one's own opinion : ABASHED ⟨feel *cheap*⟩ **5 a** : charging low prices **b** : dealing in inferior goods **6 a** : lowered in value or purchasing power (as by inflation) ⟨*cheap* dollars⟩ **b** : obtainable at a low rate of interest ⟨*cheap* money⟩ [obsolete *cheap* "bargain", from Old English *cēap* "trade", from Latin *caupo* "tradesman"] — **cheap** *adv* — **cheap•ly** *adv* — **cheap•ness** *n*

cheap•en \'chē-pən\ *vb* **cheap•ened; cheap•en•ing** \'chēp-ning, -ə-ning\ : to make or become cheap or cheaper

cheap•skate \-,skāt\ *n* : a mean or miserly person [*cheap* + *skate* "miserly person"]

[1]**cheat** \'chēt\ *n* **1** : an act of cheating : DECEPTION, FRAUD **2** : one that cheats : DECEIVER [earlier *cheat* "forfeited property", from Middle English *eschete* "escheat"]

[2]**cheat** *vb* **1** : to rob by deceit or fraud ⟨*cheated* them out of a large sum⟩ **2** : to influence or lead astray by deceit, trick, or artifice **3** : to disappoint in a hope or purpose by deceit and trickery **4 a** : to practice fraud or trickery **b** : to violate rules dishonestly (as at cards)

• **syn** CHEAT, DEFRAUD, SWINDLE mean to get something from another by deception or dishonesty. CHEAT suggests using trickery that escapes observation; DEFRAUD stresses depriving one of legitimate rights and connotes deliberate lying or deception; SWINDLE implies cheating usually on a large scale by abuse of confidence.

[1]**check** \'chek\ *n* **1** : exposure of a chess king to an attack **2 a** : a stoppage of progress : ARREST, PAUSE **b** : the act of checking a hockey or lacrosse player **3** : something that arrests, limits, or restrains : RESTRAINT ⟨constitutional *checks* and balances⟩ **4 a** : a standard for testing and evaluation : CRITERION **b** : EXAMINATION 1, INVESTIGATION, VERIFICATION; *also* : the sample used for testing **5** : an order directing a bank to pay out money in accordance with instructions written thereon **6 a** : a ticket or token that shows that the bearer has a claim to property ⟨a baggage *check*⟩ or has made payment for a previous performance that did not take place ⟨a rain *check*⟩ **b** : a slip indicating the amount due : BILL **7 a** : a pattern in squares that resembles a checkerboard **b** : a fabric with such a design **8** : a mark ✓ placed beside an item to show it has been noted **9** : CRACK, BREAK ⟨a *check* in wood or steel⟩ [Old French *eschec,* from Arabic *shāh,* from Persian, literally, "king"] — **in check** : under restraint or control

[2]**check** *vb* **1** : to put (a chess king) in check **2 a** : to bring to a sudden pause : STOP **b** : to halt through caution, uncertainty, or fear : STOP **3 a** : RESTRAIN 2, CURB **b** : to legally impede or interfere with a hockey or lacrosse player **4 a** : to make sure of the correctness or satisfactoriness of **b** : to mark printing or

writing with a check to show that something has been specially noted **5** : to mark with squares or checks ⟨a *checked* suit⟩ **6** : to leave or accept for safekeeping in a checkroom or for shipment as baggage **7** : to investigate conditions ⟨*check* up on things⟩ **8** : to correspond point for point : TALLY **9** : to develop small cracks

check•book \ˈchek-ˌbu̇k\ *n* : a book containing blank checks to be drawn on a bank

1check•er \ˈchek-ər\ *n* **1** : a square or spot resembling the markings on a checkerboard **2** : a playing piece used in checkers [Middle English *cheker* "chessboard", from Old French *eschequier,* from *eschec* "check"]

2checker *vt* **check•ered**; **check•er•ing** \ˈchek-ring, -ə-ring\ **1** : to mark with squares or spots of different colors ⟨a *checkered* tablecloth⟩ **2** : to subject to frequent changes (as of fortune) ⟨a *checkered* career⟩

3checker *n* : one that checks; *esp* : an employee who checks out purchases in a supermarket

check•er•ber•ry \ˈchek-ər-ˌber-ē, ˈchek-ə-ˌ\ *n* : the spicy red fruit of an American wintergreen; *also* : this plant [*checker* "wild service tree" + *berry*]

check•er•board \-ˌbōrd, -ˌbȯrd\ *n* : a board used in games (as checkers) and marked with 64 squares in 2 alternating colors

check•ers \ˈchek-ərz\ *n* : a game played on a checkerboard by two persons each having 12 playing pieces

check•ing account \ˈchek-ing-\ *n* : an account in a bank from which the depositor can draw money by writing checks — compare SAVINGS ACCOUNT

check•list \ˈchek-ˌlist\ *n* : a list of items that may easily be referred to (as for verifying or comparing)

1check•mate \ˈchek-ˌmāt\ *vt* **1** : to arrest or frustrate completely **2** : to check (a chess opponent's king) so that escape is impossible [Middle English, interjection announcing checkmate, from Middle French *eschec mat,* from Arabic *shāh māt,* from Persian, literally, "the king is left unable to escape"]

2checkmate *n* **1 a** : the act of checkmating **b** : the situation of a checkmated king **2** : a thorough defeat

check•off \ˈchek-ˌȯf\ *n* : an authorized practice of deducting union dues from a worker's paycheck by the employer

check out *vb* : to total or have totaled the cost of purchases in a self-service store (as a supermarket) and make or receive payment for them

check•point \ˈchek-ˌpȯint\ *n* : a point at which traffic is halted for inspection or clearance

check•rein \-ˌrān\ *n* : a short rein fastened so that it prevents a horse from lowering its head

check•room \-ˌrüm, -ˌru̇m\ *n* : a room at which baggage, parcels, or clothing is checked

check•up \ˈchek-ˌəp\ *n* : EXAMINATION; *esp* : a general physical examination

ched•dar \ˈched-ər\ *n, often cap* : a hard pressed cheese of smooth texture [*Cheddar,* England]

cheek \ˈchēk\ *n* **1** : the fleshy side of the face below the eye and above and to the side of the mouth **2 a** : something suggesting the human cheek in position or form **b** : a lateral part or side (as of a structure or opening) **3** : saucy speech or behavior : IMPUDENCE [Old English *cēace*] — **cheek by jowl** : in close proximity

cheek•bone \-ˈbōn, -ˌbōn\ *n* : the bone or the bony prominence below the eye

cheek pouch *n* : an enlargement of the cheeks in some monkeys and rodents that resembles a sac and is used for holding food

cheek tooth *n* : MOLAR

cheeky \ˈchē-kē\ *adj* **cheek•i•er**; **-est** : IMPUDENT, SAUCY — **cheek•i•ness** *n*

cheep \ˈchēp\ *vb* : 1PEEP 1 [imitative] — **cheep** *n*

1cheer \ˈchiər\ *n* **1** : state of mind or heart : SPIRIT ⟨be of good *cheer*⟩ **2** : GAIETY 2, ANIMATION **3** : food and drink for or fit for a feast **4** : something that gladdens **5** : a shout of applause or encouragement [Middle English *chere* "face, cheer", from Old French, "face"]

2cheer *vb* **1** : to give hope to or make happier : COMFORT ⟨*cheer* a sick person⟩ **2** : to urge on especially with shouts or cheers ⟨*cheer* one's team to victory⟩ **3** : to shout with joy, approval, or enthusiasm ⟨the students *cheered* loudly⟩ **4** : to grow or be cheerful : REJOICE — usually used with *up*

cheer•ful \ˈchiər-fəl\ *adj* **1 a** : full of good spirits : HAPPY **b** : WILLING 3 ⟨*cheerful* obedience⟩ **2** : pleasantly bright : likely to dispel gloom or worry ⟨a sunny *cheerful* room⟩ — **cheer•ful•ly** \-fə-lē, -flē\ *adv* — **cheer•ful•ness** \-fəl-nəs\ *n*
• **syn** CHEERY: CHEERFUL implies an inner contentment that may or may not be shown or expressed outwardly ⟨*cheerful* acceptance of responsibility⟩ CHEERY stresses the brightening or enlivening effect of behavior on others ⟨a *cheery* welcome⟩ ⟨*cheery* laughter⟩

cheer•lead•er \ˈchiər-ˌlēd-ər\ *n* : a person who directs organized cheering especially at a sports event

cheer•less \ˈchiər-ləs\ *adj* : lacking in warmth of kindliness : DEPRESSING, GLOOMY — **cheer•less•ly** *adv* — **cheer•less•ness** *n*

cheery \ˈchiər-ē\ *adj* **cheer•i•er**; **-est** : causing or suggesting cheerfulness : gay in manner or effect **syn** see CHEERFUL — **cheer•i•ly** \ˈchir-ə-lē\ *adv* — **cheer•i•ness** \ˈchir-ē-nəs\ *n*

cheese \ˈchēz\ *n* : a food made from milk especially by separating out the curd and molding or pressing and usually ripening [Old English *cēse,* from Latin *caseus*]

cheese•bur•ger \-ˌbər-gər\ *n* : a hamburger with a slice of cheese

cheese•cake \-ˌkāk\ *n* **1** : a cake made by baking a mixture of cream cheese or cottage cheese, eggs, and sugar in a pastry shell or a mold **2** : photographs of attractive usually scantily clothed girls

cheese•cloth \-ˌklȯth\ *n* : a thin loose-woven cotton cloth [from its use in making cheese]

cheesy \ˈchē-zē\ *adj* **1** : resembling or suggesting cheese (as in texture or odor) **2** *slang* : of poor quality

chee•tah \ˈchēt-ə\ *n* : a long-legged spotted swift-moving African and formerly Asian cat about the size of a small leopard that is often trained to run down game [Hindi *cītā,* from Sanskrit *citrakāya* "tiger", from *citra* "bright" + *kāya* "body"]

cheetah

chef \ˈshef\ *n* : COOK; *esp* : a head cook [French, short for *chef de cuisine* "head of the kitchen"]

chef d'oeu•vre \shā-dœvr\ *n, pl* **chefs d'oeuvre** *same*\ : a masterpiece especially in art or literature [French *chef-d'oeuvre,* literally, "leading work"]

che•la \ˈkē-lə\ *n, pl* **che•lae** \-ˌlē\ : a pincerlike organ or claw on a limb of a crustacean or arachnid [Greek *chēlē* "claw"]

chela

che•late \ˈkē-ˌlāt\ *adj* : resembling or having chelae

che•lic•era \ki-ˈlis-ə-rə\ *n, pl* **-er•as** *or* **-er•ae** \-ˌrē\ : either of the front pair of appendages of an arachnid often specialized as fangs [French *chélicère,* from Greek *chēlē* "claw" + *keras* "horn"] — **che•lic•er•al** \-ə-rəl\ *adj*

che•li•ped \ˈkē-lə-ˌped\ *n* : either of the pair of legs of a crustacean that bear chelae [Greek *chēlē* "claw" + Latin *ped-, pes* "foot"]

che•lo•ni•an \ki-ˈlō-nē-ən\ *adj* : of, relating to, or being a tortoise or turtle [Greek *chelōnē* "tortoise"] — **chelonian** *n*

chem- *or* **chemo-** *also* **chemi-** *combining form* : chemical : chemistry ⟨*chemo*reception⟩

1chem•i•cal \ˈkem-i-kəl\ *adj* **1** : of, relating to, used in, or produced by chemistry **2** : acting or operated or produced by chemicals [New Latin *chimicus* "alchemist", from Medieval Latin *alchimicus,* from *alchymia* "alchemy"] — **chem•i•cal•ly** \-i-kə-lē, -klē\ *adv*

2chemical *n* **1** : a substance (as an element or compound) obtained by a chemical process or used for producing a chemical effect

chemical engineering *n* : engineering dealing with the industrial application of chemistry

chemical warfare *n* : tactical warfare using smoke-producing substances or burning, poisonous, or smothering gases

che•mise \shə-ˈmēz, -ˈmēs\ *n* **1 :** a woman's one-piece undergarment **2 :** a loose straight-hanging dress [Old French, "shirt", from Late Latin *camisia*]

chem•ist \ˈkem-əst\ *n* **1 :** one trained or working in chemistry **2** *British* **:** PHARMACIST [New Latin *chimista* "alchemist", from Medieval Latin *alchimista*]

chem•is•try \ˈkem-ə-strē\ *n* **1 :** a science that deals with the composition, structure, and properties of substances and with the changes that they undergo **2 :** chemical composition, properties, or processes ⟨the *chemistry* of iron⟩ ⟨the *chemistry* of blood⟩

che•mo•re•cep•tion \ˌkē-mō-ri-ˈsep-shən *also* ˌkem-ō-\ *n* **:** the physiological reception of chemical stimuli — **che•mo•re•cep•tor** \-ˈsep-tər\ *n*

che•mo•syn•the•sis \-ˈsin-thə-səs, -ˈsint-\ *n* **:** formation of organic compounds (as in living cells) using energy derived from chemical reactions — **che•mo•syn•thet•ic** \-sin-ˈthet-ik\ *adj*

che•mo•tax•is \-ˈtak-səs\ *n* **:** orientation or movement of an organism in relation to chemical agents — **che•mo•tac•tic** \-ˈtak-tik\ *adj*

che•mo•ther•a•peu•tic \-ˌther-ə-ˈpyüt-ik\ *adj* **:** of or relating to chemotherapy — **che•mo•ther•a•peu•ti•cal•ly** \-ˈpyüt-i-kə-lē, -klē\ *adv*

che•mo•ther•a•py \-ˈther-ə-pē\ *n* **:** the use of chemical agents in the treatment or control of disease

che•mot•ro•pism \ki-ˈmä-trə-ˌpiz-əm, ke-\ *n* **:** orientation of cells or organisms in relation to chemical stimuli

chem•ur•gy \ˈkem-ˌər-jē, -ər-; kə-ˈmər-\ *n* **:** chemistry that deals with industrial utilization of organic raw materials especially from farm products [*chem-* + Greek *ergon* "work"] — **chem•ur•gic** \kə-ˈmər-jik, ke-\ *adj* — **chem•ur•gi•cal•ly** \-ji-kə-lē, -klē\ *adv*

che•nille \shə-ˈnēl\ *n* **:** a fabric with a deep fuzzy pile often used for bedspreads and rugs [French, literally, "caterpillar", from Latin *canicula* "little dog", from *canis* "dog"]

cheque \ˈchek\ *chiefly British variant of* CHECK 5

cher•ish \ˈcher-ish\ *vt* **1 a :** to hold dear **:** feel or show affection for ⟨*cherished* their pet⟩ **b :** to keep with care and affection ⟨*cherish* your freedom⟩ **2 :** to harbor in the mind ⟨*cherish* a hope⟩ [Middle French *cheriss-*, stem of *cherir* "to cherish", from *cher* "dear", from Latin *carus*]

cher•no•zem \ˌchər-nə-ˈzhóm, -ˈzem\ *n* **:** a dark-colored zonal soil with a deep rich humus layer found in temperate to cool climates of rather low humidity [Russian, literally, "black earth"]

Cher•o•kee \ˈcher-ə-ˌkē\ *n* **:** a member of an Iroquoian people of the southern Appalachian mountains [probably from Creek *tciloki* "people of a different speech"]

Cherokee rose *n* **:** a climbing rose with fragrant usually white blossoms native to China and Japan but widely naturalized in the southern United States

cher•ry \ˈcher-ē\ *n, pl* **cherries 1 a :** any of numerous trees and shrubs of the rose family that have rather small pale yellow to deep blackish red smooth-skinned fruits and include several grown for their edible fruits or showy flowers **b :** the fruit of a cherry **c :** the wood of a cherry **2 :** a medium red color [Old North French *cherise* (understood as plural), from Late Latin *ceresia*, from Latin *cerasus* "cherry tree", from Greek *kerasos*] — **cherry** *adj*

chert \ˈchərt, ˈchat\ *n* **:** a rock resembling flint and consisting essentially of fine crystalline quartz or fibrous chalcedony [origin unknown]

cherty \ˈchərt-ē, ˈchat-\ *adj* **chert•i•er**; **chert•i•est 1 :** resembling flint **2 :** full of flint ⟨a *cherty* soil⟩

cher•ub \ˈcher-əb\ *n* **1** *pl* **cher•u•bim** \ˈcher-yə-ˌbim,ˈker-, -ə-\ **:** an angel of high rank **2** *pl* **cherubs a :** a beautiful usually winged child in fine art **b :** a chubby rosy child [Latin, from Greek *cheroub*, from Hebrew *kĕrūbh*]

cher•vil \ˈchər-vəl\ *n* **:** an aromatic herb of the carrot family with finely divided leaves often used in soups and salads [Old English *cerfille*]

Ches•a•peake Bay retriever \ˌches-ˌpēk-ˌbā-, -ə-ˌpēk-\ *n* **:** a large powerful sporting dog that was developed in Maryland and distinguished by a short dense brown coat

Chesh•ire cat \ˌchesh-ər-\ *n* **:** a cat with a broad grin in Lewis Carroll's *Alice's Adventures in Wonderland* [*Cheshire*, England]

Cheshire cheese *n* **:** a cheese similar to cheddar made chiefly in Cheshire, England

chess \ˈches\ *n* **:** a game of strategy for 2 players each of whom plays with 16 pieces on a checkerboard [Old French *esches*, plural of *eschec* "check"] — **chess•board** \-ˌbōrd, -ˌbórd\ *n*

chess•man \-ˌman, -mən\ *n* **:** one of the 32 pieces used in chess

chest \ˈchest\ *n* **1 :** a container for storage or shipping; *esp* **:** a box with a lid **2 :** a public fund collected for some purpose **3 :** the part of the body enclosed by the ribs and breastbone [Old English *cest*, from Latin *cista* "box, basket", from Greek *kistē* "basket, hamper"] — **chest•ed** \ˈches-təd\ *adj*

ches•ter•field \ˈches-tər-ˌfēld\ *n* **:** an overcoat with a velvet collar [from a 19th century Earl of *Chesterfield*]

Ches•ter White \ˌches-tər-\ *n* **:** any of a breed of large white swine [*Chester* County, Pennsylvania]

[1]**chest•nut** \ˈches-ˌnət, -nət\ *n* **1 :** an edible nut from several trees or shrubs of the beech family; *also* **:** a plant bearing chestnuts or its wood **2 :** HORSE CHESTNUT **3 :** a horse with the body colored pure or reddish brown and the mane, tail, and points of the same or a lighter shade — compare [2]BAY 1, SORREL **4 :** a callosity on the inner side of the leg of the horse **5 :** an often repeated old joke or story [Middle French *chastaigne* "chestnut tree", from Latin *castanea*, from Greek *kastanea*]

[2]**chestnut** *adj* **:** of a grayish to reddish brown color

chestnut blight *n* **:** a destructive fungous disease of the American chestnut

chest of drawers : a piece of furniture containing a set of drawers (as for holding clothing)

che•val-de-frise \shə-ˌval-də-ˈfrēz\ *n, pl* **che•vaux-de-frise** \shə-ˌvōd-ə-\ **:** a defense consisting of a timber or barrel covered with projecting spikes and often strung with barbed wire [French, literally, "horse from Friesland"]

che•val glass \shə-ˈval-\ *n* **:** a full-length mirror that may be tilted in a frame [French *cheval* "horse, support"]

chev•a•lier \ˌshev-ə-ˈliər, *especially for 2 also* shə-ˈval-ˌyā\ *n* **1 :** CAVALIER 2 **2 :** a member of any of various orders of knighthood or of merit (as the French Legion of Honor) [Middle French, from Late Latin *caballarius* "horseman"]

chev•i•ot \ˈshev-ē-ət, ˈchev-\ *n* **1 :** any of a breed of hardy hornless British sheep **2 a :** a heavy napped woolen or worsted fabric **b :** a sturdy cotton shirting [*Cheviot* hills, England and Scotland]

chev•ron \ˈshev-rən\ *n* **1 :** a figure resembling an upside-down V **2 :** a sleeve badge usually indicating rank or service (as in the armed forces) [Middle French, "rafter, chevron"]

1 2 3
chevron 2: *1* marine, *2* air force, *3* army

[1]**chew** \ˈchü\ *vb* **:** to crush or grind with the teeth [Old English *cēowan*] — **chew•able** \-ə-bəl\ *adj* — **chew•er** *n* — **chewy** \ˈchü-ē\ *adj*

[2]**chew** *n* **1 :** the act of chewing **2 :** something for chewing

chewing gum *n* **:** gum usually of sweetened and flavored chicle prepared for chewing

che•wink \chi-ˈwingk\ *n* **:** TOWHEE 1 [imitative]

Chey•enne \shī-ˈan, -ˈen\ *n* **:** a member of an Algonquian people of the western plains [Canadian French, from Dakota *Shaiyena*, from *shaia* "to speak unintelligibly"]

chi \ˈkī\ *n* **:** the 22d letter of the Greek alphabet — Χ or χ

Chi•an•ti \kē-ˈänt-ē, -ˈant-\ *n* **:** a dry usually red table wine [*Chianti* mountain area, Italy]

chiar•oscu•ro \kē-ˌär-ə-ˈskür-ō, -ˈskyür-\ *n* **1 :** pictorial representation in terms of light and shade without regard to color **2 :** the arrangement or treatment of light and dark parts in a pictorial work of art [Italian, from *chiaro* "clear, light" + *oscuro* "obscure, dark"] — **chiar•oscu•rist** \-ˈskür-əst, -ˈskyür-\ *n*

\ə\ **abut**	\aù\ **out**	\i\ **tip**	\ȯ\ **saw**	\ù\ **foot**
\ər\ **further**	\ch\ **chin**	\ī\ **life**	\ȯi\ **coin**	\y\ **yet**
\a\ **mat**	\e\ **pet**	\j\ **job**	\th\ **thin**	\yü\ **few**
\ā\ **take**	\ē\ **easy**	\ng\ **sing**	\th\ **this**	\yù\ **cure**
\ä\ **cot, cart**	\g\ **go**	\ō\ **bone**	\ü\ **food**	\zh\ **vision**

chi•as•mus \kī-ˈaz-məs\ *n* : reversal in word order between the elements of parallel phrases (as in *we must not live to eat, but eat to live*) [Greek *chiasmos,* from *chiazein* "to mark with a chi"]

Chib•cha \ˈchib-ˌchä\ *n, pl* **Chibcha** *or* **Chibchas** : a member of an Indian people originally of central Colombia [Spanish, of American Indian origin]

[1]**chic** \ˈshēk\ *n* : STYLE 5c [French]

[2]**chic** *adj* : cleverly stylish : SMART

chi•cane \shik-ˈān, chik-\ *n* : CHICANERY [French]

chi•ca•nery \-ˈān-rē, -ə-rē\ *n, pl* **-ner•ies** : artful trickery

Chi•ca•no \chi-ˈkän-ō, shi-, -ˈkan-\ *n, pl* **-nos** : an American of Mexican descent [modification of Spanish *mejicano* "Mexican"] — **Chicano** *adj*

chi•chi \ˈshē-ˌshē, ˈchē-ˌchē\ *adj* **1** : elaborately ornamented **2** : ARTY ⟨a *chichi* film⟩ **3** : FASHIONABLE, CHIC ⟨*chichi* nightclubs⟩ [French] — **chichi** *n*

chick \ˈchik\ *n* **1 a** : CHICKEN; *esp* : one newly hatched **b** : the young of any bird **2** *slang* : a young woman

chick•a•dee \ˈchik-əd-ē\ *n* : any of several crestless American titmice usually with the crown of the head darker than the body [imitative]

chick•a•ree \ˈchik-ə-ˌrē\ *n* : RED SQUIRREL [imitative]

Chick•a•saw \ˈchik-ə-ˌsò\ *n* : a member of an Indian people of what is now northern Mississippi and Alabama and western Tennessee

chick•en \ˈchik-ən\ *n* **1** : the common domestic fowl especially when young; *also* : its flesh used as food **2** : any of various birds or their young **3** : COWARD [Old English *cicen* "young chicken"]

chicken hawk *n* : a hawk that preys or is said to prey on chickens

chick•en•heart•ed \ˌchik-ən-ˈhärt-əd\ *adj* : TIMID, COWARDLY

chicken pox *n* : a contagious virus disease especially of children marked by low fever and watery blisters on the skin

chicken snake *n* : any of several rat snakes

chick–pea \ˈchik-ˌpē\ *n* : an Asiatic leguminous herb cultivated for its short pods with one or two edible seeds; *also* : its seed [by folk etymology from Middle English *chiche,* from Middle French, from Latin *cicer*]

chick•weed \ˈchik-ˌwēd\ *n* : any of several low-growing small-leaved weedy plants of the pink family

chi•cle \ˈchik-əl, -lē\ *n* : a gum from the latex of the sapodilla used as the chief ingredient of chewing gum [Spanish, from Nahuatl *chictli*]

chic•o•ry \ˈchik-rē, -ə-rē\ *n, pl* **-ries** : a thick-rooted usually blue-flowered European perennial herb related to the daisies and grown for its roots and as a salad plant; *also* : its dried ground roasted root used to flavor or adulterate coffee [Middle French *cichorée, chicorée,* from Latin *cichoreum,* from Greek *kichoreia*]

chide \ˈchīd\ *vb* **chid** \ˈchid\ *or* **chid•ed** \ˈchīd-əd\; **chid** *or* **chid•den** \ˈchid-n\ *or* **chided**; **chid•ing** \ˈchīd-ing\ : to speak disapprovingly to : SCOLD [Old English *cīdan* "to quarrel, chide", from *cīd* "strife"]

[1]**chief** \ˈchēf\ *n* **1** : the upper part of an heraldic field **2** : the head of a group or organization : LEADER ⟨*chief* of police⟩ **3** : the principal part [Old French, "head, chief", from Latin *caput* "head"] — **in chief 1** : held or holding rights or title directly from a paramount feudal lord ⟨tenure *in chief*⟩ **2** : in the chief position or place ⟨editor *in chief*⟩

[2]**chief** *adj* **1** : highest in rank, office, or authority **2** : of greatest importance, significance, or influence

chief executive *n* : a principal officer: as **a** : the president of a republic **b** : the governor of a state

chief justice *n* : the principal judge of a court of justice

[1]**chief•ly** \ˈchē-flē\ *adv* **1** : most importantly : PRINCIPALLY **2** : for the most part : MOSTLY

[2]**chiefly** *adj* : of or relating to a chief ⟨*chiefly* duties⟩

chief master sergeant *n* : an enlisted rank in the Air Force above senior master sergeant

chief of staff 1 : the ranking officer of a military staff and principal adviser to the commander **2** : the ranking office of the Army or Air force

chief of state : the formal head of a national state as distinguished from the head of the government

chief petty officer *n* : an enlisted rank in the Navy and Coast Guard above petty officer first class and below senior chief petty officer

chief•tain \ˈchēf-tən\ *n* : a chief especially of a band, tribe, or clan [Middle French *chevetain,* from Late Latin *capitaneus* "chief"] — **chief•tain•cy** \-sē\ *n* — **chief•tain•ship** \-ˌship\ *n*

chief warrant officer *n* : any of the three warrant officer ranks in the Navy and Coast Guard and the three upper warrant officer ranks in the Army, Marine Corps, and Air Force

chif•fon \shif-ˈän, ˈshif-ˌ\ *n* : a sheer usually silk fabric [French, literally, "rag", from Middle French *chipe* "old rag", from Middle English *chip* "chip"]

chif•fo•nier \ˌshif-ə-ˈniər\ *n* : a high narrow chest of drawers often with a mirror [French *chiffonnier,* from *chiffon*]

chig•ger \ˈchig-ər, ˈjig-\ *n* **1** : CHIGOE 1 **2** : a 6-legged larval mite that sucks the blood of vertebrates and causes intense irritation [of African origin]

chi•gnon \ˈshēn-ˌyän\ *n* : a knot of hair worn at the back of the head [French]

chig•oe \ˈchig-ō, ˈchē-gō\ *n* **1** : a tropical flea of which the fertile female burrows under the skin causing great discomfort — called also *chigger* **2** : CHIGGER 2 [of American Indian origin]

Chi•hua•hua \chə-ˈwä-ˌwä, shə-, -wə\ *n* : a very small round-headed large-eared dog held to antedate Aztec civilization [*Chihuahua,* Mexico]

Chihuahua

chil•blain \ˈchil-ˌblān\ *n* : an inflammatory swelling or sore caused by exposure (as of the feet or hands) to cold

child \ˈchīld\ *n, pl* **chil•dren** \ˈchil-drən, -dərn\ **1** : an unborn or recently born person **2 a** : a young person especially between infancy and youth **b** : a childlike or childish person **c** : a person not yet of legal age **3** *usually* **childe** \ˈchīld\ *archaic* : a youth of noble birth **4 a** : a son or daughter of human parents **b** : DESCENDANT 1 **5** : one strongly influenced by another or by a place or state of affairs ⟨a *child* of the times⟩ [Old English *cild*] — **child•less** \ˈchīl-ləs, -dləs\ *adj* — **with child** : PREGNANT

child•bear•ing \ˈchīl-ˌbar-ing, ˈchīld-, -ˌber-\ *n* : the act of giving birth to children — **childbearing** *adj*

child•bed fever \ˌchīl-ˌbed-, ˌchīld-\ *n* : PUERPERAL FEVER

child•birth \ˈchīl-ˌbərth, ˈchīld-\ *n* : the act or process of giving birth to offspring — called also *parturition*

child•hood \ˈchīld-ˌhůd\ *n* : the state or time of being a child

child•ish \ˈchīl-dish\ *adj* **1** : of, resembling, or suitable to a child ⟨*childish* games⟩ **2** : marked by the less pleasing qualities (as silliness) often felt to be characteristic of the young — **child•ish•ly** *adv* — **child•ish•ness** *n*

child•like \ˈchīl-ˌlīk, -ˌdlīk\ *adj* **1** : of, relating to, or resembling a child or childhood **2** : marked by the more pleasing qualities (as simplicity, innocence, and trustfulness) often felt to be characteristic of the young — **child•like•ness** *n*

child's play *n* **1** : an extremely simple task **2** : something that is unimportant

Chile saltpeter \ˈchil-ē-\ *n* : sodium nitrate especially occurring naturally [*Chile,* South America]

chili *or* **chile** *or* **chil•li** \ˈchil-ē\ *n, pl* **chil•ies** *or* **chil•es** *or* **chil•lies 1 a** : HOT PEPPER 1 **b** *usually chilli, chiefly British* : a pepper whether hot or sweet **2** : CHILI CON CARNE [Spanish *chile,* from Nahuatl *chilli*]

chili con car•ne \ˌchil-ē-ˌkän-ˈkär-nē, -ē-kən-\ *n* : a stew of ground beef, hot peppers or chili powder, and usually beans [Spanish *chile con carne* "chili with meat"]

chili powder *n* : a seasoning made of ground hot peppers, oregano, garlic, cloves, and allspice

chili sauce *n* : a spiced tomato sauce usually made with red and green peppers

[1]**chill** \ˈchil\ *vb* **1** : to make or become cold or chilly **2** : to harden the surface of (metal) by sudden cooling [Old English *cele* "cold, frost"] — **chill•er** *n* — **chill•ing•ly** \-ing-lē\ *adv*

[2]**chill** *adj* **1 a** : fairly cold ⟨a *chill* night⟩ **b** : COLD 1, RAW ⟨a *chill* wind⟩ **2** : affected by cold **3** : cool in manner : DISTANT ⟨a *chill* greeting⟩ — **chill•ness** *n*

[3]**chill** *n* **1** : a sensation of cold accompanied by shivering **2** : a moderate but unpleasant degree of cold **3** : a depressing effect on the feelings

chilly \'chil-ē\ *adj* **chill•i•er; -est 1 :** noticeably cold **2 :** unpleasantly affected by cold **3 :** lacking warmth of feeling — **chill•i•ly** \'chil-ə-lē\ *adv* — **chill•i•ness** \'chil-ē-nəs\ *n*

[1]**chime** \'chīm\ *n* **1 :** a musically tuned set of bells **2 a :** the sound of a set of bells — usually used in pl. **b :** a musical sound suggesting that of bells [Middle English, "cymbal", from Old French *chimbe,* from Latin *cymbalum*]

[2]**chime** *vb* **1 a :** to make a musical and usually harmonious sound **b :** to make the sounds of a chime **c :** to cause to chime **2 :** to be or act in accord **3 :** to call or indicate by chiming ⟨a clock *chiming* midnight⟩ **4 :** to utter repetitively — **chim•er** *n*

chime in *vb* **:** to break into or join in a conversation

chi•me•ra *or* **chi•mae•ra** \kī-'mir-ə, kə-\ *n* **1** *cap* **:** a fire-breathing she-monster in Greek mythology usually with a lion's head, a goat's body, and a serpent's tail **2 :** an often grotesque creation of the imagination **3 :** an individual, organ, or part with tissues of diverse genetic constitution [Latin *chimaera,* from Greek *chimaira* "she-goat, chimera"]

chi•mer•i•cal \kī-'mer-i-kəl, kə-, -'mir-\ *or* **chi•mer•ic** \-ik\ *adj* **1 :** existing only in the imagination **2 :** inclined to fantastic ideas or schemes — **chi•mer•i•cal•ly** \-i-kə-lē, -klē\ *adv*

chim•ney \'chim-nē\ *n, pl* **chimneys 1 :** a passage for smoke; *esp* **:** an upright structure (as of brick or stone) extending above the roof of a building **2 :** a glass tube around a lamp flame [Middle French *cheminée,* from Late Latin *caminata,* from Latin *caminus* "furnace, fireplace", from Greek *kaminos*]

chim•ney•piece \'chim-nē-ˌpēs\ *n* **:** a decorative construction over and around a fireplace that includes the mantel

chimney pot *n* **:** a usually earthenware pipe at the top of a chimney to increase draft and carry off smoke

chimney sweep *n* **:** a person who cleans soot from chimneys

chimney swift *n* **:** a small sooty-gray bird with long narrow wings that often attaches its nest to the inside of an unused chimney

chimp \'chimp, 'shimp\ *n* **:** CHIMPANZEE

chim•pan•zee \ˌchim-ˌpan-'zē, ˌshim-; chim-'pan-zē, shim-\ *n* **:** an African anthropoid ape that is smaller, weaker, and more arboreal than the gorilla [of African origin]

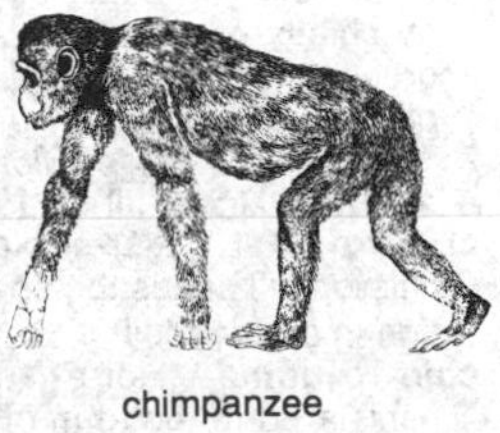
chimpanzee

[1]**chin** \'chin\ *n* **:** the lower portion of the face lying below the lower lip and including the prominence of the lower jaw [Old English *cinn*]

[2]**chin** *vb* **chinned; chin•ning 1 :** to raise (oneself) while hanging by the hands until the chin is level with the support **2** *slang* **:** to talk idly **:** CHATTER

chi•na \'chī-nə\ *n* **1 :** vitreous porcelain ware originally from the Orient; *also* **:** PORCELAIN **2 :** articles (as dishes) of porcelain or earthenware for domestic use [Persian *chīnī* "Chinese porcelain"]

chi•na•ber•ry \'chī-nə-ˌber-ē\ *n* **1 :** a soapberry of the southern United States and Mexico **2 :** a small Asiatic tree of the mahogany family naturalized in the southern United States where it is widely planted for shade or ornament

Chi•na•man \'chī-nə-mən\ *n* **:** CHINESE 1 — often taken to be offensive

Chi•na•town \-ˌtau̇n\ *n* **:** the Chinese quarter of a city

China tree *n* **:** CHINABERRY 2

chi•na•ware \'chī-nə-ˌwaər, -ˌweər\ *n* **:** tableware made of china

chinch \'chinch\ *n* **:** BEDBUG [Spanish *chinche,* from Latin *cimex*]

chinch bug *n* **:** a small black-and-white bug very destructive to cereal grasses

chin•chil•la \chin-'chil-ə\ *n* **1 :** a South American rodent the size of a large squirrel widely bred in captivity for its very soft fur of a pearly gray color; *also* **:** its fur **2 :** a heavy twilled woolen coating [Spanish]

chine \'chīn\ *n* **1 :** BACKBONE, SPINE; *also* **:** a cut of meat or fish including the backbone or part of it and the surrounding flesh **2 :** CREST 2, RIDGE **3 :** the intersection of the bottom and sides of a boat [Middle French *eschine,* of Germanic origin]

Chi•nese \chī-'nēz, -'nēs\ *n, pl* **Chinese 1 a :** a native or inhabitant of China **b :** a person of Chinese descent **2 a :** a group of related languages used by the people of China that are often mutually unintelligible in their spoken form but share a single system of writing **b :** MANDARIN 2 — **Chinese** *adj*

Chinese cabbage *n* **:** either of two Asian plants related to the common cabbage and widely used as greens

Chinese checkers *n* **:** a game in which each player in turn transfers his or her pieces from a home point to the opposite point of a 6-pointed star by means of single moves and jumps

Chinese lantern *n* **:** a collapsible lantern of thin colored paper

Chinese liver fluke *n* **:** a common and destructive Asian liver fluke that invades the human liver

Chinese puzzle *n* **1 :** an elaborate or clever puzzle **2 :** something complex and hard to solve

Ching *or* **Ch'ing** \'ching\ *n* **:** a Manchu dynasty in China dated 1644–1912 and the last imperial dynasty

[1]**chink** \'chingk\ *n* **:** a narrow slit or crack (as in a wall) [probably from Middle English *chin* "crack, fissure", from Old English *cine*]

[2]**chink** *vt* **:** to fill the chinks of (as by caulking)

[3]**chink** *n* **:** a short sharp sound [imitative]

[4]**chink** *vb* **:** to make or cause to make a short sharp sound

chi•no \'chē-nō, 'shē-\ *n, pl* **chinos 1 :** a usually khaki cotton twill fabric **2 a :** an article of clothing made of chino **b** *pl* **:** chino pants [American Spanish]

Chi•nook \shə-'nu̇k, chə-\ *n* **1 :** a member of an Indian people of the shores of the Columbia river **2** *not cap* **a :** a warm moist southwest wind of the coast from Oregon northward **b :** a warm dry wind that descends the eastern slopes of the Rocky mountains

Chinook salmon *n* **:** a large commercially important salmon of the northern Pacific ocean usually with red flesh

chin•qua•pin \'ching-ki-ˌpin\ *n* **:** an American dwarf chestnut; *also* **:** its edible nut [of American Indian origin]

chintz \'chins\ *n* **1 :** a printed calico from India **2 :** a usually glazed printed cotton fabric [earlier *chints,* plural of *chint,* from Hindi *chīṭ*]

chintzy \'chin-sē\ *adj* **chintz•i•er; -est 1 :** decorated with or as if with chintz **2 :** TAWDRY

chin-up \'chin-ˌəp\ *n* **:** the act or an instance of chinning oneself especially as a conditioning exercise

[1]**chip** \'chip\ *n* **1 a :** a small piece (as of stone) broken off by a sharp blow **:** FLAKE **b (1) :** a thin crisp slice of potato **(2) :** FRENCH FRY **2 a :** a counter used in poker **b** *pl, slang* **:** MONEY 1,2 **3 :** a piece of dried dung ⟨cow *chip*⟩ **4 :** a flaw left after a small piece has been broken off ⟨a cup with a *chip* in it⟩ **5 :** INTEGRATED CIRCUIT [Middle English] — **chip off the old block :** a child that resembles his or her parent — **chip on one's shoulder :** a challenging or belligerent attitude

[2]**chip** *vb* **chipped; chip•ping 1 a :** to cut with an edged tool ⟨*chip* ice from a sidewalk⟩ **b (1) :** to cut or break (a small piece) from something **(2) :** to cut or break a chip from ⟨*chip* a cup⟩ **2 :** to break off in small pieces

chip in *vb* **:** CONTRIBUTE ⟨everyone *chipped in* to buy the gift⟩

chip•munk \'chip-ˌməngk\ *n* **:** any of numerous small striped largely terrestrial American squirrels [of American Indian origin]

chipmunk

chipped beef \'chipt-, 'chip-\ *n* **:** smoked dried beef sliced thin

Chip•pen•dale \'chip-ən-ˌdāl\ *adj* **:** of or relating to a late 18th century English furniture style characterized by graceful outline and often ornate ornamentation [Thomas *Chippendale,* died 1779, English cabinetmaker]

chip•per \'chip-ər\ *adj* **:** SPRIGHTLY, GAY ⟨looks bright and *chip-*

\ə\ **abut**	\au̇\ **out**	\i\ **tip**	\ȯ\ **saw**	\u̇\ **foot**
\ər\ **further**	\ch\ **chin**	\ī\ **life**	\ȯi\ **coin**	\y\ **yet**
\a\ **mat**	\e\ **pet**	\j\ **job**	\th\ **thin**	\yü\ **few**
\ā\ **take**	\ē\ **easy**	\ng\ **sing**	\t͟h\ **this**	\yu̇\ **cure**
\ä\ **cot, cart**	\g\ **go**	\ō\ **bone**	\ü\ **food**	\zh\ **vision**

per every morning⟩ [perhaps from English dialect *kipper* "lively"]
Chip•pe•wa \'chip-ə-,wȯ, -,wä, -,wā\ *n* : OJIBWA
chip•ping sparrow \'chip-ing-\ *n* : a small eastern North American sparrow whose song is a monotonous trill
chiro- *combining form* : hand ⟨*chiro*practic⟩ [Greek *cheir*]
chi•rog•ra•phy \kī-'räg-rə-fē\ *n* **1** : HANDWRITING 1, PENMANSHIP **2** : CALLIGRAPHY 1 — **chi•rog•ra•pher** \-fər\ *n* — **chi•ro•graph•ic** \,kī-rə-'graf-ik\ *adj*
chi•rop•o•dy \kə-'räp-əd-ē\ *n* : PODIATRY [*chir-* + *-pod,* from its original concern with both hands and feet] — **chi•rop•o•dist** \-əd-əst\ *n*
chi•ro•prac•tic \'kī-rə-,prak-tik\ *n* : a system of therapy based on manipulation and adjustment of body structures (as the spinal column) [*chir-* + Greek *praktikos* "practical, operative"] — **chi•ro•prac•tor** \-tər\ *n*
chi•rop•ter•an \kī-'räp-tə-rən\ *n* : [3]BAT [Greek *cheir* "hand" + *pteron* "wing"]
chirp \'chərp\ *n* : the characteristic short sharp sound of a small bird or cricket [imitative] — **chirp** *vi*
chirr \'chər\ *n* : the characteristic vibrant or trilled sound of a cicada [imitative] — **chirr** *vi*
chir•rup \'chər-əp, 'chir-\ *n* : CHIRP [imitative] — **chirrup** *vb*
[1]chis•el \'chiz-əl\ *n* : a metal tool with a cutting edge at the end of a blade used to shape or chip away stone, wood, or metal [Old North French, derived from Latin *caedere* "to cut"]
[2]chisel *vb* **-eled** *or* **-elled**; **-el•ing** *or* **-el•ling** \'chiz-ling, -ə-ling\ **1** : to cut or work with or as if with a chisel **2 a** : to use shrewd sometimes unfair practices **b** : CHEAT — **chis•el•er** \'chiz-lər, -ə-lər\ *n*
chis•eled *or* **chis•elled** \'chiz-əld\ *adj* : appearing as if shaped with a chisel : finely cut ⟨sharply *chiseled* features⟩
chi–square \'kī-'skwaər, -'skweər\ *n* : a statistic that is a sum of terms each of which is a quotient obtained by dividing the square of the difference between the observed and theoretical values of a quantity by the theoretical value
chit \'chit\ *n* **1** : CHILD 2a **2** : a pert young woman [Middle English *chitte* "kitten, cub"]
chit•chat \'chit-,chat\ *n* : SMALL TALK, GOSSIP [reduplication of *chat*]
chi•tin \'kīt-n\ *n* : a horny substance that forms part of the hard outer integument of some invertebrates (as insects and crustaceans) [French *chitine,* from Greek *chitōn* "chiton, tunic"] — **chi•tin•ous** \-əs\ *adj*
chi•ton \'kīt-n, 'kī-,tän\ *n* **1** : any of a class (Amphineura) of bilaterally symmetrical marine mollusks with a dorsal shell of calcareous plates **2** : a tunic worn in ancient Greece [Greek *chitōn* "tunic", of Semitic origin]
chit•ter \'chit-ər\ *vi* **1** : TWITTER 1, CHIRP **2** : CHATTER 1 [Middle English *chiteren*]
chit•ter•lings *or* **chit•lings** *or* **chit•lins** \'chit-lənz\ *n pl* : the intestines of hogs especially when prepared as food [Middle English *chiterling*]
chi•val•ric \shə-'val-rik\ *adj* : of or relating to chivalry : CHIVALROUS
chiv•al•rous \'shiv-əl-rəs\ *adj* **1** : VALIANT **2** : of or relating to chivalry **3** : having or displaying the qualities of an ideal knight of the age of chivalry: as **a** : marked by honor, generosity, and courtesy **b** : marked by especial courtesy and consideration to women — **chiv•al•rous•ly** *adv* — **chiv•al•rous•ness** *n*
chiv•al•ry \-rē\ *n, pl* **-ries** **1** : a body of knights ⟨the *chivalry* of France⟩ **2** : the system, spirit, ways, or customs of medieval knighthood **3** : the qualities (as bravery, honor, protection of the weak, and generous treatment of foes) held to characterize an ideal knight [Old French *chevalerie,* from *chevalier*]
chive \'chīv\ *n* : a perennial herb related to the onion and used for flavoring [Old North French, from Latin *cepa* "onion"]
chlam•ydo•mo•nas \,klam-əd-ə-'mō-nəs\ *n* : any of a genus of single-celled algae that have an eyespot and two flagella and are abundant in fresh water and damp soil [Greek *chlamyd-, chlamys* "mantle" + *monas* "unit"]
chla•mydo•spore \klə-'mid-ə-,spōr, -,spȯr\ *n* : a thick-walled usually resting spore
chlor- *or* **chloro-** *combining form* **1** : green ⟨*chlor*osis⟩ **2** : chlorine ⟨*chlor*tetracycline⟩ [Greek *chlōros* "greenish yellow"]
chlo•ral hydrate \'klōr-əl-, 'klȯr-\ *n* : a bitter white crystalline drug $C_2H_3Cl_3O_2$ used to bring sleep — called also *chloral*
chlor•am•phen•i•col \,klōr-,am-'fen-i-,kȯl, klȯr-, -,kōl\ *n* : a broad-spectrum antibiotic originally isolated from cultures of a soil microorganism or prepared synthetically
chlo•rate \'klōr-,āt, 'klȯr-\ *n* : a salt of chloric acid
chlor•dane \'klōr-,dān\ *or* **chlor•dan** \-,dan\ *n* : a viscous volatile liquid insecticide $C_{10}H_6Cl_8$ [*chlor-* + *indane, indan* (C_9H_{10})]
chlor•di•az•epox•ide \,klōr-dī-,az-ə-'päk-,sīd, ,klȯr-\ *n* : a compound the hydrochloride of which is used as a tranquilizer — compare LIBRIUM
chlo•rel•la \klə-'rel-ə\ *n* : any of a genus of unicellular green algae potentially a cheap source of high-grade protein and B-complex vitamins [derived from Greek *chlōros* "greenish yellow"]
chlo•ren•chy•ma \klōr-'eng-kə-mə, klȯr-\ *n* : chlorophyll-containing tissue [*chlor-* + *-enchyma* (as in *parenchyma*)]
chlo•ric acid \,klōr-ik-, ,klȯr-\ *n* : a strong acid $HClO_3$ like nitric acid in oxidizing properties but far less stable
chlo•ride \'klōr-,īd, 'klȯr-\ *n* : a chemical compound of chlorine with another element or radical; *esp* : a salt or ester of hydrochloric acid
chloride of lime : BLEACHING POWDER
chlo•ri•nate \'klōr-ə-,nāt, 'klȯr-\ *vt* : to treat or cause to combine with chlorine especially for purifying — **chlo•ri•na•tion** \,klōr-ə-'nā-shən, ,klȯr-\ *n* — **chlo•ri•na•tor** \'klōr-ə-,nāt-ər, 'klȯr-\ *n*
chlorinated lime *n* : BLEACHING POWDER
chlo•rine \'klōr-,ēn, 'klȯr-, -ən\ *n* : a chemical element that is a heavy greenish yellow irritating gas of pungent odor used especially as a bleach, oxidizing agent, and disinfectant in water purification — see ELEMENT table
chlorine water *n* : a yellowish aqueous solution of chlorine in water used for bleaching
chlo•rite \'klōr-,īt, 'klȯr-\ *n* : any of a group of usually green minerals associated with and resembling the micas
[1]chlo•ro•form \'klōr-ə-,fȯrm, 'klȯr-\ *n* : a colorless volatile heavy poisonous liquid $CHCl_3$ with anesthetic properties that smells like ether and is used especially as a solvent [*chlor-* + *form*ic acid]
[2]chloroform *vt* : to treat with chloroform especially so as to produce anesthesia or death
chlo•ro•phyll \'klōr-ə-,fil, 'klȯr-, -fəl\ *n* : the green photosynthetic coloring matter of plants found in chloroplasts and made up chiefly of a bluish black ester $C_{55}H_{72}MgN_4O_5$ and a dark green ester $C_{55}H_{70}MgN_4O_6$ — called also respectively *chlorophyll a, chlorophyll b* [French *chlorophylle,* from *chlor-* "chlor-" + Greek *phyllon* "leaf"] — **chlo•ro•phyl•lose** \,klōr-ə-'fil-,ōs, klȯr-, -,fil-'\ *adj* — **chlo•ro•phyl•lous** \-'fil-əs\ *adj*
chlo•ro•plast \'klōr-ə-,plast, 'klȯr-\ *n* : a plastid that contains chlorophyll and is the seat of photosynthesis and starch formation in a plant cell
chlo•ro•quine \'klōr-ə-,kwēn, 'klȯr-\ *n* : a drug $C_{18}H_{26}ClN_3$ administered in the form of a phosphate for the treatment of malaria [*chlor-* + *quinine*]
chlo•ro•sis \klə-'rō-səs\ *n, pl* **-ro•ses** \-'rō-,sēz\ **1** : an anemia in which the skin is greenish **2** : a disorder of green plants marked by yellowing or blanching — **chlo•rot•ic** \-'rät-ik\ *adj*
chlor•prom•azine \klōr-'präm-ə-,zēn, klȯr-, -zən\ *n* : a phenothiazine derivative $C_{17}H_{19}ClN_2S$ used as a tranquilizer in the form of its hydrochloride — compare THORAZINE
chlor•tet•ra•cy•cline \,klōr-,te-trə-'sī-,klēn, ,klȯr-\ *n* : a yellow crystalline antibiotic $C_{22}H_{23}ClN_2O_8$ produced by a soil actinomycete, used in the treatment of diseases, and added to animal feeds for stimulating growth
[1]chock \'chäk\ *n* **1** : a wedge or block for steadying a body (as a cask) and holding it motionless, for filling in an unwanted space, or for blocking the movement of a wheel **2** : a metal fitting with two short arms curving inward between which ropes may pass for mooring or towing [origin unknown]
[2]chock *vt* : to stop or make fast with or as if with chocks
chock•a•block \'chäk-ə-,bläk\ *adj* : very full : CROWDED
chock–full \'chək-'fu̇l, 'chäk-\ *or* **chuck–full** \'chək-\ *adj* : full to the limit [Middle English *chokkefull,* probably from *choken* "to choke" + *full*]
choc•o•late \'chäk-lət, 'chȯk-, -ə-lət\ *n* **1** : a food prepared from ground roasted cacao beans **2** : a beverage of chocolate in water or milk **3** : a candy with a chocolate coating **4** : a brownish gray color [Spanish, from Nahuatl *xocoatl*] — **chocolate** *adj*
Choc•taw \'chäk-,tȯ\ *n* **1** : a member of an Indian people of

what is now Mississippi, Alabama, and Louisiana **2 :** the language of the Choctaw and Chickasaw people [Choctaw *Chahta*]

[1]**choice** \'chȯis\ *n* **1 :** the act of choosing : SELECTION **2 :** power of choosing : OPTION **3 a :** a person or thing chosen **b :** the best part : CREAM **4 :** a sufficient number and variety for wide or free selection [Old French *chois,* from *choisir* "to choose", of Germanic origin]

• **syn** CHOICE, OPTION, ALTERNATIVE, PREFERENCE mean the act or opportunity of choosing or the thing chosen. CHOICE suggests the opportunity or privilege of choosing freely; OPTION implies a power to choose that is specifically granted or guaranteed; ALTERNATIVE implies a necessity to choose one and reject another possibility; PREFERENCE suggests the guidance of choice by one's judgment or inclinations.

[2]**choice** *adj* **1 :** very fine : better than most ⟨*choice* fruits⟩ **2 :** of a grade between prime and good ⟨*choice* meat⟩ — **choice•ly** *adv* — **choice•ness** *n*

choir \'kwīr\ *n* **1 :** an organized group of singers especially in a church **2 :** the part of a church assigned to the choir and usually located between the sanctuary and the nave **3 :** any of the nine ranks of angels **4 :** a group of instruments of the same class [Old French *cuer,* from Latin *chorus* "chorus"]

choir•boy \-ˌbȯi\ *n* **:** a boy member of a church choir

choir loft *n* **:** a gallery occupied by a church choir

choir•mas•ter \-ˌmas-tər\ *n* **:** the director of a choir (as in a church)

[1]**choke** \'chōk\ *vb* **1 :** to hinder normal breathing by cutting off the supply of air **2 :** to have the windpipe stopped entirely or partly ⟨*choke* on a bone⟩ **3 :** to check the growth or action of : SUPPRESS, SMOTHER ⟨*choke* a fire⟩ ⟨*choke* back tears⟩ **4 :** to obstruct by clogging ⟨leaves *choked* the sewer⟩ **5 :** to fill to the limit ⟨the store was *choked* with customers⟩ **6 :** to decrease or shut off the air intake of the carburetor of a gasoline engine in order to make the fuel mixture richer [Old English *acēocian*]

[2]**choke** *n* **:** something that chokes: as **a :** a valve for choking a gasoline engine **b :** a narrowing toward the muzzle in the bore of a gun **c :** a coil of wire that provides inductance in an electric circuit and is used to impede the flow of current, to block surges of current, or to filter out unwanted frequencies — called also *choke coil*

choke•cher•ry \-ˌcher-ē, -'cher-\ *n* **:** any of several American wild cherries with bitter or astringent fruit; *also* **:** this fruit

choke up *vi* **1 :** to become or feel choked (as from strong emotion) **2 :** to become flustered and perform poorly

choky \'chō-kē\ *adj* **:** inclined to choke : having a tendency to choke ⟨grew *choky* with fear⟩

chol- *or* **chole-** *combining form* **:** bile : gall ⟨*chol*ine⟩ [Greek *cholē*]

cho•le•cys•ti•tis \ˌkō-lə-ˌsis-'tīt-əs\ *n* **:** inflammation of the gallbladder

cho•ler \'käl-ər, 'kō-lər\ *n* **:** a tendency toward sudden and often unreasonable irritability : IRASCIBILITY [Middle French *colere,* from Latin *cholera* "bilious disease", from Greek, from *cholē* "bile"]

chol•era \'käl-ə-rə\ *n* **:** any of several diseases usually marked by severe vomiting and dysentery; *esp* **:** ASIATIC CHOLERA [Latin, from Greek, from *cholē* "bile"] — **chol•e•ra•ic** \ˌkäl-ə-'rā-ik\ *adj*

cho•ler•ic \'käl-ə-rik, kə-'ler-ik\ *adj* **1 :** easily moved to anger : hot-tempered **2 :** showing or expressing anger : IRATE **syn** see IRASCIBLE

cho•les•ter•ol \kə-'les-tə-ˌrōl, -ˌrōl\ *n* **:** a waxy substance $C_{27}H_{45}OH$ normally present in cells and tissues, important in many bodily processes, and possibly a contributing factor to arteriosclerosis when deposits in arteries are excessive [French *cholésterine,* from *chol-* "chol-" + Greek *stereos* "solid"]

cho•line \'kō-ˌlēn\ *n* **:** a basic substance $C_5H_{15}NO_2$ that is widely distributed in animal and plant products and is a vitamin of the vitamin B complex essential to liver function

cho•lin•er•gic \ˌkō-lə-'nər-jik\ *adj* **:** liberating or activated by acetylcholine ⟨a *cholinergic* nerve fiber⟩ [acetyl*choline* + Greek *ergon* "work"]

cho•lin•es•ter•ase \ˌkō-lə-'nes-tə-ˌrās, -ˌrāz\ *n* **:** ACETYLCHOLINESTERASE

chomp \'chämp, 'chȯmp\ *vb* **:** to chew or bite on noisily or vigorously [alteration of [1]*champ*]

choose \'chüz\ *vb* **chose** \'chōz\; **cho•sen** \'chōz-n\; **choos•ing** \'chü-zing\ **1 :** to select according to preference especially after consideration ⟨*choose* a leader⟩ **2 a :** DECIDE ⟨*chose* to go by train⟩ **b :** PREFER **3 :** to see fit : INCLINE ⟨take them if you *choose*⟩ **4 :** to make a choice [Old English *cēosan*] — **choos•er** *n*

choosy *or* **choos•ey** \'chü-zē\ *adj* **choos•i•er; -est :** inclined to be very selective : FASTIDIOUS, PARTICULAR

[1]**chop** \'chäp\ *vt* **chopped; chop•ping 1 :** to cut by striking especially repeatedly with something sharp ⟨*chop* down a tree⟩ **2 :** to cut into small pieces : MINCE ⟨*chopped* vegetables⟩ **3 :** to strike (as a ball) with a short quick downward stroke [Middle English *chappen, choppen* "to chop, crack"] — **chop•per** *n*

[2]**chop** *n* **1 a :** a forceful sudden stroke with a sharp instrument **b :** a sharp downward blow or stroke especially in sports **2 :** a small cut of meat often including a part of a rib **3 :** a short quick motion (as of a wave)

[3]**chop** *vi* **chopped; chop•ping 1 :** to change direction **2 :** to veer with or as if with the wind [Old English *cēapian* "to barter"]

chop•fall•en *variant of* CHAPFALLEN

chop•house \'chäp-ˌhau̇s\ *n* **:** RESTAURANT

chop•pi•ness \'chäp-ē-nəs\ *n* **:** the quality or state of being choppy

[1]**chop•py** \'chäp-ē\ *adj* **chop•pi•er; -est :** subject to frequent changes : VARIABLE ⟨*choppy* winds⟩

[2]**choppy** *adj* **chop•pi•er; -est 1 :** rough with small waves ⟨*choppy* seas⟩ **2 :** JERKY, DISCONNECTED ⟨*choppy* sentences⟩

chops \'chäps\ *n pl* **:** the fleshy covering of the jaws ⟨the dog licked its *chops*⟩ [alteration of [4]*chap*]

chop•stick \'chäp-ˌstik\ *n* **:** one of a pair of slender sticks used chiefly in oriental countries to lift food to the mouth [Pidgin English, from *chop* "fast", of Chinese origin]

chop su•ey \chäp-'sü-ē\ *n* **:** a dish prepared chiefly from bean sprouts, bamboo shoots, water chestnuts, onions, mushrooms, and meat or fish [Chinese (Cantonese) *shap sui* "odds and ends", from *shap* "miscellaneous" + *sui* "bits"]

cho•ral \'kōr-əl, 'kȯr-\ *adj* **:** of, relating to, or performed by a chorus or choir or in chorus — **cho•ral•ly** \-ə-lē\ *adv*

cho•rale *also* **cho•ral** \kə-'ral, -'räl\ *n* **1 :** a hymn or psalm sung to a traditional or composed melody; *also* **:** a hymn tune or a harmonization of a traditional melody **2 :** CHORUS 1c, CHOIR [German *choral,* short for *choralgesang* "choral song"]

[1]**chord** \'kȯrd\ *n* **:** a combination of tones that blend harmoniously when sounded together [Middle English *cord,* short for *accord*] — **chord•al** \-l\ *adj*

[2]**chord** *vi* **:** to play chords especially on a stringed instrument

[3]**chord** *n* **1 :** CORD 3a **2 :** a straight line joining two points on a curve **3 :** an individual emotional response ⟨strike a familiar *chord*⟩ [alteration of [1]*cord*]

chor•date \'kȯrd-ət, 'kȯr-ˌdāt\ *n* **:** any of a phylum or other major group (Chordata) of animals having at least at some stage of development a notochord, paired gill slits, and a dorsally situated central nervous system and including the vertebrates, amphioxi, and tunicates — compare HEMICHORDATE — **chordate** *adj*

chore \'chōr, 'chȯr\ *n* **1** *pl* **:** the routine duties of running a household or farm **2 :** a difficult or disagreeable task ⟨reading should be fun, not a *chore*⟩ [Middle English *char* "turn, piece of work", from Old English *cierr*]

cho•rea \kə-'rē-ə\ *n* **:** a nervous disorder (as of humans or dogs) marked by spasmodic movements and lack of coordination [Latin, "dance", from Greek *choreia,* from *choros* "chorus"]

cho•re•og•ra•phy \ˌkōr-ē-'äg-rə-fē, ˌkȯr-\ *n, pl* **-phies :** the art of dancing or of composing or arranging dances and especially ballets [derived from Greek *choreia* "dance", from *choros* "chorus"] — **cho•re•o•graph** \'kōr-ē-ə-ˌgraf, 'kȯr-\ *vt* — **cho•re•og•ra•pher** \ˌkōr-ē-'äg-rə-fər, ˌkȯr-\ *n* — **cho•reo•graphic** \-ē-ə-'graf-ik\ *adj* — **cho•reo•graph•i•cal•ly** \-'graf-i-kə-lē, -klē\ *adv*

cho•ric \'kōr-ik, 'kȯr-, 'kär-\ *adj* **:** of, relating to, or being in the style of a chorus and especially a Greek chorus

cho•rine \'kōr-ˌēn, 'kȯr-\ *n* **:** CHORUS GIRL

cho•rio•al•lan•to•is \ˌkōr-ē-ō-ə-'lant-ə-wəs, ˌkȯr-\ *n* **:** a vascular fetal membrane composed of the fused chorion and adjacent wall of the allantois — **cho•rio•al•lan•to•ic** \-ō-ˌal-ən-ˈtō-ik\ *adj*

cho•ri•on \ˈkōr-ē-ˌän, ˈkȯr-\ *n* : the highly vascular outer embryonic membrane of higher vertebrates that in placental mammals joins the allantois in the formation of the placenta [Greek] — **cho•ri•on•ic** \ˌkōr-ē-ˈän-ik, ˌkȯr-\ *adj*

cho•ris•ter \ˈkōr-ə-stər, ˈkȯr-, ˈkär-\ *n* : a singer in a choir [Anglo-French *cueristre,* from Medieval Latin *chorista,* from Latin *chorus* "chorus"]

C–horizon *n* : the layer of a soil profile lying beneath the B–horizon and consisting essentially of more or less weathered parent rock

cho•roid \ˈkōr-ˌȯid, ˈkȯr-\ *also* **cho•ri•oid** \-ē-ˌȯid\ *n* : a vascular pigmented membrane of the vertebrate eye lying between the sclera and the retina [Greek *chorioeidēs,* from *chorion* "chorion"] — **choroid** *adj*

choroid coat *n* : CHOROID

chor•tle \ˈchȯrt-l\ *vi* **chor•tled**; **chor•tling** \ˈchȯrt-ling, -l-ing\ : to express often smug satisfaction by or as if by a chuckling laugh [blend of *chuckle* and *snort*] — **chortle** *n* — **chor•tler** \ˈchȯrt-lər, -l-ər\ *n*

¹cho•rus \ˈkōr-əs, ˈkȯr-\ *n* **1 a** : a group of singers and dancers in Greek drama participating in or commenting on the action **b** : a character in Elizabethan drama who speaks the prologue and epilogue and comments on the action **c** : an organized group of singers : CHOIR; *esp* : a body of singers who sing the choral parts of a work (as in opera) **d** : a group of supporting dancers and singers in a musical comedy or revue **2 a** : a recurring part of a song or hymn **b** : the part of a drama sung or spoken by the chorus **c** : a composition to be sung by a chorus **3** : something uttered simultaneously by a number of persons ⟨a *chorus* of boos⟩ [Latin, from Greek *choros*] — **in chorus** : in unison

²chorus *vb* : to sing or utter in chorus

chorus girl *n* : a young woman who sings or dances in a chorus (as of a musical comedy) — called also *chorine*

chose *past of* CHOOSE

cho•sen \ˈchōz-n\ *adj* : selected or marked for favor or special privilege ⟨privileges granted to a *chosen* few⟩ [Middle English, from past participle of *chosen* "to choose"]

Chou \ˈjō\ *n* : a Chinese dynasty traditionally dated 1122 to about 256 B.C. and marked by the development of the philosophical schools of Confucius and Lao-tzu

chough \ˈchəf\ *n* : an Old World black red-legged bird related to the crows [Middle English]

chow \ˈchau̇\ *n, slang* : FOOD, VICTUALS [perhaps from Chinese (Pekingese) *chiao*³ "meat dumpling"]

chow•chow \ˈchau̇-ˌchau̇\ *n* : a relish of chopped mixed pickles in mustard sauce [Pidgin English]

chow chow \ˈchau̇-ˌchau̇\ *n* : a thick-coated straight-legged muscular dog with a blue-black tongue and a short tail curled close to the back — called also *chow* [of Chinese origin]

chow•der \ˈchau̇d-ər\ *n* : a soup or stew made of fish, clams, or a vegetable usually stewed in milk [French *chaudière* "kettle", from Late Latin *caldaria,* from Latin *calidus* "warm"]

chow mein \ˈchau̇-ˈmān\ *n* : a thick stew of shredded or chopped meat, mushrooms, and vegetables usually served with fried noodles [Chinese (Pekingese) *ch'ao*³ *mien*⁴, from *ch'ao*³ "to fry" + *mien*⁴ "dough"]

chrism \ˈkriz-əm\ *n* : consecrated oil used especially in baptism, confirmation, and ordination [Late Latin *chrisma,* from Greek, "ointment", from *chriein* "to anoint"]

Christ \ˈkrīst\ *n* **1** : MESSIAH 1 **2** : an ideal type of humanity [Latin *Christus,* from Greek *Christos,* literally, "anointed", from *chriein* "to anoint"]

chris•ten \ˈkris-n\ *vt* **chris•tened**; **chris•ten•ing** \ˈkris-ning, -n-ing\ **1 a** : BAPTIZE 1 **b** : to name at baptism **2** : to name or dedicate (as a ship) by a ceremony suggestive of baptism [Old English *cristnian,* from *cristen* "Christian", from Latin *christianus*]

Chris•ten•dom \ˈkris-n-dəm\ *n* **1** : the entire body of Christians **2** : all the countries or peoples that are predominantly Christian

chris•ten•ing *n* : the ceremony of baptizing and naming a child

¹Chris•tian \ˈkris-chən, ˈkrish-\ *n* **1** : a person who believes or professes belief in Jesus Christ and lives according to his teachings **2** : a member of a Christian church **3** : a member of a group (as the Disciples of Christ or the Churches of Christ) seeking a return to New Testament Christianity

²Christian *adj* **1** : of or relating to Jesus Christ or the religion deriving from him **2** : of or relating to Christians ⟨a *Christian* nation⟩ **3 a** : befitting a Christian ⟨*Christian* charity⟩ **b** : KIND 1, MERCIFUL

Christian Brother *n* : a member of the Roman Catholic institute of Brothers of the Christian Schools founded in France in 1680 and devoted to primary and secondary education

Christian era *n* : the period dating from the birth of Christ

chris•ti•ania \ˌkris-chē-ˈan-ē-ə, ˌkrish-chē-, ˌkris-tē-, -ˈän-\ *n* : CHRISTIE [*Christiania,* former name of Oslo, Norway]

Chris•ti•an•i•ty \ˌkris-chē-ˈan-ət-ē, ˌkrish-, -ˈchan-; ˌkris-tē-ˈan-\ *n* **1** : the religion deriving from Jesus Christ **2** : Christian belief or practice

Chris•tian•ize \ˈkris-chə-ˌnīz, ˈkrish-\ *vt* : to make Christian — **Chris•tian•i•za•tion** \ˌkris-chə-nə-ˈzā-shən, ˌkrish-\ *n* — **Chris•tian•iz•er** *n*

christian name *n, often cap C* : the name given to a person at birth or christening as distinct from the family name

Christian Science *n* : a religion and system of healing founded by Mary Baker Eddy and taught by the Church of Christ, Scientist — **Christian Scientist** *n*

chris•tie *or* **chris•ty** \ˈkris-tē\ *n, pl* **christies** : a skiing turn made by shifting the body weight and skidding into a turn with the skis parellel — called also *christiania* [*Christiania,* former name of Oslo, Norway]

Christ•like \ˈkrīst-ˌlīk\ *adj* : resembling Christ in character or spirit

Christ•mas \ˈkris-məs\ *n* **1** : December 25 celebrated as a church festival in commemoration of the birth of Christ and observed as a legal holiday **2** : CHRISTMASTIDE [Old English *Cristes mæsse,* literally, "Christ's mass"]

Christmas club *n* : a savings account in which regular deposits are made throughout the year to provide money for Christmas shopping

Christmas fern *n* : a North American evergreen fern often used for winter decorations

Christ•mas•tide \ˈkris-mə-ˌstīd\ *n* : the festal season of Christmas

Christ•mas•time \-ˌstīm\ *n* : CHRISTMASTIDE

Christmas tree *n* : a usually evergreen tree decorated at Christmas

chrom- *or* **chromo-** *combining form* : color : colored ⟨*chromo*sphere⟩ [Greek *chrōma* "color"]

chro•ma \ˈkrō-mə\ *n* : SATURATION 2

chromat- *or* **chromato-** *combining form* : color ⟨*chromat*in⟩ ⟨*chromato*graphy⟩ [Greek *chrōmat-, chrōma*]

chro•mate \ˈkrō-ˌmāt\ *n* : a salt or ester of chromic acid

¹chro•mat•ic \krō-ˈmat-ik\ *adj* **1** : of or relating to color or color phenomena; *esp* : being a shade other than black, gray, or white ⟨*chromatic* colors like green, red, blue⟩ **2** : of, relating to, or giving all the tones of the chromatic scale — **chro•mat•i•cal•ly** \-ˈmat-i-kə-lē, -klē\ *adv*

²chromatic *n* : ACCIDENTAL

chromatic aberration *n* : aberration caused by the differences in refraction of the colored rays of the spectrum

chromatic scale *n* : a musical scale that consists entirely of half steps

chro•ma•tid \ˈkrō-mə-təd\ *n* : one of the paired longitudinal strands of a chromosome

chro•ma•tin \-tən\ *n* : a material present in chromosomes that contains the nuclear genes and stains deeply with basic dyes — **chro•ma•tin•ic** \ˌkrō-mə-ˈtin-ik\ *adj*

chro•mato•gram \krō-ˈmat-ə-ˌgram\ *n* : the pattern formed on the adsorbent medium by the layers of components separated by chromatography

chro•ma•tog•ra•phy \ˌkrō-mə-ˈtäg-rə-fē\ *n* : a separating especially of closely related compounds by allowing a solution or mixture of them to seep through an adsorbent (as clay or paper) so that each compound becomes adsorbed in a separate often colored layer — **chro•mato•graph** \krō-ˈmat-ə-ˌgraf\ *vb* — **chro•mato•graph•ic** \-ˌmat-ə-ˈgraf-ik\ *adj* — **chro•mato•graph•i•cal•ly** \-i-kə-lē, -klē\ *adv*

chro•mato•phore \krō-ˈmat-ə-ˌfōr, -ˌfȯr\ *n* : a pigment-bearing cell; *esp* : one capable of causing skin color changes in an animal by expanding or contracting

chrome \ˈkrōm\ *n* **1 a** : CHROMIUM **b** : a chromium pigment **2** : something plated with an alloy of chromium [French, from Greek *chrōma* "color"]

-chrome \ˌkrōm\ *n or adj combining form* **1** : colored thing : colored **2** : coloring matter
chrome green *n* : any of various brilliant green pigments containing or consisting of chromium compounds
chrome yellow *n* : any of various bright yellow pigments consisting essentially of a compound $PbCrO_4$ of lead, chromium, and oxygen
chro•mic \ˈkrō-mik\ *adj* : of, relating to, or derived from chromium
chromic acid *n* : an acid H_2CrO_4 analagous to sulfuric acid but known only in solution
chro•mite \ˈkrō-ˌmīt\ *n* : a mineral $FeCr_2O_4$ that consists of an oxide of iron and chromium and is an important ore of chromium
chro•mi•um \ˈkrō-mē-əm\ *n* : a blue-white metallic element found naturally only in combination and used especially in alloys and in electroplating — see ELEMENT table [New Latin, from French *chrome*]
chro•mo•mere \ˈkrō-mə-ˌmiər\ *n* : one of the small bead-shaped and heavily staining concentrations of chromatin that are linearly arranged along the chromosome
chro•mo•ne•ma \ˌkrō-mə-ˈnē-mə\ *n, pl* **-ne•ma•ta** \-ˈnē-mət-ə\ : the coiled filamentous core of a chromatid [*chrom-* + Greek *nēma* "thread"]
chro•mo•phore \ˈkrō-mə-fōr, -ˌfȯr\ *n* : a group of atoms that gives rise to color in a molecule
chro•mo•plast \-ˌplast\ *n* : a colored plastid usually containing red or yellow pigment
chro•mo•some \ˈkrō-mə-ˌsōm\ *n* : one of the usually elongated chromatin-containing bodies of a cell nucleus made up of chromatids, usually constant in number in any one kind of plant or animal, and seen especially during mitosis and meiosis — **chro•mo•som•al** \ˌkrō-mə-ˈsō-məl\ *adj*
chromosome number *n* : the usually constant number of chromosomes characteristic of a particular kind of animal or plant
chro•mo•sphere \ˈkrō-mə-ˌsfiər\ *n* : the inner part of the atmosphere of the sun composed chiefly of hydrogen
chron- *or* **chrono-** *combining form* : time ⟨chronograph⟩ [Greek *chronos*]
chron•ic \ˈkrän-ik\ *adj* **1 a** : lasting a long time or recurring frequently ⟨*chronic* indigestion⟩ — compare ACUTE 5a **b** : suffering from a chronic disease **2 a** : constantly present or encountered ⟨*chronic* financial difficulties⟩ **b** : being such habitually ⟨a *chronic* complainer⟩ — **chron•i•cal•ly** \-i-kə-lē, -klē\ *adv* — **chro•nic•i•ty** \krä-ˈnis-ətē\ *n*
[1]chron•i•cle \ˈkrän-i-kəl\ *n* **1** : a historical account of events arranged in order of time without analysis or interpretation **2** : NARRATIVE 1 [Old French *chronique*, derived from Greek *chronos* "time"]
[2]chronicle *vt* **-cled**; **-cling** \-kəling, -kling\ : to record in or as if in a chronicle : tell the story of — **chron•i•cler** \-kə-lər, -klər\ *n*
Chron•i•cles \ˈkrän-i-kəlz\ *n* — see BIBLE table
chro•no•graph \ˈkrän-ə-ˌgraf, ˈkrō-nə-\ *n* : an instrument for measuring and recording time intervals with accuracy: as **a** : an instrument having a revolving drum on which a stylus makes marks **b** : a watch with a sweep-second hand — **chron•o•graph•ic** \ˌkrän-ə-ˈgraf-ik, ˌkrō-nə-\ *adj* — **chro•nog•ra•phy** \krə-ˈnäg-rə-fē\ *n*

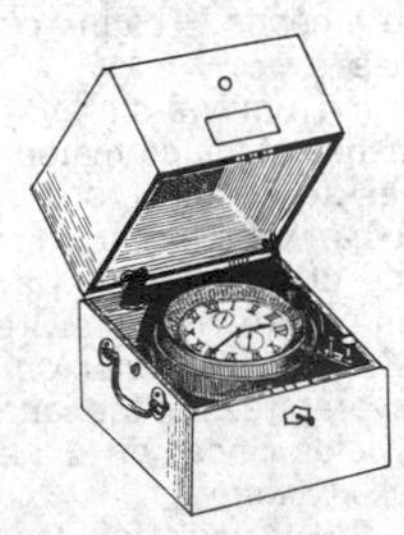
chronometer

chron•o•log•i•cal \ˌkrän-l-ˈäj-i-kəl, ˌkrōn-\ *adj* : arranged in or according to the order of time ⟨*chronological* tables of American history⟩ — **chron•o•log•i•cal•ly** \-ˈäj-i-kə-lē, -klē\ *adv*
chro•nol•o•gy \krə-ˈnäl-ə-jē\ *n, pl* **-gies** **1** : the science that deals with measuring time by regular divisions and that assigns to events their proper dates **2** : a chronological table or list **3** : an arrangement (as of events) in order of occurrence — **chro•nol•o•gist** \-jəst\ *n*
chro•nom•e•ter \krə-ˈnäm-ət-ər\ *n* : an instrument for measuring time; *esp* : one designed to keep time with great accuracy and used especially in navigation — **chron•o•met•ric** \ˌkrän-ə-ˈme-trik, ˌkrō-nə-\ *adj*
chro•no•scope \ˈkrän-ə-ˌskōp, ˈkrō-nə-\ *n* : an instrument for precise measurement of small time intervals
chrys•a•lid \ˈkris-ə-ləd\ *n* : CHRYSALIS
chrys•a•lis \ˈkris-ə-ləs\ *n, pl* **chry•sal•i•des** \krə-ˈsal-ə-ˌdēz\ *or* **chrys•a•lis•es** \ˈkris-ə-lə-səz\ : the pupa of a butterfly [Latin *chrysallis* "gold-colored pupa of butterflies", from Greek, from *chrysos* "gold", of Semitic origin]
chry•san•the•mum \kris-ˈan-thə-məm, -ant-\ *n* **1** : any of a genus of plants related to the daisies that include weeds, ornamentals grown for their brightly colored often double flower heads, and important sources of medicinals and insecticides **2** : a flower head of an ornamental chrysanthemum [Latin, from Greek *chrysanthemon*, from *chrysos* "gold" + *anthemon* "flower"]
chrys•o•phyte \ˈkris-ə-ˌfīt\ *n* : any of a major group (Chrysophyta) of algae (as diatoms) with yellowish green to golden brown pigments
chrys•o•prase \ˈkris-ə-ˌprāz\ *n* : a yellowish green chalcedony valued as a gem [derived from Greek *chrysoprasos*, from *chrysos* "gold" + *prason* "leek"]
chrys•o•tile \ˈkris-ə-ˌtīl\ *n* : a fibrous silky serpentine that is one kind of asbestos [derived from Greek *chrysos* "gold" + *tilos* "plucked hair", from *tillein* "to pluck"]
chub \ˈchəb\ *n, pl* **chub** *or* **chubs** : any of several small freshwater fishes related to the carp [Middle English *chubbe*]
chub•by \ˈchəb-ē\ *adj* **chub•bi•er**; **-est** : PLUMP ⟨*chubby* little children⟩ [*chub*] — **chub•bi•ness** *n*
[1]chuck \ˈchək\ *vt* **1** : to give a pat or a tap to ⟨*chuck* a person under the chin⟩ **2** : THROW 2, TOSS ⟨*chuck* a ball back and forth⟩ **3** : DISCARD 2 [origin unknown]
[2]chuck *n* **1** : a pat or nudge under the chin **2** : THROW 1
[3]chuck *n* **1** : a portion of a side of dressed beef including most of the neck and the parts about the shoulder blade and the first three ribs **2** *chiefly West* : FOOD **3** : a device for holding work or a tool in a machine (as a drill press or lathe) [English dialect *chuck* "lump"]
chuck-full \ˈchək-ˈfu̇l\ *variant of* CHOCK-FULL
chuck•hole \ˈchək-ˌhōl, ˈchəg-\ *n* : a hole or rut in a road [[3]*chuck*]
chuck•le \ˈchək-əl\ *vi* **chuck•led**; **chuck•ling** \ˈchək-ling, -ə-ling\ : to laugh inwardly or quietly [probably from Middle English *chukken* "to cluck"] — **chuckle** *n*
chuck•le•head \ˈchək-əl-ˌhed\ *n* : BLOCKHEAD — **chuck•le•head•ed** \ˌchək-əl-ˈhed-əd\ *adj* [*chuckle* "lumpish", from English dialect *chuck* "lump"]
chuck wagon \ˈchək-\ *n* : a wagon carrying a stove and provisions for cooking (as on a ranch)
chuck•wal•la \ˈchək-ˌwäl-ə\ *n* : a large but harmless lizard of the desert regions of the southwestern United States [Mexican Spanish *chacahuala*, of American Indian origin]
chuck-will's-wid•ow \ˌchək-ˌwilz-ˈwid-ō\ *n* : a goatsucker of the southern United States [imitative]
[1]chug \ˈchəg\ *n* : a dull explosive sound made by or as if by a laboring engine [imitative]
[2]chug *vi* **chugged**; **chug•ging** : to move or go with chugs ⟨a locomotive *chugging* along⟩
chuk•ka \ˈchək-ə\ *n* : a short usually ankle-length leather boot with two pairs of eyelets or a buckle and strap [alteration of *chukker*; from a similar polo player's boot]
chuk•ker *or* **chuk•kar** \ˈchək-ər\ *or* **chuk•ka** \ˈchək-ə\ *n* : a playing period of a polo game [Hindi *cakkar* "circular course", from Sanskrit *cakra* "wheel"]
[1]chum \ˈchəm\ *n* : a close friend : PAL [perhaps by shortening and alteration from *chamber fellow* "roommate"]
[2]chum *vi* **chummed**; **chum•ming** : to be or become chums
chum•my \ˈchəm-ē\ *adj* **chum•mi•er**; **-est** : FAMILIAR 1, INTIMATE — **chum•mi•ly** \ˈchəm-ə-lē\ *adv* — **chum•mi•ness** \ˈchəm-ē-nəs\ *n*
chump \ˈchəmp\ *n* : DUPE [perhaps blend of *chunk* and *lump*]
chunk \ˈchəngk\ *n* **1** : a short thick piece : HUNK ⟨a *chunk* of meat⟩ **2** : a significant portion ⟨food takes a *chunk* out of the budget⟩ [perhaps alteration of English dialect *chuck* "lump"]
chunky \ˈchəng-kē\ *adj* **chunk•i•er**; **-est** : STOCKY — **chunk-**

\ə\ abut	\au̇\ out	\i\ tip	\ȯ\ saw	\u̇\ foot
\ər\ further	\ch\ chin	\ī\ life	\ȯi\ coin	\y\ yet
\a\ mat	\e\ pet	\j\ job	\th\ thin	\yü\ few
\ā\ take	\ē\ easy	\ng\ sing	\t͟h\ this	\yu̇\ cure
\ä\ cot, cart	\g\ go	\ō\ bone	\ü\ food	\zh\ vision

i•ly \-kə-lē\ *adv* — **chunk•i•ness** \-kē-nəs\ *n*

1church \'chərch\ *n* **1** : a building for public and especially Christian worship **2 a** : a body or organization of religious believers **b** : the clergy of a religious body **3** : public worship especially in a church [Old English *cirice,* derived from Late Greek *kyriakon,* from Greek *kyriakos* "of the lord", from Greek *kyrios* "lord"] — **church•ly** \-lē\ *adj*

2church *vt* : to bring to church to receive one of its rites

church•go•er \-,gō-ər, -,gōr\ *n* : one that goes to church especially regularly — **church•go•ing** \-,gō-ing\ *adj or n*

church•ing *n* : a ceremony in certain churches in which a woman is received in church with prayer and blessings after childbirth

church•man \-mən\ *n* **1** : CLERGYMAN **2** : a church member

Church of England : the established episcopal church of England

church•wom•an \-,wu̇m-ən\ *n* : a woman who is a church member

church•yard \'chərch-,yärd\ *n* : a yard that belongs to a church and is often used as a burial ground

churl \'chərl\ *n* **1** : a medieval peasant **2** : RUSTIC **3** : a rude or surly person [Old English *ceorl* "man, freeman of low rank"]

churl•ish \'chər-lish\ *adj* : offensive in action or manner : RUDE, SURLY — **churl•ish•ly** *adv* — **churl•ish•ness** *n*

1churn \'chərn\ *n* : a vessel in which cream is agitated to separate the butterfat from the other parts [Old English *cyrin*]

2churn *vb* **1** : to agitate (milk or cream) in a churn in making butter : make (butter) by churning **2** : to work a churn in making butter **3** : to agitate or be agitated violently ⟨the wind *churned* up huge waves⟩

churr \'chər\ *vi* : to make a vibrant or whirring noise like that of a partridge [imitative] — **churr** *n*

chute \'shüt\ *n* **1** : a quick drop (as of a river) **2** : an inclined plane, trough, or passage down or through which things may pass ⟨a mail *chute*⟩ **3** : PARACHUTE 1 [French, "fall", from Old French, from *cheoir* "to fall", from Latin *cadere*]

chut•ney \'chət-nē\ *n, pl* **chutneys** : a relish of acid fruits, raisins, dates, and onions [Hindi *caṭnī*]

chyle \'kīl\ *n* : lymph milky from emulsified fats that is present especially in the lacteals during intestinal absorption of fats [Late Latin *chylus,* from Greek *chylos* "juice, chyle", from *chein* "to pour"]

chyme \'kīm\ *n* : the semifluid mass of partly digested food that passes from the stomach into the duodenum [Late Latin *chymus* "chyle", from Greek *chymos* "juice", from *chein* "to pour"] — **chy•mous** \'kī-məs\ *adj*

chy•mo•tryp•sin \,kī-mō-'trip-sən\ *n* : a pancreatic enzyme that acts on proteins by breaking internal peptide bonds

ci•bo•ri•um \sə-'bōr-ē-əm, -'bȯr-\ *n, pl* **-ria** \-ē-ə\ *or* **-ri•ums** **1** : a covered goblet-shaped vessel for holding eucharistic bread **2** : a vaulted canopy supported by four columns over a high altar [Latin, "cup", from Greek *kibōrion*]

ci•ca•da \sə-'kād-ə, -'käd-\ *n, pl* **-cadas** *also* **-ca•dae** \-'kād-,ē, -,käd-,ē\ : any of a family of stout-bodied insects that are related to the bugs and have a wide blunt head and large transparent wings [Latin]

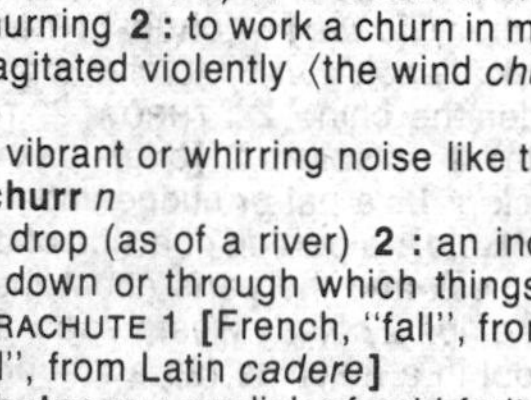

cicada

cic•a•trix \'sik-ə-,triks, sə-'kā-triks\ *n, pl* **cic•a•tri•ces** \,sik-ə-'trī-,sēz, sə-'kā-trə-,sēz\ **1** : a scar resulting from formation and contraction of fibrous tissue in a flesh wound **2** : a scar marking the previous point of attachment of a part or organ (as a leaf or seed) [Latin] — **cic•a•tri•cial** \,sik-ə-'trish-əl\ *adj*

ci•ce•ro•ne \,sis-ə-'rō-nē, ,chich-ə-\ *n, pl* **-ro•ni** \-,nē\ : GUIDE 1b [Italian, from *Cicerone* "Cicero"]

Cic•ero•nian \,sis-ə-'rō-nyən, -nē-ən\ *adj* : of, relating to, or characteristic of Cicero or his writings

cich•lid \'sik-ləd\ *n* : any of a family of mostly tropical spiny-finned freshwater fishes including several kept in tropical aquariums [derived from Greek *kichlē* "thrush, kind of fish"] — **cichlid** *adj*

-cide \,sīd\ *n combining form* **1** : killer ⟨insecti*cide*⟩ **2** : killing ⟨geno*cide*⟩ [L *-cida,* from *caedere* "to cut, kill"]

ci•der \'sīd-ər\ *n* : the fresh or fermented juice of fruit (as apples) used as a beverage or for making other products (as vinegar) [Old French *sidre,* from Late Latin *sicera* "strong drink", from Greek *sikera,* from Hebrew *shēkhār*]

ci•gar \sig-'är\ *n* : a roll of tobacco leaves for smoking [Spanish *cigarro*]

cig•a•rette *also* **cig•a•ret** \,sig-ə-'ret, 'sig-ə-,\ *n* : a small roll of cut tobacco wrapped in paper for smoking

cil•i•ary \'sil-ē-,er-ē\ *adj* **1** : of or relating to cilia **2** : of, relating to, or being the muscular body supporting the lens of the eye

1cil•i•ate \'sil-ē-ət, -,āt\ *or* **cil•i•at•ed** \-,āt-əd\ *adj* : provided with cilia

2ciliate *n* : any of a group (Ciliophora) of ciliate protozoans

cil•i•um \'sil-ē-əm\ *n, pl* **cil•ia** \-ē-ə\ **1** : EYELASH **2** : one of the tiny filaments of many cells that are capable of lashing movement [Latin, "eyelid"]

cim•me•ri•an \sə-'mir-ē-ən\ *adj, often cap* : very dark or gloomy [from *Cimmerians,* a mythical people in Homer dwelling in eternal gloom]

1cinch \'sinch\ *n* **1** : a strong girth for a pack or saddle **2** : a tight grip **3 a** : a thing done or gained with ease **b** : a certainty to happen [Spanish *cincha,* from Latin *cingula* "girdle, girth", from *cingere* "to gird"]

2cinch *vt* **1** : to put a cinch on **2** : to make certain : ASSURE ⟨*cinched* the victory⟩

cin•cho•na \sing-'kō-nə, sin-'chō-\ *n* **1** : any of a genus of South American trees and shrubs **2** : the dried bark of a cinchona containing alkaloids (as quinine) and being used as a malaria remedy — called also *cinchona bark* [countess of *Chinchón,* died 1641, wife of the Peruvian viceroy] — **cin•chon•ic** \sing-'kän-ik, sin-'chän-\ *adj*

cinc•ture \'sing-chər, 'singk-\ *n* : BELT 1, GIRDLE [Latin *cinctura,* from *cingere* "to gird"]

cin•der \'sin-dər\ *n* **1** : waste matter from the smelting of metal ores : SLAG **2 a** : a piece of partly burned coal or wood in which fire is extinct **b** : a hot coal without flame **3** *pl* : ASH 2a **4** : a fragment of solidified lava from an erupting volcano [Old English *sinder*] — **cin•dery** \-də-rē, -drē\ *adj*

cinder block *n* : a building block made of concrete using coal cinders as aggregate

cine- *combining form* : motion picture [*cinema*]

cin•e•ma \'sin-ə-mə\ *n* **1** *chiefly British* : a motion-picture theater **2** : MOVIE [short for *cinematograph,* derived from Greek *kinēma* "motion", from *kinein* "to move"] — **cin•e•mat•ic** \,sin-ə-'mat-ik\ *adj* — **cin•e•mat•i•cal•ly** \-'mat-i-kə-lē, -klē\ *adv*

cin•e•mat•o•graph \,sin-ə-'mat-ə-,graf\ *n, chiefly British* : a motion-picture camera, projector, theater, or show

cin•e•ma•tog•ra•phy \,sin-ə-mə-'täg-rə-fē\ *n* : the art or science of motion-picture photography — **cin•e•mat•o•graph•ic** \-,mat-ə-'graf-ik\ *adj*

cin•er•ar•ia \,sin-ə-'rer-ē-ə, -'rar-\ *n* : a pot plant related to the daisies that has heart-shaped leaves and clusters of bright flower heads [Latin *cinerarius* "of ashes", from *cinis* "ashes"]

cin•er•ar•i•um \-ē-əm\ *n, pl* **-ar•ia** \-ē-ə\ : a place to receive the ashes of the cremated dead [Latin, from *cinis* "ashes"] — **cin•er•ary** \'sin-ə-,rer-ē\ *adj*

cin•na•bar \'sin-ə-,bär\ *n* : a red mineral HgS that consists of a sulfide of mercury and is the only important ore of mercury [Latin *cinnabaris,* from Greek *kinnabari*]

cin•na•mon \'sin-ə-mən\ *n* **1 a** : the highly aromatic bark of any of several trees of the laurel family used as a spice **b** : a tree that yields cinnamon **2** : a light yellowish brown [Latin, from Greek *kinnamon*]

cinque•foil \'singk-,fȯil, 'sangk-\ *n* **1** : any of a genus of plants of the rose family with 5-lobed leaves **2** : a design consisting of five joined foils [Middle French *cincfoille,* from Latin *quinquefolium,* from *quinque* "five" + *folium* "leaf"]

ci•on *variant of* SCION

1ci•pher \'sī-fər\ *n* **1 a** : ZERO 1 — see NUMBER table **b** : an insignificant individual : NONENTITY **2 a** : a method of transforming a text in order to conceal its meaning — compare CODE 4 **b** : a message in code **3** : ARABIC NUMERAL **4** : a combination of symbolic letters; *esp* : the interwoven initials of a name [Middle French *cifre,* from Medieval Latin *cifra,* from Arabic *ṣifr* "empty, cipher, zero"]

2cipher *vb* **ci•phered; ci•pher•ing** \-fə-ring, -fring\ **1** : to use figures in a mathematical process **2** : ENCIPHER **3** : to compute arithmetically ⟨a sum *ciphered* out⟩

cir•ca \'sər-kə, 'kiər-,kä\ *prep* : at, in, or of approximately — used with numerals and especially with dates ⟨born *circa* 1600⟩ [Latin, from *circum* "around"]

cir•ca•di•an \sər-'kād-ē-ən, -'kad-; sər-kə-'dē-ən, -'dī-\ *adj* : being, having, or occurring in approximately 24-hour periods or cycles (as of biological activity or function) ⟨*circadian* rhythms in hatching⟩ [Latin *circa* "about" + *dies* "day" + English *-an*]

Cir•cas•sian walnut \sər-,kash-ən-\ *n* : the light brown irregularly black-veined wood of the English walnut much used for veneer and cabinetwork [*Circassia,* Russia]

cir•ci•nate \'sərs-n-,āt\ *adj* : COILED, ROUNDED; *esp* : rolled up on the axis with the apex as a center ⟨*circinate* fronds of ferns⟩ [Latin *circinare* "to round", from *circinus* "pair of compasses", from *circus* "circle, circus"] — **cir•ci•nate•ly** *adv*

[1]**cir•cle** \'sər-kəl\ *n* **1 a** : HALO 1 **b** : a closed plane curve every point of which is equidistant from a fixed point within the curve **c** : the plane surface bounded by such a curve **2** : something in the form of a circle or section of a circle: as **a** : CIRCLET, DIADEM **b** : a balcony or tier of seats in a theater or opera house **c** : a circle on the surface of a sphere (as the earth) — compare GREAT CIRCLE, SMALL CIRCLE **d** : ROTARY 2 **3** : an area of action or influence : REALM **4 a** : CYCLE 2a, ROUND **b** : fallacious reasoning in which something apparently proved is really taken for granted **5** : a group bound by a common tie; *esp* : COTERIE [Old French *cercle,* from Latin *circulus,* from *circus* "circle, circus"]

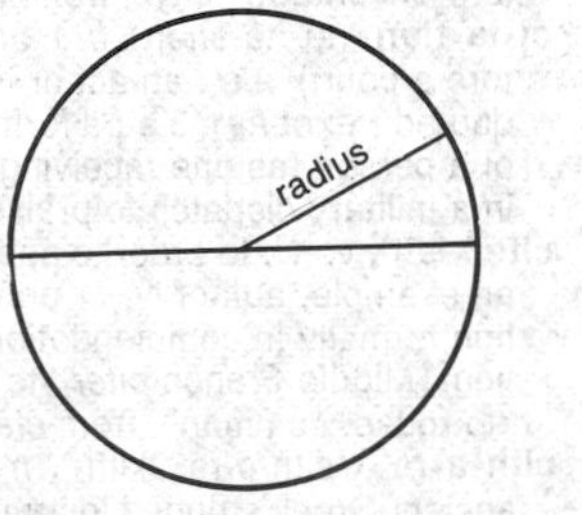

[1]circle 1b

[2]**circle** *vb* **cir•cled**; **cir•cling** \-kə-ling, -kling\ **1** : to enclose in or as if in a circle : ENCIRCLE **2** : to move or revolve around ⟨a spacecraft *circling* the earth⟩ **3** : to move in or as if in a circle — **cir•cler** \-kə-lər, -klər\ *n*

circle graph *n* : PIE CHART

cir•clet \'sər-klət\ *n* : a little circle; *esp* : a personal ornament (as a headband) in the form of a circle

cir•cuit \'sər-kət\ *n* **1** : a boundary line around an area; *also* : the space enclosed **2** : a moving or revolving around (as in a circle or orbit) : CIRCLING ⟨the *circuit* of the earth around the sun⟩ **3 a** : a regular tour (as by a judge or preacher) around an assigned territory **b** : the route traveled **4 a** : an association of similar groups : LEAGUE **b** : a group of establishments offering similar entertainment or presenting a series of contests; *esp* : a chain of theaters at which productions are successively presented **5 a** : the complete path of an electric current **b** : an assemblage of electronic elements : HOOKUP [Middle French *circuite,* from Latin *circuitus,* from *circuire* "to go around", from *circum* "around" + *ire* "to go"] — **circuit** *vb* — **cir•cuit•al** \-kət-l\ *adj*

circuit breaker *n* : a switch that automatically interrupts an electric circuit under an overload

circuit court *n* : a court that sits in two or more places in a judicial district

cir•cu•i•tous \sər-'kyü-ət-əs\ *adj* **1** : marked by a circular or winding course ⟨a *circuitous* route⟩ **2** : not being or going straight to the point : INDIRECT — **cir•cu•i•tous•ly** *adv* — **cir•cu•i•tous•ness** *n*

cir•cuit•ry \'sər-kə-trē\ *n, pl* **-ries** : the plan or the components of an electric circuit

cir•cu•i•ty \sər-'kyü-ət-ē\ *n* : INDIRECTION 1

[1]**cir•cu•lar** \'sər-kyə-lər\ *adj* **1 a** : having the form of a circle : ROUND ⟨a *circular* driveway⟩ **b** : having a circular base or bases ⟨a *circular* cone⟩ **2** : moving in or describing a circle or spiral **3** : relating to or forming part of a circle ⟨a *circular* arc⟩ **4** : CIRCUITOUS, ROUNDABOUT ⟨a *circular* explanation⟩ **5** : characterized by reasoning in a circle ⟨*circular* arguments⟩ **6** : sent around to a number of persons ⟨a *circular* letter⟩ — **cir•cu•lar•i•ty** \,sər-kyə-'lar-ət-ē\ *n* — **cir•cu•lar•ly** \'sər-kyə-lər-lē\ *adv* — **cir•cu•lar•ness** *n*

[2]**circular** *n* : a paper (as a leaflet containing an advertisement) intended for wide distribution

circular function *n* : TRIGONOMETRIC FUNCTION

cir•cu•lar•ize \'sər-kyə-lə-,rīz\ *vt* : to send circulars to — **cir•cu•lar•iza•tion** \,sər-kyə-lə-rə-'zā-shən\ *n*

circular saw *n* : a power saw having a revolving thin steel disk with teeth on its edge

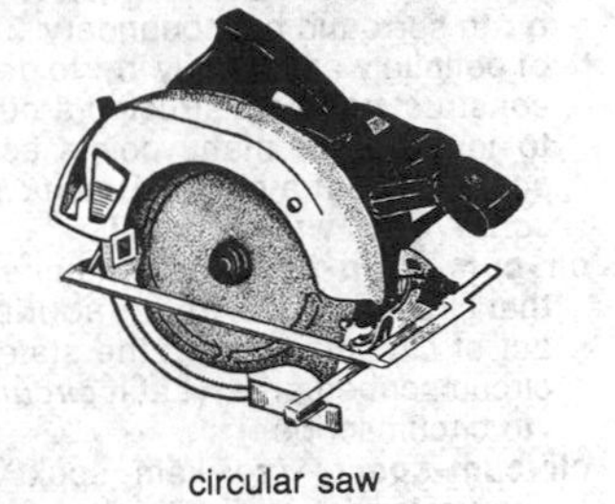
circular saw

cir•cu•late \'sər-kyə-,lāt\ *vb* **1** : to move or cause to move in a circle, circuit, or orbit; *esp* : to follow a course that returns to the starting point ⟨blood *circulates* through the body⟩ **2** : to pass from person to person or place to place: as **a** : to flow without obstruction ⟨air *circulating* through the house⟩ **b** : to become or cause to become well known or widespread ⟨*circulate* a rumor⟩ **c** : to come into the hands of readers ⟨a magazine that *circulated* widely⟩ — **cir•cu•la•tor** \-,lāt-ər\ *n*

cir•cu•la•tion \,sər-kyə-'lā-shən\ *n* **1** : orderly movement through a circuit; *esp* : the movement of blood through the vessels of the body caused by the pumping action of the heart **2 a** : passage or transmission from person to person or place to place; *esp* : the interchange of currency ⟨coins in *circulation*⟩ **b** : the extent of dissemination (as of copies of a publication sold over a given period) **3** : an active social life with different people ⟨back in *circulation* after the divorce⟩ — **cir•cu•la•tive** \'sər-kyə-,lāt-iv\ *adj*

cir•cu•la•to•ry \'sər-kyə-lə-,tōr-ē, -,tȯr-\ *adj* : of or relating to circulation (as of the blood) ⟨the *circulatory* system⟩

circum- *prefix* : around : about ⟨*circum*polar⟩ [Latin, from *circus* "circle"]

cir•cum•am•bi•ent \,sər-kəm-'am-bē-ənt\ *adj* : being on all sides : ENCOMPASSING

cir•cum•am•bu•late \-'am-byə-,lāt\ *vb* : to circle on foot especially as or as if part of a ritual

cir•cum•cen•ter \'sər-kəm-,sent-ər\ *n* : the point at which the perpendicular bisectors of the sides of a triangle intersect and which is equidistant from the three vertices

cir•cum•cise \'sər-kəm-,sīz\ *vt* : to cut off the foreskin of [Latin *circumcidere,* from *circum-* + *caedere* "to cut"]

cir•cum•ci•sion \,sər-kəm-'sizh-ən, 'sər-kəm-,\ *n* **1** : the act of circumcising or being circumcised; *esp* : a Jewish rite performed on male infants as a sign of inclusion in the covenant between God and Abraham **2** *cap* : January 1 observed as a church festival in commemoration of the circumcision of the infant Jesus

cir•cum•fer•ence \sər-'kəm-fərns, sə-, -'kəmp-, -fə-rəns, -frəns\ *n* **1** : the perimeter of a circle **2** : the external boundary or surface of a body : PERIPHERY [Middle French, from Latin *circumferentia,* from *circumferre* "to carry around", from *circum-* + *ferre* "to carry"] — **cir•cum•fer•en•tial** \-,kəm-fə-'ren-chəl, -,kəmp-\ *adj*

[1]**cir•cum•flex** \'sər-kəm-,fleks\ *adj* **1 a** : having the kind of sound indicated by a circumflex **b** : marked with a circumflex **2** : bending around ⟨a *circumflex* artery⟩ [Latin *circumflexus,* past participle of *circumflectere* "to bend around, mark with a circumflex", from *circum-* + *flectere* "to bend"]

[2]**circumflex** *n* : a mark ˆ, ˜, or ˉ used chiefly to indicate length, contraction, or a specific vowel quality

cir•cum•lo•cu•tion \,sər-kəm-lō-'kyü-shən\ *n* : use of many words to express a relatively simple idea or to avoid stating one's position directly or clearly [Latin *circumlocutio,* from *circum-* + *locutio* "speech", from *loqui* "to speak"] — **cir•cum•loc•u•to•ry** \-'läk-yə-,tōr-ē, -,tȯr-\ *adj*

cir•cum•lu•nar \,sər-kəm-'lü-nər\ *adj* : revolving about or surrounding the moon

cir•cum•nav•i•gate \-'nav-ə-,gāt\ *vt* : to go completely around (as the earth) especially by water — **cir•cum•nav•i•ga•tion** \-,nav-ə-'gā-shən\ *n* — **cir•cum•nav•i•ga•tor** \-'nav-ə-,gāt-ər\ *n*

cir•cum•po•lar \,sər-kəm-'pō-lər\ *adj* **1** : continually visible above the horizon ⟨a *circumpolar star*⟩ **2 :** surrounding or found in the vicinity of the north pole or south pole

cir·cum·scribe \'sər-kəm-ˌskrīb\ *vt* **1 a :** to draw a line around **b :** to surround by a boundary **2 a :** to limit the range or activity of definitely and clearly **b :** to define or mark off carefully **3 :** to construct or be constructed around (a geometrical figure) so as to touch at as many points as possible ⟨a triangle *circumscribed* about a circle⟩ [Latin *circumscribere,* from *circum-* + *scribere* "to write, draw"]

cir·cum·scrip·tion \ˌsər-kəm-'skrip-shən\ *n* **1 :** something that circumscribes: as **a :** BOUNDARY **b :** RESTRICTION 1 **2 :** the act of circumscribing **:** the state of being circumscribed **3 :** a circumscribed area [Latin *circumscriptio,* from *circumscribere* "to circumscribe"]

cir·cum·spect \'sər-kəm-ˌspekt\ *adj* **:** careful to consider all circumstances and possible consequences [Latin *circumspectus,* from *circumspicere* "to look around, be cautious", from *circum-* + *specere* "to look"] — **cir·cum·spect·ly** *adv*

cir·cum·spec·tion \ˌsər-kəm-'spek-shən\ *n* **:** circumspect action or behavior

cir·cum·stance \'sər-kəm-ˌstans\ *n* **1 :** a fact or event that must be considered along with another fact or event **2** *pl* **:** surrounding conditions ⟨under the *circumstances*⟩ **3** *pl* **:** condition or situation with respect to wealth ⟨in easy *circumstances*⟩ **4 :** formal ceremony accompanying an event ⟨pomp and *circumstance*⟩ **5 :** a happening or fact in a chain of events **:** DETAIL **6 :** CHANCE 1, FATE ⟨a victim of *circumstance*⟩ [Middle French, from Latin *circumstantia,* from *circumstare* "to surround", from *circum-* + *stare* "to stand"]

cir·cum·stanced \-ˌstanst\ *adj* **:** placed in particular circumstances especially in regard to property or income

cir·cum·stan·tial \ˌsər-kəm-'stan-chəl\ *adj* **1 :** consisting of or relating to circumstances **:** dependent on circumstances ⟨*circumstantial* evidence⟩ **2 :** relating to a matter but not essential to it **:** INCIDENTAL **3 :** containing full details ⟨a *circumstantial* account of what happened⟩ — **cir·cum·stan·tial·ly** \-'stanch-lē, -ə-lē\ *adv*

• **syn** PARTICULAR, MINUTE, DETAILED: CIRCUMSTANTIAL implies fullness of details that fixes something described in time and space ⟨a *circumstantial* account of our visit⟩ PARTICULAR implies a precise attention to every detail ⟨a *particular* description of the scene of the crime⟩ MINUTE implies close and searching attention to the smallest details ⟨a *minute* examination of a fossil⟩ DETAILED stresses abundance or completeness of detail ⟨a *detailed* analysis of the event⟩

cir·cum·vent \ˌsər-kəm-'vent\ *vt* **1 :** to go around **:** BYPASS ⟨*circumvent* the town⟩ **2 :** to escape from or avoid especially by skill or trickery **:** get around ⟨*circumvent* the law⟩ ⟨*circumvent* difficulties⟩ [Latin *circumvenire,* from *circum-* + *venire* "to come"] — **cir·cum·ven·tion** \-'ven-chən\ *n*

cir·cus \'sər-kəs\ *n* **1 :** a large arena enclosed by tiers of seats and used for spectacles (as athletic contests or horse races) especially in ancient Rome **2 a :** a usually traveling public entertainment that features clowns, acrobats, and animal acts **b :** a performance of a circus **c :** the company of a circus including personnel and livestock **3 :** an activity suggesting a circus especially in being a showy public display ⟨turned the campaign into a political *circus*⟩ **4** *British* **:** a usually circular area at the intersection of streets ⟨Piccadilly *Circus*⟩ [Latin, "circle, circus"]

cirque \'sərk\ *n* **1 :** something round **:** CIRCLET, CIRCLE **2 :** a deep steep-walled hollow on a mountain shaped like half a bowl [French, "circus, amphitheater", from Latin *circus*]

cir·rho·sis \sə-'rō-səs\ *n* **:** fibrosis and hardening especially of the liver [Greek *kirrhos* "orange-colored"] — **cir·rhot·ic** \-'rät-ik\ *adj or n*

cir·ri·ped \'sir-ə-ˌped\ *or* **cir·ri·pede** \-ˌpēd\ *n* **:** any of a subclass (Cirripedia) of specialized marine crustaceans (as barnacles) that swim about as larvae but are permanently attached or parasitic as adults [Latin *cirrus* "curl" + *ped-, pes* "foot"] — **cirriped** *adj*

cir·ro·cu·mu·lus \ˌsir-ō-'kyü-myə-ləs\ *n* **:** a cloud form of small white rounded masses at a high altitude usually in regular groupings

cir·ro·stra·tus \-'strāt-əs, -'strat-\ *n* **:** a fairly uniform layer of high stratus darker than cirrus

cir·rus \'sir-əs\ *n, pl* **cir·ri** \'siər-ˌī\ **1 :** a plant tendril **2 :** a slender usually flexible animal appendage **3 :** a wispy white cloud usually of minute ice crystals formed at altitudes of 6 to 12 kilometers [Latin, "curl, ringlet, tuft, bird's crest, fringe"]

cis- *prefix* **:** on this side ⟨*cis*lunar⟩ [Latin]

cis·co \'sis-kō\ *n, pl* **ciscoes :** any of various whitefishes including important food fishes of the Great Lakes region [Canadian French *ciscoette,* of American Indian origin]

cis·lu·nar \'sis-'lü-nər\ *adj* **:** lying between the earth and the moon or the moon's orbit ⟨*cislunar* space⟩

Cis·ter·cian \sis-'tər-shən\ *n* **:** a member of a monastic order founded at Cîteaux, France in 1098 under an austere rule — **Cistercian** *adj* [Medieval Latin *Cistercium* "Cîteaux"]

cis·tern \'sis-tərn\ *n* **1 :** an often underground artificial reservoir or tank for storing water and especially rainwater **2 :** a fluid-containing sac or cavity in an organism [Old French *cisterne,* from Latin *cisterna,* from *cista* "box, chest"]

cit·a·del \'sit-əd-l, -ə-ˌdel\ *n* **1 :** a fortress that commands a city **2 :** STRONGHOLD [Middle French *citadelle,* from Italian *cittadella,* from *cittade* "city", from Medieval Latin *civitas*]

ci·ta·tion \sī-'tā-shən\ *n* **1 :** an official order to appear (as before a court) **2 a :** an act or instance of quoting **b :** a passage quoted **:** EXCERPT **3 a :** a formal statement of the achievements of a person (as one receiving an award) **b :** specific reference in a military dispatch to praiseworthy performance of duty

cite \'sīt\ *vt* **1 :** to order to appear before a court **2 :** to quote as an example, authority, or proof **3 a :** to refer to; *esp* **:** to mention formally in commendation or praise **b :** to name in a citation [Middle French *citer* "to cite, summon", from Latin *citare* "to rouse, summon", from *ciēre* "to stir, move"]

cith·a·ra \'sith-ə-rə, 'kith-\ *n* **:** an ancient Greek stringed instrument of the lyre class with a wooden sounding board [Latin, from Greek *kithara*]

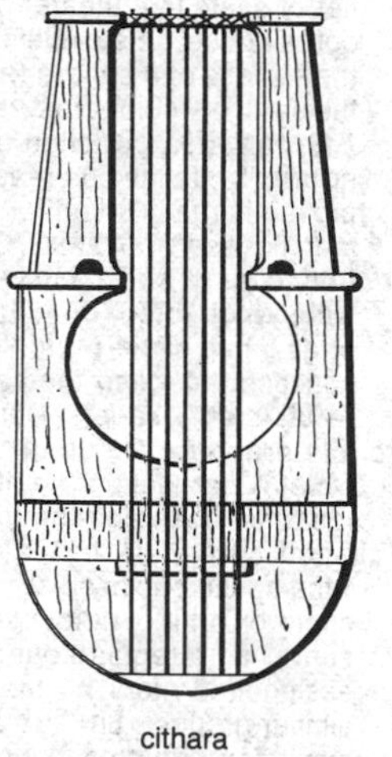

cithara

cit·i·fy \'sit-i-ˌfī\ *vt* **-fied; -fy·ing :** to accustom to urban ways

cit·i·zen \'sit-ə-zən\ *n* **1 :** an inhabitant of a city or town **2 a :** a member of a state **b :** a person who by birth or naturalization owes allegiance to a government and is entitled to protection from it **3 :** CIVILIAN [Anglo-French *citezein,* alteration of Old French *citeien,* from *cité* "city"] — **cit·i·zen·ly** \-lē\ *adj*

• **syn** CITIZEN, SUBJECT, NATIONAL mean a person owing allegiance to and entitled to the protection of a sovereign state. CITIZEN is preferred for one owing allegiance to a state in which sovereign power is retained by the people and sharing in the political rights of those people; SUBJECT implies allegiance to a personal sovereign such as a monarch; NATIONAL designates one who may claim the protection of a state whether or not he is an actual citizen or subject and applies especially to one living or traveling outside that state.

cit·i·zen·ess \-zə-nəs\ *n* **:** a woman who is a citizen

cit·i·zen·ry \-zən-rē\ *n, pl* **-ries :** the whole body of citizens

citizens band \-zənz-\ *n* **:** one of the frequency bands that in the United States is allocated officially for private radio communication

cit·i·zen·ship \-zən-ˌship\ *n* **1 :** possession of the rights and privileges of a citizen **2 :** the quality of a person's response to membership in a community

cit·rate \'si-ˌtrāt\ *n* **:** a salt or ester of citric acid

cit·ric acid \ˌsi-trik-\ *n* **:** a pleasantly sour-tasting acid $C_6H_8O_7$ occurring in cellular metabolism and obtained especially from lemon and lime juices or by fermentation of sugars and used as a flavoring [derived from Latin *citrus* "citron tree"]

citric acid cycle *n* **:** KREBS CYCLE

cit·rine \'si-ˌtrīn\ *adj* **:** resembling a citron or lemon especially in color [Middle French *citrin,* from Latin *citrus* "citron tree"]

cit·ron \'si-trən\ *n* **1 a :** a fruit like the lemon in appearance and structure but larger; *also* **:** the citrus tree producing this fruit **b :** the preserved rind of the citron used especially in fruitcake **2 :** a small hard-fleshed watermelon used mostly in pickles and preserves [Middle French, from Provençal, from Latin *citrus* "citron tree"]

cit·ro·nel·la \ˌsi-trə-'nel-ə\ *n* **:** a fragrant grass of southern

Asia that yields an oil used in perfumery and as an insect repellent; *also* : its oil [French *citronelle* "lemon balm", from *citron* "citron"]

cit•rul•line \'si-trə-ˌlēn\ *n* : an amino acid $C_6H_{13}N_3O_3$ formed especially as an intermediate in the conversion of ornithine to arginine in the living system [New Latin *Citrullus,* genus name of the watermelon, derived from Latin *citrus* "citron tree"]

cit•rus \'si-trəs\ *n, pl* **citrus** *or* **cit•rus•es** : any of a genus of often thorny trees and shrubs of the rue family grown in warm regions for their fruits (as orange, grapefruit, or lemon) with firm usually thick rind and juicy pulp; *also* : the fruit of a citrus [Latin, "citron tree"] — **citrus** *adj*

city \'sit-ē\ *n, pl* **cit•ies 1 a** : an inhabited place of greater size or importance than a town **b** : a usually large or important place in the United States governed under a charter granted by the state **2** : CITY-STATE **3** : the people of a city [Old French *cité* "capital city", from Medieval Latin *civitas,* from Latin, "citizenship, state, city of Rome", from *civis* "citizen"]

city hall *n* **1** : the chief administrative building of a city **2 a** : a municipal government **b** : city bureaucracy

city manager *n* : an official employed by an elected council to administer a city government

city–state \'sit-ē-'stāt, -ˌstāt\ *n* : a self-governing state (as of ancient Greece) consisting of a city and surrounding territory

civ•et \'siv-ət\ *n* : a thick yellowish musky-odored substance obtained from the civet cat and used in perfume [Middle French *civette,* from Italian *zibetto,* from Arabic *zabād* "civet perfume"]

civet cat *n* **1** : a long-bodied short-legged African mammal that produces most of the civet of commerce **2** : any of the small spotted skunks of western North America

civet cat 1

civ•ic \'siv-ik\ *adj* : of or relating to a citizen, a city, or citizenship ⟨*civic* pride⟩ ⟨*civic* duty⟩ [Latin *civicus,* from *civis* "citizen"] — **civ•i•cal•ly** \'siv-i-kə-lē, -klē\ *adv*

civ•ics \'siv-iks\ *n* : the study of the rights and duties of citizens

civ•il \'siv-əl\ *adj* **1** : of or relating to citizens **2** : of or relating to the state as an organized political body ⟨*civil* institutions⟩ **3** : of or relating to the general population as distinguished from the military or the church **4** : marked by courtesy or politeness ⟨give a *civil* answer⟩ **5 a** : relating to legal proceedings in connection with private rights and obligations ⟨the *civil* code⟩ ⟨a *civil* suit⟩ **b** : of or relating to the civil law [Middle French, from Latin *civilis,* from *civis* "citizen"]

• **syn** POLITE, COURTEOUS: CIVIL implies no more than barely meeting the requirements of good breeding and the avoidance of roughness or unpleasantness; POLITE implies showing good manners and thoughtfulness but may often suggest lack of warmth or cordiality; COURTEOUS implies more actively considerate or dignified politeness.

civil defense *n* : organized protective and emergency relief activities by civilians in case of attack or disaster

civil engineering *n* : engineering that deals with the designing and construction of public works (as roads or harbors) and of various private works — **civil engineer** *n*

ci•vil•ian \sə-'vil-yən\ *n* : one not on active duty in a military, police, or fire-fighting force — **civilian** *adj*

ci•vil•i•ty \sə-'vil-ət-ē\ *n, pl* **-ties 1** : POLITENESS, COURTESY **2** : a polite act or expression

civ•i•li•za•tion \ˌsiv-ə-lə-'zā-shən\ *n* **1 a** : a relatively high level of cultural and technological development **b** : the special culture of a people or a period ⟨Greek *civilization*⟩ ⟨18th century *civilization*⟩ **2** : the process of becoming civilized **3 a** : refinement of thought, manners, or taste **b** : city life and comforts

civ•i•lize \'siv-ə-ˌlīz\ *vt* : to raise out of a savage state; *esp* : to bring to an advanced and ordered stage of cultural development — **civ•i•lized** *adj*

civil law *n, often cap C & L* **1** : a body of law developed from Roman law **2** : the law of civil or private rights

civil liberty *n* : freedom from governmental interference with rights (as of free speech) especially as guaranteed by a bill of rights

civ•il•ly \'siv-ə-lē, -əl-lē\ *adv* : in a civil manner : POLITELY

civil marriage *n* : a marriage performed by a magistrate

civil rights *n pl* : the rights of personal liberty guaranteed to United States citizens by the 13th and 14th amendments to the Constitution and by acts of Congress

civil servent *n* : a member of a civil service

civil service *n* : the administrative service of a government exclusive of the armed forces

civil war *n* : a war between opposing groups of citizens of the same country or nation

clab•ber \'klab-ər\ *n, chiefly dialect* : sour milk that has thickened or curdled [short for *bonnyclabber,* from Irish Gaelic *bainne clabair,* from *bainne* "milk" + *clabar* "sour thick milk"]

[1]**clack** \'klak\ *vb* **1** : CHATTER 2, PRATTLE **2** : to make or cause to make a clatter [Middle English *clacken*] — **clack•er** *n*

[2]**clack** *n* **1** : CHATTER ⟨the *clack* of voices⟩ **2** : a sound of clacking ⟨the *clack* of a typewriter⟩

clad \'klad\ *adj* : CLOTHED, COVERED ⟨ivy-*clad* walls⟩ [past participle of *clothe*]

[1]**claim** \'klām\ *vt* **1 a** : to ask for as one's right or property ⟨*claim* an inheritance⟩ ⟨*claim* one's bags⟩ **b** : to call for : REQUIRE ⟨this matter *claims* our attention⟩ **2 a** : to state as a fact : MAINTAIN ⟨*claimed* they'd been cheated⟩ **b** : PROFESS ⟨*claimed* to know nothing of the matter⟩ [Old French *clamer,* from Latin *clamare* "to cry out"] **syn** see DEMAND — **claim•able** \'klā-mə-bəl\ *adj* — **claim•er** *n*

[2]**claim** *n* **1** : a demand for something due or believed to be due ⟨an insurance *claim*⟩ **2 a** : a right to something; *esp* : a title to something in the possession of another **b** : an assertion open to challenge ⟨a *claim* of authenticity⟩ **3** : something claimed; *esp* : a tract of land marked out by a settler or prospector

claim•ant \'klā-mənt\ *n* : a person who asserts a right to something ⟨a *claimant* to an estate⟩

clair•voy•ance \klaər-'vȯi-əns, kleər-\ *n* **1** : the professed power of seeing or knowing about things that are not present to the senses **2** : sharp insight : DISCERNMENT

[1]**clair•voy•ant** \-ənt\ *adj* **1** : unusually perceptive : DISCERNING **2** : of or relating to clairvoyance [French, from *clair* "clear" + *voyant,* present participle of *voir* "to see"] — **clair•voy•ant•ly** *adv*

[2]**clairvoyant** *n* : a person held to have the power of clairvoyance

[1]**clam** \'klam\ *n* **1** : any of numerous edible marine bivalve mollusks living in sand or mud **2** : a freshwater mussel **3** : the flesh of a clam used as food [earlier *clam* "clamp", from Old English *clamm* "bond, fetter"; from the clamping action of the shells]

[1]clam 1

[2]**clam** *vi* **clammed; clam•ming** : to gather clams especially by digging

clam•bake \'klam-ˌbāk\ *n* : a party or outing where food is cooked on heated rocks covered by seaweed; *also* : a usually loud and lively get-together

clam•ber \'klam-bər\ *vi* **clam•bered; clam•ber•ing** \'klam-bə-ring, -bring\ : to climb awkwardly (as by scrambling) ⟨*clamber* over steep rocks⟩ [Middle English *clambren*] — **clam•ber•er** \-bər-ər\ *n*

clam•my \'klam-ē\ *adj* **clam•mi•er; -est** : being damp, soft, sticky, and usually cool [Middle English, probably from *clammen* "to smear, stick", from Old English *clǣman*] — **clam•mi•ly** \'klam-ə-lē\ *adv* — **clam•mi•ness** \'klam-ē-nəs\ *n*

[1]**clam•or** \'klam-ər\ *n* **1 a** : noisy shouting **b** : a loud continuous noise **2** : insistent protest or demand ⟨public *clamor* for a

tax cut⟩ [Middle French *clamour,* from Latin *clamor,* from *clamare* "to cry out"]

2**clamor** *vb* **clam•ored; clam•or•ing** \ˈklam-riŋ, -ə-riŋ\ **1 :** to make a din ⟨gulls *clamored* overhead⟩ **2 :** to express insistently and noisily ⟨*clamoring* that they had been misunderstood⟩

clam•or•ous \ˈklam-rəs, -ə-rəs\ *adj* **:** full of clamor **:** NOISY ⟨a *clamorous* mob⟩ — **clam•or•ous•ly** *adv* — **clam•or•ous•ness** *n*

1**clamp** \ˈklamp\ *n* **:** a device that holds or presses two or more parts together firmly [probably from Dutch *klamp*]

2**clamp** *vt* **1 a :** to fasten with or as if with a clamp ⟨*clamp* two boards together⟩ **b :** to grip firmly ⟨winter *clamped* the region⟩ **2 :** to place by decree **:** IMPOSE — often used with *on* ⟨*clamped* on a curfew after the riots⟩

clamp down *vi* **:** to impose restrictions ⟨*clamping down* on speeders⟩

clam•shell \ˈklam-ˌshel\ *n* **:** a bucket or grapple (as on a dredge) having two hinged jaws

clam up *vi* **:** to become silent; *esp* **:** to refuse to talk further ⟨they *clammed up* when asked for details⟩

clam worm *n* **:** any of several large burrowing marine annelid worms often used as bait

clan \ˈklan\ *n* **1 :** a group (as in the Scottish Highlands) made up of households whose heads claim descent from a common ancestor **2 :** a group united by a common interest ⟨the whole *clan* of actors⟩ [Scottish Gaelic *clann* "offspring, clan", from Irish *cland* "plant, offspring", from Latin *planta* "plant"]

clan•des•tine \klan-ˈdes-tən\ *adj* **:** held in or conducted with secrecy **:** FURTIVE ⟨a *clandestine* meeting⟩ [Latin *clandestinus,* derived from *clam* "secretly"] **syn** see SECRET — **clan•des•tine•ly** *adv* — **clan•des•tine•ness** *n*

1**clang** \ˈklaŋ\ *vb* **:** to make or cause to make a clang [Latin *clangere*]

2**clang** *n* **:** a loud ringing metallic sound ⟨the *clang* of a fire alarm⟩

clang•or \ˈklaŋ-ər, -gər\ *n* **:** a resounding clang or series of clangs ⟨the *clangor* of hammers⟩ [Latin, from *clangere* "to clang"] — **clangor** *vi* — **clang•or•ous** \-ə-rəs, -gə-rəs\ *adj* — **clang•or•ous•ly** *adv*

1**clank** \ˈklaŋk\ *vb* **1 :** to make or cause to make a clank or series of clanks ⟨the radiator hissed and *clanked*⟩ **2 :** to move with a clank ⟨tanks *clanking* through the streets⟩ [probably imitative] — **clank•ing•ly** \ˈklaŋ-kiŋ-lē\ *adv*

2**clank** *n* **:** a sharp brief metallic ringing sound

clan•nish \ˈklan-ish\ *adj* **1 :** of or relating to a clan **2 :** tending to associate only with others of similar background or status ⟨*clannish* immigrants⟩ — **clan•nish•ly** *adv* — **clan•nish•ness** *n*

clans•man \ˈklanz-mən\ *n* **:** a member of a clan

1**clap** \ˈklap\ *vb* **clapped; clap•ping 1 :** to strike (as two flat hard surfaces) together to produce a sharp noise ⟨the door *clapped* shut⟩ **2 :** to strike the hands together repeatedly in applause **:** APPLAUD **3 :** to strike with the open hand ⟨*clapped* a friend on the shoulder⟩ **4 :** to put usually hastily or energetically ⟨*clap* on one's hat⟩ [Old English *clæppan*]

2**clap** *n* **1 :** a loud crash made by or as if by clapping ⟨a *clap* of thunder **2 :** a firm slap ⟨a *clap* on the shoulder⟩ **3 :** the sound of clapping hands; *esp* **:** APPLAUSE

3**clap** *n* **:** GONORRHEA [Middle French *clapoir* "bubo"]

clap•board \ˈklab-ərd; ˈkla-ˌbōrd, ˈklap-, -ˌbȯrd\ *n* **:** a narrow board thicker at one edge than at the other used as siding [Dutch *klaphout* "stave wood"] — **clapboard** *vt*

clap•per \ˈklap-ər\ *n* **:** one that makes a clapping sound: as **a :** the tongue of a bell **b :** a device that makes noise especially by the banging of one part against another **c :** a person who applauds

clap•trap \ˈklap-ˌtrap\ *n* **:** pretentious nonsense [1*clap;* from its being a trap for applause]

claque \ˈklak\ *n* **1 :** a group hired to applaud at a performance **2 :** a group of self-seeking flatterers [French, from *claquer* "to clap"]

clar•et \ˈklar-ət\ *n* **1 :** a dry red table wine **2 :** a dark purplish red [Middle French *vin claret* "clear wine"] — **claret** *adj*

clar•i•fy \ˈklar-ə-ˌfī\ *vb* **-fied; -fy•ing 1 :** to make or become pure or clear ⟨*clarify* a liquid⟩ **2 :** to make or become more readily understandable ⟨*clarify* an explanation⟩ [Middle French *clarifier,* from Late Latin *clarificare,* from Latin *clarus* "clear"] — **clar•i•fi•ca•tion** \ˌklar-ə-fə-ˈkā-shən\ *n* — **clar•i•fi•er** \ˈklar-ə-ˌfī-ər,-ˌfīr\ *n*

clar•i•net \ˌklar-ə-ˈnet, ˈklar-ə-nət\ *n* **:** a single-reed woodwind instrument having a cylindrical tube with moderately flaring end [French *clarinette*] — **clar•i•net•ist** *or* **clar•i•net•tist** \ˌklar-ə-ˈnet-əst\ *n*

clarinet

1**clar•i•on** \ˈklar-ē-ən\ *n* **:** a medieval trumpet with clear shrill tones [Medieval Latin *clario,* from Latin *clarus* "clear"]

2**clarion** *adj* **:** brilliantly clear ⟨a *clarion* call to action⟩

clar•i•ty \ˈklar-ət-ē\ *n* **:** CLEARNESS ⟨the *clarity* of the atmosphere⟩ [Latin *claritas,* from *clarus* "clear"]

clary \ˈklaər-ē, ˈkleər-\ *n, pl* **clar•ies :** an aromatic mint of southern Europe grown as a potherb and ornamental [Middle French *sclaree,* from Medieval Latin *sclareia*]

1**clash** \ˈklash\ *vb* **1 :** to make a clash ⟨gears *clashed* as the truck moved on⟩ **2 :** to come into conflict ⟨rebels *clashed* with the police⟩ **3 :** to cause to clash ⟨*clashed* the cymbals together⟩ [imitative] — **clash•er** *n*

2**clash** *n* **1 :** a noisy usually metallic sound of collision ⟨the *clash* of swords⟩ **2 a :** a hostile encounter ⟨a *clash* between two armies⟩ **b :** a sharp conflict ⟨a *clash* of opinion⟩

1**clasp** \ˈklasp\ *n* **1 :** a device (as a hook) for holding objects or parts together ⟨the *clasp* of a necklace⟩ **2 :** a holding with or as if with the hands **:** EMBRACE, GRASP ⟨the *clasp* of warm hands⟩ [Middle English *claspe*]

2**clasp** *vt* **1 :** to fasten with or as if with a clasp **2 :** to enclose and hold with or as if with the arms; *esp* **:** EMBRACE **3 :** to seize with or as if with the hand **:** GRASP — **clasp•er** *n*

clasp knife *n* **:** POCKETKNIFE; *esp* **:** one having a catch to hold the blade open

1**class** \ˈklas\ *n* **1 a :** a group sharing the same economic or social status ⟨the working *class*⟩ **b** *pl* **:** persons of high social or economic status ⟨the *classes* as opposed to the masses⟩ **c :** social rank or level ⟨an awareness of *class*⟩ **d :** high quality ⟨the team was competent but lacked *class*⟩ **2 a :** a course of instruction ⟨a *class* in arithmetic⟩ **b :** the group of pupils meeting regularly in a course ⟨a big *class* this year⟩ **c :** the period during which such a group meets **d :** a group of students or alumni whose year of graduation is the same ⟨*class* of '81⟩ **3 a :** a group or set alike in some way **b :** a major category in biological taxonomy ranking above the order and below the phylum or division **4 :** a division or rating based on grade or quality ⟨a *class* A movie⟩ [French *classe,* from Latin *classis* "group called to arms, class of citizens"] — **class•less** \-ləs\ *adj*

2**class** *vt* **:** CLASSIFY

class–con•scious \ˈklas-ˌkän-chəs\ *adj* **1 :** aware of one's common status with others in an economic or social class **2 :** believing in and actively aware of class struggle — **class consciousness** *n*

1**clas•sic** \ˈklas-ik\ *adj* **1 a :** serving as a standard of excellence **b :** belonging to the great accomplishments of humanity ⟨*classic* products of the imagination⟩ **c :** characterized by simple tailored lines in fashion year after year ⟨*classic* apparel⟩ **2 :** of or relating to the ancient Greeks and Romans or their culture **:** CLASSICAL **3 a :** AUTHENTIC 1 ⟨a *classic* folk dance⟩ **b :** notable as the most typical instance ⟨the *classic* study of American politics⟩ [Latin *classicus* "of the highest class of Roman citizens, of the first rank", from *classis* "class"]

2**classic** *n* **1 :** a literary work of ancient Greece or Rome **2 :** a work of enduring excellence; *also* **:** its author **3 :** something perfect of its kind **:** MODEL **4 :** a traditional event ⟨a football *classic*⟩

clas•si•cal \ˈklas-i-kəl\ *adj* **1 :** having recognized and permanent value **:** CLASSIC **2 :** of or relating to the ancient Greek and Roman world and especially to its literature and art ⟨*classical* studies⟩ ⟨a *classical* scholar⟩ **3 :** of, relating to, or being music in established European styles and forms (as the symphony and opera) **4 a :** regarded as of first historical significance **:** TRADITIONAL **b :** of or relating to the first developed form or system of a science, art, or discipline ⟨the *classical* economists⟩ **c :** conforming to a pattern of usage sanctioned by a body of literature rather than by everyday speech ⟨*classical* Latin⟩ **5** : concerned with a general study of the arts and sciences and not specializing in technical studies ⟨a *classical* high school⟩

clas·si·cal·ly \'klas-i-kə-lē, -klē\ *adv* : in a classic or classical manner

clas·si·cism \'klas-ə-ˌsiz-əm\ *n* **1 a** : the principles or style embodied in the literature, art, or architecture of ancient Greece and Rome **b** : classical scholarship **c** : a classical idiom or expression **2** : adherence to traditional standards (as of simplicity, restraint, or proportion) that are universally and permanently valid

clas·si·cist \-səst\ *n* **1** : an advocate or follower of classicism **2** : a classical scholar — **clas·si·cis·tic** \ˌklas-ə-'sis-tik\ *adj*

clas·si·fi·ca·tion \ˌklas-ə-fə-'kā-shən, ˌklas-fə-\ *n* **1** : the act or process of classifying **2 a (1)** : systematic arrangement in groups or categories according to established criteria **(2)** : TAXONOMY 2b **b** : CLASS 3a, CATEGORY — **clas·si·fi·ca·to·ry** \'klas-ə-fə-kə-ˌtōr-ē, 'klas-fə-, -ˌtòr-\ *adj*

clas·si·fied \'klas-ə-ˌfīd\ *adj* **1** : divided into classes or placed in a class ⟨*classified* ads⟩ **2** : withheld from general circulation for reasons of national security ⟨*classified* information⟩

clas·si·fy \'klas-ə-ˌfī\ *vt* **-fied**; **-fy·ing** : to arrange in or assign to a class or classes ⟨*classify* books according to subject matter⟩ — **clas·si·fi·able** \-ˌfī-ə-bəl\ *adj* — **clas·si·fi·er** \-ˌfī-ər, -ˌfīr\ *n*

class·mate \'klas-ˌmāt\ *n* : a member of the same class in a school or college

class·room \-ˌrüm, -ˌrům\ *n* : a room in a school or college in which classes meet

class struggle *n* : a basic conflict between social classes in Marxian theory — called also *class war*

[1]clat·ter \'klat-ər\ *vb* **1** : to make or cause to make a rattling sound ⟨*clattering* the dishes⟩ **2** : to move or go with a clatter ⟨*clatter* down the stairs⟩ **3** : CHATTER 2 [Middle English *clatren*] — **clat·ter·er** \-ər-ər\ *n* — **clat·ter·ing·ly** \'klat-ə-ring-lē\ *adv*

[2]clatter *n* **1** : a rattling sound (as of hard bodies striking together) **2** : COMMOTION ⟨the midday *clatter* of the business district⟩ **3** : noisy chatter — **clat·tery** \'klat-ə-rē\ *adj*

clause \'klȯz\ *n* **1** : a separate section of an article or document ⟨a *clause* in a will⟩ **2** : a group of words having its own subject and predicate but forming only part of a compound or complex sentence (as "when it rained" or "they went inside" in the sentence "when it rained, they went inside") [Old French, from Medieval Latin *clausa* "close of a rhetorical period", from Latin *claudere* "to close"] — **claus·al** \'klȯ-zəl\ *adj*

claus·tro·pho·bia \ˌklȯ-strə-'fō-bē-ə\ *n* : abnormal fear of being in closed or narrow spaces [Latin *claustrum* "bar, bolt", from *claudere* "to close"] — **claus·tro·pho·bic** \-bik\ *adj*

clave *past of* CLEAVE

clav·i·chord \'klav-ə-ˌkȯrd\ *n* : an early keyboard instrument in use before the piano [Medieval Latin *clavichordium*, from Latin *clavis* "key" + *chorda* "string"] — **clav·i·chord·ist** \-əst\ *n*

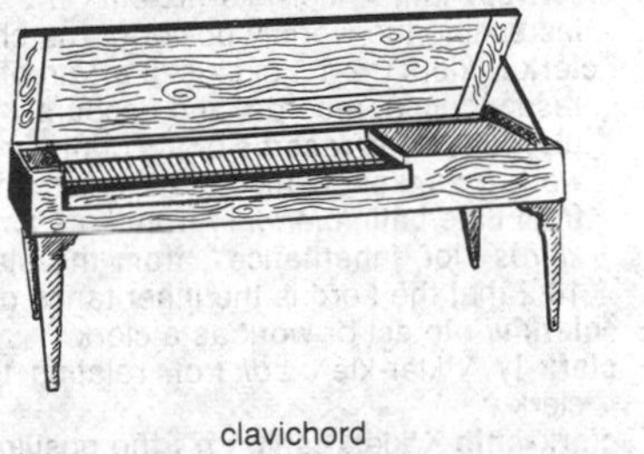

clavichord

clav·i·cle \'klav-i-kəl\ *n* : a bone of the shoulder that joins the breastbone and the shoulder blade — called also *collarbone* [French *clavicule*, derived from Latin *clavis* "key"] — **cla·vic·u·lar** \klə-'vik-yə-lər\ *adj*

cla·vier \klə-'viər; 'klāv-ē-ər, 'klav-\ *n* **1** : the keyboard of a musical instrument **2** : an early keyboard instrument [French, from Old French, "key bearer", from Latin *clavis* "key"] — **cla·vier·ist** \-əst\ *n*

[1]claw \'klȯ\ *n* **1 a** : a sharp usually slender and curved nail on the toe of an animal **b** : a sharp curved process especially if at the end of a limb (as of an insect); *also* : one of the pincerlike organs terminating some limbs of an arthropod (as a lobster or scorpion) **2** : something that resembles a claw; *esp* : the forked end of a tool (as a hammer) [Old English *clawu* "hoof, claw"] — **clawed** \'klȯd\ *adj*

[2]claw *vb* : to rake, seize, or dig with or as if with claws

clay \'klā\ *n* **1 a** : an earthy material that is plastic when moist but hard when fired, is composed chiefly of silicates of aluminum and water, and is used for brick, tile, and earthenware; *also* : soil composed chiefly of this material having particles less than a specified size **b** : earth especially when moist **2 a** : a plastic substance used for modeling **b** : the human body as distinguished from the spirit [Old English *clǣg*] — **clay·ish** \'klā-ish\ *adj*

clay·ey \'klā-ē\ *adj* **clay·i·er**; **-est** : resembling clay or containing much clay ⟨a *clayey* soil⟩

clay loam *n* : a loam consisting of from 20 to 30 percent clay

clay·more \'klā-ˌmōr, -ˌmȯr\ *n* : a large 2-edged sword formerly used by Scottish Highlanders [Scottish Gaelic *claidheamh mōr*, literally, "great sword"]

clay pigeon *n* : a saucer-shaped target thrown from a trap in skeet and trapshooting

[1]clean \'klēn\ *adj* **1 a** : free from dirt or pollution ⟨*clean* clothes⟩ ⟨*clean* air⟩ **b** : free from contamination or disease **2** : free from admixture : PURE **3 a** : characterized by moral integrity : HONORABLE ⟨a candidate with a *clean* record⟩ **b** : free from offensive treatment of sexual subjects and from the use of obscenity ⟨a *clean* joke⟩ **4** : ceremonially or spiritually pure **5 a** : so complete as to leave no remainder ⟨made a *clean* sweep⟩ **b** : well done : SKILLFUL ⟨a good *clean* job⟩ **6 a** : being trim and well-formed ⟨a ship with *clean* lines⟩ **b** : EVEN, SMOOTH ⟨a sharp knife makes a *clean* cut⟩ **7** : habitually neat [Old English *clǣne*] — **clean·ness** \'klēn-nəs\ *n*

[2]clean *adv* **1 a** : so as to clean ⟨a new broom sweeps *clean*⟩ **b** : in a clean manner ⟨fight *clean*⟩ **2** : all the way : COMPLETELY ⟨hit the ball *clean* out of the ball park⟩

[3]clean *vb* **1** : to make or become clean ⟨*clean* this room⟩ ⟨*cleaned* up for supper⟩ **2** : to remove or exhaust the contents or resources of ⟨*clean* a fish⟩ ⟨thieves *cleaned* out the safe⟩ — **clean·er** *n*

• **syn** CLEAN, CLEANSE mean to remove dirt or impurities from. CLEAN applies to any removing of dirt, litter, dust; CLEANSE applies chiefly to washing with water or a solvent; it may also apply to figurative purification ⟨*cleansed* from sin⟩

— **clean house** : to get rid of whatever is hampering, wrong, or degrading

clean–cut \'klēn-'kət\ *adj* **1** : CLEAR-CUT ⟨*clean-cut* features⟩ ⟨a *clean-cut* skyline⟩ **2** : giving an effect of wholesomeness ⟨a *clean-cut* young person⟩

[1]clean·ly \'klen-lē\ *adj* **clean·li·er**; **-est** **1** : careful to keep clean : FASTIDIOUS **2** : habitually kept clean ⟨*cleanly* surroundings⟩ — **clean·li·ness** *n*

[2]clean·ly \'klēn-lē\ *adv* : in a clean manner ⟨hit a ball *cleanly*⟩

cleanse \'klenz\ *vt* : to make clean [Old English *clǣnsian* "to purify", from *clǣne* "clean"] **syn** see CLEAN

cleans·er \'klen-zər\ *n* **1** : one that cleanses **2** : a preparation (as a scouring powder or a skin cream) used for cleaning

clean up *vi* : to make a lot of money ⟨*cleaned up* at the races⟩

[1]clear \'kliər\ *adj* **1 a** : shining brightly : LUMINOUS ⟨*clear* sunlight⟩ **b** : free from clouds, haze, or mist ⟨a *clear* day⟩ **c** : SERENE 2 ⟨a *clear* gaze⟩ **2** : CLEAN, PURE: as **a** : free of blemishes ⟨a *clear* complexion⟩ **b** : easily seen through : TRANSPARENT ⟨*clear* glass⟩ **3 a** : easily heard ⟨the sound was quite *clear*⟩ **b** : easily visible : PLAIN **c** : easily understandable : UNMISTAKABLE ⟨the meaning was *clear*⟩ **4** : free from doubt : SURE ⟨a *clear* understanding of the issue⟩ **5** : free from guile or guilt : INNOCENT ⟨a *clear* conscience⟩ **6** : unhampered by restriction or limitation: as **a** : unencumbered by debts or charges **b** : NET ⟨a *clear* profit⟩ **c** : free from qualification : ABSOLUTE ⟨a *clear* case of treason⟩ **d** : free from obstruction or entanglement ⟨the coast is *clear*⟩ [Old French *cler*, from Latin *clarus* "clear, bright"] — **clear·ly** *adv* — **clear·ness** *n*

• **syn** TRANSPARENT, TRANSLUCENT: CLEAR implies absence of cloudiness, haziness, or muddiness ⟨*clear* water⟩ TRANSPARENT implies being so clear that objects can be seen distinctly ⟨a *transparent* film of varnish⟩ TRANSLUCENT usually implies permitting the passage of light but not vision ⟨*translu-*

\ə\ **abut**	\au̇\ **out**	\i\ **tip**	\ȯ\ **saw**	\u̇\ **foot**
\ər\ **further**	\ch\ **chin**	\ī\ **life**	\ȯi\ **coin**	\y\ **yet**
\a\ **mat**	\e\ **pet**	\j\ **job**	\th\ **thin**	\yü\ **few**
\ā\ **take**	\ē\ **easy**	\ng\ **sing**	\t͟h\ **this**	\yu̇\ **cure**
\ä\ **cot, cart**	\g\ **go**	\ō\ **bone**	\ü\ **food**	\zh\ **vision**

cent frosted glass⟩ ⟨*translucent* shades for lamps⟩

[2]**clear** *adv* **1 :** in a clear manner ⟨shout loud and *clear*⟩ **2 :** all the way **:** COMPLETELY ⟨can see *clear* to the mountains on a day like this⟩

[3]**clear** *vb* **1 a :** to make or become clear or translucent ⟨*clear* the water by filtering⟩ ⟨the sky *cleared*⟩ **b :** to go away **:** DISPERSE ⟨clouds *cleared* away after the rain⟩ **2 a :** to free from accusation or blame ⟨*clear* one's name⟩ **b :** to certify as trustworthy ⟨*cleared* for top-secret work⟩ **3 :** to make intelligible **:** EXPLAIN ⟨*cleared* the matter up for me⟩ **4 :** to free from obstruction: as **a :** to submit for approval ⟨*clear* this with the boss⟩ **b :** to give approval to **:** AUTHORIZE **c :** to erase stored or displayed data from (as a computer or calculator) **5 :** to make free especially from financial obligation **:** SETTLE ⟨*clear* an account⟩ **6 :** to go through (customs) **7 :** NET ⟨*cleared* a profit⟩ **8 :** to get rid of **:** REMOVE ⟨*clear* away that trash⟩ **9 a :** to jump or go by without touching ⟨*cleared* the fence⟩ **b :** PASS 7a ⟨the bill *cleared* the legislature⟩ — **clear•able** \'klir-ə-bəl\ *adj* — **clear•er** *n* — **clear the air :** to remove tension or confusion ⟨*cleared the air* by discussing their differences⟩

[4]**clear** *n* **:** a clear space or part — **in the clear 1 :** in inside measurement **2 :** free of resistance or obstruction ⟨some nice blocking got the halfback *in the clear*⟩ **3 :** free from suspicion **4 :** not in code or cipher ⟨sent the message *in the clear*⟩

clear•ance \'klir-əns\ *n* **1 :** an act or process of clearing: as **a :** the act of clearing a ship at the customhouse; *also* **:** the papers showing that a ship has cleared **b :** the passage of checks and claims among banks through a clearinghouse **c :** certification as clear of objection ⟨was given a security *clearance*⟩ **d :** a sale to clear out stock **2 :** the distance by which one object clears another or the clear space between them

clear–cut \'kliər-'kət\ *adj* **1 :** sharply outlined **:** DISTINCT ⟨a *clear-cut* pattern⟩ **2 :** free from uncertainty **:** DEFINITE ⟨*clear-cut* victory⟩

clear•head•ed \-'hed-əd\ *adj* **:** having a clear understanding **:** PERCEPTIVE — **clear•head•ed•ly** *adv* — **clear•head•ed•ness** *n*

clear•ing \'kliər-iŋ\ *n* **1 :** the act or process of making or becoming clear **2 :** a tract of land cleared of wood and brush **3 a :** CLEARANCE 1b **b** *pl* **:** the gross amount of balances adjusted by clearance

clear•ing•house \-,haủs\ *n* **1 :** an establishment maintained by banks for settling mutual claims and accounts **2 :** a central agency for collection, classification, and distribution especially of information

clear–sight•ed \'kliər-'sīt-əd\ *adj* **1 :** having clear vision **2 :** DISCERNING — **clear–sight•ed•ly** *adv* — **clear–sight•ed•ness** *n*

[1]**cleat** \'klēt\ *n* **1 :** a wedge-shaped piece fastened to something and used as a support or check (as for a rope on the spar of a ship) **2 :** a wooden or metal device usually with projecting arms at each end around which a rope may be made fast **3 :** a strip or projecting piece fastened on or across something to give strength, to provide a grip, or to prevent slipping [Middle English *clete* "wedge"]

[2]**cleat** *vt* **1 :** to fasten to or by a cleat **2 :** to provide with a cleat

cleav•age \'klē-vij\ *n* **1 :** the quality possessed by a crystallized substance or rock of splitting along definite planes **2 :** the action of cleaving **:** the state of being cleft **3 :** cell division; *esp* **:** the series of mitotic divisions of the egg that changes the single-celled zygote into a multicellular embryo

[1]**cleave** \'klēv\ *vi* **cleaved** \'klēvd\ *or* **clove** \'klōv\ *also* **clave** \'klāv\; **cleav•ing :** CLING 1a, ADHERE [Middle English *cleven,* from Old English *clifian*]

[2]**cleave** *vb* **cleaved** \'klēvd\ *also* **cleft** \'kleft\ *or* **clove** \'klōv\; **cleaved** *also* **cleft** *or* **clo•ven** \'klō-vən\; **cleav•ing 1 a :** to split by or as if by a cutting blow ⟨some woods *cleave* along the grain easily⟩ **b :** to cause to separate ⟨the controversy *cleaved* the group into two camps⟩ **2 :** to pass through **:** PENETRATE ⟨a ship's bow *cleaving* the waves⟩ [Middle English *cleven,* from Old English *clēofan*] — **cleav•able** \'klē-və-bəl\ *adj*

cleav•er \'klē-vər\ *n* **:** one that cleaves; *esp* **:** a heavy broad-bladed knife for chopping meat or cutting through bone

cleav•ers \'klē-vərz\ *n sing or pl* **:** any of several plants of the madder family with weak prickly stems [alteration of Old English *clife* "burdock, cleavers"]

clef \'klef\ *n* **:** a sign placed on the staff in music to show what pitch is represented by each line and space [French, literally, "key", from Latin *clavis*]

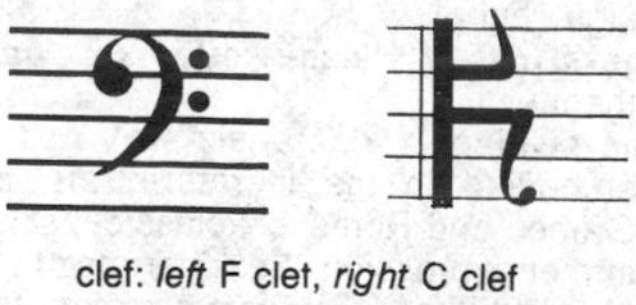

clef: *left* F clef, *right* C clef

[1]**cleft** \'kleft\ *n* **1 :** a space or opening made by splitting **:** FISSURE **2 :** a usually V-shaped indentation [Old English *geclyft*]

[2]**cleft** *adj* **1 :** partially split or divided **2 :** divided about halfway to the midrib ⟨a *cleft* leaf⟩

cleft graft *n* **:** a plant graft made by cutting the stock squarely across, splitting the cut end, and inserting one or two scions so that the cambiums of stock and scion are in contact

cleft palate *n* **:** congenital fissure of the roof of the mouth

clem•a•tis \'klem-ət-əs, kli-'mat-əs\ *n* **:** a vine or herb related to the buttercups that has leaves with three leaflets and is widely grown for its showy usually white or purple flowers [Latin, from Greek *klēmatis* "brushwood, clematis"]

clem•en•cy \'klem-ən-sē\ *n, pl* **-cies 1 a :** disposition to be merciful **b :** an act or instance of leniency **2 :** mildness of weather **syn** see MERCY

clem•ent \'klem-ənt\ *adj* **1 :** inclined to be merciful **:** LENIENT ⟨a *clement* judge⟩ **2 :** not harsh or severe ⟨*clement* weather⟩ [Latin *clemens*] — **clem•ent•ly** *adv*

[1]**clench** \'klench\ *vb* **1 :** CLINCH 1 **2 :** to hold fast **:** CLUTCH **3 :** to set or close tightly ⟨*clench* one's teeth⟩ ⟨hands *clenched* together⟩ [Old English *-clencan*]

[2]**clench** *n* **1 :** the end of a nail that is turned back in clinching it **2 :** an act or instance of clenching

clep•sy•dra \'klep-sə-drə\ *n, pl* **-dras** *or* **-drae** \-,drē, -,drī\ **:** WATER CLOCK [Latin, from Greek *klepsydra,* from *kleptein* "to steal" + *hydōr* "water"]

clere•sto•ry *or* **clear•sto•ry** \'kliər-,stōr-ē, -,stȯr-\ *n, pl* **-ries :** an outside wall of a room or building that rises above an adjoining roof and contains windows [Middle English, from *clere* "clear" + *story*]

cler•gy \'klər-jē\ *n, pl* **clergies 1 :** the body of religious officials (as priests, ministers, and rabbis) authorized to conduct services **2 :** the official or priestly class of a religion [Old French *clergie* "knowledge, learning", from *clerc* "clergyman"]

cler•gy•man \-ji-mən\ *n* **:** a member of the clergy

cler•ic \'kler-ik\ *n* **1 :** CLERGYMAN **2 :** a member of a religious order lower than the priesthood [Late Latin *clericus*]

cler•i•cal \'kler-i-kəl\ *adj* **1 :** of, relating to, or characteristic of the clergy, a clergyman, or a cleric **2 :** of or relating to a clerk or office worker — **cler•i•cal•ly** \'kler-i-kə-lē, -klē\ *adv*

clerical collar *n* **:** a narrow stiffly upright white collar buttoned at the back of the neck and worn by clergymen

cler•i•cal•ism \'kler-i-kə-,liz-əm\ *n* **:** a policy of maintaining or increasing the worldly power of the church

[1]**clerk** \'klərk\ *n* **1 :** CLERIC **2 a :** an official responsible for correspondence, records, and accounts ⟨town *clerk*⟩ **b :** one employed to keep records or accounts or to perform general office work **c :** SALESCLERK [Old English and Old French *clerc,* both from Late Latin *clericus,* from Late Greek *klērikos,* from Greek *klēros* "lot, inheritance"; from the statement in Deuteronomy 18:2 that the Lord is the inheritance of the Levite priests]

[2]**clerk** *vi* **:** to act or work as a clerk

clerk•ly \'klər-klē\ *adj* **:** of, relating to, or characteristic of a clerk

clerk•ship \'klərk-,ship\ *n* **:** the position or business of a clerk

clev•er \'klev-ər\ *adj* **1 a :** apt and skillful in using the hands or body **b :** quick in learning **2 :** marked by wit or ingenuity [Middle English *cliver*] — **clev•er•ish** \'klev-rish, -ə-rish\ *adj* — **clev•er•ly** \-ər-lē\ *adv* — **clev•er•ness** \-ər-nəs\ *n*

• **syn** CLEVER, INTELLIGENT, SMART, ALERT mean mentally quick or keen. CLEVER stresses quickness, deftness, or great aptitude; INTELLIGENT implies success in understanding and coping with the new situations and solving problems; SMART suggests alertness and quickness to learn, or it may imply pungency of wit tending often toward impudence; ALERT stresses quickness in perceiving and understanding.

clev•is \'klev-əs\ *n* **:** a usually U-shaped metal shackle with the ends drilled to receive a pin or bolt used for attaching or suspending parts [earlier *clevi,* probably of Scandinavian origin]

[1]**clew** *or* **clue** \'klü\ *n* **1 :** a ball of thread, yarn, or cord **2** *usually*

clue : something that guides a person in solving a problem; *esp* : a piece of evidence in a crime **3 :** a lower corner or the after corner of a sail [Old English *cliewen*]

[2]**clew** *or* **clue** *vt* **clewed** *or* **clued**; **clew•ing** *or* **clue•ing** *or* **clu•ing 1 :** to roll into a ball **2** *usually clue* **:** to provide with information or a clue ⟨*clue* me in on the situation⟩

cli•ché \kli-ˈshā\ *n* **1 :** a trite phrase or expression; *also* **:** the idea expressed by it **2 :** a hackneyed theme or situation [French, literally, "stereotype"] — **cliché** *adj*

[1]**click** \ˈklik\ *n* **:** a slight sharp noise [probably imitative]

[2]**click** *vb* **1 a :** to make or cause to make a click ⟨*click* one's tongue⟩ **b :** to move or strike with a click ⟨high heels *clicking* down the street⟩ ⟨*clicked* on the light⟩ **2 :** to fit or work together smoothly **3 :** SUCCEED 2 ⟨the idea *clicked*⟩

click beetle *n* **:** any of a family of elongated tapering beetles that are able when turned over to flip into the air by a sudden thoracic movement that produces a distinct click

cli•ent \ˈklī-ənt\ *n* **1 :** a person under the protection of another **:** DEPENDENT **2 a :** a person who engages the professional services of another **b :** CUSTOMER 1 [Latin *cliens*] — **cli•ent•age** \-ən-tij\ *n* — **cli•en•tal** \klī-ˈent-l, ˈklī-ənt-\ *adj*

cli•en•tele \ˌklī-ən-ˈtel\ *n* **:** a body of clients and especially of customers ⟨a store that caters to an exclusive *clientele*⟩ [French *clientèle,* from Latin *clientela,* from *cliens* "client"]

cliff \ˈklif\ *n* **:** a high steep face of rock [Old English *clif*]

cliff dweller *n, often cap C & D* **:** one of the people of the American Southwest who erected their dwellings on rock ledges or in the recesses of canyon walls and cliffs — **cliff dwelling** n

cliff–hang•er \ˈklif-ˌhang-ər\ *n* **1 :** an adventure serial or melodrama; *esp* **:** one presented in installments each ending in suspense **2 :** a contest whose outcome is in doubt up to the end

[1]**cli•mac•ter•ic** \klī-ˈmak-tə-rik, ˌklī-ˌmak-ˈter-ik\ *adj* **1 :** being or relating to a critical period (as of life) **2 :** CRUCIAL [Latin *climactericus,* from Greek *klimaktērikos,* from *klimaktēr* "critical point", literally, "rung of a ladder", from *klimax* "ladder"]

[2]**climacteric** *n* **1 :** a major turning point or critical stage **2 :** MENOPAUSE; *also* **:** a corresponding period in the male

cli•mac•tic \klī-ˈmak-tik\ *adj* **:** of, relating to, or being a climax — **cli•mac•ti•cal•ly** \-ti-kə-lē, -klē\ *adv*

cli•mate \ˈklī-mət\ *n* **1 a :** a region with specified weather conditions **b :** the average weather conditions of a place or region over a long period **2 :** the prevailing conditions or mood ⟨a favorable financial *climate*⟩ ⟨a *climate* of fear⟩ [Middle French *climat,* from Late Latin *clima,* from Greek *klima* "inclination, latitude, climate", from *klinein* "to lean"] — **cli•mat•ic** \klī-ˈmat-ik\ *adj* — **cli•mat•i•cal•ly** \-ˈmat-i-kə-lē, -klē\ *adv*

cli•ma•tol•o•gy \ˌklī-mə-ˈtäl-ə-jē\ *n* **:** the science that deals with climates — **cli•ma•to•log•i•cal** \ˌklī-mət-l-ˈäj-i-kəl\ *adj* — **cli•ma•tol•o•gist** \ˌklī-mə-ˈtäl-ə-jəst\ *n*

[1]**cli•max** \ˈklī-ˌmaks\ *n* **1 a :** a series of ideas or statements so arranged that they increase in force and power from the first to the last **b :** the highest or most forceful in a series **c :** the highest point **:** CULMINATION ⟨the storm had reached its *climax*⟩ **2 :** ORGASM **3 :** a relatively stable ecological stage or community; *esp* **:** the final stage of an ecological succession [Latin, from Greek *klimax* "ladder", from *klinein* "to lean"]

[2]**climax** *vb* **:** to come or bring to a climax

[1]**climb** \ˈklīm\ *vb* **1 a :** to go up or down by grasping or clinging with hands and feet ⟨*climb* down a ladder⟩ **b :** to ascend in growth (as by twining) ⟨a *climbing* vine⟩ **2 :** to rise gradually to a higher point ⟨*climb* from poverty to wealth⟩ **3 :** to slope upward ⟨the road *climbs* steeply⟩ [Old English *climban*] **syn** see ASCEND — **climb•able** \ˈklī-mə-bəl\ *adj* — **climb•er** \ˈklī-mər\ *n*

[2]**climb** *n* **1 :** a place where climbing is necessary **2 :** the act of climbing

climbing iron *n* **:** a steel framework with spikes that may be attached to one's boots for climbing

clime \ˈklīm\ *n* **:** CLIMATE ⟨travel to warmer *climes*⟩ [Late Latin *clima*]

[1]**clinch** \ˈklinch\ *vb* **1 a :** to turn over or flatten the protruding end of (as a driven nail) **b :** to fasten by clinching **2 :** CLENCH 2 **3 :** to make final or irrefutable ⟨*clinch* the deal⟩ **4 :** to hold a boxing opponent [probably alteration of [1]*clench*]

[2]**clinch** *n* **1 a :** a fastening by means of a clinched nail, rivet, or bolt **b :** the clinched part of a nail, bolt, or rivet **2 :** an act or instance of clinching in boxing

clinch•er \ˈklin-chər\ *n* **:** one that clinches; *esp* **:** a decisive fact, argument, act, or remark

cline \ˈklīn\ *n* **:** a graded series of differences exhibited by a group of related organisms usually along a line of environmental or geographic change [Greek *klinein* "to lean"]

cling \ˈkling\ *vi* **clung** \ˈkləng\; **cling•ing** \ˈkling-ing\ **1 a :** to adhere firmly as if glued **:** STICK ⟨the burr *clung* to the dog's tail⟩ **b :** to hold or hold on tightly ⟨*clung* desperately to the ladder⟩ **2 :** to have a strong emotional attachment or dependence ⟨*clings* to old friends⟩ [Old English *clingan*] **syn** see STICK

cling•stone \ˈkling-ˌstōn\ *n* **:** a fruit (as a peach) whose flesh clings to the pit

clin•ic \ˈklin-ik\ *n* **1 a :** a class of medical instruction in which patients are examined and discussed **b :** a facility (as of a hospital) in which persons not bedridden are diagnosed or treated **2 :** a class meeting devoted to the analysis and treatment of cases in some special field ⟨a writing *clinic* for poor students⟩ [French *clinique,* from Greek *klinikē* "medical practice at the sickbed", from *klinē* "bed", from *klinein* "to lean, recline"]

-clin•ic \ˈklin-ik\ *adj combining form* **1 :** inclining **:** dipping **2 :** having (so many) oblique intersections of the axes ⟨mono*clinic*⟩ ⟨tri*clinic*⟩ [Greek *klinein* "to lean"]

clin•i•cal \ˈklin-i-kəl\ *adj* **1 a :** of, relating to, or conducted in or as if in a clinic ⟨*clinical* examination⟩ **b :** involving or based on direct observation of the patient ⟨*clinical* studies⟩ **2 :** coolly analytical and impersonal ⟨a *clinical* analysis of the program⟩ — **clin•i•cal•ly** \ˈklin-i-kə-lē, -klē\ *adv*

clinical thermometer *n* **:** a self-registering thermometer for measuring body temperature

cli•ni•cian \klin-ˈish-ən\ *n* **:** one qualified in clinical practice (as of medicine) as distinguished from a specialist in laboratory or research techniques

[1]**clink** \ˈklingk\ *vb* **:** to make or cause to make a slight sharp short metallic sound [Middle English *clinken*]

[2]**clink** *n* **:** a clinking sound

clin•ker \ˈkling-kər\ *n* **:** stony matter fused by fire (as in a furnace from impurities in the coal) **:** SLAG [earlier *klincard,* a kind of brick, from obsolete Dutch *klinkaard,* from *klinken* "to clink"]

clin•ker–built \-ˌbilt\ *adj* **:** having the external planks or plates overlapping like clapboards on a house ⟨a *clinker-built* boat⟩ [*clinker* "clinch", from Middle English *clinken* "to clinch"]

cli•nom•e•ter \klī-ˈnäm-ət-ər\ *n* **:** an instrument for measuring angles of elevation or inclination [Greek *klinein* "to lean"]

[1]**clip** \ˈklip\ *vb* **clipped; clip•ping :** to clasp or fasten with a clip ⟨*clip* papers together⟩ [Old English *clyppan*]

[2]**clip** *n* **1 :** a device that grips, clasps, or hooks **2 :** a device to hold cartridges for charging the magazine of a rifle **3 :** a piece of jewelry held in position by a spring clip

[3]**clip** *vb* **clipped; clip•ping 1 a :** to cut or cut off or out with or as if with shears **b :** to cut off the tip or outer part of **2 a :** to make less ⟨*clip* one's influence⟩ **b :** to abbreviate in speech or writing **3 :** PUNCH 2a ⟨*clip* one on the chin⟩ **4 :** to block (an opposing player in football other than the ballcarrier) by hitting with the body from behind [Old Norse *klippa*]

[4]**clip** *n* **1 :** a 2-bladed instrument for cutting especially the nails **2 :** something that is clipped: as **a :** the sheared fleece of a sheep; *also* **:** a crop of wool **b :** a section of filmed material **3 :** an act of clipping **4 :** a sharp blow **5 :** a rapid pace ⟨move along at a good *clip*⟩

clip•board \ˈklip-ˌbōrd, -ˌbȯrd\ *n* **:** a small board with a clip at the top for holding papers

clip•per \ˈklip-ər\ *n* **1 :** one that clips **2** *pl* **:** an implement for clipping especially hair, fingernails, or toenails **3 :** a fast square-rigged ship with usually three masts, an overhanging bow, and a large sail area

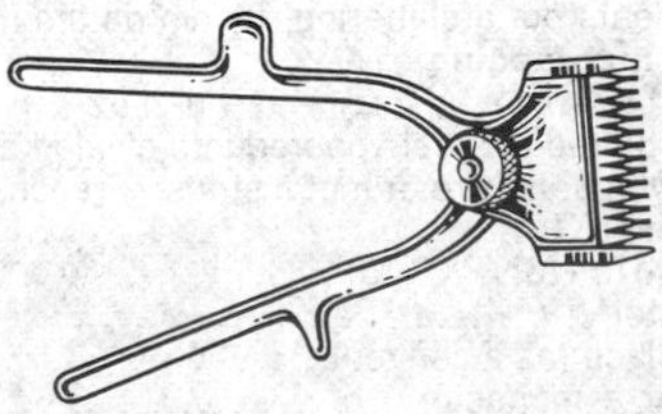

clipper 2

clip•ping \ˈklip-ing\ *n* **1 :** a cutting or shearing of something **2 :** a piece clipped or cut out or off of something ⟨a newspaper

\ə\ **abut**	\au̇\ **out**	\i\ **tip**	\ȯ\ **saw**	\u̇\ **foot**
\ər\ **further**	\ch\ **chin**	\ī\ **life**	\ȯi\ **coin**	\y\ **yet**
\a\ **mat**	\e\ **pet**	\j\ **job**	\th\ **thin**	\yü\ **few**
\ā\ **take**	\ē\ **easy**	\ng\ **sing**	\t͟h\ **this**	\yu̇\ **cure**
\ä\ **cot, cart**	\g\ **go**	\ō\ **bone**	\ü\ **food**	\zh\ **vision**

clipping⟩ ⟨swept up the hair *clippings*⟩
clique \'klēk, 'klik\ *n* : a small exclusive group of people having a shared often selfish interest [French] — **cliqu•ey** \-ē\ *adj* — **cliqu•ish** \-ish\ *adj* — **cliqu•ish•ness** *n*
cli•tel•lum \klī-'tel-əm\ *n, pl* **-la** : a thickened glandular band about the body of an earthworm that secretes a sticky sac in which the eggs are deposited [Latin *clitellae* "packsaddle"]
cli•to•ris \'klit-ə-rəs, kli-'tōr-əs\ *n, pl* **cli•to•ri•des** \kli-'tōr-ə-ˌdēz\ *or* **cli•to•ris•es** : a small organ at the anterior or ventral part of the vulva homologous to the penis [Greek *kleitoris*] — **clit•o•ral** \'klit-ə-rəl\ *adj*
clo•a•ca \klō-'ā-kə\ *n, pl* **-cae** \-ˌkē, -ˌsē\ : a chamber into which the intestinal, urinary, and reproductive canals discharge in birds, reptiles, amphibians, and many fishes; *also* : a comparable chamber of an invertebrate [Latin, "sewer"] — **clo•a•cal** \-'ā-kəl\ *adj*
[1]**cloak** \'klōk\ *n* **1** : a loose outer garment usually longer than a cape **2** : something that conceals or covers ⟨under the *cloak* of darkness⟩ [Old North French *cloque* "bell, cloak", from Medieval Latin *clocca* "bell"; from its shape] **syn** see DISGUISE
[2]**cloak** *vt* : to cover or hide with a cloak
cloak–and–dag•ger \ˌklōk-ən-'dag-ər\ *adj* : of or relating to intrigue and spying
clob•ber \'kläb-ər\ *vt* **1** : to hit with great force : SMASH **2** : to defeat overwhelmingly [origin unknown]
cloche \'klōsh\ *n* : a woman's close-fitting hat usually having a deep rounded crown and narrow brim [French, literally, "bell", from Medieval Latin *clocca*]
[1]**clock** \'kläk\ *n* **1** : a device for measuring or telling the time; *esp* : one not intended to be worn or carried about by a person **2** : a registering device (as a dial) attached to something (as a machine) to measure or record its performance **3** : TIME CLOCK **4** : BIOLOGICAL CLOCK [Dutch *clocke* "bell, clock", from Medieval Latin *clocca* "bell", of Celtic origin]
[2]**clock** *vt* **1** : to time with a stopwatch or by an electric device **2** : to register on a mechanical recording device
[3]**clock** *n* : an ornamental figure on a stocking or sock [probably from *clock* "bell"; from its original bell-like shape]
clock•wise \-ˌwīz\ *adv* : in the direction in which the hands of a clock rotate — **clockwise** *adj*
clock•work \-ˌwərk\ *n* : machinery (as in a mechanical toy) containing a train of small wheels
clod \'kläd\ *n* **1** : a lump or mass especially of earth or clay **2** : a dull or insensitive person : OAF [Middle English, alteration of *clot*] — **clod•dish** \-ish\ *adj* — **clod•dish•ness** *n* — **clod•dy** \'kläd-ē\ *adj*
clod•hop•per \'kläd-ˌhäp-ər\ *n* **1** : a clumsy and uncouth person **2** : a large heavy shoe
[1]**clog** \'kläg\ *n* **1 a** : a weight attached especially to an animal to hinder motion or prevent escape **b** : something that hinders or restrains **2** : a shoe having a thick typically wooden sole [Middle English *clogge* "log"]
[2]**clog** *vb* **clogged**; **clog•ging** **1** : to impede with a clog : HINDER **2 a** : to obstruct passage through by filling beyond capacity ⟨heavy traffic *clogged* the roads⟩ **b** : to fill or become filled ⟨pipes *clogged* with grease⟩ **3** : to become filled with extraneous matter ⟨the gutters *clogged* quickly⟩ **4** : to dance a clog dance
clog dance *n* : a dance in which the performer wears clogs and beats out a clattering rhythm on the floor — **clog dancer** *n* — **clog dancing** *n*
cloi•son•né \ˌklȯiz-n-'ā, klə-ˌwäz-\ *n* : a decoration made of colored enamels poured into divided areas in a design outlined with bent wire or metal strips [French, from *cloisonner* "to partition"]
[1]**clois•ter** \'klȯi-stər\ *n* **1 a** : a place (as a convent or a monastery) of religious seclusion **b** : life in religious seclusion **2** : a covered passage on the side of or around a court usually having one side walled and the other an open arcade or colonnade [Old French *cloistre*, from Medieval Latin *claustrum*, from Latin, "bar, bolt", from *claudere* "to close"] — **clois•tral** \-strəl\ *adj*

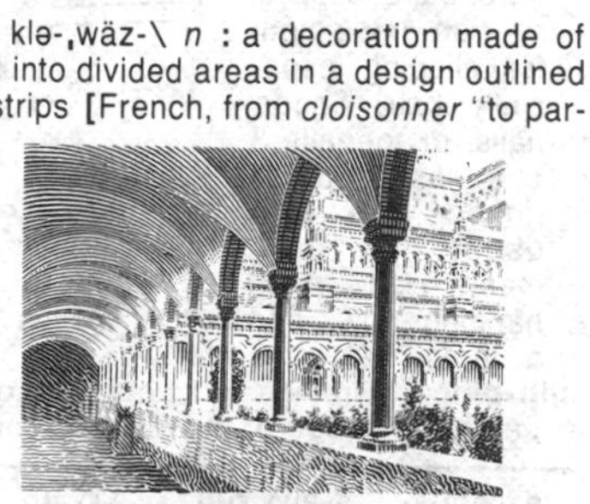

[1]cloister 2

[2]**cloister** *vt* **1** : to shut away from the world in or as if in a cloister **2** : to surround with a cloister ⟨*cloistered* gardens⟩
[1]**clone** \'klōn\ *n* : the whole asexual progeny of an individual (as a plant increased by grafting) [Greek *klōn* "twig, slip"] — **clon•al** \'klōn-l\ *adj* — **clon•al•ly** \-l-ē\ *adv*
[2]**clone** *vt* : to cause to grow as a clone
clop \'kläp\ *n* : a sound made by or as if by a hoof or wooden shoe against pavement [imitative] — **clop** *vi*
[1]**close** \'klōz\ *vb* **1 a** : to move so as to bar passage through something ⟨*close* the gate⟩ **b** : to block against entry or passage ⟨*close* a street⟩ **2** : to suspend or stop the operations of ⟨*close* school⟩ **3** : to bring or come to an end : TERMINATE ⟨*close* a meeting⟩ **4 a** : to bring or bind together the parts or edges of ⟨a *closed* fist⟩ **b** : to fill or stop up ⟨*close* a crack with plaster⟩ **5** : to fold, swing, or slide so as to leave no opening ⟨the door *closed*⟩ **6 a** : to draw near **b** : to engage in a struggle at close quarters : GRAPPLE ⟨*close* with the enemy⟩ **7** : to reach an agreement on ⟨*close* a deal⟩ [Old French *clos-*, stem of *clore*, frome Latin *claudere*] — **clos•able** \'klō-zə-bəl\ *adj* — **clos•er** *n*
• **syn** CONCLUDE, TERMINATE, END: CLOSE implies shutting off from outside forces that could cause further development or change ⟨*close* an account⟩ CONCLUDE adds a suggestion of formality; TERMINATE implies setting a limit with or without completing; END stresses finality and usually implies an achievement of progress or concluding of a sequence ⟨an armistice *ended* hostilities⟩ ⟨the years *ending* the colonial period⟩
[2]**close** \'klōz\ *n* **1 a** : a coming or bringing to a conclusion **b** : CESSATION, END **2** : the last part (as of a speech or play)
[3]**close** \'klōs\ *n* : an enclosed area
[4]**close** \'klōs\ *adj* **1** : having no openings : CLOSED **2** : confined or confining strictly ⟨*close* arrest⟩ **3** : restricted (as in membership) to a privileged group **4 a** : OUT-OF-THE-WAY 1, SECLUDED **b** : SECRETIVE **5** : STRICT 2, RIGOROUS ⟨keep *close* watch⟩ **6** : hot and stuffy **7** : reluctant to give up money or possessions **8** : having little space between items or units ⟨flying in *close* formation⟩ **9 a** : fitting tightly or exactly ⟨a *close* gown⟩ **b** : very short or near to the surface ⟨a *close* haircut⟩ **c** : matching or blending without gap ⟨ideas in *close* harmony⟩ **10** : being near in time, space, effect, or degree **11** : intimately associated : FAMILIAR ⟨*close* friends⟩ **12 a** : paying careful attention to details ⟨a *close* study⟩ **b** : marked by fidelity to an original **13** : having an even or nearly even score ⟨a *close* game⟩ **syn** see NEAR, STINGY — **close•ly** *adv* — **close•ness** *n*
[5]**close** \'klōs\ *adv* : in a close position or manner : NEAR
close call \'klōs-\ *n* : a narrow escape
closed \'klōzd\ *adj* **1 a** : not open : ENCLOSED **b** : composed entirely of closed tubes or vessels ⟨a *closed* circulatory system⟩ **2 a** : forming a self-contained unit ⟨a *closed* association⟩ **b** : not subject to immigraton or emigration ⟨the *closed* ecosystem of a spacecraft⟩ **c** : traced by a moving point that returns to an arbitrary starting point ⟨a *closed* curve⟩; *also* : so formed that every plane section is a closed curve ⟨a *closed* solid⟩ **d** : having elements that when subjected to an operation produce only elements of the same set ⟨the whole numbers are *closed* under addition and multiplication⟩ **e** : containing its endpoints ⟨a *closed* interval⟩ **3** : confined to a few ⟨a *closed* meeting⟩ **4** : ending in a consonant ⟨a *closed* syllable⟩
closed circuit *n* : a television installation in which the signal is transmitted by wire to a limited number of receivers
closed shop *n* : an establishment in which only union members in good standing are hired
close•fist•ed \'klōs-'fis-təd\ *adj* : STINGY 1, TIGHTFISTED
close–grained \-'grānd\ *adj* : having a firm smooth texture
close–hauled \-'hȯld\ *adj* : having the sails set for sailing as nearly against the wind as the vessel will go
close•mouthed \-'mau̇t͟hd, -'mau̇tht\ *adj* : cautious in speaking or disclosing information
close•out \'klō-ˌzau̇t\ *n* : a sale of leftover merchandise
close quarters \'klōs-\ *n pl* : direct contact or close range ⟨fought at *close quarters*⟩
close shave \'klōs-, 'klōsh-\ *n* : a narrow escape
[1]**clos•et** \'kläz-ət\ *n* **1** : an apartment or small room for privacy **2** : a cabinet or recess for china, household utensils, or clothing **3** : WATER CLOSET [Middle French "small enclosure", from *clos* "enclosure", from *clore* "to close"]
[2]**closet** *vt* **1** : to shut up in or as if in a closet ⟨*closeted* myself in my study⟩ **2** : to take into a private room for an interview ⟨*clos-*

eted for an hour with the governor⟩
closet drama *n* : drama suited primarily for reading
close–up \ˈklōs-ˌəp\ *n* **1** : a photograph or movie shot taken at close range **2** : an intimate view or examination
clos•ing \ˈklō-ziŋ\ *n* **1** : a concluding part (as of a speech) **2** : a closable gap (as in a garment)
clos•trid•i•um \klä-ˈstrid-ē-əm\ *n, pl* **-ia** \-ē-ə\ : any of various spore-forming mostly anaerobic soil or intestinal bacteria including some that produce deadly toxins — compare BOTULISM, TETANUS [derived from Greek *klōstēr* "spindle", from *klōthein* "to spin"]
clo•sure \ˈklō-zhər\ *n* **1** : an act of closing : the condition of being closed **2** : something that closes **3** : CLOTURE **4** : the property that a number system or a set has when it is mathematically closed under an operation
[1]clot \ˈklät\ *n* : a mass or lump made by a portion of a liquid substance thickening and sticking together ⟨a *clot* of blood⟩ [Middle English, from Old English *clott*]
[2]clot *vb* **clot•ted**; **clot•ting** : to become or cause to become a clot : form clots
cloth \ˈklȯth\ *n, pl* **cloths** \ˈklȯthz, ˈklȯths\ **1** : a pliable material made usually by weaving, felting, or knitting natural or synthetic fibers **2** : a piece of cloth used for a particular purpose; *esp* : TABLECLOTH **3** : distinctive dress of a profession or calling and especially of the clergy; *also* : CLERGY [Old English *clāth*]
clothe \ˈklōth\ *vt* **clothed** *or* **clad** \ˈklad\; **cloth•ing** **1 a** : to cover with or as if with cloth or clothing : DRESS **b** : to provide with clothes **2** : to express by suitable language : COUCH ⟨learn to *clothe* your thought effectively⟩ **3** : to endow especially with a quality ⟨*clothed* with dignity⟩ [Old English *clāthian*, from *clāth* "cloth, garment"]
clothes \ˈklōz, ˈklōthz\ *n pl* **1** : CLOTHING **2** : BEDCLOTHES
clothes•horse \-ˌhȯrs\ *n* **1** : a frame on which to hang clothes **2** : one overly concerned with fashion
clothes moth *n* : any of several small dull-colored moths whose larvae eat wool, fur, or feathers
clothes•pin \-ˌpin\ *n* : a forked piece of wood or plastic or a clamp for holding clothes on a line
clothes•press \-ˌpres\ *n* : a receptacle for clothes
clothes tree *n* : an upright stand with hooks or pegs at the top on which to hang clothes
cloth•ier \ˈklōth-yər, ˈklō-thē-ər\ *n* : one who makes or sells cloth or clothing
cloth•ing \ˈklō-thiŋ\ *n* **1** : garments or an outfit of garments **2** : an outer or protective covering ⟨the trees' green spring *clothing*⟩
clo•ture \ˈklō-chər\ *n* : the closing or limiting of debate in a legislative body especially by calling for a vote [French *clôture*, literally, "closure"] — **cloture** *vt*
[1]cloud \ˈklau̇d\ *n* **1** : a visible mass of particles of water or ice in the form of fog, mist, or haze suspended usually at a considerable height in the air **2 a** : a visible mass of minute particles in the air or a mass of obscuring matter in interstellar space **b** : an aggregate of charged particles (as electrons) **3** : a great crowd massed together : SWARM ⟨a *cloud* of mosquitoes⟩ **4** : something that appears dark or threatening ⟨war *clouds*⟩ **5** : something that obscures or blemishes ⟨worked under a *cloud* of secrecy⟩ **6** : a dark vein or spot (as in marble) [Old English *clūd* "rock, hill"] — **cloud•less** \-ləs\ *adj* — **cloud•less•ly** *adv* — **cloud•less•ness** *n*

[1]cloud 1: *top* cumulus, *middle* nimbus, *bottom* stratus

[2]cloud *vb* **1** : to grow cloudy **2** : to make or become gloomy or ominous **3** : to envelop or hide with or as if with a cloud **4** : to make unclear : OBSCURE **5** : to make or become soiled or tainted
cloud•burst \ˌ-bərst\ *n* : a sudden heavy rainfall
cloud chamber *n* : a vessel containing air saturated with water vapor whose sudden expansion reveals the passage of an ionizing particle (as an electron) by a trail of visible droplets
cloud•let \-lət\ *n* : a small cloud
cloudy \ˈklau̇d-ē\ *adj* **cloud•i•er**; **-est** **1** : of, relating to, or resembling cloud **2** : darkened by gloom or anxiety **3 a** : overcast with clouds; *esp* : six tenths to nine tenths covered with clouds **b** : having a cloudy sky **4** : obscure in meaning ⟨*cloudy* issues⟩ **5** : dimmed or dulled as if by clouds ⟨a *cloudy* mirror⟩ **6** : marked with veins or spots — **cloud•i•ly** \ˈklau̇d-l-ē\ *adv* — **cloud•i•ness** \ˈklau̇d-ē-nəs\ *n*
[1]clout \ˈklau̇t\ *n* **1** : a blow especially with the hand; *also* : a hard hit **2** : a white cloth used as a target in long-distance archery **3** : PULL 2b ⟨political *clout*⟩ [Old English *clūt* "cloth, rag"]
[2]clout *vt* : to hit forcefully
[1]clove \ˈklōv\ *n* : one of the small bulbs developed in the axils of the scales of a large bulb [Old English *clufu*]
[2]clove *past of* CLEAVE
[3]clove *n* : the dried flower bud of a tropical tree of the myrtle family that is a spice and the source of an oil used in perfumery and medicine; *also* : this tree [Old French *clou (de girofle)*, literally, "nail (of clove)" from Latin *clavus* "nail"]
clo•ven \ˈklō-vən\ *past participle of* CLEAVE
cloven foot *n* **1** : a foot (as of a sheep) divided into two parts at its outer extremity **2** : the sign of devilish character [sense 2 from the traditional representation of Satan as cloven-footed] — **clo•ven-foot•ed** \ˌklō-vən-ˈfu̇t-əd\ *adj*
cloven hoof *n* : CLOVEN FOOT — **cloven–hoofed** \ˌklō-vən-ˈhu̇ft, -ˈhu̇vd, -ˈhüft, -ˈhüvd\ *adj*
clo•ver \ˈklō-vər\ *n* : any of a genus of leguminous herbs having leaves with three leaflets and flowers in dense heads and including many valuable forage and bee plants; *also* : any of various related plants [Old English *clāfre*] — **in clover** *or* **in the clover** : in prosperity or in pleasant circumstances
clo•ver•leaf \-ˌlēf\ *n* : a road plan that in shape resembles a four-leaf clover and that is used for passing one highway over another and routing traffic for turns by turnoffs that lead around to enter the other highway from the right
[1]clown \ˈklau̇n\ *n* **1** : a rude ill-bred person : BOOR **2 a** : a fool, jester, or comedian in an entertainment; *esp* : a grotesquely dressed comedy performer in a circus **b** : one who habitually plays the buffoon : JOKER [earlier *clown* "countryman, farmer", perhaps from Middle French *coulon* "settler", from Latin *colonus* "colonist, farmer"]
[2]clown *vi* : to act like a clown
clown•ish \ˈklau̇-nish\ *adj* : of or resembling a clown (as in foolishness or ignorance) — **clown•ish•ly** *adv* — **clown•ish•ness** *n*
cloy \ˈklȯi\ *vb* **1** : to weary or disgust with an excess usually of something once pleasing **2** : to cause weariness or disgust through being in excess [Middle English *acloien* "to lame", from Middle French *encloer* "to drive in a nail", from Medieval Latin *inclavare*, from Latin *in* "in" + *clavus* "nail"] — **cloy•ing•ly** \-iŋ-lē\ *adv*
[1]club \ˈkləb\ *n* **1 a** : a heavy usually tapering staff especially of wood used as a weapon **b** : a stick or bat used for hitting a ball in a game **c** : a black figure resembling a clover leaf used to distinguish a suit of playing cards; *also* : a card of the suit bearing clubs **2 a** : an association of persons for some common object **b** : the meeting place of a club [Old Norse *klubba*]
[2]club *vb* **clubbed**; **club•bing** **1** : to beat or strike with or as if with a club **2** : to unite or combine for a common cause — often used with *together*
club•foot \ˈkləb-ˈfu̇t\ *n* : a misshapen foot twisted out of position from birth; *also* : this deformity — **club•foot•ed** \-əd\ *adj*
club fungus *n* : BASIDIOMYCETE
club•house \-ˌhau̇s\ *n* **1** : a house occupied by a club or used for club activities **2** : locker rooms used by a ball team
club moss *n* : any of an order (Lycopodiales) of low often trailing evergreen vascular plants (as the ground pine) having branching stems covered with small mosslike leaves and reproducing by spores usually borne in club-shaped cones
club sandwich *n* : a sandwich of three slices of bread and two layers of meats and lettuce, tomato, and mayonnaise

\ə\ **abut**	\au̇\ **out**	\i\ **tip**	\ȯ\ **saw**	\u̇\ **foot**
\ər\ **further**	\ch\ **chin**	\ī\ **life**	\ȯi\ **coin**	\y\ **yet**
\a\ **mat**	\e\ **pet**	\j\ **job**	\th\ **thin**	\yü\ **few**
\ā\ **take**	\ē\ **easy**	\ŋ\ **sing**	\th\ **this**	\yu̇\ **cure**
\ä\ **cot, cart**	\g\ **go**	\ō\ **bone**	\ü\ **food**	\zh\ **vision**

club steak *n* : a small steak from just behind the ribs

1**cluck** \ˈklək\ *vi* : to utter a cluck or a similar sound [imitative]

2**cluck** *n* **1** : the characteristic sound of a hen especially in calling her chicks **2** : a broody fowl

clue *variant of* CLEW

clum•ber spaniel \ˌkləm-bər-\ *n, often cap C & S* : a large massive heavyset spaniel with a dense silky largely white coat [*Clumber,* estate in Nottinghamshire, England]

1**clump** \ˈkləmp\ *n* **1** : a group of things clustered together ⟨a *clump* of bushes⟩ **2** : a compact mass : LUMP **3** : a heavy tramping sound [probably from Low German *klump*] — **clumpy** \ˈkləm-pē\ *adj*

2**clump** *vb* **1** : to walk clumsily and noisily **2** : to form or cause to form clumps

clum•sy \ˈkləm-zē\ *adj* **clum•si•er**; **-est 1 a** : lacking dexterity, nimbleness, or grace ⟨*clumsy* fingers⟩ **b** : lacking tact or subtlety ⟨a *clumsy* joke⟩ **2** : awkwardly or poorly made : UNWIELDY [probably from obsolete English *clumse* "benumbed with cold"] **syn** see AWKWARD — **clum•si•ly** \-zə-lē\ *adv* — **clum•si•ness** \-zē-nəs\ *n*

clung *past of* CLING

1**clus•ter** \ˈkləs-tər\ *n* **1** : a number of similar things growing, collected, or grouped closely together : BUNCH **2** : two or more consecutive consonants or vowels in a segment of speech [Old English *clyster*]

2**cluster** *vb* **clus•tered**; **clus•ter•ing** \-tə-ring, -tring\ : to grow, collect, or assemble in a cluster

1**clutch** \ˈkləch\ *vb* **1** : to grasp or hold with or as if with the hand or claws usually strongly, tightly, or suddenly **2** : to try to grasp and hold ⟨*clutch* at a swinging rope⟩ [Old English *clyccan*]

2**clutch** *n* **1 a** : the claws or a hand in the act of grasping or seizing firmly **b** : an often cruel or unrelenting control **2** : a device for gripping an object **3 a** : a coupling used to connect and disconnect a driving and a driven part of a mechanism **b** : a lever operating a clutch **4** : a tight or critical situation : PINCH

3**clutch** *n* : a nest or batch of eggs or a brood of chicks [alteration of English dialect *cletch* "hatching, brood"]

1**clut•ter** \ˈklət-ər\ *vt* : to fill or cover with a disorderly scattering of things ⟨*clutter* up a room⟩ [Middle English *clotteren* "to clot", from *clot*]

2**clutter** *n* : a crowded or disorderly collection ⟨a *clutter* of useless facts⟩

Clydes•dale \ˈklīdz-ˌdāl\ *n* : a heavy draft horse of a breed originally from Clydesdale, Scotland

clyp•e•us \ˈklip-ē-əs\ *n, pl* **-ei** \-ē-ˌī, -ē-ˌē\ : a plate on the front central part of an insect's head [Latin, "round shield"]

co- *prefix* **1** : with : together : joint : jointly ⟨*coexist*⟩ **2** : in or to the same degree ⟨*coextensive*⟩ **3** : fellow : partner ⟨*coauthor*⟩ [Latin, from *com-*]

See *co-* and 2d element

coact	**coexecutor**	**copresident**
coagency	**cofinance**	**coprincipal**
coagent	**cofound**	**coprisoner**
co-anchor	**cofounder**	**coproduce**
coannouncer	**coheir**	**coproducer**
coarchitect	**coheiress**	**coproduction**
coauthor	**coholder**	**copromote**
cobuilder	**cohost**	**copromoter**
cocaptain	**cohostess**	**coproprietor**
co-chairman	**coinvent**	**coproprietorship**
co-chairperson	**coinventor**	**copublish**
cochampion	**coinvestigator**	**copublisher**
cocomposer	**coleader**	**corecipient**
coconspirator	**comanagement**	**coreligionist**
cocreator	**comanager**	**coresident**
codefendant	**co-officiate**	**cosponsor**
codesign	**co-organizer**	**cowarrior**
codesigner	**co-own**	**cowinner**
codiscoverer	**co-owner**	**co-worker**
coedit	**copastor**	**cowrite**
coeditor		

co•ac•er•vate \kō-ˈas-ər-ˌvāt\ *n* : an aggregate of colloidal droplets held together by electrostatic forces [Latin *coacervatus,* past participle of *coacervare* "to heap up", from *co-* + *acervus* "heap"] — **co•ac•er•va•tion** \ˌkō-ˌas-ər-ˈvā-shən\ *n*

1**coach** \ˈkōch\ *n* **1 a** : a large usually closed four-wheeled carriage having doors in the sides and a raised seat in front for the driver **b** : a railroad passenger car intended primarily for day travel **c** : BUS 1a **d** : an automobile body especially of a closed model **e** : a class of passenger air transportation at a lower fare than first class **2 a** : a private tutor **b** : one who instructs or trains a performer or a team of performers; *esp* : one who instructs players in the fundamentals of a competitive sport and directs team strategy [Middle French *coche,* from German *kutsche;* sense 2 from the concept that the tutor conveys the student through his examinations]

2**coach** *vb* **1** : to go in a horse-drawn coach **2** : to instruct, direct, or prompt as a coach — **coach•er** *n*

coach dog *n* : DALMATIAN

coach•man \ˈkōch-mən\ *n* : a person whose business is driving a coach or carriage

co•ac•tion \kō-ˈak-shən\ *n* : joint action

co•ad•ju•tor \ˌkō-ə-ˈjüt-ər, kō-ˈaj-ət-ər\ *n* **1** : one who works together with another : ASSISTANT **2** : a bishop assisting a diocesan bishop and often having the right of succession [Middle French *coadjuteur,* from Latin *coadjutor,* from *co-* + *adjutor* "aid", from *adjuvare* "to help"] — **coadjutor** *adj*

co•ag•u•la•ble \kō-ˈag-yə-lə-bəl\ *adj* : capable of being coagulated — **co•ag•u•la•bil•i•ty** \-ˌag-yə-lə-ˈbil-ət-ē\ *n*

co•ag•u•lant \-ˈag-yə-lənt\ *n* : something that produces coagulation

co•ag•u•lase \-ˌlās, -ˌlāz\ *n* : an enzyme that promotes coagulation

co•ag•u•late \-ˌlāt\ *vb* : to become or cause to become viscous or thickened into a coherent mass : CLOT [Latin *coagulare* "to curdle", from *coagulum* "curdling agent", from *cogere* "to drive together", from *co-* + *agere* "to drive"] — **co•ag•u•la•tion** \ˌkō-ˌag-yə-ˈlā-shən\ *n*

1**coal** \ˈkōl\ *n* **1** : a piece of glowing or charred wood : EMBER **2** : a black or brownish black solid combustible mineral substance formed by the partial decay of vegetable matter under the influence of moisture and often increased pressure and temperature that is widely used as a natural fuel [Old English *col*]

2**coal** *vb* **1** : to supply with coal **2** : to take in coal

co•a•lesce \ˌkō-ə-ˈles\ *vi* : to unite by growth into one body [Latin *coalescere,* from *co-* + *alescere* "to grow"] **syn** see MIX — **co•a•les•cence** \-ˈles-ns\ *n* — **co•a•les•cent** \-nt\ *adj*

coal•field \ˈkōl-ˌfēld\ *n* : a region where deposits of coal occur

coal gas *n* : gas from coal; *esp* : gas made by distilling bituminous coal and used for heating

co•a•li•tion \ˌkō-ə-ˈlish-ən\ *n* **1** : the union of separate items into a body or group; *also* : a body or group so formed : COMBINATION **2** : a temporary alliance of persons, parties, or countries for joint action [Middle French, from Latin *coalitus,* past participle of *coalescere* "to coalesce"] — **co•a•li•tion•ist** \-ˈlish-nəst, -ə-nəst\ *n*

coal measures *n pl* : beds of coal with the associated rocks

coal oil *n* **1** : a refined oil prepared from petroleum : PETROLEUM **2** : KEROSENE

coal tar *n* : tar obtained by distilling bituminous coal and used in making drugs, dyes, and explosives

coam•ing \ˈkō-ming\ *n* : a raised frame around a hatchway to keep out water [probably derived from *comb*]

coarse \ˈkōrs, ˈkȯrs\ *adj* **1** : of ordinary or inferior quality or appearance : COMMON **2 a** : made up of fairly large parts or particles ⟨*coarse* porous soil⟩ **b** : rough in texture ⟨*coarse* skin⟩ **c** : designed for heavy, fast, or less delicate work ⟨a *coarse* saw with large teeth⟩ **d** : not precise or detailed in adjustment or discrimination **3** : crude in taste, manner, or language ⟨*coarse* humor⟩ **4** : harsh or rough in tone ⟨a *coarse* voice⟩ [Middle English *cors,* from *course, cors* "course"] — **coarse•ly** *adv* — **coarse•ness** *n*

• **syn** VULGAR, RIBALD, OBSCENE: COARSE implies roughness, rudeness, or crudeness of spirit, behavior, or language; VULGAR implies actual offensiveness to good taste or decency; RIBALD applies to what is amusingly or picturesquely vulgar or irreverent or mildly indecent; OBSCENE may apply to whatever strongly offends the sense of decency or propriety but especially implies flagrant violation of taboo in sexual matters.

coarse adjustment *n* : a knob on a microscope used for making relatively large changes in focus — compare FINE ADJUSTMENT

coarse–grained \-ˈgrānd\ *adj* **1** : having a coarse grain or texture **2** : lacking in culture : CRUDE

coars•en \ˈkōrs-ᵊn, ˈkȯrs-\ *vb* **coars•ened**; **coars•en•ing** \ˈkōrs-niŋ, ˈkȯrs-, -ᵊn-iŋ\ : to make or become coarse ⟨hands *coarsened* by hard labor⟩

¹coast \ˈkōst\ *n* **1** : the land near a shore : SEASHORE **2 :** a slope suited to sliding (as on a sled) downhill; *also* : a slide down such a slope [Middle French *coste,* from Latin *costa* "rib, side"]

²coast *vi* **1 :** to sail along a coast **2 a :** to slide, run, or glide (as over snow on a sled) downhill by the force of gravity **b :** to move along (as on a bicycle when not pedaling) without applying power

coast•al \ˈkōst-ᵊl\ *adj* : of or relating to a coast : located on, near, or along a coast ⟨*coastal* waters⟩

coastal plain *n* : a plain extending inland from a seashore

coast•er \ˈkō-stər\ *n* **1** : one that coasts; *esp* : a ship engaged in coastal trade **2 a :** a tray often on wheels that is used for passing a decanter **b :** a shallow container or a plate or mat to protect a surface ⟨tea *coasters*⟩ **c :** a small vehicle (as a sled) used in coasting

coaster brake *n* : a brake in the hub of the rear wheel of a bicycle operated by reverse pressure on the pedals

coast guard *n* : a military force concerned with enforcing marine laws and traffic regulations, maintaining aids to navigation, and performing rescue service — **coast•guards•man** \ˈkōst-ˌgärdz-mən, ˈkōs-ˌ\ *or* **coast•guard•man** \-ˌgärd-mən\ *n*

coast•line \ˈkōst-ˌlīn\ *n* : the outline or shape of a coast

coast•ward \ˈkōs-twərd\ *or* **coast•wards** \-twərdz\ *adv* : toward the coast — **coastward** *adj*

¹coat \ˈkōt\ *n* **1** : an outer garment varying in length and style according to fashion and use **2 :** the external growth (as of fur) on an animal **3 :** a layer of one substance covering another ⟨a *coat* of paint⟩ [Old French *cote,* of Germanic origin] — **coat•ed** \-əd\ *adj*

²coat *vt* : to cover with a coat and especially with a finishing, protecting, or enclosing layer

co•a•ti \kə-ˈwät-ē, ˌkō-ə-ˈtē\ *n* : a tropical American mammal related to the raccoon but with a longer body and tail and a long flexible snout [Portuguese *coati,* from Tupi]

coati

coat•ing \ˈkōt-iŋ\ *n* **1** : a layer covering a surface : COAT ⟨a *coating* of ice on a pond⟩ **2 :** cloth for coats

coat of arms : heraldic arms (as of a person or family) displayed on a shield or surface

coat of mail : a garment of metal scales or rings worn as armor

coax \ˈkōks\ *vb* **1** : to influence or influence a person by gentle urging, caressing, or flattering **2 :** to gain by gentle persuasion or flattery ⟨*coax* a dollar from one's father⟩ [obsolete *cokes* "simpleton"] — **coax•er** *n*

co•ax•i•al \kō-ˈak-sē-əl, ˈkō-\ *adj* **1** : having coincident axes **2** : mounted on concentric shafts — **co•ax•i•al•ly** \-sē-ə-lē\ *adv*

coaxial cable *n* : a transmission line that consists of a central conductor surrounded by and insulated from a tube of conducting material

cob \ˈkäb\ *n* **1** : a male swan **2 :** CORNCOB 1 **3 :** a short-legged stocky horse usually with a high stylish action [Middle English *cobbe* "leader"]

co•balt \ˈkō-ˌbȯlt\ *n* : a tough shiny silver-white magnetic metallic element found with iron and nickel — see ELEMENT table [German *kobalt,* from *kobold* "goblin"; from its occurrence in silver ore, once believed to be due to goblins] — **co•bal•tic** \kō-ˈbȯl-tik\ *adj* — **co•bal•tous** \-təs\ *adj*

cobalt chloride *n* : the dichloride of cobalt $CoCl_2$ that is blue when dehydrated but turns red in the presence of moisture

co•balt•ite \ˈkō-ˌbȯl-ˌtīt\ *or* **co•balt•ine** \-ˌtēn\ *n* : a grayish to silver-white mineral CoAsS that consists of cobalt, arsenic, and sulfur and is an important ore of cobalt

cobalt 60 *n* : a heavy radioactive isotope of cobalt of the mass number 60 produced in nuclear reactors and used as a source of gamma rays

¹cob•ble \ˈkäb-əl\ *vt* **cob•bled**; **cob•bling** \ˈkäb-liŋ, -ə-liŋ\ : to make or put together roughly or hastily ⟨a shed *cobbled* up out of scraps⟩ [Middle English *coblen*]

²cobble *n* : a naturally rounded stone larger than a pebble and smaller than a boulder; *esp* : such a stone used in paving a street [back-formation from *cobblestone*]

³cobble *vt* : to pave with cobblestones

cob•bler \ˈkäb-lər\ *n* **1** : one that mends or makes shoes **2** *archaic* : a clumsy worker **3 :** a deep-dish fruit pie with a thick top crust [Middle English *cobelere*]

cob•ble•stone \ˈkäb-əl-ˌstōn\ *n* : COBBLE [Middle English]

CO•BOL \ˈkō-ˌbȯl\ *n* : a language for programming a computer to work business problems [*co*mmon *b*usiness *o*riented *l*anguage]

co•bra \ˈkō-brə\ *n* : any of several venomous Asian and African snakes that when excited expand the skin of the neck into a hood; *also* : any of several related African snakes [Portuguese *cobra (de capello),* literally, "serpent (with a hood)", from Latin *colubra* "snake"]

cob•web \ˈkäb-ˌweb\ *n* **1** : the network spread by a spider; *also* : a single thread spun by a spider or insect larva **2 :** something resembling a spiderweb ⟨*cobwebs* of intrigue⟩ [Middle English *coppeweb,* from *coppe* "spider" (from Old English *atorcoppe)* + *web*] — **cob•webbed** \-ˌwebd\ *adj* — **cob•web•by** \-ˌweb-ē\ *adj*

co•ca \ˈkō-kə\ *n* : a South American shrub with leaves that are chewed by the natives to impart endurance and are the source of cocaine; *also* : its dried leaves [Spanish, from Quechua *kúka*]

co•caine \kō-ˈkān\ *n* : a bitter drug obtained from coca leaves that is used as a local anesthetic and can result in psychological dependence

coc•cid \ˈkäk-səd\ *n* : SCALE INSECT, MEALYBUG [derived from Greek *kokkos* "grain, kermes"]

coc•cus \ˈkäk-əs\ *n, pl* **coc•ci** \ˈkäk-ˌsī, -ˌī\ : a spherical bacterium [Greek *kokkos* "grain"] — **coc•cal** \ˈkäk-əl\ *adj*

coc•cyx \ˈkäk-siks\ *n, pl* **coc•cy•ges** \ˈkäk-sə-ˌjēz\ *also* **coc•cyx•es** : the end of the vertebral column beyond the sacrum in humans and tailless apes that consists of four reduced fused vertebrae [Greek *kokkyx* "cuckoo, coccyx"; from its resemblance to a cuckoo's beak] — **coc•cyg•eal** \käk-ˈsij-ē-əl, -ˈsij-əl\ *adj*

coch•i•neal \ˈkäch-ə-ˌnēl, ˈkō-chə-\ *n* : a red dyestuff consisting of the dried bodies of female cochineal insects used especially as a biological stain [Spanish *cochinilla* "wood louse, cochineal"]

cochineal insect *n* : a small bright red insect that is related to and resembles the mealybug, feeds on cactus, and yields cochineal

co•chlea \ˈkō-klē-ə, ˈkäk-lē-\ *n, pl* **co•chle•as** *or* **co•chle•ae** \ˈkō-klē-ˌē, ˈkäk-lē-, -ˌī\ : a part of the inner ear of higher vertebrates that is usually coiled like a snail shell and is the seat of the hearing organ [Latin, "snail, snail shell", from Greek *kochlias,* from *kochlos* "land snail"] — **co•chle•ar** \ˈkō-klē-ər, ˈkäk-lē-\ *adj*

¹cock \ˈkäk\ *n* **1** : the adult male of a bird and especially the domestic fowl **2 :** a device (as a faucet or valve) for regulating the flow of a liquid **3 :** the cocked position of the hammer of a firearm [Old English *cocc*]

²cock *vt* **1 a :** to draw back the hammer of (a firearm) and set for firing **b :** to draw or bend back in preparation to throw or hit ⟨*cock* one's fist⟩ **c :** to set a mechanism (as a camera shutter) for tripping **2 :** to turn, tip, or tilt usually to one side **3 :** to turn up (as a hat brim)

³cock *n* : TILT 3a, SLANT ⟨a *cock* of the head⟩

⁴cock *n* : a small pile (as of hay) [Middle English *cok,* of Scandinavian origin]

⁵cock *vt* : to put (as hay) into cocks

cock•ade \kä-ˈkād\ *n* : an ornament (as a rosette) worn on the hat as a badge [French *cocarde,* from *cocard* "vain", from *coq* "cock"]

Cock•aigne \kä-ˈkān\ *n* : an imaginary land of great luxury and ease [Middle French *pais de cocaigne* "land of plenty"]

cock-and-bull story \ˌkäk-ən-ˈbu̇l-\ *n* : an absurd, incredible, or highly improbable story told as true

cock•a•tiel \ˌkäk-ə-ˈtēl\ *n* **:** a small gray crested Australian parrot with a yellow head [Dutch *kaketielje,* from Malay *kakatua*]

cock•a•too \ˈkäk-ə-ˌtü\ *n, pl* **-toos :** any of numerous large noisy usually showy and crested chiefly Australasian parrots [Malay *kakatua,* from *kakak* "elder sibling" + *tua* "old"]

cock•a•trice \ˈkäk-ə-trəs, -ˌtrīs\ *n* **:** a legendary serpent with a deadly glance hatched by a reptile from a cock's egg [Middle French *cocatris* "ichneumon, cockatrice", from Medieval Latin *cocatrix* "ichneumon"]

cock•crow \ˈkäk-ˌkrō\ *n* **:** the time of day when roosters first crow **:** DAWN

cocked hat \ˈkäkt-\ *n* **:** a hat with brim turned up to give a 3-cornered appearance

cock•er•el \ˈkäk-rəl, -ə-rəl\ *n* **:** a young male domestic fowl [Old French dialect *kokerel* "small cock", from Old French *coc* "cock"]

cock•er spaniel \ˌkäk-ər-\ *n* **:** a small spaniel with long ears, square muzzle, and silky coat [*cocking* "woodcock hunting"]

cock•eye \ˈkäk-ˈī, -ˌī\ *n* **:** a squinting eye

cock•eyed \ˈkäk-ˈīd\ *adj* **1 :** having a cockeye **2 a :** being out of line **:** ASKEW **b :** slightly foolish or absurd ⟨a *cockeyed* idea⟩ **c :** DRUNK 1, INTOXICATED

cock•fight \ˈkäk-ˌfīt\ *n* **:** a combat of gamecocks usually fitted with metal spurs — **cock•fight•ing** \-iŋ\ *adj or n*

cock•horse \ˈkäk-ˌhȯrs\ *n* **:** ROCKING HORSE [perhaps from *cock* "male" + *horse*]

[1]cock•le \ˈkäk-əl\ *n* **:** any of several grainfield weeds; *esp* **:** CORN COCKLE [Old English *coccel*]

[2]cockle *n* **1 :** an edible mollusk with a heart-shaped 2-valved shell **2 :** COCKLESHELL [Middle French *coquille* "shell", from Latin *conchylium,* from Greek *konchylion,* from *konchē* "conch"]

cock•le•bur \ˈkäk-əl-ˌbər, ˈkək-\ *n* **:** any of a genus of prickly-fruited plants related to the thistles; *also* **:** one of its fruits

cock•le•shell \ˈkäk-əl-ˌshel\ *n* **1 a :** a shell or shell valve of a cockle **b :** a shell (as a scallop) suggesting a cockleshell **2 :** a light flimsy boat

cock•les of the heart \ˌkäk-əlz-\ **:** the deepest part of one's being — usually used in the phrase *warm the cockles of the heart*

cock•ney \ˈkäk-nē\ *n, pl* **cockneys** *often cap* **1 :** a native of London and especially of the East End of London **2 :** the dialect used by cockneys [Middle English *cokeney* "spoiled child", literally, "cocks' egg", from *cok* "cock" + *ey* "egg"] — **cockney** *adj*

cock•pit \ˈkäk-ˌpit\ *n* **1 :** a pit for cockfights **2 a :** an open space aft of a decked area from which a boat or yacht is steered **b :** a space in the fuselage of an airplane for the pilot or the pilot and passengers or in large passenger planes the pilot and crew

cock•roach \ˈkäk-ˌrōch\ *n* **:** any of an order (Blattaria) of mostly nocturnal insects which have flattened bodies and long antennae and some of which are domestic pests [by folk etymology from Spanish *cucaracha,* derived from *cuca* "caterpillar"]

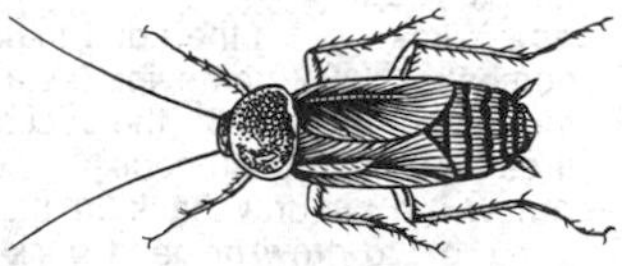

cockroach

cocks•comb \ˈkäk-ˌskōm\ *n* **1 :** COXCOMB **2 :** a garden plant of the amaranth family grown for its showy flower clusters

cock•sure \ˈkäk-ˈshu̇r\ *adj* **1 :** perfectly sure **:** CERTAIN **2 :** marked by overconfidence **:** COCKY — **cock•sure•ly** *adv* — **cock•sure•ness** *n*

cock•tail \ˈkäk-ˌtāl\ *n* **1 :** an iced drink of distilled liquor mixed with flavoring ingredients **2 :** an appetizer (as tomato juice) served as a first course at a meal

cocky \ˈkäk-ē\ *adj* **cock•i•er; -est 1 :** arrogantly self-confident **2 :** jaunty in behavior or appearance — **cock•i•ly** \ˈkäk-ə-lē\ *adv* — **cock•i•ness** \ˈkäk-ē-nəs\ *n*

[1]co•co \ˈkō-kō\ *n, pl* **cocos :** the coconut palm or its fruit [Spanish, from Portuguese *côco,* literally, "bogeyman"]

[2]coco *adj* **:** made from the fibrous husk of the coconut

co•coa \ˈkō-kō\ *n* **1 :** a cacao tree **2 a :** chocolate freed of some of its fat and ground **b :** a beverage made by heating cocoa powder with water or milk [Spanish *cacao*]

cocoa bean *n* **:** CACAO 2

cocoa butter *n* **:** a pale fat with a low melting point obtained from cacao beans and used in foods and cosmetics

co•co•nut *also* **co•coa•nut** \ˈkō-kə-ˌnət, -nət\ *n* **:** the fruit of the coconut palm with an outer fibrous husk yielding coir and a nut containing thick edible meat and coconut milk

coconut oil *n* **:** a nearly colorless oil or soft white fat extracted from coconuts or copra and used in soaps and foods

coconut palm *n* **:** a tall pinnate-leaved tropical palm probably of American origin

co•coon \kə-ˈkün\ *n* **1 a :** a usually largely silken envelope which an insect larva (as a caterpillar) forms about itself and in which it passes the pupal stage **b :** any of various other protective coverings produced by animals **2 :** a covering suggesting a cocoon [French *cocon,* from Provencal *coucoun,* from *coco* "shell", from Latin *coccum* "excrescence on a tree", from Greek *kokkos* "grain, seed, kermes berry"]

cod \ˈkäd\ *n, pl* **cod** *also* **cods :** a soft-finned fish of the colder parts of the North Atlantic that is a major food fish; *also* **:** any of several related fishes [Middle English]

co•da \ˈkōd-ə\ *n* **:** a distinctive formal closing section in a musical composition [Italian, literally, "tail", from Latin *cauda*]

cod•dle \ˈkäd-l\ *vt* **cod•dled; cod•dling** \ˈkäd-liŋ, -l-iŋ\ **1 :** to cook slowly in water just below the boiling point ⟨*coddle* eggs⟩ **2 :** to treat with extreme care **:** PAMPER [perhaps from *caudle*] — **cod•dler** \ˈkäd-lər, -l-ər\ *n*

[1]code \ˈkōd\ *n* **1 :** a systematic statement of a body of law; *esp* **:** one having the force of statute ⟨a criminal *code*⟩ **2 :** a system of principles or rules ⟨moral *codes*⟩ **3 :** a system of signals for communicating **4 :** a system (as of letters or symbols) used to represent assigned and often secret meanings **5 :** GENETIC CODE [Middle French, from Latin *codex* "tree trunk, wood writing tablet covered with wax, book"]

[2]code *vt* **:** to put into the form of a code — **cod•er** *n*

co•deine *or* **co•dein** \ˈkō-ˌdēn, ˈkōd-ē-ən\ *n* **:** a drug that is obtained from opium, is weaker than morphine, and is used in cough remedies [French *codéine,* from *kōdeia* "poppy capsule", from *kōos* "cavity"]

co•dex \ˈkō-ˌdeks\ *n, pl* **co•di•ces** \ˈkōd-ə-ˌsēz, ˈkäd-\ **:** a manuscript book (as of the Scriptures) [Latin]

cod•fish \ˈkäd-ˌfish\ *n* **:** COD; *also* **:** its flesh used as food

cod•ger \ˈkäj-ər\ *n* **:** an odd or cranky individual [probably alteration of *cadger*]

cod•i•cil \ˈkäd-ə-səl, -ˌsil\ *n* **:** a supplementary document that modifies an earlier will [Middle French *codicille,* from Latin *codex* "book"]

cod•i•fy \ˈkäd-ə-ˌfī, ˈkōd-\ *vt* **-fied; -fy•ing 1 :** to reduce (as laws) to a code **2 :** to arrange in a systematic and understandable order — **cod•i•fi•ca•tion** \ˌkäd-ə-fə-ˈkā-shən, ˌkōd-\ *n*

[1]cod•ling \ˈkäd-liŋ\ *n* **1 :** a young cod **2 :** HAKE

[2]cod•ling \ˈkäd-liŋ\ *or* **cod•lin** \-lən\ *n* **:** a small immature apple; *also* **:** any of several elongated greenish English cooking apples [Middle English *querdlyng*]

codling moth *n* **:** a small moth whose larva lives in apples, pears, quinces, and English walnuts

cod–liver oil *n* **:** an oil obtained from the liver of the cod and related fishes and used as a source of vitamins A and D

co•don \ˈkō-ˌdän\ *n* **:** a triplet of nucleotides that is part of the genetic code and that specifies a particular amino acid in a protein or starts or stops protein synthesis

[1]co•ed \ˈkō-ˌed\ *n* **:** a female student in a coeducational school

[2]coed *adj* **1 :** COEDUCATIONAL ⟨a *coed* college⟩ **2 :** of or relating to a coed

co•ed•u•ca•tion \ˌkō-ˌej-ə-ˈkā-shən\ *n* **:** the education of students of both sexes at the same school or college — **co•ed•u•ca•tion•al** \-ˈkā-shnəl, -shən-l\ *adj*

co•ef•fi•cient \ˌkō-ə-ˈfish-ənt\ *n* **1 :** any of the factors of a product considered in relation to a specific factor; *esp* **:** a constant factor of a term as distinguished from a variable ⟨in $5xy^2$, 5 is the *coefficient* of xy^2⟩ **2 :** a number that serves as a measure of a property or characteristic (as of a substance or device)

coel•acanth \ˈsē-lə-ˌkanth\ *n* **:** a fish or fossil of a family of mostly extinct fishes — compare LATIMERIA [Greek *koilos* "hollow" + *akantha* "thorn"] — **coelacanth** *adj*

-coele *or* **-coel** \ˌsēl\ *n combining form* **:** cavity **:** chamber ⟨blasto*coel*⟩ ⟨entero*coele*⟩ [Greek *koilos,* adjective, "hollow"]

coel•en•ter•ate \si-ˈlent-ə-ˌrāt, -rət\ *n* : any of a phylum (Coelenterata) of invertebrate animals that include the corals, sea anemones, jellyfishes, and hydroids and have radial body symmetry [Greek *koilos* "hollow" + *enteron* "intestine"] — **coelenterate** *adj*

coe•li•ac \ˈsē-lē-ˌak\ *adj* : of or relating to the abdominal cavity [Latin *coeliacus,* from Greek *koiliakos,* from *koilia* "cavity", from *koilos* "hollow"]

coe•lom \ˈsē-ləm\ *n, pl* **coe•loms** *or* **coe•lo•ma•ta** \si-ˈlō-mət-ə\ : the usually epithelium-lined body cavity of animals above the lower worms [German, from Greek *koilōma* "cavity", from *koilos* "hollow"] — **coe•lo•mate** \ˈsē-lə-ˌmāt\ *adj or n* — **coe•lo•mic** \si-ˈläm-ik, -ˈlō-mik\ *adj*

coen- *or* **coeno-** *combining form* : common : general ⟨*coenocytic*⟩ [Greek *koinos*]

coe•no•bite \ˈsē-nə-ˌbīt\ *variant of* CENOBITE

coe•no•cyt•ic \ˌsē-nə-ˈsit-ik\ *adj* : containing several or many nuclei ⟨a *coenocytic* cell⟩

co•en•zyme \ˈkō-ˈen-ˌzīm\ *n* : a substance (as a vitamin) closely associated with an enzyme and essential for its normal function

coenzyme A *n* : a coenzyme $C_{21}H_{36}N_7O_{16}P_3S$ that occurs in all living cells and is essential to the metabolism of carbohydrates, fats, and some amino acids — compare ACETYL COENZYME A

co•equal \ˈkō-ˈē-kwəl\ *adj* : equal with one another — **co•equal•i•ty** \ˌkō-ē-ˈkwäl-ət-ē\ *n* — **co•equal•ly** \ˈkō-ˈē-kwə-lē\ *adv*

co•erce \kō-ˈərs\ *vt* **1** : to restrain or dominate by negating individual will **2** : to compel to an act or a choice ⟨*coerced* them to cheat⟩ **3** : to enforce by force or threat ⟨*coerce* obedience to an order⟩ [Latin *coercēre,* from *co-* + *arcēre* "to shut up, enclose"] **syn** see FORCE — **co•erc•ible** \-ˈər-sə-bəl\ *adj*

co•er•cion \kō-ˈər-zhən, -shən\ *n* : the act, process, or power of coercing

co•er•cive \-ˈər-siv\ *adj* : serving or intended to coerce — **co•er•cive•ly** *adv* — **co•er•cive•ness** *n*

co•eval \kō-ˈē-vəl\ *adj* : of the same or equal age or duration [Latin *coaevus,* from *co-* + *aevum* "age, lifetime"] — **coeval** *n*

co•ex•ist \ˌkō-ig-ˈzist\ *vi* **1** : to exist together or at the same time **2** : to live in peace with each other especially as a matter of policy — **co•ex•is•tence** \-ˈzis-təns\ *n* — **co•ex•is•tent** \-tənt\ *adj*

co•ex•ten•sive \ˌkō-ik-ˈsten-siv\ *adj* : having the same scope or extent in space or time — **co•ex•ten•sive•ly** *adv*

cof•fee \ˈkȯ-fē, ˈkäf-ē\ *n* **1** : a drink made from the roasted and ground or pounded seeds of a tropical tree or shrub of the madder family; *also* : these seeds or a plant producing them **2** : a cup of coffee ⟨two *coffees*⟩ [Italian *caffè,* from Turkish *kahve,* from Arabic *qahwah*]

cof•fee•house \-ˌhau̇s\ *n* : a place where refreshments (as coffee) are sold

cof•fee•pot \-ˌpät\ *n* : a covered container for preparing or serving coffee

coffee shop *n* : a small restaurant

coffee table *n* : a low table usually placed in front of a sofa and used for serving refreshments

cof•fer \ˈkȯ-fər, ˈkäf-ər\ *n* **1** : a box or chest usually used for valuables; *esp* : STRONGBOX **2** : monetary funds : TREASURY — usually used in pl. **3** : COFFERDAM **4** : a recessed panel in a vault or ceiling [Old French *coffre,* from Latin *cophinus* "basket", from Greek *kophinos*]

cof•fer•dam \-ˌdam\ *n* : a watertight enclosure from which water is pumped to expose the bottom of a body of water and permit construction

cof•fin \ˈkȯ-fən\ *n* : a box into which a corpse is placed for burial [Middle English, "basket, receptacle", from Middle French *cofin,* from Latin *cophinus*]

coffin bone *n* : the bone enclosed within the hoof of the horse

co•func•tion \kō-ˈfəng-shən, -ˈfəngk-, ˈkō-ˌ\ *n* : a trigonometric function whose value for the complement of an angle is equal to the value of a given trigonometric function for the angle itself ⟨the sine is the *cofunction* of the cosine⟩

cog \ˈkäg\ *n* : a tooth on the rim of a wheel or gear [Middle English *cogge,* of Scandinavian origin]

co•gent \ˈkō-jənt\ *adj* **1** : having power to compel or constrain ⟨a *cogent* motive⟩ **2** : appealing forcibly to the mind or reason : CONVINCING ⟨*cogent* evidence⟩ [Latin *cogere* "to drive together, compel", from *co-* + *agere* "to drive"] **syn** see VALID — **co•gen•cy** \-jən-sē\ *n* — **co•gent•ly** *adv*

cog•i•tate \ˈkäj-ə-ˌtāt\ *vb* : to think over carefully or deeply : PONDER [Latin *cogitare* "to think, think about", from *co-* + *agitare* "to drive, agitate"] — **cog•i•ta•tion** \ˌkäj-ə-ˈtā-shən\ *n* — **cog•i•ta•tive** \ˈkäj-ə-ˌtāt-iv\ *adj*

co•gnac \ˈkōn-ˌyak\ *n* : a French brandy [*Cognac,* district in France]

cog•nate \ˈkäg-ˌnāt\ *adj* **1** : related by descent from the same ancestral language ⟨Spanish and French are *cognate* languages⟩ ⟨Spanish *madre* meaning "mother" and French *mère* meaning "mother" are *cognate* words⟩ **2 a** : related by processes of derivation within a single language ⟨English *boyish* and *boyhood* are *cognate* words⟩ **b** : related by adoption from one source language into two or more other languages ⟨English *tobacco* and French *tabac* are *cognate* words⟩ **3** : being a substantive that is related usually in derivation to the verb of which it is the object ⟨*song* in "sang the song" is a *cognate* object⟩ **4** : the same or similar nature ⟨illustrated books and *cognate* reference materials⟩ [Latin *cognatus* "related by birth", from *co-* + *gnatus, natus,* past participle of *nasci* "to be born"] — **cognate** *n* — **cog•nate•ly** *adv*

cog•ni•tion \käg-ˈnish-ən\ *n* **1** : the act or process of knowing including both awareness and judgment; *also* : something known by this process **2** : a cognitive activity [Latin *cognitio,* from *cognoscere* "to know, become acquainted with", from *co-* + *gnoscere* "to come to know"] — **cog•ni•tion•al** \-ˈnish-nəl, -ˈnish-ən-l\ *adj*

cog•ni•tive \ˈkäg-nət-iv\ *adj* : of, relating to, or being conscious intellectual activities (as thinking, reasoning, remembering, imagining, learning words, or using language) — **cog•ni•tive•ly** *adv*

cog•ni•zance \ˈkäg-nə-zəns\ *n* **1 a** : conscious recognition ⟨had no *cognizance* of the crime⟩ **b** : range of understanding or awareness ⟨an idea beyond a child's *cognizance*⟩ **c** : a noting of something : HEED ⟨take *cognizance* of what is happening⟩ **2 a** : the right and power to hear and decide controversies : JURISDICTION **b** : the judicial hearing of a matter [Old French *conoissance,* from *conoistre* "to know", from Latin *cognoscere*]

cog•ni•zant \-zənt\ *adj* : having cognizance

cog•no•men \käg-ˈnō-mən, ˈkäg-nə-\ *n, pl* **-nomens** *or* **-no•mi•na** \-ˈnäm-ə-nə, -ˈnō-mə-\ **1** : SURNAME; *esp* : the third of the usual three names of an ancient Roman **2** : NAME 1; *esp* : NICKNAME [Latin, from *co-* + *nomen* "name"]

co•gno•scen•te \ˌkän-yə-ˈshent-ē, -ə-, ˌkäg-nə-\ *n, pl* **-scen•ti** \-ˈshent-ē\ : CONNOISSEUR [obsolete, Italian, from Latin *cognoscere* "to know"]

cog•wheel \ˈkäg-ˌhwēl, -ˌwēl\ *n* : a wheel with cogs on the rim

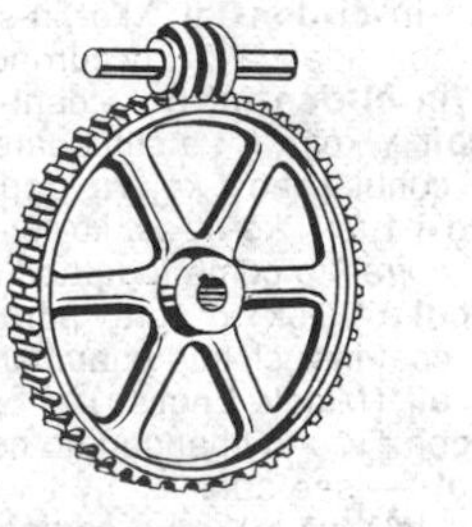

cogwheel

co•hab•it \kō-ˈhab-ət\ *vi* : to live together as husband and wife [Late Latin *cohabitare,* from Latin *co-* + *habitare* "to inhabit"] — **co•hab•i•ta•tion** \ˌkō-ˌhab-ə-ˈtā-shən\ *n*

co•here \kō-ˈhiər\ *vi* **1** : to hold together firmly as parts of the same mass **2** : to consist of parts that cohere **3 a** : to become united in principles, relationships, or interests **b** : to be consistent [Latin *cohaerēre,* from *co-* + *haerēre* "to stick"] **syn** see STICK — **co•her•ence** \-ˈhir-əns, -ˈher-\ *or* **co•her•en•cy** \-ən-sē\ *n*

co•her•ent \kō-ˈhir-ənt, -ˈher-\ *adj* **1** : having the quality of cohering **2** : logically consistent — **co•her•ent•ly** *adv*

co•he•sion \kō-ˈhē-zhən\ *n* **1** : the action of sticking together tightly **2** : union between similar plant parts or organs **3** : molecular attraction by which the particles of a body are united throughout the mass [Latin *cohaesus,* past participle of *cohaerēre* "to cohere"]

co•he•sive \kō-ˈhē-siv, -ziv\ *adj* : exhibiting or producing cohesion — **co•he•sive•ly** *adv* — **co•he•sive•ness** *n*

\ə\ **abut**	\au̇\ **out**	\i\ **tip**	\ȯ\ **saw**	\u̇\ **foot**
\ər\ **further**	\ch\ **chin**	\ī\ **life**	\ȯi\ **coin**	\y\ **yet**
\a\ **mat**	\e\ **pet**	\j\ **job**	\th\ **thin**	\yü\ **few**
\ā\ **take**	\ē\ **easy**	\ng\ **sing**	\t͟h\ **this**	\yu̇\ **cure**
\ä\ **cot, cart**	\g\ **go**	\ō\ **bone**	\ü\ **food**	\zh\ **vision**

co•ho \'kō-,hō\ *n, pl* **cohos** *or* **coho** : a small salmon with light-colored flesh [origin unknown]

co•hort \'kō-,hȯrt\ *n* **1 a** : one of 10 divisions of an ancient Roman legion **b** : a group of warriors or followers **2** : [1]COMPANION 1 [Latin *cohors* "enclosure, throng, cohort"]

[1]**coif** \'kȯif, *in sense 2 usually* 'kwäf\ *n* **1** : a close-fitting cap **2** : COIFFURE [Middle French *coife,* from Latin *cofea*]

[2]**coif** \'kȯif, 'kwäf\ *or* **coiffe** \'kwäf\ *vt* **coiffed** *or* **coifed**; **coiff•ing** *or* **coif•ing** : to provide with a coif

coif•fure \kwä-'fyu̇r\ *n* : a manner of arranging the hair [French, from *coiffer* "to cover with a coif, arrange (hair)", from *coife* "coif"]

coign of van•tage \,kȯin-ə-'vant-ij\ : an advantageous position [Middle English *coyn, coigne* "projecting corner, coin"]

[1]**coil** \'kȯil\ *n* **1** : TUMULT 1 **2** : TROUBLE 1 [origin unknown]

[2]**coil** *vb* **1** : to wind into rings or spirals **2** : to move in a circular, spiral, or winding course **3** : to form or lie in a coil [Middle French *coillir* "to gather", from Latin *colligere* "to collect"]

[3]**coil** *n* **1 a** : a series of loops : SPIRAL **b** : a single loop of a coil **2** : a number of turns of wire especially in spiral form usually for electromagnetic effect or for providing electrical resistance **3** : a series of connected pipes (as in water-heating apparatus) in rows, layers, or windings

[1]**coin** \'kȯin\ *n* **1** : a piece of metal issued by governmental authority as money **2** : metal money [Middle English *coyn, coigne* "wedge, corner, coin", from Middle French *coing, coin* "wedge, corner", from Latin *cuneus* "wedge"]

[2]**coin** *vt* **1 a** : to make (a coin) especially by stamping : MINT **b** : to convert (metal) into coins **2** : INVENT ⟨*coin* a phrase⟩ — **coin•er** *n*

coin•age \'kȯi-nij\ *n* **1** : the act or process of coining **2 a** : COINS **b** : something (as a word) made up or invented

co•in•cide \,kō-ən-'sīd\ *vi* **1** : to occupy the same place in space or time ⟨his birthday *coincides* with Christmas⟩ **2** : to be the same shape and cover the same area **3** : to correspond or agree exactly ⟨an opinion that *coincides* with my own⟩ [Medieval Latin *coincidere,* from Latin *co-* + *incidere* "to fall on", from *in-* + *cadere* "to fall"]

co•in•ci•dence \kō-'in-səd-əns\ *n* **1** : the act or condition of coinciding **2** : two things that happen at the same time by accident but seem to have some connection; *also* : either one of these things

co•in•ci•dent \-səd-ənt\ *adj* **1** : occupying the same space or time ⟨*coincident* events⟩ **2** : of similar nature : HARMONIOUS ⟨a theory *coincident* with the facts⟩ **syn** see CONTEMPORARY — **co•in•ci•dent•ly** *adv*

co•in•ci•den•tal \kō-,in-sə-'dent-l\ *adj* **1** : resulting from a coincidence **2** : occurring or existing at the same time — **co•in•ci•den•tal•ly** \-'dent-l-ē, -'dent-lē\ *adv*

coir \'kȯir\ *n* : a stiff coarse fiber from the outer husk of the coconut [Tamil *kayiṟu* "rope"]

co•i•tus \'kō-ət-əs, kō-'ēt-\ *n* : sexual intercourse [Latin, from *coire* "to come together", from *co-* + *ire* "to go"]

[1]**coke** \'kōk\ *n* : gray porous lumps of fuel made by heating soft coal in a closed chamber until some of its gases have passed off [Middle English]

[2]**coke** *vt* : to change into coke

col- — see COM-

co•la \'kō-lə\ *n* : a carbonated soft drink containing sugar, caffeine, phosphoric acid or citric acid, caramel, and a characteristic flavoring [from *Coca-Cola,* a trademark]

col•an•der \'kəl-ən-dər, 'käl-\ *n* : a perforated utensil for draining food [Middle English *colyndore,* derived from Latin *colare* "to strain", from *colum* "sieve"]

col•chi•cine \'käl-chə-,sēn, 'käl-kə-\ *n* : a poisonous substance from the corms or seeds of the meadow saffron used to induce polyploidy in cells and to treat gout

col•chi•cum \'käl-chi-kəm, 'käl-ki-\ *n* : MEADOW SAFFRON; *also* : its dried corm or dried ripe seeds containing colchicine [Latin, a kind of plant with a poisonous root, from Greek *kolchikon,* literally, "product of Colchis"]

[1]**cold** \'kōld\ *adj* **1** : having a low temperature or one decidedly below normal ⟨a *cold* day⟩ ⟨a *cold* drink⟩ **2** : lacking warmth of feeling : UNFRIENDLY ⟨a *cold* welcome⟩ **3** : suffering or uncomfortable from lack of warmth ⟨feel *cold*⟩ [Old English *ceald, cald*] — **cold•ly** *adv* — **cold•ness** \'kōld-nəs, 'kōl-\ *n* — **in cold blood** : with premeditation : DELIBERATELY

[2]**cold** *n* **1 a** : a condition of low temperature **b** : cold weather **2** : bodily sensation produced by loss or lack of heat : CHILL **3** : a bodily disorder popularly associated with chilling; *esp* : COMMON COLD

cold–blood•ed \'kōld-'bləd-əd, 'kōl-\ *adj* **1** : lacking or showing a lack of natural human feelings : not moved by sympathy ⟨a *cold-blooded* criminal⟩ **2** : having cold blood; *esp* : having a body temperature not internally regulated but approximating that of the environment **3** *or* **cold•blood** \-'bləd\ : of mixed or inferior breeding **4** : sensitive to cold — **cold–blood•ed•ly** *adv* — **cold–blood•ed•ness** *n*

cold chisel *n* : a strong steel chisel for chipping and cutting cold metal

cold cream *n* : a creamy preparation for cleansing, softening, and soothing the skin

cold cuts *n pl* : sliced assorted cold meats

cold frame *n* : a usually glass-covered frame without artificial heat used to protect plants and seedlings

cold front *n* : an advancing edge of a cold air mass

cold shoulder *n* : intentionally cold or unsympathetic treatment — **cold–shoulder** *vt*

cold sore *n* : a group of blisters about or within the mouth caused by a common virus

cold sweat *n* : concurrent perspiration and chill usually associated with fear, pain, or shock

cold war *n* : a conflict between nations carried on by methods (as propaganda or economic pressure) short of actual military action and usually without breaking off diplomatic relations

cold wave *n* : a period of unusually cold weather

cole \'kōl\ *n* : any of a genus of herbaceous plants that includes the cabbage and turnip [Old English *cāl,* from Latin *caulis* "stem, cabbage"]

cole•man•ite \'kōl-mə-,nīt\ *n* : a mineral $Ca_2B_6O_{11}\cdot 5H_2O$ consisting of a hydrous borate of calcium occurring in brilliant colorless or white massive crystals [William T. *Coleman,* died 1893, American mine owner]

co•le•op•tera \,kō-lē-'äp-tə-rə\ *n pl* : insects that are beetles [Greek *koleon* "sheath" + *pteron* "wing"] — **co•le•op•ter•ist** \-tə-rəst\ *n* — **co•le•op•ter•ous** \-tə-rəs\ *adj*

co•le•op•ter•an \-tə-rən\ *n* : [1]BEETLE 1 — **coleopteran** *adj*

co•le•op•tile \-'äp-tl\ *n* : the first leaf of a monocot seedling forming a protective sheath about the plumule [Greek *koleon* "sheath" + *ptilon* "down, feather"]

cole•slaw \'kōl-,slȯ\ *n* : a salad made of sliced or shredded raw cabbage [Dutch *koolsla,* from *kool* "cabbage" + *sla* "salad"]

co•le•us \'kō-lē-əs\ *n* : any of a large genus of herbs of the mint family often grown for their varicolored leaves [Greek *koleos, koleon* "sheath"]

col•ic \'käl-ik\ *n* : sharp sudden pain in the abdomen [Middle French *colique,* from Latin *colicus* "colicky", from Greek *kōlikos,* from *kolon* "colon"] — **col•icky** \'käl-i-kē\ *adj*

co•li•form \'kō-lə-,fȯrm\ *adj* : relating to, resembling, or being the colon bacillus [New Latin *Escherichia coli* "colon bacillus" + English *-form*] — **coliform** *n*

col•i•se•um \,käl-ə-'sē-əm\ *n* : a large building, amphitheater, or stadium for athletic contests or public entertainments [Medieval Latin *Colosseum, Coliseum* "the Colosseum"]

co•li•tis \kō-'līt-əs, kə-\ *n* : inflammation of the colon

col•lab•o•rate \kə-'lab-ə-,rāt\ *vi* **1** : to work jointly with others (as in writing a book) **2** : to cooperate with or assist an enemy force occupying one's country — **col•lab•o•ra•tion** \-,lab-ə-'rā-shən\ *n* — **col•lab•o•ra•tion•ist** \-shə-nəst, -shnəst\ *n* — **col•lab•o•ra•tor** \-'lab-ə-,rāt-ər\ *n*

col•lage \kə-'läzh, kȯ-, kō-\ *n* **1** : an artistic composition of fragments of materials (as printed matter) pasted on a surface **2** : the art of making collages [French, "gluing", from *coller* "to glue", from *colle* "glue", from Greek *kolla*]

col•la•gen \'käl-ə-jən\ *n* : an insoluble fibrous protein that is the chief constituent of connective tissue fibrils and yields gelatin and glue on prolonged heating with water [Greek *kolla* "glue"] — **col•lag•e•nous** \kə-'laj-ə-nəs\ *adj*

[1]**col•lapse** \kə-'laps\ *vb* **1** : to break down completely : DISINTEGRATE **2** : to shrink together abruptly and completely ⟨a *collapsed* balloon⟩ **3** : to fall in : give way ⟨the tunnel *collapsed*⟩ **4** : to suddenly lose value or effectiveness ⟨the country's currency *collapsed*⟩ **5** : to break down physically or mentally through exhaustion or disease; *esp* : to fall helpless or unconscious **6** : to fold down into a more compact shape ⟨*collapse* a card table⟩ [Latin *collabi,* from *com-* + *labi* "to fall, slide"] — **col•laps•ible** \-'lap-sə-bəl\ *adj*

[2]**collapse** *n* : the act or an instance of collapsing : BREAKDOWN

[1]**col•lar** \'käl-ər\ *n* **1 a :** a band, strip, or chain worn around the neck or the neckline of a garment **b :** a part of the harness of a draft animal fitted over the shoulders and taking strain when a load is drawn **2 :** something resembling a collar (as a ring or round flange to restrain motion or hold something in place) [Old French *coler,* from Latin *collare,* from *collum* "neck"] — **col•lar•less** \-ər-ləs\ *adj*

[2]**collar** *vt* **1 a :** to seize by the collar **b :** to take prisoner : NAB **2 :** to put a collar on

col•lar•bone \'käl-ər-ˌbōn, ˌkäl-ər-'\ *n* : CLAVICLE

collar cell *n* **:** a flagellated cell (as of a sponge) with a protoplasmic collar about the base of its flagellum

col•lard \'käl-ərd\ *n* **:** a stalked smooth-leaved kale — usually used in pl. [alteration of *colewort* "cole, kale"]

collared lizard *n* **:** a brightly colored iguana of the south-central United States and Mexico

col•late \kə-'lāt, kä-, kō-; 'käl-ˌāt, 'kōl-\ *vt* **:** to collect and compare carefully in order to verify and often to unify or arrange in order [back-formation from *collation*] — **col•la•tor** \-'lāt-ər, -ˌāt-\ *n*

[1]**col•lat•er•al** \kə-'lat-ə-rəl, -'la-trəl\ *adj* **1 :** associated but of secondary or supporting importance ⟨a main question and *collateral* questions⟩ **2 :** descended from the same ancestors but not in the same line ⟨cousins are *collateral* relatives⟩ **3 a :** of, relating to, or being collateral used as security **b :** secured by collateral [Medieval Latin *collateralis,* from Latin *com-* + *lateralis* "lateral"] — **col•lat•er•al•ly** \-ē\ *adv*

[2]**collateral** *n* **1 :** property (as stocks, bonds, or a mortgage) handed over or pledged as security for the repayment of a loan **2 :** a branch of a bodily part (as a vein)

col•la•tion \kə-'lā-shən, kä-, kō-\ *n* **1 :** a light meal **2 :** the act, process, or result of collating [Medieval Latin *collatio,* from Latin, "bringing together, comparison", from *collatus,* past participle of *conferre* "to bring together", from *com-* + *ferre* "to carry"]

col•league \'käl-ˌēg\ *n* **:** an associate in a profession or office; *also* **:** a fellow worker [Middle French *collegue,* from Latin *collega,* from *com-* + *legare* "to appoint, delegate"]

[1]**col•lect** \'käl-ikt, -ˌekt\ *n* **:** a short prayer consisting of an invocation, petition, and conclusion [Old French *collecte,* from Medieval Latin *collecta,* short for *oratio ad collectam* "prayer upon assembly"]

[2]**col•lect** \kə-'lekt\ *vb* **1 a :** to bring together into one body or place **b :** to gather from a number of sources ⟨*collect* taxes⟩ **2 :** to gain or regain control of ⟨*collect* one's thoughts⟩ **3 :** to claim as due and receive payment for **4 a :** ASSEMBLE ⟨a crowd *collected* at the scene of the accident⟩ **b :** ACCUMULATE ⟨dust *collects* on the furniture⟩ **5 :** to simplify mathematically by carrying out addition and subtraction of (terms containing the same variables) ⟨when terms are *collected* $8x - 3x + 5$ becomes $5x + 5$⟩ [Latin *collectus,* past participle of *colligere* "to collect", from *com-* + *legere* "to gather"] **syn** see GATHER — **col•lect•able** *or* **col•lect•ible** \-'lek-tə-bəl\ *adj*

[3]**col•lect** \kə-'lekt\ *adv or adj* **:** to be paid for by the receiver ⟨we telephoned *collect*⟩

col•lect•ed \kə-'lek-təd\ *adj* **:** SELF-POSSESSED, CALM — **col•lect•ed•ly** *adv* — **col•lect•ed•ness** *n*

collecting tubule *n* **:** the part of a nephron by which urine is collected

col•lec•tion \kə-'lek-shən\ *n* **1 :** the act or process of collecting **2 :** something collected; *esp* **:** an accumulation of objects gathered for study, comparison, or exhibition **3 :** a gathering of money (as for charitable purposes)

[1]**col•lec•tive** \kə-'lek-tiv\ *adj* **1 :** denoting a number of persons or things considered as one group ⟨*flock* is a *collective* noun⟩ **2 :** formed by collecting **:** AGGREGATED **3 :** of or relating to a group of individuals ⟨*collective* needs⟩ **4 :** collectivized or characterized by collectivism **5 :** shared or assumed by all members of the group ⟨*collective* leadership⟩ — **col•lec•tive•ly** *adv*

[2]**collective** *n* **1 :** a collective body **:** GROUP **2 :** a cooperative unit or organization; *esp* **:** COLLECTIVE FARM

collective bargaining *n* **:** negotiation between an employer and union representatives usually on wages, hours, and working conditions

collective farm *n* **:** a farm in a communist country formed from many small holdings collected into a single unit for joint operation under governmental supervision

collective fruit *n* **:** MULTIPLE FRUIT

collective mark *n* **:** a trademark or a service mark of a group (as a cooperative or other association)

col•lec•tiv•ism \kə-'lek-ti-ˌviz-əm\ *n* **:** a political or economic theory advocating collective control especially over production and distribution; *also* **:** a system marked by such control — **col•lec•tiv•ist** \-vəst\ *adj or n* — **col•lec•tiv•is•tic** \-ˌlek-ti-'vis-tik\ *adj*

col•lec•tiv•i•ty \kə-ˌlek-'tiv-ət-ē, ˌkäl-ˌek-\ *n, pl* **-ties :** a collective whole

col•lec•tiv•ize \kə-'lek-ti-ˌvīz\ *vt* **:** to organize under collective control — **col•lec•tiv•iza•tion** \-ˌlek-ti-və-'zā-shən\ *n*

col•lec•tor \kə-'lek-tər\ *n* **:** one that collects: as **a :** an official or agent who collects funds or money due **b :** one that makes a collection ⟨a stamp *collector*⟩ **c :** an object, device, or substance that collects — **col•lec•tor•ship** \-ˌship\ *n*

col•leen \kä-'lēn, 'käl-ˌēn\ *n* **:** an Irish girl [Irish Gaelic *cailīn* "young girl"]

col•lege \'käl-ij\ *n* **1 :** a building used for an educational or religious purpose **2 a :** a subordinate school in a university **b :** a school higher than a high school; *esp* **:** a 4-year school offering courses in the sciences and humanities leading to a bachelor's degree **c :** an institution offering instruction usually in a professional, vocational, or technical field ⟨business *college*⟩ ⟨barber *college*⟩ **3 :** an organized body of persons having common interests or duties ⟨the *college* of cardinals⟩ [Middle French, "body of clergy", from Latin *collegium* "society", from *collega* "colleague"]

col•le•gian \kə-'lē-jən, -jē-ən\ *n* **:** a student or recent graduate of a college

col•le•giate \kə-'lē-jət, -jē-ət\ *adj* **1 :** of or relating to a college **2 :** of, relating to, or characteristic of college students ⟨*collegiate* clothes⟩

col•le•gi•um \kə-'leg-ē-əm, -'lāg-\ *n, pl* **-gia** \-ē-ə\ *or* **-gi•ums :** a governing group in which each member has approximately equal power and authority [Russian *kollegya,* from Latin *collegium* "society"] — **col•le•gial** \-'lē-jē-əl, -jəl; -gē-əl\ *adj*

col•lem•bo•lan \kə-'lem-bə-lən\ *n* **:** SPRINGTAIL [Greek *kolla* "glue" + *embolos* "wedge, stopper"] — **collembolan** *adj*

col•len•chy•ma \kə-'leng-kə-mə\ *n* **:** a plant tissue of living usually elongated cells with thickened walls — compare SCLERENCHYMA [Greek *kolla* "glue" + *-enchyma* (as in *parenchyma*)] — **col•len•chy•ma•tous** \ˌkäl-ən-'kim-ət-əs, -'kī-mət-\ *adj*

col•lide \kə-'līd\ *vi* **1 :** to come together with solid impact **2 :** to come into conflict **:** CLASH [Latin *collidere,* from *com-* + *laedere* "to injure by striking"]

col•lie \'käl-ē\ *n* **:** a large long-coated dog developed in Scotland especially for herding sheep [probably from English dialect *colly* "black"]

collie

col•lier \'käl-yər\ *n* **1 :** a coal miner **2 :** a ship for carrying coal [Middle English *colier,* from *col* "coal"]

col•liery \'käl-yə-rē\ *n, pl* **-lier•ies :** a coal mine and the buildings connected with it

col•li•mate \'käl-ə-ˌmāt\ *vt* **:** to make (as rays of light) parallel [Latin *collimare,* from *collineare* "to make straight", from *com-* + *linea* "line"] — **col•li•ma•tor** \-ˌmāt-ər\ *n*

col•lin•e•ar \kə-'lin-ē-ər, kä-\ *adj* **:** lying on the same straight line — **col•lin•ear•i•ty** \-ˌlin-ē-'ar-ət-ē\ *n*

col•li•sion \kə-'lizh-ən\ *n* **:** an act or instance of colliding **:** CRASH [Latin *collisio,* from *collidere* "to collide"]

col•lo•ca•tion \ˌkäl-ə-'kā-shən\ *n* **:** the act or result of placing together

col•lo•di•on \kə-'lōd-ē-ən\ *n* **:** a viscous solution of pyroxylin used especially as a coating for wounds and in cements [Greek *kollōdēs* "glutinous", from *kolla* "glue"]

\ə\ **abut**	\au̇\ **out**	\i\ **tip**	\ȯ\ **saw**	\u̇\ **foot**
\ər\ **further**	\ch\ **chin**	\ī\ **life**	\ȯi\ **coin**	\y\ **yet**
\a\ **mat**	\e\ **pet**	\j\ **job**	\th\ **thin**	\yü\ **few**
\ā\ **take**	\ē\ **easy**	\ng\ **sing**	\t͟h\ **this**	\yu̇\ **cure**
\ä\ **cot, cart**	\g\ **go**	\ō\ **bone**	\ü\ **food**	\zh\ **vision**

col•loid \'käl-,òid\ *n* : a substance in a fine state of division with particles that are not visible in an ordinary microscope but that when in suspension in a liquid or gas are made visible by a beam of light and do not settle out; *also* : a system consisting of such a substance together with the gaseous, liquid, or solid substance in which it is dispersed [Greek *kolla* "glue"] — **col•loi•dal** \kə-'lòid-l, kä-\ *adj* — **col•loi•dal•ly** \-l-ē\ *adv*

col•lo•qui•al \kə-'lō-kwē-əl\ *adj* **1** : used in or characteristic of familiar and informal conversation **2** : using conversational style — **col•lo•qui•al•ly** \-kwē-ə-lē\ *adv*

col•lo•qui•al•ism \-kwē-ə-,liz-əm\ *n* **1** : a colloquial expression **2** : colloquial style

col•lo•qui•um \kə-'lō-kwē-əm\ *n, pl* **-qui•ums** *or* **-quia** \-kwē-ə\ : CONFERENCE; *esp* : a seminar that several lecturers take turns in leading [Latin, "colloquy"]

col•lo•quy \'käl-ə-kwē\ *n, pl* **-quies** : CONVERSATION; *esp* : a formal conversation or conference [Latin *colloquium*, from *colloqui* "to converse", from *com-* + *loqui* "to speak"]

col•lu•sion \kə-'lü-zhən\ *n* : secret agreement or cooperation for a deceitful purpose [Middle French, from Latin *collusio*, from *colludere* "to conspire", from *com-* + *ludere* "to play", from *ludus* "game"] — **col•lu•sive** \-'lü-siv, -ziv\ *adj* — **col•lu•sive•ly** *adv*

co•log•a•rithm \'kō-'lòg-ə-,rith-əm, -'läg-\ *n* : the logarithm of the reciprocal of a number

co•logne \kə-'lōn\ *n* : a perfumed toilet water composed of alcohol and aromatic oils [*Cologne*, Germany]

[1]**co•lon** \'kō-lən\ *n* : the part of the large intestine that extends from the cecum to the rectum [Latin, from Greek *kolon*] — **co•lon•ic** \kō-'län-ik\ *adj*

[2]**colon** *n* : a punctuation mark : used chiefly to direct attention to what follows (as a list, explanation, or quotation) [Latin, "part of a poem", from Greek *kōlon* "limb, clause"]

[3]**co•lon** \kə-'lōn\ *n, pl* **co•lo•nes** \-'lō-,nās\ **1** : the basic monetary unit of Costa Rica and El Salvador **2** : a coin or note representing one colon [Spanish *colón*, from Cristóbal *Colón* "Christopher Columbus"]

colon bacillus *n* : a bacillus regularly present in the intestine and used as an index of fecal contamination (as of water)

col•o•nel \'kərn-l\ *n* : an officer rank in the Army, Marine Corps, and Air Force above lieutenant colonel and below brigadier general [from earlier *coronel*, from Middle French, from Italian *colonnello* "column of soldiers, colonel", from *colonna* "column", from Latin *columna*] — **col•o•nel•cy** \-l-sē\ *n*

△ **origin** English *colonel* is pronounced the same as *kernel*. A review of the history of *colonel* shows how this difference between spelling and pronunciation came about. In many languages when a word contains two identical or similar sounds, one of these sounds will often change over a period of time. This kind of change is called *dissimilation*. When the Italian word *colonello* was taken into French, it became *coronel;* and the word was borrowed by the English from the French in this form. Later the spelling *colonel* came to be used in order to reflect the Italian origin of the word. But by then the pronunciation with *r* was well established.

[1]**co•lo•nial** \kə-'lō-nē-əl, -nyəl\ *adj* **1** : of, relating to, or characteristic of a colony **2** *often cap* : of or relating to the original 13 colonies forming the United States **3** : possessing, forming, or composed of colonies ⟨a *colonial* nation and its *colonial* empire⟩ — **co•lo•nial•ly** \-ē\ *adv* — **co•lo•nial•ness** *n*

[2]**colonial** *n* : COLONIST 1

co•lo•nial•ism \-nē-ə-,liz-əm, -nyə-,liz-\ *n* : control by one power over a dependent area or people; *also* : a policy advocating or based on such control — **co•lo•nial•ist** \-ləst\ *n or adj*

col•o•nist \'käl-ə-nəst\ *n* **1** : an inhabitant or member of a colony **2** : a person who takes part in founding a colony

col•o•nize \'käl-ə-,nīz\ *vb* **1** : to establish a colony in or on ⟨England *colonized* Australia⟩ **2** : to establish in a colony **3** : to make or establish a colony : SETTLE — **col•o•ni•za•tion** \,käl-ə-nə-'zā-shən\ *n* — **col•o•niz•er** *n*

col•on•nade \,käl-ə-'nād\ *n* : a row of columns set at regular intervals and usually supporting the base of the roof structure [French, from Italian *colonnata*, from *colonna* "column", from Latin *columna*] — **col•on•nad•ed** \-'nād-əd\ *adj*

col•o•ny \'käl-ə-nē\ *n, pl* **-nies 1 a** : a body of people sent out by a state to a new territory **b** : the territory inhabited by people sent to new territory **c** : a distant territory belonging to or under the control of a nation **2 a** : a distinguishable localized population within a species ⟨a *colony* of termites⟩ **b** : a circumscribed mass of microorganisms usually growing in or on a solid medium **c** : the aggregation of zooids of a compound animal **3** : a group of individuals with common characteristics or interests situated in close association; *also* : the section occupied by such a group ⟨an artist *colony*⟩ [Latin *colonia*, from *colonus* "farmer, colonist", from *colere* "to cultivate"]

col•o•phon \'käl-ə-fən, -,fän\ *n* **1** : an inscription placed at the end of a book with facts relative to its production **2** : an identifying device used by a printer or a publisher [Latin, from Greek *kolophōn* "summit, finishing touch"]

colophon 2

[1]**col•or** \'kəl-ər\ *n* **1 a** : a phenomenon of light (as red, brown, pink, gray) or visual perception that enables one to differentiate otherwise identical objects **b** : the aspect of objects and light sources that may be described in terms of hue, lightness, and saturation for objects and hue, brightness, and saturation for light sources **c** : a hue as contrasted with black, white, or gray **2 a** ; an outward often deceptive show : APPEARANCE ⟨the story has the *color* of truth⟩ **b** : an appearance of authenticity : PLAUSIBILITY **3 a** : COMPLEXION 2; *esp* : a healthy complexion **b** : BLUSH 2 **4** : vividness or variety of effects of language **5** : the use or combination of colors **6** *pl* **a** : an identifying flag, ensign, or pennant **b** : service in the armed forces ⟨a call to the *colors*⟩ **7** : VITALITY 2b, INTEREST **8** : something used to give color : PIGMENT **9** : skin pigmentation other than white characteristic of race ⟨overcome prejudice toward *color*⟩ [Old French *colour*, from Latin *color*]

• **syn** HUE, TINT, SHADE: COLOR is the general term for any distinguishable quality of light but specifically implies the property of things seen as red, yellow, blue, and so on as distinguished from white, black, or gray; HUE usually implies some modification of or a finer discrimination of a primary color ⟨a reddish orange *hue*⟩ TINT applies especially to a color modified toward white; SHADE to one modified toward black; but all four terms are frequently interchangeable.

[2]**color** *vb* **1 a** : to give color to ⟨the wind *colored* our cheeks⟩ **b** : to change the color of : PAINT **2** : MISREPRESENT, DISTORT ⟨a story *colored* by prejudice⟩ **3** : to take on or change color; *esp* : BLUSH — **col•or•er** \'kəl-ər-ər\ *n*

Col•o•ra•do blue spruce \,käl-ə-'rad-ō-, -'räd-\ *n* : a tall wide-spreading spruce usually with bluish green needles that is native to the Rocky Mountain region of the United States but is often planted elsewhere as an ornamental [*Colorado*, state of the United States]

Colorado potato beetle *n* : a black-and-yellow striped beetle that feeds on the leaves of the potato — called also *potato beetle, potato bug*

col•or•ation \,kəl-ə-'rā-shən\ *n* : use or arrangement of colors or shades : COLORING ⟨the *coloration* of a flower⟩

col•or•a•tu•ra \,kəl-ə-rə-'tür-ə, -'tyùr-\ *n* **1** : showy style in singing (as in opera) **2** : a soprano specializing in coloratura [obsolete Italian, literally, "coloring", from Latin *colorare* "to color", from *color* "color"]

col•or–blind \'kəl-ər-,blīnd\ *adj* : affected with partial or total inability to distinguish one or more chromatic colors — **color blindness** *n*

col•or•cast \-,kast\ *n* : a television broadcast in color — **colorcast** *vb*

col•ored \'kəl-ərd\ *adj* **1** : having color ⟨*colored* pictures⟩ **2** : marked by exaggeration or bias : SLANTED **3 a** : of a race other than the white; *esp* : NEGRO **b** : of or relating to colored persons

col•or•fast \'kəl-ər-,fast\ *adj* : having color that does not fade or run — **col•or•fast•ness** \-,fas-nəs, -,fast-\ *n*

color filter *n* : FILTER 3b

col•or•ful \'kəl-ər-fəl\ *adj* **1** : having striking colors **2** : full of variety or interest — **col•or•ful•ly** \-fə-lē, -flē\ *adv* — **col•or•ful•ness** \-fəl-nəs\ *n*

color guard *n* : a guard of honor for the colors of an organization

col•or•im•e•ter \,kəl-ə-'rim-ət-ər\ *n* : a device for determining colors; *esp* : one used for chemical analysis by comparison of a liquid's color with standard colors — **col•or•i•met•ric** \ˌkəl-ə-rə-ˈme-trik\ *adj* — **col•or•i•met•ri•cal•ly** \-tri-kə-lē, -klē\ *adv* — **col•or•im•e•try** \ˌkəl-ə-ˈrim-ə-trē\ *n*

col•or•ing \ˈkəl-ə-ring\ *n* **1** : the act of applying colors **2** : something that produces color **3 a** : the effect produced by applying or combining colors **b** : natural color **c** : COMPLEXION 2, COLORATION **4** : a false appearance especially of something better ⟨an explanation that gave the lie a *coloring* of truth⟩

col•or•less \ˈkəl-ər-ləs\ *adj* **1** : lacking color **2** : DULL, UNINTERESTING ⟨a *colorless* story⟩ — **col•or•less•ly** *adv* — **col•or•less•ness** *n*

co•los•sal \kə-ˈläs-əl\ *adj* **1** : of, relating to, or resembling a colossus; *esp* : of very great size **2** : EXCEPTIONAL, ASTONISHING ⟨*colossal* growth⟩ — **co•los•sal•ly** \-ə-lē\ *adv*

col•os•se•um \ˌkäl-ə-ˈsē-əm\ *n* **1** *cap* : an amphitheater built in Rome in the first century A.D. **2** : COLISEUM [Medieval Latin, from Latin *colosseus* "colossal", from *colossus* "colossus"]

Co•los•sians \kə-ˈläsh-ənz, -ˈläs-ē-ənz\ *n* — *see* BIBLE table

co•los•sus \kə-ˈläs-əs\ *n, pl* **-los•sus•es** *or* **-los•si** \-ˈläs-ˌī, -ˌē\ **1** : a statue of gigantic size and proportions **2** : one that resembles a colossus in size or scope [Latin, from Greek *kolossos*]

co•los•trum \kə-ˈläs-trəm\ *n* : milk secreted for a few days after parturition and characterized by a high content of proteins and antibodies [Latin, "colostrum of a cow"]

col•our \ˈkəl-ər\ *chiefly British variant of* COLOR

colt \ˈkōlt\ *n* **1 a** : FOAL **b** : a young male horse **2** : a young untried person [Old English]

col•ter \ˈkōl-tər\ *n* : a cutter on a plow to cut the turf [Old English *culter* and Old French *coltre,* both from Latin *culter* "plowshare"]

colt•ish \ˈkōl-tish\ *adj* **1** : FRISKY, PLAYFUL **2** : of, relating to, or resembling a colt — **colt•ish•ly** *adv*

col•um•bine \ˈkäl-əm-ˌbīn\ *n* : any of a genus of plants related to the buttercups that have showy flowers with usually five spurred petals [Medieval Latin *columbina,* from Latin *columba* "dove"]

columbine

co•lum•bi•um \kə-ˈləm-bē-əm\ *n* : NIOBIUM [New Latin, from *Columbia* "United States", from Christopher *Columbus*]

Co•lum•bus Day \kə-ˈləm-bəs-\ *n* : a day, formerly October 12 and now the second Monday in October, observed as a legal holiday in many states of the United States in commemoration of the landing of Columbus in the Bahamas in 1492

col•u•mel•la \ˌkäl-yə-ˈmel-ə, ˌkäl-ə-\ *n, pl* **-mel•lae** \-ˈmel-ˌē, -ˌī\ : any of various plant or animal parts resembling a column [Latin, "small column", from *columna* "column"]

col•umn \ˈkäl-əm\ *n* **1 a** : a printed or written vertical arrangement of items ⟨a *column* of figures⟩ **b** : one of two or more vertical sections of a printed page **c** : a special department in a newspaper or periodical **2** : a supporting pillar; *esp* : one consisting of a usually round shaft, a capital, and a base **3** : something resembling a column in form, position, or function ⟨a *column* of water⟩ **4** : a long row (as of soldiers) **5** : one of the vertical lines of elements of a determinant or matrix [Middle French *colomne,* from Latin *columna,* from *columen* "top"] — **co•lum•nar** \kə-ˈləm-nər\ *adj* — **col•umned** \ˈkäl-əmd\ *adj*

col•um•nist \ˈkäl-əm-nəst, -əm-əst\ *n* : a person who writes a newspaper or magazine column

col•za \ˈkäl-zə, ˈkōl-\ *n* : a cole (as rape) producing seed used as a source of oil [French, from Dutch *koolzaad,* literally, "cabbage seed"]

com- *or* **col-** *or* **con-** *prefix* : with : together : jointly — usually *com-* before *b, p,* or *m* ⟨*com*mingle⟩, *col-* before *l* ⟨*col*linear⟩, and *con-* before other sounds ⟨*con*centrate⟩ [Latin, "with, together, thoroughly"]

[1]co•ma \ˈkō-mə\ *n* : a state of profound unconsciousness caused by disease, injury, or poison [Greek *kōma* "deep sleep"] — **co•ma•tose** \-ˌtōs\ *adj*

[2]coma *n, pl* **co•mae** \-ˌmē, -ˌmī\ : the head of a comet usually containing a nucleus [Latin, "hair", from Greek *komē*]

Co•man•che \kə-ˈman-chē\ *n* : a member of an Indian people of the southwestern plains having an Aztec-related language [Spanish, of American Indian origin]

Co•man•che•an \-chē-ən\ *n* : the period of the Mesozoic era between the Jurassic and the Upper Cretaceous; *also* : the corresponding system of rocks [*Comanche,* Texas] — **Comanchean** *adj*

[1]comb \ˈkōm\ *n* **1 a** : a toothed implement to smooth and arrange the hair or worn in the hair to hold it in place **b** : a toothed instrument for separating fibers (as of wool or flax) **2** : a fleshy crest on the head of the domestic fowl and some related birds **3** : HONEYCOMB [Old English *camb*] — **combed** \ˈkōmd\ *adj*

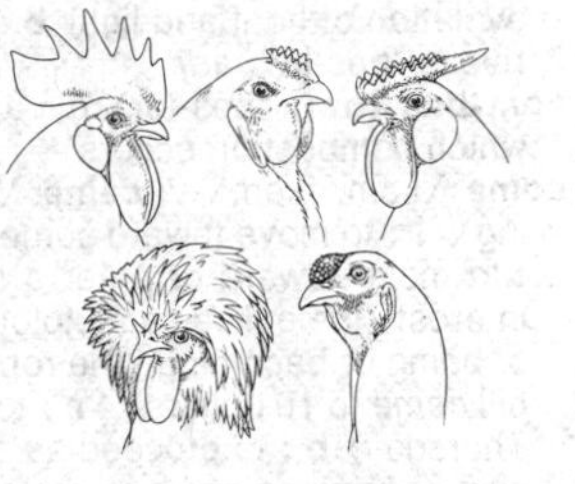

[1]comb 2

[2]comb *vb* **1** : to smooth, arrange, or untangle with a comb ⟨*comb* one's hair⟩ ⟨*comb* wool⟩ **2** : to go over or through carefully in search of something : search thoroughly ⟨*combed* the woods for the lost child⟩

[1]com•bat \kəm-ˈbat, ˈkäm-ˌ\ *vb* **-bat•ed** *or* **-bat•ted; bat•ing** *or* **-bat•ting 1** : to fight with : BATTLE **2** : to struggle against; *esp* : to strive to reduce or eliminate ⟨*combat* disease⟩ [Middle French *combattre,* from Latin *com-* + *battuere* "to beat"]

[2]com•bat \ˈkäm-ˌbat\ *n* **1** : a fight or contest between individuals or groups **2** : CONFLICT 2, CONTROVERSY **3** : active fighting in a war : ACTION

com•bat•ant \kəm-ˈbat-nt, ˈkäm-bət-ənt\ *adj* : engaging in or ready to engage in combat — **combatant** *n*

combat fatigue *n* : a neurotic or psychotic reaction to intense stress under combat conditions in wartime

com•bat•ive \kəm-ˈbat-iv\ *adj* : eager to fight : PUGNACIOUS — **com•bat•ive•ly** *adv* — **com•bat•ive•ness** *n*

comb•er \ˈkō-mər\ *n* **1** : one that combs fibers (as of wool or flax) **2** : a long curling wave rolling in from the ocean

com•bi•na•tion \ˌkäm-bə-ˈnā-shən\ *n* **1** : a result or product of combining; *esp* : an alliance of persons or groups to achieve some end **2 a** : a sequence of letters or numbers chosen in setting a lock **b** : any of the different sets of individuals (as letters) that can be chosen from a population without regard to the order of the individuals within the set **3** : a one-piece undergarment for the upper and lower parts of the body **4 a** : the act or process of combining; *esp* : that of uniting to form a chemical compound **b** : the quality or state of being combined — **com•bi•na•tion•al** \-ˈnā-shnəl, -shən-l\ *adj*

com•bi•na•to•ri•al \ˌkäm-bə-nə-ˈtōr-ē-əl, kəm-bī-nə-, -ˈtȯr-\ *adj* : of or relating to the arrangement, operation on, and selection of mathematical elements within finite sets and configurations ⟨*combinatorial* mathematics⟩

[1]com•bine \kəm-ˈbīn\ *vb* **1 a** : to bring into close relationship : UNIFY **b** : to unite or cause to unite into a chemical compound **2** : to cause to mix together : BLEND **3** : to become one **4** : to act together [Middle French *combiner,* from Late Latin *combinare,* from Latin *com-* + *bini* "two by two"] **syn** see JOIN — **com•bin•able** \-ˈbī-nə-bəl\ *adj* — **com•bin•er** *n*

[2]com•bine \ˈkäm-ˌbīn\ *n* **1** : a combination to gain an often illicit end **2** : a harvesting machine that harvests, threshes, and cleans grain while moving over a field

[3]com•bine \ˈkäm-ˌbīn\ *vt* : to harvest with a combine

comb•ings \ˈkō-mingz\ *n pl* : loose hairs or fibers removed by a comb

com•bin•ing form \kəm-ˌbī-ning-\ *n* : a linguistic form that occurs only in compounds or derivatives (as *electro-* in *electromagnetic* or *mal-* in *malodorous*)

comb jelly *n* : CTENOPHORE

com•bo \ˈkäm-ˌbō\ *n, pl* **combos 1** : COMBINATION **2** : a small jazz or dance band [alteration of *combination*]

com•bust \kəm-ˈbəst\ *vb* : BURN [Latin *combustus,* past participle of *comburere* "to burn up", from *com-* + *urere* "to burn"]

com•bus•ti•ble \kəm-ˈbəs-tə-bəl\ *adj* **1** : capable of being burned **2** : catching fire or burning easily — **com•bus•ti•bil•i•ty** \-ˌbəs-tə-ˈbil-ət-ē\ *n* — **combustible** *n* — **com•bus•ti•bly** \-ˈbəs-tə-blē\ *adv*

com•bus•tion \kəm-ˈbəs-chən\ *n* **1** : the process of burning **2 a** : a chemical process (as an oxidation) accompanied by the evolution of heat and light **b** : a slower oxidation — **com•bus•tive** \-ˈbəs-tiv\ *adj*

com•bus•tor \-ˈbəs-tər\ *n* : a chamber (as in a jet engine) in which combustion occurs

come \kəm, ˈkəm\ *vi* **came** \ˈkām\; **come**; **com•ing** \ˈkəm-ing\ **1** : to move toward something : APPROACH ⟨*come* here⟩ **2** : to move toward or enter a scene of action or into a field of interest ⟨the police *came* to our rescue⟩ **3 a** : to reach the point of being or becoming ⟨the rope *came* untied⟩ **b** : AMOUNT ⟨the bill *came* to 10 dollars⟩ **4 a** : to take place ⟨the holiday *came* on Thursday⟩ **b** : to proceed as a consequence, effect, or conclusion ⟨our plans *came* to naught⟩ **5** : ORIGINATE, ARISE ⟨*comes* from sturdy stock⟩ **6** : to be obtainable ⟨an article that *comes* in three sizes⟩ **7** : to be attainable ⟨success *came* after hard work⟩ **8** : EXTEND, REACH ⟨a coat that *comes* to the knees⟩ **9 a** : to arrive at a particular place, end, result, or conclusion ⟨*came* home tired⟩ **b** : HAPPEN, OCCUR ⟨no harm will *come* to you⟩ **10** : to fall within a scope ⟨*comes* under the terms of the treaty⟩ **11** : BECOME ⟨things will *come* clear if we are patient⟩ [Old English *cuman*] — **come across** : to meet or find by chance — **come by** : ACQUIRE — **come into** : to acquire as an inheritance — **come into one's own** : to approach or reach one's appropriate level of importance, skill, or recognition — **come to be** : to arrive at or attain to being : BECOME — **come to pass** : HAPPEN — used with *it*

come about *vi* **1** : to come to pass : HAPPEN **2** : to change direction ⟨the wind has *come about* into the north⟩ **3** : to turn a boat onto a new tack

come around *vi* : to come round

come•back \ˈkəm-ˌbak\ *n* **1** : ²RETORT **2** : a return to a former position or condition (as of health or prosperity) : RECOVERY

co•me•di•an \kə-ˈmēd-ē-ən\ *n* **1** : an actor who plays in comedy **2** : a comical individual; *esp* : a professional entertainer who uses various physical or verbal means to be amusing

co•me•di•enne \kə-ˌmēd-ē-ˈen\ *n* : a woman who is a comedian [French *comédienne,* feminine of *comédien* "comedian", from *comédie* "comedy"]

com•e•do \ˈkäm-ə-ˌdō\ *n, pl* **com•e•do•nes** \ˌkäm-ə-ˈdō-ˌnēz\ : BLACKHEAD [Latin, "glutton", from *comedere* "to eat"]

come•down \ˈkəm-ˌdaun\ *n* : a descent in rank or dignity

come down \ˌkəm-ˈdaun\ *vi* : to become sick ⟨*came down* with the measles⟩

com•e•dy \ˈkäm-əd-ē\ *n, pl* **-dies** **1 a** : a light amusing play with a happy ending **b** : dramatic literature dealing with the comic or with the serious in a light or satirical manner **2 a** : a medieval narrative that ends happily ⟨Dante's Divine *Comedy*⟩ **b** : a literary work written in a comic style or treating a comic theme **3** : an amusing or ludicrous event [Middle French *comedie,* from Latin *comoedia,* from Greek *kōmōidia,* from *kōmos* "revel" + *aidein* "to sing"]

come in *vi* **1** : to be among the finishers (as of a race) **2** : to come into use or be useful **3** : to be the recipient of — used with *for* **4** : to reach maturity, fruitfulness, or production — **come in handy** : to be useful

come•ly \ˈkəm-lē\ *adj* **come•li•er**; **-est** : pleasing to look at : good-looking ⟨*comely* people⟩ [Old English *cȳmlic* "glorious", from *cȳme* "lively, fine"]

come–on \ˈkəm-ˌȯn, -ˌän\ *n* : INDUCEMENT 2, LURE

come out *vi* **1** : to come into public view **2** : to declare oneself ⟨*come out* for a candidate⟩ **3** : to turn out ⟨the cake *came out* splendidly⟩ **4** : to make one's debut **5** : SAY 1a — usually used with *with* ⟨*come out* with the truth⟩

com•er \ˈkəm-ər\ *n* **1** : one that comes ⟨all *comers*⟩ **2** : a promising newcomer

come round *vi* **1** : to return to a former condition; *esp* : to regain consciousness **2** : to change direction or opinion

¹co•mes•ti•ble \kə-ˈmes-tə-bəl\ *adj* : suitable for eating : EATABLE, EDIBLE [Middle French, derived from Latin *comedere* "to eat up", from *com-* + *edere* "to eat"]

²comestible *n* : FOOD 3 — usually used in pl.

com•et \ˈkäm-ət\ *n* : a celestial body that orbits the sun, that consists of a diffuse head usually surrounding a bright nucleus, and that often when in the part of its orbit near the sun develops a long tail which points away from the sun [Latin *cometa,* from Greek *komētēs,* literally, "long-haired", from *komē* "hair"]

come to *vi* : to recover consciousness

come•up•pance \kə-ˈməp-əns, ˌkə-\ *n* : a deserved rebuke or penalty : DESERTS

com•fit \ˈkəm-fət, ˈkäm-, ˈkəmp-, ˈkämp-\ *n* : a confection consisting of a piece of fruit, a root, or a seed coated and preserved with sugar [Middle French *confit,* from *confire* "to prepare", from Latin *conficere,* from *com-* + *facere* "to make"]

¹com•fort \ˈkəm-fərt, ˈkəmp-\ *n* **1** : acts or words that comfort **2** : the feeling of the one that is comforted ⟨find *comfort* in a parent's love⟩ **3** : something that makes a person comfortable ⟨the *comforts* of home⟩ — **com•fort•less** \-ləs\ *adj*

²comfort *vt* **1** : to give strength and hope to : CHEER **2** : to ease the grief or trouble of : CONSOLE [Old French *conforter,* from Late Latin *confortare* "to strengthen greatly", from Latin *com-* + *fortis* "strong"]

• **syn** CONSOLE, SOLACE: COMFORT implies giving cheer, strength, or encouragement as well as lessening pain; CONSOLE stresses the lessening of grief or sense of loss rather than giving relief or pleasure; SOLACE may suggest relieving loneliness or despondency as well as pain or grief.

com•fort•able \ˈkəm-fərt-ə-bəl, ˈkəmp-; ˈkəmf-tə-bəl, ˈkəmp-, ˈkəmpf-, ˈkəm-, -tər-\ *adj* **1** : giving comfort; *esp* : providing physical comfort **2** : more than adequate ⟨a *comfortable* income⟩ **3** : physically or mentally at ease — **com•fort•able•ness** *n* — **com•fort•ably** \-blē\ *adv*

com•fort•er \ˈkəm-fərt-ər, ˈkəmp-, -fət-\ *n* **1** : one that gives comfort **2 a** : a long narrow neck scarf **b** : QUILT 1

com•fy \ˈkəm-fē, ˈkəmp-\ : COMFORTABLE [alteration of *comfortable*]

¹com•ic \ˈkäm-ik\ *adj* **1 a** : of or relating to comedy **b** : acting in comedies **2** : causing laughter or amusement : FUNNY **3** : of or relating to comic strips [Latin *comicus,* from Greek *kōmikos,* from *kōmos* "revel"]

• **syn** COMIC, COMICAL mean causing laughter. COMIC applies especially to what arouses thoughtful amusement and particularly applies to comedy as a literary form ⟨a *comic* masterpiece of wit and satire⟩ COMICAL suggests the provoking of unrestrained spontaneous hilarity ⟨*comical* frustrations of a circus clown⟩

²comic *n* **1** : COMEDIAN 2 **2 a** : COMIC STRIP **b** *pl* : the part of a newspaper devoted to comic strips

com•i•cal \ˈkäm-i-kəl\ *adj* : provoking spontaneous laughter or amusement : DROLL **syn** see COMIC — **com•i•cal•i•ty** \ˌkäm-i-ˈkal-ət-ē\ *n* — **com•i•cal•ly** \ˈkäm-i-kə-lē, -klē\ *adv*

comic book *n* : a magazine made up of a series of comic strips

comic opera *n* : a musical dramatic work with spoken dialogue that is usually of light and amusing character

comic strip *n* : a sequence of cartoons that tell a story or part of a story

com•ing \ˈkəm-ing\ *adj* **1** : APPROACHING, NEXT ⟨the *coming* year⟩ **2** : gaining importance ⟨a *coming* young star⟩

Com•in•tern \ˈkäm-ən-ˌtərn\ *n* : the Communist International established in 1919 in an attempt to supersede the Second International of Socialist organizations [Russian *Komintern,* from *Kommunisticheskiĭ Intern*atsional "Communist International"]

co•mi•ty \ˈkäm-ət-ē, ˈkō-mət-\ *n, pl* **-ties** : courteous behavior : CIVILITY [Latin *comitas,* from *comis* "courteous"]

comity of nations : the code of courtesy and friendship by which nations get along together; *also* : the group of nations observing such a code

com•ma \ˈkäm-ə\ *n* : a punctuation mark , used chiefly to show separation of words or word groups within a sentence [Latin, "part of a sentence", from Greek *komma* "segment, clause", from *koptein* "to cut"]

comma bacillus *n* : the bacterium that causes Asiatic cholera

comma fault *n* : the careless or unjustified use of a comma between coordinate main clauses not connected by a conjunction — called also *comma splice*

¹com•mand \kə-ˈmand\ *vb* **1 a** : to direct authoritatively : ORDER, GOVERN **b** : to have authority and control of a military force or post : be commander of **2 a** : to have at one's disposal **b** : to demand as one's due : EXACT ⟨*commands* a high fee⟩ **c**

: to overlook from a strategic position ⟨the hill *commands* the town⟩ [Old French *comander,* from Latin *commendare* "to commit to one's charge, commend"]

[2]**command** *n* **1 :** the act of commanding ⟨march on *command*⟩ **2 :** an order given **3 a :** the ability to control **:** MASTERY ⟨has *command* of the subject⟩ **b :** the authority or right to command **c :** the power to dominate **d :** facility in using ⟨a good *command* of French⟩ **4 :** the personnel, area, or unit under a commander **5 :** a position from which military operations are directed — called also *command post*

[3]**command** *adj* **:** done on command or request ⟨a *command* performance⟩

com•man•dant \ˈkäm-ən-ˌdant, -ˌdänt\ *n* **:** COMMANDING OFFICER

com•man•deer \ˌkäm-ən-ˈdiər\ *vt* **:** to take arbitrary or forcible possession of especially for military purposes [Afrikaans *kommandeer,* from French *commander* "to command"]

com•mand•er \kə-ˈman-dər\ *n* **1 :** one in official command; *esp* **:** COMMANDING OFFICER **2 :** an officer rank in the Navy and Coast Guard above lieutenant commander and below captain — **com•mand•er•ship** \-ˌship\ *n*

commander in chief : one who holds the supreme command of an armed force

commanding officer *n* **:** a military or naval officer in command of a unit or post

com•mand•ment \kə-ˈman-mənt, -ˈmand-\ *n* **:** something commanded; *esp* **:** one of the biblical Ten Commandments

command module *n* **:** a space vehicle module designed to carry the crew, the chief communication equipment, and the equipment for reentry

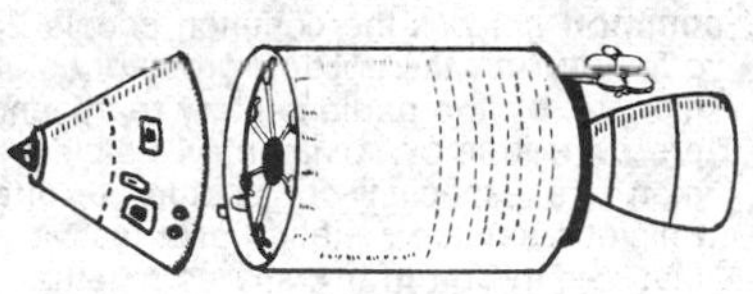
command module separating from service module

com•man•do \kə-ˈman-dō\ *n, pl* **-dos** *or* **-does 1 :** a military unit trained and organized for surprise raids into enemy territory **2 :** a member of a specialized raiding unit [Afrikaans *kommando,* from Dutch *commando* "command", from Spanish *comando,* from *comander* "to command", from French *commander*]

command sergeant major *n* **:** an enlisted rank in the Army above first sergeant

comme il faut \ˌkəm-ˌēl-ˈfō, -ˌē-\ *adj* **:** conforming to accepted standards **:** PROPER [French, literally, "as it should be"]

com•mem•o•rate \kə-ˈmem-ə-ˌrāt\ *vt* **1 :** to call to remembrance **2 :** to mark by a ceremony **:** OBSERVE **3 :** to be a memorial of [Latin *commemorare,* from *com-* + *memorare* "to remind of", from *memor* "mindful"] **syn** see KEEP — **com•mem•o•ra•tor** \-ˌrāt-ər\ *n*

com•mem•o•ra•tion \kə-ˌmem-ə-ˈrā-shən\ *n* **1 :** the act of commemorating **2 :** something (as a ceremony) that commemorates

com•mem•o•ra•tive \kə-ˈmem-ə-ˌrāt-iv, -rət-\ *adj* **:** intended to commemorate ⟨a *commemorative* stamp⟩ — **commemorative** *n* — **com•mem•o•ra•tive•ly** *adv*

com•mence \kə-ˈmens\ *vb* **:** to bring or come into activity, being, or operation ⟨*commence* firing⟩ ⟨work will *commence* next week⟩ [Middle French *comencer,* from Latin *com-* + *initiare* "to initiate"] — **com•menc•er** *n*

com•mence•ment \-ˈmens-mənt\ *n* **1 :** an act, instance, or time of commencing **2 a :** the ceremonies or the day for conferring degrees or diplomas on graduates of a school or college **b :** the period of activities at this time

com•mend \kə-ˈmend\ *vt* **1 :** to give into another's care **:** ENTRUST **2 :** to speak of with approval **:** PRAISE [Latin *commendare,* from *com-* + *mandare* "to entrust"] — **com•mend•able** \-ˈmen-də-bəl\ *adj* — **com•mend•ably** \-də-blē\ *adv*

com•men•da•tion \ˌkäm-ən-ˈdā-shən, -ˌen-\ *n* **1 :** an act of commending **2 :** something (as a formal citation) that commends — **com•men•da•to•ry** \kə-ˈmen-də-ˌtōr-ē, -ˌtȯr-\ *adj*

com•men•sal \kə-ˈmen-səl\ *adj* **:** relating to or living in a state of commensalism [Medieval Latin *commensalis* "of those who habitually eat together", from Latin *com-* + *mensa* "table"] — **commensal** *n* — **com•men•sal•ly** \-sə-lē\ *adv*

com•men•sal•ism \-sə-ˌliz-əm\ *n* **:** a relation between two kinds of organisms in which one obtains a benefit (as food) from the other without either damaging or benefiting it

com•men•su•ra•ble \kə-ˈmens-rə-bəl, -ˈmench-, -ə-rə-\ *adj* **:** having a common measure; *esp* **:** divisible by a common unit a whole number of times — **com•men•su•ra•bly** \-blē\ *adv*

com•men•su•rate \kə-ˈmens-rət, -ˈmench-, -ə-rət\ *adj* **1 :** equal in measure or extent **2 :** PROPORTIONATE ⟨a job *commensurate* with one's abilities⟩ [Late Latin *commensuratus,* from Latin *com-* + *mensura* "measure"] — **com•men•su•rate•ly** *adv* — **com•men•su•ra•tion** \-ˌmen-sə-ˈrā-shən, -ˌmench-ə-ˈrā-\ *n*

[1]**com•ment** \ˈkäm-ˌent\ *n* **1 :** an expression of opinion either in speech or writing **2 :** a usually critical or explanatory remark [Late Latin *commentum,* from Latin, "invention", from *commentus,* past participle of *comminisci* "to invent"]

[2]**comment** *vi* **:** to make a comment **:** REMARK

com•men•tary \ˈkäm-ən-ˌter-ē\ *n, pl* **-tar•ies :** a series of comments or notes; *also* **:** a book composed of such material ⟨Caesar's *Commentaries*⟩

com•men•tate \ˈkäm-ən-ˌtāt\ *vb* **:** to give a commentary on **:** act as a commentator

com•men•ta•tor \-ˌtāt-ər\ *n* **:** one that gives a commentary; *esp* **:** one who reports and discusses news on radio or television

com•merce \ˈkäm-ˌərs, -ərs\ *n* **1 :** interchange of ideas, opinions, or sentiments **2 :** the exchange or buying and selling of goods on a large scale involving transportation from place to place **:** TRADE [Middle French, from Latin *commercium,* from *com-* + *merx* "merchandise"] **syn** see BUSINESS

[1]**com•mer•cial** \kə-ˈmər-shəl\ *adj* **1 a :** of or relating to commerce **b :** engaged in commerce ⟨a *commercial* city⟩ **2 a :** viewed with regard to profit ⟨a *commercial* success⟩ **b :** designed for profit; *esp* **:** designed for mass appeal ⟨the *commercial* theater⟩ **3 :** emphasizing skills and subjects useful in business ⟨*commercial* education⟩ **4 :** paid for by advertisers ⟨*commercial* TV⟩ — **com•mer•cial•ly** \-ˈmərsh-lē, -ə-lē\ *adv*

[2]**commercial** *n* **:** an advertisement broadcast on radio or television

commercial bank *n* **:** a bank that accepts deposits withdrawable without notice and creates credit through short-term loans mainly to business

com•mer•cial•ism \kə-ˈmər-shə-ˌliz-əm\ *n* **:** a spirit, method, or practice characteristic of business — **com•mer•cial•is•tic** \-ˌmər-shə-ˈlis-tik\ *adj*

com•mer•cial•ize \kə-ˈmər-shə-ˌlīz\ *vt* **1 :** to manage on a business basis for profit **2 :** to exploit for profit ⟨*commercialize* Christmas⟩ — **com•mer•cial•iza•tion** \-ˌmər-shə-lə-ˈzā-shən\ *n*

commercial paper *n* **:** short-term negotiable instruments arising out of commercial transactions

commercial traveler *n* **:** TRAVELING SALESMAN

com•mi•na•tion \ˌkäm-ə-ˈnā-shən\ *n* **:** DENUNCIATION [Latin *comminatio,* from *comminari* "to threaten", from *com-* + *minari* "to threaten"] — **com•mi•na•to•ry** \ˈkäm-ə-nə-ˌtōr-ē, -ˌtȯr-; kə-ˈmin-ə-, -ˈmīn-\ *adj*

com•min•gle \kə-ˈming-gəl\ *vb* **:** MINGLE 1, MIX ⟨*commingle* two liquids⟩

com•mi•nute \ˈkäm-ə-ˌnüt, -nyüt\ *vt* **:** to reduce to minute particles **:** PULVERIZE [Latin *comminuere,* from *com-* + *minuere* "to lessen"] — **com•mi•nu•tion** \ˌkäm-ə-nü-shən, -ˈnyü-\ *n*

com•mis•er•ate \kə-ˈmiz-ə-ˌrāt\ *vb* **:** to feel or express sorrow, compassion, or sympathy for **:** SYMPATHIZE [Latin *commiserari,* from *com-* + *miserari* "to pity", from *miser* "wretched"] — **com•mis•er•a•tion** \-ˌmiz-ə-ˈrā-shən\ *n* — **com•mis•er•a•tive** \-ˈmiz-ə-ˌrāt-iv\ *adj*

com•mis•sar \ˈkäm-ə-ˌsär\ *n* **1 :** a Communist party official assigned to a military unit to teach party principles and policies and to ensure party loyalty **2 :** the head of a government department in the Soviet Union from 1917 to 1946 [Russian *komissar,* from German *kommissar* "commissary", from Medieval Latin *commissarius*]

com•mis•sar•i•at \ˌkäm-ə-ˈser-ē-ət, -ˈsar-, *especially for 2* -ˈsär-\ *n* **1 :** a system for supplying an army with food **2 :** a government department in the Soviet Union from 1917 to 1946 [New Latin *commissariatus,* from Medieval Latin *commissarius*

\ə\ **abut**	\au̇\ **out**	\i\ **tip**	\ȯ\ **saw**	\u̇\ **foot**
\ər\ **further**	\ch\ **chin**	\ī\ **life**	\ȯi\ **coin**	\y\ **yet**
\a\ **mat**	\e\ **pet**	\j\ **job**	\th\ **thin**	\yü\ **few**
\ā\ **take**	\ē\ **easy**	\ng\ **sing**	\t͟h\ **this**	\yu̇\ **cure**
\ä\ **cot, cart**	\g\ **go**	\ō\ **bone**	\ü\ **food**	\zh\ **vision**

"commissary"; sense 2 from Russian *komissariat,* from German *kommissariat,* from New Latin *commissariatus*]

com•mis•sary \'käm-ə-,ser-ē\ *n, pl* **-sar•ies 1 :** a person to whom a duty or office is entrusted by a superior **2 :** a store supplying provisions especially to military personnel and dependents **3 :** a lunchroom in a motion-picture studio [Medieval Latin *commissarius,* from Latin *commissus,* past participle of *committere* "to commit"]

[1]com•mis•sion \kə-'mish-ən\ *n* **1 a :** a formal order granting the power to perform various acts or duties **b :** a certificate conferring military rank and authority; *also* **:** the rank and authority conferred **2 :** an authorization or command to act in a prescribed manner or to perform prescribed acts **3 a :** authority to act as agent for another **b :** a task or matter entrusted to an agent **4 a :** a group of persons directed to perform a duty **b :** a government agency having administrative, legislative, or judicial powers **c :** a city council having legislative and executive functions **5 :** an act of committing something (as a crime) **6 :** a fee paid to an agent or employee for transacting a piece of business or performing a service ⟨a brokerage *commission*⟩ [Middle French, from Latin *commissio* "act of bringing together", from *committere* "to commit"] — **in commission 1 :** ready for active service — used of a ship **2 :** in use or ready for use — **out of commission 1 :** out of service or use **2 :** out of working order

[2]commission *vt* **-mis•sioned; -mis•sion•ing** \-'mish-ning, -ə-ning\ **1 :** to confer a commission on **2 :** to order to be made **3 :** to put (a ship) in commission

com•mis•sion•aire \kə-,mish-ə-'naər, -'neər\ *n, chiefly British* **:** a uniformed attendant [French *commissionnaire,* from *commission* "commission"]

com•mis•sion•er \kə-'mish-nər, -ə-nər\ *n* **1 :** a member of a commission **2 :** an official in charge of a government department ⟨*Commissioner* of Public Safety⟩

commission merchant *n* **:** one who buys or sells another's goods for a commission

com•mis•sure \'käm-ə-,shùr\ *n* **:** a connecting band of nerve tissue in the brain or spinal cord [Latin *commissura* "a joining", from *committere* "to connect, commit"] — **com•mis•sur•al** \,käm-ə-'shùr-əl\ *adj*

com•mit \kə-'mit\ *vt* **com•mit•ted; com•mit•ting 1 a :** to give in trust ⟨*commit* power to the legislature⟩ **b :** to place in a prison or mental institution **c :** to consign for preservation, disposal, or safekeeping ⟨*commit* it to memory⟩ **d :** to refer (as a legislative bill) to a committee for consideration and report **2 :** to bring about **:** PERFORM ⟨*commit* a crime⟩ **3 a :** OBLIGATE, BIND ⟨was *committed* to defend them⟩ **b :** to pledge or assign to a particular course or use **c :** to express the opinion of ⟨refused to *commit* themselves on the issue⟩ [Latin *committere* "to connect, entrust", from *com-* + *mittere* "to send"] — **com•mit•ta•ble** \-'mit-ə-bəl\ *adj*

com•mit•ment \kə-'mit-mənt\ *n* **1 :** an act of committing: as **a :** a consignment to a penal or mental institution **b :** an act of referring a matter to a legislative committee **2 a :** an agreement or pledge to do something in the future **b :** something pledged

com•mit•tal \kə-'mit-l\ *n* **:** COMMITMENT 1a

com•mit•tee \kə-'mit-ē\ *n* **1 :** a body of persons delegated or elected to consider or take action on some matter **2 :** a self-constituted organization for the promotion of a common goal

com•mit•tee•man \-mən, -,man\ *n* **1 :** a member of a committee **2 :** a party leader of a ward or precinct

committee of the whole : the whole membership of a legislative house sitting as a committee and operating under informal rules

com•mit•tee•wom•an \-,wùm-ən\ *n* **1 :** a woman member of a committee **2 :** a woman party leader of a ward or precinct

com•mix \kə-'miks, kä-\ *vb* **:** to mix or mingle together **:** BLEND

com•mix•ture \-chər\ *n* **:** MIXTURE 2a, COMPOUND

com•mode \kə-'mōd\ *n* **1 a :** a low chest of drawers **b :** a movable washstand with a cupboard underneath **2 :** TOILET 2b [French *commode* "suitable, convenient", from Latin *commodus,* from *com-* + *modus* "measure"]

com•mo•di•ous \kə-'mōd-ē-əs\ *adj* **1** *archaic* **:** HANDY, SERVICEABLE **2 :** comfortably or conveniently spacious **:** ROOMY [Middle French *commodieux,* from Medieval Latin *commodiosus,* from Latin *commodum* "convenience", from *commodus* "convenient"] — **com•mo•di•ous•ly** *adv* — **com•mo•dious•ness** *n*

com•mod•i•ty \kə-'mäd-ət-ē\ *n, pl* **-ties :** an economic good: as **a :** a product of agriculture or mining **b :** an article exchanged in commerce [Middle French *commodité* "convenience, advantage", from Latin *commoditas,* from *commodus* "convenient"]

com•mo•dore \'käm-ə-,dōr, -,dòr\ *n* **1 :** a former officer rank in the Navy above captain and below rear admiral **2 :** the senior captain of a line of merchant ships **3 :** the chief officer of a yacht club [probably from Dutch *commandeur* "commander", from French]

[1]com•mon \'käm-ən\ *adj* **1 :** having to do with, belonging to, or used by everybody **:** PUBLIC ⟨work for the *common* good⟩ **2 a :** belonging to or shared by two or more individuals or by the members of a group ⟨a *common* ancestor⟩ **b :** belonging equally to two or more mathematical entities ⟨two angles with a *common* side⟩ **c :** formed of or dividing into two or more branches ⟨*common* carotid artery⟩ **3 :** widely or generally known, met, or seen ⟨facts of *common* knowledge⟩ **4 :** FREQUENT, FAMILIAR ⟨a *common* sight⟩ **5 a :** not above the average in rank, merit, or social position ⟨a *common* soldier⟩ ⟨the *common* people⟩ **b :** falling below ordinary standards **:** SECOND-RATE **c :** lacking refinement **:** VULGAR **6 a :** being either masculine or feminine ⟨*common* gender⟩ **b :** being a noun that designates any of a class of beings or things **c :** being a grammatical case used both for the subject and the object ⟨the word *man* in "the man is tall", "watch the man", and "with the man" is in the *common* case⟩ [Old French *commun,* from Latin *communis*] **syn** see RECIPROCAL — **com•mon•ly** *adv* — **com•mon•ness** \-ən-nəs\ *n*

[2]common *n* **1** *pl* **:** the common people **2** *pl* **:** a dining hall **3** *pl, often cap* **a :** the political group or estate comprising the commoners **b :** the parliamentary representatives of the commoners **c :** HOUSE OF COMMONS **4 :** a piece of land subject to common use especially for pasture — often used in pl. **5 a :** a religious service suitable for a festival **b :** the ordinary of the Mass — **in common :** shared together

com•mon•al•i•ty \,käm-ə-'nal-ət-ē\ *or* **com•mon•al•ty** \'käm-ə-nəl-tē\ *n, pl* **-ties :** the common people

common carrier *n* **:** an individual or corporation engaged in transporting persons, goods, or messages for money

common cold *n* **:** an acute virus disease of the upper respiratory tract marked by congestion and inflammation of mucous membranes and usually accompanied by excessive secretion of mucus and coughing and sneezing

common denominator *n* **1 :** a common multiple of the denominators of a number of fractions **2 :** a common trait or theme

common difference *n* **:** the difference between two consecutive terms of an arithmetic progression

common divisor *n* **:** a number or expression that divides two or more numbers or expressions without remainder — called also *common factor*

com•mon•er \'käm-ə-nər\ *n* **:** one of the common people **:** a person not of noble rank

common fraction *n* **:** a fraction in which both numerator and denominator are expressed as integers

common law *n* **:** the body of law developed in England primarily from judicial decisions based on custom and precedent, unwritten in statute or code, and forming the basis of the legal system in most jurisdictions of the United States and parts of the world under British control or influence

common-law marriage *n* **:** a marriage relationship created by agreement and usually cohabitation between a man and a woman without religious or civil ceremony

common logarithm *n* **:** a logarithm whose base is 10

common market *n* **:** an economic unit formed to remove trade barriers among member nations

common multiple *n* **:** a multiple of each of two or more numbers or expressions

common noun *n* **:** a noun (as *chair* or *fear*) that names a class of persons or things or any individual of a class

[1]com•mon•place \'käm-ən-,plās\ *n* **1 :** an obvious or trite remark **2 :** a thing so commonly encountered as to be taken for granted

[2]commonplace *adj* **:** lacking originality, freshness, or interest

common ratio *n* **:** the ratio of each term of a geometric progression to the term preceding it

common room *n* **1 :** a lounge available to all members of a residential community **2 :** a room in a college for the use of the faculty

common salt *n* : SALT 1a
common school *n* : a free public school
common sense *n* : sound and prudent but often unsophisticated judgment
common stock *n* : capital stock other than preferred stock
common time *n* : four beats to a measure in music
common touch *n* : the gift of appealing to or arousing the sympathetic interest of people of all walks of life
com•mon•weal \ˈkäm-ən-ˌwēl\ *n* **1** : the general welfare **2** *archaic* : COMMONWEALTH
com•mon•wealth \-ˌwelth\ *n* **1** : a political unit whose aim is the common good of all the people **2** *cap* : the English state from the death of Charles I in 1649 to the Restoration in 1660 **3** : a state of the United States — used officially of Kentucky, Massachusetts, Pennsylvania, and Virginia **4** *cap* : a federal union of states — used officially of Australia **5** *often cap* : an association of self-governing states having a common political and cultural background and united by a common allegiance ⟨the British *Commonwealth*⟩ **6** *often cap* : a political unit having local self-government but voluntarily united with the United States — used officially of Puerto Rico
com•mo•tion \kə-ˈmō-shən\ *n* **1** : disturbed or violent motion : AGITATION **2 a** : noisy excitement and confusion **b** : a confused noisy disturbance : TUMULT [Middle French, from Latin *commotio,* from *commovēre* "to agitate", from *com-* + *movēre* "to move"]
com•mu•nal \kə-ˈmyün-l, ˈkäm-yən-l\ *adj* **1** : of or relating to a commune or community **2 a** : characterized by collective ownership and use of property **b** : shared, participated in, or used in common by members of a group or community
[1]**com•mune** \kə-ˈmyün\ *vi* **1** : to receive Communion **2** : to communicate intimately ⟨went off into the woods to *commune* with nature⟩ [Middle French *comunier* "to converse, administer or receive Communion", from Latin *communicare* "to impart, participate", from *communis* "common"]
[2]**com•mune** \ˈkäm-ˌyün; kə-ˈmyün, kä-\ *n* **1** : the smallest administrative district of many countries especially in Europe **2 a** : a medieval municipality **b** : a rural community (as the Russian mir) organized on a communal basis **3** *cap* **a** : the French government elected by representatives of the communes in 1792 **b** : a revolutionary government in Paris from March 18 to May 28, 1871 **4** : a large collectivized farm in the People's Republic of China [French, from Middle French *comugne,* from Medieval Latin *communia,* from Latin *communis* "common"]
com•mu•ni•ca•ble \kə-ˈmyü-ni-kə-bəl\ *adj* : capable of being communicated : TRANSMITTABLE ⟨*communicable* diseases⟩ — **com•mu•ni•ca•bil•i•ty** \-ˌmyü-ni-kə-ˈbil-ət-ē\ *n* — **com•mu•ni•ca•ble•ness** \-ˈmyü-ni-kə-bəl-nəs\ *n* — **com•mu•ni•ca•bly** \-blē\ *adv*
com•mu•ni•cant \kə-ˈmyü-ni-kənt\ *n* **1 a** : a person who receives Communion **b** : a church member **2** : a person who communicates — **communicant** *adj*
com•mu•ni•cate \kə-ˈmyü-nə-ˌkāt\ *vb* **1 a** : to make known ⟨*communicate* the news⟩ **b** : TRANSFER, TRANSMIT ⟨*communicate* a disease⟩ **2** : to receive Communion **3** : to be in communication **4** : JOIN, CONNECT ⟨the rooms *communicate*⟩ [Latin *communicare* "to impart, participate", from *communis* "common"] — **com•mu•ni•ca•tor** \-ˌkāt-ər\ *n*
com•mu•ni•ca•tion \kə-ˌmyü-nə-ˈkā-shən\ *n* **1** : an act or instance of transmitting **2 a** : information communicated **b** : MESSAGE 1 **3** : an exchange of information **4** *pl* **a** : a system (as of telephones) for communicating **b** : a system of routes for moving troops, supplies, and vehicles **5** *pl* : the business or technology of the transmission of information **6** : the interchange of ideas and opinions
com•mu•ni•ca•tive \kə-ˈmyü-nə-ˌkāt-iv, -ni-kət-\ *adj* **1** : tending to communicate : TALKATIVE **2** : of or relating to communication — **com•mu•ni•ca•tive•ly** *adv* — **com•mu•ni•ca•tive•ness** *n*
com•mu•nion \kə-ˈmyü-nyən\ *n* **1 a** : *cap* : a Christian sacrament in which bread and wine are partaken of as a commemoration of the death of Christ **b** : the act of receiving the sacrament **c** *cap* : the part of a religious service in which the sacrament is received **2** : COMMUNICATION 1 **3** : a body of Christians having a common faith
com•mu•ni•qué \kə-ˈmyü-nə-ˌkā, -ˌmyü-nə-ˈ\ *n* : an official communication : BULLETIN [French, from *communiquer* "to communicate", from Latin *communicare*]
com•mu•nism \ˈkäm-yə-ˌniz-əm\ *n* **1** : a social system in which property and goods are owned in common; *also* : a theory advocating such a system **2** *cap* **a** : a doctrine based upon revolutionary Marxian socialism and Marxism-Leninism that is the official ideology of the Union of Soviet Socialist Republics, the Chinese People's Republic, and several satellite nations **b** : a totalitarian system of government in which a single party controls state-owned means of production with the professed aim of establishing a stateless society
com•mu•nist \ˈkäm-yə-nəst\ *n* **1** : an adherent or advocate of communism **2** *cap* : a member or adherent of a Communist party or movement — **communist** *adj, often cap* — **com•mu•nis•tic** \ˌkäm-yə-ˈnis-tik\ *adj, often cap* — **com•mu•nis•ti•cal•ly** \-ti-kə-lē, -klē\ *adv*
com•mu•ni•ty \kə-ˈmyü-nət-ē\ *n, pl* **-ties 1 a** : the people living in an area; *also* : the area itself **b** : an interacting population of various kinds of individuals (as species) in a common location **c** : a group of people with common interests living together within a larger society ⟨the Christian *community*⟩ **d** : a body of persons or nations having a history or social, economic, or political interests or policies in common ⟨the European Coal and Steel *Community*⟩ **2 a** : joint ownership or participation ⟨*community* of goods⟩ **b** : LIKENESS ⟨their works showed a *community* of style⟩ **c** : shared activity **d** : a social state or condition
community center *n* : a building or group of buildings for a community's educational and recreational activities
community chest *n* : a general fund made up of individual subscriptions in a community to provide public aid
community college *n* : a public junior college that designs its instruction to meet the needs of the community
com•mu•nize \ˈkäm-yə-ˌnīz\ *vb* **1** : to place under common ownership **2** : to organize according to Communist principles — **com•mu•ni•za•tion** \ˌkam-yə-nə-ˈzā-shən\ *n*
com•mu•ta•tion \ˌkäm-yə-ˈtā-shən\ *n* **1** : EXCHANGE 2, REPLACEMENT; *esp* : a substitution of one form of payment for another **2** : a reduction of a legal penalty **3** : an act of commuting **4** : the process of reversing the direction of an electric circuit
commutation ticket *n* : a transportation ticket sold at a reduced rate for a fixed number of trips over the same route during a limited period
com•mu•ta•tive \ˈkäm-yə-ˌtāt-iv, kə-ˈmyüt-ət-\ *adj* : combining elements or having elements that combine in such a manner that the result is independent of the order in which the elements are taken ⟨addition of the real numbers is *commutative* but subtraction is not⟩ — **com•mu•ta•tiv•i•ty** \kə-ˌmyüt-ə-ˈtiv-ət-ē\ *n*
com•mu•ta•tor \ˈkäm-yə-ˌtāt-ər\ *n* : a device for reversing the direction of an electric current so that the alternating currents generated in the armature of a dynamo are converted to direct current
com•mute \kə-ˈmyüt\ *vb* **1 a** : INTERCHANGE, SUBSTITUTE **b** : CHANGE 1, ALTER **2** : to substitute one form of obligation for another **3** : to substitute a less severe penalty for a greater one ⟨*commute* a death sentence to life imprisonment⟩ **4 a** : to travel by use of a commutation ticket **b** : to travel back and forth regularly [Latin *commutare* "to change, exchange", from *com-* + *mutare* "to change"] — **com•mut•able** \-ˈmyüt-ə-bəl\ *adj* — **com•mut•er** *n*
[1]**com•pact** \kəm-ˈpakt, ˈkäm-ˌ\ *adj* **1** : closely united, collected, or packed **2** : arranged or designed so as to save space ⟨a *compact* house⟩ **3** : not wordy : CONCISE **4** : not rangy or lanky in appearance ⟨a *compact* body⟩ [Latin *compactus* "firmly put together", from past participle of *compingere* "to put together", from *com-* + *pangere* "to fasten"] — **com•pact•ly** *adv* — **com•pact•ness** \-ˈpakt-nəs, -ˈpak-; -ˌpakt-, -ˌpak-\ *n*
[2]**compact** *vb* **1** : CONSOLIDATE 3 **2** : FORM 1, COMPOSE **3** : to make or become compact — **com•pac•tor** *or* **com•pact•er** *n*
[3]**com•pact** \ˈkäm-ˌpakt\ *n* **1** : a small case for cosmetics **2** : a relatively small automobile
[4]**com•pact** \ˈkäm-ˌpakt\ *n* : an agreement (as a contract or treaty) between two or more parties [Latin *compactum,* from *compacisci* "to make an agreement", from *com-* + *pacisci* "to contract"]

\ə\ **abut**	\aú\ **out**	\i\ **tip**	\ó\ **saw**	\ú\ **foot**
\ər\ **further**	\ch\ **chin**	\ī\ **life**	\ói\ **coin**	\y\ **yet**
\a\ **mat**	\e\ **pet**	\j\ **job**	\th\ **thin**	\yü\ **few**
\ā\ **take**	\ē\ **easy**	\ng\ **sing**	\th\ **this**	\yú\ **cure**
\ä\ **cot, cart**	\g\ **go**	\ō\ **bone**	\ü\ **food**	\zh\ **vision**

com·pac·tion \kəm-ˈpak-shən\ *n* : the act or process of compacting : the state of being compacted

[1]**com·pan·ion** \kəm-ˈpan-yən\ *n* **1** : one much in the company of another : COMRADE **2 a** : one of a pair of matching things **b** : one employed to live with and serve another [Old French *comagnon,* from Late Latin *companio,* from Latin *com-* + *panis* "bread, food"]

[2]**companion** *n* **1** : a covering at the top of a companionway **2** : COMPANIONWAY [by folk etymology from Dutch *kampanje* "poop deck"]

com·pan·ion·able \kəm-ˈpan-yə-nə-bəl\ *adj* : fitted to be a companion : SOCIABLE — **com·pan·ion·ably** \-blē\ *adv*

companion cell *n* : a living nucleated cell adjacent to a sieve tube of a vascular plant

com·pan·ion·ship \kəm-ˈpan-yən-ˌship\ *n* : FELLOWSHIP

com·pan·ion·way \-ˌwā\ *n* : a ship's stairway from one deck to another

com·pa·ny \ˈkəmp-nē, -ə-nē\ *n, pl* **-nies 1 a** : association with another : FELLOWSHIP **b** : persons with whom one regularly associates **c** : VISITORS **2 a** : a group of persons or things **b** : a body of soldiers; *esp* : a unit especially of infantry consisting usually of a headquarters and two or more platoons **c** : an organization of musical or dramatic performers ⟨an opera *company*⟩ **d** : the officers and men of a ship **e** : a fire-fighting unit **3 a** : an association of persons carrying on a commercial or industrial enterprise **b** : those members of a partnership whose names do not appear in the firm name ⟨Doe and *Company*⟩ [Old French *compagnie,* from *compain* "companion", from Late Latin *companio*]

company union *n* : an unaffiliated labor union of the employees of a single firm; *esp* : one dominated by the employer

com·pa·ra·ble \ˈkäm-pə-rə-bəl, -prə-\ *adj* **1** : capable of being compared **2** : EQUIVALENT, SIMILAR ⟨fabrics of *comparable* quality⟩ — **com·pa·ra·bly** \-blē\ *adv*

[1]**com·par·a·tive** \kəm-ˈpar-ət-iv\ *adj* **1** : of, relating to, or constituting the degree of grammatical comparison that denotes increase in the quality, quantity, or relation expressed by an adjective or adverb **2 a** : measured by comparison : RELATIVE ⟨a *comparative* stranger⟩ **b** : involving systematic study of comparable elements ⟨*comparative* anatomy⟩ — **com·par·ative·ly** *adv* — **com·par·a·tive·ness** *n*

[2]**comparative** *n* : the comparative degree or a comparative form in a language ⟨*taller* is the *comparative* of *tall*⟩

com·par·a·tor \kəm-ˈpar-ət-ər, ˈkäm-pə-ˌrāt-\ *n* : an instrument for comparing something with a like thing or with a standard measure

[1]**com·pare** \kəm-ˈpaər, -ˈpeər\ *vb* **1** : to represent as similar : LIKEN ⟨*compare* an anthill to a town⟩ **2** : to examine in order to discover likenesses or differences ⟨*compare* two bicycles⟩ **3** : to be worthy of comparison ⟨roller-skating does not *compare* with ice-skating⟩ **4** : to inflect or modify (an adjective or adverb) according to the degrees of comparison [Middle French *comparer,* from Latin *comparare* "to couple, compare", from *compar* "like", from *com-* + *par* "equal"]

• **syn** COMPARE, CONTRAST mean to set side by side in order to show differences and likenesses. COMPARE implies an aim of showing relative values and stresses similarities; CONTRAST implies an emphasis on differences or especially opposite qualities.

[2]**compare** *n* : the possibility of comparing ⟨beauty beyond *compare*⟩

com·par·i·son \kəm-ˈpar-ə-sən\ *n* **1** : the act of comparing : the state of being compared **2** : an examination of two or more objects to find the likenesses and differences between them **3** : change in the form of an adjective or an adverb (as by having *-er* or *-est* added or *more* or *most* prefixed) to show different levels of quality, quantity, or relation

com·part·ment \kəm-ˈpärt-mənt\ *n* **1** : one of the parts into which an enclosed space is divided **2** : a separate division or section — **com·part·ment·ed** \-ˌment-əd\ *adj*

com·part·men·tal·ize \kəm-ˌpärt-ˈment-l-ˌīz\ *vt* : to separate into compartments — **com·part·men·tal·iza·tion** \-ˌment-l-ə-ˈzā-shən\ *n*

[1]**com·pass** \ˈkəm-pəs, ˈkäm-\ *vt* **1** : to travel entirely around **2 a** : to bring about : ACHIEVE **b** : to get into one's power or possession : OBTAIN **3** : to understand fully : COMPREHEND [Old French *compasser* "to measure", from Latin *com-* + *passus* "pace"]

[2]**compass** *n* **1 a** : an often rounded or curved boundary limit : CIRCUMFERENCE **b** : an enclosed space **c** : RANGE, SCOPE ⟨the *compass* of a voice⟩ **2 a** : a device for determining directions by means of a magnetic needle turning freely on a pivot and pointing to the magnetic north **b** : any of various nonmagnetic devices that indicate direction **c** : an instrument for making circles or transferring measurements that consists of two pointed branches joined at the top by a pivot — usually used in pl.; called also *pair of compasses*

compass card *n* : the circular card attached to the needles of a mariner's compass on which are marked 32 points of the compass and the 360° of the circle

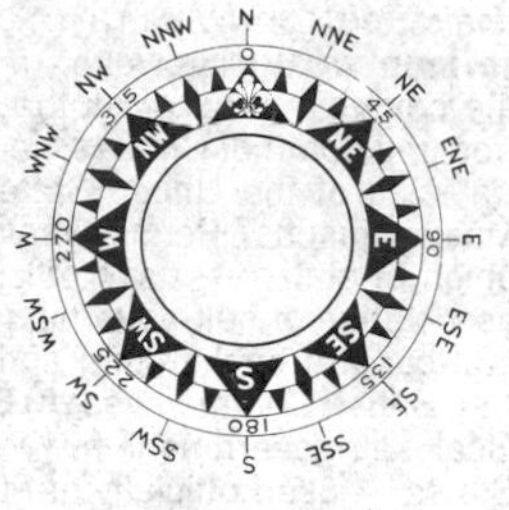

compass card

com·pas·sion \kəm-ˈpash-ən\ *n* : sorrow or pity aroused by the suffering or misfortune of another : SYMPATHY, MERCY [Late Latin *compassio,* from *compati* "to sympathize", from Latin *com-* + *pati* "to suffer"]

com·pas·sion·ate \kəm-ˈpash-nət, -ə-nət\ *adj* : having or showing compassion : SYMPATHETIC — **com·pas·sion·ate·ly** *adv*

com·pat·i·ble \kəm-ˈpat-ə-bəl\ *adj* **1** : capable of existing together in harmony ⟨*compatible* colors⟩ **2** : able to cross-fertilize freely ⟨*compatible* plants⟩ **3** : free from adverse or unwanted effects when present together ⟨*compatible* drugs⟩ [Middle French, from Medieval Latin *compatibilis* "sympathetic", from Latin *compati* "to sympathize"] — **com·pat·i·bil·i·ty** \-ˌpat-ə-ˈbil-ət-ē\ *n* — **com·pat·i·bly** \-ˈpat-ə-blē\ *adv*

com·pa·tri·ot \kəm-ˈpā-trē-ət, -ˌät\ *n* **1** : a fellow countryman **2** : COLLEAGUE, COMPANION

com·pel \kəm-ˈpel\ *vt* **com·pelled; com·pel·ling 1** : to drive or urge forcefully or irresistibly : CONSTRAIN **2** : to cause to do or occur by overwhelming pressure ⟨*compel* obedience⟩ [Middle French *compellir,* from Latin *compellere,* from *com-* + *pellere* "to drive"] **syn** see FORCE — **com·pel·ler** *n*

com·pend \ˈkäm-ˌpend\ *n* : COMPENDIUM

com·pen·di·ous \kəm-ˈpen-dē-əs\ *adj* : marked by brief expression of a comprehensive matter : CONCISE — **com·pen·di·ous·ly** *adv* — **com·pen·di·ous·ness** *n*

com·pen·di·um \-dē-əm\ *n, pl* **-di·ums** *or* **-dia** \-dē-ə\ : a brief summary of a larger work or of a field of knowledge : ABSTRACT [Latin, "saving, shortcut", from *compendere* "to weigh together", from *com-* + *pendere* "to weigh"]

com·pen·sate \ˈkäm-pən-ˌsāt\ *vb* **1** : to be equivalent to in value or effect : make up for : COUNTERBALANCE **2** : to make amends or amends to ⟨nothing can *compensate* for the loss of reputation⟩ **3** : to make equal return to : PAY ⟨*compensate* workers for their labor⟩ [Latin *compensare,* from *compensus,* past participle of *compendere* "to weigh together"] — **com·pen·sa·tor** \ˈkäm-pən-ˌsāt-ər\ *n* — **com·pen·sa·to·ry** \kəm-ˈpen-sə-ˌtōr-ē, -ˌtȯr-\ *adj*

• **syn** COMPENSATE, BALANCE, OFFSET mean to make up in one thing what is deficient or excessive in another. COMPENSATE implies making up a lack or making amends for loss or injury; BALANCE suggests the equalizing or adjusting of two things so that neither outweighs the other in effect; OFFSET implies neutralizing one thing's good or bad effect by something exerting an opposite effect. **syn** see in addition PAY

com·pen·sa·tion \ˌkäm-pən-ˈsā-shən\ *n* **1** : the act of compensating : the state of being compensated **2 a** : something that compensates; *esp* : payment to an unemployed or injured worker or his or her dependents **b** : SALARY, WAGES — **com·pen·sa·tion·al** \-shnəl, -shən-l\ *adj*

com·pete \kəm-ˈpēt\ *vi* : to vie with another for an objective (as a prize, profits, or an environmental resource) [Late Latin *competere* "to seek together", from Latin *com-* + *petere* "to go to, seek"]

com·pe·tence \ˈkäm-pət-əns\ *n* **1** : means sufficient for the necessities of life **2** : the quality or state of being competent

com·pe·ten·cy \-ən-sē\ *n* : COMPETENCE

com·pe·tent \ˈkäm-pət-ənt\ *adj* **1** : having the necessary ability or qualities : FIT **2** : legally qualified [Latin *competens,* from *competere* "to come together, be suitable", from *com-* + *petere* "to go to, seek"] **syn** see ABLE — **com·pe·tent·ly** *adv*

com•pe•ti•tion \ˌkäm-pə-ˈtish-ən\ *n* **1** : the act or process of competing **2** : a contest between rivals; *also* : one's competitors **3** : the effort of two or more persons or firms acting independently to secure business by offering the most favorable terms **4** : active demand by two or more organisms or kinds of organisms for some environmental resource in short supply — **com•pet•i•to•ry** \kəm-ˈpet-ə-ˌtōr-ē, -ˌtȯr-\ *adj*

com•pet•i•tive \kəm-ˈpet-ət-iv\ *adj* : relating to, characterized by, or based on competition ⟨*competitive* sports⟩ — **com•pet•i•tive•ly** *adv* — **com•pet•i•tive•ness** *n*

com•pet•i•tor \kəm-ˈpet-ət-ər\ *n* : one that competes: as **a** : RIVAL 1a **b** : one selling or buying goods or services in the same market as another **c** : an organism that lives in competition with another

com•pi•la•tion \ˌkäm-pə-ˈlā-shən\ *n* **1** : the act or process of compiling **2** : something compiled; *esp* : a book composed of materials gathered from other books or documents

com•pile \kəm-ˈpīl\ *vt* **1** : to collect into a volume **2** : to compose out of materials from other documents ⟨*compile* a history of India⟩ [Middle French *compiler,* from Latin *compilare* "to plunder"] — **com•pil•er** *n*

com•pla•cence \kəm-ˈplās-ns\ *n* : calm or secure satisfaction with one's self or lot : SELF-SATISFACTION

com•pla•cen•cy \-n-sē\ *n* : COMPLACENCE

com•pla•cent \kəm-ˈplās-nt\ *adj* : **1** : SELF-SATISFIED ⟨a *complacent* smile⟩ **2** : feeling or showing complaisance [Latin *complacēre* "to please greatly", from *com-* + *placēre* "to please"] — **com•pla•cent•ly** *adv*

com•plain \kəm-ˈplān\ *vi* **1** : to express grief, pain, or discontent **2** : to make a formal accusation or charge [Middle French *complaindre,* from Latin *com-* + *plangere* "to lament"] — **com•plain•er** *n* — **com•plain•ing•ly** \-ˈplā-ning-lē\ *adv*

com•plain•ant \kəm-ˈplā-nənt\ *n* : one that makes a complaint in a legal action or proceeding

com•plaint \kəm-ˈplānt\ *n* **1** : expression of grief, pain, or resentment **2 a** : a cause or reason for complaining **b** : a bodily ailment or disease **3** : a formal charge against a person

com•plai•sance \kəm-ˈplās-ns, -ˈplāz-; ˌkäm-plā-ˈzans\ *n* : inclination to please or oblige

com•plai•sant \-nt; -ˈzant\ *adj* **1** : marked by an inclination to please or oblige **2** : tending to consent to others' wishes [French, from Middle French *complaire* "to gratify, acquiesce", from Latin *complacēre* "to please greatly"] — **com•plai•sant•ly** *adv*

com•plect•ed \kəm-ˈplek-təd\ *adj* : COMPLEXIONED ⟨dark-*complected*⟩ [derived from *complexion*]

1com•ple•ment \ˈkäm-plə-mənt\ *n* **1** : something that fills up, completes, or makes perfect **2** : full quantity, number, or amount ⟨a ship's *complement* of officers and men⟩ **3 a** : an angle or arc that when added to a given angle or arc equals a right angle **b** : a subset that contains all the elements of a set that are not contained in a particular one of its subsets **4** : an added word or group of words by which the predicate of a sentence is made complete ⟨*president* in "they elected me president" and *good* in "that is good" are different kinds of *complements*⟩ **5** : a heat-sensitive substance in normal blood that in combination with antibodies destroys antigens (as bacteria and foreign blood corpuscles) [Latin *complementum,* from *complēre* "to complete"]

• **syn** COMPLEMENT, COMPLIMENT are not synonyms but are easily confused. COMPLEMENT applies to a thing, quantity, or part required to make something complete or full; COMPLIMENT is an often formal expression of approval, praise, or greeting.

2com•ple•ment \-ˌment\ *vt* : to be complementary to ⟨a salad that *complements* the roast⟩

com•ple•men•tal \ˌkäm-plə-ˈment-l\ *adj* : relating to or being a complement : COMPLEMENTARY

com•ple•men•ta•ry \ˌkäm-plə-ˈment-ə-rē, -ˈmen-trē\ *adj* **1** : forming or serving as a complement **2** : of or relating to the precise pairing of purine to pyrimidine bases between strands of DNA and sometimes RNA through which the structure of one strand determines the other — **complementary** *n*

complementary angles *n pl* : two angles whose sum is 90 degrees

complementary colors *n pl* : a pair of colors that when mixed in proper proportions produce a neutral color

1com•plete \kəm-ˈplēt\ *adj* **1 a** : possessing all necessary parts : ENTIRE **b** : having all four sets of floral organs **2** : brought to an end : CONCLUDED **3** : highly proficient ⟨a *complete* artist⟩ **4 a** : fully carried out : THOROUGH **b** : TOTAL, ABSOLUTE ⟨*complete* silence⟩ [Middle French *complet,* from Latin *completus,* from *complēre* "to complete", from *com-* + *plēre* "to fill"] — **com•plete•ly** *adv* — **com•plete•ness** *n*

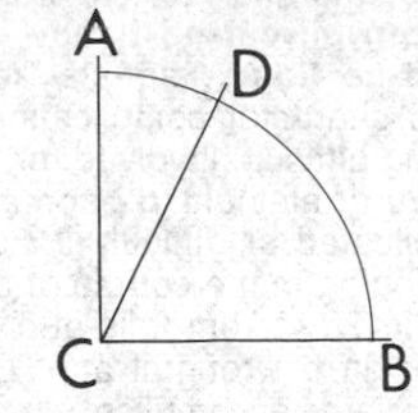

complementary angles: ∠*ACD* and ∠*DCB* are complementary

2complete *vt* **1** : to bring to an end : accomplish or achieve fully **2** : to make whole or perfect; *esp* : to provide with all lacking parts **syn** see FINISH

com•ple•tion \kəm-ˈplē-shən\ *n* : the act or process of completing : the state of being complete ⟨a job near *completion*⟩

1com•plex \käm-ˈpleks, kəm-ˈ, ˈkäm-ˌ\ *adj* **1** : composed of two or more parts ⟨a *complex* mixture⟩: as **a** : consisting of a main clause and one or more subordinate clauses ⟨*complex* sentence⟩ **b** : formed by union of simpler substances ⟨a *complex* protein⟩ **2** : having many interrelated parts, patterns, or elements that are usually hard to separate, analyze, or solve ⟨a *complex* problem⟩ **3** : of or relating to complex numbers ⟨*complex* plane⟩ [Latin *complexus,* past participle of *complecti* "to embrace, comprise", from *com-* + *plectere* "to braid"] — **com•plex•ly** *adv* — **com•plex•ness** *n*

• **syn** COMPLEX, COMPLICATED, INTRICATE, INVOLVED mean having confusingly interrelated parts. COMPLEX suggests an unavoidable and necessary lack of simplicity and does not imply a fault or failure in designing or arranging; COMPLICATED applies to what offers difficulty in understanding, explaining, or solving; INTRICATE implies an interlacing of parts that can scarcely be grasped or traced separately; INVOLVED implies extreme complication and often suggests disorder.

2com•plex \ˈkäm-ˌpleks\ *n* **1** : a whole made up of complicated or interrelated parts ⟨the military-industrial *complex*⟩ **2 a** : a group of culture traits usually associated with a particular activity or process **b** : a system of repressed desires and memories that exerts a dominating influence upon the personality; *also* : an exaggerated reaction to a subject or situation **c** : a group of obviously related units of which the degree and nature of the relationship is imperfectly known

complex fraction *n* : a fraction with a fraction or mixed number in the numerator or denominator or both — compare SIMPLE FRACTION

com•plex•ion \kəm-ˈplek-shən\ *n* **1** : natural disposition : TEMPERAMENT **2** : the hue or appearance of the skin especially of the face **3** : general appearance or impression : CHARACTER ⟨information that changes the whole *complexion* of a situation⟩ [Middle French "combination of qualities that determines temperament", from Latin *complexio* "combination", from *complexus,* past participle of *complecti* "to comprise"] — **com•plex•ioned** \-shənd\ *adj*

com•plex•i•ty \kəm-ˈplek-sət-ē, käm-\ *n, pl* **-ties** **1** : the quality or state of being complex **2** : something complex ⟨the *complexities* of the English language⟩

complex number *n* : a number (as $3 + 4\sqrt{-1}$) formed by adding a real number to the product of a real number and the square root of minus one

complex plane *n* : a plane whose points are identified by means of complex numbers

com•pli•ance \kəm-ˈplī-əns\ *n* **1** : the act or process of complying **2** : a readiness or disposition to yield to others — **in compliance with** : in accordance with : in obedience to ⟨*in compliance with* a court order⟩

com•pli•an•cy \-ən-sē\ *n* : COMPLIANCE

com•pli•ant \-ənt\ *adj* : ready or disposed to comply : SUBMISSIVE — **com•pli•ant•ly** *adv*

com•pli•cate \ˈkäm-plə-ˌkāt\ *vb* : to make or become complex, intricate, or difficult [Latin *complicare* "to fold together", from *com-* + *plicare* "to fold"]

com•pli•cat•ed *adj* **1** : consisting of parts intricately combined **2**

\ə\ abut	\au̇\ out	\i\ tip	\ȯ\ saw	\u̇\ foot
\ər\ further	\ch\ chin	\ī\ life	\ȯi\ coin	\y\ yet
\a\ mat	\e\ pet	\j\ job	\th\ thin	\yü\ few
\ā\ take	\ē\ easy	\ng\ sing	\t͟h\ this	\yu̇\ cure
\ä\ cot, cart	\g\ go	\ō\ bone	\ü\ food	\zh\ vision

: difficult to analyze, understand, or explain **syn** see COMPLEX — **com•pli•cat•ed•ly** *adv* — **com•pli•cat•ed•ness** *n*

com•pli•ca•tion \ˌkäm-plə-ˈkā-shən\ *n* **1 a** : a situation or a detail of character complicating the main thread of a plot **b** : a making difficult, involved, or intricate **c** : a complex or intricate feature or element **d** : something that makes a situation more complicated or difficult **2** : a secondary disease or condition developing in the course of a primary disease

com•plic•i•ty \kəm-ˈplis-ət-ē\ *n, pl* **-ties** : association or participation in a wrongful act [French *complicité,* from *complice* "associate, accomplice", from Late Latin *complex* "partner", from *com-* + *plicare* "to fold"]

[1]**com•pli•ment** \ˈkäm-plə-mənt\ *n* **1** : an expression of esteem, respect, affection, or admiration; *esp* : a flattering remark **2** *pl* : best wishes : REGARDS [French, from Italian *complimento,* from Spanish *cumplimiento,* from *cumplir* "to comply, be courteous"] **syn** see COMPLEMENT

[2]**com•pli•ment** \-ˌment\ *vt* : to pay a compliment to

com•pli•men•ta•ry \ˌkäm-plə-ˈment-ə-rē, -ˈmen-trē\ *adj* **1** : expressing or containing a compliment **2** : given free as a courtesy or favor ⟨a *complimentary* ticket⟩ — **com•pli•mentar•i•ly** \-ˌmen-ˈter-ə-lē\ *adv*

com•pline \ˈkäm-plən, -ˌplīn\ *n, often cap* : the last of the canonical hours [Old French *complie,* from Late Latin *completa,* from Latin *completus* "complete"]

com•ply \kəm-ˈplī\ *vi* **com•plied**; **com•ply•ing** : to conform or adapt one's actions to another's wishes, to a rule, or to necessity ⟨*comply* with a request⟩ [Italian *complire,* from Spanish *cumplir* "to perform what is due, comply, be courteous", from Latin *complēre* "to complete"] — **com•pli•er** \-ˈplī-ər, -ˈplīr\ *n*

[1]**com•po•nent** \kəm-ˈpō-nənt, ˈkäm-ˌ, käm-ˈ\ *n* **1** : a constituent part : INGREDIENT ⟨the *components* of a solution⟩ **2 a** : any one of the vector terms added to form a vector sum or resultant **b** : a coordinate of a vector [Latin *componere* "to put together", from *com-* + *ponere* "to put"] **syn** see ELEMENT — **com•po•nen•tial** \ˌkäm-pə-ˈnen-chəl\ *adj*

[2]**component** *adj* : being or forming a part : CONSTITUENT ⟨the *component* parts of a machine⟩

com•port \kəm-ˈpōrt, -ˈpȯrt\ *vb* **1** : to be fitting : ACCORD ⟨acts that *comport* with ideals⟩ **2** : CONDUCT ⟨*comport* oneself with dignity⟩ [Middle French *comporter* "to bear, conduct", from Latin *comportare* "to bring together", from *com-* + *portare* "to carry"]

com•port•ment \kəm-ˈpōrt-mənt, -ˈpȯrt-\ *n* : BEHAVIOR, BEARING

com•pose \kəm-ˈpōz\ *vb* **1 a** : to form by putting together : FASHION **b** : to make up : CONSTITUTE ⟨a cake *composed* of many ingredients⟩ **c** : to assemble the characters of (text) in order for printing : SET **2** : to create by mental or artistic labor ⟨*compose* a song⟩ **3** : to reduce to a minimum ⟨*compose* their differences⟩ **4** : to arrange in proper form **5** : to free from agitation : CALM ⟨try to *compose* their feelings⟩ [Middle French *composer,* from Latin *componere,* from *com-* + *ponere* "to put"]

com•posed \-ˈpōzd\ *adj* : free from agitation : CALM; *esp* : SELF-POSSESSED — **com•pos•ed•ly** \-ˈpō-zəd-lē\ *adv* — **com•pos•ed•ness** \-ˈpō-zəd-nəs\ *n*

com•pos•er \kəm-ˈpō-zər\ *n* : one that composes; *esp* : a person who writes music

[1]**com•pos•ite** \käm-ˈpäz-ət, kəm-\ *adj* **1** : made up of various distinct parts or elements ⟨a *composite* photograph⟩ **2** : of or relating to a large family (Compositae) of dicotyledonous trees, shrubs, and herbs (as the dandelion, sunflower, and ragweed) often considered to be the most highly evolved plants and characterized by florets arranged in dense heads that resemble single flowers ⟨the daisy and other *composite* plants⟩ [Latin *compositus,* past participle of *componere* "to compose"] — **com•pos•ite•ly** *adv*

[2]**composite** *n* **1** : something that is made up of different parts : COMPOUND **2** : a composite plant

composite number *n* : an integer that can be factored into two or more whole numbers each greater than 1

com•po•si•tion \ˌkäm-pə-ˈzish-ən\ *n* **1** : a composing: as **a** : a putting words together to make sentences : the art or practice of writing **b** : the composing of matter to be printed **2** : the manner in which the parts of a thing are put together : MAKEUP ⟨the *composition* of a painting⟩ **3** : the makeup of a compound or mixture ⟨the *composition* of rubber⟩ **4** : a product of combining various ingredients : COMBINATION ⟨a *composition* made of several different metals⟩ **5** : a literary, musical, or artistic production; *esp* : a short piece of writing done as an educational exercise ⟨must write one *composition* each week⟩ — **com•po•si•tion•al** \-ˈzish-nəl, -ən-l\ *adj*

com•pos•i•tor \kəm-ˈpäz-ət-ər\ *n* : one that composes matter to be printed

[1]**com•post** \ˈkäm-ˌpōst\ *n* : a mixture largely of decayed organic matter used for fertilizing and conditioning land [Middle French, from Medieval Latin *compostum,* from Latin *componere* "to put together"]

[2]**compost** *vt* : to convert (as plant debris) to compost

com•po•sure \kəm-ˈpō-zhər\ *n* : calmness or repose especially of mind, bearing, or appearance : SELF-POSSESSION

com•pote \ˈkäm-ˌpōt\ *n* **1** : fruits cooked in syrup **2** : a bowl usually with a base and stem from which compotes, fruits, nuts, or sweets are served [French, from Old French *composte,* from Latin *componere* "to put together, compose"]

[1]**com•pound** \käm-ˈpau̇nd, kəm-ˈ, ˈkäm-ˌ\ *vb* **1** : to put together or be joined to form a whole : COMBINE **2** : to form by combining parts ⟨*compound* a medicine⟩ **3** : to settle peaceably : COMPROMISE **4 a** : to pay (interest) on both the accrued interest and the principal ⟨*compound* interest quarterly⟩ **b** : to add to **5** : to agree for a consideration not to prosecute (an offense) ⟨*compound* a felony⟩ [Middle French *compondre,* from Latin *componere* "to put together, compose"] — **com•pound•able** \-ə-bəl\ *adj* — **com•pound•er** *n*

[2]**com•pound** \ˈkäm-ˌpau̇nd, käm-ˈ, kəm-ˈ\ *adj* **1 a** : made up of or by the union of separate elements or parts ⟨a *compound* substance⟩ **b** : composed of united similar elements especially of a kind usually independent ⟨a *compound* fruit⟩ **c** : having the blade divided to the midrib and forming two or more leaflets on a common axis ⟨a *compound* leaf⟩ **2** : involving or used in a combination : COMPOSITE **3 a** : being a word that is a compound ⟨the *compound* noun *steamboat*⟩ **b** : consisting of two or more main clauses ⟨a *compound* sentence⟩

[3]**com•pound** \ˈkäm-ˌpau̇nd\ *n* **1 a** : a word consisting of components that are words ⟨*rowboat, high school,* and *light-year* are *compounds*⟩ **b** : a word consisting of any of various combinations of words, word elements, or affixes ⟨*anthropology, kilocycle,* and *builder* are *compounds*⟩ **2** : something formed by a union of elements, ingredients, or parts; *esp* : a distinct substance formed by the union of two or more chemical elements in definite proportion by weight

[4]**com•pound** \ˈkäm-ˌpau̇nd\ **1** : an enclosure of European residences and commercial buildings especially in the Orient **2** : a large fenced or walled-in area [by folk etymology from Malay *kampong* "group of buildings, village"]

compound–complex *adj* : having two or more main clauses and one or more subordinate clauses ⟨*compound-complex* sentence⟩

compound eye *n* : an eye (as of an insect) made up of many separate visual units

compound fracture *n* : a breaking of a bone in such a way as to produce an open wound through which bone fragments stick out

compound interest *n* : interest paid or to be paid both on the principal and on accumulated interest

compound microscope *n* : a microscope consisting of an objective and an eyepiece mounted in a drawtube

com•pre•hend \ˌkäm-pri-ˈhend\ *vt* **1** : to grasp the meaning of : UNDERSTAND **2** : to take in : EMBRACE [Latin *comprehendere,* from *com-* + *prehendere* "to grasp"] **syn** see COMPRISE, INCLUDE — **com•pre•hend•ible** \-ˈhen-də-bəl\ *adj*

com•pre•hen•si•ble \-ˈhen-sə-bəl\ *adj* : capable of being comprehended : INTELLIGIBLE — **com•pre•hen•si•bil•i•ty** \-ˌhen-sə-ˈbil-ət-ē\ *n* — **com•pre•hen•si•bly** \-ˈhen-sə-blē\ *adv*

com•pre•hen•sion \ˌkäm-pri-ˈhen-chən\ *n* **1 a** : the act or process of including or comprising **b** : COMPREHENSIVENESS **2 a** : the act or action of grasping with the intellect **b** : knowledge gained by comprehending **c** : the capacity for understanding [Latin *comprehensio,* from *comprehendere* "to comprehend"]

com•pre•hen•sive \-ˈhen-siv\ *adj* **1** : covering broadly or completely : INCLUSIVE ⟨*comprehensive* insurance⟩ ⟨a *comprehensive* examination⟩ **2** : having wide mental comprehension — **com•pre•hen•sive•ly** *adv* — **com•pre•hen•sive•ness** *n*

[1]**com•press** \kəm-ˈpres\ *vb* **1** : to press or become pressed together **2** : to reduce the volume of by pressure [Late Latin *compressare* "to press hard", from Latin *compressus,* past

participle of *comprimere* "to compress", from *com-* + *premere* "to press"] **syn** see CONDENSE

[2]**com•press** \'käm-ˌpres\ *n* **1** : a folded cloth or pad applied so as to press upon a body part ⟨a cold *compress*⟩ **2** : a machine for compressing cotton into bales

com•pressed \kəm-'prest, 'käm-ˌ\ *adj* : flattened as though subjected to compression: **a** : flattened laterally ⟨petioles *compressed*⟩ **b** : narrow from side to side and deep in a dorsoventral direction

compressed air *n* : air under pressure greater than that of the atmosphere

com•press•ible \kəm-'pres-ə-bəl\ *adj* : capable of being compressed — **com•press•ibil•i•ty** \-ˌpres-ə-'bil-ət-ē\ *n*

com•pres•sion \kəm-'presh-ən\ *n* **1** : the act or process of compressing : the state of being compressed **2** : the process of compressing the fuel mixture in the cylinders of an internal-combustion engine (as of an automobile) — **com•pres•sion•al** \-'presh-nəl, -ən-l\ *adj* — **com•pres•sive** \-'pres-iv\ *adj*

com•pres•sor \-'pres-ər\ *n* **1** : one that compresses **2** : a machine that compresses gases and especially air

com•prise \kəm-'prīz\ *vt* **1** : to include especially within a particular scope : CONTAIN **2** : to be made up of **3** : to make up : CONSTITUTE [Middle French *compris,* past participle of *comprendre* "to include, comprehend", from Latin *comprehendere*]

• **syn** COMPRISE, INCLUDE, COMPREHEND, EMBRACE mean to take in or contain within one unit or boundary. COMPRISE implies that the list of parts or members is complete ⟨New York City *comprises* the boroughs Manhattan, Brooklyn, Queens, Staten Island, and the Bronx⟩ INCLUDE does not imply that all constituent members are presently specified ⟨the United States now *includes* Alaska and Hawaii⟩ COMPREHEND implies that something falls within the scope of a whole ⟨true love *comprehends* loyalty and much more⟩ EMBRACE implies a gathering of several items into a whole ⟨their philosophy *embraced* several schools of thought⟩

[1]**com•pro•mise** \'käm-prə-ˌmīz\ *n* **1** : a settlement of a dispute by mutual concessions **2** : a concession that is wrong or degrading ⟨a *compromise* of one's principles⟩ **3** : an agreement reached by mutual concessions ⟨the Missouri *Compromise*⟩ [Middle French *compromis,* from Latin *compromissum,* from *compromittere* "to promise mutually", from *com-* + *promittere* "to promise"]

[2]**compromise** *vb* **1** : to adjust or settle differences by mutual concessions **2** : to expose to discredit, suspicion, or danger **3** : to make unworthy concessions — **com•pro•mis•er** *n*

comp•trol•ler \kən-'trō-lər, 'käm-ˌ, 'kämp-ˌ, käm-', kämp-'\ *n* **1** : a public official who audits government accounts and sometimes certifies expenditures **2** : CONTROLLER 1b [Middle English, alteration of *conterroller* "controller"] — **comp•trol•lership** \-ˌship\ *n*

com•pul•sion \kəm-'pəl-shən\ *n* **1 a** : an act of compelling : the state of being compelled **b** : a force or agency that compels **2** : an irresistible impulse to do something [Late Latin *compulsio,* from Latin *compulsus,* past participle of *compellere* "to compel"]

com•pul•sive \-'pəl-siv\ *adj* **1** : having power to compel **2** : of, relating to, or caused by compulsion — **com•pul•sive•ly** *adv* — **com•pul•sive•ness** *n*

com•pul•so•ry \-'pəls-rē, -ə-rē\ *adj* **1** : required by authority **2** : having the power of compelling

com•punc•tion \kəm-'pəng-shən, -'pəngk-\ *n* **1** : sharp uneasiness caused by a sense of guilt : REMORSE **2** : a passing feeling of regret for some slight wrong [Middle French *componction,* from Late Latin *compunctio,* from Latin *compunctus,* past participle of *compungere* "to prick hard, sting", from *com-* + *pungere* "to prick"] **syn** see QUALM — **com•punc•tious** \-shəs\ *adj*

com•pu•ta•tion \ˌkäm-pyu̇-'tā-shən\ *n* **1** : the act or action of computing : CALCULATION **2** : a system of reckoning **3** : an amount computed — **com•pu•ta•tion•al** \-shnəl, -shən-l\ *adj*

com•pute \kəm-'pyüt\ *vb* : to determine or calculate especially by mathematical means [Latin *computare,* from *com-* + *putare* "to consider"] — **com•put•able** \-'pyüt-ə-bəl\ *adj*

com•put•er \-'pyüt-ər\ *n* : one that computes; *esp* : an automatic electronic machine that can store, retrieve, and process data

com•put•er•ize \-ə-ˌrīz\ *vt* **1** : to carry out, control, or conduct by means of a computer **2** : to equip with computers — **com•put•er•iza•tion** \-ˌpyüt-ə-rə-'zā-shən\ *n*

com•rade \'käm-ˌrad, -rəd\ *n* **1 a** : an intimate friend or associate : COMPANION **b** : a fellow soldier **2** : COMMUNIST [Middle French *camarade* "group of roommates, companion", from Spanish *camarada,* from *cámara* "room", from Late Latin *camera;* sense 2 from its use as a form of address by Communists]

com•rade•ship \-ˌship\ *n* : association as comrades : FELLOWSHIP, FRIENDSHIP

[1]**con** \'kän\ *vt* **conned; con•ning 1** : to study carefully : PERUSE **2** : MEMORIZE [Middle English *connen* "to know, study", alteration of *cunnen* "to know", infinitive of *can*]

[2]**con** *adv* : on the negative side : in opposition [short for *contra*]

[3]**con** *n* **1** : an opposing argument, person, or position **2** : the negative position or one holding it

[4]**con** *vt* **conned; con•ning 1** : SWINDLE **2** : COAX, CAJOLE [*confidence game*]

[5]**con** *n, slang* : a destructive disease of the lungs; *esp* : TUBERCULOSIS [short for *consumption*]

con- — see COM-

con amo•re \ˌkän-ə-'mōr-ē, ˌkō-nə-'mōr-ˌā, -'mȯr-\ *adv* **1** : with love, devotion, or zest **2** : TENDERLY — used as a direction in music [Italian, "with love"]

con•cat•e•nate \kän-'kat-ə-ˌnāt\ *vt* : to link together in a series or chain [Late Latin *concatenare,* from Latin *com-* + *catena* "chain"] — **con•cat•e•na•tion** \ˌkän-ˌkat-ə-'nā-shən\ *n*

con•cave \kän-'kāv, 'kän-ˌ\ *adj* : hollowed or rounded inward like the inside of a bowl [Middle French, from Latin *concavus,* from *com-* + *cavus* "hollow"] — **con•cave•ly** *adv* — **con•cave•ness** *n*

con•cav•i•ty \kän-'kav-ət-ē\ *n, pl* **-ties 1** : a concave surface or space : HOLLOW **2** : the quality or state of being concave

con•cavo-con•vex \kän-ˌkā-vō-kän-'veks, -kən-, -'kän-ˌveks\ *adj* **1** : concave on one side and convex on the other **2** : having the concave side of greater curvature than the convex

con•ceal \kən-'sēl\ *vt* **1** : to hide from sight **2** : to keep secret [Middle French *conceler,* from Latin *concelare,* from *com-* + *celare* "to hide"] — **con•ceal•able** \-ə-bəl\ *adj*

con•ceal•ment \-mənt\ *n* **1** : the act of hiding : the state of being hidden **2** : a hiding place

con•cede \kən-'sēd\ *vb* **1** : to grant as a right or privilege **2** : to acknowledge or admit grudgingly : YIELD [Latin *concedere,* from *com-* + *cedere* "to yield, cede"] **syn** see GRANT — **con•ced•ed•ly** \-'sēd-əd-lē\ *adv* — **con•ced•er** *n*

con•ceit \kən-'sēt\ *n* **1** : excessive pride in one's own worth or virtue **2 a** : a fanciful idea **b** : an elaborate metaphor [Middle English, "judgment", from *conceiven* "to conceive"]

con•ceit•ed \-'sēt-əd\ *adj* : having a very high opinion of onself — **con•ceit•ed•ly** *adv* — **con•ceit•ed•ness** *n*

con•ceiv•able \kən-'sē-və-bəl\ *adj* : capable of being conceived : IMAGINABLE — **con•ceiv•ably** \-blē\ *adv*

con•ceive \kən-'sēv\ *vb* **1** : to become pregnant **2 a** : to take into the mind ⟨*conceived* a liking for the student⟩ **b** : to form an idea of : IMAGINE ⟨*conceive* a new system⟩ **3** : to have an opinion : THINK ⟨not likely to *conceive* of me as a genius⟩ [Middle English *conceiven,* from Old French *conceivre,* from Latin *concipere,* from *com-* + *capere* "to take"] — **con•ceiv•er** *n*

[1]**con•cen•trate** \'kän-sən-ˌtrāt\ *vb* **1 a** : to bring, direct, or come toward a common center or objective **b** : to gather into one body, mass, or force **2** : to make stronger by removing something unwanted ⟨*concentrate* ore⟩ **3** : to fix one's powers, efforts, or attention on one thing ⟨*concentrate* on a problem⟩ [*com-* + Latin *centrum* "center"] — **con•cen•tra•tor** \-ˌtrāt-ər\ *n*

[2]**concentrate** *n* : something concentrated

con•cen•tra•tion \ˌkän-sən-'trā-shən\ *n* **1** : the act or process of concentrating : the state of being concentrated; *esp* : direction of attention on a single object **2** : a concentrated mass **3** : the relative amount of an ingredient : STRENGTH ⟨the *concentration* of salt in a solution⟩

concentration camp *n* : a camp where persons (as prisoners of

\ə\ **abut**	\au̇\ **out**	\i\ **tip**	\ȯ\ **saw**	\u̇\ **foot**
\ər\ **further**	\ch\ **chin**	\ī\ **life**	\ȯi\ **coin**	\y\ **yet**
\a\ **mat**	\e\ **pet**	\j\ **job**	\th\ **thin**	\yü\ **few**
\ā\ **take**	\ē\ **easy**	\ng\ **sing**	\th̲\ **this**	\yu̇\ **cure**
\ä\ **cot, cart**	\g\ **go**	\ō\ **bone**	\ü\ **food**	\zh\ **vision**

war or political prisoners) are detained or confined

con·cen·tric \kən-'sen-trik, 'kän-\ *adj* : having a common center ⟨*concentric* circles⟩ [Medieval Latin *concentricus,* from Latin *com-* + *centrum* "center"] — **con·cen·tri·cal·ly** \-tri-kə-lē, -klē\ *adv* — **con·cen·tric·i·ty** \ˌkän-ˌsen-'tris-ət-ē\ *n*

con·cept \'kän-ˌsept\ *n* **1** : something conceived in the mind : THOUGHT, NOTION **2** : an abstract idea generalized from particular instances [Latin *conceptus,* past participle of *concipere* "to conceive"] **syn** see IDEA

con·cep·ta·cle \kən-'sep-ti-kəl\ *n* : an external cavity containing reproductive cells in some algae [Latin *conceptaculum* "receptacle", from *concipere* "to take in, conceive"]

con·cep·tion \kən-'sep-shən\ *n* **1 a** (1) : the act of becoming pregnant (2) : the process of forming a viable zygote **b** : EMBRYO, FETUS **c** *archaic* : BEGINNING **2 a** : the function or process of forming or understanding ideas or abstractions or their symbols **b** : a general idea : CONCEPT **3** : the originating of something (as a plan) in the mind **syn** see IDEA — **con·cep·tion·al** \-shnəl, -shən-l\ *adj* — **con·cep·tive** \-'sep-tiv\ *adj*

con·cep·tu·al \kən-'sep-chə-wəl, -chəl\ *adj* : of, relating to, or consisting of concepts — **con·cep·tu·al·ly** \-ē\ *adv*

[1]**con·cern** \kən-'sərn\ *vt* **1** : to relate to : be about ⟨the novel *concerns* three soldiers⟩ **2** : to be the business or affair of : AFFECT ⟨the problem *concerns* us all⟩ **3** : to make anxious or worried ⟨our mother's illness *concerns* us all⟩ **4** : to take up the interest or energies of : INVOLVE ⟨*concern* oneself with business⟩ [Medieval Latin *concernere,* from Late Latin, "to sift together, mingle", from Latin *com-* + *cernere* "to sift"]

[2]**concern** *n* **1** : something that relates to or involves one : AFFAIR ⟨the usual *concerns* of the day⟩ **2 a** : marked regard or care ⟨showed deep *concern* for their friend's welfare⟩ **b** : a state of uncertainty and apprehension ⟨public *concern* over the threat of war⟩ **3** : a business or manufacturing establishment

con·cerned \-'sərnd\ *adj* **1** : ANXIOUS 1 **2** : interestedly engaged

con·cern·ing \-'sər-ning\ *prep* : relating to ⟨news *concerning* friends⟩

con·cern·ment \-'sərn-mənt\ *n* **1** : something in which one is concerned **2** : IMPORTANCE 1

[1]**con·cert** \kən-'sərt\ *vb* : to plan or arrange together : settle by agreement ⟨the allies *concerted* their tactics⟩ [Middle French *concerter,* from Italian *concertare,* from Late Latin, from Latin, "to contend", from *com-* + *certare* "to strive", from *certus* "determined, certain"]

[2]**con·cert** \'kän-ˌsərt, -sərt\ *n* **1** : agreement in design or plan ⟨work in *concert*⟩ **2** : musical harmony : CONCORD **3** : a musical performance of some length by several voices or instruments or both

con·cert·ed \kən-'sərt-əd\ *adj* **1 a** : mutually planned or agreed on ⟨*concerted* effort⟩ **b** : performed in unison ⟨*concerted* artillery fire⟩ **2** : arranged in parts for several voices ⟨*concerted* music⟩

con·cer·ti·na \ˌkän-sər-'tē-nə\ *n* : a musical instrument of the accordion family

concertina

con·cer·ti·no \ˌkän-chər-'tē-nō\ *n, pl* **-nos** : a short concerto

con·cert·mas·ter \'kän-sərt-ˌmas-tər\ *or* **con·cert·meis·ter** \-ˌmī-stər\ *n* : the leader of the first violins and assistant conductor

con·cer·to \kən-'chert-ō\ *n, pl* **-tos** *or* **-ti** \-ē\ : a piece for one or more soloists and orchestra usually in symphonic form with three contrasting movements [Italian, from *concerto* "concert"]

con·ces·sion \kən-'sesh-ən\ *n* **1** : the act or an instance of conceding **2** : something conceded: **a** : ACKNOWLEDGMENT, ADMISSION ⟨a *concession* of guilt⟩ **b** : a grant of property or of a right by a government ⟨a mining *concession*⟩ **c** : a lease of a part of premises for some purpose ⟨a soft-drink *concession*⟩; *also* : the part leased or the activities carried on [Latin *concessio,* from *concessus,* past participle of *concedere* "to concede"]

con·ces·sion·aire \kən-ˌsesh-ə-'naər, -'neər\ *n* : one that owns or operates a concession [French *concessionnaire,* from *concession* "concession"]

con·ces·sive \kən-'ses-iv\ *adj* : tending toward, expressing, or being a concession — **con·ces·sive·ly** *adv*

conch \'kängk, 'känch\ *n, pl* **conchs** \'kängks\ *or* **conch·es** \'kän-chəz\ **1** : a large spiral-shelled marine gastropod mollusk; *also* : its shell used especially for cameos **2** : CONCHA [Latin *concha* "mussel, mussel shell", from Greek *konchē*]

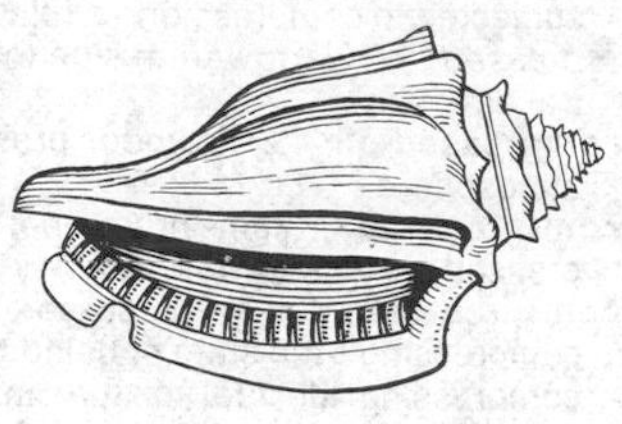
conch 1

con·cha \'käng-kə\ *n, pl* **con·chae** \-ˌkē, -ˌkī\ : the largest and deepest concavity of the external ear [Latin, "shell"]

con·chol·o·gy \käng-'käl-ə-jē\ *n* : a branch of zoology that deals with shells

con·cierge \kōn-'syerzh\ *n* : an attendant at the entrance of a building especially in France who oversees people coming or going, handles mail, and acts as a janitor or porter [French, from Latin *conservus* "fellow slave", from *com-* + *servus* "slave"]

con·cil·i·ate \kən-'sil-ē-ˌāt\ *vt* **1** : to bring into agreement or harmony : RECONCILE **2** : to gain the goodwill or favor of [Latin *conciliare* "to assemble, unite, win over", from *concilium* "assembly, council"] — **con·cil·i·a·tion** \-ˌsil-ē-'ā-shən\ *n* — **con·cil·i·a·tor** \-'sil-ē-ˌāt-ər\ *n* — **con·cil·ia·to·ry** \-'sil-yə-ˌtōr-ē, -'sil-ē-ə-, -ˌtȯr-\ *adj*

con·cise \kən-'sīs\ *adj* : marked by brevity of expression or statement ⟨a *concise* review of the year's work⟩ [Latin *concisus,* from *concidere* "to cut up", from *com-* + *caedere* "to cut"] — **con·cise·ly** *adv* — **con·cise·ness** *n*

con·clave \'kän-ˌklāv\ *n* **1** : a private meeting or secret assembly; *esp* : a meeting of Roman Catholic cardinals to choose a pope **2** : a gathering of a group : CONVENTION [Medieval Latin, from Latin, "room that can be locked up", from *com-* + *clavis* "key"] — **con·clav·ist** \-ˌklā-vəst\ *n*

con·clude \kən-'klüd\ *vb* **1** : to bring or come to an end : FINISH ⟨*conclude* a speech⟩ **2** : to form an opinion : decide by reasoning ⟨*conclude* that a statement is true⟩ **3** : to bring about as a result : ARRANGE ⟨*conclude* an agreement⟩ [Latin *concludere* "to shut up, end, infer", from *com-* + *claudere* "to shut"] **syn** see CLOSE — **con·clud·er** *n*

con·clu·sion \kən-'klü-zhən\ *n* **1 a** : a reasoned judgment : INFERENCE **b** : the necessary consequence of two or more propositions taken as premises **2** : the last part of something: as **a** : a final result : OUTCOME **b** : a final summing up **3** : an act or instance of concluding [Middle French, from Latin *conclusio,* from *concludere* "to conclude"]

con·clu·sive \kən-'klü-siv, -ziv\ *adj* : involving a conclusion or decision : DECISIVE, FINAL ⟨*conclusive* proof⟩ — **con·clu·sive·ly** *adv* — **con·clu·sive·ness** *n*

con·coct \kən-'käkt, kän-\ *vt* **1** : to prepare by combining various ingredients ⟨*concoct* a stew⟩ **2** : to make up : INVENT ⟨*concoct* a likely story⟩ [Latin *concoquere* "to cook together", from *com-* + *coquere* "to cook"] — **con·coct·er** *n* — **con·coc·tion** \-'käk-shən\ *n* — **con·coc·tive** \-'käk-tiv\ *adj*

con·com·i·tant \kən-'käm-ət-ənt, kän-\ *adj* : accompanying especially in a subordinate or incidental way [Latin *concomitari* "to accompany", from *com-* + *comit-, comes* "companion"] — **concomitant** *n* — **con·com·i·tant·ly** *adv*

con·cord \'kän-ˌkȯrd, 'käng-\ *n* **1 a** : a state of agreement : HARMONY **b** : a harmonious combination of tones heard together **2** : agreement by covenant or treaty [Old French *concorde,* from Latin *concordia,* from *com-* + *cord-, cor* "heart"]

con·cor·dance \kən-'kȯrd-ns\ *n* **1** : an alphabetical index of the principal words in a book or in the works of an author with their contexts **2** : a state of concord

con·cor·dant \-nt\ *adj* : marked by harmony : CONSONANT — **con·cor·dant·ly** *adv*

con·cor·dat \kən-'kȯr-ˌdat\ *n* : a compact or covenant especially between a pope and a government about church affairs [French, derived from Latin *com-* + *cor* "heart"]

con·course \'kän-ˌkōrs, 'käng-, -ˌkȯrs\ *n* **1** : a gathering together ⟨a great *concourse* of people⟩ **2** : a place (as a boulevard, open area, or hall) where many people pass or congregate ⟨met in the *concourse* of the bus terminal⟩ [Latin *concursus,* from *concurrere* "to run together, concur"]

con•cres•cence \kən-ˈkres-ⁿs, kän-\ *n* **:** a growing together **:** COALESCENCE [Latin *concrescentia,* from *concrescere* "to grow together"] — **con•cres•cent** \-ⁿt\ *adj*

[1]**con•crete** \kän-ˈkrēt, ˈkän-ˌ\ *adj* **1 :** naming a real thing or class of things **:** not abstract ⟨a *concrete* noun⟩ **2 a :** belonging to or derived from actual experience ⟨*concrete* examples⟩ **b :** existing in fact **:** REAL ⟨*concrete* evidence⟩ **3** \ˈkän-ˌ, kän-ˈ\ **:** relating to or made of concrete ⟨a *concrete* mixer⟩ [Latin *concretus* "formed by coalition of particles, concrete", from *concrescere* "to grow together", from *com-* + *crescere* "to grow"] — **con•crete•ly** *adv* — **con•crete•ness** *n*

[2]**con•crete** \ˈkän-ˌkrēt, kän-ˈ\ *n* **:** a hard strong building material made by mixing cement, sand, and gravel or broken rock with sufficient water to cause the cement to set and bind the entire mass

[3]**con•crete** \ˈkän-ˌkrēt, kän-ˈ\ *vb* **1 :** to form into a solid mass **:** SOLIDIFY **2 :** to cover with, form of, or set in concrete

con•cre•tion \kän-ˈkrē-shən, kən-\ *n* **1 :** the act or process of solidifying **2 :** something solidified; *esp* **:** a hard usually inorganic mass formed in a living body — **con•cre•tion•ary** \-shə-ˌner-ē\ *adj*

con•cu•bine \ˈkäng-kyə-ˌbīn, ˈkän-\ *n* **:** a woman who lives with a man and among some peoples has a legally recognized position in his household less than that of a wife [Old French, from Latin *concubina,* from *com-* + *cubare* "to lie"] — **con•cu•bi•nage** \kän-ˈkyü-bə-nij, kən-\ *n*

con•cu•pis•cence \kän-ˈkyü-pə-səns, kən-\ *n* **:** ardent desire; *esp* **:** sexual desire [Middle French, derived from Latin *concupiscere* "to desire ardently", from *com-* + *cupere* "to desire"] — **con•cu•pis•cent** \-sənt\ *adj*

con•cur \kən-ˈkər, kän-\ *vi* **con•curred; con•cur•ring 1 :** to happen together **:** COINCIDE **2 :** to act together to a common end or single effect **3 :** to be in agreement **:** ACCORD ⟨four justices *concurred* in the decision⟩ [Latin *concurrere,* from *com-* + *currere* "to run"]

con•cur•rence \kən-ˈkər-əns, -ˈkə-rəns\ *n* **1 a :** agreement in action, opinion, or intent **:** COOPERATION **b :** CONSENT **2 :** a coming together **:** CONJUNCTION

con•cur•rent \-ˈkər-ənt, -ˈkə-rənt\ *adj* **1 a :** coming together; esp **:** meeting in a point ⟨*concurrent* lines⟩ **b :** running parallel **2 :** operating at the same time ⟨*concurrent* expeditions to the Antarctic⟩ **3 :** acting in conjunction **4 :** exercised over the same matter or area by two different authorities ⟨*concurrent* jurisdiction⟩ **syn** see CONTEMPORARY — **concurrent** *n* — **con•current•ly** *adv*

concurrent resolution *n* **:** a resolution that is passed by both houses of a legislative body and lacks the force of law

con•cuss \kən-ˈkəs\ *vt* **:** to affect with concussion

con•cus•sion \kən-ˈkəsh-ən\ *n* **1 :** a violent irregular motion **2 :** a smart or hard blow or collision **3 :** bodily injury especially of the brain resulting from a sudden sharp jar (as from a blow) [Latin *concussio,* from *concutere* "to shake violently", from *com-* + *quatere* "to shake"] — **con•cus•sive** \-ˈkəs-iv\ *adj*

con•demn \kən-ˈdem\ *vt* **1 :** to declare to be wrong **:** CENSURE **2 a :** to pronounce guilty **:** CONVICT **b :** SENTENCE 1a **3 :** to declare officially to be unfit for use or consumption **4 :** to take for public use under the right of eminent domain [Old French *condemner,* from Latin *condemnare,* from *com-* + *damnare* "to damn"] **syn** see BLAME — **con•dem•nable** \-ˈdem-nə-bəl, -ˈdem-ə-bəl\ *adj* — **con•demn•er** *or* **con•dem•nor** \-ˈdem-ər\ *n*

con•dem•na•tion \ˌkän-ˌdem-ˈnā-shən, -dəm-\ *n* **1 :** CENSURE 1 **2 :** the act of judicially condemning **3 :** the state of being condemned — **con•dem•na•to•ry** \kən-ˈdem-nə-ˌtōr-ē, -ˌtȯr-\ *adj*

con•den•sa•tion \ˌkän-ˌden-ˈsā-shən, -dən-\ *n* **1 :** the act or process of condensing **2 :** a chemical reaction involving union between molecules often with elimination of a simple molecule (as water) to form a new and more complex compound **3 :** the quality or state of being condensed **4 :** a product of condensing; *esp* **:** an abridgment of a literary work — **con•den•sa•tion•al** \-shnəl, -shən-l\ *adj*

con•dense \kən-ˈdens\ *vb* **1 :** to make or become more close, compact, concise, or dense **:** CONCENTRATE, COMPRESS ⟨*condense* a paragraph into a sentence⟩ **2 :** to change from a less dense to a denser form ⟨steam *condenses* into water⟩ **3 :** to subject to or undergo condensation ⟨a chemical that *condenses* to form a plastic⟩ [Middle French *condenser,* from Latin *condensare,* from *com-* + *densus* "dense"] — **con•dens•able** \-ˈden-sə-bəl\ *adj*

• syn CONDENSE, CONTRACT, CONSTRICT, COMPRESS mean to decrease in bulk or volume. CONDENSE implies reduction to greater compactness usually of material all of the same kind ⟨*condense* gas into liquid⟩ CONTRACT applies to the drawing together of surfaces or particles or a reduction of area or length ⟨molten iron *contracts* as it cools⟩ CONSTRICT implies a tightening that reduces diameter ⟨a *constricted* throat⟩ COMPRESS implies reduction by pressure from without ⟨*compress* a bale of cotton⟩

condensed milk *n* **:** evaporated milk with sugar added

con•dens•er \kən-ˈden-sər\ *n* **1 :** one that condenses: as **a :** a lens or mirror used to concentrate light on an object **b :** an apparatus in which gas or vapor is condensed **2 :** CAPACITOR

con•de•scend \ˌkän-di-ˈsend\ *vi* **1 :** to descend to a level considered less dignified or humbler than one's own **2 :** to grant favors with a superior air [Middle French *condescendre,* from Late Latin *condescendere,* from Latin *com-* + *descendere* "to descend"] **syn** see STOOP

con•de•scend•ing *adj* **:** showing or characterized by condescension **:** PATRONIZING — **con•de•scend•ing•ly** \-ˈsen-ding-lē\ *adv*

con•de•scen•sion \ˌkän-di-ˈsen-chən\ *n* **:** a patronizing attitude

con•dign \kən-ˈdīn, ˈkän-ˌ\ *adj* **:** especially deserved or appropriate ⟨*condign* punishment⟩ [Middle French *condigne,* from Latin *condignus* "very worthy", from *com-* + *dignus* "worthy"] — **con•dign•ly** *adv*

con•di•ment \ˈkän-də-mənt\ *n* **:** something used to give an appetizing taste to food; *esp* **:** a pungent seasoning [Middle French, from Latin *condimentum,* from *condire* "to pickle", from *condere* "to build, store up"]

[1]**con•di•tion** \kən-ˈdish-ən\ *n* **1 :** a provision upon which the carrying out of an agreement depends **:** STIPULATION ⟨*conditions* of employment⟩ **2 :** something essential to another **:** PREREQUISITE **3 :** a restricting factor **:** LIMITATION **4 a :** a state of being **b :** social status **:** RANK **c** *pl* **:** attendant circumstances **5 :** state of health or fitness [Middle French *condicion,* from Latin *condicio* "terms of agreement, condition", from *condicere* "to agree", from *com-* + *dicere* "to say"]

[2]**condition** *vt* **-di•tioned; -di•tion•ing** \-ˈdish-ning, -ə-ning\ **1 :** to put into a proper or desired condition **2 a :** to adapt, modify, or mold to respond in a particular way **b :** to modify the behavior of so that a response previously associated with one stimulus becomes associated with another — **con•di•tion•er** \-ˈdish-nər, -ə-nər\ *n*

[1]**con•di•tion•al** \kən-ˈdish-nəl, -ən-l\ *adj* **1 :** subject to, implying, or dependent upon a condition ⟨a *conditional* promise⟩ **2 :** expressing, containing, or implying a supposition ⟨a *conditional* clause⟩ — **con•di•tion•al•ly** \-ē\ *adv*

[2]**conditional** *n* **:** IMPLICATION 3

con•di•tioned *adj* **1 :** CONDITIONAL 1 **2 :** brought or put into a specified state **3 :** determined or established by conditioning ⟨a *conditioned* response to a stimulus⟩

conditioned reflex *n* **:** a learned reflex reaction caused by repeated exposure to one stimulus in association with another for which the first comes to be a substitute ⟨a flow of saliva occurring in a dog when a bell is rung after the dog has learned to associate the sound with food is a classic *conditioned reflex*⟩

con•dole \kən-ˈdōl\ *vi* **:** to express sympathetic sorrow ⟨*condole* with a new-made orphan⟩ [Late Latin *condolēre* "to suffer with", from Latin *com-* + *dolēre* "to feel pain"]

con•do•lence \kən-ˈdō-ləns, ˈkän-də-\ *n* **:** expression of sympathy with another in sorrow or grief ⟨sent our *condolences* to the family⟩

con•do•min•i•um \ˌkän-də-ˈmin-ē-əm\ *n* **1 :** joint sovereignty by two or more nations **2 :** a politically dependent territory under condominium **3 :** individual ownership of a unit in a multi-unit structure (as an apartment building); *also* **:** a unit so owned [Latin *com-* + *dominium* "domain"]

\ə\ **abut**	\au̇\ **out**	\i\ **tip**	\ȯ\ **saw**	\u̇\ **foot**
\ər\ **further**	\ch\ **chin**	\ī\ **life**	\ȯi\ **coin**	\y\ **yet**
\a\ **mat**	\e\ **pet**	\j\ **job**	\th\ **thin**	\yü\ **few**
\ā\ **take**	\ē\ **easy**	\ng\ **sing**	\t͟h\ **this**	\yu̇\ **cure**
\ä\ **cot, cart**	\g\ **go**	\ō\ **bone**	\ü\ **food**	\zh\ **vision**

con•done \kən-ˈdōn\ *vt* **:** to pardon or overlook voluntarily ⟨*condone* a friend's faults⟩ [Latin *condonare* "to forgive", from *com-* + *donare* "to give"] **syn** see EXCUSE — **con•do•na•tion** \ˌkän-dō-ˈnā-shən, -də-\ *n* — **con•don•er** \kən-ˈdō-nər\ *n*

con•dor \ˈkän-dər, -ˌdȯr\ *n* **1 :** a very large South American vulture having the head and neck bare and the plumage dull black with a downy white neck ruff **2 :** CALIFORNIA CONDOR [Spanish *cóndor,* from Quechua *kúntur*]

condor 1

con•duce \kən-ˈdüs, -ˈdyüs\ *vi* **:** to lead or tend to a usually desirable result [Latin *conducere* "to conduct, conduce", from *com-* + *ducere* "to lead"]

con•du•cive \kən-ˈdü-siv, -ˈdyü-\ *adj* **:** tending to promote or aid **:** CONTRIBUTING ⟨action *conducive* to success⟩ — **con•du•cive•ness** *n*

¹con•duct \ˈkän-ˌdəkt, -dəkt\ *n* **1 :** the act, manner, or process of carrying on **:** MANAGEMENT ⟨the *conduct* of foreign affairs⟩ **2 :** personal behavior ⟨marked down for bad *conduct*⟩ [derived from Medieval Latin *conductus* "act of leading", from Latin *conducere* "to conduct, conduce"]

²con•duct \kən-ˈdəkt\ *vb* **1 :** GUIDE 1, ESCORT **2 :** to carry on or out usually from a position of command or control ⟨*conduct* a business⟩ **3 a :** to convey in a channel **b :** to act as a medium for conveying ⟨copper *conducts* electricity⟩ **4 :** to cause (oneself) to act in an indicated manner ⟨*conducted* themselves badly⟩ **5 :** to act as leader or director **6 :** to have the quality of transmitting light, heat, sound, or electricity — **con•duct•i•bil•i•ty** \-ˌdək-tə-ˈbil-ət-ē\ *n* — **con•duct•ible** \-ˈdək-tə-bəl\ *adj*

• syn MANAGE, CONTROL, DIRECT: CONDUCT implies guiding or leading in person ⟨*conduct* an orchestra⟩ ⟨selected to *conduct* negotiations⟩ MANAGE implies handling of details and maneuvering toward a desired result; CONTROL implies a regulating or restraining so as to keep on a desired course; DIRECT implies constant guidance and suggests the issuance of orders.

con•duc•tance \kən-ˈdək-təns\ *n* **1 :** conducting power **2 a :** the readiness with which a conductor transmits an electric current **b :** the reciprocal of electrical resistance

con•duc•tion \kən-ˈdək-shən\ *n* **1 :** the act of conducting or conveying **2 :** transmission through a conductor; *also* **:** CONDUCTIVITY **3 :** the transmission of excitation through living and especially nervous tissue

con•duc•tive \kən-ˈdək-tiv\ *adj* **:** having conductivity

con•duc•tiv•i•ty \ˌkän-ˌdək-ˈtiv-ət-ē\ *n, pl* **-ties :** the quality or power of conducting or transmitting

con•duc•tor \kən-ˈdək-tər\ *n* **:** one that conducts: as **a :** a person in charge of a public conveyance (as a bus or railroad train) **b :** the leader of a musical ensemble **c :** a substance or body capable of readily transmitting electricity, heat, or sound — **con•duc•to•ri•al** \ˌkän-ˌdək-ˈtōr-ē-əl, -ˈtȯr-\ *adj*

con•duc•tress \kən-ˈdək-trəs\ *n* **:** a woman who is a conductor

con•duit \ˈkän-ˌdü-ət, -ˌdyü-ət, -dət\ *n* **1 :** a natural or artificial channel through which water or other fluid is conveyed **2** *archaic* **:** FOUNTAIN **3 :** a pipe or tube for protecting electric wires or cables [Middle French, literally, "act of leading", from Medieval Latin *conductus*]

con•dy•larth \ˈkän-də-ˌlärth\ *n* **:** any of an order (Condylarthra) of primitive extinct ungulate mammals [Greek *kondylos* "knuckle, joint" + *arthron* "joint"]

con•dyle \ˈkän-ˌdīl, -dl\ *n* **:** a prominence at the end of a bone that forms part of a joint; *esp* **:** one of a pair like knuckles [Latin *condylus* "knuckle", from Greek *kondylos*]

cone \ˈkōn\ *n* **1 :** a mass of overlapping woody scales that especially in trees of the pine family are arranged on an axis and bear seeds between them; *also* **:** any of several flower or fruit clusters resembling such cones **2 :** a solid figure tapering evenly to a point from a closed curve (as a circle) in a plane; *esp* **:** a surface generated by a straight line through a fixed point as it moves along a closed curve (as a circle) in a plane — compare RIGHT CIRCULAR CONE **3 :** something that resembles a cone in shape: as **a :** a sensory end organ of the retina that functions in color vision **b :** a crisp cone-shaped wafer for holding ice cream [Latin *conus,* from Greek *kōnos*]

cone•nose \ˈkōn-ˌnōz\ *n* **:** any of various large bloodsucking bugs

Con•es•to•ga \ˌkän-ə-ˈstō-gə\ *n* **:** a broad-wheeled covered wagon used by American pioneers especially for transporting freight across the prairies — called also *Conestoga wagon* [*Conestoga,* Pennsylvania]

Conestoga

co•ney *or* **co•ny** \ˈkō-nē\ *n, pl* **coneys** *or* **conies 1 a** (1) **:** RABBIT; *esp* **:** the common European rabbit (2) **:** PIKA **b :** HYRAX **c :** rabbit fur **2 :** any of several fishes; *esp* **:** a dusky reddish-finned grouper of the tropical Atlantic [Old French *conil,* from Latin *cuniculus*]

con•fab \kən-ˈfab, ˈkän-ˌ\ *vi* **con•fabbed; con•fab•bing :** CONFABULATE — **con•fab** \ˈkän-ˌfab, kən-ˈ\ *n*

con•fab•u•late \kən-ˈfab-yə-ˌlāt\ *vi* **1 :** CHAT 2 **2 :** CONFER 2 [Latin *confabulari,* from *com-* + *fabulari* "to talk", from *fabula* "story"] — **con•fab•u•la•tion** \-ˌfab-yə-ˈlā-shən\ *n* — **con•fab•u•la•tor** \-ˈfab-yə-ˌlāt-ər\ *n*

con•fect \kən-ˈfekt\ *vt* **:** to put together from varied material [Latin *confectus,* past participle of *conficere* "to prepare", from *com-* + *facere* "to make"]

con•fec•tion \kən-ˈfek-shən\ *n* **1 :** the act or process of confecting **2 :** something confected: as **a :** a fancy dish or sweetmeat **b :** a piece of fine craftsmanship

con•fec•tion•er \-shə-nər, -shnər\ *n* **:** a manufacturer of or dealer in confections

con•fec•tion•ery \-shə-ˌner-ē\ *n, pl* **-er•ies 1 :** sweet edibles (as candy) **2 :** the confectioner's art or business **3 :** a confectioner's shop

con•fed•er•a•cy \kən-ˈfed-rə-sē, -ə-rə-\ *n, pl* **-cies 1 :** a loose league of persons, parties, or states **:** ALLIANCE, CONFEDERATION **2 :** a group united in a league; *esp, cap* **:** the Confederate States of America composed of the 11 southern states that seceded from the United States in 1860 and 1861 — **con•fed•er•al** \-ˈfed-rəl, -ə-rəl\ *adj*

¹con•fed•er•ate \kən-ˈfed-rət, -ə-rət\ *adj* **1 :** united in a league **:** ALLIED **2** *cap* **:** of or relating to the Confederate States of America [Late Latin *confoederare* "to unite by a league", from Latin *com-* + *foedus* "compact"]

²confederate *n* **1 :** ALLY 2a, ACCOMPLICE **2** *cap* **:** a soldier, citizen, or supporter of the Confederate States of America or their cause

³con•fed•er•ate \-ˈfed-ə-ˌrāt\ *vb* **:** to unite in a confederacy

Confederate Memorial Day *n* **:** any of several days appointed for the commemoration of servicemen of the Confederacy: **a :** April 26 in Alabama, Florida, Georgia, and Mississippi **b :** May 10 in North and South Carolina **c :** May 30 in Virginia **d :** June 3 in Kentucky, Louisiana, and Texas

con•fed•er•a•tion \kən-ˌfed-ə-ˈrā-shən\ *n* **1 :** an act of confederating **:** a state of being confederated **:** ALLIANCE **2 :** LEAGUE 1

con•fer \kən-ˈfər\ *vb* **con•ferred; con•fer•ring 1 :** to grant from or as if from a position of superiority **2 :** to compare views **:** CONSULT ⟨*confer* with the committee⟩ [Latin *conferre* "to bring together", from *com-* + *ferre* "to carry"] — **con•fer•ral** \-ˈfər-əl\ *n* — **con•fer•rer** \-ˈfər-ər\ *n*

con•fer•ee *or* **con•fer•ree** \ˌkän-fə-ˈrē\ *n* **1 :** one conferred with **2 :** one on whom something (as a degree) is conferred

con•fer•ence \ˈkän-fə-rəns, -frəns, -fərns\ *n* **1 :** a meeting for formal discussion or exchange of opinions; *also* **:** the discussion itself **2 :** a meeting of members of the two branches of a legislature to adjust differences **3 :** an association of athletic teams

con•fess \kən-ˈfes\ *vb* **1 :** to tell of or make known (as something wrong) ⟨*confess* a crime⟩ **2 a :** to acknowledge one's sins to God or to a priest **b :** to receive the confession of ⟨the priest *confessed* the penitents⟩ **3 :** to declare faith in **:** PROFESS [Middle French *confesser,* from Latin *confessus,* past participle of *confitēri* "to confess", from *com-* + *fatēri* "to confess"] **syn** see ACKNOWLEDGE

con•fess•ed•ly \-'fes-əd-lē, -'fest-lē\ *adv* : by confession : ADMITTEDLY

con•fes•sion \kən-'fesh-ən\ **1** : an act of confessing; *esp* : a disclosure of one's sins in the sacrament of penance **2** : a statement of something confessed: as **a** : a written acknowledgment of guilt by one accused of an offense **b** : a formal statement of religious beliefs : CREED **3** : an organized religious body having a common creed — **con•fes•sion•al** \-'fesh-nəl, -ən-l\ *adj*

con•fes•sion•al \-'fesh-nəl, -ən-l\ *n* **1** : a place where a priest hears confessions **2** : the practice of confessing to a priest

con•fes•sor \kən-'fes-ər\ *n* **1** : one that confesses **2** : a Christian who gives heroic evidence of faith but does not suffer martyrdom **3** : a priest who hears confessions

con•fet•ti \kən-'fet-ē\ *n* : small bits of brightly colored paper made for throwing (as at weddings) [Italian, plural of *confetto* "sweetmeat", from Medieval Latin *confectum,* from Latin *conficere* "to prepare"]

con•fi•dant \'kän-fə-ˌdant, -ˌdänt\ *n* : one to whom secrets are entrusted; *esp* : an intimate friend with whom one feels free to discuss private or secret matters [French *confident,* derived from Latin *confidere* "to confide"]

con•fi•dante \'kän-fə-ˌdant, -ˌdänt\ *n* : a female confidant [French *confidente,* feminine of *confident* "confidant"]

con•fide \kən-'fīd\ *vb* **1** : to have confidence : TRUST ⟨*confide* in a doctor's skill⟩ **2** : to show confidence by imparting secrets ⟨*confided* in one's mother⟩ **3** : to tell confidentially ⟨*confide* a secret to a friend⟩ **4** : ENTRUST 1 ⟨*confide* one's safety to the police⟩ [Latin *confidere,* from *com-* + *fidere* "to trust"] — **con•fid•er** *n*

con•fi•dence \'kän-fəd-əns, -fə-ˌdens\ *n* **1** : FAITH, TRUST ⟨had *confidence* in the leader⟩ **2** : consciousness of feeling sure : ASSURANCE ⟨spoke with great *confidence*⟩ **3 a** : reliance on another's discretion ⟨told a friend in *confidence*⟩ **b** : legislative support ⟨a vote of *confidence*⟩ **4** : a communication made in confidence : SECRET ⟨*confidences* between lawyer and client⟩

confidence game *n* : a swindle in which the swindler takes advantage of the trust he has persuaded the victim to place in him — called also *con game*

confidence man *n* : a swindler in a confidence game — called also *con man*

con•fi•dent \'kän-fəd-ənt, -fə-ˌdent\ *adj* : having or showing confidence; *esp* : SELF-ASSURED ⟨*confident* of their welcome⟩ — **con•fi•dent•ly** *adv*

con•fi•den•tial \ˌkän-fə-'den-chəl\ *adj* **1** : known only to a few people : PRIVATE ⟨*confidential* information⟩ **2** : marked by intimacy : FAMILIAR ⟨a *confidential* tone of voice⟩ **3** : trusted with secret matters ⟨a *confidential* secretary⟩ — **con•fi•den•tial•ly** \-'dench-lē, -ə-lē\ *adv* — **con•fi•den•tial•ness** \-'den-chəl-nəs\ *n*

con•fid•ing \kən-'fīd-ing\ *adj* : tending to confide : TRUSTFUL — **con•fid•ing•ly** \-ing-lē\ *adv*

con•fig•u•ra•tion \kən-ˌfig-yə-'rā-shən, -ˌfig-ə-\ *n* : relative arrangement of parts; *also* : something (as a figure, contour, or pattern) produced by such arrangement [Late Latin *configuratio* "similar formation", from Latin *configurare* "to form from or after", from *com-* + *figurare* "to form", from *figura* "figure"] — **con•fig•u•ra•tion•al** \-shnəl, -shən-l\ *adj* — **con•fig•u•ra•tion•al•ly** \-ē\ *adv* — **con•fig•u•ra•tive** \-'fig-yə-ˌrāt-iv, -'fig-ə-, -rət-\ *adj*

con•fine \kən-'fīn\ *vt* **1** : to keep within limits : RESTRICT ⟨*confined* to quarters⟩ **2 a** : to shut up : IMPRISON ⟨*confined* for life⟩ **b** : to keep indoors ⟨*confined* with a cold⟩ — **con•fin•er** *n*

con•fine•ment \kən-'fīn-mənt\ *n* : an act of confining : the state of being confined; *esp* : LYING-IN

con•fines \'kän-ˌfīnz\ *n pl* **1** : BOUNDARY; *also* : outlying parts **2** : [2]BOUND 3 [Latin *confine* "border", from *confinis* "adjacent", from *com-* + *finis* "end"]

con•firm \kən-'fərm\ *vt* **1** : to make firm or firmer (as in a habit, in faith, or in intention) **2** : to give approval to : RATIFY ⟨*confirm* a treaty⟩ **3** : to administer the rite of confirmation to **4** : to make sure of the truth of : VERIFY ⟨*confirm* a suspicion by careful investigation⟩ [Old French *confirmer,* from Latin *confirmare,* from *com-* + *firmus* "firm"] — **con•firm•able** \-'fər-mə-bəl\ *adj*

• **syn** CONFIRM, CORROBORATE, AUTHENTICATE, VERIFY mean to support the truth or validity of something. CONFIRM implies removing doubts by an authoritative statement or an indisputable fact; CORROBORATE suggests the strengthening of what is already partly established; AUTHENTICATE implies establishing genuineness by showing legal or official documents or presenting expert opinion; VERIFY implies the authentication of something supposed or presumed with appropriate facts or events.

con•fir•ma•tion \ˌkän-fər-'mā-shən\ *n* **1** : an act or process of confirming: as **a** : a Christian rite or sacrament conferring the gifts of the Holy Spirit and also entitling the recipient to full church privileges **b** : a ceremony confirming Jewish youths in their ancestral faith **c** : the ratification of an executive act by a legislative body **2** : something that confirms : PROOF — **con•fir•ma•to•ry** \kən-'fər-mə-ˌtōr-ē, -ˌtȯr-\ *adj*

con•firmed \kən-'fərmd\ *adj* **1 a** : made firm : STRENGTHENED **b** : deeply ingrained ⟨*confirmed* distrust of change⟩ **c** : HABITUAL, CHRONIC ⟨a *confirmed* drunkard⟩ **2** : having received the rite of confirmation — **con•firm•ed•ly** \-'fər-məd-lē\ *adv*

con•fis•cate \'kän-fə-ˌskāt\ *vt* : to seize by or as if by authority ⟨smuggled goods may be *confiscated*⟩ [Latin *confiscare,* from *com-* + *fiscus* "treasury"] — **con•fis•ca•tion** \ˌkän-fə-'skā-shən\ *n* — **con•fis•ca•tor** \'kän-fə-ˌskāt-ər\ *n* — **con•fis•ca•to•ry** \kən-'fis-kə-ˌtōr-ē, -ˌtȯr-\ *adj*

con•fi•te•or \kən-'fēt-ē-ər\ *n* : a confession of fault or error; *esp* : a liturgical form in the Mass in which sinfulness is admitted [Latin, "I confess", from *confitēri* "to confess"]

con•fla•gra•tion \ˌkän-flə-'grā-shən\ *n* : FIRE; *esp* : a large disastrous fire [Latin *conflagratio,* from *conflagrare* "to burn up", from *com-* + *flagrare* "to burn"]

[1]**con•flict** \'kän-ˌflikt\ *n* **1** : a hostile encounter : FIGHT, BATTLE **2** : a clashing or sharp disagreement (as between ideas, interests, or purposes) [Latin *conflictus* "act of striking together", from *confligere* "to strike together", from *com-* + *fligere* "to strike"]

[2]**con•flict** \kən-'flikt, 'kän-ˌ\ *vi* : to show antagonism : CLASH ⟨duty and desire often *conflict*⟩

con•flu•ence \'kän-ˌflü-əns\ *n* **1** : a coming or flowing together at one point ⟨the *confluence* of scholarship that produced the atomic bomb⟩ **2** : a flowing together or place of meeting especially of two or more streams

con•flu•ent \'kän-ˌflü-ənt, kən-'\ *adj* **1** : flowing or coming together ⟨*confluent* rivers⟩ **2** : run together ⟨a *confluent* rash⟩ [Latin *confluere* "to flow together", from *com-* + *fluere* "to flow"]

con•form \kən-'fȯrm\ *vb* **1** : to bring into harmony ⟨*conform* one's behavior to the circumstances⟩ **2** : to be similar or identical ⟨the data *conform* to the pattern⟩ **3** : to be obedient or compliant; *esp* : to adapt oneself to prevailing standards or customs ⟨found it easier to *conform* than rebel⟩ [Middle French *conformer,* from Latin *conformare,* from *com-* + *forma* "form"] **syn** see ADAPT — **con•form•er** *n* — **con•form•ism** \-'fȯr-ˌmiz-əm\ *n* — **con•form•ist** \-məst\ *n*

con•form•able \kən-'fȯr-mə-bəl\ *adj* **1** : corresponding in form or character : SIMILAR — usually used with *to* **2** : giving compliance : SUBMISSIVE — **con•form•ably** \-blē\ *adv*

con•for•mal \kən-'fȯr-məl, kän-\ *adj* **1** : leaving the size of the angle between corresponding curves unchanged; *esp* : representing small areas in their true shape ⟨a *conformal* map⟩

con•form•ance \kən-'fȯr-məns\ *n* : CONFORMITY 2, 3

con•for•ma•tion \ˌkän-fȯr-'mā-shən, -fər-\ *n* **1** : the act of conforming or producing conformity : ADAPTATION **2** : formation of something by an assembling into a whole **3 a** : STRUCTURE ⟨*conformation* of the ocean bed⟩ **b** : the proportionate shape or contour especially of an animal

con•for•mi•ty \kən-'fȯr-mət-ē\ *n, pl* **-ties** **1** : correspondence in form, manner, or character : AGREEMENT ⟨behaved in *conformity* with his beliefs⟩ **2** : an act or instance of conforming **3** : action in accordance with some standard or authority : OBEDIENCE ⟨*conformity* to social custom⟩

con•found \kən-'faund, kän-\ *vt* **1** *archaic* : to bring to ruin : DEFEAT **2** : to put to shame : DISCOMFIT **3** : to swear at : DAMN, CURSE **4** : to throw into disorder : mix up : CONFUSE [Old French *confondre,* from Latin *confundere* "to pour togeth-

er, confuse", from *com-* + *fundere* "to pour"]
con·found·ed \kən-ˈfau̇n-dəd, ˈkän-ˈfau̇n-\ *adj* **1** : filled with confusion : PERPLEXED **2** : DAMNED 1 — **con·found·ed·ly** *adv*
con·fra·ter·ni·ty \ˌkän-frə-ˈtər-nət-ē\ *n, pl* **-ties** : a society devoted to a religious or charitable cause
con·frere \ˈkōn-ˌfreər, ˈkän-\ *n* : COLLEAGUE, COMRADE [Middle French, translation of Medieval Latin *confrater* "fellow, brother", from Latin *com-* + *frater* "brother"]
con·front \kən-ˈfrənt\ *vt* **1** : to face especially in challenge : OPPOSE ⟨*confront* an enemy⟩ **2** : to bring face-to-face : cause to meet ⟨*confront* one with a problem⟩ [Middle French *confronter* "to border on, confront", derived from Latin *com-* + *frons* "forehead, front"] — **con·fron·ta·tion** \ˌkän-frən-ˈtā-shən, -ˌfrən-\ *n*
Con·fu·cian \kən-ˈfyü-shən\ *adj* : of or relating to the Chinese philosopher Confucius or his teachings or followers — **Confucian** *n* — **Con·fu·cian·ism** \-shə-ˌniz-əm\ *n* — **Con·fu·cian·ist** \-shə-nəst\ *n or adj*
con·fuse \kən-ˈfyüz\ *vt* **1 a** : to make embarrassed **b** : to disturb in mind or purpose : throw off ⟨this complicated problem *confused* me⟩ **2 a** : to make indistinct : BLUR ⟨stop *confusing* the issue⟩ **b** : to mix up : JUMBLE ⟨their motives were hopelessly *confused*⟩ **c** : to fail to distinguish between ⟨teachers always *confused* the twins⟩ [back-formation from Middle English *confused* "perplexed", from Middle French *confus*, from Latin *confusus*, past participle of *confundere* "to confuse, confound"] — **con·fused·ly** \-ˈfyüz-əd-lē\ *adv* — **con·fus·ing·ly** \-ˈfyü-zing-lē\ *adv*
con·fu·sion \kən-ˈfyü-zhən\ *n* **1** : an act or instance of confusing **2** : the quality or state of being confused — **con·fu·sion·al** \-ˈfyüzh-nəl, -ˈfyü-zhən-l\ *adj*
con·fute \kən-ˈfyüt\ *vt* : to overwhelm in argument : refute conclusively [Latin *confutare*] — **con·fu·ta·tion** \ˌkän-fyu̇-ˈtā-shən\ *n* — **con·fu·ta·tive** \kən-ˈfyüt-ət-iv\ *adj* — **con·fut·er** \kən-ˈfyüt-ər\ *n*
con·ga \ˈkäng-gə\ *n* **1** : a Cuban dance of African origin performed by a group usually in single file **2** : a tall narrow bass drum beaten with the hands [American Spanish, from *Congo*, region in Africa]
con game \ˈkän-\ *n* : CONFIDENCE GAME
con·gé \kōn-ˈzhā, ˈkän-ˌjā\ *n* **1** : DISMISSAL **2** : FAREWELL 2 [French]
con·geal \kən-ˈjēl\ *vb* **1** : to change from a fluid to a solid state by or as if by cold **2** : to make or become viscid or curdled : COAGULATE **3** : to make or become rigid or inflexible [Middle French *congeler*, from Latin *congelare*, from *com-* + *gelare* "to freeze"] — **con·geal·ment** \-mənt\ *n*
con·ge·ner \ˈkän-jə-nər, kən-ˈjē-\ *n* **1** : a member of the same taxonomic genus as another plant or animal **2** : a person or thing resembling another in nature or action [Latin, "of the same kind", from *com-* + *genus* "kind"] — **con·ge·ner·ic** \ˌkän-jə-ˈner-ik\ *adj*
con·ge·nial \kən-ˈjē-nyəl\ *adj* **1** : having the same nature, disposition, or tastes **2 a** : existing together harmoniously **b** : PLEASANT; *esp* : agreeably suited to one's nature, tastes, or outlook **c** : characterized by friendly sociability : GENIAL ⟨the innkeeper was a most *congenial* host⟩ [*com-* + *genius*] — **con·ge·nial·i·ty** \-ˌjē-nē-ˈal-ət-ē, -ˌjēn-ˈyal-\ *n* — **con·ge·nial·ly** \-ˈjē-nyə-lē\ *adv*
con·gen·i·tal \kən-ˈjen-ə-tl\ *adj* **1** : existing at or dating from birth but usually not hereditary ⟨*congenital* disease⟩ **2** : being such by nature : INHERENT ⟨a *congenital* liar⟩ [Latin *congenitus*, from *com-* + *genitus*, past participle of *gignere* "to bring forth"] **syn** see INNATE — **con·gen·i·tal·ly** \-tl-ē\ *adv*
con·ger eel \ˌkäng-gər-\ *n* : a scaleless saltwater eel that sometimes grows to a length of eight feet and is an important food fish of Europe [Old French *congre*, from Latin *conger*, from Greek *gongros*]
con·ge·ries \ˈkän-jə-rēz, -ˌrēz\ *n, pl* **congeries** *same*\ : a collection of entities : AGGREGATION [Latin, from *congerere* "to bring together"]
con·gest \kən-ˈjest\ *vb* **1** : to cause an excessive fullness of the blood vessels of (as an organ) **2** : CLOG 2 ⟨traffic *congested* the streets⟩ **3** : to concentrate in a small or narrow space [Latin *congestus*, past participle of *congerere* "to bring together", from *com-* + *gerere* "to carry"] — **con·ges·tion** \-ˈjes-chən\ *n* — **con·ges·tive** \-ˈjes-tiv\ *adj*

1con·glom·er·ate \kən-ˈgläm-rət, -ə-rət\ *adj* : made up of parts from various sources or of various kinds ⟨an ethnically *conglomerate* culture⟩ [Latin *conglomerare* "to roll together", from *com-* + *glomus* "ball"]
2con·glom·er·ate \-ˈgläm-ə-ˌrāt\ *vb* : to gather into a mass
3con·glom·er·ate \-ˈgläm-rət, -ə-rət\ *n* **1** : a composite mass or mixture; *esp* : rock composed of rounded fragments varying from small pebbles to large boulders in a cement (as of hardened clay) **2** : a widely diversified corporation
con·glom·er·a·tion \kən-ˌgläm-ə-ˈrā-shən, ˌkän-\ *n* **1** : the act of conglomerating : the state of being conglomerated **2** : something that is conglomerated
Con·go red \ˌkäng-ˌgō-\ *n* : an azo dye red in alkaline and blue in acid solution [*Congo*, region in Africa]
con·go snake \ˈkäng-ˌgō-\ *n* : a long bluish black amphibian of the southeastern United States that has two pairs of very short limbs — called also *congo eel*
con·grat·u·late \kən-ˈgrach-ə-ˌlāt\ *vt* : to express pleasure to on account of success or good fortune ⟨*congratulated* the winner⟩ [Latin *congratulari* "to wish joy", from *com-* + *gratus* "pleasing"] — **con·grat·u·la·to·ry** \-ˈgrach-lə-ˌtōr-ē, -ə-lə-, -ˌtȯr-\ *adj*
con·grat·u·la·tion \-ˌgrach-ə-ˈlā-shən\ *n* **1** : the act of congratulating **2** : an expression of pleasure at another's success, happiness, or good fortune — usually used in pl.
con·gre·gate \ˈkäng-gri-ˌgāt\ *vb* : to collect into a group or crowd : ASSEMBLE [Latin *congregare*, from *com-* + *greg-*, *grex* "flock"] **syn** see GATHER — **con·gre·ga·tor** \-ˌgāt-ər\ *n*
con·gre·ga·tion \ˌkäng-gri-ˈgā-shən\ *n* **1 a** : an assembly of persons; *esp* : one gathered for religious worship **b** : a religious community: as (1) : an organized body of believers in a particular locality (2) : a Roman Catholic religious society with only simple vows **2** : the action of congregating : the state of being congregated; *also* : a collection of separate things **3** : a body of cardinals and officials forming an administrative division of the papal curia
con·gre·ga·tion·al \-ˈgā-shnəl, -shən-l\ *adj* **1** : of or relating to a congregation **2** *cap* : of or relating to a body of Protestant churches affirming the essential importance and the autonomy of the local congregation **3** : of or relating to church government placing final authority in the assembly of the local congregation — **con·gre·ga·tion·al·ism** \-ˌiz-əm\ *n, often cap* — **con·gre·ga·tion·al·ist** \-əst\ *n or adj, often cap*
con·gress \ˈkäng-grəs\ *n* **1 a** : the act or action of coming together and meeting **b** : COITUS **2** : a formal meeting of delegates for discussion and action **3** : the supreme legislative body of a nation and especially of a republic **4** : an association of constituent organizations **5** : a single meeting or session of a group [Latin *congressus*, from *congredi* "to come together", from *com-* + *gradi* "to step, go"] — **con·gres·sion·al** \kən-ˈgresh-nəl, -ən-l\ *adj* — **con·gres·sion·al·ly** \-ē\ *adv*
con·gress·man \ˈkäng-grəs-mən\ *n* : a member of a congress; *esp* : a member of the United States House of Representatives
con·gress·wom·an \-ˌwu̇m-ən\ *n* : a female member of a congress; *esp* : a female member of the United States House of Representatives
con·gru·ence \kən-ˈgrü-əns, ˈkäng-grə-wəns\ *n* **1** : the quality or state of agreeing or coinciding **2** : a statement that two numbers are congruent with respect to a modulus
con·gru·en·cy \-ən-sē, -wən-sē\ *n* : CONGRUENCE 1
con·gru·ent \kən-ˈgrü-ənt, ˈkäng-grə-wənt\ *adj* **1** : being in agreement ⟨the report proved to be *congruent* with the facts⟩ **2** : capable of being placed over one another so that all points of one correspond to all points of the other : having the same size and shape ⟨*congruent* triangles⟩ **3** : having the difference divisible by a given modulus ⟨12 is *congruent* to 2 with respect to a modulus of 5 since 12−2=(2)·(5)⟩ [Latin *congruere* "to come together, agree"] — **con·gru·ent·ly** *adv*
con·gru·i·ty \kən-ˈgrü-ət-ē, kän-\ *n, pl* **-i·ties** **1** : the quality or state of being congruent or congruous : AGREEMENT **2** : a point of agreement
con·gru·ous \ˈkäng-grə-wəs\ *adj* **1 a** : being in agreement, harmony, or correspondence **b** : conforming to the circumstances of a situation : APPROPRIATE **2** : marked by harmony among parts [Latin *congruus*, from *congruere* "to come together, agree"] — **con·gru·ous·ly** *adv* — **con·gru·ous·ness** *n*

[1]**con•ic** \'kän-ik\ *adj* **1 :** CONICAL **2 :** of or relating to a cone

[2]**conic** *n* **:** CONIC SECTION

con•i•cal \'kän-i-kəl\ *adj* **:** resembling a cone especially in shape ⟨*conical* roots⟩ — **con•i•cal•ly** \-i-kə-lē, -klē\ *adv*

conic section *n* **:** a plane section of a cone **:** a curve (as an ellipse, parabola, hyperbola, or circle) generated by a point which always moves so that the ratio of its distance from a fixed point to its distance from a fixed line is constant

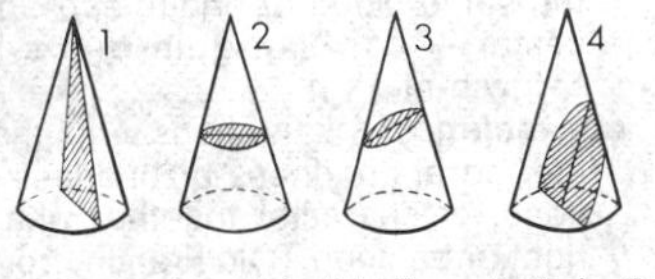

conic section: *1* straight lines, *2* circle, *3* ellipse, *4* parabola

co•nid•io•phore \kə-'nid-ē-ə-,fōr, -,fȯr\ *n* **:** a plant structure (as a special hypha) that bears conidia

co•nid•i•um \kə-'nid-ē-əm\ *n, pl* **-ia** \-ē-ə\ **:** an asexual spore produced on a conidiophore **[**Greek *konis* "dust"**]** — **co•nid•i•al** \-ē-əl\ *adj*

co•ni•fer \'kän-ə-fər *also* 'kō-nə-\ *n* **:** any of an order (Coniferales) of mostly evergreen trees and shrubs that are gymnosperms and include forms (as pines) with true cones **[**Latin *conifer* "cone-bearing", from *conus* "cone"**]** — **co•nif•er•ous** \kō-'nif-rəs, kə-, -ə-rəs\ *adj*

con•jec•tur•al \kən-'jek-chə-rəl, -'jeksh-rəl\ *adj* **1 :** of the nature of, involving, or based on conjecture **2 :** given to conjectures — **con•jec•tur•al•ly** \-ē\ *adv*

[1]**con•jec•ture** \kən-'jek-chər\ *n* **1 :** inference from inadequate evidence **2 :** a conclusion reached by surmise or guesswork ⟨a mistaken *conjecture*⟩ **[**Latin *conjectura,* from *conjectus,* past participle of *conicere* "to throw together, conjecture", from *com-* + *jacere* "to throw"**]**

[2]**conjecture** *vb* **-jec•tured; -jec•tur•ing** \-chə-ring, 'jek-shring\ **1 :** to arrive at by conjecture **2 :** to make conjectures as to **:** SURMISE — **con•jec•tur•er** \-'jek-chər-ər\ *n*

• **syn** SURMISE, GUESS: CONJECTURE implies forming an opinion on what is recognized as insufficient evidence; SURMISE implies even slighter evidence and suggests the influence of suspicion or imagination; GUESS stresses hitting on a conclusion at random or from very uncertain evidence.

con•join \kən-'jȯin, kän-\ *vb* **:** to join together for a common purpose

con•joint \-'jȯint\ *adj* **1 :** being or coming together so as to unite **2 :** related to, made up of, or carried on by two or more in combination **:** JOINT — **con•joint•ly** *adv*

con•ju•gal \'kän-ji-gəl, kən-'jü-\ *adj* **:** of or relating to the married state or matrimonial relations **[**Latin *conjugalis,* from *conjux* "spouse", from *conjungere* "to join, unite in marriage", from *com-* + *jungere* "to join"**]** **syn** see MATRIMONIAL — **con•ju•gal•ly** *adv*

con•ju•gant \'kän-ji-gənt\ *n* **:** either of a pair of conjugating gametes or organisms

[1]**con•ju•gate** \'kän-ji-gət, -jə-,gāt\ *adj* **1 a :** joined together especially in pairs **b :** acting or operating as if joined **2 :** having features in common but opposite or inverse in some particular; *esp* **:** being complex numbers that are conjugates **[**Latin *conjugare* "to unite", from *com-* + *jugum* "yoke"**]** — **con•ju•gate•ly** *adv* — **con•ju•gate•ness** *n*

[2]**con•ju•gate** \'kän-jə-,gāt\ *vb* **1 :** to give the various inflectional forms of (a verb) in a prescribed order **2 :** to join together **:** COUPLE **3 :** to unite chemically so that the product is easily broken down into the original compounds **4 :** to pair and fuse in conjugation

[3]**con•ju•gate** \-gət, -,gāt\ *n* **1 :** something conjugate **:** a product of conjugating **2 :** one of two complex numbers (as $a + bi$ and $a - bi$) differing only in the sign of the imaginary part

conjugated protein *n* **:** a compound of a protein with a nonprotein

con•ju•ga•tion \,kän-jə-'gā-shən\ *n* **1 :** the act of conjugating **:** the state of being conjugated **2 a :** an orderly arrangement of the inflectional forms of a verb **b :** verb inflection **c :** a class of verbs having the same type of inflectional forms ⟨the weak *conjugation*⟩ **3 a :** fusion of usually similar gametes that among lower thallophytes replaces the typical fertilization of higher forms **b :** temporary cytoplasmic union with exchange of nuclear material that is the usual sexual process in ciliated protozoans — **con•ju•ga•tion•al** \-shnəl, -shən-l\ *adj* — **con•ju•ga•tion•al•ly** \-ē\ *adv* — **con•ju•ga•tive** \'kän-jə-,gāt-iv\ *adj*

con•junct \kən-'jəngt, kän-, -'jəngkt\ *adj* **:** bound together **:** JOINED, UNITED **[**Latin *conjunctus,* past participle of *conjungere* "to join", from *com-* + *jungere* "to join"**]**

con•junc•tion \kən-'jəng-shən, -'jəngk-\ *n* **1 :** the act or an instance of conjoining **:** the state of being conjoined **2 :** occurrence together in time or space **:** CONCURRENCE **3 :** the apparent meeting or passing of two or more celestial bodies in the same degree of the zodiac **4 :** an uninflected word or expression that joins together sentences, clauses, phrases, or words **5 :** a statement formed by joining two or more statements together with the word *and* that is true only if all its components are true — **con•junc•tion•al** \-shnəl, -shən-l\ *adj* — **con•junc•tion•al•ly** \-ē\ *adv*

con•junc•ti•va \,kän-,jəngk-'tī-və, -'tē-\ *n, pl* **-tivas** *or* **-ti•vae** \-'tī-,vē, -'tē-,vī\ **:** the mucous membrane that lines the inner surface of the eyelids and is continued over the front part of the eyeball **[**derived from Latin *conjungere* "to join"**]** — **con•junc•ti•val** \-vəl\ *adj*

con•junc•tive \kən-'jəng-tiv, -'jəngk-\ *adj* **1 :** CONNECTIVE **2 :** done or existing in conjunction **:** CONJUNCT **3 :** being or functioning like a conjunction ⟨*conjunctive* adverbs such as *hence, however,* and *therefore*⟩ — **conjunctive** *n* — **con•junc•tive•ly** *adv*

con•junc•ti•vi•tis \kən-,jəng-ti-'vīt-əs, -,jəngk-\ *n* **:** inflammation of the conjunctiva

con•junc•ture \kən-'jəng-chər, -'jəngk-\ *n* **1 :** CONJUNCTION 1, UNION **2 :** a combination of circumstances usually producing a crisis **:** JUNCTURE

con•ju•ra•tion \,kan-jə-'rā-shən, ,kən-\ *n* **1 :** the act of conjuring **:** INCANTATION **2 :** an expression or trick used in conjuring

con•jure \'kän-jər, 'kən-; *in sense 1* kən-'jür\ *vb* **1 :** to entreat earnestly or solemnly **:** BESEECH **2 a :** to summon by invocation or incantation **b :** to create or bring about as if by magic ⟨*conjure* up a scheme⟩ **3 a :** to practice magical arts **b :** to use a conjuror's tricks **[**Old French *conjurer,* from Latin *conjurare* "to swear together", from *com-* + *jurare* "to swear"**]**

con•jur•er *or* **con•ju•ror** \'kän-jər-ər, 'kən-\ *n* **1 :** one that practices magic arts **:** WIZARD **2 :** one that performs tricks involving sleight of hand and illusion **:** MAGICIAN

conk *vi* **:** to break down; *esp* **:** STALL ⟨the motor *conked* out⟩ **[**probably imitative**]**

con man \'kän-\ *n* **:** CONFIDENCE MAN

con•nate \kä-'nāt, 'kän-,āt\ *adj* **1 :** INNATE 1 **2 :** agreeing in nature **:** CONGENIAL ⟨*connate* spirits⟩ **3 :** born or originated together **4 :** congenitally or firmly united ⟨*connate* leaves⟩ **5 :** entrapped in sediments at the time of deposition ⟨*connate* water⟩ **[**Late Latin *connatus,* past participle of *connasci* "to be born together", from Latin *com-* + *nasci* "to be born"**]** — **connate•ly** *adv*

con•nect \kə-'nekt\ *vb* **1 :** to join or link together directly or by something coming between ⟨*connect* two wires⟩ ⟨towns *connected* by a railroad⟩ **2 :** to join by personal relationship or association ⟨*connected* by marriage⟩ **3 :** to associate in the mind ⟨*connect* two ideas⟩ **4 :** to be related (as by cause or logic) ⟨an event *connected* with the fire⟩ **5 :** to meet at a time and place suitable for transferring passengers or freight ⟨*connecting* trains⟩ **[**Latin *connectere,* from *com-* + *nectere* "to bind"**]** **syn** see JOIN — **con•nec•tor** \-'nek-tər\ *n*

connecting rod *n* **:** a rod that transmits power from one rotating part of a machine to another in reciprocating motion

con•nec•tion \kə-'nek-shən\ *n* **1 :** the act of connecting **2 :** the fact or condition of being connected **:** RELATIONSHIP ⟨the *connection* between two ideas⟩ **3 a :** a thing that connects **:** BOND, LINK ⟨a loose *connection* in a radio⟩ **b :** a means of communication **4 a :** a person connected with others especially by marriage or kinship ⟨an uncle and some family *connections*⟩ **b :** a social, professional, or commercial relationship ⟨business *connections* in the city⟩ **5 :** a means of continuing a journey by transferring to another conveyance ⟨make a *connection* for New York at Chicago⟩ **6 :** a set of persons associated together: as **a :** DENOMINATION 3 **b :** a large family **:** CLAN — **con•nec-**

\ə\ **abut**	\au̇\ **out**	\i\ **tip**	\ȯ\ **saw**	\u̇\ **foot**
\ər\ **further**	\ch\ **chin**	\ī\ **life**	\ȯi\ **coin**	\y\ **yet**
\a\ **mat**	\e\ **pet**	\j\ **job**	\th\ **thin**	\yü\ **few**
\ā\ **take**	\ē\ **easy**	\ng\ **sing**	\th̲\ **this**	\yu̇\ **cure**
\ä\ **cot, cart**	\g\ **go**	\ō\ **bone**	\ü\ **food**	\zh\ **vision**

tion·al \-shnəl, -shən-ᵊl\ *adj*

[1]**con·nec·tive** \kə-ˈnek-tiv\ *adj* : connecting or tending to connect — **con·nec·tive·ly** *adv* — **con·nec·tiv·i·ty** \ˌkä-ˌnek-ˈtiv-ət-ē\ *n*

[2]**connective** *n* : something that connects; *esp* : a word or expression (as a conjunction or a relative pronoun) that connects words or word groups

connective tissue *n* : a tissue of mesodermal origin with much intercellular substance or many interlacing processes that forms a supporting framework (as of bone, cartilage, and fibrous tissue) for the body and its parts

connector neuron *n* : an internuncial neuron

conn·ing tower \ˈkän-iŋ-\ *n* **1** : an armored pilothouse (as on a battleship) **2** : a raised structure on the deck of a submarine that contains observation and communications equipment for use when the submarine is on the surface [*conn* "to direct the steering of a ship", from Middle English *condien* "to conduct", from Middle French *conduire,* from Latin *conducere*]

conning tower 2

con·nip·tion \kə-ˈnip-shən\ *n* : a fit of rage, hysteria, or alarm [origin unknown]

con·niv·ance \kə-ˈnī-vəns\ *n* : the act of conniving; *esp* : knowledge of and active or passive consent to wrongdoing

con·nive \kə-ˈnīv\ *vi* **1** : to pretend ignorance of something that one ought to oppose or stop **2** : to cooperate secretly or have a secret understanding **3** : PLOT 3, CONSPIRE [Latin *conivēre, connivēre* "to close the eyes, connive"] — **con·niv·er** *n*

con·nois·seur \ˌkän-ə-ˈsər *also* -ˈsu̇r\ *n* : a person qualified to act as a judge in matters involving taste and appreciation : EXPERT ⟨a *connoisseur* of French painting⟩ [obsolete French, from Old French *connoistre* "to know", from Latin *cognoscere,* from *com-* + *gnoscere, noscere* "to know"] — **con·nois·seur·ship** \-ˌship\ *n*

con·no·ta·tion \ˌkän-ə-ˈtā-shən\ *n* **1** : a meaning or significance suggested by a word apart from and in addition to the thing it explicitly names or describes ⟨the word *home* with all its heart-warming *connotations*⟩ — compare DENOTATION 2 **2** : something implied : IMPLICATION ⟨a speech with political *connotations*⟩ — **con·no·ta·tion·al** \-shnəl, -shən-ᵊl\ *adj*

con·no·ta·tive \ˈkän-ə-ˌtāt-iv, kə-ˈnōt-ət-iv\ *adj* **1** : connoting or tending to connote **2** : relating to connotation — **con·no·ta·tive·ly** *adv*

con·note \kə-ˈnōt\ *vt* : to suggest or mean along with or in addition to the explicit meaning ⟨the word *home* usually *connotes* comfort and security⟩ [Medieval Latin *connotare,* from Latin *com-* + *notare* "to note"] **syn** see DENOTE

con·nu·bi·al \kə-ˈnü-bē-əl, -ˈnyü-\ *adj* : of or relating to marriage : CONJUGAL [Latin *connubium* "marriage", from *com-* + *nubere* "to marry"] — **con·nu·bi·al·ly** \-bē-ə-lē\ *adv*

co·noid \ˈkō-ˌnȯid\ *or* **co·noi·dal** \kō-ˈnȯid-ᵊl\ *adj* : shaped like or nearly like a cone — **conoid** *n*

con·quer \ˈkäŋ-kər\ *vb* **con·quered**; **con·quer·ing** \-kə-riŋ, -kriŋ\ **1** : to gain or acquire by force of arms : SUBJUGATE ⟨*conquer* a country⟩ **2** : to overcome by force of arms : VANQUISH ⟨*conquered* all their enemies⟩ **3** : to master or win by overcoming obstacles or opposition ⟨*conquered* the mountain⟩ **4** : to overcome by mental or moral power ⟨*conquer* one's fear⟩ **5** : to be victorious [Old French *conquerre,* from Latin *conquirere* "to search for, collect", from *com-* + *quaerere* "to seek, ask"] — **con·quer·or** *n*

• **syn** SUBDUE, SUBJUGATE, VANQUISH: CONQUER implies gaining mastery of after a prolonged effort and with more or less permanent result; SUBDUE implies overpowering and suppressing; SUBJUGATE stresses a bringing under oppressive or humiliating rule or control; VANQUISH implies a complete or final overpowering.

con·quest \ˈkän-ˌkwest, ˈkäŋ-\ *n* **1** : the act or process of conquering **2 a** : something conquered; *esp* : territory seized in war **b** : a person whose affections have been won [Old French, from Latin *conquisitus,* past participle of *conquirere* "to search for, collect"] **syn** see VICTORY

con·quis·ta·dor \kȯŋ-ˈkēs-tə-ˌdȯr; kän-ˈkis-, -ˈkwis-; kən-\ *n, pl* **con·quis·ta·do·res** \kȯŋ-ˌkēs-tə-ˈdȯr-ēz, -ˈdȯr-ˌās, -ˈdōr-; kän-ˌkis-, -kwis-; kən-\ *or* **con·quis·ta·dors** : one that conquers; *esp* : a leader in the Spanish conquest of America and especially of Mexico and Peru in the 16th century [Spanish, from *conquista* "conquest"]

con·san·guin·e·ous \ˌkän-ˌsan-ˈgwin-ē-əs, -ˌsaŋ-\ *adj* : of the same blood or origin; *esp* : descended from the same ancestor — **con·san·guin·e·ous·ly** *adv* — **con·san·guin·i·ty** \-ˈgwin-ət-ē\ *n*

con·science \ˈkän-chəns\ *n* : the sense or consciousness of the moral goodness or badness of one's own conduct, intentions, or character together with a feeling of obligation to do right or be good [Old French, from Latin *conscientia,* from *conscire* "to be conscious, be conscious of guilt", from *com-* + *scire* "to know"] — **in all conscience** *or* **in conscience 1** : in all fairness **2** : beyond a doubt : to be sure

conscience money *n* : money paid to relieve the conscience by restoring what has been wrongfully acquired

con·sci·en·tious \ˌkän-chē-ˈen-chəs\ *adj* **1** : governed by or in accordance with one's conscience : SCRUPULOUS **2** : marked by or done with exactness and thought : CAREFUL ⟨*conscientious* workmanship⟩ — **con·sci·en·tious·ly** *adv* — **con·sci·en·tious·ness** *n*

conscientious objector *n* : a person who refuses to serve in the armed forces or bear arms on the grounds of moral or religious principles

con·scious \ˈkän-chəs\ *adj* **1** : perceiving or noticing facts or feelings **2** : personally felt ⟨*conscious* guilt⟩ **3** : capable of or marked by thought, will, design, or perception **4** : marked by self-consciousness **5** : mentally alert or active : AWAKE **6** : done or acting with critical awareness ⟨a *conscious* effort⟩ [Latin *conscius,* from *com-* + *scire* "to know"] — **con·scious·ly** *adv*

con·scious·ness \ˈkän-chəs-nəs\ *n* **1** : awareness of something ⟨*consciousness* of evil⟩ **2** : the condition of having ability to feel, think, and react : MIND **3** : the normal state of conscious life as distinguished from sleep or insensibility **4** : the part of mental life that is characterized by conscious thought and awareness

[1]**con·script** \ˈkän-ˌskript\ *adj* **1** : enrolled into service by compulsion : DRAFTED **2** : made up of conscripted persons ⟨a *conscript* army⟩ [Middle French, from Latin *conscribere* "to enroll", from *com-* + *scribere* "to write"]

[2]**conscript** *n* : a person who has been conscripted

[3]**con·script** \kən-ˈskript\ *vt* : to enroll into service by compulsion : DRAFT

con·scrip·tion \kən-ˈskrip-shən\ *n* **1** : compulsory enrollment of persons especially for military service : DRAFT **2** : a forced contribution (as of money) imposed by a government in time of emergency (as war)

[1]**con·se·crate** \ˈkän-sə-ˌkrāt\ *adj* : dedicated to a sacred purpose

[2]**consecrate** *vb* **1** : to induct into a permanent office with a religious rite; *esp* : to ordain to the office of bishop **2** : to make or declare sacred : set apart for the service of God **3** : to devote to a purpose with deep solemnity or dedication ⟨*consecrate* one's life to the dance⟩ **4** : to make inviolate or venerable ⟨rules *consecrated* by time⟩ [Latin *consecrare,* from *com-* + *sacrare* "to consecrate", from *sacer* "sacred"] — **con·se·cra·tor** \-ˌkrāt-ər\ *n*

con·se·cra·tion \ˌkän-sə-ˈkrā-shən\ *n* **1** : the act or ceremony of consecrating **2** : the state of being consecrated **3** *often cap* : the part of a Communion rite in which the bread and wine are consecrated

con·sec·u·tive \kən-ˈsek-yət-iv, -ət-\ *adj* : following one after the other in order without gaps [Latin *consecutus,* past participle of *consequi* "to follow along"] — **con·sec·u·tive·ly** *adv* — **con·sec·u·tive·ness** *n*

• **syn** CONSECUTIVE, SUCCESSIVE mean following one after the other. CONSECUTIVE stresses immediacy in following and implies that no interruption or interval occurs in the series ⟨three *consecutive* terms in office⟩ SUCCESSIVE may apply to things of the same kind that follow each other regardless of length of interval between ⟨rain fell on three *successive* weekends⟩

con·sen·sus \kən-ˈsen-səs\ *n* **1** : general agreement (as in opinion or testimony) : ACCORD **2** : the trend of opinion [Latin, from *consentire* "to agree in feeling"]

[1]**con·sent** \kən-ˈsent\ *vi* : to give assent or approval : AGREE

[Latin *consentire* "to agree in feeling", from *com-* + *sentire* "to feel"]

[2]**consent** *n* : compliance in or approval of what is asked or proposed : ACQUIESCENCE

con•se•quence \'kän-sə-,kwens, -si-kwəns\ *n* **1** : something produced by a cause or necessarily following from a set of conditions **2** : a conclusion that results from reason or argument **3 a** : importance with respect to power to produce an effect : MOMENT ⟨a mistake of no *consequence*⟩ **b** : social importance ⟨a person of *consequence*⟩ **syn** see EFFECT

[1]**con•se•quent** \-si-kwənt, -sə-,kwent\ *n* **1** : the conclusion of a conditional sentence **2** : the second term of a ratio

[2]**consequent** *adj* **1** : following as a result or effect **2** : observing logical sequence : RATIONAL [Middle French, from Latin *consequi* "to follow along", from *com-* + *sequi* "to follow"]

con•se•quen•tial \,kän-sə-'kwen-chəl\ *adj* **1** : of the nature of a consequence or result : following as a consequence **2** : having significant consequences : IMPORTANT **3** : having or displaying self-importance ⟨a *consequential* manner⟩ — **con•se•quen•tial•ly** \-'kwench-lē, -ə-lē\ *adv* — **con•se•quen•tial•ness** \-'kwen-chəl-nəs\ *n*

con•se•quent•ly \'kän-sə-,kwent-lē, -kwənt-\ *adv* : as a result : ACCORDINGLY

con•ser•van•cy \kən-'sər-vən-sē\ *n, pl* **-cies** : an organization or area designated to conserve and protect natural resources

con•ser•va•tion \,kän-sər-'vā-shən\ *n* : a careful preservation and protection of something; *esp* : planned management of a natural resource to prevent exploitation, destruction, or neglect — **con•ser•va•tion•al** \-shnəl, -shən-l\ *adj*

con•ser•va•tion•ist \-'vā-shə-nəst, -shnəst\ *n* : one who advocates conservation especially of natural resources

conservation of energy : a principle in physics: the total energy of an isolated system remains constant irrespective of whatever internal changes may take place

conservation of mass : a principle in classical physics: the total mass of any material system is neither increased nor diminished by reactions between the parts — called also *conservation of matter*

con•ser•va•tism \kən-'sər-və-,tiz-əm\ *n* **1 a** : disposition in politics to preserve what is established **b** : a political philosophy supporting tradition, social stability, and established institutions and preferring gradual development to abrupt change **2** : the tendency to prefer an existing situation and to be suspicious of change

[1]**con•ser•va•tive** \kən-'sər-vət-iv\ *adj* **1** : tending to conserve or preserve **2 a** : of or relating to conservatism **b** *often cap* : of or constituting a political party professing conservatism **3 a** : tending or disposed to maintain existing views, conditions, or institutions : TRADITIONAL **b** : MODERATE, CAUTIOUS ⟨a *conservative* investment⟩ **c** : marked by traditional standards of taste, elegance, or manners ⟨a *conservative* suit⟩ — **con•ser•va•tive•ly** *adv* — **con•ser•va•tive•ness** *n*

[2]**conservative** *n* **1 a** : an adherent or advocate of conservatism **b** *often cap* : a member or supporter of a conservative political party **2** : a cautious or discreet person

Conservative Judaism *n* : a movement in Judaism that holds sacred the Torah and the religious traditions but accepts some liturgical and ritual change

con•ser•va•tor \kən-'sər-vət-ər, -və-,tȯr; 'kän-sər-,vāt-ər\ *n* **1** : one that preserves or guards : PROTECTOR **2** : one designated to take over and protect the interests of an incompetent **3** : an official charged with the protection of something affecting public welfare and interests

con•ser•va•to•ry \kən-'sər-və-,tōr-ē, -,tȯr-\ *n, pl* **-ries** **1** : a greenhouse for growing or displaying plants **2** : a school specializing in one of the fine arts

[1]**con•serve** \kən-'sərv\ *vt* **1** : to keep in a safe or sound state : PRESERVE ⟨*conserve* natural resources⟩ **2** : to preserve with sugar [Middle French *conserver,* from Latin *conservare,* from *com-* + *servare* "to keep, guard, observe"] — **con•serv•er** *n*

[2]**con•serve** \'kän-,sərv\ *n* **1** : CONFECTION; *esp* : a candied fruit **2** : PRESERVE; *esp* : one prepared from a mixture of fruits

con•sid•er \kən-'sid-ər\ *vb* **-sid•ered**; **-sid•er•ing** \-'sid-ring, -ə-ring\ **1** : to think over carefully : PONDER **2** : to regard highly : ESTEEM **3** : to think of in a certain way : regard as being ⟨*consider* the price too high⟩ [Middle French *considerer,* from Latin *considerare,* literally, "to observe the stars", from *com-* + *sider-, sidus* "star"]

con•sid•er•able \kən-'sid-ər-bəl, -ər-ə-bəl, -'sid-rə-bəl\ *adj* **1** : worth consideration : IMPORTANT **2** : large in extent or degree ⟨a *considerable* area⟩ ⟨a *considerable* number⟩ — **con•sid•er•ably** \-blē\ *adv*

con•sid•er•ate \kən-'sid-rət, -ə-rət\ *adj* **1** : marked by or given to careful consideration : CIRCUMSPECT **2** : thoughtful of the rights and feelings of others **syn** see THOUGHTFUL — **con•sid•er•ate•ly** *adv* — **con•sid•er•ate•ness** *n*

con•sid•er•ation \kən-,sid-ə-'rā-shən\ *n* **1** : careful thought : DELIBERATION **2** : something considered as a ground : REASON **3** : thoughtfulness for other people **4** : RESPECT 3a, REGARD ⟨a person of *consideration* in that field⟩ **5** : a payment made in return for something : COMPENSATION

con•sid•er•ing \-'sid-ring,-ə-ring\ *prep* : in view of : taking into account

con•sign \kən-'sīn\ *vt* **1** : to give over to another's care : ENTRUST **2** : to give, transfer, or deliver formally ⟨*consign* a body to the grave⟩ **3** : to send or address to an agent to be cared for or sold [Middle French *consigner,* from Latin *consignare,* from *com-* + *signum* "sign, mark, seal"] — **con•sign•able** \-'sī-nə-bəl\ *adj* — **con•sign•ee** \kən-,sī-'nē, ,kän-,sī-, ,kän-sə-\ *n* — **con•sign•or** \kən-'sī-nər; kən-,sī-'nȯr, ,kän-,sī-, ,kän-sə-\ *n*

con•sign•ment \kən-'sīn-mənt\ *n* **1** : the act or process of consigning **2** : something consigned especially in a single shipment

con•sist \kən-'sist\ *vi* **1** : to be contained : LIE — used with *in* ⟨honesty *consists* in telling the truth⟩ **2** : to be composed — used with *of* ⟨breakfast *consisted* of bacon and eggs⟩ [Latin *consistere,* literally, "to stand together", from *com-* + *sistere* "to take a stand"]

con•sis•tence \kən-'sis-təns\ *n* : CONSISTENCY

con•sis•ten•cy \kən-'sis-tən-sē\ *n, pl* **-cies** **1** : the degree of density, firmness, viscosity, or resistance to movement or separation of constituent particles ⟨mud with the *consistency* of glue⟩ **2 a** : agreement or harmony of parts or features to one another or a whole **b** : harmony of conduct or practice with past performance or stated aims

con•sis•tent \kən-'sis-tənt\ *adj* **1** : marked by harmony, regularity, or steady continuity ⟨*consistent* statements⟩ **2** : conforming steadily to one's own belief, professions, or character ⟨were *consistent* in their opposition⟩ **3** : having a common solution ⟨*consistent* linear equations⟩ — **con•sis•tent•ly** *adv*

con•sis•to•ry \kən-'sis-tə-rē, -trē\ *n, pl* **-ries** : a solemn meeting of Roman Catholic cardinals presided over by the pope [Medieval Latin *consistorium* "church tribunal", from Latin *consistere* "to stand together, consist"] — **con•sis•to•ri•al** \,kän-,sis-'tōr-ē-əl, -'tȯr-, kən-\ *adj*

con•so•la•tion \,kän-sə-'lā-shən\ *n* **1** : the act or an instance of consoling : the state of being consoled : COMFORT **2** : a contest held for those who have lost early in a tournament — **con•sol•a•to•ry** \kən-'sō-lə-,tōr-ē, -'säl-ə-, -,tȯr-\ *adj*

consolation prize *n* : a prize given to a runner-up or a loser in a contest

[1]**con•sole** \kən-'sōl\ *vt* : to lessen the grief or sense of loss of [French *consoler,* from Latin *consolari,* from *com-* + *solari* "to console"] **syn** see COMFORT — **con•sol•able** \-'sō-lə-bəl\ *adj*

[2]**con•sole** \'kän-,sōl\ *n* **1** : an architectural bracket used for ornament or support **2 a** : the desk from which an organ is played and which contains the keyboards, pedal board, and controls **b** : a panel or cabinet on which are mounted dials and switches used in controlling an electronic or mechanical device or system **3** : a cabinet (as for a radio or television set) designed to rest directly on the floor [French, from Middle French, short for *consolateur* "bracket in human shape", literally, "consoler", from Latin *consolator,* from *consolari* "to console"]

console table \'kän-,sōl-\ *n* **1** : a table fixed to a wall with its top supported by brackets or bracket-shaped legs **2** : a table designed to fit against a wall

con•sol•i•date \kən-'säl-ə-,dāt\ *vb* **1** : MERGE 2 **2** : to make firm or secure : STRENGTHEN ⟨*consolidate* a beachhead⟩ **3** : to form into a compact mass [Latin *consolidare* "to make solid", from *com-* + *solidus* "solid"]

consolidated school *n* : a public school formed by merging other schools

con·sol·i·da·tion \kən-ˌsäl-ə-ˈdā-shən\ *n* **1** : the act or process of consolidating : the state of being consolidated **2** : the merger of two or more corporations into one

con·som·mé \ˌkän-sə-ˈmā\ *n* : a clear soup chiefly of meat stock [French, from *consommer* "to complete, boil down", from Latin *consummare* "to complete"]

con·so·nance \ˈkän-sə-nəns, -snəns\ *n* **1** : harmony or agreement of parts **2 a** : an agreeable combination or correspondence of musical tones or speech sounds **b** : a musical interval included in a major or minor triad and its inversions

[1]**con·so·nant** \ˈkän-sə-nənt, -snənt\ *n* **1** : a speech sound (as \p\, \n\, or \s\) characterized by narrowing or stoppage at one or more points in the breath channel **2** : a letter representing a consonant; *esp* : any letter of the English alphabet except *a, e, i, o,* and *u* [Latin *consonans,* from *consonare* "to sound together, agree", from *com-* + *sonare* "to sound"]

[2]**consonant** *adj* **1** : being in agreement or harmony ⟨*consonant* with the truth⟩ **2** : marked by musical consonances **3** : having like sounds ⟨*consonant* words⟩ — **con·so·nant·ly** *adv*

con·so·nan·tal \ˌkän-sə-ˈnant-l\ *adj* : relating to, being, or marked by a consonant or group of consonants

[1]**con·sort** \ˈkän-ˌsȯrt\ *n* **1** : a ship sailing in company with another ship **2** : a married person : SPOUSE [Middle French, "associate", from Latin *consors,* literally, "one who shares a common lot", from *com-* + *sors* "lot, share"]

[2]**con·sort** \kən-ˈsȯrt\ *vb* **1** : to keep company : ASSOCIATE ⟨*consorting* with criminals⟩ **2** : to be or come into accord : HARMONIZE

con·sor·tium \kən-ˈsȯr-shē-əm, -shəm\ *n, pl* **-tia** \-shē-ə, -shə\ : an international business or banking agreement or combination [Latin, "fellowship", from *consors* "associate"]

con·spe·cif·ic \ˌkän-spi-ˈsif-ik\ *adj* : of the same species

con·spec·tus \kən-ˈspek-təs\ *n* **1** : a brief survey or summary **2** : a condensed version of a larger work : SYNOPSIS [Latin, "sight", from *conspicere* "to get sight of"]

con·spic·u·ous \kən-ˈspik-yə-wəs\ *adj* **1** : obvious to the eye or mind **2** : attracting attention : STRIKING **3** : noticeably violating good taste [Latin *conspicuus,* from *conspicere* "to get sight of", from *com-* + *specere* "to look"] — **con·spic·u·ous·ly** *adv* — **con·spic·u·ous·ness** *n*

con·spir·a·cy \kən-ˈspir-ə-sē\ *n, pl* **-cies** **1** : the act of conspiring together **2 a** : an agreement among conspirators **b** : a group of conspirators **syn** see PLOT

con·spir·a·tor \kən-ˈspir-ət-ər\ *n* : one that conspires : PLOTTER

con·spir·a·to·ri·al \kən-ˌspir-ə-ˈtōr-ē-əl, -ˈtȯr-\ *adj* : of, relating to, or characteristic of a conspiracy — **con·spir·a·to·ri·al·ly** \-ē\ *adv*

con·spire \kən-ˈspīr\ *vi* **1** : to agree secretly to do an unlawful or wrongful act or to use such means to accomplish a lawful end ⟨*conspire* against the state⟩ **2** : to act in harmony ⟨events *conspired* to defeat their efforts⟩ [Middle French *conspirer,* from Latin *conspirare* "to breathe together, agree, conspire", from *com-* + *spirare* "to breathe"]

con·sta·ble \ˈkän-stə-bəl, ˈkən-\ *n* **1** : a high officer of a medieval royal or noble household **2** : the warden of a royal castle or a fortified town **3 a** : a public officer responsible for keeping the peace **b** : a British policeman [Old French *conestable,* from Late Latin *comes stabuli,* literally, "officer of the stable"]

△ **origin** When the word *constable* first came into English from French in the Middle Ages, a *conestable* was the chief officer of a king's household. His office was one of great power: he was commander of the army and supreme judge, subordinate only to the king himself. Latin *comes stabuli,* which is the ancestor of *constable,* means literally "officer of the stable". But the title was transferred from stable to court. The increase in prestige was not as great as it may seem. All the king's horses were scarcely less valuable to the king than all his men, and being in charge of them was a very important duty.

con·stab·u·lary \kən-ˈstab-yə-ˌler-ē\ *n, pl* **-lar·ies** **1** : an organized body of police **2** : an armed police force organized on military lines but distinct from the regular army

con·stan·cy \ˈkän-stən-sē\ *n* **1 a** : firmness in one's beliefs : STEADFASTNESS **b** : steadiness in attachments : LOYALTY **2** : freedom from change : STABILITY

[1]**con·stant** \ˈkän-stənt\ *adj* **1** : marked by firm resolution or faithfulness : STEADFAST **2** : remaining unchanged : UNIFORM **3** : continually occurring or recurring : REGULAR [Middle French, from Latin *constans,* from *constare* "to stand firm", from *com-* + *stare* "to stand"] **syn** see CONTINUAL, FAITHFUL — **con·stant·ly** *adv*

[2]**constant** *n* : something invariable or unchanging: as **a** : a number that has a fixed value (as the velocity of light) in a given situation or universally or that is a characteristic (as the refractive index of glass) of some substance or instrument **b** : a number whose value does not change in a given mathematical discussion

con·stan·tan \ˈkän-stən-ˌtan\ *n* : an alloy of copper and nickel used for electrical resistors and in thermocouples [from the fact that its resistance remains constant under change of temperature]

con·stel·la·tion \ˌkän-stə-ˈlā-shən\ *n* : any of 88 groups of stars forming patterns (as the Big Dipper) or an area of the heavens covering one of these groups [Middle French, from Late Latin *constellatio,* from Latin *com-* + *stella* "star"]

con·ster·nate \ˈkän-stər-ˌnāt\ *vt* : to fill with consternation

con·ster·na·tion \ˌkän-stər-ˈnā-shən\ *n* : amazement or dismay that hinders or throws into confusion [Latin *consternatio,* from *consternare* "to bewilder, alarm"]

con·sti·pate \ˈkän-stə-ˌpāt\ : to cause constipation in [Medieval Latin *constipare,* from Latin, "to crowd together", from *com-* + *stipare* "to press together"]

con·sti·pa·tion \ˌkän-stə-ˈpā-shən\ *n* : abnormally delayed or infrequent passage of dry hardened feces

con·stit·u·en·cy \kən-ˈstich-wən-sē, -ə-wən-\ *n, pl* **-cies** **1** : a body of citizens entitled to elect a representative to a legislative or other public body **2 a** : the residents in an electoral district **b** : an electoral district **3** : a group of supporters

[1]**con·stit·u·ent** \kən-ˈstich-wənt, -ə-wənt\ *n* **1** : an essential part : COMPONENT, ELEMENT ⟨flour is the chief *constituent* of bread⟩ **2 a** : one of a group who elects another as a representative in public office **b** : a resident in a constituency [French *constituant,* from Middle French *constituer* "to constitute", from Latin *constituere*] **syn** see ELEMENT

[2]**constituent** *adj* **1** : forming a part of a whole : COMPONENT **2** : having the power to create a government or to frame or amend a constitution ⟨a *constituent* assembly⟩ — **con·stit·u·ent·ly** *adv*

con·sti·tute \ˈkän-stə-ˌtüt, -ˌtyüt\ *vt* **1** : to appoint to an office or duty ⟨a duly *constituted* representative⟩ **2** : to set up : ESTABLISH ⟨a fund was *constituted* to help needy students⟩ **3** : to make up : FORM ⟨twelve months *constitute* a year⟩ [Latin *constituere* "to set up, constitute", from *com-* + *statuere* "to set, fix", from *status* "standing, status"]

con·sti·tu·tion \ˌkän-stə-ˈtü-shən, -ˈtyü-\ *n* **1** : the act of establishing, making, or setting up **2 a** : the physical makeup of an individual : PHYSIQUE **b** : the structure, composition, or nature of something **3 a** : the basic principles and laws of a nation, state, or social group that determine the powers and duties of the government and guarantee certain rights to the people in it **b** : a document containing a constitution

[1]**con·sti·tu·tion·al** \-shnəl, -shən-l\ *adj* **1** : of, relating to, or affecting a person's physical or mental makeup **2** : of, relating to, or entering into the fundamental makeup of something : ESSENTIAL **3** : of, relating to, or in accordance with the constitution of a nation or state ⟨a *constitutional* amendment⟩ ⟨*constitutional* rights⟩ — **con·sti·tu·tion·al·ly** \-ē\ *adv*

[2]**constitutional** *n* : a walk taken for one's health

con·sti·tu·tion·al·ism \-ˌiz-əm\ *n* : adherence to or government according to constitutional principles — **con·sti·tu·tion·al·ist** \-əst\ *n*

con·sti·tu·tion·al·i·ty \ˌkän-stə-ˌtü-shə-ˈnal-ət-ē, -ˌtyü-\ *n* : the quality or state of being in accordance with the provisions of a constitution

con·sti·tu·tive \ˈkän-stə-ˌtüt-iv, -ˌtyüt-; kən-ˈstich-ət-iv\ *adj* : forming part of the structure of a thing : CONSTITUENT, ESSENTIAL — **con·sti·tu·tive·ly** *adv*

con·strain \kən-ˈstrān\ *vt* **1** : to force by imposed restriction or limitation **2** : to force or produce in an unnatural or strained manner ⟨a *constrained* smile⟩ **3** : to secure by or as if by bond : CONFINE **4** : to hold back by force : RESTRAIN [Middle French *constraindre,* from Latin *constringere* "to constrict, constrain", from *com-* + *stringere* "to draw tight"] **syn** see FORCE — **con·strained·ly** \-ˈstrān-əd-lē, -ˈstrān-dlē\ *adv*

con·straint \kən-ˈstrānt\ *n* **1 a** : the act of constraining : the state of being constrained **b** : a constraining agency or force

: CHECK ⟨legal *constraints*⟩ **2 a :** a holding back of one's feelings, behavior, or actions **b :** a sense of being constrained : EMBARRASSMENT

con•strict \kən-ˈstrikt\ *vb* **1 a :** to make or become smaller in bulk or volume by means of compression; *also* : SQUEEZE 1a, COMPRESS ⟨snakes that kill by *constricting* their prey⟩ **b :** to make or become narrow or narrower ⟨the pupil of the eye *constricts* in bright light⟩ **2 :** to slow down, stop, or cause to falter : INHIBIT **[**Latin *constrictus,* past participle of *constringere* "to constrict, constrain"**]** — **con•stric•tive** \-ˈstrik-tiv\ *adj*

con•stric•tion \kən-ˈstrik-shən\ *n* **1 :** an act of constricting : the state of being constricted **2 :** something that constricts : a part that is constricted

con•stric•tor \kən-ˈstrik-tər\ *n* **1 :** one that constricts **2 :** a snake that kills prey by compression in its coils

con•struct \kən-ˈstrəkt\ *vt* **1 :** to make or form by combining parts **2 :** to draw (a geometrical figure) with suitable instruments and under specified conditions **[**Latin *constructus,* past participle of *construere* "to construct", from *com-* + *struere* "to build"**]** — **con•struct•ible** \-ˈstrək-tə-bəl\ *adj* — **con•struc•tor** \-ˈstrək-tər\ *n*

con•struc•tion \kən-ˈstrək-shən\ *n* **1 :** the arrangement and connection of words or groups of words in a sentence **2 :** the process, art, or manner of constructing; *also* **:** a thing constructed : STRUCTURE **3 :** an interpretation or explanation of a statement or a fact ⟨put the wrong *construction* on a remark⟩ — **con•struc•tion•al** \-shnəl, -shən-ᵊl\ *adj* — **con•struc•tion•al•ly** \-ē\ *adv*

con•struc•tion•ist \kən-ˈstrək-shə-nəst, -shnəst\ *n* **:** one who construes a legal document (as the United States Constitution) in a specific way ⟨a strict *constructionist*⟩

construction paper *n* **:** a thick colored paper used especially for school art work

con•struc•tive \kən-ˈstrək-tiv\ *adj* **1 :** fitted for or given to constructing ⟨Edison was a *constructive* genius⟩ **2 :** helping to develop or improve something ⟨*constructive* criticism⟩ — **con•struc•tive•ly** *adv* — **con•struc•tive•ness** *n*

con•strue \kən-ˈstrü\ *vb* **1 :** to explain the grammatical relationships of the words in a sentence, clause, or phrase **2 :** to understand or explain the sense or intention of : INTERPRET **[**Late Latin *construere,* from Latin, "to construct"**]** — **con•stru•able** \-ˈstrü-ə-bəl\ *adj*

con•sul \ˈkän-səl\ *n* **1 :** either of two chief magistrates of the Roman republic **2 :** an official appointed by a government to live in a foreign country to represent the commercial interests of citizens of the appointing country **[**Latin, from *consulere* "to consult"**]** — **con•sul•ar** \-sə-lər, -slər\ *adj* — **con•sul•ship** \-səl-ˌship\ *n*

con•sul•ate \ˈkän-sə-lət, -slət\ *n* **1 :** a government by consuls **2 :** the office, term of office, or jurisdiction of a consul **3 :** the residence or official premises of a consul

con•sult \kən-ˈsəlt\ *vb* **1 :** to ask the advice or opinion of ⟨*consult* a doctor⟩ **2 :** to seek information from ⟨*consult* a dictionary⟩ **3 :** to have regard to : CONSIDER ⟨*consult* one's best interests⟩ **4 :** to deliberate together : CONFER **[**Latin *consultare,* from *consultus,* past participle of *consulere* "to deliberate, counsel, consult"**]** — **con•sult•er** *n*

con•sult•ant \kən-ˈsəlt-ⁿt\ *n* **1 :** one who consults another **2 :** one who gives professional advice or services

con•sul•ta•tion \ˌkän-səl-ˈtā-shən\ *n* **1 :** CONFERENCE 1, COUNCIL; *esp* **:** a deliberation between physicians on a case or its treatment **2 :** the act of consulting or conferring

con•sul•ta•tive \kən-ˈsəl-tət-iv\ *adj* **:** of, relating to, or intended for consultation : ADVISORY

con•sul•tor \kən-ˈsəl-tər\ *n* **:** one that consults or advises; *esp* **:** a member of a Roman Catholic diocesan advisory council

con•sume \kən-ˈsüm\ *vb* **1 :** to destroy or be destroyed by or as if by fire **2 a :** to spend wastefully : SQUANDER **b :** to use up : EXPEND ⟨hard work *consumed* our energy⟩ **3 :** to eat or drink up **4 :** to engage one's interest or attention ⟨*consumed* with curiosity⟩ **[**Latin *consumere,* from *com-* + *sumere* "to take up, take", from *sub-* "up" + *emere* "to take"**]** — **con•sum•able** \-ˈsü-mə-bəl\ *adj*

con•sum•er \kən-ˈsü-mər\ *n* **:** one that consumes: as **a :** one that buys and uses economic goods **b :** an organism requiring complex organic compounds for food which it obtains by preying on other organisms or by eating particles of organic matter — compare PRODUCER 3

consumer credit *n* **:** credit granted to an individual especially to finance purchase of consumer goods or defray personal or family expenses

consumer goods *n pl* **:** goods that directly satisfy human wants

con•sum•er•ism \kən-ˈsü-mə-ˌriz-əm\ *n* **:** concern for or protection of the consumer's welfare — **con•sum•er•ist** \-rəst\ *n*

[1]**con•sum•mate** \kən-ˈsəm-ət, ˈkän-sə-mət\ *adj* **1 :** complete in every detail : PERFECT **2 :** of the highest degree or quality ⟨*consummate* skill⟩ **[**Latin *consummare* "to sum up, finish", from *com-* + *summa* "sum"**]** — **con•sum•mate•ly** *adv*

[2]**con•sum•mate** \ˈkän-sə-ˌmāt\ *vt* **1 a :** to bring to completion : FINISH ⟨*consummate* a deal⟩ **b :** to make perfect **2 :** to make (marital union) complete by sexual intercourse — **con•sum•ma•tion** \ˌkän-sə-ˈmā-shən\ *n*

con•sump•tion \kən-ˈsəm-shən, -ˈsəmp-\ *n* **1 a :** the act or process of consuming **b :** the amount consumed ⟨yearly fuel *consumption*⟩ **2 a :** a progressive wasting away of the body especially from pulmonary tuberculosis **b :** TUBERCULOSIS **[**Latin *consumptio,* from *consumere* "to consume"**]**

[1]**con•sump•tive** \kən-ˈsəm-tiv, -ˈsəmp-\ *adj* **1 :** tending to consume **2 :** of, relating to, or affected with consumption — **con•sump•tive•ly** *adv*

[2]**consumptive** *n* **:** a person affected with consumption

[1]**con•tact** \ˈkän-ˌtakt\ *n* **1 a :** union or junction of surfaces **b** (1) **:** the junction of two electrical conductors through which a current passes (2) **:** a special part made for such a junction or connection **2 a :** a social or business connection ⟨has *contacts* in the government⟩ **b :** a condition or instance of meeting, connecting, or communicating ⟨let's keep in *contact*⟩ **c :** direct visual observation of the earth's surface made from an airplane especially as an aid to navigation **d :** an establishing of communication with someone or an observing or receiving of a significant signal from a person or object **[**Latin *contactus,* from *contingere* "to have contact with", from *com-* + *tangere* "to touch"**]**

[2]**con•tact** \ˈkän-ˌtakt, kən-ˈ\ *vb* **:** to bring or come into contact

[3]**con•tact** \ˈkän-ˌtakt\ *adj* **:** maintaining, involving, or caused by contact ⟨*contact* sports⟩

contact lens *n* **:** a thin lens designed to fit over the cornea

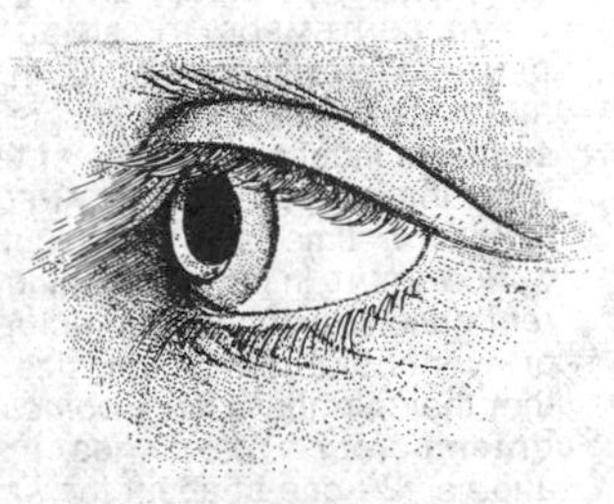
contact lens

contact print *n* **:** a photographic print made with the negative in contact with the sensitized paper, plate, or film

con•ta•gion \kən-ˈtā-jən\ *n* **1 :** the passing of a disease from one individual to another by direct or indirect contact **2 :** a contagious disease or its causative agent **3 a :** rapid communication of an influence (as an idea or doctrine) **b :** an influence that spreads rapidly **[**Latin *contagio,* from *contingere* "to have contact with"**]**

con•ta•gious \kən-ˈtā-jəs\ *adj* **1 :** communicable by contact : CATCHING **2 :** bearing contagion ⟨a person who is *contagious*⟩ **3 :** used for contagious diseases ⟨a *contagious* ward⟩ — **con•ta•gious•ly** *adv* — **con•ta•gious•ness** *n*

con•tain \kən-ˈtān\ *vt* **1 :** to keep within limits : hold back : RESTRAIN ⟨*contain* one's anger⟩ **2 a :** to have within : HOLD **b :** COMPRISE, INCLUDE ⟨a gallon *contains* four quarts⟩ **3 :** to be divisible by especially without a remainder ⟨12 *contains* 3⟩ **[**Old French *contenir,* from Latin *continēre* "to hold together, hold in, contain", from *com-* + *tenēre* "to hold"**]** — **con•tain•able** \-ˈtā-nə-bəl\ *adj*

• syn HOLD, ACCOMMODATE: CONTAIN implies the actual presence of a specified substance or quantity within something; HOLD may imply only the capacity or usual function of containing or keeping; ACCOMMODATE stresses capacity to hold without crowding or inconvenience.

con•tain•er \kən-ˈtā-nər\ *n* **:** one that contains; *esp* : RECEPTACLE

\ə\ **abut**	\au̇\ **out**	\i\ **tip**	\ȯ\ **saw**	\u̇\ **foot**
\ər\ **further**	\ch\ **chin**	\ī\ **life**	\ȯi\ **coin**	\y\ **yet**
\a\ **mat**	\e\ **pet**	\j\ **job**	\th\ **thin**	\yü\ **few**
\ā\ **take**	\ē\ **easy**	\ng\ **sing**	\t͟h\ **this**	\yu̇\ **cure**
\ä\ **cot, cart**	\g\ **go**	\ō\ **bone**	\ü\ **food**	\zh\ **vision**

con•tain•ment \kən-ˈtān-mənt\ *n* **1 :** the act or process of containing **2 :** the policy, process, or result of preventing the expansion of a hostile power or ideology

con•tam•i•nant \kən-ˈtam-ə-nənt\ *n* **:** something that contaminates

con•tam•i•nate \kən-ˈtam-ə-ˌnāt\ *vt* **1 :** to soil, stain, or infect by contact or association **2 :** to make unfit for use by introduction of unwholesome or undesirable elements [Latin *contaminare*] — **con•tam•i•na•tion** \-ˌtam-ə-ˈnā-shən\ *n* — **con•tam•i•na•tive** \-ˌnāt-iv\ *adj* — **con•tam•i•na•tor** \-ˈtam-ə-ˌnāt-ər\ *n*

con•temn \kən-ˈtem\ *vt* **:** to view or treat with contempt **:** SCORN [Middle French *contempner,* from Latin *contemnere,* from *com-* + *temnere* "to despise"] **syn** see DESPISE — **con•tem•ner** \-ˈtem-ər, -ˈtem-nər\ *n*

con•tem•plate \ˈkänt-əm-ˌplāt, ˈkän-ˌtem-\ *vb* **1 :** to consider long and carefully **:** MEDITATE **2 :** to look forward to **:** have in mind **:** INTEND [Latin *contemplari,* from *com-* + *templum* "temple, space marked out for observation of auguries"] — **con•tem•pla•tor** \-ˌplāt-ər\ *n*

con•tem•pla•tion \ˌkänt-əm-ˈplā-shən, ˌkän-ˌtem-\ *n* **1 :** concentration on spiritual things as a form of private devotion **2 :** an act of considering with attention **:** STUDY **3 :** the act of regarding steadily **4 :** the act of considering a future event **:** EXPECTATION

con•tem•pla•tive \kən-ˈtem-plət-iv; ˈkänt-əm-ˌplāt-, ˈkän-ˌtem-\ *adj* **1 :** marked by or given to contemplation **2 :** of or relating to a religious order devoted to prayer and penance — **con•tem•pla•tive•ly** *adv* — **con•tem•pla•tive•ness** *n*

con•tem•po•ra•ne•ous \kən-ˌtem-pə-ˈrā-nē-əs\ *adj* **:** existing, occurring, or originating during the same time [Latin *contemporaneus,* from *com-* + *tempor-, tempus* "time"] — **con•tem•po•ra•ne•ous•ly** *adv* — **con•tem•po•ra•ne•ous•ness** *n*

¹**con•tem•po•rary** \kən-ˈtem-pə-ˌrer-ē\ *adj* **1 :** living or occurring during the same time **:** CONTEMPORANEOUS ⟨*contemporary* events in different countries⟩ **2 :** of the same age **3 :** existing in the present **:** CURRENT ⟨our *contemporary* writers⟩ [*com-* + Latin *tempor-, tempus* "time"]

• **syn** CONTEMPORARY, SIMULTANEOUS, CONCURRENT, COINCIDENT mean existing or occurring at the same time. CONTEMPORARY applies chiefly to people and what relates to them and suggests indefinite lengths of time ⟨playwrights *contemporary* with Shakespeare⟩ SIMULTANEOUS implies correspondence in instant of time ⟨the two shots were almost *simultaneous*⟩ CONCURRENT implies beginning and ending together ⟨*concurrent* prison sentences⟩ COINCIDENT stresses simultaneousness of events and may emphasize lack of causal relation ⟨found that their birthdays were *coincident*⟩

²**contemporary** *n, pl* **-rar•ies 1 :** one that is contemporary with another **2 :** one of about the same age as another

con•tempt \kən-ˈtemt, -ˈtempt\ *n* **1 a :** the act of despising **b :** the state of mind of one who despises **:** DISDAIN **2 :** the state of being despised **3 :** disobedience to or open disrespect for a court, judge, or legislative body [Latin *contemptus,* from *contemnere* "to contemn"]

con•tempt•ible \kən-ˈtem-tə-bəl, -ˈtemp-\ *adj* **:** deserving contempt ⟨a *contemptible* lie⟩ — **con•tempt•ibly** \-blē\ *adv*

• **syn** DESPICABLE, SCURVY: CONTEMPTIBLE may apply to whatever is worthy of contempt; DESPICABLE implies arousing scornful often indignant moral disapproval; SCURVY implies extreme meanness and the arousing of disgust.

con•temp•tu•ous \kən-ˈtem-chə-wəs, -ˈtemp-, -chəs; -ˈtemsh-wəs, -ˈtempsh-\ *adj* **:** feeling or showing contempt ⟨a *contemptuous* sneer⟩ — **con•temp•tu•ous•ly** *adv* — **con•temp•tu•ous•ness** *n*

con•tend \kən-ˈtend\ *vb* **1 :** to strive in opposition to someone or something ⟨*contending* against temptation⟩ **2 :** MAINTAIN 2, ARGUE ⟨*contend* that their opinions are right⟩ **3 :** RIVAL 2, COMPETE ⟨*contend* for a prize⟩ [Latin *contendere,* from *com-* + *tendere* "to stretch"] — **con•tend•er** *n*

¹**con•tent** \kən-ˈtent\ *adj* **:** being satisfied ⟨*content* to wait⟩ [Middle French, from Latin *contentus,* from *continēre* "to hold in, contain"]

²**content** *vt* **:** to appease the desires of **:** SATISFY

³**content** *n* **:** CONTENTMENT; *esp* **:** freedom from care of discomfort

⁴**con•tent** \ˈkän-ˌtent\ *n* **1 :** something contained — usually used in pl. ⟨the *contents* of a jar⟩ **2 a :** the topics or matter treated in a written work ⟨table of *contents*⟩ **b :** essential meaning or significance **3 :** the amount of specified material contained **:** PROPORTION ⟨the sulfur *content* in a coal sample⟩ [Latin *contentus,* past participle of *continēre* "to contain"]

con•tent•ed \kən-ˈtent-əd\ *adj* **:** satisfied or showing satisfaction with one's possessions, status, or situation ⟨a *contented* smile⟩ — **con•tent•ed•ly** *adv* — **con•tent•ed•ness** *n*

con•ten•tion \kən-ˈten-chən\ *n* **1 :** an act or instance of contending **:** STRIFE, DISPUTE **2 :** a point advanced or maintained in a debate or argument [Middle French *contencioun,* from Latin *contentio,* from *contendere* "to contend"]

con•ten•tious \kən-ˈten-chəs\ *adj* **:** inclined to quarrels and disputes often over unimportant matters — **con•ten•tious•ly** *adv* — **con•ten•tious•ness** *n*

con•tent•ment \kən-ˈtent-mənt\ *n* **:** the state of being contented **:** peaceful satisfaction

con•ter•mi•nous \kən-ˈtər-mə-nəs, kän-\ *adj* **1 :** having the same or a common boundary **2 :** enclosed within one common boundary ⟨the 48 *conterminous* states of the United States⟩ [Latin *conterminus,* from *com-* + *terminus* "boundary"] — **con•ter•mi•nous•ly** *adv*

¹**con•test** \kən-ˈtest, ˈkän-ˌ\ *vb* **1 :** to make the subject of dispute or litigation; *esp* **:** CHALLENGE 3b ⟨*contest* a divorce⟩ **2 :** to struggle over or for ⟨a *contested* territory⟩ **3 :** RIVAL 2, VIE ⟨*contested* for the prize⟩ [Middle French *contester,* from Latin *contestari* "to call to witness, contest (a lawsuit)", from *com-* + *testis* "witness"] — **con•test•able** \-ə-bəl\ *adj* — **con•test•er** *n*

²**con•test** \ˈkän-ˌtest\ *n* **1 :** a struggle for victory or superiority ⟨a spelling *contest*⟩ **2 :** COMPETITION, RIVALRY ⟨meet in friendly *contest*⟩

con•tes•tant \kən-ˈtes-tənt, ˈkän-ˌtes-\ *n* **:** one that takes part in a contest

con•text \ˈkän-ˌtekst\ *n* **1 :** the parts of a written or spoken passage that are near a certain word or group of words and that help to explain its meaning **2 :** the circumstances surrounding an act or event [Latin *contextus* "connection of words, coherence", from *contexere* "to weave together", from *com-* + *texere* "to weave"] — **con•tex•tu•al** \kän-ˈteks-chə-wəl, -chəl\ *adj* — **con•tex•tu•al•ly** \-ē\ *adv*

con•ti•gu•i•ty \ˌkänt-ə-ˈgyü-ət-ē\ *n, pl* **-ties :** the quality or state of being contiguous **:** PROXIMITY

con•tig•u•ous \kən-ˈtig-yə-wəs\ *adj* **1 :** being in contact **:** TOUCHING **2 :** very near though not in actual contact **:** NEIGHBORING **3 :** CONTERMINOUS 2 [Latin *contiguus,* from *contingere* "to have contact with"] — **con•tig•u•ous•ly** *adv* — **con•tig•u•ous•ness** *n*

con•ti•nence \ˈkänt-n-əns\ *n* **:** self-restraint especially in the face of bodily temptation

¹**con•ti•nent** \ˈkänt-n-ənt\ *adj* **:** exercising continence [Middle French, from Latin *continens,* from *continēre* "to hold together, hold in, contain"] — **con•ti•nent•ly** *adv*

²**con•ti•nent** \ˈkänt-n-ənt, ˈkänt-nənt\ *n* **1 :** a continuous mass of land **2 a :** one of the great divisions of land (as North America, South America, Europe, Asia, Africa, Australia, or Antarctica) on the globe **b** *often cap* **:** the continent of Europe

¹**con•ti•nen•tal** \ˌkänt-n-ˈent-l\ *adj* **1 :** of, relating to, or characteristic of a continent ⟨*continental* waters⟩; *esp* **:** of or relating to the continent of Europe **2** *often cap* **:** of or relating to the colonies later forming the United States ⟨*Continental* Congress⟩ — **con•ti•nen•tal•ly** \-l-ē\ *adv*

²**continental** *n* **1 a** *often cap* **:** an American soldier of the Revolution in the Continental army **b :** a piece of paper currency issued by the Continental Congress **c :** an inhabitant of a continent and especially the continent of Europe **2 :** the least bit ⟨not worth a *continental*⟩ [sense 2 from the doubtful value of Continental currency]

continental drift *n* **:** a slow movement of the continents on a deep viscous zone within the earth **:** PLATE TECTONICS

continental shelf *n* **:** a shallow submarine plain of varying width forming a border to a continent and typically ending in a steep slope to the depths of the ocean

con•tin•gen•cy \kən-ˈtin-jən-sē\ *n, pl* **-cies 1 :** the state of being contingent **2 :** a chance happening or event **3 :** a possible event or one foreseen as possible if another occurs

¹**con•tin•gent** \-jənt\ *adj* **1 :** likely but not certain to happen **:** POSSIBLE **2 a :** happening by chance or unforeseen causes **b :** intended for use in circumstances not completely foreseen ⟨*contingent* funds⟩ **3 :** dependent on or conditioned by something else ⟨plans *contingent* on the weather⟩ [Middle French,

from Latin *contingere* "to have contact with, happen to"] — **con·tin·gent·ly** *adv*

[2]contingent *n* **1** : a chance occurrence : CONTINGENCY **2** : a number of persons representing or drawn from an area or group ⟨a *contingent* of troops from each regiment⟩

con·tin·u·al \kən-ˈtin-yə-wəl, -ˈtin-yəl\ *adj* **1** : continuing indefinitely without interruption ⟨*continual* fear⟩ **2** : recurring in rapid succession ⟨*continual* interruptions⟩ **3** : forming a continuous series — **con·tin·u·al·ly** \-ē\ *adv*

• **syn** CONTINUAL, CONTINUOUS, INCESSANT, CONSTANT mean marked by continued occurrence or recurrence. CONTINUAL implies prolonged succession or recurrence ⟨*continual* showers⟩ CONTINUOUS implies uninterrupted flow ⟨*continuous* roar of the falls⟩ INCESSANT implies ceaseless activity of varying intensity ⟨*incessant* quarreling⟩ CONSTANT implies uniform or persistent occurrence or recurrence ⟨a *constant* supply of work⟩

con·tin·u·ance \kən-ˈtin-yə-wəns\ *n* **1** : the act of continuing in a state, condition, or course of action ⟨during the *continuance* of the illness⟩ **2** : unbroken succession : CONTINUATION **3** : postponement of court proceedings to a specified day

con·tin·u·a·tion \kən-ˌtin-yə-ˈwā-shən\ *n* **1** : continuance in or extension of a state or activity **2** : resumption after an interruption **3** : something that continues, increases, or adds ⟨a *continuation* of last week's story⟩

con·tin·ue \kən-ˈtin-yü\ *vb* **1** : to remain in a place or a condition : STAY ⟨*continue* in one's present job⟩ **2** : ENDURE, LAST ⟨cold weather *continued*⟩ **3** : to go on or carry forward in a course ⟨*continue* to study hard⟩ **4** : to go on or carry on after an interruption : RESUME ⟨the play *continued* after the intermission⟩ **5** : to postpone a legal proceeding to a later date **6** : to allow or cause to remain especially in a position ⟨the town officials were *continued* in office⟩ [Middle French *continuer,* from Latin *continuare,* from *continuus* "continuous"] — **con·tin·u·er** *n*

continued fraction *n* : an expression in the form of a fraction whose numerator is an integer and whose denominator is an integer plus a fraction whose numerator is an integer and whose denominator is an integer plus a fraction and so on

con·ti·nu·ity \ˌkänt-n-ˈü-ət-ē, -ˈyü-\ *n, pl* **-ties 1 a** : uninterrupted connection, succession, or union **b** : persistence without change **2 a** : a motion-picture, radio, or television script **b** : transitional spoken or musical matter for a radio or television program

con·tin·u·ous \kən-ˈtin-yə-wəs\ *adj* : being without break or interruption : CONTINUED, UNBROKEN ⟨a *continuous* line⟩ [Latin *continuus,* from *continēre* "to hold together, contain"] **syn** see CONTINUAL — **con·tin·u·ous·ly** *adv* — **con·tin·u·ous·ness** *n*

con·tin·u·um \-yə-wəm\ *n, pl* **-ua** \-wə\ *also* **-u·ums 1** : something that is continuous and the same throughout **2** : something in which a common characteristic is observable in a series of imperceptible or indefinite variations [Latin, neuter of *continuus* "continuous"]

con·tort \kən-ˈtȯrt\ *vb* : to twist into an unusual appearance or unnatural shape : DEFORM, DISTORT [Latin *contortus,* past participle of *contorquēre* "to contort", from *com-* + *torquēre* "to twist"] — **con·tor·tion** \-ˈtȯr-shən\ *n*

con·tor·tion·ist \-shə-nəst, -shnəst\ *n* : one that contorts; *esp* : an acrobat who specializes in contortion of the body — **con·tor·tion·is·tic** \-ˌtȯr-shə-ˈnis-tik\ *adj*

con·tour \ˈkän-ˌtu̇r\ *n* **1** : the outline of a figure or body; *also* : a line or a drawing representing such an outline ⟨sketch the *contour* of a coast⟩ **2** : SHAPE, FORM ⟨*contour* of the land⟩ [French, from Italian *contorno,* from *contornare* "to round off, outline", from Latin *com-* + *tornare* "to turn in a lathe", from *tornus* "lathe"]

[2]contour vt **1** : to shape the contour of **2** : to shape to fit contours

[3]contour *adj* : following or fitted to the contour of something ⟨*contour* farming⟩

contour feather *n* : one of the medium-sized feathers that form the general covering of a bird and determine the external contour

contour line *n* : a line (as on a map) connecting the points on a land surface that have the same elevation

contour map *n* : a map having contour lines

contra- *prefix* **1** : against : contrary : contrasting ⟨*contra*distinction⟩ **2** : pitched below normal bass [Latin, from *contra* "against, opposite"]

con·tra·band \ˈkän-trə-ˌband\ *n* **1** : goods or merchandise whose importation, exportation, or possession is forbidden **2** : smuggled goods [Italian *contrabbando,* from Medieval Latin *contrabannum,* from *contra-* + *bannum* "decree, ban"] — **contraband** *adj*

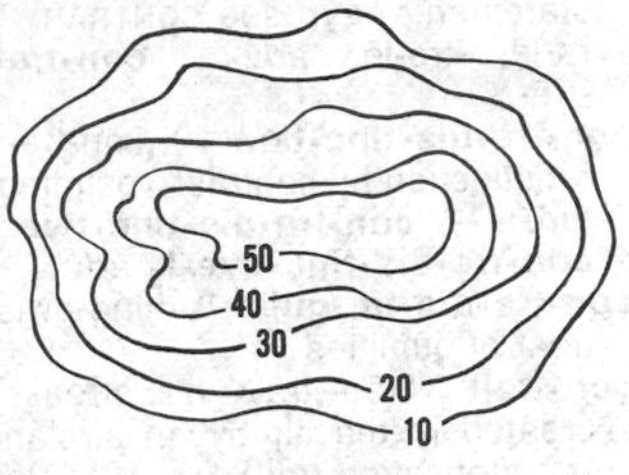

contour line

con·tra·bass \ˈkän-trə-ˌbās\ *n* : DOUBLE BASS

con·tra·bas·soon \ˌkän-trə-bə-ˈsün, -ba-\ *n* : the largest member of the oboe family an octave lower in pitch than the bassoon

con·tra·cep·tion \ˌkän-trə-ˈsep-shən\ n : voluntary prevention of conception [*contra-* + *conception*]

[1]con·tra·cep·tive \-ˈsep-tiv\ *adj* : relating to or used for contraception

[2]contraceptive *n* : a contraceptive agent or device

[1]con·tract \ˈkän-ˌtrakt\ *n* **1 a** : a legally binding agreement between two or more persons or parties : COVENANT **b** : a document containing the terms and conditions of a contract **2** : an undertaking to win a specified number of tricks or points in bridge [Latin *contractus,* from *contrahere* "to draw together, make a contract, reduce in size", from *com-* + *trahere* "to draw"]

[2]con·tract \kən-ˈtrakt, *oftenest for 2* ˈkän-ˌ\ *vb* **1** : to enter into or undertake by contract ⟨*contract* to build a bridge⟩ **2** : to draw together or draw up so as to make or become shorter and broader ⟨*contract* a muscle⟩ **3 a** : to reduce to smaller size by or as if by squeezing or forcing together **b** : to shorten (as a word) by omitting one or more sounds or letters ⟨*contract secretary* into *secy*⟩ **4 a** : GET, CATCH ⟨*contract* a cold⟩ **b** : FORM ⟨it is easier to *contract* a habit than to break one⟩ **syn** see CONDENSE — **con·tract·ibil·i·ty** \kən-ˌtrak-tə-ˈbil-ət-ē, ˌkän-\ *n* — **con·tract·ible** \kən-ˈtrak-tə-bəl, ˈkän-ˌ\ *adj*

contract bridge \ˌkän-ˌtrakt-, -ˌtrak-\ *n* : a card game for four players in two partnerships in which players bid for the right to name a trump suit and contract to win a specific number of tricks

con·trac·tile \kən-ˈtrak-tl\ *adj* : having the power or property of contracting ⟨*contractile* fibers⟩ — **con·trac·til·i·ty** \ˌkän-ˌtrak-ˈtil-ət-ē\ *n*

contractile vacuole *n* : a vacuole in a unicellular organism that contracts regularly to discharge fluid from the body and that probably has an excretory or hydrostatic function

con·trac·tion \kən-ˈtrak-shən\ *n* **1 a** : the act or process of contracting : the state of being contracted **b** : the shortening and thickening of a functioning muscle or muscle fiber **2** : a shortening of a word, syllable, or word group by omission of a sound or letter; *also* : a form produced by such shortening ⟨*aren't* is a *contraction* of *are not*⟩ — **con·trac·tion·al** \-ˈtrak-shnəl, -shən-l\ *adj* — **con·trac·tive** \-ˈtrak-tiv\ *adj*

con·trac·tor \ˈkän-ˌtrak-tər, kən-ˈ\ *n* : one that enters into a contract; *esp* : one that agrees to perform work or provide supplies at a given price or within a given time ⟨a building *contractor*⟩

con·trac·tu·al \kən-ˈtrak-chə-wəl, kän-, -chəl\ *adj* : of, relating to, or constituting a contract ⟨*contractual* agreements⟩ — **con·trac·tu·al·ly** \-ē\ *adv*

con·tra·dict \ˌkän-trə-ˈdikt\ *vt* **1** : to deny the truth of ⟨*contradict* a story⟩ **2** : to state the opposite of what another has said **3** : to be contrary or opposed to ⟨your actions *contradict* your words⟩ [Latin *contradicere,* from *contra-* + *dicere* "to say"] — **con·tra·dict·able** \-ˈdik-tə-bəl\ *adj* — **con·tra·dic·tor** \-tər\ *n*

con·tra·dic·tion \-ˈdik-shən\ *n* **1 a** : a statement that contradicts another **b** : denial of the truth of something said **2** : opposition between things ⟨a *contradiction* between desire and reality⟩

con·tra·dic·to·ry \ˌkän-trə-ˈdik-tə-rē, -trē\ *adj* **1** : tending to

\ə\ **abut**	\au̇\ **out**	\i\ **tip**	\ȯ\ **saw**	\u̇\ **foot**
\ər\ **further**	\ch\ **chin**	\ī\ **life**	\ȯi\ **coin**	\y\ **yet**
\a\ **mat**	\e\ **pet**	\j\ **job**	\th\ **thin**	\yü\ **few**
\ā\ **take**	\ē\ **easy**	\ng\ **sing**	\t͟h\ **this**	\yu̇\ **cure**
\ä\ **cot, cart**	\g\ **go**	\ō\ **bone**	\ü\ **food**	\zh\ **vision**

contradict **2 :** involving contradiction **:** OPPOSED ⟨*contradictory* statements⟩ **syn** see CONTRARY — **con•tra•dic•to•ri•ly** \-tə-rə-lē, -trə-lē\ *adv* — **con•tra•dic•to•ri•ness** \-tə-rē-nəs, -trē-\ *n*

con•tra•dis•tinc•tion \ˌkän-trə-dis-ˈting-shən, -ˈtingk-\ *n* **:** distinction by contrast ⟨painting in *contradistinction* to sculpture⟩ — **con•tra•dis•tinc•tive** \-ˈting-tiv, -ˈtingk-\ *adj* — **con•tra•dis•tinc•tive•ly** *adv*

con•tra•dis•tin•guish \-ˈting-gwish\ *vt* **:** to distinguish by contrast of qualities

con•trail \ˈkän-ˌtrāl\ *n* **:** streaks of condensed water vapor created in the air by an airplane or rocket at high altitudes [*con*densation *trail*]

con•tral•to \kən-ˈtral-tō\ *n, pl* **-tos 1 a :** the lowest female singing voice **b :** a singer having such a voice **2 :** the part sung by a contralto [Italian, from *contra-* + *alto* "high"]

con•tra•pos•i•tive \ˌkän-trə-ˈpäz-ət-iv, -ˈpäz-tiv\ *n* **:** the statement obtained by interchanging the hypothesis and conclusion of a conditional statement and denying both clauses ⟨the *contrapositive* of "if A, then B" is "if not B, then not A"⟩

con•trap•tion \kən-ˈtrap-shən\ *n* **:** CONTRIVANCE 2, GADGET [perhaps blend of *contrivance, trap,* and *invention*]

con•tra•pun•tal \ˌkän-trə-ˈpənt-l\ *adj* **1 :** of or relating to counterpoint **2 :** consisting of or relating to two or more melodies combined into a unified musical composition **:** POLYPHONIC [Italian *contrappunto* "counterpoint", from Medieval Latin *contrapunctus*] — **con•tra•pun•tal•ly** \-l-ē\ *adv*

con•tra•pun•tist \-ˈpənt-əst\ *n* **:** one who writes counterpoint

con•trari•wise \ˈkän-ˌtrer-ē-ˌwīz, kən-ˈ\ *adv* **1 :** on the contrary **2 :** vice versa **:** CONVERSELY **3 :** in a contrary manner **:** PERVERSELY

¹con•trary \ˈkän-ˌtrer-ē\ *n, pl* **-trar•ies 1 :** a fact or condition incompatible with another **:** OPPOSITE **2 :** one of a pair of opposites **3 :** a proposition in logic related to another in such a way that though both may be false they cannot both be true

²con•trary \ˈkän-ˌtrer-ē, *4 is often* kən-ˈtreər-ē\ *adj* **1 :** exactly opposite **:** wholly different ⟨*contrary* opinions⟩ **2 :** OPPOSED ⟨an act *contrary* to law⟩ **3 :** UNFAVORABLE ⟨a *contrary* wind⟩ **4 :** inclined to oppose or resist **:** WAYWARD ⟨a *contrary* child⟩ [Middle French *contraire,* from Latin *contrarius,* from *contra* "against, opposite"] — **con•trar•i•ly** \-ˌtrer-ə-lē, -ˈtrer-\ *adv* — **con•trar•i•ness** \-ˌtrer-ē-nəs, -ˈtrer-\ *n*

• **syn** OPPOSITE, CONTRADICTORY: CONTRARY implies extreme divergence and often antagonism; OPPOSITE applies to things in sharp contrast or reversed positions; CONTRADICTORY implies the impossibility of two things being true or valid at the same time.

³con•trary *like* ²CONTRARY\ *adv* **:** in a contrary manner **:** CONTRARILY

¹con•trast \ˈkän-ˌtrast\ *n* **1 :** the act or process of contrasting **:** the state of being contrasted **2 :** a person or thing that exhibits differences when contrasted **3 :** difference especially when sharp or striking between associated things ⟨the *contrast* between light and dark⟩

²con•trast \kən-ˈtrast, ˈkän-ˌ\ *vb* **1 :** to show noticeable differences ⟨black and gold *contrast* sharply⟩ **2 :** to compare especially so as to show differences ⟨*contrast* winter and summer⟩ [French *contraster,* derived from Latin *contra-* + *stare* "to stand"] **syn** see COMPARE — **con•trast•able** \-ə-bəl\ *adj*

con•tra•vene \ˌkän-trə-ˈvēn\ *vt* **1 :** to go or act contrary to ⟨*contravene* a law⟩ **2 :** to oppose in argument **:** CONTRADICT ⟨*contravene* a proposition⟩ [Late Latin *contravenire,* from Latin *contra-* + *venire* "to come"] — **con•tra•ven•er** *n*

con•tra•ven•tion \ˌkän-trə-ˈven-chən\ *n* **:** the act of contravening **:** VIOLATION [Middle French, from Late Latin *contravenire* "to contravene"]

con•tre•danse *or* **con•tra dance** \ˈkän-trə-ˌdans\ *n* **1 :** a folk dance in which couples face each other in two lines or in a square **2 :** a piece of music for a contredanse [French *contredanse,* by folk etymology (influenced by French *contre-* "counter-") from English *country-dance*]

con•tre•temps \ˈkän-trə-ˌtäⁿ\ *n, pl* **con•tre•temps** \-ˌtäⁿ, -ˌtäⁿz\ **:** an untimely and embarrassing occurrence **:** MISHAP [French, from *contre-* "counter-" + *temps* "time"]

con•trib•ute \kən-ˈtrib-yət\ *vb* **1 :** to give along with others ⟨*contribute* to charities⟩ **2 :** to have a share in something ⟨factors *contributing* to an accident⟩ **3 :** to supply for publication ⟨*contributed* a poem to the school paper⟩ [Latin *contribuere,* from *com-* + *tribuere* "to grant"] — **con•trib•u•tive** \-yət-iv\ *adj* — **con•trib•u•tor** \-yət-ər\ *n*

con•tri•bu•tion \ˌkän-trə-ˈbyü-shən\ *n* **1 :** LEVY 1, TAX **2 a :** the act of contributing **b :** the sum or thing contributed **3 :** a writing for publication especially in a periodical

con•trib•u•to•ry \kən-ˈtrib-yə-ˌtōr-ē, -ˌtȯr-ē\ *adj* **1 :** contributing or serving to contribute; *esp* **:** helping to accomplish a result ⟨carelessness *contributory* to an accident⟩ **2 a :** of, relating to, or forming a contribution **b :** supported by contributions ⟨a *contributory* pension plan⟩

con•trite \ˈkän-ˌtrīt, kən-ˈ\ *adj* **1 :** sorrowful for a wrong that one has done **:** deeply repentant **2 :** resulting from or expressing repentance ⟨*contrite* tears⟩ [Middle French *contrit,* from Medieval Latin *contritus,* from Latin *conterere* "to bruise", from *com-* + *terere* "to rub"] — **con•trite•ly** *adv* — **con•trite•ness** *n*

con•tri•tion \kən-ˈtrish-ən\ *n* **:** the state of being contrite **syn** see PENITENCE

con•triv•ance \kən-ˈtrī-vəns\ *n* **1 :** the act or faculty of contriving **:** the state of being contrived **2 :** something contrived; *esp* **:** a mechanical device

con•trive \kən-ˈtrīv\ *vb* **1 :** PLAN, SCHEME ⟨*contrive* a means of escape⟩ **2 :** to form or make in a skillful or ingenious way **:** INVENT **3 :** to bring about **:** MANAGE ⟨*contriving* to make ends meet⟩ [Middle English *controven, contreven,* from Middle French *controver,* from Late Latin *contropare* "to compare"] — **con•triv•er** *n*

con•trived *adj* **:** ARTIFICIAL 3, UNNATURAL ⟨the *contrived* ending of a play⟩

¹con•trol \kən-ˈtrōl\ *vt* **con•trolled; con•trol•ling 1 :** to check, test, or verify by evidence or experiments **2 a :** to exercise restraining or directing influence over **:** REGULATE ⟨*control* one's temper⟩ **b :** to have power over **:** RULE ⟨*control* a territory⟩ [Middle French *contreroller,* from *contrerolle* "audit", from *contre-* "counter-" + *rolle* "roll, account"] **syn** see CONDUCT — **con•trol•la•ble** \-ˈtrō-lə-bəl\ *adj*

²control *n* **1 :** the power or authority to control or command ⟨children under their parents' *control*⟩ **2 :** ability to control ⟨lose *control* of a car⟩ **3 :** a means or method of controlling **:** one that controls: as **a** (1) **:** CONTROL EXPERIMENT (2) **:** one (as an organism, culture, or group) that is part of a control **b :** a mechanism used to regulate or guide the operation of a machine, apparatus, or system ⟨the *controls* of an airplane⟩ ⟨price *controls*⟩ **c :** a personality or spirit believed to actuate the utterances or performances of a spiritualist medium

control experiment *n* **:** an experiment in which the subjects of experimentation are treated as in a parallel experiment except for omission of the procedure or agent under test and which is used as a standard of comparison in judging experimental effects

con•trol•ler \kən-ˈtrō-lər, ˈkän-ˌ\ *n* **1 a :** COMPTROLLER 1 **b :** the chief accounting officer of a business or institution **2 :** one that controls ⟨air traffic *controller*⟩ — **con•trol•ler•ship** \-ˌship\ *n*

con•tro•ver•sial \ˌkän-trə-ˈvər-shəl, -ˈvər-sē-əl\ *adj* **1 :** of, relating to, or arousing controversy ⟨a *controversial* public figure⟩ **2 :** fond of controversy **:** ARGUMENTATIVE — **con•tro•ver•sial•ist** \-əst\ *n* — **con•tro•ver•sial•ly** \-ē\ *adv*

con•tro•ver•sy \ˈkän-trə-ˌvər-sē\ *n, pl* **-sies 1 :** a discussion marked especially by expression of opposing views **:** DISPUTE **2 :** QUARREL 2, STRIFE [Latin *controversia,* from *controversus* "disputable", literally, "turned opposite", from *contro-* "opposite" + *versus,* past participle of *vertere* "to turn"]

con•tro•vert \ˈkän-trə-ˌvərt, ˌkän-trə-ˈ\ *vt* **:** to dispute or oppose by reasoning ⟨*controvert* a point in a discussion⟩ [derived from *controversy*] — **con•tro•vert•er** *n* — **con•tro•vert•ible** \-ə-bəl\ *adj*

con•tume•ly \kän-ˈtyü-mə-lē, kən-, -ˈtü-; ˈkän-tyə-ˌmē-lē, -tə-; ˈkän-tyüm-lē\ *n, pl* **-lies :** rude language or treatment arising from arrogance and contempt; *also* **:** an instance of such language or treatment [Middle French *contumelie,* from Latin *contumelia*]

con•tuse \kən-ˈtüz, -ˈtyüz\ *vt* **:** to injure (tissue) usually without breaking the skin **:** BRUISE [Middle French *contuser,* from Latin *contundere* "to crush, bruise", from *com-* + *tundere* "to beat"] — **con•tu•sion** \-ˈtü-zhən, -ˈtyü-\ *n*

co•nun•drum \kə-ˈnən-drəm\ *n* **1 :** a riddle whose answer is or involves a pun **2 :** an intricate and difficult problem [origin unknown]

con•ur•ba•tion \ˌkän-ər-ˈbā-shən\ *n* **:** a continuous network of urban communities [*com-* + Latin *urbs* "city"]

co•nus ar•te•ri•o•sus \ˈkō-nə-sär-ˌtir-ē-ˈō-səs\ *n* **1 :** an extension of the ventricle of amphibians and some fishes that has a spiral valve separating venous blood going to the respiratory arteries from blood going to the aorta and systemic arteries **2 :** a conical extension of the right ventricle in mammals from which the pulmonary arteries emerge — called also *conus* [New Latin, literally, "arterial cone"]

con•va•lesce \ˌkän-və-ˈles\ *vi* **:** to recover health and strength gradually after illness or weakness [Latin *convalescere,* from *com-* + *valescere* "to grow strong", from *valēre* "to be strong, be well"]

con•va•les•cence \ˌkän-və-ˈles-ns\ *n* **:** the process or period of convalescing — **con•va•les•cent** \-nt\ *adj or n*

con•vec•tion \kən-ˈvek-shən\ *n* **:** the circulatory motion that occurs in a gas or liquid at a nonuniform temperature owing to currents caused by differences in density with the warmer portions rising and the colder denser portions sinking; *also* **:** the transfer of heat by this automatic circulation of a fluid [Late Latin *convectio,* from Latin *convehere* "to bring together", from *com-* + *vehere* "to carry"] — **con•vec•tion•al** \-shnəl, -shən-l\ *adj* — **con•vec•tive** \-ˈvek-tiv\ *adj*

con•vec•tor \-ˈvek-tər\ *n* **:** a heating unit in which air heated by contact with a heating device in a casing circulates by convection

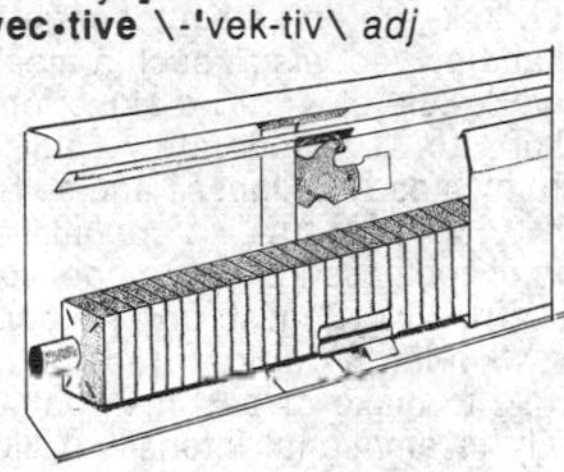

convector

con•vene \kən-ˈvēn\ *vb* **1 :** to come together in a body **:** MEET ⟨the legislature *convened* Tuesday⟩ **2 :** to cause to assemble **:** call together ⟨the chairman *convened* the meeting⟩ [Middle French *convenir,* from Latin *convenire,* from *com-* + *venire* "to come"] — **con•ven•er** *n*

con•ve•nience \kən-ˈvē-nyəns\ *n* **1 :** fitness or suitability for meeting a requirement ⟨took the house because of the *convenience* of its location⟩ **2 :** personal comfort **:** EASE ⟨thought only of their own *convenience*⟩ **3 :** a suitable time **:** OPPORTUNITY ⟨come at your earliest *convenience*⟩ **4 :** something (as a device or a service) that gives comfort or advantage ⟨a house with all modern *conveniences*⟩

con•ve•nient \kən-ˈvē-nyənt\ *adj* **1 a :** suited to personal comfort or to easy use ⟨a *convenient* location⟩ ⟨a *convenient* time⟩ **b :** suited to a particular situation ⟨found it *convenient* not to be at home⟩ **2 :** near at hand **:** HANDY ⟨schools, churches, and stores are all *convenient*⟩ [Latin *conveniens,* from *convenire* "to come together, agree, be suitable"] — **con•ve•nient•ly** *adv*

con•vent \ˈkän-vənt, -ˌvent\ *n* **:** a local community or house of a religious order or congregation; *esp* **:** an establishment of nuns [Old French *covent,* from Medieval Latin *conventus,* from Latin, "assembly", from *convenire* "to convene"] — **con•ven•tu•al** \kən-ˈvench-ə-wəl, kän-\ *adj*

con•ven•tion \kən-ˈven-chən\ *n* **1 :** AGREEMENT 2, COVENANT ⟨an international *convention* for treatment of prisoners of war⟩ **2 :** generally accepted custom, practice, or belief; *also* **:** something accepted by convention as true, useful, or convenient ⟨the *convention* of driving on the right⟩ **3 :** an assembly of persons met for a common purpose ⟨a constitutional *convention*⟩ **4 :** a practice in bidding or playing that conveys information between partners in a card game (as bridge) [Latin *conventio,* from *convenire* "to convene, be suitable"]

con•ven•tion•al \kən-ˈvench-nəl, -ˈven-chən-l\ *adj* **1 :** behaving according to convention ⟨a very *conventional* person⟩ **2 :** settled or prescribed by convention **:** CUSTOMARY ⟨*conventional* signs and symbols⟩ **3 a :** ORDINARY 1, COMMONPLACE ⟨*conventional* remarks⟩ **b :** conforming to established rules or traditions **:** not showing originality — **con•ven•tion•al•ly** \-ē\ *adv*

con•ven•tion•al•i•ty \kən-ˌven-chə-ˈnal-ət-ē\ *n, pl* **-ties 1 :** the quality or state of being conventional especially in social behavior **2 :** a conventional practice, custom, or rule **:** CONVENTION

con•ven•tion•al•ize \kən-ˈvench-nə-ˌlīz, -ˈven-chən-l-ˌīz\ *vt* **:** to make conventional — **con•ven•tion•al•iza•tion** \-ˌvench-nə-lə-ˈzā-shən, -ˌven-chən-l-ə-ˈzā-\ *n*

con•verge \kən-ˈvərj\ *vb* **1 :** to tend or move toward one point or one another **:** MEET **2 :** to come together and unite in a common interest or focus **3 :** to cause to come together [Medieval Latin *convergere,* from Latin *com-* + *vergere* "to bend, incline"]

con•ver•gence \kən-ˈvər-jəns\ *n* **1 :** the act or condition of converging especially toward union or uniformity **2 :** independent development of similar characters (as of bodily structure or cultural traits) often associated with similarity of habits or environment — **con•ver•gent** \-jənt\ *adj*

convergent evolution *n* **:** convergence of two or more biological species — called also *parallel evolution*

con•ver•sant \kən-ˈvərs-nt\ *adj* **:** having knowledge or experience **:** FAMILIAR ⟨they were *conversant* with the facts⟩ — **con•ver•sant•ly** *adv*

con•ver•sa•tion \ˌkän-vər-ˈsā-shən\ *n* **:** oral exchange of sentiments, observations, opinions, or ideas; *also* **:** an instance of such exchange **:** TALK

con•ver•sa•tion•al \ˌkän-vər-ˈsā-shnəl, -shən-l\ *adj* **1 :** of, relating to, or suitable for informal friendly talk ⟨written in *conversational* style⟩ **2 :** fond of or given to conversation — **con•ver•sa•tion•al•ly** \-ē\ *adv*

con•ver•sa•tion•al•ist \-shnə-ləst, -shən-l-əst\ *n* **:** a person who is fond of or good at conversation

1con•verse \kən-ˈvərs\ *vi* **:** to exchange thoughts and opinions in speech **:** TALK [Middle French *converser,* from Latin *conversari* "to live, keep company with", from *convertere* "to turn around, convert"] — **con•vers•er** *n*

2con•verse \ˈkän-ˌvərs\ *n* **:** CONVERSATION

3con•verse \kən-ˈvərs, ˈkän-ˌ\ *adj* **:** reversed in order, relation, or action; *also* **:** being a converse ⟨a *converse* theorem in geometry⟩ [Latin *conversus,* past participle of *convertere* "to turn around"] — **con•verse•ly** *adv*

4con•verse \ˈkän-ˌvərs\ *n* **:** something that is the opposite of something else **:** as **a :** a theorem formed by the interchange of the hypothesis and the conclusion in a given theorem **b :** the statement obtained by interchanging the subject and predicate of a logical proposition

con•ver•sion \kən-ˈvər-zhən\ *n* **1 :** the act of converting **:** the state of being converted **2 :** a change in the nature or form of a thing ⟨the *conversion* of water into steam by boiling⟩ **3 :** a spiritual change in a person associated with a change of religious belief or with the adoption of religion **4 :** the taking and using of another's property without right as one's own **5 :** the making of an an extra point in football or a successful free throw in basketball — **con•ver•sion•al** \-ˈvərzh-nəl, -ən-l\ *adj*

1con•vert \kən-ˈvərt\ *vb* **1 :** to bring over from one belief, view, or party to another **2 a :** to change from one form or function to another **:** TRANSFORM ⟨*convert* starch into sugar⟩ **b :** to exchange for an equivalent ⟨*convert* diamonds into cash⟩ **3 :** to take over without right **4 :** to undergo conversion **5 :** to make good on an extra point attempt, on a free throw, or on a penalty kick [Old French *convertir,* from Latin *convertere* "to turn around, convert", from *com-* + *vertere* "to turn"]

2con•vert \ˈkän-ˌvərt\ *n* **:** one that is converted

con•vert•er \kən-ˈvərt-ər\ *n* **:** one that converts: as **a :** the furnace used in the Bessemer process **b** *or* **con•ver•tor** \-ˈvərt-ər\ **:** a device employing mechanical rotation for changing alternating current to direct current **c :** a device for adapting a television receiver to receive channels for which it was not originally designed

1con•vert•ible \kən-ˈvərt-ə-bəl\ *adj* **1 :** capable of being converted **2 :** having a top that may be lowered or removed ⟨a *convertible* coupe⟩ — **con•vert•ibil•i•ty** \-ˌvərt-ə-ˈbil-ət-ē\ *n* — **con•vert•ibly** \-ˈvərt-ə-blē\ *adv*

2convertible *n* **:** something convertible; *esp* **:** a convertible automobile

con•vex \kän-ˈveks, ˈkän-ˌ, kən-ˈ\ *adj* **1 :** curved or rounded like the exterior of a sphere or circle **2 :** being a set containing every straight line joining two points belonging to the set; *also* **:** having the property that the union of its perimeter and its interior comprises a convex set ⟨*convex* polygons⟩ [Latin *con-*

vexus] — **con•vex•ly** *adv* — **con•vex•ness** *n*

con•vex•i•ty \kən-ˈvek-sət-ē, kän-\ *n, pl* **-ties** **1** : the quality or state of being convex **2** : a convex surface or part

con•vexo–con•cave \kən-ˌvek-sō-kän-ˈkāv, -ˈkän-ˌ\ *adj* : having the convex side of greater curvature than the concave

con•vey \kən-ˈvā\ *vt* **con•veyed**; **con•vey•ing** **1** : to carry from one place to another : TRANSPORT ⟨*convey* passengers by bus⟩ **2** : to serve as a means of transferring ⟨an infection *conveyed* by insects⟩ **3** : to communicate or serve as a means of communicating ⟨a red light *conveys* a warning⟩ **4** : to transfer or deliver to another; *esp* : to transfer title to real estate by a legal document [Old French *conveier* "to accompany, escort", from Latin *com-* + *via* "way"]

con•vey•ance \kən-ˈvā-əns\ *n* **1** : the act of conveying **2** : a means or way of conveying: as **a** : a legal document by which title to property is conveyed **b** : a means of transport : VEHICLE

con•vey•er *or* **con•vey•or** \kən-ˈvā-ər\ *n* **1** : one that conveys **2** *usually conveyor* : a mechanical apparatus for carrying (as by an endless moving belt or a chain of receptacles) packages or bulk material from place to place

[1]**con•vict** \kən-ˈvikt\ *vt* : to find or prove to be guilty [Latin *convictus,* past participle of *convincere* "to refute, convict", from *com-* + *vincere* "to conquer"]

[2]**con•vict** \ˈkän-ˌvikt\ *n* **1** : a person convicted of a crime **2** : a person serving a prison sentence usually for a long term

con•vic•tion \kən-ˈvik-shən\ *n* **1** : the act or process of convicting especially of a crime in a court of law : the state of being convicted **2** : the state of being convinced : CERTITUDE ⟨speaks with *conviction*⟩ **3** : a strong belief or opinion ⟨a person with firm *convictions*⟩ **syn** see CERTAINTY, OPINION

con•vince \kən-ˈvins\ *vt* : to bring by argument or evidence to agreement or belief : overcome the disbelief or objections of ⟨*convinced* me that they were qualified⟩ [Latin *convincere* "to refute, convict, prove"] — **con•vinc•er** *n*

con•vinc•ing \-ˈvin-siŋ\ *adj* : having the power or the effect of overcoming objection or disbelief : strongly persuasive ⟨a *convincing* argument⟩ — **con•vinc•ing•ly** \-siŋ-lē\ *adv* — **con•vinc•ing•ness** *n*

con•viv•ial \kən-ˈviv-yəl, -ˈviv-ē-əl\ *adj* : relating to, occupied with, or fond of good company and festivity [Latin *convivium* "banquet", from *com-* + *vivere* "to live"] — **con•viv•i•al•i•ty** \-ˌviv-ē-ˈal-ət-ē\ *n* — **con•viv•ial•ly** \-ē\ *adv*

con•vo•ca•tion \ˌkän-və-ˈkā-shən\ *n* **1** : a summons to a meeting **2** : ASSEMBLY 1, MEETING — **con•vo•ca•tion•al** \-shnəl, -shən-l\ *adj*

con•voke \kən-ˈvōk\ *vt* : to call together to a meeting [Middle French *convoquer,* from Latin *convocare,* from *com-* + *vocare* "to call"]

con•vo•lute \ˈkän-və-ˌlüt\ *vb* : COIL 1, TWIST [Latin *convolutus,* past participle of *convolvere* "to roll up, enfold", from *com-* + *volvere* "to roll"]

con•vo•lut•ed *adj* **1** : having elaborately curved or twisted windings; *esp* : having convolutions **2** : elaborately organized : INTRICATE

con•vo•lu•tion \ˌkän-və-ˈlü-shən\ *n* **1** : one of the irregular ridges on the surface of the brain and especially of the cerebrum of higher mammals **2** : a convoluted form or structure — **con•vo•lu•tion•al** \-shnəl, -shən-l\ *adj*

con•vol•vu•lus \kən-ˈväl-vyə-ləs, -ˈvȯl-\ *n, pl* **-lus•es** *or* **-li** \-ˌlī, -ˌlē\ : any of a genus of erect, trailing, or twining herbs and shrubs of the morning-glory family [Latin *convolvere* "to roll up, enfold"]

[1]**con•voy** \ˈkän-ˌvȯi, kən-ˈ\ *vt* : to accompany for protection either by land or by sea : ESCORT ⟨a destroyer *convoying* merchant shipping⟩ [Middle French *conveier, convoier,* from Latin *com-* + *via* "way"]

[2]**con•voy** \ˈkän-ˌvȯi\ *n* **1** : a protective escort for ships, persons, or goods **2** : the act of convoying : the state of being convoyed ⟨ships traveling in *convoy*⟩ **3** : a group convoyed ⟨a *convoy* of freighters⟩

con•vulse \kən-ˈvəls\ *vt* : to shake or agitate violently; *esp* : to shake with or as if with irregular spasms ⟨*convulsed* with laughter⟩ ⟨land *convulsed* by an earthquake⟩ [Latin *convulsus,* past participle of *convellere* "to pluck up, convulse", from *com-* + *vellere* "to pluck"]

con•vul•sion \-ˈvəl-shən\ *n* **1** : an abnormal violent and involuntary contraction or series of contractions of the muscles **2 a** : a violent disturbance **b** : an uncontrolled fit : PAROXYSM — **con•vul•sion•ary** \-shə-ˌner-ē\ *adj*

con•vul•sive \-ˈvəl-siv\ *adj* **1** : constituting or producing a convulsion **2** : accompanied by or affected with convulsions — **con•vul•sive•ly** *adv* — **con•vul•sive•ness** *n*

co•ny *variant of* CONEY

coo \ˈkü\ *vi* **1** : to utter the low soft cry characteristic of a dove or pigeon or a similar sound **2** : to talk fondly or amorously [imitative] — **coo** *n*

[1]**cook** \ˈku̇k\ *n* : one who prepares food for eating [Old English *cōc,* from Latin *coquus,* from *coquere* "to cook"]

[2]**cook** *vb* **1** : to prepare food for eating by a heating process **2** : to undergo cooking **3 a** : to go on : HAPPEN ⟨what's *cooking*⟩ **b** : CONCOCT, DEVISE ⟨*cook* up a scheme⟩ **4** : to subject to the action of heat or fire — **cook•er** *n* — **cook one's goose** : to ruin (one) beyond recovery

cook•book \ˈku̇k-ˌbu̇k\ *n* : a book of cooking directions and recipes

cook•ery \ˈku̇k-rē, -ə-rē\ *n* : the art or practice of cooking

cook•ie *or* **cooky** \ˈku̇k-ē\ *n, pl* **cook•ies** : any of various small sweet crisp or slightly raised cakes [Dutch *koekje* "small cake", from *koek* "cake"]

cook•out \ˈku̇k-ˌau̇t\ *n* : an outdoor gathering at which a meal is cooked and served; *also* : such a meal

cook•stove \ˈku̇k-ˌstōv\ *n* : a stove for cooking : RANGE

[1]**cool** \ˈkül\ *adj* **1** : moderately cold : lacking in warmth **2 a** : marked by steady calmness and self-control **b** : restrained in emotion **3** : WHOLE, FULL ⟨a *cool* million⟩ **4** : producing an impression of coolness ⟨blue is a *cool* color⟩ **5** *slang* : very good : EXCELLENT [Old English *cōl*] — **cool•ish** \ˈkü-lish\ *adj* — **cool•ly** \ˈkül-lē, -ē\ *adv* — **cool•ness** \ˈkül-nəs\ *n*

[2]**cool** *vb* **1** : to make or become cool **2** : to moderate or calm especially in emotional intensity ⟨allow tempers to *cool*⟩ — **cool it** : to calm down

[3]**cool** *n* : a cool time or place ⟨the *cool* of the night⟩

cool•ant \ˈkü-lənt\ *n* : a usually fluid cooling agent

cool•er \ˈkü-lər\ *n* **1** : one that cools: as **a** : a container for cooling liquids **b** : REFRIGERATOR **2** : LOCKUP, JAIL

cool•head•ed \ˈkül-ˈhed-əd\ *adj* : not easily excited : CALM

coo•lie \ˈkü-lē\ *n* : an unskilled laborer or porter usually in or from the Far East [Hindi *kulī*]

coon \ˈkün\ *n* : RACCOON

coon•skin \-ˌskin\ *n* : the fur or pelt of the raccoon

[1]**coop** \ˈküp, ˈku̇p\ *n* **1** : a cage or small enclosure or building for housing poultry or small animals **2** : a confined place [Middle English *cupe*]

[2]**coop** *vt* : to place or keep in or as if in a coop : PEN

co–op \ˈkō-ˌäp, kō-ˈäp\ *n* : COOPERATIVE

[1]**coo•per** \ˈkü-pər, ˈku̇p-ər\ *n* : one that makes or repairs wooden casks or tubs [derived from Latin *cupa* "cask"]

[2]**cooper** *vb* : to work or work on as a cooper

coo•per•age \ˈkü-pə-rij, -prij; ˈku̇p-rij, -ə-rij\ *n* **1** : a cooper's place of business **2** : a cooper's work or products

co•op•er•ate \kō-ˈäp-ˌrāt, -ə-ˌrāt\ *vi* : to act, work, or associate with others especially for mutual benefit [Late Latin *cooperari,* from Latin *co-* + *operari* "to work"]

co•op•er•a•tion \kō-ˌäp-ə-ˈrā-shən\ *n* **1** : the act or process of cooperating **2** : association of individuals or groups for mutual benefit

[1]**co•op•er•a•tive** \kō-ˈäp-rət-iv, -ə-rət-, -ə-ˌrāt-\ *adj* **1** : marked by cooperation or a willingness to cooperate ⟨*cooperative* neighbors⟩ **2** : of, relating to, or organized as a cooperative ⟨a *cooperative* store⟩ — **co•op•er•a•tive•ly** *adv* — **co•op•er•a•tive•ness** *n*

[2]**cooperative** *n* : an association formed to enable its members to buy, sell, or perform other economic functions to better advantage

Coo•per's hawk \ˌkü-pərz-, ˌku̇p-ərz-\ *n* : a common American hawk that has a rounded tail and is slightly smaller than a crow [William *Cooper,* died 1864, American naturalist]

co–opt \kō-ˈäpt\ *vt* **1** : to choose or elect as a fellow member or colleague **2** : ASSIMILATE 1a ⟨protesters were *co-opted* by the establishment⟩ [Latin *cooptare,* from *co-* + *optare* "to choose"] — **co–op•ta•tion** \ˌkō-ˌäp-ˈtā-shən\ *n* — **co–op•tion** \-ˈäp-shən\ *n*

[1]**co•or•di•nate** \kō-ˈȯrd-nət, -n-ət\ *adj* **1** : equal in rank or order ⟨*coordinate* branches of government⟩ **2 a** : being of equal rank in a compound sentence ⟨*coordinate* clauses⟩ **b** : joining words or word groups of the same grammatical rank ⟨the word *and* is a *coordinate* conjunction⟩ [back-formation from *coordi-*

nation] — **co•or•di•nate•ly** *adv* — **co•or•di•nate•ness** *n*

[2]coordinate *n* **1 :** one who has the same rank, authority, or importance as another **2 :** any of a set of numbers used in specifying the location of a point on a line or surface or in space — compare ABSCISSA, ORDINATE

[3]co•or•di•nate \kō-ˈȯrd-n-ˌāt\ *vb* **1 :** to make or become coordinate **2 :** to bring into a common action, movement, or condition ⟨*coordinated* the efforts of all three agencies⟩ — **co•or•di•na•tor** \-ˌāt-ər\ *n*

coordinate axis *n* **:** a line in a coordinate system along which coordinates are measured — compare X-AXIS, Y-AXIS

coordinate geometry *n* **:** ANALYTIC GEOMETRY

coordinate plane *n* **1 :** a plane whose points are labeled by means of a coordinate system **2 :** one of three mutually perpendicular planes in three-dimensional space with reference to which coordinates are measured

coordinate system *n* **:** any of various systems for locating points by means of lines; *esp* **:** CARTESIAN COORDINATE SYSTEM

co•or•di•nat•ing *adj* **:** COORDINATE 2b

co•or•di•na•tion \kō-ˌȯrd-n-ˈā-shən\ *n* **1 :** the act of coordinating **2 :** the state of being coordinate **:** harmonious working together ⟨muscular *coordination*⟩ [Late Latin *coordinatio,* from Latin *co-* + *ordinatio* "arrangement", from *ordo* "order"]

coot \ˈküt\ *n* **1 :** any of various sluggish slow-flying slaty-black birds of the rail family that somewhat resemble ducks **2 :** a North American scoter **3 :** FELLOW 4a [Middle English *coote*]

coo•tie \ˈküt-ē\ *n* **:** BODY LOUSE [perhaps from Malay *kutu*]

[1]cop \ˈkäp\ *vt* **copped; cop•ping 1** *slang* **:** to get hold of **:** CATCH **2** *slang* **:** STEAL [perhaps from Dutch *kapen* "to steal"] — **cop a plea :** to plead guilty to a lesser charge in order to avoid standing trial for a more serious one

[2]cop *n* **:** POLICEMAN [short for *[3]copper*]

co•pa•ce•tic *or* **co•pe•se•tic** \ˌkō-pə-ˈset-ik\ *adj* **:** very satisfactory [origin unknown]

co•pal \ˈkō-pəl, -ˌpal; kō-ˈpal\ *n* **:** a recent or fossil resin from various tropical trees used in making varnishes [Spanish, from Nahuatl *capalli* "resin"]

co•part•ner \ˈkō-ˈpärt-nər\ *n* **:** PARTNER — **co•part•ner•ship** \-ˌship\ *n*

[1]cope \ˈkōp\ *n* **1 :** a long enveloping ecclesiastical vestment **2 :** something (as the sky) resembling a cope (as in concealing or covering) [Old English *-cāp,* from Late Latin *cappa* "head covering, cloak"]

[1]cope 1

[2]cope *vt* **:** to cover or furnish with a cope or coping

[3]cope *vi* **:** to struggle or contend especially with some success ⟨a difficult situation to *cope* with⟩ [Middle English *copen* "to strike, fight with", from Middle French *couper* "to strike", from *coup* "blow, coup"]

co•pe•pod \ˈkō-pə-ˌpäd\ *n* **:** any of a large group (Copepoda) of usually tiny freshwater and marine crustaceans [Greek *kōpē* "oar" + *pod-, pous* "foot"]

Co•per•ni•can \kō-ˈpər-ni-kən\ *adj* **:** of or relating to Copernicus or his theory that the earth rotates daily on its axis and the planets revolve in orbits round the sun

copi•er \ˈkäp-ē-ər\ *n* **:** one that copies; *esp* **:** a machine for making copies of graphic matter

co•pi•lot \ˈkō-ˌpī-lət\ *n* **:** an assistant airplane pilot

cop•ing \ˈkō-piŋ\ *n* **:** the covering course of a wall usually with a sloping top [*[1]cope*]

coping saw *n* **:** a handsaw with a very narrow blade held in a U-shaped frame for cutting curves in wood [from *cope* "to notch", probably from French *couper* "to cut"]

co•pi•ous \ˈkō pē-əs\ *adj* **1 a :** full of thought, information, or matter **b :** profuse or exuberant in words, expression, or style **2 :** very plentiful **:** ABUNDANT [Latin *copiosus,* from *copia* "abundance", from *co-* + *ops* "wealth"] **syn** see PLENTIFUL — **co•pi•ous•ly** *adv* — **co•pi•ous•ness** *n*

co•pla•nar \ˈkō-ˈplā-nər\ *adj* **:** lying in the same plane ⟨*coplanar* lines⟩

co•pol•y•mer \ˈkō-ˈpal-ə-mər\ **:** a product of copolymerization

co•po•ly•mer•ize \ˌkō-pə-ˈlim-ə-ˌrīz, ˈkō-ˈpäl-ə-mə-\ *vb* **:** to polymerize (as two different monomers) together — **co•po•ly•mer•iza•tion** \ˌkō-pə-ˌlim-ə-rə-ˈzā-shən, ˌkō-ˌpäl-ə-mə-rə-\ *n*

cop out \käp-ˈau̇t, ˈkäp-ˈ\ *vi* **:** to withdraw from unwanted responsibility — **cop–out** \ˈkäp-ˌau̇t\ *n*

[1]cop•per \ˈkäp-ər\ *n* **1 :** a reddish chiefly univalent and bivalent metallic element that is ductile and malleable and one of the best conductors of heat and electricity — see ELEMENT table **2 :** a copper or bronze coin **3 :** any of various small butterflies usually with copper-colored wings [Old English *coper,* from Late Latin *cuprum,* from Latin *aes Cyprium,* literally, "metal of Cyprus"] — **cop•pery** \ˈkäp-rē, -ə-rē\ *adj*

[2]copper *vt* **:** to cover with copper

[3]copper *n* **:** POLICEMAN [*[1]cop*]

cop•per•as \ˈkäp-rəs, -ə-rəs\ *n* **:** a green sulfate of iron $FeSO_4 \cdot 7H_2O$ used in making inks and in dyeing [Middle French *coperose,* from Late Latin *cuprum* "copper" + Latin *rosa* "rose"]

cop•per•head \ˈkäp-ər-ˌhed\ *n* **1 :** a common largely coppery brown pit viper of the eastern United States **2 :** a person in the northern states who sympathized with the South during the Civil War

cop•per•plate \ˌkäp-ər-ˈplāt\ *n* **:** an engraved or etched copper printing plate; *also* **:** a print made from such a plate

cop•per•smith \ˈkäp-ər-ˌsmith\ *n* **:** a worker in copper

copper sulfate *n* **:** a crystalline compound $CuSO_4$ that is white when anhydrous but that is usually encountered in the blue hydrated form $CuSO_4 \cdot 5H_2O$ and that is used in solutions to destroy algae and fungi, in dyeing and printing, and in electric batteries

cop•pice \ˈkäp-əs\ *n* **1 :** a thicket, grove, or growth of small trees **2 :** forest originating mainly from sprouts or root suckers [Middle French *copeiz,* from *couper* "to cut"]

co•pra \ˈkō-prə\ *n* **:** dried coconut meat yielding coconut oil [Portuguese, from Malayalam (a Dravidian language of India) *koppara*]

cop•ro•lite \ˈkäp-rə-ˌlīt\ *n* **:** fossil excrement [derived from Greek *kopros* "dung"]

copse \ˈkäps\ *n* **:** COPPICE 1 [by alteration]

Copt \ˈkäpt\ *n* **1 :** a member of a people descended from the ancient Egyptians **2 :** a member of the ancient Christian church of Egypt [Arabic *qubṭ* "Copts", from Coptic *gyptios* "Egyptian", from Greek *aigyptios*] — **Coptic** \ˈkäp-tik\ *adj*

cop•u•la \ˈkäp-yə-lə\ *n* **:** a word or expression (as a form of the verb *to be* that links a subject with its predicate [Latin, "bond"]

cop•u•late \ˈkäp-yə-ˌlāt\ *vi* **:** to engage in sexual intercourse — **cop•u•la•tion** \ˌkäp-yə-ˈlā-shən\ *n* — **cop•u•la•to•ry** \ˈkäp-yə-lə-ˌtōr-ē, -ˌtȯr-\ *adj*

[1]cop•u•la•tive \ˈkäp-yə-lət-iv, -ˌlāt-\ *adj* **1 :** joining together coordinate words or word groups and indicating that their meanings are to be added ⟨*copulative* conjunctions⟩ **2 :** being a copula ⟨a *copulative* verb⟩ — **cop•u•la•tive•ly** *adv*

[2]copulative *n* **:** a copulative word or expression

[1]copy \ˈkäp-ē\ *n, pl* **cop•ies 1 :** an imitation, transcript, or reproduction of an original work **2 :** one of the printed reproductions of an original text, engraving, or photograph **3 :** text to be composed for printing [Middle French *copie,* from Medieval Latin *copia,* from Latin, "abundance"] **syn** see DUPLICATE

[2]copy *vb* **cop•ied; copy•ing 1 :** to make a copy **:** DUPLICATE **2 :** to model oneself on **:** IMITATE

copy•book \-ˌbu̇k\ *n* **:** a book containing copies especially of penmanship for learners to imitate

copy•boy \-ˌbȯi\ *n* **:** one that carries copy and runs errands (as in a newspaper office)

copy•cat \-ˌkat\ *n* **:** a person who imitates the behavior or work of another

copy•desk \-ˌdesk\ *n* **:** the desk at which newspaper copy is edited

copy•ist \ˈkäp-ē-əst\ *n* **1 :** a person who makes copies **2 :** IMITATOR

copy•read•er \ˈkäp-ē-ˌrēd-ər\ *n* **1 :** one that edits and writes

\ə\ **abut**	\au̇\ **out**	\i\ **tip**	\ȯ\ **saw**	\u̇\ **foot**
\ər\ **further**	\ch\ **chin**	\ī\ **life**	\ȯi\ **coin**	\y\ **yet**
\a\ **mat**	\e\ **pet**	\j\ **job**	\th\ **thin**	\yü\ **few**
\ā\ **take**	\ē\ **easy**	\ŋ\ **sing**	\t͟h\ **this**	\yu̇\ **cure**
\ä\ **cot, cart**	\g\ **go**	\ō\ **bone**	\ü\ **food**	\zh\ **vision**

headlines for newspaper copy **2** : one that reads and corrects manuscript copy in a publishing house

[1]**copy•right** \-ˌrīt\ *n* : the sole legal right to reproduce, publish, and sell the matter and form of a literary, musical, or artistic work — **copyright** *adj*

[2]**copyright** *vt* : to secure a copyright on

co•quet *or* **co•quette** \kō-ˈket\ *vi* **co•quet•ted**; **co•quet•ting** : FLIRT 2a [French *coquet* "man who indulges in coquetry", from *coq* "cock"]

co•que•try \ˈkō-kə-trē, kō-ˈke-trē\ *n, pl* **-tries** : the conduct or art of a coquette : FLIRTATION

co•quette \kō-ˈket\ *n* : FLIRT 2 — **co•quett•ish** \-ˈket-ish\ *adj* — **co•quett•ish•ly** *adv* — **co•quett•ish•ness** *n*

co•qui•na \kō-ˈkē-nə\ *n* **1** : a small marine clam used for broth or chowder **2** : a soft whitish limestone formed of broken shells and corals cemented together and used for building [Spanish]

cor•a•cle \ˈkór-ə-kəl, ˈkär-\ *n* : a boat made of horsehide or tarpaulin stretched over a wicker frame [Welsh *corwgl*]

cor•a•coid \ˈkór-ə-ˌkóid, ˈkär-\ *adj* : of, relating to, or being a process or bone that in many vertebrates extends from the scapula to or toward the sternum [Greek *korax* "raven"] — **coracoid** *n*

cor•al \ˈkór-əl, ˈkär-\ *n* **1 a** : the stony or horny skeletal deposit produced by various polyps; *esp* : a richly red material used in jewelry **b** : a polyp or polyp colony together with its membranes and skeleton **2** : a deep pink [Middle French, from Latin *corallium,* from Greek *korallion*] — **coral** *adj*

[1]**cor•al•line** \ˈkór-ə-ˌlīn, ˈkär-\ *adj* : of, relating to, or resembling coral or a coralline

[2]**coralline** *n* : any of various plants or animals (as some red algae and bryozoans) that resemble corals

coral reef *n* : a reef made up of corals, other organic deposits, and the solid limestone resulting from their fusion

coral snake *n* : any of several poisonous chiefly tropical New World snakes brilliantly banded in red, black, and yellow or white; *also* : any of several harmless snakes resembling the coral snakes

[1]**cor•bel** \ˈkór-bəl\ *n* : a bracket-shaped architectural member that projects from a wall and supports a weight [Middle French, from *corp* "raven", from Latin *corvus*]

[2]**corbel** *vt* **-beled** *or* **-belled**; **-bel•ing** *or* **-bel•ling** : to furnish with or make into a corbel

[1]**cord** \ˈkórd\ *n* **1** : a string or small rope consisting of several strands woven or twisted together **2** : a moral, spiritual, or emotional bond **3 a** : an anatomical structure (as a tendon or nerve) resembling a cord **b** : a small flexible insulated electrical cable with fittings for connecting an appliance (as a lamp) with a receptacle **4** : a unit of wood cut for fuel equal to a stack 4×4×8 feet or 128 cubic feet (about 3.6 cubic meters) **5 a** : a rib like a cord on a textile; *also* : a fabric with such ribs **b** *pl* : trousers made of this fabric [Old French *corde,* from Latin *chorda* "string", from Greek *chordē*]

[2]**cord** *vt* **1** : to furnish, bind, or connect with a cord **2** : to pile up (wood) in cords — **cord•er** *n*

cord•age \ˈkórd-ij\ *n* **1** : ropes or cords; *esp* : the ropes in the rigging of a ship **2** : the number of cords (as of wood) on a given area

cord•ed \ˈkórd-əd\ *adj* **1** : having or drawn into ridges or cords ⟨a *corded* seam⟩ ⟨*corded* muscles⟩ **2** : bound or wound about with cords

[1]**cor•dial** \ˈkór-jəl\ *adj* **1** : tending to revive, cheer, or invigorate **2** : HEARTFELT, HEARTY ⟨a *cordial* greeting⟩ [Medieval Latin *cordialis* "of the heart, hearty", from Latin *cord-, cor* "heart"] — **cor•di•al•i•ty** \ˌkór-jē-ˈal-ət-ē\ *n* — **cor•dial•ly** \ˈkórj-lē, -ə-lē\ *adv* — **cor•dial•ness** \ˈkór-jəl-nəs\ *n*

[2]**cordial** *n* **1** : a stimulating medicine or drink **2** : LIQUEUR

cor•dil•le•ra \ˌkórd-l-ˈyer-ə, -ˈer-; kór-ˈdil-ə-rə\ *n* : a system of mountain ranges often consisting of a number of more or less parallel chains [Spanish] — **cor•dil•le•ran** \-ˈyer-ən, -ˈer-ən; -ə-rən\ *adj*

cord•ite \ˈkór-ˌdīt\ *n* : a smokeless gunpowder composed of nitroglycerin, guncotton, and a stabilizing jelly

cor•do•ba \ˈkórd-ə-bə, -ə-və\ *n* **1** : the basic monetary unit of Nicaragua **2** : a note representing one cordoba [Francisco Fernández de *Córdoba,* died 1526, Spanish explorer]

cor•don \ˈkórd-n, ˈkór-ˌdän\ *n* **1 a** : an ornamental cord used especially on costumes **b** : a cord or ribbon worn as a badge or decoration **2** : a line of persons or things around a person or place ⟨a *cordon* of police⟩ [French, from *corde* "cord"]

cor•do•van \ˈkórd-ə-vən\ *n* : a fine-grained colored leather usually made of split horsehide [Spanish *Córdova* (now *Córdoba*), Spain] — **cordovan** *adj*

cor•du•roy \ˈkórd-ə-ˌrói\ *n, pl* **-roys 1 a** : a durable ribbed usually cotton fabric **b** *pl* : trousers of corduroy **2** : a road built of logs laid crosswise side by side [perhaps from the name *Corderoy*] — **corduroy** *adj*

cord•wain•er \ˈkór-ˌdwā-nər\ *n* : SHOEMAKER [Middle English *cordwane* "cordovan leather"]

cord•wood \-ˌwu̇d\ *n* : wood cut for fuel and sold by the cord

[1]**core** \ˈkōr, ˈkór\ *n* **1** : a central or inmost part: as **a** : the usually inedible central part of some fruits (as a pineapple or apple) **b** : a bar of iron or a bundle of wires used to intensify an induced magnetic field (as in a transfer or an armature) **c** : the central part of the earth that displays different properties from the surrounding mantle and crust **2** : a basic, essential, or enduring part **3** : the internal memory of a computer [Middle English]

[2]**core** *vt* : to remove the core from — **cor•er** *n*

co•re•op•sis \ˌkōr-ē-ˈäp-səs, ˌkór-\ *n* : any of a genus of herbs related to the daisies and widely grown for their showy flower heads [Greek *koris* "bedbug" + *opsis* "apperance"]

co•re•spon•dent \ˌkō-ri-ˈspän-dənt\ *n* : a person named as guilty of adultery with the defendant in a divorce suit

co•ri•an•der \ˈkōr-ē-ˌan-dər, ˈkór-\ *n* : an Old World herb of the carrot family with aromatic fruits; *also* : its dried ripened fruit [Old French *coriandre,* from Latin *coriandrum,* from Greek *koriandron*]

Co•rin•thi•an \kə-ˈrin-thē-ən\ *adj* : of or relating to the lightest and most ornate of the three Greek types of architecture characterized especially by its bell-shaped capital enveloped with acanthuses [*Corinth,* Greece]

Cor•in•thi•ans \-ənz\ *n* — see BIBLE table

Co•ri•o•lis force \ˌkōr-ē-ˌō-ləs-, ˌkór-, -ē-ə-ˌlēs-\ *n* : an apparent force that as a result of the earth's rotation deflects moving objects (as projectiles) or air currents to the right in the northern hemisphere and to the left in the southern hemisphere [Gaspard G. *Coriolis,* died 1843, French civil engineer]

co•ri•um \ˈkōr-ē-əm, ˈkór-\ *n, pl* **-ria** \-ē-ə\ : DERMIS [Latin, "leather"]

[1]**cork** \ˈkórk\ *n* **1 a** : the elastic tough outer tissue of a European oak used especially for stoppers and insulation **b** : the tissue of a woody plant making up most of the bark and arising from an inner cambium — called also *phellem* **2** : a usually cork stopper for a bottle or jug [Middle English, probably from Arabic *qurq,* from Latin *cortex* "bark, cork"]

[2]**cork** *vt* **1** : to furnish, fit, or seal with a cork **2** : to blacken with burnt cork

cork cambium *n* : PHELLOGEN

cork•er \ˈkór-kər\ *n* **1** : one that corks containers **2** *slang* : an outstanding person or thing

cork•ing \ˈkór-king\ *adj, slang* : extremely fine

cork oak *n* : an oak of southern Europe and northern Africa that is the source of the cork of commerce

[1]**cork•screw** \ˈkórk-ˌskrü\ *n* : a pointed spiral piece of metal with a handle that is used to draw corks from bottles

[2]**corkscrew** *adj* : resembling a corkscrew : SPIRAL

corky \ˈkór-kē\ *adj* **cork•i•er**; **-est 1** : resembling cork especially in dry porous quality **2** : tasting of cork ⟨*corky* wine⟩

corm \ˈkórm\ *n* : a thick fleshy underground stem (as of the crocus or gladiolus) that resembles a bulb and bears membranous or scaly leaves and buds — compare BULB, TUBER [Greek *kormos* "tree trunk"]

cor•mo•rant \ˈkórm-rənt, -ə-rənt\ *n* **1** : any of various dark-colored web-footed seabirds with a long neck, a wedge-shaped tail, a hooked bill, and a patch of bare often brightly colored skin under the mouth **2** : a greedy or gluttonous person [Middle French, from Old French *cormareng,* from *corp* "raven" + *marenc* "of the sea", from Latin *marinus*]

[1]**corn** \ˈkórn\ *n* **1 a** : the seeds of a cereal grass and especially of the important cereal crop of a particular region (as in Britain wheat, in Scotland and Ireland oats, and in the New World and Australia Indian corn) **b** : sweet corn served as a vegetable while the kernels are still soft and milky **2** : a plant that produces corn **3** : corny actions or speech [Old English]

[2]**corn** *vb* : to preserve by packing with salt or by soaking in brine ⟨*corned* beef⟩

[3]**corn** *n* : a local hardening and thickening of skin (as on a toe)

[Middle French *corne* "horn, corner", from Latin *cornu* "horn, point"]

corn borer *n* : any of several insects that bore in corn; *esp* : a moth whose larva is a major pest especially in the stems and crowns of Indian corn, dahlias, and potatoes

cormorant 1

corn bread *n* : bread made with cornmeal

corn chip *n* : a piece of a dry crisp snack food prepared from a seasoned cornmeal batter

corn•cob \ˈkȯrn-ˌkäb\ *n* **1** : the woody axis on which the kernels of Indian corn are arranged **2** : a tobacco pipe with a bowl made from a hollowed out piece of corncob

corn cockle *n* : an annual hairy weed with purplish red flowers found in grainfields

corn•crib \ˈkȯrn-ˌkrib\ *n* : a crib for storing ears of Indian corn

cor•nea \ˈkȯr-nē-ə\ *n* : the transparent part of the coat of the eyeball that covers the iris and pupil and admits light to the interior [Medieval Latin, from Latin *corneus* "horny", from *cornu* "horn"] — **cor•ne•al** \-nē-əl\ *adj*

corn earworm *n* : a large striped yellow-headed moth larva especially destructive to the ear of Indian corn and to cotton bolls; *also* : any other stage of this insect

cor•nel \ˈkȯrn-l\ *n* : any of several shrubs or trees of the dogwood family; *esp* : DOGWOOD [derived from Latin *cornus*, a kind of dogwood]

¹cor•ner \ˈkȯr-nər, ˈkȯ-nər\ *n* **1 a** : the point or place where converging lines, edges, or sides meet : ANGLE **b** : the place of intersection of two streets or roads **c** : a piece designed to form, mark, or protect a corner **2** : a usually remote area, region, or part **3** : a position from which escape or retreat is difficult or impossible **4** : control or ownership of enough of the available supply of something to control its price [Old French *cornere*, from *corne* "horn, corner", from Latin *cornu* "horn"] — **cor•nered** \-nərd\ *adj*

²corner *vb* **1** : to drive into a corner **2** : to get a corner on ⟨*corner* the wheat market⟩ **3** : to turn a corner ⟨a car that *corners* well⟩

³corner *adj* **1** : situated at a corner **2** : used or fitted for use in or on a corner

cor•ner•back \-ˌbak\ *n* : a defensive halfback in football who defends the flank

corner kick *n* : a free kick in soccer from the corner of the field awarded to the attacking team after the defending team drives the ball out of bounds over the goal line

cor•ner•stone \-ˌstōn\ *n* **1** : a stone forming part of a corner in a wall; *esp* : such a stone laid at the formal beginning of the erection of a building **2** : something of basic importance ⟨a *cornerstone* of foreign policy⟩

cor•net \kȯr-ˈnet\ *n* **1** : a brass instrument resembling the trumpet but having a shorter tube and a more mellow tone **2** : something (as a piece of paper twisted for use as a container) shaped like a cone [Middle French, from *corn* "horn", from Latin *cornu*]

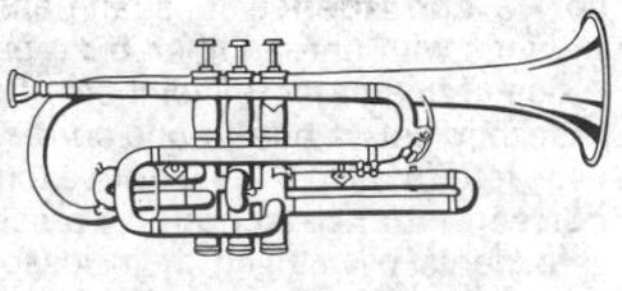

cornet 1

cor•net•ist *or* **cor•net•tist** \kȯr-ˈnet-əst\ *n* : one that plays the cornet

corn•flow•er \ˈkȯrn-ˌflau̇-ər, -ˌflau̇r\ *n* **1** : CORN COCKLE **2** : BACHELOR'S BUTTON

cor•nice \ˈkȯr-nəs\ *n* **1** : the ornamental projecting piece that forms the top edge of the front of a building or of a pillar **2** : an ornamental molding placed where the walls meet the ceiling of a room **3** : a decorative band of metal or wood to conceal curtain fixtures [Middle French, from Italian]

¹Cor•nish \ˈkȯr-nish\ *adj* : of, relating to, or characteristic of Cornwall, Cornishmen, or Cornish

²Cornish *n* **1** : a Celtic language of Cornwall extinct since the late 18th century **2** : any of an English breed of domestic fowls much used in crossbreeding for meat production

Cor•nish•man \-mən\ *n* : a native or inhabitant of Cornwall, England

corn•meal \ˈkȯrn-ˈmēl, -ˌmēl\ *n* : meal ground from Indian corn

corn oil *n* : a yellow fatty oil obtained from the germ of Indian corn kernels and used chiefly in salad oil, in soft soap, and in margarine

corn pone *n, South & Midland* : CORN BREAD; *esp* : fried corn bread

corn smut *n* : a smut attacking Indian corn; *esp* : a common smut caused by a fungus and characterized by grayish white swellings that rupture to expose a black mass of spores

corn snow *n* : granular snow formed by alternate thawing and freezing

corn•stalk \ˈkȯrn-ˌstȯk\ *n* : a stalk of Indian corn

corn•starch \-ˌstärch\ *n* : a fine starch made from Indian corn and used in cooking as a thickening agent

corn sugar *n* : sugar made by hydrolysis of cornstarch

corn syrup *n* : a syrup made from cornstarch and used in baked goods and candy

cor•nu•co•pia \ˌkȯr-nyə-ˈkō-pē-ə, -nə-\ *n* **1** : a horn-shaped container overflowing with fruits and flowers used as a symbol of abundance **2** : a great abundance **3** : a container shaped like a horn or a cone [Late Latin, from Latin *cornu copiae* "horn of plenty"]

corn whiskey *n* : whiskey distilled from a mash made up of not less than 80 percent Indian corn

corny \ˈkȯr-nē\ *adj* **corn•i•er**; **-est** : tastelessly old-fashioned or countrified : tiresomely simple or sentimental ⟨a play full of *corny* jokes⟩

co•rol•la \kə-ˈräl-ə\ *n* : the inner floral envelope of a flower consisting of petals and enclosing the stamens and pistil [Latin, "small crown, garland", from *corona* "crown"] — **co•rol•late** \-ˈräl-ət\ *adj*

cor•ol•lary \ˈkȯr-ə-ˌler-ē, ˈkär-\ *n, pl* **-lar•ies** **1** : something that follows directly from something that has been proved **2** : something that naturally follows : RESULT [Late Latin *corollarium*, from Latin, "money paid for a garland, gratuity", from *corolla* "crown, garland"] — **corollary** *adj*

co•ro•na \kə-ˈrō-nə\ *n* **1** : a usually colored circle often seen around and close to a luminous body (as the sun or moon) **2** : the outermost part of the atmosphere of the sun appearing as a gray halo around the moon's black disk during a total eclipse of the sun **3** : the upper portion of a body part (as a tooth or the skull) **4** : an appendage on the inner side of the corolla in some flowers (as the daffodil) **5** : a discharge of electricity seen as a faint glow adjacent to the surface of an electrical conductor at high voltage [Latin, "garland, crown"]

Corona Bo•re•al•is \-ˌbōr-ē-ˈal-əs, -ˌbȯr-\ *n* : a northern constellation between Hercules and Boötes [Latin, literally, "northern crown"]

cor•o•nach \ˈkȯr-ə-nək, ˈkär-\ *n* : DIRGE [Scottish Gaelic *corranach* and Irish Gaelic *corānach*]

¹cor•o•nal \ˈkȯr-ən-l, ˈkär-\ *n* : a circlet for the head

²cor•o•nal \ˈkȯr-ən-l, ˈkär-; kə-ˈrōn-\ *adj* : of or relating to a corona or crown

¹cor•o•nary \ˈkȯr-ə-ˌner-ē, ˈkär-\ *adj* : of, relating to, or being the arteries or veins that supply blood to the heart; *also* : of or relating to the heart

²coronary *n, pl* **-nar•ies** **1** : a coronary artery or vein **2** : CORONARY THROMBOSIS

coronary artery *n* : either of the two arteries, right and left, that arise from the aorta and supply the tissues of the heart

coronary occlusion *n* : the partial or complete blocking (as by a thrombus, by spasm, or by sclerosis) of a coronary artery

coronary sclerosis *n* : hardening of the coronary arteries of the heart

coronary thrombosis *n* : the blocking of an artery of the heart by a thrombus

coronary vein *n* : any of several veins that drain the tissues of the heart

cor•o•na•tion \ˌkȯr-ə-ˈnā-shən, ˌkär-\ *n* : the act or ceremony of crowning a sovereign or his consort

cor•o•ner \ˈkȯr-ə-nər, ˈkär-\ *n* : a public officer whose chief duty is to discover the causes of any death possibly not due to natural causes [Middle English, "officer of the crown", from Old French *corone* "crown", from Latin *corona*]

cor•o•net \ˌkȯr-ə-ˈnet, ˌkär-\ *n* **1** : a small crown worn by a person of noble but not of royal rank **2** : an ornamental wreath or band worn around the head

[1]**cor•po•ral** \ˈkȯr-pə-rəl, -prəl\ *n* : a linen cloth on which the eucharistic elements are placed at mass [Middle French, derived from Latin *corporalis* "of the body"; from the doctrine that the bread of the Eucharist becomes or represents the body of Christ]

[2]**corporal** *adj* : of or relating to the body ⟨whipping and other *corporal* punishments⟩ [Middle French, from Latin *corporalis,* from *corpor-, corpus* "body"] — **cor•po•ral•ly** \-pə-rə-lē, -prə-lē\ *adv*

[3]**corporal** *n* : an enlisted rank in the Army above private first class and below sergeant and in the Marine Corps above lance corporal and below sergeant [Middle French, alteration of *caporal,* from Italian *caporale,* from *capo* "head", from Latin *caput*]

cor•po•rate \ˈkȯr-pə-rət, -prət\ *adj* **1 a** : INCORPORATED **b** : of or relating to a corporation **2** : of or relating to a whole composed of individuals : COLLECTIVE [Latin *corporare* "to form into a body", from *corpus* "body"] — **cor•po•rate•ly** *adv*

cor•po•ra•tion \ˌkȯr-pə-ˈrā-shən\ *n* **1** : the municipal authorities of a town or city **2** : a body authorized by law to carry on an activity (as a business enterprise) with the rights and duties of a single person although constituted by one or more persons and having an identity that survives its incorporators

cor•po•re•al \kȯr-ˈpōr-ē-əl, -ˈpȯr-\ *adj* : having, consisting of, or relating to a physical material body: as **a** : not spiritual **b** : not immaterial or intangible : SUBSTANTIAL **c** : of or relating to a human body : BODILY **syn** see MATERIAL — **cor•po•re•al•i•ty** \-ˌpōr-ē-ˈal-ət-ē, -ˌpȯr-\ *n* — **cor•po•re•al•ly** \-ˈpōr-ē-ə-lē, -ˈpȯr-\ *adv* — **cor•po•re•al•ness** *n*

corps \ˈkōr, ˈkȯr\ *n, pl* **corps** \ˈkōrz, ˈkȯrz\ **1 a** : an organized branch of a military establishment ⟨Marine *Corps*⟩ **b** : a tactical unit consisting of two or more divisions and supporting forces **2** : a group of persons associated together or acting under common direction ⟨diplomatic *corps*⟩ [French, from Latin *corpus* "body"]

corps de bal•let \ˌkōrd-ə-ba-ˈlā, ˌkȯrd-\ *n, pl* **corps de ballet** *same*\ : the chorus of a ballet company [French]

corpse \ˈkȯrps\ *n* : a dead body [Middle French *corps* "body", from Latin *corpus*]

corps•man \ˈkōr-mən, ˈkȯr-, ˈkōrz-, ˈkȯrz-\ *n* : an enlisted man in the Navy trained to give first aid

cor•pu•lent \ˈkȯr-pyə-lənt\ *adj* : having a large bulky body : OBESE [Latin *corpulentus,* from *corpus* "body"] — **cor•pu•lence** \-ləns\ *or* **cor•pu•len•cy** \-lən-sē\ *n* — **cor•pu•lent•ly** *adv*

cor•pus \ˈkȯr-pəs\ *n, pl* **cor•po•ra** \-pə-rə, -prə\ **1** : the main or central part of a bodily structure ⟨the *corpus* of the jaw⟩ **2** : the main body or principal substance (as of a field of study) [Latin, "body"]

Cor•pus Chris•ti \ˌkȯr-pəsˈkris-tē\ *n* : the Thursday after Trinity Sunday observed as a Roman Catholic festival in honor of the Eucharist [Medieval Latin, literally, "body of Christ"]

cor•pus•cle \ˈkȯr-ˌpəs-əl\ *n* **1** : a minute particle **2** : a living cell; *esp* : one (as a blood or cartilage cell) not aggregated into continuous tissues [Latin *corpusculum* "small body", from *corpus* "body"] — **cor•pus•cu•lar** \kȯr-ˈpəs-kyə-lər\ *adj*

cor•pus de•lic•ti \ˌkȯr-pəs-di-ˈlik-ˌtī, -ˌtē\ *n, pl* **cor•po•ra delicti** \ˌkȯr-pə-rə-, -prə-\ **1** : the substantial fact necessary to prove the commission of a crime **2** : the body of a murder victim [New Latin, literally, "body of the crime"]

cor•pus lu•te•um \ˌkȯr-pəs-ˈlüt-ē-əm\ *n, pl* **cor•po•ra lu•tea** \ˌkȯr-pə-rə-ˈlüt-ē-ə, -prə-\ : a yellowish mass of endocrine tissue formed in an ovarian follicle after the egg is shed [New Latin, literally, "yellowish body"]

[1]**cor•ral** \kə-ˈral\ *n* **1** : a pen or enclosure for confining or capturing livestock **2** : an enclosure made with wagons for defense of an encampment [Spanish, derived from Latin *currus* "cart", from *currere* "to run"]

[2]**corral** *vt* **cor•ralled**; **cor•ral•ling** **1** : to confine in or as if in a corral **2** : to arrange (as wagons) so as to form a corral **3** : to round up : GATHER

[1]**cor•rect** \kə-ˈrekt\ *vt* **1 a** : to make or set right : AMEND **b** : COUNTERACT, NEUTRALIZE **c** : to alter or adjust so as to bring to some standard or required condition **2 a** : REBUKE, PUNISH **b** : to point out the errors or faults of ⟨*correct* a student's composition⟩ [Latin *correctus,* past participle of *corrigere* "to correct", from *com-* + *regere* "to lead straight"] — **cor•rect•able** \-ˈrek-tə-bəl\ *adj* — **cor•rec•tor** \-ˈrek-tər\ *n*

• **syn** CORRECT, RECTIFY, AMEND, EMEND mean to make right what is wrong. CORRECT implies taking action to remove errors, faults, or deviations; RECTIFY suggests bringing into a straight line or one direction; AMEND implies improving or restoring by making slight changes; EMEND especially applies to the correction of a text.

[2]**correct** *adj* **1** : conforming to an approved or conventional standard **2** : agreeing with fact, logic, or known truth : ACCURATE — **cor•rect•ly** *adv* — **cor•rect•ness** \-ˈrek-nəs, -ˈrekt-\ *n*

• **syn** CORRECT, ACCURATE, EXACT, PRECISE mean conforming to fact, truth, or standard. CORRECT implies little more than freedom from fault or error ⟨*correct* dress for the occasion⟩ ACCURATE implies greater fidelity to truth or fact attained by exercise of care ⟨*accurate* description of a situation⟩ EXACT stresses a very strict agreement with fact or truth ⟨a suit tailored to *exact* measurements⟩ PRECISE adds to EXACT an emphasis on sharpness of definition or delimitation ⟨*precise* terms of a contract⟩

cor•rec•tion \kə-ˈrek-shən\ *n* **1** : the action or an instance of correcting **2** : a change that corrects something **3** : punishment or discipline intended to correct faults of character or behavior **4** : the treatment of offenders through a program involving penal custody, parole, and probation — **cor•rec•tion•al** \-shnəl, -shən-l\ *adj*

cor•rec•tive \kə-ˈrek-tiv\ *adj* : serving to correct : having the power of making right, normal, or regular ⟨*corrective* exercises⟩ — **corrective** *n* — **cor•rec•tive•ly** *adv* — **cor•rec•tive•ness** *n*

cor•re•late \ˈkȯr-ə-ˌlāt, ˈkär-\ *vb* **1** : to have reciprocal or mutual relations **2** : to establish a mutual or reciprocal relation of **3** : to relate so that to each member of one set or series a corresponding member of another is assigned

cor•re•la•tion \ˌkȯr-ə-ˈlā-shən, ˌkär-\ *n* **1** : the act or process of correlating **2** : the state of being correlated; *esp* : a mutual relation existing between things ⟨the apparent *correlation* between the degree of poverty in a society and the crime rate⟩ [Medieval Latin *correlatio,* from Latin *com-* + *relatio* "relation"] — **cor•re•la•tion•al** \-shnəl, -shən-l\ *adj*

[1]**cor•rel•a•tive** \kə-ˈrel-ət-iv\ *adj* **1** : mutually related **2** : having a mutual grammatical relation and regularly used together ⟨*either* and *or* are *correlative* conjunctions⟩ — **cor•rel•a•tive•ly** *adv*

[2]**correlative** *n* : either of two correlative things

cor•re•spond \ˌkȯr-ə-ˈspänd, ˌkär-\ *vi* **1 a** : to be in conformity or agreement : SUIT **b** : to compare closely : MATCH **c** : to be equivalent or parallel **d** : to be in correspondence and especially in a one-to-one correspondence ⟨the real numbers *correspond* to points on the number line⟩ **2** : to communicate with a person by exchange of letters [Medieval Latin *correspondēre,* from Latin *com-* + *respondēre* "to respond"]

cor•re•spon•dence \-ˈspän-dəns\ *n* **1 a** : the agreement of things with one another **b** : a particular similarity **c** : association of one or more members of one set with each member of a second set ⟨a one-to-one *correspondence*⟩ **2** : communication by letters; *also* : the letters exchanged

correspondence school *n* : a school that teaches non-resident students by mailing them lessons and exercises which upon completion are returned to the school for grading

[1]**cor•re•spon•dent** \ˌkȯr-ə-ˈspän-dənt, ˌkär-\ *adj* **1** : SIMILAR 1 **2** : being in agreement : FITTING

[2]**correspondent** *n* **1** : something that corresponds or conforms to something else **2 a** : one who communicates with another by letter **b** : one who has regular commercial relations with another **c** : one who contributes news or comment to a newspaper often from a distant place

corresponding *adj* : having the same relationship (as kind, degree, position, or function) to the same or like wholes (as a geometric figure) ⟨*corresponding* parts of similar triangles⟩

cor•re•spond•ing•ly \-ˈspän-ding-lē\ *adv* : in a corresponding manner : in such a way as to correspond

cor•ri•da \kō-'rē-t͟hə\ *n* : BULLFIGHT [Spanish, literally, "act of running"]

cor•ri•dor \'kȯr-əd-ər, 'kär-, -ə-,dȯr\ *n* **1** : a passageway into which compartments or rooms open (as in a hotel or school) **2** : a narrow strip of land especially through foreign-held territory **3** : an air route (as over a foreign country) to which aircraft are restricted [Middle French, from Italian *corridore,* from *correre* "to run", from Latin *currere*]

cor•ri•gen•dum \,kȯr-ə-'jen-dəm, ,kär-\ *n, pl* **-da** \-də\ : an error in a printed work discovered after printing and shown with its correction on a separate sheet [Latin, "thing to be corrected", from *corrigere* "to correct"]

cor•ri•gi•ble \'kȯr-ə-jə-bəl, 'kär-\ *adj* : capable of being set right [Middle French, derived from Latin *corrigere* "to correct"] — **cor•ri•gi•bil•i•ty** \,kȯr-ə-jə-'bil-ət-ē, ,kär-\ *n* — **cor•ri•gi•bly** \'kȯr-ə-jə-blē, 'kär-\ *adv*

cor•rob•o•rate \kə-'räb-ə-,rāt\ *vt* : to support with evidence or authority : make more certain [Latin *corroborare* "to strengthen", from *com-* + *robur* "strength"] **syn** see CONFIRM — **cor•rob•o•ra•tor** \-,rāt-ər\ *n*

cor•rob•o•ra•tion \kə-,räb-ə-'rā-shən\ *n* **1** : the act of corroborating **2** : something that corroborates

cor•rob•o•ra•tive \kə-'räb-ə-,rāt-iv, -'räb-rət-, -ə-rət-\ *adj* : serving or tending to corroborate : CONFIRMING ⟨*corroborative* evidence⟩ — **cor•rob•o•ra•tive•ly** *adv*

cor•rob•o•ra•to•ry \kə-'räb-rə-,tōr-ē, -ə-rə-, -,tȯr-\ *adj* : CORROBORATIVE

cor•rode \kə-'rōd\ *vb* : to destroy or be destroyed gradually as if by gnawing ⟨lungs *corroded* by disease⟩; *esp* : to wear away gradually usually by chemical action [Latin *corrodere* "to gnaw to pieces", from *com-* + *rodere* "to gnaw"] — **cor•rod•ible** \-'rōd-ə-bəl\ *adj*

cor•ro•sion \kə-'rō-zhən\ *n* : the action, process, or effect of corroding [Late Latin *corrosio* "act of gnawing", from Latin *corrodere* "to gnaw"]

[1]**cor•ro•sive** \-'rō-siv, -ziv\ *adj* : tending or having the power to corrode ⟨*corrosive* acids⟩ — **cor•ro•sive•ly** *adv* — **cor•ro•sive•ness** *n*

[2]**corrosive** *n* : something corrosive

corrosive sublimate *n* : MERCURIC CHLORIDE

cor•ru•gate \'kȯr-ə-,gāt, 'kär-\ *vb* : to form or shape into parallel wrinkles or folds or ridges and grooves ⟨*corrugated* paper⟩ [Latin *corrugare,* from *com-* + *ruga* "wrinkle"]

cor•ru•ga•tion \,kȯr-ə-'gā-shən, ,kär-\ *n* **1** : the act of corrugating : the state of being corrugated **2** : a ridge or groove of a corrugated surface

[1]**cor•rupt** \kə-'rəpt\ *vb* **1 a** : to change from good to bad in morals, manners, or actions **b** : to influence a public official improperly : BRIBE **2** : TAINT 2, ROT **3** : to alter from an original or correct form or version ⟨*corrupt* a text⟩ **4** : to become debased [Latin *corruptus,* past participle of *corrumpere* "to corrupt", from *com-* + *rumpere* "to break"] **syn** see DEBASE — **corrupt•er** *or* **cor•rup•tor** \-'rəp-tər\ *n*

[2]**corrupt** *adj* **1** : morally debased : DEPRAVED **2** : characterized by improper conduct (as the selling of political favors) ⟨a *corrupt* administration⟩ — **cor•rupt•ly** *adv* — **cor•rupt•ness** \-'rəpt-nəs, -'rəp-\ *n*

cor•rupt•ible \kə-'rəp-tə-bəl\ *adj* : capable of being corrupted — **cor•rupt•ibil•i•ty** \-,rəp-tə-'bil-ət-ē\ *n*

cor•rup•tion \kə-'rəp-shən\ *n* **1 a** : physical decay or rotting **b** : moral debasement : DEPRAVITY **c** : inducement to do wrong by unlawful or improper means (as bribery) **d** : a departure from what is pure or correct **2** *archaic* : an agency or influence that corrupts

cor•rup•tive \kə-'rəp-tiv\ *adj* : producing corruption

cor•sage \kȯr-'säzh, -'säj, 'kȯr-,\ *n* **1** : the waist or bodice of a woman's dress **2** : an arrangement of flowers to be worn by a woman [French, "bust, bodice", from Old French, "bust", from *cors* "body", from Latin *corpus*]

cor•sair \'kȯr-,saər, -,seər\ *n* : PIRATE; *esp* : a privateer of the Barbary coast [Middle French *corsaire,* derived from Medieval Latin *cursarius,* from Latin *cursus* "course"]

corse \'kȯrs\ *n, archaic* : CORPSE [Old French *cors* "body"]

corse•let *n* **1** *or* **cors•let** \'kȯr-slət\ : the body armor worn by a knight especially on the upper part of the body **2** \,kȯr-sə-'let\ : a woman's undergarment somewhat like a corset [Middle French, from *cors* "body, bodice"]

[1]**cor•set** \'kȯr-sət\ *n* : a tight-fitting stiffened undergarment worn to support or give shape to waist and hips [Old French, a kind of jacket, from *cors* "body"]

[2]**corset** *vt* : to dress in or fit with a corset

cor•tege *also* **cor•tège** \kȯr-'tezh, 'kȯr-,\ *n* **1** : a train of attendants : RETINUE **2** : PROCESSION; *esp* : a funeral procession [French *cortège,* from Italian *corteggio,* from *corte* "court", from Latin *cohors* "throng"]

cor•tes \'kȯr-,tez, -,tes\ *n, pl* **cor•tes** \-,tez\ : a Spanish parliament [Spanish, plural of *corte* "court", from Latin *cohors* "throng"]

cor•tex \'kȯr-,teks\ *n, pl* **cor•ti•ces** \'kȯrt-ə-,sēz\ *or* **cor•tex•es** : an outer or surrounding layer of an organism or one of its parts ⟨the *cortex* of the kidney⟩: as **a** : the outer layer of gray matter of the brain **b** : the layer of tissue outside the vascular tissue and inside the corky or epidermal tissues of a vascular plant; *also* : all tissues external to the xylem [Latin *cortic-, cortex* "bark"] — **cor•ti•cal** \'kȯrt-i-kəl\ *adj* — **cor•ti•cal•ly** \-i-kə-lē, -klē\ *adv*

cor•ti•co•tro•pin \,kȯrt-i-kō-'trō-pən\ *n* : ACTH; *also* : a preparation of ACTH that is used especially in the treatment of rheumatoid arthritis and rheumatic fever

cor•tin \'kȯrt-n\ *n* : a hormone mixture from the adrenal cortex

cor•ti•sol \'kȯrt-ə-,sȯl, -,zȯl, -,sōl, -,zōl\ *n* : a hormone of the adrenal cortex that is derived from cortisone and has a similar use — called also *hydrocortisone*

cor•ti•sone \-,sōn, -,zōn\ *n* : a steroid hormone of the adrenal cortex used especially in the treatment of rheumatoid arthritis

co•run•dum \kə-'rən-dəm\ *n* : a very hard mineral Al_2O_3 that consists of aluminum oxide occurring in massive form and as variously colored crystals including the ruby and sapphire and that is used as an abrasive [Tamil *kuruntam,* from Sanskrit *kuruvinda* "ruby"]

cor•us•cate \'kȯr-ə-,skāt, 'kär-\ *vi* : to give off flashes of light : SPARKLE [Latin *coruscare*] — **cor•us•ca•tion** \,kȯr-ə-'skā-shən, ,kär-\ *n*

cor•vée \'kȯr-,vā, kȯr-'\ *n* : unpaid labor on public works (as roads) required usually in place of taxes [Middle French *corvee,* from Medieval Latin *corrogata,* from Latin *corrogare* "to collect, requisition", from *com-* + *rogare* "to ask"]

cor•vette \kȯr-'vet\ *n* **1** : a warship of the old sailing navies smaller than a frigate **2** : a highly maneuverable armed escort ship smaller than a destroyer [French]

Cor•vus \'kȯr-vəs\ *n* : a small constellation adjoining Virgo on the south [Latin, literally, "raven"]

Cor•y•bant \'kȯr-ə-,bant, 'kär-\ *n, pl* **Cor•y•bants** *or* **Cor•y•ban•tes** \,kȯr-ə-'ban-,tēz, ,kär-\ : one of the attendants or priests of the ancient goddess Cybele noted for their orgiastic rites [French *Corybante,* from Latin *Corybas,* from Greek *Korybas*] — **cor•y•ban•tic** \,kȯr-ə-'bant-ik, ,kär-\ *adj*

cor•ymb \'kȯr-,im, 'kär-\ *n* : a flat-topped indeterminate inflorescence in which the flower stalks arise at different levels on the main axis and reach about the same height [French *corymbe,* from Latin *corymbus* "cluster of fruit or flowers", from Greek *korymbos*]

corymb

co•se•cant \'kō-'sē-,kant, kō-, -kənt\ *n* : the trigonometric function that for an acute angle is the ratio between the hypotenuse of a right triangle of which the angle is considered part and the side opposite the angle — abbreviation *csc*

co•sig•na•to•ry \'kō-'sig-nə-,tōr-ē, -,tȯr-\ *n, pl* **-ries** : a joint signer

cosily, cosiness *variant of* COZILY, COZINESS

co•sine \'kō-,sīn\ *n* : the trigonometric function that for an acute angle is the ratio between the side adjacent to the angle when it is considered part of a right triangle and the hypotenuse — abbreviation *cos*

\ə\ **abut**	\au̇\ **out**	\i\ **tip**	\ȯ\ **saw**	\u̇\ **foot**
\ər\ **further**	\ch\ **chin**	\ī\ **life**	\ȯi\ **coin**	\y\ **yet**
\a\ **mat**	\e\ **pet**	\j\ **job**	\th\ **thin**	\yü\ **few**
\ā\ **take**	\ē\ **easy**	\ng\ **sing**	\t͟h\ **this**	\yu̇\ **cure**
\ä\ **cot, cart**	\g\ **go**	\ō\ **bone**	\ü\ **food**	\zh\ **vision**

1cos•met•ic \käz-'met-ik\ *n* **:** a cosmetic preparation for external use

2cosmetic *adj* **1 :** intended to beautify the hair or complexion **2 :** correcting defects especially of the face [Greek *kosmein* "to arrange, adorn", from *kosmos* "order"]

cos•me•tol•o•gist \ˌkäz-mə-'täl-ə-jəst\ *n* **:** a person who gives beauty treatments (as to skin and hair) — **cos•me•tol•o•gy** \-jē\ *n*

cos•mic \'käz-mik\ *adj* **1 :** of or relating to the cosmos ⟨*cosmic* theories⟩ **2 :** extremely vast **:** GRAND ⟨a topic of *cosmic* proportions⟩ — **cos•mi•cal•ly** \-mi-kə-lē, -klē\ *adv*

cosmic dust *n* **:** very fine particles of solid matter in any part of the universe and especially in interstellar space

cosmic ray *n* **:** a stream of atomic nuclei of extremely penetrating character that enter the earth's atmosphere from outer space at speeds approaching that of light

cos•mog•o•ny \käz-'mäg-ə-nē\ *n, pl* **-nies 1 :** the creation or origination of the world or universe **2 :** a theory of the origin of the universe [Greek *kosmogonia,* from *kosmos* "order, universe" + *gonos* "offspring"] — **cos•mog•o•nist** \-nəst\ *n*

cos•mog•ra•phy \käz-'mäg-rə-fē\ *n, pl* **-phies 1 :** a general description of the world or of the universe **2 :** the science that deals with the constitution of the whole order of nature — **cos•mog•ra•pher** \-fər\ *n* — **cos•mo•graph•ic** \ˌkäz-mə-'graf-ik\ *adj*

cos•mol•o•gy \käz-'mäl-ə-jē\ *n, pl* **-gies :** a study that deals with the origin, structure, and space-time relationships of the universe — **cos•mo•log•i•cal** \ˌkäz-mə-'läj-i-kəl\ *adj* — **cos•mol•o•gist** \käz-'mäl-ə-jəst\ *n*

cos•mo•naut \'käz-mə-ˌnȯt, -ˌnät\ *n* **:** a Soviet astronaut [Russian *kosmonavt,* from Greek *kosmos* "universe" + Russian *-navt* (as in *aeronavt* "aeronaut")]

cos•mo•pol•i•tan \ˌkäz-mə-'päl-ət-n\ *adj* **1 :** having a worldwide scope or outlook **:** not limited or parochial ⟨*cosmopolitan* world travelers⟩ **2 :** composed of persons or elements from many parts of the world ⟨a *cosmopolitan* city⟩ **3 :** found in most parts of the world and under varied ecological conditions ⟨a *cosmopolitan* herb⟩ [derived from Greek *kosmos* "world, cosmos" + *politēs* "citizen", from *polis* "city, state"] — **cosmopolitan** *n* — **cos•mo•pol•i•tan•ism** \-n-ˌiz-əm\ *n*

cos•mop•o•lite \käz-'mäp-ə-ˌlīt\ *n* **:** a cosmopolitan person or organism

cos•mos \'käz-məs, *1 & 2 also* -ˌmōs, -ˌmäs\ *n* **1 :** the orderly systematic universe **2 :** a complex harmonious system **3 :** a tall garden plant that is related to the daisies and has showy white, pink, or rose-colored flower heads with usually yellow centers [German *kosmos,* from Greek, "order, adornment, universe"]

cos•sack \'käs-ˌak, -ək\ *n* **:** a member of a group of frontiersmen of southern Russia organized as cavalry in the czarist army [Russian *kazak* and Ukrainian *kozak,* from Turkish *kazak* "free person"]

1cos•set \'käs-ət\ *n* **:** a pet lamb; *also* **:** PET [origin unknown]

2cosset *vt* **:** to treat as a pet **:** PAMPER

1cost \'kȯst\ *n* **1 a :** the amount paid or charged for something **:** PRICE **b :** the outlay made or loss suffered to achieve an object ⟨won the battle at the *cost* of many lives⟩ **2** *pl* **:** expenses charged to a party before a court of law ⟨fined $50 and *costs*⟩

2cost *vb* **cost; cost•ing 1 :** to have a price of **:** require payment ⟨each ticket *costs* one dollar⟩ **2 :** to cause one to pay, spend, or lose ⟨selfishness *cost* them many friends⟩ [Middle French *coster,* from Latin *constare* "to stand firm, cost", from *com-* + *stare* "to stand"]

cos•ta \'käs-tə\ *n, pl* **cos•tae** \-ˌtē, -ˌtī\ **:** a rib or a body part (as the midrib of a leaf) resembling a rib [Latin, "rib, side"] — **cos•tal** \'käst-l\ *adj*

co–star \'kō-ˌstär\ *n* **:** a performer whose role (as in a play) is equal in importance to that of the star — **co–star** *vb*

cos•tard \'käs-tərd\ *n* **1 :** any of several large English cooking apples **2** *archaic* **:** HEAD, NODDLE [Middle English]

cos•ter \'käs-tər\ *n, British* **:** COSTERMONGER

cos•ter•mon•ger \'käs-tər-ˌməng-gər, -ˌmäng-\ *n, British* **:** a person who sells fruit or vegetables in the street from a stand or cart [*costard,* a kind of apple + *monger*]

cos•tive \'käs-tiv, 'kȯs-\ *adj* **1 :** CONSTIPATED **2 :** causing constipation ⟨a *costive* diet⟩ [Middle French *costiver* "to constipate", from Latin *constipare*] — **cos•tive•ly** *adv* — **cos•tive•ness** *n*

cost•ly \'kȯst-lē\ *adj* **cost•li•er; -est 1 :** very expensive or valuable ⟨*costly* furs⟩ **2 :** gained at great cost or sacrifice ⟨a *costly* victory⟩ — **cost•li•ness** *n*

• syn EXPENSIVE, VALUABLE, DEAR: COSTLY implies high price and may suggest luxury or rarity; EXPENSIVE may imply a price beyond the thing's value or the buyer's means; VALUABLE suggests worth measured in usefulness as well as price; DEAR implies a relatively high or excessive price often due to factors other than the thing's intrinsic value.

cost•mary \'kȯst-ˌmer-ē\ *n, pl* **-mar•ies :** an aromatic herb related to the daisies and used as a potherb and in flavoring [Middle English *coste* "costmary" + *Marie,* the Virgin Mary]

1cos•tume \'käs-ˌtüm, -ˌtyüm *also* -təm *or* -chəm\ *n* **1 :** the prevailing fashion in hair style, jewelry, and apparel of a period, country, or class **2 :** a suit or dress characteristic of a period, country, or class **3 :** a person's ensemble of outer garments; *esp* **:** a woman's ensemble of dress with coat or jacket [French, from Italian, "custom, dress", from Latin *consuetudo* "custom"]

2cos•tume \käs-'tüm, -'tyüm *also* -'chüm; *or like* 1\ *vt* **1 :** to provide with a costume **2 :** to design costumes for

3cos•tume *like* 1\ *adj* **1 :** characterized by use of costumes ⟨a *costume* ball⟩ **2 :** suitable for or enhancing the effect of a particular costume ⟨a *costume* handbag⟩

cos•tum•er \'käs-ˌtü-mər, -ˌtyü-\ *or* **cos•tu•mi•er** \käs-'tü-mē-ər, -'tyü-\ *n* **1 :** one that makes, sells, or rents costumes **2 :** CLOTHES TREE

co•sy \'kō-zē\ *chiefly British variant of* COZY

1cot \'kät\ *n* **:** a small house **:** COTTAGE [Old English]

2cot *n* **:** a small often collapsible bed usually of fabric stretched on a frame [Hindi *khāṭ* "bedstead"]

co•tan•gent \'kō-'tan-jənt, kō-\ *n* **:** the trigonometric function that for an acute angle is the ratio between the side adjacent to the angle and the side opposite when the angle is considered part of a right triangle — abbreviation *cot*

cote \'kōt, 'kät\ *n* **:** a shed or coop for small domestic animals (as sheep or pigeons) [Old English *cot, cote* "cottage"]

co•te•rie \'kōt-ə-rē, ˌkōt-ə-'\ *n* **:** a small close group of persons with a shared interest or purpose [French, from Middle French, "tenants", from Medieval Latin *cotarius* "cotter"]

co•ter•mi•nal \'kō-'tər-mən-l, kō-\ *adj* **:** having the same or coincident boundaries or sides ⟨*coterminal* angles⟩

co•ter•mi•nous \'kō-'tər-mə-nəs, kō-\ *adj* **1 :** having the same boundaries **2 :** having the same scope or duration — **co•ter•mi•nous•ly** *adv*

co•til•lion *also* **co•til•lon** \kō-'til-yən\ *n* **1 :** an elaborate dance with frequent changing of partners led by one couple at formal balls **2 :** a formal ball [French *cotillon,* literally, "petticoat", from Old French, from *cote* "coat"]

co•to•neas•ter \kə-'tō-nē-ˌas-tər, 'kät-n-ˌēs-\ *n* **:** any of a genus of Old World flowering shrubs of the rose family often used in hedges [derived from Latin *eydonia, cotoneum* "quince"]

cot•ta \'kät-ə\ *n* **:** a waist-length surplice [Medieval Latin, of Germanic origin]

cot•tage \'kät-ij\ *n* **1 :** a small usually frame one-family house **2 :** a small house for vacation use [Middle English *cotage,* from *cot*]

cottage cheese *n* **:** a soft uncured cheese made from soured skim milk

cottage pudding *n* **:** plain cake covered with a hot sweet sauce

cot•tag•er \'kät-ij-ər\ *n* **:** one who lives in a cottage; *esp* **:** one occupying a private house at a vacation resort

1cot•ter *or* **cot•tar** \'kät-ər\ *n* **:** a peasant or rural laborer occupying a small holding [Medieval Latin *cotarius,* from Middle English *cot* "cottage"]

2cot•ter \'kät-ər\ *n* **:** a wedge-shaped or tapered piece used to fasten together parts of a structure [origin unknown]

cotter pin *n* **:** a half-round metal strip bent into a pin whose ends can be flared after insertion through a slot or hole

1cot•ton \'kät-n\ *n* **1 a :** a soft usually white fibrous substance composed of the hairs surrounding the seeds of various erect freely branching tropical plants of the mallow family **b :** a plant producing cotton **c :** a crop of cotton **2 a :** fabric made of cotton **b :** yarn spun from cotton [Middle French *coton,* from Arabic *quṭn*] — **cotton** *adj*

2cotton *vi* **cot•toned; cot•ton•ing** \'kät-ning, -n-ing\ **:** to take a liking ⟨*cottoned* to them at first sight⟩

cotton candy *n* **:** a candy made of spun sugar

cotton gin *n* **:** a machine that separates the seeds, hulls, and foreign material from cotton

cot•ton•mouth \'kät-n-,maüth\ *also* **cotton-mouth moccasin** *n* : WATER MOCCASIN

cot•ton•seed \-,sēd\ *n* : the seed of the cotton plant which yields a protein-rich meal and a fixed oil used especially in cooking

cottontail

cot•ton•tail \-,tāl\ *n* : any of several small brownish gray rabbits with white-tufted tail

cot•ton•wood \-,wu̇d\ *n* : a poplar that produces a tuft of cottony hairs on the seed; *esp* : one of the eastern and central United States noted for its rapid growth and luxuriant foliage

cotton wool *n* : raw cotton; *esp* : cotton batting

cot•tony \'kät-nē, -n-ē\ *adj* : resembling cotton in appearance or character: as **a** : covered with soft hairs : DOWNY **b** : SOFT 1e

-cotyl \,kät-l\ *n combining form* : cotyledon ⟨epi*cotyl*⟩

cot•y•le•don \,kät-l-'ēd-n\ *n* **1** : a small lobe of a placenta **2** : the first leaf or one of the first pair or whorl of leaves developed by the embryo of a seed plant [Greek *kotylēdōn* "cup-shaped hollow", from *kotylē* "cup"] — **cot•y•le•don•ary** \-'ēd-n-,er-ē\ *adj*

cot•y•lo•saur \'kät-l-ō-,sȯr\ *n* : any of an order (Cotylosauria) of ancient extinct primitive reptiles that were probably the earliest truly terrestrial vertebrate animals [Greek *kotylē* "cup" + *sauros* "lizard"]

[1]**couch** \'kau̇ch\ *vb* **1** : to recline for rest or sleep **2** : to bring down : LOWER ⟨a knight charging with *couched* lance⟩ **3** : to phrase in a specified manner ⟨a letter *couched* in polite terms⟩ **4** : to lie in ambush [Middle French *coucher,* from Latin *collocare* "to set in place", from *com-* + *locus* "place"]

[2]**couch** *n* : an article of furniture (as a sofa) for sitting or reclining

couch•ant \'kau̇-chənt\ *adj* : lying down especially with the head up ⟨a heraldic lion *couchant*⟩

couch grass \'kau̇ch-, 'küch-\ *n* : QUACK GRASS [*couch,* alteration of *quitch* "couch grass" from Old English *cwice*]

cou•gar \'kü-gər, -,gär\ *n, pl* **cougars** *also* **cougar** : a large powerful tawny brown cat formerly widespread in the Americas but now extinct in many areas — called also *mountain lion, panther, puma* [French *couguar,* derived from Tupi *suasuarana,* literally, "false deer", from *suasú* "deer" + *rana* "false"]

cougar

[1]**cough** \'kȯf\ *vb* **1** : to force air from the lungs with a sharp short noise or series of noises **2** : to get rid of by coughing ⟨*cough* up phlegm⟩ [Middle English *coughen*]

[2]**cough** *n* **1** : a condition marked by repeated or frequent coughing **2** : an act or sound of coughing

cough drop *n* : a medicated tablet or candy used to relieve coughing

cough up *vt* : DELIVER, PAY ⟨*cough up* the money⟩

could \kəd, 'ku̇d, 'ku̇d\ *past of* CAN — used as an auxiliary verb in the past ⟨we found we *could* go⟩ ⟨we said we would go if we *could*⟩ and as a polite or less forceful alternative to *can* ⟨*could* you do this for me⟩ [Old English *cūthe*]

could•est \'ku̇d-əst\ *archaic past 2d sing of* CAN

couldn't \'ku̇d-nt\ : could not

couldst \kədst, ku̇dst, 'ku̇dst\ *archaic past 2d sing of* CAN

cou•lee \'kü-lē\ *n* **1 a** : a dry creek bed **b** : a steep-walled valley **2** : a thick sheet or stream of lava [Canadian French *coulée,* from French, "flowing, flow of lava", from *couler* "to flow", from Latin *colare* "to strain", from *colum* "sieve"]

cou•lomb \'kü-,läm, -,lōm, kü-'\ *n* : the practical mks unit of electric charge equal to the quantity of electricity transferred by a current of one ampere in one second [Charles A. de *Coulomb,* died 1806, French physicist]

coun•cil \'kau̇n-səl\ *n* **1** : a meeting for consultation, advice, or discussion **2** : an advisory or legislative body ⟨governor's *council*⟩ **3** : an administrative body (as of a town) **4** : deliberation in a council **5 a** : a federation of or a central body uniting a group of organizations or other bodies **b** : a local chapter of an organization **c** : CLUB 2a, SOCIETY [Old French *concile,* from Latin *concilium,* from *com-* + *calare* "to call"]

coun•cil•lor *or* **coun•cil•or** \'kau̇n-sə-lər, -slər\ *n* : a member of a council — **coun•cil•lor•ship** \-,ship\ *n*

coun•cil•man \'kau̇n-səl-mən\ *n* : a member of a council especially in a city government

[1]**coun•sel** \'kau̇n-səl\ *n* **1 a** : advice given especially as a result of consultation **b** : a policy or plan of action or behavior **2** : DELIBERATION, CONSULTATION ⟨take *counsel* together⟩ **3** *pl* **counsel** : a lawyer who gives advice in law or manages cases for clients in court [Old French *conseil,* from Latin *consilium,* from *consulere* "to consult"]

[2]**counsel** *vb* **-seled** *or* **-selled**; **-sel•ing** *or* **-sel•ling** \-sə-ling, -sling\ **1** : to give counsel : ADVISE ⟨*counsel* a student on a choice of studies⟩ **2** : to seek counsel : CONSULT ⟨*counsel* with friends⟩

coun•sel•or *or* **coun•sel•lor** \'kau̇n-sə-lər, -slər\ *n* **1** : ADVISER **2** : LAWYER; *esp* : one that manages cases for clients in court **3** : a supervisor of campers or activities at a summer camp — **coun•sel•or•ship** \-,ship\ *n*

[1]**count** \'kau̇nt\ *vb* **1 a** : to find the total number of by naming units or groups ⟨*count* the apples in a box⟩ **b** : to name the consecutive numbers up to and including ⟨*count* ten⟩ **c** : to recite the numbers in order by units or groups ⟨*count* to one hundred by fives⟩ **d** : to include in a tally ⟨40 present, *counting* children⟩ **2 a** : CONSIDER ⟨*count* oneself lucky⟩ **b** : to include or exclude by or as if by counting ⟨*counted* themselves out⟩ **3 a** : RELY, DEPEND ⟨a person you can *count* on⟩ **b** : RECKON, PLAN ⟨*counted* on going⟩ **4** : to have value, significance, or importance ⟨every vote *counts*⟩ [Middle French *compter,* from Latin *computare,* from *com-* + *putare* "to consider"] — **count•able** \-ə-bəl\ *adj*

[2]**count** *n* **1** : the act or process of counting; *also* : a total obtained by counting : TALLY **2** : ALLEGATION, CHARGE; *esp* : one stating a separate cause of action in a legal declaration or indictment ⟨guilty on all *counts*⟩ **3 a** : the calling off of the seconds from one to ten when a boxer has been knocked down **b** : the number of balls and strikes called on a baseball batter

[3]**count** *n* : a European nobleman whose rank corresponds to that of a British earl [Middle French *comte,* from Late Latin *comes,* from Latin, "companion", from *com-* + *ire* "to go"]

count•down \'kau̇nt-,dau̇n\ *n* : an audible backward counting off in fixed units (as seconds) from an arbitrary starting number to mark the time remaining before an event (as the launching of a rocket)

[1]**coun•te•nance** \'kau̇nt-n-əns, 'kau̇nt-nəns\ *n* **1 a** : calm expression **b** : mental composure **c** : LOOK 2a, EXPRESSION **2** : FACE, VISAGE; *esp* : facial expression as an indication of mood, emotion, or character **3** : a show of approval ⟨gave no *countenance* to the plan⟩ [Middle French *contenance* "demeanor, bearing", from Latin *continentia* "restraint", from *continens* "continent"]

[2]**countenance** *vt* : TOLERATE 1, SANCTION ⟨refused to *countenance* such habitual lateness⟩

[1]**count•er** \'kau̇nt-ər\ *n* **1** : a piece (as of metal or plastic) used in counting or in games **2** : a level surface (as a table or board) over which transactions are conducted or food is served or on which goods are displayed

[2]**count•er** *n* : one that counts; *esp* : a device for indicating a number or amount

[3]**coun•ter** \'kau̇nt-ər\ *vb* **coun•tered**; **coun•ter•ing** \'kau̇nt-ə-ring, 'kau̇n-tring\ **1** : to act in opposition to : OPPOSE ⟨*countering* the claim for damages⟩ **2** : RETALIATE ⟨*countered* with a left hook⟩

[4]**coun•ter** *adv* : in a contrary manner or direction ⟨acted *counter* to our orders⟩ [Middle French *contre,* from Latin *contra* "against, opposite"]

[5]**coun•ter** *n* **1** : the after portion of a boat from the waterline to

\ə\ **abut**	\au̇\ **out**	\i\ **tip**	\ȯ\ **saw**	\u̇\ **foot**
\ər\ **further**	\ch\ **chin**	\ī\ **life**	\ȯi\ **coin**	\y\ **yet**
\a\ **mat**	\e\ **pet**	\j\ **job**	\th\ **thin**	\yü\ **few**
\ā\ **take**	\ē\ **easy**	\ng\ **sing**	\t͟h\ **this**	\yu̇\ **cure**
\ä\ **cot, cart**	\g\ **go**	\ō\ **bone**	\ü\ **food**	\zh\ **vision**

the extreme outward swell or overhang **2 :** the act of giving a retaliatory blow; *also* **:** the blow given **3 :** a stiffener giving shape to the upper of a shoe or boot around the heel

[6]**coun•ter** *adj* **1 :** moving in an opposite direction ⟨ships slowed by *counter* tides⟩ **2 :** designed to oppose

counter- *prefix* **1 a :** contrary **:** opposite ⟨*counter*clockwise⟩ **b :** opposing **:** retaliatory ⟨*counter*offensive⟩ **2 :** complementary **:** corresponding ⟨*counter*weight⟩ **3 :** duplicate **:** substitute ⟨*counter*foil⟩ [Middle French *contre*]

See *counter-* and 2d element

counteraccusation	**counterembargo**	**counterraid**
counteraggression	**counterevidence**	**counterrally**
counterargue	**counterguerrilla**	**counterrebuttal**
counterassault	**counterinflationary**	**counterreform**
counterbid	**counterinfluence**	**counterresponse**
counterblockade	**counterintrigue**	**counterretaliation**
counterblow	**countermeasure**	**counterstrategy**
countercampaign	**countermove**	**counterstyle**
counterchallenge	**countermovement**	**countersue**
countercharge	**counteroffer**	**countersuggestion**
countercomplaint	**counterpetition**	**countersuit**
countercoup	**counterploy**	**countertendency**
countercriticism	**counterpower**	**counterterror**
counter–demand	**counterpressure**	**counterterrorism**
counterdemonstration	**counterpropaganda**	**counterterrorist**
counterdemonstrator	**counterproposal**	**counterthreat**
countereffect	**counterprotest**	**counterthrust**
counter–effort	**counterquestion**	**countertrend**

coun•ter•act \ˌkau̇nt-ə-ˈrakt\ *vt* **:** to lessen the force of **:** OFFSET ⟨a drug that *counteracts* the effect of a poison⟩ ⟨*counteract* an evil influence⟩ — **coun•ter•ac•tion** \-ˈrak-shən\ *n* — **coun•ter•ac•tive** \-ˈrak-tiv\ *adj*

coun•ter•at•tack \ˈkau̇nt-ə-rə-ˌtak\ *n* **:** an attack made against an enemy's attack — **counterattack** *vb*

[1]**coun•ter•bal•ance** \ˈkau̇nt-ər-ˌbal-əns, ˌkau̇nt-ər-ˈ\ *n* **1 :** a weight that balances another **2 :** a force or influence that offsets or checks an opposing force

[2]**counterbalance** \ˌkau̇nt-ər-ˈ, ˈkau̇nt-ər-ˌ\ *vt* **:** to oppose with an equal weight or force

[1]**coun•ter•check** \ˈkau̇nt-ər-ˌchek\ *n* **:** a check or restraint often operating against something that is itself a check

[2]**countercheck** *vt* **:** to check a second time for verification

counter check *n* **:** a blank check obtainable at a bank; *esp* **:** one to be cashed at the bank by the drawer

coun•ter•claim \ˈkau̇nt-ər-ˌklām\ *n* **:** an opposing claim especially in law — **counterclaim** *vb*

coun•ter•clock•wise \ˌkau̇nt-ər-ˈkläk-ˌwīz\ *adv* **:** in a direction opposite to that in which the hands of a clock rotate — **counterclockwise** *adj*

coun•ter•cur•rent \ˈkau̇nt-ər-ˌkər-ənt, -ˌkə-rənt\ *n* **:** a current flowing in a direction opposite to that of another one

coun•ter•es•pi•o•nage \ˌkau̇nt-ə-ˈres-pē-ə-ˌnäzh, -nij, -ˌnäj\ *n* **:** activities intended to discover and defeat enemy espionage

coun•ter•ex•am•ple \ˈkau̇nt-ə-rig-ˌzam-pəl\ *n* **:** an example that disproves a theorem or proposition

[1]**coun•ter•feit** \ˈkau̇nt-ər-ˌfit\ *vb* **1 :** to imitate or copy especially with intent to deceive ⟨*counterfeiting* money⟩ **2 :** PRETEND 2, FEIGN ⟨*counterfeit* an air of indifference⟩ — **coun•ter•feit•er** *n*

[2]**counterfeit** *adj* **1 :** made in imitation of something else with intent to deceive ⟨*counterfeit* money⟩ **2 :** not real **:** SHAM ⟨a *counterfeit* interest⟩ [Middle French *contrefait,* from *contrefaire* "to imitate", from *contre-* "counter-" + *faire* "to make", from Latin *facere*]

[3]**counterfeit** *n* **1 :** something counterfeit **:** FORGERY **2 :** something that is likely to be confused with the genuine thing

coun•ter•foil \ˈkau̇nt-ər-ˌfȯil\ *n* **:** a detachable stub usually serving as a record or receipt [*counter-* + *foil* "leaf"]

coun•ter•in•tel•li•gence \ˌkau̇nt-ə-rin-ˈtel-ə-jəns\ *n* **:** organized activities of an intelligence service intended to foil the activities of an enemy's intelligence service by blocking its sources of information and by deceiving the enemy through tricks and misinformation

coun•ter•ir•ri•tant \ˌkau̇nt-ə-ˈrir-ə-tənt\ *n* **:** something (as a mustard plaster) used to produce surface inflammation in order to reduce inflammation in deeper nearby structures — **counterirritant** *adj*

count•er•man \ˈkau̇nt-ər-ˌman, -mən\ *n* **:** one who tends a counter (as in a lunchroom)

coun•ter•mand \ˈkau̇nt-ər-ˌmand, ˌkau̇nt-ər-ˈ\ *vt* **1 :** to cancel (a command) by a contrary order **2 :** to recall or order back by a superseding contrary order [Middle French *contremander,* from *contre-* "counter-" + *mander* "to command", from Latin *mandare*] — **countermand** *n*

coun•ter•march \ˈkau̇nt-ər-ˌmärch\ *n* **:** a marching back; *esp* **:** a maneuver by which a unit of troops reverses direction but keeps the same order — **countermarch** *vi*

coun•ter•of•fen•sive \ˈkau̇nt-ə-rə-ˌfen-siv\ *n* **:** a large-scale counterattack

coun•ter•pane \ˈkau̇nt-ər-ˌpān\ *n* **:** BEDSPREAD [Middle English *countrepointe,* from Middle French *coute pointe,* literally, "embroidered quilt"]

coun•ter•part \ˈkau̇nt-ər-ˌpärt\ *n* **1 :** a part or thing corresponding to another ⟨the left arm is the *counterpart* of the right arm⟩ **2 :** something that serves to complete something else **:** COMPLEMENT **3 :** one closely resembling another ⟨the twins were *counterparts* of each other⟩

[1]**coun•ter•plot** \-ˌplät\ *vb* **:** to plot against (a plot or plotter) **:** INTRIGUE

[2]**counterplot** *n* **:** a plot in opposition to another plot

coun•ter•point \ˈkau̇nt-ər-ˌpȯint\ *n* **1 :** one or more melodies added above or below a given melody **2 :** combination of two or more melodies into a single harmonic texture [Middle French *contrepoint,* from Medieval Latin *contrapunctus,* from Latin *contra-* "counter-" + Medieval Latin *punctus* "musical note, melody"]

[1]**coun•ter•poise** \-ˌpȯiz\ *vt* **:** COUNTERBALANCE

[2]**counterpoise** *n* **1 :** COUNTERBALANCE **2 :** a state of balance

Coun•ter–Ref•or•ma•tion \ˌkau̇nt-ər-ˌref-ər-ˈmā-shən\ *n* **:** the reform movement in the Roman Catholic Church following the Reformation

coun•ter•rev•o•lu•tion \-ˌrev-ə-ˈlü-shən\ *n* **:** a revolution intended to undo a current or earlier one — **coun•ter•rev•o•lu•tion•ary** \-shə-ˌner-ē\ *adj or n* — **coun•ter•rev•o•lu•tion•ist** \-shə-nəst, -shnəst\ *n*

coun•ter•shaft \ˈkau̇nt-ər-ˌshaft\ *n* **:** a shaft that receives motion from a main shaft and transmits it to a working part

[1]**coun•ter•sign** \-ˌsīn\ *n* **1 :** a signature confirming the authenticity of a document already signed by another **2 :** a sign used in reply to another; *esp* **:** a secret signal that must be given by one wishing to pass a guard

[2]**countersign** *vt* **:** to add one's signature to (a document) after another's to confirm authenticity — **coun•ter•sig•na•ture** \ˌkau̇nt-ər-ˈsig-nə-ˌchu̇r, -chər\ *n*

[1]**coun•ter•sink** \ˈkau̇nt-ər-ˌsiŋk\ *vt* **-sunk** \-ˌsəŋk\; **-sink•ing 1 :** to make a countersink on **2 :** to set the head of (as a screw, bolt, or nail) at or below the surface

[2]**countersink** *n* **1 :** a funnel-shaped enlargement at the outer end of a drilled hole **2 :** a bit or drill for making a countersink

coun•ter•spy \-ˌspī\ *n* **:** a spy employed in counterintelligence

coun•ter•ten•or \-ˌten-ər\ *n* **:** a tenor with an unusually high range

coun•ter•weight \-ˌwāt\ *n* **:** COUNTERBALANCE 1 — **counterweight** *vt*

count•ess \ˈkau̇nt-əs\ *n* **1 :** the wife or widow of a count or an earl **2 :** a woman who holds the rank of a count or an earl in her own right

count•ing•house \ˈkau̇nt-iŋ-ˌhau̇s\ *n* **:** a building, room, or office used for keeping books and transacting business

counting number *n* **:** NATURAL NUMBER

counting room *n* **:** COUNTINGHOUSE

count•less \ˈkau̇nt-ləs\ *adj* **:** too numerous to be counted **:** INNUMERABLE **syn** see MANY

coun•tri•fied *or* **coun•try•fied** \ˈkən-tri-ˌfīd\ *adj* **:** looking or acting as if from the country **:** RUSTIC

[1]**coun•try** \ˈkən-trē\ *n, pl* **countries 1 :** an indefinite usually large or open stretch of land **:** REGION ⟨hill *country*⟩ **2 a :** the land of a person's birth, residence, or citizenship **b :** a political state or nation or its territory **3 :** the people of a state or district **:** POPULACE **4 :** rural as distinguished from urban areas ⟨lives out in the *country*⟩ [Old French *contrée,* from Medieval Latin *contrata,* from Latin *contra* "against, on the opposite side"]

△ **origin** English *country* is derived from Latin *contra,* which means "against" or "on the opposite side". In Medieval Latin the noun *contrata* was formed from *contra. Contrata* was literally "that which is situated opposite the beholder". But that which is opposite the beholder is just what he or she sees. So *contrata* meant "landscape". It also came to mean "expanse of land, region". This was the original meaning of English *country,* which over the years has itself developed a number of new meanings.

2country *adj* : of, relating to, or characteristic of the country

country club *n* : a suburban club for social life and recreation

coun•try–dance \'kən-trē-ˌdans\ *n* : an English dance in which partners face each other especially in rows

coun•try•man \'kən-trē-mən, *3 is often* -ˌman\ *n* **1** : an inhabitant or native of a specified country ⟨a north *countryman*⟩ **2** : COMPATRIOT 1 **3** : one living in the country or marked by country ways : RUSTIC

country music *n* : music derived from or imitating the folk style of the southern United States or of the Western cowboy

coun•try•seat \ˌkən-trē-'sēt\ *n* : a mansion or estate in the country

coun•try•side \'kən-trē-ˌsīd\ *n* : a rural area or its people

coun•ty \'kaůnt-ē\ *n, pl* **counties** **1** : the domain of a count **2 a** : one of the chief territorial divisions of Great Britain and Ireland for administrative, judicial, and political purposes **b** : the largest territorial division for local government within a state of the United States [Old French *conté,* from Medieval Latin *comitatus,* from Late Latin, "office of a count", from *comit-, comes* "count"]

county agent *n* : a government agent employed to provide information about agriculture and home economics in rural areas

county seat *n* : a town that is the seat of county administration

coup \'kü\ *n, pl* **coups** \'küz\ **1** : a brilliant, sudden, and usually highly successful act **2** : COUP D'ETAT [French, "blow, stroke", from Late Latin *colpus,* from Latin *colaphus,* from Greek *kolaphos* "slap"]

coup de grace \ˌküd-ə-'gräs\ *n, pl* **coups de grace** \ˌküd-ə-\ **1** : a death blow or shot administered to end the suffering of one mortally wounded **2** : a decisive finishing blow or event [French *coup de grâce,* literally, "stroke of mercy"]

coup d'e•tat \ˌküd-ə-'tä, ˌküd-ā-\ *n, pl* **coups d'e•tat** \-'tä, -'täz\ : a sudden decisive political move; *esp* : the overthrow of an existing government by a small group [French *coup d'état,* literally, "stroke of state"]

cou•pé *or* **coupe** \kü-'pā, *2 is often* 'küp\ *n* **1** : a four-wheeled closed horse-drawn carriage for two persons inside with an outside seat for the driver in front **2** *usually coupe* **a** : a closed 2-door automobile for usually two persons **b** : a usually closed 2-door automobile with a full-width rear seat [French *coupé,* from *couper* "to cut, strike", from *coup* "blow, coup"]

1cou•ple \'kəp-əl\ *vb* **cou•pled**; **cou•pling** \'kəp-ling, -ə-ling\ **1** : to join together : CONNECT ⟨freight cars *coupled* end to end⟩ **2** : COPULATE **3** : to bring (two electric circuits) into such close proximity as to permit mutual influence

2couple *n* **1 a** : a man and woman married, engaged, or otherwise paired **b** : two persons paired together **2** : BRACE 1, PAIR **3** : two equal and opposite forces that act along parallel lines **4** : an indefinite small number ⟨a *couple* of days ago⟩ [Old French *cople* "pair, bond", from Latin *copula* "bond"]

3couple *adj* : TWO; *also* : SEVERAL 2 ⟨a *couple* days ago⟩

cou•pler \'kəp-lər, -ə-lər\ *n* **1** : one that couples **2** : a device on a keyboard instrument by which keyboards or keys are connected to play together

cou•plet \'kəp-lət\ *n* : two successive lines of verse forming a unit; *esp* : two rhyming lines of the same length — compare HEROIC COUPLET

cou•pling \'kəp-ling (*usual for 2*), -ə-ling\ *n* **1** : the act of bringing or coming together : PAIRING **2** : something that joins or connects two parts or things ⟨a car *coupling*⟩ ⟨a pipe *coupling*⟩ **3** : the joining of or the part of the body that joins the hindquarters to the forequarters of a quadruped **4** : means of electric connection of two electric circuits by having a part common to both

cou•pon \'kü-ˌpän, 'kyü-\ *n* **1** : a statement of due interest to be cut from a bond and presented for payment on a stated date **2 a** : one of a series of attached tickets to be detached and presented as needed **b** : a ticket or form authorizing purchases of rationed commodities **c** : a certificate or similar evidence of a purchase redeemable in premiums **d** : a part of a printed advertisement to be cut off for use as an order blank or inquiry form [French, from *couper* "to cut"]

cour•age \'kər-ij, 'kə-rij\ *n* : mental or moral strength to venture, persevere, and withstand danger, fear, or difficulty [Old French *corage,* from *cuer* "heart", from Latin *cor*]

• **syn** COURAGE, BRAVERY, VALOR, HEROISM mean greatness of heart in facing danger or difficulty. COURAGE implies strength in overcoming fear and in persisting against odds or difficulties; BRAVERY stresses bold and daring defiance of danger; VALOR applies especially to bravery in fighting a dangerous enemy; HEROISM suggests bravery and boldness in accepting risk or sacrifice for a noble or generous purpose.

cou•ra•geous \kə-'rā-jəs\ *adj* : having or characterized by courage : BRAVE — **cou•ra•geous•ly** *adv* — **cou•ra•geous•ness** *n*

cou•ri•er \'kůr-ē-ər, 'kər-ē-, 'kə-rē-\ *n* : MESSENGER: as **a** : a member of a diplomatic service entrusted with bearing messages **b** : a member of the armed services who carries mail, information, or supplies [Middle French *courrier,* from Italian *corriere,* from *correre* "to run", from Latin *currere*]

1course \'kōrs, 'kȯrs\ *n* **1 a** : the act or action of moving in a path from point to point **b** : LIFE HISTORY 2, CAREER **2** : the path over which something moves: as **a** : RACECOURSE **b** : the direction of flight of an airplane **c** : WATERCOURSE **d** : land laid out for golf **3 a** : accustomed procedure or action ⟨the law taking its *course*⟩ **b** : a manner of conducting oneself : BEHAVIOR ⟨the wisest *course* is to retreat⟩ **c** : progression through a series of acts or events or a development or period ⟨in the *course* of one's career⟩ **4 a** : an ordered process or succession **b** : a series of lectures or discussions dealing with a subject; *also* : a number of such courses constituting a curriculum **5 a** : a part of a meal served at one time **b** : ROW, LAYER; *esp* : a continuous level range of brick or masonry throughout a wall [Old French, from Latin *cursus,* from *currere* "to run"] — **of course** **1** : following the ordinary way or procedure ⟨did it as a matter *of course*⟩ **2** : as might be expected

2course *vb* **1 a** : to hunt or pursue (game) with hounds **b** : to cause (dogs) to run (as after game) **2** : to run through or over ⟨when buffalo *coursed* the plains⟩ **3** : to move rapidly : RACE ⟨blood *coursing* through the veins⟩

cours•er \'kōr-sər, 'kȯr-\ *n* : a swift or spirited horse

1court \'kōrt, 'kȯrt\ *n* **1 a** : the residence of a dignitary and especially a sovereign **b** : a sovereign's formal assembly of his or her councillors and officers **c** : the sovereign and his or her officials who constitute the governing power **d** : the family and retinue of a sovereign **e** : a reception held by a sovereign **2 a** : an open space wholly or partly surrounded by buildings **b** : a space arranged for playing any of various games with a ball ⟨a tennis *court*⟩ **c** : a short street or lane **3 a** : an assembly for the transaction of judicial business **b** : a session of a judicial assembly ⟨*court* is now adjourned⟩ **c** : a place (as a chamber) for the administration of justice **d** : a judge in session **e** : a faculty or agency of judgment or evaluation **4 a** : as assembly or board with legislative or administrative powers **b** : LEGISLATURE, PARLIAMENT **5** : attention designed to win favor or dispel hostility ⟨pay *court* to the king⟩ [Old French, from Latin *cohors* "enclosure, throng, cohort"]

2court *vb* **1 a** : to try to gain ⟨*courting* favor with the higher-ups⟩ **b** : to act so as to provoke ⟨was *courting* disaster⟩ **2** : to seek the affections of ⟨*courted* a college student⟩ **3** : to try to get the support of ⟨both candidates *courted* the independent voters⟩ **4 a** : to engage in social relationship and activities usually leading to marriage **b** : to engage in activity leading to mating ⟨a pair of robins *courting*⟩

cour•te•ous \'kərt-ē-əs\ *adj* **1** : marked by polished manners, gallantry, or ceremonial usage of a court **2** : marked by respect for and consideration of others **syn** see CIVIL — **cour•te•ous•ly** *adv* — **cour•te•ous•ness** *n*

cour•te•san \'kōrt-ə-zən, 'kȯrt- *also* 'kərt-\ *n* : a prostitute with an upper-class clientele [Middle French *courtisane,* from Italian *cortigiana* "female courtier", from *corte* "court", from Latin *cohors* "throng"]

cour•te•sy \'kərt-ə-sē\ *n, pl* **-sies** **1** : courtly politeness ⟨old-world *courtesy*⟩ **2** : a favor courteously performed **3** : consideration and generosity in providing ⟨flowers given through the *courtesy* of a florist⟩

courtesy title *n* : a title (as "Professor" for any teacher) taken by the user and commonly accepted without consideration of official right

court•house \'kōrt-ˌhau̇s, 'kȯrt-\ *n* **1 a :** a building in which courts of law are held **b :** a building in which county offices are housed **2 :** COUNTY SEAT

court•ier \'kōrt-ē-ər, 'kȯrt-\ *n* **1 :** a person in attendance at a royal court **2 :** a person who practices flattery

court•ly \'kōrt-lē, 'kȯrt-\ *adj* **court•li•er; -est 1 a :** of a quality befitting a royal court **:** ELEGANT ⟨*courtly* manners⟩ **b :** insincerely flattering **2 :** favoring the policy or party of the court — **court•li•ness** *n*

[1]**court-mar•tial** \'kōrt-ˌmär-shəl, 'kȯrt-\ *n, pl* **courts-martial** *also* **court-martials 1 :** a military court for the trial of members of the armed forces or others within its jurisdiction **2 :** a trial by court-martial

[2]**court-martial** *vt* **-mar•tialed** *also* **-mar•tialled; -mar•tial•ing** *also* **-mar•tial•ling** \-ˌmärsh-ling, -ə-ling\ **:** to subject to trial by court-martial

Court of St. James's \-sānt-'jāmz, -sənt-\ **:** the British court [from *Saint James's* Palace, London, former seat of the British court]

court plaster *n* **:** an adhesive plaster especially of silk coated with isinglass and glycerin [from its use for beauty spots by ladies at royal courts]

court•room \'kōrt-ˌrüm, 'kȯrt-, -ˌru̇m\ *n* **:** a room in which a court of law is held

court•ship \-ˌship\ *n* **:** the act, process, or period of courting

court tennis *n* **:** a game similar to tennis played with a ball and racket in an enclosed court

court•yard \'kōrt-ˌyärd, 'kȯrt-\ *n* **:** a court or enclosure attached to a building

cous•in \'kəz-n\ *n* **1 a :** a child of one's uncle or aunt **b :** a relative descended from a common ancestor in a different line **2 :** a person belonging to an ethnically or culturally related group ⟨our English *cousins*⟩ [Old French *cosin,* from Latin *consobrinus,* from *com-* + *sobrinus* "cousin on the mother's side", from *soror* "sister"]

cous•in-ger•man \ˌkəz-n-'jər-mən\ *n, pl* **cousins-german** \ˌkəz-nz-\ **:** COUSIN 1a [Middle English *germain* "closely related", derived from Latin *germanus* "having the same parents", from *germen* "bud, sprout, germ"]

co•va•lence \'kō-'vā-ləns, kō-\ *or* **co•va•len•cy** \-lən-sē\ *n* **:** valence characterized by the sharing of electrons in pairs by two atoms in a chemical compound; *also* **:** the number of pairs of electrons an atom can share with its neighbors — **co•va•lent** \-lənt\ *adj* — **co•va•lent•ly** *adv*

cove \'kōv\ *n* **1 a :** an architectural member with a concave cross section **b :** a trough for concealed lighting at the upper part of a wall **2 :** a small sheltered inlet or bay **3 :** a level area sheltered by hills or mountains [Old English *cofa* "den, cave"]

cov•en \'kəv-ən\ *n* **:** a meeting or band of witches [Middle French *covin* "band", derived from Latin *convenire* "to come together"]

[1]**cov•e•nant** \'kəv-nənt, -ə-nənt\ *n* **1 :** a solemn and binding agreement **:** COMPACT **2 a :** a written agreement or promise usually under seal between parties **b :** a promise incidental to and contained in an agreement (as a deed) [Old French, from *covenir,* from Latin *convenire* "to come together, agree", from *com-* + *venire* "to come"] — **cov•e•nan•tal** \ˌkəv-ə-'nant-l\ *adj*

[2]**cov•e•nant** \'kəv-nənt, -ə-nənt, -ə-nant\ *vb* **1 :** to promise by a covenant **:** PLEDGE **2 :** to enter into a covenant **:** CONTRACT — **cov•e•nant•er** \-ə-ˌnant-ər\ *n*

Cov•en•try \'kəv-ən-trē, 'käv-\ *n* **:** a state of ostracism or exclusion ⟨sent to *Coventry*⟩ [*Coventry,* England]

[1]**cov•er** \'kəv-ər\ *vb* **cov•ered; cov•er•ing** \'kəv-ring, -ə-ring\ **1 a :** to guard from attack **b :** to have within gunshot range **c** (1) **:** to provide protection or security to **:** INSURE ⟨this insurance *covers* the traveler in any accident⟩ (2) **:** to provide protection against or compensation for ⟨the policy *covered* all water damage⟩ **d :** to maintain a check on especially by patrolling ⟨state police *covering* the highways⟩ **2 a :** to hide from sight or knowledge ⟨*cover* up a scandal⟩ **b :** to conceal something illicit, blameworthy, or embarrassing from notice ⟨*cover* for a friend in an investigation⟩ **c :** to act as a substitute or replacement during an absence ⟨*covered* for me during my vacation⟩ **3 :** to overlay so as to protect or shelter ⟨*cover* the plants with mulch⟩ **4 a :** to spread or lie over or on ⟨water *covered* the floor⟩ ⟨snow *covering* the hills⟩ **b :** DOT 2 ⟨resort area *covered* with lakes⟩ **5 :** to put something protective or concealing over ⟨*cover* your head⟩ **6 :** to sit on and incubate (eggs) **7 :** to have sufficient scope to include or take into account ⟨an exam *covering* a semester's work⟩ **8 :** to have as one's territory or field of activity ⟨one salesperson *covers* the whole state⟩ **9 :** to pass over or through ⟨*covering* 500 kilometers a day⟩ **10 :** to accept an offered bet **11 :** to buy securities or commodities for delivery against (an earlier short sale) [Old French *covrir,* from Latin *cooperire,* from *co-* + *operire* "to close, cover"] — **cov•er•er** \-ər-ər\ *n*

[2]**cover** *n* **1 :** something that protects, shelters, or guards: as **a :** natural shelter for an animal or the factors that provide such shelter **b :** a position or situation affording protection from enemy fire **2 :** something that is placed over or about another thing: **a :** LID 1, TOP **b :** a binding or case for a book; *also* **:** the front or back of such a binding **c :** an overlay or outer layer especially for protection ⟨a mattress *cover*⟩ **d :** tableware laid out for one person **e :** ROOF **f :** a cloth (as a blanket or bedspread) used on a bed **g :** something (as vegetation or snow) that covers the ground **3 :** something that conceals or obscures ⟨under *cover* of darkness⟩ **4 :** an envelope or wrapper for mail

cov•er•age \'kəv-rij, -ə-rij\ *n* **1 :** the act or fact of covering or something that covers: as **a :** inclusion within the scope of protection (as of an insurance policy) **b :** inclusion within the scope of discussion or reporting ⟨*coverage* of a political convention⟩ **2 a :** the number or amount covered **:** SCOPE **b :** all the risks covered by the terms of an insurance contract ⟨a policy with an extensive *coverage*⟩

cov•er•all \'kəv-ər-ˌȯl\ *n* **:** a one-piece outer garment worn to protect one's clothes — usually used in pl.

cover charge *n* **:** a charge made by a restaurant or nightclub in addition to the charge for food and drink

cover crop *n* **:** a crop planted to prevent soil erosion and to provide humus

covered wagon *n* **:** a wagon with a canvas top supported by bows

cover glass *n* **:** a piece of very thin transparent material used to cover material mounted on a glass microscope slide

cov•er•ing \'kəv-ring, -ə-ring\ *n* **:** something that covers or conceals

cov•er•let \'kəv-ər-lət\ *n* **:** BEDSPREAD [Middle English, alteration of *coverlite,* from Old French *covrir* "to cover" + *lit* "bed"]

cov•er•slip \'kəv-ər-ˌslip\ *n* **:** COVER GLASS

[1]**co•vert** \'kō-ˌvərt, -vərt, kō-'; 'kəv-ərt\ *adj* **1 :** not openly shown, engaged in, or avowed ⟨a *covert* alliance⟩ **2 :** covered over **:** SHELTERED ⟨a *covert* nook⟩ [Old French, past participle of *covrir* "to cover"] **syn** see SECRET — **co•vert•ly** *adv* — **co•vert•ness** *n*

[2]**co•vert** \'kəv-ər, -ərt; 'kō-vərt\ *n* **1 a :** hiding place **:** SHELTER **b :** a thicket affording cover for game **2 :** a feather covering the bases of the quills of the wings and tail of a bird **3 :** a firm durable twilled sometimes waterproofed cloth

cov•et \'kəv-ət\ *vb* **:** to wish enviously especially for what belongs to another [Old French *coveitier,* from *coveitié* "desire", from Latin *cupiditas* "desire, cupidity"] — **cov•et•able** \-ə-bəl\ *adj* — **cov•et•er** \-ər\ *n* — **cov•et•ing•ly** \-ing-lē\ *adv*

cov•et•ous \'kəv-ət-əs\ *adj* **:** marked by a too eager desire for wealth or possessions or for another's possessions — **cov•et•ous•ly** *adv* — **cov•et•ous•ness** *n*

• **syn** AVARICIOUS, GREEDY, GRASPING: COVETOUS implies excessive desire especially for what belongs to another; AVARICIOUS implies a strong desire to gain and keep money; GREEDY stresses lack of restraint and often of discrimination in desire; GRASPING adds the implications of selfishness and ruthlessness.

cov•ey \'kəv-ē\ *n, pl* **coveys 1 :** a mature bird or pair of birds with a brood of young; *also* **:** a small flock **2 :** COMPANY 2a, GROUP [Middle French *covee,* from *cover* "to sit on, brood over", from Latin *cubare* "to lie"]

[1]**cow** \'kau̇\ *n* **1 :** the mature female of cattle or of any animal (as the moose) the male of which is called *bull* **2 :** a domestic bovine animal regardless of sex or age [Old English *cū*] — **cowy** \-ē\ *adj*

[2]**cow** *vt* **:** to subdue the spirits or courage of **:** INTIMIDATE ⟨*cowed* by threats⟩ [probably of Scandinavian origin]

cow·ard \ˈkau̇-ərd, ˈkau̇rd\ *n* : one who shows disgraceful fear or timidity [Old French *coart,* from *coe* "tail", from Latin *cauda*] — **coward** *adj*

△ **origin** A frightened animal may draw its tail between its hind legs, or it may simply turn its tail and run. In such an animal as the hare, the white flash of the fleeing tail is especially remarkable. But even a tailless animal like a human being can turn tail and flee when afraid. And unless an army is in retreat, it is in the tail of the army that you can expect to find the cowards. Whether it is the idea of an animal's tail or an army's that is responsible, it is certain that the Old French *coart,* from which we get our *coward,* is a derivative of *coe,* "tail".

cow·ard·ice \-əs\ *n* : lack of courage or resolution

[1]**cow·ard·ly** \-lē\ *adv* : in a cowardly manner

[2]**cowardly** *adj* **1** : disgracefully timid ⟨a *cowardly* rascal⟩ **2** : resembling or befitting a coward ⟨a *cowardly* retreat⟩ — **cow·ard·li·ness** *n*

cow·bane \ˈkau̇-ˌbān\ *n* : any of several poisonous plants (as a water hemlock) of the carrot family

cow·bell \-ˌbel\ *n* : a bell hung about the neck of a cow to indicate its whereabouts

cow·bird \-ˌbərd\ *n* : a small North American blackbird that lays its eggs in the nests of other birds

cow·boy \-ˌbȯi\ *n* **1** : one who tends or drives cattle; *esp* : a usually mounted cattle ranch hand **2** : a participant in rodeos

cow·catch·er \-ˌkach-ər, -ˌkech-\ *n* : an inclined frame on the front of a railroad locomotive for throwing obstacles off the track

cow·er \ˈkau̇-ər, ˈkau̇r\ *vi* : to shrink away or cringe (as from fear) ⟨*cowered* at the sight of a whip⟩ [Middle English *couren,* of Scandinavian origin]

cow·fish \ˈkau̇-ˌfish\ *n* : any of various small brightly colored fishes with projections resembling horns over the eyes

cow·girl \-ˌgərl\ *n* : a girl or woman who works as a cowboy

cow·hand \-ˌhand\ *n* : COWBOY

cow·herd \-ˌhərd\ *n* : one who tends cows

[1]**cow·hide** \-ˌhīd\ *n* **1** : the hide of a cow or leather made from it **2** : a coarse whip of rawhide or braided leather

[2]**cowhide** *vt* : to flog with a cowhide whip

cowl \ˈkau̇l\ *n* **1** : a hood or long hooded cloak especially of a monk **2 a** : a chimney covering for improving the draft **b** : the top portion of the front part of an automobile body forward of the two front doors to which are attached the windshield and instrument panel **c** : COWLING [Old English *cugele,* from Late Latin *cuculla* "monk's hood", from Latin *cucullus* "hood"] — **cowled** \ˈkau̇ld\ *adj*

C cowl 1

cow·lick \ˈkau̇-ˌlik\ *n* : a turned-up tuft of hair growing in a direction different from the rest of the hair [from its appearance of having been licked by a cow]

cowl·ing \ˈkau̇-ling\ *n* : a removable metal covering for the engine and sometimes a portion of the fuselage or nacelle of an airplane; *also* : a metallic cover for any engine

cow·man \ˈkau̇-mən, -ˌman\ *n* **1** : COWHERD, COWBOY **2** : a cattle owner or rancher

co–work·er \ˈkō-ˌwər-kər\ *n* : a fellow worker

cow·pea \ˈkau̇-ˌpē\ *n* : a sprawling herb related to the bean and grown in the southern United States especially for forage and green manure; *also* : its edible seed

Cow·per's gland \ˌkau̇-pərz-, ˌkü-pərz-, ˌku̇p-ərz-\ *n* : either of two small glands discharging into the male urethra [William *Cowper,* died 1709, English surgeon]

cow·poke \ˈkau̇-ˌpōk\ *n* : COWBOY [*cow* + *poke* "to punch"]

cow pony *n* : a light saddle horse trained for herding cattle

cow·pox \ˈkau̇-ˌpäks\ *n* : a mild rash-producing virus disease of the cow that when communicated to a human protects against smallpox

cow·punch·er \-ˌpən-chər\ *n* : COWBOY

cow·rie *or* **cow·ry** \ˈkau̇r-ē\ *n, pl* **cowries** : any of numerous small snails of warm seas with glossy often brightly colored shells; *also* : the shell of a cowrie [Hindi *kaurī*]

cow·slip \ˈkau̇-ˌslip\ *n* **1** : a common Old World primrose with fragrant yellow or purplish flowers **2** : MARSH MARIGOLD [Old English *cūslyppe,* literally, "cow dung"]

cox \ˈkäks\ *n* : COXSWAIN 2 — **cox** *vb*

coxa \ˈkäk-sə\ *n, pl* **cox·ae** \-ˌsē, -ˌsī\ : the segment of an arthropod limb nearest the body [Latin, "hip"] — **cox·al** \-səl\ *adj*

cox·comb \ˈkäk-ˌskōm\ *n* : a conceited foppish person [Middle English *cokkes comb,* literally, "cock's comb"] — **cox·comb·ical** \käk-ˈskō-mi-kəl, -ˈkäm-i-\ *adj*

cox·swain \ˈkäk-sən, -ˌswān\ *n* **1** : a sailor who has charge of a ship's boat and its crew **2** : one who steers a racing shell [Middle English *cokswayne,* from *cok* "small boat" + *swain* "servant"]

coy \ˈkȯi\ *adj* **1 a** : BASHFUL 1 **b** : pretending shy or demure reserve **2** : showing reluctance to make a definite commitment ⟨politicians *coy* about their plans⟩ [Middle French *coi* "quiet, calm", from Latin *quietus*] **syn** see SHY — **coy·ly** *adv* — **coy·ness** *n*

coy·ote \ˈkī-ˌōt, kī-ˈōt-ē\ *n, pl* **coyotes** *or* **coyote** : a small wolf native to western North America [Mexican Spanish, from Nahuatl *coyotl*]

coy·pu \ˈkȯi-ˌpü\ *n* **1** : a South American aquatic rodent with webbed feet, mammary glands on its back, and a fur of some commercial value **2** : NUTRIA 2 [American Spanish *coipú,* of American Indian origin]

coypu 1

coz·en \ˈkəz-n\ *vb* : to deceive by artful coaxing ⟨tried to *cozen* their opponent's supporters⟩ [obsolete Italian *cozzonare,* from Italian *cozzone* "horse trader", from Latin *cocio* "trader"] — **coz·en·age** \-n-ij\ *n* — **coz·en·er** *n*

[1]**co·zy** \ˈkō-zē\ *adj* **co·zi·er; -est 1** : enjoying or affording warmth and ease : SNUG **2** : marked by a cautious attitude ⟨a *cozy* waiting game⟩ [probably of Scandinavian origin] — **co·zi·ly** \-zə-lē\ *adv* — **co·zi·ness** \-zē-nəs\ *n*

[2]**cozy** *adv* : in a cautious manner ⟨play it *cozy*⟩

[3]**cozy** *n, pl* **cozies** : a padded covering for a vessel (as a teapot) to keep the contents hot

[1]**crab** \ˈkrab\ *n* **1** : a crustacean with a short broad usually flattened shell, a small abdomen curled forward beneath the body, and a front pair of limbs with strong pincers; *also* : any of various other crustaceans resembling true crabs in having a small abdomen **2** : any of various machines for raising or hauling heavy weights [Middle English *crabbe,* from Old English *crabba*]

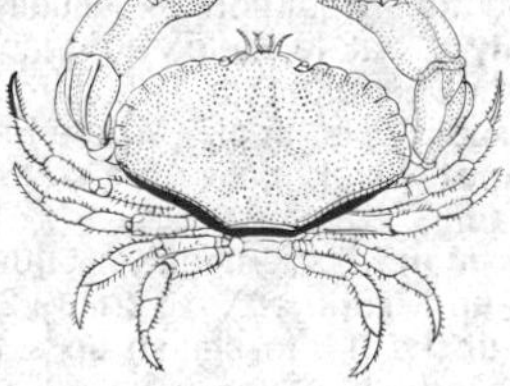
[1]crab 1

[2]**crab** *vi* **crabbed; crab·bing** : to fish for crabs — **crab·ber** *n*

[3]**crab** *vb* **crabbed; crab·bing** : to find fault : COMPLAIN

[4]**crab** *n* **1** : CRAB APPLE **2** : a disagreeable ill-tempered person [Middle English *crabbe,* perhaps from *crabbe* "[1]crab"]

crab apple *n* **1** : a small wild sour apple **2** : a cultivated apple with small usually brightly colored acid fruit

crab·bed \ˈkrab-əd\ *adj* **1** : CROSS 3 **2** : difficult to read or understand — **crab·bed·ly** *adv* — **crab·bed·ness** *n*

crab·by \ˈkrab-ē\ *adj* **crab·bi·er; -est** : ILL-NATURED ⟨a *crabby* disposition⟩

crab·grass \ˈkrab-ˌgras\ *n* : a weedy grass with creeping or sprawling stems that root freely at the nodes

crab louse *n* : a louse infesting the human pubic region

[1]**crack** \ˈkrak\ *vb* **1 a** : to break or cause to break with a sudden

sharp sound : SNAP **b** : to make or cause to make such a sound ⟨*crack* a whip⟩ **2** : to break with or without total separation of parts ⟨the ice *cracked* in several places⟩ **3** : to tell especially in a clever or witty way ⟨*crack* jokes⟩ **4 a** : to lose control **b** : to fail in tone ⟨their voices *cracked*⟩ **c** : to give or receive a sharp blow ⟨*crack* one's head⟩ **5 a** : to puzzle out and solve or discover the secret of ⟨*crack* a code⟩ **b** : to break into ⟨*crack* a safe⟩ **c** : to break through (as a barrier) **6 a** : to subject (hydrocarbons) to cracking ⟨*crack* petroleum⟩ **b** : to produce by cracking ⟨*cracked* gasoline⟩ [Old English *cracian*]

[2]**crack** *n* **1** : a sudden sharp noise **2** : a sharp witty remark : QUIP **3 a** : a narrow break **b** : a narrow opening ⟨open the window a *crack*⟩ **4 a** : a weakness or flaw caused by decay, age, or shortcoming **b** : a broken tone of the voice **5** : MOMENT ⟨the *crack* of dawn⟩ **6** : a sharp resounding blow **7** : TRY ⟨take a *crack* at it⟩

[3]**crack** *adj* : of superior quality ⟨*crack* troops⟩

crack•brain \'krak-,brān\ *n* : an erratic or unbalanced person — **crack•brained** \-'brānd\ *adj*

crack•down \'krak-,daůn\ *n* : an act or instance of cracking down ⟨a *crackdown* on gambling⟩

crack down \'krak-'daůn\ *vi* : to take positive disciplinary action

cracked \'krakt\ *adj* **1** : broken into coarse pieces ⟨*cracked* wheat⟩ **2** : mentally disturbed

crack•er \'krak-ər\ *n* **1** : something (as a firecracker) that makes a cracking noise **2** : a dry thin crisp bakery product made of flour and water **3** : the equipment in which cracking is carried out

crack•er•jack \'krak-ər-,jak\ *n* : something very excellent — **crackerjack** *adj*

Cracker Jack *trademark* — used for a candied popcorn confection

crack•ing *n* : a process in which relatively heavy hydrocarbons (as oils from petroleum) are broken up by heat into lighter products (as gasoline)

[1]**crack•le** \'krak-əl\ *vi* **crack•led**; **crack•ling** \'krak-ling, -ə-ling\ **1 a** : to make small sharp sudden repeated noises **b** : to show spirit : SPARKLE **2** : to develop a surface network of fine cracks [derived from [1]*crack*]

[2]**crackle** *n* **1** : the noise of repeated small cracks **2** : a network of fine cracks on an otherwise smooth surface

crack•ling *n* **1** \'krak-ling, -ə-ling\ : a series of small sharp crackling sounds **2** \'krak-lən, -ling\ : the crisp remainder left after the fat has been separated from the fibrous tissue (as in frying the skin of pork) — usually used in pl.

crack•ly \'krak-lē, -ə-lē\ *adj* : inclined to crackle : CRISP

crack•nel \'krak-nl\ *n* **1** : a hard brittle biscuit **2** : CRACKLING 2 — usually used in pl. [Middle English *krakenelle*]

crack•pot \'krak-,pät\ *n* : a crazy or peculiar person — **crackpot** *adj*

cracks•man \'krak-smən\ *n* : BURGLAR; *also* : SAFECRACKER

crack–up \'krak-,əp\ *n* : CRASH 2, WRECK

crack up *vb* **1** : to smash up a vehicle (as by losing control) ⟨*cracked up* on a curve⟩ **2** : to assert the excellence of : PRAISE ⟨it's not all it's *cracked up* to be⟩

-c•ra•cy \k-rə-sē\ *n combining form* **1** : form of government; *also* : state having such a government **2** : social or political class (as of powerful persons) [Middle French *-cratie*, from Greek *-kratia*, from *kratos* "strength, power"]

[1]**cra•dle** \'krād-l\ *n* **1** : a bed for a baby usually on rockers **2** : place of origin **3** : something serving as a framework or support: as **a** : the support for a telephone receiver or handset **b** : an implement with rods like fingers attached to a scythe and used formerly for harvesting grain **c** : a low frame on casters on which mechanics lie while working under an automobile **4** : a rocking device used in panning for gold [Old English *cradol*]

[2]**cradle** *vt* **cra•dled**; **cra•dling** \'krād-ling, -l-ing\ **1 a** : to place or keep in or as if in a cradle **b** : to shelter in childhood : REAR **c** : to protect and cherish lovingly **2** : to cut (grain) with a cradle scythe **3** : to place, raise, support, or transport on a cradle **4** : to wash in a miner's cradle

cra•dle•land \'krād-l-,land, -,and\ *n* : region of origin : BIRTHPLACE

cra•dle•song \'krād-l-,sȯng\ *n* : LULLABY

craft \'kraft\ *n* **1** : skill in planning, making, or executing **2** : an occupation or trade requiring artistic skill or ease in using the hands **3** : skill in deceiving to gain an end **4** : the members of a trade or trade association **5** *pl usually* **craft a** : a boat especially of small size **b** : AIRCRAFT [Old English *cræft* "strength, skill"] **syn** see ART

crafts•man \'kraf-smən, 'kraft-\ *n* **1** : a worker who practices a trade or handicraft **2** : a highly skilled worker in any field — **crafts•man•ship** \-,ship\ *n*

craft union *n* : a labor union with membership limited to workers of the same craft — compare INDUSTRIAL UNION

crafty \'kraf-tē\ *adj* **craft•i•er**; **-est** : skillful at deceiving others : CUNNING **syn** see SLY — **craft•i•ly** \-tə-lē\ *adv* — **craft•i•ness** \-tē-nəs\ *n*

crag \'krag\ *n* : a steep rugged rock or cliff [Middle English, of Celtic origin] — **crag•gy** \-ē\ *adj*

crake \'krāk\ *n* : any of various rails; *esp* : one with a short bill [Middle English, probably from Old Norse *krāka* "crow" or *krākr* "raven"]

cram \'kram\ *vb* **crammed**; **cram•ming** **1** : to stuff or crowd in ⟨*cram* clothes into a bag⟩ **2** : to fill full ⟨barns *crammed* with hay⟩ **3** : to study hastily in preparation for an examination **4** : to eat greedily : STUFF [Old English *crammian*] — **cram•mer** *n*

[1]**cramp** \'kramp\ *n* **1** : a sudden painful involuntary contraction of muscle **2** : a temporary paralysis of muscles from overuse — compare WRITER'S CRAMP **3** : sharp abdominal pain — usually used in pl. [Middle French *crampe*, of Germanic origin]

[2]**cramp** *n* **1** : a usually iron device bent at the ends and used to hold timbers or blocks of stone together **2** : [1]CLAMP [Low German or obsolete Dutch *krampe* "hook"] — **cramp** *adj*

[3]**cramp** *vt* **1** : to affect with or as if with cramp **2 a** : CONFINE ⟨felt *cramped* in the tiny room⟩ **b** : HAMPER — used in the phrase *cramp one's style* **3** : to turn (the front wheels of a vehicle) to right or left **4** : to fasten or hold with a cramp

cram•pon \'kram-,pän\ *n* **1** : a hooked clutch or dog for raising heavy objects — usually used in pl. **2** : a framework that fits the bottom of a climbing boot and has spikes which grip on slopes of hard ice or snow [Middle French *crampon*, of Germanic origin]

cran•ber•ry \'kran-,ber-ē, -bə-rē, -brē\ *n* : the bright red sour berry of any of several trailing plants related to the blueberry; *also* : a plant producing these [Low German *kraanbere*, from *kraan* "crane" + *bere* "berry"]

cranberry bush *n* : a viburnum that has leaves with three lobes and bears red fruit

[1]**crane** \'krān\ *n* **1** : any of a family of tall wading birds related to the rails **2** : any of several herons **3 a** : a machine for raising, shifting, and lowering heavy weights by means of a projecting swinging arm or with the hoisting apparatus supported on an overhead track **b** : an iron arm in a fireplace for supporting kettles **c** : a long movable support for a motion-picture or television camera [Old English *cran*]

[2]**crane** *vb* **1** : to raise or lift by a crane **2** : to stretch one's neck forward to see better

crane fly *n* : any of numerous long-legged slender two-winged flies that resemble large mosquitoes but do not bite

cranes•bill \'krānz-,bil\ *n* : GERANIUM 1

cra•ni•al \'krā-nē-əl\ *adj* **1** : of or relating to the cranium **2** : CEPHALIC — **cra•ni•al•ly** \-ə-lē\ *adv*

cranial nerve *n* : any of the paired nerves that arise from the lower surface of the brain and pass through openings in the skull

cra•ni•um \'krā-nē-əm\ *n, pl* **-ni•ums** *or* **-nia** \-nē-ə\ : SKULL; *esp* : the part that encloses the brain [Medieval Latin, from Greek *kranion*]

[1]**crank** \'krangk\ *n* **1** : a bent part of an axle or shaft or an arm at right angles to the end of a shaft by which circular motion is imparted to or received from the axle or shaft **2 a** : WHIM **b** : an eccentric person **c** : a bad-tempered person : GROUCH [Old English *cranc-* (as in *crancstæf*, a weaving instrument)]

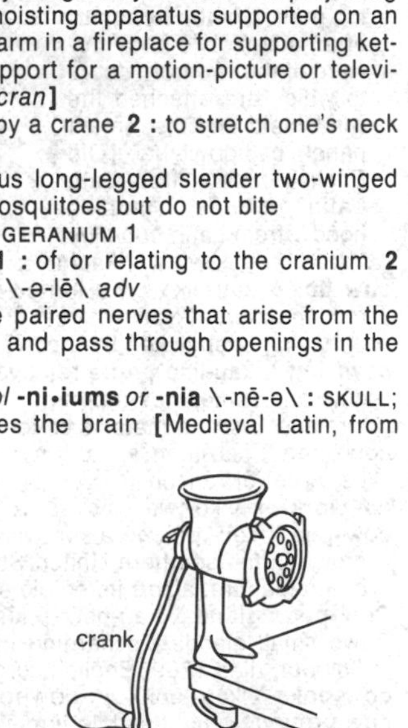

[1]crank 1

[2]**crank** *vb* **1** : to move with a winding course : ZIGZAG **2** : to bend into the shape of a crank **3** : to start or operate by turning a crank

crank•case \'krangk-,kās\ *n* : the housing of a crankshaft

crank•pin \-,pin\ *n* : the cylindrical piece which forms the handle of a crank or to which the connecting rod is attached

crank•shaft \-ˌshaft\ *n* : a shaft turning or driven by a crank

cranky \ˈkrang-kē\ *adj* **crank•i•er**; **-est** **1** : not in good working order ⟨a *cranky* old tractor⟩ **2** : IRRITABLE — **crank•i•ness** *n*

cran•ny \ˈkran-ē\ *n, pl* **crannies** : a small break or slit [Middle French *cren, cran* "notch"]

crape \ˈkrāp\ *n* **1** : CREPE 1 **2** : a band of crepe worn on a hat or sleeve as a sign of mourning [alteration of French *crêpe*]

crape myrtle *n* : an East Indian shrub of the loosestrife family widely grown in warm regions for its showy flowers

crap•pie \ˈkräp-ē\ *n* **1** : BLACK CRAPPIE **2** : WHITE CRAPPIE [Canadian French *crapet*]

craps \ˈkraps\ *n pl* : a gambling game played with two dice [French, from English *crabs* "lowest throw at hazard", from 1crab]

crap•shoot•er \ˈkrap-ˌshüt-ər\ *n* : a person who plays craps — **crap•shoot•ing** \-ˌshüt-ing\ *n*

1crash \ˈkrash\ *vb* **1 a** : to break violently and noisily : SMASH **b** : to damage an airplane in landing **2 a** : to make or cause to make a loud noise **b** : to force through with loud crashing noises **3** : to enter or attend without invitation or without paying ⟨*crash* a party⟩ **4** : to decline or fail suddenly [Middle English *crasschen*] — **crash•er** *n*

2crash *n* **1** : a loud sound (as of things smashing) **2** : a breaking to pieces by or as if by collision; *also* : an instance of crashing **3** : a sudden decline or failure (as of a business or prices) ⟨stock-market *crash*⟩

3crash *adj* : effected hastily on an emergency basis with all available means ⟨a *crash* program⟩

4crash *n* : a coarse fabric used for draperies, toweling, and clothing [probably from Russian *krashenina* "colored linen"]

crash dive *n* : a dive made by a submarine in the least possible time — **crash–dive** \ˈkrash-ˈdīv\ *vi*

crash helmet *n* : a padded helmet that is worn (as by motorcyclists) as protection against head injury

crash–land \ˈkrash-ˈland\ *vb* : to land an aircraft under emergency conditions usually with damage to the craft — **crash landing** *n*

crass \ˈkras\ *adj* : GROSS, INSENSITIVE ⟨*crass* ignorance⟩ [Latin *crassus* "thick, gross"] — **crass•ly** *adv* — **crass•ness** *n*

-crat \ˌkrat\ *n combining form* **1** : advocate or partisan of a (specified) form of government **2** : member of a (specified) dominant class [French *-crate,* back-formation from *-cratie* "-cracy"]

1crate \ˈkrāt\ *n* **1** : a box usually ventilated and made of thin wooden slats for packing fruit or vegetables **2** : an enclosing framework for protecting something (as in shipment) [Latin *cratis* "wickerwork, hurdle"]

2crate *vt* : to pack in a crate

cra•ter \ˈkrāt-ər\ *n* : a bowl-shaped depression: as **a** : one around the opening of a volcano **b** : one formed by the impact of a meteorite **c** : a hole in the ground made by the explosion of a bomb or shell [Latin, "mixing bowl, crater", from Greek *kratēr,* from *kerannynai* "to mix"]

cra•vat \krə-ˈvat\ *n* : NECKTIE [French *cravate,* from *Cravate* "Croatian"]

crave \ˈkrāv\ *vb* **1** : to ask for earnestly : BEG **2** : to have a strong desire or need for [Old English *crafian*]

1cra•ven \ˈkrā-vən\ *adj* : COWARDLY [Middle English *cravant*] — **cra•ven•ly** *adv* — **cra•ven•ness** \-vən-nəs\ *n*

2craven *n* : COWARD

crav•ing \ˈkrā-ving\ *n* : a great desire or longing; *esp* : an abnormal desire (as for a habit-forming drug)

craw \ˈkrȯ\ *n* **1** : the crop of a bird or insect **2** : the stomach especially of a lower animal [Middle English *crawe*]

craw•fish \ˈkrȯ-ˌfish\ *n* **1** : CRAYFISH 1 **2** : SPINY LOBSTER [by folk etymology from Middle English *crevis*]

1crawl \ˈkrȯl\ *vb* **1** : to move slowly with the body close to the ground : CREEP **2** : to drag along slowly or feebly **3** : to advance by cunning or servility **4** : to be swarming with or have the sensation of swarming with creeping things [Old Norse *krafla*] **syn** see CREEP — **crawl•er** *n*

2crawl *n* **1** : the act or motion of crawling **2** : a racing stroke in which a swimmer lying flat in the water moves forward by overarm strokes and a flutter kick

3crawl *n* : an enclosure in shallow waters (as for confining lobsters) [Afrikaans *kraal* "pen"]

crawly \ˈkrȯ-lē\ *adj* : having the sensation of being swarmed with crawling things

cray•fish \ˈkrā-ˌfish\ *n* **1** : any of numerous freshwater crustaceans resembling but usually much smaller than the lobster **2** : SPINY LOBSTER [by folk etymology from Middle English *crevis,* from Middle French *crevice,* of Germanic origin]

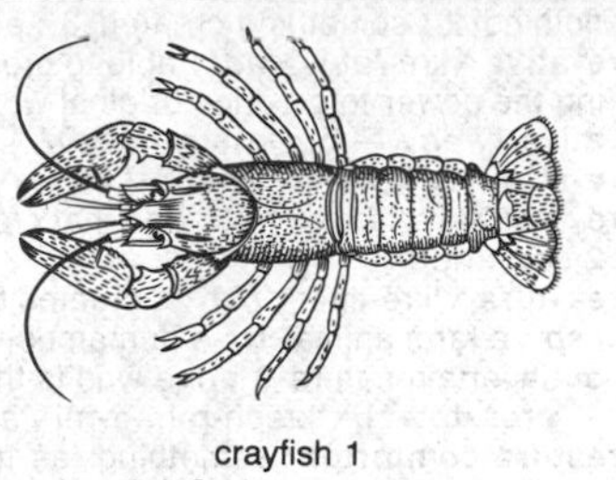

crayfish 1

1cray•on \ˈkrā-ˌän, -ən; ˈkran\ *n* **1** : a stick of white or colored chalk or of colored wax used for writing or drawing **2** : a crayon drawing [French, "crayon, pencil", from *craie* "chalk", from Latin *creta*]

2crayon *vt* : to draw or color with a crayon — **cray•on•ist** \ˈkrā-ə-nəst\ *n*

1craze \ˈkrāz\ *vb* **1** : to make or become insane **2** : to develop a network of fine cracks [Middle English *crasen* "to crush, craze", of Scandinavian origin]

2craze \ˈkrāz\ *n* **1** : a strong but temporary interest in something or the object of such an interest : FAD ⟨the latest *craze* among high school students⟩ **2** : a fine crack in glaze or enamel or on a painted surface

cra•zy \ˈkrā-zē\ *adj* **cra•zi•er**; **-est** **1 a** : full of cracks or flaws : UNSOUND **b** : CROOKED 1 **2 a** : mentally disordered : INSANE **b** (1) : wildly impractical (2) : ERRATIC **3** : distracted with desire or excitement **syn** see INSANE — **cra•zi•ly** \-zə-lē\ *adv* — **cra•zi•ness** \-zē-nəs\ *n*

crazy bone *n* : FUNNY BONE 1

crazy quilt *n* : a patchwork quilt without a design

1creak \ˈkrēk\ *vi* : to make a prolonged grating or squeaking sound [Middle English *creken* "to croak"]

2creak *n* : a rasping or grating noise — **creak•i•ly** \ˈkrē-kə-lē\ *adv* — **creaky** \ˈkrē-kē\ *adj*

1cream \ˈkrēm\ *n* **1** : the yellowish part of milk containing butterfat **2 a** : a food prepared with cream **b** : something (as a food, or a medicinal or cosmetic preparation) having the consistency of cream **3** : the choicest part ⟨the *cream* of the crop⟩ **4** : a pale yellow [Middle French *craime,* from Late Latin *cramum,* of Celtic origin] — **creamy** \ˈkrē-mē\ *adj*

2cream *vb* **1** : to form cream **2 a** : SKIM 1b **b** : to take the choicest part of something **3** : to furnish, prepare, or treat with cream **4 a** : to beat into a creamy froth **b** : to work or blend to the consistency of cream

cream cheese *n* : an unripened soft white cheese made from whole milk enriched with cream

cream•er \ˈkrē-mər\ *n* **1** : a device for separating cream from milk **2** : a small pitcher or jug for serving cream

cream•ery \ˈkrēm-rē, -ə-rē\ *n, pl* **-er•ies** : an establishment where butter and cheese are made or where milk and cream are sold or prepared

cream of tartar : a white crystalline salt $C_4H_5KO_6$ used especially in baking powder and in galvanic tinning of metals

cream puff *n* : a round shell of light pastry filled with whipped cream or a cream filling

cream sauce *n* : WHITE SAUCE

1crease \ˈkrēs\ *n* **1** : a line or mark made by or as if by folding **2** : a specially marked area around a goal (as in hockey) [probably from Middle English *creste* "crest"]

2crease *vb* **1** : to make a crease in or on **2** : to wound slightly especially by grazing **3** : to become creased — **creas•er** *n*

cre•ate \krē-ˈāt, ˈkrē-ˌ\ *vt* **1** : to bring into existence **2** : to install in a new office or rank ⟨was *created* a lieutenant⟩ **3 a** : to bring about : CAUSE, MAKE, PRODUCE ⟨*create* a disturbance⟩ **b** : DESIGN ⟨*creates* evening dresses⟩ [Latin *creare*]

cre•atine \ˈkrē-ə-ˌtēn, -ət-n\ *n* : a white crystalline nitrogenous substance $C_4H_9N_3O_2$ found especially in the muscles of vertebrates [Greek *kreat-, kreas* "flesh"]

cre•ation \krē-ˈā-shən\ *n* **1** : the act of creating or fact of being created; *esp* : the bringing of the world into existence out of nothing **2 :** something created **3 :** all created things **:** WORLD

cre•ative \krē-'āt-iv\ *adj* **:** able to create; *esp* **:** having or showing the power to produce original work (as in literature) — **cre•ative•ly** *adv* — **cre•ative•ness** *n*

cre•ativ•i•ty \,krē-ā-'tiv-ət-ē, ,krē-ə-\ *n* **:** ability to create

cre•ator \krē-'āt-ər\ *n* **1 :** one that creates or produces **:** MAKER **2** *cap* **:** GOD 1

crea•ture \'krē-chər\ *n* **1 :** a created being **2 a :** a lower animal; *esp* **:** a farm animal **b :** a human being **c :** a being of abnormal or uncertain nature **3 :** one who is the obedient tool of another — **crea•tur•al** \'krēch-rəl, -ə-rəl\ *adj*

creature comfort *n* **:** something (as food or warmth) that gives bodily comfort

crèche \'kresh\ *n* **1 :** a day nursery or foundling home **2 :** a representation of the Nativity scene in the stable at Bethlehem [French, from Old French *creche* "manger, crib", of Germanic origin]

cre•dence \'krēd-ns\ *n* **1 :** mental acceptance as true or real **:** BELIEF ⟨give *credence* to gossip⟩ **2 :** a small table where the bread and wine rest before consecration [Medieval Latin *credentia,* from Latin *credere* "to believe, trust"]

cre•den•tial \kri-'den-chəl\ *n* **1 :** something that gives a title to credit or confidence **2** *pl* **:** documents showing that a person is entitled to confidence or has a right to exercise official power

cre•den•za \kri-'den-zə\ *n* **:** a sideboard, buffet, or bookcase; *esp* **:** one without legs [Italian, literally, "belief, confidence", from Medieval Latin *credentia*]

cred•i•ble \'kred-ə-bəl\ *adj* **:** capable of being believed **:** deserving to be believed ⟨a *credible* story⟩ [Latin *credibilis,* from *credere* "to believe"] **syn** see PLAUSIBLE — **cred•i•bil•i•ty** \,kred-ə-'bil-ət-ē\ *n* — **cred•i•bly** \'kred-ə-blē\ *adv*

[1]cred•it \'kred-ət\ *n* **1 a :** a favorable balance in a bank account **b :** an entry in an account representing an addition of income or net worth ⟨debits and *credits*⟩ **c :** a sum of money placed at one's disposal by a bank **d** (1) **:** the right or privilege of taking present possession of money, goods, or services in exchange for a promise to pay for them at a future date ⟨long-term *credit*⟩ (2) **:** faith in the willingness of one to whom credit is extended to perform his or her promise ⟨buy on *credit*⟩ (3) **:** reputation for fulfilling financial obligations ⟨keep your *credit* good⟩ **2 a :** reliance on the truth or reality of something ⟨a story that deserves little *credit*⟩ **b :** reputation for honesty or integrity **:** good name **3 :** something that adds to a person's reputation or honor ⟨give a person *credit* for a discovery⟩ **4 :** a source of honor ⟨a *credit* to the school⟩ **5 a :** official certification of the completion of a course of study **b :** a unit of academic work for which such acknowledgment is made [Middle French, derived from Latin *creditum* "something entrusted to another, loan", from *credere* "to believe, trust"]

[2]credit *vt* **1 :** to trust in the truth of **:** BELIEVE **2 :** to enter upon the credit side of an account **3 a :** to give credit to **b :** to attribute to some person **syn** see ASCRIBE

cred•it•able \'kred-ət-ə-bəl\ *adj* **1 :** worthy of belief **2 :** worthy of praise — **cred•it•abil•i•ty** \,kred-ət-ə-'bil-ət-ē\ *n* — **cred•it•ably** \'kred-ət-ə-blē\ *adv*

credit card *n* **:** a card authorizing purchases on credit

cred•i•tor \'kred-ət-ər\ *n* **:** a person to whom a debt is owed; *esp* **:** a person to whom money or goods are due

cre•do \'krēd-ō, 'krād-\ *n, pl* **credos :** CREED [Latin, "I believe"]

cre•du•li•ty \kri-'dü-lət-ē, -'dyü-\ *n* **:** a willingness to believe especially on little or no evidence

cred•u•lous \'krej-ə-ləs\ *adj* **:** ready to believe especially on slight or uncertain evidence [Latin *credulus,* from *credere* "to believe"] — **cred•u•lous•ly** *adv* — **cred•u•lous•ness** *n*

Cree \'krē\ *n, pl* **Cree** *or* **Crees :** a member of an Algonquian people of what is now Manitoba and Saskatchewan [Canadian French *Christino,* probably from Ojibwa *Kenistenoag*]

creed \'krēd\ *n* **1 :** a statement of the essential beliefs of a religious faith **2 :** a set of guiding principles or beliefs [Old English *crēda,* from Latin *credo* "I believe" (first word of the Apostles' and Nicene creeds), from *credere* "to believe"] — **creed•al** *or* **cre•dal** \'krēd-l\ *adj*

creek \'krēk, 'krik\ *n* **1** *chiefly British* **:** a small narrow inlet extending farther inland than a cove **2 :** a natural stream of water usually smaller than a river [Middle English *crike, creke,* from Old Norse *-kriki* "bend"]

Creek \'krēk\ *n* **:** a member of a confederacy of Indian peoples formerly occupying most of what is now Alabama and Georgia and parts of Florida

creel \'krēl\ *n* **:** a wickerwork container (as for fish) [Middle English *creille, crele*]

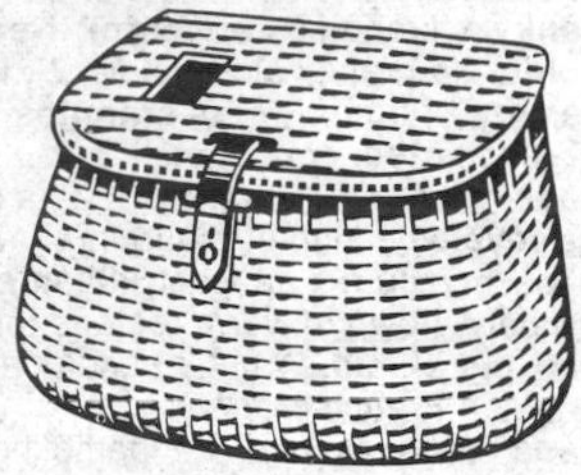

creel

[1]creep \'krēp\ *vi* **crept** \'krept\; **creep•ing 1 :** to move along with the body prone and close to the ground; *also* **:** to move slowly on hands and knees **2 :** to go slowly ⟨the hours *crept* by⟩ **3 a :** to move or stir slightly by swelling or shrinking ⟨the scream made my skin *creep*⟩ **b :** to spread or grow over a surface usually rooting at intervals ⟨*creeping* vines⟩ **4 :** to slip or gradually shift position ⟨soil *creeping* down a slope⟩ [Old English *crēopan*]

• **syn** CREEP, CRAWL mean to move slowly in a prone or crouching posture. CREEP often suggests the furtive, noiseless movement of one capable of rapid movement ⟨the cat *crept* closer to the bird⟩ CRAWL suggests the laborious progress of legless insects or reptiles or of maimed animals. CREEP connotes stealth or insinuation ⟨*crept* into favor⟩ CRAWL often connotes abjectness or submission.

[2]creep *n* **1 :** a creeping movement **2 a :** a distressing sensation like that of insects creeping over one's flesh **b :** a feeling of horror — usually used in pl. **3 :** an enclosure that young animals (as calves) can enter while adults are excluded

creep•er \'krē-pər\ *n* **1 :** one that creeps: as **a :** a creeping plant **b :** a bird that creeps about on trees or bushes searching for insects **2 :** a device with iron points worn on a shoe to prevent slipping

creepy \'krē-pē\ *adj* **creep•i•er; -est :** feeling or producing nervous shivery apprehension ⟨a *creepy* horror story⟩ — **creep•i•ness** *n*

cre•mate \'krē-,māt, kri-'\ *vt* **:** to reduce (a corpse) to ashes by burning [Latin *cremare*] — **cre•ma•tion** \kri-'mā-shən\ *n*

cre•ma•to•ri•um \,krē-mə-'tōr-ē-əm, ,krem-ə-, -'tȯr-\ *n, pl* **-ri•ums** *or* **-ria** \-ē-ə\ **:** CREMATORY

cre•ma•to•ry \'krē-mə-,tōr-ē, 'krem-ə-, -,tȯr-\ *n, pl* **-ries :** a furnace for cremating; *also* **:** a structure containing such a furnace — **crematory** *adj*

crème de ca•cao \,krēm-də-'kō-kō, ,krem-də-kə-'kau̇, -kə-'kā-ō\ *n* **:** a sweet liqueur flavored with cacao beans and vanilla [French, literally, "cream of cacao"]

crème de menthe \,krem-də-'menth, ,krēm-, -'mint\ *n* **:** a sweet mint-flavored liqueur [French, literally, "cream of mint"]

cre•nate \'krē-,nāt, 'kren-,āt\ *or* **cre•nat•ed** \-əd\ *adj* **:** having the margin (as of a leaf or a shrunken red blood cell) cut into rounded scallops [Medieval Latin *crena* "notch"] — **cre•na•tion** \kri-'nā-shən\ *n*

cren•el•late *or* **cren•el•ate** \'kren-l-,āt\ *vt* **:** to furnish with battlements [Middle French *crenel* "embrasure in a battlement", from Old French *cren* "notch"] — **cren•el•la•tion** \,kren-l-'ā-shən\ *n*

cre•o•dont \'krē-ə-,dänt\ *n* **:** any of a group (Creodonta) of extinct primitive carnivorous mammals that form a link between modern carnivores and the ungulates [Greek *kreas* "flesh" + *odont-, odous* "tooth"] — **creodont** *adj*

Cre•ole \'krē-,ōl\ *n* **1 :** a white person descended from early French or Spanish settlers in the United States Gulf states or in Latin America and preserving their speech and culture **2 :** a person of mixed French or Spanish and Black descent speaking a dialect of French or Spanish [French *créole,* from Spanish *criollo,* from Portuguese *crioulo* "white person born in the colonies"] — **Creole** *adj*

cre•o•sol \'krē-ə-,sȯl, -,sōl\ *n* **:** a colorless liquid $C_8H_{10}O_2$ obtained from the tar made from beech and a resin

cre•o•sote \'krē-ə-,sōt\ *n* **1 :** a clear or yellowish oily liquid mixture of compounds obtained by the distillation of wood tar especially from beechwood **2 :** a brownish oily liquid obtained by distillation of coal tar and used especially as a wood preservative [German *kreosot,* from Greek *kreas* "flesh" + *sōtēr* "preserver", from *sōzein* "to preserve", from *sōs* "safe"]

cresosote bush *n* **:** a desert shrub of the southwestern United States and adjacent Mexico with aromatic foliage and small bright yellow flowers

crepe *or* **crêpe** \ˈkrāp\ *n* **1 :** a thin crinkled fabric (as of silk, wool, or cotton) **2 :** a small very thin pancake [French *crêpe,* from Middle French *crespe* "curly", from Latin *crispus*] — **crepe** *adj*

crepe de chine \ˌkrāp-də-ˈshēn\ *n, often cap 2d C* **:** a soft fine clothing crepe [French *crêpe de Chine,* literally, "crepe of China"]

crepe paper *n* **:** paper with a crinkled or puckered texture

crepe rubber *n* **:** crude rubber in the form of nearly white to brown crinkled sheets used especially for shoe soles

crepe su•zette \ˌkrāp-sü-ˈzet\ *n, pl* **crepes suzette** \ˌkrāp-sü-, ˌkrāps-\ *or* **crepe suzettes** \ˌkrāp-sü-ˈzets\ **:** a thin folded or rolled pancake in a hot orange-butter sauce that is sprinkled with a liqueur and set ablaze for serving [French *crêpe Suzette,* from *crêpe* "pancake" + *Suzette* "Susy"]

crept *past of* CREEP

cre•pus•cu•lar \kri-ˈpəs-kyə-lər\ *adj* **1 :** of, relating to, or resembling twilight **:** DIM **2 :** active in the twilight ⟨*crepuscular* insects⟩ [Latin *crepusculum* "twilight"]

cre•scen•do \kri-ˈshen-dō\ *n, pl* **-dos** *or* **-does 1 :** a gradual increase in volume of sound in music; *also* **:** a passage so performed **2 :** a gradual increase (as in physical or emotional force); *also* **:** the peak of such an increase [Italian, from *crescendo* "increasing", from *crescere* "to increase", from Latin] — **crescendo** *adv or adj*

cres•cent \ˈkres-nt\ *n* **1 a :** the moon at any stage between new moon and first quarter and between last quarter and the succeeding new moon **b :** the figure of the moon defined by a convex and a concave edge **2 :** an object shaped like a crescent [Middle French *creissant,* from *creistre* "to grow, increase", from Latin *crescere*] — **cres•cen•tic** \kre-ˈsent-ik\ *adj*

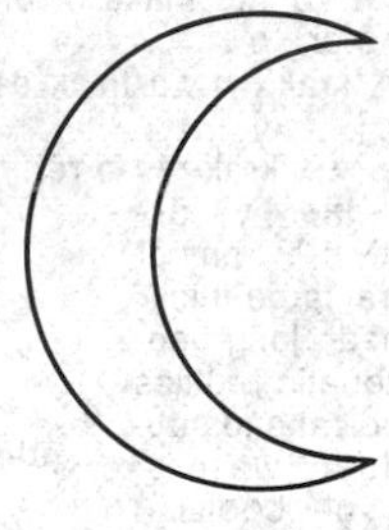

crescent 1b

cre•sol \ˈkrē-ˌsȯl, -ˌsōl\ *n* **:** any of three isomeric poisonous colorless crystalline or liquid organic substances C_7H_8O obtained from coal tar and used as disinfectants or in making resins [derived from *creosote*]

cress \ˈkres\ *n* **:** any of numerous plants of the mustard family with leaves used in salads [Old English *cressa*]

[1]crest \ˈkrest\ *n* **1 a :** a showy tuft or process on the head of an animal (as a bird) **b :** a plume worn on a knight's helmet **c :** a heraldic design above the escutcheon in a coat of arms **2 :** an upper part, edge, or limit ⟨the *crest* of a hill⟩ **3 :** a high point of an action or process **:** CLIMAX, CULMINATION ⟨at the *crest* of their fame⟩ [Middle French *creste,* from Latin *crista*] — **crestless** *adj*

[2]crest *vb* **1 :** to furnish with a crest **:** CROWN **2 :** to reach the crest of ⟨*crest* the hill⟩ **3 :** to rise to a crest ⟨the river *crested* at eight feet⟩

crest•ed \ˈkres-təd\ *adj* **:** having a crest ⟨a *crested* bird⟩

crest•fall•en \ˈkrest-ˌfȯ-lən, ˈkres-\ *adj* **:** feeling shame or humiliation **:** DEJECTED — **crest•fall•en•ness** *n*

Cre•ta•ceous \kri-ˈtā-shəs\ *n* **:** the 3d and latest period of the Mesozoic era during which chalk and most of the coal of the United States west of the Great Plains were formed; *also* **:** the corresponding system of rocks — see GEOLOGIC TIME table [Latin *cretaceus* "chalky", from *creta* "chalk"] — **Cretaceous** *adj*

cre•tin \ˈkrēt-n\ *n* **:** one affected with cretinism; *also* **:** one having a marked mental deficiency [French *crétin,* from French dialect *cretin* "Christian, human being, kind of idiot found in the Alps", from Latin *christianus* "Christian"] — **cre•tin•ous** \-əs\ *adj*

△ **origin** Most mountainous regions cannot provide an iodine-rich diet. Iodine deficiency in a mother may result in the birth of mentally and physically retarded children, who become dwarfish idiots when fully grown. Such dwarfs were once common in certain Alpine valleys of French Switzerland. They were called *cretins* in the local dialect. A *cretin* was originally simply a "Christian". The term came to be used, as well, to differentiate human beings from other animals, since the possession of a Christian soul was considered to be what gave humans dominion over the rest of creation. The specific use of *cretin* for these unfortunate idiots emphasized their humanity.

cre•tin•ism \-ˌiz-əm\ *n* **:** a usually congenital abnormal condition marked by physical and mental stunting and caused by deficient functioning of the thyroid gland

cre•tonne \ˈkrē-ˌtän, kri-ˈ\ *n* **:** a strong unglazed cotton or linen cloth used especially for curtains and upholstery [French, from *Creton,* Normandy]

cre•vasse \kri-ˈvas\ *n* **1 :** a deep crevice or fissure (as in a glacier) **2 :** a breach in a levee [French, from Middle French *crevace*]

crev•ice \ˈkrev-əs\ *n* **:** a narrow opening that results from a split or crack **:** FISSURE, CLEFT ⟨a *crevice* in a rock⟩ [Middle French *crevace,* from *crever* "to split", from Latin *crepare* "to crack"]

[1]crew \ˈkrü\ *chiefly British past of* CROW

[2]crew \ˈkrü\ *n* **1 :** a group of persons ⟨a happy *crew* on a picnic⟩ **2 :** a group of people associated in joint work ⟨a train *crew*⟩ **3 :** the group of persons who operate a ship **4 a :** the rowers and coxswain of a racing shell ⟨rowed on the college *crew*⟩ **b :** the sport of rowing **5 :** the persons who operate an aircraft in flight [Middle English *crue,* literally, "reinforcement", from Middle French *creue* "increase", from *creistre* "to increase", from Latin *crescere*]

crew cut *n* **:** a very short haircut in which the hair resembles the bristles of a brush

crew•el \ˈkrü-əl\ *n* **:** loosely twisted worsted yarn used for embroidery [Middle English *crule*]

[1]crib \ˈkrib\ *n* **1 :** a manger for feeding animals **2 :** a small child's bedstead with high enclosing usually slatted sides **3 :** a building for storage **4 :** the cards discarded in cribbage for the dealer to use in scoring **5 a :** a literal translation; *esp* **:** PONY 3 **b :** a device used for cheating in an examination **6 :** CRÈCHE 2 [Old English *cribb*]

[2]crib *vb* **cribbed; crib•bing 1 :** to copy (as an idea or passage) and use as one's own **:** PLAGIARIZE **2 :** to make use of a translation or notes dishonestly — **crib•ber** *n*

crib•bage \ˈkrib-ij\ *n* **:** a card game for two players in which each player attempts to form various counting combinations of the cards [[1]*crib*]

crick \ˈkrik\ *n* **:** a painful spasm of muscles (as of the neck or back) [Middle English *cryk*] — **crick** *vt*

[1]crick•et \ˈkrik-ət\ *n* **:** any of a family of small leaping insects with leathery fore wings and thin hind wings that are related to the grasshoppers and are noted for the chirping notes of the males [Middle French *criquet*]

[2]cricket *n* **1 :** a game played with a ball and bat by two sides of 11 players each on a large field centering upon 2 wickets **2 :** fair and honorable behavior [Middle French *criquet* "goal stake in a bowling game"] — **crick•et•er** *n*

cri•er \ˈkrī-ər, ˈkrīr\ *n* **:** one that cries; *esp* **:** one who proclaims orders or announcements

crime \ˈkrīm\ *n* **1 :** the doing of an act forbidden by law or the failure to do an act required by law **2 :** a serious offense especially against morality **3 :** criminal activity ⟨led a life of *crime*⟩ **4 :** something shameful, foolish, or regrettable ⟨a *crime* to waste food⟩ [Middle French, from Latin *crimen* "accusation, fault, crime"]

[1]crim•i•nal \ˈkrim-ən-l\ *adj* **1 :** involving or being a crime ⟨a *criminal* act⟩ **2 :** relating to crime ⟨*criminal* courts⟩ **3 :** guilty of crime [Late Latin *criminalis,* from Latin *crimen* "crime"] — **crim•i•nal•i•ty** \ˌkrim-ə-ˈnal-ət-ē\ *n* — **crim•i•nal•ly** \ˈkrim-ən-l-ē\ *adv*

[2]criminal *n* **:** one that has committed or has been convicted of a crime

crim•i•nol•o•gy \ˌkrim-ə-ˈnäl-ə-jē\ *n* **:** a scientific study of crime, criminals, and their punishment or correction — **crim•i•no•log•i•cal** \ˌkrim-ən-l-ˈäj-i-kəl\ *adj* — **crim•i•nol•o•gist** \ˌkrim-ə-ˈnäl-ə-jəst\ *n*

[1]crimp \ˈkrimp\ *vt* **1 :** to make wavy, bent, or warped **2 :** to put a crimp in **:** INHIBIT [Dutch or Low German *krimpen* "to shrivel"] — **crimp•er** *n*

[2]crimp *n* **1 :** something produced by or as if by crimping **2**

: something that cramps or inhibits

crimpy \'krim-pē\ *adj* **crimp•i•er; -est** : having a crimped appearance : FRIZZY

1crim•son \'krim-zən\ *n* : deep purplish red [Spanish *cremesín,* from Arabic *qirmizī,* from *qirmiz* "kermes"] — **crimson** *adj*

2crimson *vb* : to make or become crimson

1cringe \'krinj\ *vi* **cringed; cring•ing 1** : to draw in or contract one's muscles involuntarily **2** : to shrink in fear : COWER **3** : to behave in a servile way [Middle English *crengen*] — **cring•er** *n*

2cringe *n* : an act of cringing

1crin•kle \'kring-kəl\ *vb* **crin•kled; crin•kling** \-kə-ling, -kling\ **1** : to form many short bends or turns : RIPPLE **2** : to emit a thin crackling sound : RUSTLE ⟨*crinkling* silk⟩ [Middle English *crynkelen*]

2crinkle *n* : CREASE 1, WRINKLE ⟨*crinkles* around the eyes⟩ — **crin•kly** \-kə-lē, -klē\ *adj*

cri•noid \'krī-ˌnȯid\ *n* : any of a large class (Crinoidea) of echinoderms having usually a cup-shaped body with five or more feathery arms [Greek *krinon* "lily"] — **crinoid** *adj*

crin•o•line \'krin-l-ən\ *n* **1** : a cloth originally of horsehair and linen thread used for stiffening and lining **2 a** : HOOPSKIRT **b** : a full stiff skirt or underskirt [French, from Italian *crinolino,* from *crino* "horsehair" + *lino* "flax, linen"] — **crinoline** *adj*

1crip•ple \'krip-əl\ *n* : a lame or partly disabled individual [Old English *crypel*]

2cripple *vt* **crip•pled; crip•pling** \'krip-ling, -ə-ling\ **1** : to deprive of the use of a limb and especially a leg **2** : to deprive of strength, efficiency, wholeness, or capability for service — **crip•pler** \-lər\ *n*

cri•sis \'krī-səs\ *n, pl* **cri•ses** \'krī-ˌsēz\ **1** : the turning point for better or worse in an acute disease or fever **2** : a decisive moment (as in the plot of a story) **3** : an unstable or crucial time or state of affairs ⟨a political *crisis*⟩ [Latin, from Greek *krisis,* literally, "decision", from *krinein* "to judge, decide"] **syn** see JUNCTURE

1crisp \'krisp\ *adj* **1** : CURLY 1, WAVY ⟨*crisp* hair⟩ **2** : easily crumbled : FLAKY ⟨*crisp* pastry⟩ **3** : being firm and fresh ⟨*crisp* lettuce⟩ **4 a** : being sharp, clean, and concise ⟨a *crisp* illustration⟩ **b** : noticeably neat **c** : keenly alert and lively : INCISIVE ⟨a *crisp* retort⟩ **d** : SNAPPY 2b ⟨*crisp* weather⟩ [Old English, from Latin *crispus*] **syn** see BRITTLE — **crisp•ly** *adv* — **crisp•ness** *n*

2crisp *vb* : to make or become crisp — **crisp•er** *n*

3crisp *n* : something crisp or brittle ⟨dinner burned to a *crisp*⟩

crispy \'kris-pē\ *adj* **crisp•i•er; -est** : CRISP 2 — **crisp•i•ness** *n*

1criss•cross \'kris-ˌkrȯs\ *n* : a pattern formed by or as if by crossed lines [obsolete *christcross* "mark of a cross", from *Christ* + *cross*] — **crisscross** *adj or adv*

2crisscross *vb* **1** : to mark with intersecting lines **2** : to go or pass back and forth

cris•ta \'kris-tə\ *n, pl* **cris•tae** \-ˌtē, -ˌtī\ : any of the inwardly projecting ridges of the inner membrane of a mitochondrion [Latin, "crest"]

cri•te•ri•on \krī-'tir-ē-ən\ *n, pl* **-ria** \-ē-ə\ *also* **-ri•ons** : a standard on which a judgment or decision may be based [Greek *kritērion,* from *krinein* "to judge, decide"] **syn** see STANDARD

crit•ic \'krit-ik\ *n* **1** : a person who judges the value, worth, beauty, or excellence of something; *esp* : one whose profession is to express trained judgment on work in art, music, drama, or literature **2** : one inclined to harsh or unfair criticism : FAULTFINDER [Latin *criticus,* from Greek *kritikos,* from *krinein* "to judge"]

crit•i•cal \'krit-i-kəl\ *adj* **1 a** : inclined to criticize harshly and unfavorably **b** : consisting of or involving criticism ⟨*critical* writings⟩ **c** : using or involving careful judgment **2 a** (1) : of, relating to, or being a turning point ⟨the *critical* phase of a fever⟩ (2) : critically ill **b** : relating to or being a state in which or a measurement or point at which a quality, property, or phenomenon suffers a definite change ⟨*critical* temperature⟩ **c** : CRUCIAL ⟨a *critical* test⟩ **3 a** : of sufficient size to sustain a chain reaction — used of a mass of fissionable material **b** : sustaining a chain reaction — used of a nuclear reactor — **crit•i•cal•ly** \-i-kə-lē, -klē\ *adv* — **crit•i•cal•ness** \-kəl-nəs\ *n*

critical angle *n* : the least angle of incidence at which total reflection takes place

crit•i•cism \'krit-ə-ˌsiz-əm\ *n* **1 a** : the act of criticizing; *esp* : FAULTFINDING **b** : a critical remark or observation **c** : CRITIQUE **2** : the art of judging expertly the merits and faults of works of art or literature

crit•i•cize \'krit-ə-ˌsīz\ *vb* **1** : to examine and judge as a critic : EVALUATE **2** : to express criticism especially of an unfavorable kind **3** : to find fault or find fault with ⟨some people are too quick to *criticize*⟩ — **crit•i•ciz•er** *n*

cri•tique \krə-'tēk\ *n* : an act or instance of criticizing; *esp* : a critical estimate or discussion

1croak \'krōk\ *vb* **1 a** : to utter a croak or similar sound **b** : to speak in a hoarse throaty voice **2** : to grumble dourly : COMPLAIN **3** *slang* : DIE 1 [Middle English *croken*]

2croak *n* : the characteristic hoarse harsh cry of a frog

croak•er \'krō-kər\ *n* **1** : an animal that croaks **2** : any of various fishes that produce croaking or grunting noises **3** : one that habitually grumbles or predicts evil

Croat \'krōt, 'krō-ˌat\ *n* : CROATIAN

Cro•a•tian \krō-'ā-shən\ *n* **1** : a native or inhabitant of Croatia **2** : a south Slavic language spoken by the Croatian people and distinct from Serbian chiefly in its use of the Latin alphabet — **Croatian** *adj*

1cro•chet \krō-'shā\ *n* : needlework consisting of interlocked looped stitches formed with a single thread and a hooked needle [French, from *croche* "hook", of Scandinavian origin]

2crochet *vb* : to make of or work with crochet — **cro•chet•er** \-'shā-ər\ *n*

crock \'kräk\ *n* : a thick earthenware pot or jar [Old English *crocc*]

crock•ery \'kräk-rē, -ə-rē\ *n* : EARTHENWARE

croc•o•dile \'kräk-ə-ˌdīl\ *n* **1** : any of several large thick-skinned long-bodied aquatic reptiles of tropical and subtropical waters; *also* : CROCODILIAN — compare ALLIGATOR **2** : the skin or hide of a crocodile [Latin *crocodilus,* from Greek *krokodilos* "lizard, crocodile", from *krokē* "pebble" + *drilos* "worm"]

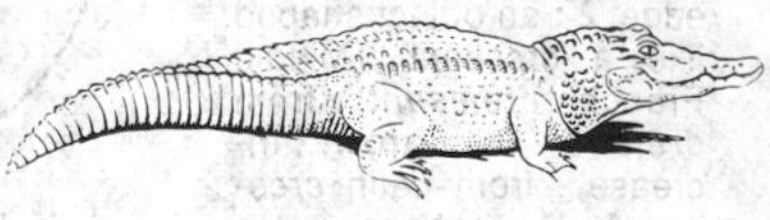

crocodile 1

crocodile tears *n pl* : false or pretended tears : insincere sorrow [from the ancient belief that crocodiles weep in sympathy for their victims]

croc•o•dil•ian \ˌkräk-ə-'dil-ē-ən, -'dil-yən\ *n* : any of an order (Loricata) of reptiles including the crocodiles, alligators, and related extinct forms — **crocodilian** *adj*

cro•cus \'krō-kəs\ *n, pl* **cro•cus•es 1** *pl also* **cro•ci** \-ˌkē, -ˌkī, -ˌsī\ : any of a large genus of small herbs of the iris family with showy solitary long-tubed flowers and slender linear leaves **2** : SAFFRON 1b [Latin, "saffron", from Greek *krokos,* of Semitic origin]

croft \'krȯft\ *n* **1** *chiefly British* : a small enclosed field **2** *chiefly British* : a small farm worked by a tenant [Old English] — **croft•er** *n, chiefly Brit*

crois•sant \krə-ˌwä-'sä^n, ˌkwä-\ *n, pl* **croissants** \-'sä^n, -'sä^{n}z\ : a rich crescent-shaped roll [French, literally, "crescent", from Middle French *creissant*]

Cro-Mag•non \krō-'mag-nən, -'man-yən\ *n* : any of a race of tall erect people known from skeletal remains chiefly from southern France and often placed in the same species as recent human beings [*Cro-Magnon,* a cave near Les Eyzies, France] — **Cro-Magnon** *adj*

crom•lech \'kräm-ˌlek\ *n* **1** : DOLMEN **2** : a circle of monoliths enclosing a dolmen [Welsh, literally, "bent stone"]

crone \'krōn\ *n* : HAG 2 [Old North French *carogne,* literally, "carrion"]

cro•ny \'krō-nē\ *n, pl* **cronies** : a close friend : CHUM [perhaps from Greek *chronios* "long-lasting", from *chronos* "time"]

1crook \'kru̇k\ *n* **1** : an implement having a bent or hooked form: as **a** : a shepherd's staff **b** : CROSIER **2** : a dishonest person; *esp* : CRIMINAL **3** : BEND 2, CURVE **4** : a hook-shaped, curved, or bent part [Old Norse *krōkr* "hook"]

2crook *vb* : to turn from a straight line : BEND, CURVE

crook•ed \'kru̇k-əd\ *adj* **1** : having a crook or curve : BENT **2** : DISHONEST — **crook•ed•ly** *adv* — **crook•ed•ness** *n*

• **syn** CROOKED, AWRY, ASKEW mean not straight. CROOKED applies to what is itself not straight but curving, bent, or twisted; AWRY applies to what is out of a straight line in relation to something else; ASKEW implies having a decided slant away from a straight course.

crook•neck \ˈkru̇k-ˌnek\ *n* **:** a squash with a long curved neck

croon \ˈkrün\ *vb* **:** to hum or sing in a gentle murmuring way ⟨*croon* a lullaby⟩ [Dutch *cronen* "to bellow"] — **croon•er** *n*

[1]crop \ˈkräp\ *n* **1 :** the stock or handle of a whip; *also* **:** a riding whip with a short straight stock and a loop **2 :** a pouched enlargement of the gullet of a bird or insect that receives food and prepares it for digestion **3 a :** an earmark on an animal; *esp* **:** one made by removing the upper part of the ear **b :** a close haircut **4 a :** a plant or animal or plant or animal product that can be grown and harvested **b :** the product or yield especially of a harvested crop **c :** BATCH 3, LOT ⟨a new *crop* of students⟩ [Old English *cropp* "craw, cluster, head of a plant"]

[2]crop *vb* **cropped; crop•ping 1 a :** to remove the upper or outer parts of ⟨*crop* a hedge⟩ **b :** to cut off short **:** CLIP **2 a :** to cause (land) to bear produce; *also* **:** to grow as a crop **b :** HARVEST ⟨fishermen *cropped* a huge number of trout⟩ **3 :** to feed by cropping something ⟨sheep *cropping* in the meadow⟩ **4 :** to yield or make a crop ⟨the apple trees *cropped* well⟩ **5 :** to appear unexpectedly or casually ⟨problems *crop* up daily⟩

crop•land \ˈkräp-ˌland\ *n* **:** land devoted to the production of plant crops

[1]crop•per \ˈkräp-ər\ *n* **:** one that raises crops; *esp* **:** SHARECROPPER

[2]cropper *n* **1 :** a severe fall **2 :** a sudden or violent failure or collapse [probably from English dialect *crop* "neck", from [1]*crop*]

crop rotation *n* **:** the practice of growing different crops in succession on the same land chiefly to preserve the capacity of the soil to produce crops

cro•quet \krō-ˈkā\ *n* **:** a game in which the players use mallets to drive wooden balls through a series of hoops set in the ground [French dialect, "hockey stick", from Old North French, "crook"]

cro•quette \krō-ˈket\ *n* **:** a small roll or ball of minced meat, fish, or vegetables fried in deep fat [French, from *croquer* "to crunch"]

cro•sier *or* **cro•zier** \ˈkrō-zhər\ *n* **:** a staff resembling a shepherd's crook carried by bishops and abbots as a symbol of office [Middle French *crossier* "crosier bearer", from *crosse* "crosier", of Germanic origin]

[1]cross \ˈkrȯs\ *n* **1 a :** a structure consisting of an upright beam and a crossbar used especially by the ancient Romans for execution **b** *often cap* **:** the cross on which Jesus was crucified **2 :** a trying affliction **3 :** a cruciform sign made to invoke the blessing of Christ especially by touching the forehead, breast, and shoulders **4 :** a cross-shaped mark or structure; *esp* **:** one used as a Christian emblem **5 :** the intersection of two ways or lines **:** CROSSING **6 a :** an act of crossing unlike individuals **b :** a crossbred individual or kind **7 :** a hook crossed over an opponent's lead in boxing [Old English, derived from Latin *crux*]

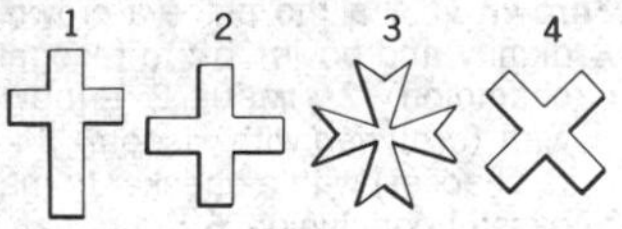

[1]cross 4: *1* Latin, *2* Greek, *3* Maltese, *4* Saint Andrew's

[2]cross *vb* **1 a :** to lie or be located across **b :** INTERSECT ⟨where two roads *cross*⟩ **2 :** to make the sign of the cross on or over **3 :** to cancel by marking a cross on or drawing a line through ⟨*cross* names off a list⟩ **4 :** to place or fold crosswise one over the other ⟨*cross* the arms⟩ **5 a :** to run counter to **:** OPPOSE ⟨gets angry when *crossed*⟩ **b :** to turn against **:** BETRAY **6 a :** to extend across **:** TRAVERSE ⟨a highway *crossing* the state⟩ **b :** to go from one side to the other of ⟨*cross* a street⟩ **7 :** to draw a line across ⟨*cross* a *t*⟩ **8 :** INTERBREED, HYBRIDIZE **9 :** to meet and pass on the way ⟨our letters *crossed* in the mail⟩

[3]cross *adj* **1 :** lying or moving across ⟨*cross* traffic⟩ **2 :** running counter **:** OPPOSITE ⟨*cross* winds⟩ **3 :** marked by bad temper **:** GRUMPY — **cross•ly** *adv* — **cross•ness** *n*

cross•bar \ˈkrȯs-ˌbär\ *n* **:** a transverse bar or stripe

cross•bill \-ˌbil\ *n* **:** any of a genus of finches with mandibles strongly curved and crossing each other

cross•bones \-ˌbōnz\ *n pl* **:** two leg or arm bones placed or depicted crosswise — compare SKULL AND CROSSBONES

cross•bow \-ˌbō\ *n* **:** a weapon that consists of a short bow mounted crosswise near the end of a wooden stock and that discharges stones or short arrows

cross•bow•man \mən\ *n, pl* **-men** \-mən\ **:** a person who uses a crossbow

cross•bred \ˈkrȯs-ˈbred\ *adj* **:** HYBRID; *esp* **:** produced by interbreeding two pure but different breeds, strains, or varieties — **cross•bred** \-ˌbred\ *n*

[1]cross•breed \-ˌbrēd, -ˈbrēd\ *vb* **1 :** HYBRIDIZE; *esp* **:** to interbreed two varieties or breeds of the same species **2 :** to engage in or undergo crossbreeding

[2]cross•breed \-ˌbrēd\ *n* **:** HYBRID 1

cross–coun•try \-ˈkən-trē\ *adj* **1 :** extending across a country ⟨a *cross-country* tour⟩ **2 :** proceeding over countryside and not by roads **3 :** of or relating to racing over the countryside — **cross–country** *adv*

cross•cur•rent \-ˈkər-ənt, -ˈkə-rənt\ *n* **1 :** a current running counter to another **2 :** a conflicting tendency

[1]cross•cut \-ˌkət, -ˈkət\ *vt* **-cut; -cut•ting 1 :** to cut with a crosscut saw **2 :** to cut, go, or move across or through

[2]crosscut *adj* **1 :** made or used for crosscutting ⟨a saw with *crosscut* teeth⟩ **2 :** cut across or transversely ⟨a *crosscut* incision⟩

[3]cross•cut \-ˌkət\ *n* **:** something (as a walk) that cuts across or through ⟨took a *crosscut* through the park⟩

crosscut saw *n* **:** a saw designed chiefly to cut across the grain of wood

crosse \ˈkrȯs\ *n* **:** the stick used in lacrosse [French, literally, "crosier"]

cross–ex•am•i•na•tion \ˌkrȯs-ig-ˌzam-ə-ˈnā-shən\ *n* **:** the questioning of a witness called by the opposing party to a legal action in order to check or discredit his or her testimony — **cross–ex•am•ine** \-ˈzam-ən\ *vt* — **cross–ex•am•in•er** *n*

cross–eye \ˈkrȯs-ˌī\ *n* **1 :** an abnormality in which the eye turns inward toward the nose **2** *pl* **:** eyes affected with cross-eye — **cross–eyed** \-ˈīd\ *adj*

cross–fer•til•i•za•tion \ˈkrȯs-ˌfərt-l-ə-ˈzā-shən\ *n* **1 :** fertilization between gametes produced by separate individuals or sometimes by individuals of different kinds **2 :** CROSS-POLLINATION — **cross–fer•tile** \-ˈfərt-l\ *adj* — **cross–fer•til•ize** \-ˈfərt-l-ˌīz\ *vb*

cross fire *n* **1 :** firing (as in combat) from two or more points so that the lines of fire cross; *also* **:** a situation in which forces of opposing factions meet or cross **2 :** rapid or heated interchange (as of words)

cross–grained \ˈkrȯs-ˈgrānd\ *adj* **1 :** having the grain or fibers running diagonally, transversely, or irregularly **2 :** difficult to deal with **:** CONTRARY

cross hair *n* **:** one of the fine wires or threads in the focus of the eyepiece of an optical instrument used as a reference line

cross•hatch \ˈkrȯs-ˌhach\ *vt* **:** to mark with a series of parallel lines that cross — **crosshatch** *n* — **cross–hatch•ing** *n*

cross•ing \ˈkrȯ-siŋ\ *n* **1 a :** the act or action of one that crosses **b :** a traversing or going across ⟨a channel *crossing*⟩ **c :** the act or process of interbreeding or hybridizing **2 :** a place or structure (as on a street or over a river) where pedestrians or vehicles cross **3 :** a point of intersection (as of streets)

cross•ing–over \ˌkrȯ-siŋ-ˈō-vər\ *n* **:** an exchange of genes or segments between associated parts of homologous chromosomes in synapsis during meiosis

cross–legged \ˈkrȯs-ˈleg-əd, -ˈlegd\ *adv or adj* **1 :** with legs crossed and knees spread wide **2 :** with one leg placed over and across the other

cross•over \ˈkrȯs-ˌō-vər\ *n* **1 :** CROSSING 2 **2 :** an instance or product of genetic crossing-over

cross•piece \ˈkrȯs-ˌpēs\ *n* **:** a horizontal member (as of a figure or a structure)

cross–pol•li•nate \-ˈpäl-ə-ˌnāt\ *vt* **:** to subject to cross-pollination

cross–pol•li•na•tion \ˌkrȯs-ˌpäl-ə-ˈnā-shən\ *n* **:** the transfer of

\ə\ **abut**	\au̇\ **out**	\i\ **tip**	\ȯ\ **saw**	\u̇\ **foot**
\ər\ **further**	\ch\ **chin**	\ī\ **life**	\ȯi\ **coin**	\y\ **yet**
\a\ **mat**	\e\ **pet**	\j\ **job**	\th\ **thin**	\yü\ **few**
\ā\ **take**	\ē\ **easy**	\ŋ\ **sing**	\t͟h\ **this**	\yu̇\ **cure**
\ä\ **cot, cart**	\g\ **go**	\ō\ **bone**	\ü\ **food**	\zh\ **vision**

pollen from one flower to the stigma of another
cross–pur•pose \ˈkrȯs-ˈpər-pəs\ *n* : an opposing or conflicting purpose ⟨working at *cross-purposes*⟩
cross–ques•tion \-ˈkwes-chən\ *vt* : to subject to close questioning; *esp* : CROSS-EXAMINE — **cross–question** *n*
cross–re•fer \ˌkrȯs-ri-ˈfər\ *vt* : to refer (a reader) by a notation or direction from one place to another (as in a book) — **cross–ref•er•ence** \ˈkrȯs-ˈref-ərns, -ˈref-rəns, -ə-rəns\ *n*
cross•road \ˈkrȯs-ˌrōd, -ˈrōd\ *n* **1** : a road that crosses a main road or runs cross-country between main roads **2** *usually pl* **a** : an intersection of two or more roads **b** : a small community located at a crossroads **3** : a crucial point where a decision must be made
cross•ruff \ˈkrȯs-ˌrəf, -ˈrəf\ *n* : a series of plays in a card game (as bridge) in which partners alternately trump different suits — **crossruff** *vb*
cross section *n* **1 a** : a cutting made across something (as a log) **b** : a representation of a cutting made across something **c** : a section cut off at right angles to an axis by a plane ⟨a *cross section* of a right circular cone is a circle⟩ **2** : a number of persons or things selected to represent the general nature of a group ⟨a *cross section* of society⟩ — **cross–sec•tion•al** \ˈkrȯs-ˈsek-shnəl, -shən-l\ *adj*
cross–stitch \ˈkrȯs-ˌstich\ *n* **1** : a needlework stitch that forms an X **2** : work done with cross-stitch — **cross–stitch** *vb*
cross•town \ˈkrȯs-ˌtau̇n, -ˈtau̇n\ *adj* **1** : situated at opposite points of a town **2** : extending or running across a town ⟨a *crosstown* street⟩ — **crosstown** *adv*
cross•trees \ˈkrȯs-ˌtrēz\ *n pl* : two horizontal crosspieces near the top of a ship's mast to spread apart the upper ropes that support the mast
cross•walk \ˈkrȯs-ˌwȯk\ *n* : a specially paved or marked path for pedestrians crossing a street or road
cross•way \-ˌwā\ *n* : CROSSROAD 2a — often used in pl.
cross•ways \-ˌwāz\ *adv* : CROSSWISE 2, DIAGONALLY
[1]**cross•wise** \-ˌwīz\ *adv* **1** *archaic* : in the form of a cross **2** : so as to cross something : ACROSS
[2]**crosswise** *adj* : extended or lying across
cross•word puzzle \ˌkrȯs-ˌwərd-\ *n* : a puzzle in which words are filled into a pattern of numbered squares in answer to similarly numbered clues and in such a way that they read across and down
crotch \ˈkräch\ *n* **1** : an angle formed by the parting of two branches or parts **2** : the region of the human body between the legs where the legs join the trunk [probably alteration of *crutch*]
crotch•et \ˈkräch-ət\ *n* : a peculiar opinion or habit [Middle French *crochet* "small hook", from *croche* "hook"] **syn** see CAPRICE
crotch•ety \ˈkräch-ət-ē\ *adj* : marked by or given to whims or ill temper — **crotch•et•i•ness** *n*
cro•ton \ˈkrōt-n\ *n* : any of several herbs and shrubs of the spurge family; *esp* : an East Indian plant yielding an oil used as a strong purgative [Greek *krotōn* "castor-oil plant"]
Cro•ton bug \ˈkrōt-n-\ *n* : a small active winged cockroach common where food and moisture are found [*Croton* river, New York]
crouch \ˈkrau̇ch\ *vb* **1** : to lower the body especially by bending the legs **2** : to bend or bow servilely : CRINGE [Middle English *crouchen*] — **crouch** *n*
[1]**croup** \ˈkrüp\ *n* : the rump of a four-footed animal [Old French *croupe*, of Germanic origin]
[2]**croup** *n* : a laryngitis especially of infants marked by episodes of difficult breathing and a hoarse metallic cough [English dialect *croup* "to cry hoarsely, cough"] — **croup•ous** \ˈkrü-pəs\ *adj* — **croupy** \-pē\ *adj*
crou•pi•er \ˈkrü-pē-ər, -pē-ˌā\ *n* : an employee of a gambling casino who collects and pays bets at a gaming table [French, literally, "rider on the croup of a horse"]
crou•ton \ˈkrü-ˌtän, krü-ˈ\ *n* : a small cube of toasted or crisply fried bread [French *croûton* "small crust", from *croûte* "crust"]
[1]**crow** \ˈkrō\ *n* **1** : any of various large usually entirely glossy black perching birds related to the jays **2** : CROWBAR **3** : a member of a Siouan people of what is now southeastern Montana [Old English *crāwe*] — **as the crow flies** : in a straight line
[2]**crow** *vi* **crowed** \ˈkrōd\ *also in sense 1 chiefly British* **crew** \ˈkrü\; **crow•ing** **1** : to utter the characteristic loud shrill cry of a cock or a similar sound **2** : to utter a sound expressive of pleasure **3 a** : to exult gloatingly especially over the distress of another **b** : to brag exultantly or blatantly [Old English *crāwan*]

[1]crow 1

[3]**crow** *n* **1** : the cry of a cock or a similar loud shrill sound **2** : a triumphant cry
crow•bar \ˈkrō-ˌbär\ *n* : a metal bar usually wedge-shaped at the working end for use as a pry or lever
crow•ber•ry \ˈkrō-ˌber-ē\ *n* **1** : any of several low shrubby evergreen plants; *esp* : a shrub of arctic and alpine regions with an insipid black berry **2** : the fruit of a crowberry
[1]**crowd** \ˈkrau̇d\ *vb* **1** : to press onward : HURRY **2** : to press close ⟨*crowd* around the speaker⟩ **3** : to collect in numbers : THRONG **4** : to fill by pressing or thronging together : PACK ⟨*crowd* a room⟩ ⟨*crowd* children into a bus⟩ [Old English *crūdan*]
[2]**crowd** *n* **1** : a large number of persons collected into a body without order **2** : the great body of the people : POPULACE ⟨books that appeal to the *crowd*⟩ **3** : a large number of things close together **4** : a group of people having a common interest **syn** see MULTITUDE
crow•foot \ˈkrō-ˌfu̇t\ *n, pl* **crow•feet** \-ˌfēt\ **1** *pl usually* **crowfoots** : any of numerous plants having leaves with cleft lobes; *esp* : BUTTERCUP **2** : CROW'S-FOOT 1 — usually used in pl.
[1]**crown** \ˈkrau̇n\ *n* **1** : a wreath or band for the head; *esp* : one worn as a mark of victory or honor **2** : a royal headdress : DIADEM **3** : the highest part: as **a** : the topmost part of the skull or head **b** : the summit of a mountain **c** : the head of foliage of a tree or shrub **d** : the part of a hat covering the crown of the head **e** : the part of a tooth external to the gum or an artificial substitute for this **4** : something (as the corona of a flower) resembling a crown **5 a** (1) *often cap* : imperial or regal power : SOVEREIGNTY (2) *often cap* : the government under a constitutional monarchy **b** : MONARCH 1 **6** : the highest point of development : CULMINATION **7 a** : a former British monetary unit equal to five shillings **b** : any of several coins representing this unit **8 a** : the region of a seed plant in which stem and root merge **b** : the thick arching end of the shank of an anchor where the arms join it [Old French *corone*, from Latin *corona* "wreath, crown", from Greek *korōnē* "anything curved"] — **crown** *adj, often cap* — **crowned** \ˈkrau̇nd\ *adj*
[2]**crown** *vt* **1 a** : to place a crown on; *esp* : to invest with regal dignity and power **b** : to recognize officially as ⟨was *crowned* champion⟩ **2** : IMBUE 2, ENDOW, ADORN — usually used with *with* ⟨*crowned* with wisdom⟩ **3** : SURMOUNT 1, TOP; *esp* : to top (a checker) with a checker to make a king **4** : to bring to a successful conclusion **5** : to put an artificial crown upon (a tooth)
crown glass *n* : a very clear glass with a low index of refraction that is used for optical instruments
crown prince *n* : the heir apparent to a crown or throne
crown princess *n* **1** : the wife of a crown prince **2** : a woman who is an heir apparent to a crown or throne
crow's–foot \ˈkrōz-ˌfu̇t\ *n, pl* **crow's–feet** \-ˌfēt\ **1** : any of the wrinkles around the outer corners of the eyes — usually used in pl. **2** : CROWFOOT 1
crow's nest *n* : a partly enclosed platform high on a ship's mast for a lookout; *also* : any similar lookout
cro•zier *variant of* CROSIER
cruces *pl of* CRUX
cru•cial \ˈkrü-shəl\ *adj* : of the utmost importance ⟨a *crucial* moment in the game⟩; *esp* : DECISIVE 2 ⟨this experiment would be *crucial*⟩ [French, literally, "cruciform", from Latin *cruc-, crux* "cross"] — **cru•cial•ly** *adv*
cru•ci•ble \ˈkrü-sə-bəl\ *n* **1** : a pot made of a heat-resistant material and used for holding a substance for treatment in a process that requires high temperature **2** : a severe test [Medieval Latin *crucibulum*, from Old French *croiseul*]
cru•ci•fer \ˈkrü-sə-fər\ *n* **1** : one who carries a cross especially at the head of a church procession **2** : any of a family of plants (as the cabbage or mustard) that produce flowers with four petals in the shape of a cross and six stamens — **cru•cif•er•ous** \krü-ˈsif-rəs, -ə-rəs\ *adj*

cru•ci•fix \ˈkrü-sə-ˌfiks\ *n* : a representation of Christ on the cross [Late Latin *crucifixus* "the crucified Christ", from *crucifigere* "to crucify", from Latin *cruc-, crux* "cross" + *figere* "to fasten, fix"]

cru•ci•fix•ion \ˌkrü-sə-ˈfik-shən\ *n* : an act of crucifying; *esp, cap* : the crucifying of Christ

cru•ci•form \ˈkrü-sə-ˌfȯrm\ *adj* : forming or arranged in a cross — **cru•ci•form•ly** *adv*

cru•ci•fy \ˈkrü-sə-ˌfī\ *vt* **-fied**; **-fy•ing** **1** : to put to death by nailing or binding the hands and feet to a cross **2** : to treat cruelly : TORTURE, PERSECUTE

crud \ˈkrəd\ *n* **1** : a deposit of something filthy, greasy, or sticky ⟨machinery covered with *crud*⟩ **2** *slang* : something disagreeable or contemptible [Middle English *curd, crudd* "curd"]

1crude \ˈkrüd\ *adj* **1** : existing in a natural state and unaltered by processing : not refined ⟨*crude* oil⟩ **2** : lacking refinement, good manners, or tact; *esp* : marked by grossness or vulgarity **3** : rough in plan or execution : RUDE ⟨a *crude* shelter⟩ **4** : not concealed or glossed over : BARE ⟨the *crude* facts⟩ [Latin *crudus* "raw"] — **crude•ly** *adv* — **crude•ness** *n* — **cru•di•ty** \ˈkrüd-ət-ē\ *n*

2crude *n* : a substance in its natural unprocessed state; *esp* : unrefined petroleum

cru•el \ˈkrü-əl\ *adj* **cru•el•er** *or* **cru•el•ler**; **cru•el•est** *or* **cru•el•lest** **1** : disposed to inflict pain **2 a** : causing or helping to cause injury, grief, or pain **b** : devoid of leniency : MERCILESS [Old French, from Latin *crudelis*, from *crudus* "raw"] — **cru•el•ly** \ˈkrü-ə-lē\ *adv* — **cru•el•ness** *n*

cru•el•ty \ˈkrü-əl-tē\ *n, pl* **-ties** **1** : the quality or state of being cruel **2 a** : a cruel action **b** : inhuman treatment

cru•et \ˈkrü-ət\ *n* : a small glass bottle for holding vinegar, oil, or sauce [Anglo-French, from Old French *crue*, of Germanic origin]

1cruise \ˈkrüz\ *vb* **1** : to sail about touching at a series of ports **2** : to travel for the sake of traveling **3** : to go about the streets at random but on the lookout for possible developments **4** : to travel at an efficient operating speed ⟨the *cruising* speed of an airplane⟩ **5** : to travel over or about [Dutch *kruisen* "to make a cross, cruise", derived from Latin *crux* "cross"]

2cruise *n* : an act or an instance of cruising

cruis•er \ˈkrü-zər\ *n* **1** : a boat or vehicle that cruises; *esp* : SQUAD CAR **2** : a warship intermediate in size between a battleship and a destroyer **3** : a motorboat with arrangements necessary for living aboard — called also *cabin cruiser*

crul•ler \ˈkrəl-ər\ *n* **1** : a small sweet cake formed in a twisted strip and fried in deep fat **2** *North & Midland* : a doughnut made without yeast [Dutch *krulle*, a twisted cake, from *krul* "curly"]

1crumb \ˈkrəm\ *n* **1** : a small fragment especially of bread **2** : PARTICLE 2 ⟨not a *crumb* of comfort⟩ [Old English *cruma*]

2crumb *vt* **1** : to break into crumbs : CRUMBLE **2** : to cover or thicken with crumbs **3** : to remove crumbs from ⟨*crumb* a table⟩

crum•ble \ˈkrəm-bəl\ *vb* **crum•bled**; **crum•bling** \-bə-ling, -bling\ : to break into small pieces : DISINTEGRATE ⟨*crumble* bread⟩ ⟨the wall *crumbled*⟩ [derived from Old English *cruma* "crumb"]

crum•bly \-bə-lē, -blē\ *adj* **crum•bli•er**; **-est** : easily crumbled — **crum•bli•ness** *n*

crum•my \ˈkrəm-ē\ *adj* **crum•mi•er**; **-est** **1** : MISERABLE 1a ⟨a *crummy* tenement⟩ **2** : CHEAP 2 ⟨a *crummy* piece of equipment⟩ [Middle English *crumme* "crumbly"]

crum•pet \ˈkrəm-pət\ *n* : a small round cake made of unsweetened batter cooked on a griddle [perhaps from Middle English *crompid cake*, "wafer", literally, "curled-up cake"]

1crum•ple \ˈkrem-pəl\ *vb* **crum•pled**; **crum•pling** \-pə-ling, -pling\ **1** : to press, bend, or crush out of shape **2** : to become crumpled **3** : to cause the collapse of or undergo collapse [Middle English *crumpen* "to curve, curl up", from *crump* "crooked", from Old English]

2crumple *n* : a wrinkle or crease made by crumpling

1crunch \ˈkrənch\ *vb* : to chew, grind, or press with a crushing or grinding noise [probably of imitative origin]

2crunch *n* : an act or sound of crunching — **crunchy** \ˈkrən-chē\ *adj*

crup•per \ˈkrəp-ər, ˈkrüp-\ *n* **1** : a leather loop passing under a horse's tail and buckled to the saddle of the harness **2** : the rump of a horse : CROUP [Old French *crupiere*, from *croupe* "croup"]

1cru•sade \krü-ˈsād\ *n* **1** *cap* : any of the military expeditions undertaken by Christian powers in the 11th, 12th, and 13th centuries to win the Holy Land from the Muslims **2** : a campaign undertaken with zeal and enthusiasm ⟨a *crusade* against corruption⟩ [Middle French *croisade* and Spanish *cruzada*, both derived from Latin *crux* "cross"]

2crusade *vi* : to engage in a crusade — **cru•sad•er** *n*

cruse \ˈkrüz, ˈkrüs\ *n* : a small vessel (as a jar or pot) for holding a liquid (as water or oil) [Middle English]

1crush \ˈkrəsh\ *vb* **1 a** : to squeeze or force by pressure so as to alter or destroy structure **b** : to squeeze together into a mass **2** : to embrace strongly : HUG **3** : to reduce to particles by pounding or grinding **4 a** : SUPPRESS 1 ⟨*crush* a rebellion⟩ **b** : to oppress or burden seriously ⟨a *crushing* burden of guilt⟩ **c** : to subdue completely : DEFEAT **5** : CROWD 4, PUSH ⟨people *crushed* into an elevator⟩ **6** : to become crushed [Middle French *cruisir*, of Germanic origin] — **crush•er** *n*

2crush *n* **1** : an act of crushing **2** : a tightly packed crowd **3** : an intense infatuation; *also* : the object of this

crust \ˈkrəst\ *n* **1 a** : the hardened exterior surface of bread **b** : a piece of dry hard bread **2** : the pastry portion of a pie **3 a** : a hard external covering or surface layer ⟨*crust* of snow⟩ **b** : the outer part of the earth composed essentially of crystalline rocks **c** : SCAB 2 [Latin *crusta*] — **crust** *vb*

crus•ta•cea \ˌkrəs-ˈtā-shē-ə, -shə\ *n pl* : CRUSTACEANS

crus•ta•cean \ˌkrəs-ˈtā-shən\ *n* : any of a large class (Crustacea) of mostly aquatic arthropods (as lobsters, shrimps, crabs, wood lice, water fleas, and barnacles) that have an exoskeleton of chitin or of a compound of chitin and calcium [derived from Latin *crusta* "crust, shell"] — **crustacean** *adj*

crust•al \ˈkrəst-l\ *adj* : relating to a crust and especially to that of the earth or the moon

crust•ose \ˈkrəs-ˌtōs\ *adj* : forming a firm thin crust ⟨*crustose* lichens⟩ — compare FOLIOSE, FRUTICOSE

crusty \ˈkrəs-tē\ *adj* **crust•i•er**; **-est** **1** : having or being a crust **2** : giving an effect of bluff incivility — **crust•i•ly** \-tə-lē\ *adv* — **crust•i•ness** \-tē-nəs\ *n*

crutch \ˈkrəch\ *n* **1** : a support typically fitting under the armpit for use by a disabled person in walking **2** : a usually forked support [Old English *crycc*]

crux \ˈkrəks, ˈkrüks\ *n, pl* **crux•es** *also* **cru•ces** \ˈkrü-ˌsēz\ **1 a** : a puzzling or difficult problem : an unsolved question **b** : a crucial or critical point ⟨the *crux* of the problem⟩ **2** : a main or central feature (as of an argument) [Latin, "cross, torture"]

cru•zei•ro \krü-ˈzeər-ō, -ü\ *n, pl* **-ros** **1** : the basic monetary unit of Brazil **2** : a coin representing one cruzeiro [Portuguese]

1cry \ˈkrī\ *vb* **cried**; **cry•ing** **1** : to call loudly : SHOUT **2** : WEEP 1, SOB **3** : to utter a characteristic sound or call **4** : BESEECH, BEG **5** : to proclaim publicly : call out [Old French *crier*, from Latin *quiritare* "to cry out to a citizen for help", from *Quirit-, Quiris* "Roman citizen"] — **cry havoc** : to sound an alarm — **cry wolf** : to give alarm without occasion

2cry *n, pl* **cries** **1** : a loud call or shout (as of pain, fear, or joy) **2** : APPEAL ⟨the *cries* of the poor⟩ **3** : a fit of weeping **4** : the characteristic sound uttered by an animal (as a bird) **5** : SLOGAN, WATCHWORD — **a far cry** : a great distance : a great change — **in full cry** : in full pursuit

cry•ba•by \ˈkrī-ˌbā-bē\ *n* : one who cries or complains easily or often

cry down *vt* : BELITTLE, DISPARAGE

cry•ing \ˈkrī-ing\ *adj* **1** : calling for attention and correction ⟨a *crying* need⟩ **2** : NOTORIOUS ⟨a *crying* evil⟩

cryo•gen•ics \ˌkrī-ə-ˈjen-iks\ *n* : a branch of physics that relates to the production and effects of very low temperatures [Greek *kryos* "cold, freezing"]

cryo•lite \ˈkrī-ə-ˌlīt\ *n* : a mineral Na_3AlF_6 consisting of sodium, aluminum, and fluorine found in Greenland and used in making aluminum

crypt \ˈkript\ *n* **1** : an underground vault or room; *esp* : one under the floor of a church used as a burial place **2** : a simple gland, glandular pit, or recess : FOLLICLE [Latin *crypta*, from Greek *kryptē*, from *kryptos* "hidden", from *kryptein* "to hide"]

cryp•tic \ˈkrip-tik\ *adj* **1** : SECRET 1a, OCCULT **2** : having or

\ə\ **abut**	\au̇\ **out**	\i\ **tip**	\ȯ\ **saw**	\u̇\ **foot**
\ər\ **further**	\ch\ **chin**	\ī\ **life**	\ȯi\ **coin**	\y\ **yet**
\a\ **mat**	\e\ **pet**	\j\ **job**	\th\ **thin**	\yü\ **few**
\ā\ **take**	\ē\ **easy**	\ng\ **sing**	\t͟h\ **this**	\yu̇\ **cure**
\ä\ **cot, cart**	\g\ **go**	\ō\ **bone**	\ü\ **food**	\zh\ **vision**

seeming to have a hidden meaning ⟨a *cryptic* remark⟩ **3** : serving to conceal ⟨*cryptic* coloration in animals⟩ **4** : employing cipher or code **syn** see OBSCURE — **cryp•ti•cal•ly** \-ti-kə-lē, -klē\ *adv*

cryp•to•gam \'krip-tə-ˌgam\ *n* : a plant (as a fern, moss, alga, or fungus) reproducing by spores and not producing flowers or seed [derived from Greek *kryptos* "hidden" + *-gamia* "-gamy"] — **cryp•to•gam•ic** \ˌkrip-tə-'gam-ik\ *adj*

cryp•to•gram \'krip-tə-ˌgram\ *n* : a writing in cipher or code

cryp•to•graph \-ˌgraf\ *n* : CRYPTOGRAM — **cryp•to•graph•ic** \ˌkrip-tə-'graf-ik\ *adj* — **cryp•to•graph•i•cal•ly** \-'graf-i-kə-lē, -klē\ *adv*

cryp•tog•ra•phy \krip-'täg-rə-fē\ *n* : the enciphering and deciphering of messages in secret code — **cryp•tog•ra•pher** \-fər\ *n*

1crys•tal \'kris-tl\ *n* **1** : quartz that is transparent or nearly so and that is either colorless or only slightly tinged **2** : something resembling crystal in transparency and colorlessness **3** : a body that is formed by the solidification of a substance or mixture and has a regularly repeating internal arrangement of its atoms and often external plane faces ⟨a *crystal* of quartz⟩ ⟨a snow *crystal*⟩ **4** : a clear colorless glass of superior quality **5** : the transparent cover over a watch or clock dial **6** : powdered methamphetamine [Old French *cristal,* from Latin *crystallum,* from Greek *krystallos* "ice, crystal"]

1crystal 3

2crystal *adj* **1** : consisting of or resembling crystal : CLEAR **2** : relating to or using a crystal ⟨a *crystal* radio receiver⟩

crys•tal•line \'kris-tə-lən\ *adj* **1** : made of crystal or composed of crystals **2** : resembling crystal : TRANSPARENT **3** : of or relating to a crystal — **crys•tal•lin•i•ty** \ˌkris-tə-'lin-ət-ē\ *n*

crystalline lens *n* : the lens of the vertebrate eye

crys•tal•lize \'kris-tə-ˌlīz\ *vb* **1** : to cause to form crystals or assume crystalline form **2** : to give a definite form to ⟨try to *crystallize* your thoughts⟩ **3** : to become crystallized — **crys•tal•liz•able** \-ˌlī-zə-bəl\ *adj* — **crys•tal•li•za•tion** \ˌkris-tə-lə-'zā-shən\ *n*

crys•tal•log•ra•phy \ˌkris-tə-'läg-rə-fē\ *n* : a science that deals with the form and structure of crystals — **crys•tal•log•ra•pher** \-fər\ *n* — **crys•tal•lo•graph•ic** \-tə-lō-'graf-ik\ *adj*

crys•tal•loid \'kris-tə-ˌlȯid\ *n* : a substance that forms a true solution and is capable of being crystallized

crystal set *n* : a radio receiver having a crystal for a detector and no vacuum tubes

cteno•phore \'ten-ə-ˌfōr, -ˌfȯr\ *n* : any of a phylum (Ctenophora) of nearly globe-shaped marine animals that superficially resemble jellyfishes but swim by means of eight bands of ciliated plates — called also *comb jelly* [derived from Greek *kten-, kteis* "comb" + *pherein* "to carry"] — **cte•noph•o•ran** \ti-'näf-ə-rən\ *adj or n*

cub \'kəb\ *n* **1 a** : a young flesh-eating mammal ⟨bear *cubs*⟩ ⟨lion *cubs*⟩ **b** : a young shark **2** : a young person **3** : APPRENTICE; *esp* : an inexperienced newspaper reporter [origin unknown]

cub•by•hole \'kəb-ē-ˌhōl\ *n* : a snug or confined place (as for hiding or storing things) [obsolete English *cub* "pen", from Dutch *kub* "thatched roof"]

1cube \'kyüb\ *n* **1** : a regular solid that has six equal square sides **2** : the product obtained by taking a number three times as a factor ⟨the *cube* of 2 is 8⟩ [Latin *cubus,* from Greek *kybos*]

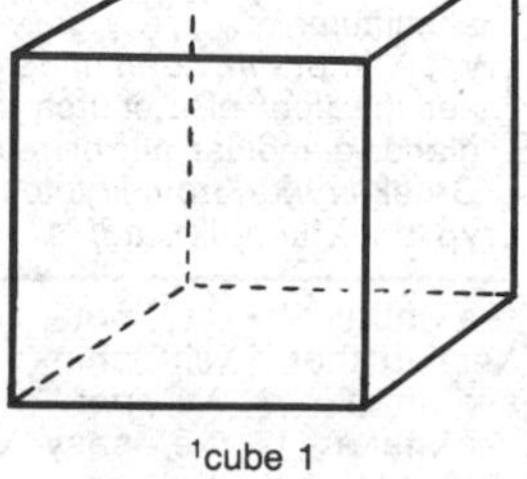

1cube 1

2cube *vt* **1** : to raise to the third power ⟨2 *cubed* is 8⟩ **2** : to form or cut into cubes

cu•beb \'kyü-ˌbeb\ *n* : the dried unripe berry of a tropical shrub of the pepper family that was formerly used in medicine as a stimulant and diuretic [Middle French *cubebe,* from Medieval Latin *cubeba,* from Arabic *kubābah*]

cube root *n* : a number whose cube is a given number ⟨the *cube root* of 27 is 3⟩

cu•bic \'kyü-bik\ *also* **cu•bi•cal** \'kyü-bi-kəl\ *adj* **1** : having the shape of a cube **2** : having, being, or relating to volume; *esp* : being the volume of a cube whose edge is a specified unit ⟨a *cubic* inch⟩

cubic equation *n* : a polynomial equation in which the sum of the exponents of the variables in any term is no greater than three ⟨$x^3 + 2x^2y + 5xy^2 + 10y^3 + 6 = 0$ is a cubic equation⟩ — called also *cubic*

cu•bi•cle \'kyü-bi-kəl\ *n* : a small partitioned compartment especially for sleeping [Latin *cubiculum,* from *cubare* "to lie, recline"]

cubic measure *n* : a unit (as a cubic inch or cubic centimeter) for measuring volume — see MEASURE table, METRIC SYSTEM table

cub•ism \'kyü-ˌbiz-əm\ *n* : a 20th century art form characterized by the abstraction of natural forms into fragmented geometric shapes — **cub•ist** \-bəst\ *adj or n*

cu•bit \'kyü-bət\ *n* : a unit of length based on the length of the forearm from the elbow to the tip of the middle finger and usually equal to about 46 centimeters [Latin *cubitum* "elbow, cubit"]

cu•boi•dal \kyü-'bȯid-l\ *adj* : somewhat cubical : made up of nearly cubical elements ⟨*cuboidal* epithelium⟩

cub scout *n* : a member of the Boy Scouts of America program for boys of the age range 8-10

1cuck•old \'kək-əld, -ōld\ *n* : a man whose wife is unfaithful [Middle English *cokewold*] — **cuck•old•ry** \-əl-drē\ *n*

2cuckold *vt* : to make a cuckold of

1cuck•oo \'kük-ü, 'ku̇k-\ *n, pl* **cuckoos** **1** : a largely grayish brown European bird that lays its eggs in the nests of other birds for them to hatch; *also* : any of various related birds **2** : the call of a cuckoo [Middle English *cuccu*]

2cuckoo *adj* **1** : of or resembling the cuckoo **2** : SILLY 1, CRAZY

cuckoo spit *n* **1** : a frothy secretion exuded upon plants by the nymphs of spittlebugs **2** : SPITTLEBUG

cu•cum•ber \'kyü-ˌkəm-bər, -kəm-\ *n* : the long fleshy many-seeded fruit of a vine of the gourd family grown as a garden vegetable; *also* : this vine [Middle French *cocombre,* from Latin *cucumis*]

cu•cur•bit \kyü-'kər-bət\ *n* : a plant of the gourd family [Middle French *cucurbite,* from Latin *cucurbita* "gourd"]

cud \'kəd, 'ku̇d\ *n* : food brought up into the mouth by a ruminating animal (as a cow) from its rumen to be chewed again [Old English *cwudu*]

cud•dle \'kəd-l\ *vb* **cud•dled**; **cud•dling** \'kəd-ling, -l-ing\ **1** : to hold close for warmth or comfort or in affection **2** : to lie close : SNUGGLE [origin unknown] — **cuddle** *n* — **cud•dly** \'kəd-lē, -l-ē\ *adj*

1cud•gel \'kəj-əl\ *n* : a short heavy club [Old English *cycgel*]

2cudgel *vt* **-geled** *or* **-gelled**; **-gel•ing** *or* **-gel•ling** : to beat with or as if with a cudgel

1cue \'kyü\ *n* **1** : a word, phrase, or action in a play serving as a signal for the next actor to speak or act **2** : something serving as a signal or suggestion : HINT [probably from *qu,* abbreviation (used as a direction in actors' copies of plays) of Latin *quando* "when"]

2cue *n* **1** : QUEUE 2 **2 a** : a tapering rod for striking a ball in games (as billiards or pool) **b** : a long-handled stick with a concave head for shoving disks in shuffleboard [French *queue,* literally, "tail", from Latin *cauda*]

cue ball *n* : the ball struck with the cue and driven into the object ball in billiards and pool

1cuff \'kəf\ *n* **1** : something (as a part of a sleeve) encircling the wrist **2** : the turned-back hem of a trouser leg [Middle English]

2cuff *vt* : to strike with or as if with the palm of the hand : SLAP

3cuff *n* : a blow with the hand especially when open : SLAP

cui•rass \kwi-'ras, kyu̇-\ *n* **1** : a piece of armor covering the body from neck to waist; *also* : the breastplate of such a piece **2** : something (as a plaster cast on the trunk and neck) resembling a cuirass [Middle French *curasse,* from Late Latin *coreaceus* "leathern", from Latin *corium* "skin, leather"]

cuir•as•sier \ˌkwir-ə-'siər, ˌkyu̇r-\ *n* : a mounted soldier wearing a cuirass

cui•sine \kwi-ˈzēn\ *n* : manner of preparing food; *also* : the food prepared [French, literally, "kitchen", from Late Latin *coquina,* from Latin *coquere* "to cook"]

cu•lex \ˈkyü-ˌleks\ *n* : any of a large cosmopolitan genus of mosquitoes that includes the mosquito commonly found in or about buildings in Europe and North America [Latin, "gnat"] — **cu•li•cine** \ˈkyü-lə-ˌsīn\ *adj or n*

cu•li•nary \ˈkəl-ə-ˌner-ē, ˈkyü-lə-\ *adj* : of or relating to the kitchen or cookery [Latin *culina* "kitchen", from *coquere* "to cook"]

[1]**cull** \ˈkəl\ *vt* **1** : to select from a group : CHOOSE **2** : to identify and remove the culls from [Middle French *cuillir,* from Latin *colligere* "to bind together, collect"] — **cull•er** *n*

[2]**cull** *n* : something rejected as inferior or worthless

[1]**culm** \ˈkəlm\ *n* : refuse coal screenings : SLACK [Middle English]

[2]**culm** *n* : the stem of a monocotyledonous plant [Latin *culmus* "stalk"]

cul•mi•nate \ˈkəl-mə-ˌnāt\ *vi* : to reach the highest or climactic point [Medieval Latin *culminare,* from Latin *culmen* "top, summit"]

cul•mi•na•tion \ˌkəl-mə-ˈnā-shən\ *n* **1** : the action of culminating **2** : the culminating position : CLIMAX

cu•lotte \ˈkü-ˌlät, ˈkyü-; kü-ˈ, kyü-ˈ\ *n* : a divided skirt or a garment with a divided skirt — often used in pl. [French, "breeches", from *cul* "backside"]

cul•pa•ble \ˈkəl-pə-bəl\ *adj* : deserving condemnation or blame ⟨*culpable* negligence⟩ [Middle French, from Latin *culpabilis,* from *culpare* "to blame", from *culpa* "fault, guilt"] — **cul•pa•bil•i•ty** \ˌkəl-pə-ˈbil-ət-ē\ *n* — **cul•pa•ble•ness** \ˈkəl-pə-bəl-nəs\ *n* — **cul•pa•bly** \-pə-blē\ *adv*

cul•prit \ˈkəl-prət, -ˌprit\ *n* **1** : one accused of or charged with a crime **2** : one guilty of a crime or fault [Anglo-French *cul.* (abbreviation of *culpable* "guilty") + *prest, prit* "ready" (that is, to prove it), from Latin *praestus*]

cult \ˈkəlt\ *n* **1** : formal religious veneration : WORSHIP **2** : a system of religious beliefs and ritual or those who practice it **3 a** : enthusiastic and usually temporary devotion to a person, idea, or thing **b** : a group of persons showing such devotion [Latin *cultus* "care, adoration", from *colere* "to cultivate, worship"] — **cult•ist** \ˈkəl-təst\ *n*

cul•ti•gen \ˈkəl-tə-jən\ *n* : a cultivated organism (as Indian corn) of a variety or species for which a wild ancestor is unknown

cul•ti•va•ble \ˈkəl-tə-və-bəl\ *adj* : capable of being cultivated

cul•ti•vate \ˈkəl-tə-ˌvāt\ *vt* **1 a** : to prepare or prepare and use for the raising of crops : TILL **b** : to loosen or break up the soil about (growing plants) **2 a** : to foster the growth of ⟨*cultivate* vegetables⟩ **b** : CULTURE 2 **c** : REFINE, IMPROVE ⟨*cultivate* the mind⟩ **3** : FURTHER, ENCOURAGE ⟨*cultivate* the arts⟩ **4** : to seek the society of [Medieval Latin *cultivare,* from *cultivus* "cultivated", from Latin *colere* "to cultivate"] — **cul•ti•vat•able** \-ˌvāt-ə-bəl\ *adj*

cul•ti•vat•ed *adj* **1** : subjected to or produced under cultivation ⟨*cultivated* farms⟩ ⟨*cultivated* fruits⟩ **2** : REFINED, EDUCATED ⟨*cultivated* speech⟩

cul•ti•va•tion \ˌkəl-tə-ˈvā-shən\ *n* **1** : the act or art of cultivating; *esp* : TILLAGE **2** : CULTURE 3, REFINEMENT

cul•ti•va•tor \ˈkəl-tə-ˌvāt-ər\ *n* : one that cultivates; *esp* : an implement to loosen the soil while crops are growing

cul•tur•al \ˈkəlch-rəl, -ə-rəl\ *adj* **1** : of or relating to culture **2** : produced by breeding ⟨a *cultural* variety⟩ — **cul•tur•al•ly** \-ē\ *adv*

cultural anthropology *n* : a division of anthropology that deals with human culture

[1]**cul•ture** \ˈkəl-chər\ *n* **1** : CULTIVATION 1, TILLAGE **2 a** : the rearing or development of a particular product, stock, or crop ⟨bee *culture*⟩ ⟨the *culture* of grapes⟩ **b** : professional or expert care and training ⟨voice *culture*⟩ **3** : the state of being cultivated; *esp* : refinement in manners, taste, and thought **4** : the characteristic features of a civilization including its beliefs, its artistic and material products, and its social institutions ⟨ancient Greek *culture*⟩; *also* : a stage in the history of a civilization **5** : cultivation of living material in prepared nutrient media; *also* : a product of such cultivation [Middle French, from Latin *cultura,* from *colere* "to cultivate"]

[2]**culture** *vt* **cul•tured**; **cul•tur•ing** \ˈkəlch-ring, -ə-ring\ **1** : CULTIVATE 1 **2** : to grow in a prepared medium

cul•tured \ˈkəl-chərd\ *adj* **1** : CULTIVATED ⟨*cultured* fields⟩ ⟨*cultured* speech⟩ **2** : produced under artificial conditions ⟨*cultured* pearls⟩

cul•vert \ˈkəl-vərt\ *n* **1** : a drain crossing under a road or railroad **2** : a conduit for a culvert **3** : a bridge over a culvert [origin unknown]

cum•ber \ˈkəm-bər\ *vt* **cum•bered**; **cum•ber•ing** \-bə-ring, -bring\ **1** : to hinder by being in the way **2** : to weigh down : BURDEN ⟨*cumbered* with cares⟩ [Middle English *cumbren*]

cum•ber•some \ˈkəm-bər-səm\ *adj* **1** : UNWIELDY, CLUMSY **2** : slow-moving : LUMBERING — **cum•ber•some•ly** *adv* — **cum•ber•some•ness** *n*

cum•brous \ˈkəm-brəs\ *adj* : CUMBERSOME — **cum•brous•ly** *adv* — **cum•brous•ness** *n*

cum•in \ˈkəm-ən\ *n* : a low plant of the carrot family grown for its aromatic seeds [Old English *cymen,* from Latin *cuminum,* from Greek *kyminon,* of Semitic origin]

cum lau•de \kům-ˈlaůd-ə, -ē; ˌkəm-ˈlȯd-ē\ *adv or adj* : with academic distinction ⟨graduated *cum laude*⟩ [New Latin, "with praise"]

cum•mer•bund \ˈkəm-ər-ˌbənd\ *n* : a broad sash worn as a waistband [Hindi *kamarband,* from Persian, from *kamar* "waist" + *band* "band"]

cu•mu•late \ˈkyü-myə-ˌlāt\ *vb* : ACCUMULATE [Latin *cumulare,* from *cumulus* "mass, heap"] — **cu•mu•la•tion** \ˌkyü-myə-ˈlā-shən\ *n*

cu•mu•la•tive \ˈkyü-myə-lət-iv, -ˌlāt-\ *adj* **1 a** : increasing (as in force, strength, or amount) by successive additions **b** : composed of a series of increases ⟨*cumulative* evidence⟩ **2** : increasing in severity with repetition of the offense ⟨*cumulative* penalty⟩ **3** : bearing interest or dividends that must be added to a future payment if not paid when due ⟨*cumulative* stock⟩ **4** : formed by addition of new material of the same kind ⟨a *cumulative* book index⟩ — **cu•mu•la•tive•ly** *adv* — **cu•mu•la•tive•ness** *n*

cu•mu•lo•nim•bus \ˌkyü-myə-lō-ˈnim-bəs\ *n* : a cumulus often spread out in the shape of an anvil extending to great heights

cu•mu•lo•stra•tus \-ˈstrāt-əs, -ˈstrat-\ *n* : a cumulus whose base extends horizontally as a stratus cloud

cu•mu•lous \ˈkyü-myə-ləs\ *adj* : resembling a cumulus

cu•mu•lus \-ləs\ *n, pl* **cu•mu•li** \-ˌlī, -ˌlē\ **1** : HEAP 2, ACCUMULATION **2** : a massive cloud form having a flat base and rounded outlines often piled up like a mountain [Latin, "heap, mass"]

cu•ne•ate \ˈkyü-nē-ˌāt, -nē-ət\ *adj* : narrowly triangular with the acute angle toward the base ⟨a *cuneate* leaf⟩ [Latin *cuneatus,* from *cuneus* "wedge"]

[1]**cu•ne•i•form** \kyů-ˈnē-ə-ˌfȯrm; ˈkyü-nə-ˌfȯrm, -nē-ə-\ *adj* **1** : having the shape of a wedge **2** : composed of or written in wedge-shaped characters ⟨*cuneiform* alphabet⟩ [derived from Latin *cuneus* "wedge"]

[2]**cuneiform** *n* : cuneiform writing (as of ancient Assyria and Babylonia)

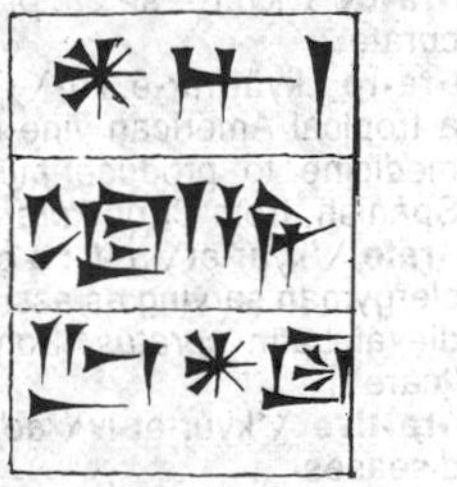

[2]cuneiform

cun•ner \ˈkən-ər\ *n* : a small American food fish that is abundant on the rocky shores of New England [origin unknown]

[1]**cun•ning** \ˈkən-ing\ *adj* **1** : dexterous or crafty in the use of resources (as skill or knowledge) ⟨*cunning* schemers⟩ **2** : marked by wily artfulness ⟨a *cunning* plot⟩ **3** : prettily appealing : CUTE [Middle English, from *can* "know, can"] — **cun•ning•ly** \-ing-lē\ *adv*

[2]**cunning** *n* **1** : SKILL 1, DEXTERITY **2** : SLYNESS, CRAFTINESS

[1]**cup** \ˈkəp\ *n* **1** : an open bowl-shaped drinking vessel usually with a handle **2 a** : the contents of a cup : CUPFUL **b** : the consecrated wine of the Communion **3** : a large ornamental cup offered as a prize **4 a** : something (as the corolla of a flower) resembling a cup **b** : a usually plastic-reinforced athletic supporter **c** : the metal case inside a hole in golf; *also* : the hole

\ə\ **abut**	\aů\ **out**	\i\ **tip**	\ȯ\ **saw**	\ů\ **foot**
\ər\ **further**	\ch\ **chin**	\ī\ **life**	\ȯi\ **coin**	\y\ **yet**
\a\ **mat**	\e\ **pet**	\j\ **job**	\th\ **thin**	\yü\ **few**
\ā\ **take**	\ē\ **easy**	\ng\ **sing**	\t͟h\ **this**	\yů\ **cure**
\ä\ **cot, cart**	\g\ **go**	\ō\ **bone**	\ü\ **food**	\zh\ **vision**

itself **5 :** a food served in a cup-shaped vessel ⟨fruit *cup*⟩ **6 :** the symbol ∪ indicating the union of two sets — compare CAP 5 [Old English *cuppe,* from Late Latin *cuppa,* from Latin *cupa* "tub"] — **cup•like** \'kəp-,līk\ *adj* — **in one's cups :** DRUNK

[2]cup *vt* **cupped; cup•ping 1 :** to treat by cupping **2 a :** to curve into the shape of a cup ⟨*cupped* my hands⟩ **b :** to place in or as if in a cup — **cup•per** *n*

cup•bearer \'kəp-,bar-ər, -,ber-\ *n* **:** one who has the duty of filling and distributing cups of drink (as at a feast)

cup•board \'kəb-ərd\ *n* **1 :** a closet with shelves for cups, dishes, or food **2 :** a small closet

cup•cake \'kəp-,kāk\ *n* **:** a small cake baked in a cuplike mold

cu•pel \kyü-'pel, 'kyü-pəl\ *n* **:** a small shallow porous cup especially of bone ash used in assaying to separate precious metals from lead [French *coupelle* "small cup", from *coupe* "cup", from Late Latin *cuppa*]

cup•ful \'kəp-,fu̇l\ *n, pl* **cup•fuls** \-,fu̇lz\ *or* **cups•ful** \'kəps-,fu̇l\ **1 :** the amount held by a cup **2 :** a half pint **:** eight ounces (about 236 milliliters)

cup fungus *n* **:** any of an order of mostly saprophytic fungi bearing a cuplike fleshy or horny spore-bearing structure that is often colored

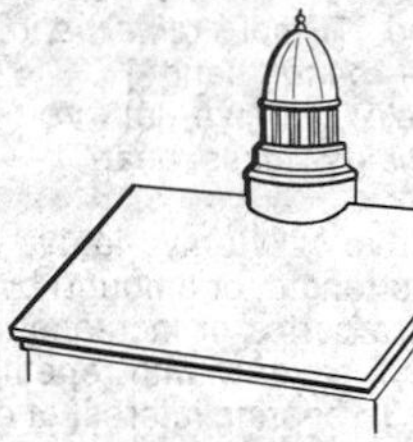

cupola 2

cu•pid \'kyü-pəd\ *n* **:** a winged naked figure of an infant often with a bow and arrow that represents the Roman god of love

cu•pid•i•ty \kyu̇-'pid-ət-ē\ *n* **:** excessive desire especially for wealth **:** GREED [Middle French *cupidité,* from Latin *cupiditas,* from *cupidus* "desirous", from *cupere* "to desire"]

cu•po•la \'kyü-pə-lə, -,lō\ *n* **1 :** a rounded roof or ceiling **2 :** a small structure built on top of a roof [Italian, from Latin *cupula* "small tub", from *cupa* "tub"]

cup•ping *n* **:** a technique formerly used for drawing blood to the surface of the body by application of a glass vessel from which air had been evacuated by heat forming a partial vacuum

cu•pric \'kü-prik, 'kyü-\ *adj* **:** of, relating to, or containing bivalent copper [Late Latin *cuprum* "copper"]

cu•prite \'kü-,prīt, 'kyü-\ *n* **:** a mineral Cu_2O that consists of oxide of copper and is an ore of copper

cu•prous \-prəs\ *adj* **:** of, relating to, or containing univalent copper

cur \'kər\ *n* **1 :** a mongrel dog **2 :** a low contemptible person [Middle English]

cur•able \'kyu̇r-ə-bəl\ *adj* **:** capable of being cured

cu•ra•cy \'kyu̇r-ə-sē\ *n, pl* **-cies :** the office or term of office of a curate

cu•ra•re \kyu̇-'rär-ē, ku̇-\ **:** a dried aqueous extract especially of a tropical American vine used in native arrow poisons and in medicine to produce muscular relaxation [Portuguese and Spanish, from Carib *kurari*]

cu•rate \'kyu̇r-ət\ *n* **1 :** a clergyman in charge of a parish **2 :** a clergyman serving as assistant (as to a rector) in a parish [Medieval Latin *curatus,* from *cura* "cure of souls", from Latin, "care"]

cu•ra•tive \'kyu̇r-ət-iv\ *adj* **:** relating to or used in the cure of diseases

cu•ra•tor \kyu̇-'rāt-ər, 'kyu̇r-,āt-\ *n* **:** one that has the care and supervision of something; *esp* **:** one in charge of a museum or zoo [Latin, from *curare* "to care", from *cura* "care"] — **cu•ra•to•ri•al** \,kyu̇r-ə-'tōr-ē-əl, -'tȯr-\ *adj* — **cu•ra•tor•ship** \kyu̇-'rāt-ər-,ship, 'kyu̇r-ət-\ *n*

[1]curb \'kərb\ *n* **1 :** a chain or strap on a bit used to restrain a horse **2 :** RESTRAINT 2, CHECK ⟨price *curbs*⟩ **3 :** a frame or a raised edge or margin to strengthen or confine ⟨the *curb* of a well⟩ **4 :** an edging built along a street to form part of a gutter [Middle French *courbe* "curve, curved piece of wood or iron", from Latin *curvus* "curved"]

[2]curb *vt* **1 :** to furnish with a curb **2 :** to check or control with or as if with a curb ⟨*curb* your impulses⟩

curb•ing \'kər-bing\ *n* **1 :** the material for a curb **2 :** CURB 3, 4

curb•stone \'kərb-,stōn\ *n* **:** a stone forming a curb

cur•cu•lio \kər-'kyü-lē-,ō\ *n, pl* **-li•os :** any of various weevils; *esp* **:** one that injures fruit [Latin, "grain weevil"]

[1]curd \'kərd\ *n* **1 :** the thick casein-rich part of coagulated milk **2 :** something resembling the curd of milk [Middle English] — **curdy** \-ē\ *adj*

[2]curd *vb* **:** COAGULATE, CURDLE

cur•dle \'kərd-l\ *vb* **cur•dled; cur•dling** \'kərd-ling, -l-ing\ **1 :** to cause curds to form in **2 :** to form curds **:** COAGULATE **3 :** SOUR, SPOIL

[1]cure \'kyu̇r\ *n* **1 :** spiritual charge of a parish **2 a :** recovery or relief from a disease **b :** something (as a drug or treatment) that cures a disease **c :** a course, system, or period of treatment **3 :** a process or method of curing ⟨a brine *cure* for meat⟩ [Old French, from Medieval Latin *cura* "cure of souls", from Latin, "care"] — **cure•less** \-ləs\ *adj*

[2]cure *vb* **1 a :** to restore to health, soundness, or normality **b :** to bring about recovery from **2 :** to eliminate or free from something objectionable or harmful ⟨the snub *cured* them of being nosy⟩ **3 :** to prepare by or undergo chemical or physical processing for keeping or use ⟨*cure* bacon⟩ ⟨hay *curing* in the sun⟩ — **cur•er** \'kyu̇r-ər\ *n*

• **syn** CURE, HEAL, REMEDY mean to rectify an unhealthy or undesirable condition. CURE applies to restoring to health after disease; HEAL may also apply to this but more commonly suggests restoring a wounded or sore part to soundness; REMEDY in extended use suggests correction or relief of a morbid or evil condition.

cu•ré \kyü-'rā, 'kyu̇r-,ā\ *n* **:** a parish priest [Old French, from Medieval Latin *curatus*]

cure–all \'kyu̇r-,ȯl\ *n* **:** a remedy for all ills **:** PANACEA

cur•few \'kər-,fyü\ *n* **1 :** a regulation requiring persons of a usually specified kind to be off the streets at a stated time **2 :** a signal (as the ringing of a bell) to announce the beginning of a curfew **3 a :** the time when a curfew begins **b :** the period during which a curfew is in effect [Middle French *covrefeu* "signal given to bank the hearth fire, curfew", from *covrir* "to cover" + *feu* "fire"]

△ **origin** In Europe in the Middle Ages people were required to put out or cover their hearth fires by a certain time in the evening. A hearth fire left unattended overnight might spread and destroy the house or even the town. A bell was rung to let people know they must cover their fires. In Middle French this signal was called *covrefeu,* a compound of *covrir,* "to cover", and *feu,* "fire". Even when hearth fires were no longer regulated, many towns had other rules that called for the ringing of an evening bell, and this signal was still called *covrefeu.* A common *covrefeu* regulation required that certain people be off the streets by a given time. The English borrowed *curfew* from the French *covrefeu.*

cu•ria \'kyu̇r-ē-ə, 'ku̇r-\ *n, pl* **cu•ri•ae** \'kyu̇r-ē-,ē, 'ku̇r-ē-,ī\ **1 :** a division of an ancient Roman tribe **2 :** a medieval royal court or court of justice **3** *often cap* **:** the group of administrative and judicial bodies through which the pope governs the Roman Catholic Church [Latin] — **cu•ri•al** \'kyu̇r-ē-əl\ *adj*

cu•rie \'kyu̇r-,ē, kyu̇-'rē\ *n* **1 :** a unit quantity of any radioactive element in which 37 billion disintegrations occur per second **2 :** a unit of radioactivity equal to 37 billion disintegrations per second [Marie *Curie*]

cu•rio \'kyu̇r-ē-,ō\ *n, pl* **-ri•os :** a rare or unusual article **:** CURIOSITY [short for *curiosity*]

cu•ri•os•i•ty \,kyu̇r-ē-'äs-ət-ē\ *n, pl* **-ties 1 :** an eager desire to learn and often to learn what does not concern one **:** INQUISITIVENESS **2 :** something strange or unusual; *esp* **:** an object valued because of its strangeness or rarity

cu•ri•ous \'kyu̇r-ē-əs\ *adj* **1 :** eager to learn ⟨children are *curious* about everything⟩ **2 :** eager to learn about others' concerns **:** NOSY **3 :** exciting attention as strange or novel ⟨a *curious* insect⟩ ⟨*curious* notions⟩ [Middle French *curios,* from Latin *curiosus* "careful, inquisitive", from *cura* "care"] — **cu•ri•ous•ly** *adv* — **cu•ri•ous•ness** *n*

• **syn** INQUISITIVE, PRYING: CURIOUS implies an eager desire to learn or observe that may be either justifiable or objectionable; INQUISITIVE implies habitual curiosity especially about the personal affairs of others; PRYING implies officious, active inquisitiveness.

cu•ri•um \'kyu̇r-ē-əm\ *n* **:** a metallic radioactive element artificially produced — see ELEMENT table [New Latin, from Marie and Pierre *Curie*]

[1]curl \'kərl\ *vb* **1 :** to form into coils or ringlets **2 :** to form into a curved shape **:** TWIST **3 a :** to grow in coils or spirals **b :** to move in curves or spirals **4 :** to play the game of curling [Middle English *curlen,* from *crul* "curly"]

[2]**curl** *n* **1 :** a lock of hair that coils : RINGLET **2 :** something having a spiral or winding form : COIL **3 :** the action of curling : the state of being curled **4 :** an abnormal rolling or curling of leaves

curl•er \'kər-lər\ *n* **1 :** one that curls; *esp* **:** a device for putting a curl into hair **2 :** a player in the game of curling

cur•lew \'kər-ˌlü, 'kərl-ˌyü\ *n, pl* **curlews** *or* **curlew :** any of various largely brownish mostly migratory birds related to the woodcocks and distinguished by long legs and a long slender down-curved bill [Middle French *corlieu*]

curli•cue *also* **curly•cue** \'kər-li-ˌkyü\ *n* **:** a fancifully curved or spiral figure (as a flourish in handwriting) [*curly* + *cue* "braid of hair"]

curl•ing \'kər-ling\ *n* **:** a game in which two teams of four men each slide special stones over ice toward a target circle

curly \'kər-lē\ *adj* **curl•i•er; -est 1 :** tending to curl; *also* **:** having curls **2 :** having the grain composed of wavy fibers that do not cross and that often form alternating light and dark lines ⟨*curly* maple⟩ — **curl•i•ness** *n*

cur•mudg•eon \kər-'məj-ən\ *n* **:** a bad-tempered and often old man [origin unknown] — **cur•mudg•eon•ly** *adj*

cur•rant \'kər-ənt, 'kə-rənt\ *n* **1 :** a small seedless raisin grown chiefly in the Levant **2 :** the acid edible fruit of any of several shrubs related to the gooseberries; *also* **:** a plant bearing currants [Middle English *raison of Coraunte,* literally, "raisin of Corinth"]

cur•ren•cy \'kər-ən-sē, 'kə-rən-\ *n, pl* **-cies 1 :** general use or acceptance ⟨a story that gained wide *currency*⟩ **2 :** coins, government notes, and bank notes circulating as a medium of exchange **:** money in circulation

[1]**cur•rent** \'kər-ənt, 'kə-rənt\ *adj* **1 a :** presently elapsing ⟨the *current* month⟩ **b :** occurring in or belonging to the present time ⟨the *current* crisis⟩ **2 :** generally accepted, used, or practiced ⟨*current* theories of government⟩ [derived from Latin *currere* "to run"] **syn** see PREVAILING — **cur•rent•ly** *adv* — **cur•rent•ness** *n*

[2]**current** *n* **1 a :** the part of a fluid body moving continuously in a certain direction **b :** the swiftest part of a stream **c :** a strong or forceful flow **2 :** general course or movement **:** TREND ⟨changed the *current* of our lives⟩ **3 :** a movement of electricity analogous to the flow of a stream of water; *also* **:** the rate of such movement

cur•ri•cle \'kər-i-kəl, 'kə-ri-\ *n* **:** a 2-wheeled chaise usually drawn by two horses [Latin *curriculum* "running, chariot"]

cur•ric•u•lum \kə-'rik-yə-ləm\ *n, pl* **-la** \-lə\ *or* **-lums :** a course of study; *esp* **:** the body of courses offered in a school or college or in one of its departments [Latin, "running, racecourse, chariot", from *currere* "to run"] — **cur•ric•u•lar** \-lər\ *adj*

[1]**cur•ry** \'kər-ē, 'kə-rē\ *vt* **cur•ried; cur•ry•ing 1 :** to dress the coat of (as a horse) with a currycomb **2 :** to treat (tanned leather) especially by incorporating oil or grease [Old French *correer* "to prepare, curry"] — **cur•ri•er** *n* — **curry fa•vor** \-'fā-vər\ **:** to seek to gain favor by flattery or attentions

[2]**cur•ry** *also* **cur•rie** \'kər-ē, 'kə-rē\ *n, pl* **curries 1 :** CURRY POWDER **2 :** a food seasoned with curry powder ⟨shrimp *curry*⟩ [of Dravidian origin]

[3]**curry** *vt* **cur•ried; cur•ry•ing :** to flavor or cook with curry

cur•ry•comb \-ˌkōm\ *n* **:** a comb with rows of metallic teeth or ridges used especially to curry horses — **currycomb** *vt*

curry powder *n* **:** a sharp seasoning consisting of ground spices

[1]**curse** \'kərs\ *n* **1 :** a prayer that harm or injury may come upon someone or something **2 :** a word or an expression used in cursing or swearing **3 :** evil or misfortune that comes as if in answer to a curse **:** a cause of great harm or evil ⟨floods are the *curse* of this region⟩ [Old English *curs*]

[2]**curse** *vb* **1 :** to call upon divine or supernatural power to send injury upon **2 a :** to use profanely insolent language against **:** BLASPHEME **b :** to utter profane or obscene words **:** SWEAR **3 :** to bring great evil upon **:** AFFLICT

cursed \'kər-səd, 'kərst\ *also* **curst** \'kərst\ *adj* **:** being under or deserving a curse — **cursed•ly** *adv* — **cursed•ness** *n*

[1]**cur•sive** \'kər-siv\ *adj* **1 :** written or formed with the strokes of the letters joined together and most of the angles rounded ⟨*cursive* handwriting⟩ **2 :** having a flowing easy character [Medieval Latin *cursivus,* literally, "running", from Latin *currere* "to run"] — **cur•sive•ly** *adv* — **cur•sive•ness** *n*

[2]**cursive** *n* **:** a style of printed letter imitating handwriting

cur•sor \'kər-sər\ *n* **:** a part of a mathematical instrument (as a slide rule) that moves back and forth on another part and usually has a hairline for the purpose of making accurate readings [Latin, "runner", from *currere* "to run"]

cur•so•ry \'kərs-rē, -ə-rē\ *adj* **:** rapidly and often superficially performed **:** HASTY ⟨a *cursory* reading of the book⟩ [Late Latin *cursorius* "of running", from Latin *currere* "to run"] **syn** see SUPERFICIAL — **cur•so•ri•ly** \'kərs-rə-lē, -ə-rə-\ *adv* — **cur•so•ri•ness** \'kərs-rē-nəs, -ə-rē-\ *n*

curt \'kərt\ *adj* **:** rudely abrupt or brief ⟨a *curt* reply⟩ [Latin *curtus* "shortened"] — **curt•ly** *adv* — **curt•ness** *n*

cur•tail \kər-'tāl\ *vt* **:** to shorten or reduce by cutting away the end or another part of [derived from Latin *curtus* "shortened"] **syn** see SHORTEN — **cur•tail•er** *n* — **cur•tail•ment** \-'tāl-mənt\ *n*

[1]**cur•tain** \'kərt-n\ *n* **1 a :** a piece of material hung (as at a window) for decoration, privacy, or control of light and drafts **b :** the screen separating the stage from the auditorium of a theater **2 a :** the ascent or descent of a theater curtain **b :** the time at which a theatrical performance begins **3 :** something that covers, conceals, or separates like a curtain — compare IRON CURTAIN **4 :** CURTAIN WALL [Old French *curtine,* from Late Latin *cortina,* from Latin *cohors* "enclosure, court"] — **curtain** *vt*

curtain call *n* **:** an appearance by a performer usually at a final curtain (as of a play) in response to the applause of the audience

curtain raiser *n* **1 :** a short play used to open a performance **2 :** a usually short and unimportant preliminary to a main event

curtain wall *n* **:** an exterior enclosing wall (as of a skyscraper) that does not support any weight but its own

[1]**curt•sy** *or* **curt•sey** \'kərt-sē\ *n, pl* **curtsies** *or* **curtseys :** a gesture of respect made chiefly by women that consists of a slight lowering of the body and bending of the knees [alteration of *courtesy*]

[2]**curtsy** *or* **curtsey** *vi* **curt•sied** *or* **curt•seyed; curt•sy•ing** *or* **curt•sey•ing :** to make a curtsy

cur•va•ceous \ˌkər-'vā-shəs\ *adj* **:** having a well-proportioned feminine figure marked by full curves

cur•va•ture \'kər-və-ˌchu̇r, -chər\ *n* **1 :** the act of curving **:** the state of being curved **2 :** a measure of the amount of curving of a curved line or surface **3 a :** an abnormal curving (as of a bodily structure) ⟨*curvature* of the spine⟩ **b :** a curved surface (as of an organ)

[1]**curve** \'kərv\ *vb* **1 :** to turn, change, or deviate gradually from a straight line **2 :** to cause to curve **:** BEND [Latin *curvare,* from *curvus* "curved"]

[2]**curve** *n* **1 :** a curving line or surface **:** BEND **2 :** something curved ⟨a *curve* in the road⟩ **3 :** a ball thrown so that it swerves from its normal course — called also *curve ball* **4 :** a line connecting points on a graph or in a coordinate system that are determined by an equation or are plotted from data **5 :** the path of a moving point — **curved** \'kərvd\ *adj*

[1]**cur•vet** \ˌkər-'vet\ *n* **:** a prancing leap of a horse in which first the forelegs and then the hind are raised so that for an instant all the legs are in the air [Italian *corvetta,* from Middle French *courbette,* from *courber* "to curve", from Latin *curvare*]

[2]**curvet** *vi* **cur•vet•ted** *or* **cur•vet•ed; cur•vet•ting** *or* **cur•vet•ing :** to make a curvet; *also* **:** CAPER, PRANCE

cur•vi•lin•ear \ˌkər-və-'lin-ē-ər\ *adj* **:** consisting of, characterized by, or bounded by curved lines

[1]**cush•ion** \'ku̇sh-ən\ *n* **1 :** a soft pillow or pad to rest on or against **2 :** something resembling a cushion in use, shape, or softness **3 :** a pad of springy rubber along the inside of the rim of a billiard table **4 :** something serving to lighten the effects of disturbances or disorders ⟨saved money as a *cushion* against hard times⟩ [Middle French *coissin,* derived from Latin *coxa* "hip"]

[2]**cushion** *vt* **cush•ioned; cush•ion•ing** \'ku̇sh-ning, -ə-ning\ **1 :** to seat or place on a cushion **2 :** to furnish with a cushion ⟨*cushion* the bench⟩ **3 a :** to lighten the effects of ⟨*cushion* the

\ə\ **abut**	\au̇\ **out**	\i\ **tip**	\ȯ\ **saw**	\u̇\ **foot**
\ər\ **further**	\ch\ **chin**	\ī\ **life**	\ȯi\ **coin**	\y\ **yet**
\a\ **mat**	\e\ **pet**	\j\ **job**	\th\ **thin**	\yü\ **few**
\ā\ **take**	\ē\ **easy**	\ng\ **sing**	\t͟h\ **this**	\yu̇\ **cure**
\ä\ **cot, cart**	\g\ **go**	\ō\ **bone**	\ü\ **food**	\zh\ **vision**

blow⟩ **b** : to shield from harm or injury : PROTECT ⟨*cushioned* the children from harsh realities⟩

Cush•it•ic \ˌkəsh-ˈit-ik, ku̇sh-\ *n* : a subfamily of the Afro-Asiatic language family comprising various languages spoken in East Africa and especially in Ethiopia and Somaliland [*Cush* (Kush), ancient country in the Nile valley] — **Cushitic** *adj*

cushy \ˈku̇sh-ē\ *adj* **cushi•er**; **cushi•est** : EASY ⟨a *cushy* job⟩ [Hindi *khush* "pleasant", from Persian *khūsh*] — **cushi•ly** \ˈku̇sh-ə-lē\ *adv*

cusk \ˈkəsk\ *n, pl* **cusk** *or* **cusks** : a large edible marine fish related to the cod [probably alteration of *tusk,* a kind of codfish]

cusp \ˈkəsp\ *n* : APEX 1, POINT: as **a** : either of the pointed ends of a crescent moon **b** : a pointed projection formed by or arising from the intersection of two arcs **c** : a point on the grinding surface of a tooth **d** : a fold or flap of a cardiac valve [Latin *cuspis* "point"]

cus•pid \ˈkəs-pəd\ *n* : CANINE [back-formation from *bicuspid*]

cus•pi•dor \ˈkəs-pə-ˌdȯr\ *n* : SPITTOON [Portuguese *cuspidouro,* from *cuspir* "to spit", from Latin *conspuere,* from *com-* + *spuere* "to spit"]

[1]**cuss** \ˈkəs\ *n* **1** : CURSE **2** : FELLOW ⟨an obstinate *cuss*⟩ [alteration of *curse*]

[2]**cuss** *vb* : CURSE 1, 2 — **cuss•er** *n*

cuss•ed \ˈkəs-əd\ *adj* **1** : CURSED **2** : PERVERSE 2, 3, OBSTINATE — **cuss•ed•ly** *adv*

cuss•ed•ness \-əd-nəs\ *n* : disposition to perversity : OBSTINACY

cus•tard \ˈkəs-tərd\ *n* : a usually sweetened mixture of milk and eggs baked, boiled, or frozen [Middle English, a kind of pie]

custard apple *n* **1** : any of several chiefly tropical American soft-fleshed edible fruits; *also* : a tree or shrub bearing such fruit **2** : PAPAW 2

cus•to•di•al \ˌkə-ˈstōd-ē-əl\ *adj* : of or relating to custody, custodians, or custodianship

cus•to•di•an \ˌkə-ˈstōd-ē-ən\ *n* : one that guards and protects or maintains: as **a** : one entrusted with guarding prisoners or inmates **b** : one entrusted with guarding and keeping property or records; *esp* : JANITOR — **cus•to•di•an•ship** \-ˌship\ *n*

cus•to•dy \ˈkəs-təd-ē\ *n* : immediate charge and control (as of a ward or suspect) exercised by a person or an authority [Latin *custodia* "guarding", from *custos* "guardian"]

[1]**cus•tom** \ˈkəs-təm\ *n* **1 a** : a usage or practice common to many or habitual with an individual **b** : long-established practice considered as unwritten law **2** *pl* : duties, tolls, or imposts imposed by the law of a country on imports or exports **3** : support given to a business by its customers : CUSTOMERS [Old French *costume, custume,* from Latin *consuetudo,* from *consuescere* "to accustom" from *com-* + *suescere* "to accustom"] **syn** see HABIT

[2]**custom** *adj* **1** : made or performed according to personal order ⟨*custom* clothes⟩ **2** : specializing in custom work or operation ⟨*custom* tailor⟩

cus•tom•ary \ˈkəs-tə-ˌmer-ē\ *adj* **1** : based on or established by custom ⟨*customary* rent⟩ **2** : commonly practiced or observed : HABITUAL ⟨*customary* courtesy⟩ **syn** see USUAL — **cus•tom•ar•i•ly** \ˌkəs-tə-ˈmer-ə-lē\ *adv* — **cus•tom•ar•i•ness** \ˈkəs-tə-ˌmer-ē-nəs\ *n*

cus•tom–built \ˌkəs-təm-ˈbilt\ *adj* : built to individual order

cus•tom•er \ˈkəs-tə-mər\ *n* **1** : one that buys from or patronizes a business especially on a regular basis **2** : PERSON, FELLOW ⟨a queer *customer*⟩

cus•tom•house \ˈkəs-təm-ˌhau̇s\ *also* **cus•toms•house** \-təmz-\ *n* : a building where customs are collected and where ships are entered and cleared at a port

cus•tom–made \ˌkəs-təm-ˈmād, -ˈād\ *adj* : made to individual order

[1]**cut** \ˈkət\ *vb* **cut**; **cut•ting** **1 a** : to penetrate with or as if with an edged instrument : GASH **b** : to function as or like an edged tool ⟨the knife *cuts* well⟩ **c** : to allow being shaped, penetrated, or divided with an edged tool ⟨cheese *cuts* easily⟩ **d** : to work with or as if with an edged tool ⟨a tailor busy *cutting*⟩ **e** : to experience the growth of (a tooth) through the gum **2 a** : to hurt emotionally **b** (1) : to strike sharply (2) : to strike or strike at (as a ball) with a glancing stroke **c** : to have validity or effect ⟨that argument *cuts* both ways⟩ **3 a** : to make less in amount ⟨*cut* costs⟩ **b** : to shorten by omissions ⟨*cut* a manuscript⟩ **c** : DILUTE ⟨*cut* whiskey with water⟩ **4 a** : TRIM 3a, PARE ⟨*cut* hair⟩ **b** : MOW, REAP ⟨*cut* hay⟩ **c** : to divide into parts with an edged tool ⟨*cut* the pie⟩ **d** : FELL, HEW ⟨*cut* timber⟩ **5** : to remove or separate from a group ⟨*cut* two players from the squad⟩ **6 a** : to turn sharply ⟨*cut* right to avoid a collision⟩ ⟨*cut* the wheels⟩ **b** : to move fast ⟨*cut* along the road⟩ **c** : to take a short or direct route ⟨*cut* across the campus⟩ **d** : INTERSECT, CROSS ⟨lines *cutting* other lines⟩ **e** : BREAK, INTERRUPT ⟨*cut* our supply line⟩ **f** : to divide a deck of cards or separate a group of cards from the deck **g** : to divide (as money) into shares : SPLIT **h** : to make a sudden transition from one sound or image to another (as in a film) **7 a** : CEASE, STOP ⟨*cut* the nonsense⟩ **b** : to refuse to recognize (an acquaintance) **c** : to fail to attend (as a meeting or class) **d** : to stop (a motor) by opening a switch **e** : to cease photographing a motion picture **8 a** : to make or give shape to with or as if with an edged tool ⟨*cut* a hole in the wall⟩ ⟨the floodwaters *cut* new channels⟩ ⟨*cut* a diamond⟩ **b** : to record sounds on (a phonograph record) **9 a** : to engage in : PERFORM ⟨*cut* a caper⟩ **b** : to give the appearance of ⟨*cuts* a fine figure⟩ [Middle English *cutten*] — **cut corners** : to reduce cost, time, or difficulty often at the expense of quality — **cut short** : to interrupt or end abruptly

[2]**cut** *n* **1** : something cut or cut off: as **a** : a yield of products cut especially during one harvest **b** : a part of a meat carcass ⟨a rib *cut*⟩ **c** : an allotted part : SHARE ⟨took our *cut* and left⟩ **2** : an effect produced by or as if by cutting: as **a** : a wound made by something sharp : GASH **b** : a surface or outline made by cutting ⟨a smooth *cut* in a board⟩ **c** : a passage made by cutting ⟨a railroad *cut*⟩ **d** : a grade or step especially in a social scale ⟨a *cut* above the neighbors⟩ **e** : a pictorial illustration **3** : the act or an instance of cutting: as **a** : a gesture or expression that wounds the feelings ⟨an unkind *cut*⟩ **b** : a straight path or course **c** : STROKE, BLOW ⟨took a *cut* at the ball⟩ **d** : the act of reducing or removing a part ⟨a *cut* in pay⟩ **e** : the act of or a turn at cutting cards ⟨it's your *cut*⟩ **4** : a voluntary absence from a class **5** : an abrupt transition from one sound or image to another in motion pictures, radio, or television **6** : the shape and style in which a thing is cut, formed, or made ⟨clothes of the latest *cut*⟩ **7** : BAND 5e

cut–and–dried \ˌkət-n-ˈdrīd\ *also* **cut–and–dry** \-ˈdrī\ *adj* : being or done according to a plan, set procedure, or formula : ROUTINE

cu•ta•ne•ous \kyu̇-ˈtā-nē-əs\ *adj* : of, relating to, or affecting the skin ⟨*cutaneous* infection⟩ [Latin *cutis* "skin"] — **cu•ta•ne•ous•ly** *adv*

[1]**cut•away** \ˈkət-ə-ˌwā\ *adj* : having or showing parts removed ⟨a *cutaway* model of a beehive showing its inner structure⟩

[2]**cutaway** *n* **1** : a coat with skirts tapering from the front waistline to form tails at the back **2** : a cutaway picture or representation

cut•back \ˈkət-ˌbak\ *n* **1** : something cut back **2** : DECREASE ⟨a *cutback* in employment⟩

cut back \ˈkət-ˈbak, ˌkət-\ *vb* **1** : to shorten by cutting : PRUNE **2** : DECREASE, REDUCE ⟨*cut back* production⟩ **3** : to interrupt the sequence of a plot by introducing events prior to those last presented

cut down *vb* **1** : to remake in a smaller size ⟨*cut down* the coat⟩ **2** : to strike down by or as if by cutting **3 a** : REDUCE 1b ⟨*cut down* the accident rate⟩ **b** : to reduce or curtail volume or activity ⟨*cut down* on smoking⟩

cute \ˈkyüt\ *adj* **1** : SHREWD, WILY **2** : attractive or pretty especially in a dainty or delicate way **3** : obviously straining for effect [short for *acute*] — **cute•ly** *adv* — **cute•ness** *n*

cute•sy *also* **cute•sie** \ˈkyüt-sē\ *adj* **cute•si•er**; **-est** : self-consciously cute ⟨*cutesy* mannerisms⟩

cut glass *n* : glass ornamented with patterns cut into its surface and polished

cu•ti•cle \ˈkyüt-i-kəl\ *n* **1** : SKIN, PELLICLE: as **a** : an external sheathing layer secreted usually by epidermal cells **b** : the epidermis when it is the outermost layer **c** : a thin continuous fatty film on the external surface of many higher plants **2** : dead or horny epidermis [Latin *cuticula,* from *cutis* "skin"] — **cu•tic•u•lar** \kyu̇-ˈtik-yə-lər\ *adj*

cut•ie *or* **cut•ey** \ˈkyüt-ē\ *n, pl* **cuties** *or* **cuteys** : one that is cute; *esp* : a pretty girl

cu•tin \ˈkyüt-n\ *n* : an insoluble substance containing waxes, fatty acids, soaps, and resinous matter that forms a continuous layer on the outer epidermal wall of a plant [Latin *cutis* "skin"] — **cu•tin•ized** \-n-ˌīzd\ *adj*

cut in *vb* **1** : to thrust oneself into a position between others or belonging to another **2** : to join in something suddenly ⟨*cut in* on the conversation⟩ **3 :** to interrupt a dancing couple and take one of them as a partner **4 :** INCLUDE ⟨*cut* me *in* on the profits⟩

cut•lass \'kət-ləs\ *n* **:** a short curved sword formerly used by sailors on warships **[**Middle French *coutelas,* from *coutel* "knife", from Latin *culter* "knife, plowshare"**]**

cut•ler \'kət-lər\ *n* **:** one that makes, deals in, or repairs cutlery **[**Middle French *coutelier,* from Late Latin *cultellarius,* from Latin *cultellus* "knife"**]**

cut•lery \'kət-lə-rē\ *n* **1 :** edged or cutting tools; *esp* **:** implements for cutting and eating food **2 :** the business of a cutler

cut•let \'kət-lət\ *n* **:** a small slice of meat for broiling or frying **[**French *côtelette,* from Old French *costelette,* from *coste* "rib, side", from Latin *costa***]**

cut•off \'kət-,ȯf\ *n* **1 :** the action of cutting off **2 a :** the channel formed when a stream cuts through the neck of an oxbow **b :** SHORTCUT 1 **3 :** a device for cutting off — **cutoff** *adj*

cut off \,kət-'ȯf, 'kət-\ *vt* **1 :** to kill usually suddenly or prematurely **2 :** to stop the passage of ⟨*cut off* our supplies⟩ **3 :** SEPARATE, ISOLATE ⟨*cut off* by the sudden attack⟩ **4 :** DISINHERIT **5 a :** to stop the operation of ⟨*cut off* a motor⟩ **b :** to stop or interrupt while in communication ⟨the operator *cut* me *off*⟩ **6 :** INTERCEPT 2 ⟨an angle whose rays *cut off* an arc on a circle⟩

cut•out \'kət-,au̇t\ *n* **:** something cut out or prepared for cutting out from something else ⟨a page of animal *cutouts*⟩ — **cutout** *adj*

[1]**cut out** \,kət-'au̇t, 'kət-\ *vb* **1 :** to be all that one can handle ⟨they have their work *cut out* for them⟩ **2 :** SUPPLANT 1 ⟨*cut out* a competitor⟩ **3 :** to remove from a series or circuit **:** DISCONNECT **4 :** to cease operating ⟨the engine *cut out*⟩ **5 :** ELIMINATE ⟨*cut out* the waste⟩

[2]**cut out** *adj* **:** fitted by nature ⟨not *cut out* to be a lawyer⟩

cut•over \,kət-,ō-vər\ *adj* **:** having most of its salable timber cut ⟨*cutover* land⟩

cut•purse \'kət-,pərs\ *n* **:** PICKPOCKET

cut–rate \'kət-'rāt\ *adj* **1 :** selling or offered at a reduced rate or price ⟨a *cut-rate* store⟩ **2 :** SECOND-RATE, CHEAP

cut•ter \'kət-ər\ *n* **1 :** one that cuts ⟨a diamond *cutter*⟩ ⟨a cookie *cutter*⟩ **2 a :** a boat used by warships for carrying passengers and stores to and from the shore **b :** a small one-masted sailing boat that usually carries two headsails **c :** a small armed boat in the coast guard **3 :** a small sleigh

[1]**cut•throat** \'kət-,thrōt\ *n* **:** a murderous person **:** MURDERER

[2]**cutthroat** *adj* **1 :** MURDEROUS, CRUEL ⟨a *cutthroat* rogue⟩ **2 :** MERCILESS, RUTHLESS ⟨*cutthroat* competition⟩

cut time *n* **:** ALLA BREVE

[1]**cut•ting** *n* **1 :** something cut or cut off or out: as **a :** a section of a plant capable of developing into a new plant **b :** HARVEST 2 **2 :** something made by cutting; *esp* **:** RECORD 4

[2]**cutting** *adj* **1 :** designed for cutting **:** SHARP ⟨the *cutting* edge of a knife⟩ **2 :** piercingly cold ⟨a *cutting* wind⟩ **3 :** SARCASTIC **syn** see INCISIVE — **cut•ting•ly** \-ing-lē\ *adv*

cut•tle•bone \'kət-l-,bōn\ *n* **:** the hard internal shell of cuttlefishes used for making polishing powder or for supplying birds housed in cages with lime and salts **[**Middle English *cotul* "cuttlefish"**]**

cut•tle•fish \-,fish\ *n* **:** a 10-armed marine mollusk differing from the related squid in having an internal shell composed of compounds of calcium **[**Middle English *cotul* "cuttlefish", from Old English *cudele***]**

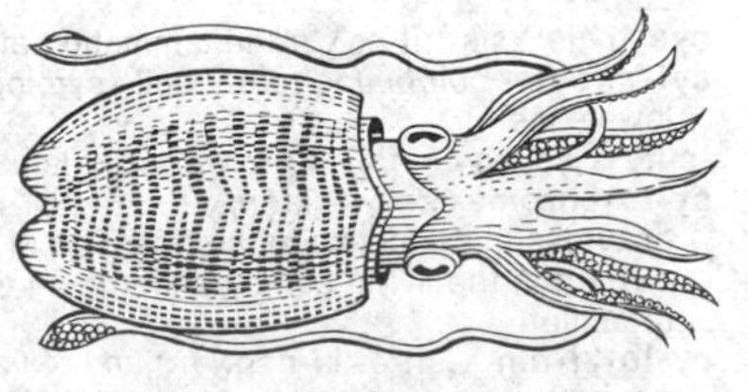

cuttlefish

cut•up \'kət-,əp\ *n* **:** one who clowns or acts boisterously

cut up \,kət-'əp, 'kət-\ *vb* **1 a :** to cut or be cut into parts or pieces **b :** to distress deeply ⟨*cut up* by the criticism⟩ **2 :** to damage by or as if by cutting ⟨the truck *cut up* the lawn⟩ **3 :** to clown or act boisterously

cut•wa•ter \-,wȯt-ər, -,wät-\ *n* **:** the forepart of a ship's stem

cut•worm \-,wərm\ *n* **:** any of various smooth-bodied moth caterpillars that hide by day and feed especially on plant stems near ground level at night

-cy \sē\ *n suffix, pl* **-cies :** action **:** practice ⟨mendicancy⟩ **:** rank **:** office ⟨chaplaincy⟩ **:** body **:** class ⟨magistracy⟩ **:** state **:** quality ⟨accuracy⟩ ⟨bankruptcy⟩ — often replacing a final *-t* or *-te* of the base word **[**Old French *-cie,* from Latin *-tia***]**

cyan- *or* **cyano-** *combining form* **1 :** dark blue **:** blue ⟨*cyanosis*⟩ **2 :** cyanogen ⟨*cyanide*⟩ **3 :** cyanide **[**Greek *kyanos* "dark blue enamel"**]**

cy•an•a•mide \sī-'an-ə-məd\ *n* **1 :** a caustic acidic compound CH_2N_2 that consists of carbon, hydrogen, and nitrogen **2 :** a grayish black lumpy or powdered substance $CaCN_2$ consisting of calcium, carbon, and nitrogen that is used as a fertilizer — called also *calcium cyanamide*

cy•a•nide \'sī-ə-,nīd, -nəd\ *n* **:** a compound of cyanogen with an element or another radical: as **a :** POTASSIUM CYANIDE **b :** SODIUM CYANIDE

cy•an•o•gen \sī-'an-ə-jən\ *n* **1 :** a univalent radical –CN that consists of carbon and nitrogen and is present in simple and complex cyanides **2 :** a colorless flammable poisonous gas $(CN)_2$

cy•a•no•sis \,sī-ə-'nō-səs\ *n* **:** a bluish or purplish discoloration (as of skin) due to lack of oxygen in the blood — **cy•a•not•ic** \,sī-ə-'nät-ik\ *adj*

cy•ber•net•ics \,sī-bər-'net-iks\ *n* **:** the science of communication and control theory that is concerned especially with the comparative study of automatic control systems (as the nervous system and brain and mechanical-electrical communication systems) **[**Greek *kybernētēs* "pilot, governor", from *kybernan* "to steer, govern"**]** — **cy•ber•net•ic** \-ik\ *adj*

cy•cad \'sī-kəd\ *n* **:** any of a family of tropical evergreen plants that resemble palms but are actually gymnosperms **[**New Latin *Cycad-, Cycas,* genus name**]**

cycl- *or* **cyclo-** *combining form* **:** circle ⟨*cyclo*meter⟩ **[**Greek *kyklos***]**

cy•cla•men \'sī-klə-mən, 'sik-lə-\ *n* **:** any of a genus of plants of the primrose family grown as pot plants for their showy nodding flowers **[**Greek *kyklaminos***]**

[1]**cy•cle** \'sī-kəl, *6 is also* 'sik-əl\ *n* **1 :** a period of time taken up by a series of events or actions that repeat themselves regularly and in the same order ⟨the *cycle* of the seasons⟩ **2 a :** a course or series of events or activities that recur regularly and usually lead back to the starting point ⟨the *cycle* of the blood from the heart, through the blood vessels, and back again⟩ **b :** one complete performance of a series of recurring events: as (1) **:** one complete series of changes in voltage and current direction of an alternating electric current (2) **:** one complete set of consecutive changes in value of a sequence of numbers or digits which repeats itself **3 :** a circular or spiral arrangement; *esp* **:** a whorl of floral leaves **4 :** a long period of time **:** AGE **5 a :** a group of poems, plays, novels, or songs treating the same theme **b :** a series of narratives dealing typically with the exploits of a legendary hero **6 a :** BICYCLE **b :** TRICYCLE **c :** MOTORCYCLE **[**Late Latin *cyclus,* from Greek *kyklos* "circle, wheel, cycle"**]** — **cy•clic** \'sī-klik, 'sik-lik\ *or* **cy•cli•cal** \'sī-kli-kəl, 'sik-li-\ *adj* — **cy•cli•cal•ly** \-kə-lē, -klē\ *adv*

[2]**cy•cle** \'sī-kəl, *2 is also* 'sik-əl\ *vb* **cy•cled; cy•cling** \'sī-kə-ling, -kling; 'sik-ling, -ə-ling\ **1 a :** to pass or cause to go through a cycle **b :** to recur in cycles **2 :** to ride a cycle — **cy•cler** \'sī-kə-lər, -klər; 'sik-lər, -ə-lər\ *n*

cyclic AMP *n* **:** a nucleotide formed from ATP that is believed to be an important message carrier to cells and a regulator of biological activities at the cellular level

cycling : the sport of bicycle riding and especially bicycle racing

cy•clist \'sī-kə-ləst, -kləst; 'sik-ləst, -ə-ləst\ *n* **:** one who rides a cycle and especially a bicycle

cy•cloid \'sī-,klȯid\ *n* **:** a curve traced out by a point on the circumference of a circle that is rolling along a straight line — **cy•cloi•dal** \sī-'klȯid-l\ *adj*

cy•clom•e•ter \sī-'kläm-ət-ər\ *n* **:** a device designed to record revolutions of a wheel and often used to register distance traversed by a wheeled vehicle

cy•clone \'sī-,klōn\ *n* **1 :** a storm or system of winds that rotates about a center of low atmospheric pressure counterclockwise in the northern hemisphere, advances at a speed of 30 to

\ə\ **abut**	\au̇\ **out**	\i\ **tip**	\ȯ\ **saw**	\u̇\ **foot**
\ər\ **further**	\ch\ **chin**	\ī\ **life**	\ȯi\ **coin**	\y\ **yet**
\a\ **mat**	\e\ **pet**	\j\ **job**	\th\ **thin**	\yü\ **few**
\ā\ **take**	\ē\ **easy**	\ng\ **sing**	\th\ **this**	\yu̇\ **cure**
\ä\ **cot, cart**	\g\ **go**	\ō\ **bone**	\ü\ **food**	\zh\ **vision**

50 kilometers an hour, and often brings abundant rain **2** : TORNADO [Greek *kyklōma* "wheel, coil", from *kykloun* "to go around", from *kyklos* "circle"] — **cy•clon•ic** \sī-'klän-ik\ *adj* — **cy•clon•i•cal•ly** \-'klän-i-kə-lē, -klē\ *adv*

cy•clo•pe•an \,sī-klə-'pē-ən, sī-'klō-pē-\ *adj* **1** *often cap* : of, relating to, or characteristic of a Cyclops **2** : HUGE a, MASSIVE

cy•clo•pe•dia *or* **cy•clo•pae•dia** \,sī-klə-'pēd-ē-ə\ *n* : ENCYCLOPEDIA — **cy•clo•pe•dic** \-'pēd-ik\ *adj*

cy•clops \'sī-,kläps\ *n* **1** *pl* **cy•clo•pes** \sī-'klō-,pēz\ *cap* : one of a race of giants in Greek mythology with a single eye in the middle of the forehead **2** *pl* **cyclops** : any of a genus of small pear-shaped water fleas [Greek *Kyklōps*, from *kyklos* "circle" + *ōps* "eye"]

cy•clo•ra•ma \,sī-klə-'ram-ə, -'räm-\ *n* : a large pictorial representation encircling the spectator and often having real objects as a foreground [*cycl-* + *-orama* (as in *panorama*)] — **cy•clo•ram•ic** \-'ram-ik\ *adj*

cy•clo•sis \sī-'klō-səs\ *n* : the streaming of protoplasm within a cell

cy•clo•stome \'sī-klə-,stōm\ *n* : any of a class (Cyclostomi or Cyclostomata) of lower vertebrates with a large sucking mouth and no jaws [Greek *kyklos* "circle" + *stoma* "mouth"] — **cyclostome** *adj*

cy•clo•thy•mic \,sī-klə-'thī-mik\ *adj* : having a temperament marked by alternate lively and depressed moods [derived from Greek *kyklos* "circle" + *thymos* "mind"]

cy•clo•tron \'sī-klə-,trän\ *n* : an accelerator in which particles (as protons or ions) are propelled by an alternating electric field in a constant magnetic field

cyg•net \'sig-nət\ *n* : a young swan [Middle French *cygne* "swan", from Latin *cygnus*, from Greek *kyknos*]

Cyg•nus \'sig-nəs\ *n* : a northern constellation between Lyra and Pegasus in the Milky Way [Latin, literally, "swan"]

cyl•in•der \'sil-ən-dər\ *n* **1** : the surface traced by a straight line moving parallel to a fixed straight line and intersecting a fixed curve; *also* : the space bounded by any such surface and two parallel planes cutting all the elements **2** : a long round solid or hollow body (as the piston chamber of an engine, the barrel of a pump, or the part of a revolver which turns and holds the cartridges) [Latin *cylindrus*, from Greek *kylindros*, from *kylindein* "to roll"] — **cyl•in•dered** \-dərd\ *adj*

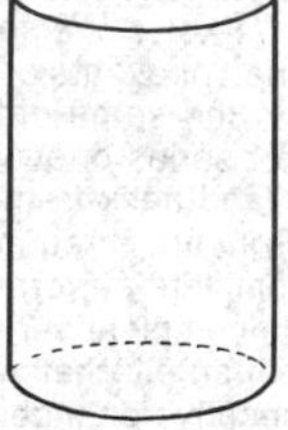

cylinder 1

cy•lin•dri•cal \sə-'lin-dri-kəl\ *or* **cy•lin•dric** \-drik\ *adj* : of, relating to, or having the form or properties of a cylinder — **cy•lin•dri•cal•ly** \-dri-kə-lē, -klē\ *adv*

cym•bal \'sim-bəl\ *n* : a brass plate that is struck with a drumstick or is used in pairs struck glancingly together to make a clashing sound [Old English, from Latin *cymbalum*, from Greek *kymbalon*, from *kymbē* "bowl"]

cym•bid•i•um \sim-'bid-ē-əm\ *n* : any of a genus of tropical Old World orchids with showy boat-shaped flowers [Latin *cymba* "boat", from Greek *kymbē* "bowl, boat"]

cyme \'sīm\ *n* : a broad branching often flat-topped cluster of flowers with a single flower at the end of each branch and with the individual flowers opening in sequence from the center toward the margin of the cluster [Latin *cyma* "cabbage sprout", from Greek *kyma* "swell, cabbage sprout", from *kyein* "to be pregnant"] — **cy•mose** \'sī-,mōs\ *adj*

[1]**Cym•ric** \'kəm-rik, 'kim-\ *adj* **1** : of, relating to, or characteristic of the non-Gaelic Celtic people of Britain or their language **2** : WELSH [Welsh *Cymry* "Welshmen"]

[2]**Cymric** *n* **1** : the non-Gaelic Celtic languages **2** : WELSH 2

cyn•ic \'sin-ik\ *n* **1** *cap* : an adherent or advocate of the view held by some ancient Greek philosophers that virtue is the only good and that its essence lies in self-control and independence **2** : one who believes that human conduct is motivated wholly by self-interest [Latin *cynicus*, a member of a school of ancient Greek philosophers, from Greek *kynikos*, from *kynikos* "like a dog", from *kyōn* "dog"] — **cynic** *adj*

△ **origin** The ancient Greek philosopher Antisthenes taught that virtue is the only goal worth striving for. He and his followers were devoted to an ascetic life and made great show of their contempt for wealth and pleasure. Such a philosopher was called *kynikos*, which means literally "doglike". It is likely that one reason for the name was that Antisthenes taught in a school outside Athens which was called *Kynosarges*. It is likely, however, that most Greeks who applied *kynikos* to these philosophers had been offended by their surly reproaches. *Cynic* has been used in English since the 16th century as a word for a philosopher of this school. The word had not been long in English before it was applied to any faultfinding critic, especially to one who doubts the sincerity of all human motives except self-interest.

cyn•i•cal \'sin-i-kəl\ *adj* : having the attitude or temper of a cynic; *esp* : contemptuously distrustful of human nature and motives ⟨*cynical* remarks about politicians⟩ — **cyn•i•cal•ly** \-kə-lē, -klē\ *adv*

cyn•i•cism \'sin-ə-,siz-əm\ *n* **1** : cynical character or quality **2** : a cynical remark

cy•no•sure \'sī-nə-,shu̇r, 'sin-ə-\ *n* **1** *cap* : the northern constellation Ursa Minor; *also* : NORTH STAR **2** : a center of attraction or attention ⟨the *cynosure* of all eyes⟩ [Latin *cynosura*, from Greek *kynosoura*, from *kynos oura* "dog's tail"]

cy•pher *chiefly British variant of* CIPHER

cy•press \'sī-prəs\ *n* **1** : any of a genus of mostly evergreen trees of the pine family that have overlapping scalelike leaves **2** : either of two large swamp trees of the southern United States with hard red wood **3** : the wood of a cypress tree [Old French *ciprès*, from Latin *cyparissus*, from Greek *kyparissos*]

cyp•ri•pe•di•um \,sip-rə-'pēd-ē-əm\ *n* : any of a genus of leafy-stemmed terrestrial orchids that have large usually showy drooping flowers in the form of a pouch [Late Latin *Cypris*, a name for Venus + Greek *pedilon* "sandal"]

Cy•ril•lic \sə-'ril-ik\ *adj* : of, relating to, or constituting an alphabet used for Russian and various other Slavic languages [Saint *Cyril*, died 869, apostle of the Slavs, reputed inventor of the Cyrillic alphabet]

cyst \'sist\ *n* **1** : a closed sac developing abnormally in a cavity or structure of the body **2** : a covering (as of an internal parasite) resembling a cyst; *also* : a body (as a spore) with such a covering [Greek *kystis* "bladder, pouch"]

cyst- *or* **cysti-** *or* **cysto-** *combining form* : bladder ⟨*cyst*itis⟩ : sac [Greek *kystis*]

-cyst \,sist\ *n combining form* : bladder : sac ⟨blasto*cyst*⟩

cys•te•ine \'sis-tə-,ēn\ *n* : a sulfur-containing amino acid $C_3H_7NO_2S$ that is readily oxidized to cystine [derived from *cystine*]

cys•tic \'sis-tik\ *adj* **1** : of, relating to, or containing cysts **2** : of or relating to the urinary bladder or the gallbladder

cys•ti•cer•cus \,sis-tə-'sər-kəs\ *n, pl* **-cer•ci** \-'sər-,sī\ : a tapeworm larva consisting of a head in a fluid-filled sac [*cyst-* + Greek *kerkos* "tail"]

cystic fibrosis *n* : a hereditary glandular disorder that appears usually in early childhood and is marked especially by defective functioning of the pancreas, respiratory disease, and excessive loss of salt in the sweat

cys•tine \'sis-,tēn\ *n* : an amino acid $C_6H_{12}N_2O_4S_2$ widespread in proteins (as keratins) [from its discovery in bladder stones]

cys•ti•tis \sis-'tīt-əs\ *n* : inflammation of the urinary bladder

cyt- *or* **cyto-** *combining form* : cell ⟨*cyto*logy⟩ [Greek *kytos* "hollow vessel"]

-cyte \,sīt\ *n combining form* : cell ⟨leuko*cyte*⟩

cy•to•chrome \'sīt-ə-,krōm\ *n* : any of several iron-containing enzymes that function in the transport of electrons to molecular oxygen in the living cell by undergoing alternate oxidation and reduction

cy•to•ki•nin \,sīt-ə-'kī-nən\ *n* : any of various substances that promote growth in plants [*cyt-* + *kinin*, a plant growth factor, from Greek *kinein* "to move, stimulate"]

cy•tol•o•gy \sī-'täl-ə-jē\ *n* : a branch of biology dealing with cells — **cy•to•log•i•cal** \,sīt-l-'äj-i-kəl\ *or* **cy•to•log•ic** \-'äj-ik\ *adj* — **cy•to•log•i•cal•ly** \-'äj-i-kə-lē, -klē\ *adv* — **cy•tol•o•gist** \sī-'täl-ə-jəst\ *n*

cy•to•plasm \'sīt-ə-,plaz-əm\ *n* : the protoplasm of the living part of a cell outside the nucleus and its membrane — **cy•to•plas•mic** \,sīt-ə-'plaz-mik\ *adj* — **cy•to•plas•mi•cal•ly** \-mi-kə-lē, -klē\ *adv*

cy•to•plast \'sīt-ə-,plast\ *n* : the cytoplasmic part of a cell — compare PROTOPLAST

cy•to•sine \'sīt-ə-,sēn\ *n* : a pyrimidine base $C_4H_5N_3O$ that codes genetic information in the polynucleotide chain of DNA and RNA — compare ADENINE, GUANINE, THYMINE, URACIL

czar \'zär\ *n* **1** *or* **tsar** *also* **tzar** : the ruler of Russia until the 1917 revolution **2** *also* **tsar** : one having great power or authority ⟨baseball *czar*⟩ [Russian *tsar'*, from Gothic *kaisar* "emperor", from Latin *Caesar*] — **czar•dom** \'zärd-əm\ *n* — **czar•ism** \'zär-,iz-əm\ *n* — **czar•ist** \'zär-əst\ *adj or n*

czar•e•vitch \'zär-ə-,vich\ *n* : an heir of a Russian czar

cza•ri•na \zä-'rē-nə\ *n* **1** : the wife of a czar **2** : a woman who has the rank of czar in her own right

Czech \'chek\ *n* **1** : a native or inhabitant of Czechoslovakia; *esp* : a native or inhabitant of the provinces of Bohemia, Moravia, or Silesia **2** : the Slavic language of the Czechs — **Czech** *adj* — **Czech•ish** \-ish\ *adj*

D d — dystrophy

d \'dē\ *n, pl* **d's** *or* **ds** \'dēz\ *often cap* **1** : the 4th letter of the English alphabet **2** : five hundred in Roman numerals **3** : the musical tone D **4** : a grade rating a student's work as poor

'd \d, əd\ *vb* **1** : HAD ⟨they'*d* gone⟩ **2 a** : WOULD ⟨we'*d* go⟩ **b** : SHOULD ⟨I'*d* go⟩ **3** : DID ⟨where'*d* they go?⟩

-d *symbol* — used after the figure 2 or 3 to indicate the ordinal number second or third ⟨2*d*⟩ ⟨23*d*⟩

[1]**dab** \'dab\ *n* **1** : a sudden blow or thrust : POKE **2** : a gentle touch or stroke : PAT [Middle English *dabbe*]

[2]**dab** *vb* **dabbed**; **dab•bing** **1** : to strike or touch lightly ⟨*dab* at one's eyes with a handkerchief⟩ **2** : to apply lightly or irregularly : DAUB — **dab•ber** *n*

[3]**dab** *n* : DAUB 1 **2** : a small amount

[4]**dab** *n* : FLATFISH; *esp* : any of several flounders [Anglo-French *dabbe*]

dab•ble \'dab-əl\ *vb* **dab•bled**; **dab•bling** \'dab-ling, -ə-ling\ **1** : to wet by splashing : SPATTER **2** : to paddle or play in or as if in water **3** : to work or concern oneself lightly or superficially [perhaps from [2]*dab*] — **dab•bler** \'dab-lər, -ə-lər\

da ca•po \dä-'käp-ō\ *adv or adj* : from the beginning — used as a direction in music to repeat [Italian]

dace \'dās\ *n, pl* **dace** : any of various small North American freshwater fishes related to the carp [Middle French *dars*, from Medieval Latin *darsus*]

da•cha \'däch-ə\ *n* : a Russian country house [Russian, literally, "gift"; from its frequently being the gift of a ruler]

dachs•hund \'däks-,hu̇nt, 'däk-sənt\ *n, pl* **dachs•hunds** *or* **dachs•hun•de** \-,hu̇n-də\ : a small dog of a breed of German origin with a long body, short legs, and long drooping ears [German, from *dachs* "badger" + *hund* "dog"]

dachshund

Da•cron \'dā-,krän, 'dak-,rän\ *trademark* — used for a synthetic polyester textile fiber

dac•tyl \'dak-tl\ *n* : a metrical foot consisting of one accented syllable followed by two unaccented syllables (as in *tenderly)* [Latin *dactylus* "foot of one long syllable followed by two short syllables", from Greek *daktylos*, literally, "finger"; from the fact that the three syllables have the first one longest like the joints of the finger] — **dac•tyl•ic** \dak-'til-ik\ *adj*

dad \'dad\ *n* : FATHER 1a [probably baby talk]

dad•dy \'dad-ē\ *n, pl* **daddies** : FATHER 1a

dad•dy long•legs \,dad-ē-'lông-,legz\ *n* : any of various animals with long slender legs: as **a** : CRANE FLY **b** : an arachnid (order Phalangida) that resembles a true spider but has a small rounded body and long slender legs — called also *harvestman*

da•do \'dād-ō\ *n, pl* **dadoes** **1** : the part of the pedestal of a column between the base and the top moldings **2** : the lower part of an interior wall when specially decorated or faced [Italian, "die, plinth"]

dae•mon *variant of* DEMON

daf•fo•dil \'daf-ə-,dil\ *n* : any of a genus of bulbous herbs with long slender leaves and yellow, white, or pinkish flowers borne in spring; *esp* : one with flowers whose inner parts are arranged to form a trumpet-shaped tube — compare JONQUIL [probably from Dutch *de affodil* "the asphodel"]

daf•fy \'daf-ē\ *adj* **daf•fi•er**; **-est** **1** : CRAZY 2a, INSANE **2** : SILLY 1,2, FOOLISH [obsolete English *daff* "fool"]

daft \'daft\ *adj* **1** : SILLY 1, 2, FOOLISH **2** : CRAZY 2a, INSANE [Middle English *dafte* "gentle, stupid"] — **daft•ly** *adv* — **daft•ness** \'daft-nəs, 'daf-\ *n*

dag•ger \'dag-ər\ *n* **1** : a short weapon for stabbing **2** : a character † used as a reference mark or to indicate a death date [Middle English]

da•guerre•o•type \də-'ger-ē-ə-,tīp, -'gər-ə-,\ *n* : an early photograph produced on a plate of silver or silver-covered copper; *also* : the process of producing such pictures [French *daguerréotype*, from L. J. M. *Daguerre*, died 1851, French painter]

dahl•ia \'dal-yə, 'däl-\ *n* : any of a genus of American tuberous-rooted herbs related to the daisies that have flower heads with brightly colored rays [Anders *Dahl*, died 1789, Swedish botanist]

[1]**dai•ly** \'dā-lē\ *adj* **1 a** : occurring, done, produced, or used every day or every weekday ⟨a *daily* newspaper⟩ **b** : of or relating to every day ⟨a *daily* visitor⟩ **2** : computed in terms of one day ⟨*daily* wages⟩ — **daily** *adv*

[2]**daily** *n, pl* **dailies** : a newspaper published every weekday

daily double *n* : a system of betting (as on horse races) in which the bettor must pick the winners of two stipulated races in order to win

dai•mon \'dī-,mōn\ *n, pl* **dai•mo•nes** \'dī-mə-,nēz\ *or* **daimons** : DEMON 1,3 [Greek *daimōn*]

dai•myo *or* **dai•mio** \'dī-mē-,ō, dī-'myō\ *n, pl* **daimyos** *or* **daimios** : a Japanese feudal baron [Japanese *daimyō*]

[1]**dain•ty** \'dānt-ē\ *n, pl* **dainties** : something that tastes delicious : DELICACY [Old French *deintié*, from Latin *dignitas* "dignity, worth"]

[2]**dainty** *adj* **dain•ti•er**; **-est** **1** : TASTY 1, DELICIOUS **2** : delicately pretty ⟨a *dainty* flower⟩ **3** : having or showing delicate or discriminating taste : FASTIDIOUS ⟨a *dainty* eater⟩ — **dain•ti•ly** \'dānt-l-ē\ *adv* — **dain•ti•ness** \'dānt-ē-nəs\ *n*

dai•qui•ri \'dī-kə-rē, 'dak-ə-\ : a cocktail made of rum, lime juice, and sugar [*Daiquiri*, Cuba]

dairy \'deər-ē, 'daər-\ *n, pl* **dair•ies** **1** : a place where milk is kept and butter or cheese is made **2** : a farm devoted to the production of milk **3** : an establishment for the sale or distribution of milk and milk products [Middle English *deye* "dairymaid", from Old English *dǣge* "kneader of dough"]

△ **origin** *Dairy* is related to *dough*. Old English *dǣge*, a relative of Old English *dāg*, "dough", meant "a kneader of bread" or "a maid". The Middle English form *deye* meant "maid" or, more specifically, "dairymaid". A dairy, then, is the place where the (dairy)maid works.

dairy breed *n* : a cattle breed developed chiefly for milk production

dairy•ing \'der-ē-ing\ *n* : the business of operating a dairy

dairy•maid \-ē-,mād\ *n* : a woman employed in a dairy

dairy•man \-ē-mən, -,man\ *n* : one who operates a dairy farm or works in a dairy

da•is \'dā-əs, 'dī-\ *n* : a raised platform in a hall or large room

[Old French *deis,* from Latin *discus* "dish, quoit"]
dai•sy \'dā-zē\ *n, pl* **daisies 1 :** any of numerous plants of the composite family having flower heads with well-developed ray flowers usually in one or a few whorls: as **a :** a low-growing European herb with white or pink ray flowers — called also *English daisy* **b :** a tall leafy-stemmed American wild flower with a yellow center and long white ray flowers — called also *oxeye daisy* **2 :** the flower head of a daisy [Old English *dægesēage,* from *dæg* "day" + *ēage* "eye"]
Da•ko•ta \də-'kōt-ə\ *n, pl* **Dakotas** *also* **Dakota :** a member of a Siouan people of the northern Mississippi valley
Da•lai La•ma \,däl-,ī-'läm-ə\ *n* **:** the spiritual head of Lamaism [Mongolian *dalai* "ocean"]
dale \'dāl\ *n* **:** VALLEY 1 [Old English *dæl*]
dal•li•ance \'dal-ē-əns\ *n* **:** an act of dallying: as **a :** amorous play (as flirting or caressing) **b :** frivolous wasting of time **:** TRIFLING ⟨a short *dalliance* with radical ideas⟩
dal•ly \'dal-ē\ *vi* **dal•lied; dal•ly•ing 1 a :** to act playfully; *esp* **:** to play amorously **b :** to deal lightly **:** TOY ⟨*dally* with a problem⟩ **2 a :** to waste time ⟨*dally* at one's work⟩ **b :** DAWDLE 2 ⟨*dally* on the way home⟩ [Anglo-French *dalier*] — **dal•li•er** *n*
dal•ma•tian \dal-'mā-shən\ *n, often cap* **:** a large dog of a breed characterized by a white short-haired coat with black or brown spots [from the supposed origin of the breed in Dalmatia]

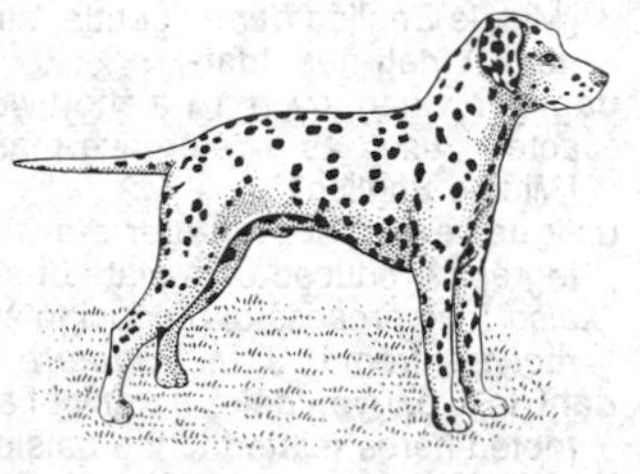
dalmatian

dal•mat•ic \dal-'mat-ik\ *n* **:** a wide-sleeved vestment with slit sides worn by a deacon or prelate [Late Latin *dalmatica,* from Latin *dalmaticus* "of Dalmatia"]
dal se•gno \däl-'sān-yō\ *adv* — used as a direction in music to return to the sign that marks the beginning of a repeat [Italian, "from the sign"]
¹dam \'dam\ *n* **:** a female parent especially of a domestic animal [Middle English *dam, dame* "lady, dam"]
²dam *n* **1 :** a barrier preventing the flow of water or of loose solid materials; *esp* **:** a barrier built across a watercourse **2 :** a body of water confined by a dam [Middle English]
³dam *vt* **dammed; dam•ming 1 :** to provide or restrain with a dam ⟨*dam* a stream⟩ **2 :** to stop up **:** BLOCK ⟨*dam* up an emotion⟩
¹dam•age \'dam-ij\ *n* **1 :** a loss or harm resulting from injury to person, property, or reputation **2** *pl* **:** compensation in money imposed by law for loss or injury [Old French, from *dam* "damage", from Latin *damnum* "damage, penalty"] **syn** see INJURY
²damage *vt* **:** to cause damage to
dam•a•scene \'dam-ə-,sēn\ *vt* **:** to ornament (as iron or steel) with wavy patterns or with inlaid work of precious metals [Middle French *damasquiner,* from *damasquin* "of Damascus"]
dam•ask \'dam-əsk\ *n* **1 :** a firm lustrous reversible figured fabric used especially for household linen **2 :** a tough steel having decorative wavy lines — called also *damask steel* **3 :** a grayish red [Medieval Latin *damascus,* from *Damascus*] — **damask** *adj*
damask rose *n* **:** a large hardy fragrant pink rose grown in Asia Minor as a source of attar of roses [obsolete *Damask* "of Damascus"]
dame \'dām\ *n* **1 :** a woman of rank, station, or authority: as **a** *archaic* **:** the mistress of a household **b :** the wife or daughter of a lord **c** *often cap* **:** a woman who is a member of an order of knighthood — used as a title before a full name or a given name **2 a :** an elderly woman **b :** WOMAN 1 [Middle English, from Old French, from Latin *domina,* feminine of *dominus* "master"]
dam•mar *or* **dam•ar** \'dam-ər\ *n* **:** a clear to yellow resin obtained from Malayan trees and used in varnishes and inks [Malay *damar*]
¹damn \'dam\ *vb* **1 :** to condemn to a punishment or fate; *esp* **:** to condemn to hell **2 :** to condemn as bad or as a failure **3 :** to swear at **:** CURSE [Old French *dampner,* from Latin *damnare,* from *damnum* "damage, penalty"]
²damn *n* **1 :** the utterance of the word *damn* as a curse **2 :** the least bit ⟨not worth a *damn*⟩
³damn *adj or adv* **:** DAMNED
dam•na•ble \'dam-nə-bəl\ *adj* **1 :** liable to or deserving condemnation ⟨*damnable* conduct⟩ **2 :** very bad **:** DETESTABLE ⟨*damnable* weather⟩ — **dam•na•bly** \-blē\ *adv*
dam•na•tion \dam-'nā-shən\ *n* **1 :** the act of damning **2 :** the state of being damned
¹damned \'damd\ *adj* **damned•er** \'dam-dər\; **damned•est** *or* **damnd•est** \'dam-dəst\ **1 :** DAMNABLE ⟨this *damned* smog⟩ **2 :** COMPLETE, UTTER ⟨*damned* nonsense⟩ **3 :** EXTRAORDINARY 1b — used in the superlative ⟨the *damnedest* thing I ever saw⟩
²damned \'damd, 'dam\ *adv* **:** VERY 1, EXTREMELY ⟨a *damned* good job⟩
¹damp \'damp\ *n* **1 :** a harmful gas especially in a coal mine **2 :** slight or moderate wetness **3 :** DAMPER 2 [Dutch or Low German, "vapor"]
²damp *vb* **1 a :** to lessen the activity or intensity of — often used with *down* ⟨failure *damped* their enthusiasm⟩ ⟨*damp* down a furnace⟩ **b :** to check the vibration or oscillation of **2 :** DAMPEN 2
³damp *adj* **1 :** lacking in vigor or spirit **:** DEPRESSED **2 :** slightly or moderately wet **:** MOIST ⟨a *damp* cellar⟩ — **damp•ly** *adv* — **damp•ness** *n*
damp•en \'dam-pən\ *vb* **damp•ened; damp•en•ing** \'damp-ning, -ə-ning\ **1 :** to check or diminish in activity or vigor **:** DEADEN **2 :** to make or become damp — **damp•en•er** \'damp-nər, -ə-nər\ *n*
damp•er \'dam-pər\ *n* **1 :** a device that damps: as **a :** a valve or plate (as in the flue of a furnace) for regulating the draft **b :** a small felted block to stop the vibration of a piano string **c :** a device for checking oscillation **2 :** a dulling or deadening influence ⟨put a *damper* on the celebration⟩
dam•sel \'dam-zəl\ *n* **:** a young woman [Old French *dameisele,* derived from Latin *domina* "lady"]
dam•sel•fly \'dam-zəl-,flī\ *n* **:** any of numerous insects that are closely related to the dragonflies but have laterally projecting eyes and fold the wings over the body when at rest
dam•son \'dam-zən\ *n* **:** an Asian plum grown for its small acid purple fruit; *also* **:** this fruit [Latin *prunum damascenum,* literally, "plum of Damascus"]
¹dance \'dans\ *vb* **1 :** to perform a rhythmic and patterned succession of bodily movements usually to music **2 :** to move quickly up and down or about **3 :** to perform or take part in as a dancer **4 :** to cause to dance [Old French *dancier*] — **danc•er** *n*
²dance *n* **1 :** an act or instance of dancing **2 :** a social gathering for dancing **3 :** a piece of music by which dancing may be guided **4 :** the art of dancing
dan•de•li•on \'dan-dl-,ī-ən\ *n* **:** any of a genus of yellow-flowered herbs of the daisy family; *esp* **:** one with long deeply toothed stemless leaves sometimes grown as a potherb [Middle French *dent de lion,* literally, "lion's tooth"]
dan•der \'dan-dər\ *n* **1 :** minute scales from hair, feathers, or skin that may cause allergy **2 :** TEMPER 4d, ANGER ⟨get one's *dander* up⟩ [alteration of *dandruff*]
dan•di•fy \'dan-di-,fī\ *vt* **-fied; -fy•ing :** to cause to resemble a dandy — **dan•di•fi•ca•tion** \,dan-di-fə-'kā-shən\ *n*
dan•dle \'dan-dl\ *vt* **dan•dled; dan•dling** \-dling, -dl-ing\ **:** to move (as a baby) up and down in one's arms or on one's knee [origin unknown]
dan•druff \'dan-drəf\ *n* **:** a thin whitish flaky crust that forms especially on the scalp and is shed as scales [origin unknown]
¹dan•dy \'dan-dē\ *n, pl* **dandies 1 :** a man who gives exaggerated attention to dress **2 :** something excellent in its class [origin unknown] — **dan•dy•ish** \-dē-ish\ *adj* — **dan•dy•ish•ly** *adv*
²dandy *adj* **dan•di•er; -est :** very good **:** FIRST-RATE
Dane \'dān\ *n* **1 :** a native or inhabitant of Denmark **2 :** a person of Danish descent [Old Norse *Danr*]
dane•geld \'dān-,geld\ *n, often cap* **:** an annual tax once imposed in England supposedly to buy off Danish invaders or to maintain forces to oppose them [Middle English, from *Dan* "Dane" + *geld* "tribute, payment", from Old English *gield*]
Dane•law \'dān-,lȯ\ *n* **1 :** the law in force in the part of England held by the Danes before the Norman Conquest **2 :** the part of England under the Danelaw
dan•ger \'dān-jər\ *n* **1 :** exposure or liability to injury, harm, or evil ⟨their lives were in *danger*⟩ **2 :** a case or cause of danger ⟨the *dangers* of mining⟩ [Middle English *daungier* "jurisdiction, liability", from Old French *dongier, dangier* "jurisdiction", de-

rived from Latin *dominium* "dominion, ownership"]
• **syn** DANGER, PERIL, HAZARD, RISK mean a threat of loss, injury, or death. DANGER implies possible but not necessarily inescapable harm; PERIL suggests imminent danger and cause for fear; HAZARD implies danger from chance or something beyond one's control; RISK implies danger following on a chance voluntarily taken.

dan•ger•ous \'dānj-rəs, -ə-rəs\ *adj* **1** : exposing to or involving danger ⟨a *dangerous* mission⟩ **2** : able or likely to inflict injury ⟨*dangerous* weapons⟩ — **dan•ger•ous•ly** *adv* — **dan•ger•ous•ness** *n*

dan•gle \'dang-gəl\ *vb* **dan•gled**; **dan•gling** \-gə-ling, -gling\ **1** : to hang loosely especially with a swinging motion **2** : to be a hanger-on or dependent **3** : to be left without proper grammatical connection in a sentence ⟨a *dangling* participle⟩ **4** : to cause to dangle : SWING **5** : to keep hanging uncertainly : hold suspended [probably of Scandinavian origin] — **dan•gler** \-gə-lər, -glər\ *n* — **dan•gling•ly** \-gə-ling-lē, -gling-\ *adv*

Dan•iel \'dan-yəl\ *n* — *see* BIBLE table

[1]**Dan•ish** \'dā-nish\ *adj* : of, relating to, or characteristic of Denmark, the Danes, or the Danish language

[2]**Danish** *n* : the Germanic language of the Danes

Danish pastry *n* : a pastry made of rich yeast-raised dough

dank \'dangk\ *adj* : unpleasantly moist or wet [Middle English *danke*] — **dank•ly** *adv* — **dank•ness** *n*

dan•seur \dä^{n}-'sər, dän-\ *n* : a male ballet dancer [French, from *danser* "to dance"]

dan•seuse \dä^{n}-'süz, -'sərz, dän-'süz\ *n* : a female ballet dancer [French, from *danser* "to dance"]

daph•nia \'daf-nē-ə\ *n* : any of a genus of tiny water fleas [New Latin, genus name]

dap•per \'dap-ər\ *adj* **1** : being neat and trim in dress or appearance : SPRUCE **2** : being alert and lively in movement and manners [Dutch, "quick, strong"] — **dap•per•ly** *adv* — **dap•per•ness** *n*

[1]**dap•ple** \'dap-əl\ *n* **1** : a dappled state **2** : a dappled animal [Middle English *dappel-gray* "gray with spots of a different color"]

[2]**dapple** *vb* **dap•pled**; **dap•pling** \'dap-ling, -ə-ling\ : to mark or become marked with numerous usually cloudy and rounded spots of a color or shade different from their background ⟨a *dappled* horse⟩

[1]**dare** \'daər, 'deər\ *vb* **1 a** : to have sufficient courage : be bold enough to ⟨try it if you *dare*⟩ **b** — used as an auxiliary verb ⟨no one *dared* say a word⟩ **2** : to confront boldly ⟨*dared* the dangerous crossing⟩ **3** : to challenge to perform an action especially as proof of courage ⟨I *dare* you⟩ [Old English *dear* "I dare, he dares"]

[2]**dare** *n* : an act or instance of daring : CHALLENGE ⟨dived from the bridge on a *dare*⟩

dare•dev•il \'daər-,dev-əl, 'deər-\ *n* : a recklessly bold person — **daredevil** *adj*

[1]**dar•ing** *adj* : fearlessly ready to take risks — **dar•ing•ly** \-ing-lē\ *adv* — **dar•ing•ness** *n*
• **syn** DARING, RASH, RECKLESS, FOOLHARDY mean exposing oneself to danger more than is sensible or courageous. DARING stresses fearlessness; RASH implies imprudent hastiness; RECKLESS implies complete heedlessness of consequences; FOOLHARDY suggests recklessness and foolish daring. **syn** see in addition ADVENTUROUS

[2]**daring** *n* : venturesome boldness

[1]**dark** \'därk\ *adj* **1 a** : being without light or without much light ⟨in winter it gets *dark* early⟩ **b** : not giving off light ⟨the *dark* side of the moon⟩ **2** : not light in color ⟨a *dark* suit⟩; *esp* : of low or very low lightness ⟨*dark* blue⟩ **3** : not bright and cheerful : GLOOMY ⟨look on the *dark* side of things⟩ **4** : lacking knowledge and culture **5** : not clear to the understanding ⟨*dark* sayings⟩ **6** : SWARTHY ⟨their *dark* good looks⟩ **7** : SECRET 1a ⟨kept their plans *dark*⟩ [Old English *deorc*] **syn** see OBSCURE — **dark•ish** \'där-kish\ *adj* — **dark•ly** \-klē\ *adv* — **dark•ness** \'därk-nəs\ *n*

[2]**dark** *n* **1** : absence of light : DARKNESS **2 a** : a place or time of little or no light **b** : NIGHT, NIGHTFALL ⟨get home before *dark*⟩ **3** : a dark or deep color — **in the dark 1** : in secrecy **2** : in ignorance

dark adaptation *n* : the process by which the eye adapts to seeing in weak light — **dark–adapt•ed** \,därk-ə-'dap-təd\ *adj*

Dark Ages *n pl* : the period from about A.D. 476 to about 1000; *also* : MIDDLE AGES

dark•en \'där-kən\ *vb* **dark•ened**; **dark•en•ing** \'därk-ning, -ə-ning\ **1** : to make or grow dark or darker ⟨*darken* a room⟩ ⟨the sky is *darkening*⟩ **2** : to make less clear : OBSCURE ⟨ignorance *darkens* the understanding⟩ **3** : BESMIRCH, TARNISH ⟨*darken* a reputation⟩ **4** : to make or become gloomy or forbidding ⟨*darkened* their hopes⟩ ⟨a face *darkened* in anger⟩ — **dark•en•er** \'därk-ner, -ə-nər\ *n*

dark horse *n* : a contestant or a political figure whose abilities and chances as a contender are not known ⟨the convention nominated a *dark horse*⟩
△ **origin** Sometimes in a horse race a horse whose name and ability are not widely known puts on a surprisingly good show and defeats his more famous rivals. Such a horse is called *dark,* not because of his color (which might be anything), but because of his obscurity. The use of the term *dark horse* has been extended from racehorses to obscure competitors who do unexpectedly well in contests of other kinds. It is most often used to refer to a little known political candidate who will surprise people if he or she wins.

dark lantern *n* : a lantern that can be closed to conceal the light

darkling *adj* **1** : DARK 1a, 3 **2** : done or taking place in the dark

dark reaction *n* : the part of photosynthesis that does not require light and that uses carbon dioxide in the formation of carbohydrate

dark•room \'därk-,rüm, -,rům\ *n* : a usually small lightproof room used in developing sensitive photographic plates and film

dark•some \'därk-səm\ *adj* : gloomily somber : DARK

[1]**dar•ling** \'där-ling\ *n* **1** : a dearly loved person **2** : FAVORITE [Old English *dēorling,* from *dēore* "dear"]

[2]**darling** *adj* **1** : dearly loved : FAVORITE **2** : very pleasing : CHARMING — **dar•ling•ly** \-ling-lē\ *adv*

[1]**darn** \'därn\ *vb* : to mend with interlacing stitches ⟨*darn* socks⟩ [probably from French dialect *darner*]

[2]**darn** *n* : a place (as in a sock) that has been darned

[3]**darn** *vb* : DAMN 3 [euphemism] — **darn** \'därn\ *or* **darned** \'därnd, 'därn\ *adj or adv*

[4]**darn** *n* : [2]DAMN 2 ⟨don't give a *darn*⟩

dar•nel \'där-nl\ *n* : any of several usually weedy grasses with bristly flower clusters [Middle English]

darning needle *n* **1** : a long needle with a large eye for use in darning **2** : DRAGONFLY, DAMSELFLY

[1]**dart** \'därt\ *n* **1 a** : a small missile usually pointed at one end and feathered on the other **b** *pl* : a game in which darts are thrown at a target **2 a** : something projected with sudden speed; *esp* : a sharp glance **b** : something causing a sudden pain or distress ⟨*darts* of sarcasm⟩ **3** : a stitched tapering fold in a garment **4** : a quick movement ⟨made a *dart* for the door⟩ [Middle French, of Germanic origin]

[1]dart 1a

[2]**dart** *vb* **1** : to throw with a sudden movement ⟨*dart* a javelin⟩ **2** : to thrust or move suddenly or rapidly

dart•er \'därt-ər\ *n* : any of numerous small American freshwater fishes closely related to the perches

Dar•win•ian \där-'win-ē-ən\ *adj* : of or relating to Charles Darwin, his theories, or his followers — **Darwinian** *n*

Dar•win•ism \'där-wə-,niz-əm\ *n* : a theory of evolution that explains how species of plants and animals arose and continue to arise by variation among offspring of a given plant or animal, by the survival of well-adapted variations in the process of natural selection, and by the gradual accumulation of differences over time — **Dar•win•ist** \-wə-nəst\ *n or adj*

[1]**dash** \'dash\ *vb* **1** : to knock, hurl, or thrust violently ⟨the storm *dashed* the boat against a reef⟩ **2** : to break by striking or knocking ⟨the statue was *dashed* to pieces when it fell⟩ **3** : SPLASH 1b, SPATTER ⟨clothes *dashed* with mud⟩ **4 a**

\ə\ abut	\aů\ **out**	\i\ **tip**	\ȯ\ **saw**	\ů\ **foot**
\ər\ further	\ch\ **chin**	\ī\ **life**	\ȯi\ **coin**	\y\ **yet**
\a\ mat	\e\ pet	\j\ **job**	\th\ **thin**	\yü\ **few**
\ā\ take	\ē\ **easy**	\ng\ **sing**	\t͟h\ **this**	\yů\ **cure**
\ä\ cot, cart	\g\ **go**	\ō\ **bone**	\ü\ **food**	\zh\ **vision**

: FRUSTRATE 1 ⟨our hopes were *dashed* every time⟩ **b :** to lower in spirit or mood : DEPRESS **5 :** to affect by mixing in something different ⟨oil *dashed* with vinegar⟩ **6 :** to perform or finish hastily ⟨*dash* off a letter⟩ **7 :** to move with sudden speed [Middle English *dasshen*] — **dash•er** *n*

[2]dash *n* **1 :** a sudden burst or splash ⟨a *dash* of cold water⟩ **2 a :** a stroke of a pen **b :** a punctuation mark — used chiefly to indicate a break in the thought or structure of a sentence **3 :** a small usually distinctive addition ⟨a *dash* of salt⟩ **4 :** a flashy display **5:** animation in style and action ⟨a leader of *dash* and vigor⟩ **6 a :** a sudden rush or attempt ⟨made a *dash* for the exit⟩ **b :** a short fast race **7 :** a long click or buzz forming a letter or part of a letter (as in the Morse code) **8 :** DASHBOARD 2

dash•board \ˈdash-ˌbōrd, -ˌbȯrd\ *n* **1 :** a screen on the front of a vehicle (as a carriage) to keep out water, mud, or snow **2 :** a panel extending across an automobile or aircraft below the windshield and usually containing dials and controls

da•shi•ki \də-ˈshē-kē\ *n* **:** a usually brightly colored loose-fitting pullover garment [Yoruba (a language of western Africa) *danshiki*]

dash•ing *adj* **1 :** marked by vigorous action ⟨a *dashing* attack⟩ **2 :** marked by smartness especially in dress and manners ⟨made a *dashing* appearance⟩ — **dash•ing•ly** \-ing-lē\ *adv*

das•tard \ˈdas-tərd\ *n* **:** COWARD; *esp* **:** one who commits dastardly acts [Middle English]

das•tard•ly \-lē\ *adj* **:** mean and treacherously cowardly — **das•tard•li•ness** *n*

da•ta \ˈdāt-ə, ˈdat-, ˈdät-\ *n sing or pl* **1 :** factual information (as measurements or statistics) used as a basis for reasoning, discussion, or calculation **2 :** DATUM [plural of *datum*]

data processing *n* **:** the process of turning raw data into a form that a computer can use and then having the computer perform useful operations on the data

[1]date \ˈdāt\ *n* **:** the oblong edible fruit of a tall Old World palm; *also* **:** this palm [Old French, derived from Latin *dactylus,* from Greek *daktylos,* literally, "finger"]

△ **origin** The *date* that means "the fruit of the date palm" is not related to the *date* that means "a time". The earlier *date* is descended from Greek *daktylos.* The primary meaning of *daktylos* is "finger", but the word was also used for the fruit. The reason for this extension of meaning is debated. Some suggest that the pinnately divided leaves of the date palm look rather like fingers and that this fact gave the fruit its name. This account would be more convincing if the tree, rather than its fruit, had been named *daktylos.* It is more likely that the clustered dates themselves were felt to resemble fingers.

[2]date *n* **1 a :** the time at which an event occurs **b :** a statement giving the time of execution or making ⟨the *date* on the check⟩ **2 :** DURATION 2 **3 :** the period of time to which something belongs ⟨sculptures of an early *date*⟩ **4 a :** APPOINTMENT 3; *esp* **:** a social engagement between two persons **b :** a person with whom one has a social engagement [Middle French, from Late Latin *data,* from *data* "given" (as in *data Romae* "given at Rome"), from Latin *dare* "to give"]

△ **origin** The English word *date* has nothing to do etymologically with *day* but is descended from Latin *dare,* "to give". In ancient Rome, the date of a letter was written in this manner: "Dabam Romae Kal. Aprilis." (I gave [this letter] at Rome April 1 — the calends of April.) A later formula used *data Romae,* "given at Rome", instead of *dabam Romae,* "I gave at Rome". By the 6th century A.D., *data* had become a noun used for the date on a letter. In French its descendant *date* was used not only for the date on a letter, but also for the actual time that such a date indicated or indeed for any given point in time.

—to date : up to the present moment

[3]date *vb* **1 :** to determine the date of ⟨*date* an antique⟩ **2 :** to record the date of or on ⟨*date* a letter⟩ **3 :** to mark with characteristics typical of a particular period ⟨the architecture *dates* the house⟩ **4 :** to make or have a date with **5 a :** ORIGINATE 2 ⟨that chair *dates* from the 16th century⟩ **b :** to extend in time **:** CONTINUE ⟨a friendship *dating* from childhood⟩ — **dat•able** *or* **date•able** \ˈdāt-ə-bəl\ *adj* — **dat•er** *n*

dat•ed *adj* **1 :** having a date **2 :** OLD-FASHIONED 1 ⟨*dated* formalities⟩ — **dat•ed•ly** *adv* — **dat•ed•ness** *n*

date•less \ˈdāt-ləs\ *adj* **1 :** ENDLESS 1 **2 :** having no date **3 :** too ancient to be dated **4 :** TIMELESS 1b, 2 ⟨the play's *dateless* theme⟩

date•line \ˈdāt-ˌlīn\ *n* **1 :** a line in a publication giving the date and place of composition or issue **2** *usually* **date line :** a hypothetical line approximately along the 180th meridian designated as the place where each calendar day begins — **dateline** *vt*

da•tive \ˈdāt-iv\ *adj* **:** of, relating to, or being the grammatical case that marks typically the indirect object of a verb or the object of some prepositions [Latin *dativus,* from *dare* "to give"] — **dative** *n*

da•tum \ˈdāt-əm, ˈdat-, ˈdät-\ *n, pl* **da•ta** \-ə\ *or* **datums :** a single piece of data **:** FACT [Latin, "something given", from *datus,* past participle of *dare* "to give"]

[1]daub \ˈdȯb, ˈdäb\ *vb* **1 :** to cover with soft adhesive matter **:** PLASTER **2 :** to coat with a dirty substance **3 :** to apply (as paint) crudely [Old French *dauber*] — **daub•er** *n*

[2]daub *n* **1 :** something daubed on **:** SMEAR **2 :** a crudely painted picture

[1]daugh•ter \ˈdȯt-ər\ *n* **1 a :** a female offspring especially of human beings **b :** woman or girl having a specified ancestor or belonging to a group of common ancestry **2 :** something considered as a daughter [Old English *dohtor*] — **daugh•ter•ly** \-lē\ *adj*

[2]daughter *adj* **1 :** having the characteristics or relationship of a daughter ⟨*daughter* cities⟩ **2 :** belonging to the first generation of offspring, cells, parts of cells, or molecules produced by reproduction, division, or formation of replicas ⟨*daughter* cells⟩ ⟨*daughter* DNA molecules⟩

daugh•ter–in–law \ˈdȯt-ə-rən-ˌlȯ, -ərn-ˌlȯ\ *n, pl* **daughters–in–law** \-ər-zən-\ **:** the wife of one's son

daunt \ˈdȯnt, ˈdänt\ *vt* **:** to lessen the courage of **:** make afraid [Old French *donter, danter,* from Latin *domitare* "to tame", from *domare* "to tame"]

daunt•less \-ləs\ *adj* **:** FEARLESS, UNDAUNTED ⟨a *dauntless* hero⟩ — **daunt•less•ly** *adv* — **daunt•less•ness** *n*

dau•phin \ˈdȯ-fən\ *n, often cap* **:** the eldest son of a king of France [Middle French *dalfin,* from Old French, title of lords of the Dauphiné, from *Dalfin,* a surname]

dav•en•port \ˈdav-ən-ˌpōrt, ˈdav-m-,-ˈpȯrt\ *n* **:** a large upholstered sofa [probably from the name *Davenport*]

da•vit \ˈdā-vət, ˈdav-ət\ *n* **:** one of a pair of crane arms used for carrying small boats (as lifeboats or dinghies) aboard ships or yachts and for raising and lowering them to the water; *also* **:** a similar hoist (as over a hatchway) [probably from the name *David*]

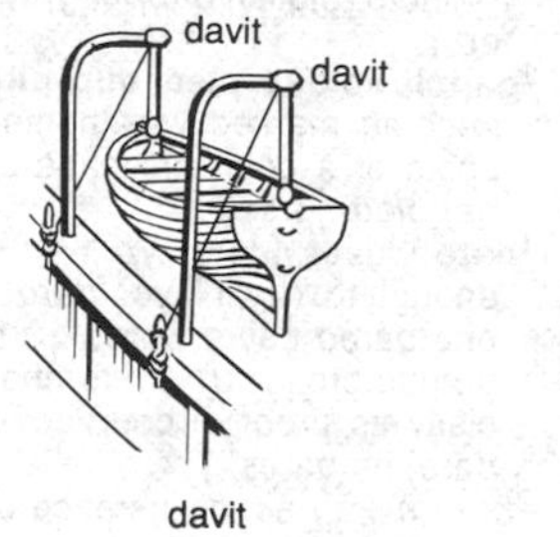

davit

Da•vy Jones's locker \ˌdā-vē-ˌjōnz, -ˌjōnz-əz-\ *n* **:** the bottom of the sea **:** a grave in the sea [*Davy Jones,* legendary spirit of the sea]

daw \ˈdȯ\ *n* **:** JACKDAW [Middle English *dawe*]

daw•dle \ˈdȯd-l\ *vb* **daw•dled; daw•dling** \ˈdȯd-ling, -l-ing\ **1 :** to spend time wastefully or idly **:** LINGER ⟨*dawdle* over homework⟩ **2 :** to move lackadaisically **:** LOITER ⟨*dawdles* on the way back⟩ **3 :** IDLE 3 ⟨*dawdle* the time away⟩ [origin unknown] — **daw•dler** \ˈdȯd-lər, -l-ər\ *n*

[1]dawn \ˈdȯn, ˈdän\ *vi* **1 :** to become dawn **:** begin to grow light as the sun rises **2 :** to begin to appear or develop ⟨the space age *dawned* with the first sputnik⟩ **3 :** to begin to be perceived or understood ⟨the truth *dawned* on them⟩ [Middle English *dawnen*]

[2]dawn *n* **1 :** the first appearance of light in the morning **2 :** a first appearance **:** BEGINNING ⟨the *dawn* of a new era⟩

day \ˈdā\ *n* **1 a :** the time of light between one night and the next **b :** DAYLIGHT 1 **2 :** the period of the earth's rotation on its axis **3 :** a period of 24 hours beginning at midnight **4 :** a specified day or date ⟨the *day* of the picnic⟩ **5 :** a specified time or period **:** AGE ⟨in our parents' *day*⟩ **6 :** the conflict or contention of the day ⟨played hard and carried the *day*⟩ **7 :** the time set apart by usage or law for work ⟨the 8-hour *day*⟩ [Old English *dæg*]

day•bed \ˈdā-ˌbed\ *n* **:** a couch with low head and foot pieces

day•book \-ˌbu̇k\ *n* **:** JOURNAL 1b, DIARY

day•break \-ˌbrāk\ *n* **:** DAWN 1

day–care \-ˌkeər, -ˌkaər\ *adj* **:** of, relating to, or providing care for preschool children during the day ⟨*day-care* centers⟩

[1]day•dream \-ˌdrēm\ *n* **:** a dreamy sequence of usually happy or pleasant imaginings

[2]daydream *vi* **:** to have a daydream — **day•dream•er** *n*

day laborer *n* : one who works for daily wages especially as an unskilled laborer

day letter *n* : a telegram sent during the day that has a lower priority than a regular telegram — compare NIGHT LETTER

day•light \'dā-ˌlīt\ *n* **1** : the light of day **2** : DAWN 1 **3** : understanding of something that has been unclear ⟨began to see *daylight* on the problem⟩ **4** *pl* : mental soundness or stability : WITS ⟨scared the *daylights* out of them⟩

daylight saving time *n* : time usually one hour ahead of standard time — called also *daylight* time

day lily *n* : any of various plants of the lily family with short-lived flowers that are widespread in cultivation and naturalized in the wild

day–neutral *adj* : flowering or developing to maturity regardless of relative length of alternating light and dark periods — compare LONG-DAY, SHORT-DAY

day nursery *n* : a public center for the care and training of young children; *also* : NURSERY SCHOOL

Day of Atonement : YOM KIPPUR

days \'dāz\ *adv* : in the daytime repeatedly ⟨work *days*⟩

day school *n* : an elementary or secondary school held on weekdays; *esp* : a private school without boarding facilities

day•star \'dā-ˌstär\ *n* **1** : MORNING STAR **2** : SUN 1a

day•time \'dā-ˌtīm\ *n* : the time during which there is daylight

daze \'dāz\ *vt* **1** : to stupefy especially by a blow : STUN **2** : to dazzle with light [Old Norse *dasask* "to become exhausted"] — **daze** *n*

daz•zle \'daz-əl\ *vt* **daz•zled**; **daz•zling** \'daz-ling, -ə-ling\ **1** : to overpower with light ⟨the desert sunlight *dazzled* them⟩ **2** : to impress greatly or confound with brilliance ⟨*dazzled* the crowd with their performances⟩ [derived from *daze*] — **dazzle** *n* — **daz•zler** \'daz-lər, -ə-lər\ *n* — **daz•zling•ly** \'daz-ling-lē, -ə-ling-\ *adv*

D day *n* : a day set for launching an operation [*D*, abbreviation for *day*]

DDT \ˌdē-ˌdē-'tē\ *n* : a colorless odorless water-insoluble compound formerly used widely as an insecticide that tends to accumulate in the environment and has toxic effects on many vertebrates [from the initial letters of its chemical components]

de- *prefix* **1 a** : do the opposite of ⟨*de*vitalize⟩ **b** : reverse of **2** : remove (a specified thing) from ⟨*de*louse⟩ : remove from (a specified thing) ⟨*de*throne⟩ **3** : reduce ⟨*de*value⟩ **4** : something derived from (a specified thing) : derived from something (of a specified nature) ⟨*de*nominative⟩ **5** : get off of (a specified thing) ⟨*de*plane⟩ [Latin *de-* "down, away, from"]

dea•con \'dē-kən\ *n* : a subordinate officer in a Christian church: as **a** : a clergyman next below a priest **b** : a clergyman or layman with particular duties in various Christian churches [Old English *dēacon*, from Late Latin *diaconus*, from Greek *diakonos*, literally, "servant"]

dea•con•ess \'dē-kə-nəs\ *n* : a woman chosen to assist in the church ministry; *esp* : one in a Protestant order

de•ac•ti•vate \dē-'ak-tə-ˌvāt\ *vt* : to make inactive or ineffective — **de•ac•ti•va•tion** \ˌdē-ˌak-tə-'vā-shən\ *n*

[1]**dead** \'ded\ *adj* **1** : deprived of life : having died : LIFELESS **2 a** : having the appearance of death : DEATHLY ⟨in a *dead* faint⟩ **b** : lacking the power to move, feel, or respond : NUMB **c** : very tired **d** : UNRESPONSIVE ⟨*dead* to pity⟩ **e** : grown cold : burned out ⟨*dead* coals⟩ **3 a** : not naturally endowed with life : INANIMATE ⟨*dead* matter⟩ **b** : no longer producing or functioning ⟨a *dead* battery⟩ **4 a** : lacking power, significance, or effect ⟨a *dead* law⟩ **b** : no longer in use : OBSOLETE ⟨a *dead* language⟩ **c** : no longer active : EXTINCT ⟨a *dead* volcano⟩ **d** : lacking in gaiety or animation ⟨a *dead* party⟩ **e** (1) : lacking in commercial activity : QUIET (2) : commercially idle or unproductive ⟨*dead* capital⟩ **f** : lacking elasticity ⟨a *dead* tennis ball⟩ **g** : being out of action or out of use; *esp* : free from any connection to a source of voltage and free from electric charges ⟨a *dead* telephone line⟩ **h** : being out of play ⟨a *dead* ball⟩ ⟨*dead* cards⟩ **5 a** : not circulating : STAGNANT ⟨*dead* air⟩ **b** : lacking warmth, vigor, or taste ⟨a *dead* wine⟩ **6 a** : absolutely uniform ⟨the *dead* level of the prairie⟩ **b** : UNERRING, EXACT ⟨a *dead* shot⟩ ⟨*dead* center of the target⟩ **c** : SUDDEN 1a, ABRUPT ⟨a *dead* stop⟩ **d** : ABSOLUTE 4, TOTAL ⟨a *dead* loss⟩ [Old English *dēad*]

[2]**dead** *n, pl* **dead 1** : one that is dead — usually used collectively ⟨the living and the *dead*⟩ **2** : the time of greatest quiet ⟨the *dead* of night⟩

[3]**dead** *adv* **1** : WHOLLY 1 ⟨*dead* right⟩ **2** : suddenly and completely ⟨stopped *dead*⟩ **3** : DIRECTLY ⟨*dead* ahead⟩

dead•beat \'ded-ˌbēt\ *n* : one who persistently fails to pay debts

dead•en \'ded-n\ *vt* **dead•ened**; **dead•en•ing** \'ded-ning, -n-ing\ **1** : to impair in vigor or sensation : BLUNT ⟨*deaden* pain with drugs⟩ **2 a** : to deprive of brilliance or spirit **b** : to make (as a wall) soundproof

dead–end \ˌded-ˌend\ *adj* : leading nowhere ⟨a *dead-end* job⟩ ⟨a *dead-end* street⟩

dead end *n* **1** : an end (as of a street) without an exit **2** : a position, situation, or course of action that leads to nothing further

dead•eye \'ded-ˌī\ *n* : an expert marksman

dead heat *n* : a contest in which two or more contestants tie (as by crossing the finish line simultaneously)

dead letter *n* **1** : something that has lost its force or authority without being formally abolished **2** : a letter that is undeliverable and unreturnable by the post office

dead•line \'ded-ˌlīn\ *n* : a date or time before which something must be done

dead•lock \'ded-ˌläk\ *n* : a stoppage of action because both sides in a struggle are equally powerful and neither will give in — **deadlock** *vt*

[1]**dead•ly** \'ded-lē\ *adj* **dead•li•er**; **-est 1** : likely to cause or capable of causing death ⟨a *deadly* disease⟩ **2 a** : aiming to kill or destroy : IMPLACABLE ⟨a *deadly* enemy⟩ **b** : very accurate : UNERRING ⟨a *deadly* marksman⟩ **3 a** : tending to deprive of force or vitality ⟨a *deadly* habit⟩ **b** : DEATHLY 2 ⟨a *deadly* chill⟩ **4** : very great : EXTREME ⟨a *deadly* bore⟩ — **dead•li•ness** *n*

• **syn** DEADLY, MORTAL, FATAL, LETHAL mean causing or capable of causing death. DEADLY applies to an established or very likely cause of death ⟨a *deadly* disease⟩ MORTAL implies that death has occurred or is inevitable ⟨a *mortal* wound⟩ FATAL stresses the inevitability of what has in fact resulted in death or destruction ⟨*fatal* consequences⟩ LETHAL applies only to something that is bound to cause death or exists for the destruction of life ⟨*lethal* gas⟩

[2]**deadly** *adv* **1** : in a manner suggesting death ⟨*deadly* pale⟩ **2** : EXTREMELY, VERY ⟨*deadly* dull⟩

deadly nightshade *n* : the belladonna plant

deadly sin *n* : one of seven sins of pride, covetousness, lust, anger, gluttony, envy, and sloth believed to be fatal to spiritual progress

dead man's float *n* : a floating position in which a person lies face down in the water with the arms extended forward

dead march *n* : a solemn march for a funeral

dead•pan \'ded-ˌpan\ *adj* : marked by an impassive manner, style, or expression [English slang *pan* "face", from [1]*pan*] — **deadpan** *adv*

dead reckoning *n* : the determination without the aid of celestial observations of the position of a ship or aircraft from the record of the courses sailed or flown and the distance made from the last known position

dead•weight \'ded-'wāt\ *n* : the unrelieved weight of an inert mass

dead•wood \'ded-ˌwu̇d\ *n* **1** : wood dead on the tree : dead branches **2** : useless personnel or material

deaf \'def\ *adj* **1** : wholly or partly unable to hear **2** : unwilling to hear or listen ⟨*deaf* to all suggestions⟩ [Old English *dēaf*] — **deaf•ness** *n*

deaf•en \'def-ən\ *vb* **deaf•ened**; **deaf•en•ing** \'def-ning, -ə-ning\ **1** : to make deaf **2** : to cause deafness : stun one with noise — **deaf•en•ing•ly** \-lē\ *adv*

deaf–mute \'def-ˌmyüt\ *n* : a deaf person who cannot speak — **deaf–mute** *adj* — **deaf–mut•ism** \-ˌmyüt-ˌiz-əm\ *n*

[1]**deal** \'dēl\ *n* **1** : a usually large or indefinite quantity or degree ⟨means a great *deal*⟩ ⟨a good *deal* faster⟩ **2 a** : the act or right of distributing cards to players in a card game **b** : HAND 11b [Old English *dǣl* "part, quantity"]

[2]**deal** *vb* **dealt** \'delt\; **deal•ing** \'de-ling\ **1** : to give as one's portion : DISTRIBUTE ⟨*deal* out sandwiches⟩ ⟨*deal* the cards⟩ **2** : DELIVER 5, BESTOW ⟨*dealt* the dog a blow⟩ **3** : to have to do ⟨the book *deals* with art⟩ **4** : to take action ⟨*deal* with offenders⟩ **5 a** : to engage in bargaining : TRADE **b** : to sell or distrib-

ute something as a business ⟨*deals* in insurance⟩ — **deal•er** *n*

[3]**deal** *n* **1 a** : an act of dealing : BARGAINING **b** : the result of bargaining : a mutual agreement ⟨make a *deal* for a used car⟩ **2** : treatment received ⟨a dirty *deal*⟩ **3** : a secret or underhand agreement **4** : a purchase at a fair or very low price : BARGAIN ⟨a good *deal* in a new car⟩

[4]**deal** *n* : wood or a board of fir or pine [Dutch or Low German *dele* "plank"] — **deal** *adj*

deal•ing *n* **1** *pl* : social or business interactions ⟨it's foolish to have *dealings* with such people⟩ **2** : a way of acting or of doing business ⟨believed in fair *dealing*⟩

de•am•i•nase \dē-ˈam-ə-ˌnās\ *n* : an enzyme that promotes removal of amino groups

de•am•i•nate \-ˌnāt\ *vt* : to remove the amino group from (a compound) — **de•am•i•na•tion** \ˌdē-ˌam-ə-ˈnā-shən\ *n*

dean \ˈdēn\ *n* **1 a** : the head of the chapter of a collegiate or cathedral church **b** : a Roman Catholic priest who supervises one district of a diocese **2 a** : the head of a division, faculty, college, or school of a university **b** : a college or secondary school administrator in charge of counseling and disciplining students **3** : the senior member of a group ⟨the *dean* of the diplomatic corps⟩ [Middle French *deien,* from Late Latin *decanus,* literally, "chief of ten", from Latin *decem* "ten"] — **dean•ship** \-ˌship\ *n*

dean•ery \ˈdēn-rē, -ə-rē\ *n, pl* **-er•ies** : the office, jurisdiction, or official residence of a clerical dean

[1]**dear** \ˈdiər\ *adj* **1** : highly valued : PRECIOUS ⟨a *dear* memory⟩ **2** : feeling or expressing love : AFFECTIONATE **3** : high-priced : EXPENSIVE **4** : HEARTFELT ⟨my *dearest* wish⟩ [Old English *dēore*] **syn** see COSTLY — **dear** *adv* — **dear•ly** *adv* — **dear•ness** *n*

[2]**dear** *n* **1** : a loved one : DARLING **2** : a lovable person

dearth \ˈdərth\ *n* **1** : scarcity that makes dear; *esp* : FAMINE **2** : inadequate supply : LACK

death \ˈdeth\ *n* **1** : a permanent cessation of all vital functions : the end of life **2** : the cause of loss of life **3** *often cap* : the destroyer of life represented usually as a skeleton with a scythe **4** : the state of being dead **5** : the passing or destruction of something inanimate of intangible ⟨the *death* of feudalism⟩ [Old English *dēath*] — **death•like** \-ˌlīk\ *adj*

death•bed \ˈdeth-ˈbed\ *n* **1** : the bed in which a person dies **2** : the last hours of life — **on one's deathbed** : near death

death•blow \-ˈblō\ *n* : a destructive or killing stroke or event

death camas *n* : any of several plants of the lily family that cause poisoning of livestock in the western United States

death knell *n* : an action or event foretelling death or destruction

death•less \ˈdeth-ləs\ *adj* : IMMORTAL 3, IMPERISHABLE ⟨*deathless* fame⟩ — **death•less•ly** *adv* — **death•less•ness** *n*

death•ly \ˈdeth-lē\ *adj* **1** : DEADLY 1, FATAL **2** : of, relating to, or suggestive of death ⟨a *deathly* pallor⟩ — **deathly** *adv*

death mask *n* : a cast taken from the face of a dead person

death's–head \ˈdeths-ˌhed\ *n* : a human skull symbolizing death

death trap *n* : a structure or situation that is potentially very dangerous to life

[1]**death•watch** \ˈdeth-ˌwäch\ *n* : any of several small insects that make a ticking sound [from the superstition that its ticking presages death]

[2]**deathwatch** *n* : a vigil kept with the dead or dying

deb \ˈdeb\ *n* : DEBUTANTE

de•ba•cle \di-ˈbäk-əl, -ˈbak-\ *n* **1** : a tumultuous breaking up of ice in a river **2** : a violent disruption (as of any army) : ROUT **3 a** : a great disaster ⟨the stock market *debacle*⟩ **b** : a complete failure : FIASCO [French *débâcle*]

de•bar \di-ˈbär\ *vt* : to bar from having or doing something : PRECLUDE — **de•bar•ment** \-mənt\ *n*

de•bark \di-ˈbärk\ *vb* : DISEMBARK [Middle French *debarquer,* from *de-* "de-" + *barque* "bark"] — **de•bar•ka•tion** \ˌdē-ˌbär-ˈka-shən\ *n*

de•base \di-ˈbās\ *vt* : to lower in status, dignity, value, quality, or character — **de•base•ment** \-mənt\ *n* — **de•bas•er** *n*

• **syn** DEBASE, DEGRADE, CORRUPT, DEPRAVE mean to cause deterioration or lowering in quality or character. DEBASE implies loss of worth, value, or dignity; DEGRADE adds shamefulness or degeneracy to debasement; CORRUPT implies loss of soundness, purity, or integrity through forces that break down, pollute, or destroy; DEPRAVE implies moral deterioration or perversion.

de•bat•able \di-ˈbāt-ə-bəl\ *adj* **1** : open to debate : QUESTIONABLE ⟨a *debatable* conclusion⟩ **2** : capable of being debated

[1]**de•bate** \di-ˈbāt\ *n* : a verbal argument: as **a** : the formal discussion of a motion before a deliberative body **b** : a regulated discussion of a proposition between two matched sides

[2]**debate** *vb* **1** : to discuss or examine a question by presenting and considering arguments on both sides **2** : to take part in a debate **3** : to present or consider the reasons for and against : CONSIDER [Middle French *debatre* "to fight, contend", from *de-* "de-" + *batre* "to beat", from Latin *battuere,* of Celtic origin] **syn** see DISCUSS — **de•bat•er** *n*

[1]**de•bauch** \di-ˈbȯch, -ˈbäch\ *vt* : to lead away from virtue or morality : CORRUPT [Middle French *debaucher* "to make disloyal"] — **de•bauch•er** *n*

[2]**debauch** *n* **1** : an act or occasion of debauchery **2** : ORGY 2

de•bauch•ee \di-ˌbȯch-ˈē, -ˌbäch-\ *n* : one given to debauchery

de•bauch•ery \di-ˈbȯch-rē, -ˈbäch-, -ə-rē\ *n, pl* **-er•ies** : extreme indulgence in sensual pleasure

de•ben•ture \di-ˈben-chər\ *n* : a bond secured only by the general assets of the issuing government or corporation [Latin *debentur* "they are due", from *debēre* "to owe"]

de•bil•i•tate \di-ˈbil-ə-ˌtāt\ *vt* : to impair the strength of : WEAKEN — **de•bil•i•ta•tion** \di-ˌbil-ə-ˈtā-shən\ *n*

de•bil•i•ty \di-ˈbil-ət-ē\ *n, pl* **-ties** : an infirm or weakened state [Middle French *debilité,* from Latin *debilitas,* from *debilis* "weak"]

[1]**deb•it** \ˈdeb-ət\ *n* **1** : an entry in an account representing an amount paid out or owed **2** : something regarded as unfavorable : DRAWBACK [Latin *debitum* "debt"]

[2]**debit** *vt* : to enter as a debit : charge with or as a debt

deb•o•nair \ˌdeb-ə-ˈnaər, -ˈneər\ *adj* : gaily and gracefully charming ⟨a *debonair* manner⟩ [Old French *debonaire,* from *de bonne aire* "of good family or nature"] — **deb•o•nair•ly** *adv* — **deb•o•nair•ness** *n*

de•bouch \di-ˈbüsh\ *vi* : to come out (as from a narrow passage) into an open area ⟨crowds *debouched* from side streets into the square⟩ [French *déboucher,* from *dé-* "de-" + *bouche* "mouth", from Latin *bucca* "cheek"] — **de•bouch•ment** \-mənt\ *n*

de•brief \di-ˈbrēf, ˈdē-\ *vt* : to interrogate (as an astronaut back from a mission) in order to obtain useful information

de•bris \də-ˈbrē, ˈdā-ˌbrē\ *n, pl* **de•bris** \-ˈbrēz, -ˌbrēz\ **1** : the remains of something broken down or destroyed **2** : an accumulation of fragments of rock [French *débris,* from Old French *debrisier* "to break to pieces", from *de-* "de-" + *brisier* "to break"]

debt \ˈdet\ *n* **1** : SIN 1, TRESPASS **2** : a state of owing ⟨hopelessly in *debt*⟩ **3** : something owed : OBLIGATION ⟨pay a *debt* of $10⟩ [Old French *dette* "something owed", from Latin *debitum,* from *debēre* "to owe", from *de-* + *habēre* "to have"]

debt•or \ˈdet-ər\ *n* **1** : SINNER **2** : one that owes a debt

de•bug \ˈdē-ˈbəg, dē-\ *vt* : to eliminate errors or malfunctions in ⟨*debug* a computer program⟩

de•bunk \dē-ˈbəngk, ˈdē-\ *vt* : to expose the sham or falseness of ⟨*debunk* a hero legend⟩ — **de•bunk•er** *n*

de•but \ˈdā-ˌbyü, dā-ˈ\ *n* **1** : a first public appearance **2** : a formal entrance into society ⟨sixteen is the usual age for making one's *debut*⟩ [French *début,* from *débuter* "to begin"]

deb•u•tante \ˈdeb-yu̇-ˌtänt\ *n* : a young woman making her formal entrance into society [French *débutante,* from *débuter* "to begin"]

deca- *or* **dec-** *or* **deka-** *or* **dek-** *combining form* : ten [Greek *deka*]

de•cade \ˈdek-ˌād, -əd; de-ˈkād; *3 is usually* ˈdek-əd\ *n* **1** : a group or set of 10 **2** : a period of 10 years **3** : a division of the rosary that is made up primarily of 10 Hail Marys

dec•a•dence \ˈdek-əd-əns, di-ˈkād-ns\ *n* **1** : the process of becoming decadent : the quality or state of being decadent **2** : a period of decline [Middle French, from Medieval Latin *decadentia,* from Late Latin *decadere* "to fall, sink", from Latin *de-* + *cadere* "to fall"]

dec•a•dent \ˈdek-əd-ənt, di-ˈkād-nt\ *adj* : marked by decay or decline — **decadent** *n* — **dec•a•dent•ly** *adv*

deca•gon \ˈdek-ə-ˌgän\ *n* : a polygon of 10 angles and 10 sides

deca•gram \ˈdek-ə-ˌgram\ *n* : DEKAGRAM

de•cal \'dē-ˌkal, di-'kal, 'dek-əl\ *n* : a picture or design made to be transferred (as to glass) from specially prepared paper [short for *decalcomania*]

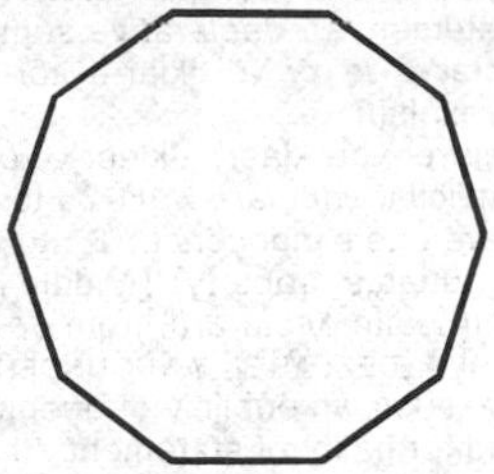
decagon

de•cal•co•ma•nia \di-ˌkal-kə-'mā-nē-ə\ *n* **1** : the art or process of transferring or ornamenting with decals **2** : DECAL [French *décalcomanie,* from *décalquer* "to copy by tracing" + *manie* "mania"]

deca•li•ter \'dek-ə-ˌlēt-ər\ *n* : DEKALITER

deca•logue \'dek-ə-ˌlȯg\ *n* **1** *cap* : TEN COMMANDMENTS **2** : a basic set of rules carrying binding authority [Late Latin *decalogus,* from Greek *dekalogos,* from *deka* "ten" + *logos* "speech, word"]

deca•me•ter \'dek-ə-ˌmēt-ər\ *n* : DEKAMETER

de•camp \di-'kamp\ *vi* **1** : to break up a camp **2** : to depart suddenly : ABSCOND ⟨*decamped* with the funds⟩ — **de•camp•ment** \-mənt\ *n*

de•cant \di-'kant\ *vt* **1** : to pour from one vessel into another **2** : to draw off without disturbing any sediment ⟨*decant* wine⟩ [New Latin *decantare,* from Latin *de-* + Medieval Latin *cantus* "side", from Latin *canthus* "iron tire"] — **de•can•ta•tion** \ˌdē-ˌkan-'tā-shən\ *n*

de•cant•er \di-'kant-ər\ *n* : a vessel used to decant liquids or to receive decanted liquids; *esp* : an ornamental bottle used for serving wine

de•cap•i•tate \di-'kap-ə-ˌtāt\ *vt* : to cut off the head of : BEHEAD [Late Latin *decapitare,* from Latin *de-* + *caput* "head"] — **de•cap•i•ta•tion** \di-ˌkap-ə-'tā-shən\ *n*

deca•pod \'dek-ə-ˌpäd\ *n* **1** : any of an order (Decapoda) of crustaceans (as shrimps, lobsters, crabs) with five pairs of appendages attached to the thorax one or more of which are modified into pincers **2** : any of an order (Decapoda) of cephalopod mollusks including forms (as the cuttlefishes and squids) with 10 arms — **decapod** *adj* — **de•cap•o•dan** \di-'kap-əd-ən\ *adj or n*

deca•stere \'dek-ə-ˌstiər\ *n* : DEKASTERE

deca•syl•lab•ic \ˌdek-ə-sə-'lab-ik\ *adj* : having 10 syllables or composed of verses of 10 syllables — **decasyllabic** *n*

de•cath•lon \di-'kath-lən, -ˌlän\ *n* : an athletic contest in which each competitor participates in each of a series of 10 track-and-field events [French *décathlon,* from *déca-* "deca-" + Greek *athlon* "contest"]

¹de•cay \di-'kā\ *vb* **1** : to decline from a sound or prosperous condition **2** : to decrease gradually in quantity, activity, or force **3** : to fall into ruin **4** : to decline in health, strength, or vigor **5** : to undergo or cause to undergo decomposition [Old North French *decaïr,* from Late Latin *decadere* "to fall, sink", from Latin *de-* + *cadere* "to fall"]

• **syn** DECAY, DECOMPOSE, ROT, SPOIL mean to undergo disintegration or dissolution. DECAY implies a deterioration, often gradual, from soundness or perfection; DECOMPOSE stresses a breaking down into components or dissolution through corruption ⟨to *decompose* water into oxygen and hydrogen⟩ ⟨bacteria *decompose* organic products⟩ ROT implies decay with corruption and often suggests offensiveness; SPOIL applies chiefly to the decomposition of foods.

²decay *n* **1** : gradual decline in strength, soundness, prosperity, excellence, or value **2** : ROT; *esp* : decomposition of proteins in the presence of oxygen chiefly by bacteria **3** : a decline in health or vigor **4 a** : spontaneous decrease in the number of radioactive atoms in radioactive material **b** : spontaneous disintegration (as of an atom or a meson)

de•cease \di-'sēs\ *n* : DEATH 1 [Middle French *deces,* from Latin *decessus* "departure, death", from *decedere* "to depart, die", from *de-* + *cedere* "to go"] — **decease** *vi*

de•ceased \-'sēst\ *n, pl* **deceased** : a dead person

de•ce•dent \di-'sēd-nt\ *n* : a deceased person — used chiefly in law

de•ceit \di-'sēt\ *n* **1** : the act or practice of deceiving : DECEPTION **2** : a statement or act intended to deceive **3** : DECEITFULNESS [Old French *deceite,* derived from Latin *decipere* "to deceive"]

de•ceit•ful \-fəl\ *adj* **1** : using or tending to use deceit **2** : marked by deceit ⟨a *deceitful* answer⟩ — **de•ceit•ful•ly** \-fə-lē\ *adv* — **de•ceit•ful•ness** *n*

de•ceive \di-'sēv\ *vb* **1** : to cause to believe what is untrue : MISLEAD **2** : to use trickery [Old French *deceivre,* from Latin *decipere,* from *de-* + *capere* "to take"] — **de•ceiv•er** *n* — **de•ceiv•ing•ly** \-'sē-ving-lē\ *adv*

• **syn** DECEIVE, MISLEAD, DELUDE, BEGUILE mean to lead astray or frustrate usually by underhandedness. DECEIVE implies imposing a false idea or belief that causes ignorance, bewilderment, or helplessness; MISLEAD implies a leading astray that may or may not be intentional; DELUDE implies deceiving so thoroughly that the truth is obscured; BEGUILE stresses the use of charm and persuasion in deceiving.

de•cel•er•ate \dē-'sel-ə-ˌrāt\ *vb* : to slow down or cause to slow down [*de-* + *accelerate*] — **de•cel•er•a•tion** \ˌdē-ˌsel-ə-'rā-shən\ *n* — **de•cel•er•a•tor** \dē-'sel-ə-ˌrāt-ər\ *n*

De•cem•ber \di-'sem-bər\ *n* : the 12th month of the year [Old French *Decembre,* from Latin *December,* from *decem* "ten"; from its having been originally the tenth month of the Roman calendar]

de•cem•vir \di-'sem-vər\ *n* : one of a body of 10 magistrates in ancient Rome [derived from Latin *decem* "ten" + *vir* "man"] — **de•cem•vi•rate** \-və-rət\ *n*

de•cen•cy \'dēs-n-sē\ *n, pl* **-cies** **1 a** : the quality or state of being decent : PROPRIETY **b** : conformity to standards of taste, propriety, or quality **2** : standard of propriety — usually used in pl.

de•cen•ni•al \di-'sen-ē-əl\ *adj* **1** : consisting of 10 years **2** : happening every 10 years ⟨*decennial* census⟩ [Latin *decennium* "period of 10 years", from *decem* "ten" + *annus* "year"] — **decennial** *n* — **de•cen•ni•al•ly** \-ē-ə-lē\ *adv*

de•cent \'dēs-nt\ *adj* **1 a** : conforming to standards of propriety, good taste, or morality **b** : modestly clothed **2** : free from immodesty or obscenity **3** : fairly good : ADEQUATE ⟨*decent* housing⟩ [Latin *decens,* present participle of *decēre* "to be fitting"] — **de•cent•ly** *adv*

de•cen•tral•ize \dē-'sen-trə-ˌlīz\ *vt* **1** : to disperse or distribute among various regional or local authorities ⟨*decentralize* the administration of flood relief⟩ **2** : to cause to withdraw from urban centers to outlying areas ⟨*decentralize* industries⟩ — **de•cen•tral•i•za•tion** \ˌdē-ˌsen-trə-lə-'zā-shən\ *n*

de•cep•tion \di-'sep-shən\ *n* **1 a** : the act of deceiving **b** : the fact or condition of being deceived **2** : something that deceives : TRICK [Middle French, from Late Latin *deceptio,* from Latin *decipere* "to deceive"]

• **syn** FRAUD, TRICKERY: DECEPTION may suggest deliberate cheating or merely legitimate tactical resource; FRAUD always implies guilt and often criminality; TRICKERY implies ingenious ways of fooling or cheating.

de•cep•tive \di-'sep-tiv\ *adj* : tending or having power to deceive — **de•cep•tive•ly** *adv* — **de•cep•tive•ness** *n*

deci- *combining form* : tenth part [Latin *decimus* "tenth", from *decem* "ten"]

deci•bel \'des-ə-ˌbel, -bəl\ *n* **1** : a unit for expressing the ratio of two amounts of electric or acoustic signal power equal to 10 times the common logarithm of this ratio **2** : a unit for measuring the relative intensity of sounds on a scale from zero for the average least perceptible sound to about 130 for the average pain level — abbreviation *db*

de•cide \di-'sīd\ *vb* **1** : to arrive at a solution that ends uncertainty or dispute about ⟨*decided* the case in favor of the defendant⟩ **2** : to bring to a definitive end ⟨one blow *decided* the fight⟩ **3** : to induce to come to a choice ⟨what *decided* your mind⟩ **4** : to make a choice or judgment ⟨*decided* to go⟩ [Middle French *decider,* from Latin *decidere,* literally, "to cut off", from *de-* + *caedere* "to cut"] — **de•cid•able** \-'sīd-ə-bəl\ *adj* — **de•cid•er** *n*

de•cid•ed \-'sīd-əd\ *adj* **1** : free from ambiguity : CLEAR, UNMISTAKABLE ⟨a *decided* smell of gas⟩ **2** : free from doubt or wavering : DETERMINED ⟨a *decided* tone of voice⟩ — **de•cid•ed•ly** *adv* — **de•cid•ed•ness** *n*

de•cid•u•ous \di-'sij-ə-wəs\ *adj* **1** : falling off or shed (as at the end of a growing period or stage of development) ⟨antlers are *deciduous*⟩ ⟨the first or milk teeth are *deciduous*⟩ **2 :** having deciduous parts or members with deciduous parts ⟨*deciduous* trees⟩ ⟨*deciduous* forests are typical of the temperate zones⟩ — compare EVERGREEN **3 :** of only passing interest or importance [Latin *deciduus,* from *decidere* "to fall off", from *de-* + *cadere* "to fall"] — **de•cid•u•ous•ly** *adv* — **de•cid•u•ous•ness** *n*

deci•gram \'des-ə-ˌgram\ *n* — see METRIC SYSTEM table

deci•li•ter \'des-ə-ˌlēt-ər\ *n* — see METRIC SYSTEM table

de•cil•lion \di-'sil-yən\ *n* — see NUMBER table [Latin *decem* "ten" + English *-illion* (as in *million*)]

[1]**dec•i•mal** \'des-məl, -ə-məl\ *adj* **1 :** based on the number 10 ⟨a *decimal* system of writing numerals⟩ ⟨*decimal* coinage⟩ **2 :** expressed as a decimal fraction ⟨¼ in *decimal* form is .25⟩ [derived from Latin *decimus* "tenth", from *decem* "ten"] — **dec•i•mal•ly** \-mə-lē\ *adv*

[2]**decimal** *n* **1 :** a proper fraction in which the denominator is a power of 10 usually not expressed but signified by a point placed at the left of the numerator (as .2 = 2/10, .25 = 25/100, .025 = 25/1000) **2 :** a mixed number (as 3.025) written as the combination of an integer and a decimal

decimal fraction *n* **:** DECIMAL

decimal notation *n* **:** expression of a number with a base of 10 using the first nine positive integers and 0 with each place representing a power of 10 — compare BINARY NOTATION

decimal point *n* **:** the dot at the left of a decimal fraction

dec•i•mate \'des-ə-ˌmāt\ *vt* **1 :** to take or destroy the tenth part of **2 :** to destroy a large part of ⟨disease and starvation *decimated* the population of the besieged city⟩ [Latin *decimare,* from *decimus* "tenth"] — **dec•i•ma•tion** \ˌdes-ə-'mā-shən\ *n*

deci•me•ter \'des-ə-ˌmēt-ər\ *n* — see METRIC SYSTEM table

de•ci•pher \dē-'sī-fər\ *vt* **1 a :** to convert into intelligible form **b :** DECODE ⟨*decipher* a message⟩ **2 :** to make out the meaning of despite indistinctness or obscurity ⟨*decipher* bad handwriting⟩ — **de•ci•pher•a•ble** \-fə-rə-bəl, -frə-\ *adj* — **de•ci•pher•ment** \-fər-mənt\ *n*

de•ci•sion \di-'sizh-ən\ *n* **1 :** the act or result of deciding especially by giving judgment ⟨the *decision* of the court⟩ **2 :** promptness and firmness in deciding **:** DETERMINATION ⟨people of courage and *decision*⟩ [Middle French, from Latin *decisio,* from *decidere* "to decide"]

de•ci•sive \di-'sī-siv\ *adj* **1 :** having the power to decide ⟨the chairperson has the *decisive* vote⟩ **2 :** of such nature as to settle a question or dispute ⟨a *decisive* victory⟩ **3 :** marked by or showing decision ⟨a *decisive* manner⟩ — **de•ci•sive•ly** *adv* — **de•ci•sive•ness** *n*

deci•stere \'des-ə-ˌstiər, -ˌsteər\ *n* **:** a metric unit of volume equal to 1/10 cubic meter

[1]**deck** \'dek\ *n* **1 :** a platform within or over the hull of a boat or ship forming a structural element and serving as a floor or a covering (as for a cabin) **2 :** something resembling the deck of a ship: as **a :** the roadway of a bridge **b :** a flat floored roofless area adjoining a house **3 :** a pack of playing cards [probably derived from Low German *decken* "to cover"] — **on deck :** next in line

[2]**deck** *vt* **1 a :** to clothe elegantly **:** ARRAY ⟨*decked* out in a new suit⟩ **b :** DECORATE 1 **2 :** to furnish with a deck **3 :** to knock down forcibly [Dutch *dekken* "to cover"]

deck chair *n* **:** a folding chair often having an adjustable leg rest

deck•er \'dek-ər\ *n* **:** something having a deck or a specified number of levels, floors, or layers — often used in combination ⟨the buses are double-*deckers*⟩

deck•hand \'dek-ˌhand\ *n* **:** a sailor who performs manual duties

deck•le edge \ˌdek-əl-\ *n* **:** the rough untrimmed edge of paper [derived from German *decken* "to cover"] — **deck•le–edged** \-'ejd\ *adj*

de•claim \di-'klām\ *vb* **:** to speak or deliver in the manner of a formal oration [Latin *declamare,* from *de-* + *clamare* "to cry out"] — **de•claim•er** *n* — **dec•la•ma•tion** \ˌdek-lə-'mā-shən\ *n*

de•clam•a•to•ry \di-'klam-ə-ˌtōr-ē, -ˌtȯr-\ *adj* **:** of, relating to, or marked by declamation or rhetorical display

dec•la•ra•tion \ˌdek-lə-'rā-shən\ *n* **1 :** the act of declaring **:** ANNOUNCEMENT **2 a :** something declared **b :** a document containing such a declaration ⟨the *Declaration* of Independence⟩

de•clar•a•tive \di-'klar-ət-iv\ *adj* **:** making a declaration or statement ⟨a *declarative* sentence⟩

de•clar•a•to•ry \di-'klar-ə-ˌtōr-ē, -ˌtȯr-\ *adj* **:** serving to declare or explain

de•clare \di-'klaər, -'kleər\ *vb* **1 :** to make known formally or explicitly ⟨*declare* war⟩ **2 :** to state emphatically **:** AFFIRM ⟨*declare* one's innocence⟩ **3 :** to make a full statement of (taxable or dutiable property) [Middle French *declarer* "to make clear", from Latin *declarare,* from *de-* + *clarus* "clear"]

• syn DECLARE, ANNOUNCE, PUBLISH, PROCLAIM mean to make known publicly or openly. DECLARE suggests a plainness and formality of statement ⟨the referee *declared* the contest a draw⟩; ANNOUNCE implies a declaration for the first time of something of interest or intended to satisfy curiosity ⟨*announce* an engagement⟩ ⟨*announce* the winner⟩ PUBLISH denotes a making public especially through print; PROCLAIM suggests a clear, forceful, and authoritative declaration ⟨the president *proclaimed* a national day of mourning⟩ **syn** see in addition ASSERT

de•clar•er \-'klar-ər, -'kler-\ *n* **1 :** one that declares **2 :** the bridge player who plays both his or her own hand and that of the dummy

de•clas•si•fy \dē-'klas-ə-ˌfī, 'dē-\ *vt* **:** to remove or reduce the security classification of ⟨*declassify* a secret document⟩

de•clen•sion \di-'klen-chən\ *n* **1 a :** inflection of a noun, adjective, or pronoun especially in some prescribed order of the forms **b :** a class of nouns or adjectives having the same inflectional forms **2 :** a falling off or away **:** DETERIORATION **3 :** a downward slope **:** DESCENT [derived from Latin *declinare* "to inflect, turn aside"] — **de•clen•sion•al** \-'klench-nəl, -ən-l\ *adj*

dec•li•na•tion \ˌdek-lə-'nā-shən\ *n* **1 :** angular distance north or south from the celestial equator measured along a great circle passing through the celestial poles ⟨the *declination* of a star⟩ **2 :** DETERIORATION ⟨moral *declination*⟩ **3 :** a bending downward **:** INCLINATION **4 :** a formal refusal **5 :** the angle that the magnetic needle makes with a true north and south line — **dec•li•na•tion•al** \-'nā-shnəl, -shən-l\ *adj*

[1]**de•cline** \di-'klīn\ *vb* **1 a :** to slope downward **:** DESCEND **b :** to bend down **:** DROOP ⟨*decline* one's head⟩ **2 :** to reach or pass toward a lower level **:** RECEDE **3 :** to draw toward a close **:** WANE **4 a :** to withhold consent **b :** to refuse to undertake, engage in, or comply with **c :** to decide not to accept **5 :** to give in a prescribed order the inflectional forms of a noun, pronoun, or adjective [derived from Latin *declinare* "to turn aside, inflect", from *de-* + *clinare* "to incline"] — **de•clin•able** \-'klī-nə-bəl\ *adj*

[2]**decline** *n* **1 :** the process of declining: **a :** a gradual wasting away **b :** a change to a lower state or level ⟨business activity showed a sharp *decline* last month⟩ **2 :** the time when something is approaching its end **3 :** a downward slope **:** DECLIVITY **4 :** a disease characterized by gradual loss of strength and health; *esp* **:** pulmonary tuberculosis

de•cliv•i•ty \di-'kliv-ət-ē\ *n, pl* **-ties 1 :** downward inclination **2 :** a descending slope [Latin *declivitas,* from *declivis* "sloping down", from *de-* + *clivus* "slope"]

de•coc•tion \di-'käk-shən\ *n* **:** an extracting (as of a flavor or active principle) by boiling in water; *also* **:** a product of this process [Late Latin *decoctio,* from Latin *decoquere* "to cook down", from *de-* + *coquere* "to cook"]

de•code \dē-'kōd, 'dē-\ *vt* **:** to convert (a coded message) into ordinary language — **de•cod•er** *n*

dé•col•le•tage \ˌdā-ˌkäl-ə-'täzh, ˌdek-lə-\ *n* **1 :** the low-cut neckline of a dress **2 :** a décolleté dress [French]

dé•col•le•té \ˌdā-ˌkäl-ə-'tā, ˌdek-lə-\ *adj* **1 :** wearing a strapless or low-necked dress **2 :** having a low-cut neckline [French]

de•col•or•ize \dē-'kəl-ə-ˌrīz, 'dē-\ *vt* **:** to remove color from — **de•col•or•iza•tion** \ˌdē-ˌkəl-ə-rə-'zā-shən\ *n* — **de•col•or•iz•er** *n*

de•com•mis•sion \ˌdē-kə-'mish-ən\ *vt* **:** to take out of commission ⟨a *decommissioned* battleship⟩

de•com•pose \ˌdē-kəm-'pōz\ *vb* **1 :** to separate into parts or elements or into simpler compounds **2 :** to break down through chemical change **:** ROT **syn** see DECAY — **de•com•pos•able** \-'pō-zə-bəl\ *adj* — **de•com•po•si•tion** \ˌdē-ˌkäm-pə-'zish-ən\ *n*

de•com•pos•er \ˌdē-kəm-'pō-zər\ *n* **:** an organism (as a bacterium or a fungus) that breaks down dead protoplasm

de·com·press \ˌdē-kəm-ˈpres\ *vt* : to release (as a diver) from pressure or compression — **de·com·pres·sion** \-ˈpresh-ən\ *n*

de·con·tam·i·nate \ˌdē-kən-ˈtam-ə-ˌnāt\ *vt* : to free from contamination — **de·con·tam·i·na·tion** \-ˌtam-ə-ˈnā-shən\ *n*

de·cor *or* **dé·cor** \dā-ˈkȯr, ˈdā-ˌ\ *n* : DECORATION; *esp* : the arrangement of accessories in interior decoration [French *décor,* from *décorer* "to decorate", from Latin *decorare*]

dec·o·rate \ˈdek-ə-ˌrāt\ *vt* **1** : to make more attractive by adding something beautiful or becoming ⟨*decorate* a room⟩ **2** : to award a decoration of honor to [Latin *decorare,* from *decor-, decus* "ornament"] **syn** see ADORN

dec·o·ra·tion \ˌdek-ə-ˈrā-shən\ *n* **1** : the act or process of decorating **2** : something that adorns or beautifies **3** : a badge of honor (as a medal)

Decoration Day *n* : MEMORIAL DAY

dec·o·ra·tive \ˈdek-rət-iv, -ə-rət-; ˈdek-ə-ˌrāt-\ *adj* : serving to decorate; *esp* : purely ornamental — **dec·o·ra·tive·ly** *adv* — **dec·o·ra·tive·ness** *n*

dec·o·ra·tor \ˈdek-ə-ˌrāt-ər\ *n* : one that decorates; *esp* : a person who designs or executes the interiors of buildings and their furnishings

dec·o·rous \ˈdek-ə-rəs; di-ˈkōr-əs, -ˈkȯr-\ *adj* : marked by propriety and good taste : CORRECT ⟨*decorous* conduct⟩ [Latin *decorus,* from *decor* "beauty, grace"] — **dec·o·rous·ly** *adv* — **dec·o·rous·ness** *n*

de·co·rum \di-ˈkōr-əm, -ˈkȯr-\ *n* **1** : conformity to accepted standards of conduct : proper behavior ⟨social *decorum*⟩ **2** : ORDERLINESS [Latin, from *decorus* "decorous"]
· **syn** PROPRIETY, DIGNITY: DECORUM suggests conduct according with good taste often formally prescribed; PROPRIETY suggests an artificial standard of what is correct in conduct or speech; DIGNITY implies reserve or restraint in conduct prompted by a sense of personal integrity or social importance.

[1]**de·coy** \ˈdē-ˌkȯi, di-ˈ\ *n* **1** : something intended to lure into a trap; *esp* : an artificial bird used to attract live birds within shooting range **2** : a person used to lead another into a trap [probably from Dutch *de kooi,* literally, "the cage"]

[2]**decoy** *vt* : to lure by or as if by a decoy : ENTICE

[1]**de·crease** \di-ˈkrēs, ˈdē-ˌ\ *vb* : to become or cause to become less [Latin *decrescere,* from *de-* + *crescere* "to grow"]
· **syn** DECREASE, LESSEN, DIMINISH, DWINDLE mean to grow or make less. DECREASE suggests progressive reduction in size, amount, or number; LESSEN suggests a decline in amount rather than in number; DIMINISH stresses loss, as in numbers or amount, and implies subtraction from the whole; DWINDLE implies progressive lessening, especially of things growing visibly smaller.

[2]**de·crease** \ˈdē-ˌkrēs, di-ˈ\ *n* **1** : a process of decreasing ⟨a *decrease* in automobile accidents⟩ **2** : the amount by which a thing decreases : REDUCTION ⟨a *decrease* of three dollars in wages⟩

[1]**de·cree** \di-ˈkrē\ *n* **1** : an order usually having the force of law : EDICT **2 a** : a religious ordinance enacted by a church assembly or head **b** : the will of the Deity **c** : something allotted by fate **3** : a judicial decision especially in an equity or probate court ⟨a divorce *decree*⟩ [Middle French *decré,* from Latin *decretum,* from *decernere* "to decide", from *de-* + *cernere* "to sift, decide"]

[2]**decree** *vb* **de·creed**; **de·cree·ing 1** : to order authoritatively ⟨*decree* an amnesty⟩ **2** : to determine or order judicially ⟨*decree* a punishment⟩ — **de·cre·er** \-ˈkrē-ər\ *n*

dec·re·ment \ˈdek-rə-mənt\ *n* : DECREASE [Latin *decrementum,* from *decrescere* "to decrease"]

de·crep·it \di-ˈkrep-ət\ *adj* : broken down or weakened by age [Middle French, from Latin *decrepitus*] — **de·crep·it·ly** *adv* — **de·crep·it·ness** *n*

de·crep·i·tude \di-ˈkrep-ə-ˌtüd, -ˌtyüd\ *n* : the quality or state of being decrepit : infirmity especially from old age

[1]**de·cre·scen·do** \ˌdā-krə-ˈshen-dō\ *adv or adj* : with diminishing volume — used as a direction in music [Italian, literally, "decreasing", from Latin *decrescere* "to decrease"]

[2]**decrescendo** *n, pl* **-dos 1** : a lessening in volume of sound **2** : a decrescendo musical passage

de·cry \di-ˈkrī\ *vt* **1** : to speak slightingly of : belittle publicly ⟨*decry* a hero's deeds⟩ **2** : to find fault with : express strong disapproval of ⟨*decried* the waste of natural resources⟩ [French *décrier,* from Old French *descrier,* from *des-* "de-" + *crier* "to cry"] — **de·cri·er** \-ˈkrī-ər, -ˈkrīr\ *n*

de·cum·bent \di-ˈkəm-bənt\ *adj* : lying down [Latin *decumbere* "to lie down", from *de-* + *-cumbere* "to lie down"] — **de·cum·ben·cy** \-bən-sē\ *n*

ded·i·cate \ˈded-i-ˌkāt\ *vt* **1** : to set apart for some purpose and especially a sacred or serious purpose : DEVOTE ⟨*dedicate* one's life to helping others⟩ **2** : to address or inscribe as a compliment ⟨*dedicate* a book to a friend⟩ [Latin *dedicare,* from *de-* + *dicare* "to proclaim, dedicate"] — **ded·i·ca·tor** \-ˌkāt-ər\ *n*

ded·i·ca·tion \ˌded-i-ˈkā-shən\ *n* **1 a** : an act or rite of dedicating to a divine being or to a sacred use **b** : a setting aside for a particular purpose **2** : an inscription dedicating a literary work **3** : self-sacrificing devotion — **ded·i·ca·tive** \ˈded-i-ˌkāt-iv\ *adj* — **ded·i·ca·to·ry** \ˈded-i-kə-ˌtōr-ē, -ˌtȯr-\ *adj*

de·duce \di-ˈdüs, -ˈdyüs\ *vt* **1** : to trace the course or derivation of **2** : to draw (an inevitable conclusion) from known facts [Latin *deducere,* literally, "to lead away", from *de-* + *ducere* "to lead"] — **de·duc·i·ble** \-ˈdü-sə-bəl, -ˈdyü-\ *adj*

de·duct \di-ˈdəkt\ *vt* : to take away (an amount) from a total : SUBTRACT [Latin *deductus,* past participle of *deducere* "to deduce, lead away"]

de·duct·ible \di-ˈdək-tə-bəl\ *adj* : capable of being deducted : allowable as a deduction — **de·duct·ibil·i·ty** \di-ˌdək-tə-ˈbil-ət-ē\ *n*

de·duc·tion \di-ˈdək-shən\ *n* **1** : an act of taking away **2 a** : the forming of a conclusion by reasoning; *esp* : inference in which the conclusion follows necessarily from the facts given **b** : a conclusion reached by mental deduction **3** : something that is or may be subtracted ⟨*deductions* from taxable income⟩ : ABATEMENT — **de·duc·tive** \-ˈdək-tiv\ *adj* — **de·duc·tive·ly** *adv*

[1]**deed** \ˈdēd\ *n* **1** : something that is done : ACT; *esp* : a brave or noteworthy act ⟨judge them by their *deeds*⟩ **2** : a legal document by which one person transfers real property to another [Old English *dǣd*] — **deed·less** \-ləs\ *adj*

[2]**deed** *vt* : to convey or transfer by legal deed

deem \ˈdēm\ *vb* : to come to think or judge : have an opinion : BELIEVE, SUPPOSE [Old English *dēman*]

[1]**deep** \ˈdēp\ *adj* **1 a** : extending far downward ⟨a *deep* well⟩ : having a great distance between the top and bottom surfaces ⟨*deep* water⟩ : not shallow **b** : extending well inward from an outer surface ⟨a *deep* gash⟩ **c** : extending well back from a front surface ⟨a *deep* closet⟩ **d** : extending far outward from a center ⟨*deep* space⟩ **e** : occurring or located near the outer limits ⟨*deep* right field⟩ **2** : having a specified extension downward, inward, or backward ⟨a shelf 40 centimeters *deep*⟩ **3 a** : difficult to understand ⟨a *deep* book⟩ **b** : MYSTERIOUS, OBSCURE ⟨a *deep* dark secret⟩ **c** : WISE ⟨a *deep* thinker⟩ **d** : ENGROSSED, INVOLVED ⟨*deep* in thought⟩ **e** : of great intensity : PROFOUND ⟨*deep* sleep⟩ **4 a** : high in saturation and low in lightness ⟨a *deep* red⟩ **b** : having a low musical pitch or range ⟨a *deep* voice⟩ **5 a** : coming from or situated well within ⟨a *deep* sigh⟩ **b** : covered, enclosed, or filled often to a specified degree ⟨knee-*deep* in water⟩ [Old English *dēop*] — **deep·ly** *adv*

[2]**deep** *adv* **1** : to a great depth : DEEPLY **2** : far on : LATE ⟨*deep* in the night⟩

[3]**deep** *n* **1** : an extremely deep place or part; *esp* : OCEAN **2** : the middle or most intense part ⟨the *deep* of winter⟩

deep–dish pie *n* : a pie baked in a deep dish and having no bottom crust

deep·en \ˈdē-pən\ *vb* **deep·ened**; **deep·en·ing** \ˈdēp-ning, -ə-ning\ : to make or become deep or deeper

deep–root·ed \ˈdēp-ˈrüt-əd, -ˈru̇t-\ *adj* : deeply implanted or established ⟨a *deep-rooted* loyalty⟩

deep–sea \ˈdēp-ˈsē\ *adj* : of, relating to, or occurring in the deeper parts of the sea ⟨*deep-sea* fishing⟩

deep–seat·ed \ˈdēp-ˈsēt-əd\ *adj* **1** : situated far below the surface **2** : firmly established ⟨a *deep-seated* tradition⟩

deep–set \ˈdēp-ˈset\ *adj* : set far in ⟨*deep-set* eyes⟩

deer \ˈdiər\ *n, pl* **deer** : any of a family of cloven-hoofed cud-chewing mammals with antlers borne by the males of nearly all and by the females of a few forms [Old English *dēor* "wild animal, beast"]

△ **origin** The development of a word's meaning is often from the general to the specific. For instance, *deer* is used in modern English to denote numerous species, including white-tailed deer, reindeer, caribou, elk, and moose, all belonging to the same natural family. The Old English *dēor,* however, could refer to any beast or wild animal, or to wild animals in general. In time, *deer* came to be restricted to the animal that was the primary object of the hunt in England. From that usage the term has spread to other members of the same family and become somewhat more general again though not so general as once.

deer•hound \-,haůnd\ *n* : a large tall slender dog of a breed developed in Scotland and formerly used in hunting deer

deer mouse *n* : any of numerous North American mice occurring in fields and woods

deer mouse

deer•skin \'diər-,skin\ *n* : leather made from the skin of a deer; *also* : a garment of such leather

de–es•ca•late \dē-'es-kə-,lāt, 'dē-\ *vb* : to make less (as in extent or scope) — **de–es•ca•la•tion** \,dē-,es-kə-'lā-shən\ *n*

de•face \di-'fās\ *vt* : to destroy or mar the face or surface of [Middle French *desfacier,* from *des-* "de-" + *face* "face"] — **de•face•ment** \-'fās-mənt\ *n* — **de•fac•er** *n*

• **syn** DEFACE, DISFIGURE mean to mar the appearance of. DEFACE suggests superficial injuries or the removal of some part or detail; DISFIGURE implies deeper or more permanent injury that impairs beauty or attractiveness.

de fac•to \di-'fak-,tō, dā-\ *adj or adv* **1** : actually exercising power ⟨a *de facto* government⟩ — compare DE JURE **2** : existing in fact ⟨a *de facto* state of war⟩ [New Latin, adverb, "in fact"]

de•fal•ca•tion \,dē-,fal-'kā-shən, -fȯl-; ,def-əl-\ *n* : a misuse or theft of money placed in one's keeping [Medieval Latin *defalcatio* "deduction", from *defalcare* "to deduct", from Latin *de-* + *falx* "sickle"] — **de•fal•cate** \di-'fal-,kāt, -'fȯl-, 'def-əl-\ *vi* — **de•fal•ca•tor** \-,kāt-ər\ *n*

def•a•ma•tion \,def-ə-'mā-shən\ *n* : the act of defaming : injury to the good name of another : SLANDER, LIBEL — **de•fam•a•to•ry** \di-'fam-ə-,tōr-ē, -,tȯr-\ *adj*

de•fame \di-'fām\ *vt* : to injure or destroy the good name of : speak evil of **syn** see SLANDER — **de•fam•er** *n*

[1]**de•fault** \di-'fȯlt\ *n* : failure to do something required by law or duty [Old French *defaute,* derived from Latin *de-* + *fallere* "to deceive"]

[2]**default** *vb* : to fail to carry out a contract, obligation, or duty; *also* : to forfeit something by such failure — **de•fault•er** *n*

[1]**de•feat** \di-'fēt\ *vt* **1** : NULLIFY, FRUSTRATE ⟨*defeat* a hope⟩ **2** : to win victory over : BEAT [Middle French *deffait,* past participle of *deffaire* "to destroy", from Medieval Latin *disfacere,* from Latin *dis-* + *facere* "to do"]

[2]**defeat** *n* **1** : frustration by prevention of success ⟨the *defeat* of our plans⟩ **2 a** : an overthrow of an army in battle **b** : loss of a contest (as by a team)

de•feat•ism \-,iz-əm\ *n* : an attitude of expecting the defeat of one's own cause or of accepting such defeat on the ground that further effort would be useless or unwise — **de•feat•ist** \-əst\ *n or adj*

def•e•cate \'def-i-,kāt\ *vb* **1** : to free from impurity or corruption : REFINE **2** : to discharge feces from the bowels [Latin *defaecare,* from *de-* + *faex* "dregs, lees"] — **def•e•ca•tion** \,def-i-'kā-shən\ *n*

[1]**de•fect** \'dē-,fekt, di-'\ *n* : a lack of something necessary for completeness or perfection : FAULT, IMPERFECTION [Middle French, from Latin *defectus* "lack", from *deficere* "to be wanting, fail, desert", from *de-* + *facere* "to do"] **syn** see BLEMISH

[2]**de•fect** \di-'fekt\ *vi* : to desert a cause or party often in order to take up another — **de•fec•tion** \-'fek-shən\ *n* — **de•fec•tor** \-'fek-tər\ *n*

[1]**de•fec•tive** \di-'fek-tiv\ *adj* **1** : lacking something essential : FAULTY **2** : lacking one or more of the usual forms of grammatical inflection ⟨*must* is a *defective* verb⟩ — **de•fec•tive•ly** *adv* — **de•fec•tive•ness** *n*

[2]**defective** *n* : a person who is subnormal physically or mentally

de•fend \di-'fend\ *vb* **1** : to repel danger or attack **2** : to act as attorney for **3** : to oppose the claim of another in a lawsuit : CONTEST **4** : to uphold against opposition ⟨*defend* an idea⟩ [Old French *defendre,* from Latin *defendere,* from *de-* + *-fendere* "to strike"] — **de•fend•er** *n*

• **syn** DEFEND, PROTECT, SHIELD, GUARD mean to keep secure from danger or against attack. DEFEND denotes warding off actual or threatened attack; PROTECT implies something, as a covering, that serves as a bar to the admission or impact of that which may attack or injure ⟨*protect* one's eyes with dark glasses⟩ ⟨a bird sanctuary *protected* by state law⟩ SHIELD suggests protective intervention in imminent danger or actual attack; GUARD implies protecting with vigilance and force against expected danger.

de•fend•ant \di-'fen-dənt\ *n* : a person called on to answer an accusation in a legal action — compare PLAINTIFF

de•fense *or* **de•fence** \di-'fens\ *n* **1** : the act of defending : resistance against attack **2** : capability of resisting attack **3 a** : means or method of defending **b** : an argument in support or justification **4 a** : a defending party or group (as in a court of law) **b** : a defensive team **5** : the answer made by the defendant in a legal action [Old French, derived from Latin *defendere* "to defend"] — **de•fense•less** \-ləs\ *adj* — **de•fense•less•ly** *adv* — **de•fense•less•ness** *n*

defense mechanism *n* **1** : a defensive reaction by an organism **2** : a mental process (as rationalization or repression) by which one avoids becoming aware of unpleasant thoughts, feelings, or emotions

de•fen•si•ble \di-'fen-sə-bəl\ *adj* : capable of being defended — **de•fen•si•bil•i•ty** \-,fen-sə-'bil-ət-ē\ *n* — **de•fen•si•bly** \-'fen-sə-blē\ *adv*

[1]**de•fen•sive** \di-'fen-siv\ *adj* : of or relating to defense: as **a** : serving or intended to defend or protect ⟨a *defensive* move⟩ **b** : of or relating to the attempt to keep an opponent from scoring in a game or contest — **de•fen•sive•ly** *adv* — **de•fen•sive•ness** *n*

[2]**defensive** *n* : a defensive position — **on the defensive** : in a state of readiness to oppose attack

[1]**de•fer** \di-'fər\ *vt* **de•ferred**; **de•fer•ring** : to put off : DELAY ⟨*defer* payment for goods⟩ [Middle French *differer,* from Latin *differre* "to postpone, be different"] — **de•fer•ra•ble** \-'fər-ə-bəl\ *adj* — **de•fer•rer** *n*

• **syn** DEFER, POSTPONE mean to delay an action or proceeding. DEFER may imply a deliberate putting off until a later usually indefinite time or may imply a delay in fulfillment ⟨*defer* college plans⟩ POSTPONE implies an intentional deferring usually to a definite time ⟨*postpone* the meeting until Monday⟩

[2]**defer** *vi* **de•ferred**; **de•fer•ring** : to yield to another's wish or opinion [Middle French *deferer,* from Latin *deferre* "to bring down", from *de-* + *ferre* "to carry"]

def•er•ence \'def-rəns, -ə-rəns\ *n* : courteous respectful regard for another or another's wishes

• **syn** DEFERENCE, RESPECT, REVERENCE, HONOR mean esteem shown to another. DEFERENCE implies a courteous yielding of one's own opinion or preference to that of another; RESPECT implies regard for a person or quality or achievement as worthy of honor or confidence; REVERENCE implies profound respect mingled with awe or devotion; HONOR implies that the recognition shown is entirely due.

— **in deference to** : in consideration of or out of respect for

def•er•en•tial \,def-ə-'ren-chəl\ *adj* : showing or expressing deference — **def•er•en•tial•ly** \-'rench-lē, -ə-lē\ *adv*

de•fer•ment \di-'fər-mənt\ *n* : the act of delaying; *esp* : official postponement of military service

de•fi•ance \di-'fī-əns\ *n* **1** : the act or an instance of defying : CHALLENGE **2** : disposition to resist : contempt of opposition — **in defiance of** : contrary to ⟨worked *in defiance of* doctor's orders⟩

de•fi•ant \-ənt\ *adj* : full of defiance : BOLD — **de•fi•ant•ly** *adv*

de•fi•cien•cy \di-'fish-ən-sē\ *n, pl* **-cies** **1** : the quality or state of being deficient **2** : shortage of something needed; *esp* : a shortage of substances necessary to health

deficiency disease *n* : a disease (as scurvy) caused by a lack of essential dietary elements and especially a vitamin or mineral

[1]**de•fi•cient** \di-'fish-ənt\ *adj* : lacking something necessary for

completeness : below a standard : DEFECTIVE ⟨a diet *deficient* in proteins⟩ [Latin *deficiens,* present participle of *deficere* "to be wanting, fail", from *de-* + *facere* "to do"] — **de·fi·cient·ly** *adv*

2deficient *n* : one that is deficient ⟨a mental *deficient*⟩

def·i·cit \'def-ə-sət\ *n* : a deficiency in amount; *esp* : an excess of expenses over income [French *déficit,* from Latin *deficit* "it is wanting", from *deficere* "to be wanting"]

1de·file \di-'fīl\ *vt* **1** : to make filthy : DIRTY **2** : to corrupt the purity or perfection of: as **a** : RAPE 2, VIOLATE **b** : DESECRATE ⟨invaders *defiled* the shrine⟩ **c** : TARNISH, ABASE ⟨*defile* a hero's record with lies⟩ [Old French *defouler* "to trample", from *de-* "de-" + *fouler* "to trample"] — **de·file·ment** \-mənt\ *n* — **de·fil·er** *n*

2de·file \di-'fīl, 'dē-,\ *vi* : to march off in a single line [French *défiler,* from *dé-* "de-" + *filer* "to move in a column"]

3de·file \di-'fīl, 'dē-,\ *n* : a narrow passage or gorge

de·fine \di-'fīn\ *vt* **1 a** : to fix or mark the limits of **b** : to make distinct in outline **2 a** : to determine the essential qualities of ⟨*define* the concept of loyalty⟩ **b** : to discover and set forth the meaning of ⟨*define* a word⟩ **c** : to assign a value or values to [Latin *definire,* from *de-* + *finis* "boundary, end"] — **de·fin·able** \-'fī-nə-bəl\ *adj* — **de·fin·er** *n*

def·i·nite \'def-nət, -ə-nət\ *adj* **1** : having certain or distinct limits : FIXED ⟨a *definite* period of time⟩ **2** : clear in meaning : EXACT, EXPLICIT ⟨a *definite* answer⟩ **3** : typically designating an identified or immediately identifiable person or thing ⟨the *definite* article *the*⟩ [Latin *definitus,* past participle of *definire* "to define"] — **def·i·nite·ly** *adv* — **def·i·nite·ness** *n*

• **syn** DEFINITE, DEFINITIVE are sometimes confused. DEFINITE denotes that which has limits so clearly fixed, defined, or stated there can be no doubt about the range or meaning ⟨a *definite* sum of money⟩ DEFINITIVE denotes supplying an answer as final and serving to end dispute and doubt ⟨a *definitive* statement of religious belief⟩ **syn** see in addition EXPLICIT

def·i·ni·tion \,def-ə-'nish-ən\ *n* **1** : an act of determining or settling the limits **2 a** : a statement of the meaning of a word or word group or of a sign or symbol **b** : the action or process of stating such a meaning **3 a** : the action or the power of making definite and clear **b** : the state of being clear ⟨the *definition* of the hills⟩ — **def·i·ni·tion·al** \-'nish-nəl, -'nish-ən-l\ *adj*

de·fin·i·tive \di-'fin-ət-iv\ *adj* **1** : providing a final solution : CONCLUSIVE ⟨a *definitive* victory⟩ **2** : authoritative and apparently completely informative ⟨the *definitive* book on the subject⟩ **3** : defining or limiting precisely **syn** see DEFINITE — **de·fin·i·tive·ly** *adv* — **de·fin·i·tive·ness** *n*

de·flate \di-'flāt, 'dē-\ *vb* **1** : to release air or gas from **2** : to cause to contract from a high level : reduce from a state of inflation ⟨*deflate* the currency⟩ **3** : to become deflated : COLLAPSE [*de-* + *-flate* (as in *inflate*)] — **de·fla·tor** \-'flāt-ər\ *n*

de·fla·tion \di-'flā-shən, 'dē-\ *n* **1** : an act or instance of deflating : the state of being deflated **2** : a shrinking in the volume of available money or credit that results in a decline of the general price level — **de·fla·tion·ary** \-shə-,ner-ē\ *adj*

de·flect \di-'flekt\ *vb* : to take or cause to take a new course : turn aside ⟨*deflect* a stream from its bed⟩ ⟨do not let your mind *deflect* from reason⟩ [Latin *deflectere* "to bend down, turn aside", from *de-* + *flectere* "to bend"] — **de·flec·tion** \-'flek-shən\ *n*

de·fo·li·ant \'dē-'fō-lē-ənt\ *n* : a chemical applied to plants to cause the leaves to drop off prematurely

de·fo·li·ate \'dē-'fō-lē-,āt\ *vt* : to deprive of leaves especially prematurely [Latin *defoliare,* from *de-* + *folium* "leaf"] — **de·fo·li·a·tion** \,dē-,fō-lē-'ā-shən\ *n* — **de·fo·li·a·tor** \'dē-'fō-lē-,āt-ər\ *n*

de·for·est \'dē-'fȯr-əst, -'fär-\ *vt* : to clear of forests — **de·for·es·ta·tion** \,dē,fȯr-ə-'stā-shən, -,fär-\ *n*

de·form \di-'fȯrm, 'dē-\ *vb* **1** : to spoil the form or natural appearance of : DISFIGURE ⟨a leg *deformed* by an injury⟩ ⟨a face *deformed* by grief⟩ **2** : to become misshapen or changed in shape — **de·for·ma·tion** \,dē-,fȯr-'mā-shən, ,def-ər-\ *n*

de·for·mi·ty \di-'fȯr-mət-ē\ *n, pl* **-ties** **1** : the state of being deformed **2** : a physical blemish or distortion **3** : a moral or aesthetic flaw

de·fraud \di-'frȯd\ *vt* : to deprive of something by trickery, deception, or fraud ⟨were *defrauded* of their money⟩ **syn** see CHEAT — **de·frau·da·tion** \,dē-,frȯ-'dā-shən\ *n* — **de·fraud·er** \di-'frȯd-ər\ *n*

de·fray \di-'frā\ *vt* : to pay or provide for the payment of ⟨needs more money to *defray* expenses⟩ [Middle French *deffrayer,* from *des-* "de-" + *frayer* "to expend", derived from Latin *frangere* "to break"] — **de·fray·able** \-'frā-ə-bəl\ *adj* — **de·fray·al** \-'frā-əl, -'frāl\ *n*

de·frost \di-'frȯst, 'dē-\ *vb* : to free from ice or a frozen state : thaw out ⟨*defrost* meat⟩ ⟨*defrost* a refrigerator⟩ — **de·frost·er** *n*

deft \'deft\ *adj* : quick and neat in action : SKILLFUL ⟨dressing the wound with *deft* fingers⟩ [Middle English *defte*] **syn** see DEXTEROUS — **deft·ly** *adv* — **deft·ness** *n*

de·funct \di-'fəngt, -'fəngkt\ *adj* : no longer living or existing ⟨a *defunct* factory⟩ [Latin *defunctus,* from *defungi* "to finish, die", from *de-* + *fungi* "to perform"]

de·fy \di-'fī\ *vt* **de·fied**; **de·fy·ing** **1** : to challenge to do something considered impossible ⟨the magician *defied* the audience to explain the trick⟩ **2** : to refuse boldly to yield or conform to ⟨*defy* public opinion⟩ ⟨*defy* the law⟩ **3** : to resist attempts at : BAFFLE ⟨a scene that *defies* description⟩ [Old French *defier* "to renounce faith in, challenge", from *de-* "de-" + *fier* "to entrust", from Latin *fidere* "to trust"] — **de·fi·er** \-'fī-ər, -'fīr\ *n*

de·gas \'dē-'gas\ *vt* : to free from gas

de·gauss \'dē-'gau̇s\ *vt* : DEMAGNETIZE

de·gen·er·a·cy \di-'jen-rə-sē, -ə-rə-\ *n, pl* **-cies** **1** : the state of being or process of becoming degenerate **2** : sexual perversion

1de·gen·er·ate \di-'jen-rət, -ə-rət\ *adj* : having sunk to a lower state or level: as **a** : having declined (as in structure or function) from an ancestral or earlier state ⟨a *degenerate* eye⟩ **b** : fallen below what is normal or desirable; *esp* : fallen to a corrupt, evil, or vicious state [Latin *degeneratus,* past participle of *degenerare* "to deteriorate", from *de-* + *genus* "race, kind"]

2degenerate *n* : a degenerate person; *esp* : a sexual pervert

3de·gen·er·ate \di-'jen-ə-,rāt\ *vi* **1** : to pass from a higher to a lower type or condition ⟨the road *degenerated* into a rough track⟩ **2** : to undergo change toward an earlier or less highly organized biological type

de·gen·er·a·tion \di-,jen-ə-'rā-shən, ,dē-\ *n* **1** : a lowering (as of power, vitality, or quality) to a feebler and poorer kind or state **2** : a change in a tissue or an organ resulting in lessened activity or usefulness ⟨fatty *degeneration* of the heart⟩; *also* : a condition marked by such changes and especially by loss of organs present in related forms ⟨tapeworms exhibit extreme *degeneration*⟩

de·gen·er·a·tive \di-'jen-ə-,rāt-iv\ *adj* : of, relating to, or tending to cause degeneration ⟨a *degenerative* disease⟩

deg·ra·da·tion \,deg-rə-'dā-shən\ *n* **1** : a reduction in rank, dignity, or standing **b** : removal from office **2** : loss of honor or reputation : HUMILIATION **3** : moral or intellectual decay : DEGENERATION

de·grade \di-'grād\ *vb* **1** : DEMOTE; *also* : DEPOSE 1 **2** : to drag down in moral or intellectual character ⟨*degraded* by a life of crime⟩ **3** : to reduce the complexity of : DECOMPOSE **syn** see DEBASE — **de·grad·er** *n*

de·gree \di-'grē\ *n* **1** : a step or stage in a process, course, or order of classification ⟨advance by *degrees*⟩ **2 a** : the extent, intensity, or scope of something especially as measured by a graded series ⟨murder in the first *degree*⟩ **b** : one of the forms or sets of forms used in the comparison of an adjective or adverb **3 a** : a rank or grade of official or social position **b** : the civil condition or status of a person **4 a** : a grade of membership attained in a ritualistic order or society **b** : the formal ceremonies observed in the awarding of a ritualistic distinction **c** : a title conferred upon students by a college, university, or professional school upon completion of a program of

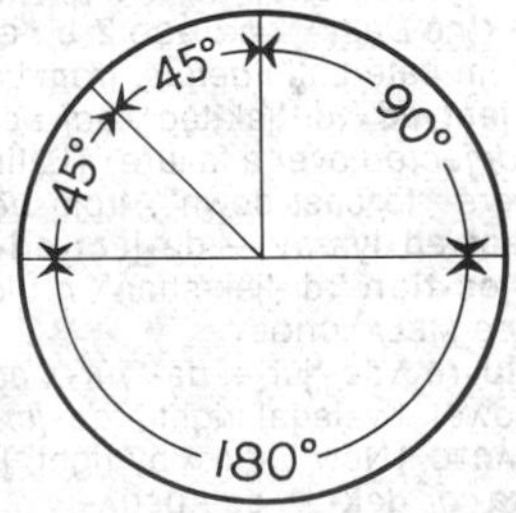

degree 5

\ə\ **abut**	\au̇\ **out**	\i\ **tip**	\ȯ\ **saw**	\u̇\ **foot**
\ər\ **further**	\ch\ **chin**	\ī\ **life**	\ȯi\ **coin**	\y\ **yet**
\a\ **mat**	\e\ **pet**	\j\ **job**	\th\ **thin**	\yü\ **few**
\ā\ **take**	\ē\ **easy**	\ng\ **sing**	\t͟h\ **this**	\yu̇\ **cure**
\ä\ **cot, cart**	\g\ **go**	\ō\ **bone**	\ü\ **food**	\zh\ **vision**

study **d** : an academic title conferred honorarily **5** : one of the divisions or intervals marked on a scale of a measuring instrument — symbol ° **6** : a 360th part of the circumference of a circle **7 a** : the sum of the exponents of the variable factors in a mathematical expression containing a single term ⟨the *degree* of $3x^2y$ is 3⟩ **b** : the degree of the term of highest degree in a polynomial ⟨the *degree* of $3x^3 + 2x^2y + 5x$ is 3⟩ **8 a** : a line or space of the musical staff **b** : a step, note, or tone of a musical scale [Old French *degré* "step, stair", from Latin *de-* + *gradus* "step, grade"] — **to a degree 1** : to a remarkable extent **2** : in a small way

degree–day *n* : a unit that represents one degree of departure from a given point (as 65°F or 18°C) in the mean daily outdoor temperature and is usually used to measure heat requirements

de•hisce \di-'his\ *vi* : to split open along a natural line especially with discharge of contents ⟨seedpods *dehiscing* at maturity⟩ [Latin *dehiscere* "to split open", from *de-* + *hiscere* "to gape"] — **de•his•cence** \-'his-ns\ *n* — **de•his•cent** \-nt\ *adj*

de•horn \dē-'hȯrn, 'dē-\ *vt* : to deprive of horns — **de•horn•er** *n*

de•hu•man•ize \dē-'hyü-mə-,nīz, dē-'yü-, 'dē-\ *vt* : to strip of human qualities or personality — **de•hu•man•iza•tion** \dē-,hyü-mə-nə-'zā-shən, dē-,yü-, 'dē-\ *n*

de•hu•mid•i•fy \,dē-hyü-'mid-ə-,fī, ,dē-yü-\ *vt* : to remove moisture from (as the air) — **de•hu•mid•i•fi•ca•tion** \-,mid-ə-fə-'kā-shən\ *n* — **de•hu•mid•i•fi•er** \-'mid-ə-,fī-ər, -,fīr\ *n*

de•hy•drate \dē-'hī-,drāt, 'dē-\ *vb* **1** : to remove water from (as foods) **2** : to lose water or body fluids — **de•hy•dra•tion** \,dē-,hī-'drā-shən\ *n*

de•hy•drog•e•nase \,dē-,hī-'dräj-ə-,nās, dē-'hī-drə-jə-\ *n* : an enzyme that accelerates the removal and transfer of hydrogen

de•hy•dro•ge•nate \,dē-,hī-'dräj-ə-,nāt, dē-'hī-drə-jə-\ *vt* : to remove hydrogen from — **de•hy•dro•ge•na•tion** \,dē-,hī-,dräj-ə-'nā-shən, ,dē-,hī-drə-jə-\ *n*

de•ice \dē-'īs, 'dē-\ *vt* : to keep free or rid of ice — **de•ic•er** *n*

de•i•fy \'dē-ə-,fī\ *vt* **-fied; -fy•ing 1 a** : to make a god of **b** : to take as an object of worship **2** : to treat as an object of supreme regard ⟨*deify* money⟩ [Middle French *deifier,* from Late Latin *deificare,* from Latin *deus* "god"] — **de•i•fi•ca•tion** \,dē-ə-fə-'kā-shən\ *n*

deign \'dān\ *vi* : to condescend reluctantly ⟨barely *deigned* to acknowledge their greeting⟩ [Old French *deignier,* from Latin *dignare,* from *dignus* "worthy"] **syn** see STOOP

de•ion•ize \dē-'ī-ə-,nīz, 'dē-\ *vt* : to remove ions from — **de•ion•iza•tion** \,dē-,ī-ə-nə-'zā-shən\ *n*

de•ism \'dē-,izəm\ *n* : a movement or system of thought advocating natural religion based on human reason rather than revelation, emphasizing morality, and in the 18th century denying the interference of the Creator with the laws of the universe — **de•ist** \'dē-əst\ *n*

de•i•ty \'dē-ət-ē, 'dā-\ *n, pl* **-ties 1 a** : DIVINITY 1 **b** *cap* : GOD 1 ⟨the *Deity*⟩ **2 a** : GOD 2 **b** : GODDESS 1 [Middle French *deité,* from Late Latin *deitas,* from Latin *deus* "god"]

de•ject•ed \di-'jek-təd\ *adj* : cast down in spirits : DEPRESSED ⟨*dejected* over a failure⟩ [Latin *dejectus,* past participle of *deicere* "to cast down", from *de-* + *jacere* "to throw"] — **de•ject•ed•ly** *adv* — **de•ject•ed•ness** *n*

de•jec•tion \di-'jek-shən\ *n* : lowness of spirits : SADNESS **syn** see MELANCHOLY

de ju•re \dē-'jür-ē, dā-'yür-\ *adj or adv* : existing or exercising power by legal right ⟨*de jure* government⟩ — compare DE FACTO [New Latin, "by right"]

deka- *or* **dek-** — see DECA-

deka•gram \'dek-ə-,gram\ *n* — see METRIC SYSTEM table

deka•li•ter \-,lēt-ər\ *n* — see METRIC SYSTEM table

deka•me•ter \-,mēt-ər\ *n* — see METRIC SYSTEM table

deka•stere \'dek-ə-,stiər, -,steər\ *n* : a metric unit of volume equal to 10 cubic meters

de•lam•i•na•tion \,dē-,lam-ə-'nā-shən\ *n* : separation or splitting into distinct layers — **de•lam•i•nate** \dē-'lam-ə-,nāt\ *vi*

Del•a•ware \'del-ə-,waər, -,weər, -wər\ *n* : a member of an Algonquian people of the Delaware valley

[1]de•lay \di-'lā\ *n* **1** : the act of delaying : the state of being delayed **2** : the time during which something is delayed

[2]delay *vb* **1** : to put off : POSTPONE **2** : to stop, detain, or hinder for a time ⟨*delayed* by a storm⟩ **3** : to move or act slowly [Old French *delaier,* from *de-* + *laier* "to leave", alteration of *laissier,* from Latin *laxare* "to slacken"] — **de•lay•er** *n*

de•lec•ta•ble \di-'lek-tə-bəl\ *adj* **1** : highly pleasing : DELIGHTFUL **2** : DELICIOUS ⟨a *delectable* meal⟩ [Middle French, derived from Latin *delectare* "to delight"] — **de•lec•ta•bly** \-blē\ *adv*

del•e•ga•cy \'del-i-gə-sē\ *n, pl* **-cies 1 a** : the act of delegating **b** : appointment as delegate **2** : a body of delegates : BOARD

[1]del•e•gate \'del-i-gət, -,gāt\ *n* : a person sent with power to act for another: as **a** : a representative to a convention, conference, or assembly **b** : a representative of a United States territory in the House of Representatives **c** : a member of the lower house of the legislature of Maryland, Virginia, or West Virginia [derived from Latin *delegare* "to delegate", from *de-* + *legare* "to send"]

[2]del•e•gate \-,gāt\ *vt* **1** : to entrust to another ⟨*delegate* responsibility⟩ **2** : to appoint as one's delegate

del•e•ga•tion \,del-i-'gā-shən\ *n* **1** : the act of delegating (as power or authority) to another **2** : one or more persons chosen to represent others

de•lete \di-'lēt\ *vt* : to eliminate especially by blotting out, cutting out, or erasing [Latin *delēre* "to wipe out, destroy"]

del•e•te•ri•ous \,del-ə-'tir-ē-əs\ *adj* : having a harmful effect [Greek *dēlētērios,* from *dēleisthai* "to hurt"] — **del•e•te•ri•ous•ly** *adv* — **del•e•te•ri•ous•ness** *n*

de•le•tion \di-'lē-shən\ *n* **1** : an act of deleting **2** : something deleted

delft \'delft\ *or* **delft•ware** \'delf-,twaər, -,tweər\ *n* **1** : a Dutch pottery covered with an opaque white glaze upon which a predominantly blue decoration is painted **2** : glazed pottery especially when blue and white [*Delft,* Netherlands]

deli \'del-ē\ *n, pl* **del•is** : DELICATESSEN

[1]de•lib•er•ate \di-'lib-rət, -ə-rət\ *adj* **1** : marked by or resulting from thorough and careful consideration ⟨a *deliberate* judgment⟩ **2** : showing awareness of the significance or nature of the thing done or said ⟨a *deliberate* lie⟩ **3** : weighing facts and arguments : careful and slow in deciding ⟨a *deliberate* person⟩ **4** : slow in action : not hurried ⟨*deliberate* movements⟩ [Latin *deliberatus,* past participle of *deliberare* "to weigh in mind", from *de-* + *libra* "scale, pound"] **syn** see VOLUNTARY — **de•lib•er•ate•ly** *adv* — **de•lib•er•ate•ness** *n*

[2]de•lib•er•ate \di-'lib-ə-,rāt\ *vb* : to think about deliberately : CONSIDER ⟨*deliberate* before answering⟩

de•lib•er•a•tion \di-,lib-ə-'rā-shən\ *n* **1** : the act of deliberating **2** : a discussion and consideration of the reasons for and against a measure or question **3** : the quality of being deliberate : DELIBERATENESS

de•lib•er•a•tive \di-'lib-ə-,rāt-iv; -'lib-rət-, -ə-rət-\ *adj* : of or relating to deliberation : engaged in or devoted to deliberation ⟨a *deliberative* assembly⟩ — **de•lib•er•a•tive•ly** *adv* — **de•lib•er•a•tive•ness** *n*

del•i•ca•cy \'del-i-kə-sē\ *n, pl* **-cies 1** : something pleasing to eat because it is rare or luxurious **2 a** : FINENESS, DAINTINESS ⟨lace of great *delicacy*⟩ **b** : FRAILTY 1 **3** : nicety or subtle expressiveness of touch (as in painting or music) **4 a** : precise and refined perception and discrimination **b** : extreme sensitivity : PRECISION **5** : SQUEAMISHNESS **6** : the quality or state of requiring delicate treatment ⟨the *delicacy* of a situation⟩

del•i•cate \'del-i-kət\ *adj* **1 a** : pleasing to the senses ⟨a *delicate* breeze⟩ ⟨a *delicate* aroma⟩ **2** : marked by keen sensitivity or fine discrimination **3** : exhibiting extreme sensitivity ⟨a *delicate* instrument⟩ **4** : calling for or involving extremely careful treatment ⟨a *delicate* balance of power⟩ **5** : marked by fineness of structure, workmanship, or texture ⟨*delicate* lace⟩ **6** : easily torn or hurt ⟨a *delicate* butterfly wing⟩; *also* : WEAK 1a, SICKLY **7** : marked by tact; *also* : requiring tact ⟨*delicate* negotiations⟩ [Latin *delicatus*] — **del•i•cate•ly** *adv* — **del•i•cate•ness** *n*

del•i•ca•tes•sen \,del-i-kə-'tes-n\ *n pl* **1** : ready-to-eat food products (as cooked meats and prepared salads) **2** *sing, pl* **delicatessens** : a store where delicatessen are sold [obsolete German (now *delikatessen),* plural of *delicatesse* "delicacy", from French *délicatesse,* derived from Latin *delicatus* "delicate"]

△ **origin** Near the end of the 19th century, the word *delicatessen* began to appear in English. Its earliest sense is "delicacies" or "ready-to-eat food products". In this sense *delicatessen* is a plural noun, reflecting its origin in a German word now spelled *Delikatessen,* the plural of *Delikatesse.* The German is a borrowing from French *délicatesse,* meaning "delicacy". In English a second sense of *delicatessen* developed when the word was understood as a singular noun used for a store where delicacies are sold. In spite of the widespread popular belief to the contrary, *delicatessen* has no etymological connection with the German verb *essen,* "to eat".

de•li•cious \di-'lish-əs\ *adj* **:** giving great pleasure **:** DELIGHTFUL; *esp* **:** very pleasing to the taste or smell [Old French, derived from Latin *delicere* "to allure"] — **de•li•cious•ly** *adv* — **de•li•cious•ness** *n*

[1]**de•light** \di-'līt\ *n* **1 :** extreme pleasure or satisfaction **:** JOY **2 :** something that gives great pleasure

[2]**delight** *vb* **1 :** to take great pleasure **2 :** to give joy or satisfaction to **:** please greatly [Old French *delitier* from Latin *delectare,* derived from *delicere* "to allure", from *de-* + *lacere* "to allure"]

de•light•ed *adj* **:** highly pleased **:** GRATIFIED — **de•light•ed•ly** *adv* — **de•light•ed•ness** *n*

de•light•ful \di-'līt-fəl\ *adj* **:** highly pleasing **:** giving delight ⟨a *delightful* vacation⟩ — **de•light•ful•ly** \-fə-lē\ *adv* — **de•light•ful•ness** *n*

de•lim•it \di-'lim-ət\ *vt* **:** to fix the limits of **:** BOUND — **de•lim•i•ta•tion** \-ˌlim-ə-'tā-shən\ *n* — **de•lim•i•ta•tive** \-'lim-əˌtāt-iv\ *adj*

de•lin•eate \di-'lin-ē-ˌāt\ *vt* **1 :** to indicate by lines drawn in the form or figure of **:** PORTRAY **2 :** to describe in usually sharp or vivid detail ⟨*delineate* the characters in a story⟩ [Latin *delineare,* from *de-* + *linea* "line"] — **de•lin•ea•tion** \di-ˌlin-ē-'ā-shən\ *n* — **de•lin•ea•tor** \-ē-ˌāt-ər\ *n*

de•lin•quen•cy \di-'ling-kwən-sē\ *n, pl* **-cies :** the quality or state of being delinquent

[1]**de•lin•quent** \-kwənt\ *n* **:** a delinquent person

[2]**delinquent** *adj* **1 :** offending by neglect or violation of duty or of law **2 :** overdue for payment ⟨a *delinquent* charge account⟩ [Latin *delinquere* "to fail, offend", from *de-* + *linquere* "to leave"] — **de•lin•quent•ly** *adv*

del•i•quesce \ˌdel-ə-'kwes\ *vi* **:** to melt away: **a :** to dissolve gradually by absorbing moisture from the air ⟨a *deliquescing* substance⟩ **b :** to become soft or liquid ⟨*deliquescing* mushrooms⟩ [Latin *deliquescere,* derived from *de-* + *liquēre* "to be fluid"] — **del•i•ques•cence** \-'kwes-ns\ *n*

del•i•ques•cent \-'kwes-nt\ *adj* **1 :** marked by or undergoing deliquescence **2 :** having repeated division into branches ⟨elms are *deliquescent* trees⟩ — compare EXCURRENT

de•lir•i•ous \di-'lir-ē-əs\ *adj* **1 :** of or relating to delirium **2 :** marked by delirium; *also* **:** wildly excited — **de•lir•i•ous•ly** *adv* — **de•lir•i•ous•ness** *n*

de•lir•i•um \-'lir-ē-əm\ *n* **1 :** a mental disturbance characterized by confusion, disordered speech, and hallucinations **2 :** frenzied excitement [Latin, from *delirare* "to deviate, be crazy", from *de-* + *lira* "furrow"]

delirium tre•mens \-'trē-mənz, -'trem-ənz\ *n* **:** a violent delirium with tremors that is induced by excessive and prolonged use of alcoholic liquors — called also *D.T.'s* [New Latin, literally, "trembling delirium"]

de•liv•er \di-'liv-ər\ *vb* **-liv•ered; -liv•er•ing** \-'liv-ring, -ə-ring\ **1 :** to set free **:** SAVE **2 :** to hand over **:** CONVEY, TRANSFER ⟨*deliver* a letter⟩ **3 :** to assist in giving birth; *also* **:** to aid in the birth of **4 :** UTTER, COMMUNICATE ⟨*deliver* a speech⟩ **5 :** to send to an intended target or destination ⟨*deliver* a pitch⟩ **6 :** to produce the promised, desired, or expected result ⟨*deliver* on a promise⟩ [Old French *delivrer,* from Late Latin *deliberare,* from Latin *de-* + *liberare* "to liberate"] **syn** see RESCUE — **de•liv•er•able** \-'liv-rə-bəl, -ə-rə-\ *adj* — **de•liv•er•er** \-'liv-ər-ər\ *n*

de•liv•er•ance \di-'liv-rəns, -ə-rəns\ *n* **1 :** a delivering or a being delivered **:** RESCUE **2 :** something delivered or communicated; *esp* **:** a publicly expressed opinion

de•liv•ery \di-'liv-rē, -ə-rē\ *n, pl* **-er•ies 1 :** a delivering from restraint **2 a :** the act of handing over **b :** a legal conveyance of right or title **c :** something delivered at one time or in one unit **3 :** the act of giving birth **4 :** a delivering especially of a speech; *also* **:** manner or style of uttering in speech or song **5 :** the act or manner of sending forth or throwing

dell \'del\ *n* **:** a secluded small valley usually covered with trees or turf [Middle English *delle*]

de•louse \dē-'laůs, 'dē-, -'laůz\ *vt* **:** to remove lice from

Del•phi•an \'del-fē-ən\ *or* **Del•phic** \-fik\ *adj* **1 :** of or relating to ancient Delphi or its oracle **2 :** AMBIGUOUS, OBSCURE

del•phin•i•um \del-'fin-ē-əm\ *n* **:** any of a large genus of chiefly perennial erect branching herbs related to the buttercups and widely grown for their irregular flowers in showy spikes — compare LARKSPUR [Greek *delphinion* "larkspur", from *delphis* "dolphin"]

Del•phi•nus \del-'fī-nəs, -'fē-\ *n* **:** a northern constellation nearly west of Pegasus [Latin, literally, "dolphin"]

del•ta \'del-tə\ *n* **1 :** the 4th letter of the Greek alphabet — Δ or δ **2 :** something shaped like a capital Δ; *esp* **:** the triangular or fan-shaped piece of land made by deposits of mud and sand at the mouth of a river — **del•ta•ic** \del-'tā-ik\ *adj*

del•toid \'del-ˌtȯid\ *n* **:** a large triangular muscle that covers the shoulder joint and serves to raise the arm laterally [Greek *deltoeidēs* "shaped like a delta"]

del•toi•de•us \del-'tȯid-ē-əs\ *n, pl* **del•toi•dei** \-ē-ˌī\ **:** DELTOID [New Latin, from Greek *deltoeidēs* "shaped like a delta"]

de•lude \di-'lüd\ *vt* **:** to mislead the mind or judgment of ⟨*deluded* by false promises⟩ [Latin *deludere, from de-* + *ludere* "to play"] **syn** see DECEIVE — **de•lud•er** *n* — **de•lud•ing•ly** \-'lüd-ing-lē\ *adv*

[1]**del•uge** \'del-ˌyüj\ *n* **1 a :** an overflowing of the land by water **:** FLOOD **b :** a drenching rain **2 :** an overwhelming amount or number ⟨a *deluge* of Christmas mail⟩ [Middle French, from Latin *diluvium,* from *diluere* "to wash away", from *dis-* + *lavere* "to wash"]

[2]**deluge** *vt* **1 :** to overflow with water **:** INUNDATE, FLOOD **2 :** to overwhelm as if with a deluge ⟨was *deluged* with inquiries⟩

de•lu•sion \di-'lü-zhən\ *n* **1 :** the act of deluding **:** the state of being deluded **2 a :** something that is falsely or delusively believed **b :** a false belief regarding the self or persons or objects outside the self that persists despite the facts and is common in some abnormal mental states [Latin *delusio,* from *deludere* "to delude"] — **de•lu•sion•al** \-'lüzh-nəl, -'lü-zhən-l\ *adj*

• syn DELUSION, ILLUSION mean something accepted as true or real that is actually false or unreal. DELUSION implies persistent self-deception concerning facts or situations and usually suggests a disordered state of mind; ILLUSION implies an attributing of truth or reality to something that seems to normal perception to be true and real but in fact is not.

de•lu•sive \-'lü-siv, -'lü-ziv\ *adj* **:** deluding or apt to delude — **de•lu•sive•ly** *adv* — **de•lu•sive•ness** *n*

de•luxe \di-'lüks, -'ləks, -'lůks\ *adj* **:** notably luxurious or elegant ⟨a *deluxe* edition⟩ [French *de luxe,* literally, "of luxury"]

delve \'delv\ *vi* **1 :** to dig or labor with a spade **2 :** to make a careful or detailed search for information ⟨*delve* into the past⟩ [Old English *delfan*] — **delv•er** *n*

de•mag•ne•tize \dē-'mag-nə-ˌtīz\ *vt* **:** to deprive of magnetic properties — **de•mag•ne•ti•za•tion** \ˌdē-ˌmag-nət-ə-'zā-shən\ *n* — **de•mag•ne•tiz•er** \dē-'mag-nə-ˌtī-zər\ *n*

dem•a•gogue *or* **dem•a•gog** \'dem-ə-ˌgäg\ *n* **:** a person who appeals to the emotions and prejudices of people in order to arouse discontent and advance personal political ends [Greek *dēmagōgos,* from *dēmos* "people" + *agein* "to lead"] — **dem•a•gog•ic** \ˌdem-ə-'gäj-ik, -'gäg-\ *or* **dem•a•gog•i•cal** \-i-kəl\ *adj* — **dem•a•gogu•ery** \'dem-ə-ˌgäg-rē, -ə-rē\ *n* — **dem•a•gogy** \-ˌgäj-ē, -ˌgäg-ē\ *n*

[1]**de•mand** \di-'mand\ *n* **1 a :** an act of demanding or asking especially with authority **b :** something claimed as due **2 a :** an expressed desire to own or use something ⟨the *demand* for new cars⟩ **b :** the ability and desire to purchase goods or services at a specified time and price **c :** the quantity of an article or service that is wanted at a stated price **3 :** a seeking or state of being sought after ⟨tickets are in great *demand*⟩ **4 :** a pressing need or requirement ⟨*demands* that tax one's energy⟩ — **on demand :** upon request for payment

[2]**demand** *vb* **1 :** to ask or call for with authority **:** claim as one's right ⟨*demand* payment of a debt⟩ **2 :** to ask earnestly or in the manner of a command ⟨the sentry *demanded* the password⟩ **3 :** to call for **:** REQUIRE ⟨an illness that *demands* constant care⟩ [Middle French *demander,* from Medieval Latin *demandare,* from Latin *de-* + *mandare* "to enjoin"] — **de•mand•able** \-'man-də-bəl\ *adj* — **de•mand•er** *n*

\ə\ **abut**	\aů\ **out**	\i\ **tip**	\ȯ\ **saw**	\ů\ **foot**
\ər\ **further**	\ch\ **chin**	\ī\ **life**	\ȯi\ **coin**	\y\ **yet**
\a\ **mat**	\e\ **pet**	\j\ **job**	\th\ **thin**	\yü\ **few**
\ā\ **take**	\ē\ **easy**	\ng\ **sing**	\t͟h\ **this**	\yů\ **cure**
\ä\ **cot, cart**	\g\ **go**	\ō\ **bone**	\ü\ **food**	\zh\ **vision**

• **syn** DEMAND, CLAIM, REQUIRE, EXACT mean to ask or call for something as due or as necessary. DEMAND carries a suggestion of authoritativeness, insistence, and a right to make a request that is to be regarded as a command; CLAIM implies a demand for the concession of something due as one's own or one's right; REQUIRE strictly implies imperativeness arising from inner necessity or the compulsion of law or the urgency of the case; EXACT implies not only demanding but getting what one demands ⟨*exact* payment of an overdue debt⟩

de•mand•ing *adj* : EXACTING — **de•mand•ing•ly** \-'man-ding-lē\ *adv*

de•mar•cate \di-'mär-,kāt, 'dē-,mär-\ *vt* **1** : to mark the limits of **2** : to set apart : SEPARATE [back-formation from *demarcation,* derived from Spanish and Portuguese *demarcar* "to delimit", from *de-* "de-" + *marcar* "to mark"] — **de•mar•ca•tion** \,dē-,mär-'kā-shən\ *n*

deme \'dēm\ *n* : a unit of local government in ancient Attica [Greek *dēmos,* literally, "people"]

[1]**de•mean** \di-'mēn\ *vt* : to conduct or behave (oneself) usually in a proper manner [Old French *demener* "to conduct", from *de-* "de-" + *mener* "to drive", from Latin *minare,* from *minari* "to threaten"]

[2]**demean** *vt* : DEGRADE, DEBASE ⟨refused to *demean* themselves by cheating⟩ [*de-* + *mean*]

de•mean•or \di-'mē-nər\ *n* : outward manner or behavior : CONDUCT, BEARING

de•ment•ed \di-'ment-əd\ *adj* : mentally disordered : INSANE — **de•ment•ed•ly** *adv* — **de•ment•ed•ness** *n*

de•men•tia \di-'men-chə\ *n* **1** : a condition of deteriorated mentality **2** : INSANITY 3a ⟨the *dementia* of racial hatred⟩ [Latin, from *demens* "mad", from *de-* + *mens* "mind"]

de•mer•it \di-'mer-ət\ *n* **1** : a quality that deserves blame : FAULT **2** : a mark placed against a person's record for some fault or offense

de•mesne \di-'mān, -'mēn\ *n* **1** : manorial land possessed by the lord and not held by free tenants **2 a** : the land attached to a mansion **b** : landed property : ESTATE **c** : a geographical area : REGION **3** : realm or range especially of interests or activity [Old French *demaine,* from Latin *dominium* "domain"]

demi- *prefix* **1** : half **2** : one that partly belongs to (a specified type or class) ⟨*demigod*⟩ [Middle French *demi,* from Latin *dimidius,* from *dis-* + *medius* "middle"]

demi•god \'dem-ē-,gäd\ *n* : a mythological being with more power than a mortal but less than a god

demi•john \-,jän\ *n* : a large bottle of glass or stoneware enclosed in wickerwork [by folk etymology from French *dame-jeanne,* literally, "Lady Jane"]

demijohn

de•mil•i•ta•rize \dē-'mil-ə-tə,rīz\ *vt* : to strip of military forces, weapons, or fortification ⟨a *demilitarized* zone⟩ — **de•mil•i•ta•ri•za•tion** \,dē-,mil-ə-tə-rə-'zā-shən\ *n*

demi•mon•daine \,dem-ē-,män-'dān\ *n* : a woman of the demimonde [French *demi-mondaine,* from *demi-monde*]

demi•monde \'dem-ē-,mänd\ *n* **1** : a class of women on the fringes of respectable society supported by wealthy lovers **2** : a group engaged in activity of doubtful legality or propriety [French *demi-monde,* from *demi-* + *monde* "world", from Latin *mundus*]

[1]**de•mise** \di-'mīz\ *vt* : to convey (property) for a period of time : LEASE

[2]**demise** *n* **1** : a letting of property : LEASE **2** : transfer of sovereignty to a successor ⟨*demise* of the crown⟩ **3 a** : DEATH 1 **b** : an end of existence or activity [Middle French *demis,* past participle of *demettre* "to dismiss", from Latin *demittere* "to send down", from *de-* + *mittere* "to send"]

demi•tasse \'dem-ē-,tas, -,täs\ *n* : a small cup of black coffee; *also* : the cup used to serve it [French *demi-tasse,* from *demi-* + *tasse* "cup", from Arabic *ṭass,* from Persian *tast*]

de•mo•bi•lize \di-'mō-bə-,līz\ *vt* **1** : to discharge from military service ⟨*demobilize* an army⟩ **2** : to change from a state of war to a state of peace — **de•mo•bi•li•za•tion** \-,mō-bə-lə-'zā-shən\ *n*

de•moc•ra•cy \di-'mäk-rə-sē\ *n, pl* **-cies 1 a** : government by the people; *esp* : rule of the majority **b** : government in which the supreme power is vested in the people and exercised by them directly or indirectly through representation **2** : a political unit that has a democratic government **3 a** : the absence of hereditary or arbitrary class distinctions or privileges **b** : belief in or practice of social or economic equality for all people [Middle French *democratie,* derived from Greek *dēmokratia,* from *dēmos* "people" + *-kratia* "-cracy"]

dem•o•crat \'dem-ə-,krat\ *n* **1 a** : an adherent of democracy **b** : one who practices social equality **2** *cap* : a member of the Democratic party of the United States

dem•o•crat•ic \,dem-ə-'krat-ik\ *adj* **1** : of, relating to, or favoring political, social, or economic democracy **2** *often cap* : of or relating to a major United States political party evolving from the anti-federalists and the Democratic-Republican party and associated with policies of broad social reform and internationalism **3** : of, relating to, or appealing to the broad masses of the people ⟨*democratic* art⟩ **4** : favoring social equality : not snobbish — **dem•o•crat•i•cal•ly** \-i-kə-lē, -klē\ *adv*

Democratic–Republican *adj* : of or relating to an early 19th century American political party favoring strict interpretation of the constitution and emphasizing states' rights

de•moc•ra•tize \di-'mäk-rə-,tīz\ *vt* : to make democratic — **de•moc•ra•ti•za•tion** \-,mäk-rət-ə-'zā-shən\ *n*

de•mod•u•late \dē-'mäj-ə-,lāt\ *vt* : to extract from (a transmitted radio signal) the wave by which the sound or picture is reproduced — **de•mod•u•la•tion** \,dē-,mäj-ə-'lā-shən\ *n*

de•mog•ra•phy \di-'mäg-rə-fē\ *n* : the statistical study of human populations and especially their size and distribution and the number of births and deaths [French *démographie,* from Greek *dēmos* "people" + French *-graphie* "-graphy"] — **de•mog•ra•pher** \-fər\ *n* — **de•mo•graph•ic** \,dē-mə-'graf-ik, ,dem-ə-\ *adj* — **de•mo•graph•i•cal•ly** \-'graf-i-kə-lē, -klē\ *adv*

dem•oi•selle \,dem-wə-'zel, -ə-\ *n* : a young lady [French]

de•mol•ish \di-'mäl-ish\ *vt* **1 a** : to tear down : RAZE **b** : to break to pieces : SMASH **2** : to do away with : put an end to [Middle French *demoliss-,* stem of *demolir,* from Latin *demoliri,* from *de-* + *moliri* "to construct", from *moles* "mass"] **syn** see DESTROY — **de•mol•ish•er** *n* — **de•mol•ish•ment** \-ish-mənt\ *n*

dem•o•li•tion \,dem-ə-'lish-ən, ,dē-mə-\ *n* : the act of demolishing; *esp* : destruction by means of explosives — **dem•o•li•tion•ist** \-'lish-nəst, -ə-nəst\ *n*

de•mon *or* **dae•mon** \'dē-mən\ *n* **1** *usually daemon* : an attendant power or spirit **2 a** : an evil spirit **b** : an evil or undesirable emotion, trait, or state **3** *usually daemon* : a demigod of Greek mythology [Latin *daemon* "divinity, spirit", from Greek *daimōn*]

de•mon•e•tize \dē-'män-ə-,tīz, -'mən-\ *vt* : to stop using as money or as a monetary standard ⟨*demonetize* silver⟩ [French *démonétiser,* from *dé-* "de-" + Latin *moneta* "coin"] — **de•mon•e•ti•za•tion** \,dē-,män-ət-ə-'zā-shən, -,mən-\ *n*

[1]**de•mo•ni•ac** \di-'mō-nē-,ak\ *also* **de•mo•ni•a•cal** \,dē-mə-'nī-ə-kəl\ *adj* **1** : possessed or influenced by a demon **2** : of, relating to, or suggestive of a demon : FIENDISH — **de•mo•ni•a•cal•ly** \,dē-mə-'nī-ə-kə-lē, -klē\ *adv*

[2]**demoniac** *n* : one held to be possessed by a demon

de•mon•ic \di-'män-ik\ *adj* : DEMONIAC 2

de•mon•ol•o•gy \,dē-mə-'näl-ə-jē\ *n* **1** : the study of demons **2** : belief in demons

de•mon•stra•ble \di-'män-strə-bəl, 'dem-ən-strə-\ *adj* **1** : capable of being demonstrated or proved **2** : APPARENT 2, EVIDENT — **de•mon•stra•bil•i•ty** \di-,män-strə-'bil-ət-ē, ,dem-ən-strə-\ *n* — **de•mon•stra•ble•ness** \di-'män-strə-bəl-nəs, 'dem-ən-strə-\ *n* — **de•mon•stra•bly** \-blē\ *adv*

dem•on•strate \'dem-ən-,strāt\ *vb* **1** : to show clearly **2 a** : to prove or make clear by reasoning or evidence **b** : to illustrate and explain especially with many examples **3** : to show publicly the good qualities of a product ⟨*demonstrate* a new car⟩ **4** : to make a public display (as of feelings or military force) ⟨citizens *demonstrated* in protest⟩ [Latin *demonstrare,* from *de-* + *monstrare* "to show", from *monstrum* "portent, monster"]

dem•on•stra•tion \,dem-ən-'strā-shən\ *n* **1** : an outward expression or display ⟨a *demonstration* of joy⟩ **2** : an act, process, or means of demonstrating to the intelligence: **a** : convincing evidence : PROOF **b** : an explanation (as of a theory) by experiment **c** : a course of reasoning intended to prove that a conclusion must follow when certain conditions are accepted **d** : a showing to a prospective buyer of the merits of a product **3** : a show of armed force **4** : a public display of group feelings especially in support or protest — **dem·on·stra·tion·al** \-shnəl, -shən-l\ *adj*

[1]**de·mon·stra·tive** \di-'män-strət-iv\ *adj* **1 a** : demonstrating as real or true **b** : characterized or established by demonstration ⟨*demonstrative* reasoning⟩ **2** : pointing out the one referred to and distinguishing it from others of the same class ⟨the *demonstrative* pronoun *this* in "this is my hat"⟩ ⟨the *demonstrative* adjective *that* in "that chair"⟩ **3** : marked by display of feeling ⟨a *demonstrative* greeting⟩ — **de·mon·stra·tive·ly** *adv* — **de·mon·stra·tive·ness** *n*

[2]**demonstrative** *n* : a demonstrative word; *esp* : a demonstrative pronoun

dem·on·stra·tor \'dem-ən-ˌstrāt-ər\ *n* **1** : a person who makes or takes part in a demonstration **2** : a product (as an automobile) used for purposes of demonstration

de·mor·al·ize \di-'mȯr-ə-ˌlīz, -'mär-\ *vb* **1** : to corrupt in morals : make bad **2** : to destroy the morale of : weaken in discipline or spirit ⟨fear *demoralized* the army⟩ — **de·mor·al·iza·tion** \di-ˌmȯr-ə-lə-'zā-shən, -ˌmär-\ *n* — **de·mor·al·iz·er** \-'mȯr-ə-ˌlī-zər, -'mär-\ *n*

de·mote \di-'mōt, 'dē-\ *vt* : to reduce to a lower grade or rank [*de-* + *-mote* (as in *promote*)] — **de·mo·tion** \-'mō-shən\ *n*

də·mot·ic \di-'mät-ik\ *adj* **1** : of or relating to the general public : POPULAR, COMMON **2** : of, relating to, or written in a simplified form of the ancient Egyptian writing **3** : of or relating to the form of Modern Greek that is based on conversational use [Greek *dēmotikos,* from *dēmos* "people"]

de·mount \dē-'mau̇nt\ *vt* **1** : to remove from a mounted position **2** : DISASSEMBLE — **de·mount·able** \-ə-bəl\ *adj*

[1]**de·mul·cent** \di-'məl-sənt\ *adj* : SOOTHING [Latin *demulcēre* "to soothe", from *de-* + *mulcēre* "to soothe"]

[2]**demulcent** *n* : a usually oily or somewhat thick and jellylike preparation used to soothe or protect an abraded mucous membrane

[1]**de·mur** \di-'mər\ *vi* **de·murred**; **de·mur·ring** **1** : to enter a demurrer **2** : to take exception : OBJECT **3** *archaic* : DELAY 1, HESITATE [Old French *demorer* "to linger", from Latin *demorari,* from *de-* + *morari* "to linger", from *mora* "delay"]

[2]**demur** *n* **1** : HESITATION **2** : the act of objecting : PROTEST ⟨accepted without *demur*⟩

de·mure \di-'myu̇r\ *adj* **1** : marked by quiet modesty **2** : affectedly modest, reserved, or serious [Middle English] — **de·mure·ly** *adv* — **de·mure·ness** *n*

de·mur·rage \di-'mər-ij, -'mə-rij\ *n* **1** : the detention of a ship by the shipper or receiver beyond a time specified for loading, unloading, or sailing **2** : a charge for detaining a ship, freight car, or truck beyond a time specified for loading or unloading

[1]**de·mur·rer** \di-'mər-ər, -'mə-rər\ *n* **1** : a claim by the defendant in a legal action that the pleadings of the plaintiff are insufficient or defective **2** : OBJECTION

[2]**de·mur·rer** \-'mər-ər\ *n* : one that demurs

[1]**den** \'den\ *n* **1** : the shelter or resting place of a wild animal **2 a** : a hiding place (as for thieves) **b** : a center of secret activity ⟨a gambling *den*⟩ **3** : a small usually squalid dwelling ⟨*dens* of misery⟩ **4** : a quiet snug room; *esp* : one set apart for reading and relaxation **5** : a subdivision of a cub-scout pack [Old English *denn*]

[2]**den** *vb* **denned**; **den·ning** **1** : to live in or retire to a den **2** : to drive into a den

de·nar·i·us \di-'nar-ē-əs, -'ner-\ *n, pl* **de·nar·ii** \-ē-ˌī, -ē-ˌē\ : a small silver coin of ancient Rome; *also* : a gold coin equal to 25 silver denarii [Latin, a coin worth ten asses, from *deni* "ten each", from *decem* "ten"]

de·na·tion·al·ize \dē-'nash-nə-ˌlīz, -'nash-ən-l-ˌīz\ *vt* **1** : to strip of national character or rights **2** : to remove from ownership or control by the national government

de·nat·u·ral·ize \dē-'nach-rə-ˌlīz, -ə-rə-\ *vt* **1** : to make unnatural **2** : to deprive of the rights and duties of a citizen

de·na·tur·ant \dē-'nāch-rənt, -ə-rənt\ *n* : a denaturing agent

de·na·ture \dē-'nā-chər\ *vt* **de·na·tured**; **de·na·tur·ing** \-'nāch-ring, -ə-ring\ : to deprive of natural qualities: as **a** : to make (alcohol) unfit for drinking without impairing usefulness for other purposes **b** : to modify (as a native protein) so as to diminish or destroy some of the original properties — **de·na·tur·ation** \ˌdē-ˌnā-chə-'rā-shən\ *n*

dendr- *or* **dendro-** *combining form* : tree ⟨*dendro*chronology⟩ : resembling a tree ⟨*dendr*ite⟩ [Greek *dendron* "tree"]

den·drite \'den-ˌdrīt\ *n* **1** : a branching figure (as in a mineral or stone) resembling a tree **2** : any of the usually branching processes of a nerve cell that conduct impulses toward its body — **den·drit·ic** \den-'drit-ik\ *adj*

den·dro·chro·nol·o·gy \ˌden-drō-krə-'näl-ə-jē\ *n* : the science of dating events by comparative study of growth rings in trees and aged wood — **den·dro·chron·o·log·i·cal** \-ˌkrän-l-'äj-i-kəl, -ˌkrōn-\ *adj* — **den·dro·chron·o·log·i·cal·ly** \-kə-lē, -klē\ *adv*

den·drol·o·gy \den-'dräl-ə-jē\ *n* : the study of trees

Den·eb \'den-ˌeb, -əb\ *n* : the brightest star in the constellation Cygnus [Arabic *dhanab al-dajāja,* literally, "tail of the hen"]

den·gue \'deng-gē, -ˌgā\ *n* : an acute virus disease characterized by headache, severe joint pain, and rash [Spanish]

de·ni·al \di-'nī-əl, -'nīl\ *n* **1** : a refusal to grant something asked for **2** : a refusal to admit the truth of a statement ⟨a flat *denial* of the charges⟩ **3** : a refusal to acknowledge something; *esp* : a statement of disbelief or rejection **4** : a cutting down or limiting : RESTRICTION ⟨*denial* of one's appetite⟩

[1]**de·ni·er** \di-'nī-ər, -'nīr\ *n* : one that denies

[2]**de·nier** *n* **1** \də-'niər, dən-'yā\ : a small originally silver coin of France and western Europe from the 8th to the 19th century **2** \'den-yər\ : a unit of fineness for silk, rayon, or nylon yarn equal to the fineness of a yarn weighing one gram for each 9000 meters [Middle French, from Latin *denarius* "denarius"]

den·i·grate \'den-i-ˌgrāt\ *vt* : to cast aspersions on : DEFAME [Latin *denigrare,* from *de-* + *nigrare* "to blacken", from *niger* "black"] — **den·i·gra·tion** \ˌden-i-'grā-shən\ *n* — **den·i·gra·tor** \'den-i-ˌgrāt-ər\ *n* — **den·i·gra·to·ry** \-grə-ˌtōr-ē, -ˌtȯr-\ *adj*

den·im \'den-əm\ *n* **1** : a firm durable twilled usually cotton fabric **2** *pl* : overalls or trousers of usually blue denim [French *serge de Nîmes,* "serge of Nîmes, France"]

△ **origin** Many fabrics have been named for the places where they originated or were manufactured. *Denim* comes from the French *de Nîmes,* meaning "of Nîmes". It was originally used in the phrase *serge de Nîmes,* which appeared in English in the 17th century as *serge denim. Serge,* from the Latin adjective *sericus,* "of silk", is a durable twilled fabric, and Nîmes is a city of southern France where textiles are still an important industry.

de·ni·tri·fy \dē-'nī-trə-ˌfī\ *vt* **1** : to remove nitrogen or its compound from **2** : to convert (a nitrate or a nitrite) into a compound of a lower state of oxidation especially as a step in the nitrogen cycle — **de·ni·tri·fi·ca·tion** \ˌdē-ˌnī-trə-fə-'kā-shən\ *n* — **de·ni·tri·fi·er** \ˌdē-'nī-trə-ˌfī-ər, -ˌfīr\ *n*

den·i·zen \'den-ə-zən\ *n* : INHABITANT; *esp* : a person, animal, or plant found or naturalized in a particular region or environment ⟨*denizens* of the forest⟩ [Middle French *denzein,* from Old French *denz* "within", from Late Latin *deintus,* from Latin *de-* + *intus* "within"]

de·nom·i·nate \di-'näm-ə-ˌnāt\ *vt* : to give a name to

de·nom·i·nate number \di-ˌnäm-ə-nət-\ *n* : a number (as *7* in 7 meters) that specifies a quantity in terms of a unit of measurement

de·nom·i·na·tion \di-ˌnäm-ə-'nā-shən\ *n* **1** : an act of denominating **2** : NAME, DESIGNATION; *esp* : a general name for a class of things **3** : a religious body comprising a number of congregations with similar beliefs **4** : one of a series of related values each having a special name ⟨bills in $5 and $10 *denominations*⟩ — **de·nom·i·na·tion·al** \-shnəl, -shən-l\ *adj* — **de·nom·i·na·tion·al·ly** \-ē\ *adv*

de·nom·i·na·tion·al·ism \-shnəl-ˌiz-əm, -shən-l-ˌiz-\ *n* : devotion to the principles or interests of a denomination

de·nom·i·na·tive \di-'näm-nət-iv, -ə-nət-\ *adj* : derived from a noun or adjective ⟨*denominative* verbs⟩

de·nom·i·na·tor \di-'näm-ə-ˌnāt-ər\ *n* : the part of a fraction that is below the line signifying division and that in fractions with 1 as the numerator indicates into how many parts the unit is divided

de·no·ta·tion \ˌdē-nō-'tā-shən\ *n* **1** : an act or process of denoting **2** : MEANING; *esp* : a direct specific meaning as distin

from connotations **3** : a denoting term or label : NAME, SIGN
de•no•ta•tive \ˈdē-nō-ˌtāt-iv, di-ˈnōt-ət-iv\ *adj* **1** : denoting or tending to denote **2** : relating to denotation
de•note \di-ˈnōt\ *vt* **1** : to serve as an indication of ⟨red flares *denoting* danger⟩ **2** : to have the meaning of : MEAN, NAME ⟨in the United States the word *corn denotes* Indian corn⟩
• **syn** DENOTE and CONNOTE, when used of words, together equal *mean.* DENOTE implies all that strictly belongs to the definition of the word; CONNOTE implies all the ideas or emotions suggested by the word ⟨*home denotes* the place where one lives, but it *connotes* the comforts, the privacy, and a whole range of experience one enjoys there⟩
de•noue•ment \ˌdā-ˌnü-ˈmä^{n}, -ˈnü-ˌ\ *n* **1** : the final untangling of the conflicts or difficulties that make up the plot of a literary work **2** : a solution or working out especially of a complex or difficult situation [French *dénouement,* literally, "untying", derived from Old French *desnoer* "to untie", from *des-* "de-" + *noer* "to tie", from Latin *nodare,* from *nodus* "knot"]
de•nounce \di-ˈnaụns\ *vt* **1** : to point out as deserving blame or punishment **2** : to inform against : ACCUSE **3** : to announce formally the ending of (as a treaty) [Old French *denoncier* "to proclaim", from Latin *denuntiare,* from *de-* + *nuntiare* "to report"] — **de•nounce•ment** \-mənt\ *n* — **de•nounc•er** *n*
de no•vo \di-ˈnō-vō, dā-\ *adv* : over again : ANEW [Latin]
dense \ˈdens\ *adj* **1** : marked by compactness or crowding together of parts ⟨a *dense* forest⟩ **2** : mentally dull **3** : having high opacity ⟨*dense* fog⟩ [Latin *densus*] **syn** see STUPID — **dense•ly** *adv* — **dense•ness** *n*
den•si•ty \ˈden-sət-ē\ *n, pl* **-ties 1** : the quality or state of being dense **2** : the quantity of something per unit volume, unit area, or unit length: as **a** : the mass of a substance per unit volume ⟨*density* expressed in grams per cubic centimeter⟩ **b** : the average number of individuals or units in a unit of area or volume ⟨population *density*⟩ **3** : STUPIDITY 1 **4** : the degree of opacity of a translucent medium
[1]**dent** \ˈdent\ *n* **1** : a hollow made by a blow or by pressure **2 a** : an impression or effect often having a weakening influence **b** : initial progress [Middle English, "blow", alteration of *dint*]
[2]**dent** *vb* **1** : to make a dent in or on **2** : to become marked by a dent
dent- *or* **denti-** *or* **dento-** *combining form* : tooth : teeth [Latin *dent-, dens* "tooth"]
[1]**den•tal** \ˈdent-l\ *adj* **1** : of or relating to the teeth or to dentistry **2** : pronounced with the tip or blade of the tongue against or near the upper front teeth — **den•tal•ly** \-l-ē\ *adv*
[2]**dental** *n* : a dental consonant
dental floss *n* : a thread used to clean between the teeth
dental hygienist *n* : one who assists a dentist especially in cleaning teeth
den•tate \ˈden-ˌtāt\ *adj* : having pointed conical projections ⟨a *dentate* margin of a leaf⟩
den•til \ˈdent-l\ *n* : one of a series of small projecting rectangular blocks especially under a cornice [obsolete French *dentille,* from *dent* "tooth"]
dent corn *n* : an Indian corn having kernels that contain both hard and soft starch and that become indented at maturity
den•ti•cle \ˈdent-i-kəl\ *n* : a small conical pointed projection (as a tooth) [Latin *denticulus* "small tooth", from *dens* "tooth"]
den•ti•frice \ˈdent-ə-frəs\ *n* : a powder, paste, or liquid for cleaning the teeth [Latin *dentifricium,* from *dens* "tooth" + *fricare* "to rub"]
den•tine \ˈden-ˌtēn, den-ˈ\ *also* **den•tin** \ˈdent-n\ *n* : a calcium-containing material like bone but harder and denser that composes the principal mass of a tooth — **den•tin•al** \den-ˈtēn-l, ˈdent-n-əl\ *adj*
den•tist \ˈdent-əst\ *n* : one whose profession is the care and treatment of the teeth and gums and the fitting of false teeth
den•tist•ry \ˈdent-ə-strē\ *n* : the profession or practice of a dentist
den•ti•tion \den-ˈtish-ən\ *n* **1** : the development and cutting of teeth **2** : the number, kind, and arrangement of teeth (as of a person)
den•ture \ˈden-chər\ *n* **1** : a set of teeth **2** : an artificial replacement for one or more teeth; *esp* : a set of false teeth
de•nude \di-ˈnüd, -ˈnyüd\ *vt* : to strip of covering : lay bare ⟨erosion that *denudes* the rocks of soil⟩ — **de•nu•da•tion** \ˌdē-ˌnü-ˈdā-shən, -ˌnyü-; ˌden-yụ-ˈdā-\ *n* — **de•nu•da•tion•al** \-shnəl, -shən-l\ *adj* — **de•nud•er** \di-ˈnüd-ər, -ˈnyüd-\ *n*
de•nu•mer•a•ble \di-ˈnüm-rə-bəl, -ˈnyüm-, -ə-rə-\ *adj* : capable of being put into one-to-one correspondence with the positive integers — **de•nu•mer•a•bly** \-rə-blē\ *adv*

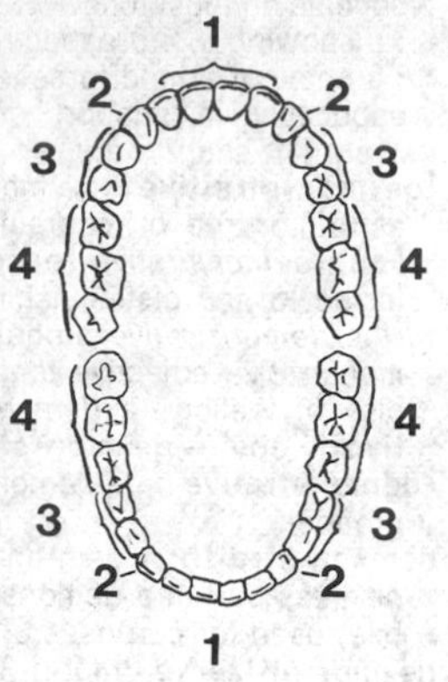

dentition 2: *top* upper jaw, *bottom* lower jaw, *1* incisors, *2* canines, *3* premolars, *4* molars

de•nun•ci•a•tion \di-ˌnən-sē-ˈā-shən\ *n* : the act of denouncing; *esp* : a public accusation — **de•nun•ci•a•to•ry** \-ˈnən-sē-ə-ˌtōr-ē, -ˌtȯr-\ *adj*
de•ny \di-ˈnī\ *vt* **de•nied; de•ny•ing 1** : to declare not to be true : CONTRADICT ⟨*deny* a report⟩ **2** : to refuse to acknowledge : DISOWN ⟨*deny* one's faith⟩ **3** : to refuse to grant ⟨*deny* a request⟩ **4** : to reject as false ⟨*deny* a theory⟩ [Old French *denier,* from Latin *denegare,* from *de-* + *negare* "to deny"] — **de•ny•ing•ly** \-ˈnī-ing-lē\ *adv*
de•o•dar \ˈdē-ə-ˌdär\ *n* : an East Indian cedar valued as an ornamental and timber tree [Hindi *deodār,* from Sanskrit *devadāru,* literally, "timber of the gods"]
de•odor•ant \dē-ˈōd-ə-rənt\ *n* : a preparation that eliminates or masks unpleasant odors — **deodorant** *adj*
de•odor•ize \dē-ˈōd-ə-ˌrīz\ *vt* : to eliminate or prevent offensive odor of or in ⟨*deodorize* a room⟩ — **de•odor•iza•tion** \ˌdē-ˌōd-ə-rə-ˈzā-shən\ *n* — **de•odor•iz•er** \dē-ˈōd-ə-ˌrī-zər\ *n*
Deo vo•len•te \ˌdā-ō-və-ˈlent-ē, ˌdē-\ : God being willing [Latin]
de•ox•i•dize \dē-ˈäk-sə-ˌdīz, ˈdē-\ *vt* : to remove oxygen from — **de•ox•i•diz•er** *n*
de•ox•y•gen•at•ed \-ˈäk-si-jə-ˌnāt-əd\ *adj* : having the hemoglobin in the reduced state
de•oxy•ri•bo•nu•cle•ic acid \ˌdē-ˌäk-sē-ˈrī-bō-nụ-ˌklē-ik-, -nyụ-, -ˌklā-\ *n* : DNA
de•oxy•ri•bose \dē-ˌäk-sē-ˈrī-ˌbōs\ *n* : a sugar that has five carbon atoms in the molecule and is a constituent of DNA
de•part \di-ˈpärt\ *vb* **1 a** : to go away or go away from : LEAVE **b** : DIE **2** : to turn aside : DEVIATE [Old French *departir* "to divide, go away", from *de-* "de-" + *partir* "to divide", from Latin *partire,* from *pars* "part"]
de•part•ed *adj* **1** : BYGONE **2** : no longer living
de•part•ment \di-ˈpärt-mənt\ *n* **1** : a distinct sphere : PROVINCE **2 a** : a major administrative division of a government or business **b** : a major territorial administrative division **c** : a division of a college or school giving instruction in a particular subject **d** : a section of a department store — **de•part•men•tal** \di-ˌpärt-ˈment-l, ˌdē-\ *adj* — **de•part•men•tal•ly** *adv*
de•part•men•tal•ize \di-ˌpärt-ˈment-l-ˌīz, ˌdē-\ *vt* : to divide into departments — **de•part•men•tal•iza•tion** \-ˌment-l-ə-ˈzā-shən\ *n*
department store *n* : a store having separate departments for different kinds of goods
de•par•ture \di-ˈpär-chər\ *n* **1 a** : the act of going away **b** *archaic* : DEATH **2** : a setting out (as on a new course) **3** : DIVERGENCE 3
de•pend \di-ˈpend\ *vi* **1** : to be determined by or based on some action, condition, or variable ⟨success of the picnic will *depend* on the weather⟩ ⟨the value of the polynomial $x^2 + 2x + 2$ *depends* on the value of *x*⟩ **2** : to place reliance or trust ⟨you can *depend* on me⟩ **3** : to rely for support ⟨children *depend* on their parents⟩ **4** : to hang down ⟨a vine *depending* from a tree⟩ [Middle French *dependre,* from Latin *dependēre,* from *de-* + *pendēre* "to hang"]
de•pend•able \di-ˈpen-də-bəl\ *adj* : capable of being depended on : TRUSTWORTHY, RELIABLE — **de•pend•abil•i•ty** \-ˌpen-də-ˈbil-ət-ē\ *n* — **de•pend•ably** \-ˈpen-də-blē\ *adv*
de•pen•dence \di-ˈpen-dəns\ *n* **1** : the quality or state of being dependent; *esp* : the quality or state of being influenced by or subject to another **2** : RELIANCE, TRUST ⟨*dependence* on friends⟩ **3** : something on which one relies **4 a** : drug addiction **b** : HABITUATION 2
de•pen•den•cy \-dən-sē\ *n, pl* **-cies 1** : DEPENDENCE 1, 4 **2** : something that is dependent on something else; *esp* : a territory under the jurisdiction of a nation but not formally annexed by it
[1]**de•pen•dent** \di-ˈpen-dənt\ *adj* **1** : hanging down **2 a** : deter-

mined or conditioned by another **b :** relying on another for support ⟨*dependent* children⟩ **c :** subject to another's jurisdiction ⟨a *dependent* territory⟩ **3 :** SUBORDINATE 3a — **de•pen•dent•ly** *adv*

²dependent *also* **de•pend•ant** *n* **:** one that is dependent; *esp* **:** a person who relies on another for support

de•pict \di-ˈpikt\ *vt* **1 :** to represent by a picture **2 :** to describe in words [Latin *depictus,* past participle of *depingere* "to depict", from *de-* + *pingere* "to paint"] — **de•pic•tion** \-ˈpik-shən\ *n*

dep•i•la•tion \ˌdep-ə-ˈlā-shən\ *n* **:** the removal of hair, wool, or bristles by chemical or mechanical methods [derived from Latin *depilare* "to remove hair from", from *de-* + *pilus* "hair"] — **dep•i•late** \ˈdep-ə-ˌlāt\ *vt*

de•pil•a•to•ry \di-ˈpil-ə-ˌtōr-ē, -ˌtȯr-\ *n, pl* **-ries :** a preparation for removing hair, wool, or bristles — **depilatory** *adj*

de•plane \ˈdē-ˈplān\ *vi* **:** to get off an airplane

de•plete \di-ˈplēt\ *vt* **:** to reduce in amount by using up **:** exhaust especially of strength or resources ⟨soil *depleted* of minerals⟩ ⟨a *depleted* treasury⟩ [Latin *deplēre,* from *de-* + *plēre* "to fill"] — **de•ple•tion** \-ˈplē-shən\ *n* — **de•ple•tive** \-ˈplēt-iv\ *adj*

de•plor•able \di-ˈplōr-ə-bəl, -ˈplȯr-\ *adj* **1 :** deserving to be deplored **:** LAMENTABLE ⟨a *deplorable* accident⟩ **2 :** very bad **:** WRETCHED ⟨*deplorable* conditions⟩ — **de•plor•able•ness** *n* — **de•plor•ably** \-blē\ *adv*

de•plore \di-ˈplōr, -ˈplȯr\ *vt* **1 a :** to feel or express grief for **b :** to regret strongly **2 :** to consider unfortunate or deserving of disapproval [Latin *deplorare,* from *de-* + *plorare* "to wail"] — **de•plor•er** *n* — **de•plor•ing•ly** \-ing-lē\ *adv*

de•ploy \di-ˈplȯi\ *vb* **:** to spread out or place in position for some purpose ⟨troops *deployed* for battle⟩ [French *déployer,* from Latin *displicare* "to scatter", from *dis-* + *plicare* "to fold"] — **de•ploy•ment** \-mənt\ *n*

de•po•lar•ize \dē-ˈpō-lə-ˌrīz, ˈdē-\ *vt* **:** to prevent, reduce, or remove polarization of (as a dry cell or the membrane of a nerve cell) — **de•po•lar•iza•tion** \ˌdē-ˌpō-lə-rə-ˈzā-shən\ *n* — **de•po•lar•iz•er** \dē-ˈpō-lə-ˌrī-zər, ˈdē-\ *n*

¹de•po•nent \di-ˈpō-nənt\ *adj* **:** occurring with passive or middle voice forms but with active voice meaning ⟨*deponent* verbs in Latin and Greek⟩ [Late Latin *deponens,* from Latin *deponere* "to put down", from *de-* + *ponere* "to put"]

²deponent *n* **1 :** a deponent verb **2 :** one who gives evidence

de•pop•u•late \dē-ˈpäp-yə-ˌlāt, ˈdē-\ *vt* **:** to reduce greatly the population of (as a city or region) by destroying or driving away the inhabitants ⟨*depopulated* by a plague⟩ — **de•pop•u•la•tion** \ˌdē-ˌpäp-yə-ˈlā-shən\ *n*

de•port \di-ˈpōrt, -ˈpȯrt\ *vt* **1 :** CONDUCT, BEHAVE ⟨*deported* themselves with dignity⟩ **2 :** to force (an alien whose presence is unlawful or harmful) to leave a country [Middle French *deporter,* from Latin *deportare* "to carry away", from *de-* + *portare* "to carry"] — **de•por•ta•tion** \ˌdē-ˌpōr-ˈtā-shən, -ˌpȯr-\ *n* — **de•por•tee** \ˌdē-ˌpōr-ˈtē, -ˌpȯr-\ *n*

de•port•ment \di-ˈpōrt-mənt, -ˈpȯrt-\ *n* **:** manner of conducting oneself **:** BEHAVIOR

de•pose \di-ˈpōz\ *vb* **1 :** to remove from a throne or other high position **2 :** to testify under oath or by affidavit [Old French *deposer,* derived from Latin *deponere* "to put down", from *de-* + *ponere* "to put"]

¹de•pos•it \di-ˈpäz-ət\ *vb* **1 :** to place for safekeeping; *esp* **:** to put money in a bank **2 :** to give as a pledge that a purchase will be made or a service used ⟨*deposit* $10 on a new bicycle⟩ **3 :** to lay down **:** PLACE, PUT ⟨*deposit* a parcel on a table⟩ **4 :** to let fall or sink ⟨sand and silt *deposited* by a flood⟩ **5 :** to become deposited **:** SETTLE [Latin *depositus,* past participle of *deponere* "to put down"] — **de•pos•i•tor** \-ˈpäz-ət-ər, -ˈpäz-tər\ *n*

²deposit *n* **1 :** the state of being deposited ⟨money on *deposit*⟩ **2 a :** something placed for safekeeping; *esp* **:** money deposited in a bank **b :** money given as a pledge **3 :** an act of depositing **4 :** something laid or thrown down ⟨a *deposit* of silt left by the flood⟩ **5 :** an accumulation of mineral matter (as iron ore, oil, or gas) in nature

de•pos•i•tary \di-ˈpäz-ə-ˌter-ē\ *n, pl* **-tar•ies 1 :** a person to whom something is entrusted **2 :** DEPOSITORY 2

dep•o•si•tion \ˌdep-ə-ˈzish-ən, ˌdē-pə-\ *n* **1 :** the act of deposing a person from high office ⟨the *deposition* of the dictator⟩ **2 :** a statement especially in writing made under oath **3 :** the action or process of depositing ⟨the *deposition* of silt by a stream⟩ **4 :** material deposited **:** SEDIMENT 2 — **dep•o•si•tion•al** \-ˈzish-nəl, -ˈzish-ən-l\ *adj*

de•pos•i•to•ry \di-ˈpäz-ə-ˌtōr-ē, -ˌtȯr-\ *n, pl* **-ries 1 :** DEPOSITARY 1 **2 :** a place where something is deposited especially for safekeeping

de•pot *1 & 2 are* ˈdep-ˌō *also* ˈdē-ˌpō, *3 is* ˈdē-ˌpō *sometimes* ˈdep-ˌō\ *n* **1 :** a place where military supplies are kept or where troops are assembled and trained **2 :** a place of deposit for goods **:** STOREHOUSE **3 :** a building for railroad or bus passengers or freight **:** STATION [French *dépôt,* derived from Latin *deponere* "to put down"]

de•prave \di-ˈprāv\ *vt* **:** to make bad **:** corrupt the morals of **:** PERVERT [Middle French *depraver* "to speak ill of", from Latin *depravare* "to pervert", from *de-* + *pravus* "crooked, bad"] **syn** see DEBASE

de•praved \-ˈprāvd\ *adj* **:** marked by corruption, unwholesomeness, or evil — **de•praved•ly** \-ˈprā-vəd-lē, -ˈprāv-dlē\ *adv* — **de•praved•ness** \-ˈprā-vəd-nəs, -ˈprāvd-nəs\ *n*

de•prav•i•ty \di-ˈprav-ət-ē\ *n, pl* **-ties 1 :** the quality or state of being depraved **2 :** a depraved act or practice

dep•re•cate \ˈdep-ri-ˌkāt\ *vt* **1 :** to express disapproval of **2 :** DEPRECIATE 2 [Latin *deprecari* "to avert by prayer", from *de-* + *precari* "to pray"] — **dep•re•cat•ing•ly** \-ˌkāt-ing-lē\ *adv* — **dep•re•ca•tion** \ˌdep-ri-ˈkā-shən\ *n*

dep•re•ca•to•ry \ˈdep-ri-kə-ˌtōr-ē, -ˌtȯr-\ *adj* **1 :** seeking to avert disapproval **:** APOLOGETIC **2 :** serving to deprecate **:** DISAPPROVING

de•pre•ci•ate \di-ˈprē-shē-ˌāt\ *vb* **1 :** to lower the price or value of **2 :** to represent as of little value **:** DISPARAGE **3 :** to fall in value [Late Latin *depretiare,* from Latin *de-* + *pretium* "price"] — **de•pre•cia•tive** \-shē-ˌāt-iv, -shē-ət, -shət-\ *adj* — **de•pre•cia•to•ry** \-shē-ə-ˌtōr-ē, -shə-, -ˌtȯr-\ *adj*

de•pre•ci•a•tion \di-ˌprē-shē-ˈā-shən\ *n* **1 :** a decline in the purchasing power or exchange value of money **2 :** the act of belittling **:** DISPARAGEMENT **3 :** a decline (as from age or wear and tear) in the value of something

dep•re•da•tion \ˌdep-rə-ˈdā-shən\ *n* **:** the action or an act of plundering or laying waste **:** RAVAGING, PILLAGING [Late Latin *depraedatio,* from *depraedari* "to plunder", from Latin *de-* + *praedari* "to plunder"] — **dep•re•date** \ˈdep-rə-ˌdāt\ *vb*

de•press \di-ˈpres\ *vt* **1 a :** to press down **b :** to cause to sink to a lower position **2 :** to lessen the activity or strength of **3 :** to make sad or downcast **:** DISCOURAGE **4 :** to lessen in price or value **:** DEPRECIATE [Middle French *depresser* "to repress", from Latin *depressus,* past participle of *deprimere* "to press down", from *de-* + *premere* "to press"] — **de•press•ible** \-ə-bəl\ *adj* — **de•press•ing•ly** \-ing-lē\ *n*

• **syn** DEPRESS, OPPRESS mean to press or weigh down heavily. DEPRESS stresses the resulting state of inactivity or dullness or dejection ⟨*depressed* by failure⟩ OPPRESS emphasizes the burden imposed that may or may not be successfully borne or withstood ⟨*oppressed* by the hot weather⟩

de•pres•sant \di-ˈpres-nt\ *n* **:** one that depresses; *esp* **:** an agent (as alcohol) that reduces activity of bodily functions — **depressant** *adj*

de•pressed *adj* **1 a :** low in spirits **:** SAD **b :** affected with psychological depression **2 :** FLATTENED; *esp* **:** lying flat or prostrate ⟨a *depressed* shrub⟩ **3 :** suffering from economic depression

de•pres•sion \di-ˈpresh-ən\ *n* **1 :** an act of depressing **:** a state of being depressed: as **a :** a pressing down **:** LOWERING **b :** DEJECTION; *also* **:** a mental disorder marked by sadness, inactivity, difficulty in thinking and concentration, and feelings of dejection **c** (1) **:** a reduction in activity, amount, quality, or force (2) **:** a lowering of vitality or functional activity **2 :** a depressed place or part **:** HOLLOW **3 :** a region of low barometric pressure **4 :** a period of low general economic activity with widespread unemployment **syn** see MELANCHOLY

de•pres•sive \-ˈpres-iv\ *adj* **:** of or relating to psychological depression

de•pres•sor \-ˈpres-ər\ *n* **:** one that depresses: as **a :** a muscle that draws down a part — compare LEVATOR **b :** a device for pressing a part down or aside

de•pres•sur•ize \dē-'presh-ə-ˌrīz, 'dē-\ *vt* : to release (as a pressurized aircraft) from pressure

de•prive \di-'prīv\ *vt* **1** : to take something away from ⟨*deprive* a person of citizenship⟩ **2** : to stop from having something ⟨*deprived* of a college education by lack of funds⟩ [Medieval Latin *deprivare,* from Latin *de-* + *privare* "to deprive"] — **de•pri•va•tion** \ˌdep-rə-'vā-shən, ˌdē-ˌprī-\ *n*

depth \'depth\ *n, pl* **depths** \'depts, 'deps, 'depths\ **1 a** (1) : something that is deep : a deep place or part (2) : ABYSS **b** : a part that is far from the outside or surface ⟨the *depths* of the woods⟩ **c** (1) : the middle of a time ⟨the *depth* of winter⟩ (2) : an extreme state (as of despair) (3) : the worst part **2** : the distance from top to bottom or from front to back **3** : the quality of being deep **4** : degree of intensity ⟨the *depth* of a color⟩ [Middle English, probably from *dep* "deep"] — **depth•less** \'depth-ləs\ *adj*

depth charge *n* : an explosive projectile for use underwater especially against submarines — called also *depth bomb*

dep•u•ta•tion \ˌdep-yə-'tā-shən\ *n* **1** : the act of appointing a deputy **2** : a group of people appointed to represent others

de•pute \di-'pyüt\ *vt* : DELEGATE [Middle French *deputer* "to appoint", from Late Latin *deputare* "to assign", from Latin *de-* + *putare* "to consider"]

dep•u•tize \'dep-yə-ˌtīz\ *vb* **1** : to appoint as deputy **2** : to act as deputy

dep•u•ty \'dep-yət-ē\ *n, pl* **-ties** **1** : a person appointed to act for or in place of another **2** : an assistant empowered to act as a substitute in the absence of his or her superior **3** : a member of a lower house of a legislative assembly — **deputy** *adj*

de•rail \di-'rāl\ *vb* : to leave or cause to leave the rails — **de•rail•ment** \-mənt\ *n*

de•rail•leur \di-'rā-lər\ *n* : a mechanism for shifting gears on a bicycle that operates by moving the chain from one set of exposed gears to another [French *dérailleur,* from *dérailler* "to throw off the track", from *dé-* "de-" + *rail* "rail", from English]

de•range \di-'rānj\ *vt* **1** : to put out of order : DISARRANGE, UPSET **2** : to disturb the operation or functions of **3** : to make insane [French *déranger,* from Old French *de-* "de-" + *reng* "place", of Germanic origin] — **de•range•ment** \-mənt\ *n*

der•by \'dər-bē, *especially British* 'där-\ *n, pl* **der•bies** **1** : any of several horse races held annually and usually restricted to 3-year-olds **2** : a race or contest open to all comers **3** : a man's stiff felt hat with dome-shaped crown and narrow brim [Edward Stanley, died 1834, 12th earl of *Derby*]

derby 3

[1]**der•e•lict** \'der-ə-ˌlikt\ *adj* **1** : abandoned by the owner or occupant ⟨a *derelict* ship⟩ **2** : NEGLECTFUL, NEGLIGENT [Latin *derelictus,* past participle of *derelinquere* "to abandon", from *de-* + *relinquere* "to leave, relinquish"]

[2]**derelict** *n* **1** : something voluntarily abandoned; *esp* : a ship abandoned on the high seas **2** : a person without apparent means of support : VAGRANT

der•e•lic•tion \ˌder-ə-'lik-shən\ *n* **1** : the act of abandoning : the state of being abandoned ⟨the *dereliction* of a cause by its leaders⟩ **2** : neglect of one's duty : DELINQUENCY

de•ride \di-'rīd\ *vt* : to laugh at scornfully : make fun of [Latin *deridēre,* from *de-* + *ridēre* "to laugh"] **syn** see RIDICULE — **de•rid•er** *n* — **de•rid•ing•ly** \-'rīd-ing-lē\ *adv*

de ri•gueur \də-ˌrē-'gər\ *adj* : prescribed or required by fashion, etiquette, or custom : PROPER [French]

de•ri•sion \di-'rizh-ən\ *n* **1** : scornful or contemptuous ridicule **2** : an object of ridicule [Middle French, from Late Latin *derisio,* from Latin *deridēre* "to deride"]

de•ri•sive \di-'rī-siv\ *adj* : expressing or characterized by derision ⟨*derisive* laughter⟩ — **de•ri•sive•ly** *adv* — **de•ri•sive•ness** *n*

de•ri•so•ry \di-'rī-sə-rē, -zə-\ *adj* : DERISIVE

der•i•va•tion \ˌder-ə-'vā-shən\ *n* **1 a** : the formation (as by the addition of an affix) of a word from an earlier word or root **b** : ETYMOLOGY 1 **2 a** : a point of origin : SOURCE **b** : development from a source : DESCENT **c** : an act or process of deriving — **der•i•va•tion•al** \-shnəl, -shən-l\ *adj*

[1]**de•riv•a•tive** \di-'riv-ət-iv\ *adj* **1** : formed by derivation **2** : made up of or characterized by elements derived from something else ⟨*derivative* poetry⟩ — **de•riv•a•tive•ly** *adv*

[2]**derivative** *n* **1** : a word formed by derivation **2** : something derived **3** : a substance that can be made from another substance in one or more steps ⟨a *derivative* of coal tar⟩

de•rive \di-'rīv\ *vb* **de•rived; de•riv•ing** **1 a** : to receive or obtain from a source **b** : to obtain (as a chemical substance) from a parent substance **2** : to trace the origin, descent, or derivation of **3** : to come from a certain source **4** : INFER 1, DEDUCE [Middle French *deriver,* from Latin *derivare,* from *de-* + *rivus* "stream"] — **de•riv•able** \di-'rī-və-bəl\ *adj*

-derm \ˌdərm\ *n combining form* : skin : covering : layer ⟨ecto*derm*⟩ [Greek *derma* "skin", from *derein* "to skin"]

der•mal \'dər-məl\ *adj* : of or relating to the dermis or epidermis : CUTANEOUS

dermat- *or* **dermato-** *combining form* : skin ⟨*dermato*logy⟩ [Greek *dermat-, derma*]

der•ma•ti•tis \ˌdər-mə-'tīt-əs\ *n* : inflammation of the skin

der•ma•tol•o•gy \ˌdər-mə-'täl-ə-jē\ *n* : a branch of science dealing with the skin — **der•ma•to•log•ic** \-mət-l-'äj-ik\ *or* **der•ma•to•log•i•cal** \-i-kəl\ *adj* — **der•ma•tol•o•gist** \ˌdər-mə-'täl-ə-jəst\ *n*

der•mes•tid \dər-'mes-təd\ *n* : any of a family of beetles that are very destructive to dried meat, fur, wool, and insect collections [derived from Greek *dermēstēs,* a leather-eating worm, literally, "skin-eater"] — **dermestid** *adj*

der•mis \'dər-məs\ *n* : the sensitive vascular inner layer of the skin — called also *corium* [New Latin, from Greek *derma* "skin"]

der•o•gate \'der-ə-ˌgāt\ *vb* **1** : to cause to seem inferior : BELITTLE **2** : to take away a part so as to impair : DETRACT [Latin *derogare* "to annul (a law), detract", from *de-* + *rogare* "to ask, propose (a law)"] — **der•o•ga•tion** \ˌder-ə-'gā-shən\ *n* — **de•rog•a•tive** \di-'räg-ət-iv, 'der-ə-ˌgāt-\ *adj*

de•rog•a•to•ry \di-'räg-ə-ˌtōr-ē, -ˌtȯr-\ *adj* : intended to lower the reputation of a person or thing : DISPARAGING — **de•rog•a•to•ri•ly** \-ˌräg-ə-'tōr-ə-lē, -'tȯr-\ *adv*

der•rick \'der-ik\ *n* **1** : any of various machines for moving or hoisting heavy weights by means of a long beam fitted with pulleys and ropes or cables **2** : a framework or tower built over a deep drill hole (as of an oil well) for supporting machinery [obsolete *derrick* "hangman, gallows", from *Derick,* name of a 17th century English hangman]

△ **origin** In the reign of Queen Elizabeth I of England an executioner named *Derick* achieved some notoriety because of his position. The common people therefore named the gallows at London after Derick the hangman. This usage spread, and throughout the 17th century *derrick* was a term for both a hangman and a gallows. These senses eventually died out, but in the next century *derrick* began to be used for a hoisting apparatus resembling a gallows. Subsequently, *derrick* has become a term for a framework or tower over an oil well.

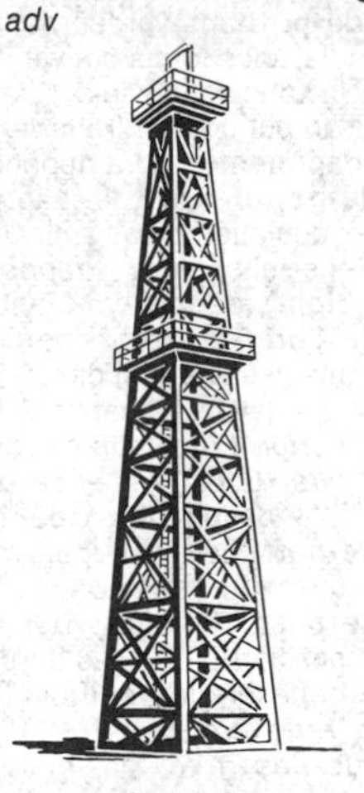

derrick 2

der•ri•ere *or* **der•ri•ère** \ˌder-ē-'eər\ *n* : BUTTOCK 2 [French *derrière,* derived from Latin *de retro* "behind"]

der•ring–do \ˌder-ing-'dü\ *n* : daring action : DARING [Middle English *dorring don* "daring to do"]

der•rin•ger \'der-ən-jər\ *n* : a short-barreled pocket pistol [Henry *Deringer,* 19th century American inventor]

der•ris \'der-əs\ *n* : any of a large genus of tropical Old World shrubs and woody vines of the pea family including commercial sources of rotenone; *also* : a derris insecticide [Greek, "skin"]

der•vish \'dər-vish\ *n* : a member of a Muslim religious order noted for devotional exercises (as bodily movements leading to a trance) [Turkish *derviş,* literally, "beggar", from Persian *darvēsh*]

de•sa•li•nate \dē-ˈsal-ə-ˌnāt\ *vt* : DESALT — **de•sa•li•na•tion** \ˌdē-ˌsal-ə-ˈnā-shən\ *n* — **de•sa•li•na•tor** \dē-ˈsal-ə-ˌnāt-ər\ *n*

de•salt \dē-ˈsólt, ˈdē-\ *vt* : to remove salt from — **de•salt•er** *n*

[1]des•cant \ˈdes-ˌkant\ *n* **1** : a melody sung above a principal melody **2** : the art of composing or singing part music; *also* : a piece of music so composed **3** : a strain of melody : SONG **4** : a discourse or comment on a subject [Medieval Latin *discantus,* from Latin *dis-* + *cantus* "song"]

[2]des•cant \ˈdes-ˌkant, des-ˈ\ *vi* **1** : to sing or play a descant **2** : to talk or write at length

de•scend \di-ˈsend\ *vb* **1 a** : to pass from a higher to a lower place or level **b** : to pass, move, or climb down or down along **2 a** : to come down from a stock or source : DERIVE **b** : to pass by inheritance **c** : to pass by transmission **3** : to incline, lead, or extend downward **4** : to swoop down in a sudden attack **5** : to sink in status or condition [Old French *descendre,* from Latin *descendere,* from *de-* + *scandere* "to climb"] — **de•scend•ible** \-ˈsen-də-bəl\ *adj*

[1]de•scen•dant *or* **de•scen•dent** \di-ˈsen-dənt\ *adj* **1** : moving or directed downward **2** : proceeding from an ancestor or source

[2]descendant *or* **descendent** *n* **1** : one descended from another or from a common stock **2** : one deriving directly from a precursor or prototype

de•scent \di-ˈsent\ *n* **1** : the act or process of descending **2** : a downward step (as in status or value) : DECLINE **3** : derivation from an ancestor : BIRTH, LINEAGE **4 a** : an inclination downward : SLOPE **b** : a descending way (as a downgrade or stairway) **5** : a sudden hostile raid or assault

de•scribe \di-ˈskrīb\ *vt* **1** : to represent or give an account of in words **2** : to trace or traverse the outline of ⟨*describe* a circle⟩ [Latin *describere,* from *de-* + *scribere* "to write"] — **de•scrib•able** \-ˈskrī-bə-bəl\ *adj* — **de•scrib•er** *n*

de•scrip•tion \di-ˈskrip-shən\ *n* **1 a** : an act or instance of describing **b** : an account that presents a picture to a person who reads or hears it **2** : KIND, SORT ⟨people of every *description*⟩ [Latin *descriptio,* from *describere* "to describe"]

de•scrip•tive \-ˈskrip-tiv\ *adj* : serving to describe — **de•scrip•tive•ly** *adv* — **de•scrip•tive•ness** *n*

de•scry \di-ˈskrī\ *vt* **de•scried**; **de•scry•ing** **1** : to catch sight of **2** : to discover or detect by observation or investigation [Old French *descrier* "to proclaim, decry"]

des•e•crate \ˈdes-i-ˌkrāt\ *vt* : to violate the sanctity of : PROFANE — **des•e•crat•er** *or* **des•e•cra•tor** \-ˌkrāt-ər\ *n* — **des•e•cra•tion** \ˌdes-i-ˈkrā-shən\ *n* [*de-* + *-secrate* (as in *consecrate*)]

de•seg•re•gate \dē-ˈseg-ri-ˌgāt, ˈdē-\ *vb* : to eliminate segregation in or from — **de•seg•re•ga•tion** \dē-ˌseg-ri-ˈgā-shən\ *n*

de•sen•si•tize \dē-ˈsen-sə-ˌtīz, ˈdē-\ *vt* : to make (an individual) insensitive or nonreactive to a sensitizing agent (as pollen) — **de•sen•si•ti•za•tion** \dē-ˌsen-sət-ə-ˈzā-shən\ *n* — **de•sen•si•tiz•er** *n*

[1]des•ert \ˈdez-ərt\ *n* : an arid barren tract incapable of supporting a considerable population without an artificial water supply [Old French, from Late Latin *desertum,* from Latin *deserere* "to desert"]

[2]des•ert \ˈdez-ərt\ *adj* : of, relating to, or resembling a desert; *esp* : being barren and uninhabited ⟨a *desert* island⟩

[3]de•sert \di-ˈzərt\ *n* **1** : worthiness of reward or punishment ⟨rewarded according to their *deserts*⟩ **2** : a just reward or punishment [Old French *deserte,* from *deservir* "to deserve"]

[4]de•sert \di-ˈzərt\ *vb* **1** : to withdraw from : LEAVE **2** : to leave in the lurch : FORSAKE **3** : to fail one in time of need **4** : to quit one's post without permission especially with the intent to remain away permanently [French *déserter,* derived from Latin *deserere* "to desert", from *de-* + *serere* "to join together"] **syn** see ABANDON — **de•sert•er** *n*

de•ser•tion \di-ˈzər-shən\ *n* **1** : an act of deserting; *esp* : the abandonment of a person (as a wife or child) to whom one has legal and moral duties and obligations **2** : a state of being deserted or forsaken : DESOLATION

de•serve \di-ˈzərv\ *vb* : to be worthy of : MERIT ⟨*deserves* another chance⟩ [Old French *deservir,* from Latin *deservire* "to serve zealously", from *de-* + *servire* "to serve"] — **de•serv•er** *n*

de•serv•ed•ly \di-ˈzər-vəd-lē\ *adv* : according to merit

deserving *adj* : MERITORIOUS, WORTHY

des•ha•bille *variant of* DISHABILLE

des•ic•cant \ˈdes-i-kənt\ *n* : a drying agent

des•ic•cate \-ˌkāt\ *vb* **1** : to dry up or become dried up **2** : to preserve (a food) by drying : DEHYDRATE [Latin *desiccare,* from *de-* + *siccare* "to dry", from *siccus* "dry"] — **des•ic•ca•tion** \ˌdes-i-ˈkā-shən\ *n* — **des•ic•ca•tor** \ˈdes-i-ˌkāt-ər\ *n*

de•sid•er•a•tum \di-ˌsid-ə-ˈrät-əm, -ˌzid-, -ˈrāt-\ *n, pl* **-ta** \-ə\ : something sought for or aimed at [Latin]

[1]de•sign \di-ˈzīn\ *vt* **1** : to conceive and plan out in the mind **2 a** : to have as a purpose or destiny : INTEND **b** : to devise for a specific function or end **3 a** : to make a pattern or sketch of **b** : to conceive and draw the plans for ⟨*design* an airplane⟩ [Middle French *designer,* from Latin *designāre,* from *de-* + *signare* "to mark, mark out"] — **de•sign•er** *n*

[2]design *n* **1** : a project or scheme in which means to an end are laid down **2 a** : a planned purpose or intention ⟨my *design* is to write a trilogy⟩ **b** : goal-directed planning **3 a** : a secret project or scheme : PLOT **b** *pl* : aggressive or evil intent — used with *on* or *against* **4** : a sketch or plan showing the main features of something to be done **5** : the arrangement of elements that make up a structure or a work of art **6** : a decorative pattern **syn** see INTENTION, PLAN

[1]des•ig•nate \ˈdez-ig-ˌnāt, -nət\ *adj* : chosen for an office but not yet installed ⟨ambassador *designate*⟩

[2]des•ig•nate \-ˌnāt\ *vt* **1** : to mark or point out : INDICATE **2** : to appoint or choose by name for a special purpose ⟨*designate* someone as supervisor⟩ **3** : to call by a name or title [Latin *designare* "to design, designate"] — **des•ig•na•tive** \-ˌnāt-iv\ *adj* — **des•ig•na•tor** \-ˌnāt-ər\ *n* — **des•ig•na•to•ry** \-nə-ˌtōr-ē, -ˌtór-\ *adj*

designated hitter *n* : a baseball player designated at the start of a game to bat in place of the pitcher without causing the pitcher to be removed from the game

des•ig•na•tion \ˌdez-ig-ˈnā-shən\ *n* **1** : the act of designating or identifying **2** : a distinguishing name, sign, or title **3** : appointment to or selection for an office, post, or service

de•sign•ed•ly \di-ˈzī-nəd-lē\ *adv* : INTENTIONALLY, PURPOSELY ⟨came late *designedly*⟩

de•sign•ing *adj* : CRAFTY, SCHEMING

de•sir•able \di-ˈzī-rə-bəl\ *adj* **1** : having pleasing qualities or properties : ATTRACTIVE ⟨a *desirable* location⟩ **2** : worth seeking or doing as advantageous, beneficial, or wise ⟨*desirable* legislation⟩ — **de•sir•abil•i•ty** \-ˌzī-rə-ˈbil-ət-ē\ *n* — **de•sir•able•ness** \-ˈzī-rə-bəl-nəs\ *n* — **de•sir•ably** \-blē\ *adv*

[1]de•sire \di-ˈzīr\ *vb* **1** : to long for : wish for earnestly ⟨*desire* peace⟩ **2** : to express a wish for : REQUEST ⟨the librarian *desires* us to return the books⟩ **3** : to have desire ⟨you can, if you *desire,* stay here⟩ [Old French *desirer,* from Latin *desiderare,* from *de-* + *sider-, sidus* "star"]

• **syn** WISH, WANT: DESIRE usually emphasizes ardor and sometimes striving; WISH, less formal than DESIRE, often connotes longing for the unattainable; WANT may stress need or lack but is often used instead of WISH ⟨they *want* (or *wish*) to leave early⟩ ⟨do you *want* (or *wish*) tea or coffee?⟩

[2]desire *n* **1** : a strong wish : LONGING **2** : an expressed wish : REQUEST **3** : something desired

de•sir•ous \di-ˈzīr-əs\ *adj* : eagerly wishing : DESIRING ⟨*desirous* of an invitation⟩ — **de•sir•ous•ly** *adv*

de•sist \di-ˈzist, -ˈsist\ *vi* : to cease to proceed or act [Middle French *desister,* from Latin *desistere,* from *de-* + *sistere* "to stand, stop"] **syn** see STOP

desk \ˈdesk\ *n* **1 a** : a table, frame, or case with a flat or sloping surface especially for writing and reading **b** : a counter at which a person performs his or her duties **c** : a music stand **2** : a specialized division of an organization (as a newspaper) ⟨city *desk*⟩ [Medieval Latin *desca,* from Italian *desco* "table", from Latin *discus* "dish, disc"]

des•mid \ˈdez-məd\ *n* : any of numerous one-celled or colonial green algae (order Zygnematales) [Greek *desmos* "bond, ligature"]

[1]des•o•late \ˈdes-ə-lət, ˈdez-\ *adj* **1** : lacking inhabitants and visitors : DESERTED **2** : disconsolate from being left alone **3 a** : showing the effects of abandonment and neglect : DILAPIDATED b : lacking signs of life : BARREN ⟨a *desolate* landscape⟩ c : lacking warmth, comfort, or hope : GLOOMY [Latin *desolatus*, past participle of *desolare* "to abandon", from *de-* + *solus* "alone"] **syn** see SOLITARY — **des•o•late•ly** *adv* — **des•o•late•ness** *n*

²des•o•late \-ˌlāt\ *vt* : to make desolate: **a** : to lay waste **b** : to make miserable

des•o•la•tion \ˌdes-ə-ˈlā-shən, ˌdez-\ *n* **1** : the action of desolating **2** : the condition of being desolated : DEVASTATION, RUIN **3** : a barren wasteland **4 a** : GRIEF 1, SADNESS **b** : LONELINESS

des•oxy•ri•bo•nu•cle•ic acid \de-ˌzäk-sē-ˈrī-bō-nu̇-ˌklē-ik-, -nyu̇-, -ˌklā-\ *n* : DNA

¹de•spair \di-ˈspaər, -ˈspeər\ *vi* : to lose all hope or confidence [Middle French *desperer*, from Latin *desperare*, from *de-* + *sperare* "to hope"]

²despair *n* **1** : utter loss of hope **2** : a cause of hopelessness **syn** see DESPONDENCY

de•spair•ing *adj* : given to, arising from, or marked by despair — **de•spair•ing•ly** \-ing-lē\ *adv*

des•patch \dis-ˈpatch\ *variant of* DISPATCH

des•per•a•do \ˌdes-pə-ˈräd-ō, -ˈrād-\ *n, pl* **-does** *or* **-dos** : a bold or reckless criminal [probably derived from *desperate*]

des•per•ate \ˈdes-pə-rət, -prət\ *adj* **1** : being beyond or almost beyond hope ⟨a *desperate* illness⟩ **2** : reckless because of despair : RASH ⟨a *desperate* attempt⟩ **3** : extremely intense : OVERPOWERING ⟨*desperate* poverty⟩ [Latin *desperatus*, past participle of *desperare* "to despair"] — **des•per•ate•ly** *adv* — **des•per•ate•ness** *n*

des•per•a•tion \ˌdes-pə-ˈrā-shən\ *n* **1** : a loss of hope and surrender to misery or dread **2** : a state of hopelessness leading to extreme recklessness **syn** see DESPONDENCY

de•spi•ca•ble \di-ˈspik-ə-bəl, ˈdes-ˌpik-\ *adj* : deserving to be despised ⟨a *despicable* traitor⟩ [Late Latin *despicabilis*, from Latin *despicari* "to despise"] **syn** see CONTEMPTIBLE — **de•spi•ca•ble•ness** *n* — **de•spi•ca•bly** \-blē\ *adv*

de•spise \di-ˈspīz\ *vt* **1** : to look down on with contempt or scorn ⟨*despised* liars⟩ **2** : to regard as negligible, worthless, or distasteful [Old French *despis-*, stem of *despire* "to despise", from Latin *despicere*, from *de-* + *specere* "to look"] — **de•spis•er** *n*

• **syn** SCORN, DISDAIN, CONTEMN: DESPISE may cover a range of feeling from indifferent disdain to active loathing; SCORN suggests either a lively and indignant or a profound and passionate contempt; DISDAIN implies an arrogant or haughty aversion to what is regarded as unworthy; CONTEMN suggests vehement condemnation of a person or thing.

¹de•spite \di-ˈspīt\ *n* **1** : the feeling or attitude of despising : CONTEMPT **2** : MALICE, SPITE **3 a** : an act of contempt or defiance **b** : HARM 1, INJURY [Old French *despit*, from Latin *despectus*, from *despicere* "to despise"] — **in despite of** : in spite of

²despite *prep* : in spite of ⟨walked to town *despite* the rain⟩

de•spite•ful \di-ˈspīt-fəl\ *adj* : expressing malice or hate — **de•spite•ful•ly** \-fə-lē\ *adv* — **de•spite•ful•ness** *n*

de•spoil \di-ˈspȯil\ *vt* : to strip of belongings, possessions, or value : PLUNDER, PILLAGE — **de•spoil•er** *n* — **de•spoil•ment** \-ˈspȯil-mənt\ *n*

de•spo•li•a•tion \di-ˌspō-lē-ˈā-shən\ *n* : the act of despoiling : the state of being despoiled

¹de•spond \di-ˈspänd\ *vi* : to become discouraged or disheartened [Latin *despondēre* "to give up, despond", from *de-* + *spondēre* "to promise solemnly"]

²despond *n* : DESPONDENCY

de•spon•den•cy \di-ˈspän-dən-sē\ *n* : the state of being despondent : DEJECTION, DISCOURAGEMENT

• **syn** DESPAIR, DESPERATION: DESPONDENCY may imply a temporary mood of depression and apathy; DESPAIR implies utter loss of hope and suggests a final ceasing of effort or resistance; DESPERATION implies an urgency that drives one to any action offering immediate success regardless of consequences.

de•spon•dent \-dənt\ *adj* : feeling extreme discouragement, dejection, or depression — **de•spon•dent•ly** *adv*

des•pot \ˈdes-pət, -ˌpät\ *n* **1** : a ruler with absolute power and authority **2** : a person exercising power abusively, oppressively, or tyrannously [Greek *despotēs* "master, lord"] — **des•pot•ic** \des-ˈpät-ik\ *adj* — **des•pot•i•cal•ly** \-i-kə-lē, -klē\ *adv*

des•po•tism \ˈdes-pə-ˌtiz-əm\ *n* **1 a** : rule by a despot : TYRANNY **b** : despotic exercise of power **2** : a state or a system of government in which the ruler has unlimited power

des•sert \di-ˈzərt\ *n* : a course of sweet food, fruit, or cheese served at the close of a meal [Middle French, from *desservir* "to clear the table", from *des-* "de-" + *servir* "to serve"]

des•ti•na•tion \ˌdes-tə-ˈnā-shən\ *n* **1** : an act of appointing, setting aside for a purpose, or predetermining **2** : the purpose for which something is destined **3** : a place which is the goal of a journey or to which something is sent

des•tine \ˈdes-tən\ *vt* **1** : to determine the fate of in advance ⟨a plan *destined* to fail⟩ **2** : to designate, assign, or dedicate in advance ⟨*destined* their children for college⟩ **3** : to be bound or directed ⟨a ship *destined* for New York⟩ [Old French *destiner*, from Latin *destinare*]

des•ti•ny \ˈdes-tə-nē\ *n, pl* **-nies 1** : something to which a person or thing is destined : FORTUNE **2** : a predetermined course of events often held to be an irresistible power or agency **syn** see FATE

des•ti•tute \ˈdes-tə-ˌtüt, -ˌtyüt\ *adj* **1** : lacking something needed or desirable ⟨*destitute* of common sense⟩ **2** : extremely poor : suffering great want ⟨a *destitute* family⟩ [Latin *destitutus*, past participle of *destituere* "to abandon, deprive", from *de-* + *statuere* "to set up"] — **des•ti•tute•ness** *n*

des•ti•tu•tion \ˌdes-tə-ˈtü-shən, -ˈtyü-\ *n* : the state of being destitute; *esp* : extreme poverty

de•stroy \di-ˈstrȯi\ *vb* **1** : to ruin the structure, organic existence, or condition of ⟨a house *destroyed* by fire⟩ **2** : KILL ⟨have a sick animal *destroyed*⟩ [Old French *destruire*, from Latin *destruere*, from *de-* + *struere* "to build"]

• **syn** DEMOLISH, ANNIHILATE: DESTROY implies any force that wrecks, kills, annihilates, or tears down or apart ⟨*destroy* a friendship by deceit⟩ DEMOLISH implies a pulling or smashing to pieces or a tearing down to the point of ruin ⟨*demolish* a building⟩ ANNIHILATE suggests destruction so complete as to make any restoration impossible ⟨*annihilate* a city by nuclear attack⟩

de•stroy•er \-ˈstrȯi-ər, -ˈstrȯir\ *n* **1** : a destroying agent or agency **2** : a small fast warship armed with guns, depth charges, torpedoes, and sometimes guided missiles

destroyer escort *n* : a warship similar to but smaller than a destroyer

de•struct \di-ˈstrəkt\ *n* : the deliberate destruction of a rocket after launching

de•struc•ti•ble \di-ˈstrək-tə-bəl\ *adj* : capable of being destroyed — **de•struc•ti•bil•i•ty** \-ˌstrək-tə-ˈbil-ət-ē\ *n*

de•struc•tion \di-ˈstrək-shən\ *n* **1** : the action or process of destroying something **2** : the state or fact of being destroyed : RUIN **3** : something that destroys [Middle French, from Latin *destructio*, from *destruere* "to destroy"]

de•struc•tive \di-ˈstrək-tiv\ *adj* **1** : causing destruction : RUINOUS ⟨*destructive* storms⟩ **2** : designed or tending to destroy or discredit ⟨*destructive* criticism⟩ — **de•struc•tive•ly** *adv* — **de•struc•tive•ness** *n*

destructive distillation *n* : decomposition of a substance (as coal or oil) by heat in a closed container and collection of the volatile products produced

de•struc•tor \di-ˈstrək-tər\ *n* **1** : a furnace for burning refuse : INCINERATOR **2** : a device for destroying a missile in flight

des•ue•tude \ˈdes-wi-ˌtüd, -ˌtyüd, di-ˈsü-ə-ˌ\ *n* : discontinuance from use or exercise : DISUSE [Latin *desuetudo*, from *desuescere* "to become unaccustomed", from *de-* + *suescere* "to become accustomed"]

des•ul•to•ry \ˈdes-əl-ˌtōr-ē, -ˌtȯr-\ *adj* : marked by lack of definite plan, regularity, or purpose : AIMLESS ⟨*desultory* reading⟩ [Latin *desultorius*, from *desilire* "to leap down", from *de-* + *salire* "to leap"] — **des•ul•to•ri•ly** \ˌdes-əl-ˈtōr-ə-lē, -ˈtȯr-\ *adv* — **des•ul•to•ri•ness** \ˈdes-əl-ˌtōr-ē-nəs, -ˌtȯr-\ *n*

de•tach \di-ˈtach\ *vt* **1** : to separate especially from a larger mass and usually without violence or damage **2** : DISENGAGE, WITHDRAW [French *détacher*, from Old French *destachier*, from *des-* "de-" + *-tachier* (as in *atachier* "to attach")] — **de•tach•able** \-ə-bəl\ *adj* — **de•tach•ably** \-blē\ *adv*

de•tached \-ˈtacht\ *adj* **1** : not joined or connected : SEPARATE ⟨a *detached* house⟩ **2** : UNBIASED, IMPARTIAL ⟨a *detached* appraisal⟩ **3** : ALOOF, UNCONCERNED — **de•tached•ly** \-ˈtach-əd-lē, -ˈtach-tlē\ *adv* — **de•tached•ness** \-ˈtach-əd-nəs; -ˈtacht-nəs, -ˈtach-\ *n*

de•tach•ment \di-ˈtach-mənt\ *n* **1** : the action or process of detaching : SEPARATION **2 a** : the dispatching of a body of troops or part of a fleet from the main body for a special service **b** : the part so dispatched **c** : a small permanent military unit having a special task or function **3 a** : indifference to worldly concerns : UNWORLDLINESS **b** : freedom from bias or prejudice : IMPARTIALITY

[1]**de·tail** \di-ˈtāl, ˈdē-ˌ\ *n* **1 a** : a dealing with something item by item ⟨go into *detail* about an adventure⟩ **b** : a small part : ITEM ⟨the *details* of a story⟩ **2 a** : selection (as of a group of soldiers) for some special service **b** : a soldier or group of soldiers appointed for special duty [French *détail,* from Old French *detail* "slice, piece", from *detaillier* "to cut in pieces"]

[2]**detail** *vt* **1** : to report in detail **2** : ENUMERATE 2, SPECIFY **3** : to assign to a task — **de·tail·er** *n*

de·tailed \di-ˈtāld, ˈdē-ˌ\ *adj* **1 a** : including many details **b** : marked by careful attention to details **2** : furnished with finely finished details ⟨beautifully *detailed* clothes⟩ **syn** see CIRCUMSTANTIAL — **de·tailed·ly** \di-ˈtāl-əd-lē, -ˈtāld-lē, ˈdē-ˌ\ *adv* — **de·tailed·ness** \di-ˈtā-ləd-nəs, -ˈtāld-nəs, -ˈtāl-nəs-, ˈdē-ˌ\ *n*

de·tain \di-ˈtān\ *vt* **1** : to hold or keep in or as if in custody **2** : to keep back (as something due) : WITHHOLD **3** : to restrain especially from proceeding : STOP [Middle French *detenir,* from Latin *detinēre,* from *de-* + *tenēre* "to hold"] — **de·tain·ment** \-mənt\ *n*

de·tect \di-ˈtekt\ *vt* **1** : to discover the nature, existence, presence, or fact of ⟨*detect* smoke⟩ **2** : DEMODULATE [Latin *detectus,* past participle of *detegere* "to uncover"] — **de·tect·able** \-ˈtek-tə-bəl\ *adj*

de·tec·tion \di-ˈtek-shən\ *n* **1** : the act of detecting : the state or fact of being detected : DISCOVERY **2** : the extraction of information from a radio, laser, or computer signal

[1]**de·tec·tive** \di-ˈtek-tiv\ *adj* **1** : fitted for or used in detecting something ⟨a *detective* device for coal gas⟩ **2** : of or relating to detectives or their work ⟨a *detective* story⟩

[2]**detective** *n* : an individual (as a policeman) whose business is solving crimes and catching criminals or gathering information that is not readily accessible

de·tec·tor \di-ˈtek-tər\ *n* **1** : one that detects **2** : a device for demodulating a radio signal

de·tent \ˈdē-ˌtent, di-ˈ\ *n* : a mechanism that locks or unlocks a movement : PAWL [French *détente,* from Old French *destendre* "to slacken", from *des-* "de-" + *tendre* "to stretch", from Latin *tendere*]

dé·tente \dā-ˈtänt, -ˈtäⁿt\ *n* : a relaxation of strained relations or tensions (as between nations) [French]

de·ten·tion \di-ˈten-chən\ *n* : the act of detaining : the state of being detained: as **a** : CONFINEMENT; *esp* : temporary custody preceding trial **b** : a forced delay [Late Latin *detentio,* from Latin *detinēre* "to detain"]

de·ter \di-ˈtər\ *vt* **de·terred**; **de·ter·ring** : to turn aside, discourage, or prevent from acting (as by fear) [Latin *deterrēre,* from *de-* + *terrēre* "to frighten"] — **de·ter·ment** \-ˈtər-mənt\ *n*

de·ter·gen·cy \di-ˈtər-jən-sē\ *n* : cleansing quality or power

[1]**de·ter·gent** \-jənt\ *adj* : CLEANSING ⟨*detergent* oil for engines⟩ [Latin *detergēre* "to wash off", from *de-* + *tergēre* "to wipe"]

[2]**detergent** *n* : a cleansing agent; *esp* : any of numerous synthetic organic preparations that are chemically different from soaps but resemble them in the ability to emulsify oils and hold dirt in suspension

de·te·ri·o·rate \di-ˈtir-ē-ə-ˌrāt\ *vb* : to make or become worse or of less value : DEGENERATE [Late Latin *deteriorare,* from Latin *deterior* "worse"] — **de·te·ri·o·ra·tion** \-ˌtir-ē-ə-ˈrā-shən\ *n* — **de·te·ri·o·ra·tive** \-ˈtir-ē-ə-ˌrāt-iv\ *adj*

de·ter·min·able \di-ˈtərm-ə-nə-bəl, -ˈtərm-nə-\ *adj* : capable of being determined or ascertained — **de·ter·min·able·ness** *n* — **de·ter·min·ably** \-blē\ *adv*

de·ter·mi·nant \di-ˈtərm-ə-nənt, -ˈtərm-nənt\ *n* **1** : something that determines or conditions : FACTOR **2** : a square array of numbers bordered on either side by a straight line whose value is the algebraic sum of all the products that can be formed by taking as factors one element from each row and column such that no two elements in a given product are in the same row or column and giving the products a sign by rule

de·ter·mi·nate \-mə-nət\ *adj* **1** : having fixed limits : DEFINITE **2** : definitely settled ⟨arranged in a *determinate* order⟩ **3** : having a single flower terminating the main or central stalk and opening before those below or around it : CYMOSE ⟨a *determinate* inflorescence⟩ — **de·ter·mi·nate·ly** *adv* — **de·ter·mi·nate·ness** *n*

de·ter·mi·na·tion \di-ˌtər-mə-ˈnā-shən\ *n* **1** : the act of coming to a decision; *also* : the decision or conclusion reached **2** : the act of fixing the extent, position, or character of something ⟨*determination* of the position of a ship⟩ **3** : accurate measurement (as of length or volume) **4** : firm or fixed purpose : FIRMNESS **5** : an identification of the taxonomic position of a plant or animal

[1]**de·ter·mi·na·tive** \-ˈtər-mə-ˌnāt-iv\ *adj* : having power or tendency to determine — **de·ter·mi·na·tive·ly** *adv* — **de·ter·mi·na·tive·ness** *n*

[2]**determinative** *n* : one that serves to determine

de·ter·mine \di-ˈtər-mən\ *vb* **1 a** : to fix conclusively or authoritatively ⟨two points *determine* a straight line⟩ **b** : to bring about as a result ⟨demand *determines* the price⟩ **2** : to come to a decision : DECIDE ⟨*determine* whom to invite⟩ **3** : to find out the limits, nature, dimensions, or scope of : gain definite knowledge about ⟨*determine* the direction of the wind⟩ **4** : to be the cause of or reason for ⟨the quality of your work *determines* your mark⟩ **5** : to discover the taxonomic position or the generic and specific names of [Middle French *determiner,* from Latin *determinare,* from *de-* + *terminare* "to limit, terminate"]

de·ter·mined \-mənd\ *adj* **1** : marked by a decided purpose : RESOLVED ⟨*determined* to succeed⟩ **2** : marked by firmness or resoluteness ⟨a *determined* attack⟩ — **de·ter·mined·ly** \-mən-dlē, -mə-nəd-lē\ *adv* — **de·ter·mined·ness** \-mənd-nəs, -mən-\ *n*

de·ter·min·er \-mə-nər\ *n* : one that determines: as **a** : GENE, DETERMINANT **b** : a word belonging to a group of noun modifiers characterized by occurrence before descriptive adjectives modifying the same noun ⟨*my* in "my new car" is a *determiner*⟩

de·ter·min·ism \-mə-ˌniz-əm\ *n* : a doctrine that acts of the will, natural events, or social changes are determined by preceding causes — **de·ter·min·ist** \-mə-nəst\ *n or adj* — **de·ter·min·is·tic** \-ˌtər-mə-ˈnis-tik\ *adj*

de·ter·rence \di-ˈtər-əns, -ˈter-\ *n* : the act, process, or capacity of deterring

de·ter·rent \-ənt\ *adj* **1** : serving to deter **2** : relating to deterrence — **deterrent** *n* — **de·ter·rent·ly** *adv*

de·test \di-ˈtest\ *vt* : to dislike intensely : LOATHE, ABHOR [Latin *detestari* "to curse while calling a deity to witness, detest", from *de-* + *testari* "to call to witness"] **syn** see HATE — **de·test·er** *n*

de·test·able \di-ˈtes-tə-bəl\ *adj* : arousing or deserving intense dislike : ABOMINABLE — **de·test·able·ness** *n* — **de·test·ably** \-blē\ *adv*

de·tes·ta·tion \ˌdē-ˌtes-ˈtā-shən\ *n* **1** : intense hatred or dislike : LOATHING **2** : an object of hatred or contempt

de·throne \di-ˈthrōn\ *vt* : to remove from a throne : DEPOSE — **de·throne·ment** \-mənt\ *n* — **de·thron·er** *n*

det·o·nate \ˈdet-n-ˌāt, ˈdet-ə-ˌnāt\ *vb* : to explode or cause to explode with sudden violence [Latin *detonare* "to thunder down", from *de-* + *tonare* "to thunder"] — **det·o·na·tion** \ˌdet-n-ˈā-shən, ˌdet-ə-ˈnā-shən\ *n*

det·o·na·tor \ˈdet-n-ˌāt-ər, ˈdet-ə-ˌnāt-\ *n* : a device or small quantity of explosive used for detonating a high explosive

[1]**de·tour** \ˈdē-ˌtu̇r, di-ˈ\ *n* : a deviation from a direct course or the usual procedure; *esp* : a roundabout way temporarily replacing part of a regular route [French *détour,* from Old French *destorner* "to divert", from *des-* "de-" + *torner* "to turn"]

[2]**detour** *vb* **1** : to send or proceed by a detour ⟨*detour* around a pit⟩ **2** : to avoid by going around : BYPASS

de·tox·i·fy \dē-ˈtäk-sə-ˌfī\ *vt* **-fied**; **-fy·ing** : to remove a poison or toxin or the effect of such from — **de·tox·i·fi·ca·tion** \ˌdē-ˌtäk-sə-fə-ˈkā-shən\ *n*

de·tract \di-ˈtrakt\ *vb* **1** : to lessen in importance, value, or praiseworthiness ⟨*detract* from a person's reputation⟩ **2** : DISTRACT 1 ⟨*detract* attention⟩ [Latin *detractus,* past participle of *detrahere* "to withdraw, disparage", from *de-* + *trahere* "to draw"] — **de·trac·tor** \-ˈtrak-tər\ *n*

de·trac·tion \di-ˈtrak-shən\ *n* : a lessening of reputation or esteem especially by malicious or petty criticism : BELITTLING — **de•trac•tive** \-'trak-tiv\ *adj* — **de•trac•tive•ly** *adv*

de•train \dē-'trān, 'dē-\ *vb* : to leave or cause to leave a railroad train — **de•train•ment** \-mənt\ *n*

det•ri•ment \'de-trə-mənt\ *n* : injury or damage or its cause : HURT [Latin *detrimentum,* from *deterere* "to wear away, impair", from *de-* + *terere* "to rub"]

det•ri•men•tal \,de-trə-'ment-l\ *adj* : causing detriment : DAMAGING — **det•ri•men•tal•ly** \-l-ē\ *adv*

de•tri•tus \di-'trīt-əs\ *n* **1** : loose material that results directly from rock disintegration or abrasion **2** : a product of disintegration or wearing away [French *détritus,* from Latin *detritus,* past participle of *deterere* "to wear away"] — **de•tri•tal** \-'trīt-l\ *adj*

[1]**deuce** \'düs, 'dyüs\ *n* **1 a** (1) : the face of dice that bears two spots (2) : a playing card bearing the number two **b** : a cast of dice yielding a point of two **2** : a tie in tennis with each side having a score of 40 **3** : DEVIL 1,DICKENS — used chiefly as a mild oath [Middle French *deus* "two"; from Latin *duo;* sense 3 from obsolete English *deuce* "bad luck"]

[1]deuce 1a (2)

[2]**deuce** *vt* : to bring the score of (a tennis game or set) to deuce

deuc•ed \'dü-səd, 'dyü-\ *adj* : DAMNED, CONFOUNDED ⟨in a *deuced* fix⟩ — **deuced** *or* **deuc•ed•ly** *adv*

deu•te•ri•um \dü-'tir-ē-əm, dyü-\ *n* : the hydrogen isotope that is of approximately twice the mass of ordinary hydrogen and that occurs in water — called also *heavy hydrogen*; symbol *D* [New Latin, from Greek *deuteros* "second"]

deuterium oxide *n* : heavy water D_2O composed of deuterium and oxygen

deu•ter•on \'düt-ə-,rän, 'dyüt-\ *n* : the nucleus of the deuterium atom that consists of one proton and one neutron

Deu•ter•on•o•my \,düt-ə-'rän-ə-mē, ,dyüt-\ *n* — see BIBLE table [Greek *Deuteronomion,* from *deuteros* "second" + *nomos* "law"]

deut•sche mark \,dòi-chə-'märk\ *n* **1** : the basic monetary unit of West Germany **2** : a coin representing one deutsche mark [German]

de•val•ue \dē-'val-yü, 'dē-\ *vb* : to reduce the international exchange value of a currency — **de•val•u•a•tion** \,dē-,val-yə-'wā-shən\ *n*

dev•as•tate \'dev-ə-,stāt\ *vt* **1** : to reduce to ruin : lay waste **2** : OVERPOWER, OVERWHELM ⟨*devastated* by grief⟩ [Latin *devastare,* from *de-* + *vastare* "to lay waste"] **syn** see RAVAGE — **dev•as•tat•ing•ly** \-,stāt-ing-lē\ *adv* — **dev•as•ta•tor** \-,stāt-ər\ *n*

dev•as•ta•tion \,dev-ə-'stā-shən\ *n* : the action of devastating : the state of being devastated : DESOLATION

de•vel•op \di-'vel-əp\ *vb* **1 a** : to unfold gradually or in detail **b** : to subject (exposed photographic material) especially to a chemical treatment to produce a visible image **c** : to elaborate (a musical theme) by working out rhythmic and harmonic changes **2** : to bring to a more advanced or more nearly perfect state ⟨study to *develop* the mind⟩ **3** : to make more available or usable ⟨*develop* resources⟩ **4** : to acquire gradually ⟨*develop* a taste for olives⟩ **5 a** : to go through a process of natural growth, differentiation, or evolution ⟨a blossom *develops* from a bud⟩ **b** : to acquire secondary sex characters **6** : to become apparent [French *développer,* from Old French *desvoloper,* from *des-* "de-" + *voloper* "to wrap"] — **de•vel•op•able** \-'vel-ə-pə-bəl\ *adj*

de•vel•op•er \-'vel-ə-pər\ *n* : one that develops; *esp* : a chemical used to develop exposed photographic materials

de•vel•op•ment \di-'vel-əp-mənt\ *n* **1** : the act, process, or result of developing **2** : the state of being developed **3** : the elaboration of a musical theme, subject, or idea — **de•vel•op•men•tal** \-,vel-əp-'ment-l\ *adj* — **de•vel•op•men•tal•ly** \-l-ē\ *adv*

de•vi•ant \'dē-vē-ənt\ *adj* **1** : deviating especially from an accepted norm **2** : characterized by deviation — **de•vi•ance** \-əns\ *n* — **deviant** *n*

[1]**de•vi•ate** \'dē-vē-,āt\ *vb* : to turn aside especially from an established way [Late Latin *deviare,* from Latin *de-* + *via* "way"]

[2]**de•vi•ate** \-vē-ət, -vē-,āt\ *adj* : DEVIANT — **deviate** *n*

de•vi•a•tion \,dē-vē-'ā-shən\ *n* : an act or instance of deviating: as **a** : the difference found by subtracting some fixed number (as the arithmetic mean of a series of statistical data) from any item of the series **b** : departure from an established ideology or party line **c** : noticeable departure from accepted norms (as of behavior) — **de•vi•a•tion•ism** \-shə-,niz-əm\ *n* — **de•vi•a•tion•ist** \-shə-nəst, -shnəst\ *n*

de•vice \di-'vīs\ *n* **1 a** : a scheme to deceive : STRATAGEM **b** : a piece of equipment or a mechanism designed to serve a special purpose **2** *pl* : a way of doing or acting : unsupervised activities ⟨left to their own *devices*⟩ **3** : an emblematic design used especially as a heraldic bearing [Old French *devis* "division, intention", from *deviser* "to divide, regulate, tell"]

[1]**dev•il** \'dev-əl\ *n* **1** *often cap* : the personified supreme spirit of evil often represented in Jewish and Christian belief as the ruler of hell — often used with *the* as a mild imprecation or expression of surprise, vexation, or emphasis **2** : DEMON 2a **3 a** : an extremely wicked person **b** : a reckless or dashing person **c** : a pitiable person — usually used in the phrase *poor devil* [Old English *dēofol,* from Late Latin *diabolus,* from Greek *diabolos,* literally, "slanderer", from *diaballein* "to throw across, slander", from *dia-* + *ballein* "to throw"]

[2]**devil** *vt* **dev•iled** *or* **dev•illed**; **dev•il•ing** *or* **dev•il•ling** \'dev-ling, -ə-ling\ **1** : ANNOY; *esp* : to press, beg, or urge persistently **2** : to season highly ⟨*deviled* eggs⟩

dev•il•fish \'dev-əl-,fish\ *n* **1** : any of several extremely large rays widely distributed in warm seas — called also *manta* **2** : OCTOPUS 1

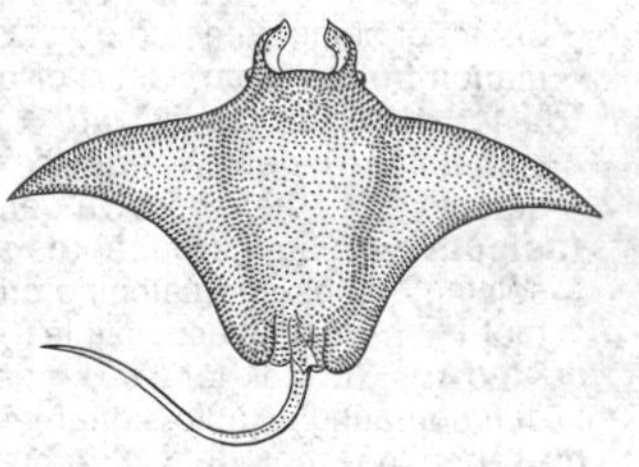

devilfish 1

dev•il•ish \'dev-lish, -ə-lish\ *adj* **1** : characteristic of or resembling the devil ⟨*devilish* tricks⟩ **2** : EXTREME 1, EXCESSIVE ⟨in a *devilish* hurry⟩ — **devilish** *adv* — **dev•il•ish•ly** *adv* — **dev•il•ish•ness** *n*

dev•il–may–care \,dev-əl-,mā-'keər, -'kaər\ *adj* : heedless of authority : RECKLESS

dev•il•ment \'dev-əl-mənt, -,ment\ *n* : reckless mischief

dev•il•ry \'dev-əl-rē\ *or* **dev•il•try** \-əl-trē\ *n, pl* **-ries** *or* **-tries** **1** : action performed with the help of the devil : WITCHCRAFT **2** : reckless unrestrained conduct : MISCHIEF

devil's advocate *n* **1** : a Roman Catholic official whose duty is to examine critically the evidence on which a demand for beatification or canonization rests **2** : a person who supports a less accepted or approved cause for the sake of argument

devil's darning needle *n* **1** : DRAGONFLY **2** : DAMSELFLY

dev•il's food cake \'dev-əlz-,füd-,kāk\ *n* : a rich chocolate cake

devil's paintbrush *n* : any of various hawkweeds found in the eastern United States

de•vi•ous \'dē-vē-əs\ *adj* **1** : deviating from a straight line : TWISTING **2 a** : ERRANT 2b **b** : UNDERHAND 1, SNEAKY [Latin *devius,* from *de-* + *via* "way"] — **de•vi•ous•ly** *adv* — **de•vi•ous•ness** *n*

de•vise \di-'vīz\ *vt* **1** : to form in the mind by new combinations or applications of ideas or principles : INVENT ⟨*devise* an engine⟩ **2** : to lay plans to obtain or bring about : PLOT ⟨*devise* the death of an enemy⟩ [Old French *deviser* "to divide, regulate, tell", from Latin *divisus,* past participle of *dividere* "to divide"] — **de•vis•er** *n*

de•vi•tal•ize \dē-'vīt-l-,īz, 'dē-\ *vt* : to deprive of life or vitality

de•void \di-'vòid\ *adj* : wholly lacking : DESTITUTE ⟨a book *devoid* of interest⟩

de•voir \dəv-'wär, 'dev-,\ *n* **1** : an assigned or required task : DUTY **2** : RESPECT 3c — usually used in pl. [Old French *deveir,* from *devoir, deveir* "to owe, be obliged", from Latin *debēre*]

dev•o•lu•tion \,dev-ə-'lü-shən, ,dē-və-\ *n* : transference (as of rights or powers) from one individual to another [Medieval Latin *devolutio,* from Latin *devolvere* "to roll down"] — **dev•o•lu-**

tion•ary \-shə-ˌner-ē\ *adj* — **dev•o•lu•tion•ist** \-shə-nəst, -shnəst\ *n*

de•volve \di-ˈvälv, -ˈvȯlv\ *vb* **:** to pass by transmission or succession from one person to another [Latin *devolvere* "to roll down", from *de-* + *volvere* "to roll"]

dev•on \ˈdev-ən\ *n, often cap* **:** any of a breed of vigorous red dual-purpose cattle of English origin [*Devon,* England]

De•vo•ni•an \di-ˈvō-nē-ən\ *n* **1 :** the period of the Paleozoic era between the Silurian and Mississippian — called also *Age of Fishes;* see GEOLOGIC TIME table **2 :** the system of rocks corresponding to the Devonian period [*Devon,* England] — **Devonian** *adj*

de•vote \di-ˈvōt\ *vt* **1 :** to set apart for a special use ⟨*devote* land to farming⟩ **2 :** to center the attention or activities of (oneself) ⟨*devoted* themselves to restoring the house⟩ [Latin *devotus,* past participle of *devovēre* "to dedicate, devote", from *de-* + *vovēre* "to vow"]

de•vot•ed *adj* **1 :** dedicated to a purpose **:** DEVOUT, ZEALOUS ⟨*devoted* admirers⟩ **2 :** LOVING ⟨*devoted* parents⟩ — **de•vot•ed•ly** *adv* — **de•vot•ed•ness** *n*

dev•o•tee \ˌdev-ə-ˈtē, -ˈtā\ *n* **1 :** an ardent follower of a religion or deity **2 :** a zealous follower, supporter, or enthusiast ⟨a *devotee* of sports⟩

de•vo•tion \di-ˈvō-shən\ *n* **1 a :** religious fervor **:** PIETY **b :** an act of prayer — usually used in pl. **c :** a religious exercise or practice other than the regular worship of a church **2 a :** the act of devoting or the quality of being devoted **b :** ardent love, affection, or dedication — **de•vo•tion•al** \-shnəl, -shən-ᵊl\ *adj* — **de•vo•tion•al•ly** \-ē\ *adv*

de•vo•tion•al \-shnəl, -shən-ᵊl\ *n* **:** a short worship service

de•vour \di-ˈvau̇r\ *vt* **1 :** to eat up greedily **2 :** to seize upon and destroy **:** CONSUME ⟨fire *devoured* the building⟩ **3 :** to enjoy avidly ⟨*devour* a book⟩ [Middle French *devourer,* from Latin *devorare,* from *de-* + *vorare* "to devour"]

de•vout \di-ˈvau̇t\ *adj* **1 :** devoted to religion or to religious duties or exercises **2 :** expressing devotion or piety **3 :** warmly devoted **:** SINCERE ⟨*devout* thanks⟩ [Old French *devot,* from Late Latin *devotus,* from Latin *devovēre* "to devote"] — **de•vout•ly** *adv* — **de•vout•ness** *n*

• **syn** DEVOUT, PIOUS, RELIGIOUS mean showing fervor and reverence in religious practice. DEVOUT stresses an attitude that leads to frequent but not necessarily outward prayer and reverent worship; PIOUS emphasizes the faithful performance of one's religious duties; RELIGIOUS implies devoutness and piety but stresses faith in God or gods and adherence to a way of life conforming to that faith.

dew \ˈdü, ˈdyü\ *n* **1 :** moisture condensed upon cool surfaces at night **2 :** something resembling dew in purity, freshness, or power to refresh **3 :** moisture especially when appearing in minute droplets [Old English *dēaw*] — **dew** *vt*

dew•ber•ry \-ˌber-ē\ *n* **:** any of several sweet edible berries related to and resembling blackberries; *also* **:** a trailing bramble that bears these

dew•claw \-ˌklȯ\ *n* **:** a vestigial digit on the foot of a mammal or a claw or hoof on such a digit — **dew•clawed** \-ˌklȯd\ *adj*

dew•drop \-ˌdräp\ *n* **:** a drop of dew

Dew•ey decimal classification \ˌdü-ē-, ˌdyü-\ *n* **:** a system of classifying publications whereby main classes are designated by a 3-digit number and subdivisions are shown by numbers after a decimal point [Melvil *Dewey,* died 1931, American librarian]

dew•fall \ˈdü-ˌfȯl, ˈdyü-\ *n* **:** formation of dew; *also* **:** the time when dew begins to form

dew•lap \-ˌlap\ *n* **:** a hanging fold of skin under the neck especially of a cud-chewing animal — **dew•lapped** \-ˌlapt\ *adj*

dew point *n* **:** the temperature at which the moisture in the air begins to condense

dewy \ˈdü-ē, ˈdyü-\ *adj* **dew•i•er; -est :** moist with, affected by, or suggestive of dew ⟨eyes *dewy* with tears⟩ — **dew•i•ly** \ˈdü-ə-lē, ˈdyü-\ *adv* — **dew•i•ness** \-ē-nəs\ *n*

Dex•e•drine \ˈdek-sə-ˌdrēn, -drən\ *trademark* — used for dextroamphetamine

dex•ter \ˈdek-stər\ *adj* **1 :** relating to or situated on the right **2 :** being or related to the side of a heraldic shield at the right of the person bearing it [Latin, "dextral, skillful"] — **dexter** *adv*

dex•ter•i•ty \dek-ˈster-ət-ē\ *n, pl* **-ties 1 :** readiness and grace in physical activity; *esp* **:** skill and ease in using the hands **2 :** mental skill or quickness

dex•ter•ous *or* **dex•trous** \ˈdek-stə-rəs, -strəs\ *adj* **1 :** skillful and competent with the hands **2 :** mentally quick and skillful **:** EXPERT **3 :** done with skillfulness — **dex•ter•ous•ly** *adv* — **dex•ter•ous•ness** *n*

• **syn** DEXTEROUS, ADROIT, DEFT mean ready and skilled in physical or mental movement. DEXTEROUS implies expertness with facility and agility in manipulation or movement ⟨a *dexterous* pianist⟩ ⟨*dexterous* diplomacy⟩ ADROIT adds artfulness and resourcefulness to dexterity ⟨an *adroit* magician⟩ DEFT stresses lightness, neatness, and sureness of touch ⟨*deft* handling of suspense in a mystery novel⟩

dextr- *or* **dextro-** *combining form* **1 :** right **:** on or toward the right **2 :** turning the plane of polarization of light to the right ⟨*dextrose*⟩ [Latin *dextr-, dexter*]

dex•tral \ˈdek-strəl\ *adj* **:** of, relating to, or inclined to the right; *esp* **:** RIGHT-HANDED — **dex•tral•i•ty** \dek-ˈstral-ət-ē\ *n* — **dex•tral•ly** \ˈdek-strə-lē\ *adv*

dex•trin \ˈdek-strən\ *also* **dex•trine** \-ˌstrēn, -strən\ *n* **:** any of various soluble gummy substances obtained from starch by the action of heat, acids, or enzymes

dex•tro•am•phet•amine \ˈdek-ˌstrō-am-ˈfet-ə-ˌmēn, -mən\ *n* **:** a stimulant of the central nervous system that is a derivative of amphetamine — compare DEXEDRINE

dex•trose \ˈdek-ˌstrōs\ *n* **:** a sugar $C_6H_{12}O_6$ that is a kind of glucose, occurs in plants, fruits, and blood, is a source of energy for living things, may be obtained by hydrolysis of starch in acid solution, and is used in making candy [from the fact that it turns the plane of polarization of light to the right]

dey \ˈdā\ *n* **:** a ruling official of the Ottoman Empire in northern Africa [French, from Turkish *dayı,* literally, "maternal uncle"]

dhar•ma \ˈdər-mə\ *n* **1 :** custom or law regarded as duty in Hinduism **2 a :** the basic principles of cosmic or individual existence in Hinduism and Buddhism **b :** conformity to one's duty and nature in Hinduism and Buddhism [Sanskrit, from *dhārayati* "he holds"]

dhow \ˈdau̇\ *n* **:** any of a number of typically lateen-rigged Arab sailing vessels [Arabic *dāwa*]

dhow

di- *combining form* **1 :** twice **:** twofold **:** double ⟨*dichromatic*⟩ **2 :** containing two atoms, radicals, or groups ⟨*dichromate*⟩ [Greek]

dia- *also* **di-** *prefix* **:** through **:** across [Greek, "through, apart", from *dia*]

di•a•be•tes \ˌdī-ə-ˈbēt-ēz, -ˈbēt-əs\ *n* **:** any of various abnormal conditions characterized by the secretion and excretion of excessive amounts of urine; *esp* **:** DIABETES MELLITUS [Latin, from Greek *diabētēs,* from *diabainein* "to cross over", from *dia-* + *bainein* "to go"] — **di•a•bet•ic** \ˌdī-ə-ˈbet-ik\ *adj or n*

diabetes in•sip•i•dus \-in-ˈsip-əd-əs\ *n* **:** a disorder of the pituitary gland characterized by intense thirst and by the excretion of large amounts of urine [New Latin, literally, "insipid diabetes"]

diabetes mel•li•tus \-ˈmel-ət-əs\ *n* **:** an endocrine disorder characterized by inadequate secretion or utilization of insulin, by the discharge of abnormal amounts of urine, by large amounts of sugar in the blood and urine, and by thirst, hunger, and loss of weight [New Latin, literally "honey-sweet diabetes"]

di•a•bol•ic \ˌdī-ə-ˈbäl-ik\ *adj* **:** of, relating to, or characteristic of the devil **:** FIENDISH [Middle French *diabolique,* from Late Latin *diabolicus,* from *diabolus* "devil"] — **di•a•bol•i•cal** \-ˈbäl-i-kəl\ *adj* — **di•a•bol•i•cal•ly** \-i-kə-lē, -klē\ *adv* — **di•a•bol•i•cal•ness** \-i-kəl-nəs\ *n*

di•ac•o•nate \dī-ˈak-ə-nət, dē-, -ˌnāt\ *n* **1 :** the office or period of office of a deacon or deaconess **2 :** an official body of deacons [Late Latin *diaconatus,* from *diaconus* "deacon"]

di•a•crit•ic \ˌdī-ə-ˈkrit-ik\ *n* **:** a mark used with a letter or group of letters and indicating a sound value different from that given the unmarked or otherwise marked letter or combination of letters — called also *diacritical mark*

di·a·crit·i·cal \ˌdī-ə-ˈkrit-i-kəl\ *also* **di·a·crit·ic** \-ˈkrit-ik\ *adj* **:** serving as a diacritic [Greek *diakritikos* "separative", from *diakrinein* "to distinguish", from *dia-* + *krinein* "to separate"]

di·a·dem \ˈdī-ə-ˌdem, -əd-əm\ *n* **1 :** CROWN; *esp* **:** an ornamental headband worn as a badge of royalty **2 :** regal power or dignity [Old French *diademe,* derived from Greek *diadēma,* from *diadein* "to bind around", from *dia-* + *dein* "to bind"]

di·aer·e·sis \dī-ˈer-ə-səs\ *n, pl* **-e·ses** \-ˌsēz\ **:** a mark ¨ placed over a vowel to show that it is pronounced in a separate syllable (as in *Brontë*) [Late Latin, from Greek *diairesis,* from *diairein* "to divide", from *dia-* + *hairein* "to take"]

di·ag·nose \ˈdī-ig-ˌnōs, -ˌnōz, ˌdī-ig-ˈ\ *vb* **:** to recognize (as a disease) by signs and symptoms **:** make a diagnosis ⟨*diagnose* a play in football⟩ [back-formation from *diagnosis*] — **di·ag·nos·able** \ˌdī-ig-ˈnō-sə-bəl, -zə-\ *adj*

di·ag·no·sis \ˌdī-ig-ˈnō-səs\ *n, pl* **-no·ses** \-ˈnō-ˌsēz\ **1 :** the art or act of identifying a disease from its signs and symptoms **2 :** a concise technical description of a taxonomic group or entity **3 a :** a careful critical study of something especially to determine its nature or importance **b :** the conclusion reached after a critical study [Greek *diagnōsis,* from *diagignōskein* "to distinguish", from *dia-* + *gignōskein* "to know"] — **di·ag·nos·tic** \-ˈnäs-tik\ *adj* — **di·ag·nos·ti·cal·ly** \-ˈnäs-ti-kə-lē, -klē\ *adv* — **di·ag·nos·ti·cian** \-ˌnäs-ˈtish-ən\ *n*

[1]**di·ag·o·nal** \dī-ˈag-ən-l\ *adj* **1 :** joining two nonadjacent corners of a plane figure composed of straight lines or of a solid bounded by plane faces in three dimensions **2 a :** running in a slanting direction **b :** having diagonal markings or parts ⟨a *diagonal* weave⟩ [Latin *diagonalis,* from Greek *diagōnios* "from angle to angle", from *dia-* + *gōnia* "angle"] — **di·ag·o·nal·ly** \-ˈag-ən-l-ē, -ˈag-nə-lē\ *adv*

[2]**diagonal** *n* **1 :** a diagonal line or plane **2 a :** a diagonal direction **b :** a diagonal row, arrangement, or pattern **3 :** a mark / used chiefly to denote "or" (as in *and/or*), "and or" (as in *straggler/deserter*), or "per" (as in *feet /second*) — called also *slant, slash, virgule*

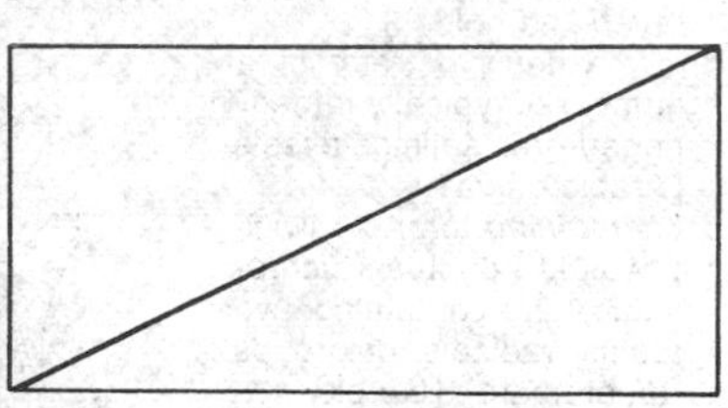

[2]diagonal 1

[1]**di·a·gram** \ˈdī-ə-ˌgram\ *n* **:** a drawing, sketch, plan, or chart that makes something clearer or easier to understand [Greek *diagramma,* from *diagraphein* "to mark out by lines", from *dia-* + *graphein* "to write"] — **di·a·gram·mat·ic** \ˌdī-ə-grə-ˈmat-ik\ *adj* — **di·a·gram·mat·i·cal·ly** \-ˈmat-i-kə-lē, -klē\ *adv*

[2]**diagram** *vt* **-gramed** *or* **-grammed** \-ˌgramd\; **-gram·ing** *or* **-gram·ming** \-ˌgram-ing\ **:** to represent by or put into the form of a diagram ⟨*diagram* a sentence⟩

[1]**di·al** \ˈdī-əl, ˈdīl\ *n* **1 a :** the face of a watch or clock **b :** SUNDIAL **2 a :** a face or scale upon which some measurement or other number is registered or indicated usually by means of numbers and a pointer ⟨the *dial* of a pressure gauge⟩ **b :** a disk usually with a knob or slots that may be turned to make electrical connections (as on a telephone) or to regulate the operation of a device (as a radio) and that usually has guiding marks around its border [Latin *dies* "day"]

[2]**dial** *vt* **di·aled** *or* **di·alled**; **di·al·ing** *or* **di·al·ling :** to manipulate a dial so as to operate, regulate, or select ⟨*dialed* a wrong number⟩ ⟨*dial* your favorite program⟩

di·a·lect \ˈdī-ə-ˌlekt\ *n* **1 :** a regional variety of a language usually transmitted orally and differing distinctively from the standard language ⟨the Lancashire *dialect* of English⟩ **2 :** a special vocabulary or idiom used by the members of an occupational group ⟨the *dialect* of the atomic physicist⟩ **3 :** a variety of language whose identity is fixed by a factor (as social class) other than geography [Middle French *dialecte,* from Latin *dialectus,* from Greek *dialektos* "conversation, dialect", from *dialegesthai* "to converse", from *dia-* + *legein* "to speak"] — **di·a·lec·tal** \ˌdī-ə-ˈlek-tl\ *adj* — **di·a·lec·tal·ly** \ˌdī-ə-ˈlek-tl-ē\ *adv*

• **syn** DIALECT, LINGO, JARGON, SLANG mean language not recognized as standard. DIALECT applies to a form of language persisting regionally or among the uneducated; LINGO is mildly contemptuous for any language not readily understood; JARGON applies to a special or technical language used by a trade, profession, or cult, and may also be a stronger term than LINGO for language that sounds outlandish; SLANG designates a class of mostly recently coined and often short-lived terms or usages informally preferred to standard usage as being forceful, novel, or fashionable.

di·a·lec·tic \ˌdī-ə-ˈlek-tik\ *n* **:** a process of reasoning based on the clash of one idea with its opposite leading to a resolution of these ideas in the form of a truer or more comprehensive concept

di·a·lec·ti·cal \ˌdī-ə-ˈlek-ti-kəl\ *also* **di·a·lec·tic** \-tik\ *adj* **1 :** of, relating to, or in accordance with dialectic **2 :** of, relating to, or characteristic of a dialect — **di·a·lec·ti·cal·ly** \-ti-kə-lē, -klē\ *adv*

di·a·lec·tol·o·gy \ˌdī-ə-ˌlek-ˈtäl-ə-jē\ *n* **:** the systematic study of dialect — **di·a·lec·tol·o·gist** \-jəst\ *n*

di·a·logue *or* **di·a·log** \ˈdī-ə-ˌlȯg\ *n* **1 a :** a conversation between two or more persons **b :** an exchange of ideas and opinions **2 :** the parts of a literary or dramatic composition that represent conversation [Middle French, from Latin *dialogus,* from Greek *dialogos,* from *dialegesthai* "to converse", from *dia-* + *legein* "to speak"]

di·al·y·sis \dī-ˈal-ə-səs\ *n, pl* **-y·ses** \-ə-ˌsēz\ **:** the separation of substances in solution by means of their unequal diffusion through semipermeable membranes; *esp* **:** such a separation of colloids from soluble substances [Greek, "separation", from *dialyein* "to dissolve", from *dia-* + *lyein* "to loosen"]

di·a·lyze \ˈdī-ə-ˌlīz\ *vt* **:** to subject to dialysis

dia·mag·net·ic \ˌdī-ə-ˌmag-ˈnet-ik\ *adj* **:** slightly repelled by a magnet — **dia·mag·ne·tism** \-ˈmag-nə-ˌtiz-əm\ *n*

di·am·e·ter \dī-ˈam-ət-ər\ *n* **1 :** a chord passing through the center of a figure or body **2 :** the length of a straight line through the center of an object [Middle French *diametre,* from Latin *diametros,* from Greek, from *dia-* + *metron* "measure"] — **di·am·e·tral** \-ˈam-ə-trəl\ *adj*

di·a·met·ric \ˌdī-ə-ˈme-trik\ *or* **di·a·met·ri·cal** \-tri-kəl\ *adj* **1 :** of, relating to, or being a diameter **2 :** completely opposed or opposite ⟨a *diametric* contradiction⟩ — **di·a·met·ri·cal·ly** \-tri-kə-lē, -klē\ *adv*

di·a·mond \ˈdī-ə-mənd, ˈdī-mənd\ *n* **1 a :** native crystalline carbon that is usually nearly colorless, that when transparent and free from flaws is highly valued as a precious stone, and that is used industrially as an abrasive powder and in rock drills; *also* **:** a piece of this substance especially when cut and polished **b :** crystallized carbon produced artificially **2 :** a square or rhombus-shaped configuration usually upright or oriented on a diagonal axis **3 :** a red diamond-shaped mark used to distinguish a suit of playing cards; *also* **:** a card of the suit so marked **4 a :** INFIELD 1 **b :** the entire playing field in baseball or softball [Middle French *diamant,* from Late Latin *diamas,* alteration of Latin *adamas* "hardest metal, diamond", from Greek]

[1]**di·a·mond·back** \ˈdī-mənd-ˌbak, -ə-mənd-, -mən-\ *also* **di·a·mond–backed** \-ˈbakt\ *adj* **:** having marks like diamonds on the back

[2]**diamondback** *n* **:** a large and deadly rattlesnake of the southern United States

diamondback terrapin *n* **:** any of several edible terrapins of coastal salt marshes of the southeastern United States

di·a·pa·son \ˌdī-ə-ˈpāz-n, -ˈpās-\ *n* **1 :** a full deep burst of harmonious sound **2 :** one of two principal stops in an organ extending through the complete scale of the instrument **3 :** the full range of musical tones [Latin, from Greek (*hē*) *dia pasōn* (*chordōn symphōnia*) "(the concord) through all (the notes)"]

dia·pause \ˈdī-ə-ˌpȯz\ *n* **:** a period of dormancy (as in some insects) in which development slows down or in which activity is decreased

[1]**di·a·per** \ˈdī-pər, -ə-pər\ *n* **1 :** a usually white linen or cotton fabric woven in a pattern formed by the repetition of a simple usually geometric design; *also* **:** the design on such cloth **2 :** a basic garment for infants comprising a piece of absorbent material drawn up between the legs and fastened at the waist [Middle French *diapre,* from Medieval Latin *diasprum*]

[2]**diaper** *vt* **1 :** to ornament with diaper designs **2 :** to put a diaper on ⟨*diaper* a baby⟩

di·aph·a·nous \dī-ˈaf-ə-nəs\ *adj* **:** having a very fine delicate texture **:** TRANSPARENT ⟨*diaphanous* chiffon⟩ [Medieval Latin *diaphanus,* from Greek *diaphanēs,* from *diaphainein* "to show through", from *dia-* + *phainein* "to show"] — **di•aph•a•nous•ly** *adv* — **di•aph•a•nous•ness** *n*

di•a•phragm \'dī-ə-,fram\ *n* **1 :** a body partition of muscle and connective tissue; *esp* **:** the partition separating the chest and abdominal cavities in mammals **2 :** a dividing membrane or thin partition (as in a tube) **3 :** a device that limits (as in a camera) the aperture of a lens or optical system **4 :** a thin flexible disk that vibrates (as in a microphone) [Late Latin *diaphragma,* from Greek, from *diaphrassein* "to barricade", from *dia-* + *phrassein* "to enclose"] — **di•a•phrag•mat•ic** \,dī-ə-,frag-'mat-ik\ *adj* — **di•a•phrag•mat•i•cal•ly** \-'mat-i-kə-lē, -klē\ *adv*

di•a•rist \'dī-ə-rəst\ *n* **:** one who keeps a diary

di•ar•rhea *or* **di•ar•rhoea** \,dī-ə-'rē-ə\ *n* **:** an abnormally frequent or abundant discharge of loose or fluid material from the bowels [Late Latin *diarrhoea,* from Greek *diarrhoia,* from *diarrhein* "to flow through", from *dia-* + *rhein* "to flow"] — **di•ar•rhe•al** \-'rē-əl\ *or* **di•ar•rhe•ic** \-'rē-ik\ *adj*

di•a•ry \'dī-ə-rē, 'dī-rē\ *n, pl* **-ries :** a daily record especially of personal experiences, observations, and thoughts; *also* **:** a book intended or used as a diary [Latin *diarium,* from *dies* "day"]

Di•as•po•ra \dī-'as-pə-rə, -prə\ *n* **1 :** the settling of scattered colonies of Jews outside Palestine after the Babylonian exile **2 :** the Jews living outside Palestine or modern Israel [Greek, "dispersion", from *diaspeirein* "to scatter", from *dia-* + *speirein* "to sow"]

di•a•stase \'dī-ə-,stās\ *n* **:** AMYLASE; *esp* **:** a mixture of amylases from malt [French, from Greek *diastasis* "separation", from *diistanai* "to separate", from *dia-* + *histanai* "to cause to stand"] — **di•a•stat•ic** \,dī-ə-'stat-ik\ *adj*

di•as•to•le \dī-'as-tə-,lē\ *n* **:** the relaxation of the heart during which its cavities fill with blood [Greek *diastolē* "stretching", from *diastellein* "to expand", from *dia-* + *stellein* "to send"] — **di•a•stol•ic** \,dī-ə-'stäl-ik\ *adj*

di•as•tro•phism \dī-'as-trə-,fiz-əm\ *n* **:** the process of deformation that produces in the earth's crust its continents and ocean basins, plateaus and mountains, folds of strata, and faults [Greek *diastrophē* "twisting", from *diastrephein* "to distort", from *dia-* + *strephein* "to twist"] — **di•a•stroph•ic** \,dī-ə-'sträf-ik\ *adj*

dia•ther•my \'dī-ə-,thər-mē\ *n* **:** the production of heat in tissue by electric currents for medical or surgical purposes — **dia•ther•mic** \,dī-ə-'thər-mik\ *adj*

di•ath•e•sis \dī-'ath-ə-səs\ *n, pl* **-e•ses** \-ə-,sēz\ **:** a constitutional predisposition toward an abnormality or disease [Greek, literally, "arrangement", from *diatithenai* "to arrange" from *dia-* + *tithenai* "to set"]

di•a•tom \'dī-ə-,täm\ *n* **:** any of a class (Bacillariophyceae) of minute floating single-celled or colonial algae that are abundant in fresh and salt water and in soil and have a cell wall of silica that persists as a skeleton after death [derived from Greek *diatomos* "cut in half", from *diatemnein* "to cut through", from *dia-* + *temnein* "to cut"] — **di•a•to•ma•ceous** \,dī-ət-ə-'mā-shəs\ *adj*

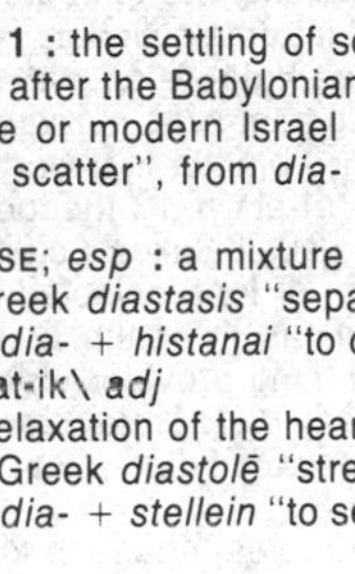

diatom

diatomaceous earth *n* **:** DIATOMITE

di•atom•ic \,dī-ə-'täm-ik\ *adj* **:** having two atoms in the molecule

di•at•o•mite \dī-'at-ə-,mīt\ *n* **:** a light crumbly silica-containing material derived chiefly from diatom remains and used especially as a filter and as an adsorbent and for heat insulation

dia•ton•ic \,dī-ə-'tän-ik\ *adj* **:** relating to or being a standard major or minor scale of eight tones to the octave without chromatic deviation [Late Latin *diatonicus,* from Greek *diatonikos,* from *diatonos* "stretching", from *diateinein* "to stretch out", from *dia-* + *teinein* "to stretch"] — **dia•ton•i•cal•ly** \-'tän-i-kə-lē, -klē\ *adv*

di•a•tribe \'dī-ə-,trīb\ *n* **:** a bitter and abusive speech or writing [Latin *diatriba* "discourse", from Greek *diatribē* "pastime, discourse", from *diatribein* "to spend (time), wear away", from *dia-* + *tribein* "to rub"]

di•az•e•pam \dī-'az-ə-,pam\ *n* **:** a tranquilizer $C_{16}H_{13}ClN_2O$ used especially to relieve anxiety and tension and to relax muscles — compare VALIUM

di•ba•sic \dī-'bā-sik, 'dī-\ *adj* **1 :** having two replaceable hydrogen atoms — used of acids **2 :** having two hydroxyl groups — used of bases and basic salts

[1]**dib•ble** \'dib-əl\ *n* **:** a small hand tool for making holes in the ground for plants, seeds, or bulbs [Middle English *debylle*]

[2]**dibble** *vt* **dib•bled; dib•bling** \'dib-ling, -ə-ling\ **1 :** to plant with a dibble **2 :** to make holes in (soil) with or as if with a dibble

[1]**dice** \'dīs\ *n, pl* **dice 1 :** DIE 1 **2 :** a gambling game played with dice [Middle English *dees, dyce,* pl. of *dee* "die"] — **no dice :** nothing doing **:** no use

[2]**dice** *vb* **1 :** to cut into small cubes ⟨*dice* carrots⟩ **2 :** to play games with dice — **dic•er** *n*

di•chlo•ride \dī-'klōr-,īd, -'klȯr-\ *n* **:** a binary compound containing two atoms of chlorine combined with an element or radical — called also *bichloride*

di•chot•o•mous \dī-'kät-ə-məs\ *adj* **1 :** dividing into two parts **2 :** relating to, involving, or proceeding from dichotomy — **di•chot•o•mous•ly** *adv*

dichotomous key *n* **:** a key to biological classification based on successive choices between pairs of alternate characters

di•chot•o•my \dī-'kät-ə-mē\ *n, pl* **-mies :** a division or the process of dividing into two groups that are mutually exclusive or contradictory [Greek *dichotomia,* from *dicha* "in two" + *temnein* "to cut"]

di•chro•ic \dī-'krō-ik\ *adj* **:** having the property of dichroism [Greek *dichroos* "two-colored", from *di-* + *chrōs* "color"]

di•chro•ism \'dī-krə-,wiz-əm\ *n* **1 :** the property according to which the colors are unlike when a crystal is viewed in the direction of two different axes **2 :** the property of a surface of reflecting light of one color and transmitting light of other colors

di•chro•mate \dī-'krō-,māt, 'dī-\ *n* **:** a usually orange to red chromium salt containing the radical Cr_2O_7 — called also *bichromate*

di•chro•mat•ic \,dī-krō-'mat-ik\ *adj* **:** having or exhibiting two colors

dick•cis•sel \dik-'sis-əl\ *n* **:** a common migratory black-throated finch of the central United States [imitative]

dick•ens \'dik-ənz\ *n* **:** DEVIL 1, DEUCE — used chiefly as a mild oath [euphemism]

Dick•en•si•an \dik-'en-zē-ən, -sē-\ *adj* **:** of, relating to, or characteristic of Charles Dickens or his writings

dick•er \'dik-ər\ *vi* **dick•ered; dick•er•ing** \'dik-ring, -ə-ring\ **:** HAGGLE 2, BARGAIN ⟨buyers *dickering* for lower prices⟩ [origin unknown] — **dicker** *n*

dick•ey *or* **dicky** \'dik-ē\ *n, pl* **dick•eys** *or* **dick•ies 1 :** any of various articles of clothing: as **a :** a separate or detachable shirtfront **b :** a small cloth insert worn to fill in a neckline **2 :** a small bird [*Dicky,* nickname for *Richard*]

Dick test \'dik-\ *n* **:** a test to determine whether one can contract scarlet fever made by an injection of scarlet fever toxin [George F. *Dick,* died 1967, and Gladys H. *Dick,* died 1963, American physicians]

di•cli•nous \dī-'klī-nəs,'dī-\ *adj* **:** having the stamens and pistils in separate flowers — compare MONOCLINOUS [*di-* + Greek *klinē* "bed"]

di•cot \'dī-,kät\ *n* **:** DICOTYLEDON — **dicot** *adj*

di•cot•y•le•don \,dī-,kät-l-'ēd-n\ *n* **:** any of a group (Dicotyledones) of flowering plants (as an aster, an oak, or a cabbage) having an embryo with two cotyledons and usually net-veined leaves and flower parts not in threes — **di•cot•y•le•don•ous** \-n-əs\ *adj*

Dic•ta•phone \'dik-tə-,fōn\ *trademark* — used for a dictating machine

[1]**dic•tate** \'dik-,tāt\ *vb* **1 :** to speak or read for a person to transcribe or for a machine to record ⟨*dictate* a letter⟩ **2 :** to say or state with authority **:** give orders ⟨*dictate* terms of surrender⟩ [Latin *dictare,* from *dicere* "to say"]

[2]**dictate** *n* **:** an authoritative rule, prescription, or injunction

\ə\ **abut**	\au̇\ **out**	\i\ **tip**	\ȯ\ **saw**	\u̇\ **foot**
\ər\ **further**	\ch\ **chin**	\ī\ **life**	\ȯi\ **coin**	\y\ **yet**
\a\ **mat**	\e\ **pet**	\j\ **job**	\th\ **thin**	\yü\ **few**
\ā\ **take**	\ē\ **easy**	\ng\ **sing**	\th\ **this**	\yu̇\ **cure**
\ä\ **cot, cart**	\g\ **go**	\ō\ **bone**	\ü\ **food**	\zh\ **vision**

: COMMAND ⟨the *dictates* of conscience⟩ ⟨the *dictates* of good taste⟩

dictating machine *n* : a machine used especially for the recording of dictated matter

dic•ta•tion \dik-'tā-shən\ *n* **1** : the act or process of giving arbitrary commands **2 a** : the dictating of words ⟨write from *dictation*⟩ **b** : something that is dictated or is taken down as dictated ⟨take *dictation*⟩

dic•ta•tor \'dik-ˌtāt-ər, dik-'\ *n* **1 a** : a person given absolute emergency power by the ancient Roman senate **b** : one holding complete autocratic and often oppressive control **2** : one that dictates

dic•ta•to•ri•al \ˌdik-tə-'tōr-ē-əl, -'tȯr-\ *adj* **1** : of, relating to, or characteristic of a dictator or a dictatorship ⟨a *dictatorial* manner⟩ ⟨a *dictatorial* regime⟩ **2** : oppressive to or contemptuously overbearing toward others — **dic•ta•to•ri•al•ly** \-ē-ə-lē\ *adv* — **dic•ta•to•ri•al•ness** *n*

• **syn** DICTATORIAL, DOGMATIC, DOCTRINAIRE mean imposing one's will or opinions on others. DICTATORIAL stresses autocratic, high-handed methods and a domineering manner; DOGMATIC implies being unduly and offensively positive in laying down principles and expressing opinions; DOCTRINAIRE implies a disposition to follow abstract theories in framing laws or policies affecting people.

dic•ta•tor•ship \dik-'tāt-ər-ˌship\ *n* **1** : the office or term of office of a dictator **2** : autocratic rule, control, or leadership **3** : a government, form of government, or country in which absolute power is held by a dictator or a small clique

dictatorship of the proletariat : the assumption of political power by the proletariat held in Marxism to be an essential part of the transition from capitalism to communism

dic•tion \'dik-shən\ *n* **1** : choice of words especially as to correctness, clearness, or effectiveness : WORDING ⟨careless *diction* in the essay⟩ **2** : quality of vocal expression : ENUNCIATION ⟨a singer with excellent *diction*⟩ [Latin *dictio* "speaking, style", from *dicere* "to say"]

• **syn** STYLE: DICTION applies to choice of words in reference to their effectiveness in expressing ideas or emotions ⟨poetic *diction*⟩ STYLE refers to a manner of expression characteristic of its author and having artistic distinction ⟨Hemingway's terse *style*⟩

dic•tio•nary \'dik-shə-ˌner-ē\ *n, pl* **-nar•ies** **1** : a reference book containing words usually alphabetically arranged along with information about their forms, pronunciations, functions, etymologies, meanings, and syntactical and idiomatic uses **2** : a reference book listing alphabetically terms or names important to a particular subject or activity along with discussion of their meanings and applications ⟨a law *dictionary*⟩ **3** : a reference book giving for words of one language equivalents in another ⟨an English-French *dictionary*⟩ [Medieval Latin *dictionarium*, from Late Latin *dictio* "word", from Latin, "speaking"]

dic•tum \'dik-təm\ *n, pl* **dic•ta** \-tə\ *also* **dic•tums** : a formal authoritative statement : PRONOUNCEMENT [Latin, from *dictus*, past participle of *dicere* "to say"]

did *past of* DO

di•dac•tic \dī-'dak-tik\ *adj* **1** : intended primarily to instruct rather than to entertain; *esp* : intended to teach a moral lesson ⟨*didactic* literature⟩ **2** : having or showing a tendency to instruct or lecture others ⟨a *didactic* manner⟩ [Greek *didaktikos*, from *didaskein* "to teach"] — **di•dac•ti•cal** \-ti-kəl\ *adj* — **di•dac•ti•cal•ly** \-ti-kə-lē, -klē\ *adv* — **di•dac•ti•cism** \-tə-ˌsiz-əm\ *n*

di•dac•tics \-tiks\ *n sing or pl* : systematic instruction : PEDAGOGY, TEACHINGS

didn't \'did-nt\ : did not

di•do \'dīd-ō\ *n, pl* **didoes** *or* **didos** **1** : a foolish or mischievous act ⟨cutting *didoes*⟩ **2** : something frivolous or showy [origin unknown]

didst \didst, 'didst\ *archaic past 2d sing of* DO

[1]**die** \'dī\ *vi* **died**; **dy•ing** \'dī-ing\ **1** : to stop living : EXPIRE ⟨*died* of old age⟩ **2 a** : to pass out of existence ⟨a *dying* race⟩ **b** : to disappear or subside gradually ⟨the wind *died* down⟩ **3** : to long keenly or desperately ⟨*dying* to go⟩ **4** : STOP ⟨the motor *died*⟩ [Middle English *dien*]

[2]**die** \'dī\ *n, pl* **dice** \'dīs\ *or* **dies** \'dīz\ **1** *pl dice* : a small cube marked on each face with from one to six spots and used usually in pairs in various games **2** *pl dies* : any of various tools or devices for imparting a desired shape, form, or finish to a material or for impressing an object or material : as **a** : the larger of a pair of cutting or shaping tools that when moved toward each other produce a certain desired form in or impress a desired device on an object **b** : a hollow screw-cutting tool for forming screw threads **c** : a perforated block through which metal or plastic is drawn or extruded [Middle English *dee*, from Middle French *dé*]

die•hard \'dī-ˌhärd\ *n* : an irreconcilable opponent of change — **die-hard** *adj*

diel•drin \'dēl-drən\ *n* : a white crystalline chlorine-containing insecticide [*Diels-Alder* reaction, from Otto *Diels*, died 1954, and Kurt *Alder*, died 1958, German chemists]

di•elec•tric \ˌdī-ə-'lek-trik\ *n* : a nonconductor of direct electric current [*dia-* + *electric*] — **dielectric** *adj*

di•en•ceph•a•lon \ˌdī-ˌen-'sef-ə-ˌlän\ *n* : the posterior subdivision of the forebrain [*dia-* + *encephalon*] — **di•en•ce•phal•ic** \ˌdī-ˌen-sə-'fal-ik\ *adj*

die•sel \'dē-zəl, -səl\ *n* **1** : DIESEL ENGINE **2** : a vehicle driven by a diesel engine [Rudolf *Diesel*, died 1913, German engineer]

diesel engine *n* : an internal-combustion engine in which air is compressed to a temperature sufficiently high to ignite fuel injected into the cylinder

Di•es Irae \ˌdē-ˌā-'sē-ˌrā\ *n* : a medieval Latin hymn on the Day of Judgment sung in requiem masses [Medieval Latin, "day of wrath"; from the first words of the hymn]

[1]**di•et** \'dī-ət\ *n* **1** : the food and drink that a person, animal, or group usually takes : customary nourishment **2** : the kind and amount of food selected for a person or animal for a special reason (as ill health or overweight) ⟨a high-protein *diet*⟩ **3** : something provided especially habitually (as for enjoyment) ⟨a steady *diet* of television⟩ [Old French *diete*, from Latin *diaeta* "prescribed diet", from Greek *diaita*, literally, "manner of living"]

[2]**diet** *vb* : to eat or cause to eat less or according to set rules — **di•et•er** *n*

[3]**diet** *n* : a formal deliberative assembly; *esp* : any of various national or provincial legislatures [Medieval Latin *dieta* "day's journey, assembly", from Latin *dies* "day"]

dietary *adj* : of or relating to a diet or to the rules of diet

di•e•tet•ic \ˌdī-ə-'tet-ik\ *adj* : of or relating to diet or dietetics — **di•e•tet•i•cal•ly** \-'tet-i-kə-lē, -klē\ *adv*

di•e•tet•ics \-'tet-iks\ *n* : the science or art of applying the principles of nutrition to feeding

di•e•ti•tian *or* **di•e•ti•cian** \ˌdī-ə-'tish-ən\ *n* : a person qualified in or practicing dietetics ⟨a hospital *dietitian*⟩

dif•fer \'dif-ər\ *vi* **dif•fered**; **dif•fer•ing** \'dif-ring, -ə-ring\ **1** : to be not the same : be unlike ⟨children who *differ* in looks⟩ **2** : DISAGREE 1, 2 ⟨they *differ* about what should be done⟩ [Latin *differre* "to postpone, be different", from *dis-* + *ferre* "to carry"]

dif•fer•ence \'dif-ərns, 'dif-rəns, -ə-rəns\ *n* **1** : unlikeness between persons or things ⟨the striking *difference* in the children's looks⟩ **2** : the degree or amount by which things differ in quantity or measure; *esp* : the number or mathematical expression that is obtained by subtracting one number or expression from another ⟨the *difference* between 4 and 6 is 2⟩ **3** : a disagreement in opinion : DISPUTE ⟨persons unable to settle their *differences*⟩

dif•fer•ent \'dif-ərnt, 'dif-rənt, -ə-rənt\ *adj* **1** : partly or totally unlike another in nature, form, or quality ⟨this apple is *different* from the others⟩ **2** : not the same: as **a** : DISTINCT ⟨*different* age groups⟩ **b** : VARIOUS ⟨*different* members of the class⟩ **c** : ANOTHER ⟨switch to a *different* channel⟩

• **syn** DIFFERENT, DIVERSE, DISPARATE, DIVERGENT mean unlike in kind or character. DIFFERENT often implies little more than separateness but may also suggest contrast or contrariness; DIVERSE implies both distinctness and marked contrast ⟨a person of *diverse* interests⟩ DISPARATE stresses incongruity or incompatibility; DIVERGENT implies movement apart or along different courses with little chance for an ultimate meeting.

dif•fer•en•tia \ˌdif-ə-'ren-chē-ə, -chə\ *n, pl* **-ti•ae** \-chē-ˌē, -chē-ˌī\ : the element, feature, or factor that distinguishes one thing, state, or class from another [Latin, "difference", from *differre* "to differ"]

[1]**dif•fer•en•tial** \ˌdif-ə-'ren-chəl\ *adj* **1 a** : of, relating to, or constituting a distinction : DISTINGUISHING ⟨the *differential* character of voice timbre⟩ **b** : making a distinction between individuals or classes ⟨*differential* legislation⟩ **c** : based upon or

resulting from a differential ⟨*differential* freight charges⟩ **d** : functioning or proceeding differently or at a different rate ⟨*differential* melting in a glacier⟩ **2 :** relating to quantitative differences ⟨*differential* readings on a scale⟩ — **dif•fer•en•tial•ly** \-'rench-lē, -ə-lē\ *adv*

[2]differential *n* **1 :** an amount or degree of difference between comparable individuals or classes ⟨price *differential* between gasoline grades⟩ ⟨a wage *differential* for night work⟩ **2 :** DIFFERENTIAL GEAR

differential calculus *n* **:** a branch of mathematics dealing chiefly with the rate of change of functions with respect to their variables — compare INTEGRAL CALCULUS

differential gear *n* **:** an arrangement of gears in an automobile that allows one of the driving wheels to turn (as in going around a curve) faster than the other

dif•fer•en•ti•ate \ˌdif-ə-'ren-chē-ˌāt\ *vb* **1 :** to make a person or a thing different in some way ⟨the color of their eyes *differentiates* the twins⟩ **2 :** to undergo or cause to undergo differentiation in the course of development **3 :** to recognize or state the difference or differences ⟨*differentiate* between two plants⟩

dif•fer•en•ti•a•tion \-ˌren-chē-'ā-shən\ *n* **1 :** the act or process of differentiating **2 :** development from the one to the many, the simple to the complex, or the homogeneous to the heterogeneous ⟨the *differentiation* of Latin into the modern Romance languages⟩ **3 :** the developmental processes by which cells, tissues, and structures attain their specialized adult form and function; *also* **:** the result of these processes

dif•fer•ent•ly \'dif-ərnt-lē, 'dif-rənt-, -ə-rənt-\ *adv* **1 :** in a different manner ⟨they talk *differently* from us⟩ **2 :** to the contrary ⟨thought they would win but learned *differently*⟩

dif•fi•cult \'dif-i-ˌkəlt, -kəlt\ *adj* **1 :** hard to do, make, or carry out ⟨a *difficult* climb⟩ **2 a :** hard to deal with, manage, or overcome ⟨a *difficult* child⟩ **b :** hard to understand ⟨*difficult* reading⟩ **[**back-formation from *difficulty***]** — **dif•fi•cult•ly** *adv*

dif•fi•cul•ty \-ˌkəl-tē, -kəl-\ *n, pl* **-ties 1 :** difficult nature ⟨slowed up by the *difficulty* of a task⟩ **2 :** great effort ⟨accomplish a task with *difficulty*⟩ **3 :** something that is hard to do or deal with ⟨overcome *difficulties*⟩ **4 :** a difficult or distressing situation ⟨in financial *difficulties*⟩ **5 :** a disagreement in opinion ⟨finally cleared up their *difficulties*⟩ **[**Latin *difficultas,* from *difficilis* "difficult", from *dis-* + *facilis* "easy"**]**

dif•fi•dent \-əd-ənt, -ə-ˌdent\ *adj* **1 :** lacking confidence **:** TIMID **2 :** RESERVED 1, UNASSERTIVE **[**Latin *diffidens,* present participle of *diffidere* "to distrust", from *dis-* + *fidere* "to trust"**]** — **dif•fi•dence** \-əd-əns, -ə-ˌdens\ *n* — **dif•fi•dent•ly** *adv*

dif•fract \dif-'rakt\ *vt* **:** to cause to undergo diffraction ⟨*diffract* light⟩ **[**back-formation from *diffraction***]**

dif•frac•tion \dif-'rak-shən\ *n* **:** a modification which light undergoes in passing by the edges of opaque bodies or through narrow slits or in being reflected from ruled surfaces and in which the rays appear to be deflected and produce a series of parallel light and dark or colored bands; *also* **:** a similar modification of other waves **[**Latin *diffractus,* past participle of *diffringere* "to break apart", from *dis-* + *frangere* "to break"**]**

diffraction grating *n* **:** GRATING 2

[1]dif•fuse \dif-'yüs\ *adj* **1 :** poured or spread out **:** SCATTERED **2 :** marked by wordiness **:** VERBOSE ⟨a *diffuse* writer⟩ **[**Latin *diffusus,* past participle of *diffundere* "to spread out", from *dis-* + *fundere* "to pour"**]** — **dif•fuse•ly** *adv* — **dif•fuse•ness** *n*

[2]dif•fuse \dif-'yüz\ *vb* **1 :** to pour out and spread freely **2 :** to subject to or undergo diffusion ⟨gases *diffuse* at different rates⟩ — **dif•fus•er** *also* **dif•fu•sor** \-'yü-zər\ *n*

dif•fus•ible \dif-'yü-zə-bəl\ *adj* **:** capable of diffusing or of being diffused — **dif•fus•ibil•i•ty** \-ˌyü-zə-'bil-ət-ē\ *n*

dif•fu•sion \dif-'yü-zhən\ *n* **1 :** a diffusing or a being diffused; *also* **:** the state of being diffused **2 :** the intermingling of the particles of liquids, gases, or solids as a result of their spontaneous movement so that in dissolved substances they move from a region of higher to one of lower concentration **3 :** the reflection of light from a rough surface or the transmission of light through a translucent material (as frosted glass) — **dif•fu•sion•al** \-'yüzh-nəl, -'yü-zhən-l\ *adj*

dif•fu•sive \dif-'yü-siv, -ziv\ *adj* **:** tending to diffuse **:** characterized by diffusion — **dif•fu•sive•ly** *adv* — **dif•fu•sive•ness** *n*

[1]dig \'dig\ *vb* **dug** \'dəg\; **dig•ging 1 a :** to turn up the soil (as with a spade) **b :** to hollow out or form by removing earth ⟨*dig* a hole⟩ ⟨*dig* a cellar⟩ **2 :** to uncover or seek by turning up earth ⟨*dig* potatoes⟩ ⟨*dig* for gold⟩ **3 :** to bring to light **:** DISCOVER ⟨*dig* up information⟩ **4 :** JAB ⟨*dig* a person in the ribs⟩ **5 :** to work hard **6** *slang* **a :** to pay attention to **b :** UNDERSTAND 1, GRASP **[**Middle English *diggen***]** — **dig•ger** *n*

[2]dig *n* **1 :** POKE 1, JAB **2 :** a cutting remark **:** GIBE **3 :** a place where an excavation is made for ancient relics; *also* **:** the excavation itself

[1]di•gest \'dī-ˌjest\ *n* **:** a summary or condensation of a body of information or of a literary work ⟨a *digest* of the laws⟩ **[**Latin *digesta* "collection of writings arranged under headings", from *digerere* "to arrange, digest", from *dis-* + *gerere* "to carry"**]**

[2]di•gest \dī-'jest, də-\ *vb* **1 :** to think over and arrange in the mind **:** take in mentally **2 :** to convert food into simpler forms that can be taken in and used by the body **3 :** to soften or decompose or to extract soluble ingredients from by heat and moisture **4 :** to condense into a short summary **5 :** to become digested — **di•gest•er** *n* — **di•gest•ible** \-'jes-tə-bəl\ *adj* — **di•gest•ibil•i•ty** \-ˌjes-tə-'bil-ət-ē\ *n*

di•ges•tion \dī-'jes-chən, də-, -'jesh-\ *n* **:** the process or power of digesting something and especially food

[1]di•ges•tive \-'jes-tiv\ *n* **:** something that aids digestion

[2]digestive *adj* **1 :** of or relating to digestion **2 :** having the power to cause or promote digestion ⟨*digestive* enzymes⟩ — **di•ges•tive•ly** *adv*

digger wasp *n* **:** a burrowing wasp; *esp* **:** one that digs nest burrows in the soil and provisions them with insects or spiders paralyzed by stinging

dig•gings \'dig-ingz\ *n pl* **1 :** a place where ore, metals, or precious stones are dug **2** *chiefly British* **:** LODGING 2

dight \'dīt\ *vt* **dight•ed** *or* **dight**; **dight•ing** *archaic* **:** DRESS, ADORN **[**Old English *dihtan* "to arrange, compose", from Latin *dictare* "to dictate, compose"**]**

dig in *vi* **1 :** to dig and take position in defensive trenches **2 :** to go to work **3 :** to begin eating

dig•it \'dij-ət\ *n* **1 a :** any of the arabic numerals 1 to 9 and usually the symbol 0 **b :** one of the elements that combine to form numbers in a system other than the decimal system **2 :** a finger or toe **[**Latin *digitus* "finger, toe"**]**

dig•i•tal \'dij-ət-l\ *adj* **1 :** of or relating to the fingers or toes **2 :** of or relating to calculation directly with digits rather than through measurable physical quantities **3 :** providing a readout in numerical digits ⟨a *digital* watch⟩ — **dig•i•tal•ly** \-l-ē\ *adv*

digital computer *n* **:** a computer that operates numbers in the form of digits — compare ANALOG COMPUTER

dig•i•tal•is \ˌdij-ə-'tal-əs\ *n* **1 :** FOXGLOVE **2 :** a powerful drug used as a heart stimulant and prepared from the dried leaves of the common foxglove **[**Latin, "of a finger", from *digitus* "finger, toe"; from its finger-shaped corolla**]**

dig•i•tate \'dij-ə-ˌtāt\ *adj* **1 :** having digits **2 :** having divisions arranged like fingers on a hand ⟨*digitate* leaves⟩

dig•i•ti•grade \'dij-ət-ə-ˌgrād\ *adj* **:** walking on the toes with the back part of the foot raised **[**French, from Latin *digitus* "finger, toe" + *gradi* "to step, go"**]**

dig•ni•fied \'dig-nə-ˌfīd\ *adj* **:** showing or expressing dignity

dig•ni•fy \-ˌfī\ *vt* **-fied**; **-fy•ing :** to give dignity or distinction to **:** HONOR **[**Middle French *dignifier,* from Late Latin *dignificare,* from Latin *dignus* "worthy"**]**

dig•ni•tary \'dig-nə-ˌter-ē\ *n, pl* **-tar•ies :** a person of high position or honor ⟨*dignitaries* of the church⟩

dig•ni•ty \'dig-nət-ē\ *n, pl* **-ties 1 :** the quality or state of being worthy, honored, or esteemed **2 :** high rank, office, or position **3 :** formal reserve of manner or language **[**Old French *digneté,* from Latin *dignitas,* from *dignus* "worthy"**]** **syn** see DECORUM

di•graph \'dī-ˌgraf\ *n* **:** a group of two successive letters representing a single sound or a complex sound which is not a combination of the sounds ordinarily represented by each in other occurrences ⟨*ea* in *bread* and *ch* in *chin* are *digraphs*⟩ — **di•graph•ic** \dī-'graf-ik\ *adj*

di•gress \dī-'gres, də-\ *vi* **:** to turn aside especially from the main subject in writing or speaking **[**Latin *digressus,* past participle of *digredi* "to digress", from *dis-* + *gradi* "to step, go"**]** — **di•gres•sion** \-'gresh-ən\ *n*

\ə\ **abut**	\au̇\ **out**	\i\ **tip**	\ȯ\ **saw**	\u̇\ **foot**
\ər\ **further**	\ch\ **chin**	\ī\ **life**	\ȯi\ **coin**	\y\ **yet**
\a\ **mat**	\e\ **pet**	\j\ **job**	\th\ **thin**	\yü\ **few**
\ā\ **take**	\ē\ **easy**	\ng\ **sing**	\th\ **this**	\yu̇\ **cure**
\ä\ **cot, cart**	\g\ **go**	\ō\ **bone**	\ü\ **food**	\zh\ **vision**

di•gres•sive \-ˈgres-iv\ *adj* : characterized by digressions ⟨a *digressive* book⟩ — **di•gres•sive•ly** *adv* — **di•gres•sive•ness** *n*

di•he•dral angle \dī-ˌhē-drəl-\ *n* : the figure formed by two half planes meeting along a common line

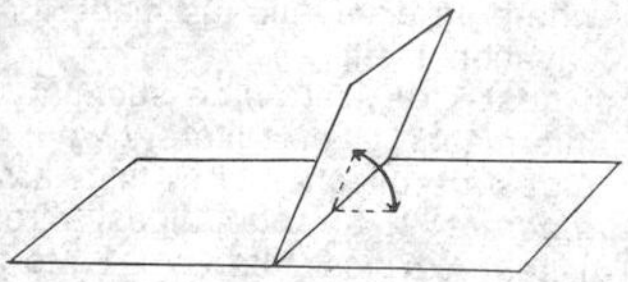

dihedral angle

di•hy•brid \dī-ˈhī-brəd, ˈdī-\ *adj* : heterozygous with respect to two pairs of genes — **dihybrid** *n*

1dike *or* **dyke** \ˈdīk\ *n* **1** : an artificial watercourse : DITCH **2** : a bank of earth constructed to control or confine water : LEVEE **3** : a long usually vertical body of igneous rock that has been forced while molten into a fissure [Old English *dīc* "ditch, dike"]

2dike *or* **dyke** *vt* : to surround or protect with a dike; *also* : to drain by a dike — **dik•er** *n*

di•lap•i•dat•ed \də-ˈlap-ə-ˌdāt-əd\ *adj* : partly ruined or decayed ⟨a *dilapidated* old house⟩ [Latin *dilapidare* "to destroy", from *dis-* + *lapidare* "to throw stones", from *lapis* "stone"]

di•lap•i•da•tion \də-ˌlap-ə-ˈdā-shən\ *n* : partial ruin (as from neglect)

di•la•ta•tion \ˌdil-ə-ˈtā-shən, ˌdī-lə-\ *n* **1** : the condition of being stretched beyond normal dimensions especially as a result of overwork or disease ⟨*dilatation* of the heart⟩ **2** : the action of dilating an organ or part of the body **3** : a dilated part or formation — **di•la•ta•tion•al** \-shnəl, -shən-l\ *adj*

di•late \dī-ˈlāt, ˈdī-ˌ\ *vb* : to make or grow larger or wider : SWELL, DISTEND ⟨eyes *dilated* with fear⟩ ⟨lungs *dilated* with air⟩ [Middle French *dilater*, from Latin *dilatare*, literally, "to spread wide", from *dis-* + *latus* "wide"] **syn** see EXPAND — **di•lat•able** \dī-ˈlāt-ə-bəl\ *adj* — **di•la•tor** \dī-ˈlāt-ər, ˈdī-ˌ\ *n*

di•la•tion \dī-ˈlā-shən\ *n* : the act of dilating : the state of being dilated : EXPANSION ⟨*dilation* of the pupils of the eyes⟩

dil•a•to•ry \ˈdil-ə-ˌtōr-ē, -ˌtȯr-\ *adj* **1** : tending or intended to cause delay ⟨*dilatory* tactics⟩ **2** : characterized by dawdling or delay [Late Latin *dilatorius*, from Latin *dilatus*, past participle of *differre* "to postpone, differ", from *dis-* + *ferre* "to carry"] — **dil•a•to•ri•ly** \ˌdil-ə-ˈtōr-ə-lē, -ˈtȯr-\ *adv* — **dil•a•to•ri•ness** \ˈdil-ə-ˌtōr-ē-nəs, -ˌtȯr-\ *n*

di•lem•ma \də-ˈlem-ə *also* dī-\ *n* : a choice or a situation in which one has to choose between two or more things, ways, or plans that are equally unsatisfactory : a difficult choice [Late Latin, from Late Greek *dilēmma*, from Greek *di-* + *lēmma* "assumption"] **syn** see PREDICAMENT

dil•et•tante \ˈdil-ə-ˌtänt, -ˌtant; ˌdil-ə-ˈ; -ˈtänt-ē, -ˈtant-ē\ *n, pl* **-tantes** *or* **-tan•ti** \-ˈtänt-ē, -ˈtant-ē\ **1** : an admirer or lover of the arts **2** : a person who engages usually superficially in an art or branch of knowledge as a pastime [Italian, from *dilettare* "to delight", from Latin *dilectare*] — **dilettante** *adj* — **dil•et•tan•tism** \-ˌtän-ˌtiz-əm, -ˌtan-, -ˈtän-, -ˈtan-\ *n*

1dil•i•gence \ˈdil-ə-jəns\ *n* : careful and continued work : conscientious effort : INDUSTRY

2dil•i•gence \ˈdil-ə-ˌzhäⁿs, ˈdil-ə-jəns\ *n* : STAGECOACH [French, "industry, haste, stagecoach"]

dil•i•gent \ˈdil-ə-jənt\ *adj* : characterized by steady, earnest, and energetic application and effort : PAINSTAKING [Middle French, from Latin *diligens*, from *diligere* "to esteem, love", from *di-* (from *dis-* "apart") + *legere* "to select"] — **dil•i•gent•ly** *adv*

dill \ˈdil\ *n* : any of several plants of the carrot family; *esp* : a European herb with aromatic foliage and seeds used especially in flavoring pickles [Old English *dile*]

dill pickle *n* : a pickle seasoned with dill or dill juice

dil•ly•dal•ly \ˈdil-ē-ˌdal-ē\ *vi* : to waste time by loitering or delay : DAWDLE ⟨*dillydallied* too long before making a decision⟩ [reduplication of *dally*]

dil•u•ent \ˈdil-yə-wənt\ *n* : a diluting agent

1di•lute \dī-ˈlüt, də-\ *vt* **1** : to make more liquid by admixture (as with water) **2** : to lessen the strength, flavor, or quality of by admixture **3** : to make smaller or less ⟨*dilute* profits⟩ [Latin *diluere* "to wash away, dilute", from *dis-* + *lavere* "to wash"] — **di•lut•er** *or* **di•lu•tor** *n*

2dilute *adj* : that has been diluted ⟨a *dilute* acid⟩ — **di•lute•ness** *n*

di•lu•tion \dī-ˈlü-shən, də-\ *n* **1** : the action of diluting : the state of being diluted **2** : something (as a solution) that is diluted

di•lu•vi•al \də-ˈlü-vē-əl, dī-\ *or* **di•lu•vi•an** \-vē-ən\ *adj* : of, relating to, or brought about by a flood [Latin *diluvium* "deluge"]

1dim \ˈdim\ *adj* **dim•mer**; **dim•mest** **1** : not bright or distinct : OBSCURE, FAINT ⟨a *dim* light⟩ **2** : being without luster : DULL **3 a** : not seen or understood clearly **b** : characterized by a skeptical or unfavorable attitude ⟨took a *dim* view of the proceedings⟩ **4** : not seeing or understanding clearly ⟨eyes grown *dim* with age⟩ [Old English] — **dim•ly** *adv* — **dim•ness** *n*

2dim *vb* **dimmed**; **dim•ming** **1** : to make or become dim **2** : to reduce the light from (headlights) by switching to the low beam

dime \ˈdīm\ *n* : a United States coin worth 1/10 dollar [Middle French, "tenth part", from Latin *decima*, from *decimus* "tenth", from *decem* "ten"]

1di•men•sion \də-ˈmen-chən *also* dī-\ *n* **1 a** : one of three or four coordinates determining a position in space or space and time **b** : magnitude of extension in one direction or in all directions ⟨find the *dimensions* of the rectangle⟩ **2** : the number of rows or columns in a matrix or determinant **3** : the range over which something extends : SCOPE [Middle French, from Latin *dimensio*, from *dimetiri* "to measure out", from *dis-* + *metiri* "to measure"] — **di•men•sion•al** \-ˈmench-nəl, -ˈmen-chən-l\ *adj* — **di•men•sion•al•i•ty** \-ˌmen-chə-ˈnal-ət-ē\ *n* — **di•men•sion•al•ly** \-ˈmench-nə-lē, -ˈmen-chən-l-ē\ *adv* — **di•men•sion•less** \-ˈmen-chən-ləs\ *adj*

2dimension *vt* **1** : to form to the required dimensions **2** : to indicate the dimensions on (a drawing)

dim•e•ter \ˈdim-ət-ər\ *n* : a line of verse consisting of two metrical feet [Late Latin, from Greek *dimetros* "being a dimeter", from *di-* + *metron* "measure"]

di•min•ish \də-ˈmin-ish\ *vb* **1** : to make less or cause to appear less **2** : to lessen the authority, dignity, or reputation of : BELITTLE **3** : to become gradually less : DWINDLE ⟨interest in the project was *diminishing*⟩ [Middle English *deminishen*, alteration of *diminuen*, from Middle French *diminuer*, from Latin *deminuere*, from *de-* + *minuere* "to lessen"] **syn** see DECREASE — **di•min•ish•able** \-ish-ə-bəl\ *adj* — **di•min•ish•ment** \-ish-mənt\ *n*

di•min•ished *adj* : made one half step less than perfect or minor ⟨the musical interval of a *diminished* fifth⟩

di•min•u•en•do \də-ˌmin-yə-ˈwen-dō, -ˌmin-ə-\ *adv or adj* : DECRESCENDO [Italian, literally, "diminishing", from Latin *deminuere* "to diminish"] — **diminuendo** *n*

dim•i•nu•tion \ˌdim-ə-ˈnü-shən, -ˈnyü-\ *n* : the act, process, or an instance of diminishing : DECREASE

1di•min•u•tive \də-ˈmin-yət-iv\ *n* **1** : a diminutive word or affix **2** : a diminutive individual

2diminutive *adj* **1** : indicating small size and sometimes the state or quality of being lovable, pitiable, or contemptible ⟨the *diminutive* suffixes *-ette* and *-ling*⟩ ⟨the *diminutive* nouns *kitchenette* and *duckling*⟩ **2** : extremely small : TINY — **di•min•u•tive•ly** *adv* — **di•min•u•tive•ness** *n*

dim•i•ty \ˈdim-ət-ē\ *n, pl* **-ties** : a sheer usually corded cotton fabric of plain weave in checks or stripes [Middle English *demyt*]

dim•mer \ˈdim-ər\ *n* **1** : one that dims **2** *pl* **a** : small lights on an automobile for use in parking **b** : headlights that have been dimmed

di•mor•phic \dī-ˈmȯr-fik\ *adj* : DIMORPHOUS ⟨a *dimorphic* butterfly⟩

di•mor•phism \-ˌfiz-əm\ *n* : the condition or property of being dimorphous; *esp* : occurrence of individuals that might be expected to be similar or identical in two distinguishable forms ⟨sexual *dimorphism* in birds⟩

di•mor•phous \-fəs\ *adj* : occurring or crystallizing in two distinct forms

1dim•ple \ˈdim-pəl\ *n* **1** : a slight natural indentation in the surface of some part of the human body **2** : a slight hollow [Middle English *dympull*]

2dimple *vb* **dim•pled**; **dim•pling** \-pə-ling, -pling\ : to mark with or form dimples ⟨you *dimple* when you smile⟩

1din \ˈdin\ *n* : a loud noise; *esp* : a jumble of confused or discordant sounds [Old English *dyne*]

2din *vb* **dinned; din•ning 1 a :** to make a loud noise **b :** to deafen with loud noise **2 :** to impress by insistent repetition ⟨*dinning* the lesson into their heads⟩

di•nar \di-'när, 'dē-ˌ\ *n* **1 :** a gold coin formerly used in Muslim countries **2 a :** the basic monetary unit of Algeria, Bahrain, Iraq, Jordan, Kuwait, Libya, Tunisia, Southern Yemen, and Yugoslavia **b :** a coin or note representing one dinar **3 :** an Irani monetary unit equal to 1/100 rial [Arabic *dīnār,* from Greek *dēnarion* "denarius", from Latin *denarius*]

dine \'dīn\ *vb* **1 :** to eat dinner **2 :** to give a dinner to **:** FEED ⟨wined and *dined* their friends⟩ [Old French *diner,* derived from Latin *dis-* + *jejunus* "fasting"]

din•er \'dī-nər\ *n* **1 :** one that dines **2 a :** DINING CAR **b :** a restaurant usually in the shape of a railroad car

di•nette \dī-'net\ *n* **:** a small space usually off a kitchen used for dining

ding \'diŋ\ *vi* **:** to make a ringing sound [imitative]

1ding•dong \'diŋ-ˌdȯŋ, -ˌdäŋ\ *n* **:** the sound of repeated strokes especially on a bell [imitative]

2dingdong *adj* **1 :** of, relating to, or resembling the ringing sound made by a bell **2 :** vigorously contested ⟨a *dingdong* battle⟩

din•ghy \'diŋ-ē, -gē, -kē\ *n, pl* **dinghies 1 :** an East Indian rowboat or sailboat **2 :** a small sailboat **3 :** a small boat used as a tender or lifeboat for a larger boat or yacht **4 :** a rubber life raft [Bengali *ḍiṅgi* and Hindi *ḍiṅgī*]

din•gle \'diŋ-gəl\ *n* **:** a small narrow wooded valley [Middle English, "abyss"]

din•go \'diŋ-ˌgō\ *n, pl* **dingoes :** a reddish brown bushy-tailed wild dog of Australia [native name in Australia]

dingo

din•gus \'diŋ-gəs, -əs\ *n* **:** something whose common name is unknown or forgotten [Dutch *dinges* or German *dings,* from *ding* "thing"]

din•gy \'din-jē\ *adj* **din•gi•er; -est 1 :** not fresh or clean **:** GRIMY ⟨*dingy* wallpaper⟩ **2 :** dull or drab in color ⟨a *dingy* unlighted room⟩ [origin unknown] — **din•gi•ly** \-jə-lē\ *adv* — **din•gi•ness** \-jē-nəs\ *n*

dining car *n* **:** a railroad car in which meals are served

din•key *or* **din•ky** \'diŋ-kē\ *n, pl* **dinkeys** *or* **dinkies :** a small locomotive used especially for hauling freight, logging, and shunting ⟨probably from *dinky* "small"⟩

din•ky \'diŋ-kē\ *adj* **din•ki•er; -est :** SMALL, INSIGNIFICANT ⟨a *dinky* two-room apartment⟩ [Scottish *dink* "neat"]

din•ner \'din-ər\ *n* **1 a :** the main meal of the day **b :** the food provided for a dinner **2 :** a formal banquet [Old French *diner,* from *diner* "to dine"]

dinner jacket *n* **:** a single-breasted or double-breasted usually black or blackish blue jacket

di•no•flag•el•late \ˌdī-nō-'flaj-ə-lət, -ˌlāt\ *n* **:** any of an order (Dinoflagellata) of chiefly marine floating organisms that resemble both algae and protozoa and are important in marine food chains [Greek *dinos* "rotation, eddy"]

di•no•saur \'dī-nə-ˌsȯr\ *n* **:** any of a group (Dinosauria) of extinct chiefly land-dwelling long-tailed reptiles with limbs adapted for walking [Greek *deinos* "terrible" + *sauros* "lizard"] — **di•no•sau•ri•an** \ˌdī-nə-'sȯr-ē-ən\ *adj or n*

1dint \'dint\ *n* **1 :** FORCE, POWER — used chiefly in the phrase *by dint of* **2 :** a mark left by a blow **:** DENT [Old English *dynt*]

2dint *vt* **:** DENT1

di•oc•e•san \dī-'äs-ə-sən\ *n* **:** a bishop having jurisdiction over a diocese

di•o•cese \'dī-ə-səs, -ˌsēz, -ˌsēs\ *n, pl* **di•o•ces•es** \-sə-səz, -ˌsē-zəz, -ˌsē-səz; 'dī-ə-ˌsēz\ **:** the district over which a bishop has authority [Middle French *diocise,* derived from Greek *dioikēsis* "administration, administrative division", from *dia-* + *oikein* "to dwell, manage", from *oikos* "house"] — **di•oc•e•san** \dī-'äs-ə-sən\ *adj*

di•ode \'dī-ˌōd\ *n* **1 :** a 2-electrode electron tube having a cathode and an anode **2 :** a rectifier consisting of a semiconducting crystal with two terminals

di•oe•cious \dī-'ē-shəs\ *adj* **:** having male and female flowers borne on different plants [Greek *di-* + *oikos* "house"] — **di•oe•cious•ly** *adv* — **di•oe•cism** \-'ē-ˌsiz-əm\ *n*

Di•o•ny•sia \ˌdī-ə-'nizh-ē-ə, -'niz-, -'nish-, -'nis-\ *n pl* **:** any of the ancient Greek festivals held in honor of Dionysus; *esp* **:** an autumn festival from which the Greek drama is held to have developed

di•o•rama \ˌdī-ə-'ram-ə, -'räm-\ *n* **:** a scenic representation in which a partly transparent painting is seen from a distance through an opening or in which lifelike sculptured figures and surrounding details are realistically illuminated against a painted background [French, from *dia-* "dia-" + *-orama* (as in *panorama,* from English)]

di•o•rite \'dī-ə-ˌrīt\ *n* **:** a granular crystalline igneous rock [French, from Greek *diorizein* "to distinguish", from *dia-* + *horizein* "to define"]

di•ox•ide \dī-'äk-ˌsīd\ *n* **:** an oxide containing two atoms of oxygen in the molecule

1dip \'dip\ *vb* **dipped; dip•ping 1 a :** to plunge momentarily or partially under the surface (as of a liquid) so as to moisten, cool, or coat **b :** to thrust in a way to suggest immersion **2 :** to lift a portion of by reaching below the surface with something shaped to hold liquid **:** LADLE ⟨*dip* water from a pail⟩ **3 :** to lower and then raise again ⟨*dip* a flag in salute⟩ **4 a :** to plunge into a liquid and quickly emerge ⟨oars *dipping* rhythmically⟩ **b :** to immerse something into a processing liquid or finishing material **5 a :** to suddenly drop down or out of sight ⟨the road *dipped* below the crest⟩ **b :** to decrease moderately and usually temporarily ⟨prices *dipped*⟩ **6 :** to reach down inside or as if inside or below a surface especially to withdraw a part of the contents ⟨*dipped* into their savings⟩ **7 :** to examine something casually or tentatively; *esp* **:** to read superficially ⟨*dip* into a book⟩ [Old English *dyppan*]

2dip *n* **1 :** an act of dipping; *esp* **:** a brief plunge into the water for sport or exercise **2 a :** inclination downward **b :** a sharp or slight downward course **:** DROP **3 :** something obtained by or used in dipping **4 a :** a sauce or soft mixture into which food may be dipped **b :** a liquid preparation into which an object may be dipped (as for coloring)

di•pep•tide \dī-'pep-ˌtīd\ *n* **:** a peptide composed of two molecules of amino acid

di•phos•pho•gly•cer•ic acid \dī-'fäs-fō-glis-ˌer-ik-\ *n* **:** a phosphate of glyceric acid that is important in photosynthesis and in glycolysis and fermentation

diph•the•ria \dif-'thir-ē-ə, dip-\ *n* **:** a contagious bacterial disease with fever in which the air passages become coated with a membranous layer that often obstructs breathing [French *diphthérie,* from Greek *diphthera* "leather"; from the toughness of the membranous layer] — **diph•the•rit•ic** \ˌdif-thə-'rit-ik, ˌdip-\ *adj*

diph•thong \'dif-ˌthȯŋ, 'dip-\ *n* **1 :** a 2-element speech sound that begins with the tongue position for one vowel and ends with the tongue position for another all within one syllable ⟨the sounds of *ou* in *out* and of *oy* in *boy* are *diphthongs*⟩ **2 :** DIGRAPH [Middle French *diptongue,* from Late Latin *diphthongus,* from Greek *diphthongos,* from *di-* + *phthongos* "voice, sound"] — **diph•thon•gal** \dif-'thȯŋ-əl, dip-, -gəl\ *adj*

diph•thong•ize \-ˌthȯŋ-ˌīz\ *vb* **:** to change into or pronounce as a diphthong — **diph•thong•iza•tion** \ˌdif-thȯŋ-ə-'zā-shən, ˌdip-\ *n*

dipl- *or* **diplo-** *combining form* **:** double **:** twofold ⟨*diploid*⟩ [Greek *diploos,* from *di-* + *-ploos* "-fold"]

dip•lo•blas•tic \ˌdip-lō-'blas-tik\ *adj* **:** being an embryo or an invertebrate (as a hydra or a sponge) that has only two germ layers and lacks a true mesoderm

dip•lo•coc•cus \ˌdip-lō-'käk-əs\ *n, pl* **-coc•ci** \-'käk-ˌsī, -ˌī, -ˌsē, -ˌē\ **:** any of a genus of parasitic bacteria that occur usually in pairs in a capsule and include serious disease-causing agents — **dip•lo•coc•cal** \-'käk-əl\ *adj*

di•plod•o•cus \də-'pläd-ə-kəs, dī-\ *n* **:** any of a genus of very large plant-eating dinosaurs from what are now Colorado and Wyoming [*dipl-* + Greek *dokos* "beam"]

dip•loid \'dip-ˌlȯid\ *adj* **:** having or being the basic chromosome number doubled ⟨a *diploid* cell⟩ ⟨the *diploid* number of chro-

\ə\ **abut**	\au̇\ **out**	\i\ **tip**	\ȯ\ **saw**	\u̇\ **foot**
\ər\ **further**	\ch\ **chin**	\ī\ **life**	\ȯi\ **coin**	\y\ **yet**
\a\ **mat**	\e\ **pet**	\j\ **job**	\th\ **thin**	\yü\ **few**
\ā\ **take**	\ē\ **easy**	\ŋ\ **sing**	\th\ **this**	\yu̇\ **cure**
\ä\ **cot, cart**	\g\ **go**	\ō\ **bone**	\ü\ **food**	\zh\ **vision**

mosomes) — **diploid** *n* — **dip·loi·dy** \-ˌlȯid-ē\ *n*

di·plo·ma \də-ˈplō-mə\ *n* **1 :** a document conferring a privilege or honor **2 :** an official paper bearing record of graduation from or of a degree conferred by an educational institution **[**Latin, "passport, diploma", from Greek *diplōma* "folded paper, passport", from *diploun* "to double", from *diploos* "double"**]**

di·plo·ma·cy \də-ˈplō-mə-sē\ *n* **1 :** the art and practice of conducting negotiations between nations **2 :** skill in handling affairs without arousing hostility **:** TACT

dip·lo·mat \ˈdip-lə-ˌmat\ *n* **:** a person employed or skilled in diplomacy

dip·lo·mat·ic \ˌdip-lə-ˈmat-ik\ *adj* **1 :** of, relating to, or concerned with diplomacy or diplomats ⟨*diplomatic* relations⟩ **2 :** TACTFUL ⟨found a *diplomatic* way to say it⟩ **[**French *diplomatique,* from Latin *diploma* "document, diploma"**]** — **dip·lo·mat·i·cal·ly** \-ˈmat-i-kə-lē, -klē\ *adv*

di·plo·ma·tist \də-ˈplō-mət-əst\ *n* **:** DIPLOMAT

di·pole \ˈdī-ˌpōl\ *n* **1 a :** a pair of equal and opposite electric charges or magnetic poles of opposite sign separated by a small distance **b :** a body (as a molecule) having such charges or poles **2 :** a radio antenna consisting of two horizontal rods in line with each other with their ends slightly separated — **di·po·lar** \dī-ˈpō-lər, ˈdī-\ *adj*

dip·per \ˈdip-ər\ *n* **1 :** one that dips; *esp* **:** something (as a long-handled cup) used for dipping **2** *cap* **a :** the seven principal stars in the constellation of Ursa Major arranged in a form resembling a dipper **b :** the seven principal stars in Ursa Minor similarly arranged with the North Star forming the outer end of the handle **3 :** any of several birds (as a bufflehead or water ouzel) skilled in diving

dipper 1

dip·so·ma·nia \ˌdip-sə-ˈmā-nē-ə, -nyə\ *n* **:** an uncontrollable craving for alcoholic liquors **[**Greek *dipsa* "thirst"**]** — **dip·so·ma·ni·ac** \-nē-ˌak\ *n* — **dip·so·ma·ni·a·cal** \ˌdip-sō-mə-ˈnī-ə-kəl\ *adj*

dip·stick \ˈdip-ˌstik\ *n* **:** a graduated rod for indicating depth (as of oil in a crankcase)

dip·tera \ˈdip-tə-rə\ *n pl* **:** insects that are two-winged flies

dip·ter·an \ˈdip-tə-rən\ *adj* **:** of, relating to, or being a two-winged fly — **dipteran** *n*

dip·ter·ous \-rəs\ *adj* **:** of or relating to the two-winged flies **[**Greek *dipteros* "two-winged", from *di-* + *pteron* "wing"**]**

dip·tych \ˈdip-tik\ *n* **1 :** a picture or series of pictures (as an altarpiece) painted on two hinged tablets **2 :** a work made up of two matching parts **[**derived from Greek *di-* + *ptychē* "fold"**]**

dire \ˈdīr\ *adj* **1 :** exciting horror **:** DREADFUL ⟨*dire* suffering⟩ **2 :** warning of disaster ⟨a *dire* forecast⟩ **3 :** EXTREME ⟨*dire* poverty⟩ ⟨*dire* need⟩ **[**Latin *dirus***]** — **dire·ly** *adv* — **dire·ness** *n*

[1]di·rect \də-ˈrekt, dī-\ *vt* **1 :** to mark with a name and address ⟨*direct* a letter⟩ **2 :** to cause to turn, move, or point or to follow a straight course **3 :** to point, extend, or project in a specified line, course, or direction **4 :** to show or point out the way for **5 a :** to regulate the activities or course of ⟨*directed* the project⟩ **b :** to guide the organizing, supervising, or performance of ⟨*direct* a play⟩ ⟨*direct* an orchestra⟩ **6 :** to request or instruct with authority ⟨use only as *directed*⟩ **[**Latin *directus,* past participle of *dirigere* "to set straight, direct", from *dis-* + *regere* "to lead straight"**]** **syn** see CONDUCT

[2]direct *adj* **1 :** proceeding from one point to another in time or space without deviation or interruption **2 a :** stemming immediately from a source ⟨a *direct* result⟩ **b :** being or passing in a straight line of descent from parent to offspring **:** LINEAL ⟨a *direct* ancestor⟩ **3 :** NATURAL, STRAIGHTFORWARD ⟨a *direct* manner⟩ **4 :** operating without an intervening agency or step ⟨*direct* action⟩ **5 a :** effected by the action of the people or the electorate and not by representatives **b :** consisting of or reproducing the exact words of a speaker ⟨*direct* discourse⟩ ⟨a *direct* quotation⟩ — **direct** *adv* — **di·rect·ness** \-ˈrekt-nəs, -ˈrek-\ *n*

direct current *n* **:** an electric current flowing in one direction only — abbreviation *DC*

di·rect·ed *adj* **:** proceeding or measured in a direction designated as positive or negative ⟨a *directed* line segment⟩

di·rec·tion \də-ˈrek-shən, dī-\ *n* **1 :** guidance or supervision of action or conduct **2 :** the art and technique of directing an orchestra or a theatrical production **3 :** an authoritative instruction, indication, or order **4 :** the line or course along which something moves, lies, points, or is measured **5 :** a course of progress or development **:** TREND

di·rec·tion·al \-shnəl, -shən-l\ *adj* **1 :** relating to or indicating direction in space ⟨the *directional* signal lights on an automobile⟩: **a :** suitable for sending out or receiving radio signals in one direction only ⟨a *directional* antenna⟩ **b :** operating in a particular direction ⟨a *directional* microphone⟩ **2 :** relating to direction or guidance especially of thought or effort

[1]di·rec·tive \də-ˈrek-tiv, dī-\ *adj* **:** serving to direct, guide, or influence ⟨the *directive* power of conscience⟩

[2]directive *n* **:** something that serves to direct, guide, and usually impel toward an action or goal; *esp* **:** an authoritative instruction issued by a high-level body or official

di·rec·tiv·i·ty \də-ˌrek-ˈtiv-ət-ē, ˌdī-\ *n* **:** the property of being directional

di·rect·ly \də-ˈrek-tlē, dī-, -lē, *in sense 2 also* ˈdrek-lē\ *adv* **1 :** in a direct manner ⟨spoke *directly*⟩ **2 :** without delay **:** IMMEDIATELY ⟨go *directly* home⟩

direct object *n* **:** a grammatical object representing the primary goal or the result of the action of its verb ⟨*me* in "you hit me" and *house* in "we built a house" are *direct objects*⟩

di·rec·tor \də-ˈrek-tər, dī-\ *n* **:** one that directs: as **a :** the head of an organized group or administrative unit (as a school) **b :** one of a group of persons who direct the affairs of a corporation **c :** one that supervises the production of a show **d :** CONDUCTOR b — **di·rec·to·ri·al** \də-ˌrek-ˈtōr-ē-əl, ˌdī-, -ˈtȯr-\ *adj* — **di·rec·tor·ship** \də-ˈrek-tər-ˌship, dī-\ *n*

di·rec·tor·ate \də-ˈrek-tə-rət, dī-, -trət\ *n* **1 :** the office of director **2 :** a board of directors (as of a corporation)

di·rec·to·ry \-tə-rē, -trē\ *n, pl* **-ries 1 :** an alphabetical or classified list containing names and addresses **2 :** a body of directors (as of a government)

direct primary *n* **:** a primary in which nominations of candidates for office are made by direct vote

di·rec·trix \də-ˈrek-triks, dī-\ *n* **:** a fixed curve with which a generatrix keeps a constant relationship as it traces out a geometric figure; *esp* **:** a straight line for which the distance from any point on a conic section is in fixed ratio to the distance from the same point to the focus

dire·ful \ˈdīr-fəl\ *adj* **:** producing dire effects — **dire·ful·ly** \-fə-lē\ *adv*

dire wolf *n* **:** a large extinct mammal related to the wolf whose remains are found in Pleistocene deposits of North America

dirge \ˈdərj\ *n* **:** a song or hymn of grief; *esp* **:** one intended for funeral or memorial rites **[**Latin *dirige* (the first word of a Late Latin antiphon), imperative of *dirigere* "to direct"**]**

△ **origin** The meaning of English *dirge* is not directly related to the meaning of the Latin word it comes from. *Dirge* and its earlier form *dirige,* meaning "a song or hymn of lamentation", come from the first word of a Latin chant used in the church service for the dead: "Dirige, Domine deus meus, in conspectu tuo viam meam." (Direct, O Lord my God, my way in thy sight.) The first word of the Latin chant became the common English term for a funeral hymn and later for any slow, solemn, and mournful piece of music.

[1]di·ri·gi·ble \ˈdir-ə-jə-bəl, də-ˈrij-ə-\ *adj* **:** capable of being steered **[**Latin *dirigere* "to direct"**]**

[2]dirigible *n* **:** AIRSHIP

dirk \ˈdərk\ *n* **:** a long straight-bladed dagger **[**Scottish *durk***]** — **dirk** *vt*

dirndl \ˈdərn-dl\ *n* **1 :** a dress with tight bodice and gathered skirt **2 :** a full skirt with a tight waistband **[**short for German *dirndlkleid,* from German dialect *dirndl* "girl" + German *kleid* "dress"**]**

dirt \ˈdərt\ *n* **1 a :** a filthy or soiling substance (as mud, dust, or grime) **b :** a contemptible person **2 :** loose or packed earth **:** SOIL **3 a :** CORRUPTION 1c **b :** obscene language or theme **4 :** scandalous gossip **[**Old Norse *drit* "excrement"**]**

[1]dirty \ˈdərt-ē\ *adj* **dirt·i·er; -est 1 :** not clean **:** FILTHY, SOILED ⟨*dirty* clothes⟩ **2 :** characterized by unfairness **:** LOW-DOWN ⟨a *dirty* trick⟩ **3 :** OBSCENE 2, SMUTTY ⟨*dirty* talk⟩ **4 :** STORMY 1 ⟨*dirty* weather⟩ **5 :** not clear in color **:** DULL ⟨a *dirty* red⟩ **6 :** conveying ill-natured resentment ⟨gave them a *dirty* look⟩ — **dirt·i·ly** \ˈdərt-l-ē\ *adv* — **dirt·i·ness** \ˈdərt-ē-nəs\ *n*

• **syn** DIRTY, FILTHY, FOUL, NASTY mean conspicuously unclean or impure, literally or figuratively. DIRTY applies generally to whatever is soiled by dirt of any kind ⟨*dirty* hands⟩ or is capable of soiling ⟨*dirty* jokes⟩ FILTHY suggests offensiveness and a besmeared, cluttered state ⟨*filthy* rags⟩ FOUL adds to the offensiveness an implication of rottenness or loathsomeness ⟨*foul* sewers⟩ NASTY applies to something that is unpleasant or repugnant to one who is fastidious about cleanliness, sweetness, or freshness ⟨a *nasty* smell⟩ or it may imply mere disagreeableness ⟨received a *nasty* shock⟩

²dirty *vb* **dirt•ied**; **dirty•ing 1 :** to make or become dirty **2 :** to stain with dishonor **:** SULLY

dis- *prefix* **1 a :** do the opposite of ⟨*dis*establish⟩ **b :** deprive of (a specified quality, rank, or object) ⟨*dis*able⟩ ⟨*dis*mast⟩ **c :** exclude or expel from ⟨*dis*bar⟩ **2 :** opposite or absence of ⟨*dis*union⟩ **3 :** not ⟨*dis*agreeable⟩ **4 :** DYS- **[**Latin, literally, "apart"; sense 4 by folk etymology from *dys-***]**

dis•abil•i•ty \ˌdis-ə-ˈbil-ət-ē\ *n, pl* **-ties 1 :** the condition of being disabled **:** lack of ability, power, or fitness to do something and especially to hold employment **2 :** a source of disability (as a physical injury); *also* **:** a legal disqualification that prevents a person from doing something ⟨a law placing severe *disabilities* on immigrants⟩ **syn** see INABILITY

dis•able \dis-ˈā-bəl\ *vt* **dis•abled**; **dis•abling** \-bə-liŋ, -bliŋ\ **1 :** to disqualify legally **2 :** to make unable or incapable; *esp* **:** to deprive of physical, moral, or intellectual strength **:** CRIPPLE — **dis•able•ment** \-bəl-mənt\ *n*

dis•abuse \ˌdis-ə-ˈbyüz\ *vt* **:** to free from error (as in reasoning or judgment) **:** UNDECEIVE **[**French *désabuser,* from *dés-* "dis-" + *abuser* "to abuse"**]**

di•sac•cha•ride \dī-ˈsak-ə-ˌrīd\ *n* **:** any of a class of sugars (as sucrose) that yield on hydrolysis two monosaccharide molecules

dis•ac•cus•tom \ˌdis-ə-ˈkəs-təm\ *vt* **:** to make no longer accustomed

¹dis•ad•van•tage \ˌdis-əd-ˈvant-ij\ *n* **1 :** loss or damage especially to reputation or finances ⟨the deal worked to our *disadvantage*⟩ **2 a :** an unfavorable or prejudicial condition ⟨was at a *disadvantage* in educated company⟩ **b :** HANDICAP ⟨the machine has two serious *disadvantages*⟩

²disadvantage *vt* **:** to place at a disadvantage **:** HARM

dis•ad•van•taged *adj* **:** lacking essentials (as standard housing or civil rights) held to be necessary for an equal position in society

dis•ad•van•ta•geous \ˌdis-ˌad-ˌvan-ˈtā-jəs, -vən-\ *adj* **:** constituting a disadvantage — **dis•ad•van•ta•geous•ly** *adv* — **dis•ad•van•ta•geous•ness** *n*

dis•af•fect \ˌdis-ə-ˈfekt\ *vt* **:** to alienate the affection or loyalty of **:** cause discontent in ⟨the troops were *disaffected*⟩ — **dis•af•fec•tion** \ˌdis-ə-ˈfek-shən\ *n*

dis•agree \ˌdis-ə-ˈgrē\ *vi* **1 :** to fail to agree ⟨the two accounts *disagree*⟩ **2 :** to differ in opinion ⟨*disagree* over the price⟩ **3 :** to be unsuitable ⟨fried foods *disagree* with me⟩

dis•agree•able \-ˈgrē-ə-bəl\ *adj* **1 :** causing discomfort **:** UNPLEASANT ⟨a *disagreeable* taste⟩ **2 :** marked by ill temper — **dis•agree•able•ness** *n* — **dis•agree•ably** \-blē\ *adv*

dis•agree•ment \ˌdis-ə-ˈgrē-mənt\ *n* **1 :** the act of disagreeing **2 a :** the state of being different or at odds **b :** QUARREL 2

dis•al•low \ˌdis-ə-ˈlau̇\ *vt* **:** to refuse to admit or recognize **:** REJECT ⟨*disallow* a claim⟩ — **dis•al•low•ance** \-ˈlau̇-əns\ *n*

dis•ap•pear \ˌdis-ə-ˈpiər\ *vi* **1 :** to pass from view or thought **2 :** to pass from existence ⟨dinosaurs *disappeared* ages ago⟩ — **dis•ap•pear•ance** \-ˈpir-əns\ *n*

dis•ap•point \ˌdis-ə-ˈpȯint\ *vt* **:** to fail to come up to the expectation or hope of **[**Middle French *desapointier,* from *des-* "dis-" + *apointier* "to arrange"**]**

dis•ap•point•ed *adj* **:** defeated in expectation or hope

dis•ap•point•ment \ˌdis-ə-ˈpȯint-mənt\ *n* **1 :** the act or an instance of disappointing **:** the state of being disappointed **2 :** one that disappoints ⟨the play was a *disappointment*⟩

dis•ap•pro•ba•tion \ˌdis-ˌap-rə-ˈbā-shən\ *n* **:** DISAPPROVAL

dis•ap•prov•al \ˌdis-ə-ˈprü-vəl\ *n* **1 :** the act of disapproving ⟨frowned in *disapproval*⟩ **2 :** unfavorable opinion or judgment **:** CENSURE ⟨the plan met with *disapproval*⟩

dis•ap•prove \-ˈprüv\ *vb* **1 :** to pass unfavorable judgment on **:** CONDEMN ⟨I *disapprove* your conduct⟩ **2 :** to refuse approval to **:** REJECT ⟨*disapproved* the architect's plans⟩ **3 :** to feel or express disapproval ⟨*disapproves* of smoking⟩ — **dis•ap•prov•ing•ly** \-ˈprü-viŋ-lē\ *adv*

dis•arm \dis-ˈärm\ *vb* **1 :** to deprive of arms **:** take arms or weapons from **2 :** to disband or reduce the size and strength of the armed forces of a country **3 :** to make harmless, peaceable, or friendly **:** remove dislike or suspicion ⟨a *disarming* smile⟩ — **dis•ar•ma•ment** \-ˈär-mə-mənt\ *n*

dis•ar•range \ˌdis-ə-ˈrānj\ *vt* **:** to disturb the arrangement or order of — **dis•ar•range•ment** \-mənt\ *n*

¹dis•ar•ray \ˌdis-ə-ˈrā\ *n* **1 :** a lack of order or sequence **:** CONFUSION **2 :** disorderly dress

²disarray *vt* **:** to throw into disorder

dis•as•sem•ble \ˌdis-ə-ˈsem-bəl\ *vt* **:** to take apart ⟨*disassemble* an engine⟩

dis•as•so•ci•ate \ˌdis-ə-ˈsō-shē-ˌāt, -sē-\ *vt* **:** to detach from association **:** DISSOCIATE — **dis•as•so•ci•a•tion** \-ˌsō-sē-ˈā-shən, -ˌsō-shē-\ *n*

di•sas•ter \diz-ˈas-tər, dis-\ *n* **:** a sudden great misfortune; *esp* **:** one bringing with it destruction of life or property or causing complete ruin **[**Middle French *desastre* "unfavorable aspect of a star", from Italian *disastro,* from *dis-* "dis-" + *astro* "star", from Latin *astrum***]**

• **syn** DISASTER, CATASTROPHE, CALAMITY, CATACLYSM mean an event or situation that is a terrible misfortune. DISASTER is an unforeseen, ruinous, and often sudden misfortune that happens either through lack of foresight or through some hostile external agency; CATASTROPHE implies a disastrous conclusion, emphasizing finality; CALAMITY heightens the personal reaction to a great public loss; CATACLYSM, originally a deluge or geological convulsion, applies to an event or situation that produces an upheaval or complete reversal.

di•sas•trous \-ˈas-trəs\ *adj* **:** accompanied by or producing suffering or disaster **:** CALAMITOUS — **di•sas•trous•ly** *adv*

dis•avow \ˌdis-ə-ˈvau̇\ *vt* **:** to refuse to acknowledge **:** deny responsibility for — **dis•avow•al** \-ˈvau̇-əl, -ˈvau̇l\ *n*

dis•band \dis-ˈband\ *vb* **:** to break up the organization of **:** DISPERSE ⟨*disband* an army⟩ — **dis•band•ment** \-ˈband-mənt, -ˈban-\ *n*

dis•bar \dis-ˈbär\ *vt* **dis•barred**; **dis•bar•ring :** to deprive (a lawyer) of the rights and privileges of membership in the legal profession — **dis•bar•ment** \-ˈbär-mənt\ *n*

dis•be•lief \ˌdis-bə-ˈlēf\ *n* **:** the act of disbelieving **:** mental rejection of a statement as untrue **syn** see UNBELIEF

dis•be•lieve \-ˈlēv\ *vb* **1 :** to hold not to be true or real **2 :** to withhold or reject belief — **dis•be•liev•er** *n*

dis•bud \dis-ˈbəd, ˈdis-\ *vt* **:** to remove some flower buds from in order to improve the remaining flowers

dis•burse \dis-ˈbərs\ *vt* **:** to pay out **:** EXPEND **[**Middle French *desbourser,* from *des-* "dis-" + *bourse* "purse", from Medieval Latin *bursa***]** — **dis•burs•er** *n*

dis•burse•ment \-ˈbər-smənt\ *n* **:** the act of disbursing; *also* **:** funds paid out

disc *variant of* DISK

¹dis•card \dis-ˈkärd, ˈdis-ˌ\ *vb* **1 a :** to remove a playing card from one's hand **b :** to play (a card) from a suit other than trump but different from the one led **2 :** to get rid of as useless or unwanted

²dis•card \ˈdis-ˌkärd\ *n* **1 :** the act of discarding **2 :** a person or thing cast off or rejected

disc brake *n* **:** a brake that operates by the friction of two plates pressing against the sides of a rotating disc

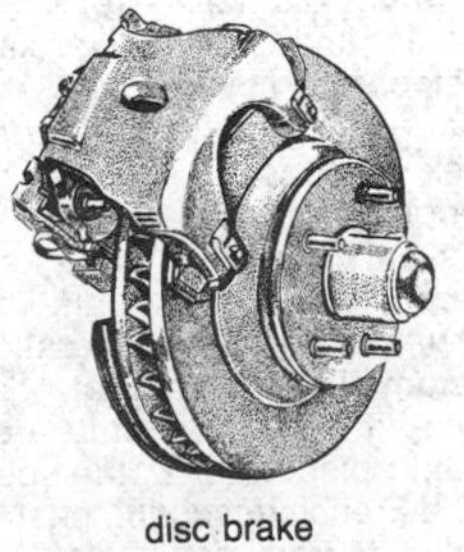
disc brake

dis•cern \dis-ˈərn, diz-\ *vt* **1 :** to detect with the eyes **:** DISTINGUISH ⟨*discern* an airplane in the clouds⟩ **2 :** to come to know, recognize, or discriminate mentally ⟨*discern* the basic issue⟩ **[**Middle French *discerner,* from Latin *discernere* "to distinguish between", from *dis-* + *cernere* "to sift"**]** — **dis•cern•ible** \-ˈər-nə-bəl\ *adj* — **dis•cern•ibly** \-blē\ *adv*

\ə\ **abut**	\au̇\ **out**	\i\ **tip**	\ȯ\ **saw**	\u̇\ **foot**
\ər\ **further**	\ch\ **chin**	\ī\ **life**	\ȯi\ **coin**	\y\ **yet**
\a\ **mat**	\e\ **pet**	\j\ **job**	\th\ **thin**	\yü\ **few**
\ā\ **take**	\ē\ **easy**	\ŋ\ **sing**	\t͟h\ **this**	\yu̇\ **cure**
\ä\ **cot, cart**	\g\ **go**	\ō\ **bone**	\ü\ **food**	\zh\ **vision**

dis•cern•ing *adj* : revealing insight and understanding : PERCEPTIVE ⟨a *discerning* critic⟩ — **dis•cern•ing•ly** \-ˈər-niŋ-lē\ *adv*

dis•cern•ment \dis-ˈərn-mənt, diz-\ *n* : skill in discerning or discriminating : keenness of insight

[1]**dis•charge** \dis-ˈchärj, ˈdis-ˌ\ *vb* **1** : to relieve of a charge, load, or burden : UNLOAD **2** : SHOOT ⟨*discharge* a gun⟩ **3** : to set free ⟨*discharge* a prisoner⟩ **4** : to dismiss from service or employment ⟨*discharge* a soldier⟩ **5** : to let go or let off ⟨*discharge* passengers⟩ **6** : to give forth fluid or other contents ⟨this river *discharges* into the ocean⟩ **7** : to get rid of by paying or doing ⟨*discharge* a debt⟩ **syn** see FREE — **dis•charg•er** *n*

[2]**dis•charge** \ˈdis-ˌchärj, dis-ˈ\ *n* **1 a** : the act of discharging, unloading, or releasing **b** : something that discharges; *esp* : a certification of release or payment **2** : a firing off of a weapon or missile **3 a** : a flowing or issuing out; *also* : a rate of flow **b** : something that is emitted **4 a** : release or dismissal especially from an office or employment **b** : complete separation from military service **5 a** : the equalization of electric potential between two points by a flow of electricity **b** : the conversion of the chemical energy of a battery into electrical energy

discharge tube *n* : an electron tube which contains gas or vapor at low pressure and through which electrical conduction takes place when a high voltage is applied

dis•ci•ple \dis-ˈī-pəl\ *n* **1 a** : a pupil or follower who accepts and helps to spread the teachings of another **b** : a convinced adherent **2** *cap* : a member of the Disciples of Christ founded in the United States in 1809 **[**derived from Latin *discipulus* "pupil"**]** — **dis•ci•ple•ship** \-ˌship\ *n*

dis•ci•pli•nar•i•an \ˌdis-ə-plə-ˈner-ē-ən\ *n* : one that disciplines or enforces order — **disciplinarian** *adj*

dis•ci•plin•ary \ˈdis-ə-plə-ˌner-ē\ *adj* : of or relating to discipline : CORRECTIVE ⟨take *disciplinary* action⟩

[1]**dis•ci•pline** \ˈdis-ə-plən\ *n* **1** : a field of study : SUBJECT **2** : training that corrects, molds, or perfects **3** : PUNISHMENT 1 **4** : control gained by obedience or training : orderly conduct **5** : a system of rules governing conduct or practice **[**Latin *disciplina* "teaching, learning", from *discipulus* "pupil"**]**

[2]**discipline** *vt* **1** : to punish or penalize for the sake of discipline **2** : to train or develop by instruction and exercise especially in self-control **3** : to bring (a group) under control ⟨*discipline* troops⟩ **syn** see PUNISH — **dis•ci•plin•er** *n*

disc jockey *n* : a person who conducts and announces a radio program of musical recordings often with interspersed comments not related to the music

dis•claim \dis-ˈklām\ *vt* : to deny having a connection with or responsibility for

dis•claim•er \-ˈklā-mər\ *n* : an act of disclaiming : a statement that discliams : DENIAL

disc•like *variant of* DISKLIKE

dis•close \dis-ˈklōz\ *vt* : to expose to view : make known : REVEAL ⟨*disclose* secrets⟩ — **dis•clos•er** *n*

dis•clo•sure \-ˈklō-zhər\ *n* **1** : the act or an instance of disclosing : EXPOSURE **2** : something disclosed : REVELATION

dis•co \ˈdis-kō\ *n, pl* **discos** : DISCOTHEQUE

dis•cog•ra•phy \dis-ˈkäg-rə-fē\ *n, pl* **-phies** : a descriptive list of phonograph recordings

dis•coid \ˈdis-ˌkȯid\ *adj* **1** : resembling a disk especially in being flat and circular **2** : relating to, forming, or being part of a disk or disk flower

dis•coi•dal \dis-ˈkȯid-l\ *adj* : of, resembling, or producing a disk ⟨a *discoidal* sponge⟩

dis•col•or \dis-ˈkəl-ər\ *vb* : to alter or change in hue or color — **dis•col•or•a•tion** \ˌdis-ˌkəl-ə-ˈrā-shən\ *n*

dis•com•bob•u•late \ˌdis-kəm-ˈbäb-yə-ˌlāt, -ə-\ *vt* : UPSET 4, CONFUSE **[**probably alteration of *discompose***]**

dis•com•fit \dis-ˈkəm-fət, -ˈkəmp- *especially in the South* ˌdis-kəm-ˈfit\ *vt* : to put into a state of perplexity and embarrassment : DISCONCERT ⟨the speaker was *discomfited* by hecklers⟩ **[**Old French *desconfit,* past participle of *desconfire* "to destroy, defeat", from *des-* "dis-" + *confire* "to prepare"**]** **syn** see EMBARRASS — **dis•com•fi•ture** \dis-ˈkəm-fə-ˌchu̇r, -ˈkəmp-, -fə-chər\ *n*

[1]**dis•com•fort** \dis-ˈkəm-fərt, -ˈkəmp-\ *vt* : to make uncomfortable or uneasy

[2]**discomfort** *n* : physical or mental uneasiness : DISTRESS

dis•com•mode \ˌdis-kə-ˈmōd\ *vt* : to cause inconvenience to **[**Middle French *discommoder,* from *dis-* "dis-" + *commode* "convenient"**]**

dis•com•pose \ˌdis-kəm-ˈpōz\ *vt* **1** : to disturb the calmness or peace of : AGITATE ⟨*discomposed* by the bad news⟩ **2** : DISARRANGE ⟨hair *discomposed* by the wind⟩ — **dis•com•po•sure** \-ˈpō-zhər\ *n*

dis•con•cert \ˌdis-kən-ˈsərt\ *vt* **1** : to throw into confusion ⟨the unexpected event *disconcerted* their plans⟩ **2** : to disturb the composure of ⟨the verdict *disconcerted* the defendant⟩ **syn** see EMBARRASS — **dis•con•cert•ing•ly** *adv*

dis•con•nect \ˌdis-kə-ˈnekt\ *vt* : to undo or break the connection of ⟨*disconnect* two pipes⟩ ⟨*disconnect* a telephone⟩ — **dis•con•nec•tion** \-ˈnek-shən\ *n*

dis•con•nect•ed *adj* **1** : not connected : SEPARATE **2** : DISCURSIVE, INCOHERENT ⟨*disconnected* thoughts⟩ — **dis•con•nect•ed•ly** *adv* — **dis•con•nect•ed•ness** *n*

dis•con•so•late \dis-ˈkän-sə-lət\ *adj* **1** : DEJECTED, DOWNCAST ⟨the team was *disconsolate* after three straight losses⟩ **2** : causing or suggestive of dejection : CHEERLESS ⟨a *disconsolate* row of empty houses⟩ **[**Medieval Latin *disconsolatus,* from Latin *dis-* + *consolari* "to console"**]** — **dis•con•so•late•ly** *adv* — **dis•con•so•late•ness** *n*

[1]**dis•con•tent** \ˌdis-kən-ˈtent\ *adj* : DISCONTENTED

[2]**discontent** *vt* : to make discontented — **dis•con•tent•ment** \-mənt\ *n*

[3]**discontent** *n* **1** : lack of contentment : UNEASINESS **2** : a yearning for improvement or perfection **syn** see DISSATISFACTION

dis•con•tent•ed *adj* : not satisfied : MALCONTENT — **dis•con•tent•ed•ly** *adv* — **dis•con•tent•ed•ness** *n*

dis•con•tinu•ance \ˌdis-kən-ˈtin-yə-wəns\ *n* : the act or an instance of discontinuing

dis•con•tin•ue \ˌdis-kən-ˈtin-yü\ *vb* **1** : to break the continuity of : cease to operate, use, or take **2** : END; *esp* : to cease publication

dis•con•tin•u•ous \ˌdis-kən-ˈtin-yə-wəs\ *adj* : not continuous : having interruptions or gaps : BROKEN ⟨*discontinuous* sleep⟩ — **dis•con•ti•nu•i•ty** \ˌdis-ˌkänt-n-ˈü-ət-ē, -ˈyü-\ *n* — **dis•con•tin•u•ous•ly** \ˌdis-kən-ˈtin-yə-wəs-lē\ *adv*

dis•cord \ˈdis-ˌkȯrd\ *n* **1** : lack of agreement or accord : CONFLICT **2 a** : a harsh combination of musical sounds **b** : a harsh or unpleasant sound **[**derived from Latin *discordia,* from *discors* "discordant", from *dis-* + *cor* "heart"**]**

dis•cor•dance \dis-ˈkȯrd-ns\ *n* **1** : the state or an instance of being discordant **2** : discordant sound or noises : DISSONANCE

dis•cor•dant \-nt\ *adj* **1 a** : being at variance : DISAGREEING **b** : QUARRELSOME **2** : relating to or producing a discord : JARRING **syn** see DISSONANT — **dis•cor•dant•ly** *adv*

dis•co•theque \ˈdis-kə-ˌtek, ˌdis-kə-ˈ\ *n* : a nightclub for dancing to recorded music **[**French *discothèque,* from *disque* "disk, record" + *-othèque* (as in *bibliothèque* "library")**]**

[1]**dis•count** \ˈdis-ˌkau̇nt\ *n* **1** : a reduction made from a regular or list price ⟨two percent *discount* for cash⟩ **2** : a deduction of interest in advance when lending money

[2]**dis•count** \ˈdis-ˌkau̇nt, dis-ˈ\ *vt* **1 a** : to reduce or deduct from the amount of a bill, debt, or charge **b** : to sell or offer for sale at a discount **2** : to lend money on (a note) after deducting the discount **3 a** : MINIMIZE ⟨*discounted* the value of experience⟩ **b** : to make allowance for bias or exaggeration in ⟨*discount* a romantic tale⟩ **c** : to take into account (as a future event) in present calculations ⟨the stock market has already *discounted* the company's better prospects for next year⟩ — **dis•count•able** \-ə-bəl\ *adj*

dis•coun•te•nance \dis-ˈkau̇nt-n-əns, -ˈkau̇nt-nəns\ *vt* **1** : to put to shame : EMBARRASS **2** : to look with disfavor on

discount store *n* : a store where merchandise is sold at a discount from list price — called also *discount house*

dis•cour•age \dis-ˈkər-ij, -ˈkə-rij\ *vt* **1** : to lessen the courage or confidence of ⟨*discouraged* by a single failure⟩ **2 a** : to hinder by inspiring fear of consequences : DETER ⟨laws that *discourage* speeding⟩ **b** : to attempt to dissuade ⟨*discouraged* their children from becoming musicians⟩ — **dis•cour•ag•ing•ly** \-ˈkər-i-jiŋ-lē, -ˈkə-ri-\ *adv*

dis•cour•age•ment \-ˈkər-ij-mənt, -ˈkə-rij-\ *n* **1** : an act of discouraging : the state of being discouraged **2** : something that discourages

[1]**dis•course** \ˈdis-ˌkōrs, -ˌkȯrs, dis-ˈ\ *n* **1** : verbal interchange of ideas : CONVERSATION **2** : formal and orderly and usually extended expression of thought on a subject **[**Late Latin *discursus* "conversation", from Latin *discurrere* "to run about", from *dis-* + *currere* "to run"**]**

²**dis•course** \dis-ˈkōrs, -ˈkȯrs, ˈdis-ˌ\ *vi* **1 :** to express oneself especially in oral discourse **2 :** TALK 5, CONVERSE
dis•cour•te•ous \dis-ˈkərt-ē-əs\ *adj* **:** lacking courtesy **:** RUDE — **dis•cour•te•ous•ly** *adv* — **dis•cour•te•ous•ness** *n*
dis•cour•te•sy \-ˈkərt-ə-sē\ *n* **1 :** rudeness of behavior or language **2 :** a rude act
dis•cov•er \dis-ˈkəv-ər\ *vt* **dis•cov•ered**; **dis•cov•er•ing** \-ˈkəv-ring, -ə-ring\ **1 :** to make known or visible **2 a :** to obtain sight or knowledge of for the first time **b :** to detect the presence of **:** FIND **c :** to find out — **dis•cov•er•able** \-ˈkəv-rə-bəl, -ə-rə-\ *adj* — **dis•cov•er•er** \-ˈkəv-ər-ər\ *n*
• syn DISCOVER, INVENT mean to bring something new into being. DISCOVER implies the finding of something that preexisted but had been unknown ⟨Newton *discovered* the law of gravity⟩ INVENT suggests fabrication as a result of experiment, study, or ingenuity ⟨the cotton gin was *invented* by Eli Whitney⟩
dis•cov•ery \dis-ˈkəv-rē, -ə-rē\ *n, pl* **-er•ies 1 :** the act or process of discovering **2 :** something discovered
¹**dis•cred•it** \dis-ˈkred-ət\ *vt* **1 :** to refuse to accept as true or accurate **:** DISBELIEVE ⟨*discredit* a rumor⟩ **2 :** to cause disbelief in the accuracy or authority of ⟨*discredit* a witness⟩ **3 :** to destroy the reputation of **:** DISGRACE ⟨involvement in graft *discredited* them⟩
²**discredit** *n* **1 :** loss of credit or reputation ⟨knew something to their *discredit*⟩ **2 :** lack or loss of belief or confidence **:** DOUBT ⟨bring a story into *discredit*⟩
dis•cred•it•able \-ə-bəl\ *adj* **:** injurious to reputation — **dis•cred•it•ably** \-blē\ *adv*
dis•creet \dis-ˈkrēt\ *adj* **:** having or showing good judgment in conduct and especially in speech **:** PRUDENT; *esp* **:** capable of observing prudent silence **[**Middle French *discret,* from Latin *discretus,* past participle of *discernere* "to distinguish, discern"**]** — **dis•creet•ly** *adv* — **dis•creet•ness** *n*
dis•crep•an•cy \dis-ˈkrep-ən-sē\ *n, pl* **-cies 1 :** the quality or state of being discrepant **:** DIFFERENCE ⟨the extent of *discrepancy* between two reports⟩ **2 :** an instance of being discrepant ⟨*discrepancies* in the firm's financial statements⟩
dis•crep•ant \-ənt\ *adj* **:** being at variance **:** DISAGREEING **[**Latin *discrepare* "to sound discordantly", from *dis-* + *crepare* "to rattle, creak"**]** — **dis•crep•ant•ly** *adv*
dis•crete \dis-ˈkrēt, ˈdis-ˌ\ *adj* **1 :** individually distinct **:** SEPARATE ⟨radiation composed of *discrete* particles⟩ **2 :** consisting of unconnected elements **:** DISCONTINUOUS ⟨a *discrete* series⟩ **[**Latin *discretus,* past participle of *discernere* "to separate, distinguish, discern"**]** — **dis•crete•ly** *adv* — **dis•crete•ness** *n*
dis•cre•tion \dis-ˈkresh-ən\ *n* **1 :** the quality of being discreet **:** PRUDENCE **2 a :** individual choice or judgment ⟨left the decision to your *discretion*⟩ **b :** power of free decision ⟨reached the age of *discretion*⟩ — **dis•cre•tion•ary** \-ˈkresh-ə-ˌner-ē\ *adj*
dis•crim•i•nant \dis-ˈkrim-ə-nənt\ *n* **:** a mathematical expression from which it is possible to make statements about the value of another more complicated expression, relation, or set of relations
dis•crim•i•nate \dis-ˈkrim-ə-ˌnāt\ *vb* **1 a :** to perceive the distinguishing features of ⟨*discriminate* the geological features of a terrain⟩ **b :** DIFFERENTIATE 3, DISTINGUISH ⟨*discriminate* hundreds of colors⟩ **2 :** to see and note the differences ⟨*discriminate* among values⟩; *esp* **:** to distinguish one like object from another ⟨*discriminate* between a maple and an oak⟩ **3 :** to make a distinction in favor of or against one person or thing as compared with others ⟨*discriminated* against because of race⟩ **[**Latin *discriminare,* from *discrimen* "distinction", from *discernere* "to distinguish, discern"**]** — **dis•crim•i•na•ble** \-ˈkrim-nə-bəl, -ə-nə-\ *adj*
dis•crim•i•nat•ing *adj* **:** marked by discrimination; *esp* **:** DISCERNING, JUDICIOUS ⟨a *discriminating* taste⟩ — **dis•crim•i•nat•ing•ly** \-ˌnāt-ing-lē\ *adv*
dis•crim•i•na•tion \dis-ˌkrim-ə-ˈnā-shən\ *n* **1 :** the act of discriminating **:** DIFFERENTIATION **2 :** the quality or power of finely distinguishing **3 :** distinction and especially unjust distinction made against one person or group in favor of another ⟨racial *discrimination*⟩ — **dis•crim•i•na•tion•al** \-shnəl, -shən-l\ *adj*
dis•crim•i•na•tive \dis-ˈkrim-ə-ˌnāt-iv\ *adj* **1 :** making distinctions **2 :** DISCRIMINATORY — **dis•crim•i•na•tive•ly** *adv*
dis•crim•i•na•to•ry \dis-ˈkrim-nə-ˌtōr-ē, -ə-nə-, -ˌtȯr-\ *adj* **:** marked by unjust discrimination ⟨*discriminatory* treatment⟩
dis•cur•sive \dis-ˈkər-siv\ *adj* **:** passing from one topic to another **:** RAMBLING **[**Medieval Latin *discursivus,* from Latin *discurrere* "to run about", from *dis-* + *currere* "to run"**]**
dis•cur•sive•ly *adv* — **dis•cur•sive•ness** *n*
dis•cus \ˈdis-kəs\ *n, pl* **dis•cus•es :** a disk (as of wood or plastic) thicker in the center than at the edge that is hurled for distance in track-and-field competition **[**Latin, "disk, dish"**]**

discus

dis•cuss \dis-ˈkəs\ *vt* **1 :** to investigate or consider carefully by reasoning or argument ⟨*discuss* a proposal⟩ **2 :** to talk about ⟨*discuss* the weather⟩ **[**Latin *discussus,* past participle of *discutere* "to shake apart, scatter", from *dis-* + *quatere* "to shake"**]**
• syn DISCUSS, ARGUE, DEBATE, DISPUTE mean to talk about in order to reach conclusions or to convince others. DISCUSS implies a presentation of considerations pro and con and suggests an interchange of opinion for the sake of clarifying issues; ARGUE implies the marshaling of evidence and reasons to support a proposition or proposal; DEBATE stresses formal or public argument between opposing parties; DISPUTE implies quarrelsome or heated argument.
dis•cus•sion \dis-ˈkəsh-ən\ *n* **1 :** consideration of a question in open usually informal debate **2 :** a formal treatment of a topic
¹**dis•dain** \dis-ˈdān\ *n* **:** a feeling of contempt for something regarded as beneath one **:** SCORN
²**disdain** *vt* **1 :** to look with scorn on **2 :** to reject or refrain from because of disdain **[**Middle French *desdeignier,* derived from Latin *dis-* + *dignare* "to deign"**] syn** see DESPISE
dis•dain•ful \-fəl\ *adj* **:** full of or expressing disdain **:** SCORNFUL — **dis•dain•ful•ly** \-fə-lē\ *adv* — **dis•dain•ful•ness** *n*
dis•ease \diz-ˈēz\ *n* **1 :** a condition of the living animal or plant body in which the normal state is altered and the performance of the vital functions is impaired **:** ILLNESS **2 :** a harmful development **[**Middle French *desaise* "trouble", from *des-* "dis-" + *aise* "ease"**]** — **dis•eased** \-ˈēzd\ *adj*
dis•em•bark \ˌdis-əm-ˈbärk\ *vb* **1 :** to put ashore (as cargo) from a ship **2 :** to leave a vehicle (as a ship or plane) — **dis•em•bar•ka•tion** \ˌdis-ˌem-ˌbär-ˈkā-shən, -bər-\ *n*
dis•em•bar•rass \ˌdis-əm-ˈbar-əs\ *vt* **:** to free from something troublesome or unnecessary
dis•em•body \ˌdis-əm-ˈbäd-ē\ *vt* **:** to deprive of bodily existence
dis•em•bow•el \ˌdis-əm-ˈbau̇-əl, -ˈbau̇l\ *vt* **-eled** *or* **-elled**; **-el•ing** *or* **-el•ling :** to take out the bowels of — **dis•em•bow•el•ment** \-mənt\ *n*
dis•en•chant \ˌdis-n-ˈchant\ *vt* **:** to free from illusion — **dis•en•chant•ment** \-mənt\ *n*
dis•en•cum•ber \ˌdis-n-ˈkəm-bər\ *vt* **:** to free from something that burdens or obstructs
dis•en•fran•chise \ˌdis-n-ˈfran-ˌchīz\ *vt* **:** to deprive of a franchise, a legal right, or a privilege or immunity; *esp* **:** to deprive of the right to vote — **dis•en•fran•chise•ment** \-ˌchīz-mənt, -chəz-\ *n*
dis•en•gage \ˌdis-n-ˈgāj\ *vb* **:** to free or release from an engagement, entanglement, or encumbrance ⟨*disengage* an automobile clutch⟩; *esp* **:** to remove oneself from military commitments, alliances, or positions — **dis•en•gage•ment** \-ˈgāj-mənt\ *n*
dis•en•tan•gle \ˌdis-n-ˈtang-gəl\ *vb* **:** to free or become free from entanglement **syn** see EXTRICATE — **dis•en•tan•gle•ment** \-mənt\ *n*
dis•equi•lib•ri•um \ˌdis-ˌē-kwə-ˈlib-rē-əm, -ˌek-wə-\ *n* **:** loss or lack of equilibrium
dis•es•tab•lish \ˌdis-ə-ˈstab-lish\ *vt* **:** to end the establishment of; *esp* **:** to deprive of the status and privileges of an estab-

lished church — **dis•es•tab•lish•ment** \-mənt\ *n*

[1]dis•es•teem \ˌdis-ə-ˈstēm\ *vt* : to regard with disfavor

[2]disesteem *n* : lack of esteem : DISFAVOR, DISREPUTE

[1]dis•fa•vor \dis-ˈfā-vər, ˈdis-\ *n* **1** : DISAPPROVAL, DISLIKE ⟨practices looked on with *disfavor*⟩ **2** : the state or fact of being deprived of favor ⟨in *disfavor* at school⟩

[2]disfavor *vt* : to regard with disfavor

dis•fig•ure \dis-ˈfig-yər, *especially British* -ˈfig-ər\ *vt* : to spoil the appearance of ⟨*disfigured* by a scar⟩ **syn** see DEFACE — **dis•fig•ure•ment** \-mənt\ *n*

dis•fran•chise \dis-ˈfran-ˌchīz\ *vt* : DISENFRANCHISE — **dis•fran•chise•ment** \-ˌchīz-mənt, -chəz-\ *n*

dis•gorge \dis-ˈgȯrj, ˈdis-\ *vb* **1** : VOMIT 1 **2** : to discharge violently, confusedly, or as a result of force **3** : to discharge contents

[1]dis•grace \dis-ˈgrās\ *vt* : to bring reproach or shame to — **dis•grac•er** *n*

[2]disgrace *n* **1** : the condition of being out of favor : loss of respect ⟨in *disgrace* with one's schoolmates⟩ **2** : SHAME, DISHONOR ⟨the *disgrace* of being a coward⟩ **3** : a cause of shame ⟨that child's manners are a *disgrace*⟩

dis•grace•ful \-fəl\ *adj* : bringing or involving shame or disgrace — **dis•grace•ful•ly** \-fə-lē\ *adv* — **dis•grace•ful•ness** *n*

dis•grun•tle \dis-ˈgrənt-l\ *vt* **dis•grun•tled**; **dis•grun•tling** \-ˈgrənt-ling, -l-ing\ : to put in bad humor **[***dis-* + Middle English *gruntlen* "to grumble", from *grunten* "to grunt"**]** — **dis•grun•tle•ment** \-l-mənt\ *n*

[1]dis•guise \dis-ˈgīz\ *vt* **1** : to change the dress or looks of so as to conceal the identity or so as to resemble another ⟨*disguised* themselves with wigs⟩ **2 a** : HIDE, CONCEAL ⟨*disguised* their true feelings⟩ **b** : ALTER ⟨tried to *disguise* my voice⟩ — **dis•guised•ly** \-ˈgīz-əd-lē, -ˈgīzd-lē\ *adv* — **dis•guis•er** \-ˈgī-zər\ *n*

[2]disguise *n* **1** : clothing put on to conceal one's identity or counterfeit another's **2 a** : an outward form hiding or misrepresenting the true nature or identity of a person or thing **b** : an artificial manner : PRETENSE **3** : the act of disguising

• **syn** DISGUISE, CLOAK, MASK mean an appearance that hides one's true identity or nature. DISGUISE implies a change in appearance or behavior that misleads by presenting a different apparent identity; CLOAK suggests a means of hiding a movement or an intention completely; MASK suggests some usually obvious means of preventing recognition and does not always imply deception or pretense.

[1]dis•gust \dis-ˈgəst\ *n* : marked aversion to something distasteful or loathsome : REPUGNANCE

[2]disgust *vt* : to provoke to loathing, repugnance, or aversion : be offensive to **[**Middle French *desgouster*, from *des-* "dis-" + *goust* "taste"; from Latin *gustus***]** — **dis•gust•ed** *adj* — **dis•gust•ed•ly** *adv* — **dis•gust•ing** \-ˈgəs-ting\ *adj* — **dis•gust•ing•ly** \-ting-lē\ *adv*

[1]dish \ˈdish\ *n* **1** : a usually concave vessel from which food is served **2 a** : the food served in a dish ⟨ate a *dish* of strawberries⟩ **b** : food prepared in a particular way **3** : something resembling a dish especially in being shallow and concave **[**Old English *disc* "plate", from Latin *discus* "quoit, disk, dish", from Greek *diskos*, from *dikein* "to throw"**]**

[2]dish *vt* **1** : to put into a dish or set of dishes **2** : to make concave like a dish ⟨a *dished* metal disk⟩

dis•ha•bille *or* **des•ha•bille** \ˌdis-ə-ˈbēl\ *n* : the state of being dressed in a casual or careless style **[**French *déshabillé*, from *déshabiller* "to undress", from *dés-* "dis-" + *habiller* "to dress"**]**

dis•har•mo•ny \dis-ˈhär-mə-nē\ *n* : lack of harmony : DISCORD

dish•cloth \ˈdish-ˌklȯth\ *n* : a cloth for washing dishes

dis•heart•en \dis-ˈhärt-n\ *vt* : to deprive of courage and hope : DISCOURAGE — **dis•heart•en•ing** \-ˈhärt-ning, -n-ing\ *adj* — **dis•heart•en•ing•ly** \-ning-lē, -n-ing-lē\ *adv* — **dis•heart•en•ment** \-ˈhärt-n-mənt\ *n*

di•shev•el \dish-ˈev-əl\ *vt* **di•shev•eled** *or* **di•shev•elled**; **di•shev•el•ing** *or* **di•shev•el•ling** \-ˈev-ling, -ə-ling\ : to put into disorder or disarray **[**Middle French *descheveler* "to disarrange the hair", from *des-* "dis-" + *chevel* "hair", from Latin *capillus***]** — **di•shev•el•ment** \-əl-mənt\ *n*

di•shev•eled *or* **di•shev•elled** *adj* : marked by disorder or disarray

dis•hon•est \dis-ˈän-əst, ˈdis-\ *adj* **1** : not honest : UNTRUSTWORTHY **2** : marked by fraud : DECEITFUL, CORRUPT ⟨*dishonest* dealings⟩ — **dis•hon•est•ly** *adv*

dis•hon•es•ty \-ə-stē\ *n* : lack of honesty or integrity : disposition to defraud or deceive

[1]dis•hon•or \dis-ˈän-ər, ˈdis-\ *n* **1 a** : loss of honor or reputation **b** : the state of one who has lost honor or prestige **c** : a cause of disgrace **2** : the refusal to accept or pay (as a bill or check)

[2]dishonor *vt* **1** : to bring shame on : DISGRACE **2** : to refuse to accept or pay (as a bill or check) — **dis•hon•or•er** *n*

dis•hon•or•able \dis-ˈän-rə-bəl, -ˈän-ə-rə-bəl, -ˈän-ər-bəl\ *adj* : not honorable : DISGRACEFUL, SHAMEFUL — **dis•hon•or•ably** \-blē\ *adv*

dish•rag \ˈdish-ˌrag\ *n* : DISHCLOTH

dish towel *n* : a cloth for drying dishes

dish•wash•er \ˈdish-ˌwȯsh-ər, -ˌwäsh-\ *n* : a person or a machine that washes dishes

dish•wa•ter \-ˌwȯt-ər, -ˌwät-\ *n* : water in which dishes have been or are to be washed

[1]dis•il•lu•sion \ˌdis-ə-ˈlü-zhən\ *n* : the loss of illusions or hopes

[2]disillusion *vt* **-lu•sioned**; **-lu•sion•ing** \-ˈlüzh-ning, -ə-ning\ : to leave without illusion — **dis•il•lu•sion•ment** \-ˈlü-zhən-mənt\ *n*

dis•in•cline \ˌdis-n-ˈklīn\ *vb* : to make or be unwilling — **dis•in•cli•na•tion** \ˌdis-ˌin-klə-ˈnā-shən, -ˌing-\ *n*

dis•in•fect \ˌdis-n-ˈfekt\ *vt* : to free from infection especially by destroying harmful germs; *also* : CLEANSE — **dis•in•fec•tion** \-ˈfek-shən\ *n*

dis•in•fec•tant \-ˈfek-tənt\ *n* : a substance that destroys harmful germs but not ordinarily spores of bacteria — **disinfectant** *adj*

dis•in•gen•u•ous \ˌdis-n-ˈjen-yə-wəs\ *adj* : lacking in candor : neither frank nor naive — **dis•in•gen•u•ous•ly** *adv* — **dis•in•gen•u•ous•ness** *n*

dis•in•her•it \ˌdis-n-ˈher-ət\ *vt* : to deprive of the right to inherit

dis•in•te•grate \dis-ˈint-ə-ˌgrāt\ *vb* **1** : to break or decompose into constituent elements, parts, or particles **2 a** : to destroy the unity or integrity of **b** : to lose unity or integrity by or as if by breaking into parts **3** : to undergo a change in composition ⟨an atomic nucleus that *disintegrates* because of radioactivity⟩ — **dis•in•te•gra•tion** \ˌdis-ˌint-ə-ˈgrā-shən\ *n* — **dis•in•te•gra•tor** \dis-ˈint-ə-ˌgrāt-ər\ *n*

dis•in•ter \ˌdis-n-ˈtər\ *vt* **1** : to take out of the grave or tomb **2** : to bring to light : UNEARTH — **dis•in•ter•ment** \-mənt\ *n*

dis•in•ter•est•ed \dis-ˈint-ə-ˌres-təd, ˈdis-; -ˈin-trəs-, -ˌtres-; -ˈint-ərs-, -ˈint-ə-rəs-\ *adj* **1** : not interested **2** : free from selfish motive or interest : UNBIASED ⟨a *disinterested* decision⟩ **syn** see UNINTERESTED — **dis•in•ter•est•ed•ly** *adv* — **dis•in•ter•est•ed•ness** *n*

dis•join \dis-ˈjȯin, ˈdis-\ *vb* : to end the union of or become separated ⟨chromosome pairs *disjoin* in meiosis⟩

[1]dis•joint \dis-ˈjȯint, ˈdis-\ *adj* : completely separate; *esp* : having no elements in common ⟨*disjoint* mathematical sets⟩

[2]disjoint *vb* **1** : to separate the parts of **2** : to take apart or become parted at the joints

dis•joint•ed *adj* **1** : separated at or as if at the joint **2** : lacking coherence or orderly sequence ⟨*disjointed* conversation⟩ — **dis•joint•ed•ly** *adv* — **dis•joint•ed•ness** *n*

dis•junc•tion \dis-ˈjəng-shən, -ˈjəngk-\ *n* **1** : DISUNION, SEPARATION **2** : a proposition composed of two or more statements joined by the connective *or* or its equivalent; *esp* : one in which one and only one of the statements is true at a time

[1]dis•junc•tive \-ˈjəng-tiv, -ˈjəngk-\ *n* : a disjunctive conjunction

[2]disjunctive *adj* **1** : tending to disjoin **2** : expressing an alternative between the meanings of the words connected ⟨the *disjunctive* conjunction *or*⟩

[1]disk *or* **disc** \ˈdisk\ *n* **1** : the seemingly flat figure of a celestial body ⟨solar *disk*⟩ **2 a** : the central part of the flower head of a typical composite plant made up of closely packed tubular flowers **b** : any of various rounded and flattened animal anatomical structures **3 a** : a thin circular object : an object that appears to be thin and circular **b** *usually disc* : a phonograph record **c** : a round, flat plate coated with a magnetic substance on which data for a computer may be stored **4** *usually disc* : a tilling implement (as a harrow or plow) with sharp-edged circular concave cutting blades; *also* : one of these blades **[**Latin *discus* "dish, disk"**]** — **disk•like** *or* **disc•like** \-ˌlīk\ *adj*

[2]disk *or* **disc** *vt* **:** to cultivate (land) with a disc

disk flower *n* **:** one of the tubular flowers in the disk of a composite plant — called also *disk floret*

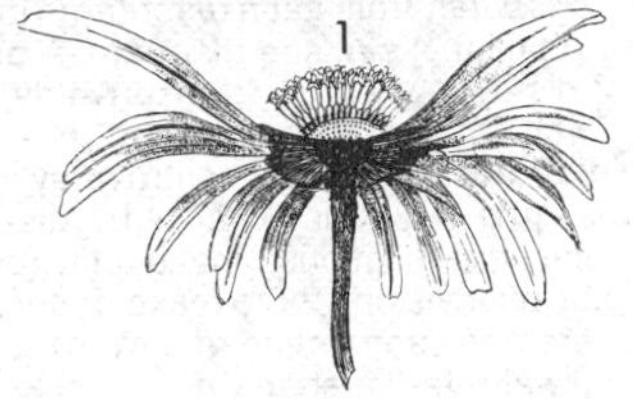

1 [1]disk 2a

[1]dis•like \dis-ˈlīk, ˈdis-\ *vt* **:** to regard with dislike **:** DISAPPROVE

[2]dislike *n* **:** a feeling of distaste or disapproval

dis•lo•cate \ˈdis-lō-ˌkāt, dis-ˈlō-\ *vt* **1 :** to put out of place; *esp* **:** to displace (a bone) from normal connections with another bone **2 :** DISRUPT 2 — **dis•lo•ca•tion** \ˌdis-ˌlō-ˈkā-shən\ *n*

dis•lodge \dis-ˈläj, ˈdis-\ *vt* **1 :** to force out of a resting place **2 :** to drive from a place of hiding or defense

dis•loy•al \dis-ˈlȯi-əl, -ˈlȯil\ *adj* **:** lacking in loyalty **syn** see FAITHLESS — **dis•loy•al•ly** \-ˈlȯi-ə-lē\ *adv*

dis•loy•al•ty \-ˈlȯi-əl-tē, -ˈlȯil-\ *n* **:** lack of loyalty

dis•mal \ˈdiz-məl\ *adj* **:** showing or causing gloom or depression ⟨a *dismal* voice⟩ ⟨*dismal* winter afternoons⟩ [derived from Medieval Latin *dies mali* "evil days"] — **dis•mal•ly** \-mə-lē\ *adv*

△ **origin** Medieval calendars marked two days in every month as *dies mali,* "evil days". They were considered unlucky. English *dismal* was originally a noun meaning "the set of evil days". By the 15th century *dismal* was often being used before another noun. A "dismal day" was one of the 24 that belonged to the dismal. It was not long before the word was reinterpreted as an adjective, meaning at first "unlucky" but eventually "gloomy" or "depressing".

dis•man•tle \dis-ˈmant-l\ *vt* **dis•man•tled; dis•man•tling** \-ˈmant-ling, -l-ing\ **1 :** to strip of furniture and equipment **2 :** to take apart ⟨*dismantled* the engine to repair it⟩ [Middle French *desmanteler* "to strip of dress", from *des-* "dis-" + *mantel* "mantle"] — **dis•man•tle•ment** \-ˈmant-l-mənt\ *n*

dis•mast \dis-ˈmast, ˈdis-\ *vt* **:** to remove or break off the mast of ⟨a ship *dismasted* in a storm⟩

[1]dis•may \dis-ˈmā, diz-\ *vt* **:** to cause to lose courage or resolution through alarm or fear **:** DAUNT [Middle English *dismayen,* derived from Old French *des-* "dis-" + *-maiier* (as in *esmaiier* "to dismay")] — **dis•may•ing•ly** \-ing-lē\ *adv*

[2]dismay *n* **1 :** sudden loss of courage or resolution from alarm or fear **2 :** a feeling of alarm or disappointment

dis•mem•ber \dis-ˈmem-bər, ˈdis-\ *vt* **dis•mem•bered; dis•mem•ber•ing** \-bə-ring, -bring\ **1 :** to cut off or separate the limbs, members, or parts of **2 :** to break up or tear into pieces — **dis•mem•ber•ment** \-bər-mənt\ *n*

dis•miss \dis-ˈmis\ *vt* **1 :** to permit or cause to leave ⟨*dismiss* the class⟩ **2 :** to discharge from office, service, or employment **3 :** to put aside or out of mind ⟨*dismiss* the thought⟩ **4 :** to refuse further judicial consideration to ⟨the judge *dismissed* the charge⟩ [Latin *dimissus,* past participle of *dimittere* "to dismiss", from *dis-* "apart" + *mittere* "to send"]

dis•miss•al \-ˈmis-əl\ *n* **:** the act of dismissing **:** the fact or state of being dismissed

dis•mount \dis-ˈmau̇nt, ˈdis-\ *vb* **1 :** to get down from something (as a horse or bicycle) **2 :** to throw down from a horse **:** UNHORSE **3 :** to take down or apart from an assembled condition **:** DISASSEMBLE

dis•obe•di•ence \ˌdis-ə-ˈbēd-ē-əns\ *n* **:** neglect or refusal to obey — **dis•obe•di•ent** \-ənt\ *adj* — **dis•obe•di•ent•ly** *adv*

dis•obey \ˌdis-ə-ˈbā\ *vb* **:** to fail to obey **:** be disobedient

dis•oblige \ˌdis-ə-ˈblīj\ *vt* **1 :** to go counter to the wishes of **2 :** to cause inconvenience to

[1]dis•or•der \dis-ˈȯrd-ər, ˈdis-\ *vt* **1 :** to disturb the order of **2 :** to disturb the regular or normal functions of

[2]disorder *n* **1 a :** lack of order **b :** a disturbing, neglecting, or breaking away from a normal order **2 :** an abnormal physical or mental condition **:** AILMENT — **dis•or•dered** \-ˈȯrd-ərd\ *adj*

dis•or•der•ly \-ər-lē\ *adj* **1 a :** UNRULY, TURBULENT **b** (1) **:** offensive to public order or decency ⟨*disorderly* behavior⟩ (2) **:** guilty of disorderly conduct ⟨*disorderly* persons⟩ **2 :** not in an orderly condition **:** DISARRANGED ⟨a *disorderly* mass of papers⟩ — **dis•or•der•li•ness** *n*

dis•or•ga•nize \ˈdis-ˈȯr-gə-ˌnīz\ *vt* **:** to break up the regular arrangement or system of **:** throw into disorder **:** CONFUSE — **dis•or•ga•ni•za•tion** \ˌdis-ˌȯrg-ə-nə-ˈzā-shən, -ˌȯrg-nə-\ *n*

dis•ori•ent \dis-ˈōr-ē-ˌent, -ˈȯr-\ *vt* **:** to cause to lose bearings **:** deprive of the normal sense of position or relationship — **dis•ori•en•ta•tion** \ˌdis-ˌōr-ē-ən-ˈtā-shən, -ˌȯr-\ *n*

dis•own \dis-ˈōn, ˈdis-\ *vt* **:** to refuse to acknowledge as one's own **:** REPUDIATE

dis•par•age \dis-ˈpar-ij\ *vt* **1 :** to lower in rank or reputation **:** DEGRADE **2 :** to speak slightingly of **:** BELITTLE ⟨*disparaged* their achievements⟩ [Middle French *desparagier* "to marry below one's class", from *des-* "dis-" + *parage* "lineage", from *per* "peer"] — **dis•par•age•ment** \-mənt\ *n* — **dis•par•ag•ing•ly** \-ij-ing-lē\ *adv*

dis•par•ate \dis-ˈpar-ət; ˈdis-pə-rət, -prət\ *adj* **:** markedly distinct in quality or character [Latin *disparatus,* past participle of *disparare* "to separate", from *dis-* + *parare* "to prepare"] **syn** see DIFFERENT — **dis•par•ate•ly** *adv* — **dis•par•ate•ness** *n* — **dis•par•i•ty** \dis-ˈpar-ət-ē\ *n*

dis•pas•sion•ate \dis-ˈpash-nət, -ə-nət\ *adj* **:** not influenced by strong feeling **:** IMPARTIAL — **dis•pas•sion•ate•ly** *adv*

[1]dis•patch *or* **des•patch** \dis-ˈpach\ *vt* **1 :** to send away promptly or rapidly to a particular place or for a particular purpose ⟨*dispatch* a messenger⟩ ⟨*dispatch* a train⟩ **2 :** KILL 1 **3 :** to attend to or dispose of speedily ⟨*dispatch* business⟩ [Spanish *despachar* or Italian *dispacciare,* from Provençal *despacher* "to get rid of", from Middle French *despeechier* "to set free"] — **dis•patch•er** *n*

[2]dispatch *or* **despatch** *n* **1 a :** the sending of a message or messenger **b :** the shipment of goods **2 :** MESSAGE; *esp* **:** an important official message **3 :** the act of killing **4 :** a news item sent in by a correspondent to a newpaper **5 :** promptness and efficiency in performing a task

dis•pel \dis-ˈpel\ *vt* **dis•pelled; dis•pel•ling :** to drive away by or as if by scattering **:** DISSIPATE [Latin *dispellere,* from *dis-* + *pellere* "to drive, beat"] **syn** see SCATTER

dis•pens•able \dis-ˈpen-sə-bəl\ *adj* **:** capable of being dispensed with **:** NONESSENTIAL — **dis•pens•abil•i•ty** \-ˌpen-sə-ˈbil-ət-ē\ *n*

dis•pen•sa•ry \dis-ˈpens-rē, -ə-rē\ *n, pl* **-ries :** a place where medical or dental aid is dispensed

dis•pen•sa•tion \ˌdis-pən-ˈsā-shən, -ˌpen-\ *n* **1 a :** a system of rules for ordering affairs **b :** a particular arrangement or provision especially of nature **2 :** an exemption from a rule or from a vow or oath **3 a :** the act of dispensing **b :** something dispensed or distributed — **dis•pen•sa•tion•al** \-shnəl, -shən-l\ *adj*

dis•pen•sa•to•ry \dis-ˈpen-sə-ˌtōr-ē, -ˌtȯr-\ *n, pl* **-ries :** a book containing descriptions of medicines

dis•pense \dis-ˈpens\ *vt* **1 a :** to deal out in portions **b :** ADMINISTER ⟨*dispense* justice⟩ **2 :** to prepare and distribute (medication) [Latin *dispensare* "to distribute", from *dispendere* "to weigh out", from *dis-* + *pendere* "to weigh"] — **dispense with 1 :** to suspend the operation of **2 :** to do or get along without

dis•pens•er \dis-ˈpen-sər\ *n* **:** one that dispenses; *esp* **:** a container that releases its contents in convenient amounts ⟨a soap *dispenser*⟩

dis•pers•al \dis-ˈpər-səl\ *n* **:** the act or result of dispersing

dis•perse \dis-ˈpərs\ *vb* **1 a :** to cause to break up and go in different ways **b :** to cause to become spread widely **c :** to drive or clear away **2 a :** to subject (as light) to dispersion **b :** to distribute more or less evenly throughout a medium ⟨*disperse* particles in water⟩ **3 :** to move in different directions **:** SCATTER [Middle French *disperser,* from Latin *dispergere* "to scatter", from *dis-* + *spargere* "to scatter"] **syn** see SCATTER — **dis•pers•ible** \-ˈpər-sə-bəl\ *adj*

dis•per•sion \dis-ˈpər-zhən\ *n* **1 :** the act or process of dispersing **:** the state of being dispersed **2 :** the separation of light into colors by refraction or diffraction with formation of a spectrum **3 a :** a result or product of dispersing **:** something dispersed **b :** a system consisting of a dispersed substance and the medium in which it is dispersed ⟨a *dispersion* of fine particles in water⟩ — **dis•per•sive** \-ˈpər-siv, -ziv\ *adj* — **dis•per•sive•ly** *adv* — **dis•per•sive•ness** *n*

\ə\ **abut**	\au̇\ **out**	\i\ **tip**	\ȯ\ **saw**	\u̇\ **foot**
\ər\ **further**	\ch\ **chin**	\ī\ **life**	\ȯi\ **coin**	\y\ **yet**
\a\ **mat**	\e\ **pet**	\j\ **job**	\th\ **thin**	\yü\ **few**
\ā\ **take**	\ē\ **easy**	\ng\ **sing**	\t͟h\ **this**	\yu̇\ **cure**
\ä\ **cot, cart**	\g\ **go**	\ō\ **bone**	\ü\ **food**	\zh\ **vision**

dispir•it \dis-'pir-ət, 'dis-\ *vt* : to deprive of morale or enthusiasm : DISHEARTEN [*dis-* + *spirit*] — **dispir•it•ed** *adj* — **dispir•it•ed•ly** *adv* — **dispir•it•ed•ness** *n*

dis•place \dis-'plās, 'dis-\ *vt* **1** : to remove from a usual or proper place; *esp* : to expel or force to flee from home or homeland ⟨*displaced* persons⟩ **2 a** : to remove physically out of position ⟨water *displaced* by a floating object⟩ **b** : to take the place of : REPLACE — **dis•place•able** \-ə-bəl\ *adj*

dis•place•ment \-'plās-mənt\ *n* **1** : the act of displacing : the state of being displaced **2 a** : the volume or weight of a fluid (as water) displaced by a floating body (as a ship) with the weight of the displaced fluid being equal to that of the displacing body ⟨a ship of 3000 tons *displacement*⟩ **b** : the difference between the initial position of an object and any later position

1dis•play \dis-'plā\ *vb* **1 a** : to spread before the view ⟨*display* the flag⟩ **b** : to make evident : SHOW **2** : to make a display [Anglo-French *despleier,* from Latin *displicare* "to scatter", from *dis-* + *plicare* "to fold"] **syn** see SHOW

2display *n* **1 a** : a displaying of something; *esp* : a device that gives information in visual form in communications ⟨a radar *display*⟩ **b** : unnecessary show especially for effect **c** : an eye-catching exhibition **2** : a pattern of behavior exhibited especially by male birds in the breeding season

dis•please \dis-'plēz, 'dis-\ *vb* **1** : to arouse the disapproval and dislike of **2** : to be offensive to **3** : to give displeasure

dis•plea•sure \dis-'plezh-ər, 'dis-, -'plāzh-\ *n* : the feeling of one who is displeased : DISSATISFACTION

dis•port \dis-'pōrt, -'pȯrt\ *vb* **1 a** : DIVERT, AMUSE ⟨*disporting* themselves on the beach⟩ **b** : FROLIC **2** : DISPLAY 1b [Middle French *desporter,* from *des-* "dis-" + *porter* "to carry"]

dis•pos•al \dis-'pō-zəl\ *n* **1** : an orderly distribution : ARRANGEMENT ⟨the *disposal* of troops for battle⟩ **2** : MANAGEMENT 1, ADMINISTRATION **3** : a discarding or destroying especially in a systematic way ⟨trash *disposal*⟩ **4** : the transfer of something into new hands ⟨a *disposal* of property⟩ **5** : the power to dispose of something : CONTROL, COMMAND ⟨the car was at my *disposal*⟩ **6** : a device used to reduce waste matter (as by grinding)

dis•pose \dis-'pōz\ *vt* **1** : to give a tendency to : INCLINE ⟨they were *disposed* to refuse⟩ **2** : to put in order : ARRANGE [Middle French *disposer,* from Latin *disponere* "to arrange", from *dis-* + *ponere* "to put"] — **dis•pos•able** \-'pō-zə-bəl\ *adj* — **dispose of 1** : to settle or determine the fate, condition, or use of : deal with conclusively ⟨has the right to *dispose of* the personal property⟩ **2 a** : to get rid of ⟨*dispose of* rubbish⟩ **b** : to treat or handle so as to finish with ⟨*dispose of* the morning's mail⟩ **3** : to transfer to the control of another ⟨we had to *dispose of* the house before we moved⟩

dis•po•si•tion \,dis-pə-'zish-ən\ *n* **1 a** : the act or power of disposing : DISPOSAL ⟨money at their *disposition*⟩ **b** : a final settlement ⟨the *dispositon* of the case⟩ **2** : the giving up or transferring of something ⟨*disposition* of real estate⟩ **3** : ARRANGEMENT ⟨the *disposition* of furniture in a room⟩ **4 a** : TENDENCY, INCLINATION ⟨a natural *disposition* to avoid pain⟩ **b** : natural attitude toward things ⟨a cheerful *dispostion*⟩

dis•pos•sess \,dis-pə-'zes\ *vt* : to deprive of possession or occupancy (as of land or houses) — **dis•pos•ses•sion** \-'zesh-ən\ *n*

dis•praise \dis-'prāz, 'dis-\ *vt* : to comment on with disapproval or censure — **dispraise** *n* — **dis•prais•er** *n* — **dis•prais•ingly** \-'prā-zing-lē\ *adv*

dis•proof \dis-'prüf, 'dis-\ *n* **1** : the action of disproving **2** : evidence that disproves

dis•pro•por•tion \,dis-prə-'pōr-shən, -'pȯr-\ *n* : lack of proportion, symmetry, or proper relation : DISPARITY; *also* : an instance of this — **disproportion** *vt* — **dis•pro•por•tion•al** \-shnəl, -shən-l\ *adj* — **dis•pro•por•tion•ate** \-shə-nət, -shnət\ *adj* — **dis•pro•por•tion•ate•ly** *adv*

dis•prove \dis-'pruv\ *vt* : to prove to be false : REFUTE — **dis•prov•able** \-'prü-və-bəl\ *adj*

dis•pu•ta•tion \,dis-pyu̇-'tā-shən\ *n* **1** : the act of disputing : DEBATE **2** : an oral defense of an academic thesis

dis•pu•ta•tious \,dis-pyu̇-'tā-shəs\ *adj* : inclined to dispute : ARGUMENTATIVE — **dis•pu•ta•tious•ly** *adv* — **dis•pu•ta•tious•ness** *n*

1dis•pute \dis-'pyüt\ *vb* **1** : to engage in argument : DEBATE; *esp* : to argue irritably or with irritating persistence **2** : WRANGLE 1 **3 a** : to engage in controversy over : argue about **b** : to deny the truth or rightness of : QUESTION **4 a** : to struggle against : OPPOSE **b** : to struggle over : CONTEST [Old French *desputer,* from Latin *disputare* "to discuss", from *dis-* + *putare* "to think"] **syn** see DISCUSS — **dis•put•able** \dis-'pyüt-ə-bəl, 'dis-pyət-\ *adj* — **dis•put•ably** \-blē\ *adv* — **dis•pu•tant** \dis-'pyüt-nt, 'dis-pyət-ənt\ *n* — **dis•put•er** *n*

2dispute *n* **1** : verbal controversy : DEBATE **2** : QUARREL 2

dis•qual•i•fy \dis-'kwäl-ə-,fī, 'dis-\ *vt* **1** : to deprive of necessary qualifications : make unfit ⟨*disqualified* for military service by poor vision⟩ **2** : to make or declare ineligible ⟨*disqualify* voters who cannot read and write⟩ — **dis•qual•i•fi•ca•tion** \,dis-,kwäl-ə-fə-'kā-shən\ *n*

1dis•qui•et \dis-'kwī-ət\ *vt* : to make uneasy or restless : DISTURB — **dis•qui•et•ing** \-ing\ *adj* — **dis•qui•et•ing•ly** \-ing-lē\ *adv*

2disquiet *n* : DISQUIETUDE

dis•qui•etude \dis-'kwī-ə-,tüd, -,tyüd\ *n* : lack of peace and tranquillity : a state of unrest or anxiety

dis•qui•si•tion \,dis-kwə-'zish-ən\ *n* : a formal inquiry or discussion : DISCOURSE [Latin *disquisitio,* from *disquirere* "to inquire diligently", from *dis-* + *quaerere* "to seek"]

1dis•re•gard \,dis-ri-'gärd\ *vt* : to pay no attention to : treat as unworthy of regard or notice

2disregard *n* : the act of disregarding : the state of being disregarded — **dis•re•gard•ful** \-fəl\ *adj*

1dis•rel•ish \dis-'rel-ish\ *vt* : to find objectionable or distasteful

2disrelish *n* : lack of relish : DISTASTE, DISLIKE

dis•re•pair \,dis-ri-'paər, -'peər\ *n* : the state of being in need of repair

dis•rep•u•ta•ble \dis-'rep-yət-ə-bəl, 'dis-\ *adj* : not reputable; *esp* : having a bad reputation — **dis•rep•u•ta•ble•ness** *n* — **dis•rep•u•ta•bly** \-blē\ *adv*

dis•re•pute \,dis-ri-'pyüt\ *n* : loss or lack of esteem or reputation : DISCREDIT

dis•re•spect \,dis-ri-'spekt\ *n* : lack of respect : DISCOURTESY — **dis•re•spect•ful** \-fəl\ *adj* — **dis•re•spect•ful•ly** \-fə-lē\ *adv*

dis•robe \dis-'rōb, 'dis-\ *vb* : UNDRESS

dis•rupt \dis-'rəpt\ *vt* **1** : to break apart : RUPTURE **2** : to throw into disorder : break up **3** : to interrupt the unity or continuity of ⟨the storm *disrupted* communications⟩ [Latin *disruptus,* past participle of *disrumpere* "to break apart", from *dis-* + *rumpere* "to break"] — **dis•rupt•er** *n* — **dis•rup•tion** \-'rəp-shən\ *n* — **dis•rup•tive** \-'rəp-tiv\ *adj* — **dis•rup•tive•ly** *adv* — **dis•rup•tive•ness** *n*

dis•sat•is•fac•tion \,dis-,sat-əs-'fak-shən, ,dis-,at-\ *n* : the quality or state of being dissatisfied

• **syn** DISCONTENT: DISSATISFACTION has usually a definite cause and is often temporary ⟨*dissatisfaction* with the trend of business⟩ DISCONTENT is more general, personal, and deep-rooted ⟨the *discontent* of colonial peoples⟩

dis•sat•is•fac•to•ry \-'fak-tə-rē, -trē\ *adj* : causing dissatisfaction

dis•sat•is•fied \dis-'sat-əs-,fīd, 'dis-,-'at-\ *adj* : expressing or showing dissatisfaction ⟨a *dissatisfied* look⟩ ⟨*dissatisfied* customers⟩

dis•sat•is•fy \dis-'sat-əs-,fī, 'dis-, -'at-\ *vt* : to fail to satisfy

dis•sect \dis-'ekt; dī-'sekt, 'dī-,\ *vt* **1** : to divide (as a plant or animal) into separate parts for examination and study **2** : to analyze thoroughly ⟨*dissect* a proposed plan⟩ [Latin *dissecare* "to cut apart", from *dis-* + *secare* "to cut"] — **dis•sec•tion** \dis-'ek-shən; dī-sek-, 'dī-,\ *n* — **dis•sec•tor** \-ər\ *n*

dis•sect•ed *adj* : cut deeply into fine lobes ⟨a *dissected* leaf⟩

dis•sem•ble \dis-'em-bəl\ *vb* **-bled**; **-bling** \-bə-ling, -bling\ **1** : to hide under or put on a false appearance : conceal facts, intentions, or feelings under some pretense **2** : to put on the appearance of : SIMULATE [Middle French *dissimuler,* from Latin *dissimulare* "to dissimulate"] — **dis•sem•bler** \-bə-lər, -blər\ *n*

dis•sem•i•nate \dis-'em-ə-,nāt\ *vt* : to spread abroad as though sowing seed ⟨*disseminate* ideas⟩ [Latin *disseminare,* from *dis-* + *seminare* "to sow", from *semen* "seed"] — **dis•sem•i•na•tion** \-,em-ə-'nā-shən\ *n* — **dis•sem•i•na•tor** \-'em-ə-,nāt-ər\ *n*

dis•sen•sion \dis-'en-chən\ *n* : disagreement in opinion : DISCORD, QUARRELING [Middle French, from Latin *dissensio,* from *dissentire* "to dissent"]

1dis•sent \dis-'ent\ *vi* **1** : to withhold assent **2** : to differ in opinion [Latin *dissentire,* from *dis-* + *sentire* "to feel"]

[2]dissent *n* **1 :** difference of opinion; *esp* **:** religious nonconformity **2 :** a written statement in which a justice disagrees with the opinion of the majority — called also *dissenting opinion*

dis•sent•er \dis-ˈent-ər\ *n* **1 :** one that dissents **2** *cap* **:** an English Nonconformist

dis•ser•ta•tion \ˌdis-ər-ˈtā-shən\ *n* **:** an extended usually written treatment of a subject; *esp* **:** one submitted for a doctorate [Latin *dissertatio* "discussion", derived from *disserere* "to discourse", from *dis-* + *serere* "to join, arrange"]

dis•ser•vice \dis-ˈsər-vəs, -ˈər-\ *n* **:** an act that adversely affects someone or something **:** INJURY, HARM

dis•si•dence \ˈdis-əd-əns\ *n* **:** DISSENT 1, DISAGREEMENT

dis•si•dent \-ənt\ *adj* **:** openly differing with an opinion or a group **:** expressing dissent [Latin *dissidēre* "to sit apart, disagree", from *dis-* + *sedēre* "to sit"] — **dissident** *n*

dis•sim•i•lar \dis-ˈsim-ə-lər, -ˈim-\ *adj* **:** UNLIKE a — **dis•sim•i•lar•i•ty** \ˌdis-ˌsim-ə-ˈlar-ət-ē, -ˌim-\ *n* — **dis•sim•i•lar•ly** \dis-ˈsim-ə-lər-lē, -ˈim-\ *adv*

dis•sim•i•la•tion \ˌdis-ˌim-ə-ˈlā-shən\ *n* **:** the change or omission of one of two identical or closely related sounds in a word — **dis•sim•i•la•tive** \dis-ˈim-ə-ˌlāt-iv\ *adj*

dis•si•mil•i•tude \ˌdis-sə-ˈmil-ə-ˌtüd, ˌdis-ə-, -ˌtyüd\ *n* **:** lack of resemblance

dis•sim•u•late \dis-ˈim-yə-ˌlāt\ *vb* **:** to hide under a false appearance **:** DISSEMBLE [Latin *dissimulare,* from *dis-* + *simulare* "to simulate"] — **dis•sim•u•la•tion** \ˌdis-ˌim-yə-ˈlā-shən\ *n* — **dis•sim•u•la•tor** \dis-ˈim-yə-ˌlāt-ər\ *n*

dis•si•pate \ˈdis-ə-ˌpāt\ *vb* **1 a :** to break up and drive off (as a crowd) **b :** to cause to spread out to the point of vanishing **:** DISSOLVE ⟨the breeze *dissipated* the fog⟩ **2 a :** to expend aimlessly or foolishly ⟨*dissipate* our energies⟩ **b :** SQUANDER ⟨*dissipated* a fortune in gambling⟩ **3 :** to separate into parts and scatter or vanish **4 :** to be extravagant or uncontrolled in the pursuit of pleasure; *esp* **:** to drink to excess [Latin *dissipare,* from *dis-* + *supare* "to throw"] **syn** see SCATTER

dis•si•pat•ed *adj* **:** given to dissipation — **dis•si•pat•ed•ly** *adv* — **dis•si•pat•ed•ness** *n*

dis•si•pa•tion \ˌdis-ə-ˈpā-shən\ *n* **:** the act of dissipating **:** the state of being dissipated: **a :** DISPERSION 1, DIFFUSION **b :** wasteful expenditure **c :** intemperate living; *esp* **:** excessive drinking

dis•so•ci•ate \dis-ˈō-sē-ˌāt, -shē-ˌāt\ *vb* **1 :** to separate from association or union with another **:** DISCONNECT **2 :** DISUNITE; *esp* **:** to subject to chemical dissociation **3 :** to undergo dissociation ⟨salts and acids *dissociate* in water⟩ [Latin *dissociare,* from *dis-* + *sociare* "to join", from *socius* "companion"]

dis•so•ci•a•tion \ˌdis-ˌō-sē-ˈā-shən, -ˌō-shē-\ *n* **:** the act or process of dissociating **:** the state of being dissociated; *esp* **:** the process by which a chemical combination breaks up into simpler constituents — **dis•so•cia•tive** \dis-ˈō-sē-ˌāt-iv, -sē-ˌāt-, -shət-iv\ *adj*

dis•sol•u•ble \dis-ˈäl-yə-bəl\ *adj* **:** capable of being dissolved — **dis•sol•u•bil•i•ty** \dis-ˌäl-yə-ˈbil-ət-ē\ *n*

dis•so•lute \ˈdis-ə-ˌlüt\ *adj* **:** lacking restraint; *esp* **:** loose in morals or conduct [Latin *dissolutus,* from *dissolvere* "to loosen, dissolve"] — **dis•so•lute•ly** *adv* — **dis•so•lute•ness** *n*

dis•so•lu•tion \ˌdis-ə-ˈlü-shən\ *n* **1 :** the action or process of dissolving: as **a :** separation into component parts **b :** DECAY 1 **2 :** the termination or breaking up of an assembly or a partnership or corporation

[1]dis•solve \diz-ˈälv, -ˈȯlv\ *vb* **1 :** to break up into component parts **2 :** to pass or cause to pass into solution ⟨sugar *dissolves* in water⟩ **3 :** to bring to an end **:** TERMINATE ⟨*dissolve* parliament⟩ **4 :** to waste or fade away as if by breaking up or melting ⟨their courage *dissolved* in the face of danger⟩ **5 :** to fade out (a motion-picture shot) in a dissolve **6 :** to be overcome emotionally ⟨*dissolved* into tears⟩ [Latin *dissolvere,* from *dis-* + *solvere* "to loosen"] — **dis•solv•able** \-ə-bəl\ *adj* — **dis•solv•er** *n*

[2]dissolve *n* **:** a gradual superimposing of one motion-picture or television shot upon another on a screen

dis•so•nance \ˈdis-ə-nəns\ *n* **1 :** a harsh or unpleasant sound or combination of sounds **2 :** lack of agreement **:** DISCORD **3 :** an unresolved musical note or chord

dis•so•nant \ˈdis-ə-nənt\ *adj* **1 :** marked by dissonance in sound **2 :** not being in harmony or agreement ⟨*dissonant* viewpoints⟩ [Latin *dissonare* "to be discordant", from *dis-* + *sonare* "to sound"] — **dis•so•nant•ly** *adv*

• **syn** DISCORDANT: DISSONANT may apply to lack of harmony intended as a contrast to consonant sounds; DISCORDANT commonly suggests an unpleasant or disagreeable effect on the listener.

dis•suade \dis-ˈwād\ *vt* **:** to advise against a course of action **:** persuade or try to persuade not to do something [Latin *dissuadēre,* from *dis-* + *suadēre* "to urge"] — **dis•sua•sion** \-ˈwā-zhən\ *n* — **dis•sua•sive** \-ˈwā-siv, -ziv\ *adj* — **dis•sua•sive•ly** *adv* — **dis•sua•sive•ness** *n*

[1]dis•taff \ˈdis-ˌtaf\ *n, pl* **dis•taffs** \-ˌtafs, -ˌtavz\ **1 :** a staff for holding the flax, tow, or wool in spinning **2 :** the female branch or side of a family [Old English *distæf*]

[1]distaff 1

△ **origin** A distaff is a small staff used in spinning yarn or thread. Because spinning was in former times an important activity of most women, the distaff became a symbol for woman's work. Activity that was felt to be proper to men rather than to women was symbolized by the spear, and the male side of a family was known as the "spear side". This term is now used very rarely, if at all, but the female side of a family is still commonly called the "distaff side" or simply the "distaff".

[2]distaff *adj* **:** FEMALE

dis•tal \ˈdist-l\ *adj* **1 :** far from the point of attachment or origin (as of a bone or limb) — compare PROXIMAL **2 :** of, relating to, or being the surface of a tooth that is most distant from the middle of the front of the jaw and is usually next to the tooth behind it [*distant* + *-al*] — **dis•tal•ly** \-l-ē\ *adv*

[1]dis•tance \ˈdis-təns\ *n* **1 :** separation in time **2 :** separation in space **:** the amount of space between two points, lines, surfaces, or objects ⟨the *distance* from the earth to the moon⟩ **3 a :** a measurable advance along a route or course ⟨walked a *distance* of five kilometers⟩ **b :** an amount or degree of progress ⟨have come quite a *distance* toward achieving peace⟩ **c :** a full course or extent ⟨go the *distance*⟩ **4 :** the quality or state of being distant: **a :** remoteness in space ⟨their parents sought to keep them at a *distance*⟩ **b :** COLDNESS, RESERVE ⟨they keep their *distance*⟩ **5 :** a distant point or region ⟨saw a car off in the *distance*⟩

[2]distance *vt* **:** to leave far behind **:** OUTSTRIP

dis•tant \ˈdis-tənt\ *adj* **1 a :** separated in space **:** AWAY ⟨a point 100 meters *distant*⟩ **b :** situated at a great distance **:** FAR-OFF ⟨travel to *distant* lands⟩ **2 :** not close in relationship ⟨a *distant* cousin⟩ **3 :** reserved or aloof in personal relationship **:** COLD ⟨they have recently been very *distant* toward me⟩ **4 :** coming from or going to a distance ⟨*distant* voyages⟩ [Middle French, from Latin *distare* "to stand apart, be distant", from *dis-* + *stare* "to stand"] — **dis•tant•ly** *adv* — **dis•tant•ness** *n*

• **syn** DISTANT, FAR, REMOTE, REMOVED mean not close or near in space, time, or relationship. DISTANT is the opposite of *close* and implies separation in space or time; FAR is the opposite of *near* and implies a relatively long distance away; REMOTE applies to what is far removed especially from what is regarded as a center of interest ⟨a *remote* corner of the world⟩ REMOVED implies separateness and often a contrast in character or quality as well as time or space.

dis•taste \dis-ˈtāst, ˈdis-\ *n* **:** DISLIKE, AVERSION ⟨a *distaste* for work⟩

dis•taste•ful \-fəl\ *adj* **:** distinctly unpleasant **:** DISAGREEABLE — **dis•taste•ful•ly** \-fə-lē\ *adv* — **dis•taste•ful•ness** *n*

[1]dis•tem•per \dis-ˈtem-pər\ *n* **1 :** a bad humor or temper **2 :** a disordered or abnormal bodily state: as **a :** a highly contagious virus disease especially of dogs marked by fever and by respiratory and sometimes nervous symptoms **b :** PANLEUCOPENIA

[2]distemper *n* **:** a water-based paint in which the pigments are usually mixed with size or a casein binder and which is used for scene painting and mural decoration [Middle French *distemprer* "to dilute", from Latin *dis-* + *temperare* "to temper"]

dis•tend \dis-ˈtend\ *vb* : to stretch out or bulge out in all directions : SWELL [Latin *distendere,* from *dis-* + *tendere* "to stretch"] **syn** see EXPAND

dis•ten•sion *or* **dis•ten•tion** \dis-ˈten-chən\ *n* : the act of distending : the state of being distended especially unduly or abnormally

dis•till *also* **dis•til** \dis-ˈtil\ *vb* **dis•tilled; dis•till•ing 1** : to fall or let fall in drops **2 a** : to subject to or transform by distillation ⟨*distill* water⟩ **b** : to obtain by distillation ⟨*distill* brandy from wine⟩ **3** : to extract the essence of : CONCENTRATE ⟨*distilled* the information in the report⟩ **4** : to undergo distillation : condense from a still after distillation [Middle French *distiller,* from Latin *destillare,* from *de-* + *stilla* "drop"]

dis•til•late \ˈdis-tə-ˌlāt, dis-ˈtil-ət\ *n* : a liquid product condensed from vapor during distillation

dis•til•la•tion \ˌdis-tə-ˈlā-shən\ *n* **1** : a process that consists of driving gas or vapor from liquids or solids by heating and condensing to liquid products and that is used especially for purification, separation, or the formation of new substances **2** : something obtained by or as if by a process of distilling : ESSENCE

dis•till•er \dis-ˈtil-ər\ *n* : one that distills especially alcoholic liquors

dis•till•ery \dis-ˈtil-rē, -ə-rē\ *n, pl* **-er•ies** : a place where distilling especially of alcoholic liquors is carried on

dis•tinct \dis-ˈtingt, -tingkt\ *adj* **1** : distinguished from others : SEPARATE ⟨guilty of three *distinct* crimes⟩ **2** : clearly seen, heard, or understood : UNMISTAKABLE ⟨*distinct* footprints⟩; *also* : NOTABLE ⟨a *distinct* improvement⟩ [Middle French, from Latin *distinctus,* from *distinguere* "to distinguish"] — **dis•tinct•ly** *adv* — **dis•tinct•ness** *n*

dis•tinc•tion \dis-ˈting-shən, -ˈtingk-\ *n* **1** : the act of distinguishing a difference **2** : the quality or state of being different or distinct : DIFFERENCE ⟨the *distinction* between good and evil⟩ **3** : something that makes a difference : a distinguishing quality or mark ⟨the *distinction* of being the tallest building in town⟩ **4** : SIGNIFICANCE, EMINENCE ⟨a speaker of *distinction*⟩ **5** : special honor or recognition ⟨graduated with *distinction*⟩

dis•tinc•tive \dis-ˈting-tiv, -ˈtingk-\ *adj* : clearly marking a person or a thing as different from others ⟨a *distinctive* way of speaking⟩ **syn** see CHARACTERISTIC — **dis•tinc•tive•ly** *adv* — **dis•tinc•tive•ness** *n*

dis•tin•gué \ˌdēs-ˌtang-ˈgā\ *adj* : distinguished especially in manner or bearing [French, from *distinguer* "to distinguish"]

dis•tin•guish \dis-ˈting-gwish, -wish\ *vb* **1** : to recognize as different by some mark or quality ⟨*distinguish* the sound of a piano in an orchestra⟩ **2** : to make distinctions ⟨*distinguish* between right and wrong⟩ **3** : to mark as different or distinct : set apart ⟨a church *distinguished* by the absence of a steeple⟩ **4** : to perceive clearly : make out ⟨*distinguish* a light in the distance⟩ **5** : to separate from others by a mark of honor : single out; *also* : to make (oneself) prominent ⟨*distinguished* themselves in Congress⟩ [Middle French *distinguer,* from Latin *distinguere,* literally, "to separate by pricking"] — **dis•tin•guish•able** \-ə-bəl\ *adj* — **dis•tin•guish•ably** \-ə-blē\ *adv*

dis•tin•guished *adj* **1** : marked by eminence, distinction, or excellence **2** : befitting an eminent person

dis•tort \dis-ˈtȯrt\ *vt* **1** : to twist out of the true meaning : MISREPRESENT **2** : to twist out of a natural, normal, or original shape or condition [Latin *distortus,* past participle of *distorguēre* "to distort", from *dis-* + *torquēre* "to twist"] — **dis•tort•er** *n*

dis•tor•tion \dis-ˈtȯr-shən\ *n* **1** : the act of distorting **2** : the condition of being distorted or a product of distortion: as **a** : a misshapen condition of an image caused by defects in a lens **b** : inaccurate reproduction of a sound in radio or of an image in television — **dis•tor•tion•al** \-shnəl, -shən-l\ *adj*

dis•tract \dis-ˈtrakt\ *vt* **1** : to turn aside : DIVERT; *esp* : to draw (the attention or mind) to a different object **2** : to stir up or confuse with conflicting emotions or motives : HARASS [Latin *distractus,* past participle of *distrahere* "to draw apart, distract", from *dis-* + *trahere* "to draw"]

dis•trac•tion \dis-ˈtrak-shən\ *n* **1** : the act of distracting or the state of being distracted; *esp* : mental confusion **2** : something that distracts; *esp* : AMUSEMENT — **dis•trac•tive** \-ˈtrak-tiv\ *adj*

dis•traught \dis-ˈtrȯt\ *adj* **1** : troubled with doubt or mental conflict **2** : being or acting insane : CRAZED [Middle English, from Latin *distractus* "distracted"]

¹dis•tress \dis-ˈtres\ *n* **1** : great suffering of body or mind : PAIN, ANGUISH ⟨suffer *distress* from loss of a friend⟩ **2** : MISFORTUNE, TROUBLE ⟨unemployment and economic *distress*⟩ **3** : a condition of danger or desperate need ⟨a ship in *distress*⟩ [Old French *destresse,* derived from Latin *distringere* "to draw apart, detain"]

• **syn** DISTRESS, SUFFERING, MISERY, AGONY mean the state of being in physical or mental anguish. DISTRESS implies conditions or circumstances that cause physical or mental stress or strain and suggests the need of assistance ⟨the *distress* of war orphans⟩ SUFFERING applies to human beings and connotes conscious awareness and endurance of pain; MISERY stresses the unhappy or wretched conditions attending distress or suffering; AGONY suggests suffering too intense to be borne.

²distress *vt* **1** : to subject to great strain or difficulties **2** : to cause to worry or be troubled : UPSET — **dis•tress•ing•ly** \-ing-lē\ *adv*

dis•tress•ful \-fəl\ *adj* : causing distress : full of distress — **dis•tress•ful•ly** \-fə-lē\ *adv* — **dis•tress•ful•ness** *n*

dis•trib•u•tary \dis-ˈtrib-yə-ˌter-ē\ *n, pl* **-taries** : a river branch flowing away from the main stream

dis•trib•ute \dis-ˈtrib-yət\ *vt* **1** : to divide among several or many : APPORTION ⟨*distribute* food packages to the needy⟩ **2 a** : to spread out so as to cover something : SCATTER ⟨*distribute* grass seed over a lawn⟩ **b** : to hand out : DELIVER ⟨*distributing* handbills to passersby⟩ **3** : to divide or separate especially into kinds **4** : to market (a line of goods) in a particular area usually as a wholesaler [Latin *distribuere,* from *dis-* + *tribuere* "to allot"] — **dis•trib•ut•able** \-yət-ə-bəl\ *adj*

dis•tri•bu•tion \ˌdis-trə-ˈbyü-shən\ *n* **1** : the act or process of distributing **2 a** : the position, arrangement, or frequency of occurrence (as of the members of a group) over an area or throughout a space or unit of time ⟨the *distribution* of iron ore in the United States⟩ **b** : the natural geographic range of an organism **3 a** : something distributed **b** : FREQUENCY DISTRIBUTION **4** : the marketing or merchandising of commodities — **dis•tri•bu•tion•al** \-shnəl, -shən-l\ *adj*

dis•trib•u•tive \dis-ˈtrib-yət-iv\ *adj* **1** : of or relating to distribution **2** : referring singly and without exception to the members of a group ⟨the *distributive* adjectives *each* and *every*⟩ **3 a** : being an operation (as multiplication in $a(b + c) = ab + ac$) that produces the same result when operating on the whole mathematical expression as when operating on each part and collecting the results **b** : being or relating to a rule or property concerning a distributive operation ⟨the *distributive* axiom for multiplication⟩ — **dis•trib•u•tive•ly** *adv* — **dis•trib•u•tive•ness** *n*

distributive education *n, often cap D & E* : a vocational program set up between schools and employers in which students receive both classroom instruction and on-the-job training

dis•trib•u•tor \dis-ˈtrib-yət-ər\ *n* **1** : one that distributes **2** : an agent or agency for marketing goods **3** : a device for distributing electric current to the spark plugs of an engine

¹dis•trict \ˈdis-trikt\ *n* **1** : a territorial division marked off or defined (as for administrative or electoral purposes) ⟨school *districts*⟩ ⟨a judicial *district*⟩ **2** : a distinctive area or region ⟨residential *district*⟩ [French, from Medieval Latin *districtus* "jurisdiction, district", from Latin *distringere* "to draw apart, detain"]

²district *vt* : to divide or organize into districts

district attorney *n* : a public official who is the prosecuting officer for a judicial district

district court *n* : a trial court with jurisdiction over certain cases within a specified judicial district

¹dis•trust \dis-ˈtrəst, ˈdis-\ *vt* : to have no confidence in : SUSPECT

²distrust *n* : a lack of trust or confidence : SUSPICION, WARINESS **syn** see DOUBT — **dis•trust•ful** \-fəl\ *adj* — **dis•trust•ful•ly** \-fə-lē\ *adv* — **dis•trust•ful•ness** *n*

dis•turb \dis-ˈtərb\ *vt* **1 a** : to interfere with : INTERRUPT **b** : to alter the position or arrangement of **2 a** : to destroy the tranquillity or composure of : make uneasy **b** : to throw into disorder **c** : to put to inconvenience [Latin *disturbare,* from *dis-* + *turbare* "to throw into disorder"] — **dis•turb•er** *n*

• **syn** PERTURB: DISTURB implies the distracting or distorting effect of worry, conflict, or strain on mental processes; PERTURB applies to the deeper unsettling of the mind by uncertainty, disappointment, or danger.

dis•tur•bance \dis-ˈtər-bəns\ *n* **1** : the act of disturbing : the state of being disturbed **2** : mental confusion : UPSET ⟨an emotional *disturbance*⟩ **3** : public disorder : COMMOTION

dis•turbed *adj* : showing symptoms of mental or emotional illness

di•sul•fide \dī-'səl-,fīd\ *n* : a compound containing two atoms of sulfur combined with an element or radical

dis•union \dis-'ü-nyən, dis-, -'yü-\ *n* : lack of union or agreement : SEPARATION

dis•unite \,dish-ü-'nīt, ,dis-, -yü-\ *vt* : DIVIDE 1, SEPARATE

dis•uni•ty \dish-'ü-nət-ē, dis-, -'yü-\ *n* : lack of unity; *esp* : DISSENSION

1dis•use \dish-'üz, dis-, -'yüz\ *vt* : to discontinue the use or practice of : ABANDON

2dis•use \dish-'üs, dis-, -'yüs\ *n* : cessation of use or practice

di•syl•lab•ic \,dī-sə-'lab-ik\ *adj* : having two syllables — **di•syl•la•ble** \'dī-,sil-ə-bəl, dī-'\ *n*

1ditch \'dich\ *n* : a long narrow excavation dug in the earth for defense, drainage, or irrigation [Old English *dīc* "dike, ditch"]

2ditch *vt* **1 a** : to enclose with a ditch **b** : to provide with ditches (as for drainage or irrigation) **2** : to drive (a car) into a ditch **3** : to get rid of : DISCARD **4** : to make a forced landing of (an airplane) on water

dith•er \'dith-ər\ *n* : a highly nervous, excited, or agitated state [Middle English *didderen*] — **dith•ery** \-ə-rē\ *adj*

dith•y•ramb \'dith-i-,ram\ *n* **1** : a short poem in a wild inspired strain **2** : an exalted or impassioned statement or writing [Greek *dithyrambos*] — **dith•y•ram•bic** \,dith-i-'ram-bik\ *adj*

dit•to \'dit-ō\ *n, pl* **dittos 1** : SAME : more of the same : ANOTHER — used to avoid repeating a word ⟨lost: one shirt (white); *ditto* (blue)⟩ **2** : a mark composed of a pair of inverted commas or apostrophes used as a symbol for the word *ditto* [Italian dialect, past participle of Italian *dire* "to say", from Latin *dicere*]

dit•ty \'dit-ē\ *n, pl* **ditties** : SONG; *esp* : a short simple song [Old French *ditié* "poem", from *ditier* "to compose", from Latin *dictare* "to dictate, compose"]

dit•ty bag \'dit-ē-\ *n* : a small bag used especially by sailors to hold odds and ends of gear (as thread, needles, or tape) [origin unknown]

di•uret•ic \,dī-yü-'ret-ik\ *adj* : tending to increase the flow of urine [Late Latin *diureticus*, from Greek *diourētikos*, from *diourein* "to urinate", from *dia-* + *ourein* "to urinate"] — **diuretic** *n*

di•ur•nal \dī-'ərn-l\ *adj* **1 a** : recurring every day ⟨a *diurnal* task⟩ **b** : having a daily cycle ⟨*diurnal* rotation of the heavens⟩ **2 a** : of, relating to, occurring in, or active during the daytime ⟨a *diurnal* organism⟩ **b** : opening during the day and closing at night ⟨*diurnal* flowers⟩ [Latin *diurnalis*, from *diurnus* "of the day", from *dies* "day"] — **di•ur•nal•ly** \-l-ē\ *adv*

di•va \'dē-və\ *n, pl* **di•vas** *or* **di•ve** \-,vā\ : PRIMA DONNA 1 [Italian, literally, "goddess", from Latin, from *divus* "divine, god"]

di•va•gate \'dī-və-,gāt, 'div-ə-\ *vi* : to wander about : STRAY [Late Latin *divagari*, from Latin *dis-* + *vagari* "to wander"] — **di•va•ga•tion** \,dī-və-'gā-shən, ,div-ə-\ *n*

di•va•lent \dī-'vā-lənt, 'dī-\ *adj* : BIVALENT

di•van \di-'van, 'dī-,van\ *n* : a large couch or sofa usually without back or arms and often designed for use as a bed [Turkish, "council", from Persian *dīwān* "account book"]

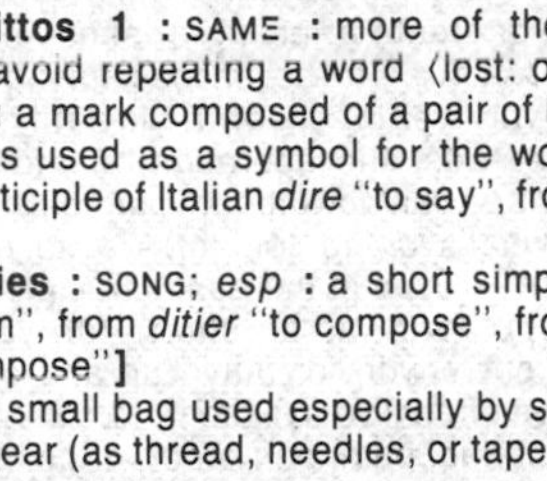

divan

1dive \'dīv\ *vi* **dived** \'dīvd\ *or* **dove** \'dōv\; **div•ing 1 a** : to plunge into water headfirst; *esp* : to execute a dive **b** : SUBMERGE **2 a** : PLUNGE 3b **b** : to descend in a dive **3** : to plunge into some matter or activity **4** : DART, LUNGE [Old English *dȳfan* "to dip" and *dūfan* "to dive"]

2dive *n* **1** : the act or an instance of diving: as **a** : a plunge into water executed in a prescribed manner **b** : a submerging of a submarine **c** : a steep descent of an airplane with or without power **2** : a sharp decline

dive–bomb \'dīv-,bäm\ *vt* : to bomb from an airplane by making a steep dive toward the target before releasing the bomb — **dive–bomb•er** *n*

div•er \'dī-vər\ *n* **1** : one that dives **2 a** : a person who stays under water for long periods by having air supplied from the surface or by carrying a supply of compressed air **b** : any of various diving birds; *esp* : LOON

di•verge \də-'vərj, dī-\ *vi* **1 a** : to move or extend in different directions from a common point : draw apart ⟨*diverging* rays of light⟩ **b** : to differ in character, form, or opinion **2** : to turn aside from a path or course : DEVIATE [Medieval Latin *divergere*, from Latin *dis-* + *vergere* "to incline"]

di•ver•gence \-'vər-jəns\ *n* **1** : a drawing apart (as of lines extending from a common center) **2** : DIFFERENCE 3, DISAGREEMENT **3** : a deviation from a course or standard

di•ver•gent \-jənt\ *adj* **1** : drawing apart from each other : SPREADING **2** : differing from each other or from a standard : DEVIANT **syn** see DIFFERENT — **di•ver•gent•ly** *adv*

di•vers \'dī-vərz\ *adj* : VARIOUS 3 [Middle English *divers, diverse*]

di•verse \dī-'vərs, də-, 'dī-,\ *adj* **1** : differing from one another : UNLIKE **2** : having various forms or qualities ⟨a *diverse* personality⟩ [Middle English, from Latin *diversus*, from *divertere* "to divert"] **syn** see DIFFERENT — **di•verse•ly** *adv* — **di•verse•ness** *n*

di•ver•si•fy \də-'vər-sə-,fī, dī-\ *vb* **-fied**; **-fy•ing 1** : to make diverse : give variety to ⟨*diversify* an educational program by adding new subjects⟩ **2** : to produce variety; *esp* : to engage in a variety of operations ⟨manufacturers *diversifying* into new fields⟩ — **di•ver•si•fi•ca•tion** \də-,vər-sə-fə-'kā-shən, ,dī-\ *n*

di•ver•sion \də-'vər-zhən, dī-\ *n* **1** : the act or an instance of diverting from a course, activity, or use : DEVIATION **2** : something that diverts or amuses : PASTIME **3** : an attack made to draw the attention of an enemy from the point of a principal operation — **di•ver•sion•ary** \-zhə-,ner-ē\ *adj*

di•ver•si•ty \də-'vər-sət-ē, dī-\ *n, pl* **-ties 1** : the condition of being different or having differences **2** : an instance or a point of difference **3** : VARIETY ⟨*diversity* of opinion⟩

di•vert \də-'vərt, dī-\ *vb* **1 a** : to turn from one course or use to another : DEFLECT **b** : DISTRACT **2** : to give pleasure to by causing the time to pass pleasantly [Latin *divertere* "to turn in opposite directions", from *dis-* + *vertere* "to turn"] **syn** see AMUSE

di•ver•tic•u•lum \,dī-vər-'tik-yə-ləm\ *n, pl* **-la** \-lə\ : a pocket or closed branch opening off a main passage ⟨intestinal *diverticula*⟩ [Latin, "bypath", probably from *devertere* "to turn aside", from *de-* + *vertere* "to turn"]

di•ver•ti•men•to \di-,vərt-ə-'ment-ō, -,vert-\ *n, pl* **-men•ti** \-'ment-ē\ *or* **-men•tos** : a light instrumental musical work in several movements [Italian, literally, "diversion"]

di•vest \dī-'vest, də-\ *vt* **1** : to strip especially of clothing, ornament, or equipment **2** : to deprive especially of a right [Middle French *desvestir*, derived from Latin *dis-* + *vestire* "to clothe"]

1di•vide \də-'vīd\ *vb* **1 a** : to separate into two or more parts, areas, or groups **b** : to separate into classes, categories, or divisions **2 a** : to give out in shares : DISTRIBUTE **b** : to possess or make use of in common : SHARE **3** : to cause to be separate, distinct, or apart from one another **4 a** : to mark divisions on : GRADUATE ⟨*divide* a sextant⟩ **b** (1) : to subject (a number or quantity) to the operation of finding how many times it contains another number or quantity ⟨*divide* 42 by 14⟩ (2) : to use as a divisor ⟨*divide* 14 into 42⟩ **5 a** : to become separated into parts **b** : to branch out : DIVERGE [Latin *dividere*] **syn** see SEPARATE

2divide *n* : a dividing ridge between drainage areas : WATERSHED

di•vid•ed *adj* **1 a** : separated into parts or pieces ⟨finely *divided* particles of iron⟩ **b** : cut into distinct parts by incisions extending to the base or to the midrib ⟨a *divided* leaf⟩ **c** : having the opposing streams of traffic separated ⟨a *divided* highway⟩ **2 a** : disagreeing with each other : DISUNITED ⟨sharply *divided*

\ə\ **abut**	\au̇\ **out**	\i\ **tip**	\ȯ\ **saw**	\u̇\ **foot**
\ər\ **further**	\ch\ **chin**	\ī\ **life**	\ȯi\ **coin**	\y\ **yet**
\a\ **mat**	\e\ **pet**	\j\ **job**	\th\ **thin**	\yü\ **few**
\ā\ **take**	\ē\ **easy**	\ng\ **sing**	\t͟h\ **this**	\yu̇\ **cure**
\ä\ **cot, cart**	\g\ **go**	\ō\ **bone**	\ü\ **food**	\zh\ **vision**

over the issue⟩ **b** : directed or moved toward conflicting goals ⟨*divided* loyalties⟩
div•i•dend \'div-ə-,dend, -əd-ənd\ *n* **1** : a sum or amount to be distributed or an individual share of such a sum: as **a** : a share of profits distributed to stockholders or of surplus to an insurance policyholder **b** : interest paid on a bank account **2** : BONUS **3** : a number to be divided by another
di•vid•er \də-'vīd-ər\ *n* **1** : one that divides or separates ⟨a room *divider*⟩ **2** *pl* : an instrument that consists of two pointed branches joined at a pivot for measuring or marking (as in dividing lines and transferring dimensions)
div•i•na•tion \,div-ə-'nā-shən\ *n* **1** : the art or practice that seeks to foresee or foretell future events or discover hidden knowledge usually by interpreting omens or by means of supernatural powers **2** : unusual insight or intuitive perception
¹di•vine \də-'vīn\ *adj* **1 a** : of, relating to, or proceeding directly from deity ⟨*divine* law⟩ **b** : being deity ⟨the *divine* Savior⟩ **c** : directed to deity ⟨*divine* worship⟩ **2 a** : supremely good : SUPERB ⟨this pie is *divine*⟩ **b** : having a sublime quality ⟨*divine* beauty⟩ [Middle French *divin,* from Latin *divinus,* from *divus* "god"] — **di•vine•ly** *adv*
²divine *n* **1** : CLERGYMAN **2** : THEOLOGIAN
³divine *vb* **1** : to discover or perceive intuitively : INFER **2** : to practice divination : PROPHESY [Latin *divinare,* from *divinus* "soothsayer", from *divinus,* adjective, "divine"] — **di•vin•er** *n*
Divine Liturgy *n* : the eucharistic rite of Eastern churches
Divine Office *n* : the daily devotional readings prescribed for priests
divine right *n* : a theory that a monarch receives his right to rule from God and not from the people
diving bell *n* : a diving apparatus consisting of a container open only at the bottom and supplied with compressed air by a hose
diving board *n* : a flexible board secured at one end and extending over water (as at a swimming pool or a lake) that is used to gain height in diving
diving duck *n* : any of various ducks that frequent deep waters and obtain their food by diving
diving suit *n* : a waterproof suit with a helmet that is worn for underwater work by a person who is supplied with air through a tube from the surface
divining rod *n* : a forked rod believed to indicate the presence of water or minerals by dipping downward when held over a vein
di•vin•i•ty \də-'vin-ət-ē\ *n, pl* **-ties** **1** : the quality or state of being divine **2 a** *often cap* : GOD 1 **b** (1) : GOD 2 (2) : GODDESS 1 **c** : DEMIGOD
di•vis•i•ble \də-'viz-ə-bəl\ *adj* : capable of being separated or divided — **di•vis•i•bil•i•ty** \-,viz-ə-'bil-ət-ē\ *n*
di•vi•sion \də-'vizh-ən\ *n* **1 a** : the act, process, or operation of dividing : the state of being divided **b** : DISTRIBUTION ⟨agreed on the *division* of profits⟩ **2** : one of the parts, sections, or groupings into which a whole is divided: as **a** : a large self-contained military unit capable of independent action **b** : an administrative or operating unit of a governmental, business, or educational organization **3** : a group of organisms forming part of a larger group; *esp* : a primary category of the plant kingdon **4** : something that divides, separates, or marks off ⟨the *divisions* of the compass⟩ **5** : difference in opinion or interest : DISAGREEMENT [Middle French, from Latin *divisio,* from *dividere* "to divide"] — **di•vi•sion•al** \-'vizh-nəl, -ən-l\ *adj*
division of labor : the distribution of tasks among members of a group or to different areas to increase efficiency
di•vi•sive \də-'vī-siv *also* -'viz-iv\ *adj* : creating disunity or dissension — **di•vi•sive•ly** *adv* — **di•vi•sive•ness** *n*
di•vi•sor \də-'vī-zər\ *n* : the number by which a dividend is divided
¹di•vorce \də-'vōrs, -'vȯrs\ *n* **1** : a complete legal dissolution of a marriage **2** : complete separation [Middle French *divorse,* from Latin *divortium,* from *divertere, divortere* "to divert, leave one's husband"]
²divorce *vt* **1 a** : to obtain a divorce from (one's spouse) **b** : to dissolve the marriage between (two spouses) **2** : SEPARATE, DISUNITE ⟨*divorce* church from state⟩ — **di•vorce•ment** \-mənt\ *n*
di•vor•cée \də-,vōr-'sā, -,vȯr-, -'sē\ *n* : a divorced woman [French]
div•ot \'div-ət\ *n* : a piece of turf dug from a golf fairway in making a stroke [origin unknown]
di•vulge \də-'vəlj, dī-\ *vt* : to make known : DISCLOSE, REVEAL ⟨*divulge* a secret⟩ [Latin *divulgare,* from *dis-* + *vulgare* "to spread abroad", from *vulgus* "mob, common people"] — **di•vul•gence** \-'vəl-jəns\ *n*
Dix•ie \'dik-sē\ *n* : the southern states of the United States [name for the southern states in the song *Dixie* (1859) by Daniel D. Emmett]
Dix•ie•crat \-,krat\ *n* : a dissident southern Democrat; *esp* : a supporter of a 1948 presidential ticket opposing the civil rights stand of the regular Democrats — **Dix•ie•crat•ic** \,dik-sē-'krat-ik\ *adj*
¹diz•zy \'diz-ē\ *adj* **diz•zi•er; -est** **1 a** : having a whirling sensation in the head : GIDDY **b** : mentally confused **2 a** : causing or associated with a whirling sensation or a feeling of falling ⟨a *dizzy* height⟩ **b** : extremely rapid ⟨works at a *dizzy* pace⟩ [Old English *dysig* "stupid"] — **diz•zi•ly** \'diz-ə-lē\ *adv* — **diz•zi•ness** \'diz-ē-nəs\ *n*
²dizzy *vt* **diz•zied; diz•zy•ing** : to cause to feel dizzy
DNA \,dē-,en-'ā\ *n* : any of various nucleic acids that are found especially in cell nuclei, are the molecular basis of heredity in many organisms, and are constructed of a double helix held together by hydrogen bonds in an arrangement much like a rope ladder coiled like a corkscrew — compare RNA [deoxyribonucleic acid]
¹do \dü, 'dü\ *vb* **did** \did, 'did, dəd\; **done** \'dən\; **do•ing** \'dü-ing\; **does** \dəz, 'dəz\ **1 a** : to carry out : PERFORM ⟨*do* some work⟩ ⟨*do* me a favor⟩ **b** : to work on ⟨*doing* a puzzle⟩ **2** : ACT, BEHAVE ⟨*do* as I say, not as I *do*⟩ **3 a** : to affect in a usually specified way ⟨it might *do* you good⟩ **b** : to act so as to cause or create a feeling or sense of ⟨*do* honor to a soldier's memory⟩ **4 a** : to be successful : get along : FLOURISH ⟨not *doing* very well in school⟩ **b** : to be in regard to health : FEEL ⟨*doing* well after the operation⟩ **5** : to carry on in one's affairs : MANAGE ⟨can *do* without your help⟩ **6** : to take place : HAPPEN ⟨see what's *doing* tonight⟩ **7** : to come or bring to an end : FINISH — used in the past participle ⟨the work is finally *done*⟩ **8** : to put forth (as an effort) ⟨*do* your best to win⟩ **9** : to be about one's work or duty ⟨up and *doing*⟩ **10** : to produce by creative effort ⟨*do* a sketch⟩ **11** : to deal with or treat in a sense of preparing, putting in order, or giving care and attention ⟨*did* the dishes⟩ ⟨must *do* my hair⟩ **12** : DECORATE, FURNISH ⟨*did* the bedroom in blue⟩ **13** : to work at as a vocation ⟨what do you *do* for a living⟩ **14 a** : to travel at a speed of ⟨I was only *doing* 55, officer⟩ **b** : to visit and explore as or as if sightseeing : enjoy the sights and attractions of ⟨*did* Europe last fall⟩ ⟨*doing* the town⟩ **15** : to be suitable to the needs of : be adequate or fitting : SERVE ⟨worms will *do* us for bait⟩ **16** : to endure (as a term) in prison ⟨*doing* 20 years for armed robbery⟩ **17** : to be approved of especially by custom, propriety, or opinion : be fitting or appropriate — usually used in the negative ⟨it just won't *do* to be late⟩ **18** — used with *so* or a pronoun object as a substitute verb to avoid repetition ⟨if you must make a racket, *do* it somewhere else⟩ **19** — used as an auxiliary verb (1) before the subject of an interrogative sentence ⟨*do* you work?⟩ and after certain adverbs ⟨rarely *do* I go out⟩ ⟨they work and so *do* I⟩, (2) in a negative statement ⟨you *don't* look well⟩, (3) for emphasis ⟨*do* be careful⟩, and (4) as a substitute for a preceding verb or verb phrase ⟨this looks better than that *does*⟩ [Old English *dōn*] — **do away with** **1** : to put an end to : ABOLISH **2** : to put to death : KILL — **do by** : to deal with : TREAT ⟨*did* well *by* us⟩ — **do for** **1** : to bring about the death or ruin of **2** : to attend to the wants and needs of — **do one proud** : to give cause for pride or gratification — **do one's thing** : to engage in an activity or pursuit that is personally satisfying or rewarding
²do \'dō\ *n* : the 1st note of the diatonic scale [Italian]
do•able \'dü-ə-bəl\ *adj* : capable of being done
dob•bin \'däb-ən\ *n* **1** : a farm horse **2** : a quiet plodding horse [*Dobbin,* nickname for *Robert*]
Do•ber•man pin•scher \,dō-bər-mən-'pin-chər\ *n* : a short-haired medium-sized working dog of a breed of German origin [Ludwig *Dobermann,* 19th century German dog breeder]
dob•son \'däb-sən\ *n* : HELLGRAMMITE [probably from the name *Dobson*]
dob•son•fly \-,flī\ *n* : a large-eyed winged insect with a large carnivorous aquatic larva — compare HELLGRAMMITE
do•cent \'dōs-nt; dō-'sent, dōt-\ *n* : TEACHER, LECTURER [obsolete German, from Latin *docēre* "to teach"]
doc•ile \'däs-əl\ *adj* : easily taught, led, or managed : TRACTABLE ⟨a *docile* child⟩ [Latin *docilis,* from *docēre* "to

teach"] — **do•cile•ly** \'däs-əl-lē, -ə-lē\ *adv* — **do•cil•i•ty** \dä-'sil-ət-ē, dō-\ *n*

[1]**dock** \'däk\ *n* : any of a genus of coarse weedy plants related to buckwheat that are used as potherbs and in folk medicine [Old English *docce*]

[2]**dock** *n* : the solid part of an animal's tail as distinguished from the hair [Old English *-docca* (as in *fingirdocca* "finger muscle")]

[3]**dock** *vt* **1** : to cut off the end of : cut short ⟨a *docked* tail⟩ **2** : to take away a part of : make a deduction from ⟨*dock* one's wages⟩

[4]**dock** *n* **1** : an artificial basin to receive ships that has gates to keep the water in or out **2** : a slip or waterway usually between two piers to receive ships **3** : a wharf or platform for the loading or unloading of materials ⟨a ship moored to the *dock*⟩ ⟨a loading *dock* for trucks⟩ **4** : a place or scaffolding for the inspection and repair of aircraft [probably from Dutch *docke* "dock, ditch", derived from Latin *ducere* "to lead"]

[5]**dock** *vb* **1** : to haul or guide into a dock **2** : to come or go into dock **3** : to join (as two spacecraft) mechanically while in space

[6]**dock** *n* : the place in a criminal court where a defendant stands or sits during trial [Flemish *docke* "cage"]

dock•age \'däk-ij\ *n* **1** : a charge for the use of a dock **2** : docking facilities **3** : the docking of ships

[1]**dock•et** \'däk-ət\ *n* **1 a** : a formal abridged record of the proceedings in a legal action **b** : a register of such records **2** : a list of legal causes to be tried **3** : a calendar of matters to be acted on : AGENDA [Middle English *doggette* "brief summary, abstract"]

[2]**docket** *vt* **1** : to mark with an identifying statement : LABEL **2** : to make a brief abstract of (as a legal matter) and enter it in a list **3** : to place on the docket for legal action

dock•hand \'däk-,hand\ *n* : LONGSHOREMAN

dock•yard \'däk-,yärd\ *n* : SHIPYARD

[1]**doc•tor** \'däk-tər\ *n* **1 a** : an eminent theologian declared a sound expounder of doctrine by the Roman Catholic Church — called also *doctor of the church* **b** : a learned or authoritative teacher **c** : a person holding one of the highest academic degrees (as a PhD) conferred by a university **2 a** : one skilled or specializing in healing; *esp* : a physician, surgeon, dentist, or veterinarian licensed to practice **b** : MEDICINE MAN [Medieval Latin, from Latin, "teacher", from *docēre* "to teach"] — **doc•tor•al** \-tə-rəl, -trəl\ *adj*

[2]**doctor** *vb* **doc•tored**; **doc•tor•ing** \-tə-ring, -tring\ **1 a** : to give medical treatment to **b** : to practice medicine **c** : to restore to good condition : REPAIR ⟨*doctor* an old clock⟩ **2 a** : to adapt or modify for a desired end ⟨*doctored* the play by abridging the last act⟩ **b** : to alter deceptively ⟨*doctored* the election returns⟩

doc•tor•ate \'däk-tə-rət, -trət\ *n* : the degree, title, or rank of a doctor

doc•tri•naire \,däk-trə-'naər, -'neər\ *n* : one who attempts to put an abstract theory into effect without regard to practical difficulties [French, from *doctrine* "doctrine"] **syn** see DICTATORIAL — **doctrinaire** *adj*

doc•trine \'däk-trən\ *n* **1** : something that is taught **2** : a principle or position or the body of principles in a branch of knowledge or system of belief **3** : a principle of law established through past decisions [Latin *doctrina* "teaching, instruction", from *doctor* "teacher"] — **doc•tri•nal** \-trən-l\ *adj* — **doc•tri•nal•ly** \-l-ē\ *adv*

• **syn** DOCTRINE, DOGMA, TENET mean a principle accepted as authoritative. DOCTRINE strictly implies authoritative teaching accepted by a body of believers or adherents of a philosophy or school ⟨Christian *doctrine*⟩ ⟨a mathematical *doctrine*⟩ but also denotes a theory supported by evidence and proposed for acceptance ⟨the *doctrine* of evolution⟩ DOGMA implies a doctrine laid down as true and beyond dispute; TENET stresses acceptance and belief of a principle and implies a body of adherents ⟨the *tenets* of socialism are not identical with the *doctrines* of Marx⟩

[1]**doc•u•ment** \'däk-yə-mənt\ *n* : a usually original or official paper furnishing information or used as proof of something [Middle French, from Latin *documentum* "lesson, proof", from *docēre* "to teach"] — **doc•u•men•tal** \,däk-yə-'ment-l\ *adj*

[2]**doc•u•ment** \'däk-yə-,ment\ *vt* : to furnish documentary evidence of ⟨*document* a case with an adversary's own statements⟩ — **doc•u•ment•able** \-ə-bəl, ,däk-yə-'ment-\ *adj*

[1]**doc•u•men•ta•ry** \,däk-yə-'ment-ə-rē, -'men-trē\ *adj* **1** : consisting of or being documents; *also* : contained or certified in writing ⟨*documentary* proof⟩ **2** : giving factual material in artistic form ⟨a *documentary* film⟩ — **doc•u•men•tar•i•ly** \-mən-'ter-ə-lē, -,men-\ *adv*

[2]**documentary** *n, pl* **-ries** : a documentary presentation (as a film)

doc•u•men•ta•tion \,däk-yə-mən-'tā-shən, -,men-\ *n* **1** : the providing or the using of documents in proof of something **2** : evidence in the form of documents or references (as in footnotes) to documents

[1]**dod•der** \'däd-ər\ *n* : any of a genus of leafless herbs deficient in chlorophyll and parasitic on other plants [Middle English *doder*]

[2]**dodder** *vi* **dod•dered**; **dod•der•ing** \'däd-ring, -ə-ring\ **1** : to tremble from weakness or age **2** : to progress feebly [Middle English *dadiren*]

dod•der•ing *adj* : feeble and dull especially from age

do•deca•gon \dō-'dek-ə-,gän\ *n* : a polygon of 12 angles and 12 sides [Greek *dōdekagōnon*, from *dōdeka* "twelve" + *-gōnon* "-gon"]

do•deca•he•dron \,dō-,dek-ə-'hē-drən\ *n, pl* **-drons** *or* **-dra** \-drə\ : a solid having 12 plane faces

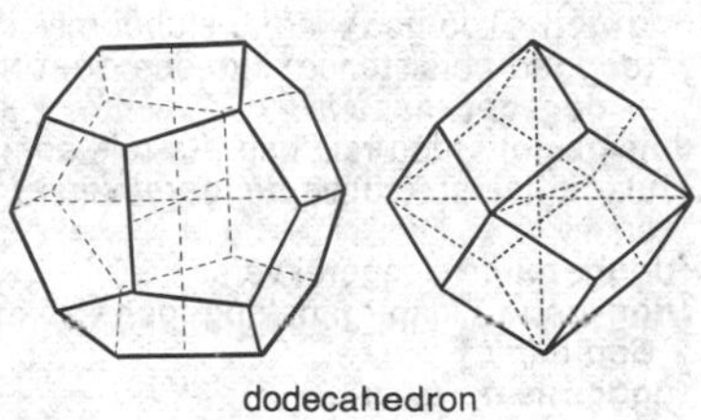

dodecahedron

[1]**dodge** \'däj\ *vb* **1 a** : to move suddenly aside **b** : to avoid by moving quickly aside ⟨*dodge* a batted ball⟩ **2** : to avoid by trickery or evasion ⟨*dodge* work⟩ [origin unknown]

[2]**dodge** *n* **1** : an act of evading by sudden bodily movement **2 a** : an artful device to evade, deceive, or trick ⟨crafty legal *dodges*⟩ **b** : EXPEDIENT 2

dodge ball *n* : a game in which players stand in a circle and attempt to hit a player within the circle with a large inflated ball

dodg•er \'däj-ər\ *n* **1** : one that dodges; *esp* : one that uses trickery **2** : a small handbill **3** : a cake made of cornmeal

do•do \'dōd-ō\ *n, pl* **dodoes** *or* **dodos** **1** : a large heavy flightless extinct bird related to the pigeons and formerly found on some of the islands of the Indian ocean **2 a** : a person hopelessly behind the times **b** : a stupid person [Portuguese *doudo*, from *doudo* "silly, stupid"]

doe \'dō\ *n, pl* **does** *or* **doe** : an adult female deer; *also* : the female especially when adult of any mammal (as an antelope or hare) of which the male is called *buck* [Old English *dā*]

do•er \'dü-ər\ *n* : one that does; *esp* : a person who gets things done

does *present 3d sing of* DO

doe•skin \'dō-,skin\ *n* **1** : the skin of does or leather made of it; *also* : soft leather from sheepskins or lambskins **2** : a soft firm cloth

doesn't \'dəz-nt\ : does not

do•est \'dü-əst\ *archaic present 2d sing of* DO

do•eth \'dü-əth\ *archaic present 3d sing of* DO

doff \'däf, 'dȯf\ *vt* **1** : to take off (one's clothes); *esp* : to take off or lift up (the hat) **2** : to rid oneself of : put aside [Middle English *doffen*, from *don* "to do" + *of* "off"]

[1]**dog** \'dȯg\ *n* **1 a** : a variable flesh-eating domesticated mammal probably descended form the common wolf **b** : an animal of the family to which the domesticated dog belongs **c** : a male dog **2 a** : a worthless fellow **b** : FELLOW, CHAP ⟨a lazy *dog*⟩ **3** : any of various devices for holding, gripping, or fastening that consist of a spike, rod, or bar **4** : affected stylishness or dignity ⟨put on the *dog*⟩ **5** *pl, slang* : FEET **6** *pl* : RUIN ⟨go to the *dogs*⟩ [Old English *docga*] — **dog•like** \-,līk\ *adj*

[2]**dog** *vt* **dogged**; **dog•ging** **1** : to hunt or track like a hound **2** : HOUND ⟨*dogged* by bad luck⟩

dog•bane \'dȯg-,bān\ *n* : any of a genus of chiefly tropical and

\ə\ abut	\au̇\ **out**	\i\ **tip**	\ȯ\ **saw**	\u̇\ **foot**
\ər\ **further**	\ch\ **chin**	\ī\ **life**	\ȯi\ **coin**	\y\ **yet**
\a\ **mat**	\e\ **pet**	\j\ **job**	\th\ **thin**	\yü\ **few**
\ā\ **take**	\ē\ **easy**	\ng\ **sing**	\t͟h\ **this**	\yu̇\ **cure**
\ä\ **cot, cart**	\g\ **go**	\ō\ **bone**	\ü\ **food**	\zh\ **vision**

often poisonous plants with milky juice and small white or pink flowers

dog·cart \-ˌkärt\ *n* **1 :** a cart drawn by a dog **2 :** a light one-horse carriage with two seats back to back

dog·catch·er \-ˌkach-ər, -ˌkech-\ *n* **:** a community official assigned to catch and dispose of stray dogs

dog days *n pl* **:** the hot sultry period of summer between early July and early September **[**from their beginning at the date when the Dog Star (Sirius) rises just before the sun**]**

doge \ˈdōj\ *n* **:** the chief magistrate in the republics of Venice and Genoa **[**Italian dialect, from Latin *dux* "leader"**]**

dog–ear \ˈdȯ-ˌgiər\ *n* **:** the turned-down corner of a page of a book — **dog–ear** *vt*

dog–eared \-ˌgiərd\ *adj* **1 :** having dog-ears ⟨a *dog-eared* book⟩ **2 :** SHABBY 1, WORN, RUN-DOWN

dog–eat–dog \ˌdȯ-ˌgēt-ˈdȯg\ *adj* **:** marked by ruthless self-interest ⟨a *dog-eat-dog* business⟩

dog·face \ˈdȯg-ˌfās\ *n, slang* **:** SOLDIER; *esp* **:** INFANTRYMAN

dog·fight \-ˌfīt\ *n* **:** a fight between two or more fighter planes usually at close quarters

dog·fish \-ˌfish\ *n* **:** any of various small sharks that often appear in schools near shore

dog·ged \ˈdȯ-gəd\ *adj* **:** stubbornly determined **:** TENACIOUS ⟨*dogged* persistence⟩ **syn** see OBSTINATE — **dog·ged·ly** *adv* — **dog·ged·ness** *n*

dog·ger·el \ˈdȯg-rəl, ˈdäg-, -ə-rəl\ *adj* **:** loose in style and irregular in meter ⟨comic *doggerel* verse⟩ **[**Middle English *dogerel*]

[2]**doggerel** *n* **:** doggerel verse

[1]**dog·gone** \ˈdäg-ˈgän, ˈdȯg-ˈgȯn\ *vb* **:** DAMN 3 **[**euphemism for *God damn*]

[2]**doggone** *n* **:** DAMN 2

dog·goned *or* **dog·gone** \ˌdäg-ˌgän, -ˌgänd; ˌdȯg-ˌgȯn, -ˌgȯnd\ *adj or adv* **:** DAMNED

[1]**dog·gy** \ˈdȯ-gē\ *adj* **dog·gi·er**; **-est 1 :** of or resembling a dog **2 :** STYLISH, SHOWY

[2]**dog·gy** *or* **dog·gie** \ˈdȯ-gē\ *n, pl* **doggies :** a small dog

dog·house \ˈdȯg-ˌhau̇s\ *n* **:** a shelter for a dog — **in the doghouse :** in a state of disfavor

do·gie \ˈdō-gē\ *n, chiefly West* **:** a motherless calf in a range herd **[**origin unknown**]**

dog in the manger : a person who selfishly withholds from others something useless to himself **[**from the fable of the dog who prevented an ox from eating hay which he did not want himself**]**

dog·ma \ˈdȯg-mə, ˈdäg-\ *n, pl* **dog·mas** *also* **dog·ma·ta** \-mət-ə\ **1 a :** something held as an established opinion; *esp* **:** a tenet set forth as authoritative **b :** a point of view or opinion set forth as authoritative without adequate grounds **2 :** a doctrine or body of doctrines concerning faith or morals laid down by a church **[**Latin *dogmat-, dogma,* from Greek, from *dokein* "to seem, seem good"**] syn** see DOCTRINE

dog·mat·ic \dȯg-ˈmat-ik, däg-\ *adj* **1 :** characterized by or given to the use of dogmatism ⟨a *dogmatic* critic⟩ **2 :** of or relating to dogma **syn** see DICTATORIAL — **dog·mat·i·cal·ly** \-ˈmat-i-kə-lē, -klē\ *adv*

dog·ma·tism \ˈdȯg-mə-ˌtiz-əm, ˈdäg-\ *n* **1 :** positiveness in assertion of opinion especially when unwarranted or arrogant **2 :** a viewpoint or system of ideas based on inadequate study or knowledge

dog·ma·tist \-mət-əst\ *n* **:** one who dogmatizes

dog·ma·tize \-mə-ˌtīz\ *vb* **:** to speak or write dogmatically — **dog·ma·tiz·er** *n*

do–good·er \ˈdü-ˌgu̇d-ər\ *n* **:** an earnest usually impractical and often naive and ineffectual humanitarian or reformer

dog paddle *n* **:** an elementary form of swimming in which the head is kept out of the water and the arms paddle in the water while the legs maintain a kicking motion

Dog Star *n* **1 :** SIRIUS **2 :** PROCYON

dog tag *n* **1 :** a tag worn on a dog's neck bearing a license registration number **2 :** a military identification tag

dog·tooth violet \ˌdȯg-ˌtüth-\ *n* **:** any of a genus of small spring-flowering bulbous herbs of the lily family

[1]**dog·trot** \ˈdȯg-ˌträt\ *n* **:** an easy gait suggesting that of a dog

[2]**dogtrot** *vi* **:** to move or progress at a dogtrot

dog watch *n* **1 :** either of two shipboard watches from 4 to 6 and from 6 to 8 p.m. **2 :** any of various night shifts; *esp* **:** the last shift

dog·wood \ˈdȯg-ˌwu̇d\ *n* **:** any of a genus of trees and shrubs with clusters of small flowers often surrounded by four broad leaves resembling petals

doi·ly \ˈdȯi-lē\ *n, pl* **doilies 1 :** a small napkin **2 :** a small often decorative mat **[***Doily* or *Doyley,* 18th century London draper**]**

do in *vt* **1 :** to bring about the defeat or destruction of **:** RUIN ⟨*done in* by the stock-market crash⟩ **2 :** KILL ⟨tried to *do* them *in* with a club⟩ **3 :** to wear out **:** EXHAUST ⟨*done in* after work⟩

do·ing \ˈdü-ing\ *n* **1 :** the act of performing or executing **:** ACTION ⟨it will take some *doing* to beat this record⟩ **2** *pl* **a :** things that are done or that occur ⟨everyday *doings*⟩ **b** *dial* **:** social activities ⟨big *doings* tonight⟩

doit \ˈdȯit\ *n* **1 :** an old Dutch coin equal to about ¼ cent **2 :** TRIFLE 1 **[**Dutch *duit*]

do–it–your·self \ˌdü-ə-chər-ˈself\ *adj* **:** of, relating to, or designed for use in construction, repair, or artistic work done by an amateur or hobbyist ⟨*do-it-yourself* tools⟩

dol·ce \ˈdōl-chā\ *adv or adj* **:** SOFT 1b, SMOOTH — used as a direction in music **[**Italian, literally, "sweet", from Latin *dulcis*]

dol·ce far nien·te \ˈdōl-chē-ˌfär-nē-ˈent-ē\ *n* **:** delightful relaxation in carefree idleness **[**Italian, literally, "a sweet doing nothing"**]**

dol·drums \ˈdōl-drəmz, ˈdäl-\ *n pl* **1 :** a spell of listlessness or despondency **2 :** a part of the ocean near the equator abounding in calms and light shifting winds **3 :** a state of inactivity, stagnation, or slump **[**probably related to Old English *dol* "foolish"**]**

[1]**dole** \ˈdōl\ *n* **1 a** (1) **:** a giving out of food, money, or clothing to the needy (2) **:** money, food, or clothing so given **b :** a grant of government funds to the unemployed **2 :** something portioned out and distributed **[**Old English *dāl* "portion"**]**

[2]**dole** *vt* **1 :** to distribute as charity ⟨*doled* out blankets and clothing to the flood victims⟩ **2 :** to give out in small portions or gradually ⟨*dole* out stories each evening⟩

[3]**dole** *n, archaic* **:** GRIEF 1, SORROW **[**Old French *dol,* from Latin *dolor*]

dole·ful \ˈdōl-fəl\ *adj* **:** full of grief **:** SAD — **dole·ful·ly** \-fə-lē\ *adv* — **dole·ful·ness** *n*

doll \ˈdäl, ˈdȯl\ *n* **1 :** a small-scale figure of a human being used especially as a child's plaything **2 a :** a pretty but often scatterbrained young woman **b** *slang* **:** WOMAN 1 **c** *slang* **:** DARLING 1, SWEETHEART **d :** an attractive person **[**probably from *Doll,* nickname for *Dorothy*]

dol·lar \ˈdäl-ər\ *n* **1 :** TALER **2 :** a coin (as a Spanish piece of eight) patterned after the taler **3 a :** a basic monetary unit (as of the United States and Canada) **b :** a coin, note, or token representing one dollar **[**Dutch or Low German *daler,* from German *taler*]

△ **origin** In the mountains of northwestern Bohemia is the small town of Jáchymov. In the early 16th century the town was known by its German name, Sankt Joachimstal. At that time a silver mine was opened nearby, and coins were minted to which the name *joachimstaler* was applied. In German this was shortened to *taler.* Shortly afterward the Dutch or Low German form *daler* was borrowed into English to refer to the taler and other coins that were patterned after it. Our modern word *dollar* is a different spelling of this *daler.*

dollar diplomacy *n* **:** diplomacy held to be designed primarily to further private financial and commercial interests

dol·lop \ˈdäl-əp\ *n* **:** LUMP 1, BLOB ⟨a *dollop* of jelly⟩ **[**origin unknown**]**

doll up *vb* **:** to dress or decorate formally or elegantly

[1]**dolly** \ˈdäl-ē, ˈdȯ-lē\ *n, pl* **doll·ies 1 :** DOLL 1 **2 :** a platform on a roller or on wheels for transporting heavy objects; *esp* **:** a wheeled platform for a television or motion-picture camera

[2]**dolly** *vi* **doll·ied**; **doll·y·ing :** to move a motion-picture or television dolly about while shooting a scene

dol·man \ˈdōl-mən, ˈdȯl-, ˈdäl-\ *n* **:** a woman's coat made with dolman sleeves **[**French *doliman,* a kind of Turkish robe, from Turkish *dolama*]

dolman sleeve *n* **:** a sleeve that is very wide at the armhole and tight at the wrist

dol·men \ˈdōl-mən, ˈdȯl-, ˈdäl-\ *n* **:** a prehistoric monument consisting of two or more upright stones supporting a horizontal stone slab **[**French, from Breton *tolmen,* from *tol* "table" + *men* "stone"**]**

do·lo·mite \ˈdō-lə-ˌmīt, ˈdäl-ə-\ *n* **:** a mineral $CaMg(CO_3)_2$ consisting of a calcium magnesium carbonate found in crystals and in extensive beds as a compact limestone **[**Déodat de *Dolo-*

ieu, died 1801, French geologist] — **do•lo•mit•ic** \ˌdō-lə-ˈmit-ik, ˌdäl-ə-\ *adj*

do•lor \ˈdō-lər, ˈdäl-ər\ *n* : mental suffering or grief : SORROW [Middle French *dolour,* from Latin *dolor* "pain, grief", from *dolēre* "to feel pain, grieve"]

do•lor•ous \ˈdō-lə-rəs, ˈdäl-ə-\ *adj* : causing, marked by, or expressive of misery or grief — **do•lor•ous•ly** *adv* — **do•lor•ous•ness** *n*

dol•phin \ˈdäl-fən, ˈdȯl-\ *n* **1 a** : any of various small long-nosed toothed whales **b** : PORPOISE 1 **2** : either of two active spiny-finned marine food fishes noted for their brilliant colors when taken out of the water **3** *cap* : DELPHINUS [Middle French *dophin,* derived from Latin *delphinus,* from Greek *delphis*]

dolt \ˈdōlt\ *n* : a stupid person [probably related to Old English *dol* "foolish"] — **dolt•ish** \ˈdōl-tish\ *adj* — **dolt•ish•ly** *adv* — **dolt•ish•ness** *n*

Dom *n* **1** \ˌdäm\ — used as a title prefixed to the name of some monks and canons regular **2** \ˌdō^{n}\ — used as a title prefixed to the Christian name of a Portuguese or Brazilian man of rank [Latin *dominus* "master"]

-dom \dəm\ *n suffix* **1 a** : dignity : office ⟨duke*dom*⟩ **b** : realm : jurisdiction ⟨king*dom*⟩ **2** : state or fact of being ⟨free*dom*⟩ **3** : those having a (specified) office, occupation, interest, or character ⟨official*dom*⟩ [Old English *-dōm*]

do•main \dō-ˈmān, də-\ *n* **1 a** : complete and absolute ownership of land — compare EMINENT DOMAIN **b** : land completely owned **2** : a territory over which dominion is exercised **3** : a sphere of influence or activity ⟨the widening *domain* of science⟩ **4** : the set of values to which a mathematical variable is limited; *esp* : the set on which a function is defined — compare RANGE 8 **5** : a small region of a magnetic substance that contains a group of atoms all aligned in the same direction so that each group has the effect of a tiny magnet pointing in one direction [Middle French *domaine,* from Latin *dominium,* from *dominus* "master"]

[1]**dome** \ˈdōm\ *n* **1** *archaic* : a stately building : MANSION **2** : a large hemispherical roof or ceiling **3** : a natural formation that resembles the dome or cupola of a building ⟨elevated rock *domes*⟩ [Medieval Latin *domus* "church", from Latin, "house"]

[2]**dome** *vb* **1** : to cover with or as if with a dome **2** : to form into or swell upward or outward like a dome

[1]**do•mes•tic** \də-ˈmes-tik\ *adj* **1** : of or relating to the household or the family ⟨*domestic* life⟩ **2** : of, relating to, produced, or carried on within one country ⟨*domestic* trade⟩ **3 a** : living near or about human habitations ⟨*domestic* vermin⟩ **b** : adapted to life with and to the advantage of humans : TAME **4** : devoted to home duties and pleasures [Middle French *domestique,* from Latin *domesticus,* from *domus* "house, home"] — **do•mes•ti•cal•ly** \-ti-kə-lē, -klē\ *adv*

[2]**domestic** *n* : a household servant

domestic animal *n* : any of various animals (as the horse or sheep) adapted by humans to live and breed in domestication

do•mes•ti•cate \də-ˈmes-ti-ˌkāt\ *vt* **1** : to bring into domestic use : ADOPT ⟨European customs *domesticated* in America⟩ **2** : to fit for domestic life **3** : to adapt to life in intimate association with and to the advantage of human beings ⟨who *domesticated* the dog is unknown⟩ — **do•mes•ti•ca•tion** \də-ˌmes-ti-ˈkā-shən\ *n*

do•mes•tic•i•ty \ˌdō-ˌmes-ˈtis-ət-ē, də-\ *n, pl* **-ties 1** : the quality or state of being domestic or domesticated **2** : domestic activities or life **3** *pl* : domestic affairs

domestic prelate *n* : a priest having permanent honorary membership in the papal household

domestic science *n* : instruction in domestic management and the household arts (as cooking and sewing)

domestic system *n* : a system of manufacturing in the home with raw materials supplied by an employer

dom•i•cal \ˈdō-mi-kəl, ˈdäm-i-\ *adj* : relating to, shaped like, or having a dome

[1]**do•mi•cile** \ˈdäm-ə-ˌsīl, ˈdō-mə-; ˈdäm-ə-səl\ *n* **1** : a dwelling place : place of residence : HOME **2** : a person's fixed, permanent, and principal home for legal purposes [Middle French, from Latin *domicilium,* from *domus* "house"] — **do•mi•cil•i•ary** \ˌdäm-ə-ˈsil-ē-ˌer-ē, ˌdō-mə-\ *adj*

[2]**domicile** *vt* : to establish in or provide with a domicile

do•mi•cil•i•ate \ˌdäm-ə-ˈsil-ē-ˌāt, ˌdō-mə-\ *vb* **1** : DOMICILE **2** : DOMESTICATE 3 **3** : RESIDE

dom•i•nance \ˈdäm-nəns, -ə-nəns\ *n* : the fact or state of being dominant: as **a** (1) : dominant position in an order of forcefulness : AUTHORITY (2) : the relative position of an individual in a social hierarchy (as a pecking order) **b** : the condition of being the one of a pair of contrasting genes or traits controlled by genes that is expressed in preference to the other when both are represented in the genetic material **c** : the influence or control exerted over an ecological community by a dominant organism

[1]**dom•i•nant** \-nənt\ *adj* **1** : commanding, controlling, or prevailing over all others ⟨a *dominant* political figure⟩ **2** : overlooking from a higher elevation ⟨a *dominant* hill⟩ **3** : being the more effective or predominant in action of a pair of bodily structures ⟨*dominant* eye⟩ **4** : exhibiting genetic dominance — **dom•i•nant•ly** *adv*

[2]**dominant** *n* **1 a** : a dominant genetic gene or trait **b** : a kind of organism (as a species) that exerts a controlling influence on an ecological community **2** : the 5th note of the diatonic scale

dom•i•nate \ˈdäm-ə-ˌnāt\ *vb* **1** : to exert dominance over : be dominant ⟨refuse to be *dominated* by friends⟩ **2** : to have a commanding position or controlling power over ⟨the rock of Gibraltar *dominates* the straits⟩ **3** : to rise high above ⟨the mountain range was *dominated* by a single snow-capped peak⟩ [Latin *dominari,* from *dominus* "master"] — **dom•i•na•tive** \-ˌnāt-iv\ *adj* — **dom•i•na•tor** \-ˌnāt-ər\ *n*

dom•i•na•tion \ˌdäm-ə-ˈnā-shən\ *n* **1** : supremacy over another **2** : exercise of authority or power

dom•i•neer \ˌdäm-ə-ˈniər\ *vb* **1** : to rule in a haughty manner **2** : to be overbearing

dom•i•neer•ing *adj* : inclined to domineer **syn** see MASTERFUL — **dom•i•neer•ing•ly** \-iŋ-lē\ *adv* — **dom•i•neer•ing•ness** *n*

Do•min•i•can \də-ˈmin-i-kən\ *n* : a member of a mendicant Order of Preachers founded in 1215 [Saint *Dominic*] — **Dominican** *adj*

do•mi•nie *1 oftenest* ˈdäm-ə-nē, *2 oftenest* ˈdō-mə-\ *n* **1** *chiefly Scottish* : SCHOOLMASTER **2** : CLERGYMAN [derived from Latin *dominus* "master"]

do•min•ion \də-ˈmin-yən\ *n* **1** : supreme authority **2** : DOMAIN 2 **3** *often cap* : a self-governing nation of the British Commonwealth other than the United Kingdom that acknowledges the British monarch as chief of state [Middle French, from Latin *dominium,* from *dominus* "master"]

Dominion Day *n* : July 1 observed in Canada as a legal holiday in commemoration of the proclamation of dominion status in 1867

dom•i•no \ˈdäm-ə-ˌnō\ *n, pl* **-noes** *or* **-nos 1** : a long loose hooded cloak usually worn with a half mask as a masquerade costume **2 a** : a small rectangular block (as of wood or plastic) whose face is divided into two equal parts that are blank or bear from one to usually six dots arranged as on dice faces **b** *pl* : any of several games played with a set of usually 28 dominoes [French, probably derived from Latin *dominus* "master"]

△ **origin** English *domino* was borrowed from French but is ultimately derived from Latin *dominus,* which means "lord" or "master". The hooded cape worn in masquerades was given its French name of *domino* because it looks rather like the hooded capes worn by members of some religious orders. The name of the garment was probably derived from the Latin phrase "Benedicamus Domino" (Let us bless the Lord), used in prayers.

Another meaning of *domino* is "a rectangular block used in games". This *domino* came into our language from Italian, by way of French. Formerly, the winner of a game of dominoes would exclaim "Domino!" It is likely that this Italian exclamation originally meant "(I am) master!" Italian *domino,* meaning "master" or "lord", was derived from Latin *dominus.*

[1]**don** \ˈdän\ *n* **1** : a Spanish nobleman or gentleman — used as a title prefixed to the Christian name **2** : a head, tutor, or fellow in a college of Oxford or Cambridge University [Spanish, from Latin *dominus* "master"]

[2]**don** *vt* **donned; don•ning** : to put on : dress oneself in ⟨*don* an apron for washing dishes⟩ [*do* + *on*]

do•ña \ˌdō-nyə\ *n* : a Spanish woman of rank — used as a title

\ə\ **abut**	\au̇\ **out**	\i\ **tip**	\ȯ\ **saw**	\u̇\ **foot**
\ər\ **further**	\ch\ **chin**	\ī\ **life**	\ȯi\ **coin**	\y\ **yet**
\a\ **mat**	\e\ **pet**	\j\ **job**	\th\ **thin**	\yü\ **few**
\ā\ **take**	\ē\ **easy**	\ŋ\ **sing**	\t͟h\ **this**	\yu̇\ **cure**
\ä\ **cot, cart**	\g\ **go**	\ō\ **bone**	\ü\ **food**	\zh\ **vision**

prefixed to the Christian name [Spanish, from Latin *domina* "lady", from *dominus* "master"]

do•nate \'dō-,nāt, dō-'\ *vb* : to make a gift of; *esp* : to contribute to a public or charitable cause ⟨*donate* a site for a park⟩ ⟨*donate* to the scholarship fund⟩ [back-formation from *donation*] **syn** see GIVE — **do•na•tor** \-,nāt-ər, -'nāt-\ *n*

do•na•tion \dō-'nā-shən\ *n* **1** : the action of donating something **2** : a free contribution : GIFT [Latin *donatio,* from *donare* "to present", from *donum* "gift"]

[1]done \'dən\ *past participle of* DO

[2]done *adj* **1** : socially acceptable ⟨that's not the *done* thing⟩ **2** : physically exhausted : SPENT ⟨felt completely *done* at the end of the hike⟩ **3** : gone by : FINISHED **4** : doomed to failure, defeat, or death **5** : cooked sufficiently

do•nee \dō-'nē\ *n* : one that receives a gift [*don*or + *-ee*]

done for \'dən-,fȯr\ *adj* **1** : having no hope of surviving ⟨were *done for* when the boat sank⟩ **2** : WASHED-UP 1 ⟨that blunder means you are *done for* as a politician⟩

don•jon \'dän-jən, 'dən-\ *n* : a massive inner tower in a medieval castle [Middle French, derived from Latin *dominus* "lord, master"]

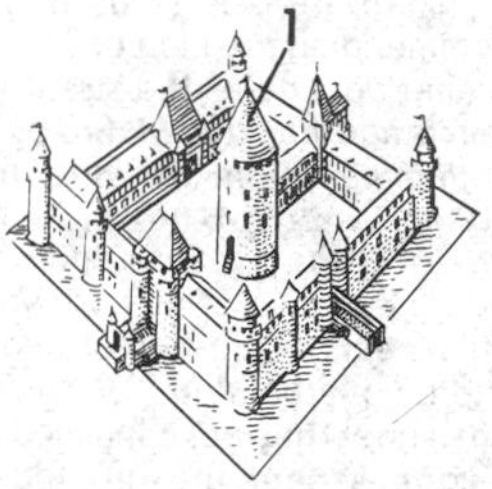

1 donjon

Don Juan \'dän-'wän, -'hwän; dän-'jü-ən\ *n* : [5]RAKE [*Don Juan,* unprincipled nobleman of Spanish legend]

don•key \'däng-kē, 'dəng-, 'dȯng-\ *n, pl* **donkeys 1** : the domestic ass **2** : a stupid or stubborn person [perhaps from [1]*dun* + *-key* (as in *monkey*)]

donkey engine *n* **1** : a small usually portable auxiliary engine **2** : a small locomotive used in switching

don•na \,dän-ə\ *n, pl* **don•ne** \-ā\ : an Italian woman usually of rank — used as a title prefixed to the Christian name [Italian, from Latin *domina* "lady"]

don•nish \'dän-ish\ *adj* : suggestive of a university don ⟨a prim *donnish* greeting⟩ — **don•nish•ly** *adv* — **don•nish•ness** *n*

don•ny•brook \'dän-ē-,brůk\ *n, often cap* : an uproarious brawl [*Donnybrook* Fair, annual Irish event known for its brawls]

do•nor \'dō-nər, -,nȯr\ *n* **1** : one that donates **2** : one used as a source of biological material ⟨a blood *donor*⟩ [Middle French *doneur,* from Latin *donator,* from *donare* "to present"] — **do•nor•ship** \-,ship\ *n*

do-noth•ing \'dü-,nəth-ing\ *adj* : marked by inactivity; *esp* : marked by lack of ambition, unwillingness to disturb the existing state of affairs, or failure to make positive progress ⟨a *do-nothing* government⟩ — **do-noth•ing•ism** \-ing-,iz-əm\ *n*

don't \dōnt, 'dōnt\ : do not

do•nut *variant of* DOUGHNUT

doo•dad \'dü-,dad\ *n* : a small article whose common name is unknown or forgotten [origin unknown]

[1]doo•dle \'düd-l\ *vb* **doo•dled; doo•dling** \'düd-ling, -l-ing\ : to draw or scribble aimlessly while occupied with something else [perhaps from earlier *doodle* "to ridicule", from *doodle* "fool"] — **doo•dler** \'düd-lər, -l-ər\ *n*

[2]doodle *n* : something produced by doodling

doo•dle•bug \'düd-l-,bəg\ *n* **1** : the larva of an ant lion **2** : a device (as a divining rod) used in attempting to locate underground gas, water, oil, or ores [probably from *doodle* "fool"]

doo•hick•ey \'dü-,hik-ē\ *n* : DOODAD [probably from *doodad* + *hickey* "gadget", of unknown origin]

[1]doom \'düm\ *n* **1 a** : a judicial decision; *esp* : a judicial sentence **b** (1) : a final determining of what is just (2) : JUDGMENT DAY **2 a** : an inevitable and usually calamitous state or end **b** : DEATH 2, RUIN [Old English *dōm* "law, judgment"] **syn** see FATE

[2]doom *vt* **1** : to give judgment against : CONDEMN **2 a** : to fix the fate of : DESTINE **b** : to ensure the failure or destruction of

dooms•day \'dümz-,dā\ *n* : JUDGMENT DAY

door \'dōr, 'dȯr\ *n* **1 a** : a usually swinging or sliding barrier by which an entry (as in a building) is closed and opened **b** : a similar part of a piece of furniture **2** : DOORWAY **3** : a means of access ⟨the *door* to success⟩ [Old English *duru* "door" and *dor* "gate"]

door•bell \'dōr-,bel, 'dȯr-\ *n* : a bell, gong, or set of chimes to be rung usually by a push button at an outside door

door•jamb \-,jam\ *n* : an upright piece forming the side of a door opening

door•keep•er \-,kē-pər\ *n* : one that tends a door

door•knob \-,näb\ *n* : a knob that when turned releases a door latch

door•man \-,man, -mən\ *n* **1** : DOORKEEPER **2** : one who tends a door (as of a hotel) and assists people by calling taxis and helping them in and out of cars

door•mat \-,mat\ *n* : a mat placed before or inside a door for wiping dirt from the shoes

door•nail \-,nāl, -'nāl\ *n* : a large-headed nail — used chiefly in the phrase *dead as a doornail*

door•plate \-,plāt\ *n* : a nameplate on a door

door•post \-,pōst\ *n* : DOORJAMB

door•sill \-,sil\ *n* : SILL 1b

door•step \-,step\ *n* : a step or series of steps before an outer door

door•way \-,wā\ *n* **1** : the opening that a door closes **2** : a means of gaining access

door•yard \-,yärd\ *n* : a yard outside the door of a house

[1]dope \'dōp\ *n* **1 a** : a thick liquid or pasty preparation **b** : a preparation for giving a desired quality to a substance or surface; *esp* : an antiknock added to gasoline **2 a** : a restricted or illicit drug (as heroin) **b** : a stupid person **3** : information especially from a reliable source [Dutch *doop* "sauce", from *dopen* "to dip"]

[2]dope *vt* **1** : to treat or affect with dope; *esp* : to give a narcotic to **2** *slang* : to guess the result of : predict (an outcome) especially by means of special information or skill ⟨*dope* out which team will win⟩ — **dop•er** *n*

dope•ster \'dōp-stər\ *n* : a forecaster of the outcome of future events (as sports contests or elections)

dop•ey \'dō-pē\ *adj* **dop•i•er; -est 1** : dulled by or as if by alcohol or a narcotic **2** : DULL 1, 2, 3 — **dop•i•ness** *n*

Dopp•ler effect \'däp-lər-\ *n* : a change in the frequency with which waves (as of sound or light) from a given source reach an observer when the source and observer are in rapid motion with respect to each other [Christian J. *Doppler,* died 1853, Austrian physicist and mathematician]

Do•ri•an \'dōr-ē-ən, 'dȯr-\ *n* : one of a Hellenic race that completed the overthrow of Mycenaean civilization and settled especially in the Peloponnesus and Crete [*Doris,* region of ancient Greece] — **Dorian** *adj*

Dor•ic \'dȯr-ik, 'där-\ *adj* **1** : of, relating to, or characteristic of the Dorians **2** : belonging to the oldest and simplest Greek architectural order

dorm \'dȯrm\ *n* : DORMITORY 2

dor•mant \'dȯr-mənt\ *adj* **1** : not active but capable of resuming activity ⟨a *dormant* volcano⟩ **2 a** : sleeping or appearing to be asleep : SLUGGISH **b** : biologically inactive; *esp* : not actively growing ⟨a *dormant* bud⟩ **3** : of, relating to, or used during a period of inactivity or lack of growth ⟨a *dormant* condition⟩ ⟨*dormant* sprays⟩ [Middle French, "stationary", from *dormir* "to sleep", from Latin *dormire*] **syn** see LATENT — **dor•man•cy** \-mən-sē\ *n*

dor•mer \'dȯr-mər\ *n* : a window placed upright in a sloping roof; *also* : a roofed structure containing such a window [Middle French *dormeor* "dormitory", from Latin *dormitorium*]

dor•mi•to•ry \'dȯr-mə-,tōr-ē, -,tȯr-\ *n, pl* **-ries 1** : a room for sleeping; *esp* : a large room containing a number of beds **2** : a residence hall providing sleeping rooms [Latin *dormitorium,* from *dormire* "to sleep"]

dor•mouse \'dȯr-,maůs\ *n, pl* **dor•mice** \-,mīs\ : any of numerous Old World rodents that resemble small squirrels [perhaps from Middle French *dormir* "to sleep"]

dors- *or* **dorsi-** *or* **dorso-** *combining form* : back : dorsal ⟨*dorsad*⟩ ⟨*dorso*ventral⟩ [Latin *dorsum*]

dor•sad \'dȯr-,sad\ *adv* : toward the back : DORSALLY

dor•sal \'dȯr-səl\ *adj* : relating to or situated near or on the back (as of an animal) — **dor•sal•ly** \-sə-lē\ *adv*

dorsal fin *n* : a fin on the ridge along the middle of the back of a fish

dorsal lip *n* : the dorsal margin of the blastopore of a gastrula

dor•so•ven•tral \,dȯr-sō-'ven-trəl\ *adj* : extending from the dorsal toward the ventral side — **dor•so•ven•tral•ly** \-trə-lē\ *adv*

dor•sum \'dȯr-səm\ *n, pl* **dor•sa** \-sə\ : the dorsal surface (as of an animal or one of its parts) [Latin, "back"]

do•ry \'dōr-ē, 'dȯr-\ *n, pl* **dories** : a flat-bottomed rowboat with a sharp bow and high sides that curve upward and outward [of American Indian origin]

dos•age \ˈdō-sij\ *n* **1 a** : the giving of medicine in doses **b** : the amount of a single dose **2 a** : the addition of a substance or the application of an agent in a measured dose **b** : the presence and relative representation or strength of a factor or agent

1dose \ˈdōs\ *n* **1 a** : the measured amount of a medicine to be taken at one time **b** : the quantity of radiation administered or absorbed **2** : a portion of a substance added during a process **3** : an experience to which one is exposed ⟨a *dose* of defeat⟩ [French, from Late Latin *dosis,* from Greek, literally, "act of giving", from *didonai* "to give"]

2dose *vt* **1** : to give medicine to **2** : to divide (as a medicine) into doses **3** : to treat with an application or agent

do•sim•e•ter \dō-ˈsim-ət-ər\ *n* : an instrument for measuring doses of X rays or of radioactivity

dos•sier \ˈdȯs-ˌyā, ˈdȯs-ē-ˌā, ˈdäs-\ *n* : a file of papers containing a detailed report or detailed information [French, "bundle of documents labeled on the back, dossier", from *dos* "back", from Latin *dorsum*]

dost \dəst, ˈdəst\ *archaic present 2d sing of* DO

1dot \ˈdät\ *n* **1** : a small spot : SPECK **2 a** : a small point made with or as if with a pen **b** (1) : a point after a note or rest in music indicating increase of the time value by one half (2) : a point over or under a note indicating staccato **c** : DECIMAL POINT **d** : a centered point used as a sign of multiplication **3** : a precise point in time or space **4** : a short click or buzz forming a letter or part of a letter (as in the Morse code) [Old English *dott* "head of a boil"]

2dot *vt* **dot•ted; dot•ting 1** : to mark with a dot ⟨*dot* an *i*⟩ **2** : to cover with or as if with dots ⟨a lake *dotted* with boats⟩ — **dot•ter** *n*

3dot \ˈdȯt\ *n* : DOWRY [French, from Latin *dot-, dos*] — **do•tal** \ˈdōt-l\ *adj*

dot•age \ˈdōt-ij\ *n* : SECOND CHILDHOOD, SENILITY

dot•ard \ˈdōt-ərd\ *n* : a person in his or her dotage

dote \ˈdōt\ *vi* **1** : to be feebleminded especially from old age **2** : to show excessive or foolish affection or fondness ⟨*doted* on their grandchildren⟩ [Middle English *doten*] — **dot•er** *n* — **dot•ing•ly** \-ing-lē\ *adv*

doth \dəth, ˈdəth\ *archaic present 3d sing of* DO

dotted swiss *n* : a sheer light muslin ornamented with evenly spaced raised dots

dot•ter•el \ˈdät-ə-rəl, ˈdä-trəl\ *n* : a Eurasian plover formerly common in England; *also* : any of several related birds [Middle English *dotrelle,* from *doten* "to dote"]

dotterel

dot•tle \ˈdät-l\ *n* : unburned and partly burned tobacco caked in the bowl of a pipe [Middle English *dottel* "plug"]

dot•ty \ˈdät-ē\ *adj* **dot•ti•er; -est** : mentally unbalanced : CRAZY [derived from Middle English *doten* "to dote"]

1dou•ble \ˈdəb-əl\ *adj* **1** : TWOFOLD, DUAL ⟨serving a *double* function⟩ **2** : consisting of two members or parts **3** : being twice as great or as many **4** : DECEITFUL 1 **5** : folded in two **6** : having more than the usual number of floral leaves ⟨*double* roses⟩ [Old French, from Latin *duplus,* from *duo* "two" + *-plus* "-fold"] — **dou•ble•ness** *n*

2double *n* **1 a** : something twice another ⟨12 is the *double* of 6⟩ **b** : a base hit in baseball that enables the batter to reach second base **2** : COUNTERPART; *esp* : a person who closely resembles another **3** : a sharp turn : REVERSAL **4 a** : something that is folded in two **b** : a combined bet placed on two different contests **5** *pl* : a game between two pairs of players **6** : an act of doubling in a card game

3double *adv* **1** : to twice the extent or amount : DOUBLY **2** : two together ⟨sleep *double*⟩

4double *vb* **dou•bled; dou•bling** \ˈdəb-ling, -ə-ling\ **1 a** : to make, be, or become twice as great or as many **b** : to make a call in bridge that increases the value of tricks over or less than (an opponent's bid) **2 a** : to make double by bending one part over another **b** : CLENCH 3 ⟨*double* one's fist⟩ **c** : to cause to stoop **d** : to become bent or folded usually in the middle **3** : to sail around (as a cape) by reversing direction **4** : to take the place of another **5** : to make a double in baseball **6** : to turn sharply and go back on one's course — **dou•bler** \ˈdəb-lər, -ə-lər\ *n*

double bar *n* : two vertical lines or a heavy single line separating principal sections of a musical composition

double bass *n* : the largest instrument of the viol family

double bassoon *n* : CONTRABASSOON

double bed *n* : a bed designed to sleep two persons

double boiler *n* : a cooking utensil consisting of two saucepans fitting into each other so that the contents of the upper can be cooked or heated by boiling water in the lower

double bond *n* : a chemical bond consisting of two covalent bonds between two atoms in a molecule

dou•ble–breast•ed \ˌdəb-əl-ˈbres-təd\ *adj* : having one half of the front lapped over the other and usually two rows of buttons

dou•ble–check \ˌdəb-əl-ˈchek, ˈdəb-əl-ˌ\ *vb* : to make or subject to a double check

double check *n* : a careful checking to determine accuracy, condition, or progress especially of something already checked

double chin *n* : a fleshy or fatty fold under the chin — **dou•ble–chinned** \ˌdəb-əl-ˈchind\ *adj*

double cross *n* **1** : an act of betraying or cheating especially an associate **2** : a cross between first-generation hybrids of four separate inbred lines — **dou•ble–cross** \ˌdəb-əl-ˈkrȯs\ *vt* — **dou•ble–cross•er** *n*

double dagger *n* : a character ‡ used as a reference mark

dou•ble–deal•ing \ˌdəb-əl-ˈdē-ling\ *n* : DUPLICITY — **dou•ble–deal•er** *n* — **double–dealing** *adj*

dou•ble–deck•er \-ˈdek-ər\ *n* **1** : something (as a ship, bus, or bed) having two decks **2** : a 2-layered sandwich

double dribble *n* : an illegal action in basketball that occurs when a player resumes a dribble after allowing the ball to come to rest in his or her hand or dribbles the ball with both hands simultaneously

dou•ble entendre \ˌdüb-ˌlän-ˈtändr, ˌdəb-, -ə-ˌlän-\ *n, pl* **dou•ble entendres** \-ˈtändr, -ˈtänd-rəz\ : a word or expression capable of two interpretations one of which is usually indelicate [obsolete French, literally, "double meaning"]

double entry *n* : a method of bookkeeping that debits the amount of a business transaction to one account and credits it to another so that the total debits equal the total credits

double fertilization *n* : fertilization characteristic of seed plants in which one of the two sperm nuclei fuses with the egg nucleus to form an embryo and the other fuses with the two separate or fused polar nuclei to form endosperm

dou•ble•head•er \ˌdəb-əl-ˈhed-ər\ *n* **1** : a train pulled by two locomotives **2** : two games, contests, or events held consecutively on the same program

double hyphen *n* : a punctuation mark ⸗ used in place of a hyphen at the end of a line to indicate that the word so divided is normally hyphenated

dou•ble–joint•ed \ˌdəb-əl-ˈjȯint-əd\ *adj* : having a joint that permits an exceptional degree of freedom of motion of the parts joined

double knit *n* : a knitted fabric made with a double set of needles to produce a double thickness of fabric with each thickness joined by interlocking stitches

double negative *n* : a nonstandard syntactic construction that contains two negatives and is intended to have a negative meaning (as in "I didn't hear nothing" instead of "I didn't hear anything")

dou•ble–park \ˌdəb-əl-ˈpärk\ *vb* : to park beside a row of vehicles already parked parallel to the curb

double play *n* : a single play in baseball in which two players are put out

double pneumonia *n* : pneumonia involving both lungs

dou•ble–quick \ˈdəb-əl-ˌkwik\ *n* : DOUBLE TIME — **dou•ble–quick** *vi*

dou•ble–space \ˌdəb-əl-ˈspās\ *vb* **1** : to type (copy) leaving every other line blank **2** : to type on every second line

double star *n* **1** : BINARY STAR **2** : two stars that appear as one to

the naked eye but can be seen as separate when viewed with a telescope
double sugar *n* : DISACCHARIDE
dou•blet \'dəb-lət\ *n* **1** : a close-fitting jacket worn by men of western Europe chiefly in the 16th century **2** : one of two similar or identical things **3** : one of two or more words in the same language derived by different routes from the same source ⟨*dish* and *disk* are *doublets*⟩ [Middle French, from *double* "double"]

D doublet 1

dou•ble–talk \'dəb-əl-ˌtȯk\ *n* **1** : language that appears to be meaningful but in fact is a mixture of sense and nonsense **2** : deliberately ambiguous language
dou•ble–time \'dəb-əl-ˌtīm\ *vi* : to move at double time
double time *n* **1** : a marching cadence of 180 36-inch steps per minute **2** : payment of a worker at twice the regular wage rate
double vision *n* : vision in which an object is seen as double due to unequal action of the eye muscles
dou•bloon \ˌdə-'blün\ *n* : an old gold coin of Spain and Spanish America worth 16 pieces of eight [Spanish *doblón*, derived from Latin *duplus* "double"]
dou•bly \'dəb-lē\ *adv* **1** : to twice the degree **2** : in a twofold manner
[1]**doubt** \'dau̇t\ *vb* **1** : to be uncertain about **2** : to lack confidence in : DISTRUST **3** : to consider unlikely [Old French *douter*, from Latin *dubitare*] — **doubt•able** \-ə-bəl\ *adj* — **doubter** *n* — **doubt•ing•ly** \-ing-lē\ *adv*
[2]**doubt** *n* **1** : uncertainty of belief or opinion **2** : a state of affairs that causes uncertainty or suspense ⟨the outcome is in *doubt*⟩ **3 a** : a lack of confidence : DISTRUST **b** : an inclination not to believe or accept
• **syn** DOUBT, UNCERTAINTY, DISTRUST, SUSPICION mean lack of sureness about someone or something. DOUBT implies uncertainty about the truth or reality of something and an inability to make a decision; UNCERTAINTY may range from a falling short of certainty to an almost complete lack of knowledge about an outcome or result; DISTRUST implies lack of trust or confidence on vague or general grounds; SUSPICION stresses lack of faith in the truth or reality of someone or something and implies an often unfounded charge of wrongdoing.
doubt•ful \'dau̇t-fəl\ *adj* **1** : not clear or certain as to fact ⟨a *doubtful* claim⟩ **2** : questionable in character ⟨*doubtful* intentions⟩ **3** : not settled in opinion : UNDECIDED ⟨*doubtful* about what to do⟩ **4** : not certain in outcome ⟨a *doubtful* battle⟩ — **doubt•ful•ly** \-fə-lē\ *adv* — **doubt•ful•ness** *n*
doubting Thom•as \-'täm-əs\ *n* : a habitually doubtful person [*Thomas*, apostle of Jesus who doubted Jesus' resurrection until he had proof of it (John 20:24–29)]
[1]**doubt•less** \'dau̇t-ləs\ *adv* **1** : without doubt **2** : PROBABLY
[2]**doubtless** *adj* : free from doubt : CERTAIN
douche \'düsh\ *n* **1 a** : a jet of fluid (as water) directed against a part or into a cavity of the body **b** : a cleansing with a douche **2** : a device for giving douches [French] — **douche** *vb*
dough \'dō\ *n* **1 a** : a soft mass of moistened flour or meal thick enough to knead or roll **b** : a comparably soft pasty mass **2** : MONEY 1, 2 [Old English *dāg*] — **doughy** \'dō-ē\ *adj*
dough•boy \'dō-ˌbȯi\ *n* : an American infantryman especially in World War I
dough•nut *or* **do•nut** \'dō-nət, -ˌnət\ *n* : a small usually ring-shaped cake fried in fat
dough•ty \'dau̇t-ē\ *adj* **dough•ti•er**; **-est** : being strong and valiant : BOLD [Old English *dohtig*] — **dough•ti•ly** \'dau̇t-l-ē\ *adv* — **dough•ti•ness** \'dau̇t-ē-nəs\ *n*
Doug•las fir \ˌdəg-ləs-\ *n* : a tall evergreen cone-bearing timber tree of the western United States; *also* : its wood [David *Douglas*, died 1834, Scottish botanist]
do up *vt* **1** : to put in order; *also* : REPAIR ⟨planned to *do up* the house⟩ **2** : WRAP 1b ⟨*do up* holiday packages⟩ **3** : ARRAY, CLOTHE ⟨all *done up* in a pirate costume⟩
dour \'dau̇r, 'du̇r\ *adj* **1** : STERN 3, HARSH **2** : MOROSE 1 [Latin *durus* "hard"] — **dour•ly** *adv* — **dour•ness** *n*
[1]**douse** \'dau̇s\ *vt* : to take in ⟨*douse* a sail⟩ [earlier *douse* "blow, stroke"]
[2]**douse** \'dau̇s, 'dau̇z\ *vt* **1 a** : to plunge into water **b** : to throw a liquid on : DRENCH **2** : to put out : EXTINGUISH
[1]**dove** \'dəv\ *n* **1** : any of numerous pigeons; *esp* : a small wild pigeon **2** : a person who advocates negotiations and compromise in a dispute; *esp* : an opponent of war — compare HAWK [Middle English] — **dov•ish** \'dəv-ish\ *adj*
[2]**dove** \'dōv\ *past of* DIVE
dove•cote \'dəv-ˌkōt, -ˌkät\ *or* **dove•cot** \-ˌkät\ *n* : a small raised house or box with compartments for domestic pigeons
dove•kie \'dəv-kē\ *n* : a small short-billed auk breeding on arctic coasts and ranging south in winter [derived from *dove*]
dove•tail \'dəv-ˌtāl\ *n* : something resembling a dove's tail; *esp* : a flaring projection on a board and a slot into which it fits tightly making an interlocking joint between two pieces
[2]**dovetail** *vb* **1 a** : to join by means of dovetails **b** : to cut to a dovetail **2** : to fit skillfully together to form a whole
dow•a•ger \'dau̇-i-jər\ *n* **1** : a widow holding property or a title received from her deceased husband **2** : a dignified elderly woman [Middle French *douagiere*, from *douage* "dower", from *douer* "to endow", from Latin *dotare*, from *dot-*, *dos* "gift, dower"]
[1]**dowdy** \'dau̇d-ē\ *n, pl* **dowd•ies** : a dowdy woman [Middle English *doude*]
[2]**dowdy** *adj* **dowd•i•er**; **-est** : not neatly or becomingly dressed or cared for : SHABBY, UNTIDY; *also* : lacking in smartness or taste — **dowd•i•ly** \'dau̇d-l-ē\ *adv* — **dowd•i•ness** \'dau̇d-ē-nəs\ *n*
[1]**dow•el** \'dau̇-əl, 'dau̇l\ *n* : a pin or peg projecting from one of two parts or surfaces (as of wood) to be fastened together and fitting into a hole prepared in the other part; *also* : a rod for cutting into dowels [Middle English *dowle*]
[2]**dowel** *vt* **-eled** *or* **-elled**; **-el•ing** *or* **-el•ling** : to fasten by or furnish with dowels
[1]**dow•er** \'dau̇-ər, 'dau̇r\ *n* **1** : the part of or interest in the real estate of a deceased husband given by law to his widow during her life **2** : DOWRY
[2]**dower** *vt* : to supply with a dower or dowry : ENDOW
[1]**down** \'dau̇n\ *n* : an undulating usually treeless upland with sparse soil — usually used in pl. [Old English *dūn* "hill"]
[2]**down** *adv* **1 a** (1) : toward or in a lower physical position (2) : to a lying or sitting position (3) : toward or to the ground, floor, or bottom **b** : in cash ⟨paid $10 *down*⟩ **2** : in a direction that is the opposite of up: as **a** : SOUTH **b** : away from a center (as of activity) ⟨went *down* to the country⟩ **3** : to or in a lower or worse condition, level, or status **4** : from a past time ⟨heirlooms handed *down*⟩ **5** : to or in a state of less activity ⟨excitement died *down*⟩ **6** : to a concentrated state ⟨boil *down* a report⟩ [Old English *dūne*, short for *adūne*, from *a-* "off, from" + *dūn* "hill"]
[3]**down** *adj* **1 a** : occupying a low position; *esp* : lying on the ground **b** : directed or going downward ⟨a *down* car⟩ **c** : being at a lower level ⟨sales were *down* because of bad weather⟩ **2 a** : being in a state of reduced or low activity **b** (1) : DEJECTED, DEPRESSED ⟨felt *down* after losing the game⟩ (2) : SICK ⟨*down* with flu⟩ (3) : having a low opinion or dislike ⟨was *down* on me for not helping⟩ **3** : DONE 3, FINISHED ⟨eight *down* and two to go⟩
[4]**down** *prep* : down along : down through : down toward : down in : down into : down on ⟨*down* the road⟩
[5]**down** *n* **1** : a low or falling period (as in activity, emotional life, or fortunes) ⟨have their ups and *downs*⟩ **2 a** : a complete play to advance the ball in football **b** : one of a series of four attempts to advance a football 10 yards
[6]**down** *vb* : to go or cause to go or come down
[7]**down** *n* **1** : a covering of soft fluffy feathers **2** : something soft and fluffy like down [Old Norse *dūnn*]
down•beat \'dau̇n-ˌbēt\ *n* : the downward stroke of a conductor indicating the principally accented note of a measure of music
down•cast \-ˌkast\ *adj* **1** : low in spirit : DISCOURAGED ⟨a *downcast* manner⟩ **2** : directed down ⟨*downcast* eyes⟩
down•draft \-ˌdraft\ *n* : a downward current of gas (as air in a chimney or during a thunderstorm)
down•er \'dau̇-nər\ *n* : a depressant drug; *esp* : BARBITURATE
down•fall \'dau̇n-ˌfȯl\ *n* **1** : FALL 2c; *esp* : a sudden or heavy fall (as of rain) **2** : a sudden descent (as from a high position) : RUIN ⟨the *downfall* of the beaten champion⟩ **3** : the cause of a

downfall ⟨drink was their *downfall*⟩ — **down•fall•en** \-ˌfo̊-lən\ *adj*

[1]**down•grade** \-ˌgrād\ *n* **1** : a downward grade or slope **2** : a decline toward a worse condition ⟨a neighborhood on the *downgrade*⟩ — **down•grade** \-ˈgrād\ *adv*

[2]**down•grade** \-ˌgrād\ *vt* : to lower in grade, rank, position, or status

down•heart•ed \ˈdau̇n-ˈhärt-əd\ *adj* : DEJECTED, DOWNCAST — **down•heart•ed•ly** *adv* — **down•heart•ed•ness** *n*

[1]**down•hill** \ˈdau̇n-ˈhil\ *adv* **1** : toward the bottom of a hill **2** : toward a lower state or level

[2]**down•hill** \-ˌhil\ *adj* : sloping downhill

[3]**downhill** *n* : a ski race in which individuals competing one at a time try to find the fastest most direct route down a long steep course

down payment *n* : a part of the full price paid at the time of purchase with the balance to be paid later

down•pour \ˈdau̇n-ˌpōr, -ˌpo̊r\ *n* : a heavy rain

down•range \-ˈrānj\ *adv* : toward the target area of a firing range ⟨a missile landing 5000 kilometers *downrange*⟩ — **down•range** *adj*

[1]**down•right** \-ˌrīt\ *adv* : OUTRIGHT 1 ⟨*downright* mean⟩

[2]**downright** *adj* **1** : ABSOLUTE 4, UTTER ⟨a *downright* lie⟩ **2** : PLAIN 4b, BLUNT ⟨a straightforward *downright* person⟩ — **down•right•ly** *adv* — **down•right•ness** *n*

Down's syndrome \ˈdau̇nz-\ *n* : an inherited condition marked by moderate to severe mental deficiency, by distinctive physical characteristics (as slanting eyes and broad hands with short fingers), and by the presence of three chromosomes of the chromosome pair numbered 21 in human beings — called also *mongolism* **[**J.L.H. *Down*, died 1896, English physician**]**

down•stage \-ˈstāj\ *adv or adj* : toward or at the front of a theatrical stage

[1]**down•stairs** \ˈdau̇n-ˈstaərz, -ˈsteərz\ *adv* : down the stairs : on or to a lower floor

[2]**down•stairs** \-ˌstaərz, -ˌsteərz\ *adj* : located on the main, lower, or ground floor of a building

[3]**down•stairs** \ˈdau̇n-ˈ, ˈdau̇n-ˌ\ *n* : the lower floor of a building

down•stream \ˈdau̇n-ˈstrēm\ *adv or adj* : in the direction of flow of a stream

down•stroke \-ˌstrōk\ *n* : a stroke made in a downward direction

down•swing \-ˌswing\ *n* **1** : a swing downward **2** : DOWNTURN 2

down–to–earth \ˌdau̇n-tə-ˈərth, -ˈwərth\ *adj* : free from frills or foibles : PRACTICAL

[1]**down•town** \ˈdau̇n-ˈtau̇n\ *adv* : to, toward, or in the lower part or business center of a town or city — **downtown** *adj*

[2]**down•town** \-ˌtau̇n\ *n* : an urban business center

down•trod•den \ˈdau̇n-ˈträd-n\ *adj* : crushed by superior power : OPPRESSED

down•turn \-ˌtərn\ *n* **1** : a turning downward **2** : a decline especially in business activity

[1]**down•ward** \ˈdau̇n-wərd\ *also* **down•wards** \-wərdz\ *adv* **1** : from a higher to a lower place or condition **2 a** : from an earlier time **b** : from an ancestor or predecessor

[2]**downward** *adj* **1** : moving or extending downward **2** : descending from a head, origin, or source

down•wind \ˈdau̇n-ˈwind\ *adv or adj* : in the direction that the wind is blowing

downy \ˈdau̇-nē\ *adj* **down•i•er**; **-est** **1** : suggesting a bird's down (as in softness or lightness) **2** : covered with or made of down

downy mildew *n* : a parasitic mold that bears whitish masses of spore-producing bodies on the undersurface of the leaves of the host; *also* : a plant disease caused by a downy mildew

dow•ry \ˈdau̇r-ē\ *n, pl* **dowries** **1** : the property that a woman brings to her husband in marriage **2** : a gift of money or property by a man to or for his bride **[**Anglo-French *dowarie*, from Medieval Latin *dotarium*, from Latin *dot-*, *dos* "gift, dower"**]**

dowse \ˈdau̇z\ *vb* : to use a divining rod especially to find water **[**origin unknown**]** — **dows•er** *n*

dox•ol•o•gy \däk-ˈsäl-ə-jē\ *n, pl* **-gies** : a usually liturgical expression of praise to God **[**Medieval Latin *doxologia*, from Late Greek, from Greek *doxa* "opinion, glory" + *-logia* "-logy"**]**

doze \ˈdōz\ *vi* : to sleep lightly **[**probably of Scandinavian origin**]** — **doze** *n* — **doz•er** *n*

doz•en \ˈdəz-n\ *n, pl* **dozens** *or* **dozen** : a group of twelve **[**Old French *dozaine*, from *doze* "twelve", from Latin *duodecim*, from *duo* "two" + *decem* "ten"**]** — **dozen** *adj* — **doz•enth** \-nth, -ntth\ *adj*

DP \ˈdē-ˈpē\ *n, pl* **DP's** *or* **DPs** : a displaced person

[1]**drab** \ˈdrab\ *n* : a light olive brown **[**Middle French *drap* "cloth", from Late Latin *drappus***]**

[2]**drab** *adj* **drab•ber**; **drab•best** **1** : of the color drab **2** : characterized by dullness and monotony : CHEERLESS ⟨they lead *drab* lives⟩ — **drab•ly** *adv* — **drab•ness** *n*

drachm \ˈdram\ *n* **1** : DRACHMA 2a **2** : DRAM 1, 2b

drach•ma \ˈdrak-mə\ *n, pl* **drach•mas** *or* **drach•mae** \-ˌmē, -ˌmī\ *or* **drach•mai** \-ˌmī\ **1 a** : any of various ancient Greek units of weight **b** : any of various modern units of weight; *esp* : DRAM 1 **2 a** : an ancient Greek silver coin equivalent to 6 obols **b** : the basic monetary unit of modern Greece; *also* : a coin representing this unit **[**Latin, "drachma, dram", from Greek *drachmē***]**

Dra•co \ˈdrā-kō\ *n* : a northern circumpolar constellation between the Big Dipper and Little Dipper **[**Latin, literally, "dragon"**]**

[1]**draft** \ˈdraft, ˈdráft\ *n* **1** : the act of drawing a net; *also* : the quantity of fish taken at one drawing **2** : the act of moving loads by drawing or pulling **3 a** : the force required to pull an implement **b** : load-pulling capacity **4 a** : the act or an instance of drinking or inhaling; *also* : the portion drunk or inhaled **b** : a potion prepared for drinking : DOSE **5 a** : DELINEATION, REPRESENTATION; *esp* : a construction plan ⟨the *draft* of a future building⟩ **b** : a preliminary sketch, outline, or version ⟨a rough *draft* of a thesis⟩ **6** : the act or result of drawing out or stretching **7** : the act of drawing (as from a cask); *also* : a portion of liquid so drawn **8** : the depth of water a ship draws especially when loaded **9 a** : the selection of a person especially for compulsory military service **b** : a group of persons selected **10 a** : an order (as a check) issued by one party to another (as a bank) to pay money to a third party **b** : a heavy demand : STRAIN ⟨a *draft* on national resources⟩ **11 a** : a current of air in an enclosed space **b** : a device for regulating the flow of air (as in a fireplace) **12** : ANGLE, TAPER; *esp* : the taper given to a pattern or die so that the work can be easily withdrawn **13** : a narrow border along the edge of a stone or across its face serving as a stonecutter's guide **14** : a system whereby exclusive rights to selected new players are apportioned among professional teams **[**Middle English *draght***]** — **on draft** : ready to be drawn from a receptacle ⟨beer *on draft*⟩

[2]**draft** *adj* **1** : used for drawing loads ⟨*draft* animals⟩ **2** : constituting a preliminary or tentative version, sketch, or outline ⟨a *draft* treaty⟩ **3** : being on draft ⟨*draft* beer⟩

[3]**draft** *vt* **1** : to select usually on a compulsory basis; *esp* : to conscript for military service **2 a** : to draw up a preliminary sketch, version, or plan of **b** : to draw up : COMPOSE ⟨*draft* a constitution⟩ **3** : to draw off or away ⟨water *drafted* by pumps⟩ — **draft•er** *n*

draft•ee \draf-ˈtē, dráf-\ *n* : a person who is drafted especially into the armed forces

drafts•man \ˈdraf-smən, ˈdráf-, ˈdraft-, ˈdráft-\ *n* : one who draws plans and sketches (as for machinery) — **drafts•man•ship** \-ˌship\ *n*

drafty \ˈdraf-tē, ˈdráf-\ *adj* **draf•ti•er**; **-est** : having or exposed to a draft ⟨a *drafty* hall⟩ — **draft•i•ly** \-tə-lē\ *adv* — **draft•i•ness** \-tē-nəs\ *n*

[1]**drag** \ˈdrag\ *n* **1** : something that is dragged, pulled, or drawn along or over a surface: as **a** : HARROW **b** : a sledge for carrying heavy loads **2** : something used to drag with; *esp* : a device for dragging under water to detect or obtain objects **3 a** : something that retards motion **b** : the retarding force acting on a body (as an airplane) moving through a fluid (as air) **c** : friction between engine parts **d** : something that hinders or obstructs progress **4 a** : the act or an instance of dragging or drawing **b** : a drawing along or over a surface with effort or pressure **c** : motion achieved with slowness or difficulty; *also* : the condition of having or seeming to have such motion **d** : a draw on a pipe, cigarette, or cigar : PUFF; *also* : a draft of liquid **5** : a movement, inclination, or retardation caused by or as if by

dragging **6** *slang* **:** influence securing special favor **7** *slang* **:** STREET 1, ROAD ⟨the main *drag*⟩ **8 :** one that is boring ⟨the movie was a *drag*⟩

[2]**drag** *vb* **dragged**; **drag•ging 1 a :** to draw slowly or heavily **:** HAUL **b :** to move or cause to move with painful slowness or difficulty ⟨*drags* one leg⟩ ⟨the story *drags*⟩ **c :** to bring by force or compulsion ⟨*dragged* them to the theater⟩ **d :** to pass (time) in lingering pain, tedium, or unhappiness **e :** PROTRACT ⟨*drag* a story out⟩ **2 :** to hang or lag behind **3 :** to trail along a surface **4 :** to explore, search, or fish with a drag **5 :** to inhale deeply ⟨*drag* on a cigarette⟩ [Old Norse *draga* or Old English *dragan*]

drag•ger \ˈdrag-ər\ *n* **:** one that drags; *esp* **:** a fishing boat operating a trawl or dragnet

drag•gle \ˈdrag-əl\ *vb* **drag•gled**; **drag•gling** \ˈdrag-ling, -ə-ling\ **1 :** to make or become wet and dirty by dragging **2 a :** to follow slowly **:** STRAGGLE **b :** to move along slowly [derived from *drag*]

drag•gy \ˈdrag-ē\ *adj* **drag•gi•er**; **-est 1 :** DULL 3 **2 :** TEDIOUS

drag•net \ˈdrag-ˌnet\ *n* **1 a :** a net drawn along the bottom of a body of water **:** TRAWL **b :** a net used (as to capture small game) on the ground **2 :** a network of planned actions for pursuing and catching a criminal

drag•o•man \ˈdrag-ə-mən\ *n, pl* **-mans** *or* **-men** \-mən\ **:** an interpreter chiefly of Arabic, Turkish, or Persian employed especially in the Near East [Middle French *drogman*, from Italian *dragomanno*, from Middle Greek *dragomanos*, from Arabic *tarjumān*, from Aramaic *tūrgĕmānā*]

drag•on \ˈdrag-ən\ *n* **1 :** an imaginary animal usually represented as a huge winged and scaly serpent or lizard with a crested head and enormous claws **2** *cap* **:** DRACO **3 :** a fierce or very strict person [Old French, from Latin *draco* "serpent, dragon", from Greek *drakōn* "serpent"]

drag•on•fly \-ˌflī\ *n* **:** any of an order (Odonata) of large harmless insects that have four long wings and feed especially on flies, gnats, and mosquitoes — compare DAMSELFLY

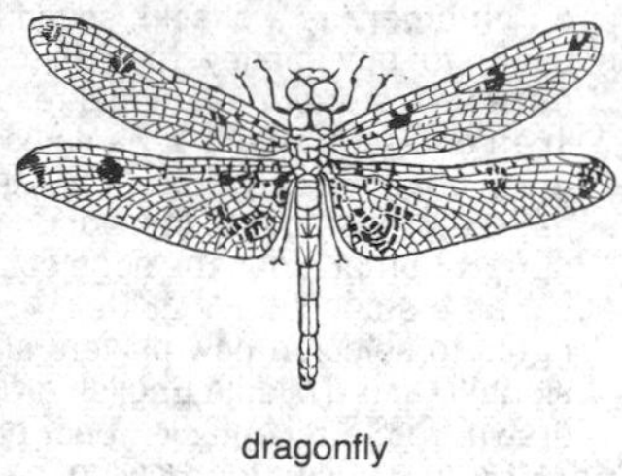
dragonfly

[1]**dra•goon** \drə-ˈgün, dra-\ *n* **:** a cavalry soldier [French *dragon* "dragon, dragoon"]

[2]**dragoon** *vt* **:** to force or attempt to force into submission by violent measures

drag race *n* **:** an acceleration contest between motor vehicles

[1]**drain** \ˈdrān\ *vb* **1 a :** to draw off or flow off gradually or completely ⟨*drain* water from a tank⟩ **b :** to cause the gradual disappearance of **:** DWINDLE **c :** to exhaust physically or emotionally **2 a :** to make or become gradually dry or empty ⟨let the dishes *drain*⟩ **b :** to carry away the surface water of **:** discharge surface or surplus water [Old English *drēahnian*] — **drain•er** *n*

[2]**drain** *n* **1 :** a means by which usually liquid matter is drained **2 a :** the act of draining **b :** a gradual outflow or withdrawal **:** DEPLETION **3 :** something that causes depletion **:** BURDEN ⟨a *drain* on one's resources⟩ — **down the drain :** used wastefully or brought to nothing

drain•age \ˈdrā-nij\ *n* **1 :** the act, process, or mode of draining; *also* **:** something drained off **2 :** a means for draining; *also* **:** a system of drains **3 :** an area drained

drain•pipe \ˈdrān-ˌpīp\ *n* **:** a pipe for drainage

drake *n* **:** a male duck [Middle English]

dram \ˈdram\ *n* **1 a** — see MEASURE table **b :** FLUIDRAM **2 a :** a small portion of something to drink **b :** a small amount [Late Latin *dragma* "dram, drachma", from Latin *drachma*, from Greek *drachmē*, literally, "handful", from *drassesthai* "to grasp"]

dra•ma \ˈdräm-ə, ˈdram-\ *n* **1 :** a composition telling a story through action and dialogue and designed for theatrical performance **:** PLAY **2 :** dramatic art, literature, or affairs **3 a :** a series of events involving interesting or intense conflict of forces ⟨the *drama* of a hockey game⟩ **b :** dramatic effect or quality [Late Latin *dramat-, drama*, from Greek, "deed, drama", from *dran* "to do"]

Dram•a•mine \ˈdram-ə-ˌmēn\ *trademark* — used for a crystalline compound used in the prevention or treatment of motion sickness

dra•mat•ic \drə-ˈmat-ik\ *adj* **1 :** of or relating to the drama **2 a :** suitable to or characteristic of the drama **b :** striking in appearance or effect — **dra•mat•i•cal•ly** \-ˈmat-i-kə-lē, -klē\ *adv*

• **syn** DRAMATIC, THEATRICAL, HISTRIONIC, MELODRAMATIC mean having a character or an effect like that of acted plays. DRAMATIC applies to situations in life and literature when they give evidence of power to stir the imagination and emotions deeply ⟨a *dramatic* meeting of leaders⟩ THEATRICAL implies a crude appeal through artificiality or exaggeration in gesture or vocal expression ⟨a *theatrical* oration⟩ HISTRIONIC applies to tones, gestures, and motions and suggests a deliberate affectation or staginess ⟨a *histrionic* show of grief⟩ MELODRAMATIC suggests an exaggerated emotionalism or an inappropriate theatricalism ⟨making a *melodramatic* scene in public⟩

dra•mat•ics \-iks\ *n sing or pl* **1 a :** performance of plays especially as an extracurricular activity in school or college **b :** theatrical technique ⟨studying *dramatics*⟩ **2 :** dramatic behavior or expression

dra•ma•tis per•so•nae \ˌdram-ət-ə-spər-ˈsō-ˌnē, ˌdräm-, -ˌnī\ *n pl* **:** the characters or actors in a drama [New Latin]

dra•ma•tist \ˈdram-ət-əst, ˈdräm-\ *n* **:** PLAYWRIGHT

dra•ma•tize \ˈdram-ə-ˌtīz, ˈdräm-\ *vt* **1 :** to adapt for theatrical presentation **2 :** to present or represent in a dramatic manner — **dra•ma•ti•za•tion** \ˌdram-ət-ə-ˈzā-shən, ˌdräm-\ *n*

dra•ma•tur•gy \ˈdram-ə-ˌtər-jē, ˈdräm-\ *n* **:** the art or technique of dramatic composition and theatrical representation [German *dramaturgie*, from Greek *dramatourgia* "dramatic composition", derived from *drama* "drama" + *ergon* "work"] — **dra•ma•tur•gic** \ˌdram-ə-ˈtər-jik, ˌdräm-\ *adj*

drank *past of* DRINK

[1]**drape** \ˈdrāp\ *vb* **1 :** to cover or adorn with or as if with folds of cloth **2 :** to cause to hang or stretch out loosely or carelessly ⟨*drape* oneself over a chair⟩ **3 :** to arrange or become arranged in flowing lines or folds ⟨a cleverly *draped* suit⟩ [Middle French *draper* "to weave", from *drap* "cloth", from Late Latin *drappus*]

[2]**drape** *n* **1 :** a drapery especially for a window **:** CURTAIN **2 :** arrangement in or of folds **3 :** the cut or hang of clothing ⟨the *drape* of a jacket⟩

drap•er \ˈdrā-pər\ *n, chiefly British* **:** a dealer in cloth and sometimes also in clothing and dry goods

drap•ery \ˈdrā-pə-rē, -prē\ *n, pl* **-er•ies 1** *British* **:** DRY GOODS **2 a :** a decorative fabric usually hung in loose folds and arranged in a graceful design **b :** a hanging of heavy fabric used as a curtain **3 :** the draping or arranging of materials

dras•tic \ˈdras-tik\ *adj* **1 :** acting rapidly or violently ⟨a *drastic* purgative⟩ **2 :** extreme in effect **:** SEVERE ⟨*drastic* changes in the law⟩ [Greek *drastikos*, from *dran* "to do"] — **dras•ti•cal•ly** \-ti-kə-lē, -klē\ *adv*

draught \ˈdraft, ˈdräft\ *chiefly British variant of* DRAFT

draughts \ˈdrafs, ˈdräfs, ˈdrafts, ˈdräfts\ *n, British* **:** CHECKERS [Middle English *draghtes*, from *draght* "draft, move in chess"]

Dra•vid•i•an \drə-ˈvid-ē-ən\ *n* **1 :** a member of an ancient Australoid race of southern India **2 :** any of several languages of India, Sri Lanka, and Pakistan constituting a language family [Sanskrit *Draviḍa*] — **Dravidian** *adj*

[1]**draw** \ˈdrȯ\ *vb* **drew** \ˈdrü\; **drawn** \ˈdrȯn\; **draw•ing 1 :** to cause to move continuously toward or after a force applied in advance **:** HAUL, DRAG **2 a :** to cause to go in a certain direction (as by leading) ⟨*drew* us aside⟩ **b :** to move or go steadily or gradually ⟨night *draws* near⟩ **3 a :** ATTRACT, ENTICE ⟨honey *draws* flies⟩ **b :** to bring on oneself **:** PROVOKE ⟨*drew* enemy fire⟩ **4 :** INHALE ⟨*drew* a deep breath⟩ **5 a :** to bring or pull out by effort ⟨*draw* a sword⟩ **b :** to extract the essence from ⟨*draw* tea⟩ **c :** EVISCERATE ⟨a *drawn* and plucked hen⟩ **6 :** to require (a specified depth) to float in ⟨a ship that *draws* four meters of water⟩ **7 a :** ACCUMULATE, GAIN ⟨*draw* interest⟩ **b :** to take (money) from a place of deposit **:** WITHDRAW **c :** to receive regularly from a source ⟨*draw* a salary⟩ **8 a :** to take (cards) from a stack or the dealer **b :** to receive or take at random ⟨*drew* a winning number⟩ **9 :** to bend (a bow) by pulling back the string **10 a :** to cause to shrink or tighten **b :** to change shape by or as if by pulling or stretching ⟨a face *drawn* with fatigue⟩ **11 :** to strike (a ball) so as to impart a backward spin **12 :** to leave (a contest) undecided **:** TIE **13 a :** to produce a likeness of by or as if by making lines on a surface **:** DELINEATE **b :** to write out in due form **:** DRAFT ⟨*draw* up a will⟩ **c :** express in detail **:** FORMULATE ⟨*draw* comparisons⟩ **14 :** to infer from evidence

or premises ⟨*draw* a conclusion⟩ **15 :** to spread or elongate (metal) by hammering or by pulling through dies **16 a :** to produce or allow a draft or current of air ⟨the furnace *draws* well⟩ **b :** to swell out in a wind ⟨all sails *drawing*⟩ [Old English *dragan*] — **draw a bead on :** to take aim at

[2]draw *n* **1 :** the act, process, or result of drawing **2 :** a lot or chance drawn at random ⟨a win at the first *draw*⟩ **3 :** the movable part of a drawbridge **4 :** a contest left undecided or deadlocked : TIE **5 :** something that draws attention or patronage **6 :** a gully shallower than a ravine

draw away *vi* **:** to move ahead (as of an opponent in a race) ⟨the brown horse soon *drew away* from the others⟩

draw•back \\'drȯ-ˌbak\\ *n* **:** an objectionable feature : SHORTCOMING

draw•bar \\-ˌbär\\ *n* **:** a beam across the rear of a tractor to which implements are hitched

draw•bridge \\-ˌbrij\\ *n* **:** a bridge made to be raised up, let down, or drawn aside so as to permit or hinder passage

drawbridge

draw•ee \\drȯ-'ē\\ *n* **:** the party (as a bank) ordered to pay a draft

draw•er \\'drȯ-ər, 'drȯr\\ *n* **1 :** one that draws: as **a :** a person who draws liquor **b :** DRAFTSMAN **c :** one who executes a draft or makes a promissory note **2 :** a sliding box or receptacle (as in a table or desk) opened by pulling out and closed by pushing in **3** *pl* **:** an undergarment for the lower part of the body

draw•ing \\'drȯ-ing\\ *n* **1 a :** an act or instance of drawing **b :** the deciding of something by drawing lots **2 :** the act, art, or technique of representing an object by means of lines **3 :** something drawn or capable of being drawn; *esp* **:** a representation formed by drawing

drawing board *n* **:** a board on which paper to be drawn on is fastened

drawing card *n* **:** something or someone that attracts attention or patronage

drawing room *n* **1 a :** a formal reception room **b :** a private room on a railroad passenger car with three berths and an enclosed toilet **2 :** a formal reception ⟨at the queen's *drawing room*⟩ [short for *withdrawing room*]

draw•knife \\'drȯ-ˌnīf\\ *n* **:** a woodworker's tool having a blade with a handle at each end used to shave off surfaces

[1]drawl \\'drȯl\\ *vb* **:** to speak slowly with vowels greatly prolonged : utter in a slow lengthened tone [probably derived from *draw*] — **drawl•er** *n* — **drawl•ing•ly** \\'drȯ-ling-lē\\ *adv*

[2]drawl *n* **:** a drawling manner of speaking

drawn butter *n* **:** melted and often seasoned butter

drawn•work \\'drȯn-ˌwərk\\ *n* **:** decoration on cloth made by drawing out threads according to a pattern

draw on *vb* **1 a :** APPROACH 1a ⟨night *draws on*⟩ **b :** to bring on : CAUSE **2 :** to take funds from ⟨*draw on* a bank account⟩

draw out *vt* **1 :** EXTRACT 1 ⟨*draw out* a confession⟩ **2 :** to cause to speak freely ⟨tried to *draw* them *out* on the subject⟩ **3 :** PROLONG 1 ⟨refused to *draw out* the interview⟩

draw•shave \\'drȯ-ˌshāv\\ *n* **:** DRAWKNIFE

draw•string \\-ˌstring\\ *n* **:** a string, cord, or tape run through a hem, a casing, or eyelets and used to close a bag or to control fullness in garments and curtains

draw•tube \\-ˌtüb, -ˌtyüb\\ *n* **:** a telescoping tube (as for the eyepiece of a microscope)

draw up *vb* **1 :** to arrange (as troops) in order **2 :** to straighten (oneself) to an erect posture **3 :** to bring or come to a halt : STOP

[1]dray \\'drā\\ *n* **:** a vehicle used to haul goods; *esp* **:** a strong low cart or wagon without sides [Middle English *draye,* a wheelless vehicle, from Old English *dræge* "dragnet"]

[2]dray *vt* **:** to carry or transport on a dray

dray•age \\'drā-ij\\ *n* **:** the work or cost of draying

dray•man \\'drā-mən\\ *n* **:** one whose work is draying

[1]dread \\'dred\\ *vb* **1 a :** to fear greatly : be apprehensive or fearful **b** *archaic* **:** to regard with awe **2 :** to feel extreme reluctance to meet or face [Old English *drǣdan*]

[2]dread *n* **1 a :** great fear especially in the face of impending evil or harm **b** *archaic* **:** AWE 1 **2 :** one causing fear or awe **syn** see FEAR

[3]dread *adj* **:** causing dread : DREADFUL

dread•ful \\'dred-fəl\\ *adj* **1 :** inspiring dread or awe : FRIGHTENING **2 :** extremely distasteful, unpleasant, or shocking — **dread•ful•ly** \\-fə-lē, -flē\\ *adv* — **dread•ful•ness** \\-fəl-nəs\\ *n*

dread•nought \\'dred-ˌnȯt, -ˌnät\\ *n* **:** a battleship whose main armament consists entirely of big guns all of the same caliber [*Dreadnought,* a British battleship]

[1]dream \\'drēm\\ *n* **1 :** a series of thoughts, images, or emotions occurring during sleep **2 a :** a visionary creation of the imagination : DAYDREAM **b :** a state of mind in which a person is lost in fancies or reveries **c :** an object seen in a dreamlike state : VISION **3 :** something notable for its beauty, excellence, or enjoyable quality **4 :** a goal or purpose strongly desired [Old English *drēam* "noise, joy"] — **dream•like** \\-ˌlīk\\ *adj*

△ **origin** Not until the 13th century was our word *dream* used in the sense of "a series of thoughts, images, or emotions occurring during sleep". But the word itself is considerably older. In Old English *dream* means "joy", "noise", or "music". Yet the shift in sense did not come simply from the development of a more specialized sense. Rather it appears that after many Scandinavian conflicts, conquests, and settlements in Britain the Old Norse *draumr,* meaning "a dream during sleep", influenced the meaning of the similar and probably related English word. By the end of the 14th century the earlier meanings had been entirely replaced.

[2]dream \\'drēm\\ *vb* **dreamed** \\'dremt, 'drēmd\\ *or* **dreamt** \\'dremt\\; **dream•ing** \\'drē-ming\\ **1 :** to have a dream **2 :** to indulge in daydreams : pass (time) in reverie **3 :** to conceive as possible, fitting, or proper : IMAGINE ⟨*dreamed* of success⟩

dream•er \\'drē-mər\\ *n* **1 :** one that dreams **2 a :** one that lives in a world of fancy and imagination **b :** one that constantly conceives of impractical projects

dream•land \\'drēm-ˌland\\ *n* **:** an unreal delightful country existing only in imagination or in dreams

dream•world \\-ˌwərld\\ *n* **:** DREAMLAND; *also* **:** a world of illusion or fantasy

dreamy \\'drē-mē\\ *adj* **dream•i•er; -est 1 :** full of dreams ⟨*dreamy* sleep⟩ **2 :** given to or marked by dreaming or fantasy **3 a :** having the quality or characteristics of a dream **b :** quiet and soothing ⟨*dreamy* music⟩ **c :** DELIGHTFUL ⟨a *dreamy* car⟩ — **dream•i•ly** \\-mə-lē\\ *adv* — **dream•i•ness** \\-mē-nəs\\ *n*

drea•ry \\'driər-ē\\ *adj* **drea•ri•er** \\'drir-ē-ər\\; **-est :** causing feelings of cheerlessness : GLOOMY ⟨a *dreary* landscape⟩ [Old English *drēorig* "sad, bloody", from *drēor* "gore"] — **drea•ri•ly** \\'drir-ə-lē\\ *adv* — **drea•ri•ness** \\'drir-ē-nəs\\ *n*

[1]dredge \\'drej\\ *n* **1 :** an oblong iron frame with an attached bag net used especially for gathering fish and shellfish **2 :** a machine for removing earth usually by buckets on an endless chain or by a suction tube **3 :** a barge used in dredging [probably from Scottish *dreg-* (in *dregbot* "dredge boat")]

[2]dredge *vb* **1 :** to dig, gather, or pull out with or as if with a dredge ⟨*dredge* a channel⟩ ⟨*dredge* up something from one's memory⟩ **2 :** to search with or as if with a dredge ⟨*dredging* for oysters⟩ — **dredg•er** *n*

[3]dredge *vt* **:** to coat (food) by sprinkling (as with flour) [Middle English *drage, drege* "sweetmeat", from Middle French *dragie,* from Latin *tragemata* "sweetmeats", from Greek *tragēmata,* pl. of *tragēma* "sweetmeat", from *trōgein* "to gnaw"] — **dredg•er** *n*

dreg \\'dreg\\ *n* **1 :** sediment contained in a liquid or precipitated from it : LEES — usually used in pl. **2 :** the most undesirable part — usually used in pl. ⟨the *dregs* of society⟩ **3 :** the last remaining part : VESTIGE [Old Norse *dregg*]

[1]drench \\'drench\\ *n* **1 :** a medicinal potion for a domestic animal **2 a :** something that drenches **b :** a quantity sufficient to drench or saturate

[2]drench *vt* **1 a** *archaic* **:** to force to drink **b :** to administer a drench to (an animal) **2 :** to wet thoroughly : SATURATE [Old English *drencan*]

[1]dress \\'dres\\ *vb* **1 :** to make or set straight (as troops in formation) : ALIGN **2 a** : to put clothes on **b** : to provide with clothing **c** : to put on or wear formal or fancy clothes **3** : to add decorative details to : EMBELLISH ⟨*dress* a store window⟩ **4** : to prepare for use or service **5 a** : to apply dressings or medication to **b** : to arrange (the hair) by combing, brushing, or curling **c** : to prepare (an animal) by grooming and currying **d** : to kill and prepare for market ⟨*dress* a chicken⟩ **e** : CULTIVATE, TEND; *esp* : to apply manure or fertilizer to **6** : SMOOTH, FINISH ⟨*dress* timber⟩ [Middle French *dresser,* derived from Latin *directus* "straight, direct"]

[2]**dress** *n* **1** : APPAREL, CLOTHING **2** : an outer garment with a skirt used by women or girls **3** : covering, adornment, or appearance appropriate or peculiar to a particular time **4** : the particular style in which something is presented : GUISE

[3]**dress** *adj* **1** : relating to or used for a dress ⟨*dress* goods⟩ **2** : suitable for a formal occasion ⟨*dress* clothes⟩ **3** : requiring or permitting formal dress ⟨a *dress* affair⟩

dres•sage \drə-ˈsäzh, dre-\ *n* : the execution by a horse of complex maneuvers in response to barely perceptible movements of a rider's hands, legs, and weight

dress circle *n* : the first or lowest curved tier of seats in a theater

dress down *vt* : to reprove severely

[1]**dress•er** \ˈdres-ər\ *n* **1** *obsolete* : a table or sideboard for preparing and serving food **2** : a cupboard to hold dishes and cooking utensils **3** : a chest of drawers or bureau with a mirror

[2]**dresser** *n* : one that dresses ⟨a window *dresser*⟩

dress•ing *n* **1 a** : the act or process of one that dresses **b** : an instance of dressing **2 a** : a sauce for adding to a dish **b** : a seasoned mixture usually used as a stuffing (as for poultry) **3 a** : material used to cover an injury **b** : fertilizing material

dressing gown *n* : a loose robe worn especially while dressing or resting

dressing room *n* : a room used chiefly for dressing; *esp* : a room in a theater for changing costumes and makeup

dressing station *n* : a station for giving first aid to the wounded

dressing table *n* : a low table with a mirror at which one sits while dressing

dress•mak•er \ˈdres-ˌmā-kər\ *n* : one that does dressmaking

dress•mak•ing \-king\ *n* : the process or occupation of making dresses

dress rehearsal *n* : a full rehearsal of a play in costume and with stage properties shortly before the first performance

dress shirt *n* : a man's shirt especially for wear with evening dress

dress suit *n* : a suit worn for full dress

dress uniform *n* : a uniform for formal wear

dressy \ˈdres-ē\ *adj* **dress•i•er**; **-est** **1** : showy in dress **2** : SMART 6a, STYLISH

drew *past of* DRAW

[1]**drib•ble** \ˈdrib-əl\ *vb* **drib•bled**; **drib•bling** \ˈdrib-ling, -ə-ling\ **1** : to fall or flow or let fall in drops : TRICKLE **2** : DROOL 1, SLOBBER **3** : to come or issue little by little ⟨replies *dribbled* in⟩ **4** : to propel by tapping, bouncing, or kicking ⟨*dribble* a basketball⟩ [derived from *drib* "to dribble", probably alteration of *drip*] — **drib•bler** \ˈdrib-lər, -ə-lər\ *n*

[2]**dribble** *n* **1 a** : a small trickling stream or flow **b** : a drizzling shower **2** : a tiny or insignificant quantity **3** : an act or instance of dribbling a ball or puck

drib•let \ˈdrib-lət\ *n* **1** : a small amount **2** : a drop of liquid

dri•er *also* **dry•er** \ˈdrī-ər, ˈdrīr\ *n* **1** : something that extracts or absorbs moisture **2** : a substance that accelerates drying (as of oils, paints, and printing inks) **3** *usually dryer* : a device for drying (as clothes) by heat or air

[1]**drift** \ˈdrift\ *n* **1 a** : the act of driving something along **b** : the flow of a river or ocean stream **2 a** : wind-driven snow, rain, or smoke usually near the ground surface **b** : a mass of matter (as sand) deposited together by or as if by wind or water **c** : a deposit of clay, sand, gravel, and boulders transported by a glacier or by running water from a glacier **3 a** : a general underlying design or tendency **b** : the meaning, import, or purport of what is spoken or written **4 a** : a ship's deviation from its course caused by currents **b** : the lateral motion of an airplane due to air currents **5 a** : a gradual shift in attitude, opinion, or position **b** : an aimless course [Middle English] **syn** see TENDENCY

[2]**drift** *vb* **1 a** : to be or cause to be driven or carried along by a current (as of water or air) **b** : to move or float smoothly and effortlessly **2 a** : to move along a line of least resistance **b** : to travel about in a random way especially in search of work **c** : to become carried along subject to no guidance or control ⟨the conversation *drifted* from one topic to another⟩ **3 a** : to accumulate or cause to accumulate in a mass ⟨*drifting* snow blocked the road⟩ **b** : to cover or become covered with a drift ⟨the road was *drifted* shut⟩ **4 a** : to vary or deviate from a set adjustment **b** : to vary sluggishly — **drift•er** *n* — **drift•ing•ly** \ˈdrif-ting-lē\ *adv*

drift•age \ˈdrif-tij\ *n* **1** : a drifting of some object especially through action of wind or water **2** : deviation from a set course due to drifting **3** : something that drifts

drift•wood \ˈdrift-ˌwu̇d\ *n* **1** : wood drifted or floated by water **2** : someone or something that drifts aimlessly

[1]**drill** \ˈdril\ *vb* **1** : to pierce or bore with or as if with a drill ⟨*drill* a tooth⟩ ⟨*drill* a hole⟩ **2 a** : to instruct thoroughly ⟨*drill* a class⟩ **b** : to impart or communicate by repetition ⟨*drill* some sense into their heads⟩ **c** : to train or exercise in military skill and discipline ⟨*drill* soldiers⟩ [Dutch *drillen*] — **drill•er** *n*

[2]**drill** *n* **1** : a tool for making holes in hard substances by revolving or by a succession of blows **2** : the training of soldiers in military skill and discipline **3** : a physical or mental exercise regularly and repeatedly practiced **4** : a marine snail that destroys oysters by boring through their shells and feeding on the soft parts

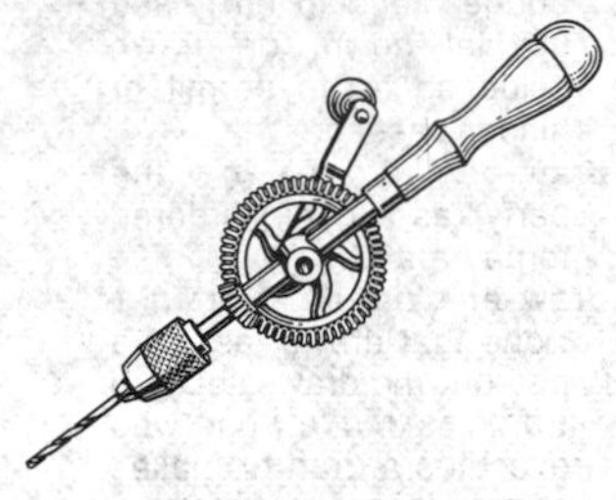

[2]drill 1

[3]**drill** *n* : a west African baboon closely related to the typical mandrills [probably native name in West Africa]

[4]**drill** *n* **1** : a shallow furrow or trench into which seed is sown **2** : a planting implement that opens a drill, drops in seed, and covers it with earth [perhaps from earlier *drill* "small brook"]

[5]**drill** *vt* : to sow with or as if with a drill

[6]**drill** *n* : a durable cotton fabric in twill weave [derived from German *drillich,* from Middle High German *drilich* "fabric woven with a threefold thread", from Latin *trilix* "made up of three threads", from *tri-* + *licium* "thread"]

drill•mas•ter \ˈdril-ˌmas-tər\ *n* : one who drills; *esp* : an instructor in military drill

drill press *n* : an upright drilling machine in which the drill is pressed to the work by a hand lever or by power

drily *variant of* DRYLY

[1]**drink** \ˈdringk\ *vb* **drank** \ˈdrangk\; **drunk** \ˈdrəngk\ *or* **drank**; **drink•ing** **1 a** : to swallow liquid : IMBIBE **b** : to take in or suck up : ABSORB **c** : to take in or receive avidly ⟨*drink* in the scenery⟩ **2** : to give or join in a toast ⟨*drink* to our leader⟩ **3 a** : to drink alcoholic beverages **b** : to spend in or waste on consumption of alcoholic beverages ⟨*drank* the hours away⟩ **c** : to bring to a specified state by taking drink [Old English *drincan*]

[2]**drink** *n* **1 a** : liquid suitable for swallowing : BEVERAGE **b** : alcoholic liquor **2** : a draft or portion of liquid **3** : excessive consumption of alcoholic beverages

[1]**drink•able** \ˈdring-kə-bəl\ *adj* : suitable or safe for drinking

[2]**drinkable** *n* : a liquid suitable for drinking : BEVERAGE

drink•er \ˈdring-kər\ *n* **1** : one that drinks **2** : one that drinks alcoholic beverages especially to excess

[1]**drip** \ˈdrip\ *vb* **dripped**; **drip•ping** **1** : to fall or let fall in drops **2 a** : to let fall drops of moisture or liquid ⟨a *dripping* faucet⟩ **b** : to overflow with or as if with moisture [Old English *dryppan*] — **drip•per** *n*

[2]**drip** *n* **1 a** : a falling in drops **b** : liquid that falls, overflows, or is extruded in drops **2** : the sound made by or as if by falling drops **3** : a part of a cornice or other member that projects to throw off rainwater; *also* : an overlapping metal strip serving the same purpose **4** *slang* : a dull or unattractive person

drip–dry \ˈdrip-ˈdrī\ *vi* : to dry with few or no wrinkles when hung dripping wet — **drip–dry** \-ˌdrī\ *adj*

drip•ping \ˈdrip-ing\ *n* : fat and juices that drip from meat during cooking — often used in pl.

[1]**drive** \ˈdrīv\ *vb* **drove** \ˈdrōv\; **driv•en** \ˈdriv-ən\; **driv•ing** \ˈdrī-ving\ **1 a** : to urge, push, or force onward **b** : to cause to penetrate with force ⟨*drive* a nail⟩ **2 a** (1) : to direct the movement or course of ⟨*drive* a car⟩ (2) : to operate a vehicle ⟨learn how to *drive*⟩ **b** : to convey or transport in a vehicle ⟨*drove* us

to the airport⟩ **c :** to ride in a vehicle ⟨we *drove* into town⟩ **3 :** to set or keep in motion ⟨*drive* machinery by electricity⟩ **4 :** to carry through strongly ⟨*drive* a hard bargain⟩ **5 a :** to force to act ⟨*driven* by hunger to steal⟩ **b :** to project, inject, or impress forcefully ⟨*drove* the lesson home⟩ **6 :** to bring into a specified condition ⟨the noise is *driving* me crazy⟩ **7 :** to produce by opening a way (as by drilling) ⟨*drive* a well⟩ **8 :** to rush and press with violence ⟨the police *drove* into the mob⟩ **9 :** to hit a golf ball from the tee [Old English *drīfan*] **syn** see MOVE, RIDE

[2]drive *n* **1 :** an act of driving or being driven: as **a :** a trip in a vehicle (as an automobile) **b :** a driving together of animals **c :** the guiding of logs downstream to a mill **d :** the act of driving a ball **e :** the flight of a ball **2 a :** DRIVEWAY 2 **b :** a public road for driving **3 a :** an offensive or aggressive move; *esp* **:** a strong sustained military attack **b :** an intensive group effort ⟨a membership *drive*⟩ **4 :** the state of being hurried and under pressure **5 a :** an urgent, basic, or instinctual need or longing ⟨the sex *drive*⟩ **b :** dynamic quality ⟨full of *drive*⟩ **6 a :** the means for giving motion to a machine or machine part ⟨a chain *drive*⟩ **b :** the means by which the motive power of an automotive vehicle is applied to the road ⟨front wheel *drive*⟩ **7 :** a device including both driving and sensing mechanisms for reading or writing on a magnetic medium (as magnetic tape)

drive–in \ˈdrīv-ˌin\ *adj* **:** arranged and equipped to accommodate patrons while they remain in their vehicles ⟨a *drive-in* theater⟩ ⟨*drive-in* banks⟩ — **drive–in** *n*

[1]driv•el \ˈdriv-əl\ *vb* **driv•eled** *or* **driv•elled; driv•el•ing** *or* **driv•el•ling** \ˈdriv-ling, -ə-ling\ **1 :** to let saliva dribble from the mouth **:** SLAVER **2 :** to talk or utter stupidly, carelessly, or in an infantile way [Old English *dreflian*] — **driv•el•er** *or* **driv•el•ler** \ˈdriv-lər, -ə-lər\ *n*

[2]drivel *n* **:** NONSENSE 1

driv•er \ˈdrī-vər\ *n* **:** one that drives: as **a :** the operator of a motor vehicle **b :** a golf club having a wooden head with a nearly straight face used in driving

driver ant *n* **:** ARMY ANT

driver's seat *n* **:** the position of top authority or dominance

drive•way \ˈdrīv-ˌwā\ *n* **1 :** a road or way along which animals are driven **2 :** a short private road leading from a public street to a house, garage, or parking lot

driving iron *n* **:** a golf iron with a nearly vertical head for distance and little loft

[1]driz•zle \ˈdriz-əl\ *vb* **driz•zled; driz•zling** \ˈdriz-ling, -ə-ling\ **1 :** to rain in very small drops **:** SPRINKLE **2 :** to shed in minute drops or particles [perhaps from Middle English *drysnen* "to fall"]

[2]drizzle *n* **:** a fine misty rain — **driz•zly** \ˈdriz-lē, -ə-lē\ *adj*

drogue \ˈdrōg\ *n* **:** a small attached parachute for slowing down or stabilizing something (as an astronaut's capsule) [probably alteration of [1]*drag*]

droll \ˈdrōl\ *adj* **:** having a humorous, whimsical, or odd quality ⟨a *droll* expression⟩ [French *drôle*] — **droll•ness** \ˈdrōl-nəs\ *n* — **drol•ly** \ˈdrōl-lē\ *adv*

droll•ery \ˈdrōl-rē, -ə-rē\ *n, pl* **-er•ies 1 :** something droll; *esp* **:** an amusing story or gesture **2 :** droll behavior **3 :** whimsical humor

-drome \ˌdrōm\ *n combining form* **1 :** racecourse **2 :** large specially prepared place ⟨aero*drome*⟩ [*hippodrome*]

drom•e•dary \ˈdräm-ə-ˌder-ē *also* ˈdrəm-\ *n, pl* **-dar•ies 1 :** a camel of unusual speed bred and trained especially for riding **2 :** the one-humped camel of western Asia and northern Africa [Middle French *dromedaire,* from Late Latin *dromedarius,* from Latin *dromas,* from Greek, "running"]

dromedary 2

[1]drone \ˈdrōn\ *n* **1 :** the stingless male bee (as of the honeybee) that gathers no honey **2 :** one that lives on the labors of others **:** PARASITE **3 :** a pilotless airplane or ship controlled by radio signals [Old English *drān*]

[2]drone *vb* **:** to make or speak with a low dull monotonous humming sound

[3]drone *n* **1 :** one of the pipes on a bagpipe that sound fixed continuous tones **2 :** a deep monotonous sound **:** HUM

drone fly *n* **:** a large two-winged fly resembling a honeybee

drool \ˈdrül\ *vb* **1 a :** to water at the mouth **b :** to let saliva or some other substance flow from the mouth **:** SLAVER **2 a :** to talk foolishly **b :** to express in a sentimental or effusive way [perhaps alteration of *drivel*]

[1]droop \ˈdrüp\ *vb* **1 :** to hang or incline downward **2 :** to sink gradually **3 :** to become depressed or weakened **:** LANGUISH **4 :** to let droop [Old Norse *drūpa*] — **droop•ing•ly** \ˈdrü-ping-lē\ *adv*

[2]droop *n* **:** the condition or appearance of drooping

droopy \ˈdrü-pē\ *adj* **droop•i•er; -est 1 :** drooping or tending to droop **2 :** GLOOMY 2, DOWNCAST

[1]drop \ˈdräp\ *n* **1 a** (1) **:** the quantity of fluid that falls in one spherical mass (2) *pl* **:** a dose of medicine measured by drops **b :** a small quantity of drink **c :** the smallest practical unit of liquid measure **2 :** something (as a hanging ornament on jewelry) shaped like a drop **3 a :** the act or an instance of dropping **:** FALL **b :** a decline in quantity or quality ⟨a *drop* in water pressure⟩ **c :** a descent by parachute; *also* **:** the persons or equipment dropped by parachute **4 :** the distance through which something drops **5 :** a slot into which something is to be dropped **6 :** an unframed piece of cloth scenery in a theater [Old English *dropa*]

[2]drop *vb* **dropped; drop•ping 1 :** to fall or let fall in drops **2 a :** to let fall ⟨*drop* a book⟩ **b :** to let fall gradually **:** LOWER ⟨*drop* one's voice⟩ **3 :** SEND ⟨*drop* me a letter⟩ **4 :** to let go **:** DISMISS ⟨*drop* the subject⟩ ⟨*drop* several workers⟩ **5 :** to knock down **:** cause to fall ⟨*drop* an opponent in a fight⟩ **6 :** to go lower ⟨prices *dropped*⟩ **7 :** to come or go unexpectedly or informally ⟨*drop* in for a chat⟩ **8 :** to pass into a less active state ⟨*drop* off to sleep⟩ **9 :** to move downward or with a current **10 :** to withdraw from participation or membership **:** QUIT — usually used with *out* ⟨*drop* out of school⟩ **11 :** to leave (a letter representing a speech sound) unsounded ⟨*drop* the first *r* in *surprise*⟩ **12 :** to give birth to ⟨the cow *dropped* a fine calf⟩ **13 :** to draw from an external point (as from a point to a line or plane) ⟨*drop* a perpendicular to a plane⟩

drop–forge \ˈdräp-ˈfōrj, -ˈfȯrj\ *vt* **:** to forge between dies by a drop hammer or punch press — **drop forger** *n*

drop hammer *n* **:** a power hammer raised and then released to drop (as on metal resting on an anvil or die)

drop•kick \ˈdräp-ˈkik\ *n* **:** a kick made by dropping a football to the ground and kicking it at the moment it starts to rebound — **drop–kick** *vb* — **drop–kick•er** *n*

drop leaf *n* **:** a hinged leaf on a table that can be folded down

drop•let \ˈdräp-lət\ *n* **:** a very small drop

droplet infection *n* **:** infection transmitted by airborne droplets of sputum containing infectious organisms

drop•out \ˈdräp-ˌau̇t\ *n* **:** one who drops out (as from school)

dropped egg *n* **:** a poached egg

drop•per \ˈdräp-ər\ *n* **1 :** one that drops **2 :** a short glass or plastic tube with a rubber bulb used to measure out liquids by drops

drop•pings \ˈdräp-ingz\ *n pl* **:** animal dung

drop•sy \ˈdräp-sē\ *n* **:** EDEMA [Old French *ydropesie,* from Latin *hydropisis,* from Greek *hydrōps,* from *hydōr* "water"] — **drop•si•cal** \-si-kəl\ *adj*

dro•soph•i•la \drō-ˈsäf-ə-lə\ *n* **:** any of a genus of small two-winged flies used especially in the study of inheritance [Greek *drosos* "dew" + *-philos* "-phil"]

dross \ˈdräs, ˈdrȯs\ *n* **1 :** the scum that forms on the surface of molten metal **2 :** waste or foreign matter **:** IMPURITY [Old English *drōs* "dregs"]

drought *or* **drouth** \ˈdrau̇th, ˈdrau̇t\ *n* **:** a long period of dry weather [Old English *drūgath,* from *drūgian* "to dry up"] — **droughty** \-ē\ *adj*

drove \ˈdrōv\ *n* **1 :** a group of animals driven or moving in a body **2 :** a crowd of people moving or acting together [Old English *drāf,* from *drīfan* "to drive"]

drov•er \ˈdrō-vər\ *n* **:** one that drives cattle or sheep

drown \ˈdrau̇n\ *vb* **1 a :** to suffocate by submersion especially in water **b :** to become drowned **2 :** to cover with water

: INUNDATE **3** : OVERWHELM 1, OVERPOWER [Middle English *drounen*]

drowse \'draủz\ *vi* : to sleep lightly : DOZE [probably related to Old English *drūsian* "to droop, become sluggish"] — **drowse** *n*

drowsy \'draủ-zē\ *adj* **drows•i•er**; **-est** **1** : ready to fall asleep **2** : making one sleepy — **drows•i•ly** \-zə-lē\ *adv* — **drows-i•ness** \-zē-nəs\ *n*

drub \'drəb\ *vt* **drubbed**; **drub•bing** **1** : to beat severely with or as if with a stick **2** : to defeat decisively [perhaps from Arabic *daraba*]

[1]drudge \'drəj\ *vi* : to do hard, menial, or monotonous work [Middle English *druggen*] — **drudg•er** *n*

[2]drudge *n* : one engaged in drudgery

drudg•ery \'drəj-rē, -ə-rē\ *n, pl* **-er•ies** : tiresome or menial work

[1]drug \'drəg\ *n* **1** : a substance used as a medicine or in making medicines **2** : something for which there is little demand ⟨a *drug* on the market⟩ **3** : a narcotic substance or preparation

[2]drug *vb* **drugged**; **drug•ging** **1** : to affect or treat with a drug; *esp* : to stupefy by a narcotic drug **2** : to lull or stupefy as if with a drug

drug•gist \'drəg-əst\ *n* : one who sells or dispenses drugs and medicines: as **a** : PHARMACIST **b** : an owner or manager of a drugstore

drug•store \'drəg-,stōr, -,stȯr\ *n* : a retail shop where medicines and miscellaneous articles are sold : PHARMACY

dru•id \'drü-əd\ *n, often cap* : one of an ancient Celtic priesthood of Gaul, Britain, and Ireland appearing in legends as magicians and wizards [Latin *druides* "druids", from Gaulish] — **dru•id•ic** \drü-'id-ik\ *adj, often cap* — **dru•id•ism** \'drü-ə-,diz-əm\ *n, often cap*

[1]drum \'drəm\ *n* **1** : a musical percussion instrument usually consisting of a hollow cylinder with a skin head stretched over each end that is beaten with a stick or pair of sticks in playing **2** : EARDRUM **3** : the sound of a drum; *also* : a similar sound **4** : a drum-shaped object: as **a** : a cylindrical machine or mechanical device or part **b** : a cylindrical container; *esp* : a metal barrel with a capacity of 45 to 416 liters **c** : a disk-shaped magazine for an automatic weapon **5** : any of various spiny-finned fishes that make a drumming noise [probably from Dutch *trom*]

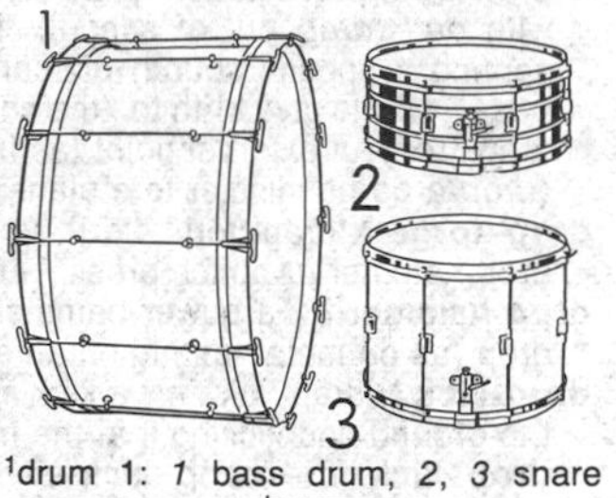

[1]drum 1: *1* bass drum, *2, 3* snare drums

[2]drum *vb* **drummed**; **drum•ming** **1** : to beat a drum **2** : to sound rhythmically : THROB, BEAT **3** : to stir up interest : SOLICIT — usually used with *up* ⟨*drum* up customers⟩ **4** : to dismiss dishonorably : EXPEL — usually used with *out* **5** : to drive or force by steady effort or reiteration ⟨*drum* a lesson into one's head⟩ **6** : to strike or tap repeatedly so as to produce rhythmic sounds

drum•beat \'drəm-,bēt\ *n* : a stroke on a drum or its sound

drum•lin \'drəm-lən\ *n* : a long or oval hill of glacial drift [Irish Gaelic *druim* "back, ridge"]

drum major *n* : the marching leader of a band or drum corps

drum ma•jor•ette \,drəm-,mā-jə-'ret\ *n* : a girl who is a drum major

drum•mer \'drəm-ər\ *n* **1** : one that plays a drum **2** : TRAVELING SALESMAN

drum•stick \'drəm-,stik\ *n* **1** : a stick for beating a drum **2** : the lower segment of a fowl's leg

[1]drunk \'drəngk\ *adj* **1** : having the faculties impaired by alcohol **2** : controlled by an intense feeling ⟨*drunk* with power⟩ **3** : DRUNKEN 2 [Middle English *drunke*, alteration of *drunken*]

[2]drunk *n* **1 a** : a person who is drunk **b** : DRUNKARD **2** : a period of excessive drinking : SPREE

drunk•ard \'drəng-kərd\ *n* : one who is habitually drunk

drunk•en \'drəng-kən\ *adj* **1 a** : DRUNK 1 **b** : given to habitual excessive use of alcohol **2** : of, relating to, or resulting from intoxication ⟨a *drunken* brawl⟩ **3** : unsteady or lurching as if from intoxication [Old English *druncen*, from past participle of *drincan* "to drink"] — **drunk•en•ly** *adv* — **drunk•en•ness** \-kən-nəs\ *n*

drupe \'drüp\ *n* : a fruit (as the plum, cherry, or peach) having one seed enclosed in a hard bony stone that is usually covered by pulpy flesh with a firm skin [Latin *drupa* "overripe olive", from Greek *dryppa* "olive"] — **dru•pa•ceous** \drü-'pā-shəs\ *adj*

drupe•let \'drüp-lət\ *n* : a small drupe; *esp* : one of the individual parts of an aggregate fruit (as the raspberry)

[1]dry \'drī\ *adj* **dri•er** \'drī-ər, 'drīr\; **dri•est** \'drī-əst\ **1** : free or freed from water or liquid **2** : characterized by loss or lack of water: as **a** : lacking precipitation and humidity ⟨a *dry* climate⟩ **b** : lacking freshness : STALE **c** : low in or deprived of tissue moisture ⟨*dry* hay⟩ ⟨achenes and other *dry* fruits⟩ **3** : not being in or under water ⟨*dry* land⟩ **4 a** : THIRSTY 1 **b** : marked by the absence of alcoholic beverages **c** : no longer liquid or sticky ⟨the ink is *dry*⟩ **5** : containing or employing no liquid (as water) ⟨a *dry* creek⟩ ⟨*dry* heat⟩ **6** : not giving milk ⟨a *dry* cow⟩ **7** : lacking natural lubrication ⟨a *dry* cough⟩ **8** : solid as opposed to liquid ⟨*dry* groceries⟩ **9** : not productive **10** : marked by a matter-of-fact, ironic, or terse manner of expression ⟨*dry* humor⟩ **11** : UNINTERESTING, WEARISOME ⟨*dry* reading⟩ **12** : not sweet ⟨*dry* wines⟩ **13** : relating to, favoring, or practicing prohibition of alcoholic beverages ⟨a *dry* state⟩ [Old English *drȳge*] — **dry•ly** *adv* — **dry•ness** *n*

[2]dry *vb* **dried**; **dry•ing** : to make or become dry

[3]dry *n, pl* **drys** : PROHIBITIONIST

dry•ad \'drī-əd, -,ad\ *n* : WOOD NYMPH [Latin *dryas*, from Greek, from *drys* "tree"]

dry cell *n* : a small battery whose contents are not spillable

dry–clean \'drī-,klēn\ *vt* : to subject to dry cleaning — **dry clean•er** \-,klē-nər\ *n*

dry clean•ing \-,klē-ning\ *n* : the cleansing of fabrics with organic solvents (as naphtha)

dry dock \'drī-,däk\ *n* : a dock that can be kept dry for use during the construction or repairing of ships

dry•er *variant of* DRIER

dry farm \'drī-'färm\ *n* : a farm on dry land operated without irrigation on the basis of moisture-conserving tillage and drought-resistant crops — **dry–farm** *vt* — **dry farmer** *n* — **dry farming** *n*

dry fly *n* : an artificial angling fly designed to float upon the surface of the water

dry goods \'drī-,gu̇dz\ *n pl* : textiles, ready-to-wear clothing, and notions as distinguished from other goods

dry ice *n* : solidified carbon dioxide usually in the form of blocks that at −78.5° C changes directly to a gas and that is used chiefly as a refrigerant

drying oil *n* : an oil (as linseed oil) that changes readily to a hard tough elastic substance when exposed in a thin film to air

dry measure *n* : a series of units of capacity for dry commodities — see MEASURE table, METRIC SYSTEM table

dry•point \'drī-,pȯint\ *n* : an engraving made with a pointed instrument (as a needle) on the metal plate without the use of acid

dry rot *n* : a fungous decay of seasoned timber in which the cellulose of wood is consumed leaving a soft skeleton readily reduced to powder — **dry–rot** *vb*

dry run *n* **1** : a practice firing without ammunition **2** : a practice exercise : REHEARSAL

dry wash *n, West* : WASH 3d

d.t.'s \dē-'tēz\ *n pl, often cap D&T* : DELIRIUM TREMENS

du•al \'dü-əl, 'dyü-\ *adj* **1** : consisting of two parts or elements : having two like parts **2** : having a double character or nature [Latin *dualis*, from *duo* "two"] — **du•al•i•ty** \dü-'al-ət-ē, dyü-\ *n* — **du•al•ly** \'dü-ə-lē, 'dyü-\ *adv*

du•al•ism \'dü-ə-,liz-əm, 'dyü-\ *n* : a doctrine that the universe is made up of or governed by two opposing principles (as good and evil) — **du•al•ist** \-ləst\ *n*

du•al–pur•pose \,dü-əl-'pər-pəs, ,dyü-\ *adj* : intended for or serving two purposes ⟨*dual-purpose* cattle⟩

[1]dub \'dəb\ *vt* **dubbed**; **dub•bing** **1 a** : to confer knighthood upon **2** : to call by a descriptive name : NICKNAME [Old English *dubbian*]

[2]dub *vt* **dubbed**; **dub•bing** **1** : to provide (a motion-picture film) with a new sound track **2** : to add (sound effects) to a film or broadcast [from *double*]

du•bi•ous \'dü-bē-əs, 'dyü-\ *adj* **1** : causing doubt : UNCERTAIN **2** : feeling doubt : UNDECIDED **3** : of doubtful promise or uncertain outcome ⟨a *dubious* battle⟩ **4** : of questionable value, quality, or propriety ⟨a *dubious* bargain⟩ ⟨won by *dubious* means⟩ [Latin *dubius,* from *dubare* "to vacillate"] — **du•bi•ous•ly** *adv* — **du•bi•ous•ness** *n*

du•bi•ta•ble \'dü-bət-ə-bəl, 'dyü-\ *adj* : open to doubt or question

du•cal \'dü-kəl, 'dyü-\ *adj* : of or relating to a duke or duchy

duc•at \'dək-ət\ *n* : a gold coin formerly used in Austria, Czechoslovakia, and the Netherlands [Middle French, from Italian *ducato* "coin with the doge's portrait on it", from *duca* "doge", from Late Greek *doux* "leader", from Latin *dux*]

duch•ess \'dəch-əs\ *n* **1** : the wife or widow of a duke **2** : a woman who holds a ducal title in her own right [Middle French *duchesse,* from *duc* "duke"]

duchy \'dəch-ē\ *n, pl* **duch•ies** : the territory of a duke or duchess : DUKEDOM [Middle French *duché,* from *duc* "duke"]

1**duck** \'dək\ *n, pl* **duck** *or* **ducks** : any of various swimming birds with the neck and legs short, the body heavy, the bill often broad and flat, and the sexes almost always different from each other in plumage *also* : a female duck — compare DRAKE [Old English *dūce*]

2**duck** *vb* **1** : to thrust or plunge under water **2** : to lower the head or body suddenly **3 a** : to move quickly : DODGE **b** : to evade a duty, question, or responsibility ⟨*duck* the issue⟩ [Middle English *douken*] — **duck•er** *n*

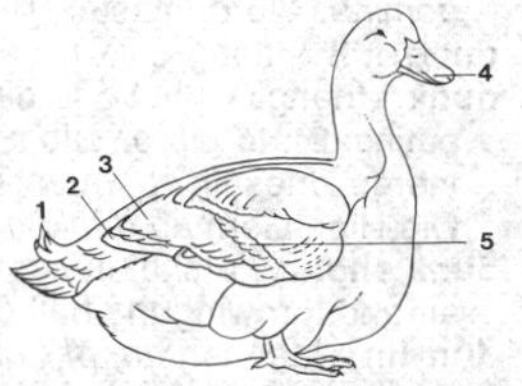

1duck: *1* drake feathers, *2* primaries, *3* secondaries, *4* bill, *5* coverts

3**duck** *n* **1** : a durable closely woven usually cotton fabric **2** *pl* : clothes made of duck [Dutch *doek* "cloth"]

4**duck** *n* : an amphibious truck [*DUKW,* its code designation]

duck•bill \'dək-,bil\ *n* : PLATYPUS

duck•billed dinosaur \,dək-,bild-\ *n* : any of numerous plant-eating dinosaurs with the front part of the jaws covered by a horny bill resembling that of a bird

duckbilled platypus *n* : PLATYPUS

duck•board \'dək-,bōrd, -,bȯrd\ *n* : a boardwalk or slatted flooring laid on a wet, muddy, or cold surface — usually used in pl.

duck•ling \'dək-ling\ *n* : a young duck

duck•pin \'dək-,pin\ *n* **1** : a small bowling pin shorter and wider in the middle than a tenpin **2** *pl* : a bowling game using duckpins

ducks and drakes *n* : the pastime of skimming flat stones or shells along the surface of calm water

duck•weed \-,wēd\ *n* : a tiny free-floating stemless plant that grows on the surface of bodies of still water (as a pond)

duct \'dəkt\ *n* **1** : a tube or vessel carrying a bodily fluid (as the secretion of a gland) **2 a** : a pipe, tube, or channel that conveys a fluid (as air or water) **b** : a pipe or tubular passage for conductors (as an electric power line or telephone cables) [Latin *ductus* "act of leading", from *ducere* "to lead"] — **duct•less** \'dəkt-ləs\ *adj*

duc•tile \'dək-tl\ *adj* **1** : capable of being drawn out (as into a wire) or hammered thin ⟨*ductile* metal⟩ **2** : easily led or influenced — **duc•til•i•ty** \,dək-'til-ət-ē\ *n*

ductless gland *n* : ENDOCRINE GLAND

duc•tus ar•te•ri•o•sus \'dək-təs-är-,tir-ē-'ō-səs\ *n* : a short broad vessel in the fetus that conducts most of the blood directly from the right ventricle to the aorta bypassing the lungs [New Latin, literally, "arterial duct"]

dud \'dəd\ *n* **1** *pl* **a** : CLOTHES 1 **b** : personal belongings **2** : one that fails completely **3** : a missile (as a bomb or shell) that fails to explode [Middle English *dudde*]

dude \'düd, 'dyüd\ *n* **1** : an extremely fastidious man : DANDY **2** : a city man; *esp* : an Easterner in the West **3** : FELLOW 4a, MAN [origin unknown] — **dud•ish** \'düd-ish, 'dyüd-\ *adj* — **dud•ish•ly** *adv*

dude ranch *n* : a vacation resort offering horseback riding and other activities typical of western ranches

1**due** \'dü, 'dyü\ *adj* **1** : owed or owing as a debt or right **2** : according to accepted notions or procedures : APPROPRIATE **3 a** : SUFFICIENT, ADEQUATE ⟨arrived in *due* time⟩ **b** : REGULAR, LAWFUL ⟨*due* process of law⟩ **4** : ATTRIBUTABLE, ASCRIBABLE — used with *to* ⟨an accident *due* to negligence⟩ **5** : having reached the date at which payment is required : PAYABLE **6** : required or expected to happen : SCHEDULED ⟨*due* to arrive any time⟩ [Middle French *deu,* past participle of *devoir* "to owe", from Latin *debēre*]

2**due** *n* **1** : something owed : DEBT ⟨pay them their *due*⟩ **2** *pl* : a regular or legal charge or fee ⟨membership *dues*⟩

3**due** *adv* : DIRECTLY, EXACTLY ⟨*due* north⟩

1**du•el** \'dü-əl, 'dyü-\ *n* **1** : a combat between two persons; *esp* : one fought with weapons in the presence of witnesses **2** : a conflict between antagonistic persons, ideas, or forces [Medieval Latin *duellum,* from Latin *duellum, bellum* "war"]

2**duel** *vb* **du•eled** *or* **du•elled**; **du•el•ing** *or* **du•el•ling** : to fight in a duel — **du•el•er** *n* — **du•el•ist** \'dü-ə-ləst, 'dyü-\ *n*

du•en•na \dü-'en-ə, dyü-\ *n* **1** : an elderly woman in charge of the younger ladies in a Spanish or Portuguese family **2** : GOVERNESS, CHAPERON [Spanish *dueña,* from Latin *domina* "mistress, lady"]

du•et \dü-'et, dyü-\ *n* : a composition for or performance by two performers [Italian *duetto,* from *duo,* from Latin, "two"]

due to *prep* : because of

duff \'dəf\ *n* **1** : a steamed pudding usually containing raisins and currants **2** : partly decayed organic matter on the forest floor [English dialect, alteration of *dough*]

duf•fel \'dəf-əl\ *n* : an outfit of supplies (as for camping) : KIT [Dutch *duffel,* a kind of cloth, from *Duffel,* Belgium]

duffel bag *n* : a large cylindrical fabric bag for personal belongings

duf•fer \'dəf-ər\ *n* : an incompetent or clumsy person [origin unknown]

1**dug** *past of* DIG

2**dug** \'dəg\ *n* : UDDER 1, BREAST; *also* : TEAT 1, NIPPLE [perhaps of Scandinavian origin]

du•gong \'dü-,gäng, -,gȯng\ *n* : an aquatic plant-eating mammal related to the manatees but having a 2-lobed tail and tusks in the male — called also *sea cow* [Malay and Tagalog *duyong*]

dug•out \'dəg-,aůt\ *n* **1** : a boat made by hollowing out a large log **2** : a shelter dug in a hillside or in the ground or in the side of a trench **3** : a low shelter facing a baseball diamond and containing the players' bench

dui•ker \'dī-kər\ *n* : any of several small African antelopes [Afrikaans, literally, "diver"]

duke \'dük, 'dyük\ **1** : a sovereign ruler of a duchy **2** : a noble of the highest rank; *esp* : a member of the highest grade of the British peerage **3** *slang* : FIST 1, HAND — usually used in pl. [Old French *duc,* from Latin *duc-, dux* "leader", from *ducere* "to lead"] — **duke•dom** \-dəm\ *n*

dul•cet \'dəl-sət\ *adj* : sweet to the ear : MELODIOUS [Middle French *doucet* "sweet to the taste", from *douz* "sweet", from Latin *dulcis*]

dul•ci•mer \'dəl-sə-mər\ *n* **1** : a wire-stringed instrument played with light hammers held in the hands **2** *or* **dul•ci•more** \-,mōr, -,mȯr\ : an American folk instrument with three or four strings stretched over an elongate fretted sound box held on the lap and played by strumming or plucking [Middle French *doulcemer,* from Italian *dolcimelo*]

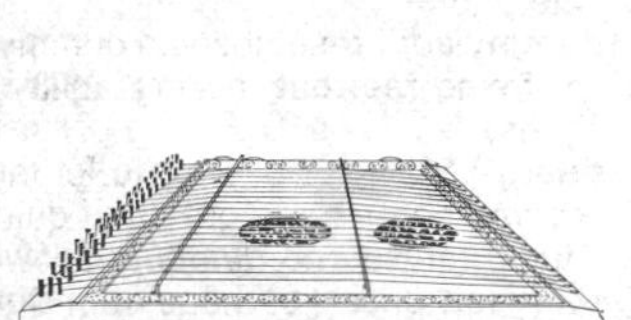

dulcimer 1

1**dull** \'dəl\ *adj* **1** : mentally slow : STUPID **2 a** : slow in perception or sensibility ⟨were *dull* to what went on around them⟩ **b** : lacking zest or vivacity : LISTLESS **3** : slow in action : SLUGGISH ⟨a *dull* market⟩ **4** : lacking sharpness of edge or point **5** : lacking brilliance or luster **6** : not resonant or ringing **7** : CLOUDY 3a, OVERCAST **8** : TEDIOUS, UNINTERESTING ⟨*dull* sermons⟩ **9** : low in saturation and lightness ⟨a *dull* shade of

\ə\ **abut**	\aů\ **out**	\i\ **tip**	\ȯ\ **saw**	\ů\ **foot**
\ər\ **further**	\ch\ **chin**	\ī\ **life**	\ȯi\ **coin**	\y\ **yet**
\a\ **mat**	\e\ **pet**	\j\ **job**	\th\ **thin**	\yü\ **few**
\ā\ **take**	\ē\ **easy**	\ng\ **sing**	\th\ **this**	\yů\ **cure**
\ä\ **cot, cart**	\g\ **go**	\ō\ **bone**	\ü\ **food**	\zh\ **vision**

blue⟩ [Middle English *dul*] **syn** see BLUNT, STUPID — **dull·ness** *or* **dul·ness** \ˈdəl-nəs\ *n* — **dul·ly** \ˈdəl-lē, -ē\ *adv*

[2]dull *vb* : to make or become dull

dull·ard \ˈdəl-ərd\ *n* : a stupid person

dulse \ˈdəls\ *n* : any of several coarse red seaweeds especially of northern seas that are used as food [Scottish Gaelic and Irish Gaelic *duilseag*]

du·ly \ˈdü-lē, ˈdyü-\ *adv* : in a due manner, time, or degree ⟨*duly* authorized⟩ ⟨will be *duly* considered⟩

du·ma \ˈdü-mə\ *n* : a representative council in Russia; *esp* : the principal legislative assembly in czarist Russia [Russian, of Germanic origin]

dumb \ˈdəm\ *adj* **1 a** : lacking the normal power of speech ⟨deaf and *dumb* from birth⟩ **b** : naturally incapable of speech **2** : not willing to speak **3** : STUPID 1, FOOLISH [Old English] — **dumb·ly** \ˈdəm-lē\ *adv* — **dumb·ness** *n*

• **syn** MUTE, SPEECHLESS: DUMB stresses lack of power to speak that may be natural and permanent ⟨*dumb* animals⟩ or temporary ⟨struck *dumb* with wonder⟩ MUTE stresses the fact of not speaking from whatever cause ⟨stood *mute* and ashamed before the accusers⟩ SPEECHLESS implies especially inability to find words because of shock or confusion of mind.

dumb·bell \ˈdəm-ˌbel\ *n* **1** : a weight consisting of a short bar with a sphere or weighted disk at each end and used usually in pairs for calisthenic exercise **2** : a dull or stupid person

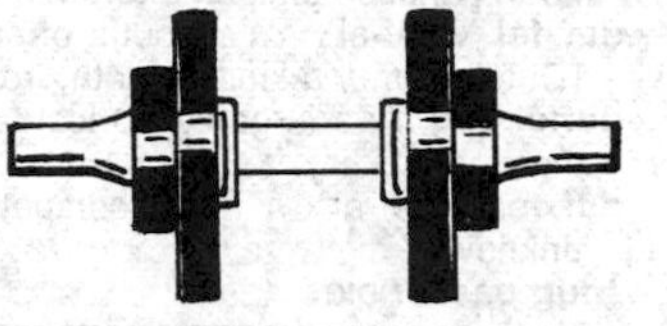
dumbbell 1

dumb·found *or* **dum·found** \ˌdəm-ˈfau̇nd\ *vt* : to astonish greatly [*dumb* + *-found* (as in *confound*)]

dumb show *n* : signs and gestures without words : PANTOMIME

dumb·wait·er \ˈdəm-ˈwāt-ər\ *n* **1** : a portable serving table **2** : a small elevator for conveying food and dishes or small goods from one story of a building to another

dum·dum \ˈdəm-ˌdəm\ *n* : a soft-nosed bullet that expands upon hitting an object [*Dum-Dum*, arsenal near Calcutta, India]

[1]dum·my \ˈdəm-ē\ *n, pl* **dum·mies 1** : a person who lacks or seems to lack the power of speech **2** : one (as a person or group) that though seeming to act independently is actually a front for another **3** : a stupid person **4** : an imitation of something to be used as a substitute or model ⟨the *dummies* in a store window⟩ **5 a** : an exposed hand in bridge played by one of the players in addition to his own hand **b** : a bridge player whose hand is a dummy **6** : a set of pages (as for a newspaper or magazine) with the position of text and artwork indicated for the printer

[2]dummy *adj* : resembling a dummy; *esp* : having the appearance of being real but lacking ability to function ⟨*dummy* wooden guns⟩

[1]dump \ˈdəmp\ *vb* **1 a** : to let fall in a heap or mass : UNLOAD ⟨*dump* coal⟩ **b** : to get rid of quickly or unceremoniously **c** : to dump refuse ⟨no *dumping* allowed⟩ **2** : to sell in quantity at a very low price [perhaps from Dutch *dompen* "to immerse, topple"] — **dump·er** *n*

[2]dump *n* **1** : a place where discarded materials are dumped **2** : a place where reserve military supplies are stored **3** : a disorderly, slovenly, or dilapidated place

dump·ling \ˈdəm-pliŋ\ *n* **1** : a small mass of dough cooked by boiling or steaming **2** : a dessert of fruit baked in biscuit dough [perhaps alteration of *lump*]

dumps \ˈdəmps\ *n pl* : a dull gloomy state of mind : low spirits ⟨in the *dumps*⟩ [probably from Dutch *domp* "haze"]

dump truck *n* : a truck for transporting and dumping loose materials

dumpy \ˈdəm-pē\ *adj* **dump·i·er; -est** : short and thick in build : SQUAT [English dialect *dump* "lump"] — **dump·i·ness** *n*

[1]dun \ˈdən\ *adj* **1** : having a dun color **2** : marked by dullness and drabness [Old English *dunn*] — **dun·ness** \ˈdən-nəs\ *n*

[2]dun *n* **1** : a pale horse usually with a dark mane and tail and a dorsal stripe **2** : a nearly neutral slightly brownish dark gray **3** : an immature winged mayfly

[3]dun *vt* **dunned; dun·ning 1** : to make persistent demands upon for payment **2** : to plague or pester constantly ⟨*dunned* by financial problems⟩ [origin unknown]

[4]dun *n* **1** : a person who duns another **2** : an urgent request; *esp* : a demand for payment

dunce \ˈdəns\ *n* : a dull-witted and stupid person [John *Duns* Scotus, died about 1308, Scottish scholastic theologian, whose once accepted writings were ridiculed in the 16th century]

dun·der·head \ˈdən-dər-ˌhed\ *n* : DUNCE, BLOCKHEAD [perhaps from Dutch *donder* "thunder"] — **dun·der·head·ed** \ˌdən-dər-ˈhed-əd\ *adj*

dune \ˈdün, ˈdyün\ *n* : a hill or ridge of sand piled up by the wind [French, from Old French, from Dutch]

[1]dung \ˈdəŋ\ *n* : the excrement of an animal : MANURE [Old English] — **dungy** \ˈdəŋ-ē\ *adj*

[2]dung *vt* : to fertilize or dress with manure

dun·ga·ree \ˌdəŋ-gə-ˈrē\ *n* **1** : a heavy coarse durable cotton twill woven from colored yarns; *esp* : blue denim **2** *pl* : trousers made of dungaree [Hindi *dūgrī*]

dung beetle *n* : a beetle (as a tumblebug) that rolls balls of dung in which it lays eggs and on which the larvae feed

dun·geon \ˈdən-jən\ *n* **1** : DONJON **2** : a close dark usually underground prison [Middle French *donjon*, derived from Latin *dominus* "lord, master"]

dung·hill \ˈdəŋ-ˌhil\ *n* : a manure pile

dunk \ˈdəŋk\ *vb* **1** : to dip (as bread or cake) into liquid while eating **2** : to dip or submerge temporarily in liquid **3** : to submerge oneself in water [Pennsylvania German *dunke*, from Old High German *dunkōn*]

dunk shot *n* : a shot in basketball made by leaping high into the air and throwing the ball down through the basket

dun·lin \ˈdən-lən\ *n, pl* **dunlins** *or* **dunlin** : a widely distributed small sandpiper largely brown above and white below with a black patch on the belly [[1]*dun* + *-lin* (alteration of *-ling*)]

dun·nage \ˈdən-ij\ *n* **1** : loose materials used around a cargo to prevent damage; *also* : padding in a shipping container **2** : baggage or personal effects especially of a sailor [origin unknown]

duo \ˈdü-ō, ˈdyü-\ *n, pl* **du·os 1** : DUET; *esp* : a composition for two performers at two pianos **2** : PAIR 3 [Italian, from Latin, "two"]

duo·dec·i·mal \ˌdü-ə-ˈdes-ə-məl, ˌdyü-\ *adj* **1** : of, relating to, or proceeding by 12 **2** : relating to, expressed in, or being a system of numeration with a base of 12 [Latin *duodecim* "twelve"] — **duodecimal** *n*

du·o·de·num \ˌdü-ə-ˈdē-nəm, ˌdyü-; du̇-ˈäd-n-əm, dyu̇-\ *n, pl* **-de·na** \-ˈdē-nə, -n-ə\ *or* **-denums** : the first part of the small intestine extending from the pylorus to the jejunum [Medieval Latin, from Latin *duodeni* "twelve each", from *duodecim* "twelve"; from its length, about 12 fingers' breadth] — **du·o·de·nal** \-ˈdēn-l, -n-əl\ *adj*

duo·logue \ˈdü-ə-ˌlȯg, ˈdyü-\ *n* : a dialogue between two persons

[1]dupe \ˈdüp, ˈdyüp\ *n* : one who is easily deceived or cheated [French]

[2]dupe *vt* : to make a dupe of : DECEIVE — **dup·er** *n*

du·ple \ˈdü-pəl, ˈdyü-\ *adj* **1** : taken by twos : TWOFOLD **2** : having two beats or a multiple of two beats per measure of music ⟨*duple* time⟩ [Latin *duplus* "double"]

[1]du·plex \ˈdü-ˌpleks, ˈdyü-\ *adj* : DOUBLE 2, TWOFOLD; esp : having two parts that act at the same time or in the same way ⟨a *duplex* lathe⟩ [Latin, from *duo* "two" + *-plex* "-fold"]

[2]duplex *n* : something duplex; *esp* : a 2-family house

duplex apartment *n* : an apartment having rooms on two floors

[1]du·pli·cate \ˈdü-pli-kət, ˈdyü-\ *adj* **1** : having or being two corresponding or identical parts or examples **2** : being the same as another **3** : of or relating to a card game in which players play identical hands in order to compare scores ⟨*duplicate* bridge⟩ [Latin *duplicare* "to double", from *duplex* "double"]

[2]duplicate *n* **1** : a thing that exactly resembles another in appearance, pattern, or content : COPY **2** : two copies both alike ⟨typed in *duplicate*⟩

• **syn** DUPLICATE, COPY, FACSIMILE, REPRODUCTION mean a thing made to resemble another or an original closely. DUPLICATE suggests exact sameness of pattern and usually of material; COPY applies to anything reproduced mechanically or without intentional changes; FACSIMILE implies exact and detailed reproduction of pattern that may differ in scale or material; REPRODUCTION implies an exact or very close imitation of an original in all respects.

[3]du·pli·cate \ˈdü-pli-ˌkāt, ˈdyü-\ *vt* **1** : to make double or twofold **2** : to make a duplicate of — **du·pli·ca·tive** \-ˌkāt-iv\ *adj*

du·pli·ca·tion \ˌdü-pli-ˈkā-shən, ˌdyü-\ *n* **1 a** : an act or process of duplicating **b** : the quality or state of being duplicated **2** : DUPLICATE, COUNTERPART

duplication of the cube : the mathematical problem of constructing the edge of a cube having twice the volume of a cube whose edge is given

du·pli·ca·tor \ˈdü-pli-ˌkāt-ər, ˈdyü-\ *n* : one that duplicates; *esp* : a machine for making copies of graphic matter

du·plic·i·ty \du̇-ˈplis-ət-ē, dyu̇-\ *n, pl* **-ties** : deception by pretending to feel and act one way while acting another

du·ra·ble \ˈdu̇r-ə-bəl\ *adj* : able to last a long time ⟨*durable* clothing⟩ [Middle French, from Latin *durare* "to last"] **syn** see LASTING — **du·ra·bil·i·ty** \ˌdu̇r-ə-ˈbil-ət-ē, ˌdyu̇r-\ *n* — **du·ra·ble·ness** *n* — **du·ra·bly** \ˈdu̇r-ə-blē, ˈdyu̇r-\ *adv*

du·ral·u·min \du̇-ˈral-yə-mən, dyu̇-; ˌdu̇r-ə-ˈlü-mən, ˌdyu̇r-\ *n* : a strong light alloy of aluminum, copper, manganese, and magnesium [German, from *Düren*, Germany + *aluminium* "aluminum"]

du·ra ma·ter \ˈdu̇r-ə-ˌmāt-ər, ˈdyu̇r-, -ˌmät-\ *n* : the outermost and tough fibrous membrane that envelops the brain and spinal cord [Medieval Latin, literally, "hard mother"]

du·rance \ˈdu̇r-əns, ˈdyu̇r-\ *n* : IMPRISONMENT [Middle French, "endurance", from *durer* "to endure"]

du·ra·tion \du̇-ˈrā-shən, dyu̇-\ *n* **1** : continuance in time ⟨a storm of short *duration*⟩ **2** : the time during which something lasts ⟨the *duration* of the war⟩ [Medieval Latin *duratio*, from Latin *durare* "to last"]

du·ress \du̇-ˈres, dyu̇-\ *n* **1** : forcible restraint **2** : compulsion by threat ⟨a confession obtained under *duress*⟩ [Middle French *duresce* "hardness, severity", from Latin *duritia*, from *durus* "hard"]

Dur·ham \ˈdər-əm, ˈdə-rəm, ˈdu̇r-əm\ *n* : SHORTHORN [County *Durham*, England]

du·ri·an \ˈdu̇r-ē-ən, ˈdyu̇r-\ *n* : a large oval tasty but foul-smelling fruit with a prickly rind and soft pulp; *also* : the East Indian tree that bears it [Malay]

dur·ing \ˌdu̇r-ing, ˌdyu̇r-\ *prep* **1** : throughout the duration of ⟨*during* their whole lifetimes⟩ **2** : at some time or times in the course of ⟨occasional showers *during* the day⟩ [Middle English, from *duren* "to last", from Old French *durer*, from Latin *durare*, from *durus* "hard"]

dur·ra \ˈdu̇r-ə\ *n* : any of several grain sorghums grown in warm dry regions [Arabic *dhurah*]

du·rum wheat \ˌdu̇r-əm-, ˌdyu̇r-\ *n* : a wheat that yields a flour that is rich in gluten and is used especially in macaroni and spaghetti — called also *durum* [Latin *durum*, neuter of *durus* "hard"]

[1]**dusk** \ˈdəsk\ *vb* : to make or become dark or gloomy [Middle English *dosk* "dusky", alteration of Old English *dox*]

[2]**dusk** *n* **1** : the darker part of twilight especially at night **2** : GLOOM

dusky \ˈdəs-kē\ *adj* **dusk·i·er**; **-est 1** : somewhat dark in color; *esp* : having dark skin **2** : marked by slight or deficient light : SHADOWY — **dusk·i·ly** \-kə-lē\ *adv* — **dusk·i·ness** \-kē-nəs\ *n*

[1]**dust** \ˈdəst\ *n* **1** : fine particles (as of earth or in space); *also* : a fine powder **2** : the earthy remains of bodies once alive; *esp* : the human corpse **3 a** : a place (as in the earth) of burial **b** : the surface of the ground **4 a** : something worthless **b** : a low or miserable condition : state of humiliation [Old English *dūst*] — **dust·less** \ˈdəst-ləs\ *adj*

[2]**dust** *vb* **1 a** : to free from dust **b** : to brush or wipe away dust **2** : to sprinkle with fine particles or in the form of dust ⟨*dust* a pan with flour⟩ ⟨*dust* an insecticide on plants⟩

dust·bin \ˈdəst-ˌbin, ˈdəs-\ *n, British* : a trash or garbage can

dust bowl *n* : a region that suffers from prolonged droughts and dust storms

dust devil *n* : a small whirlwind containing sand or dust

dust·er \ˈdəs-tər\ *n* **1** : one that dusts: as **a** : something (as a cloth) with which dust is removed **b** : a device for applying insecticidal or fungicidal dusts to crops **2 a** : a light outer garment to protect clothing from dust **b** : a dress-length housecoat

dust jacket *n* : a removable usually decorative paper cover for a book

dust·man \ˈdəst-mən, ˈdəs-\ *n, British* : a trash or garbage collector

dust·pan \-ˌpan\ *n* : a shovel-shaped pan for sweepings

dust storm *n* : strong turbulent winds bearing clouds of dust across a dry region

dusty \ˈdəs-tē\ *adj* **dust·i·er**; **-est 1** : filled or covered with dust **2** : consisting of or resembling dust : POWDERY — **dust·i·ly** \-tə-lē\ *adv* — **dust·i·ness** \-tē-nəs\ *n*

dutch \ˈdəch\ *adv, often cap* : with each person paying his own way

[1]**Dutch** \ˈdəch\ *adj* **1** *slang* : GERMAN **2** : of or relating to the Netherlands, its inhabitants, or their language

[2]**Dutch** *n* **1** : the Germanic language of the Netherlands **2** *pl in construction* : the people of the Netherlands **3** : DISFAVOR, TROUBLE ⟨was in *Dutch* with the teacher⟩ [Middle English *Duche*, from Dutch *duutsch*]

Dutch clover *n* : WHITE CLOVER

Dutch door *n* : a door divided horizontally so that the lower part can be shut while the upper part remains open

Dutch elm disease *n* : a fungous disease of elms characterized by yellowing of the foliage, loss of leaves, and death

Dutch·man \ˈdəch-mən\ *n* **1 a** : a native or inhabitant of the Netherlands **b** : a person of Dutch descent **2** *slang* : GERMAN

Dutch·man's–breech·es \ˌdəch-mənz-ˈbrich-əz\ *n pl* : a delicate spring-flowering herb of the eastern United States resembling the related bleeding heart but having cream-white double-spurred flowers

Dutchman's-breeches

Dutch oven *n* **1** : a metal shield for roasting before an open fire **2** : a brick oven in which cooking is done by the preheated walls **3 a** : a cast-iron kettle with a tight cover used for baking in an open fire **b** : a heavy pot with a tight-fitting domed cover

Dutch treat *n* : something (as a meal) for which each participant pays his or her own way

Dutch uncle *n* : one who admonishes sternly and bluntly

du·te·ous \ˈdüt-ē-əs, ˈdyüt-\ *adj* : DUTIFUL, OBEDIENT — **du·te·ous·ly** *adv* — **du·te·ous·ness** *n*

du·ti·able \ˈdüt-ē-ə-bəl, ˈdyüt-\ *adj* : subject to a duty ⟨*dutiable* imports⟩

du·ti·ful \ˈdüt-i-fəl, ˈdyüt-\ *adj* **1** : motivated by a sense of duty ⟨a *dutiful* son⟩ **2** : coming from or showing a sense of duty ⟨*dutiful* affection⟩ — **du·ti·ful·ly** \-fə-lē\ *adv* — **du·ti·ful·ness** *n*

du·ty \ˈdüt-ē, ˈdyüt-\ *n, pl* **duties 1** : conduct due to parents and superiors : RESPECT **2 a** : the action required by one's position or occupation **b** : assigned service or business; *esp* : active military service **3 a** : a moral or legal obligation **b** : the force of moral obligation ⟨obey the call of *duty*⟩ **4** : TAX; *esp* : a tax on imports **5** : the service required (as of a machine) : USE ⟨a drill designed to withstand heavy *duty*⟩ [Anglo-French *dueté*, from Old French *deu* "due"] **syn** see TASK

du·um·vir \du̇-ˈəm-vər, dyu̇-\ *n* : either of two Roman officers or magistrates jointly constituting a board or court [Latin, from *duum* (genitive of *duo* "two") + *vir* "man"]

du·um·vi·rate \-və-rət\ *n* **1** : two people associated in high office **2** : government or control by two people

[1]**dwarf** \ˈdwȯrf\ *n, pl* **dwarfs** \ˈdwȯrfs\ *also* **dwarves** \ˈdwȯrvz\ **1** : a person, lower animal, or plant much below normal size **2** : a small legendary humanlike being usually misshapen and ugly and skilled at metalwork **3** : a star of ordinary or low luminosity and relatively small mass and size [Old English *dweorg*, *dweorh*] — **dwarf** *adj* — **dwarf·ish** \ˈdwȯr-fish\ *adj* — **dwarf·ness** *n*

[2]**dwarf** *vb* **1** : to restrict the growth or development of : STUNT ⟨*dwarf* a tree⟩ **2** : to cause to appear smaller

dwarf·ism \ˈdwȯr-ˌfiz-əm\ *n* : a condition of stunted growth

dwell \'dwel\ *vi* **dwelt** \'dwelt\ *or* **dwelled** \'dweld, 'dwelt\; **dwell·ing 1 :** to remain for a time **2 :** to live as a resident **:** RESIDE **3 a :** to linger over something (as with the eyes or mind) **:** keep the attention directed ⟨*dwelt* on the scene before them⟩ **b :** to write or speak at length or insistently **[**Old English *dwellan* "to go astray, hinder"**]** — **dwell·er** *n*

dwell·ing \'dwel-ing\ *n* **:** a building or other shelter in which people live **:** HOUSE

dwin·dle \'dwin-dl\ *vb* **dwin·dled**; **dwin·dling** \'dwin-dling, -dl-ing\ **:** to make or become gradually less ⟨a *dwindling* supply of coal⟩ **[**probably from *dwine* "to waste away"**]** **syn** see DECREASE

dyb·buk \'dib-ək\ *n* **:** a wandering soul believed in Jewish folklore to enter and control a person **[**Hebrew *dibbūq***]**

¹dye \'dī\ *n* **1 :** color from dyeing **2 :** a material used for dyeing or staining **[**Old English *dēah, dēag***]**

²dye *vb* **dyed**; **dye·ing 1 :** to stain or color usually permanently **2 :** to impart (a color) by dyeing **3 :** to take up or impart color in dyeing — **dy·er** \'dī-ər, 'dīr\ *n*

dyed-in-the-wool \,dīd-n-thə-'wu̇l\ *adj* **:** THOROUGHGOING, UNCOMPROMISING ⟨a *dyed-in-the-wool* conservative⟩

dye·stuff \'dī-,stəf\ *n* **:** DYE 2

dy·ing \'dī-ing\ *adj* **1 :** being about to die **:** being in the act of dying or dying out ⟨a *dying* child⟩ ⟨a *dying* fire⟩ **2 :** of or relating to dying or death ⟨a *dying* wish⟩ **[**from present participle of *die***]**

dyke *variant of* DIKE

dy·nam·ic \dī-'nam-ik\ *adj* **1 a :** of or relating to physical force or energy **b :** of or relating to dynamics **:** ACTIVE **2 a :** marked by continuous activity or change **b :** marked by energy **:** FORCEFUL ⟨a *dynamic* personality⟩ **[**French *dynamique,* from Greek *dynamis* "power", from *dynasthai* "to be able"**]** — **dy·nam·i·cal** \-'nam-i-kəl\ *adj* — **dy·nam·i·cal·ly** \-i-kə-lē, -klē\ *adv*

dy·nam·ics \dī-'nam-iks\ *n sing or pl* **1 :** a branch of mechanics that deals with the motion of bodies and the action of forces in producing or changing their motion **2 :** physical, moral, or intellectual forces or the laws relating to them **3 :** the pattern of change or growth typical of something **4 :** variation and contrast in force or intensity (as in music)

dy·na·mism \'dī-nə-,miz-əm\ *n* **1 a :** a theory that explains the universe in terms of forces and their interplay **b :** DYNAMICS 3 **2 :** a dynamic quality

¹dy·na·mite \'dī-nə-,mīt\ *n* **:** a blasting explosive that is made chiefly of nitroglycerin absorbed in a porous material; *also* **:** any of various blasting explosives that contain no nitroglycerin

²dynamite *vt* **:** to blow up with dynamite — **dy·na·mit·er** *n*

dy·na·mo \'dī-nə-,mō\ *n, pl* **-mos 1 :** GENERATOR 3 **2 :** a forceful energetic person **[**short for *dynamoelectric machine***]**

dy·na·mom·e·ter \,dī-nə-'mäm-ət-ər\ *n* **:** an apparatus for measuring mechanical power (as of an engine) — **dy·na·mo·met·ric** \,dī-nə-mō-'me-trik\ *adj* — **dy·na·mom·e·try** \,dī-nə-'mäm-ə-trē\ *n*

dy·na·mo·tor \'dī-nə-,mōt-ər\ *n* **:** a motor generator combining the electric motor and generator

dy·nas·ty \'dī-nə-stē, -,nas-tē\ *n, pl* **-ties 1 :** a succession of rulers of the same line of descent **2 :** a powerful group or family that maintains its position for a considerable time **[**Greek *dynasteia* "power, lordship," from *dynastēs* "ruler", from *dynasthai* "to be able"**]** — **dy·nas·tic** \dī-'nas-tik\ *adj* — **dy·nas·ti·cal·ly** \-ti-kə-lē, -klē\ *adv*

dyne \'dīn\ *n* **:** the unit of force in the cgs system equal to the force that would give a free mass of one gram an acceleration of one centimeter per second per second that is equivalent to 10^{-5} newton **[**French, from Greek *dynamis* "power"**]**

dys- *combining form* **1 :** abnormal **2 :** difficult ⟨*dys*menorrhea⟩ — compare EU- **3 :** impaired ⟨*dys*function⟩ **[**Greek, "bad, difficult"**]**

dys·en·tery \'dis-n-,ter-ē\ *n* **1 :** a disease characterized by severe diarrhea with passage of mucus and blood and usually caused by infection **2 :** DIARRHEA **[**Latin *dysenteria,* from Greek, from *dys-* + *enteron* "intestine"**]** — **dys·en·ter·ic** \,dis-n-'ter-ik\ *adj*

dys·func·tion \dis-'fəng-shən, -'fəngk-\ *n* **:** impaired or abnormal functioning — **dys·func·tion·al** \-shnəl, -shən-l\ *adj*

dys·lex·ia \dis-'lek-sē-ə\ *n* **:** a disturbance of the ability to read **[***dys-* + Greek *lexis* "word, speech"**]** — **dys·lex·ic** \-sik\ *adj*

dys·men·or·rhea \,dis-,men-ə-'rē-ə\ *n* **:** painful menstruation **[***dys-* + *meno-* "menstruation" + *-rrhea***]** — **dys·men·or·rhe·ic** \-'rē-ik\ *adj*

dys·pep·sia \dis-'pep-shə, -sē-ə\ *n* **:** INDIGESTION **[**Latin, from Greek, from *dys-* + *pepsis* "digestion", from *peptein, pessein* "to cook, digest"**]**

dys·pep·tic \-'pep-tik\ *adj* **1 :** relating to or having dyspepsia **2 :** GLOOMY 2, CROSS — **dys·pep·ti·cal·ly** \-ti-kə-lē, -klē\ *adv*

dys·pro·si·um \dis-'prō-zē-əm\ *n* **:** a chemical element that forms highly magnetic compounds — see ELEMENT table **[**New Latin, from Greek *dysprositos* "hard to get at", from *dys-* + *prositos* "approachable"**]**

dys·tro·phy \'dis-trə-fē\ *n, pl* **-phies :** imperfect nutrition; *esp* **:** any of several disorders involving nerves and muscles — compare MUSCULAR DYSTROPHY — **dys·tro·phic** \dis-'trō-fik\ *adj*

E e—Ezra

e \'ē\ *n, pl* **e's** *or* **es** \ēz\ *often cap* **1 :** the 5th letter of the English alphabet **2 :** the musical tone E **3 :** the base of the system of natural logarithms having the approximate numerical value 2.71828 **4 :** a grade rating a student's work as poor and usually constituting a conditional pass

e- \ē, 'ē, i\ *prefix* **1 :** not **2 :** out, forth, away **[**Latin, "out, forth, away", from *ex-***]**

¹each \'ēch\ *adj* **:** being one of two or more distinct individuals **[**Old English *ǣlc***]**

²each *pron* **:** each one ⟨*each* of us had a twin⟩

³each *adv* **:** to or for each **:** APIECE

each other *pron* **:** each of two or more in reciprocal action or relation ⟨looked at *each other*⟩

ea·ger \'ē-gər\ *adj* **:** marked by enthusiastic or sharply expectant desire or interest **[**Old French *aigre* "keen, sharp", from Latin *acer***]** — **ea·ger·ly** *adv* — **ea·ger·ness** *n*

• **syn** ANXIOUS: EAGER implies ardor and enthusiasm and suggests impatience at delay or restraint; ANXIOUS stresses fear of frustration or failure or disappointment.

eager beaver *n* **:** one who is unduly zealous in performing his assigned duties and in volunteering for more

ea·gle \'ē-gəl\ *n* **1 :** any of various large day-flying sharp-eyed predatory birds that have a powerful flight and are related to the hawks **2 :** a seal or standard or an insignia shaped like or bearing an eagle **3 :** a 10-dollar gold coin of the United States bearing an eagle on the reverse **4 :** a golf score of two strokes less than par on a hole **[**Old French *aigle,* from Latin *aquila***]**

ea·glet \'ē-glət\ *n* **:** a young eagle

eagle 1

-ean — see -AN

¹ear \'iər\ *n* **1 a :** the vertebrate organ of hearing and balance consisting in the typical mammal of a sound-collecting outer ear separated by a membranous drum from a sound-transmitting middle ear that in turn is separated from a sensory inner ear **b :** the outer ear **c :** any of various organs capable of detecting vibrations **2 a :** the sense or act of hearing **b :** sensitivity to musical tone and pitch **3** : ATTENTION; *esp* : sympathetic attention **4** : something resembling an ear in shape or position [Old English *ēare*] — **eared** \ˈiərd\ *adj* — **ear•less** \ˈiər-ləs\ *adj*

[2]ear *n* : the fruiting spike of a cereal (as Indian corn) including both the seeds and protective structures [Old English *ēar*] — **ear** *vi*

ear•ache \ˈiər-ˌāk\ *n* : an ache or pain in the ear

ear•drum \ˈiər-ˌdrəm\ *n* : the thin membrane that separates the outer and middle ear and transmits sound waves as vibrations to the chain of tiny bones in the middle ear

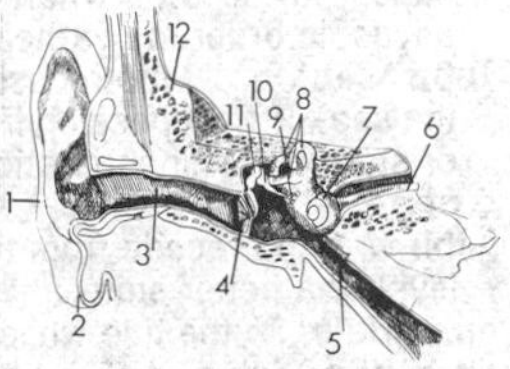

[1]ear 1a: *1* pinna, *2* lobe, *3* auditory canal, *4* eardrum, *5* eustachian tube, *6* auditory nerve, *7* cochlea, *8* semicircular canals, *9* stapes, *10* incus, *11* malleus, *12* bones of skull

eared seal *n* : any of a family of seals including the sea lions and fur seals and having small well-developed external ears

ear•ful \-ˌfu̇l\ *n* **1** : an outpouring of news or gossip **2** : a sharp reprimand

earl \ˈərl\ *n* : a member of the British peerage ranking below a marquess and above a viscount [Old English *eorl* "warrior, nobleman"] — **earl•dom** \-dəm\ *n*

earless seal *n* : any of a family of seals with hairy coats and no external ears

ear•lobe \ˈiər-ˌlōb\ *n* : the pendent part of the ear of human beings or some fowls

[1]ear•ly \ˈər-lē\ *adv* **ear•li•er**; **-est** **1** : near the beginning of a period of time or of a process or series **2** : before the usual or expected time [Old English *ǣrlīce*, from *ǣr* "early, soon"]

[2]early *adj* **ear•li•er**; **-est** **1 a** : of, relating to, or occurring near the beginning of a period of time, a development, or a series **b** : PRIMITIVE ⟨*early* art forms⟩ **2 a** : occurring before the usual or expected time ⟨spring was *early* this year⟩ **b** : occurring in the near future **c** : maturing or producing sooner than related forms ⟨an *early* peach⟩ — **ear•li•ness** *n*

[1]ear•mark \ˈiər-ˌmärk\ *n* **1** : a mark of identification on the ear of an animal **2** : a distinguishing characteristic ⟨all the *earmarks* of poverty⟩

[2]earmark *vt* **1** : to mark with or as if with an earmark **2** : to set aside (as funds) for a specific use

ear•muff \ˈiər-ˌməf\ *n* : one of a pair of ear coverings connected by a flexible band and worn as protection against cold or noises

earn \ˈərn\ *vt* **1 a** : to get for services given ⟨*earn* a good salary⟩ **b** : RETURN 6, YIELD ⟨investments *earning* 8%⟩ **2** : to deserve as a result of labor or service ⟨you *earned* every cent you were paid⟩ [Old English *earnian*] — **earn•er** *n*

[1]ear•nest \ˈər-nəst\ *n* : a serious and intent state of mind ⟨in *earnest*⟩ [Old English *eornost*]

[2]earnest *adj* **1** : characterized by or proceeding from a serious and intense state of mind **2** : not trivial : IMPORTANT **syn** see SERIOUS — **ear•nest•ly** *adv* — **ear•nest•ness** \-nəst-nəs, -nəs-nəs\ *n*

[3]earnest *n* **1** : something of value given by a buyer to a seller to bind a bargain **2** : a token of what is to come : PLEDGE [Old French *erres*, pl. of *erre* "earnest," from Latin *arra*, short for *arrabo*, from Greek *arrhabōn*, from Hebrew *'ērābhōn*]

earn•ings \ˈər-ningz\ *n pl* : something earned: as **a** : WAGE **b** : revenue after deduction of expenses

ear•phone \ˈiər-ˌfōn\ *n* : a device that converts electrical energy into sound waves and is worn over or inserted into the ear ⟨a radio *earphone*⟩

ear•ring \ˈiər-ˌring\ *n* : an ornament for the earlobe

ear•shot \ˈiər-ˌshät\ *n* : the range within which the unaided voice may be heard

ear•split•ting \-ˌsplit-ing\ *adj* : intolerably loud or shrill

[1]earth \ˈərth\ *n* **1** : the soft or granular material composing part of the surface of the globe; *esp* : cultivable soil **2** : the sphere of mortal life as distinguished from heaven and hell **3** : areas of land as distinguished from sea and air : GROUND **4** *often cap* : the planet on which we live and which is 3d in order of distance from the sun — see PLANET table **5** : the lair of a burrowing animal **6** : any of several metallic oxides (as alumina) [Old English *eorthe*] — **earth•like** \-ˌlīk\ *adj*

• **syn** EARTH, WORLD, UNIVERSE mean the entire area in which humanity thinks of itself as living. EARTH denotes the material global body, the planet of the sun, but often means the immediate sphere of human action in contrast to the religious concepts of heaven and hell; WORLD often equals EARTH but may apply to space, earth, and all visible celestial bodies within our present range of knowledge; UNIVERSE denotes the entire system of created things and physical phenomena regarded as a unit in its arrangement and operation.

[2]earth *vt* : to draw soil about (plants)

earth•en \ˈər-thən, -t͟hən\ *adj* : made of earth or of baked clay ⟨an *earthen* floor⟩ ⟨*earthen* dishes⟩

earth•en•ware \-ˌwaər, -ˌweər\ *n* : articles (as utensils or ornaments) made of baked clay

earth•ling \ˈərth-ling\ *n* : an inhabitant of the earth

earth•ly \ˈərth-lē\ *adj* **1 a** : of, relating to, or characteristic of the earth **b** : relating to human life on the earth ⟨*earthly* joys⟩ **2** : POSSIBLE, IMAGINABLE ⟨that tool is of no *earthly* use⟩ — **earth•li•ness** *n*

• **syn** WORLDLY, MUNDANE: EARTHLY often implies contrast with heavenly or spiritual ⟨*earthly* love⟩ WORLDLY and MUNDANE both imply a relation to the immediate concerns and activities of human beings, WORLDLY suggesting tangible personal gain or gratification ⟨*worldly* goods⟩ and MUNDANE suggesting reference to the immediate and practical ⟨a *mundane* discussion of finances⟩

earth•quake \ˈərth-ˌkwāk\ *n* : a shaking or trembling of a portion of the earth caused by movement of rock masses or by volcanic shocks

earth science *n* : any of the sciences (as geology or geography) that deal with the earth or one of its parts

earth•shine \-ˌshīn\ *n* : sunlight reflected by the earth that illuminates the dark part of the moon — called also *earthlight*

earth•work \-ˌwərk\ *n* : an embankment or other construction of earth; *esp* : one made as a fortification

earth•worm \-ˌwərm\ *n* : a long slender worm with segmented body that lives in damp earth and moves with the aid of setae

earthy \ˈər-thē, -t͟hē\ *adj* **earth•i•er**; **-est** **1** : consisting of or resembling earth ⟨an *earthy* flavor⟩ **2 a** : DOWN-TO-EARTH, PRACTICAL **b** : CRUDE, GROSS ⟨*earthy* humor⟩ — **earth•i•ness** *n*

ear•wax \ˈiər-ˌwaks\ *n* : a brownish yellow or orange waxlike substance produced by the glands of the external ear — called also *cerumen, wax*

ear•wig \-ˌwig\ *n* : any of numerous insects (order Dermaptera) with slender many-jointed antennae and a pair of large terminal appendages arranged like forceps [Old English *ēarwicga*, from *ēare* "ear" + *wicga* "insect"]

[1]ease \ˈēz\ *n* **1** : the state of being comfortable: as **a** : freedom from pain or discomfort **b** : freedom from care **c** : freedom from a sense of difficulty or embarrassment : NATURALNESS ⟨speak with *ease*⟩ **2** : EFFORTLESSNESS ⟨rides a horse with *ease*⟩ [Old French *aise* "convenience, comfort", from Latin *adjacens* "neighborhood", from *adjacēre* "to lie near", from *ad-* + *jacēre* "to lie"] — **ease•ful** \-fəl\ *adj*

[2]ease *vb* **1** : to free from something that disquiets or burdens ⟨*ease* you of your troubles⟩ **2** : to make less painful : ALLEVIATE ⟨*ease* your suffering⟩ **3** : to make less tight or difficult : LOOSEN, SLACKEN ⟨*ease* credit⟩ ⟨*ease* up on a rope⟩

ea•sel \ˈē-zəl\ *n* : a frame for supporting something (as an artist's canvas) [Dutch *ezel* "ass", from Latin *asinus*]

△ **origin** An easel is a frame for supporting something, such as an artist's painting or a blackboard. The word was borrowed into English from the Dutch *ezel*, which was used for the same piece of equipment. This sense of *ezel* was a metaphorical extension of the literal meaning "ass, donkey", probably because an easel, like a beast of burden, is used to hold things.

eas•i•ly \ˈēz-lē, -ə-lē\ *adv* **1** : in an easy manner ⟨won the game *easily*⟩ **2** : by far ⟨*easily* the best candidate⟩

[1]east \ˈēst\ *adv* : to, toward, or in the east [Old English *ēast*]

[2]east *adj* **1** : situated toward or at the east **2** : coming from the east

\ə\ **abut**	\au̇\ **out**	\i\ **tip**	\ȯ\ **saw**	\u̇\ **foot**
\ər\ **further**	\ch\ **chin**	\ī\ **life**	\ȯi\ **coin**	\y\ **yet**
\a\ **mat**	\e\ **pet**	\j\ **job**	\th\ **thin**	\yü\ **few**
\ā\ **take**	\ē\ **easy**	\ng\ **sing**	\t͟h\ **this**	\yu̇\ **cure**
\ä\ **cot, cart**	\g\ **go**	\ō\ **bone**	\ü\ **food**	\zh\ **vision**

[3]**east** *n* **1 a :** the general direction of sunrise **b :** the compass point directly opposite to west **2** *cap* **:** regions or countries east of a specified or implied point **3 :** the altar end of a church
east•bound \'ēst-,baùnd, 'ēs-\ *adj* **:** headed east
Eas•ter \'ē-stər\ *n* **:** a feast that commemorates Christ's resurrection and is observed on the first Sunday after the full moon on or next after March 21 or one week later if the full moon falls on Sunday [Old English *ēastre*]
Easter lily *n* **:** any of several white cultivated lilies that bloom in early spring
east•er•ly \'ē-stər-lē\ *adv or adj* **1 :** from the east **2 :** toward the east
east•ern \'ē-stərn\ *adj* **1** *often cap* **:** of, relating to, or characteristic of a region conventionally designated East **2** *cap* **a :** of, relating to, or being the Christian churches originating in the church of the Eastern Roman Empire **b :** Eastern Orthodox **3 :** lying toward or coming from the east [Old English *ēasterne*] — **east•ern•most** \-,mōst\ *adj*
East•ern•er \'ē-stər-nər, -stə-nər\ *n* **:** a native or inhabitant of the East (as of the United States)
eastern hemisphere *n* **:** the half of the earth to the east of the Atlantic ocean including Europe, Asia, and Africa
Eastern Orthodox *adj* **:** of or consisting of the Eastern churches that form a loose federation according primacy of honor to the patriarch of Constantinople and adhering to the decisions of the first seven ecumenical councils and to one rite
Eastern time *n* **:** the time of the 5th time zone west of Greenwich that includes the eastern United States
East Goth *n* **:** OSTROGOTH
east•ing \'ē-sting\ *n* **1 :** difference in longitude to the east from the last preceding point of reckoning **2 :** easterly progress
east–northeast *n* **:** two points north of east **:** N67°30′E
east–southeast *n* **:** two points south of east **:** S67°30′E
[1]**east•ward** \'ēs-twərd\ *adv or adj* **:** toward the east — **east•wards** \-twərdz\ *adv*
[2]**eastward** *n* **:** eastward direction or part
easy \'ē-zē\ *adj* **eas•i•er; -est 1 :** not hard to do ⟨an *easy* lesson⟩ **2 a :** not severe **:** LENIENT ⟨an *easy* teacher⟩ **b :** not steep or abrupt ⟨*easy* slopes⟩ **3 a :** marked by peace and comfort **b :** not hurried ⟨an *easy* pace⟩ **4 a :** free from pain, trouble or worry **b :** showing ease **:** NATURAL ⟨an *easy* manner⟩ **5 a :** giving comfort or relaxation ⟨an *easy* chair⟩ **b :** not imposing hardship ⟨buying on *easy* terms⟩ **syn** see SIMPLE — **eas•i•ness** *n*
easy•go•ing \,ē-zē-'gō-ing\ *adj* **:** taking life easily **:** CAREFREE — **easy•go•ing•ness** *n*
easy street *n* **:** a situation with no financial worries
eat \'ēt\ *vb* **ate** \'āt\; **eat•en** \'ēt-n\; **eat•ing 1 :** to take into the mouth as food **:** chew and swallow in turn **2 :** to take a meal **3 :** to destroy, use up, or waste by or as if by eating ⟨locusts *ate* the country bare⟩ ⟨rust *eats* away metal⟩ **4 a :** to affect something by gradual destruction or consumption — used with *into* ⟨acid *ate* into the metal⟩ **b :** BOTHER ⟨what's *eating* you⟩ [Old English *etan*] — **eat•er** *n* — **eat crow :** to accept what one has fought against — **eat one's heart out :** to suffer deep distress (as from grief or envy) — **eat one's words :** to take back what one has said
[1]**eat•able** \'ēt-ə-bəl\ *adj* **:** fit to be eaten
[2]**eatable** *n* **1 :** something to eat **2** *pl* **:** FOOD 2
eau de cologne \,ōd-ə-kə-'lōn\ *n, pl* **eaux de cologne** \,ōd-ə-, ,ōzd-ə-\ **:** COLOGNE [French, literally, "water from Cologne"]
eau–de–vie \,ōd-ə-'vē\ *n, pl* **eaux–de–vie** \,ōd-ə-, ,ōzd-ə-\ **:** BRANDY [French, literally, "water of life"]
eaves \'ēvz\ *n sing or pl* **:** the overhanging lower edge of a roof projecting beyond the wall of a building [Old English *efes*, singular]

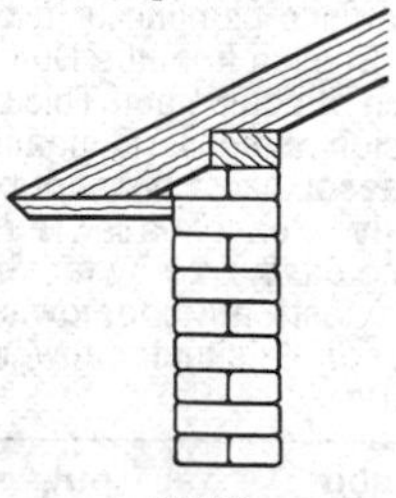
eaves

eaves•drop \'ēvz-,dräp\ *vi* **:** to listen secretly to what is said in private [probably back-formation from *eavesdropper*, literally, "one standing under the drip from the eaves"] — **eaves•drop•per** *n*
△ **origin** The verb *eavesdrop* is probably a back-formation from the noun *eavesdropper*. In Middle English the water that falls from the eaves of a house was called *evesdrop*, spelled *eavesdrop* in modern English (the noun is now very rare). *Eavesdropper* was originally used for a person who stood close to a house, in the area where water, or eavesdrop, falls from the eaves, in order to overhear what was going on inside.
[1]**ebb** \'eb\ *n* **1 :** the recession of the tide ⟨the *ebb* and flow of the sea⟩ **2 a :** a passing from a high to a low point **b :** a period or state of decline ⟨relations were at a low *ebb*⟩ [Old English *ebba*]
[2]**ebb** *vi* **1 :** to recede from the flood **2 :** to decline from a higher level or a better state
ebb tide *n* **1 :** the tide while ebbing **2 :** EBB 2b
eb•o•nite \'eb-ə-,nīt\ *n* **:** hard rubber especially when black
[1]**eb•o•ny** \'eb-ə-nē\ *n, pl* **-nies :** a hard heavy wood yielded by various Old World tropical trees related to the persimmon; *also* **:** a tree yielding ebony [derived from Greek *ebenos*, from Egyptian *hbnj*]
[2]**ebony** *adj* **1 :** made of or resembling ebony **2 :** BLACK 1, DARK
ebul•lient \i-'bùl-yənt\ *adj* **:** intensely agitated **:** BOILING **2 :** characterized by enthusiastic expression of thoughts or feelings **:** EXUBERANT [Latin *ebullire* "to bubble out", from *e-* + *bullire* "to bubble, boil"] — **ebul•lience** \-yəns\ *n* — **ebul•lient•ly** *adv*
eb•ul•li•tion \,eb-ə-'lish-ən\ *n* **:** the process or state of boiling or bubbling up
[1]**ec•cen•tric** \ik-'sen-trik, ek-\ *adj* **1 :** not having the same center ⟨*eccentric* spheres⟩ **2 :** deviating from some established pattern or from accepted usage or conduct **3 a :** deviating from a circular path ⟨an *eccentric* orbit⟩ **b :** located elsewhere than at the geometrical center [Medieval Latin *eccentricus*, from Greek *ekkentros*, from *ex* "out of" + *kentron* "center"] — **ec•cen•tri•cal•ly** \-tri-kə-lē, -klē\ *adv*
[2]**eccentric** *n* **1 :** a disklike device that turns around a shaft not at its center and is used in machinery for changing circular motion into back-and-forth motion **2 :** an eccentric person

echidna

ec•cen•tric•i•ty \,ek-,sen-'tris-ət-ē\ *n, pl* **-ties 1 a :** the quality or state of being eccentric **b :** deviation from an established pattern, rule, or norm; *esp* **:** odd or whimsical behavior **2 :** the degree of deviation from a circular path ⟨a planet's *eccentricity*⟩
• **syn** ECCENTRICITY, IDIOSYNCRASY mean a peculiar trait, trick, or habit. ECCENTRICITY stresses divergence from the usual or customary and suggests whimsicality or mild mental aberration; IDIOSYNCRASY stresses the following of one's particular bent or temperament and connotes strong individuality and independence of action.
Ec•cle•si•as•tes \ik-,lē-zē-'as-,tēz\ *n* — *see* BIBLE table [Greek *Ekklēsiastēs*, literally, "preacher"]
ec•cle•si•as•tic \-'as-tik\ *n* **:** a member of the clergy
ec•cle•si•as•ti•cal \-ti-kəl\ *or* **ec•cle•si•as•tic** \-tik\ *adj* **:** of or relating to a church especially as an established institution ⟨*ecclesiastical* law⟩ [Late Latin *ecclesiasticus*, derived from Greek *ekklēsia* "assembly of citizens, church", from *ekkalein* "to summon", from *ex* "out of" + *kalein* "to call"] — **ec•cle•si•as•ti•cal•ly** \-ti-kə-lē, -klē\ *adv*
Ec•cle•si•as•ti•cus \-ti-kəs\ *n* — *see* BIBLE table
ec•dy•sis \'ek-də-səs\ *n, pl* **-dy•ses** \-də-,sēz\ **:** the act of molting or of shedding (as by insects and crustaceans) an outer layer of cuticle [Greek *ekdysis* "act of getting out"]
ech•e•lon \'esh-ə-,län\ *n* **1 a :** a formation of units (as troops or airplanes) resembling a series of steps **b :** any of several military units in echelon formation **2 a :** one of a series of levels or grades especially of authority **b :** the individuals at such a level ⟨policies determined by the higher *echelons*⟩ [French *échelon*, literally, "rung of a ladder"]
echid•na \i-'kid-nə\ *n* **:** a spiny-coated toothless burrowing egg-laying mammal of Australia with a tapering snout and long tongue for eating ants [Latin, "viper", from Greek]
echi•no•derm \i-'kī-nə-,dərm\ *n* **:** any of a phylum (Echinodermata) of marine animals (as the starfishes and sea urchins) that have true coeloms and have similar parts arranged sym-

metrically around a central axis [*echin-* "prickle" (from Greek *echinos* "sea urchin") + Greek *derma* "skin"] — **echi•no•der•ma•tous** \i-ˌkī-nə-ˈdər-mət-əs\ *adj*

echi•noid \i-ˈkī-ˌnȯid, ˈek-ə-ˌnȯid\ *n* : SEA URCHIN

echi•nus \i-ˈkī-nəs\ *n, pl* **-ni** \-ˌnī\ : SEA URCHIN [Latin, from Greek *echinos* "hedgehog, sea urchin"]

[1]**echo** \ˈek-ō\ *n, pl* **ech•oes** **1** : the repetition of a sound caused by reflection of sound waves **2 a** : a repetition or imitation of another **b** : REPERCUSSION, RESULT ⟨the economic collapse had political *echoes*⟩ **3** : one who closely imitates or repeats another **4 a** : the repetition of a received radio signal due especially to reflection **b** (1) : the reflection of transmitted radar signals by an object (2) : the visual indication of this reflection on a radarscope [Latin, from Greek *ēchō*] — **echo•ic** \i-ˈkō-ik, e-\ *adj*

[2]**echo** *vb* **1** : to resound with echoes **2** : to produce an echo : send back or repeat a sound **3** : REPEAT, IMITATE ⟨*echoing* the words of the teacher⟩

echo•lo•ca•tion \ˌek-ō-lō-ˈkā-shən\ *n* : a process for locating distant or invisible objects by means of sound waves reflected back to the sender by the objects

echo sounder *n* : an instrument for determining the depth of a body of water or of an object below the surface by means of sound waves

éclair \ā-ˈklaər, -ˈkleər, ˈā-ˌ\ *n* : an oblong cream puff with whipped cream or custard filling [French, literally "lightning"]

eclamp•sia \e-ˈklam-sē-ə, -ˈklamp-\ *n* : a convulsive state; *esp* : an attack of convulsions during pregnancy or during the process of giving birth [Greek *eklampsis* "sudden flashing", from *eklampein* "to shine forth", from *ex* "out" + *lampein* "to shine"]

éclat \ā-ˈklä\ *n* **1** : brilliance especially in performance or achievement **2** : demonstration of approval : ACCLAIM [French, "splinter, burst, éclat"]

eclec•tic \e-ˈklek-tik, i-\ *adj* **1** : selecting what appears to be best from various doctrines, methods, or styles **2** : composed of elements drawn from various sources [Greek *eklektikos*, from *eklegein* "to select", from *ex* "out" + *legein* "to gather"] — **eclectic** *n* — **eclec•ti•cal•ly** \-ti-kə-lē, -klē\ *adv* — **eclec•ti•cism** \-tə-ˌsiz-əm\ *n*

[1]**eclipse** \i-ˈklips\ *n* **1** : a complete or partial hiding or darkening of one celestial body by another **2** : a falling into obscurity or decline [Old French, from Latin *eclipsis*, from Greek *ekleipsis*, from *ekleipein* "to omit, suffer eclipse", from *ex-* "out" + *leipein* "to leave"]

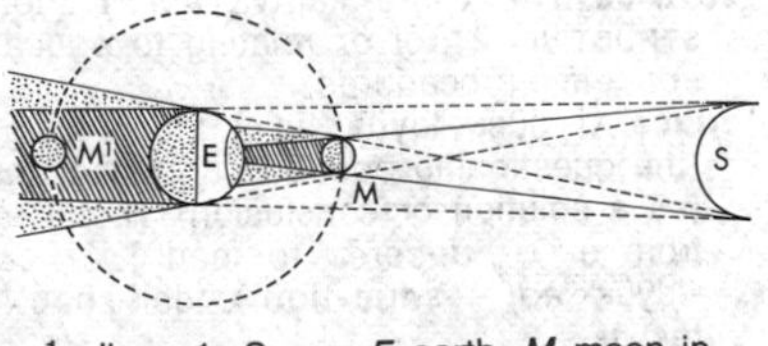

[1]eclipse 1: *S* sun, *E* earth, *M* moon in solar eclipse, *M'* moon in lunar eclipse

[2]**eclipse** *vt* **1** : to cause an eclipse of **2** : to reduce in fame **3** : to surpass greatly : OUTSHINE

[1]**eclip•tic** \i-ˈklip-tik\ *n* : the great circle of the celestial sphere that is the apparent path of the sun among the stars [Late Latin *ecliptica linea*, literally, "line of eclipses"]

[2]**ecliptic** *adj* : of or relating to the ecliptic or an eclipse

ec•logue \ˈek-ˌlȯg\ *n* : a poem in which shepherds converse [Latin *Eclogae*, title of Vergil's pastorals, literally, "selections"]

eco- *combining form* **1** : habitat or environment ⟨*eco*system⟩ **2** : ecology [Greek *oikos* "house"]

eco•log•i•cal \ˌē-kə-ˈläj-i-kəl, ˌek-ə-\ *also* **eco•log•ic** \-ik\ *adj* : of, relating to, concerned with, or affecting ecology or the ecology of a particular group of organisms or an environment — **eco•log•i•cal•ly** \-i-kə-lē,-klē\ *adv*

ecol•o•gy \i-ˈkäl-ə-jē, e-\ *n* **1** : a branch of science concerned with the interrelationship of organisms and their environments **2** : the pattern of relations between one or more organisms and the environment [German *ökologie*, from *öko-* "eco-" + *-logie* "-logy"] — **ecol•o•gist** \i-ˈkäl-ə-jəst, e-\ *n*

ec•o•nom•ic \ˌek-ə-ˈnäm-ik, ˌē-kə-\ *adj* **1 a** : of or relating to economics **b** : of, relating to, or based on the production, distribution, and consumption of goods and services **c** : of or relating to an economy **2** : having practical or industrial significance or uses : affecting material resources ⟨*economic* pests⟩

ec•o•nom•i•cal \-ˈnäm-i-kəl\ *adj* **1** : given to thrift : FRUGAL **2** : operating with little waste or at a saving ⟨an *economical* car⟩ — **ec•o•nom•i•cal•ly** \-ˈnäm-i-kə-lē, -klē\ *adv*

ec•o•nom•ics \ˌek-ə-ˈnäm-iks, ˌē-kə-\ *n sing or pl* **1** : a social science concerned chiefly with description and analysis of the production, distribution, and consumption of goods and services **2** : economic aspect or significance ⟨the *economics* of buying a small car⟩ — **econ•o•mist** \i-ˈkän-ə-məst\ *n*

econ•o•mize \i-ˈkän-ə-ˌmīz\ *vb* **1** : to practice economy : be frugal ⟨*economize* on fuel⟩ **2** : to use more economically : SAVE — **econ•o•miz•er** *n*

econ•o•my \i-ˈkän-ə-mē\ *n, pl* **-mies** **1 a** : thrifty use of material resources : frugality in expenditures; *also* : an act of economizing **b** : efficient and sparing use of nonmaterial resources (as effort or language) **2** : systematic arrangement of something : ORGANIZATION **3** : the structure of economic life in a country, area, or period; *esp* : an economic system [Middle French *yconomie*, from Medieval Latin *oeconomia*, from Greek *oikonomia*, derived from *oikos* "house" + *nemein* "to manage"]

eco•sys•tem \ˈē-kō-ˌsis-təm, ˈek-ō-\ *n* : a complex system composed of an ecological community of organisms interacting with their environment

ec•ru \ˈek-rü, ˈā-krü\ *adj* : BEIGE [French *écru* "unbleached"]

ec•sta•sy \ˈek-stə-sē\ *n, pl* **-sies** **1** : a state of being beyond reason and self-control **2** : a state of overwhelming emotion; *esp* : rapturous delight [Middle French *ecstasie*, derived from Greek *ekstasis*, from *existanai* "to derange", from *ex* "out" + *histanai* "to cause to stand"]

ec•stat•ic \ek-ˈstat-ik\ *adj* : of, relating to, or marked by ecstasy — **ec•stat•i•cal•ly** \-i-kə-lē, -klē\ *adv*

ect- *or* **ecto-** *combining form* : outside : external ⟨*ecto*derm⟩ — compare END-, EXO- [Greek *ektos*, from *ex* "out, out of"]

ec•to•derm \ˈek-tə-ˌdərm\ *n* **1** : the outer cellular layer of a 2-layered animal (as a jellyfish) **2** : the outermost of the three primary germ layers of an embryo; *also* : a tissue (as skin or nerve) derived from this — **ec•to•der•mal** \ˌek-tə-ˈdər-məl\ *adj*

ec•to•mor•phic \ˌek-tə-ˈmȯr-fik\ *adj* : having a light and slender body build — **ec•to•morph** \ˈek-tə-ˌmȯrf\ *n* — **ec•to•mor•phy** \ˈek-tə-ˌmȯr-fē\ *n*

-ec•to•my \ˈek-tə-mē\ *n combining form, pl* **-mies** : surgical removal ⟨tonsill*ectomy*⟩ [Greek *ektemnein* "to cut out", from *ex-* "out" + *temnein* "to cut"]

ec•to•plasm \ˈek-tə-ˌplaz-əm\ *n* **1** : the outer relatively rigid layer of the cytoplasm usually held to be reversibly convertible from a gel to a sol — compare ENDOPLASM **2** : a substance held to be the material form of a ghost — **ec•to•plas•mic** \ˌek-tə-ˈplaz-mik\ *adj*

ec•u•men•i•cal \ˌek-yə-ˈmen-i-kəl\ *adj* **1** : worldwide or general in extent, influence, or application **2** : of, relating to, or representing the whole of a body of churches **3** : promoting Christian unity or cooperation [Late Latin *oecumenicus*, derived from Greek *oikoumenē* "the inhabited world", from *oikein* "to inhabit", from *oikos* "house"] — **ec•u•men•i•cal•ly** \-i-kə-lē, -klē\ *adv* — **ec•u•me•nic•i•ty** \-mə-ˈnis-ət-ē\ *n*

ec•ze•ma \ig-ˈzē-mə, ˈek-sə-mə, ˈeg-zə-\ *n* : a skin inflammation marked by redness, itching, and scaly or crusted lesions [Greek *ekzema*, from *ekzein* "to erupt, from *ex* "out" + *zein* "to boil"] — **ec•zem•a•tous** \ig-ˈzem-ət-əs\ *adj*

[1]**-ed** \d *after a vowel or* b, g, j, l, m, n, ng, r, t͟h, v, z, zh; əd, id *after* d, t; t *after other sounds; exceptions are pronounced at their subentries or entries*\ *vb suffix or adj suffix* **1** — used to form the past participle of regular weak verbs ⟨end*ed*⟩ ⟨fad*ed*⟩ ⟨tri*ed*⟩ ⟨patt*ed*⟩ **2** — used to form adjectives of identical meaning from Latin-derived adjectives ending in *-ate* ⟨umbilicat*ed*⟩ **3 a** : having : characterized by ⟨cultur*ed*⟩ ⟨two-fac*ed*⟩ **b** : having the characteristics of ⟨bigot*ed*⟩ [Old English *-ed, -od, -ad*]

[2]**-ed** *vb suffix* — used to form the past tense of regular weak verbs ⟨judg*ed*⟩ ⟨deni*ed*⟩ ⟨dropp*ed*⟩ [Old English *-de, -ede, -ode, -ade*]

Edam \ˈēd-əm, ˈē-ˌdam\ *n* : a Dutch pressed cheese of yellow color and mild flavor [*Edam*, Netherlands]

edaph•ic \i-ˈdaf-ik\ *adj* : of, relating to, or resulting from the soil

\ə\ **abut**	\au̇\ **out**	\i\ **tip**	\ȯ\ **saw**	\u̇\ **foot**
\ər\ **further**	\ch\ **chin**	\ī\ **life**	\ȯi\ **coin**	\y\ **yet**
\a\ **mat**	\e\ **pet**	\j\ **job**	\th\ **thin**	\yü\ **few**
\ā\ **take**	\ē\ **easy**	\ng\ **sing**	\t͟h\ **this**	\yu̇\ **cure**
\ä\ **cot, cart**	\g\ **go**	\ō\ **bone**	\ü\ **food**	\zh\ **vision**

[Greek *edaphos* "bottom, ground"] — **edaph•i•cal•ly** \-'daf-i-kə-lē, -klē\ *adv*

Ed•dic \'ed-ik\ *adj* **:** of, relating to, or resembling the Old Norse *Edda* which is a 13th century collection of chiefly mythological poems in alliterative verse

1ed•dy \'ed-ē\ *n, pl* **eddies 1 :** a current of air or water running contrary to the main current; *esp* **:** a current moving in a circle like a whirlpool **2 :** a substance moving like an eddy ⟨*eddies* of dust⟩ [Middle English (Scottish dialect) *ydy*]

2eddy *vb* **ed•died**; **ed•dy•ing :** to move in an eddy or so as to form an eddy ⟨the stream *eddied* about a large rock⟩

eddy current *n* **:** an electric current induced by an alternating magnetic field

edel•weiss \'ād-l-ˌwīs\ *n* **:** a small perennial woolly herb that is related to the thistles and grows high in the Alps [German, from *edel* "noble" + *weiss* "white"]

ede•ma \i-'dē-mə\ *n* **:** abnormal accumulation of watery fluid in a bodily tissue or cavity [Greek *oidēma* "swelling", from *oidein* "to swell"] — **edem•a•tous** \i-'dem-ət-əs\ *adj*

edelweiss

Eden \'ēd-n\ *n* **:** PARADISE 3 [from *Eden,* the garden where Adam and Eve are held to have lived first, from Late Latin, from Hebrew *'Edhen*] — **Eden•ic** \i-'den-ik\ *adj*

eden•tate \ē-'den-ˌtāt\ *n* **:** any of an order (Edentata) of mammals having few or no teeth and including the sloths, armadillos, and New World anteaters — **edentate** *adj*

1edge \'ej\ *n* **1 a :** the cutting side of a blade **b :** the sharpness of a blade **c :** penetrating power **:** KEENNESS ⟨a voice with a sarcastic *edge*⟩ **2 a :** the line where an object or surface begins or ends; *also* **:** the narrow adjacent part **b :** the intersection of two plane faces of a solid or of two planes **3 :** a favorable margin **:** ADVANTAGE [Old English *ecg*] **syn** see BORDER — **edged** \'ejd\ *adj* — **on edge :** ANXIOUS 1, NERVOUS

2edge *vb* **1 :** to give an edge to ⟨*edge* an axe⟩ ⟨a voice *edged* with anger⟩ **2 :** to move or advance slowly or by short moves ⟨the crowd *edged* along⟩ ⟨*edge* one's chair closer⟩ **3 :** to incline (a ski) sideways

edge tool *n* **:** a tool (as a chisel, knife, plane, or gouge) with a sharp cutting edge

edge•ways \'ej-ˌwāz\ *adv* **:** with the edge foremost **:** SIDEWAYS

edge•wise \-ˌwīz\ *adv* **:** EDGEWAYS

edg•ing \'ej-ing\ *n* **:** something that forms an edge or border ⟨a lace *edging*⟩

edgy \'ej-ē\ *adj* **edg•i•er**; **-est 1 :** having an edge **:** SHARP ⟨an *edgy* tone⟩ **2 :** being on edge **:** TENSE — **edg•i•ly** \'ej-ə-lē\ *adv* — **edg•i•ness** \'ej-ē-nəs\ *n*

ed•i•ble \'ed-ə-bəl\ *adj* **:** fit or safe to be eaten [Late Latin *edibilis,* from Latin *edere* "to eat"] — **ed•i•bil•i•ty** \ˌed-ə-'bil-ət-ē\ *n* — **edible** *n* — **ed•i•ble•ness** *n*

edict \'ē-ˌdikt\ *n* **:** a decree or order proclaimed by an authority (as a sovereign) that has the force of law [Latin *edictum,* from *edicere* "to decree", from *e-* + *dicere* "to say"] — **edic•tal** \i-'dik-tl\ *adj*

ed•i•fice \'ed-ə-fəs\ *n* **:** BUILDING; *esp* **:** a large or impressive building (as a church) [Middle French, from Latin *aedificium,* from *aedificare* "to erect a house"]

ed•i•fy \'ed-ə-ˌfī\ *vt* **-fied**; **-fy•ing :** to instruct and improve especially by good example **:** benefit morally or spiritually ⟨plays that *edify* the audience⟩ [Middle French *edifier,* from Late Latin *aedificare,* from Latin, "to erect a house", from *aedes* "temple, house"] — **ed•i•fi•ca•tion** \ˌed-ə-fə-'kā-shən\ *n*

ed•it \'ed-ət\ *vt* **1 a :** to correct, revise, and prepare especially for publication ⟨*edit* Poe's works⟩ **b :** to assemble (as a motion-picture film or tape recording) for use or publication by cutting and rearranging **2 :** to supervise the publication of [back-formation from *editor*]

edi•tion \i-'dish-ən\ *n* **1 :** the form in which a text (as a printed book) is published **2 :** the whole number of copies printed or published at one time ⟨a third *edition*⟩ **3 :** one of the several issues of a newspaper for a single day [Middle French, from Latin *editio* "publication, edition", from *edere* "to bring forth, publish"]

ed•i•tor \'ed-ət-ər\ *n* **1 :** one that edits especially as an occupation **2 :** a person who writes editorials [Late Latin, "publisher", from Latin *edere* "to bring forth, publish"] — **ed•i•tor•ship** \-ˌship\ *n*

1ed•i•to•ri•al \ˌed-ə-'tōr-ē-əl, -'tòr-\ *adj* **1 :** of or relating to an editor ⟨an *editorial* staff⟩ **2 :** being or resembling an editorial ⟨an *editorial* statement⟩ — **ed•i•to•ri•al•ly** \-ē-ə-lē\ *adv*

2editorial *n* **:** a newspaper or magazine article that gives the opinions of its editors or publishers

ed•i•to•ri•al•ist \-ē-ə-ləst\ *n* **:** a writer of editorials

ed•i•to•ri•al•ize \ˌed-ə-'tōr-ē-ə-ˌlīz, -'tòr-\ *vi* **1 :** to express an opinion in the form of an editorial **2 :** to introduce opinion into the reporting of facts — **ed•i•to•ri•al•iza•tion** \-ˌtōr-ē-ə-lə-'zā-shən, -ˌtòr-\ *n* — **ed•i•to•ri•al•iz•er** \-'tōr-ē-ə-ˌlī-zər, -'tòr-\ *n*

ed•u•ca•ble \'ej-ə-kə-bəl\ *also* **ed•u•cat•able** \-ˌkāt-ə-bəl\ *adj* **:** capable of being educated

ed•u•cate \'ej-ə-ˌkāt\ *vt* **1 :** to provide schooling for **2 a :** to develop mentally and morally especially by formal instruction **b :** TRAIN [Latin *educare* "to rear, educate"] **syn** see TEACH — **ed•u•ca•tor** \-ˌkāt-ər\ *n*

ed•u•cat•ed *adj* **1 :** having an education; *esp* **:** having an education beyond the average **2 :** giving evidence of education ⟨*educated* speech⟩ **3 :** based on some knowledge of fact ⟨an *educated* guess⟩

ed•u•ca•tion \ˌej-ə-'kā-shən\ *n* **1 a :** the action or process of educating or of being educated **b :** the knowledge and development resulting from an educational process ⟨a person of little *education*⟩ **2 :** the field of study that deals mainly with methods and problems of teaching — **ed•u•ca•tion•al** \-shnəl, -shən-l\ *adj* — **ed•u•ca•tion•al•ly** \-ē\ *adv*

• syn TRAINING, EDUCATION is the general term for institutional learning and implies the guidance and training intended to develop a person's full capacities and intelligence; TRAINING suggests exercise or practice to gain skill, endurance, or facility in a specific field.

ed•u•ca•tive \'ej-ə-ˌkāt-iv\ *adj* **1 :** tending to educate **:** INSTRUCTIVE **2 :** of or relating to education ⟨improvements in *educative* procedures⟩

educe \i-'düs, -'dyüs\ *vt* **1 :** to bring out **:** draw forth **:** ELICIT ⟨the questioning *educed* surprising answers⟩ **2 :** to arrive at (as a solution or conclusion) [Latin *educere* "to draw out", from *e-* + *ducere* "to lead"] — **educ•ible** \-'dü-sə-bəl, -'dyü-\ *adj* — **educ•tion** \-'dək-shən\ *n* — **educ•tor** \-'dək-tər\ *n*

Ed•war•di•an \ed-'wärd-ē-ən\ *adj* **:** of, relating to, or characteristic of Edward VII of England or his age — **Edwardian** *n*

1-ee \'ē, ˌē, ē\ *n suffix* **1 :** recipient or beneficiary of (a specified action or thing) ⟨appointee⟩ ⟨grantee⟩ ⟨patentee⟩ **2 :** one who performs (a specified action) ⟨escapee⟩ [Middle French *-é,* from *-é,* past participle ending, from Latin *-atus*]

2-ee *n suffix* **1 :** a particular especially small kind of ⟨bootee⟩ **2 :** one resembling or suggestive of ⟨goatee⟩ [probably alteration of *-y*]

eel \'ēl\ *n, pl* **eels** *or* **eel 1 :** any of numerous long snakelike fishes with smooth slimy skin and no pelvic fins **2 :** EELWORM [Old English *ǣl*] — **eel•like** \'ēl-ˌlīk\ *adj* — **eely** \'ē-lē\ *adj*

eel•grass \'ēl-ˌgras\ *n* **:** a plant that grows underwater and has long narrow leaves

eel•pout \-ˌpaůt\ *n* **1 :** any of various marine fishes resembling blennies **2 :** BURBOT

eel•worm \-ˌwərm\ *n* **:** a nematode worm; *esp* **:** one living in soil or parasitic on plants

e'en \ēn, 'ēn\ *adv* **:** EVEN

-eer \'iər\ *n suffix* **:** one that is concerned with professionally, conducts, or produces ⟨auctioneer⟩ ⟨pamphleteer⟩ — often in words with derogatory meaning ⟨profiteer⟩ [Middle French *-ier,* from Latin *-arius*]

e'er \eər, 'eər, aər, 'aər\ *adv* **:** EVER

ee•rie *also* **ee•ry** \'iər-ē\ *adj* **ee•ri•er**; **-est 1 :** frightening because of strangeness or gloominess **2 :** STRANGE, MYSTERIOUS ⟨*eerie* lights shone from the swamp⟩ [Old English *earg* "cowardly, wretched"] **syn** see WEIRD — **ee•ri•ly** \'ir-ə-lē\ *adv* — **ee•ri•ness** \'ir-ē-nəs\ *n*

ef•face \i-ˈfās, e-\ *vt* **1 :** to wipe out **:** OBLITERATE **2 :** to make indistinct by or as if by rubbing out **:** ERASE ⟨*efface* an inscription⟩ **3 :** to make (oneself) inconspicuous or modestly unnoticeable [Middle French *effacer,* from *ex-* "ex-" + *face* "face"] — **ef•face•able** \-ˈfā-sə-bəl\ *adj* — **ef•face•ment** \-ˈfās-mənt\ *n* — **ef•fac•er** *n*

[1]**ef•fect** \i-ˈfekt\ *n* **1 :** an event, condition, or state of affairs that is produced by a cause **2 :** EXECUTION, OPERATION ⟨the law went into *effect* today⟩ **3 :** REALITY, FACT ⟨an excuse that was in *effect* a plain refusal⟩ **4 :** the act of making a particular impression ⟨talked merely for *effect*⟩ **5 :** INFLUENCE ⟨the *effect* of climate on growth⟩ **6** *pl* **:** GOODS, POSSESSIONS ⟨household *effects*⟩ [Latin *effectus,* from *efficere* "to bring about", from *ex-* + *facere* "to make, do"]

• **syn** EFFECT, CONSEQUENCE, RESULT mean a condition or occurrence traceable to a cause. EFFECT designates something that necessarily and directly follows or occurs by reason of a cause ⟨the *effect* of the medicine was drowsiness⟩ CONSEQUENCE implies a looser or remoter connection with a cause that may no longer be operating ⟨the loss of prestige was a *consequence* of this ill-advised action⟩ RESULT often applies to the last in a series of effects.

[2]**effect** *vt* **:** to bring about **:** ACCOMPLISH **syn** see AFFECT — **ef•fect•er** *n*

[1]**ef•fec•tive** \i-ˈfek-tiv\ *adj* **1 a :** producing a decided, decisive, or desired effect **b :** IMPRESSIVE, STRIKING ⟨an *effective* window display⟩ **2 :** ready for service or action **3 :** being in effect **:** OPERATIVE — **ef•fec•tive•ly** *adv* — **ef•fec•tive•ness** *n*

• **syn** EFFECTUAL, EFFICIENT, EFFICACIOUS: EFFECTIVE stresses the actual production of an effect when in use or force ⟨the law becomes *effective* immediately⟩ EFFECTUAL suggests the decisive accomplishment of a result or fulfillment of an intention ⟨*effectual* methods of pest control⟩ EFFICIENT suggests having given proof of power to produce maximum results with minimum effort ⟨an *efficient* worker⟩ ⟨an *efficient* machine⟩ EFFICACIOUS implies possession of special qualities giving effective power ⟨this fluid is *efficacious* in removing ink spots⟩

[2]**effective** *n* **:** one that is effective; *esp* **:** a soldier equipped for duty

ef•fec•tor \i-ˈfek-tər\ *n* **:** a bodily organ (as a gland or muscle) that becomes active in response to stimulation

ef•fec•tu•al \i-ˈfek-chə-wəl, -ˈfek-chəl, -ˈfeksh-wəl\ *adj* **:** producing or capable of producing a desired effect ⟨an *effectual* remedy⟩ **syn** see EFFECTIVE — **ef•fec•tu•al•ly** \-ē\ *adv* — **ef•fec•tu•al•ness** *n*

ef•fec•tu•ate \i-ˈfek-chə-ˌwāt\ *vt* **:** to bring about **:** EFFECT

ef•fem•i•nate \ə-ˈfem-ə-nət\ *adj* **1 :** marked by qualities held to be more characteristic of and suited to women than to men **:** UNMANLY **2 :** marked by weakness and love of ease ⟨an *effeminate* civilization⟩ [Latin *effeminatus,* from *effeminare* "to make effeminate", from *ex-* + *femina* "woman"] — **ef•fem•i•na•cy** \-nə-sē\ *n* — **ef•fem•i•nate•ly** *adv* — **ef•fem•i•nate•ness** *n*

ef•fen•di \e-ˈfen-dē, ə-\ *n* **:** a man of property, authority, or education in an eastern Mediterranean country [Turkish *efendi* "master", derived from Greek *authentēs*]

ef•fer•ent \ˈef-ə-rənt; ˈef-ˌer-ənt, ˈē-ˌfer-\ *adj* **:** conducting outward from a part or organ; *esp* **:** conveying nervous impulses to an effector — compare AFFERENT [French *efférent,* from Latin *efferre* "to carry outward", from *ex-* + *ferre* "to carry"] — **efferent** *n*

ef•fer•vesce \ˌef-ər-ˈves\ *vi* **1 :** to bubble, hiss, and foam as gas escapes ⟨ginger ale *effervesces*⟩ **2 :** to show liveliness or exhilaration ⟨*effervesced* with excitement⟩ [Latin *effervescere,* from *ex-* + *fervescere* "to begin to boil", from *fervēre* "to boil"] — **ef•fer•ves•cence** \-ˈves-nts\ *n* — **ef•fer•ves•cent** \-nt\ *adj* — **ef•fer•ves•cent•ly** *adv*

ef•fete \e-ˈfēt, i-\ *adj* **1 :** no longer productive **2 :** worn out **:** EXHAUSTED; *also* **:** marked by weakness or decadence ⟨an *effete* civilization⟩ [Latin *effetus,* from *ex-* + *fetus* "fruitful"] — **ef•fete•ly** *adv* — **ef•fete•ness** *n*

ef•fi•ca•cious \ˌef-ə-ˈkā-shəs\ *adj* **:** having the power to produce a desired effect ⟨an *efficacious* remedy⟩ [Latin *efficax,* from *efficere* "to bring about"] **syn** see EFFECTIVE — **ef•fi•ca•cious•ly** *adv* — **ef•fi•ca•cious•ness** *n*

ef•fi•ca•cy \ˈef-i-kə-sē\ *n, pl* **-cies :** power to produce effects **:** EFFECTIVENESS ⟨a medicine of tested *efficacy*⟩

ef•fi•cien•cy \i-ˈfish-ən-sē\ *n, pl* **-cies 1 :** the quality or degree of being efficient **2 a :** efficient operation **b :** effective operation as measured by a comparison of production with cost (as in energy, time, and money) **3 :** the ratio of the useful energy delivered by a dynamic system (as a machine) to the energy supplied to it

efficiency engineer *n* **:** one who analyzes methods, procedures, and jobs in order to secure maximum efficiency

ef•fi•cient \i-ˈfish-ənt\ *adj* **:** capable of producing desired effects ⟨an *efficient* worker⟩; *esp* **:** productive without waste ⟨*efficient* machinery⟩ [Latin *efficiens,* from *efficere* "to bring about"] **syn** see EFFECTIVE — **ef•fi•cient•ly** *adv*

ef•fi•gy \ˈef-ə-jē\ *n, pl* **-gies :** an image or likeness especially of a person: as **a :** a sculptured image on a tomb **b :** a crude figure representing a hated person [Latin *effigies,* from *effingere* "to form", from *ex-* + *fingere* "to shape"]

ef•flo•resce \ˌef-lə-ˈres\ *vi* **1 :** to burst forth or appear as if by flowering **2 a :** to change to a powder from loss of water of crystallization ⟨a salt that *effloresces*⟩ **b :** to form or become covered with a powdery crust ⟨a brick that *effloresces*⟩ [Latin *efflorescere,* from *ex-* + *florescere* "to begin to blossom"]

ef•flo•res•cence \-ˈres-ns\ *n* **1 :** the act, process, period, or result of developing or unfolding **2 :** fullness of manifestation **:** CULMINATION **3 :** the process or product of efflorescing chemically **4 :** a redness of the skin **:** ERUPTION — **ef•flo•res•cent** \-nt\ *adj*

ef•flu•ence \ˈef-ˌlü-əns; e-ˈflü-, ə-ˈ\ **1 :** something that flows out **2 :** an action or process of flowing out [Latin *effluere* "to flow out", from *ex-* + *fluere* "to flow"] — **ef•flu•ent** \-ənt\ *adj or n*

ef•flu•vi•um \e-ˈflü-vē-əm\ *n, pl* **-via** \-vē-ə\ *or* **-vi•ums :** an invisible emanation; *esp* **:** an offensive exhalation or smell [Latin, "act of flowing out", from *effluere* "to flow out"]

ef•fort \ˈef-ərt, -ˌōrt\ *n* **1 :** conscious exertion of power **2 :** a serious attempt **:** TRY **3 :** something produced especially by creative or artistic exertion [Middle French, from Old French *esfort,* from *esforcier* "to force", from *ex-* "ex-" + *forcier* to force"]

• **syn** EFFORT, EXERTION, PAINS, TROUBLE mean the active use of energy in producing a result. EFFORT stresses the calling up or directing of energy by the conscious will and suggests a single action or attempt; EXERTION suggests sustained, laborious, or exhausting effort; PAINS implies toilsome or solicitous effort; TROUBLE suggests that the effort inconveniences one.

ef•fort•less \ˈef-ərt-ləs\ *adj* **:** showing or requiring little or no effort **:** EASY — **ef•fort•less•ly** *adv* — **ef•fort•less•ness** *n*

ef•fron•tery \i-ˈfrənt-ə-rē, e-\ *n, pl* **-ter•ies :** shameless boldness **:** INSOLENCE ⟨had the *effrontery* to deny all guilt⟩ [French *effronterie,* derived from Late Latin *effrons* "shameless", from Latin *ex-* + *frons* "forehead"]

ef•ful•gence \i-ˈfu̇l-jəns, e-, -ˈfəl-\ *n* **:** radiant splendor **:** BRILLIANCE [Late Latin *effulgentia,* from Latin *effulgēre* "to shine forth", from *ex-* + *fulgēre* "to shine"] — **ef•ful•gent** \-jənt\ *adj*

[1]**ef•fuse** \i-ˈfyüz, e-\ *vb* **1 :** to pour out (a liquid) **2 :** to give off **:** RADIATE **3 :** to flow out **:** EMANATE [Latin *effusus,* past participle of *effundere* "to pour out", from *ex-* + *fundere* "to pour"]

[2]**ef•fuse** \-ˈfyüs\ *adj* **:** poured out freely **:** OVERFLOWING ⟨*effuse* praise⟩

ef•fu•sion \i-ˈfyü-zhən, e-\ *n* **1 :** an act of effusing **2 :** unrestrained expression of words or feelings **3 a :** escape of a fluid from containing vessels (as a blood vessel) **b :** the fluid that escapes

ef•fu•sive \i-ˈfyü-siv, e-, -ziv\ *adj* **1 :** excessively demonstrative or emotional **:** GUSHING ⟨*effusive* thanks⟩ **2 :** characterized or formed by a nonexplosive outpouring of lava — **ef•fu•sive•ly** *adv* — **ef•fu•sive•ness** *n*

eft \ˈeft\ *n* **:** NEWT [Old English *efete*]

egad \i-ˈgad\ *interj* — used as a mild oath [probably euphemism for *oh God*]

egal•i•tar•i•an \i-ˌgal-ə-ˈter-ē-ən\ *adj* **:** asserting, promoting, or marked by egalitarianism [French *égalitaire,* from *égalité* "equality", from Latin *aequalitas,* from *aequalis* "equal"] — **egalitarian** *n*

egal•i•tar•i•an•ism \-ē-ə-ˌniz-əm\ *n* **1 :** a belief in human equality especially in social, political, and economic affairs **2** : a social philosophy advocating the removal of social, political and economic inequalities

egest \i-ˈjest\ *vt* : to rid the body of (waste); *esp* : DEFECATE [Latin *egestus,* past participle of *egerere* "to carry outside, discharge", from *e-* + *gerere* "to carry"] — **eges•tion** \-ˈjes-chən\ *n* — **eges•tive** \-ˈjes-tiv\ *adj*

[1]**egg** \ˈeg\ *vt* : to incite to action : URGE — usually used with *on* ⟨bystanders *egged* them on to fight⟩ [Old Norse *eggja*]

[2]**egg** *n* **1 a** : the hard-shelled reproductive body produced by a bird and especially by domestic poultry **b** : an animal reproductive body consisting of an ovum with its nutritive and protective envelopes and being capable of development into a new individual **c** : OVUM **2** : something resembling an egg **3** : PERSON, INDIVIDUAL ⟨a good *egg*⟩ [Old Norse]

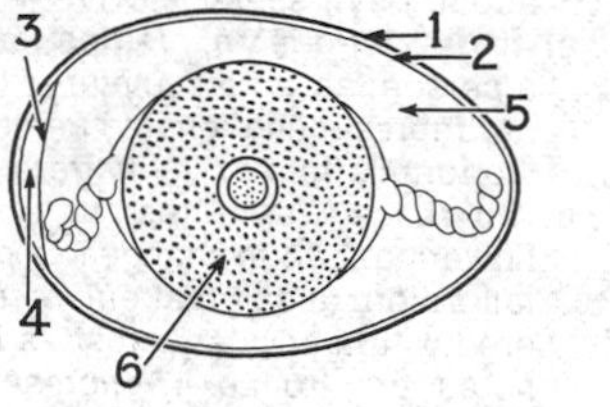

[2]egg 1a: *1* shell, *2* outer shell membrane, *3* inner shell membrane, *4* air space, *5* albumen or white, *6* yolk

egg•beat•er \ˈeg-ˌbēt-ər\ *n* : a rotary beater operated by hand for beating eggs or liquids (as cream)

egg cell *n* : OVUM

egg•head \ˈeg-ˌhed\ *n* : INTELLECTUAL, HIGHBROW

egg•nog \-ˌnäg\ *n* : a drink consisting of eggs beaten up with sugar, milk or cream, and often alcoholic liquor

egg•plant \-ˌplant\ *n* : a widely cultivated perennial herb that is related to the potato and yields edible fruit; *also* : its usually smooth and purple ovoid fruit

[1]**egg•shell** \-ˌshel\ *n* : the hard exterior covering of an egg

[2]**eggshell** *adj* **1** : being thin and fragile ⟨*eggshell* china⟩ **2** : slightly glossy

egg tooth *n* : a hard sharp prominence on the beak of an unhatched bird or the nose of an unhatched reptile that is used to break through the eggshell

eg•lan•tine \ˈeg-lən-ˌtīn, -ˌtēn\ *n* : SWEETBRIER [Middle French *aiglent*]

ego \ˈē-gō\ *n, pl* **egos 1** : the self especially as contrasted with another self or the world **2 a** : EGOTISM 2 **b** : SELF-ESTEEM 2 **3** : the one of the three divisions of the personality in psychoanalytic theory that acts as a go-between between demands of the outside world and basic inner drives — compare ID, SUPEREGO [Latin, "I"]

ego•cen•tric \ˌē-gō-ˈsen-trik\ *adj* : overly concerned with the self; *esp* : SELF-CENTERED, SELFISH — **egocentric** *n*

ego•ism \ˈē-gə-ˌwiz-əm\ *n* **1** : excessive interest in oneself : a self-centered attitude **2** : EGOTISM

ego•ist \ˈē-gə-wəst\ *n* : a self-centered person — **ego•is•tic** \ˌē-gə-ˈwis-tik\ *adj* — **ego•is•ti•cal•ly** \-ˈwis-ti-kə-lē, -klē\ *adv*

• **syn** EGOTIST: EGOIST implies a person whose self-centered concentration on his own desires and aspirations excludes interest in others; EGOTIST may indicate a tendency to attract attention and center interest on oneself and one's achievements.

ego•tism \ˈē-gə-ˌtiz-əm\ *n* **1** : too frequent reference (as by use of the word *I*) to oneself **2** : an exaggerated sense of self-importance : CONCEIT [Latin *ego* "I" + English *-tism* (as in *idiotism* "idiocy", from *idiot* + *-ism*)]

ego•tist \ˈē-gə-təst\ *n* : a conceited person **syn** see EGOIST — **ego•tis•tic** \ˌē-gə-ˈtis-tik\ *or* **ego•tis•ti•cal** \-ˈtis-ti-kəl\ *adj* — **ego•tis•ti•cal•ly** \-ˈtis-ti-kə-lē, -klē\ *adv*

ego trip *n* : an act that satisfies one's ego

egre•gious \i-ˈgrē-jəs\ *adj* : conspicuously bad : FLAGRANT ⟨*egregious* errors⟩ [Latin *egregius* "distinguished", from *e-* + *greg-, grex* "herd"] — **egre•gious•ly** *adv* — **egre•gious•ness** *n*

△ **origin** English *egregious* comes from Latin *egregius,* which means "distinguished" or "eminent". The Latin word was derived from *e-,* "out of", and *grex* "herd, flock". An egregious person, then, has some quality that sets him or her apart from others. Originally this was a remarkably good quality that placed one above others. In 16th century English, however, *egregious* began to be used for one that was conspicuously bad. This shift to a pejorative sense may have resulted from the ironic use of the original sense. In any case, the pejorative meaning is the one that persists in common use today.

egress \ˈē-ˌgres\ *n* **1** : the act or right of going or coming out **2** : a place or means of going out : EXIT [Latin *egressus,* from *egredi* "to go out", from *e-* + *gradi* "to go"]

egret \ˈē-grət, i-ˈgret, ˈē-ˌgret, ˈeg-rət\ *n* : any of various herons that bear long plumes during the breeding season [Middle French *aigrette*]

egret

Egyp•tian \i-ˈjip-shən\ *n* **1** : a native or inhabitant of Egypt **2** : the language spoken by the ancient Egyptians from earliest times to about the 3d century A.D. — **Egyptian** *adj*

Egyptian cotton *n* : a fine often somewhat brownish cotton with relatively long fibers that is grown chiefly in Egypt

Egyp•tol•o•gy \ˌē-jip-ˈtäl-ə-jē\ *n* : the study of Egyptian antiquities — **Egyp•tol•o•gist** \-jəst\ *n*

eh \ˈā, ˈe, ˈa, ˈai, *also with* h *preceding and/or with nasalization*\ *interj* — used to ask for confirmation or to express inquiry [Middle English *ey*]

ei•der \ˈīd-ər\ *n* **1** : any of several large northern sea ducks having fine soft down that is used by the female for lining the nest — called also *eider duck* **2** : EIDERDOWN 1 [derived from Old Norse *æthr*]

ei•der•down \-ˌdau̇n\ *n* **1** : the down of the eider **2** : a comforter filled with eiderdown

ei•det•ic \ī-ˈdet-ik\ *adj* : marked by or involving peculiarly vivid recall especially of visual images ⟨an *eidetic* memory⟩ [Greek *eidētikos* "of a form", from *eidos* "form"]

eight \ˈāt\ *n* **1** : one more than seven; *also* : a symbol representing this — see NUMBER table **2** : the eighth in a set or series **3** : something having eight units or members: as **a** : an 8-oared racing boat or crew **b** : an 8-cylinder engine or automobile [Old English *eahta*] — **eight** *adj or pron*

eight ball *n* **1** : a black pool ball numbered 8 **2** : a pool game in which the eight ball is to be pocketed last — **behind the eight ball** : in a highly disadvantageous position or baffling situation

eigh•teen \ā-ˈtēn, āt-, ˈā-, ˈāt-\ *n* : one more than 17; *also* : a symbol representing this — see NUMBER table [Old English *eahtatīene*] — **eighteen** *adj or pron* — **eigh•teenth** \-ˈtēnth, -ˈtēntth\ *adj or n*

eighth \ˈātth\ *n, pl* **eighths** \ˈāts, ˈātths\ : number eight in a countable series — see NUMBER table — **eighth** *adj or adv*

eighth note *n* : a musical note with the time value of one eighth of a whole note

eighty \ˈāt-ē\ *n, pl* **eight•ies** : ten more than 70; *also* : a symbol representing this — see NUMBER table [Old English *eahtatig*] — **eighty** *adj or pron* — **eight•i•eth** \ˈāt-ē-əth\ *adj or n*

ein•stei•ni•um \īn-ˈstī-nē-əm\ *n* : a adioactive element produced artificially — see ELEMENT table [New Latin, from Albert *Einstein*]

[1]**ei•ther** \ˈē-thər *also* ˈī-\ *adj* **1** : the one and the other of two : EACH ⟨flowers blooming on *either* side of the walk⟩ **2** : the one or the other of two ⟨take *either* road⟩ [Old English *ǣghwæther* "both, each"]

[2]**either** *pron* : the one or the other

[3]**either** *conj* — used before the first of two or more words or word groups of which the last is preceded by *or* to indicate that they represent alternatives ⟨a statement is *either* true or false⟩

[4]**either** *adv* **1** : LIKEWISE 2, MOREOVER — used for emphasis after a negative ⟨not wise or handsome *either*⟩ **2** : as far as that is concerned — used for emphasis after an alternative following a question or conditional clause especially where negation is implied ⟨if their father had come or their mother *either* all would have gone well⟩

ejac•u•late \i-ˈjak-yə-ˌlāt\ *vb* **1** : to utter or eject suddenly and vigorously **2** : to eject a fluid and especially semen [Latin *ejaculari* "to throw out", from *e-* + *jaculari* "to throw", from *jaculum* "dart", from *jacere* "to throw"] — **ejac•u•la•to•ry** \-yə-lə-ˌtōr-ē, -ˌtȯr-\ *adj*

ejac•u•la•tion \i-ˌjak-yə-ˈlā-shən\ *n* **1** : an act or process of ejaculating; *esp* : a sudden discharging of a fluid from a duct **2** : something ejaculated; *esp* : a short sudden emotional utterance (as an exclamation)

eject \i-ˈjekt\ *vt* **1 a** : to drive out especially by physical force **b** : to evict from property **2** : to throw out or off from within [Latin *ejectus,* past participle of *eicere* "to eject", from *e-* + *jacere* "to throw"] — **ejec•tion** \-ˈjek-shən\ *n* — **ejec•tor** \-ˈjek-tər\ *n*

• **syn** EJECT, EXPEL, EVICT, OUST mean to drive or force out. EJECT carries a strong implication of throwing or thrusting out from within as a physical action ⟨hot lava *ejected* from a volcano⟩ EXPEL stresses a thrusting out or driving away especially permanently ⟨*expelled* from school⟩ EVICT chiefly applies to turning out of house and home; OUST implies removal or dispossession by power of the law or by compulsion of necessity.

ejection seat *n* : an emergency escape seat for propelling an occupant out and away from an airplane by means of an explosive charge

eke out \ˌē-ˈkau̇t\ *vt* **1 a** : SUPPLEMENT ⟨*eked out* a small income by doing odd jobs⟩ **b** : to make (a supply) last by economy **2** : to make (a living) by difficult or uncertain means [Old English *īecan, ēcan* "to increase, lengthen"]

el \ˈel\ *n* : ELEVATED RAILROAD

1elab•o•rate \i-ˈlab-rət, -ə-rət\ *adj* **1** : planned or carried out with great care ⟨*elaborate* preparations⟩ **2** : marked by complexity, fullness of detail, or ornateness ⟨an *elaborate* design⟩ [Latin *elaboratus,* from *elaborare* "to work out", from *e-* + *laborare* "to work"] — **elab•o•rate•ly** *adv* — **elab•o•rate•ness** *n*

2elab•o•rate \i-ˈlab-ə-ˌrāt\ *vb* **1** : to build up (complex organic compounds) from simple ingredients ⟨a substance *elaborated* by a gland⟩ **2** : to work out in detail : DEVELOP ⟨*elaborate* an idea⟩ **3** : to give especially additional details ⟨*elaborate* on a story⟩ — **elab•o•ra•tion** \-ˌlab-ə-ˈrā-shən\ *n* — **elab•o•ra•tive** \-ˈlab-ə-ˌrāt-iv\ *adj*

élan \ā-ˈlä^{n}\ *n* : vigorous spirit or enthusiasm [French]

eland \ˈē-lənd\ *n* : either of two large African antelopes resembling oxen and having short spirally twisted horns in both sexes [Afrikaans, "elk", from Dutch]

eland

elapse \i-ˈlaps\ *vi* : to slip or glide away : PASS ⟨years *elapsed*⟩ [Latin *elapsus,* past participle of *elabi* "to elapse", from *e-* + *labi* "to slip"]

elas•mo•branch \i-ˈlaz-mə-ˌbrangk\ *n, pl* **-branchs** : any of a class (Chondrichthyes) of fishes (as a shark or ray) with skeletons of cartilage and with platelike gills [Greek *elasmos* "metal plate" + Latin *branchia* "gill"] — **elasmobranch** *adj*

1elas•tic \i-ˈlas-tik\ *adj* **1 a** : capable of recovering shape or size after being stretched, pressed, or squeezed together : SPRINGY ⟨sponges are *elastic*⟩ **b** : capable of indefinite expansion — used of a gas **2** : able to recover quickly especially from depression or fatigue ⟨a youthful, *elastic* spirit⟩ **3** : FLEXIBLE, ADAPTABLE ⟨a plan *elastic* enough to be changed at any time⟩ [Late Greek *elastos* "ductile, beaten", from Greek *elaunein* "to beat out"] — **elas•ti•cal•ly** \-ti-kə-lē, -klē\ *adv*

• **syn** ELASTIC, RESILIENT, BUOYANT mean quick to recover from depression or a setback. ELASTIC may indicate an ability to recover quickly from discouragement or dejection ⟨an *elastic* power of throwing off painful memories⟩ RESILIENT may stress speed of return to usual good or high spirits after strain, depression, or setback ⟨the *resilient* energy of the storm-wracked villagers⟩ BUOYANT may stress a lightness of spirit incapable of lasting dejection.

2elastic *n* **1 a** : an elastic fabric usually made of yarns containing rubber **b** : something made from elastic fabric **2** : easily stretched rubber; *esp* : a rubber band

elas•tic•i•ty \i-ˌlas-ˈtis-ət-ē, ˌē-ˌlas-\ *n, pl* **-ties** : the quality or state of being elastic : RESILIENCE, ADAPTABILITY

elas•ti•cized \i-ˈlas-tə-ˌsīzd\ *adj* : made with elastic thread or inserts

elas•to•mer \i-ˈlas-tə-mər\ *n* : any of various elastic substances resembling rubber [*elastic* + *-o-* + Greek *meros* "part"] — **elas•to•mer•ic** \i-ˌlas-tə-ˈmer-ik\ *adj*

elate \i-ˈlāt\ *vt* : to fill with joy or pride [Latin *elatus,* past participle of *efferre* "to carry out, elevate", from *e-* + *ferre* "to carry"]

elat•ed \i-ˈlāt-əd\ *adj* : marked by high spirits : EXULTANT ⟨*elated* over the team's victory⟩ — **elat•ed•ly** *adv* — **elat•ed•ness** *n*

el•a•ter \ˈel-ət-ər\ *n* : CLICK BEETLE [Greek *elatēr* "driver", from *elaunein* "to beat out, drive"]

ela•tion \i-ˈlā-shən\ *n* : the quality or state of being elated ⟨alternating moods of *elation* and despair⟩

E layer *n* : a layer of the ionosphere that occurs at about 100 kilometers above the earth's surface and is capable of reflecting radio waves

1el•bow \ˈel-ˌbō\ *n* **1 a** : the joint of the arm; *also* : the outer curve of a bent arm **b** : a corresponding joint in the front limb of an animal **2** : something resembling an elbow; *esp* : an angular pipe fitting [Old English *elboga*]

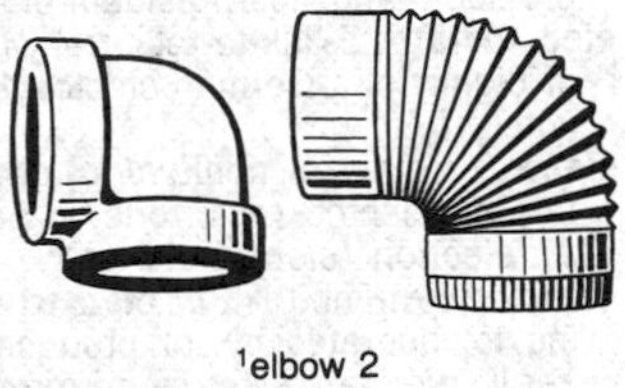

1elbow 2

2elbow *vb* **1** : to push or shove aside with the elbow : JOSTLE **2** : to force or advance by or as if by pushing with the elbow ⟨*elbowed* their way through the crowd⟩

elbow grease *n* : energy vigorously exerted especially in physical labor

el•bow•room \-ˌrüm, -ˌru̇m\ *n* **1** : room for moving the elbows freely **2** : enough space for work or operation

1el•der \ˈel-dər\ *n* : any of a genus of shrubs or trees of the honeysuckle family with flat clusters of small white or pink flowers and black or red drupes resembling berries [Old English *ellærn*]

2elder *adj* : of earlier birth or greater age : OLDER [Old English *ieldra,* comparative of *eald* "old"]

3elder *n* **1** : one who is older : SENIOR **2** : a person having authority by virtue of age and experience ⟨the village *elders*⟩ **3** : any of various church officers — **el•der•ship** \-ˌship\ *n*

el•der•ber•ry \ˈel-dər-ˌber-ē, -də-\ *n* **1** : the edible fruit of an elder **2** : 1ELDER

el•der•ly \ˈel-dər-lē\ *adj* **1** : rather old; *esp* : past middle age **2** : of, relating to, or characteristic of later life ⟨*elderly* pursuits⟩ — **el•der•li•ness** *n*

elder statesman *n* : an eminent senior member of a group or organization; *esp* : a retired statesman who unofficially advises current leaders

el•dest \ˈel-dəst\ *adj* : OLDEST

El Dorado \ˌel-də-ˈräd-ō, -ˈrād-\ *n* **1** : a city or country of fabulous riches held by 16th century explorers to exist in South America **2** : a place of great wealth, abundance, or opportunity [Spanish, literally, "the gilded one"]

ele•cam•pane \ˌel-i-ˌkam-ˈpān\ *n* : a coarse yellow-flowered European herb related to the daisies and naturalized in the United States [Medieval Latin *enula campana,* literally, "field elecampane", from *enula* "elecampane" + *campana* "of the field"]

1elect \i-ˈlekt\ *adj* **1** : carefully selected : CHOSEN **2** : chosen for salvation through divine mercy **3** : chosen for office or position but not yet installed ⟨president-*elect*⟩ [Latin *electus* "choice", from *eligere* "to select", from *e-* + *legere* "to choose"]

2elect *n pl* : a carefully chosen group — usually used with *the*

3elect *vb* **1** : to select usually by vote for an office, position, or membership **2** : to choose especially by preference

elec•tion \i-ˈlek-shən\ *n* **1 a** : an act or process of electing; *esp* : the process of voting to choose a person for office **b** : the fact of being elected **2** : predestination to salvation **3** : the power or privilege of making a choice

\ə\ **abut**	\au̇\ **out**	\i\ **tip**	\ȯ\ **saw**	\u̇\ **foot**
\ər\ **further**	\ch\ **chin**	\ī\ **life**	\ȯi\ **coin**	\y\ **yet**
\a\ **mat**	\e\ **pet**	\j\ **job**	\th\ **thin**	\yü\ **few**
\ā\ **take**	\ē\ **easy**	\ng\ **sing**	\t͟h\ **this**	\yu̇\ **cure**
\ä\ **cot, cart**	\g\ **go**	\ō\ **bone**	\ü\ **food**	\zh\ **vision**

elec•tion•eer \i-ˌlek-shə-ˈniər\ *vi* **:** to work for the election of a candidate or party

[1]**elec•tive** \i-ˈlek-tiv\ *adj* **1 :** chosen by election ⟨an *elective* official⟩ **2 :** filled by a person who is elected ⟨the presidency is an *elective* office⟩ **3 :** of, relating to, or based on elections ⟨an *elective* government⟩ **4 :** followed or taken by choice **:** not required ⟨an *elective* course in school⟩ — **elec•tive•ly** *adv* — **elec•tive•ness** *n*

[2]**elective** *n* **:** an elective course or subject in school

elec•tor \i-ˈlek-tər, -ˌtȯr\ *n* **1 :** one qualified to vote in an election **2 :** one entitled by his office to participate in an election: as **a :** one of the German princes entitled to take part in choosing the Holy Roman emperor **b :** a member of the electoral college in the United States

elec•tor•al \i-ˈlek-tə-rəl, -trəl\ *adj* **:** of or relating to an election or electors

electoral college *n* **:** a body of electors; *esp* **:** one that elects the president and vice-president of the United States

elec•tor•ate \i-ˈlek-tə-rət, -trət\ *n* **1 :** the territory, jurisdiction, or dignity of a German elector **2 :** a body of people entitled to vote

electr- *or* **electro-** *combining form* **1 a :** electricity ⟨*electro*meter⟩ **b :** electric ⟨*electr*ode⟩ **c :** electric and ⟨*electro*chemical⟩ **2 :** electron ⟨*electro*valence⟩

[1]**elec•tric** \i-ˈlek-trik\ *or* **elec•tri•cal** \-tri-kəl\ *adj* **1 :** of, relating to, operated by, or produced by electricity **2 :** EXCITING, THRILLING ⟨an *electric* performance⟩ **[**New Latin *electricus* "produced from amber by friction, electric", from Latin *electrum* "amber", from Greek *ēlektron***]** — **elec•tri•cal•ly** \-tri-kə-lē, -klē\ *adv*

△ **origin** Only in modern times has practical use been made of electricity, but some electrical phenomena have been known since ancient times. Certain philosophers of ancient Greece found that, by rubbing amber with a piece of cloth, they could enable the amber to pick up light objects, such as feathers. In the 17th century, students of natural science began to discover that other natural phenomena were related to the effect of friction on amber. The word *electric,* used to refer to such phenomena, is derived from the Greek word for amber, *ēlektron.*

[2]**electric** *n* **:** something operated by electricity; *esp* **:** an electric automobile

electrical engineering *n* **:** engineering that deals with the practical applications of electricity — **electrical engineer** *n*

electrical storm *n* **:** THUNDERSTORM

electrical transcription *n* **1 :** a phonograph record or tape recording especially designed for use in radiobroadcasting **2 :** a radio program broadcast from an electrical transcription

electric chair *n* **1 :** a chair used in legal electrocution **2 :** the penalty of death by electrocution

electric eel *n* **:** a large South American eel-shaped fish able to give a severe electric shock

electric eye *n* **:** PHOTOELECTRIC CELL

elec•tri•cian \i-ˌlek-ˈtrish-ən\ *n* **:** one who installs, operates, or repairs electrical equipment

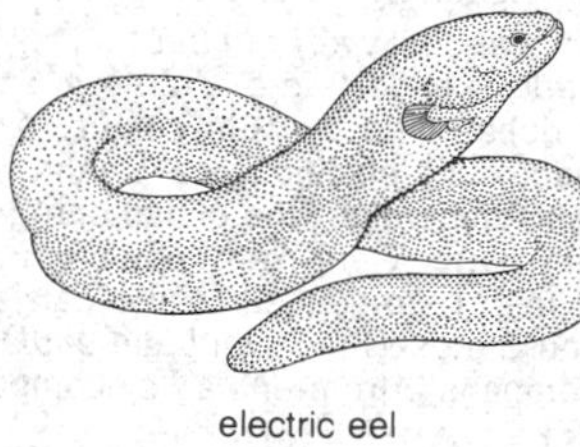
electric eel

elec•tric•i•ty \i-ˌlek-ˈtris-ət-ē, -ˈtris-tē\ *n* **1 a :** a fundamental phenomenon of nature consisting of negative and positive kinds composed respectively of electrons and protons, observable in the attractions and repulsions of bodies electrified by friction and in natural phenomena (as lightning), and usually utilized as a source of energy in the form of electric currents **b :** electric current **2 :** a science that deals with the phenomena and laws of electricity **3 :** keen contagious excitement

electric ray *n* **:** any of various round-bodied short-tailed rays of warm seas able to give a severe electric shock

elec•tri•fy \i-ˈlek-trə-ˌfī\ *vt* **-fied; -fy•ing 1 a :** to charge with electricity **b** (1) **:** to equip for use of electric power (2) **:** to supply with electric power **2 :** to excite intensely or suddenly **:** THRILL ⟨the acrobat *electrified* the audience⟩ — **elec•tri•fi•ca•tion** \i-ˌlek-trə-fə-ˈkā-shən\ *n*

elec•tro•car•dio•gram \i-ˌlek-trō-ˈkärd-ē-ə-ˌgram\ *n* **:** the tracing made by an electrocardiograph

elec•tro•car•dio•graph \-ˌgraf\ *n* **:** an instrument for recording the changes of electrical potential occurring during the heartbeat — **elec•tro•car•dio•graph•ic** \-ˌkärd-ē-ə-ˈgraf-ik\ *adj* — **elec•tro•car•dio•graph•i•cal•ly** \-ˈgraf-i-kə-lē, -klē\ *adv* — **elec•tro•car•di•og•ra•phy** \-ē-ˈäg-rə-fē\ *n*

elec•tro•chem•is•try \i-ˌlek-trō-ˈkem-ə-strē\ *n* **:** a science that deals with the relation of electricity to chemical changes and with the mutual conversion of chemical and electrical energy — **elec•tro•chem•i•cal** \-ˈkem-i-kəl\ *adj* — **elec•tro•chem•i•cal•ly** \-i-kə-lē, -klē\ *adv*

elec•tro•con•vul•sive therapy \i-ˌlek-trō-kən-ˌvəl-siv-\ *n* **:** ELECTROSHOCK THERAPY

elec•tro•cute \i-ˈlek-trə-ˌkyüt\ *vt* **:** to kill by electric shock; *esp* **:** to execute (a criminal) in this way **[***electr-* + *-cute* (as in *execute*)**]** — **elec•tro•cu•tion** \i-ˌlek-trə-ˈkyü-shən\ *n*

elec•trode \i-ˈlek-ˌtrōd\ *n* **:** a conductor (as a metal or carbon) used to establish electrical contact with a nonmetallic part of a circuit (as in a storage battery, electron tube, or arc lamp)

elec•tro•de•pos•it \i-ˌlek-trō-di-ˈpäz-ət\ *vt* **:** to deposit (as a metal or rubber) by electrolysis — **elec•tro•dep•o•si•tion** \-ˌdep-ə-ˈzish-ən, -ˌdē-pə-\ *n*

elec•tro•dy•nam•ics \-dī-ˈnam-iks\ *n* **:** physics that deals with the effects arising from the interactions of electric currents with magnets, with other currents, or with themselves — **elec•tro•dy•nam•ic** \-ik\ *adj*

elec•tro•en•ceph•a•lo•gram \-en-ˈsef-ə-lō-ˌgram\ *n* **:** the tracing of brain waves that is made by an electroencephalograph

elec•tro•en•ceph•a•lo•graph \-ˌgraf\ *n* **:** an apparatus for detecting and recording brain waves — **elec•tro•en•ceph•a•lo•graph•ic** \-en-ˌsef-ə-lō-ˈgraf-ik\ *adj* — **elec•tro•en•ceph•a•log•ra•phy** \-ˌsef-ə-ˈläg-rə-fē\ *n*

elec•tro•form \i-ˈlek-trə-ˌfȯrm\ *vb* **:** to form (shaped articles) by electrodeposition on a mold

elec•trol•y•sis \i-ˌlek-ˈträl-ə-səs\ *n* **1 a :** the producing of chemical changes by passage of an electric current through an electrolyte with the ions carrying the current by migrating to the electrodes where they may form new substances that are given off as gases or deposited as solids **b :** subjection to this action **2 :** the destruction of hair roots with an electric current

elec•tro•lyte \i-ˈlek-trə-ˌlīt\ *n* **1 :** a nonmetallic electric conductor in which current is carried by the movement of ions **2 :** a substance that when dissolved in a suitable solvent or when fused becomes an ionic conductor

elec•tro•lyt•ic \i-ˌlek-trə-ˈlit-ik\ *adj* **:** of or relating to electrolysis or an electrolyte — **elec•tro•lyt•i•cal•ly** \-i-kə-lē, -klē\ *adv*

elec•tro•lyze \i-ˈlek-trə-ˌlīz\ *vt* **:** to subject to chemical electrolysis

elec•tro•mag•net \i-ˌlek-trō-ˈmag-nət\ *n* **:** a core of magnetic material (as soft iron) surrounded by a coil of wire through which an electric current is passed to magnetize the core

elec•tro•mag•net•ic radiation \-mag-ˌnet-ik-\ *n* **:** a series of electromagnetic waves

electromagnetic spectrum *n* **:** the entire range of wavelengths or frequencies of electromagnetic waves extending from gamma rays to the longest radio waves and including visible light

electromagnetic wave *n* **:** a wave (as a radio wave, infrared wave, wave of visible light, or X ray) that travels at the speed of light and that consists of an associated magnetic and electric effect

elec•tro•mag•ne•tism \i-ˌlek-trō-ˈmag-nə-ˌtiz-əm\ *n* **1 :** magnetism developed by a current of electricity **2 :** physical science that deals with the physical relations between electricity and magnetism — **elec•tro•mag•net•ic** \-mag-ˈnet-ik\ *adj* — **elec•tro•mag•net•i•cal•ly** \-ˈnet-i-kə-lē, -klē\ *adv*

elec•trom•e•ter \i-ˌlek-ˈträm-ət-ər\ *n* **:** an instrument for detecting or measuring electric-potential differences or ionizing radiations — **elec•tro•met•ric** \i-ˌlek-trə-ˈme-trik\ *adj*

elec•tro•mo•tive force \i-ˌlek-trə-ˌmōt-iv-\ *n* **:** a force that moves or tends to move electricity — abbreviation *emf*

elec•tron \i-ˈlek-ˌträn\ *n* **:** a negatively charged elementary particle that revolves around the nucleus of an atom and that is of the kind of particles whose flow along a conductor is an electric current

elec•tro•neg•a•tive \i-ˌlek-trō-ˈneg-ət-iv\ *adj* **1 :** charged with negative electricity **2 :** capable of acting as the negative electrode of a voltaic cell **3 :** having a tendency to attract electrons — **elec•tro•neg•a•tiv•i•ty** \-ˌneg-ə-ˈtiv-ət-ē\ *n*

electron gun *n* **:** the part of a cathode-ray tube that produces, accelerates, and focuses a stream of electrons

elec•tron•ic \i-ˌlek-ˈträn-ik\ *adj* **1 :** of or relating to electrons **2 :** of, relating to, or utilizing devices constructed or working by principles of electronics — **elec•tron•i•cal•ly** \-ˈträn-i-kə-lē, -klē\ *adv*

elec•tron•ics \-ˈträn-iks\ *n* **:** a branch of physics that deals with the emission, behavior, and effects of electrons (as in electron tubes and transistors) and with electronic devices

electron micrograph *n* **:** a micrograph made with an electron microscope

electron microscope *n* **:** an instrument in which a beam of electrons is used to produce an enlarged image of a minute object in a way similar to that in which light is used to form the image in an ordinary microscope

electron tube *n* **:** a device in which a controlled electron current flows through a vacuum or a gas within a sealed glass or metal container and which has various common uses (as in radio and television)

electron volt *n* **:** a unit of energy equal to the energy gained by an electron in passing from a point of low potential to a point one volt higher in potential that is equivalent to 1.60 x 10^{-19} joule

elec•tro•pho•re•sis \i-ˌlek-trə-fə-ˈrē-səs\ *n* **:** the movement of suspended particles through a fluid under the action of an electromotive force applied to electrodes in contact with the suspension [Greek *phorein* "to carry"] — **elec•tro•pho•ret•ic** \-ˈret-ik\ *adj*

elec•tro•plate \i-ˈlek-trə-ˌplāt\ *vt* **:** to cover with a coating (as of metal or rubber) by means of electrolysis

elec•tro•pos•i•tive \i-ˌlek-trō-ˈpäz-ət-iv, -ˈpäz-tiv\ *adj* **1 a :** charged with positive electricity **b :** capable of acting as the positive electrode of a voltaic cell **2 :** having a tendency to release electrons ⟨an *electropositive* atom⟩

elec•tro•scope \i-ˈlek-trə-ˌskōp\ *n* **:** any of various instruments for detecting the presence of an electric charge on a body, for determining whether the charge is positive or negative, or for indicating and measuring intensity of radiation

elec•tro•shock therapy \-ˌshäk-\ *n* **:** the treatment of mental disorder by the induction of coma with an electric current — called also *electroconvulsive therapy, electroshock*

elec•tro•stat•ic \i-ˌlek-trə-ˈstat-ik\ *adj* **:** of or relating to static electricity or electrostatics — **elec•tro•stat•i•cal•ly** \-ˈstat-i-kə-lē, -klē\ *adv*

electrostatic generator *n* **:** an apparatus for the production of electrical discharges at high voltage commonly consisting of an insulated hollow conducting sphere on which is accumulated large quantities of electric charge

elec•tro•stat•ics \i-ˌlek-trə-ˈstat-iks\ *n* **:** physics that deals with phenomena due to attractions or repulsions of electric charges but not dependent upon their motion

elec•tro•ther•mal \-ˈthər-məl\ *or* **elec•tro•ther•mic** \-mik\ *adj* **:** relating to the generation of heat by electricity

elec•tro•type \i-ˈlek-trə-ˌtīp\ *n* **1 :** a plate for use in printing made by making a mold of the matter to be printed, covering this mold with a thin shell of metal by electrolysis, and putting on a backing (as of heavy metal or plastic) **2 :** a print made from an electrotype — **elec•tro•typ•er** \-ˌtī-pər\ *n*

elec•tro•va•lence \i-ˌlek-trō-ˈvā-ləns\ *or* **elec•tro•va•len•cy** \-lən-sē\ *n* **:** valence characterized by the transfer of electrons from one atom to another with the formation of ions; *also* **:** the number of charges acquired by an atom by the loss or gain of electrons — **elec•tro•va•lent** \-lənt\ *adj*

elec•trum \i-ˈlek-trəm\ *n* **:** a naturally occurring pale yellow alloy of gold and silver [Latin, "amber, electrum", from Greek *ēlektron*]

elec•tu•ary \i-ˈlek-chə-ˌwer-ē\ *n, pl* **-ar•ies :** a medicinal preparation made as a paste with honey or syrup [Latin *electuarium*]

el•ee•mos•y•nary \ˌel-i-ˈmäs-n-ˌer-ē, -ˈmäz-\ *adj* **:** of, relating to, or supported by charity [Medieval Latin *eleemosynarius*, from Late Latin *eleemosyna* "alms", from Greek *eleēmosynē* "mercy, alms", from *eleein* "to have mercy"]

el•e•gance \ˈel-i-gəns\ *n* **1 :** refined gracefulness **2 :** tasteful richness of design or decoration

el•e•gan.cy \-gən-sē\ *n, pl* **-cies :** ELEGANCE

el•e•gant \ˈel-i-gənt\ *adj* **1 :** marked by elegance **2 :** EXCELLENT, FIRST-RATE [Latin *elegans*] — **el•e•gant•ly** *adv*

el•e•gy \ˈel-ə-jē\ *n, pl* **-gies 1 :** a poem expressing sorrow for one who is dead **2 :** a poem that is sad or mournful [Latin *elegia*, from Greek *elegeia*, from *elegos* "song of mourning"] — **el•e•gi•ac** \ˌel-ə-ˈjī-ək, i-ˈlē-jē-ˌak\ *adj* — **el•e•gize** \ˈel-ə-ˌjīz\ *vb*

el•e•ment \ˈel-ə-mənt\ *n* **1 a :** one of the four substances air, water, fire, or earth formerly believed to compose the physical universe **b** *pl* **:** forces of nature; *esp* **:** stormy or cold weather **c :** the state or sphere natural or suited to a person or thing **2 :** a constituent part: as **a** *pl* **:** the simplest principles of a subject of study **:** RUDIMENTS **b** (1) **:** a generator of a geometric figure (as a cone) (2) **:** a member of a mathematical set (3) **:** one of the numbers that make up a matrix or determinant **c :** any of more than 100 fundamental substances that consist of atoms of only one kind ⟨gold and carbon are *elements*⟩ **d :** a distinct part of a composite device **e :** a subdivision of a military unit **3** *pl* **:** the bread and wine used in the sacrament of Communion [Latin *elementum*]

• **syn** COMPONENT, CONSTITUENT, INGREDIENT: ELEMENT applies to anything that is a part of a compound or complex whole and often connotes irreducible simplicity; COMPONENT and CONSTITUENT are often interchangeable in designating any of the substances or qualities that enter into a compound or complex product; COMPONENT applies to one of the parts that make up a compounded or complex thing ⟨the *components* of a carburetor⟩ CONSTITUENT implies the essential or formative character of the parts ⟨atoms are the *constituents* of molecules⟩ INGREDIENT is applicable to any substance that combines with others to form something else and may also apply to intangible matters ⟨*ingredients* of a chocolate cake⟩ ⟨*ingredients* of successful comedy⟩

CHEMICAL ELEMENTS

Those weights shown in parentheses are for the most stable or best known isotopes

ELEMENT & SYMBOL	ATOMIC NUMBER	ATOMIC WEIGHT (C = 12)
actinium (Ac)	89	(227)
aluminum (Al)	13	26.98154
americium (Am)	95	(243)
antimony (Sb)	51	121.75
argon (Ar)	18	39.948
arsenic (As)	33	74.9216
astatine (At)	85	(210)
barium (Ba)	56	137.33
berkelium (Bk)	97	(247)
beryllium (Be)	4	9.01218
bismuth (Bi)	83	208.9808
boron (B)	5	10.81
bromine (Br)	35	79.904
cadmium (Cd)	48	112.41
calcium (Ca)	20	40.08
californium (Cf)	98	(251)
carbon (C)	6	12.011
cerium (Ce)	58	140.12
cesium (Cs)	55	132.9054
chlorine (Cl)	17	35.453
chromium (Cr)	24	51.996
cobalt (Co)	27	58.9332
columbium (Cb)	(see niobium)	
copper (Cu)	29	63.546
curium (Cm)	96	(247)
dysprosium (Dy)	66	162.50
einsteinium (Es)	99	(254)
erbium (Er)	68	167.26
europium (Eu)	63	151.96
fermium (Fm)	100	(257)
fluorine (F)	9	18.998403
francium (Fr)	87	(223)
gadolinium (Gd)	64	157.25
gallium (Ga)	31	69.72
germanium (Ge)	32	72.59

gold (Au)	79	196.9665
hafnium (Hf)	72	178.49
helium (He)	2	4.00260
holmium (Ho)	67	164.9304
hydrogen (H)	1	1.0079
indium (In)	49	114.82
iodine (I)	53	126.9045
iridium (Ir)	77	192.22
iron (Fe)	26	55.847
krypton (Kr)	36	83.80
lanthanum (La)	57	138.9055
lawrencium (Lr)	103	(260)
lead (Pb)	82	207.2
lithium (Li)	3	6.941
lutetium (Lu)	71	174.97
magnesium (Mg)	12	24.305
manganese (Mn)	25	54.9380
mendelevium (Md)	101	(258)
mercury (Hg)	80	200.59
molybdenum (Mo)	42	95.94
neodymium (Nd)	60	144.24
neon (Ne)	10	20.179
neptunium (Np)	93	237.0482
nickel (Ni)	28	58.71
niobium (Nb)	41	92.9064
nitrogen (N)	7	14.0067
nobelium (No)	102	(259)
osmium (Os)	76	190.2
oxygen (O)	8	15.9994
palladium (Pd)	46	106.4
phosphorus (P)	15	30.9738
platinum (Pt)	78	195.09
plutonium (Pu)	94	(244)
polonium (Po)	84	(210)
potassium (K)	19	39.0983
praseodymium (Pr)	59	140.9077
promethium (Pm)	61	(145)
protactinium (Pa)	91	231.0359
radium (Ra)	88	226.0254
radon (Rn)	86	(222)
rhenium (Re)	75	186.2
rhodium (Rh)	45	102.9055
rubidium (Rb)	37	85.4678
ruthenium (Ru)	44	101.07
samarium (Sm)	62	150.4
scandium (Sc)	21	44.9559
selenium (Se)	34	78.96
silicon (Si)	14	28.0855
silver (Ag)	47	107.868
sodium (Na)	11	22.9898
strontium (Sr)	38	87.62
sulfur (S)	16	32.06
tantalum (Ta)	73	180.9479
technetium (Tc)	43	98.9062
tellurium (Te)	52	127.60
terbium (Tb)	65	158.9254
thallium (Tl)	81	204.37
thorium (Th)	90	232.0381
thulium (Tm)	69	168.9342
tin (Sn)	50	118.69
titanium (Ti)	22	47.90
tungsten (W)	74	183.85
uranium (U)	92	238.029
vanadium (V)	23	50.9414
wolfram (W)	(see tungsten)	
xenon (Xe)	54	131.30
ytterbium (Yb)	70	173.04
yttrium (Y)	39	88.9059
zinc (Zn)	30	65.38
zirconium (Zr)	40	91.22

el•e•men•tal \ˌel-ə-'ment-l\ *adj* **1 a :** of, relating to, or being an element; *esp* **:** existing as an uncombined chemical element **b :** of, relating to, or being an ultimate constituent **:** FUNDAMENTAL **c :** ELEMENTARY 1a **d :** forming an integral part **:** INHERENT **2 :** of, relating to, or resembling a great force of nature — **el•e•men•tal•ly** \-l-ē\ *adv*

el•e•men•ta•ry \ˌel-ə-'ment-ə-rē, -'men-trē\ *adj* **1 a :** of or relating to the simplest principles of something (as a subject) **b :** of or relating to an elementary school ⟨an *elementary* curriculum⟩ **2 :** ELEMENTAL 1a

elementary particle *n* **:** any of the ultimate constituents (as the electron, proton, or neutron) of matter

elementary school *n* **:** a school usually including the first six or sometimes the first four or eight grades

el•e•phant \'el-ə-fənt\ *n* **:** any of several huge thickset nearly hairless mammals having the snout prolonged as a trunk and two upper incisors developed into long outward-curving pointed tusks which furnish ivory: **a :** one with large ears that occurs in tropical Africa **b :** one with relatively small ears that occurs in southeastern Asia [Latin *elephantus,* from Greek *elephas*]

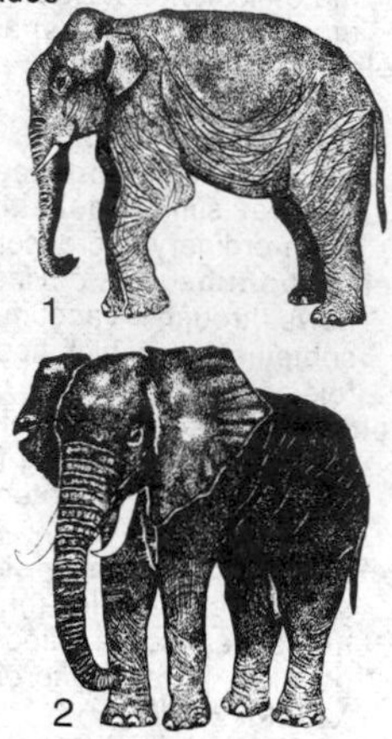

elephant a, b: *1* Asian, *2* African

elephant bird *n* **:** a gigantic extinct flightless bird of Madagascar

el•e•phan•ti•a•sis \ˌel-ə-fən-'tī-ə-səs, -ˌfan-\ *n, pl* **-a•ses** \-ə-ˌsēz\ **:** enlargement and thickening of tissues caused by obstruction (as by filarial worms) of vessels that carry lymph [Latin, a kind of leprosy, from Greek, from *elephas* "elephant"]

el•e•phan•tine \ˌel-ə-'fan-ˌtēn, -ˌtīn, 'el-ə-fən-\ *adj* **1 :** of or relating to an elephant **2 a :** IMMENSE 1, HUGE **b :** lacking grace or ease **:** PONDEROUS

el•e•vate \'el-ə-ˌvāt\ *vt* **1 :** to lift up **:** RAISE **2 :** to raise in rank or status **:** EXALT **3 :** to improve morally, intellectually, or culturally **4 :** to raise the spirits of **:** ELATE [Latin *elevare,* from *e-* + *levare* "to raise"]

el•e•vat•ed \-ˌvāt-əd\ *adj* **1 :** raised especially above the ground ⟨an *elevated* freeway⟩ **2 a :** morally or intellectually on a high plane ⟨an *elevated* mind⟩ **b :** FORMAL, DIGNIFIED ⟨*elevated* diction⟩

elevated railroad *n* **:** a railroad supported by a structure of trestles and girders high enough to permit movement of traffic underneath — called also *elevated railway*

el•e•va•tion \ˌel-ə-'vā-shən\ *n* **1 :** the height to which something is elevated: as **a :** the angular distance of a celestial object above the horizon **b :** the degree to which a gun is aimed above the horizon **c :** the height above sea level **:** ALTITUDE **2 :** an act or instance of elevating **3 a :** something that is elevated **b :** an elevated place or station **4 :** the quality or state of being elevated **5 :** a scale drawing showing a vertical section (as of a building) **syn** see HEIGHT

el•e•va•tor \'el-ə-ˌvāt-ər\ *n* **1 a :** an endless belt or chain conveyor with cleats, scoops, or buckets for raising material **b :** a cage or platform and its hoisting machinery for conveying something to different levels **c :** a building for elevating, storing, discharging, and sometimes processing grain **2 :** a movable airfoil usually attached to the tail plane of an airplane for producing motion up or down

elev•en \i-'lev-ən\ *n* **1 :** one more than 10; *also* **:** a symbol representing this — see NUMBER table **2 :** the 11th in a set or series **3 :** something having 11 units or members [Old English *endleofan*] — **eleven** *adj or pron* — **elev•enth** \-ənth, -əntth\ *n* — **eleventh** *adj or adv*

eleventh hour *n* **:** the latest possible time ⟨was saved at the *eleventh hour*⟩

el•e•von \'el-ə-ˌvän\ *n* **:** an airplane control surface that combines the functions of elevator and aileron [*elevator* + *aileron*]

elf \'elf\ *n, pl* **elves** \'elvz\ **:** a small legendary humanlike being [Old English *ælf*] — **elf•ish** *adj* — **elf•ish•ly** \'el-fish-lē\ *adv*

elf•in \'el-fən\ *adj* **1 :** of or relating to an elf or elves **2 :** resembling an elf; *esp* **:** having a strange beauty or charm

elic•it \i-'lis-ət\ *vt* **:** to draw forth or bring out often by skillful questioning or discussion ⟨*elicit* the truth from an unwilling witness⟩ [Latin *elicitus,* past participle of *elicere* "to elicit", from *e-* + *lacere* "to allure"] — **elic•i•ta•tion** \i-ˌlis-ə-'tā-shən\ *n* — **elic•i•tor** \i-'lis-ət-ər\ *n*

elide \i-'līd\ *vt* **1 :** to suppress or alter (as a vowel) by elision **2**

: to leave out of consideration : IGNORE [Latin *elidere* "to strike out", from *e-* + *laedere* "to injure by striking"]

el•i•gi•ble \'el-ə-jə-bəl\ *adj* **1 :** qualified to be chosen or to serve ⟨*eligible* candidates for office⟩ **2 :** having a right to something : ENTITLED ⟨*eligible* to retire⟩ ⟨*eligible* for benefits⟩ [Late Latin *eligibilis,* from Latin *eligere* "to choose"] — **el•i•gi•bil•i•ty** \,el-i-jə-'bil-ət-ē\ *n* — **eligible** *n* — **el•i•gi•bly** \'el-i-jə-blē\ *adv*

elim•i•nate \i-'lim-ə-,nāt\ *vt* **1 a :** to cast out or get rid of : REMOVE **b :** to set aside as unimportant : IGNORE **2 :** to expel (as waste) from the living body **3 :** to cause (a variable) to disappear by combining two or more equations [Latin *eliminare,* from *e-* + *limen* "threshold"] — **elim•i•na•tion** \i-,lim-ə-'nā-shən\ *n* — **elim•i•na•tive** \i-'lim-ə-,nāt-iv\ *adj* — **elim•i•na•tor** \-,nāt-ər\ *n*

eli•sion \i-'lizh-ən\ *n* **1 a :** the omission of a final or initial sound of a word ⟨*is* has become *'s* in *there's* by *elision*⟩ **b :** the omission of an unstressed vowel or syllable in a verse to achieve a uniform rhythm **2 :** the act or an instance of dropping out or omitting something [Late Latin *elisio,* from Latin *elidere* "to strike out"]

elite \ā-'lēt, i-\ *n* **1 a :** the choice part; *esp* **:** a socially superior group **b :** a powerful minority group ⟨a power *elite* inside the government⟩ **2 :** a typewriter type providing 12 characters to the inch [French *élite,* from Old French *eslite,* from *eslire* "to choose", from Latin *eligere*] — **elite** *adj*

elix•ir \i-'lik-sər\ *n* **1 a :** a substance held to be capable of changing metals into gold **b :** a substance held to be capable of prolonging life indefinitely **c :** CURE-ALL **2 :** a sweetened usually alcoholic liquid used as a vehicle for medicinal agents [Medieval Latin, from Arabic *al-iksīr* "the elixir"]

Eliz•a•be•than \i-,liz-ə-'bē-thən\ *adj* **:** of, relating to, or characteristic of Elizabeth I of England or her age — **Elizabethan** *n*

elk \'elk\ *n, pl* **elk** *or* **elks 1 a :** the largest existing deer of Europe and Asia resembling but not so large as the moose of North America **b :** a large North American deer with curved antlers having many branches — called also *wapiti* **c :** any of various large Asian deer **2** *cap* **:** a member of a major benevolent and fraternal order [Middle English]

elk 1b

[1]ell \'el\ *n* **:** a former English unit of length for cloth equal to 45 inches (about 1.14 meters) [Old English *eln*]

[2]ell *n* **:** an extension at right angles to a building [from the resulting shape like the letter *L*]

el•lipse \i-'lips, e-\ *n* **1 :** an elongated circle : OVAL **2 :** a closed plane curve generated by a point moving in such a way that the sums of its distances from two fixed points is a constant : a conic section that is a closed curve but not a circle [Greek *elleipsis*]

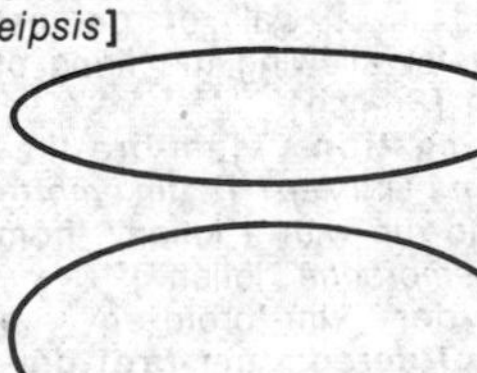
ellipse 1

el•lip•sis \i-'lip-səs, e-\ *n, pl* **-lip•ses** \-'lip-,sēz\ **1 :** the omission of one or more words from a phrase when such omission does not affect its meaning ⟨"fire when ready" for "fire when you are ready" is an example of *ellipsis*⟩ **2 :** marks or a mark (as ... or *** or —) used to show the omission especially of letters or words [Latin, from Greek *elleipsis* "ellipsis, ellipse", from *elleipein* "to leave out, fall short", from *en-* "in-" + *leipein* "to leave"]

el•lip•soid \i-'lip-,sȯid, e-\ *n* **:** a surface all plane sections of which are ellipses or circles; *esp* **:** SPHEROID — **ellipsoid** *or* **el•lip•soi•dal** \i-,lip-'sȯid-l\ *adj*

el•lip•tic \i-'lip-tik, e-\ *or* **el•lip•ti•cal** \-ti-kəl\ *adj* **1 :** of, relating to, or shaped like an ellipse **2 :** of, relating to, or marked by ellipsis — **el•lip•ti•cal•ly** \-ti-kə-lē, -klē\ *adv*

elm \'elm\ *n* **1 :** any of a genus of large trees that have alternate toothed leaves, small flowers without petals, and nearly circular one-seeded winged fruits and are often grown as shade trees **2 :** the wood of an elm [Old English]

el•o•cu•tion \,el-ə-'kyü-shən\ *n* **1 :** the art of effective public speaking **2 :** a style of speaking especially in public [Latin *elocutio,* from *eloqui* "to speak out"] — **el•o•cu•tion•ary** \-shə-,ner-ē\ *adj* — **el•o•cu•tion•ist** \-shə-nəst, -shnəst\ *n*

elo•dea \i-'lōd-ē-ə\ *n* **:** any of a small genus of American aquatic herbs [Greek *helōdēs* "marshy", from *helos* "marsh"]

[1]elon•gate \i-'lȯng-,gāt\ *vb* **1 :** to extend the length of **2 :** to grow in length — **elon•ga•tion** \,ē-,lȯng-'gā-shən\ *n*

[2]elongate *adj* **1 :** stretched out : LENGTHENED **2 :** long in proportion to width

elon•gat•ed *adj* **:** ELONGATE

elope \i-'lōp\ *vi* **1 :** to run away secretly with the intention of getting married usually without parental consent **2 :** to slip away : ESCAPE [Anglo-French *aloper*] — **elope•ment** \-mənt\ *n* — **elop•er** *n*

el•o•quence \'el-ə-kwəns\ *n* **:** discourse marked by force and persuasiveness; *also* **:** the art or power of using such discourse

el•o•quent \-kwənt\ *adj* **1 :** marked by forceful and fluent expression **2 :** vividly or movingly expressive or revealing [Middle French, from Latin *eloquens,* from *eloqui* "to speak out", from *e-* + *loqui* "to speak"] — **el•o•quent•ly** adv

[1]else \'els\ *adv* **1 a :** in a different manner or place or at a different time ⟨how *else* can we act⟩ ⟨when *else* can they come⟩ **b :** in an additional place or manner or at an additional time **2 :** if not : OTHERWISE [Old English *elles*]

[2]else *adj* **:** OTHER: **a :** being different in identity ⟨somebody *else*⟩ **b :** being in addition ⟨what *else*⟩

else•where \-,hweər, -,hwaər, -,weər, -,waər\ *adv* **:** in or to another place

elu•ci•date \i-'lü-sə-,dāt\ *vt* **:** to make clear or plain : EXPLAIN [Late Latin *elucidare,* from Latin *e-* + *lucidus* "lucid"] — **elu•ci•da•tion** \i-,lü-sə-'dā-shən\ *n* — **elu•ci•da•tive** \i-'lü-sə-,dāt-iv\ *adj* — **elu•ci•da•tor** \-,dāt-ər\ *n*

elude \ē-'lüd\ *vt* **:** to avoid or escape adroitly; *esp* **:** to evade by baffling ⟨the identity of the disease *eluded* researchers⟩ [Latin *eludere,* from *e-* + *ludere* "to play"] **syn** see EVADE

elu•sion \ē-'lü-zhən\ *n* **:** an act of eluding : ESCAPE, EVASION [Medieval Latin *elusio,* derived from Latin *eludere* "to elude"]

elu•sive \ē-'lü-siv, -ziv\ *adj* **1 :** tending to elude : EVASIVE **2 :** hard to comprehend or define ⟨an *elusive* idea⟩ — **elu•sive•ly** *adv* — **elu•sive•ness** *n*

elute \ē-'lüt\ *vt* **:** to extract especially by means of a solvent [Latin *eluere* "to wash out", from *e-* + *lavere* "to wash"]

elu•vi•al \ē-'lü-vē-əl\ *adj* **:** of or relating to eluvium

elu•vi•um \-vē-əm\ *n* **1 :** fine material produced where found by weathering of rock **2 :** fine soil material deposited by wind [New Latin, from Latin *eluere* "to wash out"]

el•ver \'el-vər\ *n* **:** a young eel [alteration of *eelfare* "migration of eels"]

elves *pl of* ELF

elv•ish \'el-vish\ *adj* **:** MISCHIEVOUS 2, 3

Ely•si•um \i-'lizh-ē-əm, -'liz-\ *n* **1 :** the abode of the good after death in classical mythology **2 :** PARADISE 3 [Latin, from Greek *Elysion*] — **Ely•sian** \i-'lizh-ən\ *adj*

el•y•tron \'el-ə-,trän\ *also* **el•y•trum** \-trəm\ *n, pl* **-tra** \-trə\ **:** one of the thick modified front wings in beetles and some other insects that protect the pair of functional hind wings [Greek *elytron* "sheath, wing cover", from *eilyein* "to roll, wrap"]

em \'em\ *n* **1 :** the width of a piece of type about as wide as it is tall used as a unit of measure of printed matter **2 :** PICA 2 [from the size of the quad used for the letter *m*]

em- — see EN-

ema•ci•ate \i-'mā-shē-,āt\ *vt* **1 :** to cause to lose flesh so as to become very thin **2 :** to make feeble [Latin *emaciare,* from *e-* + *macies* "leanness", from *macer* "lean"] — **ema•ci•a•tion** \i-,mā-shē-'ā-shən, -sē-'ā-\ *n*

em•a•nate \'em-ə-,nāt\ *vb* **1 :** to come out from a source **2 :** to give out : EMIT [Latin *emanare,* from *e-* + *manare* "to flow"]

em•a•na•tion \ˌem-ə-ˈnā-shən\ *n* **1** : the action of emanating **2** : something that emanates or is produced by emanation — **em•a•na•tion•al** \-shnəl, -shən-l\ *adj* — **em•a•na•tive** \ˈem-ə-ˌnāt-iv\ *adj*

eman•ci•pate \i-ˈman-sə-ˌpāt\ *vt* : to free from restraint, control, or the power of another; *esp* : to free from slavery [Latin *emancipare,* from *e-* + *mancipare* "to transfer ownership of", from *manceps* "purchaser", from *manus* "hand" + *capere* "to take"] — **eman•ci•pa•tion** \i-ˌman-sə-ˈpā-shən\ *n* — **eman•ci•pa•tor** \i-ˈman-sə-ˌpāt-ər\ *n*

emas•cu•late \i-ˈmas-kyə-ˌlāt\ *vt* **1** : CASTRATE **2** : to deprive of vigor or spirit : WEAKEN [Latin *emasculare,* from *e-* + *masculus* "male"] — **emas•cu•la•tion** \i-ˌmas-kyə-ˈlā-shən\ *n* — **emas•cu•la•tor** \i-ˈmas-kyə-ˌlāt-ər\ *n*

em•balm \im-ˈbäm, -ˈbälm\ *vb* **1** : to treat a corpse with special preparations to preserve it from decay **2** : to preserve as if by embalming [Middle French *embaumer,* from Old French *embasmer,* from *en-* + *basme* "balm"] — **em•balm•er** *n* — **embalm•ment** \-ˈbäm-mənt, -ˈbälm-\ *n*

em•bank \im-ˈbangk\ *vt* : to enclose or confine by an embankment

em•bank•ment \-mənt\ *n* **1** : the action of embanking **2** : a raised bank or wall to carry a roadway or to hold back water

em•bar•go \im-ˈbär-gō\ *n, pl* **-goes** **1** : an order of a government prohibiting the departure of commercial ships from its ports **2** : legal prohibition or restriction of commerce **3** : IMPEDIMENT 1, STOPPAGE; *esp* : PROHIBITION 2 [Spanish, from *embargar* "to bar"] — **embargo** *vt*

em•bark \im-ˈbärk\ *vb* **1** : to go or put on board a ship or airplane **2** : to enter into an enterprise or undertaking ⟨*embark* on a career⟩ [Middle French *embarquer,* from Provençal *embarcar,* from *em-* "en-" + *barca* "bark"] — **em•bar•ka•tion** \ˌem-ˌbär-ˈkā-shən\ *n* — **em•bark•ment** \im-ˈbärk-mənt\ *n*

em•bar•rass \im-ˈbar-əs\ *vt* **1** : to hinder the freedom of movement of : IMPEDE ⟨soldiers *embarrassed* by heavy packs⟩ **2 a** : to involve in financial difficulties **b** : to make confused or upset in mind : cause a feeling of uneasiness in : DISCONCERT ⟨unexpected laughter *embarrassed* the speaker⟩ [French *embarrasser,* from Spanish *embarazar,* from Portuguese *embaraçar*] — **em•bar•rass•ing•ly** \-ə-sing-lē\ *adv*

• **syn** ABASH, DISCONCERT, DISCOMFIT: EMBARRASS implies an influence or circumstance that checks or constrains one's freedom of action, speech, or choice and causes uneasiness or confusion of mind; ABASH suggests producing feelings of shame, shyness, or unworthiness by suddenly destroying self-confidence; DISCONCERT implies producing uncertainty, hesitancy, or confusion especially through an unexpected discovery or turn of events; DISCOMFIT implies a hampering or frustrating accompanied by confusion.

em•bar•rass•ment \im-ˈbar-ə-smənt\ *n* **1** : the state of being embarrassed: as **a** : confusion or discomposure of mind **b** : difficulty arising from a lack of money to pay debts **2 a** : something that embarrasses : IMPEDIMENT **b** : an excessive quantity from which to select — used especially in the phrase *embarrassment of riches*

em•bas•sy \ˈem-bə-sē\ *n, pl* **-sies** **1** : the function or position of an ambassador **2** : a mission abroad undertaken by an ambassador **3** : a body of diplomatic representatives **4** : the official residence or office of an ambassador [Middle French *ambassee,* of Germanic origin]

em•bat•tle \im-ˈbat-l\ *vt* **1** : to arrange in battle order : prepare for battle **2** : FORTIFY a

em•bed *or* **im•bed** \im-ˈbed\ *vb* **1** : to enclose closely in or as if in a surrounding mass : set solidly in or as if in a bed ⟨*embed* a post in concrete⟩ **2** : to become embedded

em•bel•lish \im-ˈbel-ish\ *vt* **1** : to make beautiful with ornamentation : DECORATE **2** : to heighten the attractiveness of by adding ornamental details [Middle French *embeliss-,* stem of *embelir* "to embellish", from *en-* + *bel* "beautiful"] **syn** see ADORN — **em•bel•lish•ment** \-mənt\ *n*

em•ber \ˈem-bər\ *n* **1** : a glowing piece of coal or wood from a fire; *esp* : such a piece smoldering in ashes **2** *pl* : smoldering remains (as of a fire or a romance) [Old Norse *eimyrja*]

em•ber day \ˈem-bər-\ *n* : a Wednesday, Friday, or Saturday following the first Sunday in Lent, Whitsunday, September 14, or December 13 and set apart for fasting and prayer [Old English *ymbrendæg,* from *ymbrene* "anniversary" + *dæg* "day"]

em•bez•zle \im-ˈbez-əl\ *vt* **em•bez•zled; em•bez•zling** \-ˈbez-ling, -ə-ling\ : to take (property entrusted to one's care) dishonestly for one's own use [Anglo-French *embeseiller,* from Middle French *en-* + *besillier* "to destroy"] — **em•bez•zle•ment** \-ˈbez-əl-mənt\ *n* — **em•bez•zler** \-ˈbez-lər, -ə-lər\ *n*

em•bit•ter \im-ˈbit-ər\ *vt* : to make bitter or more bitter; *esp* : to arouse bitter feeling in — **em•bit•ter•ment** \-mənt\ *n*

em•bla•zon \im-ˈblāz-n\ *vt* **1** : to inscribe or ornament with markings or emblems used in heraldry **2 a** : to deck in bright colors **b** : CELEBRATE 3, EXTOL

em•blem \ˈem-bləm\ *n* **1** : an object or a likeness used to suggest a thing that cannot be pictured : SYMBOL ⟨the flag is the *emblem* of one's country⟩ **2** : a device, symbol, design, or figure used as an identifying mark [Latin *emblema* "inlaid work", from Greek *emblēma,* from *emballein* "to insert", from *en-* + *ballein* "to throw"]

em•blem•at•ic \ˌem-blə-ˈmat-ik\ *also* **em•blem•at•i•cal** \-ˈmat-i-kəl\ *adj* : of, relating to, or constituting an emblem : SYMBOLIC

em•bod•i•ment \im-ˈbäd-i-mənt\ *n* **1** : the act of embodying : the state of being embodied **2** : one that embodies something ⟨the *embodiment* of all our hopes⟩

em•body \im-ˈbäd-ē\ *vt* **-bod•ied; -body•ing** **1** : to make a part of a body or system : INCORPORATE ⟨*embodied* a tax provision in the new law⟩ **2** : to express in a concrete or definite form ⟨embody one's ideas in words⟩ **3** : to represent in visible form ⟨a person who *embodies* courage⟩ — **em•bod•i•er** *n*

em•bold•en \im-ˈbōl-dən\ *vt* : to make bold

em•bo•lism \ˈem-bə-ˌliz-əm\ *n* **1** : the sudden obstruction of a blood vessel by an embolus **2** : EMBOLUS — **em•bol•ic** \em-ˈbäl-ik\ *adj*

em•bo•lus \ˈem-bə-ləs\ *n, pl* **-li** \-ˌlī, -ˌlē\ : an abnormal particle (as an air bubble) circulating in the blood — compare THROMBUS [Greek *embolos* "wedge-shaped object, stopper", from *emballein* "to insert, intercalate"]

em•bo•som \im-ˈbu̇z-əm\ *vt* : to shelter closely : ENCLOSE

em•boss \im-ˈbäs, -ˈbȯs\ *vt* : to ornament with a raised pattern or design [Middle French *embocer,* from *en-* + *boce* "boss"] — **em•boss•er** *n* — **em•boss•ment** \-mənt\ *n*

em•bou•chure \ˌäm-bu̇-ˈshu̇r\ *n* **1** : the position and use of the lips in producing a musical tone on a wind instrument **2** : the mouthpiece of a musical instrument [French, from *(s')emboucher* "to flow into", from *en-* + *bouche* "mouth"]

em•bow•er \im-ˈbau̇-ər, -ˈbau̇r\ *vt* : to shelter or enclose in or as if in a bower

[1]**em•brace** \im-ˈbrās\ *vb* **1** : to clasp in the arms : HUG **2** : ENCIRCLE 1, ENCLOSE **3 a** : to take up readily or gladly ⟨*embrace* a cause⟩ **b** : to avail oneself of : WELCOME ⟨*embrace* an opportunity⟩ **4** : to take in : INCLUDE [Middle French *embracer,* from Old French *embracier,* from *en-* + *brace* "two arms", from Latin *bracchia,* pl. of *bracchium* "arm"] **syn** see COMPRISE — **em•brace•able** \-ˈbrā-sə-bəl\ *adj* — **embrace•ment** \-ˈbrās-mənt\ *n* — **em•brac•er** *n*

[2]**embrace** *n* : a gathering into one's arms and holding close

em•bra•sure \im-ˈbrā-zhər\ *n* **1** : a recess of a door or window **2** : an opening with sides flaring outward in a wall or parapet usually for allowing the firing of cannon [French]

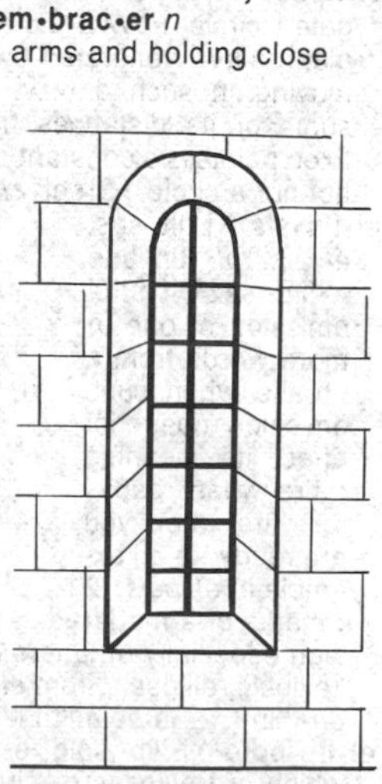

embrasure 1

em•bro•ca•tion \ˌem-brə-ˈkā-shən\ *n* : LINIMENT [Latin *embrocare* "to rub with a lotion", from Greek *embrochē* "lotion"]

em•broi•der \im-ˈbrȯid-ər\ *vb* **em•broi•dered; em•broi•der•ing** \-ˈbrȯid-ring, -ə-ring\ **1** : to make or fill in a design with needlework **2** : to ornament with needlework **3** : to elaborate with often fictitious details : EXAGGERATE [Middle French *embroder*] — **em•broi•der•er** \-ˈbrȯid-ər-ər\ *n*

em•broi•dery \im-ˈbrȯid-rē, -ə-rē\ *n, pl* **-der•ies** **1 a** : the process or art of embroidering **b** : decorative needlework **2** : elaboration in details

em•broil \im-ˈbrȯil\ *vt* **1** : to throw into disorder or confusion **2**

: to involve in conflict or difficulties [French *embrouiller,* from *en-* + *brouiller* "to broil"] — **em•broil•ment** \-mənt\ *n*

em•bryo \'em-brē-,ō\ *n, pl* **em•bry•os** **1 :** an animal in the early stages of development that are characterized by cleavage, the laying down of fundamental tissues, and the formation of primitive organs and organ systems — compare FETUS **2 :** a rudimentary plant within a seed **3 :** a beginning or undeveloped stage — used especially in the phrase *in embryo* [Medieval Latin, from Greek *embryon,* from *en-* + *bryein* "to swell"]

em•bry•ol•o•gy \,em-brē-'äl-ə-jē\ *n* **1 :** a branch of biology dealing with embryos and their development **2 :** the events and processes involved in the formation and development of an embryo — **em•bry•o•log•ic** \,em-brē-ə-'läj-ik\ *or* **em•bry•o•log•i•cal** \-'läj-i-kəl\ *adj* — **em•bry•o•log•i•cal•ly** \-i-kə-lē, -klē\ *adv* — **em•bry•ol•o•gist** \,em-brē-'äl-ə-jəst\ *n*

em•bry•on•ic \,em-brē-'än-ik\ *adj* **1 :** of or relating to an embryo **2 :** being in an early or undeveloped stage : being in embryo ⟨an *embryonic* idea⟩ — **em•bry•on•i•cal•ly** \-i-kə-lē, -klē\ *adv*

embryo sac *n* **:** the individual that produces female germ cells in the sexually reproducing generation of a seed plant and that consists of a thin-walled sac containing the egg nucleus and other nuclei which form nutritive tissue upon fertilization

[1]**em•cee** \'em-'sē\ *n* **:** MASTER OF CEREMONIES [*M.C.*]

[2]**emcee** *vb* **em•ceed; em•cee•ing :** to act as master of ceremonies : HOST

emend \ē-'mend\ *vt* **:** to correct usually by textual changes [Latin *emendare* "to emend, amend"] **syn** see CORRECT — **emend•able** \-'men-də-bəl\ *adj*

emen•da•tion \,ē-,men-'dā-shən, ,em-ən-\ *n* **1 :** the act of emending **2 :** a change designed to correct or improve

[1]**em•er•ald** \'em-rəld, -ə-rəld\ *n* **1 :** a rich green beryl prized as a gemstone **2 :** a green gemstone (as synthetic corundum) [Middle French *esmeralde,* from Latin *smaragdus,* from Greek *smaragdos*]

[2]**emerald** *adj* **:** brightly or richly green

emerald green *n* **1 :** a clear bright green resembling that of the emerald **2 :** a strong green

emerge \i-'mərj\ *vi* **1 :** to rise from or as if from an enveloping fluid : come out into view **2 :** to become known or apparent **3 :** to rise from an obscure or inferior condition [Latin *emergere,* from *e-* + *mergere* "to plunge"]

emer•gence \i-'mər-jəns\ *n* **:** the act or an instance of emerging

emer•gen•cy \i-'mər-jən-sē\ *n, pl* **-cies 1 :** an unforeseen combination of circumstances or the resulting state that calls for immediate action **2 :** a pressing need **syn** see JUNCTURE

[1]**emer•gent** \i-'mər-jənt\ *adj* **:** rising out of or as if out of a fluid ⟨cattails are *emergent* plants⟩

[2]**emergent** *n* **:** a plant rooted in shallow water and having most of its growth above water

emer•i•tus \i-'mer-ət-əs\ *adj* **1 :** holding after retirement an honorary title corresponding to that held last during active service ⟨professor *emeritus*⟩ **2 :** retired from an office or position [Latin, past participle of *emereri* "to serve out one's term", from *e-* + *mereri, merēre* "to earn, serve"] — **emeritus** *n*

emer•sion \ē-'mər-zhən\ *n* **:** an act of emerging : EMERGENCE [Latin *emersus,* past participle of *emergere* "to emerge"]

em•ery \'em-rē, -ə-rē\ *n, pl* **em•er•ies :** a dark corundum used especially in the form of powder or grains for grinding and polishing [Middle French *emeri,* from Italian *smiriglio,* from Medieval Latin *smiriglum,* from Greek *smyris* "powdered emery"]

emet•ic \i-'met-ik\ *n* **:** an agent that induces vomiting [Latin *emetica,* from Greek *emetikē,* from *emein* "to vomit"] — **emetic** *adj* — **emet•i•cal•ly** \-'met-i-kə-lē, -klē\ *adv*

-emia *or* **-ae•mia** \'ē-mē-ə\ *n combining form* **1 :** condition of having (such) blood ⟨septic*emia*⟩ **2 :** condition of having (a specified thing) in the blood ⟨ur*emia*⟩ [Greek *haima* "blood"]

em•i•grant \'em-i-grənt\ *n* **1 :** one that emigrates **2 :** a migrant plant or animal — **emigrant** *adj*

• **syn** EMIGRANT, IMMIGRANT mean one who leaves his or her country to settle in another. EMIGRANT applies to the person leaving a country; IMMIGRANT applies to the same person entering and settling in another country.

em•i•grate \'em-ə-,grāt\ *vi* **:** to leave one's residence or country to live or reside elsewhere [Latin *emigrare,* from *e-* + *migrare* "to migrate"] — **em•i•gra•tion** \,em-ə-'grā-shən\ *n*

émi•gré *or* **emi•gré** \'em-i-,grā, ,em-i-'\ *n* **:** EMIGRANT; *esp* **:** a person forced to emigrate for political reasons [French *émigré,* from *émigrer* "to emigrate", from Latin *emigrare*]

em•i•nence \'em-ə-nəns\ *n* **1 :** a condition or station of prominence or superiority **2** *often cap* — used as a form of address for a Roman Catholic cardinal ⟨His *Eminence* Terence Cardinal Cooke⟩ ⟨Your *Eminence*⟩ **3 a :** a person of high rank or achievement **b :** a natural elevation : HEIGHT

em•i•nent \-nənt\ *adj* **:** standing above all others especially in rank, merit, or virtue : NOTABLE ⟨an *eminent* physician⟩ [Latin *eminens,* from *eminēre* "to stand out"] — **em•i•nent•ly** *adv*

eminent domain *n* **:** a right of a government to buy private property for public use even if the owner is unwilling to sell

emir *or* **amir** \i-'miər, ā-\ *n* **:** a ruler in parts of Asia and Africa [Arabic *amīr* "commander" — see ADMIRAL *origin*] — **emir•ate** \-'miər-ət, -,āt\ *n*

em•is•sary \'em-ə-,ser-ē\ *n, pl* **-sar•ies 1 :** one sent on a mission as the agent of another **2 :** a secret agent [Latin *emissarius,* from *emittere* "to send out"]

emis•sion \ē-'mish-ən\ *n* **1 :** an act or instance of emitting **2 :** DISCHARGE 6 — **emis•sive** \ē-'mis-iv\ *adj*

emit \ē-'mit\ *vt* **emit•ted; emit•ting 1 a :** to throw or give off or out (as light) **b :** to send out : EJECT **2 :** to issue (as a decree) with authority **3 :** to give voice to : EXPRESS ⟨*emitted* a groan⟩ [Latin *emittere* "to send out", from *e-* + *mittere* "to send"] — **emit•ter** *n*

em•mer \'em-ər\ *n* **:** a hard red wheat having spikelets with two kernels [German]

Em•my \'em-ē\ *n, pl* **Emmys :** a statuette awarded annually for notable achievement in television [from *Immy,* nickname for *image orthicon,* a camera tube used in television]

[1]**emol•lient** \i-'mäl-yənt\ *adj* **:** making soft or supple; *also* **:** soothing especially to the skin or mucous membrane [Latin *emollire* "to soften", from *e-* + *mollis* "soft"]

[2]**emollient** *n* **:** something that softens or soothes

emol•u•ment \i-'mäl-yə-mənt\ *n* **:** profit from one's employment or from an office held : SALARY, WAGES [Latin *emolumentum,* literally, "miller's fee", from *emolere* "to grind up", from *e-* + *molere* "to grind"]

emote \i-'mōt\ *vi* **:** to express emotion in or as if in a play [backformation from *emotion*]

emo•tion \i-'mō-shən\ *n* **1 :** strong feeling : EXCITEMENT ⟨spoke with *emotion*⟩ **2 :** a mental and bodily reaction (as anger, joy, hate, or fear) marked by strong feeling and physiological responses that prepare the body for action [Middle French, from *emouvoir* "to stir up", from Latin *exmovēre* "to move away, disturb", from *ex-* + *movēre* "to move"] **syn** see FEELING

emo•tion•al \i-'mō-shnəl, -shən-l\ *adj* **1 :** of or relating to the emotions ⟨an *emotional* upset⟩ **2 :** inclined to show or express emotion : easily moved ⟨an *emotional* person⟩ **3 :** appealing to or arousing emotion — **emo•tion•al•ly** \-ē\ *adv*

emo•tive \i-'mōt-iv\ *adj* **1 :** EMOTIONAL 1 **2 :** EMOTIONAL 3 — **emo•tive•ly** *adv*

em•pa•thy \'em-pə-thē\ *n* **:** the capacity for experiencing as one's own the feelings of another — **em•path•ic** \em-'path-ik\ *adj* — **em•pa•thize** \'em-pə-,thīz\ *vi*

em•pen•nage \,äm-pə-'näzh, ,em-\ *n* **:** the tail assembly of an airplane [French, "feathers of an arrow, empennage"]

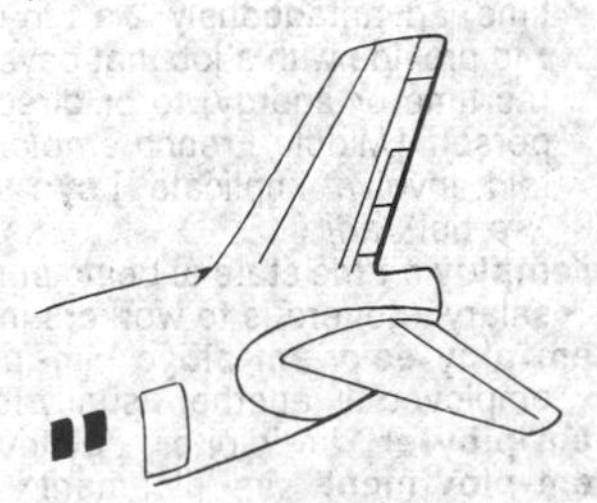

empennage

em•per•or \'em-pər-ər, -prər\ *n* **:** the sovereign ruler of an empire — compare MONARCH [Old French *empereor,* from Latin *imperator,* literally, "commander", from *imperare* "to command", from *in-* + *parare* "to prepare, arrange"]

em•pery \'em-pə-rē, -prē\ *n* **:** wide dominion : EMPIRE

em•pha•sis \'em-fə-səs, 'emp-\ *n, pl* **-pha•ses** \-fə-,sēz\ **1 a :** forcefulness of expression ⟨spoke with *emphasis*⟩ **b :** prominence given to a word or syllable in reading or speaking **2** : special stress or insistence on something ⟨put great *emphasis* on cleanliness⟩ [Latin, from Greek, "exposition, emphasis", from *emphainein* "to indicate", from *en-* + *phainein* "to show"]

em•pha•size \'em-fə-,sīz, 'emp-\ *vt* : to place emphasis on : STRESS

em•phat•ic \im-'fat-ik, em-\ *adj* **1** : uttered with or marked by emphasis **2** : tending to express oneself in forceful speech or action **3** : attracting special attention ⟨an *emphatic* contrast⟩ **4** : constituting or belonging to a set of verb forms in English that have the auxiliary *do* and are used rarely for emphasis and regularly to take the place of a simple verb form in questions or negative statements ⟨the *emphatic* form "do know" or "do...know" in "but I tell you I do know him", "do you know him?", and "I do not know him"⟩ [Greek *emphatikos,* from *emphainein* "to indicate"] — **em•phat•i•cal•ly** \-'fat-i-kə-lē, -klē\ *adv*

em•phy•se•ma \,em-fə-'sē-mə, ,emp-, -'zē-\ *n* : a disorder marked by air-filled expansions of tissues especially of the lung [Greek *emphysēma* "bodily inflation"] — **em•phy•se•ma•tous** \-mət-əs\ *adj*

em•pire \'em-,pīr\ *n* **1 a** (1) : a major political unit with a great extent of territory or a number of territories or peoples under one sovereign authority; *esp* : one having an emperor as chief of state (2) : the territory of such a unit **b** : something held to resemble a political empire; *esp* : an extensive territory or enterprise under one control **2** : imperial sovereignty, rule, or dominion [Old French, from Latin *imperium,* from *imperare* "to command"]

Em•pire \'äm-,piər, 'em-,pīr\ *adj* : of or relating to an early 19th century French style (as of clothing or furniture) characterized by elaborateness and formality [French, from *le premier Empire* "the first Empire (of France)"]

em•pir•ic \im-'pir-ik, em-\ *n* : one who relies on practical experience [Latin *empiricus* "doctor relying on experience alone", from Greek *empeirikos,* from *empeiria* "experience", from *en-* + *peiran* "to attempt"]

em•pir•i•cal \-'pir-i-kəl\ *or* **em•pir•ic** \-'pir-ik\ *adj* **1** : relying on experience or observation usually without due regard for system and theory ⟨*empirical* medicine⟩ **2** : originating in or based on observation or experience **3** : capable of being verified or disproved by observation or experiment ⟨*empirical* laws⟩ — **em•pir•i•cal•ly** \-'pir-i-kə-lē, -klē\ *adv*

empirical formula *n* : a chemical formula showing the simplest ratio of elements in a compound

em•pir•i•cism \im-'pir-ə-,siz-əm, em-\ *n* **1** : reliance on observation and experiment especially in the natural sciences **2** : a theory that knowledge originates in experience — **em•pir•i•cist** \-səst\ *adj or n*

em•place \im-'plās\ *vt* : to put into place

em•place•ment \im-'plā-smənt\ *n* **1** : a prepared position for weapons or military equipment **2** : a putting into position : PLACEMENT

1em•ploy \im-'plȯi\ *vt* **1 a** : to make use of **b** : to occupy (as time) advantageously **2 a** : to use or engage the services of **b** : to provide with a job that pays wages or a salary **3** : to devote (as time or energy) to or direct toward a particular activity or person [Middle French *emploier,* from Latin *implicare* "to enfold, involve, implicate"] **syn** see HIRE, USE — **em•ploy•able** \-ə-bəl\ *adj*

2employ *n* : the state of being employed especially for wages or a salary ⟨generous to workers in their *employ*⟩

em•ploy•ee *or* **em•ploye** \im-,plȯi-'ē, ,em-; im-'plȯi-,ē\ *n* : one employed by another usually for wages or a salary

em•ploy•er \im-'plȯi-ər, -'plȯir\ *n* : one that employs others

em•ploy•ment \im-'plȯi-mənt\ *n* **1** : USE 1a, PURPOSE; *also* : the action of using **2 a** : the act of engaging a person for work : HIRING **b** : the work at which one is employed : OCCUPATION **c** : the state of being employed ⟨*employment* in the machine trade⟩ **d** : the extent or degree to which a labor force is employed ⟨*employment* is high⟩

em•po•ri•um \im-'pōr-ē-əm, em-, -'pȯr-\ *n, pl* **-ri•ums** *or* **-ria** \-ē-ə\ **1** : a place of trade : MARKETPLACE; *esp* : a commercial center **2** : a store carrying a wide variety of merchandise [Latin, from Greek *emporion,* from *emporos* "traveler, trader", from *en* "in" + *poros* "passage"]

em•pow•er \im-'pau̇-ər, -'pau̇r\ *vt* : to give official authority or legal power to **syn** see ENABLE

em•press \'em-prəs\ *n* **1** : the wife or widow of an emperor **2** : a woman who holds an imperial title in her own right

em•prise \em-'prīz\ *n* : UNDERTAKING 1, ENTERPRISE; *esp* : a chivalric enterprise [Middle French, from Old French, from *emprendre* "to undertake"]

1emp•ty \'em-tē, 'emp-\ *adj* **emp•ti•er**; **-est** **1** : containing nothing ⟨an *empty* box⟩ **2** : UNOCCUPIED, VACANT ⟨an *empty* house⟩ **3** : being without reality or substance ⟨*empty* dreams⟩ **4** : lacking in value, sense, effect, or sincerity ⟨*empty* pleasures⟩ **5** : HUNGRY ⟨feel *empty* before dinner⟩ **6** : NULL 4 [Old English *ǣmettig* "unoccupied", from *ǣmetta* "leisure"] — **emp•ti•ly** \-tə-lē\ *adv* — **emp•ti•ness** \-tē-nəs\ *n*

• **syn** VACANT, VOID, BLANK: EMPTY implies a complete lack or absence of usual content or significance ⟨*empty* jars⟩ ⟨an *empty* promise⟩ VACANT implies lack of what is considered as or intended to be the usual occupant, tenant, or attribute ⟨a *vacant* store⟩ ⟨a *vacant* look⟩ VOID intensifies emptiness ⟨*void* of compassion⟩ BLANK stresses what is free from writing or marking and implies lack of signs of expression, comprehension, or meaning ⟨a *blank* page⟩ ⟨*blank* surprise⟩

2empty *vb* **emp•tied**; **emp•ty•ing** **1** : to make or become empty by removal of contents ⟨*empty* a barrel⟩ ⟨the theater *emptied* quickly⟩ **2** : to transfer by emptying ⟨*empty* the trash⟩ **3** : to discharge its contents ⟨the river *empties* into the ocean⟩

3empty *n, pl* **empties** : an empty container

emp•ty–hand•ed \,em-tē-'han-dəd, ,emp-\ *adj* **1** : having nothing in the hands **2** : having acquired or gained nothing

em•pur•ple \im-'pər-pəl\ *vb* **em•pur•pled**; **em•pur•pling** \-'pər-pə-ling, -pling\ : to tinge or color purple

em•py•re•an \,em-,pī-'rē-ən, -pə-; em-'pir-ē-ən, -'pī-rē-\ *n* **1** : the highest heaven or heavenly sphere **2** : FIRMAMENT, HEAVENS [Late Latin *empyreus* "celestial", from Late Greek *empyrios,* from Greek *en* "in" + *pyr* "fire"] — **em•py•re•al** \-əl\ *adj* — **empyrean** *adj*

emu \'ē-,myü\ *n* : a swift-running Australian bird with undeveloped wings that is related to but smaller than the ostrich [Portuguese *ema* "rhea"]

emu

em•u•late \'em-yə-,lāt\ *vt* **1** : to strive to equal or excel **2** : to equal or approach equality with : RIVAL [Latin *aemulari,* from *aemulus* "rivaling"] — **em•u•la•tor** \-,lāt-ər\ *n*

em•u•la•tion \,em-yə-'lā-shən\ *n* : effort or desire to equal or excel — **em•u•la•tive** \'em-yə-,lāt-iv\ *adj*

em•u•lous \'em-yə-ləs\ *adj* : eager or ambitious to equal or excel another — **em•u•lous•ly** *adv* — **em•u•lous•ness** *n*

emul•si•fi•er \i-'məl-sə-,fī-ər, -'fīr\ *n* : an agent (as a soap) promoting the formation and stabilization of an emulsion

emul•si•fy \-,fī\ *vt* **-fied**; **-fy•ing** : to convert (as an oil) into an emulsion — **emul•si•fi•able** \-,fī-ə-bəl\ *adj* — **emul•si•fi•ca•tion** \i-,məl-sə-fə-'kā-shən\ *n*

emul•sion \i-'məl-shən\ *n* **1** : a material consisting of a mixture of liquids that do not dissolve in each other and having droplets of one liquid dispersed throughout the other ⟨an *emulsion* of oil in water⟩ **2** : a light-sensitive coating on photographic plates, film, or paper consisting of particles of a silver salt suspended in a thick substance (as a gelatin solution) [Latin *emulsus,* past participle of *emulgēre* "to milk out", from *e-* + *mulgēre* "to milk"] — **emul•sive** \-siv\ *adj*

emul•soid \-,sȯid\ *n* : a colloid consisting of one liquid dispersed in another

en \'en\ *n* : one half of an em [from the size of the quad used for the letter *n*]

1en- *also* **em-** \e *also occurs in these prefixes although only* i *may be shown as in "engage"*\ *prefix* **1** : put into or onto ⟨*en*throne⟩ : go into or onto ⟨*en*train⟩ — in verbs formed from nouns **2** : cause to be ⟨*en*able⟩ ⟨*en*slave⟩ — in verbs formed from adjectives or nouns **3** : provide with ⟨*em*power⟩ — in verbs formed from nouns **4** : so as to cover ⟨*en*wrap⟩ : thoroughly ⟨*en*tangle⟩ — in verbs formed from verbs; in all senses usually *em-* before *b, m,* or *p* [Old French, from Latin *in-*]

²en- *also* **em-** *prefix* : in : within ⟨*em*pathy⟩ — usually *em-* before *b, m,* or *p* [Greek, from *en* "in"]

¹-en \ən, ᵊn\ *also* **-n** \n\ *adj suffix* : made of : consisting of ⟨earth*en*⟩ ⟨silver*n*⟩ ⟨wool*en*⟩ [Old English]

²-en *vb suffix* **1** : become or cause to be ⟨sharp*en*⟩ **2** : cause or come to have ⟨strength*en*⟩ [Old English *-nian*]

en•able \in-ˈā-bəl\ *vt* **en•abled**; **en•abling** \-bə-liŋ, -bliŋ\ **1 a** : to make able ⟨glasses *enable* me to read⟩ **b** : to make possible, practical, or easy **2** : to give a legal power or right to **• syn** ENABLE, EMPOWER mean to make one able to do something. ENABLE implies provision of the means or opportunity for doing; EMPOWER implies the granting of power or delegation of authority to do.

en•act \in-ˈakt\ *vt* **1** : to make (as a bill) into law **2** : to act out : REPRESENT — **en•ac•tor** \-ˈak-tər\ *n*

en•act•ment \-ˈakt-mənt, -ˈak-\ *n* **1** : the act of enacting : the state of being enacted **2** : something (as a law) that has been enacted

¹enam•el \in-ˈam-əl\ *vt* **enam•eled** *or* **enam•elled**; **enam•el•ing** *or* **enam•el•ling** \-ˈam-liŋ, -ə-liŋ\ **1** : to cover or inlay with enamel **2** : to form a glossy surface on [Middle French *enamailler,* from *en-* + *esmail* "enamel", of Germanic origin]

²enamel *n* **1** : a usually opaque glassy composition applied by fusion to the surface of metal, glass, or pottery **2** : a surface that resembles enamel **3** : a usually glossy paint that flows out to a smooth hard coat when applied **4** : a very hard outer layer covering the crown of a tooth

enam•el•ware \-ˌwaər, -ˌweər\ *n* : metal utensils (as pots and pans) coated with enamel

en•am•or \in-ˈam-ər\ *vt* : to fill with love or delight ⟨*enamored* with the charm of the scene⟩ [Old French *enamourer,* from *en-* + *amour* "love"]

en bloc \äⁿ-ˈbläk\ *adv or adj* : as a whole : in a mass [French]

en•camp \in-ˈkamp\ *vb* **1** : to set up and occupy a camp : CAMP **2** : to place or establish in a camp ⟨*encamp* troops⟩

en•camp•ment \-mənt\ *n* **1** : the act of encamping : the state of being encamped **2** : CAMP 1a, b, d, 2a

en•cap•su•late \in-ˈkap-sə-ˌlāt\ *vb* **1** : to encase in a capsule **2** : to become encapsulated ⟨parasites that *encapsulate* in muscle⟩ — **en•cap•su•la•tion** \-ˌkap-sə-ˈlā-shən\ *n*

en•case *also* **in•case** \in-ˈkās\ *vt* : to enclose in or as if in a case — **en•case•ment** \-ˈkā-smənt\ *n*

en•caus•tic \in-ˈkȯ-stik\ *n* : a paint mixed with melted beeswax and after application fixed by heat [derived from Greek *enkaustos* "painted in encaustic", from *enkaiein* "to burn in, paint in encaustic", from *en-* + *kaiein* "to burn"]

-ence \əns, ᵊns\ *n suffix* **1** : action or process : instance of an action or process ⟨emerg*ence*⟩ ⟨refer*ence*⟩ **2** : quality or state ⟨coexist*ence*⟩ [Old French, from Latin *-entia,* from *-ent-, -ens,* present participle ending + *-ia* "-y"]

encephal- *or* **encephalo-** *combining form* : brain ⟨*encephal*itis⟩ [Greek *enkephalos,* from *en* "in" + *kephalē* "head"]

en•ceph•a•li•tis \ˌen-ˌsef-ə-ˈlīt-əs\ *n* : inflammation of the brain — **en•ceph•a•lit•ic** \-ˈlit-ik\ *adj*

en•ceph•a•lo•my•e•li•tis \en-ˌsef-ə-lō-ˌmī-ə-ˈlīt-əs\ *n* : concurrent inflammation of the brain and spinal cord

en•ceph•a•lon \en-ˈsef-ə-ˌlän, -lən\ *n, pl* **-la** \-lə\ : the vertebrate brain — **en•ce•phal•ic** \ˌen-sə-ˈfal-ik\ *adj*

en•chain \in-ˈchān\ *vt* **1** : to bind with or as if with chains **2** : to attract and hold (as the attention) — **en•chain•ment** \-mənt\ *n*

en•chant \in-ˈchant\ *vt* **1** : to influence by charms and incantation : BEWITCH **2** : THRILL 1 [Middle French *enchanter,* from Latin *incantare,* from *in-* + *cantare* "to sing"]

en•chant•er \-ər\ *n* : one that enchants; *esp* : SORCERER

en•chant•ing *adj* : ATTRACTIVE, CHARMING — **en•chant•ing•ly** \-iŋ-lē\ *adv*

en•chant•ment \in-ˈchant-mənt\ *n* **1** : the act or art of enchanting : the state of being enchanted **2** : something that enchants : SPELL, CHARM

en•chant•ress \in-ˈchan-trəs\ *n* **1** : a woman who practices magic : SORCERESS **2** : a fascinating woman

enchase \in-ˈchās\ *vt* **1** : SET ⟨*enchase* a gem⟩ **2** : ORNAMENT: as **a** : to cut or carve in relief **b** : INLAY [Middle French *enchasser* "to enshrine, set", from *en-* + *chasse* "reliquary", from Latin *capsa* "case"]

en•chi•la•da \ˌen-chə-ˈläd-ə\ *n* : a tortilla rolled with meat or cheese filling and served with tomato sauce seasoned with chili [American Spanish]

en•ci•pher \in-ˈsī-fər, en-\ *vt* : to convert (a message) into cipher

en•cir•cle \in-ˈsər-kəl\ *vt* **1** : to form a circle around : SURROUND **2** : to pass completely around — **en•cir•cle•ment** \-kəl-mənt\ *n*

en•clave \ˈen-ˌklāv, ˈän-, ˈäŋ-\ *n* : a territorial or culturally distinct unit enclosed within foreign territory [French, from Middle French *enclaver* "to enclose", from Latin *in-* + *clavis* "key"]

en•clit•ic \en-ˈklit-ik\ *adj* : being without independent accent and treated in pronunciation as forming a part of the preceding word ⟨*thee* in *prithee* and *not* in *cannot* are *enclitic*⟩ [Latin *encliticus,* from Greek *enklitikos,* from *enklinesthai* "to lean on", from *en-* + *klinein* "to lean"] — **enclitic** *n*

en•close *or* **in•close** \in-ˈklōz\ *vt* **1 a** : to close in : SURROUND; *esp* : to mark off (land) by or as if by a fence **b** : to hold in : CONFINE **2** : to place in a parcel or envelope

en•clo•sure *or* **in•clo•sure** \in-ˈklō-zhər\ *n* **1** : the act of enclosing : the state of being enclosed **2** : an enclosed space **3** : something (as a fence) that encloses **4** : something enclosed ⟨a letter with two *enclosures*⟩

en•code \in-ˈkōd\ *vt* : to transfer from one system of communication into another; *esp* : to put (a message) in the form of a code

en•co•mi•ast \en-ˈkō-mē-ˌast, -mē-əst\ *n* : one that praises — **en•co•mi•as•tic** \-ˌkō-mē-ˈas-tik\ *adj*

en•co•mi•um \en-ˈkō-mē-əm\ *n, pl* **-mi•ums** *or* **-mia** \-mē-ə\ : warm or high praise especially when formally expressed [Latin, from Greek *enkōmion,* from *en* "in" + *kōmos* "celebration"]

en•com•pass \in-ˈkəm-pəs, -ˈkäm-\ *vt* **1** : to form a circle about : ENCLOSE **2 a** : ENVELOP **b** : INCLUDE ⟨a plan that *encompasses* a number of aims⟩ — **en•com•pass•ment** \-mənt\ *n*

¹en•core \ˈän-ˌkōr, -ˌkȯr\ *n* : a demand for repetition or reappearance made by an audience; *also* : a further performance in response to such a demand [French, "again"]

²encore *vt* : to call for a further performance or appearance of or by

¹en•coun•ter \in-ˈkau̇nt-ər\ *vt* **en•coun•tered**; **en•coun•ter•ing** \-ˈkau̇nt-ə-riŋ, -ˈkau̇n-triŋ\ **1** : to meet as an enemy : engage in conflict with **2** : to come upon face to face **3** : to come upon unexpectedly ⟨*encounter* difficulties⟩ [Old French *encontrer,* derived from Latin *in-* + *contra* "against"]

²encounter *n* **1 a** : a meeting between unfriendly factions or persons **b** : a sudden often violent clash : COMBAT **2 a** : a chance meeting **b** : a meeting face to face

en•cour•age \in-ˈkər-ij, -ˈkə-rij\ *vt* **1** : to inspire with courage, spirit, or hope : HEARTEN **2** : to spur on **3** : to give help to : FOSTER — **en•cour•ag•ing•ly** \-iŋ-lē\ *adv*

en•cour•age•ment \-mənt\ *n* **1** : the act of encouraging : the state of being encouraged **2** : something that encourages

en•croach \in-ˈkrōch\ *vi* **1** : to enter or force oneself gradually upon another's property or rights : TRESPASS **2** : to advance beyond the usual or proper limits ⟨the gradually *encroaching* sea⟩ [Middle French *encrochier* "to get, seize", from *en-* + *croche* "hook"] — **en•croach•ment** \-mənt\ *n*

en•crust *also* **in•crust** \in-ˈkrəst\ *vb* **1** : to cover with a crust **2** : to form a crust

en•crus•ta•tion \in-ˌkrəs-ˈtā-shən, ˌen-\ *variant of* INCRUSTATION

en•cum•ber *also* **in•cum•ber** \in-ˈkəm-bər\ *vt* **en•cum•bered**; **en•cum•ber•ing** \-bə-riŋ, -briŋ\ **1** : to weigh down : BURDEN **2** : to hamper the function or activity of : HINDER **3** : to burden with a legal claim (as a mortgage) ⟨*encumber* an estate⟩ [Middle French *encombrer*]

en•cum•brance \in-ˈkəm-brəns\ *n* **1** : something that encumbers : LOAD, BURDEN **2** *or* **in•cum•brance** : a legal claim (as a mortgage) against property

-en•cy \ən-sē, ᵊn-sē\ *n suffix* : quality or state ⟨despond*ency*⟩ [Latin *-entia* "-ency, -ence"]

¹en•cyc•li•cal \in-ˈsik-li-kəl, en-\ *adj* : addressed to all the individuals of a group : GENERAL [Late Latin *encyclicus,* from Greek *enkyklios* "circular, general", from *en* "in" + *kyklos* "circle"]

[2]**encyclical** *n* : an encyclical letter; *esp* : a papal letter to the bishops of the church as a whole or to those in one country

en•cy•clo•pe•dia *also* **en•cy•clo•pae•dia** \in-,sī-klə-'pēd-ē-ə\ *n* : a work that contains information on all branches of knowledge or treats comprehensively a particular branch of knowledge usually in articles arranged alphabetically by subject [Medieval Latin *encyclopaedia* "course of general education", from Greek *enkyklios paideia* "general education"]

en•cy•clo•pe•dic *also* **en•cy•clo•pae•dic** \-'pēd-ik\ *adj* **1** : of or relating to an encyclopedia **2** : covering a wide range of subjects ⟨*encyclopedic* knowledge⟩ — **en•cy•clo•pe•di•cal•ly** \-'pēd-i-kə-lē, -klē\ *adv*

en•cyst \in-'sist, en-\ *vi* : to form or become enclosed in a cyst — **en•cyst•ment** \-'sist-mənt, -'sis-\ *n*

[1]**end** \'end\ *n* **1 a** : the part of an area that lies at the boundary **b** : a point that marks the extent or limit of something **c** : the point where something ceases to exist ⟨world without *end*⟩ **d** : the extreme or last part lengthwise : TIP **e** : a football lineman whose position is at the extremity of the line **2 a** : cessation of a course of action or activity **b** : DEATH, DESTRUCTION ⟨meet one's *end* bravely⟩ **c** (1) : the final state (2) : RESULT, ISSUE **d** : the complex of events, parts, or sections that forms a finish **3** : something left over **4** : the goal toward which an agent acts or should act **5** : a particular phase of an undertaking [Old English *ende*] — **end•ed** \'en-dəd\ *adj*

• **syn** END, TERMINATION, ENDING mean the point or line beyond which a thing does not or cannot go. END implies the final limit in time, space, extent, influence, or range of possibility; TERMINATION applies to the end of something complete or finished or having a set limit ⟨the *termination* of the treaty⟩ ENDING also includes the portion leading to the actual final point ⟨the *ending* of a play⟩ ⟨a long *ending* to a symphony⟩

[2]**end** *vb* **1 a** : to bring or come to an end : STOP **b** : DESTROY 1 **2** : to make up the end of **syn** see CLOSE

end- *or* **endo-** *combining form* **1** : within : inside ⟨*endo*skeleton⟩ — compare ECT-, EXO- **2** : taking in ⟨*endo*thermal⟩ [Greek *endon* "within"]

en•dan•ger \in-'dān-jər\ *vt* **en•dan•gered**; **en•dan•ger•ing** \-'dānj-ring, -ə-ring\ : to bring into danger or peril

en•dan•gered *adj* : threatened with extinction ⟨an *endangered* species of bird⟩

end brush *n* : END PLATE

en•dear \in-'diər\ *vt* : to cause to become dear or beloved

en•dear•ment \-mənt\ *n* : a word or an act (as a caress) showing love or affection

[1]**en•deav•or** \in-'dev-ər\ *vb* **en•deav•ored**; **en•deav•or•ing** \-'dev-ring, -ə-ring\ : to make an effort : work for a particular end : TRY ⟨*endeavor* to do better⟩ [Middle English *en-* + *dever* "duty", from Old French *devoir* "to owe", from Latin *debēre*]

[2]**endeavor** *n* : a serious determined effort

[1]**en•dem•ic** \en-'dem-ik\ *adj* : restricted or peculiar to a locality or region ⟨*endemic* diseases⟩ ⟨an *endemic* plant⟩ [French *endémique,* derived from Greek *endēmos,* from *en* "in" + *dēmos* "people, populace"] **syn** see NATIVE — **en•dem•i•cal•ly** \-'dem-i-kə-lē, -klē\ *adv* — **en•de•mic•i•ty** \,en-,dem-'is-ət-ē, -də-'mis-\ *n*

[2]**endemic** *n* : NATIVE 2b

end•er•gon•ic \,en-dər-'gän-ik\ *adj* : requiring outlay of energy ⟨an *endergonic* biochemical reaction⟩ [*end-* + Greek *ergon* "work"]

end•ing \'en-ding\ *n* **1** : CONCLUSION, END ⟨a novel with a happy *ending*⟩ **2** : one or more sounds or letters added at the end of a word especially in inflection **syn** see END

en•dive \'en-,dīv\ *n* **1** : an annual or biennial herb closely related to chicory and widely grown as a salad plant — called also *escarole* **2** : the developing crown of chicory when blanched for use as salad [Middle French, from Late Latin *endivia,* from Late Greek *entubion,* from Latin *intubus*]

end•less \'en-dləs, -ləs\ *adj* **1** : being or seeming to be without end ⟨waited *endless* hours⟩ ⟨the *endless* prairie⟩ **2** : joined at the ends : CONTINUOUS ⟨an *endless* belt⟩ **syn** see ETERNAL — **end•less•ly** *adv* — **end•less•ness** *n*

end line *n* : a line at each end of a playing area (as a court or field) perpendicular to the sidelines marking a boundary

end man *n* : a comedian at either end of the line of performers in a minstrel show

end•most \'end-,mōst, 'en-\ *adj* : situated at the very end : FARTHEST

en•do•car•di•tis \,en-dō-kär-'dīt-əs\ *n* : inflammation of the lining of the heart and its valves

en•do•car•di•um \,en-dō-'kärd-ē-əm\ *n* : a thin membrane lining the cavities of the heart [New Latin, from *end-* + Greek *kardia* "heart"]

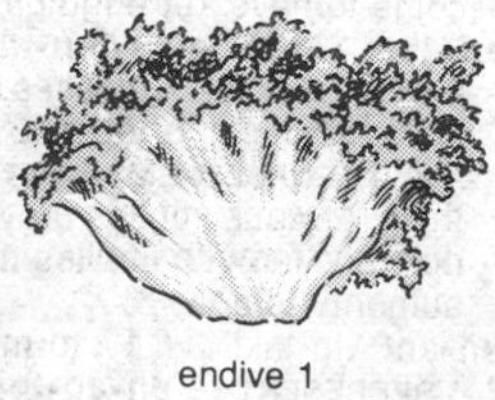
endive 1

en•do•carp \'en-də-,kärp\ *n* : the inner layer of the pericarp of a fruit (as the stony wall enclosing the seed of a peach) — compare EPICARP, MESOCARP

[1]**en•do•crine** \'en-də-krən, -,krīn, -,krēn\ *adj* **1** : of, relating to, being, or resembling that of an endocrine gland **2** : HORMONAL [*end-* + Greek *krinein* "to separate"]

[2]**endocrine** *n* **1** : HORMONE **2** : ENDOCRINE GLAND

endocrine gland *n* : any of various glands (as the thyroid) that have no duct and pour their secretions directly into the blood or lymph

en•do•cri•nol•o•gy \,en-də-kri-'näl-ə-jē, -krī-\ *n* : a science dealing with the endocrine glands — **en•do•cri•no•log•i•cal** \-,krin-l-'äj-i-kəl, -,krīn-\ *adj* — **en•do•cri•nol•o•gist** \-kri-'näl-ə-jəst, -krī-\ *n*

en•do•derm \'en-də-,dərm\ *n* : the innermost of the three primary germ layers of an embryo giving rise to the epithelium of the digestive tract and its derivatives; *also* : a tissue derived from this layer

en•do•der•mal \,en-də-'dər-məl\ *adj* : of or derived from endoderm or from endodermis

en•do•der•mis \,en-də-'dər-məs\ *n* : the innermost tissue of the cortex in many roots and stems

en•dog•a•my \en-'däg-ə-mē\ *n* : mating between members of a social group or population usually consisting of genetically related individuals — **en•dog•a•mous** \-məs\ *adj*

en•dog•e•nous \en-'däj-ə-nəs\ *adj* : developing or originating within the cell or body — **en•dog•e•nous•ly** *adv*

en•do•lymph \'en-də-,limf, -,limpf\ *n* : the watery fluid in the inner ear

en•do•mor•phic \,en-də-'mȯr-fik\ *adj* : broad and heavy in build [*endo*derm + *-morphic;* from the predominance in such people of structures developed from the endoderm] — **en•do•morph** \'en-də-,mȯrf\ *n* — **en•do•mor•phy** \-,mȯr-fē\ *n*

en•do•plasm \'en-də-,plaz-əm\ *n* : the inner relatively fluid part of the cytoplasm — compare ECTOPLASM — **en•do•plas•mic** \,en-də-'plaz-mik\ *adj*

endoplasmic reticulum *n* : a system of cavities and minute connecting canals that occupy much of the cytoplasm of the cell and are studded with ribosomes in some places

end organ *n* : a structure forming the end of a path of nerve conduction and consisting of an effector or a receptor with its associated nerve terminations

en•dorse *or* **in•dorse** \in-'dȯrs\ *vt* **1** : to sign the back of (a commercial document) for some special purpose ⟨*endorse* a check⟩ **2** : to express approval of publicly ⟨*endorse* a candidate⟩ [Middle French *endosser,* from Old French, "to put on the back", from *en-* + *dos* "back", from Latin *dorsum*] **syn** see APPROVE — **en•dors•ee** \in-,dȯr-'sē, ,en-\ *n* — **en•dors•er** \in-'dȯr-sər\ *n*

en•dorse•ment *or* **in•dorse•ment** \in-'dȯr-smənt\ *n* **1** : the act or process of endorsing **2** : something written in the process of endorsing **3** : APPROVAL ⟨*endorsement* of a plan⟩

en•do•skel•e•ton \,en-dō-'skel-ət-n\ *n* : an internal skeleton or supporting framework in an animal — compare EXOSKELETON — **en•do•skel•e•tal** \-ət-l\ *adj*

en•do•sperm \'en-də-,spərm\ *n* : a nutritive tissue in seed plants formed within the embryo sac

en•do•spore \'en-də-,spōr, -,spȯr\ *n* : an asexual spore developed within the cell especially in bacteria

en•do•the•li•um \,en-də-'thē-lē-əm\ *n, pl* **-lia** \-lē-ə\ : an inner layer (as of epithelium or of a seed coat) [*end-* + *epithelium*] — **en•do•the•li•al** \-lē-əl\ *adj*

en•do•ther•mic \,en-də-'thər-mik\ *or* **en•do•ther•mal** \-məl\

adj : characterized by or formed with absorption of heat ⟨*endothermic* chemical reactions⟩

en·do·tox·in \ˌen-dō-ˈtäk-sən\ *n* : a poisonous substance of a bacterium (as one causing typhoid fever) separable from the cell only on its disintegration

en·dow \in-ˈdau̇\ *vt* **1** : to furnish with money for support or maintenance ⟨*endow* a hospital⟩ **2** : to furnish with something freely or naturally ⟨human beings are *endowed* with reason⟩ [Anglo-French *endouer*, from Middle French *en-* + *douer* "to endow", from Latin *dotare*, from *dot-*, *dos* "gift"]

en·dow·ment \-mənt\ *n* **1** : the providing of a permanent fund for support or the fund provided ⟨a college with a large *endowment*⟩ **2** : natural ability or talent

endowment policy *n* : a life-insurance policy that provides for payment of a sum to the policyholder at the end of a stated period or to the beneficiary if the policyholder dies during that period

end·pa·per \ˈend-ˌpā-pər, ˈen-\ *n* : a sheet of paper folded once with one half pasted flat against the inside of the front or back cover of a book and the other pasted to the base of the front or last page

end plate *n* : a treelike ending of a motor nerve fiber

end·point \ˈend-ˌpȯint, ˈen-\ *n* **1** : a point marking the end of a process or a stage in a process **2** : either of two points that mark the ends of a line segment or a point that marks the end of a ray

end product *n* : the final product of a series of processes or activities

end run *n* : a football play in which the ballcarrier attempts to run wide around the end

end table *n* : a small table used beside a larger piece of furniture

en·due *also* **in·due** \in-ˈdü, -ˈdyü\ *vt* : to provide with a quality or power ⟨*endued* with grace⟩ [Middle French *enduire* "to bring in, introduce", from Latin *inducere*, from *in-* + *ducere* "to lead"]

en·dur·ance \in-ˈdu̇r-əns, -ˈdyu̇r-\ *n* **1** : PERMANENCE, DURATION **2** : the ability to withstand hardship, misfortune, or stress **3** : TRIAL 3, SUFFERING

en·dure \in-ˈdu̇r, -ˈdyu̇r\ *vb* **1** : to continue in the same state : LAST **2 a** : to remain firm under suffering or misfortune without yielding **b** : to bear patiently : SUFFER **3** : to put up with : PERMIT [Middle French *endurer*, from Latin *indurare* "to harden", from *in-* + *durare* "to harden, endure"] — **en·dur·able** \-ə-bəl\ *adj* — **en·dur·ably** \-ə-blē\ *adv*

en·dur·ing *adj* : LASTING, DURABLE — **en·dur·ing·ly** \-ing-lē\ *adv* — **en·dur·ing·ness** *n*

end·ways \ˈen-ˌdwāz\ *adv or adj* **1** : with the end forward **2** : in or toward the direction of the ends : LENGTHWISE **3** : on end : UPRIGHT

end·wise \-ˌdwīz\ *adv or adj* : ENDWAYS

end zone *n* : the area at each end of a football field bounded by the end line, the goal line, and the sidelines

-ene \ˌēn\ *n suffix* : unsaturated carbon compound ⟨benz*ene*⟩; *esp* : carbon compound with one double bond ⟨ethyl*ene*⟩ [Greek *-ēnē*, feminine of *-ēnos*, adj. suffix]

en·e·ma \ˈen-ə-mə\ *n* : the injection of liquid into the intestine by way of the anus; *also* : the material injected [Late Latin, from Greek, from *enienai* "to inject", from *en-* + *hienai* "to send"]

en·e·my \ˈen-ə-mē\ *n, pl* **-mies 1** : one that hates another : one that attacks or tries to harm another **2** : something that harms **3 a** : a nation with which a country is at war **b** : a hostile unit or force [Old French *enemi*, from Latin *inimicus*, from *in-* "[1]in-" + *amicus* "friend"]

• **syn** ENEMY, FOE mean one who shows hostility or ill will. ENEMY stresses antagonism showing itself in hatred or destructive attitude or action; FOE stresses active fighting or struggle and is used poetically for an enemy in war

en·er·get·ic \ˌen-ər-ˈjet-ik\ *adj* : having or showing energy : ACTIVE, FORCEFUL ⟨an *energetic* salesman⟩ [Greek *energētikos*, from *energein* "to be active", from *energos* "active"] **syn** see VIGOROUS — **en·er·get·i·cal·ly** \-ˈjet-i-kə-lē, -klē\ *adv*

en·er·gize \ˈen-ər-ˌjīz\ *vb* **1** : to put forth energy : ACT **2 a** : to impart energy to **b** : to make energetic or vigorous **3** : to apply voltage to — **en·er·giz·er** *n*

en·er·gy \ˈen-ər-jē\ *n, pl* **-gies 1** : power or capacity to be active : strength of body or mind to do things or to work ⟨a person of great intellectual *energy*⟩ **2** : natural power vigorously exerted : vigorous action ⟨work with *energy*⟩ **3** : the capacity for performing work : usable power; *also* : the resources for producing such power — compare KINETIC ENERGY, POTENTIAL ENERGY [Late Latin *energia*, from Greek *energeia* "activity", from *energos* "active", from *en* "in" + *ergon* "work"] **syn** see POWER

energy level *n* : one of the stable states of constant energy that may be assumed by a physical system — used especially of electrons in atoms

en·er·vate \ˈen-ər-ˌvāt\ *vt* : to cause to lose strength or vigor : WEAKEN [Latin *enervare*, from *e-* + *nervus* "sinew"] — **en·er·va·tion** \ˌen-ər-ˈvā-shən\ *n*

en·fant ter·ri·ble \äⁿ-fäⁿ-te-rēbl\ *n* : a person whose remarks or actions cause embarrassment [French, literally, "terrifying child"]

en·fee·ble \in-ˈfē-bəl\ *vt* **en·fee·bled**; **en·fee·bling** \-bə-ling, -bling\ : to make feeble — **en·fee·ble·ment** \-bəl-mənt\ *n*

[1]en·fi·lade \ˈen-fə-ˌlād, -ˌläd\ *n* : gunfire directed along the length of an enemy battle line [French, from *enfiler* "to thread, enfilade", from *en-* + *fil* "thread"]

[2]enfilade *vt* : to rake or be in a position to rake with gunfire in a lengthwise direction

en·fold \in-ˈfōld\ *vt* **1 a** : to cover with folds **b** : to surround with a covering : CONTAIN **2** : to clasp within the arms

en·force \in-ˈfōrs, -ˈfȯrs\ *vt* **1** : FORCE, COMPEL ⟨*enforce* obedience⟩ **2** : to carry out effectively ⟨*enforce* the law⟩ — **en·force·able** \-ə-bəl\ *adj* — **en·force·ment** \-mənt\ *n* — **en·forc·er** *n*

en·fran·chise \in-ˈfran-ˌchīz\ *vt* **1** : to set free (as from slavery) **2** : to grant the privileges of a citizen to; *esp* : to grant the right of suffrage to [Middle French *enfranchiss-*, stem of *enfranchir* "to enfranchise", from *en-* + *franc* "free"] — **en·fran·chise·ment** \-ˌchīz-mənt, -chəz-\ *n*

en·gage \in-ˈgāj\ *vb* : **1** : to interlock with : MESH; *also* : to cause to mesh **2** : to bind oneself to do something; *esp* : to bind by a pledge to marry **3 a** : to arrange to obtain the use or services of : HIRE **b** : ENGROSS, OCCUPY ⟨the task *engaged* my attention⟩ **4** : to enter into contest with ⟨*engage* the enemy⟩ **5 a** : to begin and carry on an enterprise ⟨*engaged* in sales⟩ **b** : PARTICIPATE [Middle French *engagier*, from *en-* + *gage* "[1]gage"]

en·gaged \in-ˈgājd\ *adj* **1** : OCCUPIED, EMPLOYED, BUSY ⟨*engaged* in conversation⟩ **2** : pledged to be married

en·gage·ment \in-ˈgāj-mənt\ *n* **1 a** : the act of engaging : the state of being engaged **b** : an agreement to marry **2** : PLEDGE, OBLIGATION ⟨financial *engagements* to fulfill⟩ **3 a** : a promise to be present at a specified time and place **b** : employment especially for a stated time **4** : the state of being in gear **5** : a hostile encounter between military forces

en·gag·ing \in-ˈgā-jing\ *adj* : ATTRACTIVE, PLEASING — **en·gag·ing·ly** \-jing-lē\ *adv*

en·gen·der \in-ˈjen-dər\ *vt* **en·gen·dered**; **en·gen·der·ing** \-də-ring, -dring\ **1** : BEGET 1 **2** : to cause to exist : PRODUCE ⟨angry words *engender* strife⟩ [Middle French *engendrer*, from Latin *ingenerare*, from *in-* + *generare* "to generate"]

en·gine \ˈen-jən\ *n* **1 a** : a mechanical tool (as an instrument of war or torture) **b** : a mechanical appliance — compare FIRE ENGINE **2** : a machine for converting energy into mechanical force and motion **3** : a railroad locomotive [Old French *engin* "ingenuity", from Latin *ingenium* "natural disposition, talent", from *in-* + *gignere* "to beget"]

[1]en·gi·neer \ˌen-jə-ˈniər\ *n* **1** : a member of a military group devoted to engineering work **2 a** : a designer or builder of engines **b** : a person who is trained in or follows as a profession a branch of engineering **c** : a person who skillfully carries out an enterprise **3** : a person who runs or supervises an engine or an apparatus

[2]engineer *vt* **1** : to plan, build, or manage as an engineer **2** : to guide the course of ⟨*engineer* a fund-raising campaign⟩

en·gi·neer·ing *n* **1** : the art of managing engines **2** : the application of science and mathematics by which the properties of matter and the sources of energy in nature are made useful to human beings

¹En·glish \'iŋ-glish *also* 'iŋ-lish\ *adj* : of, relating to, or characteristic of England, the English people, or the English language [Old English *englisc,* from *Engle* "Angles"] — **En·glish·man** \-mən\ *n* — **En·glish·wom·an** \-ˌwu̇m-ən\ *n*

²English *n* **1 a** : the language of the people of England, the United States, and many areas now or formerly under British control **b** : English language, literature, or composition as a subject of study **2** *pl in construction* : the people of England **3** : a sideways spin given to a ball

³English *vt* : to translate into English

English daisy *n* : DAISY 1a

English horn *n* : a double-reed woodwind instrument similar to the oboe but a fifth lower in pitch

English horn

English ivy *n* : IVY 1

English setter *n* : any of a breed of bird dogs with a flat silky coat of white or white with color

English shepherd *n* : any of a breed of medium-sized dogs with a long and glossy black coat and usually tan to brown markings

English sonnet *n* : a sonnet consisting of three quatrains and a couplet with a rhyme scheme of *abab cdcd efef gg*

English sparrow *n* : an Old World sparrow widely naturalized in the New World — called also *house sparrow*

English walnut *n* : an Old World walnut valued for its large edible nut and its hard richly figured wood; also : its nut

en·gorge \in-'gȯrj\ *vb* **1** : GORGE, GLUT **2** : to fill with blood : CONGEST — **en·gorge·ment** \-mənt\ *n*

en·grave \in-'grāv\ *vt* **1 a** : to form (as letters or devices) by cutting into a surface **b** : to impress deeply ⟨the incident was *engraved* in my memory⟩ **2 a** : to cut figures, letters, or devices upon especially for printing; *also* : to print from an engraved plate **b** : PHOTOENGRAVE — **en·grav·er** *n*

en·grav·ing \in-'grā-viŋ\ *n* **1** : the art of cutting figures, letters, or devices in wood, stone, or metal **2** : something engraved: as **a** : an engraved printing surface **b** : engraved work **3** : a print made from an engraved surface

en·gross \in-'grōs\ *vt* **1 a** : to copy or write in a large hand **b** : to prepare the usually final handwritten or printed text of (an official document) **2** : to take up the whole interest of : occupy fully : ABSORB [sense 1 from Anglo-French *engrosser,* probably from Medieval Latin *ingrossare,* from Latin *in* "in" + Medieval Latin *grossa* "large handwriting", from Latin *grossus* "thick"; sense 2 from Middle French *en gros* "in large quantities", from *gros* "thick", from Latin *grossus*] — **en·gross·er** *n* — **en·gross·ment** \-'grō-smənt\ *n*

en·gulf \in-'gəlf\ *vt* : to flow over and enclose; *also* : to take in (food) by such means — **en·gulf·ment** \-mənt\ *n*

en·hance \in-'hans\ *vt* : to make greater (as in value, desirability, or attractiveness) : HEIGHTEN [Anglo-French *enhauncer,* from Old French *enhaucier,* derived from Latin *in* "in" + *altus* "high"] **syn** see INTENSIFY — **en·hance·ment** \-mənt\ *n*

enig·ma \i-'nig-mə\ *n* : something hard to understand or explain : PUZZLE [Latin *aenigma,* from Greek *ainigmat-, ainigma,* from *ainissesthai* "to speak in riddles", from *ainos* "fable, riddle"] **syn** see MYSTERY — **enig·mat·ic** \ˌen-ig-'mat-ik *also* ˌē-nig-\ *or* **enig·mat·i·cal** \-'mat-i-kəl\ *adj* — **enig·mat·i·cal·ly** \-i-kə-lē, -klē\ *adv*

en·isle \in-'īl\ *vt* **1** : ISOLATE 1 **2** : to make an island of

en·jamb·ment *or* **en·jambe·ment** \in-'jam-mənt\ *n* : the running over of a sentence from one verse or couplet into another so that closely related words fall in different lines [French *enjambement,* from *enjamber* "to straddle", from *en-* + *jambe* "leg"]

en·join \in-'jȯin\ *vt* **1** : to direct or impose by authoritative order **2** : FORBID 1, PROHIBIT

en·joy \in-'jȯi\ *vt* **1** : to take pleasure or satisfaction in **2** : to have for one's use, benefit, or lot — **en·joy·able** \-ə-bəl\ *adj* — **en·joy·able·ness** n — **en·joy·ably** \-ə-blē\ *adv*

en·joy·ment \in-'jȯi-mənt\ *n* **1** : the condition of enjoying something : possession and use of something with satisfaction ⟨the *enjoyment* of good health⟩ **2** : PLEASURE, SATISFACTION ⟨find *enjoyment* in skating⟩ **3** : something that gives pleasure

en·kin·dle \in-'kin-dl\ *vb* : KINDLE 1, 2

en·lace \in-'lās\ *vt* **1** : ENCIRCLE, ENFOLD **2** : ENTWINE, INTERLACE

en·large \in-'lärj\ *vb* **1** : to make or grow larger **2** : ELABORATE ⟨*enlarge* on a story⟩ — **en·larg·er** *n*

en·large·ment \in-'lärj-mənt\ *n* **1** : an act or instance of enlarging : the state of being enlarged **2** : a photographic print that is larger than the negative and is made by projecting an image of the negative upon a photographic printing surface

en·light·en \in-'līt-n\ *vt* **en·light·ened**; **en·light·en·ing** \-'līt-niŋ, -n-iŋ\ **1** : to furnish knowledge to : INSTRUCT **2** : to give spiritual insight to — **en·light·en·ment** \-'līt-n-mənt\ *n*

en·list \in-'list\ *vb* **1** : to enroll for military or naval service; *esp* : to join one of the armed services voluntarily **2** : to obtain the help or support of ⟨*enlisted* friends in the campaign⟩; *also* : to participate heartily (as in a cause) — **en·list·ment** \-'list-mənt, -'lis-\ *n*

en·list·ed *adj* : of, relating to, or constituting the part of a military or naval force below commissioned or warrant officers

en·liv·en \in-'lī-vən\ *vt* : to give life, action, or spirit to : ANIMATE

en masse \äⁿ-'mas, äⁿ-\ *adv* : in a body : as a whole [French]

en·mesh \in-'mesh\ *vt* : to entangle in or as if in meshes ⟨was *enmeshed* in disputes with the neighbors⟩

en·mi·ty \'en-mət-ē\ *n, pl* **-ties** : positive, active, and typically mutual hatred or ill will [Middle French *enemité,* from *enemi* "enemy"]

• **syn** HOSTILITY, ANIMOSITY, ANTAGONISM: ENMITY suggests positive hatred which may be open or concealed; HOSTILITY suggests enmity showing itself in attacks or aggression; ANIMOSITY implies intense ill will and vindictiveness that threaten to kindle hostility; ANTAGONISM suggests a clash of temperaments leading readily to hostility.

en·no·ble \in-'ō-bəl\ *vt* **-bled**; **-bling** \-bə-liŋ, -bliŋ\ **1** : to make noble : ELEVATE **2** : to raise to the rank of nobility — **en·no·ble·ment** \-bəl-mənt\ *n*

en·nui \'än-'wē\ *n* : a feeling of weariness and dissatisfaction : BOREDOM [French, from Old French *enui* "annoyance", from *enuier* "to annoy"]

enor·mi·ty \i-'nȯr-mət-ē\ *n, pl* **-ties** **1** : great wickedness : OUTRAGEOUSNESS ⟨the *enormity* of the offense⟩ **2** : an outrageous act or offense **3** : very large size; *also* : something very large

enor·mous \i-'nȯr-məs\ *adj* **1** *archaic* **a** : ABNORMAL, INORDINATE **b** : exceedingly wicked : OUTRAGEOUS **2** : very great in size, number, or degree [Latin *enormis,* from *e, ex* "out of" + *norma* "norm"] — **enor·mous·ly** *adv* — **enor·mous·ness** *n*

• **syn** IMMENSE, HUGE, VAST: ENORMOUS implies exceeding ordinary bounds in size, amount, or degree ⟨the *enormous* expenditures for war⟩ IMMENSE suggests size far in excess of ordinary measurements or concepts ⟨an *immense* waste of natural resources⟩ HUGE suggests immensity of bulk, size, or capacity ⟨*huge* wine vats⟩ VAST usually suggests immensity of extent ⟨*vast* stretches of desert⟩

¹enough \i-'nəf; *after* t, d, s, z *often* ᵊn-'əf\ *adj* : occurring in such quantity, quality, or scope as to fully satisfy demands or needs [Middle English *ynough,* from Old English *genōg*] **syn** see SUFFICIENT

²enough *adv* **1** : in sufficient amount or degree : SUFFICIENTLY ⟨did not run fast *enough*⟩ **2** : FULLY, QUITE ⟨ready *enough* to admit the truth⟩ **3** : PASSABLY, TOLERABLY ⟨sang well *enough*⟩

³enough *n* : a sufficient quantity ⟨we have *enough* to eat⟩

enow \i-'nau̇\ *adv or adj, archaic* : ENOUGH [Middle English *inow,* from Old English *genōg*]

en·plane \in-'plān\ *vi* : to board an airplane

en·quire \in-'kwīr\, **en·qui·ry** \'in-ˌkwīr-ē, in-'; 'in-kwə-rē, 'iŋ-\ *variant of* INQUIRE, INQUIRY

en·rage \in-'rāj\ *vt* : to fill with rage : MADDEN

en·rapt \in-'rapt\ *adj* : RAPT 1, ENRAPTURED

en·rap·ture \in-'rap-chər\ *vt* **-rap·tured**; **-rap·tur·ing** \-'rap-chə-riŋ, -'rap-shriŋ\ : to fill with delight

en·rich \in-'rich\ *vt* **1** : to make rich or richer ⟨*enrich* the mind⟩ **2** : ADORN, ORNAMENT **3 a** : to make (soil) more fertile **b** : to improve (a food) in nutritive value by adding vitamins and minerals in processing **4** : to expand (a course of study) by increasing the variety of subjects and depth of treatment — **en·rich·ment** \-mənt\ *n*

en·robe \in-ˈrōb\ *vt* : to invest or adorn with a robe

en·roll *or* **en·rol** \in-ˈrōl\ *vb* **en·rolled**; **en·roll·ing** **1** : to enter in a list, catalog, or roll **2** : ENTER, JOIN ⟨*enroll* in school⟩ — **en·roll·ment** \-ˈrōl-mənt\ *n*

en route \än-ˈrüt, en-, in-\ *adv* : on or along the way [French]

en·sconce \in-ˈskäns\ *vt* **1** : to place or hide securely : CONCEAL **2** : to establish comfortably : settle snugly

en·sem·ble \än-ˈsäm-bəl, ä^{n}-\ *n* : a group constituting a whole or producing a single effect: as **a** : SET 3 **b** : concerted music of two or more parts or the musicians that perform it **c** : a complete costume of harmonizing clothes **d** : a group of supporting performers [French, from *ensemble* "together", from Latin *insimul* "at the same time", from *in-* + *simul* "at the same time"]

en·sheathe \in-ˈshēth\ *vt* : to cover with or as if with a sheath

en·shrine \in-ˈshrīn\ *vt* **1** : to enclose in or as if in a shrine **2** : to preserve or cherish as sacred

en·shroud \in-ˈshrau̇d\ *vt* : SHROUD

en·sign \ˈen-sən, *in senses 1 & 2 also* ˈen-ˌsīn\ *n* **1** : a flag flown as the symbol of nationality **2** : a badge of office, rank, or power **3** : an officer rank in the Navy and Coast Guard below lieutenant junior grade [Middle French *enseigne,* from Latin *insignia* "insignia, flags"]

en·si·lage \ˈen-sə-lij\ *n* : SILAGE

en·sile \en-ˈsīl, in-\ *vt* : to prepare and store (fodder) for silage [French *ensiler,* from *en-* + *silo* "silo", from Spanish]

en·slave \in-ˈslāv\ *vt* : to reduce to slavery : SUBJUGATE — **en·slave·ment** \-mənt\ *n* — **en·slav·er** *n*

en·snare \in-ˈsnaər, -ˈsneər\ *vt* : SNARE 1, ENTRAP

en·sue \in-ˈsü\ *vi* : to come after in time or as a result ⟨*ensuing* effects⟩ [Middle French *ensuivre,* from *en-* + *suivre* "to follow"] **syn** see FOLLOW

en·sure \in-ˈshu̇r\ *vt* : to make sure, certain, or safe : GUARANTEE [Anglo-French *enseurer*]

en·tab·la·ture \in-ˈtab-lə-ˌchu̇r, -chər\ *n* : the upper section of a wall or story usually supported on columns or pilasters and in classical orders consisting of architrave, frieze, and cornice [obsolete French, derived from Latin *in-* + *tabula* "board, table"]

[1]**en·tail** \in-ˈtāl\ *vt* **1** : to limit the inheritance of (property) to the owner's direct descendants or to a class of these **2** : to impose, involve, or imply as a necessary accompaniment or result [derived from Middle French *taille* "limitation", from Old French *taillier* "to cut, limit"] — **en·tail·ment** \-mənt\ *n*

[2]**en·tail** \ˈen-ˌtāl, in-ˈtāl\ *n* **1 a** : an entailing especially of lands **b** : an entailed estate **2** : the rule by which the descent of property is fixed

en·tan·gle \in-ˈtang-gəl\ *vt* **1** : to make tangled, complicated, or confused **2** : to involve in or as if in a tangle — **en·tan·gle·ment** \-gəl-mənt\ *n*

en·tente \än-ˈtänt\ *n* **1** : an international understanding providing for a common course of action **2** : a coalition of parties to an entente [French, from Old French, "intent, understanding"]

en·ter \ˈent-ər\ *vb* **en·tered**; **en·ter·ing** \ˈent-ə-ring, ˈen-tring\ **1** : to go or come into : go or come in ⟨*enter* a room⟩ ⟨*enter* and leave by the same door⟩ **2** : to pass into or through usually by overcoming resistance : PIERCE **3** : to cause to be admitted to ⟨*enter* a child in kindergarten⟩ **4** : to become a member of : JOIN ⟨*enter* the hikers' club⟩ **5** : to make a beginning ⟨*enter* into business⟩ **6** : to take part or play a part ⟨*enter* into a discussion⟩ **7** : to take possession ⟨*entered* upon their inheritance⟩ **8** : to set down in a book or list ⟨*enter* words in a dictionary⟩ **9** : to make a report to customs officials of (a ship or its cargo) upon arrival in port **10** : to put formally on record ⟨*enter* a complaint⟩ [Old French *entrer,* from Latin *intrare,* from *intra* "within"] — **en·ter·able** \ˈent-ə-rə-bəl\ *adj*

• syn ENTER, PENETRATE, PIERCE mean to make way into something. ENTER is the general term and may imply going in or forcing a way in; PENETRATE carries a strong implication of an impelling force or compelling power that achieves entrance; PIERCE adds an implication of running through with a sharp-pointed instrument.

enter- *or* **entero-** *combining form* : intestine ⟨*enter*itis⟩ [Greek *enteron*]

en·ter·ic \en-ˈter-ik\ *adj* : of or relating to the alimentary canal : INTESTINAL

en·ter·i·tis \ˌent-ə-ˈrīt-əs\ *n* : inflammation of the intestine or a disease marked by this

en·tero·coc·cus \ˌent-ə-rō-ˈkäk-əs\ *n* : STREPTOCOCCUS; *esp* : one normally present in the intestine — **en·tero·coc·cal** \-ˈkäk-əl\ *adj*

en·tero·coele *or* **en·tero·coel** \ˈent-ə-rō-ˌsēl\ *n* : a coelom originating by outgrowth from the cavity of the gastrula — **en·tero·coe·lic** \ˌent-ə-rō-ˈsē-lik\ *adj* — **en·tero·coe·lous** \-ləs\ *adj*

en·tero·ki·nase \ˌent-ə-rō-ˈkīn-ˌās, -ˌnāz\ *n* : an intestinal enzyme that converts trypsinogen to trypsin [*enter-* + *kin*etic + *-ase*]

en·ter·on \ˈent-ə-ˌrän, -rən\ *n* : an embryonic alimentary canal

en·ter·prise \ˈent-ər-ˌprīz, ˈent-ə-ˌ\ *n* **1** : a difficult, complicated, or risky project or undertaking **2** : a business organization **3** : readiness to engage in daring or difficult action : INITIATIVE [Middle French *entreprise,* from *entreprendre* "to undertake", from *entre-* "inter-" + *prendre* "to take", from Latin *prehendere* 'to seize"] — **en·ter·pris·er** \-ˌprī-zər\ *n*

en·ter·pris·ing \-ˌprī-zing\ *adj* : marked by an independent energetic spirit and by readiness to undertake or experiment

en·ter·tain \ˌent-ər-ˈtān\ *vb* **1** : to receive and provide for as host : have as a guest ⟨*entertain* friends over the weekend⟩ **2** : to provide entertainment especially for guests **3** : to have in mind : CONSIDER ⟨*entertained* thoughts of quitting the job⟩ **4** : to provide entertainment for ⟨*entertain* the class with a play⟩ [Middle French *entretenir,* from *entre-* "inter-" + *tenir* "to hold", from Latin *tenēre*] **syn** see AMUSE

en·ter·tain·er \-ˈtā-nər\ *n* : one that entertains; *esp* : one that gives or takes part in public entertainments

en·ter·tain·ment \-ˈtān-mənt\ *n* **1** : provision for guests especially in public places (as hotels and inns) **2** : AMUSEMENT 3, RECREATION **3** : a means of amusement or recreation; *esp* : a public performance

en·thrall *or* **en·thral** \in-ˈthrȯl\ *vt* **en·thralled**; **en·thrall·ing** **1** : ENSLAVE **2** : to hold spellbound : CHARM — **en·thrall·ment** \-ˈthrȯl-mənt\ *n*

en·throne \in-ˈthrōn\ *vt* **1** : to seat ceremonially on a throne **2** : to regard as of supreme virtue or value : EXALT — **en·throne·ment** \-mənt\ *n*

en·thuse \in-ˈthüz, -ˈthyüz\ *vb* **1** : to make or grow enthusiastic **2** : to show enthusiasm [back-formation from *enthusiasm*]

en·thu·si·asm \in-ˈthü-zē-ˌaz-əm, -ˈthyü-\ *n* **1** : strong excitement of feeling : FERVOR **2** : something inspiring zeal or fervor [Greek *enthousiasmos,* from*enthousiazein* "to be inspired", from *entheos* "inspired", from *en-* + *theos* "god"] **syn** see ZEAL

en·thu·si·ast \-zē-ˌast, -əst\ *n* : a person filled with enthusiasm

en·thu·si·as·tic \in-ˌthü-zē-ˈas-tik, -ˌthyü-\ *adj* : filled with or marked by enthusiasm ⟨an *enthusiastic* welcome⟩ — **en·thu·si·as·ti·cal·ly** \-ti-kə-lē, -klē\ *adv*

en·tice \in-ˈtīs\ *vt* : to attract by arousing hope or desire : TEMPT [Old French *enticier*] — **en·tice·ment** \-mənt\ *n*

en·tire \in-ˈtīr, ˈen-ˌ\ *adj* **1** : having no element or part left out **2** : COMPLETE, TOTAL ⟨an *entire* regiment was lost⟩ **3** : consisting of one piece **4** : having the margin continuous and free from indentations ⟨an *entire* leaf⟩ [Middle French *entir,* from Latin *integer,* literally, "untouched", from *in-* + *tangere* "to touch"] **syn** see WHOLE — **entire** *adv* — **en·tire·ly** *adv* — **en·tire·ness** *n*

en·tire·ty \in-ˈtī-rət-ē, -ˈtīrt-ē\ *n* **1** : the state of being entire or complete **2** : sum total : WHOLE

en·ti·tle \in-ˈtīt-l\ *vt* **en·ti·tled**; **en·ti·tling** \-ˈtīt-ling, -l-ing\ **1** : to give a title to : DESIGNATE **2 a** : to give a legal right to **b** : to qualify for something — **en·ti·tle·ment** \-ˈtīt-l-mənt\ *n*

en·ti·ty \ˈent-ət-ē\ *n, pl* **-ti·ties** : something existing or thought of as existing : BEING [Medieval Latin *entitas,* from Latin *ent-, ens* "existing thing", from coined present participle of *esse* "to be"]

en·tomb \in-ˈtüm\ *vt* : to place in a tomb : BURY — **en·tomb·ment** \-ˈtüm-mənt\ *n*

\ə\ **abut**	\au̇\ **out**	\i\ **tip**	\ȯ\ **saw**	\u̇\ **foot**
\ər\ **further**	\ch\ **chin**	\ī\ **life**	\ȯi\ **coin**	\y\ **yet**
\a\ **mat**	\e\ **pet**	\j\ **job**	\th\ **thin**	\yü\ **few**
\ā\ **take**	\ē\ **easy**	\ng\ **sing**	\th\ **this**	\yu̇\ **cure**
\ä\ **cot, cart**	\g\ **go**	\ō\ **bone**	\ü\ **food**	\zh\ **vision**

en•to•mol•o•gy \ˌent-ə-ˈmäl-ə-jē\ *n* **:** a branch of zoology that deals with insects [French *entomologie,* from Greek *entomon* "insect", from *entomos* "cut up", from *en-* + *temnein* "to cut" — see INSECT *origin*] — **en•to•mo•log•i•cal** \ˌent-ə-mə-ˈläj-i-kəl\ *adj* — **en•to•mo•log•i•cal•ly** \-i-kə-lē, -klē\ *adv* — **en•to•mol•o•gist** \ˌent-ə-ˈmäl-ə-jəst\ *n*

en•tou•rage \ˌän-tü-ˈräzh\ *n* **:** one's attendants or associates **:** RETINUE [French]

en•tr'acte \ˈän-ˌtrakt, ˈäⁿ-; än-ˈ, äⁿ-ˈ\ *n* **1 :** the interval between two acts of a play **2 :** a dance. piece of music, or interlude performed between two acts of a play [French, from *entre-* "inter-" + *acte* "act"]

en•trails \ˈen-trəlz, -ˌtrālz\ *n pl* **:** internal parts **:** VISCERA; *esp* **:** INTESTINES [Middle French *entrailles,* from Medieval Latin *intralia,* alteration of Latin *interanea* from *interaneus* "interior"]

en•train \in-ˈtrān\ *vb* **:** to put or go aboard a railroad train

[1]**en•trance** \ˈen-trəns\ *n* **1 :** the act of entering **2 :** the means or place of entry **3 :** power or permission to enter **:** ADMISSION

[2]**en•trance** \in-ˈtrans\ *vt* **1 :** to put into a trance **2 :** to fill with delight, wonder, or rapture — **en•trance•ment** \-mənt\ *n*

en•trant \ˈen-trənt\ *n* **:** one that enters; *esp* **:** one that enters a contest

en•trap \in-ˈtrap\ *vt* **1 :** to catch in or as if in a trap **2 :** to lure into a compromising statement or act — **en•trap•ment** \-mənt\ *n*

en•treat \in-ˈtrēt\ *vb* **:** to ask earnestly or urgently **:** PLEAD [Middle French *entraitier* "to treat", from *en-* + *traitier* "to treat"] **syn** see BEG — **en•treat•ing•ly** \-ing-lē\ *adv*

en•treaty \in-ˈtrēt-ē\ *n, pl* **-treat•ies :** an earnest request **:** PLEA

en•trée *or* **en•tree** \ˈän-ˌtrā\ *n* **1 a :** the act or manner of entering **:** ENTRANCE **b :** freedom of entry or access **2 :** the principal dish of a meal in the United States [French *entrée*]

en•trench *or* **in•trench** \in-ˈtrench\ *vb* **1 a :** to dig, place within, surround with, or occupy a trench especially for defense **b :** to establish solidly **2 :** to cut into **:** FURROW; *esp* **:** to erode downward so as to form a trench **3 :** ENCROACH 1 — used with *on* or *upon*

en•trench•ment \in-ˈtrench-mənt\ *n* **1 :** the act of entrenching **:** the state of being entrenched **2 :** DEFENSE; *esp* **:** a defensive work consisting of a trench and a wall of earth

en•tre•pre•neur \ˌän-trə-prə-ˈnər, -pə-, -ˈnu̇r, -ˈnyu̇r\ *n* **:** one who organizes, manages, and assumes the risks of a business or enterprise [French]

en•tro•py \ˈen-trə-pē\ *n* **1 :** a measure of the unavailable energy in a closed thermodynamic system **2 :** the degradation of the matter and energy in the universe to an ultimate state of inert uniformity [German *entropie,* from Greek *en-* + *trepein* "to turn, change"]

en•trust *or* **in•trust** \in-ˈtrəst\ *vt* **1 :** to give into the care of another (as for safekeeping) **2 :** to give custody, care, or charge of something to as a trust ⟨*entrusted* a bank with their savings⟩ — **en•trust•ment** \-ˈtrəst-mənt, -ˈtrəs-\ *n*

en•try \ˈen-trē\ *n, pl* **entries 1 :** the act of entering **:** ENTRANCE **2 :** a place through which entrance is made **:** HALL 3a, VESTIBULE **3 a :** the act of making (as in a book or list) a written record of something **b :** the thing thus recorded: as (1) **:** HEADWORD (2) **:** a headword with its definition or identification (3) **:** VOCABULARY ENTRY **4 :** a person, thing, or group entered in a contest or race

en•twine \in-ˈtwīn\ *vb* **:** to twine together or around

enu•mer•ate \i-ˈnü-mə-ˌrāt, -ˈnyü-\ *vt* **1 :** to ascertain the number of **:** COUNT **2 :** to specify one after another **:** LIST [Latin *enumerare,* from *e-* + *numerare* "to count", from *numerus* "number"] — **enu•mer•a•ble** \-ˈnüm-rə-bəl, ˈnyüm-, -ə-rə-\ *adj* — **enu•mer•a•tion** \-ˌnü-mə-ˈrā-shən, -ˌnyü-\ *n* — **enu•mer•a•tor** \-ˈnü-mə-ˌrāt-ər, -ˈnyü-\ *n*

enun•ci•ate \ē-ˈnən-sē-ˌāt\ *vt* **1 :** to make known publicly **:** PROCLAIM ⟨*enunciate* the aims of a program⟩ **2 :** to utter distinctly **:** PRONOUNCE ⟨*enunciate* your words clearly⟩ [Latin *enuntiare* "to report, declare", from *e-* + *nuntiare* "to report", from *nuntius* "messenger"] — **enun•ci•a•tion** \-ˌnən-sē-ˈā-shən\ *n*

en•ure•sis \ˌen-yü-ˈrē-səs\ *n* **:** involuntary discharge of urine **:** bed wetting [New Latin, from Greek *enourein* "to urinate in, wet the bed", from *en-* + *ourein* "to urinate"] — **en•uret•ic** \-ˈret-ik\ *adj or n*

en•vel•op \in-ˈvel-əp\ *vt* **:** to enclose or enfold completely with or as if with a covering [Middle French *enveloper,* from Old French *envoloper,* from *en-* + *voloper* "to wrap"] — **en•vel•op•ment** \-mənt\ *n*

en•ve•lope \ˈen-və-ˌlōp, ˈän-\ *n* **1 :** something that envelops **2 :** a flat usually paper container (as for a letter) **3 :** the bag containing the gas in a balloon or airship **4 :** a natural enclosing covering (as a membrane)

en•ven•om \in-ˈven-əm\ *vt* **1 :** to taint or fill with poison **2 :** EMBITTER

en•vi•a•ble \ˈen-vē-ə-bəl\ *adj* **:** highly desirable — **en•vi•a•ble•ness** *n* — **en•vi•a•bly** \-blē\ *adv*

en•vi•ous \ˈen-vē-əs\ *adj* **:** feeling or showing envy ⟨*envious* of a neighbor's wealth⟩ — **en•vi•ous•ly** *adv* — **en•vi•ous•ness** *n*

• **syn** JEALOUS: ENVIOUS suggests a spiteful or malicious grudging of another's possessions and accomplishments; JEALOUS implies a grudging of something regarded as properly belonging to oneself; it may also indicate a vigilant guarding ⟨*jealous* of one's good name and honor⟩

en•vi•ron•ment \in-ˈvī-rən-mənt, -ˈvī-ərn-, -ˈvīrn-\ *n* **1 :** the circumstances, objects, or conditions by which one is surrounded **2 :** surrounding conditions or forces that influence or change: as **a :** the whole complex of factors (as soil, climate, and living things) that determine the form and survival of an organism or ecological community **b :** the social and cultural conditions that influence the life of a person or human community [*environ* "to surround", from Middle French *environner,* from *environ* "around", from *en* "in" + *viron* "circle"] — **en•vi•ron•men•tal** \in-ˌvī-rən-ˈment-l, -ˌvī-ərn-, -ˌvīrn-\ *adj* — **en•vi•ron•men•tal•ly** \-l-ē\ *adv*

en•vi•ron•men•tal•ist \-ˌvī-rən-ˈment-l-əst, -ˌvī-ərn-, -ˌvīrn-\ *n* **:** one concerned about the quality of the human environment

en•vi•rons \in-ˈvī-rənz, -ˈvī-ərnz, -ˈvīrnz\ *n pl* **1 :** the districts around a city **2 :** ENVIRONMENT 1

en•vis•age \in-ˈviz-ij\ *vt* **:** to have a mental picture of especially in advance of realization **:** VISUALIZE

en•vi•sion \in-ˈvizh-ən\ *vt* **:** to picture to oneself

en•voy \ˈen-ˌvȯi, ˈän-\ *n* **1 a :** a diplomatic representative who ranks between an ambassador and a minister **b :** a representative sent by one government to another **2 :** REPRESENTATIVE 2a, MESSENGER [French *envoyé,* from *envoyer* "to send", from Latin *in-* + *via* "way"]

[1]**en•vy** \ˈen-vē\ *n, pl* **envies 1 :** painful or resentful awareness of an advantage enjoyed by another joined with a desire to possess the same advantage **2 :** an object of envy ⟨their new car was the *envy* of the neighborhood⟩ [Old French *envie,* from Latin *invidia,* from *invidus* "envious", from *invidēre* "to look askance at, envy", from *in-* + *vidēre* "to see"]

[2]**envy** *vt* **en•vied; en•vy•ing :** to feel envy toward or on account of — **en•vi•er** *n* — **en•vy•ing•ly** \-ing-lē\ *adv*

en•wrap \in-ˈrap\ *vt* **1 :** to wrap in a covering **:** ENFOLD **2 :** to hold one's interest **:** ENGROSS

en•zy•mat•ic \ˌen-zə-ˈmat-ik\ *adj* **:** of, relating to, or produced by an enzyme — **en•zy•mat•i•cal•ly** \-i-kə-lē, -klē\ *adv*

en•zyme \ˈen-ˌzīm\ *n* **:** any of various complex proteins produced by living cells that bring about or accelerate reactions (as in the digestion of food at body temperatures) without being permanently altered [German *enzym,* derived from Greek *en-* + *zymē* "leaven"]

en•zy•mic \en-ˈzī-mik\ *adj* **:** ENZYMATIC — **en•zy•mi•cal•ly** \-mi-kə-lē, -klē\ *adv*

eo- *combining form* **:** earliest **:** oldest ⟨*Eocene*⟩ [Greek *ēōs* "dawn"]

Eo•cene \ˈē-ə-ˌsēn\ *n* **:** the epoch of the Tertiary between the Paleocene and the Oligocene; *also* **:** the corresponding system of rocks — **Eocene** *adj*

eo•hip•pus \ˌē-ō-ˈhip-əs\ *n* **:** any of a genus of small primitive horses from the lower Eocene of the western United States with four toes on each forelimb [Greek *hippos* "horse"]

eo•lian *also* **ae•o•lian** \ē-ˈō-lē-ən, -ˈōl-yən\ *adj* **:** borne, deposited, produced, or eroded by the wind ⟨*eolian* sand⟩ [Latin *Aeolus,* god of the winds]

eo•lith \ˈē-ə-ˌlith\ *n* **:** a very crudely chipped flint from the earliest phase of human culture

Eo•lith•ic \ˌē-ə-ˈlith-ik\ *adj* **:** of or relating to the early period of the Stone Age marked by the use of eoliths — compare NEOLITHIC, PALEOLITHIC

eon *variant of* AEON

eo•sin \ˈē-ə-sən\ *or* **eo•sine** \-sən, -ˌsēn\ *n* **:** a red synthetic fluorescent dye used especially in cosmetics and as a toner;

also : a salt of this dye used chiefly in red pigments and as a stain for biological tissue [Greek *ēōs* "dawn"]

-eous *adj suffix* : like : resembling [Latin *-eus*]

ep•au•let *also* **ep•au•lette** \ˌep-ə-ˈlet\ *n* : a shoulder ornament on a uniform especially of a military or naval officer [French *épaulette,* from *épaule* "shoulder", from Late Latin *spatula* "shoulder blade, spoon", from Latin *spatha* "spoon, sword"]

épée \ˈep-ˌā, ā-ˈpā\ *n* : a fencing or dueling sword having a bowl-shaped guard and a tapering rigid blade with no cutting edge [French, from Latin *spatha* "spoon, sword"]

ephah \ˈē-fə, ˈef-ə\ *n* : an ancient Hebrew unit of dry measure equal to a little more than a bushel (about 35 liters) [Hebrew *ēphāh,* from Egyptian *ipt*]

ephed•rine \i-ˈfed-rən\ *n* : a crystalline basic substance extracted from Chinese woody plants or synthesized and used as a salt in relieving hay fever, asthma, and nasal congestion [New Latin *Ephedra,* genus of shrubs]

ephem•era \i-ˈfem-rə, -ə-rə\ *n pl* : ephemeral things

ephem•er•al \i-ˈfem-rəl, -ə-rəl\ *adj* **1** : lasting one day only **2** : lasting a very short time [Greek *ephēmeros* "lasting a day daily", from *epi-* + *hēmera* "day"] — **ephem•er•al•ly** \-rə-lē\ *adv*

ephem•er•is \-rəs\ *n, pl* **eph•e•mer•i•des** \ˌef-ə-ˈmer-ə-ˈdēz\ : a tabular statement of the assigned places of a celestial body for regular intervals [Latin, "diary, ephemeris", from Greek *ephēmeris,* from *ephēmeros* "daily"]

Ephe•sians \i-ˈfē-zhənz\ *n* — see BIBLE table

eph•or \ˈef-ər, -ˌȯr\ *n* : one of five ancient Spartan magistrates having power over the king [Latin *ephorus,* from Greek *ephoros,* from *ephoran* "to oversee", from *epi-* + *horan* "to see"]

epi- *or* **ep-** *prefix* : upon ⟨*epi*phyte⟩ : near to : over ⟨*epi*center⟩ : outer ⟨*epi*carp⟩ : after ⟨*epi*genesis⟩ [Greek, from *epi* "on"]

1ep•ic \ˈep-ik\ *adj* **1** : of, relating to, or having the characteristics of an epic **2** : unusually long especially in size or scope [Latin *epicus,* from Greek *epikos,* from *epos* "word, speech, poem"]

2epic *n* **1** : a long serious narrative poem in a dignified style relating the deeds of a legendary or historical hero **2** : a work of art that resembles or suggests an epic **3** : a series of events or body of tradition held to form the proper subject of an epic ⟨the winning of the West was a great American *epic*⟩

epi•carp \ˈep-ə-ˌkärp\ *n* : the usually thin membranous outermost layer of the pericarp of a fruit (as the skin of a peach) — compare ENDOCARP, MESOCARP

epi•cen•ter \ˈep-ə-ˌsent-ər\ *n* **1** : the part of the earth's surface directly above the focus of an earthquake **2** : CENTER 2a ⟨the *epicenter* of cultural activity⟩

ep•i•cot•yl \ˈep-ə-ˌkät-l\ *n* : the part of a plant embryo or seedling above the cotyledons

ep•i•cure \ˈep-i-ˌkyu̇r\ *n* : a person with sensitive and discriminating tastes in food or wine [*Epicurus,* died 270 B.C., Greek philosopher]

1ep•i•cu•re•an \ˌep-i-kyu̇-ˈrē-ən, -ˈkyu̇r-ē-\ *adj* **1** *cap* : of or relating to Epicurus or Epicureanism **2** : of, relating to, or suited to an epicure

2epicurean *n* **1** *cap* : a follower of Epicurus **2** : EPICURE

Ep•i•cu•re•an•ism \-ə-ˌniz-əm\ *n* : the philosophy of Epicurus that pleasure is the only good and the pleasures of wise, just, and moderate living are the best

1ep•i•dem•ic \ˌep-ə-ˈdem-ik\ *adj* **1** : affecting many individuals at one time ⟨an *epidemic* disease⟩ **2** : widespread especially to an excessive degree ⟨crime had reached *epidemic* proportions⟩ [French *épidémique,* derived from Greek *epidēmia* "visit, epidemic", from *epi-* + *dēmos* "people"] — **ep•i•dem•i•cal•ly** \-ˈdem-i-kə-lē, -klē\ *adv* — **ep•i•de•mic•i•ty** \-ˌdem-ˈis-ət-ē\ *n*

2epidemic *n* **1** : an outbreak of epidemic disease **2** : a sudden rapidly spreading outbreak

ep•i•de•mi•ol•o•gy \ˌep-ə-ˌdē-mē-ˈäl-ə-jē\ *n* **1** : a branch of medical science that deals with the rate of occurrence, distribution, and control of disease in a population **2** : the sum of the factors controlling the presence or absence of a particular disease — **ep•i•de•mi•o•log•ic** \-mē-ə-ˈläj-ik\ *or* **ep•i•de•mi•o•log•i•cal** \-ˈläj-i-kəl\ *adj* — **ep•i•de•mi•o•log•i•cal•ly** \-i-kə-lē, -klē\ *adv* — **ep•i•de•mi•ol•o•gist** \-mē-ˈäl-ə-jəst\ *n*

epi•der•mis \ˌep-ə-ˈdər-məs\ *n* **1** : the thin outer layer of the animal body that in vertebrates forms an insensitive covering over the dermis **2** : a thin surface layer of protecting cells in seed plants and ferns **3** : any of various covering layers resembling the epidermis of the skin [Late Latin, from Greek, from *epi-* + *derma* "skin"] — **epi•der•mal** \-məl\ *adj*

ep•i•did•y•mis \ˌep-ə-ˈdid-ə-məs\ *n, pl* **-mi•des** \-mə-ˌdēz\ : a mass at the back of the testis composed of coiled tubes in which sperms are stored [Greek, from *epi-* + *didymos* "testicle", from *dyo* "two"] — **epi•did•y•mal** \-ˈdid-ə-məl\ *adj*

epi•gen•e•sis \ˌep-ə-ˈjen-ə-səs\ *n, pl* **-e•ses** \-ˌsēz\ : development in which an initially unspecialized entity (as a spore) gradually develops specialized characters (as of a whole plant) — **ep•i•ge•net•ic** \-jə-ˈnet-ik\ *adj*

epi•glot•tis \ˌep-ə-ˈglät-əs\ *n* : a thin plate of flexible cartilage in front of the glottis that folds back over and protects the glottis during swallowing — **epi•glot•tal** \-ˈglät-l\ *adj*

ep•i•gram \ˈep-ə-ˌgram\ *n* **1** : a short often satirical poem ending with a clever turn of thought **2** : a brief witty saying [Latin *epigramma,* from Greek, from *epigraphein* "to write on, inscribe", from *epi-* + *graphein* "to write"] — **ep•i•gram•ma•tist** \ˌep-ə-ˈgram-ət-əst\ *n*

ep•i•gram•mat•ic \ˌep-i-grə-ˈmat-ik\ *adj* **1** : of, relating to, or resembling an epigram **2** : marked by or given to the use of epigrams — **ep•i•gram•mat•i•cal** \-ˈmat-i-kəl\ *adj* — **ep•i•gram•mat•i•cal•ly** \-i-kə-lē, -klē\ *adv*

epig•ra•phy \i-ˈpig-rə-fē, e-\ *n* : the study of inscriptions and especially of ancient inscriptions [Greek *epigraphein* "to inscribe", from *epi-* + *graphein* "to write"]

epig•y•nous \i-ˈpij-ə-nəs, e-\ *adj* **1** : grown to and appearing to arise from the top of a plant ovary ⟨*epigynous* stamens⟩ **2** : having epigynous floral organs

ep•i•lep•sy \ˈep-ə-ˌlep-sē\ *n* : a disorder marked by disturbed electrical rhythms of the central nervous system and characterized by convulsive fits and loss of consciousness [Middle French *epilepsie,* from Late Latin *epilepsia,* from Greek *epilēpsia,* from *epilambanein* "to seize", from *epi-* + *lambanein* "to take, seize"] — **ep•i•lep•tic** \ˌep-ə-ˈlep-tik\ *adj or n*

ep•i•logue \ˈep-ə-ˌlȯg, -ˌläg\ *n* **1** : a concluding section that rounds out the design of a literary work **2** : a speech often in verse addressed to the audience by an actor at the end of a play **3** : a concluding event or development [Middle French, from Latin *epilogus,* from Greek *epilogos,* from *epilegein* "to say in addition", from *epi-* + *legein* "to say"]

ep•i•neph•rine *also* **epi•neph•rin** \ˌep-ə-ˈnef-rən\ *n* : a hormone of the adrenal gland acting especially on smooth muscle, causing narrowing of blood vessels, and raising blood pressure — called also *adrenaline* [derived from Greek *epi-* + *nephros* "kidney"]

epiph•a•ny \i-ˈpif-ə-nē\ *n, pl* **-nies** **1** *cap* : January 6 observed as a church festival in commemoration of the coming of the three wise men to Jesus at Bethlehem **2** : an appearance or manifestation especially of a divine being [Middle French *epiphanie,* from Late Latin *epiphania,* from Late Greek, plural, probably from Greek *epiphaneia* "appearance, manifestation", from *epi-* + *phainein* "to show"]

epiph•y•sis \i-ˈpif-ə-səs\ *n, pl* **-y•ses** \-ə-ˌsēz\ : the end of a long bone [Greek, "growth", from *epi-* + *physesthai* "to grow"] — **epiph•y•se•al** \i-ˌpif-ə-ˈsē-əl\ *adj*

ep•i•phyte \ˈep-ə-ˌfīt\ *n* : a plant that derives its moisture and nutrients from the air and rain and grows usually on another plant

ep•i•phyt•ic \ˌep-ə-ˈfit-ik\ *adj* **1** : of, relating to, or being an epiphyte **2** : living on the surface of plants ⟨*epiphytic* algae on kelps⟩ — **ep•i•phyt•i•cal•ly** \-ˈfit-i-kə-lē, -klē\ *adv*

epi•scia \i-ˈpish-ē-ə, -ˈpish-ə\ *n* : any of a genus of tropical American herbs often grown for their showy hairy foliage and reddish flowers [Greek *episkios* "shaded", from *epi-* + *skia* "shadow"]

epis•co•pa•cy \i-ˈpis-kə-pə-sē\ *n, pl* **-cies** **1** : government of the church by bishops **2** : EPISCOPATE 2

epis•co•pal \i-ˈpis-kə-pəl\ *adj* **1** : of or relating to a bishop or episcopacy **2** *cap* : of or relating to the Protestant Episcopal Church [Late Latin *episcopalis,* from *episcopus* "bishop", from Greek *episkopos,* literally, "overseer", from *epi-* + *skeptesthai* "to look at"] — **epis•co•pal•ly** \-pə-lē, -plē\ *adv*

Epis•co•pa•lian \i-ˌpis-kə-ˈpāl-yən\ *n* **1** : an adherent of epis-

\ə\ **abut**	\au̇\ **out**	\i\ **tip**	\ȯ\ **saw**	\u̇\ **foot**
\ər\ **further**	\ch\ **chin**	\ī\ **life**	\ȯi\ **coin**	\y\ **yet**
\a\ **mat**	\e\ **pet**	\j\ **job**	\th\ **thin**	\yü\ **few**
\ā\ **take**	\ē\ **easy**	\ng\ **sing**	\t͟h\ **this**	\yu̇\ **cure**
\ä\ **cot, cart**	\g\ **go**	\ō\ **bone**	\ü\ **food**	\zh\ **vision**

copacy **2 :** a member of the Protestant Episcopal Church — **Episcopalian** *adj* — **Epis•co•pa•lian•ism** \-yə-ˌniz-əm\ *n*

epis•co•pate \i-ˈpis-kə-pət\ *n* **1 :** the rank, office, or term of office of a bishop **2 :** the whole body of bishops

ep•i•sode \ˈep-ə-ˌsōd\ *n* **1 a :** a developed situation integral to but separable from a continuous narrative **:** INCIDENT **b :** one of a series of loosely connected stories or scenes **2 :** an event that is distinctive and separate especially in history or in a life ⟨an *episode* of the war⟩ ⟨an *episode* of coughing⟩ **3 :** a digressive subdivision in a musical composition [Greek *epeisodion,* from *epeisodios* "coming in besides", from *epi-* + *eisodios* "coming in", from *eis* "into + *hodos* "road"] **syn** see OCCURRENCE — **ep•i•sod•ic** \ˌep-ə-ˈsäd-ik\ *also* **ep•i•sod•i•cal** \-ˈsäd-i-kəl\ *adj* — **ep•i•sod•i•cal•ly** \-i-kə-lē, -klē\ *adv*

epis•tle \i-ˈpis-əl\ *n* **1** *cap* **a :** any of the letters of the New Testament **b :** a liturgical reading usually from one of the New Testament Epistles **2 :** LETTER 2; *esp* **:** a formal or elegant letter [Old French, literally, "letter", from Latin *epistula, epistola,* from Greek *epistolē,* from *epi-* + *stellein* "to send"]

epis•to•lary \i-ˈpis-tə-ˌler-ē\ *adj* **1 :** of, relating to, or suitable to a letter **2 :** contained in or carried on by letters **3 :** written in the form of a series of letters ⟨an *epistolary* novel⟩

ep•i•taph \ˈep-ə-ˌtaf\ *n* **:** an inscription (as on a tombstone) in memory of a dead person [Middle French *epitaphe,* from Latin *epitaphium* "funeral oration", from Greek *epitaphion,* from *epi-* + *taphos* "tomb, funeral"]

ep•i•the•li•um \ˌep-ə-ˈthē-lē-əm\ *n, pl* **-lia** \-lē-ə\ **1 :** a membranous cellular tissue that covers a free surface or lines a tube or cavity of an animal body and usually encloses parts of the body, produces secretions and excretions, or functions in assimilation **2 :** a usually thin layer of parenchyma that lines a cavity or tube of a plant [*epi-* + Greek *thēlē* "nipple"] — **ep•i•the•li•al** \-lē-əl\ *adj* — **ep•i•the•li•oid** \-lē-ˌȯid\ *adj*

ep•i•thet \ˈep-ə-ˌthet\ *n* **1 :** a word or phrase (as *Lion-Hearted* in "Richard the Lion-Hearted") that expresses a quality held to be characteristic of a person or thing **2 :** a disparaging or abusive word or phrase **3 :** the part of a taxonomic name identifying a subunit (as a species or variety) within a genus [Latin *epitheton,* from Greek, from *epitithenai* "to put on, add", from *epi-* + *tithenai* "to put"] — **ep•i•thet•ic** \ˌep-ə-ˈthet-ik\ *adj*

epit•o•me \i-ˈpit-ə-mē\ *n* **1 :** a summary of a written work **2 :** a typical or ideal example **:** EMBODIMENT ⟨the *epitome* of good taste⟩ [Latin, from Greek *epitomē,* from *epitemnein* "to cut short", from *epi-* + *temnein* "to cut"]

epit•o•mize \i-ˈpit-ə-ˌmīz\ *vt* **1 :** to form or give an epitome of **:** SUMMARIZE **2 :** TYPIFY 2, EXEMPLIFY

¹epi•zo•ot•ic \ˌep-ə-zə-ˈwät-ik\ *adj* **:** of, relating to, or being a disease that affects many animals of one kind at the same time

²epizootic *n* **:** an epizootic disease

e plu•ri•bus unum \ˌē-ˌplu̇r-ə-bəs-ˈyü-nəm; ˌā-ˌplu̇r-, -bə-ˈsü-\ **:** one composed of many — used on the seal of the United States and on several United States coins [Latin, "one out of many"]

ep•och \ˈep-ək, -ˌäk\ *n* **1 :** an instant of time selected as a point of reference in astronomy **2 a :** an event or a time that begins a new period or development **b :** a memorable event or date **3 a :** an extended period of time characterized by a distinctive development or by a memorable series of events **b :** a division of geologic time less than a period and greater than an age [Medieval Latin *epocha,* from Greek *epochē* "cessation, fixed point", from *epechein* "to pause, hold back", from *epi-* + *echein* "to hold"] **syn** see PERIOD — **ep•och•al** \-əl\ *adj* — **ep•och•al•ly** \-ə-lē\ *adv*

epon•y•mous \i-ˈpän-ə-məs, e-\ *adj* **:** of, relating to, or being the person for whom something is named or is believed to be named [Greek *epōnymos,* from *epi-* + *onyma* "name"]

ep•oxy resin \ˌep-ˌäk-sē-\ *n* **:** a flexible usually thermosetting resin made by polymerization of an oxygen-containing compound and used chiefly in coatings and adhesives — called also *epoxy* [*epi-* + *oxygen*]

ep•si•lon \ˈep-sə-ˌlän, -lən\ *n* **:** the 5th letter of the Greek alphabet — Ε or ϵ

Ep•som salt \ˌep-səm-\ *n* **:** a bitter colorless or white crystalline salt $MgSO_4 \cdot 7H_2O$ that is a hydrated sulfate of magnesium and is used especially as a cathartic — usually used in pl. [*Epsom,* England]

eq•ua•ble \ˈek-wə-bəl, ˈē-kwə-\ *adj* **:** EVEN 2, UNIFORM; *esp* **:** free from extremes or sudden or harsh changes ⟨an *equable* temper⟩ ⟨an *equable* climate⟩ [Latin *aequabilis,* from *aequare* "to make level or equal", from *aequus* "level, equal"] — **eq•ua•bly** \-blē\ *adv*

¹equal \ˈē-kwəl\ *adj* **1 a** (1) **:** of the same measure, quantity, amount, or number as another **:** LIKE (2) **:** identical in value **:** EQUIVALENT **b :** like in quality, nature, or status **c :** like for all; *esp* **:** not restricted to a particular ethnic, social, or sexual group ⟨*equal* job opportunities⟩ **d :** not varying **:** UNIFORM **2 :** FAIR 5a, IMPARTIAL **3 a :** free from extremes **b :** tranquil of mind or mood **4 :** capable of meeting requirements ⟨was *equal* to the task⟩ [Latin *aequalis,* from *aequus* "level, equal"]

²equal *n* **1 :** one that is equal ⟨has no *equal* at chess⟩ **2 :** an equal quantity

³equal *vt* **equaled** *or* **equalled; equal•ing** *or* **equal•ling 1 :** to be equal to; *esp* **:** to be identical in value to **2 :** to produce something equal to **:** MATCH

equal–area *adj* **:** preserving the true extent of area of the forms represented although with distortion of shape ⟨*equal-area* maps⟩

equal•i•ty \i-ˈkwäl-ət-ē\ *n, pl* **-ties 1 :** the quality or state of being equal **2 :** EQUATION 2a

equal•ize \ˈē-kwə-ˌlīz\ *vt* **1 :** to make equal **2 :** to make uniform; *esp* **:** to distribute evenly or uniformly **:** BALANCE — **equal•iza•tion** \ˌē-kwə-lə-ˈzā-shən\ *n* — **equal•iz•er** \ˈē-kwə-ˌlī-zər\ *n*

equal•ly \ˈē-kwə-lē\ *adv* **1 :** in an equal manner **:** EVENLY **2 :** to an equal degree **:** ALIKE

equa•nim•i•ty \ˌē-kwə-ˈnim-ət-ē, ˌek-wə-\ *n* **:** evenness of mind **:** calm temper **:** COMPOSURE ⟨accept misfortunes with *equanimity*⟩ [Latin *aequanimitas,* from *aequo animo* "with even mind"]

equate \i-ˈkwāt\ *vt* **:** to make or treat as equal **:** represent or express as equal or equivalent

equa•tion \i-ˈkwā-zhən, -shən\ *n* **1 a :** the act or process of equating **b :** a state of being equated; *esp* **:** the regarding of two or more things as identical or similar **2 a :** a statement of the equality of two mathematical expressions ⟨solve the *equation* $x^2 - 6x + 9 = 0$ for *x*⟩ **b :** an expression representing a chemical reaction by means of chemical symbols

equa•tion•al \i-ˈkwāzh-nəl, -ˈkwāsh-, -ən-l\ *adj* **:** of, using, or involving equations or the equating of elements

equa•tor \i-ˈkwāt-ər, ˈē-ˌkwāt-\ *n* **1 :** the great circle of the celestial sphere whose plane is perpendicular to the axis of the earth **2 :** a great circle of the earth that is everywhere equally distant from the two poles and divides the earth's surface into the northern and southern hemispheres **3 :** a circle or roughly circular cross section dividing a body into two usually equal and symmetrical parts ⟨chromosomes move to the *equator* of a dividing cell⟩ [Medieval Latin *aequator,* literally, "equalizer", from Latin *aequare* "to make equal"; from its containing the equinoxes]

equa•to•ri•al \ˌē-kwə-ˈtōr-ē-əl, ˌek-wə-, -ˈtȯr-\ *adj* **1 :** of, relating to, or located at the equator or an equator **2 :** of, originating in, or suggesting the region around the geographic equator ⟨*equatorial* heat⟩

equatorial plate *n* **:** METAPHASE PLATE

eq•uer•ry \ˈek-wə-rē, i-ˈkwer-ē\ *n, pl* **-ries 1 :** an officer in charge of the horses of a prince or noble **2 :** a personal attendant of a member of the British royal family [Middle French *escuirie* "office of a squire, stable", from *escuier* "squire"]

¹eques•tri•an \i-ˈkwes-trē-ən\ *adj* **1 :** of, relating to, or featuring horseback riding **2 :** representing a person on horseback ⟨an *equestrian* statue⟩ [Latin *equester* "of a horseman", from *eques* "horseman", from *equus* "horse"]

²equestrian *n* **:** one who rides on horseback

equi- *combining form* **:** equal **:** equally ⟨*equi*poise⟩ ⟨*equi*potential⟩ [Latin *aequus* "equal"]

See *equi-* and 2d element

equiamplitude	**equidensity**	**equipotent**
equianalgesic	**equidimensional**	**equiprobability**
equiareal	**equiedged**	**equiprobable**
equicaloric	**equieffective**	**equispaced**
equiconcave	**equiluminous**	**equisweet**
equicontinuous	**equinumerous**	**equitoxic**
equiconvex	**equipossible**	**equivalue**
equidense		

equi•an•gu•lar \ˌē-kwi-ˈaŋ-gyə-lər, ˌek-wi-\ *adj* : having all or corresponding angles equal ⟨an *equiangular* triangle⟩

equi•dis•tant \ˌē-kwə-ˈdis-tənt, ˌek-wə-\ *adj* : equally distant ⟨two points *equidistant* from a line⟩

equi•lat•er•al \ˌē-kwə-ˈlat-ə-rəl, ˌek-wə-, -ˈla-trəl\ *adj* : having all sides or all faces equal ⟨*equilateral* triangle⟩

equil•i•brate \i-ˈkwil-ə-ˌbrāt\ *vb* **1** : to bring into or keep in equilibrium **2** : to bring about, come to, or be in equilibrium — **equil•i•bra•tion** \i-ˌkwil-ə-ˈbrā-shən\ *n*

equi•lib•ri•um \ˌē-kwə-ˈlib-rē-əm, ˌek-wə-\ *n, pl* **-ri•ums** *or* **-ria** \-rē-ə\ **1** : a static or dynamic state of balance between opposing forces or actions **2** : a state of intellectual or emotional balance : POISE **3** : the normal oriented state of the animal body in respect to the ground beneath it **[**Latin *aequilibrium,* from *aequi-* "equi-" + *libra* "weight, balance"**]**

equine \ˈē-ˌkwīn, ˈek-ˌwīn\ *adj* : of, relating to, or resembling a horse or the horse family **[**Latin *equinus,* from *equus* "horse"**]** — **equine** *n*

[1]equi•noc•tial \ˌē-kwə-ˈnäk-shəl, ˌek-wə-\ *adj* **1** : of, relating to, or occurring at or near an equinox ⟨*equinoctial* storms⟩ **2** : of or relating to the regions or climate of the equator ⟨*equinoctial* lands⟩ ⟨*equinoctial* heat⟩

[2]equinoctial *n* **1** : EQUATOR 1 **2** : an equinoctial storm

equinoctial circle *n* : EQUATOR 1 — called also *equinoctial line*

equi•nox \ˈē-kwə-ˌnäks, ˈek-wə-\ *n* **1** : either of the two times each year when the sun crosses the equator and day and night are everywhere of equal length that occur about March 21 and September 23 **2** : either of the two points on the celestial sphere where the celestial equator intersects the ecliptic **[**Medieval Latin *equinoxium,* from Latin *aequinoctium,* from *aequi-* "equi-" + *noct-, nox* "night"**]**

equip \i-ˈkwip\ *vt* **equipped; equip•ping** : to provide with what is necessary for service or action **[**Middle French *equiper,* from Old French *eschiper* "to equip a ship", of Germanic origin**]**

eq•ui•page \ˈek-wə-pij\ *n* **1** : material or articles used in equipment : OUTFIT **2** : a horse-drawn carriage with its attendants or the carriage alone

equip•ment \i-ˈkwip-mənt\ *n* **1 a** : the equipping of a person or thing **b** : the state of being equipped **2 a** : the articles or resources serving to equip a person or thing: as (1) : the implements used in an operation or activity : APPARATUS (2) : the rolling stock of a railway **b** : a piece of such equipment

eq•ui•poise \ˈek-wə-ˌpȯiz, ˈē-kwə-\ *n* **1** : a state of balance : EQUILIBRIUM **2** : a weight used to balance another weight

equi•pon•der•ate \ˌē-kwə-ˈpän-də-ˌrāt\ *vb* : to be or make equal in weight or force

equi•po•ten•tial \-pə-ˈten-chəl\ *adj* : having the same electrical potential ⟨*equipotential* points⟩ : of uniform potential throughout

eq•ui•se•tum \ˌek-wə-ˈsēt-əm\ *n* : any of a genus of primitive perennial vascular plants with leaves reduced to sheaths at the nodes on the hollow jointed grooved shoots — called also *horsetail, scouring rush* **[**Latin *equisaetum,* from *equus* "horse" + *saeta* "bristle"**]**

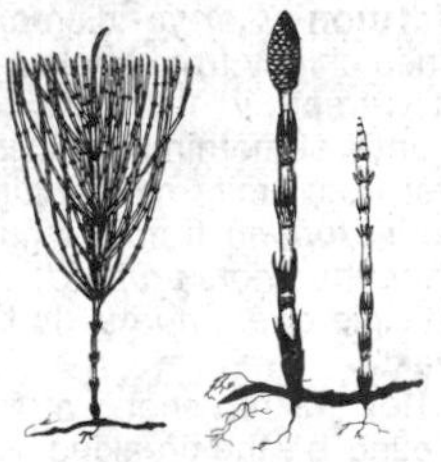

equisetum

eq•ui•ta•ble \ˈek-wət-ə-bəl\ *adj* : having or exhibiting equity : JUST **syn** see FAIR — **eq•ui•ta•ble•ness** *n* — **eq•ui•ta•bly** \-blē\ *adv*

eq•ui•ta•tion \ˌek-wə-ˈtā-shən\ *n* : the act or art of riding on horseback **[**Latin *equitare* "to ride on horseback", from *eques* "horseman", from *equus* "horse"**]**

eq•ui•ty \ˈek-wət-ē\ *n, pl* **-ties 1** : fairness or justice in dealings between persons **2** : a system of law that is a more flexible supplement to common and statute law and is intended to protect legal rights and enforce legal duties **3** : the value of an owner's interest in a property in excess of claims against it

equivalence relation *n* : a relation (as equality) that for a given set of elements (as the real numbers) is symmetric, reflexive, and transitive and for any two elements may or may not hold

equiv•a•lent \i-ˈkwiv-lənt, -ə-lənt\ *adj* **1 a** : alike or equal in number, numerical value, or meaning ⟨*equivalent* fractions⟩ **b** : having the same solution set ⟨*equivalent* equations⟩ **c** : equal in area or volume but not capable of superposition ⟨a square *equivalent* to a triangle⟩ **2** : corresponding or virtually identical in effect or function **3** : having the same chemical combining capacity **[**Late Latin *aequivalēre* "to have equal power", from Latin *aequi-* "equi-" + *valēre* "to be strong"**]** — **equiv•a•lence** \-ləns\ *n* — **equivalent** *n* — **equiv•a•lent•ly** *adv*

equiv•o•cal \i-ˈkwiv-ə-kəl\ *adj* **1** : having two or more possible meanings : AMBIGUOUS ⟨an *equivocal* answer⟩ **2** : DOUBTFUL 1, 4, UNCERTAIN ⟨an *equivocal* result⟩ **3** : QUESTIONABLE 2, SUSPICIOUS ⟨*equivocal* behavior⟩ **[**Late Latin *aequivocus,* from Latin *aequi-* "equi-" + *voc-, vox* "voice"**]** — **equiv•o•cal•ly** \-kə-lē, -klē\ *adv* — **equiv•o•cal•ness** \-kəl-nəs\ *n*

equiv•o•cate \i-ˈkwiv-ə-ˌkāt\ *vi* **1** : to use equivocal language especially with intent to deceive : QUIBBLE **2** : to avoid committing oneself in what one says — **equiv•o•ca•tion** \i-ˌkwiv-ə-ˈkā-shən\ *n* — **equiv•o•ca•tor** \i-ˈkwiv-ə-ˌkāt-ər\ *n*

[1]-er \ər; *after some vowels, often* r; *after* ŋ, *usually* gər\ *adj suffix or adv suffix* — used to form the comparative degree of adjectives and adverbs of one syllable ⟨hott*er*⟩ ⟨dri*er*⟩ and of some adjectives and adverbs of two syllables ⟨kindli*er*⟩ and sometimes of longer ones **[**Old English *-ra* (in adjectives), *-or* (in adverbs)**]**

[2]-er \ər; *after some vowels, often* r\ *also* **-ier** \ē-ər, yər\ *or* **-yer** \yər\ *n suffix* **1 a** : a person occupationally connected with ⟨furri*er*⟩ ⟨hatt*er*⟩ ⟨law*yer*⟩ **b** : person or thing belonging to or associated with ⟨old-tim*er*⟩ **c** : native of : resident of ⟨cottag*er*⟩ ⟨New York*er*⟩ **d** : one that has ⟨three-deck*er*⟩ **e** : one that produces or yields ⟨pork*er*⟩ **2 a** : one that does or performs (a specified action) ⟨report*er*⟩ — sometimes added to both elements of a compound ⟨build*er*-upp*er*⟩ **b** : one that is a suitable object of (a specified action) ⟨fry*er*⟩ **3** : one that is ⟨foreign*er*⟩ **[**Middle English, partly from Old English *-ere,* partly from Old French *-ier,* both from Latin *-arius* "-ary"**]**

era \ˈir-ə, ˈer-ə, ˈē-rə\ *n* **1** : a period of time reckoned from a special date or event ⟨the Christian *era* is computed from the birth of Christ⟩ **2** : an important or distinctive period of history ⟨the Revolutionary *era*⟩ **3** : one of the five major divisions of geologic time **[**Late Latin *aera,* from Latin, "counters", plural of *aer-, aes* "copper, money"**]** **syn** see PERIOD

erad•i•cate \i-ˈrad-ə-ˌkāt\ *vt* : to remove by or as if by uprooting : ELIMINATE ⟨*eradicate* weeds⟩ **[**Latin *eradicare,* from *e-* + *radix* "root"**]** — **erad•i•ca•ble** \-ˈrad-i-kə-bəl\ *adj* — **erad•i•ca•tion** \-ˌrad-ə-ˈkā-shən\ *n* — **erad•i•ca•tor** \-ˈrad-ə-ˌkāt-ər\ *n*

erase \i-ˈrās\ *vb* **1 a** : to rub or scrape out (as something written) **b** : to remove (recorded matter) from a magnetic tape **2** : to remove as if by erasing ⟨*erased* the event from their memories⟩ **3** : to yield to being erased **[**Latin *erasus,* past participle of *eradere* "to erase", from *e-* + *radere* "to scratch, scrape"**]** — **eras•abil•i•ty** \-ˌrā-sə-ˈbil-ət-ē\ *n* — **eras•able** \-ˈrā-sə-bəl\ *adj*

• **syn** CANCEL, OBLITERATE, EXPUNGE: ERASE implies rubbing or wiping out symbols or impressions often for correction or insertion of new matter; CANCEL implies an action (as marking, revoking, or neutralizing) that makes a thing no longer effective or usable; OBLITERATE implies a covering up or defacing that removes all distinct traces of a thing's existence; EXPUNGE stresses a removal or destruction that leaves no trace.

eras•er \i-ˈrā-sər\ *n* : one that erases; *esp* : a device used to erase marks (as of chalk or ink)

era•sure \i-ˈrā-shər, -zhər\ *n* : an act or instance of erasing

er•bi•um \ˈər-bē-əm\ *n* : a soft rare earth element that occurs with yttrium — see ELEMENT table **[**New Latin, from *Ytterby,* Sweden**]**

[1]ere \ˌeər, ˌaər\ *prep* : [2]BEFORE 2 **[**Old English *ǣr* "early, soon"**]**

[2]ere *conj* : [3]BEFORE 2

[1]erect \i-ˈrekt\ *adj* **1 a** : vertical in position : UPRIGHT ⟨an *erect* pole⟩ **b** : straight in posture ⟨*erect* bearing⟩ **c** : standing up or out from the body ⟨a porcupine with quills *erect*⟩ **2** : directed upward ⟨a tree with *erect* branches⟩ **3** : being in a state of physiological erection **[**Latin *erectus,* past participle of *erigere* "to erect", from *e-* + *regere* "to lead straight"] — **erect·ly** *adv* — **erect·ness** \-ˈrekt-nəs, -ˈrek-\ *n*

2erect *vt* **1 a :** to put up by the fitting together of materials **:** BUILD ⟨*erect* a building⟩ **b :** to fix in an upright position ⟨*erect* a flagpole⟩ **c :** to cause to stand up or out **2 :** to elevate in status **3 :** to set up **:** ESTABLISH ⟨*erect* social barriers⟩ **4 :** to construct (as a perpendicular) upon a given base — **erec·tor** \-ˈrek-tər\ *n*

erec·tile \i-ˈrek-tl, -ˌtīl\ *adj* **1 :** capable of being raised to an erect position **2 :** capable of undergoing physiological erection

erec·tion \i-ˈrek-shən\ *n* **1 :** the process of erecting **:** the state of being erected **2 a :** a state marked by firm turgid form and erect position of a previously limp and flabby bodily part whose tissue becomes dilated with blood **b :** an occurrence of such a state **3 :** something erected

ere·long \eər-ˈlȯŋ, aər-\ *adv* **:** before long **:** SOON

er·e·mite \ˈer-ə-ˌmīt\ *n* **:** HERMIT 1 [Middle English]

erep·sin \i-ˈrep-sən\ *n* **:** a mixture of peptide-digesting enzymes from the intestinal juice [*er-* (probably from Latin *eripere* "to sweep away") + *pepsin*]

erg \ˈərg\ *n* **:** a cgs unit of work equal to the work done by a force of one dyne acting through a distance of one centimeter and equivalent to 10^{-7} joule [Greek *ergon* "work"]

er·go \ˈeər-ˌgō, ˈər-\ *adv* **:** THEREFORE, HENCE [Latin]

er·gos·ter·ol \ˌər-ˈgäs-tə-ˌrȯl, -ˌrōl\ *n* **:** a steroid alcohol that occurs especially in yeast, molds, and ergot and is converted by ultraviolet irradiation into vitamin D [*ergot* + *sterol*]

er·got \ˈər-gət, -ˌgät\ *n* **1 a :** the dark club-shaped fruiting body of several fungi that replaces the seed of a grass (as rye) **b :** a disease of cereals (as rye) caused by ergot-producing fungi **2 :** dried ergots that are used medicinally for their contractile effect on smooth muscle [French, literally, "cock's spur"]

er·got·ism \ˈər-gət-ˌiz-əm\ *n* **:** a toxic condition caused by consumption of ergot (as in grain or bread)

Erie \ˈiər-ē\ *n* **:** a member of an Iroquoian people of the Lake Erie region

Er·len·mey·er flask \ˌər-lən-ˌmī-ər-, ˌer-lən-, -ˌmīr-\ *n* **:** a flat-bottomed conical laboratory flask [Emil *Erlenmeyer*, died 1909, German chemist]

er·mine \ˈər-mən\ *n, pl* **ermine** *or* **ermines 1 a :** any of several weasels that assume a white winter coat usually with more or less black on the tail **b :** the white fur of an ermine **2 :** a rank or office whose robe is ornamented with ermine [Old French, of Germanic origin] — **er·mined** \-mənd\ *adj*

ermine 1a

erne *or* **ern** \ˈərn, ˈeərn\ *n* **:** EAGLE; *esp* **:** a white-tailed sea eagle [Old English *earn*]

erode \i-ˈrōd\ *vb* **1 :** to diminish or destroy by degrees: **a :** to eat into or away by slow destruction of substance **:** CORRODE **b :** to wear away by or as if by the action of water, wind, or glacial ice ⟨corruption that *eroded* confidence in government⟩ **2 :** to undergo erosion [Latin *erodere* "to eat away", from *e-* + *rodere* "to gnaw"] — **erod·ible** \-ˈrōd-ə-bəl\ *adj*

ero·sion \i-ˈrō-zhən\ *n* **:** the process of eroding **:** the state of being eroded [Middle French, from Latin *erosio*, from *erodere* "to erode"] — **ero·sion·al** \-ˈrōzh-nəl, -ˈrō-zhən-l\ *adj*

ero·sive \i-ˈrō-siv, -ziv\ *adj* **:** eating or wearing away ⟨the *erosive* effect of water⟩ ⟨an *erosive* ulcer⟩ — **ero·sive·ness** *n* — **ero·siv·i·ty** \i-ˌrō-ˈsiv-ət-ē\ *n*

erot·ic \i-ˈrät-ik\ *adj* **:** of, relating to, or marked by sexual love or desire [Greek *erōtikos*, from *erōt-*, *erōs* "love"] — **erot·i·cal·ly** \-i-kə-lē, -klē\ *adv* — **erot·i·cism** \-ˈrät-ə-ˌsiz-əm\ *n*

err \ˈeər, ˈər\ *vi* **1 :** to make a mistake ⟨*err* in one's calculations⟩ **2 :** to violate an accepted standard of conduct [Old French *errer* "to stray", from Latin *errare*]

er·ran·cy \ˈer-ən-sē\ *n, pl* **-cies :** the state or an instance of erring

er·rand \ˈer-ənd\ *n* **:** a short trip taken to do something often for another; *also* **:** the object or purpose of such a trip [Old English *ǣrend* "message, business"]

er·rant \ˈer-ənt\ *adj* **1 :** wandering especially in search of adventure ⟨an *errant* knight⟩ **2 a :** straying outside the proper bounds ⟨an *errant* calf⟩ **b :** deviating from an accepted pattern or standard ⟨an *errant* child⟩ — **er·rant·ry** \-ən-trē\ *n*

er·ra·ta \e-ˈrät-ə, -ˈrāt-, -ˈrat-\ *n* **:** a list of corrigenda [from plural of *erratum*]

er·rat·ic \ir-ˈat-ik\ *adj* **1 :** having no fixed course **:** WANDERING ⟨an *erratic* comet⟩ **2 :** marked by lack of consistency or regularity **:** ECCENTRIC ⟨*erratic* behavior⟩ [Latin *erraticus*, from *errare* "to stray"] — **er·rat·i·cal·ly** \-i-kə-lē, -klē\ *adv*

er·ra·tum \e-ˈrät-əm, -ˈrāt-, -ˈrat-\ *n, pl* **-ta** \-ə\ **:** CORRIGENDUM [Latin, from *errare* "to stray"]

er·ro·ne·ous \ir-ˈō-nē-əs, e-ˈrō-\ *adj* **:** containing or characterized by error [Latin *erroneus* "wandering", from *erro* "wanderer", from *errare* "to stray"] — **er·ro·ne·ous·ly** *adv* — **er·ro·ne·ous·ness** *n*

er·ror \ˈer-ər\ *n* **1 a :** deviation from a code of behavior ⟨saw the *error* of their ways⟩ **b :** an act involving an unintentional deviation from truth or accuracy ⟨an arithmetic *error*⟩ **c :** an act that through ignorance, deficiency, or accident fails to achieve what should be done ⟨an *error* in judgment⟩ **d :** a defensive misplay made by a baseball player **2 :** the quality or state of erring **3 :** a false belief or a set of false beliefs **4 :** something produced by mistake **5 :** the difference between an observed or calculated value and the true value; *esp* **:** variation in measurements, calculations, or observations of a quantity due to mistakes or to uncontrollable factors [Old French *errour*, from Latin *error*, from *errare* "to stray"] — **er·ror·less** \-ləs\ *adj*

• syn ERROR, MISTAKE, BLUNDER, SLIP mean a departure from what is true, right, or proper. ERROR is a deviation from what is right, correct, or sanctioned ⟨an *error* in reasoning⟩ ⟨an *error* in addition⟩ MISTAKE implies misunderstanding or an oversight or unintentional wrongdoing and connotes less severe judgment than ERROR; BLUNDER suggests ignorance, stupidity, carelessness, or lack of foresight and sometimes implies blame; SLIP carries a strong implication of inadvertence or accident producing trivial mistakes.

er·satz \ˈer-ˌzäts, er-ˈ\ *adj* **:** being a usually artificial and inferior substitute ⟨*ersatz* cream⟩ [German, noun, "substitute"] **syn** see ARTIFICIAL

Erse \ˈərs\ *n* **1 :** SCOTTISH GAELIC **2 :** IRISH GAELIC [Middle English *Erisch* "Irish", alteration of *Irish*] — **Erse** *adj*

erst·while \ˈərst-ˌhwīl, -ˌwīl\ *adv* **:** in the past **:** FORMERLY [Old English *ǣrest*, superlative of *ǣr* "early"] — **erstwhile** *adj*

eruct \i-ˈrəkt\ *vb* **:** BELCH [Latin *eructare*, from *e-* + *ructare* "to belch"] — **eruc·ta·tion** \i-ˌrək-ˈtā-shən, ˌē-ˌrək-\ *n*

er·u·dite \ˈer-yə-ˌdīt, -ə-\ *adj* **:** characterized by erudition [Latin *eruditus*, from *erudire* "to instruct", from *e-* + *rudis* "rude, 2Hignorant"] — **er·u·dite·ly** *adv*

er·u·di·tion \ˌer-yə-ˈdish-ən, -ə-\ *n* **:** extensive knowledge gained chiefly from books **:** LEARNING

erupt \i-ˈrəpt\ *vi* **1 a :** to force out or release suddenly and often violently something pent up ⟨the volcano *erupted*⟩ **b** (1) **:** to burst from limits or restraint (2) **:** to break through a surface ⟨teeth *erupting* from the gum⟩ **c :** to become active or violent **:** EXPLODE ⟨riots *erupted*⟩ **2 :** to break out [Latin *eruptus*, past participle of *erumpere* "to burst forth", from *e-* + *rumpere* "to break"]

erup·tion \i-ˈrəp-shən\ *n* **1 a :** an act, process, or instance of erupting **b :** the breaking out of a rash on the skin **2 :** a product (as a skin rash) of erupting — **erup·tive** \-ˈrəp-tiv\ *adj*

-ery \ə-rē, rē\ *n suffix, pl* **-eries 1 :** qualities collectively **:** character **:** -HOOD 1 ⟨snobb*ery*⟩ **2 :** art **:** practice ⟨cook*ery*⟩ **3 :** place of doing, keeping, producing, or selling (a specified thing) ⟨bak*ery*⟩ ⟨fish*ery*⟩ **4 :** collection **:** aggregate ⟨fin*ery*⟩ **5 :** state or condition ⟨slav*ery*⟩ [Old French *-erie*, from *-ier* "-er" + *-ie* "-y"]

er·y·sip·e·las \ˌer-ə-ˈsip-ləs, ˌir-, -ə-ləs\ *n* **:** an acute disease marked by fever and intense local inflammation of the skin and underlying tissues and caused by a streptococcus [Latin, from Greek]

eryth·ro·cyte \i-ˈrith-rə-ˌsīt\ *n* **:** RED BLOOD CELL [Greek *erythros* "red"] — **eryth·ro·cyt·ic** \-ˌrith-rə-ˈsit-ik\ *adj*

eryth·ro·my·cin \i-ˌrith-rə-ˈmīs-n\ *n* **:** an antibiotic produced by an actinomycete and active against some bacteria

1-es \əz, iz *after* s, z, sh, ch; z *after* v *or a vowel*\ *n pl suffix* **1 —** used to form the plural of most nouns that end in *s* ⟨glass*es*⟩, *z* ⟨fuzz*es*⟩, *sh* ⟨bush*es*⟩, *ch* ⟨peach*es*⟩, or a final *y* that changes to *i* ⟨lad*ies*⟩ and of some nouns ending in *f* that changes to *v*

⟨loaves⟩ — compare 1-s 1 **2 :** 1-s 2 [Old English *-as,* nominative and accusative plural ending of some masculine nouns]

2-es *vb suffix* — used to form the third person singular present of most verbs that end in *s* ⟨blesses⟩, *z* ⟨fizzes⟩, *sh* ⟨hushes⟩, *ch* ⟨catches⟩, or a final *y* that changes to *i* ⟨defies⟩ — compare 2-s [Old English *-es, -as*]

es•ca•drille \'es-kə-ˌdril, -ˌdrē\ *n* **:** a unit of a European air command containing usually six airplanes [French, "flotilla, escadrille", from Spanish *escuadrilla,* from *escuadra* "squadron, squad"]

es•ca•late \'es-kə-ˌlāt\ *vb* **:** to increase or be increased in extent, number, intensity, or scope [back-formation from *escalator*] — **es•ca•la•tion** \ˌes-kə-'lā-shən\ *n*

1es•ca•la•tor \'es-kə-ˌlāt-ər\ *n* **:** a power-driven set of stairs arranged like an endless belt that ascend or descend continuously [from *Escalator,* a former trademark]

2escalator *adj* **:** providing for a periodic proportional upward or downward adjustment (as of prices or wages)

es•cal•lop \is-'käl-əp, -'kal-\ *variant of* SCALLOP

es•cap•able \is-'kā-pə-bəl\ *adj* **:** capable of being escaped **:** AVOIDABLE

es•ca•pade \'es-kə-ˌpād\ *n* **:** an unconventional adventure or experience **:** PRANK

1es•cape \is-'kāp\ *vb* **1 a :** to get away (as by flight) ⟨*escape* from prison⟩ **b :** to leak out from confinement ⟨gas is *escaping*⟩ **c :** to run wild from cultivation **2 :** to get out of the way of **:** AVOID ⟨*escaped* the plague by moving to the country⟩ **3 :** to fail to be noticed or recallable by ⟨the name *escapes* me⟩ **4 :** to issue from or be uttered involuntarily by ⟨a sigh *escaped* me⟩ [Old North French *escaper,* derived from Latin *ex-* + Late Latin *cappa* "head covering, cloak"] — **es•cap•er** *n*

△ **origin** A fugitive may sometimes get away from pursuers, even if they are close enough to clutch the fugitive, by slipping out of a coat or cloak and leaving the would-be captors holding an empty garment. This is the idea behind the word *escape. Escape* is derived from Latin *ex,* which means "out of", and Late Latin *cappa,* which means "head covering" or "cloak". This *cappa* is also the ancestor of English *cap* and *cape.*

2escape *n* **1 :** an act or instance of escaping **2 :** a means of escaping **3 :** a cultivated plant run wild

3escape *adj* **:** providing a means of escape ⟨an *escape* hatch⟩ ⟨an *escape* clause⟩

es•cap•ee \ˌes-ˌkā-'pē, is-ˌkā-, ˌes-kə-\ *n* **:** one that has escaped; *esp* **:** an escaped prisoner

escape mechanism *n* **:** a mode of behavior or thinking adopted to evade unpleasant facts or responsibilities

es•cape•ment \is-'kāp-mənt\ *n* **1 :** a device in a timepiece through which the energy of the weight or spring is transmitted to the pendulum or balance by means of impulses that permit one tooth on a wheel to escape from a projecting part at regular intervals **2 :** a device (as the spacing mechanism of a typewriter) that permits motion in one direction only and in equal steps

escapement 1

escape velocity *n* **:** the minimum velocity that a moving body (as a rocket) must have to escape from the gravitational field of the earth or of a celestial body and move outward into space

es•cap•ism \is-'kā-ˌpiz-əm\ *n* **:** habitual thinking about imaginary or entertaining things in order to escape from reality or routine — **es•cap•ist** \-pəst\ *adj or n*

es•ca•role \'es-kə-ˌrōl\ *n* **:** ENDIVE 1 [French, from Late Latin *escariola,* from Latin *esca* "food", from *edere* "to eat"]

es•carp•ment \is-'kärp-mənt\ *n* **1 :** a steep slope in front of a fortification **2 :** a long cliff [French *escarpement,* from *escarper* "to scarp"]

-escent \'es-nt\ *adj suffix* **1 :** beginning **:** beginning to be **:** slightly ⟨iridescent⟩ **2 :** reflecting or emitting light (in a specified way) ⟨opalescent⟩ ⟨phosphorescent⟩ [Latin *-escent-, -escens,* present participle ending of verbs in *-escere*]

1es•cheat \is-'chēt\ *n* **:** the reversion of property to the state when there are no persons (as heirs) legally entitled to hold it; *also* **:** the property that reverts [Middle English *eschete,* from Old French, from *escheoir* "to fall, devolve", derived from Latin *ex-* + *cadere* "to fall"]

2escheat *vb* **:** to revert or cause to revert by escheat — **es•cheat•able** \-ə-bəl\ *adj*

es•chew \is-'chü, ish-\ *vt* **:** to abstain or refrain from **:** SHUN [Middle French *eschiuver,* of Germanic origin]

1es•cort \'es-ˌkȯrt\ *n* **1 a :** a person or group of persons accompanying another to give protection or show courtesy **b :** the man who goes on a date with a woman **c :** a protective screen of vehicles, warships, or airplanes **2 :** accompaniment by a person or an armed protector [French *escorte,* from Italian *scorta,* from *scorgere* "to guide", from Latin *ex-* + *corrigere* "to make straight, correct"]

2es•cort \is-'kȯrt, es-', 'es-ˌ\ *vt* **:** to accompany as an escort

es•crow \'es-ˌkrō, es-'\ *n* **:** something (as a deed or a sum of money) delivered by one person to another to be delivered by the second to a third party only upon the fulfillment of a condition [Middle French *escroue* "scroll"] — **in escrow :** in trust as an escrow

es•cu•do \is-'küd-ō\ *n, pl* **-dos 1 :** any of various former gold or silver coins of Hispanic countries **2 a :** the basic monetary unit of Portugal **b :** a coin representing this unit [Spanish and Portuguese, literally, "shield"]

es•cu•lent \'es-kyə-lənt\ *adj* **:** fit to be eaten **:** EDIBLE [Latin *esculentus,* from *esca* "food", from *edere* "to eat"] — **esculent** *n*

es•cutch•eon \is-'kəch-ən\ *n* **:** the usually shield-shaped surface on which a coat of arms is shown [Middle French *escuchon,* from Latin *scutum* "shield"]

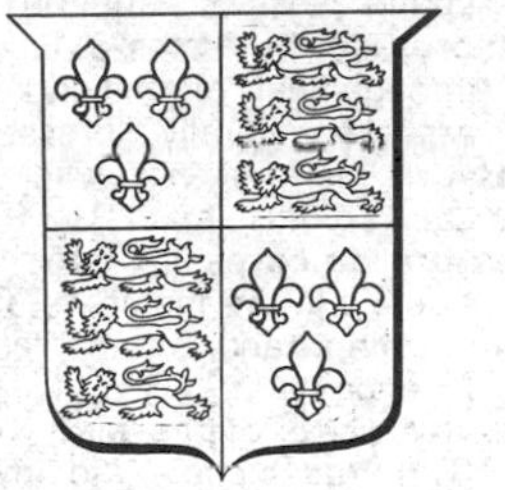
escutcheon

Es•dras \'ez-drəs\ *n* — see BIBLE table

1-ese \'ēz, 'ēs\ *adj suffix* **:** of, relating to, or originating in (a specified place or country) ⟨Japanese⟩ [Portuguese *-ês* and Italian *-ese,* from Latin *-ensis*]

2-ese *n suffix, pl* **-ese 1 :** native or resident of (a specified place or country) ⟨Chinese⟩ **2 a :** language of (a specified place, country, or nationality) ⟨Japanese⟩ **b :** speech, literary style, or diction peculiar to (a specified place, person, or group) — usually in words applied in depreciation ⟨journalese⟩

es•ker \'es-kər\ *n* **:** a long narrow mound of material deposited by a stream flowing on, within, or beneath a stagnant glacier [Irish Gaelic *eiscir* "ridge"]

Es•ki•mo \'es-kə-ˌmō\ *n* **1 :** a member of a group of peoples of what is now northern Canada, Greenland, Alaska, and eastern Siberia **2 :** the language of the Eskimo people [Danish, of American Indian origin]

Eskimo dog *n* **1 :** a broad-chested powerful dog native to Greenland and Labrador that has a heavy double coat **2 :** a sled dog of American origin

esoph•a•gus *also* **oesoph•a•gus** \i-'säf-ə-gəs\ *n, pl* **-gi** \-ˌgī, -ˌjī, -ˌgē\ **:** a muscular tube that leads from the pharynx to the stomach in vertebrates; *also* **:** a part of the muscular tube between the mouth and the stomach in some invertebrates [Greek *oisophagos,* from *oisein* "to be going to carry" + *phagein* "to eat"] — **esoph•a•ge•al** \i-ˌsäf-ə-'jē-əl\ *adj*

es•o•ter•ic \ˌes-ə-'ter-ik\ *adj* **1 :** designed for or understood by the specially initiated alone ⟨an *esoteric* ritual⟩ **2 :** of or relating to knowledge that is restricted to a small group **:** RECONDITE ⟨*esoteric* writings⟩ **3 :** PRIVATE 2b, CONFIDENTIAL ⟨an *esoteric* purpose⟩ [Late Latin *esotericus,* from Greek *esōterikos,* from *esōterō,* comparative of *eisō, esō* "within"] — **es•o•ter•i•cal•ly** \-'ter-i-kə-lē, -klē\ *adv*

ESP \ˌē-ˌes-'pē\ *n* **:** EXTRASENSORY PERCEPTION

es•pa•drille \'es-pə-ˌdril\ *n* **:** a flat sandal usually having a fabric upper and a flexible sole [French]

es•pal•ier \is-'pal-yər, -ˌyā\ *n* **:** a plant (as a fruit tree) trained to grow flat against a support (as a wall or trellis) [French] — **espalier** *vt*

es•par•to \is-'pärt-ō\ *n, pl* **-tos** : either of two Spanish and Algerian grasses from which cordage, shoes, baskets, and paper are made — called also *esparto grass* [Spanish]

es•pe•cial \is-'pesh-əl\ *adj* : SPECIAL 1, 2 — **es•pe•cial•ly** \-'pesh-lē, -ə-lē\ *adv*

Es•pe•ran•to \,es-pə-'rant-ō, -'ränt-\ *n* : an artificial international language based as far as possible on words common to the chief European languages [Dr. *Esperanto,* pseudonym of L. L. Zamenhof, died 1917, Polish oculist, its inventor]

es•pi•al \is-'pī-əl, -'pīl\ *n* **1** : an act of spying or watching **2** : an act of noticing

es•pi•o•nage \'es-pē-ə-,näzh, -nij, -,näj\ *n* : the practice of spying or the use of spies to obtain information about the plans and activities (as of a foreign government or a business competitor) [French *espionnage,* from Middle French *espionner* "to spy", from *espion* "spy", from Italian *spione,* from *spia* "spy", of Germanic origin]

es•pla•nade \'es-plə-,näd, -,nād\ *n* : a level open stretch or area; *esp* : one designed for walking or driving along a shore [French]

es•pous•al \is-'paù-zəl *also* -səl\ *n* **1 a** : BETROTHAL **b** : WEDDING 1 **c** : MARRIAGE 2a; *also* : a union resembling marriage **2** : a taking up of a cause or belief

es•pouse \is-'paùz *also* -'paùs\ *vt* **1** : MARRY 1b, c **2** : to take up the cause of : SUPPORT — **es•pous•er** *n*

espres•so \e-'spres-ō\ *n* : coffee brewed by forcing steam through finely ground darkly roasted coffee beans [Italian *caffè espresso,* literally, "pressed out coffee"]

es•prit \is-'prē\ *n* : vivacious cleverness or wit [French, from Latin *spiritus* "spirit"]

es•prit de corps \is-,prēd-ə-'kōr, -'kȯr\ *n* : the common spirit existing in the members of a group and inspiring enthusiasm, devotion, and strong regard for the honor of the group [French]

es•py \is-'pī\ *vt* **es•pied** \-'pīd\; **es•py•ing** : to catch sight of [Old French *espier* "to spy", of Germanic origin]

-esque \'esk\ *adj suffix* : in the manner or style of : like ⟨Romanesque⟩ ⟨statuesque⟩ [French, from Italian *-esco,* of Germanic origin]

es•quire \'es-,kwīr, is-'\ *n* **1** : a member of the English gentry ranking immediately below a knight **2** : a candidate for knighthood serving as attendant to a knight **3** *often cap* — used as a courtesy title usually placed in its abbreviated form after a surname (as of an attorney) ⟨John M. Doe, *Esq.*⟩ [Middle French *esquier* "squire"]

-ess \əs, is *also* ,es\ *n suffix* : female ⟨poetess⟩ [Old French *-esse,* from Late Latin *-issa,* from Greek]

[1]**es•say** \e-'sā, 'es-,ā\ *vt* : to make an often tentative effort to perform ⟨*essayed* the role of mediator⟩

[2]**es•say** \'es-,ā, *in sense 1 also* e-'sā\ *n* **1** : ATTEMPT; *esp* : an initial tentative effort **2** : a nonfictional usually short literary composition dealing with its subject from a limited or personal point of view [Middle French *essai,* from Late Latin *exagium* "act of weighing", from Latin *ex-* + *agere* "to drive"]

es•say•ist \'es-,ā-əst\ *n* : a writer of essays

es•sence \'es-ns\ *n* **1** : the basic nature of a thing : the quality or qualities that make a thing what it is ⟨the *essence* of honesty is truthfulness⟩ **2** : a substance extracted (as from a plant or drug) that retains the special qualities of its source ⟨*essence* of peppermint⟩ **3** : PERFUME 1, SCENT [Latin *essentia,* from *esse* "to be"]

Es•sene \is-'ēn, 'es-,\ *n* : a member of a monastic brotherhood of Jews in Palestine from the 2d century B.C. to the 2d century A.D. [Greek *Essēnos*]

[1]**es•sen•tial** \i-'sen-chəl\ *adj* **1** : forming or belonging to the fundamental nature of a thing ⟨free speech is an *essential* right of citizenship⟩ **2** : containing or having the character of a volatile essence ⟨*essential* oils⟩ **3** : important in the highest degree : NECESSARY ⟨food is *essential* to life⟩ — **es•sen•ti•al•i•ty** \-,sen-chē-'al-ət-ē\ *n* — **es•sen•tial•ly** \-'sench-lē, -ə-lē\ *adv* — **es•sen•tial•ness** \-əl-nəs\ *n*

• **syn** ESSENTIAL, FUNDAMENTAL, VITAL mean so important as to be indispensable. ESSENTIAL implies belonging to the very nature of a thing and therefore being incapable of removal without destroying the thing itself or its character; FUNDAMENTAL suggests something that is of the nature of a foundation without which an entire system or complex whole would collapse ⟨the *fundamental* principles of a democracy⟩ VITAL suggests that which is as necessary to continuance as air, food, and water are to living things ⟨resources *vital* to security⟩ **syn** see in addition NECESSARY

[2]**essential** *n* : something basic, necessary, or indispensable ⟨the *essentials* for success⟩

essential amino acid *n* : an amino acid that is necessary for proper growth of the animal body and that cannot be manufactured by the body unassisted but must be obtained from protein food

[1]**-est** \əst, ist\ *adj suffix or adv suffix* — used to form the superlative degree of adjectives andadverbs of one syllable ⟨fatt*est*⟩ ⟨lat*est*⟩, of some adjectives and adverbs of two syllables ⟨luck*iest*⟩, and less often of longer ones [Old English]

[2]**-est** \əst, ist\ *or* **-st** \st\ *vb suffix* — used to form the archaic second person singular of verbs (with *thou*) ⟨get*test*⟩ ⟨did*st*⟩ [Old English]

es•tab•lish \is-'tab-lish\ *vb* **1** : to make firm or stable ⟨*establish* a gun on its base⟩ **2** : to enact permanently ⟨*establish* a constitution⟩ **3 a** : to bring into existence : FOUND ⟨*establish* a republic⟩ **b** : to bring about : EFFECT ⟨*establish* a good relationship⟩ **4 a** : to set on a firm basis ⟨*establish* one's children in business⟩ **b** : to put into a favorable position ⟨the *established* order⟩ **c** : to gain full recognition or acceptance of ⟨*establish* a claim⟩ **5** : to put beyond doubt : PROVE ⟨*establish* one's innocence⟩ **6** : to become naturalized ⟨a grass that *establishes* on poor soil⟩ [Middle French *establiss-,* stem of *establir* "to establish", from Latin *stabilire,* from *stabilis* "stable"] — **es•tab•lish•er** *n*

established church *n* : a church recognized by law as the official church of a nation

es•tab•lish•ment \is-'tab-lish-mənt\ *n* **1 a** : the act of establishing : the state or fact of being established **b** : the granting of a privileged position ⟨*establishment* of a church⟩ **2** : a permanent civil or military organization **3** : a place of business or residence with its furnishings and staff ⟨a dry-cleaning *establishment*⟩ **4** : an established order of society; *also, often cap* : the social, economic, and political leaders of such an order

es•tate \is-'tāt\ *n* **1** : STATE 1a, CONDITION **2** : social standing or rank especially of a high order **3** : a social or political class; *esp* : one of the great classes (as the nobility, clergy, and commons) formerly having distinct political powers **4 a** : the nature and extent of one's interest in property **b** : POSSESSIONS, PROPERTY; *esp* : a person's property in land and tenements **c** : the assets and liabilities left by a person at death **5** : a usually extensive landed property often with a large house [Middle French *estat,* from Latin *status* "state"]

[1]**es•teem** \is-'tēm\ *n* : high regard

[2]**esteem** *vt* **1 a** : to view as : CONSIDER ⟨*esteem* it a privilege⟩ **b** : THINK 3a, BELIEVE **2** : to set a high value on : PRIZE [Middle French *estimer* "to estimate", from Latin *aestimare*] **syn** see REGARD

es•ter \'es-tər\ *n* : an organic compound formed by the reaction between an acid and an alcohol [German, from *essigäther* "ethyl acetate", from *essig* "vinegar" + *äther* "ether"]

es•ter•ase \'es-tə-,rās\ *n* : an enzyme that accelerates the breakdown or synthesis of esters

es•ter•i•fy \e-'ster-ə-,fī\ *vt* **-fied**; **-fy•ing** : to convert into an ester — **es•ter•i•fi•ca•tion** \-,ster-ə-fə-'kā-shən\ *n*

Es•ther \'es-tər\ *n* — *see* BIBLE table

esthete, esthetic, esthetics *variant of* AESTHETE, AESTHETIC, AESTHETICS

es•ti•ma•ble \'es-tə-mə-bəl\ *adj* : worthy of esteem — **es•ti•ma•ble•ness** *n*

[1]**es•ti•mate** \'es-tə-,māt\ *vt* **1** : to judge or determine tentatively or approximately the value, size, or cost of ⟨*estimate* a painting job⟩ **2** : to form an opinion of : JUDGE, CONCLUDE [Latin *aestimare* "to value, estimate"] — **es•ti•ma•tor** \-,māt-ər\ *n*

• **syn** ESTIMATE, APPRAISE, EVALUATE, ASSESS mean to judge a thing with respect to its worth. ESTIMATE implies a judgment, considered or casual, that precedes or takes the place of actual measuring, counting, or testing; APPRAISE implies the fixing of the monetary worth of a thing by an expert; EVALUATE suggests an attempt to determine the relative or intrinsic worth of something in terms other than of money ⟨*evaluate* a new novel⟩ ASSESS implies a critical appraisal for the purpose of understanding or interpreting or as a guide in taking action ⟨*assess* the deterrent effect of punishment⟩ ⟨*assess* taxable real estate⟩

[2]**es•ti•mate** \'es-tə-mət\ *n* **1** : the act of appraising or valuing **2** : an opinion or judgment of the nature, character, or quality of a thing **3** : a rough or approximate calculation **4** : a statement of the cost of a job
es•ti•ma•tion \ˌes-tə-'mā-shən\ *n* **1** : an opinion formed or expressed **2 a** : the act of estimating **b** : ESTIMATE **3** : ESTEEM, HONOR
estivate, estivation *variant of* AESTIVATE, AESTIVATION
Es•to•nian \e-'stō-nē-ən, -nyən\ *n* **1** : a member of a Finno-Ugric-speaking people chiefly of Estonia **2** : the Finno-Ugric language of the Estonians — **Estonian** *adj*
estr- *or* **estro-** *or* **oestr-** *or* **oestro-** *combining form* : estrus ⟨*estrogen*⟩
es•tra•di•ol \ˌes-trə-'dī-ˌȯl, -ˌōl\ *n* : a powerful estrogenic hormone usually made synthetically for medicinal use
es•trange \is-'trānj\ *vt* **1** : to remove from customary environment or associations **2** : to destroy the affection of : ALIENATE ⟨friends *estranged* by gossip⟩ [Middle French *estranger*, from Medieval Latin *extraneare*, from Latin *extraneus* "strange"] — **es•trange•ment** \-mənt\ *n*
es•trin \'es-trən\ *n* : an estrogenic hormone
es•tri•ol \'es-ˌtrī-ˌȯl, e-'strī-, -ˌōl\ *n* : an estrogenic hormone usually obtained from the urine of pregnant women
es•tro•gen \'es-trə-jən\ *n* : a substance (as a sex hormone) tending to promote estrus and stimulate the development of secondary sex characteristics in the female — **es•tro•gen•ic** \ˌes-trə-'jen-ik\ *adj*
es•trone \'es-ˌtrōn\ *n* : an estrogenic hormone from the urine of pregnant females
estrous cycle *n* : the series of physiological changes of the endocrine and reproductive systems of a female mammal from the beginning of one period of estrus to the beginning of the next
es•trus \'es-trəs\ *or* **es•trum** \-trəm\ *n* **1** : a regularly recurrent state of sexual excitability during which the female of most mammals will accept the male and is capable of conceiving : HEAT **2** : ESTROUS CYCLE [Latin *oestrus* "gadfly, frenzy", from Greek *oistros*] — **es•trous** \-trəs\ *adj*
es•tu•a•rine \'es-chə-wə-ˌrīn\ *adj* : of, relating to, or formed in an estuary
es•tu•ary \'es-chə-ˌwer-ē\ *n, pl* **-ar•ies** : a water passage where the tide meets a river current; *esp* : an arm of the sea at the lower end of a river [Latin *aestuarium*, from *aestus* "boiling, time"]
-et \'et, ˌet, ət, it\ *n suffix* **1** : small one : lesser one ⟨baron*et*⟩ ⟨isl*et*⟩ **2** : group ⟨oct*et*⟩ [Old French, from Latin *-itus*]
eta \'āt-ə\ *n* : the 7th letter of the Greek alphabet — Η or η
et cetera \et-'set-ə-rə, -'se-trə\ : and others especially of the same kind : and so forth [Latin]
etch \'ech\ *vt* **1** : to produce (as a design) especially on metal or glass by the corrosive action of an acid; *also* : to subject to such etching **2** : to impress (as on the mind) sharply or clearly [Dutch *etsen*, from German *ätzen*, literally, "to feed"] — **etcher** *n*
etch•ing *n* **1** : the art of producing pictures or designs by printing from an etched metal plate **2** : an impression from an etched plate
eter•nal \i-'tərn-l\ *adj* **1** : having no beginning and no end : lasting forever **2** : continuing without interruption : UNCEASING ⟨that dog's *eternal* barking⟩ [Middle French, from Late Latin *aeternalis*, from Latin *aeternus* "eternal"] — **eter•nal•ly** \-l-ē\ *adv* — **eter•nal•ness** *n*
• **syn** ETERNAL, EVERLASTING, ENDLESS mean continuing on and on without end. ETERNAL implies being without either beginning or end and so unaffected by time or change ⟨*eternal* truths⟩ EVERLASTING and ENDLESS apply to what exists and endures in time without end or limit, EVERLASTING stressing the quality of permanence or the fact of duration and ENDLESS frequently suggesting a wearisome stretching out without conclusion or final rest ⟨*endless* arguments about money⟩ ⟨*endless* punishment⟩
Eternal *n* : GOD 1 — used with *the*
eter•ni•ty \i-'tər-nət-ē\ *n, pl* **-ties** **1** : the quality or state of being eternal **2** : infinite time **3** : the state after death : IMMORTALITY **4** : a seemingly endless time : AGE [Middle French *eternité*, from Latin *aeternitas*, from *aeternus* "eternal"]
[1]**-eth** \əth, ith\ *or* **-th** \th\ *vb suffix* — used to form the archaic 3d person sing. present of verbs ⟨go*eth*⟩ ⟨do*th*⟩ [Old English]
[2]**-eth** — see -TH
eth•ane \'eth-ˌān\ *n* : a colorless odorless gas C_2H_6 that consists of carbon and hydrogen, is found in natural gas, and is used especially as a fuel [*eth*yl + *-ane*]
eth•a•nol \'eth-ə-ˌnȯl, -ˌnōl\ *n* : ALCOHOL 1a
ether \'ē-thər\ *n* **1** : the upper regions of space : HEAVENS **2 a** : a medium formerly held to permeate all space and transmit transverse waves (as light) **b** : the medium that transmits radio waves **3 a** : a light volatile flammable liquid $C_4H_{10}O$ obtained by the distillation of alcohol with sulfuric acid and used chiefly as a solvent especially of fats and as an anesthetic **b** : any of various organic compounds characterized by an oxygen atom attached to two carbon atoms [Latin *aether*, from Greek *aithēr*, from *aithein* "to ignite"]
ethe•re•al \i-'thir-ē-əl\ *adj* **1** : HEAVENLY 1 ⟨*ethereal* spirits⟩ **2** : being light and airy : DELICATE ⟨*ethereal* music⟩ — **ethe•re•al•i•ty** \i-ˌthir-ē-'al-ət-ē\ *n* — **ethe•re•al•ly** \-'thir-ē-ə-lē\ *adv* — **ethe•re•al•ness** *n*
ether•ize \'ē-thə-ˌrīz\ *vt* : to treat or anesthetize with ether — **ether•iza•tion** \ˌē-thə-rə-'zā-shən\ *n* — **ether•iz•er** *n*
eth•i•cal \'eth-i-kəl\ *or* **eth•ic** \-ik\ *adj* **1** : of or relating to ethics **2** : conforming to accepted and especially professional standards of conduct ⟨*ethical* practices⟩ **3** : sold only on a doctor's prescription ⟨*ethical* drugs⟩ [Latin *ethicus*, from Greek *ēthikos*, from *ēthos* "character"] **syn** see MORAL — **eth•i•cal•ly** \'eth-i-kə-lē, -klē\ *adv*
eth•ics \'eth-iks\ *n sing or pl* **1** : a branch of philosophy dealing with what is good and bad and with moral duty and obligation **2** : the principles of moral conduct governing an individual or a group
Ethi•o•pi•an \ˌē-thē-'ō-pē-ən\ *n* **1** : a member of any of the mythical or actual peoples usually described by the ancient Greeks as dark-skinned and living far to the south **2** : a native or inhabitant of Ethiopia — **Ethiopian** *adj*
Ethi•op•ic \-'äp-ik, -'ō-pik\ *n* : a Semitic language formerly spoken in Ethiopia and still used in church services there
eth•moid \'eth-ˌmȯid\ *or* **eth•moi•dal** \eth-'mȯid-l\ *adj* : of, relating to, adjoining, or being one or more bones of the walls of the nasal cavity [French *ethmoïde*, from Greek *ēthmoeidēs*, literally, "like a strainer", from *ēthmos* "strainer"] — **ethmoid** *n*
[1]**eth•nic** \'eth-nik\ *adj* : of or relating to races or large groups of people classed according to common traits and customs ⟨*ethnic* minorities⟩ [Late Latin *ethnicus* "heathen", from Greek *ethnikos* "national", from *ethnos* "nation"] — **eth•ni•cal•ly** \-ni-kə-lē, -klē\ *adv*
[2]**ethnic** *n* : a member of an ethnic group; *esp* : one retaining traditional customs, outlook, and language
ethno- *combining form* : race : people : cultural group ⟨*ethno*centric⟩ [Greek *ethnos* "nation"]
eth•no•cen•tric \ˌeth-nō-'sen-trik\ *adj* : favoring especially one's own ethnic group ⟨*ethnocentric* views⟩
eth•nol•o•gy \eth-'näl-ə-jē\ *n* **1** : a science that deals with the origin, distribution, relations, and characteristics of human races **2** : the comparative study of cultures — **eth•no•log•ic** \ˌeth-nə-'läj-ik\ *or* **eth•no•log•i•cal** \-i-kəl\ *adj* — **eth•no•log•i•cal•ly** \-i-kə-lē, -klē\ *adv* — **eth•nol•o•gist** \eth-'näl-ə-jəst\ *n*
ethol•o•gy \ē-'thäl-ə-jē\ *n* : the scientific study of animal behavior [Latin *ethologia* "art of depicting character", from Greek *ēthologia*, from *ēthos* "character" + *-logia* "-logy"] — **etho•log•i•cal** \ˌē-thə-'läj-i-kəl, ˌeth-ə-\ *adj* — **ethol•o•gist** \ē-'thäl-ə-jəst\ *n*
eth•yl \'eth-əl\ *n* : a chemical radical C_2H_5 consisting of carbon and hydrogen [*ether* + *-yl*]
ethyl alcohol *n* : ALCOHOL 1a
ethyl cellulose *n* : any of various thermoplastic substances used especially in plastics and lacquers
eth•yl•ene \'eth-ə-ˌlēn\ *n* **1** : a colorless flammable gas C_2H_4 found in coal gas or obtained from petroleum hydrocarbons and used to ripen fruits or as an anesthetic **2** : a bivalent hydrocarbon radical C_2H_4 derived from ethane — **eth•yl•enic** \ˌeth-ə-'lē-nik\ *adj*

ethylene gly•col \-'glī-ˌkȯl, -ˌkōl\ *n* **:** a thick liquid alcohol $C_2H_6O_2$ used especially as an antifreeze

-et•ic \'et-ik\ *adj suffix* **:** -IC ⟨limnetic⟩ — often in adjectives corresponding to nouns ending in *-esis* ⟨genetic⟩ [Greek *-etikos, -ētikos*, from *-etos, -ētos*, ending of certain verbals]

eti•o•late \'ēt-ē-ə-ˌlāt\ *vt* **1 :** to make (a green plant) pale and spindling by lack of light **2 :** to make pale and sickly [French *étioler*] — **eti•o•la•tion** \ˌēt-ē-ə-'lā-shən\ *n*

eti•ol•o•gy \ˌēt-ē-'äl-ə-jē\ *n* **:** the cause or origin especially of a disease [Medieval Latin *aetiologia* "statement of causes", from Greek *aitiologia*, from *aitia* "cause"] — **eti•o•log•ic** \ˌēt-ē-ə-'läj-ik\ *or* **eti•o•log•i•cal** \-i-kəl\ *adj* — **eti•o•log•i•cal•ly** \-i-kə-lē, -i-klē\ *adv*

et•i•quette \'et-i-kət, -ˌket\ *n* **:** the body of rules governing the way in which people behave socially, ceremonially, or in public life [French *étiquette*, literally, "ticket"]

△ **origin** The primary meaning of French *étiquette* is "ticket, label attached to something for description or identification". It was once the practice in royal palaces of France to post notices that set down the proper forms to be observed at court. Such notices were called *étiquettes*. The word came to be used for the court ceremonial itself as well as the document that described it. It was this sense of French *étiquette* that English borrowed.

Eton collar \ˌēt-n-\ *n* **:** a large stiff turnover collar [*Eton* College, English public school]

Eton jacket *n* **:** a short black jacket with long sleeves, wide lapels, and an open front

Eton jacket

Etrus•can \i-'trəs-kən\ *n* **1 :** a native or inhabitant of ancient Etruria **2 :** the language of the Etruscans — **Etruscan** *adj*

-ette \'et, ˌet, ət, it\ *n suffix* **1 :** little one ⟨kitchenette⟩ **2 :** female ⟨drum majorette⟩ [Middle French, feminine of *-et*]

étude \'ā-ˌtüd, -ˌtyüd\ *n* **1 :** a piece of music for practice to develop technical skill **2 :** a composition built on a technical motif but played for its artistic value [French, literally, "study", from Middle French *estude, estudie*]

et•y•mol•o•gy \ˌet-ə-'mäl-ə-jē\ *n, pl* **-gies 1 :** the history of a word as shown by identifying its related forms in other languages and tracing these to their origin in a common form in an earlier parent language or by tracing the transmission of a word from one language to another **2 :** a branch of language study concerned with etymologies [Latin *etymologia*, from Greek, from *etymon* "the literal meaning of a word according to its origin", from *etymos* "true"] — **et•y•mo•log•i•cal** \-mə-'läj-i-kəl\ *adj* — **et•y•mo•log•i•cal•ly** \-'läj-i-kə-lē, -klē\ *adv* — **et•y•mol•o•gist** \ˌet-ə-'mäl-ə-jəst\ *n*

eu- *combining form* **1 :** well **:** easily **:** good — compare DYS- **2 :** true, truly ⟨*eu*caryote⟩ [Greek, "well, good"]

eu•ca•lypt \'yü-kə-ˌlipt\ *n* **:** EUCALYPTUS

eu•ca•lyp•tus \ˌyü-kə-'lip-təs\ *n, pl* **-ti** \-ˌtī, -ˌtē\ *or* **-tus•es :** any of a genus of mostly Australian evergreen trees of the myrtle family including many that are widely cultivated for their gums, resins, oils, and useful woods [*eu-* + Greek *kalyptos* "covered", from *kalyptein* "to conceal"; from the conical covering of the buds]

Eu•cha•rist \'yü-kə-rəst, -krəst\ *n* **:** COMMUNION 1a; *esp* **:** a Roman Catholic sacrament renewing Christ's sacrifice of his body and blood [Middle French *eucharistie*, from Late Latin *eucharistia*; from Greek, "gratitude, Eucharist", from *eu-* + *charis* "favor, grace, gratitude"] — **eu•cha•ris•tic** \ˌyü-kə-'ris-tik\ *adj, often cap*

eu•chre \'yü-kər\ *n* **:** a card game in which each player is dealt five cards and the player making trump must take three tricks to win a hand [origin unknown]

eu•clid•e•an \yu̇-'klid-ē-ən\ *adj, often cap* **:** of or relating to the geometry of Euclid

eu•gen•ic \yu̇-'jen-ik\ *adj* **1 :** relating to or fitted for the production of good offspring **2 :** of or relating to eugenics — **eu•gen•i•cal•ly** \-'jen-i-kə-lē, -klē\ *adv*

eu•gen•ics \yu̇-'jen-iks\ *n* **:** a science that deals with the improvement of hereditary qualities of a race or breed and especially of human beings — **eu•gen•ist** \yu̇-'jen-əst, 'yü-jə-nəst\ *also* **eu•gen•i•cist** \yu̇-'jen-ə-səst\ *n*

eu•gle•na \yu̇-'glē-nə\ *n* **:** any of a large genus of green freshwater flagellates often classed as algae [*eu-* + Greek *glēnē* "eyeball"] — **eu•gle•noid** \-ˌnȯid\ *adj or n*

euglenoid movement *n* **:** writhing protoplasmic movement typical of some euglenoid flagellates

eu•kary•ote *or* **eu•cary•ote** \yü-'kar-ē-ˌōt, -ē-ət\ *n* **:** an organism composed of one or more cells with visibly evident nuclei — compare PROKARYOTE [*eu-* + *kary-* + *-ote* (as in *zygote*)] — **eu•kary•ot•ic** *or* **eu•cary•ot•ic** \ˌyü-ˌkar-ē-'ät-ik\ *adj*

eu•lo•gize \'yü-lə-ˌjīz\ *vt* **:** to speak or write in high praise of **:** EXTOL — **eu•lo•gist** \-jəst\ *n* — **eu•lo•gis•tic** \ˌyü-lə-'jis-tik\ *adj* — **eu•lo•gis•ti•cal•ly** \-ti-kə-lē, -klē\ *adv*

eu•lo•gy \'yü-lə-jē\ *n, pl* **-gies 1 :** a speech or a writing in praise of a person or thing; *esp* **:** a formal speech in praise of a dead person **2 :** high praise

eu•nuch \'yü-nək\ *n* **:** a castrated man; *esp* **:** one placed in charge of a harem or employed as a court official [Latin *eunuchus*, from Greek *eunouchos*, from *eunē* "bed" + *echein* "to have, have charge of"]

eu•on•y•mus \yu̇-'än-ə-məs\ *n* **:** any of a genus of shrubs and small trees often grown as ornamentals [Latin *euonymos*, from Greek *euōnymos*, literally, "having an auspicious name", from *eu-* + *onyma* "name"]

eu•phe•mism \'yü-fə-ˌmiz-əm\ *n* **:** the substitution of an agreeable or inoffensive expression for one that may offend or suggest something unpleasant; *also* **:** an expression so substituted ⟨*pass away* is a widely used *euphemism* for *die*⟩ [Greek *euphēmismos*, from *eu-* + *phēmē* "speech", from *phanai* "to speak"] — **eu•phe•mis•tic** \ˌyü-fə-'mis-tik\ *adj* — **eu•phe•mis•ti•cal•ly** \-ti-kə-lē, -klē\ *adv*

eu•pho•ni•ous \yu̇-'fō-nē-əs\ *adj* **:** pleasing to the ear **:** smooth-sounding — **eu•pho•ni•ous•ly** *adv* — **eu•pho•ni•ous•ness** *n*

eu•pho•ni•um \-nē-əm\ *n* **:** a tenor tuba like a baritone but mellower in tone

euphonium

eu•pho•ny \'yü-fə-nē\ *n, pl* **-nies :** pleasing or sweet sound; *esp* **:** the effect of words so combined as to please the ear [French *euphonie*, from Late Latin *euphonia*, from Greek *euphōnia*, from *eu-* + *phōnē* "voice"] — **eu•phon•ic** \yu̇-'fän-ik\ *adj* — **eu•phon•i•cal•ly** \-'fän-i-kə-lē, -klē\ *adv*

eu•phor•bia \yu̇-'fȯr-bē-ə\ *n* **:** any of a genus of spurges that have milky juice and flowers without a calyx [Latin *euphorbea*, from *Euphorbus*, 1st century A.D. physician]

eu•pho•ria \yu̇-'fōr-ē-ə, -'fȯr-\ *n* **:** a strong feeling of well-being or elation [Greek, from *euphoros* "healthy", from *eu-* + *pherein* "to bear"] — **eu•phor•ic** \-'fȯr-ik, -'fär-\ *adj*

Eur•asian \yu̇-'rā-zhən, -shən\ *adj* **1 :** of or relating to Eurasia **2 :** of mixed European and Asian origin — **Eurasian** *n*

eu•re•ka \yu̇-'rē-kə\ *interj* — used to express triumph on a discovery [Greek *heurēka* "I have found", from *heuriskein* "to find"; from the exclamation attributed to Archimedes on his discovering a method for determining the purity of gold]

Eu•ro•pe•an \ˌyu̇r-ə-'pē-ən\ *n* **1 :** a native or inhabitant of Europe **2 :** a person of European descent — **European** *adj*

European corn borer *n* **:** an Old World moth whose larva is a major pest in eastern North America especially in the stems and crowns of Indian corn, dahlias, and potatoes

European plan *n* **:** a hotel plan whereby the daily rate covers only the cost of the room — compare AMERICAN PLAN

eu•ro•pi•um \yu̇-'rō-pē-əm\ *n* **:** a gray soft rare earth element — see ELEMENT table [New Latin, from *Europa* "Europe"]

eury- *combining form* **:** broad **:** wide ⟨*eury*haline⟩ [Greek *eurys*]

eu•ry•ha•line \ˌyu̇r-i-'hā-ˌlīn, -'hal-ˌīn\ *adj* **:** able to live in waters of a wide range of salinity

eu•ryp•ter•id \yu̇-'rip-tə-rəd\ *n* **:** any of an order (Eurypterida) of usually large aquatic Paleozoic arthropods related to the horseshoe crabs [derived from Greek *eurys* "broad" + *pteron* "wing"] — **eurypterid** *adj*

eu•sta•chian tube \yü-ˌstā-shən- *also* -ˌstā-kē-ən-\ *n, often cap E* : a tube connecting the middle ear with the throat and equalizing air pressure on both sides of the eardrum [Bartolommeo *Eustachio*, died 1574, Italian anatomist]

eu•stat•ic \yü-ˈstat-ik\ *adj* : relating to or characterized by worldwide change of sea level

eu•tha•na•sia \ˌyü-thə-ˈnā-zhə, -zhē-ə\ *n* : MERCY KILLING [Greek, "easy death", from *eu-* + *thanatos* "death"]

eu•tro•phic \yü-ˈtrō-fik\ *adj* : being a body of water rich in dissolved nutrients (as phosphates) but often shallow and seasonally deficient in oxygen [derived from Greek *eutrophos* "well nourished, nourishing", from *eu-* + *trephein* "to nourish"] — **eu•tro•phi•ca•tion** \-ˌtrō-fə-ˈkā-shən\ *n*

evac•u•ate \i-ˈvak-yə-ˌwāt\ *vb* **1** : to make empty **2** : to discharge waste matter from the body : VOID **3** : to remove something from especially by pumping **4 a** : to remove or withdraw from a military or occupation zone or from a dangerous area **b** : VACATE 2 [Latin *evacuare*, from *e-* + *vacuus* "empty"] — **evac•u•a•tion** \i-ˌvak-yə-ˈwā-shən\ *n* — **evac•u•a•tive** \i-ˈvak-yə-ˌwāt-iv\ *adj*

evac•u•ee \i-ˌvak-yə-ˈwē\ *n* : an evacuated person

evade \i-ˈvād\ *vb* **1** : to get away or avoid by skill or trickery ⟨*evade* a question⟩ **2** : to avoid facing up to ⟨*evade* responsibility⟩ **3** : BAFFLE, FOIL ⟨the problem *evades* all efforts at solution⟩ [Latin *evadere*, from *e-* + *vadere* "to go, walk"] — **evad•able** \i-ˈvād-ə-bəl\ *adj* — **evad•er** *n*

• **syn** ELUDE: EVADE implies adroitness, ingenuity, or lack of scruple in escaping or avoiding a pursuer or attacker, ELUDE implies a slippery or elusive quality that baffles attempts to seize or keep or identify the person or thing that escapes.

evag•i•nate \i-ˈvaj-ə-ˌnāt\ *vt* : to turn inside out [Latin *evaginare* "to unsheathe", from *e-* + *vagina* "sheath"] — **evag•i•na•tion** \i-ˌvaj-ə-ˈnā-shən\ *n*

eval•u•ate \i-ˈval-yə-ˌwāt\ *vt* **1** : to determine or fix the value of **2** : to examine and judge the quality or degree of **syn** see ESTIMATE — **eval•u•a•tion** \-ˌval-yə-ˈwā-shən\ *n* — **eval•u•a•tive** \-ˈval-yə-ˌwāt-iv\ *adj*

ev•a•nesce \ˌev-ə-ˈnes\ *vi* : to dissipate like vapor [Latin *evanescere*, from *e-* + *vanus* "empty"]

ev•a•nes•cence \ˌev-ə-ˈnes-ns\ *n* **1** : the process or fact of evanescing **2** : evanescent quality

ev•a•nes•cent \-nt\ *adj* : tending to vanish like vapor : not lasting : quickly passing ⟨*evanescent* pleasures⟩

evan•gel \i-ˈvan-jəl\ *n* : GOSPEL [Middle French *evangile*, from Late Latin *evangelium*, from Greek *euangelion* "good news, gospel", from *eu-* + *angelos* "messenger"]

evan•gel•i•cal \ˌē-ˌvan-ˈjel-i-kəl, ˌev-ən-\ *also* **evan•gel•ic** \-ˈjel-ik\ *adj* **1** : of, relating to, or in agreement with the Christian gospel especially as it is presented in the four Gospels **2** : PROTESTANT 1b **3** : emphasizing salvation by faith in the atoning death of Jesus Christ through personal conversion, the authority of Scripture, and the importance of preaching as contrasted with ritual **4** *often cap* **a** : FUNDAMENTALIST **b** : Low Church **5** : ZEALOUS — **Evan•gel•i•cal•ism** \-i-kə-ˌliz-əm\ *n* — **evan•gel•i•cal•ly** \-i-kə-lē, -klē\ *adv*

Evangelical *n* : one holding evangelical principles or belonging to an evangelical party or church

evan•ge•lism \i-ˈvan-jəˌliz-əm\ *n* **1** : the winning or revival of personal commitments to Christ **2** : militant or crusading zeal — **evan•ge•lis•tic** \i-ˌvan-jə-ˈlis-tik\ *adj* — **evan•ge•lis•ti•cal•ly** \-ti-kə-lē\ *adv*

evan•ge•list \i-ˈvan-jə-ləst\ *n* **1** *often cap* : a writer of any of the four Gospels **2** : one who evangelizes; *esp* : a preacher who goes about from place to place trying to awake religious enthusiasm

evan•ge•lize \i-ˈvan-jə-ˌlīz\ *vb* **1** : to preach the gospel **2** : to convert to Christianity — **evan•ge•li•za•tion** \-ˌvan-jə-lə-ˈzā-shən\ *n* — **evan•ge•liz•er** \-ˈvan-jə-ˌlī-zər\ *n*

evap•o•rate \i-ˈvap-ə-ˌrāt\ *vb* **1** : to change into vapor ⟨ether *evaporates* rapidly in air⟩; *also* : to pass off or cause to pass off in usually invisible minute particles **2 a** : to pass off or away : DISAPPEAR **b** : to diminish quickly **3** : to expel moisture from (as by heat) ⟨*evaporate* apples⟩ — **evap•o•ra•tion** \-ˌvap-ə-ˈrā-shən\ *n* — **evap•o•ra•tive** \-ˈvap-ə-ˌrāt-iv\ *adj* — **evap•o•ra•tor** \-ˌrāt-ər\ *n*

evaporated milk *n* : milk concentrated by evaporation without the addition of sugar to one half or less of its bulk

evap•o•rite \i-ˈvap-ə-ˌrīt\ *n* : a sedimentary rock (as gypsum) that originates by evaporation of seawater in an enclosed basin

eva•sion \i-ˈvā-zhən\ *n* **1** : the act or an instance of evading : ESCAPE ⟨tax *evasion*⟩ **2** : a means of evading [Late Latin *evasio*, from Latin *evadere* "to evade"]

eva•sive \i-ˈvā-siv, -ziv\ *adj* : tending or intended to evade : EQUIVOCAL — **eva•sive•ly** *adv* — **eva•sive•ness** *n*

eve \ˈēv\ *n* **1** : EVENING **2** : the evening or the day before a special day ⟨Christmas *Eve*⟩ **3** : the period immediately preceding an event [Middle English *even, eve*]

¹even \ˈē-vən\ *n, archaic* : EVENING [Middle English, from Old English *ǣfen*]

²even *adj* **1 a** : having a horizontal surface : FLAT ⟨*even* ground⟩ **b** : being without break or irregularity : SMOOTH **c** : being in the same plane or line ⟨houses *even* with each other⟩ **2** : being without variation : UNIFORM **3 a** : EQUAL, FAIR ⟨an *even* exchange⟩ **b** : leaving nothing due on either side : SQUARE **c** : BALANCED; *esp* : showing neither profit nor loss **4** : being exactly divisible by 2 ⟨*even* numbers⟩ **5** : EXACT, PRECISE ⟨an *even* dozen⟩ **6** : FIFTY-FIFTY 2 ⟨stands an *even* chance of winning⟩ [Old English *efen*] **syn** see STEADY — **even•ly** *adv* — **even•ness** \-vən-nəs\ *n*

³even *adv* **1 a** : PRECISELY, EXACTLY ⟨*even* as you and I⟩ **b** : at the very time ⟨*even* as the clock struck⟩ **2 a** — used as an intensive to indicate something unexpected ⟨respected *even* by their enemies⟩ **b** — used as an intensive to stress the comparative degree ⟨did *even* better⟩

⁴even *vb* **evened**; **even•ing** \ˈēv-ning, -ə-ning\ : to make or become even — **even•er** \ˈēv-nər, -ə-nər\ *n*

even•hand•ed \ˌē-vən-ˈhan-dəd\ *adj* : FAIR 5a, IMPARTIAL

eve•ning \ˈēv-ning\ *n* **1** : the latter part and close of the day and early part of the night **2** : the latter part ⟨the *evening* of life⟩ [derived from Old English *ǣfen* "evening"]

evening dress *n* : conventional dress for formal or semiformal evening social occasions

evening prayer *n, often cap E&P* : an evening service of the Anglican liturgy

evening primrose *n* : a coarse biennial herb with yellow flowers that open in the evening; *also* : any of several related plants

eve•nings \ˈēv-ningz\ *adv* : in the evening repeatedly ⟨goes bowling *evenings*⟩

evening star *n* : a bright planet (as Venus) seen in the western sky at or after sunset

even•song \ˈē-vən-ˌsȯng\ *n, often cap* **1** : VESPERS 1 **2** : EVENING PRAYER

event \i-ˈvent\ *n* **1 a** : something that happens : OCCURRENCE **b** : a noteworthy happening **c** : a social occasion or activity **2** : CASE 4, EVENTUALITY ⟨in the *event* of rain the picnic will be postponed⟩ **3** : any of the contests in a program of sports **4** : a subset of the possible outcomes of a statistical experiment ⟨7 is an *event* in the throwing of two dice⟩ [Latin *eventus*, from *evenire* "to happen", from *e-* + *venire* "to come"] **syn** see OCCURRENCE — **at all events** : in any case — **in any event** : in any case

event•ful \-fəl\ *adj* **1** : full of or rich in events ⟨an *eventful* day⟩ **2** : MOMENTOUS — **event•ful•ly** \-fə-lē\ *adv* — **event•ful•ness** *n*

even•tide \ˈē-vən-ˌtīd\ *n* : EVENING

even•tu•al \i-ˈvench-wəl, -ə-wəl; -ˈven-chəl\ *adj* : taking place at an unspecified later time : ULTIMATE ⟨*eventual* success⟩ — **even•tu•al•ly** \-ē\ *adv*

even•tu•al•i•ty \i-ˌven-chə-ˈwal-ət-ē\ *n, pl* **-ties** : something that may happen : POSSIBILITY

even•tu•ate \i-ˈven-chə-ˌwāt\ *vt* : to come out finally

ev•er \ˈev-ər\ *adv* **1** : ALWAYS ⟨*ever* faithful⟩ **2 a** : at any time ⟨seldom if *ever* home⟩ **b** : in any way ⟨how can I *ever* repay you⟩ **3** — used as an intensive especially with *so* ⟨*ever* so angry⟩ [Old English *ǣfre*]

ev•er•bloom•ing \ˌev-ər-ˈblü-ming\ *adj* : blooming more or less continuously throughout the growing season

ev•er•glade \ˈev-ər-ˌglād\ *n* : a low-lying tract of swampy or marshy land [the *Everglades*, Florida]

1**ev•er•green** \'ev-ər-ˌgrēn\ *adj* : having foliage that remains green and functional through more than one growing season ⟨most conifers are *evergreen* trees⟩ — compare DECIDUOUS

2**evergreen** *n* **1** : an evergreen plant; *also* : CONIFER **2** *pl* : twigs and branches of evergreen plants used for decoration

1**ev•er•last•ing** \ˌev-ər-'las-ting\ *adj* **1** : lasting or enduring through all time : ETERNAL **2 a** (1) : continuing long or indefinitely : PERPETUAL (2) : retaining form or color when dried ⟨*everlasting* flowers⟩ **b** : tediously persistent **3** : wearing indefinitely : DURABLE **syn** see ETERNAL — **ev•er•last•ing•ly** \-ting-lē\ *adv* — **ev•er•last•ing•ness** *n*

2**everlasting** *n* **1** *cap* : GOD 1 — used with *the* **2** : ETERNITY ⟨from *everlasting*⟩ **3 a** : a plant especially of the daisy family with everlasting flowers **b** : an everlasting flower

ev•er•more \ˌev-ər-'mōr, -'mȯr\ *adv* : at all times : FOREVER

evert \i-'vərt\ *vt* : to turn outward or inside out [Latin *evertere* "to overturn" (past participle *eversus*), from *e-* + *vertere* "to turn"] — **ever•si•ble** \-'vər-sə-bəl\ *adj* — **ever•sion** \-'vər-zhən\ *n*

ev•ery \'ev-rē\ *adj* **1** : being each individual or part of a group without exception **2** : COMPLETE, ENTIRE ⟨I have *every* confidence in you⟩ [Middle English *everich, every,* from Old English *ǣfre ǣlc,* from *ǣfre* "ever" + *ǣlc* "each"]

ev•ery•body \'ev-ri-ˌbäd-ē, -bəd-\ *pron* : every person

ev•ery•day \ˌev-rē-ˌdā\ *adj* : encountered or used routinely or typically : ORDINARY ⟨*everyday* clothes⟩

ev•ery•one \'ev-rē-wən, -ˌwən\ *pron* : EVERYBODY

ev•ery•thing \'ev-rē-ˌthing\ *pron* **1 a** : all that exists **b** : all that relates to the subject ⟨tell *everything*⟩ **2** : something that is most important or excellent : all that counts ⟨money isn't *everything*⟩

ev•ery•where \-ˌhweər, -ˌhwaər\ *adv* : in every place or part

evict \i-'vikt\ *vt* : to put (an occupant) out from property by legal process [Late Latin *evictus,* past participle of *evincere* "to evict", from Latin, "to vanquish", from *e-* + *vincere* "to conquer"] **syn** see EJECT — **evic•tion** \-'vik-shən\ *n* — **evic•tor** \-'vik-tər\ *n*

1**ev•i•dence** \'ev-əd-əns, -ə-ˌdens\ *n* **1 a** : an outward sign : INDICATION **b** : something that furnishes proof : TESTIMONY; *esp* : material legally submitted to a tribunal to determine the truth of a matter **2** : one who bears witness; *esp* : one who voluntarily confesses a crime and testifies for the prosecution against his accomplices — **ev•i•den•tial** \ˌev-ə-'den-chəl\ *adj* — **in evidence** : to be seen : CONSPICUOUS

2**evidence** *vt* : to offer evidence of : PROVE

ev•i•dent \'ev-əd-ənt, -ə-ˌdent\ *adj* : clear to the sight or understanding : PLAIN ⟨was *evident* that the children were twins⟩ [Middle French, from Latin *evidens,* from *e-* + *videns,* present participle of *vidēre* "to see"] **syn** see APPARENT — **ev•i•dent•ly** *adv*

1**evil** \'ē-vəl\ *adj* **evil•er** *or* **evil•ler; evil•est** *or* **evil•lest** **1 a** : not good morally : WICKED **b** : arising from bad character or conduct ⟨a person of *evil* reputation⟩ **2 a** : causing discomfort or repulsion : OFFENSIVE **b** : DISAGREEABLE ⟨in an *evil* temper⟩ **3 a** : causing harm : PERNICIOUS **b** : marked by misfortune : UNLUCKY ⟨an *evil* day⟩ [Old English *yfel*] — **evil•ly** \-vəl-lē, -və-\ *adv*

2**evil** *n* **1** : something that brings sorrow, distress, or calamity **2** : the fact of suffering, misfortune, and wrongdoing — **evil•do•er** \ˌē-vəl-'dü-ər\ *n* — **evil•do•ing** \-'dü-ing\ *n*

evil eye *n* : an eye or glance held to be capable of inflicting harm

evil–mind•ed \ˌē-vəl-'mīn-dəd\ *adj* : having an evil disposition or evil thoughts

evince \i-'vins\ *vt* **1** : to be evidence of : SHOW **2** : to display clearly : REVEAL [Latin *evincere* "to vanquish, win a point", from *e-* + *vincere* "to conquer"] — **evinc•i•ble** \i-'vin-sə-bəl\ *adj*

evis•cer•ate \i-'vis-ə-ˌrāt\ *vt* **1** : to take out the entrails of **2** : to deprive of vital content or force — **evis•cer•a•tion** \i-ˌvis-ə-'rā-shən\ *n*

evo•ca•tion \ˌē-vō-'kā-shən, ˌev-ə-\ *n* : the act or fact of evoking

evoke \i-'vōk\ *vt* **1** : to call forth or up: as **a** : CONJURE 2a ⟨*evoke* evil spirits⟩ **b** : to cite especially with approval : INVOKE **c** : to bring to mind ⟨this place *evokes* happy memories⟩ **2** : to recreate imaginatively [French *évoquer,* from Latin *evocare,* from *e-* + *vocare* "to call"] — **ev•o•ca•ble** \'ev-ə-kə-bəl, i-'vō-kə-\ *adj* — **evoc•a•tive** \i-'väk-ət-iv\ *adj* — **evoc•a•tive•ly** *adv* — **evo•ca•tor** \'ē-vō-ˌkāt-ər, 'ev-ə-\ *n*

ev•o•lu•tion \ˌev-ə-'lü-shən, ˌē-və-\ *n* **1 a** : a process of evolving or emitting ⟨*evolution* of a gas⟩ **b** : a process of change especially from a lower to a higher state : GROWTH **c** : something evolved **2** : one of a set of prescribed movements (as of a dancer) **3** : the process of working out or developing something (as an idea) **4** : the extraction of a mathematical root **5 a** : PHYLOGENY **b** : a theory that the various types of animals and plants have their origin in other preexisting types and that the distinguishable differences are due to changes in successive generations **6** : a process in which the whole universe is a progression of interrelated phenomena [Latin *evolutio* "unrolling", from *evolvere* "to unroll"] — **ev•o•lu•tion•ary** \-shə-ˌner-ē\ *adj* — **ev•o•lu•tion•ism** \-shə-ˌniz-əm\ *n* — **ev•o•lu•tion•ist** \-shə-nəst, -shnəst\ *n or adj*

evolve \i-'välv, -'vȯlv\ *vb* **1** : to give off : EMIT **2 a** : to arrive at through thought or study : work out ⟨*evolve* a plan⟩ **b** : to produce by natural evolutionary processes ⟨insects *evolved* wings⟩ **3** : to undergo evolutionary change ⟨species *evolve* continuously⟩ [Latin *evolvere* "to unroll", from *e-* + *volvere* "to roll"] — **evolve•ment** \-mənt\ *n*

ewe \'yü, 'yō\ *n* : the female of the sheep or a related animal especially when mature [Old English *ēowu*]

ew•er \'yü-ər, 'yu̇-ər, 'yu̇r\ *n* : a vase-shaped pitcher or jug [Anglo-French, from Old French *evier,* from Latin *aquarius* "of water", from *aqua* "water"]

ewer

ex \eks, ˌeks\ *prep* **1 a** : out of : FROM ⟨goods supplied *ex* stock⟩ **b** : from a specified dam ⟨a promising colt by Ranger *ex* Margot⟩ **2** : without an indicated value or right — used especially of securities ⟨*ex* dividend⟩ [Latin]

1**ex-** *prefix* **1** \e *also occurs in this prefix where only* i *is shown in entries below and* ks *sometimes occurs where only* gz *is shown*\ : out of : outside ⟨*exurb*⟩ **2** \eks, ˌeks, 'eks\ : former ⟨*ex*-president⟩ [Latin, "out, out of, thoroughly", from *ex* "out of, from"]

2**ex-** — see EXO-

ex•ac•er•bate \ig-'zas-ər-ˌbāt, ek-'sas-\ *vt* : to make more violent, bitter, or severe [Latin *exacerbare,* from *ex-* + *acerbus* "harsh, bitter", from *acer* "sharp"] — **ex•ac•er•ba•tion** \ig-ˌzas-ər-'bā-shən, ek-ˌsas-\ *n*

1**ex•act** \ig-'zakt\ *vt* **1** : to call for forcibly or urgently and obtain ⟨*exact* the full penalty of the law⟩ **2** : to call for as necessary, appropriate, or desirable [Latin *exactus,* past participle of *exigere* "to drive out, demand", from *ex-* + *agere* "to drive"] **syn** see DEMAND — **ex•act•able** \-'zak-tə-bəl\ *adj*

2**exact** *adj* **1** : showing strict, particular, and complete accordance with fact ⟨*exact* knowledge⟩ **2 a** : marked by thorough consideration or minute measurement of small factual details ⟨build an *exact* replica⟩ **b** : not incomplete or approximate ⟨*exact* measurements⟩ **syn** see CORRECT — **exact•ness** \-'zakt-nəs -'zak-\ *n*

ex•act•ing \ig-'zak-ting\ *adj* **1** : making severe demands upon a person : TRYING ⟨an *exacting* teacher⟩ **2** : requiring precise accuracy ⟨*exacting* work⟩ — **ex•act•ing•ly** \-ting-lē\ *adv* — **ex•act•ing•ness** *n*

ex•ac•tion \ig-'zak-shən\ *n* **1** : the act or process of exacting especially by way of extortion **2** : something exacted; *esp* : something demanded with compelling force

ex•ac•ti•tude \ig-'zak-tə-ˌtüd, -ˌtyüd\ *n* : the quality or an instance of being exact

ex•act•ly \ig-'zak-tlē, -lē\ *adv* **1 a** : in an exact manner : PRECISELY ⟨copy *exactly*⟩ **b** : ALTOGETHER ⟨not *exactly* what I had in mind⟩ **2** : quite so — used to express agreement

exact science *n* : a science (as physics, chemistry, or astronomy) whose laws are capable of expression in accurately measured quantities

ex•ag•ger•ate \ig-'zaj-ə-ˌrāt\ *vb* **1** : to enlarge a fact beyond what is actual or true : OVERSTATE **2** : to enlarge or increase especially beyond the normal [Latin *exaggerare,* literally, "to heap up", from *ex-* + *agger* "heap"] — **ex•ag•ger•at•ed•ly**

\-ˌrāt-əd-lē\ *adv* — **ex•ag•ger•a•tion** \-ˌzaj-ə-ˈrā-shən\ *n* — **ex•ag•ger•a•tor** \-ˈzaj-ə-ˌrāt-ər\ *n*

ex•alt \ig-ˈzȯlt\ *vt* **1** : to raise high : ELEVATE **2** : to raise in rank, power, or character **3** : to elevate by praise or in estimation : GLORIFY [Latin *exaltare,* from *ex-* + *altus* "high"] — **ex•alt•er** *n*

ex•al•ta•tion \ˌeg-ˌzȯl-ˈtā-shən\ *n* **1** : the act of exalting : the state of being exalted **2** : a greatly heightened sense of well-being, power, or importance

ex•am \ig-ˈzam\ *n* : EXAMINATION

ex•am•i•na•tion \ig-ˌzam-ə-ˈnā-shən\ *n* **1** : the act or process of examining : the state of being examined **2** : an exercise designed to examine progress or test qualification or knowledge **3** : a formal interrogation — **ex•am•i•na•tion•al** \-shnəl, -shən-l\ *adj*

ex•am•ine \ig-ˈzam-ən\ *vb* **1 a** : to inspect closely ⟨*examine* rock specimens⟩ **b** : to test the condition of ⟨have your eyes *examined*⟩ **c** : to inquire into carefully : INVESTIGATE **2** : to question closely in order to determine progress, fitness, or knowledge ⟨*examine* a class in arithmetic⟩ [Middle French *examiner,* from Latin *examinare,* from *examen* "tongue of a balance, examination", from *exigere* "to drive out, weigh"] **syn** see SCRUTINIZE — **ex•am•in•er** *n*

ex•am•ple \ig-ˈzam-pəl\ *n* **1** : a sample of something taken to show what the whole is like ⟨a striking *example* of scientific method⟩ **2** : something to be imitated : MODEL ⟨a good *example*⟩ ⟨avoid bad *examples*⟩ **3** : punishment inflicted on someone as a warning to others **4** : a problem to be solved in order to show how a rule works ⟨an *example* in arithmetic⟩ [Middle French, from Latin *exemplum,* from *eximere* "to take out", from *ex-* + *emere* "to take"] **syn** see INSTANCE

ex•arch \ˈek-ˌsärk\ *n* : an Eastern bishop ranking below a patriarch and above a metropolitan; *esp* : the head of an independent church [Late Latin *exarchus,* from Greek *exarchos* "leader", from *ex-* "ex-" + *archein* "to begin, rule"] — **ex•ar•chal** \ek-ˈsär-kəl\ *adj* — **ex•arch•ate** \ˈek-ˌsär-kət\ *n* — **ex•ar•chy** \ˈek-ˌsär-kē\ *n*

ex•as•per•ate \ig-ˈzas-pə-ˌrāt\ *vt* **1** : to make angry : ENRAGE **2** : to cause irritation or annoyance to [Latin *exasperare,* from *ex-* + *asper* "rough"] **syn** see IRRITATE

ex•as•per•a•tion \ig-ˌzas-pə-ˈrā-shən\ *n* **1** : the state of being exasperated **2** : the action or an instance of exasperating

Ex•cal•i•bur \ek-ˈskal-ə-bər\ *n* : the legendary sword of King Arthur [Old French *Escalibor,* from Medieval Latin *Caliburnus*]

ex ca•the•dra \ˌeks-kə-ˈthē-drə\ *adv or adj* : officially and with authority ⟨*ex cathedra* pronouncements⟩ [New Latin, literally, "from the chair"]

ex•ca•vate \ˈek-skə-ˌvāt\ *vt* **1** : to hollow out : form a hole in ⟨*excavate* a hillside⟩ **2** : to make by hollowing out ⟨*excavate* a tunnel⟩ **3** : to dig out and remove ⟨*excavate* sand⟩ **4** : to uncover by digging away covering earth [Latin *excavare,* from *ex-* + *cavare* "to make hollow", from *cavus* "hollow"] — **ex•ca•va•tor** \-ˌvāt-ər\ *n*

ex•ca•va•tion \ˌek-skə-ˈvā-shən\ *n* **1** : the act or process of excavating **2** : a hollowed-out place formed by excavating

ex•ceed \ik-ˈsēd\ *vt* **1** : to extend outside of ⟨the river will *exceed* its banks⟩ **2** : to be greater than or superior to : SURPASS ⟨the cost *exceeded* our funds⟩ **3** : to go beyond a limit set by ⟨*exceed* one's authority⟩ [Middle French *exceder,* from Latin *excedere,* from *ex-* + *cedere* "to go"]

• **syn** EXCEL, SURPASS, TRANSCEND: EXCEED implies going beyond a limit or standard set by authority, custom, or previous achievement ⟨*exceed* last year's production⟩ EXCEL implies preeminence in achievement or quality ⟨*excelling* in athletics⟩ ⟨*excels* in writing dialogue⟩ SURPASS suggests superiority in quality, merit, or skill; TRANSCEND implies a rising or extending notably above or beyond ordinary limits ⟨writing that *transcends* prosaic statement⟩

ex•ceed•ing *adj* : exceptional in amount, quality, or degree

ex•ceed•ing•ly \ik-ˈsēd-ing-lē\ *or* **ex•ceed•ing** *adv* : to an extreme degree : EXTREMELY

ex•cel \ik-ˈsel\ *vb* **ex•celled; ex•cel•ling** : to outdo others (as in good qualities or ability) : SURPASS ⟨*excel* in math⟩ ⟨a jump *excelling* the previous record⟩ [Latin *excellere,* from *ex-* + *-cellere* "to rise, project"] **syn** see EXCEED

ex•cel•lence \ˈek-sə-ləns, -sləns\ *n* **1** : the quality of being excellent **2** : an excellent or valuable quality : VIRTUE **3** *cap* : EXCELLENCY 2

ex•cel•len•cy \-sə-lən-sē, -slən-\ *n, pl* **-cies 1** : outstanding or valuable quality — usually used in pl. **2** *cap* — used as a form of address for a high dignitary of state (as a foreign ambassador) or church (as a Roman Catholic bishop) ⟨Your *Excellency*⟩ ⟨His *Excellency*⟩ ⟨Her *Excellency*⟩

ex•cel•lent \ˈek-sə-lənt, -slənt\ *adj* : very good of its kind : FIRST-CLASS — **ex•cel•lent•ly** *adv*

ex•cel•si•or \ik-ˈsel-sē-ər\ *n* : fine curled wood shavings used especially for packing fragile items [trade name, from Latin, "higher", from *excelsus* "high", from *excellere* "to excel"]

[1]**ex•cept** \ik-ˈsept\ *vt* : to take or leave out from a number or a whole : EXCLUDE [Middle French *excepter,* from Latin *exceptare,* from *excipere* "to take out, except", from *ex-* + *capere* "to take"]

[2]**except** *also* **ex•cept•ing** *prep* : with the exclusion or exception of ⟨everybody *except* you⟩

[3]**except** *also* **excepting** *conj* **1** : UNLESS ⟨*except* you repent⟩ **2** : [3]ONLY b ⟨I would go *except* it's too far⟩

ex•cep•tion \ik-ˈsep-shən\ *n* **1** : the act of excepting : EXCLUSION **2** : one that is excepted **3** : something offered as objection or taken as objectionable

ex•cep•tion•able \ik-ˈsep-shə-nə-bəl, -shnə-\ *adj* : likely to cause objection : OBJECTIONABLE — **ex•cep•tion•ably** \-blē\ *adv*

ex•cep•tion•al \ik-ˈsep-shnəl, -shən-l\ *adj* **1** : forming an exception : RARE **2** : better than average : SUPERIOR **3** : deviating from the norm; *esp* : below average ⟨schools for *exceptional* children⟩ — **ex•cep•tion•al•ly** \-ē\ *adv* — **ex•cep•tion•al•ness** *n*

[1]**ex•cerpt** \ek-ˈsərpt, eg-ˈzərpt, ˈek-ˌ, ˈeg-ˌ\ *vt* : to select (a passage) for quoting : EXTRACT [Latin *excerpere,* from *ex-* + *carpere* "to gather, pluck"]

[2]**ex•cerpt** \ˈek-ˌsərpt, ˈeg-ˌzərpt\ *n* : a passage selected or copied : EXTRACT

[1]**ex•cess** \ik-ˈses, ˈek-ˌ\ *n* **1 a** : the state or an instance of surpassing usual limits : SUPERFLUITY **b** : the amount or degree by which one thing or quantity exceeds another **2** : INTEMPERANCE [Late Latin *excessus,* from Latin *excedere* "to exceed"]

[2]**excess** *adj* : being more than the usual, proper, or specified amount ⟨charges for *excess* baggage⟩

ex•ces•sive \ik-ˈses-iv\ *adj* : exceeding the usual, proper, or normal — **ex•ces•sive•ly** *adv* — **ex•ces•sive•ness** *n*

• **syn** EXCESSIVE, EXORBITANT, INORDINATE, EXTRAVAGANT mean going beyond a normal limit. EXCESSIVE implies an amount or degree too great to be reasonable or acceptable ⟨*excessive* bail was required⟩ EXORBITANT applies to what is grossly excessive ⟨*exorbitant* demands⟩ INORDINATE implies an exceeding of the limits dictated by reason or good judgment ⟨an *inordinate* appetite⟩ ⟨*inordinate* desire for power⟩ EXTRAVAGANT implies an indifference to restraints imposed by truth, prudence, or good taste ⟨*extravagant* purchases⟩

[1]**ex•change** \iks-ˈchānj, ˈeks-ˌ\ *n* **1** : a giving or taking one thing in return for another : TRADE **2** : the act of substituting one thing for another **3** : something offered, given, or received in an exchange **4 a** : funds payable currently at a distant point in foreign or domestic currency **b** (1) : interchange of two kinds of money (as money of two different countries) with allowance for difference in value (2) : the amount of one currency that will buy a given amount of another **5** : a place where things or services are exchanged: as **a** : an organized market or center for trading in securities or commodities **b** : a central office in which telephone lines are connected to permit communication

[2]**exchange** *vt* **1 a** : to give in exchange : TRADE ⟨*exchange* a knife for a book⟩ **b** : to replace by other merchandise ⟨*exchange* this shirt for one in a larger size⟩ **2** : to part with for a substitute ⟨*exchange* future security for immediate pleasure⟩ — **ex•change•able** \-ə-bəl\ *adj* — **ex•chang•er** *n*

exchange student *n* : a student from a usually foreign country received into an educational institution in exchange for a student sent to that foreign country

ex•che•quer \ˈeks-ˌchek-ər, iks-ˈ\ *n* **1** : the department of the British government concerned with the receipt and care of the

\ə\ **abut**	\aù\ **out**	\i\ **tip**	\ȯ\ **saw**	\ù\ **foot**
\ər\ **further**	\ch\ **chin**	\ī\ **life**	\ȯi\ **coin**	\y\ **yet**
\a\ **mat**	\e\ **pet**	\j\ **job**	\th\ **thin**	\yü\ **few**
\ā\ **take**	\ē\ **easy**	\ng\ **sing**	\t͟h\ **this**	\yù\ **cure**
\ä\ **cot, cart**	\g\ **go**	\ō\ **bone**	\ü\ **food**	\zh\ **vision**

national revenue **2 :** TREASURY; *esp* **:** a national or royal treasury **3 :** money available **:** FUNDS **[**Anglo-French *escheker,* from Old French *eschequier* "chessboard, counting table", from *eschec* "check"**]**

1ex•cise \ˈek-ˌsīz, -ˌsīs\ *n* **:** an internal tax levied on the manufacture, sale, or consumption of a commodity within a country **[**obsolete Dutch *excijs***]**

2ex•cise \ek-ˈsīz\ *vt* **:** to remove by cutting out ⟨*excise* a tumor⟩ **[**Latin *excisus,* past participle of *excidere* "to excise", from *ex-* + *caedere* "to cut"**]** — **ex•ci•sion** \-ˈsizh-ən\ *n*

ex•cit•able \ik-ˈsīt-ə-bəl\ *adj* **:** readily roused into action or an active state; *esp* **:** capable of activation by and reaction to stimuli — **ex•cit•abil•i•ty** \-ˌsīt-ə-ˈbil-ət-ē\ *n*

ex•ci•ta•tion \ˌek-ˌsī-ˈtā-shən, ˌek-sə-\ *n* **:** EXCITEMENT; *esp* **:** the irritability induced in protoplasm by a stimulus

ex•cit•ato•ry \ik-ˈsīt-ə-ˌtōr-ē, -ˌtȯr-\ *adj* **:** tending to produce or marked by usually physiological excitation

ex•cite \ik-ˈsīt\ *vt* **1 a :** to call to activity **b :** to rouse to feeling **2 a :** ENERGIZE **b :** to produce a magnetic field in **3 a :** to increase the activity of (as nervous tissue) **b :** to arouse (as an emotional response) by appropriate stimuli **4 :** to raise (as an atom) to a higher energy level **[**Middle French *exciter,* from Latin *excitare,* from *ex-* + *citare* "to rouse"**] syn** see PROVOKE — **ex•cit•er** \-ˈsīt-ər\ *n*

ex•cit•ed \-ˈsīt-əd\ *adj* **:** having or showing strong feeling **:** worked up — **ex•cit•ed•ly** *adv*

ex•cite•ment \ik-ˈsīt-mənt\ *n* **1 :** the act of exciting **:** the state of being excited **2 :** something that excites

ex•cit•ing \-ˈsīt-ing\ *adj* **:** causing excitement **:** STIRRING — **ex•cit•ing•ly** \-ing-lē\ *adv*

ex•claim \iks-ˈklām\ *vb* **1 :** to speak or cry out in strong or sudden emotion **2 :** to speak loudly or forcefully **[**Middle French *exclamer,* from Latin *exclamare,* from *ex-* + *clamare* "to cry out"**]**

ex•cla•ma•tion \ˌeks-klə-ˈmā-shən\ *n* **1 :** a sharp or sudden utterance **:** OUTCRY **2 :** forceful expression of protest or complaint

exclamation point *n* **:** a punctuation mark ! used chiefly after an exclamation to show forceful utterance or strong feeling

ex•clam•a•to•ry \iks-ˈklam-ə-ˌtōr-ē, -ˌtȯr-\ *adj* **:** containing, expressing, using, or relating to exclamation

ex•clude \iks-ˈklüd\ *vt* **1 a :** to shut out **b :** to bar from participation, consideration, or inclusion **2 :** to put out **:** EXPEL **[**Latin *excludere* (past participle *exclusus*), from *ex-* + *claudere* "to close"**]** — **ex•clud•able** \-ˈklüd-ə-bəl\ *adj* — **ex•clud•er** *n* — **ex•clu•sion** \-ˈklü-zhən\ *n*

ex•clu•sive \iks-ˈklü-siv, -ziv\ *adj* **1 :** excluding or inclined to exclude certain persons or classes (as from ownership, membership, or privileges) **:** catering to a distinct and especially a fashionable class ⟨an *exclusive* neighborhood⟩ **2 :** SOLE, SINGLE ⟨*exclusive* use of a beach⟩ **3 :** COMPLETE, UNDIVIDED ⟨give me your *exclusive* attention⟩ **4 :** not taking account **:** not inclusive ⟨for five days *exclusive* of today⟩ — **ex•clu•sive•ly** *adv* — **ex•clu•sive•ness** *n*

ex•cog•i•tate \eks-ˈkäj-ə-ˌtāt\ *vt* **:** to think out **:** DEVISE — **ex•cog•i•ta•tion** \ˌeks-ˌkäj-ə-ˈtā-shən\ *n* — **ex•cog•i•ta•tive** \eks-ˈkäj-ə-ˌtāt-iv\ *adj*

ex•com•mu•ni•cate \ˌeks-kə-ˈmyü-nə-ˌkāt\ *vt* **:** to deprive officially of the rights of church membership — **ex•com•mu•ni•ca•tion** \-ˌmyü-nə-ˈkā-shən\ *n* — **ex•com•mu•ni•ca•tor** \-ˈmyü-nə-ˌkāt-ər\ *n*

ex•co•ri•ate \ek-ˈskōr-ē-ˌāt, -ˈskȯr-\ *vt* **1 :** to wear off the skin of **:** ABRADE **2 :** to censure scathingly **[**Late Latin *excoriare,* from Latin *ex-* + *corium* "skin, hide"**]** — **ex•co•ri•a•tion** \ek-ˌskōr-ē-ˈā-shən, -ˌskȯr-\ *n*

ex•cre•ment \ˈek-skrə-mənt\ *n* **:** waste matter discharged from the body and especially from the alimentary canal **[**Latin *excrementum,* from *excernere* "to discharge"**]** — **ex•cre•men•tal** \ˌek-skrə-ˈment-l\ *adj*

ex•cres•cence \ek-ˈskres-ns\ *n* **:** OUTGROWTH; *esp* **:** an abnormal outgrowth (as a wart) on the body

ex•cres•cent \-nt\ *adj* **:** being or forming an excrescence **[**Latin *excrescere* "to grow out", from *ex-* + *crescere* "to grow"**]** — **ex•cres•cent•ly** *adv*

ex•cre•ta \ek-ˈskrēt-ə\ *n pl* **:** waste matter eliminated or separated from an organism

ex•crete \ek-ˈskrēt\ *vt* **:** to separate and eliminate (waste) from the blood or tissues or from the active protoplasm usually in the form of sweat or urine **[**Latin *excretus,* past participle of *excernere* "to sift out, discharge", from *ex-* + *cernere* "to sift"**]** — **ex•cret•er** *n*

ex•cre•tion \ek-ˈskrē-shən\ *n* **1 :** the act or process of excreting **2 :** excreted matter

ex•cre•to•ry \ˈek-skrə-ˌtōr-ē, -ˌtȯr-\ *adj* **:** of, relating to, or functioning in excretion

ex•cru•ci•ate \ik-ˈskrü-shē-ˌāt\ *vt* **:** to subject to intense pain or mental distress **[**Latin *excruciare,* from *ex-* + *cruciare* "to crucify", from *cruc-, crux* "cross"**]** — **ex•cru•ci•a•tion** \-ˌskrü-shē-ˈā-shən, -sē-ˈā-\ *n*

ex•cru•ci•at•ing \-ˈskrü-shē-ˌāt-ing\ *adj* **1 :** causing great pain or mental distress **:** AGONIZING **2 :** very intense **:** EXTREME — **ex•cru•ci•at•ing•ly** \-ing-lē\ *adv*

ex•cul•pate \ˈek-skəl-ˌpāt, -ˌskəl-, ek-ˈ\ *vt* **:** to clear from alleged fault or guilt **[**derived from Latin *ex-* + *culpa* "blame"**]** — **ex•cul•pa•tion** \ˌek-skəl-ˈpā-shən, -ˌskəl-\ *n* — **ex•cul•pa•to•ry** \ek-ˈskəl-pə-ˌtōr-ē, -ˌtȯr-\ *adj*

ex•cur•rent \ek-ˈskər-ənt, -ˈskə-rənt\ *adj* **1 :** having a straight main stem that extends without forking to the top ⟨the spruce is an *excurrent* tree⟩ — compare DELIQUESCENT **2 :** characterized by a current that flows outward ⟨*excurrent* canals of a sponge⟩

ex•cur•sion \ik-ˈskər-zhən\ *n* **1 a :** a going out or forth **:** EXPEDITION **b :** a usually brief pleasure trip; *esp* **:** such a trip at special reduced rates **2 :** departure from a direct or proper course; *esp* **:** DIGRESSION **[**Latin *excursio,* from *excurrere* "to run out", from *ex-* + *currere* "to run"**]**

ex•cur•sion•ist \ik-ˈskərzh-nəst, -ə-nəst\ *n* **:** a person who goes on an excursion

ex•cur•sive \ik-ˈskər-siv\ *adj* **:** constituting a digression **:** characterized by digression — **ex•cur•sive•ly** *adv* — **ex•cur•sive•ness** *n*

ex•cur•sus \ik-ˈskər-səs\ *n, pl* **ex•cur•sus•es** *also* **ex•cur•sus** \-səs, -ˌsüs\ **:** an appendix or a digression containing further exposition of some point or topic **[**Latin, "digression", from *excurrere* "to run out"**]**

1ex•cuse \ik-ˈskyüz\ *vt* **1 :** to make apology for **:** try to remove blame from ⟨*excuse* oneself for being late⟩ **2 :** to accept an excuse for **:** PARDON **3 :** to free or let off from doing something ⟨*excuse* a person from a debt⟩ **4 :** to serve as an acceptable reason or explanation for (something said or done) **:** JUSTIFY ⟨nothing can *excuse* dishonesty⟩ **[**Old French *excuser,* from Latin *excusare,* from *ex-* + *causa* "cause, explanation"**]** — **ex•cus•able** \-ˈskyü-zə-bəl\ *adj* — **ex•cus•ably** \-blē\ *adv* — **ex•cus•er** *n*

• **syn** CONDONE, PARDON, FORGIVE: EXCUSE implies an overlooking of a fault, omission, or failure without censure or due punishment; CONDONE suggests accepting without protest or censure a reprehensible act or condition ⟨*condone* the use of drugs⟩ PARDON implies freeing from penalty due for admitted or proved offense; FORGIVE implies a sincere change of feeling that makes no claim to retaliation and gives up resentment or desire for revenge.

2ex•cuse \ik-ˈskyüs\ *n* **1 :** the act of excusing **2 a :** something offered as justification or as grounds for being excused **b :** a note of explanation of an absence **3 :** JUSTIFICATION 2b, REASON **syn** see APOLOGY

ex•ec \ig-ˈzek\ *n* **:** EXECUTIVE OFFICER

ex•e•cra•ble \ˈek-si-krə-bəl\ *adj* **:** DETESTABLE — **ex•e•cra•ble•ness** *n* — **ex•e•cra•bly** \-blē\ *adv*

ex•e•crate \ˈek-sə-ˌkrāt\ *vt* **1 :** to declare to be evil or detestable **2 :** to detest utterly **[**Latin *exsecrari* "to put under a curse", from *ex-* + *sacer* "sacred"**]** — **ex•e•cra•tion** \ˌek-sə-ˈkrā-shən\ *n* — **ex•e•cra•tor** \ˈek-sə-ˌkrāt-ər\ *n*

ex•e•cute \ˈek-sə-ˌkyüt\ *vt* **1 :** to put into effect **:** carry out **:** PERFORM **2 :** to do what is provided or required by ⟨execute a *decree*⟩ **3 :** to put to death according to legal orders **4 :** to make or produce especially by carrying out a design **5 :** to perform what is required to give legal force to ⟨*execute* a deed⟩ **[**Middle French *executer,* derived from Latin *exsequi,* from *ex-* + *sequi* "to follow"**]**

ex•e•cu•tion \ˌek-sə-ˈkyü-shən\ *n* **1 :** the act or process of executing **:** PERFORMANCE ⟨put a plan into *execution*⟩ **2 :** a putting to death as a legal penalty **3 :** a judicial writ empowering an officer to carry out a judgment **4 :** the act or mode or result of performance in something requiring special skill **5 :** effective or destructive action

ex•e•cu•tion•er \-ˈkyü-shə-nər, -shnər\ *n* **:** one that executes; *esp* **:** one who puts into effect a sentence of death

[1]**ex•ec•u•tive** \ig-ˈzek-yət-iv, -ˈzek-ət-\ *adj* **1 :** designed for or relating to the execution of affairs ⟨*executive* ability⟩ **2 :** of or relating to the execution of the laws and the conduct of public affairs **3 :** of or relating to an executive

[2]**executive** *n* **1 :** the executive branch of a government **2 :** an individual or group that directs an organization **3 :** one who holds a position of administrative or managerial responsibility

executive officer *n* **:** the officer second in command of a military or naval unit

executive session *n* **:** a usually closed session (as of a legislative body)

ex•ec•u•tor \ig-ˈzek-yət-ər, -ˈzek-ət-, *in sense 1 also* ˈek-sə-ˌkyüt-\ *n* **1 :** one that executes something **2 :** the person named in a will to carry out its provisions

ex•ec•u•trix \ig-ˈzek-yə-ˌtriks, -ˈzek-ə-\ *n, pl* **ex•ec•u•trix•es** *or* **ex•ec•u•tri•ces** \-ˌzek-yə-ˈtrī-ˌsēz, -ˌzek-ə-\ **:** a woman who is an executor

ex•e•ge•sis \ˌek-sə-ˈjē-səs\ *n, pl* **-ge•ses** \-ˈjē-ˌsēz\ **:** explanation or critical interpretation of a text [Greek *exēgēsis,* from *exēgeisthai* "to explain, interpret", from *ex-* "ex-" + *hēgeisthai* "to lead"] — **ex•e•get•ic** \-ˈjet-ik\ *or* **ex•e•get•i•cal** \-ˈjet-i-kəl\ *adj* — **ex•e•get•i•cal•ly** \-i-kə-lē, -klē\ *adv*

ex•e•gete \ˈek-sə-ˌjēt\ *n* **:** one who practices exegesis

ex•em•plar \ig-ˈzem-ˌplär, -plər\ *n* **1 a :** one that serves as a model or pattern; *esp* **:** an ideal model **b :** ARCHETYPE **2 :** a typical instance **:** EXAMPLE; *esp* **:** a typical or standard specimen [Latin, from *exemplum* "example"]

ex•em•pla•ry \ig-ˈzem-plə-rē\ *adj* **1 a :** serving as a pattern **b :** deserving imitation **2 :** serving as a warning **3 :** serving as an example, instance, or illustration — **ex•em•plar•i•ly** \ˌeg-zəm-ˈpler-ə-lē\ *adv* — **ex•em•pla•ri•ness** \ig-ˈzem-plə-rē-nəs\ *n*

ex•em•pli•fy \ig-ˈzem-plə-ˌfī\ *vt* **-fied; -fy•ing 1 :** to show or illustrate by example **2 :** to serve as an example of — **ex•em•pli•fi•ca•tion** \-ˌzem-plə-fə-ˈkā-shən\ *n*

ex•em•pli gra•tia \ig-ˌzem-plē-ˈgrät-ē-ˌä\ *adv* **:** for example [Latin]

[1]**ex•empt** \ig-ˈzempt\ *adj* **:** free or released from an obligation or requirement to which others are subject [Latin *exemptus,* past participle of *eximere* "to take out", from *ex-* + *emere* "to take"]

[2]**exempt** *vt* **:** to make exempt

ex•emp•tion \ig-ˈzem-shən, -ˈzemp-\ *n* **1 :** the act of exempting **:** the state of being exempt **2 :** something exempted; *esp* **:** a source or an amount of income exempted from taxation

ex•e•quy \ˈek-sə-kwē\ *n, pl* **-quies :** a funeral rite — usually used in pl. [Latin *exsequiae,* pl., from *exsequi* "to follow out"]

[1]**ex•er•cise** \ˈek-sər-ˌsīz\ *n* **1 :** the act of bringing into play or realizing in action **:** USE **2 a :** regular or repeated use of a mental faculty or bodily organ **b :** bodily exertion for the sake of physical fitness **3 :** something performed or practiced in order to develop, improve, or display a specific power or skill **:** EXAMPLE ⟨10 *exercises* for math homework⟩ **4 a :** a drill carried out for training and discipline **b** *pl* **:** a program including speeches, announcements of awards and honors, and various traditional practices [Middle French *exercice,* from Latin *exercitium,* from *exercēre* "to drive on, keep busy", from *ex-* + *arcēre* "to hold off"]

[2]**exercise** *vb* **1 :** to bring to bear **:** EXERT ⟨*exercise* patience⟩ **2 a :** to use repeatedly in order to strengthen or develop ⟨*exercise* one's wits⟩ **b :** to train (as troops) by drills **c :** to go or put through exercises **:** give or take exercise ⟨*exercise* a dog⟩ **3 :** to engage the attention of; *esp* **:** to cause anxiety, alarm, or indignation in ⟨citizens *exercised* about pollution⟩ — **ex•er•cis•able** \-ˈsī-zə-bəl\ *adj* — **ex•er•cis•er** *n*

ex•ert \ig-ˈzərt\ *vt* **1 :** to put forth (as strength, force, power, or influence) **:** bring into play **2 :** to put (oneself) into action or to tiring effort [Latin *exsertus,* past participle of *exserere* "to thrust out", from *ex-* + *serere* "to join"]

ex•er•tion \ig-ˈzər-shən\ *n* **:** the act or an instance of exerting; *esp* **:** laborious or perceptible effort **syn** see EFFORT

ex•e•unt \ˈek-sē-ənt, -sē-ˌənt\ — used as a stage direction to specify that all or certain named characters leave the stage [Latin, "they go out", from *exire* "to go out", from *ex-* + *ire* "to go"]

ex•fo•li•ate \eks-ˈfō-lē-ˌāt, ˈeks-\ *vb* **:** to shed or remove in thin layers or scales — **ex•fo•li•a•tion** \ˌeks-ˌfō-lē-ˈā-shən\ *n* — **ex•fo•li•a•tive** \eks-ˈfō-lē-ˌāt-iv\ *adj*

ex•hal•ant \eks-ˈhā-lənt\ *adj* **:** bearing out or outward ⟨an *exhalant* siphon of a clam⟩

ex•ha•la•tion \ˌeks-ə-ˈlā-shən, -hə-ˈlā-\ *n* **:** an act or product of exhaling

ex•hale \eks-ˈhāl\ *vb* **1 :** to breathe out **2 :** to send forth (as gas or odor) **:** EMIT ⟨the fragrance that flowers *exhale*⟩ **3 :** to rise or be given off as vapor [Latin *exhalare,* from *ex-* + *halare* "to breathe"]

[1]**ex•haust** \ig-ˈzȯst\ *vb* **1 a :** to draw off or let out completely ⟨*exhaust* the air from the jar⟩ **b :** to empty by drawing something from; *esp* **:** to create a vacuum in **2 a :** to use up the whole supply of **b :** to deprive wholly of (as strength, patience, or resources) **3 a :** to develop (a subject) completely **b :** to try out the whole number of ⟨had *exhausted* all possibilities⟩ **4 :** to destroy the fertility of (soil) **5 :** to pass or flow out **:** EMPTY [Latin *exhaustus,* past participle of *exhaurire* "to exhaust", from *ex-* + *haurire* "to draw"] — **ex•haust•er** *n* — **ex•haust•ibil•i•ty** \-ˌzȯ-stə-ˈbil-ət-ē\ *n* — **ex•haust•ible** \-ˈzȯ-stə-bəl\ *adj*

[2]**exhaust** *n* **1 a :** the escape of used steam or gas from an engine **b :** the gas thus escaping **2 a :** a conduit through which used gases escape **b :** an arrangement for withdrawing fumes, dusts, or odors from an enclosure

ex•haus•tion \ig-ˈzȯs-chən\ *n* **1 :** the act or process of exhausting **2 :** the state of being exhausted; *esp* **:** extreme weariness or fatigue

ex•haus•tive \ig-ˈzȯ-stiv\ *adj* **1 :** serving or tending to exhaust **2 :** THOROUGH 1, COMPLETE ⟨an *exhaustive* discussion⟩ — **ex•haus•tive•ly** *adv* — **ex•haus•tive•ness** *n*

ex•haust•less \ig-ˈzȯst-ləs\ *adj* **:** INEXHAUSTIBLE

[1]**ex•hib•it** \ig-ˈzib-ət\ *vt* **1 :** to show outwardly ⟨*exhibit* an interest in music⟩ **2 :** to put on display ⟨*exhibit* a collection of paintings⟩ **3 :** to present in legal form (as to a court) [Latin *exhibitus,* past participle of *exhibēre* "to exhibit", from *ex-* + *habēre* "to have, hold"] **syn** see SHOW — **ex•hib•i•tor** \-ət-ər\ *n*

[2]**exhibit** *n* **1 :** an act or instance of exhibiting **2 :** something exhibited; *esp* **:** a document or material object produced and identified (as in a court) for use as evidence

ex•hi•bi•tion \ˌek-sə-ˈbish-ən\ *n* **1 :** an act or instance of exhibiting **2** *British* **:** a grant drawn from the funds of a school or university to help maintain a student **3 :** a public showing (as of works of art, objects of manufacture, or athletic skill)

ex•hi•bi•tion•er \-ˈbish-nər, -ə-nər\ *n, British* **:** one who holds an exhibition (sense 2)

ex•hi•bi•tion•ism \-ˈbish-ə-ˌniz-əm\ *n* **1 a :** a compulsive tendency to expose one's body and especially the sex organs in a public place where such exposure is regarded as indecent **b :** an act of such exposure **2 :** the act or practice of behaving so as to attract attention to oneself — **ex•hi•bi•tion•ist** \-ˈbish-nəst, -ə-nəst\ *n or adj* — **ex•hi•bi•tion•is•tic** \-ˌbish-ə-ˈnis-tik\ *adj*

ex•hil•a•rate \ig-ˈzil-ə-ˌrāt\ *vt* **1 :** to make cheerful **2 :** to fill with a lively sense of well-being ⟨an *exhilarating* autumn day⟩ [Latin *exhilarare,* from *ex-* + *hilarare* "to gladden", from *ex-* + *hilarus* "cheerful"] — **ex•hil•a•ra•tive** \-ˌrāt-iv\ *adj*

ex•hil•a•ra•tion \ig-ˌzil-ə-ˈrā-shən\ *n* **1 :** the action of exhilarating **2 :** the state or the feeling of being exhilarated **:** high spirits **:** LIVELINESS

ex•hort \ig-ˈzȯrt\ *vb* **:** to arouse by words (as of advice, encouragement, or warning) **:** urge or appeal strongly [Middle French *exhorter,* from Latin *exhortari,* from *ex-* + *hortari* "to incite"] — **ex•hort•er** *n*

ex•hor•ta•tion \ˌeks-ˌȯr-ˈtā-shən, ˌegz-\ *n* **1 :** an act or instance of exhorting **2 :** a speech intended to exhort **:** earnestly spoken words of urgent advice or warning

ex•hor•ta•tive \ig-ˈzȯrt-ət-iv\ *adj* **:** serving to exhort

ex•hor•ta•to•ry \-ə-ˌtōr-ē, -ˌtȯr-\ *adj* **:** giving exhortation

ex•hume \igz-ˈüm, -ˈyüm; iks-ˈyüm, -ˈhyüm\ *vt* **1 :** to dig out of the ground; *esp* **:** to uncover and take out of a place of burial **2 :** to bring back from neglect or obscurity [Medieval Latin *exhumare,* from Latin *ex* "out of" + *humus* "earth"] — **ex•hu•ma•tion** \ˌeks-yü-ˈmā-shən, -hyü-; ˌegz-ü-, -yü-\ *n* — **ex•hum•er** *n*

ex•i•gence \ˈek-sə-jəns\ *n* **:** EXIGENCY

\ə\ **abut**	\au̇\ **out**	\i\ **tip**	\ȯ\ **saw**	\u̇\ **foot**
\ər\ **further**	\ch\ **chin**	\ī\ **life**	\ȯi\ **coin**	\y\ **yet**
\a\ **mat**	\e\ **pet**	\j\ **job**	\th\ **thin**	\yü\ **few**
\ā\ **take**	\ē\ **easy**	\ng\ **sing**	\t͟h\ **this**	\yu̇\ **cure**
\ä\ **cot, cart**	\g\ **go**	\ō\ **bone**	\ü\ **food**	\zh\ **vision**

ex•i•gen•cy \'ek-sə-jən-sē, ig-'zij-ən-\ *n, pl* **-cies** **1 :** a case or a state of affairs demanding immediate action or remedy **2 :** an urgent need **syn** see NEED

ex•i•gent \'ek-sə-jənt\ *adj* **1 :** requiring immediate aid or action **:** URGENT **2 :** requiring or calling for much **:** DEMANDING, EXACTING **[**Latin *exigere* "to demand", from *ex-* + *agere* "to drive"**]** — **ex•i•gent•ly** *adv*

ex•ig•u•ous \eg-'zig-yə-wəs\ *adj* **:** scanty in amount **[**Latin *exiguus,* from *exigere* "to demand"**]** — **ex•i•gu•ity** \,ek-sə-'gyü-ət-ē\ *n* — **ex•ig•u•ous•ly** \eg-'zig-yə-wəs-lē\ *adv* — **ex•ig•u•ous•ness** *n*

[1]**ex•ile** \'eg-,zīl, 'ek-,sīl\ *n* **1 :** forced removal or voluntary absence from one's native country; *also* **:** the state of one so absent **2 :** a person expelled from his or her country by authority **[**Middle French *exil,* from Latin *exilium***]**

[2]**exile** *vt* **:** to expel from one's own country or home

ex•ist \ig-'zist\ *vi* **1 :** to have actuality or reality **:** be real **:** BE ⟨do unicorns *exist*⟩ **2 :** to continue to be **:** LIVE ⟨earn hardly enough to *exist* on⟩ **3 :** to be found **:** OCCUR ⟨a disease that no longer *exists*⟩ **[**Latin *exsistere* "to come into being, exist", from *ex-* + *sistere* "to stand"**]**

ex•ist•ence \ig-'zis-təns\ *n* **1 a :** the fact or the state of being real and not imaginary ⟨believed in the *existence* of dragons⟩ **b :** objective reality **:** BEING ⟨the largest animal in *existence*⟩ **2 :** continuance in living or way of living **:** LIFE ⟨a happy *existence*⟩ **3 :** actual occurrence ⟨recognized the *existence* of a state of war⟩ **4 a :** the sum total of existing things **b :** a particular being

ex•ist•ent \-tənt\ *adj* **1 :** having being **:** EXISTING **2 :** existing now **:** PRESENT

ex•is•ten•tial \,eg-zis-'ten-chəl, ,ek-sis-\ *adj* **1 :** of, relating to, or dealing with existence **2 a :** grounded in existence or the experience of existence **b :** having being in time and space **3 :** concerned with or involving human existence or its nature

[1]**ex•it** \'eg-zət, 'ek-sət\ — used as a stage direction to specify who goes off stage **[**Latin, "he, she, or it goes out", from *exire* "to go out", from *ex-* + *ire* "to go"**]**

[2]**exit** *n* **1 :** a departure from a stage **2 :** the act of going out or going away **3 :** a way out of an enclosed place or space

[3]**exit** *vi* **:** to go out **:** LEAVE

ex li•bris \ek-'slē-brəs\ *n, pl* **ex libris :** BOOKPLATE **[**New Latin, "from the books"; used before the owner's name on bookplates**]**

exo- *or* **ex-** *combining form* **:** outside ⟨*exo*gamy⟩ **:** outer ⟨*exo*skeleton⟩ — compare ECT-, END- **[**Greek *exō* "out, outside", from *ex* "out of"**]**

exo•crine \'ek-sə-krən, -,krīn, -,krēn\ *adj* **:** secreting or secreted externally **[***exo-* + Greek *krinein* "to separate"**]**

exocrine gland *n* **:** a gland (as a salivary gland or a sweat gland) that produces an exocrine secretion

ex•o•dus \'ek-səd-əs\ *n* **1** *cap* — see BIBLE table **2 :** a mass departure **[**Latin, from Greek *Exodos,* literally, "road out", from *ex-* + *hodos* "road"**]**

ex of•fi•cio \,eks-ə-'fish-ē-,ō\ *adv or adj* **:** because of an office ⟨*ex officio* chairman⟩ **[**Late Latin**]**

ex•og•a•my \ek-'säg-ə-mē\ *n* **:** marriage outside a specific group especially as required by custom or law — **ex•og•a•mous** \-məs\ *adj*

ex•og•e•nous \ek-'säj-ə-nəs\ *adj* **:** developing or originating outside the cell or body — **ex•og•e•nous•ly** *adv*

ex•on•er•ate \ig-'zän-ə-,rāt\ *vt* **:** to clear from a charge of wrongdoing or from blame **:** declare innocent **[**Latin *exonerare* "to unburden", from *ex-* + *oner-, onus* "load"**]** — **ex•on•er•a•tion** \ig-,zän-ə-'rā-shən\ *n* — **ex•on•er•a•tive** \ig-'zän-ə-,rāt-iv\ *adj*

ex•or•bi•tant \ig-'zȯr-bət-ənt\ *adj* **:** going beyond the limits of what is fair, reasonable, or expected ⟨*exorbitant* prices⟩ **[**Middle French, from Late Latin *exorbitare* "to deviate", from Latin *ex-* + *orbita* "track, rut"**]** **syn** see EXCESSIVE — **ex•or•bi•tance** \-bət-əns\ *n* — **ex•or•bi•tant•ly** *adv*

ex•or•cise \'ek-,sȯr-,sīz, -sər-\ *vt* **1 a :** to drive (an evil spirit) off or out by religious exercises or spells **b :** to get rid of (something that troubles or menaces) **2 :** to free (as a person or place) from an evil spirit **[**Middle French *exorciser,* from Late Latin *exorcizare,* from Greek *exorkizein,* from *ex-* + *horkizein* "to bind by oath", from *horkos* "oath"**]** — **ex•or•cis•er** *n*

ex•or•cism \-,siz-əm\ *n* **1 :** the act or practice of exorcising **2 :** a spell or formula used in exorcising — **ex•or•cist** \-,sist, -səst\ *n*

exo•skel•e•ton \,ek-sō-'skel-ət-n\ *n* **:** a hard supporting or protective structure (as of a crustacean) developed on the outside of the body — compare ENDOSKELETON — **exo•skel•e•tal** \-ət-l\ *adj*

exo•sphere \'ek-sō-,sfiər\ *n* **:** the outermost region of the atmosphere

exo•ther•mic \,ek-sō-'thər-mik\ *or* **exo•ther•mal** \-məl\ *adj* **:** characterized by or formed by the giving off of heat ⟨an *exothermic* chemical reaction⟩

[1]**ex•ot•ic** \ig-'zät-ik\ *adj* **1 :** introduced from another country ⟨*exotic* plants⟩ **2 :** strikingly or excitingly different or unusual (as in color or design) **[**Latin *exoticus,* from Greek *exōtikos,* from *exō* "outside", from *ex* "out of"**]** — **ex•ot•i•cal•ly** \-'zät-i-kə-lē, -klē\ *adv* — **ex•ot•ic•ness** \-ik-nəs\ *n*

[2]**exotic** *n* **:** something (as a plant) that is exotic

exo•tox•in \,ek-sō-'täk-sən\ *n* **:** a soluble poisonous substance given off by a microorganism

ex•pand \ik-'spand\ *vb* **1 :** to open wide **:** UNFOLD ⟨a bird with wings *expanded*⟩ **2 :** to take up or cause to take up more space ⟨metals *expand* under heat⟩ **3 :** to develop more fully **:** work out in greater detail ⟨*expand* an argument⟩ **4 :** to state in enlarged form or in the form of a series **:** write out in full ⟨*expand* an equation⟩ **5 :** to increase in quantity or scope ⟨*expand* a business⟩ **[**Latin *expandere,* from *ex-* + *pandere* "to spread"**]** — **ex•pand•able** \-'span-də-bəl\ *adj* — **ex•pand•er** *n*

• syn EXPAND, DILATE, DISTEND, INFLATE mean to increase in size or volume. EXPAND applies to any enlarging that comes from within or outside or in any way, as in growth, unfolding, or addition of parts; DILATE suggests expansion of diameter or circumference ⟨the pupil of the eye *dilates* in dim light⟩ DISTEND implies swelling or stretching caused by pressure from within forcing extension outward ⟨*distended* nostrils⟩ INFLATE implies distension by the introduction of air or something insubstantial and suggests a liability to sudden collapse ⟨an *inflated* balloon⟩ ⟨*inflated* currency⟩

ex•panse \ik-'spans\ *n* **:** a wide space, area, or stretch ⟨the vast *expanse* of the ocean⟩ **[**Latin *expansus,* past participle of *expandere* "to expand"**]**

ex•pan•si•ble \ik-'span-sə-bəl\ *adj* **:** capable of being expanded

ex•pan•sion \ik-'span-chən\ *n* **1 :** the act or process of expanding **2 :** the quality or state of being expanded **3 a :** an expanded part **b :** something that results from an act of expanding **4 :** the result of an indicated operation **:** the result of expanding a mathematical expression or function (as into a sequence of terms)

ex•pan•sive \ik-'span-siv\ *adj* **1 :** having a capacity or a tendency to expand ⟨gases are *expansive*⟩ **2 :** causing or tending to cause expansion ⟨an *expansive* force⟩ **3 :** characterized by high spirits or benevolent inclinations ⟨in an *expansive* mood⟩ **4 :** having considerable extent **:** BROAD ⟨too *expansive* a subject for brief treatment⟩ — **ex•pan•sive•ly** *adv* — **ex•pan•sive•ness** *n*

ex par•te \ek-'spärt-ē, 'ek-\ *adj or adv* **:** from a one-sided or partisan point of view **[**Medieval Latin, "on behalf"**]**

ex•pa•ti•ate \ek-'spā-shē-,āt\ *vi* **:** to speak or write at length or in detail **[**Latin *exspatiari* "to wander, digress", from *ex-* + *spatium* "space, course"**]** — **ex•pa•ti•a•tion** \ek-,spā-shē-'ā-shən\ *n*

[1]**ex•pa•tri•ate** \ek-'spā-trē-,āt\ *vb* **1 :** to drive into exile **:** BANISH **2 :** to leave one's native country; *esp* **:** to renounce allegiance to one's native country **[**Medieval Latin *expatriare* "to leave one's country", from Latin *ex-* + *patria* "native country", derived from *pater* "father"**]** — **ex•pa•tri•a•tion** \ek-,spā-trē-'ā-shən\ *n*

[2]**ex•pa•tri•ate** \ek-'spā-trē-,āt, -trē-ət\ *adj* **:** living in a foreign country **:** EXPATRIATED — **expatriate** *n*

ex•pect \ik-'spekt\ *vb* **1 :** to anticipate or look forward to the coming or occurrence of ⟨*expect* rain⟩ ⟨*expect* a phone call⟩ **2 :** to be pregnant **3 :** SUPPOSE 2, THINK **4 a :** to consider probable or certain ⟨*expect* to be forgiven⟩ **b :** to consider reasonable, due, or necessary ⟨*expect* an honest day's work⟩ **c :** to consider obligated or in duty bound ⟨*expect* you to pay your dues⟩ **[**Latin *exspectare* "to look forward to", from *ex-* + *spectare* "to look at", from *specere* "to look"**]** — **ex•pect•able** \-'spek-tə-bəl\ *adj* — **ex•pect•ably** \-blē\ *adv*

ex•pect•ance \ik-'spek-təns\ *n* **:** EXPECTATION

ex•pect•an•cy \ik-'spek-tən-sē\ *n, pl* **-cies** **1 :** EXPECTATION 1 **2 a :** EXPECTATION 3 **b :** the expected amount (as of years of

life) based on statistical probability
ex•pect•ant \-tənt\ *adj* **1** : characterized by or being in a state of expectation **2** : expecting the birth of a child ⟨*expectant* parents⟩; *esp* : PREGNANT — **expectant** *n* — **ex•pect•ant•ly** *adv*
ex•pec•ta•tion \ˌek-ˌspek-ˈtā-shən, ik-\ *n* **1** : the act or state of expecting : a looking forward to or waiting for something **2** : prospect of good or bad fortune; *esp* : prospects of inheriting — usually used in pl. **3** : something expected
ex•pec•to•rant \ik-ˈspek-tə-rənt\ *adj* : tending to promote discharge of mucus from the respiratory tract — **expectorant** *n*
ex•pec•to•rate \ik-ˈspek-tə-ˌrāt\ *vb* **1** : to discharge (as phlegm) from the throat or lungs by coughing and spitting **2** : SPIT 1a [Latin *expectorare* "to cast out of the mind", from *ex-* + *pector, pectus* "breast, soul"] — **ex•pec•to•ra•tion** \-ˌspek-tə-ˈrā-shən\ *n*
ex•pe•di•ence \ik-ˈspēd-ē-əns\ *n* : EXPEDIENCY
ex•pe•di•en•cy \ik-ˈspēd-ē-ən-sē\ *n, pl* **-cies** **1** : the quality or state of being suited to the end in view : SUITABILITY **2** : the use of means and methods advantageous to oneself without regard to principles of fairness and rightness
[1]ex•pe•di•ent \ik-ˈspēd-ē-ənt\ *adj* **1** : appropriate to and efficient in attaining an end **2** : seeking or concerned with immediate advantage rather than with what is just or right [Latin *expediens,* present participle of *expedire* "to extricate, be advantageous", from *ex-* + *ped-, pes* "foot"] — **ex•pe•di•ent•ly** *adv*
• **syn** POLITIC, ADVISABLE: EXPEDIENT usually applies to what is immediately advantageous often without regard for ethics; POLITIC may apply to what is judicious and of tactical value and sometimes suggests an artful ulterior motive ⟨thought it *politic* to keep out of that argument⟩ ADVISABLE applies to what is practical, prudent, or advantageous without derogatory implication ⟨*advisable* to drive carefully⟩
[2]expedient *n* **1** : something expedient **2** : a means to accomplish an end; *esp* : one used in place of a better means that is not available
ex•pe•dite \ˈek-spə-ˌdīt\ *vt* **1** : to carry out rapidly : execute promptly **2** : to accelerate the process or progress of **3** : to send out : DISPATCH [Latin *expedire* "to extricate, arrange, be advantageous"]
ex•pe•dit•er *also* **ex•pe•di•tor** \-ˌdīt-ər\ *n* : one that expedites; *esp* : one employed to ensure adequate supplies of raw materials and equipment or to coordinate the flow of materials, tools, parts, and processed goods within a plant
ex•pe•di•tion \ˌek-spə-ˈdish-ən\ *n* **1 a** : a journey or trip undertaken for a specific purpose (as war or exploring) **b** : a group making such a journey **2** : efficient promptness : SPEED
ex•pe•di•tion•ary \-ˈdish-ə-ˌner-ē\ *adj* : of, relating to, or constituting an expedition; *esp* : sent on military service abroad ⟨an *expeditionary* force⟩
ex•pe•di•tious \ˌek-spə-ˈdish-əs\ *adj* : characterized by or acting with promptness and efficiency : SPEEDY — **ex•pe•di•tious•ly** *adv* — **ex•pe•di•tious•ness** *n*
ex•pel \ik-ˈspel\ *vt* **ex•pelled**; **ex•pel•ling** **1** : to drive or force out ⟨*expel* air from the lungs⟩ **2** : to drive away; *esp* : DEPORT **3** : to cut off from membership ⟨*expelled* from college⟩ [Latin *expellere,* from *ex-* + *pellere* "to drive"] **syn** see EJECT — **ex•pel•la•ble** \-ˈspel-ə-bəl\ *adj*
ex•pend \ik-ˈspend\ *vt* **1** : to pay out : SPEND **2** : to consume by use : use up ⟨*expended* countless hours on the project⟩ [Latin *expendere* "to weigh out, expend", from *ex-* + *pendere* "to weigh, pay"]
ex•pend•able \ik-ˈspen-də-bəl\ *adj* : that may be used up in an ordinary way or sacrificed to accomplish a mission ⟨*expendable* ammunition⟩ — **ex•pend•abil•i•ty** \-ˌpen-də-ˈbil-ət-ē\ *n* — **expendable** *n* — **ex•pend•ably** \-ˈpen-də-blē\ *adv*
ex•pen•di•ture \ik-ˈspen-di-chər, -də-ˌchu̇r\ *n* **1** : the act or process of expending **2** : an amount (as of money or time) expended
ex•pense \ik-ˈspens\ *n* **1 a** : something expended to secure a benefit or bring about a result **b** : financial burden or outlay : COST **2** : a cause of expenditure ⟨a car is a great *expense*⟩ **3** : SACRIFICE 3 — usually used in the phrase *at the expense of* [Late Latin *expensa,* from Latin *expendere* "to expend"]
expense account *n* : an account of expenses reimbursable to an employee
ex•pen•sive \ik-ˈspen-siv\ *adj* **1** : involving expense ⟨an *expensive* journey⟩ **2** : high-priced : DEAR **syn** see COSTLY — **ex•pen•sive•ly** *adv* — **ex•pen•sive•ness** *n*

[1]ex•pe•ri•ence \ik-ˈspir-ē-əns\ *n* **1 a** : the usually conscious perception or understanding of reality or of an event **b** : the sum total of the conscious events that make up an individual life or the past of a community, nation, or humankind generally **2 a** : the actual living through an event or series of events ⟨learn by *experience*⟩ **b** : something that one has actually done or lived through ⟨a soldier's *experiences* in war⟩ **3 a** : the skill or knowledge gained by actually doing or feeling a thing ⟨a job that requires *experience*⟩ **b** : the amount or kind of work one has done or the time during which work has been done ⟨a person with five years' *experience*⟩ [Middle French, from Latin *experientia* "act of trying", from *experiri* "to try"] — **ex•pe•ri•en•tial** \-ˌspir-ē-ˈen-chəl\ *adj*
[2]experience *vt* **1** : to have experience of : UNDERGO **2** : to learn by experience
ex•pe•ri•enced \ik-ˈspir-ē-ənst\ *adj* : having experience : made skillful or wise through experience ⟨an *experienced* pilot⟩
[1]ex•per•i•ment \ik-ˈsper-ə-mənt\ *n* **1 a** : TEST 1a, TRIAL **b** : a tentative procedure or policy **c** : an operation carried out under controlled conditions in order to discover an unknown effect or law, to test or establish a hypothesis, or to illustrate a known law **2** : the process of testing : EXPERIMENTATION [Middle French, from Latin *experimentum,* from *experiri* "to try"]
[2]ex•per•i•ment \-ˌment\ *vi* : to make experiments — **ex•per•i•men•ta•tion** \ik-ˌsper-ə-mən-ˈtā-shən, -ˌmen-\ *n* — **ex•per•i•ment•er** \-ˈsper-ə-ˌment-ər\ *n*
[1]ex•per•i•men•tal \ik-ˌsper-ə-ˈment-l\ *adj* **1** : of, relating to, or based on experience **2** : founded on or derived from experiment ⟨an *experimental* finding⟩ **3** : serving the ends of or used for experimentation ⟨*experimental* apparatus⟩ **4** : relating to or having the characteristics of experiment : TENTATIVE ⟨*experimental* flights⟩ — **ex•per•i•men•tal•ly** \-l-ē\ *adv*
[2]experimental *n* : a plant or animal actually subjected to an experimental condition as contrasted to one kept for a control
experiment station *n* : an establishment for scientific research (as in agriculture) especially of practical application and for the spread of information
[1]ex•pert \ˈek-ˌspərt, ik-ˈ\ *adj* : having, involving, or displaying special skill or knowledge derived from training or experience [Latin *expertus,* from *experiri* "to try"] **syn** see PROFICIENT — **ex•pert•ly** *adv* — **ex•pert•ness** *n*
[2]ex•pert \ˈek-ˌspərt\ *n* : one who has acquired special skill in or knowledge of a subject
ex•per•tise \ˌek-spər-ˈtēz, -ˌspər-, *also* -ˈtēs\ *n* **1** : expert opinion or commentary **2** : skill in a particular field : KNOW-HOW [French, from *expert* "expert"]
ex•pi•ate \ˈek-spē-ˌāt\ *vt* **1** : to atone for : pay the penalty for **2** : to make amends for [Latin *expiare* "to atone for", from *ex-* + *piare* "to appease"] — **ex•pi•a•ble** \-spē-ə-bəl\ *adj* — **ex•pi•a•tor** \-ˌāt-ər\ *n*
ex•pi•a•tion \ˌek-spē-ˈā-shən\ *n* **1** : the act of making atonement **2** : the means by which atonement is made
ex•pi•a•to•ry \ˈek-spē-ə-ˌtōr-ē, -ˌtȯr-\ *adj* : serving to expiate
ex•pi•ra•tion \ˌek-spə-ˈrā-shən\ *n* **1 a** : the expelling of air from the lungs in breathing **b** : air or vapor expelled from the lungs **2** : the fact of coming to an end : TERMINATION
ex•pi•ra•to•ry \ek-ˈspī-rə-ˌtōr-ē, -ˌtȯr-\ *adj* : of, relating to, or used in respiratory expiration
ex•pire \ik-ˈspīr, *oftenest for 3* ek-\ *vb* **1** : DIE 1 **2** : to come to an end : STOP **3 a** : to emit the breath **b** : to breathe out from or as if from the lungs [Latin *exspirare,* from *ex-* + *spirare* "to breathe"]
ex•pi•ry \ik-ˈspīr-ē, ˈek-spə-rē\ *n, pl* **-ries** **1** : DEATH 1 **2** : TERMINATION; *esp* : the termination of a time or period fixed by law, contract, or agreement
ex•plain \ik-ˈsplān\ *vb* **1** : to make plain or understandable **2** : to give the reason for or cause of **3** : to show the logical development or relationships of [Latin *explanare,* literally, "to make level", from *ex-* + *planus* "level"] — **ex•plain•able** \-ˈsplā-nə-bəl\ *adj* — **ex•plain•er** *n*
• **syn** EXPOUND, EXPLICATE, INTERPRET: EXPLAIN implies making plain or intelligible; EXPOUND implies a careful, often elabo-

rate explanation ⟨*expounding* one's philosophy of life⟩ EXPLICATE adds the idea of a developed or detailed analysis ⟨*explicate* the plot of a novel⟩ INTERPRET adds the use of the imagination, sympathy, or special knowledge to clarify something of more than obvious difficulty ⟨*interpret* a poem⟩ ⟨*interpret* the law⟩

ex•pla•na•tion \ˌek-splə-ˈnā-shən\ *n* **1 :** the act or process of explaining **2 :** something that explains; *esp* **:** a statement that makes something clear

ex•plan•a•to•ry \ik-ˈsplan-ə-ˌtōr-ē, -ˌtȯr-\ *adj* **:** serving to explain ⟨*explanatory* notes⟩ — **ex•plan•a•to•ri•ly** \-ˌsplan-ə-ˈtōr-ə-lē, -ˈtȯr-\ *adv*

ex•plant \ek-ˈsplant, ˈek-\ *vt* **:** to remove (living tissue) especially to a tissue culture medium

ex•ple•tive \ˈek-splət-iv\ *n* **1 :** a syllable, word, or phrase inserted to fill a vacancy (as in a sentence or a line of verse) without adding to the sense; *esp* **:** a word that occupies the position of the subject or object of a verb in normal English word order and anticipates a subsequent word or phrase that supplies the needed meaningful content ⟨*it* in "it is easy to say so" and in "make it clear which you prefer" is an *expletive*⟩ **2 :** an exclamatory word or phrase; *esp* **:** one that is obscene or profane **[**Late Latin *expletivus* "serving to fill up", from Latin *explēre* "to fill out", from *ex-* + *plēre* "to fill"**]** — **expletive** *adj*

ex•pli•cate \ˈek-splə-ˌkāt\ *vt* **:** to give a detailed explanation of **[**Latin *explicare,* literally, "to unfold", from *ex-* + *plicare* "to fold"**] syn** see EXPLAIN — **ex•pli•ca•ble** \ek-ˈsplik-ə-bəl, ˈek-splik-\ *adj* — **ex•pli•ca•tion** \ˌek-splə-ˈkā-shən\ *n* — **ex•pli•ca•tive** \ek-ˈsplik-ət-iv, ˈek-splə-ˌkāt-\ *adj* — **ex•pli•ca•tor** \ˈek-splə-ˌkāt-ər\ *n* — **ex•pli•ca•to•ry** \ek-ˈsplik-ə-ˌtōr-ē, ˈek-splik-, -ˌtȯr-\ *adj*

ex•plic•it \ik-ˈsplis-ət\ *adj* **:** so clear in statement that there is no doubt about the meaning **:** fully stated ⟨*explicit* instructions⟩ — compare IMPLICIT **[**Medieval Latin *explicitus,* from Latin *explicare* "to explicate"**]** — **ex•plic•it•ly** *adv* — **ex•plic•it•ness** *n*

• **syn** EXPLICIT, DEFINITE, EXPRESS, SPECIFIC mean perfectly clear in meaning. EXPLICIT implies such verbal plainness and distinctness that there is no room for doubt or difficulty in understanding; DEFINITE stresses precise, clear statement or arrangement that leaves no doubt or indecision; EXPRESS implies explicitness and utterance with directness and positiveness ⟨*express* denial of the charges⟩ SPECIFIC applies to what is precisely and fully treated in detail or particular.

ex•plode \ik-ˈsplōd\ *vb* **1 :** to cause to be given up or rejected **:** DISCREDIT ⟨science has *exploded* many old ideas⟩ **2 a :** to burst or cause to burst violently and noisily **b :** to burn suddenly so that there is a violent expansion of hot gases with great disruptive force and a loud noise; *also* **:** to undergo an atomic nuclear reaction with similar but more violent effects **3 :** to burst forth (as with anger or laughter) **[**Latin *explodere* "to drive off the stage by clapping", from *ex-* + *plaudere* "to clap"**]**

△ **origin** A modern audience often expresses its disapproval of a performance by hissing, but in ancient Rome audiences showed their low opinion of an actor, and might even drive him from the stage, by loud clapping. Latin *explodere,* a compound of *ex,* "out of, from", and *plaudere,* "to clap", means "to drive off by clapping". The Latin verb was borrowed into English with 2Hthe meaning "to drive from the stage by noisy disapproval". From this sense developed the now current senses "to reject or discredit" and "to burst noisily". *Explode* is no longer used in its original sense.

ex•plod•ed *adj* **:** showing the parts separated but in correct relationship to each other ⟨an *exploded* view of a carburetor⟩

¹ex•ploit \ˈek-ˌsplȯit, ik-ˈ\ *n* **:** a deed notable especially for heroism **[**Old French, "outcome, success", derived from Latin *explicare* "to explicate, unfold"**] syn** see FEAT

²ex•ploit \ik-ˈsplȯit, ˈek-ˌ\ *vt* **1 :** to extract value or use from **:** UTILIZE ⟨*exploit* a mine⟩ **2 :** to make use of unfairly for one's own advantage — **ex•ploit•able** \-ə-bəl\ *adj* — **ex•ploi•ta•tion** \ˌek-ˌsplȯi-ˈtā-shən\ *n* — **ex•ploit•er** \ik-ˈsplȯit-ər, ˈek-ˌ\ *n*

ex•plo•ra•tion \ˌek-splə-ˈrā-shən\ *n* **:** the act or an instance of exploring — **ex•plor•ative** \ik-ˈsplōr-ət-iv, -ˈsplȯr-\ *adj* — **ex•plor•ato•ry** \-ə-ˌtōr-ē, -ˌtȯr-\ *adj*

ex•plore \ik-ˈsplōr, -ˈsplȯr\ *vb* **1 a :** to search through or into **b :** to examine carefully and in detail especially for diagnostic purposes ⟨*explore* a wound⟩ **c :** to penetrate into or range over for purposes of discovery ⟨*explore* an uncharted sea⟩ **2 :** to make or conduct a systematic search ⟨*explore* for oil⟩ **[**Latin *explorare* "to seek for", from *ex-* + *plorare* "to cry out"; probably from the outcry of hunters on sighting game**]**

ex•plor•er \ik-ˈsplōr-ər, -ˈsplȯr-\ *n* **:** one that explores; *esp* **:** a person who travels in search of geographical or scientific information

ex•plo•sion \ik-ˈsplō-zhən\ *n* **1 :** the act or an instance of exploding **2 :** a large-scale, rapid, and spectacular expansion, outbreak, or upheaval **3 :** a violent outburst of feeling **[**Latin *explosio* "act of driving off by clapping", from *explodere* "to drive off by clapping"**]**

¹ex•plo•sive \ik-ˈsplō-siv, -ziv\ *adj* **1 :** relating to, characterized by, or operated by explosion **2 :** likely to explode — **ex•plo•sive•ly** *adv* — **ex•plo•sive•ness** *n*

²explosive *n* **:** an explosive substance

ex•po•nent \ik-ˈspō-nənt, ˈek-ˌ\ *n* **1 :** a symbol written above and to the right of a mathematical expression to indicate the operation of raising to a power ⟨in the expression a^3, the *exponent 3* indicates that *a* is to be taken as a factor three times⟩ **2 a :** one that expounds or interprets **b :** one that champions or advocates **[**Latin *exponere* "to set forth, explain", from *ex-* + *ponere* "to put"**]**

ex•po•nen•tial \ˌek-spə-ˈnen-chəl\ *adj* **1 a :** of or relating to an exponent **b :** expressed in a form using exponents **2 :** involving a variable exponent ⟨a function of the form $y = 10^x$ is an *exponential* function⟩ — **ex•po•nen•tial•ly** \-ˈnench-lē, -ə-lē\ *adv*

¹ex•port \ek-ˈspōrt, -ˈspȯrt, ˈek-ˌ\ *vt* **:** to carry or send (as a commodity) to another country or place especially for sale **[**Latin *exportare,* from *ex-* + *portare* "to carry"**]** — **ex•port•able** \-ə-bəl\ *adj* — **ex•por•ta•tion** \ˌek-ˌspōr-ˈtā-shən, -ˌspȯr-, -spər-\ *n* — **ex•port•er** \ek-ˈspōrt-ər, -ˈspȯrt-, ˈek-ˌ\ *n*

²ex•port \ˈek-ˌspōrt, -ˌspȯrt\ *n* **1 :** something exported; *esp* **:** a commodity conveyed from one country or region to another for purposes of trade **2 :** an act of exporting **:** EXPORTATION

³export \ˈek-ˌ\ *adj* **1 :** of or relating to exportation or exports ⟨*export* duties⟩ **2 :** intended for export ⟨*export* goods⟩

ex•pose \ik-ˈspōz\ *vt* **1 a :** to deprive of shelter, protection, or care ⟨*expose* troops needlessly⟩ **b :** to submit or subject to an action or influence; *esp* **:** to subject (a sensitive photographic film, plate, or paper) to the action of radiant energy (as light) **c :** to abandon (an infant) especially in the open **2 :** to lay open to view **:** DISPLAY **3 :** to bring to light **:** UNMASK ⟨*expose* a murderer⟩ **[**Middle French *exposer,* from Latin *exponere* "to set forth, explain", from *ex-* + *ponere* "to put, place"**]** — **ex•pos•er** *n*

ex•po•sé \ˌek-spō-ˈzā\ *n* **:** an exposure of something discreditable ⟨a newspaper *exposé* of illegal gambling⟩ **[**French, from *exposer* "to expose"**]**

ex•po•si•tion \ˌek-spə-ˈzish-ən\ *n* **1 :** an explaining of the meaning or purpose of something (as a piece of writing) **2 :** a composition that explains something **3 :** a public exhibition or show **4 :** the first part of a musical composition in sonata form in which the thematic material of the movement is presented — **ex•pos•i•to•ry** \ik-ˈspäz-ə-ˌtōr-ē, -ˌtȯr-\ *adj*

ex•pos•i•tor \ik-ˈspäz-ət-ər\ *n* **:** one that expounds or explains **[**Middle French *expositeur,* from Late Latin *expositor,* from Latin *exponere* "to set forth, explain"**]**

ex post fac•to \ˌek-ˌspōst-ˈfak-tō\ *adj* **:** affecting something (as status or an action) having prior existence ⟨got *ex post facto* approval of the plan⟩ **[**Late Latin, "from a thing done afterward"**]**

ex•pos•tu•late \ik-ˈspäs-chə-ˌlāt\ *vi* **:** to reason earnestly with a person for purposes of dissuasion or protest **[**Latin *expostulare* "to demand, dispute", from *ex-* + *postulare* "to ask for"**]** — **ex•pos•tu•la•tion** \-ˌspäs-chə-ˈlā-shən\ *n* — **ex•pos•tu•la•to•ry** \-ˈspäs-chə-lə-ˌtōr-ē, -ˌtȯr-\ *adj*

ex•po•sure \ik-ˈspō-zhər\ *n* **1 :** the act or an instance of exposing: as **a :** disclosure to view **b :** disclosure of something usually shameful or criminal **c :** an act of abandoning especially in the open **d** (1) **:** a section of a film for a single picture (2) **:** the time during which a sensitive photographic film is exposed **2 a :** a condition or an instance of being exposed; *esp* **:** the condition of being exposed to the elements **b :** a position with respect to direction or to weather conditions ⟨a southern *exposure*⟩

ex•pound \ik-ˈspau̇nd\ *vt* **1 a :** to set forth **:** STATE **b :** to defend (as a theory) with argument **2** : to make clear the meaning of : INTERPRET [Middle French *expondre,* from Latin *exponere* "to explain"] **syn** see EXPLAIN — **ex·pound·er** *n*

[1]ex·press \ik-'spres\ *adj* **1 a** : directly and distinctly stated : EXPLICIT **b** : exactly represented : PRECISE **2** : of a particular sort : SPECIAL **3 a** : traveling at high speed; *esp* : traveling with few or no stops ⟨an *express* train⟩ **b** : adapted or suitable for travel at high speed ⟨an *express* route⟩ [Middle French *expres,* from Latin *expressus,* past participle of *exprimere* "to press out", from *ex-* + *premere* "to press"] **syn** see EXPLICIT

[2]express *adv* : by express ⟨send a package *express*⟩

[3]express *n* **1 a** : a system for the prompt transportation of goods at an extra charge **b** : a company operating such a service **c** : the goods or shipments so transported **2** : an express vehicle

[4]express *vt* **1 a** : to represent especially in words or symbols **b** : to give expression to the opinions, feelings, or abilities of (oneself) **c** : SYMBOLIZE ⟨the sign = *expresses* equality⟩ **2** : to press or squeeze out ⟨*express* juice from a lemon⟩ **3** : to send by express — **ex·press·er** *n* — **ex·press·ible** \-ə-bəl\ *adj*

ex·pres·sion \ik-'spresh-ən\ *n* **1** : the act or process of expressing especially in words or symbols **2 a** : a word, phrase, or sign that expresses a thought, feeling, or quality; *esp* : a significant word or phrase **b** : a mathematical symbol or a combination of symbols and signs representing a quantity or operation **3** : a way of speaking or of singing or playing an instrument so as to show mood or feeling **4** : LOOK 2a, APPEARANCE ⟨a pleased *expression*⟩ **5** : the detectable effect of a gene **6** : an act or product of pressing out — **ex·pres·sion·less** \-ləs\ *adj*

ex·pres·sion·ism \ik-'spresh-ə-ˌniz-əm\ *n* : a theory or practice in art of trying to depict the artist's personal responses to objects and events — **ex·pres·sion·ist** \-'spresh-nəst, -ə-nəst\ *n or adj* — **ex·pres·sion·is·tic** \-ˌspresh-ə-'nis-tik\ *adj*

ex·pres·sive \ik-'spres-iv\ *adj* **1** : of or relating to expression **2** : serving to express **3** : full of expression : SIGNIFICANT — **ex·pres·sive·ly** *adv* — **ex·pres·sive·ness** *n*

ex·press·ly \ik-'spres-lē\ *adv* **1** : in an express manner : EXPLICITLY **2** : for the express purpose : PARTICULARLY

ex·press·way \ik-'spres-ˌwā\ *n* : a high-speed divided highway with controlled access

ex·pro·pri·ate \ek-'sprō-prē-ˌāt\ *vt* : to take away from a person the possession of or right to (property) [Medieval Latin *expropriare,* from Latin *ex-* + *proprius* "own"] — **ex·pro·pri·a·tion** \ˌek-ˌsprō-prē-'ā-shən\ *n* — **ex·pro·pri·a·tor** \ek-'sprō-prē-ˌāt-ər\ *n*

ex·pul·sion \ik-'spəl-shən\ *n* : the act of expelling : the state of being expelled [Latin *expulsio,* from *expellere* "to expel"] — **ex·pul·sive** \-'spəl-siv\ *adj*

ex·punge \ik-'spənj\ *vt* **1** : to strike out, obliterate, or mark for deletion **2** : to efface completely [Latin *expungere* "to mark for deletion by dots", from *ex-* + *pungere* "to prick"] **syn** see ERASE — **ex·pung·er** *n*

ex·pur·gate \'ek-spər-ˌgāt\ *vt* : to clear of something wrong or objectionable; *esp* : to clear (as a book) of objectionable words or passages [Latin *expurgare,* from *ex-* + *purgare* "to purge"] — **ex·pur·ga·tion** \ˌek-spər-'gā-shən\ *n* — **ex·pur·ga·tor** \'ek-spər-ˌgāt-ər\ *n*

ex·quis·ite \ek-'skwiz-ət; 'ek-skwiz-, -ˌskwiz-\ *adj* **1** : marked by flawless craftsmanship or delicate execution **2** : keenly appreciative : DISCRIMINATING **3** : pleasing through beauty or excellence **4** : ACUTE 3, INTENSE [Latin *exquisitus,* from *exquirere* "to search out", from *ex-* + *quaerere* "to seek"] — **ex·quis·ite·ly** *adv* — **ex·quis·ite·ness** *n*

ex·tant \'ek-stənt, ek-'stant\ *adj* : currently existing : not destroyed or lost [Latin *exstare* "to stand out, be in existence", from *ex-* + *stare* "to stand"]

ex·tem·po·ra·ne·ous \ek-ˌstem-pə-'rā-nē-əs\ *adj* **1** : composed, performed, or uttered on the spur of the moment : IMPROMPTU **2** : carefully prepared but delivered without notes or text **3** : provided, made, or put to use as an expedient : MAKESHIFT [Late Latin *extemporaneus,* from Latin *ex tempore* "on the spur of the moment"] — **ex·tem·po·ra·ne·ous·ly** *adv* — **ex·tem·po·ra·ne·ous·ness** *n*

ex·tem·po·rary \ik-'stem-pə-ˌrer-ē\ *adj* : EXTEMPORANEOUS — **ex·tem·po·rar·i·ly** \-ˌstem-pə-'rer-ə-lē\ *adv*

ex·tem·po·re \ik-'stem-pə-rē\ *adv* : EXTEMPORANEOUSLY

ex·tem·po·rize \ik-'stem-pə-ˌrīz\ *vb* : to do, make, or utter extemporaneously : IMPROVISE — **ex·tem·po·ri·za·tion** \ik-ˌstem-pə-rə-'zā-shən\ *n* — **ex·tem·po·riz·er** \-'stem-pə-ˌrī-zər\ *n*

ex·tend \ik-'stend\ *vb* **1** : to spread out or stretch forth ⟨*extend* one's arm⟩ **2** : to exert (oneself) to full capacity ⟨*extended* themselves to meet the deadline⟩ **3** : to increase the bulk of (a product) by the addition of a cheaper substance **4 a** : to make the offer of : PROFFER **b** : to make available **5** : to cause to be longer; *esp* : to prolong in time **6 a** : to cause to be of greater area or volume : ENLARGE **b** : to increase the scope, meaning, or application of : BROADEN **7** : to stretch out in distance, space, or time : REACH ⟨the bridge *extends* across the river⟩ **8** : to span an interval of distance, space, or time [Latin *extendere,* from *ex-* + *tendere* "to stretch"] — **ex·ten·si·ble** \-'sten-sə-bəl\ *or* **ex·tend·ible** \-'sten-də-bəl\ *adj*

• **syn** EXTEND, LENGTHEN, PROLONG, PROTRACT mean to draw out or add to so as to increase in length. EXTEND and LENGTHEN imply a drawing out in space or time; EXTEND may also imply increase in width, scope, area, or range ⟨*extend* a vacation⟩ ⟨*extend* welfare services⟩ ⟨*lengthen* a skirt⟩ ⟨*lengthen* the workweek⟩ PROLONG suggests chiefly increase in duration especially beyond usual limits ⟨*prolonged* illness⟩ PROTRACT adds to PROLONG implications of needlessness, vexation, or indefiniteness ⟨*protracted* litigation⟩

ex·tend·er \ik-'sten-dər\ *n* : something added to another thing usually to dilute or modify

ex·ten·sion \ik-'sten-chən\ *n* **1 a** : the act of extending : the state of being extended **b** : something extended **2** : the total range over which something extends : COMPASS **3** : the property of occupying space **4** : an increase in time; *esp* : a granting of extra time to fulfill an obligation **5** : an educational program with special arrangements for persons unable to attend a school **6 a** : a part constituting an addition **b** : a section forming an additional length **c** : an extra telephone connected to the principal line [Late Latin *extensio,* from Latin *extendere* "to extend"]

extension cord *n* : an electric cord fitted with a plug at one end and a receptacle at the other

ex·ten·sive \ik-'sten-siv\ *adj* : having wide or considerable extent — **ex·ten·sive·ly** *adv* — **ex·ten·sive·ness** *n*

ex·ten·sor \ik-'sten-sər\ *n* : a muscle serving to extend a bodily part (as a limb) — compare FLEXOR

ex·tent \ik-'stent\ *n* **1 a** : the range, distance, or space over which something extends : SCOPE **b** : the point, degree, or limit to which something extends ⟨using talents to the greatest *extent*⟩ **2** : an extended tract or region [Middle French *extente* "area", from *extendre* "to extend", from Latin *extendere*]

ex·ten·u·ate \ik-'sten-yə-ˌwāt\ *vt* : to lessen or try to lessen the seriousness or extent of by making partial excuses ⟨pleading the youth of the offender to *extenuate* the offense⟩ [Latin *extenuare,* from *ex-* + *tenuis* "thin"] — **ex·ten·u·a·tion** \-ˌsten-yə-'wā-shən\ *n* — **ex·ten·u·a·tor** \-'sten-yə-ˌwāt-ər\ *n* — **ex·ten·u·a·to·ry** \-wə-ˌtōr-ē, -ˌtȯr-\ *adj*

[1]ex·te·ri·or \ek-'stir-ē-ər\ *adj* **1** : EXTERNAL 2, OUTER **2 a** : happening or coming from outside **b** : suitable for use on outside surfaces ⟨*exterior* paint⟩ [Latin, comparative of *exter, exterus* "being on the outside", from *ex* "out of"] — **ex·te·ri·or·ly** *adv*

[2]exterior *n* **1 a** : an exterior part or surface : OUTSIDE **b** : outward manner or appearance **2** : a representation of an outdoor scene

exterior angle *n* **1** : the angle between a side of a polygon and an extended adjacent side **2** : an angle formed by a transversal cutting two lines and lying outside them

ex·ter·mi·nate \ik-'stər-mə-ˌnāt\ *vt* : to destroy utterly : ANNIHILATE [Latin *exterminare,* from *ex-* + *terminus* "boundary"] — **ex·ter·mi·na·tion** \-ˌstər-mə-'nā-shən\ *n* — **ex·ter·mi·na·tor** \-'stər-mə-ˌnāt-ər\ *n*

[1]ex·ter·nal \ek-'stərn-l\ *adj* **1 a** : outwardly visible ⟨*external* signs⟩ **b** : having only the outward appearance of : SUPERFICIAL **2 a** : of, relating to, or connected with the outside or an outer part **b** : applied or applicable to the outside **3 a** (1) : situated outside, apart, or beyond (2) : arising or acting from outside ⟨*external* force⟩ **b :** of or relating to relationships with foreign countries **[**Latin *externus,* from *exter* "being on the outside"**]** — **ex·ter·nal·ly** \-l-ē\ *adv*

[2]ex·ter·nal *n* **:** an external feature or aspect — usually used in pl.

external-combustion engine *n* **:** a heat engine (as a steam engine) that derives its heat from fuel consumed outside the engine cylinder

external ear *n* **:** the outer part of the ear consisting of the sound-collecting pinna and the canal leading from this to the eardrum

external respiration *n* **:** exchange of gases between the external environment and a distributing system of the animal body (as gills or lungs) or between the alveoli of the lungs and the blood — compare INTERNAL RESPIRATION

ex·tinct \ik-ˈstiŋt, ˈek-ˌ, -ˈstiŋkt\ *adj* **1 :** no longer burning **:** EXTINGUISHED **2 :** no longer active ⟨an *extinct* volcano⟩ **3 :** no longer existing ⟨an *extinct* animal⟩ **[**Latin *extinctus,* past participle of *extinguere* "to extinguish"**]** — **ex·tinc·tion** \ik-ˈstiŋ-shən, -ˈstiŋk-\ *n*

ex·tin·guish \ik-ˈstiŋ-gwish\ *vt* **1 a :** to put out (as a fire or a light) **b :** EXTERMINATE, ANNIHILATE **c :** to dim the brightness of **:** ECLIPSE **2 :** to cause to be void **:** NULLIFY ⟨*extinguish* a claim⟩ **[**Latin *extinguere* (from *ex-* + *stinguere* "to extinguish") + English *-ish* (as in *abolish*)**]** — **ex·tin·guish·able** \-ə-bəl\ *adj* — **ex·tin·guish·er** \-ər\ *n* — **ex·tin·guish·ment** \-mənt\ *n*

ex·tir·pate \ˈek-stər-ˌpāt, ek-ˈ\ *vt* **1 :** to pull up by the roots **2 a :** to eradicate (as by surgery) **b :** to destroy wholly **[**Latin *exstirpare,* from *ex-* + *stirps* "trunk, root"**]**

ex·tol *also* **ex·toll** \ik-ˈstōl\ *vt* **ex·tolled; ex·tol·ling :** to praise highly **:** GLORIFY **[**Latin *extollere,* from *ex-* + *tollere* "to lift up"**]** — **ex·tol·ler** *n* — **ex·tol·ment** \-ˈstōl-mənt\ *n*

ex·tort \ik-ˈstȯrt\ *vt* **:** to obtain (as money or a confession) from a person by force or threats **[**Latin *extortus,* past participle of *extorquēre* "to wrench out, extort", from *ex-* + *torquēre* "to twist"**]** — **ex·tort·er** *n* — **ex·tor·tive** \-ˈstȯrt-iv\ *adj*

ex·tor·tion \ik-ˈstȯr-shən\ *n* **1 :** the act or practice of extorting; *esp* **:** the offense committed by an official engaging in this practice **2 :** something extorted; *esp* **:** a gross overcharge — **ex·tor·tion·er** \-ˈstȯr-shə-nər, -shnər\ *n* — **ex·tor·tion·ist** \-shə-nəst, -shnəst\ *n*

ex·tor·tion·ate \ik-ˈstȯr-shə-nət, -shnət\ *adj* **1 :** characterized by extortion **2 :** grossly excessive **:** EXORBITANT ⟨*extortionate* prices⟩ — **ex·tor·tion·ate·ly** *adv*

[1]ex·tra \ˈek-strə\ *adj* **1 a :** more than is due, usual, or necessary **:** ADDITIONAL ⟨*extra* work⟩ **b :** subject to an additional charge **2 :** SUPERIOR ⟨*extra* quality⟩ **[**probably short for *extraordinary***]**

[2]extra *n* **:** something extra or additional: as **a :** an added charge **b :** a special edition of a newspaper **c :** an additional worker; *esp* **:** one hired to act in a group scene in a motion picture or stage production

[3]extra *adv* **:** beyond the usual size, extent, or degree ⟨*extra* long⟩

extra- *prefix* **:** outside **:** beyond ⟨*extra*curricular⟩ **[**Latin, from *extra* "outside, except, beyond"**]**

See *extra-* and 2d element

extra-academic
extra-archeological
extra-atmospheric
extrabiblical
extrabiological
extrabuccal
extracampus
extraclass
extraclassroom
extracommunity
extracompany
extraconjugal
extraconstitutional
extra-continental
extracorporeal
extracourtroom
extradepartmental
extradimensional
extradiocesan
extradomestic
extradramatic
extraeconomic
extraeducational
extraexperimental
extrafamilial
extrafamily
extragalactic
extragovernmental
extrahistorical
extrahospital
extrahuman
extra-institutional
extrajudicial
extralegal
extralinguistic
extraliterary
extralunar
extramarital
extramaritally
extramedical
extramusical
extranational
extraparliamentary
extraparochial
extraplanetary
extrapolitical
extraprofessional
extrarational
extrareligious
extrascholastic
extrascholastically
extrascientific
extra-sexual
extrasocial
extrasomatic
extra-systemic
extratribal
extratropical
extra-university
extra-urban

extra-base hit *n* **:** a base hit in baseball that enables the batter to take more than one base

ex·tra·cel·lu·lar \ˌek-strə-ˈsel-yə-lər\ *adj* **:** situated, acting, or occurring outside a cell or the cells of the body ⟨*extracellular* digestion⟩ — **ex·tra·cel·lu·lar·ly** *adv*

[1]ex·tract \ik-ˈstrakt, *oftenest in sense 5* ˈek-ˌ\ *vt* **1 a :** to draw forth ⟨the magician *extracted* a rabbit from the hat⟩ **b :** to pull out forcibly ⟨*extract* a tooth⟩ **c :** to obtain by effort from or as if from someone unwilling ⟨*extract* a confession⟩ ⟨*extract* information from a book⟩ **2 :** to separate or otherwise obtain (as a juice or a constituent element) by physical or chemical process **3 :** to separate (a metal) from an ore **4 :** to determine (a mathematical root) by calculation **5 :** to select (excerpts) and copy out or cite **[**Latin *extractus,* past participle of *extrahere* "to extract", from *ex-* + *trahere* "to draw"**]** — **ex·tract·able** \-ə-bəl\ *adj* — **ex·trac·tor** \-ər\ *n*

[2]ex·tract \ˈek-ˌstrakt\ *n* **1 :** a selection from a writing or discourse **:** EXCERPT **2 :** a product (as an essence or concentrate) prepared by extracting; *esp* **:** a solution of essential constituents of a complex material (as meat or an aromatic plant)

ex·trac·tion \ik-ˈstrak-shən\ *n* **1 :** the act or process of extracting ⟨a tooth *extraction*⟩ **2 :** ANCESTRY 1, LINEAGE **3 :** something extracted

[1]ex·trac·tive \ik-ˈstrak-tiv\ *adj* **1 a :** of, relating to, or involving extraction ⟨*extractive* processes⟩ **b :** capable of being extracted ⟨*extractive* by-products of coal tar⟩ **2 :** drawing on natural and especially irreplaceable resources ⟨*extractive* industries such as mining and lumbering⟩

[2]extractive *n* **:** an extractive substance

ex·tra·cur·ric·u·lar \ˌek-strə-kə-ˈrik-yə-lər\ *adj* **1 :** not falling within a regular curriculum; *esp* **:** of, relating to, or being those activities (as athletics) connected with school but usually not carrying academic credit **2 :** being outside one's regular duties or routine

ex·tra·dite \ˈek-strə-ˌdīt\ *vt* **1 :** to deliver up to extradition **2 :** to obtain the extradition of **[**back-formation from *extradition***]** — **ex·tra·dit·able** \-ˌdīt-ə-bəl\ *adj*

ex·tra·di·tion \ˌek-strə-ˈdish-ən\ *n* **:** the surrender of an alleged criminal by one authority (as a state) to another for trial **[**French, from *ex-* "ex-" + Latin *traditio* "act of handing over"**]**

ex·tra·dos \ˈek-strə-ˌdäs, -ˌdō; ek-ˈstrā-ˌdäs\ *n, pl* **extrados** \-ˌdōz, -ˌdäs\ *or* **ex·tra·dos·es** \-ˌdäs-əz\ **:** the exterior curve of an arch **[**French, from Latin *extra* "outside" + French *dos* "back"**]**

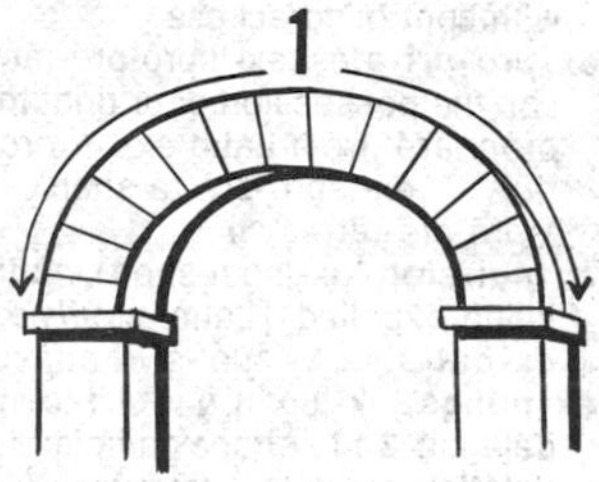

1 extrados

ex·tra·em·bry·on·ic \ˌek-strə-ˌem-brē-ˈän-ik\ *adj* **:** situated outside the embryo proper; *esp* **:** developed from the fertilized egg but not part of the embryo itself ⟨*extraembryonic* membranes⟩

ex·tra·ne·ous \ek-ˈstrā-nē-əs\ *adj* **1 :** existing or coming from the outside **2 a :** not forming an essential or vital part **b :** having no relevance **[**Latin *extraneus* "external, strange", from *extra* "outside"**]** — **ex·tra·ne·ous·ly** *adv* — **ex·tra·ne·ous·ness** *n*

ex·traor·di·nary \ik-ˈstrȯrd-n-ˌer-ē, ˌek-strə-ˈȯrd-\ *adj* **1 a :** going beyond what is usual, regular, or customary ⟨*extraordinary* powers⟩ **b :** very exceptional **:** REMARKABLE ⟨*extraordinary* beauty⟩ **2 :** employed for or sent on a special function or service ⟨an ambassador *extraordinary*⟩ — **ex·traor·di·nar·i·ly** \ik-ˌstrȯrd-n-ˈer-ə-lē, ˌek-strə-ˌȯrd-\ *adv* — **ex·traor·di·nar·i·ness** \ik-ˈstrȯrd-n-ˌer-ē-nəs, ˌek-strə-ˈȯrd-\ *n*

extra point *n* **1 :** a point scored in football after a touchdown by drop-kicking or placekicking **2** *pl* **:** a score of two points scored after a touchdown by advancing the ball across the goal line in one play

ex·trap·o·late \ik-ˈstrap-ə-ˌlāt\ *vb* **:** to infer or infer facts and data from known facts and data **[**Latin *extra* "outside" + English *-polate* (as in *interpolate*)**]** — **ex·trap·o·la·tion** \-ˌstrap-ə-ˈlā-shən\ *n*

ex·tra·sen·so·ry perception \ˌek-strə-ˌsens-rē-, -ə-rē-\ *n* **:** an awareness of events or facts held to involve communication outside all the known senses

ex·tra·ter·res·tri·al \ˌek-strə-tə-ˈres-trē-əl, -ˈresh-chəl\ *adj* : originating, existing, or taking place outside the earth or its atmosphere ⟨*extraterrestrial* life⟩

ex·tra·ter·ri·to·ri·al \-ˌter-ə-ˈtōr-ē-əl, -ˈtȯr-\ *adj* : located outside the territorial limits of a jurisdiction — **ex·tra·ter·ri·to·ri·al·ly** \-ē-ə-lē\ *adv*

ex·tra·ter·ri·to·ri·al·i·ty \-ˌtōr-ē-ˈal-ət-ē, -ˌtȯr-\ *n* : exemption from the application or jurisdiction of local law or tribunals ⟨diplomats enjoy *extraterritoriality*⟩

ex·trav·a·gance \ik-ˈstrav-i-gəns\ *n* **1 a :** an extravagant act; *esp* : excessive spending of money **b :** something extravagant **2 :** the quality or fact of being extravagant

ex·trav·a·gant \-gənt\ *adj* **1 :** going beyond what is reasonable or suitable ⟨*extravagant* praise⟩ **2 :** wasteful especially of money **3 :** too high in price **[**Middle French, from Medieval Latin *extravagans,* from Latin *extra-* + *vagari* "to wander about"**]** **syn** see EXCESSIVE — **ex·trav·a·gant·ly** *adv*

△ **origin** *Extravagant* is derived from Medieval Latin *extravagans,* formed from the prefix *extra-,* meaning "outside" or "beyond", and the verb *vagari,* "to wander about". Something that is *extravagant,* then, wanders beyond the borders of its usual home. Developing from its literal sense, "wandering", *extravagant* came to mean "exceeding the limits of reason or necessity" and "lacking in moderation, balance, and restraint". From these is derived the related wasteful sense of *extravagant,* that is, "spending much more than necessary".

ex·trav·a·gan·za \ik-ˌstrav-ə-ˈgan-zə\ *n* **1 :** a literary or musical work marked by extreme freedom of style and structure **2 :** a spectacular show **[**Italian *estravaganza,* literally, "extravagance"**]**

ex·tra·ve·hic·u·lar \ˌek-strə-vē-ˈhik-yə-lər\ *adj* : taking place outside a vehicle (as a spacecraft)

ex·tra·vert *or* **ex·tro·vert** \ˈek-strə-ˌvərt\ *n* : a person whose attention and interests are directed wholly or predominantly toward what is outside the self — **ex·tra·ver·sion** \ˌek-strə-ˈvər-zhən, -shən\ *n* — **extravert** *adj* — **ex·tra·vert·ed** \ˈek-strə-ˌvərt-əd\ *adj*

[1]**ex·treme** \ik-ˈstrēm\ *adj* **1 a :** existing in a very high degree ⟨*extreme* poverty⟩ **b :** going to great or exaggerated lengths **c :** exceeding the ordinary, usual, or expected ⟨*extreme* measures⟩ **2 :** most distant from a center ⟨an *extreme* outpost⟩ **3 :** farthest advanced : UTMOST ⟨the *extreme* edge of the cliff⟩ **[**Middle French, from Latin *extremus,* superlative of *exter, exterus* "being on the outside"**]** — **ex·treme·ly** *adv* — **ex·treme·ness** *n*

[2]**extreme** *n* **1 :** an extreme state, condition, or degree **2 a :** something situated at or marking one end or the other of a range ⟨*extremes* of heat and cold⟩ **b :** the first term or the last term of a mathematical proportion **3 :** highest degree : MAXIMUM **4 :** an extreme measure or expedient ⟨go to *extremes*⟩

extremely high frequency *n* : a ratio frequency in the range between 30,000 and 300,000 megahertz — abbreviation *EHF*

extreme unction *n* : ANOINTING OF THE SICK

ex·trem·ism \ik-ˈstrē-ˌmiz-əm\ *n* : advocacy or practice of extreme measures especially in politics; *esp* : RADICALISM — **ex·trem·ist** \-məst\ *n or adj*

ex·trem·i·ty \ik-ˈstrem-ət-ē\ *n, pl* **-ties 1 a :** the farthest or most remote part, section, or point **b :** a limb of the body; *esp* : a human hand or foot **2 a :** extreme danger or critical need **b :** a moment of such danger or need **3 :** the utmost degree (as of emotion or pain) **4 :** a drastic or desperate act or measure

ex·tri·cate \ˈek-strə-ˌkāt\ *vt* : to free or remove from an entanglement or difficulty **[**Latin *extricare,* from *ex-* + *tricae* "trifles, perplexities"**]** — **ex·tri·ca·ble** \ek-ˈstrik-ə-bəl, ˈek-strik-\ *adj* — **ex·tri·ca·tion** \ˌek-strə-ˈkā-shən\ *n*

• **syn** EXTRICATE, DISENTANGLE, UNTANGLE mean to free from what binds or holds back. EXTRICATE implies the use of care or ingenuity in freeing from a difficult position or situation; DISENTANGLE implies a painstaking separating of two or more things that are confused together or closely interrelated; UNTANGLE suggests straightening out something whose parts are confusingly tangled or disordered.

ex·trin·sic \ek-ˈstrin-zik, -ˈstrin-sik\ *adj* **1 a :** not forming part of or belonging to a thing : EXTRANEOUS **b :** originating from or on the outside **2 :** EXTERNAL 2a **[**Latin *extrinsecus* "from without"**]** — **ex·trin·si·cal·ly** \-zi-kə-lē, -si, -klē\ *adv*

ex·trude \ik-ˈstrüd\ *vb* **1 :** to force, press, or push out ⟨volcanoes *extrude* lava⟩ **2 :** to shape (as metal) by forcing through a die **3 :** to become extruded **[**Latin *extrudere,* from *ex-* + *trudere* "to thrust"**]** — **ex·trud·er** *n*

ex·tru·sion \ik-ˈstrü-zhən\ *n* : the act or process of extruding; *also* : a form produced by this process **[**Medieval Latin *extrusio,* from Latin *extrudere* "to extrude"**]**

ex·tru·sive \-ˈstrü-siv, -ziv\ *adj* : formed by crystallization of lava poured out on the earth's surface ⟨*extrusive* rock⟩

ex·u·ber·ant \ig-ˈzü-bə-rənt, -brənt\ *adj* **1 :** joyously unrestrained and enthusiastic **2 :** extreme or excessive in degree, size, or extent **3 :** produced in great abundance **[**Middle French, from Latin *exuberare* "to be abundant", from *ex-* + *uber* "fruitful", from *uber* "udder"**]** — **ex·u·ber·ance** \-bə-rəns, -brənts\ *n* — **ex·u·ber·ant·ly** *adv*

ex·u·date \ˈeks-ə-ˌdāt, ˈegz-\ *n* : exuded matter

ex·ude \ig-ˈzüd\ *vb* **1 :** to discharge slowly through pores or cuts : OOZE ⟨*exude* sweat⟩ ⟨sap *exuding* from a cut stem⟩ **2 :** to give off or out conspicuously or abundantly ⟨*exuded* charm⟩ **[**Latin *exsudare,* from *ex-* + *sudare* "to sweat"**]** — **ex·u·da·tion** \ˌek-sü-ˈdā-shən, -syü-, -shü-\ *n* — **ex·u·da·tive** \ig-ˈzüd-ət-iv\ *adj*

ex·ult \ig-ˈzəlt\ *vi* : to be extremely and often triumphantly joyful **[**Middle French *exulter,* from Latin *exsultare,* literally, "to leap up", from *ex-* + *saltare* "to leap"**]** — **ex·ult·ing·ly** \-ˈzəl-ting-lē\ *adv*

ex·ult·ant \ig-ˈzəlt-nt\ *adj* : filled with or expressing great joy : JUBILANT — **ex·ult·ant·ly** *adv*

ex·ul·ta·tion \ˌeks-əl-ˈtā-shən, ˌegz-, -ˌəl-\ *n* : the act of exulting : the state of being exultant

ex·urb \ˈek-ˌsərb, ˈeg-ˌzərb\ *n* : a region or district outside a city and usually beyond its suburbs inhabited chiefly by well-to-do families **[***ex-* + *-urb* (as in *suburb*)**]** — **ex·ur·bia** \ek-ˈsər-bē-ə, eg-ˈzər-\ *n*

ex·ur·ban·ite \ek-ˈsər-bə-ˌnīt, eg-ˈzər-\ *n* : one who lives in an exurb

-ey — see -Y

[1]**eye** \ˈī\ *n* **1 a :** an organ of sight; *esp* : a rounded hollow organ lined with a sensitive retina and lodged in a bony orbit in the vertebrate skull **b :** the ability to see with the eyes **c :** the ability to perceive or appreciate ⟨an *eye* for beauty⟩ **d :** LOOK, GLANCE ⟨gave them the *eye*⟩ **e :** very close watching or observation ⟨kept an *eye* on them⟩ **f :** POINT OF VIEW, JUDGMENT — often used in pl. ⟨guilty in the *eyes* of the law⟩ **2 :** something suggestive of an eye: as **a :** the hole through the head of a needle **b :** a loop to receive a hook **c :** an undeveloped bud (as on a potato) **3 :** something central : CENTER ⟨the *eye* of a hurricane⟩ **[**Old English *ēage***]** — **eyed** \ˈīd\ *adj* — **eye·less** \ˈī-ləs\ *adj* — **eye·like** \ˈī-ˌlīk\ *adj*

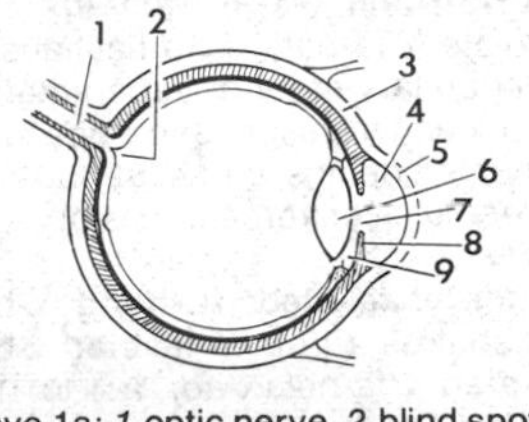

[1]eye 1a: *1* optic nerve, *2* blind spot, *3* sclera, *4* anterior chamber, *5* cornea, *6* lens, *7* pupil, *8* iris, *9* posterior chamber

[2]**eye** *vt* **eyed; eye·ing** *or* **ey·ing :** to fix the eyes on : watch closely

eye·ball \ˈī-ˌbȯl\ *n* : the vertebrate eye

eye·brow \ˈī-ˌbrau̇\ *n* : the ridge over the eye or hair growing on it

eye–catch·er \ˈī-ˌkach-ər, -ˌkech-\ *n* : something that strongly attracts the eye — **eye–catch·ing** \-ing\ *adj*

eye·cup \ˈī-ˌkəp\ *n* : a small oval cup with a rim curved to fit the orbit of the eye used for applying liquid remedies to the eyes

eye doctor *n* : a specialist (as an optometrist or ophthalmologist) in the examination, treatment, or care of the eyes

eye·drop·per \ˈī-ˌdräp-ər\ *n* : DROPPER 2

eye·ful \ˈī-ˌfu̇l\ *n* **1 :** a satisfying view **2 :** one that is visually attractive

eye·glass \ˈī-ˌglas\ *n* **1 a :** a glass lens used to improve faulty eyesight **b** *pl* : GLASS 2c **2 :** EYEPIECE

eye·lash \ˈī-ˌlash\ *n* **1** *pl* : the fringe of hair edging the eyelid **2 :** a single hair of the eyelashes

eye·let \ˈī-lət\ *n* **1 :** a small hole designed to receive a cord or

\ə\ **abut**	\au̇\ **out**	\i\ **tip**	\ȯ\ **saw**	\u̇\ **foot**
\ər\ **further**	\ch\ **chin**	\ī\ **life**	\ȯi\ **coin**	\y\ **yet**
\a\ **mat**	\e\ **pet**	\j\ **job**	\th\ **thin**	\yü\ **few**
\ā\ **take**	\ē\ **easy**	\ng\ **sing**	\t͟h\ **this**	\yu̇\ **cure**
\ä\ **cot, cart**	\g\ **go**	\ō\ **bone**	\ü\ **food**	\zh\ **vision**

used for decoration (as in embroidery) **2 :** GROMMET 2
eye•lid \'ī-ˌlid\ *n* **:** one of the movable lids of skin and muscle that can be closed over the eyeball
eye•lin•er \'ī-ˌlī-nər\ *n* **:** makeup used to emphasize the contour of the eyes
eye–open•er \'ī-ˌōp-nər, -ə-nər\ *n* **:** something startling or surprising — **eye–open•ing** \-ning\ *adj*
eye•piece \'ī-ˌpēs\ *n* **:** the lens or combination of lenses at the eye end of an optical instrument
eye shadow *n* **:** tinted makeup applied to the eyelids to accent the eyes
eye•sight \'ī-ˌsīt\ *n* **:** SIGHT, VISION ⟨keen *eyesight*⟩
eye socket *n* **:** ORBIT 1
eye•sore \'ī-ˌsōr, -ˌsȯr\ *n* **:** something displeasing to the sight
eye•spot \'ī-ˌspät\ *n* **:** a simple or primitive visual organ
eye•stalk \'ī-ˌstȯk\ *n* **:** a movable stalk bearing an eye at the tip in a crustacean
eye•strain \'ī-ˌstrān\ *n* **:** weariness or a strained state of the eye
eye•tooth \'ī-'tüth\ *n* **:** a canine tooth of the upper jaw
eye•wash \'ī-ˌwȯsh, -ˌwäsh\ *n* **1 :** an eye lotion **2 :** misleading or deceptive statements, actions, or procedures
eye•wit•ness \'ī-'wit-nəs\ *n* **:** a person who sees an occurrence and is able to give a firsthand account of it ⟨an *eyewitness* to an accident⟩
ey•rie \'īər-ē, *or like* AERIE\ *variant of* AERIE
Eze•chiel \i-zē-kyəl, -kē-əl\ *n* — see BIBLE table
Eze•kiel \i-'zē-kyəl, -kē-əl\ *n* — see BIBLE table
Ez•ra \'ez-rə\ *n* — see BIBLE table

F f—-fying

f \'ef\ *n, pl* **f's** *or* **fs** \'efs\ *often cap* **1 :** the 6th letter of the English alphabet **2 :** the musical tone F **3 :** a grade rating a student's work as failing
fa \'fä\ *n* **:** the 4th note of the diatonic scale **[**Medieval Latin**]**
Fa•bi•an \'fā-bē-ən\ *adj* **:** of, relating to, or being a society of socialists organized in England in 1884 to spread socialist principles gradually **[**the *Fabian* Society, from Quintus *Fabius* Maximus, died 203 B. C., Roman general**]** — **Fabian** *n* — **Fa•bi•an•ism** \-ə-ˌniz-əm\ *n*
¹fa•ble \'fā-bəl\ *n* **:** a fictitious narrative or statement: as **a :** a legendary story of supernatural happenings **b :** a story meant to teach a lesson; *esp* **:** one in which animals speak and act like human beings **c :** FALSEHOOD 1, LIE **[**Middle French, from Latin *fabula* "conversation, story", from *fari* "to speak"**] syn** see MYTH
²fable *vt* **fa•bled; fa•bling** \-bə-ling, -bling\ **:** to talk or write about as if true — **fa•bler** \-bə-lər, -blər\ *n*
fa•bled \'fā-bəld\ *adj* **1 :** FICTITIOUS **2 :** told or mentioned in fable **:** LEGENDARY
fab•ric \'fab-rik\ *n* **1 :** underlying structure **:** FRAMEWORK ⟨the *fabric* of society⟩ **2 a :** a woven or knitted cloth ⟨cotton *fabrics*⟩ **b :** a material that resembles cloth **[**Middle French *fabrique,* from Latin *fabrica* "workshop, structure", from *faber* "artisan, smith"**]**
fab•ri•cate \'fab-ri-ˌkāt\ *vt* **1 :** to construct especially from standardized parts **2 :** to make up in order to deceive **syn** see FICTION — **fab•ri•ca•tion** \ˌfab-ri-'kā-shən\ *n* — **fab•ri•ca•tor** \'fab-ri-ˌkāt-ər\ *n*
fab•u•list \'fab-yə-ləst\ *n* **:** a creator or teller of fables
fab•u•lous \'fab-yə-ləs\ *adj* **1 :** told about in fable ⟨*fabulous* animals⟩ **2 :** resembling a fable especially in incredible, marvelous, or exaggerated quality ⟨the *fabulous* adventures of an explorer⟩ **3 :** especially pleasing or satisfactory ⟨had a *fabulous* meal⟩ — **fab•u•lous•ly** *adv* — **fab•u•lous•ness** *n*
• syn FABULOUS, LEGENDARY, MYTHICAL mean having the character of what is invented or imagined. FABULOUS stresses marvelousness or incredibility often without implying actual nonexistence or impossibility ⟨the company made *fabulous profits*⟩ LEGENDARY suggests having a fabulous character created by the distortions or exaggerations of historical fact by popular tradition ⟨*legendary* deeds of Robin Hood⟩ MYTHICAL applies to what is or has been popularly believed but does not in fact exist ⟨*mythical* wood nymphs⟩
fa•cade *also* **fa•çade** \fə-'säd\ *n* **1 :** the front of a building especially when given special architectural treatment **2 :** a false, superficial, or artificial appearance ⟨a *facade* of wealth⟩ **[**French *façade***]**
¹face \'fās\ *n* **1 :** the front part of the head including the chin, mouth, nose, cheeks, eyes, and usually the forehead **2 :** PRESENCE ⟨brave in the *face* of danger⟩ **3 a :** LOOK 2a, EXPRESSION ⟨put a sad *face* on⟩ **b :** GRIMACE **4 a :** outward appearance ⟨suspicious on the *face* of it⟩ **b :** ASSURANCE 2, CONFIDENCE **c :** DIGNITY, PRESTIGE ⟨afraid to lose *face*⟩ **5 :** SURFACE: **a :** a front, upper, or outer surface; *esp* **:** an exposed surface of rock **b :** any of the plane surfaces that bound a geometric solid or a dihedral angle **c :** a surface or side that is marked or specially prepared ⟨the *face* of a clock⟩ **6 :** an end or wall (as of a mine tunnel) at which work is progressing **[**Old French, derived from Latin *facies* "make, form, face", from *facere* "to make"**]**

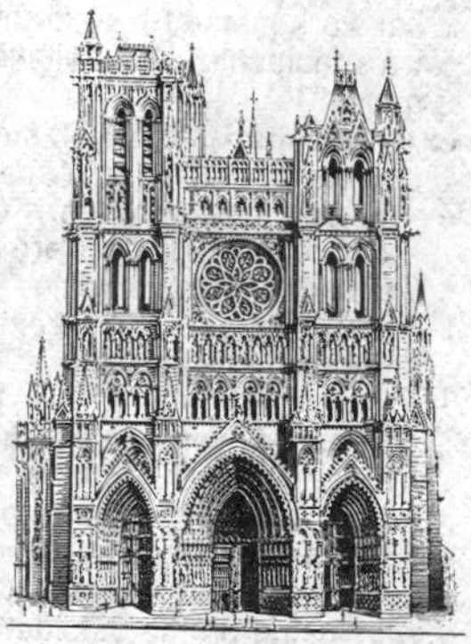
facade 1

²face *vb* **1 :** to confront brazenly ⟨*face* out a compromising situation⟩ **2 a :** to line near the edge especially with a different material **b :** to cover the front or surface of ⟨*faced* the building with marble⟩ **3 :** to bring face to face ⟨*face* one with the evidence⟩ **4 a :** to stand or sit with the face toward ⟨*face* the class⟩ **b :** to front on ⟨a house *facing* the park⟩ **5 a :** to oppose firmly ⟨*faces* danger bravely⟩ **b :** to master by confronting with determination ⟨*faced* down the critics of their policy⟩ **6 :** to turn or cause to turn the face or body in a specified direction
face card *n* **:** a playing card that is a king, queen, or jack
-faced \fāst\ *adj combining form* **:** having (such) a face or (so many) faces
face•down \'fās-'daun\ *adv* **:** with the face downward
face–lift•ing \'fās-ˌlif-ting\ *n* **1 :** plastic surgery for removal of facial defects (as wrinkles or sagging) **2 :** an alteration intended to modernize
face–off \'fā-ˌsȯf\ *n* **:** a method of putting the puck in play in ice hockey by dropping it between two opposing players
face•plate \'fā-ˌsplāt\ *n* **:** a disk fixed with its face at right angles to the live spindle of a lathe for the attachment of the work
fac•et \'fas-ət\ *n* **1 :** a small plane surface (as on a cut gem) **2 :** ASPECT 2, PHASE **3 :** the external surface of a unit of a compound eye (as of an insect) **[**French *facette,* from *face* "face"**]** — **fac•et•ed** \'fas-ət-əd\ *adj*
fa•ce•tious \fə-'sē-shəs\ *adj* **1 :** jocular in an awkward or inappropriate way **2 :** marked by often unseemly flippancy **[**Middle French *facetieux,* from *facetie* "jest", from Latin *facetia***]** — **fa•ce•tious•ly** *adv* — **fa•ce•tious•ness** *n*
face–to–face *adj* **:** being within each other's sight or presence ⟨a *face-to-face* interview⟩
face value *n* **1 :** the value indicated on the face (as of a bill or a stock certificate) **2 :** the apparent worth ⟨can't take a braggart's statements at *face value*⟩
¹fa•cial \'fā-shəl\ *adj* **:** of or relating to the face — **fa•cial•ly** \-shə-lē\ *adv*
²facial *n* **:** a facial treatment or massage
facial nerve *n* **:** either of the 7th pair of cranial nerves that control

facial and ear movements and transmit sensations of taste

fa·cies \'fā-shēz, -shē-,ēz\ *n, pl* **facies** : a particular form or appearance; *esp* : a rock or group of rocks that can be distinguished (as by composition) in a single rock mass [Latin, "face"]

fac·ile \'fas-əl\ *adj* **1 a** : easily accomplished or attained ⟨a *facile* success⟩ **b** : SPECIOUS, SUPERFICIAL ⟨too *facile* a solution to a complex problem⟩ **c** : easily produced and often insincere ⟨*facile* tears⟩ **2** : mild or yielding in disposition : PLIANT **3** : READY, FLUENT ⟨a *facile* writer⟩ [Middle French, from Latin *facilis,* from *facere* "to do, make"] — **fac·ile·ly** \-əl-lē, -ə-lē\ *adv* — **fac·ile·ness** \-əl-nəs\ *n*

fa·cil·i·tate \fə-'sil-ə-,tāt\ *vt* : to make easier — **fa·cil·i·ta·tion** \-,sil-ə-'tā-shən\ *n*

fa·cil·i·ty \fə-'sil-ət-ē\ *n, pl* **-ties 1** : the quality of being easily performed **2** : ease in performance : APTITUDE **3** : readiness to be influenced : PLIANCY **4 a** : something that makes an action, operation, or course of conduct easier — usually used in pl. ⟨library *facilities*⟩ ⟨*facilities* for graduate study⟩ **b** : something built, installed, or established to serve a particular purpose ⟨a hospital *facility*⟩

fac·ing \'fā-sing\ *n* **1 a** : a lining along an edge (as of a garment) **b** *pl* : the collar, cuffs, and trimmings of a uniform coat **2** : an ornamental or protective layer ⟨a frame house with brick *facing*⟩ **3** : material for facing

fac·sim·i·le \fak-'sim-ə-lē\ *n* **1** : an exact copy **2** : the transmission of graphic matter by wire or radio and its reproduction [Latin *fac simile* "make similar"] **syn** see DUPLICATE

fact \'fakt\ *n* **1 a** : a thing done : DEED **b** : CRIME 1 **2** : something that exists, happens, or has objective reality ⟨spaceflight is now a *fact*⟩ **3** : information or an item of information that is accurate and true ⟨they do not know *fact* from fancy⟩ [Latin *factum,* from *facere* "to make, do"] — **in fact** : in truth : ACTUALLY

fac·tion \'fak-shən\ *n* **1** : a group or combination acting together within and usually against a larger body (as in a state, political party, or church) : CLIQUE **2** : dissension within a group [Latin *factio* "act of making, faction", from *facere* "to make, do"] — **fac·tion·al** \-shnəl, -shən-l\ *adj* — **fac·tion·al·ism** \-,iz-əm\ *n* — **fac·tion·al·ist** \-shnəl-əst, -shən-l-\ *n*

fac·tious \'fak-shəs\ *adj* **1** : of, relating to, or caused by faction ⟨*factious* disputes⟩ **2** : inclined to faction or the formation of factions ⟨*factious* politicians⟩ — **fac·tious·ly** *adv* — **fac·tious·ness** *n*

fac·ti·tious \fak-'tish-əs\ *adj* : not natural or genuine : ARTIFICIAL ⟨a *factitious* display of grief⟩ [Latin *facticius,* from *facere* "to make, do"] **syn** see FICTITIOUS — **fac·ti·tious·ly** *adv* — **fac·ti·tious·ness** *n*

[1]**fac·tor** \'fak-tər\ *n* **1 a** : one that buys or sells property for another **b** : an agent in charge of a trading post **2** : something that actively contributes to the production of a result ⟨hard work was a *factor* in their success⟩ **3** : GENE **4** : any of two or more numbers or mathematical expressions that when multiplied together form a product [Middle French *facteur,* from Latin *factor* "doer", from *facere* "to do, make"] — **fac·tor·ship** \-,ship\ *n*

[2]**factor** *vb* **fac·tored; fac·tor·ing** \-tə-ring, -tring\ **1** : to resolve into factors **2** : to work as a factor — **fac·tor·able** \-tə-rə-bəl, -trə-\ *adj*

[1]**fac·to·ri·al** \fak-'tōr-ē-əl, -'tȯr-\ *n* **1** : the product of all the positive integers from 1 to a given number **2** : the quantity that is obtained by substituting 0 in the notation for a factorial and that is arbitrarily defined as equal to 1

[2]**factorial** *adj* : of or relating to factors, factoring, or factorials

fac·tor·iza·tion \,fak-tə-rə-'zā-shən\ *n* : the process or result of taking factors

fac·to·ry \'fak-tə-rē, -trē\ *n, pl* **-ries 1** : a trading station where resident factors trade **2** : a building or set of buildings used or suitable for manufacturing

factory system *n* : a system of manufacturing based on concentration of industry into large establishments that began with the Industrial Revolution

fac·to·tum \fak-'tōt-əm\ *n* : an employee with numerous varied duties [Latin *fac* "do" + *totum* "everything"]

fac·tu·al \'fak-chə-wəl, -chəl\ *adj* **1** : of or relating to fact or facts ⟨*factual* evidence⟩ **2** : restricted to or based on fact ⟨little *factual* knowledge of ancient civilizations⟩ — **fac·tu·al·i·ty** \,fak-chə-'wal-ət-ē\ *n* — **fac·tu·al·ly** \'fak-chə-wə-lē, -chə-lē\ *adv* — **fac·tu·al·ness** *n*

fac·u·la \'fak-yə-lə\ *n, pl* **-lae** \-,lē, -,lī\ : any of the brighter regions of the sun's photosphere [New Latin, from Latin *fac-, fax* "torch"]

fac·ul·ta·tive \'fak-əl-,tāt-iv\ *adj* **1** : taking place under some conditions but not under others ⟨*facultative* diapause⟩ **2** : showing the typical mode of life under some environmental conditions but not under others ⟨*facultative* anaerobes⟩ — **fac·ul·ta·tive·ly** *adv*

fac·ul·ty \'fak-əl-tē\ *n, pl* **-ties 1** : ability to do something : TALENT ⟨a *faculty* for making friends⟩ **2** : one of the powers of the mind or body ⟨the *faculty* of hearing⟩ **3** : the teachers in a school or college or in one of its departments **4** : the members of a profession [Middle French *faculté,* from Latin *facultas,* from *facilis* "facile"]

fad \'fad\ *n* : a practice or interest followed for a time with great zeal : CRAZE [origin unknown] — **fad·dist** \'fad-əst\ *n*

[1]**fade** \'fād\ *vb* **1** : to lose freshness or vitality : WITHER **2** : to lose or cause to lose freshness or brilliance of color **3** : to grow dim or disappear gradually ⟨their hopes *faded*⟩ **4** : to change gradually in loudness or visibility — used of a motion-picture image or of an electronics signal and usually with *in* or *out* [Middle French *fader,* from *fade* "feeble, insipid", derived from Latin *fatuus* "fatuous, insipid"]

[2]**fade** *n* : a gradual changing of one picture to another in a motion-picture or television sequence

fade·less \'fād-ləs\ *adj* : not susceptible to fading

fae·cal, fae·ces *variant of* FECAL, FECES

fa·er·ie *also* **fa·ery** \'fā-rē, 'fā-ə-rē, 'faər-ē, 'feər-ē\ *n, pl* **fa·er·ies 1** : FAIRYLAND **2** : FAIRY [Middle French *faerie*] — **faery** *adj*

[1]**fag** \'fag\ *vb* **fagged; fag·ging 1** : DRUDGE **2** : to act as a fag **3** : to tire by strenuous activity : EXHAUST [obsolete *fag* "to droop"]

[2]**fag** *n* **1** : an English public-school boy who acts as servant to another **2** : MENIAL, DRUDGE

[3]**fag** *n* : CIGARETTE [*fag end*]

fag end *n* **1 a** : the last part or coarser end of a web of cloth **b** : the untwisted end of a rope **2 a** : a poor or worn-out end **b** : the extreme end [Middle English *fagge* "flap"]

fag·ot *or* **fag·got** \'fag-ət\ *n* : a bundle of sticks or twigs used especially for fuel [Middle French *fagot*]

fag·ot·ing *or* **fag·got·ing** \'fag-ət-ing\ *n* : an embroidery produced by tying threads in hourglass-shaped clusters

Fahr·en·heit \'far-ən-,hīt\ *adj* : relating or conforming to a temperature scale on which under standard atmospheric pressure the boiling point of water is at 212 degrees above the zero of the scale and the freezing point is at 32 degrees above zero — abbreviation *F* [Gabriel D. *Fahrenheit*]

fa·ience *or* **fa·ïence** \fā-'äns\ *n* : earthenware decorated with opaque colored glazes [French, from *Faenza,* Italy]

[1]**fail** \'fāl\ *vb* **1 a** : to lose strength : WEAKEN ⟨as one's eyesight *fails*⟩ **b** : to stop functioning ⟨the engine *failed*⟩ **2 a** : to fall short ⟨failed in their duty⟩ **b** : to prove inadequate : give way or break down ⟨the water supply *failed*⟩ **c** (1) : to be unsuccessful in passing ⟨*failed* the exam⟩ (2) : to grade as not passing ⟨*fail* a student⟩ **d** : to become insolvent ⟨the bank *failed*⟩ **3** : DISAPPOINT, DESERT ⟨*fail* a friend⟩ **4 a** : to be such as not ⟨the play *failed* to excite me⟩ **b** : to act, behave, or exist so as not ⟨the valve *failed* to function⟩ ⟨*failed* to see the red light⟩ [Old French *faillir,* from Latin *fallere* "to deceive, disappoint"]

[2]**fail** *n* : FAILURE — usually used in the phrase *without fail*

[1]**fail·ing** \'fā-ling\ *n* : a slight defect in character or conduct **syn** see FAULT

[2]**failing** *prep* : in the absence or lack of ⟨*failing* specific instructions, use your own judgment⟩

faille \'fīl\ *n* : a somewhat shiny closely woven ribbed fabric [French]

fail–safe \'fāl-,sāf\ *adj* : incorporating some feature for automatically counteracting the effect of an anticipated possible failure

fail·ure \'fāl-yər\ *n* **1 a** : a failing to do or perform ⟨their *failure* to appear⟩ **b** : a state of inability to perform a normal function adequately ⟨heart *failure*⟩ **2 a** : lack of satisfactory performance or effect ⟨our *failure* in the campaign⟩ **b :** a lack of commercial or financial success ⟨a business *failure*⟩ **3 a :** a falling short **:** DEFICIENCY ⟨crop *failure*⟩ **b :** DETERIORATION, BREAKDOWN ⟨a *failure* of memory⟩ **4 :** one that has failed

¹fain \'fān\ *adj* **1** *archaic* **:** GLAD **2** *archaic* **:** INCLINED 1 **3** *archaic* **:** OBLIGED [Old English *fægen*]

²fain *adv* **1** *archaic* **:** WILLINGLY **2** *archaic* **:** RATHER 1

¹faint \'fānt\ *adj* **1 :** lacking courage and spirit **:** COWARDLY ⟨*faint* heart⟩ **2 :** being weak, dizzy, and likely to faint ⟨feel *faint* at the sight of blood⟩ **3 :** lacking strength **:** FEEBLE ⟨a *faint* attempt⟩ **4 :** lacking distinctness **:** barely perceptible ⟨a *faint* sound⟩ [Old French *feint, faint,* from *feindre, faindre* "to feign, shirk"] — **faint•ly** *adv* — **faint•ness** *n*

²faint *vi* **1** *archaic* **:** to lose courage or spirit **2 :** to lose consciousness because of a temporary decrease in the blood supply to the brain

³faint *n* **:** an act or condition of fainting

faint•heart•ed \'fānt-'härt-əd\ *adj* **:** lacking courage or resolution **:** TIMID — **faint•heart•ed•ly** *adv* — **faint•heart•ed•ness** *n*

¹fair \'faər, 'feər\ *adj* **1 :** attractive in appearance **:** BEAUTIFUL ⟨*fair* lady⟩ ⟨our *fair* city⟩ **2 :** deceptively agreeable **:** SPECIOUS ⟨don't trust those *fair* words⟩ **3 a :** CLEAN, PURE ⟨sully a *fair* name⟩ **b :** CLEAR, LEGIBLE ⟨make a *fair* copy⟩ **4 :** not stormy or cloudy ⟨*fair* weather⟩ **5 a :** marked by impartiality and honesty **:** JUST **b :** conforming with the rules **:** ALLOWED ⟨*fair* play⟩ **c :** open to legitimate pursuit or attack ⟨*fair* game⟩ **6 a :** PROMISING, LIKELY ⟨a *fair* chance of winning⟩ **b :** favorable to a ship's course ⟨a *fair* wind⟩ **7 :** not dark ⟨a *fair* complexion⟩ **8 :** moderately good ⟨made a *fair* grade⟩ [Old English *fæger*] — **fair•ness** *n*

• **syn** FAIR, EQUITABLE, IMPARTIAL, UNBIASED mean free from favor toward either or any side. FAIR implies eliminating one's own feelings, prejudices, or desires so as to achieve a proper balance of conflicting interests ⟨a *fair* settlement of property claims⟩ EQUITABLE stresses equal treatment of all concerned ⟨*equitable* sharing in the profits of a venture⟩ IMPARTIAL implies absence or suppression of favor or prejudice in making a judgment ⟨an *impartial* referee⟩ UNBIASED stresses more definitely complete absence of prejudice or predisposition ⟨*unbiased* history⟩ **syn** see in addition BEAUTIFUL

²fair *adv* **1 :** in a fair way **2 :** so as to be a fair ball

³fair *n* **1 :** a gathering of buyers and sellers at a particular place and time for trade **2 :** a competitive exhibition (as of farm products) usually with accompanying entertainment and amusements **3 :** a sale of a collection of articles usually for a charitable purpose [Old French *feire,* from Medieval Latin *feria,* from Latin *feriae* (pl.) "holidays"]

fair ball *n* **:** a batted baseball that settles within the foul lines in the infield, that first touches the ground within the foul lines in the outfield, or that is within the foul lines when bounding to the outfield past first or third base or when going beyond the outfield for a home run

fair catch *n* **:** a catch of a kicked football by a player who having given a prescribed signal gives up his right to advance the ball and may not be tackled

fair•ground \'faər-,graünd, 'feər-\ *n* **:** an area set aside for the holding of fairs

¹fair•ing \'faər-ing, 'feər-\ *n, British* **:** GIFT; *esp* **:** a present bought or given at a fair

²fairing *n* **:** a structure (as on an aircraft or missile) whose function is to produce a smooth outline and reduce resistance to motion through the air

fair•ish \'faər-ish, 'feər-\ *adj* **:** fairly good or large

fair•lead \'faər-,lēd, 'feər-\ *n* **:** a block or ring that serves as a guide for a line on board a boat or ship and prevents it from chafing

fair•ly \'faər-lē, 'feər-\ *adv* **1 :** HANDSOMELY, FAVORABLY ⟨*fairly* situated⟩ **2 :** QUITE, COMPLETELY ⟨*fairly* bursting with pride⟩ **3 :** in a fair manner **:** JUSTLY ⟨treat each person *fairly*⟩ **4 :** MODERATELY ⟨a *fairly* easy job⟩

fair–spo•ken \'faər-'spō-kən, 'feər-\ *adj* **:** pleasant and courteous in speech

fair–trade \-'trād\ *adj* **:** of, relating to, or being an agreement between a producer and a seller of an item that it will not be sold below a certain price — **fair–trade** *vt*

fair•way \-,wā\ *n* **1 :** a navigable part of a river, bay, or harbor **2 :** a path or line of travel **3 :** the mowed part of a golf course between a tee and a green

fair–weather *adj* **:** loyal only when things are going well ⟨a *fair-weather* friend⟩

fairy \'faər-ē, 'feər-\ *n, pl* **fairies :** a usually small humanlike being of folklore and romance endowed with magical powers [Old French *faerie* "fairyland, fairy people, from *feie, fee* "fairy", from Latin *Fata,* goddess of fate, from *fatum* "fate"] — **fairy•like** \-,līk\ *adj*

fairy•land \-,land\ *n* **1 :** a land of fairies **2 :** a place of delicate beauty or magical charm

fairy ring *n* **:** a ring of mushrooms in a lawn or meadow growing outward from a central point

fairy shrimp *n* **:** any of several delicate transparent freshwater crustaceans (order Anostraca)

fairy tale *n* **1 :** a simple children's story about supernatural beings — called also *fairy story* **2 :** a made-up story usually meant to mislead

fait ac•com•pli \'fāt-,ak-,ōⁿ-'plē, ,fe-,tak-, -,ōⁿm-\ *n, pl* **faits accomplis** *same, or* -'plēz\ **:** a thing accomplished and presumably irreversible [French, "accomplished fact"]

faith \'fāth\ *n* **1 a :** allegiance to duty or a person **:** LOYALTY **b :** fidelity to one's promises **2 a** (1) **:** belief and trust in and loyalty to God (2) **:** belief in the traditional doctrines of a religion **b** (1) **:** firm belief in something for which there is no proof (2) **:** complete confidence **3 :** something that is believed especially with strong conviction; *also* **:** a system of religious beliefs [Old French *feid, foi,* from Latin *fides*] **syn** see BELIEF — **in faith :** by my faith **:** TRULY

¹faith•ful \'fāth-fəl\ *adj* **1 :** full of faith especially in God **2 :** steadfast in keeping promises or in fulfilling duties ⟨a *faithful* worker⟩ **3 :** steady, firm, and dependable in allegiance or devotion **:** LOYAL ⟨a *faithful* friend⟩ **4 :** true to the facts **:** ACCURATE ⟨a *faithful* copy⟩ — **faith•ful•ly** \-fə-lē\ *adv* — **faith•ful•ness** *n*

• **syn** LOYAL, CONSTANT, STEADFAST: FAITHFUL implies unswerving adherence to a person or to an oath or promise; LOYAL implies a firm resistance to any temptation to desert or betray; CONSTANT implies continuing firmness of emotional attachment; STEADFAST stresses a steady and unwavering adherence.

²faithful *n, pl* **faith•ful** *or* **faith•fuls :** one that is faithful: as **a :** a member of a religious body ⟨the *faithful* observe the holy days⟩ **b :** a loyal follower or member ⟨party *faithfuls* gather on election night⟩

faith•less \'fāth-ləs\ *adj* **1 :** not having faith **2 :** not worthy of trust or reliance **:** DISLOYAL — **faith•less•ly** *adv* — **faith•less•ness** *n*

• **syn** FALSE, DISLOYAL, PERFIDIOUS: FAITHLESS may apply to any failure to keep a promise or pledge or to any breach of allegiance or loyalty; FALSE often implies a degree of premeditation and deception in betrayal or treachery ⟨*false* friends⟩ DISLOYAL implies a lack of complete faithfulness to a friend, cause, leader, or country ⟨*disloyal* officers⟩ PERFIDIOUS implies an inability to be faithful or reliable.

¹fake \'fāk\ *vt* **1 :** to treat so as to falsify **:** DOCTOR ⟨*faked* the statistics to prove a point⟩ **2 :** COUNTERFEIT ⟨*fake* a rare edition⟩ **3 :** PRETEND, SIMULATE ⟨*fake* surprise⟩ [origin unknown] — **fak•er** \'fā-kər\ *n* — **fak•ery** \-kə-rē, -krē\ *n*

²fake *n* **1 :** an imitation that is passed off as genuine **:** FRAUD, COUNTERFEIT ⟨the supposed antique was a *fake*⟩ **2 :** IMPOSTOR, CHARLATAN

³fake *adj* **:** COUNTERFEIT, PHONY

fa•kir \fə-'kiər, fä-, fa-, 'fā-kər\ *n* **1 :** a Muslim beggar **:** DERVISH **2 :** a wandering Hindu ascetic or wonder-worker [Arabic *faqīr,* literally, "poor man"]

fal•chion \'fȯl-chən\ *n* **:** a broad-bladed slightly curved medieval sword [Old French *fauchon,* from *fauchier* "to mow", from Latin *falc-, falx* "sickle, scythe"]

fal•con \'fal-kən *also* 'fȯl- *sometimes* 'fȯ-kən\ *n* **1 :** a hawk trained for use in falconry; *esp* **:** a female peregrine falcon — compare TIERCEL **2 :** any of various hawks with long wings and a notch and tooth on the upper half of the bill [Old French, from Late Latin *falco*]

fal•con•er \-kə-nər\ *n* **:** one that hunts with hawks or breeds or trains hawks for hunting

fal•con•ry \'fal-kən-rē *also* 'fȯl- *sometimes* 'fȯ-kən-\ *n* **1 :** the art of training falcons to pursue game **2 :** the sport of hunting with falcons

fal•de•ral \'fäl-də-,räl\ *variant of* FOLDEROL

¹fall \'fȯl\ *vi* **fell** \'fel\; **fall•en** \'fȯ-lən\; **fall•ing 1 a :** to descend freely by the force of gravity **b :** to hang freely ⟨the drapes *fall* quite gracefully⟩ **c :** to drop oneself to a lower position ⟨*fall* to one's knees⟩ **d :** to come as if by descending ⟨darkness *falls* early in winter⟩ **2 a :** to go down ⟨the temperature *fell* 10 degrees⟩ **b :** to drop in pitch or volume **c :** to become uttered ⟨as the words *fell* from my lips⟩ **d :** to become lowered ⟨her eyes *fell*⟩ **3 a :** to tip over from an erect position ⟨the lamp *fell* on its side⟩ **b :** to enter as if unaware **:** STUMBLE ⟨*fell* into error⟩ **c :** to drop down wounded or dead; *esp* **:** to die in battle **d :** to become captured or defeated ⟨the fortress *fell*⟩ **e :** to suffer ruin or failure **4 :** to commit a wrong or immoral act **5 a :** to move or extend in a downward direction ⟨the ground *falls* away to the east⟩ **b :** SUBSIDE 4, ABATE **c :** to decline in quality, activity, quantity, or value **d :** to lose weight — used with *off* or *away* **e :** to assume a look of shame or dejection ⟨my face *fell* when I lost⟩ **6 a :** to occur at a certain time **b :** to come by chance ⟨*fell* in with a bad crowd⟩ **c :** DEVOLVE ⟨it *fell* to us to break the news⟩ **d :** to have the proper place or station ⟨the accent *falls* on the second syllable⟩ **7 :** to come within the scope of something **8 :** to pass from one condition of body or mind to another ⟨*fall* ill⟩ ⟨*fall* asleep⟩ **9 :** to set about heartily or actively ⟨*fell* to work⟩ [Old English *feallan*] — **fall flat :** to produce no response or result **:** FAIL — **fall for 1 :** to fall in love with **2 :** to become a victim of — **fall foul 1 :** to have a collision — used chiefly of ships **2 :** to have a quarrel **:** CLASH — often used with *of* — **fall from grace 1 :** to lapse morally **:** SIN **2 :** BACKSLIDE — **fall into line :** to comply with a certain course of action — **fall over oneself :** to display excessive eagerness — **fall short 1 :** to be deficient **2 :** to fail to attain

[2]**fall** *n* **1 :** the act of falling by the force of gravity ⟨a *fall* from a horse⟩ **2 a :** a falling out, off, or away **:** DROPPING ⟨the *fall* of the leaves⟩ **b :** AUTUMN **c :** a thing or quantity that falls ⟨a heavy *fall* of snow⟩ **3 a :** loss of greatness **:** COLLAPSE **b :** the surrender or capture of a besieged place **c :** lapse or departure from innocence or goodness; *esp, often cap* **:** the act of Adam and Eve in eating the forbidden fruit **d :** loss of chastity **4 a :** the descent of land or a hill **:** SLOPE **b :** WATERFALL — usually used in pl. **5 :** a decrease in size, quantity, degree, activity, or value **6 :** the distance which something falls **7 a :** an act of forcing a wrestler's shoulders to the mat **b :** a bout of wrestling

fal•la•cious \fə-'lā-shəs\ *adj* **1 :** embodying a fallacy ⟨a *fallacious* argument⟩ **2 :** DELUSIVE, MISLEADING ⟨cherish a *fallacious* hope⟩ — **fal•la•cious•ly** *adv* — **fal•la•cious•ness** *n*

fal•la•cy \'fal-ə-sē\ *n, pl* **-cies 1 :** a false or mistaken idea ⟨the popular *fallacy* that poets are impractical⟩ **2 :** false or illogical reasoning or an instance of this [Latin *fallacia,* from *fallac-, fallax* "deceptive", from *fallere* "to deceive"]

fall back *vi* **:** RETREAT 1, RECEDE

fall•er \'fó-lər\ *n* **:** a logger who fells trees

fall guy *n* **1 :** one that is easily duped **2 :** SCAPEGOAT 2

fal•li•ble \'fal-ə-bəl\ *adj* **:** liable to err or be erroneous ⟨even experts are *fallible*⟩ ⟨a *fallible* generalization⟩ [Medieval Latin *fallibilis,* from Latin *fallere* "to deceive"] — **fal•li•bil•i•ty** \,fal-ə-'bil-ət-ē\ *n* — **fal•li•bly** \'fal-ə-blē\ *adv*

fall in *vi* **:** to take one's proper place in a military formation

fall•ing–out \,fó-ling-'aůt\ *n, pl* **fallings–out** *or* **falling–outs :** QUARREL 2

falling star *n* **:** METEOR

fal•lo•pi•an tube \fə-,lō-pē-ən-\ *n, often cap F* **:** either of the pair of tubes that conduct the egg from the ovary to the uterus [Gabriel *Fallopius,* died 1562, Italian anatomist]

fall•out \'fó-,laůt\ *n* **:** the often radioactive particles resulting from a nuclear explosion and descending through the atmosphere

fall out \'fó-,laůt, 'fó-\ *vi* **1 :** CHANCE 1, HAPPEN **2 :** to have a quarrel **3 a :** to leave one's place in the ranks **b :** to leave a building to take one's place in a military formation

[1]**fal•low** \'fal-ō\ *adj* **:** of a light yellowish brown [Old English *fealu*]

[2]**fallow** *n* **1 :** land for crops allowed to lie idle during the growing season **2 :** the state or period of being fallow ⟨fields in summer *fallow*⟩ [Old English *fealg* "plowed land"]

[3]**fallow** *vt* **:** to till (land) without seeding

[4]**fallow** *adj* **1 :** left untilled or if tilled left unsown **2 :** DORMANT 1, INACTIVE — **fal•low•ness** *n*

fallow deer *n* **:** a small European deer with broad antlers and a pale yellow coat spotted white in the summer

[1]**false** \'fóls\ *adj* **1 :** ARTIFICIAL 1 ⟨*false* teeth⟩ **2 a :** intentionally untrue ⟨*false* testimony⟩ **b :** adjusted or made so as to deceive ⟨*false* scales⟩ **c :** tending to mislead ⟨a *false* promise⟩ **3 :** not genuine or sincere ⟨*false* modesty⟩ ⟨a *false* prophet⟩ **4 :** not faithful or loyal **:** TREACHEROUS **5 :** not essential to structure ⟨a *false* ceiling⟩ **6 :** inaccurate in pitch ⟨a *false* note⟩ **7 a :** based on mistaken ideas ⟨*false* pride⟩ **b :** inconsistent with the true facts ⟨a *false* sense of security⟩ [Latin *falsus,* from *fallere* "to deceive"] **syn** see FAITHLESS — **false•ly** *adv* — **false•ness** *n*

fallow deer

[2]**false** *adv* **:** in a false or faithless manner **:** TREACHEROUSLY ⟨they played us *false*⟩

false•hood \'fóls-,hůd\ *n* **1 :** an untrue statement **:** LIE **2 :** absence of truth or accuracy **3 :** the practice of lying

false rib *n* **:** a rib whose cartilages unite indirectly or not at all with the sternum — compare FLOATING RIB

[1]**fal•set•to** \fól-'set-ō\ *n, pl* **-tos 1 :** an artifically high voice; *esp* **:** an artificial singing voice that extends above the range of the full voice especially of a tenor **2 :** a singer who uses falsetto [Italian, from *falso* "false", from Latin *falsus*]

[2]**falsetto** *adv* **:** in falsetto

fal•si•fy \'fól-sə-,fī\ *vb* **-fied; -fy•ing 1 :** to make false **:** change so as to deceive ⟨*falsify* financial accounts⟩ **2 a :** to tell lies **:** LIE **b :** MISREPRESENT **3 :** to prove to be false ⟨promises *falsified* by events⟩ — **fal•si•fi•ca•tion** \,fól-sə-fə-'kā-shən\ *n* — **fal•si•fi•er** \'fól-sə-,fī-ər, -,fīr\ *n*

fal•si•ty \'fól-sət-ē, -stē\ *n, pl* **-ties 1 :** something false **:** LIE **2 :** the quality or state of being false

falt•boat \'fält-,bōt\ *n* **:** FOLDBOAT [German *faltboot,* from *falten* "to fold" + *boot* "boat"]

[1]**fal•ter** \'fól-tər\ *vb* **fal•tered; fal•ter•ing** \'fól-tə-ring, -tring\ **1 :** to move unsteadily **:** WAVER **2 :** to stumble or hesitate in speech **:** STAMMER **3 :** to hesitate in purpose or action ⟨courage that never *falters*⟩ [Middle English *falteren*] **syn** see HESITATE — **fal•ter•er** \-tər-ər\ *n* — **fal•ter•ing•ly** \-tə-ring-lē, -tring-\ *adv*

[2]**falter** *n* **:** an act or instance of faltering

fame \'fām\ *n* **:** the fact or condition of being known to the public **:** RENOWN [Old French, from Latin *fama* "report, fame"]

famed \'fāmd\ *adj* **:** FAMOUS 1, WELL-KNOWN, RENOWNED

fa•mil•ial \fə-'mil-yəl\ *adj* **:** of, relating to, or characteristic of a family

[1]**fa•mil•iar** \fə-'mil-yər\ *n* **1 :** an intimate associate **:** COMPANION **2 :** a spirit held to attend and serve or guard a person — called also *familiar spirit* **3 :** one that frequents a place

[2]**familiar** *adj* **1 :** closely acquainted **:** INTIMATE ⟨*familiar* friends⟩ **2 :** INFORMAL 1, CASUAL ⟨spoke in a *familiar* manner⟩ **3 :** overly intimate **:** FORWARD, PRESUMPTUOUS **4 a :** frequently seen or experienced **b :** of everyday occurrence **5 :** having a good knowledge ⟨*familiar* with the rules of soccer⟩ [Old French *familier,* from Latin *familiaris,* from *familia* "family"] — **fa•mil•iar•ly** *adv*

fa•mil•iar•i•ty \fə-,mil-'yar-ət-ē, -,mil-ē-'ar-\ *n, pl* **-ties 1 :** close friendship **:** INTIMACY **2 :** close acquaintance with or knowledge of something ⟨acquire a *familiarity* with French⟩ **3 :** lack of formality **:** freedom and ease in personal relations **4 :** an unduly bold or forward act or expression

fa•mil•iar•ize \fə-'mil-yə-,rīz\ *vt* **1 :** to make thoroughly acquainted **:** ACCUSTOM ⟨*familiarize* oneself with a new job⟩ **2 :** to make well known ⟨advertising *familiarizes* the name of a product⟩ — **fa•mil•iar•iza•tion** \-,mil-yə-rə-'zā-shən\ *n*

fam•i•ly \'fam-lē, -ə-lē\ *n, pl* **-lies 1 :** a group of persons of common ancestry **:** CLAN **2 :** a group of individuals living under one roof and under one head **:** HOUSEHOLD **3 :** a group of things having common characteristics or properties **4 :** a social group composed of parents and their children **5 :** a group of related plants or animals ranking in biological classification above a genus and below an order [Latin *familia* "household (including servants as well as kin of the householder)", from *famulus* "servant"]

family name *n* : SURNAME

family tree *n* **1** : GENEALOGY 1 **2** : a diagram showing family relationships

fam•ine \ˈfam-ən\ *n* **1** : an extreme general scarcity of food **2** : a great shortage [Middle French, from Latin *fames* "hunger"]

fam•ish \ˈfam-ish\ *vb* **1** : to suffer or cause to suffer from extreme hunger **2** : to suffer for lack of something ⟨*famished* for news from home⟩ — **fam•ish•ment** \-mənt\ *n*

fa•mous \ˈfā-məs\ *adj* **1** : widely and favorably known ⟨a *famous* explorer⟩ **2** : deserving to be remembered : EXCELLENT
• **syn** RENOWNED, CELEBRATED: FAMOUS may imply no more than being widely and favorably known for any reason and any length of time; RENOWNED implies glory and acclamation ⟨heroes *renowned* in song and story⟩ CELEBRATED stresses frequent public notice and mention especially in print ⟨a *celebrated* murder trial⟩

fa•mous•ly \ˈfā-məs-lē\ *adv* : very well ⟨got along *famously* together⟩

[1]fan \ˈfan\ *n* **1** : any of various devices for winnowing grain **2** : a device for producing a current of air: as **a** : a device that consists of material (as paper or silk) often in the shape of a segment of a circle and is waved to and fro by hand **b** : a device that consists of a series of vanes radiating from a hub rotated on its axle by a motor **3** : something shaped like or suggesting a hand fan [Old English *fann,* from Latin *vannus*]

[1]fan 2a

[2]fan *vb* **fanned**; **fan•ning** **1** : to drive away the chaff from grain by winnowing **2** : to move or impel air with a fan **3 a** : to direct a current of air upon with a fan **b** : to stir up to activity as if by fanning : STIMULATE **4** : to spread out or move like a fan **5** : to strike out in baseball **6** : to fire a gun by squeezing the trigger and striking the hammer to the rear with the free hand — **fan•ner** *n*

[3]fan *n* **1** : an enthusiastic follower of a sport or entertainment **2** : an enthusiastic admirer (as of an athlete or movie star) [probably short for *fanatic*]

fa•nat•ic \fə-ˈnat-ik\ *adj* : marked or moved by excessive enthusiasm and intense uncritical devotion [Latin *fanaticus* "inspired by a deity, frenzied", from *fanum* "temple"] — **fanatic** *n* — **fa•nat•i•cal** \-i-kəl\ *adj* — **fa•nat•i•cal•ly** \-i-kə-lē, -klē\ *adv* — **fa•nat•i•cism** \-ˈnat-ə-ˌsiz-əm\ *n*

△ **origin** The Latin adjective *fanaticus,* a derivative of the noun *fanum,* "temple", originally meant "of or relating to a temple". It was later used to refer to those pious individuals who were thought to have been inspired by a god or goddess. In time the sense "frantic, frenzied, mad" arose because it was thought that persons behaving in such a manner were possessed by a deity. This was the first meaning of the English word *fanatic.* This sense is now obsolete, but it led to the development of the sense "excessively enthusiastic, especially about religious matters". The word later became less specific, meaning simply "excessively enthusiastic or unreasonable". The noun *fan,* meaning "enthusiast", is probably a shortening of *fanatic.*

fan•ci•er \ˈfan-sē-ər\ *n* : one with a special liking or interest; *esp* : a person who breeds or grows a particular animal or plant for points of excellence

fan•ci•ful \ˈfan-si-fəl\ *adj* **1 a** : full of fancy ⟨a *fanciful* tale of an imaginary kingdom⟩ **b** : guided by fancy ⟨a *fanciful* impractical person⟩ **2** : coming from the fancy rather than from the reason ⟨a *fanciful* scheme for getting rich⟩ **3** : curiously made or shaped ⟨*fanciful* forms of ice on a windowpane⟩ — **fan•ci•ful•ly** \-fə-lē, -flē\ *adv* — **fan•ci•ful•ness** \-fəl-nəs\ *n*

[1]fan•cy \ˈfan-sē\ *n, pl* **fancies** **1** : the power of the mind to think of things not present : IMAGINATION **2** : LIKING ⟨take a *fancy* to a person⟩ **3** : WHIM, NOTION ⟨changed plans at the slightest *fancy*⟩ **4** : taste or judgment especially in art, literature, or decoration **5** : enthusiasts over something (as an art or pursuit) : FANCIERS [Middle English *fantasie, fantsy* "fantasy, fancy", from Middle French *fantasie*]

[2]fancy *vt* **fan•cied**; **fan•cy•ing** **1** : to have a fancy for : LIKE **2** : to form a conception of : IMAGINE **3** : to believe without evidence

[3]fancy *adj* **fan•ci•er**; **-est** **1** : based on fancy : WHIMSICAL **2 a** : not plain : SHOWY **b** : of particular excellence **c** : bred primarily for showiness **3** : executed with technical skill and superior grace ⟨*fancy* diving⟩ — **fan•ci•ly** \ˈfan-sə-lē\ *adv* — **fan•ci•ness** \-sē-nəs\ *n*

fancy dress *n* : a costume (as for a masquerade) chosen to suit the wearer's fancy — **fancy-dress** *adj*

fan•cy-free \ˈfan-sē-ˈfrē\ *adj* : not centering the attention on any one person or thing; *esp* : not in love

fan•cy•work \-ˌwərk\ *n* : ornamental needlework (as embroidery)

fan•dan•go \fan-ˈdang-gō\ *n, pl* **-gos** : a lively Spanish or Spanish-American dance [Spanish]

fane \ˈfān\ *n* : a place of worship [Latin *fanum*]

fan•fare \ˈfan-ˌfaər, -ˌfeər\ *n* **1** : a flourish of trumpets **2** : a showy outward display [French]

fang \ˈfang\ *n* : a long sharp tooth: as **a** : one by which an animal's prey is seized and held or torn **b** : one of the long hollow or grooved poison-injecting teeth of a venomous snake [Old English] — **fanged** \ˈfangd\ *adj*

fan-jet \ˈfan-ˌjet\ *n* **1** : a jet engine having a fan that operates in a duct and draws in extra air whose compression and expulsion provide extra thrust **2** : an airplane powered by a fan-jet engine

fan•light \ˈfan-ˌlīt\ *n* : a semicircular window with radiating sash bars like the ribs of a fan placed over a door or window

fan mail *n* : letters sent to a public figure by admirers

fan•tail \ˈfan-ˌtāl\ *n* **1** : a fan-shaped tail or end **2 a** : a domestic pigeon having a broad rounded tail **b** : a fancy goldfish with the tail fins double **3** : an architectural part resembling a fan **4** : the part of the stern of a ship that overhangs the water

fan-tan \ˈfan-ˌtan\ *n* **1** : a Chinese gambling game **2** : a card game in which players play in sequence upon sevens [Chinese (Pekingese dialect) *fan¹-t'an¹*]

fan•ta•sia \fan-ˈtā-zhə, ˌfant-ə-ˈzē-ə\ *n* : an instrumental composition in a form determined by the composer's fancy [Italian *fantasia,* literally, "fancy"]

fan•ta•size \ˈfant-ə-ˌsīz\ *vb* : to create mental images by daydreaming

fan•tas•tic \fan-ˈtas-tik, fən-\ *also* **fan•tas•ti•cal** \-ti-kəl\ *adj* **1** : produced or seemingly produced by unrestrained fancy ⟨*fantastic* dreams⟩ ⟨a *fantastic* scheme⟩ **2** : going beyond belief : incredible or hardly credible ⟨airplanes now travel at *fantastic* speeds⟩ **3** : extremely individual or eccentric ⟨*fantastic* behavior⟩ [Late Latin *phantasticus,* from Greek *phantastikos* "producing mental images", from *phantazein* "to present to the mind"] — **fan•tas•ti•cal•ly** \-ti-kə-lē, -klē\ *adv*
• **syn** FANTASTIC, BIZARRE, GROTESQUE mean conceived or produced without reference to reality, truth, or common sense. FANTASTIC may connote unrestrained extravagance in conception ⟨a *fantastic* theory⟩ ⟨*fantastic* prices⟩ or merely elaborateness of decorative invention; BIZARRE implies strangeness produced by violence of contrast or incongruity of combination ⟨*bizarre* architecture of an amusement park⟩ GROTESQUE implies violent distortion of the natural with a comic, startling, or pathetic result ⟨*grotesque* masks⟩ ⟨made *grotesque* attempts at operatic roles⟩

fan•ta•sy *or* **phan•ta•sy** \ˈfant-ə-sē, -ə-zē\ *n, pl* **-sies** **1** : IMAGINATION 1, FANCY **2** : something produced by a person's imagination: as **a** : a mental image produced to fill a psychological need : DAYDREAM **b** : FANTASIA [Middle French *fantasie* "fancy", from Latin *phantasia,* from Greek, "imagination", from *phantazein* "to present to the mind", from *phainein* "to show"]

[1]far \ˈfär\ *adv* **far•ther** \-thər\ *or* **fur•ther** \ˈfər-\; **far•thest** *or* **fur•thest** \-thəst\ **1** : at or to a considerable distance in space or time ⟨*far* from home⟩ ⟨*far* in the future⟩ **2** : by a broad interval : WIDELY ⟨this is *far* better⟩ **3** : to or at a definite distance, point, or degree ⟨as *far* as I know⟩ **4** : to an advanced point or extent : a long way ⟨a field in which one can go *far*⟩ [Middle English *fer,* from Old English *feorr*] — **by far** : GREATLY — **far and away** : DECIDEDLY

[2]far *adj* **farther** *or* **further**; **farthest** *or* **furthest** **1** : remote in space or time **2** : LONG 1 ⟨a *far* journey⟩ **3** : the more distant of two ⟨on the *far* side of the lake⟩ **syn** see DISTANT

far•ad \'far-,ad, -əd\ *n* : the unit of capacitance equal to the capacitance of a capacitor between whose plates there appears a potential of one volt when it is charged by one coulomb of electricity [Michael *Faraday*]

far•away \,fär-ə-,wā\ *adj* **1** : DISTANT 1 ⟨*faraway* lands⟩ **2** : PENSIVE 1, DREAMY ⟨a *faraway* look⟩

farce \'färs\ *n* **1** : a play about ridiculous and absurd situations intended to make people laugh **2** : humor characteristic of a farce **3** : a ridiculous action, display, or pretense [Middle French, "stuffing, farce", from Latin *farcire* "to stuff"] — **far•ci•cal** \'fär-si-kəl\ *adj*

far•ceur \fär-'sər\ *n* : a writer or actor of farce [French]

1fare \'faər, 'feər\ *vi* **1** : GO, TRAVEL ⟨*fare* forth on a journey⟩ **2** : to get along : SUCCEED ⟨how did you *fare*⟩ **3** : EAT 2, DINE [Old English *faran*]

2fare *n* **1** : the money a person pays to travel on a public conveyance **2** : a person paying a fare **3** : FOOD 3

1fare•well \faər-'wel, feər-\ *imperative verb* : get along well — used interjectionally to or by one departing

2farewell *n* **1** : a wish of welfare at parting : GOOD-BYE **2** : an act of departure : LEAVE-TAKING

3fare•well \,faər-,wel, ,feər-\ *adj* : FINAL

far•fetched \'fär-'fecht\ *adj* : not natural or plausible : IMPROBABLE

far–flung \'fär-'fləng\ *adj* : covering a great area ⟨a *far-flung* empire⟩

fa•ri•na \fə-'rē-nə\ *n* : a fine meal (as of nuts or a cereal grain) used especially as a breakfast cereal [Latin, "meal, flour", from *far* "spelt"]

far•i•na•ceous \,far-ə-'nā-shəs\ *adj* **1** : containing or rich in starch **2** : having a mealy texture or surface

1farm \'färm\ *n* **1 a** : a tract of land devoted to raising crops or livestock **b** : a tract of water used for the cultivation of aquatic animals ⟨oyster *farms*⟩ **2** : a minor-league subsidiary of a major-league baseball club to which recruits are assigned for training [Middle English *ferme* "rent, lease", from Old French, "lease", from *fermer* "to make a contract", from Latin *firmare* "to make firm", from *firmus* "firm"]

2farm *vb* **1** : to turn over for performance or use usually on contract or for an agreed payment — usually used with *out* **2 a** : to devote to agriculture ⟨*farm* 60 hectares⟩ **b** : to engage in raising crops or livestock — **farm•er** *n*

farm•hand \'färm-,hand\ *n* : a farm laborer

farm•house \-,haůs\ *n* : a dwelling on a farm

farm•ing \'fär-ming\ *n* : the occupation or business of a person who farms : AGRICULTURE

farm•land \'färm-,land\ *n* : land used or suitable for farming

farm•stead \-,sted\ *n* : the building and adjacent service areas of a farm

farm•yard \-,yärd\ *n* : space around or enclosed by farm buildings

faro \'faər-ō, 'feər-\ *n, pl* **far•os** : a gambling game in which players bet on cards drawn from a dealing box [probably alteration of earlier *pharaoh*]

far–off \'fär-'ȯf\ *adj* : remote in time or space

fa•rouche \fə-'rüsh\ *adj* : marked by shyness and lack of polish; *also* : UNRESTRAINED 1, WILD [French, "wild, shy", from Late Latin *forasticus* "belonging outside", from Latin *foras* "outdoors"]

far–out \'fär-'aůt\ *adj* : departing considerably from the conventional or traditional : EXTREME

far•ra•go \fə-'räg-ō, -'rā-gō\ *n, pl* **-goes** : a confused collection : MIXTURE [Latin, "mixed fodder, mixture", from *far* "spelt"]

far–reach•ing \'fär-'rē-ching\ *adj* : having a wide range, influence, or effect ⟨a *far-reaching* decision⟩

far•ri•er \'far-ē-ər\ *n* : a blacksmith who shoes horses

1far•row \'far-ō\ *vb* : to give birth to pigs [Middle English *farwen,* derived from Old English *fearh* "young pig"]

2farrow *n* : a litter of pigs

far•see•ing \'fär-'sē-ing\ *adj* : FARSIGHTED

far•sight•ed \-'sīt-əd\ *adj* **1** : able to see distant things more clearly than near ones **2** : able to judge how something will work out in the future — **far•sight•ed•ly** *adv* — **far•sight•ed•ness** *n*

1far•ther \'fär-t͟hər\ *adv* **1** : at or to a greater distance or more advanced point **2** : more completely [Middle English *ferther,* alteration of *further*]

2farther *adj* **1** : more distant : REMOTER **2** : 2FURTHER 2

far•ther•most \-,mōst\ *adj* : most distant : FARTHEST

1far•thest \'fär-t͟həst\ *adj* : most distant in space or time

2farthest *adv* **1** : to or at the greatest distance in space or time : REMOTEST **2** : to the most advanced point **3** : by the greatest degree or extent : MOST

far•thing \'fär-t͟hing\ *n* : a former British monetary unit equal to 1/4 of a penny; *also* : a coin representing this unit [Old English *fēorthung*]

far•thin•gale \'fär-t͟hən-,gāl, -thing-\ *n* : a support (as of hoops) worn especially in the 16th century to swell out a skirt [Middle French *verdugale,* from Spanish *verdugado,* from *verdugo* "young shoot of a tree", from *verde* "green", from Latin *viridis*]

fas•ces \'fas-,ēz\ *n sing or pl* : a bundle of rods surrounding an ax with projecting blade borne before ancient Roman magistrates as a badge of authority [Latin, from plural of *fascis* "bundle"]

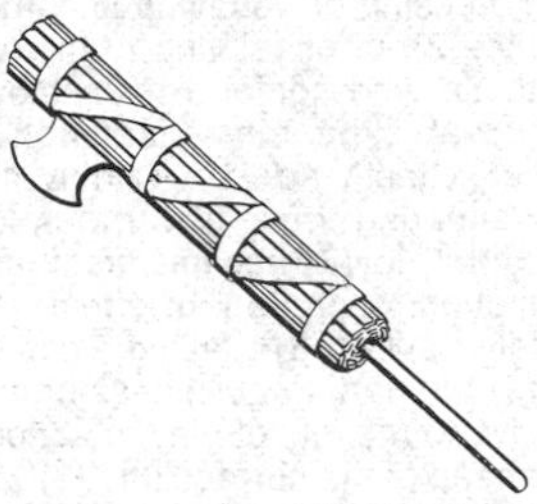

fasces

fas•cia \'fash-ə, 'fash-ē-ə, 'fāsh-\ *n, pl* **fas•ci•ae** \-ē-,ē\ *or* **fas•cias** : a sheet of connective tissue covering or binding together body structures [Latin, "band, bandage"]

fas•ci•cle \'fas-i-kəl\ *n* **1** : a small bundle or cluster (as of flowers or roots) **2** : one of the divisions of a book published in parts [Latin *fasciculus,* from *fascis* "bundle"] — **fas•ci•cled** \-kəld\ *adj* — **fas•cic•u•lar** \fə-'sik-yə-lər, fa-\ *adj* — **fas•cic•u•late** \-lət\ *adj*

fas•ci•nate \'fas-n-,āt\ *vb* **1** : to grip the attention of especially so as to take away the power to move, act, or think for oneself **2** : to allure and hold by charming qualities : CAPTIVATE [Latin *fascinare,* from *fascinum* "witchcraft"] — **fas•ci•na•tion** \,fas-n-'ā-shən\ *n*

fas•ci•na•tor \'fas-n-,āt-ər\ *n* **1** : one that fascinates **2** : a crocheted head covering for women

fas•cine \fa-'sēn, fə-\ *n* : a long bundle of sticks of wood bound together and used for such purposes as filling ditches and making parapets [French, from Latin *fascina,* from *fascis* "bundle"]

fas•cism \'fash-,iz-əm\ *n, often cap* **1** : the principles of an Italian political organization headed by Mussolini that governed Italy 1922–1943 and that advocated nationalism, a centralized dictatorial regime, severe economic and social regimentation, and forcible suppression of opposition; *also* : the movement advocating or the regime following these principles **2** : a political philosophy, movement, or regime (as Nazism) similar to Fascism [Italian *fascismo,* from *fascio* "bundle, fasces, group", from Latin *fascis* "bundle" and *fasces* "fasces"] — **fas•cist** \'fash-əst\ *n or adj, often cap* — **fas•cis•tic** \fa-'shis-tik\ *adj, often cap*

△ **origin** The English words *fascism* and *fascist* are borrowings from Italian *fascismo* and *fascista,* derivatives of *fascio,* "bundle, fasces, group". *Fascista* was first used in 1919, when Benito Mussolini organized a political group, the *Partito Nazionale Fascista* ("National Fascist Party"), to oppose communism. The fasces, a bundle of rods with an ax among them, was taken to symbolize the power of many people united and obedient to the single authority of the state. The English word *fascist* was first used for members of the Italian Fascisti, but it has since been generalized to those of similar beliefs.

Fa•sci•sta \fä-'shē-stä\ *n, pl* **-sti** \-stē\ : a member of the Italian Fascist movement [Italian]

1fash•ion \'fash-ən\ *n* **1** : the make or form of something **2** : MANNER, WAY ⟨behaving in a strange *fashion*⟩ **3 a** : a prevailing custom, usage, or style **b** : the prevailing style (as in dress) during a particular time or among an especially innovative group ⟨*fashions* in women's hats⟩ [Old French *façon* "shape, manner", from Latin *factio* "act of making, faction"]

\ə\ **abut**	\aů\ **out**	\i\ **tip**	\ȯ\ **saw**	\ů\ **foot**
\ər\ **further**	\ch\ **chin**	\ī\ **life**	\ȯi\ **coin**	\y\ **yet**
\a\ **mat**	\e\ **pet**	\j\ **job**	\th\ **thin**	\yü\ **few**
\ā\ **take**	\ē\ **easy**	\ng\ **sing**	\t͟h\ **this**	\yů\ **cure**
\ä\ **cot, cart**	\g\ **go**	\ō\ **bone**	\ü\ **food**	\zh\ **vision**

• syn STYLE, MODE, VOGUE: FASHION may apply to any way of dressing, behaving, writing, or performing that is favored at any one time or place; STYLE often implies the fashion approved by the wealthy or socially prominent; MODE suggests the fashion among those anxious to appear elegant and sophisticated; VOGUE applies to a temporary widespread style.

— **after a fashion :** in a rough or approximate way ⟨did the job *after a fashion*⟩

2fashion *vt* **fash•ioned; fash•ion•ing** \ˈfash-ning, -ə-ning\ **:** to give shape or form to **:** MOLD, CONSTRUCT — **fash•ion•er** \ˈfash-nər, -ə-nər\ *n*

fash•ion•able \ˈfash-nə-bəl, -ə-nə-\ *adj* **1 a :** following the fashion or established style **:** STYLISH ⟨*fashionable* clothes⟩ **b :** dressing or behaving according to fashion ⟨*fashionable* people⟩ **2 :** of or relating to the world of fashion **:** popular among those who conform to fashion ⟨*fashionable* stores⟩ — **fash•ion•able•ness** *n* — **fash•ion•ably** \-blē\ *adj*

1fast \ˈfast\ *adj* **1 a :** firmly fixed or bound **b :** tightly shut **c :** adhering firmly **d :** UNCHANGEABLE ⟨hard and *fast* rules⟩ **2 :** firmly loyal ⟨became *fast* friends⟩ **3 a :** characterized by quick motion, operation, or effect: (1) **:** moving or able to move rapidly **:** SWIFT (2) ; taking a comparatively short time ⟨a *fast* trip⟩ (3) **:** imparting quickness of motion ⟨a *fast* bowler⟩ **b :** conducive to rapidity of play or action ⟨a *fast* track⟩ **c** (1) **:** indicating ahead of the correct time (2) **:** according to daylight saving time **d :** contributing to a shortening of photographic exposure time ⟨a *fast* lens⟩ **4 :** not easily loosened or disturbed **5 a :** permanently dyed **b :** proof against fading by a particular agency **6 a :** DISSIPATED, WILD **b :** daringly unconventional especially in sexual matters **[**Old English *fæst***]**

• syn RAPID, SWIFT, FLEET: FAST and RAPID are very close in meaning but FAST applies especially to the thing that moves ⟨a *fast* horse⟩ and RAPID to the movement ⟨a series of *rapid* blows⟩ SWIFT suggests great rapidity together with ease of movement ⟨*swift* play of the imagination⟩ FLEET adds an implication of lightness and nimbleness ⟨*fleet* little ponies⟩

2fast *adv* **1 :** in a fast or fixed manner ⟨stuck *fast* in the mud⟩ **2 :** SOUNDLY, DEEPLY ⟨*fast* asleep⟩ **3 a :** in a rapid manner **b :** in quick succession **4 :** in a dissipated manner **:** RECKLESSLY

3fast *vi* **1 :** to eat no food **2 :** to eat sparingly or avoid some foods **[**Old English *fæstan***]**

4fast *n* **1 :** the act or practice of fasting **2 :** a time of fasting

fast•back \ˈfast-ˌbak, ˈfas-\ *n* **:** an automobile roof with a long curving downward slope to the rear; *also* **:** an automobile with such a roof

fast•ball *n* **:** a baseball pitch thrown at full speed

fast break *n* **:** a quick offensive drive toward a goal (as in basketball) in an attempt to score before the defense can get into position

fas•ten \ˈfas-n\ *vb* **fas•tened; fas•ten•ing** \ˈfas-ning, -n-ing\ **1 :** to attach or join by or as if by pinning, tying, or nailing ⟨*fasten* clothes on a line⟩ ⟨*fastened* the blame on the runaway⟩ **2 :** to make fast **:** fix securely ⟨*fasten* a door⟩ **3 :** to fix or set steadily ⟨*fasten* one's eyes on the view⟩ **4 :** to become fixed or joined ⟨a shoe that *fastens* with a buckle⟩ — **fas•ten•er** \ˈfas-nər, -n-ər\ *n*

fas•ten•ing \ˈfas-ning, -n-ing\ *n* **:** something that fastens **:** FASTENER

fas•tid•i•ous \fa-ˈstid-ē-əs\ *adj* **:** very difficult to please especially in matters of taste or cleanliness **[**Latin *fastidiosus* "disgusted, fastidious", from *fastidium* "disgust"**]** — **fas•tid•i•ous•ly** *adv* — **fas•tid•i•ous•ness** *n*

fast•ness \ˈfast-nəs, ˈfas-\ *n* **1 :** the quality or state of being fast **2 :** a fortified or secure place **:** STRONGHOLD

1fat \ˈfat\ *adj* **fat•ter; fat•test 1 a :** PLUMP, FLESHY **b :** OILY 2, GREASY **2 :** well stocked **:** ABUNDANT ⟨a *fat* purse⟩ **3 :** richly rewarding **:** PROFITABLE **[**Old English *fætt*, from *fǣtan* "to cram"**]** — **fat•ness** *n*

2fat *n* **1 :** animal tissue consisting chiefly of cells containing much greasy or oily matter **2 a :** any of numerous compounds of carbon, hydrogen, and oxygen that are esters of glycerol and fatty acids, the chief constituents of plant and animal fat, and a major class of energy-rich food, and that are soluble in ether but not in water **b :** a solid or semisolid fat (as lard) as distinguished from an oil **3 :** the best or richest part ⟨lived on the *fat* of the land⟩ **4 :** excess matter

3fat *vt* **fat•ted; fat•ting :** to make fat **:** FATTEN

fa•tal \ˈfāt-l\ *adj* **1 :** causing death or ruin ⟨a *fatal* accident⟩ **2 :** determining one's fate ⟨a *fatal* day in our lives⟩ **[**Latin *fatalis*, from *fatum* "fate"**] syn** see DEADLY — **fa•tal•ly** \-l-ē\ *adv*

fa•tal•ism \ˈfāt-l-ˌiz-əm\ *n* **:** the belief that events are determined in advance by powers beyond human control; *also* **:** the attitude of mind of a person holding this belief — **fa•tal•ist** \-l-əst\ *n* — **fa•tal•is•tic** \ˌfāt-l-ˈis-tik\ *adj* — **fa•tal•is•ti•cal•ly** \-ˈis-ti-kə-lē, -klē\ *adv*

fa•tal•i•ty \fā-ˈtal-ət-ē, fə-\ *n, pl* **-ties 1 a :** the quality or state of causing death **:** DEADLINESS **b :** the quality or condition of being destined for disaster **2 :** FATE 1a **3 :** a death resulting from a disaster or accident

fat•back \ˈfat-ˌbak\ *n* **:** a fatty strip from the back of the hog usually cured by salting and drying

fat body *n* **:** a mass of fatty tissue attached to each germ-cell producing gland in amphibians

1fate \ˈfāt\ *n* **1 a :** a power beyond human control that is held to determine what happens **:** DESTINY ⟨blamed the failure on *fate*⟩ **b** *cap* **:** any of three goddesses of classical mythology who determine the course of human life **2 :** something that happens as though determined by fate **:** FORTUNE ⟨it was their *fate* to outlive their children⟩ **3 :** an unavoidable and often unpleasant outcome, condition, or end ⟨awaited news of the *fate* of the polar expedition⟩ **4 :** DISASTER; *esp* **:** DEATH **[**Latin *fatum*, literally, "what has been spoken", from *fari* "to speak"**]**

• syn FATE, DESTINY, LOT, DOOM mean a predetermined state or end. FATE implies an inevitable and usually adverse outcome or end; DESTINY implies something foreordained and usually suggests a great or notable course or end; LOT implies a distribution of success or happiness by fate or destiny according to blind chance; DOOM implies a grim or calamitous fate.

2fate *vt* **:** DESTINE 1; *also* **:** DOOM

fate•ful \ˈfāt-fəl\ *adj* **1 :** having or marked by serious consequences **:** IMPORTANT ⟨a *fateful* decision⟩ ⟨that *fateful* day⟩ **2 :** OMINOUS, PROPHETIC ⟨the *fateful* circling of the vultures overhead⟩ — **fate•ful•ly** \-fə-lē\ *adv* — **fate•ful•ness** *n*

1fa•ther \ˈfäth-ər, ˈfȧth-\ *n* **1 a :** a male parent **b** *cap* (1) **:** GOD 1 (2) **:** the first person of the Trinity **2 :** FOREFATHER **3 a :** one who cares for another as a father might **b :** one deserving the respect and love given to a father **4** *often cap* **:** a pre-Scholastic Christian writer accepted by the church as an authoritative witness to its teaching and practice **5 :** AUTHOR 2, ORIGINATOR **6** *often cap* **:** PRIEST — used especially as a title ⟨*Father* Smith⟩ **7 :** one of the leading men (as of a city) — usually used in pl. **[**Old English *fæder***]**

2father *vt* **fa•thered; fa•ther•ing** \ˈfäth-ring, ˈfȧth-, -ə-ring\ **1 a :** BEGET **b :** to be the founder, producer, or author of **2 :** to treat or care for as a father

fa•ther•hood \ˈfäth-ər-ˌhu̇d, ˈfȧth-\ *n* **:** the condition of being a father

fa•ther-in-law \ˈfäth-rən-ˌlȯ, ˈfȧth-, -ə-rən-ˌlȯ, -ərn-ˌlȯ\ *n, pl* **fathers-in-law** \ˈfäth-ər-zən-\ **:** the father of one's spouse

fa•ther•land \ˈfäth-ər-ˌland, ˈfȧth-\ *n* **1 :** one's native land **2** 2 H:the native land of one's ancestors

fa•ther•less \-ləs\ *adj* **:** having no father **:** ORPHAN

fa•ther•ly \-lē\ *adj* **1 :** of or resembling a father ⟨a *fatherly* old man⟩ **2 :** showing the affection or concern of a father ⟨*fatherly* advice⟩ — **fa•ther•li•ness** *n*

Father's Day *n* **:** the 3d Sunday in June appointed for the honoring of fathers

1fath•om \ˈfath-əm\ *n* **:** a unit of length equal to 6 feet (about 1.83 meters) that is used especially for measuring the depth of water **[**Old English *fæthm* "outstretched arms, length of the outstretched arms"**]**

2fathom *vb* **1 :** to measure by a sounding line **:** take soundings; *also* **:** PROBE **2 :** to penetrate and come to understand ⟨failed to *fathom* the problem⟩ — **fath•om•able** \ˈfath-ə-mə-bəl\ *adj*

Fa•thom•e•ter \fa-ˈthäm-ət-ər; ˈfath-əm-ˌmēt-, ˈfath-ə-ˌ\ *trademark* — used for a sonic depth finder

fath•om•less \ˈfath-əm-ləs\ *adj* **:** incapable of being fathomed

1fa•tigue \fə-ˈtēg\ *n* **1 a :** weariness from labor or exertion **b :** temporary loss of power to respond (as of a sense organ) after prolonged stimulation **2 a :** manual or menial work performed by military personnel **b** *pl* **:** the uniform or work clothing worn on fatigue and in the field **3 :** the tendency of a material (as metal) to break under repeated stress (as bending) **[**French, from *fatiguer* "to fatigue", from Latin *fatigare***]**

2fatigue *vb* **1 :** to weary or become weary with labor or exertion **2 :** to induce a condition of fatigue in

fat•ling \ˈfat-ling\ *n* **:** a young animal fattened for slaughter

fats•hed•era \fats-ˈhed-ə-rə, -ˈed-\ *n* **:** a hybrid plant grown as a houseplant for its glossy deeply lobed leaves [New Latin *Fatsia,* genus of shrubs + *Hedera,* genus of vines, from Latin, "ivy"]

fat–soluble *adj* : soluble in fats or fat solvents

fat•ten \'fat-n\ *vb* **fat•tened; fat•ten•ing** \'fat-ning, -n-ing\ **1 a** : to make or become fat or fatter ⟨cattle *fattening* on the range⟩ **b** : to make larger ⟨*fatten* profits⟩ **2** : to make (as land) fertile : ENRICH — **fat•ten•er** \'fat-nər, -n-ər\ *n*

fat•ty \'fat-ē\ *adj* **fat•ti•er; -est 1** : containing fat especially in unusual amounts; *also* : unduly stout **2** : GREASY — **fat•ti•ly** \'fat-l-ē\ *adv* — **fat•ti•ness** \'fat-ē-nəs\ *n*

fatty acid *n* : any of numerous saturated or unsaturated acids that contain only carbon, hydrogen, and oxygen and that occur naturally in the form of glycerides in fats and various oils

fa•tu•ity \fə-'tü-ət-ē, fa-, -'tyü-\ *n, pl* **-ities** : FOOLISHNESS, STUPIDITY ⟨the *fatuity* of such a remark⟩

fat•u•ous \'fach-wəs, -ə-wəs\ *adj* : complacently or inanely foolish : SILLY [Latin *fatuus*] — **fat•u•ous•ly** *adv* — **fat•u•ous•ness** *n*

fau•bourg \fō-'bu̇r\ *n* **1** : SUBURB 1; *esp* : a suburb of a French city **2** : a city quarter [Middle French *fauxbourg,* from Old French *forsborc,* from *fors* "outside" + *borc* "town"]

fau•ces \'fȯ-,sēz\ *n pl* : the narrow passage between the soft palate and the base of the tongue that joins the mouth to the pharynx [Latin, "throat, fauces"] — **fau•cial** \'fȯ-shəl\ *adj*

fau•cet \'fȯ-sət, 'fäs-ət\ *n* : a fixture for drawing a liquid (as from a pipe or cask) [Middle French *fausset* "bung", from *fausser* "to damage", from Late Latin *falsare* "to falsify", from *falsus* "false"]

△ **origin** English *faucet* is descended from Latin *falsus,* "false". In Late Latin a verb was formed from this adjective, *falsare,* "to falsify". In course of time it became French *fausser.* In medieval French the verb developed new meanings. As well as "to falsify", *fausser* could mean "to be false to" or even "to damage or break". A cask which is made to hold liquids usually has a hole through which it may be emptied. Although this bunghole is present by intention, the stopper that plugs it may be looked on a bit fancifully as piercing or breaking into the cask. So such a stopper was called a *fausset.* The English borrowing, *faucet,* was used not only for the stopper in a cask but also for a fixture used to draw liquid from a cask, pipe, or other container.

[1]fault \'fȯlt\ *n* **1 a** : a weakness in character : FAILING; *esp* : a moral weakness less serious than a vice **b** : a physical or intellectual imperfection or impairment **c** : an error in a service in tennis **2 a** : a trivial misdeed **b** : MISTAKE 2 **3** : responsibility for wrongdoing or failure **4** : a fracture in the earth's crust accompanied by a displacement of rock masses in a direction parallel to the fracture [Old French *faute,* derived from Latin *fallere* "to deceive, disappoint"]

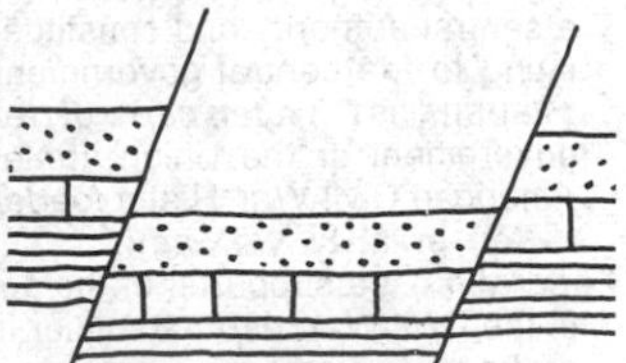
[1]fault 4

• **syn** FAULT, FAILING, FOIBLE, FRAILTY mean a weakness or imperfection of character. FAULT applies to any failure, serious or trivial, to attain a standard of perfection in action, disposition, or habit; FAILING suggests a minor shortcoming in character; FOIBLE implies a harmless or even endearing weakness; FRAILTY implies weakness in the face of temptation.

— **at fault** : open to blame : RESPONSIBLE — **to a fault** : EXCESSIVELY ⟨generous *to a fault*⟩

[2]fault *vb* **1** : to commit a fault : ERR **2** : to fracture so as to produce a geologic fault **3** : to find a fault in ⟨could not *fault* that argument⟩

fault•find•er \'fȯlt-,fīn-dər\ *n* : a person who is inclined to complain or criticize — **fault•find•ing** \-ding\ *n or adj*

fault•less \'fȯlt-ləs\ *adj* : free from fault : including no error or imperfection : PERFECT — **fault•less•ly** *adv* — **fault•less•ness** *n*

faulty \'fȯl-tē\ *adj* **fault•i•er; -est** : marked by fault, blemish, or defect : IMPERFECT — **fault•i•ly** \-tə-lē\ *adj* — **fault•i•ness** \-tē-nəs\ *n*

faun \'fȯn, 'fän\ *n* : an ancient Italian deity of fields and herds represented as part goat and part man [Latin *faunus,* from *Faunus,* god of animals]

fau•na \'fȯn-ə, 'fän-\ *n, pl* **faunas** *also* **fau•nae** \-,ē, -,ī\ : animals or animal life especially of a region, period, or environment — compare FLORA [Late Latin *Fauna,* sister of Faunus, god of animals] — **fau•nal** \'fȯn-l, 'fän-\ *adj* — **fau•nal•ly** \-l-ē\ *adv*

fau•vism \'fō-,viz-əm\ *n, often cap* : a movement in painting typified by the work of Matisse and characterized by vivid colors, free treatment of form, and a resulting vibrant and decorative effect [French *fauvisme,* from *fauve* "wild animal"] — **fau•vist** \-vəst\ *n, often cap*

faux pas \'fō-'pä\ *n, pl* **faux pas** \-'pä, -'päz\ : BLUNDER; *esp* : a social blunder [French, literally, "false step"]

fa•va bean \,fäv-ə-\ *n* : BROAD BEAN [Italian *fava,* from Latin *faba* "bean"]

[1]fa•vor \'fā-vər\ *n* **1 a** : friendly regard shown toward another especially by a superior ⟨enjoyed the *favor* of the king⟩ **b** : APPROVAL, APPROBATION ⟨look with *favor* on a project⟩ **c** : PARTIALITY ⟨the judge showed *favor* to the defendant⟩ **d** : POPULARITY ⟨a fad loses *favor* quickly⟩ **2** : gracious kindness ⟨treated the child with *favor*⟩; also : an act of such kindness **3 a** : a token of love (as a ribbon) usually worn conspicuously **b** : a small gift or decorative item given out at a party **4** : a special privilege or right granted or conceded **5** *archaic* : LETTER **6** : BEHALF, INTEREST [Old French, "friendly regard", from Latin, from *favēre* "to be favorable"] — **in favor of 1** : in accord or sympathy with **2** : in support of — **out of favor** : not now popular ⟨study seems *out of favor* today⟩

[2]favor *vt* **fa•vored; fa•vor•ing** \'fāv-ring, -ə-ring\ **1 a** : to regard or treat with favor **b** (1) : to do a kindness for : OBLIGE (2) : ENDOW ⟨*favored* by nature⟩ **c** : to treat gently or carefully : SPARE ⟨*favor* a lame leg⟩ **2** : PREFER 1 **3 a** : to give support to : SUSTAIN **b** : to offer chances for success to : FACILITATE ⟨darkness *favors* attack⟩ **4** : to bear a resemblance to ⟨children who *favor* their parents⟩ — **fa•vor•er** \'fā-vər-ər\ *n*

fa•vor•able \'fāv-rə-bəl, -ə-rə-; 'fā-vər-bəl\ *adj* **1** : showing favor : APPROVING ⟨a *favorable* opinion⟩ **2** : tending to promote or advance something ⟨*favorable* weather for the fair⟩ — **fa•vor•able•ness** *n* — **fa•vor•ably** \-blē\ *adv*

[1]fa•vor•ite \'fāv-rət, -ə-rət\ *n* **1** : a person or a thing that is favored above others **2** : the contestant regarded as having the best chance to win [Italian *favorito,* past participle of *favorire* "to favor", from *favore* "favor", from Latin *favor*]

[2]favorite *adj* : being a favorite; *esp* : best-liked ⟨our *favorite* show⟩

favorite son *n* : a candidate supported by the delegates of his state at a presidential nominating convention

fa•vor•it•ism \'fā-rət-,iz-əm, -ə-rət-\ *n* : unfairly favorable treatment of one or some to the neglect of others : PARTIALITY

[1]fawn \'fȯn, 'fän\ *vi* **1** : to show affection — used especially of a dog **2** : to try to win favor by behavior that shows lack of self-respect [Old English *fagnian* "to rejoice", from *fægen* "glad, fain"] — **fawn•er** *n* — **fawn•ing•ly** \-ing-lē\ *adv*

[2]fawn *n* **1** : a young deer; *esp* : one in its first year **2** : a light grayish brown [Middle French *feon, faon* "young of an animal", derived from Latin *fetus* "offspring"]

[1]fay \'fā\ *n* **1** : FAIRY **2** : ELF [Middle French *feie, fee*]

[2]fay *adj* : ELFIN 2

faze \'fāz\ *also* **feaze** \'fēz, 'fāz\ *vt* : to disturb the composure or courage of : DAUNT [Old English *fēsian* "to drive away"]

F clef *n* : BASS CLEF

fe•al•ty \'fē-əl-tē, 'fēl-\ *n* **1** : the loyalty of a feudal vassal to his lord **2** : ALLEGIANCE 2 [Old French *feelté, fealté,* from Latin *fidelitas* "fidelity"] **syn** see FIDELITY

[1]fear \'fiər\ *n* **1 a** : an unpleasant often strong emotion caused by expectation or awareness of danger **b** : an instance of fear or a state marked by fear **2** : anxious concern : WORRY **3** : reverential awe especially toward God [Old English *fǣr* "sudden danger"]

• **syn** FEAR, DREAD, FRIGHT, PANIC mean a painful emotion in the presence or expectation of danger. FEAR is the general term and implies great anxiety and usually loss of courage; DREAD adds the idea of intense aversion and reluctance to face something; FRIGHT suggests the shock of sudden, startling appear-

\ə\ **abut**	\au̇\ **out**	\i\ **tip**	\ȯ\ **saw**	\u̇\ **foot**
\ər\ **further**	\ch\ **chin**	\ī\ **life**	\ȯi\ **coin**	\y\ **yet**
\a\ **mat**	\e\ **pet**	\j\ **job**	\th\ **thin**	\yü\ **few**
\ā\ **take**	\ē\ **easy**	\ng\ **sing**	\th̲\ **this**	\yu̇\ **cure**
\ä\ **cot, cart**	\g\ **go**	\ō\ **bone**	\ü\ **food**	\zh\ **vision**

ance of danger or threat; PANIC implies completely dominating fear that causes hysterical activity.

[2]fear *vb* **1 :** to have a reverential awe of ⟨*fear* God⟩ **2 :** to be afraid of : have fear **3 :** to be apprehensive ⟨*feared* they would miss the train⟩ — **fear·er** *n*

fear·ful \ˈfiər-fəl\ *adj* **1 :** causing fear ⟨the *fearful* roar of a lion⟩ **2 :** filled with fear ⟨*fearful* of danger⟩ **3 :** showing or caused by fear ⟨a *fearful* glance⟩ **4 :** extremely bad, large, or intense ⟨*fearful* cold⟩ — **fear·ful·ly** \-fə-lē\ *adv* — **fear·ful·ness** *n*

fear·less \ˈfiər-ləs\ *adj* : free from fear : BRAVE — **fear·less·ly** *adv* — **fear·less·ness** *n*

fear·some \ˈfiər-səm\ *adj* **1 :** causing fear **2 :** TIMID — **fear·some·ly** *adv* — **fear·some·ness** *n*

fea·si·ble \ˈfē-zə-bəl\ *adj* **1 :** capable of being done or carried out ⟨a *feasible* plan⟩ **2 :** capable of being used or dealt with successfully : SUITABLE ⟨a *feasible* new energy source⟩ **3 :** PLAUSIBLE 1, LIKELY ⟨a *feasible* story⟩ [Middle French *faisible,* from *fais-,* stem of *faire* "to make, do", from Latin *facere*] **syn** see POSSIBLE — **fea·si·bil·i·ty** \ˌfē-zə-ˈbil-ət-ē\ *n* — **fea·si·ble·ness** \ˈfē-zə-bəl-nəs\ *n* — **fea·si·bly** \-blē\ *adv*

[1]feast \ˈfēst\ *n* **1 a :** an elaborate meal : BANQUET **b :** something that gives great pleasure ⟨a *feast* of wit⟩ **2 :** a religious festival : HOLY DAY [Old French *feste* "festival", from Latin *festum,* from *festus* "solemn, festal"]

[2]feast *vb* **1 :** to eat plentifully : participate in a feast **2 :** to entertain with rich and plentiful food — **feast·er** *n* — **feast one's eyes on :** to take pleasure in (something seen) ⟨*feast one's eyes on* autumn colors⟩

[1]feat \ˈfēt\ *adj* **1** *archaic* **:** BECOMING, NEAT **2** *archaic* **:** SKILLFUL, DEXTEROUS [Middle French *fait,* past participle of *faire* "to make, do"]

[2]feat *n* **1 :** ACT 1, DEED **2 a :** a deed notable especially for courage **b :** an act or product of skill, endurance, or ingenuity [Middle French *fait,* from Latin *factum,* from *facere* "to make, do"]

• **syn** FEAT, EXPLOIT, ACHIEVEMENT mean a remarkable deed. FEAT implies strength or dexterity or daring in achieving; EXPLOIT applies to an adventurous or heroic act that brings fame; ACHIEVEMENT implies hard-won success in the face of difficulty or opposition.

[1]feath·er \ˈfet͟h-ər\ *n* **1 a :** one of the light horny outgrowths that form the external covering of the body of a bird **b :** the vane of an arrow **2 a :** KIND 1b, SORT **b :** CLOTHING, DRESS **c** (1) **:** CONDITION 5 (2) **:** MOOD **3 :** a feathery tuft or fringe of hair **4 :** a projecting strip, rib, fin, or flange **5 :** the act of feathering an oar [Old English *fether*] — **feath·ered** \-ərd\ *adj* — **feath·er·less** \ˈfet͟h-ər-ləs\ *adj* — **a feather in one's cap :** a mark of distinction : HONOR

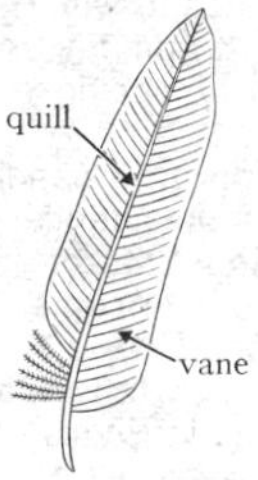

[1]feather 1a

[2]feather *vb* **feath·ered; feath·er·ing** \ˈfet͟h-ring, -ə-ring\ **1 a :** to furnish (as an arrow) with feathers **b :** to cover, clothe, or adorn with feathers **2 a :** to turn (an oar blade) almost horizontal when lifting from the water at the end of a stroke in order to reduce air resistance while moving it forward for the next stroke **b :** to rotate (the blades of an aircraft propeller) about their base-to-tip axis in order to decrease wind resistance **3 :** to grow or form feathers **4 :** to move, spread, or grow like feathers — **feather one's nest :** to provide for oneself especially by taking advantage of a position of trust

feath·er bed \ˈfet͟h-ər-ˌbed\ *n* **:** a mattress filled with feathers; *also* **:** a bed with such a mattress

feath·er·bed·ding \-ˌbed-ing\ *n* **:** the requiring of an employer usually under a union rule or safety statute to employ more workers than are needed or to limit production

feath·er·brain \ˈfet͟h-ər-ˌbrān\ *n* **:** a foolish scatterbrained person — **feath·er·brained** \ˌfet͟h-ər-ˈbrānd\ *adj*

feath·er·edge \ˈfet͟h-ə-ˌrej, ˌfet͟h-ə-ˈ\ *n* **:** a very thin sharp edge; *esp* **:** one that is easily broken or bent — **featheredge** *vt*

feath·er·weight \-ər-ˌwāt\ *n* **1 :** one that is very light in weight; *esp* **:** a boxer in a weight division having the approximate range of 54 to 57 kilograms **2 :** a person of limited intelligence or effectiveness

feath·ery \ˈfet͟h-rē, -ə-rē\ *adj* **:** resembling, suggesting, or covered with feathers

[1]fea·ture \ˈfē-chər\ *n* **1 a :** the shape or appearance of the face ⟨stern of *feature*⟩ **b :** a single part of the face (as the nose or the mouth) **2 :** something especially noticeable **:** a prominent part or detail **:** CHARACTERISTIC ⟨such earth *features* as mountains and rivers⟩ **3 :** a main or outstanding attraction: as **a :** the principal motion picture on a program **b :** a special column or section in a newspaper or magazine [Middle French *feture,* from Latin *factura* "act of making", from *facere* "to make, do"]

[2]feature *vb* **fea·tured; fea·tur·ing** \ˈfēch-ring, -ə-ring\ **1 :** to picture in the mind **:** IMAGINE ⟨*feature* wearing such a hat⟩ **2 :** to give special prominence to ⟨*feature* a story in a newspaper⟩ **3 :** to play an important part

fea·ture·less \ˈfē-chər-ləs\ *adj* **:** having no distinctive features

feaze \ˈfēz, ˈfāz\ *variant of* FAZE

feb·ri·fuge \ˈfeb-rə-ˌfyüj\ *n* **:** a medicine for relieving fever [French *fébrifuge,* derived from Latin *febris* "fever" + *fugare* "to put to flight"] — **febrifuge** *adj*

fe·brile \ˈfeb-ˌrīl *also* ˈfēb-\ *adj* **:** affected with or as if with fever **:** FEVERISH [Medieval Latin *febrilis,* from Latin *febris* "fever"]

Feb·ru·ary \ˈfeb-yə-ˌwer-ē, ˈfeb-ə-, ˈfeb-rə-\ *n* **:** the 2d month of the year [Latin *Februarius,* from *Februa,* a festival held during the month]

fe·ces *also* **fae·ces** \ˈfē-ˌsēz\ *n, pl* **:** bodily waste discharged through the anus **:** EXCREMENT [Middle English, "sediment, dregs", from Latin *faeces,* pl. of *faex*] — **fe·cal** \ˈfē-kəl\ *adj*

feck·less \ˈfek-ləs\ *adj* **1 :** INEFFECTUAL, WEAK **2 :** lacking qualities needed for efficiency or success [Scottish *feck* "effect", from Middle English *fek,* alteration of *effect*] — **feck·less·ly** *adv* — **feck·less·ness** *n*

fe·cund \ˈfek-ənd, ˈfēk-\ *adj* **1 :** fruitful in offspring or vegetation **:** PROLIFIC **2 :** intellectually creative to a marked degree [Middle French *fecond,* from Latin *fecundus*] **syn** see FERTILE — **fe·cun·di·ty** \fi-ˈkən-dət-ē\ *n*

fe·cun·date \ˈfek-ən-ˌdāt, ˈfē-kən-\ *vt* **:** FERTILIZE — **fe·cun·da·tion** \ˌfek-ən-ˈdā-shən, ˌfē-kən-\ *n*

fed·er·al \ˈfed-rəl, -ə-rəl\ *adj* **1 a :** formed by a compact between political units that give up individual sovereignty to a central authority but retain certain limited powers **b :** of or being a form of government in which power is distributed between a central authority and constituent territorial units **c :** of or relating to the central government of a federation **2** *often cap* **:** FEDERALIST **3** *often cap* **:** of, relating to, or loyal to the federal government or the Union armies of the United States in the American Civil War [Latin *foeder-, foedus* "compact, league"] — **fed·er·al·ly** \-ē\ *adv*

Federal *n* **1 :** a supporter of the government of the United States in the Civil War; *esp* **:** a soldier in the federal armies **2 :** a federal agent or officer

federal district *n* **:** a district (as the District of Columbia) set apart as the seat of the central government of a federation

fed·er·al·ism \ˈfed-rə-ˌliz-əm, -ə-rə-\ *n* **1 a** *often cap* **:** the federal principle of organization **b :** support or advocacy of this principle **2** *cap* **:** the principles of the Federalists

fed·er·al·ist \-ləst\ *n* **1 :** an advocate of federalism; *esp, often cap* **:** an advocate of a federal union between the American colonies after the Revolution and of the adoption of the United States Constitution **2** *cap* **:** a member of a major political party in the early years of the United States favoring a strong centralized national government — **federalist** *adj, often cap*

fed·er·al·ize \ˈfed-rə-ˌlīz, -ə-rə-\ *vt* **1 :** to unite in or under a federal system **2 :** to bring under the jurisdiction of a federal government — **fed·er·al·i·za·tion** \ˌfed-rə-lə-ˈzā-shən, -ə-rə-\ *n*

Federal Reserve Bank *n* **:** a bank of the Federal Reserve system

Federal Reserve system *n* **:** a system of 12 central banks in the United States that serve as a depository for reserves of affiliated banks, engage in rediscounting, and serve as a clearinghouse for checks

fed·er·ate \ˈfed-ə-ˌrāt\ *vb* **:** to join in a federation

fed·er·a·tion \ˌfed-ə-ˈrā-shən\ *n* **1 :** the act of federating; *esp* **:** the formation of a federal union **2 :** something formed by federation: as **a :** a federal government **b :** a union of organizations

fed·er·a·tive \ˈfed-ə-ˌrāt-iv; ˈfed-rət-, -ə-rət-\ *adj* **:** involving or arising from federation

fe•do•ra \fi-ˈdōr-ə, -ˈdȯr-\ *n* **:** a low soft felt hat with the crown creased lengthwise [*Fédora* (1882), drama by V. Sardou in which a type of fedora was introduced]

fedora

fed up *adj* **:** utterly worn out and disgusted ⟨*fed up* with their mistakes⟩

fee \ˈfē\ *n* **1 a :** an estate in land held from a feudal lord in return for homage and service paid him **b :** an inherited or heritable estate in land **2 a :** a fixed charge ⟨an admission *fee*⟩ ⟨license *fees*⟩ **b :** a charge for a professional service ⟨a doctor's *fees*⟩ **c :** GRATUITY, TIP [Old French *fé, fief,* of Germanic origin] **syn** see WAGE

fee•ble \ˈfē-bəl\ *adj* **fee•bler** \-bə-lər, -blər\; **-blest** \-bə-ləst, -bləst\ **1 a :** greatly deficient in physical strength ⟨a *feeble* invalid⟩ **b :** showing weakness ⟨*feeble* steps⟩ **2 :** not strong or effective (as in quality, character, or mind) **:** INADEQUATE ⟨*feeble* imagery⟩ ⟨a *feeble* attempt⟩ [Old French *feble,* from Latin *flebilis* "lamentable, wretched", from *flēre* "to weep" — **fee•ble•ness** \-bəl-nəs\ *n* — **fee•bly** \-blē\ *adv*

fee•ble•mind•ed \ˌfē-bəl-ˈmīn-dəd\ *adj* **:** lacking normal intelligence **:** mentally deficient — **fee•ble•mind•ed•ness** *n*

1**feed** \ˈfēd\ *vb* **fed** \ˈfed\; **feed•ing 1 a :** to give food to **b :** to give as food **c :** to consume food **:** EAT **d :** PREY — used with *on, upon,* or *off* **2 a :** to furnish with something essential to growth, sustenance, or operation **b :** to become nourished or satisfied as if by food **3 :** to give satisfaction to **:** GRATIFY ⟨praise only *fed* their vanity⟩ **4 a :** to supply (as material) for use or consumption **b :** to supply (a signal) to an electronic circuit **5 :** to supply (a performer) with cues and situations that make a role more effective [Old English *fēdan*]

2**feed** *n* **1 a :** an act of eating **b :** MEAL; *esp* **:** a large meal **2 a :** food for livestock **b :** the amount given at one feeding **3 a :** material supplied (as to a furnace) **b :** a mechanism by which the action of feeding is effected

feed•back \ˈfēd-ˌbak\ *n* **1 :** the return to the input of a part of the output of a machine, system, or process **2 :** transmission to the original or controlling source of information about an action or process ⟨asked for student *feedback* about course content⟩; *also* **:** the information so transmitted

feed•er \ˈfēd-ər\ *n* **:** one that feeds: as **a :** a device or apparatus for supplying food **b :** TRIBUTARY **c :** a source of supply **d :** an animal being fattened or suitable for fattening **e :** an actor or role that serves as a foil for another — **feeder** *adj*

feed•lot \ˈfēd-ˌlät\ *n* **:** a plot of land on which cattle are fattened for market

feed•stuff \-ˌstəf\ *n* **:** FEED 2a; *also* **:** any of the nutrients in an animal ration

1**feel** \ˈfēl\ *vb* **felt** \ˈfelt\; **feel•ing 1 a :** to perceive as a result of physical contact ⟨*feel* a blow⟩ **b :** to examine or test by touching **:** HANDLE ⟨*feel* a fabric with one's fingers⟩ **2 a :** EXPERIENCE ⟨*felt* their scorn⟩ **b :** to suffer from ⟨*feel* the heat⟩ **3 :** to ascertain by cautious trial — often used with *out* **4 a :** to be aware or aware of ⟨*feel* the joy of victory⟩ **b :** BELIEVE 4, THINK **5 :** to search for something with the fingers **6 :** to seem especially to the sense of touch ⟨*feels* like wool⟩ **7 :** to have sympathy or pity ⟨I *feel* for you⟩ [Old English *fēlan*] — **feel in one's bones :** to be sure for no evident reason

2**feel** *n* **1 :** the sense of touch **2 :** SENSATION, FEELING ⟨success brought them a *feel* of power⟩ **3 :** the quality of a thing as imparted through touch

feel•er \ˈfē-lər\ *n* **1 :** one that feels; *esp* **:** a movable organ (as an antenna) of an animal that usually functions for touch **2 :** a proposal or remark made to find out the views of other people

1**feel•ing** \ˈfē-liŋ\ *n* **1 a :** a sense whose receptors are chiefly in the skin and by which the hardness or softness, hotness or coldness, or heaviness or lightness of things is determined; *esp* **:** TOUCH 3 **b :** a sensation experienced through this sense **2 a :** an often indefinite state of mind ⟨a *feeling* of loneliness⟩; *also* **:** such a state with regard to someone or something ⟨a *feeling* of dislike⟩ **b** *pl* **:** general emotional condition **:** SENSIBILITIES ⟨hurt one's *feelings*⟩ **3 a :** the overall quality of one's awareness **b :** conscious recognition **:** SENSE **4 a :** OPINION, BELIEF ⟨it's my *feeling* we will win⟩ **b :** unreasoned attitude **:** SENTIMENT ⟨public *feeling* was aroused by the crime⟩ **5 :** capacity to respond emotionally especially with the higher emotions **:** SYMPATHY **6 :** the quality of a work of art that conveys the emotion of the artist

• syn EMOTION, SENTIMENT, PASSION: FEELING applies to any response or awareness marked by pleasure, pain, attraction, or repulsion; it may suggest the existence of a response without implying anything definite about its nature or intensity; EMOTION implies a clearly defined feeling and usually greater excitement or agitation; SENTIMENT may imply emotion inspired by an idea or belief ⟨argued more from grounds of moral *sentiment* than cold logic⟩ PASSION suggests a very powerful or controlling emotion.

2**feeling** *adj* **:** SENSITIVE 1; *esp* **:** easily moved emotionally — **feel•ing•ly** \ˈfē-liŋ-lē\ *adv* — **feel•ing•ness** *n*

feet *pl of* FOOT

feet•first \ˈfēt-ˈfərst\ *adv* **:** with the feet foremost ⟨jumped into the water *feetfirst*⟩

feign \ˈfān\ *vb* **1 :** to give a false appearance of **:** SHAM ⟨*feign* illness⟩ **2 :** to assert as if true **:** PRETEND ⟨*feign* an excuse⟩ [Old French *feindre,* from Latin *fingere* "to shape, feign"] — **feign•er** *n*

feint \ˈfānt\ *n* **:** something feigned; *esp* **:** a mock blow or attack at one point in order to distract attention from the point one really intends to attack [French *feinte,* from *feindre* "to feign"] — **feint** *vi*

feist \ˈfīst\ *n, chiefly dialect* **:** a small dog [obsolete *fisting hound,* from obsolete *fist,* "to break wind"]

feisty \ˈfī-stē\ *adj* **feist•i•er**; **-est :** SCRAPPY

feld•spar \ˈfeld-ˌspär, ˈfel-\ *n* **:** any of a group of crystalline minerals that consist of silicates of aluminum with either potassium, sodium, calcium, or barium and that are an essential constituent of nearly all crystalline rocks [German *feldspat,* from *feld* "field" + *spat* "spar"]

fe•lic•i•tate \fi-ˈlis-ə-ˌtāt\ *vt* **:** to offer congratulations to — **fe•lic•i•ta•tion** \-ˌlis-ə-ˈtā-shən\ *n* — **fe•lic•i•ta•tor** \-ˈlis-ə-ˌtāt-ər\ *n*

fe•lic•i•tous \fi-ˈlis-ət-əs\ *adj* **1 :** suitably expressed **:** APT ⟨*felicitous* wording⟩ **2 :** having a talent for apt expression ⟨a *felicitous* speaker⟩ — **fe•lic•i•tous•ly** *adv* — **fe•lic•i•tous•ness** *n*

fe•lic•i•ty \fi-ˈlis-ət-ē\ *n, pl* **-ties 1 :** the quality or state of being happy; *esp* **:** great happiness **2 :** something that causes happiness **3 a :** a talent for apt expression **b :** an apt expression [Middle French *felicité,* from Latin *felicitas,* from *felix* "fruitful, happy"]

fe•line \ˈfē-ˌlīn\ *adj* **1 a :** belonging to the family of soft-furred flesh-eating mammals that includes the cats, lions, tigers, leopards, pumas, and lynxes **b :** of or resembling a cat **:** characteristic of cats **2 a :** SLY 1, TREACHEROUS **b :** STEALTHY 1 [Latin *felinus,* from *felis* "cat"] — **feline** *n*

1**fell** \ˈfel\ *n* **:** 2HIDE, PELT [Old English]

2**fell** *vt* **1 a :** to cut, beat, or knock down ⟨*fell* trees for lumber⟩ **b :** KILL 1 **2 :** to sew (a seam) by folding one edge under the other [Old English *fellan*] — **fell•able** \-ə-bəl\ *adj*

3**fell** *past of* FALL

4**fell** *adj* **:** FIERCE 1, CRUEL; *also* **:** GRAVE 1b [Old French *fel,* from Medieval Latin *fello* "villain, felon"]

fel•lah \ˈfel-ə, fə-ˈlä\ *n, pl* **fel•la•hin** \ˌfel-ə-ˈhēn, fə-ˌlä-ˈhēn\ **:** a peasant or agricultural laborer in Arab countries (as Egypt or Syria) [Arabic *fallāḥ*]

fel•low \ˈfel-ō\ *n* **1 :** COMRADE 1a, ASSOCIATE **2 a :** an equal in rank, power, or character **:** PEER **b :** one of a pair **:** MATE **3 :** a member of an incorporated literary or scientific society **4 a :** a male human being ⟨played cards with the *fellows*⟩ **b :** INDIVIDUAL 2, PERSON ⟨won't give a *fellow* a chance⟩ **c :** BOYFRIEND ⟨on a date with her *fellow*⟩ **5 :** a person granted funds for advanced study [Old English *fēolaga,* from Old Norse *fēlagi,* from *fēlag* "partnership", from *fē* "cattle, money" + *lag* "act of laying"] — **fellow** *adj*

△ **origin** The Old Norse word for a partner, *fēlagi,* means literally "fee-layer". Such people were those who laid together their property (fee) for some common purpose. Old English bor-

\ə\ **abut**	\au̇\ **out**	\i\ **tip**	\ȯ\ **saw**	\u̇\ **foot**
\ər\ **further**	\ch\ **chin**	\ī\ **life**	\ȯi\ **coin**	\y\ **yet**
\a\ **mat**	\e\ **pet**	\j\ **job**	\th\ **thin**	\yü\ **few**
\ā\ **take**	\ē\ **easy**	\ŋ\ **sing**	\t͟h\ **this**	\yu̇\ **cure**
\ä\ **cot, cart**	\g\ **go**	\ō\ **bone**	\ü\ **food**	\zh\ **vision**

rowed *fēlagi* from Old Norse and called a partner a *fēolaga.* This word has come down to us, through several centuries and the development of a number of senses, as modern English *fellow.* Perhaps its most common use today is its very general one, in which it is applied to any boy or man.

fel•low•man \ˌfel-ō-ˈman\ *n* : a kindred human being

fel•low•ship \ˈfel-ō-ˌship\ *n* **1** : the condition of friendly relationship existing among persons **2** : a community of interest, activity, or feeling **3** : a group with similar interests **4 a** : the position of a fellow (as of a university) **b** : the funds granted a fellow

fellow traveler *n* : a person who sympathizes with and often furthers the ideals and program of an organized group (as the Communist party) without joining it or regularly participating in its activities [translation of Russian *poputchik*]

fel•ly \ˈfel-ē\ *or* **fel•loe** \-ō\ *n, pl* **fellies** *or* **felloes** : the outside rim or a part of the rim of a wheel supported by the spokes [Old English *felg*]

fel•on \ˈfel-ən\ *n* **1** : one who has committed a felony **2** : a deep inflammation of the finger or toe especially near the end or around the nail and usually with pus [Old French *felon, fel* "villain, inflammation", from Medieval Latin *fello* "evildoer, villain"]

fel•o•ny \ˈfel-ə-nē\ *n, pl* **-nies** : a serious crime usually punishable by a sentence heavier than that for a misdemeanor — **fe•lo•ni•ous** \fə-ˈlō-nē-əs\ *adj* — **fe•lo•ni•ous•ly** *adv* — **fe•lo•ni•ous•ness** *n*

¹felt \ˈfelt\ *n* **1** : an unwoven cloth (as of wool and fur) made by matting the fibers with heat, moisture, and pressure **2** : an article made of felt **3** : a material resembling felt [Old English]

²felt *vt* **1** : to make into felt **2** : to cause to adhere and mat together **3** : to cover with felt

³felt *past of* FEEL

felt•ing \ˈfel-ting\ *n* **1** : the process by which felt is made **2** : FELT 1

fe•luc•ca \fə-ˈlü-kə, -ˈlək-ə\ *n* : a narrow fast lateen-rigged sailing vessel of the Mediterranean [Italian *feluca*]

¹fe•male \ˈfe-ˌmāl\ *n* : a female plant or animal [Middle English *femelle,* from Medieval Latin *femella,* from Latin, "girl", from *femina* "woman"]

△ **origin** In the 14th century *female* appeared in English with spellings such as *femel, femelle,* and *female.* It is derived from the Latin *femella,* "young woman, girl", which is a diminutive of *femina,* "woman". In English the similarity in form and pronunciation between the words *female* and *male* led to the retention only of the spelling *female.* It also gave rise to the popular belief that *female* is derived from or somehow related to *male.* Apart from the influence on the spelling, however, there is no etymological connection between them.

²female *adj* **1 a** : of, relating to, or being the sex that bears young or produces eggs **b** : having only seed-producing flowers : PISTILLATE ⟨a *female* holly⟩ **2 a** : of, relating to, or characteristic of the female sex **b** : made up of females ⟨a large *female* population⟩ **3** : designed with a hollow into which a corresponding male part fits ⟨a *female* hose coupling⟩ — **fe•male•ness** *n*

¹fem•i•nine \ˈfem-ə-nən\ *adj* **1** : of the female sex **2** : characteristic of or belonging to women : WOMANLY **3** : of, relating to, or constituting the class of words that ordinarily includes most of those referring to females ⟨a *feminine* noun⟩ ⟨the *feminine* gender⟩ **4** : having or occurring in an unstressed extra final syllable ⟨*feminine* rhyme⟩ [Middle French *feminin,* from Latin *femininus,* from *femina* "woman"]

²feminine *n* **1** : a word or form of the feminine gender **2** : the feminine gender

fem•i•nin•i•ty \ˌfem-ə-ˈnin-ət-ē\ *n* **1** : the quality or nature of the female sex **2** : EFFEMINACY **3** : female human beings : WOMANKIND

fem•i•nism \ˈfem-ə-ˌniz-əm\ *n* **1** : a doctrine advocating political, economic, and social equality of the sexes **2** : organized activity on behalf of women's rights and interests — **fem•i•nist** \-nəst\ *n or adj* — **fem•i•nis•tic** \ˌfem-ə-ˈnis-tik\ *adj*

fem•o•ral \ˈfem-rəl, -ə-rəl\ *adj* : of, relating to, or situated in or near the femur or thigh ⟨*femoral* artery⟩

femto- \ˌfem-tō\ *combining form* : one quadrillionth (10^{-15}) part of [Danish or Norwegian *femten* "fifteen"]

fe•mur \ˈfē-mər\ *n, pl* **fe•murs** *or* **fem•o•ra** \ˈfem-rə, -ə-rə\ **1** : the long bone of the hind or lower limb extending from the hip to the knee and supporting the thigh — called also *thighbone* **2** : the segment of an insect's leg that is third from the body [Latin *femor-, femur* "thigh"]

fen \ˈfen\ *n* : low land covered naturally in whole or in part with water [Old English *fenn*]

¹fence \ˈfens\ *n* **1** : a barrier intended to prevent escape or intrusion or to mark a boundary **2** : a person who receives stolen goods or a shop where stolen goods are disposed of [Middle English *fens* "defense", short for *defens*] — **fence•less** \-ləs\ *adj* — **on the fence** : being neutral or undecided

²fence *vb* **1 a** : to enclose with a fence **b** : to keep in or out with a fence **2** : to engage in fencing — **fenc•er** *n*

fence•row \ˈfens-ˌrō\ *n* : the land occupied by a fence including the uncultivated land on each side

fenc•ing *n* **1** : the art or sport of attack and defense with a foil, épée, or saber **2 a** : the fences of a property or region **b** : material used for building fences

fend \ˈfend\ *vb* **1** : to keep or ward off : REPEL **2** : to try to get along without help : SHIFT ⟨*fend* for yourself⟩ [Middle English *fenden,* short for *defenden*]

fend•er \ˈfen-dər\ *n* : a device that protects: as **a** : a cushion hung over the side of a boat to protect it when two boats are together or when alongside a dock **b** : RAILING **c** : a device in front of a locomotive or streetcar to lessen injury to animals or pedestrians in case of collision **d** : a guard over the wheel of a motor vehicle **e** : a screen or a low metal frame before an open fireplace

fe•nes•tra \fi-ˈnes-trə\ *n, pl* **-trae** \-ˌtrē, -ˌtrī\ : a small opening; *esp* : either of two membrane-covered apertures in the bone between the middle and inner ear [Latin, "window"] — **fe•nes•tral** \-trəl\ *adj*

fen•es•tra•tion \ˌfen-əs-ˈtrā-shən\ *n* : the arrangement, proportioning, and design of windows and doors in a building

Fe•ni•an \ˈfē-nē-ən\ *n* **1** : one of a legendary band of Irish warriors of the 2d and 3d centuries A.D. **2** : a member of a secret 19th century Irish and Irish-American organization dedicated to the overthrow of British rule in Ireland [Irish Gaelic *Fiann,* legendary band of warriors] — **Fenian** *adj*

fen•nec \ˈfen-ik\ *n* : a small large-eared African fox [Arabic *fanak*]

fennec

fen•nel \ˈfen-l\ *n* : a perennial European herb of the carrot family grown for its aromatic seeds and foliage; *also* : its seed [Old English *finugl,* from Latin *feniculum,* from *fenum* "hay"]

fen•ny \ˈfen-ē\ *adj* **1** : characteristic of a fen : BOGGY **2** : peculiar to or found in a fen

fen•u•greek \ˈfen-yə-ˌgrēk\ *n* : a white-flowered Old World legume with aromatic seeds once used in medicine [Middle French *fenugrec,* from Latin *fenum Graecum,* literally, "Greek hay"]

-fer \fər\ *n combining form* : one that bears ⟨aquifer⟩ [Latin, from *ferre* "to carry, bear"]

fe•ral \ˈfir-əl, ˈfer-\ *adj* **1** : of, relating to, or suggestive of a wild beast : SAVAGE **2** : having escaped from domestication and become wild [Medieval Latin *feralis,* from Latin *fera* "wild animal", from *ferus* "wild"]

fer-de-lance \ˌferd-l-ˈans, -ˈäns\ *n, pl* **fer-de-lance** : a large extremely poisonous pit viper of Central and South America [French, literally, "lance iron"]

fe•ria \ˈfir-ē-ə, ˈfer-\ *n* : a weekday of a church calendar on which no feast is celebrated [Medieval Latin, "weekday, fair"] — **fe•ri•al** \-ē-əl\ *adj*

¹fer•ment \fər-ˈment\ *vb* : to undergo or cause to undergo fermentation — **fer•ment•able** \-ə-bəl\ *adj* — **fer•ment•er** *n*

²fer•ment \ˈfər-ˌment\ *n* **1** : an agent (as an enzyme or a yeast) capable of bringing about fermentation **2 a** : FERMENTATION 1 **b** : a state of intense activity or unrest : AGITATION [Latin *fermentum* "yeast"]

fer•men•ta•tion \ˌfər-mən-ˈtā-shən, -ˌmen-\ *n* **1** : chemical breaking down of an organic substance (as in the souring of milk or the formation of alcohol from sugar) produced by an enzyme and often accompanied by the evolution of a gas; *esp* : such an energy-yielding reaction proceeding without the aid of free oxygen **2 :** FERMENT 2b — **fer•men•ta•tive** \fər-ˈment-ət-iv\ *adj*

fer•mi•um \ˈfer-mē-əm, ˈfər-\ *n* **:** a radioactive metallic element artificially produced (as by bombardment of plutonium with neutrons) — see ELEMENT table [Enrico *Fermi,* died 1954, Italian physicist]

fern \ˈfərn\ *n* **:** any of a class (Filicineae) of flowerless seedless vascular plants; *esp* **:** any of an order (Filicales) resembling seed plants in having root, stem, and leaflike fronds but reproducing by spores [Old English *fearn*] — **fern•like** \-ˌlīk\ *adj* — **ferny** \ˈfər-nē\ *adj*

fern•ery \ˈfərn-rē, -ə-rē\ *n, pl* **-er•ies 1 :** a place for growing ferns **2 :** a collection of growing ferns

fe•ro•cious \fə-ˈrō-shəs\ *adj* **1 :** showing or given to extreme fierceness, violence, and brutality **2 :** unbearably intense ⟨*ferocious* heat⟩ [Latin *feroc-, ferox*] **syn** see FIERCE — **fe•ro•cious•ly** *adv* — **fe•ro•cious•ness** *n*

fe•roc•i•ty \fə-ˈräs-ət-ē\ *n, pl* **-ties :** the quality or state of being ferocious

-f•er•ous \f-rəs, f-ə-rəs\ *adj combining form* **:** bearing **:** producing ⟨carboni*ferous*⟩

fer•re•dox•in \ˌfer-ə-ˈdäk-sən\ *n* **:** an iron-containing plant protein that functions as an electron carrier especially in photosynthesis [Latin *ferrum* "iron" + English *redox* + *-in*]

1fer•ret \ˈfer-ət\ *n* **:** a partially domesticated usually albino European polecat used especially for hunting rodents [Middle French *furet,* from Latin *fur* "thief"]

1ferret

2ferret *vb* **1 :** to hunt game with ferrets **2 a :** to drive out of a hiding place **b :** to find and bring to light by searching — usually used with *out* — **fer•ret•er** *n*

fer•ric \ˈfer-ik\ *adj* **1 :** of, relating to, or containing iron **2 :** being or containing iron usually with a valence of three [Latin *ferrum* "iron"]

ferric oxide *n* **:** the red or black oxide of iron Fe_2O_3 that is found in nature as hematite and as rust, is obtained synthetically, and is used as a pigment and for polishing

Fer•ris wheel \ˈfer-əs-\ *n* **:** an amusement device consisting of a large upright power-driven wheel carrying seats around its rim [G. W. G. *Ferris,* died 1896, American engineer]

ferro- *combining form* **:** iron **:** iron and ⟨*ferro*magnetic⟩ [Latin *ferrum*]

fer•ro•mag•net•ic \ˌfer-ō-mag-ˈnet-ik\ *adj* **:** of or relating to substances (as iron and nickel) that are easily magnetized

fer•ro•type \ˈfer-ə-ˌtīp\ *vt* **:** to give a gloss to (a photographic print) by pressing with the face down while wet on a metal plate and allowing to dry

fer•rous \ˈfer-əs\ *adj* **1 :** of, relating to, or containing iron **2 :** being or containing bivalent iron

ferrous oxide *n* **:** the monoxide of iron FeO

ferrous sulfate *n* **:** a salt $FeSO_4$ that consists of iron, sulfur, and oxygen and is used in making pigments and ink, in treating industrial wastes, and in medicine

fer•ru•gi•nous \fə-ˈrü-jə-nəs, fe-\ *or* **fer•ru•gin•e•ous** \ˌfer-ü-ˈjin-ē-əs, -yü-\ *adj* **1 :** of, relating to, or containing iron **2 :** resembling iron rust in color [Latin *ferruginus,* from *ferrugo* "iron rust", from *ferrum* "iron"]

fer•rule \ˈfer-əl\ *n* **:** a metal ring or cap placed around the end of a slender shaft of wood (as a cane) or around a tool handle to prevent splitting or to provide a strong well-fitting joint [Middle English *virole,* from Middle French, from Latin *viriola* "little bracelet", from *viria* "bracelet", of Celtic origin]

1fer•ry \ˈfer-ē\ *vb* **fer•ried; fer•ry•ing 1 a :** to carry by boat over a body of water (as a river) **b :** to cross by a ferry **2 a :** to fly (an airplane) from the shipping point to a delivery point **b :** to transport in an airplane [Old English *ferian* "to carry, convey"]

2ferry *n, pl* **ferries 1 :** a place where persons or things are carried across a body of water in a boat **2 :** FERRYBOAT **3 :** an organized service and route for flying airplanes — **fer•ry•man** \-mən\ *n*

fer•ry•boat \-ˌbōt\ *n* **:** a boat used to ferry passengers, vehicles, or goods

fer•tile \ˈfərt-l\ *adj* **1 :** producing or bearing fruit in great quantities **:** PRODUCTIVE **2 a** (1) **:** favorable to plant growth (2) **:** affording abundant possibilities for development ⟨a *fertile* area for research⟩ **b :** capable of growing or developing ⟨a *fertile* egg⟩ **c :** capable of reproducing or of producing reproductive cells ⟨a *fertile* bull⟩ ⟨*fertile* fungous hyphae⟩ [Latin *fertilis,* from *ferre* "to bear"] — **fer•tile•ly** \-l-lē, -l-ē\ *adv* — **fer•tile•ness** \-l-nəs\ *n* — **fer•til•i•ty** \fər-ˈtil-ət-ē\ *n*

• **syn** FRUITFUL, PROLIFIC, FECUND: FERTILE implies having the inherent power to reproduce in kind or to assist in reproduction and growth ⟨*fertile* soil⟩ FRUITFUL adds the implication of actually producing desirable and useful results ⟨*fruitful* methods⟩ PROLIFIC stresses the power of multiplying and spreading rapidly ⟨*prolific* rabbits⟩ or of creating freely ⟨a *prolific* writer⟩ FECUND emphasizes abundance or rapidity in bearing fruit or offspring.

fer•til•iza•tion \ˌfərt-l-ə-ˈzā-shən\ *n* **:** an act or process of making fertile: as **a :** the application of fertilizer **b :** union of male and female germ cells to form a zygote

fer•til•ize \ˈfərt-l-ˌīz\ *vt* **:** to make fertile: as **a :** to cause the fertilization of **b :** to apply a fertilizer to ⟨*fertilize* land⟩ — **fer•til•iz•able** \-ˌī-zə-bəl\ *adj*

fer•til•iz•er \-ˌī-zər\ *n* **:** one that fertilizes; *esp* **:** a substance (as manure or a chemical mixture) used to make soil more fertile

fer•ule \ˈfer-əl\ *n* **:** a rod or ruler used in punishing children [Latin *ferula*]

fer•ven•cy \ˈfər-vən-sē\ *n* **:** FERVOR 2

fer•vent \ˈfər-vənt\ *adj* **1 :** very hot **:** GLOWING **2 :** marked by great warmth of feeling **:** ARDENT [Latin *fervens,* present participle of *fervere* "to boil, glow"] — **fer•vent•ly** *adv*

fer•vid \ˈfər-vəd\ *adj* **:** FERVENT [Latin *fervidus,* from *fervēre* "to boil, glow"] — **fer•vid•ly** *adv* — **fer•vid•ness** *n*

fer•vor \ˈfər-vər\ *n* **1 :** intense heat **2 :** warm steady intensity of feeling or expression [Latin, from *fervēre* "to boil, glow"] **syn** see PASSION

fes•cue \ˈfes-kyü\ *n* **:** any of numerous tufted perennial grasses [Middle French *festu* "stalk, straw", derived from Latin *festuca*]

-fest \ˌfest\ *n combining form* **:** meeting or occasion marked by (such) activity ⟨gab*fest*⟩ [German *fest* "celebration", from Latin *festum*]

fes•tal \ˈfest-l\ *adj* **:** of or relating to a feast or festival **:** FESTIVE [Latin *festum* "feast, festival"] — **fes•tal•ly** \-l-ē\ *adv*

1fes•ter \ˈfes-tər\ *n* **:** a pus-filled sore **:** PUSTULE [Middle French *festre,* from Latin *fistula* "pipe, fistula"]

2fester *vb* **fes•tered; fes•ter•ing** \-tə-ring, -tring\ **1 :** to form pus **2 :** PUTREFY, ROT **3 :** to grow or cause to grow increasingly more irritating **:** RANKLE ⟨let resentment *fester* in one's mind⟩

fes•ti•val \ˈfes-tə-vəl\ *n* **1 :** a time of celebration marked by special observances **2 :** a periodic season or program of cultural events or entertainment ⟨a music *festival*⟩ — **festival** *adj*

fes•tive \ˈfes-tiv\ *adj* **1 :** of, relating to, or suitable for a feast or festival **2 :** GAY 1, MERRY — **fes•tive•ly** *adv* — **fes•tive•ness** *n*

fes•tiv•i•ty \fe-ˈstiv-ət-ē\ *n, pl* **-ties 1 :** FESTIVAL 1 **2 :** the quality or state of being festive **:** GAIETY **3 :** festive activity

1fes•toon \fe-ˈstün\ *n* **1 :** a decorative chain or strip hanging between two points **2 :** a carved, molded, or painted ornament representing a decorative chain [French *feston,* from Italian *festone,* from *festa* "festival", from Latin *festum*]

2festoon *vt* **1 :** to hang or form festoons on **2 :** to shape into festoons

1fetch \ˈfech\ *vb* **1 :** to go after and bring back ⟨*fetch* a glass of water⟩ **2 :** to cause to come ⟨*fetch* tears to one's eyes⟩ **3 :** to bring as a price **:** sell for **4 :** to arrive at [Old English *feccan*] — **fetch•er** *n*

2fetch *n* **:** an act or instance of fetching

fetch•ing *adj* **:** ATTRACTIVE, PLEASING ⟨a *fetching* smile⟩ — **fetch•ing•ly** \-ing-lē\ *adv*

1fete *or* **fête** \ˈfāt\ *n* **1 :** FESTIVAL 1 **2 :** a lavish entertainment or party [French *fête,* from Old French *feste*]

\ə\ **abut**	\au̇\ **out**	\i\ **tip**	\ȯ\ **saw**	\u̇\ **foot**
\ər\ **further**	\ch\ **chin**	\ī\ **life**	\ȯi\ **coin**	\y\ **yet**
\a\ **mat**	\e\ **pet**	\j\ **job**	\th\ **thin**	\yü\ **few**
\ā\ **take**	\ē\ **easy**	\ng\ **sing**	\t͟h\ **this**	\yu̇\ **cure**
\ä\ **cot, cart**	\g\ **go**	\ō\ **bone**	\ü\ **food**	\zh\ **vision**

[2]**fete** *or* **fête** *vt* **1 :** to honor or commemorate with a fete **2 :** to pay high honor to

fet·id \ˈfet-əd\ *adj* **:** having an offensive smell [Latin *foetidus,* from *foetēre* "stink"] — **fet·id·ly** *adv* — **fet·id·ness** *n*

fet·ish *also* **fet·ich** \ˈfet-ish, ˈfēt-\ *n* **1 :** an object (as an idol or image) believed to have supernatural or magical powers **2 :** an object of unreasoning devotion or concern ⟨make a *fetish* of secrecy⟩ [French *fétiche,* from Portuguese *feitiço,* from *feitiço* "artificial", from Latin *facticius* "factitious"] — **fet·ish·ism** \-ˌiz-əm\ *n*

fet·lock \ˈfet-ˌläk\ *n* **1 :** a projection with a tuft of hair on the back of a horse's leg above the hoof **2 :** the tuft of hair growing out of the fetlock [Middle English *fitlok*]

[1]**fet·ter** \ˈfet-ər\ *n* **1 :** a chain or shackle for the feet **2 :** something that confines **:** RESTRAINT [Old English *feter*]

[2]**fetter** *vt* **1 :** to put fetters on **:** SHACKLE **2 :** to restrain from motion or action **:** CONFINE **syn** see HAMPER

fet·tle \ˈfet-l\ *n* **:** a state of fitness or order **:** CONDITION ⟨in fine *fettle*⟩ [Middle English *fetlen*]

fe·tus *also* **foe·tus** \ˈfēt-əs\ *n* **:** a young animal while in the body of its mother or in the egg especially in the later stages of development — compare EMBRYO [Latin, "act of bearing young, offspring"] — **fe·tal** \ˈfēt-l\ *adj*

[1]**feud** \ˈfyüd\ *n* **:** a prolonged quarrel; *esp* **:** a lasting conflict between families or clans marked by violent attacks undertaken for revenge [Middle French *feide,* of Germanic origin] — **feud** *vi*

[2]**feud** *n* **:** FEE 1a [Medieval Latin *feodum, feudum,* of Germanic origin]

feu·dal \ˈfyüd-l\ *adj* **1 :** of, relating to, or having the characteristics of a medieval fee **2 :** of, relating to, or characteristic of feudalism — **feu·dal·ly** \-l-ē\ *adv*

feu·dal·ism \-ˌiz-əm\ *n* **:** a system of political organization in medieval Europe in which a vassal gave service to a lord and received protection and land in return; *also* **:** any of various similar political or social systems — **feu·dal·is·tic** \ˌfyüd-l-ˈis-tik\ *adj*

[1]**feu·da·to·ry** \ˈfyüd-ə-ˌtōr-ē, -ˌtȯr-\ *adj* **:** owing feudal allegiance

[2]**feudatory** *n, pl* **-ries 1 :** one who holds lands by feudal law or usage **2 :** FIEF

fe·ver \ˈfē-vər\ *n* **1 a :** a rise of body temperature above the normal **b :** a disease of which fever is a prominent symptom **2 a :** a state of heightened or intense emotion or activity **b :** CRAZE 1 [Old English *fēfer,* from Latin *febris*] — **fe·vered** \-vərd\ *adj*

fever blister *n* **:** COLD SORE

fe·ver·few \ˈfē-vər-ˌfyü\ *n* **:** a perennial European herb related to the daisies [Late Latin *febrifugia,* a plant related to the gentians]

fe·ver·ish \ˈfēv-rish, -ə-rish\ *adj* **1 a :** having a fever **b :** relating to or indicative of fever **c :** tending to cause fever **2 :** marked by intense emotion, activity, or instability — **fe·ver·ish·ly** *adv* — **fe·ver·ish·ness** *n*

[1]**few** \ˈfyü\ *pron, pl in construction* **:** not many persons or things ⟨*few* were present⟩ ⟨*few* of those stories are true⟩ [Old English *fēawa*]

[2]**few** *adj* **1 :** consisting of or amounting to a small number ⟨one of our *few* pleasures⟩ **2 :** not many but some ⟨caught a *few* fish⟩ — **few·ness** *n*

[3]**few** *n pl* **1 :** a small number of units or individuals ⟨a *few* of them⟩ **2 :** a special limited number ⟨the discriminating *few*⟩

[1]**few·er** \ˈfyü-ər\ *pron, pl in construction* **:** a smaller number of persons or things ⟨*fewer* came than were expected⟩

[2]**few·er** *adj, comparative of* FEW

• **syn** LESS: FEWER is applied to countable things ⟨*fewer* dollars⟩ ⟨*fewer* hours⟩ LESS may refer to amount, degree, or value ⟨*less* pay⟩ ⟨*less* heat⟩ ⟨*less* beauty⟩

fey \ˈfā\ *adj* **1** *chiefly Scottish* **:** fated to die; *also* **:** marked by a foreboding of death or calamity **2 :** CRAZY 2, TOUCHED **3 :** having an unworldly air **:** ELFIN [Old English *fǣge*]

fez \ˈfez\ *n, pl* **fez·zes :** a brimless flat-crowned hat that usually has a tassel, is made of red felt, and is worn especially by men in eastern Mediterranean countries [French, from *Fez,* Morocco]

fi·an·cé \ˌfē-ˌän-ˈsā, fē-ˈän-ˌsā\ *n* **:** a man engaged to be married [French, from *fiancer* "to betroth"]

fi·an·cée \ˌfē-ˌän-ˈsā, fē-ˈän-ˌsā\ *n* **:** a woman engaged to be married [French, feminine of *fiancé*]

fi·as·co \fē-ˈas-kō\ *n, pl* **-coes :** a complete and often ridiculous failure [French, from Italian, literally, "bottle"]

fez

fi·at \ˈfē-ət, -ˌat, -ˌät; ˈfī-ət, -ˌat\ *n* **:** an authoritative often arbitrary order or decree [Latin, "let it be done", from *fieri* "to be done, become"]

[1]**fib** \ˈfib\ *n* **:** a trivial or harmless lie [perhaps from *fable*]

[2]**fib** *vi* **fibbed; fib·bing :** to tell a fib — **fib·ber** *n*

fi·ber *or* **fi·bre** \ˈfī-bər\ *n* **1 :** a thread or a structure or object resembling a thread: as **a :** a slender root (as of a grass) **b :** a long tapering thick-walled plant cell especially of vascular tissue **c** (1) **:** a strand of nerve tissue **:** AXON, DENDRITE (2) **:** a muscle cell **d :** a slender and greatly elongated natural or synthetic unit of material (as wool, cotton, asbestos, gold, glass, or rayon) typically capable of being spun into yarn **2 :** material made of fibers; *esp* **:** a tough hard or flexible material made from cellulose fibers and used for luggage **3 a :** an element that gives texture or substance **b :** basic toughness **:** STRENGTH [French *fibre,* from Latin *fibra*]

fi·ber·board \ˈfī-bər-ˌbōrd, -ˌbȯrd\ *n* **:** a material made by compressing fibers (as of wood) into stiff sheets

fi·ber·glass \ˈfī-bər-ˌglas\ *n* **:** glass in fibrous form used in making various products (as yarn and insulation)

fibr- *or* **fibro-** *combining form* **:** fiber **:** fibrous tissue **:** fibrous and ⟨*fibroid*⟩ [Latin *fibra*]

fi·bril \ˈfīb-rəl, ˈfib-\ *n* **:** a small filament or fiber (as a root hair) — **fi·bril·lar** \-rə-lər\ *adj* — **fi·bril·lose** \-rə-ˌlōs\ *adj*

fi·bril·la·tion \ˌfib-rə-ˈlā-shən, ˌfīb-\ *n* **:** rapid irregular contractions of muscle fibers of the heart

fi·brin \ˈfī-brən\ *n* **:** a white insoluble fibrous protein formed in the clotting of blood — **fi·brin·ous** \ˈfib-rə-nəs, ˈfīb-\ *adj*

fi·brin·o·gen \fī-ˈbrin-ə-jən\ *n* **:** a soluble protein produced in the liver, present especially in blood plasma, and converted into fibrin during clotting of blood

fi·bro·blast \ˈfī-brə-ˌblast\ *n* **:** a cell giving rise to connective tissue [Greek *blastos* "bud, shoot"] — **fi·bro·blas·tic** \ˌfī-brə-ˈblas-tik\ *adj*

fi·broid \ˈfī-ˌbrȯid\ *adj* **:** resembling, forming, or consisting of fibrous tissue ⟨*fibroid* tumors⟩

fi·bro·sis \fī-ˈbrō-səs\ *n* **:** an abnormal condition in which increased amounts of fibrous tissue form in other tissues — **fi·brot·ic** \-ˈbrät-ik\ *adj*

fi·brous \ˈfī-brəs\ *adj* **1 :** containing, consisting of, or resembling fibers **2 :** TOUGH 1, STRINGY

fibrous root *n* **:** a root that is one of many similar slender roots branching directly from the base of the stem of a plant — compare TAPROOT

fibrous tissue *n* **:** a connective tissue rich in fibers that forms in and supports body structures and is prominent in healing wounds

fi·bro·vas·cu·lar bundle \ˌfī-brō-ˌvas-kyə-lər-\ *n* **:** VASCULAR BUNDLE

fib·u·la \ˈfib-yə-lə\ *n, pl* **-lae** \-ˌlē, -ˌlī\ *or* **-las :** the outer and usually the smaller of the two bones of the hind limb below the knee [Latin, "clasp, brace"] — **fib·u·lar** \-lər\ *adj*

-fic \fik\ *adj suffix* **:** making **:** causing ⟨sudorific⟩ [Latin *-ficus,* from *facere* "to make, do"]

-fi·ca·tion \fə-ˈkā-shən\ *n suffix* **:** making **:** production ⟨syllabification⟩ [Latin *-fication-, -ficatio,* derived from *-ficus* "-fic"]

fichu \ˈfish-ü\ *n* **:** a woman's light triangular scarf draped over the shoulders and fastened in front [French]

fick·le \ˈfik-əl\ *adj* **:** not firm or steadfast in attitude or character **:** INCONSTANT ⟨*fickle* friends⟩ [Old English *ficol* "deceitful"] — **fick·le·ness** *n*

fic·tion \ˈfik-shən\ *n* **1 :** something told or written that is not fact **:** something made up ⟨both fact and *fiction* in that story⟩ **2 :** a made-up story about real or imaginary persons or events; *also* **:** such stories as a class ⟨a writer of *fiction*⟩ [Middle French, from Latin *fictio* "act of fashioning, fiction", from *fingere* "to shape, fashion, feign"] — **fic·tion·al** \ˈfik-shnəl, -shən-l\ *adj* — **fic·tion·al·ly** \-ē\ *adv*

• **syn** FICTION, FIGMENT, FABRICATION mean something that is an invention of the human mind. FICTION implies imaginative creation of events, characters, or circumstances with or more often without intent to deceive ⟨King Arthur belongs to *fiction* rather than to history⟩ FIGMENT suggests a creation of the imagination that deceives its own creator ⟨this *figment* of a fevered brain⟩ FABRICATION implies something deliberately made up to deceive or mislead ⟨their story of being robbed was pure *fabrication*⟩

fic•tion•al•ize \ˈfik-shnəl-ˌīz, -shən-l-\ *vb* **:** to make into fiction ⟨*fictionalize* a war diary⟩ — **fic•tion•al•iza•tion** \ˌfik-shnəl-ə-ˈzā-shən, -shən-l-\ *n*

fic•tion•ize \ˈfik-shə-ˌnīz\ *vt* **:** FICTIONALIZE — **fic•tion•iza•tion** \ˌfik-shə-nə-ˈzā-shən\ *n*

fic•ti•tious \fik-ˈtish-əs\ *adj* **1 :** of, relating to, or suggestive of fiction **:** IMAGINARY ⟨*fictitious* values⟩ **2 :** not genuinely felt or expressed **:** SIMULATED [Latin *ficticius* "artificial, feigned", from *fingere* "to feign"]
• syn FICTITIOUS, FACTITIOUS are easily confused. FICTITIOUS applies to what is invented by the imagination ⟨a child's *fictitious* playmate⟩ ⟨*fictitious* characters in a novel⟩ FACTITIOUS applies to what has actual existence but an artificial rather than natural origin or cause ⟨a *factitious* show of enthusiasm⟩ ⟨a *factitious* scarcity of goods created by unfounded rumors⟩

fid \ˈfid\ *n* **:** a pin usually of hard wood that tapers to a point and is used in opening the strands of rope [origin unknown]

1fid•dle \ˈfid-l\ *n* **:** VIOLIN [Old English *fithele*]

2fiddle *vb* **fid•dled; fid•dling** \ˈfid-ling, -l-ing\ **1 :** to play on a fiddle **2 a :** to move the hands or fingers restlessly **b :** to spend time in aimless activity **:** PUTTER **c :** TAMPER 2, MEDDLE — usually used with *with* — **fid•dler** \ˈfid-lər, -l-ər\ *n*

fid•dle•head \ˈfid-l-ˌhed\ *n* **:** one of the young unfurling fronds of some ferns that are often eaten as greens

fiddler crab *n* **:** any of numerous burrowing crabs with one claw much larger than the other in the male

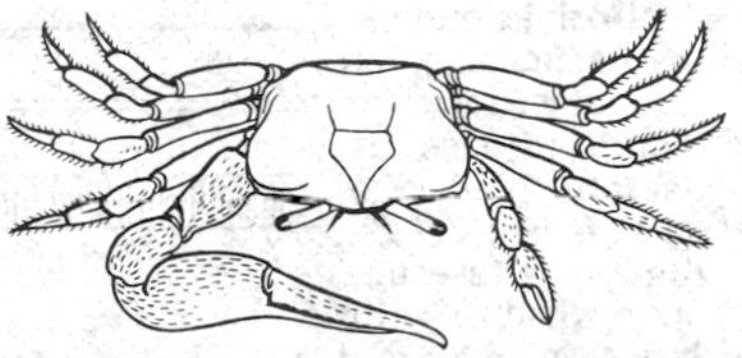

fiddler crab

fid•dle•sticks \ˈfid-l-ˌstiks\ *n pl* **:** NONSENSE — used as an interjection

fi•del•i•ty \fə-ˈdel-ət-ē, fī-\ *n, pl* **-ties 1 a :** the quality or state of being faithful **b :** accuracy in details **:** EXACTNESS **2 :** the degree to which an electronic device (as a radio or phonograph) accurately reproduces its effect (as sound) [Middle French *fidelité,* from Latin *fidelitas,* from *fidelis* "faithful", from *fides* "faith"]
• syn ALLEGIANCE, FEALTY, LOYALTY: FIDELITY implies strict and continuous faithfulness to an obligation, trust, or duty; ALLEGIANCE implies the formal obedient adherence of a subject to a sovereign or a citizen to a state; FEALTY implies an individual compelling fidelity; LOYALTY implies personal steadfast adherence in the face of any temptation to desert or betray.

1fidg•et \ˈfij-ət\ *n* **1** *pl* **:** uneasiness or restlessness as shown by nervous movements **2 :** one that fidgets [Scottish *fidge* "to fidget"] — **fidg•ety** \-ət-ē\ *adj*

2fidget *vb* **:** to move or cause to move or act nervously or restlessly

1fi•du•cia•ry \fə-ˈdü-shē-ˌer-ē, fī-, -ˈdyü-, -shə-rē\ *n, pl* **-ries 1 :** one that acts as a trustee for another **2 :** one that acts in a confidential capacity

2fiduciary *adj* **1 :** involving a confidence or trust ⟨employed in a *fiduciary* capacity⟩ **2 :** held or holding in trust for another ⟨*fiduciary* accounts⟩ [Latin *fiduciarius,* from *fiducia* "confidence, trust", from *fidere* "to trust"]

fie \ˈfī\ *interj* — used to express mild disapproval or feigned shock [Old French *fi*]

fief \ˈfēf\ *n* **:** a feudal estate **:** FEE [French, from Old French *fief, fé,* of Germanic origin]

1field \ˈfēld\ *n* **1 a :** open country — usually used in pl. **b :** a piece of open land **c :** a piece of land put to a special use or yielding a special product ⟨an athletic *field*⟩ ⟨a gas *field*⟩ **d :** a place where a battle is fought **:** the region in which military operations are carried on **e :** an open space or expanse ⟨a *field* of ice⟩ **2 :** a sphere or range of activity or influence ⟨the *field* of science⟩ **3 :** a background on which something is drawn, painted, or mounted ⟨the American flag has white stars on a blue *field*⟩ **4 :** the individuals that make up all or part of a sports activity: as **a :** all the participants in a contest or sporting event (as a golf tournament) **b :** the baseball team not at bat **5 :** a region or space in which a given effect (as gravity, electricity, or magnetism) exists **6 :** the area visible through the lens of an optical instrument [Old English *feld*]

2field *vb* **1 :** to catch, stop, or throw a ball as a fielder ⟨*field* a ground ball⟩ **2 :** to put into the field ⟨*field* an army⟩

3field *adj* **:** of or relating to a field: as **a :** growing or living in open country ⟨*field* flowers⟩ **b :** made, conducted, used, or operating in the field

field artillery *n* **:** artillery other than antiaircraft artillery used with armies in the field

field corn *n* **:** an Indian corn with starchy kernels grown for feeding livestock or for market grain

field day *n* **1 :** a day devoted to outdoor sports and athletic competition **2 :** a time of unusual pleasure or unexpected success

field•er \ˈfēl-dər\ *n* **:** one that fields; *esp* **:** a baseball player stationed in the outfield

field event *n* **:** an event in a track meet other than a race

field glasses *n pl* **:** a hand-held magnifying optical instrument consisting of two simple telescopes mounted side-by-side in a frame which permits simultaneous focusing; *also* **:** BINOCULARS

field goal *n* **1 :** a score of three points in football made by drop-kicking or place-kicking the ball over the crossbar from ordinary play **2 :** a score of two points in basketball on a goal made while the ball is in play

field hockey *n* **:** a game played on a field between two teams of 11 players whose object is to knock a ball into the opponent's goal with a curved stick

field magnet *n* **:** a magnet for producing and maintaining a magnetic field especially in a generator or electric motor

field marshal *n* **:** an officer (as in the British army) of the highest rank

field mouse *n* **:** any of various mice that inhabit open fields

field pea *n* **:** a small-seeded pea widely grown chiefly for forage

field piece \ˈfēld-ˌpēs\ *n* **:** a gun or howitzer for use in the field

field trial *n* **:** a trial of sporting dogs in actual performance

field trip *n* **:** a visit (as to a factory, farm, or museum) made by students and usually a teacher for purposes of firsthand observation

fiend \ˈfēnd\ *n* **1 a :** DEVIL 1 **b :** DEMON 2a **2 :** an extremely wicked or cruel person **3 a :** a person excessively devoted to a pursuit **:** FANATIC ⟨a golf *fiend*⟩ **b :** a person who uses immoderate quantities of something **:** ADDICT ⟨a dope *fiend*⟩ [Old English *fīend,* literally, "enemy"]

fiend•ish \ˈfēn-dish\ *adj* **:** extremely cruel or wicked **:** DIABOLICAL — **fiend•ish•ly** *adv* — **fiend•ish•ness** *n*

fierce \ˈfiərs\ *adj* **1 a :** violently hostile or aggressive in temperament **b :** given to fighting or killing **:** PUGNACIOUS **2 :** marked by unrestrained zeal or vehemence **:** INTENSE **3 :** furiously active or determined **4 :** wild or menacing in aspect [Old French *fiers,* from Latin *ferus* "wild, savage"] — **fierce•ly** *adv* — **fierce•ness** *n*
• syn FEROCIOUS: FIERCE implies inspiring fear because of a wild and menacing aspect or display of fury in attack ⟨*fierce* mountain tribes⟩ FEROCIOUS implies extreme fierceness and unrestrained violence and brutality.

fi•ery \ˈfī-rē, -ə-rē\ *adj* **fi•eri•er; -est 1 a :** consisting of fire **b :** BURNING, BLAZING ⟨a *fiery* furnace⟩ **c :** FLAMMABLE ⟨a *fiery* vapor⟩ **2 a :** hot like fire **b** (1) **:** INFLAMED ⟨a *fiery* boil⟩ (2) **:** feverish and flushed **3 a :** of the color of fire **:** RED **b :** intensely or unnaturally red **4 a :** full of emotion or spirit **b :** easily provoked **:** IRRITABLE — **fi•eri•ness** *n*

fi•es•ta \fē-ˈes-tə\ *n* **:** FESTIVAL; *esp* **:** a saint's day celebrated in Spain and Latin America with processions and dances [Spanish, from Latin *festa,* pl. of *festum*]

fife \ˈfīf\ *n* **:** a small shrill musical instrument resembling a flute [German *pfeife* "pipe, fife"]

fif•teen \fif-ˈtēn, ˈfif-\ *n* **1 :** one more than 14; *also* **:** a symbol representing this — see NUMBER table **2 :** the 1st point scored by a side in a game of tennis — called also *five* [Old English *fīftēne*] — **fifteen** *adj or pron* — **fif•teenth** \-'tēnth, -'tēntth\ *adj or n*

fifth \'fifth, 'fiftth\ *n, pl* **fifths** \'fifths, 'fiftths, 'fifts, 'fifs\ **1** : number five in a countable series — see NUMBER table **2 a** : the musical interval embracing five diatonic degrees **b** : the harmonic combination of two tones at this interval **3** : a unit of measure for liquor equal to one fifth of a United States gallon (about .75 liter) — **fifth** *adj or adv* — **fifth•ly** *adv*

fifth column *n* : a group of secret sympathizers or supporters of a nation's enemy that engage in espionage or sabotage within the country [name applied to rebel sympathizers in Madrid in 1936 when four rebel columns were advancing on the city] — **fifth columnist** *n*

fifth wheel *n* : one that is unnecessary or superfluous

fif•ty \'fif-tē\ *n, pl* **fifties** : ten more than 40; *also* : a symbol representing this — see NUMBER table [Old English *fīftig*] — **fifty** *adj or pron* — **fif•ti•eth** \-tē-əth\ *adj or n*

fif•ty–fif•ty \ˌfif-tē-'fif-tē\ *adj* **1** : shared equally ⟨a *fifty-fifty* proposition⟩ **2** : half favorable and half unfavorable ⟨a *fifty-fifty* chance to live⟩ — **fifty–fifty** *adv*

fig \'fig\ *n* **1** : the usually edible oblong or pear-shaped fruit of a tree of the mulberry family; *also* : a tree bearing figs **2** : TRIFLE 1 [Old French *fige, figue,* derived from Latin *ficus* "fig tree, fig"]

[1]**fight** \'fīt\ *vb* **fought** \'fȯt\; **fight•ing 1 a** : to contend against another in battle or physical combat **b** : to engage in boxing : BOX **2** : to try hard **3 a** : to act in opposition : STRUGGLE, CONTEND ⟨*fight* for the right⟩ **b** : to attempt to prevent the success or effectiveness of **4** : to carry on : WAGE ⟨*fight* a war⟩ **5** : to gain by struggle ⟨*fought* their way through⟩ [Old English *feohtan*]

[2]**fight** *n* **1 a** : a hostile encounter : BATTLE **b** : a boxing match **c** : a verbal disagreement **2** : a struggle for a goal or an objective **3** : strength or disposition for fighting ⟨full of *fight*⟩

fight•er \'fīt-ər\ *n* : one that fights: **a** : SOLDIER 1, WARRIOR **b** : [1]BOXER **c** : an airplane of high speed and maneuverability with armament for destroying enemy aircraft.

fig•ment \'fig-mənt\ *n* : something imagined or made up ⟨a *figment* of a fevered imagination⟩ [Latin *figmentum,* from *fingere* "to shape, feign"] **syn** see FICTION

fig•u•ra•tion \ˌfig-yə-'rā-shən, ˌfig-ə-'\ *n* **1** : OUTLINE 1, FORM **2** : an act or instance of representation in figures and shapes

fig•u•ra•tive \'fig-yə-rət-iv, 'fig-ə-; 'fig-yərt-iv, -ərt-\ *adj* **1** : representing by a figure : EMBLEMATIC **2 a** : expressing one thing in terms normally denoting another : METAPHORICAL **b** : characterized by figures of speech — **fig•u•ra•tive•ly** *adv* — **fig•u•ra•tive•ness** *n*

[1]**fig•ure** \'fig-yər, *especially British* 'fig-ər\ *n* **1 a** : a number symbol : NUMERAL **b** *pl* : arithmetical calculations **c** : a written or printed character **d** : value especially as expressed in numbers : PRICE **2 a** : the shape or outline of something **b** : bodily shape especially of a person **c** : an object noticeable only as a shape ⟨*figures* moving in the dusk⟩ **3 a** : the graphic representation of a form especially of a person **b** : a diagram or pictorial illustration of a text **c** : a combination of points, lines, or surfaces in geometry ⟨a circle is a closed plane *figure*⟩ **4** : FIGURE OF SPEECH **5** : PATTERN 5a, 6, DESIGN **6** : impression produced ⟨the couple cut quite a *figure*⟩ **7 a** : a series of movements in a dance **b** : an outline representation of a form traced by a series of evolutions (as with skates on ice) **8** : a prominent personality : PERSONAGE [Old French, from Latin *figura,* from *fingere* "to shape, feign"] **syn** see FORM

[2]**figure** *vb* **1** : to represent by or as if by a figure or outline : PORTRAY **2** : to decorate with a pattern **3 a** : to indicate or represent by numerals **b** : CONCLUDE, DECIDE ⟨*figured* there was no use⟩ **c** : REGARD, CONSIDER ⟨*figure* oneself a good candidate⟩ **4** : to be or appear important or conspicuous ⟨*figure* in the news⟩ **5** : COMPUTE, CALCULATE — **fig•ur•er** \-yər-ər, -ər-ər\ *n* — **figure on 1** : to take into consideration **2** : to rely on **3** : PLAN 2

fig•ured *adj* **1** : being represented : PORTRAYED **2** : adorned with, formed into, or marked with a figure **3** : indicated by figures

figure eight *n* : something (as a skating figure) resembling the Arabic numeral 8 in shape

fig•ure•head \'fig-yər-ˌhed, -ər-\ *n* **1** : a figure, statue, or bust on the bow of a ship **2** : a head or chief in name only

figure of speech : a form of expression (as a simile or metaphor) in which words are intentionally used in other than a plain or literal way so as to produce fresh, vivid, or poetic effects

figure out *vt* : SOLVE

figure skating *n* : skating in which the skater performs figures and special jumps and turns

fig•u•rine \ˌfig-yə-'rēn, fig-ə-\ *n* : a small carved or molded figure

fig•wort \'fig-ˌwərt, -ˌwȯrt\ *n* : any of a genus of chiefly erect herbs with toothed leaves and clustered flowers

fil•a•ment \'fil-ə-mənt\ *n* : a single thread or a thin flexible threadlike object, process, or appendage: as **a** : a wire (as in an electric lamp) made incandescent by the passage of an electric current; *esp* : a cathode in the form of a metal wire in an electron tube **b** : the anther-bearing stalk of a stamen [Middle French, from Medieval Latin *filamentum,* from Late Latin *filare* "to spin", from Latin *filum* "thread"] — **fil•a•men•tous** \ˌfil-ə-'ment-əs\ *adj*

fi•lar•ia \fə-'lar-ē-ə, -'ler-\ *n, pl* **-i•ae** \-ē-ˌē, -ē-ˌī\ : any of numerous slender threadlike nematodes that as adults are parasites in the blood or tissues of mammals and as larvae usually develop in biting insects [derived from Latin *filum* "thread"] — **fi•lar•i•al** \-ē-əl\ *adj*

fil•a•ri•a•sis \ˌfil-ə-'rī-ə-səs\ *n, pl* **-a•ses** \-ˌsēz\ : infestation with or disease caused by filariae

fil•bert \'fil-bərt\ *n* **1** : either of two European hazels; *also* : the sweet thick-shelled nut of a filbert **2** : HAZELNUT [Anglo-French *philber,* from Saint Philibert, died 684, Frankish abbot whose feast day falls in the nutting season]

filch \'filch\ *vt* : to steal furtively : PILFER [Middle English *filchen*]

[1]**file** \'fīl\ *n* : a usually steel tool with sharp ridges or teeth on its surface for smoothing or rubbing down a hard substance (as metal) [Old English *fēol*]

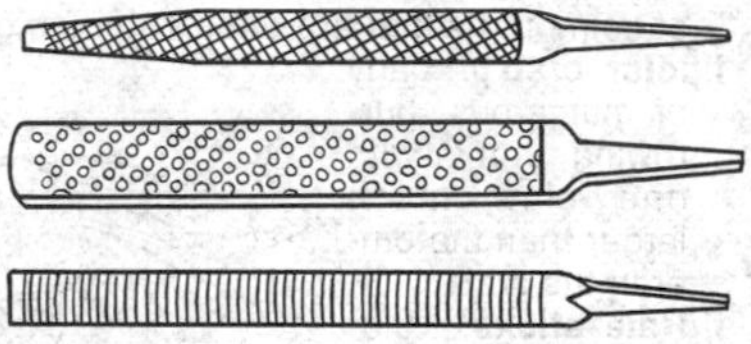

[1]file

[2]**file** *vt* : to rub, smooth, or cut away with a file

[3]**file** *vb* **1** : to arrange in order for preservation or reference **2 a** : to enter or record as prescribed by law ⟨*file* a mortgage⟩ **b** : to send (copy) to a newspaper ⟨*file* a story⟩ **3** : to register as a candidate especially in a primary election [Middle French *filer* "to string documents on a string or wire", from *fil* "thread", from Latin *filum*]

[4]**file** *n* **1** : a device (as a folder, case, or cabinet) in which records are kept in order **2** : a collection of material kept in a file

[5]**file** *n* : a row of persons, animals, or things arranged one behind the other [Middle French, derived from Latin *filum* "thread"]

[6]**file** *vi* : to march or proceed in file

file•fish \'fīl-ˌfish\ *n* : any of various fishes with rough granular leathery skins

fi•let \fi-'lā\ *n* : a lace with a square mesh and geometric designs [French, literally, "net"]

fi•let mi•gnon \ˌfil-ˌā-mēn-'yō^{n}, fi-ˌlā-\ *n, pl* **filets mignons** *same or* -'yō^{n}z\ : a fillet of beef cut from the thick end of a beef tenderloin [French, literally, "dainty fillet"]

fil•ial \'fil-ē-əl, 'fil-yəl\ *adj* **1** : of, relating to, or befitting a son or daughter **2** : having or assuming the relation of a child or offspring [Late Latin *filialis,* from Latin *filius* "son"] — **fil•ial•ly** \-ē\ *adv*

filial generation *n* : a generation of offspring in a breeding experiment that is produced by the parents in the original cross by their offspring

[1]**fil•i•bus•ter** \'fil-ə-ˌbəs-tər\ *n* **1** : an irregular mercenary; *esp* : an American engaged in stirring up rebellions in Latin America in the mid-19th century **2 a** : the use of delaying tactics (as extremely long speeches) in an attempt to delay or prevent action especially in a legislative assembly **b** : an instance of this practice [Spanish *filibustero,* derived from English *freebooter*]

△ **origin** The Dutch word *vrijbuiter,* "plunderer", has left its mark on the English vocabulary not once but twice. It first appeared in the 16th century as *freebooter.* Though the spelling had changed, the meaning remained the same. From English it passed into Spanish and became *filibustero.* In the middle of the 19th century bands of adventurers organized in the United States were active in Central America and the West Indies stirring up revolutions. Such an adventurer came to be called in English a *filibuster*, from the Spanish *filibustero*, and so *vrijbuiter* made its second appearance in a very different guise. Later in the 19th century, the use of delaying tactics became very common in the United States Senate. Senators who practiced such tactics were compared with the troublesome *filibusters* and were said to be *filibustering*.

²filibuster *vb* **fil•i•bus•tered**; **fil•i•bus•ter•ing** \-tə-riŋ, -triŋ\ **1** : to carry out revolutionary activities in a foreign country **2** : to engage in a legislative filibuster — **fil•i•bus•ter•er** \-tər-ər\ *n*

fil•i•form \ˈfil-ə-ˌfȯrm, ˈfī-lə-\ *adj* : shaped like a thread

fil•i•gree \ˈfil-ə-ˌgrē\ *n* **1** : ornamental work especially of fine wire applied chiefly to gold and silver surfaces **2 a** : ornamental openwork of delicate or intricate design **b** : a pattern or design resembling this openwork [French *filigrane*, from Italian *filigrana*, from Latin *filum* "thread" + *granum* "grain"]

fil•ing \ˈfī-liŋ\ *n* **1** : the act of one who files **2** : a small piece scraped off by a file ⟨iron *filings*⟩

Fil•i•pi•no \ˌfil-ə-ˈpē-nō\ *n, pl* **-nos** **1** : a native or inhabitant of the Philippines **2** : a person of Filipino descent [Spanish] — **Filipino** *adj*

¹fill \ˈfil\ *vb* **1** : to put into as much as can be held or conveniently contained **2** : to become full **3** : FULFILL 2 ⟨*fill* all requirements⟩ **4** : to take up whatever space there is **5** : to spread through ⟨laughter *filled* the room⟩ **6** : to stop up (as crevices or holes) : PLUG ⟨*fill* a crack with putty⟩ ⟨*fill* a tooth⟩ **7 a** : to have and perform the duties of : OCCUPY ⟨*fill* the office of president⟩ **b** : to put a person in ⟨*filled* several vacancies⟩ **8** : to supply according to directions ⟨*fill* a prescription⟩ [Old English *fyllan*] — **fill one's shoes** : to take one's place or position — **fill the bill** : to serve the purpose satisfactorily

²fill *n* **1** : a full supply; *esp* : a quantity that satisfies or satiates **2** : material used especially for filling a ditch or hollow in the ground

fill•er \ˈfil-ər\ *n* : one that fills: as **a** : a substance added to a product (as to increase bulk, weight, viscosity, opacity, or strength) **b** : a material used for filling cracks and pores in wood before painting **c** : a pack of paper for insertion in a binder

¹fil•let \ˈfil-ət\ *also* **fi•let** \fi-ˈlā, ˈfil-ā\ *n* **1** : a narrow strip of material (as a ribbon) used as a headband **2 a** : a thin narrow strip of material **b** : a piece or slice of boneless meat or fish **3 a** : a flat molding separating other moldings **b** : the space between two flutings in a shaft [Middle French *filet*, from *fil* "thread", from Latin *filum*]

²fillet *vt* **1** : to bind or adorn with or as if with a fillet **2** : to cut into fillets

fill in *vb* **1** : to furnish with specified information ⟨*fill in* an application⟩ **2** : to fill a vacancy usually temporarily : SUBSTITUTE ⟨*filled in* during the emergency⟩

fill•ing \ˈfil-iŋ\ *n* **1** : material that is used to fill something ⟨a *filling* for a tooth⟩ **2** : something that completes: as **a** : the yarn interlacing the warp in a fabric **b** : a food mixture used to fill pastry or sandwiches

filling station *n* : SERVICE STATION

¹fil•lip \ˈfil-əp\ *n* **1** : a blow or gesture made by the sudden forcible straightening of a finger curled up against the thumb **2** : something tending to arouse or excite [probably imitative]

²fillip *vt* **1** : to tap with the finger by flicking the fingernail outward across the end of the thumb **2** : to urge on : STIMULATE

fill out *vi* : to put on flesh

fil•ly \ˈfil-ē\ *n, pl* **fillies** : a young female horse usually less than four years old [Old Norse *fylja*]

¹film \ˈfilm\ *n* **1** : a thin skin or membrane **2** : a thin coating or layer **3** : a roll or strip of thin flexible transparent material coated with a chemical substance sensitive to light and used in taking pictures **4** : MOVIE [Old English *filmen*]

²film *vb* **1** : to cover or become covered with film ⟨eyes *filmed* with tears⟩ **2** : to photograph on film; *esp* : to make a motion picture of ⟨*film* a battle scene⟩

film•ic \ˈfil-mik\ *adj* : of, relating to, or resembling motion pictures

film•strip \ˈfilm-ˌstrip\ *n* : a strip of usually 35 millimeter film bearing photographs, diagrams, or graphic matter for still projection upon a screen

filmy \ˈfil-mē\ *adj* **film•i•er**; **-est** **1** : of, resembling, or composed of film **2** : covered with a haze or film — **film•i•ness** *n*

fi•lo•plume \fil-ə-ˌplüm, ˈfī-lə-\ *n* : a slender threadlike feather with a tuft at the end [Latin *filum* "thread" + English *-o-* + *plume*]

¹fil•ter \ˈfil-tər\ *n* **1** : a porous article or mass through which a gas or liquid is passed to separate out matter in suspension **2** : an apparatus containing a filter medium **3 a** : a device or material for suppressing or minimizing waves or oscillations of certain frequencies (as of electricity, light, or sound) **b** : a transparent material (as colored glass) that absorbs light of certain colors and is used for modifying the light which reaches a sensitized photographic material [Medieval Latin *filtrum* "piece of felt used as a filter", of Germanic origin]

²filter *vb* **fil•tered**; **fil•ter•ing** \-tə-riŋ, -triŋ\ **1** : to subject to the action of a filter **2** : to remove by means of a filter **3** : to pass through or as if through a filter

fil•ter•able *also* **fil•tra•ble** \ˈfil-tə-rə-bəl, -trə-bəl\ *adj* : capable of being separated by or of passing through a filter ⟨*filterable* microorganisms⟩ ⟨a *filterable* liquid⟩ — **fil•ter•abil•i•ty** \ˌfil-tə-rə-ˈbil-ət-ē, -trə-ˈ\ *n*

filterable virus *n* : VIRUS 1a

filter bed *n* : a bed of sand or gravel for filtering water or sewage

filter paper *n* : porous paper used for filtering

filter tip *n* : a cigar or cigarette with a tip designed to filter the smoke

filth \ˈfilth\ *n* **1** : foul or putrid matter; *esp* : disgusting dirt or refuse **2 a** : moral corruption **b** : something that tends to corrupt or disgust [Old English *fȳlth*, from *fūl* "foul"]

filthy \ˈfil-thē\ *adj* **filth•i•er**; **-est** **1** : covered with or containing filth : disgustingly dirty **2 a** : morally polluted : EVIL ⟨*filthy* politics⟩ **b** : OBSCENE **syn** see DIRTY — **filth•i•ly** \-thə-lē\ *adv* — **filth•i•ness** \-thē-nəs\ *n*

fil•trate \ˈfil-ˌtrāt\ *n* : fluid that has passed through a filter

fil•tra•tion \fil-ˈtrā-shən\ *n* : the act or process of filtering

fin \ˈfin\ *n* **1** : a thin external process of an aquatic animal (as a fish or whale) used in propelling or guiding the body **2 a** : a fin-shaped part (as on an airplane, boat, or automobile) **b** : FLIPPER 2 **c** : a projecting rib on a radiator or an engine cylinder [Old English *finn*] — **fin•like** \-ˌlīk\ *adj* — **finned** \ˈfind\ *adj*

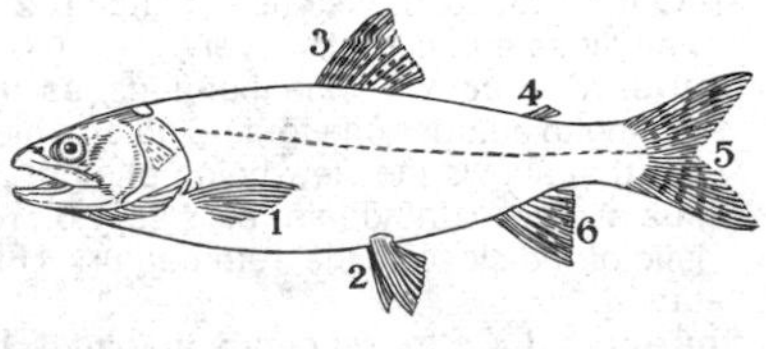

fin 1: *1* pectoral, *2* pelvic, *3, 4* dorsal, *5* caudal, *6* anal

fi•na•gle \fə-ˈnā-gəl\ *vb* **fi•na•gled**; **fi•na•gling** \-ˈnā-gə-liŋ, -gliŋ\ : WANGLE 1a [perhaps from *fainaigue* "to renege"] — **fi•na•gler** \-gə-lər, -glər\ *n*

¹fi•nal \ˈfīn-l\ *adj* **1 a** : bringing something (as conflict or uncertainty) to an end ⟨the *final* war that destroyed life⟩ **b** : not to be altered or undone ⟨reached a *final* decision⟩ ⟨all sales are *final*⟩ **2** : being the last stage of a series or process ⟨paid their *final* debt to nature⟩ **3** : being or relating to an end or purpose ⟨*final* causes⟩ **4** : coming after all others ⟨the *final* chapter of a book⟩ [Middle French, from Latin *finalis*, from *finis* "end, boundary"] **syn** see LAST — **fi•nal•ly** \ˈfīn-l-ē, ˈfīn-lē\ *adv*

²final *n* : something final: as **a** : a deciding match, game, or trial **b** : the last examination in a course — usually used in pl.

fi•na•le \fə-ˈnal-ē, fi-ˈnäl-\ *n* : the close or termination of something; *esp* : the last section of an instrumental musical composition [Italian, from Latin *finalis* "final"]

fi•nal•ist \ˈfīn-l-əst\ *n* : a contestant in the finals of a competition

fi•nal•i•ty \fī-ˈnal-ət-ē, fə-\ *n, pl* **-ties** **1** : the character or condition of being final, settled, or complete **2** : something final

fi•nal•ize \ˈfīn-l-ˌīz\ *vt* : to put in final or finished form

¹fi•nance \fə-ˈnans, ˈfī-ˌ, fī-ˈ\ *n* **1** *pl* : liquid resources (as money) of a government, business, group, or individual **2** : the system that includes the circulation of money, the granting of cred-

\ə\ **abut**	\au̇\ **out**	\i\ **tip**	\ȯ\ **saw**	\u̇\ **foot**
\ər\ **further**	\ch\ **chin**	\ī\ **life**	\ȯi\ **coin**	\y\ **yet**
\a\ **mat**	\e\ **pet**	\j\ **job**	\th\ **thin**	\yü\ **few**
\ā\ **take**	\ē\ **easy**	\ŋ\ **sing**	\t͟h\ **this**	\yu̇\ **cure**
\ä\ **cot, cart**	\g\ **go**	\ō\ **bone**	\ü\ **food**	\zh\ **vision**

it, the making of investments, and the provision of banking facilities **3 :** the obtaining of funds or capital **:** FINANCING **[**Middle English, "payment, ransom", from Middle French, from *finer* "to end, pay", from *fin* "end", from Latin *finis***]**

[2]finance *vt* **1 :** to raise or provide funds or capital for ⟨*finance* a new car⟩ **2 :** to sell to or supply on credit ⟨*finance* farmers until harvest⟩

finance company *n* **:** a company that specializes in making small loans usually to individuals

fi•nan•cial \fə-ˈnan-chəl, fī-\ *adj* **:** having to do with finance or with finances — **fi•nan•cial•ly** \-ˈnanch-lē, -ə-lē\ *adv*

• **syn** MONETARY, PECUNIARY, FISCAL: FINANCIAL implies money matters involving a large scale or some degree of complexity ⟨*financial* aspects of a business⟩ MONETARY refers to money as coined, distributed, or circulating ⟨*monetary* reform⟩ PECUNIARY implies reference to money matters affecting the individual ⟨*pecuniary* rewards of an office⟩ FISCAL applies to the financial affairs of a corporation, institution, or state.

fin•an•cier \ˌfin-ən-ˈsiər, fə-ˌnan-, ˌfī-ˌnan-\ *n* **:** a person who deals with finance and investment on a large scale

fin•back \ˈfin-ˌbak\ *n* **:** RORQUAL; *esp* **:** a large whale of the Atlantic

finch \ˈfinch\ *n* **:** any of numerous songbirds (as sparrows, grosbeaks, crossbills, goldfinches, linnets, and buntings) having a short stout conical bill adapted for crushing seeds **[**Old English *finc***]**

[1]find \ˈfīnd\ *vb* **found** \ˈfau̇nd\; **find•ing 1 :** to encounter someone or something by chance ⟨*find* a kitten on the porch⟩ **2 :** to come upon by searching or study **:** DISCOVER **3 :** to obtain by effort or management ⟨*find* time to do it⟩ **4 :** to arrive at **:** REACH ⟨*find* one's place in the world⟩ **5 :** to make a decision and declare it ⟨*find* a verdict⟩ **6 :** to know by experience ⟨people *found* them honest⟩ **7 :** to gain or regain the use of ⟨*find* one's feet after an illness⟩ **8 :** PROVIDE, SUPPLY ⟨*find* room for a guest⟩ **[**Old English *findan***]** — **find fault :** to criticize unfavorably

[2]find *n* **1 :** an act or instance of finding **2 :** something found; *esp* **:** a valuable item of discovery

find•er \ˈfīn-dər\ *n* **:** one that finds: as **a :** a small telescope attached to a larger one for finding an object **b :** a lens on a camera that shows the view being photographed by the camera

fin de si•ècle \ˌfa^{n}-də-sē-ˈekl\ *adj* **:** of, relating to, or characteristic of the close of the 19th century **[**French, "end of the century"**]**

find•ing *n* **1 a :** the act of one that finds **b :** FIND 2 **2 :** the result of a judicial proceeding or investigation

find out *vt* **1 :** to learn by study or observation **2 :** DETECT 1, DISCOVER

[1]fine \ˈfīn\ *n* **:** a sum of money imposed as punishment for an offense **[**Old French *fin* "end, fine", from Latin *finis* "end, limit, boundary"**]**

[2]fine *vt* **:** to impose a fine on **:** punish by a fine

[3]fine *adj* **1 a :** free from impurity **b :** having a stated proportion of pure metal in the composition ⟨silver 800/1000 *fine*⟩ **2 a :** very thin in gauge or texture ⟨*fine* thread⟩ **b :** not coarse ⟨*fine* sand⟩ **c :** very small ⟨*fine* print⟩ **3 :** subtle or sensitive in perception or discrimination ⟨a *fine* distinction⟩ **4 :** superior in quality, conception, or appearance **:** EXCELLENT ⟨a *fine* musician⟩ **5 :** marked by or affecting elegance or refinement ⟨*fine* manners⟩ **6 :** to one's liking **:** AGREEABLE ⟨that's *fine* with me⟩ **[**Old French *fin,* from Latin *finis* "end, limit"**]** — **fine•ly** *adv* — **fine•ness** \ˈfīn-nəs\ *n*

[4]fine *adv* **:** FINELY

[5]fi•ne \ˈfē-ˌnā\ *n* **:** END — used as a direction in music to mark the closing point after a repeat **[**Italian, from Latin *finis* "end"**]**

fine adjustment *n* **:** a knob on a microscope used for making small changes in focus — compare COARSE ADJUSTMENT

fine art *n* **:** art (as painting, sculpture, or music) concerned primarily with the creation of beautiful objects — usually used in pl.

fin•ery \ˈfīn-rē, -ə-rē\ *n, pl* **-er•ies :** ORNAMENT 1, DECORATION; *esp* **:** showy clothing and jewels

fines \ˈfīnz\ *n pl* **:** finely crushed or powdered material (as ore or coal)

[1]fi•nesse \fə-ˈnes\ *n* **1 :** refinement or delicacy of workmanship or composition ⟨a painting done with *finesse*⟩ **2 :** skillful handling of a situation **:** CUNNING, SUBTLETY **3 :** the withholding of one's highest card or trump in the hope that a lower card will take the trick because the only opposing higher card is in the hand of an opponent who has already played **[**Middle French, from *fin* "fine"**]**

[2]finesse *vb* **1 a :** to make a finesse in playing cards **b :** to play (a card) as a finesse **2 a :** to bring about by shrewd maneuvering **b :** to get the better of **:** TRICK

[1]fin•ger \ˈfing-gər\ *n* **1 :** one of the five divisions of the end of the hand; *esp* **:** one other than the thumb **2 a :** something that resembles or does the work of a finger **b :** a part of a glove into which a finger is inserted **3 :** the breadth of a finger **[**Old English**]** — **fin•ger•like** \-ˌlīk\ *adj*

[2]finger *vb* **fin•gered**; **fin•ger•ing** \ˈfing-gə-ring, -gring\ **1 :** to touch with the fingers **:** HANDLE **2 :** to perform with the fingers or with a certain fingering **3 :** to mark the notes of a piece of music to show what fingers are to be used **4 :** to point out **:** IDENTIFY

fin•ger•board \ˈfing-gər-ˌbōrd, -ˌbȯrd\ *n* **:** the part of a stringed instrument against which the fingers press the strings to vary the pitch

finger bowl *n* **:** a small bowl to hold water for rinsing the fingers at the table

finger hole *n* **:** a hole in a wind instrument by means of which the pitch of the tone is changed when it is left open or closed by the finger

fin•ger•ing *n* **1 :** the act or process of handling or touching with the fingers **2 a :** the act or method of using the fingers in playing an instrument **b :** the marking of the method of fingering

fin•ger•ling \ˈfing-gər-ling\ *n* **:** a young fish especially up to one year of age

fin•ger•nail \ˈfing-gər-ˌnāl, ˌfing-gər-ˈ\ *n* **:** the nail of a finger

finger painting *n* **1 :** a technique of spreading pigment on paper with the fingertips **2 :** a picture produced by finger painting

fin•ger•post \ˈfing-gər-ˌpōst\ *n* **:** a post bearing one or more signs often terminating in a pointing finger

fin•ger•print \ˈfing-gər-ˌprint\ *n* **:** the pattern of marks made by pressing the tip of a finger or thumb on a surface; *esp* **:** an ink impression of the lines on the tip of a finger or thumb taken for the purpose of identification — **fingerprint** *vt*

fin•ger•tip \-ˌtip\ *n* **:** the tip of a finger

fin•i•al \ˈfin-ē-əl\ *n* **:** an ornamental projection or end (as on a spire or topping a lamp shade) **[**Middle English, from *final, finial* "final"**]**

finial

fin•icky \ˈfin-i-kē\ *adj* **:** very particular or exacting in taste or standards **:** FUSSY **[**probably derived from *[3]fine***]** — **fin•ick•i•ness** *n*

fi•nis \fin-əs, ˈfī-nəs\ *n* **:** END 1b, CONCLUSION **[**Latin**]**

[1]fin•ish \ˈfin-ish\ *vb* **1 a :** to bring or come to an end **:** TERMINATE **b :** to use or dispose of entirely **2 a :** to bring to completion **:** PERFECT **b :** to put a final coat or surface on **3 :** to bring about the death of **4 :** to come to the end of a course, task, or undertaking **[**Middle French *finiss-,* stem of *finir* "to finish", from Latin *finire,* from *finis* "end"**]** — **fin•ish•er** *n*

• **syn** COMPLETE: FINISH implies accomplishing the final act or stage in producing, performing, or perfecting something ⟨needed more paint to *finish* the job⟩ COMPLETE stresses a bringing of something to a state of wholeness, fullness, or soundness ⟨still another link was needed to *complete* the circle⟩

[2]finish *n* **1 :** END 1b, CONCLUSION ⟨a close *finish* in a race⟩ **2 :** the final treatment or coating of a surface **3 :** cultivation in manners and speech **:** social polish

finishing school *n* **:** a private school for girls that emphasizes cultural studies and prepares students especially for social activities

finish line *n* **:** a line marking the end of a racecourse

fi•nite \ˈfī-ˌnīt\ *adj* **1 :** having definite or definable limits **:** limited in scope or nature **2 :** not infinite but limited in number or extent; *esp* **:** having the number of elements or terms equal to zero or some positive integer ⟨a *finite* set⟩ **3 :** showing distinction of grammatical person and number ⟨a *finite* verb⟩ **[**Latin *finitus,* past participle of *finire* "to limit, finish"**]** — **fi•nite•ly** *adv* — **fi•nite•ness** *n*

Finn \ˈfin\ *n* **1 :** a member of a people speaking Finnish or a related language **2 a :** a native or inhabitant of Finland **b :** a person of Finnish descent [Swedish *Finne*]

1Finn•ish \ˈfin-ish\ *adj* **:** of, relating to, or characteristic of Finland, the Finns, or Finnish

2Finnish *n* **:** a Finno-Ugric language spoken in Finland, Karelia, and small areas of Sweden and Norway

Fin•no–Ugric \ˌfin-ō-ˈyü-grik, -ˈü-\ *adj* **1 :** of or relating to any of various peoples including the Finnish, Hungarian, and Bulgarian peoples and the Lapps and Estonians **2 :** of, relating to, or constituting a subfamily of the Uralic family of languages comprising various languages spoken in Hungary, Finland, Estonia, and northwestern Russia [derived from *Finn* + Old Russian *Ugre* "Hungarians"] — **Finno–Ugric** *n*

fin•ny \ˈfin-ē\ *adj* **1 :** resembling or having fins **2 :** of, relating to, or full of fish

fiord *variant of* FJORD

fip•ple flute \ˌfip-əl-\ *n* **:** a wind instrument (as the recorder) in which air is blown through a flue in the mouthpiece [origin unknown]

fir \ˈfər\ *n* **1 :** any of various usually large symmetrical evergreen trees of the pine family which have cones growing upward on the branches and some of which yield useful lumber or resins **2 :** the wood of a fir [Old English *fyrh*]

1fire \ˈfīr\ *n* **1 :** the light and heat and especially the flame produced by burning **2 :** fuel that is burning (as in a fireplace or stove) **3 :** the destructive burning of something (as a building or a forest) **4 :** ardent liveliness **:** ENTHUSIASM **5 :** the discharge of firearms [Old English *fȳr*] — **on fire 1 a :** in a state of combustion **b :** very hot **2 :** EAGER — **under fire 1 :** exposed to the firing of an enemy's guns **2 :** under attack

2fire *vb* **1 a :** to set on fire **:** KINDLE, IGNITE **b :** STIR, ENLIVEN ⟨*fire* the imagination⟩ **2 :** to dismiss from employment **3 :** to cause to explode ⟨*fire* dynamite⟩ **4 :** to propel from or as if from a gun ⟨*fire* an arrow⟩: **a :** DISCHARGE ⟨*fire* a gun⟩ **b :** LAUNCH ⟨*fire* a rocket⟩ **c :** to throw with speed **:** HURL ⟨*fired* the ball to first base⟩ **5 a :** to subject to intense heat ⟨*fire* pottery⟩ **b :** to feed or serve the fire of ⟨*fire* a furnace⟩ **6 a :** to take fire **:** KINDLE **b :** to have the explosive charge ignite at the proper time ⟨a cylinder that does not *fire* right⟩ **7 a :** to discharge a firearm **b :** to emit or let fly an object — **fir•er** *n*

fire•arm \ˈfīr-ˌärm\ *n* **:** a weapon from which a shot is discharged by gunpowder — usually used only of a small arm (as a rifle or pistol)

fire•ball \-ˌbȯl\ *n* **1 :** a ball of fire **2 :** a brilliant meteor **3 :** the highly luminous cloud of vapor and dust created by a nuclear explosion (as of an atom bomb)

fire blight *n* **:** a destructive highly infectious disease especially of apples and pears that is caused by a bacterium

fire•boat \ˈfīr-ˌbōt\ *n* **:** a boat or ship equipped with apparatus (as pumps) for fighting fire

fire•bomb \-ˌbäm\ *n* **:** an incendiary bomb — **firebomb** *vt*

fire•box \-ˌbäks\ *n* **1 :** a chamber (as of a furnace or steam boiler) that contains a fire **2 :** a box containing an apparatus for transmitting an alarm to a fire station

fire•brand \-ˌbrand\ *n* **1 :** a piece of burning wood **2 :** a person who creates unrest or strife **:** AGITATOR

fire•break \-ˌbrāk\ *n* **:** a barrier of cleared or plowed land intended to check a forest or grass fire

fire•brick \-ˌbrik\ *n* **:** a brick capable of withstanding great heat and used for lining furnaces or fireplaces

fire•bug \-ˌbəg\ *n* **:** a person who deliberately sets destructive fires **:** ARSONIST

fire•clay \-ˌklā\ *n* **:** clay capable of withstanding high temperatures and used especially for firebrick and crucibles

fire•crack•er \-ˌkrak-ər\ *n* **:** a paper cylinder containing an explosive and a fuse that is usually set off for amusement to make a noise

fire•damp \-ˌdamp\ *n* **:** a combustible mine gas that consists chiefly of methane; *also* **:** the explosive mixture of this gas with air

fire•dog \-ˌdȯg\ *n* **:** ANDIRON

fire drill *n* **:** a practice drill in extinguishing fires or in the conduct and manner of exit in case of fire

fire engine *n* **:** an apparatus for directing water or an extinguishing chemical on fires; *esp* **:** a motortruck equipped with such an apparatus

fire escape *n* **:** a stairway or ladder for escape from a burning building

fire extinguisher *n* **:** something used to put out a fire; *esp* **:** a portable apparatus for ejecting fire-extinguishing chemicals

fire fighter *n* **:** one that fights fires **:** FIREMAN — **fire fighting** *n*

fire•fly \ˈfīr-ˌflī\ *n* **:** a winged nocturnal insect producing a bright soft flashing light; *esp* **:** the male of various long flat beetles — called also *lightning bug*

fire•house \-ˌhau̇s\ *n* **:** FIRE STATION

fire irons *n pl* **:** implements for tending a fire especially in a fireplace

fire•light \ˈfīr-ˌlīt\ *n* **:** the light of a fire (as in a fireplace)

fire•man \-mən\ *n* **1 :** a member of a company organized to fight fires **2 :** one who tends or feeds fires **:** STOKER

fire•place \-ˌplās\ *n* **:** a structure (as a recess opening into a chimney) with a hearth on which an open fire can be built for heat or especially outdoors for cooking

fire•plug \-ˌpləg\ *n* **:** HYDRANT

fire•pow•er \-ˌpau̇-ər, -ˌpau̇r\ *n* **:** the ability (as of a military unit) to deliver gunfire or missiles on a target

1fire•proof \-ˈprüf\ *adj* **:** proof against or resistant to fire

2fireproof *vt* **:** to make fireproof

fire sale *n* **:** a sale of merchandise damaged by fire

fire screen *n* **:** a protecting screen before a fireplace

fire•side \ˈfīr-ˌsīd\ *n* **1 :** a place near the fire or hearth **2 :** HOME 1a

fire station *n* **:** a building housing fire apparatus and usually fire fighters

fire tower *n* **1 :** a tower from which a watch for fires is kept (as in a forest) **2 :** a fireproof compartment extending from top to bottom of a building and containing a stairway

fire•trap \ˈfīr-ˌtrap\ *n* **:** a place (as a building) apt to catch on fire or difficult to escape from in case of fire

fire wall *n* **:** a wall for preventing the spread of fire

fire•wa•ter \-ˌwȯt-ər, -ˌwät\ *n* **:** intoxicating liquor

fire•weed \-ˌwēd\ *n* **1 :** a tall perennial with long spikes of pinkish purple flowers that is related to the evening primrose and tends to spring up in clearings or burned areas **2 :** any of several plants similar or related to the fireweed

fire•wood \-ˌwu̇d\ *n* **:** wood cut for fuel

fire•work \-ˌwərk\ *n* **1 :** a device for producing a striking display (as of light, noise, or smoke) by the combustion of explosive or flammable compositions **2** *pl* **:** a display of fireworks **3** *pl* **:** a display of temper or hostility

firing line *n* **1 :** a line from which gunfire is directed at a target **2 :** the forefront of an activity

firing pin *n* **:** a pin that strikes the cartridge primer in the breech mechanism of a firearm

firing squad *n* **1 :** a detachment detailed to fire volleys over the grave of one buried with military honors **2 :** a detachment detailed to carry out a death sentence by shooting

fir•kin \ˈfər-kən\ *n* **1 :** a small wooden vessel or cask **2 :** any of various British units of capacity usually equal to 1/4 barrel [derived from Dutch *veerdel* "fourth"]

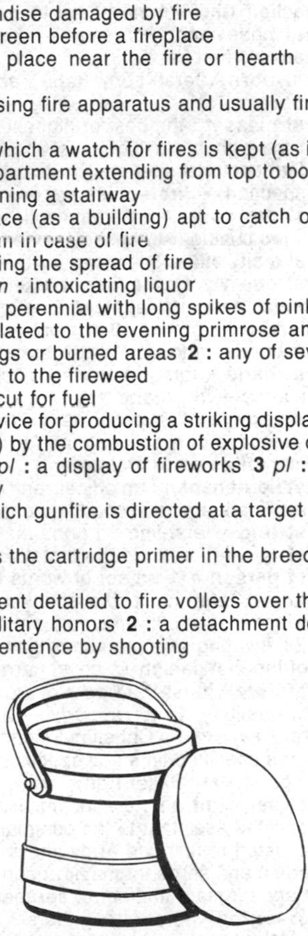

firkin 1

1firm \ˈfərm\ *adj* **1 a :** securely or solidly fixed in place **b :** not weak or uncertain **:** VIGOROUS **c :** having a solid or compact texture **2 a :** not subject to change or fluctuation ⟨a *firm* price⟩ **b :** not easily moved or disturbed **:** STEADFAST **c :** WELL-FOUNDED **3 :** indicating firmness or resolution ⟨a *firm* mouth⟩ [Middle French *ferm,* from Latin *firmus*] — **firm•ly** *adv* — **firm•ness** *n*

2firm *vb* **1 a :** to make secure ⟨*firm* one's grip on a racket⟩ **b :** to make solid or compact ⟨*firm* the soil⟩ **2 :** to become firm

3firm *n* **1 :** the name under which a company does business **2 :** a business partnership of two or more persons **3 :** a business enterprise [German *firma,* from Italian, "signature", derived from Latin *firmare* "to make firm, confirm", from *firmus* "firm"]

\ə\ **abut**	\au̇\ **out**	\i\ **tip**	\ȯ\ **saw**	\u̇\ **foot**
\ər\ **further**	\ch\ **chin**	\ī\ **life**	\ȯi\ **coin**	\y\ **yet**
\a\ **mat**	\e\ **pet**	\j\ **job**	\th\ **thin**	\yü\ **few**
\ā\ **take**	\ē\ **easy**	\ng\ **sing**	\t͟h\ **this**	\yu̇\ **cure**
\ä\ **cot, cart**	\g\ **go**	\ō\ **bone**	\ü\ **food**	\zh\ **vision**

fir•ma•ment \'fər-mə-mənt\ *n* **:** the arch of the sky **:** HEAVENS [Latin *firmamentum* "support", from *firmare* "to make firm"]

firn \'firn\ *n* **:** NÉVÉ [German]

[1]first \'fərst\ *adj* **1 :** being number one in a countable series ⟨the *first* day of spring⟩ **2 :** preceding all others (as in time, order, or importance) ⟨caught the *first* train⟩ **3 :** being the lowest forward gear or speed of a motor vehicle **4 :** highest or most prominent in carrying the melody ⟨*first* violin⟩ [Old English *fyrst*]

[2]first *adv* **1 a :** before any other ⟨we got there *first*⟩ **b :** for the first time **2 :** in preference to something else **:** SOONER

[3]first *n* **1 :** number one in a countable series ⟨the *first* of the month⟩ — see NUMBER table **2 :** something that is first: as **a :** the lowest gear or speed of a motor vehicle **b :** the winning place in a competition or contest

first aid *n* **:** emergency care or treatment given to an ill or injured person — **first–aid•er** \'fər-'stād-ər\ *n*

first base *n* **1 :** the base that must be touched first by a base runner in baseball **2 :** the position of the player defending the area around first base **3 :** the first step or stage in a course of action ⟨the plan never got to *first base*⟩

first base•man \'bā-smən\ *n* **:** the player defending the area around first base

first•born \'fərst-'bȯrn, 'fərs-\ *adj* **:** born first **:** ELDEST — **firstborn** *n*

first class *n* **:** the best or highest group in a classification: as **a :** the highest class of travel accommodations **b :** a class of mail that comprises letters, postcards, or matter sealed against inspection — **first–class** *adj or adv*

first day cover *n* **:** a stamp collector's cover bearing a newly issued postage stamp that is postmarked on the first day of issue at a city officially chosen for the first day of sale

first down *n* **1 :** the first of a series of four downs in football in which a team must make a net gain of 10 yards (about 9.1 meters) **2 :** a gain of 10 or more yards within four downs that permits a team to start a new series of four downs

first•hand \'fərst-'hand\ *adj* **:** coming directly from the original source — **firsthand** *adv*

first lady *n, often cap F&L* **1 :** the wife or hostess of the chief executive of a political unit (as a country) **2 :** the leading woman of an art or profession

first lieutenant *n* **:** an officer rank in the Army, Marine Corps, and Air Force above second lieutenant and below captain

first•ling \'fərst-liŋ\ *n* **:** one that comes or is produced first

first•ly \-lē\ *adv* **:** in the first place

first person *n* **1 :** a set of words or forms (as pronouns or verb forms) referring to the speaker or writer of the utterance in which they occur; *also* **:** a word or form belonging to such a set **2 :** a writing style marked by general use of verbs and pronouns of the first person ⟨a novel narrated in the *first person*⟩

first–rate \'fərst-'rāt\ *adj* **:** of the first order of size, importance, or quality — **first–rate** *adv* — **first–rat•er** \-'rāt-ər\ *n*

First Reader *n* **:** a Christian Scientist chosen to conduct meetings for a specified time and specifically to read aloud from the writings of Mary Baker Eddy

first sergeant *n* **1 :** a noncommissioned officer serving as chief enlisted assistant to the commander (as of a company) **2 :** an enlisted rank in the Army above a platoon sergeant and below command sergeant major and in the Marine Corps above gunnery sergeant and below sergeant major

first–string \'fərst-'striŋ, 'fərs-\ *adj* **:** being a regular as distinguished from a substitute (as on a football team)

first water *n* **1 :** the purest luster — used of gems **2 :** the highest grade, degree, or quality ⟨a novel of the *first water*⟩

firth \'fərth\ *n* **:** a narrow arm of the sea; *also* **:** ESTUARY [Old Norse *fjörthr*]

fis•cal \'fis-kəl\ *adj* **1 :** of or relating to taxation, public revenues, or public debt **2 :** of or relating to financial matters [Latin *fiscalis,* from *fiscus* "basket, treasury"] **syn** see FINANCIAL — **fis•cal•ly** \-kə-lē\ *adv*

[1]fish \'fish\ *n, pl* **fish** *or* **fish•es 1 a :** an aquatic animal — usually used in combination ⟨star*fish*⟩ ⟨cuttle*fish*⟩ **b :** any of numerous cold-blooded aquatic water-breathing vertebrates with a usually long scaly body, limbs developed as fins, and a vertical tail fin **2 :** the flesh of fish used as food **3 :** INDIVIDUAL 2 ⟨an odd *fish*⟩ **4 :** a piece of wood or iron fastened alongside another member to strengthen it [Old English *fisc*] — **fish•like** \'fish-ˌlīk\ *adj*

[2]fish *vb* **1 :** to catch fish **2 :** to catch or try to catch fish in ⟨*fish* the stream⟩ **3 :** to search (as with a hook) for something underwater **4 :** to seek something by or as if by groping or feeling

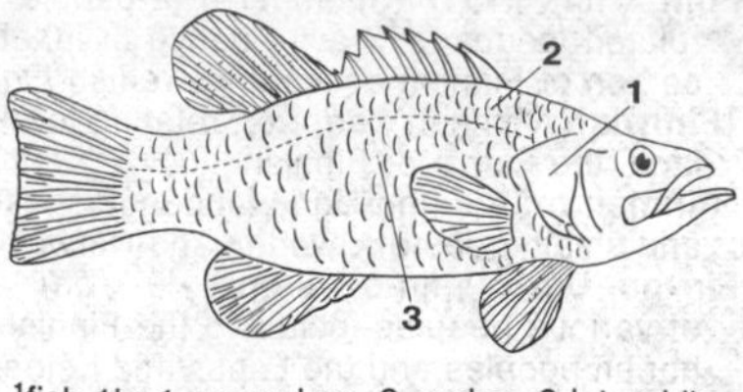

[1]fish 1b: *1* operculum, *2* scales, *3* lateral line

fish–and–chips \ˌfish-ən-'chips\ *n pl* **:** fried fish and french fried potatoes

fish cake *n* **:** a round fried cake made of shredded fish and mashed potato — called also *fish ball*

fish•er \'fish-ər\ *n* **1 :** one that fishes **2 :** a large dark brown North American flesh-eating mammal related to the weasels; *also* **:** its valuable fur or pelt

fish•er•man \-mən\ *n* **1 :** one who engages in fishing as an occupation or for pleasure **2 :** a ship used in commercial fishing

fish•ery \'fish-rē, -ə-rē\ *n, pl* **-er•ies 1 :** the activity or business of taking fish or other aquatic animals **2 :** a place or establishment for catching fish or other aquatic animals

fish hawk *n* **:** OSPREY

fish•hook \'fish-ˌhu̇k\ *n* **:** a usually barbed hook for catching fish

fish•ing *n* **:** the sport or business of catching fish

fish ladder *n* **:** a series of pools arranged like steps by which fishes can pass over or around a dam in going upstream

fish meal *n* **:** ground dried fish and fish waste used as fertilizer and animal food

fish•mon•ger \'fish-ˌməŋ-gər, -ˌmäŋ-\ *n, chiefly British* **:** a fish dealer

fish•net \-ˌnet\ *n* **:** netting fitted with floats and weights or a supporting frame for catching fish

fish•plate \-ˌplāt\ *n* **:** a steel plate used to lap a butt joint

fish•pond \-ˌpänd\ *n* **:** a pond stocked with edible fish

fish stick *n* **:** a small elongated breaded fillet of fish

fish story *n* **:** an extravagant or incredible story

fish•wife \'fish-ˌwīf\ *n* **1 :** a woman who sells fish **2 :** a coarsely abusive woman

fishy \'fish-ē\ *adj* **fish•i•er; -est 1 :** of, relating to, or resembling fish ⟨a *fishy* odor⟩ **2 :** creating doubt or suspicion **:** QUESTIONABLE ⟨that story sounds *fishy* to me⟩

fis•sile \'fis-əl, -ˌīl\ *adj* **1 :** capable of being split or divided along the grain or along planes ⟨a *fissile* crystal⟩ **2 :** FISSIONABLE

[1]fis•sion \'fish-ən *also* 'fizh-\ *n* **1 :** a splitting or breaking up into parts **2 :** reproduction by spontaneous division of a body or a cell into two or more parts each of which grows into a complete individual **3 :** the splitting of an atomic nucleus resulting in the release of large amounts of energy [Latin *fissio,* from *findere* "to split"]

[2]fission *vb* **:** to undergo or cause to undergo fission

fis•sion•able \'fish-nə-bəl, 'fizh, -ə-nə-\ *adj* **:** capable of undergoing fission ⟨*fissionable* material⟩

fission bomb *n* **:** ATOM BOMB 1 — compare FUSION BOMB

fis•sip•a•rous \fis-'ip-ə-rəs\ *adj* **:** tending to break something up into parts **:** DIVISIVE [Latin *fissus,* past participle of *findere* "to split" + *parere* "to give birth to, produce"]

[1]fis•sure \'fish-ər\ *n* **:** a narrow opening or crack of some length and depth ⟨a *fissure* in rock⟩

[2]fissure *vb* **1 :** to break into fissures **:** CLEAVE **2 :** CRACK 2, DIVIDE

fist \'fist\ *n* **1 :** the hand clenched with fingers doubled into the palm **2 :** CLUTCH 1a, GRASP **3 :** INDEX 5 [Old English *fȳst*]

fist•ic \'fis-tik\ *adj* **:** of or relating to boxing or to fist fighting

fist•i•cuffs \'fis-ti-ˌkəfs\ *n pl* **:** a fight with the fists [alteration of *fisty cuff,* from *fisty* "fistic" + *cuff*]

fis•tu•la \'fis-chə-lə\ *n, pl* **-las** *or* **-lae** \-ˌlē, -ˌlī\ **:** an abnormal passage leading from an abscess or hollow organ to the body surface or from one hollow organ to another [Latin, "reed, pipe, fistula"] — **fis•tu•lous** \-ləs\ *adj*

[1]fit \'fit\ *n* **1 :** a sudden violent attack of a disorder (as epilepsy) especially when marked by convulsions or loss of consciousness **2 :** a sudden flurry (as of activity) ⟨completed the assignment in a *fit* of efficiency⟩ **3 :** an emotional outburst ⟨a *fit* of anger⟩ [Old English *fitt* "strife"] — **by fits** *or* **by fits and starts :** in an impulsive and irregular manner

[2]fit *adj* **fit•ter; fit•test 1 a :** adapted to an end or design

: APPROPRIATE ⟨water *fit* for drinking⟩ **b** : adapted to the environment so as to be capable of surviving **2** : SEEMLY 3, PROPER **3** : put into a suitable state ⟨a house *fit* to live in⟩ **4** : QUALIFIED 1, COMPETENT **5** : sound physically and mentally : HEALTHY [Middle English] — **fit•ly** *adv* — **fit•ness** *n*

• **syn** FIT, SUITABLE, PROPER, APPROPRIATE mean right with respect to the nature, condition, or use of the thing qualified. FIT stresses adaptability to the end in view or special readiness for a particular activity ⟨*fit* to teach young children⟩ SUITABLE implies answering the demands or requirements of an occasion ⟨*suitable* clothes for the reception⟩ PROPER suggests a suitability through essential nature ⟨a *proper* diet⟩ or in accordance with custom ⟨a request made in *proper* form⟩ APPROPRIATE implies a marked or distinctive fitness or suitability ⟨*appropriate* words of congratulation⟩

^{3}fit *vb* **fit•ted**; **fit•ting** **1** : to be suitable for or to : BEFIT **2 a** : to be correctly adjusted to or shaped for **b** : to insert or adjust until correctly in place **c** : to make a place or room for **3** : to be in agreement or accord with ⟨the theory *fits* the facts⟩ **4 a** : to make ready : PREPARE **b** : to bring to a required form and size : ADJUST **c** : to cause to conform to or suit something else **5** : SUPPLY, EQUIP ⟨*fitted* the ship with new engines⟩ **6** : to be in harmony or accord : BELONG [Middle English *fitten*] — **fit•ter** \ˈfit-ər\ *n*

^{4}fit *n* **1** : the quality, state, or manner of being fitted **2** : the manner in which clothing fits the wearer **3** : the degree of closeness with which surfaces are brought together in an assembly of parts

fitch \ˈfich\ *or* **fitch•ew** \ˈfich-ü\ *n* : POLECAT 1; *also* : its fur or pelt [Middle French *fichau,* from Dutch *vitsau*]

fit•ful \ˈfit-fəl\ *adj* : not regular : INTERMITTENT ⟨a *fitful* breeze⟩ — **fit•ful•ly** \-fə-lē\ *adv* — **fit•ful•ness** *n*

^{1}fit•ting *adj* : of a kind appropriate to the situation : SUITABLE — **fit•ting•ly** \-ing-lē\ *adv* — **fit•ting•ness** *n*

^{2}fitting *n* **1 a** : the action or act of one that fits **b** : a trying on of clothes being made or altered **2** : a small often standardized accessory ⟨an electrical *fitting*⟩

five \ˈfīv\ *n* **1** : one more than four; *also* : a symbol representing this — see NUMBER table **2** : the fifth in a set or series **3** : something having five units or members; *esp* : a basketball team **4** : a 5-dollar bill **5** : FIFTEEN 2 [Old English *fīf*] — **five** *adj or pron*

five–and–ten \ˌfī-vən-ˈten\ *also* **five–and–dime** \-ˈdīm\ *n* : a variety store that carries chiefly inexpensive items

five–year plan *n* : one of a series of detailed plans for development (as economic) each of which covers a 5-year period

^{1}fix \ˈfiks\ *vb* **1 a** : to make firm, stable, or fast **b** : to give a permanent or final form to: as (1) : to change into a stable or available form ⟨bacteria that *fix* nitrogen⟩ (2) : to kill, harden, and preserve for microscopic study (3) : to make the image of (a photographic film or print) permanent by chemical treatment **c** : AFFIX 1, ATTACH **2** : to hold or direct steadily ⟨*fixed* their eyes on the horizon⟩ **3 a** : to set or place definitely : ESTABLISH ⟨*fix* the date of a meeting⟩ **b** : ASSIGN ⟨*fix* blame⟩ **4** : to set in order : ADJUST **5** : to get ready : PREPARE ⟨*fix* lunch⟩ **6 a** : to make sound or whole again: (1) : REPAIR, MEND ⟨*fix* the clock⟩ (2) : RESTORE, CURE ⟨the doctor *fixed* me up⟩ **b** : SPAY, CASTRATE **7** : to influence the actions, outcome, or effect of by improper or illegal methods ⟨*fix* a horse race⟩ [Latin *fixus,* past participle of *figere* "to fasten"] — **fix•able** \ˈfik-sə-bəl\ *adj* — **fix•er** *n*

• **syn** FIX, REPAIR mean to restore to sound condition or working order. FIX tends to stress the arranging, straightening out, or adjusting of parts ⟨*fix* a clock⟩ ⟨get one's teeth *fixed*⟩ REPAIR usually stresses the replacing or remaking of damaged or lost parts ⟨*repair* a damaged automobile⟩

^{2}fix *n* **1** : a position of difficulty or embarrassment : PREDICAMENT **2** : the position (as of a ship) determined by bearings, observations, or radio; *also* : a precise determination of one's position **3** : a shot of a narcotic

fix•ate \ˈfik-ˌsāt\ *vb* **1** : to make unchanging : FIX **2 a** : to focus one's eyes upon **b** : to concentrate one's attention

fix•a•tion \fik-ˈsā-shən\ *n* **1** : the act, process, or result of fixing or fixating ⟨*fixation* of nitrogen⟩ **2** : an unhealthy or abnormally persistent state of concern or attachment

fix•a•tive \ˈfik-sət-iv\ *n* : something that stabilizes or sets: as **a** : a substance added to a perfume especially to prevent too rapid evaporation **b** : a varnish used especially for the protection of pencil or charcoal drawings — **fixative** *adj*

fixed \ˈfikst\ *adj* **1 a** : securely placed or fastened : STATIONARY **b** (1) : NONVOLATILE ⟨*fixed* oil⟩ (2) : COMBINED ⟨*fixed* nitrogen⟩ **c** : not subject to change or fluctuation : SETTLED ⟨a *fixed* income⟩ **d** : recurring on the same date from year to year ⟨*fixed* holidays⟩ **e** : INTENT ⟨a *fixed* stare⟩ **2** : supplied with something (as money) needed or desirable — **fix•ed•ly** \ˈfik-səd-lē\ *adv* — **fix•ed•ness** \ˈfik-səd-nəs\ *n*

fixed–point *adj* : involving or being a mathematical notation (as in a decimal system) in which the point separating integers and fractions is fixed — compare FLOATING-POINT

fixed star *n* : a star so distant that its motion can be measured only by very precise long-term observations

fix•ing \ˈfik-sing, *2 is often* -sənz\ *n* **1** : a putting in permanent form **2** *pl* : TRIMMINGS ⟨a turkey dinner with all the *fixings*⟩

fix•i•ty \ˈfik-sət-ē\ *n* : the quality or state of being fixed or stable

fix•ture \ˈfiks-chər\ *n* **1** : the act of fixing : the state of being fixed **2** : something attached to another thing as a permanent part ⟨bathroom *fixtures*⟩ **3** : one firmly established in a place

^{1}fizz \ˈfiz\ *vi* : to make a hissing or sputtering sound [probably imitative]

^{2}fizz *n* **1** : a hissing sound **2** : an effervescent beverage — **fizzy** \ˈfiz-ē\ *adj*

^{1}fiz•zle \ˈfiz-əl\ *vi* **fiz•zled**; **fiz•zling** \ˈfiz-ling, -ə-ling\ **1** : FIZZ **2** : to fail or end feebly especially after a promising start [probably alteration of *fist* "to break wind"]

^{2}fizzle *n* : an abortive effort : FAILURE

fjord *or* **fiord** \fē-ˈörd\ *n* : a narrow inlet of the sea between cliffs or steep slopes [Norwegian, from Old Norse *fjörthr*]

flab•ber•gast \ˈflab-ər-ˌgast\ *vt* : to overwhelm with shock, surprise, or wonder : ASTOUND [origin unknown]

flab•by \ˈflab-ē\ *adj* **flab•bi•er**; **-est** **1** : lacking resilience or firmness **2** : being weak and ineffective : FEEBLE [alteration of *flappy* "tending to flap"] **syn** see LIMP — **flab•bi•ly** \ˈflab-ə-lē\ *adv* — **flab•bi•ness** \ˈflab-ē-nəs\ *n*

flac•cid \ˈflak-səd, ˈflas-əd\ *adj* : FLABBY ⟨a *flaccid* muscle⟩; *also* : deficient in turgor ⟨*flaccid* stems⟩ [Latin *flaccidus*] **syn** see LIMP — **flac•cid•i•ty** \flak-ˈsid-ət-ē, fla-\ *n* — **flac•cid•ly** \ˈflak-səd-lē, ˈflas-əd-\ *adv*

fla•con \ˈflak-ən, -ˌän; fla-ˈkō^{n}\ *n* : a small usually ornamental bottle with a tight cap [French]

^{1}flag \ˈflag\ *n* : any of various plants with long narrow leaves: as **a** : IRIS; *esp* : a wild iris **b** : SWEET FLAG [Middle English *flagge* "reed, rush"]

^{2}flag *n* **1** : a hard stone that is composed of even layers and splits into flat pieces suitable for paving **2** : a thin piece of flag used for paving [Old Norse *flaga* "slab"]

^{3}flag *vt* **flagged**; **flag•ging** : to pave (as a walk) with flags

^{4}flag *n* **1** : a usually rectangular piece of fabric of distinctive design that is used as a symbol (as of a nation) or as a signaling device **2 a** : something used like a flag to attract attention **b** : one of the cross strokes of a musical note less than a quarter note in value [perhaps from ^{1}*flag*]

^{5}flag *vt* **flagged**; **flag•ging** **1** : to put a flag on ⟨*flagged* the important pages with red tabs⟩ **2** : to signal with or as if with a flag; *esp* : to signal to stop ⟨*flag* a taxi⟩

^{6}flag *vi* **flagged**; **flag•ging** **1** : to hang loose without stiffness; *also* : to droop especially from lack of water ⟨plants *flagging* under the summer sun⟩ **2 a** : to become weak ⟨our interest *flagged*⟩ **b** : to decline in interest or attraction ⟨the topic *flagged*⟩ [origin unknown]

Flag Day *n* : June 14 observed in various states in commemoration of the adoption in 1777 of the official United States flag

fla•gel•lant \ˈflaj-ə-lənt, flə-ˈjel-ənt\ *n* : one that whips; *esp* : a person who scourges himself as a public penance

^{1}flag•el•late \ˈflaj-ə-ˌlāt\ *vt* : to punish by whipping : WHIP [Latin *flagellare,* from *flagellum* "small whip", from *flagrum* "whip"] — **flag•el•la•tion** \ˌflaj-ə-ˈlā-shən\ *n*

^{2}fla•gel•late \ˈflaj-ə-lət, -ˌlāt; flə-ˈjel-ət\ *adj* **1 a** *or* **flag•el•lat•ed** \ˈflaj-ə-ˌlāt-əd\ : having flagella **b** : resembling a flagellum **2** : of, relating to, or caused by flagellates

^{3}flagellate *like*^{2}\ *n* : a protozoan or alga having flagella

fla•gel•lum \flə-ˈjel-əm\ *n, pl* **-gel•la** \-ˈjel-ə\ *also* **-gellums**

\ə\ **abut**	\au̇\ **out**	\i\ **tip**	\ȯ\ **saw**	\u̇\ **foot**
\ər\ **further**	\ch\ **chin**	\ī\ **life**	\ȯi\ **coin**	\y\ **yet**
\a\ **mat**	\e\ **pet**	\j\ **job**	\th\ **thin**	\yü\ **few**
\ā\ **take**	\ē\ **easy**	\ng\ **sing**	\t͟h\ **this**	\yu̇\ **cure**
\ä\ **cot, cart**	\g\ **go**	\ō\ **bone**	\ü\ **food**	\zh\ **vision**

: a tapering process that projects singly or in groups from a cell and is the primary organ of motion of many microorganisms [Latin, "whip, shoot of a plant"] — **fla•gel•lar** \-ˈjel-ər\ *adj*

fla•geo•let \ˌflaj-ə-ˈlet\ *n* : a small woodwind instrument belonging to the flute class [French]

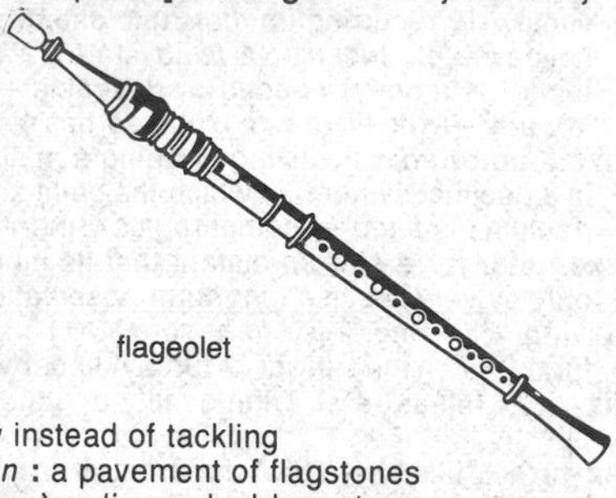
flageolet

flag football *n* : a variation of football in which a player pulls a flag or handkerchief from the ballcarrier's clothing to stop play instead of tackling

flag•ging \ˈflag-ing\ *n* : a pavement of flagstones

fla•gi•tious \flə-ˈjish-əs\ *adj* : marked by outrageous or scandalous crime or vice : VILLAINOUS [Latin *flagitiosus,* from *flagitium* "shameful thing"] — **fla•gi•tious•ly** *adv* — **fla•gi•tious•ness** *n*

flag•man \ˈflag-mən\ *n* : one who signals with or as if with a flag

flag of truce : a white flag carried or displayed to an enemy to signal a desire to negotiate or surrender

flag•on \ˈflag-ən\ *n* : a container for liquids that has a handle, spout, and often a lid [Middle French *flascon, flacon* "bottle", from Late Latin *flasco*]

flag•pole \ˈflag-ˌpōl\ *n* : a pole on which to display a flag

flag rank *n* : any of the ranks in the Navy or Coast Guard above captain

fla•grant \ˈflā-grənt\ *adj* : conspicuously bad or objectionable : OUTRAGEOUS, NOTORIOUS ⟨*flagrant* abuse of power⟩ [Latin *flagrare* "to blaze, burn"] — **fla•gran•cy** \-grən-sē\ *n* — **fla•grant•ly** *adv*

• **syn** FLAGRANT, GLARING, GROSS, RANK mean conspicuously bad or objectionable. FLAGRANT applies to behavior, errors, or offenses so bad that they cannot escape notice or be excused ⟨*flagrant* disobedience⟩ GLARING suggests painful or damaging obtrusiveness ⟨*glaring* imperfection⟩ GROSS applies to utterly inexcusable faults or offenses ⟨*gross* dishonesty⟩ ⟨*gross* carelessness⟩ RANK applies to what is openly and extremely objectionable and utterly condemned ⟨*rank* corruption in public office⟩

fla•gran•te de•lic•to \flə-ˌgrant-ē-di-ˈlik-ˌtō\ *adv* : in the very act of committing a misdeed [Medieval Latin, literally, "while the crime is blazing"]

flag•ship \ˈflag-ˌship\ *n* **1** : the ship that carries the commander of a fleet or subdivision thereof and flies his flag **2** : the finest, largest, or most important of a series or group

flag•staff \-ˌstaf\ *n* : FLAGPOLE

flag•stone \-ˌstōn\ *n* : [2]FLAG 2

flag–wav•ing \ˈflag-ˌwā-ving\ *n* : passionate appeal to patriotic or partisan sentiment : political chauvinism

[1]flail \ˈflāl\ *n* : a hand threshing tool consisting of a wooden handle with a free-swinging stout short stick at the end [Middle French *flaiel,* from Latin *flagellum* "whip"]

[2]flail *vb* : to strike with or as if with a flail

flair \ˈflaər, ˈfleər\ *n* **1** : instinctive discernment ⟨relying on *flair* more than careful study⟩ **2** : natural aptitude : BENT **3** : a uniquely attractive quality ⟨a car with real *flair*⟩ [French, literally, "sense of smell", from Old French, "odor", from *flairier* "to give off an odor", from Late Latin *flagrare,* alteration of Latin *fragrare*] **syn** see PENCHANT

flak \ˈflak\ *n* **1** : antiaircraft guns or the bursting shells fired from them **2** : severe criticism [German, from *fliegerabwehrkanonen,* from *flieger* "flyer" + *abwehr* "defense" + *kanonen* "cannons"]

[1]flake \ˈflāk\ *n* : a thin flattened usually loose piece ⟨a *flake* of snow⟩ ⟨soap *flakes*⟩ [Middle English, of Scandinavian origin]

[2]flake *vb* : to form or separate into flakes : make or become flaky ⟨this paint *flakes* badly⟩

flaky \ˈflā-kē\ *adj* **flak•i•er**; **-est 1** : consisting of flakes **2** : tending to flake ⟨pie with a crisp *flaky* crust⟩ — **flak•i•ness** *n*

flam•beau \ˈflam-ˌbō\ *n, pl* **flam•beaux** \-ˌbōz\ *or* **flambeaus** : a flaming torch [French]

flam•boy•ant \flam-ˈbȯi-ənt\ *adj* **1** *often cap* : characterized by waving curves suggesting flames ⟨flamboyant window tracery⟩ **2** : FLORID 1, ORNATE; *also* : brightly colored **3** : given to dashing display : SHOWY [French, from *flamboyer* "to flame", from Old French, from *flambe* "flame"] — **flam•boy•ance** \-əns\ *also* **flam•boy•an•cy** \-ən-sē\ *n* — **flam•boy•ant•ly** *adv*

[1]flame \ˈflām\ *n* **1** : the glowing gaseous part of a fire **2 a** : a state of blazing combustion **b** : a condition or appearance suggesting a flame **3** : burning zeal or passion **4** : SWEETHEART [Middle French *flamme, flambe,* derived from Latin *flamma*]

[2]flame *vb* **1** : to burn with a flame : BLAZE **2** : to burst or break out violently or passionately ⟨*flaming* with anger⟩ **3** : to shine brightly : GLOW **4** : to treat or affect with flame — **flam•er** *n*

flame cell *n* : a hollow excretory cell of various lower invertebrates that has a tuft of cilia

fla•men•co \flə-ˈmeng-kō\ *n, pl* **-cos** : a vigorous rhythmic dance style of the Andalusian Gypsies [Spanish, "Flemish, like a Gypsy", from Dutch *Vlaminc* "Fleming"]

△ **origin** The Spanish homonyms *Flamenco,* "Fleming", and *flamenco,* "flamingo", are not related. From the first of these we get our English word *flamenco,* "a vigorous dance style of Gypsy origin". In the early 16th century the Holy Roman Emperor Charles V, who was also King Charles I of Spain, had several Flemish ministers unpopular with the king's Spanish subjects. It was probably because these particular Flemings were so detestable that *Flamenco,* the Spanish word for Fleming, became a disparaging term for any foreigner. Inhabitants of southern Spain used the term derisively for the Gypsies who came into that region in the 16th century. *Flamenco* was also applied to the dance style typical of these Gypsies.

flame•out \ˈflā-ˌmau̇t\ *n* : the unintentional cessation of operation of a jet airplane engine

flame•proof \ˈflām-ˈprüf\ *adj* **1** : resistant to the action of flame **2** : not burning on contact with flame

flame•throw•er \-ˌthrō-ər, -ˌthrōr\ *n* : a device that expels from a nozzle a burning stream of liquid or semiliquid fuel under pressure

flam•ing \ˈflā-ming\ *adj* **1** : producing flames **2** : suggesting a flame in brilliance or wavy outline **3** : ARDENT 1, PASSIONATE — **flam•ing•ly** \-ming-lē\ *adv*

fla•min•go \flə-ˈming-gō\ *n, pl* **-gos** *also* **-goes** : any of several aquatic long-legged and long-necked birds with a broad bill bent downward at the end and usually rosy-white plumage with scarlet on the wings [Portuguese, from Spanish *flamenco,* derived from Latin *flamma* "flame"]

flamingo

△ **origin** English *flamingo* is a derivative, by way of Portuguese, of Spanish *flamenco,* "flamingo". This *flamenco* comes from Latin *flamma* "flame". Most flamingos are pale pink or rosy white. When standing at rest or wading about in search of food, they do not seem to justify their vivid name. But when they take flight, the sudden flash of their scarlet wing coverts against the coal black of their quill feathers is like a burst of flame.

flam•ma•ble \ˈflam-ə-bəl\ *adj* : capable of being easily ignited and of burning with extreme rapidity — **flam•ma•bil•i•ty** \ˌflam-ə-ˈbil-ət-ē\ *n* — **flam•mable** *n*

fla•neur \flä-ˈnər\ *n* : an aimless person: as **a** : MAN-ABOUT-TOWN **b** : an intellectual trifler [French *flâneur* "idler"]

[1]flange \ˈflanj\ *n* : a rib or rim used for strength, for guiding, or for attachment to another object ⟨a *flange* on a pipe⟩ [perhaps derived from Middle French *flanche* "flank", from *flanc*]

[2]flange *vt* : to furnish with a flange

[1]flank \ˈflangk\ *n* **1 a** : the fleshy part of the side between the ribs and the hip; *also* : the side of a four-footed animal **b** : a cut of meat from this part of an animal **2 a** : SIDE 2 **b** : the right or left of a formation [Old French *flanc,* of Germanic origin]

[2]flank *vt* **1 a** : to attack or threaten the flank of **b** : to turn the flank of **2** : to be situated at the side of : BORDER

flank•er \ˈflang-kər\ *n* **1** : one that flanks **2** : a football player stationed wide of the formation; *esp* : an offensive halfback who lines up on the flank and serves chiefly as a pass receiver — called also *flanker back*

flan•nel \ˈflan-ᵊl\ *n* **1 a :** a soft twilled wool or worsted fabric with a napped surface **b :** a stout cotton fabric napped on one side **2** *pl* **:** flannel underwear or trousers [Middle English *flaunneol* "woolen cloth or garment"]

flan•nel•ette \ˌflan-ᵊl-ˈet\ *n* **:** a cotton flannel napped on one or both sides

1flap \ˈflap\ *n* **1 :** a stroke with something broad **:** SLAP **2 :** something broad, limber, or flat and usually thin that hangs loose: as **a :** a piece on a garment that hangs free **b :** an extended part forming the closure (as of an envelope) **3 :** the motion of something broad and limber **4 :** a movable auxiliary airfoil attached to the trailing edge of an airplane wing permitting a steeper gliding angle in landing **5 :** a state of excitement or agitation **:** UPROAR ⟨created a *flap* by denying the workers their raises⟩ [Middle English *flappe*]

2flap *vb* **flapped; flap•ping 1 :** to beat with something broad and flat **2 :** to move or cause to move with a beating motion ⟨birds *flapping* their wings⟩ **3 :** to sway loosely usually with a noise of striking ⟨the flag *flapped* in the wind⟩ **4 :** to talk foolishly and persistently

flap•jack \ˈflap-ˌjak\ *n* **:** PANCAKE

flap•per \ˈflap-ər\ *n* **1 :** one that flaps **2 :** a young woman especially of the 1920s who shows bold freedom from conventions in conduct and dress

1flare \ˈflaər, ˈfleər\ *vb* **1 :** to burn with an unsteady flame **2 a :** to shine with a sudden light **b :** to become suddenly exicted or angry ⟨*flare* up⟩ **3 :** to open or spread outward [origin unknown]

2flare *n* **1 :** an unsteady glaring light **2 a :** a fire or blaze of light used to signal, illuminate, or attract attention; *also* **:** a device or composition used to produce such a flare **b :** a temporary outburst of energy from a small area of the sun's surface **3 :** a sudden outburst (as of sound, excitement, or anger) **4 :** a spreading outward; *also* **:** a place or part that spreads ⟨the *flare* of a skirt⟩ ⟨the *flare* of a trumpet⟩

flare-up \-ˌəp\ *n* **:** a sudden burst (as of flame or anger)

1flash \ˈflash\ *vb* **1 :** to shine in or like a sudden flame ⟨lightning *flashed*⟩ **2 :** to send out in or as if in flashes ⟨*flash* a message⟩ **3 :** to appear or pass very suddenly ⟨a car *flashed* by⟩ **4 :** to make a sudden display (as of brilliance or feeling) ⟨their eyes *flashed* with excitement⟩ **5 :** to give off light suddenly or in brief bursts **6 :** to expose briefly to view ⟨*flash* a badge⟩ [Middle English *flaschen*]

• **syn** FLASH, GLANCE, GLINT, SPARKLE mean to send forth light. FLASH implies a sudden brief outburst of bright light; GLANCE suggests a darting light reflected from a quickly moving surface ⟨sunlight *glancing* from the ripples⟩ GLINT suggests a cold glancing light; SPARKLE implies innumerable moving points of bright light

2flash *n* **1 a :** a sudden burst of light **b :** a movement of a flag or light in signaling **2 :** a sudden and brilliant burst (as of wit) **3 :** a brief time **4 a** SHOW 2, DISPLAY **b :** one that attracts notice; *esp* **:** an outstanding athlete **5 :** something flashed: as **a :** GLIMPSE 1, LOOK **b :** a first brief news report **c :** FLASHLIGHT 2 **d :** a quick-spreading flame or momentary intense outburst of radiant heat

3flash *adj* **1 :** FLASHY, SPORTY **2 :** of sudden origin and short duration ⟨a *flash* fire⟩

flash•back \ˈflash-ˌbak\ *n* **:** introduction into the chronological sequence of events in a literary or theatrical work of an event of earlier occurrence; *also* **:** an event so introduced

flash•bulb \-ˌbəlb\ *n* **:** an electric flash lamp in which metal foil or wire is burned

flash card *n* **:** a card bearing words, numbers, or pictures briefly displayed by a teacher to a class during drills (as in reading, spelling, or arithmetic)

flash•cube \ˈflash-ˌkyüb\ *n* **:** a cubical device incorporating four flashbulbs for taking four pictures in succession

flash•er \ˈflash-ər\ *n* **:** one that flashes; *esp* **:** BLINKER

flash flood *n* **:** a local flood of great volume and short duration generally resulting from nearby heavy rainfall

flash•gun \ˈflash-ˌgən\ *n* **:** a device for holding and operating a flash lamp

flash•ing \ˈflash-ing\ *n* **:** sheet metal used in waterproofing roof valleys or the angle between a chimney or wall and a roof

flash lamp *n* **:** a usually electric lamp for producing a brief but intense flash of light for taking photographs

flash•light \ˈflash-ˌlīt\ *n* **1 :** a flash of light or a light that flashes **2 a :** a sudden bright artificial light used in taking photographic pictures **b :** a photograph taken by such a light **3 :** a small battery-operated portable electric light

flash•over \-ˌō-vər\ *n* **:** an abnormal electrical discharge (as through the air to the ground) from a high potential source

flash point *n* **:** the lowest temperature at which vapors above a volatile combustible substance ignite in air when exposed to flame

flash•tube \ˈflash-ˌtüb, -ˌtyüb\ *n* **:** a gas discharge tube that produces very brief intense flashes of light and is used especially in photography

flashy \ˈflash-ē\ *adj* **flash•i•er; -est 1 :** momentarily dazzling **2 a :** superficially attractive **:** BRIGHT **b :** tastelessly showy **syn** see GAUDY — **flash•i•ly** \ˈflash-ə-lē\ *adv* — **flash•i•ness** \ˈflash-ē-nəs\ *n*

flask \ˈflask\ *n* **:** a bottle-shaped container often somewhat narrowed toward the outlet and often fitted with a closure: **a :** a broad flat container (as for liquor) sometimes curved to fit a hip pocket **b :** a round or conical glass container with a narrow opening used in a laboratory [Middle French *flasque* "powder flask", derived from Late Latin *flasco* "bottle", of Germanic origin]

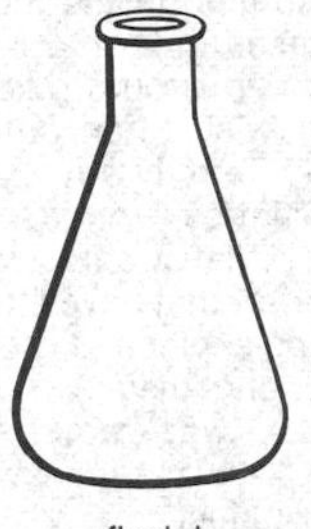

flask b

1flat \ˈflat\ *adj* **flat•ter; flat•test 1 :** having a smooth level horizontal surface ⟨*flat* ground⟩ **2 :** being smooth and even or having a smooth even surface ⟨a *flat* rock⟩ **3 :** spread out on or along a surface ⟨was *flat* on the ground⟩ **4 :** having opposite major surfaces essentially parallel ⟨a *flat* board⟩ **5 :** DOWNRIGHT, POSITIVE ⟨a *flat* refusal⟩ **6 :** FIXED, UNCHANGING ⟨charge a *flat* rate⟩ **7 :** EXACT ⟨a *flat* four minutes⟩ **8 :** DULL, UNINTERESTING, INSIPID ⟨a *flat* story⟩ ⟨water that tastes *flat*⟩ **9 :** DEFLATED — used of tires **10 a :** lower than the true pitch **b :** lower by a half step ⟨tone of A *flat*⟩ **c :** having a flat in the signature ⟨key of B *flat*⟩ **11 :** pronounced like the vowel of *hat* ⟨a *flat a*⟩ **12 :** being an adverb with no distinctive ending **13 a :** having little or no illusion of depth ⟨a *flat* painting⟩ **b :** lacking contrast ⟨a *flat* photographic negative⟩ **c :** free from gloss ⟨*flat* paint⟩ [Old Norse *flatr*] — **flat•ly** *adv* — **flat•ness** *n*

2flat *n* **1 :** a level surface of land with little or no relief **:** PLAIN **2 :** a flat part or surface **3 a :** a musical note or tone one half step lower than a specified note or tone **b :** a character ♭ on a line or space of the staff indicating such a note or tone **4 :** something flat: as **a :** a flat piece of theatrical scenery **b :** a shoe or slipper having a flat heel or no heel **5 :** a deflated tire

3flat *adv* **:** in a flat manner: as **a :** on or against a flat surface ⟨lie *flat*⟩ **b :** EXACTLY ⟨four minutes *flat*⟩ **c :** below the true musical pitch ⟨sing *flat*⟩

4flat *vb* **flat•ted; flat•ting 1 :** FLATTEN **2 a :** to lower in pitch especially by a half step **b :** to sing or play below the true pitch

5flat *n* **1 :** a floor or story in a building **2 :** an apartment on one floor

flat•bed \ˈflat-ˌbed\ *n* **:** a motortruck or trailer with a body in the form of a platform or shallow box

flat•boat \-ˌbōt\ *n* **:** a large flat-bottomed boat with square ends used for transporting heavy freight on rivers

flat•car \-ˌkär\ *n* **:** a railroad freight car without permanent sides, ends, or covering

flat•fish \-ˌfish\ *n* **:** any of an order (Heterosomata) of marine fishes (as halibuts, flounders, or soles) that as adults swim on one side of the laterally compressed body and have both eyes on the upper side

flat•foot \-ˌfu̇t, *1,2 also* -ˈfu̇t\ *n, pl* **flat•feet 1 :** a condition in which the main arch of the foot is so flattened that the entire sole rests upon the ground **2 :** a foot affected with flatfoot **3** *or pl* **flatfoots** *slang* **:** POLICE OFFICER; *esp* **:** PATROLMAN — **flat-foot•ed** \-ˈfu̇t-əd\ *adj*

flat•iron \ˈflat-ˌī-ərn, -ˌīrn\ *n* **:** an iron for pressing clothes

\ə\ **abut**	\au̇\ **out**	\i\ **tip**	\ȯ\ **saw**	\u̇\ **foot**
\ər\ **further**	\ch\ **chin**	\ī\ **life**	\ȯi\ **coin**	\y\ **yet**
\a\ **mat**	\e\ **pet**	\j\ **job**	\th\ **thin**	\yü\ **few**
\ā\ **take**	\ē\ **easy**	\ng\ **sing**	\t͟h\ **this**	\yu̇\ **cure**
\ä\ **cot, cart**	\g\ **go**	\ō\ **bone**	\ü\ **food**	\zh\ **vision**

flat•ten \ˈflat-ⁿn\ *vb* **flat•tened**; **flat•ten•ing** \ˈflat-ning, -ⁿn-ing\ : to make or become flat

flat•ter \ˈflat-ər\ *vt* **1** : to praise too much or without sincerity especially out of self-interest **2** : to represent too favorably ⟨the picture *flatters* us⟩ **3** : to judge (oneself) favorably or too favorably especially in respect to an accomplishment or ability ⟨I *flatter* myself on my skill as a swimmer⟩ [Middle English *flateren,* from Old French *flater* "to lick, flatter", of Germanic origin] — **flat•ter•er** \ˈflat-ər-ər\ *n* — **flat•ter•ing•ly** \ˈflat-ə-ring-lē\ *adv*

flat•tery \ˈflat-ə-rē\ *n, pl* **-ter•ies 1** : the act of flattering **2** : flattering speech or attentions : insincere or excessive praise

flat•top \ˈflat-ˌtäp\ *n* : AIRCRAFT CARRIER

flat•u•lent \ˈflach-ə-lənt\ *adj* **1 a** : marked by or affected with gases formed in the intestine or stomach **b** : likely to cause such gases to form **2** : pretentious without real worth or substance : POMPOUS [Middle French, from Latin *flatus* "act of blowing, wind", from *flare* "to blow"] — **flat•u•lence** \-ləns\ *n* — **flat•u•lent•ly** *adv*

fla•tus \ˈflāt-əs\ *n* : gas formed in the intestine or stomach

flat•ware \ˈflat-ˌwaər, -ˌweər\ *n* **1** : ceramic objects (as plates or saucers) that have little depth and are usually formed or cast in a single piece **2** : eating and serving utensils (as forks, spoons, and knives)

flat•ways \-ˌwāz\ *adv* : FLATWISE

flat•wise \-ˌwīz\ *adv* : with the flat side downward or next to another object

flat•worm \-ˌwərm\ *n* : any of a phylum (Platyhelminthes) of flat bilaterally symmetrical unsegmented worms (as a planaria, a liver fluke, or a tapeworm) that lack a body cavity

flaunt \ˈflȯnt, ˈflänt\ *vb* **1** : to wave or flutter showily **2** : to call public attention to onself **3** : to display ostentatiously or boldly : PARADE ⟨the winners *flaunted* their victory⟩ [probably of Scandinavian origin] — **flaunt** *n* — **flaunt•ing•ly** \-ing-lē\ *adv*

• **syn** FLAUNT, FLOUT are often confused. FLAUNT implies displaying something shamelessly, boastfully, or offensively ⟨*flaunting* their criminal exploits in the tabloids⟩ FLOUT implies scoffing or jeering at in contempt or defiance ⟨openly *flouting* the nation's laws⟩

flau•tist \ˈflȯt-əst, ˈflaut-\ *n* : FLUTIST [Italian *flautista,* from *flauto* "flute"]

fla•vo•pro•tein \ˌflā-vō-ˈprō-ˌtēn, -ˈprōt-ē-ən\ *n* : an enzyme that serves in the removal and transport of hydrogen and plays a major role in biological oxidations [derived from Latin *flavus* "yellow"]

[1]**fla•vor** \ˈflā-vər\ *n* **1 a** : the quality of something that affects the sense of taste : SAVOR **b** : the blend of taste and smell sensations evoked by a substance in the mouth **2** : a substance that flavors **3** : characteristic or predominant quality [Middle French *flaor, flavor,* from Latin *flare* "to blow"] — **fla•vored** \-vərd\ *adj* — **fla•vor•ful** \-vər-fəl\ *adj* — **fla•vor•less** \-ləs\ *adj*

[2]**flavor** *vt* **fla•vored**; **fla•vor•ing** \ˈflāv-ring, -ə-ring\ : to give or add flavor to

fla•vor•ing *n* : FLAVOR 2

fla•vour \ˈflā-vər\ *chiefly British variant of* FLAVOR

[1]**flaw** \ˈflȯ\ *n* **1** : an often hidden defect that may cause failure ⟨a *flaw* in a plan⟩ **2** : a marred or imperfect part ⟨a diamond with a *flaw*⟩ [Middle English] **syn** see BLEMISH — **flaw•less** \-ləs\ *adj* — **flaw•less•ly** *adv* — **flaw•less•ness** *n*

[2]**flaw** *vb* : to make or become defective

flax \ˈflaks\ *n* : a slender erect blue-flowered plant grown for its fiber and seeds; *also* : its fiber especially prepared for spinning — compare LINEN [Old English *fleax*]

flax•en \ˈflak-sən\ *adj* **1** : made of flax **2** : resembling flax especially in pale soft straw color

flax•seed \ˈflak-ˌsēd\ *n* : the seed of flax used as a source of linseed oil and medicinally

flay \ˈflā\ *vt* **1** : to strip off the skin or surface of : SKIN **2** : to criticize harshly : SCOLD [Old English *flēan*]

F layer *n* : the highest and most densely ionized regular layer of the ionosphere

flea \ˈflē\ *n* : any of an order (Siphonaptera) of wingless blood-sucking insects with a hard laterally compressed body and legs adapted to leaping [Old English *flēa*]

flea•bane \-ˌbān\ *n* : any of various plants related to the daisies

flea beetle *n* : any of various small beetles that leap like fleas, feed on foliage, and sometimes transmit virus diseases of plants

flea–bit•ten \ˈflē-ˌbit-ⁿn\ *adj* : bitten by or infested with fleas

flea collar *n* : a collar for an animal (as a dog or a cat) that contains insecticide for killing fleas

flea market *n* : a usually open-air market for secondhand articles and antiques [translation of French *Marché aux Puces,* a market in Paris]

[1]**fleck** \ˈflek\ *vt* : STREAK, SPOT ⟨yellow bananas *flecked* with brown⟩ [back-formation from *flecked* "spotted", from Middle English]

[2]**fleck** *n* **1** : SPOT 2a, MARK **2** : FLAKE, PARTICLE

flec•tion \ˈflek-shən\ *n* : FLEXION — **flec•tion•al** \-shnəl, -shən-ˡl\ *adj*

fledge \ˈflej\ *vb* **1** : to develop the feathers necessary for flying **2** : to furnish with feathers ⟨*fledge* an arrow⟩ [Old English *-flycge* "capable of flying"]

fledg•ling \ˈflej-ling\ *n* **1** : a young bird just fledged **2** : an immature or inexperienced person

flee \ˈflē\ *vb* **fled** \ˈfled\; **flee•ing 1 a** : to run away from danger or evil : FLY **b** : to run away from : SHUN **2** : to pass away swiftly : VANISH [Old English *flēon*]

[1]**fleece** \ˈflēs\ *n* **1** : the coat of wool covering an animal (as a sheep) **2** : a soft or woolly covering [Old English *flēos*]

[2]**fleece** *vt* **1** : to remove the fleece from : SHEAR **2** : to rob by fraud or extortion

fleecy \ˈflē-sē\ *adj* **fleec•i•er**; **-est** : covered with, made of, or resembling fleece — **fleec•i•ness** *n*

[1]**fleet** \ˈflēt\ *vi* : to fly swiftly : pass rapidly ⟨time is *fleeting*⟩ [Old English *flēotan* "to float, flow"]

[2]**fleet** *n* **1** : a group of warships under one command **2** : a group of ships or vehicles that move together or are operated under one management ⟨a *fleet* of trucks⟩ ⟨a *fleet* of airplanes⟩ [Old English *flēot* "ship", from *flēotan* "to float"]

[3]**fleet** *adj* **1** : swift in motion : NIMBLE **2** : not enduring : MOMENTARY [probably from [1]*fleet*] **syn** see FAST — **fleet•ly** *adv* — **fleet•ness** *n*

Fleet Admiral *n* : a commissioned officer of highest rank in the Navy whose insignia is five stars

fleet–foot•ed \ˈflēt-ˌfu̇t-əd\ *adj* : swift of foot — **fleet–foot•ed•ness** *n*

Flem•ing \ˈflem-ing\ *n* : a member of the Germanic people inhabiting northern Belgium and a small section of northern France bordering on Belgium [Dutch *Vlaminc*]

Flem•ish \ˈflem-ish\ *n* **1** : the Germanic language of the Flemings that is made up of dialects of Dutch **2** *pl in construction* : FLEMINGS — **Flemish** *adj*

[1]**flesh** \ˈflesh\ *n* **1 a** : the soft parts of the body of an animal; *esp* : skeletal muscle of a vertebrate **b** : sleek well-fatted condition of body **2** : parts of an animal used as food **3** : the physical being of a person as distinguished from the soul **4 a** : HUMAN BEINGS **b** : living beings **c** : STOCK 5b, KINDRED **5** : a fleshy plant part used as food; *esp* : the fleshy part of a fruit [Old English *flǣsc*] — **fleshed** \ˈflesht\ *adj*

[2]**flesh** *vb* **1** : to give substance to ⟨*flesh* out a story with details⟩ **2** : to remove flesh from **3** : to become fleshy — often used with *up* or *out*

flesh fly *n* : a two-winged fly whose maggots feed on flesh

flesh•ing \ˈflesh-ing\ *n* : the distribution of the lean and fat on an animal

flesh•ly \ˈflesh-lē\ *adj* **1** : CORPOREAL c, BODILY **2 a** : CARNAL, SENSUAL ⟨*fleshly* desires⟩ **b** : not spiritual : WORLDLY

flesh wound *n* : an injury involving penetration of body muscles without damage to other soft parts or to bones

fleshy \ˈflesh-ē\ *adj* **flesh•i•er**; **-est 1 a** : resembling or consisting of flesh **b** : having abundant flesh; *esp* : FAT **2** : SUCCULENT 1 ⟨*fleshy* fruits⟩ — **flesh•i•ness** *n*

fleur–de–lis *or* **fleur–de–lys** \ˌflərd-ˡl-ˈē, ˌflu̇rd-\ *n, pl* **fleurs–de–lis** *or* **fleur–de–lis** *or* **fleurs–de–lys** *or* **fleur–de–lys** *same or* -ˈēz\ **1** : IRIS 3 **2** : a conventionalized iris in art and heraldry

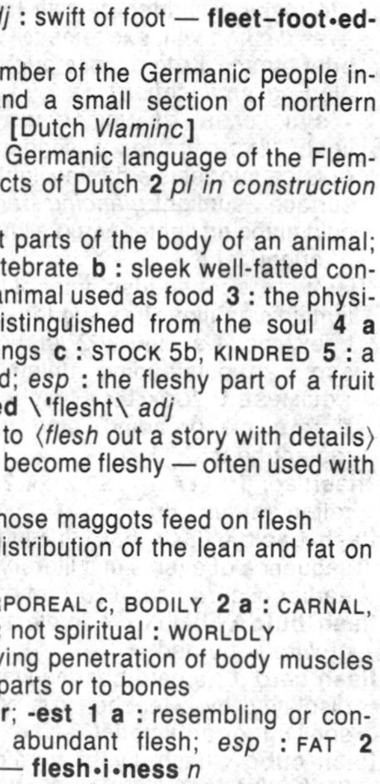

fleur-de-lis 2

[Middle French *flor de lis,* literally, "lily flower"]

flew *past of* FLY

flews \'flüz\ *n pl* : the drooping lateral parts of a dog's upper lip [origin unknown]

flex \'fleks\ *vb* : to bend especially repeatedly : cause flexion of [Latin *flexus,* past participle of *flectere* "to bend, flex"]

flex•i•ble \'flek-sə-bəl\ *adj* **1** : capable of being flexed : PLIANT **2** : readily changed or changing : ADAPTABLE ⟨a *flexible* mind⟩ — **flex•i•bil•i•ty** \ˌflek-sə-'bil-ət-ē\ *n* — **flex•i•bly** \'flek-sə-blē\ *adv*

flex•ion \'flek-shən\ *n* : muscular movement that lessens the angle between bones or parts; *also* : the resulting state or relation of parts

flex•or \'flek-sər\ *n* : a muscle that produces flexion — compare EXTENSOR — **flexor** *adj*

flex•ure \'flek-shər\ *n* **1** : the quality or state of being flexed **2** : TURN, FOLD ⟨the *flexure* between thigh and abdomen⟩ — **flex•ur•al** \-shə-rəl, -shrəl\ *adj*

[1]**flick** \'flik\ *n* **1** : a light sharp jerky stroke or movement **2** : a sound produced by a flick **3** : DAUB 1, SPLOTCH [imitative]

[2]**flick** *vb* **1** : to strike lightly with a quick sharp motion ⟨*flicked* a speck off the table⟩ **2** : FLICKER 1

[3]**flick** *n, slang* : MOVIE [short for [2]*flicker*]

[1]**flick•er** \'flik-ər\ *vb* **flick•ered; flick•er•ing** \'flik-ring, -ə-ring\ **1** : to move irregularly or unsteadily : FLUTTER **2** : to burn fitfully or with a fluctuating light ⟨a *flickering* candle⟩ [Old English *flicorian*]

[2]**flicker** *n* **1** : a brief interval of brightness **2** : a flickering light **3** : a brief stirring ⟨a *flicker* of interest⟩ — **flick•ery** \'flik-rē, -ə-rē\ *adj*

[3]**flicker** *n* : a common large brightly marked woodpecker of eastern North America; *also* : a related bird of the southern and western United States [probably from [2]*flick*]

[3]flicker

flied *past of* FLY 5

fli•er *or* **fly•er** \'flī-ər, 'flīr\ *n* **1** : one that flies; *esp* : AVIATOR **2** : a speculative undertaking; *esp* : an attempt to gain large profits in a business venture by one who is inexperienced or uninformed **3** : a printed notice or message (as an advertising leaflet) distributed in large numbers

[1]**flight** \'flīt\ *n* **1** : an act or instance of passing through the air by the use of wings ⟨a *flight* in a plane⟩ ⟨the *flight* of birds⟩ **2 a** : a passing through the air or through space outside the earth's atmosphere ⟨the *flight* of a bullet⟩ ⟨a moon *flight*⟩ **b** : the distance covered in a flight **c** : swift movement **3** : an airplane making a scheduled flight **4** : a group of similar things flying through the air together ⟨a *flight* of ducks⟩ ⟨a *flight* of bombers⟩ **5** : a brilliant, imaginative, or unrestrained exercise or display ⟨a *flight* of fancy⟩ **6** : a continuous series of stairs from one landing or floor to another [Old English *flyht*]

[2]**flight** *n* : an act or instance of running away [Middle English *fliht*]

flight control *n* : the control from a ground station of an airplane or spacecraft especially by radio

flight engineer *n* : a member of a flight crew responsible for mechanical operation

flight feather *n* : one of the quills of a bird's wing or tail that support it in flight

flight•less \'flīt-ləs\ *adj* : unable to fly ⟨*flightless* birds⟩

flight line *n* : a parking and servicing area for airplanes

flight path *n* : the path made or followed by something (as a spacecraft, airplane, or particle) in flight

flighty \'flīt-ē\ *adj* **flight•i•er; -est 1** : easily upset : VOLATILE ⟨a *flighty* temper⟩ **2** : easily excited : SKITTISH ⟨*flighty* horses⟩ **3** : SCATTERBRAINED, SILLY — **flight•i•ly** \'flīt-l-ē\ *adv* — **flight•i•ness** \'flīt-ē-nəs\ *n*

flim•flam \'flim-ˌflam\ *n* **1** : DECEPTION 1, FRAUD **2** : HANKY-PANKY [probably of Scandinavian origin] — **flimflam** *vb*

flim•sy \'flim-zē\ *adj* **flim•si•er; -est 1 a** : lacking strength or substance **b** : of inferior materials and workmanship **2** : having little worth or plausibility ⟨a *flimsy* excuse⟩ [perhaps derived from [1]*film*] — **flim•si•ly** \-zə-lē\ *adv* — **flim•si•ness** \-zē-nəs\ *n*

flinch \'flinch\ *vi* : to shrink from or as if from physical pain : WINCE [Middle French *flenchir* "to bend"] — **flinch** *n* — **flinch•er** *n*

[1]**fling** \'fling\ *vb* **flung** \'fləng\; **fling•ing** \'fling-ing\ **1** : to move in a brusque or headlong manner ⟨*flung* out of the room⟩ **2** : to kick or plunge vigorously **3 a** : to throw or swing with force or recklessness **b** : to cast aside : DISCARD **4** : to place or put suddenly and unexpectedly into a state or condition ⟨*flung* the troops into confusion⟩ [Middle English *flingen,* of Scandinavian origin] **syn** see THROW — **fling•er** \'fling-ər\ *n*

[2]**fling** *n* **1** : an act or instance of flinging **2** : a casual try : ATTEMPT **3** : a period of self-indulgence

flint \'flint\ *n* **1** : a grayish or dark hard quartz that produces a spark when struck by steel **2** : an alloy (as of iron and cerium) used for producing a spark in cigarette lighters [Old English]

flint glass *n* : heavy glass that contains an oxide of lead and is used for optical structures (as lenses)

flint•lock \'flint-ˌläk\ *n* **1** : a lock for a 17th and 18th century firearm using a flint to ignite the charge **2** : a firearm fitted with a flintlock

flinty \'flint-ē\ *adj* **flint•i•er; -est 1** : composed of or covered with flint **2 a** : notably hard ⟨*flinty* seeds⟩ **b** : UNYIELDING, STERN ⟨a strong *flinty* character⟩ — **flint•i•ly** \'flint-l-ē\ *adv* — **flint•i•ness** \'flint-ē-nəs\ *n*

[1]**flip** \'flip\ *vb* **flipped; flip•ping 1** : to turn by tossing ⟨*flip* a coin⟩ **2** : to turn quickly ⟨*flip* the pages of a book⟩ **3** : FLICK ⟨*flip* a light switch⟩ **4** : to lose self-control [probably imitative]

[2]**flip** *n* **1** : an act or instance of flipping : TOSS, FLICK **2** : a somersault performed in the air

[3]**flip** *adj* : FLIPPANT

flip•pant \'flip-ənt\ *adj* : treating lightly something serious or worthy of respect : lacking earnestness [probably from [1]*flip*] — **flip•pan•cy** \-ən-sē\ *n* — **flip•pant•ly** *adv*

flip•per \'flip-ər\ *n* **1** : a broad flat limb (as of a seal) adapted for swimming **2** : a flat rubber shoe with the front expanded into a paddle used in skin diving

[1]**flirt** \'flərt\ *vi* **1** : to move erratically : FLIT **2 a** : to behave amorously without serious intent **b** : TOY ⟨*flirted* with the idea of getting a job⟩ [origin unknown] — **flir•ta•tion** \ˌflər-'tā-shən\ *n* — **flir•ta•tious** \-shəs\ *adj* — **flir•ta•tious•ness** *n* — **flirt•er** \'flərt-ər\ *n*

[2]**flirt** *n* **1** : an act or instance of flirting **2** : a person who flirts

flit \'flit\ *vi* **flit•ted; flit•ting** : to move or progress in quick erratic darts [Middle English *flitten,* of Scandinavian origin] — **flit** *n*

flit•ter \'flit-ər\ *vi* : FLUTTER 1, FLICKER [derived from *flit*]

fliv•ver \'fliv-ər\ *n* : a small cheap usually old automobile [origin unknown]

[1]**float** \'flōt\ *n* **1** : an act or instance of floating **2** : something that floats in or on the surface of a fluid: as **a** : a cork or bob buoying up the baited end of a fishing line **b** : a floating platform anchored near a shoreline for use by swimmers or boats **c** : a hollow ball that controls the flow or level of the liquid it floats on (as in a tank or cistern) **d** : a watertight structure giving an airplane buoyancy on water **3** : a vehicle carrying an exhibit in a parade **4** : a drink consisting of ice cream floating in a beverage [Middle English *flote* "boat, float", from Old English *flota* "ship"]

[2]**float** *vb* **1** : to rest or cause to rest in or on the surface of a fluid **2 a** : to drift or cause to drift on or through or as if on or through a fluid ⟨dust *floating* through the air⟩ ⟨*float* logs down a river⟩ **b** : WANDER ⟨*floating* from town to town⟩ **3 a** : to offer (an issue of stocks or bonds) in order to finance an enterprise **b** : to finance (an enterprise) by floating an issue of stocks or bonds **c** : to arrange for ⟨*float* a loan⟩

float•er \'flōt-ər\ *n* **1 a** : one that floats **b** : a person who floats something **2** : a person without a permanent home or job : VAGRANT

float•ing *adj* **1** : buoyed on or in a fluid **2 a** : not settled or committed : not established ⟨*floating* capital⟩ ⟨a *floating* population⟩ **b** : short-term and usually not funded ⟨a *floating* debt⟩ **3** : connected or constructed so as to operate and adjust smoothly ⟨a *floating* axle⟩

floating-point *adj* : involving or being a mathematical notation in which a quantity is denoted by one number multiplied by a power of the number base ⟨the fixed-point value 99.9 could be expressed in a *floating-point* system as .999 × 10^2⟩ — compare FIXED-POINT

floating rib *n* : a rib (as one of the last two pairs in human beings) that has no attachment to the sternum — compare FALSE RIB

floc•cu•late \ˈfläk-yə-ˌlāt\ *vb* : to collect or cause to collect into a flocculent mass — **floc•cu•la•tion** \ˌfläk-yə-ˈlā-shən\ *n*

floc•cu•lent \ˈfläk-yə-lənt\ *adj* : resembling wool especially in loose fluffy texture [Latin *floccus* "flock of wool"]

¹flock \ˈfläk\ *n* **1** : a group of birds or mammals assembled or herded together **2** : a group under the guidance of a leader **3** : a large number [Old English *flocc* "crowd, band"]

²flock *vi* : to gather or move in a crowd ⟨they *flocked* to the beach⟩

³flock *n* **1** : a tuft of wool or cotton fiber **2** : woolen or cotton refuse used for stuffing furniture and mattresses **3** : very short or pulverized fiber used to form a pattern on cloth or paper or a protective covering on metal [Middle English]

⁴flock *vt* **1** : to fill with flock **2** : to decorate with flock

flock•ing \ˈfläk-ing\ *n* : a design in flock

floe \ˈflō\ *n* : a sheet or mass of floating ice [probably from Norwegian *flo* "flat layer"]

flog \ˈfläg\ *vt* **flogged**; **flog•ging** : to beat severely with a rod or whip [perhaps from Latin *flagellare* "to whip"] — **flog•ger** *n*

¹flood \ˈfləd\ *n* **1 a** : a great flow of water that rises and spreads over the land **b** *cap* : a flood described in the Bible as covering the earth in the time of Noah **2** : the flowing in of the tide **3** : an overwhelming quantity or volume ⟨a *flood* of mail⟩ [Old English *flōd*]

²flood *vb* **1** : to cover or become filled with a flood ⟨the river *flooded* the lowlands⟩ ⟨the cellar *floods* after a rain⟩ **2** : to fill abundantly or excessively ⟨a room *flooded* with light⟩ ⟨*flood* a carburetor⟩ **3** : to pour forth in a flood

flood•gate \ˈfləd-ˌgāt\ *n* **1** : a gate (as in a canal) for shutting out, admitting, or releasing a body of water : SLUICE **2** : something serving to restrain an outburst

flood•light \-ˌlīt\ *n* **1** : artificial illumination in a broad beam **2** : a lighting unit for projecting a beam of light — **floodlight** *vt*

flood•plain \-ˌplān\ *n* **1** : low flat land along a stream that may flood **2** : a plain built up by deposits of earth from floodwaters

flood tide *n* **1** : the tide while rising or at its greatest height **2 a** : an overwhelming quantity **b** : a high point : PEAK ⟨our success was at *flood tide*⟩

flood•wa•ter \ˈfləd-ˌwȯt-ər, -ˌwät-\ *n* : the water of a flood

flood•way \-ˌwā\ *n* : a channel for diverting floodwaters

¹floor \ˈflōr, ˈflȯr\ *n* **1** : the part of a room on which one stands **2 a** : the lower inside surface of a hollow structure **b** : a ground surface ⟨the ocean *floor*⟩ ⟨the *floor* of a forest⟩ **3 a** : a structure dividing a building into stories **b** : STORY ⟨they live on the first *floor*⟩ **c** : the occupants of a story **4** : the surface of a structure on which one travels ⟨the *floor* of a bridge⟩ **5 a** : a main level space (as in a legislative chamber) distinguished from a platform or gallery **b** : the right to speak from one's place in an assembly ⟨the senator has the *floor*⟩ **6** : a lower limit (as of prices) [Old English *flōr*]

²floor *vt* **1** : to cover with a floor or flooring **2 a** : to knock to the floor **b** : SHOCK, OVERWHELM ⟨the news *floored* us⟩

floor•board \ˈflōr-ˌbōrd, ˈflȯr-ˌbȯrd\ *n* **1** : a board in a floor **2** : the floor of an automobile

floor exercise *n* : a gymnastic event in which participants perform various ballet and tumbling feats on a floor mat

floor•ing \ˈflōr-ing, ˈflȯr-\ *n* **1** : FLOOR 1 **2** : material for floors

floor lamp *n* : a tall lamp that stands on the floor

floor leader *n* : a member of a legislative body chosen by a party to have charge of its organization and strategy on the floor

floor show *n* : a series of acts presented in a nightclub

floor•walk•er \ˈflōr-ˌwȯ-kər, ˈflȯr-\ *n* : a person employed in a retail store to oversee the sales force and aid customers

floo•zy \ˈflü-zē\ *n, pl* **floozies** : a tawdry or immoral woman [origin unknown]

¹flop \ˈfläp\ *vb* **flopped**; **flop•ping** **1** : to swing or bounce loosely : flap about ⟨a hat brim *flopping* in the wind⟩ **2 a** : to throw oneself down heavily, clumsily, or in a completely relaxed manner ⟨*flop* into the chair⟩ **b** : to throw or drop suddenly and usually heavily or noisily ⟨*flopped* the bundles onto the table⟩ **3** : to fail completely ⟨the play *flopped*⟩ [alteration of ²*flap*]

²flop *n* **1** : an act or sound of flopping **2** : a complete failure : DUD ⟨the play was a *flop*⟩

³flop *adv* : RIGHT, SQUARELY ⟨fall *flop* on one's face⟩

flop•house \-ˌhau̇s\ *n* : a cheap rooming house or hotel

flop•py \ˈfläp-ē\ *adj* **flop•pi•er**; **-est** : tending to flop; *esp* : being soft and flexible ⟨a hat with a *floppy* brim⟩

flo•ra \ˈflōr-ə, ˈflȯr-\ *n, pl* **floras** *also* **flo•rae** \-ˌē, -ˌī\ : plants or plant life especially of a region, period, or environment — compare FAUNA [Latin *Flora*, Roman goddess of flowers]

flo•ral \ˈflōr-əl, ˈflȯr-\ *adj* : of or relating to flowers or a flora [Latin *flor-*, *flos* "flower"] — **flo•ral•ly** \-ə-lē\ *adv*

Flor•ence flask \ˌflȯr-əns-, ˌflär-\ *n* : a round usually flat-bottomed glass laboratory vessel with a long neck [*Florence*, Italy; from the use of flasks of this shape for certain Italian wines]

flo•res•cence \flȯ-ˈres-ns, flə-\ *n* : a state or period of being in bloom or flourishing ⟨the highest *florescence* of a civilization⟩ [Latin *florescere* "to begin to bloom", from *florēre* "to blossom, flourish"] — **flo•res•cent** \-nt\ *adj*

flo•ret \ˈflōr-ət, ˈflȯr-\ *n* : a small flower; *esp* : one of the small flowers forming the head of a plant of the daisy family

flori- *combining form* : flower or flowers ⟨*flori*gen⟩ [Latin *flor-*, *flos* "flower"]

flor•id \ˈflȯr-əd, ˈflär-\ *adj* **1** : excessively flowery in style : ORNATE ⟨*florid* writing⟩ **2** : tinged with red : RUDDY ⟨a *florid* complexion⟩ [Latin *floridus* "blooming, flowery", from *florēre* "to blossom, flourish"] — **flo•rid•i•ty** \flə-ˈrid-ət-ē, flȯ-\ *n* — **flor•id•ly** \ˈflȯr-əd-lē, ˈflär-\ *adv* — **flor•id•ness** *n*

flo•rif•er•ous \flȯ-ˈrif-rəs, -ə-rəs\ *adj* : bearing flowers; *esp* : blooming freely — **flo•rif•er•ous•ness** *n*

flo•ri•gen \ˈflōr-ə-jən, ˈflȯr-, ˈflär-\ *n* : a plant hormone that promotes flowering

flor•in \ˈflȯr-ən, ˈflär-, ˈflōr-\ *n* **1 a** : an old gold coin first struck at Florence in 1252 **b** : any of various former gold coins of European countries patterned after the Florentine florin **2 a** : a former British silver coin worth two shillings **b** : any of several similar coins issued in British Commonwealth countries **3** : GULDEN [Middle French, from Italian *fiorino*, from *fiore* "flower", from Latin *flor-*, *flos*; from the lily on the first florins]

flo•rist \ˈflōr-əst, ˈflȯr-, ˈflär-\ *n* : a seller of flowers and ornamental plants

flo•ris•tic \flȯ-ˈris-tik\ *adj* : of or relating to flowers or a flora — **flo•ris•ti•cal•ly** \-ti-kə-lē, -klē\ *adv*

¹floss \ˈfläs, ˈflȯs\ *n* **1** : waste or short silk fibers that cannot be reeled **2 a** : soft thread of silk or mercerized cotton used for embroidery **b** : DENTAL FLOSS **c** : a lightweight wool knitting yarn **3** : fluffy fibrous material; *esp* : SILK COTTON [Dutch *vlos*]

²floss *vb* : to use or clean with dental floss ⟨*floss* daily⟩

flossy \ˈfläs-ē, ˈflȯs-\ *adj* **floss•i•er**; **-est** **1 a** : of, relating to, or having the characteristics of floss **b** : DOWNY 2 **2** : stylish or glamorous especially at first impression ⟨slick *flossy* writing⟩

flo•ta•tion \flō-ˈtā-shən\ *n* **1** : the act, process, or state of floating **2** : the separation of the particles of a mass of pulverized ore according to their relative capacity for floating on a given liquid

flo•til•la \flō-ˈtil-ə\ *n* : a fleet of ships; *esp* : a fleet of small ships [Spanish, from *flota* "fleet", from Old French *flote*, from Old Norse *floti*]

flot•sam \ˈflät-səm\ *n* : floating wreckage of a ship or its cargo [Anglo-French *floteson*, from Old French *floter* "to float", of Germanic origin]

¹flounce \ˈflau̇ns\ *vi* **1** : to move with exaggerated jerky motions **2** : to go with sudden determination ⟨*flounced* out of the room in anger⟩ [perhaps of Scandinavian origin]

²flounce *n* : an act or instance of flouncing

³flounce *n* : a strip of fabric attached by the upper edge ⟨a wide *flounce* at the bottom of the skirt⟩ [alteration of Middle English *frouncen* "to curl"]

⁴flounce *vt* : to trim or finish with a flounce

¹floun•der \ˈflau̇n-dər\ *n, pl* **flounder** *or* **flounders** : FLATFISH; *esp* : any of various important marine food fishes [Middle English, of Scandinavian origin]

²flounder *vi* **floun•dered**; **floun•der•ing** \-də-ring, -dring\ : to struggle or proceed clumsily ⟨*flounder* in the deep mud⟩ [probably alteration of *founder*]

^{1}**flour** \ˈflau̇r\ *n* **1 a :** finely ground powdery meal of wheat usually largely freed from bran **b :** a similar meal of any cereal grain or edible seed **2 :** a fine soft powder [Middle English, "flower, best of anything, flour"]
• **syn** FLOUR, MEAL mean the product of grinding cereal grain or other seeds. FLOUR used alone denotes wheat kernels finely ground and sifted to remove the bran; MEAL applies to any grain or seed coarsely ground and unsifted.

^{2}**flour** *vt* **:** to coat with flour

flour beetle *n* **:** any of several usually elongated flattened brown beetles that are economic pests especially in flour or meal

^{1}**flour•ish** \ˈflər-ish, ˈflə-rish\ *vb* **1 :** to grow luxuriantly **:** THRIVE **2 a :** to achieve success **:** PROSPER **b :** to be active or prominent ⟨*flourished* around 1850⟩ **3 :** to make bold and sweeping gestures **4 :** to wield with dramatic gestures **:** BRANDISH ⟨*flourish* a sword⟩ [Middle French *floriss-*, stem of *florir* "to flourish", from Latin *florēre*, from *flor-*, *flos* "flower"]

^{2}**flourish** *n* **1 :** a period of thriving **2 a :** a flowery embellishment or passage ⟨handwriting with *flourishes*⟩ **b :** an act or instance of brandishing **:** WAVE ⟨gave a *flourish* of the cane⟩ **c :** a dramatic action ⟨introduced them with a *flourish*⟩

floury \ˈflau̇r-ē\ *adj* **1 :** of, relating to, or resembling flour **2 :** covered with flour

flout \ˈflau̇t\ *vb* **1 :** to treat with contemptuous disregard **:** SCORN ⟨*flouting* their parents' advice⟩ **2 :** to indulge in scornful behavior [probably from Middle English *flouten* "to play the flute", from *floute* "flute"] **syn** see FLAUNT — **flout•er** *n*

^{1}**flow** \ˈflō\ *vi* **1 a :** to issue or move in a stream **b :** to move with a continual shifting of the constituent particles ⟨the molasses *flowed* slowly⟩ **2 :** RISE ⟨the tide ebbs and *flows*⟩ **3 :** ABOUND ⟨a land that *flows* with milk and honey⟩ **4 a :** to proceed smoothly and readily ⟨the words *flowed* from my mouth⟩ **b :** to have a smooth uninterrupted continuity **5 :** to hang loose and billowing ⟨a flag *flowing* in the breeze⟩ **6 :** to come from as a source **7 :** MENSTRUATE [Old English *flōwan*] — **flow•ing•ly** \-iŋ-lē\ *adv*

^{2}**flow** *n* **1 :** an act of flowing **2 :** FLOOD 1a, 2 **3 a :** a smooth uninterrupted movement **b :** a stream of fluid; *also* **:** a mass of matter that has flowed ⟨a lava *flow*⟩ **4 :** the quantity that flows in a certain time ⟨the *flow* of water over a dam⟩ **5 a :** MENSTRUATION **b :** OUTPUT 1, YIELD **6 :** a continuous transfer of energy ⟨a *flow* of electricity⟩

flow chart *n* **:** a diagram showing step-by-step progression through a procedure or system

^{1}**flow•er** \ˈflau̇-ər, ˈflau̇r\ *n* **1 a :** BLOSSOM, INFLORESCENCE **b :** a shoot of the spore-producing generation of a higher plant that is specialized for reproduction and consists of a shortened axis bearing modified leaves (as petals and sporophylls) **c :** a plant cultivated or valued for its blossoms **2 a :** the best part or example ⟨the *flower* of the family⟩ **b :** the finest most vigorous period **c :** a state of blooming or flourishing ⟨when knighthood was in *flower*⟩ **3** *pl* **:** a finely divided powder produced especially by condensation or sublimation ⟨*flowers* of sulfur⟩ [Middle English *flour*, from Old French, from Latin *flor-*, *flos*] — **flow•er•less** \-ləs\ *adj* — **flow•er•like** \-ˌlīk\ *adj*

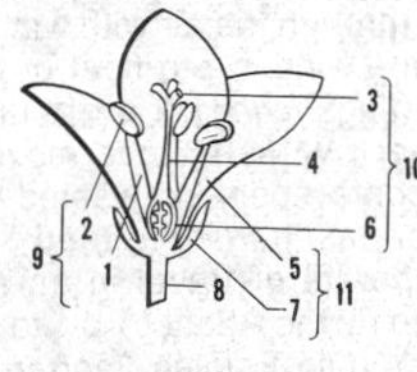

^{1}flower 1a: *1* filament, *2* anther, *3* stigma, *4* style, *5* petal, *6* ovary, *7* sepal, *8* pedicel, *9* stamen, *10* pistol, *11* perianth

^{2}**flower** *vb* **1 :** to produce flowers **:** BLOOM **2 a :** DEVELOP ⟨*flowered* into a real scholar⟩ **b :** FLOURISH 2 **3 :** to decorate with floral designs

flow•ered \ˈflau̇-ərd, ˈflau̇rd\ *adj* **1 :** having or bearing flowers **2 :** decorated with flowers or flowerlike figures ⟨*flowered* silk⟩

flow•er•et \ˈflau̇-ər-ət, ˈflau̇r-ət\ *n* **:** FLORET

flower girl *n* **:** a little girl who carries flowers at a wedding

flower head *n* **:** a tight cluster of small stemless flowers that looks like a single flower

flowering plant *n* **:** any of a major group (Angiospermae) of higher plants that comprises those which produce flowers, fruits, and seeds with the seeds in a closed ovary — called also *angiosperm;* compare SEED PLANT

flow•er•pot \ˈflau̇-ər-ˌpät, ˈflau̇r-\ *n* **:** a pot in which to grow plants

flow•ery \ˈflau̇-ər-ē, flau̇r-\ *adj* **flow•er•i•er; -est 1 :** full of or covered with flowers **2 :** full of fine words or phrases **:** FLORID ⟨*flowery* language⟩ — **flow•er•i•ness** *n*

flown *past participle of* FLY

flu \ˈflü\ *n* **1 :** INFLUENZA 1 **2 :** any of several virus diseases marked especially by respiratory symptoms

flub \ˈfləb\ *vb* **flubbed; flub•bing 1 :** to make a mess of **:** BOTCH ⟨the actor *flubbed* the line⟩ **2 :** BLUNDER 2 [origin unknown] — **flub** *n*

fluc•tu•ate \ˈflək-chə-ˌwāt\ *vi* **1 :** to move up and down or back and forth like a wave **2 :** to be changing constantly and irregularly (as between points, levels, or conditions) ⟨the market *fluctuated* wildly⟩ ⟨one's health may *fluctuate* with the weather⟩ [Latin *fluctuare*, from *fluctus* "flow, wave", from *fluere* "to flow"] — **fluc•tu•a•tion** \ˌflək-chə-ˈwā-shən\ *n*

flue \ˈflü\ *n* **:** an enclosed passageway for directing a current: as **a :** a channel in a chimney for conveying flame and smoke to the outer air **b :** a pipe for conveying flame and hot gases around or through water in a steam boiler **c :** FLUE PIPE [origin unknown]

flu•en•cy \ˈflü-ən-sē\ *n* **:** the quality or state of being fluent especially in speech

flu•ent \ˈflü-ənt\ *adj* **1 :** capable of flowing **:** FLUID **2 a :** ready or easy in speech ⟨*fluent* in Spanish⟩ **b :** effortlessly smooth and rapid **:** POLISHED ⟨*fluent* speech⟩ [Latin *fluere* "to flow"] — **flu•ent•ly** *adv*

flue pipe *n* **:** an organ pipe whose tone is produced by an air current striking the lip and causing the air within to vibrate

flue stop *n* **:** an organ stop made up of flue pipes

^{1}**fluff** \ˈfləf\ *n* **1 :** ^{3}NAP, DOWN ⟨soft *fluff* from a pillow⟩ **2 :** something fluffy **3 :** something unimportant **4 :** BLUNDER; *esp* **:** an actor's lapse of memory [probably alteration of *flue* "fluff", from Flemish *vluwe*, from French *velu* "shaggy"]

^{2}**fluff** *vb* **1 :** to make or become fluffy ⟨*fluff* up a pillow⟩ **2 :** to spoil by or make a mistake **:** BOTCH **3 :** to deliver badly or fail to remember (one's lines in a play)

fluffy \ˈfləf-ē\ *adj* **fluff•i•er; -est 1 a :** having, covered with, or resembling fluff or down ⟨*fluffy* fur⟩ **b :** being light and soft or airy ⟨a *fluffy* omelet⟩ **2 :** SILLY 3 — **fluff•i•ness** *n*

^{1}**flu•id** \ˈflü-əd\ *adj* **1 a :** capable of flowing like a liquid or gas **b :** likely or tending to change or move **2 :** characterized by or employing a smooth easy style **3 a :** available for various uses **b :** easily converted into cash ⟨*fluid* assets⟩ [Latin *fluidus*, from *fluere* "to flow"] — **flu•id•i•ty** \flü-ˈid-ət-ē\ *n* — **flu•id•ly** \ˈflü-əd-lē\ *adv* — **flu•id•ness** *n*

^{2}**fluid** *n* **:** a substance tending to flow or conform to the outline of its container ⟨liquids and gases are *fluids*⟩

fluid mechanics *n sing or pl* **:** a branch of mechanics that deals with the properties of liquids and gases

flu•id•ounce \ˌflü-əd-ˈau̇ns\ *n* **:** a unit of liquid capacity equal to 1/16 pint (about 29.6 milliliters) — see MEASURE table

flu•idram \ˌflü-əd-ˈdram, ˌflü-ə-\ *n* **:** a unit of liquid capacity equal to 1/8 fluid ounce (about 3.7 milliliters) — see MEASURE table [blend of *fluid* and *dram*]

^{1}**fluke** \ˈflük\ *n* **1 :** FLATFISH **2 :** any of a group of trematodes; *also* **:** TREMATODE [Old English *flōc*]

^{2}**fluke** *n* **1 :** the part of an anchor that digs into the ground **2 :** a barbed head (as of a harpoon) **3 :** one of the lobes of a whale's tail

^{3}**fluke** *n* **1 :** an accidentally successful stroke at billiards or pool **2 :** a stroke of luck ⟨won by a *fluke*⟩ [origin unknown]

fluky \ˈflü-kē\ *adj* **fluk•i•er; -est 1 :** happening by or depending on chance **2 :** being unsteady or uncertain **:** CHANGEABLE ⟨a *fluky* wind⟩

flume \ˈflüm\ *n* **1 :** a ravine or gorge with a stream running through it **2 :** an inclined channel for conveying water (as for power) [probably from Middle English *flum* "river", from Old French, from Latin *flumen*, from *fluere* "to flow"]

flum•mery \ˈfləm-rē, -ə-rē\ *n, pl* **-mer•ies 1 a :** a soft jelly or porridge made with flour or meal **b :** any of several sweet desserts **2 a :** something trashy **b :** empty compliment **:** HUMBUG [Welsh *llymru*]

flum•mox \ˈfləm-əks, -iks\ *vt* **:** CONFUSE 1 [origin unknown]

flung *past of* FLING
flunk \ˈfləŋk\ *vb* **1 :** to fail an examination or course **2 :** to give a failing grade to [perhaps blend of *flinch* and *funk*] — **flunk** *n*
flunk out *vb* **:** to dismiss or be dismissed from a school or college for failure
flun•ky *or* **flun•key** \ˈfləŋ-kē\ *n, pl* **flunkies** *or* **flunkeys 1 a :** a servant in livery **b :** one doing menial duties **2 :** TOADY, YES-MAN [Scottish]
fluor- *or* **fluoro-** *combining form* **1 :** fluorine ⟨*fluor*ide⟩ **2** *also* **fluori- :** fluorescence ⟨*fluoro*scope⟩
flu•o•resce \flu̇r-ˈes, ˌflu̇-ər-\ *vi* **:** to produce, undergo, or exhibit fluorescence [back-formation from *fluorescence*]
flu•o•res•ce•in \-ˈes-ē-ən\ *n* **:** a yellow or red crystalline dye with a bright yellow-green fluorescence in alkaline solution
flu•o•res•cence \-ˈes-ns\ *n* **:** the property of a substance of emitting radiation usually as visible light when exposed to radiation from another source; *also* **:** the radiation emitted — **flu•o•res•cent** \-nt\ *adj*
fluorescent lamp *n* **:** an electric lamp in which light is produced on the inside fluorescent coating of a glass tube by the action of ultraviolet light
flu•o•ri•date \ˈflu̇r-ə-ˌdāt\ *vt* **:** to add a fluoride to ⟨*fluoridate* drinking water⟩ — **flu•o•ri•da•tion** \ˌflu̇r-ə-ˈdā-shən\ *n*
flu•o•ride \ˈflu̇-ər-ˌīd, ˈflu̇r-ˌ\ *n* **:** a compound of fluorine with another chemical element or a radical
flu•o•ri•nate \ˈflu̇r-ə-ˌnāt\ *vt* **:** to treat or cause to combine with fluorine or a compound of fluorine — **flu•o•ri•na•tion** \ˌflu̇r-ə-ˈnā-shən\ *n*
flu•o•rine \ˈflu̇r-ˌēn, ˈflu̇-ər-\ *n* **:** a nonmetallic univalent chemical element that is normally a pale yellowish flammable irritating toxic gas — see ELEMENT table [French, from New Latin *fluor* "mineral belonging to a group including fluorite and used as fluxes", from Latin, "flow", from *fluere* "to flow"]
flu•o•rite \ˈflu̇r-ˌīt, ˈflu̇-ər-\ *n* **:** a transparent or translucent mineral CaF_2 of different colors that consists of a fluoride of calcium and is used as a flux and in making glass
flu•o•ro•car•bon \ˈflu̇r-ō-ˌkär-bən, ˈflu̇-ər-\ *n* **:** any of various inert compounds of carbon and fluorine used chiefly as lubricants and refrigerants
[1]**flu•o•ro•scope** \ˈflu̇r-ə-ˌskōp\ *n* **:** an instrument that is used especially in examining inner parts of the body (as the lungs) by observing light and dark shadows produced on a screen by the action of X rays — **flu•o•ro•scop•ic** \ˌflu̇r-ə-ˈskäp-ik\ *adj* — **flu•o•ros•co•py** \ˌflu̇r-ˈäs-kə-pē, ˌflu̇-ər-ˈ\ *n*
[2]**fluoroscope** *vt* **:** to examine by a fluoroscope
flu•or•spar \ˈflu̇r-ˌspär, ˈflu̇-ər-\ *n* **:** FLUORITE
[1]**flur•ry** \ˈflər-ē, ˈflə-rē\ *n, pl* **flurries 1 a :** a gust of wind **b :** a brief light snowfall **2 :** nervous commotion **3 :** a brief outburst of activity ⟨a *flurry* of trading in the stock exchange⟩ [probably from *flurr* "to strew"]
[2]**flurry** *vb* **flur•ried; flur•ry•ing :** to become or cause to become agitated and confused
[1]**flush** \ˈfləsh\ *vb* **:** to take flight or cause to take flight suddenly ⟨*flushed* a covey of quail⟩ [Middle English *flusshen*]
[2]**flush** *n* **1 :** a sudden flow (as of water) **2 a :** a sudden increase (as of growth) ⟨a spring *flush* of grass⟩ **b :** a surge of emotion ⟨a *flush* of anger⟩ **3 a :** a tinge of red **:** BLUSH **b :** a fresh and vigorous state ⟨in the *flush* of youth⟩ **4 :** a brief sensation of extreme heat [perhaps from Latin *fluxus* "flow"]
[3]**flush** *vb* **1 :** to flow and spread suddenly and freely **2 a :** to glow brightly **b :** BLUSH 1, 3 **3 :** to pour liquid over or through; *esp* **:** to wash out with a rush of liquid **4 :** INFLAME, EXCITE ⟨troops *flushed* with victory⟩ **5 :** to make red or hot ⟨a face *flushed* with fever⟩
[4]**flush** *adj* **1 a :** filled to overflowing **b :** fully supplied especially with money **2 a :** full of life and vigor **:** LUSTY **b :** of a ruddy healthy color **3 :** readily available **:** ABUNDANT **4 a :** having an unbroken continuous surface ⟨*flush* paneling⟩ **b :** directly abutting or immediately adjacent **c :** set even with an edge of a type page or column — **flush•ness** *n*
[5]**flush** *adv* **1 :** in a flush manner **2 :** SQUARELY ⟨was hit *flush* on the chin⟩
[6]**flush** *vt* **:** to make flush ⟨*flush* the headings on a page⟩
[7]**flush** *n* **:** a hand of playing cards all of the same suit [Middle French *flus,* from Latin *fluxus* "flow"]
[1]**flus•ter** \ˈfləs-tər\ *vt* **flus•tered; flus•ter•ing** \-tə-ring, -tring\ **1 :** BEFUDDLE 1 **2 :** to make nervous and unsure **:** UPSET ⟨*flustered* by their rudeness⟩ [probably of Scandinavian origin]
[2]**fluster** *n* **:** a state of agitated confusion
[1]**flute** \ˈflüt\ *n* **1 a :** RECORDER 3 **b :** a woodwind instrument consisting of a tube with keys that is played by blowing across a hole near the closed end **2 a :** a grooved pleat **b :** a rounded groove; *esp* **:** one of the vertical parallel grooves on a classical architectural column [Middle English *floute,* from Middle French *flahute,* from Provençal *flaut*] — **flute•like** \-ˌlīk\ *adj*

[1]flute.1b

[2]**flute** *vb* **1 :** to play a flute **2 :** to make a sound like that of a flute **3 :** to form flutes in ⟨*fluted* columns⟩
flut•ing \ˈflüt-iŋ\ *n* **:** fluted decoration
flut•ist \ˈflüt-əst\ *n* **:** a flute player
[1]**flut•ter** \ˈflət-ər\ *vb* **1 :** to move or cause the wings to move rapidly without flying or in short flights ⟨butterflies *flutter*⟩ **2 a :** to move with quick wavering or flapping motions ⟨flags *fluttered* in the breeze⟩ **b :** to vibrate in irregular spasms ⟨a *fluttering* pulse⟩ **3 :** to move about or behave in an agitated aimless way [Old English *floterian,* from *flotian* "to float"] — **flut•tery** \ˈflət-ə-rē\ *adj*
[2]**flutter** *n* **1 :** an act of fluttering **2 a :** a state of nervous confusion or excitement **b :** FLURRY 3 **3 :** a distortion in reproduced sound similar to but of a higher pitch than wow
flutter kick *n* **:** an alternating whipping motion of the legs used in various swimming strokes (as the crawl)
flu•vi•al \ˈflü-vē-əl\ *adj* **:** produced by stream action ⟨a *fluvial* plain⟩ [Latin *fluvialis,* from *fluvius* "river", from *fluere* "to flow"]
[1]**flux** \ˈfləks\ *n* **1 :** an excessive fluid discharge from the body and especially the bowels **2 a :** a flowing in ⟨*flux* of the tide⟩ **b :** a series of changes **:** a state of continuous change **3 :** a substance used to promote fusion especially of metals or minerals **4 :** the rate of flow of fluid, particles, or energy across a given surface [Latin *fluxus* "flow", from *fluere* "to flow"]
[2]**flux** *vb* **1 :** to become or cause to become fluid **:** FUSE **2 :** to treat with a flux
[1]**fly** \ˈflī\ *vb* **flew** \ˈflü\; **flown** \ˈflōn\; **fly•ing 1 a :** to move in or pass through the air with wings **b :** to move through the air or before the wind **c :** to float or cause to float, wave, or soar in the air ⟨flags *flying*⟩ **2 a :** to take flight **:** FLEE **b :** to fade and disappear **:** VANISH **3 :** to move or pass swiftly ⟨time *flies*⟩ **4 :** to become spent or wasted rapidly ⟨our money just *flew*⟩ **5** *past or past participle* **flied** \ˈflīd\ **:** to hit a fly in baseball **6 a :** to operate or travel in an aircraft **b :** to journey over by flying ⟨to *fly* the Atlantic⟩ **c :** to transport by aircraft ⟨to *fly* passengers⟩ [Old English *flēogan*] — **fly at :** to assail suddenly and violently — **fly blind :** to fly an airplane solely by instruments — **fly contact :** to fly an airplane with the aid of visible landmarks or reference points — **fly high :** to be elated — **fly in the face of** *or* **fly in the teeth of :** to act forthrightly or brazenly in defiance or disobedience of
[2]**fly** *n, pl* **flies 1 :** the action or process of flying **:** FLIGHT **2 :** a horse-drawn public coach or delivery wagon **3** *pl* **:** the space over a theater stage **4 :** something attached by one edge: as **a :** a garment closing concealed by a fold of cloth extending over the fastener **b :** the outer fabric of a tent with a double top **c :** the length of an extended flag from its staff or support; *also* **:** the outer or loose end of a flag **5 :** a baseball hit high into the air — **on the fly 1 :** continuously active **:** very busy **2 :** while still in the air
[3]**fly** *n, pl* **flies 1 :** a winged insect **2 :** a winged or rarely wingless insect (order Diptera) **:** TWO-WINGED FLY; *esp* **:** one (as a housefly or horsefly) that is relatively large and stout-bodied — compare GNAT **3 :** a fishhook dressed to suggest an insect [Old English *flēoge*] — **fly in the ointment :** a detracting factor or element
fly•able \ˈflī-ə-bəl\ *adj* **:** suitable for flying or being flown
fly agaric *n* **:** a poisonous mushroom with a usually bright red cap
fly ash *n* **:** fine solid particles of noncombustible ash carried out of a bed of burning solid fuel by the draft
fly ball *n* **:** [2]FLY 5

fly•blown \ˈflī-ˌblōn\ *adj* **1 :** infested with the eggs or young larvae of a flesh fly or blowfly ⟨*flyblown* sheep⟩ **2 :** not pure **:** TAINTED, CORRUPT

fly•by \-ˌbī\ *n, pl* **flybys :** a usually low-altitude flight past an appointed place by an aircraft or spacecraft

fly–by–night \ˈflī-bə-ˌnīt\ *adj* **1 :** given to making quick profits by shady or irresponsible acts **2 :** SHORT-LIVED, TRANSITORY ⟨*fly-by-night* fashions⟩

fly casting *n* **:** the casting of artificial flies in fly-fishing or as a competitive sport

fly•catch•er \ˈflī-ˌkach-ər, -ˌkech-\ *n* **:** a small bird that feeds on insects that it captures in the air

fly•er *variant of* FLIER

fly–fishing \ˈflī-ˌfish-iŋ\ *n* **:** fishing with artificial flies cast by means of a large flexible pole and a relatively heavy line

¹fly•ing \ˈflī-iŋ\ *adj* **1 a :** rapidly moving **b :** HASTY 1a ⟨a *flying* visit⟩ **2 :** ready to move or act quickly **:** MOBILE

²flying *n* **1 :** travel by air **2 :** the operation of an aircraft or spacecraft

flying boat *n* **:** a seaplane with a hull adapted for floating

flying buttress *n* **:** a projecting arched structure to support a wall or building

flying colors *n pl* **:** complete success ⟨passed the exam with *flying colors*⟩

flying fish *n* **:** any of numerous sea fishes that have long fins suggesting wings and are able to glide for a distance through the air

flying fox *n* **:** FRUIT BAT

flying jib *n* **:** a sail forward of the jib set on an extension of the jibboom

flying machine *n* **:** AIRCRAFT

flying saucer *n* **:** any of various unidentified moving objects repeatedly reported as seen in the air and usually represented as being saucer-shaped or disk-shaped

1 flying buttress

flying squirrel *n* **:** a squirrel with folds of skin connecting the forelegs and hind legs and enabling it to make long gliding leaps

flying start *n* **:** a start in racing in which the participants are moving when they receive the starting signal

fly•leaf \ˈflī-ˌlēf\ *n* **:** the half of the endpaper of a book that is not pasted down to the cover

flying squirrel

fly•pa•per \-ˌpā-pər\ *n* **:** paper poisoned or coated with a sticky substance for killing or catching flies

fly•speck \-ˌspek\ *n* **1 :** a speck of fly dung **2 :** something small and insignificant — **flyspeck** *vt*

fly•swat•ter \-ˌswät-ər\ *n* **:** a device for killing insects that consists of a flat piece of perforated rubber or plastic or fine-mesh wire netting attached to a handle

fly•way \-ˌwā\ *n* **:** an established air route of migratory birds

fly•weight \-ˌwāt\ *n* **:** a boxer in a weight division having the approximate range of 48 to 51 kilograms

fly•wheel \-ˌhwēl, -ˌwēl\ *n* **:** a heavy wheel attached to the shaft of a revolving machine that reduces fluctuation in shaft speed through its inertia

f–number \ˈef-ˌnəm-bər\ *n* **:** a number following the symbol f/ that expresses the ratio of the focal length of a camera or telescope lens to the aperture and that determines the range of sharpness and the brightness of the image so that the smaller the number the brighter the image but the larger the number the greater the range of sharpness [*f*ocal length]

¹foal \ˈfōl\ *n* **:** the young of an animal of the horse family; *esp* **:** one under one year [Old English *fola*]

²foal *vb* **:** to give birth to a foal

¹foam \ˈfōm\ *n* **1 :** a light frothy mass of fine bubbles formed in or on a liquid **2 :** a froth formed (as by a horse) in salivating or sweating **3 :** a stabilized froth produced chemically and used especially in fighting oil fires **4 :** a material (as rubber) in a lightweight cellular form resulting from introduction of gas bubbles during manufacture [Old English *fām*]

²foam *vb* **1 a :** to produce or form foam **b :** to froth at the mouth especially in anger; *also* **:** to be angry **2 :** to gush out in foam **3 :** to cause to form foam; *esp* **:** to cause air bubbles to form in **4 :** to convert (as a plastic) into a foam

foam rubber *n* **:** spongy rubber of fine texture made from latex by foaming before vulcanization

foamy \ˈfō-mē\ *adj* **foam•i•er; -est 1 :** covered with foam **:** FROTHY **2 :** full of, consisting of, or resembling foam — **foam•i•ly** \-mə-lē\ *adv* — **foam•i•ness** \-mē-nəs\ *n*

fob \ˈfäb\ *n* **1 :** a watch chain or ribbon; *esp* **:** one hanging from a small watch pocket near the waistband in trousers **2 :** a small ornament worn on a watch chain [earlier *fob* "watch pocket"]

fob off *vt* **1 :** to put off with a trick or excuse **2 :** to offer as genuine **3 :** to put aside [Middle English *fobben* "to cheat"]

fo•cal \ˈfō-kəl\ *adj* **:** of, relating to, or having a focus — **fo•cal•ly** \-kə-lē\ *adv*

focal infection *n* **:** a persistent localized infection especially when causing symptoms elsewhere in the body

focal length *n* **:** the distance of the focus from the surface of a lens or concave mirror

fo'•c'sle *variant of* FORECASTLE

¹fo•cus \ˈfō-kəs\ *n, pl* **fo•cus•es** *or* **fo•ci** \-ˌsī\ **1 :** a point at which rays (as of light, heat, or sound) converge or from which they diverge or appear to diverge; *esp* **:** the point at which an image is formed by a mirror, lens, or optical system **2 a :** FOCAL LENGTH **b :** adjustment (as of the eye or field glasses) for distinct vision; *also* **:** the area that may be seen distinctly or resolved into a clear image **3 :** a fixed point or one of the fixed points used in defining a circle, ellipse, parabola, or hyperbola **4 :** a center of activity, attraction, or attention **5 :** the place of origin of an earthquake [Latin, "hearth"]

²focus *vb* **fo•cused** *also* **fo•cussed; fo•cus•ing** *also* **fo•cus•sing 1 :** to bring to a focus ⟨*focus* rays of light⟩ **2 :** to cause to be concentrated ⟨*focus* public attention on a problem⟩ **3 :** to adjust the focus of ⟨*focus* the eyes⟩ ⟨*focus* a telescope⟩ **4 :** to come to a focus **5 :** to adjust one's eye or a camera to a particular range ⟨*focus* at 3 meters⟩

fod•der \ˈfäd-ər\ *n* **:** coarse dry food (as cornstalks) for livestock [Old English *fōdor*] — **fodder** *vt*

foe \ˈfō\ *n* **1 :** one who hates another **:** ENEMY **2 :** an enemy in war **:** ADVERSARY **3 :** one who opposes on principle ⟨a *foe* to waste⟩ **4 :** something injurious ⟨a *foe* to health⟩ [Old English *fāh*] **syn** see ENEMY

foehn *or* **föhn** \ˈfœn, ˈfərn, ˈfān\ *n* **:** a warm dry wind blowing down the side of a mountain [German *föhn*]

foe•tal, foe•tus *variant of* FETAL, FETUS

¹fog \ˈfȯg, ˈfäg\ *n* **1 a :** fine particles of water suspended in the lower atmosphere that differ from cloud only in being near the ground **b :** a fine spray or a foam for fire fighting **2 :** a murky condition of the atmosphere or a substance causing it **3 :** a state of mental confusion **4 :** cloudiness in a developed photographic image caused by chemical action or stray radiation [probably of Scandinavian origin]

²fog *vb* **fogged; fog•ging 1 :** to cover or become covered with or as if with fog **2 :** to make obscure or confusing **3 :** to make confused

fog•bound \ˈfȯg-ˌbau̇nd, ˈfäg-\ *adj* **1 :** covered with or surrounded by fog ⟨a *fogbound* coast⟩ **2 :** unable to move because of fog ⟨*fogbound* ships⟩

fog•gy \ˈfȯg-ē, ˈfäg-\ *adj* **fog•gi•er; -est 1 a :** filled or abounding with fog **b :** covered or made opaque by moisture or grime **2 :** VAGUE 2 — **fog•gi•ly** \-ə-lē\ *adv* — **fog•gi•ness** \-ē-nəs\ *n*

fog•horn \ˈfȯg-ˌhȯrn, ˈfäg-\ *n* **:** a horn (as on a ship) sounded in foggy weather to give warning

fo•gy *also* **fo•gey** \ˈfō-gē\ *n, pl* **fogies** *also* **fogeys :** a person with old-fashioned ideas — usually used with *old* [origin unknown] — **fo•gy•ish** \-gē-ish\ *adj* — **fo•gy•ism** \-gē-ˌiz-əm\ *n*

foi•ble \ˈfȯi-bəl\ *n* : a minor flaw or shortcoming in personal character or behavior : WEAKNESS [obsolete French, from Old French *feble* "feeble"] **syn** see FAULT

¹foil \ˈfȯil\ *vt* : to prevent from attaining an end : DEFEAT ⟨*foil* a plot⟩ [Middle English *foilen* "to trample, full cloth", from Middle French *fouler*] **syn** see FRUSTRATE

²foil *n* **1** : a fencing weapon with a flat guard and a light flexible blade tapering to a blunt point **2** : the art or practice of fencing with foils — often used in pl.

³foil *n* **1** : a leaf-shaped architectural ornamentation or one of the arcs or rounded spaces between its projections **2** : a very thin sheet of metal ⟨tin or aluminum *foil*⟩ **3** : a thin leaf of polished and colored metal placed under an inferior or paste gem to add color and brilliance **4** : one that serves as a contrast to another ⟨acted as a *foil* for a comedian⟩ [Middle French, from Latin *folium* "leaf"]

foils•man \ˈfȯilz-mən\ *n* : one that fences with a foil

foist \ˈfȯist\ *vt* : to pass off as genuine or worthy [probably from Dutch *vuisten* "to take into one's hand", from *vuist* "fist"]

¹fold \ˈfōld\ *n* **1** : an enclosure for sheep **2 a** : a flock of sheep **b** : a group of people with a common faith, belief, or interest [Old English *falod, fald*]

²fold *vt* : to pen up or confine (as sheep) in a fold

³fold *vb* **1** : to lay one part over or against another part ⟨*fold* a blanket⟩ **2** : to clasp together ⟨*fold* one's hands⟩ **3** : EMBRACE 1 **4** : to incorporate (a food ingredient) into a mixture by overturning repeatedly without stirring or beating **5** : to become doubled or pleated ⟨the map *folds* into its case⟩ **6** : to fail completely ⟨the business *folded*⟩ [Old English *fealdan*]

⁴fold *n* **1** : a doubling or folding over **2** : a part doubled or laid over another part

-fold \ˌfōld, ˈfōld\ *adj suffix or adv suffix* **1** : multiplied by (a specified number) : times ⟨a twelve*fold* increase⟩ ⟨repay you ten*fold*⟩ **2** : having (so many) parts ⟨three*fold* solution to the problem⟩ [Old English *-feald*]

fold•boat \ˈfōld-ˌbōt, ˈfōl-\ *n* : a collapsible kayak made of rubberized fabric stretched over a framework

fold•er \ˈfōl-dər\ *n* **1** : one that folds **2** : a printed circular of folded sheets **3** : a folded cover or large envelope for holding loose papers

fol•de•rol *also* **fal•de•ral** \ˈfäl-də-ˌräl\ *n* **1** : a useless trifle **2** : NONSENSE 1 [*fol-de-rol,* a refrain in some old songs]

fo•li•a•ceous \ˌfō-lē-ˈā-shəs\ *adj* : of, relating to, or resembling a plant leaf

fo•li•age \ˈfō-lē-ij, -lyij, -lij\ *n* : the mass of leaves of a plant : LEAFAGE [Middle French *fuellage,* from *foille* "leaf", from Latin *folium*] — **fo•li•aged** \-lē-ijd, -lyjd, -lijd\ *adj*

foliage plant *n* : a plant grown for its decorative foliage

fo•li•ar \ˈfō-lē-ər\ *adj* : consisting of or relating to leaves

¹fo•li•ate \ˈfō-lē-ət\ *adj* : having or made up of leaves ⟨3-*foliate*⟩

²fo•li•ate \-lē-ˌāt\ *vb* **1** : to number the leaves of (as a manuscript) **2** : to ornament with foils **3** : to divide into layers or leaves — **fo•li•at•ed** \-ˌāt-əd\ *adj*

fo•li•a•tion \ˌfō-lē-ˈā-shən\ *n* **1** : the leafing out of a plant : the state of being in leaf **2** : the act of numbering the leaves of a book; *also* : the total count of leaves numbered **3** : a decoration resembling a leaf **4** : foliated texture

fo•lic acid \ˌfō-lik-\ *n* : a vitamin of the B complex used especially in the treatment of nutritional anemias [Latin *folium* "leaf"]

fo•lio \ˈfō-lē-ˌō\ *n, pl* **fo•li•os** **1** : a leaf of a manuscript or book **2 a** : a book made of sheets of paper each folded once to make two leaves or four pages **b** : a very large book [Latin, ablative of *folium* "leaf"]

fo•li•o•late \ˈfō-lē-ə-ˌlāt\ *adj* : having or made up of leaflets — usually used in combination [Late Latin *foliolum* "leaflet", from Latin *folium* "leaf"]

fo•li•ose \ˈfō-lē-ˌōs\ *adj* : suggesting a leaf or an arrangement of leaves ⟨*foliose* lichens⟩ — compare CRUSTOSE, FRUTICOSE

¹folk \ˈfōk\ *n, pl* **folk** *or* **folks** **1** : a group of people forming a tribe or nation; *also* : the largest number or most characteristic part of such a group **2** *pl* : people of a specified kind or class ⟨country *folk*⟩ ⟨old *folks*⟩ **3** *folks pl* : people generally **4** *folks pl* : the persons of one's own family ⟨visit your *folks*⟩ [Old English *folc*]

²folk *adj* : of, relating to, or originating among the common people ⟨*folk* dances⟩

folk etymology *n* : the transformation of words so as to give them an apparent relationship to other better-known or better-understood words (as the change of *chaise longue* to *chaise lounge*)

folk•lore \ˈfōk-ˌlōr, -ˌlȯr\ *n* : customs, beliefs, stories, and sayings of a people handed down from generation to generation — **folk•lor•ist** \-ˌlōr-əst, -ˌlȯr-\ *n*

folk medicine *n* : traditional medicine involving especially the empirical and nonprofessional use of vegetable remedies

folk song *n* : a song originated or traditional among the common people of a country or region — **folk•sing•er** \ˈfōk-ˌsing-ər\ *n*

folksy \ˈfōk-sē\ *adj* **folks•i•er**; **-est** **1** : SOCIABLE 1, FRIENDLY **2** : informal, casual, or familiar in manner or style — **folks•i•ly** \-sə-lē\ *adv* — **folks•i•ness** \-sē-nəs\ *n*

folk•tale \ˈfōk-ˌtāl\ *n* : an anonymous tale circulated orally among a people

folk•way \ˈfōk-ˌwā\ *n* : a way of thinking, feeling, or acting common to a people or to a social group

fol•li•cle \ˈfäl-i-kəl\ *n* **1 a** : a small anatomical cavity or deep narrow-mouthed depression (as from which a hair grows) **b** : GRAAFIAN FOLLICLE **2** : a dry one-celled fruit (as in the peony, larkspur, or milkweed) that splits open by only one seam [Latin *folliculus* "small bag", from *follis* "bellows, bag"] — **fol•lic•u•lar** \fə-ˈlik-yə-lər, fä-\ *adj*

follicle–stimulating hormone *n* : a hormone from the pituitary gland that stimulates the growth of ovarian follicles

¹fol•low \ˈfäl-ō\ *vb* **1** : to go or come after or behind **2** : to accept as authority : OBEY ⟨*follow* your conscience⟩ ⟨*follow* instructions⟩ **3** : to go after or on the track of ⟨*follow* that car⟩ **4** : to proceed along ⟨*follow* a path⟩ **5** : to engage in as a calling or a way of life ⟨*follow* the sea⟩ **6** : to come after in order of rank or natural sequence ⟨two *follows* one⟩ **7** : to result from something ⟨disaster *followed* the blunder⟩ **8** : to keep one's eyes or attention fixed on ⟨*follow* a lesson⟩ [Old English *folgian*]

• **syn** FOLLOW, SUCCEED, ENSUE mean to come after or later than something or someone. FOLLOW may apply to a coming after in time, position, or logical sequence ⟨continue the sentence on the *following* page⟩ ⟨the punishment that *follows* crime⟩ SUCCEED may add a stronger implication of displacing or replacing ⟨hoped to *succeed* the president in office⟩ ENSUE commonly suggests a logical consequence or naturally expected development ⟨after the talk a lively debate *ensued*⟩ **syn** see in addition CHASE

— **follow suit** **1** : to play a card of the same suit as the card led **2** : to follow an example set

²follow *n* : the act or process of following

fol•low•er \ˈfäl-ə-wər\ *n* **1** : one in the service of another : RETAINER **2** : one that follows the opinions or teachings of another **3** : one that imitates another

¹fol•low•ing \ˈfäl-ə-wing\ *adj* **1** : next after : SUCCEEDING ⟨the *following* day⟩ **2** : that immediately follows ⟨trains will leave at the *following* times⟩

²following *n* : a group of followers, adherents, or partisans

³following *prep* : subsequent to ⟨*following* the lecture tea was served⟩

follow out *vt* **1** : to follow to the end or to a conclusion **2** : to carry out : EXECUTE

fol•low–through \ˈfäl-ō-ˌthrü, ˌfäl-ō-ˈ, -ə-\ *n* **1** : the act or an instance of following through **2** : the part of a stroke or swing following the striking of an object

follow through *vi* **1** : to continue a stroke or swing to the end of its arc **2** : to press on in an activity to a conclusion ⟨*follow through* with a study⟩

fol•low–up \ˈfäl-ə-ˌwəp\ *n* **1** : the act or an instance of following up **2** : something that follows up — **follow–up** *adj*

follow up \ˌfäl-ə-ˈwəp\ *vt* : to follow with something similar, related, or additional ⟨*follow up* an idea with action⟩

fol•ly \ˈfäl-ē\ *n, pl* **follies** **1** : lack of good sense or normal prudence and foresight **2 a** : a foolish act or idea **b** : foolish actions or conduct **3** : an excessively costly or unprofitable undertaking [Old French *folie,* from *fol* "fool"]

Fol•som \ˈfōl-səm\ *adj* : of or relating to a prehistoric culture of North America on the east side of the Rocky mountains characterized especially by a leaf-shaped flint projectile point [*Folsom,* New Mexico]

fo•ment \fō-ˈment\ *vt* : to stir up : ROUSE, INSTIGATE ⟨*foment* rebellion⟩ [Late Latin *fomentare,* from Latin *fomentum* "fomentation", from *fovēre* "to warm, fondle, foment"] **syn** see INCITE — **fo•ment•er** \fō-'ment-ər\ *n*

fo•men•ta•tion \ˌfō-mən-'tā-shən, -ˌmen-\ *n* **1 :** a warm or hot moist material (as a hot damp cloth) applied to the body to ease pain **2 :** the act of fomenting **:** INSTIGATION

fond \'fänd\ *adj* **1 :** FOOLISH, SILLY ⟨*fond* pride⟩ **2 a :** prizing highly **:** DESIROUS ⟨*fond* of praise⟩ **b :** having an affection or liking ⟨*fond* of music⟩ **3 :** LOVING, AFFECTIONATE ⟨a *fond* family⟩ **4 :** doted on **:** DEAR ⟨their *fondest* hopes⟩ [Middle English, from *fonne* "fool"] — **fond•ly** *adv* — **fond•ness** \'fänd-nəs, 'fän-\ *n*

fon•dant \'fän-dənt\ *n* **1 :** a creamy preparation of sugar used as a basis for candies or icings **2 :** a candy consisting chiefly of fondant [French, from *fondre* "to melt"]

fon•dle \'fän-dl\ *vt* **fon•dled; fon•dling** \-dling, -dl-ing\ **:** to touch or handle in a tender or loving manner **:** CARESS [derived from *fond*] — **fon•dler** \-dlər, -dl-ər\ *n*

fon•due \fän-'dü, -'dyü\ *n* **1 :** a preparation of melted cheese flavored with wine or brandy **2 :** a dish consisting of small pieces of food (as meat) cooked in or dipped into a hot liquid [French, from *fondre* "to melt"]

[1]**font** \'fänt\ *n* **1 :** a basin for baptismal or holy water **2 :** SOURCE 2b (1), FOUNTAIN [Old English, from Latin *font-, fons* "fountain"]

[2]**font** *n* **:** an assortment of type all of one size and style [Middle French *fonte* "act of founding", derived from Latin *fundere* "to found, pour"]

fon•ta•nel *also* **fon•ta•nelle** \ˌfänt-n-'el\ *n* **:** a membrane-covered opening in bone or between bones; *esp* **:** one between the bones of a fetal or young skull [Middle English *fontinelle* "bodily hollow or pit", from Middle French *fontenele* "little spring", from *fontaine* "spring, fountain"]

food \'füd\ *n* **1 a :** material containing or consisting of carbohydrates, fats, proteins, and supplementary substances (as minerals) used in the body of an animal to sustain growth, repair, and vital processes and to furnish energy **b (1) :** inorganic substances absorbed by plants in gaseous form or in water solution **(2) :** organic material produced by green plants and used by them as building material and as a source of energy **2 :** nourishment in solid form **3 :** something that nourishes, sustains, or supplies [Old English *fōda*] — **food•less** \-ləs\ *adj* — **food•less•ness** *n*

food chain *n* **:** a sequence of the organisms of an ecological community in which each uses the next usually lower member of the sequence for food

food poisoning *n* **:** an acute digestive disorder caused by bacteria or their toxic products or by chemicals in food

food pyramid *n* **:** a system of ecological food relationships arranged by levels in which a chief predator is at the top, each level preys on the next lower level, and usually green plants are at the bottom

food stamp *n* **:** a government-issued coupon that can be used as currency to buy food

food•stuff \'füd-ˌstəf\ *n* **:** a substance with food value; *esp* **:** a specific nutrient (as protein or fat)

food vacuole *n* **:** a vacuole (as in an amoeba) in which ingested food is digested

food web *n* **:** the totality of interacting food chains in an ecological community

[1]**fool** \'fül\ *n* **1 :** a person who lacks sense or judgment **2 a :** a person formerly kept in a noble or royal household for casual entertainment — called also *jester* **b :** DUPE **3 :** a person lacking in common powers of understanding [Old French *fol,* derived from Latin *follis* "bellows, bag"]

[2]**fool** *vb* **1 a :** to spend time idly or aimlessly **b :** to meddle or tamper thoughtlessly or ignorantly ⟨don't *fool* with that gun⟩ **2 :** to speak or act in jest **:** JOKE ⟨I was only *fooling*⟩ **3 :** to make a fool of **:** DECEIVE **4 :** to spend on trifles or without advantage **:** FRITTER — used with *away*

fool•ery \'fül-rē, -ə-rē\ *n, pl* **-er•ies 1 :** foolish behavior **2 :** a foolish act, utterance, or belief

fool•har•dy \'fül-ˌhärd-ē\ *adj* **:** foolishly adventurous and bold **:** RASH **syn** see DARING — **fool•har•di•ly** \-ˌhärd-l-ē\ *adv* — **fool•har•di•ness** \-ˌhärd-ē-nəs\ *n*

fool•ish \'fü-lish\ *adj* **1 :** lacking in sense, judgment, or discretion **2 :** amusingly absurd ⟨a *foolish* little hat⟩ — **fool•ish•ly** *adv* — **fool•ish•ness** *n*

fool•proof \'fül-'prüf\ *adj* **:** so simple, plain, or reliable as to leave no opportunity for error, misuse, or failure

fool's gold *n* **1 :** PYRITE **2 :** CHALCOPYRITE

fool's paradise *n* **:** a state of delusory happiness

[1]**foot** \'fu̇t\ *n, pl* **feet** \'fēt\ *also* **foot 1 a :** the terminal part of the vertebrate leg upon which an individual stands **b :** an invertebrate organ of locomotion or attachment; *esp* **:** a ventral muscular part of a mollusk **2 :** any of various units of length based on the length of the human foot; *esp* **:** a unit equal to 1/3 yard and comprising 12 inches (.3048 meter) ⟨a 10-*foot* pole⟩ ⟨6 *feet* tall⟩ — see MEASURE table **3 :** the basic unit of verse meter consisting of a group of accented and unaccented syllables **4 :** something resembling an animal's foot in position or use or in being opposite to the head ⟨the *foot* of a mountain⟩ ⟨the *foot* of a bed⟩ **5 :** the lower edge (as of a sail) **6 foots** *pl* **:** material deposited especially on aging or refining **:** DREGS [Old English *fōt*] — **footlike** \'fu̇t-ˌlīk\ *adj* — **on foot 1 :** by walking **2 :** under way **:** in progress

[2]**foot** *vb* **1 :** DANCE 1 — often used with *it* **2 :** to go on foot **3 a :** to add up ⟨*foot* up an account⟩ **b :** to pay or provide for paying ⟨*foot* the bill⟩

foot•age \'fu̇t-ij\ *n* **:** length expressed in feet

foot-and-mouth disease *n* **:** an acute virus disease especially of cattle marked by fever and by ulcers in the mouth, about the hooves, and on the udder

foot•ball \'fu̇t-ˌbȯl\ *n* **1 :** any of several games that are played with an inflated ball on a rectangular field having two goalposts at each end by two teams whose object is to get the ball over a goal line or between goalposts by running, passing, or kicking: as **a** *British* **:** SOCCER **b** *British* **:** RUGBY **c :** an American game played between two teams of 11 players each in which the ball is advanced by running or passing **2 :** the ball used in football **3 :** something shifted rapidly from one party to another with no one wanting responsibility for it ⟨a political *football*⟩

foot•board \'fu̇t-ˌbōrd, -ˌbȯrd\ *n* **1 :** a narrow platform on which to stand or brace the feet **2 :** a board forming the foot of a bed

foot•bridge \-ˌbrij\ *n* **:** a bridge for pedestrians

foot-can•dle \'fu̇t-'kan-dl\ *n* **:** a unit for measuring illumination that equals the illumination on a surface all parts of which are one foot from a light having an intensity of one candle and that amounts to about 10.76 lux

foot•ed \'fu̇t-əd\ *adj* **:** having a foot or feet especially of a specified kind or number ⟨a *footed* stand⟩ ⟨a four-*footed* animal⟩

foot•fall \'fu̇t-ˌfȯl\ *n* **:** FOOTSTEP 1a; *also* **:** the sound of a footstep

foot•gear \-ˌgiər\ *n* **:** FOOTWEAR

foot•hill \-ˌhil\ *n* **:** a hill at the foot of higher hills or mountains

foot•hold \-ˌhōld\ *n* **1 :** a hold for the feet **:** FOOTING **2 :** a position usable as a base for further advance

foot•ing \'fu̇t-ing\ *n* **1 :** the placing of one's feet in a stable position **2 :** the act of moving on foot **3 a :** a place for standing **:** FOOTHOLD **b :** position with respect to one another **:** STATUS ⟨nations on a friendly *footing*⟩ **c :** BASIS ⟨put the enterprise on a firm *footing*⟩ **4 :** the sum of a column of figures

foot•lights \'fu̇t-ˌlīts\ *n pl* **1 :** a row of lights set across the front of a stage floor **2 :** the stage as a profession

foot•ling \-ling\ *adj* **1 :** INEPT ⟨*footling* amateurs⟩ **2 :** TRIVIAL 2 [*footle* "to trifle"]

foot•lock•er \-ˌläk-ər\ *n* **:** a small trunk designed to be placed at the foot of a bed (as in barracks)

foot•loose \-ˌlüs\ *adj* **:** having no ties **:** free to roam

foot•man \'fu̇t-mən\ *n* **:** a male servant who attends a carriage, waits on table, admits visitors, and runs errands

foot•mark \-ˌmärk\ *n* **:** FOOTPRINT

foot•note \-ˌnōt\ *n* **1 :** a note of reference, explanation, or comment often placed below the text on a printed page **2 :** something that is subordinately related to a larger event or work — **footnote** *vt*

foot•path \-ˌpath, -ˌpȧth\ *n* **:** a narrow path for pedestrians

foot-pound \-'pau̇nd\ *n, pl* **foot-pounds :** a unit of work that equals the work done by a force of one pound acting through a distance of one foot and that amounts to about 1.36 joule

foot-pound-second *adj* **:** being or relating to a system of units based upon the foot as the unit of length, the pound as the unit of weight or mass, and the second as the unit of time — abbreviation *fps*

foot•print \'fu̇t-,print\ *n* : an impression left by a foot

foot•race \-,rās\ *n* : a race run by humans on foot

foot•rest \-,rest\ *n* : a support for the feet

foot soldier *n* : INFANTRYMAN

foot•sore \'fu̇t-,sōr, -,sȯr\ *adj* : having sore or tender feet (as from much walking)

foot•step \-,step\ *n* **1 a** : a step of the foot **b** : distance covered by a step : PACE **2** : the mark of the foot : TRACK **3** : a step on which to ascend or descend **4** : a way of life, conduct, or action

foot•stone \-,stōn\ *n* : a stone placed at the foot of a grave

foot•stool \-,stül\ *n* : a low stool to support the feet

foot•way \-,wā\ *n* : a narrow way or path for pedestrians

foot•wear \-,waər, -,weər\ *n* : covering (as shoes) for the feet

foot•work \-,wərk\ *n* : the movement of the feet (as in boxing)

foo•zle \'fü-zəl\ *vt* **foo•zled**; **foo•zling** \'füz-ling, -ə-ling\ : to manage or play awkwardly : BUNGLE [perhaps from German dialect *fuseln* "to work carelessly"] — **foozle** *n*

fop \'fäp\ *n* : a man who is vain about his dress or appearance : DANDY [Middle English] — **fop•pish** \'fäp-ish\ *adj* — **fop•pish•ly** *adv* — **fop•pish•ness** *n*

fop•pery \'fäp-rē, -ə-re\ *n, pl* **-per•ies** **1** : foolish character or action : FOLLY **2** : the behavior or dress of a fop

[1]**for** \fər, fȯr, 'fȯr\ *prep* **1** — used as a function word to indicate purpose ⟨money *for* studying⟩, intended destination ⟨left *for* home⟩, or an object of one's desire ⟨now *for* a good rest⟩ **2** : as being ⟨do you take me *for* a fool⟩ **3** : because of ⟨cried *for* joy⟩ **4 a** : in support of ⟨fighting *for* their country⟩ **b** — used as a function word to indicate appropriateness or belonging ⟨medicine *for* a cold⟩ **c** : so as to bring about a certain state ⟨shouted the news *for* all to hear⟩ **5 a** : in place of ⟨Doe batting *for* Roe⟩ **b** : as the equal or equivalent of ⟨paid $10 *for* a hat⟩ **6** : in spite of ⟨unconvinced *for* all the clever arguments⟩ **7** : CONCERNING ⟨a stickler *for* detail⟩ **8** — used as a function word to indicate equality or proportion ⟨point *for* point⟩ ⟨tall *for* their age⟩ **9** — used as a function word to indicate duration of time or extent of space ⟨waited *for* several hours⟩ **10** : [2]AFTER 3b ⟨named *for* my grandfather⟩ [Old English]

[2]**for** *conj* : for this reason : on this ground

for- *prefix* **1** : so as to involve prohibition, exclusion, omission, failure, neglect, or refusal ⟨*for*bid⟩ **2** : destructively or detrimentally ⟨*for*do⟩ **3** : completely : excessively : to exhaustion : to pieces ⟨*for*lorn⟩ [Old English]

fora *pl of* FORUM

[1]**for•age** \'fȯr-ij, 'fär-\ *n* **1** : food for animals especially when taken by browsing or grazing **2** : the act of foraging : search for provisions [Middle French, from *forre* "fodder", of Germanic origin]

[2]**forage** *vb* **1** : to collect forage from **2** : to seek forage or provisions ⟨*forage* through the refrigerator⟩ **3** : to get by foraging ⟨*forage* a chicken⟩ — **for•ag•er** *n*

fo•ram \'fōr-əm, 'fȯr-\ *n* : FORAMINIFER

fo•ra•men \fə-'rā-mən\ *n, pl* **-ram•i•na** \-'ram-ə-nə\ *or* **-ra•mens** \-'rā-mənz\ : a small opening, perforation, or orifice [Latin *foramin-, foramen,* from *forare* "to bore"]

fo•ra•men mag•num \fə-,rā-mən-'mag-nəm\ *n* : the opening in the skull through which the spinal cord joins the brain [New Latin, literally, "great opening"]

foramen ova•le \-ō-'val-ē, -'väl-, -'vāl-\ *n* : a small opening between the two atria of the heart that is normally present only in the fetus [New Latin, literally, "oval opening"]

for•a•min•i•fer \,fȯr-ə-'min-ə-fər, ,fär-\ *n* : any of an order (Foraminifera) of large chiefly marine amoeboid protozoans usually having perforated shells containing calcium that are important sources of chalk and limestone — **fo•ra•mi•nif•er•al** \fə-,ram-ə-'nif-rəl, -ə-rəl; ,fȯr-ə-mə-'nif-, ,fär-\ *adj* — **fo•ra•mi•nif•er•an** \-rən\ *adj or n*

for•as•much as \'fȯr-əz-,məch-əz\ *conj* : in view of the fact that : SINCE

for•ay \'fȯr-,ā\ *vb* : to raid especially in search of plunder : PILLAGE [Middle French *forrer,* from *forre* "fodder"] — **foray** *n*

forb \'fȯrb\ *n* : an herb other than a grass [Greek *phorbe* "fodder, food", from *pherbein* "to graze"]

[1]**for•bear** \fȯr-baər, fər-, -'beər\ *vb* **-bore** \-bōr, -'bȯr\; **-borne** \-bōrn, -'bȯrn\; **-bear•ing** **1** : to refrain or desist from : ABSTAIN **2** : to control oneself when provoked : be patient [Old English *forberan* "to endure, do without", from *for-* + *beran* "to bear"] **syn** see REFRAIN — **for•bear•er** *n*

[2]**forbear** *variant of* FOREBEAR

for•bear•ance \'fȯr-'bar-əns, fər-, -'ber-\ *n* **1** : the act of forbearing **2** : the quality of being forbearing : PATIENCE

for•bid \fər-'bid, fȯr-\ *vt* **-bade** \-'bad, -'bād\ *or* **-bad** \-'bad\; **-bid•den** \-'bid-n\; **-bid•ding** **1** : to order not to do something or not to be done or used : PROHIBIT ⟨they *forbade* us to leave⟩ ⟨loitering is *forbidden*⟩ **2** : to hinder or prevent as if by command ⟨space *forbids* quoting in full⟩ [Old English *forbēodan,* from *for-* + *bēodan* "to bid"] — **for•bid•der** *n*

• **syn** PROHIBIT, INHIBIT, BAN: FORBID implies absolute proscription with expectation of obedience; PROHIBIT implies more generality and suggests the effect of statutes or ordinances; INHIBIT implies hampering or restricting by authority or more often by circumstances or involuntary self-restraint; BAN adds the implication of condemnation or disapproval along with prohibition.

for•bid•ding *adj* : frightening away : REPELLENT ⟨a stern *forbidding* manner⟩ — **for•bid•ding•ly** \-ing-lē\ *adv* — **for•bid•ding•ness** *n*

forbode *variant of* FOREBODE

[1]**force** \'fōrs, 'fȯrs\ *n* **1 a** : strength or energy exerted : active power ⟨*forces* of nature⟩ **b** : moral or mental strength **c** (1) : capacity to persuade or convince ⟨the *force* of this argument⟩ (2) : legal effectiveness ⟨that law is still in *force*⟩ **2 a** : military strength **b** (1) : a body (as of troops or ships) assigned to a military purpose (2) *pl* : ARMED FORCES **c** : a body of persons available for a particular end ⟨the labor *force*⟩ **3** : violence, compulsion, or constraint exerted on or against a person or thing **4** : an influence (as a push or pull) that if applied to a material free body results chiefly in an acceleration of the body and sometimes in other effects (as deformation) [Middle French, derived from Latin *fortis* "strong"] **syn** see POWER — **force•less** \-ləs\ *adj*

[2]**force** *vt* **1** : to compel by force : COERCE ⟨*forced* them to quit⟩ **2** : to make or cause through natural or logical necessity ⟨*forced* to admit I am wrong⟩ **3** : to attain to or effect against resistance ⟨*force* a bill through the legislature⟩ **4 a** : to gain by struggle or violence ⟨*force* one's way in⟩ **b** : to break open or through ⟨*force* a lock⟩ **5 a** : to raise or accelerate to the utmost ⟨*forcing* the pace⟩ **b** : to produce with unnatural effort ⟨*forced* a laugh⟩ **6 a** : to hasten the rate of progress or growth of **b** : to bring (as plants) to maturity out of the normal season ⟨*forcing* lilies for the Easter trade⟩ — **forc•er** *n*

• **syn** COMPEL, COERCE, CONSTRAIN: FORCE implies the use of physical power to overcome resistance of persons or things ⟨*forced* them to submit⟩ ⟨*forced* the door with a crowbar⟩ COMPEL and COERCE take only personal objects, COMPEL implying the working of an irresistible force ⟨hunger *compelled* them to surrender⟩ and COERCE suggesting the use of threatened violence or other injury; CONSTRAIN suggests the effect of a force or circumstance that limits action or choice ⟨*constrained* by hunger to yield⟩

forced \'fōrst, 'fȯrst\ *adj* **1** : compelled by force : INVOLUNTARY ⟨a *forced* landing⟩ **2** : done or produced with effort, exertion, or pressure ⟨*forced* laughter⟩ — **forc•ed•ly** \'fōr-səd-lē, 'fȯr-\ *adv*

force•ful \'fōrs-fəl, 'fȯrs-\ *adj* : possessing much force : VIGOROUS — **force•ful•ly** \-fə-lē\ *adv* — **force•ful•ness** *n*

force•meat \'fōrs-,mēt, 'fȯrs-\ *n* : chopped and seasoned meat or fish served alone or used as a stuffing [*force* (alteration of *farce* "stuffing") + *meat*]

for•ceps \'fȯr-səps\ *n, pl* **forceps** : an instrument for grasping, holding, or moving objects especially for delicate operations (as by jewelers or surgeons) [Latin, from *formus* "warm" + *capere* "to take"] — **for•ceps•like** \-,līk\ *adj*

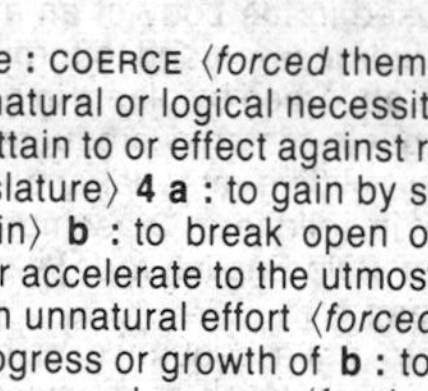

forceps

forc•ible \'fōr-sə-bəl, 'fȯr-\ *adj* **1** : got, made, or done by force or violence ⟨a *forcible* entrance⟩ **2** : showing force or energy — **forc•ibly** \-blē\ *adv*

[1]**ford** \'fōrd, 'fȯrd\ *n* : a shallow part of a body of water that may be crossed by wading [Old English]
[2]**ford** *vt* : to cross (a body of water) by wading — **ford•able** \-ə-bəl\ *adj*
for•do *or* **fore•do** \fȯr-'dü, fōr-\ *vt* **-did** \-did\; **-done** \-'dən\; **-do•ing** : to overcome with fatigue : EXHAUST [Old English *fordōn* "to destroy", from *for-* + *dōn* "to do"]
[1]**fore** \'fōr, 'fȯr\ *adv* : in, toward, or adjacent to the front : FORWARD ⟨the shell hit *fore* of the mast⟩ [Old English]
[2]**fore** *adj* : being or coming before in time, order, or space
[3]**fore** *n* : something that occupies a front position — **to the fore** : in or into a prominent position
[4]**fore** *interj* — used by a golfer to warn anyone within range of the probable line of flight of the ball [probably short for *before*]
fore- *combining form* **1** : earlier : beforehand ⟨*fore*named⟩ ⟨*fore*see⟩ **2 a** : situated at the front : in front ⟨*fore*leg⟩ **b** : front part of (something specified) ⟨*fore*brain⟩ [Old English, from *fore,* adv.]
fore–and–aft \,fōr-ə-'naft, ,fȯr-\ *adj* **1** : lying, running, or acting in the general line of the length of a construction (as a ship) ⟨*fore-and-aft* sails⟩ **2** : having no square sails
fore and aft *adv* : lengthwise of a ship : from stem to stern
fore–and–aft•er \-'naf-tər\ *n* : a ship with a fore-and-aft rig; *esp* : SCHOONER
fore–and–aft rig *n* : a sailing-ship rig in which most or all of the sails are not attached to yards but are bent to gaffs or set on the masts or on stays in a fore-and-aft line — **fore–and–aft rigged** *adj*
[1]**fore•arm** \fōr-'ärm, 'fōr-, 'fȯr-\ *vt* : to arm in advance : PREPARE
[2]**fore•arm** \'fōr-,ärm, 'fȯr-\ *n* : the part of the arm between the elbow and the wrist
fore•bear *or* **for•bear** \'fōr-,baer, 'fȯr-, -,beər\ *n* : ANCESTOR 1, FOREFATHER [Middle English *forebear,* from *fore-* + *-bear* "one that is", from *been* "to be"]
fore•bode *also* **for•bode** \fōr-'bōd, fȯr-\ *vb* **1** : FORETELL, PORTEND ⟨such heavy air *forebodes* a storm⟩ **2** : to have a premonition of (as misfortune) — **fore•bod•er** *n*
[1]**fore•bod•ing** *n* : an omen, prediction, or presentiment especially of coming evil : PORTENT
[2]**foreboding** *adj* : indicative of or marked by foreboding — **fore•bod•ing•ly** \-ing-lē\ *adv* — **fore•bod•ing•ness** *n*
fore•brain \'fōr-,brān, 'fȯr-\ *n* : the front division of the embryonic vertebrate brain or the parts (as the cerebrum and olfactory lobes) developed from it
[1]**fore•cast** \'fōr-,kast, 'fȯr-\ *vb* **forecast** *or* **fore•cast•ed**; **fore•cast•ing** **1** : to calculate or predict (a future event or condition) usually as a result of study and analysis of data; *esp* : to predict (weather conditions) on the basis of meterological observations **2** : to indicate as likely to occur ⟨*forecast* an easy victory at the polls⟩ **syn** see FORETELL — **fore•cast•er** *n*
[2]**forecast** *n* : a prophecy, estimate, or prediction of a future happening or condition ⟨weather *forecasts*⟩
fore•cas•tle \'fōk-səl; 'fōr-,kas-əl, 'fȯr-\ *or* **fo'•c'sle** \'fōk-səl\ *n* **1** : the part of the upper deck of a ship forward of the foremast **2** : the part of a merchantman where the crew is housed
fore•close \fōr-'klōz, fȯr-\ *vb* **1** : to rule out ⟨didn't *foreclose* the possibility of a second term⟩ **2** : to take legal measures to end a mortgage and take possession of the mortgaged property because the conditions of the mortgage have not been met by the mortgagor [Old French *forclore,* from *fors* "outside" + *clore* "to close"]
fore•clo•sure \-'klō-zhər\ *n* : the act of foreclosing; *esp* : the legal procedure of foreclosing a mortgage
fore•deck \'fōr-,dek, 'fȯr-\ *n* : the forepart of a ship's main deck
foredo *variant of* FORDO
fore•doom \fōr-'düm, fȯr-\ *vt* : to doom beforehand ⟨efforts *foredoomed* to failure⟩
fore•fa•ther \'fōr-,fäth-ər, 'fȯr-, -,fäth-\ *n* **1** : ANCESTOR 1 **2** : a person of an earlier period and common heritage
fore•fin•ger \'fōr-,fing-gər, 'fȯr-\ *n* : the finger next to the thumb
fore•foot \-,fu̇t\ *n* **1** : one of the front feet of a four-footed animal **2** : the forward part of a ship where the stem and keel meet
fore•front \-,frənt\ *n* : the foremost part or place : the place of greatest activity or interest ⟨an event in the *forefront* of the news⟩
foregather *variant of* FORGATHER
[1]**fore•go** \fōr-'gō, fȯr-\ *vb* **-went** \-'went\; **-gone** \-'gȯn, -'gän\; **-go•ing** \-'gō-ing\ : to go before : PRECEDE — **fore•go•er** \-'gō-ər, -'gōr\ *n*
[2]**forego** *variant of* FORGO
fore•go•ing \fōr-'gō-ing, fȯr-\ *adj* : going before; *esp* : said, written, or listed before or above **syn** see PRECEDING
fore•gone \,fōr-,gȯn, ,fȯr-, -,gän\ *adj* : determined or settled in advance ⟨success was a *foregone* conclusion⟩
fore•ground \'fōr-,grau̇nd, 'fȯr-\ *n* **1** : the part of a scene or representation that is nearest to and in front of the spectator **2** : a position of prominence : FOREFRONT
fore•gut \-,gət\ *n* : the part of the alimentary canal of a vertebrate embryo that develops into the pharynx, esophagus, stomach, and first part of the intestine
[1]**fore•hand** \'fōr-,hand, 'fȯr-\ *n* : a stroke made with the palm of the hand turned in the direction of movement
[2]**forehand** *adv* : with a forehand
[3]**forehand** *adj* : using or made with a forehand
fore•hand•ed \'fōr-'han-dəd, 'fȯr-\ *adj* **1** : mindful of the future : THRIFTY, PRUDENT **2** : FOREHAND — **fore•hand•ed•ly** *adv* — **fore•hand•ed•ness** *n*
fore•head \'fȯr-əd, 'fär-; 'fōr-,hed, 'fȯr-\ *n* **1** : the part of the face above the eyes **2** : the front or forepart of something
for•eign \'fȯr-ən, 'fär-\ *adj* **1** : situated outside a place or country; *esp* : situated outside one's own country ⟨*foreign* nations⟩ **2** : born in, belonging to, or characteristic of some place or country other than the one under consideration ⟨a *foreign* language⟩ **3** : alien in character : not connected or pertinent ⟨material *foreign* to the topic under discussion⟩ **4** : related to or dealing with other nations ⟨*foreign* affairs⟩ **5** : occurring in an abnormal situation in the living body and commonly introduced from outside ⟨a *foreign* body in the eye⟩ [Old French *forein,* from Late Latin *foranus* "being outside", from Latin *foris* "outside"] — **for•eign•ness** \-ən-nəs\ *n*
for•eign•er \'fȯr-ə-nər, 'fär-\ *n* : a person belonging to or owing allegiance to a foreign country : ALIEN
foreign exchange *n* **1** : a process of settling accounts or debts between persons living in different countries **2** : foreign currency or current short-term credit instruments payable in such currency
for•eign•ism \'fȯr-ə-,niz-əm, 'fär-\ *n* : something peculiar to a foreign language or people; *esp* : a foreign idiom or custom
foreign minister *n* : a governmental minister for foreign affairs
fore•know \fōr-'nō, fȯr-, 'fōr-, 'fȯr-\ *vt* **-knew** \-'nu, -'nyu\; **-known** \-'nōn\; **-know•ing** : to have previous knowledge of : know beforehand **syn** see FORESEE — **fore•knowl•edge** \-'näl-ij\ *n*
fore•la•dy \'fōr-,lād-ē, 'fȯr-\ *n* : a woman in charge of a group of workers
fore•land \-lənd\ *n* : PROMONTORY, HEADLAND
fore•leg \-,leg\ *n* : a front leg
fore•limb \-,lim\ *n* : an arm, fin, wing, or leg that is one of a front pair of limbs
fore•lock \-,läk\ *n* : a lock of hair growing from the front of the head
fore•man \'fōr-mən, 'fȯr-\ *n* **1** : a member of a jury who acts as chairperson and spokesperson **2** : a person in charge of a group of workers
fore•mast \-,mast, -məst\ *n* : the mast nearest the bow of a ship
[1]**fore•most** \'fōr-,mōst, 'fȯr-\ *adj* : first in time, place, or order; *also* : most important [Old English *formest,* superlative of *forma* "first"]
[2]**foremost** *adv* : in the first place
fore•name \-,nām\ *n* : a first name
fore•named \-,nāmd\ *adj* : previously named : AFORESAID
fore•noon \'fōr-,nün, 'fȯr-\ *n* : the early part of the day ending with noon : MORNING
[1]**fo•ren•sic** \fə-'ren-sik, -'ren-zik\ *adj* : belonging to, used in, or suitable to courts of law or to public discussion and debate [Latin *forensis,* from *forum* "forum"] — **fo•ren•si•cal•ly** \-si-kə-lē, -zi-, -klē\ *adv*

\ə\ **abut**	\au̇\ **out**	\i\ **tip**	\ȯ\ **saw**	\u̇\ **foot**
\ər\ **further**	\ch\ **chin**	\ī\ **life**	\ȯi\ **coin**	\y\ **yet**
\a\ **mat**	\e\ **pet**	\j\ **job**	\th\ **thin**	\yü\ **few**
\ā\ **take**	\ē\ **easy**	\ng\ **sing**	\th\ **this**	\yu̇\ **cure**
\ä\ **cot, cart**	\g\ **go**	\ō\ **bone**	\ü\ **food**	\zh\ **vision**

[2]forensic *n* **1 :** an argumentative exercise **2** *pl* **:** the art or study of argumentative discourse
fore•or•dain \ˌfōr-ȯr-ˈdān, ˌfȯr-\ *vt* **:** to ordain or decree in advance **:** PREDESTINE ⟨a *foreordained* course of events⟩ — **fore•or•di•na•tion** \-ˌȯrd-n-ˈā-shən\ *n*
fore•part \ˈfōr-ˌpärt, ˈfȯr-\ *n* **:** the part most advanced or first in place or in time ⟨the *forepart* of the day⟩
fore•paw \-ˌpȯ\ *n* **:** the paw of a foreleg
fore•quar•ter \-ˌkwȯrt-ər, -ˌkwȯt-\ *n* **:** the left or right half of the front half of the body or carcass of a four-footed animal ⟨a *forequarter* of beef⟩
fore•reach \fōr-ˈrēch, fȯr-\ *vb* **1 :** to gain ground in tacking **2 :** to gain on or overhaul and go ahead of (a ship) when close-hauled
fore•run•ner \ˈfōr-ˌrən-ər, ˈfȯr-\ *n* **1 :** one that precedes and indicates the approach of another ⟨the dark clouds were *forerunners* of a storm⟩ **2 :** one that precedes another (as in office or an activity) ⟨*forerunners* of the modern cartoon⟩
fore•sail \ˈfōr-ˌsāl, ˈfȯr-, -səl\ *n* **1 :** the lowest sail on the foremast of a square-rigged ship **2 :** the lower sail set on the foremast of a schooner

1 foresail 1

fore•see \fōr-ˈsē, fȯr-\ *vt* **-saw** \-ˈsȯ\; **-seen** \-ˈsēn\; **-see•ing :** to see or realize (as a development) beforehand **:** EXPECT — **fore•see•able** \-ə-bəl\ *adj* — **fore•se•er** \-ˈsē-ər\ *n*
• **syn** FORESEE, FOREKNOW, ANTICIPATE mean to know beforehand. FORESEE may apply to ordinary reasoning and of itself implies nothing concerning either action or feeling; FOREKNOW usually implies the involvement of supernatural forces; ANTICIPATE implies responding emotionally to or taking action about something before it happens.
fore•shad•ow \-ˈshad-ō\ *vt* **:** to give a hint of beforehand ⟨trends that *foreshadow* future trouble⟩ — **fore•shad•ow•er** *n*
fore•sheet \-ˌshēt\ *n* **1 :** one of the sheets of a foresail **2** *pl* **:** the forward part of an open boat
fore•shore \-ˌshōr, -ˌshȯr\ *n* **:** the part of a seashore between high-water and low-water marks
fore•short•en \fōr-ˈshȯrt-n, fȯr-\ *vt* **:** to shorten (a detail) in a drawing or painting so that the composition appears to have depth
fore•show \-ˈshō\ *vt* **:** FORETELL, FORESHADOW
fore•side \ˈfōr-ˌsīd, ˈfōr-\ *n* **:** the front side or part **:** FRONT
fore•sight \ˈfōr-ˌsīt, ˈfȯr-\ *n* **1 :** the act or power of foreseeing **:** knowledge of something before it happens **2 :** the act of looking forward; *also* **:** a view forward **3 :** care or provision for the future **:** PRUDENCE — **fore•sight•ed** \-ˌsīt-əd\ *adj* — **fore•sight•ed•ly** *adv* — **fore•sight•ed•ness** *n*
fore•skin \-ˌskin\ *n* **:** a fold of skin that covers the end of the penis — called also *prepuce*
for•est \ˈfȯr-əst, ˈfär-\ *n* **1 :** a dense growth of trees and underbrush covering a large tract; *also* **:** an area covered by forest **2 :** something resembling a forest especially in profusion ⟨a *forest* of masts⟩ **[**Old French, "forest, hunting preserve", from Medieval Latin *forestis,* from Latin *foris* "outside"**]** — **for•est•ed** \ˈfȯr-ə-stəd, ˈfär-\ *adj*
fore•stage \ˈfōr-ˌstāj, ˈfȯr-\ *n* **:** APRON 2
fore•stall \fōr-ˈstȯl, fȯr-\ *vt* **:** to keep out, hinder, or prevent by measures taken in advance ⟨*forestall* unnecessary questions by giving careful directions⟩ **syn** see PREVENT — **fore•stall•er** *n* — **fore•stall•ment** \-ˈstȯl-mənt\ *n*
for•es•ta•tion \ˌfȯr-ə-ˈstā-shən, ˌfär-\ *n* **:** the planting and care of a forest
fore•stay \ˈfōr-ˌstā, ˈfȯr-\ *n* **:** a stay from the top of a ship's foremast to the deck
for•est•er \ˈfȯr-ə-stər, ˈfär-\ *n* **:** a person who practices or is trained in forestry
forest floor *n* **:** the upper layer of mixed soil and organic debris typical of forested land
forest green *n* **:** a dark yellowish or moderate olive green
forest ranger *n* **:** an officer in charge of forest protection (as by preventing, detecting, and fighting fires) and management (as supervision of lumbering and recreation)
for•est•ry \ˈfȯr-ə-strē, ˈfär-\ *n* **:** scientific management of forests including development, care, and often economic harvesting
foreswear *variant of* FORSWEAR
[1]fore•taste \ˈfōr-ˌtāst, ˈfȯr-\ *n* **:** a preliminary or partial experience of something that will not be fully experienced until later ⟨through maneuvers a soldier gets a *foretaste* of war⟩
[2]fore•taste \fōr-ˈtāst, fȯr-ˈ, ˈfōr-ˌ, ˈfȯr-ˌ\ *vt* **:** to have a foretaste of
fore•tell \fōr-ˈtel, fȯr-\ *vt* **-told** \-ˈtōld\; **-tell•ing :** to tell of or describe beforehand — **fore•tell•er** *n*
• **syn** FORETELL, PREDICT, FORECAST, PROPHESY mean to tell beforehand. FORETELL often implies seeing the future through occult or unexplained powers ⟨a sorcerer *foretold* their evil end⟩ PREDICT implies often exact foretelling through scientific methods ⟨*predict* an eclipse⟩ FORECAST commonly deals in probabilities and eventualities rather than certainties ⟨*forecasting* the week's weather⟩ PROPHESY suggests the presence of inspired or mystic knowledge in predicting ⟨*prophesying* the end of the world⟩
fore•thought \ˈfōr-ˌthȯt, ˈfȯr-\ *n* **1 :** a thinking or planning out in advance **:** PREMEDITATION **2 :** thoughtful care for the future — **fore•thought•ful** \-fəl\ *adj* — **fore•thought•ful•ly** \-fə-lē\ *adv* — **fore•thought•ful•ness** *n*
[1]fore•to•ken \ˈfōr-ˌtō-kən, ˈfȯr-\ *n* **:** a premonitory sign
[2]fore•to•ken \fōr-ˈtō-kən, fȯr-\ *vt* **-to•kened**; **-to•ken•ing** \-ˈtōk-ning, -ə-ning\ **:** to indicate in advance ⟨the bright sunset *foretokened* good weather⟩
for•ev•er \fə-ˈrev-ər, fō-\ *adv* **1 :** for a limitless time **:** EVERLASTINGLY **2 :** at all times **:** CONSTANTLY ⟨a dog that was *forever* chasing cars⟩
for•ev•er•more \-ˌrev-ər-ˈmōr, -ˌrev-ə-ˈ, -ˈmȯr\ *adv* **:** FOREVER 1
fore•warn \fōr-ˈwȯrn, fȯr-\ *vt* **:** to warn in advance ⟨*forewarned* of danger⟩
fore wing *n* **:** either of the front wings of a 4-winged insect
fore•wom•an \ˈfōr-ˌwu̇m-ən, ˈfȯr-\ *n* **1 :** FORELADY **2 :** a woman member of a jury who acts as foreman
fore•word \ˈfōr-wərd, ˈfȯr-, -ˌwərd\ *n* **:** PREFACE 2
[1]for•feit \ˈfȯr-fət\ *n* **1 :** something lost by or taken away from a person because of an offense or error committed **:** PENALTY, FINE **2** *pl* **:** a game in which the players redeem personal articles by paying amusing or embarrassing penalties **[**Middle French *forfait,* from *forfaire* "to commit a crime, forfeit"**]**
[2]forfeit *vt* **:** to lose or lose the right to by some error, offense, or crime — **for•feit•er** *n*
[3]forfeit *adj* **:** forfeited or subject to forfeiture ⟨the spy's life was *forfeit*⟩
for•fei•ture \ˈfȯr-fə-ˌchu̇r, -chər\ *n* **1 :** the act of forfeiting **2 :** something forfeited **:** PENALTY
for•fend \fȯr-ˈfend\ *vt* **1 a** *archaic* **:** FORBID 1 **b :** to ward off **2 :** PRESERVE 1, PROTECT
for•gath•er *or* **fore•gath•er** \fȯr-ˈgath-ər, fōr-\ *vi* **1 :** to come together **:** ASSEMBLE **2 :** to meet someone usually by chance
[1]forge \ˈfōrj, ˈfȯrj\ *n* **1 :** a furnace or a shop with its furnace where metal is heated and worked **2 :** a workshop where wrought iron is produced or where iron is made malleable **[**Old French, from Latin *fabrica* "workshop", from *faber* "artisan, smith"**]**
[2]forge *vt* **1 a :** to form (as metal) by heating and hammering **b :** to form (metal) by a mechanical or hydraulic press **2 :** to form or shape in any way **:** FASHION ⟨*forge* ties of friendship⟩ **3 :** to make or imitate falsely especially with intent to defraud **:** COUNTERFEIT ⟨*forge* a check⟩
[3]forge *vi* **:** to move forward steadily but gradually ⟨*forge* ahead in the election⟩
forg•er \ˈfōr-jər, ˈfȯr-\ *n* **:** one that forges; *esp* **:** a person guilty of forgery
forg•ery \ˈfōrj-rē, ˈfȯrj-, -ə-rē\ *n, pl* **-er•ies 1 :** the crime of falsely making or changing a written paper or signing someone else's name **2 :** something (as a signature) that has been forged
for•get \fər-ˈget, fȯr-\ *vb* **-got** \-ˈgät\; **-got•ten** \-ˈgät-n\ *or* **-got**; **-get•ting 1 :** to be unable to think of or recall ⟨*forgot* the address⟩ **2 a :** to fail to recall at the proper time ⟨*forgot* about paying the bill⟩ **b :** NEGLECT ⟨*forget* old friends⟩ **[**Old English *forgietan***]** — **for•get•ter** *n* — **forget oneself :** to lose one's dignity, temper, or self-control

for•get•ful \-'get-fəl\ *adj* **1 :** having a poor memory **2 :** CARELESS, NEGLECTFUL ⟨*forgetful* of responsibilities⟩ — **for•get•ful•ly** \-'get-fə-lē\ *adv* — **for•get•ful•ness** *n*

for•get–me–not \fər-'get-mē-,nät, fȯr-\ *n* **:** any of a genus of small herbs with bright blue, pink, or white flowers usually in a curved spike

for•get•ta•ble \-'get-ə-bəl\ *adj* **:** likely to be forgotten

forg•ing \'fōr-jing, 'fȯr-\ *n* **:** a piece of forged work ⟨aluminum *forgings*⟩

for•give \fər-'giv, fȯr-\ *vb* **-gave** \-'gāv\; **-giv•en** \-'giv-ən\; **-giv•ing** **1 :** to cease to feel resentment against (an offender) **:** PARDON ⟨*forgive* your enemies⟩ **2 a :** to give up resentment of or claim to requital for ⟨*forgive* an insult⟩ **b :** to grant relief from payment of ⟨*forgive* a debt⟩ [Old English *forgifan,* from *for-* + *gifan* "to give"] **syn** see EXCUSE — **for•giv•able** \-'giv-ə-bəl\ *adj* — **for•giv•er** *n*

for•give•ness \-'giv-nəs\ *n* **:** the act of forgiving **:** PARDON

for•giv•ing \-'giv-ing\ *adj* **:** showing forgiveness **:** inclined or ready to forgive ⟨a person with a *forgiving* nature⟩ — **for•giv•ing•ly** \-ing-lē\ *adv* — **for•giv•ing•ness** *n*

for•go *or* **fore•go** \fȯr-'gō, fōr-\ *vt* **-went** \-'went\; **-gone** \-'gȯn, -'gän\; **-go•ing** \-'gō-ing\ **:** to give up **:** let pass **:** go without ⟨*forgo* lunch⟩ ⟨*forgo* an opportunity⟩ [Old English *forgān* "to pass by, forgo", from *for-* + *gān* "to go"]

¹fork \'fȯrk\ *n* **1 :** an implement with two or more prongs used especially for taking up (as in eating), pitching, or digging **2 :** a forked part, tool, or piece of equipment **3 a :** a dividing into branches or the place where something divides into branches ⟨a *fork* in the road⟩ **b :** a branch of a fork ⟨take the left *fork* at the crossroads⟩ [Old English *forca* and Old North French *forque,* both from Latin *furca*]

²fork *vb* **1 :** to divide into two or more branches ⟨the road *forks*⟩ **2 :** to give the form of a fork to ⟨*fork* one's fingers⟩ **3 :** to raise or pitch with a fork ⟨*fork* hay⟩ — **fork•er** *n*

forked \'fȯrkt, 'fȯr-kəd\ *adj* **:** having a fork **:** shaped like a fork ⟨*forked* lightning⟩

fork•ful \'fȯrk-,fu̇l\ *n, pl* **forkfuls** \'fȯrk-,fu̇lz\ *or* **forks•ful** \'fȯrks-,fu̇l\ **:** as much as a fork will hold

fork•lift \'fȯrk-,lift\ *n* **:** a machine for hoisting and transporting heavy objects by means of steel fingers inserted under the load

for•lorn \fər-'lȯrn\ *adj* **1 :** seeming sad and lonely especially because empty or abandoned **2 :** being or feeling deserted or neglected **:** WRETCHED **3 :** nearly hopeless ⟨a *forlorn* cause⟩ [Old English *forloren,* past participle of *forlēosan* "to lose, abandon", from *for-* + *lēosan* "to lose"] **syn** see SOLITARY — **for•lorn•ly** *adv* — **for•lorn•ness** \-'lȯrn-nəs\ *n*

forlorn hope *n* **1 :** a body of men selected to perform a perilous service **2 :** a desperate or extremely difficult enterprise [by folk etymology from Dutch *verloren hoop,* literally, "lost band"]

¹form \'fȯrm\ *n* **1 a :** the shape and structure of something as distinguished from its material **b :** a body (as of a person) especially in its external appearance or as distinguished from the face **2 :** the essential nature of a thing as distinguished from its matter **3 :** an established manner of doing or saying something ⟨the *forms* of worship⟩ **4 :** a printed or typed document with blank spaces for insertion of required information ⟨a tax *form*⟩ **5 a :** conduct regulated by custom or etiquette **:** CEREMONY, CONVENTION; *also* **:** show without substance ⟨outward *forms* of mourning⟩ **b :** manner of performing according to recognized standards ⟨such behavior is bad *form*⟩ **6 :** a long seat **:** BENCH **7 a :** a supporting frame model of the human figure used for displaying clothes **b :** a mold in which concrete is placed to set **8 :** printing type or matter arranged and secured ready for printing **9 :** one of the different manifestations of a particular thing or substance ⟨coal is a *form* of carbon⟩ **10 a :** orderly method of arrangement (as in the presentation of ideas or artistic elements); *also* **:** a particular kind or instance of such arrangement ⟨the sonnet is a poetical *form*⟩ **b :** the structural element, plan, or design of a work of art **c :** a visible and measurable unit defined by a contour **:** a bounded surface or volume **11 :** a grade in a British secondary school or in some American private schools **12 a :** known ability to perform **b :** condition suitable for performing (as in athletic competition) **13 a :** a meaningful unit of speech (as a morpheme, word, or sentence) **b :** any of the different pronunciations or spellings a word may take in inflection or compounding **14 :** a particular kind of mathematical expression ⟨the number 2.5 can be written in fractional *form* as $5/2$⟩ [Old French *forme,* from Latin *forma*]

• **syn** FIGURE, SHAPE: FORM may refer both to internal structure and external outline and often suggests the principle giving unity to the whole ⟨early *forms* of animal life⟩ FIGURE applies chiefly to the bounding or enclosing lines of a form ⟨cutting doll *figures* out of paper⟩ SHAPE may also suggest an outline, but carries a stronger implication of a three-dimensional body ⟨the *shape* of the monument was pyramidal⟩

²form *vb* **1 :** to give form or shape to **:** FASHION, MAKE ⟨*form* a letter of the alphabet⟩ **2 :** TRAIN, INSTRUCT ⟨education *forms* the mind⟩ **3 :** DEVELOP, ACQUIRE ⟨*form* a habit⟩ **4 :** to make up **:** CONSTITUTE ⟨bonds *formed* the bulk of the estate⟩ **5 :** to arrange in order ⟨*form* a battle line⟩ **6 :** to take form **:** ARISE ⟨fog *forms* in the valleys⟩ **7 :** to take a definite form, shape, or arrangement ⟨each column of soldiers marched away as soon as it *formed*⟩ — **form•er** *n*

-form \,fȯrm\ *adj combining form* **:** in the form or shape of **:** resembling ⟨reni*form*⟩ [Latin *-formis,* from *forma* "form"]

¹for•mal \'fȯr-məl\ *adj* **1 :** relating to, concerned with, or constituting the outward form of something as distinguished from its content ⟨the *formal* features of a thing can be misleading⟩ **2 a :** CONVENTIONAL 2 ⟨paying *formal* attention to his hostess⟩ ⟨a *formal* dinner⟩ **b :** done in due or lawful form ⟨a *formal* contract⟩ **3 :** characterized by punctilious respect for form ⟨very *formal* in all their dealings⟩ **4 :** NOMINAL 3a ⟨a purely *formal* requirement⟩ — **for•mal•ly** \-mə-lē\ *adv*

²formal *n* **:** something (as a social event) formal in character

form•al•de•hyde \fȯr-'mal-də-,hīd, fər-\ *n* **:** a colorless gas CH_2O that consists of carbon, hydrogen, and oxygen, has a sharp irritating odor, and is used as a disinfectant and preservative [*form*ic acid + *aldehyde*]

for•ma•lin \'fȯr-mə-lən, -,lēn\ *n* **:** a clear water solution of formaldehyde containing a small amount of methanol

for•mal•ism \'fȯr-mə-,liz-əm\ *n* **:** the strict observance of forms or conventions (as in religion or art) — **for•mal•ist** \-ləst\ *n* — **for•mal•is•tic** \,fȯr-mə-'lis-tik\ *adj* — **for•mal•is•ti•cal•ly** \-ti-kə-lē, -klē\ *adv*

for•mal•i•ty \fȯr-'mal-ət-ē\ *n, pl* **-ties** **1 :** the quality or state of being formal **2 :** compliance with formal or conventional rules **:** CEREMONY **3 :** an established form that is required or conventional

for•mal•ize \'fȯr-mə-,līz\ *vt* **1 :** to make formal **2 :** to give formal status or approval to — **for•mal•iz•er** *n*

for•mat \'fȯr-,mat\ *n* **1 :** the shape, size, and general makeup of a publication **2 :** the general plan of organization or arrangement of something [German, from Latin *formare* "to form", from *forma* "form"]

for•ma•tion \fȯr-'mā-shən\ *n* **1 :** a forming of something ⟨the *formation* of good habits during childhood⟩ **2 :** something that is formed ⟨new word *formations*⟩ **3 :** the manner in which a thing is formed **:** STRUCTURE, SHAPE ⟨an abnormal *formation* of the jaw⟩ **4 :** an arrangement or grouping of persons, ships, or airplanes ⟨battle *formation*⟩ ⟨planes flying in *formation*⟩ **5 :** a bed of rocks or series of beds recognizable as a unit — **for•ma•tion•al** \-shnəl, -shən-l\ *adj*

for•ma•tive \'fȯr-mət-iv\ *adj* **1 :** giving or capable of giving form **:** CONSTRUCTIVE ⟨a *formative* influence⟩ **2 :** of, relating to, or characterized by important growth or formation ⟨*formative* years⟩ — **for•ma•tive•ly** *adv* — **for•ma•tive•ness** *n*

form class *n* **:** a class of linguistic forms that can be used in the same position in a construction and that have one or more morphological or syntactical features in common

for•mer \'fȯr-mər\ *adj* **1 :** coming before in time; *esp* **:** of, relating to, or occurring in the past ⟨our *former* correspondence⟩ **2 :** preceding in place or arrangement **:** FOREGOING ⟨the *former* part of the chapter⟩ **3 :** first mentioned or in order of two things mentioned or understood ⟨of these two evils the *former* is the lesser⟩ [Middle English, from *forme* "first", from Old English *forma*]

for•mer•ly \-mər-lē, -mə-lē\ *adv* **:** at an earlier time **:** PREVIOUSLY

form•fit•ting \'fȯrm-,fit-ing\ *adj* **:** conforming to the outline of the body ⟨a *formfitting* sweater⟩

For•mi•ca \fȯr-'mī-kə, fər-\ *trademark* — used for any of various laminated plastic products used especially for surface finish

for•mic acid \ˌfȯr-mik-\ *n* : a colorless strong-smelling liquid acid CH_2O_2 that irritates the skin, is found in insects (as ants) and in many plants, and is used chiefly in dyeing and finishing textiles [Latin *formica* "ant"]

for•mi•cary \ˈfȯr-mə-ˌker-ē\ *n, pl* **-car•ies** : an ant nest

for•mi•da•ble \ˈfȯr-məd-ə-bəl, fȯr-ˈmid-\ *adj* **1** : arousing fear ⟨a *formidable* foe⟩ **2** : imposing serious difficulties or hardships ⟨the mountains were a *formidable* barrier⟩ **3** : tending to inspire awe or wonder ⟨the *formidable* accomplishments of science⟩ [Latin *formidabilis,* from *formidare* "to fear", from *formido* "fear"] — **for•mi•da•bil•i•ty** \ˌfȯr-məd-ə-ˈbil-ət-ē, fȯr-ˌmid-\ *n* — **for•mi•da•ble•ness** *n* — **for•mi•da•bly** \-blē\ *adv*

form•less \ˈfȯrm-ləs\ *adj* : having no regular form or shape — **form•less•ly** *adv* — **form•less•ness** *n*

for•mu•la \ˈfȯr-myə-lə\ *n, pl* **-las** *also* **-lae** \-ˌlē, -ˌlī\ **1** : a set form of words for use in a ceremony or ritual **2 a** : RECIPE, PRESCRIPTION ⟨our *formula* for happiness⟩ **b** : a milk mixture or substitute for a baby **3 a** : a symbolic expression of the composition or constitution of a substance ⟨the *formula* for water is H_2O⟩ **b** : a group of mathematical symbols used to express briefly a single concept **4** : a prescribed or set form or method [Latin, "small form", from *forma* "form"] — **for•mu•la•ic** \ˌfȯr-myə-ˈlā-ik\ *adj* — **for•mu•la•ical•ly** \-ˈlā-ə-kə-lē, -klē\ *adv*

for•mu•la•rize \ˈfȯr-myə-lə-ˌrīz\ *vt* : to state in or reduce to a formula : FORMULATE — **for•mu•la•riz•er** *n*

for•mu•lary \ˈfȯr-myə-ˌler-ē\ *n, pl* **-lar•ies** **1** : a book or collection of stated and prescribed forms **2** : a prescribed form or model : FORMULA **3** : a book containing a list of medicinal substances and formulas — **formulary** *adj*

for•mu•late \ˈfȯr-myə-ˌlāt\ *vt* **1** : to express in a formula **2** : to put in systematic form : state definitely and clearly ⟨*formulate* a plan⟩ — **for•mu•la•tion** \ˌfȯr-myə-ˈlā-shən\ *n* — **for•mu•la•tor** \ˈfȯr-myə-ˌlāt-ər\ *n*

for•ni•cate \ˈfȯr-nə-ˌkāt\ *vi* : to commit fornication [Late Latin *fornicare,* from Latin *fornix* "arch, vaulted basement, brothel"] — **for•ni•ca•tor** \-ˌkāt-ər\ *n*

for•ni•ca•tion \ˌfȯr-nə-ˈkā-shən\ *n* : human sexual intercourse other than between a husband and wife and especially between unmarried persons — used in some translations (as AV, DV) of the Bible (as in Matthew 5:32) for *unchastity* (as in RSV) or *immorality* (as in NCE) to cover all sexual intercourse except between husband and wife or concubine; compare ADULTERY

for•nix \ˈfȯr-niks\ *n, pl* **for•ni•ces** \-nə-ˌsēz\ : an anatomical arch or fold [Latin, "arch"]

for•sake \fər-ˈsāk, fȯr-\ *vt* **for•sook** \-ˈsu̇k\; **for•sak•en** \-ˈsā-kən\; **for•sak•ing** **1** : to give up : RENOUNCE **2** : to quit or leave entirely : withdraw from ⟨*forsook* the theater for other work⟩ ⟨*forsaken* by false friends⟩ [Old English *forsacan,* from *for-* + *sacan* "to dispute"] **syn** see ABANDON

for•sooth \fər-ˈsüth\ *adv* : in truth : INDEED

for•swear *or* **fore•swear** \fȯr-ˈswaər, fōr-, -ˈsweər\ *vb* **-swore** \-ˈswōr, -ˈswȯr\; **-sworn** \-ˈswōrn, -ˈswȯrn\; **-swear•ing** **1** : to swear falsely : commit perjury **2** : to pledge oneself to give up ⟨*forswear* gambling⟩

for•syth•ia \fər-ˈsith-ē-ə\ *n* : any of a genus of shrubs of the olive family widely grown for their yellow bell-shaped flowers appearing before the leaves in early spring [William *Forsyth,* died 1804, British botanist]

fort \ˈfōrt, ˈfȯrt\ *n* **1** : a strong or fortified place; *esp* : a place surrounded with defenses and occupied by soldiers **2** : a permanent army post [Middle French, from *fort* "strong", from Latin *fortis*]

[1]forte \ˈfōrt, ˈfȯrt, ˈfȯr-ˌtā\ *n* : something in which a person shows special ability : a strong point ⟨music was always your *forte*⟩ [Middle French *fort,* from *fort* "strong"]

[2]for•te \ˈfȯr-ˌtā, ˈfȯrt-ē\ *adv or adj* : LOUDLY, POWERFULLY — used as a direction in music [Italian, from *forte* "strong", from Latin *fortis*]

forth \ˈfōrth, ˈfȯrth\ *adv* **1** : FORWARD, ONWARD ⟨from that time *forth*⟩ ⟨and so *forth*⟩ ⟨back and *forth*⟩ **2** : out into view : OUT ⟨plants putting *forth* leaves⟩ [Old English]

[1]forth•com•ing \fōrth-ˈkəm-ing, fȯrth-\ *adj* **1** : being about to appear : APPROACHING ⟨the *forthcoming* holidays⟩ **2 a** : readily available ⟨the needed supplies were *forthcoming*⟩ **b** : RESPONSIVE 2

[2]forthcoming *n* : a coming forth : APPROACH

forth•right \ˈfōrth-ˌrīt, ˈfȯrth-\ *adj* : STRAIGHTFORWARD, DIRECT ⟨a *forthright* answer⟩ — **forth•right•ly** *adv* — **forth•right•ness** *n*

forth•with \fōrth-ˈwith, fȯrth-, -ˈwith\ *adv* : IMMEDIATELY ⟨expect an answer *forthwith*⟩

for•ti•fi•ca•tion \ˌfȯrt-ə-fə-ˈkā-shən\ *n* **1** : the act of fortifying **2 a** : a construction built for the defense of a place : FORT **b** *pl* : defensive works

for•ti•fy \ˈfȯrt-ə-ˌfī\ *vt* **-fied**; **-fy•ing** : to make strong: as **a** : to strengthen and secure by military defenses ⟨*fortify* a town⟩ **b** : to give physical strength, courage, or endurance to ⟨*fortify* the body against illness⟩ **c** : to add mental or moral strength to : ENCOURAGE **d** : to add material to for strengthening or improving : ENRICH ⟨*fortify* a soil with fertilizer⟩ [Middle French *fortifier,* from Late Latin *fortificare,* from Latin *fortis* "strong"] — **for•ti•fi•er** \-ˌfī-ər, -ˌfīr\ *n*

for•tis•si•mo \fȯr-ˈtis-ə-ˌmō\ *adv or adj* : very loudly — used as a direction in music [Italian, superlative of *forte* "strong"]

for•ti•tude \ˈfȯrt-ə-ˌtüd, -ˌtyüd\ *n* : strength of mind that enables a person to meet danger or bear pain or adversity with courage [Latin *fortitudo* "strength", from *fortis* "strong"]

fort•night \ˈfȯrt-ˌnīt, ˈfȯrt-\ *n* : the space of 14 days : two weeks [Middle English *fourtenight,* alteration of *fourtene night* "fourteen nights"]

[1]fort•night•ly \-lē\ *adj* : occurring or appearing once in a fortnight

[2]fortnightly *adv* : once in a fortnight

[3]fortnightly *n, pl* **-lies** : a publication issued fortnightly

FOR•TRAN \ˈfȯr-ˌtran\ *n* : an algebraic and logical language for programming a computer [*formula translation*]

for•tress \ˈfȯr-trəs\ *n* : a fortified place; *esp* : a large and permanent fortification sometimes including a town [Middle French *forteresce,* derived from Latin *fortis* "strong"]

for•tu•i•tous \fȯr-ˈtü-ət-əs, fər-, -ˈtyü-\ *adj* : occurring by chance [Latin *fortuitus*] **syn** see ACCIDENTAL — **for•tu•i•tous•ly** *adv* — **for•tu•i•tous•ness** *n*

for•tu•i•ty \-ət-ē\ *n, pl* **-ties** **1** : the quality or state of being fortuitous **2** : a chance event or occurrence

for•tu•nate \ˈfȯrch-nət, -ə-nət\ *adj* **1** : coming or happening by good luck : bringing a benefit or good that was not expected or was not forseen as certain **2** : receiving some unexpected good : LUCKY **syn** see LUCKY — **for•tu•nate•ly** *adv* — **for•tu•nate•ness** *n*

for•tune \ˈfȯr-chən\ *n* **1** : an apparent cause of something that happens to one suddenly and unexpectedly : CHANCE, LUCK **2** : what happens to a person : good or bad luck ⟨the *fortunes* of war⟩ ⟨have the good *fortune* to be elected class president⟩ **3** : a person's destiny or fate ⟨tell one's *fortune*⟩ **4 a** : possession of material goods : WEALTH ⟨people of *fortune*⟩ **b** : a store of material possessions : RICHES ⟨the family *fortune*⟩ [Middle French, from Latin *fortuna*]

fortune cookie *n* : a thin folded cookie containing a slip of paper on which is printed a fortune, proverb, or humorous statement

fortune hunter *n* : a person who seeks wealth especially by marriage

for•tune–tell•er \-ˌtel-ər\ *n* : a person who professes to foretell future events — **for•tune–tell•ing** \-ˌtel-ing\ *n or adj*

for•ty \ˈfȯrt-ē\ *n, pl* **forties** **1** : ten more than 30; *also* : a symbol representing this — see NUMBER table **2** : the 3d point scored by a side in a game of tennis [Old English *fēowertig*] — **for•ti•eth** \-ē-əth\ *adj or n* — **forty** *adj or pron*

for•ty–five \ˌfȯrt-ē-ˈfīv\ *n* **1** : a .45 caliber pistol — usually written .45 **2** : a phonograph record for play at 45 revolutions per minute

Forty Hours *n sing or pl* : a Roman Catholic devotion in which the churches of a diocese in two-day turns maintain continuous daytime prayer before the exposed Blessed Sacrament

for•ty–nin•er \ˌfȯrt-ē-ˈnī-nər\ *n* : a person in California in the gold rush of 1849

forty winks *n sing or pl* : a short sleep : NAP

fo•rum \ˈfōr-əm, ˈfȯr-\ *n, pl* **forums** *also* **fo•ra** \-ə\ **1 a** : the marketplace or public place of an ancient Roman city serving as the center of judicial and public business **b** : a medium of open discussion **2** : a judicial body or assembly : COURT **3 a** : a public meeting or lecture involving audience discussion **b** : a program (as on radio or television) involving discussion of a problem usually by several authorities [Latin]

[1]for•ward \ˈfȯr-wərd\ *adj* **1** : near, being at, or belonging to the front **2 a** : strongly inclined : READY **b** : tending to push oneself : BRASH **3** : notably advanced or developed **4** : moving, tend-

ing, or leading toward a position in front ⟨*forward* movement⟩ **5** : of, relating to, or getting ready for the future ⟨*forward* buying of produce⟩ [Old English *foreweard,* from *fore-* + *-weard* "-ward"] — **for·ward·ly** *adv* — **for·ward·ness** *n*
²forward *adv* : to or toward what is before or in front
³forward *n* : a mainly offensive player in a game (as basketball or soccer) who is stationed near the goal that the opposing team is defending
⁴forward *vt* **1** : to help onward : ADVANCE ⟨*forward* a friend's career⟩ **2 a** : to send forward **b** : to send or ship onward from an intermediate post or station in transit
for·ward·er \'fȯr-wərd-ər\ *n* : one that forwards; *esp* : an agent who forwards goods ⟨a freight *forwarder*⟩
for·ward·ing \-wərd-ing\ *n* : the act of one that forwards; *esp* : the business of a forwarder of goods
forward pass *n* : a pass in football thrown in the direction of the opponents' goal
for·wards \'fȯr-wərdz\ *adv* : FORWARD
fos·sa \'fäs-ə\ *n, pl* **fos·sae** \'fäs-ˌē, -ˌī\ : an anatomical pit or depression [Latin, "ditch"]
fosse *or* **foss** \'fäs\ *n* : DITCH, MOAT [Old French *fosse,* from Latin *fossa,* from *fodere* "to dig"]
¹fos·sil \'fäs-əl\ *n* **1** : a trace or impression or the remains of a plant or animal of a past age preserved in the earth's crust **2 a** : a person whose ideas are out-of-date **b** : something that has become rigidly fixed [Latin *fossilis* "dug up", from *fodere* "to dig"]
²fossil *adj* **1** : ultimately derived from living things of past geologic ages ⟨*fossil* fuels such as coal⟩ **2** : being or resembling a fossil ⟨*fossil* plants⟩
fos·sil·if·er·ous \ˌfäs-ə-'lif-rəs, -ə-rəs\ *adj* : containing fossils
fos·sil·ize \'fäs-ə-ˌlīz\ *vb* **1** : to convert or become converted into a fossil **2** : to make outmoded, rigid, or fixed — **fos·sil·iza·tion** \ˌfäs-ə-lə-'zā-shən\ *n*
fos·so·ri·al \fä-'sōr-ē-əl, -'sȯr-\ *adj* : adapted to or occupied in digging ⟨a *fossorial* foot⟩ ⟨*fossorial* animals⟩
¹fos·ter \'fȯs-tər, 'fäs-\ *adj* : affording, receiving, or sharing nurture or parental care though not related by blood or legal ties ⟨*foster* parent⟩ ⟨*foster* child⟩ [Old English *fōstor-,* from *fōstor* "food, feeding"]
²foster *vt* **fos·tered**; **fos·ter·ing** \-tə-ring, -tring\ **1** : to give parental care to : NURTURE **2** : to promote the growth or development of : ENCOURAGE ⟨*foster* the spread of higher education⟩ — **fos·ter·er** \-tər-ər\ *n*
fos·ter·age \'fȯs-tə-rij, 'fäs-\ *n* : the act of fostering
foster home *n* : a household in which an orphaned, neglected, or delinquent child or a mentally ill person is placed for care
fos·ter·ling \-tər-ling\ *n* : a foster child
fought *past of* FIGHT
¹foul \'fau̇l\ *adj* **1 a** : offensive to the senses ⟨a *foul* sewer⟩ **b** : clogged or covered with dirt **2** : morally or spiritually odious : DETESTABLE ⟨*foul* crimes⟩ **3** : OBSCENE, ABUSIVE ⟨*foul* language⟩ **4** : being wet and stormy ⟨*foul* weather⟩ **5 a** : grossly unfair : DISHONORABLE **b** : violating a rule in a game or sport ⟨a *foul* blow in boxing⟩ **6** : marked up or defaced by changes ⟨*foul* manuscript⟩ **7** : being outside the foul lines in baseball ⟨a *foul* grounder⟩ [Old English *fūl*] **syn** see DIRTY — **foul·ly** \'fau̇l-lē, fau̇-\ *adv*
²foul *n* **1** : an entanglement or collision especially in angling or sailing **2** : an infringement of the rules in a game or sport **3** : FOUL BALL
³foul *adv* : FOULLY
⁴foul *vb* **1** : to make or become foul or filthy ⟨*foul* the air⟩ ⟨*foul* a stream⟩ **2** : DISGRACE ⟨*foul* one's good name⟩ **3 a** : to commit a violation of the rules in a sport or game **b** : to hit a foul ball **4** : to entangle or become entangled ⟨*foul* a rope⟩ **5** : to collide with ⟨*foul* a launch in moving away from the dock⟩
fou·lard \fü-'lärd\ *n* **1** : a lightweight plain-woven or twilled silk usually decorated with a printed pattern **2** : an article of clothing (as a scarf) made of foulard [French]
foul ball *n* : a baseball hit into foul territory
foul line *n* **1** : either of two straight lines extending from the rear corner of home plate through the outer corners of first and third bases and continued to the boundary of a baseball field **2** : a line across a bowling alley that a player must not step over when delivering the ball **3** : either of 2 lines on a basketball court behind which a player stands to shoot a free throw
foul·mouthed \'fau̇l-'mau̇thd, -'mau̇tht\ *adj* : inclined to use dirty, profane, or abusive language
foul·ness \'fau̇l-nəs\ *n* **1** : the quality or state of being foul **2** : something that is foul
foul play *n* : unfair play or dealing : dishonest conduct; *esp* : VIOLENCE ⟨a victim of *foul play*⟩
foul shot *n* : a free throw in basketball
foul tip *n* : a pitched baseball that is slightly deflected by the bat
foul–up \'fau̇-ˌləp\ *n* **1** : a state of confusion caused by bungling, carelessness, or mismanagement **2** : a mechanical difficulty
foul up \fau̇-'ləp, 'fau̇-\ *vb* **1** : to make dirty **2** : to spoil by making mistakes or using poor judgment : CONFUSE **3** : to become confused : get into difficulty : BUNGLE
¹found \'fau̇nd\ *past of* FIND
²found *vt* **1** : to take the first steps in building ⟨*found* a colony⟩ **2** : to set or ground on something solid : BASE ⟨a house *founded* on rock⟩ **3** : to establish and often to provide for the future maintenance of ⟨*found* a college⟩ [Old French *fonder,* from Latin *fundare,* from *fundus* "bottom"]
³found *vt* : to melt (metal) and pour into a mold [Middle French *fondre* "to pour, melt", from Latin *fundere*]
foun·da·tion \fau̇n-'dā-shən\ *n* **1** : the act of founding **2** : the base or basis upon which something stands or is supported ⟨a house with a cinder-block *foundation*⟩ ⟨suspicions with no *foundation* in fact⟩ **3** : funds given for the permanent support of an institution : ENDOWMENT; *also* : an organization or institution so endowed — **foun·da·tion·al** \-shnəl, -shən-l\ *adj*
¹found·er \'fau̇n-dər\ *n* : one that founds or establishes something ⟨the *founders* of the town⟩
²foun·der \'fau̇n-dər\ *vb* **foun·dered**, **foun·der·ing** \-də-ring, -dring\ **1** : to go or cause to go lame ⟨the horse *foundered*⟩ **2** : to give way ⟨the building *foundered* in the fire⟩ **3** : to sink or cause to sink below the surface of the water ⟨a *foundering* ship⟩ **4** : to come or cause to come to grief : FAIL ⟨their efforts all *foundered*⟩ [Middle French *fondrer* "to send to the bottom, collapse", derived from Latin *fundus* "bottom"]
³found·er *n* : one that founds metal
found·ling \'fau̇n-dling\ *n* : an infant found after its unknown parents have abandoned it
foundry \'fau̇n-drē\ *n, pl* **foundries** **1** : the act, process, or art of casting metals; *also* : CASTINGS **2** : an establishment where founding is carried on
fount \'fau̇nt\ *n* : FOUNTAIN, SOURCE ⟨a *fount* of information⟩
foun·tain \'fau̇nt-n\ *n* **1** : a spring of water issuing from the earth **2** : SOURCE 2b **3** : an artificially produced jet of water; *also* : the structure from which it rises **4** : a reservoir containing a liquid that can be drawn off as needed [Middle French *fontaine,* from Late Latin *fontana,* derived from Latin *font-, fons*]
foun·tain·head \-ˌhed\ *n* **1** : a fountain or spring that is the source of a stream **2** : a primary source : ORIGIN ⟨a *fountainhead* of wisdom⟩
fountain pen *n* : a pen with a reservoir that automatically feeds the writing point with ink
four \'fōr, 'fȯr\ *n* **1** : one more than three; *also* : a symbol representing this — see NUMBER table **2** : the 4th in a set or series **3** : something having four units or members [Old English *fēower*] — **four** *adj or pron*
four–dimensional *adj* : relating to or having four dimensions; *esp* : consisting of or relating to mathematical elements requiring four coordinates to determine them
four–flush \'fōr-ˌfləsh, 'fȯr-\ *vi* : to make a false claim : BLUFF [earlier *four-flush* "to bluff in poker holding four cards of the same suit in a five-card hand"] — **four–flush·er** *n*
four·fold \-ˌfōld, -'fōld\ *adj* **1** : having four units or members **2** : being four times as great or as many — **fourfold** *adv*
four–foot·ed \-'fu̇t-əd\ *adj* : having four feet : QUADRUPED
4–H \-'āch\ *adj* : of or relating to a program set up by the United States Department of Agriculture to help young people become productive citizens by instructing them in useful skills, community service, and personal development ⟨*4-H* club⟩ [from the fourfold aim of improving the head, heart, hands, and health] — **4–H'er** \-'ā-chər\ *n*

four-hand \'fōr-ˌhand, 'fȯr-\ *adj* : FOUR-HANDED

four-hand•ed \-'han-dəd\ *adj* **1** : designed for four hands **2** : engaged in by four persons ⟨a *four-handed* card game⟩

Four Horsemen *n pl* : war, famine, pestilence, and death personified as the four major plagues of mankind [from the apocalyptic vision in Revelation 6:2–8]

Four Hundred or 400 *n* : the exclusive social set of a community — used with *the* [from the idea that a social elite must necessarily be small in number]

four-in-hand \'fōr-ən-ˌhand, 'fȯr-\ *n* **1 a** : a team of four horses driven by one person **b** : a vehicle drawn by such a team **2** : a necktie tied in a slipknot with long ends overlapping vertically in front

four–letter word *n* : any of a group of dirty or abusive words typically made up of four letters

four–o'clock \-ə-ˌkläk\ *n* : an American garden plant with fragrant yellow, red, or white flowers opening late in the afternoon

four–post•er \-'pō-stər\ *n* : a bed with tall corner posts originally designed to support curtains or a canopy

four•ra•gère \ˌfu̇r-ə-'zheər\ *n* : a braided cord worn (as by a soldier in uniform) usually around the left shoulder [French]

four•score \'fōr-ˌskōr, 'fȯr-ˌskȯr\ *adj* : being four times twenty : EIGHTY

four•some \'fōr-səm, 'fȯr-\ *n* **1** : a group of four members **2** : a group of four golfers playing together

four•square \-'skwaər, -'skwer\ *adj* **1** : SQUARE 1a **2** : marked by boldness and conviction : FORTHRIGHT — **foursquare** *adv*

four•teen \fōr-'tēn, fȯr-, fōrt-, fȯrt-, 'fōr-, 'fȯr-, 'fōrt-, 'fȯrt-\ *n* : one more than 13; *also* : a symbol representing this — see NUMBER table [Old English *fēowertīene*] — **fourteen** *adj or pron* — **fourteenth** \-'tēnth, -'tēntth\ *adj or n*

four•teen•er \-'tē-nər\ *n* : a verse consisting of 14 syllables or especially of 7 iambic feet

fourth \'fōrth, 'fȯrth\ *n* **1** : number four in a countable series — see NUMBER table **2 a** : the musical interval embracing four diatonic degrees **b** : the harmonic combination of two tones a fourth apart **3** : the 4th forward gear or speed of a motor vehicle — **fourth** *adj or adv* — **fourth•ly** *adv*

fourth class *n* **1** : a class or group ranking fourth in a series **2** : a class of mail in the United States that comprises merchandise and non-second-class printed matter and is not sealed against inspection

fourth dimension *n* **1** : a dimension in addition to length, width, and depth; *esp* : a coordinate in addition to three rectangular coordinates **2** : something outside the range of ordinary experience

fourth estate *n, often cap F&E* : the public press

△ **origin** In Europe, in earlier days, the people who participated in the government of a country were generally divided into three classes or estates. In England the three traditional estates were the nobility, the clergy, and the commons. Occasionally the term *fourth estate* was used for some other group, like the mob or the public press, that had unofficial but often great influence on government. In time *fourth estate* came to refer exclusively to the press.

Fourth of July : INDEPENDENCE DAY

four–wheel \'fōr-ˌhwēl, 'fȯr-, -ˌwēl\ *or* **four–wheeled** \-'hwēld, -'wēld\ *adj* **1** : having four wheels **2** : acting on or by means of four wheels of an automotive vehicle ⟨*four-wheel* drive⟩

fo•vea \'fō-vē-ə\ *n, pl* **-ve•ae** \-vē-ˌē, -vē-ˌī\ : an area of the retina containing only cones and affording acute vision [Latin, "pit"] — **fo•ve•al** \-vē-əl\ *adj* — **fo•ve•ate** \-vē-ˌāt\ *adj*

[1]**fowl** \'fau̇l\ *n, pl* **fowl** *or* **fowls** **1** : BIRD 1: as **a** : a domestic cock or hen; *esp* : an adult hen **b** : any of several domesticated or wild birds related to the common domestic cock and hen **2** : the flesh of fowls used as food [Middle English *foul,* from Old English *fugel*]

[2]**fowl** *vi* : to seek, catch, or kill wildfowl — **fowl•er** *n*

fowling piece *n* : a light gun for shooting birds or small mammals

[1]**fox** \'fäks\ *n, pl* **fox•es** *or* **fox** **1 a** : any of various flesh-eating mammals related to the wolves but smaller and with shorter legs and more pointed muzzle **b** : the fur of a fox **2** : a clever crafty person [Old English]

[2]**fox** *vt* : to trick by cleverness or cunning : OUTWIT

foxed \'fäkst\ *adj* : discolored with yellowish brown stains ⟨the *foxed* pages of an old book⟩

fox fire *n* : an eerie phosphorescent light (as of decaying wood); *also* : a luminous fungus that causes decaying wood to glow

fox•glove \'fäks-ˌgləv\ *n* : any of a genus of erect herbs of the snapdragon family; *esp* : a common biennial or perennial plant that bears showy spikes of dotted white or purple tubular flowers and is a source of digitalis

fox grape *n* : any of several native grapes of eastern North America with sour or musky fruit

fox•hole \'fäks-ˌhōl\ *n* : a pit dug hastily during combat for individual cover against enemy fire

fox•hound \-ˌhau̇nd\ *n* : any of various large swift powerful hounds used in hunting foxes

foxhound

fox•tail \'fäk-ˌstāl\ *n* : any of several grasses with spikes resembling brushes

foxtail millet *n* : a coarse drought-resistant but frost-sensitive annual grass grown for grain, hay, and forage

fox terrier *n* : a small lively terrier formerly used to dig out foxes and known in smooth-haired and wirehaired varieties

fox–trot \'fäks-ˌträt\ *n* **1** : a short broken slow trotting gait of the horse **2** : a ballroom dance in duple time that includes slow walking steps and quick running steps — **fox–trot** *vi*

foxy \'fäk-sē\ *adj* **fox•i•er**; **-est** **1 a** : resembling a fox in appearance or disposition : WILY **b** : being alert and knowing : CLEVER **2** : having the color of a fox **3** : FOXED **4** : being good-looking : ATTRACTIVE — **fox•i•ly** \-sə-lē\ *adv* — **fox•i•ness** \-sē-nəs\ *n*

foy•er \'fȯiər, 'fȯir; 'fȯi-ˌā, -ˌyā\ *n* : an anteroom or lobby especially of a theater; *also* : an entrance hallway [French, literally, "fireplace", from Medieval Latin *focarius,* from Latin *focus* "hearth"]

fra•cas \'frā-kəs, 'frak-əs\ *n* : a noisy quarrel : BRAWL [French]

frac•tion \'frak-shən\ *n* **1** : a mathematical expression (as 1/2 or 3/4) that represents one or more equal parts or the division of one number by another; *also* : a number (as 3.323) consisting of a decimal or a whole number and a decimal **2 a** : a piece broken off : FRAGMENT **b** : PORTION, SECTION ⟨a small *fraction* of the voters⟩ [Late Latin *fractio* "act of breaking", from Latin *frangere* "to break"]

frac•tion•al \-shnəl, -shən-l\ *adj* **1** : of, relating to, or being a fraction **2** : relatively small : INCONSIDERABLE **3** : of, relating to, or involving a separating of components from a mixture through differences in physical or chemical properties ⟨*fractional* distillation⟩ — **frac•tion•al•ly** \-ē\ *adv*

fractional equation *n* : an equation containing the unknown in the denominator of one or more terms ⟨ $\frac{a}{x} + \frac{b}{x+1} = c$ is a *fractional equation*⟩

frac•tion•ate \'frak-shə-ˌnāt\ *vt* : to separate into different portions; *esp* : to subject to fractional distillation — **frac•tion•ation** \ˌfrak-shə-'nā-shən\ *n*

frac•tious \'frak-shəs\ *adj* **1** : hard to handle or control ⟨a *fractious* horse⟩ **2** : QUARRELSOME [*fraction* ("discord") + *-ous*] — **frac•tious•ly** *adv* — **frac•tious•ness** *n*

[1]**frac•ture** \'frak-chər\ *n* **1** : the act or process of breaking or the state of being broken; *esp* : the breaking of a bone — compare SIMPLE FRACTURE, COMPOUND FRACTURE **2** : the result of fracturing; *esp* : an injury resulting from the fracture of a bone [Latin *fractura,* from *frangere* "to break"]

• **syn** FRACTURE, RUPTURE mean a break in tissue. FRACTURE applies to the cracking of hard substance ⟨*fractured* bones⟩ RUPTURE applies to the tearing or bursting of soft tissues ⟨a *ruptured* blood vessel⟩

[2]**fracture** *vb* **frac•tured**; **frac•tur•ing** \-chə-ring, -shring\ **1** : to cause a fracture in : BREAK **2** : to damage or destroy as if by breaking ⟨*fractured* families⟩ **3** : to undergo fracture

frae \frā, 'frā\ *prep, Scottish* : FROM [Old Norse *frā*]

frag•ile \'fraj-əl, -ˌīl\ *adj* **1** : easily broken or destroyed : DELICATE **2** : TENUOUS, SLIGHT ⟨*fragile* evidence⟩ [Middle French, from Latin *fragilis,* from *frangere* "to break"] **syn** see BRITTLE — **fra•gil•i•ty** \frə-'jil-ət-ē\ *n*

frag•ment \'frag-mənt\ *n* **1** : a part broken off, detached, or incomplete **2** : SENTENCE FRAGMENT [Latin *fragmentum,* from frangere "to break"] — **frag•ment** \-,ment\ *vb*

frag•men•tal \frag-'ment-l\ *adj* : FRAGMENTARY — **frag•men•tal•ly** \-l-ē\ *adv*

frag•men•tary \'frag-mən-,ter-ē\ *adj* : consisting of fragments : INCOMPLETE ⟨*fragmentary* evidence⟩ ⟨a *fragmentary* report⟩ — **frag•men•tar•i•ness** *n*

frag•men•tate \'frag-mən-,tāt\ *vb* : to break or fall into pieces [back-formation from *fragmentation*] — **frag•men•ta•tion** \,frag-mən-'tā-shən, -,men-\ *n*

frag•men•tize \'frag-mən-,tīz\ *vb* : FRAGMENTATE

fra•grance \'frā-grəns\ *n* **1** : a sweet, pleasing and often flowery or fruity odor — compare AROMA **2** : a particular odor (as of a perfume or toilet water)

fra•grant \-grənt\ *adj* : having fragrance [Latin *fragrans,* from *fragrare* "to be fragrant"] — **fra•grant•ly** *adv*

frail \'frāl\ *adj* **1** : morally weak ⟨*frail* humanity⟩ **2** : FRAGILE 1 **3 a** : physically weak **b** : UNSUBSTANTIAL [Middle French *fraile,* from Latin *fragilis* "fragile"] — **frail•ly** \'frāl-lē\ *adv* — **frail•ness** *n*

frail•ty \'frā-əl-tē, 'frāl-\ *n, pl* **frailties 1** : the quality or state of being frail **2** : a fault due to weakness especially of moral character **syn** see FAULT

[1]**frame** \'frām\ *vt* **1 a** : PLAN 1, CONTRIVE **b** : to give expression to : FORMULATE **c** : SHAPE 1, CONSTRUCT **d** : to draw up ⟨*frame* a constitution⟩ **2** : to fit or adjust for a purpose **3** : to construct by fitting and uniting the parts of the skeleton of (a structure) **4** : to enclose in a frame ⟨*frame* a picture⟩ **5** : to make (an innocent person) appear guilty [Old English *framian* "to benefit, make progress"] — **fram•er** *n*

[2]**frame** *n* **1 a** : something composed of parts fitted together and united **b** : the physical makeup of an animal and especially a human body : PHYSIQUE **2 a** : an arrangement of structural parts that gives form or support to something ⟨the *frame* of a cart⟩ ⟨the bony *frame* of the body⟩; *esp* : one (as of girders, beams, and joists) that forms the main support of a structure (as a building) **b** : a structural unit on or in which something rests ⟨the *frame* of a bucksaw⟩; *also* : a machine built on or in a frame **c** : a supporting or enclosing border or open case (as for a window or a picture) **d** : matter or an area enclosed by a border: as (1) : one of the squares in which scores for each round are recorded (as in bowling); *also* : a turn in bowling (2) : one picture of the series on a length of film (3) : a complete image being transmitted by television **3** : a particular state of mind

[3]**frame** *adj* : having a wood frame ⟨*frame* houses⟩

frame of reference : a set or system (as of facts or ideas) serving to orient or give particular meaning

frame–up \'frā-,məp\ *n* : a scheme to cause an innocent person to be accused of a crime; *also* : the result of such a scheme

frame•work \'frām-,wərk\ *n* **1** : a structural or skeletal frame **2** : a basic structure (as of ideas)

fram•ing \'frā-ming\ *n* : FRAME 2, FRAMEWORK

franc \'frangk\ *n* **1** : the basic monetary unit of any of several countries (as France, Belgium, or Switzerland) **2** : a coin representing one franc [French, from Medieval Latin *Francorum Rex* "king of the French", words on 14th century francs]

fran•chise \'fran-,chīz\ *n* **1 a** : a special privilege or exemption granted (as by a government); *esp* : the right to exist and function as a corporation **b** : a right or license to market a company's goods or services in a particular territory; *also* : the territory covered by such a right or license **2** : a legal right or privilege; *esp* : the right to vote [Old French, "freedom from a restriction", from *franchir* "to free", from *franc* "free, frank"]

[1]**Fran•cis•can** \fran-'sis-kən\ *adj* : of or relating to Saint Francis of Assisi or one of the orders under his monastic rule [Medieval Latin *Franciscus* "Francis"]

[2]**Franciscan** *n* : a member of a religious order established by Saint Francis of Assisi and engaging chiefly in preaching and in missionary and charitable work

fran•ci•um \'fran-sē-əm\ *n* : a radioactive chemical element obtained artificially by the bombardment of thorium with protons — see ELEMENT table [New Latin, from *France*]

Franco- *combining form* **1** : French and ⟨*Franco*-American⟩ **2** : French ⟨*Francophile*⟩ [Medieval Latin *Francus* "Frenchman", from Late Latin, "Frank"]

fran•co•lin \'frang-kə-lən\ *n* : any of various African or Asian partridges [French, from Italian *francolino*]

Fran•co•phile \'frang-kə-,fīl\ *adj* : admiring or favoring France or French culture — **Francophile** *n*

fran•gi•ble \'fran-jə-bəl\ *adj* : easily broken : FRAGILE [Medieval Latin *frangibilis,* from Latin *frangere* "to break"] — **fran•gi•bil•i•ty** \,fran-jə-'bil-ət-ē\ *n*

fran•gi•pani *also* **fran•gi•pan•ni** \,fran-jə-'pan-ē\ *n, pl* **-pani** *or* **-pan•is** *also* **-pan•ni** *or* **pan•nis** : a perfume derived from or imitating the odor of the flower of the red jasmine; *also* : red jasmine or a related tropical American shrub or small tree [Italian *frangipane,* from Marquis Muzio *Frangipane,* 16th century Italian nobleman]

[1]**frank** \'frangk\ *adj* **1** : free and forthright in expressing one's feelings and opinions : OUTSPOKEN **2** : unmistakably evident : DOWNRIGHT ⟨*frank* treason⟩ [Old French *franc* "free, frank", from Medieval Latin *francus,* from Late Latin *Francus* "Frank"] — **frank•ly** *adv* — **frank•ness** *n*

△ **origin** The word *frank* comes from the name of the Franks, a West Germanic people who lived long ago. In the early Middle Ages the Franks were in power in France. (It was from them that the country got its name.) At that time the Franks were the only people in the country who enjoyed complete freedom. So their name (*Francus* in Latin) came to mean "free". From the English adjective *frank,* which means "free" or "forthright", we get the verb *frank,* which means "to mark mail with an official sign so that it may be mailed free".

• **syn** FRANK, CANDID, OPEN, PLAIN mean showing willingness to tell one's thoughts or feelings. FRANK implies absence of the evasiveness that springs from considerations of tact or of expedience ⟨*frank* declaration of selfish motives⟩ CANDID stresses sincerity and honesty of expression especially in offering unwelcome criticism or opinion ⟨gave a *candid* appraisal of my faults⟩ OPEN implies frankness but suggests more indiscretion than *frank* and less earnestness than CANDID ⟨*open* betrayal of a friend⟩ PLAIN suggests outspokenness and freedom from affectation or subtlety in expression ⟨*plain* talk⟩

[2]**frank** *vt* : to mark (a piece of mail) with an official signature or sign indicating the right of the sender to free mailing; *also* : to mail in this manner

[3]**frank** *n* **1** : a signature, mark, or stamp on a piece of mail indicating that it can be mailed free **2** : the privilege of sending mail free of charge

Frank \'frangk\ *n* : a member of a West Germanic people entering the Roman provinces in A.D. 253 and establishing themselves in the Netherlands, in Gaul, and along the Rhine [Old French *Franc,* from Late Latin *Francus,* of Germanic origin] — **Frank•ish** \'frang-kish\ *adj*

Fran•ken•stein \'frang-kən-,stīn, -,stēn\ *n* **1** : a work or agency that ruins its originator **2** : a monster in the shape of a man [from *Frankenstein,* a student of physiology in Mary W. Shelley's novel *Frankenstein* whose life is ruined by a monster he creates]

frank•furt•er *or* **frank•fort•er** \'frangk-fərt-ər, -fət-ər\ or **frank•furt** *or* **frank•fort** \-fərt\ *n* : a seasoned beef or beef and pork sausage [German *frankfurter* "of Frankfurt", from *Frankfurt am Main,* Germany]

frank•in•cense \'frang-kən-,sens\ *n* : a fragrant gum resin from African or Arabian trees that is burned as incense [Middle English *frank* "frank, free, pure" + *incense*]

frank•lin \'frang-klən\ *n* : a free medieval English landowner not of noble birth [Anglo-French *fraunclein,* from Old French *franc* "free"]

Franklin stove

Frank•lin stove \,frangklən-\ *n* : a metal heating stove resembling an open fireplace but designed to conserve and radiate heat [Benjamin *Franklin,* its inventor]

fran•tic \'frant-ik\ *adj* : wildly or uncontrollably excited ⟨*frantic* with pain⟩ ⟨*frantic* cries for help⟩ [Middle English *frenetik, frantik* "insane", from Middle French *frenetique,* from Latin *phreneticus,* from Greek *phrenitikos,* from *phrenitis* "inflammation of the brain", from *phrēn* "mind"] — **fran•ti•cal•ly** \-i-kə-lē,

-klē\ *adv* — **fran•tic•ly** \-i-klē\ *adv* — **fran•tic•ness** *n*

frap•pé \fra-ˈpā\ *or* **frappe** \ˈfrap, fra-ˈpā\ *n* **1** : an iced or frozen mixture or drink **2** : a thick milk shake [French *frappé* "iced, chilled", from *frapper* "to strike, chill"] — **frappé** *adj*

fra•ter•nal \frə-ˈtərn-l\ *adj* **1 a** : of, relating to, or involving brothers **b** : of, relating to, or being a fraternity or society **2** : BROTHERLY 2, FRIENDLY [Medieval Latin *fraternalis,* from Latin *fraternus,* from *frater* "brother"] — **fra•ter•nal•ism** \-l-ˌiz-əm\ *n* — **fra•ter•nal•ly** \-l-ē\ *adv*

fraternal twin *n* : either member of a pair of twins that are produced from different fertilized egg cells, usually differ in some or many genes, and are often not physically similar

fra•ter•ni•ty \frə-ˈtər-nət-ē\ *n, pl* **-ties** **1** : a social, honorary, or professional organization; *esp* : a social club of male college students **2** : BROTHERHOOD 1, BROTHERLINESS **3** : persons of the same class, profession, character, or tastes ⟨the legal *fraternity*⟩

frat•er•nize \ˈfrat-ər-ˌnīz\ *vi* **1** : to associate or mingle as brothers or friends **2** : to associate on friendly terms with citizens or troops of a hostile nation — **frat•er•ni•za•tion** \ˌfrat-ər-nə-ˈzā-shən\ *n* — **frat•er•niz•er** \ˈfrat-ər-ˌnī-zər\ *n*

frat•ri•cide \ˈfra-trə-ˌsīd\ *n* **1** : one who murders his or her own brother or sister **2** : the act of a fratricide [derived from Latin *fratr-, frater* "brother"] — **frat•ri•cid•al** \ˌfra-trə-ˈsīd-l\ *adj*

Frau \ˈfrau̇\ *n, pl* **Frau•en** \ˈfrau̇-ən\ — used by German-speaking people as a courtesy title equivalent to *Mrs.* [German]

fraud \ˈfrȯd\ *n* **1 a** : DECEIT; *esp* : misrepresentation intended to induce another to part with something of value or to surrender a legal right **b** : an act of deceiving or misrepresenting : TRICK **2 a** : one who is not what he pretends to be : IMPOSTOR **b** : one who defrauds : CHEAT [Middle French *fraude,* from Latin *fraus*]
syn see DECEPTION

fraud•u•lent \ˈfrȯ-jə-lənt\ *adj* : characterized by, based on, or done by fraud : DECEITFUL ⟨*fraudulent* claims of injury⟩ — **fraud•u•lence** \-ləns\ *n* — **fraud•u•lent•ly** *adv* — **fraud•u•lent•ness** *n*

fraught \ˈfrȯt\ *adj* : full of or accompanied by something specified ⟨a situation *fraught* with danger⟩ [Middle English, "laden", from *fraughten* "to load", from *fraught* "freight, load", from Dutch or Low German *vracht, vrecht*]

Fräu•lein \ˈfrȯi-ˌlīn\ *n* — used by German-speaking people as a courtesy title equivalent to *Miss* [German]

¹fray \ˈfrā\ *n* **1** : a noisy quarrel or fight : BRAWL **2** : a heated dispute [Middle English, short for *affray*]

²fray *vb* **1 a** : to wear (as an edge of cloth) by rubbing **b** : to separate the threads at the edge of **c** : to wear out or into shreds **2** : STRAIN, IRRITATE ⟨tempers were *frayed*⟩ [Middle French *frayer* "to rub", from Latin *fricare*]

fraz•zle \ˈfraz-əl\ *vb* **fraz•zled**; **fraz•zling** \ˈfraz-ling, -ə-ling\ **1** : FRAY 1 **2** : to exhaust physically or emotionally ⟨*frazzled* by hard work⟩ [alteration of English dialect *fazle* "to tangle, fray"] — **frazzle** *n*

¹freak \ˈfrēk\ *n* **1 a** : WHIM **b** : a seemingly capricious action or event **2** : one that is very unusual or abnormal; *esp* : a person with a physical oddity who appears in a circus sideshow **3** *slang* : a person who uses an illicit drug **4** *slang* : an ardent enthusiast [origin unknown] — **freak•ish** \ˈfrē-kish\ *adj* — **freak•ish•ly** *adv* — **freak•ish•ness** *n*

²freak *adj* : having the character of a freak; *esp* : very unusual ⟨a *freak* accident⟩

freak–out \ˈfrē-ˌkau̇t\ *n* : a drug-induced state of mind characterized by nightmarish hallucinations; *also* : a person in such a state

freak out \frē-ˈkau̇t\ *vb* **1** : to experience a freak-out **2** : to behave irrationally under or as if under the influence of drugs **3** : to put into a state of intense excitement

¹freck•le \ˈfrek-əl\ *n* : a small brownish spot in the skin usually due to precipitation of pigment on exposure to sunlight [Middle English *freken, frekel,* of Scandinavian origin] — **freck•ly** \ˈfrek-lē, -ə-lē\ *adv*

²freckle *vb* **freck•led**; **freck•ling** \ˈfrek-ling, -ə-ling\ : to mark or become marked with freckles or small spots

¹free \ˈfrē\ *adj* **fre•er** \ˈfrē-ər\; **fre•est** \ˈfrē-əst\ **1 a** : having liberty : not being a slave or prisoner **b** : not controlled by others : INDEPENDENT ⟨a *free* state⟩ **2** : not subject to a duty, tax, or other charge **3** : released or not suffering from something unpleasant or painful ⟨*free* from worry⟩ **4** : given without charge ⟨*free* tickets⟩ **5** : made or done voluntarily ⟨a *free* choice⟩ **6** : LAVISH ⟨a *free* spender⟩ **7** : PLENTIFUL, COPIOUS ⟨a *free* flow of goods⟩ **8** : not held back by fear or distrust : OPEN, FRANK ⟨*free* expression of opinion⟩ **9** : not restricted by conventional forms ⟨*free* verse⟩ **10** : not literal or exact ⟨a *free* translation⟩ **11 a** : not obstructed : CLEAR ⟨a road *free* of ice⟩ **b** : not being used or occupied ⟨*free* time⟩ **c** : not fastened or bound : able to act, move, or turn ⟨*free* electrons⟩ **12** : not restricted or interfered with by an opponent ⟨a *free* kick⟩ ⟨let a player get *free*⟩ **13** : chemically uncombined ⟨*free* oxygen⟩ **14** : capable of being used meaningfully apart from another linguistic form ⟨the word *hats* is a *free* form⟩ — compare bound [Old English *frēo*] — **free•ly** *adv*

• **syn** FREE, INDEPENDENT, SOVEREIGN mean not subject to the rule or control of another. FREE stresses the complete absence of external rule and the full right to make decisions ⟨a *free* society of equals⟩ INDEPENDENT implies standing alone; applied to a state it implies that no other state has power to interfere with its citizens, laws, or policies; SOVEREIGN stresses supremacy within one's own domain or sphere and implies the absence of any superior power.

²free *adv* **1** : in a free manner **2** : without charge ⟨was admitted *free*⟩

³free *vt* **freed**; **free•ing** **1** : to cause to be free : set free ⟨*free* a prisoner⟩ **2** : RELIEVE, RID ⟨was *freed* from pain⟩ **3** : to clear of obstacles ⟨*free* a road of debris⟩

• **syn** FREE, RELEASE, LIBERATE, DISCHARGE mean to set loose from restraint or constraint. FREE implies usually permanent removal from whatever binds, entangles, or oppresses; RELEASE suggests a setting loose from confinement or from a state of pressure or tension; LIBERATE stresses the state resulting from freeing or releasing; DISCHARGE may imply removing from a lighter degree of restraint or constraint.

free association *n* **1** : expression of thoughts as they come to mind without control or censorship **2** : the reporting of the first thought that comes to mind in response to a given stimulus and especially a word

free•board \ˈfre-ˌbōrd, -ˌbȯrd\ *n* : the vertical distance between the waterline and the deck of a ship on the upper edge of the side of a boat

free•boo•ter \ˈfrē-ˌbüt-ər\ *n* : PIRATE, PLUNDERER [Dutch *vrijbuiter,* from *vrijbuit* "plunder", from *vrij* "free" + *buit* "booty" — see FILIBUSTER *origin*]

free•born \ˈfrē-ˈbȯrn\ *adj* **1** : not born in vassalage or slavery **2** : relating to or befitting one that is freeborn

freed•man \ˈfrēd-mən\ *n* : a person freed from slavery

free•dom \ˈfrēd-əm\ *n* **1** : the quality or state of being free: as **a** : the absence of necessity, coercion, or constraint in choice or action **b** : liberation from slavery or restraint or from the power of another : INDEPENDENCE **c** : EXEMPTION, RELEASE ⟨*freedom* from care⟩ **d** : EASE, FACILITY ⟨*freedom* of movement⟩ **e** : the quality of being outspoken **f** : unrestricted use ⟨the dog had the *freedom* of the yard⟩ **2** : PRIVILEGE, RIGHT; *esp* : one guaranteed by fundamental law

• **syn** FREEDOM, LIBERTY, LICENSE mean the power or condition of acting without compulsion. FREEDOM has a broad range of application from total absence of restraint to merely a sense of not being unduly hampered or frustrated; LIBERTY suggests release from former restraint or compulsion; LICENSE implies freedom specially granted or conceded and may connote an abuse of freedom.

freed•wom•an \ˈfrēd-ˌwu̇m-ən\ *n* : a woman freed from slavery

free enterprise *n* : freedom of private business to organize and operate for profit in competition with other businesses with a minimum of interference by the government; *also* : an economic system providing this freedom

free–for–all \ˈfrē-fə-ˌrȯl\ *n* : a competition, dispute, or fight open to all comers and usually with no rules

free•hand \ˈfrē-ˌhand\ *adj* : done without mechanical aids or devices ⟨*freehand* drawing⟩ — **freehand** *adv*

free hand \-ˈhand\ *n* : freedom of action or decision ⟨given a *free hand* to get the job done⟩

free•hand•ed \-ˈhan-dəd\ *adj* : OPENHANDED, GENEROUS

free•hold \ˈfrē-ˌhōld\ *n* : ownership of real estate for life usually with the right of leaving it to one's heirs; *also* : an estate so owned — **free•hold•er** \-ˌhōl-dər\ *n*

free lance *n* **1** : a knight whose services could be bought by any ruler or state **2** : one who pursues a profession (as writing, art, or acting) without being committed to work for one employer for a long period — **free–lance** *adj* — **free–lance** *vb* — **free–lanc•er** *n*

free–liv•ing \'frē-'liv-iŋ\ *adj* : being neither parasitic nor symbiotic

free•load \-'lōd\ *vi* : SPONGE 3 — **free•load•er** *n*

free•man \'frē-mən\ *n* **1** : a person enjoying civil or political liberty **2** : one having the full rights of a citizen

free•mar•tin \-,märt-n\ *n* : a sexually imperfect usually sterile female calf born in the same birth with a male [origin unknown]

Free•ma•son \-'mās-n\ *n* : a member of a secret fraternal society called Free and Accepted Masons

free•ma•son•ry \-rē\ *n* **1** *cap* : the principles, institutions, or practices of Freemasons — called also *Masonry* **2** : natural or instinctive fellowship or sympathy

free on board *adv or adj* : delivered without charge onto a means of transportation

free port *n* **1** : a port or section of a port where goods are received and shipped free of customs duty **2** : a port open to all vessels on equal terms

free•sia \'frē-zhə, -zhē-ə\ *n* : any of a genus of sweet-scented African herbs with showy red, white, or yellow flowers [F.H.T. *Freese,* died 1876, German physician]

free silver *n* : the free coinage of silver often at a fixed ratio with gold

free–soil *adj* **1** : characterized by free soil **2** *cap F&S* : of, relating to, or constituting a minor United States political party prior to the Civil War opposing the extension of slavery into United States territories and the admission of slave states into the Union — **Free–Soil•er** \-,sȯi-lər\ *n*

free soil *n* : United States territory where slavery was prohibited before the Civil War

free–spo•ken \'frē-'spō-kən\ *adj* : OUTSPOKEN

free•stand•ing \-'stan-diŋ\ *adj* : standing alone or on its own foundation free of attachment or support ⟨a *freestanding* tower⟩

free•stone \'frē-,stōn\ *n* **1** : a stone that may be cut without splitting **2 a** : a fruit stone to which the flesh does not cling **b** : a fruit (as a peach or cherry) having a freestone

free•style \-,stīl\ *n* : competition in which each competitor is free to use a style, method, or performance of his or her choice

free•think•er \-'thiŋ-kər\ *n* : one who forms opinions independently and on the basis of reason; *esp* : one who doubts or denies religious dogma **syn** see ATHEIST — **free•think•ing** \-kiŋ\ *n or adj*

free throw *n* : an unhindered shot in basketball made from behind a fixed line and awarded because of a foul by an opponent

free trade *n* : trade based on the unrestricted international exchange of goods without high tariffs

free•way \'frē-,wā\ *n* **1** : an expressway with fully controlled access **2** : a toll-free highway

free•wheel \'frē-'hwēl, -'wēl\ *vi* : to move or live freely or irresponsibly

free•will \,frē-,wil\ *adj* : VOLUNTARY ⟨a *freewill* offering⟩

free will *n* : the power of directing one's own actions without restraint by necessity or fate that is held to be inherent in moral beings

free world *n* : the part of the world where political democracy and capitalism or moderate socialism rather than totalitarian or Communist political and economic systems prevail

1freeze \'frēz\ *vb* **froze** \'frōz\; **fro•zen** \'frōz-n\; **freez•ing** **1** : to harden into or be hardened into ice or a like solid by loss of heat ⟨the river *froze* over⟩ ⟨*freeze* cream⟩ **2 a** : to chill or become chilled with cold ⟨almost *froze* to death⟩ **b** : to become coldly formal in manner **c** : to act toward in a stiff and formal way **3 a** : to act on usually destructively by frost ⟨*froze* the tomato plants⟩ **b** : to anesthetize by cold **4 a** : to adhere solidly by freezing **b** : to cause to grip tightly or remain in immovable contact ⟨fear *froze* the driver to the wheel⟩ **5** : to clog or become clogged with ice ⟨the water pipes *froze*⟩ **6** : to become fixed or motionless; *esp* : to make or become incapable of acting or speaking ⟨fear *froze* them in their tracks⟩ **7** : to fix at a certain stage or level ⟨*freeze* rents⟩ [Old English *frēosan*]

2freeze *n* **1** : a state of weather marked by low temperature **2 a** : an act or instance of freezing **b** : the state of being frozen

freeze–dry \'frēz-,drī\ *vt* : to dry in a frozen state under high vacuum especially for preservation

freez•er \'frē-zər\ *n* : one that freezes or keeps cool; *esp* : an insulated compartment or room for keeping food at a temperature below freezing or for freezing perishable food rapidly

freezing point *n* : the temperature at which a liquid solidifies ⟨the *freezing point* of water is 0°C or 32°F⟩

F region *n* : the highest region of the atmosphere occurring from 140 to more than 400 kilometers above the earth

1freight \'frāt\ *n* **1** : the amount paid to a common carrier for carrying goods **2** : goods or cargo carried by a common carrier; *also* : the ordinary carrying of goods from one place to another by a common carrier especially as distinguished from express **3** : a train that carries freight [Dutch or Low German *vracht, vrecht*]

2freight *vt* **1 a** : to load with goods for transportation **b** : to weigh down : BURDEN ⟨*freighted* with fear⟩ **2** : to transport or ship by freight

freight•er \'frāt-ər\ *n* **1** : one that loads or charters and loads a ship **2** : SHIPPER **3** : a ship or airplane used chiefly to carry freight

1French \'french\ *adj* : of, relating to, or characteristic of France, its people, or their language [Old English *frencisc,* from *Franca* "Frank"] — **French•man** \-mən\ *n* — **French•wom•an** \-,wu̇m-ən\ *n*

2French *n* **1** : a Romance language developing out of the Vulgar Latin of Transalpine Gaul and becoming the literary and official language of France **2** *pl in construction* : the French people

French Canadian *n* : one of the descendants of French settlers in lower Canada — **French–Canadian** *adj*

French cuff *n* : a shirt cuff that is made by turning back part of a wide cuff and is fastened with a cuff link

French door *n* : a door with glazed rectangular panels extending the full length; *also* : one of a pair of such doors in a single frame

1french fry *vt, often cap 1st F* : to fry (as strips of potato) in deep fat until brown

2french fry *n, often cap 1st F* : a strip of potato fried in deep fat — usually used in pl.

French horn *n* : a brass wind instrument consisting of a long curved conical tube with a narrow funnel-shaped mouthpiece at one end and a flaring bell at the other

French leave *n* : an informal, hasty, or secret departure [from an 18th century French custom of leaving a reception without taking leave of the host or hostess]

French toast *n* : bread dipped in a mixture of egg and milk and then fried

French window *n* **1** : a French door placed in an outside wall **2** : a casement window

French horn

fre•net•ic \fri-'net-ik\ *adj* : HECTIC 2, FRANTIC [Middle French *frenetique* "insane", from Latin *phreneticus* "insane, frantic"] — **fre•net•i•cal•ly** \-'net-i-kə-lē, -klē\ *adv*

fre•num \'frē-nəm\ *n, pl* **frenums** *or* **fre•na** \-nə\ : a fold of membrane (as beneath the tongue) that supports or restrains [Latin, literally, "bridle"]

fren•zied \'fren-zēd\ *adj* : marked by frenzy : wildly excited — **fren•zied•ly** *adv*

fren•zy \'fren-zē\ *n, pl* **frenzies** **1** : a temporary madness or violent agitation **2** : intense and usually wild activity [Middle French *frenesie,* derived from Latin *phrenesis,* from *phreneticus* "insane, frantic"] — **frenzy** *vt*

Fre•on \'frē-,än\ *trademark* — used for any of various nonflammable gaseous and liquid hydrocarbons used as refrigerants

fre•quen•cy \'frē-kwən-sē\ *n, pl* **-cies** **1** : the fact or condition of occurring frequently **2 a** : rate or proportion of occurrence ⟨*frequency* of a gene in a population⟩ **b** : the number of individuals or objects in a particular class when classified according to variation in one or more qualities **3 :** the number of repetitions of a periodic process in a unit of time: as **a :** the number of complete alternations per second of an alternating current ⟨a current having a *frequency* of 60 hertz⟩ **b :** the number of sound waves per second produced by a sounding body ⟨a sound having a frequency of 1500 hertz⟩ **c :** the number of complete oscillations per second of an electromagnetic wave ⟨the *frequency* of a radio wave⟩ ⟨the *frequency* of yellow light⟩

frequency distribution *n* **:** an arrangement of statistical data that exhibits the frequency of the occurrence of the values of a variable

frequency modulation *n* **:** modulation of the frequency of a carrier wave in accordance with speech or a signal; *esp* **:** a system of broadcasting using this method of modulation — abbreviation *FM*

1fre·quent \'frē-kwənt\ *adj* **1 :** happening often or at short intervals ⟨made *frequent* trips to town⟩ **2 :** HABITUAL, CONSTANT ⟨a *frequent* visitor⟩ [Latin *frequens* "crowded, frequent"] — **fre·quent·ly** *adv* — **fre·quent·ness** *n*

2fre·quent \frē-'kwent, 'frē-kwənt\ *vt* **:** to visit often **:** associate with, be in, or resort to habitually ⟨*frequented* the library⟩ — **fre·quent·er** *n*

fres·co \'fres-,kō\ *n, pl* **frescoes** *or* **frescos 1 :** the art of painting on freshly spread moist lime plaster with pigments suspended in water **2 :** a painting executed in fresco [Italian, from *fresco* "fresh", of Germanic origin] — **fresco** *vt*

1fresh \'fresh\ *adj* **1 a :** not salt ⟨*fresh* water⟩ **b :** PURE, INVIGORATING ⟨*fresh* air⟩ **c :** fairly strong **:** BRISK ⟨a *fresh* breeze⟩ **2 a :** not stored, cured, or preserved ⟨*fresh* vegetables⟩ **b :** having its original qualities unimpaired: as (1) **:** full of or renewed in vigor **:** REFRESHED (2) **:** not stale, sour, or decayed ⟨*fresh* bread⟩ (3) **:** not faded (4) **:** not worn or rumpled **3 a** (1) **:** experienced, made, or received newly or anew (2) **:** ADDITIONAL, ANOTHER ⟨make a *fresh* start⟩ **b :** not trite or hackneyed **c :** INEXPERIENCED, RAW **d :** newly arrived ⟨*fresh* out of college⟩ **4 :** showing disrespect **:** IMPUDENT [Old French *freis,* of Germanic origin] **syn** see NEW — **fresh·ly** *adv* — **fresh·ness** *n*

2fresh *adv* **:** just recently **:** FRESHLY ⟨a *fresh* laid egg⟩

fresh·en \'fresh-ən\ *vb* **fresh·ened**; **fresh·en·ing** \'fresh-ning, -ə-ning\ **1 :** to make or become fresh: as **a :** to become brisk or strong ⟨the wind *freshened*⟩ **b :** to make or become fresh in appearance or vitality ⟨*freshen* up with a shower⟩ **2 :** to begin giving milk ⟨when the cow *freshens*⟩ — **fresh·en·er** \'fresh-nər, -ə-nər\ *n*

fresh·et \'fresh-ət\ *n* **:** a great rise or overflowing of a stream caused by heavy rains or melted snow [from *fresh* "increased flow, freshet, stream of fresh water", from 1*fresh*]

fresh·man \'fresh-mən\ *n* **1 :** a newcomer to an occupation or activity **:** NOVICE **2 :** a student in the first year (as of high school or college)

fresh·wa·ter \,fresh-,wȯt-ər, -,wät-\ *adj* **1 :** of, relating to, or living in fresh water **2 :** accustomed to navigating only in fresh waters ⟨a *freshwater* sailor⟩

1fret \'fret\ *vb* **fret·ted**; **fret·ting 1 :** to suffer or cause to suffer emotional strain **:** WORRY, VEX ⟨*fretted* over petty problems⟩ **2 a :** to eat into or wear away ⟨rock *fretted* by rainwater⟩ **b :** FRAY 1a **c :** to cause by wearing away ⟨the stream *fretted* a channel⟩ **3 :** to affect something as if by gnawing or biting **:** GRATE ⟨the siren *fretted* at their nerves⟩ **4 :** to cause (water) to ripple [Old English *fretan* "to devour"]

2fret *n* **:** an irritated or worried state ⟨be in a *fret*⟩

3fret *vt* **fret·ted**; **fret·ting :** to decorate with interlaced designs [Middle French *freter* "to bind with a ferrule, fret", from *frete* "ferrule"]

4fret *n* **:** ornamental work consisting of small straight intersecting bars

5fret *n* **:** one of a series of ridges fixed across the fingerboard of a stringed musical instrument [probably from Middle French *frete* "ferrule"] — **fret·ted** \'fret-əd\ *adj*

fret·ful \'fret-fəl\ *adj* **1 :** inclined to fret **:** IRRITABLE **2 a :** marked by turbulence **:** TROUBLED ⟨*fretful* waters⟩ **b :** GUSTY ⟨a *fretful* wind⟩ — **fret·ful·ly** \-fə-lē\ *adv* — **fret·ful·ness** *n*

fret·saw \'fret-,sȯ\ *n* **:** a narrow-bladed fine-toothed saw for cutting curved outlines

fret·work \-,wərk\ *n* **1 :** decoration consisting of work adorned with frets **2 :** ornamental openwork or work in relief

Freud·ian \'frȯid-ē-ən\ *adj* **:** of, relating to, or according with the theories of psychology or practices of psychotherapy of Sigmund Freud — **Freudian** *n* — **Freud·ian·ism** \-ē-ə-,niz-əm\ *n*

fri·a·ble \'frī-ə-bəl\ *adj* **:** easily crumbled or pulverized [Latin *friabilis,* from *friare* "to crumble"] **syn** see BRITTLE — **fri·a·bil·i·ty** \,frī-ə-bil-ət-ē\ *n* — **fri·a·ble·ness** \'frī-ə-bəl-nəs\ *n*

fri·ar \'frī-ər, 'frīr\ *n* **:** a member of one of several Roman Catholic religious orders for men in which monastic life is combined with preaching and other priestly duties — compare MONK [Old French *frere,* literally, "brother", from Latin *frater*]

fri·ary \'frī-ə-rē, 'frī-rē\ *n, pl* **-ar·ies :** a monastery of friars

1fric·as·see \'frik-ə-,sē, ,frik-ə-'\ *n* **:** a dish of meat (as chicken or veal) cut into pieces and stewed in a gravy [Middle French]

2fricassee *vt* **-seed**; **-see·ing :** to cook as a fricassee

fric·a·tive \'frik-ət-iv\ *n* **:** a consonant characterized by frictional passage of the expired breath through a narrowing at some point in the mouth or throat ⟨\f v th t͟h s z sh zh h\ are *fricatives*⟩ [Latin *fricare* "to rub"] — **fricative** *adj*

fric·tion \'frik-shən\ *n* **1 a :** the rubbing of one body against another **b :** resistance to motion between two bodies in contact ⟨the *friction* of a box sliding along the floor⟩ **2 :** discord between two persons or parties [Latin *frictio,* from *fricare* "to rub"] — **fric·tion·less** \-ləs\ *adj*

fric·tion·al \'frik-shnəl, -shən-l\ *adj* **1 :** of or relating to friction **2 :** moved or produced by friction — **fric·tion·al·ly** \-ē\ *adv*

friction tape *n* **:** a usually cloth tape impregnated with insulating material and an adhesive and used especially to protect and insulate electrical conductors

Fri·day \'frīd-ē\ *n* **:** the 6th day of the week [Old English *frīgedæg,* derived from a translation of Latin *Veneris dies* "day of Venus"; from the fact that Frig, or Fria, was the Germanic goddess of love]

fried cake \'frīd-,kāk\ *n* **:** DOUGHNUT, CRULLER

friend \'frend\ *n* **1 a :** one attached to another by affection or esteem **b :** ACQUAINTANCE 2 **2 :** one who is not hostile ⟨are you *friend* or foe⟩ **3 :** one who supports or favors something ⟨a *friend* of liberal education⟩ **4** *cap* **:** a member of a Christian group that stresses Inner Light, rejects ostentation, outward rites, and an ordained ministry, and opposes war — called also *Quaker* [Old English *frēond*] — **friend·less** \'fren-dləs\ *adj* — **friend·less·ness** *n*

friend·ly \'fren-dlē, -lē\ *adj* **friend·li·er**; **-est :** of, relating to, or befitting a friend: as **a :** showing kindly interest and goodwill ⟨a *friendly* gesture⟩ **b :** not hostile ⟨*friendly* natives⟩ **c :** serving a beneficial or helpful purpose **:** FAVORABLE ⟨a *friendly* breeze⟩ **d :** COMFORTING, CHEERFUL ⟨the *friendly* glow of the fire⟩ — **friend·li·ness** *n*

friend·ship \'frend-,ship, 'fren-\ *n* **1 :** the state of being friends **2 :** a friendly feeling **:** FRIENDLINESS

fri·er *variant of* FRYER

1frieze \'frēz, frē-'zā\ *n* **:** a woolen cloth with a shaggy surface [Middle French *frise,* from Dutch *vriese*]

2frieze \'frēz\ *n* **1 :** the part of an entablature between the architrave and the cornice **2 :** a sculptured or richly ornamented band (as around a building) [Middle French *frise,* perhaps derived from Latin *Phrygius* "Phrygian"]

frig·ate \'frig-ət\ *n* **1 :** a square-rigged warship intermediate between a corvette and a ship of the line **2 :** a British or Canadian escort ship between a corvette and a destroyer in size **3 :** a United States warship smaller than a cruiser and larger than a destroyer [Middle French, from Italian *fregata*]

frigate bird *n* **:** any of several chiefly tropical seabirds noted for their power of flight and the habit of robbing other birds of fish — called also *man-o'-war bird*

1fright \'frīt\ *n* **1 :** fear or alarm caused by sudden danger ⟨cry out in *fright*⟩ **2 :** something that frightens **3 :** something that is grotesque or shocking ⟨you look a *fright*⟩ [Old English *fyrhto, fryhto*] **syn** see FEAR

2fright *vt* **:** to alarm suddenly **:** FRIGHTEN

fright·en \'frīt-n\ *vb* **fright·ened**; **fright·en·ing** \'frīt-ning, -n-ing\ **1 :** to make afraid **:** TERRIFY **2 :** to drive away or out by frightening **3 :** to become frightened — **fright·en·ing·ly** \-ning-lē, -n-ing-\ *adv*

fright·ful \'frīt-fəl\ *adj* **1 :** causing fear or alarm **:** TERRIFYING **2 :** causing shock or horror **:** STARTLING **3 :** EXTREME ⟨*frightful* thirst⟩ — **fright·ful·ly** \-fə-lē\ *adv* — **fright·ful·ness** *n*

frig•id \'frij-əd\ *adj* **1 :** intensely cold **2 :** lacking warmth or ardor **:** INDIFFERENT [Latin *frigidus,* from *frigere* "to be cold"] — **fri•gid•i•ty** \frij-'id-ət-ē\ *n* — **frig•id•ly** \'frij-əd-lē\ *adv* — **frig•id•ness** *n*

frigid zone *n* **:** the area or region between the arctic circle and the north pole or between the antarctic circle and the south pole

fri•jol \frē-'hōl\ *also* **fri•jo•le** \-'hō-lē\ *n, pl* **fri•jo•les** \-'hō-lēz\ *chiefly Southwest* **:** BEAN 1b [American Spanish *frijol*]

1frill \'fril\ *vt* **:** to provide or decorate with a frill

2frill *n* **1 :** a gathered, pleated, or ruffled edging (as of lace) **2 :** a ruff of hair or feathers about the neck of an animal **3 :** something decorative but not essential [perhaps from Flemish *frul*] — **frilly** \'fril-ē\ *adj*

1fringe \'frinj\ *n* **1 :** an ornamental border consisting of short straight or twisted threads or strips hanging from cut or raveled edges or from a separate band **2 :** something resembling a fringe **:** BORDER **3 a :** something that is secondary or supplementary to what is basic **b :** a group with marginal or extremist views [Middle French *frenge,* from Latin *fimbriae* (pl.) "fibers, fringe"]

2fringe *vt* **1 :** to furnish or adorn with a fringe **2 :** to serve as a fringe for **:** BORDER

fringe area *n* **:** a region in which reception from a broadcasting station is weak or subject to serious distortion

fringe benefit *n* **:** an employment benefit paid for by an employer without affecting basic wage rates

frip•pery \'frip-rē, -ə-rē\ *n, pl* **-per•ies 1 :** cheap showy finery **2 :** affected elegance **:** pretentious display [Middle French *friperie* "cast-off clothes", derived from Medieval Latin *faluppa* "piece of straw"] — **frippery** *adj*

Fris•bee \'friz-bē\ *trademark* — used for a plastic disk sailed between players in games of catch

Fri•sian \'frizh-ən, 'frē-zhən\ *n* **1 :** a member of a people that inhabit principally the Netherlands province of Friesland and the Frisian islands in the North sea **2 :** the Germanic language of the Frisian people [Latin *Frisii* "Frisians"] — **Frisian** *adj*

frisk \'frisk\ *vb* **1 :** to leap, skip, or dance in a lively or playful way **:** GAMBOL **2 :** to search (a person) rapidly especially for concealed weapons by running the hand over the clothing [obsolete *frisk* "lively", from Middle French *frisque,* of Germanic origin] — **frisk•er** *n*

frisky \'fris-kē\ *adj* **frisk•i•er; -est :** inclined to frisk **:** FROLICSOME — **frisk•i•ly** \-kə-lē\ *adv* — **frisk•i•ness** \-kē-nəs\ *n*

frit•il•lar•ia \ˌfrit-l-'er-ē-ə, -'ar-\ *n* **:** any of a genus of bulbous herbs of the lily family with mottled or checkered flowers [Latin *fritillus* "dice cup"; from its spotted markings]

frit•il•lary \'frit-l-ˌer-ē\ *n, pl* **-laries 1 :** FRITILLARIA **2 :** any of numerous butterflies that are usually orange spotted with black

1frit•ter \'frit-ər\ *n* **:** a small quantity of fried or sautéed batter often containing fruit, vegetables, or meat [Middle French *friture,* derived from Latin *frigere* "to fry"]

2fritter *vb* **1 :** to reduce or waste little by little ⟨*frittering* away their time⟩ **2 :** to break into small fragments **3 :** to dwindle away [*fritter,* n., "fragment"] — **frit•ter•er** \-ər-ər\ *n*

fri•vol•i•ty \friv-'äl-ət-ē\ *n, pl* **-ties 1 :** the quality or state of being frivolous **2 :** a frivolous act or thing

friv•o•lous \'friv-ləs, -ə-ləs\ *adj* **1 :** of little importance **:** TRIVIAL **2 :** not serious or practical ⟨a *frivolous* attitude⟩ [Latin *frivolus*] — **friv•o•lous•ly** *adv* — **friv•o•lous•ness** *n*

1frizz \'friz\ *vb* **:** to curl in small tight curls [French *friser*]

2frizz *n* **:** a small tight curl or hair that is tightly curled — **frizzy** \'friz-ē\ *adj*

1friz•zle \'friz-əl\ *vb* **friz•zled; friz•zling** \'friz-ling, -ə-ling\ **:** FRIZZ, CURL [probably related to Old English *frīs* "curly"] — **frizzle** *n* — **friz•zly** \'friz-lē, -ə-lē\ *adj*

2frizzle *vb* **1 :** to fry until crip and curled **2 :** to cook with a sizzling noise [*fry* + *sizzle*]

fro \'frō\ *adv* **:** BACK 2a, AWAY — used in the phrase *to and fro* [Middle English *fra, fro* "from", from Old Norse *frā*]

frock \'fräk\ *n* **1 :** a friar's habit **2 :** an outer garment worn by men **3 :** a woman's or child's dress [Middle French *froc,* of Germanic origin]

frock coat *n* **:** a man's usually double-breasted knee-length coat

frog \'frȯg, 'fräg\ *n* **1 a :** any of various smooth-skinned web-footed largely aquatic tailless leaping amphibians — compare TOAD **b :** a condition in the throat that produces hoarseness ⟨a *frog* in one's throat⟩ **2 :** the triangular elastic horny pad on the sole of the hoof of a horse **3 :** an ornamental braiding for fastening the front of a garment by a loop through which a button passes **4 :** a device permitting the wheels on one rail of a track to cross an intersecting rail **5 :** a small holder with perforations or spikes for holding flowers in place in a bowl or vase [Old English *frogga*]

frog 3

frog kick *n* **:** a kick used in swimming in which the legs are moved up, out, and back in the manner of a frog

frog•man \-ˌman, -mən\ *n* **:** a swimmer having equipment (as face mask, flippers, and air supply) that permits an extended stay under water usually for observation or demolition; *esp* **:** a member of a military unit so equipped

frog spit *n* **:** CUCKOO SPIT 1 — called also *frog spittle*

1frol•ic \'fräl-ik\ *vi* **frol•icked; frol•ick•ing 1 :** to make merry **2 :** to play about boisterously **:** ROMP ⟨children *frolicking* on the beach⟩ [Dutch *vroolijk,* from earlier Dutch *vro* "happy"]

2frolic *n* **1 :** a playful mischievous action **2 :** GAIETY 2, MERRIMENT

frol•ic•some \'fräl-ik-səm\ *adj* **:** full of gaiety **:** PLAYFUL

from \frəm, 'frəm, 'främ\ *prep* **1** — used as a function word to indicate a starting point ⟨came here *from* the city⟩ ⟨cost *from* $5 to $10⟩ ⟨an avid reader *from* childhood⟩ **2** — used as a function word to indicate separation: as (1) physical separation ⟨a child taken *from* its mother⟩ (2) an act or condition of removal, abstention, exclusion, release, or differentiation ⟨refrain *from* interrupting⟩ ⟨far *from* safe⟩ **3** — used as a function word to indicate the source, cause, agent, or basis ⟨reading aloud *from* a book⟩ ⟨suffering *from* a cold⟩ [Old English]

frond \'fränd\ *n* **:** a leaf or leaflike part: as **a :** a palm leaf **b :** a fern leaf **c :** a leaflike thallus or shoot (as of a lichen or seaweed) [Latin *frond-, frons* "foliage"] — **frond•ed** \'frän-dəd\ *adj*

1front \'frənt\ *n* **1 a :** FOREHEAD; *also* **:** the whole face **b :** DEMEANOR, BEARING **c :** external often feigned appearance ⟨put up a good *front*⟩ **2 a :** a region in which active warfare is taking place **b :** a sphere of activity **c :** the lateral space occupied by a military unit ⟨advanced on a 4-kilometer *front*⟩ **3 :** the side of a building containing the principal entrance **4 a :** the forward part or surface ⟨the *front* of a shirt⟩ **b :** FRONTAGE 1 **c :** the boundary between two dissimilar air masses **5 a :** a position directly before or ahead of something else **b :** a position of leadership or superiority ⟨at the *front* of the profession⟩ **6 :** a person, group, or thing used to mask the identity or true character or activity of the actual controlling agent ⟨the candy store was a *front* for a bookie joint⟩ **7 :** a political coalition [Old French, from Latin *front-, frons*]

2front *vb* **1 :** FACE ⟨the cottage *fronts* on the lake⟩ ⟨the house *fronts* the street⟩ **2 :** to serve as a front **3 :** CONFRONT

3front *adj* **1 :** of, relating to, or situated at the front **2 :** pronounced with closure or narrowing at or toward the front of the oral passage ⟨the *front* vowels \i\ and \e\⟩ — **front** *adv*

front•age \'frənt-ij\ *n* **1 a :** a piece of land that fronts something (as on a river or road) **b :** the front side of a building **2 :** the extent or measure of a frontage ⟨the United States has an Atlantic *frontage* of over 3000 kilometers⟩

front•al \'frənt-l\ *adj* **1 :** of, relating to, or adjacent to the forehead or the frontal bone **2 a :** of, relating to, or situated at the front **b :** directed against the front or at the main point or issue ⟨a *frontal* assault⟩ — **fron•tal•ly** \-l-ē\ *adv*

frontal bone *n* **:** either of a pair of bones that unite to form the human forehead and the upper part of the cavities of the eye and nose

frontal lobe *n* **:** the front part of each cerebral hemisphere

fron•tier \ˌfrən-'tiər, frän-\ *n* **1 :** a border between two countries

2 **a** : a region that forms the margin of settled territory in a country being populated **b** : the outer limits of knowledge or achievement ⟨the *frontiers* of science⟩ [Middle French *frontiere,* from *front* "front"] — **frontier** *adj*

fron•tiers•man \-'tiərz-mən\ *n* : a person living on a frontier

fron•tiers•wom•an \-wu̇m-ən\ *n* : a woman living on a frontier

fron•tis•piece \'frənt-ə-ˌspēs\ *n* : an illustration preceding and usually facing the title page of a book [Middle French *frontispice* "front of a building", from Late Latin *frontispicium,* from Latin *front-, frons* "front" + *specere* "to look at"]

△ **origin** The process of folk etymology changes unfamiliar words to give them an apparent relationship to more familiar ones. This obscured the true origin of *frontispiece,* which has nothing to do with the word *piece* at all. The earliest known form of the word in English is *frontispice.* Latin *frons, frontis* originally meant "forehead" or "brow" and then came to mean "front" in general. This word combined with *specere,* "to look at", is the source of *frontispiece.* The earliest sense of *frontispice* was architectural: "the part of a building most easily seen, front". The word came to be used as well for the title page of a book, probably because of the once common practice of decorating title pages with columns and other architectural details. From this sense developed its current meaning.

front•let \'frənt-lət\ *n* **1** : a band worn on the forehead **2** : the forehead especially of a bird when distinctively marked

front man *n* : a person serving as a front or figurehead

front–runner \-'rən-ər\ *n* **1** : a competitor who is most effective when running in the lead **2** : the leader in a contest

¹frost \'fro̍st\ *n* **1 a** : the process of freezing **b** : the temperature that causes freezing **c** : a covering of minute ice crystals on a cold surface **2** : coldness of manner or feeling : INDIFFERENCE [Old English]

²frost *vb* **1 a** : to cover with or as if with frost; *esp* : to put icing on (as cake) **b** : to produce a fine-grained slightly roughened surface on (as glass) **2** : to injure or kill by frost : FREEZE

¹frost•bite \'fro̍st-ˌbīt, 'fro̍s-\ *vt* : to blight or nip with frost

²frostbite *n* : the freezing or the local effect of a partial freezing of some part of the body

frost•ed \'fro̍-stəd\ *adj* **1** : covered with frost or with something resembling frost ⟨*frosted* glass⟩ **2** : decorated with frosting ⟨a *frosted* cake⟩ **3** : QUICK-FROZEN ⟨*frosted* foods⟩

frost heave *n* : an upthrust of ground or pavement caused by freezing of moist soil — called also *frost heaving*

frost•ing \'fro̍-sting\ *n* **1** : ¹ICING **2** : dull finish on metal or glass

frosty \'fro̍-stē\ *adj* **frost•i•er**; **-est 1** : attended with or producing frost : FREEZING ⟨a *frosty* night⟩ **2** : covered or appearing as if covered with frost **3** : marked by coolness or extreme reserve in manner ⟨a *frosty* reception⟩ — **frost•i•ly** \-stə-lē\ *adv* — **frost•i•ness** \-stē-nəs\ *n*

¹froth \'fro̍th\ *n, pl* **froths** \'fro̍ths, 'fro̍t͟hz\ **1 a** : bubbles formed in or on a liquid by fermentation or agitation **b** : the foam produced by saliva that sometimes accompanies disease or exhaustion **2** : something light or frivolous and of little value [Old Norse *frotha*]

²froth \'fro̍th, 'fro̍t͟h\ *vb* **1** : to cause to foam **2** : to cover with froth **3** : to produce or throw up froth

frothy \'fro̍-thē, -t͟hē\ *adj* **froth•i•er**; **-est 1** : full of or consisting of froth **2** : gaily frivolous or light in content or treatment — **froth•i•ly** \-thə-lē, -t͟hə-\ *adv* — **froth•i•ness** \-thē-nəs, -t͟hē-\ *n*

frou•frou \frü-ˌfrü\ *n* **1** : a rustling especially of a woman's skirts **2** : frilly ornamentation especially in clothing [French]

fro•ward \'frō-wərd, -ərd\ *adj* : inclined to disobey and oppose : CONTRARY [Middle English, "turned away, froward", from *fro* + *-ward*] — **fro•ward•ly** *adv* — **fro•ward•ness** *n*

frown \'frau̇n\ *vb* **1** : to wrinkle the forehead (as in anger, displeasure, or concentration) **2** : to look with disapproval ⟨parents *frown* on rudeness⟩ **3** : to express with a frown ⟨*frown* one's disapproval⟩ [Middle French *froigner* "to snort, frown"] — **frown** *n* — **frown•er** *n* — **frown•ing•ly** \'frau̇-ning-lē\ *adv*

frow•sy *also* **frow•zy** \'frau̇-zē\ *adj* **frow•si•er** *also* **frow•zi•er**; **-est** : having a slovenly or uncared-for appearance [origin unknown]

froze *past of* FREEZE

fro•zen \'frōz-n\ *adj* **1 a** : affected or crusted over by freezing **b** : subject to long and severe cold ⟨the *frozen* north⟩ **2 a** : expressing or characterized by cold unfriendliness ⟨a *frozen* stare⟩ **b** : incapable of being changed, moved, or undone ⟨wages were *frozen*⟩ **c** : not available for present use ⟨*frozen* capital⟩ — **fro•zen•ly** *adv* — **fro•zen•ness** \-n-nəs, -əs\ *n*

frozen food *n* : food that has been subjected to rapid freezing and is kept frozen until used

fruc•ti•fy \'frək-tə-ˌfī, 'fru̇k-\ *vb* **-fied**; **-fy•ing 1** : to bear fruit **2** : to make fruitful or productive [Middle French *fructifier,* derived from Latin *fructus* "fruit"] — **fruc•ti•fi•ca•tion** \ˌfrək-tə-fə-'kā-shən, fru̇k-\ *n*

fruc•tose \'frək-ˌtōs, 'fru̇k-\ *n* : a very sweet soluble sugar $C_6H_{12}O_6$ that occurs especially in fruit juices and honey [Latin *fructus* "fruit"]

fru•gal \'frü-gəl\ *adj* : characterized by or reflecting economy in the use of resources : THRIFTY [Latin *frugalis* "virtuous, frugal", derived from *frux* "fruit, value"] — **fru•gal•i•ty** \frü-'gal-ət-ē\ *n* — **fru•gal•ly** \'frü-gə-lē\ *adv*

¹fruit \'früt\ *n* **1 a** : a usually useful product of plant growth (as grain, vegetables, or cotton) ⟨*fruits* of the earth⟩ **b** : the usually edible reproductive body of a seed plant; *esp* : one (as a strawberry) having a sweet pulp **c** : a product of fertilization in a plant with its envelopes or appendages; *esp* : the ripened ovary of a seed plant, its contents, and inseparably associated parts (as the pod of a pea) **2** : CONSEQUENCE, RESULT ⟨the *fruits* of their labors⟩ [Old French, from Latin *fructus* "fruit, use", from *frui* "to enjoy, have the use of"] — **fruit•ed** \-əd\ *adj*

²fruit *vb* : to bear or cause to bear fruit

fruit•age \'früt-ij\ *n* **1** : the condition or process of bearing fruit **2** : yield or amount of fruit

fruit bat *n* : any of numerous large Old World fruit-eating bats of warm regions — called also *flying fox*

fruit•cake \'früt-ˌkāk\ *n* : a rich cake containing nuts, dried or candied fruits, and spices

fruit•er•er \'früt-ər-ər\ *n* : one that deals in fruit

fruit fly *n* : any of various small two-winged flies (as a drosophila) whose larvae feed on fruit or decaying vegetable matter

fruit•ful \'früt-fəl\ *adj* **1** : yielding or producing fruit **2** : abundantly productive : bringing results **syn** see FERTILE — **fruit•ful•ly** \-fə-lē\ *adv* — **fruit•ful•ness** *n*

fruiting body *n* : a plant organ specialized for producing spores

fru•i•tion \frü-'ish-ən\ *n* **1** : the state of bearing fruit **2** : REALIZATION, ACCOMPLISHMENT ⟨brought the project to *fruition*⟩ [Late Latin *fruitio* "enjoyment", derived from Latin *frui* "to enjoy"]

fruit•less \'früt-ləs\ *adj* **1** : lacking or not bearing fruit **2** : producing no good effect : UNSUCCESSFUL ⟨a *fruitless* attempt⟩ — **fruit•less•ly** *adv* — **fruit•less•ness** *n*

fruit sugar *n* : FRUCTOSE

fruity \'früt-ē\ *adj* **fruit•i•er**; **-est** : relating to or suggesting fruit

frus•trate \'frəs-ˌtrāt\ *vt* **1** : to prevent from carrying out a purpose ⟨*frustrate* a person⟩ **2** : to make ineffective ⟨*frustrate* a plan⟩ [Latin *frustrare,* from *frustra* "in vain"] — **frus•tra•tion** \ˌfrəs-'trā-shən, frəs-\ *n*

• **syn** THWART, BAFFLE, FOIL: FRUSTRATE implies making even the best or most persistent efforts vain and ineffectual; THWART implies frustrating or checking especially by deliberately crossing or opposing; BAFFLE implies frustrating by confusing or puzzling; FOIL implies checking or defeating so as to discourage further effort.

frus•tum \'frəs-təm\ *n, pl* **frustums** *or* **frus•ta** \-tə\ : the part of a cone or pyramid formed by cutting off the top by a plane parallel to the base [Latin, "piece, bit"]

fru•ti•cose \'früt-i-ˌkōs\ *adj* : having a shrubby bushy thallus with flattened or cylindrical branches ⟨*fruticose* lichens⟩ — compare CRUSTOSE, FOLIOSE [Latin *fruticosus,* from *frutex* "shrub"]

¹fry \'frī\ *vb* **fried**; **fry•ing** : to cook in a pan or on a griddle over a fire especially in fat [Old French *frire,* from Latin *frigere*]

²fry *n, pl* **fries 1** : a dish of something fried **2** : a social gathering where fried food is eaten

³fry *n, pl* **fry 1 a** : recently hatched fishes **b** : the young of animals other than fish **2** : very small adult fishes **3** : members of a group or class : PERSONS ⟨small *fry*⟩ [Middle English, probably from Old North French *fri,* from Old French *frier* "to rub, spawn"]

fry•er *also* **fri•er** \'frī-ər, 'frīr\ *n* : something intended for or used in frying: as **a** : a young chicken **b** : a deep utensil for frying foods

f–stop \'ef-ˌstäp\ *n* : a camera lens aperture setting indicated by an f-number

fuch•sia \'fyü-shə\ *n* **1 :** any of a genus of shrubs of the evening-primrose family that have showy nodding flowers usually in deep pinks, reds, and purples **2 :** a vivid reddish purple [Leonhard *Fuchs,* died 1566, German botanist]

fuch•sine *or* **fuch•sin** \'fyük-sən, -,sēn\ *n* **:** a synthetic dye that yields a brilliant bluish red [French *fuchsine,* probably from *fuchsia* "fuchsia"]

fu•co•xan•thin \,fyü-kō-'zan-thən\ *n* **:** a brown pigment occurring especially in the ova of brown algae [derived from Greek *phykos* "seaweed" + *xanthos* "yellow"]

fu•cus \'fyü-kəs\ *n* **:** ROCKWEED [Latin, a kind of lichen, from Greek *phykos* "seaweed"]

fud•dle \'fəd-l\ *vt* **fud•dled; fud•dling** \'fəd-ling, -l-ing\ **:** to make confused **:** MUDDLE [origin unknown]

fud•dy–dud•dy \'fəd-ē-,dəd-ē\ *n, pl* **-dies :** one that is old-fashioned, pompous, unimaginative, or concerned about trifles [perhaps reduplication of Scottish *fuddy* "short-tailed animal, tail", from *fud* "tail"]

[1]**fudge** \'fəj\ *vb* **1 :** to act dishonestly **2 :** to avoid commitment **:** HEDGE **3 a :** to devise as a substitute **:** FAKE **b :** FALSIFY ⟨*fudged* the figures⟩ [origin unknown]

[2]**fudge** *n* **1 :** foolish nonsense **2 :** a soft creamy candy of sugar, milk, butter, and flavoring

[1]**fu•el** \'fyü-əl\ *n* **1 a :** a material used to produce heat or power by burning **b :** a material from which atomic energy can be produced especially in a reactor **2 :** a source of support **:** REINFORCEMENT [Old French *fouaille,* from *feu* "fire", derived from Latin *focus* "hearth"]

[2]**fuel** *vb* **-eled** *or* **-elled; -el•ing** *or* **-el•ling 1 :** to provide with or take in fuel **2 :** SUPPORT, STIMULATE ⟨*fuel* research with federal grants⟩

fuel cell *n* **:** a cell that continuously changes the chemical energy of a fuel and oxidant to electrical energy

fuel oil *n* **:** an oil that is used for fuel and that usually ignites at a higher temperature than kerosene

[1]**fu•gi•tive** \'fyü-jət-iv\ *adj* **1 :** running away or trying to escape ⟨a *fugitive* slave⟩ **2 :** likely to vanish suddenly **:** not fixed or lasting ⟨*fugitive* thoughts⟩ [Latin *fugitivus,* from *fugere* "to flee"] — **fu•gi•tive•ly** *adv* — **fu•gi•tive•ness** *n*

[2]**fugitive** *n* **1 :** one that flees or tries to escape **2 :** something elusive or hard to find

fugue \'fyüg\ *n* **:** a musical composition in which one or two themes are repeated or imitated by successively entering voices and developed in a continuous interweaving of the voice parts [probably from Italian *fuga* "flight, fugue", from Latin, "flight", from *fugere* "to flee"] — **fu•gal** \'fyü-gəl\ *adj*

füh•rer *or* **fueh•rer** \'fyür-ər, 'fir-\ *n* **:** LEADER 2c — used chiefly of the leader of the German Nazis [German]

[1]**-ful** \fəl\ *adj suffix, sometimes* **-ful•ler;** *sometimes* **-ful•lest 1 :** full of ⟨eventful⟩ **2 :** characterized by ⟨peaceful⟩ **3 :** having the qualities of ⟨masterful⟩ **4 :** tending, given, or liable to ⟨mournful⟩

[2]**-ful** \,fúl\ *n suffix* **:** number or quantity that fills or would fill ⟨roomful⟩

ful•crum \'fúl-krəm, 'fəl-\ *n, pl* **fulcrums** *or* **ful•cra** \-krə\ **:** the support about which a lever turns [Latin, "bedpost", from *fulcire* "to prop"]

F fulcrum

ful•fill *or* **ful•fil** \fúl-'fil\ *vt* **ful•filled; ful•fill•ing 1 :** to put into effect ⟨*fulfill* a promise⟩ **2 :** to measure up to **:** SATISFY ⟨*fulfill* a need⟩ [Old English *fullfyllan,* from *full* + *fyllan* "to fill"] — **ful•fill•er** *n* — **ful•fill•ment** \-mənt\ *n*

[1]**full** \'fúl\ *adj* **1 :** containing as much or as many as is possible or normal ⟨a bin *full* of corn⟩ **2 a :** complete as to number, amount, or duration ⟨a *full* share⟩ **b :** having all the distinguishing characteristics ⟨a *full* member⟩ **c :** being at the highest degree **:** MAXIMUM ⟨*full* strength⟩ **3 a :** plump and rounded in outline ⟨a *full* figure⟩ **b :** having an abundance of material ⟨a *full* skirt⟩ **4 a :** possessing or containing an abundance ⟨a *full* life⟩ **b :** rich in detail ⟨a *full* report⟩ **5 :** satisfied especially with food or drink **6 :** having both parents in common ⟨*full* sisters⟩ **7 :** having volume or depth of sound ⟨*full* tones⟩ **8 :** completely occupied especially with a thought or plan ⟨*full* of one's own concerns⟩ [Old English] — **full•ness** *also* **ful•ness** *n*

[2]**full** *adv* **1 a :** VERY, EXTREMELY ⟨knew *full* well they were lying⟩ **b :** ENTIRELY ⟨fill a glass *full*⟩ **2 :** EXACTLY, SQUARELY ⟨was hit *full* in the face⟩

[3]**full** *n* **1 a :** the utmost extent ⟨enjoy life to the *full*⟩ **b :** the highest or fullest state or degree ⟨the *full* of the moon⟩ **2 :** the requisite or complete amount ⟨paid in *full*⟩

[4]**full** *vt* **:** to shrink and thicken (woolen cloth) by moistening, heating, and pressing [Middle French *fouler,* from Latin *fullo* "fuller"]

full•back \'fúl-,bak\ *n* **1 :** an offensive football back who usually lines up between the halfbacks **2 :** a primarily defensive player stationed usually near his own goal (as in soccer or field hockey)

full–blood•ed \'fúl-'bləd-əd\ *adj* **:** of unmixed ancestry **:** PUREBRED — **full–blood•ed•ness** *n*

full–blown \-'blōn\ *adj* **1 :** being at the height of bloom ⟨a *full-blown* rose⟩ **2 :** fully mature or developed ⟨a *full-blown* scandal⟩

full–bod•ied \-'bäd-ēd\ *adj* **:** marked by richness and fullness ⟨a *full-bodied* wine⟩

full dress *n* **:** formal or ceremonial dress — **full–dress** *adj*

full•er \'fúl-ər\ *n* **:** one that fulls cloth

fuller's earth *n* **:** a clayish earthy substance used in fulling cloth, as a filter medium, and as a catalyst

fuller's teasel *n* **:** TEASEL 1a

full–fledged \'fúl-'flejd\ *adj* **1 :** fully developed **:** MATURE **2 :** having full plumage

full–grown \-'grōn\ *adj* **:** having reached full growth or development **:** MATURE

full house *n* **:** a poker hand containing three cards of one rank plus a pair of cards of another rank

full moon *n* **:** the moon with its whole apparent disk illuminated

full–scale \'fúl-'skāl\ *adj* **1 :** identical to an original in proportion and size ⟨*full-scale* drawing⟩ **2 :** involving full use of available resources ⟨a *full-scale* biography⟩

full tilt *adv* **:** at high speed

full time *n* **:** the standard working time for a given job or period — **full–time** *adj*

ful•ly \'fúl-lē, -ē\ *adv* **1 :** in a full manner or degree **:** COMPLETELY **2 :** at least ⟨*fully* nine tenths of us⟩

ful•mar \'fúl-mər, -,mär\ *n* **:** an Arctic seabird closely related to the petrels [of Scandinavian origin]

ful•mi•nate \'fúl-mə-,nāt, 'fəl-\ *vb* **1 :** to utter or send out censure or condemnation **2 :** to make a sudden loud noise **:** EXPLODE [Medieval Latin *fulminare,* from Latin, "to flash with lightning, strike with lightning", from *fulmen* "lightning"] — **ful•mi•na•tion** \,fúl-mə-'nā-shən, ,fəl-\ *n* — **ful•mi•na•tor** \-,nāt-ər\ *n*

ful•some \'fúl-səm\ *adj* **:** offensive especially from insincerity or baseness of motive ⟨*fulsome* praise⟩ [Middle English *fulsome* "copious, cloying", from *ful* "full" + *-som* "-some"] — **ful•some•ly** *adv* — **ful•some•ness** *n*

fu•ma•role \'fyü-mə-,rōl\ *n* **:** a hole in a volcanic region from which hot gases and vapors issue [Italian *fumarola,* derived from Latin *fumus* "fume"]

[1]**fum•ble** \'fəm-bəl\ *vb* **fum•bled; fum•bling** \-bə-ling, -bling\ **1 :** to feel or grope about clumsily ⟨*fumbled* for the key⟩ **2 :** to handle or manage something clumsily **:** fail to grasp firmly; *esp* **:** to fail to hold, catch, or handle the ball properly in a game (as baseball or football) [probably of Scandinavian origin] — **fum•bler** \-bə-lər, -blər\ *n*

[2]**fumble** *n* **1 :** an act or instance of fumbling **2 :** a fumbled ball

[1]**fume** \'fyüm\ *n* **1 :** a usually irritating or offensive smoke, vapor, or gas — usually used in pl. ⟨engine exhaust *fumes*⟩ ⟨acid *fumes*⟩ **2 :** a state of excited irritation or anger [Middle French *fum,* from Latin *fumus* "smoke, fume"] — **fumy** \'fyü-mē\ *adj*

[2]**fume** *vb* **1 :** to expose to or treat with fumes **2 :** to give off fumes **3 a :** to be in a fume **b :** to express irritable annoyance ⟨*fume* at a delay⟩

fu•mi•gant \'fyü-mi-gənt\ *n* **:** a substance used for fumigating

\ə\ **abut**	\aü\ **out**	\i\ **tip**	\ó\ **saw**	\ú\ **foot**
\ər\ **further**	\ch\ **chin**	\ī\ **life**	\ói\ **coin**	\y\ **yet**
\a\ **mat**	\e\ **pet**	\j\ **job**	\th\ **thin**	\yü\ **few**
\ā\ **take**	\ē\ **easy**	\ng\ **sing**	\t͟h\ **this**	\yú\ **cure**
\ä\ **cot, cart**	\g\ **go**	\ō\ **bone**	\ü\ **food**	\zh\ **vision**

fu•mi•gate \'fyü-mə-ˌgāt\ *vt* : to apply smoke, vapor, or gas to especially for the purpose of disinfecting or of destroying pests [Latin *fumigare,* from *fumus* "fume"] — **fu•mi•ga•tion** \ˌfyü-mə-'gā-shən\ *n* — **fu•mi•ga•tor** \'fyü-mə-ˌgāt-ər\ *n*

fu•mi•to•ry \'fyü-mə-ˌtōr-ē, -ˌtȯr-\ *n, pl* **-ries** : any of a genus of erect or climbing herbs with showy irregular flowers [Middle French *fumeterre,* from Medieval Latin *fumus terrae,* literally, "smoke of the earth"]

¹fun \'fən\ *n* **1** : something that provides amusement or enjoyment; *esp* : playful boisterous action or speech **2** : AMUSEMENT, ENJOYMENT ⟨sickness takes the *fun* out of life⟩ [English dialect *fun* "to hoax"]

²fun *vi* **funned**; **fun•ning** : to indulge in banter or play : JOKE

¹func•tion \'fəng-shən, 'fəngk-\ *n* **1** : professional position or duties : OCCUPATION **2** : the action for which a person or thing is specially fitted or used or for which a thing exists **3** : an impressive, elaborate, or formal ceremony or social gathering **4** : one of a group of related actions contributing to a larger action; *esp* : the normal and specific contribution of a bodily part to the economy of a living organism **5 a** : a mathematical relationship that assigns to each element of one set one and usually only one element of the same or another set **b** : quality, trait, or fact dependent on and varying with another [Latin *functio* "performance", from *fungi* "to perform"] — **func•tion•less** \-ləs\ *adj*

²function *vi* **func•tioned**; **func•tion•ing** \-shə-ning, -shning\ **1** : to have a function : SERVE **2** : to be in action : OPERATE

func•tion•al \'fəng-shnəl, 'fəngk-, -shən-l\ *adj* **1 a** : of, connected with, or being a function **b** : affecting functions but not structure ⟨*functional* heart disease⟩ — compare ORGANIC 1b **2** : serving in a larger whole; *also* : designed or developed chiefly from the point of view of use ⟨*functional* architecture⟩ **3** : performing or able to perform a regular function **4** : organized by functions — **func•tion•al•ly** \-ē\ *adv*

func•tion•ary \'fəng-shə-ˌner-ē, 'fəngk-\ *n, pl* **-ar•ies** : a person charged with the performance of a certain function; *esp* : OFFICIAL

function word *n* : a word expressing primarily grammatical relationship

¹fund \'fənd\ *n* **1** : an available quantity of material or intangible resources : SUPPLY **2 a** : a sum of money or other resources the principal or interest of which is set apart for a specific objective **b** *pl* : available money **3** : an organization administering a special fund [Latin *fundus* "bottom, piece of landed property"]

²fund *vt* **1** : to provide funds for ⟨the government *funded* the project⟩ **2** : to convert (a short-term obligation) into a debt payable at a distant date or at no definite date and bearing a fixed interest ⟨*fund* a debt⟩

fun•da•ment \'fən-də-mənt\ *n* **1** : FOUNDATION 2, BASE **2** : BUTTOCK 2 [Old French *fondement,* from Latin *fundamentum,* from *fundare* "to found", from *fundus* "bottom"]

¹fun•da•men•tal \ˌfən-də-'ment-l\ *adj* **1 a** : serving as an origin or source : PRIMARY **b** : serving as a basic support or essential structure or function : BASIC **2** : of or relating to essential structure or function : RADICAL ⟨a *fundamental* change⟩ **3** : of, relating to, or produced by the lowest component of a complex vibration **4** : of central importance : PRINCIPAL ⟨the *fundamental* purpose⟩ **syn** see ESSENTIAL — **fun•da•men•tal•ly** \-l-ē\ *adv*

²fundamental *n* **1** : something fundamental; *esp* : one of the basic constituents essential to a thing or system **2** : the harmonic component of a wave that has the lowest frequency and commonly the greatest amplitude

fun•da•men•tal•ism \-l-ˌiz-əm\ *n* **1** *often cap* : a movement in 20th century Protestantism emphasizing the literally interpreted Bible as fundamental to Christian life and teaching **2 a** : the beliefs associated with fundamentalism **b** : adherence to such beliefs — **fun•da•men•tal•ist** \-l-əst\ *adj or n*

fundamental particle *n* : ELEMENTARY PARTICLE

¹fu•ner•al \'fyün-rəl, -ə-rəl\ *adj* **1** : of, relating to, or constituting a funeral **2** : FUNEREAL 2 [Late Latin *funeralis,* from Latin *funer-, funus,* n., "funeral"]

²funeral *n* **1** : a ceremony held for a dead person usually before burial or cremation **2** : a funeral party in transit

funeral director *n* : a person who manages funerals and is usually an embalmer

funeral home *n* : a set of rooms with facilities for the preparation of the dead for burial or cremation, for the viewing of the body, and for funerals — called also *funeral parlor*

fu•ne•re•al \fyü-'nir-ē-əl\ *adj* **1** : of or relating to a funeral **2** : suggesting a funeral ⟨*funereal* gloom⟩ [Latin *funereus,* from *funer-, funus* "funeral"] — **fu•ne•re•al•ly** \-ē-ə-lē\ *adv*

fun•gal \'fəng-gəl\ *adj* : FUNGOUS

fungi- *combining form* : fungus ⟨*fungi*cide⟩

fun•gi•cide \'fən-jə-ˌsīd, ˌfəng-gə-\ *n* : a substance that destroys fungi or inhibits their growth — **fun•gi•cid•al** \ˌfən-jə-'sīd-l, fəng-gə-\ *adj* — **fun•gi•cid•al•ly** \-l-ē\ *adv*

fun•go \'fəng-gō\ *n, pl* **fungoes** : a fly ball hit by a player who tosses a ball in the air and hits it as it comes down [origin unknown]

fun•goid \'fəng-ˌgȯid\ *adj* : resembling, characteristic of, or being a fungus — **fungoid** *n*

fun•gous \'fəng-gəs\ *adj* **1** : of, relating to, or resembling fungi **2** : caused by a fungus

fun•gus \'fəng-gəs\ *n, pl* **fun•gi** \'fən-ˌjī, 'fəng-ˌgī\ *also* **fun•gus•es** **1** : any of a major group (Fungi) of lower plants (as molds, rusts, mildews, smuts, mushrooms, and usually bacteria) that lack chlorophyll and are saprophytic or parasitic **2** : infection with a fungus [Latin] — **fungus** *adj*

fu•nic•u•lar \fyü-'nik-yə-lər, fə-\ *n* : a cable railway ascending a mountain; *esp* : one in which an ascending car counterbalances a descending car [derived from Latin *funiculus* "small rope"]

¹funk \'fəngk\ *n* **1** : a state of paralyzing fear **2** : a depressed state of mind [probably from obsolete Flemish *fonck*]

²funk *vb* **1** : to become frightened and shrink back **2** : to be afraid of : DREAD

¹fun•nel \'fən-l\ *n* **1** : a utensil usually shaped like a hollow cone with a tube extending from the point to catch and direct a downward flow (as of liquid) **2** : a stack or flue (as of a ship) for the escape of smoke or for ventilation [Provençal *fonilh,* from Medieval Latin *fundibulum,* from Latin *infundibulum,* from *infundere* "to pour in", from *in-* + *fundere* "to pour"]

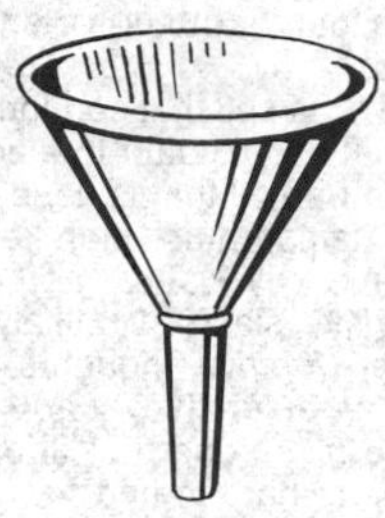

¹funnel 1

²funnel *vb* **-neled** *also* **-nelled**; **-nel•ing** *also* **-nel•ling** **1** : to form, take, or give the shape of a funnel ⟨*funneling* clouds⟩ **2** : to pass through or as if through a funnel ⟨funds were *funneled* into the project⟩

fun•ny \'fən-ē\ *adj* **fun•ni•er**; **-est** **1 a** : affording light mirth and laughter : AMUSING **b** : seeking or intended to amuse **2** : differing from the ordinary in a suspicious way : QUEER **3** : involving trickery or deception — **fun•ni•ly** \'fən-l-ē\ *adv* — **fun•ni•ness** \'fən-ē-nəs\ *n*

funny bone *n* **1** : a place at the back of the elbow where a blow may compress a nerve and cause a painful tingling sensation **2** : a sense of humor ⟨a joke that tickles my *funny bone*⟩

¹fur \'fər\ *vt* **furred**; **fur•ring** : to cover, line, trim, or clothe with fur [Middle French *fourrer,* from Old French *fuerre* "sheath", of Germanic origin]

△ **origin** The hairy coat of a mammal is called *fur.* But originally this coat could not be called *fur* until it had been removed from the animal and used to adorn a human being. The well-to-do of the late Middle Ages wore robes *furred* (lined and trimmed) with the pelts of animals. These trimmings and linings were called *furs.* The word was soon used for the soft hair of animals, even of living animals. But when robes were first *furred,* it was the act of lining rather than the material used that the verb *fur* suggested. Middle French *fourrer,* "to line a garment", which is the source of English *fur,* originally meant "to encase". *Fourrer* was derived from the noun *fuerre,* a Germanic loanword in Old French which meant "sheath".

²fur *n* **1** : a piece of the dressed pelt of an animal used to make, trim, or line wearing apparel **2** : an article of clothing made of or with fur **3** : the hairy coat of a mammal especially when fine, soft, and thick **4** : a coating (as on the tongue) resembling fur — **fur•less** \'fər-ləs\ *adj* — **furred** \'fərd\ *adj*

fur•bear•er \'fər-ˌbar-ər, -ˌber-\ *n* : an animal that bears fur especially of a commerically desired quality

fur•be•low \'fər-bə-ˌlō\ *n* **1** : a pleated or gathered piece of material (as a ruffle or flounce) **2** : showy trimming [by folk etymology from French dialect *farbella*]

fur•bish \'fər-bish\ *vt* **1** : to make lustrous : POLISH **2** : to give a new look to : RENOVATE [Middle French *fourbiss-*, stem of *fourbir* "to furbish", of Germanic origin]

fu•ri•ous \'fyu̇r-ē-əs\ *adj* **1** : being in a fury : FIERCE, ANGRY **2** : VIOLENT ⟨a *furious* wind⟩ — **fu•ri•ous•ly** *adv*

[1]**furl** \'fərl\ *vt* : to wrap or roll (as a sail or a flap) close to or around something [Middle French *ferler*, from Old North French *ferlier* "to tie tightly", from Old French *ferm, fer* "tight" (from Latin *firmus* "firm") + *lier* "to tie", from Latin *ligare*]

[2]**furl** *n* **1** : the act of furling **2** : something that is furled

fur•long \'fər-,lȯng\ *n* : a unit of distance equal to 220 yards (about 201.2 meters) [Old English *furlang*, from *furh* "furrow" + *lang* "long"]

[1]**fur•lough** \'fər-lō\ *n* : a leave of absence from duty; *esp* : one granted to a soldier [Dutch *verlof*, literally, "permission"]

[2]**furlough** *vt* **1** : to grant a furlough to **2** : to lay off from work

fur•nace \'fər-nəs\ *n* : an enclosed structure in which heat is produced (as for heating a house or melting metals) [Old French *fornaise*, from Latin *fornax*]

fur•nish \'fər-nish\ *vt* **1** : to provide with what is needed; *esp* : to equip with furniture **2** : SUPPLY, GIVE ⟨*furnished* them with food⟩ [Middle French *fourniss-*, stem of *fournir* "to complete, equip", of Germanic origin] — **fur•nish•er** *n*

fur•nish•ings \-nish-ingz\ *n pl* **1** : articles or accessories of dress **2** : objects that tend to increase comfort or utility; *esp* : articles of furniture for a room

fur•ni•ture \'fər-ni-chər\ *n* : equipment that is necessary, useful, or desirable; *esp* : movable articles (as chairs, tables, or beds) needed to fit a room for use [Middle French *fourniture*, from *fournir* "to equip"]

fu•ror \'fyu̇r-,ȯr, -,ōr\ *n* **1** : a fit of anger : RAGE **2** : a fashionable craze : VOGUE **3** : an outburst of public excitement or indignation : UPROAR [Latin, from *furere* "to rage"]

fu•rore \-,ōr, -,ȯr\ *n* : FUROR 2, 3

fur•ri•er \'fər-ē-ər\ *n* : a person who prepares or deals in furs — **fur•ri•ery** \-ē-ə-rē\ *n*

fur•ring \'fər-ing\ *n* **1** : a fur trimming or lining **2** : the application of thin wood, brick, or metal to joists, studs, or walls to form a level surface or an air space; *also* : the material used in this process

[1]**fur•row** \'fər-ō, 'fə-rō\ *n* **1** : a trench in the earth made by or as if by a plow **2** : something (as a groove or wrinkle) that resembles the track of a plow [Old English *furh*]

[2]**furrow** *vb* **1** : to make furrows in **2** : to form furrows

fur•ry \'fər-ē\ *adj* **fur•ri•er**; **-est** **1** : consisting of or resembling fur **2** : covered with fur

fur seal *n* : any of various seals with a dense soft undercoat used as a fur — compare HAIR SEAL

[1]**fur•ther** \'fər-t͟hər\ *adv* **1** : [1]FARTHER 1 **2** : in addition : MOREOVER **3** : to a greater degree or extent [Old English *furthor*, comparative of *forth*]

[2]**further** *adj* **1** : [2]FARTHER 1 **2** : going or extending beyond : ADDITIONAL ⟨*further* education⟩

[3]**further** *vt* **fur•thered**; **fur•ther•ing** \'fərt͟h-ring, -ə-ring\ : to help forward : PROMOTE ⟨*furthered* medical research⟩ — **fur•ther•er** \'fər-t͟hər-ər\ *n*

fur•ther•ance \'fərt͟h-rəns, -ə-rəns\ *n* : the act of furthering : ADVANCEMENT

fur•ther•more \'fər-t͟hər-,mōr, -t͟hə-, -,mȯr\ *adv* : in addition to what precedes : BESIDES

fur•ther•most \-,mōst\ *adj* : most distant : FARTHEST

fur•thest \'fər-t͟həst\ *adv or adj* : FARTHEST

fur•tive \'fərt-iv\ *adj* : done by stealth : SLY, SECRET ⟨a *furtive* look⟩ [Latin *furtivus*, from *furtum* "theft", from *fur* "thief"] — **fur•tive•ly** *adv* — **fur•tive•ness** *n*

fu•run•cle \'fyu̇r-,əng-kəl\ *n* : a localized inflammatory swelling of the skin and underlying tissues : BOIL [Latin *furunculus* "petty thief, sucker, furuncle", derived from *fur* "thief"]

fu•ry \'fyu̇r-ē\ *n, pl* **furies** **1** : an intense and often destructive rage **2 a** *cap* : one of the avenging spirits in classical mythology **b** : a violent, angry, or spiteful person **3** : extreme fierceness or violence ⟨the *fury* of the storm⟩ [Latin *furia*, from *furere* "to rage"] **syn** see ANGER

furze \'fərz\ *n* : a prickly evergreen shrub of the pea family with yellow flowers [Old English *fyrs*]

[1]**fuse** \'fyüz\ *n* **1** : a continuous train (as of gunpowder) enclosed in a cord or cable for setting off an explosive charge by transmitting fire to it **2** *usually* **fuze** : a mechanical or electrical detonating device for setting off the bursting charge of a projectile, bomb, or torpedo [Italian *fuso* "spindle", from Latin *fusus*]

[2]**fuse** *or* **fuze** *vt* : to equip with a fuse

[3]**fuse** *vb* **1** : to reduce to a liquid or plastic state by heat **2** : to become fluid with heat **3** : to unite by or as if by melting together : BLEND, INTEGRATE [Latin *fusus*, past participle of *fundere* "to pour, melt"]

[4]**fuse** *n* : an electrical safety device consisting of or including a wire or strip of fusible metal that melts and interrupts the circuit when the current becomes too strong

fu•see *or* **fu•zee** \fyü-'zē\ *n* **1** : a friction match with a bulbous head not easily blown out **2** : a red signal flare used especially for protecting stalled trains and trucks

fu•se•lage \'fyü-sə-,läzh, 'fyü-zə-\ *n* : the central body portion of an airplane which holds the crew, passengers, and cargo [French, from *fuselé* "spindle-shaped", derived from Latin *fusus* "spindle"]

fu•sel oil \'fyü-zəl-\ *n* : an acrid oily liquid occurring in insufficiently distilled alcoholic liquors and consisting chiefly of amyl alcohol [German *fusel* "bad liquor"]

fus•ible \'fyü-zə-bəl\ *adj* : capable of being fused and especially liquefied by heat — **fus•ibil•i•ty** \,fyü-zə-'bil-ət-ē\ *n*

fu•si•form \'fyü-zə-,fȯrm\ *adj* : tapering toward each end ⟨*fusiform* swelling of the fingers⟩ [Latin *fusus* "spindle"]

fu•sil \'fyü-zəl\ *n* : a light flintlock musket [French, "steel for striking fire, fusil", derived from Late Latin *focus* "fire", from Latin, "hearth"]

fu•sil•ier *or* **fu•sil•eer** \,fyü-zə-'liər\ *n* **1** : a soldier armed with a fusil **2** : a member of a British regiment formerly armed with fusils

fu•sil•lade \'fyü-sə-,läd, -zə-, -,lād\ *n* **1** : a number of shots fired simultaneously or in rapid succession **2** : a spirited outburst especially of criticism

fu•sion \'fyü-zhən\ *n* **1** : the act or process of making fluid by heat **2** : union by or as if by melting; *esp* : a merging of diverse elements into a unified whole **3** : the union of atomic nuclei to form heavier nuclei resulting in the release of enormous quantities of energy when certain light elements unite

fusion bomb *n* : a bomb in which nuclei of a light chemical element unite to form nuclei of heavier elements with a release of energy; *esp* : HYDROGEN BOMB — compare FISSION BOMB

[1]**fuss** \'fəs\ *n* **1 a** : needless bustle or excitement : COMMOTION **b** : a show of flattering attention ⟨made a big *fuss* over their grandchildren⟩ **2** : a state of agitation especially over a trivial matter [perhaps of imitative origin]

[2]**fuss** *vi* **1 a** : to create or be in a state of restless activity; *esp* : to shower flattering attentions **b** : to pay undue attention to small details **2** : to become upset : WORRY — **fuss•er** *n*

fuss•budg•et \'fəs-,bəj-ət\ *n* : one who fusses about trifles

fussy \'fəs-ē\ *adj* **fuss•i•er**; **-est** **1** : easily upset : IRRITABLE **2 a** : requiring or giving close attention to details **b** : too particular : FINICKY ⟨*fussy* about food⟩ — **fuss•i•ly** \'fəs-ə-lē\ *adv* — **fuss•i•ness** \'fəs-ē-nəs\ *n*

fus•tian \'fəs-chən\ *n* **1** : a strong cotton and linen fabric **2** : pretentious writing or speech [Old French *fustaine*, from Medieval Latin *fustaneum*] — **fustian** *adj*

fus•tic \'fəs-tik\ *n* : the wood of a tropical American tree of the mulberry family that yields a yellow dye; *also* : a tree yielding fustic [Middle French *fustoc*, from Arabic *fustuq*, from Greek *pistakē* "pistachio tree"]

fus•ty \'fəs-tē\ *adj* **fus•ti•er**; **-est** **1** : saturated with dust and stale odors **2** : rigidly conservative : OLD-FASHIONED [Middle English, from *fust* "wine cask", from Middle French, "club, cask", from Latin *fustis* "club, staff"] — **fus•ti•ly** \-tə-lē\ *adv* — **fus•ti•ness** \-tē-nəs\ *n*

fu•tile \'fyüt-l, 'fyü-,tīl\ *adj* : having no result or effect : useless ⟨a *futile* struggle⟩ **2** : UNIMPORTANT, TRIVIAL ⟨*futile* pleasures⟩ [Latin *futilis*, literally, "that pours out easily"] **syn** see VAIN — **fu•tile•ly** \-l-lē, -,tīl-lē\ *adv* — **fu•til•i•ty** \fyü-'til-ət-ē\ *n*

[1]**fu•ture** \'fyü-chər\ *adj* **1 a** : that is to be **b** : existing after death **2** : of, relating to, or constituting a verb tense formed in

glish with *will* and *shall* and expressive of time yet to come [Latin *futurus* "about to be"]

[2]**future** *n* **1 a :** time that is to come **b :** what is going to happen **2 :** expectation of advancement or development ⟨a promising *future*⟩ **3 :** something (as a commodity) bought or sold for delivery at a future time — usually used in pl. **4 a :** the future tense **b :** a verb form in the future tense

fu•ture•less \-ləs\ *adj* **:** having no prospect of future success or accomplishment ⟨a *futureless* job⟩

future perfect *adj* **:** of, relating to, or constituting a verb tense formed in English with *will have* and *shall have* and expressing completion of an action by a specified time that is yet to come — **future perfect** *n*

fu•tur•ism \'fyü-chə-ˌriz-əm\ *n* **:** a movement in art, music, and literature begun in Italy about 1910 and marked especially by an effort to give formal expression to the dynamic energy and movement of mechanical processes — **fu•tur•ist** \'fyüch-rəst, -ə-rəst\ *n*

fu•tur•is•tic \ˌfyü-chə-'ris-tik\ *adj* **:** of or relating to the future or to futurism — **fu•tur•is•ti•cal•ly** \-ti-kə-lē, -klē\ *adv*

fu•tu•ri•ty \'fyü-'tür-ət-ē, -'tyür-, -'chür-\ *n, pl* **-ties 1 :** FUTURE 1 **2 :** the quality or state of being future **3** *pl* **:** future events

fuze, fuzee *variant of* FUSE, FUSEE

fuzz \'fəz\ *n* **:** fine light particles or fibers (as of down or fluff) [probably back-formation from *fuzzy*]

fuzzy \'fəz-ē\ *adj* **fuzz•i•er; -est 1 :** covered with or resembling fuzz **2 :** not clear **:** INDISTINCT [perhaps from Low German *fussig* "loose, spongy"] — **fuzz•i•ly** \'fəz-ə-lē\ *adv* — **fuzz•i•ness** \'fəz-ē-nəs\ *n*

-fy \ˌfī\ *vb suffix* **-fied; -fying 1 :** make **:** form into ⟨dandify⟩ **2 :** invest with the attributes of **:** make similar to ⟨citify⟩ [Old French *-fier,* from Latin *-ficare,* from *-ficus* "-fic"]

G

g—gyve

g \'jē\ *n, pl* **g's** *or* **gs** \'jēz\ *often cap* **1 :** the 7th letter of the English alphabet **2 :** the musical tone G **3 :** a unit of force equal to the force exerted by gravity on a body at rest and used to express the force to which a body is subjected when accelerated ⟨a force of three *G's*⟩ [sense 3 from *gravity*]

gab \'gab\ *vi* **gabbed; gab•bing :** to talk idly **:** CHATTER [probably short for *gabble*] — **gab** *n*

gab•ar•dine \'gab-ər-ˌdēn\ *n* **1 :** GABERDINE 1 **2 a :** a firm durable twilled fabric having diagonal ribs **b :** a garment of gabardine [Middle French *gaverdine*]

gab•ble \'gab-əl\ *vb* **gab•bled; gab•bling** \'gab-ling, -ə-ling\ **:** to talk fast or foolishly **:** JABBER, BABBLE [probably imitative] — **gabble** *n* — **gab•bler** \'gab-lər, -ə-lər\ *n*

gab•bro \'gab-rō\ *n, pl* **gabbros :** a granular igneous rock containing much magnesium and little quartz [Italian] — **gab•bro•ic** \ga-'brō-ik\ *adj*

gab•by \'gab-ē\ *adj* **gab•bi•er; -est :** TALKATIVE, GARRULOUS

gab•er•dine \'gab-ər-ˌdēn\ *n* **1 a :** a long smock worn chiefly by Jews in medieval times **b :** an English laborer's smock **2 :** GABARDINE 2 [Middle French *gaverdine*]

gab•fest \'gab-ˌfest\ *n* **1 :** an informal gathering for general talk **2 :** a long conversation

ga•ble \'gā-bəl\ *n* **:** the triangular part of an outside wall of a building that is formed by the sides of the roof sloping down from the ridgepole to the eaves; *also* **:** a similar triangular structure (as over a door or window) [Middle French, of Germanic origin] — **ga•bled** \-bəld\ *adj*

gable roof *n* **:** a roof having two sides sloping from a ridge and forming a gable at each end

[1]**gad** \'gad\ *vi* **gad•ded; gad•ding :** to be on the go mainly for pleasure ⟨too busy *gadding* to work⟩ [Middle English *gadden*] — **gad•der** *n*

[2]**gad** *interj* — used as a mild oath [euphemism for *God*]

gad•about \'gad-ə-ˌbaüt\ *n* **:** a person who flits about in social activity — **gadabout** *adj*

gad•fly \'gad-ˌflī\ *n* **1 :** any of various flies (as a horsefly or botfly) that bite or harass livestock **2 :** a person who annoys or criticizes others in an attempt to provoke or stimulate them [Middle English *gad* "spike", from Old Norse *gaddr*]

gad•get \'gaj-ət\ *n* **:** DEVICE 1b, CONTRIVANCE ⟨a *gadget* for peeling potatoes⟩ [origin unknown] — **gad•ge•teer** \ˌgaj-ə-'tiər\ *n* — **gad•get•ry** \'gaj-ə-trē\ *n*

gad•o•lin•i•um \ˌgad-l-'in-ē-əm\ *n* **:** a magnetic metallic chemical element occurring in several minerals — see ELEMENT table [Johann *Gadolin,* died 1852, Finnish chemist]

gad•wall \'gad-ˌwöl\ *n, pl* **gadwalls** *or* **gadwall :** a grayish brown duck about the size of the mallard [origin unknown]

Gael \'gāl\ *n* **1 :** a Scottish Highlander **2 :** a Celtic especially Gaelic-speaking inhabitant of Ireland, Scotland, or the Isle of Man [Scottish Gaelic *Gāidheal* and Irish Gaelic *Gaedheal*]

Gael•ic \'gā-lik\ *adj* **1 :** of or relating to the Gaels and especially the Celtic Highlanders of Scotland **2 :** of, relating to, or constituting the Goidelic speech of the Celts in Ireland, the Isle of Man, and the Scottish Highlands — **Gaelic** *n*

[1]**gaff** \'gaf\ *n* **1 a :** a spear or spearhead for taking fish or turtles **b :** a handled hook for holding or lifting heavy fish **c :** a metal spur for a gamecock **2 :** the spar upon which the head of a fore-and-aft sail is extended **3 :** rough treatment **:** ABUSE [French *gaffe*]

[2]**gaff** *vt* **:** to strike, take, or handle with a gaff

gaffe \'gaf\ *n* **:** a social blunder [French, "gaff, gaffe"]

gaf•fer \'gaf-ər\ *n* **:** an old man [probably alteration of *godfather*]

[1]**gag** \'gag\ *vb* **gagged; gag•ging 1 a :** to prevent from speaking or crying out by stopping up the mouth **b :** to prevent from speaking freely **2 :** to retch or cause to retch **3 :** to make quips [Middle English *gaggen* "to strangle"]

[2]**gag** *n* **1 a :** something thrust into the mouth especially to prevent speech or outcry **b :** CLOTURE **c :** a check to free speech **2 :** a laugh-provoking remark or act **3 :** something (as a story or an action) intended to deceive **:** HOAX

ga•ga \'gä-ˌgä\ *adj* **1 :** CRAZY 2, FOOLISH **2 :** INFATUATED [French, from *gaga* "fool"]

[1]**gage** \'gāj\ *n* **1 :** a token of defiance; *esp* **:** a glove or cap cast on the ground as a pledge of combat **2 :** PLEDGE 2a [Middle French, of Germanic origin]

[2]**gage** *variant of* GAUGE

gag•man \'gag-ˌman\ *n* **1 :** a writer of gags **2 :** a comedian who uses gags

gag rule *n* **:** a rule restricting freedom of debate or expression especially in a legislative body

gag•ster \'gag-stər\ *n* **:** GAGMAN

gai•ety *or* **gay•ety** \'gā-ət-ē\ *n, pl* **-ties 1 :** MERRYMAKING 1 **2 :** gay spirits or manner **3 :** bright showy appearance

gail•lar•dia \gə-'lärd-ē-ə, -'lärd-ə\ *n* **:** any of a genus of chiefly western American herbs of the sunflower family with showy flower heads [*Gaillard* de Marentonneau, 18th century French botanist]

gai•ly *or* **gay•ly** \'gā-lē\ *adv* **:** in a gay manner

[1]**gain** \'gān\ *n* **1 :** resources or advantage acquired or increased **:** PROFIT **2 :** the obtaining of profit or possessions **3 :** an increase in amount, magnitude, or degree [Middle French *gaigne,* from Old French *gaaignier* "to till, earn, gain", of Germanic origin]

[2]**gain** *vb* **1 a :** to get possession of **:** PROCURE **b :** to win in competition or conflict ⟨*gain* a victory⟩ **c :** to get by a natural development or process **:** ACHIEVE ⟨*gain* strength⟩ **d :** to arrive at ⟨*gained* the river that night⟩ **2 :** to win to one's side **:** PERSUADE **3 :** to increase in ⟨*gain* momentum⟩ **4 :** to run fast ⟨my watch *gains* a minute a day⟩ **5 :** to get advantage **:** PROFIT ⟨hoped to *gain* from their crime⟩ **6 a :** INCREASE 1 **b :** to improve in health — **gain ground :** to make progress

gain•er \'gā-nər\ *n* **1 :** one that gains **2 :** a fancy dive in which the diver from a forward position rotates backward and enters the water feetfirst and facing away from the board

gain•ful \'gān-fəl\ *adj* **:** producing gain **:** PROFITABLE ⟨*gainful*

employment⟩ — **gain•ful•ly** \-fə-lē\ *adv* — **gain•ful•ness** *n*
gain•say \gān-'sā\ *vt* **gain•said** \-'sād, -'sed\; **gain•say•ing** \-'sā-ing\ **1** : DENY 4, DISPUTE **2** : to speak against : CONTRADICT [Middle English *gainsayen,* from *gain-* "against" + *sayen* "to say"] — **gain•say•er** *n*
gait \'gāt\ *n* : manner of moving on foot ⟨a slow unsteady *gait*⟩; *also* : a particular pattern or style of such movement ⟨the walk, trot, and canter are *gaits* of the horse⟩ [Middle English *gate* "way, path", from Old Norse *gata*] — **gait•ed** \-əd\ *adj*
gai•ter \'gāt-ər\ *n* **1** : a cloth or leather leg covering reaching from the instep to ankle, mid calf, or knee **2 a** : an ankle-high shoe with elastic gores in the sides **b** : an overshoe with fabric upper [French *guêtre*]
ga•la \'gā-lə, 'gal-ə\ *n* : a gay celebration : FESTIVITY [Italian, from Middle French *gale* "festivity, pleasure"] — **gala** *adj*
ga•lac•tic \gə-'lak-tik\ *adj* : of or relating to a galaxy
ga•lac•tose \gə-'lak-ˌtōs\ *n* : a sugar $C_6H_{12}O_6$ less soluble and less sweet than glucose [French, from Greek *galakt-, gala* "milk"]
ga•la•go \gə-'lā-gō, -'läg-ō\ *n, pl* **-gos** : any of several small active leaping African primates with long ears, a long tail, and long hind limbs [perhaps from Wolof (a language of western Africa) *golokh* "monkey"]

galago

Ga•la•tians \gə-'lā-shənz\ *n — see* BIBLE table
ga•lax \'gā-ˌlaks\ *n* : an evergreen herb related to the heaths that has shiny leaves used in decorations [probably from Greek *galaxias* "Milky Way, galaxy"]
gal•axy \'gal-ək-sē\ *n, pl* **-ax•ies 1 a** *often cap* : MILKY WAY GALAXY **b** : one of billions of systems each including stars, nebulae, clusters of stars, gas, and dust that make up the universe **2** : an assemblage of brilliant or notable persons or things [Late Latin *galaxias,* from Greek, from *galakt-, gala* "milk"]
△ **origin** The system of stars that includes our sun looks, in the night sky, like a broad band of light. We call this band the *Milky Way.* The idea of the whiteness of the Milky Way being similar to that of milk is much older than the English language, however. *Galaxias,* the Greek word for the Milky Way, was derived from the Greek *gala,* "milk". English *galaxy,* derived from Greek *galaxias,* was not used until the 19th century as a generic term for other star systems as well as the one in which we live.
gale \'gāl\ *n* **1** : a strong current of air; *esp* : a wind of from 13.9 to 24.4 meters per second **2** : an emotional outburst ⟨*gales* of laughter⟩ [origin unknown]
ga•le•na \gə-'lē-nə\ *n* : a bluish gray mineral PbS with metallic luster consisting of sulfide of lead and constituting the principal ore of lead [Latin, "lead ore"]
[1]**gall** \'gȯl\ *n* **1** : BILE 1 **2** : something hard to bear **3** : EFFRONTERY, IMPUDENCE [Old English *gealla*]
[2]**gall** *n* **1** : a skin sore (as on a horse's back) caused by chronic irritation **2** : a cause or state of exasperation [Old English *gealla,* from Latin *galla* "gall on a plant"]
[3]**gall** *vb* **1 a** : to fray and wear away by friction : CHAFE **b** : to become sore or worn by rubbing **2** : IRRITATE 1, VEX **3** : HARASS ⟨*galled* by enemy fire⟩
[4]**gall** *n* : a swelling or growth of plant tissue usually caused by fungi or insect parasites [Middle French *galle,* from Latin *galla*]
[1]**gal•lant** \gə-'lant, gə-'länt, 'gal-ənt\ *n* **1** : a fashionable young man **2 a** : a man who shows a marked fondness for the company of women and who is especially attentive to them **b** : SUITOR 3
[2]**gal•lant** \'gal-ənt *(usual in sense 2b)*; gə-'lant, gə-'länt *(usual in sense 3)*\ *adj* **1** : showy in dress or bearing : SMART **2 a** : SPLENDID, STATELY ⟨a *gallant* ship⟩ **b** : SPIRITED, BRAVE **c** : CHIVALROUS 3a, NOBLE **3** : polite and attentive to women [Middle French *galant,* from *galer* "to have a good time", from *gale* "pleasure", of Germanic origin] — **gal•lant•ly** *adv*
gal•lant•ry \'gal-ən-trē\ *n, pl* **-ries 1** *archaic* : gallant appearance **2 a** : an act of marked courtesy **b** : courteous attention to a woman **3** : conspicuous bravery
gall•blad•der \'gȯl-ˌblad-ər\ *n* : a membranous muscular sac in which bile from the liver is stored
gal•le•on \'gal-ē-ən\ *n* : a heavy square-rigged sailing ship of the 15th to early 18th centuries used for war or commerce especially by the Spanish [Spanish *galeón,* from Middle French *galion,* from Old French *galie* "galley"]

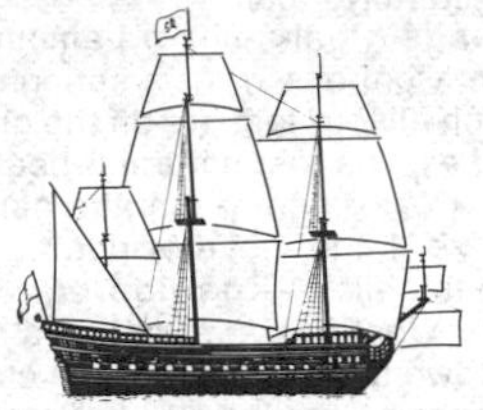
galleon

gal•lery \'gal-rē, -ə-rē\ *n, pl* **gal•ler•ies 1 a** : a roofed promenade : COLONNADE **b** : an outdoor balcony **c** *South & Midland* : PORCH, VERANDA **d** : a structure projecting from one or more interior walls of an auditorium to seat additional people; *esp* : the highest such structure in a theater or the people who sit there **e** : a body of spectators at a tennis or golf match **2 a** : a long narrow room, hall, or passage; *esp* : one having windows along one side **b** : a subterranean passageway (as in a mine) **c** : a passage (as in earth or wood) made by an animal and especially an insect **3 a** : a room or building devoted to the exhibition of works of art **b** : an institution or business exhibiting or dealing in works of art **4** : a photographer's studio [Medieval Latin *galeria*] — **gal•ler•ied** \-rēd\ *adj*
gal•ley \'gal-ē\ *n, pl* **galleys 1** : a large low ship propelled by oars and sails and used in ancient times and in the Middle Ages chiefly in the Mediterranean sea **2** : the kitchen of a ship or airplane **3 a** : an oblong tray with upright sides to hold printer's type that has been set **b** : a proof from type in a galley [Old French *galie,* derived from Middle Greek *galea*]
galley slave *n* **1** : a slave or criminal acting as a rower on a galley **2** : DRUDGE
gall•fly \'gȯl-ˌflī\ *n* : an insect (as a gall wasp) that deposits its eggs in plants and causes galls in which the larvae feed
Gal•lic \'gal-ik\ *adj* : of or relating to Gaul or France [Latin *Gallicus,* from *Gallia* "Gaul"]
gal•li•cism \'gal-ə-ˌsiz-əm\ *n, often cap* : a characteristic French idiom, expression, or trait
gal•li•gas•kins \ˌgal-i-'gas-kənz\ *n pl* **1** : loose wide breeches worn in the 16th and 17th centuries **2** : *chiefly dialect* : LEGGINGS [probably from Middle French *garguesques,* from Spanish *gregüescos,* from *griego* "Greek"]
gal•li•na•ceous \ˌgal-ə-'na-shəs\ *adj* : of or relating to an order (Galliformes) of heavy-bodied largely land-dwelling birds including the pheasants, turkeys, grouse, and the common domestic fowl [Latin *gallinaceus* "of domestic fowl", from *gallina* "hen", from *gallus* "cock"]
gall•ing \'gȯ-ling\ *adj* : very irritating : VEXING
gal•li•nip•per \'gal-ə-ˌnip-ər\ *n* : a large American mosquito [origin unknown]
gal•li•nule \'gal-ə-ˌnül, -ˌnyül\ *n* : any of several aquatic birds related to the rails but having unlobed feet and a shield on the front of the head [Latin *gallinula* "pullet", from *gallina* "hen"]

gallinule

gal•li•um \'gal-ē-əm\ *n* : a rare bluish white metallic chemical element that is hard and brittle at low temperatures but melts just above room temperature — see ELEMENT table [Latin *gallus* "cock" (intended as translation of Paul *Lecoq* de Boisbaudran, died 1912, French chemist)]
gal•li•vant \'gal-əˌvant\ *vi* : to travel or roam about for pleasure [perhaps derived from *gallant*]

\ə\ **abut**	\au̇\ **out**	\i\ **tip**	\ȯ\ **saw**	\u̇\ **foot**
\ər\ **further**	\ch\ **chin**	\ī\ **life**	\ȯi\ **coin**	\y\ **yet**
\a\ **mat**	\e\ **pet**	\j\ **job**	\th\ **thin**	\yü\ **few**
\ā\ **take**	\ē\ **easy**	\ng\ **sing**	\t͟h\ **this**	\yu̇\ **cure**
\ä\ **cot, cart**	\g\ **go**	\ō\ **bone**	\ü\ **food**	\zh\ **vision**

gal•lon \'gal-ən\ *n* — *see* MEASURE table [Middle English *galon,* a liquid measure, from Old North French, from Medieval Latin, literally, "pail"]

gal•lon•age \'gal-ə-nij\ *n* **:** amount in gallons

[1]gal•lop \'gal-əp\ *n* **1 :** a springing gait of a four-footed animal in which all four feet are off the ground at one time once in each stride; *esp* **:** a fast natural 3-beat gait of the horse — compare CANTER **2 :** a ride or run at a gallop [Middle French *galop*]

[2]gallop *vb* **1 :** to move or ride at a gallop **2 :** to run fast **3 :** to cause to gallop — **gal•lop•er** *n*

gal•lows \'gal-ōz\ *n, pl* **gallows** *or* **gal•lows•es :** a frame usually of two upright posts and a crosspiece from which criminals are hanged — called also *gallows tree* [Middle English *galwes,* pl. of *galwe,* from Old English *gealga*]

gall•stone \'gȯl-ˌstōn\ *n* **:** a hard mass formed in the gallbladder or bile passages

gall wasp *n* **:** a wasp that is a gallfly

ga•loot \gə-'lüt\ *n, slang* **:** a person who is odd or foolish [origin unknown]

ga•lore \gə-'lōr, -'lȯr\ *adj* **:** ABUNDANT, PLENTIFUL — used after the word it modifies ⟨bargains *galore*⟩ [Irish Gaelic *go leor* "enough"]

ga•losh \gə-'läsh\ *n* **:** a high overshoe worn especially in snow and slush [Middle French *galoche,* a kind of heavy-soled shoe]

gal•van•ic \gal-'van-ik\ *adj* **1 :** of, relating to, or producing a direct current of electricity ⟨a *galvanic* cell⟩ **2 :** having an electric effect **:** STIMULATING ⟨a *galvanic* personality⟩ — **gal•van•i•cal•ly** \-i-kə-lē, -klē\ *adv*

gal•va•nism \'gal-və-ˌniz-əm\ *n* **:** a direct current of electricity produced by chemical action [Luigi *Galvani,* died 1798, Italian physician and physicist]

gal•va•nize \'gal-və-ˌnīz\ *vt* **1 a :** to subject to the action of an electric current **b :** to stimulate or excite by or as if by an electric shock **2 :** to coat (as iron) with zinc for protection — **gal•va•ni•za•tion** \ˌgal-və-nə-'zā-shən\ *n*

gal•va•nom•e•ter \ˌgal-və-'näm-ət-ər\ *n* **:** an instrument for detecting or measuring a small electric current by movements of a magnetic needle or of a coil in a magnetic filed — **gal•va•no•met•ric** \ˌgal-və-nō-'me-trik\ *adj*

gal•vano•scope \gal-'van-ə-ˌskōp\ *n* **:** an instrument for detecting the presence and direction of an electric current by the deflection of a magnetic needle

gam•bit \'gam-bət\ *n* **1 :** a chess opening in which a player risks one or more minor pieces to gain an advantage in position **2 :** a carefully thought-out move **:** STRATAGEM [Italian *gambetto,* literally, "act of tripping someone", from *gamba* "leg", from Late Latin *gamba, camba,* from Greek *kampē* "bend"]

[1]gam•ble \'gam-bəl\ *vb* **gam•bled**; **gam•bling** \-bə-ling, -bling\ **1 a :** to play a game for money or other stakes **b :** to bet on an uncertain outcome **2 :** to stake something on a doubtful event **:** BET, WAGER **3 :** RISK 1, HAZARD [probably derived from obsolete English *gamen* "to play", from *game*] — **gambler** \-blər\ *n*

[2]gamble *n* **:** a risky undertaking

gam•boge \gam-'bōj, -'büzh\ *n* **:** an orange to brown gum resin from southeast Asian trees that is used as a yellow pigment and purgative [derived from *Cambodia*]

gam•bol \'gam-bəl\ *vi* **-boled** *or* **-bolled**; **-bol•ing** *or* **-bol•ling** \-bə-ling, -bling\ **:** to skip about in play **:** FRISK [Middle French *gambade* "spring of a horse, gambol"] — **gambol** *n*

gam•brel roof \ˌgam-brəl-\ *n* **:** a roof having a double slope on each side with a lower steeper slope and an upper flatter one [Old North French *gamberel* "stick for suspending slaughtered animals", from *gambe* "leg", from Late Latin *gamba*]

gam•bu•sia \gam-'byü-zhē-ə, -zhə\ *n* **:** any of several topminnows used to exterminate mosquito larvae in warm fresh waters [American Spanish *gambusino*]

[1]game \'gām\ *n* **1 a :** activity engaged in for amusement **b :** FUN 1, SPORT **c :** the equipment for a game **2 a :** a procedure for gaining an end **b :** a line of work ⟨the newspaper *game*⟩ **3 a** (1) **:** a physical or mental contest (2) **:** a division of a larger contest (3) **:** the number of points necessary to win (4) **:** the manner of playing in a contest **b :** a situation that involves contest, rivalry, or struggle **4 a** (1) **:** animals pursued or taken in hunting especially for sport or food (2) **:** the flesh of game animals **b :** an object of ridicule or attack — often used in the phrase *fair game* [Old English *gamen*]

[2]game *vb* **:** to play for a stake **:** GAMBLE

[3]game *adj* **1 :** having a resolute unyielding spirit ⟨*game* to the end⟩ **2 :** of, relating to, or being game ⟨*game* laws⟩ ⟨a *game* bird⟩ — **game•ly** *adv* — **game•ness** *n*

[4]game *adj* **:** LAME ⟨a *game* leg⟩

game•cock \'gām-ˌkäk\ *n* **:** a male game fowl

gamecock

game fish *n* **:** a fish of the trout family; *also* **:** a fish regularly sought by anglers for sport

game fowl *n* **:** a domestic fowl of a strain developed for the production of fighting cocks

game•keep•er \'gām-ˌkē-pər\ *n* **:** a person who has charge of the breeding and protection of game animals or birds on a private preserve

game of chance : a game (as a dice game) in which chance rather than skill determines the outcome

game•ster \'gām-stər\ *n* **:** a person who plays games; *esp* **:** GAMBLER

gam•etan•gi•um \ˌgam-ə-'tan-jē-əm\ *n, pl* **-gia** \-jē-ə\ **:** a cell or organ in which gametes are developed [*gamete* + Greek *angeion* "vessel"]

ga•mete \gə-'mēt, 'gam-ˌēt\ *n* **:** a mature germ cell capable of developing into a new individual upon uniting with another such cell [Greek *gametēs* "husband," from *gamein* "to marry", from *gamos* "marriage"] — **ga•met•ic** \gə-'met-ik\ *adj* — **ga•met•i•cal•ly** \-'met-i-kə-lē, -klē\ *adv*

ga•me•to•cyte \gə-'mēt-ə-ˌsīt\ *n* **:** a cell that divides to produce gametes

ga•me•to•gen•e•sis \gə-ˌmēt-ə-'jen-ə-səs\ *n* **:** the production of gametes

ga•me•to•phyte \gə-'mēt-ə-ˌfīt\ *n* **:** the individual or generation of a plant with alternating sexual and asexual generations that produces the gametes from which the asexual sporophyte develops — **ga•me•to•phyt•ic** \-ˌmēt-ə-'fit-ik\ *adj*

gam•in \'gam-ən\ *n* **1 :** a boy who hangs out on the streets **2 :** URCHIN 2 **3 :** GAMINE 2 [French]

ga•mine \ga-'mēn\ *n* **1 :** a girl who hangs out on the streets **2 :** a girl of typically slight build and elfish charm [French, feminine of *gamin*]

gam•ing \'gā-ming\ *n* **:** the practice of gambling

gam•ma \'gam-ə\ *n* **:** the 3d letter of the Greek alphabet — Γ or γ

gamma globulin *n* **:** any of several proteins of blood plasma that include most antibodies

gamma radiation *n* **:** a continuous stream of gamma rays

gamma ray *n* **:** a very penetrating radiation of the same nature as X rays but of shorter wavelength emitted by various radioactive atomic nuclei

gam•mer \'gam-ər\ *n* **:** an old woman [probably alteration of *godmother*]

gam•ut \'gam-ət\ *n* **1 :** the whole series of recognized musical notes **2 :** an entire range or series [Medieval Latin *gamma,* lowest note of a medieval musical scale (from Late Latin, 3d letter of the Greek alphabet) + *ut,* lowest note of each group of six notes in the scale]

△ **origin** In the 11th century, Guido d'Arezzo, a musician and former Benedictine monk, devised a system of musical notation that was later adopted throughout Europe. Guido's system consisted of groups of six notes, which he named *ut, re, mi, fa, sol,* and *la.* Guido called the first line of the bass staff *gamma,* and we can assume that *gamma ut* was the term his followers used for the note falling on this line, that is, the first note of the lowest group of six. This was later contracted to *gamut* and used for the whole scale as well as the lowest note. The term was further generalized to mean the whole range of a voice or instrument. Eventually *gamut* came to be used for an entire range of any sort.

gamy \'gā-mē\ *adj* **gam•i•er**; **-est 1 :** [3]GAME, PLUCKY **2 :** having the flavor of game especially when slightly tainted ⟨*gamy* meat⟩ — **gam•i•ly** \'gā-mə-lē\ *adv* — **gam•i•ness** \'gā-mē-nəs\ *n*

-g•a•my \g-ə-mē\ *n combining form, pl* **-gamies 1 :** marriage ⟨exo*gamy*⟩ **2 :** union for propagation or reproduction ⟨syn*gamy*⟩ [Greek *-gamia,* from *gamos* "marriage"]

Gan•da \'gan-də\ *n, pl* **Ganda** *or* **Gandas** **1 :** a member of a Bantu-speaking people of Uganda **2 :** the Bantu language of the Ganda people

[1]**gan•der** \'gan-dər\ *n* **:** a male goose [Old English *gandra*]

[2]**gander** *n, slang* **:** a usually appraising look [probably from [1]*gander;* from the outstretched neck of a person craning to look at something]

gan•dy dancer \'gan-dē-\ *n* **:** a laborer in a railroad section gang [perhaps from the *Gandy* Manufacturing Company, Chicago, Illinois, toolmakers]

[1]**gang** \'gang\ *n* **1 :** a group of persons working or going about together ⟨a *gang* of laborers⟩ ⟨a *gang* of children playing⟩ **2 :** a group of persons associated together for unlawful or antisocial purposes ⟨a *gang* of thieves⟩ **3 :** two or more similar implements or devices arranged to work together ⟨a *gang* of saws⟩ [Middle English, "journey, set of things or persons", from Old English, "act of going, journey"]

[2]**gang** *vi* **:** to form into or move or act as a gang

[3]**gang** *vi, Scottish* **:** GO, WALK [Old English *gangan*]

gang•land \'gang-ˌland\ *n* **:** the world of organized crime

gan•gling \'gang-gling, -glən\ *adj* **:** LANKY, SPINDLY [perhaps from Scottish *gangrel* "vagrant, lanky person"]

gan•gli•on \'gang-glē-ən\ *n, pl* **-glia** \-glē-ə\ *also* **-gli•ons :** a mass of neural tissue lying outside the brain or spinal cord and containing nerve cells; *also* **:** NUCLEUS c [Greek] — **gan•gli•on•at•ed** \'gang-glē-ə-ˌnāt-əd\ *adj* — **gan•gli•on•ic** \ˌgang-glē-'än-ik\ *adj*

gan•gly \'gang-glē\ *adj* **gan•gli•er; -est :** LANKY, GANGLING

gang•plank \'gang-ˌplangk\ *n* **:** a movable bridge used in boarding or leaving a ship at a pier [English dialect *gang* "passage, journey"]

gang•plow \-ˌplau̇\ *n* **:** a plow designed to turn two or more furrows at one time

[1]**gan•grene** \'gang-ˌgrēn, gang-', 'gan-ˌ, gan-'\ *n* **:** local death of soft tissues due to loss of blood supply [Latin *gangraena,* from Greek *gangraina*] — **gan•gre•nous** \'gang-grə-nəs\ *adj*

[2]**gangrene** *vb* **:** to make or become gangrenous

gang•ster \'gang-stər\ *n* **:** a member of a gang of criminals — **gang•ster•ism** \-stə-ˌriz-əm\ *n*

gangue \'gang\ *n* **:** the rock or earth in which valuable metals or minerals occur [French, from German *gang* "vein of metal"]

gang up *vi* **:** to combine for a specific and often hostile purpose ⟨*ganged up* to fix prices⟩ ⟨*ganged up* on them and beat them⟩

gang•way \'gang-ˌwā\ *n* **1 :** a passage into, through, or out of an enclosed place **2 :** GANGPLANK **3 :** a clear passage through a crowd — often used as an interjection

gan•net \'gan-ət\ *n, pl* **gannets** *also* **gannet :** any of several large fish-eating seabirds that remain at sea for long periods and breed chiefly on offshore islands [Old English *ganot*]

gan•oid \'gan-ˌȯid\ *adj* **:** of or relating to a group (Ganoidei) of teleost fishes with usually hard enameled scales [derived from Greek *ganos* "brightness"] — **ganoid** *n*

gant•let \'gȯnt-lət, 'gänt-\ *variant of* GAUNTLET

gan•try \'gan-trē\ *n, pl* **gantries 1 :** a platform made to carry a traveling crane and supported by towers or side frames running on parallel tracks; *also* **:** a movable structure with platforms at different levels used for erecting and servicing rockets before launching **2 :** a structure spanning several railroad tracks and displaying signals for each [perhaps from Old North French *gantier* "frame for supporting barrels", from Latin *cantherius* "trellis"]

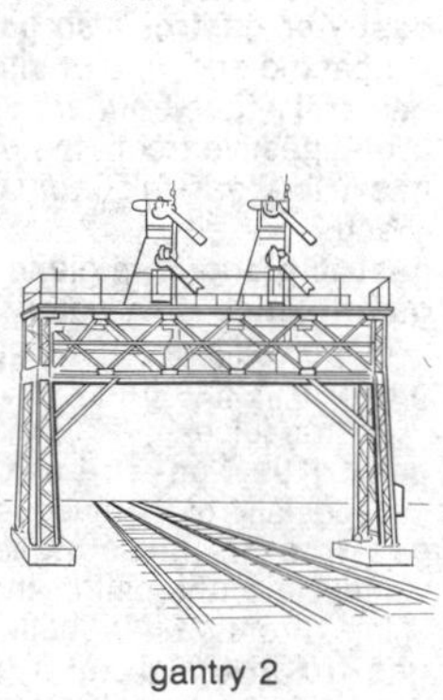
gantry 2

gaol \'jāl\, **gaol•er** *chiefly British variant of* JAIL, JAILER

gap \'gap\ *n* **1 :** an opening made by a break or a parting **:** BREACH, CLEFT **2 :** a mountain pass **3 :** a break in continuity **:** a blank space ⟨a *gap* where the tooth had been⟩ **4 :** a wide difference (as in amount, character, or attitude) [Old Norse, "chasm, hole"] — **gap** *vb*

[1]**gape** \'gāp\ *vi* **1 a :** to open the mouth wide **b :** to open or part widely **2 :** to stare openmouthed **3 :** YAWN 2 [Old Norse *gapa*] — **gap•er** *n* — **gap•ing•ly** *adv*

[2]**gape** *n* **1 :** an act of gaping **2 :** the line along which the mandibles of a bird close **3** *pl* **:** a disease of young birds in which gapeworms invade and irritate the trachea

gape•worm \'gāp-ˌwərm\ *n* **:** a nematode worm that causes gapes in birds

gar \'gär\ *n* **:** any of various fishes with a long body like that of a pike and long narrow jaws; *esp* **:** any of several predatory North American freshwater ganoid fishes with edible but tough flesh [short for *garfish*]

[1]**ga•rage** \gə-'räzh, -'räj\ *n* **:** a building where automobiles are housed or repaired [French] — **ga•rage•man** \-ˌman\ *n*

[2]**garage** *vt* **:** to keep or put in a garage

[1]**garb** \'gärb\ *n* **1 :** a style of clothing **2 :** APPAREL, CLOTHING [Middle French *garbe* "grace", from Italian *garbo*]

[2]**garb** *vt* **:** CLOTHE 1a, ARRAY

gar•bage \'gär-bij\ *n* **:** unwanted or useless material; *esp* **:** food waste [Middle English, "animal entrails"]

gar•ble \'gär-bəl\ *vt* **gar•bled; gar•bling** \-bə-ling, -bling\ **:** to distort the meaning or sound of ⟨*garble* a story⟩ ⟨*garble* words⟩ [Middle English *garbelen* "to cull", from Italian *garbellare* "to sift", from Arabic *ghirbāl* "sieve", from Late Latin *cribellum*] — **gar•bler** \-bə-lər, -blər\ *n*

gar•çon \gär-'sōⁿ\ *n, pl* **garçons** \-'sōⁿ, -'sōⁿz\ **:** WAITER 1 [French, "boy, servant"]

[1]**gar•den** \'gärd-n\ *n* **1 :** a plot of ground where herbs, fruits, flowers, or vegetables are grown **2 a :** a public recreation area or park; *esp* **:** one for the exhibition of plants or animals ⟨a botanical *garden*⟩ **b :** an open-air eating or drinking place [Old North French *gardin,* of Germanic origin]

[2]**garden** *vb* **gar•dened; gar•den•ing** \'gärd-ning, -n-ing\ **1 :** to lay out or work in a garden **2 :** to make into a garden — **gar•den•er** \'gärd-nər, -n-ər\ *n*

[3]**garden** *adj* **1 :** of, relating to, or frequenting gardens **2 :** of a kind grown under cultivation especially in the open **3 :** ORDINARY, COMMONPLACE

garden heliotrope *n* **:** a tall Old World valerian widely grown for its fragrant tiny flowers and for its roots which yield the drug valerian

gar•de•nia \gär-'dē-nyə\ *n* **:** any of various Old World tropical trees and shrubs of the madder family with leathery leaves and fragrant white or yellow flowers; *also* **:** one of the flowers [Alexander *Garden,* died 1791, Scottish naturalist]

gar•fish \'gär-ˌfish\ *n* **:** GAR [Middle English *garfysshe*]

gar•gan•tu•an \gär-'ganch-wən, -ə-wən\ *adj, often cap* **:** of tremendous size or volume **:** GIGANTIC [*Gargantua,* gigantic king in the novel *Gargantua* by Rabelais]

[1]**gar•gle** \'gär-gəl\ *vb* **gar•gled; gar•gling** \-gə-ling, -gling\ **:** to rinse the throat with a liquid kept in motion by air forced through it from the lungs [Middle French *gargouiller*]

[2]**gargle** *n* **1 :** a liquid used in gargling **2 :** a gargling sound

gar•goyle \'gär-ˌgȯil\ *n* **:** a spout in the form of a grotesque human or animal figure projecting from a roof gutter to throw rainwater away from a building [Middle French *gargouille*] — **gar•goyled** \-ˌgȯild\ *adj*

gargoyle

gar•ish \'gaər-ish, 'geər-\ *adj* **1 a :** excessively vivid **:** FLASHY ⟨*garish* colors⟩ **b :** offensively bright **:** GLARING ⟨*garish* lighting⟩ **2 :** tastelessly showy ⟨a *garish* display of wealth⟩ [origin unknown] **syn** see GAUDY — **gar•ish•ly** *adv* — **gar•ish•ness** *n*

[1]**gar•land** \'gär-lənd\ *n* **:** a wreath or rope of leaves or flowers [Middle French *garlande*]

[2]**garland** *vt* **:** to form into or deck with a garland

gar•lic \'gär-lik\ *n* **:** a European bulbous herb of the lily family widely grown for its pungent compound bulbs used in cooking; *also* **:** one of the bulbs [Old English *gārlēac,* from *gār* "spear" + *lēac* "leek"] — **gar•licky** \-li-kē\ *adj*

[1]**gar•ment** \'gär-mənt\ *n* **:** an article of clothing [Middle French *garnement,* from Old French *garnir* "to equip"]

[2]**garment** *vt* **:** to clothe with or as if with a garment

[1]**gar•ner** \'gär-nər\ *n* **:** a bin or building for storing grain [Old French *grenier,* from Latin *granarium,* from *granum* "grain"]

[2]**garner** *vt* **1 :** to gather into or as if into a granary **2 a :** to acquire by effort **:** EARN ⟨*garnered* notoriety with displays of temper⟩ **b :** ACCUMULATE, COLLECT ⟨*garnered* many souvenirs on their travels⟩

gar•net \'gär-nət n **1 :** a brittle and more or less transparent usually red silicate mineral that occurs mainly in crystals and is used as a semiprecious stone and as an abrasive **2 :** a deep red color [Middle French *grenat,* from *grenat,* adj., "red like a pomegranate", from *pomme grenate* "pomegranate"]

gar•net•if•er•ous \,gär-nət-'if-rəs, -ə-rəs\ *adj* **:** containing garnets

garnet paper *n* **:** an abrasive paper with crushed garnet as the abrasive

[1]**gar•nish** \'gär-nish\ *vt* **1 :** DECORATE 1, EMBELLISH **2 :** to add decorative or savory touches to (food) **3 :** GARNISHEE [Middle French *garniss-,* stem of *garnir* "to warn, equip, garnish", of Germanic origin]

[2]**garnish** *n* **1 :** ORNAMENT 1, EMBELLISHMENT **2 :** a savory and usually decorative accompaniment to food

gar•nish•ee \,gär-nə-'shē\ *vt* **-eed; -ee•ing :** to take (as a debtor's wages) by legal authority

gar•nish•ment \'gär-nish-mənt\ *n* **1 :** GARNISH **2 :** a legal warning to a party holding property of a debtor to give it to a creditor; *also* **:** the attachment of such property (as a bank account or pending wages) to satisfy a creditor

gar•ni•ture \'gär-ni-chər, -nə-,chür\ *n* **:** a decorative accessory **:** EMBELLISHMENT [Middle French, "equipment", from Old French *garnesture,* from *garnir* "to equip, garnish"]

gar•ret \'gar-ət\ *n* **:** a room or unfinished part of a house just under the roof [Middle French *garite* "watchtower"]

[1]**gar•ri•son** \'gar-ə-sən\ *n* **1 :** a military post; *esp* **:** a permanent military installation **2 :** the troops stationed at a garrison [Old French *garison* "protection", from *garir* "to protect", of Germanic origin]

[2]**garrison** *vt* **1 :** to furnish (as a fort, town, or region) with troops or military installations for defense **2 :** to assign as a garrison

garrison house *n* **1 :** a house fortified against Indian attack **2 :** a house having the second story overhanging the first in the front

[1]**gar•rote** *or* **ga•rotte** \gə-'rät, -'rōt; 'gar-ət\ *n* **1 a :** a method of execution by strangling with an iron collar **b :** the collar used **2 a :** strangulation especially for the purpose of robbery **b :** an implement (as a length of wire with handles) for this purpose [Spanish *garrote*]

[2]**garrote** *or* **garotte** *vt* **1 :** to execute with or as if with a garrote **2 :** to strangle from behind especially in order to rob — **gar•rot•er** *n*

gar•ru•lous \'gar-ə-ləs\ *adj* **:** very talkative especially about trifles **:** WORDY [Latin *garrulus,* from *garrire* "to chatter"] **syn** see TALKATIVE — **gar•ru•li•ty** \gə-'rü-lət-ē\ *n* — **gar•ru•lous•ly** \'gar-ə-ləs-lē\ *adv* — **gar•ru•lous•ness** *n*

[1]**gar•ter** \'gärt-ər\ *n* **:** a band or strap worn to hold up a stocking or sock [Old North French *gartier,* from *garet* "bend of the knee", of Celtic origin]

[2]**garter** *vt* **:** to support with or as if with a garter

garter snake *n* **:** any of numerous harmless viviparous American snakes with stripes along the back

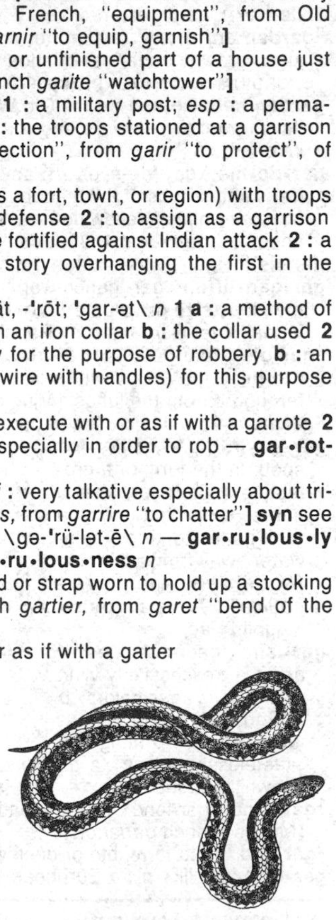

garter snake

[1]**gas** \'gas\ *n, pl* **gas•es** *also* **gas•ses 1 :** a fluid (as hydrogen or air) that has neither independent shape nor volume but tends to expand indefinitely **2 a :** a gas or gaseous mixture used as a fuel or as an anesthetic **b :** a gaseous, liquid, or solid substance (as tear gas or mustard gas) that can be used to produce a poisonous, asphyxiating, or irritant atmosphere **3** *slang* **:** empty talk **4 :** GASOLINE [New Latin, alteration of Latin *chaos* "space, chaos"]

[2]**gas** *vb* **gassed; gas•sing 1 a :** to treat chemically with gas **b :** to poison with gas **2 :** to supply with gas or especially gasoline ⟨*gas* up the automobile⟩ **3** *slang* **:** to talk idly

gas chamber *n* **:** a room in which people are executed by poison gas

gas•con \'gas-kən\ *n* **1** *cap* **:** a native of Gascony **2 :** a boastful swaggering person — **Gascon** *adj*

gas•con•ade \,gas-kə-'nād\ *n* **:** arrogant boastful talk [French *gasconnade,* from *gasconner* "to boast", from *gascon* "gascon, boaster"] — **gasconade** *vi*

gas•eous \'gas-ē-əs, 'gash-əs\ *adj* **1 :** having the form of or being gas; *also* **:** of or relating to gas **2 :** lacking substance or solidity

gas fitter *n* **:** a worker who installs or repairs gas pipes or fittings

gas gangrene *n* **:** progressive gangrene marked by gas in the dead and dying tissue and caused by toxin-producing bacteria

gash \'gash\ *vb* **:** to make a long deep cut in **:** CUT [Old North French *garser,* derived from Greek *charassein* "to scratch, engrave"] — **gash** *n*

gas•hold•er \'gas-,hōl-dər\ *n* **:** a large cylindrical tank for storing fuel gas under pressure

gas•ify \'gas-ə-,fī\ *vb* **-fied; -fy•ing 1 :** to convert into gas **2 :** to become gaseous — **gas•ifi•ca•tion** \,gas-ə-fə-'kā-shən\ *n*

gas•ket \'gas-kət\ *n* **1 :** a line or band used to lash a furled sail **2 :** material (as asbestos, rubber, or metal) used to make a joint leakproof [probably from French *garcette*]

gas•light \'gas-,līt\ *n* **1 :** light made by burning illuminating gas **2 a :** a gas flame **b :** a gas lighting fixture — **gas•light•ing** \-ing\ *n* — **gas•lit** \-,lit\ *adj*

gas mask *n* **:** a mask connected to a chemical air filter and used to protect the face and lungs against harmful gases

gas•ogene \'gas-ə-,jēn\ **1 :** an apparatus carried by a vehicle to produce gas for fuel by partial burning of charcoal or wood **2 :** a portable apparatus for carbonating liquids [French *gazogène,* from *gaz* "gas" + *-o-* + *-gène* "-gen"]

gas•o•line \'gas-ə-,lēn, ,gas-ə-'\ *n* **:** a flammable liquid that evaporates easily, consists of a mixture of hydrocarbons produced by blending products from natural gas and petroleum, and is used especially as a motor fuel [*gas* + *-ol* + *-ine*]

gasoline engine *n* **:** an internal-combustion engine using gasoline as fuel

gas•om•e•ter \ga-'säm-ət-ər\ *n* **:** a laboratory apparatus for holding and measuring gases

gasp \'gasp\ *vb* **1 :** to draw in a breath sharply with shock or other emotion **2 :** to breathe laboriously **:** PANT **3 :** to utter in a gasping manner [Middle English *gaspen*] — **gasp** *n*

gas•ser \'gas-ər\ *n* **:** an oil well that yields gas

gas station *n* **:** SERVICE STATION

gas•sy \'gas-ē\ *adj* **gas•si•er; -est 1 :** full of or containing gas **2 :** having the characteristics of gas **3 :** FLATULENT 1a — **gas•si•ness** *n*

gastr- *or* **gastro-** *also* **gastri- 1 :** belly **:** stomach ⟨*gastr*itis⟩ **2 :** gastric and ⟨*gastro*intestinal⟩ [Greek *gastr-, gastēr*]

gas•tral \'gas-trəl\ *adj* **:** of, relating to, or serving as a stomach or digestive tract ⟨the *gastral* cavity of a sponge⟩

gas•tric \'gas-trik\ *adj* **:** of, relating to, or located near the stomach

gastric gland *n* **:** a gland secreting gastric juice

gastric juice *n* **:** a watery acid digestive fluid secreted by glands in the walls of the stomach

gas•trin \'gas-trən\ *n* **:** a hormone that induces secretion of gastric juice

gas•tri•tis \ga-'strīt-əs\ *n* **:** inflammation of the stomach and especially of its mucous membrane

gas•troc•ne•mi•us \,gas-träk-'nē-mē-əs, -trək-\ *n* **:** the largest muscle of the calf of the leg [Greek *gastroknēmē* "calf of the leg", from *gastēr* "belly" + *knēmē* "shank"]

gas•tro•in•tes•ti•nal \,gas-trō-in-'tes-tən-l, -'tes-nəl\ *adj* **:** of, relating to, or including both stomach and intestine

gas•tron•o•my \ga-'strän-ə-mē\ *n* **:** the art of appreciating fine food [French *gastronomie,* from Greek *gastronomia,* from *gastēr* "belly" + *nomos* "law"] — **gas•tro•nom•ic** \,gas-trə-'näm-ik\ *adj* — **gas•tro•nom•i•cal** \-'näm-i-kəl\ *adj*

gas•tro•pod \'gas-trə-,päd\ *n* **:** any of a large class (Gastropoda) of mollusks (as snails) having a muscular ventral foot and usually a distinct head bearing sensory organs — **gastro·pod** *adj*

gas·tro·trich \'gas-trə-,trik\ *n* : any of a small group (Gastrotricha) of minute freshwater many-celled animals that resemble infusorians [derived from Greek *gastēr* "belly" + *trich-*, *thrix* "hair"]

gas·tro·vas·cu·lar \,gas-trō-'vas-kyə-lər\ *adj* : functioning in both digestion and circulation ⟨the *gastrovascular* cavity of a starfish⟩

gas·tru·la \'gas-trə-lə\ *n, pl* **-las** *or* **-lae** \-,lē, -,lī\ : an early embryo typically consisting of a double cup-shaped layer of cells produced by a folding in of the wall of the blastula [New Latin, from *gastr-*] — **gas·tru·lar** \-lər\ *adj*

gas·tru·late \-,lāt\ *vi* : to become or form a gastrula — **gas·tru·la·tion** \,gas-trə-'lā-shən\ *n*

gas turbine *n* : an engine in which turbine blades are driven by hot compressed gases produced during combustion

gas·works \'gas-,wərks\ *n pl* : a plant for manufacturing gas

¹gat \gat, 'gat\ *archaic past of* GET

²gat \'gat\ *n, slang* : PISTOL [short for *Gatling gun*]

gate \'gāt\ *n* **1** : an opening in a wall or fence **2** : a city or castle entrance often with towers or other defensive structures **3** : the frame or door that closes a gate **4** : a means of entrance or exit **5** : a door, valve, or other device for controlling the passage especially of fluid **6** : the total admission receipts or the number of spectators at a sports event **7** *slang* : DISMISSAL ⟨got the *gate* for loafing⟩ [Old English *geat*]

gate–crash·er \'gāt-,krash-ər\ *n* : one who enters without paying admission or attends without invitation — **gate–crash·ing** \-ing\ *n*

gate·leg table \,gāt-,leg-\ *n* : a table with drop leaves supported by movable paired legs

gate·post \'gāt-,pōst\ *n* : the post to which a gate is hung or the one against which it closes

gate·way \-,wā\ *n* **1** : an opening for a gate in a wall or fence **2** : a passage into or out of a place or state ⟨Gibraltar is the *gateway* to the Mediterranean⟩ ⟨knowledge is the *gateway* to wisdom⟩

¹gath·er \'ga<u>th</u>-ər, 'ge<u>th</u>-\ *vb* **gath·ered**; **gath·er·ing** \'ga<u>th</u>-ring, 'ge<u>th</u>-, -ə-ring\ **1** : to come together in a body **2** : to bring together : COLLECT ⟨*gather* a crowd⟩ **3 a** : PICK 2b, HARVEST ⟨*gather* flowers⟩ **b** : to pick up little by little ⟨*gather* souvenirs⟩ **c** : to accumulate and place in order or readiness ⟨*gathered* up their tools⟩ **4 a** : GROW, INCREASE ⟨the storm *gathered* in intensity as it advanced⟩ **b** : to swell and fill with pus **5 a** : to summon up ⟨*gather* courage to dive⟩ **b** : to prepare (as oneself) by mustering strength **c** : to gain by gradual increase ⟨*gather* speed⟩ **6** : GUESS 1, INFER **7 a** : to draw about or close to something ⟨*gather* a cloak about oneself⟩ **b** : to pull (fabric) along a line of stitching into puckers [Old English *gaderian*]
• **syn** COLLECT, ASSEMBLE, CONGREGATE: GATHER is the general term for bringing or coming together from a spread-out or scattered state ⟨a crowd *gathered* at the scene of the accident⟩ ⟨*gather* all the leaves into one pile⟩ COLLECT often implies careful selection or orderly arrangement ⟨*collect* rare coins⟩ ASSEMBLE implies an ordered gathering for a definite purpose often into a unified whole ⟨*assembled* a team of experts for an antarctic expedition⟩ CONGREGATE implies a spontaneous flocking together into a crowd or huddle ⟨people *congregating* on street corners⟩

²gather *n* : a drawing together; *esp* : a puckering in cloth made by gathering

gath·er·ing *n* **1 a** : the action or an instance of gathering **b** : ASSEMBLY 1, MEETING **c** : a pus-filled swelling (as an abscess) **2** : the collecting of food and raw materials from the wild **3** : something that is gathered: as **a** : COLLECTION 3 **b** : COMPILATION 2 **c** : a gather in cloth

Gat·ling gun \'gat-ling-\ *n* : an early machine gun with a revolving cluster of barrels fired once each per revolution [Richard J. *Gatling*, died 1903, American inventor]

gauche \'gōsh\ *adj* : lacking social experience or grace : CRUDE [French, literally, "left"] **syn** see AWKWARD — **gauche·ness** *n*

gau·che·rie \,gōsh-'rē, -ə-'rē\ *n* : a tactless or awkward action

gau·cho \'gaù-chō\ *n, pl* **gauchos** : a cowboy of the South American pampas [American Spanish]

gaud \'gȯd, 'gäd\ *n* : a showy ornament or trinket [Middle English *gaude*]

gaudy \-ē\ *adj* **gaud·i·er**; **-est** : showily or tastelessly ornamented — **gaud·i·ly** \-l-ē\ *adv* — **gaud·i·ness** \-ē-nəs\ *n*
• **syn** GARISH, FLASHY, TAWDRY: GAUDY implies a tasteless use of overly bright colors or lavish ornamentation; GARISH stresses an unpleasant brightness; FLASHY applies to what is momentarily dazzling but soon revealed to be shallow and vulgar; TAWDRY implies both gaudiness and cheapness of quality.

¹gauge *or* **gage** \'gāj\ *n* **1 a** : measurement according to some standard or system **b** : SIZE 1, DIMENSIONS **2** : an instrument for measuring, testing, or registering ⟨a steam *gauge*⟩ **3** : the distance between the rails of a railroad **4** : the size of a shotgun expressed as the number of lead balls of the same size as the interior diameter of the barrel required to make a pound ⟨a 12-*gauge* shotgun⟩ **5** : the thickness of sheet metal or the diameter of wire or a screw **6** : the fineness of a knitted fabric in loops per 1½ inch (3.81 centimeters) [Old North French] **syn** see STANDARD

²gauge *or* **gage** *vt* **1 a** : to measure exactly the size, dimensions, or other measurable quantity of **b** : to determine the capacity or contents of **2** : JUDGE 5, ESTIMATE ⟨*gauge* the response of the audience⟩ — **gauge·able** \'gā-jə-bəl\ *adj* — **gaug·er** *n*

Gaul \'gȯl\ *n* **1** : a Celt of ancient Gaul **2** : FRENCHMAN

¹Gaul·ish \'gȯ-lish\ *adj* : of or relating to the ancient Gauls or their language or land

²Gaulish *n* : the Celtic language of the ancient Gauls

gaunt \'gȯnt, 'gänt\ *adj* **1** : excessively thin and angular often as a result of suffering or weariness **2** : grim and forbidding : DESOLATE [Middle English] **syn** see LANK — **gaunt·ly** *adv* — **gaunt·ness** *n*

¹gaunt·let \'gȯnt-lət, 'gänt-\ *n* **1** : a protective glove worn with medieval armor **2** : a protective glove used in industry **3** : a dress glove extending above the wrist [Middle French *gantelet*, from *gant* "glove", of Germanic origin] — **gaunt·let·ed** \-lət-əd\ *adj*

²gaunt·let *or* **gant·let** \'gȯnt-lət, 'gänt-\ *n* **1** : a double row of people armed with clubs who strike at a person forced to run between them **2** : CROSS FIRE 1; *also* : ORDEAL 2 [by folk etymology from earlier *gantelope*, from Swedish *gatlopp*]

gaur \'gaùr\ *n* : an East Indian wild ox [Hindi, from Sanskrit *gaura*]

gauss \'gaùs\ *n, pl* **gauss** *also* **gauss·es** : a cgs unit of magnetic induction that is equal to 1 × 10^{-4} tesla [Karl F. *Gauss*]

gauze \'gȯz\ *n* **1** : a thin often transparent fabric **2** : a loosely woven cotton surgical dressing **3** : a woven fabric of metal or plastic filaments [Middle French *gaze*] — **gauz·i·ness** \'gȯ-zē-nəs\ *n* — **gauzy** \'gȯ-zē\ *adj*

gave *past of* GIVE

gav·el \'gav-əl\ *n* : the mallet of a presiding officer or auctioneer [origin unknown]

ga·votte \gə-'vät\ *n* : a lively dance in 4/4 time of French peasant origin [French] — **gavotte** *vi*

¹gawk \'gȯk\ *vi* : to gape or stare stupidly [perhaps from obsolete *gaw* "to stare"]

²gawk *n* : a clumsy stupid person : LOUT [probably from English dialect *gawk* "left-handed"]

gawky \'gȯ-kē\ *adj* **gawk·i·er**; **-est** : CLUMSY 1a, AWKWARD ⟨a tall *gawky* youth⟩ — **gawk·i·ly** \-kə-lē\ *adv* — **gawk·i·ness** \-kē-nəs\ *n*

gay \'gā\ *adj* **1** : happily excited : MERRY **2 a** : BRIGHT ⟨a *gay* sunny meadow⟩ **b** : brilliant in color **3** : given to social pleasures; *also* : LICENTIOUS **4** : HOMOSEXUAL [Middle French *gai*] — **gay·ness** *n*

gay·e·ty *variant of* GAIETY

gay·ly *variant of* GAILY

gaze \'gāz\ *vi* : to fix the eyes in a steady intent look [Middle English *gazen*] — **gaze** *n* — **gaz·er** *n*

ga·ze·bo \gə-'zā-bō, -'zē-\ *n, pl* **-bos** : a freestanding roofed structure usually open on the sides [perhaps from *gaze* + Latin *-ebo* (as in *videbo* "I shall see")]

gaze·hound \'gāz-,haùnd\ *n* : a dog that hunts chiefly by sight; *esp* : GREYHOUND

ga·zelle \gə-'zel\ *n, pl* **gazelles** *also* **gazelle** : any of numerous small graceful swift antelopes [French, from Arabic *ghazāl*]

1ga·zette \gə-ˈzet\ *n* **1** : NEWSPAPER **2** : an official journal [French, from Italian *gazetta*]

2gazette *vt, chiefly British* : to announce or publish in a gazette

gaz·et·teer \ˌgaz-ə-ˈtiər\ *n* : a geographical dictionary [from *The Gazetteer's: or, Newsman's Interpreter* (1693), a geographical index, from earlier *gazetteer* "journalist"]

G clef *n* : TREBLE CLEF

ge- *or* **geo-** *combining form* **1** : earth : ground : soil ⟨*geo*centric⟩ **2** : geographical : geography and ⟨*geo*politics⟩ [Greek *gē-*, *gēo-*, from *gē* "earth"]

1gear \ˈgiər\ *n* **1** : CLOTHING, GARMENTS **2** : EQUIPMENT, PARAPHERNALIA ⟨camping *gear*⟩ ⟨electronic *gear*⟩ **3** : the rigging of a ship or boat **4 a** (1) : a mechanism that performs a specific function in a complete machine ⟨steering *gear*⟩ (2) : a toothed wheel : COGWHEEL (3) : working relation or adjustment ⟨in *gear*⟩ **b** : one of two or more adjustments of a motor-vehicle transmission that determine the direction of travel and the relative speed between the engine and the motion of the vehicle [probably from Old Norse *gervi*] — **gear·less** \-ləs\ *adj*

2gear *vb* **1 a** : to provide with gearing **b** : to connect by gearing **c** : to put into gear **2 a** : to make ready for effective operation ⟨*gear* up for a new season⟩ **b** : to adjust or become adjusted so as to match or satisfy something ⟨*geared* to the needs of the blind⟩ **3** : to be in or come into gear

gear·box \ˈgiər-ˌbäks\ *n* : TRANSMISSION

gear·ing *n* **1** : the act or process of providing or fitting with gears **2** : the parts by which motion is transmitted from one portion of machinery to another; *esp* : a train of gear wheels

gear·shift \ˈgiər-ˌshift\ *n* : a mechanism by which the transmission gears in a power-transmission system are engaged and disengaged

gear wheel *n* : a toothed wheel that gears with another piece of a mechanism; *esp* : COGWHEEL

Geat \ˈgēt, ˈyaət\ *n* : a member of a Scandinavian people of southern Sweden subjugated by the Swedes in the 6th century [Old English *Gēat*] — **Geat·ish** \-ish\ *adj*

gecko \ˈgek-ō\ *n, pl* **geck·os** *or* **geck·oes** : any of numerous small harmless chiefly tropical and nocturnal insect-eating lizards [Malay *ge'kok*]

gecko

1gee \ˈjē\ *imperative verb* — used as a direction to turn to the right or move ahead; compare 4HAW [origin unknown]

2gee *interj* — used to express surprise or enthusiasm [euphemism for *Jesus*]

geese *pl of* GOOSE

gee whiz \jē-ˈhwiz, ˈjē-, -ˈwiz\ *interj* : 2GEE

gee·zer \ˈgē-zər\ *n* : FELLOW 4a, GUY [probably from Scottish *guiser* "one in disguise"]

ge·gen·schein \ˈgā-gən-ˌshīn\ *n, often cap* : a faint light on the celestial sphere opposite the sun [German, from *gegen* "against, counter-" + *schein* "shine"]

Ge·hen·na \gi-ˈhen-ə\ *n* **1** : HELL 2 **2** : a place or state of misery [Late Latin, from Greek *Geenna*, from Hebrew *Gê' Hinnōm*, literally, "valley of Hinnom"]

Gei·ger counter \ˈgī-gər-\ *or* **Geiger–Mül·ler counter** \-ˈmyül-ər-, -ˈmil-, -ˈməl-\ *n* : an electronic instrument for detecting the presence of cosmic rays or radioactive substances [Hans *Geiger*, died 1945, German physicist, and W. Müller, 20th century German physicist]

gei·sha \ˈgā-shə, ˈgē-\ *n, pl* **geisha** *or* **geishas** : a Japanese girl who is trained to entertain men usually with music, dancing, or conversation [Japanese, from *gei* "art" + *-sha* "person"]

1gel \ˈjel\ *n* : a colloid in a more solid form than a sol ⟨fruit jelly and gelatin dessert are *gels*⟩ [*gelatin*]

2gel *vi* **gelled**; **gel·ling** : to change into or take on the form of a gel — **gel·able** \ˈjel-ə-bəl\ *adj*

gel·ate \ˈjel-ˌāt\ *vi* : GEL — **ge·la·tion** \ji-ˈlā-shən\ *n*

gel·a·tin *also* **gel·a·tine** \ˈjel-ət-n\ *n* **1** : gummy or sticky material obtained from animal tissues by boiling; *esp* : a colloidal protein used as a food, in photography, and in medicine **2 a** : any of various substances resembling gelatin **b** : an edible jelly formed with gelatin **c** : a thin colored transparent sheet used to color a stage light [French *gélatine*, from Italian *gelatina*, from *gelare* "to freeze", from Latin]

ge·lat·i·nous \jə-ˈlat-nəs, -n-əs\ *adj* **1** : resembling gelatin or jelly ⟨a *gelatinous* precipitate⟩ **2** : of, relating to, or containing gelatin — **ge·lat·i·nous·ly** *adv* — **ge·lat·i·nous·ness** *n*

geld \ˈgeld\ *vt* : CASTRATE; *also* : SPAY [Old Norse *gelda*]

geld·ing \ˈgel-ding\ *n* : a castrated animal; *esp* : a castrated male horse

1gem \ˈjem\ *n* **1 a** : JEWEL 3 **b** : a precious or sometimes semiprecious stone cut and polished for ornament **2** : something usually small or brief that is prized for great beauty or perfection [Middle French *gemme*, from Latin *gemma* "bud, gem"]

2gem *vt* **gemmed**; **gem·ming** : to adorn with or as if with gems

Ge·ma·ra \gə-ˈmär-ə, -ˈmȯr-\ *n* : a commentary on the Mishnah forming the second part of the Talmud [Aramaic *gĕmārā* "completion"]

gem·i·nate \ˈjem-ə-ˌnāt\ *vb* : DOUBLE 1a [Latin *geminare*, from *geminus* "twin"] — **gem·i·na·tion** \ˌjem-ə-ˈnā-shən\ *n*

Gem·i·ni \ˈjem-ə-nē, -ˌnī\ *n* **1** : the 3d zodiacal constellation pictorially represented as the twins Castor and Pollux sitting together and located on the opposite side of the Milky Way from Taurus and Orion **2** : the 3d sign of the zodiac; *also* : one born under this sign [Latin, literally, "the twins" (Castor and Pollux)]

gem·ma \ˈjem-ə\ *n, pl* **gem·mae** \ˈjem-ˌē\ : BUD; *also* : a many-celled asexual reproductive body that becomes detached from a parent plant [Latin] — **gem·ma·tion** \je-ˈmā-shən\ *n*

gem·ol·o·gy *or* **gem·mol·o·gy** \je-ˈmäl-ə-jē\ *n* : the science of gems — **gem·olog·i·cal** *or* **gem·mo·log·i·cal** \ˌjem-ə-ˈläj-i-kəl\ *adj*

gem·mule \ˈjem-yül\ *n* : a small bud; *esp* : an internal reproductive bud (as of a sponge) [French, from Latin *gemmula*, from *gemma* "bud"]

gems·bok \ˈgemz-ˌbäk\ *n, pl* **gemsbok** *also* **gemsboks** : a large oryx formerly abundant in southern Africa [Afrikaans, literally, "male chamois", from German *gemsbock*, from *gems* "chamois" + *bock* "male goat"]

gemsbok

gem·stone \ˈjem-ˌstōn\ *n* : a mineral or petrified material that when cut and polished can be used in jewelry

1gen- *or* **geno-** *combining form* **1** : race ⟨*geno*cide⟩ **2** : genus : kind [Greek *genos* "birth, race, kind"]

2gen- *or* **geno-** *combining form* : gene ⟨*geno*type⟩

-gen \jən, ˌjen\ *also* **-gene** \ˌjēn\ *n combining form* **1** : producer ⟨andro*gen*⟩ **2** : one that is (so) produced ⟨culti*gen*⟩ ⟨phos*gene*⟩ [Greek *-genēs* "born"]

gen·darme \ˈzhän-ˌdärm *also* ˈjän-\ *n* : a police officer especially in France [French, derived from Middle French *gent d'armes*, literally, "armed people"]

gen·dar·mer·ie *or* **gen·dar·mery** \jän-ˈdärm-ə-rē, zhän-, -ˈdäm-\ *n, pl* **-mer·ies** : a body of gendarmes [French *gendarmerie*, from *gendarme*]

gen·der \ˈjen-dər\ *n* **1** : SEX 1 **2** : any of two or more classes of words (as nouns or pronouns) or of forms of words (as adjectives) that are usually partly based on sex and that determine agreement with other words or grammatical forms [Middle French *genre*, *gendre*, from Latin *gener-*, *genus* "birth, race, kind, gender"]

gene \ˈjēn\ *n* : a specific sequence of nucleotides in DNA or sometimes RNA that transmits a hereditary character and is usually located in a chromosome in the cell nucleus [German *gen*, short for *pangen*, from *pan-* + *-gen*]

ge·ne·al·o·gy \ˌjē-nē-ˈäl-ə-jē, ˌjen-ē-, -ˈal-\ *n, pl* **-gies** **1** : a history of the descent of a person or family from an ancestor **2** : the descent of a person or family from an ancestor : PEDIGREE, LINEAGE **3** : the study of family pedigrees [Middle French *genealogie*, from Late Latin *genealogia*, from Greek, from *genea* "race, family" + *-logia* "-logy"] — **ge·ne·a·log·i·cal** \ˌjē-nē-ə-ˈläj-i-kəl, ˌjen-ē-\ *adj* — **ge·ne·a·log·i·cal·ly** \-ˈläj-i-kə-lē, -klē\ *adv* — **ge·ne·al·o·gist** \-ˈäl-ə-jəst, -ˈal-\ *n*

gene pool *n* : the whole body of genes in an interbreeding population

genera *pl of* GENUS

[1]**gen•er•al** \'jen-rəl, -ə-rəl\ *adj* **1** : of or relating to the whole : not local ⟨a *general* election⟩ **2** : taken as a whole ⟨the *general* body of citizens⟩ **3** : relating to or covering all instances or individuals of a class or group ⟨a *general* conclusion⟩ **4** : not limited in meaning : not specific or in detail ⟨a *general* outline⟩ **5** : common to many ⟨a *general* custom⟩ **6** : not special or specialized ⟨a *general* surgeon⟩ **7** : not precise or definite ⟨*general* comments⟩ **8** : superior in rank ⟨*general* manager⟩ ⟨inspector *general*⟩ [Middle French, from Latin *generalis,* from *gener-, genus* "kind, class"] **syn** see UNIVERSAL

[2]**general** *n* **1** : something that involves or is applicable to the whole **2 a** : GENERAL OFFICER **b** : an officer rank in the Army, Marine Corps, and Air Force above lieutenant general — **in general** : for the most part : GENERALLY

general assembly *n* **1** : a legislative assembly; *esp* : a United States state legislature **2** *cap G&A* : the supreme deliberative body of the United Nations

General Court *n* : the state legislature in Massachusetts and New Hampshire

general delivery *n* : a department of a post office that can be used by individuals as a mailing address

gen•er•a•lis•si•mo \ˌjen-rə-'lis-ə-ˌmō, -ə-rə-\ *n, pl* **-mos** : the chief commander of an army : COMMANDER IN CHIEF [Italian, from *generale* "general"]

gen•er•al•i•ty \ˌjen-ə-'ral-ət-ē\ *n, pl* **-ties 1** : the quality or state of being general **2 a** : GENERALIZATION 2 **b** : a vague or inadequate statement **3** : the greatest part : BULK

gen•er•al•i•za•tion \ˌjen-rə-lə-'zā-shən, -ə-rə-\ *n* **1** : the act or process of generalizing **2** : a general statement, law, principle, or proposition

gen•er•al•ize \'jen-rə-ˌlīz, -ə-rə-\ *vb* **1** : to make general : give a general form to **2** : to draw general conclusions from ⟨*generalized* their experiences⟩ **3** : to reach a general conclusion especially from particular instances — **gen•er•al•iz•er** *n*

gen•er•al•ized *adj* : made general; *esp* : not highly specialized biologically nor strictly adapted (as to an environment)

gen•er•al•ly \'jen-rə-lē, -ə-rə-, 'jen-ər-lē\ *adv* : in a general manner: as **a** : in disregard of specific instances and with regard to an overall picture ⟨*generally* speaking⟩ **b** : as a rule : USUALLY

general officer *n* : an officer ranking above a colonel in the Army, Marine Corps, or Air Force

General of the Air Force : a commissioned officer of highest rank in the Air Force whose insignia is five stars

General of the Army : a commissioned officer of highest rank in the Army whose insignia is five stars

general paresis *n* : insanity caused by syphilis of the brain that leads to dementia and paralysis

general practitioner *n* : a physician or veterinarian who does not limit his or her practice to a specialty

gen•er•al•ship \'jen-rəl-ˌship, -ə-rəl-\ *n* **1** : office or tenure of office of a general **2** : military skill as a high commander **3** : LEADERSHIP

general staff *n* : a group of officers who assist a high-level commander in planning, coordinating, and supervising military operations

general store *n* : a retail store that carries a wide variety of goods but is not divided into departments

general strike *n* : a strike by workers in all industries and enterprises of an area

gen•er•ate \'jen-ə-ˌrāt\ *vt* : to bring into existence: as **a** : to originate especially by a vital or chemical process : PRODUCE ⟨*generate* an electric current⟩ ⟨heat *generated* by friction⟩ **b** : to trace out mathematically (a line, surface, or solid) by a moving point, line, or surface [Latin *generare,* from *gener-, genus* "birth, kind"] — **gen•er•a•tive** \-ə-ˌrāt-iv, -rət-\ *adj*

gen•er•a•tion \ˌjen-ə-'rā-shən\ *n* **1 a** : a group of living beings constituting a single step in the line of descent from an ancestor **b** : a group of individuals born and living at the same time **c** : a type or class of objects developed from an earlier type **2** : the average span of time between the birth of parents and that of their offspring **3** : the action or process of generating ⟨*generation* of an electric current⟩ — **gen•er•a•tion•al** \-shnəl, -shən-l\ *adj*

generative nucleus *n* : the nucleus of a developing pollen grain that produces sperm nuclei — compare TUBE NUCLEUS

gen•er•a•tor \'jen-ə-ˌrāt-ər\ *n* **1** : one that generates **2** : an apparatus in which vapor or gas is formed **3** : a machine by which mechanical energy is changed into electrical energy

gen•er•a•trix \ˌjen-ə-'rā-triks\ *n, pl* **-tri•ces** \-trə-ˌsēz\ : a point, line, or surface whose motion generates a line, surface, or solid

ge•ner•ic \jə-'ner-ik\ *adj* **1 a** : of, relating to, or characteristic of a whole group or class : not specific : GENERAL **b** : not protected by a trademark registration ⟨*generic* drugs⟩ **2** : of, relating to, or ranking as a biological genus — **ge•ner•i•cal•ly** \-'ner-i-kə-lē, -klē\ *adv*

gen•er•os•i•ty \ˌjen-ə-'räs-ət-ē\ *n, pl* **-ties 1 a** : liberality in spirit or act; *esp* : liberality in giving **b** : a generous act **2 a** : ABUNDANCE 1 **b** : LARGENESS

gen•er•ous \'jen-rəs, -ə-rəs\ *adj* **1** : free in giving or sharing : not mean or stingy ⟨a *generous* giver⟩ **2** : HIGH-MINDED, NOBLE ⟨*generous* in dealing with a defeated enemy⟩ **3** : ABUNDANT, PLENTIFUL, AMPLE ⟨a *generous* supply⟩ [Latin *generosus* "highborn, magnanimous", from *gener-, genus* "birth, family, kind"] — **gen•er•ous•ly** *adv* — **gen•er•ous•ness** *n*
• **syn** GENEROUS, BOUNTIFUL, MUNIFICENT mean giving freely and unstintingly. GENEROUS stresses unselfish warmheartedness in giving rather than the size or importance of the gift; BOUNTIFUL implies giving lavishly from ample means or an inexhaustible source of supply; MUNIFICENT suggests a scale of giving appropriate to lords and princes.

gen•e•sis \'jen-ə-səs\ *n, pl* **-e•ses** \-ə-ˌsēz\ : the origin or coming into being of something [Latin, from Greek, from *gignesthai* "to be born"]

Genesis — see BIBLE table

gen•et \'jen-ət\ *n* : an Old World flesh-eating mammal related to the civets [Middle French *genete,* from Arabic *jarnayt*]

ge•net•ic \jə-'net-ik\ *adj* **1** : of or relating to the origin, development, or causes of something **2 a** : of, relating to, or involving genetics **b** : GENIC — **ge•net•i•cal** \-i-kəl\ *adj* — **ge•net•i•cal•ly** \-i-kə-lē, -klē\ *adv*

genetic code *n* **1** : the chemical basis of heredity consisting of specific chemical groupings which make up DNA and RNA and each kind of which determines a particular amino acid in proteins or controls a genetic process (as starting or stopping protein synthesis) **2** : the specific arrangement of the chemical groupings of the genetic code in the hereditary material of an organism

ge•net•ics \jə-'net-iks\ *n* **1** : a branch of biology that deals with heredity and variation of organisms **2** : the heredity and genetic processes of an organism, a group of organisms, or a condition (as a disease) — **ge•net•i•cist** \-'net-ə-səst\ *n*

ge•nial \'jē-nyəl\ *adj* **1** : favorable to growth or comfort ⟨a *genial* climate⟩ **2** : being cheerful and cheering : FRIENDLY [Latin *genialis,* from *genius*] — **ge•nial•i•ty** \ˌjē-nē-'al-ət-ē, jēn-'yal-\ *n* — **ge•nial•ly** \'jē-nyə-lē\ *adv* — **ge•nial•ness** *n*

gen•ic \'jēn-ik, 'jen-\ *adj* : of, relating to, produced by, or being a gene — **gen•i•cal•ly** \-i-kə-lē, -klē\ *adv*

-gen•ic \'jen-ik *sometimes* 'jē-nik\ *adj combining form* **1** : producing : forming ⟨carcino*genic*⟩ **2** : produced by : formed from ⟨nephro*genic*⟩ **3** : suitable for production or reproduction by (such) a medium ⟨tele*genic*⟩ [*-gen* and *-geny* + *-ic;* sense 3 from *photogenic*]

ge•nie \'jē-nē *also* 'jen-ē\ *n, pl* **genies** : JINN [French *génie,* from Arabic *jinnīy*]

[1]**gen•i•tal** \'jen-ə-tl\ *adj* : of or relating to reproduction or the sexual organs [Latin *genitalis,* from *genitus,* past participle of *gignere* "to beget"]

[2]**genital** *n* : one of the genitalia

gen•i•ta•lia \ˌjen-ə-'tāl-yə\ *n pl* : reproductive organs; *esp* : the external genital organs [Latin, from *genitalis* "genital"] — **gen•i•tal•ic** \-'tal-ik, -'tāl-\ *adj*

gen•i•tive \'jen-ət-iv\ *adj* : of, relating to, or being a grammatical case marking typically a relationship especially of possessor or source — compare POSSESSIVE [Latin *genitivus,* literally "of generation", from *genitus,* past participle of *gignere* "to beget"] — **gen•i•ti•val** \ˌjen-ə-'tī-vəl\ *adj* — **genitive** *n*

gen•i•to•uri•nary \ˌjen-ə-tō-'yůr-ə-ˌner-ē\ *adj* : of or relating to

\ə\ **abut**	\aů\ **out**	\i\ **tip**	\ȯ\ **saw**	\ů\ **foot**
\ər\ **further**	\ch\ **chin**	\ī\ **life**	\ȯi\ **coin**	\y\ **yet**
\a\ **mat**	\e\ **pet**	\j\ **job**	\th\ **thin**	\yü\ **few**
\ā\ **take**	\ē\ **easy**	\ng\ **sing**	\th\ **this**	\yů\ **cure**
\ä\ **cot, cart**	\g\ **go**	\ō\ **bone**	\ü\ **food**	\zh\ **vision**

GEOLOGIC TIME AND FORMATIONS

ERAS	PERIODS AND SYSTEMS	EPOCHS AND SERIES	APPROXIMATE NUMBER OF YEARS AGO	EARLIEST RECORD OF ANIMALS	EARLIEST RECORD OF PLANTS
Cenozoic	Quaternary	Holocene (Recent) Pleistocene (Glacial)			
	Tertiary	Pliocene Miocene Oligocene Eocene Paleocene	70,000,000	mankind placental mammals	
Mesozoic	Cretaceous	Upper			
		Lower			grasses and cereals
	Jurassic		160,000,000	birds mammals	flowering plants
	Triassic				
Paleozoic	Permian		230,000,000		ginkgoes cycads and conifers
	Pennsylvanian			insects	primitive gymnosperms
	Mississippian			reptiles	
	Devonian		390,000,000	amphibians	seed ferns vascular plants: lycopods, equisetums, ferns, etc.
	Silurian				
	Ordovician			fishes	
	Cambrian		500,000,000		mosses
Proterozoic	not divided into periods		620,000,000 1,420,000,000	invertebrates	spores of uncertain relationship marine algae
Archeozoic			2,300,000,000		

the genital and urinary organs or functions

ge•nius \'jē-nyəs, -nē-əs\ *n, pl* **ge•nius•es** *or* **ge•nii** \-nē-,ī\ **1** *pl genii* **:** an attendant spirit of a person or place **2 :** a strong leaning or inclination **:** PENCHANT **3 a :** a peculiar, distinctive, or identifying character or spirit **b :** the associations and traditions of a place **4** *pl genii* **a :** JINN **b :** a person who influences another for good or bad ⟨my cousin was my evil *genius*⟩ **5** *pl geniuses* **a :** a single strongly marked capacity or aptitude **b :** extraordinary intellectual power especially as manifested in creative activity **c :** a person endowed with such power; *esp* **:** one with a very high intelligence quotient [Latin, "tutelary spirit, fondness for social enjoyment", from *gignere* "to beget"] **syn** see TALENT

△ **origin** According to ancient mythology, there are supernatural beings whose nature is intermediate between that of a god and that of a human being. It was believed that at birth each person is assigned one of these spirits to act as a guardian throughout life. The Latin name for such a spirit was *genius,* from *gignere* "to beget". *Genius,* in the sense of "attendant spirit", was borrowed from Latin into English in the early 15th century. Part of the role of such a genius was to guard a person's character, and in the 16th century *genius* came to be used for a person's inclination or character. Later this led to the sense of "a strongly marked aptitude", and eventually *genius* came to mean "an extraordinary native intellectual power".

geno- — see GEN-

geno•cide \'jen-ə-,sīd\ *n* **:** the deliberate and systematic destruction of a racial, political, or cultural group — **geno•cid•al** \,jen-ə-'sīd-l\ *adj*

ge•nome \'jē-,nōm\ *or* **ge•nom** \-,näm\ *n* **:** one haploid set of chromosomes with the genes they contain [German *genom,* from *gen* "gene" + chromosom "chromosome"] — **ge•no•mic** \ji-'nō-mik, -'näm-ik\ *adj*

ge•no•type \'jē-nə-,tīp, 'jen-ə-\ *n* **:** the genetic constitution of an individual or group — **ge•no•typ•ic** \,jē-nə-'tip-ik, ,jen-ə-\ *adj* — **ge•no•typ•i•cal•ly** \-i-kə-lē, -klē\ *adv*

-g•e•nous \j-ə-nəs\ *adj combining form* **1 :** producing **:** yielding **2 :** having (such) an origin ⟨endo*genous*⟩ [*-gen* + *-ous*]

genre \'zhän-rə, 'zhä^n-, 'zhäng-; 'zhä^{n}r, 'zhä^n-ər\ *n* **1 :** KIND 1b, SORT **2 :** paintings that depict scenes or events from everyday life usually realistically; *also* **:** the style of painting featuring such subject matter **3 :** a distinctive type or category of literary or musical composition [French, from Middle French, "kind, gender"]

gens \'jenz, 'gens\ *n, pl* **gen•tes** \'jen-,tēz, 'gen-,tās\ **:** a Roman clan embracing the families of the same stock in the male line [Latin]

gent \'jent\ *n* **:** FELLOW 4a [short for *gentleman*]

gen•teel \jen-'tēl\ *adj* **1 :** of or relating or appropriate to an upper class (as in elegance, refinement, or style) **2 a :** maintaining the appearance of superior or middle-class social status or respectability **b :** marked by false delicacy, prudery, or affectation [Middle French *gentil* "gentle"] — **gen•teel•ly** \-'tēl-lē\ *adv* — **gen•teel•ness** *n*

gen•tian \'jen-chən\ *n* **:** any of various herbs with opposite smooth leaves and showy usually blue flowers [Middle French *gentiane,* from Latin *gentiana*]

gentian violet *n, often cap G&V* **:** a violet dye in the form of a green powder produced chemically and used as a biological stain and as an antiseptic in bacterial and fungus infections

gen•tile \'jen-,tīl\ *n* **1** *often cap* **:** a person who is not Jewish **2 :** HEATHEN 1, PAGAN **3** *often cap* **:** a person who is not a Mormon [Late Latin *gentilis* "heathen", from Latin *gent-, gens* "clan, nation"] — **gentile** *adj, often cap*

gen•til•i•ty \jen-'til-ət-ē\ *n, pl* **-ties** **1 :** good birth and family **2 a :** the qualities and manners characteristic of a well-bred person **b :** affectedly delicate or prudish attitude or behavior **3 :** maintenance of the appearance of superior or middle-class social status

[1]**gen•tle** \'jent-l\ *adj* **gen•tler** \'jent-lər, -l-ər\; **gen•tlest** \'jent-ləst, -l-əst\ **1 a :** belonging or suitable to a family of high social station **b :** NOBLE, DISTINGUISHED ⟨of *gentle* blood⟩ **c :** AMIABLE, KIND ⟨*gentle* reader⟩ **2 a :** TRACTABLE 1, DOCILE ⟨a *gentle* horse⟩ **b :** not harsh or stern ⟨*gentle* words⟩ **3 :** SOFT, DELICATE ⟨a *gentle* touch⟩ **4 :** MODERATE ⟨a *gentle* slope⟩ [Old French *gentil,* from Latin *gentilis* "of a clan, of the same clan", from *gent-, gens* "clan, nation"] — **gen•tle•ness** \'jent-l-nəs\ *n* — **gent•ly** \'jent-lē\ *adv*

[2]**gentle** *vt* **gen•tled**; **gen•tling** \'jent-ling, -l-ing\ **1 :** to make mild, docile, soft, or moderate **2 :** PLACATE, MOLLIFY

gen•tle•folk \'jent-l-,fōk\ *also* **gen•tle•folks** \-,fōks\ *n pl* **:** persons of good family and breeding

gen•tle•man \'jent-l-mən\ *n* **1 :** a man of good family **2 a :** a well-bred man of good education and social position **b :** a thoughtful, polite, well-mannered male ⟨that cabdriver was a real *gentleman*⟩ **3 :** MAN — used in the pl. as a form of address in speaking to a group of men

gen•tle•man•ly \-lē\ *adj* **:** characteristic of or having the character of a gentleman — **gen•tle•man•li•ness** *n*

gentleman's agreement *n* **:** an unwritten agreement secured only by the honor of the participants — called also *gentlemen's agreement*

gen•tle•wom•an \'jent-l-,wu̇m-ən\ *n* **1 :** a woman of good family or breeding **2 :** a woman attending a lady of rank

gen•try \'jen-trē\ *n* **1 :** people of good birth, breeding, and education **:** ARISTOCRACY **2 :** the class of British people between the nobility and the yeomanry **3 :** PEOPLE; *esp* **:** persons of a designated class ⟨the academic *gentry*⟩ [Old French *genterise,* alteration of *gentelise,* from *gentil* "gentle"]

gen•u•flect \'jen-yə-,flekt\ *vi* **:** to kneel on one knee and then rise again especially as an act of reverence [Late Latin *genuflectere,* from Latin *genu* "knee" + *flectere* "to bend"] — **gen•u•flec•tion** \,jen-yə-'flek-shən\ *n*

gen•u•ine \'jen-yə-wən\ *adj* **1 :** being actually what it seems to be **:** REAL ⟨*genuine* gold⟩ ⟨a *genuine* antique⟩ **2 :** SINCERE, HONEST ⟨a *genuine* interest in classical music⟩ [Latin *genuinus* "native, genuine"] **syn** see AUTHENTIC — **gen•u•ine•ly** *adv* — **gen•u•ine•ness** *n*

ge•nus \'jē-nəs\ *n, pl* **gen•era** \'jen-ə-rə\ **1 :** a category of biological classification ranking between the family and the species, comprising structurally or genetically related species and being designated by a capitalized singular noun formed in Latin **2 :** a class of objects divided into several subordinate groups [Latin *gener-, genus* "birth, race, kind"]

-g•e•ny \j-ə-nē\ *n combining form, pl* **-genies** **:** generation **:** production ⟨phylo*geny*⟩ [Greek *-geneia* "act of being born", from *-genēs* "born"]

geo — see GE-

geo•cen•tric \,jē-ō-'sen-trik\ *adj* **1 :** relating to or measured from the earth's center **2 :** having or relating to the earth as a center — compare HELIOCENTRIC

geo•chem•is•try \-'kem-ə-strē\ *n* **:** a science that deals with the chemical composition of and chemical changes in the crust of the earth — **geo•chem•i•cal** \-'kem-i-kəl\ *adj*

geo•chro•nol•o•gy \,jē-ō-krə-'näl-ə-jē\ *n* **:** the chronology of the past as indicated by geologic data — **geo•chro•no•log•i•cal** \-,krän-l-'äj-i-kəl, -,krōn-\ *adj*

ge•ode \'je-,ōd\ *n* **:** a nodule of stone having a cavity lined with crystals or mineral matter; *also* **:** the cavity in a geode [Latin *geodes,* a kind of gem, from Greek *geōdēs* "earthlike", from *gē* "earth"]

[1]**ge•o•de•sic** \,jē-ə-'des-ik, -'dēs-, -'dez-, -'dēz-\ *adj* **:** made of a framework of light straight-sided polygons in tension ⟨a *geodesic* dome⟩ [derived from Greek *geōdaisia* "measuring or surveying of land", from *geō-* "ge-" + *daiesthai* "to divide"]

[2]**geodesic** *n* **:** the shortest line between two points on a surface

geo•det•ic survey \,jē-ə-,det-ik-\ *n* **:** a survey of a large land area in which corrections are made for the curvature of the earth's surface [*geodetic* derived from Greek *geōdaisia* "land measuring"] — **geodetic surveying** *n*

ge•og•ra•pher \jē-'äg-rə-fər\ *n* **:** a specialist in geography

ge•o•graph•ic \,jē-ə-'graf-ik\ *or* **geo•graph•i•cal** \-i-kəl\ *adj* **1 :** of or relating to geography **2 :** belonging to or characteristic of a particular region ⟨*geographic* features of the plains⟩ — **ge•o•graph•i•cal•ly** \-i-kə-lē, -klē\ *adv*

geographical mile *n* **:** NAUTICAL MILE

ge•og•ra•phy \jē-'äg-rə-fē\ *n, pl* **-phies** **1 :** a science that deals with the distribution and interaction of the diverse physical and cultural features of the earth's surface **2 :** the natural features of an area

geologic time *n* **:** the long period of time marked by the sequence of events in the earth's geological history

ge•ol•o•gy \jē-'äl-ə-jē\ *n, pl* **-gies 1 a :** a science that deals with the history of the earth and its life especially as recorded in rocks **b :** a study of the features of a celestial body (as the moon) **2 :** the geologic features of an area — **geo•log•ic** \ˌjē-ə-'läj-ik\ *or* **geo•log•i•cal** \-i-kəl\ *adj* — **geo•log•i•cal•ly** \-i-kə-lē, -klē\ *adv* — **ge•ol•o•gist** \jē-'äl-ə-jəst\ *n*

geo•mag•net•ic \ˌjē-ō-mag-'net-ik\ *adj* **:** of or relating to the magnetism of the earth — **geo•mag•ne•tism** \-'mag-nə-ˌtiz-əm\ *n*

ge•om•e•ter \jē-'äm-ət-ər\ *n* **:** a specialist in geometry

geo•met•ric \ˌjē-ə-'me-trik\ *also* **geo•met•ri•cal** \-'me-tri-kəl\ *adj* **1 :** of, relating to, or based on the methods or principles of geometry **2 :** utilizing rectilinear or simple curvilinear motifs or outlines in design — **geo•met•ri•cal•ly** \-tri-kə-lē, -klē\ *adv*

geo•me•tri•cian \jē-ˌäm-ə-'trish-ən, ˌjē-ə-mə-\ *n* **:** GEOMETER

geometric mean *n* **1 :** the square root of the product of two terms; *also* **:** the *n*th root of the product of *n* numbers **2 :** a term between any two terms of a geometric progression

geometric progression *n* **:** a progression (as 1, 1/2, 1/4) in which the ratio of a term to the preceding one is always the same

geo•met•rid \jē-'äm-ə-trəd, ˌjē-ə-'me-trəd\ *n* **:** any of a family of medium-sized moths with large wings and larvae that are loopers — **geometrid** *adj*

ge•om•e•try \jē-'äm-ə-trē\ *n* **1 a :** a branch of mathematics that deals with the measurement, properties, and relationships of points, lines, angles, surfaces, and solids **b :** a particular type or system of geometry **2 a :** the arrangement of the parts of a device ⟨the *geometry* of an electron tube⟩ **b :** SHAPE ⟨the *geometry* of a crystal⟩ **[**Middle French *geometrie,* from Latin *geometria,* from Greek *geōmetria,* from *geōmetrein* "to measure the earth", from *geō-* "ge-" + *metron* "measure"**]**

geo•mor•phol•o•gy \ˌjē-ə-mȯr-'fäl-ə-jē\ *n* **:** a science that deals with the land and submarine relief features of the earth's surface — **geo•mor•pho•log•i•cal** \-ˌmȯr-fə-'läj-i-kəl\ *adj*

geo•phys•ics \ˌjē-ə-'fiz-iks\ *n* **:** the physics of the earth including the fields of meteorology, hydrology, oceanography, seismology, volcanology, magnetism, and geodesy — **geo•phys•i•cal** \-'fiz-i-kəl\ *adj* — **geo•phys•i•cist** \-'fiz-ə-səst\ *n*

geo•pol•i•tics \ˌjē-ō-'päl-ə-ˌtiks\ *n* **:** study of the influence of such factors as geography, economics, and population on the politics and especially the foreign policy of a state — **geo•po•lit•i•cal** \-pə-'lit-i-kəl\ *adj*

geor•gette \jȯr-'jet\ *n* **:** a thin strong clothing crepe having a dull pebbly surface **[**from *Georgette,* a former trademark**]**

[1]**Geor•gian** \'jȯr-jən\ *adj* **1 :** of, relating to, or characteristic of the reigns of the first four Georges of Great Britain ⟨*Georgian* architecture⟩ **2 :** of, relating to, or characteristic of the reign of George V of Great Britain

[2]**Georgian** *n* **:** one belonging to either of the Georgian periods

geo•sci•ence \ˌjē-ō-'sī-əns\ *n* **:** any of the sciences dealing with the earth

geo•syn•cline \-'sin-ˌklīn\ *n* **:** a great elongate subsidence of the earth's crust

geo•tax•is \-'tak-səs\ *n* **:** a taxis in which the force of gravity is the controlling stimulus — **geo•tac•tic** \-'tak-tik\ *adj* — **geo•tac•ti•cal•ly** \-ti-kə-lē, -klē\ *adv*

geo•ther•mal \-'thər-məl\ *or* **geo•ther•mic** \-mik\ *adj* **:** of or relating to the heat of the earth's interior; *also* **:** produced by such heat ⟨*geothermal* steam⟩

ge•ot•ro•pism \jē-'ä-trə-ˌpiz-əm\ *n* **:** a tropism involving turning or movement toward the earth — **geo•tro•pic** \ˌjē-ə-'trō-pik, -'träp-ik\ *adj* — **geo•tro•pi•cal•ly** \-'trō-pi-kə-lē, -'träp-i-, -klē\ *adv*

ge•ra•ni•um \jə-'rā-nē-əm\ *n* **1 :** any of a widely distributed genus of herbs with usually deeply cut leaves, regular flowers in which glands alternate with the petals, and long slender dry fruits **2 :** any of a genus of herbs that are distinguished by clusters of scarlet, pink, or white flowers with the sepals joined at the base into a hollow spur and that are popular as window plants — called also *pelargonium* **[**Latin, from Greek *geranion,* from *geranos* "crane"**]**

ger•bil *also* **ger•bille** \'jər-bəl\ *n* **:** any of numerous Old World burrowing desert rodents with long hind legs adapted for leaping **[**French *gerbille***]**

ger•i•at•ric \ˌjer-ē-'a-trik\ *adj* **:** of or relating to geriatrics, the old, or the process of aging **[**Greek *gēras* "old age" + *iatros* "physician"**]**

ger•i•at•rics \ˌjer-ē-'a-triks\ *n* **:** a branch of medicine that deals with the problems and diseases of old age and aging people — compare GERONTOLOGY — **ger•i•a•tri•cian** \ˌjer-ē-ə-'trish-ən\ *n*

germ \'jərm\ *n* **1 :** a small mass of living substance capable of developing into an organism or one of its parts **2 :** something that serves or may serve as an origin **:** RUDIMENT ⟨the *germ* of an idea⟩ **3 :** MICROBE; *esp* **:** one causing disease **[**French *germe,* from Latin *germen,* from *gignere* "to beget"**]**

Ger•man \'jər-mən\ *n* **1 a :** a native or inhabitant of Germany **b :** a person of German descent **2 :** the Germanic language of Germany, Austria, and parts of Switzerland **3** *often not cap* **a :** a dance consisting of capriciously involved figures intermingled with waltzes **b** *chiefly Midland* **:** a dancing party; *esp* **:** one at which the german is danced **[**Latin *Germanus,* any member of the Germanic peoples**]** — **German** *adj*

ger•man•der \jər-'man-dər, ˌjər-\ *n* **:** a plant of the mint family with dense spikes of purple flowers **[**derived from Greek *chamaidrys,* from *chamai* "on the ground" + *drys* "tree"**]**

ger•mane \jər-'mān, ˌjər-\ *adj* **:** having a significant connection **:** PERTINENT **[**Middle English *germain* "closely related", derived from Latin *germanus* "having the same parents", from *germen* "bud, sprout, germ"**]** — **ger•mane•ly** *adv*

[1]**Ger•man•ic** \jər-'man-ik, ˌjər-\ *adj* **1 :** GERMAN **2 :** of, relating to, or characteristic of the Germanic-speaking peoples **3 :** of, relating to, or constituting Germanic

[2]**Germanic** *n* **:** a branch of the Indo-European language family containing English, German, Dutch, Afrikaans, Flemish, Frisian, the Scandinavian languages, and Gothic

ger•ma•ni•um \jər-'mā-nē-əm, ˌjər-\ *n* **:** a grayish white hard brittle chemical element that resembles silicon and is used as a semiconductor — see ELEMENT table **[**New Latin, from Medieval Latin *Germania* "Germany"**]**

ger•man•ize \'jər-mə-ˌnīz\ *vt, often cap* **:** to cause to acquire German characteristics — **ger•man•iza•tion** \ˌjər-mə-nə-'zā-shən\ *n, often cap*

German measles *n sing or pl* **:** an acute contagious virus disease that is usually milder than typical measles but is likely to cause damage to the fetus when occurring early in pregnancy

Ger•mano- \jər-'man-ō, ˌjər-\ *combining form* **1 :** German **2 :** German and

German shepherd *n* **:** a large erect-eared dog of a breed originating in northern Europe that is often used in police work and as a guide dog for the blind

German silver *n* **:** NICKEL SILVER

germ cell *n* **:** an egg or sperm or one of the cells from which they arise

ger•mi•cid•al \ˌjər-mə-'sīd-l\ *adj* **:** of or relating to a germicide; *also* **:** destroying germs

ger•mi•cide \'jər-mə-ˌsīd\ *n* **:** an agent that destroys germs

ger•mi•nal \'jər-mən-l\ *adj* **1 :** of or relating to a germ or germ cell; *also* **:** EMBRYONIC **2 :** CREATIVE ⟨*germinal* ideas⟩ — **ger•mi•nal•ly** \-l-ē\ *adv*

ger•mi•nate \'jər-mə-ˌnāt\ *vb* **1 :** to cause to sprout or develop **2 :** to begin to grow **:** SPROUT **3 :** to come into being **:** EVOLVE ⟨an idea that *germinated* slowly⟩ **[**Latin *germinare* "to sprout", from *germin-, germen* "bud, sprout, germ"**]** — **ger•mi•na•tion** \ˌjər-mə-'nā-shən\ *n*

ger•mi•na•tive \'jər-mə-ˌnāt-iv\ *adj* **:** having the power to germinate or to develop

germ layer *n* **:** any of the three primary layers of cells formed in most embryos during and immediately following gastrulation — called also *primary germ layer*; compare ECTODERM, ENDODERM, MESODERM

germ plasm *n* **1 :** germ cells viewed as the bearers of hereditary material **2 :** GENES

germ theory *n* **:** a theory that infectious and contagious disorders result from the action of living organisms

germ warfare *n* **:** the use of harmful microorganisms (as bacteria) as weapons in war

ger•on•tol•o•gy \ˌjer-ən-'täl-ə-jē\ *n* **:** a branch of knowledge dealing with aging and the problems of the old — compare GERIATRICS **[**Greek *geront-, gerōn* "old man"**]** — **ger•on•to•log•i•cal** \ˌjer-ˌänt-l-'äj-i-kəl\ *adj* — **ger•on•tol•o•gist** \ˌjer-ən-'täl-ə-jəst\ *n*

[1]**ger•ry•man•der** \ˌjer-ē-'man-dər, 'jer-ē-, *also* ˌger-, 'ger-\ *n* **1 :** the act or method of gerrymandering **2 :** a district or pattern of districts varying greatly in size or population as a result of gerrymandering **[**Elbridge *Gerry,* died 1814, American statesman + *-mander* (as in *salamander*); from the shape of an election district formed during Gerry's governorship of Massachusetts**]**

[2]**gerrymander** *vt* **-dered; -der•ing** \-də-riŋ, -driŋ\ **:** to divide (as a state or county) into election districts so as to give one political party an advantage over its opponents

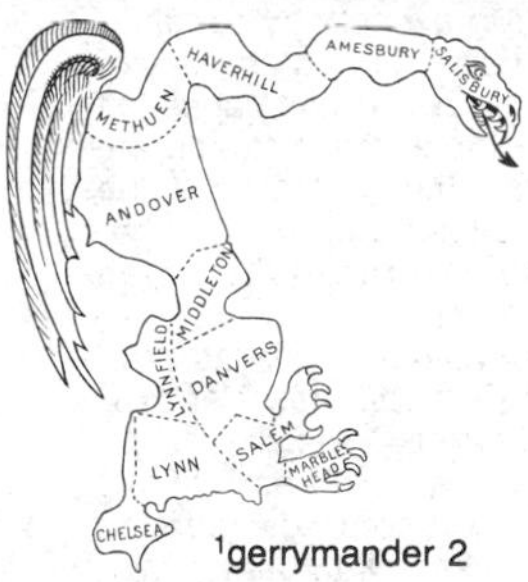

[1]gerrymander 2

ger•und \'jer-ənd\ *n* **1 :** a verbal noun in Latin that expresses generalized or uncompleted action **2 :** an English verbal noun in *-ing* used as a substantive and at the same time capable of taking adverbial modifiers and having an object **[**Late Latin *gerundium,* from Latin *gerere* "to carry, carry on"**]**

ge•run•dive \jə-'rən-div\ *n* **:** a Latin verbal adjective that expresses necessity or fitness and has the same suffix as the gerund

ges•so \'jes-ō\ *n* **:** plaster of paris or gypsum mixed with a binder for use as a surface for painting or in making bas-reliefs **[**Italian, literally, "gypsum", from Latin *gypsum***]**

gest *or* **geste** \'jest\ *n* **1 :** a remarkable deed **:** EXPLOIT **2 :** a tale of adventures; *esp* **:** a medieval tale in verse **[**Old French *geste,* from Latin *gesta* "exploits", from *gerere* "to carry, carry on, perform"**]**

Ge•sta•po \gə-'stäp-ō\ *n* **1 :** the state secret police of Nazi Germany **2 :** a group whose tactics resemble those of the Gestapo **[**German, from *Ge*heime *Sta*ats *po*lizei, literally, "secret state police"**]**

ges•tate \'jes-ˌtāt\ *vt* **1 :** to carry in the uterus during pregnancy **2 :** to conceive and gradually develop in the mind **[**back-formation from *gestation***]**

ges•ta•tion \je-'stā-shən\ *n* **1 :** the carrying of young in the uterus **:** PREGNANCY **2 :** conception and development especially in the mind **[**Latin *gestatio,* from *gestare* "to bear", from *gestus,* past participle of *gerere* "to bear, carry"**]** — **ges•ta•tion•al** \-shnəl, -shən-l\ *adj*

ges•tic•u•late \je-'stik-yə-ˌlāt\ *vi* **:** to make gestures especially when speaking **[**Latin *gesticulari,* from *gestus,* past participle of *gerere* "to carry"**]** — **ges•tic•u•la•tor** \-ˌlāt-ər\ *n*

ges•tic•u•la•tion \je-ˌstik-yə-'lā-shən\ *n* **1 :** the action of making gestures **2 :** GESTURE; *esp* **:** an expressive gesture made in showing strong feeling or in enforcing an argument

ges•tic•u•la•tive \je-'stik-yə-ˌlāt-iv\ *adj* **:** inclined to or marked by gesticulation

[1]**ges•ture** \'jes-chər, 'jesh-\ *n* **1 :** the use of motions of the limbs or body as a means of communication; *also* **:** an instance of such communication ⟨their *gesture* of defiance cheered us⟩ **2 :** something said or done by way of formality or courtesy, as a symbol or token, or for its effect on the attitudes of others ⟨a political *gesture*⟩ **[**Medieval Latin *gestura* "mode of action", from Latin *gestus,* past participle of *gerere* "to carry, carry on"**]**

[2]**gesture** *vb* **1 :** to make a gesture **2 :** to express or direct by a gesture

ge•sund•heit \gə-'zu̇nt-ˌhīt\ *interj* — used to wish good health especially to one who has just sneezed **[**German, literally, "health"**]**

[1]**get** \get, 'get; *often* git, *without stress, when a heavily stressed syllable follows, as in "get up"*\ *vb* **got** \gät, 'gät\; **got** *or* **got•ten** \'gät-n\; **get•ting 1 a :** to gain possession of (as by receiving, acquiring, earning, buying, or winning) ⟨*get* a present⟩ ⟨*got* first prize⟩ ⟨*get* a dog⟩ **b :** to seek out and obtain ⟨planned to *get* dinner at the inn⟩ **c :** FETCH ⟨*get* your father his slippers⟩ **d :** to acquire wealth ⟨those that have, *get*⟩ **2 a :** to succeed in coming or going ⟨*got* to the city on time⟩ ⟨*got* home early⟩ **b :** to cause to come or go ⟨*got* the dog out in a hurry⟩ **3 :** BEGET 1 **4 a :** to cause to be in a certain condition ⟨*got* his hair cut⟩ ⟨*got* his feet wet⟩ **b :** BECOME ⟨*get* sick⟩ ⟨*get* better⟩ **c :** PREPARE ⟨started *getting* dinner⟩ **5 a :** SEIZE ⟨*got* the thief by the leg⟩ **b :** to move emotionally ⟨a song that always *got* them⟩ **c :** BAFFLE, PUZZLE ⟨the third question *got* everybody⟩ **d :** IRRITATE ⟨don't let it *get* you⟩ **e :** HIT ⟨*got* the dog in the leg⟩ **f :** KILL ⟨swore to *get* a deer⟩ **6 a :** to be subjected to ⟨*get* a broken nose⟩ ⟨*got* the measles⟩ **b :** to receive as punishment ⟨*got* six months for larceny⟩ **7 a :** to find out by calculation ⟨*got* the right answer⟩ **b :** to hear correctly ⟨I didn't *get* your name⟩ **c :** UNDERSTAND 1 **8 :** PERSUADE, INDUCE ⟨couldn't *get* them to agree⟩ **9 a :** HAVE — used in the present perfect form with present meaning ⟨I've *got* no money⟩ **b :** to be obliged — used in the present perfect form with present meaning ⟨we have *got* to leave⟩ **10 :** to establish communication with ⟨*got* me on the telephone⟩ **11 :** to be able **:** CONTRIVE, MANAGE ⟨never *got* to go to college⟩ **12 :** to leave at once **:** clear out ⟨told them to *get*⟩ **[**Old Norse *geta* "to get, beget"**]** — **get ahead :** to achieve success — **get around 1 :** to get the better of **2 :** EVADE — **get at 1 :** to reach effectively **2 :** to influence corruptly **3 :** to turn one's attention to **4 :** to try to prove or make clear ⟨what are you *getting at*⟩ — **get away with :** to perform without suffering unpleasant consequences — **get back at :** to get even with — **get even :** to get revenge — **get even with :** to repay in kind — **get it :** to receive a scolding or punishment — **get one's goat :** to make one angry or annoyed — **get over 1 :** OVERCOME ⟨*get over* difficulties⟩ **2 :** to recover from — **get through 1 :** to reach the end of **:** COMPLETE **2 :** to while away — **get to 1 :** BEGIN **2 :** to have an effect on **:** INFLUENCE — **get together 1 :** to bring together **:** ACCUMULATE **2 :** to come together **:** ASSEMBLE **3 :** to reach agreement — **get wind of :** to become aware of

[2]**get** \'get\ *n* **1 :** something begotten **:** OFFSPRING, PROGENY **2 :** a difficult return of a shot in tennis

get along *vi* **1 a :** PROGRESS **b :** to approach old age **2 :** to meet one's needs **:** MANAGE **3 :** to be or remain on congenial terms

get•at•able \get-'at-ə-bəl\ *adj* **:** ACCESSIBLE

get•away \'get-ə-ˌwā\ *n* **1 :** the action or fact of getting away **:** ESCAPE **2 :** the action of starting or getting under way (as in a race)

get by *vi* **1 :** to avoid failure or catastrophe **:** barely succeed **2 :** to proceed without being discovered, criticized, or punished

Geth•sem•a•ne \geth-'sem-ə-nē\ *n* **:** a place or occasion of great suffering especially in mind or spirit **[**from *Gethsemane,* the garden outside Jerusalem mentioned in the New Testament as the scene of the agony and arrest of Jesus, from Greek *Gethsēmanē***]**

get off *vb* **1 :** UTTER ⟨*get off* a joke⟩ **2 :** START 5a, LEAVE **3 :** to escape or help to escape **4 :** to leave work with permission

get on *vi* **1 :** to get along ⟨they *get on* well⟩ **2 :** to gain knowledge or understanding ⟨*got on* to the racket⟩

get out *vb* **1 :** to escape or cause to escape ⟨hoping to *get out* alive⟩ ⟨*get* oneself *out* of trouble⟩ **2 :** to become or cause to become known or public ⟨let a secret *get out*⟩; *esp* **:** PUBLISH

get•ter \'get-ər\ *n* **1 :** one that gets **2 :** a substance introduced into a vacuum tube or incandescent electric lamp to remove traces of gas

get-to•geth•er \'get-tə-ˌgeth-ər\ *n* **:** MEETING; *esp* **:** an informal social gathering

get•up \'get-ˌəp\ *n* **:** COSTUME 3, OUTFIT

get up \get-'əp, git-\ *vb* **1 a :** to arise from bed **b :** to rise to one's feet **2 :** to go ahead or faster — used as a command to a horse **3 :** to make preparations for **:** ORGANIZE ⟨*get up* a party⟩ **4 :** to arrange as to external appearance **:** DRESS ⟨was *got up* as a pirate⟩

gew•gaw \'gü-ˌgȯ, 'gyü-\ *n* **:** a showy trifle **:** BAUBLE, TRINKET **[**origin unknown**]**

gey•ser \'gī-zər\ *n* **:** a spring that throws forth intermittent jets of heated water and steam **[**Icelandic *geysir* "gusher"**]**

gey•ser•ite \'gī-zə-ˌrīt\ *n* **:** a variety of opal that is deposited around some hot springs and geysers

[1]**ghast•ly** \'gast-lē\ *adj* **ghast•li•er; -est 1 :** terrifyingly horrible to the mind or senses ⟨a *ghastly* crime⟩ **2 :** resembling a ghost **:** DEATHLIKE, PALE ⟨a *ghastly* face⟩ **[**Middle English *gastly,* from *gasten* "to terrify"**]** — **ghast•li•ness** *n*

• **syn** GHASTLY, GRUESOME, GRIM, LURID mean horrifying and repellent in appearance or aspect. GHASTLY suggests the horrifying aspects of corpses or skeletons; GRUESOME suggests additionally the effects of cruelty or extreme violence; GRIM implies a fierce and forbidding aspect; LURID adds to GRUESOME the suggestion of shuddering fascination with violent death and especially with murder.

[2]**ghastly** *adv* **:** in a ghastly manner ⟨turned *ghastly* pale⟩

\ə\ **abut**	\au̇\ **out**	\i\ **tip**	\ȯ\ **saw**	\u̇\ **foot**
\ər\ **further**	\ch\ **chin**	\ī\ **life**	\ȯi\ **coin**	\y\ **yet**
\a\ **mat**	\e\ **pet**	\j\ **job**	\th\ **thin**	\yü\ **few**
\ā\ **take**	\ē\ **easy**	\ŋ\ **sing**	\t͟h\ **this**	\yu̇\ **cure**
\ä\ **cot, cart**	\g\ **go**	\ō\ **bone**	\ü\ **food**	\zh\ **vision**

ghat \ˈgȯt, ˈgät\ *n* : a landing place with stairs descending to a river in India [Hindi *ghāṭ*]

gher•kin \ˈgər-kən\ *n* **1** : a small prickly cucumber used for pickling; *also* : the vine that bears it **2** : the immature fruit of the common cucumber [Dutch *gurken,* pl. of *gurk* "cucumber"]

ghet•to \ˈget-ō\ *n, pl* **ghettos** *or* **ghettoes** **1** : a quarter of a city in which Jews were formerly required to live **2** : a quarter of a city in which members of a minority group live because of social, legal, or economic pressure [Italian]

ghillie *variant of* GILLIE

[1]**ghost** \ˈgōst\ *n* **1** : the seat of life : SOUL ⟨give up the *ghost*⟩ **2** : a disembodied soul; *esp* : the soul of a dead person believed to be an inhabitant of the unseen world or to appear to the living in bodily likeness **3** : SPIRIT 2b, DEMON **4** : a faint shadowy trace or suggestion ⟨a *ghost* of a smile⟩ **5** : a false image in a photographic negative or on a television screen caused especially by reflection **6** : one who ghostwrites [Old English *gāst*] — **ghost•like** \-ˌlīk\ *adj* — **ghosty** \ˈgo-stē\ *adj*

[2]**ghost** *vb* **1** : to haunt like a ghost **2** : to move silently like a ghost **3** : GHOSTWRITE

ghost•ly \ˈgōst-lē\ *adj* **ghost•li•er**; **-est** **1** : of or relating to the soul : SPIRITUAL **2** : of, relating to, or having the characteristics of a ghost : SPECTRAL — **ghost•li•ness** *n*

ghost town *n* : a once flourishing town deserted or nearly so usually after exhaustion of some natural resource

ghost•write \ˈgōst-ˌrīt\ *vb* : to write for and in the name of another [back-formation from *ghost-writer*] — **ghost–writ•er** *n*

ghoul \ˈgül\ *n* **1** : a legendary evil being that robs graves and feeds on corpses **2** : a person (as a grave robber) whose activities suggest those of a ghoul [Arabic *ghūl*] — **ghoul•ish** \ˈgü-lish\ *adj* — **ghoul•ish•ly** *adv* — **ghoul•ish•ness** *n*

[1]**GI** \jē-ˈī, ˈjē-\ *adj* **1** : provided by an official United States military supply department ⟨*GI* shoes⟩ **2** : of, relating to, or characteristic of United States military personnel **3** : conforming to military regulations or customs ⟨a *GI* haircut⟩ [*g*alvanized *i*ron; from abbreviation used in listing such articles as garbage cans, but taken as abbreviation for *government issue*]

[2]**GI** *n* : a member or former member of the United States forces; *esp* : an enlisted person

[3]**GI** *vt* **GI'd**; **GI'ing** : to prepare for military inspection by cleaning

[1]**gi•ant** \ˈjī-ənt\ *n* **1** : a legendary being of great stature and strength and of more than mortal but less than godlike power **2** **a** : a living being of great size **b** : a person of extraordinary powers ⟨a literary *giant*⟩ **3** : something unusually large or powerful [Middle French *geant,* from Latin *gigant-, gigas,* from Greek]

[2]**giant** *adj* : characterized by extremely large size, proportion, or power

giant cactus *n* : SAGUARO

gi•ant•ess \ˈjī-ənt-əs\ *n* : a female giant; *esp* : an unusually large woman

gi•ant•ism \ˈjī-ənt-ˌiz-əm\ *n* **1** : the quality or state of being a giant **2** : GIGANTISM 2

giant panda *n* : PANDA 2

giant sequoia *n* : BIG TREE

giant squid *n* : any of a group of very large squids that include the largest mollusks known with some being 12 meters long including the arms

giant star *n* : a star of great luminosity and of large mass

giaour \ˈjau̇r\ *n* : one outside the Muslim faith : INFIDEL [Turkish *gâvur*]

gib \ˈgib\ *n* : a plate (as of metal) machined to hold other parts in place, to afford a bearing surface, or to take up wear [origin unknown]

gib•ber \ˈjib-ər\ *vi* **gib•bered**; **gib•ber•ing** \ˈjib-ring, -ə-ring\ : to speak gibberish : CHATTER [imitative] — **gibber** *n*

gib•ber•el•lic acid \ˌjib-ə-ˌrel-ik-\ *n* : a crystalline organic acid associated with and similar in effect to the gibberellins

gib•ber•el•lin \-ˈrel-ən\ *n* : any of several plant-growth regulators that in low concentrations promote shoot growth [New Latin *Gibberella,* genus of fungi]

gib•ber•ish \ˈjib-rish, ˈgib-, -ə-rish\ *n* : obscure, confused, or meaningless speech or language [probably from *gibber*]

[1]**gib•bet** \ˈjib-ət\ *n* **1** : GALLOWS **2** : an upright post with a projecting arm for hanging the bodies of executed criminals as a warning [Old French *gibet*]

[2]**gibbet** *vt* **1** **a** : to hang on a gibbet **b** : to expose to public scorn **2** : to execute by hanging

gib•bon \ˈgib-ən\ *n* : any of several tailless apes of southeastern Asia and the East Indies that are the smallest and most arboreal anthropoid apes [French]

gibbon

gib•bos•i•ty \jib-ˈäs-ət-ē, gib-\ *n, pl* **-ties** : PROTUBERANCE, SWELLING

gib•bous \ˈjib-əs, ˈgib-\ *adj* **1** : convexly rounded **2** : seen with more than half but not all of the apparent disk illuminated ⟨*gibbous* moon⟩ [Middle French *gibbeux* "protuberant, gibbous", from Late Latin *gibbosus* "humpbacked", from Latin *gibbus* "hump"]

[1]**gibe** *or* **jibe** \ˈjīb\ *vb* : to utter or reproach with taunting or sarcastic words [perhaps from Middle French *giber* "to shake, handle roughly"] — **gib•er** *n*

[2]**gibe** *or* **jibe** *n* : JEER, TAUNT

gib•lets \ˈjib-ləts\ *n pl* : the edible viscera of a bird [Middle English *gibelet* "entrails, garbage", from Middle French, "stew of wildfowl"] — **gib•let** \-lət\ *adj*

gid \ˈgid\ *n* : a disease usually of sheep caused by a tapeworm larva in the brain [back-formation from *giddy*]

gid•dap \gid-ˈap\ *imperative verb* — a command to a horse to go ahead or go faster [alteration of *get up*]

gid•dy \ˈgid-ē\ *adj* **gid•di•er**; **-est** **1** : having a feeling of whirling or reeling about : DIZZY **2** : causing dizziness ⟨a *giddy* height⟩ **3** : lightheartedly silly : FRIVOLOUS [Old English *gydig* "possessed, mad"] — **gid•di•ly** \ˈgid-l-ē\ *adv* — **gid•di•ness** \ˈgid-ē-nəs\ *n*

gie \ˈgē\ *chiefly Scottish variant of* GIVE

gift \ˈgift\ *n* **1** : the act or power of giving ⟨the appointment was not in my *gift*⟩ **2** : something given : PRESENT **3** : a special ability : TALENT ⟨a *gift* for music⟩ [Old Norse, "something given, talent"]

gift•ed \ˈgif-təd\ *adj* : having great natural ability ⟨a class for *gifted* children⟩

gift wrap *vt* : to wrap (merchandise intended as a gift) in specially attractive or fancy wrappings

[1]**gig** \ˈgig\ *n* **1** **a** : a long light ship's boat propelled by oars, sail, or motor and usually reserved for use by the captain **b** : a rowboat designed for speed rather than for work **2** : a light 2-wheeled one-horse carriage [earlier *gig* "something that whirls, top", from Middle English *gigg* "top"]

[2]**gig** *n* : a pronged spear for catching fish [short for earlier *fizgig, fishgig,* of unknown origin]

[3]**gig** *vb* **gigged**; **gig•ging** : to spear or fish with a gig

[4]**gig** *n* : a military demerit [origin unknown]

[5]**gig** *vt* **gigged**; **gig•ging** : to give a military gig to ⟨*gigged* for dirty shoes⟩

giga- \ˈjig-ə, ˈgig-ə\ *combining form* : billion [Greek *gigas* "giant"]

gi•gan•tesque \ˌjī-ˌgan-ˈtesk, -gən-\ *adj* : of huge proportions

gi•gan•tic \jī-ˈgant-ik\ *adj* : extremely large or great : HUGE ⟨*gigantic* industry⟩ [Greek *gigantikos,* from *gigant-, gigas* "giant"] — **gi•gan•ti•cal•ly** \-ˈgant-i-kə-lē, -klē\ *adv*

gi•gan•tism \jī-ˈgan-ˌtiz-əm, jə-; ˈjī-gən-\ *n* **1** : GIANTISM 1 **2** : development to abnormally large size; *esp* : excessive bodily growth with delayed or inhibited reproduction

[1]**gig•gle** \ˈgig-əl\ *vi* **gig•gled**; **gig•gling** \ˈgig-ling, -ə-ling\ : to laugh in a silly manner [imitative] — **gig•gler** \ˈgig-lər, -ə-lər\ *n*

[2]**giggle** *n* : the act of giggling : a light silly laugh

gig•gly \ˈgig-lē, -ə-lē\ *adj* : given to giggling

gig•o•lo \ˈjig-ə-ˌlō\ *n, pl* **-los** **1** : a man supported by a woman in return for sexual favors **2** : a professional dancing partner or male escort [French]

gi•got \ˈjig-ət, zhē-ˈgō\ *n, pl* **gigots** \-əts, -ˈgō, -ˈgōz\ **1** : a leg (as of lamb) especially when cooked **2** : a leg-of-mutton sleeve [Middle French, from *gigue* "fiddle"; from its shape]

Gi•la monster \ˌhē-lə-\ *n* : a large orange and black venomous lizard of the southwestern United States; *also* : a related Mexican lizard [*Gila* river, Arizona]

[1]**gild** \ˈgild\ *vt* **gild•ed** *or* **gilt** \ˈgilt\; **gild•ing** **1** : to cover with or as if with a thin coating of gold **2** : to give a falsely attractive

appearance to [Old English *gyldan*] — **gild•er** *n* — **gild the lily** : to add unnecessary ornamentation to something beautiful in its own right

Gila monster

[2]gild *variant of* GUILD

[1]gill \ˈjil\ *n* — see MEASURE table [Middle English *gille*]

[2]gill \ˈgil\ *n* **1** : an organ (as of a fish) for obtaining oxygen from water **2** *pl* : the flesh under or about the chin or jaws **3** : one of the radiating plates forming the undersurface of the cap of a mushroom [Middle English *gile, gille*] — **gilled** \ˈgild\ *adj*

gill arch *n* : one of the several bars of bone or cartilage that are paired on either side of the throat and support the gills of water-breathing vertebrates

gill filament *n* : one of the threadlike processes making up a gill

gil•lie *or* **gil•ly** *or* **ghil•lie** \ˈgil-ē\ *n, pl* **gillies** *or* **ghillies** **1** : a male attendant on a Scottish Highland chief **2** *Scottish & Irish* : a fishing and hunting guide **3** *usually ghillie* : a low-cut shoe with decorative lacing [Scottish Gaelic *gille* "boy"]

gill net *n* : a net that allows the head of a fish to pass but entangles it as it seeks to withdraw — **gill•net** \ˈgil-ˌnet\ *vt*

gill raker *n* : one of the bony processes on each gill arch that divert debris

gill slit *n* **1** : any of the openings in vertebrates with gills through which water taken in at the mouth moves to the outside bathing the gills **2** : a rudiment of a gill slit that occurs at some stage of development in all vertebrate embryos

gil•ly•flow•er \ˈjil-ē-ˌflau̇-ər, -ˌflau̇r\ *n* : an Old World pink that is grown for its clove-scented flowers and is the source of garden carnations [by folk etymology from Middle English *gilofre* "clove", from Middle French *girofle, gilofre,* from Latin *caryophyllum,* from Greek *karyophyllon,* from *karyon* "nut" + *phyllon* "leaf"]

[1]gilt \ˈgilt\ *adj* : of the color of gold [from past participle of [1]*gild*]

[2]gilt *n* **1** : gold or something that resembles gold laid on a surface **2** : superficial brilliance

[3]gilt *n* : a young female swine [Old Norse *gyltr*]

gilt–edged \ˈgilt-ˈejd\ *or* **gilt–edge** \-ˈej\ *adj* **1** : having a gilt edge **2** : of the best quality; *esp* : extremely safe for investment ⟨*gilt-edged* securities⟩

gim•bal \ˈgim-bəl, ˈjim-\ *n* : a device that permits a body to incline freely in any direction or suspends something (as a ship's compass) so that it will remain level when its support is tipped — usually used in pl.; called also *gimbal ring* [from obsolete *gemel* "double hinge", derived from Latin *geminus* "twin"]

gim•crack \ˈjim-ˌkrak\ *n* : a showy object of little use or value : GEWGAW [origin unknown] — **gimcrack** *adj* — **gim•crack•ery** \-ˌkrak-rē, -ə-rē\ *n*

gim•let \ˈgim-lət\ *n* : a small tool with a screw point, grooved shank, and cross handle for boring holes [Middle French *guimbelet*]

gim•mick \ˈgim-ik\ *n* **1** : an ingenious or novel mechanical device : GADGET **2 a** : an important feature that is not immediately apparent : CATCH **b** : a new and ingenious scheme [origin unknown]

[1]gimp \ˈgimp\ *n* : an ornamental flat braid or round cord used as a trimming [perhaps from Dutch]

[2]gimp *n* : CRIPPLE; *also* : LIMP — **gimpy** \ˈgim-pē\ *adj*

[1]gin \ˈjin\ *n* : a mechanical tool or device: as **a** : a snare or trap for game **b** : COTTON GIN [Old French *engin* "engine"]

[2]gin *vt* **ginned**; **gin•ning** **1** : SNARE 1 **2** : to separate (cotton fiber) from seeds and waste material — **gin•ner** *n*

[3]gin *n* **1** : a usually colorless alcoholic liquor flavored with juniper berries **2 a** : GIN RUMMY **b** : the act of laying down a full hand of matched cards in gin rummy [from earlier *geneva,* from obsolete Dutch *genever,* literally, "juniper", derived from Latin *juniperus*]

gin•ger \ˈjin-jər\ *n* **1** : any of a genus of tropical Old World herbs with pungent aromatic underground stems used for flavoring and in medicine; *also* : the underground stem **2** : high spirit : PEP [Old English *gingifer,* from Medieval Latin *gingiber,* from Latin *zingiber,* from Greek *zingiberi*] — **gin•gery** \ˈjinj-rē, -ə-rē\ *adj*

ginger ale *n* : a carbonated nonalcoholic drink flavored with ginger extract

ginger beer *n* : a carbonated nonalcoholic drink heavily flavored with ginger or capsicum or both

gin•ger•bread \ˈjin-jər-ˌbred\ *n* **1** : a cake made with molasses and flavored with ginger **2** : lavish or superfluous ornament — **gin•ger•bready** \-ē\ *adj*

gin•ger•ly \ˈjin-jər-lē\ *adj* : very cautious or careful [perhaps from *ginger*] — **gin•ger•li•ness** *n* — **gingerly** *adv*

gin•ger•snap \-ˌsnap\ *n* : a thin brittle cookie flavored with ginger

ging•ham \ˈging-əm\ *n* : a fabric usually of yarn-dyed cotton in plain weave [Malay *genggang* "checkered cloth"]

gin•gi•vi•tis \ˌjin-jə-ˈvīt-əs\ *n* : inflammation of the gums [Latin *gingiva* "gum"]

gink•go \ˈging-kō\ *n, pl* **ginkgoes** *or* **ginkgos** : a large Chinese tree with fan-shaped leaves and foul-smelling fruit that is often grown as a shade tree — called also *maidenhair tree* [Japanese *ginkyo*]

gin rummy *n* : a rummy game for two players in which each player is dealt 10 cards and a player may win by matching all cards in the hand in sets or may end play when unmatched cards count up to 10 or less [[3]*gin*]

gin•seng \ˈjin-ˌsang, -ˌseng\ *n* **1** : a perennial Chinese herb with small greenish flowers in a rounded cluster and scarlet berries; *also* : a closely related North American herb **2** : the forked aromatic root of the ginseng used as a medicine in China [Chinese (Pekingese dialect) *jen[2]-shen[1]*]

Gipsy *variant of* GYPSY

gi•raffe \jə-ˈraf\ *n, pl* **giraffe** *or* **giraffes** : a large fleet African ruminant mammal that is the tallest living four-footed animal and that has a very long neck and a short coat with dark blotches separated by pale lines [Italian *giraffa,* from Arabic *zirāfah*] — **gi•raff•ish** \-ˈraf-ish\ *adj*

giraffe

gird \ˈgərd\ *vb* **gird•ed** *or* **girt** \ˈgərt\; **gird•ing** **1** : to encircle or fasten with or as if with a belt ⟨*gird* on a sword⟩ **2** : to invest especially with power or authority **3** : to get ready ⟨*girded* themselves for a fight⟩ [Old English *gyrdan*]

gird•er \ˈgərd-ər\ *n* : a horizontal main supporting beam

[1]gir•dle \ˈgərd-l\ *n* : something that encircles or confines: as **a** : a belt or sash encircling the waist **b** : a woman's supporting undergarment that extends from the waist to below the hips **c** : a bony arch for the support of a limb — compare PECTORAL GIRDLE, PELVIC GIRDLE **d** : a ring made by the removal of the bark and cambium around a plant stem [Old English *gyrdel*]

[2]girdle *vt* **gir•dled**; **gir•dling** \ˈgərd-ling, -l-ing\ **1** : to encircle with a girdle **2** : to move around : CIRCLE **3** : to cut a girdle around (a plant)

girl \ˈgərl\ *n* **1 a** : a female child **b** : a typically young woman **2** : a female servant or employee **3** : GIRL FRIEND 2 [Middle English *girle* "young person of either sex"] — **girl•hood** \-ˌhu̇d\ *n*

girl friend *n* **1** : a female friend **2** : a frequent or regular female companion of a boy or man

girl guide *n* : a member of the British Girl Guides

girl•ish \ˈgər-lish\ *adj* : of, relating to, or having the characteristics of a female child — **girl•ish•ly** *adv* — **girl•ish•ness** *n*

girl scout *n* : a member of the Girl Scouts of the United States of America

Gi•rond•ist \jə-ˈrän-dəst\ *n* : a member of the moderate repub-

\ə\ **abut**	\au̇\ **out**	\i\ **tip**	\ȯ\ **saw**	\u̇\ **foot**
\ər\ **further**	\ch\ **chin**	\ī\ **life**	\ȯi\ **coin**	\y\ **yet**
\a\ **mat**	\e\ **pet**	\j\ **job**	\th\ **thin**	\yü\ **few**
\ā\ **take**	\ē\ **easy**	\ng\ **sing**	\t͟h\ **this**	\yu̇\ **cure**
\ä\ **cot, cart**	\g\ **go**	\ō\ **bone**	\ü\ **food**	\zh\ **vision**

lican party in the French legislative assembly in 1791 [French *girondiste,* from *Gironde,* a political party, from *Gironde,* department of France]

girt \'gərt\ *vt* **1 :** GIRD 1, 2 **2 :** to fasten by means of a girth [Middle English *girten,* alteration of *girden*]

[1]**girth** \'gərth\ *n* **1 :** a band or strap that encircles the body of an animal to fasten something (as a saddle) upon its back **2 :** a measure around a body [Old Norse *gjörth*]

[2]**girth** *vt* **1 :** ENCIRCLE 2 **2 :** to bind or fasten with a girth

gist \'jist\ *n* **:** the main point of a matter **:** ESSENCE [Anglo-French, "it lies" (in *cest action gist* "this action lies", statement laying the foundation of a legal action)]

[1]**give** \'giv\ *vb* **gave** \'gāv\; **giv•en** \'giv-ən\; **giv•ing 1 :** to make a present of **2 a :** GRANT, ACCORD ⟨*give* citizens the right to vote⟩ **b :** to offer or yield to another ⟨*gave* them my confidence⟩ **3 a :** to put into the possession or keeping of another **b :** to offer to another **:** PROFFER ⟨give one's hand to a visitor⟩ **4 a :** to present in public performance ⟨*give* a concert⟩ **b :** to present to view ⟨*gave* the signal⟩ **5 :** to provide by way of entertainment ⟨*give* a party⟩ **6 :** to designate as a share or portion **:** ALLOT **7 :** ATTRIBUTE, ASCRIBE ⟨*gave* all the glory to God⟩ **8 :** to grant as true **:** ASSUME **9 :** to yield as a product or result ⟨cows *give* milk⟩ **10 :** PAY ⟨*give* a fair price⟩ **11 a :** to deliver by bodily action ⟨*gave* it a push⟩ **b :** to carry out (a movement) **:** EXECUTE ⟨*gave* a sudden leap⟩ **c :** to award by formal verdict ⟨*give* judgment⟩ **12 :** to offer for consideration or acceptance ⟨*give* a reason⟩ **13 :** to apply fully **:** DEVOTE ⟨*give* oneself to a cause⟩ **14 :** to cause one to have or receive ⟨*gave* pleasure to the reader⟩ **15 :** to make gifts or presents **16 a :** to yield to physical force or strain **b :** to collapse from the application of force or pressure [Middle English *given,* of Scandinavian origin] — **giv•er** \'giv-ər\ *n*

• **syn** PRESENT, DONATE: GIVE is the general term applying to delivering, passing over, or transmitting in any manner; PRESENT implies more ceremony or formality and suggests a degree of complexity or value in what is given; DONATE implies a free but usually publicized giving, as to charity.

— **give ground :** to withdraw before superior force **:** RETREAT — **give it to :** to attack vigorously — **give way 1 a :** RETREAT **b :** to yield the right of way **2 :** to yield oneself without restraint or control **3 a :** COLLAPSE 3, FAIL **b :** CONCEDE 2

[2]**give** *n* **1 :** capacity or tendency to yield to force or strain **2 :** the quality or state of being springy

give–and–take \,giv-ən-'tāk\ *n* **1 :** the practice of making mutual concessions **2 :** good-natured exchange of ideas

give•away \'giv-ə-,wā\ *n* **1 :** an unintentional revelation or betrayal **2 :** something given away free; *esp* **:** PREMIUM

give away \,giv-ə-'wā\ *vt* **1 :** to deliver (a bride) to the bridegroom at a wedding **2 a :** to expose to detection or ridicule **:** BETRAY **b :** REVEAL 1, DISCLOSE

give back *vb* **1 :** RETREAT 1 **2 :** RETURN 5, RESTORE

give in *vi* **:** YIELD 5, SURRENDER

giv•en \'giv-ən\ *adj* **1 :** DISPOSED, INCLINED ⟨*given* to gossiping⟩ **2 :** FIXED 1C, SPECIFIED ⟨at a *given* time⟩ **3 :** granted as true **:** ASSUMED

given name *n* **:** CHRISTIAN NAME

give off *vt* **:** EMIT 1a

give out *vb* **1 :** EMIT 1a **2 :** ISSUE 2b **3 :** to become exhausted **:** COLLAPSE **4 :** to break down

give up *vb* **1 :** to hand over to another **:** SURRENDER **2 :** to abandon (oneself) to a feeling, influence, or activity **3 :** to withdraw from an activity or course of action

giz•mo *or* **gis•mo** \'giz-mō\ *n, pl* **gizmos** *or* **gismos :** CONTRIVANCE 2, GADGET [origin unknown]

giz•zard \'giz-ərd\ *n* **:** a muscular enlargement of the digestive canal (as of a bird) that usually follows the crop and has a horny lining for grinding the food [Middle English *giser,* from Old North French *guisier,* from Latin *gigeria* "giblets"]

gla•brous \'glā-brəs\ *adj* **:** having a surface without hairs or projections **:** SMOOTH [Latin *glaber* "smooth, bald"] — **gla•brous•ness** *n*

gla•cé \gla-'sā\ *adj* **1 :** made or finished so as to have a smooth glossy surface **2 :** coated with a glaze **:** CANDIED [French, from *glacer* "to freeze, ice, glaze", derived from Latin *glacies* "ice"]

gla•cial \'glā-shəl\ *adj* **1 a :** extremely cold **:** FRIGID **b :** lacking warmth and cordiality **2 a :** of, relating to, or produced by glaciers **b** (1) **:** of, relating to, or being any of those parts of geologic time when a large portion of the earth was covered by glaciers (2) *cap* **:** PLEISTOCENE — **gla•cial•ly** \-shə-lē\ *adv*

gla•ci•ate \'glā-shē-,āt\ *vt* **1 :** to cover with a glacier **2 :** to subject to glacial action; *also* **:** to produce glacial effects in or on — **gla•ci•a•tion** \,glā-shē-'ā-shən, -sē-\ *n*

gla•cier \'glā-shər\ *n* **:** a large body of ice moving slowly down a slope or valley or spreading outward on a land surface [French dialect, from Middle French *glace* "ice", from Latin *glacies*]

gla•ci•ol•o•gy \,glā-shē-'äl-ə-jē, -sē-\ *n* **:** a branch of geology dealing with snow or ice accumulation, glaciation, and glacial epochs — **gla•ci•ol•o•gist** \-jəst\ *n*

[1]**glad** \'glad\ *adj* **glad•der; glad•dest 1 a :** experiencing pleasure, joy, or delight **:** made happy **b :** very willing ⟨*glad* to do it⟩ **2 :** causing happiness and joy **:** PLEASANT ⟨*glad* tidings⟩ **3 :** full of brightness and cheerfulness [Old English *glæd* "shining, glad"] — **glad•ly** *adv* — **glad•ness** *n*

[2]**glad** *n* **:** GLADIOLUS

glad•den \'glad-n\ *vt* **glad•dened; glad•den•ing** \'glad-ning, -n-ing\ **:** to make glad

glade \'glād\ *n* **:** a grassy open space in a forest [perhaps from [1]*glad*]

glad•i•a•tor \'glad-ē-,āt-ər\ *n* **1 :** a person engaged in a fight to the death for public entertainment in ancient Rome **2 :** a person engaging in a fierce fight or controversy [Latin, from *gladius* "sword", of Celtic origin] — **glad•i•a•to•ri•al** \,glad-ē-ə-'tōr-ē-əl, -'tȯr-\ *adj*

glad•i•o•lus \,glad-ē-'ō-ləs\ *n, pl* **-o•li** \-lē, -,lē, -,lī\ *or* **-o•lus** *or* **-o•lus•es :** any of a genus of chiefly African plants of the iris family with erect sword-shaped leaves and spikes of brilliantly colored irregular flowers [Latin, from *gladius* "sword"]

gladiolus

glad•some \'glad-səm\ *adj* **:** giving or showing joy **:** CHEERFUL — **glad•some•ly** *adv* — **glad•some•ness** *n*

glad•stone \'glad-,stōn\ *n, often cap* **:** a traveling bag with flexible sides on a rigid frame that opens flat into two compartments [W. E. *Gladstone,* died 1898, British statesman]

glam•or•ize \'glam-ə-,rīz\ *vt* **1 :** to make glamorous **2 :** to look upon as glamorous — **glam•or•iza•tion** \,glam-ə-rə-'zā-shən\ *n* — **glam•or•iz•er** *n*

glam•or•ous \'glam-rəs, -ə-rəs\ *adj* **:** full of glamour — **glam•or•ous•ly** *adv* — **glam•or•ous•ness** *n*

glam•our *or* **glam•or** \'glam-ər\ *n* **:** a romantic, exciting, and often illusory attractiveness; *esp* **:** alluring or fascinating personal attraction [Scottish *glamour* "magic spell", alteration of English *grammar*]

△ **origin** In the Middle Ages the meaning of *grammar* was not restricted to the study of language but included learning in general. Since almost all learning was couched in language not spoken or understood by the unschooled populace, it was commonly believed that such subjects as magic and astrology were included in this broad sense of *grammar.* Scholars were often viewed with awe and more than a little suspicion by ordinary people. This connection between grammar and magic was evident in a number of languages, and in Scotland by the 18th century a form of *grammar,* altered to *glamer* or *glamour,* meant "a magic spell or enchantment". As *glamour* passed into more extended English usage, it came to mean "an elusive, mysteriously exciting attractiveness".

[1]**glance** \'glans\ *vi* **1 :** to strike something and fly off at an angle ⟨the bullet *glanced* off the wall⟩ **2 :** to flash or gleam with quick intermittent rays of light ⟨the pond *glanced* in the sunlight⟩ **3 a :** to take a quick or hasty look ⟨*glanced* up from the book⟩ **b :** to refer briefly to a subject [Middle English *glencen, glenchen*] **syn** see FLASH — **glanc•ing•ly** \-ing-lē\ *adv*

[2]**glance** *n* **1 :** a quick intermittent flash or gleam **2 :** a deflected impact or blow **3 a :** a swift movement of the eyes **b :** a quick or cursory look — **at first glance :** on first consideration

• **syn** GLANCE, GLIMPSE are not synonymous even though both mean a brief view or viewing. GLANCE implies that one looks at something only briefly when he or she could have looked longer ⟨gave the paper hardly a *glance*⟩ GLIMPSE implies that only a brief look is possible ⟨got a *glimpse* of the deer before it vanished into the woods⟩

gland \ˈgland\ *n* **1 :** a cell or group of cells that prepares and secretes a product for further use in or for elimination from the plant or animal body **2 :** LYMPH GLAND **[**French *glande,* derived from Latin *gland-, glans* "acorn"**]** — **gland** *adj*

glan·ders \ˈglan-dərz\ *n sing or pl* **:** a destructive bacterial disease especially of horses characterized by nodules that tend to ulcerate **[**Middle French *glandre* "glandular swelling on the neck", derived from Latin *glans* "acorn"**]** — **glan·dered** \-dərd\ *adj*

glan·du·lar \ˈglan-jə-lər\ *adj* **1 :** of, relating to, or involving glands, gland cells, or their products **2 :** having the characteristics or function of a gland — **glan·du·lar·ly** *adv*

glans \ˈglanz\ *n, pl* **glan·des** \ˈglan-ˌdēz\ **:** the conical vascular extremity of the penis or clitoris **[**Latin, literally, "acorn"**]**

glans cli·to·ri·dis \-klə-ˈtȯr-əd-əs\ *n* **:** the glans of the clitoris

glans penis *n* **:** the glans of the penis

1**glare** \ˈglaər, ˈgleər\ *vb* **1 :** to shine with a harsh uncomfortably brilliant light **2 a :** to stare angrily or fiercely **b :** to express (as hostility) by staring angrily **[**Middle English *glaren***]**

2**glare** *n* **1 :** a harsh uncomfortably bright light; *esp* **:** painfully bright sunlight **2 :** an angry or fierce stare

3**glare** *n* **:** a smooth slippery surface or sheet of ice

glar·ing *adj* **1 :** having a fixed look of hostility, fierceness, or anger **2 a :** shining with or reflecting an uncomfortably bright light **b** (1) **:** GARISH 1b (2) **:** vulgarly ostentatious **3 :** painfully obvious ⟨a *glaring* error⟩ **syn** see FLAGRANT — **glar·ing·ly** \-ing-lē\ *adv* — **glar·ing·ness** *n*

glary \ˈglaər-ē, ˈgleər-\ *adj* **glar·i·er; -est :** having a dazzling brightness **:** GLARING

1**glass** \ˈglas\ *n* **1 a :** a hard brittle usually transparent or translucent noncrystalline inorganic substance formed by melting a mixture (as of silica sand and metallic oxides) and cooling to a rigid condition **b :** a substance (as a rock formed by the rapid cooling of molten minerals) resembling glass **2 a :** something (as a water tumbler, lens, mirror, barometer, or telescope) that is made of glass or has a glass lens **b** *pl* **:** BINOCULARS **c** *pl* **:** a pair of glass lenses used to correct defects of vision — called also *eyeglasses, spectacles* **3 :** the quantity held by a glass container **[**Old English *glæs***]**

2**glass** *vt* **:** to fit or protect with glass

glass·blow·ing \-ˌblō-ing\ *n* **:** the art of shaping a mass of glass that has been softened by heat by blowing air into it through a tube — **glass·blow·er** \-ˌblō-ər, -ˌblōr\ *n*

glass·ful \ˈglas-ˌfu̇l\ *n* **:** the quantity held by a glass

glass·mak·ing \-ˌmā-king\ *n* **:** the art or process of manufacturing glass

glass snake *n* **:** a limbless lizard of the southern United States resembling a snake and having a fragile tail that readily breaks into pieces

glass sponge *n* **:** a sponge with a glassy skeleton of silica

glass·ware \ˈglas-ˌwaər, -ˌweər\ *n* **:** articles made of glass

glass wool *n* **:** glass fibers in a mass resembling wool used especially for thermal insulation and air filters

glassy \ˈglas-ē\ *adj* **glass·i·er; -est 1 :** resembling glass **2 :** DULL, LIFELESS ⟨*glassy* eyes⟩ — **glass·i·ly** \ˈglas-ə-lē\ *adv* — **glass·i·ness** \ˈglas-ē-nəs\ *n*

Glau·ber's salt \ˌglau̇-bərz-ˈsȯlt\ *also* **Glau·ber salt** \ˌglau̇-bər-\ *n* **:** a colorless crystalline sulfate of sodium $Na_2SO_4 \cdot 10H_2O$ used especially as a cathartic **[**Johann R. *Glauber,* died 1668, German chemist**]**

glau·co·ma \glau̇-ˈkō-mə, glȯ-\ *n* **:** an abnormal condition of the eye marked by increased pressure within the eye that causes damage to the retina and gradual loss of vision **[**Latin, "cataract", from Greek *glaukōma,* from *glaukos* "gray"**]**

glau·cous \ˈglȯ-kəs\ *adj* **1 a :** of a pale yellow green color **b :** of a light bluish gray or bluish white color **2 :** having a powdery or waxy coating ⟨*glaucous* fruits like plums or grapes⟩ **[**Latin *glaucus* "gleaming, gray", from Greek *glaukos***]** — **glau·cous·ness** *n*

1**glaze** \ˈglāz\ *vb* **1 :** to furnish or fit with glass **2 a :** to coat with or as if with glass **b :** to apply a glaze to **3 :** to give a smooth glossy surface to **4 :** to become glazed **[**Middle English *glasen,* from *glas* "glass"**]** — **glaz·er** *n*

2**glaze** *n* **1 :** a smooth slippery coating of thin ice **2 a :** a transparent or translucent substance used as a coating (as on food or pottery) to produce a gloss **b :** a smooth glossy or lustrous surface or finish

gla·zier \ˈglā-zhər, -zē-ər\ *n* **:** a person who sets glass in window frames

glaz·ing \ˈglā-zing\ *n* **:** GLAZE

1**gleam** \ˈglēm\ *n* **1 a :** a transient subdued or partly obscured light **b :** a small bright light **:** GLINT **2 :** a brief or faint appearance **:** TRACE ⟨a *gleam* of hope⟩ **[**Old English *glǣm***]**

2**gleam** *vi* **1 :** to shine with subdued light or moderate brightness **2 :** to appear briefly or faintly

glean \ˈglēn\ *vb* **1 :** to gather from a field or vineyard what has been left by harvesters **2 :** to gather little by little ⟨*glean* knowledge from books⟩ **[**Middle French *glener,* from Late Latin *glennare***]** — **glean·er** *n*

glean·ings \ˈglē-ningz\ *n pl* **:** things gotten by gleaning

glee \ˈglē\ *n* **1 :** exultant high-spirited joy **:** HILARITY **2 :** an unaccompanied song for three or more voices **[**Old English *glēo* "entertainment, music"**]** **syn** see MIRTH

glee club *n* **:** a chorus organized for singing usually short choral pieces

glee·ful \ˈglē-fəl\ *adj* **:** full of glee **:** MERRY — **glee·ful·ly** \-fə-lē\ *adv* — **glee·ful·ness** *n*

gleet \ˈglēt\ *n* **:** chronic inflammation about a bodily opening accompanied by an abnormal discharge; *also* **:** this discharge **[**Middle French *glete* "mucous matter", from Latin *glittus* "viscous"**]**

glen \ˈglen\ *n* **:** a small secluded narrow valley **[**Middle English (Scottish dialect), "valley", of Scottish Gaelic origin**]**

glen·gar·ry \glen-ˈgar-ē\ *n, often cap* **:** a woolen cap of Scottish origin **[***Glengarry,* valley in Scotland**]**

glib \ˈglib\ *adj* **glib·ber; glib·best :** marked by careless ease and fluency and often trickiness in speaking or writing ⟨a *glib* talker⟩ ⟨a *glib* excuse⟩ **[**probably from Low German *glibberig* "slippery"**]** — **glib·ly** *adv* — **glib·ness** *n*

1**glide** \ˈglīd\ *vi* **1 :** to move smoothly, continuously, and effortlessly **2 :** to pass gradually and imperceptibly ⟨hours *gliding* by⟩ **3 :** to descend gradually without engine power sufficient for level flight ⟨*glide* in an airplane⟩ **[**Old English *glīdan***]**

2**glide** *n* **1 :** the act or action of gliding **2 a :** PORTAMENTO **b :** a transitional sound produced by the passing of the vocal organs to or from the position for the articulation of a speech sound

glid·er \ˈglīd-ər\ *n* **:** one that glides: as **a :** an aircraft without an engine that glides on air currents **b :** a porch seat suspended from a frame by short chains or straps

1**glim·mer** \ˈglim-ər\ *vi* **glim·mered; glim·mer·ing** \ˈglim-ring, -ə-ring\ **:** to shine faintly or unsteadily **[**Middle English *glimeren***]**

2**glimmer** *n* **1 a :** a feeble or intermittent light **b :** a soft shimmer **2 a :** a faint idea **:** INKLING **b :** a small amount **:** BIT

1**glimpse** \ˈglimps\ *vb* **:** to take a brief look **:** see momentarily or incompletely **[**Middle English *glimsen***]** — **glimps·er** *n*

2**glimpse** *n* **1 :** a short hurried view ⟨catch a *glimpse* of someone rushing by⟩ **2 :** GLIMMER 2a **syn** see GLANCE

1**glint** \ˈglint\ *vi* **1** *archaic* **:** GLANCE 1 **2 :** to shine by reflection: **a :** to shine with small bright flashes **:** SPARKLE **b :** GLITTER 1a **c :** GLEAM 1 **3 :** to appear briefly or faintly ⟨fear *glinted* in their eyes⟩ **[**Middle English *glinten* "to dart obliquely, glint", of Scandinavian origin**]** **syn** see FLASH

2**glint** *n* **1 :** a small bright flash of light **:** SPARKLE **2 :** a brief or faint manifestation ⟨a *glint* of interest⟩

glis·san·do \gli-ˈsän-dō\ *n, pl* **-di** \-ˌdē\ *or* **-dos :** a rapid sliding up or down the musical scale **[**probably from French *glissade* "slide", from *glisser* "to slide"**]**

glis·ten \ˈglis-n\ *vi* **glis·tened; glis·ten·ing** \ˈglis-ning, -n-ing\ **:** to shine by reflection with a soft luster or sparkle **[**Old English *glisnian***]** — **glisten** *n*

• **syn** GLISTEN, GLITTER, SCINTILLATE mean to give out bright flashes of light. GLISTEN implies a subdued shining as from a wet or oily surface; GLITTER implies a dancing brightness often with a suggestion of coldness or evil ⟨eyes *glittering* with greed⟩ SCINTILLATE suggests a series of quick flashes caused by or as if by the emission of sparks ⟨clear sky with *scintillating* stars⟩ ⟨*scintillating* conversation⟩

glis·ter \'glis-tər\ *vi* **glis·tered**; **glis·ter·ing** \-tə-ring, -tring\ : GLISTEN [Middle English *glistren*] — **glister** *n*

1glit·ter \'glit-ər\ *vi* **1 a** : to shine with brilliant or metallic luster ⟨*glittering* sequins⟩ **b** : to shine with a cold glassy brilliance ⟨eyes *glittered* cruelly⟩ **2** : to be brilliantly attractive especially in a superficial way [Old Norse *glitra*] **syn** see GLISTEN

2glitter *n* **1** : sparkling brilliancy, showiness, or attractiveness **2** : small glittering objects used for decoration — **glit·tery** \'glit-ə-rē\ *adj*

gloam·ing \'glō-ming\ *n* : DUSK 1, TWILIGHT [Old English *glōming*, from *glōm* "twilight"]

gloat \'glōt\ *vi* : to think about something with great and often malicious delight ⟨*gloat* over a rival's misfortune⟩ [probably of Scandinavian origin] — **gloat·er** *n* — **gloat·ing·ly** \-ing-lē\ *adv*

glob \'gläb\ *n* : a small drop : BLOB [perhaps blend of *globe* and *blob*]

glob·al \'glō-bəl\ *adj* **1** : GLOBULAR **2** : WORLDWIDE ⟨*global* war⟩ — **glob·al·ly** \-bə-lē\ *adv*

globe \'glōb\ *n* : something spherical or rounded: as **a** : a spherical representation of the earth or heavens **b** : EARTH 4 — usually used with *the* or *this* [Middle French, from Latin *globus*]

globe·fish \-,fish\ *n* : PUFFER 2

globe–trot·ter \-,trät-ər\ *n* : one that travels widely — **globe–trot·ting** \-,trät-ing\ *n or adj*

glob·u·lar \'gläb-yə-lər\ *adj* : having the shape of a globe

glob·ule \'gläb-yül\ *n* : a tiny globe or ball ⟨*globules* of fat⟩

glob·u·lin \'gläb-yə-lən\ *n* : any of a class of simple proteins insoluble in pure water but soluble in dilute salt solutions that occur widely in plant and animal tissues

glock·en·spiel \'gläk-ən-,shpēl, -,spēl\ *n* : a percussion instrument consisting of a series of graduated metal bars tuned to the chromatic scale and played with two hammers [German, from *glocke* "bell" + *spiel* "play"]

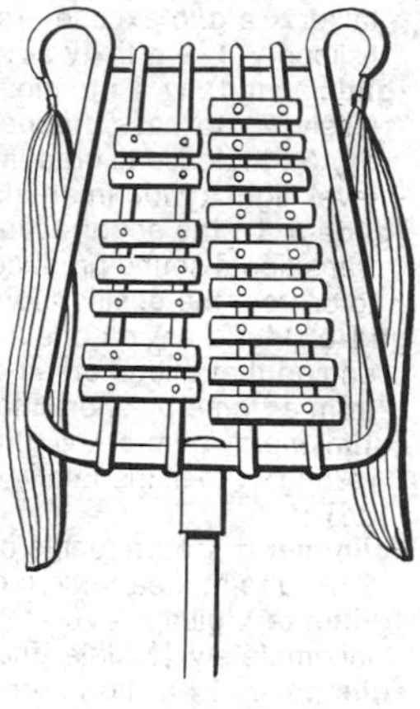
glockenspiel

glo·mer·u·lus \glä-'mer-ə-ləs, -yə-ləs\ *n, pl* **-li** \-lī, -lē\ : a clump of capillaries surrounded by the expanded sac-shaped end of each functional tubule of the vertebrate kidney [New Latin, from Latin *glomus* "ball"] — **glo·mer·u·lar** \-lər\ *adj*

1gloom \'glüm\ *vi* **1** : to look sullen or despondent **2** : to be or become overcast [Middle English *gloumen*]

2gloom *n* **1** : partial or total darkness **2 a** : lowness of spirits : DEJECTION **b** : an atmosphere of despondency

gloomy \'glü-mē\ *adj* **gloom·i·er**; **-est 1** : dismally dark ⟨a *gloomy* cave⟩ **2** : low in spirits **3 a** : causing gloom ⟨*gloomy* weather⟩ ⟨*gloomy* news⟩ **b** : PESSIMISTIC 1 — **gloom·i·ly** \-mə-lē\ *adv* — **gloom·i·ness** \-mē-nəs\ *n*

Glo·ria \'glōr-ē-ə, 'glòr-\ *n* : either of two Christian doxologies: **a** *or* **Gloria in Ex·cel·sis** \-,in-eks-'chel-səs, -ek-'shel-\ : one beginning "Glory be to God on high" **b** *or* **Gloria Pa·tri** \-'pä-trē\ : one beginning "Glory be to the Father" [Latin *gloria* "glory"]

glo·ri·fy \'glōr-ə-,fī, 'glòr-\ *vt* **-fied**; **-fy·ing 1** : to make glorious by bestowing honor, praise, or admiration **2** : to present in a highly often overly favorable light ⟨*glorify* war⟩ **3** : to give glory to (as in worship) — **glo·ri·fi·ca·tion** \,glōr-ə-fə-'kā-shən, ,glòr-\ *n* — **glo·ri·fi·er** \'glōr-ə-,fī-ər, 'glòr-, -,fīr\ *n*

glo·ri·ous \'glōr-ē-əs, 'glòr-\ *adj* **1 a** : having or deserving glory **b** : conferring glory ⟨a *glorious* victory⟩ **2** : marked by great beauty, excellence, or splendor ⟨*glorious* weather⟩ **3** : extremely pleasant ⟨had a *glorious* time⟩ **syn** see SPLENDID — **glo·ri·ous·ly** *adv* — **glo·ri·ous·ness** *n*

1glo·ry \'glōr-ē, 'glòr-\ *n, pl* **glories 1 a** : praise, honor, or distinction extended by common consent : RENOWN **b** : worshipful praise, honor, and thanksgiving ⟨giving *glory* to God⟩ **2 a** : something that brings praise or renown **b** : a brilliant asset ⟨was a *glory* to the profession⟩ **3 a** : RESPLENDENCE, MAGNIFICENCE ⟨the *glory* of ancient Greece⟩ **b** : the splendor and bliss of heaven **4** : a height of prosperity, achievement, or gratification ⟨in your *glory* when you're acting⟩ [Latin *gloria*]

2glory *vi* : to rejoice proudly or intensely : EXULT

1gloss \'gläs, 'glòs\ *n* **1** : brightness from a smooth surface : LUSTER, SHEEN **2** : a deceptively attractive appearance ⟨a *gloss* of good manners⟩ [probably of Scandinavian origin]

2gloss *vt* **1** : to give a false appearance of acceptableness or adequacy to ⟨*gloss* over faults⟩ **2** : to make glossy

3gloss *n* **1** : a brief explanation (as in the margin of a text) of a hard or unusual word or expression **2 a** : GLOSSARY **b** : an interlinear translation **c** : a continuous commentary accompanying a text [Old French *glose*, from Latin *glossa* "unusual word requiring explanation", from Greek *glōssa*, *glōtta*, literally, "tongue, language"]

4gloss *vt* : to furnish glosses for

glos·sa·ry \'gläs-rē, 'glòs-, -ə-rē\ *n, pl* **-ries 1** : a list in the back of a book of the hard or unusual words found in the text **2** : a dictionary of the special terms found in a particular field of study — **glos·sar·i·al** \gläs-'sar-ē-əl, -'ser-\ *adj*

glos·so·pha·ryn·geal nerve \,gläs-ō-,far-ən-'jē-əl-, ,glòs-; -fə-'rin-jē-əl-, -jəl-\ *n* : either of a pair of cranial nerves that supply chiefly the pharynx, posterior tongue, and parotid gland — called also *glossopharyngeal* [Greek *glōssa* "tongue"]

glossy \'gläs-ē, 'glòs-\ *adj* **gloss·i·er**; **-est 1** : having surface luster ⟨*glossy* leather⟩ **2** : superficially sophisticated and attractive ⟨*glossy* advertisements⟩ — **gloss·i·ness** *n*

glot·tis \'glät-əs\ *n, pl* **glot·tis·es** *or* **glot·ti·des** \'glät-ə-,dēz\ : the elongated space in the larynx between the vocal cords; *also* : the structures that surround this space — compare EPIGLOTTIS [Greek *glōttis*, from *glōtta* "tongue"] — **glot·tal** \'glät-l\ *adj*

glove \'gləv\ *n* **1 a** : a covering for the hand having separate sections for each finger **b** : GAUNTLET 1 **2 a** : a padded leather covering for the hand used in baseball **b** : BOXING GLOVE [Old English *glōf*] — **gloved** \'gləvd\ *adj*

1glow \'glō\ *vi* **1 a** : to shine with or as if with an intense heat **b** (1) : to have a rich warm usually ruddy color (2) : FLUSH, BLUSH **2 a** : to experience a sensation of heat **b** : to show exuberance or elation ⟨*glow* with pride⟩ [Old English *glōwan*]

2glow *n* **1** : brightness or warmth of color; *esp* : REDNESS **2 a** : warmth of feeling or emotion **b** : a sensation of warmth **3** : light that is emitted by something intensely hot but not flaming or by something seemingly hot ⟨the *glow* of embers⟩ ⟨a firefly's *glow*⟩

glow·er \'glaủ-ər, 'glaủr\ *vi* [Middle English *glowren*] — **glower** *n*

glow·worm \'glō-,wərm\ *n* : an insect or insect larva that gives off light

glox·in·ia \gläk-'sin-ē-ə\ *n* : any of a genus of Brazilian tuberous herbs related to the African violets; *esp* : one often grown for its showy bell-shaped or slipper-shaped flowers [B. P. *Gloxin*, 18th century German botanist]

gloze \'glōz\ *vt* : 2GLOSS 1 [Middle English *glosen* "to gloss, flatter", from *glose* "gloss"]

glu·ca·gon \'glü-kə-,gän\ *n* : a protein hormone secreted by the pancreas that increases the content of sugar in the blood [derived from *glucose*]

glu·cose \'glü-,kōs\ *n* **1** : a sugar $C_6H_{12}O_6$ known in three different forms; *esp* : DEXTROSE **2** : CORN SYRUP [French, from Greek *gleukos* "must, sweet wine"]

glu·co·side \'glü-kə-,sīd\ *n* : GLYCOSIDE

1glue \'glü\ *n* **1** : any of various strong adhesive substances; *esp* : a hard protein substance that absorbs water to form a viscous solution with strong adhesive properties **2** : a solution of glue used to stick things together [Middle French *glu*, from Late Latin *glus*] — **glu·ey** \'glü-ē\ *adj* — **glu·i·ly** \'glü-ə-lē\ *adv*

2glue *vt* **glued**; **glu·ing** *also* **glue·ing** : to make fast with or as if with glue

glum \'gləm\ *adj* **glum·mer**; **glum·mest 1** : SULLEN 1 **2** : DREARY, GLOOMY ⟨a *glum* look⟩ [probably related to Middle English *gloumen* "to gloom"] — **glum·ly** *adv* — **glum·ness** *n*

glume \'glüm\ *n* : either of two empty bracts at the base of the spikelet in a grass [Latin *gluma* "hull, husk"]

1glut \'glət\ *vt* **glut·ted**; **glut·ting 1** : to fill especially with food to excess : STUFF **2** : to flood with goods so that supply exceeds demand ⟨the market was *glutted* with fruit⟩ [Middle English *glouten*]

²glut *n* : an excessive quantity : OVERSUPPLY

glu•ta•mate \'glüt-ə-ˌmāt\ *n* : a salt or ester of glutamic acid

glu•tam•ic acid \glü-ˌtam-ik-\ *n* : an amino acid $C_5H_9NO_4$ widely distributed in plant and animal proteins and used in the form of a sodium salt as a seasoning [*glu*ten + *amino* + *-ic*]

glu•ta•mine \'glüt-ə-ˌmēn\ *n* : an amino acid that is found in plant and animal proteins and that yields glutamic acid and ammonia on hydrolysis

glu•ten \'glüt-n\ *n* : a tough elastic protein substance in flour especially from wheat that holds dough together and makes it sticky [Latin, "glue"] — **glu•ten•ous** \'glüt-nəs, -n-əs\ *adj*

glu•te•us \'glüt-ē-əs\ *n, pl* **-tei** \-ē-ˌī\ : any of the large muscles of the buttocks [New Latin, from Greek *gloutos* "buttock"] — **glu•te•al** \-ē-əl\ *adj*

glu•ti•nous \'glüt-nəs, -n-əs\ *adj* : resembling glue : STICKY [Latin *glutinosus,* from *gluten* "glue"] — **glu•ti•nous•ly** *adv*

glut•ton \'glət-n\ *n* **1** : one that eats too much **2 a** : a shaggy thickset flesh-eating mammal of northern Europe and Asia related to the marten and the sable **b** : WOLVERINE [Old French *gloton,* from Latin *glutto*] — **glut•ton•ous** \'glət-nəs, -n-əs\ *adj* — **glut•ton•ous•ly** *adv*

glut•tony \'glət-nē, -n-ē\ *n, pl* **-ton•ies** : excess in eating or drinking

glyc•er•al•de•hyde \ˌglis-ə-'ral-də-ˌhīd\ *n* : a sweet crystalline compound $C_3H_6O_3$ that is formed as an intermediate in carbohydrate metabolism by the breakdown of sugars

gly•cer•ic acid \glis-ˌer-ik-\ *n* : a syrupy acid $C_3H_6O_4$ obtainable by oxidation of glycerol

glyc•er•ide \'glis-ə-ˌrīd\ *n* : an ester of glycerol especially with fatty acids — **glyc•er•id•ic** \ˌglis-ə-'rid-ik\ *adj*

glyc•er•in *or* **glyc•er•ine** \'glis-rən, -ə-rən\ *n* : GLYCEROL [French *glycérine,* from Greek *glykeros* "sweet"]

glyc•er•ol \'glis-ə-ˌrȯl, -ˌrōl\ *n* : a sweet colorless syrupy alcohol $C_3H_8O_3$ usually obtained by the hydrolysis of fats and oils and used especially as a solvent and plasticizer

gly•cine \'glī-ˌsēn, 'glīs-n\ *n* : a sweet amino acid $C_2H_5NO_2$ formed especially by hydrolysis of proteins [Greek *glykys* "sweet"]

gly•co•gen \'glī-kə-jən\ *n* : a white tasteless substance that is the chief storage carbohydrate of animals — called also *animal starch* [Greek *glykys* "sweet"]

gly•col•y•sis \glī-'käl-ə-səs\ *n* : energy-producing breakdown of carbohydrate (as glucose) by enzymes by way of phosphate derivatives — **gly•co•lyt•ic** \ˌglī-kə-'lit-ik\ *adj*

gly•co•side \'glī-kə-ˌsīd\ *n* : any of numerous derivatives of sugars that on hydrolysis yield a sugar (as glucose) — **gly•co•sid•ic** \ˌglī-kə-'sid-ik\ *adj*

gly•cos•uria \ˌglī-kō-'shu̇r-ē-ə, -kəs-'yu̇r-\ *n* : the presence of abnormal amounts of sugar in the urine [derived from Greek *glykys* "sweet" + *ouron* "urine"]

G–man \'jē-ˌman\ *n* : a special agent of the Federal Bureau of Investigation [probably from *government man*]

gnarl \'närl\ *n* : a hard knob with twisted grain on a tree [probably from *knurl*] — **gnarled** \'närld\ *adj* — **gnarly** \'när-lē\ *adj*

gnash \'nash\ *vt* : to strike or grind (the teeth) together [Middle English *gnasten*]

gnat \'nat\ *n* : any of various small usually biting two-winged flies — compare ³FLY 2 [Old English *gnæt*]

gnaw \'nȯ\ *vb* **1 a** : to bite or chew with the teeth; *esp* : to wear away by persistent biting or nibbling ⟨a dog *gnawing* a bone⟩ **b** : to make by gnawing ⟨rats *gnawed* a hole⟩ **2 a** : to be a source of vexation to : PLAGUE **b** : to affect like gnawing ⟨*gnawing* hunger⟩ **3** : ERODE 1a, CORRODE [Old English *gnagan*] — **gnaw•er** \'nȯ-ər, 'nȯr\ *n*

gneiss \'nīs\ *n* : a metamorphic rock occurring in layers that is similar in composition to granite or feldspar [German *gneis*]

gnome \'nōm\ *n* : a legendary dwarf living inside the earth and guarding precious ore or treasure [French] — **gnom•ish** \'nō-mish\ *adj*

gno•mon \'nō-ˌmän, -mən\ *n* : an object that by the position or length of its shadow serves as an indicator of the hour of the day: *esp* : the style of an ordinary sundial [Latin, from Greek *gnōmōn* 'interpreter, pointer on a sundial", from *gignōskein* "to know"]

gnu \'nü, 'nyü\ *n, pl* **gnu** *or* **gnus** : any of several large African antelopes with a head like that of an ox, short mane, long tail, and horns in both sexes that curve downward and outward [Bushman *nqu*]

¹go \'gō\ *vb* **went** \'went\; **gone** \'gȯn, 'gän\; **go•ing** \'gō-ing\; **goes** \'gōz\ **1** : to move on a course : PROCEED ⟨*go* slow⟩ **2** : to move away from one point to or toward another : LEAVE, DEPART **3 a** : to take a certain course or follow a certain procedure ⟨reports *go* through channels⟩ **b** : to pass by a process like journeying ⟨the message *went* by wire⟩ **c** (1) : EXTEND, RUN ⟨our land *goes* to the river⟩ (2) : to give access : LEAD ⟨that door *goes* to the cellar⟩ **4** : to be habitually in a certain state ⟨*goes* bareheaded⟩ **5 a** : to become lost, consumed, or spent **b** : ELAPSE, PASS ⟨the evening *went* well⟩ **c** : to pass by sale ⟨*went* for a good price⟩ **d** : to become impaired or weakened ⟨my hearing started to *go*⟩ **e** : to give way under force or pressure : BREAK **6 a** : to be in general or on an average ⟨cheap, as yachts *go*⟩ **b** : to become especially as the result of a contest ⟨the decision *went* against them⟩ **7 a** : to apply oneself ⟨*went* to fighting among themselves⟩ **b** : to put or subject oneself ⟨*went* to great expense⟩ **8** : to have recourse : RESORT ⟨*go* to court to recover damages⟩ **9 a** : to begin or maintain an action or motion ⟨drums *going* strong⟩ **b** : to function properly ⟨get the motor to *go*⟩ **10** : to have currency : CIRCULATE ⟨the report *goes*⟩ **11 a** : to act in accordance ⟨a good rule to *go* by⟩ **b** : to come to be applied ⟨part of the budget *goes* for schools⟩ **c** : to pass by award, assignment, or lot ⟨the prize *went* to a sophomore⟩ **d** : to contribute to a result ⟨qualities that *go* to make a hero⟩ **12 a** : to be about, intending, or expecting something ⟨is *going* to leave town⟩ **b** : to come or arrive at a certain state or condition ⟨*go* to sleep⟩ **c** : to come to be ⟨the tire *went* flat⟩ **13 a** : FIT 2a ⟨these clothes will *go* in your suitcase⟩ **b** : to have a usual or proper place or position : BELONG ⟨these books *go* on the top shelf⟩ **c** : to be contained in another quantity when used as a divisor ⟨5 *goes* into 60 12 times⟩ **14** : TEND, CONDUCE ⟨*goes* to show they can be trusted⟩ **15** : to be acceptable : DO ⟨any kind of dress *goes*⟩ **16 a** : to proceed along or according to : FOLLOW ⟨if I was *going* your way⟩ **b** : TRAVERSE 2 **17** : to make a wager or offer of ⟨willing to *go* $50⟩ **18 a** : to assume the function or obligation of ⟨*go* bail for a friend⟩ **b** : to participate to the extent of ⟨*go* halves⟩ **19** : WEIGH 1b [Old English *gan*] — **go at 1** : to make an attack on **2** : UNDERTAKE 1 — **go back on 1** : ABANDON 2, 3 **2** : BETRAY 2 **3** : FAIL 2a — **go by the board** : to be discarded — **go down the line** : to give wholehearted support — **go for 1** : to pass for or serve as **2** : to be attracted to : LIKE **3** : ATTACK 1 — **go one better** : SURPASS 1, OUTDO — **go over 1 a** : CONSIDER 1 **b** : EXAMINE 1 **2 a** : REPEAT 1a **b** : REVIEW 1 — **go places** : to be on the way to success — **go steady** : to date one person exclusively — **go through 1** : to subject to thorough examination, consideration, or study **2** : EXPERIENCE 1, UNDERGO **3** : to carry out : PERFORM ⟨*went through* the act perfectly⟩ — **go to bat for** : to give active support or help to — **go to one's head** : to cause one to become conceited or overconfident — **go to pieces** : to become shattered (as in nerves or health) — **go to town 1** : to act rapidly or efficiently **2** : to be very successful — **go with** : DATE 4 — **go without saying** : to be self-evident

gnu

²go, *n, pl* **goes 1** : the act or manner of going **2** : the height of fashion **3** : an often unexpected turn of affairs **4** : ENERGY 1 **5** : TRY ⟨give it a *go*⟩ **6** : a spell of activity — **no go** : to no avail : USELESS — **on the go** : constantly or restlessly active

³go *adj* : ready to go ⟨declared all systems *go*⟩

⁴go *n* : an Oriental board game played between two players who alternately place black and white stones on a board checkered by 19 vertical and 19 horizontal lines in an attempt to enclose the opponent's stones [Japanese]

goad \'gōd\ *n* **1** : a pointed rod used to urge an animal on **2** : something that urges : SPUR [Old English *gād* "spear, goad"] — **goad** *vt*

go–ahead \ˈgō-ə-ˌhed\ *n* : GREEN LIGHT
goal \ˈgōl, *in children's games sometimes* ˈgül\ *n* **1** : the terminal point of a race **2** : the end toward which effort is directed : AIM **3 a** : an area or object toward which players in various games attempt to advance a ball or puck to score points **b** : the score resulting from such an act [Middle English *gol* "boundary, limit"]
goal•ie \ˈgō-lē\ *n* : GOALKEEPER
goal•keep•er \ˈgōl-ˌkē-pər\ *n* : a player who defends the goal in various games
goal line *n* : a line at or near one end of the playing area which marks the goal or on which the goal sits
goal•post \ˈgōl-ˌpōst\ *n* : one of two vertical posts that with a crossbar constitute the goal in various games
goal•ten•der \ˈgōl-ˌten-dər\ *n* : GOALKEEPER
goat \ˈgōt\ *n, pl* **goat** *or* **goats** **1** : any of various hollow-horned ruminant mammals related to the sheep but of lighter build and with backwardly arching horns, a short tail, and usually straight hair **2** : SCAPEGOAT 2 [Old English *gāt*] — **goat•like** \-ˌlīk\ *adj*
goa•tee \gō-ˈtē\ *n* : a small pointed or tufted beard on a man's chin [from its resemblance to the beard of a he-goat]
goat•fish \ˈgōt-ˌfish\ *n* : MULLET 2
goat•skin \-ˌskin\ *n* **1** : the skin of a goat **2** : leather made from goatskin
goat•suck•er \-ˌsək-ər\ *n* : any of various medium-sized long-winged nocturnal birds (as the whippoorwills and nighthawks) having a short wide bill, short legs, and soft mottled plumage and feeding on insects which they catch on the wing [from the belief that it sucks milk from goats]
1gob \ˈgäb\ *n* **1** : LUMP 1, MASS **2** : a large amount — usually used in pl. ⟨*gobs* of money⟩ [Middle French *gobe* "large piece of food", from *gobet*]
2gob *n* : SAILOR 1a [origin unknown]
gob•bet \ˈgäb-ət\ *n* : LUMP 1, MASS [Middle French *gobet* "mouthful, piece"]
1gob•ble \ˈgäb-əl\ *vt* **gob•bled**; **gob•bling** \ˈgäb-ling, -ə-ling\ **1** : to swallow or eat greedily **2** : to take eagerly : GRAB — usually used with *up* [probably from 1*gob*]
2gobble *vi* : to utter the characteristic guttural cry of a male turkey [imitative] — **gobble** *n*
gob•ble•dy•gook *or* **gob•ble•de•gook** \ˌgäb-əl-dē-ˈgu̇k\ *n* : wordy and generally unintelligible jargon [from *gobble,* n.]
gob•bler \ˈgäb-lər\ *n* : a male turkey
go–be•tween \ˈgō-bə-ˌtwēn\ *n* : a person who acts as a messenger or an intermediary between two parties
gob•let \ˈgäb-lət\ *n* : a drinking glass with a foot and stem — compare TUMBLER [Middle French *gobelet*]
goblet cell *n* : a mucus-secreting cell swollen at the free end by secretion [from its shape]
gob•lin \ˈgäb-lən\ *n* : an ugly grotesque sprite with evil or mischievous ways [Middle French *gobelin,* from Medieval Latin *gobelinus,* derived from Greek *kobalos* "rogue"]
go•by \ˈgō-bē\ *n, pl* **gobies** *also* **goby** : any of numerous spiny-finned fishes with the pelvic fins often united to form a sucking disk [Latin *gobius,* a kind of fish, from Greek *kōbios*]
go–cart \ˈgō-ˌkärt\ *n* **1** : STROLLER 2 **2** : a light open carriage
god \ˈgäd *also* ˈgȯd\ *n* **1** *cap* : the supreme or ultimate reality; *esp* : the Being perfect in power, wisdom, and goodness whom humans worship as creator and ruler of the universe **2** : a being held to possess more than human powers ⟨ancient peoples worshipped many *gods*⟩ **3** : a natural or man-made physical object (as an image or idol) worshipped as divine **4** : something held to be the most important thing in existence ⟨make a *god* of money⟩ [Old English]
god•child \-ˌchīld\ *n* : a person for whom another person stands as sponsor at baptism
god•daugh•ter \-ˌdȯt-ər\ *n* : a female godchild
god•dess \ˈgäd-əs\ *n* **1** : a female god **2** : a woman whose great charm or beauty arouses adoration
god•fa•ther \ˈgäd-ˌfäth-ər *also* ˈgȯd-\ *n* : a man who stands as sponsor for a child at its baptism
god•head \-ˌhed\ *n* **1** : divine nature or essence : DIVINITY **2** *cap* **a** : GOD 1 **b** : the nature of God especially as existing in three persons — used with *the* [Middle English *godhed,* from *god* + *-hed* "-hood"]
god•hood \-ˌhu̇d\ *n* : DIVINITY 1
god•less \ˈgäd-ləs *also* ˈgȯd-\ *adj* : not acknowledging a deity or divine law — **god•less•ness** *n*
god•like \-ˌlīk\ *adj* : resembling or having the qualities of God or a god : DIVINE — **god•like•ness** *n*
god•ling \-ling\ *n* : an inferior or local god
god•ly \-lē\ *adj* **god•li•er**; **-est** : PIOUS, DEVOUT ⟨*godly* people⟩ — **god•li•ness** *n*
god•moth•er \-ˌməth-ər\ *n* : a woman who stands as sponsor for a child at its baptism
god•par•ent \-ˌpar-ənt, -ˌper-\ *n* : a sponsor at baptism
God's acre *n* : CHURCHYARD; *esp* : a churchyard burial ground
god•send \ˈgäd-ˌsend *also* ˈgȯd-\ *n* : a desirable or needed thing or event that comes unexpectedly [back-formation from *god-sent*]
god•son \-ˌsən\ *n* : a male godchild
God•speed \-ˈspēd\ *n* : a prosperous journey : SUCCESS ⟨wished them *Godspeed*⟩ [Middle English *god speid,* from the phrase *God spede you* "God prosper you"]
god•wit \ˈgäd-ˌwit\ *n* : any of a genus of long-billed wading birds related to the snipes but similar to curlews [origin unknown]
go•er \ˈgō-ər, ˈgōr\ *n* : one that goes
go–get•ter \ˈgo-ˌget-ər\ *n* : an aggressively enterprising person : HUSTLER — **go–get•ting** \-ˌget-ing\ *adj or n*
1gog•gle \ˈgäg-əl\ *vi* **gog•gled**; **gog•gling** \ˈgäg-ling, -ə-ling\ : to stare with wide or protuberant eyes [Middle English *gogelen* "to squint"] — **gog•gler** \ˈgäg-lər, -ə-lər\ *n*
2goggle *adj* : PROTUBERANT, STARING ⟨*goggle* eyes⟩ — **gog•gly** \ˈgäg-lē, -ə-lē\ *adj*
gog•gle–eyed \ˌgäg-əl-ˈīd\ *adj* : having bulging or rolling eyes
gog•gles \ˈgäg-əlz\ *n pl* : protective eyeglasses typically with shields at the side
Goi•del•ic \gȯi-ˈdel-ik\ *n* : a branch of the Celtic languages that includes Irish Gaelic, Scottish Gaelic, and Manx [Irish *Gōidel* "Gael"] — **Goidelic** *adj*
go in *vi* : to enter some place — **go in for** **1** : to make one's particular interest or specialty **2** : to take part in out of interest or liking ⟨*go in for* track⟩
1go•ing \ˈgō-ing\ *n* **1** : the condition of the ground especially for walking or driving **2** : advance toward an objective : PROGRESS
2going *adj* **1** : EXISTING, LIVING ⟨the best novelist *going*⟩ **2** : CURRENT, PREVAILING ⟨*going* prices⟩ **3** : being successful and likely to remain so ⟨a *going* concern⟩
go•ing–over \ˌgō-ing-ˈō-vər\ *n* **1** : a thorough examination or investigation **2** : a severe scolding or beating : DRUBBING
go•ings–on \ˌgō-ingz-ˈȯn, -ˈän\ *n pl* : usually undesirable actions or events
goi•ter *also* **goi•tre** \ˈgȯit-ər\ *n* : an enlargement of the thyroid gland visible as a swelling of the front of the neck — compare HYPERTHYROIDISM, HYPOTHYROIDISM [French *goitre,* from Middle French *goitron* "throat", from Latin *guttur*] — **goi•trous** \ˈgȯi-trəs, ˈgȯit-ə-rəs\ *adj*
gold \ˈgōld\ *n* **1** : a malleable ductile yellow metallic element that occurs chiefly free but also in a few minerals and is used especially in coins and jewelry — see ELEMENT table **2 a** : gold coins **b** : RICHES, MONEY **3** : a deep yellow [Old English] — **gold** *adj*
1gold•brick \ˈgōld-ˌbrik, gōl-\ *n* : a person who habitually shirks assigned work [earlier *goldbrick* "worthless brick that appears to be of gold"]
2goldbrick *vi* : to shirk duty or responsibility
gold digger *n* : a woman who uses her charm to get money or gifts from men
gold•en \ˈgōl-dən\ *adj* **1** : consisting of, relating to, or containing gold **2** : having the color of gold ⟨*golden* hair⟩ **3** : FLOURISHING, PROSPEROUS ⟨a *golden* age⟩ **4** : radiantly youthful and vigorous **5** : of precious rarity ⟨a *golden* opportunity⟩ **6** : MELLOW, RESONANT ⟨a smooth *golden* tenor⟩ — **gold•en•ly** *adv* — **gold•en•ness** \-dən-nəs\ *n*
golden–brown alga *n* : any of a major group (Chrysophyta) of algae with golden brown pigments usually hiding the chlorophyll — called also *golden alga*
gold•en•eye \ˈgōl-də-ˌnī\ *n* **1** : a northern diving duck having the male strikingly marked in black and white **2** : LACEWING
golden glow *n* : a tall branching herb related to the daisies that has showy yellow very double flower heads
golden mean *n* : the medium between extremes : MODERATION
gold•en•rod \ˈgōl-dən-ˌräd\ *n* : any of numerous chiefly North American biennial or perennial plants that are related to the daisies and that have stems resembling wands and heads of

small yellow or sometimes white flowers usually in loosely branched clusters

golden rule *n* : a rule that one should do to others as one would do to oneself

gol•den•seal \'gōl-dən-,sēl\ *n* : a perennial American herb of the buttercup family with a thick knotted yellow rhizome and large rounded leaves

golden section *n* : division of a line segment such that the ratio of the smaller part to the larger is equal to the ratio of the larger to the whole segment

gold•field \'gōld-,fēld, 'gōl-\ *n* : a gold-mining district

gold–filled \-'fild\ *adj* : covered with a layer of gold ⟨a *gold-filled* bracelet⟩

gold•finch \-,finch\ *n* **1** : a small largely red, black, and yellow European finch often kept as a cage bird **2** : any of several small American finches usually having the male in summer plumage yellow with black wings, tail, and crown

gold•fish \-,fish\ *n* : a small usually golden yellow or orange carp much used as an aquarium and pond fish

gold leaf *n* : a thin sheet of gold used especially for gilding

gold•smith \'gōld-,smith, 'gōl-\ *n* : a maker of or dealer in articles of gold

gold standard *n* : a monetary standard under which the basic unit of currency is defined by a stated quantity of gold

golf \'gälf, 'gȯlf, 'gäf, 'gȯf\ *n* : a game in which a player using special clubs tries to sink a ball into each of 9 or 18 holes around a course using as few strokes as possible [Middle English (Scottish dialect)] — **golf** *vi* — **golf•er** *n*

Gol•gi apparatus \'gȯl-jē-\ *n* : a cytoplasmic component that probably plays a part in the formation and secretion of cell products — called also *Golgi complex* [Camillo *Golgi*, died 1926, Italian physician]

Golgi body *n* : a single particle of the Golgi apparatus

golly \'gäl-ē\ *interj* — used as a mild oath or to express surprise [euphemism for *God*]

gon- or gono- *combining form* : sexual : generative : semen : seed ⟨*gono*coccus⟩ [Greek *gonos* "procreation, seed", from *gignesthai* "to be born"]

-gon \,gän *also* gən\ *n combining form* : figure having (so many) angles ⟨nona*gon*⟩ [Greek *-gōnon,* from *gōnia* "angle"]

go•nad \'gō-,nad\ *n* : a sperm- or egg-producing gland ⟨testes and ovaries are *gonads*⟩ [New Latin *gonad-, gonas,* from Greek *gonos*] — **go•nad•al** \gō-'nad-l\ *adj*

go•nad•o•tro•phic \gō-,nad-ə-'trō-fik\ *or* **go•nad•o•trop•ic** \-'träp-ik\ *adj* : acting on or stimulating the gonads ⟨a *gonadotropic* hormone⟩

go•nad•o•tro•phin \-'trō-fən\ *or* **go•nad•o•tro•pin** \-pən\ *n* : a gonadotrophic hormone

gon•do•la \'gän-də-lə (*usual for sense 1*), gän-'dō-\ *n* **1** : a long narrow flat-bottomed boat with a high bow and stern used on the canals of Venice **2** : a railroad car with flat bottom, fixed sides, and no top used chiefly for hauling heavy bulk commodities **3 a** : an elongated car attached to the underside of an airship **b** : an enclosure or metal-frame basket suspended from a balloon for carrying passengers or instruments **c** : an enclosed car suspended from a cable used especially as a ski lift [Italian]

gondola 1

gon•do•lier \,gän-də-'liər\ *n* : a boatman who handles a gondola

gone \'gȯn, 'gän\ *adj* **1** : PAST 2 **2 a** : ADVANCED, ABSORBED ⟨far *gone* in hysteria⟩ **b** : INFATUATED ⟨they're *gone* on each other⟩ **c** : PREGNANT 1a **3 a** : DEAD 1 **b** : WEAK 1a ⟨a *gone* feeling from hunger⟩ [from past participle of *go*]

gon•er \'gȯn-ər, 'gän-\ *n* : one whose case is hopeless

gon•fa•lon \'gän-fə-,län\ *n* **1** : the ensign of certain princes or states (as the medieval republics of Italy) **2** : a flag that hangs from a crosspiece or frame [Italian *gonfalone*]

gong \'gäng, 'gȯng\ *n* **1** : a metallic disk that produces a resounding tone when struck **2** : a flat saucer-shaped bell [Malay]

go•nid•i•um \gō-'nid-ē-əm\ *n, pl* **-ia** \-ē-ə\ : an asexual reproductive cell or group of cells of a gametophyte — **go•nid•i•al** \-ē-əl\ *adj*

gono•coc•cus \,gän-ə-'käk-əs\ *n, pl* **-coc•ci** \-'käk-,sī, -,ī, -sē, -ē\ : the bacterium that causes gonorrhea [*gon-* + Greek *kokkos* "grain, seed, berry"] — **gono•coc•cal** \-'käk-əl\ *or* **gono•coc•cic** \-'käk-sik, -ik\

gon•or•rhea \,gän-ə-'rē-ə\ *n* : a contagious inflammatory disease of the genitourinary tract caused by the gonococcus — called also *clap* — **gon•or•rhe•al** \-'rē-əl\ *adj*

-g•o•ny \g-ə-nē\ *n combining form, pl* **-gonies** : reproduction [Greek *-gonia,* from *gonos* "procreation, seed"]

goo \'gü\ *n* : a viscid or sticky substance [perhaps alteration of *glue*] — **goo•ey** \'gü-ē\ *adj*

goo•ber \'gü-bər, 'gu̇b-ər\ *n, South & Midland* : PEANUT 1 [of African origin]

1good \'gu̇d\ *adj* **bet•ter** \'bet-ər\; **best** \'best\ **1 a** (1) : of a favorable character or tendency ⟨*good* news⟩ (2) : BOUNTIFUL, FERTILE ⟨*good* land⟩ (3) : COMELY, ATTRACTIVE ⟨*good* looks⟩ **b** (1) : SUITABLE, FIT ⟨*good* to eat⟩ (2) : SOUND, WHOLE ⟨one *good* arm⟩ (3) : not depreciated ⟨bad money drives out *good*⟩ (4) : commercially reliable ⟨a *good* risk⟩ (5) : certain to last or live ⟨*good* for another year⟩ (6) : certain to pay or contribute ⟨*good* for a hundred dollars⟩ (7) : certain to elicit a specified result ⟨always *good* for a laugh⟩ **c** (1) : AGREEABLE, PLEASANT ⟨a *good* time⟩ (2) : SALUTARY, WHOLESOME ⟨*good* for a cold⟩ **d** (1) : CONSIDERABLE, AMPLE ⟨a *good* margin⟩ (2) : FULL ⟨a *good* four hours⟩ **e** (1) : WELL-FOUNDED, COGENT ⟨*good* reasons⟩ (2) : TRUE ⟨holds *good* for society at large⟩ (3) : recognized or valid especially in law ⟨members in *good* standing⟩ ⟨a *good* title⟩ **f** (1) : ADEQUATE, SATISFACTORY ⟨*good* care⟩ (2) : conforming to a standard ⟨*good* English⟩ (3) : DISCRIMINATING, CHOICE ⟨*good* taste⟩ **2 a** (1) : COMMENDABLE, VIRTUOUS, JUST ⟨a *good* man⟩ (2) : RIGHT ⟨*good* conduct⟩ (3) : KIND, BENEVOLENT ⟨*good* intentions⟩ **b** : UPPER-CLASS ⟨a *good* family⟩ **c** : COMPETENT, SKILLFUL ⟨a *good* doctor⟩ **d** : LOYAL, FAITHFUL ⟨a *good* member of the party⟩ ⟨a *good* Catholic⟩ **3** : containing less fat and being less tender than higher grades — used of meat and especially beef [Old English *gōd*] — **as good as** : in effect : VIRTUALLY ⟨*as good as* dead⟩ — **good and** : VERY, ENTIRELY ⟨was *good and* mad⟩

2good *n* **1 a** : what is good or moral ⟨know *good* from evil⟩ **b** : praiseworthy character : GOODNESS **2** : PROSPERITY, BENEFIT, WELFARE ⟨for the *good* of the community⟩ **3 a** : something that has economic utility or satisfies an economic need or desire **b** *pl* : PERSONAL PROPERTY **c** *pl* : CLOTH 1 **d** *pl* : WARES, COMMODITIES ⟨canned *goods*⟩ **4** : good persons — used with *the* ⟨the *good* die young⟩ **5** *pl* : proof of wrongdoing ⟨got the *goods* on them⟩

3good *adv* : WELL

good book *n, often cap G&B* : BIBLE 1

good–bye *or* **good–by** \gu̇d-'bī, gəd-, gə-\ *n* : a concluding remark at parting ⟨said their *good-byes* and left⟩ — often used interjectionally as a farewell [alteration of *God be with you*]

good day *interj* — used as a greeting or farewell in the daytime

good evening *interj* — used as a greeting or farewell in the evening

good fellow *n* : an affable companionable person — **good–fel•low•ship** *n*

1good–for–nothing \'gu̇d-fər-,nəth-ing\ *adj* : of no value : USELESS, WORTHLESS ⟨a *good-for-nothing* bum⟩

2good–for–nothing *n* : a good-for-nothing person

Good Friday *n* : the Friday before Easter observed as the anniversary of the crucifixion of Christ [from its special sanctity]

good–heart•ed \'gu̇d-'härt-əd\ *adj* : having a kindly generous disposition — **good–heart•ed•ly** *adv* — **good–heart•ed•ness** *n*

good–hu•mored \-'hyü-mərd, -'yü-\ *adj* : AMIABLE, CHEERFUL — **good–hu•mored•ly** *adv* — **good–hu•mored•ness** *n*

good•ish \'gu̇d-ish\ *adj* **1** : fairly good **2** : fairly large or long

good•looking \'gu̇d-lu̇k-ing\ *adj* : having an attractive appearance — **good–looker** *n*

good•ly \'gu̇d-lē\ *adj* **good•li•er**; **-est** **1** : of pleasing appear-

ance **2** : LARGE, CONSIDERABLE ⟨a *goodly* number⟩
good•man \'gu̇d-mən\ *n* **1** *archaic* : the head of a household : HUSBAND **2** *archaic* : MISTER 1
good morning *interj* — used as a greeting or farewell in the morning
good–na•tured \'gu̇d-'nā-chərd\ *adj* : of a pleasant cheerful disposition — **good–na•tured•ly** *adv* — **good–na•tured•ness** *n*
good–neighbor policy *n* : a policy of friendship, cooperation, and noninterference in the affairs of another country
good•ness \'gu̇d-nəs\ *n* **1** : the quality or state of being good; *esp* : excellence of character **2** : the nutritious, flavorful, or beneficial portion or element
good–sized \'gu̇d-'sīzd\ *adj* : fairly large
good–tem•pered \-'tem-pərd\ *adj* : having an even temper — **good–tem•pered•ly** *adv* — **good–tem•pered•ness** *n*
good•wife \'gu̇d-,wīf\ *n* **1** *archaic* : the mistress of a household **2** *archaic* : MRS. 1
good•will \'gu̇d-'wil\ *n* **1** : kindly feeling : BENEVOLENCE **2** : the value of the custom a business has built up over a period of time **3 a** : cheerful consent **b** : willing effort
¹goody \'gu̇d-ē\ *n, pl* **good•ies** : something that is particularly good to eat or otherwise attractive
²goody *interj* — used as an expression of delight especially by children
goody–goody \,gu̇d-ē-'gu̇d-ē\ *adj* : affectedly or self-righteously good — **goody–goody** *n*
goo•ey \'gü-ē\ *adj* **goo•i•er**; **-est** **1** : STICKY 1 **2** : very emotional or sentimental
goof \'güf\ *vb* : BUNGLE [earlier *goof* "ridiculous or stupid person", probably from English dialect *goff* "simpleton"] — **goof** *n*
goof•ball \'güf-,bȯl\ *n* **1** *slang* : a barbiturate sleeping pill **2** *slang* : a mentally abnormal person
go off *vi* **1** : EXPLODE 2 **2** : to undergo decline or deterioration **3** : to follow the expected or desired course
goofy \'gü-fē\ *adj* **goof•i•er**; **-est** : CRAZY 2b, SILLY — **goof•i•ly** \-fə-lē\ *adv* — **goof•i•ness** *n*
goon \'gün\ *n* **1** *slang* : DOPE 2b, SAP **2** : a man hired to terrorize or eliminate opponents [probably from English dialect *gooney* "simpleton"]
goo•ney \'gü-nē\ *n, pl* **gooneys** : an albatross of the Pacific that is chiefly blackish with a dusky bill and black feet and legs — called also *gooney bird* [probably from English dialect *gooney* "simpleton"]
goose \güs\ *n, pl* **geese** \'gēs\ **1 a** : any of numerous long-necked birds intermediate in size between the related swans and ducks **b** : a female goose as distinguished from a gander **2** : SIMPLETON, DOLT **3** *pl* **goos•es** : a tailor's smoothing iron with a goosened handle [Old English *gōs*]

goose 1a

goose•ber•ry \'güs-,ber-ē, 'güz-\ *n* : the acid usually prickly fruit of any of several shrubs related to the currant
goose bumps *n pl* : GOOSEFLESH
goose•flesh \'güs-,flesh\ *n* : a roughening of the skin caused usually by cold or fear
goose•foot \-,fu̇t\ *n, pl* **goosefoots** : any of numerous mostly weedy smooth herbs with branched clusters of small petalless greenish or whitish flowers — compare BEET, SPINACH
goose•neck \-,nek\ *n* : something (as a flexible or jointed metal tube) curved like the neck of a goose or U-shaped — **goose-necked** \-,nekt\ *adj*
goose pimples *n pl* : GOOSEFLESH
goose step *n* : a straight-legged stiff-kneed step used by troops of some armies when passing in review — **goose–step** \'güs-,step\ *vi*
go out *vi* **1** : to go forth; *esp* : to leave one's house **2** : to become extinguished ⟨the hall light *went out*⟩ **3** : to go on strike **4** : to become a candidate ⟨*went out* for the football team⟩
go•pher \'gō-fər\ *n* **1** : a burrowing American land tortoise — called also *gopher tortoise* **2 a** : any of several burrowing American rodents with large cheek pouches — called also *pocket gopher* **b** : a small striped ground squirrel of the prairie region of the United States [origin unknown]
Gor•di•an knot \,gȯrd-ē-ən-\ *n* : a very intricate and difficult problem or task [*Gordius,* king of Phrygia, who tied a knot held to be capable of being untied only by the future ruler of Asia, and cut by Alexander the Great with his sword]
¹gore \'gōr, 'gȯr\ *n* : BLOOD; *esp* : clotted blood [Old English *gor* "filth"]
²gore *n* : a tapering or triangular piece (as of cloth in a skirt) [Old English *gāra* "triangular piece of land"]
³gore *vt* **1** : to cut into a tapering triangular form **2** : to provide with a gore
⁴gore *vt* : to pierce or wound with a horn or tusk [Middle English *goren*]
¹gorge \'gȯrj\ *n* **1** : THROAT 1 **2** : a narrow passage (as between two mountains) **3** : a mass of matter that chokes up a passage ⟨an ice *gorge* in the river⟩ [Middle French, from Late Latin *gurges,* from Latin, "whirlpool"]
△ **origin** *Gurges,* the Latin word for "whirlpool", came in Late Latin to mean "throat" as well. The notions of downward passage and of voraciousness must have suggested to speakers of Late Latin that a word meaning "whirlpool" was an apt term for the throat. *Gurges* eventually became Middle French *gorge,* which was borrowed into English in the late 14th century, later developing such familiar meanings as "a ravine with steep, rocky walls", by metaphorical extension from the original "throat".
²gorge *vb* : to eat greedily : stuff to capacity — **gorg•er** *n*
gor•geous \'gȯr-jəs\ *adj* : resplendently beautiful ⟨a *gorgeous* sunset⟩ [Middle French *gorgias* "elegant", from *gorgias* "wimple", from *gorge* "throat"] — **syn** see SPLENDID — **gor•geous•ly** *adv* — **gor•geous•ness** *n*
△ **origin** In the late Middle Ages, a standard article of feminine dress was the wimple, a cloth headdress that surrounded the neck and head, leaving only the face uncovered. Middle French *gorgias,* derived from *gorge,* "throat", was, strictly speaking, the name for the part of this garment that covered the throat and shoulders. But the word was also applied to the whole wimple. An elegant and elaborate wimple, or *gorgias,* was so much the mark of a well-to-do and fashionable lady that *gorgias* became an adjective meaning "elegant" or "fond of dress". In English it gradually came to emphasize "beauty" more than "elegance".
gor•get \'gȯr-jət\ *n* : a piece of armor protecting the throat and shoulders [Middle French, from *gorge* "throat"]
gor•gon \'gȯr-gən\ *n* **1** *cap* : any of three snaky-haired sisters in Greek mythology capable of turning to stone any who behold them **2** : an ugly or repulsive woman [Greek *Gorgōn*]
Gor•gon•zo•la \,gȯr-gən-'zō-lə\ *n* : a blue cheese of Italian origin usually made of cow's milk [*Gorgonzola,* Italy]
go•ril•la \gə-'ril-ə\ *n* **1** : an anthropoid ape of west equatorial Africa related to but much larger than the chimpanzee **2** : THUG, GOON [Greek *Gorillai,* African creatures believed to be hairy women]
gor•man•dize \'gȯr-mən-,dīz\ *vb* : to eat greedily or ravenously [*gormand,* alteration of *gourmand*] — **gor•man•diz•er** *n*

gorilla 1

gorse \'gȯrs\ *n* : FURZE [Old English *gorst*] — **gorsy** \'gȯr-sē\ *adj*
gory \'gōr-ē, 'gȯr-\ *adj* **gor•i•er**; **-est** **1** : covered with blood : BLOODSTAINED **2** : involving much bloodshed ⟨a *gory* fight⟩ **3** : BLOODCURDLING
gosh \'gäsh *also* 'gȯsh\ *interj* — used as a mild oath or to express surprise [euphemism for *God*]
gos•hawk \'gäs-,hȯk\ *n* : any of several long-tailed short-winged hawks noted for their powerful flight, activity, and vigor [Old English *gōshafoc,* from *gōs* "goose" + *hafoc* "hawk"]
gos•ling \'gäz-ling, 'gȯz-, -lən\ *n* : a young goose [Middle English, from *gos* "goose"]
¹gos•pel \'gäs-pəl\ *n* **1 a** *often cap* : the Christian message concerning Christ, the kingdom of God, and salvation **b** *cap*

: any of the first four New Testament books that tell of the life, death, and resurrection of Jesus Christ; *also* : a similar apocryphal book **2** *cap* : a liturgical reading from one of the New Testament Gospels **3** : the message or teachings of a religious teacher **4** : something accepted as infallible truth or as a guiding principle [Old English *gōdspel,* from *gōd* "good" + *spell* "tale, news"]

²gospel *adj* **1** : relating to or in accordance with the gospel : EVANGELICAL **2** : EVANGELISTIC ⟨a *gospel* team⟩ **3** : of or relating to religious songs associated with evangelism and popular devotion ⟨a *gospel* singer⟩

gospel truth *n* : something absolutely and completely true

Gos•plan \ˈgäs-ˌplan, ˈgȯs-ˌplän\ *n* : a Soviet governmental agency that makes long-term economic and social plans [Russian *Gos*udarstvennaya *Plan*ovaya Komissiya "State Planning Commission"]

gos•sa•mer \ˈgäs-ə-mər, ˈgäz-\ *n* **1** : a film of cobwebs floating in air **2** : something light, delicate, or tenuous [Middle English *gossomer,* from *gos* "goose" + *somer* "summer"] — **gossamer** *adj* — **gos•sa•mery** \-mə-rē\ *adj*

¹gos•sip \ˈgäs-əp\ *n* **1** : a person who habitually reveals personal or sensational facts **2 a** : rumor or report of an intimate nature **b** : chatty talk **c** : the subject matter of gossip [Middle English *gossib* "crony, godparent", from Old English *godsibb* "godparent", from *god* + *sibb* "kinsman"] — **gos•sipy** \-ə-pē\ *adj*

△ **origin** Old English *sibb,* meaning "relative" or "kinsman", came from the adjective *sibb,* "related by blood" (the ancestor of modern English *sibling*). Old English *godsibb* was a person spiritually related to another, specifically by being a sponsor at baptism. Today we call such a person a *godparent.* Over the centuries *godsibb* changed both in form and in meaning. Middle English *gossib* came to be used for a close friend or crony as well as for a godparent. From there it was only a short step to the *gossip* of today, a person no longer necessarily friend, relative, or sponsor, but someone filled with irresistible tidbits of rumor.

²gossip *vi* : to relate gossip — **gos•sip•er** *n*

got *past of* GET

Goth \ˈgäth\ *n* : a member of a Germanic people that in the early centuries of the Christian era overran the Roman Empire [Late Latin *Gothi* "Goths"]

¹Goth•ic \ˈgäth-ik\ *adj* **1** : of, relating to, or resembling the Goths, their civilization, or their language **2** : of or relating to a style of architecture prevalent in western Europe from the middle 12th to the early 16th century and characterized by weights and stresses converging at isolated points on slender vertical piers and counterbalancing buttresses and by pointed arches and vaulting **3** *often not cap* : of or relating to a literary style characterized by the use of desolate or remote settings and macabre, mysterious, or violent incidents — **goth•i•cal•ly** \-i-kə-lē, -klē\ *adv* — **Goth•ic•ness** *n*

²Gothic *n* **1** : the Germanic language of the Goths **2** : the Gothic architectural style or decoration

gotten *past participle of* GET

gouache \ˈgwäsh\ *n* **1** : painting with watercolors that have been mixed with white pigment to produce an opaque effect **2** : a picture painted by gouache [French]

Gou•da \ˈgau̇d-ə, ˈgüd-\ *n* : a mild cheese of Dutch origin resembling Edam but containing more fat [*Gouda,* Netherlands]

¹gouge \ˈgau̇j\ *n* **1** : a chisel with a curved blade for scooping or cutting holes **2** : a hole or groove made with or as if with a gouge [Middle French, from Late Latin *gulbia,* of Celtic origin]

²gouge *vt* **1** : to cut holes or grooves in with or as if with a gouge **2** : to force out (an eye) with the thumb **3** : to charge excessively : DEFRAUD, CHEAT — **goug•er** *n*

gou•lash \ˈgü-ˌläsh, -ˌlash\ *n* : a beef stew usually with onion, paprika, and caraway [Hungarian *gulyás* "herdsman, herdsman's stew"]

gourd \ˈgōrd, ˈgȯrd, ˈgu̇rd\ *n* **1** : any of a family of chiefly herbaceous tendril-bearing vines including the cucumber, melon, squash, and pumpkin **2** : the fruit of a gourd; *esp* : any of various hard-shelled inedible fruits often used for ornament or for vessels and utensils [Middle French *gourde,* from Latin *cucurbita*]

gourde \ˈgu̇rd\ *n* **1** : the basic monetary unit of Haiti **2** : a coin representing one gourde [American French]

gour•mand \ˈgu̇r-ˌmänd\ *n* **1** : one who is excessively fond of eating and drinking **2** : a person heartily interested in good food and drink [Middle French *gourmant*] — **gour•mand•ism** \ˈgu̇r-ˌmän-ˌdiz-əm, -mən-\ *n*

gour•met \-ˌmā\ *n* : a connoisseur of food and drink [French, from Middle French *gromet* "groom, wine merchant's assistant", from Middle English *grom* "groom"]

gout \ˈgau̇t\ *n* **1** : a metabolic disease marked by a painful inflammation and swelling of the joints with deposits of salts of uric acid in and around the joints **2** : a drop or clot (as of blood) [Old French *goute* "drop, gout", from Latin *gutta* "drop"] — **gouty** \-ē\ *adj*

gov•ern \ˈgəv-ərn\ *vb* **1** : to exercise authority or authority over : RULE; *esp* : to control and direct the making and administration of policy in **2** : to control the speed of by automatic means **3 a** : to control, direct, or strongly influence the actions and conduct of **b** : to hold in check : RESTRAIN **4** : to require a word to be in a certain case or mood ⟨in English a transitive verb *governs* a pronoun in the objective case⟩ **5** : to constitute a rule or law for [Old French *governer,* from Latin *gubernare* "to steer, govern", from Greek *kybernan*] — **gov•ern•able** \-ər-nə-bəl\ *adj*

• **syn** GOVERN, RULE mean to exercise power or authority over others. GOVERN implies the aim of keeping in a straight course or smooth operation for the common good; RULE more often suggests the exercise of arbitrary or despotic power.

gov•ern•ance \ˈgəv-ər-nəns\ *n* : the exercise of control

gov•ern•ess \ˈgəv-ər-nəs\ *n* : a woman who teaches and trains a child especially in a private home

gov•ern•ment \ˈgəv-ər-mənt; ˈgəb-m-ənt, ˈgəv-; ˈgəv-ərn-mənt\ *n* **1** : the act or process of governing; *esp* : authoritative direction or control **2 a** : the exercise of authority over a political unit : RULE **b** : the making of policy as distinguished from the administration of policy decisions **3 a** : the organization, machinery, or agency through which a political unit exercises authority and performs functions **b** : manner of governing : the institutions, laws, and customs through which a political unit is governed ⟨republican *government*⟩ **4** : the body of persons that constitutes the governing authority of a political unit: as **a** : the officials comprising the governing body of a political unit **b** *cap* : the executive branch of the United States federal government **5** : POLITICAL SCIENCE — **government** *adj* — **gov•ern•men•tal** \ˌgəv-ərn-ˈment-l, -ər-\ *adj* — **gov•ern•men•tal•ly** \-l-ē\ *adv*

gov•er•nor \ˈgəv-ə-nər, -ər-\ *n* **1** : one that governs: as **a** : one that exercises authority especially over an area or group **b** : an official elected or appointed to act as ruler, chief executive, or nominal head of a political unit (as a colony, state, or province) **c** : COMMANDANT ⟨*governor* of a fortress⟩ **d** : the managing director and usually the principal officer of an institution or organization ⟨the *governor* of a bank⟩ **e** : a member of a group that directs or controls an institution or society ⟨a board of *governors*⟩ **2** : TUTOR **3** : an attachment to a machine for automatic control of speed

gov•er•nor–gen•er•al \ˌgəv-ə-nər-ˈjen-rəl, -ər-nər, -ə-rəl\ *n, pl* **governors–general** *or* **governor–generals** : a governor of high rank; *esp* : one who governs a large territory or has deputy governors under him

governor's council *n* : an executive or legislative council chosen to advise or assist a governor

gov•er•nor•ship \ˈgəv-ə-nər-ˌship, -ər-nər-\ *n* **1** : the office or position of governor **2** : the term of office of a governor

gown \ˈgau̇n\ *n* **1 a** : a loose flowing outer garment formerly worn by men **b** : an official robe worn especially by a judge, clergyman, or teacher **c** : a woman's dress; *esp* : one suitable for afternoon or evening wear **d** : a loose robe (as a nightgown) **e** : a coverall worn in an operating room **2 a** : an office or profession symbolized by a distinctive robe **b** : a body of college students and faculty [Middle French *goune,* from Late Latin *gunna,* a kind of fur garment] — **gown** *vt*

Graaf•ian follicle \ˌgräf-ē-ən-, ˌgraf-\ *n* : a fluid-filled sac in a mammal ovary enclosing a developing egg — called also *follicle*

[1]**grab** \ˈgrab\ *vb* **grabbed; grab•bing :** to take hastily : CLUTCH, SNATCH [obsolete Dutch or Low German *grabben*] — **grab•ber** *n*

[2]**grab** *n* **1 a :** a sudden snatch **b :** an unlawful seizure ⟨a land *grab*⟩ **c :** something grabbed **2 a :** a device for clutching an object **b :** CLAMSHELL

[1]**grace** \ˈgrās\ *n* **1 a :** help held to be given man by God especially in overcoming temptation or in leading a good life **b :** a state of freedom from sin and of love for God held to be enjoyed through divine grace **2 :** a short prayer at a meal asking a blessing or giving thanks **3 a :** a disposition to kindness or mercy **b :** a temporary delay granted from the performance of an obligation (as the payment of a debt) **c :** APPROVAL, ACCEPTANCE ⟨stay in one's good *graces*⟩ **4 a :** a charming trait or accomplishment **b** (1) **:** BEAUTY, ATTRACTIVENESS (2) **:** fitness or proportion of line or expression (3) **:** ease of movement **:** charm of bearing **5 :** a musical trill, turn, or appoggiatura **6** *cap* — used as a form of address for a duke, a duchess, or an archbishop **7** *cap* **:** any of three sister goddesses who personify charm and beauty in Greek mythology [Old French, from Latin *gratia* "favor, thanks", from *gratus* "pleasing, grateful"] — **grace•ful** \-fəl\ *adj* — **grace•ful•ly** \-fə-lē\ *adv* — **grace•ful•ness** *n*

[2]**grace** *vt* **1 :** HONOR 1b **2 :** ADORN, EMBELLISH

grace•less \ˈgrās-ləs\ *adj* **:** lacking grace, charm, or elegance; *esp* **:** showing lack of feeling for what is fitting ⟨*graceless* behavior⟩ — **grace•less•ly** *adv* — **grace•less•ness** *n*

grace note *n* **:** a musical note added as an ornament; *esp* **:** APPOGGIATURA

gra•cious \ˈgrā-shəs\ *adj* **1 a :** marked by kindness and courtesy **b :** GRACEFUL **c :** characterized by charm, good taste, and urbanity ⟨*gracious* living⟩ **2 :** MERCIFUL, COMPASSIONATE — used conventionally of royalty and high nobility — **gra•cious•ly** *adv* — **gra•cious•ness** *n*

grack•le \ˈgrak-əl\ *n* **1 :** any of various Old World starlings **2 :** any of several rather large American blackbirds with glossy iridescent black plumage [derived from Latin *graculus* "jackdaw"]

grackle 2

gra•da•tion \grā-ˈdā-shən, grə-\ *n* **1 a :** a series forming successive stages **b :** a step, degree, or stage in a series **2 :** an advance by regular degrees **3 :** the act or process of arranging in grades — **gra•da•tion•al** \-shnəl, -shən-l\ *adj* — **gra•da•tion•al•ly** \-ē\ *adv*

[1]**grade** \ˈgrād\ *n* **1 :** a stage, step, or degree in a series, order, or ranking **2 :** position in a scale of rank, quality, or order ⟨the *grade* of sergeant⟩ ⟨leather of the highest *grade*⟩ **3 :** a class of things that are of the same rank, quality, or order **4 a :** a division of the school course representing a year's work ⟨finish the fourth *grade*⟩ **b :** the pupils in a school division **c** *pl* **:** the elementary school system ⟨teach in the *grades*⟩ **5 :** a mark or rating especially of accomplishment in school ⟨a *grade* of 90 in a test⟩ **6 :** a standard of quality ⟨government *grades* for meat⟩ **7 a :** the degree of slope (as of a road, railroad track, or embankment); *also* **:** a sloping road **b :** ground level **8 :** a domestic animal with only one parent purebred [French, from Latin *gradus* "step, degree"]

[2]**grade** *vb* **1 :** to arrange in grades **:** SORT ⟨*grade* apples⟩ **2 :** to make level or evenly sloping ⟨*grade* a highway⟩ **3 :** to give a grade to ⟨*grade* a pupil in arithmetic⟩ **4 :** to assign to a grade or assign a grade to ⟨*grade* lumber⟩ **5 :** to form a series having only slight differences ⟨colors that *grade* into one another⟩

grade crossing *n* **:** a crossing (as of highways, railroad tracks, or pedestrian walks) on the same level

grad•er \ˈgrād-ər\ *n* **1 :** one that grades **2 :** a machine for leveling earth **3 :** a pupil in a school grade ⟨a 5th *grader*⟩

grade school *n* **:** a public school including usually the first six or the first eight grades

gra•di•ent \ˈgrād-ē-ənt\ *n* **1 a :** the rate of ascent or descent **:** INCLINATION ⟨the *gradient* of a rock layer⟩ **b :** a part (as of a road) sloping upward or downward **:** GRADE **2 :** change in the value of a quantity per unit distance in a specified direction ⟨vertical temperature *gradient*⟩ [Latin *gradiens,* present participle of *gradi* "to step, go"]

[1]**grad•u•al** \ˈgraj-ə-wəl, ˈgraj-əl\ *n, often cap* **1 :** a response following the Epistle in the Mass **2** *or* **gra•du•a•le** \ˌgräd-ə-ˈwäl-ˌā\ **:** a book containing the choral parts of the Mass [Medieval Latin *graduale,* from Latin *gradus* "step"; from its being sung on the steps of the altar]

[2]**gradual** *adj* **1 :** proceeding by steps or degrees **2 :** moving or changing by slight degrees [Medieval Latin *gradualis,* from Latin *gradus* "degree, step"] — **grad•u•al•ly** \ˈgraj-ə-lē, -ə-wə-lē\ *adv* — **grad•u•al•ness** \ˈgraj-ə-wəl-nəs, ˈgraj-əl-\ *n*

grad•u•al•ism \ˈgraj-ə-wə-ˌliz-əm, -ə-ˌliz-\ *n* **:** the policy of approaching a desired end by gradual stages — **grad•u•al•ist** \-ləst\ *n or adj*

[1]**grad•u•ate** \ˈgraj-ə-wət, -ˌwāt\ *n* **1 :** a holder of an academic degree or diploma **2 :** a graduated cup, cylinder, or flask for measuring contents

[2]**graduate** *adj* **1 :** holding an academic degree or diploma **2 :** of, relating to, or engaged in studies beyond the bachelor's degree ⟨*graduate* work⟩

[3]**grad•u•ate** \ˈgraj-ə-ˌwāt\ *vb* **1 :** to grant or receive an academic degree or diploma **2 :** to admit to a particular standing or grade **3 a :** to mark with degrees of measurement ⟨*graduate* a thermometer⟩ **b :** to divide into grades, classes, or intervals ⟨a *graduated* income tax⟩ **4 :** to change gradually [Medieval Latin *graduare,* from Latin *gradus* "step, degree"] — **grad•u•a•tor** \-ˌwāt-ər\ *n*

graduate school *n* **:** a division of a university or college devoted entirely to studies beyond the bachelor's degree and having authority to grant advanced degrees

grad•u•a•tion \ˌgraj-ə-ˈwā-shən\ *n* **1 :** a mark or the marks on an instrument or vessel indicating degrees or quantity **2 a :** an act or process of graduating **b :** the ceremony or exercises marking the completion by a student of a course of study at a school or college **:** COMMENCEMENT **3 :** arrangement in degrees or ranks

Graeco- — see GRECO-

graf•fi•to \grə-ˈfēt-ō\ *n, pl* **-ti** \-ē\ **:** an inscription or drawing made on a rock or wall [Italian]

[1]**graft** \ˈgraft\ *vb* **1 a :** to unite (plants or scion and stock) to form a graft; *also* **:** to insert a shoot from a plant into (a different plant) to grow **b :** to join as if by grafting **2 :** to implant (living tissue) surgically ⟨*graft* skin over a scar⟩ **3 :** to gain money or advantage by dishonest means [Middle English *graffen, graften,* from *graffe* "grafted plant", from Middle French *grafe,* from Latin *graphium* "stylus", from Greek *grapheion,* from *graphein* "to write"] — **graft•er** *n*

[2]**graft** *n* **1 a :** a grafted plant **b :** the point of insertion of a scion upon a stock **2 a :** the act of grafting **b :** something used in grafting: as (1) **:** SCION 1 (2) **:** living tissue used in surgical grafting **3 :** the getting of money or advantage by dishonest means through misuse of an official position; *also* **:** the money or advantage gained

gra•ham cracker \ˌgrā-əm-, ˌgram-\ *n* **:** a slightly sweet cracker made chiefly of whole wheat flour

graham flour *n* **:** whole wheat flour [Sylvester *Graham,* died 1851, American dietary reformer]

Grail \ˈgrāl\ *n* **:** the cup or platter used according to medieval legend by Christ at the Last Supper and thereafter the object of knightly quests — called also *Holy Grail* [Middle French *graal* "bowl, grail", from Medieval Latin *gradalis*]

[1]**grain** \ˈgrān\ *n* **1 a :** a seed or fruit of a cereal grass **b :** the seeds or fruits of various food plants and especially the cereal grasses **c :** plants producing grain **2 :** a small hard particle or crystal (as of sand) **3 a :** a granulated surface or appearance **b :** the outer or hair side of a skin or hide **4 :** a unit of weight based on the weight of a grain of wheat — see MEASURE table **5 a :** the arrangement of fibers in wood **b :** appearance or texture due to constituent particles or fibers ⟨the *grain* of a rock⟩ **6 :** natural disposition **:** TEMPER [Middle French, from Latin *granum*] — **grained** \ˈgrānd\ *adj* — **with a grain of salt :** SKEPTICALLY ⟨take my predictions *with a grain of salt*⟩

[2]**grain** *vt* **1 :** to form into grains **:** GRANULATE **2 :** to paint in imitation of the grain of wood or stone — **grain•er** *n*

grain alcohol *n* **:** ALCOHOL 1a

grain elevator *n* **:** ELEVATOR 1c

grain•field \ˈgrān-ˌfēld\ *n* **:** a field where grain is grown

grain sorghum *n* **:** any of several sorghums cultivated primarily for grain — compare SORGO

grainy \'grā-nē\ *adj* **grain•i•er; -est 1 :** consisting of or resembling grains **:** GRANULAR **2 :** resembling the grain of wood — **grain•i•ness** *n*

gram *or* **gramme** \'gram\ *n* **:** a metric unit of mass and weight equal to 1/1000 kilogram and nearly equal to one cubic centimeter of water at its maximum density — see METRIC SYSTEM table [French *gramme,* from Late Latin *gramma,* a small weight, from Greek *gramma* "letter, writing, a small weight"]

-gram \ˌgram\ *n combining form* **:** drawing **:** writing **:** record ⟨spectro*gram*⟩ ⟨tele*gram*⟩ [Greek *gramma* "letter, writing", from *graphein* "to write"]

grama \'gram-ə\ *n* **:** a pasture grass of the western United States — called also *grama grass* [Spanish]

gram atom *n* **:** the quantity of an element that has a weight in grams numerically equal to the atomic weight — called also *gram-atomic weight*

gra•mer•cy \grə-'mər-sē\ *interj, archaic* — used to express gratitude or astonishment [Middle French *grand merci* "great thanks"]

gram•i•ci•din \ˌgram-ə-'sīd-n\ *n* **:** a toxic crystalline antibiotic produced by a soil bacterium and used against bacteria in local infections [*gram*-positive + *-i-* + *-cide* + *-in*]

gram•mar \'gram-ər\ *n* **1 :** the study of the structure of a language **2 :** the facts of language with which grammar deals **3 a :** a grammar textbook **b :** speech or writing evaluated according to its conformity to grammatical rules ⟨bad *grammar*⟩ [Middle French *gramaire,* from Latin *grammatica,* from Greek *grammatikē,* from *gramma* "letter, writing", from *graphein* "to write"] — **gram•mar•i•an** \grə-'mer-ē-ən, -'mar-\ *n*

grammar school *n* **1 a :** a secondary school emphasizing Latin and Greek in preparation for college **b :** a British college preparatory school **2 :** an elementary school

gram•mat•i•cal \grə-'mat-i-kəl\ *adj* **1 :** of or relating to grammar **2 :** conforming to the rules of grammar — **gram•mat•i•cal•ly** \-kə-lē, -klē\ *adv*

gram molecule *n* **:** the quantity of a chemical compound or element that has a weight in grams numerically equal to the molecular weight — called also *gram-molecular weight*

gram–neg•a•tive \'gram-'neg-ət-iv\ *adj* **:** not holding the purple dye when stained by the Gram stain

gram•o•phone \'gram-ə-ˌfōn\ *n* **:** PHONOGRAPH [from *Gramophone,* a former trademark]

gram–pos•i•tive \'gram-'päz-ət-iv, -'päz-tiv\ *adj* **:** holding the purple dye when stained by the Gram stain

gram•pus \'gram-pəs\ *n* **1 :** a sea mammal that is a dolphin with teeth in the lower jaw only **2 :** KILLER WHALE [Middle French *graspeis,* from *gras* "fat" + *peis* "fish"]

Gram stain \'gram-\ *also* **Gram's stain** *n* **:** a technique of staining bacteria with gentian violet such that some bacteria retain the stain and others do not — compare GRAM-NEGATIVE, GRAM-POSITIVE [Hans C. J. *Gram,* died 1938, Danish physician]

grana *pl of* GRANUM

gran•a•dil•la \ˌgran-ə-'dil-ə\ *n* **:** the edible fruit of a tropical American passionflower [Spanish]

gra•na•ry \'grān-rē, 'gran-, -ə-rē\ *n, pl* **-ries 1 :** a storehouse for threshed grain **2 :** a region producing grain in abundance [Latin *granarium,* from *granum* "grain"]

[1]**grand** \'grand\ *adj* **1 :** higher in rank than others of the same class **:** FOREMOST, PRINCIPAL ⟨the *grand* prize⟩ **2 :** INCLUSIVE, COMPLETE ⟨a *grand* total⟩ **3 :** of great size, scope, or extent ⟨*grand* ideas⟩ **4 a :** marked by magnificence or splendor **b :** tending to impress (as by wealth, dignity, or rank) ⟨a *grand* lady⟩ **5 :** making a fine show **:** STATELY ⟨a *grand* palace⟩ **6 :** very good **:** FINE ⟨have a *grand* old time⟩ [Middle French, "large, great, grand", from Latin *grandis*] — **grand•ly** \'grand-lē, -lē\ *adv* — **grand•ness** \'grand-nəs, 'gran-\ *n*

• syn MAGNIFICENT, MAJESTIC, GRANDIOSE: GRAND often adds to greatness of size implications of handsomeness and dignity; MAGNIFICENT implies an impressive largeness achieved without sacrifice of dignity or taste ⟨*magnificent* paintings⟩ MAJESTIC adds to MAGNIFICENT connotations of awe-inspiring grandeur or loftiness ⟨a *majestic* waterfall⟩ GRANDIOSE commonly implies inflated pretension or pomposity ⟨*grandiose* schemes of world conquest⟩

[2]**grand** *n* **1 :** GRAND PIANO **2** *pl* **grand,** *slang* **:** a thousand dollars

gran•dam \'gran-ˌdam, -dəm\ *or* **gran•dame** \-ˌdām, -dəm\ *n* **1 :** GRANDMOTHER **2 :** an old woman [Anglo-French *graund dame,* literally, "great lady"]

grand•aunt \'gran-'dant, -'dånt\ *n* **:** an aunt of one's father or mother

grand•child \'grand-ˌchīld, 'gran-\ *n* **:** a child of one's son or daughter

grand•daugh•ter \'gran-ˌdȯt-ər\ *n* **:** a daughter of one's son or daughter

grand duchess *n* **1 :** the wife or widow of a grand duke **2 :** a woman who rules a grand duchy in her own right

grand duchy *n* **:** the territory or dominion of a grand duke or grand duchess

grand duke *n* **1 :** the sovereign duke of any of various European states **2 :** a son or male descendant of a Russian czar

grande dame \grä^{n}d-dåm, grä^{n}-\ *n, pl* **grandes dames** *or* **grande dames** *same or* -dåmz\ **:** a usually elderly woman of great prestige [French, literally, "great lady"]

gran•dee \gran-'dē\ *n* **:** a man of high rank or station; *esp* **:** a high-ranking Spanish or Portuguese nobleman [Spanish *grande,* from *grande* "large, great", from Latin *grandis*]

gran•deur \'gran-jər\ *n* **:** the quality or state of being grand **:** awe-inspiring magnificence [Middle French, from *grand*]

grand•fa•ther \'grand-ˌfä*th*-ər, 'gran-\ *n* **:** the father of one's father or mother; *also* **:** ANCESTOR 1

grandfather clock *n* **:** a tall pendulum clock standing on the floor — called also *grandfather's clock*

grandfather clock

gran•dil•o•quence \gran-'dil-ə-kwəns\ *n* **:** lofty or pompous eloquence **:** BOMBAST [derived from Latin *grandiloquus* "using lofty language", from *grandis* "grand" + *loqui* "to speak"] — **gran•dil•o•quent** \-kwənt\ *adj* — **gran•dil•o•quent•ly** *adv*

gran•di•ose \'gran-dē-ˌōs\ *adj* **1 :** impressive because of uncommon largeness, scope, effect, or grandeur **2 :** characterized by affectation of grandeur or splendor or by absurd exaggeration [French, from Italian *grandioso,* from *grande* "great", from Latin *grandis*] **syn** see GRAND — **gran•di•ose•ly** *adv* — **gran•di•os•i•ty** \ˌgran-dē-'äs-ət-ē\ *n*

grand jury *n* **:** a jury that chiefly examines accusations made against persons and if the evidence warrants makes formal charges on which the accused persons are tried

grand•ma \'grand-ˌmä, 'gran-, -ˌmȯ; 'gram-ˌä, -ˌȯ\ *n* **:** GRANDMOTHER

grand mal \'grand-'mäl, 'gran-\ *n* **:** severe epilepsy [French, literally, "great illness"]

grand march *n* **:** a march at the opening of a ball in which all the guests participate

grand•moth•er \'grand-ˌmə*th*-ər, 'gran-\ *n* **:** the mother of one's father or mother; *also* **:** a female ancestor

grand•neph•ew \-'nef-yü\ *n* **:** a grandson of one's brother or sister

grand•niece \-'nēs\ *n* **:** a granddaughter of one's brother or sister

grand opera *n* **:** opera in which the plot is elaborated as in serious drama and the entire text set to music

grand•pa \'grand-ˌpä, 'gran-, -ˌpȯ; 'gram-ˌpä, -ˌpȯ\ *n* **:** GRANDFATHER

grand•par•ent \'grand-ˌpar-ənt, 'gran-, -ˌper-\ *n* **:** a parent of one's father or mother

grand piano *n* **:** a piano with horizontal frame and strings

grand•sire \'grand-ˌsīr, 'gran-\ *or* **grand•sir** \'gran-sər\ *n* **1** *dialect* **:** GRANDFATHER **2** *archaic* **:** an aged man

grand slam *n* **1 :** the winning of all the tricks of one hand in a card game (as bridge) **2 :** a clean sweep or total success (as in winning all of a number of specified contests) **3 :** a home run made with the bases loaded

\ə\ **abut**	\au̇\ **out**	\i\ **tip**	\ȯ\ **saw**	\u̇\ **foot**
\ər\ **further**	\ch\ **chin**	\ī\ **life**	\ȯi\ **coin**	\y\ **yet**
\a\ **mat**	\e\ **pet**	\j\ **job**	\th\ **thin**	\yü\ **few**
\ā\ **take**	\ē\ **easy**	\ng\ **sing**	*th*\ **this**	\yu̇\ **cure**
\ä\ **cot, cart**	\g\ **go**	\ō\ **bone**	\ü\ **food**	\zh\ **vision**

grand•son \ˈgrand-ˌsən, ˈgran-\ *n* : a son of one's son or daughter

grand•stand \-ˌstand\ *n* : a usually roofed stand for spectators at a racecourse or stadium

grand tour *n* : an extended European tour once a part of the education of aristocratic British youth

grand•un•cle \ˈgran-ˈdəng-kəl\ *n* : an uncle of one's father or mother

grange \ˈgrānj\ *n* **1** : FARM; *esp* : a farmhouse with out-buildings **2** *cap* : one of the lodges of a national fraternal association of farmers; *also* : the association itself [Middle French, "granary", from Medieval Latin *granica*, from Latin *granum* "grain"]

grang•er \ˈgrān-jər\ *n* : a member of a Grange

gran•ite \ˈgran-ət\ *n* : a very hard igneous rock formed essentially of quartz and orthoclase or microcline and used for building and for monuments [Italian *granito*, from *granire* "to granulate", from *grano* "grain", from Latin *granum*] — **gra•nit•ic** \gra-ˈnit-ik\ *adj*

gran•ite•ware \ˈgran-ət-ˌwaər, -ˌweər\ *n* : enameled ironware

gran•ny *or* **gran•nie** \ˈgran-ē\ *n, pl* **grannies** : GRANDMOTHER [by shortening and alteration]

granny knot *n* : an insecure knot often made instead of a square knot

[1]**grant** \ˈgrant\ *vt* **1 a** : to consent to : ALLOW **b** : to permit as a right, privilege, or favor **2** : to give the possession or benefit of formally or legally ⟨*grant* a pardon⟩ **3** : to concede (something not yet proved) to be true [Old French *creanter, graanter*, derived from Latin *credere* "to believe, trust"] — **grant•er** \-ər\ *n* — **grant•or** \ˈgrant-ər, grant-ˈȯr\ *n*

• **syn** GRANT, CONCEDE mean to give as a favor or a right. GRANT implies giving voluntarily something that could be as well withheld or denied ⟨*grant* one's assistant a week's leave⟩ CONCEDE implies yielding with reluctance to a rightful or compelling claim ⟨forced to *concede* that they were right⟩

[2]**grant** *n* **1** : the act of granting ⟨land ceded by *grant*⟩ **2** : something granted; *esp* : a gift (as of money) for a particular purpose ⟨a research *grant*⟩ **3 a** : a transfer of property by deed or writing **b** : the instrument by which such a transfer is made; *also* : the property so transferred

grant•ee \grant-ˈē\ *n* : one to whom a grant is made

gran•tia \ˈgrant-ē-ə\ *n* : a small cylindrical sponge with a skeleton containing calcium [Robert E. *Grant*, died 1874, Scottish anatomist]

grant-in-aid \ˌgrant-n-ˈād\ *n, pl* **grants-in-aid** \ˌgran-sə-ˈnād\ **1** : a grant from public funds paid to a local government in aid of a public undertaking **2** : a grant to a school or individual for an educational or artistic project

gran•u•lar \ˈgran-yə-lər\ *adj* : consisting of or appearing to consist of granules : having a grainy texture — **gran•u•lar•i•ty** \ˌgran-yə-ˈlar-ət-ē\ *n*

gran•u•late \ˈgran-yə-ˌlāt\ *vb* **1** : to form or crystallize into grains or granules **2** : to collect into grains or granules

gran•u•la•tion \ˌgran-yə-ˈlā-shən\ *n* **1** : the act or process of granulating or the condition of being granulated **2** : a product of granulating (as a tiny knot of vascular tissue in a healing wound)

granulation tissue *n* : tissue made up of granulations that temporarily replaces lost tissue in a wound

gran•ule \ˈgran-yül\ *n* : a small grain or particle ⟨*granules* of sugar⟩ [Late Latin *granulum*, from Latin *granum* "grain"]

gra•num \ˈgrā-nəm\ *n, pl* **gra•na** \-nə\ : one of the laminated stacks of chlorophyll-containing material in plant chloroplasts [Latin, "grain, seed"]

grape \ˈgrāp\ *n* **1** : a smooth-skinned juicy greenish white to deep red or purple berry eaten dried or fresh as a fruit or used to make wine **2** : a climbing woody vine whose clustered fruits are grapes **3** : GRAPESHOT [Old French] — **grapy** \ˈgrā-pē\ *adj*

grape•fruit \ˈgrāp-ˌfrüt\ *n* : a large citrus fruit with a bitter yellow rind and a highly flavored somewhat acid juicy pulp; *also* : a tree that bears grapefruit [from its growing in clusters like grapes]

grape hyacinth *n* : any of several small bulbous spring-flowering herbs of the lily family bearing spikes of clustered usually blue flowers

grape•shot \ˈgrāp-ˌshät\ *n* : a cluster of small iron balls used as shot for a cannon

grape sugar *n* : DEXTROSE

grape•vine \ˈgrāp-ˌvīn\ *n* **1** : GRAPE 2 **2 a** : an informal means of circulating information, rumor, or gossip **b** : a secret source of information

[1]**graph** \ˈgraf\ *n* **1** : a diagram that represents change in one variable factor in comparison with that of one or more other factors **2** : a pictorial representation of a set of points (as a line or curve) that satisfy a mathematical equation or belong to a given set [short for *graphic formula*]

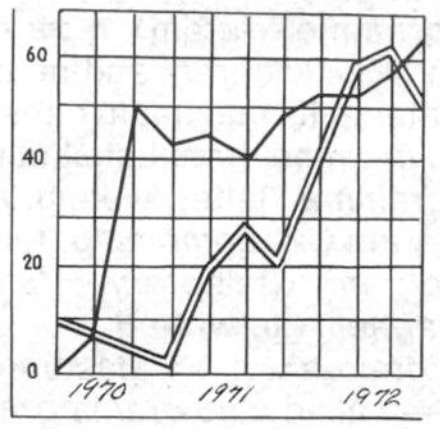

[1]graph 1

[2]**graph** *vt* **1** : to represent by a graph **2** : to plot on a graph

-graph \ˌgraf\ *n combining form* **1** : something written ⟨mono*graph*⟩ **2** : instrument for making or transmitting records ⟨chrono*graph*⟩ [Greek *graphein* "to write"]

-g•ra•pher \g-rə-fər\ *n combining form* : one that writes about (specified) material or in a (specified) way ⟨bio*grapher*⟩

[1]**graph•ic** \ˈgraf-ik\ *or* **graph•i•cal** \-i-kəl\ *adj* **1** : being written, drawn, or engraved **2 a** : described or related with vivid clarity or striking imaginative power **b** : sharply outlined or detailed **3** : of or relating to the graphic arts **4** : of, relating to, or represented by a graph **5** : of or relating to writing [Latin *graphicus*, from Greek *graphikos*, from *graphein* "to write"] — **graph•i•cal•ly** \-i-kə-lē, -klē\ *adv* — **graph•ic•ness** *n*

• **syn** GRAPHIC, VIVID, PICTURESQUE mean giving a clear visual impression through words. GRAPHIC stresses the evoking of a lifelike picture especially of an action; VIVID suggests conveying a strong or lasting impression of reality; PICTURESQUE implies the presenting of a striking or effective picture often without regard to reality ⟨a *picturesque* account of their adventures⟩

[2]**graphic** *n* **1 a** : a product of graphic art **b** *pl* : the graphic media **2** : a picture, map, or graph used for illustration or demonstration

graphic arts *n pl* : the fine and applied arts of representation, decoration, and writing or printing on flat surfaces together with the techniques and crafts associated with each

graph•ite \ˈgraf-ˌīt\ *n* : a soft black carbon with a metallic luster that conducts electricity and is used in making lead pencils, as a dry lubricant, and for electrodes [German *graphit*, from Greek *graphein* "to write"] — **gra•phit•ic** \gra-ˈfit-ik\ *adj*

graph•i•tize \ˈgraf-ə-ˌtīz\ *vt* **1** : to convert into graphite **2** : to impregnate or coat with graphite — **graph•it•iza•tion** \ˌgraf-ˌīt-ə-ˈzā-shən\ *n*

gra•phol•o•gy \gra-ˈfäl-ə-jē\ *n* : the study of handwriting especially for the purpose of character analysis — **gra•phol•o•gist** \-jəst\ *n*

graph paper *n* : paper ruled (as into small squares) for drawing graphs or making diagrams

-g•ra•phy \g-rə-fē\ *n combining form, pl* **-graphies** **1** : writing or representation in a (specified) manner or by a (specified) means or of a (specified) object ⟨phono*graphy*⟩ ⟨photo*graphy*⟩ ⟨steno*graphy*⟩ **2** : writing on a (specified) subject or in a (specified) field ⟨lexico*graphy*⟩

grap•nel \ˈgrap-nᵊl\ *n* : a small anchor with four or five claws or curved flukes used in dragging or grappling operations and for anchoring a small boat [Middle English *grapenel*, derived from Middle French *grape* "hook"]

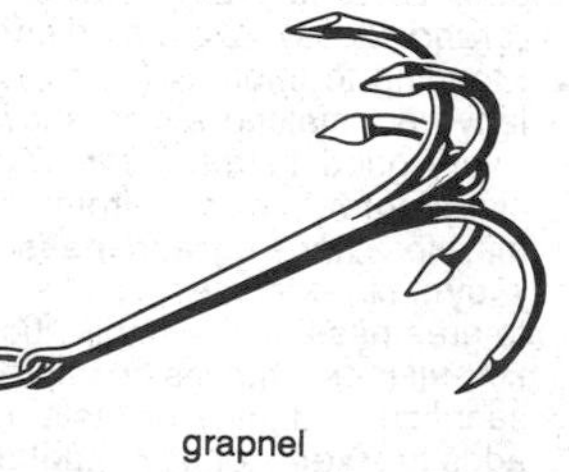

grapnel

[1]**grap•ple** \ˈgrap-əl\ *n* **1** : an implement used or designed for grappling; *esp* : GRAPNEL **2** : the act of grappling or seizing : GRIP, HOLD [Middle French *grappelle* "small hook", from *grape* "hook"]

[2]**grapple** *vb* **grap•pled**; **grap•pling** \ˈgrap-ling, -ə-ling\ **1** : to seize or hold with or as if with a hooked implement **2** : to seize one another : struggle in or as if in a close fight **3** : to attempt to deal : COPE ⟨*grapple* with a problem⟩ — **grap•pler** \ˈgrap-lər, -ə-lər\

grappling iron *n* : a hooked iron for anchoring a boat, grappling ships to each other, or recovering sunken objects

grap•to•lite \'grap-tə-ˌlīt\ *n* : any of numerous Paleozoic fossil colonial animals having individual animals in cups arranged along a support of chitin [Greek *graptos* "painted", from *graphein* "to write, paint"]

1grasp \'grasp\ *vb* **1** : to make the effort of seizing with or as if with the hand : CLUTCH ⟨*grasping* at straws⟩ **2** : to clasp or embrace with or as if with the fingers or arms ⟨*grasp* a bat⟩ **3** : UNDERSTAND 1, COMPREHEND ⟨*grasp* a new idea⟩ [Middle English *graspen*] **syn** see TAKE — **grasp•able** \'gras-pə-bəl\ *adj* — **grasp•er** *n*

2grasp *n* **1 a** : HANDLE 1 **b** : EMBRACE **2** : HOLD, CONTROL ⟨in the tyrant's *grasp*⟩ **3** : the power of seizing and holding ⟨success almost within our *grasp*⟩ **4** : UNDERSTANDING 2, COMPREHENSION

grasp•ing *adj* : ruthlessly avaricious **syn** see COVETOUS — **grasp•ing•ly** \'gras-ping-lē\ *adv* — **grasp•ing•ness** *n*

1grass \'gras\ *n* **1** : herbage suitable or used for grazing animals **2** : any of a large family of mostly herbaceous plants with jointed stems, slender sheathing leaves, and fruits consisting of seedlike grains **3** : grass-covered land **4** : MARIJUANA [Old English *græs*] — **grass•like** \-ˌlīk\ *adj*

2grass *vt* : to seed with grass

grass•hop•per \'gras-ˌhäp-ər\ *n* : any of numerous plant-eating insects (order Orthoptera) having the hind legs adapted for leaping

grass•land \-ˌland\ *n* : land covered naturally or under cultivation with grasses and other low-growing herbs

grass roots *n pl* : society at the local and popular level especially in rural areas as distinguished from the centers of political leadership ⟨*grass roots* support⟩

grass widow *n* **1** : a woman divorced or separated from her husband **2** : a woman whose husband is temporarily away

grass widower *n* **1** : a man divorced or separated from his wife **2** : a man whose wife is temporarily away

grassy \'gras-ē\ *adj* **grass•i•er**; **-est 1** : containing or covered or abounding with grass **2** : resembling a grass ⟨a *grassy* odor⟩ ⟨*grassy*-leaved⟩

1grate \'grāt\ *n* **1** : a frame containing parallel or crossed bars (as in a prison window) **2** : a frame or basket of iron bars for holding burning fuel (as in a furnace or a fireplace) [Medieval Latin *crata, grata* "hurdle", from Latin *cratis*]

2grate *vt* : to furnish with a grate

3grate *vb* **1** : to make into small particles by rubbing against something rough ⟨*grate* cheese⟩ **2** : to grind or rub against something with a rasping noise ⟨a door that *grates* on its hinges⟩ **3** : to have a harsh or rasping effect ⟨a noise that *grates* on one's nerves⟩ [Middle French *grater* "to scratch", of Germanic origin] — **grat•er** *n*

grate•ful \'grāt-fəl\ *adj* **1 a** : appreciative of benefits received **b** : expressing gratitude **2** : affording pleasure or contentment; *esp* : pleasing by reason of comfort supplied or discomfort alleviated ⟨*grateful* warmth of a fire on a frosty day⟩ [obsolete *grate* "pleasing, thankful", from Latin *gratus*] — **grate•ful•ly** \-fə-lē\ *adv* — **grate•ful•ness** *n*

• **syn** GRATEFUL, THANKFUL mean feeling or expressing gratitude. GRATEFUL applies to an appropriate sense of having received favors from other persons ⟨I was very *grateful* for your help⟩ THANKFUL suggests a more generalized acknowledgement of what is vaguely felt to be providential ⟨*thankful* for a good harvest⟩

grat•i•fi•ca•tion \ˌgrat-ə-fə-'kā-shən\ *n* **1** : the act of gratifying : the state of being gratified **2** : a source of satisfaction or pleasure

grat•i•fy \'grat-ə-ˌfī\ *vt* **-fied**; **-fy•ing 1** : to give or be a source of pleasure or satisfaction to **2** : to give in to : INDULGE ⟨*gratify* a whim⟩ [Middle French *gratifier,* from Latin *gratificari,* literally, "to make oneself pleasing", from *gratus* "pleasing" + *-ificari,* passive of *-ificare* "-ify"]

grat•ing \'grāt-ing\ *n* **1** : a partition, covering, or frame of parallel bars or crossbars : GRATE **2** : a system of close parallel lines on a polished surface used to produce spectra by diffraction

gra•tis \'grat-əs, 'grāt-\ *adv or adj* : without charge or recompense : FREE [Latin *gratiis, gratis,* from *gratia* "favor"]

grat•i•tude \'grat-ə-ˌtüd, -ˌtyüd\ *n* : the state of being grateful : THANKFULNESS [Medieval Latin *gratitudo,* from Latin *gratus* "grateful"]

gra•tu•i•tous \grə-'tü-ət-əs, -'tyü-\ *adj* **1** : done or provided without return or expectation of return or payment; *also* : acting without compensation **2** : not called for by the circumstances : UNWARRANTED ⟨a *gratuitous* insult⟩ [Latin *gratuitus,* from *gratus* "pleasing, grateful"] — **gra•tu•i•tous•ly** *adv* — **gra•tu•i•tous•ness** *n*

gra•tu•i•ty \grə-'tü-ət-ē, -'tyü-\ *n, pl* **-ties** : something given freely; *also* : something given in return for a favor or service : TIP

gra•va•men \grə-'vām-ən\ *n, pl* **-vamens** *or* **-va•mi•na** \-'vam-ə-nə\ : the significant part (as of a grievance or complaint) : BASIS [Late Latin, "burden", from Latin *gravare* "to burden", from *gravis* "heavy"]

1grave \'grāv\ *vt* **graved**; **grav•en** \'grā-vən\ *or* **graved**; **grav•ing 1 a** : to carve or shape with a chisel : SCULPTURE **b** : to carve or cut (as letters or figures) into a hard surface : ENGRAVE **2** : to impress or fix (as a thought) deeply [Old English *grafan* "to dig, engrave"]

2grave *n* **1 a** : an excavation for burial of a body **b** : TOMB 2 **2** : DEATH 1 — used with *the* [Old English *græf*]

3grave \'grāv, *in sense 4 also* 'gräv\ *adj* **1 a** : meriting serious consideration : IMPORTANT ⟨a *grave* issue⟩ **b** : threatening great harm or danger : MORTAL ⟨*grave* risks⟩ **2** : dignified in appearance or demeanor : SERIOUS **3** : drab in color : SOMBER **4** : of, marked by, or being an accent mark having the form ` [Middle French, from Latin *gravis* "heavy, grave"] **syn** see SERIOUS — **grave•ly** *adv* — **grave•ness** *n*

4gra•ve \'gräv-ā\ *adv or adj* : in a slow and solemn manner — used as a direction in music [Italian, from Latin *gravis* "grave"]

grave•clothes \'grāv-ˌklōz, -ˌklōthz\ *n pl* : the clothes in which a dead person is buried

1grav•el \'grav-əl\ *n* **1** : loose rounded fragments of rock coarser than sand **2** : a deposit of small hard masses in the kidneys and urinary bladder [Middle French *gravele,* from *grave, greve* "pebbly ground"]

2gravel *adj* : GRAVELLY 2

3gravel *vt* **grav•eled** *or* **grav•elled**; **grav•el•ing** *or* **grav•el•ling** \'grav-ling, -ə-ling\ : to cover or spread with gravel

grave•less \'grāv-ləs\ *adj* **1** : not buried ⟨*graveless* bones⟩ **2** : not requiring graves : DEATHLESS ⟨the *graveless* home of the blessed⟩

grav•el•ly \'grav-lē, -ə-lē\ *adj* **1** : of, containing, or covered with gravel **2** : having a harsh grating sound ⟨a *gravelly* voice⟩

grav•er \'grā-vər\ *n* **1** : SCULPTOR, ENGRAVER **2** : any of various cutting or shaving tools

grave•stone \'grāv-ˌstōn\ *n* : a stone marking a grave

grave•yard \-ˌyärd\ *n* : CEMETERY

grav•id \'grav-əd\ *adj* : PREGNANT 1a [Latin *gravidus,* from *gravis* "heavy"]

gra•vi•me•ter \grə-'vim-ət-ər, 'grav-ə-ˌmēt-\ *n* **1** : a device similar to a hydrometer for determining specific gravity **2** : an instrument for measuring differences in the force of gravity at different places — **gravi•met•ric** \ˌgrav-ə-'me-trik\ *adj*

grav•i•tate \'grav-ə-ˌtāt\ *vi* **1** : to move or tend to move under the influence of gravitation **2** : to be attracted to or toward something

grav•i•ta•tion \ˌgrav-ə-'tā-shən\ *n* **1** : a force of attraction between two material particles or bodies that is proportional to the product of their masses and inversely proportional to the square of the distance between them **2** : the action or process of gravitating — **grav•i•ta•tion•al** \-shnəl, -shən-l\ *adj* — **grav•i•ta•tion•al•ly** \-ē\ *adv* — **grav•i•ta•tive** \'grav-ə-ˌtāt-iv\ *adj*

grav•i•ty \'grav-ət-ē\ *n, pl* **-ties 1 a** : dignity or sobriety of bearing **b** : IMPORTANCE 1; *esp* : SERIOUSNESS ⟨the *gravity* of the crime⟩ **2** : WEIGHT — used chiefly in the phrase *center of gravity* **3 a** : the gravitational attraction of the earth's mass for bodies at or near its surface **b** : GRAVITATION 1 **c** : ACCELERATION OF GRAVITY [Latin *gravitas,* from *gravis* "heavy, grave"] — **gravity** *adj*

gra•vure \grə-'vyu̇r, grā-\ *n* : PHOTOGRAVURE [French, from

\ə\ **abut**	\au̇\ **out**	\i\ **tip**	\ȯ\ **saw**	\u̇\ **foot**
\ər\ **further**	\ch\ **chin**	\ī\ **life**	\ȯi\ **coin**	\y\ **yet**
\a\ **mat**	\e\ **pet**	\j\ **job**	\th\ **thin**	\yü\ **few**
\ā\ **take**	\ē\ **easy**	\ng\ **sing**	\th\ **this**	\yu̇\ **cure**
\ä\ **cot, cart**	\g\ **go**	\ō\ **bone**	\ü\ **food**	\zh\ **vision**

graver "to grave", of Germanic origin]
gra•vy \'grā-vē\ *n, pl* **gravies 1 :** a sauce made from the thickened and seasoned juices of cooked meat **2 :** something over and above what is ordinarily earned or expected [Middle French *gravé*]
1gray *or* **grey** \'grā\ *adj* **1 :** of the color gray; *also* **:** dull in color **2 :** having gray hair **3 :** dull or cheerless in mood or outlook **:** DISMAL ⟨a *gray* day⟩ [Old English *grǣg*] — **gray•ish** \'grā-ish\ *adj* — **gray•ness** *n*
2gray *n* **1 :** something of a gray color **2 :** one of the series of shades formed by a blending of black and white
3gray *vb* **:** to make or become gray
gray•beard \'grā-ˌbiərd\ *n* **:** an old man
gray•ling \'grā-ling\ *n, pl* **grayling** *also* **graylings :** any of several freshwater fishes related to the trouts and valued for food and sport
gray matter *n* **1 :** neural tissue especially of the brain and spinal cord that contains nerve-cell bodies as well as nerve fibers and has a brownish gray color **2 :** BRAINS, INTELLECT ⟨use one's *gray matter*⟩
gray squirrel *n* **:** a common light gray to black squirrel native to eastern North America and introduced into England
gray trout *n* **:** a common weakfish of the Atlantic coast of the United States
1graze \'grāz\ *vb* **1 :** to feed on growing herbage or the herbage of **2 :** to put cattle to feed on the herbage of ⟨we will *graze* the upper field next week⟩ **3 :** to put to graze [Old English *grasian*, from *græs* "grass"]
• syn GRAZE, BROWSE mean to feed on growing vegetation. GRAZE applies especially to animals wandering freely on open grassland; BROWSE implies specifically feeding on leaves and shoots of trees or shrubs.
2graze *n* **1 :** an act of grazing **2 :** herbage for grazing
3graze *vt* **1 :** to rub or touch lightly in passing **:** touch against and glance off ⟨*graze* the curb with the wheel of a car⟩ **2 :** to scratch or scrape by rubbing against something [perhaps from *1graze*]
4graze *n* **:** a scraping along a surface or an abrasion made by it; *esp* **:** a superficial skin injury
1grease \'grēs\ *n* **1 :** rendered animal fat **2 :** oily matter **3 :** a thick lubricant [Old French *craisse, graisse*, from Latin *crassus*, adj., "fat"]
2grease \'grēs, 'grēz\ *vt* **1 :** to smear or daub with grease **2 :** to lubricate with grease — **greas•er** *n*
grease•paint \'grēs-ˌpānt\ *n* **:** theater makeup
grease•wood \-ˌwu̇d\ *n* **:** a low stiff shrub of the goosefoot family common in alkaline soils in the western United States
greasy \'grē-sē, -zē\ *adj* **greas•i•er; -est 1 :** smeared with grease **2 :** containing grease ⟨*greasy* food⟩ **3 :** resembling grease or oil **:** SMOOTH, SLIPPERY — **greas•i•ly** \-sə-lē, -zə-\ *adv* — **greas•i•ness** \-sē-nəs, -zē-\ *n*
great \'grāt, *in South also* 'greət, 'gret\ *adj* **1 :** very large in size or extent ⟨a *great* expanse of land⟩ **2 :** large in number ⟨4 is *greater* than 2⟩ **3 :** being much beyond the average or ordinary ⟨in *great* pain⟩ ⟨once in a *great* while⟩ **4 :** EMINENT, DISTINGUISHED ⟨a *great* artist⟩ **5 :** remarkable for knowledge of or skill in something ⟨*great* at arithmetic⟩ **6 :** much favored or much used ⟨a *great* joke of my friend's⟩ **7 :** EXCELLENT, FINE ⟨a *great* time at the beach⟩ **8 :** more distant in relationship by one generation ⟨*great*-grandchildren⟩ [Old English *grēat*] **syn** see LARGE — **great•ly** *adv* — **great•ness** *n*
great ape *n* **:** any of the recent anthropoid apes
great auk *n* **:** an extinct large flightless auk formerly abundant along North Atlantic coasts
great–aunt *n* **:** GRANDAUNT
Great Bear *n* **:** URSA MAJOR
great blue heron *n* **:** a large grayish blue American heron with a crested head
great circle *n* **:** a circle formed on the surface of a sphere by the intersection of a plane that passes through the center of the sphere; *esp* **:** such a circle on the surface of the earth an arc of which constitutes the shortest distance between any two points on the earth's surface — compare SMALL CIRCLE
great•coat \'grāt-ˌkōt\ *n* **:** a heavy overcoat
Great Dane *n* **:** any of a breed of tall massive powerful smooth-coated dogs
great divide *n* **1 :** a watershed between major drainage systems **2 :** a significant point of division; *esp* **:** DEATH ⟨crossed the *great divide* bravely⟩
greatest common divisor *n* **:** the largest integer that is an exact divisor of each of two or more integers — called also *greatest common factor*

Great Dane

great•heart•ed \'grāt-'härt-əd\ *adj* **1 :** COURAGEOUS **2 :** MAGNANIMOUS 2 — **great•heart•ed•ly** *adv* — **great•heart•ed•ness** *n*
great–nephew *n* **:** GRANDNEPHEW
great–niece *n* **:** GRANDNIECE
great power *n* **:** one of the nations that figure most decisively in international affairs
Great Russian *n* **:** a member of the Russian-speaking people of central and northeastern Russian Soviet Federated Socialist Republic
great–uncle *n* **:** GRANDUNCLE
great white shark *n* **:** a large man-eating shark that is bluish gray when young but becomes whitish when older and is widespread in warm and tropical seas
greave \'grēv\ *n* **:** armor for the leg below the knee [Middle French *greve*]
grebe \'grēb\ *n* **:** any of a family of swimming and diving birds closely related to the loons [French *grèbe*]
Gre•cian \'grē-shən\ *adj* **:** GREEK 1 [Latin *Graecia* "Greece"] — **Grecian** *n*
Greco- *or* **Graeco-** \'grek-ō, 'grē-kō\ *combining form* **1 :** Greece **:** Greeks **2 :** Greek and [Latin *Graecus*]
greed \'grēd\ *n* **:** excessive or blameworthy acquisitiveness **:** AVARICE [back-formation from *greedy*]
greedy \'grēd-ē\ *adj* **greed•i•er; -est 1 :** having a driving appetite for food or drink **:** very hungry ⟨a lion *greedy* for its prey⟩ **2 :** having an eager and often selfish desire or longing ⟨*greedy* for praise⟩ **3 :** wanting more than one needs or more than one's fair share (as of food or wealth) [Old English *grǣdig*] **syn** see COVETOUS — **greed•i•ly** \'grēd-l-ē\ *adv* — **greed•i•ness** \'grēd-ē-nəs\ *n*
1Greek \'grēk\ *n* **1 a :** a native or inhabitant of ancient or modern Greece **b :** a person of Greek descent **2 a :** the Indo-European language used by the Greeks from prehistoric times to the present **b :** ancient Greek as used from the time of the earliest records to the end of the 2d century A.D. [Old English *Grēca*, from Latin *Graecus*, from Greek *Graikos*]
2Greek *adj* **1 :** of, relating to, or characteristic of Greece, the Greeks, or Greek ⟨*Greek* architecture⟩ **2 a :** Eastern Orthodox **b :** of or relating to the Orthodox church of Greece **3 :** of or relating to the Eastern rite of the Roman Catholic Church
Greek cross *n* **:** an upright cross with all arms of equal length
Greek fire *n* **:** a composition of uncertain ingredients that burns even in water [from the Byzantine Greeks who used it in warfare]
Greek Orthodox *adj* **:** Eastern Orthodox; *esp* **:** GREEK 2b
1green \'grēn\ *adj* **1 :** of the color green **2 a :** covered by green foliage or herbage ⟨*green* hills⟩ **b :** consisting of green plants or of the leafy part of a plant ⟨a *green* salad⟩ **3 :** YOUTHFUL, VIGOROUS ⟨remained young and *green* at heart⟩ **4 :** not fully grown or ripe ⟨*green* apples⟩ **5 :** appearing sickly or pale ⟨scared *green*⟩ **6 :** not fully processed, treated, or seasoned ⟨*green* lumber⟩ **7 a :** lacking training, knowledge, or experience ⟨*green* troops⟩ **b :** GULLIBLE, NAIVE ⟨too *green* to suspect a trick⟩ [Old English *grēne*] — **green•ish** \'grē-nish\ *adj* — **green•ly** *adv* — **green•ness** \'grēn-nəs\ *n*
2green *vb* **:** to make or become green
3green *n* **1 :** a color whose hue is somewhat less yellow than that of growing fresh grass or of the emerald or is that of the part of the spectrum lying between blue and yellow **2 :** something of a green color **3 a :** green vegetation **b** *pl* **:** leafy parts of plants used for some purpose (as ornament or food) **4 :** a grassy plain or plot; *esp* **:** PUTTING GREEN — **greeny** \'grē-nē\ *adj*
green alga *n* **:** an alga (especially group Chlorophyta) in which the chlorophyll is not masked by other pigments
green•back \'grēn-ˌbak\ *n* **:** a piece of paper currency issued by the United States government; *esp* **:** one without gold or silver backing issued during the Civil War
Green•back•er \-ər\ *n* **:** a member of a post-Civil War American

political party opposing reduction in the amount of greenbacks in circulation

green bean *n* : a kidney bean that is used as a snap bean while the pods are green

green•belt \ˈgrēn-ˌbelt\ *n* : a belt of parkways, parks, or farmlands that encircles a community

green•bri•er \ˈgrēn-ˌbrī-ər, -ˌbrīr\ *n* : a prickly vine of the lily family of the eastern United States with thick leaves and clusters of small greenish flowers

green•ery \ˈgrēn-rē, -ə-rē\ *n, pl* **-er•ies** : green foliage or plants : VERDURE

green gland *n* : a greenish excretory organ in the head of some crustaceans (as a lobster)

green•gro•cer \ˈgrēn-ˌgrō-sər\ *n, chiefly British* : a retailer of fresh vegetables and fruit — **green•gro•cery** \-ˌgrōs-rē, -ə-rē\ *n*

green•horn \ˈgrēn-ˌhȯrn\ *n* : an inexperienced person; *esp* : one easily tricked or cheated [obsolete *greenhorn* "animal with young horns"]

green•house \-ˌhau̇s\ *n* : a glassed enclosure used for the cultivation or protection of plants

greenhouse effect *n* : warming of the lower atmosphere as a result of absorption by carbon dioxide and water vapor of radiation received from the sun and reemitted by the earth

green light *n* : authority or permission to undertake a project [from the green traffic light which signals permission to proceed]

green•ling \ˈgrēn-ling\ *n* : any of several spiny-finned food fishes of the rocky coasts of the northern Pacific

green manure *n* : an herbaceous crop (as clover) plowed under while green to enrich the soil

green mold *n* : a green or green-spored mold (as a penicillium)

green onion *n* : a young onion pulled before the bulb has enlarged especially for use in salad

green pepper *n* : SWEET PEPPER

green revolution *n* : the great increase in the production of food grains resulting from improved plant varieties and farming methods

green•room \ˈgrēn-ˌrüm, -ˌru̇m\ *n* : a room in a theater or concert hall where actors or musicians relax before, between, or after appearances

green snake *n* : either of two bright green harmless largely insect-eating North American snakes

green soap *n* : a soft soap made from vegetable oils and used especially to treat skin diseases

green•stick fracture \ˈgrēn-ˈstik-\ *n* : a bone fracture in the young in which the bone is partly broken and partly bent

green•sward \ˈgrēn-ˌswȯrd\ *n* : turf green with growing grass

green thumb *n* : an unusual ability to make plants grow — **green–thumbed** \ˈgrēn-ˈthəmd\ *adj*

green turtle *n* : a large edible sea turtle with a smooth greenish shell

Green•wich time \ˈgrin-ij-, ˈgren-, -ich-\ *n* : the time of the meridian of Greenwich used as the basis of standard time throughout the world [*Greenwich,* England]

green•wood \ˈgrēn-ˌwu̇d\ *n* : a forest green with foliage

greet \ˈgrēt\ *vt* **1** : to address with expressions of kind wishes : HAIL **2** : to meet or react to in a specified manner ⟨*greeted* the team with cheers⟩ **3** : to be perceived by ⟨offensive odors *greeted* the nose⟩ [Old English *grētan*] — **greet•er** *n*

greet•ing *n* **1** : a salutation at meeting **2** : an expression of good wishes : REGARDS — usually used in pl.

gre•gar•i•ous \gri-ˈgar-ē-əs, -ˈger-\ *adj* **1** : tending to associate with others of one's kind : SOCIAL **2** : habitually living or moving with others of one's own kind : tending to flock together ⟨*gregarious* insects⟩ [Latin *gregarius* "of a flock or herd", from *greg-, grex* "flock, herd"] — **gre•gar•i•ous•ly** *adv* — **gre•gar•i•ous•ness** *n*

Gre•go•ri•an calendar \gri-ˌgōr-ē-ən-, -ˌgȯr-\ *n* : a calendar in general use introduced in 1582 by Pope Gregory XIII as a revision of the Julian calendar that was marked by the initial dropping of 10 days as well as the 366th day in any century year not divisible by 400 (as 1700, 1800, and 1900) and that was adopted by Great Britain and the American colonies in 1752

Gregorian chant *n* : a rhythmically free unaccompanied melody sung in unison in services of the Roman Catholic Church

grem•lin \ˈgrem-lən\ *n* : a small sprite held to be responsible for malfunction of equipment especially in an airplane [probably from *grem-* (of unknown origin) + *-lin* (as in *goblin*)]

gre•nade \grə-ˈnād\ *n* **1** : a small bomb filled with a destructive agent (as gas, high explosive, or incendiary chemicals) and made to be hurled **2** : a device containing a gaseous or volatile substance (as tear gas) that when hurled releases its contents on impact [Middle French, "pomegranate", from Late Latin *granata,* from Latin *granum* "grain"]

gren•a•dier \ˌgren-ə-ˈdiər\ *n* : a member of a European regiment formerly armed with grenades

gren•a•dine \ˌgren-ə-ˈdēn, ˈgren-ə-ˌ\ *n* : a syrup flavored with pomegranates and used in mixed drinks [French, from *grenade* "pomegranate"]

Gret•na Green \ˌgret-nə-ˈgrēn\ *n* : a place where many eloping couples are married [*Gretna Green,* village in Scotland near the English border]

grew *past of* GROW

grey *variant of* GRAY

grey friar *n, often cap G & F* : a Franciscan friar

grey•hound \ˈgrā-ˌhau̇nd\ *n* : a tall slender graceful smooth-coated dog noted for swiftness and keen sight and used for pursuing game and for racing [Old English *grīghund*]

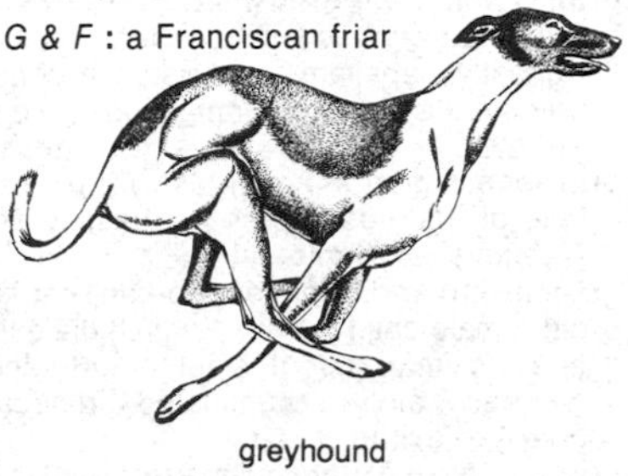
greyhound

grey•lag \-ˌlag\ *n* : the common gray wild goose of Europe [probably from *gray* + *lag* "last", from *lag* "to fall behind"]

grid \ˈgrid\ *n* **1** : GRATING 1 **2** : a perforated or ridged metal plate used as a conductor in a storage battery **3** : an electrode consisting of a mesh or a spiral of fine wire placed between two other elements of an electron tube so as to control the amount of current that flows between them **4 a** : a network of horizontal and perpendicular lines for locating points by means of coordinates ⟨a *grid* of longitude and latitude lines on a map⟩ **b** : GRIDIRON 2 [back-formation from *gridiron*]

grid•dle \ˈgrid-l\ *n* : a flat surface or pan on which food is cooked by dry heat [Old North French *gredil* "gridiron", from Latin *craticulum,* from *cratis* "wickerwork, hurdle"]

griddle cake *n* : PANCAKE

grid•iron \ˈgrid-ˌī-ərn, -ˌīrn\ *n* **1** : a grate for broiling food **2** : something consisting of or covered with a network; *esp* : a football field [Middle English *gredire*]

grief \ˈgrēf\ *n* **1** : deep sorrow : SADNESS, DISTRESS **2** : a cause of sorrow **3** : MISHAP, DISASTER ⟨the boat came to *grief* on the rocks⟩ [Old French, "heavy, grave", from Latin *gravis*] **syn** see SORROW

griev•ance \ˈgrē-vəns\ *n* **1** : a cause of distress (as an unsatisfactory working condition) affording reason for complaint or resistance **2** : the formal expression of a grievance : COMPLAINT

grieve \ˈgrēv\ *vb* **1** : to cause grief or sorrow to : cause to suffer : DISTRESS **2** : to feel grief : SORROW [Old French *grever,* from Latin *gravare* "to burden", from *gravis* "heavy, grave"] — **griev•er** *n*

griev•ous \ˈgrē-vəs\ *adj* **1** : causing suffering or sorrow : DISTRESSING ⟨*grievous* poverty⟩ ⟨*grievous* news⟩ **2** : SERIOUS, GRAVE ⟨a *grievous* fault⟩ — **griev•ous•ly** *adv* — **griev•ous•ness** *n*

grif•fin *or* **grif•fon** *also* **gryph•on** \ˈgrif-ən\ *n* : a fabulous animal typically half eagle and half lion [Middle French *grifon,* from Latin *gryphus,* from Greek *gryps,* from *grypos* "curved"]

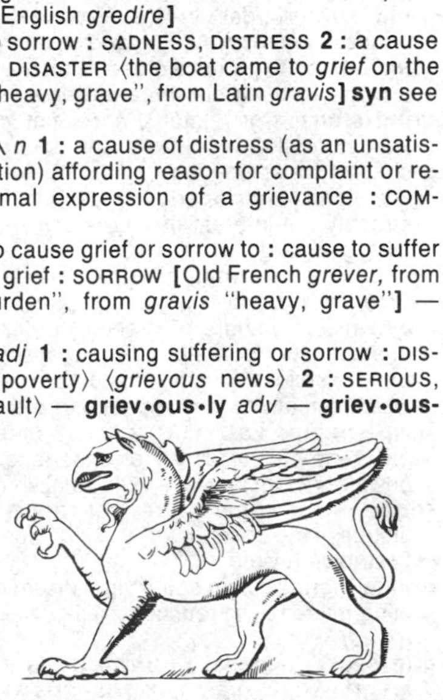
griffin

\ə\ **abut**	\au̇\ **out**	\i\ **tip**	\ȯ\ **saw**	\u̇\ **foot**
\ər\ **further**	\ch\ **chin**	\ī\ **life**	\ȯi\ **coin**	\y\ **yet**
\a\ **mat**	\e\ **pet**	\j\ **job**	\th\ **thin**	\yü\ **few**
\ā\ **take**	\ē\ **easy**	\ng\ **sing**	\th\ **this**	\yu̇\ **cure**
\ä\ **cot, cart**	\g\ **go**	\ō\ **bone**	\ü\ **food**	\zh\ **vision**

[1]**grill** \'gril\ *vt* **1** : to broil on a grill **2** : to question intensely ⟨police *grilled* the suspect⟩

[2]**grill** *n* **1** : a cooking utensil of parallel bars on which food is exposed to radiant heat (as from charcoal) **2** : food that is broiled usually on a grill **3** : a usually informal restaurant [French *gril*, from Latin *craticulum*, from *cratis* "wickerwork, hurdle"]

grille *or* **grill** \'gril\ *n* **1** : a grating forming a barrier or screen **2** : an opening covered with a grille [French *grille*, from Latin *craticula* "fine wickerwork, gridiron", from *cratis* "wickerwork, hurdle"]

grill•work \'gril-,wərk\ *n* : work constituting or resembling a grille

grilse \'grils\ *n, pl* **grilse** : a young mature Atlantic salmon returning from the sea to spawn for the first time [Middle English *grills*]

grim \'grim\ *adj* **grim•mer**; **grim•mest** **1** : SAVAGE, FIERCE ⟨a *grim* battle⟩ **2 a** : harsh and forbidding in appearance **b** : ghastly, repellent, or sinister in character **3** : UNFLINCHING, UNYIELDING ⟨*grim* determination⟩ [Old English *grimm*] **syn** see GHASTLY — **grim•ly** *adv* — **grim•ness** *n*

grim•ace \'grim-əs, grim-'ās\ *n* : a twisting or distortion of the face or features expressive usually of disgust or disapproval [French] — **grimace** *vi*

gri•mal•kin \grim-'ȯl-kən, -'ȯ-kən, -'al-kən\ *n* : CAT 1a; *esp* : an old female cat [*gray* + English dialect *malkin* "cat"]

grime \'grīm\ *n* : soot, smut, or dirt adhering to or embedded in a surface; *also* : accumulated dirtiness and disorder [Flemish *grijm*] — **grime** *vt*

grimy \'grī-mē\ *adj* **grim•i•er**; **-est** : full of or covered with grime : DIRTY — **grim•i•ness** *n*

grin \'grin\ *vi* **grinned**; **grin•ning** : to draw back the lips so as to show the teeth especially in amusement or laughter [Old English *grennian*] — **grin** *n*

[1]**grind** \'grīnd\ *vb* **ground** \'grau̇nd\; **grind•ing** **1** : to reduce to powder or small fragments by crushing (as in a mill or with the teeth) **2** : to wear down, polish, or sharpen by friction **3** : to press with a grating noise : GRIT ⟨*grind* the teeth⟩ **4** : OPPRESS, HARASS ⟨*grinding* down the peasantry⟩ **5** : to operate or produce by or as if by turning a crank **6** : to move with difficulty or friction especially so as to make a grating noise ⟨gears *grinding* in an automobile⟩ [Old English *grindan*]

[2]**grind** *n* **1** : an act of grinding **2 a** : monotonous labor or routine; *esp* : intensive study **b** : a student who studies excessively **3** : the result of grinding; *esp* : the size of particle obtained by grinding

grind•er \'grīn-dər\ *n* **1 a** : MOLAR **b** *pl* : TEETH **2** : one that grinds **3** *chiefly New England* : [2]SUBMARINE 2

grind out *vt* : to produce steadily but mechanically as if by turning a crank ⟨*ground out* three novels a year for 20 years⟩

grind•stone \'grīn-,stōn\ *n* : a flat circular stone of natural sandstone that revolves on an axle and is used for grinding, shaping, or smoothing

[1]**grip** \'grip\ *vt* **gripped**; **grip•ping** **1** : to seize firmly **2** : to hold strongly the interest of ⟨the story *grips* the reader⟩ [Old English *grippan*]

[2]**grip** *n* **1 a** : a strong or tight grasp **b** : strength in gripping **c** : manner or style of gripping; *esp* : a way of clasping the hand by which members of a secret order recognize or greet one another **2 a** : CONTROL 1, 2, MASTERY **b** : mental grasp : UNDERSTANDING **3** : a part or device for gripping **4** : a part by which something is grasped; *esp* : HANDLE **5** : SUITCASE

[1]**gripe** \'grīp\ *vb* **1** : CLUTCH 1, **2** : IRRITATE, VEX ⟨these rules *gripe* me⟩ **3** : to cause or experience spasms of pain in the bowels **4** : COMPLAIN 1 [Old English *grīpan*] — **grip•er** *n*

[2]**gripe** *n* **1 a** : GRIP 1a **b** : CONTROL 1, MASTERY **2 a** : painful distress **b** : COMPLAINT 1 **3** : a spasm of intestinal pain **4** : HANDLE 1, GRIP

grippe \'grip\ *n* : an acute virus disease identical with or resembling influenza [French, literally, "seizure"] — **grippy** \'grip-ē\ *adj*

grip•sack \'grip-,sak\ *n* : TRAVELING BAG

gris–gris \'grē-,grē\ *n, pl* **gris–gris** \-,grēz\ : an amulet or incantation used chiefly by people of African ancestry [French, of African origin]

gris•ly \'griz-lē\ *adj* **gris•li•er**; **-est** : GHASTLY 1, GRUESOME [Old English *grislic*] — **gris•li•ness** *n*

grist \'grist\ *n* : grain to be ground or already ground [Old English *grīst*]

gris•tle \'gris-əl\ *n* : tough tissue of fiber or cartilage especially in table meats [Old English] — **gris•tli•ness** \'gris-lē-nəs, -ə-lē-\ *n* — **gris•tly** \'gris-lē, -ə-lē\ *adj*

grist•mill \'grist-,mil\ *n* : a mill for grinding grain

[1]**grit** \'grit\ *n* **1** : a hard sharp granule (as of sand); *also* : material (as an abrasive) composed of such granules **2** : firmness of mind or spirit [Old English *grēot*]

[2]**grit** *vb* **grit•ted**; **grit•ting** : to grind or cause to grind : GRATE

grits \'grits\ *n pl* : coarsely ground hulled grain [Old English *grytt*]

grit•ty \'grit-ē\ *adj* **grit•ti•er**; **-est** **1** : containing or resembling grit **2** : courageously persistent : PLUCKY — **grit•ti•ness** *n*

griz•zled \'griz-əld\ *adj* : sprinkled, streaked, or mixed with gray [Middle French *grisel* "gray", from *gris*, of Germanic origin]

[1]**griz•zly** \'griz-lē\ *adj* **griz•zli•er**; **-est** : GRIZZLED

[2]**grizzly** *n, pl* **grizzlies** : GRIZZLY BEAR

grizzly bear *n* : a large powerful usually brownish yellow bear of the uplands of western North America

grizzly bear

groan \'grōn\ *vi* **1** : to utter a deep moan of pain, grief, or annoyance **2** : to make a harsh sound under sudden or prolonged strain ⟨the floor *groaned* under the weight⟩ [Old English *grānian*] — **groan** *n* — **groan•er** *n*

[1]**groat** \'grōt\ *n* **1** : hulled grain broken into fragments larger than grits **2** : a grain (as of oats) exclusive of the hull [Old English *grot*]

[2]**groat** *n* : a former British coin worth four pennies [Middle English *groot*]

gro•cer \'grō-sər\ *n* : a dealer in staple foodstuffs and household supplies [Middle French *grossier* "wholesaler", from *gros*, adj., "gross, wholesale"]

gro•cery \'grōs-rē, -ə-rē\ *n, pl* **-cer•ies** **1** *pl* : commodities sold by a grocer **2** : a grocer's store

grog \'gräg\ *n* : alcoholic liquor; *esp* : liquor (as rum) cut with water [Old *Grog*, nickname of Edward Vernon, died 1757, English admiral who ordered the sailors' rum to be diluted] — **grog•shop** \-,shäp\ *n*

△ **origin** The 18th century English admiral Edward Vernon is said to have been in the habit of wearing a cloak made of a kind of coarsely woven fabric called *grogram*. For this reason, the sailors under his command gave him the nickname "Old Grog". The Royal Navy in the West Indies had been given by custom a daily ration of rum, but in 1740 Vernon, alarmed at the damage to the physical and moral health of his men, ordered that the rum should be diluted with water. This mixture was christened *grog*, after its godfather. *Grog* is now sometimes used as a general term for any liquor, even undiluted.

grog•gy \'gräg-ē\ *adj* **grog•gi•er**; **-est** : weak and unsteady on the feet or in action [*grog*] — **grog•gi•ly** \'gräg-ə-lē\ *adv* — **grog•gi•ness** \'gräg-ē-nəs\ *n*

[1]**groin** \'grȯin\ *n* **1** : the fold or depression marking the junction of the lower abdomen and the thigh; *also* : the region of this junction **2** : the projecting curved line along which two intersecting structural vaults meet [Middle English *grynde*, from Old English, "abyss"]

[2]**groin** *vt* : to build or equip with groins

grom•met \'gräm-ət, 'grəm-\ *n* **1** : a ring of rope **2** : a small usually metal ring used to reinforce an eyelet or to protect something passed through it [perhaps from obsolete French *gormette* "curb of a bridle"]

[1]**groom** \'grüm, 'gru̇m\ *n* **1 a** *archaic* : a male servant **b** : a person in charge of horses **2** : BRIDEGROOM [Middle English *grom* "man, servant"; sense 2 short for *bridegroom*]

[2]**groom** *vt* **1** : to clean and care for (an animal) **2** : to make neat, attractive, or acceptable

grooms•man \'grümz-mən, 'gru̇mz-\ *n* : a male attendant of a bridegroom at his wedding

groove \'grüv\ *n* **1** : a long narrow channel or depression **2** : a fixed routine : RUT [Middle English *groof*] — **groove** *vt* — **in the groove** : in top form

groovy \'grü-vē\ *adj* **groov•i•er**; **-est** : MARVELOUS 3, WONDERFUL ⟨had a *groovy* time at the beach⟩

grope \'grōp\ *vi* **1 :** to feel about or cast about blindly or uncertainly in search ⟨*grope* for the right word⟩ **2 :** to feel one's way by groping ⟨*grope* along a wall⟩ [Old English *grāpian*]

gros•beak \'grōs-ˌbēk\ *n* **:** any of several finches of Europe or America having large stout conical bills [French *grosbec,* from *gros* "gross, thick" + *bec* "beak"]

gro•schen \'grō-shən, 'grò-\ *n, pl* **groschen 1 :** a unit of value equal to 1/100 schilling **2 :** an Austrian coin representing one groschen [German]

gros•grain \'grō-ˌgrān\ *n* **:** a silk or rayon fabric with crosswise cotton ribs [French *gros grain* "coarse texture"]

1gross \'grōs\ *adj* **1 a :** glaringly noticeable usually because of inexcusable badness ⟨a *gross* error⟩ **b :** OUT-AND-OUT, UTTER ⟨a *gross* fool⟩ **2 a :** BIG, BULKY; *esp* **:** excessively fat **b :** excessively luxuriant **3 a :** GENERAL 4, BROAD **b :** consisting of an overall total before any deductions ⟨*gross* earnings⟩ — compare NET **4 :** EARTHY, CARNAL ⟨*gross* pleasures⟩ **5 :** lacking knowledge or culture **6 :** crudely vulgar ⟨*gross* epithets⟩ [Middle French *gros* "thick, coarse", from Latin *grossus*] **syn** see FLAGRANT — **gross•ly** *adv* — **gross•ness** *n*

2gross *n* **:** a whole amount before any deductions

3gross *vt* **:** to earn before deductions

4gross *n, pl* **gross :** a total of 12 dozen things ⟨a *gross* of pencils⟩ [Middle French *grosse,* from *gros* "thick, coarse"]

gross national product *n* **:** the total value of the goods and services produced in a nation during a year

1gro•tesque \grō-'tesk\ *n* **1 :** decorative art featuring fanciful human and animal forms often interwoven with foliage **2 :** one that is grotesque [Italian *pittura grottesca,* literally, "cave painting", from *grotta* "cave"]

△ **origin** During the Italian Renaissance the remaining buildings of the ancient city of Rome were heavily excavated, exposing chambers that became known, familiarly, as *grotte,* "caves" (the plural of *grotta).* The walls of many *grotte* were covered with exotic paintings. *Pittura grottesca,* or simply *grottesca,* the term for such a painting, became the name for a later but similar type of painting representing fantastic combinations of human and animal forms interwoven with strange fruits and flowers. The word was soon borrowed into English. The adjective *grotesque,* first applied only to decorative art of this kind, is now used to describe anything fanciful or bizarre.

2grotesque *adj* **:** of, relating to, or characteristic of the grotesque: as **a :** FANCIFUL 3, BIZARRE **b :** absurdly awkward or incongruous **syn** see FANTASTIC — **gro•tesque•ly** *adv* — **gro•tesque•ness** *n*

grot•to \'grät-ō\ *n, pl* **grottoes** *also* **grottos 1 :** CAVE **2 :** an artificial recess or structure made to resemble a natural cave [Italian *grotta, grotto,* from Latin *crypta* "cavern, crypt"]

grouch \'grau̇ch\ *n* **1 :** a fit of bad temper **2 :** an habitually irritable or complaining person [probably from English dialect *grutch* "grudge", from Middle English *grucchen* "to grumble"] — **grouch** *vi* — **grouch•i•ly** \'grau̇-chə-lē\ *adv* — **grouch•i•ness** \-chē-nəs\ *n* — **grouchy** \-chē\ *adj*

1ground \'grau̇nd\ *n* **1 a :** the bottom of a body of water ⟨the boat struck *ground*⟩ **b** *pl* **:** sediment at the bottom of a liquid **:** LEES **2 :** a basis for belief, action, or argument ⟨*grounds* for divorce⟩ **3 a :** a surrounding area **:** BACKGROUND ⟨a picture on a gray *ground*⟩ **b :** material that serves as a base **:** FOUNDATION **4 a :** the surface of the earth **b :** an area used for a particular purpose ⟨parade *ground*⟩ **c** *pl* **:** the area around and belonging to a building ⟨the capitol *grounds*⟩ **5 :** SOIL 2, EARTH **6 a :** an object that makes an electrical connection with the earth **b :** a large conducting body (as the earth) used as a common return for an electric circuit [Old English *grund*]

2ground *vb* **1 :** to bring to or place on the ground ⟨*ground* a rifle⟩ **2 a :** to provide a reason or justification for **b :** to instruct in fundamentals ⟨well *grounded* in math⟩ **3 :** to connect electrically with a ground **4 :** to restrict to the ground ⟨*ground* a pilot⟩ **5 :** to run aground ⟨the ship *grounded* on a reef⟩ **6 :** to hit a ground ball

3ground *past of* GRIND

ground ball *n* **:** a baseball hit along the ground

ground–cher•ry \'grau̇nd-'cher-ē, 'grau̇n-\ *n* **:** a plant related to the nightshades that is sometimes grown for its edible yellow fruits enclosed in papery husks; *also* **:** its fruit

ground cover *n* **:** low-growing plants that cover the ground (as in a forest or in place of turf); *also* **:** a plant used as ground cover

ground crew *n* **:** the mechanics and technicians who maintain and service an airplane

ground•er \'grau̇n-dər\ *n* **:** GROUND BALL

ground finch *n* **:** any of several dull-colored large-billed finches of the Galapagos islands

ground floor *n* **:** the floor of a building most nearly on a level with the ground

ground glass *n* **:** glass with a roughened light-diffusing nontransparent surface

ground•hog \'grau̇nd-ˌhȯg, -ˌhäg\ *n* **:** WOODCHUCK

Groundhog Day *n* **:** February 2 that traditionally indicates six more weeks of winter if sunny or an early spring if cloudy [from the legend that the groundhog comes out and is frightened back into hibernation if he sees his shadow]

ground•less \'grau̇n-dləs\ *adj* **:** being without basis or reason ⟨*groundless* fears⟩ — **ground•less•ly** *adv* — **ground•less•ness** *n*

ground•ling \'grau̇n-dling\ *n* **1 :** a member of the masses **:** PLEBEIAN **2 :** one that lives or works on or near the ground

ground loop *n* **:** a sharp uncontrollable turn made by an airplane in landing, taking off, or taxiing

ground•mass \'grau̇nd-ˌmas, 'grau̇n-\ *n* **:** the fine-grained base of a rock in which larger crystals are embedded

ground•nut \-ˌnət\ *n* **:** a North American vine of the pea family with brownish purple fragrant flowers and an edible tuberous root; *also* **:** its root

ground pine *n* **:** any of several club mosses with long creeping stems and erect branches

ground plan *n* **1 :** a plan of a floor of a building **2 :** a basic plan

ground rule *n* **1 :** a sports rule adopted to modify play on a particular field, court, or course **2 :** a basic rule of procedure

ground•sel \'grau̇nd-səl, 'grau̇n-\ *n* **:** any of a large genus of plants of the daisy family which have mostly yellow flower heads and some of which are poisonous [Old English *grundeswelge,* from *grund* "ground" + *swelgan* "to swallow"]

ground•sheet \-ˌshēt\ *n* **:** a waterproof sheet placed on the ground for protection from moisture

ground squirrel *n* **:** any of numerous burrowing rodents (as the gophers and chipmunks) differing from true squirrels in having cheek pouches and shorter fur

ground state *n* **:** the energy level of a system (as of elementary particles) having the least energy of all its possible states

ground swell *n* **1 :** a broad deep ocean swell caused by a distant storm or earthquake **2 :** a rapid spontaneous growth (as of political opinion)

ground•wa•ter \'grau̇n-ˌdwȯt-ər, -ˌdwät-\ *n* **:** water within the earth that supplies wells and springs

ground wave *n* **:** a radio wave that is propagated along the surface of the earth

ground•work \'grau̇n-ˌdwərk\ *n* **:** FOUNDATION 2, BASIS

1group \'grüp\ *n* **1 :** two or more figures forming a complete unit (as in a painting) **2 a :** a number of individuals assembled together or having common interests **b :** a number of objects regarded as a unit **3 a :** an assemblage of related organisms **b :** an assemblage of atoms forming part of a molecule ⟨a methyl *group* (CH_3)⟩ [French *groupe,* from Italian *gruppo,* of Germanic origin]

2group *vb* **1 :** to combine in a group **2 :** to assign to a group **:** CLASSIFY **3 :** to form a group

grou•per \'grü-pər\ *n, pl* **groupers** *also* **grouper 1 :** any of numerous mostly large solitary bottom fishes of warm seas related to the sea basses **2 :** any of several rockfishes [Portuguese *garoupa*]

group•ie \'grü-pē\ *n* **:** a female fan of a rock group who usually follows it on tour

1grouse \'grau̇s\ *n, pl* **grouse :** any of numerous plump-bodied game birds usually protectively colored and less brilliant in plumage than the related pheasants [origin unknown]

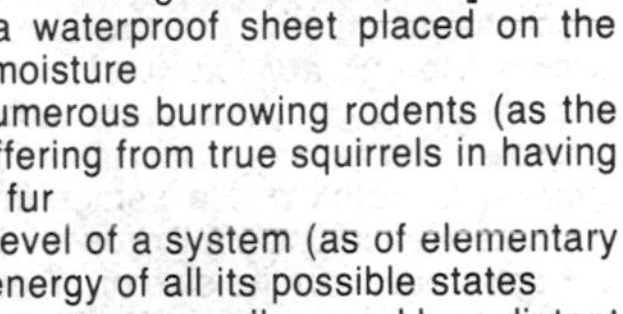

1grouse

\ə\ abut	\au̇\ out	\i\ tip	\ȯ\ saw	\u̇\ foot
\ər\ further	\ch\ chin	\ī\ life	\ȯi\ coin	\y\ yet
\a\ mat	\e\ pet	\j\ job	\th\ thin	\yü\ few
\ā\ take	\ē\ easy	\ng\ sing	\t͟h\ this	\yu̇\ cure
\ä\ cot, cart	\g\ go	\ō\ bone	\ü\ food	\zh\ vision

2grouse *vi* : COMPLAIN 1, GRUMBLE [origin unknown] — **grous·er** *n*

grout \ˈgrau̇t\ *n* **1** : thin mortar **2** : PLASTER 2 [Old English *grūt* "coarse meal"] — **grout** *vt*

grove \ˈgrōv\ *n* : a small wood; *esp* : a group of trees without underbrush [Old English *grāf*]

grov·el \ˈgräv-əl, ˈgrəv-\ *vi* **grov·eled** *or* **grov·elled**; **grov·el·ing** *or* **grov·el·ling** \ˈgräv-liŋ, ˈgrəv-, -ə-liŋ\ **1** : to lie or creep with the body prostrate especially as a sign of humbleness or abasement **2** : to abase oneself : CRINGE [back-formation from *groveling* "prone", from Middle English *gruf* "on the face" + 2*-ling*] — **grov·el·er** *or* **grov·el·ler** \-lər, -ə-lər\ *n*

grow \ˈgrō\ *vb* **grew** \ˈgrü\; **grown** \ˈgrōn\; **grow·ing** **1 a** : to spring up and develop to maturity **b** : to be able to grow in some place or situation ⟨rice *grows* in water⟩ **c** : to assume some relation through or as if through a process of natural growth ⟨a tree with limbs *grown* together⟩ **2 a** : to become larger and often more complex by addition of material either by assimilation into the living organism or by accretion in a natural inorganic process (as crystallization) **b** : INCREASE, EXPAND ⟨the city is *growing* rapidly⟩ ⟨*grow* in wisdom⟩ **3** : ORIGINATE ⟨the project *grew* out of a mere suggestion⟩ **4 a** : to pass into a condition : BECOME ⟨*grew* pale⟩ **b** : to obtain influence ⟨habit *grows* on a person⟩ **5** : to cause to grow : CULTIVATE, RAISE ⟨*grow* wheat⟩ [Old English *grōwan*] — **grow·er** \ˈgrō-ər, ˈgrōr\ *n*

growing pains *n pl* **1** : pains in the legs of growing children having no demonstrable relation to growth **2** : the stresses and strains attending a new project or development

growing point *n* : the tip of a plant shoot from which additional shoot tissues differentiate

growl \ˈgrau̇l\ *vb* **1 a** : RUMBLE 1 **b** : to utter a deep guttural threatening sound ⟨a *growling* dog⟩ **2** : to complain angrily [probably imitative] — **growl** *n* — **growl·er** *n*

grown \ˈgrōn\ *adj* : ADULT 1, MATURE

grown–up \ˈgrō-ˌnəp\ *adj* : ADULT ⟨*grown-up* behavior⟩ — **grown–up** *n*

growth \ˈgrōth\ *n* **1 a** : stage or condition attained in growing : SIZE ⟨reach one's full *growth*⟩ **b** : a process of growing: as (1) : an increase in the size or amount of something (as an organism, a crystal, or wealth) (2) : progressive development ⟨the *growth* of civilization⟩ **2** : a result or product of growing: as **a** : vegetation or a cover of vegetation ⟨a *growth* of new rye⟩ **b** : an abnormal mass of tissue (as a tumor) **3** : a producing especially by growing ⟨fruits of one's own *growth*⟩

growth factor *n* : a substance (as a vitamin) that promotes the growth of an organism

growth hormone *n* **1** : a hormone that is secreted by the pituitary gland and regulates growth — called also *somatotrophic hormone* **2** : any of various plant substances (as gibberellin) that regulate growth

growth ring *n* : a layer of wood (as an annual ring) produced during a single period of growth

1grub \ˈgrəb\ *vb* **grubbed**; **grub·bing** **1** : to clear or root out by digging ⟨*grub* up roots⟩ ⟨*grub* land for planting⟩ **2** : to work hard : DRUDGE **3 a** : to dig in the ground usually for a hidden object ⟨*grub* for potatoes⟩ **b** : to search about : RUMMAGE ⟨*grubbing* through the drawer⟩ [Middle English *grubben*] — **grub·ber** *n*

2grub *n* **1** : a soft thick wormlike larva of an insect **2** : a dull plodding person **3** : FOOD 2 [Middle English *grubbe,* from *grubben* "to grub"]

grub·by \ˈgrəb-ē\ *adj* **grub·bi·er**; **-est** **1** : DIRTY 1, GRIMY **2** : IGNOBLE 2 — **grub·bi·ly** \ˈgrəb-ə-lē\ *adv* — **grub·bi·ness** \ˈgrəb-ē-nəs\ *n*

grub·stake \ˈgrəb-ˌstāk\ *n* **1** : supplies or funds furnished a mining prospector in return for a promise of a share in his finds **2** : material assistance advanced for a project — **grubstake** *vt* — **grub·stak·er** *n*

1grudge \ˈgrəj\ *vt* : BEGRUDGE 1 [Middle English *grucchen, grudgen* "to grumble, complain", from Old French *groucier,* of Germanic origin] — **grudg·er** *n* — **grudg·ing·ly** \ˈgrəj-iŋ-lē\ *adv*

2grudge *n* : a feeling of deep-seated resentment or ill will

gru·el \ˈgrü-əl\ *n* : a thin porridge [Middle French, of Germanic origin]

gru·el·ing *or* **gru·el·ling** \ˈgrü-ə-liŋ\ *adj* : taxing to the point of exhaustion : making severe demands : PUNISHING ⟨a *grueling* race⟩ [from obsolete *gruel* "to exhaust"]

grue·some \ˈgrü-səm\ *adj* : inspiring horror or repulsion : GRISLY [Middle English *gruen* "to shiver"] **syn** see GHASTLY — **grue·some·ly** *adv* — **grue·some·ness** *n*

gruff \ˈgrəf\ *adj* **1** : rough or stern in manner, speech, or look ⟨a *gruff* reply⟩ **2** : being deep and harsh : HOARSE ⟨a *gruff* voice⟩ [Dutch *grof*] — **gruff·ly** *adv* — **gruff·ness** *n*

grum·ble \ˈgrəm-bəl\ *vb* **grum·bled**; **grum·bling** \-bə-liŋ, -bliŋ\ **1** : to mutter in discontent **2 a** : to make low indistinct noises **b** : RUMBLE 1 [probably from Middle French *grommeler*] — **grumble** *n* — **grum·bler** \-bə-lər, -blər\ *n*

grump \ˈgrəmp\ *n* **1** *pl* : a fit of bad humor **2** : a person given to complaining [obsolete *grumps* "snubs, slights"] — **grump** *vi* — **grump·i·ly** \ˈgrəm-pə-lē\ *adv* — **grump·i·ness** \-pē-nəs\ *n* — **grumpy** \-pē\ *adj*

grun·ion \ˈgrən-yən\ *n* : a small fish of the California coast that regularly comes inshore to spawn at nearly full moon [probably from Spanish *gruñón* "grunter"]

1grunt \ˈgrənt\ *vb* **1** : to utter a grunt **2** : to utter with a grunt [Old English *grunnettan*] — **grunt·er** *n*

2grunt *n* **1** : the characteristic deep short sound of a hog or a similar sound **2** : any of numerous marine fishes related to the snappers

gryph·on *variant of* GRIFFIN

G suit *n* : an aviator's or astronaut's suit designed to counteract the physiological effects of acceleration [gravity *suit*]

gua·na·co \gwə-ˈnäk-ō\ *n, pl* **-cos** *also* **-co** : a South American mammal that has a soft thick fawn-colored coat and is related to the camel [Spanish, from Quechua *huanacu*]

guanaco

gua·nine \ˈgwän-ˌēn\ *n* : a purine base $C_5H_5N_5O$ that codes genetic information in the polynucleotide chain of DNA and RNA — compare ADENINE, CYTOSINE, THYMINE, URACIL [*guano* + *-ine*; from its being found in guano]

gua·no \ˈgwän-ō\ *n, pl* **guanos** : a substance composed chiefly of the excrement of seabirds and used as a fertilizer [Spanish, from Quechua *huanu* "dung"]

gua·ra·ni \ˌgwär-ə-ˈnē\ *n, pl* **-nis** *or* **-nies** : the basic monetary unit of Paraguay; *also* : a note representing this unit [Spanish]

1guar·an·tee \ˌgar-ən-ˈtē, ˌgär-\ *n* **1** : GUARANTOR **2** : an agreement by which a person or firm guarantees something or someone **3** : something given as security : PLEDGE

2guarantee *vt* **-teed**; **-tee·ing** **1** : to undertake to answer to (a party) for the debt, failure to perform, or faulty performance of another **2** : to undertake an obligation to establish, perform, or continue ⟨*guaranteed* annual wage⟩ **3** : SECURE 1c

guar·an·tor \ˌgar-ən-ˈtȯr, ˈgar-ən-tər, ˌgär-, ˈgär-\ *n* : one that gives a guarantee

1guar·an·ty \ˈgar-ən-tē, ˈgär-\ *n, pl* **-ties** : GUARANTEE [Middle French *garantie,* from *garantir* "to guarantee", from *garant* "warrant", of Germanic origin]

2guaranty *vt* **-tied**; **-ty·ing** : GUARANTEE

1guard \ˈgärd\ *n* **1** : a defensive position (as in boxing) **2 a** : the act or duty of defending **b** : PROTECTION 1 **3 a** : a person or a body of persons on sentinel duty **b** *pl* : troops attached to the person of a sovereign **4 a** : either of two football players who line up inside the tackles and next to the center **b** : either of two players stationed usually away from the basket in basketball **5** : a protective or safety device (as on a machine) [Middle French *garde,* from *garder* "to guard", of Germanic origin]

2guard *vb* **1** : to protect from danger : DEFEND **2 a** : to watch over so as to prevent escape, disclosure, or indiscretion ⟨*guard* a prisoner⟩ ⟨*guard* a secret⟩ **b** : to attempt to prevent (an opponent) from playing effectively or scoring **3** : to be on guard : take precautions ⟨*guard* against infection⟩ **syn** see DEFEND

guard cell *n* : one of the two crescent-shaped epidermal cells that border and open and close a plant stoma

guard·ed \ˈgärd-əd\ *adj* : CAUTIOUS, CIRCUMSPECT ⟨a *guarded* answer⟩ — **guard·ed·ly** *adv*

guard hair *n* : one of the long coarse hairs forming a protective coating over the underfur of a mammal

guard•house \'gärd-ˌhau̇s\ *n* **1** : a building occupied by a guard or used as a headquarters by soldiers on guard duty **2** : a military jail

guard•i•an \'gärd-ē-ən\ *n* **1** : one that guards : CUSTODIAN **2** : one having the care of the person or property of another — **guard•i•an•ship** \-ˌship\ *n*

guard of honor : a guard assigned to greet or accompany a distinguished person or to accompany a casket at a military funeral — called also *honor guard*

guard•rail \'gär-ˌdrāl\ *n* : a railing for guarding against danger or trespass; *esp* : a barrier placed at dangerous points along a highway

guard•room \'gär-ˌdrüm, -ˌdru̇m\ *n* **1** : a room used by a military guard while on duty **2** : a room where military prisoners are confined

guards•man \'gärdz-mən\ *n* : a member of a military body organized as guards

gua•va \'gwäv-ə\ *n* **1** : any of several tropical American shrubs or small trees of the myrtle family; *esp* : one widely grown for its sweet-to-acid yellow fruit **2** : the fruit of a guava [Spanish *guayaba*, of American Indian origin]

gua•yu•le \gwī-'ü-lē, wī-\ *n* : a low shrubby plant of the daisy family that is found in Mexico and the southwestern United States and has been grown as a source of rubber [American Spanish, from Nahuatl *cuauhuli*]

gu•ber•na•to•ri•al \ˌgü-bər-nə-'tōr-ē-əl, ˌgyü-, -bə-, -'tȯr-\ *adj* : of or relating to a governor [Latin *gubernator* "governor", from *gubernare* "to govern"]

guern•sey \'gərn-zē\ *n, pl* **guernseys** *often cap* : any of a breed of fawn and white dairy cattle that are larger than jerseys and produce rich yellowish milk [*Guernsey*, Channel Islands]

guer•ril•la *or* **gue•ril•la** \gə-'ril-ə\ *n* : one who engages in irregular warfare especially as a member of an independent unit carrying out harassment and sabotage [Spanish *guerrilla*, from *guerra* "war", of Germanic origin]

guess \'ges\ *vb* **1** : to form an opinion from little or no evidence ⟨can you *guess* how many beans are in the jar⟩ **2** : to arrive at a correct conclusion about by conjecture ⟨*guessed* the answer⟩ **3** : BELIEVE, SUPPOSE ⟨I *guess* you're right⟩ [Middle English *gessen*] **syn** see CONJECTURE — **guess** *n* — **guess•er** *n* — **guess•work** \'ges-ˌwərk\ *n*

guest \'gest\ *n* **1 a** : a person entertained in one's house **b** : a person to whom hospitality is extended **c** : a patron of a commercial establishment (as a hotel or restaurant) **2** : an organism that lives in close association with another kind of organism [Old Norse *gestr*]

guf•faw \gə-'fȯ, ˌgə-\ *n* : a loud boisterous burst of laughter [imitative] — **guf•faw** *vi*

guid•ance \'gīd-ns\ *n* **1** : the act or process of guiding **2** : advice on vocational or educational problems given to students

¹guide \'gīd\ *n* **1 a** : one who leads or directs another on a course **b** : one who exhibits and explains points of interest **c** : something that provides guiding information ⟨a city *guide*⟩ **d** : one (as a teacher) that directs a person in the conduct or course of life **2 a** : a device for steadying or directing the motion of something **b** : a sheet or a card with a projecting tab for labeling that is inserted in a card index to facilitate reference [Middle French, from Provençal *guida*, of Germanic origin]

²guide *vt* **1** : to act as a guide for : CONDUCT **2 a** : MANAGE, DIRECT ⟨*guide* a car through traffic⟩ **b** : to superintend the training of — **guid•able** \'gīd-ə-bəl\ *adj*

guide•book \'gīd-ˌbu̇k\ *n* : a book of information for travelers

guid•ed missile \ˌgīd-əd-\ *n* : a missile whose course toward a target may be changed (as by radio signals or a built-in target-seeking device) during flight

guide word *n* : either of the terms at the head of a page of an alphabetical reference work (as a dictionary) indicating the alphabetically first and last words on the page

gui•don \'gīd-ˌän, -n\ *n* **1** : a small flag; *esp* : one carried by a military unit as a unit marker **2** : one who carries a guidon [Middle French]

guild *also* **gild** \'gild\ *n* : an association of people with similar interests or pursuits; *esp* : a medieval association of merchants or craftsmen [Old Norse *gildi* "payment, guild"] — **guild•ship** \-ˌship\ *n*

guil•der \'gil-dər\ *n* : GULDEN [Dutch *gulden*]

guild•hall \'gild-ˌhȯl\ *n* : a hall where a guild or corporation usually assembles

guile \'gīl\ *n* : deceitful cunning : DUPLICITY [Old French] — **guile•ful** \-fəl\ *adj* — **guile•ful•ly** \-fə-lē\ *adv* — **guile•ful•ness** *n*

guile•less \'gīl-ləs\ *adj* : free from deceit or cunning : NAIVE — **guile•less•ly** *adv* — **guile•less•ness** *n*

guil•le•mot \'gil-ə-ˌmät\ *n* : any of several narrow-billed auks of northern seas [French, from *Guillaume* "William"]

guil•lo•tine \'gil-ə-ˌtēn; ˌgē-ə-', 'gē-ə-ˌ, -yə-\ *n* : a device for beheading by means of a heavy blade that slides down between vertical guides [French, from Joseph *Guillotin*, died 1814, French physician] — **guillotine** *vt*

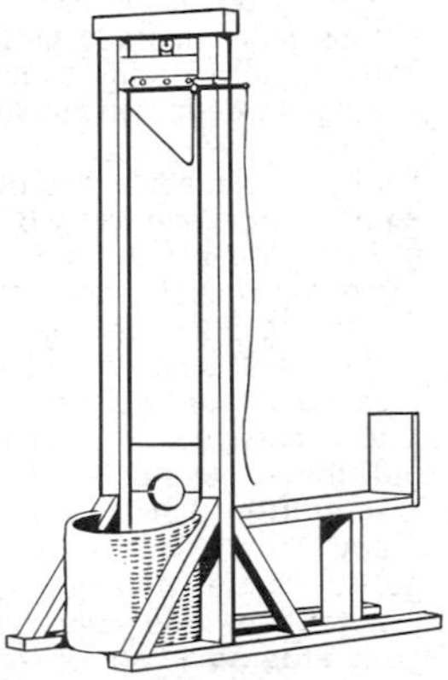
guillotine

guilt \'gilt\ *n* **1** : the fact of having committed an offense and especially one that is punishable by law **2** : the state of deserving blame **3** : a feeling of responsibility for offenses [Old English *gylt* "delinquency"] — **guilt•less** \-ləs\ *adj*

guilty \'gil-tē\ *adj* **guilt•i•er; -est** **1** : having committed a breach of conduct **2 a** : suggesting or involving guilt ⟨a *guilty* look⟩ **b** : aware of or suffering from guilt — **guilt•i•ly** \-tə-lē\ *adv* — **guilt•i•ness** \-tē-nəs\ *n*

guin•ea \'gin-ē\ *n* **1** : a former monetary unit equal to 21 shillings **2** : a British gold coin representing this unit [*Guinea*, West Africa, supposed source of the gold from which it was made]

guinea fowl *n* : an African bird related to the pheasants, widely raised for food, and marked by a bare neck and head and white-speckled usually gray plumage

guinea hen *n* : a female guinea fowl; *also* : GUINEA FOWL

guinea pig *n* **1** : a small stout-bodied short-eared nearly tailless rodent often kept as a pet and widely used in biological research — called also *cavy* **2** : one that is the subject of a scientific experiment

guinea worm *n* : a slender nematode worm attaining a length of several feet and occurring as an adult under the skin of various mammals including humans

guise \'gīz\ *n* **1** : a form or style of dress : COSTUME ⟨appeared in the *guise* of a shepherd⟩ **2** : external appearance : SEMBLANCE ⟨swindled them under the *guise* of friendship⟩ [Old French, of Germanic origin]

gui•tar \gə-'tär, gi-\ *n* : a flat-bodied stringed instrument with a long fretted neck and usually six strings plucked with a pick or with the fingers [French *guitare*, from Spanish *guitarra*, from Arabic *gītār*, from Greek *kithara* "cithara"]

guitar

gu•lar \'gü-lər, 'gyü-\ *adj* : of, relating to, or situated on the throat [Latin *gula* "throat"]

gulch \'gəlch\ *n* : RAVINE, COULEE [perhaps from English dialect *gulch* "to gulp"]

gul•den \'gül-dən, 'gu̇l-\ *n, pl* **guldens** *or* **gulden** **1** : the basic monetary unit of the Netherlands **2** : a coin or note representing one gulden [Dutch *gulden florijn* "golden florin"]

gulf \'gəlf\ *n* **1** : a part of an ocean or sea extending into the land **2** : a deep hollow in the earth : CHASM, ABYSS **3** : WHIRLPOOL **4** : an unbridgeable gap [Middle French *golfe*, from Italian *golfo*, from Late Latin *colpus*, from Greek *kolpos* "bosom, gulf"]

\ə\ **abut**	\au̇\ **out**	\i\ **tip**	\ȯ\ **saw**	\u̇\ **foot**
\ər\ **further**	\ch\ **chin**	\ī\ **life**	\ȯi\ **coin**	\y\ **yet**
\a\ **mat**	\e\ **pet**	\j\ **job**	\th\ **thin**	\yü\ **few**
\ā\ **take**	\ē\ **easy**	\ng\ **sing**	\t͟h\ **this**	\yu̇\ **cure**
\ä\ **cot, cart**	\g\ **go**	\ō\ **bone**	\ü\ **food**	\zh\ **vision**

• **syn** BAY: GULF implies a body of water of considerable size and importance and usually suggests deep penetration of the land and a relatively narrow entrance; BAY commonly implies a shallow penetration and wide entrance but may apply to a body of water of almost any size or shape that is connected with or is part of a larger one.

gulf•weed \ˈgəlf-ˌwēd\ *n* : any of several marine brown algae; *esp* : a branching olive-brown seaweed of tropical American seas with numerous air-filled sacs suggesting berries

[1]**gull** \ˈgəl\ *n* : any of numerous mostly white or gray long-winged web-footed aquatic birds [Middle English, of Celtic origin]

[2]**gull** *vt* : take advantage of : DUPE [obsolete *gull* "gullet"]

[3]**gull** *n* : a person easily deceived or cheated : DUPE

gul•let \ˈgəl-ət\ *n* **1 a** : a tube that leads from the back of the mouth to the stomach : ESOPHAGUS **b** : THROAT 1 **2** : a tubular infolding of the protoplasm in various protozoans (as a paramecium) that sometimes functions in the intake of food **3** : the space between adjacent saw teeth [Middle French *goulet* "narrow passage", from *goule* "throat", from Latin *gula*]

gull•ible \ˈgəl-ə-bəl\ *adj* : easily deceived, cheated, or duped — **gull•ibil•i•ty** \ˌgəl-ə-ˈbil-ət-ē\ *n* — **gull•ibly** \ˈgəl-ə-blē\ *adv*

gul•ly \ˈgəl-ē\ *n, pl* **gullies** : a trench worn in the earth by rainwater [obsolete *gully* "gullet"] — **gully** *vb*

gully erosion *n* : soil erosion produced by running water

gulp \ˈgəlp\ *vb* **1** : to swallow hurriedly or greedily or in one swallow **2** : to keep back as if by swallowing ⟨*gulp* down a sob⟩ **3** : to catch the breath as if in taking a long drink [Middle English *gulpen*] — **gulp** *n* — **gulp•er** *n*

[1]**gum** \ˈgəm\ *n* : the tissue along the jaws of animals that surrounds the necks of the teeth [Old English *gōma* "palate"]

[2]**gum** *vt* **gummed**; **gum•ming 1** : to enlarge gullets of (a saw) **2** : to chew with the gums

[3]**gum** *n* **1** : any of numerous complex colloidal substances (as gum arabic) that are exuded by plants or are extracted from them by solvents, that are thick or sticky when moist but harden on drying and are either soluble in water or swell up in contact with water, and that are used in pharmacy (as for emulsifiers), for adhesives, as food thickeners, and in inks; *also* : any of various gummy plant exudates including natural resins, oleoresins, rubber, and rubberlike substances **2** : a substance or deposit resembling a plant gum (as in sticky quality) **3 a** (1) : BLACK GUM (2) : SWEET GUM **b** *Australian* : EUCALYPTUS **4** : the wood of a gum **5** : CHEWING GUM [Old French *gomme*, from Latin *cummi, gummi*, from Greek *kommi*, from Egyptian *gmy·t*]

[4]**gum** *vt* **gummed**; **gum•ming** : to smear, seal, or clog with or as if with gum ⟨*gum* up the works⟩

gum arabic *n* : a water-soluble gum obtained from several acacias and used especially in adhesives, in confectionery, and in pharmacy

gum•bo \ˈgəm-ˌbō\ *n, pl* **gumbos 1** : OKRA **2** : a soup thickened with okra pods **3** : any of various silty soils that when wet become very sticky [American French *gombo*, of Bantu origin]

gum•drop \-ˌdräp\ *n* : a sugar-coated candy made usually from corn syrup with gelatin or gum arabic

gum•ma \ˈgəm-ə\ *n, pl* **gummas** *also* **gum•ma•ta** \ˈgəm-ət-ə\ : a gummy or rubbery tumor associated especially with late stages of syphilis [Late Latin *gummat-, gumma* "gum", from Latin *gummi*] — **gum•ma•tous** \-ət-əs\ *adj*

gum•my \ˈgəm-ē\ *adj* **gum•mi•er**; **-est 1** : consisting of, containing, or covered with gum **2** : VISCOUS 1, STICKY — **gum•mi•ness** *n*

gump•tion \ˈgəm-shən, ˈgəmp-\ *n* **1** : shrewd common sense **2** : ENTERPRISE 3, INITIATIVE [origin unknown]

gum resin *n* : a plant product consisting essentially of a mixture of gum and resin

gum•shoe \ˈgəm-ˌshü\ *n* : DETECTIVE — **gumshoe** *vi*

gum tragacanth *n* : TRAGACANTH

gum turpentine *n* : TURPENTINE 2a

gum•wood \ˈgəm-ˌwu̇d\ *n* : [3]GUM 4

[1]**gun** \ˈgən\ *n* **1 a** : a piece of artillery usually with high muzzle velocity and comparatively flat trajectory : CANNON **b** : a portable firearm (as a rifle or pistol) **c** : a device that throws a projectile **2 a** : a discharge of a gun **b** : a signal marking a beginning or ending ⟨the opening *gun* of a campaign⟩ **3** : one who is skilled with a gun ⟨a hired *gun*⟩ **4** : something suggesting a gun in shape or function ⟨a grease *gun*⟩ **5** : THROTTLE 2 [Middle English *gunne*] — **gunned** \ˈgənd\ *adj*

[2]**gun** *vb* **gunned**; **gun•ning 1** : to hunt or shoot with a gun **2** : to open up the throttle of quickly so as to increase speed ⟨*gun* the engine⟩

gun•boat \ˈgən-ˌbōt\ *n* : a small armed ship for patrolling coastal waters

gun•cot•ton \-ˌkät-n\ *n* : an explosive that consists of cellulose nitrate with a high nitrogen content and is used chiefly in smokeless powder

gun•fight \-ˌfīt\ *n* : a duel with guns — **gun•fight•er** *n*

gun•fire \-ˌfīr\ *n* : the firing of guns

gung ho \ˈgəŋ-ˈhō\ *adj* : very enthusiastic [*Gung ho!*, motto (supposed to mean "work together") of a United States Marine battalion in World War II, from Chinese (Pekingese dialect) *kung*^{1}*-ho*^{2}, short for *chung*^{1}*-kuo*^{2} *kung*^{1}*-yeh*^{4} *ho*^{2}*-tso*^{4} *she*^{4} "Chinese Industrial Cooperatives Society"]

△ **origin** The Chinese Industrial Cooperatives Society, whose Chinese name was *chung*^{1}*-kuo*^{2} *kung*^{1}*-yeh*^{4} *ho*^{2}*-tso*^{4} *she*^{4}, was founded in 1938. Its long name was soon abbreviated to *kung*^{1}*-ho*^{2}. In 1942 Lt. Col. Evans Fordyce Carlson of the United States Marine Corps was in China organizing the Second Raider Battalion. Trying to instill a sense of unity and purpose in his men, Carlson told them that *Gung ho* was the motto of the Chinese cooperatives, whose ardent spirit he admired, and that it meant "work together". In fact, although *kung*^{1} may be translated "work" and *ho*^{2} "together", the two do not form a Chinese phrase meaning "work together", but are only a shortened form of an unwieldy name. But the misinterpreted motto caught on and members of the battalion were soon proudly calling themselves and their spirit *gung ho*.

gun•lock \ˈgən-ˌläk\ *n* : a device on a firearm by which the charge is ignited

gun•man \-mən\ *n* : a man armed with a gun; *esp* : a professional killer

gun•met•al \ˈgən-ˌmet-l\ *n* : a bronze formerly used for making cannons; *also* : a metal treated to look like gunmetal

gun•ner \ˈgən-ər\ *n* **1** : a person (as a soldier) who operates a gun **2** : one that hunts with a gun

gun•nery \ˈgən-rē, -ə-rē\ *n* : the use of guns; *esp* : the science of the flight of projectiles and of the effective use of guns

gunnery sergeant *n* : an enlisted rank in the Marine Corps above staff sergeant and below master sergeant

gun•ny \ˈgən-ē\ *n, pl* **gunnies 1** : coarse jute sacking **2** : BURLAP [Hindi *ganī*]

gun•ny•sack \-ˌsak\ *n* : a sack made of gunny

gun•point \ˈgən-ˌpȯint\ *n* : the point of a gun — **at gunpoint** : under a threat of death by being shot

gun•pow•der \-ˌpau̇d-ər\ *n* : an explosive mixture of potassium nitrate, charcoal, and sulfur used in gunnery and blasting; *also* : any of various explosive powders used in guns

gun•shot \-ˌshät\ *n* **1** : shot or a projectile fired from a gun **2** : the range of a gun ⟨within *gunshot*⟩ **3** : the firing of a gun

gun–shy \-ˌshī\ *adj* **1** : afraid of loud noise (as that of a gun) **2** : markedly distrustful

gun•smith \-ˌsmith\ *n* : one whose business is to design, make, or repair small firearms

gun•wale *or* **gun•nel** \ˈgən-l\ *n* : the upper edge of a ship's side [from its former use as a support for guns]

gup•py \ˈgəp-ē\ *n, pl* **guppies** : a small tropical topminnow frequently kept as an aquarium fish [R. J. L. *Guppy*, died 1916, Trinidadian naturalist]

gur•gle \ˈgər-gəl\ *vi* **gur•gled**; **gur•gling** \ˈgər-gə-liŋ, -gliŋ\ **1** : to flow in a broken irregular current **2** : to make a sound like that of a gurgling liquid [probably imitative] — **gurgle** *n*

gur•nard \ˈgər-nərd\ *n, pl* **gurnard** *or* **gurnards** : any of various marine spiny-finned fishes with a spiny armored head and modified fins used especially in crawling [Middle French *gornart*]

gu•ru \gə-ˈrü, ˈgu̇r-ü\ *n* **1** : a personal religious teacher and spiritual guide in Hinduism **2** : an acknowledged leader or teacher [Hindi *gurū*, from Sanskrit *guru*, from *guru* "heavy, venerable"]

gush \ˈgəsh\ *vb* **1** : to issue or pour forth copiously or violently : SPOUT ⟨oil *gushed* from the well⟩ **2** : to make an exaggerated display of affection or enthusiasm ⟨*gushed* over the movie star⟩ [Middle English *guschen*] — **gush** *n*

gush•er \ˈgəsh-ər\ *n* : one that gushes; *esp* : an oil well with a large natural flow

gushy \ˈgəsh-ē\ *adj* **gush•i•er**; **-est** : marked by exaggerated sentimentality — **gush•i•ly** \'gəsh-ə-lē\ *adv* — **gush•i•ness** \'gəsh-ē-nəs\ *n*

gus•set \'gəs-ət\ *n* : a usually triangular or diamond-shaped insert (as in a glove) to give width or strength [Middle English, "piece of armor covering the joints in a suit of armor", from Middle French *gouchet*]

gust \'gəst\ *n* **1** : a sudden brief rush of wind **2** : a sudden outburst : SURGE ⟨a *gust* of rage⟩ [probably from Old Norse *gustr*] — **gust•i•ly** \'gəs-tə-lē\ *adv* — **gust•i•ness** \-tē-nəs\ *n* — **gusty** \-tē\ *adj*

gus•ta•tion \ˌgəs-'tā-shən\ *n* : the act or sensation of tasting [Latin *gustatio,* from *gustare* "to taste"]

gus•ta•to•ry \'gəs-tə-ˌtōr-ē, -ˌtȯr-\ *adj* : relating to, associated with, or being the sense or sensation of taste

gus•to \'gəs-ˌtō\ *n* **1** : enthusiastic vigorous enjoyment or appreciation ⟨eat with *gusto*⟩ **2** : very great vitality [Spanish, from Latin *gustus* "taste"] **syn** see TASTE

[1]**gut** \'gət\ *n* **1 a** : VISCERA, ENTRAILS — usually used in pl. **b** : the alimentary canal or part of it **c** : ABDOMEN 1, BELLY **2** *pl* : the inner essential parts ⟨the *guts* of a car⟩ **3** *pl* : COURAGE [Old English *guttas,* pl.]

[2]**gut** *vt* **gut•ted**; **gut•ting** **1** : EVISCERATE 1 **2** : to destroy the inside of ⟨fire *gutted* the building⟩

gutsy \'gət-sē\ *adj* **guts•i•er**; **-est** : COURAGEOUS ⟨a *gutsy* fighter⟩

gut•ta–per•cha \ˌgət-ə-'pər-chə\ *n* : a tough plastic substance from the latex of several Malaysian trees that resembles but contains more resin than rubber and that is used especially as insulation and in dentistry [Malay *gĕtah-pĕrcha*]

gut•ta•tion \ˌgə-'tā-shən\ *n* : physiological oozing of drops of water from a plant [Latin *gutta* "drop"]

[1]**gut•ter** \'gət-ər\ *n* **1 a** : a trough along the eaves to catch and carry off water from a roof **b** : a low area (as at a roadside) to carry off surface water **2** : a narrow channel or groove [Old French *goutiere,* from *goute* "drop", from Latin *gutta*]

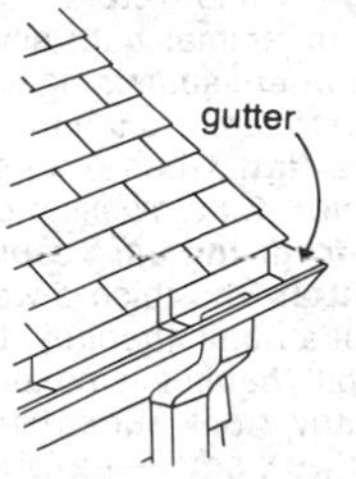

[1]gutter 1a

[2]**gutter** *vb* **1** : to form gutters in **2 a** : to flow in small streams **b** : to melt away rapidly by becoming channeled down the sides ⟨a *guttering* candle⟩ **3** : to flicker in a draft ⟨a flame *guttering* in the breeze⟩

gut•ter•snipe \-ˌsnīp\ *n* : a person of the lowest moral or economic station; *esp* : a street urchin

gut•tur•al \'gət-ə-rəl\ *adj* **1** : of or relating to the throat **2 a** : formed or pronounced in the throat ⟨*guttural* sounds⟩ **b** : VELAR 2 **c** : being or marked by an utterance that is strange or disagreeable [Middle French, derived from Latin *guttur* "throat"] — **guttural** *n* — **gut•tur•al•ly** \-rə-lē\ *adv* — **gut•tur•al•ness** *n*

gut•ty \'gət-ē\ *adj* **gut•ti•er**; **-est** **1** : COURAGEOUS ⟨a *gutty* fighter⟩ **2** : having a vigorous challenging quality ⟨*gutty* realism⟩

[1]**guy** \'gī\ *n* : a rope, chain, or wire attached to something as a brace or guide [probably from Dutch *gei* "brail"]

[2]**guy** *vt* **guyed**; **guy•ing** : to steady or reinforce with a guy

[3]**guy** *n* : FELLOW 4a [*guy* "grotesque effigy of Guy Fawkes paraded and burned in England on November 5", from *Guy* Fawkes, died 1606, English conspirator who plotted to blow up the Houses of Parliament]

△ **origin** On 4 November 1605 in London, Guy Fawkes was arrested for having planted gunpowder in the cellars of the Houses of Parliament as his part in a conspiracy to blow up the Parliament buildings on the following day. He was later executed. The failure of the conspiracy is still celebrated in England on November 5, Guy Fawkes Day. On this day fireworks are displayed and effigies of Guy Fawkes are burned on bonfires. These effigies came to be called *guys.* The use of the word was extended to other similar effigies and then to people of grotesque appearance. In the United States the word was generalized to mean simply "man" or "fellow".

[4]**guy** *vt* : to make fun of : RIDICULE

guy•ot \'gē-ō\ *n* : a flat-topped seamount [Arnold H. *Guyot,* died 1884, American geographer and geologist]

guz•zle \'gəz-əl\ *vb* **guz•zled**; **guz•zling** \'gəz-ling, -ə-ling\ : to drink greedily [origin unknown] — **guz•zler** \-lər, -ə-lər\ *n*

gybe \'jīb\ *variant of* JIBE

gym \'jim\ *n* : GYMNASIUM 1

gym•kha•na \jim-'kän-ə, -'kan-\ *n* : a meet featuring sports contests (as horseback-riding events) [probably from Hindi *gendkhāna,* court for a game similar to tennis]

gymn- *or* **gymno-** *combining form* : naked : bare ⟨*gymno*sperm⟩ [Greek *gymnos*]

gym•na•si•um *in sense 1* jim-'nā-zē-əm, *in sense 2* gim-'nä-zē-əm\ *n, pl* **-si•ums** *or* **-sia** \-zē-ə\ **1** : a room or building for indoor sports activities **2** : a German secondary school preparing students for the university [Latin, "exercise ground, school", from Greek *gymnasion,* from *gymnazein* "to exercise naked", from *gymnos* "naked"]

gym•nast \'jim-ˌnast, -nəst\ *n* : one trained in gymnastics

gym•nas•tics \jim-'nas-tiks\ *n sing or pl* : physical exercises developing or exhibiting skill, strength, and control in the use of the body — **gym•nas•tic** \-tik\ *adj* — **gym•nas•ti•cal•ly** \-ti-kə-lē, -klē\ *adv*

gym•no•din•i•um \ˌjim-nō-'din-ē-əm\ *n* : any of a genus of marine dinoflagellates some of which cause red tides [*gymn-* + Greek *dinein* "to whirl"]

gym•no•sperm \'jim-nə-ˌspərm\ *n* : any of a group (Gymnospermae) of woody vascular seed plants that produce naked seeds not enclosed in a true fruit [*gymn-* + Greek *sperma* "seed"] — **gym•no•sper•mous** \ˌjim-nə-'spər-məs\ *adj*

gyn•an•dro•morph \gīn-'an-drə-ˌmȯrf, jin-\ *n* : an abnormal individual exhibiting characters of both sexes in various parts of the body [Greek *gynō* "woman" + *andr-, anēr* "man" + *morphē* "form"] — **gyn•an•dro•mor•phic** \-ˌan-drə-'mȯr-fik\ *adj* — **gyn•an•dro•mor•phism** \-ˌfiz-əm\ *n* — **gyn•an•dro•mor•phy** \-'an-drə-ˌmȯr-fē\ *n*

gy•ne•col•o•gy \ˌgīn-i-'käl-ə-jē, ˌjin-\ *n* : a branch of medicine that deals with women, their diseases, and their hygiene [Greek *gynaik-, gynē* "woman"] — **gy•ne•co•log•ic** \-kə-'läj-ik\ *or* **gy•ne•co•log•i•cal** \-'läj-i-kəl\ *adj* — **gy•ne•col•o•gist** \-'käl-ə-jəst\ *n*

gy•noe•ci•um \jin-'ē-sē-əm, gīn-, -shē-\ *n, pl* **-cia** \-sē-ə, -shē-ə\ : the carpels in a flower [Latin *gynaeceum* "women's apartments", from Greek *gynaikeion,* from *gynaik-, gynē* "woman"]

-g•y•nous \j-ə-nəs\ *adj combining form* **1** : of, relating to, or having (such or so many) females ⟨poly*gynous*⟩ **2** : situated (in a specified place) in relation to a female organ of a plant ⟨hypo*gynous*⟩ [Greek *gynē* "woman"]

[1]**gyp** \'jip\ *n* **1** : CHEAT 2, SWINDLER **2** : FRAUD 1b, SWINDLE [probably short for *Gypsy*]

[2]**gyp** *vb* **gypped**; **gyp•ping** : CHEAT 1, 4, SWINDLE

gyp•soph•i•la \jip-'säf-ə-lə\ *n* : any of a large genus of Old World herbs of the pink family having loosely branched clusters of tiny flowers [Latin *gypsum* + *-phila* "-phil"]

gyp•sum \'jip-səm\ *n* : a colorless mineral $CaSO_4 \cdot 2H_2O$ that consists of hydrous sulfate of calcium occurring in crystals or masses and that is used especially as a soil improver and in making plaster of paris [Latin, from Greek *gypsos,* of Semitic origin]

Gyp•sy *or* **Gip•sy** \'jip-sē\ *n, pl* **Gypsies** *or* **Gipsies** **1** : one of a dark Caucasoid people coming originally from India to Europe in the 14th or 15th century and living and maintaining a migratory way of life chiefly in Europe and the United States **2** : ROMANY 2 **3** *not cap* : one that resembles a Gypsy : WANDERER [alteration of *Egyptian*]

△ **origin** In the early years of the 16th century there began to appear in Britain some members of a wandering race of people who were ultimately of Hindu origin and who called themselves and their language *Romany.* In Britain, however, it was popularly believed that they came from Egypt, so they were called *Egipcyans* or *Egyptians.* This was soon shortened to *Gipcyan,* and by 1600 the further altered form *Gipsy, Gypsey* began to appear in print.

gypsy moth *n* : an Old World tussock moth introduced about

1869 into the United States that has a hairy caterpillar which is a destructive defoliator of many trees

gyr- *or* **gyro-** *combining form* **1** : ring : circle : spiral **2** : gyroscope ⟨*gyro*compass⟩ [Greek *gyros*]

gy•rate \ˈjī-ˌrāt\ *vi* **1** : to revolve around a point or axis **2** : to oscillate with or as if with a circular or spiral motion — **gy•ra•tion** \jī-ˈrā-shən\ *n* — **gy•ra•tion•al** \-shnəl, -shən-l\ *adj*

gyr•fal•con \ˈjər-ˌfal-kən *also* -ˌfȯl- *sometimes* -ˌfȯ-kən\ *n* : an arctic falcon that occurs in several forms, is the largest of all falcons, and is more powerful though less active than the peregrine falcon [Middle French *girfaucon*]

gy•ro \ˈjī-rō\ *n, pl* **gyros 1** : GYROSCOPE **2** : GYROCOMPASS

gy•ro•com•pass \ˈjī-rō-ˌkəm-pəs, -ˌkäm-\ *n* : a compass in which the horizontal axis of a constantly spinning gyroscope points to the north and which is often used instead of a magnetic compass where metal in the vicinity (as on a ship) would interfere with the working of a magnetic compass

gy•ro•scope \ˈjī-rə-ˌskōp\ *n* : a wheel or disk mounted to spin rapidly about an axis that is free to turn in various directions [from its original use to illustrate the rotation of the earth] — **gy•ro•scop•ic** \ˌjī-rə-ˈskäp-ik\ *adj*

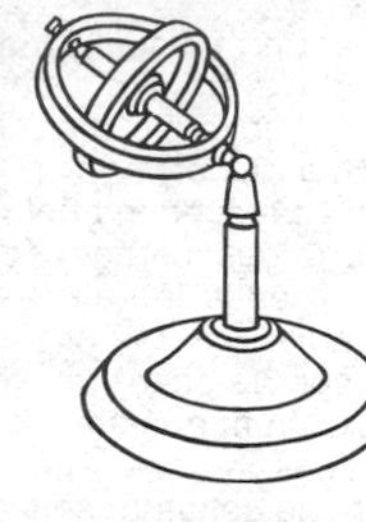
gyroscope

gy•rus \ˈjī-rəs\ *n, pl* **gy•ri** \-ˌrī\ : a convoluted ridge between anatomical grooves [Latin, "circle", from Greek *gyros*]

gyve \ˈjīv\ *n* : FETTER 1 [Middle English] — **gyve** *vt*

H h—hysterics

h \ˈāch\ *n, pl* **h's** *or* **hs** \ˈā-chəz\ *often cap* : the 8th letter of the English alphabet

ha *or* **hah** \ˈhä\ *interj* — used especially to express surprise or joy [Middle English *ha*]

Ha•ba•cuc \ˈhab-ə-ˌkək, hə-ˈbak-ək\ *n* — see BIBLE table

Hab•ak•kuk \ˈhab-ə-ˌkək, hə-ˈbak-ək\ *n* — see BIBLE table

ha•ba•ne•ra \ˌhäb-ə-ˈner-ə, ˌäb-\ *n* **1** : a Cuban dance in slow duple time **2** : the music for the habanera [Spanish *danza habanera,* literally, "dance of Havana"]

hab•da•lah \ˌhäv-də-ˈlä, häv-ˈdȯ-lə\ *n, often cap* : a Jewish ceremony that marks the close of a Sabbath or holy day [Hebrew *habhdālāh* "separation"]

ha•be•as cor•pus \ˌhā-bē-ə-ˈskȯr-pəs\ *n* **1** : any of several writs issued to bring a person before a court; *esp* : one ordering an inquiry to determine whether or not a person has been lawfully imprisoned **2** : the right of a citizen to obtain a writ of habeas corpus as a protection against illegal imprisonment [Medieval Latin, literally, "you should have the body" (the opening words of the writ)]

hab•er•dash•er \ˈhab-ər-ˌdash-ər, ˈhab-ə-ˌ\ *n* : a dealer in menswear [Anglo-French *hapertas* "petty merchandise"]

hab•er•dash•ery \-ˌdash-rē, -ə-rē\ *n, pl* **-er•ies 1** : goods sold by a haberdasher **2** : a haberdasher's shop

ha•bil•i•ment \hə-ˈbil-ə-mənt\ *n* **1** : the dress characteristic of an occupation or occasion — usually used in pl. ⟨the *habiliments* of a priest⟩ **2** : CLOTHING — usually used in pl. [Middle French *habillement,* from *habiller* "to dress a log, dress", from *bille* "log"]

[1]**hab•it** \ˈhab-ət\ *n* **1** : a costume characteristic of a calling, rank, or function ⟨riding *habit*⟩ **2** : bodily appearance or physical makeup : PHYSIQUE **3** : the prevailing disposition or character of a person's thoughts and feelings : mental makeup **4** : a usual manner of behavior : CUSTOM **5 a** : a behavior pattern acquired and fixed by frequent repetition — compare REFLEX **b** : an acquired mode of behavior that has become nearly or completely involuntary **c** : ADDICTION **6** : characteristic mode of growth or occurrence ⟨elms have a spreading *habit*⟩ [Old French, from Latin *habitus* "condition, custom, dress", from *habēre* "to have, hold"]

• **syn** HABIT, PRACTICE, USAGE, CUSTOM mean a way of acting that has become fixed through repetition. HABIT implies doing something unconsciously, often involuntarily or without forethought, and as a result of much repetition ⟨*habits* of speech⟩ ⟨pocketed the car keys by force of *habit*⟩ PRACTICE suggests an act performed with regularity and usually by choice; USAGE suggests a customary action or practice followed so generally that it has become a social norm; CUSTOM applies to practice or usage so long and continuously associated with an individual or group as to have the force of unwritten law ⟨by *custom* Saturday was bath night⟩

[2]**habit** *vt* : CLOTHE 1, DRESS

hab•it•able \ˈhab-ət-ə-bəl\ *adj* : suitable or fit to live in ⟨the *habitable* parts of the earth⟩ — **hab•it•abil•i•ty** \ˌhab-ət-ə-ˈbil-ət-ē\ *n* — **hab•it•able•ness** \ˈhab-ət-ə-bəl-nəs\ *n* — **hab•it•ably** \-blē\ *adv*

ha•bi•tant *n* **1** \ˈhab-ət-ənt\ : INHABITANT, RESIDENT **2** \ˌhab-i-ˈtä^{n}, ˌab-\ : a French settler or a farmer of French origin in Canada

hab•i•tat \ˈhab-ə-ˌtat\ *n* **1** : the place or type of site where a plant or animal naturally or normally lives or grows **2** : the place where something is commonly found [Latin, "it inhabits", from *habitare* "to inhabit"]

hab•i•ta•tion \ˌhab-ə-ˈtā-shən\ *n* **1** : the act of inhabiting : OCCUPANCY **2** : a dwelling place : RESIDENCE

hab•it–form•ing *adj* : causing addiction

ha•bit•u•al \hə-ˈbich-ə-wəl, -ˈbich-wəl\ *adj* **1** : having the nature of a habit ⟨*habitual* tardiness⟩ **2** : doing or acting by force of habit ⟨*habitual* smokers⟩ **3** : done, followed, or used often or regularly ⟨took our *habitual* path⟩ **syn** see USUAL — **ha•bit•u•al•ly** \-ē\ *adv* — **ha•bit•u•al•ness** *n*

ha•bit•u•ate \hə-ˈbich-ə-ˌwāt, ha-\ *vt* : to make used to : ACCUSTOM

ha•bit•u•a•tion \-ˌbich-ə-ˈwā-shən\ *n* **1** : the act or process of habituating **2** : psychological dependence on a drug after a period of use — compare ADDICTION

hab•i•tude \ˈhab-ə-ˌtüd, -ˌtyüd\ *n* **1** : habitual disposition or mode of behavior or procedure **2** : CUSTOM 1b

ha•bi•tué \hə-ˈbich-ə-ˌwā, ha-\ *n* : one who frequents a place or type of place [French, from *habituer* "to frequent", derived from Latin *habitus* "habit"]

hab•i•tus \ˈhab-ət-əs\ *n, pl* **habitus** \-ət-əs, -ə-ˌtüs\ : bodily habit; *also* : HABIT 6 [Latin]

Habs•burg \ˈhaps-ˌbərg ˈhäps-, -ˌbu̇rg\ *variant of* HAPSBURG

ha•chure \ha-ˈshu̇r\ *n* : a short line used for shading and in representing surfaces in relief (as in map drawing) [French]

ha•ci•en•da \ˌhäs-ē-ˈen-də, ˌäs-\ *n* **1** : a large estate especially in a Spanish-speaking country : PLANTATION **2** : the main building of a farm or ranch [Spanish]

[1]**hack** \ˈhak\ *vb* **1 a** : to cut with repeated irregular or unskillful blows **b** : to sever with repeated blows : CHOP **2** : to cough in a short dry manner **3** : to manage successfully ⟨tried sales work but couldn't *hack* it⟩ [Old English *-haccian*] — **hack•er** *n*

[2]**hack** *n* **1** : an implement for hacking **2** : NICK 1, NOTCH **3** : a short dry cough **4** : a hacking blow

[3]**hack** *n* **1 a** (1) : a horse let out for common hire (2) : a horse used in all kinds of work **b** : a horse worn out in service **c** : a light easy saddle horse; *esp* : a saddle horse trained to walk, trot, and canter **2 a** : HACKNEY 2 **b** (1) : TAXICAB (2) : CABDRIVER **3** : one who gives up individual freedom of action or professional integrity in exchange for money or other reward; *esp* : a writer who works mainly for hire [short for *hackney*]

[4]**hack** *adj* **1** : working for hire **2** : done by or characteristic of a hack ⟨*hack* writing⟩ **3** : HACKNEYED, TRITE

[5]**hack** *vi* **1** : to ride or drive at an ordinary pace or over the roads as distinguished from racing or riding across country **2** : to operate a taxicab

hack•a•more \'hak-ə-,mōr, -,mȯr\ *n* : a bridle (as of rope) that controls by a slip noose about the nose or a loop about the lower jaw (as of a horse) [by folk etymology from Spanish *jaquima*]

hack•ber•ry \'hak-,ber-ē\ *n* : any of a genus of trees and shrubs of the elm family with small often edible berries; *also* : its wood [alteration of *hagberry,* a kind of cherry]

hack•ie \'hak-ē\ *n* : CABDRIVER

[1]**hack•le** \'hak-əl\ *n* **1** : a comb for dressing fibers (as flax or hemp) **2** : one of the long narrow feathers on the neck or lower back of a bird **3** *pl* **a** : hairs that can be raised to an erect position along the neck and back especially of a dog **b** : TEMPER 4d, DANDER [Middle English *hakell*]

[2]**hackle** *vt* **hack•led**; **hack•ling** \'hak-ling, -ə-ling\ : to chop up or chop off roughly : HACK [derived from [1]*hack*]

hack•man \'hak-mən\ *n* : CABDRIVER

hack•ma•tack \'hak-mə-,tak\ **1** : TAMARACK **2** : BALSAM POPLAR [of American Indian origin]

[1]**hack•ney** \'hak-nē\ *n, pl* **hack•neys 1 a** : a horse suitable for ordinary riding or driving **b** : any of a breed of rather compact English horses with a flashy high-stepping action while trotting **2** : a carriage or automobile kept for hire [Middle English *hackeney*]

[2]**hackney** *adj* **1** : kept for public hire **2** : HACKNEYED

[3]**hackney** *vt* **1** : to make common or frequent use of **2** : to make trite, vulgar, or commonplace

hack•neyed \'hak-nēd\ *adj* : lacking in freshness or originality ⟨a *hackneyed* expression⟩ **syn** see TRITE

hack•saw \'hak-,sȯ\ *n* : a fine-tooth saw with blade under tension in a bow-shaped frame for cutting hard materials (as metal)

hack•work \-,wərk\ *n* : literary, artistic, or professional work done on order usually according to formula and in conformity with commercial standards

had *past of* HAVE

had•dock \'had-ək\ *n, pl* **haddock** *also* **haddocks** : an important Atlantic food fish usually smaller than the related common cod [Middle English *haddok*]

ha•des \'hād-ēz, -,ēz\ *n, often cap* : HELL 1 [Greek *Haidēs,* god of the underworld, abode of the dead in Greek mythology]

hadn't \'had-nt\ : had not

hadst \hadst, 'hadst, hədst, ədst\ *archaic past 2d sing of* HAVE

hae \hā, 'hā\ *chiefly Scottish variant of* HAVE

haem- *or* **haemo-** — see HEM-

haemat- *or* **haemato-** — see HEMAT-

haf•ni•um \'haf-nē-əm\ *n* : a metallic chemical element that resembles zirconium chemically and is useful because of its ready emission of electrons — see ELEMENT table [New Latin, from *Hafnia* (Copenhagen), Denmark]

[1]**haft** \'haft\ *n* : the handle of a weapon or tool (as a sword or file) [Old English *hæft*]

[2]**haft** *vt* : to set in or furnish with a haft

haf•ta•rah *or* **haf•to•rah** \,häf-tə-'rä, häf-'tō-rə\ *n* : one of the biblical selections from the Books of the Prophets read at the conclusion of the Jewish synagogue service [Hebrew *haphṭārāh* "conclusion"]

hag \'hag\ *n* **1** : WITCH 1 **2** : an ugly, slatternly, or evil-looking old woman [Middle English *hagge*]

hag•fish \'hag-,fish\ *n* : an eellike fish related to the lampreys

Hag•ga•dah \hə-'gäd-ə, -'gōd-\ *n, pl* **Hag•ga•doth** \-'gäd-,ōt, -'gōd-, -,ōth\ **1** : ancient Jewish lore forming especially the nonlegal part of the Talmud **2** : the Jewish ritual for the seder [Hebrew *haggadhah*] — **hag•gad•ic** \-'gad-ik, -'gäd-, -'gōd-\ *adj, often cap*

Hag•gai \'hag-ē-,ī, 'hag-,ī\ *n — see* BIBLE table

hag•gard \'hag-ərd\ *adj* **1** : wild in appearance **2** : having a worn or emaciated look : GAUNT [Middle French *hagard*]

hag•gis \'hag-əs\ *n* : a pudding popular especially in Scotland made of the heart, liver, and lungs of a sheep or a calf minced with suet, onions, oatmeal, and seasonings and boiled in the stomach of the animal [Middle English *hagese*]

[1]**hag•gle** \'hag-əl\ *vb* **hag•gled**; **hag•gling** \'hag-ling, -ə-ling\ **1** : to cut roughly or clumsily : HACK **2** : to argue especially over a price [derived from Middle English *haggen* "to hew"] — **hag•gler** \-lər, -ə-lər\ *n*

[2]**haggle** *n* : an act or instance of haggling

Hag•i•og•ra•pha \,hag-ē-'äg-rə-fə, ,hā-jē-\ *n sing or pl* : the third part of the Jewish scriptures — compare LAW 3b, PROPHETS [Late Latin, from Late Greek, literally, "holy writings"]

hag•i•og•ra•phy \-fē\ *n* **1** : biography of saints or venerated persons **2** : idealizing or idolizing biography [Greek *hagios* "saint", from *hagios* "holy"] — **hag•i•og•ra•pher** \-fər\ *n*

hah *variant of* HA

ha–ha \hä-'hä, 'hä-\ *interj* — used to express amusement or derision [Old English *ha ha*]

[1]**hail** \'hāl\ *n* : precipitation in the form of small balls or lumps usually consisting of concentric layers of clear ice and compact snow **2** : something that gives the effect of falling hail ⟨a *hail* of bullets⟩ [Old English *hægl*]

[2]**hail** *vb* **1** : to precipitate hail **2** : to pour down like hail **3** : to hurl forcibly ⟨*hailed* curses on them⟩

[3]**hail** *interj* **1** — used to express acclamation **2** *archaic* — used as a greeting [Old Norse *heill,* from *heill* "healthy, hale"]

[4]**hail** *vb* **1 a** : SALUTE 1, GREET **b** : to greet with enthusiastic approval : ACCLAIM ⟨*hailed* the book as a masterpiece⟩ **2** : to greet or summon by calling ⟨*hail* a taxi⟩ **3** : to call out; *esp* : to call a greeting to a passing ship — **hail from** : to come from ⟨they *hail from* New York⟩

[5]**hail** *n* **1** : an exclamation of greeting or acclamation **2** : a calling to attract attention **3** : hearing distance ⟨stayed within *hail*⟩

hail–fel•low \'hāl-,fel-ō\ *or* **hail–fellow–well–met** \-,wel-'met\ *adj* : heartily informal [from the archaic salutation "Hail, fellow! Well met!"]

Hail Mary *n* : a Roman Catholic prayer to the Virgin Mary [translation of Medieval Latin *Ave, Maria*]

hail•stone \'hāl-,stōn\ *n* : a pellet of hail

hail•storm \-,stȯrm\ *n* : a storm accompanied by hail

hair \'haər, 'heər\ *n* **1 a** : a slender threadlike outgrowth of the epidermis of an animal; *esp* : one of the usually pigmented filaments that form the characteristic coat of a mammal **b** : the hairy covering of an animal or a body part **2** : HAIRCLOTH **3 a** : a minute distance or amount : TRIFLE ⟨won by a *hair*⟩ **b** : a precise degree : NICETY ⟨aligned to a *hair*⟩ **4** : a threadlike structure that resembles hair ⟨leaf *hairs*⟩ [Old English *hǣr*] — **haired** \'haərd, 'heərd\ *adj* — **hair•less** \'haər-ləs, 'heər-\ *adj* — **hair•like** \-,līk\ *adj*

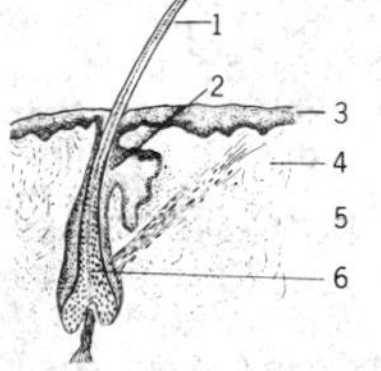

hair 1a: *1* shaft, *2* sebaceous gland, *3* epidermis, *4* dermis, *5* follicle, *6* root

[1]**hair•breadth** \'haər-,bredth, 'heər-\ *or* **hairs•breadth** \'haərz-, 'heərz-\ *n* : a very small distance or margin

[2]**hairbreadth** *adj* : very narrow : CLOSE ⟨a *hairbreadth* escape⟩

hair•brush \'haər-,brəsh, 'heər-\ *n* : a brush for the hair

hair cell *n* : a sensory cell (as of the organ of hearing) bearing hairlike processes

hair•cloth \-,klȯth\ *n* : any of various stiff wiry fabrics especially of horsehair or camel's hair used for upholstery or stiffening in garments

hair•cut \-,kət\ *n* : the act, process, or result of cutting and shaping the hair — **hair•cut•ter** \-,kət-ər\ *n* — **hair•cut•ting** \-,kət-ing\ *n*

hair•do \-,dü\ *n, pl* **hairdos** : a way of dressing a person's hair : COIFFURE

hair•dress•er \-,dres-ər\ *n* : one that dresses or cuts hair — **hair•dress•ing** \-,dres-ing\ *n*

hair follicle *n* : the tubular sheath surrounding the lower part of a hair shaft

hair•line \-,līn\ *n* **1** : a very slender line **2** : the line at which the hair meets the scalp ⟨a receding *hairline*⟩ — **hairline** *adj*

hair•pin \-,pin\ *n* **1** : a 2-pronged U-shaped pin to hold the hair in place **2** : something shaped like a hairpin; *esp* : a sharp turn in a road — **hairpin** *adj*

hair–rais•er \'haər-,rā-zər, 'heər-\ *n* : THRILLER

hair–rais•ing \-,rā-zing\ *adj* : causing terror, excitement, or astonishment ⟨a *hair-raising* adventure⟩ — **hair-rais·ing·ly** \-zing-lē\ *adv*

hair seal *n* : any of a family of seals with coarse hairy coats and no external ears — compare FUR SEAL

hair shirt *n* : a shirt made of rough animal hair worn next to the skin as a penance

hair·split·ter \'haər-,split-ər, 'heər-\ *n* : one that makes excessively fine distinctions in reasoning — **hair·split·ting** \-,split-ing\ *adj or n*

hair·spring \-,spring\ *n* : a slender spiraled spring that regulates the motion of the balance wheel of a timepiece

hair·streak \-,strēk\ *n* : any of various small usually dark butterflies with filaments projecting from the hind wings

hair trigger *n* : a trigger so adjusted as to permit a firearm to be fired by a very slight pressure

hair·worm \'haər-,wərm, 'heər-\ *n* : any of various very slender worms (as a horsehair worm)

hairy \'haər-ē, 'heər-\ *adj* **hair·i·er; -est 1** : bearing or covered with or as if with hair **2** : made of or resembling hair **3** : tending to cause nervous tension (as from danger, difficulty, or fear) ⟨a *hairy* experience⟩ — **hair·i·ness** *n*

hake \'hāk\ *n* : any of several marine food fishes related to the cod [Middle English]

hal- *or* **halo-** *combining form* **1** : salt ⟨*halo*phyte⟩ **2** : halogen ⟨*hal*ide⟩ [Greek *hals* "salt, sea"]

ha·la·kah \hä-'läk-ə, ,hä-lə-'kä\ *n, often cap* : the body of Jewish law supplementing the scriptural law and forming especially the legal part of the Talmud [Hebrew *hălākhāh*, literally, "way"] — **ha·lak·ic** \hə-'lak-ik, -'läk-\ *adj, often cap*

ha·la·tion \hā-'lā-shən\ *n* : the spreading (as in a developed photographic image) of light beyond its proper boundaries [*halo* + *-ation*]

hal·berd \'hal-bərd, 'hȯl-\ *or* **hal·bert** \-bərt\ *n* : a long-handled weapon used both as a spear and as a battle-ax especially in the 15th and 16th centuries [Middle French *hallebarde*] — **hal·berd·ier** \,hal-bər-'diər, ,hȯl-\ *n*

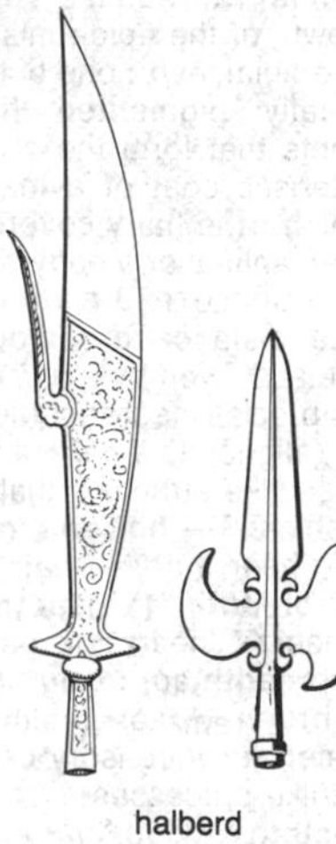
halberd

1hal·cy·on \'hal-sē-ən\ *n* **1** : a bird identified with the kingfisher and held in ancient legend to nest at sea about the time of the winter solstice and to calm the waves during incubation **2** : KINGFISHER [Latin, from Greek *halkyōn*]

2halcyon *adj* **1** : of or relating to the halcyon or its nesting period **2 a** : CALM 2, PEACEFUL **b** : HAPPY, GOLDEN ⟨the *halcyon* days of youth⟩

1hale \'hāl\ *adj* : free from defect, disease, or infirmity : SOUND, HEALTHY ⟨still *hale* at the age of 80⟩ [partly from Old English *hāl* "whole"; partly from Old Norse *heill*]

2hale *vt* **1** : HAUL 2a, PULL **2** : to compel to go ⟨*haled* them into court⟩ [Middle French *haler*]

1half \'haf, 'häf\ *n, pl* **halves** \'havz, 'hävz\ **1a** (1) : one of two equal parts into which a thing is divisible; *also* : a part of a thing approximately equal to the remainder (2) : a number which when multiplied by 2 is equal to a given number **b** : half an hour **2** : one of a pair: as **a** : PARTNER **b** : SEMESTER, TERM **c** : one of the two playing periods usually separated by an interval that together make up the playing time of various games [Old English *healf*] — **by half** : by a great deal — **by halves** : in part : HALFHEARTEDLY — **in half** : into two equal or nearly equal parts

2half *adj* **1 a** : being one of two equal parts **b** (1) : amounting to nearly half (2) : PARTIAL ⟨a *half* smile⟩ **2** : of half the usual size or extent — **half·ness** *n*

3half *adv* **1 a** : to the extent of half ⟨*half* full⟩ **b** : PARTIALLY ⟨*half* persuaded⟩ **2** : at all : by any means — used with preceding negative ⟨the song wasn't *half* bad⟩

half-and-half \,haf-ən-'haf, ,häf-ən-'häf\ *n* : something that is half one thing and half another: as **a** : a mixture of two malt beverages **b** : a mixture of cream and whole milk — **half-and-half** *adj or adv*

half·back \'haf-,bak, 'häf-\ *n* **1** : a football back who lines up on or near either flank **2** : a player stationed behind the forward line in field games (as soccer or field hockey)

half-baked \-'bākt\ *adj* **1** : imperfectly baked : UNDERDONE **2 a** : not well planned ⟨a *half-baked* scheme⟩ **b** : lacking judgment, intelligence, or common sense

half blood *n* : the relation of individuals with but one parent or parent strain in common; *also* : one related in the half blood — **half-blood·ed** \-'bləd-əd\ *adj*

half boot *n* : a boot with a top reaching above the ankle

half-breed \'haf-,brēd, 'häf-\ *n* : the offspring of parents of different races; *esp* : the offspring of an American Indian and a white person — **half-breed** *adj*

half brother *n* : a brother related through one parent only

half-caste \'haf-,kast, 'häf-\ *n* : a person of mixed racial descent : HALF-BREED — **half-caste** *adj*

half cock *n* **1** : the position of the hammer of a firearm when it is partly drawn back and locked in position so that it cannot be operated by a pull on the trigger **2** : a state of inadequate preparation or mental confusion — **half-cocked** \'haf-'käkt, 'häf-\ *adj*

half crown *n* : a former British coin worth two shillings and sixpence

half-dol·lar \'haf-'däl-ər, 'häf-\ *n* **1** : a coin representing one half of a dollar **2** : the sum of fifty cents

half eagle *n* : a 5-dollar gold piece issued by the United States 1795–1916 and in 1929

half-ev·er·green \'haf-'ev-ər-,grēn, 'häf-\ *adj* : tending to be evergreen in a mild climate but deciduous in a rigorous climate

half gainer *n* : a gainer in which the diver executes a half-backward somersault and enters the water headfirst and facing the board

half·heart·ed \'haf-'härt-əd, 'häf-\ *adj* : lacking spirit or interest — **half·heart·ed·ly** *adv* — **half·heart·ed·ness** *n*

half hitch *n* : a simple knot so made as to be easily unfastened

half hour *n* **1** : thirty minutes **2** : the middle point of an hour — **half-hour·ly** \'haf-'au̇r-lē, 'häf-\ *adv or adj*

half-knot \'haf-,nät, 'häf-\ *n* : a knot joining the ends of two cords and used in tying other knots

half-life \-,līf\ *n* : the time required for half of the atoms of a radioactive substance to disintegrate

half line *n* : a straight line extending from a point in one direction only

half-mast \'haf-'mast, 'häf-\ *n* : a point some distance but not necessarily halfway down below the top of a mast or staff or the peak of a gaff ⟨⟨flags flying at *half-mast*⟩

half-moon \-,mün\ *n* **1** : the moon when half its disk appears illuminated **2** : something shaped like a crescent **3** : the lunule of a fingernail

half note *n* : a musical note equal in value to one half of a whole note

half·pen·ny \'hāp-nē, -ə-nē, *United States also* 'haf-,pen-ē, 'häf-\ *n, pl* **half·pence** \'hā-pəns, *United States also* 'haf-,pens, 'häf-\ *or* **halfpennies 1** : a former British coin worth one half of a penny **2** : the sum of half a penny **3** : a small amount — **halfpenny** *adj*

half plane *n* : a part of a plane on one side of an indefinitely extended straight line drawn in the plane

half sister *n* : a sister related through one parent only

half-slip \'haf-,slip, 'häf-\ *n* : an underskirt with an elasticized waistband

half sole *n* : a shoe sole extending from the shank forward — **half-sole** \'haf-'sōl, 'häf-\ *vt*

half sovereign *n* : a former British gold coin worth 10 shillings

half-staff \'haf-'staf, 'häf-\ *n* : HALF-MAST

half step *n* : the pitch interval between any two adjacent tones on a keyboard instrument — called also *semitone*

half-tim·ber \'haf-'tim-bər, 'häf-\ *or* **half-tim·bered** \-bərd\ *adj* : constructed of wood framing with spaces filled with masonry ⟨a *half-timbered* house⟩

half·time \-,tīm\ *n* : an intermission marking the completion of half of a game

half·tone \-,tōn\ *n* **1** : HALF STEP **2 a** : any of the shades of gray between the darkest and the lightest parts of a photographic image **b** : a photoengraving made from an image photographed through a screen so that the details of the image are reproduced in dots

half-track \-,trak\ *n* **1** : one of the endless-chain tracks used in place of rear wheels on a heavy-duty vehicle **2** : a motor vehicle propelled by half-tracks; *esp* : such a vehicle lightly armored for military use — **half-track** *or* **half-tracked** \-ˌtrakt\ *adj*

half-truth \-ˌtrüth\ *n* : a statement that is only partially true; *esp* : one that mingles truth and falsehood with deliberate intent to deceive

half•way \-ˈwā\ *adj* **1** : midway between two points ⟨stop at the *halfway* mark⟩ **2** : PARTIAL 3 ⟨*halfway* measures⟩ — **halfway** *adv*

half-wit \-ˌwit\ *n* : a foolish or imbecilic person — **half-wit•ted** \-ˈwit-əd\ *adj*

hal•i•but \ˈhal-ə-bət, ˈhäl-\ *n, pl* **halibut** *also* **halibuts** : a marine food fish that is the largest flatfish of both the Atlantic and Pacific oceans [Middle English *halybutte,* from *haly* "holy" + *butte* "flatfish"; from its being eaten on holy days]

ha•lide \ˈhal-ˌīd, ˈhā-ˌlīd\ *n* : a compound of a halogen with another element or a radical

hal•i•dom \ˈhal-əd-əm\ *or* **hal•i•dome** \-ə-ˌdōm\ *n, archaic* : a holy place or relic [Old English *hāligdōm,* from *hālig* "holy"]

ha•lite \ˈhal-ˌīt, ˈhā-ˌlīt\ *n* : native salt : ROCK SALT

hal•i•to•sis \ˌhal-ə-ˈtō-səs\ *n* : a condition of having breath with an offensive odor [Latin *halitus* "breath", from *halare* "to breathe"]

hall \ˈhȯl\ *n* **1 a** : a large or imposing residence; *esp* : MANOR HOUSE **b** : a large building used for public purposes ⟨city *hall*⟩ **c** : one of the buildings of a college or university set apart for a special purpose ⟨Science *Hall*⟩ ⟨residence *halls*⟩ **d** : a college or a division of a college at some universities **e** : the common dining room of an English college **2** : the chief living room in a medieval castle **3 a** : the entrance room of a building : LOBBY **b** : a corridor or passage in a building **4** : a large room for assembly : AUDITORIUM **5** : a place used for public entertainment [Old English *heall*]

Hal•lel \hä-ˈlāl\ *n* : a selection comprising Psalms 113–118 chanted during a Jewish feast (as the Passover) [Hebrew *hallēl* "praise"]

1hal•le•lu•jah \ˌhal-ə-ˈlü-yə\ *interj* — used to express praise, joy, or thanks [Hebrew *hallĕlūyāh* "praise ye the Lord"]

2hallelujah *n* : a shout or song of praise or thanksgiving

halliard *variant of* HALYARD

1hall•mark \ˈhȯl-ˌmärk\ *n* **1 a** : an official mark stamped on gold and silver articles in England to attest their purity **b** : a mark placed on an article to indicate origin, purity, or genuineness **2** : a distinguishing characteristic or feature [Goldsmiths' *Hall,* London, England, where gold and silver articles were assayed and stamped]

2hallmark *vt* : to stamp with a hallmark

hal•lo \hə-ˈlō, ha-\ *or* **hal•loo** \-ˈlü\ *variant of* HOLLO

Hall of Fame 1 : a structure housing memorials to famous individuals **2** : a group of individuals selected as particularly distinguished in a field or category (as a sport) — **Hall of Fam•er**

hal•low \ˈhal-ō\ *vt* **1** : to make holy or set apart for holy use **2** : to respect greatly [Old English *hālgian,* from *hālig* "holy"]

hal•lowed \ˈhal-ōd, -əd, *in the Lord's Prayer also* ˈhal-ə-wəd\ *adj* : SACRED ⟨*hallowed* traditions⟩

Hal•low•een \ˌhal-ə-ˈwēn, ˌhäl-\ *n* : October 31 observed with merrymaking and the playing of pranks by children during the evening [short for *All Hallow even,* the eve of All Saints' Day]

Hal•low•mas \ˈhal-ō-ˌmas, -məs\ *n* : ALL SAINTS' DAY

hal•lu•ci•na•tion \hə-ˌlüs-n-ˈā-shən\ *n* : the perceiving of objects or the experiencing of feelings that have no cause outside one's mind especially as the result of a mental disorder or as the effect of a drug; *also* : something so perceived or experienced [Latin *hallucinatio,* from *hallucinari* "to wander in mind"] — **hal•lu•ci•nate** \-ˈlüs-n-ˌāt\ *vb* — **hal•lu•ci•na•to•ry** \-ˈlüs-n-ə-ˌtōr-ē, -ˌtȯr-\ *adj*

hal•lu•ci•no•gen \hə-ˈlüs-n-ə-jən\ *n* : a substance (as LSD) that induces hallucinations — **hal•lu•ci•no•gen•ic** \-ˌlüs-n-ə-ˈjen-ik\ *adj*

hal•lux \ˈhal-əks\ *n, pl* **hal•lu•ces** \ˈhal-ə-ˌsēz, -yə-\ : BIG TOE [Latin]

hall•way \ˈhȯl-ˌwā\ *n* **1** : an entrance hall **2** : CORRIDOR 1

1ha•lo \ˈhā-lō\ *n, pl* **halos** *or* **haloes 1** : a circle of light around the sun or moon caused by the presence of tiny ice crystals in the air **2** : something resembling a halo: as **a** : NIMBUS 1, 2 **b** : a differentiated zone surrounding a central object **3** : the glory surrounding an idealized person or thing [Latin *halos,* from Greek *halōs* "threshing floor, disk, halo"]

2halo *vt* : to form into or surround with a halo

halo- — see HAL-

hal•o•gen \ˈhal-ə-jən\ *n* : any of the five elements fluorine, chlorine, bromine, iodine, and astatine existing in the free state normally as diatomic molecules

hal•o•ge•ton \ˌhal-ə-ˈjē-ˌtän\ *n* : a coarse annual herb related to the goosefoots that is a noxious weed in western North America [*hal-* + Greek *geitōn* "neighbor"]

hal•o•phyte \ˈhal-ə-ˌfīt\ *n* : a plant that thrives in salty soil — **hal•o•phyt•ic** \ˌhal-ə-ˈfit-ik\ *adj*

1halt \ˈhȯlt\ *adj* : LAME [Old English *healt*]

2halt *vi* **1** : to walk or proceed lamely : LIMP **2** : to stand in perplexity or doubt between alternate courses **3** : to display weakness or fault

3halt *n* : STOP ⟨call a *halt*⟩ [German, derived from Old High German *haltan* "to hold"]

4halt *vb* **1** : to cease marching or journeying **2** : to bring or come to a stop : END

1hal•ter \ˈhȯl-tər\ *n* **1 a** : a rope or strap for leading or tying an animal **b** : a headstall to which a lead may be attached **2** : a rope for hanging criminals : NOOSE **3** : a woman's blouse that is typically held in place by straps around the neck and across the back and leaves the back, arms, and midriff bare [Old English *hælftre*]

2halter *vt* **hal•tered**; **hal•ter•ing** \-tə-ring, -tring\ **1** : to catch with or as if with a halter; *also* : to put a halter on **2** : RESTRAIN 1, HAMPER

hal•tere \ˈhȯl-ˌtiər, ˈhal-\ *also* **hal•ter** \-tər\ *n, pl* **hal•teres** \-ˌtiərz; hȯl-ˈtir-ēz, hal-\ : one of a pair of club-shaped organs that are the modified second pair of wings of a two-winged fly and serve to maintain balance in flight [Latin *halter* "jumping weight", from Greek *haltēr,* from *hallesthai* "to jump"]

halt•ing \ˈhȯl-ting\ *adj* **1** : marked by a limp **2** : UNCERTAIN, FALTERING ⟨the witness spoke in a *halting* manner⟩ — **halt•ing•ly** \-ting-lē\ *adv*

hal•vah *or* **hal•va** \häl-ˈvä, ˈhäl-ˌvä, -və\ *n* : a flaky candy made of crushed sesame seeds in a base of syrup (as of honey) [Yiddish *halva,* derived from Arabic *ḥalwā* "sweetmeat"]

halve \ˈhav, ˈhȧv\ *vt* **1 a** : to divide into two equal parts **b** : to reduce to one half ⟨*halving* the cost⟩ **c** : to share equally **2** : to play (a hole) in the same number of strokes as one's opponent at golf

halv•ers \ˈhav-ərz, ˈhȧv-\ *n pl* : half shares : HALVES

halves *pl of* HALF

hal•yard *or* **hal•liard** \ˈhal-yərd\ *n* : a rope or tackle for hoisting and lowering [Middle English *halier,* from *halen* "to pull, haul"]

1ham \ˈham\ *n* **1** : a buttock with its associated thigh — usually used in pl. **2** : a cut of meat consisting of a thigh; *esp* : one from a hog **3 a** : an unskillful but showy performer **b** : an operator of an amateur radio station [Old English *hamm* "hollow of the knee"; sense 3 short for *hamfatter,* from "The *Ham-Fat* Man," minstrel song] — **ham** *adj*

2ham *vb* **hammed**; **ham•ming** : to execute with exaggerated speech or gestures : OVERACT

hama•dry•ad \ˌham-ə-ˈdrī-əd, -ˌad\ *n* : WOOD NYMPH [Latin *hamadryas,* from Greek, from *hama* "together with" + *dryas* "dryad"]

ham•burg•er \ˈham-ˌbər-gər\ *or* **ham•burg** \-ˌbərg\ *n* **1 a** : ground beef **b** : a cooked patty of ground beef **2** : a sandwich consisting of a patty of hamburger in a split round bun [German *Hamburger* "of Hamburg"]

hame \ˈhām\ *n* : one of two curved supports which are attached to the collar of a draft horse and to which the traces are fastened [Middle English]

Ham•ite \ˈham-ˌīt\ *n* : a member of a mainly Caucasoid group of chiefly northern African peoples [*Ham,* son of Noah, their supposed ancestor]

Ham•it•ic \ha-ˈmit-ik, hə-\ *adj* : of, relating to, or characteristic of the Hamites or one of the Hamitic languages

Hamitic languages *n pl* : the Berber, Cushitic, and sometimes Egyptian branches of the Afro-Asiatic languages

\ə\ **abut**	\au̇\ **out**	\i\ **tip**	\ȯ\ **saw**	\u̇\ **foot**
\ər\ **further**	\ch\ **chin**	\ī\ **life**	\ȯi\ **coin**	\y\ **yet**
\a\ **mat**	\e\ **pet**	\j\ **job**	\th\ **thin**	\yü\ **few**
\ā\ **take**	\ē\ **easy**	\ng\ **sing**	\t͟h\ **this**	\yu̇\ **cure**
\ä\ **cot, cart**	\g\ **go**	\ō\ **bone**	\ü\ **food**	\zh\ **vision**

ham•let \'ham-lət\ *n* : a small group of houses in a rural area [Middle French *hamelet*, from *ham* "village", of Germanic origin]

¹ham•mer \'ham-ər\ *n* **1 a :** a hand tool that consists of a solid head set crosswise on a handle and is used for pounding (as in driving nails) **b :** a power tool that substitutes a metal block or a drill for the head for pounding (as in driving posts or breaking rock) **2 :** something that resembles a hammer in shape or action: as **a :** an implement consisting of a handle or lever and a striking head used to sound a musical instrument (as a bell, the strings of a piano, or a xylophone) **b :** the part of a gun whose striking action causes explosion of the charge **3 :** MALLEUS **4 :** a metal sphere weighing about 7.26 kilograms that is attached to a wire handle and is hurled in an athletic event [Old English *hamor*]

²hammer *vb* **ham•mered**; **ham•mer•ing** \'ham-ring, -ə-ring\ **1 :** to strike blows especially repeatedly with or as if with a hammer : POUND **2 a :** to make repeated efforts **b :** to emphasize (as an opinion) by repetition **3 a :** to beat, drive, or shape with repeated blows of a hammer **b :** to fasten or build with a hammer **4 :** to produce or bring about as if by repeated blows ⟨*hammer* out a policy⟩

hammer and sickle *n* : an emblem consisting of a crossed hammer and sickle used chiefly as a symbol of Soviet Communism

hammer and tongs *adv* : with great force and violence

ham•mered *adj* : having surface indentations produced or appearing to have been produced by hammering

ham•mer•head \'ham-ər-,hed\ *n* **1 :** the striking part of a hammer **2 :** BLOCKHEAD **3 :** any of several sharks with the eyes on lateral extensions of the flat head

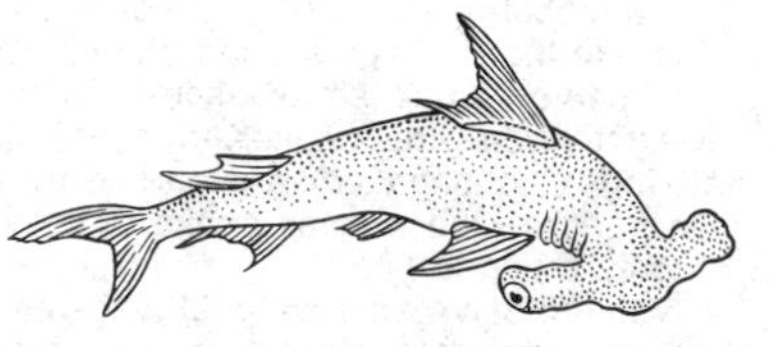

hammerhead 3

ham•mer•lock \-,läk\ *n* : a wrestling hold in which an opponent's arm is held bent behind the back

ham•mer•toe \-,tō\ *n* : a toe and especially the second deformed by having the end part permanently bent

¹ham•mock \'ham-ək\ *n* : a swinging couch or bed usually made of netting or canvas and slung by cords from supports at each end [Spanish *hamaca*, of American Indian origin]

²hammock *n* : HUMMOCK 1 [origin unknown]

ham•my \'ham-ē\ *adj* **ham•mi•er**; **-est** : characteristic of a ham actor

¹ham•per \'ham-pər\ *vt* **ham•pered**; **ham•per•ing** \-pə-ring, -pring\ **1 :** to restrict or interfere with the movement or operation of ⟨fog *hampered* the traffic⟩ **2 :** to interfere with : ENCUMBER [Middle English *hamperen*]
• **syn** FETTER, SHACKLE, MANACLE: HAMPER may imply the effect of any hindering or restraining influence; FETTER suggests a restraining so severe that freedom to move or progress is almost lost; SHACKLE and MANACLE are still stronger and suggest total loss of freedom to act or to move from one position.

²hamper *n* : a large basket usually with a cover ⟨a clothes *hamper*⟩ [Middle French *hanapier* "case to hold goblets", from *hanap* "goblet", of Germanic origin]

ham•ster \'ham-stər, 'hamp-\ *n* : any of various stocky short-tailed Old World rodents with large cheek pouches [German, of Slavic origin]

¹ham•string \'ham-,string\ *n* **1 a :** either of two groups of tendons at the back of the human knee **b :** HAMSTRING MUSCLE **2 :** a large tendon above and behind the hock of a four-footed animal

²hamstring *vt* **-strung** \-,strəng\; **-string•ing** \-,string-ing\ **1 :** to cripple by cutting the leg tendons **2 :** to make ineffective or powerless : CRIPPLE

hamstring muscle *n* : any of three muscles at the back of the thigh that function to extend the thigh when the leg is flexed

Han \'hän\ *n* : a Chinese dynasty dated 207B.C.–A.D.220 and marked by centralized bureaucratic control, a revival of learning, and the penetration of Buddhism

¹hand \'hand\ *n* **1 a :** the free end part of the forelimb when modified (as in man) for handling, grasping, and holding **b :** any of various anatomical parts (as the hind foot of an ape or the chela of a crab) that are like the hand in origin or function **2 :** something resembling a hand: as **a :** an indicator or pointer on a dial **b :** a figure of a hand with forefinger extended to point a direction or call attention to something **c :** a cluster of bananas developed from a single flower group **3 :** personal possession : CONTROL ⟨in the *hands* of the enemy⟩ **4 a :** SIDE, DIRECTION ⟨fighting on either *hand*⟩ **b :** a side or aspect of an issue or argument ⟨on the one *hand*. . . on the other *hand*⟩ **5 :** a pledge especially of marriage **6 a :** style of penmanship : HANDWRITING **b :** SIGNATURE ⟨some legal orders require a judge's *hand*⟩ **7 a :** SKILL, ABILITY ⟨try one's *hand* at chess⟩ **b :** a part or share in doing something ⟨take a *hand* in the work⟩ **c :** ASSISTANCE, AID ⟨lend a *hand*⟩ **8 :** SOURCE ⟨learn at first *hand*⟩ **9 :** a unit of measure equal to 10.16 centimeters used especially for the height of horses **10 :** a round of applause **11 a** (1) **:** a player in a card game or board game (2) **:** the cards or pieces held by a player **b :** a single round in a game **12 a :** one who performs or executes a particular work ⟨two portraits by the same *hand*⟩ **b :** a hired worker : LABORER **c :** a member of a ship's crew ⟨all *hands* on deck⟩ **d :** one skilled in a particular activity or field **13 a :** HANDIWORK 1 **b :** style of execution : WORKMANSHIP ⟨the *hand* of a master⟩ **c :** the touch or feel of something [Old English] — **at hand :** near in time or place — **by hand :** with the hands — **in hand 1 :** in one's possession or control **2 :** in preparation — **off one's hands :** out of one's care or charge — **on all hands** *or* **on every hand :** EVERYWHERE — **on hand 1 :** in present possession ⟨goods *on hand*⟩ **2 :** about to appear **3 :** in attendence : PRESENT — **out of hand 1 :** without delay : FORTHWITH **2 :** done with **3 :** out of control — **to hand 1 :** into possession **2 :** within reach **3 :** into control or subjection

²hand *vt* **1 :** to lead, guide, or assist with the hand : CONDUCT **2 a :** to give or pass with the hand ⟨*hand* a person a letter⟩ **b :** PRESENT, PROVIDE ⟨*handed* them a surprise⟩

hand and foot *adv* : TOTALLY 1, COMPLETELY ⟨waited on them *hand and foot*⟩

hand ax *n* : a prehistoric stone tool having one end pointed for cutting and the other end rounded for holding in the hand

hand•bag \'hand-,bag, 'han-\ *n* **1 :** TRAVELING BAG **2 :** a bag for carrying small personal articles and money

hand•ball \-,bȯl\ *n* : a game played in a walled court or against a single wall or board by two or four players who use their hands to strike a small rubber ball; *also* : the ball used in this game

hand•bar•row \-,bar-ō\ *n* : a flat rectangular frame with handles at both ends that is carried by two persons

hand•bill \-,bil\ *n* : a small printed sheet to be distributed by hand

hand•book \-,bu̇k\ *n* : a small book of facts or useful information usually about a particular subject : MANUAL

hand•breadth \-,bredth\ *or* **hands•breadth** \'hanz-\ *n* : any of various units of length based on the breadth of a hand varying from about 6 to 10 centimeters

hand•car \'hand-,kär, 'han-\ *n* : a small four-wheeled railroad car propelled by a hand-operated mechanism or by a small motor

hand•cart \-,kärt\ *n* : a cart drawn or pushed by hand

hand•clasp \-,klasp\ *n* : HANDSHAKE

¹hand•craft \-,kraft\ *n* : HANDICRAFT

²handcraft *vt* : to fashion by handicraft

¹hand•cuff \-,kəf\ *vt* : to apply handcuffs to : MANACLE

²handcuff *n* : a metal fastening that can be locked around a wrist and that is usually connected by a chain or bar with another handcuff

hand down *vt* **1 :** to transmit in succession ⟨*handed down* from generation to generation⟩ **2 :** to make official formulation of and express (the opinion of a court)

hand•ed \'han-dəd\ *adj* : having or using such or so many hands ⟨a right-*handed* person⟩ — **hand•ed•ness** n

hand•ful \'hand-,fu̇l,'han-\ *n, pl* **handfuls** \-,fu̇lz\ *or* **handsful** \'hanz-,fu̇l\ **1 :** as much as or as many as the hand will grasp **2 :** a small quantity or number **3 :** as much as one can control or manage

hand•glass *n* : a small mirror with a handle

hand•grip \'hand-,grip,'han-\ *n* **1 :** a grasping with the hand **2 :** HANDLE 1

hand•gun \'hand-,gən,'han-\ *n* : a firearm held and fired with one hand

hand•hold \'hand-ˌhōld\ *n* **1** : GRIP 1a **2** : HOLD 5

[1]**hand•i•cap** \'han-di-ˌkap\ *n* **1 a** : a race or contest in which an artificial advantage is given to or disadvantage imposed on a contestant to equalize chances of winning **b** : the advantage given or disadvantage imposed **2** : a disadvantage that makes progress or success more difficult [obsolete *handicap,* a game in which forfeits were held in a cap, from *hand in cap*]

△ **origin** *Handicap,* from *hand in cap,* was an old form of barter. Two people who wished to make an exchange asked a third to act as umpire. All three put forfeit money in a cap, into which each of the two barterers put a hand. The umpire described the goods to be traded and set the additional amount the owner of the inferior article should pay the other in order that the exchange might be fair. The barterers withdrew their hands from the cap empty to signify refusal of the umpire's decision, or full to indicate acceptance. If both hands were full, the exchange was made and the umpire pocketed the forfeit money. If both were empty, the umpire took the money but there was no exchange. Otherwise, each barterer kept his own property, and the one who had accepted the umpire's decision took the forfeit money as well. Later, horse races arranged in accordance with the rules of *handicap* were called *handicap races.* The umpire decided how much extra weight the better horse should carry. The term was eventually extended to other contests, and the advantage or disadvantage imposed was called *handicap.*

[2]**handicap** *vt* **-capped**; **-cap•ping 1 a** : to give a handicap to **b** : to assign handicaps to **2** : to put at a disadvantage

hand•i•craft \'han-di-ˌkraft\ *n* **1** : an occupation (as weaving or pottery making) requiring skill with the hands **2** : articles fashioned by those engaged in handicraft [alteration of *handcraft*] — **hand•i•craft•er** \-ˌkraf-tər\ *n* — **hand•i•crafts•man** \-ˌkrafs-mən\ *n*

hand•i•ly \'han-də-lē\ *adv* : in a handy manner : EASILY, CONVENIENTLY

hand•i•ness \-dē-nəs\ *n* : the quality or state of being handy

hand in glove *or* **hand and glove** *adv* : in extremely close relationship or agreement

hand in hand *adv* **1** : with one's hand clasping another's hand **2** : in close association

hand•i•work \'han-di-ˌwərk\ *n* : work done by the hands or personally ⟨showed the *handiwork* of a master criminal⟩ [Old English *handgeweorc,* from *hand* + *geweorc* "work", from *ge-,* collective prefix + *weorc* "work"]

hand•ker•chief \'hang-kər-chəf, -ˌchif, -ˌchēf\ *n, pl* **-chiefs** *also* **-chieves** \-chəfs, -ˌchifs, ˌchēvz (*used by many who have sing.* -chəf *or* -ˌchif), -ˌchēfs, -ˌchəvz, -ˌchivz\ **1** : a small piece of cloth used especially for wiping the face, nose, or eyes **2** : KERCHIEF 1

hand language *n* : communication by means of a manual alphabet

[1]**han•dle** \'han-dl\ *n* **1** : a part that is designed especially to be grasped by the hand **2** : something that resembles a handle **3** *slang* : NAME [Old English] — **han•dled** \-dld\ *adj* — **off the handle** : into a state of sudden and violent anger

[2]**handle** *vb* **han•dled**; **han•dling** \-dling, -dl-ing\ **1 a** : to affect with the hand (as by touching or feeling) **b** : to manage with the hands ⟨*handle* a horse⟩ **2 a** : to deal with in writing or speaking or in the plastic arts **b** : CONTROL, DIRECT ⟨a lawyer *handles* my affairs⟩ **c** : to train and act as second for (a prizefighter) **3** : to deal with or act on ⟨*handle* a problem⟩ **4** : to deal or trade in ⟨a store that *handles* rugs⟩ **5** : to act, behave, or feel in a certain way when managed or directed ⟨a car that *handles* well⟩ [Old English *handlian*]

han•dle•able \'han-dl-ə-bəl\ *adj* : capable of being handled

handlebar mustache *n* : a heavy mustache with long sections that curve upward at each end

han•dle•bars \'han-dl-ˌbärz\ *n pl* : a straight or bent bar with a handle (as for steering a bicycle) at each end

hand lens *n* : a magnifying glass to be held in the hands

han•dler \'han-dlər, -dl-ər\ *n* **1** : one that handles **2** : one that helps to train a prizefighter or acts as his second during a match

hand•made \'hand-'mād, 'han-\ *adj* : made by hand and not by machine

hand•maid \-ˌmād\ *or* **hand•maid•en** \-ˌmād-n\ *n* : a female servant or attendant

hand–me–down \'hand-mē-ˌdaůn,'han-\ *adj* : worn or put in use by one person or group after being discarded by another — **hand–me–down** *n*

hand•off \'han-ˌdöf\ *n* : a football play in which the ball is handed by one player to another nearby

hand on *vt* : to pass along in succession : hand down

hand organ *n* : a barrel organ operated by a hand crank

hand•out \'han-ˌdaůt\ *n* **1** : a portion of food, clothing, or money given to or as if to a beggar **2** : an information sheet for free distribution **3** : a prepared statement released to the press

hand over *vt* : to give up possession or control of

hand•pick \'hand-'pik, 'han-\ *vt* : to select personally

hand•rail \'han-ˌdrāl\ *n* : a narrow rail for grasping with the hand as a support (as on a staircase)

hand•saw \'hand-ˌsȯ, 'han-\ *n* : a saw used with one hand; *esp* : a woodworker's ripsaw or crosscut saw

hands•breadth \'handz-ˌbredth\ *variant of* HANDBREADTH

hands down *adv* : without question : EASILY

hand•sel \'han-səl\ *n* **1** : a gift made as a token of good wishes or luck especially at the beginning of a new year **2** : [3]EARNEST, FORETASTE [Middle English *hansell*]

hand•set \'hand-ˌset, han-\ *n* : a combined telephone transmitter and receiver mounted on a handle

hand•shake \-ˌshāk\ *n* : a clasping (as in greeting or farewell) of right hands by two people

hands–off \'han-'zȯf\ *adj* : marked by noninterference

hand•some \'han-səm\ *adj* **1** : fairly large : SIZABLE ⟨a *handsome* fortune⟩ **2** : marked by graciousness or generosity ⟨a *handsome* tribute⟩ **3** : having a pleasing and often impressive or dignified appearance ⟨a *handsome* young lad⟩ ⟨a *handsome* building⟩ [Middle English *handsom* "easy to manipulate"] — **hand•some•ly** adv — **hand•some•ness** n

hand•spike \'han-ˌspīk\ *n* : a bar used as a lever (as in working a windlass on a boat) [by folk etymology from Dutch *handspaak,* from *hand* "hand" + *spaak* "pole"]

hand•spring \-ˌspring\ *n* : a tumbling feat in which the body turns forward or backward in a full circle from a standing position and lands first on the hands and then on the feet

hand•stand \-ˌstand\ *n* : an act of balancing the body on the hands with the trunk and legs in the air

hand–to–hand \ˌhan-tə-ˌhand, -də-\ *adj* : involving physical contact — **hand to hand** \-'hand\ *adv*

hand–to–mouth \-tə-'maůth\ *adj* : having or providing nothing to spare ⟨a *hand-to-mouth* existence⟩

hand•wheel \'hand-ˌhwēl, 'han-, -ˌwēl\ *n* : a wheel worked by hand

hand•work \'han-ˌdwərk\ *n* : work done with the hands and not by machine

hand•wo•ven \'han-'dwō-vən\ *adj* : produced on a hand-operated loom

hand•writ•ing \'han-ˌdrīt-ing\ *n* **1** : writing done by hand; *esp* : the cast or form of writing peculiar to a particular person **2** : something written by hand : MANUSCRIPT — **hand•writ•ten** \-ˌdrit-n\ *adj*

handy \'han-dē\ *adj* **hand•i•er**; **-est 1 a** : conveniently near **b** : convenient for use ⟨a *handy* reference book⟩ **c** : easily handled ⟨a *handy* sloop⟩ **2** : clever in using the hands : DEXTEROUS ⟨*handy* with a needle⟩

handy•man \-dē-ˌman\ *n* : a person who does odd jobs

[1]**hang** \'hang\ *vb* **hung** \'həng\ *also* **hanged** \'hangd\; **hang•ing** \'hang-ing\ **1 a** : to fasten or be fastened to some elevated point without support from below **b** : to put to death or be put to death by hanging from a rope tied round the neck ⟨sentenced to be *hanged*⟩ **c** : to fasten so as to allow free motion upon a point of suspension ⟨*hang* a door⟩ **d** : to adjust the hem of (a skirt) so as to hang evenly and at a proper height when worn **2** : to cover, decorate, or furnish by hanging pictures, trophies, or drapery **3** : to hold or bear in a suspended or inclined manner : DROOP ⟨*hang* your head in shame⟩ **4** : to fasten to a wall ⟨*hang* wallpaper⟩ **5** : to display (pictures) in a gallery **6** : to remain poised or stationary in the air ⟨clouds *hanging* low overhead⟩ **7** : to stay with persistence **8** : to hover threateningly ⟨evils *hang* over the nation⟩ **9** : DEPEND ⟨(election *hangs* on one vote⟩ **10 a** : to take hold for support : CLING ⟨*hang* on my arm⟩ **b** : to be burdensome or oppressive ⟨time *hung* on our hands⟩ **11** : to be in suspense : suffer delay ⟨the

decision is still *hanging*⟩ **12 :** to lean, incline, or jut over or downward **13 :** to be in a state of close attention ⟨*hung* on their every word⟩ **14 :** to fit or fall from the figure in easy lines ⟨the coat *hangs* loosely⟩ [Old English *hōn* (v.t.) and *hanglan* (v.i. and v.t.)] — **hang•able** \'hang-ə-bəl\ *adj*
— **hang together 1 :** to remain united : stand by one another **2 :** to form a consistent or coherent whole
²hang *n* **1 :** the manner in which a thing hangs ⟨the *hang* of a skirt⟩ **2 a :** peculiar and significant meaning ⟨the *hang* of an argument⟩ **b :** the special method of doing, using, or dealing with something : KNACK ⟨get the *hang* of driving a car⟩
¹hang•ar \'hang-ər, 'hang-gər\ *n* **:** SHELTER, SHED; *esp* **:** a covered and usually enclosed area for housing and repairing aircraft [French]
²hangar *vt* **:** to place in a hangar
hang around *vb* **1 :** to pass time or stay aimlessly : loiter idly ⟨*hang around* the park⟩ **2 :** to spend one's time in company
hang back *vi* **1 :** to lag behind others **2 :** to be reluctant : HESITATE
hang•dog \'hang-,dȯg\ *adj* **1 :** ASHAMED 1, GUILTY ⟨a *hangdog* look⟩ **2 :** ABJECT 3, COWED
hang•er \'hang-ər\ *n* **1 :** one that hangs or causes to be hung or hanged **2 :** a device by which or to which something is hung or hangs; *esp* **:** a device for hanging a garment from a hook or rod
hang•er–on \'hang-ər-,ȯn, -,än\ *n, pl* **hangers–on :** one that hangs around a person, place, or institution in hope of personal gain
hang glider *n* **:** a small glider made usually in the form of a kite from which a person hangs in soaring — **hang gliding** *n*

hang glider

¹hang•ing \'hang-ing\ *n* **1 :** an execution by strangling or breaking the neck by a suspended noose **2 :** something hung (as a curtain or tapestry) — usually used in pl. **3 :** a downward slope
²hanging *adj* **1 :** situated or lying on steeply sloping ground ⟨*hanging* gardens⟩ **2 a :** jutting out or over **b :** supported only by the wall on one side ⟨a *hanging* staircase⟩ **3 :** adapted for sustaining a hanging object **4 :** punishable by death by hanging ⟨a *hanging* offense⟩
hang•man \'hang-mən\ *n* **:** a person who hangs condemned criminals
hang•nail \-,nāl\ *n* **:** a bit of skin hanging loose at the side or base of a fingernail [by folk etymology from earlier *agnail,* from Old English *angnægl* "corn on the foot or toe"]
△ **origin** Old English *angnægl* meant "a corn on the foot". The second element of the word, *-nægl,* meant "nail", but it referred to an iron nail rather than to a toenail or fingernail. A hard corn was likened to the head of a nail. The first element, *ang-,* is related to Old English *ange,* "painful". Over the centuries *angnægl* became *agnail* and was used for a variety of ailments of the fingers or toes. This usage led to the belief that the *-nail* of *agnail* meant "toenail" or "fingernail". By then the adjective *ange* was obsolete, and the first element of *agnail* was not easy to interpret. So the compound was transformed to make sense to ordinary speakers of the language. The new form, *hangnail,* was used specifically for a bit of loose skin at the base of a fingernail.
hang on *vi* **1 :** to keep hold : hold onto something **2 :** to persist stubbornly ⟨a cold that *hung on* all spring⟩ — **hang on to :** to hold, grip, or keep persistently ⟨learn to *hang on to* your money⟩
hang•out \'hang-,au̇t\ *n* **:** a favorite or usual meeting place
hang out \'hang-'au̇t, hang-\ *vi* **:** to habitually spend one's time idly ⟨*hangs out* in poolrooms⟩
hang•over \'hang-,ō-vər\ *n* **1 :** something (as a surviving custom) that remains from what is past **2 :** disagreeable aftereffects following great excitement or excess (as in consumption of alcohol)
hang–up \'hang-,əp\ *n* **:** a source of mental or emotional difficulty
hang up \'hang-'əp, hang-\ *vb* **1 a :** to place on a hook or hanger ⟨*hang up* your coat⟩ **b :** to replace (a telephone receiver) on the cradle so that the connection is broken; *also* **:** to terminate a telephone conversation **2 :** to snag or cause to snag so as to be immovable ⟨the ship *hung up* on a sandbar⟩
hank \'hangk\ *n* **:** SKEIN [Middle English, of Scandinavian origin]
han•ker \'hang-kər\ *vi* **han•kered; han•ker•ing** \-kə-ring, -kring\ **:** to have an eager or persistent desire ⟨*hanker* after fame and fortune⟩ [probably from Flemish *hankeren,* from *hangen* "to hang"] **syn** see LONG — **han•ker•er** \-kər-ər\ *n*
han•ky–pan•ky \,hang-kē-'pang-kē\ *n* **:** questionable or underhand activity [alteration of *hocus-pocus*]
Han•o•ve•ri•an \,han-ə-'vir-ē-ən, -'ver-\ *adj* **:** of, relating to, or supporting the German ducal house of Hanover or the descendant British royal house furnishing sovereigns from 1714 to 1901 [*Hanover,* Germany] — **Hanoverian** *n*
Han•sen's disease \'han-sənz-\ *n* **:** LEPROSY [Armauer *Hansen,* died 1912, Norwegian physician]
han•som \'han-səm\ *n* **:** a light 2-wheeled covered carriage with the driver's seat elevated behind [Joseph A. *Hansom,* died 1882, English architect]
Ha•nuk•kah \'k̲än-ə-kə, 'hän-\ *n* **:** an 8-day Jewish festival of lights celebrated in November or December in commemoration of the rededication of the Temple of Jerusalem after its defilement by Antiochus of Syria [Hebrew *ḥănukkāh* "dedication"]
hao•le \'hau̇-lā\ *n* **:** one who is not a member of the native race of Hawaii; *esp* **:** WHITE [Hawaiian]
¹hap \'hap\ *n* **1 :** HAPPENING **2 :** CHANCE 1, FORTUNE [Old Norse *happ* "good luck"]
²hap *vb* **happed; hap•ping :** HAPPEN 3, 4a
hap•haz•ard \hap-'haz-ərd, 'hap-\ *adj* **:** marked by lack of plan, order, or direction : AIMLESS **syn** see RANDOM — **haphazard** *adv* — **hap•haz•ard•ly** *adv* — **hap•haz•ard•ness** *n*
hap•less \'hap-ləs\ *adj* **:** having no luck : UNFORTUNATE ⟨a *hapless* child⟩ — **hap•less•ly** *adv* — **hap•less•ness** *n*
hap•loid \'hap-,lȯid\ *adj* **:** having the number of chromosomes characteristic of germ cells or half the number characteristic of body cells [Greek *haploeidēs* "single", from *haploos* "single"] — **haploid** *n* — **hap•loi•dy** \-,lȯid-ē\ *n*
hap•pen \'hap-ən, 'hap-m\ *vi* **hap•pened; hap•pen•ing** \'hapning, -ə-ning\ **1 :** to occur by chance **2 :** to take place **3 :** to have occasion or opportunity without intention : CHANCE ⟨*happened* to overhear⟩ **4 a :** to find something by chance ⟨*happened* on the right answer⟩ **b :** to appear casually or by chance **5 :** to come especially by way of injury or harm ⟨I promise nothing will *happen* to you⟩ [Middle English *happenen,* from *hap*]
• **syn** HAPPEN, CHANCE, OCCUR, TRANSPIRE mean to come about. HAPPEN applies to whatever comes about without cause or intention; CHANCE stresses lack of plan or apparent cause; OCCUR, often interchangeable with HAPPEN, stresses a being brought to sight or to mind or attention ⟨theoretically possible, but not *occurring* in reality⟩ ⟨it never *occurred* to them that we would object⟩ TRANSPIRE can imply a coming out or becoming known ⟨what *happened* that day only *transpired* much later⟩ but is often equal to OCCUR.
hap•pen•ing *n* **1 :** something that happens : OCCURRENCE **2 a :** an event or series of events designed to evoke a spontaneous reaction to sensory, emotional, or spiritual stimuli **b :** something (as an event) of special interest or importance
hap•pi•ly \'hap-ə-lē\ *adv* **1 :** FORTUNATELY, LUCKILY ⟨*happily,* no one was injured⟩ **2 :** in a happy manner or state ⟨lived *happily* ever after⟩ **3 :** APTLY, SUCCESSFULLY ⟨the remarks were *happily* worded⟩
hap•pi•ness \'hap-i-nəs\ *n* **1 a :** a state of well-being and contentment : JOY **b :** a pleasurable satisfaction **2 :** FELICITY 1, APTNESS
hap•py \'hap-ē\ *adj* **hap•pi•er; -est 1 :** favored by fortune : FORTUNATE **2 :** notably well adapted or fitting ⟨a *happy* choice for governor⟩ **3 a :** enjoying well-being and contentment ⟨*happy* in their work⟩ **b :** expressing or suggestive of happiness : PLEASANT ⟨*happy* laughter⟩ **c :** feeling satisfaction ⟨*happy* to escape⟩ [Middle English, from *hap*]
hap•py–go–lucky \,hap-ē-gō-'lək-ē\ *adj* **:** blithely unconcerned : CAREFREE
Haps•burg *also* **Habs•burg** \'haps-,bərg, 'häps-,bu̇rg\ *adj* **:** of or relating to a princely German family furnishing the rulers of Austria from 1278 to 1918 and of Spain from 1516 to 1700 and many of the Holy Roman emperors [*Habsburg,* Aargau, Switzerland] — **Hapsburg** *n*
hap•ten \'hap-,ten\ *n* **:** a substance that does not cause forma-

tion of antibodies by itself but reacts with specific chemical groups on antibodies and may stimulate antibody formation when joined with a protein [German, from Greek *haptesthai* "to touch"]

hara–kiri \ˌhar-i-ˈkir-ē, -ˈkar-ē\ *n* : suicide by disembowelment formerly practiced by the Japanese samurai [Japanese *hara-kiri*]

ha•rangue \hə-ˈrang\ *n* **1** : a speech addressed to a public assembly **2** : a ranting speech or writing [Middle French, from Italian *aringa*] — **harangue** *vb* — **ha•rangu•er** \-ˈrang-ər\ *n*

ha•rass \hə-ˈras, ˈhar-əs\ *vt* **1** : to tire out by persistent efforts : worry or annoy with repeated attacks **2** : to lay waste : HARRY [French *harasser,* from Middle French *harer* "to set a dog on", from Old French *hare,* interj. used to incite dogs, of Germanic origin] **syn** see ANNOY — **ha•rass•ment** \-mənt\ *n*

1har•bin•ger \ˈhär-bən-jər\ *n* : one that announces or shows what is coming : FORERUNNER ⟨robins are *harbingers* of spring⟩ [Middle English *herbergere* "host, one sent ahead to provide lodgings", from Old French, "host", from *herberge* "inn", of Germanic origin]

△ **origin** The modern *harbinger* is simply a forerunner. But in late medieval and early modern times a *harbinger,* or *herbergere,* was the person sent before an army, a royal progress, or the like, to find lodgings for the whole company. Still earlier English *herbergeres* were hosts, the actual providers of lodgings. The Old French word from which the English was borrowed was itself derived from an early Germanic loanword. Old French *herberge* took from its Germanic ancestor both the literal meaning, "army encampment", and the figurative extension, "hostelry, inn". Modern English *harbor* is another descendant of the same old Germanic word.

2harbinger *vt* : to be a harbinger of : PRESAGE

1har•bor \ˈhär-bər\ *n* **1** : a place of security : REFUGE **2** : a protected part of a body of water deep enough to furnish anchorage; *esp* : one with port facilities [Middle English *herberge* — see HARBINGER *origin*] — **har•bor•less** \-ləs\ *adj*

2harbor *vb* **har•bored**; **har•bor•ing** \-bə-ring, -bring\ **1 a** : to give shelter or refuge to **b** : to be the home or habitat of : CONTAIN **2** : to hold a thought or feeling of **3** : to take shelter in or as if in a harbor — **har•bor•er** *n*

har•bor•age \ˈhär-bə-rij\ *n* : SHELTER 1, HARBOR

har•bour \ˈhär-bər\ *chiefly British variant of* HARBOR

1hard \ˈhärd\ *adj* **1** : not easily penetrated, cut, or divided into parts : not soft **2 a** : strong in alcoholic content ⟨*hard* liquor⟩ **b** : characterized by the presence of salts that prevent lathering with soap ⟨*hard* water⟩ **3 a** : having high penetrating power ⟨*hard* X rays⟩ **b** : having or producing relatively great photographic contrast ⟨a *hard* negative⟩ **4 a** : metallic as distinct from paper ⟨*hard* money⟩ **b** : convertible into gold : stable in value ⟨*hard* currency⟩ **5 a** : physically fit ⟨in good *hard* condition⟩ **b** : free of weakness or flaw **6 a** (1) : FIRM, DEFINITE ⟨a *hard* agreement⟩ (2) : FACTUAL, ACTUAL ⟨*hard* evidence⟩ **b** : CLOSE, SEARCHING ⟨a *hard* look⟩ **c** : free from sentimentality or illusion : REALISTIC ⟨good *hard* sense⟩ **d** : lacking sympathy or sentiment ⟨a *hard* heart⟩ **7 a** : difficult to bear or endure : HARSH, SEVERE ⟨*hard* times⟩ **b** : RESENTFUL ⟨*hard* feelings⟩ **c** : making no concessions ⟨drive a *hard* bargain⟩ **d** : INCLEMENT ⟨a *hard* winter⟩ **e** : intense in force, manner, or degree ⟨a *hard* blow⟩ **f** : physically or mentally difficult ⟨*hard* work⟩ ⟨a *hard* question⟩ **8** : DILIGENT, ENERGETIC ⟨a *hard* worker⟩ **9 a** : sharply or harshly defined : STARK ⟨*hard* shadows⟩ **b** : sounding as in *cow* and *gun* respectively — used of *c* and *g* **10 a** : difficult to accomplish or resolve : TROUBLESOME ⟨a *hard* problem⟩ **b** : difficult to comprehend or explain ⟨*hard* words⟩ **11** : being both addictive and harmful to health ⟨*hard* drugs⟩ **12** : persisting in the environment for a long time without breaking down ⟨*hard* insecticides⟩ [Old English *heard*] — **hard up 1** : short of money : POOR ⟨family was *hard up* for years⟩ **2** : poorly provided ⟨*hard up* for friends⟩

2hard *adv* **1 a** : with great effort or energy : STRENUOUSLY ⟨*try* hard⟩ **b** : VIOLENTLY, FIERCELY ⟨the wind is blowing *hard*⟩ **c** : to the full extent — used in nautical directions **d** : in a searching, close, or concentrated manner ⟨stared *hard* at the sign⟩ **2 a** : HARSHLY, SEVERELY ⟨the recession hit them *hard*⟩ **b** : with rancor, bitterness, or grief ⟨took the defeat *hard*⟩ **3** : TIGHTLY, FIRMLY ⟨hold *hard* to something⟩ **4** : to the point of hardness **5** : close in time or space ⟨the school stood *hard* by a church⟩

hard–and–fast \ˌhärd-n-ˈfast\ *adj* : rigidly binding : STRICT ⟨a *hard-and-fast* rule⟩

hard•back \ˈhärd-ˌbak\ *n* : a book bound in hard covers

hard•ball \-ˌbȯl\ *n* : BASEBALL

hard–bit•ten \-ˈbit-n\ *adj* : seasoned or strengthened by difficult experience : TOUGH ⟨*hard-bitten* campaigners⟩

hard•board \-ˌbōrd, -ˌbȯrd\ *n* : composition board made by compressing shredded wood chips often with a binder at high temperatures

hard–boiled \-ˈbȯild\ *adj* **1** : boiled until both white and yolk become solid ⟨*hard-boiled* eggs⟩ **2 a** : lacking sentiment ⟨a *hard-boiled* drill sergeant⟩ **b** : PRACTICAL, REALISTIC ⟨*hard-boiled* business dealings⟩

hard candy *n* : a candy made of sugar and corn syrup boiled without crystallizing and often fruit-flavored

hard coal *n* : ANTHRACITE

hard–core \ˈhärd-ˌkōr, -ˌkȯr\ *adj* **1** : fanatically loyal, devoted, or committed ⟨*hard-core* supporters⟩ **2** : barely capable of being or willing to be reformed ⟨a *hard-core* criminal⟩ **3** : continuing for a long time ⟨*hard-core* unemployment⟩ — **hard core** *n*

hard•en \ˈhärd-n\ *vb* **hard•ened**; **hard•en•ing** \ˈhärd-ning, -n-ing\ **1** : to make or become hard or harder **2** : to make or become hardy or strong ⟨muscles *hardened* by exercise⟩ **3 a** : to make or become stubborn, unfeeling, or unsympathetic ⟨*harden* one's heart⟩ **b** : to become confirmed or strengthened ⟨opposition began to *harden*⟩ — **hard•en•er** \ˈhärd-nər, -n-ər\ *n*

hard•hack \ˈhärd-ˌhak\ *n* : a shrubby American spirea with rusty hairy leaves and dense terminal clusters of pink or occasionally white flowers

hard•head•ed \-ˈhed-əd\ *adj* **1** : STUBBORN 1 **2** : marked by sound judgment : REALISTIC ⟨a *hardheaded* reappraisal⟩ — **hard•head•ed•ly** *adv* — **hard•head•ed•ness** *n*

hard•heart•ed \-ˈhärt-əd\ *adj* : lacking in sympathetic understanding — **hard•heart•ed•ly** *adv* — **hard•heart•ed•ness** *n*

hard labor *n* : compulsory labor of imprisoned criminals that is a part of the prison discipline

hard•ly \ˈhärd-lē\ *adv* **1** : in a severe manner : HARSHLY **2** : with difficulty : PAINFULLY **3** : almost not : BARELY ⟨it *hardly* ever rains there⟩ **4** : certainly not ⟨that news is *hardly* surprising⟩

hard•ness *n* **1** : the quality or state of being hard **2** : the cohesion of the particles on the surface of a mineral as determined by its capacity to scratch another or be itself scratched

hard–of–hearing \ˌhärd-əv-ˈhiər-ing, -ə-ˈ\ *adj* : of or relating to a defective but functional sense of hearing

hard palate *n* : the bony front part of the palate

hard•pan \ˈhärd-ˌpan\ *n* **1** : a cemented or compacted and often clayey layer in soil that roots cannot readily penetrate **2** : a fundamental part : BASIS

hard put *adj* : barely able ⟨*hard put* to find an explanation⟩

hard rubber *n* : a firm rubber or rubber product that is relatively incapable of being stretched

hard sell *n* : aggressive high-pressure salesmanship

hard•ship \ˈhärd-ˌship\ *n* **1** : PRIVATION 2, DISTRESS **2** : something that causes or involves distress or privation

hard•stand \-ˌstand\ *n* : a hard-surfaced area for parking an airplane

hard–sur•face \-ˈsər-fəs\ *vt* : to provide (as a road) with a paved surface

hard•tack \ˈhärd-ˌtak\ *n* : a hard biscuit or bread made of flour and water without salt

hard•top \-ˌtäp\ *n* : an automobile styled to resemble a convertible but having a rigid top of metal or plastic

hard•ware \ˈhär-ˌdwaər, -ˌdweər\ *n* **1** : articles (as fittings, cutlery, tools, utensils, or parts of machines) made of metal **2** : the physical components (as electronic and electrical devices) of a vehicle (as a spacecraft) or an apparatus (as a computer)

hardware cloth *n* : galvanized screening of steel wire woven with a close mesh commonly 1/8 to 3/4 inch (3 to 19 millimeters)

hard wheat *n* : a wheat with hard flinty kernels high in gluten that yield a flour especially suitable for bread and macaroni

1hard•wood \ˈhär-ˌdwu̇d\ *n* **1** : the wood of a deciduous broad-leaved tree **2** : a tree that yields hardwood

2hardwood *adj* **1** : having or made of hardwood ⟨*hardwood*

\ə\ **abut**	\au̇\ **out**	\i\ **tip**	\ȯ\ **saw**	\u̇\ **foot**
\ər\ **further**	\ch\ **chin**	\ī\ **life**	\ȯi\ **coin**	\y\ **yet**
\a\ **mat**	\e\ **pet**	\j\ **job**	\th\ **thin**	\yü\ **few**
\ā\ **take**	\ē\ **easy**	\ng\ **sing**	\t͟h\ **this**	\yu̇\ **cure**
\ä\ **cot, cart**	\g\ **go**	\ō\ **bone**	\ü\ **food**	\zh\ **vision**

floors⟩ **2 :** consisting of mature woody tissue ⟨a *hardwood* cutting⟩
hard–wood•ed \'här-'dwu̇d-əd\ *adj* **1 :** having wood that is hard ⟨a *hard-wooded* pine⟩ **2 :** HARDWOOD 1
hard•work•ing \'här-'dwər-kiŋ\ *adj* **:** INDUSTRIOUS
har•dy \'härd-ē\ *adj* **har•di•er; -est 1 :** BOLD 1, BRAVE **2 :** full of confidence or brashness **:** BRAZEN **3 a :** used to fatigue or hardships **:** ROBUST **b :** able to withstand adverse conditions (as of weather) ⟨a *hardy* rose⟩ [Old French *hardi,* of Germanic origin] — **har•di•ly** \'härd-l-ē\ *adv* — **har•di•ness** \'härd-ē-nəs\ *n*
Har•dy–Wein•berg law \ˌhärd-ē-'wīn-ˌbərg-\ *n* **:** a fundamental principle of population genetics: population gene frequencies remain constant from generation to generation if mating is random and if mutation, selection, immigration, and emigration do not occur — called also *Hardy-Weinberg principle* [G. H. *Hardy,* died 1947, English mathematician and W. *Weinberg,* 20th century German scientist]
hare \'haər, 'heər\ *n, pl* **hare** *or* **hares :** any of various swift timid long-eared mammals (order Lagomorpha) with a divided upper lip, long hind legs, a short cocked tail, and the young open-eyed and furred at birth — compare RABBIT [Old English *hara*]

hare

hare and hounds *n* **:** a game in which some of the players scatter bits of paper for a trail and others try to find and catch them
hare•bell \'haər-ˌbel, 'heər-\ *n* **:** a slender herb with bright blue bell-shaped flowers
hare•brained \-'brānd\ *adj* **:** FLIGHTY, FOOLISH
hare•lip \-'lip\ *n* **:** a deformity in which the upper lip is divided like that of a hare — **hare•lipped** \-'lipt\ *adj*
har•em \'har-əm, 'her-\ *n* **1 a :** the rooms assigned to the women in a Muslim household **b :** the women of a Muslim household **2 :** a group of female animals (as fur seals) associated with one male [Arabic *ḥarīm*]
hark \'härk\ *vi* **:** to pay close attention [Middle English *herken*]
hark back *vi* **:** to turn back to an earlier topic or circumstance
har•le•quin \'här-li-kən, -kwən\ **1 :** BUFFOON 1, CLOWN **2 :** a variegated pattern (as of a textile) [Italian *arlecchino,* a character in comedy and pantomime with a shaved head, masked face, variegated tights, and wooden sword, from Middle French *Helquin,* a demon]
har•lot \'här-lət\ *n* **:** PROSTITUTE [Old French *herlot* "rogue"]
har•lot•ry \-lə-trē\ *n, pl* **-ries :** PROSTITUTION
1harm \'härm\ *n* **1 :** physical or mental damage **:** INJURY **2 :** MISCHIEF 2, HURT [Old English *hearm*] **syn** see INJURY
2harm *vt* **:** to cause harm to
harm•ful \'härm-fəl\ *adj* **:** INJURIOUS, DAMAGING — **harm•ful•ly** \-fə-lē\ *adv* — **harm•ful•ness** *n*
harm•less \'härm-ləs\ *adj* **1 :** free from harm, liability, or loss **2 :** lacking capacity or intent to injure ⟨a *harmless* joke⟩ — **harm•less•ly** *adv* — **harm•less•ness** *n*
1har•mon•ic \här-'män-ik\ *adj* **1 :** of or relating to musical harmony as opposed to melody or rhythm **2 :** HARMONIOUS 2 — **har•mon•i•cal•ly** \-'män-i-kə-lē, -klē\ *adv*
2harmonic *n* **1 a :** OVERTONE 1; *esp* **:** one whose frequency is a multiple of the fundamental **b :** a flutelike tone produced (as on a violin) by lightly touching a vibrating string with a finger **2 :** a component frequency of a harmonic motion (as of an electromagnetic wave) that is an integral multiple of the fundamental frequency
har•mon•i•ca \här-'män-i-kə\ *n* **:** a small rectangular wind instrument with free metallic reeds sounded by exhaling and inhaling — called also *mouth organ*
harmonic motion *n* **:** a periodic motion that has a single frequency or amplitude (as of a sounding violin string or swinging pendulum) or a vibratory motion that is composed of two or more such simple periodic motions
har•mon•ics \här-'män-iks\ *n* **:** the study of the physical characteristics of musical sounds
har•mo•ni•ous \här-'mō-nē-əs\ *adj* **1 :** musically concordant ⟨a *harmonious* song⟩ **2 :** having the parts agreeably related **:** CONGRUOUS ⟨*harmonious* colors⟩ **3 :** marked by accord in sentiment or action ⟨a *harmonious* family⟩ — **har•mo•ni•ous•ly** *adv* — **har•mo•ni•ous•ness** *n*

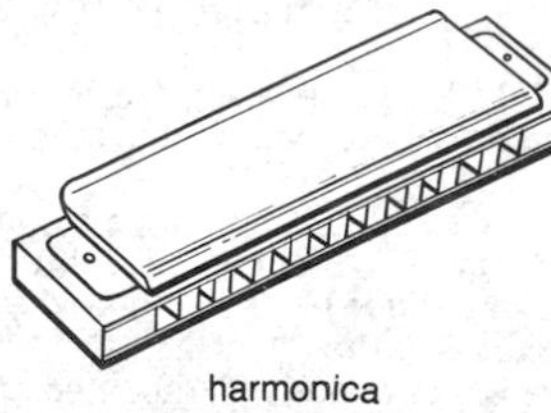
harmonica

har•mo•ni•um \-nē-əm\ *n* **:** REED ORGAN
har•mo•nize \'här-mə-ˌnīz\ *vb* **1 :** to play or sing in harmony **2 :** to be in harmony **3 :** to bring into harmony or agreement **4 :** to provide or accompany with harmony ⟨*harmonize* a melody⟩ — **har•mo•ni•za•tion** \ˌhär-mə-nə-'zā-shən\ *n* — **har•mo•niz•er** \'här-mə-ˌnī-zər\ *n*
har•mo•ny \'här-mə-nē\ *n, pl* **-nies 1** *archaic* **:** tuneful sound **2 a :** the combination of simultaneous musical notes in a chord **b :** the structure of music with respect to the composition and progression of chords **c :** the science of the structure, relation, and progression of chords **3 a :** pleasing or congruent arrangement of parts ⟨a picture showing *harmony* of color and design⟩ **b :** ACCORD, AGREEMENT ⟨live in *harmony* with one's neighbors⟩ **c :** internal calm **:** TRANQUILLITY [Middle French *armonie,* from Latin *harmonia,* from Greek, "fastening, harmony", from *harmos* "joint, fastening"]
1har•ness \'här-nəs\ *n* **1 a :** the gear of a draft animal other than a yoke **b :** TACKLE 1, EQUIPMENT; *esp* **:** military equipment for man or horse **c :** something felt to resemble an animal's harness ⟨shoulder *harness* for a motorist⟩ **2 a :** occupational surroundings or routine ⟨back in *harness* after a vacation⟩ **b :** close association ⟨doesn't work well in *harness*⟩ [Old French *herneis* "baggage, gear"]
2harness *vt* **1 a :** to put a harness on **b :** to attach by means of a harness **2 :** to join together **:** YOKE **3 :** to put to work **:** UTILIZE ⟨*harness* a waterfall⟩
harness horse *n* **:** a horse for racing or working in harness
harness racing *n* **:** the sport of racing standardbred horses harnessed to 2-wheeled sulkies
1harp \'härp\ *n* **:** an instrument having strings of graded length stretched across an open triangular frame with a curving top and played by plucking with the fingers [Old English *hearpe*] — **harp•ist** \'här-pəst\ *n*
2harp *vi* **1 :** to play on a harp **2 :** to swell on or come back to a subject tiresomely or monotonously ⟨always *harping* on my shortcomings⟩ — **harp•er** \'här-pər\ *n*
har•poon \här-'pün\ *n* **:** a barbed spear used especially in hunting large fish or whales [probably from Dutch *harpoen,* from Middle French *harpon* "clamp"] — **harpoon** *vt* — **har•poon•er** *n*
harp•si•chord \'härp-si-ˌkȯrd\ *n* **:** a keyboard instrument resembling the grand piano and producing tones by the plucking of wire strings with quills or leather points [Italian *arpicordo,* from *arpa* "harp" + *corda* "string"]

1harp

har•py \'här-pē\ *n, pl* **harpies 1** *cap* **:** a foul malign creature in Greek mythology that is part woman and part bird **2 a :** a greedy or grasping person **:** LEECH **b :** a shrewish woman [Latin *Harpyia,* from Greek]
har•que•bus \'här-kwi-bəs, -ˌbəs\ *or* **ar•que•bus** \'är-\ *n* **:** a portable firearm of the 15th and 16th centuries later replaced by the musket [Middle French *harquebuse, arquebuse*]
har•ri•dan \'har-əd-n\ *n* **:** a scolding old woman [perhaps from French *haridelle* "old horse, gaunt woman"]
1har•ri•er \'har-ē-ər\ *n* **1 :** a hunting dog that resembles a small foxhound and is used especially for hunting rabbits **2 :** a runner on a cross-country team [derived from *hare*]
2harrier *n* **1 :** one that harries **2 :** any of various slender long-legged hawks

[1]har•row \ˈhar-ō\ *n* : a cultivating implement set with spikes, spring teeth, or disks and used primarily for pulverizing and smoothing the soil [Middle English *harwe*]

[2]harrow *vt* **1** : to cultivate with a harrow **2** : TORMENT, VEX ⟨*harrowed* by grief⟩ — **har•row•er** \ˈhar-ə-wər\ *n*

har•ry \ˈhar-ē\ *vt* **har•ried**; **har•ry•ing** **1** : to make a raid on : PILLAGE **2** : to torment by or as if by constant attack ⟨*harried* by cares⟩ [Old English *hergian*]

harsh \ˈhärsh\ *adj* **1** : having a coarse uneven surface unpleasant to the touch **2** : disagreeable to one of the senses ⟨a *harsh* light⟩; *also* : physically discomforting : PAINFUL ⟨a *harsh* wind⟩ **3** : unduly exacting : SEVERE ⟨*harsh* discipline⟩ **4** : lacking in aesthetic appeal or refinement : CRUDE ⟨*harsh* gaudy colors⟩ [Middle English *harsk*, of Scandinavian origin] **syn** see ROUGH — **harsh•en** \ˈhär-shən\ *vb* — **harsh•ly** *adv* — **harsh•ness** *n*

hart \ˈhärt\ *n, chiefly British* : a male red deer especially over five years old : STAG — compare HIND [Old English *heort*]

harte•beest \ˈhärt-ˌbēst, -ə-ˌbēst\ *n* : a large nearly extinct African antelope with ringed horns [obsolete Afrikaans, from Dutch, from *hart* "deer" + *beest* "beast"]

harts•horn \ˈhärts-ˌhȯrn\ *n* : a preparation of ammonia used as smelling salts [from the former use of harts' horns as the chief source of ammonia]

har•um–scar•um \ˌhar-əm-ˈskar-əm, ˌher-əm-ˈsker-\ *adj* : casually or heedlessly careless [perhaps alteration of *helter-skelter*] — **harum–scarum** *n* — **harum–scarum** *adv*

ha•rus•pex \hə-ˈrəs-ˌpeks, ˈhar-əs-\ *n, pl* **ha•rus•pi•ces** \hə-ˈrəs-pə-ˌsēz\ : a diviner in ancient Rome basing predictions on inspection of the entrails of animals [Latin]

[1]har•vest \ˈhär-vəst\ *n* **1** : the season when grains and fruits are gathered **2** : the gathering of a crop **3** : a ripe crop; *also* : the quantity of a crop gathered in a single season **4** : the product or reward of effort [Old English *hærfest*]

[2]harvest *vb* **1 a** : to gather in a crop : REAP **b** : to gather as if by harvesting **2** : to win by achievement — **har•vest•able** \-və-stə-bəl\ *adj* — **har•vest•er** *n*

har•vest•man \ˈhär-vəst-mən, -vəs-\ *n* : DADDY LONGLEGS

harvest moon *n* : the full moon nearest the time of the September equinox

has *present 3d sing of* HAVE

has–been \ˈhaz-ˌbin\ *n* : one that has passed the peak of ability, power, effectiveness, or popularity

ha•sen•pfef•fer \ˈhäz-n-ˌpfef-ər, -ˌfef-\ *n* : a stew made of marinated rabbit meat [German, from *hase* "hare" + *pfeffer* "pepper"]

[1]hash \ˈhash\ *vt* **1 a** : to chop into small pieces **b** : CONFUSE 1, MUDDLE **2** : to talk about : REVIEW ⟨*hash* over the evidence⟩ [French *hacher*, from *hache* "ax", of Germanic origin]

[2]hash *n* **1** : chopped food; *esp* : chopped meat mixed with potatoes and browned **2** : a restatement of something that is already known **3** : JUMBLE, HODGEPODGE

[3]hash *n* : HASHISH

Hash•em•ite *or* **Hash•im•ite** \ˈhash-ə-ˌmīt\ *n* : a member of an Arab family having common ancestry with Muhammad and founding dynasties in countries of the eastern Mediterranean [*Hashim*, great-grandfather of Muhammad]

hash•ish \ˈhash-ˌēsh, -ish, -ˌish\ *n* : the resin from the flowering tops of the female hemp plant that is smoked, chewed, or drunk for its intoxicating effect — called also *charas;* compare BHANG, CANNABIS, MARIJUANA [Arabic *ḥashīsh*]

Ha•sid *or* **Cha•sid** *or* **Has•sid** *or* **Chas•sid** \ˈhas-əd, ˈk̲äs-\ *n, pl* **Ha•si•dim** *or* **Has•si•dim** \ˈhas-əd-əm, k̲ə-ˈsēd-\ : a member of a Jewish mystical sect founded in Poland about 1750 in opposition to rationalism and ritual laxity [Hebrew *ḥāsīdh* "pious"] — **Ha•sid•ic** \hə-ˈsid-ik, ha-\ *adj* — **Has•i•dism** \ˈhas-ə-ˌdiz-əm\ *n*

Has•mo•nae•an *or* **Has•mo•ne•an** \ˌhaz-mə-ˈnē-ən\ *n* : a member of the Maccabees [*Hasmon*, ancestor of the Maccabees] — **Hasmonaean** *or* **Hasmonean** *adj*

hasn't \ˈhaz-nt\ : has not

hasp \ˈhasp\ *n* : any of several devices for fastening; *esp* : a fastener (as for a door or lid) consisting of a hinged metal strap that fits over a staple and is secured by a pin or padlock [Old English *hæsp*]

has•sle \ˈhas-əl\ *n* **1** : a heated argument : WRANGLE **2** : a violent skirmish : FIGHT [perhaps blend of *haggle* and *tussle*] — **hassle** *vi*

has•sock \ˈhas-ək\ *n* **1** : a tuft of bog grass or sedge **2 a** : a cushion to kneel on in prayer **b** : a cushion that serves as a seat or as a leg rest [Old English *hassuc* "coarse grass"]

hast \hast, ˈhast, əst, həst\ *archaic present 2d sing of* HAVE

has•tate \ˈhas-ˌtāt\ *adj* : shaped like an arrow with flaring barbs ⟨a *hastate* leaf⟩ [Latin *hasta* "spear"]

[1]haste \ˈhāst\ *n* **1** : rapidity of motion or action : SWIFTNESS **2** : rash or headlong action **3** : undue eagerness to act : URGENCY [Old French, of Germanic origin]

• **syn** HASTE, HURRY, SPEED mean quickness in movement or action. HASTE implies quickness impelled by urgency, eagerness, or rashness; HURRY suggests agitation, bustle, or confusion; SPEED stresses swiftness without confusion and often with success ⟨increase the *speed* of social progress⟩

[2]haste *vb* : to move or act swiftly : HASTEN, HURRY

has•ten \ˈhās-n\ *vb* **has•tened**; **has•ten•ing** \ˈhās-ning, -n-ing\ **1** : to urge on **2** : to speed up : ACCELERATE ⟨*hasten* one's steps⟩ **3** : to move or act quickly : HURRY ⟨*hasten* home⟩ — **has•ten•er** \-nər, -n-ər\ *n*

hasty \ˈhā-stē\ *adj* **hast•i•er**; **-est** **1 a** : done or made in a hurry ⟨made a *hasty* sketch of the scene⟩ **b** : fast and often superficial ⟨a *hasty* survey of the problem⟩ **2** : acting or done without forethought : RASH **3** : quick to anger : IRRITABLE ⟨a *hasty* temper⟩ — **hast•i•ly** \-stə-lē\ *adv* — **hast•i•ness** \-stē-nəs\ *n*

hasty pudding *n* **1** *British* : a porridge of oatmeal or flour boiled in water **2** *New England* : cornmeal mush

hat \ˈhat\ *n* : a covering for the head usually having a shaped crown and brim [Old English *hæt*] — **hat in the ring** : an announcement of entry especially into a political contest

hat•box \ˈhat-ˌbäks\ *n* : a round piece of luggage especially for carrying hats

[1]hatch \ˈhach\ *n* **1** : an opening in the deck of a ship or in the floor or roof of a building; *also* : a small door or opening (as in an airplane) ⟨an escape *hatch*⟩ ⟨a cargo *hatch*⟩ **2** : the covering for a hatch [Old English *hæc* "lower part of a divided door"]

[2]hatch *vb* **1 a** : to produce (young) from the egg by applying heat ⟨the hen *hatched* chicks⟩ **b** : INCUBATE 1 ⟨the hen *hatched* the eggs⟩ **2 a** : to emerge from an egg, pupa, or chrysalis ⟨the chicks *hatched* today⟩ **b** : to give forth young ⟨the eggs *hatched* today⟩ **3** : to bring into being : ORIGINATE; *esp* : to concoct in secret ⟨*hatch* a plot⟩ [Middle English *hacchen*] — **hatch•abil•i•ty** \ˌhach-ə-ˈbil-ət-ē\ *n* — **hatch•able** \ˈhach-ə-bəl\ *adj*

[3]hatch *n* : a brood of hatched young

[4]hatch *vt* **1** : to inlay in fine lines **2** : to mark (as the shading in a picture) with fine closely spaced lines [Middle French *hacher* "to chop up, hatch", from *hache* "ax"]

[5]hatch *n* : a line used to give the effect of shading

hatch•ery \ˈhach-rē, -ə-rē\ *n, pl* **-er•ies** : a place for hatching eggs

hatch•et \ˈhach-ət\ *n* **1** : a short-handled ax for use with one hand **2** : TOMAHAWK [Middle French *hachette*, from *hache* "ax"]

hatchet face *n* : a thin sharp face — **hatch•et–faced** \ˌhach-ət-ˈfāst\ *adj*

hatchet man *n* : one hired for murder, coercion, or unscrupulous attack

hatch•ment \ˈhach-mənt\ *n* : a panel on which a coat of arms of a deceased person is temporarily displayed [perhaps alteration of *achievement*]

hatch•way \ˈhach-ˌwā\ *n* : a hatch giving access to an enclosed space (as a compartment or cellar) and usually having a ladder or stairs

[1]hate \ˈhāt\ *n* **1 a** : intense hostility and aversion **b** : distaste coupled with sustained ill will **c** : a very strong dislike : ANTIPATHY **2** : an object of hatred [Old English *hete*]

[2]hate *vt* **1** : to feel extreme enmity toward ⟨*hate* one's enemies⟩ **2 a** : to have a strong aversion to : DETEST ⟨*hate* hypocrisy⟩ **b** : to find distasteful : DISLIKE ⟨*hates* cold weather⟩ — **hat•er** *n*

• **syn** DETEST, ABHOR, LOATHE: HATE implies strong dislike coupled with enmity or malice; DETEST suggests violent or intense dislike but may lack the hostility implied in HATE; ABHOR

\ə\ **abut**	\au̇\ **out**	\i\ **tip**	\ȯ\ **saw**	\u̇\ **foot**
\ər\ **further**	\ch\ **chin**	\ī\ **life**	\ȯi\ **coin**	\y\ **yet**
\a\ **mat**	\e\ **pet**	\j\ **job**	\th\ **thin**	\yü\ **few**
\ā\ **take**	\ē\ **easy**	\ng\ **sing**	\t̲h̲\ **this**	\yu̇\ **cure**
\ä\ **cot, cart**	\g\ **go**	\ō\ **bone**	\ü\ **food**	\zh\ **vision**

suggests a deep often shuddering repugnance; LOATHE implies utter disgust and intolerance.

hate•ful \ˈhāt-fəl\ *adj* **1 :** full of hate **:** MALICIOUS ⟨*hateful* enemies⟩ **2 :** exciting or deserving hate ⟨a *hateful* crime⟩ — **hate•ful•ly** \-fə-lē\ *adv* — **hate•ful•ness** *n*

hath \hath, ˈhath, əth, həth\ *archaic present 3d sing of* HAVE

ha•tred \ˈhā-trəd\ *n* **1 :** HATE 1 **2 :** prejudiced hostility or animosity [Middle English, from *hate* + Old English *rǣden* "condition"]

hat•ter \ˈhat-ər\ *n* **:** one that makes, sells, or cleans and repairs hats

hat trick *n* **:** the scoring of three goals in one game by one player (as in hockey or soccer)

hau•berk \ˈhȯ-bərk\ *n* **:** a tunic of chain mail worn as armor from the 12th to the 14th century [Old French *hauberc,* of Germanic origin]

haugh•ty \ˈhȯt-ē, ˈhät-\ *adj* **haugh•ti•er; -est :** disdainfully proud [Middle French *haut,* literally, "high", from Latin *altus*] — **haugh•ti•ly** \-l-ē\ *adv* — **haugh•ti•ness** \-ē-nəs\ *n*

¹haul \ˈhȯl\ *vb* **1 :** to change the course of (a ship) especially so as to sail closer to the wind **2 a :** to exert traction **:** DRAW, PULL ⟨the horse *hauled* a cart⟩ **b :** to obtain or move by or as if by hauling **c :** to transport in a vehicle **3 :** SHIFT ⟨the wind *hauled* around to the south⟩ [Old French *haler* "to pull, draw", of Germanic origin] — **haul•er** *n*

²haul *n* **1 a :** the act or process of hauling **b :** a device for hauling **2 a :** an amount collected **:** TAKE ⟨a burglar's *haul*⟩ **b :** the fish taken in a single draft of a net **3 a :** transportation by hauling **b :** the distance or route over which a load is transported ⟨a long *haul*⟩ **c :** a quantity transported **:** LOAD

haul•age \ˈhȯ-lij\ *n* **1 :** the act or process of hauling **2 :** a charge made for hauling

haulm \ˈhȯm\ *n* **:** the stems or tops of a plant (as peas or potatoes) especially after the crop is gathered; *also* **:** a plant stem [Old English *healm*]

haunch \ˈhȯnch, ˈhänch\ *n* **1 a :** HIP 1 **b :** HINDQUARTER 2 — usually used in pl. **2 :** HINDQUARTER 1 [Old French *hanche,* of Germanic origin]

¹haunt \ˈhȯnt, ˈhänt\ *vb* **1 a :** to visit often **:** FREQUENT **b :** to continually seek the company of **c :** to stay around or persist **:** LINGER **2 a :** to recur constantly and spontaneously to ⟨the tune *haunted* me all day⟩ **b :** to reappear continually in **3 :** to visit or inhabit as a ghost [Old French *hanter*]

²haunt \ˈhȯnt, ˈhänt, *2 is usually* ˈhant\ *n* **1 :** a place habitually frequented or repeatedly visited ⟨a favorite *haunt* of birds⟩ **2** *chiefly dialect* **:** GHOST 2

haunt•ing \-ing\ *adj* **:** not easily forgotten ⟨a *haunting* melody⟩ — **haunt•ing•ly** \-ing-lē\ *adv*

haus•to•ri•um \hȯ-ˈstōr-ē-əm, -ˈstȯr-\ *n, pl* **-ria** \-ē-ə\ **:** a food-absorbing outgrowth of a plant organ [New Latin, from Latin *haustus,* past participle of *haurire* "to drink, drain"] — **haus•to•ri•al** \-ē-əl\ *adj*

haut•bois *or* **haut•boy** \ˈō-ˌbȯi, ˈhō-\ *n, pl* **hautbois** \-ˌbȯiz\ *or* **hautboys :** OBOE [Middle French *hautbois,* from *haut* "high" + *bois* "wood"]

haute cou•ture \ˌōt-kü-ˈtu̇r\ *n* **:** the establishments or designers that create high fashions for women; *also* **:** the fashions created [French, literally, "high sewing"]

hau•teur \hō-ˈtər\ *n* **:** ARROGANCE, HAUGHTINESS [French, from *haut* "high", from Latin *altus*]

¹have \hav, ˈhav, həv, əv, v; *before "to" usually* ˈhaf\ *vb, past & past participle* **had** \had, ˈhad, həd, əd, d\; *present participle* **hav•ing** \ˈhav-ing\; *present 3d sing* **has** \haz, ˈhaz, həz, əz, z, s; *before "to" usually* ˈhas\ **1 a :** POSSESS, OWN ⟨*have* a car⟩ **b :** to hold in one's use, service, or affection or at one's disposal ⟨can't *have* your cake and eat it too⟩ **c :** to consist of **:** CONTAIN ⟨April *has* 30 days⟩ **2 :** to feel obligation or necessity in regard to ⟨*have* to go⟩ **3 :** to stand in relationship to ⟨*have* enemies⟩ **4 a :** to get possession of **:** OBTAIN ⟨best to be *had*⟩ **b :** RECEIVE ⟨*had* bad news⟩ **c :** ACCEPT; *esp* **:** to accept in marriage **5 a :** to be marked or characterized by ⟨*have* red hair⟩ **b :** SHOW ⟨*had* the gall to refuse⟩ **c :** USE, EXERCISE ⟨*have* mercy on us⟩ **6 a :** to experience especially by submitting to, undergoing, or suffering ⟨*have* a cold⟩ **b :** to carry on **:** PERFORM, TAKE ⟨*have* a look at this⟩ ⟨*have* a fight⟩ **c :** to entertain in the mind ⟨*have* an opinion⟩ **7 a :** to cause to by persuasive or forceful means ⟨please *have* them stay⟩ **b :** to cause to be ⟨*have* the house painted⟩ **8 :** ALLOW ⟨we'll *have* no more of that⟩ **9 :** to be competent in ⟨I *have* no French⟩ **10 a :** to hold an advantage over ⟨we *have* them now⟩ **b :** TRICK, FOOL ⟨was *had* by a partner⟩ **11 :** to be able to exercise ⟨I *have* my rights⟩ **12 :** BEGET 1, BEAR ⟨*have* a baby⟩ **13 :** to partake of ⟨*have* dinner⟩ **14 :** BRIBE ⟨can be *had* for a price⟩ **15** — used as an auxiliary verb with the past participle to form the present perfect, past perfect, or future perfect ⟨*has* gone home⟩ ⟨*had* already eaten⟩ ⟨will *have* finished⟩ [Old English *habban*] — **have at :** to go at or deal with **:** ATTACK — **have done :** FINISH 1a, STOP — **have it in for :** to intend to do harm to — **have it out :** to settle a matter of contention by discussion or fighting — **have to do with 1 :** to deal with ⟨the program *has to do with* rare animals⟩ **2 :** to have a specified relationship with or effect on ⟨size *has* nothing *to do with* intelligence⟩

²have \ˈhav\ *n* **:** one that has material wealth — compare HAVE-NOT

ha•ven \ˈhā-vən\ *n* **1 :** HARBOR 2, PORT **2 a :** place of safety **:** ASYLUM [Old English *hæfen*]

have–not \ˈhav-ˌnät,-ˈnät\ *n* **:** one that is poor in material wealth — compare HAVE

haven't \ˈhav-ənt\ **:** have not

hav•er•sack \ˈhav-ər-ˌsak\ *n* **:** a bag similar to a knapsack but worn over one shoulder [French *havresac,* from German *habersack* "bag for oats", from *haber* "oats" + *sack* "bag"]

Ha•ver•sian canal \hə-ˌvər-zhən-\ *n* **:** any of the small canals by which blood vessels traverse bone [Clopton *Havers,* died 1702, English physician]

hav•oc \ˈhav-ək\ *n* **1 :** wide and general destruction **:** DEVASTATION **2 :** great confusion and disorder [Anglo-French *havok,* from Old French *havot* "plunder"]

¹haw \ˈhȯ\ *n* **1 :** a hawthorn berry **2 :** HAWTHORN [Old English *haga*]

²haw *vi* **:** to utter the sound represented by *haw* ⟨hemmed and *hawed* before answering⟩ [imitative]

³haw *n* **:** a vocalized pause in speaking or an instance of uttering this sound [imitative]

⁴haw *imperative verb* — used as a direction to turn to the left; compare GEE [origin unknown]

Ha•wai•ian \hə-ˈwä-yən; -ˈwī-yən, -ən-; -ˈwȯ-yən\ *n* **1 :** a native or resident of Hawaii; *esp* **:** one of Polynesian ancestry **2 :** the Polynesian language of the Hawaiians — **Hawaiian** *adj*

Hawaiian guitar *n* **:** a usually electric stringed instrument consisting of a long soundboard and six to eight steel strings that are plucked while being pressed with a movable steel bar

Hawaii time *n* **:** the time of the 10th time zone west of Greenwich that includes the Hawaiian islands

¹hawk \ˈhȯk\ *n* **1 :** any of numerous birds of prey including all the smaller members of this group active mostly by day — compare OWL **2 :** a person who advocates immediate vigorous action in a dispute; *esp* **:** a supporter of a war or warlike policy — compare DOVE [Old English *hafoc*] — **hawk•ish** \ˈhȯ-kish\ *adj*

²hawk *vb* **1 :** to hunt birds by means of a trained hawk **2 :** to hunt on the wing like a hawk

³hawk *vt* **:** to offer for sale by calling out in the street ⟨*hawk* vegetables⟩ [back-formation from ²*hawker*]

⁴hawk *vb* **1 :** to utter a harsh guttural sound in or as if in clearing the throat **2 :** to raise by hawking ⟨*hawk* up phlegm⟩ [imitative]

¹hawk•er \ˈhȯ-kər\ *n* **:** FALCONER

²hawker *n* **:** one that hawks wares [Low German *höker,* from *höken* "to peddle"]

hawk•moth \ˈhȯk-ˌmȯth\ *n* **:** any of numerous stout-bodied swift-flying moths with long strong narrow pointed fore wings and small hind wings

hawks•bill \ˈhȯks-ˌbil\ *n* **:** a flesh-eating sea turtle whose shell yields the best tortoiseshell of commerce

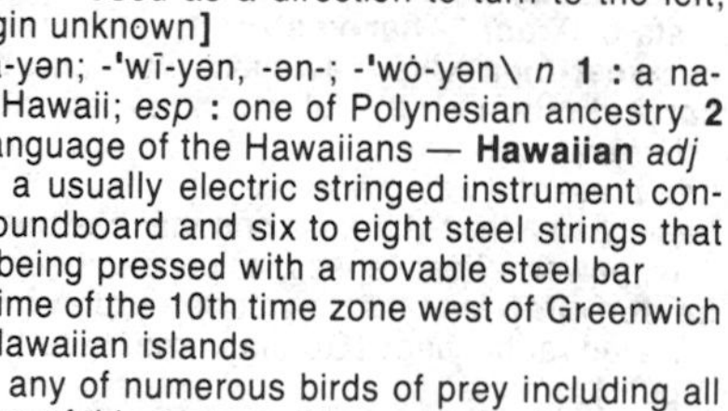
hawksbill

hawk•weed \ˈhȯ-ˌkwēd\ *n* **:** any of several plants of the daisy family that usually have flower heads with red or orange rays

hawse \ˈhȯz\ *n* **1 a :** HAWSEHOLE **b :** the part of a ship's bow that contains the hawseholes **2 :** the distance between a ship's bow and her anchor [Old Norse *hals* "neck, hawse"]

hawse•hole \-,hōl\ *n* : a hole in the bow of a ship through which a cable passes

haw•ser \'hȯ-zər\ *n* : a large rope for towing, mooring, or securing a ship [Anglo-French *hauceour,* from Middle French *haucier* "to hoist", derived from Latin *altus* "high"]

haw•thorn \'hȯ-,thȯrn\ *n* : any of a genus of spring-flowering spiny shrubs or small trees of the rose family with glossy and often lobed leaves, white or pink fragrant flowers, and small red fruits

[1]**hay** \'hā\ *n* : herbage (as grass) mowed and cured for fodder [Old English *hīeg*]

[2]**hay** *vb* **1** : to cut, cure, and store herbage for hay **2** : to feed with hay — **hay•er** *n*

hay•cock \'hā-,käk\ *n* : a conical pile of hay

hay fever *n* : an acute allergic reaction of the mucous membranes of the eyes, nose, and throat characterized especially by secretion of tears, itching, inflammation of the mucous membranes, and sneezing

hay•fork \'hā-,fȯrk\ *n* : a fork operated mechanically or by hand to load or unload hay

hay•loft \-,lȯft\ *n* : HAYMOW

hay•mak•er \-,mā-kər\ *n* **1** : one that cures or cuts and cures hay **2** : a powerful blow (as in boxing)

hay•mow \-,maů\ *n* : the upper part of a barn where hay is stored

hay•rack \-,rak\ *n* **1 a** : a frame mounted on the running gear of a wagon and used especially in hauling hay or straw **b** : a wagon mounted with a hayrack **2** : a feeding rack that holds hay for livestock

hay•rick \-,rik\ *n* : a large sometimes thatched outdoor stack of hay

hay•seed \-,sēd\ *n* **1 a** : seed shattered from hay **b** : clinging bits of straw of chaff from hay **2** : BUMPKIN, YOKEL

hay•stack \-,stak\ *n* : a stack of hay : HAYRICK

hay•wire \-,wīr\ *adj* **1** : hastily or shoddily made **2** : being out of order ⟨the radio is *haywire*⟩ **3** : emotionally or mentally upset : CRAZY ⟨went *haywire* after the accident⟩ [from the use of baling wire for makeshift repairs]

ha•zan \kə-'zän, 'käz-n\ *n, pl* **ha•za•nim** \kə-'zän-əm\ : CANTOR 2 [Hebrew *ḥazzān*]

[1]**haz•ard** \'haz-ərd\ *n* **1** : a game of chance played with two dice **2** : a source of danger **3 a** : ACCIDENT 1b, CHANCE **b** : chance that is likely to result unfavorably **4** : a golf-course obstacle [Middle French *hasard,* from Arabic *az-zahr* "the die"] **syn** see DANGER

△ *origin* *Hazard* was originally a game played with dice. The English word comes from Middle French *hasard,* which was most likely borrowed from Arabic *az-zahr,* "the die" ("one of the dice"). *Hazard* was borrowed from the French by the medieval English, and within a few centuries what had been a venture on the outcome of a throw of the dice could be any venture or risk. Now "chance" or "venture" and "risk" or "peril" are the primary meanings of *hazard.* The game of *hazard* is only infrequently played, and the modern player probably assumes that the game is so called because of the chances taken in play.

[2]**hazard** *vt* : VENTURE, RISK ⟨*hazard* a guess⟩

haz•ard•ous \'haz-ərd-əs\ *adj* : DANGEROUS, RISKY — **haz•ard•ous•ly** *adv* — **haz•ard•ous•ness** *n*

[1]**haze** \'hāz\ *vb* : to make or become hazy or cloudy [probably back-formation from *hazy*]

[2]**haze** *n* **1** : fine dust, smoke, or light vapor causing lack of transparency in the air **2** : a vague uncertain state of mind or mental perception

[3]**haze** *vt* **1** : to harass needlessly (as by exacting hard or disagreeable work or by mockery) **2** : to play abusive and humiliating tricks on by way of initiation [origin unknown] — **haz•er** *n*

ha•zel \'hā-zəl\ *n* **1** : any of a genus of shrubs or small trees of the birch family bearing edible nuts enclosed in a leafy case **2** : a light brown to a strong yellowish brown [Old English *hæsel*] — **hazel** adj

ha•zel•nut \'hā-zəl-,nət\ *n* : the nut of a hazel

hazy \'hā-zē\ *adj* **haz•i•er; -est** **1** : obscured or darkened by or as if by haze ⟨a *hazy* view⟩ **2** : VAGUE, INDEFINITE ⟨a *hazy* idea⟩ [origin unknown] — **haz•i•ly** \-zə-lē\ *adv* — **haz•i•ness** \-zē-nəs\ *n*

H-bomb \'āch-,bäm\ *n* : HYDROGEN BOMB

[1]**he** \hē, 'hē, ē\ *pron* **1** : that male one who is neither speaker nor hearer ⟨*he* is my father⟩ — compare HIM, HIS, IT, SHE, THEY **2** — used in generic sense or when the sex of the person is not specified ⟨*he* who hesitates is lost⟩ ⟨one should do the best *he* can⟩ [Old English *hē*]

[2]**he** \'hē\ *n* : a male person or animal

[1]**head** \'hed\ *n* **1** : the upper or front division of the body (as of a human or an insect) that contains the brain, the chief sense organs, and the mouth **2 a** : MIND, UNDERSTANDING ⟨a good *head* for figures⟩ **b** : mental or emotional control : POISE ⟨a level *head*⟩ **3** : the obverse of a coin **4 a** : PERSON, INDIVIDUAL ⟨count *heads*⟩ **b** *pl* **head** : a unit of number (as of livestock) **5 a** : the end that is upper or higher or opposite the foot ⟨the *head* of the bed⟩ **b** : the source of a stream **c** : either end of something (as a drum) whose two ends need not be distinguished **d** : a horizontal passage in a coal mine **6 a** : HEADMASTER **b** : a person responsible for directing the actions and duties of others : CHIEF, LEADER ⟨the *head* of a company⟩ **7 a** : an inflorescence (as of a dandelion or daisy) in the form of a rounded or flattened cluster of stemless flowers — called also *capitulum* **b** : a compact mass of plant parts (as leaves or flowers) ⟨a *head* of cabbage⟩ **8 a** : the leading element of a military column or a procession **b** : HEADWAY 1a **9 a** : the uppermost extremity or projecting part of an object : TOP **b** : the striking part of a weapon or tool **10** : a body of water kept in reserve at a height **11 a** : the difference in elevation between two points in a body of fluid **b** : the resulting pressure of the fluid at the lower point expressible as this height; *also* : pressure of a fluid ⟨a *head* of steam⟩ **12 a** : the bow and adjacent parts of a ship **b** : a ship's toilet **13** : the place of leadership or command ⟨the one at the *head* of the group⟩ **14 a** (1) : a word often in larger letters placed above a passage in order to introduce or categorize (2) : a separate part or topic **b** : a portion of a page or sheet that is above the first line of printing **15** : the foam that rises on an effervescing liquid **16 a** : the part of a boil, pimple, or abscess at which it is likely to break **b** : CRISIS ⟨events came to a *head*⟩ **17** : a part of a machine or machine tool containing a device (as a cutter, drill) ⟨a machine with a grinding *head*⟩; *also* : the part of an apparatus that performs the chief function or a particular function ⟨a shower*head*⟩ [Old English *hēafod*] — **off one's head** : CRAZY, DISTRACTED — **out of one's head** : DELIRIOUS — **over one's head** **1** : beyond one's comprehension **2** : so as to bypass or ignore one's superior standing or authority

[2]**head** *adj* **1** : of, relating to, or used for the head **2** : PRINCIPAL, CHIEF ⟨*head* cook⟩ **3** : situated at the head **4** : coming from in front ⟨*head* sea⟩

[3]**head** *vb* **1** : to cut back or off the upper or terminal growth of (a plant or plant part) **2 a** : to provide with or form a head ⟨*head* an arrow⟩ ⟨this cabbage *heads* early⟩ **b** : to form the head or top of ⟨a tower *headed* by a spire⟩ **3** : to put oneself at the head of : act as leader to ⟨*head* a revolt⟩ **4 a** : to get in front of so as to hinder, stop, or turn back ⟨*head* them off at the pass⟩ **b** : to take a lead over (as in a race) **c** : to pass (a stream) by going round above the source **5 a** : to put something at the head of (as a list) **b** : to stand as the first or leading member of ⟨*heads* the list⟩ **6** : to take or cause to take a specified course ⟨*head* for home⟩

head•ache \'hed-,āk\ *n* **1** : pain in the head **2** : an annoying or baffling situation or problem — **head•achy** \-,ā-kē\ *adj*

head•band \-,band\ *n* : a band worn on or around the head

head•board \-,bōrd, -,bȯrd\ *n* : a board forming the head (as of a bed)

head•cheese \-,chēz\ *n* : a jellied loaf or sausage made from the edible parts of the head, feet, and sometimes the tongue and heart especially of a pig

head cold *n* : a common cold centered in the nasal passages and adjacent mucous tissues

head•dress \'hed-,dres, 'he-\ *n* : a covering or ornament for the head

head•ed \'hed-əd\ *adj* **1** : having a head or a heading ⟨a *headed* bolt⟩ **2** : having such a head or so many heads ⟨curly-*headed*⟩ ⟨three-*headed* monster⟩

head•er \'hed-ər\ *n* **1** : one that removes heads; *esp* : a grain-harvesting machine that cuts off the grain heads and lifts them into a wagon **2 a :** a brick or stone laid in a wall with its end toward the face of the wall **b :** a beam fitted between trimmers and across the ends of tailpieces in a building frame **3 :** a fall or dive head foremost **4 :** a shot or pass made in soccer by hitting the ball with the head

head•first \ˈhed-ˈfərst\ *also* **head•fore•most** \-ˈfōr-ˌmōst, -fȯr-\ *adv* **:** with the head foremost **:** HEADLONG — **headfirst** *adj*

head gate *n* **:** a gate for controlling the water flowing into a channel (as an irrigation ditch)

head•gear \ˈhed-ˌgiər\ *n* **1 :** a covering or protective device for the head **2 :** harness for a horse's head

head•hunt•ing \-ˌhənt-iŋ\ *n* **:** the practice of cutting off and preserving the heads of enemies as trophies — **head•hunt•er** *n*

head•ing \ˈhed-iŋ\ *n* **1 :** the compass direction in which the longitudinal axis of a ship or aircraft points **2 :** something that forms or serves as a head; *esp* **:** an inscription, headline, or title standing at the top or beginning (as of a letter or chapter)

head•land \ˈhed-lənd, -ˌland\ *n* **:** a point of usually high land jutting out into the sea **:** PROMONTORY

head•less \-ləs\ *adj* **1 :** having no head **2 :** having no leader **3 :** lacking good sense or prudence **:** FOOLISH — **head•less•ness** *n*

head•light \-ˌlīt\ *n* **:** a light on the front of a vehicle

¹head•line \-ˌlīn\ *n* **1 :** the title over an item or article in a newspaper **2 :** a line at the top of a page (as in a book) giving a title or heading

²headline *vt* **1 :** to provide with a headline **2 :** to publicize highly **3 :** to be a leading performer or attraction in

head•lin•er \-ˌlī-nər\ *n* **:** a performer whose name is given prominent billing **:** STAR

head•lock \ˈhed-ˌläk\ *n* **:** a wrestling hold in which one encircles the opponent's head with one arm

¹head•long \-ˈlȯŋ\ *adv* **1 :** HEADFIRST **2 :** without deliberation **:** RECKLESSLY ⟨dash *headlong* into traffic⟩ **3 :** without pause or delay [Middle English *hedlong,* alteration of *hedling,* from *hed* "head" + *-ling*]

²head•long \-ˌlȯŋ\ *adj* **1 :** PRECIPITATE, RASH ⟨*headlong* flight⟩ **2 :** plunging headfirst ⟨a *headlong* dive into the pool⟩

head louse *n* **:** a louse that lives on the human scalp

head•man \ˈhed-ˈman, -ˌman\ *n* **:** one who is a leader (as of a tribe, clan, or village) **:** CHIEF

head•mas•ter \ˈhed-ˌmas-tər\ *n* **:** a man heading the staff of a private school

head•mis•tress \-ˌmis-trəs\ *n* **:** a woman heading the staff of a private school

head•most \-ˌmōst\ *adj* **:** most advanced **:** LEADING

head–on \ˈhed-ˈȯn, -ˈän\ *adj* **1 :** having the front facing in the direction of initial contact or line of sight **2 :** FRONTAL 2b — **head–on** *adv*

head over heels *adv* **1 :** in or as if in a somersault ⟨fell *head over heels* down the hill⟩ **2 :** HOPELESSLY, DEEPLY ⟨*head over heels* in love⟩

head•phone \ˈhed-ˌfōn\ *n* **:** an earphone held over the ear by a band worn on the head

head•piece \-ˌpēs\ *n* **1 :** a protective or defensive covering for the head **2 :** INTELLIGENCE 1a, BRAINS

head•pin \-ˌpin\ *n* **:** a pin that stands at the apex in a triangular arrangement of bowling pins

head•quarter \ˈhed-ˌkwȯrt-ər, -ˌkwȯt, hed-ˈ\ *vb* **1 :** to make one's headquarters **2 :** to place in headquarters

head•quar•ters \-ərz\ *n sing or pl* **1 :** a place from which a commander exercises command **2 :** the administrative center of an enterprise

head•rest \ˈhed-ˌrest\ *n* **:** a support for the head

head•sail \-ˌsāl, -səl\ *n* **:** a sail set forward of the mast

head•set \-ˌset\ *n* **:** a pair of headphones

head•ship \-ˌship\ *n* **:** the position, office, or dignity of a head

heads•man \ˈhedz-mən\ *n* **:** one that beheads **:** EXECUTIONER

head•stall \ˈhed-ˌstȯl\ *n* **:** a part of a bridle or halter that encircles the head

head•stand \-ˌstand\ *n* **:** the gymnastic feat of standing on one's head usually with support from the hands

head start *n* **1 :** an advantage allowed at the start of a race **2 :** a favorable or promising beginning

head•stock \ˈhed-ˌstäk\ *n* **:** a part of a lathe that holds the revolving spindle and its attachments

head•stone \-ˌstōn\ *n* **:** a memorial stone placed at the head of a grave

head•strong \-ˌstrȯŋ\ *adj* **1 :** not easily restrained **:** WILLFUL ⟨a *headstrong* child⟩ **2 :** directed by ungovernable will ⟨violent *headstrong* actions⟩

head•wait•er \ˈhed-ˈwāt-ər\ *n* **:** the head of the dining-room staff of a restaurant or hotel

head•wa•ters \-ˌwȯt-ərz, -ˌwät-\ *n pl* **:** the source and upper part of a stream

headset

head•way \-ˌwā\ *n* **1 a :** motion or rate of motion (as of a ship) in a forward direction **b :** ADVANCE, PROGRESS ⟨made *headway* in scientific research⟩ **2 :** clear space (as under an arch) **3 :** the time interval between two vehicles traveling in the same direction on the same route

head wind *n* **:** a wind blowing in a direction opposite to a course especially of a ship or aircraft

head•word \ˈhed-ˌwərd\ *n* **:** a word or term placed at the beginning (as of a chapter or entry)

head•work \-ˌwərk\ *n* **:** mental work **:** THINKING

heady \ˈhed-ē\ *adj* **head•i•er; -est 1 :** WILLFUL, RASH ⟨*heady* opinions⟩ **2 :** tending to make giddy ⟨*heady* wine⟩ — **head•i•ly** \ˈhed-l-ē\ *adv* — **head•i•ness** \ˈhed-ē-nəs\ *n*

heal \ˈhēl\ *vb* **1 :** to make healthy or whole **2 :** to return to a sound or healthy condition ⟨the arm *healed*⟩ ⟨the wound *healed*⟩ [Old English *hǣlan*] **syn** see CURE

heal•er \ˈhē-lər\ *n* **:** one that heals

health \ˈhelth\ *n* **1 a :** the condition of being sound in body, mind, or spirit; *esp* **:** freedom from physical disease or pain **b :** general condition of an individual ⟨in poor *health*⟩ **2 :** flourishing condition ⟨the economic *health* of a country⟩ **3 :** a toast to someone's health or prosperity [Old English *hǣlth,* from *hāl* "whole, hale"]

health•ful \-fəl\ *adj* **1 :** beneficial to health of body or mind ⟨*healthful* exercise⟩ **2 :** HEALTHY 1 — **health•ful•ly** \-fə-lē\ *adv* — **health•ful•ness** *n*

• **syn** HEALTHFUL, WHOLESOME, SALUBRIOUS, SALUTARY mean favorable to the health of mind or body. HEALTHFUL implies a positive contribution to a healthy condition ⟨a *healthful* diet⟩ WHOLESOME applies to what benefits, builds up, or sustains physically, mentally, or spiritually ⟨*wholesome* meals⟩ ⟨*wholesome* literature⟩ SALUBRIOUS applies chiefly to the helpful effects of climate or air; SALUTARY describes something corrective or beneficially effective, even though it may in itself be unpleasant ⟨the *salutary* influence of constructive criticism⟩

healthy \ˈhel-thē\ *adj* **health•i•er; -est 1 :** enjoying or typical of good health **:** WELL **2 :** conducive to health **3 a :** PROSPEROUS, FLOURISHING ⟨a *healthy* economy⟩ **b :** not small or feeble **:** CONSIDERABLE ⟨a *healthy* serving⟩ — **health•i•ly** \-thə-lē\ *adv* — **health•i•ness** \-thē-nəs\ *n*

• **syn** WELL, SOUND: HEALTHY implies full strength and vigor as well as freedom from disease; WELL implies merely freedom from disease or illness; SOUND stresses perfect health, absence of all defects, disease, or morbidity ⟨a *sound* mind in a *sound* body⟩

¹heap \ˈhēp\ *n* **1 :** a collection of things thrown one on another **:** PILE ⟨a rubbish *heap*⟩ **2 :** a great number or large quantity **:** LOT ⟨*heaps* of people⟩ ⟨a *heap* of fun⟩ [Old English *hēap*]

²heap *vt* **1 :** to throw or lay in a heap **:** PILE ⟨*heap* up leaves⟩ **2 :** to cast or bestow in large quantities ⟨*heaped* scorn on them⟩ **3 :** to fill (a measure or container) more than even full

hear \ˈhiər\ *vb* **heard** \ˈhərd\; **hear•ing** \ˈhiər-iŋ\ **1 :** to perceive or grasp by the ear ⟨*hear* music⟩; *also* **:** to have the power of perceiving sound ⟨doesn't *hear* well⟩ **2 :** to gain knowledge of by hearing **:** LEARN ⟨*heard* you're leaving⟩ **3 :** to listen to **:** HEED ⟨*hear* me out⟩ **4 a :** to give a legal hearing to ⟨*hear* a case⟩ **b :** to take testimony from ⟨*hear* witnesses⟩ **5 a :** to get news ⟨*heard* from them yesterday⟩ **b :** to have knowledge ⟨had *heard* of them⟩ **6 :** to entertain the idea ⟨wouldn't *hear* of it [Old English *hīeran*] — **hear•er** \ˈhir-ər\ *n*

• **syn** LISTEN: HEAR implies the actual sensation and response of the auditory nerves to a stimulus; LISTEN implies the conscious or voluntary effort to hear.

hear•ing *n* **1 a :** the process, function, or power of perceiving sound; *esp* **:** the special sense by which noises and tones are received as stimuli **b :** EARSHOT ⟨stay within *hearing*⟩ **2 a :** a chance to present one's case **b :** a listening to arguments or testimony **c :** a session in which testimony is heard ⟨a public *hearing* on the bill⟩

hearing aid *n* **:** an electronic device for amplifying sound usually worn by a person to assist poor hearing

hear•ken \ˈhär-kən\ *vi* **hear•kened; hear•ken•ing** \ˈhärk-ning, -ə-ning\ **1 :** LISTEN 1 **2 :** to give respectful attention [Old English *heorcnian*]

hear•say \ˈhiər-ˌsā\ *n* **:** something heard from another **:** RUMOR

hearsay evidence *n* **:** evidence based not on a witness's personal knowledge but on information given the witness by someone else

hearse \ˈhərs\ *n* **:** a vehicle for conveying the dead to the grave [Middle French *herce* "harrow, frame for holding candles", from Latin *hirpex* "harrow"]

△ **origin** In Middle French the word *herce,* meaning "harrow", was applied to a triangular frame that was used for holding candles and was similar to the ancient form of a harrow. Both the literal and extended senses were used in English when the word was borrowed. It was a widespread practice to erect an elaborate framework over the coffin or tomb of a distinguished person. Because such frameworks were often decorated with lighted candles, the term *hearse* was applied to them. A series of extensions led to the use of *hearse* for a bier and then for a vehicle to carry the dead to the grave.

heart \ˈhärt\ *n* **1 a :** a hollow muscular organ of vertebrate animals that by its rhythmic contraction acts as a force pump maintaining the circulation of the blood **b :** a structure in an invertebrate animal similar in function to the vertebrate heart **2 :** something resembling a heart in shape **3 a :** a red stylized heart used to distinguish a suit of playing cards; *also* **:** a card of the suit bearing hearts **b** *pl* **:** a card game in which the object is to avoid taking tricks containing hearts or win all of the hearts **4 a :** the whole personality including intellectual and emotional functions or traits **b :** generous disposition **:** KINDNESS ⟨a person without a *heart*⟩ **c :** COURAGE, SPIRIT ⟨take *heart*⟩ **5 a :** the central part ⟨the *heart* of the forest⟩ **b :** the most important part ⟨the *heart* of the issue⟩ [Old English *heorte*] — **by heart :** by rote — **to heart :** with deep concern

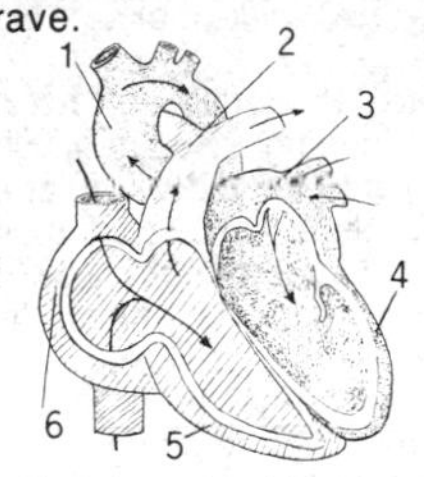

heart 1a: *1* aorta, *2* pulmonary artery, *3* left auricle, *4* left ventricle, *5* right ventricle, *6* right auricle

heart•ache \ˈhärt-ˌāk\ *n* **:** mental anguish **:** SORROW

heart attack *n* **:** an acute episode of heart disease especially when caused by a coronary thrombosis or occlusion

heart•beat \ˈhärt-ˌbēt\ *n* **:** one complete pulsation of the heart

heart block *n* **:** lack of coordination of the heartbeat so that the atria and ventricles beat independently

heart•break \ˈhärt-ˌbrāk\ *n* **:** crushing grief

heart•break•ing \-ˌbrā-king\ *adj* **:** causing crushing grief — **heart•break•ing•ly** \-king-lē\ *adv*

heart•bro•ken \-ˌbrō-kən\ *adj* **:** overcome by grief

heart•burn \-ˌbərn\ *n* **:** a burning discomfort that seems to be localized about the heart and is usually related to spasm of the lower esophagus or the upper stomach

heart•burn•ing \-ˌbər-ning\ *n* **:** intense or rancorous jealousy or resentment

heart disease *n* **:** an abnormal condition of the heart or of the heart and circulation

heart•ed \ˈhärt-əd\ *adj* **:** having a heart especially of a specified kind ⟨stout*hearted*⟩

heart•en \ˈhärt-n\ *vt* **heart•ened; heart•en•ing** \ˈhärt-ning, -n-ing\ **:** to cheer up **:** ENCOURAGE

heart•felt \ˈhärt-ˌfelt\ *adj* **:** deeply felt **:** EARNEST

hearth \ˈhärth\ *n* **1 a :** a brick, stone, or cement area in front of a fireplace **b :** the floor of a fireplace **c** (1) **:** the lowest section of a blast furnace (2) **:** the floor of a metal-processing furnace **2 :** HOME 1a, FIRESIDE [Old English *heorth*]

hearth•stone \-ˌstōn\ *n* **:** stone forming a hearth

heart•i•ly \ˈhärt-l-ē\ *adv* **1 :** with sincerity, goodwill, or enthusiasm ⟨set to work *heartily*⟩ ⟨eat *heartily*⟩ **2 :** CORDIALLY ⟨made them *heartily* welcome⟩ **3 :** COMPLETELY, THOROUGHLY ⟨*heartily* sick of the continuing complaints⟩

heart•land \ˈhärt-ˌland\ *n* **:** a central land area; *esp* **:** one thought of as economically and militarily self-sufficient

heart•less \-ləs\ *adj* **:** lacking feeling or compassion **:** PITILESS — **heart•less•ly** *adv* — **heart•less•ness** *n*

heart•rend•ing \-ˌren-ding\ *adj* **:** causing heartbreak ⟨a *heartrending* experience⟩

hearts•ease \ˈhärt-ˌsēz\ *n* **1 :** peace of mind **:** TRANQUILLITY **2 :** any of various violas; *esp* **:** WILD PANSY

heart•sick \ˈhärt-ˌsik\ *adj* **:** very despondent **:** DEPRESSED — **heart•sick•ness** *n*

heart•sore \-ˌsōr, -ˌsȯr\ *adj* **:** HEARTSICK

heart•string \-ˌstring\ *n* **:** the deepest emotions or affections ⟨pulled at their *heartstrings*⟩

heart•throb \-ˌthräb\ *n* **1 :** the throb of a heart **2 a :** sentimental emotion **:** PASSION **b :** SWEETHEART 2

heart–to–heart \ˌhärt-tə-ˌhärt\ *adj* **:** SINCERE, FRANK ⟨a *heart-to-heart* talk⟩

heart•wood \ˈhärt-ˌwu̇d\ *n* **:** the older harder usually darker wood in the central portion of a woody stem — compare SAPWOOD

[1]**hearty** \ˈhärt-ē\ *adj* **heart•i•er; -est 1 a :** giving unqualified support **:** THOROUGHGOING ⟨*hearty* agreement⟩ **b :** enthusiastically cordial ⟨a *hearty* welcome⟩ **c :** UNRESTRAINED ⟨*hearty* laughter⟩ **2 a :** exhibiting vigorous good health **b :** abundant and satisfying ⟨a *hearty* meal⟩ **c :** NOURISHING ⟨a *hearty* beef stew⟩ **3 :** ENERGETIC, STRONG ⟨gave a *hearty* pull⟩ — **heart•i•ness** *n*

[2]**hearty** *n, pl* **heart•ies :** a bold brave fellow

[1]**heat** \ˈhēt\ *vb* **1 :** to make or become warm or hot **2 :** to make or become excited or angry [Old English *hǣtan*]

[2]**heat** *n* **1 a :** a condition of being hot **:** WARMTH **b :** a high degree of hotness **c :** a hot place or period **d :** a form of energy that causes substances to rise in temperature, fuse, evaporate, expand, or undergo any of various other changes and that flows to a body by contact with or radiation from bodies at higher temperatures **2 a :** intensity of feeling; *esp* **:** ANGER ⟨answered with some *heat*⟩ **b :** the height of an action or condition ⟨the *heat* of battle⟩ **c :** sexual excitement especially in a female mammal; *esp* **:** ESTRUS **3 :** pungency of flavor **4 :** a single continuous effort: as **a :** a single course in a race **b :** one of several preliminary races held to eliminate less competent contenders **5 a** *slang* **:** POLICE FORCE — usually used with *the* **b :** PRESSURE, COERCION ⟨the *heat* was on to get the job done⟩ — **heat•less** \ˈhēt-ləs\ *adj*

heat•ed \ˈhēt-əd\ *adj* **1 :** HOT ⟨a *heated* engine⟩ **2 :** marked by emotional heat **:** ANGRY ⟨*heated* words⟩ — **heat•ed•ly** *adv*

heat engine *n* **:** a mechanism for converting heat energy into mechanical energy

heat•er \ˈhēt-ər\ *n* **:** a device that imparts heat or holds something to be heated

heat exhaustion *n* **:** a condition marked by weakness, nausea, dizziness, and profuse sweating that results from physical exertion in a hot environment — called also *heat prostration;* compare HEATSTROKE

heath \ˈhēth\ *n* **1 :** any of a family of shrubby often evergreen plants that thrive on open barren usually acid and poorly drained soil; *esp* **:** a low evergreen shrub with whorls of needlelike leaves and clusters of small flowers **2 :** a tract of usually level and poorly drained wasteland commonly overgrown with low shrubs [Old English *hǣth*] — **heath•like** \-ˌlīk\ *adj* — **heathy** \ˈhē-thē\ *adj*

[1]**hea•then** \ˈhē-t͟hən\ *adj* **:** of or relating to heathens [Old English *hǣthen*]

[2]**heathen** *n, pl* **heathens** *or* **heathen 1 :** an unconverted member of a people or nation that does not acknowledge the God of the Bible **2 :** an uncivilized or irreligious person — **hea•then•dom** \-dəm\ *n* — **hea•then•ism** \-ˌt͟hə-ˌniz-əm\ *n*

hea•then•ish \ˈhē-t͟hə-nish\ *adj* **:** resembling or characteristic of heathens **:** BARBAROUS — **hea•then•ish•ly** *adv*

[1]**heath•er** \ˈhet͟h-ər\ *n* **:** HEATH 1; *esp* **:** a common evergreen heath of northern and alpine regions with small crowded stemless leaves and tiny usually purplish pink flowers in one-sided

\ə\ **abut**	\au̇\ **out**	\i\ **tip**	\ȯ\ **saw**	\u̇\ **foot**
\ər\ **further**	\ch\ **chin**	\ī\ **life**	\ȯi\ **coin**	\y\ **yet**
\a\ **mat**	\e\ **pet**	\j\ **job**	\th\ **thin**	\yü\ **few**
\ā\ **take**	\ē\ **easy**	\ng\ **sing**	\t͟h\ **this**	\yu̇\ **cure**
\ä\ **cot, cart**	\g\ **go**	\ō\ **bone**	\ü\ **food**	\zh\ **vision**

spikes [Middle English *hather*] — **heath•ery** \'heth-rē, -ə-rē\ *adj*

[2]heather *adj* **1 :** of, relating to, or resembling heather **2 :** having flecks of various colors ⟨a soft *heather* tweed⟩

heath hen *n* **:** an extinct grouse of the northeastern United States related to the prairie chicken

heat island *n* **:** an urban area in which significantly more heat is absorbed and retained (as by buildings and streets) than in surrounding areas

heat lightning *n* **:** flashes of light without thunder seen near the horizon and caused by distant lightning reflected by high clouds

heat rash *n* **:** PRICKLY HEAT

heat•stroke \'hēt-,strōk\ *n* **:** a condition marked especially by cessation of sweating, high fever, and collapse that results from prolonged exposure to high temperature — compare HEAT EXHAUSTION

heat wave *n* **:** a period of unusually hot weather

[1]heave \'hēv\ *vb* **heaved** *or* **hove** \'hōv\; **heav•ing 1 :** to raise with an effort **:** LIFT ⟨*heave* a trunk onto a truck⟩ **2 :** THROW, HURL ⟨*heave* a rock⟩ **3 :** to utter with effort ⟨*heave* a sigh⟩ **4 :** to rise and fall repeatedly ⟨the runner's chest was *heaving*⟩ **5 :** to be thrown up or raised ⟨the ground *heaved* during the earthquake⟩ **6 :** RETCH [Old English *hebban*] — **heav•er** *n* — **heave to :** to bring a ship to a stop

[2]heave *n* **1 a :** an effort to heave or raise **b :** a forceful throw **:** CAST **2 :** an upward motion; *esp* **:** a rhythmical rising (as of the chest in breathing)

heav•en \'hev-ən\ *n* **1 :** SKY 1 — usually used in pl. **2 a** *often cap* **:** the dwelling place of God **b :** a spiritual state of everlasting communion with God **3** *cap* **:** GOD 1 **4 :** a place or condition of utmost happiness [Old English *heofon*]

heav•en•ly \'hev-ən-lē\ *adj* **1 :** of or relating to heaven or the heavens **2 :** DIVINE, SACRED ⟨*heavenly* grace⟩ **3 :** supremely delightful ⟨a *heavenly* day⟩ — **heav•en•li•ness** *n*

heav•en•ward \'hev-ən-wərd\ *adv or adj* **:** toward heaven

heav•en•wards \-wərdz\ *adv* **:** HEAVENWARD

heav•i•ly \'hev-ə-lē\ *adv* **1 :** in a heavy manner **2 :** in a slow and laborious manner ⟨breathe *heavily*⟩ **3 :** to a great degree **:** SEVERELY ⟨*heavily* punished⟩

[1]heavy \'hev-ē\ *adj* **heav•i•er**; **-est 1 a :** having great weight **b :** weighty in proportion to bulk **:** having a high specific gravity ⟨gold is a *heavy* metal⟩ **2 :** hard to bear; *esp* **:** GRIEVOUS ⟨a *heavy* sorrow⟩ **3 :** of great import **:** SERIOUS ⟨words *heavy* with meaning⟩ **4 a :** borne down by something oppressive **:** BURDENED **b :** PREGNANT 1a; *esp* **:** approaching the time for giving birth **5 a :** slow or dull from loss of vitality or resiliency **:** SLUGGISH **b :** lacking sparkle or vivacity ⟨a *heavy* writing style⟩ **c :** lacking mirth or gaiety **:** DOLEFUL **6 :** dulled with weariness **:** DROWSY **7 :** greater in volume or force than the average ⟨*heavy* traffic⟩ ⟨*heavy* seas⟩ **8 a :** OVERCAST ⟨*heavy* skies⟩ **b :** full of clay and inclined to hold water ⟨*heavy* soils⟩ **c :** coming as if from a depth **:** LOUD **d :** THICK ⟨a *heavy* growth of timber⟩ **e :** OPPRESSIVE ⟨a *heavy* odor⟩ **f :** STEEP, ACUTE ⟨a *heavy* grade⟩ **g :** LABORIOUS, DIFFICULT ⟨a *heavy* task⟩ **h :** of large capacity or output ⟨a *heavy* drinker⟩ **9 a :** digested with difficulty because of excessive richness or seasoning ⟨a *heavy* dessert⟩ **b :** not properly raised or leavened ⟨*heavy* bread⟩ **10 :** producing goods (as coal or steel) used in the production of other goods ⟨*heavy* industry⟩ **11 :** heavily armed or armored ⟨*heavy* tank⟩ **12 :** having stress ⟨*heavy* syllables⟩ [Old English *hefig*] — **heav•i•ness** *n*

[2]heavy *adv* **:** in a heavy manner **:** HEAVILY

[3]heavy *n, pl* **heav•ies 1 :** HEAVYWEIGHT 2 **2 a :** a theatrical role or an actor representing a dignified or imposing person **b :** VILLAIN 4

heavy–du•ty \,hev-ē-'düt-ē, -'dyüt-\ *adj* **:** able or designed to withstand unusual strain

heavy–foot•ed \-'fu̇t-əd\ *adj* **:** heavy and slow in movement

heavy–hand•ed \-'han-dəd\ *adj* **1 :** CLUMSY 1 **2 :** OPPRESSIVE 1,2 — **heavy–hand•ed•ly** *adv* — **heavy–hand•ed•ness** *n*

heavy•heart•ed \-'härt-əd\ *adj* **:** SAD 1, MELANCHOLY — **heavy•heart•ed•ly** *adv* — **heavy•heart•ed•ness** *n*

heavy hydrogen *n* **:** DEUTERIUM

heavy•set \,hev-ē-'set\ *adj* **:** being stocky and compact and sometimes tending to stoutness in build

heavy water *n* **:** water containing more than the usual proportion of heavy isotopes; *esp* **:** water enriched with deuterium

heavy•weight \'hev-ē-,wāt\ *n* **1 :** one above average in weight **2 :** one in the heaviest class of contestants; *esp* **:** a boxer weighing over 81 kilograms

He•bra•ic \hi-'brā-ik\ *adj* **:** of, relating to, or characteristic of the Hebrews or their language or culture

He•bra•ism \'hē-brā-,iz-əm\ *n* **1 :** a characteristic feature of Hebrew occurring in another language **2 :** the thought, spirit, or practice characteristic of the Hebrews

He•bra•ist \-,brā-əst\ *n* **:** a specialist in Hebrew and Hebraic studies

He•brew \'hē-,brü\ *n* **1 :** a member of or descendant from one of a group of northern Semitic peoples including the Israelites; *esp* **:** ISRAELITE **2 a :** the Semitic language of the ancient Hebrews **b :** any of various later forms of this language [derived from Greek *Hebraios,* from Aramaic *'Ebrai*] — **Hebrew** *adj*

He•brews \'hē-,brüz\ *n* — *see* BIBLE table

hec•a•tomb \'hek-ə-,tōm\ *n* **1 :** an ancient Greek and Roman sacrifice of 100 oxen or cattle **2 :** a great slaughter [Latin *hecatombe,* from Greek *hekatombē,* from *hekaton* "hundred" + *bous* "cow"]

heck•le \'hek-əl\ *vt* **heck•led**; **heck•ling** \'hek-ling, -ə-ling\ **:** to interrupt with questions or comments usually in order to annoy or hinder **:** BADGER ⟨*heckle* a public speaker⟩ [Middle English *hekelen,* from *heckele* "hackle"] — **heck•ler** \-lər, -ə-lər\ *n*

hect- *or* **hecto-** *combining form* **:** hundred [French, derived from Greek *hekaton*]

hect•are \'hek-,taər, -,teər, -,tär\ *n* — see METRIC SYSTEM table

hec•tic \'hek-tik\ *adj* **1 a :** characteristic of a wasting disease; *esp* **:** being a fluctuating but persistent fever (as in tuberculosis) **b :** affected by or appearing as if affected by a hectic fever; *esp* **:** FLUSHED **2 :** filled with excitement or confusion [derived from Late Latin *hecticus,* from Greek *hektikos* "habitual, consumptive", from *echein* "to have, hold"] — **hec•ti•cal•ly** \-ti-kə-lē, -klē\ *adv*

hec•to•gram \'hek-tə,gram\ *n* — see METRIC SYSTEM table

hec•to•graph \-,graf\ *n* **:** a machine for making copies of a writing or drawing — **hectograph** *vt* — **hec•to•graph•ic** \,hek-tə-'graf-ik\ *adj*

hec•to•li•ter \'hek-tə-,lēt-ər\ *n* — see METRIC SYSTEM table

hec•to•me•ter \'hek-tə-,mēt-ər\ *n* — see METRIC SYSTEM table

hec•tor \'hek-tər\ *vb* **hec•tored**; **hec•tor•ing** \-tə-ring, -tring\ **1 :** to act like a bully **:** SWAGGER **2 :** to intimidate by bluster or personal pressure [*Hector,* Trojan champion]

he'd \hēd, ,hēd, ēd\ **:** he had **:** he would

hed•dle \'hed-l\ *n* **:** one of the sets of parallel cords or wires that with their mounting compose the harness used to guide warp threads in a loom [probably derived from Old English *hefeld*]

[1]hedge \'hej\ *n* **1 a :** a fence or boundary formed by a dense row of shrubs or low trees **b :** a fence or wall marking a boundary or forming a barrier **2 :** a protection against financial loss **3 :** a statement that intentionally avoids a direct answer or a promise [Old English *hecg*]

[2]hedge *vb* **1 :** to enclose or protect with or as if with a hedge **2 :** to obstruct with or as if with a barrier **:** HINDER ⟨*hedged* in by restrictions⟩ **3 :** to protect oneself from losing by making a second balancing transaction ⟨*hedge* on a bet⟩ **4 :** to avoid giving a direct or definite answer or promise ⟨*hedged* when asked their opinion⟩ — **hedg•er** *n*

[3]hedge *adj* **:** of, relating to, or designed for a hedge

hedge•hog \'hej-,hóg, -,häg\ *n* **1 :** an Old World insect-eating mammal having sharp spines mixed with the hair on its back and able to roll itself up into a spiny ball **2 :** PORCUPINE

hedgehog 1

hedge•hop \-,häp\ *vi* **:** to fly an airplane so low that it is sometimes necessary to climb to avoid obstacles (as trees) [back-formation from *hedgehopper*] — **hedge•hop•per** *n*

hedge•row \-,rō\ *n* **:** HEDGE 1a; *esp* **:** one bounding or separating fields

he•do•nism \'hēd-n-,iz-əm\ *n* **1 :** a doctrine that pleasure or happiness is the sole or chief good in life **2 :** a way of life based on hedonism [Greek *hēdonē* "pleasure"] — **he•do•nist** \-n-əst\ *n* — **he•do•nis•tic** \ˌhēd-n-ˈis-tik\ *adj*

-he•dral \ˈhē-drəl\ *adj combining form* **:** having (such) a surface or (such or so many) surfaces ⟨di*hedral*⟩ [Greek *hedra* "seat"]

-he•dron \ˈhē-drən\ *n combining form, pl* **-hedrons** *or* **-he•dra** \-drə\ **:** crystal or geometric figure having a (specified) form or number of surfaces ⟨rhombo*hedron*⟩ [Greek *hedra* "seat"]

hee•bie–jee•bies \ˌhē-bē-ˈjē-bēz\ *n pl* **:** JITTERS, WILLIES [coined by Billy DeBeck, died 1942, American cartoonist]

1heed \ˈhēd\ *vb* **1 :** to pay attention **2 :** to concern oneself with **:** MIND [Old English *hēdan*]

2heed *n* **:** ATTENTION 1, NOTICE ⟨give *heed* to my words⟩

heed•ful \ˈhēd-fəl\ *adj* **:** taking heed ⟨*heedful* of the rights of others⟩ — **heed•ful•ly** \-fə-lē\ *adv* — **heed•ful•ness** *n*

heed•less \-ləs\ *adj* **:** not taking heed **:** INATTENTIVE ⟨*heedless* of danger⟩ — **heed•less•ly** *adv* — **heed•less•ness** *n*

hee–haw \ˈhē-ˌhȯ\ *n* **1 :** the bray of a donkey **2 :** a loud rude laugh **:** GUFFAW [imitative] — **hee–haw** *vi*

1heel \ˈhēl\ *n* **1 a :** the back part of the human foot behind the arch and below the ankle; *also* **:** the corresponding part of a lower vertebrate **b :** the part of the palm of the hand nearest the wrist **2 a :** a part (as of a shoe) that covers the human heel **b :** a solid attachment of a shoe or boot forming the back of the sole under the heel of the foot **3 :** something resembling a heel in form, function, or position: as **a** (1) **:** one of the crusty ends of a loaf of bread (2) **:** one of the rind ends of a cheese **b** (1) **:** the after end of a ship's keel (2) **:** the lower end of a mast **c :** the base of a tuber or cutting of a plant used for propagation **d :** the base of a ladder **4 :** a contemptible person [Old English *hōla*] — **heeled** \ˈhēld\ *adj* — **heel•less** \ˈhēl-ləs\ *adj*

2heel *vt* **1 :** to furnish with a heel **2 :** to supply especially with money ⟨a well-*heeled* customer⟩ **3 :** to follow closely ⟨a dog *heeling* his master⟩ — **heel•er** *n*

3heel *vb* **:** to tilt or cause to tilt to one side **:** TIP ⟨a boat *heeling* badly⟩ [Old English *hieldan*]

4heel *n* **:** a tilt to one side

heel–and–toe \ˌhē-lən-ˈtō\ *adj* **:** marked by a stride in which the heel of one foot touches the ground before the toe of the other foot leaves it ⟨a *heel-and-toe* walking race⟩

heel•tap \ˈhēl-ˌtap\ *n* **1 :** a lift for the heel of a shoe **2 :** a small quantity of liquor remaining (as in a glass after drinking)

1heft \ˈheft\ *n* **:** physical or figurative weight [derived from *heave*]

2heft *vt* **1 :** to heave up **:** HOIST **2 :** to test the weight of by lifting

hefty \ˈhef-tē\ *adj* **heft•i•er; -est 1 :** quite heavy **2 :** marked by bigness, bulk, and usually strength — **heft•i•ly** \-tə-lē\ *adv* — **heft•i•ness** \-tē-nəs\ *n*

he•gem•o•ny \hi-ˈjem-ə-nē, ˈhej-ə-ˌmō-nē\ *n* **:** dominant influence or authority especially of one nation over others [Greek *hēgemonia,* from *hēgemōn* "leader", from *hēgeisthai* "to lead"]

he•gi•ra *or* **he•ji•ra** \hi-ˈjī-rə, ˈhej-ə-rə\ *n* **:** a journey especially when undertaken to seek refuge away from a dangerous or undesirable environment [the *Hegira,* flight of Muhammad from Mecca in A.D. 622, from Medieval Latin, from Arabic *hijrah,* literally, "flight"]

Hei•del•berg man \ˌhīd-l-ˌbərg-, -ˌberg-\ *n* **:** an early Pleistocene man known only from a massive fossilized jaw with distinctly human teeth [*Heidelberg,* Germany]

heif•er \ˈhef-ər\ *n* **:** a young cow; *esp* **:** one that has not had a calf [Old English *hēahfore*]

heigh–ho \ˈhī-ˈhō,ˈhā-\ *interj* — used typically to express boredom, weariness, or sadness or sometimes as a cry of encouragement

height \ˈhīt, ˈhītth\ *n* **1 a :** the highest part **:** SUMMIT **b :** the highest or most advanced point or level ⟨the *height* of stupidity⟩ **2 a :** the distance from the bottom to the top of something standing upright **b :** the extent of elevation above a level **:** ALTITUDE **3 :** the condition of being tall or high **4 a :** an extent of land rising to a considerable degree above the surrounding country **b :** a high point or position [Old English *hiehthu*]

• syn ELEVATION, ALTITUDE: HEIGHT refers to something measured vertically whether high or low ⟨a wall 2 meters in *height*⟩ ⟨lettering not more than one centimeter in *height*⟩ ELEVATION and ALTITUDE suggest reckoning of height by angular measurement or atmospheric pressure; ALTITUDE is preferable when referring to vertical distance above the surface of the earth or above sea level and ELEVATION is used especially in reference to vertical height on land ⟨fly at an *altitude* of 10,000 meters⟩ ⟨Mexico City has a high *elevation*⟩

height•en \ˈhīt-n\ *vb* **height•ened; height•en•ing** \ˈhīt-ning, -n-ing\ **1 a :** to increase the amount or degree of **:** AUGMENT ⟨*heightened* the citizens' awareness⟩ **b :** to make or become brighter or more intense **:** DEEPEN ⟨excitement *heightened* the pinkness of their cheeks⟩ **c :** to bring out more strongly **:** point up ⟨*heighten* a contrast⟩ **2 a :** to raise high or higher **:** ELEVATE **b :** to raise above the ordinary or trite **syn** see INTENSIFY

hei•nous \ˈhā-nəs\ *adj* **:** hatefully or shockingly evil **:** ABOMINABLE [Middle French *haineus,* from *haine* "hate", from *hair* "to hate", of Germanic origin] **syn** see OUTRAGEOUS — **hei•nous•ly** *adv* — **hei•nous•ness** *n*

heir \ˈaər, ˈeər\ *n* **1 :** a person who inherits or is entitled to inherit property **2 :** a person who has legal claim to a title or a throne when the person holding it dies [Old French, from Latin *heres*] — **heir•ship** \-ˌship\ *n*

heir apparent *n, pl* **heirs apparent :** an heir who cannot legally be deprived of the right to succeed (as to a throne or a title)

heir•ess \ˈar-əs, ˈer-\ *n* **:** a woman who is an heir; *also* **:** one who is wealthy through inheritance

heir•loom \ˈaər-ˌlüm, ˈeər-\ *n* **:** a piece of personal property handed down by inheritance for several generations [Middle English *heirlome,* from *heir* + *lome* "implement"]

heir presumptive *n, pl* **heirs presumptive :** an heir whose present right to inherit could be lost through the birth of a nearer relative

1heist \ˈhīst\ *vt* **1** *chiefly dialect* **:** HOIST **2** *slang* **a :** to commit armed robbery on **b :** STEAL 2a [alteration of *hoist*]

2heist *n, slang* **:** armed robbery **:** HOLDUP; *also* **:** THEFT

held *past of* HOLD

heli- *or* **helio-** *combining form* **:** sun ⟨*helio*centric⟩ [Greek *hēlios*]

helic- *or* **helico-** *combining form* **:** helix **:** spiral ⟨*helic*al⟩ [Greek *helik-, helix* "spiral"]

hel•i•cal \ˈhel-i-kəl, ˈhē-li-\ *adj* **:** of, relating to, or having the form of a helix; *also* **:** SPIRAL 1 — **hel•i•cal•ly** \-kə-lē, -klē\ *adv*

hel•i•con \ˈhel-ə-ˌkän, -i-kən\ *n* **:** a large circular bass tuba used in military bands [probably derived from Greek *helix* "spiral"]

1he•li•cop•ter \ˈhel-ə-ˌkäp-tər, ˈhē-lə-\ *n* **:** an aircraft that is supported in the air by propellers revolving on a vertical axis [French *hélicoptère,* from Greek *helix* "helix" + *pteron* "wing"]

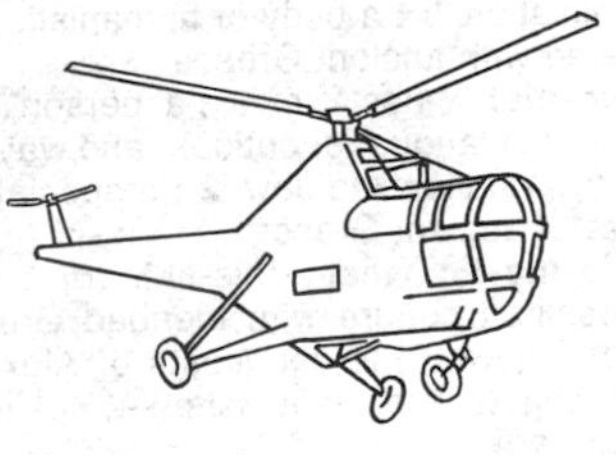

1helicopter

2helicopter *vb* **:** to travel or transport by helicopter

he•lio•cen•tric \ˌhē-lē-ō-ˈsen-trik\ *adj* **1 :** referred to or measured from the sun's center or appearing as if seen from it ⟨a *heliocentric* position⟩ **2 :** having or relating to the sun as a center ⟨a *heliocentric* theory of the solar system⟩ — compare GEOCENTRIC

he•lio•graph \ˈhē-lē-ə-ˌgraf\ *n* **:** an apparatus for signaling by means of the sun's rays reflected from a mirror — **heliograph** *vb*

he•lio•trope \ˈhēl-yə-ˌtrōp\ *n* **1 :** any of a genus of herbs or shrubs related to the forget-me-not — compare GARDEN HELIOTROPE **2 :** BLOODSTONE **3 a :** a moderate purple **b :** a moderate reddish purple [Latin *heliotropium,* from Greek *hēliotropion,* from *hēlios* "sun" + *tropos* "turn"; from its flowers turning toward the sun]

he•li•ot•ro•pism \ˌhē-lē-ˈä-trə-ˌpiz-əm\ *n* **:** phototropism in which sunlight is the orienting stimulus — **he•lio•tro•pic** \ˌhē-lē-ə-ˈtrōp-ik, -ˈträp-\ *adj*

he•li•port \ˈhel-ə-ˌpōrt, ˈhē-lə-, -ˌpȯrt\ *n* **:** a landing and takeoff place for a helicopter

he•li•um \ˈhē-lē-əm\ *n* **:** a light colorless nonflammable gaseous chemical element found in various natural gases — see ELEMENT table [New Latin, from Greek *hēlios* "sun"; from its first being observed in the sun's atmosphere]

he•lix \ˈhē-liks\ *n, pl* **he•li•ces** \ˈhel-ə-ˌsēz, ˈhē-lə-\ *also* **he•lix•es** \ˈhē-lik-səz\ **1 :** something (as a wire coiled around a cylinder, a cone-shaped wire spring, or a corkscrew) spiral in form **2 :** the incurved rim of the external ear **3 :** a curve traced on a cylinder by a point moving at a constant angle to the straight lines parallel to the axis and lying in the surface; *also;* SPIRAL 1b [Latin, from Greek]

hellbender

hell \ˈhel\ *n* **1 :** a nether world in which the dead are held to continue to exist **:** HADES **2 :** a place or state of punishment for the wicked after death **:** the home of evil spirits **3 :** a place or condition of misery or wickedness **4 :** something that causes torment; *esp* **:** a severe scolding [Old English]

he'll \hēl, ˌhēl, hil, ēl, il\ **:** he shall **:** he will

hell•ben•der \ˈhel-ˌben-dər\ *n* **:** a large aquatic salamander of the Ohio valley

hell–bent \-ˌbent\ *adj* **1 :** stubbornly and often recklessly determined **2 :** moving at full speed

hell•cat \-ˌkat\ *n* **:** a violently temperamental person; *esp* **:** SHREW 2

hel•le•bore \ˈhel-ə-ˌbōr, -ˌbȯr\ *n* **1 a :** any of a genus of herbs of the buttercup family **b :** the dried root of a hellebore formerly used in medicine **2 :** a poisonous herb of the lily family; *also* **:** its dried root or a product of this containing alkaloids used in medicine and insecticides [Latin *helleborus,* from Greek *helleboros*]

Hel•lene \ˈhel-ˌēn\ *n* **:** GREEK 1 [Greek *Hellēn*] — **Hel•len•ic** \he-ˈlen-ik, hə-\ *adj*

Hel•le•nism \ˈhel-ə-ˌniz-əm\ *n* **1 :** devotion to or imitation of especially ancient Greek thought, customs, or styles **2 :** Greek civilization **3 :** a body of humanistic and classical ideals associated with ancient Greece

Hel•le•nist \-nəst\ *n* **1 :** a person living in Hellenistic times Greek in language, outlook, and way of life but not in ancestry; *esp* **:** a hellenized Jew **2 :** a specialist in the language or culture of ancient Greece

Hel•le•nis•tic \ˌhel-ə-ˈnis-tik\ *adj* **1 :** of or relating to the cosmopolitan culture with blended Greek and eastern elements that followed the conquests of Alexander the Great **2 :** of or relating to the Hellenists — **Hel•le•nis•ti•cal•ly** \-ti-kə-lē, -klē\ *adv*

hel•le•nize \ˈhel-ə-ˌnīz\ *vb, often cap* **:** to make or become Greek or Hellenistic in form or culture — **hel•le•ni•za•tion** \ˌhel-ə-nə-ˈzā-shən\ *n, often cap*

hell•er \ˈhel-ər\ *n, chiefly dialect* **:** HELLION

hel•leri \ˈhel-ə-ˌrī, -rē\ *n* **:** a brightly colored hybrid tropical fish [C. *Heller,* 20th century tropical fish collector]

hell•gram•mite \ˈhel-grə-ˌmīt\ *n* **:** the aquatic larva of a dobsonfly much used as fish bait [origin unknown]

hel•lion \ˈhel-yən\ *n* **:** a troublesome or mischievous person [probably from earlier *hallion* "scamp"]

hell•ish \ˈhel-ish\ *adj* **:** of, resembling, or befitting hell **:** DEVILISH — **hell•ish•ly** *adv* — **hell•ish•ness** *n*

hel•lo \hə-ˈlō, he-\ *n, pl* **hellos :** an expression or gesture of greeting — used interjectionally in greeting, in answering the telephone, or to express surprise [alteration of *hollo*]

[1]helm \ˈhelm\ *n* **:** HELMET 1 [Old English]

[2]helm *vt* **:** to cover or furnish with a helmet

[3]helm *n* **1 :** a lever or wheel controlling the rudder of a ship for steering; *also* **:** the entire apparatus for steering a ship **2 :** a position of control ⟨at the *helm* of the business⟩ [Old English *helma*]

hel•met \ˈhel-mət\ *n* **1 :** a covering or enclosing headpiece of ancient or medieval armor **2 :** any of various protective head coverings usually made of a hard material to resist impact **3 :** something resembling a helmet [Middle French, from *helme* "helmet", of Germanic origin] — **hel•met•like** \-ˌlīk\ *adj*

helmet 2

hel•minth \ˈhel-ˌminth, -ˌmintth\ *n* **:** a parasitic worm; *esp* **:** an intestinal worm (as a tapeworm) [Greek *helminth-, helmis*] — **hel•min•thic** \hel-ˈmin-thik, -ˈmint-\ *adj*

hel•min•thi•a•sis \ˌhel-ˌmin-ˈthī-ə-səs\ *n* **:** infestation with or disease caused by parasitic worms

hel•min•thol•o•gy \-ˈthäl-ə-jē\ *n* **:** a branch of zoology concerned with the study of parasitic worms

helms•man \ˈhelmz-mən\ *n* **:** the person at the helm **:** STEERSMAN

hel•ot \ˈhel-ət\ *n* **1** *cap* **:** a member of a class of serfs of ancient Sparta **2 :** SLAVE 1 [Latin *Helotes,* pl., from Greek *Heilōtes*] — **hel•ot•ism** \ˈhel-ət-ˌiz-əm\ *n* — **hel•ot•ry** \-ə-trē\ *n*

[1]help \ˈhelp, *South also* ˈhep\ *vb* **1 :** to give aid or assistance ⟨*help* a child with a lesson⟩ **2 a :** REMEDY, RELIEVE ⟨rest *helps* a cold⟩ **b :** to get (oneself) out of a difficulty ⟨you must learn to *help* yourself⟩ **3 :** to further the advancement of **:** PROMOTE ⟨*helping* industrial development with loans⟩ **4 a :** to change for the better ⟨learn to live with what you can't *help*⟩ **b :** to refrain from ⟨couldn't *help* laughing⟩ **c :** to keep from occurring **:** PREVENT ⟨they couldn't *help* the accident⟩ **5 :** to serve with food or drink especially at a meal — often used with *to* **6 :** to appropriate for the use of (oneself) [Old English *helpan*] — **cannot help but :** cannot but — **so help me :** on my word **:** believe it or not

[2]help *n* **1 :** an act or instance of helping **:** AID, ASSISTANCE ⟨give *help*⟩ **2 :** the state of being helped **:** RELIEF ⟨a situation beyond *help*⟩ **3 :** a person or a thing that helps ⟨a *help* in time of trouble⟩ **4 :** a hired helper or a body of hired helpers ⟨hire additional *help* in a business⟩

help•er \ˈhel-pər\ *n* **:** one that helps; *esp* **:** a relatively unskilled worker who assists a skilled worker usually by manual labor

help•ful \ˈhelp-fəl\ *adj* **:** furnishing help ⟨a *helpful* friend⟩ ⟨a *helpful* book⟩ — **help•ful•ly** \-fə-lē\ *adv* — **help•ful•ness** *n*

help•ing \ˈhel-ping\ *n* **:** a portion of food **:** SERVING

helping verb *n* **:** an auxiliary verb

help•less \ˈhel-pləs\ *adj* **1 :** lacking protection or support **:** DEFENSELESS **2 :** lacking strength or effectiveness **:** POWERLESS ⟨was *helpless* to prevent them from going⟩ — **help•less•ly** *adv* — **help•less•ness** *n*

help•mate \ˈhelp-ˌmāt\ *n* **:** one that is a companion and helper [by folk etymology from *helpmeet*]

help•meet \-ˌmēt\ n **:** HELPMATE\ [[2]*help* + *meet,* adj.]

[1]hel•ter–skel•ter \ˌhel-tər-ˈskel-tər\ *adv* **1 :** in headlong disorder **:** FELL-MELL **2 :** in random order **:** HAPHAZARDLY [imitative]

[2]helter–skelter *n* **:** a disorderly confusion **:** TURMOIL

[3]helter–skelter *adj* **1 :** confusedly hurried **:** PRECIPITATE ⟨*helter-skelter* rush-hour traffic⟩ **2 :** HIT-OR-MISS, HAPHAZARD ⟨does things in a *helter-skelter* manner⟩

helve \ˈhelv\ *n* **:** a handle of a tool or weapon **:** HAFT [Old English *hielfe*]

Hel•ve•tian \hel-ˈvē-shən\ *adj* **:** of or relating to the Helvetii or Helvetia **:** SWISS — **Helvetian** *n*

Hel•ve•tii \-shē-ˌī\ *n pl* **:** an early Celtic people of western Switzerland in the time of Julius Caesar [Latin]

[1]hem \ˈhem\ *n* **:** a border of a garment or cloth; *esp* **:** one made by folding back an edge and sewing it down [Old English]

[2]hem *vb* **hemmed; hem•ming 1 :** to finish with or make a hem in sewing **2 :** to surround in a restrictive manner **:** CONFINE ⟨*hemmed* in by the enemy⟩ — **hem•mer** *n*

[3]hem *usually read as* ˈhem\ *interj* — often used to indicate a vocalized pause in speaking [imitative]

[4]hem \ˈhem\ *vi* **hemmed; hem•ming 1 :** to utter the sound represented by *hem* **2 :** EQUIVOCATE ⟨*hemmed* and hawed and refused to act⟩

hem- *or* **hemo-** *or* **haem-** *or* **haemo-** *combining form* **:** blood ⟨*hemocyanin*⟩ [Greek *haima*]

he–man \ˈhē-ˈman\ *n* **:** a strong virile man

hemat- *or* **hemato-** *or* **haemat-** *or* **haemato-** *combining form*

: blood ⟨*hematology*⟩ [Greek *haimat-, haima*]

he•ma•tite \'hē-mə-,tīt\ *n* : a mineral Fe_2O_3 consisting of ferric oxide, constituting an important iron ore, and occurring in crystals or in a red earthy form

he•ma•tol•o•gy \,hē-mə-'täl-ə-jē\ *n* : a branch of biology that deals with the blood and blood-forming organs — **he•ma•to•log•ic** \,hē-mət-l-'äj-ik\ *adj* — **he•ma•tol•o•gist** \,hē-mə-'täl-ə-jəst\ *n*

he•ma•to•ma \,hē-mə-'tō-mə\ *n, pl* **-mas** *or* **-ma•ta** \-mət-ə\ : a blood-containing tumor or swelling

he•ma•tox•y•lin \,hē-mə-'täk-sə-lən\ *n* : a crystalline compound found in logwood and used chiefly as a biological stain [New Latin *Haematoxylon,* genus of plants that includes the logwood]

heme \'hēm\ *n* : a deep red iron-containing pigment obtained from hemoglobin [derived from Greek *haima* "blood"]

hem•ero•cal•lis \,hem-ə-rō-'kal-əs\ *n* : DAY LILY [Greek *hēmerokalles,* from *hēmera* "day" + *kallos* "beauty"]

hemi- *prefix* : half — compare SEMI- [Greek *hēmi-*]

hemi•chor•date \,hem-i-'kord-ət, -'kor-,dāt\ *n* : any of a small group (Hemichordata) of lowly marine animals (as an acorn worm) resembling worms but having a proboscis that contains a structure held to be a degenerate notochord — compare CHORDATE

he•mip•ter•an \hi-'mip-tə-rən\ *n* : any of a large order (Hemiptera) of insects including the true bugs (as the bedbug and chinch bug) and sometimes related forms (as the plant lice) and having flattened bodies, two pairs of wings, and heads with piercing and sucking organs [Greek *pteron* "wing"] — **hemip•ter•ous** \-tə-rəs\ *adj*

hemi•sphere \'hem-ə-,sfiər\ *n* **1** : the northern or southern half of the earth divided by the equator or the eastern or western half divided by a meridian **2** : one of two half spheres formed by a plane through the sphere's center **3** : CEREBRAL HEMISPHERE — **hemi•spher•ic** \,hem-ə-'sfiər-ik, -'sfer-\ *or* **hemi•spher•i•cal** \-'sfir-i-kəl, -'sfer-\ *adj*

hemi•stitch \'hem-i-,stik\ *n* : half a poetic line usually divided by a caesura [Latin *hemistichium,* from Greek *hēmistichion,* from *hēmi-* + *stichos* "line, verse"]

hem•line \'hem-,līn\ *n* : the line formed by the lower edge of a dress, skirt, or coat

hem•lock \'hem-,läk\ *n* **1** : any of several poisonous herbs of the carrot family having finely cut leaves and small white flowers **2** : any of a genus of evergreen trees of the pine family; *also* : the soft light splintery wood of a hemlock [Old English *hemlic*]

hemo- — see HEM-

he•mo•cy•a•nin \,hē-mō-'sī-ə-nən\ *n* : a copper-containing respiratory pigment in the blood of some mollusks and arthropods

he•mo•glo•bin \'hē-mə-,glō-bən\ *n* : an iron-containing protein that is the chief means of oxygen transport in the vertebrate body where it occurs in the red blood cells and is able to combine loosely with oxygen in regions (as the lungs) of high concentration and release it in regions (as the visceral tissues) of low concentration; *also* : any of various similar iron-containing compounds [derived from Greek *haima* "blood" + Latin *globus* "globe"]

hemoglobin S *n* : a hemoglobin that occurs in the red blood cells in sickle-cell anemia and sickle-cell trait

he•mo•phil•ia \,hē-mə-'fil-ē-ə\ *n* : a usually hereditary tendency to uncontrollable bleeding — **he•mo•phil•i•ac** \-ē-,ak\ *adj or n*

hem•or•rhage \'hem-rij, -ə-rij\ *n* : a copious discharge of blood from the blood vessels [Latin *haemorrhagia,* from Greek *haimorrhagia,* from *haima* "blood" + *rhēgnynai* "to break"] — **hemorrhage** *vi* — **hem•or•rhag•ic** \,hem-ə-'raj-ik\ *adj*

hem•or•rhoid \'hem-,roid, -ə-,roid\ *n* : a swollen mass of dilated veins situated at or just within the anus — usually used in pl.; called also *piles* [derived from Greek *haimorrhoides* "hemorrhoids", from *haima* "blood" + *rhein* "to flow"] — **hem•or•rhoid•al** \,hem-ə-'roid-l\ *adj*

hemp \'hemp\ *n* : a tall Asian herb of the mulberry family widely grown for its tough bast fiber that is used especially in cordage or for its flowers and leaves that yield hashish and marijuana [Old English *hænep*] — **hemp•en** \'hem-pən\ *adj*

[1]**hem•stitch** \'hem-,stich\ *vt* : to embroider (fabric) by drawing out parallel threads and stitching the exposed threads in groups to form various designs — **hem•stitch•er** *n*

[2]**hemstitch** *n* **1** : decorative needlework **2** : a stitch used in hemstitching

hen \'hen\ *n* **1** : a female domestic fowl especially over a year old; *also* : a female bird **2** : the female of various mostly aquatic animals (as lobsters or fish) [Old English *henn*]

hen•bane \'hen-,bān\ *n* : a poisonous sticky-leaved Old World herb related to the nightshades

hence \'hens\ *adv* **1** : from this place : AWAY **2** : from this time ⟨a week *hence*⟩ **3** : CONSEQUENTLY, THEREFORE ⟨was a newcomer and *hence* had no close friends in the city⟩ [Middle English *hennes, henne,* from Old English *heonan*]

hence•forth \-,fōrth, -,forth\ *adv* : from this point on

hence•for•ward \hens-'for-wərd\ *adv* : HENCEFORTH

hench•man \'hench-mən\ *n* : a trusted follower or supporter ⟨a gangster's *henchman*⟩ [Middle English *hengestman* "groom", from *hengest* "stallion" + *man*]

hen•e•quen \'hen-i-kən, ,hen-i-'ken\ *n* : a strong hard cordage fiber from the leaves of a tropical American agave; *also* : this plant [Spanish *henequén*]

Hen•le's loop \,hen-lēz-\ *n* : LOOP OF HENLE

[1]**hen•na** \'hen-ə\ *n* **1** : an Old World tropical shrub with clusters of fragrant white flowers **2** : a reddish brown dye obtained from leaves of the henna and used especially on hair [Arabic *ḥinnā'*]

[2]**henna** *vb* **hen•naed** \'hen-əd\; **hen•na•ing** : to treat or dye with henna

hen•nery \'hen-ə-rē\ *n, pl* **-ner•ies** : a poultry farm; *also* : a poultry enclosure or house

hen party *n* : a party for women only

hen•peck \'hen-,pek\ *vt* : to subject (one's husband) to persistent nagging and domination

hen•ry \'hen-rē\ *n, pl* **henries** *also* **henrys** : the mks unit of inductance equal to the self-inductance of a circuit or the mutual inductance of two circuits in which the variation of one ampere per second results in an induced electromotive force of one volt [Joseph *Henry,* died 1878, American physicist]

hep \'hep\ *variant of* HIP

hep•a•rin \'hep-ə-rən\ *n* : a compound found especially in liver that slows the clotting of blood and is used medically [Greek *hēpar* "liver"]

he•pat•ic \hi-'pat-ik\ *adj* : of, relating to, affecting, or conveying to or away from the liver ⟨*hepatic* veins⟩ ⟨*hepatic* arteries⟩ [Latin *hepaticus,* from Greek *hēpatikos,* from *hēpar* "liver"]

he•pat•i•ca \hi-'pat-i-kə\ *n* : any of a genus of herbs of the buttercup family with lobed leaves and delicate white, pink, or bluish flowers; *also* : one of these flowers [Medieval Latin, from Latin *hepaticus* "hepatic"]

hep•a•ti•tis \,hep-ə-'tīt-əs\ *n, pl* **-tit•i•des** \-'tit-ə-,dēz\ : inflammation of the liver; *also* : an acute virus disease marked by hepatitis, jaundice, fever, and gastrointestinal symptoms

hepped up \'hep-'təp\ *adj* : ENTHUSIASTIC

Hep•ple•white \'hep-əl-,hwīt, -,wīt\ *adj* : of or relating to a style of furniture originating in late 18th century England [George *Hepplewhite,* died 1786, English cabinetmaker]

hepta- *or* **hept-** *combining form* : seven ⟨*heptameter*⟩ [Greek *hepta*]

hep•ta•gon \'hep-tə-,gän\ *n* : a polygon of seven angles and seven sides — **hep•tag•o•nal** \hep-'tag-ən-l\ *adj*

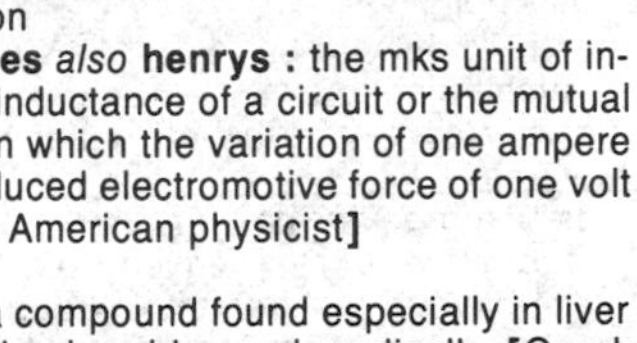

heptagon

hep•tam•e•ter \hep-'tam-ət-ər\ *n* : a line of verse consisting of seven metrical feet

[1]**her** \hər, ər, ,hər\ *adj* : of or relating to her or herself especially as possessor, agent, or object of an action ⟨*her* house⟩ ⟨*her* research⟩ ⟨*her* rescue⟩ — compare [1]SHE 1 [Old English *hiere,* genitive of *hēo* "she"]

\ə\ **abut**	\au̇\ **out**	\i\ **tip**	\ȯ\ **saw**	\u̇\ **foot**
\ər\ **further**	\ch\ **chin**	\ī\ **life**	\ȯi\ **coin**	\y\ **yet**
\a\ **mat**	\e\ **pet**	\j\ **job**	\th\ **thin**	\yü\ **few**
\ā\ **take**	\ē\ **easy**	\ng\ **sing**	\th\ **this**	\yu̇\ **cure**
\ä\ **cot, cart**	\g\ **go**	\ō\ **bone**	\ü\ **food**	\zh\ **vision**

[2]**her** \ər, hər, 'hər\ *pron, objective case of* SHE

[1]**her·ald** \'her-əld\ *n* **1 a** : an official at a medieval tournament **b** : an officer acting as messenger between leaders of warring parties **c** : an officer responsible for granting and registering coats of arms **2** : an official crier or messenger **3** : one that precedes or foreshadows : HARBINGER [Middle French *hiraut,* of Germanic origin]

[2]**herald** *vt* **1** : to give notice of : ANNOUNCE **2** : to greet especially with enthusiasm : HAIL

he·ral·dic \he-'ral-dik\ *adj* : of or relating to heralds or heraldry — **he·ral·di·cal·ly** \-di-kə-lē, -klē\ *adv*

her·ald·ry \'her-əl-drē\ *n, pl* **-ries 1** : the art or science of tracing a person's family history and determining its coat of arms **2** : PAGEANTRY 2

herb \'ərb, 'hərb\ *n* **1** : an annual, biennial, or perennial seed plant that does not develop persistent woody tissue but dies down at the end of a growing season — compare SHRUB **2** : a plant or plant part used in medicine or for seasoning [Old French *herbe,* from Latin *herba* "grass, herb"] — **her·ba·ceous** \,ər-'bā-shəs, ,hər-\ *adj* — **herb·like** \'ərb-,līk, 'hərb-\ *adj* — **herby** \'ər-bē, 'hər-\ *adj*

herb·age \'ər-bij, 'hər-\ *n* **1** : herbaceous vegetation (as grass) especially when used for grazing **2** : the juicy parts of herbaceous plants

[1]**herb·al** \'ər-bəl, 'hər-\ *n* : a book about plants and especially their medical properties

[2]**herbal** *adj* : of, relating to, or made of herbs

herb·al·ist \'ər-bə-ləst, 'hər-\ *n* : one that collects, grows, or deals in herbs

her·bar·i·um \,ər-'bar-ē-əm, ,hər-, -'ber-\ *n, pl* **-ia** \-ē-ə\ **1** : a collection of dried plant specimens **2** : a place that houses an herbarium

her·bi·cide \'ər-bə-,sīd, 'hər-\ *n* : an agent used to destroy or inhibit plant growth — **her·bi·cid·al** \,ər-bə-'sīd-l, ,hər-\ *adj*

her·biv·o·ra \,ər-'biv-ə-rə, ,hər-\ *n pl* : animals that are herbivores

her·bi·vore \'ər-bə-,vōr, 'hər-, -,vȯr\ *n* : a plant-eating animal; *esp* : UNGULATE [derived from Latin *herba* "grass" + *vorare* "to devour"] — **her·biv·o·rous** \,ər-'biv-ə-rəs, ,hər-\ *adj*

her·cu·le·an \,hər-kyə-'lē-ən, ,hər-'kyü-lē-\ *adj, often cap* : of extraordinary power, size, or difficulty ⟨a *herculean* task⟩ [*Hercules,* mythical hero]

Her·cu·les \'hər-kyə-,lēz\ *n* : a northern constellation between Corona Borealis and Lyra

Her·cu·les'–club \,hər-kyə-,lēz-'kləb\ *n* : a small prickly tree of the eastern United States that is related to the ginseng

[1]**herd** \'hərd\ *n* **1** : a number of animals of one kind kept or living together **2** : CROWD 2 [Old English *heord*]

[2]**herd** *vb* : to keep, assemble, or move in or as if in a herd — **herd·er** *n*

herds·man \'hərdz-mən\ *n* : a manager, breeder, or tender of livestock

[1]**here** \'hiər\ *adv* **1 a** : in or at this place ⟨turn *here*⟩ **b** : NOW ⟨*here* it's morning already⟩ **2** : at or in this point or particular ⟨*here* we agree⟩ **3** : in the present life or state **4** : to this place ⟨come *here*⟩ **5** — used interjectionally in rebuke or encouragement ⟨*here,* that's enough⟩ [Old English *hēr*]

[2]**here** *n* : this place ⟨get away from *here*⟩

here·abouts \'hir-ə-,bau̇ts\ *or* **here·about** \-,bau̇t\ *adv* : in this vicinity

[1]**here·af·ter** \hir-'af-tər\ *adv* **1** : after this **2** : in some future time or state

[2]**hereafter** *n, often cap* **1** : FUTURE 1a **2** : an existence beyond earthly life ⟨belief in the *hereafter*⟩

here and there *adv* : in one place and another

here·by \hir-'bī\ *adv* : by this means

her·e·dit·a·ment \,her-ə-'dit-ə-mənt\ *n* : heritable property [Medieval Latin *hereditamentum,* from Late Latin *hereditare* "to inherit", from Latin *heres* "heir"]

he·red·i·tary \hə-'red-ə-,ter-ē\ *adj* **1** : genetically transmitted from parent to offspring ⟨*hereditary* traits⟩ **2 a** : received or passing by inheritance ⟨*hereditary* rank⟩ **b** : having title or possession through inheritance ⟨*hereditary* rulers⟩ **3** : of a kind established by tradition **4** : of or relating to inheritance or heredity

he·red·i·ty \hə-'red-ət-ē\ *n, pl* **-ties 1** : the genetic traits including both genes and their expressed characters derived from one's ancestors **2** : the transmission of qualities from ancestor to descendant through genes [Middle French *heredité* "inheritance", from Latin *hereditas,* from *hered-, heres* "heir"]

Her·e·ford \'hər-fərd *sometimes* 'her-ə-\ *n* : any of an English breed of hardy red white-faced beef cattle widely raised in the western United States [*Hereford* county, England]

here·in \hir-'in\ *adv* : in this

here·of \hir-'əv, -'äv\ *adv* : of this

here·on \-'ȯn, -'än\ *adv* : on this

her·e·sy \'her-ə-sē\ *n, pl* **-sies 1** : religious opinion contrary to the doctrines of a church **2** : opinion or doctrine contrary to a dominant or generally accepted belief [Old French *heresie,* from Late Latin *haeresis,* from Greek *hairesis* "action of taking, choice, sect", from *hairein* "to take"]

her·e·tic \'her-ə-,tik\ *n* : a person who believes or teaches heretical doctrines

he·ret·i·cal \hə-'ret-i-kəl\ *also* **her·e·tic** \'her-ə-,tik, hə-'ret-ik\ *adj* : of, relating to, or characterized by heresy : UNORTHODOX **syn** see HETERODOX — **he·ret·i·cal·ly** \hə-'ret-i-kə-lē,-klē\ *adv* — **he·ret·i·cal·ness** \-kəl-nəs\ *n*

here·to \hir-'tü\ *adv* : to this document

here·to·fore \'hirt-ə-,fōr, -,fȯr\ *adv* : up to this time : HITHERTO

here·un·der \hir-'ən-dər\ *adv* : under or in accordance with this document or agreement

here·un·to \hir-'ən-tü\ *adv* : to this

here·up·on \'hir-ə-,pȯn, -,pän\ *adv* : on this : immediately after this

here·with \hir-'wit͟h, -'with\ *adv* : with this : enclosed in this

her·i·ot \'her-ē-ət\ *n* : a feudal duty or tribute due under English law to a lord on the death of a tenant [Old English *heregeatwe* "military equipment", from *here* "army" + *geatwe* "equipment"]

her·i·ta·ble \'her-ət-ə-bəl\ *adj* : HEREDITARY 1, 2 — **her·i·ta·bil·i·ty** \,her-ət-ə-'bil-ət-ē\ *n*

her·i·tage \'her-ət-ij\ *n* **1** : property that descends to an heir **2** : something transmitted by or acquired from a predecessor : LEGACY **3** : TRADITION ⟨America's Puritan *heritage*⟩ [Middle French, from *heriter* "to inherit", from Late Latin *hereditare,* from Latin *heres* "heir"]

• **syn** INHERITANCE: HERITAGE may imply anything passed on to heirs or succeeding generations, but applies usually to something other than actual property or material things ⟨our *heritage* of freedom⟩ INHERITANCE applies to anything acquired by an heir ⟨received a large *inheritance* from an aunt⟩ ⟨this optimistic nature was considered a maternal *inheritance*⟩

her·maph·ro·dite \hər-'maf-rə-,dīt\ *n* : one that has both male and female reproductive organs [Latin *hermaphroditus,* from Greek *hermaphroditos,* from *Hermaphroditos* "Hermaphroditus"] — **her·maph·ro·dit·ic** \hər-,maf-rə-'dit-ik\ *adj*

her·met·ic \hər-'met-ik\ *adj* **1** : AIRTIGHT 1 **2** : completely resistant to outside influence [New Latin *hermeticus,* from *Hermes Trismegistus,* legendary inventor of a magic seal to keep vessels airtight] — **her·met·i·cal** \-'met-i-kəl\ *adj* — **her·met·i·cal·ly** \-i-kə-lē, -klē\ *adv*

her·mit \'hər-mət\ *n* **1** : one that lives in solitude especially for religious reasons **2** : a spiced molasses cookie [Old French *eremite,* from Late Latin *eremita,* from Late Greek *erēmitēs,* from Greek *erēmia* "solitude, desert", from *erēmos* "lonely"]

her·mit·age \'hər-mət-ij\ *n* **1** : the habitation of a hermit **2** : a secluded residence : RETREAT

hermit crab *n* : any of various marine crustaceans having soft asymmetrical abdomens and occupying empty mollusk shells

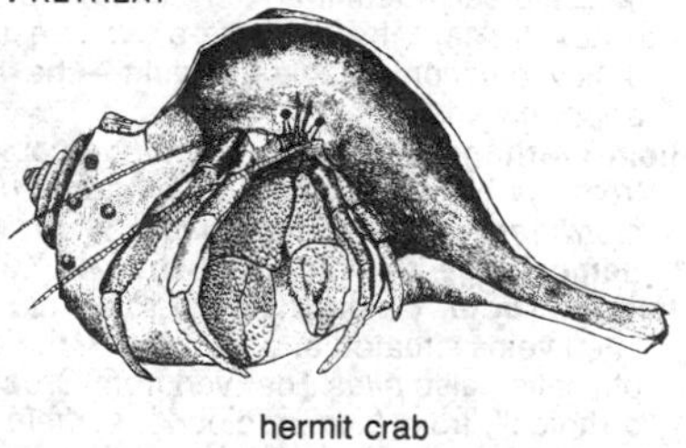
hermit crab

her·nia \'hər-nē-ə\ *n, pl* **her·ni·as** *or* **her·ni·ae** \-nē-,ē, -nē-,ī\ : a protrusion of an organ or part through connective tissue or through a wall of the cavity in which it is normally enclosed — called also *rupture* [Latin] — **her·ni·al** \-nē-əl\ *adj* — **her·ni·ate** \-nē-,āt\ *vi*

he·ro \'hē-rō, 'hiər-ō\ *n, pl* **heroes 1 a** : a mythological or legendary figure often of divine descent endowed with great strength or ability **b** : an illustrious warrior **c** : a person admired for achievements and qualities **d** : one that shows great

courage ⟨the *hero* of a rescue⟩ **2 a** : the chief male figure in a literary work or in an event or period [Latin *heros,* from Greek *hērōs*]
he•ro•ic \hi-'rō-ik\ *adj* **1** : of, relating to, or resembling heroes especially of antiquity ⟨the *heroic* age⟩ ⟨*heroic* legends⟩ **2** : exhibiting or marked by courage, daring, or desperate enterprise ⟨a *heroic* rescue⟩ **3 a** : GRAND, NOBLE ⟨a *heroic* plan for civic improvement⟩ **b** : larger than life-size ⟨a *heroic* statue⟩ — **he•ro•i•cal** \-'rō-i-kəl\ *adj* — **he•ro•i•cal•ly** \-i-kə-lē, -klē\ *adv*
heroic couplet *n* : a rhyming couplet in iambic pentameter
he•ro•ics \hi-'rō-iks\ *n pl* **1** : heroic behavior **2** : showy behavior
heroic verse *n* : the iambic pentameter used in English poetry (as epic) during the 17th and 18th centuries
her•o•in \'her-ə-wən\ *n* : a strongly addictive narcotic derived from the opium poppy and more potent than morphine [from *Heroin,* a former trademark] — **her•o•in•ism** \-wə-,niz-əm\ *n*
her•o•ine \'her-ə-wən\ *n* **1** : a woman of courage and daring **2** : a woman admired for her achievements and qualities **3** : the chief female figure in a literary work or in an event or period [Latin *heroina,* from Greek *hērōinē,* feminine of *hērōs* "hero"]
her•o•ism \'her-ə-,wiz-əm\ *n* **1** : heroic conduct or qualities **2** : great self-sacrificing courage **syn** see COURAGE
her•on \'her-ən\ *n, pl* **herons** *also* **heron** : any of various long-necked wading birds with a long tapering bill, large wings, and soft plumage [Middle French *hairon,* of Germanic origin]
hero worship *n* **1** : veneration of a hero **2** : foolish or excessive praise for an individual
her•pes \'hər-pēz\ *n* : any of several virus diseases marked by the formation of blisters on the skin or mucous membranes [Latin, from Greek *herpēs,* from *herpein* "to creep"] — **her•pet•ic** \hər-'pet-ik\ *adj*
herpes sim•plex \-'sim-,pleks\ *n* : a virus disease marked by groups of watery blisters on the skin or mucous membranes (as of the lips or genitals) [New Latin, literally, "simple herpes"]
her•pe•tol•o•gy \,hər-pə-'täl-ə-jē\ *n* : a branch of zoology dealing with reptiles and amphibians [Greek *herpeton* "reptile", from *herpein* "to creep"] — **her•pe•tol•o•gist** \,hər-pə-'täl-ə-jəst\ *n*
Herr \heər, ,heər\ *n, pl* **Her•ren** \,her-ən, heərn, ,heərn\ — used by or to German-speaking people as a courtesy title equivalent to *Mr.* [German]
her•ring \'her-ing\ *n, pl* **herring** *or* **herrings** : a valuable soft-rayed food fish abundant in the temperate and colder parts of the north Atlantic; *also* : any of various similar and related fishes [Old English *hǣring*]
her•ring•bone \'her-ing-,bōn\ *n* **1** : a pattern made up of rows of parallel lines with neighboring rows slanting in opposite directions **2** : a twilled fabric with a herringbone pattern
herring gull *n* : a common large gull of the northern hemisphere that as an adult is largely white and gray with dark wing tips
hers \'hərz\ *pron, sing or pl in construction* : that which belongs to her : those which belong to her — used without a following noun as an equivalent in meaning to the adjective *her*
her•self \hər-'self, ər-\ *pron* **1** : that identical female one — used reflexively or for emphasis ⟨she considers *herself* lucky⟩ ⟨she *herself* did it⟩; compare SHE 1 **2** : her normal, healthy, or sane condition or self ⟨was *herself* again after a good night's sleep⟩
hertz \'hərts, 'heərts\ *n* : a unit of frequency equal to one cycle per second — abbreviation *Hz* [Heinrich R. *Hertz,* died 1894, German physicist]
hertz•ian wave \,hərt-sē-ən-, ,hert-\ *n* : an electromagnetic wave produced by the oscillation of electricity in a conductor (as a radio antenna) [Heinrich R. *Hertz*]
he's \hēz, ,hēz, ēz\ : he is : he has
hes•i•tance \'hez-ə-təns\ *n* : HESITANCY
hes•i•tan•cy \-tən-sē\ *n, pl* **-cies 1** : the quality or state of being hesitant **2** : an act or instance of hesitating
hes•i•tant \'hez-ə-tənt\ *adj* : tending to hesitate — **hes•i•tant•ly** adv
hes•i•tate \'hez-ə-,tāt\ *vi* **1** : to stop or pause because of forgetfulness, uncertainty, or indecision ⟨*hesitate* before answering⟩ **2** : to be reluctant ⟨never *hesitated* to ask a favor⟩ **3** : to falter in speaking : STAMMER [Latin *haesitare* "to stick fast, hesitate", from *haesus,* past participle of *haerēre* "to stick"] — **hes•i•tat•er** n — **hes•i•tat•ing•ly** \-,tat-ing-lē\ *adv* — **hes•i•ta•tion** \,hez-ə-'tā-shən\ *n*
• **syn** HESITATE, WAVER, VACILLATE, FALTER mean to show irresolution or uncertainty. HESITATE implies a pause before deciding, acting, or choosing; WAVER implies hesitation after a decision and connotes weakness or a retreat; VACILLATE implies prolonged hesitation from inability to reach a decision; FALTER suggests a wavering or stumbling due to emotional stress, lack of courage, or fear.
Hes•per•us \'hes-pə-rəs, -prəs\ *n* : Venus when appearing as an evening star [Latin, from Greek *Hesperos*]
Hes•sian \'hesh-ən\ *n* **1** : a native or inhabitant of Hesse **2** : a German mercenary serving in the British forces during the American Revolution
Hessian fly *n* : a small two-winged fly destructive in America especially to wheat
heter- *or* **hetero-** *combining form* : other than usual : other : different ⟨*hetero*gamete⟩ [Greek *heteros* "other"]
het•ero•chro•mat•ic \,het-ə-rō-krə-'mat-ik\ *adj* : of, relating to, or having different colors especially in a complex pattern
het•ero•cyst \'het-ə-rō-,sist\ *n* : a large transparent thick-walled cell that resembles a spore and occurs at intervals along the filament of some blue-green algae
het•er•o•dox \'het-ə-rə-,däks\ *adj* **1** : differing from or contrary to prevailing opinions, beliefs, or standards; *esp* : not orthodox in religion **2** : holding or expressing unorthodox beliefs or opinions [Late Latin *heterodoxus,* from Greek *heterodoxos,* from *heteros* "other" + *doxa* "opinion"]
• **syn** HERETICAL: HETERODOX implies only not being in conformity with orthodox teachings; HERETICAL implies that such divergence is regarded as destructive of truth.
het•er•o•doxy \-,däk-sē\ *n, pl* **-dox•ies 1** : the quality or state of being heterodox **2** : a heterodox opinion or doctrine
het•ero•dyne \'het-ə-rə-,dīn\ *vt* : to combine (a radio frequency) with a different frequency so that a beat is produced — **heterodyne** *adj*
het•ero•ga•mete \,het-ə-rō-gə-'mēt, -'gam-,ēt\ *n* : either of a pair of gametes (as egg and sperm) that differ in form, size, or behavior — **het•ero•ga•met•ic** \-gə-'met-ik\ *adj*
het•er•o•ge•ne•ity \,het-ə-rō-jə-'nē-ət-ē\ *n* : the quality or state of being heterogeneous
het•er•o•ge•neous \,het-ə-rə-'jē-nē-əs, -nyəs\ *adj* : differing in kind : consisting of dissimilar ingredients or constituents : MIXED ⟨a *heterogeneous* population⟩ [Medieval Latin *heterogeneus,* from Greek *heterogenēs,* from *heteros* "other" + *genos* "kind"] — **het•er•o•ge•neous•ly** *adv* — **het•er•o•ge•neous•ness** *n*
het•er•ol•o•gous \,het-ə-'räl-ə-gəs\ *adj* : derived from a different species ⟨a *heterologous* organ transplant⟩ [*heter-* + Greek *logos* "proportion, word"]
het•er•op•ter•ous \,het-ə-'räp-tə-rəs\ *adj* : of or relating to a group (Heteroptera) of insects comprising the true bugs [*heter-* + Greek *pteron* "wing"] — **het•er•op•ter•an** \-tə-rən\ *adj or n*
het•ero•sex•u•al \,het-ə-rō-'sek-shə-wəl, -shəl\ *adj* : of, relating to, or marked by sexual orientation toward members of the opposite sex — **heterosexual** *n* — **het•ero•sex•u•al•i•ty** \-,sek-shə-'wal-ət-ē\ *n*
het•er•o•sis \,het-ə-'rō-səs\ *n* : HYBRID VIGOR — **het•er•ot•ic** \-'rät-ik\ *adj*
het•ero•troph \'het-ə-rə-,trōf, -,träf\ *n* : an organism that is unable to live and grow without complex compounds of nitrogen and carbon — **het•ero•tro•phic** \,het-ə-rə-'trō-fik\ *adj* — **het•ero•tro•phi•cal•ly** \-fi-kə-lē, -klē\ *adv*
het•ero•zy•gote \-'zī-,gōt\ *n* : a plant or animal with at least one gene pair containing different genes — **het•ero•zy•gos•i•ty** \-,zī-'gäs-ət-ē\ *n* — **het•ero•zy•gous** \,het-ə-rō-'zī-gəs\ *adj*
hew \'hyü\ *vb* **hewed**; **hewed** *or* **hewn** \'hyün\; **hew•ing 1** : to chop down : CHOP ⟨*hew* logs⟩ ⟨*hew* trees⟩ **2** : to make or shape by or as if by cutting with an ax ⟨a cabin built of rough-*hewn* logs⟩ **3** : to conform strictly : ADHERE ⟨*hew* to the line⟩ [Old English *hēawan*] — **hew•er** *n*
[1]**hex** \'heks\ *vt* **1** : to put a hex on **2** : to affect as if by an evil

spell : JINX [German *hexen,* from *hexe* "witch"] — **hex•er** *n*

2hex *n* **1 :** 1SPELL 1, JINX **2 :** a person who practices witchcraft : WITCH

3hex *adj* **:** HEXAGONAL ⟨a bolt with a *hex* head⟩

hexa- *or* **hex-** *combining form* **:** six ⟨*hexose*⟩ [Greek *hex*]

hexa•dec•i•mal \ˌhek-sə-ˈdes-ə-məl, -ˈdes-məl\ *adj* **:** of, relating to, or being a number system with a base of 16

hex•a•gon \ˈhek-sə-ˌgän\ *n* **:** a polygon of six angles and six sides

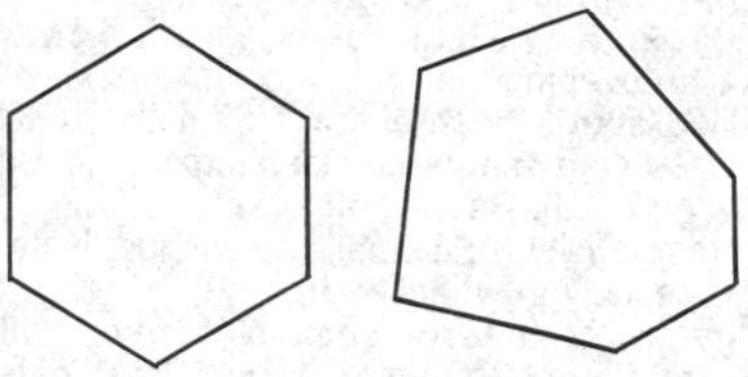

hexagon

hex•ag•o•nal \hek-ˈsag-ən-l\ *adj* **1 :** having six angles and six sides **2 :** relating to or being a crystal system characterized by three equal lateral axes intersecting at angles of 60 degrees and a vertical axis of variable length at right angles ⟨quartz occurs in *hexagonal* crystals⟩ — **hex•ag•o•nal•ly** \-l-ē\ *adv*

hex•a•he•dron \ˌhek-sə-ˈhē-drən\ *n, pl* **-drons** *also* **-dra** \-drə\ **:** a polyhedron of six faces

hex•am•e•ter \hek-ˈsam-ət-ər\ *n* **:** a line consisting of six metrical feet

hex•ane \ˈhek-ˌsān\ *n* **:** any of five isomeric volatile liquid hydrocarbons C_6H_{14} found in petroleum

1hex•a•pod \ˈhek-sə-ˌpäd\ *n* **:** INSECT 2

2hexapod *adj* **1 :** having six feet **2 :** of or relating to insects

hex•ose \ˈhek-ˌsōs\ *n* **:** a saccharide $C_6H_{12}O_6$ containing six carbon atoms in the molecule

hey \ˈhā\ *interj* — used especially to call attention or to express doubt, surprise, or joy [Middle English]

hey•day \ˈhā-ˌdā\ *n* **:** the time of greatest strength or vigor

hi \ˈhī, ˈhī-ē\ *interj* — used especially as a greeting [Middle English *hy*]

hi•a•tus \hī-ˈāt-əs\ *n* **1 :** a gap in space or in time; *esp* **:** a break where a part is missing ⟨a *hiatus* in an old manuscript⟩ **2 :** the occurrence of two vowel sounds without pause or intervening consonantal sound [Latin, from *hiare* "to gape, yawn"]

hi•ba•chi \hi-ˈbäch-ē\ *n* **:** a charcoal brazier [Japanese]

hi•ber•nate \ˈhī-bər-ˌnāt\ *vi* **:** to pass the winter in a torpid or resting state [Latin *hibernare* "to pass the winter", from *hibernus* "of winter"] — **hi•ber•na•tion** \ˌhī-bər-ˈnā-shən\ *n* — **hi•ber•na•tor** \ˈhī-bər-ˌnāt-ər\ *n*

hi•bis•cus \hī-ˈbis-kəs, hə-\ *n* **:** any of a large genus of herbs, shrubs, or small trees of the mallow family with toothed leaves and large showy flowers [Latin, "marshmallow plant"]

1hic•cup *also* **hic•cough** \ˈhik-ˌəp, -əp\ *n* **:** a spasmodic drawing in of breath that is stopped by sudden closure of the glottis and is accompanied by a peculiar sound [imitative]

2hiccup *also* **hiccough** *vi* **hic•cuped** *also* **hic•cupped; hic•cup•ing** *also* **hic•cup•ping :** to make a hiccup or be affected with hiccups

hick \ˈhik\ *n* **:** an awkward unsophisticated person : BUMPKIN [*Hick,* nickname for *Richard*]

hick•o•ry \ˈhik-rē, -ə-rē\ *n, pl* **-ries 1 :** any of a genus of North American hardwood trees of the walnut family that often produce hard-shelled sweet edible nuts **2 :** the usually tough pale wood of a hickory [of American Indian origin]

hi•dal•go \hid-ˈal-gō, ē-ˈthäl-\ *n, pl* **-gos :** a member of the lower nobility of Spain [Spanish]

hidden hunger *n* **:** a bodily disorder caused by a badly balanced diet

1hide \ˈhīd\ *vb* **hid** \ˈhid\; **hid•den** \ˈhid-n\ *or* **hid; hid•ing** \ˈhīd-ing\ **1 :** to put or get out of sight ⟨*hide* a treasure⟩ ⟨*hid* in a closet⟩ **2 :** to keep secret ⟨*hid* their grief⟩ **3 :** to screen from view ⟨a house *hidden* by trees⟩ **4 :** to seek protection or evade responsibility ⟨*hides* behind dark glasses⟩ [Old English *hȳdan*] — **hid•er** \ˈhīd-ər\ *n*

2hide *n* **:** the skin of an animal whether raw or dressed [Old English *hȳd*]

3hide *vt* **hid•ed; hid•ing :** to give a beating to : FLOG

hide–and–go–seek \ˌhīd-n-gō-ˈsēk\ *n* **:** HIDE-AND-SEEK

hide–and–seek \-n-ˈsēk\ *n* **:** a children's game in which one player gives the others time to hide and then tries to find them before they can return safely to the goal

hide•away \ˈhīd-ə-ˌwā\ *n* **:** RETREAT 2, HIDEOUT

hide•bound \ˈhīd-ˌbaund\ *adj* **1 :** having a dry skin lacking in pliancy and adhering closely to the underlying flesh ⟨a *hidebound* horse⟩ **2 :** stubbornly conservative

hid•eous \ˈhid-ē-əs\ *adj* **:** horribly ugly or disgusting : FRIGHTFUL [Old French *hidous,* from *hisde, hide* "terror"] — **hid•eous•ly** *adv* — **hid•eous•ness** *n*

hide•out \ˈhīd-ˌaut\ *n* **:** a place of refuge or concealment

1hid•ing \ˈhīd-ing\ *n* **:** a state or place of concealment ⟨go into *hiding*⟩

2hiding *n* **:** WHIPPING, FLOGGING ⟨got a severe *hiding*⟩

hie \ˈhī\ *vb* **hied; hy•ing** *or* **hie•ing :** HURRY 1, HASTEN [Old English *hīgian*]

hi•er•arch \ˈhī-ˌrärk, -ə-ˌrärk\ *n* **1 :** a religious leader in a position of authority **2 :** a person high in a hierarchy [Medieval Latin *hierarcha,* from Greek *hierarchēs,* from *hieros* "holy" + *archos* "ruler, leader"] — **hi•er•ar•chal** \ˌhī-ˈrär-kəl, -ə-ˈrär-\ *adj*

hi•er•ar•chy \ˈhī-ˌrär-kē, -ə-ˌrär-\ *n, pl* **-chies 1 :** a ruling body especially of clergy organized into ranks each subordinate to the one above it **2 a :** arrangement into a graded series **b :** persons or things arranged in ranks or classes — **hi•er•ar•chi•cal** \ˌhī-ˈrär-ki-kəl, -ə-ˈrär-\ *or* **hi•er•ar•chic** \-ˈrär-kik\ *adj* — **hi•er•ar•chi•cal•ly** \-ˈrär-ki-kə-lē, -klē\ *adv*

△ **origin** The earliest examples of the use of *hierarchy* in English are found in works of the late 14th century and refer to the ranks or orders of angels. The first element of the word is from Greek *hieros,* "holy, sacred". The second element comes from Greek *archos,* "leader, ruler". A second sense of the word, appearing only slightly later than the first, is "a form of government administered by a priesthood". Later the term was extended from government to the classification of groups of people and then to the arrangement of objects, elements, or values in graduated series.

hi•er•o•glyph \ˈhī-rə-ˌglif, -ə-rə-\ *n* **:** a character used in a system of hieroglyphic writing [French *hiéroglyphe,* from Middle French *hieroglyphique,* adj., "hieroglyphic", from Late Latin *hieroglyphicus,* from Greek *hieroglyphikos,* from *hieros* "holy" + *glyphein* "to carve"]

hi•ero•glyph•ic \ˌhī-rə-ˈglif-ik, -ə-rə-\ *n* **1 :** HIEROGLYPH **2 :** a system of hieroglyphic writing; *esp* **:** the picture script of the ancient Egyptian priesthood **3 :** characters that resemble a hieroglyphic especially in being hard to decipher — **hieroglyphic** *adj*

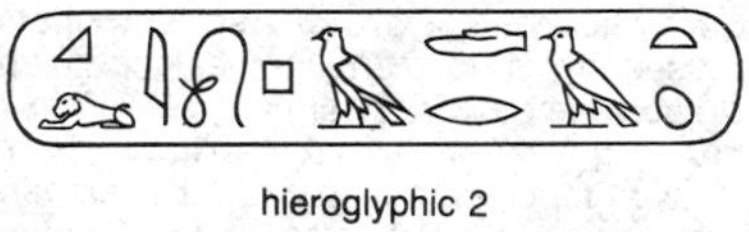

hieroglyphic 2

hi–fi \ˈhī-ˈfī\ *n* **1 :** HIGH FIDELITY **2 :** equipment for reproduction of sound with high fidelity

hig•gle•dy–pig•gle•dy \ˌhig-əl-dē-ˈpig-əl-dē\ *adv* **:** in confusion : TOPSY-TURVY [origin unknown] — **higgledy–piggledy** *adj*

1high \ˈhī\ *adj* **1 a :** extending or raised up ⟨a *high* building⟩ **b :** having a specified elevation ⟨six meters *high*⟩ **2 :** advanced toward fullness or culmination ⟨*high* summer⟩ **3 :** elevated in pitch ⟨a *high* note⟩ **4 :** relatively far from the equator ⟨*high* latitudes⟩ **5 :** exalted in character : NOBLE ⟨a person of *high* purpose⟩ **6 :** of greater degree, size, amount, or content than average or ordinary ⟨*high* pressure⟩ ⟨*high* prices⟩ **7 :** of relatively great importance: as **a :** foremost in rank, dignity, or standing ⟨*high* society⟩ **b :** SERIOUS, GRAVE ⟨*high* crimes⟩ **8 :** FORCIBLE, STRONG ⟨*high* winds⟩ **9 a :** showing elation or excitement ⟨*high* spirits⟩ **b :** INTOXICATED 1b **10 :** advanced in complexity or development ⟨*higher* mathematics⟩ ⟨*higher* algae⟩ **11 :** pronounced with some part of the tongue close to the palate ⟨\ē\ is a *high* vowel⟩ [Old English *hēah*]

2high *adv* **1 :** at or to a high place, altitude, or degree ⟨hit the ball *high* into the bleachers⟩ **2 :** RICHLY, LUXURIOUSLY ⟨lived *high* after winning the lottery⟩

3high *n* **1 :** an elevated place or region: as **a :** HILL 1, KNOLL **b :** SKY 1, HEAVEN ⟨birds wheeling on *high*⟩ **2 :** a region of high barometric pressure **3 a :** a high point or level ⟨prices reached a new *high*⟩ **b :** the transmission gear of an automotive vehicle giving the highest ratio of propeller-shaft to engine-shaft speed and consequently the highest speed of travel **4 :** an excited or

stupefied state produced by or as if by a drug
high•ball \'hī-,bȯl\ *n* : a drink of alcoholic liquor (as whiskey) with water or a carbonated beverage [earlier *highball* "fast train, signal for a train to proceed at full speed"]
high•bind•er \-,bīn-dər\ *n* **1** : a professional killer operating in the Chinese quarter of an American city **2** : a corrupt or scheming politician [the *Highbinders,* gang of vagabonds in New York City about 1806]
high blood pressure *n* : blood pressure that is abnormally high especially in the arteries; *also* : the bodily condition accompanying high blood pressure
high•born \'hī-'bȯrn\ *adj* : of noble birth
high•boy \'hī-,bȯi\ *n* : a tall chest of drawers mounted on a base with long legs
high•bred \-'bred\ *adj* : coming from superior stock
high•brow \-,braü\ *n* : a person of superior learning or culture : INTELLECTUAL — **highbrow** *adj*
high chair *n* : a child's chair with long legs, a feeding tray, and a footrest
High Church *adj* : tending to stress the ceremonial, traditional, and Catholic elements especially in Anglican worship — compare LOW CHURCH
high comedy *n* : comedy employing subtle characterizations and witty dialogue
high command *n* **1** : the supreme headquarters of a military force **2** : the highest leaders in an organization
high commissioner *n* : a principal or high-ranking commissioner; *esp* : an ambassadorial representative of the government of one country stationed in another
higher education *n* : education provided by a college or university
high•er–up \,hī-ər-'əp\ *n* : a superior officer or official
high explosive *n* : an explosive (as TNT) that generates gas with extreme rapidity and has a shattering effect
high•fa•lu•tin \,hī-fə-'lüt-n\ *adj* **1** : PRETENTIOUS 1 **2** : POMPOUS 3, BOMBASTIC ⟨*highfalutin* talk⟩ [perhaps from *high* + *fluting,* present participle of *flute*]
high fidelity *n* : the reproduction of sound with a high degree of faithfulness to the original
high–flown \'hī-'flōn\ *adj* : FLOWERY 2, EXTRAVAGANT ⟨*high-flown* language⟩
high–fly•ing \-'flī-ing\ *adj* **1** : rising to considerable height **2** : marked by extravagance, pretension, or excessive ambition
high frequency *n* : a radio frequency in the range between 3 and 30 megahertz — abbreviation *HF*
High German *n* : German as natively used in southern and central Germany
high–grade \'hī-'grād\ *adj* : of superior grade or quality
high–hand•ed \-'han-dəd\ *adj* : DOMINEERING, OVERBEARING ⟨*high-handed* actions⟩ — **high–hand•ed•ly** *adv* — **high–hand•ed•ness** *n*
high–hat \'hī-'hat\ *adj* : snobbish and supercilious in attitude — **high–hat** *vt*
High Holiday *n* : either of two important Jewish holidays: **a** : ROSH HASHANAH **b** : YOM KIPPUR
high horse *n* : an arrogant mood or attitude ⟨get off your *high horse* and start treating your classmates as equals⟩
high jump *n* : a jump for height in a track-and-field contest — **high jumper** *n*
¹high•land \'hī-lənd\ *n* : elevated or mountainous land
²highland *adj* **1** : of or relating to a highland **2** *cap* : of or relating to the Highlands of Scotland
high•land•er \-lən-dər\ *n* **1** : an inhabitant of a highland **2** *cap* : an inhabitant of the Highlands of Scotland
Highland fling *n* : a lively Scottish folk dance
¹high•light \'hī-,līt\ *n* **1 a** : one of the points or areas on an object that reflect the most light **b** : the brightest spot (as in a painting or drawing) **2** : an event or scene of major interest ⟨the *highlights* of a trip⟩
²highlight *vt* **1** : to throw a strong light on **2 a** : to center attention on : EMPHASIZE **b** : to be a highlight of ⟨a bullfight *highlighted* their trip to Mexico⟩
high•ly \'hī-lē\ *adv* **1** : to a high degree : EXTREMELY ⟨*highly* pleased⟩ **2** : with much approval ⟨speak *highly* of a person⟩
high mass *n, often cap H & M* : a mass that is sung in full ceremonial form — compare LOW MASS
high–mind•ed \'hī-'mīn-dəd\ *adj* : having or marked by elevated principles and feelings — **high–mind•ed•ly** *adv* — **high–mind•ed•ness** *n*
high–muck–a–muck \,hī-,mək-i-'mək\ *or* **high–muck•e•ty–muck** \,hī-mək-ət-ē-'mək\ *n* : an important and often arrogant person [by folk etymology from Chinook Jargon (a pidgin language used in northwestern America) *hiu muckamuck* "plenty to eat"]
high•ness \'hī-nəs\ *n* **1** : the quality or state of being high **2** *often cap* — used as a form of address for persons (as a prince, a princess, a duke, or a duchess) of exalted rank and usually of royal blood ⟨Her *Highness* Princess Anne⟩ ⟨His *Highness* the Duke of Edinburgh⟩ ⟨Your *Highness*⟩ ⟨Their *Highnesses*⟩
high–octane *adj* : having a high octane number and hence good antiknock properties ⟨*high-octane* gasoline⟩
¹high–pressure *adj* **1 a** : having or involving a high or comparatively high pressure especially greatly exceeding that of the atmosphere **b** : having a high atmospheric pressure **2 a** : using or involving aggressive and insistent sales techniques **b** : imposing or involving severe strain or tension ⟨a *high-pressure* job⟩
²high–pressure *vt* : to sell or influence by high-pressure tactics
high relief *n* : sculptural relief in which at least half the thickness of the represented form is raised from the background — compare BAS-RELIEF
high–rise \'hī-'rīz\ *adj* : having many stories and being equipped with elevators ⟨*high-rise* apartment buildings⟩
high•road \'hī-,rōd\ *n* **1** *chiefly British* : HIGHWAY **2** : the easiest course
high school *n* : a school usually including grades 9–12 or 10–12
high seas *n pl* : the open part of a sea or ocean especially outside territorial waters
high–sound•ing \'hī-'saün-ding\ *adj* : PRETENTIOUS 1, IMPOSING
high–spir•it•ed \'hī-'spir-ət-əd\ *adj* : characterized by a bold or energetic spirit — **high–spir•it•ed•ly** *adv* — **high–spir•it•ed•ness** *n*
high–strung \-'strəng\ *adj* : having an extremely nervous or sensitive temperament
high•tail \'hī-,tāl\ *vi* : to retreat at full speed ⟨*hightailed* it for home⟩
high–tension *adj* : having a high voltage; *also* : relating to apparatus to be used at high voltage
high–test *adj* : meeting a high standard; *esp* : HIGH-OCTANE ⟨*high-test* gasoline⟩
high tide *n* **1** : the tide when the water is at its greatest height **2** : the culminating point : CLIMAX
high–toned \'hī-'tōnd\ *adj* **1** : high in social, moral, or intellectual quality **2** : pretentiously fashionable
high treason *n* : TREASON 2
high•way \'hī-,wā\ *n* : a public road or way; *esp* : a main direct road
high•way•man \-mən\ *n* : a person who robs travelers on a road
hi•jack *or* **high–jack** \'hī-,jak\ *vt* **1** : to steal by stopping a vehicle on the highway ⟨*hijack* a load of furs⟩; *also* : to stop and steal from (a vehicle in transit) **2** : to commandeer a flying airplane (as by coercing the pilot at gunpoint) [origin unknown] — **hi•jack•er** *n*
¹hike \'hīk\ *vb* **1 a** : to move or raise up often with a sudden motion **b** : to increase (as prices) usually sharply or suddenly **2** : to go on a hike [perhaps related to ¹*hitch*] — **hik•er** *n*
²hike *n* **1** : a long walk especially for pleasure or exercise **2** : an upward movement : RISE ⟨a price *hike*⟩
hi•lar•i•ous \hil-'ar-ē-əs, -'er-; hī-'lar-, -'ler-\ *adj* : marked by or causing hilarity [Latin *hilarus, hilarus* "cheerful", from Greek *hilaros*] — **hi•lar•i•ous•ly** *adv* — **hi•lar•i•ous•ness** *n*
hi•lar•i•ty \-ət-ē\ *n* : high spirits usually marked by boisterous conviviality or merriment **syn** see MIRTH
¹hill \'hil\ *n* **1** : a usually rounded natural elevation of land lower than a mountain **2** : an artificial heap or mound (as of earth) **3** : several seeds or plants planted in a group rather than a row ⟨a *hill* of beans⟩ [Old English *hyll*]
²hill *vt* **1** : to form into a heap **2** : to draw earth around the roots or base of — **hill•er** *n*

\ə\ **abut**	\aü\ **out**	\i\ **tip**	\ȯ\ **saw**	\ü\ **foot**
\ər\ **further**	\ch\ **chin**	\ī\ **life**	\ȯi\ **coin**	\y\ **yet**
\a\ **mat**	\e\ **pet**	\j\ **job**	\th\ **thin**	\yü\ **few**
\ā\ **take**	\ē\ **easy**	\ng\ **sing**	\th\ **this**	\yu̇\ **cure**
\ä\ **cot, cart**	\g\ **go**	\ō\ **bone**	\ü\ **food**	\zh\ **vision**

hill•bil•ly \'hil-ˌbil-ē\ *n, pl* **-lies** : a person from a backwoods area [[1]*hill* + *Billy,* nickname for *William*]
hillbilly music *n* : COUNTRY MUSIC
hill•ock \'hil-ək\ *n* : a small hill — **hill•ocky** \-ə-kē\ *adj*
hill•side \'hil-ˌsīd\ *n* : the side of a hill
hill•top \'hil-ˌtäp\ *n* : the highest part of a hill
hilly \'hil-ē\ *adj* **hill•i•er**; **-est 1** : having many hills ⟨a *hilly* city⟩ **2** : STEEP ⟨a *hilly* climb⟩
hilt \'hilt\ *n* : a handle especially of a sword or dagger [Old English] — **to the hilt** : to the very limit : COMPLETELY
hi•lum \'hī-ləm\ *n, pl* **hi•la** \-lə\ **1** : a scar on a seed (as a bean) at the point of attachment of the ovule **2** : a notch in or opening from a bodily part suggesting the hilum of a bean [Latin, "trifle"] — **hi•lar** \-lər\ *adj*
him \im, him, 'him\ *pron, objective case of* HE
Hi•ma•la•yan \ˌhim-ə-'lā-ən; him-'äl-yən, -ə-yən\ *n* : any of a breed of small white domesticated rabbits with black nose, feet, tail, and ear tips — called also *Himalayan rabbit* [*Himalaya* mountains]
him•self \im-'self, him-\ *pron* **1 a** : that identical male one — used reflexively or for emphasis ⟨he considers *himself* lucky⟩ ⟨he *himself* did it⟩; compare [1]HE **b** — used reflexively when the sex of the antecedent is unspecified ⟨everyone must look out for *himself*⟩ **2** : his normal, healthy, or sane condition or self ⟨he's *himself* again⟩
[1]**hind** \'hīnd\ *n, pl* **hinds** *also* **hind 1** : a female red deer — compare HART **2** : any of various usually spotted groupers [Old English]
[2]**hind** *adj* : located behind : REAR ⟨*hind* legs⟩ [Middle English]
hind•brain \'hīnd-ˌbrān, 'hīn-\ *n* : the posterior division of the embryonic vertebrate brain or the parts developed from it
hin•der \'hin-dər\ *vb* **hin•dered**; **hin•der•ing** \-də-ring, -dring\ **1** : to make slow or difficult : HAMPER ⟨bad weather *hindered* the progress of the climbers⟩ **2** : to hold back : CHECK [Old English *hindrian*]
hind•gut \'hīnd-ˌgət, 'hīn-\ *n* : the posterior part of the alimentary canal
Hin•di \'hin-dē\ *n* **1** : a literary and official language of northern India **2** : a complex of Indic dialects of northern India for which Hindi is the usual literary language [Hindi *hindī,* from *Hind* "India", from Persian] — **Hindi** *adj*
hind•most \'hīnd-ˌmōst, 'hīn-\ *adj* : farthest to the rear
hind•quar•ter \-ˌkwȯrt-ər, -ˌkwȯt-\ *n* **1** : the back half of a lateral half of the body or carcass of a four-footed animal ⟨a *hindquarter* of beef⟩ **2** *pl* : the part of a four-footed animal lying behind the attachment of the hind legs to the trunk
hin•drance \'hin-drəns\ *n* **1** : the state of being hindered **2** : the action of hindering **3** : something that hinders : IMPEDIMENT
hind•sight \'hīnd-ˌsīt, 'hīn-\ *n* : the understanding of the importance of an event only after it has happened ⟨*hindsight* is easier than foresight⟩
[1]**Hin•du** *also* **Hin•doo** \'hin-ˌdü\ *n* **1** : an adherent of Hinduism **2** : a native or inhabitant of India [Persian *Hindū* "inhabitant of India", from *Hind* "India"]
[2]**Hindu** *also* **Hindoo** *adj* : of, relating to, or characteristic of the Hindus or Hinduism
Hin•du•ism \-ˌiz-əm\ *n* : a body of social, cultural, and religious beliefs and practices native to the Indian subcontinent
Hin•du•stani *also* **Hin•do•stani** \ˌhin-dü-'stan-ē, -'stän-ē\ *n* **1** : a group of Indic dialects of northern India of which literary Hindi and Urdu are considered diverse written forms **2** : a form of speech related to Urdu but less divergent from Hindi [Hindi *Hindūstānī,* from Persian *Hindūstān* "India"] — **Hindustani** *adj*
[1]**hinge** \'hinj\ *n* **1** : a jointed piece on which one surface (as a door, gate, or lid) turns or swings on another **2** : the joint between valves of a bivalve's shell — compare HINGE JOINT [Middle English *heng*]

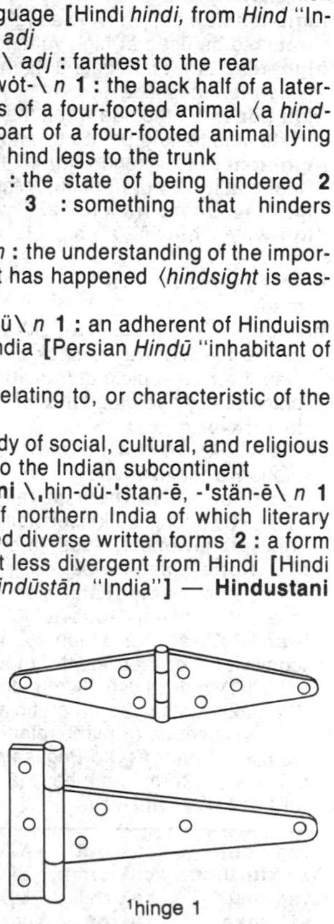

[1]hinge 1

[2]**hinge** *vb* **1** : to attach by or furnish with hinges **2** : to hang or turn as if on a hinge ⟨success *hinges* on the decision⟩
hinge joint *n* : a joint between bones (as at the elbow) that permits motion in but one plane
hin•ny \'hin-ē\ *n, pl* **hinnies** : a hybrid between a stallion and a female donkey — compare MULE [Latin *hinnus*]
[1]**hint** \'hint\ *n* **1 a** : a suggestion for action given briefly or in an indirect manner ⟨*hints* on lawn care⟩ **b** : a statement that communicates delicately and indirectly rather than directly **2 a** : a slight indication of the existence or nature of something **b** : SMIDGEN, BIT [probably from *hent* "to seize", from Old English *hentan*]
[2]**hint** *vb* : to convey by or make a hint **syn** see SUGGEST — **hint•er** *n*
hin•ter•land \'hint-ər-ˌland\ *n* **1** : a region lying inland from a coast **2** : a region remote from urban areas or cultural centers [German, from *hinter* "hind" + *land* "land"]
[1]**hip** \'hip\ *n* : the fruit of a rose [Old English *hēope*]
[2]**hip** *n* **1** : the part of the body that curves outward below the waist on either side and is formed by the side part of the pelvis and the upper part of the thigh **2** : HIP JOINT [Old English *hype*]
[3]**hip** *also* **hep** \'hep\ *adj* **hip•per**; **hip•pest** : characterized by a keen informed awareness of or interest in the newest developments [origin unknown]
hip•bone \'hip-'bōn, -ˌbōn\ *n* : either of two large flaring compound bones that make lateral halves of the pelvis in mammals, provide points of attachment for the skeleton of the leg, and fuse together in front and with the backbone in the rear to form a closed bony ring which supports the lower part of the trunk and the abdominal organs
hip girdle *n* : PELVIC GIRDLE
hip joint *n* : the articulation between the femur and the hipbone
hip•par•i•on \hip-'ar-ē-ˌän, -'er-\ *n* : any of a genus of extinct Miocene and Pliocene 3-toed horses [Greek, "pony", from *hippos* "horse"]
[1]**hipped** \'hipt\ *adj* : having hips or such hips ⟨a *hipped* roof⟩ ⟨broad-*hipped*⟩
[2]**hipped** *adj* **1** : being in low spirits : DEPRESSED **2** : extremely interested [derived from *hypochondria*]
hip•pie *or* **hip•py** \'hip-ē\ *n, pl* **hippies** : a usually young person who rejects the values and practices of established society (as by dressing unconventionally or using drugs); *also* : a long-haired unconventionally dressed young person [[3]*hip* + *-ie*]
hip•po \'hip-ō\ *n, pl* **hippos** : HIPPOPOTAMUS
Hip•po•crat•ic oath \ˌhip-ə-ˌkrat-ik-\ *n* : an oath embodying a code of medical ethics usually taken by those about to begin medical practice [*Hippocrates,* died about 377 B.C., Greek physician believed to have formulated it]
hip•po•drome \'hip-ə-ˌdrōm\ *n* **1** : an oval stadium for horse and chariot races in ancient Greece **2** : an arena for spectacles (as horse shows or circuses) [Middle French, from Latin *hippodromos,* from Greek, from *hippos* "horse" + *dromos* "racecourse"]
hip•po•pot•a•mus \ˌhip-ə-'pät-ə-məs\ *n, pl* **-mus•es** *or* **-mi** \-ˌmī, -mē\ : any of several large plant-eating 4-toed chiefly aquatic African mammals related to the swine and characterized by an extremely large head and mouth, very thick hairless skin, and short legs [Latin, from Greek *hippopotamos,* from *hippos* "horse" + *potamos* "river"]

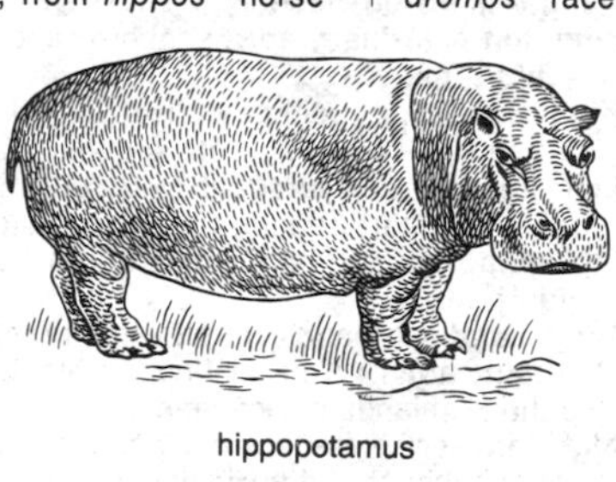

hippopotamus

△ **origin** *Hippopotamos* was the name invented by the Greeks to describe the bulky, barrel-shaped animal that spends most of the day bathing in the rivers of Africa. The two elements of the word are *hippos,* "horse", and *potamos,* "river". In fact, however, the hippopotamus is more closely related to the hog than to the horse.
hip roof *n* : a roof having sloping ends and sloping sides
hip•ster \'hip-stər\ *n* **1** : a person who is hip **2** : HIPPIE
[1]**hire** \'hīr\ *n* **1 a** : payment for temporary use **b** : payment for services : WAGES **2 a** : the act of hiring **b** : the state of being hired : EMPLOYMENT [Old English *hȳr*] — **for hire** : available for use or service at a price

²hire *vb* **1 a :** to engage the personal services of for a set sum ⟨*hire* a new crew⟩ **b :** to engage the temporary use of for a fixed sum ⟨*hire* a hall⟩ **2 :** to grant the personal services of for a fixed sum ⟨*hire* themselves out⟩ **3 :** to take employment ⟨*hire* out as a cook⟩ — **hir•er** *n*

• syn HIRE, LET, LEASE, RENT mean to engage or grant for use at a price. HIRE and LET, strictly speaking, are complementary terms, HIRE implying the act of engaging or taking for use and LET the granting of use ⟨we *hired* a car for the summer⟩ ⟨decided to *let* the cottage to a young couple⟩ LEASE strictly implies a letting under the terms of a contract but is often applied to hiring on a lease ⟨the diplomat *leased* an apartment for a year⟩ ⟨the landlord refused to *lease* to tenants with pets⟩ RENT stresses the payment of money for the full use of property and may imply either hiring or letting.

• syn HIRE, EMPLOY mean to engage for work. HIRE stresses the act of engaging a person's services for pay; EMPLOY stresses the continued or regular use of a person's services.

hire•ling \'hīr-liŋ\ *n* **:** a person who serves for pay and usually for no other reason

hiring hall *n* **:** a union-operated placement office where registered applicants are referred in rotation to jobs

hir•sute \'hər-ˌsüt, 'hiər-\ *adj* **:** HAIRY; *esp* **:** having coarse stiff hairs [Latin *hirsutus*] — **hir•sute•ness** *n*

¹his \iz, hiz, ˌhiz\ *adj* **:** of or relating to him or himself especially as possessor, agent, or object of an action ⟨*his* house⟩ ⟨*his* writings⟩ ⟨*his* confirmation⟩ — compare ¹HE [Old English, genitive of *hē* "he"]

²his \'hiz\ *pron, sing or pl in construction* **:** that which belongs to him **:** those which belong to him — used without a following noun as an equivalent in meaning to the adjective *his*

¹His•pan•ic \his-'pan-ik\ *adj* **:** of, relating to, or derived from the people, speech, or culture of Spain or Latin America [Latin *Hispania* "Iberian peninsula, Spain"]

²Hispanic *n* **:** a Hispanic person

his•pid \'his-pəd\ *adj* **:** rough or covered with bristles, stiff hairs, or minute spines ⟨*hispid* leaf⟩ [Latin *hispidus*] — **his•pid•i•ty** \his-'pid-ət-ē\ *n*

hiss \'his\ *vb* **1 :** to utter the characteristic prolonged sibilant sound of an alarmed animal (as a snake or cat) or a similar sound **2 :** to express disapproval by hissing [Middle English *hissen*] — **hiss** *n* — **hiss•er** *n*

hist \s *often prolonged and usually with* p *preceding and* t *following; often read as* 'hist\ *interj* — used to attract attention [origin unknown]

hist- *or* **histo-** *combining form* **:** tissue ⟨*histamine*⟩ [Greek *histos* "mast, loom, beam, web", from *histanai* "to cause to stand"]

his•tam•i•nase \his-'tam-ə-ˌnās, 'his-tə-mə-\ *n* **:** an enzyme that breaks down histamine

his•ta•mine \'his-tə-ˌmēn, -mən\ *n* **:** a compound occurring in many animal tissues that is believed to play an important part in allergic reactions (as hives, asthma, and hay fever) and in some respiratory diseases

his•ti•dine \'his-tə-ˌdēn\ *n* **:** a crystalline basic amino acid $C_6H_9N_3O_2$ formed in the splitting of most proteins

his•to•gram \'his-tə-ˌgram\ *n* **:** a representation of a frequency distribution by means of rectangles whose widths represent the different values included in the class and whose heights represent the number of items found within the class [Greek *histos* "mast, pole, web"]

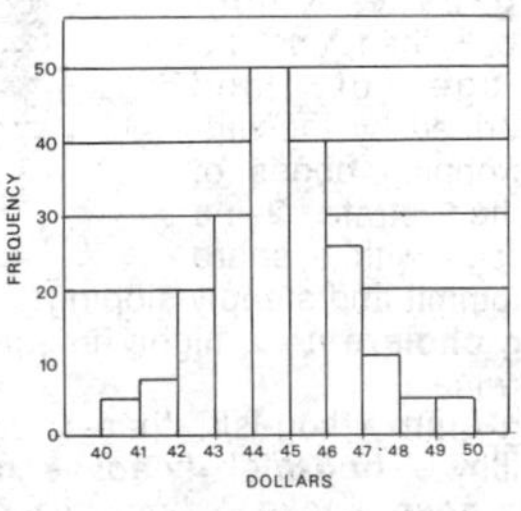

histogram

his•tol•o•gy \his-'täl-ə-jē\ *n, pl* **-gies 1 :** a branch of anatomy that deals with the structure of animal and plant tissues as revealed by the microscope **2 :** tissue structure or organization — **his•to•log•i•cal** \ˌhis-tə-'läj-i-kəl\ *adj* — **his•tol•o•gist** \his-'täl-ə-jəst\ *n*

his•to•plas•mo•sis \ˌhis-tə-plaz-'mō-səs\ *n* **:** a disease that is caused by a fungus infection of the lungs and is endemic in the Mississippi and Ohio River valleys of the United States

his•to•ri•an \his-'tōr-ē-ən, -'tòr-\ *n* **1 :** a student or writer of history; *esp* **:** one that produces a scholarly historical study **2 :** a writer of chronicles **:** CHRONICLER

his•tor•ic \his-'tòr-ik, -'tär-\ *adj* **:** HISTORICAL; *esp* **:** famous in history ⟨*historic* events⟩

his•tor•i•cal \-i-kəl\ *adj* **1 a :** of, relating to, or having the character of history ⟨*historical* fact⟩ **b :** based on history ⟨*historical* novels⟩ **2 :** famous in history ⟨*historical* personages⟩ — **his•tor•i•cal•ly** \-i-kə-lē, -klē\ *adv* — **his•tor•i•cal•ness** \-kəl-nəs\ *n*

historical present *n* **:** the present tense used to relate past events

his•to•ric•i•ty \ˌhis-tə-'ris-ət-ē\ *n* **:** historical actuality **:** FACT

his•to•ri•og•ra•pher \his-ˌtōr-ē-'äg-rə-fər, -ˌtòr-\ *n* **:** a usually official writer of history **:** HISTORIAN — **his•to•rio•graph•ic** \-ē-ə-'graf-ik\ *or* **his•to•rio•graph•i•cal** \-'graf-i-kəl\ *adj* — **his•to•rio•graph•i•cal•ly** \-i-kə-lē, -klē\ *adv* — **his•to•ri•og•ra•phy** \-ē-'äg-rə-fē\ *n*

his•to•ry \'his-tə-rē, -trē\ *n, pl* **-ries 1 :** STORY 1a, TALE **2 a :** a chronological record of significant events usually with an explanation of their causes **b :** an account of a sick person's medical background **3 :** a branch of knowledge that records and explains past events **4 a :** events that form the subject matter of a history **b :** past events [Latin *historia*, from Greek, "inquiry, history", from *istōr, histōr* "knowing, learned"]

his•tri•on•ic \ˌhis-trē-'än-ik\ *adj* **1 :** of or relating to actors, acting, or the theater **2 :** deliberately affected **:** THEATRICAL [Late Latin *histrionicus*, from Latin *histrio* "actor"] **syn** see DRAMATIC — **his•tri•on•i•cal•ly** \-'än-i-kə-lē, -klē\ *adv*

his•tri•on•ics \-'än-iks\ *n sing or pl* **1 :** theatrical performances **2 :** deliberate display of emotion for effect

¹hit \'hit\ *vb* **hit; hit•ting 1 a :** to strike usually with force ⟨*hit* a ball⟩ ⟨the ball *hit* against the house⟩ **b :** to make usually forceful contact with something ⟨fell and *hit* the ground⟩ **2 a :** ATTACK ⟨tried to guess when and where the enemy would *hit*⟩ **b :** to affect unfavorably ⟨the loss of the contract *hit* the company hard⟩ **3 :** OCCUR, HAPPEN ⟨when the storm *hit*⟩ **4 a :** COME, STUMBLE ⟨*hit* upon the solution⟩ **b :** to experience or find especially by chance ⟨*hit* a run of bad luck⟩ **c :** to get to **:** REACH ⟨*hit* town that night⟩ ⟨prices *hit* a new high⟩ **d :** to accord with accurately ⟨styles that *hit* modern taste⟩ **5 :** to fire the charge in the cylinders ⟨an automobile engine not *hitting*⟩ [Old Norse *hitta* "to meet with, hit"] — **hit•ter** *n*

²hit *n* **1 a :** a blow striking an object aimed at **b :** COLLISION **2 a :** a stroke of luck **b :** something that is conspicuously successful ⟨the show was a *hit*⟩ **3 :** a telling remark **4 :** BASE HIT

hit-and-miss \ˌhit-n-'mis\ *adj* **:** sometimes successful and sometimes not **:** HAPHAZARD

hit-and-run \-'rən\ *adj* **1 :** being or relating to a baseball play in which a base runner starts for the next base as the pitcher starts to pitch and the batter attempts to hit the ball **2 :** being or involving a motor-vehicle driver who does not stop after being involved in an accident

¹hitch \'hich\ *vb* **1 :** to move by jerks ⟨*hitch* a chair toward the table⟩ **2 a :** to catch or fasten by or as if by a hook or knot ⟨*hitch* a horse to a rail⟩ **b :** to connect to or with a hitch **3 :** HITCHHIKE [Middle English *hytchen*] — **hitch•er** *n*

²hitch *n* **1 :** a jerky movement or pull **2 :** a sudden stop **:** an unforeseen obstacle **:** HALT ⟨the plan went off without a *hitch*⟩ **3 :** the connection between something towed (as a plow or trailer) and its mover (as a tractor, automobile, or animal) **4 :** a knot used for a temporary fastening ⟨barrel *hitch*⟩ **5 :** a period of time in a specified state or activity ⟨a *hitch* in the infantry⟩

hitch•hike \'hich-ˌhīk\ *vb* **:** to travel by or secure free rides — **hitch•hik•er** *n*

hitch up *vi* **:** to harness and hitch a draft animal or team

¹hith•er \'hith-ər\ *adv* **:** to this place ⟨come *hither*⟩ [Old English *hider*]

²hither *adj* **:** being on the near or adjacent side ⟨the *hither* side of the hill⟩

hith•er•most \-ˌmōst\ *adj* **:** nearest on this side

hith•er•to \-ˌtü\ *adv* **:** up to this time

hith•er•ward \'hith-ər-wərd, -ə-\ *adv* **:** HITHER

hit off *vb* **1 :** to characterize precisely and usually satirically **2 :** HARMONIZE, AGREE

\ə\ **abut**	\aù\ **out**	\i\ **tip**	\ò\ **saw**	\ù\ **foot**
\ər\ **further**	\ch\ **chin**	\ī\ **life**	\òi\ **coin**	\y\ **yet**
\a\ **mat**	\e\ **pet**	\j\ **job**	\th\ **thin**	\yü\ **few**
\ā\ **take**	\ē\ **easy**	\ŋ\ **sing**	\th\ **this**	\yù\ **cure**
\ä\ **cot, cart**	\g\ **go**	\ō\ **bone**	\ü\ **food**	\zh\ **vision**

hit–or–miss \ˌhit-ər-ˈmis\ *adj* **:** marked by a lack of care, forethought, system, or plan

hit or miss *adv* **:** in a hit-or-miss manner **:** HAPHAZARDLY

Hit•tite \ˈhi-ˌtīt\ *n* **1 :** a member of a conquering people in Asia Minor and Syria ruling an empire in the 2d millennium B.C. **2 :** an Indo-European language of the Hittite people known from cuneiform texts [Hebrew *Ḥittī,* from Hittite *ḫatti*] — **Hittite** *adj*

[1]hive \ˈhīv\ *n* **1 a :** a container for housing honeybees **b :** a colony of bees **2 :** a place swarming with busy occupants [Old English *hȳf*] — **hive•less** \-ləs\ *adj*

[2]hive *vb* **1 a :** to collect (as bees) into a hive **b :** to enter and take over a hive **2 :** to store up in or as if in a hive ⟨*hive* honey⟩ **3 :** to live in close association

[3]hive *n* **:** an itching swelling characteristic of hives [back-formation from *hives*]

hives *n sing or pl* **:** an allergic disorder in which the skin or mucous membrane is affected by itching swellings [origin unknown]

ho \ˈhō\ *interj* — used especially to attract attention [Middle English]

hoar \ˈhōr, ˈhȯr\ *adj, archaic* **:** HOARY [Old English *hār*]

hoard \ˈhōrd, ˈhọrd\ *n* **:** a supply or fund stored up usually in secret [Old English *hord*] — **hoard** *vt* — **hoard•er** *n*

hoar•frost \ˈhōr-ˌfrȯst, ˈhȯr-\ *n* **:** FROST 1c

hoarse \ˈhōrs, ˈhȯrs\ *adj* **1 :** harsh in sound ⟨a crow's *hoarse* caw⟩ **2 :** having a rough grating voice ⟨*hoarse* from a cold⟩ [Middle English *hos, hors,* from Old English *hās*] — **hoarse•ly** *adv* — **hoarse•ness** *n*

hoary \ˈhōr-ē, ˈhȯr-\ *adj* **hoar•i•er; -est 1 :** grayish or whitish especially from age ⟨an old dog's *hoary* muzzle⟩ **2 :** very old **:** ANCIENT ⟨*hoary* legends⟩ — **hoar•i•ness** *n*

[1]hoax \ˈhōks\ *vt* **:** to trick into believing or accepting as genuine something false and often preposterous [probably from *hocus*] — **hoax•er** *n*

[2]hoax *n* **1 :** an act intended to trick or fool **2 :** something false passed off or accepted as genuine

[1]hob \ˈhäb\ *n* **1** *English dialect* **:** HOBGOBLIN 1, ELF **2 :** MISCHIEF, TROUBLE ⟨raise *hob*⟩ [Middle English *hobbe,* from *Hobbe,* nickname for *Robert*]

[2]hob *n* **1 :** a projection at the back or side of a fireplace on which something may be kept warm **2 :** a cutting tool used for cutting the teeth of worm wheels or gear wheels [origin unknown]

[3]hob *vt* **hobbed; hob•bing 1 :** to furnish with hobnails **2 :** to cut with a hob

[1]hob•ble \ˈhäb-əl\ *vb* **hob•bled; hob•bling** \ˈhäb-ling, -ə-ling\ **1 a :** to move along unsteadily or with difficulty; *esp* **:** to limp along ⟨*hobble* on crutches⟩ **b :** to cause to limp **:** make lame **:** CRIPPLE ⟨*hobbled* by an ankle injury⟩ **2 a :** to keep (as a horse) from straying by joining two legs with a short length (as of rope) **b :** to place under handicap **:** HAMPER, IMPEDE [Middle English *hoblen*] — **hob•bler** \ˈhäb-lər, -ə-lər\ *n*

[2]hobble *n* **1 :** a hobbling movement **2 :** something used to hobble an animal

hob•ble•de•hoy \ˈhäb-əl-di-ˌhȯi\ *n* **:** an awkward gawky youth [origin unknown]

hobble skirt *n* **:** a skirt very narrow at the ankles

hob•by \ˈhäb-ē\ *n, pl* **hobbies :** an interest or activity which is outside a person's regular occupation and is pursued for pleasure [short for *hobbyhorse*] — **hob•by•ist** \-ē-əst\ *n*

hob•by•horse \ˈhäb-ē-ˌhȯrs\ *n* **1 :** a stick with an imitation horse's head at one end which children pretend to ride **2 a :** a toy horse **b :** ROCKING HORSE **3 :** a topic to which one constantly returns [Middle English *hoby* "small light horse"]

hob•gob•lin \ˈhäb-ˌgäb-lən\ *n* **1 :** a mischievous elf or goblin **2 :** BOGEY 2, BUGABOO

hob•nail \ˈhäb-ˌnāl\ *n* **:** a short large-headed nail used to stud the soles of heavy shoes as a protection against wear [[2]*hob*] — **hob•nailed** \-ˌnāld\ *adj*

hob•nob \-ˌnäb\ *vi* **hob•nobbed; hob•nob•bing :** to associate familiarly ⟨*hobnobbing* with royalty⟩ [from the obsolete phrase *drink hobnob* "to drink alternately to one another"] — **hob•nob•ber** *n*

ho•bo \ˈhō-bō\ *n, pl* **hoboes** *also* **hobos 1 :** a migratory worker **2 :** TRAMP 1 [perhaps from *ho, boy*] — **hobo** *vi*

Hob•son's choice \ˌhäb-sənz-\ *n* **:** apparently free choice with no real alternative [Thomas *Hobson,* died 1631, English liveryman, who required every customer to take the horse nearest the door]

[1]hock \ˈhäk\ *n* **:** the tarsal joint or region in the hind limb of a four-footed animal (as the horse) corresponding to the human ankle [Old English *hōh* "heel"]

[2]hock *n, often cap, chiefly British* **:** RHINE WINE [German *hochheimer,* from *Hochheim,* Germany]

[3]hock *n* **:** [1]PAWN 2 ⟨got the watch out of *hock*⟩ [Dutch *hok* "pen, prison"]

[4]hock *vt* **:** PAWN ⟨*hocked* the silverware⟩

hock•ey \ˈhäk-ē\ *n* **1 :** FIELD HOCKEY **2 :** ICE HOCKEY [perhaps from Middle French *hoquet* "shepherd's crook", from *hoc* "hook", of Germanic origin]

ho•cus \ˈhō-kəs\ *vt* **ho•cused** *or* **ho•cussed; ho•cus•ing** *or* **ho•cus•sing 1 :** to play a trick on **:** DECEIVE **2 :** DRUG 1, DOPE [from *hocus-pocus*]

ho•cus–po•cus \ˌhō-kə-ˈspō-kəs\ *n* **1 :** a set form of words used by those skilled in tricks of illusion **2 :** nonsense that serves as a means of deception [probably from *hocus pocus,* imitation Latin phrase used by jugglers]

hod \ˈhäd\ *n* **1 :** a long-handled wooden tray or trough used for carrying mortar or bricks on the shoulder **2 :** a bucket for holding or carrying coal [probably from Dutch *hodde*]

hod carrier *n* **:** a laborer who carries supplies to bricklayers, stonemasons, cement finishers, or plasterers on the job

hodge•podge \ˈhäj-ˌpäj\ *n* **:** MISHMASH, JUMBLE [alteration of *hotchpotch*]

△ **origin** An earlier form of *hodgepodge,* and still a form used commonly in Britain, is *hotchpotch.* This in turn is a rhyming alteration of Middle English *hochepot.* The Old French *hochepot,* from which the English is derived, is formed from *hochier,* "to shake", and *pot,* which has the same meaning as English *pot. Hochepot,* then, was a stew with many different ingredients all shaken (and presumably cooked) together in the same pot. This mixture of many ingredients in one pot prompted the extension of meaning to any heterogeneous mixture.

Hodg•kin's disease \ˈhäj-kənz-\ *n* **:** a disease characterized by progressive enlargement of the lymph glands, spleen, and liver and by progressive anemia [Thomas *Hodgkin,* died 1866, English physician]

hoe \ˈhō\ *n* **:** a farm or garden tool with a thin flat blade at nearly a right angle to a long handle that is used for weeding, loosening the earth about plants, and hilling [Middle French *houe,* of Germanic origin] — **hoe** *vb* — **ho•er** \ˈhō-ər, ˈhōr\ *n*

hoe•cake \ˈhō-ˌkāk\ *n* **:** a small cornmeal cake [from its formerly being baked on the blade of a hoe]

hoe•down \-ˌdaun\ *n* **1 :** SQUARE DANCE **2 :** a gathering featuring hoedowns

[1]hog \ˈhȯg, ˈhäg\ *n, pl* **hogs** *also* **hog 1 :** a domestic swine especially when weighing more than 120 pounds; *also* **:** any of various animals related to the domestic swine **2 :** a selfish, gluttonous, or filthy person [Old English *hogg*]

[2]hog *vt* **hogged; hog•ging :** to take more than one's share of

ho•gan \ˈhō-ˌgän\ *n* **:** an earth-covered dwelling of the Navaho Indians [Navaho]

hogan

hog•back \ˈhȯg-ˌbak, ˈhäg-\ *n* **1 :** a ridge of land formed by the outcropping edges of tilted strata **2 :** a ridge with a sharp summit and steeply sloping sides

hog cholera *n* **:** a highly infectious often fatal virus disease of swine

hog•gish \ˈhȯg-ish, ˈhäg-\ *adj* **:** very selfish, gluttonous, or filthy — **hog•gish•ly** *adv* — **hog•gish•ness** *n*

hog•nose snake \ˌhȯg-ˌnōz-, ˌhäg-\ *or* **hog–nosed snake** \-ˌnōz-, -ˌnōzd-\ *n* **:** any of several rather small harmless stout-bodied North American snakes that protect themselves when disturbed first by a threat display and then by playing dead — called also *puff adder*

hogs•head \ˈhȯgz-ˌhed, ˈhägz-\ *n* **1 :** a large cask or barrel; *esp* **:** one containing from 63 to 140 gallons (about 238 to 530 liters) **2 :** a United States measure for liquids equal to 63 gallons (about 238 liters)

hog–tie \ˈhȯg-ˌtī, ˈhäg-\ *vt* **1 :** to tie together the feet of ⟨*hog-tie* a calf⟩ **2 :** to make helpless ⟨*hog-tied* by red tape⟩

hog•wash \-,wȯsh, -,wäsh\ *n* **1** : SWILL 1, SLOP 4a **2** : worthless or nonsensical language

Ho•hen•stau•fen \'hō-ən-,shtaů-fən, -,staů-\ *adj* : of or relating to the German royal family furnishing monarchs of the Holy Roman Empire from 1138 to 1254 and of Sicily from 1194 to 1266 — **Hohenstaufen** *n*

Ho•hen•zol•lern \'hō-ən-,zäl-ərn\ *adj* : of or relating to the German royal family furnishing kings of Prussia from 1701 to 1918 and German emperors from 1871 to 1918 — **Hohenzollern** *n*

hoi polloi \,hȯi-pə-'lȯi\ *n pl* : the common people : MASSES [Greek, "the many"]

hoise \'hȯiz\ *vt* **hoised** \'hȯizd\ *or* **hoist** \'hȯist\; **hois•ing** \'hȯi-zing\ : HOIST [origin unknown] — **hoist with one's own petard** : affected or hurt by one's own scheme

[1]hoist \'hȯist\ *vb* : to raise or become raised into position by or as if by means of tackle [alteration of *hoise*] **syn** see LIFT — **hoist•er** *n*

[2]hoist *n* **1** : an act of hoisting : LIFT **2** : an apparatus for hoisting heavy loads

hoi•ty-toi•ty \,hȯit-ē-'tȯit-ē, ,hīt-ē-'tīt-ē\ *adj* **1** : GIDDY 3, FLIGHTY **2** : HAUGHTY, PATRONIZING [derived from English dialect *hoit* "to play the fool"]

ho•key-po•key \,hō-kē-'pō-kē\ *n* : HOCUS-POCUS 2

ho•kum \'hō-kəm\ *n* **1** : a stock technique for evoking a desired response (as laughter or sentiment) from an audience **2** : pretentious nonsense : BUNKUM [probably from *hocus-pocus* + *bunkum*]

hol- *or* **holo-** *combining form* : complete : total : completely : totally ⟨*Holocene*⟩ [Greek *holos* "whole"]

[1]hold \'hōld\ *vb* **held** \'held\; **hold•ing** **1 a** : to maintain possession of : HAVE ⟨*hold* title to property⟩ **b** : to retain by force ⟨the soldiers *held* the bridge⟩ **2 a** : to impose restraint upon especially by keeping back ⟨*hold* your temper⟩ **b** : DELAY ⟨*held* the plane⟩ **c** : to keep from advancing or succeeding in attack **d** : to bind legally or morally : CONSTRAIN ⟨I'll *hold* you to your word⟩ **3 a** : to have or keep in the grasp **b** : to cause to be or remain in a particular situation, position, or relation ⟨*hold* a ladder steady⟩ **c** : SUPPORT, SUSTAIN ⟨the floor will *hold* 10 metric tons⟩ **d** : to keep in custody **e** : to have in one's keeping : RESERVE ⟨*hold* a room⟩ **4** : BEAR, CARRY, COMPORT ⟨*hold* oneself proudly⟩ **5 a** : to keep up without interruption or flagging ⟨*hold* silence⟩ **b** : to keep the uninterrupted interest, attention, or devotion of **6 a** : to receive and retain : CONTAIN, ACCOMMODATE ⟨the can *holds* 20 liters⟩ **b** : to have in store ⟨what the future *holds*⟩ **7 a** : HARBOR, ENTERTAIN ⟨*hold* a theory⟩ **b** : CONSIDER, REGARD, JUDGE ⟨truths *held* to be self-evident⟩ **8** : to schedule and carry out (as a social event or a conference) **9 a** : to have (as an office) by election or appointment ⟨*holds* a captaincy in the navy⟩ **b** : to have earned or been awarded ⟨*holds* a Ph.D.⟩ **10** : to handle (as reins or a gun) so as to guide or manage **11 a** : to maintain position : not retreat **b** (1) : to continue in the same way or state : LAST ⟨hope the weather *holds*⟩ (2) : to endure a test or trial ⟨their courage *held* against all odds⟩ **c** : to remain steadfast or faithful ⟨*held* to their beliefs⟩ **12** : to maintain a grasp on something : remain fastened to something ⟨the anchor *held* in the rough sea⟩ **13** : to bear or carry oneself ⟨asked them to *hold* still⟩ **14** : to be or remain valid : APPLY ⟨the rule *holds* in most cases⟩ **15** : to forbear an intended or threatened action : HALT, PAUSE [Old English *healdan*] **syn** see CONTAIN — **hold forth** : to talk or preach at length — **hold one's own** : to prove at least equal to opposition — **hold the bag 1** : to be left empty-handed **2** : to bear alone a responsibility that should have been shared by others — **hold water** : to stand up under criticism or analysis — **hold with** : to agree with or approve of

[2]hold *n* **1** : STRONGHOLD 1 **2** : the act or manner of holding : SEIZURE, GRASP ⟨took a firm *hold* on the rope⟩ **3** : a manner of grasping the opponent in wrestling **4** : the authority to take or keep : POWER ⟨had a strong *hold* over their children⟩ **5** : something that may be grasped or held **6** : a prolonged note or rest in music; *also* : a sign ⌒ or ⌣ denoting a hold **7** : an order or indication that something is to be reserved or delayed

[3]hold *n* **1** : the interior of a ship below decks; *esp* : the cargo deck of a ship **2** : the cargo compartment of an airplane [alteration of *hole*]

hold•all \'hōl-,dȯl\ *n* : a container for miscellaneous articles; *esp* : a traveling case or bag

hold•er \'hōl-dər\ *n* **1** : a person that holds: **a** (1) : OWNER — often used in combination ⟨job*holder*⟩ (2) : TENANT 1 **b** : a person in possession of and legally entitled to receive payment of a bill, note, or check **2** : a device that holds ⟨cigarette *holder*⟩

hold•fast \'hōld-,fast, 'hōl-\ *n* : a part by which a plant or animal clings (as to a flat surface or the body of a host)

hold•ing \'hōl-ding\ *n* **1 a** : land held (as for farming or residence) **b** : property (as bonds or stocks) owned — usually used in pl. **2** : a ruling of a court especially on an issue of law raised in a case

holding company *n* : a company that owns part or all of other companies for purposes of control

hold out \hōl-'daůt, 'hōl-\ *vb* **1** : PROFFER ⟨*held out* little chance of success⟩ **2** : REPRESENT 4 ⟨*hold* oneself *out* to be a scholar⟩ **3** : to remain unsubdued or operative : continue to cope **4** : to refuse to come to an agreement — **hold•out** \'hōl-,daůt\ *n*

hold over \hōl-'dō-vər, 'hōl-\ *vb* **1** : to continue (as in office) beyond the normal term **2** : to prolong the engagement or tenure of ⟨a smash hit *held over* by popular demand⟩ — **hold•over** \'hōl-,dō-vər\ *n*

hold up \hōl-'dəp, 'hōl-\ *vt* **1** : DELAY, IMPEDE ⟨only *holding* things *up*⟩ **2** : to rob at gunpoint — **hold•up** \'hōl-,dəp\ *n*

hole \'hōl\ *n* **1** : an opening into or through a thing ⟨a *hole* in a wall⟩ **2 a** : a hollow place (as a pit or cave) **b** : a deep place in a body of water ⟨trout *holes*⟩ **3** : an underground habitation : BURROW ⟨a fox in its *hole*⟩ **4** : FLAW, FAULT ⟨a big *hole* in your argument⟩ **5 a** : a cavity in the putting green of a golf course into which the ball is played **b** : the play or the part of the course from the tee to the hole **6** : a mean or dingy place ⟨lives in a real *hole*⟩ **7** : an awkward position : FIX [Old English *hol* and *holh*] — **hole** *vb* — **hol•ey** \'hō-lē\ *adj* — **in the hole 1** : in debt **2** : having a score below zero

hol•i•day \'häl-ə-,dā\ *n* **1** : HOLY DAY **2** : a day of freedom from work; *esp* : a day of celebration or commemoration fixed by law **3** : a period of relaxation : VACATION [Old English *hāligdæg*, from *hālig* "holy" + *dæg* "day"] — **holiday** *vi* — **hol•i•day•er** *n*

ho•li•ness \'hō-lē-nəs\ *n* **1** : the quality or state of being holy **2** *cap* — used as a form of address for various high religious dignitaries ⟨His *Holiness* Pope John Paul II⟩ ⟨Your *Holiness*⟩

hol•land \'häl-ənd\ *n* : a cotton or linen fabric in plain weave usually heavily sized or glazed and used especially for window shades [Middle English *Holand*, county in the Netherlands, from Dutch *Holland*]

hol•lan•daise sauce \,häl-ən-,dāz-\ *n* : a sauce made of butter, yolks of eggs, and lemon juice or vinegar [French *sauce hollandaise*, literally, "Dutch sauce"]

[1]hol•ler \'häl-ər\ *vb* **hol•lered**; **hol•ler•ing** \'häl-ring, -ə-ring\ **1** : to cry or call out : SHOUT **2** : COMPLAIN 1 [alteration of *hollo*, of unknown origin]

[2]holler *n* **1** : SHOUT, CRY **2** : COMPLAINT 1

hol•lo \hä-'lō, hə-; 'häl-ō\ *or* **hal•lo** \hə-'lō, ha-\ *or* **hal•loo** \-'lü\ *interj* **1** — used to attract attention **2** — used as a call of encouragement or jubilation

[1]hol•low \'häl-ō\ *adj* **1** : curved inward : SUNKEN ⟨*hollow* cheeks⟩ **2** : having a hole inside : not solid throughout ⟨a *hollow* tree⟩ **3 a** : FALSE, DECEITFUL ⟨*hollow* promises⟩ **b** : apparently but not really valuable or significant ⟨a *hollow* victory⟩ **4** : echoing like a sound made in a large empty enclosure or by beating on a hollow object [Middle English *holh, holw*, from *holh* "hole, den", from Old English, "hole, hollow"] — **hol•low•ly** *adv* — **hol•low•ness** *n*

[2]hollow *vb* : to make or become hollow

[3]hollow *n* **1** : a low spot in a surface; *esp* : VALLEY **2** : an empty space within something : HOLE ⟨the *hollow* of a tree⟩

hol•low•ware *or* **hol•lo•ware** \'häl-ə-,waər, -,weər\ *n* **1** : vessels (as cups or vases) usually of pottery or glass that have significant depth **2** : domestic metalware and especially tableware other than flatware

hol•ly \'häl-ē\ *n, pl* **hollies** : any of a genus of trees and shrubs with thick glossy spiny-margined leaves and usually bright red

\ə\ **abut**	\aů\ **out**	\i\ **tip**	\ȯ\ **saw**	\ů\ **foot**
\ər\ **further**	\ch\ **chin**	\ī\ **life**	\ȯi\ **coin**	\y\ **yet**
\a\ **mat**	\e\ **pet**	\j\ **job**	\th\ **thin**	\yü\ **few**
\ā\ **take**	\ē\ **easy**	\ng\ **sing**	\th\ **this**	\yů\ **cure**
\ä\ **cot, cart**	\g\ **go**	\ō\ **bone**	\ü\ **food**	\zh\ **vision**

berries; *also* : the foliage or branches of a holly [Old English *holegn*]

hol•ly•hock \ˈhäl-ē-ˌhäk, -ˌhȯk\ *n* : a tall widely grown perennial Chinese herb of the mallow family with large coarse rounded leaves and tall spikes of showy flowers [Middle English *holihoc*, from *holi* "holy" + *hoc* "mallow", from Old English]

Hol•ly•wood bed \ˌhäl-ē-ˌwu̇d-\ *n* : a mattress on a box spring supported by low legs sometimes with an upholstered headboard [*Hollywood*, district of Los Angeles, California]

hol•mi•um \ˈhōl-mē-əm, ˈhō-\ *n* : a metallic element that occurs with yttrium and forms highly magnetic compounds — see ELEMENT table [New Latin, from *Holmia* (Stockholm), Sweden]

holly

holo- — see HOL-

ho•lo•caust \ˈhäl-ə-ˌkȯst, ˈhō-lə- *also* ˈhȯ-lə-\ *n* **1** : a sacrifice consumed by fire **2** : a thorough destruction especially by fire [Old French *holocauste*, from Late Latin *holocaustum*, from Greek *holokauston*, from *holokaustos* "burnt whole", from *holos* "whole" + *kaustos* "burnt", from *kaiein* "to burn"]

Ho•lo•cene \ˈhō-lə-ˌsēn, ˈhäl-ə-\ *adj* : RECENT 2 — **Holocene** *n*

ho•lo•gram \ˈhō-lə-ˌgram, ˈhäl-ə-\ *n* : a three-dimensional picture that is made on a photographic film or plate without the use of a camera, that consists of a pattern of interference produced by a split coherent beam of light, and that for viewing is illuminated with coherent light from behind

ho•lo•graph \ˈhō-lə-ˌgraf, ˈhäl-ə-\ *n* : a document wholly in the handwriting of its author — **holograph** *adj* — **ho•lo•graph•ic** \ˌhō-lə-ˈgraf-ik, ˌhäl-ə-\ *adj*

ho•log•ra•phy \hō-ˈläg-rə-fē\ *n* : the process of making or using a hologram — **ho•lo•graph** \ˈhō-lə-ˌgraf, ˈhäl-ə-\ *vt* — **ho•lo•graph•ic** \ˌhō-lə-ˈgraf-ik, ˌhäl-ə-\ *adj* — **ho•lo•graph•i•cal•ly** \-i-kə-lē, -klē\ *adv*

ho•lo•thu•ri•an \ˌhō-lə-ˈthu̇r-ē-ən, ˌhäl-ə-, -ˈthyu̇r-\ *n* : SEA CUCUMBER [derived from Greek *holothourion*, a water polyp] — **holothurian** *adj*

hol•stein \ˈhōl-ˌstēn, -ˌstīn\ *n* : any of a breed of large black-and-white dairy cattle that produce large quantities of comparatively low-fat milk [short for *holstein-friesian*]

hol•stein–frie•sian \-ˈfrē-zhən\ *n* : HOLSTEIN [*Holstein*, Germany + *Friesian*, variant of *Frisian*]

hol•ster \ˈhōl-stər, ˈhōlt-\ *n* : a usually leather case for carrying a pistol [Dutch]

ho•ly \ˈhō-lē\ *adj* **ho•li•er**; **-est** **1** : set apart to the service of God or a god : SACRED **2 a** : commanding absolute adoration and reverence **b** : spiritually pure : SAINTLY **3 a** : evoking or meriting veneration or awe **b** : being awesome, frightening, or beyond belief ⟨a *holy* terror⟩ [Old English *hālig*]

Holy Communion *n* : COMMUNION 1a

holy day *n* : a day observed as a religious feast or fast

holy day of obligation : a feast on which Roman Catholics are obliged to hear mass

Holy Father *n* : POPE

Holy Ghost *n* : HOLY SPIRIT

Holy Grail *n* : GRAIL

holy orders *n pl, often cap H&O* : the rite or sacrament of ordination

Holy Roman Empire *n* : a loose confederation of German and Italian territories under an emperor that existed from the 9th or 10th century to 1806

Holy Saturday *n* : the Saturday before Easter

Holy See *n* : the see of the pope

Holy Spirit *n* : the active presence of God in human life constituting the third person of the Trinity

ho•ly•stone \ˈhō-lē-ˌstōn\ *n* : a soft sandstone used to scrub a ship's decks — **holystone** *vb*

Holy Thursday *n* : MAUNDY THURSDAY

holy water *n* : water blessed by a priest and used as a purifying sacramental

Holy Week *n* : the week before Easter

Holy Writ *n* : BIBLE 1, 2

hom- *or* **homo-** *combining form* : one and the same : similar : alike ⟨*homo*graph⟩ [Greek *homos* "same"]

hom•age \ˈäm-ij, ˈhäm-\ *n* **1** : a ceremony in which a person pledged allegiance to a lord and became his vassal **2** : something done or given as an acknowledgment of a vassal's duty to his lord **3 a** : respectful admiration : HONOR **b** : flattering attention : TRIBUTE [Old French *hommage*, from *homme* "man, vassal", from Latin *homo* "man"]

hom•bre \ˈäm-brē, -ˌbrā\ *n* : FELLOW 4a [Spanish, "man", from Latin *homo*]

hom•burg \ˈhäm-ˌbərg\ *n* : a man's felt hat with a stiff curled brim and a high crown creased lengthwise [*Homburg*, Germany]

¹home \ˈhōm\ *n* **1 a** : the house in which one lives or in which one's family lives **b** : a dwelling house ⟨new *homes* for sale⟩ **2** : the social unit formed by a family living together in one dwelling ⟨a city of 20,000 *homes*⟩ **3** : the country or place where one lives or where one's ancestors lived **4** : the place where something is usually or naturally found : HABITAT ⟨the *home* of the elephant⟩ **5** : a place for the care of persons unable to care for themselves ⟨a *home* for old people⟩ **6** : the goal or point to be reached in some games [Old English *hām* "village, home"]

²home *adv* **1** : to or at home ⟨go *home*⟩ ⟨stay *home*⟩ **2** : to a final, closed, or standard position ⟨drive a nail *home*⟩ **3** : to a vital core ⟨the truth struck *home*⟩

³home *vb* **1 a** : to go or return home **b** : to return home accurately from a distance ⟨a pigeon *homes* to its loft⟩ **c** : to proceed to or toward a source of radiated energy used as a guide ⟨missiles *home* in on radar⟩ **2** : to have a home **3** : to send to or provide with a home

home- *or* **homeo-** *also* **homoi-** *or* **homoio-** *combining form* : like : similar ⟨*homeo*stasis⟩ ⟨*homoio*thermic⟩ [Greek *homoios*, from *homos* "same"]

home•body \ˈhōm-ˌbäd-ē\ *n* : one whose life centers around the home

home•bred \-ˈbred\ *adj* : produced at home : INDIGENOUS

home brew *n* : an alcoholic beverage made at home

home•com•ing \ˈhōm-ˌkəm-iŋ\ *n* **1** : a return home **2 a** : the return of a group of people especially on a special occasion to a place formerly frequented **b** : an annual celebration for alumni at a college or university

home economics *n* : the study of the various arts and skills involved in the care and management of a household — **home economist** *n*

home front *n* : the sphere of civilian activity in war

home•grown \ˈhōm-ˈgrōn\ *adj* **1** : grown or produced at home or nearby ⟨*homegrown* corn⟩ **2** : INDIGENOUS ⟨*homegrown* politicians⟩

home•land \ˈhōm-ˌland\ *n* : native land : FATHERLAND

home•less \ˈhōm-ləs\ *adj* : having no home ⟨a *homeless* kitten⟩

home•like \-ˌlīk\ *adj* : having qualities suggestive of a home or family living

home•ly \ˈhōm-lē\ *adj* **home•li•er**; **-est** **1** : characteristic of home life : PLAIN, SIMPLE ⟨*homely* meals⟩ **2** : lacking polish or refinement ⟨*homely* manners⟩ **3** : not handsome ⟨a *homely* person⟩ — **home•li•ness** *n*

home•made \ˈhōm-ˈmād, ˈhō-\ *adj* : made in the home, on the premises, or by one's own efforts ⟨*homemade* bread⟩

home•mak•er \ˈhōm-ˌmā-kər\ *n* : a person who manages a household especially as a wife and mother — **home•mak•ing** \-kiŋ\ *n or adj*

ho•me•op•a•thy \ˌhō-mē-ˈäp-ə-thē\ *n* : a system of medical practice that treats disease especially with minute doses of material that would in healthy persons produce symptoms of the disease treated — **ho•meo•path** \ˈhō-mē-ə-ˌpath\ *n* — **ho•meo•path•ic** \ˌhō-mē-ə-ˈpath-ik\ *adj*

ho•meo•sta•sis \ˌhō-mē-ō-ˈstā-səs\ *n* : a tendency toward keeping a relatively stable internal environment in the bodies of higher animals by means of complex physiological interactions — **ho•meo•stat•ic** \-mē-ō-ˈstat-ik\ *adj*

home plate *n* : the rubber slab at the apex of a baseball diamond that the batter stands beside and must return to in order to score

hom•er \ˈhō-mər\ *n* **1** : HOMING PIGEON **2** : HOME RUN

home range *n* : the area to which an animal confines its activities — compare TERRITORY

Ho•mer•ic \hō-'mer-ik\ *adj* : of, relating to, or characteristic of the Greek poet Homer, his age, or his writings — **Ho•mer•i•cal•ly** \-i-kə-lē, -klē\ *adv*

home•room \'hōm-,rüm, -,rům\ *n* : a schoolroom where pupils of the same class report at the opening of school

home rule *n* : self-government in internal affairs by the people of a dependent political unit

home run *n* : a hit in baseball that enables the batter to round all the bases and score a run — called also *homer*

home•sick \'hōm-,sik\ *adj* : longing for home and family while absent from them — **home•sick•ness** *n*

¹home•spun \-,spən\ *adj* **1 a** : spun or made at home **b** : made of homespun **2** : SIMPLE 3a(1), HOMELY ⟨*homespun* humor⟩

²homespun *n* : a loosely woven usually woolen or linen fabric originally made from homespun yarn

¹home•stead \'hōm-,sted\ *n* **1 a** : the home and adjoining land occupied by a family **b** : an ancestral home **2** : a tract of land acquired from United States public lands by filing a record and living on and cultivating it

²homestead *vb* : to acquire or settle on land for use as a homestead ⟨*homesteaded* in Alaska⟩

home•stead•er \-,sted-ər\ *n* : one that holds a homestead; *esp* : a person with a homestead acquired under laws authorizing the sale of public lands in parcels of about 64.75 hectares to settlers

home•stretch \'hōm-'strech\ *n* **1** : the part of a racecourse between the last curve and the winning post **2** : a final stage (as of a project)

home•ward \'hōm-wərd\ *or* **home•wards** \-wərdz\ *adv* : toward or in the direction of home — **homeward** *adj*

home•work \-,wərk\ *n* : work and especially school lessons to be done at home

hom•ey \'hō-mē\ *adj* **hom•i•er**; **-est** : HOMELIKE, INTIMATE — **hom•ey•ness** *or* **hom•i•ness** *n*

hom•i•cid•al \,häm-ə-'sīd-l, ,hō-mə-\ *adj* : having or showing tendencies toward homicide : MURDEROUS — **hom•i•cid•al•ly** \-l-ē\ *adv*

hom•i•cide \'häm-ə-,sīd, 'hō-mə-\ *n* : a person who kills another **2** : a killing of one human being by another [Middle French, from Latin *homicida,* from *homo* "man" + *-cida* "-cide"]

hom•i•let•ic \,häm-ə-'let-ik\ *adj* **1** : of the nature of a homily **2** : of or relating to homiletics — **hom•i•let•i•cal** \-i-kəl\ *adj* — **hom•i•let•i•cal•ly** \-i-kə-lē, -klē\ *adv*

hom•i•let•ics \-'let-iks\ *n* : the art of preaching

hom•i•ly \'häm-ə-lē\ *n, pl* **-lies** **1** : SERMON; *esp* : an informal explanation of Scripture **2** : a moral lecture [Middle French *omelie,* from Late Latin *homilia,* from Greek, "conversation, discourse", from *homilein* "to consort with, address", from *homilos* "crowd, assembly"]

homing pigeon *n* : a racing pigeon trained to return home

hom•i•nid \'häm-ə-nəd\ *n* : any of a family (Hominidae) of 2-footed primate mammals comprising recent human beings, their immediate ancestors, and related extinct forms [derived from Latin *homin-, homo* "man"] — **hominid** *adj*

hom•i•noid \'häm-ə-,nȯid\ *adj* : resembling or related to the biological family to which human beings belong — **hominoid** *n*

hom•i•ny \'häm-ə-nē\ *n* : hulled corn with the germ removed [of American Indian origin]

ho•mo \'hō-mō\ : any of a genus (*Homo*) of primate mammals that usually includes a single recent species (*H. sapiens*) comprising all surviving human beings and various extinct ancestors [Latin, "man"]

homo- — see HOM-

ho•mog•e•nate \hō-'mäj-ə-,nāt\ *n* : a product of homogenizing

ho•mo•ge•ne•i•ty \,hō-mə-jə-'nē-ət-ē, -'nā-ət-\ *n* : the quality or state of being homogeneous

ho•mo•ge•neous \-'jē-nē-əs, -nyəs\ *adj* **1** : of the same or a similar kind or nature **2** : of uniform structure or composition throughout [Medieval Latin *homogeneus,* from Greek *homogenēs,* from *homos* "same" + *genos* "kind"] — **ho•mo•ge•neous•ly** *adv* — **ho•mo•ge•neous•ness** *n*

ho•mog•e•nize \hə-'mäj-ə-,nīz, hō-\ *vt* **1** : to make homogeneous **2 a** : to reduce to small particles of uniform size and distribute evenly ⟨*homogenize* paint⟩ **b** : to break up the fat globules of (milk) into very fine particles especially by forcing through minute openings — **ho•mog•e•ni•za•tion** \-,mäj-ə-nə-'zā-shən\ *n* — **ho•mog•e•niz•er** \-'mäj-ə-,nī-zər\ *n*

ho•mog•e•nous \-'mäj-ə-nəs\ *adj* : HOMOGENEOUS

ho•mo•graph \'häm-ə-,graf, 'hō-mə-\ *n* : one of two or more words alike in spelling but different in origin or meaning or pronunciation ⟨the noun *conduct* and the verb *conduct* are *homographs*⟩ — **ho•mo•graph•ic** \,häm-ə-'graf-ik, ,hō-mə-\ *adj*

homoi- *or* **homoio-** — see HOME-

ho•moio•ther•mic \hō-,mȯi-ə-'thər-mik\ *or* **ho•moio•ther•mal** \-məl\ *adj* : WARM-BLOODED — **ho•moio•therm** \-'mȯi-ə-,thərm\ *n*

ho•mol•o•gous \hō-'mäl-ə-gəs, hə-\ *adj* **1 a** : having the same relative position, value, or structure **b** (1) : corresponding in structure because of derivation from the same or a similar part of a remote ancestor ⟨arms and wings are *homologous* structures⟩ (2) : having the same or allelic genes with corresponding genes arranged in the same order ⟨*homologous* chromosomes⟩ **c** : belonging to or consisting of a chemical series whose members exhibit homology **2** : derived from or developed in response to organisms of the same species ⟨*homologous* tissue graft⟩ [Greek *homologos* "agreeing", from *homos* "same" + *legein* "to say"]

ho•mo•logue *or* **ho•mo•log** \'hō-mə-,lȯg, 'häm-ə-, -,läg\ *n* : something that is homologous

ho•mol•o•gy \hō-'mäl-ə-jē, hə-\ *n, pl* **-gies** **1** : a similarity often attributable to common origin **2 a** : structural likeness between corresponding parts of different organisms due to evolution from a remote common ancestor — compare ANALOGY **b** : structural likeness between different parts of the same individual **3** : the relation existing between chemical compounds in a series whose successive members have in composition a regular difference

hom•onym \'häm-ə-,nim, 'hō-mə-\ *n* **1 a** : HOMOPHONE **b** : HOMOGRAPH **2** : one of two or more words spelled and pronounced alike but different in meaning ⟨*pool* of water and *pool* (the game) are *homonyms*⟩ [Latin *homonymum,* from Greek *homōnymon,* from *homōnymos* "having the same name", from *homos* "same" + *onyma, onoma* "name"] — **hom•onym•ic** \,häm-ə-'nim-ik, ,hō-mə-\ *adj*

ho•mo•phone \'häm-ə-,fōn, 'hō-mə-\ *n* : one of two or more words pronounced alike but different in meaning or derivation or spelling ⟨*to, too,* and *two* are *homophones*⟩ — **ho•moph•o•nous** \hō-'mäf-ə-nəs\ *adj*

ho•mo•phon•ic \,häm-ə-'fän-ik, ,hō-mə-\ *adj* : of, relating to, or being music consisting of a single accompanied melodic line — **ho•moph•o•ny** \hō-'mäf-ə-nē\ *n*

ho•mop•ter•ous \hō-'mäp-tə-rəs\ *adj* : of or relating to a group (Homoptera) of insects (as cicadas, aphids, or scale insects) having sucking mouthparts [derived from Greek *homos* "same" + *pteron* "wing"] — **ho•mop•ter•an** \-rən\ *adj or n*

ho•mo sa•pi•ens \,hō-mō-'sap-ē-ənz, -'sā-pē-, -,enz\ *n* : HUMANITY 4 [New Latin, species name, from Latin *homo* "man" + *sapiens* "wise, intelligent"]

ho•mo•sex•u•al \,hō-mə-'sek-shə-wəl, -shəl\ *adj* : of, relating to, or exhibiting sexual desire toward a member of one's own sex — **homosexual** *n* — **ho•mo•sex•u•al•i•ty** \-,sek-shə-'wal-ət-ē\ *n*

ho•mo•zy•gote \-'zī-,gōt\ *n* : a plant or animal with at least one gene pair containing identical genes — **ho•mo•zy•gos•i•ty** \-zī-'gäs-ət-ē\ *n* — **ho•mo•zy•gous** \-'zī-gəs\ *adj*

¹hone \'hōn\ *n* **1** : a fine-grit whetstone; *esp* : one for sharpening razors **2** : a tool for enlarging holes to precise measurements by means of a rotated abrasive [Old English *hān* "stone"]

²hone *vt* : to sharpen, enlarge, or smooth with a hone — **hon•er** *n*

hon•est \'än-əst\ *adj* **1 a** : free from fraud or deception : TRUTHFUL ⟨an *honest* plea⟩ **b** : GENUINE, REAL ⟨made an *honest* mistake⟩ **c** : free from ornament or pretense : PLAIN **2** : virtuous in the eyes of society : RESPECTABLE **3** : of a creditable nature : PRAISEWORTHY ⟨do an *honest* job⟩ **4 a** : marked by integrity : UPRIGHT **b** : marked by frankness or sincerity : STRAIGHTFORWARD **c** : INNOCENT 4, SIMPLE [Old French *honeste,* from Latin *honestus* "honorable", from *honos, honor* "honor"] — **hon•est•ly** *adv*

hon•es•ty \'än-ə-stē\ *n* **1** : fairness and straightforwardness of

\ə\ **abut**	\au̇\ **out**	\i\ **tip**	\ȯ\ **saw**	\u̇\ **foot**
\ər\ **further**	\ch\ **chin**	\ī\ **life**	\ȯi\ **coin**	\y\ **yet**
\a\ **mat**	\e\ **pet**	\j\ **job**	\th\ **thin**	\yü\ **few**
\ā\ **take**	\ē\ **easy**	\ng\ **sing**	\t͟h\ **this**	\yu̇\ **cure**
\ä\ **cot, cart**	\g\ **go**	\ō\ **bone**	\ü\ **food**	\zh\ **vision**

conduct : INTEGRITY **2** : TRUTHFULNESS, SINCERITY ⟨*honesty* is the best policy⟩

1hon•ey \'hən-ē\ *n, pl* **honeys** **1** : a thick sugary material prepared by bees from floral nectar and stored by them in a honeycomb for food **2 a** : SWEETHEART, DEAR — often used as a term of endearment **b** : something superlative ⟨a *honey* of a play⟩ **3** : the quality or state of being sweet : SWEETNESS [Old English *hunig*] — **honey** *adj*

2honey *vb* **hon•eyed** *also* **hon•ied**; **hon•ey•ing** **1** : to sweeten with or as if with honey **2** : to speak ingratiatingly : FLATTER

hon•ey•bee \'hən-ē-ˌbē\ *n* : a social honey-producing bee; *esp* : a European bee widely kept for its honey and wax

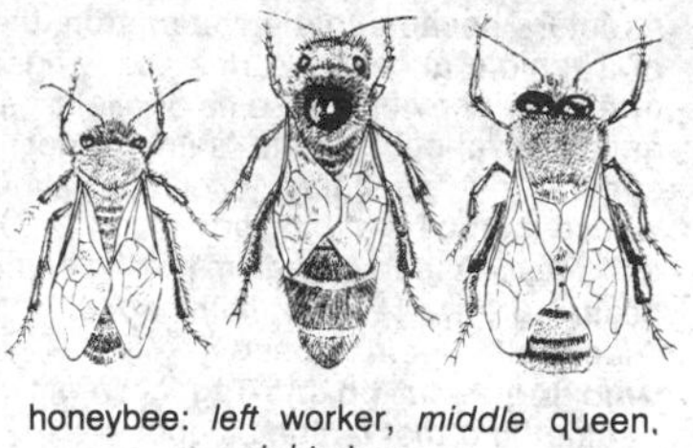

honeybee: *left* worker, *middle* queen, *right* drone

1hon•ey•comb \-ˌkōm\ *n* **1** : a mass of 6-sided wax cells built by honeybees in their nest for rearing larvae and storing honey **2** : something that resembles a honeycomb in structure or appearance

2honeycomb *vb* : to make or become full of holes like a honeycomb

hon•ey•dew \'hən-ē-ˌdü, -ˌdyü\ *n* : a sugary deposit secreted on the leaves of plants by aphids, scale insects, or fungus

honeydew melon *n* : a pale smooth-skinned muskmelon with sweet greenish flesh

honey locust *n* : a tall usually spiny North American tree of the pea family with hard durable wood and long flat twisted pods

hon•ey•moon \'hən-ē-ˌmün\ *n* **1** : the time immediately after marriage **2** : the holiday spent by a newly-married couple [from the idea that the first month of marriage is the sweetest] — **honeymoon** *vi* — **hon•ey•moon•er** *n*

hon•ey•suck•le \-ˌsək-əl\ *n* : any of a genus of shrubs with opposite leaves and often showy flowers rich in nectar; *also* : any of various plants (as a columbine or azalea) with tubular flowers rich in nectar [Old English *hunisūce*, from *hunig* "honey" + *sūcan* "to suck"]

honk \'häŋk, 'hȯŋk\ *vb* : to utter the characteristic cry of a goose or a similar sound [imitative] — **honk** *n*

hon•ky–tonk \'häŋ-kē-ˌtäŋk, 'hȯŋ-kē-ˌtȯŋk\ *n* : a cheap nightclub or dance hall [origin unknown]

1hon•or \'än-ər\ *n* **1 a** : good name : public esteem : REPUTATION **b** : a showing of usually merited respect ⟨a leader worthy of all possible *honor*⟩ **2** : PRIVILEGE ⟨whom have I the *honor* of addressing⟩ **3** *cap* — used especially as a title for a holder of high usually judicial office ⟨if Your *Honor* please⟩ **4** : one whose worth brings respect or fame : CREDIT ⟨an *honor* to your profession⟩ **5** : an evidence or symbol of distinction: as **a** : an exalted title or rank **b** : BADGE 3, DECORATION **c** : a ceremonial rite or observance ⟨buried with full military *honors*⟩ **d** *pl* : an academic distinction conferred on a superior student **e** : an award in a contest or field of competition **6** : CHASTITY, PURITY **7 a** : a keen sense of ethical conduct : INTEGRITY ⟨a person of *honor*⟩ **b** : one's word given as a guarantee of performance **8** *pl* : social courtesies or civilities extended by a host ⟨did the *honors* at the table⟩ [Old French, from Latin *honos, honor*] **syn** see DEFERENCE

2honor *vt* **hon•ored**; **hon•or•ing** \'än-riŋ, -ə-riŋ\ **1 a** : to regard or treat with honor : RESPECT ⟨*honor* your parents⟩ **b** : to confer honor on **2** : to live up to or fulfill the terms of; *esp* : to accept and pay when due ⟨*honor* a check⟩ **3** : to salute with a bow in square dancing

hon•or•able \'än-rə-bəl, -ə-rə-; 'än-ər-bəl\ *adj* **1** : deserving of honor and respect **2** : performed or accompanied with marks of honor or respect ⟨an *honorable* burial⟩ **3 a** : of great renown : ILLUSTRIOUS **b** *cap* — used as a title usually preceded by *the* and placed before the names of various high-ranking persons ⟨the *Honorable* John M. Doe⟩ ⟨the *Honorable* Jane M. Doe⟩ ⟨met the *Honorable* Mr. Doe⟩ ⟨met the *Honorable* Ms. Doe⟩ **4 a** : doing credit to the possessor **b** : consistent with an untarnished reputation **5** : characterized by integrity : ETHICAL — **hon•or•ably** \-blē\ *adv*

hon•o•rar•i•um \ˌän-ə-'rer-ē-əm\ *n, pl* **-ia** \-ē-ə\ *also* **-i•ums** : a reward usually for professional services on which custom forbids a price to be set [Latin, from *honorarius* "honorary"]

hon•or•ary \'än-ə-ˌrer-ē\ *adj* **1 a** : having or conferring distinction **b** : COMMEMORATIVE ⟨an *honorary* plaque⟩ **2** : conferred in recognition of achievement or service without the usual requirements or obligations ⟨an *honorary* degree⟩ **3** : UNPAID, VOLUNTARY ⟨*honorary* chairman⟩ [Latin *honorarius*, from *honor* "honor"] — **hon•or•ar•i•ly** \ˌän-ə-'rer-ə-lē\ *adv*

honor guard *n* : GUARD OF HONOR

1hon•or•if•ic \ˌän-ə-'rif-ik\ *adj* **1** : conferring or conveying honor **2** : belonging to or constituting a class of grammatical forms used in speaking to or about a social superior

2honorific *n* : an honorific word, phrase, or form

hon•our \'än-ər\ *chiefly British variant of* HONOR

1hood \'hu̇d\ *n* **1 a** : a flexible covering for the head and neck often attached to a coat or cape **b** : a protective covering for the head and face **2 a** (1) : an ornamental scarf worn over an academic gown (2) : an ornamental fold at the back of an ecclesiastical vestment **b** : a color marking, crest, or expandable fold on the head of an animal **3 a** : a covering that resembles a hood **b** : a cover for parts of mechanisms; *esp* : the movable metal covering over the engine of an automobile [Old English *hōd*] — **hood** *vt* — **hood•like** \-ˌlīk\ *adj*

2hood \'hu̇d, 'hüd\ *n, slang* : HOODLUM

-hood \ˌhu̇d\ *n suffix* **1** : state : condition : quality : character ⟨child*hood*⟩ ⟨hardi*hood*⟩ **2** : instance of a (specified) state or quality ⟨false*hood*⟩ **3** : individuals sharing a (specified) state or character ⟨brother*hood*⟩ [Old English *-hād*]

hood•ed \'hu̇d-əd\ *adj* : having or shaped like a hood — **hood•ed•ness** *n*

hood•lum \'hüd-ləm\ *n* **1** : THUG, MOBSTER **2** : a young ruffian [origin unknown]

hoo•doo \'hüd-ü\ *n, pl* **hoodoos** **1** : VOODOO 1 **2** : something that brings bad luck [of African origin] — **hoodoo** *vt* — **hoo•doo•ism** \-ˌiz-əm\ *n*

hood•wink \'hu̇d-ˌwiŋk\ *vt* **1** *archaic* : BLINDFOLD **2** : DECEIVE, CHEAT [1*hood* + *wink*]

hoo•ey \'hü-ē\ *n* : NONSENSE 1 [origin unknown]

1hoof \'hu̇f, 'hüf\ *n, pl* **hooves** \'hüvz, 'hu̇vz\ *or* **hoofs** **1** : a curved covering of horn that protects the front of or encloses the ends of the toes of some mammals and that corresponds to a nail or claw **2** : a hoofed foot especially of a horse [Old English *hōf*] — **hoofed** \'hu̇ft, 'hüft, 'hüvd, 'hu̇vd\ *adj* — **on the hoof** : LIVING ⟨meat animals bought *on the hoof*⟩

2hoof *vb* **1** : to move or traverse on foot : WALK **2** : DANCE 1, 3

hoof–and–mouth disease *n* : FOOT-AND-MOUTH DISEASE

hoof•beat \'hu̇f-ˌbēt, 'hüf-\ *n* : the sound of a hoof striking a hard surface (as the ground)

1hook \'hu̇k\ *n* **1** : a curved or bent implement for catching, holding, or pulling **2** : something (as a sharp bend in a road) curved or bent like a hook **3** : a path of a ball that deviates from a straight course in a direction opposite to the dominant hand of the player propelling it **4** : a short blow delivered with a circular motion by a boxer while the elbow remains bent and rigid [Old English *hōc*] — **by hook or by crook** : by any means — **off the hook** : out of trouble — **on one's own hook** : by oneself : INDEPENDENTLY

2hook *vb* **1** : to form into a hook : CROOK, CURVE **2 a** : to seize, make fast, or connect by or as if by a hook **b** : to become secured or connected by or as if by a hook **3** : to strike or pierce as if with a hook **4** : to make (as a rug) by drawing loops of thread, yarn, or cloth through a coarse fabric with a hook **5** : to propel (a ball) so that a hook results

hoo•kah \'hu̇k-ə, 'hü-kə\ *n* : a tobacco pipe with a water vessel and a long flexible tube so that the smoke is drawn through the water where it is cooled [Arabic *ḥuqqah* "bottle of a hookah"]

hook and eye *n* : a 2-part fastening device (as on a garment or a door) consisting of a wire hook that catches over a bar or into a loop of wire

hooked \'hu̇kt\ *adj* **1** : shaped like or furnished with a hook **2** : made by hooking ⟨a *hooked* rug⟩ **3 a** : addicted to narcotics **b** : fascinated by or devoted to something ⟨*hooked* on skiing⟩

1hook•er \'hu̇k-ər\ *n* : one that hooks

2hooker *n* **1** : a one-masted fishing boat **2** : an outmoded or clumsy boat [Dutch *hoeker*, derived from *hoec* "fishhook"]

hook•up \'hu̇k-ˌəp\ *n* **1** : an assemblage (as of circuits) used for a specific purpose (as in radio); *also* : the plan of such an assemblage **2** : an arrangement of mechanical parts

hook•worm \'hu̇k-ˌwərm\ *n* **1** : any of several parasitic nematode worms which have strong hooks or plates about the mouth and some of which are serious bloodsucking pests **2** : a disordered state marked by blood loss, paleness, and weakness due to hookworms in the intestine — called also *hookworm disease*

hooky *or* **hook•ey** \'hu̇k-ē\ *n, pl* **hookies** *or* **hookeys** : TRUANT — used chiefly in the phrase *play hooky* [probably from slang *hook, hook it* "to make off"]

hoo•li•gan \'hü-li-gən\ *n* : RUFFIAN, HOODLUM [perhaps from Patrick *Hooligan,* 19th century Irish hoodlum in London] — **hoo•li•gan•ism** \-gə-ˌniz-əm\ *n*

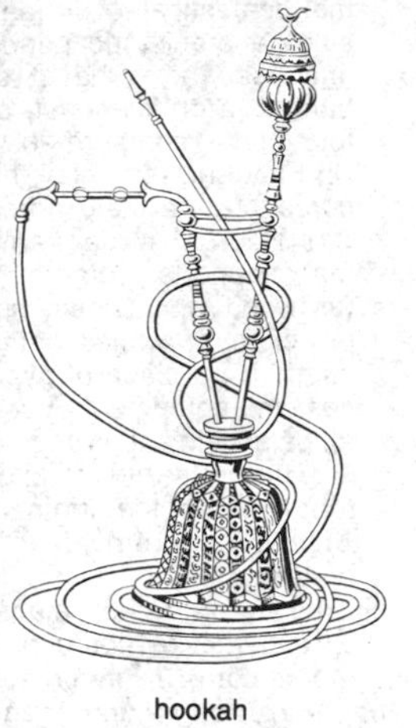

hookah

1hoop \'hu̇p, 'hüp\ *n* **1** : a circular strip used especially for holding together the staves of containers **2** : a circular figure or object : RING **3** : a circle or series of circles of flexible material used to expand a woman's skirt [Old English *hōp*]

2hoop *vt* : to bind or fasten with or as if with a hoop — **hoop•er** *n*

hoop•la \'hü-ˌplä\ *n* : great commotion and excitement : FUSS, BALLYHOO ⟨*hoopla* and fanfare of the bicentennial⟩ [French *houp-là,* interj.]

hoop•skirt \'hu̇p-'skərt, 'hüp-\ *n* : a skirt stiffened with or as if with hoops

hoo•ray \hu̇-'rā\ *variant of* HURRAH

hoose•gow \'hüs-ˌgau̇\ *n, slang* : JAIL [Spanish *juzgado* "panel of judges, courtroom", from *juzgar* "to judge", from Latin *judicare*]

1hoot \'hüt\ *vb* **1** : to utter a loud shout usually in contempt **2** : to make the characteristic cry of an owl or a similar cry **3** : to assail or drive out by hooting ⟨*hooted* the speaker off the stage⟩ **4** : to express in or by hoots ⟨*hooted* disapproval⟩ [Middle English *houten*] — **hoot•er** *n*

2hoot *n* **1** : the cry of an owl or a similar sound **2** : the least bit ⟨don't care a *hoot* about the book⟩

hoo•te•nan•ny \'hüt-n-ˌan-ē\ *n, pl* **-nies** : a gathering at which folksingers entertain often with the audience joining in [origin unknown]

1hop \'häp\ *vb* **hopped**; **hop•ping** **1** : to move by a quick springy leap or in a series of leaps; *esp* : to jump on one foot **2** : to jump over ⟨*hop* a puddle⟩ **3** : to get aboard by or as if by hopping ⟨*hop* a train⟩ **4** : to make a quick trip ⟨*hop* down to the store⟩ [Old English *hoppian*]

2hop *n* **1 a** : a short brisk leap especially on one leg **b** : BOUNCE, REBOUND ⟨fielded the ball on the first *hop*⟩ **2** : DANCE, BALL ⟨the junior *hop*⟩ **3 a** : a flight in an airplane **b** : a short trip

3hop *n* **1** : a twining vine of the mulberry family with lobed leaves and female flowers in cone-shaped catkins **2** *pl* : the ripe dried catkins of a hop used especially to impart a bitter flavor to malt liquors [Dutch *hoppe*]

4hop *vt* **hopped**; **hop•ping** **1** : to flavor with hops **2** : to increase the power of beyond an original rating — used with *up* ⟨*hop* up an engine⟩

1hope \'hōp\ *vb* **1** : to cherish a desire with expectation of fulfillment ⟨*hope* to succeed⟩ ⟨*hope* for peace⟩ **2** : to long for with expectation of obtainment **3** : to expect with desire : TRUST ⟨*hope* you'll accept the invitation⟩ [Old English *hopian*]

2hope *n* **1** : TRUST, RELIANCE ⟨our *hope* is in the Lord⟩ **2 a** : desire accompanied by expectation of or belief in fulfillment ⟨in *hope* of an early recovery⟩ **b** : someone or something on which hopes are centered ⟨a fast halfback was the team's only *hope* for victory⟩ **c** : something hoped for

hope chest *n* : a young woman's accumulation of clothes and domestic furnishings (as silver or linen) kept in or as if in a chest in anticipation of her marriage; *also* : a chest for such an accumulation

1hope•ful \'hōp-fəl\ *adj* **1** : full of or inclined to hope **2** : having qualities which inspire hope ⟨a *hopeful* sign⟩ — **hope•ful•ly** \-fə-lē\ *adv* — **hope•ful•ness** *n*

2hopeful *n* : a person who has hopes or is considered promising especially as a political candidate

hope•less \'hō-pləs\ *adj* **1 a** : having no expectation of good or success **b** : not susceptible of remedy or cure : INCURABLE **2 a** : giving no ground for hope : DESPERATE ⟨a *hopeless* situation⟩ **b** : incapable of solution, management, or accomplishment : IMPOSSIBLE ⟨a *hopeless* task⟩ — **hope•less•ly** *adv* — **hope•less•ness** *n*

Ho•pi \'hō-pē\ *n, pl* **Hopi** *also* **Hopis** **1** : a member of an Indian people of what is now northeastern Arizona **2** : the Aztec-related language of the Hopi people [Hopi *Hópi,* literally, "good, peaceful"]

hop•lite \'häp-ˌlīt\ *n* : a heavily armed infantry soldier of ancient Greece [Greek *hoplitēs,* from *hoplon* "tool, weapon"]

hop•per \'häp-ər\ *n* **1** : one that hops or leaps; *esp* : an immature hopping form of an insect (as a grasshopper) **2 a** : a usually funnel-shaped receptacle for delivering material (as grain or coal) **b** : a tank holding liquid and having a device for releasing its contents through a pipe **3** : a box in which a bill to be considered by a legislative body is dropped [sense 2 from the shaking motion of hoppers used to feed grain into a mill]

hop•scotch \'häp-ˌskäch\ *n* : a child's game in which a player tosses an object (as a stone) into areas of a figure outlined on the ground and hops through the figure and back to regain the object

ho•ra *also* **ho•rah** \'hōr-ə, 'hȯr-ə\ *n* : a circle dance of Rumania and Israel [Modern Hebrew *hōrāh,* from Rumanian *horă*]

horde \'hōrd, 'hȯrd\ *n* **1 a** : a tribal group of Mongolian nomads **b** : a nomadic people or tribe **2** : a great multitude : THRONG, SWARM ⟨*hordes* of tourists⟩ [Polish *horda,* of Mongolic origin]

hore•hound \'hōr-ˌhau̇nd, 'hȯr-\ *n* : an aromatic bitter mint with hoary downy leaves; *also* : an extract or confection made from this plant [Old English *hārhūne,* from *hār* "hoary" + *hūne* "horehound"]

ho•ri•zon \hə-'rīz-n\ *n* **1** : the apparent junction of earth and sky **2** : the limit or range of a person's outlook or experience ⟨reading broadens our *horizons*⟩ **3 a** : the geological deposit of a particular time **b** : a distinct layer of soil or its underlying material in a vertical section of land [Late Latin *horizont-, horizon,* from Greek *horizont-, horizōn,* from *horizein* "to bound", from *horos* "boundary"] — **ho•ri•zon•al** \-'rīz-nəl, -n-əl\ *adj*

1hor•i•zon•tal \ˌhȯr-ə-'zänt-l, ˌhär-\ *adj* **1 a** : of, relating to, or situated near the horizon **b** : parallel to, in the plane of, or operating in a plane parallel to the horizon or to a base line : LEVEL ⟨*horizontal* distance⟩ ⟨*horizontal* engine⟩ **2** : relating to or consisting of individuals or groups of similar level in a hierarchy ⟨*horizontal* labor unions⟩ — **hor•i•zon•tal•ly** \-l-ē\ *adv*

2horizontal *n* : something (as a line or plane) that is horizontal

horizontal bar *n* : a steel bar supported horizontally above the ground and used for swinging feats in gymnastics

hor•mone \'hȯr-ˌmōn\ *n* : a product of living cells that circulates in body fluids or sap and produces a specific and usually stimulatory effect on cells at a distance from the point of origin [Greek *hormōn,* present participle of *horman* "to stir up, set in motion"] — **hor•mon•al** \hȯr-'mōn-l\ *adj* — **hor•mon•al•ly** \-l-ē\ *adv*

horn \'hȯrn\ *n* **1 a** : one of the hard growths of bone or keratin on the head of many hoofed animals: as (1) : one of the permanent paired hollow sheaths of keratin usually present in both sexes of cattle and their relatives that function chiefly for defense and arise from a bony core anchored to the skull (2) : ANTLER **b** : a tough fibrous material that consists chiefly of keratin and forms the sheath of a true horn and horny parts (as hooves or nails) **2** : a hollow animal's horn used to hold something (as gunpowder) **3** : something resembling or suggestive of a horn: as **a** : one of the curved ends of a crescent **b** : the knob on the pommel of a western-style saddle **4** : a manufactured product (as a plastic) resembling horn **5 a** : an animal's horn used as a musical instrument **b** : a brass wind instrument; *esp* : FRENCH HORN **c** : a usually electrical device that makes a noise like that of a horn ⟨an automobile *horn*⟩ [Old English] — **horned** \'hȯrnd\ *adj* — **horn•less** \'hȯrn-ləs\ *adj* — **horn•less•ness** *n* — **horn•like** \-ˌlīk\ *adj*

horn•beam \'hȯrn-ˌbēm\ *n* : any of a genus of trees of the birch family having smooth gray bark and hard white wood

horn•bill \ˈ-ˌbil\ *n* : any of a family of large Old World birds with enormous bills

hornbill

horn•blende \ˈ-ˌblend\ *n* : a black, dark green, or brown mineral that occurs as distinct crystals and in columnar, fibrous, and granular form [German]

horn•book \ˈ-ˌbu̇k\ *n* **1** : an early primer for children consisting of a sheet of parchment or paper containing the alphabet, numbers, and often religious verses or prayers protected by a transparent sheet of horn **2** : a treatise of basic principles or skills

horned owl *n* : any of several owls with conspicuous tufts of feathers on the head

horned pout *n* : a common bullhead of the eastern United States

horned toad *n* : any of several small harmless insect-eating lizards of the western United States and Mexico having hornlike spines

hor•net \ˈhȯr-nət\ *n* : any of the larger social wasps — compare YELLOW JACKET [Old English *hyrnet*]

horn in *vi* : to participate without invitation or consent : INTRUDE ⟨*horn in* on a conversation⟩

horn of plenty : CORNUCOPIA 1

horn•pipe \ˈhȯrn-ˌpīp\ *n* **1** : a single-reed wind instrument consisting of a wooden or bone pipe with holes at intervals and a bell and mouthpiece usually of horn **2** : a lively folk dance of the British Isles originally accompanied by hornpipe playing

horn•tail \ˈ-ˌtāl\ *n* : any of a family of insects closely related to the sawflies

horn•worm \ˈ-ˌwərm\ *n* : a hawkmoth caterpillar having a hornlike tail process

horn•wort \ˈ-ˌwərt, -ˌwȯrt\ *n* : any of an order (Anthocerotales) of mostly aquatic plants related to the liverworts

horny \ˈhȯr-nē\ *adj* **horn•i•er**; **-est** **1** : made of horn or of something resembling horn **2** : HARD, CALLOUS ⟨*horny* hands⟩

ho•rol•o•gy \hə-ˈräl-ə-jē\ *n* **1** : the science of measuring time **2** : the art of constructing instruments for indicating time [Greek *hōra* "time, hour"] — **hor•o•log•ic** \ˌhȯr-ə-ˈläj-ik, ˌhär-, -ˈlōj-\ *adj* — **hor•o•log•i•cal** \-i-kəl\ *adj* — **ho•rol•o•gist** \hə-ˈräl-ə-jəst\ *n*

hor•o•scope \ˈhȯr-ə-ˌskōp, ˈhär-\ *n* **1** : a diagram of the relative positions of planets and signs of the zodiac at a specific time (as that of a person's birth) used by astrologers to infer character traits and foretell events **2** : an astrological forecast [Middle French, from Latin *horoscopus,* from Greek *horoskopos,* from *hora* "time, hour" + *skopein* "to look at"]

hor•ren•dous \hȯ-ˈren-dəs, hä-\ *adj* : DREADFUL, HORRIBLE [Latin *horrendus,* from *horrēre* "to shudder"] — **hor•ren•dous•ly** *adv*

hor•ri•ble \ˈhȯr-ə-bəl, ˈhär-\ *adj* **1** : marked by or conducive to horror **2** : extremely unpleasant or disagreeable — **hor•ri•bly** \-blē\ *adv*

hor•rid \ˈhȯr-əd, ˈhär-\ *adj* **1** : HIDEOUS, SHOCKING **2** : REPULSIVE 2, OFFENSIVE [Latin *horridus,* from *horrēre* "to shudder"] — **hor•rid•ly** *adv* — **hor•rid•ness** *n*

hor•rif•ic \hȯ-ˈrif-ik, hä-\ *adj* : causing horror

hor•ri•fy \ˈhȯr-ə-ˌfī, ˈhär-\ *vt* **-fied**; **-fy•ing** **1** : to cause to feel horror **2** : to fill with distaste : SHOCK

hor•ror \ˈhȯr-ər, ˈhär-\ *n* **1 a** : painful and intense fear, dread, or dismay **b** : intense aversion or repugnance **2 a** : the quality of inspiring horror **b** : something that inspires horror ⟨the war was a *horror*⟩ **3** *pl* : a state of extreme depression or apprehension [Middle French, from Latin, "action of trembling", from *horrēre* "to tremble, shudder"]

hors de combat \ˌȯrd-ə-kōⁿ-ˈbä\ *adv or adj* : out of combat : disabled especially from fighting [French]

hors d'oeuvre \ȯr-ˈdərv\ *n, pl* **hors d'oeuvres** *also* **hors d'oeuvre** \-ˈdərvz, -ˈdərv\ : any of various savory foods usually served as appetizers at the beginning of a meal [French *hors-d'œuvre,* literally, "outside of work"]

^{1}**horse** \ˈhȯrs\ *n, pl* **hors•es** *also* **horse** **1 a** (1) : a large solid-hoofed plant-eating mammal domesticated by man since a prehistoric period and used as a beast of burden, a draft animal, or for riding — compare PONY (2) : RACEHORSE ⟨play the *horses*⟩ **b** : a male horse : STALLION **2 a** : a frame that supports something (as wood while being cut or clothes while being dried) **b** : a piece of gymnasium equipment used for balancing and swinging movements or for vaulting exercises **3** *slang* : HEROIN [Old English *hors*] — **from the horse's mouth** : from the original source

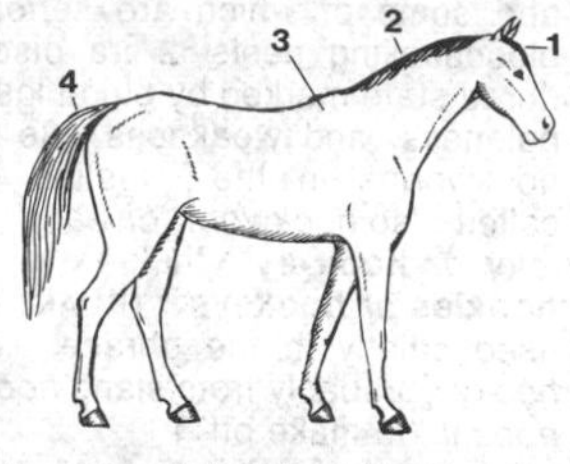

^{1}horse 1a (1): *1* forelock, *2* mane, *3* withers, *4* tail

^{2}**horse** *vt* **1** : to provide with a horse **2** : to lift, pull, or push by brute force

^{3}**horse** *adj* **1 a** : of or relating to the horse **b** : hauled or powered by a horse ⟨a *horse* barge⟩ **2** : large or coarse of its kind ⟨*horse* corn⟩ **3** : mounted on horses ⟨*horse* guards⟩

horse around *vi* : to engage in horseplay

^{1}**horse•back** \ˈhȯrs-ˌbak\ *n* : the back of a horse

^{2}**horseback** *adv* : on horseback

horse•car \ˈhȯr-ˌskär\ *n* **1** : a streetcar drawn by horses **2** : a car for transporting horses

horse chestnut *n* : a large Asian tree that has palmate leaves and erect clusters of showy flowers and is widely grown as an ornamental and shade tree; *also* : its large glossy brown seed

horse•flesh \ˈhȯrs-ˌflesh\ *n* : horses for riding, driving, or racing

horse•fly \ˈ-ˌflī\ *n* : any of a family of swift usually large two-winged flies with bloodsucking females

horse•hair \ˈ-ˌhaər, -ˌheər\ *n* **1** : the hair of a horse especially from the mane or tail **2** : cloth made from horsehair

horsehair worm *n* : any of various long slender worms whose adults live in water and whose larvae are parasites of insects — called also *horsehair snake*

horse•hide \ˈhȯrs-ˌhīd\ *n* : a horse's hide or leather made from it

horse latitudes *n pl* : either of two belts or regions in the neighborhood of 30° north and 30° south latitude characterized by high pressure, calms, and light changeable winds

horse•laugh \ˈhȯr-ˌslaf, -ˌsläf\ *n* : a loud boisterous laugh

horse•less carriage \ˌhȯr-sləs-\ *n* : AUTOMOBILE

horse mackerel *n* : any of several large fishes (as a bluefin tuna)

horse•man \ˈhȯr-smən\ *n* **1 a** : a rider on horseback **b** : one skilled in managing horses **2** : a breeder or raiser of horses — **horse•man•ship** \-ˌship\ *n*

horse•mint \ˈhȯr-ˌsmint\ *n* : any of various coarse mints

horse nettle *n* : a coarse prickly weed with bright yellow fruit that is related to the nightshades

horse opera *n* : a movie or radio or television play about western ranch life or cowboys

horse•play \ˈhȯr-ˌsplā\ *n* : rough or boisterous play

horse•pow•er \ˈhȯr-ˌspau̇-ər, -ˌspau̇r\ *n* : a unit of power equal in the United States to 746 watts

horse•rad•ish \ˈhȯrs-ˌrad-ish\ *n* : a tall coarse white-flowered herb of the mustard family; *also* : its pungent root used as a seasoning

horse sense *n* : COMMON SENSE

horse•shoe \ˈhȯrs-ˌshü, ˈhȯrsh-\ *n* **1** : a shoe for horses usually consisting of a narrow plate of iron shaped to fit the rim of a horse's hoof **2** : something (as a valley) shaped like a horseshoe **3** *pl* : a game in which horseshoes or horseshoe-shaped pieces of metal are tossed at a stake in the ground in an attempt to encircle the stake or come closer than one's opponent — **horseshoe** *vt* — **horse•sho•er** \ˈ-ˌshü-ər\ *n*

horseshoe crab *n* : any of several closely related marine arthropods with a broad crescent-shaped cephalothorax — called also *king crab, limulus*

horse•tail \ˈhȯr-ˌstāl\ *n* : EQUISETUM

horse trade *n* : negotiation accompanied by shrewd bargaining and concessions on both sides — **horse–trade** *vi* — **horse trader** *n*

horse•whip \ˈhȯr-ˌswip, ˈhȯrs-ˌhwip\ *vt* : to flog with or as if with a whip made to be used on a horse

horse•wom•an \'hȯr-ˌswu̇m-ən\ *n* **1** : a woman horseback rider **2** : a woman skilled in riding horseback or in caring for or managing horses

hors•ey *or* **horsy** \'hȯr-sē\ *adj* **hors•i•er; -est 1** : of, relating to, or suggesting a horse **2 a** : having to do with horses or horse racing ⟨the *horsey* set⟩ **b** : characteristic of horsemen and horsewomen — **hors•i•ness** *n*

hor•ta•to•ry \'hȯrt-ə-tōr-ē, -ˈtȯr-\ *adj* : given to or characterized by strong urging or encouragement [Late Latin *hortatorius,* from Latin *hortari* "to urge, exhort"]

hor•ti•cul•ture \'hȯrt-ə-ˌkəl-chər\ *n* : the science and art of growing fruits, vegetables, flowers, or ornamental plants [Latin *hortus* "garden"] — **hor•ti•cul•tur•al** \ˌhȯrt-ə-'kəlch-rəl, -ə-rəl\ *adj* — **hor•ti•cul•tur•al•ly** \-rə-lē\ *adv* — **hor•ti•cul•tur•ist** \-'kəlch-rəst, -ə-rəst\ *n*

ho•san•na \hō-'zan-ə\ *interj* — used as a cry of acclamation and adoration [Late Latin *osanna,* from Greek *hōsanna,* from Hebrew *hōshīʽāh-nnā* "pray, save (us)!"]

¹hose \'hōz\ *n, pl* **hose** *or* **hos•es 1** *pl* **hose a** (1) : a cloth leg covering that sometimes covers the foot (2) : STOCKING 1, SOCK **b** (1) : a close-fitting garment covering the legs and waist that is usually attached to a doublet by points (2) : short breeches reaching to the knee **2** : a flexible tube for conveying a fluid (as from a faucet) [Old English *hosa* "stocking, husk"]

²hose *vt* : to spray, water, or wash with a hose

Ho•sea \hō-'zē-ə, -'zā-\ *n* — see BIBLE table

ho•siery \'hōzh-rē, 'hōz-, -ə-rē\ *n* : HOSE 1a

hos•pice \'häs-pəs\ *n* : an inn for travelers; *esp* : one kept by a religious order [French, from Latin *hospitium* "lodging", from *hospit-, hospes* "host"]

hos•pi•ta•ble \hä-'spit-ə-bəl, 'häs-pit-\ *adj* **1 a** : showing hospitality : generous and cordial in receiving guests **b** : promising or suggesting generous and cordial welcome **c** : offering a pleasant or sustaining environment **2** : readily receptive : OPEN ⟨*hospitable* to new ideas⟩ — **hos•pi•ta•bly** \-blē\ *adv*

hos•pi•tal \'häs-ˌpit-l\ *n* **1** : an institution where the sick or injured are given medical or surgical care **2** : a repair shop for specified small objects ⟨doll *hospital*⟩ [Old French, derived from Late Latin *hospitale* "hospice", from Latin, "guest room", from *hospit-, hospes* "host, guest"]

Hos•pi•tal•er *or* **Hos•pi•tal•ler** \-l-ər\ *n* : a member of a religious military order established in Jerusalem in the 12th century

hos•pi•tal•i•ty \ˌhäs-pə-'tal-ət-ē\ *n, pl* **-ties 1** : cordial reception and entertainment (as of guests) **2** : an instance of hospitality

hos•pi•tal•ize \'häs-ˌpit-l-ˌīz\ *vt* : to place in a hospital for care and treatment — **hos•pi•tal•iza•tion** \ˌhäs-ˌpit-l-ə-'zā-shən\ *n*

¹host \'hōst\ *n* **1** : ARMY 1a **2** : a great number : MULTITUDE [Old French, from Late Latin *hostis,* from Latin, "stranger, enemy"]

²host *n* **1** : one who receives or entertains guests socially or as a business **2** : a living animal or plant that provides food and living space to a parasite [Old French *hoste* "host, guest", from Latin *hospit-, hospes,* from *hostis* "stranger"] — **host** *vt* — **host•al** \'hōst-l\ *adj*

³host *n, often cap* : the bread or wafer consecrated in the Mass [Middle French *hoiste,* from Latin *hostia* "sacrifice"]

hos•tage \'häs-tij\ *n* : a person held by one party in a conflict as a pledge that promises will be kept or terms met by the other party [Old French, from *hoste* "host, guest"]

hos•tel \'häst-l\ *n* **1** : INN 1 **2** : a supervised lodging for usually young travelers — called also *youth hostel* [Old French, from Late Latin *hospitale* "hospice"]

hos•tel•er \'häs-tə-lər\ *n* **1** : one that lodges guests or strangers **2** : a young traveler who stops at hostels

hos•tel•ry \'häst-l-rē\ *n, pl* **-ries** : INN 1, HOTEL

host•ess \'hō-stəs\ *n* : a woman who acts as host; *esp* : one who greets and provides service for patrons

hos•tile \'häst-l, 'häs-ˌtīl\ *adj* **1** : of or relating to an enemy ⟨*hostile* troops⟩ **2** : marked by open antagonism : UNFRIENDLY **3** : not hospitable ⟨a *hostile* environment⟩ [Latin *hostilis,* from *hostis* "enemy"] — **hos•tile•ly** \-l-lē, -ˌtīl-lē\ *adv*

hos•til•i•ty \hä-'stil-ət-ē\ *n, pl* **-ties 1 a** : a hostile state **b** (1) : hostile action (2) *pl* : overt acts of warfare **2** : antagonism, opposition, or resistance in thought or principle **syn** see ENMITY

hos•tler \'äs-lər, 'häs-\ *also* **ost•ler** \'äs-\ *n* **1** : one who takes care of horses or mules **2** : one who services a vehicle (as a locomotive or truck) or machine (as a crane) [Middle English, "innkeeper, hostler", from *hostel*]

¹hot \'hät\ *adj* **hot•ter; hot•test 1 a** : having a relatively high temperature **b** : capable of burning, scalding, or searing **2** : having or showing intense feeling: as **a** : FIERY, VEHEMENT ⟨a *hot* temper⟩ **b** : VIOLENT 1 ⟨a *hot* battle⟩ **c** : LUSTFUL **d** : ZEALOUS ⟨*hot* for reform⟩ **3** : feeling or causing an uncomfortable degree of body heat **4 a** : NEW, FRESH ⟨*hot* off the press⟩ **b** : close to an objective ⟨guess again, you're getting *hotter*⟩ **c** : in close pursuit ⟨police were *hot* on their heels⟩ **5** : PUNGENT, SPICY ⟨*hot* sauces⟩ **6 a** : causing a sensation ⟨a *hot* scandal⟩ **b** : currently popular ⟨cotton is the *hot* item for spring clothes⟩ **c** : temporarily capable of unusual performances ⟨felt *hot* with the dice⟩ **d** — used as a generalized term of approval ⟨a *hot* new lawyer⟩ **7 a** : electrically charged especially with high voltage **b** : RADIOACTIVE **8** : recently stolen ⟨the jewels are *hot*⟩ **9** : dangerously unsafe ⟨police made the town too *hot* for them⟩ [Old English *hāt*] — **hot•ly** *adv* — **hot•ness** *n*

²hot *adv* : HOTLY

hot air *n* : empty talk

hot•bed \'hät-ˌbed\ *n* **1** : a bed of soil enclosed in glass, heated usually by fermenting manure, and used for forcing or for raising seedlings **2** : an environment that favors rapid growth or development ⟨a *hotbed* of dissent⟩

hot-blood•ed \-'bləd-əd\ *adj* : easily roused or excited : PASSIONATE — **hot-blood•ed•ness** *n*

hot•box \'hät-ˌbäks\ *n* : a journal bearing (as of a railroad car) overheated by friction

hot•cake \-ˌkāk\ *n* : PANCAKE

hotch•potch \'häch-ˌpäch\ *n* : HODGEPODGE [Middle French *hochepot* "stew", from *hochier* "to shake" + *pot* "pot"]

hot cross bun *n* : a sweet bun that is marked with a cross on the top and often contains fruit (as raisins)

hot dog \'hät-ˌdȯg\ *n* : FRANKFURTER; *esp* : a cooked frankfurter usually served in a long split roll

ho•tel \hō-'tel\ *n* : an establishment that provides lodging and usually meals, entertainment, and various personal services for the public [French *hôtel,* from Old French *hostel*]

¹hot•foot \'hät-ˌfu̇t\ *adv* : in haste

²hotfoot *vi* : to go quickly : HURRY ⟨*hotfooted* it home⟩

³hotfoot *n, pl* **hotfoots** : a practical joke in which a match is secretly inserted into the side of a victim's shoe and lighted

hot•head \'hät-ˌhed\ *n* : a hotheaded person

hot•head•ed \-'hed-əd\ *adj* : RASH 2, HEADSTRONG — **hot•head•ed•ly** *adv* — **hot•head•ed•ness** *n*

hot•house \'hät-ˌhau̇s\ *n* : a heated greenhouse — **hothouse** *adj*

hot line *n* : a communications line for direct emergency use (as between heads of governments or to a counseling service)

hot pants *n pl* : very short shorts

hot pepper *n* **1** : a pungent often thin-walled and small capsicum fruit **2** : a pepper plant bearing hot peppers

hot plate *n* : a small portable appliance for heating or for cooking

hot rod *n* : an automobile rebuilt or modified for high speed and fast acceleration — **hot-rod•der** \'hät-'räd-ər\ *n*

hot•shot \'hät-ˌshät\ *n* : a spectacularly skillful or successful person

hot spring *n* : THERMAL SPRING; *esp* : a spring with water above 36.7°C

Hot•ten•tot \'hät-n-ˌtät\ *n* : a member of a people of southern Africa apparently akin to both the Bushmen and the Bantus [Afrikaans]

hot water *n* : a distressing predicament : TROUBLE ⟨got in *hot water* at school⟩

¹hound \'hau̇nd\ *n* **1 a** : DOG 1a **b** : a dog of any of various hunting breeds typically having large drooping ears and a deep voice and following its prey by scent **2** : ENTHUSIAST, FAN ⟨autograph *hounds*⟩ [Old English *hund*]

²hound *vt* **1** : to pursue with or as if with hounds **2** : HARASS 1

hour \'au̇r\ *n* **1** : a time or office for daily devotion; *esp* : CANONICAL HOUR **2** : one of the 24 divisions of a day : 60 minutes **3 a :** the time of day reckoned in two 12-hour periods ⟨the *hour* is now 10:00 a.m.⟩ **b** *pl* **:** the time reckoned in one 24-hour period ⟨in the military 4:00 p.m. is called 1600 *hours*⟩ **4 a :** a customary time ⟨the lunch *hour*⟩ **b :** a particular time ⟨in your *hour* of need⟩ **5 :** the work done or distance traveled at normal rate in an hour ⟨two *hours* away by car⟩ **6 :** the time (as 50 minutes) taken up by a class ⟨I have math this *hour*⟩ **[**Old French *heure,* from Latin *hora* "hour of the day", from Greek *hōra***]**

hour•glass \\-ˌglas\\ *n* **:** an instrument for measuring time in which sand, water, or mercury runs from the upper to the lower part of a glass container in an hour — **hourglass** *adj*

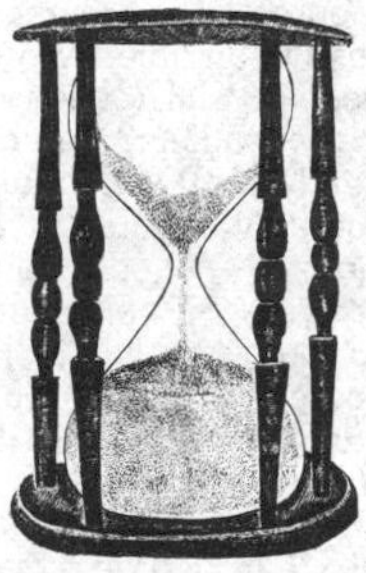

hourglass

hou•ri \\ˈhu̇r-ē, ˈhü-rē\\ *n* **:** one of the beautiful maidens that in Muslim belief live with the blessed in paradise **[**French, from Persian *hūri,* from Arabic *ḥūrīyah***]**

hour•ly \\ˈau̇r-lē\\ *adj* **1 :** occurring hour by hour **2 :** computed in terms of one hour ⟨*hourly* wages⟩ — **hourly** *adv*

[1]**house** \\ˈhau̇s\\ *n, pl* **hous•es** \\ˈhau̇-zəz\\ **1 :** a building that serves as living quarters for one or more families **2 a :** an animal's shelter or habitation **b :** a building in which something is housed ⟨carriage *house*⟩ **3 a :** one of the 12 equal sectors in which the celestial sphere is divided in astrology **b :** a zodiacal sign that is the seat of a planet's greatest influence **4 a :** HOUSEHOLD **b :** FAMILY 1; *esp* **:** a royal or noble family ⟨the *house* of Windsor⟩ **5 a :** a residence for a religious community or for students **b :** the community or students in residence **6 a :** a legislative, deliberative, or consultative assembly; *esp* **:** one constituting a division of a bicameral body **b :** the place where an assembly meets **7 a :** a place of business or entertainment ⟨the *house* was full for the opening⟩ **b** (1) **:** a business organization ⟨a publishing *house*⟩ (2) **:** the operator of a gambling establishment ⟨a percentage of the bets always goes to the *house*⟩ **c :** the audience in a theater or concert hall ⟨played to small *houses*⟩ **[**Old English *hūs***]** — **house•ful** \\ˈhau̇s-ˌfu̇l\\ *n* — **on the house :** at the expense of the management

[2]**house** \\ˈhau̇z\\ *vb* **1 a :** to provide with living quarters or shelter **b :** to store in a house **2 :** to encase, enclose, or shelter as if by putting in a house **3 :** to take shelter **:** LODGE

house•boat \\ˈhau̇s-ˌbōt\\ *n* **:** a usually flat-bottomed shallow-draft vessel with a structure resembling a house built on deck for use as a dwelling on the water

house•boy \\-ˌbȯi\\ *n* **:** a boy or man hired to act as a general household servant

house•break \\-ˌbrāk\\ *vt* **:** to make housebroken

house•break•ing \\-ˌbrā-king\\ *n* **:** the act of breaking into and entering a person's dwelling house with the intent of committing a felony — **house•break•er** \\-kər\\ *n*

house•bro•ken \\-ˌbrō-kən\\ *adj* **:** trained to excretory habits acceptable in indoor living

house•clean \\ˈhau̇-ˌsklēn\\ *vb* **1 :** to clean a house and its furniture **2 :** to clean the surfaces and furnishings of (as a room) **3 :** to get rid of unwanted or undesirable items or people — **house•clean•ing** *n*

house•coat \\ˈhau̇-ˌskōt\\ *n* **:** a woman's one-piece and often long garment for wear around the house

house•fly \\ˈhau̇s-ˌflī\\ *n* **:** a two-winged fly that is common about human habitations and can act as a carrier of disease-producing organisms

[1]**house•hold** \\ˈhau̇s-ˌhōld, ˈhau̇-ˌsōld\\ *n* **:** those who dwell under the same roof and compose a family; *also* **:** such a family and its servants or retainers

[2]**household** *adj* **1 :** of or relating to a household **:** DOMESTIC **2 :** FAMILIAR, COMMON ⟨a *household* name⟩

house•hold•er \\ˈhau̇s-ˌhōl-dər, ˈhau̇-ˌsōl-\\ *n* **:** one who occupies a dwelling alone or as the head of a household

house•keep \\ˈhau̇-ˌskēp\\ *vi* **-kept** \\-ˌskept\\; **-keep•ing :** to care for and run a home **[**back-formation from *housekeeper***]**

house•keep•er \\-ˌskē-pər\\ *n* **:** a person employed to housekeep

house•keep•ing \\-ping\\ *n* **:** the care and management of a house and home affairs

house•less \\ˈhau̇-sləs, ˈhau̇z-ləs\\ *adj* **1 :** HOMELESS **2 :** destitute of houses — **house•less•ness** *n*

house•lights \\ˈhau̇-ˌslīts\\ *n pl* **:** the lights that illuminate the parts of a theater occupied by the audience

house•maid \\-ˌsmād\\ *n* **:** a woman or girl employed to do housework

housemaid's knee *n* **:** a swelling over the knee due to an enlargement of the bursa in the front of the kneecap

house•man \\ˈhau̇-smən, -ˌsman\\ *n* **:** a man who performs general work about a house **:** HOUSEBOY

house•moth•er \\ˈhau̇-ˌsmət͟h-ər\\ *n* **:** a woman acting as hostess, chaperon, and often supervisor in a residence for young people

House of Burgesses : the representative assembly of colonial Virginia

House of Commons : the lower house of the British and Canadian parliaments

house of correction : an institution where persons are confined who have committed a minor offense and are considered capable of being reformed

House of Lords : the upper house of the British Parliament composed of the peers temporal and spiritual

house of representatives : the lower house of a legislative body (as the United States Congress)

house organ *n* **:** a periodical distributed by a business concern among its employees, sales personnel, and customers

house party *n* **:** a party lasting over one or more nights at a residence (as a home or fraternity house)

house•plant \\ˈhau̇-ˌsplant\\ *n* **:** a plant grown or kept indoors

house–rais•ing \\ˈhau̇s-ˌrā-zing\\ *n* **:** the putting up of a house or its framework by a gathering of neighbors

house sparrow *n* **:** ENGLISH SPARROW

house•top \\ˈhau̇-ˌstäp\\ *n* **:** ROOF 1

house•warm•ing \\-ˌswȯr-ming\\ *n* **:** a party to celebrate moving into a house or premises

house•wife \\ˈhau̇-ˌswīf, *2 is often* ˈhəz-əf, ˈhəs-əf\\ *n* **1 :** a usually married woman in charge of a household **2 :** a small container for small articles (as thread) — **house•wife•li•ness** \\ˈhau̇-ˌswī-flē-nəs\\ *n* — **house•wife•ly** \\-flē\\ *adj* — **house•wif•ery** \\-ˌswī-fə-rē, -frē\\ *n*

house•work \\ˈhau̇-ˌswərk\\ *n* **:** the work of housekeeping

[1]**hous•ing** \\ˈhau̇-zing\\ *n* **1 a :** SHELTER 1, LODGING **b :** dwellings provided for people ⟨*housing* for the elderly⟩ **2 a :** something that covers or protects **b :** a support (as a frame) for mechanical parts

[2]**housing** *n* **:** a usually ornamental covering for the back and sides of a horse **:** CAPARISON **[**Middle French *housse,* of Germanic origin**]**

hove *past of* HEAVE

hov•el \\ˈhəv-əl, ˈhäv-\\ *n* **1 :** an open shed or shelter **2 :** a small mean house **:** HUT **[**Middle English**]**

hov•er \\ˈhəv-ər, ˈhäv-\\ *vb* **hov•ered; hov•er•ing** \\ˈhəv-ring, ˈhäv-, -ə-ring\\ **1 :** to hang fluttering in the air or on the wing ⟨hawks *hovering* over their prey⟩ **2 a :** to move to and fro near a place ⟨waiters *hovered* about⟩ **b :** to be in a state of uncertainty, irresolution, or suspense ⟨*hovering* between life and death⟩ **3 :** to brood over ⟨a hen *hovers* her chicks⟩ **[**Middle English *hoveren***]** — **hover** *n* — **hov•er•er** \\-ər-ər\\ *n*

[1]**how** \\hau̇, ˈhau̇\\ *adv* **1 a :** in what manner or way ⟨learn *how* to study⟩ **b :** with what meaning **:** to what effect ⟨*how* do you mean that⟩ **c :** by what name or title **d :** for what reason **:** WHY ⟨*how* can you do that⟩ **2 :** to what degree or extent ⟨*how* do you like that⟩ **3 :** in what state or condition ⟨*how* are you⟩ **4 :** at what price ⟨*how* do you sell your eggs⟩ **[**Old English *hū***]** — **how about :** what do you say to or think of ⟨*how about* another game⟩ — **how come :** why is it that ⟨*how come* you're so early⟩ — **how do you do** — used to express a polite greeting

[2]**how** *conj* **1 :** in what manner or condition ⟨remember *how* they fought⟩ ⟨asked *how* they were⟩ **2 :** in whatever way or manner ⟨do it *how* you like⟩

[3]**how** \\ˈhau̇\\ *n* **:** MANNER, METHOD ⟨the *hows* and whys⟩

[1]**how•be•it** \\hau̇-ˈbē-ət\\ *adv* **:** NEVERTHELESS

[2]**howbeit** *conj* **:** ALTHOUGH

how•dah \\ˈhau̇d-ə\\ *n* **:** a seat or covered pavilion on the back of an elephant or camel **[**Hindi *hauda***]**

how•dy \\ˈhau̇-dē\\ *interj* — used to express a greeting **[**from *how do you do***]**

[1]**how•ev•er** \\hau̇-ˈev-ər\\ *conj* **:** in whatever way or manner ⟨go *however* you like⟩

[2]**however** *adv* **1 a :** to whatever degree or extent **b :** in whatever manner or way **2 :** in spite of that : on the other hand : BUT ⟨still seems possible, *however,* that conditions will improve⟩ **3 :** how in the world ⟨*however* did you do it⟩

howdah

how•it•zer \ˈhau̇-ət-sər\ *n* **:** a short cannon used to fire projectiles in a high trajectory [Dutch *houwitser,* from German *haubitze,* from Czech *houfnice,* a machine for hurling missiles]

howl \ˈhau̇l\ *vb* **1 :** to make a loud sustained doleful sound ⟨the wind *howled* all night⟩ **2 :** to cry out or exclaim without restraint under strong impulse (as pain, grief, or rage) **3 :** to utter with unrestrained outcry **4 :** to affect, effect, or drive by adverse outcry ⟨*howl* down all opposition⟩ [Middle English *houlen*] — **howl** *n*

howl•er \ˈhau̇-lər\ *n* **1 a :** one that howls **b :** HOWLER MONKEY **2 :** a stupid and ridiculous blunder

howler monkey *n* **:** any of a genus of South and Central American monkeys that have a long grasping tail and are able to make loud howling noises

how•so•ev•er \ˌhau̇-sə-ˈwev-ər\ *adv* **1 :** in whatever manner **2 :** to whatever degree or extent

hoy•den \ˈhȯid-n\ *n* **:** a girl or woman of saucy, boisterous, or carefree behavior [perhaps from obsolete Dutch *heiden* "country lout", from Dutch, "heathen"] — **hoy•den•ish** \-ish\ *adj*

hua•ra•che \wə-ˈräch-ē, hə-\ *n* **:** a low-heeled sandal having an upper made of interwoven leather thongs [Mexican Spanish]

hub \ˈhəb\ *n* **1 :** the central part of a wheel, propeller, or fan **2 :** a center of activity ⟨the *hub* of the universe⟩ [probably alteration of [2]*hob*]

hub•bub \ˈhəb-ˌəb\ *n* **1 :** a noisy confusion of sound : UPROAR **2 :** TURMOIL [probably of Celtic origin]

hu•bris \ˈhyü-brəs\ *n* **:** bold or unreasonable pride or self-confidence : ARROGANCE [Greek *hybris*]

huck•le•ber•ry \ˈhək-əl-ˌber-ē\ *n* **1 :** an American shrub related to the blueberry; *also* **:** its edible dark blue to black usually acid berry **2 :** BLUEBERRY [perhaps alteration of *hurtleberry* "whortleberry, huckleberry"]

huck•ster \ˈhək-stər\ *n* **1 :** [2]HAWKER, PEDDLER **2 :** a writer of advertising especially for radio or television [Dutch *hoekester,* from *hoeken* "to peddle"]

[1]**hud•dle** \ˈhəd-l\ *vb* **hud•dled; hud•dling** \ˈhəd-ling, -l-ing\ **1** *British* **:** to throw together, arrange, or complete carelessly or hurriedly **2 :** to crowd, push, or pile together ⟨*huddled* in a doorway⟩ **3 :** to gather in a group for conference : CONFER; *esp* **:** to gather in a huddle during a football game **4 :** to curl up : CROUCH ⟨a child *huddled* in its crib⟩ [probably from Middle English *hoderen*] — **hud•dler** \ˈhəd-lər, -l-ər\ *n*

[2]**huddle** *n* **1 :** a close-packed group : BUNCH **2 a :** CONFERENCE 1 **b :** a brief gathering of football players behind the line of scrimmage before each play to receive instructions

Hud•son seal \ˌhəd-sən-\ *n* **:** the fur of the muskrat dressed to resemble seal [*Hudson* bay, sea in Canada]

hue \ˈhyü\ *n* **1 :** outward appearance : ASPECT **2 a :** gradation of color **b :** the attribute of colors that permits them to be classed as red, yellow, green, blue, or an intermediate between any neighboring pair of these colors [Old English *hīw*] **syn** see COLOR — **hued** \ˈhyüd\ *adj*

hue and cry \ˌhyü-\ *n* **1 :** a loud outcry formerly used in the pursuit of felons **2 :** a clamor of protest [earlier *hue* "outcry", from Old French *hue,* from *huer* "to shout, hoot"]

[1]**huff** \ˈhəf\ *vi* **1 :** PUFF 1a, b ⟨tourists *huffing* up the steps behind their guide⟩ **2 a :** BLUSTER 2, RANT **b :** to react indignantly ⟨*huffed* off in a fit of anger⟩

[2]**huff** *n* **:** a fit of anger or pique

huffy \ˈhəf-ē\ *adj* **huff•i•er; -est 1 :** HAUGHTY **2 a :** aroused to indignation : OFFENDED **b :** easily offended : TOUCHY — **huff•i•ly** \ˈhəf-ə-lē\ *adv* — **huff•i•ness** *n*

hug \ˈhəg\ *vb* **hugged; hug•ging 1 :** to press tightly especially in the arms : EMBRACE **2 :** to hold fast : CHERISH ⟨*hugged* their fancied grievances⟩ **3 :** to stay close to ⟨drives along *hugging* the curb⟩ [perhaps of Scandinavian origin] — **hug** *n*

huge \ˈhyüj, ˈyüj\ *adj* **:** very large or extensive: as **a :** of great size or area **b :** of sizable scale or degree ⟨a *huge* success⟩ **c :** of limitless scope or character ⟨*huge* talent⟩ [Old French *ahuge*] **syn** see ENORMOUS — **huge•ly** *adv* — **huge•ness** *n*

hug•ger–mug•ger \ˈhəg-ər-ˌməg-ər\ *n* **1 :** SECRECY 2 **2 :** a disorderly jumble [origin unknown] — **hugger–mugger** *adj*

Hu•gue•not \ˈhyü-gə-ˌnät\ *n* **:** a French Protestant of the 16th and 17th centuries [Middle French, from Middle French dialect, "adherent of a Swiss political movement", from Besançon *Hugues,* died 1532, Swiss political leader + *eidgnot* "confederate", from German dialect *eidgnoss*]

huh *a short or a strong* h*-sound followed with varying intonation by an* m*-sound or by* ə[n]*; often read as* ˈhə\ *interj* — used to express surprise, disbelief, disgust, or interrogation [probably imitative]

hu•la \ˈhü-lə\ *or* **hu•la–hu•la** \ˌhü-lə-ˈhü-lə\ *n* **:** a Polynesian dance usually accompanied by chants and rhythmic drumming [Hawaiian]

[1]**hulk** \ˈhəlk\ *n* **1 :** a heavy clumsy ship **2 :** the body of an old ship unfit for service or of an abandoned wreck **3 :** a bulky, unwieldy, or clumsy person or thing [Old English *hulc,* from Medieval Latin *holcas,* from Greek *holkas,* from *helkein* "to pull, drag"]

[2]**hulk** *vi* **:** to appear impressively large : BULK

hulk•ing \ˈhəl-king\ *adj* **:** MASSIVE 2a, PONDEROUS

[1]**hull** \ˈhəl\ *n* **1 a :** the outer covering of a fruit or seed **b :** the persistent calyx or involucre that clings to the base of some fruits **2 :** the frame or body of a ship, flying boat, or airship **3 :** COVERING, CASING [Old English *hulu*]

[2]**hull** *vt* **:** to remove the hulls of — **hull•er** *n*

hul•la•ba•loo \ˈhəl-ə-bə-ˌlü\ *n, pl* **-loos :** a confused noise : UPROAR [perhaps from *hallo,* interj. used to attract attention + Scottish *balloo,* interj. used to hush children]

hum \ˈhəm\ *vb* **hummed; hum•ming 1 a :** to utter a sound like that of the speech sound \m\ prolonged **b :** to make the characteristic buzzing sound of an insect in motion or a similar sound **c :** to give forth a low continuous blend of sound **2 :** to sing with the lips closed and without articulation **3 :** to be busily active [Middle English *hummen*] — **hum** *n* — **hum•mer** *n*

hu•man \ˈhyü-mən, ˈyü-\ *adj* **1 :** of, relating to, or characteristic of human beings ⟨the *human* body⟩ ⟨*human* history⟩ ⟨to err is *human*⟩ **2 :** consisting of human beings ⟨the *human* race⟩ **3 :** having human form or attributes ⟨the dog's expression was almost *human*⟩ [Middle French *humain,* from Latin *humanus*] — **human** *n* — **hu•man•ness** \-mən-nəs\ *n*

• **syn** HUMANE: HUMAN applies to any feeling or quality shared by humanity in general ⟨*human* love⟩ ⟨*human* achievements⟩ HUMANE suggests the gentler side of human nature and implies compassion for people or animals in difficulty or need ⟨the growth of the *humane* treatment of prisoners in recent history⟩

human being *n* **:** an individual of the species of primate mammal that walks on two feet, is related to the great apes, and is distinguished by a greatly developed brain with capacity for speech and abstract reasoning

hu•mane \hyü-ˈmān, yü-\ *adj* **1 :** marked by compassion, sympathy, or consideration for others **2 :** characterized by broad humanistic culture ⟨*humane* studies⟩ [Middle French *humain* "human, humane"] **syn** see HUMAN — **hu•mane•ly** *adv* — **hu•mane•ness** \-ˈmān-nəs\ *n*

hu•man•ism \ˈhyü-mə-ˌniz-əm, ˈyü-\ *n* **1 :** a revival of classical letters, an individualistic and inquiring spirit, and an emphasis on secular concerns characteristic of the Renaissance **2 :** a doctrine or way of life centered on human interests or values; *esp* **:** a philosophy that asserts the dignity and worth of human beings and their capacity for self-realization through reason and that often rejects supernaturalism — **hu•man•ist** \-nəst\ *n or adj* — **hu•man•is•tic** \ˌhyü-mə-ˈnis-tik, ˌyü-\ *adj*

hu•man•i•tar•i•an \ˌhyü-ˌman-ə-ˈter-ē-ən, ˌyü-\ *n* **:** a person promoting human welfare and social reform : PHILANTHROPIST — **humanitarian** *adj* — **hu•man•i•tar•i•an•ism** \-ē-ə-ˌniz-əm\ *n*

hu•man•i•ty \hyü-ˈman-ət-ē, yü-\ *n, pl* **-ties 1 :** the quality or state of being humane : COMPASSION **2 :** the quality or state of being human ⟨the common *humanity* of all peoples⟩ **3** *pl* **:** the branches of learning having primarily a cultural character **4 :** the whole of the human race

hu•man•ize \ˈhyü-mə-ˌnīz, ˈyü-\ *vb* **1 :** to represent as human or with human attributes **2 :** to make or become humane or more humane ⟨*humanize* industry⟩ — **hu•man•iza•tion** \ˌhyü-mə-nə-ˈzā-shən, ˌyü-\ *n*

hu•man•kind \ˈhyü-mən-ˌkīnd, ˈyü-\ *n* **:** HUMANITY 4

hu•man•like \-ˌlīk\ *adj* **:** resembling a human being

hu•man•ly \ˈhyü-mən-lē, ˈyü-\ *adv* **1 a :** from the viewpoint of human beings **b :** within the range of human capacity ⟨a task not *humanly* possible⟩ **2 :** in a human manner

hu•man•oid \-mə-ˌnȯid\ *adj* **:** HUMANLIKE — **humanoid** *n*

[1]**hum•ble** \ˈhəm-bəl, ˈəm-\ *adj* **hum•bler** \-bə-lər, -blər\; **hum•blest** \-bə-ləst, -bləst\ **1 :** modest or meek in spirit or manner **:** not proud or assertive **2 :** expressing a spirit of deference or submission ⟨a *humble* apology⟩ **3 :** low in rank or status **:** UNPRETENTIOUS ⟨*humble* birth⟩ ⟨a *humble* position⟩ [Old French, from Latin *humilis* "low, humble", from *humus* "earth"] — **hum•bly** \-blē\ *adv*

[2]**humble** *vt* **hum•bled**; **hum•bling** \-bə-ling, -bling\ **1 :** to make humble in spirit or manner **2 :** to destroy the power or prestige of ⟨*humbled* their opponents with a crushing attack⟩ — **hum•bler** \-bə-lər, -blər\ *n*

hum•ble–bee \ˈhəm-bəl-ˌbē\ *n* **:** BUMBLEBEE [Middle English *humbylbee*]

hum•bug \ˈhəm-ˌbəg\ *n* **1 a :** something designed to deceive and mislead **:** FRAUD ⟨took their fervent denials as *humbug*⟩ **b :** CHARLATAN **2 :** DRIVEL, NONSENSE ⟨the speech was full of *humbug*⟩ [origin unknown] — **humbug** *vb* — **hum•bug•gery** \-ˌbəg-rē, -ə-rē\ *n*

hum•ding•er \ˈhəm-ˈding-ər\ *n* **:** a striking or extraordinary one of its kind [probably alteration of *hummer*]

hum•drum \ˈhəm-ˌdrəm\ *adj* **:** BANAL, ORDINARY [reduplication of *hum*]

hu•mec•tant \hyü-ˈmek-tənt\ *n* **:** a substance that promotes retention of moisture [Latin *humectare* "to moisten", from *humectus* "moist", from *humēre* "to be moist"]

hu•mer•al \ˈhyüm-rəl, -ə-rəl\ *adj* **:** of, relating to, or used or located in the region of the humerus or shoulder or an analogous region — **humeral** *n*

humeral veil *n* **:** an oblong vestment worn around the shoulders and over the hands by a priest or subdeacon holding a sacred vessel

hu•mer•us \ˈhyüm-rəs, -ə-rəs\ *n, pl* **hu•meri** \ˈhyü-mə-ˌrī, -ˌrē\ **:** the long bone of the upper arm or forelimb extending from the shoulder to the elbow [Latin, "upper arm, shoulder"]

hu•mic \ˈhyü-mik, ˈyü-\ *adj* **:** of, relating to, or derived from humus ⟨a *humic* acid⟩

hu•mid \ˈhyü-məd, ˈyü-\ *adj* **:** containing or characterized by perceptible moisture ⟨a *humid* day⟩ ⟨a *humid* climate⟩ [Latin *humidus,* from *humēre* "to be moist"] — **hu•mid•ly** *adv*

hu•mid•i•fy \hyü-ˈmid-ə-ˌfī, yü-\ *vt* **-fied**; **-fy•ing :** to make (as the air of a room) humid — **hu•mid•i•fi•ca•tion** \-ˌmid-ə-fə-ˈkā-shən\ *n* — **hu•mid•i•fi•er** \-ˈmid-ə-ˌfī-ər, -ˌfīr\ *n*

hu•mid•i•ty \-ˈmid-ət-ē\ *n, pl* **-ties :** DAMPNESS, MOISTURE; *esp* **:** the amount of moisture in the air — compare RELATIVE HUMIDITY

hu•mi•dor \ˈhyü-mə-ˌdȯr, ˈyü-\ *n* **:** a case usually for storing cigars in which the air is kept properly humidified [*humid* + *-or* (as in *cuspidor*)]

hu•mil•i•ate \hyü-ˈmil-ē-ˌāt, yü-\ *vt* **:** to reduce to a lower position in one's own eyes or others' eyes **:** MORTIFY ⟨the public reprimand *humiliated* the general⟩ [Late Latin *humiliare,* from Latin *humilis* "low, humble"] — **hu•mil•i•a•tion** \-ˌmil-ē-ˈā-shən\ *n*

hu•mil•i•ty \hyü-ˈmil-ət-ē, yü-\ *n* **:** the quality or state of being humble

hum•ming•bird \ˈhəm-ing-ˌbərd\ *n* **:** any of numerous tiny brightly colored American birds related to the swifts and having narrow swiftly beating wings, a slender bill, and a long tongue for sipping nectar

hum•mock \ˈhəm-ək\ *n* **1 :** a rounded mound of earth **:** KNOLL **2 :** a ridge or pile of ice [alteration of [2]*hammock*] — **hummocky** \-ə-kē\ *adj*

[1]**hu•mor** \ˈhyü-mər, ˈyü-\ *n* **1 :** a normal functioning bodily semifluid or fluid (as the blood or lymph) — compare AQUEOUS HUMOR, VITREOUS HUMOR **2 :** an often temporary state of mind induced especially by circumstances **3 :** WHIM 1, FANCY **4 :** the amusing quality of things ⟨the *humor* of a situation⟩ **5 :** the power to see or tell about the amusing side of things **:** a keen perception of the comic or the ridiculous **6 :** something comical or amusing [Middle French *humeur,* from Latin *humor* "moisture"] **syn** see MOOD, WIT — **hu•mor•less** \-ləs\ *adj* — **hu•mor•less•ness** *n*

hummingbird

△ **origin** In the Middle Ages it was believed that everything on Earth was made of different combinations of four elements: earth, air, fire, and water. These elements in turn were thought to be composed of combinations of what were known as the Four Contraries: hot, cold, moist, and dry. In people these same four contraries were thought to combine into the four humors: choler, blood, melancholy, and phlegm. The balance or imbalance of these humors determined a person's temperament. Coming from a Latin word meaning "moisture", *humor* originally reflected the combinations of heat and moisture that accounted for a person's disposition. *Humor* became a general term for "disposition" and soon came to mean "a mood or state of mind". From this developed the sense of "whim or fancy", from which are derived the senses of *humor* which refer to the comical or amusing.

[2]**humor** *vt* **hu•mored**; **hu•mor•ing** \ˈhyüm-ring, ˈyüm-, -ə-ring\ **:** to comply with the wishes or mood of

hu•mor•al \ˈhyüm-rəl, ˈyüm-, -ə-rəl\ *adj* **:** of, relating to, proceeding from, or involving a bodily humor and especially a hormone

hu•mor•esque \ˌhyü-mə-ˈresk, ˌyü-\ *n* **:** a typically whimsical or fanciful musical composition [German *humoreske,* from *humor* "humor", from English]

hu•mor•ist \ˈhyüm-rəst, ˈyüm-, -ə-rəst\ *n* **:** a person specializing in or noted for humor

hu•mor•ous \ˈhyüm-rəs, ˈyüm-, -ə-rəs\ *adj* **:** full of, characterized by, or expressive of humor **:** DROLL ⟨a *humorous* story⟩ — **hu•mor•ous•ly** *adv* — **hu•mor•ous•ness** *n*

hu•mour *chiefly British variant of* HUMOR

[1]**hump** \ˈhəmp\ *n* **1 :** a rounded bulge or lump (as on the back of a camel) **2 :** KNOLL, HUMMOCK **3 :** a difficult phase [related to Low German *hump* "bump"] — **humped** \ˈhəmpt\ *adj* — **humpy** \ˈhəm-pē\ *adj*

[2]**hump** *vb* **1 :** to exert oneself vigorously **:** HUSTLE **2 :** to make hump-shaped **:** HUNCH

hump•back \ˈhəmp-ˌbak\ *n* **1 :** a humped or crooked back **2 :** HUNCHBACK 2 **3 :** a large whalebone whale with very long flippers

hump•backed \-ˈbakt\ *or* **hump•back** \-ˌbak\ *adj* **:** having a humped back

hu•mus \ˈhyü-məs, ˈyü-\ *n* **:** the brown or black organic portion of soil formed by partial decomposition of plant or animal matter [Latin, "earth"]

Hun \ˈhən\ *n* **1 :** a member of a nomadic Mongolian people gaining control of a large part of central and eastern Europe under Attila about A.D. 450 **2** *often not cap* **:** a person who is wantonly destructive [Late Latin *Hunni* "Huns"]

[1]**hunch** \ˈhənch\ *vb* **1 :** to thrust oneself forward ⟨*hunch* nearer the fire⟩ **2 :** to assume a bent or crooked posture ⟨sat *hunched* over the table⟩ **3 :** to thrust into a hump ⟨*hunch* one's shoulders⟩ [origin unknown]

[2]**hunch** *n* **1 :** HUMP 1 **2 :** a strong intuitive feeling

hunch•back \ˈhənch-ˌbak\ *n* **1 :** HUMPBACK 1 **2 :** a person with a humpback — **hunch•backed** \-ˈbakt\ *adj*

hun•dred \ˈhən-drəd, -dərd\ *n, pl* **hundreds** *or* **hundred 1 :** ten more than 90; *also* **:** a symbol representing this — see NUMBER table **2 :** a great number ⟨*hundreds* of times⟩ [Old English] — **hundred** *adj*

hundreds digit *n* **:** the numeral (as 4 in 456) occupying the hundreds place in a number expressed in the Arabic system of writing numbers

hundreds place *n* **:** the place three to the left of the decimal point in a number expressed in the Arabic system of writing numbers

hun•dredth \ˈhən-drədth, -drətth\ *n* **1 :** one of 100 equal parts of something **2 :** one numbered 100 in a countable series —

see NUMBER table — **hundredth** *adj*

hun·dred·weight \ˈhən-drə-ˌdwāt, -dər-ˌdwāt\ *n, pl* **-weight** *or* **-weights** **1 :** a unit of weight equal to 100 pounds (about 45.6 kilograms) — called also *short hundredweight*; see MEASURE table **2** *British* **:** a unit of weight equal to 112 pounds (about 50.8 kilograms) — called also *long hundredweight*

hung *past of* HANG

Hun·gar·i·an \ˌhəng-ˈger-ē-ən, -ˈgar-\ *n* **1 a :** a native or inhabitant of Hungary **:** MAGYAR **b :** a person of Hungarian descent **2 :** MAGYAR 2 — **Hungarian** *adj*

[1]**hun·ger** \ˈhəng-gər\ *n* **1 :** a desire or a need for food; *also* **:** an uneasy feeling or weakened condition resulting from lack of food **2 :** a strong desire **:** CRAVING ⟨a *hunger* for praise⟩ [Old English *hungor*] — **hunger** *adj*

[2]**hunger** *vi* **hun·gered**; **hun·ger·ing** \-gə-ring, -gring\ **1 :** to feel or suffer hunger **2 :** to have an eager desire

hunger strike *n* **:** refusal (as by a prisoner) to eat enough to sustain life

hung jury *n* **:** a jury that fails to reach a verdict

hun·gry \ˈhəng-grē\ *adj* **hun·gri·er**; **-est** **1 :** feeling or showing hunger **2 :** EAGER, AVID **3 :** not rich or fertile **:** BARREN — **hun·gri·ly** \-grə-lē\ *adv* — **hun·gri·ness** \-grē-nəs\ *n*

hunk \ˈhəngk\ *n* **:** a large lump or piece [Flemish *hunke*]

hun·ker \ˈhəng-kər\ *vi* **:** CROUCH 1, SQUAT [perhaps of Scandinavian origin]

hun·kers \-kərz\ *n pl* **:** HINDQUARTER 2

hun·ky–do·ry \ˌhəng-kē-ˈdōr-ē, -ˈdȯr-\ *adj* **:** quite satisfactory **:** FINE [obsolete English dialect *hunk* "home base" + *-dory*, of unknown origin]

[1]**hunt** \ˈhənt\ *vb* **1 a :** to seek out and pursue (game) for food or sport ⟨*hunt* deer⟩ **b :** to use in hunting game ⟨*hunts* a pack of dogs⟩ **2 :** to pursue with intent to capture **3 a :** to attempt to find something **b :** to search out **:** SEEK **4 :** to drive or chase especially by harrying ⟨*hunt* a criminal out of town⟩ **5 :** to search through in quest of prey ⟨*hunts* the woods⟩ **6 :** to take part in a hunt [Old English *huntian*]

[2]**hunt** *n* **1 :** the act, the practice, or an instance of hunting **2 :** a group of hunters; *esp* **:** persons with horses and dogs engaged in hunting (as foxes)

hunt·er \ˈhənt-ər\ *n* **1 a :** a person who hunts game **b :** a dog or horse used or trained for hunting **2 :** a person who searches for something

hunt·ing *n* **:** the act of one that hunts; *esp* **:** the pursuit of game

hunt·ress \ˈhən-trəs\ *n* **:** a woman who is a hunter

hunts·man \ˈhənts-mən\ *n* **1 :** HUNTER 1a **2 :** a person who manages the hounds in a hunt

[1]**hur·dle** \ˈhərd-l\ *n* **1 :** a movable panel used for enclosing land or livestock **2 :** a barrier to be jumped in a race **3 :** OBSTACLE [Old English *hyrdel*]

[2]**hurdle** *vt* **hur·dled**; **hur·dling** \ˈhərd-ling, -l-ing\ **1 :** to leap over while running **2 :** OVERCOME 1, SURMOUNT — **hur·dler** \ˈhərd-lər, -l-ər\ *n*

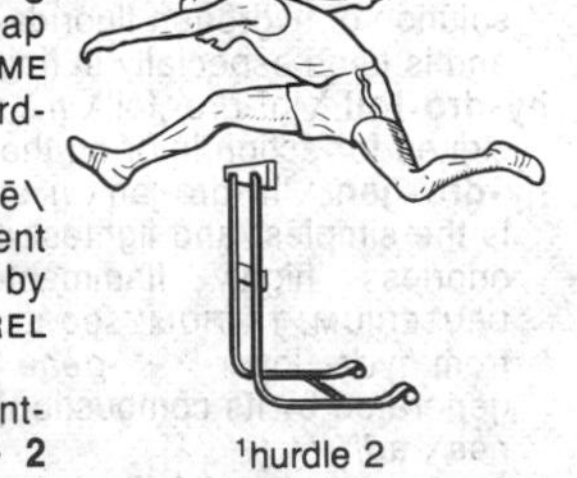

[1]hurdle 2

hur·dy–gur·dy \ˌhərd-ē-ˈgərd-ē\ *n, pl* **-dies** **:** a musical instrument in which the sound is produced by turning a crank; *esp* **:** BARREL ORGAN [probably imitative]

hurl \ˈhərl\ *vb* **1 :** to throw violently or powerfully ⟨*hurl* a spear⟩ **2 :** PITCH 2 [Middle English *hurlen*] **syn** see THROW — **hurl·er** *n*

hur·ly–bur·ly \ˌhər-lē-ˈbər-lē\ *n, pl* **-lies** **:** UPROAR, TUMULT [probably derived from *hurl*]

Hu·ron \ˈhyu̇r-ən, ˈhyu̇r-ˌän\ *n* **:** a member of an Iroquoian people originally of the St. Lawrence valley and what is now Ontario [French, literally, "boor"]

[1]**hur·rah** \hu̇-ˈrō, -ˈrä\ *or* **hoo·ray** \-ˈrā\ *also* **hur·ray** \-ˈrā\ *interj* — used to express joy, approval, or encouragement [perhaps from German *hurra*]

[2]**hur·rah** \hu̇-ˈrō, -ˈrä, ˈhü-ˌ\ *also* **hoo·ray** \-ˈrā\ *n* **1 :** FANFARE 2, EXCITEMENT **2 :** FUSS 2, CONTROVERSY

hur·ri·cane \ˈhər-ə-ˌkān, -i-kən, ˈhə-rə-, ˈhə-ri-\ *n* **:** a tropical cyclone with winds of 33.1 meters per second or greater but rarely exceeding 65 meters per second usually accompanied by rain, thunder, and lightning [Spanish *huracán*, of American Indian origin]

hurricane deck *n* **:** PROMENADE DECK

hurricane lamp *n* **:** a candlestick or an electric lamp with a glass chimney

hur·ried \ˈhər-ēd, ˈhə-rēd\ *adj* **1 :** going or working at speed ⟨the *hurried* life of the city⟩ **2 :** done in a hurry **:** HASTY ⟨a *hurried* meal⟩ — **hur·ried·ly** *adv*

[1]**hur·ry** \ˈhər-ē, ˈhə-rē\ *vb* **hur·ried**; **hur·ry·ing** **1 a :** to carry or cause to go with haste ⟨*hurry* them to the airport⟩ **b :** to move or act with haste ⟨had to *hurry* to arrive in time⟩ **2 a :** to impel to greater speed **:** PROD **b :** EXPEDITE ⟨*hurry* a repair job⟩ **c :** to perform with undue haste [perhaps from Middle English *horyen*] — **hur·ri·er** *n*

[2]**hurry** *n, pl* **hurries** **1 :** DISTURBANCE 3, COMMOTION **2 :** a recurrent agitation of sound ⟨a *hurry* of voices⟩ **3 a :** agitated and often bustling or disorderly haste **b :** a state of eagerness or urgency **:** RUSH ⟨in a *hurry* to get there⟩ **syn** see HASTE

[1]**hurt** \ˈhərt\ *vb* **hurt**; **hurt·ing** **1 a :** to afflict with physical pain **b :** to do physical harm to **:** DAMAGE ⟨the storm didn't *hurt* the house⟩ **2 a :** to cause anguish to **:** OFFEND **b :** HAMPER ⟨the scandal *hurt* their election chances⟩ **3 :** to feel or be a source of pain ⟨I *hurt* all over⟩ ⟨my tooth *hurts*⟩ [Middle English *hurten*] — **hurt·er** *n*

[2]**hurt** *n* **1 a :** a bodily injury or wound **b :** mental distress **:** SUFFERING **2 :** WRONG 1a, HARM

hurt·ful \ˈhərt-fəl\ *adj* **:** causing injury or suffering **:** DAMAGING — **hurt·ful·ly** \-fə-lē\ *adv* — **hurt·ful·ness** *n*

hur·tle \ˈhərt-l\ *vb* **hur·tled**; **hur·tling** \ˈhərt-ling, -l-ing\ **1 :** to move with or as if with a rushing sound ⟨boulders *hurtled* down the hill⟩ **2 :** HURL, FLING ⟨*hurtled* the stone through the air⟩ [Middle English *hurtlen* "to collide", from *hurten* "to cause to strike, hurt"]

[1]**hus·band** \ˈhəz-bənd\ *n* **:** a married man [Old English *hūsbonda* "master of a house", from Old Norse *hūsbōndi*, from *hūs* "house" + *bōndi* "householder"]

[2]**husband** *vt* **1 :** to manage prudently and economically **:** use carefully **:** CONSERVE ⟨*husbanded* their resources⟩ **2** *archaic* **:** to be a husband to **:** MARRY — **hus·band·er** *n*

hus·band·man \ˈhəz-bənd-mən, -bən-\ *n* **:** FARMER; *also* **:** a specialist in farm husbandry

hus·band·ry \-bən-drē\ *n* **1 :** the management or careful use of resources **:** ECONOMY **2 :** FARMING, AGRICULTURE; *esp* **:** the technical and scientific aspects of farming and especially of the care and production of domestic animals — compare ANIMAL HUSBANDRY

[1]**hush** \ˈhəsh\ *vb* **1 :** to make quiet, calm, or still **:** SOOTHE ⟨*hush* a baby⟩ **2 :** to become quiet **3 :** to keep from public knowledge **:** SUPPRESS ⟨*hush* up a scandal⟩ [Middle English *huissht*, interj. used to enjoin silence]

[2]**hush** *n* **:** a silence or calm especially following noise **:** QUIET

hush–hush \ˈhəsh-ˌhəsh\ *adj* **:** SECRET 1a, CONFIDENTIAL

[1]**husk** \ˈhəsk\ *n* **1 :** a usually thin dry outer covering of a seed or fruit **2 :** an outer layer **:** SHELL [Middle English]

[2]**husk** *vt* **:** to strip the husk from — **husk·er** *n*

husk·ing *n* **:** a gathering of farm families to husk corn — called also *husking bee*

[1]**husky** \ˈhəs-kē\ *adj* **husk·i·er**; **-est** **:** resembling, containing, or full of husks

[2]**husky** *adj* **husk·i·er**; **-est** **:** hoarse with or as if with emotion [probably from obsolete *husk* "to have a dry cough"] — **husk·i·ly** \ˈhəs-kə-lē\ *adv* — **husk·i·ness** \-kē-nəs\ *n*

[3]**husky** *adj* **husk·i·er**; **-est** **:** BURLY, ROBUST [probably from [1]*husk*]

[4]**husky** *n, pl* **husk·ies** **:** one that is husky

[5]**hus·ky** \ˈhəs-kē\ *n, pl* **hus·kies** **:** a heavy-coated working dog especially of the New World arctic region [probably alteration of *Eskimo*]

hus·sar \hə-ˈzär, ˌhə-, -ˈsär\ *n* **:** a member of any of various European military units originally of light cavalry [Hungarian *huszár* "highwayman, hussar", from Serbian *husar* "pirate", from Medieval Latin *cursarius* "corsair"]

Huss·ite \ˈhəs-ˌīt, ˈhu̇s-\ *n* **:** a member of the Bohemian reli-

\ə\ **abut**	\au̇\ **out**	\i\ **tip**	\ȯ\ **saw**	\u̇\ **foot**
\ər\ **further**	\ch\ **chin**	\ī\ **life**	\ȯi\ **coin**	\y\ **yet**
\a\ **mat**	\e\ **pet**	\j\ **job**	\th\ **thin**	\yü\ **few**
\ā\ **take**	\ē\ **easy**	\ng\ **sing**	\t͟h\ **this**	\yu̇\ **cure**
\ä\ **cot, cart**	\g\ **go**	\ō\ **bone**	\ü\ **food**	\zh\ **vision**

gious and nationalist movement originating with John Huss — **Hussite** *adj*

hus•sy \'həz-ē, 'həs-\ *n, pl* **hus•sies** **1 :** a lewd or brazen woman **2 :** a pert or mischievous girl [alteration of *housewife*]

hus•tings \'həs-tiŋz\ *n pl* **:** a place where political campaign speeches are made; *also* **:** the proceedings in an election campaign [Old English *hūsting* "local court", from Old Norse *hūsthing*, from *hūs* "house" + *thing* "assembly"]

hus•tle \'həs-əl\ *vb* **hus•tled; hus•tling** \'həs-liŋ, -ə-liŋ\ **1 :** to push, crowd, or force forward roughly ⟨*hustled* the prisoner to jail⟩ **2 a :** to move or work with energetic activity **b :** to sell something to or obtain something from by energetic and especially underhanded activity [Dutch *husselen* "to shake"] — **hustle** *n* — **hus•tler** \'həs-lər, -ə-lər\ *n*

hut \'hət\ *n* **:** an often small and temporary dwelling or shelter **:** SHACK [Middle French *hutte*, of Germanic origin] — **hut** *vb*

hutch \'həch\ *n* **1 a :** a chest or compartment for storage **b :** a low cupboard usually surmounted by open shelves **2 :** a pen or coop for an animal **3 :** SHANTY, SHACK [Old French huche]

hut•ment \'hət-mənt\ *n* **1 :** a camp of huts **2 :** HUT

huz•zah *or* **huz•za** \hə-'zä, ˌhə-\ *interj* — used to express joy or approbation [origin unknown]

hwan \'hwän\ *n, pl* **hwan** **1 :** a South Korean monetary unit equal to 1/10 won **2 :** a coin representing one hwan [Korean]

hy•a•cinth \'hī-ə-ˌsinth, -ˌsintth\ *n* **1 :** a red or brownish gem zircon or garnet **2 :** any of a genus of bulbous herbs of the lily family; *esp* **:** a common garden plant widely grown for its showy fragrant bell-shaped 6-lobed flowers **3 :** a light violet to moderate purple [Latin *hyacinthus*, a precious stone, a flowering plant, from Greek *hyakinthos*] — **hy•a•cin•thine** \ˌhī-ə-'sin-thən, -'sint-\ *adj*

hyacinth 2

Hy•a•des \'hī-ə-ˌdēz\ *n pl* **:** a V-shaped cluster of stars in the head of the constellation Taurus held by the ancients to indicate rainy weather when they rise with the sun [Latin, from Greek]

hy•ae•na *variant of* HYENA

hy•a•line \'hī-ə-lən, -ˌlīn\ *adj* **:** transparent or nearly so and usually homogeneous ⟨a *hyaline* membrane⟩ [derived from Greek *hyalos* "glass"]

hy•a•lite \'hī-ə-ˌlīt\ *n* **:** a colorless opal that is clear as glass or sometimes translucent or whitish [German *hyalit*, from Greek *hyalos* "glass"]

hy•brid \'hī-brəd\ *n* **1 :** an offspring of genetically different parents especially of different races, breeds, varieties, species, or genera **2 :** something of mixed origin or composition [Latin *hybrida*] — **hybrid** *adj* — **hy•brid•ism** \'hī-brə-ˌdiz-əm\ *n* — **hy•brid•i•ty** \hī-'brid-ət-ē\ *n*

hy•brid•ize \'hī-brə-ˌdīz\ *vb* **:** to produce or cause to produce hybrids **:** INTERBREED — **hy•brid•iza•tion** \ˌhī-brəd-ə-'zā-shən\ *n* — **hy•brid•iz•er** \'hī-brə-ˌdī-zər\ *n*

hybrid vigor *n* **:** exceptional vigor or capacity for growth on the part of a hybrid — called also *heterosis*

hy•da•tid \'hīd-ə-təd, -ˌtid\ *n* **:** a larval tapeworm that occurs in the host's tissues as a fluid-filled sac containing daughter cysts and scolices [Greek *hydatid-*, *hydatis* "watery cyst", from *hydat-*, *hydōr* "water"]

hydr- *or* **hydro-** *combining form* **1 :** water ⟨*hydro*electric⟩ ⟨*hydrous*⟩ **2 :** hydrogen ⟨*hydro*carbon⟩ [Greek, from *hydōr*]

Hy•dra \'hī-drə\ *n* **1 :** a many-headed serpent or monster of Greek mythology slain by Hercules **2 :** a southern constellation that is represented on old maps by a serpent **3** *not cap* **:** any of numerous small tubular freshwater animals related to the jellyfishes and having a mouth surrounded by tentacles at one end [Latin, from Greek]

hy•dran•gea \hī-'drān-jə\ *n* **:** any of a genus of shrubby plants of the saxifrage family with showy clusters of usually sterile white, pink, or blue flowers [*hydr-* + Greek *angeion* "vessel"]

hy•drant \'hī-drənt\ *n* **:** a discharge pipe with a valve and spout at which water may be drawn from a main

1**hy•drate** \'hī-ˌdrāt\ *n* **1 :** a compound or complex ion formed by the union of water with some other substance ⟨a *hydrate* of copper sulfate⟩ **2 :** HYDROXIDE ⟨calcium *hydrate*⟩

2**hydrate** *vt* **:** to cause to take up or combine with water or the elements of water — **hy•dra•tion** \hī-'drā-shən\ *n*

hy•drau•lic \hī-'drȯ-lik\ *adj* **1 :** operated, moved, or effected by means of water **2 :** of or relating to hydraulics ⟨*hydraulic* engineer⟩ **3 :** operated by the resistance offered or the pressure transmitted when a quantity of liquid is forced through a comparatively small orifice or through a tube ⟨*hydraulic* brakes⟩ **4 :** hardening or setting under water ⟨*hydraulic* cement⟩ [Latin *hydraulicus*, from Greek *hydraulikos*, from *hydraulis* "hydraulic organ", from *hydr-* + *aulos* "reed instrument"] — **hy•drau•li•cal•ly** \-li-kə-lē, -klē\ *adv*

hydraulic ram *n* **:** a pump that forces running water to a higher level by utilizing the kinetic energy of flow

hy•drau•lics \-liks\ *n* **:** science that deals with practical applications of liquid (as water) in motion

hy•dra•zine \'hī-drə-ˌzēn\ *n* **:** a colorless fuming corrosive liquid N_2H_4 used especially in fuels for rocket engines [*hydr-* + *az-* (from French *azote* "nitrogen", from Greek *a-* + *zōē* "life") + *-ine*]

hy•dride \'hī-ˌdrīd\ *n* **:** a compound of hydrogen usually with a more electropositive element or radical

hy•dro \'hī-drō\ *adj* **:** HYDROELECTRIC ⟨*hydro* power⟩

hy•dro•car•bon \ˌhī-drə-'kär-bən\ *n* **:** an organic compound (as acetylene or benzene) containing only carbon and hydrogen

hy•dro•ceph•a•lus \ˌhī-drō-'sef-ə-ləs\ *also* **hy•dro•ceph•a•ly** \-lē\ *n* **:** an abnormal state in which increased cerebrospinal fluid results in expansion of the cerebral ventricles, enlargement of the skull, and wasting away of the brain [derived from Greek *hydr-* + *kephalē* "head"] — **hy•dro•ce•phal•ic** \-sə-'fal-ik\ *adj or n*

hy•dro•chlo•ric acid \ˌhī-drə-ˌklōr-ik-, -ˌklȯr-\ *n* **:** an aqueous solution of hydrogen chloride HCl that is a strong corrosive liquid acid, is normally present in dilute form in gastric juice, and is widely used in industry and in the laboratory

hy•dro•chlo•ride \-'klōr-ˌīd, -'klȯr-\ *n* **:** a compound of hydrochloric acid

hy•dro•cor•ti•sone \-'kȯrt-ə-ˌsōn, -ˌzōn\ *n* **:** CORTISOL

hy•dro•cy•an•ic acid \ˌhī-drō-sī-ˌan-ik-\ *n* **:** an aqueous solution of hydrogen cyanide HCN that is a weak poisonous acid and is used in fumigating

hy•dro•dy•nam•ics \ˌhī-drō-dī-'nam-iks\ *n* **:** a science that deals with the motion of fluids and the forces acting on solid bodies immersed in fluids and in motion relative to them — **hy•dro•dy•nam•ic** \-ik\ *adj*

hy•dro•elec•tric \ˌhī-drō-i-'lek-trik\ *adj* **:** of or relating to production of electricity by waterpower — **hy•dro•elec•tric•i•ty** \-ˌlek-'tris-ət-ē, -'tris-tē\ *n*

hy•dro•flu•or•ic acid \ˌhī-drō-flu̇-ˌȯr-ik, -ˌär-\ *n* **:** an aqueous solution of hydrogen fluoride HF that is a weak poisonous acid and is used especially in finishing and etching glass

hy•dro•foil \'hī-drə-ˌfȯil\ *n* **:** a body similar to an airfoil but designed for action in or on the water

hy•dro•gen \'hī-drə-jən\ *n* **:** a univalent chemical element that is the simplest and lightest of the elements and is a colorless odorless highly flammable diatomic gas — compare DEUTERIUM, TRITIUM; see ELEMENT table [French *hydrogène*, from *hydr-* "hydr-" + *-gène* "-gen"; from the fact that water is generated by its combustion] — **hy•drog•e•nous** \hī-'dräj-ə-nəs\ *adj*

hy•dro•ge•nate \'hī-drə-jə-ˌnāt, hī-'dräj-ə-\ *vt* **:** to combine or treat with hydrogen; *esp* **:** to add hydrogen to the molecule of ⟨*hydrogenate* a vegetable oil to form a fat⟩ — **hy•dro•ge•na•tion** \ˌhī-drə-jə-'nā-shən, hī-ˌdräj-ə-\ *n*

hydrogen bomb *n* **:** a bomb whose violent explosive power is due to the sudden release of atomic energy resulting from the union of light nuclei (as of hydrogen atoms)

hydrogen chloride *n* **:** a colorless pungent poisonous gas HCl that fumes in moist air and yields hydrochloric acid when dissolved in water

hydrogen fluoride *n* **:** a colorless corrosive fuming poisonous liquid or gas HF that yields hydrofluoric acid when dissolved in water

hydrogen ion *n* **1 :** the cation H+ of acids consisting of a hydrogen atom whose electron has been transferred to the anion of the acid **2 :** HYDRONIUM

hydrogen peroxide *n* : an unstable liquid compound H_2O_2 used especially as an oxidizing and bleaching agent, an antiseptic, and a propellant

hydrogen sulfide *n* : a flammable poisonous gas H_2S of disagreeable odor found especially in many mineral waters and in decomposing matter

hy•drog•ra•phy \hī-ˈdräg-rə-fē\ *n* **1 :** the study of bodies of water (as seas, lakes, rivers) especially with reference to their use by man **2 :** the mapping of bodies of water — **hy•drog•ra•pher** \-fər\ *n* — **hy•dro•graph•ic** \ˌhī-drə-ˈgraf-ik\ *adj*

[1]**hy•droid** \ˈhī-ˌdrȯid\ *adj* : of or relating to the hydrozoans; *esp* : resembling a typical hydra

[2]**hydroid** *n* : HYDROZOAN; *esp* : a hydrozoan polyp as distinguished from a hydrozoan jellyfish

hydrologic cycle *n* : the sequence of conditions through which water naturally passes from water vapor in the atmosphere through precipitation upon land or water surfaces and finally back into the atmosphere as a result of evaporation and transpiration

hy•drol•o•gy \hī-ˈdräl-ə-jē\ *n* : a science dealing with the properties, distribution, and circulation of water on and below the surface of the land and in the atmosphere — **hy•dro•log•ic** \ˌhī-drə-ˈläj-ik\ *adj* — **hy•drol•o•gist** \hī-ˈdräl-ə-jəst\ *n*

hy•drol•y•sis \hī-ˈdräl-ə-səs\ *n* : a chemical process of decomposition involving splitting of a bond and addition of the elements of water — **hy•dro•lyt•ic** \ˌhī-drə-ˈlit-ik\ *adj*

hy•dro•lyze \ˈhī-drə-ˌlīz\ *vb* : to subject to or undergo hydrolysis

hy•drom•e•ter \hī-ˈdräm-ət-ər\ *n* : a floating instrument for determining specific gravities of liquids and hence the strength (as of alcoholic liquors, saline solutions) — **hy•dro•met•ric** \ˌhī-drə-ˈme-trik\ *adj* — **hy•drom•e•try** \hī-ˈdräm-ə-trē\ *n*

hy•dro•ni•um \hī-ˈdrō-nē-əm\ *n* : a hydrated hydrogen ion H_3O+ [*hydr-* + *-onium* (as in *ammonium*)]

hy•dro•phil•ic \ˌhī-drə-ˈfil-ik\ *adj* : of, relating to, or having a strong affinity for water

hy•dro•pho•bia \ˌhī-drə-ˈfō-bē-ə\ *n* **1 :** a morbid dread of water **2 :** RABIES

hy•dro•pho•bic \-ˈfō-bik, -ˈfäb-ik\ *adj* **1 :** of, relating to, or suffering from rabies **2 :** lacking affinity for water — **hy•dro•pho•bic•i•ty** \-fō-ˈbis-ət-ē\ *n*

hy•dro•phone \ˈhī-drə-ˌfōn\ *n* : an instrument for listening to sound transmitted through water

hy•dro•phyte \-ˌfīt\ *n* : a plant growing in water or in waterlogged soil — **hy•dro•phyt•ic** \ˌhī-drə-ˈfit-ik\ *adj*

[1]**hy•dro•plane** \ˈhī-drə-ˌplān\ *n* **1 :** a speedboat with fins or a bottom so designed that the hull is raised wholly or partly out of the water **2 :** SEAPLANE

[2]**hydroplane** *vi* **1 :** to skim over the water with the hull more or less clear of the surface **2 :** to drive or ride in a hydroplane

hy•dro•pon•ics \ˌhī-drə-ˈpän-iks\ *n* : the growing of plants in nutrient solutions [*hydr-* + *-ponics* (as in *geoponics* "agriculture", from Greek *geōponein* "to plow", from *geō-* "ge-" + *ponein* "to toil")] — **hy•dro•pon•ic** \-ik\ *adj* — **hy•dro•pon•i•cal•ly** \-ˈpän-i-kə-lē, -klē\ *adv*

hy•dro•qui•none \ˌhī-drō-kwin-ˈōn, -ˈkwin-ˌōn\ *n* : a white crystalline compound used as a photographic developer and as an antioxidant and stabilizer [derived from *hydr-* + *quinine*]

hy•dro•sphere \ˈhī-drə-ˌsfiər\ *n* **1 :** the water vapor that surrounds the earth as part of the atmosphere **2 :** the surface waters of the earth and the water vapor in the atmosphere

hy•dro•stat•ic \ˌhī-drə-ˈstat-ik\ *adj* : of or relating to liquids at rest or to the pressures they exert or transmit

hy•dro•stat•ics \-iks\ *n* : a branch of physics that deals with the characteristics of liquids at rest and especially with the pressure in a liquid or exerted by a liquid on an immersed body

hy•dro•ther•a•py \-ˈther-ə-pē\ *n* : the use of water in the treatment of disease

hy•drot•ro•pism \hī-ˈdrä-trə-ˌpiz-əm\ *n* : a tropism (as in plant roots) in which water or water vapor is the orienting factor — **hy•dro•tro•pic** \ˌhī-drə-ˈtrō-pik, -ˈträp-ik\ *adj*

hy•drous \ˈhī-drəs\ *adj* : containing water usually chemically combined

hy•drox•ide \hī-ˈdräk-ˌsīd\ *n* : a compound of hydroxyl with an element or radical

hy•drox•yl \hī-ˈdräk-səl\ *n* : the univalent group or radical OH consisting of one atom of hydrogen and one of oxygen that is characteristic of hydroxides

hy•dro•zo•an \ˌhī-drə-ˈzō-ən\ *n* : any of a class (Hydrozoa) of coelenterates including the hydras and various polyps and jellyfishes — **hydrozoan** *adj*

hy•e•na *also* **hy•ae•na** \hī-ˈē-nə\ *n* : any of several large strong nocturnal flesh-eating Old World mammals [Latin *hyaena*, from Greek *hyaina*, from *hys* "hog"]

hyena

hy•giene \ˈhī-ˌjēn\ *n* **1 :** a science dealing with the establishment and maintenance of health **2 :** conditions or practices (as of cleanliness) tending to promote or aid health [French *hygiène*, from Greek *hygienos* "healthful", from *hygiēs* "healthy"] — **hy•gien•ic** \ˌhī-jē-ˈen-ik, hī-ˈjen-, hī-ˈjēn-\ *adj* — **hy•gien•i•cal•ly** \-i-kə-lē, -klē\ *adv* — **hy•gien•ist** \hī-ˈjēn-əst, -ˈjen-, ˈhī-ˌ\ *n*

hygr- *or* **hygro-** *combining form* : humidity : moisture ⟨*hygro*graph⟩ [Greek *hygros* "wet"]

hy•gro•graph \ˈhī-grə-ˌgraf\ *n* : an instrument for automatic recording of variations in atmospheric humidity

hy•grom•e•ter \hī-ˈgräm-ət-ər\ *n* : any of several instruments for measuring the humidity of the atmosphere — **hy•gro•met•ric** \ˌhī-grə-ˈme-trik\ *adj* — **hy•grom•e•try** \hī-ˈgräm-ə-trē\ *n*

hy•gro•scop•ic \ˌhī-grə-ˈskäp-ik\ *adj* **1 :** readily taking up and retaining moisture ⟨salt is somewhat *hygroscopic*⟩ **2 :** taken up and retained ⟨*hygroscopic* moisture⟩

hying *present participle of* HIE

Hyk•sos \ˈhik-ˌsōs\ *n* : a Semitic dynasty ruling Egypt from about 1750 to 1580 B.C. [Greek *Hyksōs*, from Egyptian *hqꜣ šꜣsw* "ruler of the countries of the nomads"]

hy•la \ˈhī-lə\ *n* : any of a genus of tree frogs [Greek *hylē* "wood"]

hy•men \ˈhī-mən\ *n* : a fold of mucous membrane partly closing the opening of the vagina — called also *maidenhead* [Late Latin, from Greek *hymēn* "membrane"] — **hy•men•al** \ˈhī-mən-l\ *adj*

hy•me•nop•ter•on \ˌhī-mə-ˈnäp-tə-ˌrän, -rən\ *n, pl* **-tera** \-rə\ : any of an order (Hymenoptera) of highly specialized and often colonial insects (as bees, wasps, and ants) that have usually four membranous wings and the abdomen on a slender stalk [derived from Greek *hymēn* "membrane" + *pteron* "wing"] — **hy•me•nop•ter•an** \-rən\ *adj or n* — **hy•me•nop•ter•ous** \-rəs\ *adj*

hymn \ˈhim\ *n* **1 :** a song of praise especially to God **2 :** a religious song [Old French *ymne*, from Latin *hymnus*, from Greek *hymnos*]

hym•nal \ˈhim-nəl\ *n* : a book of hymns

hymn•book \ˈhim-ˌbu̇k\ *n* : HYMNAL

hym•no•dy \ˈhim-nəd-ē\ *n* **1 :** hymn singing **2 :** hymn writing **3 :** the hymns of a time, place, or church [Late Latin *hymnodia*, from Greek *hymnōidia*, from *hymnos* "hymn" + *aeidein* "to sing"]

hy•oid bone \ˌhī-ˌȯid-\ *n* : a bone or complex of bones supporting the tongue and its muscles [Greek *hyoeidēs* "shaped like the letter upsilon (υ)", from *hy* "upsilon"] — **hy•oid** \ˈhī-ˌȯid\ *adj or n*

hyp- — see HYPO-

hyper- *prefix* **1 :** above : beyond : SUPER- ⟨*hyper*sonic⟩ **2 a :** excessively ⟨*hyper*critical⟩ **b :** excessive ⟨*hyper*xemia⟩ [Greek *hyper*]

See *hyper-* and 2d element

hyperabundant	**hyperanxious**	**hypercivilized**
hyperacuity	**hyperaware**	**hyperclarity**
hyperacute	**hyperawareness**	**hyperclean**
hyperaggressive	**hyperbizarre**	**hypercomplex**
hyperalert	**hypercautious**	**hyperconcentration**

\ə\ **abut**	\au̇\ **out**	\i\ **tip**	\ȯ\ **saw**	\u̇\ **foot**
\ər\ **further**	\ch\ **chin**	\ī\ **life**	\ȯi\ **coin**	\y\ **yet**
\a\ **mat**	\e\ **pet**	\j\ **job**	\th\ **thin**	\yü\ **few**
\ā\ **take**	\ē\ **easy**	\ng\ **sing**	\t͟h\ **this**	\yu̇\ **cure**
\ä\ **cot, cart**	\g\ **go**	\ō\ **bone**	\ü\ **food**	\zh\ **vision**

hyperconscientious
hyperconscientiousness
hyperconscious
hyperconsciousness
hypercorrect
hypercorrection
hypercorrectly
hypercreative
hypercreativity
hyperdevelop
hyperdevelopment
hyperemotional
hyperemotionally
hyperenergetic
hyperexcitability
hyperexcitable
hyperexcitement
hyperexpressive
hyperexpressiveness
hyperfastidious
hyperfastidiousness
hyperflexible
hyperinflation
hyperintellectual
hyperintellectuality
hyperintelligent
hyperintense
hypermasculine
hypermilitant
hypermodern
hypermodernism
hypermoralistic
hypernationalistic
hyperorganize
hyperpigmented
hyperproduce
hyperproduction
hyperpure
hyperradical
hyperrational
hyperrationality
hyperreaction
hyperreactive
hyperreactivity
hyperreactor
hyperrealism
hyperrealist
hyperrealistic
hyperresponsive
hyper-romantic
hyper-romanticize
hypersaline
hypersalinity
hypersexual
hypersexuality
hyperspecialization
hyperstimulation
hypersusceptibility
hypersusceptible
hypersuspicious
hypertechnical
hypertense
hypertoxic
hypertypical
hypertypically
hypervariable
hypervigilance
hypervigilant
hypervirulent

hy•per•acid•i•ty \ˌhī-pə-rə-ˈsid-ət-ē\ *n* : the condition of containing more than the normal amount of acid — **hy•per•acid** \-ˌpə-ˈras-əd\ *adj*

hy•per•ac•tive \-ˈrak-tiv\ *adj* : excessively or abnormally active — **hy•per•ac•tiv•ity** \-ˌrak-ˈtiv-ət-ē\ *n*

hy•per•bo•la \hī-ˈpər-bə-lə\ *n, pl* **-las** *or* **-lae** \-ˌlē\ : a plane curve generated by a point moving so that the difference of the distances from two fixed points is a constant : a curve formed by the intersection of a double right circular cone with a plane that cuts both halves of the cone [Greek *hyperbolē*]

hy•per•bo•le \hī-ˈpər-bə-lē\ *n* : extravagant exaggeration [Latin, from Greek *hyperbolē* "excess, hyperbole, hyperbola", from *hyperballein* "to exceed", from *hyper* "beyond" + *ballein* "to throw"]

hy•per•bol•ic \ˌhī-pər-ˈbäl-ik\ *adj* **1** : of, characterized by, or given to hyperbole **2** : of or relating to a hyperbola — **hy•per•bol•i•cal•ly** \-i-kə-lē, -klē\ *adv*

Hy•per•bo•re•an \ˌhī-pər-ˈbōr-ē-ən, -ˈbȯr-; -bə-ˈrē-ən\ *n* **1** : a member of a people held by the ancient Greeks to live beyond the north wind in a region of perpetual sunshine **2** *often not cap* : an inhabitant of a remote northern region [Latin *Hyperborei*, pl., from Greek *Hyperboreoi*, from *hyper* "beyond" + *Boreas* "north wind"]

hy•per•crit•i•cal \ˌhī-pər-ˈkrit-i-kəl\ *adj* : excessively critical — **hy•per•crit•i•cal•ly** \-kə-lē, -klē\ *adv*

hy•per•emia \ˌhī-pə-ˈrē-mē-ə\ *n* : excess of blood in a body part : CONGESTION — **hy•per•emic** \-mik\ *adj*

hy•per•gly•ce•mia \ˌhī-pər-glī-ˈsē-mē-ə\ *n* : excess of sugar in the blood [Greek *glykys* "sweet"] — **hy•per•gly•ce•mic** \-mik\ *adv*

hy•per•opia \ˌhī-pə-ˈrō-pē-ə\ *n* : a condition in which visual images come to a focus behind the retina and the eye is farsighted

hy•per•pla•sia \ˌhī-pər-ˈplā-zhə, -zhē-ə\ *n* : an abnormal or unusual increase in the elements (as tissue cells) composing a bodily part — **hy•per•plas•tic** \-ˈplas-tik\ *adj*

hy•per•sen•si•tive \-ˈsen-sət-iv, -ˈsen-stiv\ *adj* **1** : excessively or abnormally sensitive **2** : abnormally susceptible to a drug, antigen, or other agent — **hy•per•sen•si•tive•ness** *n* — **hy•per•sen•si•tiv•i•ty** \-ˌsen-sə-ˈtiv-ət-ē\ *n*

hy•per•son•ic \-ˈsän-ik\ *adj* **1** : of or relating to speed five or more times that of sound in air — compare SONIC **2** : moving, capable of moving, or utilizing air currents that move at hypersonic speed ⟨a *hypersonic* wind tunnel⟩

hy•per•ten•sion \ˌhī-pər-ˈten-chən\ *n* : HIGH BLOOD PRESSURE — **hy•per•ten•sive** \-ˈten-siv\ *adj or n*

hy•per•thy•roid•ism \-ˈthī-ˌrȯid-ˌiz-əm, -rəd-\ *n* : excessive activity of the thyroid gland; *also* : the resulting abnormal state of health — compare GOITER — **hy•per•thy•roid** \-ˌrȯid\ *adj*

hy•per•ton•ic \-ˈtän-ik\ *adj* : having a higher osmotic pressure than a fluid under comparison — **hy•per•to•nic•i•ty** \-tə-ˈnis-ət-ē\ *n*

hy•per•tro•phy \hī-ˈpər-trə-fē\ *n, pl* **-phies** : excessive development of a bodily part; *esp* : increase in bulk (as by thickening of muscle fibers) without multiplication of constituent units — **hy•per•tro•phic** \hī-ˈpər-trə-fik, ˌhī-pər-ˈträf-ik\ *adj* — **hypertrophy** *vb*

hy•pha \ˈhī-fə\ *n, pl* **hy•phae** \-fē\ : one of the threads that make up the mycelium of a fungus [Greek *hyphē* "web"] — **hy•phal** \-fəl\ *adj*

[1]**hy•phen** \ˈhī-fən\ *n* : a punctuation mark - used to divide or to compound words or word elements [Greek, from *hyph' hen* "under one"]

[2]**hyphen** *vt* : HYPHENATE

hy•phen•ate \ˈhī-fə-ˌnāt\ *vt* : to connect or mark with a hyphen — **hy•phen•ation** \ˌhī-fə-ˈnā-shən\ *n*

hyp•no•sis \hip-ˈnō-səs\ *n, pl* **-no•ses** \-ˈnō-ˌsēz\ : an induced state which resembles sleep but in which the subject is very responsive to suggestions of the hypnotizer [derived from Greek *hypnos* "sleep"]

hyp•no•ther•a•py \ˌhip-nō-ˈther-ə-pē\ *n* : the use of hypnotism in medical or psychiatric practice

[1]**hyp•not•ic** \hip-ˈnät-ik\ *adj* **1** : tending to induce sleep : SOPORIFIC **2** : of or relating to hypnosis or hypnotism [Late Latin *hypnoticus*, from Greek *hypnōtikos*, from *hypnoun* "to put to sleep", from *hypnos* "sleep"] — **hyp•not•i•cal•ly** \-i-kə-lē, -klē\ *adv*

[2]**hypnotic** *n* : a sleep-inducing agent : SOPORIFIC

hyp•no•tism \ˈhip-nə-ˌtiz-əm\ *n* **1** : the study of or act of inducing hypnosis **2** : HYPNOSIS — **hyp•no•tist** \-təst\ *n*

hyp•no•tize \-ˌtīz\ *vt* **1** : to induce hypnosis in **2** : to deaden (judgment or resistance) by or as if by hypnotic suggestion — **hyp•no•tiz•able** \-ˌtī-zə-bəl\ *adj* — **hyp•no•ti•za•tion** \ˌhip-nət-ə-ˈzā-shən\ *n* — **hyp•no•tiz•er** \ˈhip-nə-ˌtī-zər\ *n*

[1]**hy•po** \ˈhī-pō\ *n* : sodium thiosulfate used in photography as a fixing agent [short for *hyposulfite*]

[2]**hypo** *n, pl* **hypos** : a hypodermic syringe or injection

hypo- *or* **hyp-** *prefix* **1** : under : beneath : down ⟨*hypo*dermic⟩ **2** : less than normal or normally ⟨*hypo*tension⟩ **3** : in a lower state of oxidation : in a low and usually the lowest position in a series of compounds ⟨*hypo*chlorous acid⟩ [Greek *hypo*]

hy•po•chlo•rite \ˌhī-pə-ˈklōr-ˌīt, -ˈklȯr-\ *n* : a salt or ester of hypochlorous acid

hy•po•chlo•rous acid \ˌhī-pə-ˌklōr-əs-, -ˌklȯr-\ *n* : an unstable weak acid HClO used especially in the form of salts as an oxidizing agent, bleaching agent, and disinfectant

hy•po•chon•dria \ˌhī-pə-ˈkän-drē-ə\ *n* : severe depression of mind or spirits often centered on imaginary physical ailments [Late Latin, pl., "upper abdomen" (formerly regarded as the seat of hypochondria), from Greek, literally, "the parts under the cartilage (of the breastbone)", from *hypo* "under" + *chondros* "cartilage"] — **hy•po•chon•dri•ac** \-drē-ˌak\ *adj or n* — **hy•po•chon•dri•a•cal** \-kən-ˈdrī-ə-kəl, -ˌkän-\ *adj* — **hy•po•chon•dri•a•cal•ly** \-ˈdrī-ə-kə-lē, -klē\ *adv*

△ **origin** Many ancient theories of disease have been discarded. That dire humor, black bile (or melancholy), was said to be a secretion of the spleen or kidneys and was believed to produce a morbid state of depression. This disease was named for the region below the breastbone in which it had its origin, the *hypochondria*. This Late Latin word is a derivative of Greek *hypo*, "under", and *chondros*, "cartilage of the breastbone".

hy•po•cot•yl \ˈhī-pə-ˌkät-l\ *n* : the part of the main stem of a plant embryo or seedling below the cotyledons

hy•poc•ri•sy \hip-ˈäk-rə-sē\ *n, pl* **-sies** : a pretending to be what one is not or to believe what one does not; *esp* : a pretending to be more virtuous or religious than one really is

hyp•o•crite \ˈhip-ə-ˌkrit\ *n* : a person who affects virtues or qualities he does not have : DISSEMBLER [Old French *ypocrite*, from Late Latin *hypocrita*, from Greek *hypokritēs* "actor, hypocrite", from *hypokrinesthai* "to answer, act on the stage"] — **hyp•o•crit•i•cal** \ˌhip-ə-ˈkrit-i-kəl\ *adj* — **hyp•o•crit•i•cal•ly** \-i-kə-lē, -klē\ *adv*

[1]**hy•po•der•mic** \ˌhī-pə-ˈdər-mik\ *adj* : of, relating to, or injected into the parts beneath the skin — **hy•po•der•mi•cal•ly** \-mi-kə-lē, -klē\ *adv*

[2]**hypodermic** *n* **1** : HYPODERMIC INJECTION **2** : HYPODERMIC SYRINGE

hypodermic injection *n* : an injection made into the tissues beneath the skin

hypodermic needle *n* **1** : NEEDLE 1c **2** : a hypodermic syringe complete with needle

hypodermic syringe *n* : a small syringe used with a hollow needle for injection of material into or beneath the skin

hy•po•der•mis \ˌhī-pə-ˈdər-məs\ *n* : a layer of tissue immediately beneath an outermost layer; *esp* : a layer just beneath the epidermis of a plant and often modified to serve as a supporting and protecting layer

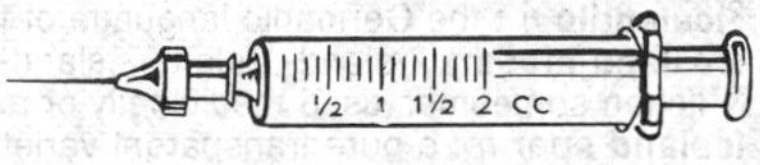

hypodermic syringe

hy•po•glos•sal nerve \ˌhī-pə-ˈgläs-əl\ *n* : either of the 12th and final pair of cranial nerves that are motor nerves arising from the medulla oblongata and supply muscles of the tongue in higher vertebrates — called also *hypoglossal* [Greek *glōssa* "tongue"]

hy•po•gly•ce•mia \ˌhī-pə-ˌglī-ˈsē-mē-ə\ *n* : abnormal decrease of sugar in the blood [Greek *glykys* "sweet"] — **hy•po•gly•ce•mic** \-mik\ *adj*

hy•poph•y•sis \hī-ˈpäf-ə-səs\ *n, pl* **-y•ses** \-ə-ˌsēz\ : PITUITARY GLAND [Greek, "attachment beneath", from *hypophyein* "to grow beneath", from *hypo* "under" + *phyein* "to grow"] — **hy•poph•y•se•al** \hī-ˌpäf-ə-ˈsē-əl\ *adj*

hy•po•style \ˈhī-pə-ˌstīl\ *adj* : having the roof resting on rows of columns [Greek *hypostylos*, from *hypo* "under" + *stylos* "pillar"]

hy•po•sul•fite \ˌhī-pō-ˈsəl-ˌfīt\ *n* : a chemical $Na_2S_2O_3$ used especially as a fixing agent in photography

hy•po•ten•sion \ˌhī-pō-ˈten-chən\ *n* : LOW BLOOD PRESSURE — **hy•po•ten•sive** \-ˈten-siv\ *adj or n*

hy•pot•e•nuse \hī-ˈpät-n-ˌüs, -ˌüz, -ˌyüs, -ˌyüz\ *n* : the side of a right triangle that is opposite the right angle [Latin *hypotenusa*, from Greek *hypoteinousa*, from *hypoteinein* "to subtend", from *hypo* "under" + *teinein* "to stretch"]

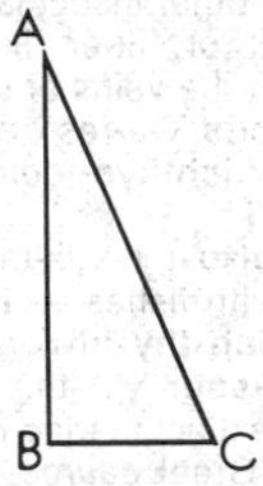

AC hypotenuse

hy•po•thal•a•mus \ˌhī-pō-ˈthal-ə-məs\ *n* : a part of the brain that lies beneath the thalamus, produces hormones which pass to the front part of the pituitary gland, and is important in the regulation of the activities of the autonomic nervous system — **hy•po•tha•lam•ic** \-thə-ˈlam-ik\ *adj*

hy•poth•e•sis \hī-ˈpäth-ə-səs\ *n, pl* **-e•ses** \-ə-ˌsēz\ **1** : something not proved but assumed to be true for purposes of argument or further study or investigation **2** : the conditional clause in a conditional statement ⟨"If P" is the *hypothesis* in the statement "If P then Q"⟩ [Greek, "supposition", from *hypotithenai* "to put under, suppose", from *hypo* "under", + *tithenai* "to put"]

• **syn** HYPOTHESIS, THEORY, LAW mean a formula derived by inference from scientific data that explains a principle operating in nature. HYPOTHESIS implies insufficient evidence to provide more than a tentative explanation; THEORY implies a greater range of evidence and greater likelihood of truth; LAW applies to a statement of order and relation in nature that has been found to be invariable under the same conditions.

hy•poth•e•size \hī-ˈpäth-ə-ˌsīz\ *vb* **1** : to make a hypothesis **2** : to adopt as a hypothesis

hy•po•thet•i•cal \ˌhī-pə-ˈthet-i-kəl\ *adj* **1** : involving hypothesis : ASSUMED **2** : of or depending on supposition : CONJECTURAL — **hy•po•thet•i•cal•ly** \-i-kə-lē, -klē\ *adv*

hy•po•thy•roid•ism \ˌhī-pō-ˈthī-ˌrȯid-ˌiz-əm\ *n* : deficient activity of the thyroid gland; *also* : the resultant condition marked especially by lowered metabolic rate and loss of vigor — compare GOITER — **hy•po•thy•roid** \-ˌrȯid\ *adj*

hy•po•ton•ic \ˌhī-pə-ˈtän-ik\ *adj* : having a lower osmotic pressure than a fluid under comparison — **hy•po•to•nic•i•ty** \-tə-ˈnis-ət-ē\ *n*

hyp•ox•ia \hip-ˈäk-sē-ə, hī-ˈpäk-\ *n* : a deficiency of oxygen reaching the tissues of the body — **hyp•ox•ic** \-sik\ *adj*

hyp•som•e•ter \hip-ˈsäm-ət-ər\ *n* : any of various instruments for determining the height of trees by triangulation [Greek *hypsos* "height"]

hy•rax \ˈhī-ˌraks\ *n, pl* **hy•rax•es** *also* **hy•ra•ces** \ˈhī-rə-ˌsēz\ : any of several small thickset Old World ungulate mammals (order Hyracoidea) — called also *coney* [Greek, "shrew"]

hys•sop \ˈhis-əp\ *n* **1** : a plant used in purificatory sprinkling rites by the ancient Hebrews **2** : a woody European mint with pungent aromatic leaves sometimes used in folk medicine for bruises [Old English *ysope*, from Latin *hyssopus*, from Greek *hyssōpos*, of Semitic origin]

hys•te•ria \his-ˈter-ē-ə, -ˈtir-\ *n* **1** : a neurosis marked by emotional excitability and a tendency to develop sensory and physical disturbances with no apparent organic basis **2** : unmanageable fear or emotional excess [derived from Greek *hystera* "womb"; from the former notion that hysterical women were suffering from disturbances of the womb] — **hys•ter•ic** \-ˈter-ik\ *n*

hys•ter•i•cal \-ˈter-i-kəl\ *also* **hys•ter•ic** \-ˈter-ik\ *adj* : of, relating to, or exhibiting hysteria or emotional excess — **hys•ter•i•cal•ly** \-i-kə-lē, -klē\ *adv*

hys•ter•ics \his-ˈter-iks\ *n sing or pl* : a fit of uncontrollable laughter or crying : HYSTERIA

i—-ize

i \ˈī\ *n, pl* **i's** *or* **is** \ˈīz\ *often cap* **1** : the 9th letter of the English alphabet **2** : one in Roman numerals **3** : a grade rating a student's work as incomplete

I \ī, ˈī, ə\ *pron* : the one who is speaking or writing ⟨*I* feel fine⟩ ⟨it wasn't *I*⟩ — *compare* ME, MINE, MY, WE [Old English *ic*]

-i- — used as a connective vowel to join word elements especially of Latin origin ⟨pesticide⟩ [Latin, stem vowel of most nouns and adjectives in combination]

-ia *n suffix* **1** : pathological condition ⟨hyster*ia*⟩ **2** : genus of plants or animals ⟨Fuchs*ia*⟩ **3** : territory : world : society ⟨suburb*ia*⟩ [New Latin, from Latin and Greek, suffix forming feminine nouns]

-ial *adj suffix* : [1]-AL ⟨manor*ial*⟩ [Latin *-ialis*, from *-i-* + *-alis* "-al"]

iamb \ˈī-ˌam, -ˌamb\ *or* **iam•bus** \ī-ˈam-bəs\ *n, pl* **iambs** \ˈī-ˌamz\ *or* **iam•bus•es** : a metrical foot consisting of one unaccented syllable followed by one accented syllable (as in *away*) [Latin *iambus* "metrical foot of one short syllable followed by one long syllable", from Greek *iambos*] — **iam•bic** \ī-ˈam-bik\ *adj*

-ian — see -AN

-iana — see -ANA

-i•a•sis \ˈī-ə-səs\ *n suffix, pl* **-i•a•ses** \-ˌsēz\ : disease having characteristics of or produced by (something specified) ⟨ame*biasis*⟩ [New Latin, from Greek, suffix of action]

iat•ro•gen•ic \ī-ˌa-trə-ˈjen-ik\ *adj* : caused by the physician ⟨*iatrogenic* illness⟩ [Greek *iatros* "physician"]

-i•a•try \ˈī-ə-trē, *in a few words* ē-ˌa-trē\ *n combining form* : medical treatment : healing ⟨psych*iatry*⟩ [Greek *iatreia* "art of healing", from *iatros* "physician"]

Ibe•ri•an \ī-ˈbir-ē-ən\ *n* **1** : a member of one or more Caucasoid peoples anciently inhabiting the peninsula comprising Spain and Portugal **2** : a native or inhabitant of Spain or Portugal [*Iberia*, peninsula in Europe] — **Iberian** *adj*

\ə\ **abut**	\au̇\ **out**	\i\ **tip**	\ȯ\ **saw**	\u̇\ **foot**
\ər\ **further**	\ch\ **chin**	\ī\ **life**	\ȯi\ **coin**	\y\ **yet**
\a\ **mat**	\e\ **pet**	\j\ **job**	\th\ **thin**	\yü\ **few**
\ā\ **take**	\ē\ **easy**	\ng\ **sing**	\t͟h\ **this**	\yu̇\ **cure**
\ä\ **cot, cart**	\g\ **go**	\ō\ **bone**	\ü\ **food**	\zh\ **vision**

ibex \ˈī-ˌbeks\ *n, pl* **ibex** *or* **ibex•es** : any of several wild goats living chiefly in high mountain areas of the Old World and having large recurved horns transversely ridged in front [Latin]

ibex

ibi•dem \ˈib-ə-ˌdem, ib-ˈīd-əm\ *adv* : in the same place [Latin]

-ibility — see -ABILITY

ibis \ˈī-bəs\ *n, pl* **ibis** *or* **ibis•es** : any of several wading birds related to the herons but distinguished by a long slender downward curving bill [Latin, from Greek, from Egyptian *hby*]

-ible — see -ABLE

1-ic \ik\ *adj suffix* **1** : having the character or form of : being : consisting of ⟨panoram*ic*⟩ ⟨run*ic*⟩ **2 a** : of or relating to ⟨alderman*ic*⟩ **b** : related to, derived from, or containing ⟨alcohol*ic*⟩ ⟨ole*ic*⟩ **3** : in the manner of : like that of : characteristic of ⟨Byron*ic*⟩ **4** : associated or dealing with : utilizing ⟨electron*ic*⟩ **5** : characterized by : exhibiting ⟨nostalg*ic*⟩ : affected with ⟨parapleg*ic*⟩ **6** : caused by ⟨amoeb*ic*⟩ **7** : tending to produce ⟨analges*ic*⟩ **8** : having a valence higher than in compounds or ions named with an adjective ending in *-ous* ⟨ferric iron⟩ [Latin *-icus*]

2-ic *n suffix* : one having the character or nature of : one belonging to or associated with : one exhibiting or affected by : one that produces [Latin *-icus,* from *-icus,* adj. suffix]

-i•cal \i-kəl\ *adj suffix* : -IC ⟨geolog*ical*⟩ ⟨symmetr*ical*⟩ — sometimes differing from *-ic* in that adjectives formed with *-ical* have a wider range of meaning than corresponding adjectives in *-ic* [Late Latin *-icalis,* from nouns in *-icus* + Latin *-alis* "-al"]

1ice \ˈīs\ *n* **1 a** : frozen water **b** : an expanse of frozen water **2** : a state of coldness (as from formality or reserve) **3** : a substance resembling ice **4** : a frozen dessert; *esp* : one containing no milk or cream [Old English *īs*] — **on ice 1** : with every likelihood of being won or accomplished **2** : in reserve or safekeeping

2ice *vb* **1 a** : to coat or become coated with ice : change into ice **b** : to chill with ice **c** : to supply with ice **2** : to cover with or as if with icing

ice age *n* **1** : a time of widespread glaciation **2** *cap I & A* : the Pleistocene glacial epoch

ice bag *n* : a waterproof bag to hold ice for local application of cold to the body

ice•berg \ˈīs-ˌbərg\ *n* : a large floating mass of ice detached from a glacier [probably from Danish or Norwegian *isberg,* from *is* "ice" + *berg* "mountain"]

ice•boat \-ˌbōt\ *n* : a skeleton boat or frame on runners propelled on ice usually by sails

iceboat

ice•bound \-ˌbau̇nd\ *adj* : surrounded or obstructed by ice

ice•box \-ˌbäks\ *n* : REFRIGERATOR

ice•break•er \-ˌbrā-kər\ *n* **1** : a ship equipped to make and maintain a channel through ice **2** : something that breaks the ice (as at a social occasion)

ice cap *n* : a glacier forming on an extensive area of relatively level land and flowing outward from its center

ice–cold \ˈī-ˈskōld\ *adj* : extremely cold

ice cream \ī-ˈskrēm, ī-ˈ, ˈī-ˌ\ *n* : a flavored and sweetened frozen food containing cream or butterfat and usually eggs

ice field *n* **1** : an extensive sheet of sea ice **2** : ICE CAP

ice floe *n* : a flat free mass of floating sea ice

ice hockey *n* : a game played on an ice rink between two teams of six players in which the players move a puck along the ice with sticks and try to shoot it past the opposing goalkeeper into the goal

ice•house \ˈīs-ˌhau̇s\ *n* : a building for storing ice

1Ice•lan•dic \ī-ˈslan-dik\ *adj* : of, relating to, or characteristic of Iceland, the Icelanders, or Icelandic

2Icelandic *n* : the Germanic language of the Icelandic people

Ice•land moss \ˌī-slənd-, -slən-, -ˌsland-, -ˌslan-\ *n* : an arctic lichen sometimes used medicinally or as food

Iceland spar *n* : a pure transparent variety of calcite

ice•man \ˈī-ˌsman\ *n* : one who sells or delivers ice

ice pack *n* : an expanse of pack ice

ice pick *n* : a hand tool ending in a spike for chipping ice

ice sheet *n* : ICE CAP

ice–skate \ˈīs-ˌskāt, ˈī-\ *vi* : to skate on ice — **ice skater** *n*

ice skate *n* : a metal runner usually attached to the bottom of a boot that is used for skating on ice

ice storm *n* : a storm in which falling rain freezes as it lands

ice water *n* : chilled or iced water especially for drinking

ich•neu•mon \ik-ˈnü-mən, -ˈnyü-\ *n* **1** : MONGOOSE **2** : ICHNEUMON FLY [Latin, from Greek *ichneumōn,* literally, "tracker", from *ichneuein* "to track", from *ichnos* "track, trail"]

△ **origin** The ancient Egyptians thought very highly of the African mongoose (a close relative of the mongoose of India) because they believed that it sought out and devoured the eggs of crocodiles. The Greeks, hearing this story, named the beast *ichneumōn,* which means "tracker". In English we call any mongoose, including the Indian, *ichneumon.* The Greek word *ichneumōn* was also used for a certain kind of small wasp that hunts spiders. We use *ichneumon* today for an insect rather distantly related to the Greek *ichneumōn.*

ichneumon fly *n* : any of numerous small insects which are related to the wasps and whose larvae are usually internal parasites of other insect larvae

ichor \ˈīk-ˌȯr, ˈīk-ər, ˈik-\ *n* : an ethereal fluid taking the place of blood in the veins of the ancient Greek gods [Greek *ichōr*] — **ichor•ous** \-ə-rəs\ *adj*

ichthy- *or* **ichthyo-** *combining form* : fish ⟨*ichthy*ology⟩ [Greek *ichthys*]

ich•thy•ol•o•gy \ˌik-thē-ˈäl-ə-jē\ *n* : a branch of zoology that deals with fishes — **ich•thy•o•log•i•cal** \ˌik-thē-ə-ˈläj-i-kəl\ *adj* — **ich•thy•ol•o•gist** \ˌik-thē-ˈäl-ə-jəst\ *n*

ich•thyo•saur \ˈik-thē-ə-ˌsȯr\ *n* : any of an order (Ichthyosauria) of extinct marine reptiles with a fish-shaped body and long snout [Greek *sauros* "lizard"] — **ich•thyo•sau•ri•an** \ˌik-thē-ə-ˈsȯr-ē-ən\ *adj or n*

-i•cian \ˈish-ən\ *n suffix* : specialist : practitioner ⟨beaut*ician*⟩ [Old French *-icien,* from Latin *-ica* "-ic, -ics" + Old French *-ien* "-ian"]

ici•cle \ˈī-ˌsik-əl\ *n* : a hanging mass of ice formed by the freezing of dripping water [Middle English *isikel,* from *is* "ice" + *ikel* "icicle", from Old English *gicel*]

△ **origin** Old English *gicel,* "icicle", became Middle English *ikyl* or *ikel* and later modern English *ickle,* which still survives as a dialect word in Yorkshire, England. The word for ice in Old English is *īs,* and in a manuscript of about the year 1000 we find Latin *stiria,* "icicle", glossed somewhat redundantly as *īses gicel,* that is, "an icicle of ice". Some three hundred years later in Middle English this became the compound we know today as *icicle,* which means precisely what it did a thousand years ago.

1ic•ing \ˈī-sing\ *n* : a sweet and usually creamy mixture used to coat baked goods — called also *frosting*

2icing *n* : the shooting of a hockey puck the length of the rink

icon \ˈī-ˌkän\ *n* **1** : a usually pictorial representation **2** *also* **ikon** : a conventional religious image typically painted on a small wooden panel and used in the devotions of Eastern Christians [Latin, from Greek *eikōn,* from *eikenai* "to resemble"] — **icon•ic** \ī-ˈkän-ik\ *adj* — **icon•i•cal•ly** \-ˈkän-i-kə-lē, -klē\ *adv*

icon•o•clasm \ī-ˈkän-ə-ˌklaz-əm\ *n* : the doctrine, practice, or attitude of an iconoclast

icon•o•clast \-ˌklast\ *n* **1** : one who destroys religious images or opposes their veneration **2** : one who attacks established beliefs or institutions [Medieval Latin *iconoclastes,* from Middle Greek *eikonoklastēs,* from Greek *eikōn* "image" + *klan* "to break"] — **icon•o•clas•tic** \ī-ˌkän-ə-ˈklas-tik\ *adj* — **icon•o•clas•ti•cal•ly** \-ti-kə-lē, -klē\ *adv*

icon•o•scope \ī-ˈkän-ə-ˌskōp\ *n* : a camera tube that transforms pictures into electrical signals for television

ico•sa•he•dron \ī-ˌkō-sə-ˈhē-drən, -ˌkäs-ə-\ *n, pl* **-drons** *or* **-dra** \-drə\ : a polyhedron having 20 faces [Greek *eikosaedron,* from *eikosi* "twenty" + *-edron* "-hedron"]

-ics \iks, ˌiks\ *n sing or pl suffix* **1** : study : knowledge : skill : practice ⟨linguist*ics*⟩ **2** : characteristic actions or activities ⟨acrobat*ics*⟩ **3** : characteristic qualities, operations, or phenomena ⟨acoust*ics*⟩

ic•ter•us \ˈik-tə-rəs\ *n* : JAUNDICE 1 [Greek *ikteros*] — **ic•ter•ic** \ik-ˈter-ik\ *adj*

ic•tus \ˈik-təs\ *n* : the recurring stress or beat in a rhythmic or metrical series of sounds [Latin *ictus,* from *icere* "to strike"]

icy \ˈī-sē\ *adj* **ic•i•er; -est 1 a** : covered with, full of, or consisting of ice ⟨*icy* roads⟩ **b** : intensely cold ⟨*icy* weather⟩ **2** : characterized by coldness : FRIGID ⟨an *icy* stare⟩ — **ic•i•ly** \-sə-lē\ *adv* — **ic•i•ness** \-sē-nəs\ *n*

id \ˈid\ *n* : the one of the three divisions of the psyche in psychoanalytic theory that is completely unconscious and is the source of psychic energy derived from instinctual needs and drives — compare EGO, SUPEREGO [Latin, 'it"]

I'd \īd, ˌīd\ : I had : I should : I would

-ide \ˌīd\ *also* **-id** \əd, id, ˌid\ *n suffix* **1** : binary chemical compound ⟨hydrogen sulf*ide*⟩ ⟨cyan*ide*⟩ **2** : chemical compound derived from or related to another (usually specified) compound ⟨anhydr*ide*⟩ ⟨glucos*ide*⟩ [French *-ide* (as in *oxide*)]

idea \ī-ˈdē-ə, ˈīd-ē-ə, *especially South* ˈīd-ē\ *n* **1** : a plan of action : INTENTION ⟨my *idea* is to study law⟩ **2** : something imagined or pictured in the mind : NOTION ⟨form an *idea* of a foreign country from reading⟩ **3** : a central meaning or purpose ⟨the *idea* of the game is to keep from getting caught⟩ [Latin, "form, notion", from Greek, from *idein* "to see"] — **idea•less** \ī-ˈdē-ə-ləs\ *adj*

• **syn** CONCEPT, CONCEPTION; IDEA may apply to a mental image of something seen, known, or imagined or to an abstraction or to something assumed or vaguely sensed ⟨the *idea* of interplanetary travel⟩ ⟨a new *idea* for redecorating a room⟩ ⟨*ideas* about the nature of democracy⟩ CONCEPT may apply to the idea formed after knowing many instances of a type or to an idea of what a thing ought to be ⟨the *concepts* of modern architecture⟩ ⟨the *concept* of the role of a citizen in a democracy⟩ CONCEPTION is often interchangeable with CONCEPT, but it may stress the act of imagining or formulating rather than the result ⟨the primitive *conception* of all nature as animate⟩

¹ide•al \ī-ˈdē-əl, -ˈdēl\ *adj* **1** : existing only in the mind : not real **2** : embodying or symbolizing an ideal : PERFECT ⟨an *ideal* place for a picnic⟩ ⟨*ideal* weather⟩

²ideal *n* **1** : a standard of perfection, beauty, or excellence **2** : a perfect type : a model for imitation **3** : an ultimate object or aim of endeavor : GOAL — **ide•al•less** \ī-ˈdē-əl-ləs, -ˈdēl-\ *adj*

ide•al•ism \ī-ˈdē-ə-ˌliz-əm, -ˈdē-ˌliz-\ *n* **1 a** : a theory that ultimate reality lies in a realm transcending phenomena **b** : a theory that reality lies essentially in consciousness or reason **2** : the practice of forming ideals or living under their influence **3** : literary or artistic theory or practice that affirms the value of imagination over the representation of objective reality — compare REALISM

ide•al•ist \ī-ˈdē-ə-ləst, -ˈdē-ləst\ *n* **1 a** : an adherent of a philosophical theory of idealism **b** : an artist or author who advocates or practices idealism in art or writing **2** : one guided by ideals; *esp* : one that places ideals before practical considerations — **ide•al•is•tic** \-ˌdē-ə-ˈlis-tik, -ˌdē-ˈlis-\ *adj* — **ide•al•is•ti•cal•ly** \-ti-kə-lē, -klē\ *adv*

ide•al•ize \ī-ˈdē-ə-ˌlīz, -ˈdē-ˌlīz\ *vt* : to think of or represent as ideal ⟨*idealize* life on a farm⟩ — **ide•al•i•za•tion** \ī-ˌdē-ə-lə-ˈzā-shən, -ˌdē-lə-\ *n* — **ide•al•iz•er** *n*

ide•al•ly \ī-ˈdē-ə-lē, -ˈdē-lē\ *adv* **1** : in idea or imagination : MENTALLY ⟨it's possible only *ideally,* not in fact⟩ **2** : conformably to an ideal : PERFECTLY ⟨*ideally* suited to the position⟩

ide•ation \ˌīd-ē-ˈā-shən\ *n* : the capacity for or the act of forming or entertaining ideas — **ide•ate** \ˈīd-ē-ˌāt\ *vb* — **ide•ation•al** \ˌīd-ē-ˈā-shnəl, -shən-l\ *adj*

idem \ˈīd-ˌem, ˈēd-, ˈid-\ *pron* : something previously mentioned : SAME [Latin, "same"]

iden•ti•cal \ī-ˈdent-i-kəl, ə-\ *adj* **1** : being the same ⟨the *identical* place we stopped before⟩ **2** : being essentially the same or exactly alike ⟨*identical* hats⟩ — **iden•ti•cal•ly** \-i-kə-lē, -klē\ *adv* — **iden•ti•cal•ness** \-kəl-nəs\ *n*

identical twin *n* : either member of a pair of twins that are produced from a single fertilized egg cell, carry the same genes, and are physically similar

iden•ti•fi•ca•tion \ī-ˌdent-ə-fə-ˈkā-shən, ə-\ *n* **1** : an act of identifying : the state of being identified **2** : evidence of identity ⟨carry *identification*⟩

iden•ti•fy \ī-ˈdent-ə-ˌfī, ə-\ *vt* **-fied; -fy•ing 1 a** : to regard as identical ⟨*identifies* democracy with capitalism⟩ **b** : to think of as united (as in principle) ⟨groups that are *identified* with conservation⟩ **2** : to establish the identity of ⟨*identified* the dog as my lost pet⟩ — **iden•ti•fi•able** \-ˌfī-ə-bəl\ *adj* — **iden•ti•fi•ably** \-blē\ *adv* — **iden•ti•fi•er** \-ˌfī-ər, -ˌfīr\ *n*

iden•ti•ty \ī-ˈdent-ət-ē, ə-\ *n, pl* **-ties 1** : the fact or condition of being exactly alike : SAMENESS ⟨an *identity* of interests⟩ **2** : distinguishing character or personality : INDIVIDUALITY **3** : the fact of being the same as something described or known to exist ⟨establish the *identity* of stolen goods⟩ **4 a** : an equation that is true for all values substituted for the variables **b** : IDENTITY ELEMENT [Middle French *identité,* from Late Latin *identitas,* from Latin *idem* "same", from *is* "that"]

identity element *n* : an element (as 0 in the set of all integers under addition) of a set that leaves any element of the set to which it belongs unchanged when combined with it by a specified operation

ideo•gram \ˈid-ē-ə-ˌgram, ˈid-\ *n* **1** : a picture of symbol used in a system of writing to represent a thing or an idea but not a particular word or phrase for it **2** : a character or symbol used in a system of writing to represent an entire word

ideo•graph \-ˌgraf\ *n* : IDEOGRAM — **ideo•graph•ic** \ˌīd-ē-ə-ˈgraf-ik, ˌid-\ *adj* — **ideo•graph•i•cal•ly** \-ˈgraf-i-kə-lē, -klē\ *adv*

ide•ol•o•gy \ˌīd-ē-ˈäl-ə-jē, ˌid-\ *n, pl* **-gies 1** : a systematic body of concepts especially about human life or culture **2** : a manner or the content of thinking characteristic of an individual, group, or culture **3** : the integrated assertions, theories, and aims that constitute a political, social and economic program [French *idéologie,* from Greek *idea* "form, notion, idea"] — **ideo•log•i•cal** \-ē-ə-ˈläj-i-kəl\ *adj* — **ideo•log•i•cal•ly** \-i-kə-lē, -klē\ *adv* — **ide•ol•o•gist** \-ē-ˈäl-ə-jəst\ *n*

ides \ˈīdz\ *n pl* : the 15th day of March, May, July, or October or the 13th day of any other month in the ancient Roman calendar [Middle French, from Latin *idus*]

idio- *combining form* : one's own : personal : separate : distinct ⟨*idio*lect⟩ [Greek *idios* "one's own, private"]

id•i•o•cy \ˈid-ē-ə-sē\ *n, pl* **-cies 1** : extreme mental deficiency commonly due to a brain defect **2** : something notably stupid or foolish

id•io•lect \ˈid-ē-ə-ˌlekt\ *n* : the speech pattern of one individual [*idio-* + *-lect* (as in *dialect*)]

id•i•om \ˈid-ē-əm\ *n* **1** : the language peculiar to a group ⟨doctors speaking in their professional *idiom*⟩ **2** : the characteristic form of expression of a language ⟨know the vocabulary of a foreign language but not its *idiom*⟩ **3** : an expression that cannot be understood from the meanings of its separate words but must be learned as a whole ⟨the expression *give way,* meaning "retreat", is an *idiom*⟩ [Late Latin *idioma* "individual peculiarity of language", from Greek *idiōmat-, idiōma,* from *idios* "one's own"] — **id•i•om•at•ic** \ˌid-ē-ə-ˈmat-ik\ *adj* — **id•i•om•at•i•cal•ly** \-ˈmat-i-kə-lē, -klē\ *adv* — **id•i•om•at•ic•ness** \-ˈmat-ik-nəs\ *n*

id•io•syn•cra•sy \ˌid-ē-ə-ˈsing-krə-sē\ *n, pl* **-sies** : characteristic peculiarity of habit or structure [Greek *idiosynkrasia,* from *idios* "one's own" + *synkerannynai* "to blend", from *syn-* + *kerannynai* "to mix"] **syn** see ECCENTRICITY — **id•io•syn•crat•ic** \ˌid-ē-ō-sin-ˈkrat-ik\ *adj* — **id•io•syn•crat•i•cal•ly** \-ˈkrat-i-kə-lē, -klē\ *adv*

id•i•ot \ˈid-ē-ət\ *n* **1** : a person affected with idiocy; *esp* : a mentally retarded person having a mental age not exceeding three years and requiring complete custodial care **2** : a silly or foolish person [Latin *idiota* "ignorant person", from Greek *idiōtēs* "one in a private station, layman, ignorant person", from *idios* "one's own, private"] — **idiot** *adj*

△ **origin** The Greek adjective *idios* means "one's own" or "private". The derivative noun *idiōtēs* means "private person". A Greek *idiōtēs* was a person who was not in the public eye, who held no public office. From this sense came the sense "common man", and later "ignorant person" — a natural extension, for the common people of ancient Greece were not, in general, particularly learned. English *idiot* originally meant "ignorant

\ə\ **abut**	\au̇\ **out**	\i\ **tip**	\ȯ\ **saw**	\u̇\ **foot**
\ər\ **further**	\ch\ **chin**	\ī\ **life**	\ȯi\ **coin**	\y\ **yet**
\a\ **mat**	\e\ **pet**	\j\ **job**	\th\ **thin**	\yü\ **few**
\ā\ **take**	\ē\ **easy**	\ng\ **sing**	\t͟h\ **this**	\yu̇\ **cure**
\ä\ **cot, cart**	\g\ **go**	\ō\ **bone**	\ü\ **food**	\zh\ **vision**

person", but this mild meaning is now obsolete. By carrying ignorance to extremes, we have arrived at the *idiot* who is mentally deficient.

• **syn** IDIOT, IMBECILE, MORON mean one who is mentally defective and technically designate three grades of mental deficiency. An IDIOT is incapable of coherent speech and of avoiding ordinary hazards and therefore requires constant care; an IMBECILE is incapable of earning a living but can be taught to attend to his basic wants and to avoid ordinary dangers; a MORON can learn a simple trade but requires constant supervision in work and play.

id•i•ot•ic \ˌid-ē-ˈät-ik\ *adj* **1** : characterized by idiocy **2** : showing complete lack of thought : FOOLISH — **id•i•ot•i•cal•ly** \-ˈät-i-kə-lē, -klē\ *adv*

[1]**idle** \ˈīd-l\ *adj* **idler** \ˈīd-lər, -l-ər\; **idlest** \ˈīd-ləst, -l-əst\ **1** : lacking worth or basis ⟨*idle* rumor⟩ **2** : not employed : doing nothing ⟨*idle* workers⟩ ⟨*idle* machines⟩ **3** : disliking work : LAZY [Old English *īdel*] **syn** see INACTIVE — **idle•ness** \ˈīd-l-nəs\ *n* — **idly** \ˈīd-lē\ *adv*

[2]**idle** *vb* **idled**; **idling** \ˈīd-ling, -l-ing\ **1 a** : to spend time in idleness **b** : to move idly **2** : to run disengaged so that power is not used for useful work ⟨the engine is *idling*⟩ **3** : to pass in idleness : WASTE — **idler** \ˈīd-lər, -l-ər\ *n*

idol \ˈīd-l\ *n* **1** : an image of a god made or used as an object of worship **2** : one that is very greatly or excessively loved and admired [Old French *idole*, from Late Latin *idolum*, from Greek *eidōlon* "phantom, idol"]

idol•a•ter \ī-ˈdäl-ət-ər\ *n* **1** : a worshiper of idols **2** : a person that admires or loves intensely and often blindly [Middle French *idolatre*, from Late Latin *idolatres*, from Greek *eidōlatrēs*, from *eidōlon* "idol" + *-latrēs* "worshiper"]

idol•a•tress \ī-ˈdäl-ə-trəs\ *n* : a female idolater

idol•a•trous \ī-ˈdäl-ə-trəs\ *adj* **1** : of or relating to idolatry **2** : having the character of idolatry **3** : given to idolatry — **idol•a•trous•ly** *adv* — **idol•a•trous•ness** *n*

idol•a•try \-trē\ *n, pl* **-tries** **1** : the worship of a physical object as a god **2** : excessive attachment or devotion to something

idol•ize \ˈīd-l-ˌīz\ *vb* **1** : to worship idolatrously **2** : to love or admire to excess — **idol•iza•tion** \ˌīd-l-ə-ˈzā-shən\ *n* — **idol•iz•er** \ˈīd-l-ˌī-zər\ *n*

idyll *or* **idyl** \ˈīd-l\ *n* **1 a** : a simple poetic or prose work descriptive of peaceful rustic life or pastoral scenes **b** : a romantic narrative poem **2** : a fit subject for an idyll [Latin *idyllium*, from Greek *eidyllion*, from *eidos* "form"] — **idyl•lic** \ī-ˈdil-ik\ *adj* — **idyl•li•cal•ly** \-ˈdil-i-kə-lē, -klē\ *adv*

-ie *also* **-y** \ē\ *n suffix, pl* **-ies** **1** : little one : dear little one ⟨las*sie*⟩ ⟨son*ny*⟩ — sometimes used in names of articles of clothing ⟨night*ie*⟩ **2** : one belonging to : one having to do with ⟨cab*by*⟩ **3** : one of (such) a kind or quality ⟨good*y*⟩ ⟨smart*y*⟩ [Middle English]

-ier — see -ER

[1]**if** \if, əf, ˌif\ *conj* **1** : in the event that ⟨come *if* you can⟩ **2** : WHETHER ⟨asked *if* the mail had come⟩ **3** — used as a function word to introduce an exclamation expressing a wish ⟨*if* it would only rain⟩ **4** : even though ⟨an interesting *if* untenable argument⟩ [Old English *gif*]

[2]**if** \ˈif\ *n* **1** : CONDITION 3, STIPULATION **2** : SUPPOSITION ⟨a theory full of *ifs*⟩

-if•er•ous \ˈif-rəs, -ə-rəs\ *adj combining form* : -FEROUS

if•fy \ˈif-ē\ *adj* : full of contingencies or unknown qualities or conditions

-i•form \ə-ˌfȯrm\ *adj combining form* : -FORM

-i•fy \ə-ˌfī\ *vb suffix* **-i•fied**; **-i•fy•ing** : -FY

ig•loo \ˈig-lü\ *n, pl* **igloos** **1** : an Eskimo house often made of snow blocks and in the shape of a dome **2** : a structure shaped like a dome [Eskimo *iglu* "house"]

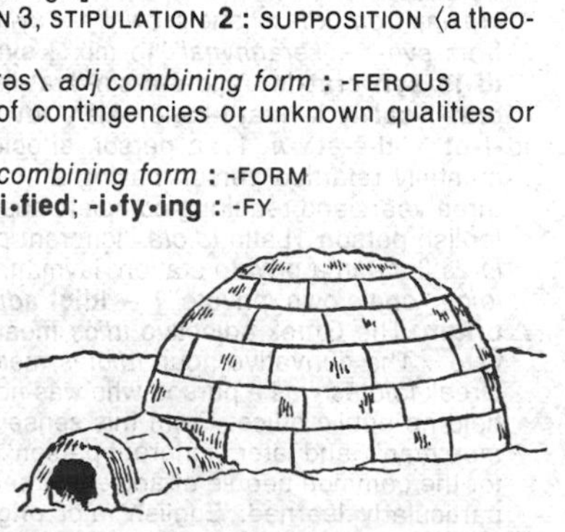

igloo 1

ig•ne•ous \ˈig-nē-əs\ *adj* **1** : of, relating to, or resembling fire : FIERY **2** : formed by solidification of magma ⟨*igneous* rock⟩ — Latin *igneus*, from *ignis* "fire"

ig•nis fatuus \ˌig-nəs-ˈfach-ə-wəs\ *n, pl* **ig•nes fat•ui** \-ˌnēz-ˈfach-ə-ˌwī\ **1** : a light that sometimes appears in the night over marshy ground and is often attributable to the combustion of gas from decomposed organic matter **2** : WILL-O'-THE-WISP 2 [Medieval Latin, literally, "foolish fire"]

ig•nite \ig-ˈnīt\ *vb* **1 a** : to set afire ⟨*ignite* a piece of paper⟩; *also* : KINDLE ⟨*ignite* a fire⟩ **b** : to cause (a fuel mixture) to burn **2** : to catch fire ⟨dry wood *ignites* quickly⟩ [Latin *ignire*, from *ignis* "fire" — **ig•nit•able** \-ˈnīt-ə-bəl\ *adj* — **ig•nit•er** *or* **ig•ni•tor** \-ˈnīt-ər\ *n*

ig•ni•tion \ig-ˈnish-ən\ *n* **1** : the act or action of igniting : KINDLING **2** : the process or means (as an electric spark) of igniting a fuel mixture

ig•no•ble \ig-ˈnō-bəl\ *adj* **1** : of low birth : PLEBEIAN **2** : characterized by baseness or meanness ⟨*ignoble* conduct⟩ [Latin *ignobilis*, from *in-* + *nobilis* "noble" — **ig•no•ble•ness** *n* — **ig•no•bly** \-blē\ *adv*

ig•no•min•i•ous \ˌig-nə-ˈmin-ē-əs\ *adj* **1** : marked by disgrace or shame : DISHONORABLE **2** : deserving of shame : DESPICABLE **3** : SHAMEFUL, DEGRADING ⟨an *ignominious* defeat⟩ — **ig•no•min•i•ous•ly** *adv* — **ig•no•min•i•ous•ness** *n*

ig•no•mi•ny \ˈig-nə-ˌmin-ē, ig-ˈnäm-ə-nē\ *n, pl* **-nies** **1** : deep personal humiliation and disgrace **2** : disgraceful conduct, quality, or action [Latin *ignominia*, from *ig-* (as in *ignorare* "to be ignorant of, ignore") + *nomen* "name, repute"]

ig•no•ra•mus \ˌig-nə-ˈrā-məs\ *n, pl* **-mus•es** : an utterly ignorant person : DUNCE [from *Ignoramus*, an ignorant lawyer in *Ignoramus (1615), a play by George Ruggle*]

ig•no•rance \ˈig-nə-rəns\ *n* : the state of being ignorant

ig•no•rant \-rənt\ *adj* **1 a** : lacking knowledge or education **b** : resulting from or showing lack of knowledge ⟨an *ignorant* mistake⟩ **2** : not knowing : UNAWARE ⟨*ignorant* of the true facts⟩ — **ig•no•rant•ly** *adv* — **ig•no•rant•ness** *n*

• **syn** ILLITERATE: IGNORANT indicates a lack of knowledge in general or of a particular thing; ILLITERATE implies inability to read or write or complete unfamiliarity with the world of learning ⟨the vast problem of teaching the *illiterate* millions of this world⟩

ig•nore \ig-ˈnōr, -ˈnȯr\ *vt* : to refuse to take notice of ⟨*ignore* an interruption⟩ [French *ignorer* "to be ignorant of", from Latin *ignorare* "to be ignorant of, ignore", from *ignarus* "ignorant, unknown", from *in-* + *gnoscere, noscere* "to know"] — **ig•nor•er** *n*

igua•na \i-ˈgwän-ə\ *n* : any of various large plant-eating tropical American lizards with a serrated crest on the back that are locally important as human food [Spanish, of American Indian origin]

iguana

IHS \ˌī-ˌā-ˈches\ — used as a Christian symbol and monogram for *Jesus* [Late Latin, part transliteration of Greek ΙΗΣ, abbreviation for ΙΗΣΟΥΣ *Iēsous* "Jesus"]

ikon *variant of* ICON

il- — see IN-

-ile \əl, ᵊl, ˌīl, ˌil\ *adj suffix* : of, relating to, or capable of ⟨contrac*tile*⟩ [Latin *-ilis*]

il•e•i•tis \ˌil-ē-ˈīt-əs\ *n* : inflammation of the ileum

il•e•um \ˈil-ē-əm\ *n, pl* **il•ea** \-ē-ə\ : the part of the small intestine between the jejunum and the large intestine [Latin, "groin, viscera"] — **il•e•al** \-ē-əl\ *adj*

ilex \ˈī-ˌleks\ *n* : HOLLY [Latin, a kind of oak]

il•i•um \ˈil-ē-əm\ *n, pl* **il•ia** \-ē-ə\ : the broad expanded upper one of the three bones composing either lateral half of the pelvis [Latin *ilium, ileum* "groin"] — **il•i•ac** \-ē-ˌak\ *adj*

ilk \ˈilk\ *n* : SORT 1, FAMILY — used chiefly in the phrase *of that ilk* [Old English *ilca* "same"]

[1]**ill** \ˈil\ *adj* **worse** \ˈwərs\; **worst** \ˈwərst\ **1** : showing or implying evil intention ⟨*ill* deeds⟩ **2 a** : causing suffering or distress : DISAGREEABLE ⟨*ill* weather⟩ **b** : not normal or sound : FAILING ⟨*ill* health⟩ **c** : not in good health ⟨an *ill* person⟩ **d** : NAUSEATED ⟨felt *ill*⟩ **3** : UNFORTUNATE, UNLUCKY ⟨an *ill* omen⟩ **4** : UNKIND, UNFRIENDLY ⟨*ill* fellings⟩ **5** : not right or proper ⟨an *ill* use of power⟩ [Old Norse *illr* "evil"] **syn** see SICK

[2]**ill** *adv* **worse**; **worst** **1 a** : with displeasure ⟨the remark was *ill* received⟩ **b** : HARSHLY ⟨*ill* treated⟩ **2** : in a reprehensible man-

ner ⟨an *ill*-spent youth⟩ **3** : SCARCELY ⟨can *ill* afford it⟩ **4** : BADLY, POORLY ⟨*ill* equipped⟩

3ill *n* **1** : EVIL, MISFORTUNE ⟨for good or *ill*⟩ **2** : SICKNESS ⟨childhood *ills*⟩ **3** : TROUBLE, AFFLICTION ⟨the *ills* of society⟩ **4** : something that reflects unfavorably ⟨spoke no *ill* of them⟩

I'll \ī, ˌīl\ : I shall : I will

ill–ad•vised \ˌil-əd-ˈvīzd\ *adj* : showing lack of wise and sufficient advice or consideration : UNWISE — **ill–ad•vis•ed•ly** \-ˈvī-zəd-lē\ *adv*

ill–bred \ˈil-ˈbred\ *adj* : badly brought up : IMPOLITE

il•le•gal \il-ˈlē-gəl, -ˈē-\ *adj* : not lawful — **il•le•gal•i•ty** \ˌil-ē-ˈgal-ət-ē\ *n* — **il•le•gal•ly** \il-ˈlē-gə-lē, -ˈē-\ *adv*

il•leg•ible \il-ˈlej-ə-bəl, -ˈej-\ *adj* : impossible or very hard to read ⟨*illegible* handwriting⟩ **syn** see UNREADABLE — **il•leg•ibil•i•ty** \il-ˌej-ə-ˈbil-ət-ē\ *n* — **il•leg•ibly** \il-ˈlej-ə-blē, -ˈej-\ *adv*

il•le•git•i•mate \ˌil-i-ˈjit-ə-mət\ *adj* **1** : born of a father and mother who are not married **2** : not correctly deduced or reasoned ⟨an *illegitimate* conclusion⟩ **3** : not lawful or proper — **il•le•git•i•ma•cy** \-ˈjit-ə-mə-sē\ *n* — **il•le•git•i•mate•ly** *adv*

ill–fat•ed \ˈil-ˈfāt-əd\ *adj* : doomed to failure or disaster ⟨an *ill-fated* expedition⟩

ill–fa•vored \-ˈfā-vərd\ *adj* : unattractive in physical appearance; *esp* : having an ugly face

ill–got•ten \-ˈgät-n\ *adj* : acquired by evil means

ill–hu•mored \ˈil-ˈhyü-mərd, -ˈyü-\ *adj* : SURLY, IRRITABLE ⟨became *ill-humored* when tired⟩ — **ill–hu•mored•ly** *adv*

il•lib•er•al \il-ˈlib-rəl, -ˈib-, -ə-rəl\ *adj* : not broad-minded : BIGOTED — **il•lib•er•al•i•ty** \il-ˌib-ə-ˈral-ət-ē\ *n* — **il•lib•er•al•ly** \-ˈlib-rə-lē, -ˈib-, -ə-rə-\ *adv* — **il•lib•er•al•ness** *n*

il•lic•it \il-ˈlis-ət, -ˈis-\ *adj* : not permitted : UNLAWFUL — **il•lic•it•ly** *adv*

il•lim•it•able \il-ˈlim-ət-ə-bəl, -ˈim-\ *adj* : incapable of being limited : BOUNDLESS — **il•lim•it•abil•i•ty** \-ˌlim-ət-ə-ˈbil-ət-ē, -ˌim-\ *n* — **il•lim•it•able•ness** \-ˈlim-ət-ə-bəl-nəs, -ˈim-\ *n* — **il•lim•it•ably** \-blē\ *adv*

il•lit•er•a•cy \il-ˈlit-ə-rə-sē, -ˈit-; -ˈli-trə-sē, -ˈi-trə-\ *n, pl* **-cies** **1** : the quality or state of being illiterate; *esp* : inability to read or write **2** : a mistake or crudity made by one who is illiterate

il•lit•er•ate \il-ˈlit-ə-rət, -ˈit-; -ˈli-trət, -ˈi-trət\ *adj* **1** : having little or no education; *esp* : unable to read or write **2 a** : showing or marked by a lack of familiarity with language and literature **b** : showing ignorance of the fundamentals of a particular field of knowledge **syn** see IGNORANT — **illiterate** *n* — **il•lit•er•ate•ly** *adv* — **il•lit•er•ate•ness** *n*

ill–man•nered \ˈil-ˈman-ərd\ *adj* : marked by bad manners : RUDE

ill–na•tured \-ˈnā-chərd\ *adj* : having a bad disposition — **ill–na•tured•ly** *adv*

ill•ness \ˈil-nəs\ *n* : an unhealthy condition of body or mind : SICKNESS

il•log•i•cal \il-ˈläj-i-kəl, -ˈäj-\ *adj* : not observing the principles of logic or good reasoning — **il•log•i•cal•ly** \-i-kə-lē, -klē\ *adv* — **il•log•i•cal•ness** \-kəl-nəs\ *n*

ill–starred \ˈil-ˈstärd\ *adj* : ILL-FATED ⟨*ill-starred* lovers⟩

ill–tem•pered \-ˈtem-pərd\ *adj* : ILL-NATURED, QUARRELSOME — **ill–tem•pered•ly** *adv*

ill–treat \-ˈtrēt\ *vt* : to treat cruelly or improperly : MALTREAT — **ill–treat•ment** \-mənt\ *n*

il•lu•mi•nant \il-ˈü-mə-nənt\ *n* : an illuminating device (as an electric lamp) or substance (as natural gas)

il•lu•mi•nate \-ˌnāt\ *vt* **1 a** : to supply or brighten with light : light up ⟨*illuminate* a building⟩ **b** : ENLIGHTEN **2** : to make clear : EXPLAIN **3** : to decorate with designs or pictures in gold or colors ⟨*illuminate* a manuscript⟩ [Latin *illuminare,* from *in-* + *luminare* "to light up", from *lumen* "light"] — **il•lu•mi•na•tive** \-ˌnāt-iv\ *adj* — **il•lu•mi•na•tor** \-ˌnāt-ər\ *n*

illuminating gas *n* : a gas that is burned for illumination

il•lu•mi•na•tion \il-ˌü-mə-ˈnā-shən\ *n* **1** : the action of illuminating or state of being illuminated: as **a** : spiritual or intellectual enlightenment **b** : decorative lighting or lighting effects **c** : decoration by the art of illuminating **2** : the quantity of light or the luminous flux per unit area on an intercepting surface at any given point

il•lu•mine \il-ˈü-mən\ *vt* : ILLUMINATE

ill–us•age \ˈil-ˈyü-sij, -ˈyü-zij\ *n* : harsh or abusive treatment

ill–use \-ˈyüz\ *vt* : to use badly : MALTREAT, ABUSE

il•lu•sion \il-ˈü-zhən\ *n* **1 a** : a misleading image (as a hallucination) presented to the vision **b** : perception of something actually existing so as to misinterpret its real nature **c** : a figure or pattern capable of being perceived in several ways — called also *optical illusion* **2** : the state or fact of being led to accept as true something unreal or imagined **3** : a misleading or inaccurate idea or impression of reality [Middle French, from Latin *illusio* "action of mocking", from *illudere* "to mock at", from *in-* + *ludere* "to play, mock"] **syn** see DELUSION — **il•lu•sion•ary** \-zhə-ˌner-ē\ *adj*

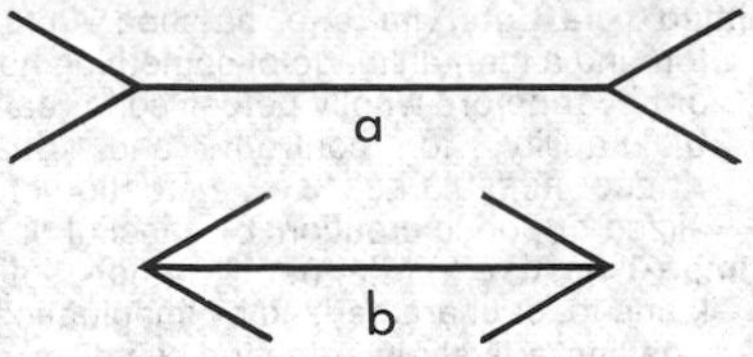

illusion 1c: *a* equals *b* in length

il•lu•sion•ist \il-ˈüzh-nəst, -ə-nəst\ *n* : one that produces illusions; *esp* : a ventriloquist or sleight-of-hand performer

il•lu•sive \il-ˈü-siv, -ˈü-ziv\ *adj* : ILLUSORY — **il•lu•sive•ly** *adv* — **il•lu•sive•ness** *n*

il•lu•so•ry \il-ˈüs-rē, -ˈüz-, -ə-rē\ *adj* : based on or producing illusion : DECEPTIVE — **il•lu•so•ri•ly** \-rə-lē\ *adv* — **il•lu•so•ri•ness** \-rē-nəs\ *n*

il•lus•trate \ˈil-ə-ˌstrāt\ *vt* **1** : to make clear especially by serving as or giving an example or instance ⟨*illustrate* a point from one's own experience⟩ **2 a** : to provide with pictures or figures intended to explain or decorate ⟨*illustrate* a book⟩ **b** : to serve to explain or decorate ⟨*illustrates* the operation of a computer⟩ [Latin *illustrare,* from *in-* + *lustrare* "to purify, make bright"] — **il•lus•tra•tor** \-ˌstrāt-ər\ *n*

il•lus•tra•tion \ˌil-ə-ˈstrā-shən\ *n* **1** : the action of illustrating : the condition of being illustrated **2 a** : an example or instance intended to make something clear **b** : a picture or diagram intended to explain or decorate

il•lus•tra•tive \il-ˈəs-trət-iv\ *adj* : serving, tending, or designed to illustrate ⟨an *illustrative* diagram⟩ — **il•lus•tra•tive•ly** *adv*

il•lus•tri•ous \il-ˈəs-trē-əs\ *adj* : notably outstanding because of rank or achievement : EMINENT — **il•lus•tri•ous•ly** *adv* — **il•lus•tri•ous•ness** *n*

ill will *n* : unfriendly feeling : MALICE

ill–wish•er \ˈil-ˈwish-ər\ *n* : one that wishes ill to another

il•ly \ˈil-lē, ˈil-ē\ *adv* : BADLY, ILL ⟨*illy* chosen⟩

il•men•ite \ˈil-mə-ˌnīt\ *n* : a metallic-black mineral composed of iron, titanium, and oxygen that is an ore of titanium [*Ilmen* range, Ural Mountains, Union of Soviet Socialist Republics]

im- — see IN-

I'm \īm, ˌīm\ : I am

1im•age \ˈim-ij\ *n* **1** : a reproduction or imitation of the form of a person or thing; *esp* : STATUE **2 a** : a picture of an object produced by a lens, a mirror, or an electronic system **b** : a likeness of an object produced on a photographic material **3** : a mental picture of something not actually present : IMPRESSION **4** : a vivid or graphic representation or description **5** : FIGURE OF SPEECH **6** : a person strikingly like another person ⟨the child is the *image* of the father⟩ **7** : a set of values of a mathematical function that corresponds to a particular subset of the domain [Old French, from Latin *imago*]

2image *vt* **1** : to describe or portray in language especially vividly **2** : to call up a mental picture of : IMAGINE **3 a** : REFLECT, MIRROR ⟨a face *imaged* in a mirror⟩ **b** : to make appear : PROJECT ⟨a film *imaged* on a screen⟩

im•ag•ery \ˈim-ij-rē, -ə-rē\ *n, pl* **-er•ies** **1** : the product of image makers : IMAGES; *also* : the art of making images **2** : figurative language ⟨*imagery* of a poem⟩ **3** : mental images; *esp* : the products of imagination

imag•in•able \im-ˈaj-nə-bəl, -ə-nə-\ *adj* : capable of being imagined : CONCEIVABLE — **imag•in•ably** \-blē\ *adv*

imag•i•nary \im-ˈaj-ə-ˌner-ē\ *adj* **1** : existing only in imagination : FANCIED **2** : of, relating to, or being an imaginary number — **imag•i•nar•i•ly** \-ˌmaj-ə-ˈner-ə-lē\ *adv* — **imag•i•nar•i•ness** \-ˈmaj-ə-ˌner-ē-nəs\ *n*

imaginary number *n* : a complex number in which the part (as $3\sqrt{-1}$ in $2+3\sqrt{-1}$) containing the positive square root of minus

\ə\ **abut**	\au̇\ **out**	\i\ **tip**	\ȯ\ **saw**	\u̇\ **foot**
\ər\ **further**	\ch\ **chin**	\ī\ **life**	\ȯi\ **coin**	\y\ **yet**
\a\ **mat**	\e\ **pet**	\j\ **job**	\th\ **thin**	\yü\ **few**
\ā\ **take**	\ē\ **easy**	\ng\ **sing**	\th\ **this**	\yu̇\ **cure**
\ä\ **cot, cart**	\g\ **go**	\ō\ **bone**	\ü\ **food**	\zh\ **vision**

1 is not equal to zero — called also *imaginary*

imag•i•na•tion \im-ˌaj-ə-ˈnā-shən\ *n* **1 :** the act or power of forming a mental image of something not present to the senses or never before wholly perceived in reality **2 a :** creative ability **b :** ability to confront and deal with a problem **:** RESOURCEFULNESS **3 a :** a creation of the mind; *esp* **:** an idealized or poetic creation **b :** fanciful or empty assumption

imag•i•na•tive \im-ˈaj-nət-iv, -ə-nət-, -ˈaj-ə-ˌnāt-\ *adj* **1 :** of, relating to, or characterized by imagination **2 :** given to imagining **:** having a lively imagination **3 :** of or relating to images; *esp* **:** showing a command of imagery — **imag•i•na•tive•ly** *adv* — **imag•i•na•tive•ness** *n*

imag•ine \im-ˈaj-ən\ *vb* **imag•ined; imag•in•ing** \-ˈaj-ning, -ə-ning\ **1 :** to form a mental image of something not present **:** use the imagination **2 :** SUPPOSE, GUESS ⟨I *imagine* it will rain⟩ [Middle French *imaginer,* from Latin *imaginari,* from *imagin-, imago* "image"]

im•ag•ism \ˈim-ij-ˌiz-əm\ *n* **:** a movement in poetry advocating free verse and the expression of ideas and emotions through clear precise images — **im•ag•ist** \-ij-əst\ *n* — **imagist** *or* **im•ag•is•tic** \ˌim-ij-ˈis-tik\ *adj* — **im•ag•is•ti•cal•ly** \ˌim-ij-ˈis-ti-kə-lē, -klē\ *adv*

ima•go \im-ˈā-gō, -ˈäg-ō\ *n, pl* **imagoes** *or* **ima•gi•nes** \-ˈā-gə-ˌnēz, -ˈäg-ə-\ **:** an insect in its final adult, sexually mature, and usually winged state [Latin, "image"] — **ima•gi•nal** \-ˈā-gən-l, -ˈäg-ən-\ *adj*

imam \i-ˈmäm, -ˈmam\ *n* **1 :** the prayer leader of a mosque **2** *cap* **:** a Muslim leader held to be a divinely appointed successor of Muhammad **3 :** any of various Muslim rulers that claim descent from Muhammad [Arabic *imām*] — **imam•ate** \-ˌāt\ *n, often cap*

im•bal•ance \im-ˈbal-əns, ˈim-\ *n* **:** lack of balance **:** the state of being out of equilibrium or out of proportion

im•be•cile \ˈim-bə-səl, -ˌsil\ *n* **1 :** a mentally deficient person; *esp* **:** a mentally retarded person having a mental age of three to seven years and requiring supervision in the performance of routine daily tasks of personal care **2 :** FOOL 1, SIMPLETON [French *imbécile,* from *imbécile* "weak, weak-minded", from Latin *imbecillus*] **syn** see IDIOT — **imbecile** *or* **im•be•cil•ic** \ˌim-bə-ˈsil-ik\ *adj* — **im•be•cile•ly** \ˈim-bə-səl-lē, -sə-lē, -ˌsil-lē\ *adv*

im•be•cil•i•ty \ˌim-bə-ˈsil-ət-ē\ *n, pl* **-ties 1 :** the quality or state of being imbecile or an imbecile **2 a :** utter foolishness; *also* **:** FUTILITY **b :** something foolish or nonsensical

imbed *variant of* EMBED

im•bibe \im-ˈbīb\ *vb* **1 :** to receive into the mind and retain ⟨*imbibe* knowledge⟩ **2 a :** DRINK 1a **b :** to take in or up **:** ABSORB ⟨sponges *imbibe* moisture⟩ [Latin *imbibere* "to drink in", from *in-* + *bibere* "to drink"] — **im•bib•er** *n*

im•bri•cate \ˈim-brə-ˌkāt\ *vb* **:** OVERLAP ⟨*imbricated* shingles⟩ [Late Latin *imbricare* "to cover with tiles", from Latin *imbrex* "roofing tile", from *imber* "rain"] — **im•bri•ca•tion** \ˌim-brə-ˈkā-shən\ *n*

im•bro•glio \im-ˈbrōl-yō\ *n, pl* **-glios 1 :** a confused mass ⟨an *imbroglio* of papers and books⟩ **2 a :** an intricate or complicated situation (as in a novel) **b :** a painful or embarrassing misunderstanding **:** EMBROILMENT ⟨an *imbroglio* between foreign ministers⟩ [Italian, from *imbrogliare* "to embroil", from French *embrouiller*]

im•bue \im-ˈbyü\ *vt* **1 :** to tinge or dye deeply **2 :** to cause to become penetrated **:** PERMEATE ⟨*imbued* with a deep sense of loyalty⟩ [Latin *imbuere*]

im•i•ta•ble \ˈim-ət-ə-bəl\ *adj* **:** capable or worthy of being imitated or copied

im•i•tate \ˈim-ə-ˌtāt\ *vt* **1 :** to follow as a pattern, model, or example **2 :** to be or appear similar to **:** RESEMBLE **3 :** to copy exactly ⟨*imitated* a dog's bark⟩ [Latin *imitari*] — **im•i•ta•tor** \-ˌtāt-ər\ *n*

• **syn** MIMIC, APE, MOCK: IMITATE suggests following a model or a pattern but may allow for some variation ⟨*imitate* a poet's style⟩ MIMIC implies a close copying as of voice or mannerism often for fun, ridicule, or lifelike imitation ⟨*mimicked* the bird's notes⟩ ⟨children *mimicking* adults⟩ APE may suggest presumptuous, slavish, or inept imitating of a superior original ⟨peasants *aping* their feudal lords⟩ MOCK usually implies imitation with derision ⟨*mocking* a crippled beggar⟩

[1]im•i•ta•tion \ˌim-ə-ˈtā-shən\ *n* **1 :** an act of imitating **2 :** something produced as a copy **3 :** the repetition in a voice part of the melodic theme, phrase, or motive previously found in another part — **im•i•ta•tion•al** \-shnəl, -shən-l\ *adv*

[2]imitation *adj* **:** resembling something else especially of greater worth **:** not real ⟨*imitation* leather⟩

im•i•ta•tive \ˈim-ə-ˌtāt-iv\ *adj* **1 a :** marked by imitation **b :** reproducing or representing a natural sound ⟨*hiss* is an *imitative* word⟩ **2 :** inclined to imitate **3 :** imitating something superior — **im•i•ta•tive•ly** *adv* — **im•i•ta•tive•ness** *n*

im•mac•u•late \im-ˈak-yə-lət\ *adj* **1 :** having no stain or blemish **:** PURE ⟨an *immaculate* heart⟩ **2 :** containing no flaw or error **3 :** spotlessly clean ⟨*immaculate* linen⟩ [Latin *immaculatus,* from *in-* + *maculare* "to stain", from *macula* "spot, stain"] — **im•mac•u•late•ly** *adv* — **im•mac•u•late•ness** *n*

im•ma•te•ri•al \ˌim-ə-ˈtir-ē-əl\ *adj* **1 :** not consisting of matter **2 :** of no consequence **:** UNIMPORTANT — **im•ma•te•ri•al•i•ty** \-ˌtir-ē-ˈal-ət-ē\ *n* — **im•ma•te•ri•al•ly** \-ˈtir-ē-ə-lē\ *adv* — **im•ma•te•ri•al•ness** *n*

im•ma•ture \ˌim-ə-ˈtu̇r, -ˈtyu̇r\ *adj* **:** not mature or fully developed **:** YOUNG, UNRIPE — **immature** *n* — **im•ma•ture•ly** *adv* — **im•ma•ture•ness** *n* — **im•ma•tu•ri•ty** \-ˈtu̇r-ət-ē, -ˈtyu̇r-\ *n*

im•mea•sur•able \im-ˈezh-rə-bəl, -ˈezh-ə-rə-, -ˈezh-ər-bəl, -ˈāzh-, ˈim-\ *adj* **:** incapable of being measured **:** indefinitely extensive ⟨the *immeasurable* sea⟩ — **im•mea•sur•able•ness** *n* — **im•mea•sur•ably** \-blē\ *adv*

im•me•di•a•cy \im-ˈēd-ē-ə-sē\ *n, pl* **-cies 1 :** the quality or state of being immediate **2 :** something that is of immediate importance — usually used in pl.

im•me•di•ate \im-ˈēd-ē-ət\ *adj* **1 :** next in line or relationship ⟨the monarch's *immediate* heir⟩ **2 :** closest in importance ⟨our *immediate* interest⟩ **3 :** acting directly and alone without anything intervening ⟨an *immediate* cause of disease⟩ **4 :** not distant or separated **:** NEXT ⟨their *immediate neighbors*⟩ **5 :** close in time ⟨the *immediate* past⟩ **6 :** made or done at once ⟨ask for an *immediate* reply⟩ [Late Latin *immediatus,* derived from Latin *in-* "[1]in-" + *medius* "middle"] — **im•me•di•ate•ness** *n*

im•me•di•ate•ly *adv* **1 :** with nothing between **:** DIRECTLY ⟨the house *immediately* beyond this one⟩ **2 :** without delay **:** STRAIGHTWAY ⟨do it *immediately*⟩

im•me•mo•ri•al \ˌim-ə-ˈmōr-ē-əl, -ˈmȯr-\ *adj* **:** extending beyond the reach of memory, record, or tradition ⟨since time *immemorial*⟩ — **im•me•mo•ri•al•ly** \-ē-ə-lē\ *adv*

im•mense \im-ˈens\ *adj* **1 :** very great in size or degree **:** HUGE **2 :** supremely good **:** EXCELLENT [Middle French, from Latin *immensus* "immeasurable", from *in-* + *mensus,* past participle of *metiri* "to measure"] **syn** see ENORMOUS — **im•mense•ly** *adv* — **im•mense•ness** *n*

im•men•si•ty \im-ˈen-sət-ē\ *n, pl* **-ties 1 :** the quality or state of being immense **2 :** something immense

im•merse \im-ˈərs\ *vt* **1 :** to plunge into something that surrounds or covers; *esp* **:** to plunge or dip into a fluid **2 :** to baptize by submerging in water **3 :** ENGROSS, ABSORB ⟨completely *immersed* in my work⟩ [Latin *immersus,* past participle of *immergere* "to immerse", from *in-* + *mergere* "to dip"]

im•mer•sion \im-ˈər-zhən, -shən\ *n* **:** an act of immersing **:** a state of being immersed

im•mi•grant \ˈim-i-grənt\ *n* **:** one that immigrates: **a :** a person who comes to a country to become a permanent resident **b :** a plant or animal that becomes established in an area where it was previously unknown **syn** see EMIGRANT — **immigrant** *adv*

im•mi•grate \ˈim-ə-ˌgrāt\ *vi* **:** to enter and usually become established; *esp* **:** to come into a country of which one is not a native to take up permanent residence — **im•mi•gra•tion** \ˌim-ə-ˈgrā-shən\ *n*

im•mi•nence \ˈim-ə-nəns\ *n* **1** *also* **im•mi•nen•cy** \-nən-sē\ **:** the quality or state of being imminent **2 :** something imminent; *esp* **:** impending evil or danger

im•mi•nent \-nənt\ *adj* **:** ready to take place; *esp* **:** hanging threateningly over one's head [Latin *imminens,* present participle of *imminēre* "to project, threaten"] **syn** see IMPENDING — **im•mi•nent•ly** *adv* — **im•mi•nent•ness** *n*

im•mis•ci•ble \im-ˈis-ə-bəl, ˈim-\ *adj* **:** incapable of mixing ⟨ether and water are *immiscible*⟩ — **im•mis•ci•bil•i•ty** \im-ˌis-ə-ˈbil-ət-ē\ *n*

im•mo•bile \im-ˈō-bəl, -ˌbēl, -ˌbīl, ˈim-\ *adj* **:** incapable of being moved **:** FIXED — **im•mo•bil•i•ty** \ˌim-ō-ˈbil-ət-ē\ *n*

im•mo•bi•lize \im-ˈō-bə-ˌlīz\ *vt* **:** to make immobile; *esp* **:** to prevent freedom of movement or effective use of — **im•mo•bi•li•za•tion** \im-ˌō-bə-lə-ˈzā-shən\ *n* — **im•mo•bi•liz•er** \im-ˈō-bə-ˌlī-zər\ *n*

im·mod·er·ate \im-'äd-rət, 'im-, -ə-rət\ *adj* **:** lacking in moderation **:** EXCESSIVE — **im·mod·er·a·cy** \-'äd-rə-sē, -ə-rə-\ *n* — **im·mod·er·ate·ly** *adv* — **im·mod·er·ate·ness** *n* — **im·mod·er·a·tion** \ˌim-ˌäd-ə-'rā-shən\ *n*

im·mod·est \'im-'äd-əst, 'im-\ *adj* **:** not modest; *esp* **:** INDECENT ⟨*immodest* clothing⟩ — **im·mod·est·ly** *adv* — **im·mod·es·ty** \-ə-stē\ *n*

im·mo·late \'im-ə-ˌlāt\ *vt* **1 :** to offer in sacrifice; *esp* **:** to kill as a sacrificial victim **2 :** KILL 1, DESTROY [Latin *immolare,* from *in-* + *mola* "meal"; from the custom of sprinkling victims with sacrificial meal] — **im·mo·la·tion** \ˌim-ə-'lā-shən\ *n* — **im·mo·la·tor** \'im-ə-ˌlāt-ər\ *n*

im·mor·al \'im-'ȯr-əl, 'im-, -'är-\ *adj* **:** not moral — **im·mor·al·ly** \-ə-lē\ *adv*

im·mor·al·ist \-ə-ləst\ *n* **:** an advocate of immorality

im·mo·ral·i·ty \ˌim-ˌȯ-'ral-ət-ē, ˌim-ə-'ral-\ *n, pl* **-ties 1 :** the quality or state of being immoral; *esp* **:** UNCHASTITY **2 :** an immoral act or practice

[1]**im·mor·tal** \im-'ȯrt-l, 'im-\ *adj* **1 :** not subject to death ⟨*immortal* gods⟩ **2 :** connected with or relating to immortality ⟨*immortal* longings⟩ **3 :** lasting forever ⟨*immortal* fame⟩ — **im·mor·tal·ly** \-l-ē\ *adv*

[2]**immortal** *n* **1 a :** one exempt from death **b** *pl, often cap* **:** the gods of the Greek and Roman pantheon **2 :** a person whose fame is lasting ⟨one of the *immortals* of baseball⟩

im·mor·tal·i·ty \ˌim-ˌȯr-'tal-ət-ē\ *n* **:** the quality or state of being immortal: **a :** unending existence **b :** lasting fame

im·mor·tal·ize \im-'ȯrt-l-ˌīz\ *vt* **:** to make immortal — **im·mor·tal·iza·tion** \-ˌȯrt-l-ə-'zā-shən\ *n* — **im·mor·tal·iz·er** \-'ȯrt-l-ˌī-zər\ *n*

im·mor·telle \ˌim-ˌȯr-'tel\ *n* **:** EVERLASTING 3 [French, from *immortel* "immortal"]

im·mov·able \im-'ü-və-bəl, 'im-\ *adj* **1 a :** incapable of being moved ⟨*immovable* mountains⟩ **b :** STATIONARY 1 **2 a :** STEADFAST, UNYIELDING ⟨an *immovable* purpose⟩ **b :** not capable of being moved emotionally — **im·mov·abil·i·ty** \ˌim-ˌü-və-'bil-ət-ē\ *n* — **im·mov·able·ness** \im-'ü-və-bəl-nəs, 'im-\ *n* — **im·mov·ably** \-blē\ *adv*

im·mune \im-'yün\ *adj* **1 :** FREE, EXEMPT ⟨*immune* from punishment⟩ **2 :** not susceptible or responsive ⟨*immune* to fatigue⟩ ⟨*immune* to persuasion⟩; *esp* **:** having a high degree of resistance to a disease ⟨*immune* to diphtheria⟩ **3 :** containing or producing antibodies ⟨an *immune* serum⟩ [Latin *immunis,* from *in-* "[1]in-" + *munia* "services, obligations"] — **immune** *n*

im·mu·ni·ty \im-'yü-nət-ē\ *n, pl* **-ties :** the quality or state of being immune; *esp* **:** bodily power to resist an infectious disease usually by preventing development of the causative microorganism or by neutralizing its poisons

im·mu·nize \'im-yə-ˌnīz\ *vt* **:** to make immune — **im·mu·ni·za·tion** \ˌim-yə-nə-'zā-shən\ *n*

im·mu·no·gen·ic \ˌim-yə-nō-'jen-ik\ *adj* **:** producing immunity — **im·mu·no·gen·i·cal·ly** \-'jen-i-kə-lē, -klē\ *adv* — **im·mu·no·ge·nic·i·ty** \-jə-'nis-ət-ē\ *n*

im·mu·nol·o·gy \ˌim-yə-'näl-ə-jē\ *n* **:** a science that deals with the processes and causes of immunity — **im·mu·no·log·ic** \-yən-l-'äj-ik\ *or* **im·mu·no·log·i·cal** \-i-kəl\ *adj* — **im·mu·no·log·i·cal·ly** \-i-kə-lē, -klē\ *adv* — **im·mu·nol·o·gist** \ˌim-yə-'näl-ə-jəst\ *n*

im·mu·no·sup·pres·sion \ˌim-yə-nō-sə-'presh-ən\ *n* **:** suppression (as by drugs) of natural immune responses — **im·mu·no·sup·pres·sant** \-'pres-nt\ *n or adj* — **im·mu·no·sup·pres·sive** \-'pres-iv\ *adj*

im·mure \im-'yu̇r\ *vt* **1 a :** to enclose within or as if within walls **b :** to shut up **:** IMPRISON **2 :** to build into a wall; *esp* **:** to entomb in a wall [Medieval Latin *immurare,* from Latin *in-* + *murus* "wall" — **im·mure·ment** \-mənt\ *n*

im·mu·ta·ble \im-'yüt-ə-bəl, 'im-\ *adj* **:** not capable of change — **im·mu·ta·bil·i·ty** \im-ˌyüt-ə-'bil-ət-ē\ *n* — **im·mu·ta·ble·ness** \im-'yüt-ə-bəl-nəs, 'im-\ *n* — **im·mu·ta·bly** \-blē\ *adv*

imp \'imp\ *n* **1 :** a small demon **2 :** a mischievous child [Old English *impa* "bud, shoot, scion"]

[1]**im·pact** \im-'pakt\ *vt* **1 a :** to fix firmly by or as if by packing or wedging **b :** to press together **2 :** to impinge upon [Latin *impactus,* past participle of *impingere* "to push against, impinge"]

[2]**im·pact** \'im-ˌpakt\ *n* **1 a :** an impinging or striking (as of one body against another) **b :** a forceful contact, collision, or onset; *also* **:** the impetus communicated in or as if in a collision **2 :** the force of impression or operation of one thing on another **:** EFFECT ⟨the *impact* of technology on society⟩

im·pact·ed \im-'pak-təd\ *adj* **:** wedged between the jawbone and another tooth

im·pac·tion \im-'pak-shən\ *n* **:** the act of becoming or the state of being impacted; *also* **:** accumulation and packing of something (as feces) in a body passage or cavity

im·pair \im-'paər, -'peər\ *vt* **:** to diminish in quantity, value, excellence, strength, or efficiency **:** DAMAGE [Middle French *empeirer,* derived from Latin *in-* "[2]in-" + *pejor* "worse"] — **im·pair·er** *n* — **im·pair·ment** \-mənt\ *n*

im·pa·la \im-'pal-ə, -'päl-\ *n* **:** a large brownish African antelope that in the male has slender curving horns [Zulu]

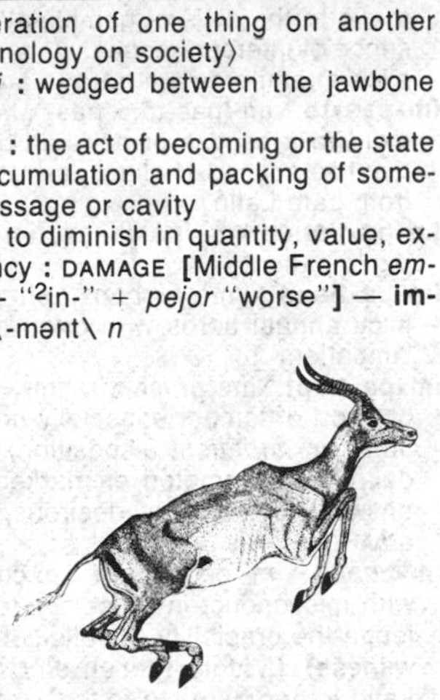
impala

im·pale \im-'pāl\ *vt* **:** to pierce with or as if with something pointed; *esp* **:** to torture or kill by fixing on a sharp stake [Medieval Latin *impalare,* from Latin *in-* + *palus* "stake"] — **im·pale·ment** \-mənt\ *n*

im·pal·pa·ble \im-'pal-pə-bəl, 'im-\ *adj* **1 :** incapable of being felt by the touch **:** INTANGIBLE **2 :** not readily discerned or understood — **im·pal·pa·bil·i·ty** \im-ˌpal-pə-'bil-ət-ē\ *n* — **im·pal·pa·bly** \'im-'pal-pə-blē, 'im-\ *adv*

im·pan·el \im-'pan-l\ *vt* **-eled** *or* **-elled; -el·ing** *or* **-el·ling :** to enter in or on a panel or list **:** ENROLL

im·par·a·dise \im-'par-ə-ˌdīs, -ˌdīz\ *vt* **:** ENRAPTURE

im·par·i·ty \im-'par-ət-ē, 'im-\ *n, pl* **-ties :** INEQUALITY 1, DISPARITY

im·part \im-'pärt\ *vt* **1 :** to give from or as if from one's store or abundance ⟨the sun *imparts* warmth⟩ **2 :** to communicate the knowledge of **:** DISCLOSE ⟨*imparted* their plans⟩ [Latin *impartire,* from *in-* + *partire* "to divide, part"] — **im·part·able** \-ə-bəl\ *adj* — **im·par·ta·tion** \ˌim-ˌpär-'tā-shən\ *n* — **im·part·ment** \im-'part-mənt\ *n*

im·par·tial \im-'pär-shəl, 'im-\ *adj* **:** not partial **:** UNBIASED **syn** see FAIR — **im·par·ti·al·i·ty** \ˌim-ˌpär-shē-'al-ət-ē, -ˌpär-'shal-\ *n* — **im·par·tial·ly** \im-'pärsh-lē, 'im-, -ə-lē\ *adv*

im·pass·able \im-'pas-ə-bəl, 'im-\ *adj* **:** incapable of being passed, traveled, crossed, or climbed — **im·pass·abil·i·ty** \ˌim-ˌpas-ə-'bil-ət-ē\ *n* — **im·pass·able·ness** \im-'pas-ə-bəl-nəs, 'im-\ *n* — **im·pass·ably** \-blē\ *adv*

im·passe \'im-ˌpas, im-'\ *n* **1 :** an impassable road or way **2 a :** a predicament from which there is no obvious escape **b :** DEADLOCK [French, from *in-* "[1]in-" + *passer* "to pass"]

im·pas·si·ble \im-'pas-ə-bəl, 'im-\ *adj* **1 a :** incapable of experiencing pain **b :** incapable of being harmed **2 :** incapable of feeling **:** IMPASSIVE [Late Latin *impassibilis,* derived from Latin *in-* + *passus,* past participle of *pati* "to suffer"] — **im·pas·si·bil·i·ty** \ˌim-ˌpas-ə-'bil-ət-ē\ *n* — **im·pas·si·bly** \im-'pas-ə-blē, 'im-\ *adv*

im·pas·sioned \im-'pash-ənd\ *adj* **:** filled with passion or zeal **:** showing great warmth or intensity of feeling ⟨*impassioned* plea for justice⟩

• **syn** IMPASSIONED, PASSIONATE mean showing intense feeling. IMPASSIONED implies warmth and intensity without violence and suggests a fluent verbal expression; PASSIONATE implies great vehemence and often violence and wasteful diffusion of emotion.

im·pas·sive \im-'pas-iv, 'im-\ *adj* **:** not feeling or not showing any emotion ⟨an *impassive* stare⟩ — **im·pas·sive·ly** *adv* — **im·pas·sive·ness** *n* — **im·pas·siv·i·ty** \ˌim-ˌpas-'iv-ət-ē\ *n*

• **syn** IMPASSIVE, APATHETIC, STOLID, PHLEGMATIC mean unresponsive to something that might normally excite interest or emotion. IMPASSIVE stresses the absence of any external sign of emotion in action or facial expression; APATHETIC may imply a puzzling or deplorable indifference or inertness ⟨people *apa-*

\ə\ **abut**	\au̇\ **out**	\i\ **tip**	\ȯ\ **saw**	\u̇\ **foot**
\ər\ **further**	\ch\ **chin**	\ī\ **life**	\ȯi\ **coin**	\y\ **yet**
\a\ **mat**	\e\ **pet**	\j\ **job**	\th\ **thin**	\yü\ **few**
\ā\ **take**	\ē\ **easy**	\ng\ **sing**	\th\ **this**	\yu̇\ **cure**
\ä\ **cot, cart**	\g\ **go**	\ō\ **bone**	\ü\ **food**	\zh\ **vision**

thetic to the evils of gambling〉 STOLID implies an habitual absence of interest, responsiveness, or curiosity; PHLEGMATIC implies a temperament hard to arouse.

im·pas·to \im-ˈpas-tō, -ˈpäs-\ *n* **:** the thick application of a pigment to a canvas or panel in painting; *also* **:** the body of pigment so applied [Italian, derived from *in-* "in" + *pasta* "paste", from Late Latin]

im·pa·tience \im-ˈpā-shəns, ˈim-\ *n* **:** the quality or state of being impatient

im·pa·tiens \im-ˈpā-shənz, -shəns\ *n* **:** any of a large genus of juicy annual herbs with often showy irregular flowers [Latin, "impatient"]

im·pa·tient \im-ˈpā-shənt, ˈim-\ *adj* **1 a :** not patient **:** restless or short of temper especially under irritation, delay, or opposition 〈an *impatient* disposition〉 **b :** INTOLERANT 〈*impatient* of delay〉 **2 :** prompted or marked by impatience 〈an *impatient* answer〉 **3 :** eagerly desirous **:** ANXIOUS — **im·pa·tient·ly** *adv*

im·peach \im-ˈpēch\ *vt* **1 :** to charge (a public official) formally with misconduct in office **2 :** to cast doubt on; *esp* **:** to challenge the credibility or validity of 〈*impeach* the testimony of a witness〉 [Middle French *empeechier* "to hinder", from Late Latin *impedicare* "to fetter", from Latin *in-* + *pedica* "fetter", from *ped-, pes* "foot"] — **im·peach·able** \-ˈpē-chə-bəl\ *adj* — **im·peach·ment** \-ˈpēch-mənt\ *n*

im·pearl \im-ˈpərl\ *vt* **:** to form into pearls; *also* **:** to form of or adorn with pearls

im·pec·ca·ble \im-ˈpek-ə-bəl, ˈim-\ *adj* **1 :** not capable of sinning or liable to sin **2 :** free from fault or blame **:** FLAWLESS 〈a person of *impeccable* character〉 [Latin *impeccabilis,* from *in-* + *peccare* "to sin"] — **im·pec·ca·bil·i·ty** \ˌim-ˌpek-ə-ˈbil-ət-ē\ *n* — **im·pec·ca·bly** \im-ˈpek-ə-blē, ˈim-\ *adv*

im·pe·cu·nious \ˌim-pi-ˈkyü-nyəs, -nē-əs\ *adj* **:** having very little or no money usually habitually **:** PENNILESS [derived from Latin *pecunia* "money"] — **im·pe·cu·ni·os·i·ty** \-ˌkyü-nē-ˈäs-ət-ē\ *n* — **im·pe·cu·ni·ous·ly** *adv* — **im·pe·cu·ni·ous·ness** *n*

im·ped·ance \im-ˈpēd-ns\ *n* **:** the apparent opposition in an electrical circuit to the flow of an alternating current as a result of a combination of resistance and reactance

im·pede \im-ˈpēd\ *vt* **:** to interfere with the progress of **:** BLOCK, HINDER 〈traffic *impeded* by heavy rain〉 [Latin *impedire,* from *in-* "2in-" + *ped-, pes* "foot"] — **im·ped·er** *n*

im·ped·i·ment \im-ˈped-ə-mənt\ *n* **1 :** something that impedes **2 :** a defect in speech

im·ped·i·men·ta \im-ˌped-ə-ˈment-ə\ *n pl* **:** things (as baggage or supplies) that impede progress or movement [Latin, "impediments"]

im·pel \im-ˈpel\ *vt* **im·pelled; im·pel·ling 1 :** to urge or drive forward or into action 〈felt *impelled* to speak up in their defense〉 **2 :** to impart motion to **:** PROPEL 〈*impel* water through a pipe〉 [Latin *impellere,* from *in-* + *pellere* "to drive"] **syn** see MOVE — **im·pel·ler** *also* **im·pel·lor** \-ˈpel-ər\ *n*

im·pend \im-ˈpend\ *vi* **:** to hover threateningly **:** MENACE 〈warning of a danger that *impends*〉 **2 :** to be about to occur [Latin *impendēre,* from *in-* + *pendēre* "to hang"]

im·pend·ing *adj* **:** threatening to occur soon **:** APPROACHING

• **syn** IMPENDING, IMMINENT mean threatening to occur very soon. IMPENDING implies signs that keep one in suspense 〈an *impending* thunderstorm kept us from going on a picnic〉 IMMINENT emphasizes the shortness of time before happening 〈execution of the death sentence was now *imminent*〉

im·pen·e·tra·bil·i·ty \im-ˌpen-ə-trə-ˈbil-ət-ē\ *n* **:** the quality or state of being impenetrable

im·pen·e·tra·ble \im-ˈpen-ə-trə-bəl, ˈim-\ *adj* **1 a :** incapable of being penetrated or pierced 〈*impenetrable* rock〉 〈*impenetrable* jungle〉 **b :** inaccessible to knowledge, reason, or sympathy **:** IMPERVIOUS **2 :** incapable of being comprehended **:** INSCRUTABLE 〈*impenetrable* mystery〉 — **im·pen·e·tra·ble·ness** *n* — **im·pen·e·tra·bly** \-blē\ *adv*

im·pen·i·tent \im-ˈpen-ə-tənt, ˈim-\ *adj* **:** not penitent **:** not sorry for having done wrong — **im·pen·i·tent·ly** *adv*

1im·per·a·tive \im-ˈper-ət-iv\ *adj* **1 a :** of, relating to, or constituting the grammatical mood that expresses a command, request, or strong encouragement **b :** expressive of a command, entreaty, or exhortation 〈an *imperative* gesture〉 **2 :** not to be avoided or evaded **:** URGENT 〈*imperative* business〉 [Late Latin *imperativus,* from Latin *imperare* "to command"] — **im·per·a·tive·ly** *adv* — **im·per·a·tive·ness** *n*

2imperative *n* **1 :** the imperative mood or a verb form expressing it **2 :** something that is imperative: **a :** COMMAND 2, ORDER **b :** an obligatory act or duty

im·pe·ra·tor \ˌim-pə-ˈrät-ər, -ˈrä-ˌtȯr\ *n* **:** a supreme leader of the ancient Romans **:** EMPEROR [Latin] — **im·per·a·to·ri·al** \ˌim-ˌper-ə-ˈtōr-ē-əl, -ˈtȯr-\ *adj*

im·per·cep·ti·ble \ˌim-pər-ˈsep-tə-bəl\ *adj* **1 :** not perceptible by a sense or by the mind **2 :** extremely slight, gradual, or subtle — **im·per·cep·ti·bil·i·ty** \-ˌsep-tə-ˈbil-ət-ē\ *n* — **im·per·cep·ti·bly** \-ˈsep-tə-blē\ *adv*

im·per·cep·tive \ˌim-pər-ˈsep-tiv\ *adj* **:** not perceptive — **im·per·cep·tive·ness** n

im·per·cip·i·ent \ˌim-pər-ˈsip-ē-ənt\ *adj* **:** not percipient **:** UNPERCEPTIVE

1im·per·fect \im-ˈpər-fikt, ˈim-\ *adj* **1 :** not perfect **:** DEFECTIVE **2 :** of, relating to, or constituting a verb tense used to designate a continuing state or an incomplete action especially in the past — **im·per·fect·ly** \-fik-lē, -tlē\ *adv* — **im·per·fect·ness** \-fik-nəs, -fikt-\ *n*

2imperfect *n* **:** the imperfect tense of a verb; *also* **:** a verb in this tense

imperfect flower *n* **:** a flower with stamens or pistils but not both

imperfect fungus *n* **:** any of an order (Fungi Imperfecti) of fungi of which only the asexual stage is known

im·per·fec·tion \ˌim-pər-ˈfek-shən\ *n* **:** the quality or state of being imperfect; *also* **:** BLEMISH, FAULT

im·per·fo·rate \im-ˈpər-fə-rət, ˈim-, -frət, -fə-ˌrāt\ *adj* **:** lacking perforations or rouletting 〈*imperforate* postage stamps〉 — **imperforate** *n*

1im·pe·ri·al \im-ˈpir-ē-əl\ *adj* **1 a :** of, relating to, or befitting an empire or an emperor 〈by *imperial* decree〉 **b :** of or relating to the British Commonwealth or Empire **2 a :** SUPREME 2 **b :** REGAL 1, IMPERIOUS **3 :** of superior or unusual size or excellence **4 :** belonging to a British series of weights and measures 〈an *imperial* gallon〉 [Middle French, from Late Latin *imperialis,* from Latin *imperium* "command, empire"] — **im·pe·ri·al·ly** \-ē-ə-lē\ *adv*

2imperial *n* **:** a pointed beard growing below the lower lip [from the beard worn by Napoleon III]

2imperial

im·pe·ri·al·ism \im-ˈpir-ē-ə-ˌliz-əm\ *n* **1 :** imperial government, authority, or system **2 :** the policy or practice of extending the power and dominion of one nation by direct territorial acquisitions or by indirect control over the political or economic life of other areas — **im·pe·ri·al·ist** \-ləst\ *n* — **imperialist** *or* **im·pe·ri·al·is·tic** \im-ˌpir-ē-ə-ˈlis-tik\ *adj* — **im·pe·ri·al·is·ti·cal·ly** \-ti-kə-lē, -klē\ *adv*

im·per·il \im-ˈper-əl\ *vt* **-iled** *or* **-illed; -il·ing** *or* **-il·ling :** to bring into peril **:** ENDANGER — **im·per·il·ment** \-əl-mənt\ *n*

im·pe·ri·ous \im-ˈpir-ē-əs\ *adj* **1 :** befitting or characteristic of one of eminent rank or attainments **2 :** marked by arrogant assurance **:** DOMINEERING **3 :** IMPERATIVE, URGENT 〈*imperious* problems〉 [Latin *imperiosus,* from *imperium* "command, empire"] **syn** see MASTERFUL — **im·pe·ri·ous·ly** *adv* — **im·pe·ri·ous·ness** *n*

im·per·ish·able \im-ˈper-ish-ə-bəl, ˈim-\ *adj* **:** not perishable or subject to decay **:** INDESTRUCTIBLE 〈*imperishable* fame〉— **im·per·ish·abil·i·ty** \ˌim-ˌper-ish-ə-ˈbil-ət-ē\ *n* — **im·per·ish·able·ness** \im-ˈper-ish-ə-bəl-nəs, ˈim-\ *n* — **im·per·ish·ably** \-blē\ *adv*

im·pe·ri·um \im-ˈpir-ē-əm\ *n* **1 a :** supreme power or dominion **b :** the right to supreme power **:** SOVEREIGNTY **2 :** EMPIRE 1a (2) [Latin]

im·per·ma·nent \im-ˈpər-mə-nənt, ˈim-\ *adj* **:** not permanent **:** TRANSIENT — **im·per·ma·nence** \-nəns\ *n* — **im·per·ma·nent·ly** adv

im·per·me·able \im-ˈpər-mē-ə-bəl, ˈim-\ *adj* **:** not permitting passage (as of a fluid) through its substance **:** IMPERVIOUS — **im·per·me·abil·i·ty** \ˌim-ˌpər-mē-ə-ˈbil-ət-ē\ *n* — **im·per·me·able·ness** \im-ˈpər-mē-ə-bəl-nəs, ˈim-\ *n* — **im·per·me·ably** \-blē\ *adv*

im•per•mis•si•ble \ˌim-pər-ˈmis-ə-bəl\ *adj* : not permissible — **im•per•mis•si•bil•i•ty** \-ˌmis-ə-ˈbil-ət-ē\ *n* — **im•per•mis•si•bly** \-ˈmis-ə-blē\ *adv*

im•per•son•al \im-ˈpərs-nəl, ˈim-, -n-əl\ *adj* **1** : of, relating to, or being a verb used with no expressed subject or with a merely formal subject ⟨*methinks* in "methinks you are wrong" and *rained* in "it rained" are *impersonal* verbs⟩ **2 a** : having no personal reference or connection ⟨*impersonal* criticism⟩ **b** : not engaging the human personality or emotions ⟨the *impersonal* attitude of a doctor⟩ **c** : not existing as a person ⟨an *impersonal* deity⟩ — **im•per•son•al•i•ty** \ˌim-ˌpərs-n-ˈal-ət-ē\ *n* — **im•per•son•al•ize** \im-ˈpərs-nə-ˌlīz ˈim-, -n-ə-ˌlīz\ *vt* — **im•per•son•al•ly** \-nə-lē, -n-ə-lē\ *adv*

im•per•son•ate \im-ˈpərs-n-ˌāt\ *vt* : to act the part of or pretend to be (some other person) ⟨*impersonate* a circus barker⟩ — **im•per•son•ation** \-ˌpərs-n-ˈā-shən\ *n* — **im•per•son•ator** \-ˈpərs-n-ˌāt-ər\ *n*

im•per•ti•nence \im-ˈpərt-n-əns, ˈim-\ *also* **im•per•ti•nen•cy** \-ən-sē\ *n, pl* **-nences** *also* **-nencies** **1** : the quality or state of being impertinent **2** : something impertinent

im•per•ti•nent \-ənt\ *adj* **1** : not pertinent : IRRELEVANT **2** : not restrained within due or proper bounds : RUDE, INSOLENT — **im•per•ti•nent•ly** *adv*

im•per•turb•able \ˌim-pər-ˈtər-bə-bəl\ *adj* : marked by extreme calm, impassivity, and steadiness : SERENE — **im•per•turb•abil•i•ty** \-ˌtər-bə-ˈbil-ət-ē\ *n* — **im•per•turb•ably** \-ˈtər-bə-blē\ *adv*

im•per•vi•ous \im-ˈpər-vē-əs, ˈim-\ *adj* **1** : not allowing entrance or passage : IMPENETRABLE ⟨a coat *impervious* to rain⟩ **2** : not capable of being affected or disturbed ⟨*impervious* to criticism⟩ — **im•per•vi•ous•ly** *adv* — **im•per•vi•ous•ness** *n*

im•pe•ti•go \ˌim-pə-ˈtē-gō, -ˈtī-\ *n* : an acute contagious skin disease characterized by small pus-filled blisters and yellowish crusts [Latin, from *impetere* "to attack"] — **im•pe•tig•i•nous** \-ˈtij-ə-nəs\ *adj*

im•pet•u•os•i•ty \im-ˌpech-ə-ˈwäs-ət-ē\ *n, pl* **-ties** **1** : the quality or state of being impetuous **2** : an impetuous action or impulse

im•pet•u•ous \im-ˈpech-wəs, -ə-wəs\ *adj* **1** : marked by force and violence **2** : marked by impulsive vehemence [Middle French *impetueux*, from Late Latin *impetuosus*, from Latin *impetus*] — **im•pet•u•ous•ly** *adv* — **im•pet•u•ous•ness** *n*

im•pe•tus \ˈim-pət-əs\ *n* **1 a** : a driving force : IMPULSE **b** : INCENTIVE, STIMULUS **2** : MOMENTUM 1 ⟨the *impetus* of a bullet [Latin, "assault, impetus", from *impetere* "to attack", from *in-* + *petere* "to go to, seek"]

im•pi•e•ty \im-ˈpī-ət-ē, ˈim-\ *n, pl* **-ties** **1** : the quality or state of being impious : IRREVERENCE **2** : an impious act

im•pinge \im-ˈpinj\ *vi* **1** : to strike or dash especially with a sharp collision ⟨sound waves *impinge* upon the eardrums⟩ **2** : to come into close contact **3** : ENCROACH, INFRINGE ⟨*impinge* on another person's rights⟩ [Latin *impingere*, from *in-* + *pangere* "to fasten, drive in"] — **im•pinge•ment** \-mənt\ *n*

im•pi•ous \ˈim-pē-əs; im-ˈpī-, ˈim-\ *adj* : lacking in reverence or proper respect — **im•pi•ous•ly** *adv*

imp•ish \ˈim-pish\ *adj* : of, relating to, or befitting an imp; *esp* : MISCHIEVOUS — **imp•ish•ly** *adv* — **imp•ish•ness** *n*

im•pla•ca•ble \im-ˈplak-ə-bəl, ˈim-, -ˈplā-kə-\ *adj* : not placable : not capable of being appeased, pacified, or mitigated ⟨an *implacable* enemy⟩ — **im•pla•ca•bil•i•ty** \ˌim-ˌplak-ə-ˈbil-ət-ē, -ˌplā-kə-\ *n* — **im•plac•a•ble•ness** \im-ˈplak-ə-bəl-nəs, ˈim-, -ˈplā-kə-\ *n* — **im•pla•ca•bly** \-blē\ *adv*

im•plant \im-ˈplant\ *vt* **1 a** : to fix or set securely or deeply **b** : to set permanently in the consciousness or habit patterns ⟨*implant* patriotism in children⟩ **2** : to insert in a living site ⟨*implant* a graft of tissue⟩ — **implant** *n* — **im•plan•ta•tion** \ˌim-ˌplan-ˈtā-shən\ *n* — **im•plant•er** *n*

im•plau•si•ble \im-ˈplȯ-zə-bəl, ˈim-\ *adj* : not plausible — **im•plau•si•bil•i•ty** \ˌim-ˌplȯ-zə-ˈbil-ət-ē\ *n* — **im•plau•si•bly** \im-ˈplȯ-zə-blē, ˈim-\ *adv*

¹im•ple•ment \ˈim-plə-mənt\ *n* **1** : a piece of equipment : TOOL **2** : one that serves as an instrument or tool [Late Latin *implementum* "action of filling up", from Latin *implēre* "to fill up", from *in-* + *plēre* "to fill"]

• **syn** IMPLEMENT, TOOL, UTENSIL, INSTRUMENT apply to a device for performing work. IMPLEMENT may apply to anything necessary to bring about an end or perform a task ⟨propaganda as an *implement* of peace and war⟩ ⟨agricultural and garden *implements*⟩ TOOL suggests an implement adapted for a specific task and implies the need of skill in its use ⟨carpenter's *tools*⟩ UTENSIL suggests a device useful for domestic tasks ⟨kitchen *utensils*⟩ or some routine unskilled activity; INSTRUMENT suggests a device capable of delicate or precise work ⟨a surgeon's *instruments*⟩

²im•ple•ment \-ˌment\ *vt* **1** : to carry out : FULFILL; *esp* : to give practical effect to by positive action ⟨*implement* the provisions of a treaty⟩ **2** : to provide implements for — **im•ple•men•ta•tion** \ˌim-plə-mən-ˈtā-shən, -ˌmen-\ *n*

im•pli•cate \ˈim-plə-ˌkāt\ *vt* : to bring into connection : INVOLVE ⟨the confession *implicated* several others in the crime⟩ [Latin *implicare*, literally, "to enfold", from *in-* + *plicare* "to fold"]

im•pli•ca•tion \ˌim-plə-ˈkā-shən\ *n* **1 a** : the act of implicating : the state of being implicated **b** : an incriminating involvement **2 a** : the act of implying : the state of being implied **b** : something implied **3** : a sentence which is composed of two parts beginning with "if" and "then" and for which the "then" part is true whenever the "if" part is true ⟨"If P then Q" is an *implication*⟩ — called also *conditional* — **im•pli•ca•tive** \ˈim-plə-ˌkāt-iv\ *adj* — **im•pli•ca•tive•ly** *adv* — **im•pli•ca•tive•ness** *n*

im•plic•it \im-ˈplis-ət\ *adj* **1** : understood though not directly stated ⟨an *implicit* agreement⟩ **2** : being without reserve : COMPLETE, UNQUESTIONING ⟨*implicit* trust⟩ — compare EXPLICIT [Latin *implicitus*, past participle of *implicare* "to enfold, implicate"] — **im•plic•it•ly** *adv* — **im•plic•it•ness** *n*

im•plode \im-ˈplōd\ *vi* : to burst inward [*in-* + *-plode* (as in *explode*)] — **im•plo•sion** \-ˈplō-zhən\ *n* — **im•plo•sive** \-ˈplō-siv, -ziv\ *adj*

im•plore \im-ˈplōr, -ˈplȯr\ *vt* **1** : to call upon in supplication : BESEECH **2** : to call or pray for earnestly [Latin *implorare*, from *in-* + *plorare* "to cry out"] **syn** see BEG

im•ply \im-ˈplī\ *vt* **im•plied**; **im•ply•ing** **1 a** : to include or involve as a natural or necessary though not definitely stated part or effect ⟨the rights of citizenship *imply* certain obligations⟩ **b** : to involve as a necessary consequence or condition ⟨"If A then B" means that A *implies* B⟩ **2** : to express indirectly : suggest rather than say plainly ⟨remarks that *implied* consent⟩ [Middle French *emplier* "to enfold", from Latin *implicare* "to enfold, implicate"]

• **syn** INFER: INFER is sometimes used for IMPLY but to most users the two words are complementary rather than synonymous. IMPLY means conveying or drawing attention to a fact or relationship by suggestion or hint rather than by direct statement ⟨their silence *implied* disapproval⟩ INFER means to arrive at a conclusion by reasoning from evidence and if the evidence is slight, comes close to *surmise* ⟨I *inferred* their disapproval from their silence⟩ ⟨a future rise in the number of college students may be *inferred* from the present population statistics⟩

im•po•lite \ˌim-pə-ˈlīt\ *adj* : not polite : RUDE — **im•po•lite•ly** *adv* — **im•po•lite•ness** *n*

im•pol•i•tic \im-ˈpäl-ə-ˌtik, ˈim-\ *adj* : not politic : UNWISE — **im•pol•i•tic•ly** *adv*

im•pon•der•able \im-ˈpän-də-rə-bəl, ˈim-, -drə-bəl\ *adj* : not capable of being weighed or evaluated with exactness — **im•pon•der•abil•i•ty** \im-ˌpän-də-rə-ˈbil-ət-ē, -drə-ˈbil-\ *n* — **imponderable** *n* — **im•pon•der•able•ness** \im-ˈpän-də-rə-bəl-nəs, ˈim-, -drə-bəl-\ *n* — **im•pon•der•ably** \-blē\ *adv*

¹im•port \im-ˈpōrt, -ˈpȯrt, ˈim-ˌ\ *vb* **1 a** : MEAN ⟨their words *imported* a need for change⟩ **b** : to be of importance : MATTER **2** : to bring in or introduce from a foreign country; *esp* : to bring in (goods) to be resold ⟨*import* coffee⟩ [Latin *importare* "to bring in", from *in-* + *portare* "to carry"] — **im•port•able** \-ə-bəl\ *adj* — **im•port•er** *n*

²im•port \ˈim-ˌpōrt, -ˌpȯrt\ *n* **1** : MEANING **2** : IMPORTANCE **3 a** : something imported **b** : IMPORTATION 1

im•por•tance \im-ˈpȯrt-ns, -əns\ *n* **1** : the quality or state of being important **2** : an important aspect or bearing

im•por•tant \im-ˈpȯrt-nt, -ənt\ *adj* **1** : having great meaning or influence ⟨an *important* change in printing methods⟩ **2** : having considerable power or authority ⟨an *important* official⟩ **3** : showing a feeling of personal importance — **im•por•tant•ly** *adv*

im•por•ta•tion \ˌim-ˌpōr-ˈtā-shən, -ˌpȯr-, -pər-\ *n* **1** : the act or practice of importing **2** : IMPORT 3a

im•por•tu•nate \im-'pȯrch-nət, -ə-nət\ *adj* **1** : BURDENSOME, TROUBLESOME **2** : overly persistent in request or demand — **im•por•tu•nate•ly** *adv* — **im•por•tu•nate•ness** *n*

¹im•por•tune \ˌim-pər-'tün, -tyün; im-'pȯr-chən\ *adj* : IMPORTUNATE [Latin *importunus,* from *in-* + *-portunus* (as in *opportunus* "opportune")] — **im•por•tune•ly** *adv*

²importune *vb* **1** : to press, beg, or urge with troublesome persistence **2** : ANNOY, TROUBLE — **im•por•tun•er** *n*

im•por•tu•ni•ty \ˌim-pər-'tü-nət-ē, -'tyü-\ *n, pl* **-ties 1** : the quality or state of being importunate **2** *pl* : importunate requests or demands

im•pose \im-'pōz\ *vb* **1 a** : to establish or apply as a charge or penalty : LEVY ⟨*impose* a fine⟩ ⟨*impose* a tax⟩ **b** : to establish by force **2** : to use trickery or deception to get what one wants ⟨*impose* on an ignorant person⟩ **3** : to arrange (as type or printing plates) in proper order for printing **4** : to take unwarranted advantage of something ⟨*impose* upon a friend's good nature⟩ [Middle French *imposer,* from Latin *imponere,* literally, "to put upon", from *in-* + *ponere* "to put"] — **im•pos•er** *n*

im•pos•ing \im-'pō-zing\ *adj* : impressive because of size, bearing, dignity, or grandeur ⟨an *imposing* building⟩ — **im•pos•ing•ly** \-zing-lē\ *adv*

im•po•si•tion \ˌim-pə-'zish-ən\ *n* **1** : the act of imposing **2** : something imposed: as **a** : LEVY 1, TAX **b** : an overly burdensome requirement or demand **3** : TRICK 1a, DECEPTION

im•pos•si•bil•i•ty \im-ˌpäs-ə-'bil-ət-ē\ *n, pl* **-ties 1** : the quality or state of being impossible **2** : something impossible

im•pos•si•ble \im-'päs-ə-bəl, 'im-\ *adj* **1 a** : not capable of being or of occurring **b** : very difficult to accomplish or deal with ⟨an *impossible* situation⟩ **2 a** : extremely undesirable : OBJECTIONABLE, UNACCEPTABLE ⟨living in *impossible* conditions⟩ — **im•pos•si•bly** \-blē\ *adv*

¹im•post \'im-ˌpōst\ *n* : TAX; *esp* : a customs duty [Middle French, from Medieval Latin *impositum,* from Latin *imponere* "to impose"]

²impost *n* : a block, capital, or molding (as of a pillar or pier) from which an arch extends

1 ²impost

im•pos•tor \im-'päs-tər\ *n* : one that practices deceit; *esp* : a person who fraudulently pretends to be someone else [Late Latin, from Latin *impositus, impostus,* past participle of *imponere* "to impose"]

im•pos•ture \im-'päs-chər\ *n* : the act or conduct of an impostor

im•po•tence \'im-pət-əns\ *n* : the quality or state of being impotent

im•po•tent \'im-pət-ənt\ *adj* **1** : not potent : lacking in power, strength, or vigor : HELPLESS **2** : unable to copulate; *also* : STERILE 1 — usually used of males — **impotent** *n* — **im•po•tent•ly** *adv*

im•pound \im-'pau̇nd\ *vt* **1** : to shut up in or as if in a pound : CONFINE **2** : to seize and hold in legal custody ⟨*impound* funds pending decision of a case⟩ **3** : to collect (water) in a reservoir

im•pound•ment \im-'pau̇nd-mənt, -'pau̇n-\ *n* **1** : the act of impounding : the state of being impounded **2** : a body of water formed by impounding

im•pov•er•ish \im-'päv-rish, -ə-rish\ *vt* **1** : to make poor **2** : to use up the strength, richness, or fertility of [Middle French *empovriss-,* stem of *empovrir,* from *en-* + *povre* "poor", from Latin *pauper*] — **im•pov•er•ish•er** *n* — **im•pov•er•ish•ment** \-mənt\ *n*

im•prac•ti•ca•ble \im-'prak-ti-kə-bəl, 'im-\ *adj* **1** : not practicable : not capable of being put into practice or use ⟨an *impracticable* plan⟩ **2** : IMPASSABLE ⟨an *impracticable* road⟩ — **im•prac•ti•ca•bil•i•ty** \im-ˌprak-ti-kə-'bil-ət-ē\ *n* — **im•prac•ti•ca•ble•ness** \im-'prak-ti-kə-bəl-nəs, 'im-\ *n* — **im•prac•ti•ca•bly** \-blē\ *adv*

im•prac•ti•cal \im-'prak-ti-kəl, 'im-\ *adj* : not practical: as **a** : not wise to put into or keep in practice or effect **b** : THEORETICAL 1, IDEALISTIC **c** : not capable of dealing sensibly with practical matters **d** : IMPRACTICABLE 1 — **im•prac•ti•cal•i•ty** \im-ˌprak-ti-'kal-ət-ē\ *n* — **im•prac•ti•cal•ness** \im-'prak-ti-kəl-nəs, 'im-\ *n*

im•pre•cate \'im-pri-ˌkāt\ *vb* : to invoke evil upon : CURSE [Latin *imprecari,* from *in-* "²in-" + *precari* "to pray"] — **im•pre•ca•tion** \ˌim-pri-'kā-shən\ *n* — **im•pre•ca•to•ry** \'im-pri-kə-ˌtōr-ē, im-'prek-ə-, -ˌtȯr-\ *adj*

im•pre•cise \ˌim-pri-'sīs\ *adj* : not precise — **im•pre•cise•ly** *adv* — **im•pre•cise•ness** *n* — **im•pre•ci•sion** \-'sizh-ən\ *n*

im•preg•na•ble \im-'preg-nə-bəl\ *adj* : not capable of being taken by assault : able to resist any attack [Middle French *imprenable,* from *in-* "not" + *prenable* "vulnerable to capture", from *prendre* "to take", from Latin *prehendere*] — **im•preg•na•bil•i•ty** \-ˌpreg-nə-'bil-ət-ē\ *n* — **im•preg•na•ble•ness** \-'preg-nə-bəl-nəs\ *n* — **im•preg•na•bly** \-blē\ *adv*

im•preg•nate \im-'preg-ˌnāt\ *vt* **1 a** (1) : to make pregnant (2) : to introduce sperm cells into **b** : to make fertile or fruitful **2** : to cause (a material or substance) to be filled, permeated, or saturated ⟨*impregnate* wood with a preservative⟩ [Late Latin *impraegnare,* from Latin *in-* + *praegnas* "pregnant"] — **im•preg•na•tion** \ˌim-ˌpreg-'nā-shən\ *n* — **im•preg•na•tor** \im-'preg-ˌnāt-ər\ *n*

im•pre•sa•rio \ˌim-prə-'sär-ē-ˌō, -'sar-, -'ser-\ *n, pl* **-rios 1** : the manager or conductor of an opera or concert company **2** : one who puts on an entertainment **3** : PRODUCER 2, MANAGER [Italian, from *impresa* "undertaking"]

¹im•press \im-'pres\ *vt* **1 a** : to apply with pressure so as to imprint **b** : to produce (as a mark) by pressure **c** : to mark by or as if by pressure or stamping **2 a** : to produce a vivid impression of **b** : to affect especially forcibly or deeply : INFLUENCE [Latin *impressus,* past participle of *imprimere* "to press into, imprint", from *in-* + *premere* "to press"]

²im•press \'im-ˌpres\ *n* **1** : the act of impressing **2 a** : a mark made by pressure **b** : an image of something formed by or as if by pressure; *esp* : SEAL **c** : a product of pressure or influence **3** : a characteristic or distinctive mark : STAMP **4** : EFFECT 4, IMPRESSION

³im•press \im-'pres\ *vt* **1** : to seize for public service; *esp* : to force into naval service **2** : to enlist the aid or services of by strong argument or appeal [*in-* + *press*]

⁴im•press \'im-ˌpres\ *n* : IMPRESSMENT

im•press•ible \im-'pres-ə-bəl\ *adj* : capable of being impressed : SENSITIVE — **im•press•ibil•i•ty** \-ˌpres-ə-'bil-ət-ē\ *n* — **im•press•ibly** \-'pres-ə-ble\ *adv*

im•pres•sion \im-'presh-ən\ *n* **1** : the act or process of impressing **2** : the effect produced by impressing: as **a** : a stamp, form, or figure resulting from physical contact **b** : an especially marked influence or effect on feeling, sense, or mind **3 a** : a characteristic trait or feature resulting from influence **b** : an effect of change or improvement **c** : a telling image impressed on the senses or the mind **4 a** : one instance of the meeting of a printing surface and the material being printed; *also* : a single print or copy so made **b** : all the copies of a publication (as a book) printed at one time **5** : a usually indistinct or imprecise notion or remembrance **6** : an imitation of outstanding features in an artistic or theatrical medium; *esp* : an imitation in caricature of a noted personality as a form of theatrical entertainment — **im•pres•sion•al** \-'presh-nəl, -ən-l\ *adj*

im•pres•sion•able \im-'presh-nə-bəl, -ə-nə-\ *adj* : capable of being easily impressed : easily molded or influenced : PLASTIC — **im•pres•sion•abil•i•ty** \-ˌpresh-nə-'bil-ət-ē, -ə-nə-\ *n* — **im•pres•sion•able•ness** \-'presh-nə-bəl-nəs, -ə-nə-\ *n* — **im•pres•sion•ably** \-blē\ *adv*

im•pres•sion•ism \im-'presh-ə-ˌniz-əm\ *n* **1** *often cap* : a theory or practice in painting especially among French painters of about 1870 of representing the effect of light on objects by means of broken strokes of unmixed pigment that blend together when viewed from a distance **2 a** : the depiction of scene, emotion, or character by details evoking impressions rather than by recreating reality **b** : a style of musical composition designed to create moods through rich and varied harmonies **3** : a practice of presenting and elaborating one's reactions to a work of art — **im•pres•sion•ist** \-'presh-nəst, -ə-nəst\ *n or adj* — **im•pres•sion•is•tic** \-ˌpresh-ə-'nis-tik\ *adj* — **im•pres•sion•is•ti•cal•ly** \-ti-kə-lē, -klē\ *adv*

im•pres•sive \im-'pres-iv\ *adj* : making or tending to make a marked impression : stirring deep feeling especially of awe or admiration ⟨an *impressive* speech⟩ — **im•pres•sive•ly** *adv* — **im•pres•sive•ness** *n*

im•press•ment \im-'pres-mənt\ *n* : the act of seizing for public use or of impressing into public service

im•pri•ma•tur \ˌim-prə-ˈmät-ər\ *n* **1 a** : a license to print or publish **b** : official approval of a publication by a censor **2** : APPROVAL 1 [New Latin, "let it be printed", from *imprimere* "to print", from Latin, "to impress, imprint"]

1im•print \im-ˈprint, ˈim-ˌ\ *vt* **1** : to mark by or as if by pressure : STAMP, IMPRESS **2** : to fix firmly (as in the memory)

2im•print \ˈim-ˌprint\ *n* : something imprinted or printed: as **a** : 2IMPRESS 2 **b** : a publisher's name often with address and date of publication printed at the foot of a title page **c** : an indelible distinguishing effect or influence

im•print•ing \ˈim-ˌprint-ing, im-ˈ\ *n* : a behavior pattern that is firmly established during a susceptible period early in the life of a social animal and involves especially the recognition of and attraction to characters of its own kind or a substitute

im•pris•on \im-ˈpriz-n\ *vt* **-pris•oned; -pris•on•ing** \-ˈpriz-ning, -n-ing\ : to confine in or as if in prison — **im•pris•on•ment** \-ˈpriz-n-mənt\ *n*

im•prob•able \im-ˈpräb-ə-bəl, ˈim-\ *adj* : unlikely to be true or to occur — **im•prob•a•bil•i•ty** \im-ˌpräb-ə-ˈbil-ət-ē\ *n* — **im•prob•a•ble•ness** \im-ˈpräb-ə-bəl-nəs, ˈim-\ *n* — **im•prob•a•bly** \-ˈpräb-ə-blē\ *adv*

im•pro•bi•ty \im-ˈprō-bət-ē, ˈim-, -ˈpräb-ət-\ *n* : DISHONESTY

im•promp•tu \im-ˈpräm-tü, -ˈprämp-, -tyü\ *adj* **1** : made or done on or as if on the spur of the moment **2** : produced without previous study or preparation ⟨an *impromptu* speech⟩ [French, from *impromptu* "extemporaneously", from Latin *in promptu* "in readiness"] — **impromptu** *adv or n*

im•prop•er \im-ˈpräp-ər, ˈim-\ *adj* **1** : not proper, fit, or suitable ⟨*improper* dress for the occasion⟩ **2** : INCORRECT, INACCURATE ⟨an *improper* deduction⟩ **3** : not in accordance with good taste or good manners ⟨*improper* language⟩ **syn** see INDECOROUS — **im•prop•er•ly** *adv* — **im•prop•er•ness** *n*

improper fraction *n* : a fraction whose numerator is equal to or larger than the denominator

improper subset *n* : a set which contains the same elements as another set ⟨every set is an *improper subset* of itself⟩

im•pro•pri•ety \ˌim-prə-ˈprī-ət-ē\ *n, pl* **-ties 1** : the quality or state of being improper **2** : an improper act or remark; *esp* : an unacceptable use of a word or of language

im•prove \im-ˈprüv\ *vb* **1** : to make greater in amount or degree : INCREASE **2 a** : to increase in value or quality : make or grow better **b** : to increase the value of (real estate) by betterment (as by cultivation or the erection of buildings) **c** : to grade and drain (a road) and apply surfacing material other than pavement **3** : to make good use of ⟨*improved* their time by studying⟩ **4** : to make improvements ⟨*improve* on the carburetor⟩ [Anglo-French *emprouer* "to invest profitably", from Old French *en-* + *prou* "advantage", from Late Latin *prode*, from Latin *prodesse* "to be advantageous"] — **im•prov•able** \-ˈprü-və-bəl\ *adj* — **im•prov•er** *n*

im•prove•ment \im-ˈprüv-mənt\ *n* **1** : the act or process of improving **2 a** : the state of being improved; *esp* : increased value or excellence **b** : an instance or result of improvement **3** : something that increases value especially of real estate ⟨make *improvements* in an old house⟩

im•prov•i•dent \im-ˈpräv-əd-ənt, ˈim-, -ə-ˌdent\ *adj* : not providing for the future : THRIFTLESS — **im•prov•i•dence** \-əd-əns, -ə-ˌdens\ *n* — **im•prov•i•dent•ly** *adv*

im•prov•i•sa•tion \im-ˌpräv-ə-ˈzā-shən, ˌim-prə-və-\ *n* **1** : the act or art of improvising **2** : something that is improvised — **im•prov•i•sa•tion•al** \-shnəl, -shən-l\ *adj*

im•prov•i•sa•tor \im-ˈpräv-ə-ˌzāt-ər\ *n* : IMPROVISER — **im•prov•i•sa•to•ri•al** \-ˌpräv-ə-zə-ˈtōr-ē-əl, -ˈtòr-\ *or* **im•prov•i•sa•to•ry** \-ˈpräv-ə-zə-ˌtōr-ē, -ˌtòr-\ *adj*

im•pro•vise \ˌim-prə-ˈvīz\ *vb* **1** : to compose, recite, or sing on the spur of the moment **2** : to make, invent, or arrange offhand [French *improviser*, from Italian *improvvisare*, from Latin *improvisus* "sudden, unforeseen", from *in-* + *providēre* "to see ahead, provide"] — **im•pro•vis•er** *n*

im•pru•dent \im-ˈprüd-nt, ˈim-\ *adj* : not prudent : RASH, UNWISE — **im•pru•dence** \-ns\ *n* — **im•pru•dent•ly** *adv*

im•pu•dent \ˈim-pyəd-ənt\ *adj* : showing contempt for or disregard of others : INSOLENT, DISRESPECTFUL [Latin *impudens* "shameless, impudent", from *in-* + *pudēre* "to feel shame"] — **im•pu•dence** \-əns\ *n* — **im•pu•dent•ly** *adv*

im•pugn \im-ˈpyün\ *vt* : to oppose or attack as false : cast doubt on [Middle French *impugner*, from Latin *impugnare*, from *in-* + *pugnare* "to fight"] — **im•pugn•er** *n*

im•puis•sance \im-ˈpwis-ns, ˈim-, -ˈpyü-ə-səns\ *n* : WEAKNESS 1, POWERLESSNESS

im•pulse \im-ˌpəls\ *n* **1 a** : a force that starts a body into motion : IMPULSION **b** : the motion produced by such an impulsion **2** : a sudden spontaneous arousing of the mind and spirit to do something : an inclination to act ⟨an *impulse* to run away⟩ ⟨acts on *impulse*⟩ **3** : NERVE IMPULSE **4** : the product of the average value of a force and the time during which it acts [Latin *impulsus*, from *impellere* "to impel"] **syn** see MOTIVE

im•pul•sion \im-ˈpəl-shən\ *n* **1 a** : the action of impelling : the state of being impelled **b** : an impelling force **c** : IMPETUS 1 **2** : IMPULSE 2 **3** : COMPULSION 2

im•pul•sive \im-ˈpəl-siv\ *adj* **1** : having the power of driving or impelling **2** : acting or liable to act on impulse : moved or caused by an impulse **syn** see SPONTANEOUS — **im•pul•sive•ly** *adv* — **im•pul•sive•ness** *n*

im•pu•ni•ty \im-ˈpyü-nət-ē\ *n* : immunity or freedom from punishment, harm, or loss [Latin *impunitas*, from *impune* "without punishment", from *in-* + *poena* "pain, penalty"]

im•pure \im-ˈpyu̇r, ˈim-\ *adj* : not pure: as **a** : UNCHASTE, OBSCENE ⟨*impure* language⟩ **b** : containing something unclean : FOUL ⟨*impure* water⟩ **c** : ritually unclean **d** : marked by an intermixture of foreign elements or by substandard, incongruous, or objectionable locutions **e** : mixed with some other substance and especially some inferior substance ⟨an *impure* chemical⟩ **f** : MIXED, BASTARD ⟨an *impure* style of ornamentation⟩ — **im•pure•ly** *adv* — **im•pure•ness** *n*

im•pu•ri•ty \im-ˈpyu̇r-ət-ē, ˈim-\ *n, pl* **-ties 1** : the quality or state of being impure **2** : something that is impure or that makes something else impure ⟨*impurities* in water⟩

im•pute \im-ˈpyüt\ *vt* **1** : to place the responsibility or blame for : CHARGE **2** : to credit to a person or a cause : ATTRIBUTE [Latin *imputare*, from *in-* "2in-" + *putare* "to reckon"] **syn** see ASCRIBE — **im•put•able** \-ˈpyüt-ə-bəl\ *adj* — **im•put•ably** \-blē\ *adv* — **im•pu•ta•tion** \ˌim-pyə-ˈtā-shən\ *n* — **im•pu•ta•tive** \im-ˈpyüt-ət-iv\ *adj* — **im•pu•ta•tive•ly** *adv*

1in \in, ˈin, ən, ᵊn\ *prep* **1a** — used as a function word to indicate inclusion, location, or position within limits ⟨*in* the lake⟩ ⟨*in* the summer⟩ **b** : INTO 1a ⟨went *in* the house⟩ **2** : by means of : WITH ⟨written *in* pencil⟩ **3a** — used as a function word to indicate manner, state, or situation ⟨alike *in* some respects⟩ ⟨left *in* a hurry⟩ **b** : INTO 2a ⟨broke *in* pieces⟩ **4** — used as a function word to indicate purpose ⟨said *in* reply⟩ [Old English]

2in \ˈin\ *adv* **1 a** : to or toward the inside ⟨went *in* and closed the door⟩ **b** : to or toward some particular place ⟨flew *in* on the first plane⟩ **c** : at close quarters : NEAR ⟨play close *in*⟩ **d** : into the midst of something ⟨mix *in* the flour⟩ **e** : to or at its proper place ⟨fit a piece *in*⟩ **f** : into line ⟨fell *in* with our plans⟩ **2 a** : within a particular place; *esp* : within the customary place of residence or business ⟨tell them I'm not *in*⟩ **b** : in the position of insider ⟨*in* on the scheme⟩ **c** : on good terms **d** : in a position of assured success; *also* : in style or season **e** : at hand or on hand ⟨the evidence is all *in*⟩ ⟨harvests are *in*⟩

3in \ˈin\ *adj* **1 a** : being inside or within ⟨the *in* part⟩ **b** : being in position, operation, or power ⟨the *in* party⟩ **2** : directed or bound inward : INCOMING ⟨the *in* train⟩ **3** : keenly aware of and responsive to what is new and smart ⟨the *in* crowd⟩ **4** : extremely fashionable ⟨the *in* thing to do⟩

4in \ˈin\ *n* **1** : one who is in office or power or on the inside **2** : INFLUENCE, PULL ⟨had an *in* with the boss⟩

1in- *or* **il-** *or* **im-** *or* **ir-** *prefix* : not : NON- : UN- — usually *il-* before *l* ⟨*il*logical⟩, *im-* before *b, m,* or *p* ⟨*im*balance⟩ ⟨*im*moral⟩ ⟨*im*practical⟩, *ir-* before *r* ⟨*ir*reducible⟩, and *in-* before other sounds ⟨*in*conclusive ⟩ [Latin]

See *in-* and 2d element

inaccessibility	**inadequateness**	**inapposite**
inaccessible	**inadmissibility**	**inappositely**
inaccessibly	**inadmissible**	**inappositeness**
inadequacy	**inadvisability**	**inappreciative**
inadequate	**inadvisable**	**inappreciatively**
inadequately	**inapparent**	**inappreciativeness**

\ə\ **abut**	\au̇\ **out**	\i\ **tip**	\ò\ **saw**	\u̇\ **foot**
\ər\ **further**	\ch\ **chin**	\ī\ **life**	\òi\ **coin**	\y\ **yet**
\a\ **mat**	\e\ **pet**	\j\ **job**	\th\ **thin**	\yü\ **few**
\ā\ **take**	\ē\ **easy**	\ng\ **sing**	\t͟h\ **this**	\yu̇\ **cure**
\ä\ **cot, cart**	\g\ **go**	\ō\ **bone**	\ü\ **food**	\zh\ **vision**

inapproachable
inappropriate
inappropriately
inappropriateness
inarguable
inarguably
inartistic
inartistically
inauspicious
inauspiciously
inauspiciousness
inauthentic
incohesive
incommensurable
incommensurably
incommodious
incommodiously
incommodiousness
incommutable
incompliant
inconsecutive
inconsumable
indecipherable
indestructibility
indestructible
indevout
indevoutly
indiscoverable
ineducable
ineffaceable
ineradicable
inessential
inexcitability
inexcitable
inexpert
inexpertly
inexpertness
inexpiable
inexplainable
inexplicit
inextinguishable
infeasibility
infeasible
injudicious
injudiciously
injudiciousness
insolvable
insurmountable
insusceptibility
insusceptible
insusceptibly

^{2}**in-** *or* **il-** *or* **im-** *or* **ir-** *prefix* **1 :** in : within : into : toward : on **2 :** ^{1}EN- ⟨*implant*⟩ — in both senses usually *il-* before *l*, *im-* before *b*, *m*, or *p*, *ir-* before *r*, and *in-* before other sounds **[**Latin, from *in* "in, into"**]**

^{1}**-in** \ən, ^{ə}n, ˌin\ *n suffix* **:** chemical compound ⟨insul*in*⟩ **[**French *-ine*, from Latin *-īna*, feminine of *-īnus* "^{1}-ine"**]**

^{2}**-in** \-ˌin\ *n combining form* **1 :** organized public protest by means of or in favor of : demonstration ⟨teach-*in*⟩ ⟨love-*in*⟩ **2 :** public group activity ⟨sing-*in*⟩ **[***in* (as in *sit-in*)**]**

in•abil•i•ty \ˌin-ə-ˈbil-ət-ē\ *n* **:** the condition of being unable : lack of ability, power, or means

• **syn** INABILITY, DISABILITY both denote lack of ability to perform a given act or to pursue a specific trade or profession. INABILITY implies lack of power to perform and suggests lack of means, health, training, or temperamental fitness ⟨*inability* to see⟩ ⟨*inability* to understand⟩ DISABILITY implies the loss of power to perform due to accident, illness, or disqualification and applies both to the resulting inability and to the cause of it ⟨because of *disabilities* many veterans failed to return to their former occupations⟩

in absentia \ˌin-ab-ˈsen-chə, -chē-ə\ *adv* **:** in one's absence : while absent ⟨was awarded the degree *in absentia*⟩ **[**Latin, "in absence"**]**

in•ac•cu•ra•cy \in-ˈak-yə-rə-sē, ˈin-\ *n, pl* **-cies 1 :** the quality or state of being inaccurate **2 :** MISTAKE, ERROR

in•ac•cu•rate \-rət\ *adj* **:** not accurate : FAULTY — **in•ac•cu•rate•ly** *adv*

in•ac•tion \in-ˈak-shən, ˈin-\ *n* **:** lack of action or activity

in•ac•ti•vate \in-ˈak-tə-ˌvāt, ˈin-\ *vt* **:** to make inactive — **in•ac•ti•va•tion** \in-ˌak-tə-ˈvā-shən\ *n*

in•ac•tive \in-ˈak-tiv, ˈin-\ *adj* **:** not active: as **a :** INDOLENT 2, SLUGGISH **b :** being out of use or activity **c :** relating to members of the armed forces who are not performing or available for military duties **d :** chemically inert — **in•ac•tive•ly** *adv* — **in•ac•tiv•i•ty** \ˌin-ak-ˈtiv-ət-ē\ *n*

• **syn** INERT, IDLE: INACTIVE applies to anyone or anything not in action or in operation or at work ⟨an *inactive* mine⟩ ⟨an *inactive* seasonal worker⟩ INERT as applied to a thing implies being powerless to move itself or to affect other things ⟨an *inert* gas⟩ ⟨*inert* drugs no longer effective⟩ and applied to a person suggests an inherent or habitual indisposition to activity ⟨politically *inert* citizens⟩ IDLE applies to people who are not busy or occupied or to their powers or implements ⟨*idle* laborers hoping for work⟩

in•ad•ver•tence \ˌin-əd-ˈvərt-ns\ *n* **:** INATTENTION; *also* **:** a result of inattention : OVERSIGHT **[**Medieval Latin *inadvertentia*, from Latin *in-* + *advertere* "to notice"**]** — **in•ad•ver•ten•cy** \-n-sē\ *n*

in•ad•ver•tent \-nt\ *adj* **1 :** INATTENTIVE **2 :** UNINTENTIONAL — **in•ad•ver•tent•ly** *adv*

in•alien•able \in-ˈāl-yə-nə-bəl, ˈin-, -ˈā-lē-ə-nə-\ *adj* **:** not capable of being taken away, given up, or transferred ⟨*inalienable* rights⟩ — **in•alien•abil•i•ty** \in-ˌāl-yə-nə-ˈbil-ət-ē, -ˌā-lē-ə-nə-\ *n* — **in•alien•ably** \in-ˈāl-yə-nə-blē, ˈin-, -ˈā-lē-ə-nə-\ *adv*

in•al•ter•a•ble \in-ˈȯl-tə-rə-bəl, ˈin-, -trə-\ *adj* **:** UNALTERABLE — **in•al•ter•abil•i•ty** \in-ˌȯl-tə-rə-ˈbil-ət-ē, -trə-\ *n* — **in•al•ter•able•ness** \in-ˈȯl-tə-rə-bəl-nəs, -trə-\ *n* — **in•al•ter•ably** \-blē\ *adv*

in•amo•ra•ta \in-ˌam-ə-ˈrät-ə\ *n* **:** a woman with whom one is in love **[**Italian *innamorata*, from *innamorare* "to inspire with love", from *in-* "^{2}in-" + *amore* "love", from Latin *amor***]**

inane \in-ˈān\ *adj* **:** lacking significance, meaning, or point : SILLY **[**Latin *inanis***]** **syn** see INSIPID — **inane•ly** *adv* — **inane•ness** \-ˈān-nəs\ *n*

in•an•i•mate \in-ˈan-ə-mət, ˈin-\ *adj* **1 :** not animate: **a :** not endowed with life or spirit **b :** lacking consciousness or power of motion **2 :** not animated or lively : DULL — **in•an•i•mate•ly** *adv* — **in•an•i•mate•ness** *n*

in•a•ni•tion \ˌin-ə-ˈnish-ən\ *n* **:** a weakened condition resulting from or as if from lack of food and water **[**Medieval Latin *inanitio*, from Latin *inanire* "to empty", from *inanis* "empty, inane"**]**

inan•i•ty \in-ˈan-ət-ē\ *n, pl* **-ties 1 :** the quality or state of being inane; *esp* **:** foolish or trivial character **2 :** something that is inane; *esp* **:** a senseless or foolish remark

in•ap•peas•able \ˌin-ə-ˈpē-zə-bəl\ *adj* **:** UNAPPEASABLE

in•ap•pe•tence \in-ˈap-ət-əns\ *n* **:** lack of appetite

in•ap•pli•ca•ble \in-ˈap-li-kə-bəl, ˈin-; ˌin-ə-ˈplik-ə-\ *adj* **:** not applicable : UNSUITABLE, IRRELEVANT — **in•ap•pli•ca•bil•i•ty** \in-ˌap-li-kə-ˈbil-ət-ē, ˌin-ə-ˌplik-ə-\ *n* — **in•ap•pli•ca•bly** \in-ˈap-li-kə-blē, ˈin-; ˌin-ə-ˈplik-ə-\ *adv*

in•ap•pre•cia•ble \ˌin-ə-ˈprē-shə-bəl\ *adj* **:** too small to be perceived : very slight — **in•ap•pre•cia•bly** \-blē\ *adv*

in•apt \in-ˈapt, ˈin-\ *adj* **1 :** not suitable **2 :** INEPT 1 — **in•apt•ly** *adv* — **in•apt•ness** \-ˈapt-nəs, -ˈap-\ *n*

in•ap•ti•tude \-ˈap-tə-ˌtüd, -ˌtyüd\ *n* **:** lack of aptitude

in•ar•tic•u•late \ˌin-är-ˈtik-yə-lət\ *adj* **1 a :** not understandable as spoken words ⟨*inarticulate* cries⟩ **b :** incapable of speech especially under emotional stress : MUTE **c :** incapable of being expressed by speech ⟨*inarticulate* longings⟩ **d :** not voiced or expressed **2 :** incapable of giving coherent, clear, or effective expression to one's ideas or feelings — **in•ar•tic•u•late•ly** *adv* — **in•ar•tic•u•late•ness** n

in•as•much as \ˌin-əz-ˌməch-əz\ *conj* **1 :** to the extent that **2 :** in view of the fact that : SINCE

in•at•ten•tion \ˌin-ə-ˈten-chən\ *n* **:** failure to pay attention

in•at•ten•tive \-ˈtent-iv\ *adj* **:** marked by inattention — **in•at•ten•tive•ly** *adv* — **in•at•ten•tive•ness** *n*

^{1}**in•au•gu•ral** \in-ˈȯ-gyə-rəl, -gə-rəl, -grəl\ *adj* **1 :** of or relating to an inauguration ⟨*inaugural* address⟩ **2 :** marking a beginning : first in a projected series ⟨*inaugural* run of a new luxury liner⟩

^{2}**inaugural** *n* **1 :** an inaugural address **2 :** INAUGURATION

in•au•gu•rate \in-ˈȯ-gyə-ˌrāt, -gə-\ *vt* **1 :** to introduce into office with suitable ceremonies : INSTALL ⟨*inaugurate* a president⟩ **2 :** to celebrate or mark the opening of ⟨*inaugurate* the new athletic field⟩ **3 :** to commence or enter upon : BEGIN ⟨*inaugurate* a reform⟩ **[**Latin *inaugurare* "to practice augury, inaugurate", from *in-* + *augur* "augur"; from the consulting of omens at inaugurations**]** — **in•au•gu•ra•tor** \-ˌrāt-ər\ *n*

in•au•gu•ra•tion \in-ˌȯ-gyə-ˈrā-shən, -gə-\ *n* **:** an act of inaugurating; *esp* **:** a ceremonial introduction into office

^{1}**in between** *adv* **:** BETWEEN ⟨were neither young nor old but fell somewhere *in between*⟩

^{2}**in between** *prep* **:** BETWEEN ⟨a meadow lies *in between* the house and the woods⟩

in•board \ˈin-ˌbōrd, -ˌbȯrd\ *adv* **1 :** inside the line of a ship's bulwarks or hull : toward the center line of a ship **2 :** in a position closer or closest to the longitudinal axis of an aircraft — **inboard** *adj*

in•born \ˈin-ˈbȯrn\ *adj* **1 :** born in or with one : not acquired by training or experience : NATURAL **2 :** HEREDITARY 1, INHERITED **syn** see INNATE

in•bound \ˈin-ˈbau̇nd\ *adj* **:** inward bound ⟨*inbound* traffic⟩

in•breathe \ˈin-ˈbrēth\ *vt* **:** INHALE 2

in•bred \ˈin-ˈbred\ *adj* **1 a :** present from birth **b :** planted in by early teaching or training : INCULCATED **2 :** subjected to or produced by inbreeding **syn** see INNATE

in•breed \ˈin-ˈbrēd\ *vb* **-bred** \-ˈbred\; **-breed•ing :** to produce by or subject to inbreeding

in•breed•ing \ˈin-ˌbrēd-ing\ *n* **1 :** the interbreeding of closely related individuals especially to preserve and fix desirable characters of and to eliminate unfavorable characters from a stock **2 :** confinement to a narrow range or a local or limited field of choice

In•ca \ˈing-kə\ *n* **1 :** a noble or a member of the Quechuan peoples of Peru maintaining an empire until the Spanish conquest **2 :** a member of any people under Inca influence **[**Spanish, from Quechua *inka* "king, prince"**]** — **In•can** \-kən\ *adj*

in•cal•cu•la•ble \in-ˈkal-kyə-lə-bəl, ˈin-\ *adj* **1 :** not capable of being calculated; *esp* : too large or numerous to be calculated **2** : not capable of being known in advance : UNCERTAIN — **in•cal•cu•la•bil•i•ty** \in-ˌkal-kyə-lə-'bil-ət-ē\ *n* — **in•cal•cu•la•bly** \-blē\ *adv*

in•can•des•cence \ˌin-kən-'des-ns\ *n* : a glowing condition of a body due to its high temperature

in•can•des•cent \-nt\ *adj* **1 a** : white or glowing with intense heat **b** : strikingly bright, radiant, or clear **c** : BRILLIANT ⟨*incandescent* wit⟩ **2 a** : of, relating to, or being light produced by incandescence **b** : producing light by incandescence [derived from Latin *incandescere* "to become hot", from *in-* + *candēre* "to glow"] — **in•can•des•cent•ly** *adv*

incandescent lamp *n* : a lamp whose light is produced by the glow of a filament heated by an electric current

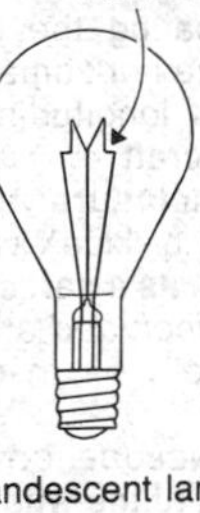

incandescent lamp

in•can•ta•tion \ˌin-ˌkan-'tā-shən\ *n* : a use of spells or charms spoken or sung as part of a ritual of magic; *also* : a formula of words so used [Middle French, from Late Latin *incantatio*, from Latin *incantare* "to enchant"] — **in•can•ta•tion•al** \-shnəl, -shən-l\ *adj* — **in•can•ta•to•ry** \in-'kant-ə-ˌtōr-ē, -ˌtȯr-\ *adj*

in•ca•pa•ble \in-'kā-pə-bəl, 'in-\ *adj* : not capable : lacking capacity, ability, or qualification for the purpose or end in view: as **a** : not in a state or of a kind to admit : INSUSCEPTIBLE ⟨*incapable* of precise measurement⟩ **b** : not able or fit : UNQUALIFIED, INCOMPETENT — **in•ca•pa•bil•i•ty** \in-ˌkā-pə-'bil-ət-ē\ *n* — **in•ca•pa•ble•ness** \in-'kā-pə-bəl-nəs, 'in-\ *n* — **in•ca•pa•bly** \-blē\ *adv*

in•ca•pac•i•tate \ˌin-kə-'pas-ə-ˌtāt\ *vt* **1** : to deprive of natural capacity or power : DISABLE **2** : to make legally incapable or ineligible — **in•ca•pac•i•ta•tion** \-ˌpas-ə-'tā-shən\ *n*

in•ca•pac•i•ty \ˌin-kə-'pas-ət-ē, -'pas-tē\ *n, pl* **-ties** : lack of ability or power ⟨a seeming *incapacity* for telling the truth⟩

in•car•cer•ate \in-'kär-sə-ˌrāt\ *vt* : IMPRISON, CONFINE [Latin *incarcerare*, from *in-* + *carcer* "prison" — see CANCEL *origin*] — **in•car•cer•a•tion** \in-ˌkär-sə-'rā-shən\ *n*

[1]**in•car•na•dine** \in-'kär-nə-ˌdīn, -ˌdēn\ *adj* : RED 1a; *esp* : BLOODRED [Middle French *incarnadin*, from Italian *incarnadino*, from *incarnato* "flesh-colored", from Late Latin *incarnare* "to incarnate"]

[2]**incarnadine** *vt* : to make incarnadine : REDDEN

[1]**in•car•nate** \in-'kär-nət, -ˌnāt\ *adj* **1** : invested with bodily and especially human nature and form **2** : EMBODIED, PERSONIFIED ⟨a fiend *incarnate*⟩ [Late Latin *incarnatus*, past participle of *incarnare* "to incarnate", from Latin *in-* + *carn-*, *caro* "flesh"]

[2]**in•car•nate** \-ˌnāt\ *vt* : to make incarnate

in•car•na•tion \ˌin-ˌkär-'nā-shən\ *n* **1** : the act of incarnating : the state of being incarnate **2 a** : the embodiment of a deity or spirit in an earthly form; *esp, cap* : the union of divinity with humanity in Jesus Christ **b** : a concrete example of a quality or concept; *esp* : a person showing a trait or typical character to a marked degree

incase *variant of* ENCASE

in•cau•tious \in-'kȯ-shəs, 'in-\ *adj* : lacking in caution : CARELESS — **in•cau•tious•ly** *adv* — **in•cau•tious•ness** *n*

in•cen•di•a•rism \in-'sen-dē-ə-ˌriz-əm\ *n* : incendiary action or behavior

[1]**in•cen•di•ary** \in-'sen-dē-ˌer-ē\ *n, pl* **-ar•ies 1 a** : a person who unlawfully sets fire to property **b** : an incendiary agent (as a bomb) **2** : a person who excites quarrels : AGITATOR [Latin *incendiarius*, from *incendium* "conflagration", from *incendere* "to set on fire"]

[2]**incendiary** *adj* **1** : of, relating to, or involving unlawful burning of property **2** : tending to excite or inflame quarrels : INFLAMMATORY **3 a** : igniting combustible materials spontaneously **b** : relating to or being a missile containing chemicals that ignite on bursting or on contact

[1]**in•cense** \'in-ˌsens\ *n* **1** : material used to produce a fragrant odor when burned **2 a** : the perfume given off by some spices and gums when burned **b** : a pleasing scent [Old French *encens*, from Late Latin *incensum*, from Latin *incendere* "to set on fire"]

[2]**in•cense** \in-'sens\ *vt* : to inflame with anger or indignation ⟨*incensed* by their bad behavior⟩ [Middle French *encenser*, from Latin *incendere*, literally, "to set on fire"]

in•cen•ter \'in-ˌsent-ər\ *n* : the point of intersection of the bisectors of the angles of a triangle

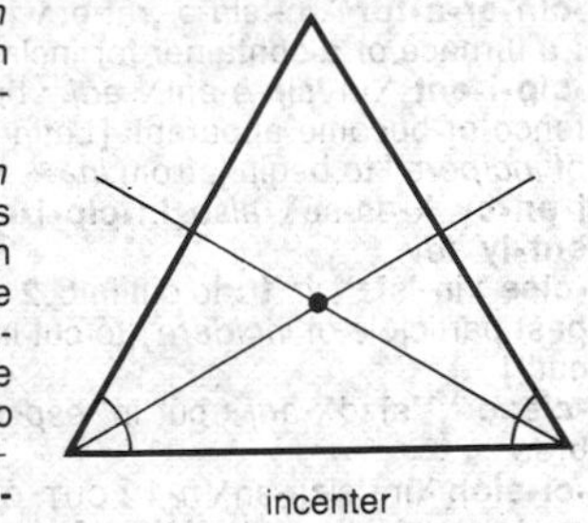
incenter

in•cen•tive \in-'sent-iv\ *n* : something that arouses or spurs one on to action or effort : STIMULUS [Late Latin *incentivum*, from Latin *incentivus* "setting the tune", from *incinere* "to set the tune", from *in-* + *canere* "to sing"] — **incentive** *adj*

in•cep•tion \in-'sep-shən\ *n* : an act, process, or instance of beginning : COMMENCEMENT ⟨the program has been a success since its *inception*⟩ [Latin *inceptio*, from *incipere* "to begin", from *in-* + *capere* "to take"] **syn** see ORIGIN

in•cep•tive \in-'sep-tiv\ *adj* : of or relating to a beginning — **in•cep•tive•ly** *adv*

in•cer•ti•tude \in-'sərt-ə-ˌtüd, 'in-, -ˌtyüd\ *n* : UNCERTAINTY: **a** : absence of assurance : DOUBT, INDECISION **b** : INSTABILITY, INSECURITY

in•ces•sant \in-'ses-nt, 'in-\ *adj* : continuing without interruption : UNCEASING ⟨*incessant* rains⟩ [Late Latin *incessans*, from Latin *in-* + *cessare* "to delay"] **syn** see CONTINUAL — **in•ces•sant•ly** *adv*

in•cest \'in-ˌsest\ *n* : sexual intercourse between persons so closely related that they are forbidden by law to marry; *also* : the statutory crime of such a relationship [Latin *incestum*, from *incestus* "impure", from *in-* + *castus* "pure"]

in•ces•tu•ous \in-'ses-chə-wəs\ *adj* **1** : constituting or involving incest **2** : guilty of incest — **in•ces•tu•ous•ly** *adv* — **in•ces•tu•ous•ness** *n*

[1]**inch** \'inch\ *n* **1** : a unit of length equal to 1/36 yard (2.54 centimeters) — see MEASURE table **2** : a small amount, distance, or degree ⟨wouldn't move an *inch*⟩ **3** *pl* : STATURE 1, HEIGHT [Old English *ynce*, from Latin *uncia* "12th part, inch, ounce"]

[2]**inch** *vb* : to move by small degrees

[3]**inch** *n, chiefly Scottish* : ISLAND 1 [Scottish Gaelic *innis*]

inch•meal \'inch-ˌmēl\ *adv* : little by little : GRADUALLY

in•cho•ate \in-'kō-ət, 'in-kə-ˌwāt\ *adj* : being recently begun or only partly in existence or operation; *esp* : imperfectly formed ⟨*inchoate* suspicions⟩ [Latin *inchoatus*, past participle of *inchoare* "to begin"] — **in•cho•ate•ly** *adv* — **in•cho•ate•ness** *n*

inch•worm \'inch-ˌwərm\ *n* : LOOPER 1

in•ci•dence \'in-səd-əns, -sə-ˌdens\ *n* **1 a** : an act or fact of affecting : OCCURRENCE **b** : rate of occurrence or influence ⟨a high *incidence* of crime⟩ **2 a** : the arrival of something (as a projectile or a ray of light) at a surface **b** : ANGLE OF INCIDENCE

[1]**in•ci•dent** \'in-səd-ənt, -sə-ˌdent\ *n* **1 a** : an occurrence that is a separate item of experience : HAPPENING **b** : an accompanying minor occurrence **2** : an action likely to lead to grave consequences especially in diplomatic matters **3** : something dependent on or subordinate to something else of greater importance [Middle French, from Medieval Latin *incidens*, from Latin *incidere* "to fall into, occur", from *in-* + *cadere* "to fall"] **syn** see OCCURRENCE

[2]**incident** *adj* **1** : occurring or likely to occur as a minor consequence or accompaniment ⟨a question *incident* to the main topic⟩ **2** : dependent on or relating to another thing **3** : falling or striking on something ⟨*incident* light rays⟩

[1]**in•ci•den•tal** \ˌin-sə-'dent-l\ *adj* **1** : occurring merely by chance or without intention **2** : being likely to happen as a chance or minor consequence ⟨*incidental* expenses of a trip⟩ — **in•ci•den•tal•ly** \-'dent-lē, -l-ē\ *adv*

[2]**incidental** *n* **1** : something incidental **2** *pl* : minor items (as of expense) that are not listed individually

\ə\ **abut**	\aů\ **out**	\i\ **tip**	\ȯ\ **saw**	\ů\ **foot**
\ər\ **further**	\ch\ **chin**	\ī\ **life**	\ȯi\ **coin**	\y\ **yet**
\a\ **mat**	\e\ **pet**	\j\ **job**	\th\ **thin**	\yü\ **few**
\ā\ **take**	\ē\ **easy**	\ng\ **sing**	\t͟h\ **this**	\yů\ **cure**
\ä\ **cot, cart**	\g\ **go**	\ō\ **bone**	\ü\ **food**	\zh\ **vision**

in•cin•er•ate \in-'sin-ə-,rāt\ *vt* **:** to burn to ashes [Medieval Latin *incinerare,* from Latin *in-* + *ciner-, cinis* "ashes"] — **in•cin•er•a•tion** \in-,sin-ə-'rā-shən\ *n*

in•cin•er•a•tor \in-'sin-ə-,rāt-ər\ *n* **:** one that incinerates; *esp* **:** a furnace or a container for incinerating waste materials

in•cip•i•ent \in-'sip-ē-ənt\ *adj* **:** beginning to come into existence or become apparent [Latin *incipiens,* present participle of *incipere* "to begin", from *in-* + *capere* "to take"] — **in•cip•i•en•cy** \-ən-sē\ *also* **in•cip•i•ence** \-əns\ *n* — **in•cip•i•ent•ly** *adv*

in•cise \in-'sīz\ *vt* **1 :** to cut into **2 :** ENGRAVE 1a [Latin *incisus,* past participle of *incidere* "to cut into", from *in-* + *caedere* "to cut"]

in•cised \-'sīzd\ *adj* **:** cut in; *esp* **:** decorated with incised figures

in•ci•sion \in-'sizh-ən\ *n* **1 :** CUT, GASH; *esp* **:** an incised wound made surgically in the body **2 :** an act of incising **3 :** incisive quality

in•ci•sive \in-'sī-siv\ *adj* **:** impressively direct and decisive ⟨an *incisive* writing style⟩ ⟨an *incisive* and convincing argument⟩ — **in•ci•sive•ly** *adv* — **in•ci•sive•ness** *n*

• **syn** INCISIVE, TRENCHANT, CUTTING, BITING mean having or manifesting a keen mind. INCISIVE implies a power to impress the mind by keen penetration, directness, and decisiveness ⟨no one could ignore that *incisive* command⟩ TRENCHANT implies an energetic cutting or deep probing so as to reveal distinctions or get to the heart of the matter ⟨a *trenchant* critic of political pretensions⟩ CUTTING suggests sarcasm or penetrating accuracy that wounds the feelings ⟨makes the most *cutting* remarks with that quiet voice⟩ BITING adds a greater implication of harsh vehemence or ironic force ⟨a *biting* commentary on the election⟩

in•ci•sor \in-'sī-zər\ *n* **:** a tooth adapted for cutting; *esp* **:** one of the cutting teeth in front of the canines of a mammal — **incisor** *adj*

in•ci•ta•tion \,in-,sī-'tā-shən, ,in-sə-\ *n* **:** INCITEMENT

in•cite \in-'sīt\ *vt* **:** to move to action **:** stir up **:** urge on [Middle French *inciter,* from Latin *incitare* "to put in motion, rouse, cite"] — **in•cit•er** *n*

• **syn** INSTIGATE, ABET, FOMENT: INCITE stresses a stirring up and urging on and may or may not imply initiative ⟨propaganda *inciting* war⟩ INSTIGATE implies responsibility for initiating another's action and often connotes dubious or evil intention ⟨pamphleteers whose writings *instigated* rebellion⟩ ABET implies both assisting and encouraging ⟨traitors *abetting* the enemy⟩ FOMENT stresses persistence in goading ⟨hawks incessantly *fomented* war⟩

in•cite•ment \in-'sīt-mənt\ *n* **1 :** the act of inciting **:** the state of being incited ⟨charged with *incitement* to riot⟩ **2 :** something that incites **:** INCENTIVE

in•ci•vil•i•ty \,in-sə-'vil-ət-ē\ *n, pl* **-ties 1 :** the quality or state of being uncivil **2 :** a rude or discourteous act

in•clem•ent \in-'klem-ənt, 'in-\ *adj* **:** physically severe **:** STORMY, ROUGH ⟨*inclement* weather⟩; *also* **:** marked by such weather ⟨an *inclement* day⟩ — **in•clem•en•cy** \-ən-sē\ *n* — **in•clem•ent•ly** *adv*

in•clin•able \in-'klī-nə-bəl\ *adj* **1 :** having a tendency or inclination **:** DISPOSED ⟨*inclinable* to idleness⟩ **2 :** favorably disposed ⟨*inclinable* to their request⟩

in•cli•na•tion \,in-klə-'nā-shən, ,ing-\ *n* **1 :** an act or the action of bending or inclining: as **a :** [2]BOW, NOD **b :** a tilting of something **2 :** a particular disposition of mind or character; *esp* **:** LIKING **3 a :** a departure from the true vertical or horizontal **:** SLANT ⟨the *inclination* of the earth's axis⟩; *also* **:** the degree of such departure **b :** an inclined surface **:** SLOPE **4 :** a tendency to a particular state, character, or action ⟨the weather showed some *inclination* to snow⟩ — **in•cli•na•tion•al** \-shnəl, -shən-l\ *adj*

[1]**in•cline** \in-'klīn\ *vb* **1 :** to bend the head or body forward **:** BOW **2 :** to lean in one's mind **:** be favorable (as toward a person, an opinion, or a course of action) **:** TEND ⟨*incline* toward the second of two proposals⟩ **3 :** to deviate from a line, direction, or course **:** SLOPE, SLANT; *esp* **:** to deviate from the vertical or horizontal **4 :** to cause to bend, bow, slope, or slant **5 :** to have influence on (as in direction, course of action, or opinion) [Middle French *incliner,* from Latin *inclinare,* from *in-* + *clinare* "to lean"] — **in•clin•er** *n*

[2]**in•cline** \'in-,klīn\ *n* **:** an inclined plane **:** GRADE, SLOPE

in•clined \in-'klīnd, *2 also* 'in-,\ *adj* **1 :** having an inclination, disposition, or tendency **2 a :** having a slant or slope **b :** making an angle with a line or plane

inclined plane *n* **:** a plane surface that makes an oblique angle with the plane of the horizon

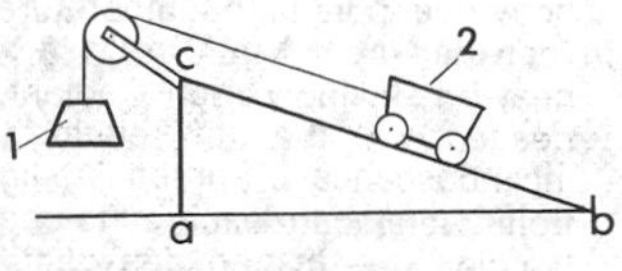

inclined plane: *ab* base, *ac* height, *cb* inclined plane, *1* force, *2* resistance

in•cli•nom•e•ter \,in-klə-'näm-ət-ər, ,ing-\ *n* **1 :** an apparatus for determining the direction of the earth's magnetic field with reference to the plane of the horizon **2 :** an instrument for indicating the inclination to the horizontal of the lateral or longitudinal axis of an aircraft

inclose, inclosure *variant of* ENCLOSE, ENCLOSURE

in•clude \in-'klüd\ *vt* **1 :** to shut up **:** ENCLOSE **2 :** to take in or comprise as a part of a whole **3 :** to contain between ⟨two sides and the *included* angle⟩ [Latin *includere,* from *in-* + *claudere* "to close"] — **in•clud•able** *or* **in•clud•ible** \-'klüd-ə-bəl\ *adj*

• **syn** INCLUDE, COMPREHEND, INVOLVE mean to contain within as a part of the whole. INCLUDE suggests containing something as a constituent or subordinate part of a larger whole ⟨most oaks are *included* in the genus *Quercus*⟩ COMPREHEND implies that something comes within the range or scope of a statement or definition ⟨in some cases the term *commerce* does not *comprehend* navigation⟩ INVOLVE suggests an intimate entangling or mingling a thing with a whole, often as an inevitable result or an essential antecedent ⟨surrender *involves* submission⟩ ⟨freedom *involves* responsibility⟩ **syn** see in addition COMPRISE

in•clu•sion \in-'klü-zhən\ *n* **1 :** the act of including **:** the state of being included **2 :** something that is included; *esp* **:** a passive product of cell activity (as a starch grain) within the protoplasm [Latin *inclusio,* from *includere* "to include"]

in•clu•sive \in-'klü-siv, -ziv\ *adj* **1 :** including the specified limits and everything in between ⟨March to June *inclusive*⟩ **2 :** broad or complete in orientation, scope, or coverage ⟨an *inclusive* insurance policy⟩ — **in•clu•sive•ly** *adv* — **in•clu•sive•ness** *n*

inclusive of *prep* **:** taking into account ⟨the cost of building *inclusive of* materials⟩

in•co•erc•ible \,in-kō-'ər-sə-bəl\ *adj* **:** incapable of being controlled, checked, or confined

[1]**in•cog•ni•to** \,in-,käg-'nēt-ō, in-'käg-nə-,tō\ *adv or adj* **:** with one's identity concealed [Italian, from Latin *incognitus* "unknown", from *in-* + *cognoscere* "to know"]

[2]**incognito** *n, pl* **-tos 1 :** one appearing or living incognito **2 :** the state or disguise of an incognito

in•co•her•ence \,in-kō-'hir-əns, -'her-\ *n* **1 :** the quality or state of being incoherent **2 :** an incoherent utterance

in•co•her•ent \-ənt\ *adj* **:** not coherent: as **a :** not sticking closely or compactly together **:** LOOSE **b :** not clearly or logically connected ⟨an *incoherent* story⟩ — **in•co•her•ent•ly** *adv*

in•com•bus•ti•ble \,in-kəm-'bəs-tə-bəl\ *adj* **:** not combustible **:** incapable of being burned

in•come \'in-,kəm\ *n* **:** a gain usually measured in money that comes from capital or labor; *also* **:** the amount of such gain received by an individual in a given period of time

income tax \,in-kəm-\ *n* **:** a tax on the net income of an individual or business concern

[1]**in•com•ing** \'in-,kəm-ing\ *n* **:** the act of coming in **:** ARRIVAL

[2]**incoming** *adj* **:** coming in: as **a :** taking a place or position formerly held by another ⟨the *incoming* president⟩ **b :** arriving at a usual or designated destination ⟨*incoming* mail⟩ **c :** just starting or beginning ⟨the *incoming* class⟩

in•com•men•su•rate \,in-kə-'mens-rət, -'mench-rət, -ə-rət\ *adj* **:** not commensurate; *esp* **:** not enough to satisfy ⟨funds *incommensurate* with need⟩

in•com•mode \,in-kə-'mōd\ *vt* **:** to give inconvenience or trouble to [Middle French *incommoder,* from Latin *incommodare,* from *incommodus* "inconvenient", from *in-* + *commodus* "convenient"]

in•com•mod•i•ty \-'mäd-ət-ē\ *n* **:** INCONVENIENCE 2, DISADVANTAGE

in•com•mu•ni•ca•ble \,in-kə-'myü-ni-kə-bəl\ *adj* **:** not capable of being communicated or imparted — **in·com·mu·ni·ca·bil·i·ty** \-ˌmyü-ni-kə-ˈbil-ət-ē\ *n* — **in·com·mu·ni·ca·bly** \-ˈmyü-ni-kə-blē\ *adv*

in·com·mu·ni·ca·do \ˌin-kə-ˌmyü-nə-ˈkäd-ō\ *adv or adj* : without means of communication with others ⟨a prisoner held *incommunicado*⟩ [Spanish *incomunicado,* from *incomunicar* "to deprive of communication"]

in·com·mu·ni·ca·tive \ˌin-kə-ˈmyü-nə-ˌkāt-iv, -ni-kət-\ *adj* : UNCOMMUNICATIVE

in·com·pa·ra·ble \in-ˈkäm-pə-rə-bəl, -prə-bəl\ *adj* **1** : having no equal (as in quality or worth) : MATCHLESS **2** : not suitable for comparison — **in·com·pa·ra·bil·i·ty** \in-ˌkäm-pə-rə-ˈbil-ət-ē, -prə-\ — **in·com·pa·ra·bly** \in-ˈkäm-pə-rə-blē, -prə-\ *adv*

in·com·pat·i·bil·i·ty \ˌin-kəm-ˌpat-ə-ˈbil-ət-ē\ *n, pl* **-ties** **1** : the quality or state of being incompatible **2** *pl* : mutually antagonistic things or qualities

in·com·pat·i·ble \ˌin-kəm-ˈpat-ə-bəl\ *adj* : incapable of or unsuitable for association ⟨were temperamentally *incompatible*⟩: as **a** : lacking harmony or congruity : DISCORDANT ⟨*incompatible* colors⟩ ⟨conduct *incompatible* with honor⟩ **b** : unsuitable for use together because of undesirable chemical or bodily effects ⟨*incompatible* blood types⟩ **c** : infertile in a particular genetic cross ⟨*incompatible* plants⟩ — **in·com·pat·i·bly** \-blē\ *adv*

in·com·pe·tence \in-ˈkäm-pət-əns, ˈin-\ *also* **in·com·pe·ten·cy** \-ən-sē\ *n, pl* **-tenc·es** *also* **-tencies** : the quality, state, or fact of being incompetent

[1]in·com·pe·tent \in-ˈkäm-pət-ənt, ˈin-\ *adj* **1** : lacking the qualities (as knowledge, skill, or ability) necessary for effective independent action **2** : not legally qualified **3** : inadequate to or unsuitable for the purpose ⟨an *incompetent* heart valve⟩ ⟨an *incompetent* system of government⟩ — **in·com·pe·tent·ly** *adv*

[2]incompetent *n* : an incompetent person

in·com·plete \ˌin-kəm-ˈplēt\ *adj* : not complete : lacking some part : UNFINISHED, IMPERFECT — **in·com·plete·ly** *adv* — **in·com·plete·ness** n

in·com·pre·hen·si·ble \in-ˌkäm-pri-ˈhen-sə-bəl\ *adj* : incapable of being understood — **in·com·pre·hen·si·bil·i·ty** \-ˌhen-sə-ˈbil-ət-ē\ *n* — **in·com·pre·hen·si·ble·ness** \-ˈhen-sə-bəl-nəs\ *n* — **in·com·pre·hen·si·bly** \-blē\ *adv*

in·com·pre·hen·sion \in-ˌkäm-pri-ˈhen-chən\ *n* : lack of understanding

in·com·press·ible \ˌin-kəm-ˈpres-ə-bəl\ *adj* : incapable of or resistant to compression — **in·com·press·ibil·i·ty** \-ˌpres-ə-ˈbil-ət-ē\ *n* — **in·com·press·ibly** \-ˈpres-ə-blē\ *adv*

in·com·put·able \ˌin-kəm-ˈpyüt-ə-bəl\ *adj* : greater than can be computed or counted — **in·com·put·ably** \-blē\ *adv*

in·con·ceiv·able \ˌin-kən-ˈsē-və-bəl\ *adj* : impossible to imagine or conceive — **in·con·ceiv·abil·i·ty** \-ˌsē-və-ˈbil-ət-ē\ *n* — **in·con·ceiv·able·ness** \-ˈsē-və-bəl-nəs\ *n* — **in·con·ceiv·ably** \-blē\ *adv*

in·con·clu·sive \ˌin-kən-ˈklü-siv, -ziv\ *adj* : leading to no conclusion or definite result — **in·con·clu·sive·ly** *adv* — **in·con·clu·sive·ness** *n*

in·con·dens·able \ˌin-kən-ˈden-sə-bəl\ *adj* : incapable of being condensed

in·con·for·mi·ty \ˌin-kən-ˈfȯr-mət-ē\ *n* : NONCONFORMITY 2

in·con·gru·ence \ˌin-kən-ˈgrü-əns; in-ˈkäng-grə-wəns, ˈin-\ *n* : INCONGRUITY

in·con·gru·ent \ˌin-kən-ˈgrü-ənt; in-ˈkäng-grə-wənt, ˈin-\ *adj* : marked by incongruity — **in·con·gru·ent·ly** *adv*

in·con·gru·i·ty \ˌin-kən-ˈgrü-ət-ē, -ˌkän-\ *n, pl* **-ties** **1** : the quality or state of being incongruous **2** : something that is incongruous

in·con·gru·ous \in-ˈkäng-grə-wəs, ˈin-\ *adj* : not consistent with or suitable to the surroundings or associations : not harmonious, appropriate, or proper ⟨*incongruous* colors⟩ ⟨an act *incongruous* with their duty⟩ — **in·con·gru·ous·ly** *adv* — **in·con·gru·ous·ness** *n*

in·con·se·quence \in-ˈkän-sə-ˌkwens, -si-kwəns, ˈin-\ *n* : the quality or state of being inconsequent

in·con·se·quent \-kwənt, -ˌkwent\ *adj* **1 a** : lacking reasonable sequence : ILLOGICAL **b** : not consecutive **2** : IRRELEVANT **3** : INCONSEQUENTIAL 2 — **in·con·se·quent·ly** \-ˌkwent-lē, -kwənt-\ *adv*

in·con·se·quen·tial \in-ˌkän-sə-ˈkwen-chəl\ *adj* **1 a** : ILLOGICAL **b** : IRRELEVANT **2** : of no significance : UNIMPORTANT — **in·con·se·quen·ti·al·i·ty** \-ˌkwen-chē-ˈal-ət-ē\ *n* — **in·con·se·quen·tial·ly** \-ˈkwench-lē, -ə-lē\ *adv*

in·con·sid·er·able \ˌin-kən-ˈsid-ər-bəl, -ˈsid-ər-ə-bəl, -ˈsid-rə-bəl\ *adj* : not worth considering : SLIGHT, TRIVIAL — **in·con·sid·er·able·ness** *n* — **in·con·sid·er·ably** \-blē\ *adv*

in·con·sid·er·ate \ˌin-kən-ˈsid-rət, -ə-rət\ *adj* **1** : acting or tending to act without due thought **2** : careless of the rights or feelings of others — **in·con·sid·er·ate·ly** *adv* — **in·con·sid·er·ate·ness** *n*

in·con·sis·ten·cy \ˌin-kən-ˈsis-tən-sē\ *n, pl* **-cies** **1** : the quality or state of being inconsistent **2** : an instance of being inconsistent

in·con·sis·tent \ˌin-kən-ˈsis-tənt\ *adj* **1 a** : not being in agreement or harmony : INCOMPATIBLE ⟨an explanation *inconsistent* with the facts⟩ **b** : containing incompatible elements ⟨an *inconsistent* argument⟩ **2** : not logical in thought or actions : CHANGEABLE ⟨a very *inconsistent* person⟩ — **in·con·sis·tent·ly** *adv*

in·con·sol·able \ˌin-kən-ˈsō-lə-bəl\ *adj* : incapable of being consoled : DISCONSOLATE — **in·con·sol·able·ness** *n* — **in·con·sol·ably** \-blē\ *adv*

in·con·so·nance \in-ˈkän-sə-nəns, ˈin-, -snəns\ *n* : lack of consonance or harmony : DISAGREEMENT

in·con·so·nant \-sə-nənt, -snənt\ *adj* : DISCORDANT

in·con·spic·u·ous \ˌin-kən-ˈspik-yə-wəs\ *adj* : not readily noticeable — **in·con·spic·u·ous·ly** *adv* — **in·con·spic·u·ous·ness** *n*

in·con·stan·cy \in-ˈkän-stən-sē, ˈin-\ *n, pl* **-cies** : the quality or state of being inconstant

in·con·stant \-stənt\ *adj* : given to changing frequently without apparent reason : CHANGEABLE — **in·con·stant·ly** *adv*

in·con·test·able \ˌin-kən-ˈtes-tə-bəl\ *adj* : not open to doubt or contest : INDISPUTABLE, UNQUESTIONABLE — **in·con·test·abil·i·ty** \-ˌtes-tə-ˈbil-ət-ē\ *n* — **in·con·test·ably** \-ˈtes-tə-blē\ *adv*

in·con·ti·nent \in-ˈkänt-n-ənt, ˈin-\ *adj* **1** : lacking in self-restraint especially in the gratification of sensuous desires **2** : unable to retain a bodily discharge (as urine) voluntarily — **in·con·ti·nence** \-əns\ *n* — **in·con·ti·nent·ly** *adv*

in·con·trol·la·ble \ˌin-kən-ˈtrō-lə-bəl\ *adj* : UNCONTROLLABLE

in·con·tro·vert·ible \in-ˌkän-trə-ˈvərt-ə-bəl\ *adj* : not open to question : INDISPUTABLE ⟨*incontrovertible* evidence⟩ — **in·con·tro·vert·ibly** \-blē\ *adv*

[1]in·con·ve·nience \ˌin-kən-ˈvē-nyəns\ *n* **1** : the quality or state of being inconvenient; *esp* : lack of suitability for personal ease or comfort **2** : something inconvenient

[2]inconvenience *vt* : to cause inconvenience to

in·con·ve·nient \-nyənt\ *adj* : not convenient : causing difficulty, discomfort, or annoyance — **in·con·ve·nient·ly** *adv*

in·con·vert·ible \ˌin-kən-ˈvərt-ə-bəl\ *adj* : not convertible into something else; *esp* : not exchangeable for a foreign currency or into specie — **in·con·vert·ibil·i·ty** \-ˌvərt-ə-ˈbil-ət-ē\ *n* — **in·con·vert·ibly** \-ˈvərt-ə-blē\ *adv*

in·con·vinc·ible \ˌin-kən-ˈvin-sə-bəl\ *adj* : incapable of being convinced

in·co·or·di·nate \ˌin-kō-ˈȯrd-nət, -n-ət\ *adj* : not coordinate : marked by incoordination

in·co·or·di·na·tion \ˌin-kō-ˌȯrd-n-ˈā-shən\ *n* : lack of coordination especially of muscular movement

[1]in·cor·po·rate \in-ˈkȯr-pə-ˌrāt\ *vb* **1** : to unite with or work into something already existent **2** : to unite or combine to form a single body or a consistent whole **3** : to give material form to : EMBODY **4** : to form, form into, or become a corporation ⟨*incorporate* a firm⟩ ⟨an *incorporated* town⟩ [Late Latin *incorporare,* from Latin *in-* + *corpor-, corpus* "body"] — **in·cor·po·ra·tion** \in-ˌkȯr-pə-ˈrā-shən\ *n* — **in·cor·po·ra·tive** \in-ˈkȯr-pə-ˌrāt-iv, -pə-rət-, -prət-\ *adj* — **in·cor·po·ra·tor** \-pə-ˌrāt-ər\ *n*

[2]in·cor·po·rate \in-ˈkȯr-pə-rət, -prət\ *adj* : INCORPORATED

in·cor·po·rat·ed \-pə-ˌrāt-əd\ *adj* : united in one body; *esp* : formed into a legal corporation

in·cor·po·re·al \ˌin-kȯr-ˈpōr-ē-əl, -ˈpȯr-\ *adj* : having no mate-

rial body or form : IMMATERIAL — **in•cor•po•re•al•ly** \-ə-lē\ *adv*
in•cor•po•re•i•ty \ˌin-ˌkȯr-pə-ˈrē-ət-ē\ *n* : the quality or state of being incorporeal : IMMATERIALITY
in•cor•rect \ˌin-kə-ˈrekt\ *adj* **1 a** : INACCURATE, FAULTY ⟨an *incorrect* copy⟩ **b** : not true : WRONG ⟨an *incorrect* answer⟩ **2** : UNBECOMING, IMPROPER ⟨*incorrect* behavior⟩ — **in•cor•rect•ly** *adv* — **in•cor•rect•ness** \-ˈrekt-nəs, -ˈrek-nəs\ *n*
¹in•cor•ri•gi•ble \in-ˈkȯr-ə-jə-bəl, ˈin-, -ˈkär-\ *adj* : not to be corrected or improved: as **a** : incapable of being reformed ⟨an *incorrigible* gambler⟩ **b** : UNRULY, UNMANAGEABLE ⟨*incorrigible* hair⟩ — **in•cor•ri•gi•bil•i•ty** \in-ˌkȯr-ə-jə-ˈbil-ət-ē, -ˌkär-\ *n* — **in•cor•ri•gi•ble•ness** \in-ˈkȯr-ə-jə-bəl-nəs, ˈin-, -ˈkär-\ *n* — **in•cor•ri•gi•bly** \-blē\ *adv*
²incorrigible *n* : an incorrigible person
in•cor•rupt•ible \ˌin-kə-ˈrəp-tə-bəl\ *adj* : not to be corrupted: as **a** : not subject to decay **b** : incapable of being bribed or morally corrupted — **in•cor•rupt•ibil•i•ty** \-ˌrəp-tə-ˈbil-ət-ē\ *n* — **in•cor•rupt•ibly** \-ˈrəp-tə-blē\ *adv*
¹in•crease \in-ˈkrēs, ˈin-ˌ\ *vb* **1** : to make or become greater (as in size, number, value, or power) ⟨*increase* speed⟩ ⟨skill *increases* with practice⟩ **2** : to multiply by the production of young [Middle French *encreistre,* from Latin *increscere,* from *in-* + *crescere* "to grow"] — **in•creas•able** \-ˈkrē-sə-bəl, -ˌkrē-\ *adj* — **in•creas•er** *n*
²in•crease \ˈin-ˌkrēs, in-ˈ\ *n* **1** : the act of increasing : addition or enlargement in size, extent, or quantity **2** : something (as offspring, produce, or profit) added to an original stock by enlargement or growth
in•creas•ing•ly \in-ˈkrē-sing-lē, ˈin-ˌkrē-\ *adv* : to an increasing degree : more and more
in•cred•i•ble \in-ˈkred-ə-bəl, ˈin-\ *adj* : too extraordinary or improbable to be believed; *also* : hard to believe — **in•cred•i•bil•i•ty** \in-ˌkred-ə-ˈbil-ət-ē\ *n* — **in•cred•i•bly** \in-ˈkred-ə-blē, ˈin-\ *adv*
in•cre•du•li•ty \ˌin-kri-ˈdü-lət-ē, -ˈdyü-\ *n* : the quality or state of being incredulous : DISBELIEF **syn** see UNBELIEF
in•cred•u•lous \in-ˈkrej-ə-ləs, ˈin-\ *adj* **1** : tending to disbelieve : SKEPTICAL **2** : indicating or caused by disbelief ⟨an *incredulous* stare⟩ — **in•cred•u•lous•ly** *adv*
in•cre•ment \ˈing-krə-mənt, ˈin-\ *n* **1** : an increasing or growth especially in quantity or value : ENLARGEMENT, INCREASE; *also* : QUANTITY **2 a** : something gained or added **b** : one of a series of regular consecutive additions **c** : a minute increase in quantity [Latin *incrementum,* from *increscere* "to increase"] — **in•cre•men•tal** \ˌing-krə-ˈment-l, ˌin-\ *adj*
in•crim•i•nate \in-ˈkrim-ə-ˌnāt\ *vt* : to charge with or involve in a crime or fault : ACCUSE [Late Latin *incriminare,* from Latin *in-* + *crimen* "crime, accusation"] — **in•crim•i•na•tion** \in-ˌkrim-ə-ˈnā-shən\ *n* — **in•crim•i•na•to•ry** \in-ˈkrim-nə-ˌtōr-ē, -ə-nə-, -ˌtȯr-\ *adj*
in•cross \ˈin-ˌkrȯs\ *n* : an individual produced by crossing inbred lines of the same breed or strain
incrust *variant of* ENCRUST
in•crus•ta•tion \ˌin-ˌkrəs-ˈtā-shən\ *or* **en•crus•ta•tion** \ˌin-, ˌen-\ *n* **1** : the act of encrusting : the state of being encrusted **2** : a hard coating : CRUST **3 a** : OVERLAY **b** : INLAY 1
in•cu•bate \ˈing-kyə-ˌbāt, ˈin-\ *vb* **1** : to sit upon (eggs) to hatch by warmth **2** : to maintain (as bacteria or a chemically active system) under conditions favorable for development or reaction **3** : to undergo incubation [Latin *incubare,* from *in-* + *cubare* "to lie"]
in•cu•ba•tion \ˌing-kyə-ˈbā-shən, ˌin-\ *n* **1** : the act or process of incubating **2** : the period between infection and the manifestation of a disease
in•cu•ba•tor \ˈing-kyə-ˌbāt-ər, ˈin-\ *n* : one that incubates; *esp* : an apparatus providing suitable conditions (as of warmth and moisture) for incubating something ⟨an *incubator* for premature babies⟩
in•cu•bus \ˈing-kyə-bəs, ˈin-\ *n, pl* **-bi** \-ˌbī, -ˌbē\ *also* **-bus•es 1** : an evil spirit held to lie upon persons in their sleep **2** : NIGHTMARE 1 **3** : one that oppresses or burdens like a nightmare [Late Latin, from Latin *incubare* "to lie on, incubate"]

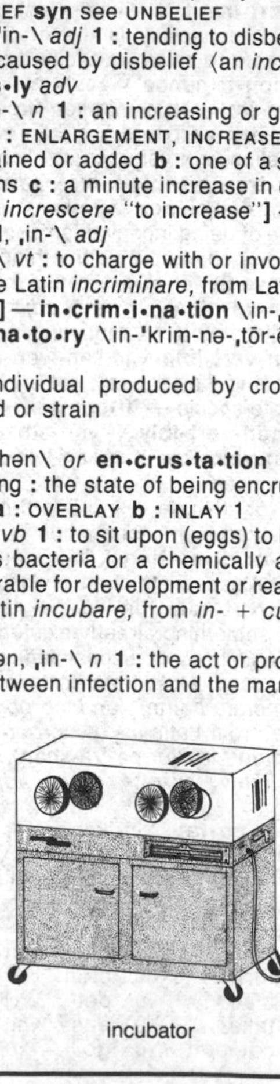
incubator

in•cul•cate \in-ˈkəl-ˌkāt, ˈin-ˌkəl-\ *vt* : to impress on the mind by frequent repetition ⟨*inculcated* high ideals in their children⟩ [Latin *inculcare,* literally, "to tread on", from *in-* + *calcare* "to trample", from *calx* "heel"] — **in•cul•ca•tion** \ˌin-ˌkəl-ˈkā-shən\ *n* — **in•cul•ca•tor** \in-ˈkəl-ˌkāt-ər, ˈin-ˌkəl-\ *n*
in•cul•pa•ble \in-ˈkəl-pə-bəl, ˈin-\ *adj* : free from guilt : BLAMELESS
in•cul•pate \in-ˈkəl-ˌpāt, ˈin-ˌkəl-\ *vt* : INCRIMINATE [derived from Latin *in-* "²in-" + *culpa* "blame, fault"] — **in•cul•pa•tion** \ˌin-ˌkəl-ˈpā-shən\ *n*
in•cum•ben•cy \in-ˈkəm-bən-sē\ *n, pl* **-cies 1** : the quality or state of being incumbent **2** : the office or period of office of an incumbent
¹in•cum•bent \-bənt\ *n* : the holder of an office or position [Latin *incumbere* "to lie down on"]
²incumbent *adj* **1** : lying or resting on something else **2** : imposed as a duty : OBLIGATORY
incumber, incumbrance *variant of* ENCUMBER, ENCUMBRANCE
in•cu•nab•u•lum \ˌin-kyə-ˈnab-yə-ləm, ˌing-\ *n, pl* **-la** \-lə\ : a book printed before 1501; *also* : a work of art or industry of an early period [New Latin, from Latin *incunabula* "swaddling clothes, cradle", from *in-* + *cunae* "cradle"]
in•cur \in-ˈkər\ *vt* **in•curred**; **in•cur•ring** : to become liable or subject to : bring down upon oneself ⟨*incur* punishment⟩ ⟨*incur* expenses⟩ [Latin *incurrere,* literally, "to run into", from *in-* + *currere* "to run"] — **in•cur•rence** \in-ˈkər-əns, -ˈkə-rəns\ *n*
¹in•cur•able \in-ˈkyu̇r-ə-bəl, ˈin-\ *adj* : not capable of being cured — **in•cur•abil•i•ty** \in-ˌkyu̇r-ə-ˈbil-ət-ē\ *n* — **in•cur•ably** \-blē\ *adv*
²incurable *n* : a person suffering from a disease that is beyond cure
in•cu•ri•ous \in-ˈkyu̇r-ē-əs, ˈin-\ *adj* : showing no interest or concern : INDIFFERENT — **in•cu•ri•ous•ly** *adv* — **in•cu•ri•ous•ness** *n*
in•cur•rent \in-ˈkər-ənt, -ˈkə-rənt\ *adj* : characterized by a current that flows inward ⟨*incurrent* canals of a sponge⟩
in•cur•sion \in-ˈkər-zhən\ *n* : a sudden usually temporary invasion : RAID [Latin *incursio,* from *incurrere* "to run into"]
in•cur•vate \ˈin-ˌkər-ˌvāt, in-ˈ\ *vt* : to cause to curve inward : BEND — **in•cur•vate** \ˈin-ˌkər-ˌvāt, in-ˈkər-vət\ *adj* — **in•cur•va•tion** \ˌin-ˌkər-ˈvā-shən\ *n* — **in•cur•va•ture** \in-ˈkər-və-ˌchu̇r, ˈin-, -chər\ *n*
in•curve \in-ˈkərv, ˈin-\ *vb* : to bend so as to curve inward
in•cus \ˈing-kəs\ *n, pl* **in•cu•des** \ing-ˈkyüd-ēz, ˈing-kyə-ˌdēz\ : the middle of a chain of three small bones in the ear of a mammal — called also *anvil*; compare MALLEUS, STAPES [Latin, "anvil"]
Ind- *or* **Indo-** *combining form* **1** : India or the East Indies **2** : Indo-European
in•debt•ed \in-ˈdet-əd\ *adj* : owing something (as money, gratitude, or recognition)
in•debt•ed•ness *n* **1** : the condition of being indebted **2** : something owed
in•de•cen•cy \in-ˈdēs-n-sē, ˈin-\ *n* **1** : lack of decency **2** : an indecent act or word
in•de•cent \-nt\ *adj* **1** : UNSEEMLY, UNBECOMING ⟨remarried in *indecent* haste⟩ **2** : morally offensive — **in•de•cent•ly** *adv*
in•de•ci•sion \ˌin-di-ˈsizh-ən\ *n* : slowness or hesitation in making up one's mind
in•de•ci•sive \-ˈsī-siv\ *adj* **1** : not decisive ⟨an *indecisive* battle⟩ **2** : characterized by indecision : UNCERTAIN ⟨an *indecisive* person⟩ — **in•de•ci•sive•ly** *adv* — **in•de•ci•sive•ness** *n*
in•de•clin•able \ˌin-di-ˈklī-nə-bəl\ *adj* : having no grammatical inflections
in•dec•o•rous \in-ˈdek-ə-rəs, ˈin-; ˌin-di-ˈkōr-əs, -ˈkȯr-\ *adj* : not decorous : UNBECOMING — **in•dec•o•rous•ly** *adv* — **in•dec•o•rous•ness** *n*
• **syn** IMPROPER, UNSEEMLY, UNBECOMING: INDECOROUS suggests a violation of accepted standards of good manners ⟨talking in church is *indecorous*⟩ IMPROPER applies to a broader range of violation of rules not only of social behavior but also of ethical practice or logical procedure ⟨inferred an *improper* conclusion from the premises⟩ ⟨telling *improper* jokes⟩ UNSEEMLY adds a suggestion of an offensiveness to good taste ⟨they married with *unseemly* haste⟩ UNBECOMING suggests behavior or language that does not suit one's character or status ⟨conduct *unbecoming* an officer⟩

in•de•co•rum \ˌin-di-ˈkōr-əm, -ˈkȯr-\ *n* : lack of decorum

in•deed \in-ˈdēd\ *adv* **1** : without any question : TRULY — often used interjectionally to express disbelief or surprise **2** : in reality **3** : as a matter of fact : all things considered

in•de•fat•i•ga•ble \ˌin-di-ˈfat-i-gə-bəl\ *adj* : capable of working a long time without tiring : TIRELESS [Middle French, from Latin *indefatigabilis,* from *in-* + *defatigare* "to fatigue", from *de-* + *fatigare* "to fatigue"] — **in•de•fat•i•ga•bil•i•ty** \-ˌfat-i-gə-ˈbil-ət-ē\ *n* — **in•de•fat•i•ga•ble•ness** \-ˈfat-i-gə-bəl-nəs\ *n* — **in•de•fat•i•ga•bly** \-blē\ *adv*

in•de•fea•si•ble \ˌin-di-ˈfē-zə-bəl\ *adj* : not capable of being abolished or annulled ⟨*indefeasible* rights⟩ [*in-* + earlier *defeasible* "capable of being annulled", from Anglo-French *defaisible,* from Old French *deffaire* "to undo, destroy", from Medieval Latin *disfacere,* from Latin *dis-* + *facere* "to do"] — **in•de•fea•si•bil•i•ty** \-ˌfē-zə-ˈbil-ət-ē\ *n* — **in•de•fea•si•bly** \-ˈfē-zə-blē\ *adv*

in•de•fec•ti•ble \ˌin-di-ˈfek-tə-bəl\ *adj* **1** : not subject to failure or decay : LASTING **2** : free of faults : FLAWLESS — **in•de•fec•ti•bil•i•ty** \-ˌfek-tə-ˈbil-ət-ē\ *n* — **in•de•fec•ti•bly** \-ˈfek-tə-blē\ *adv*

in•de•fen•si•ble \ˌin-di-ˈfen-sə-bəl\ *adj* : not capable of being defended or justified ⟨an *indefensible* position⟩ — **in•de•fen•si•bil•i•ty** \-ˌfen-sə-ˈbil-ət-ē\ *n* — **in•de•fen•si•bly** \-ˈfen-sə-blē\ *adv*

in•de•fin•able \ˌin-di-ˈfī-nə-bəl\ *adj* : incapable of being precisely described or analyzed — **in•de•fin•abil•i•ty** \-ˌfī-nə-ˈbil-ət-ē\ *n* — **in•de•fin•able•ness** \-ˈfī-nə-bəl-nəs\ *n* — **in•de•fin•ably** \-blē\ *adv*

in•def•i•nite \in-ˈdef-nət, ˈin-, -ə-nət\ *adj* **1** : typically designating an unidentified or not immediately identifiable person or thing ⟨the *indefinite* articles *a* and *an*⟩ **2** : not precise in meaning or details : VAGUE ⟨an *indefinite* answer⟩ **3** : not fixed or limited (as in amount or length) ⟨an *indefinite* period⟩ — **in•def•i•nite•ly** *adv* — **in•def•i•nite•ness** *n*

in•de•his•cent \ˌin-di-ˈhis-nt\ *adj* : remaining closed at maturity ⟨*indehiscent* fruits⟩ — **in•de•his•cence** \-ns\ *n*

in•del•i•ble \in-ˈdel-ə-bəl\ *adj* **1** : not capable of being erased, removed, or blotted out ⟨an *indelible* impression⟩ **2** : making marks not easily erased ⟨an *indelible* pencil⟩ [Latin *indelebilis,* from *in-* + *delēre* "to delete"] — **in•del•i•bil•i•ty** \in-ˌdel-ə-ˈbil-ət-ē\ *n* — **in•del•i•bly** \in-ˈdel-ə-blē\ *adv*

in•del•i•ca•cy \in-ˈdel-i-kə-sē, ˈin-\ *n* **1** : the quality or state of being indelicate **2** : something that is indelicate

in•del•i•cate \-kət\ *adj* : offensive to good manners or taste : IMMODEST, COARSE — **in•del•i•cate•ly** *adv* — **in•del•i•cate•ness** *n*

in•dem•ni•fy \in-ˈdem-nə-ˌfī\ *vt* **-fied**; **-fy•ing** **1** : to insure or protect against loss, damage, or injury **2** : to compensate for loss, damage, or injury ⟨*indemnify* victims of a disaster⟩ **3** : to make compensation for : make good ⟨have their losses *indemnified*⟩ [Latin *indemnis* "unharmed", from *in-* + *damnum* "damage"] — **in•dem•ni•fi•ca•tion** \-ˌdem-nə-fə-ˈkā-shən\ *n* — **in•dem•ni•fi•er** \-ˈdem-nə-ˌfī-ər, -ˌfīr\ *n*

in•dem•ni•ty \in-ˈdem-nət-ē\ *n, pl* **-ties** **1** : protection from loss, damage, or injury : INSURANCE **2** : freedom from penalty for past offenses **3** : compensation for loss, damage, or injury

¹in•dent \in-ˈdent\ *vt* **1 a** : to notch the edge of : make jagged **b** : to cut into for the purpose of mortising or dovetailing **2** : to set in from the margin ⟨*indent* the first line of a paragraph⟩ [Middle French *endenter,* from *en-* + *dent* "tooth", from Latin *dent-, dens*] — **in•dent•er** *n*

²indent *vt* **1** : to force inward so as to form a depression **2** : to form a dent in — **in•dent•er** *n*

³indent *n* **1** : INDENTATION 1b **2** : DENT 1

in•den•ta•tion \ˌin-ˌden-ˈtā-shən\ *n* **1 a** : an angular cut in an edge **b** : a recess in a surface **2 a** : the action of indenting : the state of being indented **b** : INDENTION 2 **3** : DENT 1

in•den•tion \in-ˈden-chən\ *n* **1** : INDENTATION 2 a **2** : the space left by indentation

¹in•den•ture \in-ˈden-chər\ *n* **1** : a written agreement : CONTRACT **2** : a contract that binds a person to serve another for a specified period — usually used in pl. [Middle French *endenture* "document carrying two or more copies and divided by an irregular notched cut so that the sections might be proved to belong to the same document by matching the divided edges", from *endenter* to indent, notch]

²indenture *vt* : to bind (as an apprentice) by indentures

in•de•pen•dence \ˌin-də-ˈpen-dəns\ *n* : the quality or state of being independent : freedom from outside control

Independence Day *n* : July 4 observed as a legal holiday in commemoration of the adoption of the Declaration of Independence in 1776

in•de•pen•den•cy \ˌin-də-ˈpen-dən-sē\ *n* : FREEDOM 1b, INDEPENDENCE

¹in•de•pen•dent \ˌin-də-ˈpen-dənt\ *adj* **1** : not subject to control or rule by another : SELF-GOVERNING, FREE ⟨an *independent* nation⟩ **2** : not having connections with another : SEPARATE ⟨*independent* conclusions⟩ **3** : not supported by or relying on another : having or providing enough money to live on ⟨a person of *independent* means⟩ **4** : not easily influenced : showing self-reliance ⟨an *independent* person⟩ **5** : having full meaning in itself and capable of standing alone as a simple sentence : MAIN ⟨an *independent* clause⟩ **6** : not committed to a political party **7** : having probabilities such that the occurrence or nonoccurrence of one event does not influence the outcome of another ⟨the outcomes of the tossing of two dice are *independent*⟩ **syn** see FREE — **in•de•pend•ent•ly** *adv*

²independent *n* : one that is independent; *esp, often cap* : one not committed to a political party

independent assortment *n* : formation of random combinations of chromosomes and genes in meiosis with one of each pair of homologous chromosomes passing into each gamete independently of each other pair

in•de•scrib•able \ˌin-di-ˈskrī-bə-bəl\ *adj* : incapable of being described : being beyond description ⟨*indescribable* beauty⟩ — **in•de•scrib•able•ness** *n* — **in•de•scrib•ably** \-bə-blē\ *adv*

in•de•ter•min•able \ˌin-di-ˈtərm-nə-bəl, -ə-nə-\ *adj* : incapable of being definitely decided or ascertained — **in•de•ter•min•able•ness** *n* — **in•de•ter•min•ably** \-blē\ *adv*

in•de•ter•mi•nate \ˌin-di-ˈtərm-nət, -ə-nət\ *adj* **1 a** : not definitely or precisely determined : VAGUE ⟨*indeterminate* plans⟩ **b** : not leading to a definite end or result **2** : having the capacity for growing in length indefinitely; *esp* : having or being an inflorescence in which the main stem continues to grow without forming a terminal flower and the lower flowers on the stem bloom first — **in•de•ter•mi•na•cy** \-nə-sē\ *n* — **in•de•ter•mi•nate•ly** *adv* — **in•de•ter•mi•nate•ness** *n*

in•de•ter•mi•na•tion \-ˌtər-mə-ˈnā-shən\ *n* : a state of mental indecision

¹in•dex \ˈin-ˌdeks\ *n, pl* **in•dex•es** *or* **in•di•ces** \-də-ˌsēz\ **1** : a guide (as a table or file) for facilitating reference; *esp* : an alphabetical list of items treated in a printed work that gives with each item the page number where it may be found **2** : POINTER, INDICATOR ⟨the *index* on a scale⟩ **3** : SIGN, INDICATION ⟨an *index* of your mood⟩ **4** *pl usually* **indices** : a mathematical figure, letter, or expression associated with another to indicate a mathematical operation to be performed or to indicate use or position in an arrangement ⟨2 is the *index* in $\sqrt[2]{5}$ to specify a square root of 5 **5** : a character ☞ used to direct attention — called also *fist* **6** : a number derived from a series of observations and used as an indicator or measure; *esp* : INDEX NUMBER [Latin *indic-, index,* from *indicare* "to indicate"] — **in•dex•i•cal** \in-ˈdek-si-kəl\ *adj*

²index *vt* **1 a** : to provide with an index **b** : to list in an index **2** : to serve as an index of — **in•dex•er** *n*

index finger *n* : the finger next to the thumb

index fossil *n* : a fossil that is found over a relatively short span of geological time and can be used in dating formations in which it is found

index number *n* : a number used to indicate change in magnitude (as of cost or price) as compared with the magnitude at some specified time usually taken as 100

index of refraction : the ratio of the velocity of light in the first of two media to its velocity in the second as it passes from one into the other

in•dia ink \ˌin-dē-ə-\ *n, often cap 1st I* **1** : a solid black pigment (as lampblack) used in drawing and lettering **2** : a fluid consisting of a fine suspension of india ink in a liquid

In•dia•man \ˈin-dē-ə-mən\ *n* : a large sailing ship formerly used in trade with India

\ə\ **abut**	\au̇\ **out**	\i\ **tip**	\ȯ\ **saw**	\u̇\ **foot**
\ər\ **further**	\ch\ **chin**	\ī\ **life**	\ȯi\ **coin**	\y\ **yet**
\a\ **mat**	\e\ **pet**	\j\ **job**	\th\ **thin**	\yü\ **few**
\ā\ **take**	\ē\ **easy**	\ng\ **sing**	\t͟h\ **this**	\yu̇\ **cure**
\ä\ **cot, cart**	\g\ **go**	\ō\ **bone**	\ü\ **food**	\zh\ **vision**

In·di·an \'in-dē-ən\ *n* **1** : a native or inhabitant of the subcontinent of India or the East Indies **2 a** : a member of any of the aboriginal peoples of the western hemisphere except the Eskimos **b** : an American Indian language [sense 2 from Columbus's belief that the lands he discovered were part of Asia] — **Indian** *adj*

Indian club *n* : a wooden club that resembles a tenpin and is swung for exercise

Indian corn *n* **1** : a tall widely cultivated American cereal grass bearing seeds on elongated ears **2** : the ears of Indian corn; *also* : its edible seeds

Indian giver *n* : one that gives something to another and then takes it back or expects an equivalent in return — **Indian giving** *n*

Indian meal *n* : CORNMEAL

Indian paintbrush *n* **1** : any of a large genus of American and northeast Asian herbs that have dense spikes of hooded flowers with brightly colored bracts **2** : ORANGE HAWKWEED

Indian pipe *n* : a waxy white leafless saprophytic herb with a solitary nodding bell-shaped flower

Indian pudding *n* : a pudding made chiefly of cornmeal, milk, and molasses

Indian summer *n* : a period of mild weather in late autumn or early winter

Indian tobacco *n* : any of several plants resembling or used in place of tobacco; *esp* : an American wild lobelia with small blue flowers

Indian turnip *n* : JACK-IN-THE-PULPIT; *also* : its acrid root

Indian wrestling *n* : any of various contests of strength or of strength and balance in which two individuals try to overcome each other using only one arm or one leg; *esp* : ARM WRESTLING

India paper *n* : a thin tough opaque printing paper

india rubber *n, often cap I* : RUBBER 2a

In·dic \'in-dik\ *adj* **1** : of or relating to the subcontinent of India : INDIAN **2** : of, relating to, or constituting the Indian branch of the Indo-European languages — **Indic** *n*

in·di·cate \'in-də-ˌkāt\ *vt* **1 a** : to point out or point to **b** : to be a sign, symptom, or index of **2** : to state or express briefly : SUGGEST [Latin *indicare,* from *in-* + *dicare* "to proclaim"]

in·di·ca·tion \ˌin-də-'kā-shən\ *n* **1** : the action of indicating **2** : something that indicates : SIGN **3** : the degree or amount indicated on a graduated instrument

¹in·dic·a·tive \in-'dik-ət-iv\ *adj* **1** : of, relating to, or constituting the grammatical mood that represents the denoted act or state as an objective fact **2** : indicating something not visible or obvious : SUGGESTIVE ⟨remarks *indicative* of anger⟩ — **in·dic·a·tive·ly** *adv*

²indicative *n* : the indicative mood of a verb or a verb in this mood

in·di·ca·tor \'in-də-ˌkāt-ər\ *n* **1** : one that indicates: as **a** : a pointer on an instrument (as a dial) **b** : a pressure gauge **2** : a substance used to show visually (as by change of color) the condition of a solution with respect to the presence of free acid, alkali, or other substance — **in·dic·a·to·ry** \in-'dik-ə-ˌtōr-ē, -ˌtȯr-\ *adj*

indices *pl of* INDEX

in·di·cia \in-'dish-ə, -'dish-ē-ə\ *n pl* **1** : distinctive marks : INDICATIONS **2** : postal markings often imprinted on mail or on labels to be affixed to mail [Latin, pl. of *indicium* "sign", from *indicare* "to indicate"]

in·dict \in-'dīt\ *vt* : ACCUSE; *esp* : to charge with a crime by the finding of a grand jury [Anglo-French *enditer,* from Old French, "to write down, indite"] — **in·dict·able** \-ə-bəl\ *adj* — **in·dict·er** *n*

in·dict·ment \in-'dīt-mənt\ *n* **1** : the act or process of indicting **2** : a formal statement charging a person with an offense that is drawn up by a prosecuting attorney and reported by a grand jury after an inquiry

in·dif·fer·ence \in-'dif-ərns, -'dif-rəns, -'dif-ə-rəns\ *n* **1** : lack of feeling for or against something **2** : lack of importance ⟨a matter of *indifference* to them⟩

• **syn** UNCONCERN: INDIFFERENCE implies neutrality of feeling from lack of inclination, preference, or prejudice; UNCONCERN suggests a lack of sensitivity or regard for others' needs or troubles.

in·dif·fer·ent \in-'dif-ərnt, -'dif-rənt, -'dif-ə-rənt\ *adj* **1** : having no preference : not interested or concerned ⟨*indifferent* to the troubles of others⟩ **2** : showing neither liking nor dislike ⟨an *indifferent* audience⟩ **3** : neither good nor bad : MEDIOCRE ⟨*indifferent* health⟩ **4** : of no special influence or value : UNIMPORTANT **5** : capable of development in more than one direction — **in·dif·fer·ent·ly** *adv*

in·di·gence \'in-di-jəns\ *n* : POVERTY 1, NEEDINESS

in·dig·e·nous \in-'dij-ə-nəs\ *adj* : originating in or produced, growing, or living naturally in a particular region or environment [Late Latin *indigenus,* from Latin *indigena,* n., "native", derived from *gignere* "to beget"] **syn** see NATIVE — **in·dig·e·nous·ly** *adv* — **in·dig·e·nous·ness** *n*

in·di·gent \'in-di-jənt\ *adj* : POOR 1, NEEDY [Middle French, from Latin *indigēre* "to need"]

in·di·gest·ible \ˌin-dī-'jes-tə-bəl, -də-\ *adj* : not digestible : hard to digest — **in·di·gest·ibil·i·ty** \-ˌjes-tə-'bil-ət-ē\ *n*

in·di·ges·tion \-'jes-chən\ *n* **1** : inability to digest or difficulty in digesting something **2** : a case or attack of indigestion — **in·di·ges·tive** \-'jes-tiv\ *adj*

in·dig·nant \in-'dig-nənt\ *adj* : filled with or marked by indignation [Latin *indignari* "to be indignant", from *indignus* "unworthy", from *in-* + *dignus* "worthy"] — **in·dig·nant·ly** *adv*

in·dig·na·tion \ˌin-dig-'nā-shən\ *n* : anger aroused by something unjust, unworthy, or mean

in·dig·ni·ty \in-'dig-nət-ē\ *n, pl* **-ties** **1** : an act that offends against a person's dignity or self-respect : INSULT **2** : humiliating treatment **syn** see AFFRONT

in·di·go \'in-di-ˌgō\ *n, pl* **-gos** *or* **-goes** **1** : a blue dye made artificially and formerly obtained from indigo plants **2** : a dark grayish blue [Italian dialect, from Latin *indicum,* from Greek *indikon,* from *indikos* "Indian", from *Indos* "India"]

indigo plant *n* : any of various mostly leguminous plants that yield indigo

indigo snake *n* : a large harmless blue-black snake of the southern United States

in·di·rect \ˌin-də-'rekt, -dī-\ *adj* **1** : not straight : not the shortest ⟨an *indirect* route⟩ **2** : not straightforward : ROUNDABOUT ⟨*indirect* methods⟩ **3** : not having a plainly seen connection ⟨an *indirect* cause⟩ **4** : not straight to the point ⟨an *indirect* answer⟩ **5** : stating what an original speaker said with changes in wording that adapt the statement grammatically to the rest of the sentence ⟨*they would come* in "they said that they would come" is in *indirect* discourse⟩ — **in·di·rect·ly** *adv* — **in·di·rect·ness** \-'rekt-nəs, -'rek-\ *n*

in·di·rec·tion \-'rek-shən\ *n* **1** : lack of straightforwardness and openness : DECEITFULNESS **2** : lack of direction : AIMLESSNESS

indirect lighting *n* : lighting in which the light emitted by a source is diffusely reflected (as by the ceiling)

indirect object *n* : a grammatical object representing the secondary goal of the action of its verb ⟨*me* in "gave me the book" is an *indirect object*⟩

indirect tax *n* : a tax exacted from a person other than the one on whom the ultimate burden of the tax is expected to fall

in·dis·cern·ible \ˌin-dis-'ər-nə-bəl, -diz-\ *adj* : incapable of being discerned

in·dis·creet \ˌin-dis-'krēt\ *adj* : not discreet : IMPRUDENT — **in·dis·creet·ly** *adv* — **in·dis·creet·ness** *n*

in·dis·crete \ˌin-dis-'krēt; in-'dis,, 'in-\ *adj* : not separated into distinct parts ⟨an *indiscrete* mass⟩

in·dis·cre·tion \ˌin-dis-'kresh-ən\ *n* **1** : lack of discretion : IMPRUDENCE **2** : an indiscreet act or remark

in·dis·crim·i·nate \ˌin-dis-'krim-nət, -ə-nət\ *adj* : showing lack of discrimination : not making careful distinctions ⟨an *indiscriminate* reader⟩ ⟨*indiscriminate* criticism⟩ — **in·dis·crim·i·nate·ly** *adv* — **in·dis·crim·i·nate·ness** *n*

in·dis·crim·i·na·tion \-ˌkrim-ə-'nā-shən\ *n* : lack of discrimination

in·dis·pens·able \ˌin-dis-'pen-sə-bəl\ *adj* : absolutely necessary ⟨an *indispensable* employee⟩ — **in·dis·pens·abil·i·ty** \-ˌpen-sə-'bil-ət-ē\ *n* — **indispensable** *n* — **in·dis·pens·able·ness** \-'pen-sə-bəl-nəs\ *n* — **in·dis·pens·ably** \-blē\ *adv*

in·dis·pose \ˌin-dis-'pōz\ *vt* **1** : to make unfit : DISQUALIFY **2** : to make averse : DISINCLINE

in·dis·posed \-'pōzd\ *adj* **1** : slightly ill **2** : UNWILLING, AVERSE

in·dis·po·si·tion \ˌin-ˌdis-pə-'zish-ən\ *n* **1** : a slight illness **2** : AVERSION 1, RELUCTANCE

in·dis·put·able \ˌin-dis-'pyüt-ə-bəl; in-'dis-pyət-, 'in-\ *adj* : not disputable : UNQUESTIONABLE ⟨*indisputable* proof⟩ — **in·dis-**

put•able•ness *n* — **in•dis•put•ably** \-blē\ *adv*

in•dis•sol•u•ble \ˌin-dis-ˈäl-yə-bəl\ *adj* : not capable of being dissolved, undone, broken up, or decomposed ⟨an *indissoluble* contract⟩ — **in•dis•sol•u•bil•i•ty** \-ˌäl-yə-ˈbil-ət-ē\ *n* — **in•dis•sol•u•ble•ness** \-ˈäl-yə-bəl-nəs\ *n* — **in•dis•sol•u•bly** \-blē\ *adv*

in•dis•tinct \ˌin-dis-ˈtingt, -ˈtingkt\ *adj* : not distinct: as **a** : BLURRED ⟨*indistinct* figures in the fog⟩ **b** : FAINT 4, DIM **c** : not clearly recognizable or understandable : UNCERTAIN — **in•dis•tinct•ly** *adv* — **in•dis•tinct•ness** *n*

in•dis•tinc•tive \-ˈting-tiv, -ˈtingk-\ *adj* : lacking distinctive qualities

in•dis•tin•guish•able \ˌin-dis-ˈting-gwish-ə-bəl\ *adj* : not capable of being clearly distinguished — **in•dis•tin•guish•able•ness** *n* — **in•dis•tin•guish•ably** \-blē\ *adv*

in•dite \in-ˈdīt\ *vt* **1** : to make up : COMPOSE ⟨*indite* a poem⟩ **2** : to put down in writing ⟨*indite* a message⟩ [Old French *enditer* "to write down, proclaim", from Latin *indictus,* past participle of *indicere* "to proclaim", from *in-* + *dicere* "to say"] — **in•dit•er** *n*

in•di•um \ˈin-dē-əm\ *n* : a malleable fusible silvery metallic chemical element — see ELEMENT table [New Latin, from Latin *indicum* "indigo"; from the indigo lines in its spectrum]

[1]**in•di•vid•u•al** \ˌin-də-ˈvij-ə-wəl, -ˈvij-əl\ *adj* **1 a** : of or relating to an individual ⟨*individual* traits⟩ **b** : intended for one person ⟨*individual* servings⟩ **2** : PARTICULAR, SEPARATE ⟨*individual* copies⟩ **3** : having marked individuality ⟨an *individual* style⟩ [Medieval Latin *individualis* "inseparable, individual", from Latin *individuus* "indivisible", from *in-* + *dividere* "to divide"] **syn** see CHARACTERISTIC — **in•di•vid•u•al•ly** \-ē\ *adv*

[2]**individual** *n* **1** : a particular being or thing as distinguished from a class, species, or collection **2** : a particular person ⟨an odd *individual*⟩

in•di•vid•u•al•ism \-ˈvij-ə-wə-ˌliz-əm, -ˈvij-ə-ˌliz-\ *n* **1** : a doctrine that the interests of the individual are primary **2** : a doctrine that the individual has certain political or economic rights with which the state must not interfere **3** : INDIVIDUALITY 1

in•di•vid•u•al•ist \-ləst\ *n* **1** : a person showing marked individuality or independence in thought or behavior **2** : a supporter of individualism — **in•di•vid•u•al•is•tic** \-ˌvij-ə-wə-ˈlis-tik, -ˌvij-ə-ˈlis-\ *adj* — **in•di•vid•u•al•is•ti•cal•ly** \-ti-kə-lē, -klē\ *adv*

in•di•vid•u•al•i•ty \ˌin-də-ˌvij-ə-ˈwal-ət-ē\ *n, pl* **-ties 1** : the qualities that distinguish one person or thing from all others **2** : the condition of having separate existence

in•di•vid•u•al•ize \-ˈvij-ə-wə-ˌlīz,-ˈvij-ə-ˌlīz\ *vt* **1** : to make individual in character **2** : to treat or notice individually **3** : to adapt to the needs of an individual — **in•di•vid•u•al•iza•tion** \-ˌvij-ə-wə-lə-ˈzā-shən, -ˌvij-ə-lə-\ *n*

in•di•vis•i•ble \ˌin-də-ˈviz-ə-bəl\ *adj* : not capable of being divided or separated — **in•di•vis•i•bil•i•ty** \-ˌviz-ə-ˈbil-ət-ē\ *n* — **in•di•vis•i•ble•ness** \-ˈviz-ə-bəl-nəs\ *n* — **in•di•vis•i•bly** \-blē\ *adv*

Indo- — see IND-

In•do-Ar•y•an \ˌin-dō-ˈar-ē-ən, -ˈer-; -ˈär-yən\ *n* **1** : a member of one of the peoples of India of Aryan speech and physique **2** : one of the early Indo-European invaders of Persia, Afghanistan, and India — **Indo-Aryan** *adj*

in•doc•ile \in-ˈdäs-əl, ˈin-\ *adj* : unwilling to be taught or disciplined : INTRACTABLE — **in•do•cil•i•ty** \ˌin-dä-ˈsil-ət-ē, -dō-\ *n*

in•doc•tri•nate \in-ˈdäk-trə-ˌnāt\ *vt* **1** : to instruct especially in fundamentals **2** : to teach the beliefs or doctrines of a particular group — **in•doc•tri•na•tion** \in-ˌdäk-trə-ˈnā-shən\ *n* — **in•doc•tri•na•tor** \in-ˈdäk-trə-ˌnāt-ər\ *n*

[1]**In•do-Eu•ro•pe•an** \ˌin-dō-ˌyu̇r-ə-ˈpē-ən\ *adj* : of, relating to, or constituting a family of languages comprising those spoken in most of Europe and in the parts of the world colonized by Europeans since 1500 and also in some parts of Asia (as Iran and the subcontinent of India)

[2]**Indo-European** *n* **1** : the Indo-European languages **2** : a member of a people whose original tongue is one of the Indo-European languages

in•dole•ace•tic acid \ˌin-ˌdōl-ə-ˌsēt-ik-\ *n* : a crystalline plant hormone that promotes growth and rooting of plants [*indole,* a crystalline compound, derived from Latin *indicum* "indigo"]

in•dole•bu•tyr•ic acid \-byü-ˌtir-ik-\ *n* : a crystalline acid similar to indoleacetic acid in its effects on plants

in•do•lent \ˈin-də-lənt\ *adj* **1** : slow to develop or heal **2** : averse to exertion : LAZY ⟨felt *indolent* every spring⟩ [Late Latin *indolens* "insensitive to pain", from Latin *in-* + *dolēre* "to feel pain"] — **in•do•lence** \-ləns\ *n* — **in•do•lent•ly** *adv*

in•dom•i•ta•ble \in-ˈdäm-ət-ə-bəl\ *adj* : incapable of being subdued : UNCONQUERABLE [Late Latin *indomitabilis,* from Latin *in-* + *domitare* "to tame, daunt"] — **in•dom•i•ta•bil•i•ty** \-ˌdäm-ət-ə-ˈbil-ət-ē\ *n* — **in•dom•i•ta•ble•ness** \-ˈdäm-ət-ə-bəl-nəs\ *n* — **in•dom•i•ta•bly** \-blē\ *adv*

• **syn** INVINCIBLE: INDOMITABLE stresses courage or determination that cannot be overcome or subdued; INVINCIBLE more often applies to a person and implies having strength and ability superior to all enemies.

In•do•ne•sian \ˌin-də-ˈnē-zhən, -shən\ *n* **1** : a native or inhabitant of the Malay archipelago **2 a** : a native or inhabitant of the Republic of Indonesia **b** : the language based on Malay that is the national language of the Republic of Indonesia — **Indonesian** *adj*

in•door \ˌin-ˌdōr, -ˌdȯr\ *adj* **1** : of or relating to the interior of a building **2** : done, living, or belonging within a building

in•doors \in-ˈdōrz, ˈin-, -ˈdȯrz\ *adv* : in or into a building

indorse, indorsement *variant of* ENDORSE, ENDORSEMENT

in•du•bi•ta•ble \in-ˈdü-bət-ə-bəl, ˈin-, -ˈdyü-\ *adj* : too evident to be doubted : UNQUESTIONABLE — **in•du•bi•ta•ble•ness** *n* — **in•du•bi•ta•bly** \-blē\ *adv*

in•duce \in-ˈdüs, -ˈdyüs\ *vt* **1** : to lead on to do something : PERSUADE **2** : to bring about : CAUSE ⟨an illness *induced* by overwork⟩ **3** : to conclude or infer by reasoning from particular instances **4** : to produce (as an electric current) by induction [Latin *inducere,* from *in-* + *ducere* "to lead"] — **in•duc•er** *n* — **in•duc•ible** \-ˈdü-sə-bəl, -ˈdyü-\ *adj*

in•duce•ment \in-ˈdü-smənt, -ˈdyü-\ *n* **1** : the act of inducing **2** : something that induces ⟨advertising gimmicks that are mere *inducements* to buy⟩

in•duct \in-ˈdəkt\ *vt* **1** : to place formally in office : INSTALL **2** : to enroll into military service [Latin *inductus,* past participle of *inducere* "to lead in, induce"] — **in•duct•ee** \ˌin-ˌdək-ˈtē\ *n*

in•duc•tance \in-ˈdək-təns\ *n* : a property of an electric circuit by which an electromotive force is induced in it by a variation of current either in the circuit itself or in a neighboring circuit

in•duc•tion \in-ˈdək-shən\ *n* **1 a** : the act or process of inducting (as into office) **b** : an initial experience : INITIATION **c** : the procedure by which a civilian is inducted into military service **2 a** : reasoning from particular instances to a general conclusion; *also* : the conclusion so reached **b** : mathematical demonstration of the validity of a law concerning all the positive integers by proving that it holds for the integer 1 and that if it holds for all the integers preceding a given integer it must hold for the next following integer **3 a** : the act of causing or bringing on or about **b** : the process by which an electrical conductor becomes electrified when near a charged body, by which a body becomes magnetized when in a magnetic field or in the flux set up by a magnetizing force, or by which an electromotive force is produced in a circuit by varying the magnetic field linked with the circuit **c** : the way in which one embryonic tissue or structure influences the development and differentiation of another

induction coil *n* : an apparatus for obtaining intermittent high voltage consisting of a primary coil through which the direct current flows, an interrupter, and a secondary coil of a larger number of turns in which the high voltage is induced

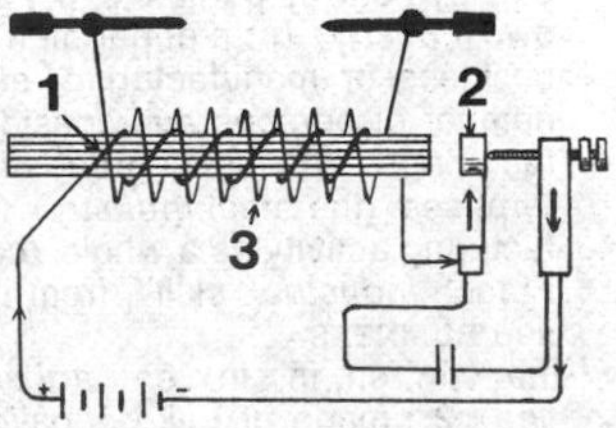

induction coil: *1* primary coil, *2* interrupter, *3* secondary coil

induction heating *n* : the heating of material by means of an electric current that is caused to flow through the material or its container by electromagnetic induction

in•duc•tive \in-ˈdək-tiv\ *adj* : relating to, employing, or based on induction — **in•duc•tive•ly** *adv* — **in•duc•tive•ness** *n*

in•duc•tor \in-'dək-tər\ *n* **1 :** one that inducts **2 :** a part of an electrical apparatus that acts upon another or is itself acted upon by induction **3 :** ORGANIZER 2

indue *variant of* ENDUE

in•dulge \in-'dəlj\ *vb* **1 :** to be tolerant toward **:** HUMOR ⟨*indulge* a child⟩ **2 :** to allow oneself to use, do, or have ⟨refused to *indulge* in liquor⟩ **[**Latin *indulgēre***]** — **in•dulg•er** *n*

in•dul•gence \in-'dəl-jəns\ *n* **1 :** a release from punishment in this world or in purgatory gained by performing pious acts authorized by the Roman Catholic Church **2 a :** the act of indulging **:** the state of being indulgent **b :** an indulgent act **c :** something indulged in

in•dul•gent \-jənt\ *adj* **:** disinclined to be severe or rigorous **:** LENIENT — **in•dul•gent•ly** *adv*

in•dult \'in-ˌdəlt, in-'\ *n* **:** a special often temporary privilege granted in the Roman Catholic Church **[**Medieval Latin *indultum,* from Latin *indultus,* past participle of *indulgēre* "to indulge"**]**

¹in•du•rate \'in-də-rət, -dyə-; in-'dür-ət, -'dyür-\ *adj* **:** physically or morally hardened

²in•du•rate \'in-də-ˌrāt, -dyə-\ *vb* **1 :** to make unfeeling, stubborn, or obdurate **2 :** to make hardy **:** INURE **3 :** to make fibrous or hard ⟨great heat *indurates* clay⟩ ⟨*indurated* tissue⟩ **4 :** to grow hard **:** HARDEN **[**Latin *indurare,* from *in-* + *durare* "to harden", from *durus* "hard"**]** — **in•du•ra•tion** \ˌin-də-'rā-shən, -dyə-\ *n* — **in•du•ra•tive** \'in-də-ˌrāt-iv, -dyə-; in-'dür-ət-, -'dyür-\ *adj*

in•dus•tri•al \in-'dəs-trē-əl\ *adj* **1 :** of, relating to, or engaged in industry **2 :** characterized by highly developed industries ⟨an *industrial* nation⟩ **3 :** derived from human industry **4 :** used in industry ⟨*industrial* diamonds⟩ — **in•dus•tri•al•ly** \-trē-ə-lē\ *adv*

industrial arts *n sing or pl* **:** a subject taught in elementary and secondary schools that aims at developing manual skill and familiarity with tools and machines

in•dus•tri•al•ism \in-'dəs-trē-ə-ˌliz-əm\ *n* **:** social organization in which large-scale industries are dominant

in•dus•tri•al•ist \-ləst\ *n* **:** one owning or engaged in the management of an industry **:** MANUFACTURER

in•dus•tri•al•ize \in-'dəs-trē-ə-ˌlīz\ *vb* **:** to make or become industrial ⟨*industrialize* an agricultural region⟩ — **in•dus•tri•al•iza•tion** \-ˌdəs-trē-ə-lə-'zā-shən\ *n*

industrial revolution *n* **:** a rapid major change in an economy (as in England in the late 18th century) marked by the general introduction of power-driven machinery or by an important change in the prevailing types and methods of use of such machines

industrial school *n* **:** a school specializing in the teaching of the industrial arts

industrial union *n* **:** a labor union that admits to membership workers in an industry irrespective of their occupation or craft — compare TRADE UNION

in•dus•tri•ous \in-'dəs-trē-əs\ *adj* **:** constantly, regularly, or habitually occupied **:** DILIGENT — **in•dus•tri•ous•ly** *adv* — **in•dus•tri•ous•ness** *n*

in•dus•try \'in-dəs-trē, -ˌdəs-\ *n, pl* **-tries 1 :** diligence in an employment or pursuit **2 a :** systematic labor ⟨live by one's own *industry*⟩ **b :** a department or branch of a craft or art or of business or manufacturing; *esp* **:** one that employs a large number of persons and considerable capital usually in manufacturing **c :** a distinct group of productive or profit-making enterprises ⟨the steel *industry*⟩ ⟨the tourist *industry*⟩ **d :** manufacturing activity as a whole ⟨commerce and *industry*⟩ **[**Middle French *industrie* "skill", from Latin *industria* "diligence"**] syn** see BUSINESS

¹-ine \ˌīn, ən, in, ˌin, ˌēn\ *adj suffix* **1 :** of or relating to ⟨alka*line*⟩ **2 :** made of **:** like ⟨opal*ine*⟩ **[**sense 1 from Latin *-īnus;* sense 2 from Latin *-ĭnus,* from Greek *-inos***]**

²-ine \ˌēn, 'ēn, ən, in, ˌin\ *n suffix* **1 :** chemical substance: as **a :** halogen element ⟨chlor*ine*⟩ **b :** basic or base-containing carbon compound that contains nitrogen ⟨cyst*ine*⟩ **c :** mixture of compounds (as of hydrocarbons) ⟨gasol*ine*⟩ **d :** hydride ⟨ar*sine*⟩ **2 :** neutral chemical compound **[**Latin *-īna,* from *-īnus,* adj. suffix**]**

ine•bri•ate \in-'ē-brē-ˌāt\ *vt* **:** to make drunk **:** INTOXICATE **[**Latin *inebriare,* from *in-* + *ebrius* "drunk"**]** — **ine•bri•ate** \-'brē-ət\ *adj or n* — **ine•bri•a•tion** \in-ˌē-brē-'ā-shən\ *n*

ine•bri•at•ed *adj* **:** exhilarated or confused by or as if by alcohol **:** INTOXICATED

in•e•bri•e•ty \ˌin-i-'brī-ət-ē\ *n* **:** the state of being inebriated **:** DRUNKENNESS

in•ed•i•ble \in-'ed-ə-bəl, 'in-\ *adj* **:** not fit or safe for food ⟨*inedible* mushrooms⟩

in•ef•fa•ble \-'ef-ə-bəl\ *adj* **:** INEXPRESSIBLE, UNUTTERABLE ⟨*ineffable* bliss⟩ **[**Middle French, from Latin *ineffabilis,* from *in-* + *effari* "to utter", from *ex-* + *fari* "to speak"**]** — **in•ef•fa•bil•i•ty** \in-ˌef-ə-'bil-ət-ē\ *n* — **in•ef•fa•ble•ness** \in-'ef-ə-bəl-nəs, 'in-\ *n* — **in•ef•fa•bly** \-blē\ *adv*

in•ef•fec•tive \ˌin-ə-'fek-tiv\ *adj* **1 :** not effective **:** INEFFECTUAL ⟨an *ineffective* law⟩ **2 :** not efficient **:** INCAPABLE ⟨an *ineffective* leader⟩ — **in•ef•fec•tive•ly** *adv* — **in•ef•fec•tive•ness** *n*

in•ef•fec•tu•al \ˌin-ə-'fek-chə-wəl, -'fek-chəl, -'feksh-wəl\ *adj* **:** not producing the proper or usual effect **:** FUTILE — **in•ef•fec•tu•al•ly** \-ē\ *adv* — **in•ef•fec•tu•al•ness** *n*

in•ef•fi•ca•cious \ˌin-ˌef-ə-'kā-shəs\ *adj* **:** lacking the power to produce a desired effect **:** INADEQUATE — **in•ef•fi•ca•cious•ly** *adv* — **in•ef•fi•ca•cious•ness** *n* — **in•ef•fi•ca•cy** \-'ef-ə-kə-sē\ *n*

in•ef•fi•cient \ˌin-ə-'fish-ənt\ *adj* **1 :** not producing the intended or desired effect **:** INEFFICACIOUS **2 :** INCAPABLE b, INCOMPETENT ⟨*inefficient* management⟩ — **in•ef•fi•cien•cy** \-'fish-ən-sē\ *n* — **in•ef•fi•cient•ly** *adv*

in•elas•tic \ˌin-ə-'las-tik\ *adj* **1 :** not elastic **2 :** slow to respond to changing conditions — **in•elas•tic•i•ty** \ˌin-i-ˌlas-'tis-ət-ē\ *n*

in•el•e•gance \in-'el-i-gəns, 'in-\ *n* **:** lack of elegance

in•el•e•gant \in-'el-i-gənt, 'in-\ *adj* **:** lacking in refinement, grace, or good taste — **in•el•e•gant•ly** *adv*

in•el•i•gi•ble \in-'el-ə-jə-bəl, 'in-\ *adj* **:** not qualified or worthy to be chosen — **in•el•i•gi•bil•i•ty** \ˌin-ˌel-ə-jə-'bil-ət-ē\ *n* — **ineligible** *n*

in•eluc•ta•ble \ˌin-i-'lək-tə-bəl\ *adj* **:** not to be avoided, changed, or resisted **:** INEVITABLE **[**Latin *ineluctabilis,* from *in-* + *eluctari* "to struggle out", from *ex-* + *luctari* "to struggle"**]** — **in•eluc•ta•bil•i•ty** \-ˌlək-tə-'bil-ət-ē\ *n* — **in•eluc•ta•bly** \-'lək-tə-blē\ *adv*

in•ept \in-'ept\ *adj* **1 :** lacking in fitness or aptitude **:** UNFIT **2 :** not suited to the occasion **:** INAPPROPRIATE **3 :** lacking sense or reason **:** FOOLISH **4 :** generally incompetent **:** BUNGLING **[**French *inepte,* from Latin *ineptus,* from *in-* + *aptus* "apt"**] syn** see AWKWARD — **in•ep•ti•tude** \-'ep-tə-ˌtüd, -ˌtyüd\ *n* — **in•ept•ly** *adv* — **in•ept•ness** \-'ept-nəs, -'ep-nəs\ *n*

in•equal•i•ty \ˌin-i-'kwäl-ət-ē\ *n* **1 :** the quality of being unequal or uneven **2 :** an instance of being unequal (as an irregularity in a surface) **3 :** a formal logical or mathematical statement that two quantities are unequal

in•eq•ui•ta•ble \in-'ek-wət-ə-bəl, 'in-\ *adj* **:** not equitable **:** UNFAIR, UNJUST — **in•eq•ui•ta•bly** \-blē\ *adv*

in•eq•ui•ty \-wət-ē\ *n* **1 :** INJUSTICE 1, UNFAIRNESS **2 :** an instance of injustice or unfairness

in•ert \in-'ərt\ *adj* **1 :** not having the power to move itself **2 :** deficient in active properties; *esp* **:** lacking a usual or anticipated chemical or biological action **3 :** very slow to move or act **:** SLUGGISH **[**Latin *inert-, iners* "unskilled, idle", from *in-* + *art-, ars* "skill, art"**] syn** see INACTIVE — **in•ert•ly** *adv* — **in•ert•ness** *n*

in•er•tia \in-'ər-shə, -shē-ə\ *n* **1 :** a property of matter by which it remains at rest or in uniform motion in the same straight line unless acted upon by some external force; *also* **:** an analogous property of other physical quantities (as electricity) **2 :** a disposition not to move, change, or exert oneself **:** INERTNESS **[**Latin, "lack of skill", from *iners* "unskilled"**]** — **in•er•tial** \-shəl\ *adj*

inertial guidance *n* **:** guidance (as of a spacecraft) by means of self-contained automatically controlling devices that respond to changes in velocity or direction

in•es•cap•able \ˌin-ə-'skā-pə-bəl\ *adj* **:** incapable of being escaped **:** INEVITABLE — **in•es•cap•ably** \-blē\ *adv*

in•es•ti•ma•ble \in-'es-tə-mə-bəl, 'in-\ *adj* **1 :** incapable of being estimated or computed ⟨the storm caused *inestimable* damage⟩ **2 :** too valuable or excellent to be measured or appreciated — **in•es•ti•ma•bly** \-blē\ *adv*

in•ev•i•ta•ble \in-'ev-ət-ə-bəl\ *adj* **:** bound to happen **:** CERTAIN **[**Latin *inevitabilis,* from *in-* + *evitare* "to avoid", from *ex-* + *vitare* "to shun"**]** — **in•ev•i•ta•bil•i•ty** \in-ˌev-ət-ə-'bil-ət-ē\ *n* — **in•ev•i•ta•ble•ness** \in-'ev-ət-ə-bəl-nəs, 'in-\ *n* — **in•ev•i•ta•bly** \-blē\ *adv*

in•ex•act \ˌin-ig-'zakt\ *adj* **:** not precisely correct or true

: INACCURATE — **in•ex•ac•ti•tude** \-'zak-tə-ˌtüd, -ˌtyüd\ *n* — **in•ex•act•ly** \-'zak-tlē, -lē\ *adv* — **in•ex•act•ness** \-'zakt-nəs, -'zak-\ *n*
in•ex•cus•able \ˌin-ik-'skyü-zə-bəl\ *adj* : not to be excused : not justifiable ⟨*inexcusable* rudeness⟩ — **in•ex•cus•able•ness** *n* — **in•ex•cus•ably** \-blē\ *adv*
in•ex•haust•ible \ˌin-ig-'zȯ-stə-bəl\ *adj* **1** : plentiful enough not to give out or be used up : UNFAILING ⟨an *inexhaustible* supply⟩ **2** : not subject to fatigue or wear — **in•ex•haust•ibil•i•ty** \-ˌzȯ-stə-'bil-ət-ē\ *n* — **in•ex•haust•ibly** \-'zȯ-stə-blē\ *adv*
in•ex•o•ra•ble \in-'eks-rə-bəl, 'in-, -ə-rə-\ *adj* : not to be persuaded or moved by entreaty : RELENTLESS [Latin *inexorabilis,* from *in-* + *exorabilis* "pliant", from *exorare* "to prevail upon", from *ex-* + *orare* "to speak"] — **in•ex•o•ra•bil•i•ty** \in-ˌeks-rə-'bil-ət-ē, -ə-rə-\ *n* — **in•ex•o•ra•ble•ness** \in-'eks-rə-bəl-nəs, -ə-rə-\ *n* — **in•ex•o•ra•bly** \-blē\ *adv*
in•ex•pe•di•ent \ˌin-ik-'spēd-ē-ənt\ *adj* : not suited to bring about a desired result : UNWISE — **in•ex•pe•di•en•cy** \-ən-sē\ *n* — **in•ex•pe•di•ent•ly** *adv*
in•ex•pen•sive \ˌin-ik-'spen-siv\ *adj* : reasonable in price : CHEAP — **in•ex•pen•sive•ly** *adv* — **in•ex•pen•sive•ness** *n*
in•ex•pe•ri•ence \ˌin-ik-'spir-ē-əns\ *n* : lack of experience or of knowledge or skill gained by experience — **in•ex•pe•ri•enced** \-ənst\ *adj*
in•ex•plic•able \ˌin-ik-'splik-ə-bəl; in-'ek-splik-, 'in-\ *adj* : incapable of being explained, interpreted, or accounted for — **in•ex•plic•abil•i•ty** \ˌin-ik-ˌsplik-ə-'bil-ət-ē, in-ˌek-splik-ə-'bil-\ *n* — **in•ex•plic•able•ness** \ˌin-ik-'splik-ə-bəl-nəs; in-'ek-splik-, 'in-\ *n* — **in•ex•plic•ably** \-blē\ *adv*
in•ex•press•ible \ˌin-ik-'spres-ə-bəl\ *adj* : being beyond one's power to express : INDESCRIBABLE ⟨*inexpressible* joy⟩ — **in•ex•press•ibil•i•ty** \-ˌspres-ə-'bil-ət-ē\ *n* — **in•ex•press•ible•ness** \-'spres-ə-bəl-nəs\ *n* — **in•ex•press•ibly** \-blē\ *adv*
in•ex•pres•sive \-'spres-iv\ *adj* : lacking expression or meaning ⟨an *inexpressive* face⟩ — **in•ex•pres•sive•ly** *adv* — **in•ex•pres•sive•ness** *n*
in ex•tre•mis \ˌin-ik-'strā-məs, -ˌmēs\ *adv* : in extreme circumstances; *esp* : at the point of death [Latin]
in•ex•tric•able \ˌin-ik-'strik-ə-bəl; in-'ek-strik-, 'in-\ *adj* **1** : forming a tangle from which one cannot free oneself **2** : not capable of being disentangled ⟨an *inextricable* knot⟩ — **in•ex•tric•ably** \-blē\ *adv*
in•fal•li•ble \in-'fal-ə-bəl, 'in-\ *adj* **1** : not capable of being wrong ⟨an *infallible* memory⟩ **2** : not liable to fail, deceive, or disappoint : CERTAIN ⟨an *infallible* remedy⟩ — **in•fal•li•bil•i•ty** \in-ˌfal-ə-'bil-ət-ē\ *n* — **in•fal•li•bly** \in-'fal-ə-blē, 'in-\ *adv*
in•fa•mous \'in-fə-məs\ *adj* **1** : having an evil reputation ⟨an *infamous* person⟩ **2** : DETESTABLE, DISGRACEFUL ⟨an *infamous* crime⟩ [Latin *infamis,* from *in-* + *fama* "fame, reputation"] — **in•fa•mous•ly** *adv*
in•fa•my \-mē\ *n, pl* **-mies** **1** : evil reputation brought about by something grossly criminal, shocking, or brutal **2 a** : an infamous act **b** : the state of being infamous
in•fan•cy \'in-fən-sē\ *n, pl* **-cies** **1** : early childhood **2** : a beginning or early period of existence **3** : the legal status of a minor
[1]**in•fant** \'in-fənt\ *n* **1** : a child in the first period of life **2** : MINOR 1 [Middle French *enfant,* from Latin *infans,* from *infans* "incapable of speech, young", from *in-* + *fari* "to speak"]
△ **origin** Latin *infans* means literally "not speaking, incapable of speech". In classical Latin the noun *infans* designated a very young child who had not yet learned to talk. But later *infans* became the most common word for any child, however talkative. In the Romance languages, too, the descendants of Latin *infans* are words that mean "child". In English the word *infant,* which was borrowed from the French, was originally used for any child. But the word usually is used now in the earlier Latin sense "a very young child, a baby"
[2]**infant** *adj* : of, relating to, or being in infancy
in•fan•ti•cide \in-'fant-ə-ˌsīd\ *n* **1** : the killing of an infant **2** : one who deliberately kills an infant
in•fan•tile \'in-fən-ˌtīl, -təl, -ˌtēl\ *adj* **1** : of, relating to, or resembling infants or infancy : CHILDISH **2** : being in a very early stage of development following an uplift or equivalent change ⟨an *infantile* river⟩ — **in•fan•til•i•ty** \ˌin-fən-'til-ət-ē\ *n*
infantile paralysis *n* : POLIOMYELITIS
in•fan•til•ism \'in-fən-ˌtīl-ˌiz-əm, -təl-, -ˌtēl-\ *n* : retention of childish qualities in adult life; *esp* : failure to attain sexual maturity
in•fan•try \'in-fən-trē\ *n, pl* **-tries** **1** : soldiers trained, armed, and equipped to fight on foot **2** : a branch of an army composed of infantry [Middle French *infanterie,* from Italian *infanteria,* from *infante* "infant, boy, foot soldier", from Latin *infans* "infant"] — **in•fan•try•man** \-mən\ *n*
△ **origin** In the Middle Ages in France, a young soldier of good family who had not yet been made a knight was called *enfant,* which means literally "child". Similarly, in Italy one of the soldiers who followed a mounted knight on foot was an *infante.* Soon foot soldiers collectively became *infanteria,* which was borrowed into French as *infanterie* and into English as *infantry.*
in•farct \'in-ˌfärkt\ *n* : an area of dead tissue (as of the heart wall) caused by blockage of local blood circulation [Latin *infarctus,* past participle of *infarcire* "to stuff in", from *in-* + *farcire* "to stuff"] — **in•farc•tion** \in-'färk-shən\ *n*
in•fat•u•ate \in-'fach-ə-ˌwāt\ *vt* : to fill with a foolish or extravagant love or admiration [Latin *infatuare,* from *in-* + *fatuus* "fatuous"] — **in•fat•u•a•tion** \in-ˌfach-ə-'wā-shən\ *n*
in•fect \in-'fekt\ *vt* **1** : to contaminate with a disease-producing substance or organism ⟨*infected* bedding⟩ **2 a** : to communicate a germ or disease to ⟨coughing people who *infect* others⟩ **b** : to enter and cause disease in ⟨bacteria that *infect* wounds⟩ **3** : to cause to share one's feelings ⟨*infected* everyone with their enthusiasm⟩ [Latin *infectus,* past participle of *inficere* "to infect", from *in-* "[3]in-" + *facere* "to make, do"] — **in•fec•tor** \-'fek-tər\ *n*
in•fec•tion \in-'fek-shən\ *n* **1** : an act or process of infecting **2** : the state produced by the establishment of a germ in or on a suitable host; *also* : a contagious or infectious disease **3** : an infective agent or material contaminated with an infective agent **4** : the communication of emotions or qualities through example or contact
in•fec•tious \in-'fek-shəs\ *adj* **1 a** : capable of causing infection **b** : communicable by infection **2** : spreading or capable of spreading rapidly to others ⟨their enthusiasm was *infectious*⟩ — **in•fec•tious•ly** *adv* — **in•fec•tious•ness** *n*
infectious mononucleosis *n* : an acute infectious disease characterized by fever, swelling of the lymph glands, and an abnormal increase in the number of lymphocytes in the blood
in•fec•tive \in-'fek-tiv\ *adj* : producing or able to produce infection — **in•fec•tiv•i•ty** \in-ˌfek-'tiv-ət-ē\ *n*
in•fe•lic•i•tous \ˌin-fi-'lis-ət-əs\ *adj* : not apt : not suitably chosen for the occasion ⟨an *infelicitous* remark⟩ — **in•fe•lic•i•tous•ly** *adv*
in•fe•lic•i•ty \-ət-ē\ *n, pl* **-ties** **1** : a lack of suitability or aptness **2** : an unsuitable or inappropriate act or utterance
• **in•fer** \in-'fər\ *vt* **in•ferred; in•fer•ring** **1** : to derive as a conclusion from facts or premises **2** : GUESS 1, SURMISE **3** : HINT, SUGGEST [Latin *inferre,* literally, "to carry into", from *in-* + *ferre* "to carry"] **syn** see IMPLY — **in•fer•able** *or* **in•fer•ri•ble** \-'fər-ə-bəl\ *adj* — **in•fer•rer** \-'fər-ər\ *n*
in•fer•ence \'in-fə-rəns, -frəns\ *n* **1** : the act or process of inferring **2** : something inferred; *esp* : a proposition arrived at by inference
in•fe•ri•or \in-'fir-ē-ər\ *adj* **1 a** : situated lower down **b** : situated below another usually similar part of the upright body ⟨*inferior* vena cava⟩ **2** : of low or lower degree or rank **3** : of little or less importance, value, or merit [Latin, comparative of *inferus* "low, situated beneath"] — **inferior** *n* — **in•fe•ri•or•i•ty** \in-ˌfir-ē-'ȯr-ət-ē, -'är-\ *n* — **in•fe•ri•or•ly** \in-'fir-ē-ər-lē\ *adv*
inferiority complex *n* : an acute sense of personal inferiority resulting either in timidity or in exaggerated aggressiveness
inferior vena cava *n* : a branch of the vena cava that returns blood to the heart from the lower parts of the body including the viscera below the lungs and the lower limbs
in•fer•nal \in-'fərn-l\ *adj* **1** : of or relating to a netherworld of the dead **2 a** : of or relating to hell **b** : suggestive of or appropriate to hell : FIENDISH **3** : DAMNABLE 2, DAMNED [Old French, from Late Latin *infernus* "hell", from Latin, "lower"] — **in•fer•nal•ly** \-l-ē\ *adv*

infernal machine *n* **:** an apparatus designed to explode and destroy life or property

in•fer•no \in-ˈfər-nō\ *n, pl* **-nos :** a place or a state that resembles or suggests hell especially in intense heat or raging fire [Italian, "hell", from Late Latin *infernus*]

in•fer•tile \in-ˈfərt-l, ˈin-\ *adj* **:** not fertile or productive **:** BARREN — **in•fer•til•i•ty** \ˌin-fər-ˈtil-ət-ē\ *n*

in•fest \in-ˈfest\ *vt* **1 :** to spread or swarm in or over in a troublesome manner **2 :** to live in or on as a parasite [Middle French *infester*, from Latin *infestare*, from *infestus* "hostile"] — **in•fes•ta•tion** \ˌin-ˌfes-ˈtā-shən\ *n* — **in•fest•er** \in-ˈfes-tər\ *n*

in•fi•del \ˈin-fəd-l, -fə-ˌdel\ *n* **:** a person who does not believe in a particular religion [Middle French *infidele*, from Latin *infidelis* "unfaithful", from *in-* + *fidelis* "faithful", from *fides* "faith"] — **infidel** *adj*

in•fi•del•i•ty \ˌin-fə-ˈdel-ət-ē, -fī-\ *n, pl* **-ties 1 :** lack of faith in a religion **2 :** unfaithfulness especially to one's spouse

in•field \ˈin-ˌfēld\ *n* **1 :** the part of a baseball field enclosed by the three bases and home plate **2 :** the area enclosed by a racetrack or running track — **in•field•er** \-ˌfēl-dər\ *n*

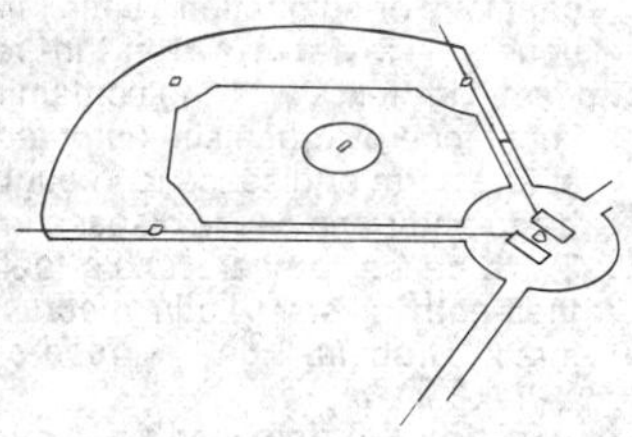

infield 1

in•fight•ing \ˈin-ˌfīt-ing\ *n* **1 :** fighting or boxing at close quarters **2 :** prolonged and often bitter disagreement among members of a group — **in•fight•er** *n*

in•fil•trate \in-ˈfil-ˌtrāt, ˈin-fil-\ *vb* **1 :** to pass into or through by filtering or permeating **2 :** to enter or become established gradually or inconspicuously — **in•fil•tra•tion** \ˌin-fil-ˈtrā-shən\ *n* — **in•fil•tra•tor** \ˈin-fil-ˌtrāt-ər, in-ˈfil-\ *n*

in•fi•nite \ˈin-fə-nət\ *adj* **1 :** being without limits of any kind **:** ENDLESS ⟨*infinite* space⟩ **2 :** seeming to be without limits **:** VAST, INEXHAUSTIBLE ⟨*infinite* patience⟩ ⟨*infinite* wealth⟩ **3 a :** extending, lying, or being beyond any preassigned value however large **b :** having an infinite number of elements or terms — **infinite** *n* — **in•fi•nite•ly** *adv* — **in•fi•nite•ness** *n*

in•fin•i•tes•i•mal \in-ˌfin-ə-ˈtes-ə-məl\ *adj* **:** immeasurably or incalculably small — **in•fin•i•tes•i•mal•ly** \-mə-lē\ *adv*

in•fin•i•tive \in-ˈfin-ət-iv\ *n* **:** an uninflected verb form serving as a noun or as a modifier and yet showing certain characteristics of a verb (as association with objects and adverbial modifiers) ⟨*have* in "let me have it" and *to run* in "able to run fast" are *infinitives*⟩ — **infinitive** *adj*

in•fin•i•tude \in-ˈfin-ə-ˌtüd, -ˌtyüd\ *n* **1 :** INFINITY 1a **2 :** something infinite especially in extent **3 :** an infinite number or quantity

in•fin•i•ty \in-ˈfin-ət-ē\ *n, pl* **-ties 1 a :** the quality of being infinite **b :** unlimited extent of time, space, or quantity **2 :** INFINITUDE 3 **3 :** a distance so great that the rays of light from a point source at that distance may be regarded as parallel ⟨a camera focused at *infinity*⟩

in•firm \in-ˈfərm\ *adj* **1 :** poor or weakened in vitality; *esp* **:** feeble from age **2 :** not solid or stable **:** INSECURE — **in•firm•ly** *adv*

in•fir•ma•ry \in-ˈfərm-rē, -ə-rē\ *n, pl* **-ries :** a place (as in a school or factory) where the infirm, sick, or hurt are lodged for care and treatment

in•fir•mi•ty \in-ˈfər-mət-ē\ *n, pl* **-ties 1 :** the quality or state of being infirm **:** FEEBLENESS, FRAILTY **2 a :** DISEASE, AILMENT **b :** a personal failing **:** FOIBLE

in•flame \in-ˈflām\ *vb* **1 :** to set on fire **:** KINDLE **2 a :** to excite to excess or unnatural action or feeling **b :** to make more heated or violent **:** INTENSIFY **3 :** to cause to redden or grow hot from anger or excitement **4 :** to cause inflammation in (bodily tissue) **5 :** to become affected with inflammation — **in•flam•er** *n*

in•flam•ma•ble \in-ˈflam-ə-bəl\ *adj* **1 :** FLAMMABLE **2 :** easily inflamed **:** EXCITABLE — **in•flam•ma•bil•i•ty** \-ˌflam-ə-ˈbil-ət-ē\ *n* — **inflammable** *n* — **in•flam•ma•ble•ness** \-ˈflam-ə-bəl-nəs\ *n* — **in•flam•ma•bly** \-blē\ *adv*

in•flam•ma•tion \ˌin-flə-ˈmā-shən\ *n* **1 :** the act of inflaming **:** the state of being inflamed **2 :** a local bodily response to injury in which an affected area becomes red, hot, painful, and congested with blood

in•flam•ma•to•ry \in-ˈflam-ə-ˌtōr-ē, -ˌtȯr-\ *adj* **1 :** tending to excite anger, disorder, or tumult **2 :** causing or accompanied by inflammation ⟨*inflammatory* diseases⟩

in•flate \in-ˈflāt\ *vb* **1 :** to swell with air or gas ⟨*inflate* a balloon⟩ **2 :** to puff up **:** ELATE ⟨*inflated* with pride⟩ **3 :** to increase abnormally ⟨*inflated* prices⟩ ⟨*inflated* currency⟩ [Latin *inflare*, from *in-* + *flare* "to blow"] **syn** see EXPAND — **in•flat•able** \in-ˈflāt-ə-bəl\ *adj* — **in•fla•tor** \-ˈflāt-ər\ *n*

in•fla•tion \in-ˈflā-shən\ *n* **1 :** an act of inflating **:** the state of being inflated **2 :** an increase in the volume of money and credit relative to available goods resulting in a substantial and continuing rise in prices

in•fla•tion•ary \-shə-ˌner-ē\ *adj* **:** of, relating to, or tending to cause inflation

in•flect \in-ˈflekt\ *vb* **1 :** to turn from a direct line or course **:** CURVE **2 :** to vary a word by inflection **3 :** to vary the pitch of the voice [Latin *inflectere*, from *in-* + *flectere* "to bend"]

in•flec•tion \in-ˈflek-shən\ *n* **1 :** the act or result of curving or bending **2 :** a change in the pitch of a person's voice **3 :** the change in the form of a word showing its case, gender, number, person, tense, mood, voice, or comparison — **in•flec•tion•al** \-shnəl, -shən-l\ *adj* — **in•flec•tion•al•ly** \-ē\ *adv*

in•flex•ible \in-ˈflek-sə-bəl, ˈin-\ *adj* **1 :** not easily bent or twisted **:** RIGID, STIFF **2 :** not easily influenced or persuaded **:** FIRM ⟨an *inflexible* judge⟩ **3 :** incapable of change ⟨*inflexible* laws⟩ — **in•flex•ibil•i•ty** \in-ˌflek-sə-ˈbil-ət-ē\ *n* — **in•flex•ibly** \in-ˈflek-sə-blē, ˈin-\ *adv*

in•flict \in-ˈflikt\ *vt* **1 :** to give by striking ⟨*inflict* a wound⟩ **2 :** to cause (something damaging or painful) to be endured **:** IMPOSE ⟨*inflict* punishment⟩ [Latin *inflictus*, past participle of *infligere* "to inflict", from *in-* + *fligere* "to strike"] — **in•flic•tion** \in-ˈflik-shən\ *n* — **in•flic•tive** \-ˈflik-tiv\ *adj*

in•flo•res•cence \ˌin-flə-ˈres-ns\ *n* **1 a :** the mode of development and arrangement of flowers on a stem **b :** a flowering stem with all its parts; *also* **:** a flower cluster or sometimes a solitary flower **2 :** the forming and unfolding of blossoms [Late Latin *inflorescere* "to begin to bloom", from Latin *in-* + *florescere* "to begin to bloom, from *florēre* "to blossom, flourish"] — **in•flo•res•cent** \-nt\ *adj*

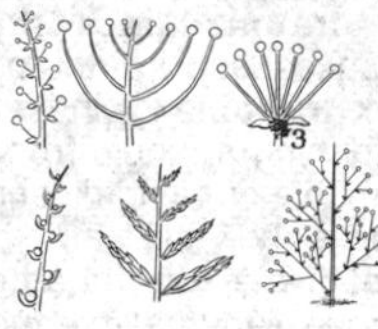

inflorescence 1a

in•flow \ˈin-ˌflō\ *n* **1 :** the act of flowing in **2 :** something that flows in

¹in•flu•ence \ˈin-ˌflü-əns\ *n* **1 :** the act or power of producing an effect without apparent exertion of force or direct exercise of command **2 :** corrupt interference with authority for personal gain **3 :** a person or thing that exerts influence [Middle French, from Medieval Latin *influentia* "ethereal fluid thought to flow from the stars and affect people's actions", from Latin *influere* "to flow in", from *in-* + *fluere* "to flow"]

²influence *vt* **1 :** to affect or alter (as behavior) by indirect or intangible means **2 :** to have an effect on the condition or development of **:** MODIFY — **in•flu•enc•er** *n*

• **syn** AFFECT, SWAY: INFLUENCE is used of a force that brings about a change or determines a course of action or behavior ⟨traditions that *influenced* resistance to change⟩ AFFECT implies a stimulus strong enough to bring about a reaction or modification without a total change ⟨rainfall *affects* the growth of plants⟩ ⟨the new law *affects* only some aspects of commerce⟩ SWAY suggests that the forces either are not resisted or are irresistible and bring about a change ⟨advertising that *sways* public taste⟩

in•flu•en•tial \ˌin-flü-ˈen-chəl\ *adj* **:** having or exerting influence — **in•flu•en•tial•ly** \-ˈench-lē, -ə-lē\ *adv*

in•flu•en•za \ˌin-flü-ˈen-zə\ *n* **1 :** an acute and very contagious virus disease with sudden onset, fever, exhaustion, severe aches and pains, and inflammation of the respiratory tract **2 :** any of various feverish usually virus diseases of humans or domestic animals typically with respiratory symptoms and inflammation and often affecting the body as a whole [Italian, literally, "influence", from Medieval Latin *influentia*]

△ **origin** Italian *influenza* has the same meaning as its English cognate *influence.* But in the 15th century sudden epidemics whose earthly causes were not apparent were blamed on the influence of the stars, so in Italy epidemic diseases were given the name *influenza.* The report of a Roman epidemic which spread through much of Europe in 1743 brought the word to England.

in•flux \ˈin-ˌfləks\ *n* **:** a flowing in **:** INFLOW [Late Latin *influxus,* from Latin *influere* "to flow in"]

in•fold *vb 1* \in-ˈfōld\ **:** ENFOLD **2** \ˈin-ˌfōld\ **:** to fold inward or toward one another

in•form \in-ˈfȯrm\ *vb* **1 :** to let a person know something **:** TELL **2 :** to give information so as to accuse or cast suspicion ⟨*inform* against someone to the police⟩ [Middle French *enformer* "to give form to, inform", from Latin *informare,* from *in-* + *forma* "form"]

in•for•mal \in-ˈfȯr-məl, ˈin-\ *adj* **1 :** conducted or carried out without formality or ceremony **2 :** appropriate for ordinary or casual use ⟨*informal* clothes⟩ — **in•for•mal•i•ty** \ˌin-fȯr-ˈmal-ət-ē, -fər-\ *n* — **in•for•mal•ly** \in-ˈfȯr-mə-lē, ˈin-\ *adv*

in•for•mant \in-ˈfȯr-mənt\ *n* **:** INFORMER

in•for•ma•tion \ˌin-fər-ˈmā-shən\ *n* **1 :** the communication or reception of knowledge or intelligence **2 a :** knowledge obtained from investigation, study, or instruction **b :** knowledge of a particular event or situation **:** NEWS **c :** FACT 3, DATA **d :** a signal or mark put into or put out by a computing machine — **in•for•ma•tion•al** \-shnəl, -shən-l\ *adj*

information theory *n* **:** a mathematical and statistical theory that deals with information, its measurement, and the efficiency of processes of communication between men and machines

in•for•ma•tive \in-ˈfȯr-mət-iv\ *adj* **:** imparting knowledge **:** INSTRUCTIVE — **in•for•ma•tive•ly** *adv* — **in•for•ma•tive•ness** *n*

in•formed \in-ˈfȯrmd\ *adj* **1 :** having information ⟨*informed* sources⟩ **2 :** EDUCATED, KNOWLEDGEABLE ⟨what an *informed* person should know about psychology⟩

in•form•er \in-ˈfȯr-mər\ *n* **:** one that informs; *esp* **:** a person who informs against someone else

infra- *prefix* **1 :** below ⟨*infra*human⟩ ⟨*infra*sonic⟩ **2 :** below in a scale or series ⟨*infra*red⟩ [Latin *infra*]

in•frac•tion \in-ˈfrak-shən\ *n* **:** the act of infringing **:** VIOLATION [Latin *infractio,* from *infractus,* past participle of *infringere* "to infringe"]

in•fra•hu•man \ˌin-frə-ˈhyü-mən, -ˈyü-\ *adj* **:** less or lower than human ⟨*infrahuman* primates⟩ — **infrahuman** *n*

in•fra•red \ˌin-frə-ˈred, -frä-\ *adj* **1 :** lying outside the visible spectrum at its red end — used of heat radiation of wavelengths longer than those of visible light **2 :** relating to, producing, or employing infrared radiation — **infrared** *n*

in•fra•son•ic \-ˈsän-ik\ *adj* **1 :** having a frequency below the audibility range of the human ear **2 :** utilizing or produced by infrasonic waves or vibrations

in•fre•quent \in-ˈfrē-kwənt, ˈin-\ *adj* **1 :** seldom happening or occurring **:** RARE **2 :** placed or occurring at considerable distances or intervals — **in•fre•quen•cy** \-kwən-sē\ *n* — **in•fre•quent•ly** *adv*

• **syn** SPORADIC, SCATTERED: INFREQUENT applies to that which occurs at wide intervals in time or space ⟨*infrequent* church attendance⟩ ⟨*infrequent* stands of pine alongside the highway⟩ SPORADIC applies to that which occurs in scattered instances without continuity or continuous existence ⟨*sporadic* cases of food poisoning⟩ ⟨*sporadic* border fighting⟩ SCATTERED more often applies to wide intervals in space and implies haphazard irregular distribution ⟨*scattered* showers⟩ ⟨*scattered* misspellings in the report⟩

in•fringe \in-ˈfrinj\ *vb* **1 :** VIOLATE, TRANSGRESS ⟨*infringe* a treaty⟩ ⟨*infringe* a patent⟩ **2 :** ENCROACH 1 ⟨*infringe* upon a person's rights⟩ [Latin *infringere,* literally, "to break off", from *in-* "^{2}in-" + *frangere* "to break"] — **infringement** *n* — **in•fring•er** *n*

in•fun•dib•u•lum \ˌin-fən-ˈdib-yə-ləm\ *n, pl* **-la** \-lə\ **:** a conical or dilated body part: as **a :** the stalk by which the pituitary body is continuous with the brain **b :** the abdominal opening of a fallopian tube [Latin, "funnel", from *infundere* "to pour in", from *in-* + *fundere* "to pour"] — **in•fun•dib•u•lar** \-lər\ *adj*

in•fu•ri•ate \in-ˈfyu̇r-ē-ˌāt\ *vt* **:** to make furious **:** ENRAGE — **in•fu•ri•at•ing•ly** \-ˌāt-ing-lē\ *adv* — **in•fu•ri•a•tion** \-ˌfyu̇r-ē-ˈā-shən\ *n*

in•fuse \in-ˈfyüz\ *vt* **1 :** to put in as if by pouring ⟨*infused* courage into their followers⟩ **2 :** to make full ⟨*infused* with a desire to help⟩ **3 :** to steep (as tea) without boiling [Latin *infusus,* past participle of *infundere* "to pour in", from *in-* + *fundere* "to pour"] — **in•fus•er** *n*

in•fus•ible \in-ˈfyü-zə-bəl, ˈin-\ *adj* **:** difficult or impossible to fuse ⟨*infusible* clays⟩ — **in•fus•ibil•i•ty** \in-ˌfyü-zə-ˈbil-ət-ē\ *n* — **in•fus•ible•ness** \in-ˈfyü-zə-bəl-nəs, ˈin-\ *n*

in•fu•sion \in-ˈfyü-zhən\ *n* **1 :** the act or process of infusing **2 :** a substance extracted especially from a plant material by infusing

in•fu•so•ri•an \ˌin-fyü-ˈzōr-ē-ən, -ˈzȯr-\ *n* **:** any of a heterogeneous group of minute organisms found especially in decomposing infusions of organic matter; *esp* **:** a ciliated protozoan — **in•fu•so•ri•al** \-ē-əl\ *or* **infusorian** *adj*

^{1}**-ing** \ing; *in some dialects usually, in other dialects informally,* ən, in, *or* (*after certain consonants*) ^{ə}n, ^{ə}m, ^{ə}ng\ *vb suffix or adj suffix* — used to form the present participle ⟨sail*ing*⟩ and sometimes to form an adjective resembling a present participle but not derived from a verb ⟨swashbuckl*ing*⟩ [Middle English, alteration of *-ende,* from Old English]

^{2}**-ing** *n suffix* **:** one of a (specified) kind ⟨sweet*ing*⟩ [Old English]

^{3}**-ing** *n suffix* **1 :** action or process ⟨runn*ing*⟩ ⟨sleep*ing*⟩ **:** instance of an action or process ⟨a meet*ing*⟩ **2 a :** product or result of an action or process ⟨an engrav*ing*⟩ — often in pl. ⟨earn*ings*⟩ **b :** something used in an action or process ⟨a bed cover*ing*⟩ **3 :** action or process connected with (a specified thing) **4 :** something connected with, consisting of, or used in making (a specified thing) ⟨roof*ing*⟩ **5 :** something related to (a specified concept) ⟨off*ing*⟩ [Old English, suffix forming nouns from verbs]

in•gath•er•ing \ˈin-ˌga*th*-ring, -ə-ring\ *n* **1 :** COLLECTION 1, HARVEST **2 :** ASSEMBLY 3

in•ge•nious \in-ˈjē-nyəs\ *adj* **:** marked by ingenuity ⟨*ingenious* planning⟩ ⟨an *ingenious* device⟩ [Middle French *ingenieux,* from Latin *ingeniosus,* from Latin *ingenium* "natural capacity", from *in-* + *gignere* "to beget"] — **in•ge•nious•ly** *adv* — **in•ge•nious•ness** *n*

• **syn** INGENIOUS, INGENUOUS are not synonymous but they are readily confused. INGENIOUS implies having inborn inventiveness and cleverness; INGENUOUS implies keeping a childlike innocence, frankness, or lack of sophistication.

in•ge•nue *or* **in•gé•nue** \ˈan-jə-ˌnü, ˈän-; ˈa^{n}-zhə-, ˈä^{n}-\ *n* **:** a naive girl or young woman; *also* **:** an actress representing such a person [French *ingénue,* from *ingénu* "ingenuous", from Latin *ingenuus*]

in•ge•nu•i•ty \ˌin-jə-ˈnü-ət-ē, -ˈnyü-\ *n, pl* **-ties 1 a :** skill or cleverness in devising or combining **:** INVENTIVENESS **b :** cleverness or aptness of design or contrivance **2 :** an ingenious device or contrivance [obsolete *ingenuity* "ingenuousness"]

in•gen•u•ous \in-ˈjen-yə-wəs\ *adj* **1 :** FRANK 1 **2 :** showing innocent or childlike simplicity **:** NAIVE [Latin *ingenuus* "native, freeborn, ingenuous", from *in-* + *gignere* "to beget"] **syn** see INGENIOUS — **in•gen•u•ous•ly** *adv* — **in•gen•u•ous•ness** *n*

in•gest \in-ˈjest\ *vt* **:** to take in for or as if for digestion [Latin *ingestus,* past participle of *ingerere* "to carry in", from *in-* + *gerere* "to carry"] — **in•gest•ible** \-ˈjes-tə-bəl\ *adj* — **in•ges•tion** \-ˈjes-chən\ *n* — **in•ges•tive** \-ˈjes-tiv\ *adj*

in•ges•ta \in-ˈjes-tə\ *n pl* **:** material taken into the body by way of the mouth [New Latin]

in•gle \ˈing-gəl, -əl\ *n* **1 :** a fire in a fireplace **2 :** an indoor fireplace [Scottish Gaelic *aingeal*]

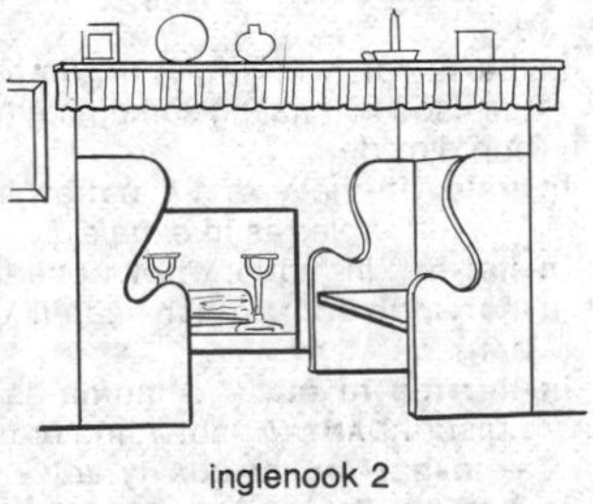

inglenook 2

in•gle•nook \-ˌnu̇k\ *n* **1 :** a corner by the fire or chimney **2 :** a high-backed wooden bench placed close to a fireplace

in•glo•ri•ous \in-ˈglōr-ē-əs, ˈin-, -ˈglȯr-\ *adj* **1 :** not glorious

: lacking fame or honor **2** : bringing disgrace : SHAMEFUL ⟨*inglorious* defeat⟩ — **in·glo·ri·ous·ly** *adv* — **in·glo·ri·ous·ness** *n*

in·got \'ing-gət\ *n* : a mass of metal cast into a convenient shape for storage or transportation [Middle English]

¹in·grain \in-'grān, 'in-\ *vt* : to work indelibly into the natural texture or mental or moral constitution : IMBUE

²in·grain \'in-,grān\ *adj* **1 a** : made of fiber that is dyed before being spun into yarn **b** : made of yarn that is dyed before being woven or knitted ⟨*ingrain* carpet⟩ **2** : thoroughly worked in : INNATE — **ingrain** *n*

in·grained \'in-,grānd, in-', 'in-'\ *adj* : worked into the grain or fiber : DEEP-SEATED ⟨*ingrained* prejudice⟩ — **in·grain·ed·ly** \-,grā-nəd-lē, -'grā-\ *adv*

in·grate \'in-,grāt\ *n* : an ungrateful person [Latin *ingratus* "ungrateful", from *in-* + *gratus* "grateful"]

in·gra·ti·ate \in-'grā-shē-,āt\ *vt* : to gain favor or favorable acceptance for by deliberate effort ⟨*ingratiate* oneself with a new boss⟩ [²*in-* + Latin *gratia* "grace"] — **in·gra·ti·a·tion** \-,grā-shē-'ā-shən\ *n* — **in·gra·tia·to·ry** \-'grā-shə-,tōr-ē, -shē-ə-, -,tȯr-\ *adj*

in·gra·ti·at·ing *adj* **1** : capable of winning favor : PLEASING ⟨an *ingratiating* smile⟩ **2** : intended or adopted in order to gain favor ⟨*ingratiating* manners⟩ — **in·gra·ti·at·ing·ly** \-,āt-ing-lē\ *adv*

in·grat·i·tude \in-'grat-ə-,tüd, 'in-, -,tyüd\ *n* : forgetfulness of or poor return for kindness received

in·gre·di·ent \in-'grēd-ē-ənt\ *n* : one of the substances that make up a mixture ⟨*ingredients* of a cake⟩ [Latin *ingrediens*, present participle of *ingredi* "to go into", from *in-* + *gradi* "to go"] **syn** see ELEMENT — **ingredient** *adj*

in·gress \'in-,gres\ *n* **1** : the act of entering : ENTRANCE **2** : the power or liberty of entrance or access ⟨free *ingress* to the circus grounds⟩ [Latin *ingressus*, from *ingredi* "to go into"]

in·grow·ing \'in-,grō-ing\ *adj* : growing or tending inward

in·grown \-,grōn\ *adj* : grown in; *esp* : having the free tip or edge embedded in the flesh ⟨an *ingrown* toenail⟩ — **in·grown·ness** \-,grōn-nəs\ *n*

in·growth \'in-,grōth\ *n* **1** : a growing inward (as to fill a void) **2** : something that grows in or into a space

in·gui·nal \'ing-gwən-l\ *adj* : of, relating to, or located in the region of the groin [Latin *inguinalis*, from *inguen* "groin"]

in·gur·gi·tate \in-'gər-jə-,tāt\ *vt* : to swallow greedily or in large quantity [Latin *ingurgitare*, from *in-* + *gurges* "whirlpool"] — **in·gur·gi·ta·tion** \-,gər-jə-'tā-shən\ *n*

in·hab·it \in-'hab-ət\ *vt* : to live or dwell in [Latin *inhabitare*, from *in-* + *habitare* "to dwell", from *habēre* "to have"] — **in·hab·it·able** \-ə-bəl\ *adj* — **in·hab·i·ta·tion** \-,hab-ə-'tā-shən\ *n* — **in·hab·it·er** \-'hab-ət-ər\ *n*

in·hab·it·an·cy \-ən-sē\ *n* : OCCUPANCY

in·hab·it·ant \in-'hab-ət-ənt\ *n* : one that lives permanently in a place

¹in·hal·ant \in-'hā-lənt\ *n* : something (as an allergen or medicated spray) that is inhaled

²inhalant *adj* **1** : of or relating to an inhalant **2** : bearing in or inward ⟨an *inhalant* siphon of a clam⟩

in·ha·la·tion \,in-hə-'lā-shən, ,in-ə-'lā-, ,in-l-'ā-\ *n* : the act or an instance of inhaling — **in·ha·la·tion·al** \-shnəl, -shən-l\ *adj*

in·ha·la·tor \'in-hə-,lāt-ər, 'in-ə-,lāt-, 'in-l-,āt-\ *n* : an apparatus used in inhaling something (as a mixture of oxygen and carbon dioxide)

in·hale \in-'hāl\ *vb* **1** : to draw in by breathing **2** : to breathe in [²*in-* + *-hale* (as in *exhale*)]

in·hal·er \in-'hā-lər\ *n* **1** : one that inhales **2** : INHALATOR

in·har·mon·ic \,in-här-'män-ik\ *adj* : not harmonic : DISCORDANT

in·har·mo·ni·ous \-'mō-nē-əs\ *adj* **1** : not harmonious : DISCORDANT **2** : not fitting or congenial ⟨*inharmonious* ideas⟩ — **in·har·mo·ni·ous·ly** *adv* — **in·har·mo·ni·ous·ness** *n*

in·har·mo·ny \in-'här-mə-nē, 'in-\ *n* : DISCORD

in·here \in-'hiər\ *vi* : to be inherent : BELONG ⟨power to make laws *inheres* in the state⟩ [*inhaerēre*, from *in-* + *haerēre* "to stick, adhere"]

in·her·ent \in-'hir-ənt, -'her-\ *adj* : belonging to or being a part of the nature of a person or thing : INTRINSIC ⟨an *inherent* sense of fair play⟩ ⟨fluidity is an *inherent* quality of gas⟩ — **in·her·ence** \-əns\ *n* — **in·her·ent·ly** *adv*

in·her·it \in-'her-ət\ *vt* **1** : to come into possession of : RECEIVE **2** : to receive by legal right from a person at the person's death **3 a** : to receive by genetic transmission ⟨*inherit* a strong constitution⟩ **b** : to have handed on to one by a predecessor ⟨the president *inherited* the problem of unemployment⟩ [Middle French *inheriter* "to make heir", from Latin *in-* + *hereditas* "inheritance", from *hered-*, *heres* "heir"] — **in·her·i·tor** \-ət-ər\ *n* — **in·her·i·tress** \-ə-trəs\ *or* **in·her·i·trix** \-ə-,triks\ *n*

in·her·it·able \in-'her-ət-ə-bəl\ *adj* : capable of being inherited — **in·her·it·able·ness** *n*

in·her·it·ance \in-'her-ət-əns\ *n* **1** : the act of inheriting **2** : something that is or may be inherited **syn** see HERITAGE

in·hib·it \in-'hib-ət\ *vt* **1** : to prohibit from doing something **2 a** : to hold in check : RESTRAIN **b** : to discourage from free or spontaneous activity : REPRESS [Latin *inhibitus*, past participle of *inhibēre* "to inhibit", from *in-* + *habēre* "to have, hold"] **syn** see FORBID — **in·hib·i·tive** \-ət-iv\ *adj* — **in·hib·i·to·ry** \-ə-,tōr-ē, -,tȯr-\ *adj*

in·hi·bi·tion \,in-ə-'bish-ən, ,in-hə-\ *n* **1 a** : the act of inhibiting : the state of being inhibited **b** : something that forbids **2** : an inner force that interferes with free activity, expression, or functioning

in·hib·i·tor *or* **in·hib·it·er** \in-'hib-ət-ər\ *n* : one that inhibits; *esp* : an agent that slows or interferes with a chemical action ⟨rust *inhibitor*⟩

in·hos·pi·ta·ble \,in-,häs-'pit-ə-bəl; in-'häs-pit-, 'in-\ *adj* **1** : not showing hospitality **2** : providing no shelter or food : BARREN ⟨miles of *inhospitable* desert⟩ — **in·hos·pi·ta·ble·ness** *n* — **in·hos·pi·ta·bly** \-blē\ *adv*

in·hos·pi·tal·i·ty \in-,häs-pə-'tal-ət-ē\ *n* : the quality or state of being inhospitable

in·hu·man \in-'hyü-mən, in-'yü-, 'in-\ *adj* **1 a** : lacking pity or kindness : SAVAGE **b** : lacking human warmth : IMPERSONAL **c** : not fit, adequate, or worthy to meet human needs ⟨living in *inhuman* conditions⟩ **2** : of or suggesting a nonhuman class of beings — **in·hu·man·ly** *adv*

in·hu·mane \,in-hyü-'mān, ,in-yü-\ *adj* : INHUMAN 1 — **in·hu·mane·ly** *adv*

in·hu·man·i·ty \-'man-ət-ē\ *n, pl* **-ties** **1** : the quality or state of being cruel or barbarous **2** : a cruel or barbarous act

in·hume \in-'hyüm\ *vt* : BURY 1, INTER [derived from Latin *inhumare*, from *in-* + *humus* "earth"]

in·im·i·cal \in-'im-i-kəl\ *adj* **1 a** : having the disposition of an enemy : HOSTILE **b** : reflecting or indicating hostility : UNFRIENDLY ⟨*inimical* stares⟩ **2** : HARMFUL, ADVERSE ⟨habits *inimical* to health⟩ [Late Latin *inimicalis*, from Latin *inimicus* "enemy"] — **in·im·i·cal·ly** \-'im-i-kə-lē, -klē\ *adv*

in·im·i·ta·ble \in-'im-ət-ə-bəl, 'in-\ *adj* : not capable of being imitated : MATCHLESS — **in·im·i·ta·bil·i·ty** \in-,im-ət-ə-'bil-ət-ē\ *n* — **in·im·i·ta·ble·ness** \in-'im-ət-ə-bəl-nəs, 'in-\ *n* — **in·im·i·ta·bly** \-blē\ *adv*

in·iq·ui·tous \in-'ik-wət-əs\ *adj* : characterized by iniquity : WICKED — **in·iq·ui·tous·ly** *adv* — **in·iq·ui·tous·ness** *n*

in·iq·ui·ty \in-'ik-wət-ē\ *n, pl* **-ties** **1** : shameful injustice : WICKEDNESS **2** : an unjust or wicked act or thing [Middle French *iniquité*, from Latin *iniquitas*, from *iniquus* "uneven, unfair", from *in-* + *aequus* "equal, fair"]

¹ini·tial \in-'ish-əl\ *adj* **1** : of, relating to, or existing at the beginning : INCIPIENT ⟨*initial* stages of a disease⟩ **2** : placed or standing at the beginning : FIRST ⟨*initial* letter of a word⟩ [Latin *initialis*, from *initium* "beginning", from *inire* "to go in", from *in-* + *ire* "to go"]

²initial *n* **1** : the first letter of a name **2** : a large letter beginning a text or a division or paragraph

³initial *vt* **ini·tialed** *or* **ini·tialled**; **ini·tial·ing** *or* **ini·tial·ling** \-'ish-ling, -ə-ling\ : to affix initials or an initial to : mark with an initial ⟨*initial* a memorandum⟩

ini·tial·ly \in-'ish-lē, -ə-lē\ *adv* : in the first place : at the beginning

initial side *n* : a straight line containing a point about which another line rotates to generate an angle

¹ini·ti·ate \in-'ish-ē-,āt\ *vt* **1** : to set going : BEGIN ⟨*initiate* a new policy⟩ **2** : to instruct in the basics or principles of something : INTRODUCE ⟨*initiate* tourists to the local customs⟩ **3** : to admit into membership by or as if by special ceremonies — **ini·ti·a·tor** \-,āt-ər\ *n*

²ini·tiate \in-'ish-ət, -ē-ət\ *adj* : INITIATED

³ini·tiate \in-'ish-ət, -ē-ət\ *n* **1** : a person who is undergoing or has passed an initiation **2** : an expert in a special field

ini·ti·a·tion \in-,ish-ē-'ā-shən\ *n* **1** : the act of initiating : the process of being initiated **2** : the ceremonies by which a person is made a member of a society or club

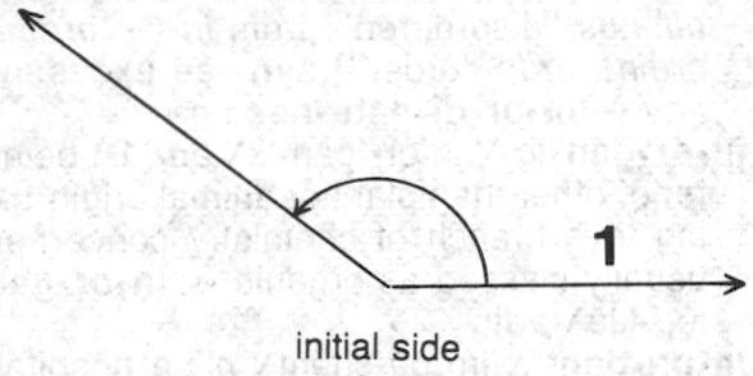

ini·tia·tive \in-ˈish-ət-iv\ *n* **1** : a first step or movement ⟨take the *initiative* in making friends⟩ **2** : energy or ability displayed in initiating something : ENTERPRISE ⟨has the desire to win but lacks *initiative*⟩ **3 a** : the right to initiate legislative action **b** : a procedure enabling a specified number of voters to propose a law for approval of the electorate or the legislature — compare REFERENDUM

ini·tia·to·ry \in-ˈish-ə-ˌtōr-ē, -ˈish-ē-ə-, -ˌtȯr-\ *adj* **1** : constituting a beginning : INTRODUCTORY ⟨*initiatory* remarks⟩ **2** : serving to initiate ⟨*initiatory* ceremonies⟩

in·ject \in-ˈjekt\ *vt* **1 a** : to throw, drive, or force into something ⟨*inject* fuel into an engine⟩ **b** : to force a fluid into especially for medical purposes **2** : to introduce as an additional element ⟨*injected* humor into the speech⟩ [Latin *injectus,* past participle of *inicere* "to inject", from *in-* + *jacere* "to throw"] — **in·ject·able** \-ˈjek-tə-bəl\ *adj* — **in·jec·tor** \-tər\ *n*

in·jec·tion \in-ˈjek-shən\ *n* **1** : an act or instance of injecting (as by a syringe or pump) **2** : something (as a medication) that is injected

in·ju·di·cious \ˌin-jü-ˈdish-əs\ *adj* : lacking sound judgment : INDISCREET, UNWISE — **in·ju·di·cious·ly** *adv* — **in·ju·di·cious·ness** *n*

in·junc·tion \in-ˈjəng-shən, -ˈjəngk-\ *n* **1** : the act or an instance of enjoining : ORDER **2** : a court order requiring a party to do or refrain from doing a specified act ⟨sought an *injunction* against the strike⟩ [Late Latin *injunctio,* from Latin *injungere* "to enjoin"] — **in·junc·tive** \-ˈjəng-tiv, -ˈjəngk-\ *adj*

in·jure \ˈin-jər\ *vt* **in·jured**; **in·jur·ing** \ˈinj-ring, -ə-ring\ **1 a** : to do an injustice to : WRONG **b** : to harm, impair, or tarnish the standing of **c** : to give pain to ⟨*injure* one's pride⟩ **2 a** : to inflict bodily hurt on **b** : to impair the soundness of **c** : to inflict material damage or loss on [back-formation from *injury*]

in·ju·ri·ous \in-ˈju̇r-ē-əs\ *adj* : causing injury : HARMFUL — **in·ju·ri·ous·ly** *adv* — **in·ju·ri·ous·ness** *n*

in·ju·ry \ˈinj-rē, -ə-rē\ *n, pl* **-ries** **1** : an act that damages or hurts : WRONG **2** : hurt, damage, or loss sustained [Latin *injuria,* from *in-* + *jur-, jus* "justice, right"]

• **syn** DAMAGE, HARM: INJURY implies an act or result detrimental to one's rights, well-being, freedom, property, or success ⟨the accident resulted in both physical and emotional *injuries*⟩ DAMAGE applies to injury involving loss ⟨the pest did considerable *damage* to the crop⟩ ⟨scandal that resulted in *damage* to the company's prestige⟩ HARM applies to any evil that injures and often suggests suffering, pain, or annoyance ⟨assured there would be no bodily *harm*⟩

in·jus·tice \in-ˈjəs-təs, ˈin-\ *n* **1** : violation of the rights of another : UNFAIRNESS **2** : an unjust act

[1]ink \ˈingk\ *n* **1** : a usually liquid and colored material for writing and printing **2** : the black protective secretion of a cephalopod [Old French *enke,* from Late Latin *encaustum,* from Latin *encaustus* "burned in", from Greek *enkaustos,* from *enkaiein* "to burn in", from *en-* + *kaiein* "to burn"]

[2]ink *vt* : to put ink on — **ink·er** *n*

ink·ber·ry \ˈingk-ˌber-ē\ *n* **1** : a black-berried American holly **2** : POKEWEED **3** : the fruit of an inkberry

ink·blot test \ˈingk-ˌblät-\ *n* : any of several psychological tests based on the interpretation of irregular figures (as blots of ink)

[1]ink·horn \ˈingk-ˌhȯrn\ *n* : a small portable bottle (as of horn) for holding ink

[2]inkhorn *adj* : ostentatiously learned : PEDANTIC ⟨*inkhorn* terms⟩

in·kling \ˈing-kling\ *n* **1** : a slight suggestion : HINT **2** : a slight knowledge or vague notion ⟨didn't have an *inkling* of what it all meant⟩ [Middle English *yngkiling*]

ink·stand \ˈingk-ˌstand\ *n* : INKWELL; *also* : a pen and inkwell

ink·well \ˈing-ˌkwel\ *n* : a container for ink

inky \ˈing-kē\ *adj* **ink·i·er**; **-est** **1** : consisting of or using ink ⟨an *inky* blot⟩ **2** : suggestive of ink: as **a** : very dark or black ⟨an *inky* cloud⟩ **b** : dark with dirt ⟨*inky* fingernails⟩ — **ink·i·ness** *n*

inky cap *n* : a small mushroom whose cap dissolves into an inky fluid after the spores mature

in·laid \ˈin-ˈlād\ *adj* **1** : set into a surface in a decorative design **2** : decorated with a design or material set into a surface ⟨a table with an *inlaid* top⟩ **3** : having a design that goes all the way through to the backing ⟨*inlaid* linoleum⟩

in·land \ˈin-ˌland, -lənd\ *n* : the land away from the coast or boundaries : INTERIOR — **inland** *adj or adv* — **in·land·er** \ˈin-ˌlan-dər, -lən-\ *n*

in-law \ˈin-ˌlȯ\ *n* : a relative by marriage [back-formation from *mother-in-law,* etc.]

[1]in·lay \in-ˈlā, ˈin-\ *vt* **in·laid**; **in·lay·ing** : to set into a surface or ground material for decoration or reinforcement — **in·lay·er** *n*

[2]in·lay \ˈin-ˌlā\ *n* **1** : inlaid work or material used in inlaying **2** : a tooth filling shaped to fit a cavity and then cemented into place

in·let \ˈin-ˌlet, -lət\ *n* **1** : a small or narrow indentation into the land formed by a body of water **2** : an opening for intake

in·mate \ˈin-ˌmāt\ *n* : one of a group occupying a single residence; *esp* : a person confined to an institution (as a hospital or prison)

in me·di·as res \in-ˌmed-ē-əs-ˈrās, -ˌmēd-ē-əs-ˈrēz\ *adv* : in or into the middle of a narrative or plot [Latin, literally, "into the midst of things"]

in me·mo·ri·am \ˌin-mə-ˈmōr-ē-əm, -ˈmȯr-\ *prep* : in memory of — used especially in epitaphs [Latin]

in·most \ˈin-ˌmōst\ *adj* : INNERMOST [Old English *innemest,* superlative of *inne* "in, within", from *in*]

inn \ˈin\ *n* **1** : a public house that provides lodging and food for travelers : HOTEL **2** : TAVERN 1 [Old English]

in·nards \ˈin-ərdz\ *n pl* **1** : the internal organs of a man or animal; *esp* : VISCERA **2** : the internal parts of a structure or mechanism [alteration of *inwards*]

in·nate \in-ˈāt, ˈin-ˌ\ *adj* **1** : existing in or belonging to an individual from birth : NATIVE **2** : belonging to the essential nature of something : INHERENT [Latin *innatus,* past participle of *innasci* "to be born in", from *in-* + *nasci* "to be born"] — **in·nate·ly** *adv* — **in·nate·ness** *n*

• **syn** INNATE, INBORN, INBRED, CONGENITAL mean not acquired after birth. INNATE applies to qualities or characteristics that are part of the essential nature of a person or thing ⟨develop the *innate* talent of the young⟩ ⟨the *innate* defect of the scheme⟩ INBORN suggests a quality or tendency either present at birth or so deep-seated as to seem so ⟨an *inborn* ability to act⟩ INBRED suggests something deeply rooted and acquired from parents by heredity or early nurture ⟨an *inbred* hatred of injustice⟩ CONGENITAL applies to something acquired during fetal development ⟨*congenital* heart defects⟩

in·ner \ˈin-ər\ *adj* **1 a** : situated farther in ⟨an *inner* room⟩ **b** : being near a center especially of influence ⟨the *inner* circle of party leaders⟩ **2** : of or relating to the mind or spirit ⟨valued a rich *inner* life⟩ — **in·ner·ly** *adv*

inner city *n* : the usually older and more densely populated central section of a city — **inner–city** *adj*

inner ear *n* : a cavity in the temporal bone that encloses a complex membranous labyrinth containing sense organs of hearing and of awareness of position in space

inner light *n, often cap I & L* : a divine presence held (as in Quaker doctrine) to enlighten and guide the soul

in·ner·most \ˈin-ər-ˌmōst\ *adj* **1** : situated farthest inward **2** : most intimate : DEEPEST ⟨one's *innermost* feelings⟩

in·ner·sole \ˌin-ər-ˈsōl\ *n* : INSOLE

inner tube *n* : an airtight tube of rubber placed inside the casing of a pneumatic tire to hold air under pressure

in·ner·vate \in-ˈər-ˌvāt, ˈin-ər-, ˈin-ˌər-\ *vt* : to supply with nerves — **in·ner·va·tion** \ˌin-ər-ˈvā-shən, ˌin-ˌər-\ *n* — **in·ner·va·tion·al** \-shnəl, -shən-l\ *adj*

in·ning \ˈin-ing\ *n* **1** : a baseball team's turn at bat ending with the 3d out; *also* : a division of a baseball game consisting of a turn at bat for each team **2** : a chance or turn for action or accomplishment ⟨time for the opposition to have its *innings*⟩ [^{2}*in*]

inn•keep•er \ˈin-ˌkē-pər\ *n* : the landlord of an inn

in•no•cence \ˈin-ə-səns\ *n* **1** : the quality or state of being innocent **2** : BLUET

in•no•cent \-sənt\ *adj* **1** : free from sin : PURE **2** : free from guilt or blame : GUILTLESS ⟨*innocent* of the crime⟩ **3** : free from evil influence or effect : HARMLESS ⟨*innocent* fun⟩ **4** : lacking or reflecting a lack of sophistication, guile, or self-consciousness [Middle French, from Latin *innocens,* from *in-* + *nocens* "wicked", from *nocēre* "to harm"] — **innocent** *n* — **in•no•cent•ly** *adv*

in•noc•u•ous \in-ˈäk-yə-wəs\ *adj* **1** : causing no injury : HARMLESS **2 a** : not likely to give offense : INOFFENSIVE ⟨an *innocuous* joke⟩ **b** : INSIPID 2, DULL ⟨*innocuous* poems⟩ [Latin *innocuus,* from *in-* + *nocēre* "to harm"] — **in•noc•u•ous•ly** *adv* — **in•noc•u•ous•ness** *n*

in•nom•i•nate \in-ˈäm-ə-nət\ *adj* : having no name; *also* : ANONYMOUS [Late Latin *innominatus,* from Latin *in-* + *nominare* "to name, nominate"]

innominate artery *n* : a short artery arising from the arched first part of the aorta and dividing into the carotid and subclavian arteries of the right side

innominate bone *n* : HIPBONE

innominate vein *n* : either of a pair of veins that receive blood from the head and upper limbs and fuse to form the superior vena cava

in•no•vate \ˈin-ə-ˌvāt\ *vb* **1** : to introduce as or as if new **2** : to make changes [Latin *innovare,* from *in-* + *novus* "new"] — **in•no•va•tive** \-ˌvāt-iv\ *adj* — **in•no•va•tor** \-ˌvāt-ər\ *n*

in•no•va•tion \ˌin-ə-ˈvā-shən\ *n* **1** : the introduction of something new **2** : a new idea, method, or device

in•nu•en•do \ˌin-yə-ˈwen-dō\ *n, pl* **-dos** *or* **-does** : a subtle or indirect suggestion; *esp* : an unfavorable insinuation [Latin, "by hinting", from *innuere* "to hint", from *in-* + *nuere* "to nod"]

in•nu•mer•a•ble \in-ˈüm-rə-bəl, -ˈyüm-, -ə-rə-\ *adj* : too many to be numbered : COUNTLESS — **in•nu•mer•a•ble•ness** *n* — **in•nu•mer•a•bly** \-blē\ *adv*

in•nu•mer•ous \in-ˈüm-rəs, -ˈyüm-, -ə-rəs\ *adj* : INNUMERABLE

in•ob•ser•vance \ˌin-əb-ˈzər-vəns\ *n* **1** : lack of attention : HEEDLESSNESS **2** : failure to fulfill : NONOBSERVANCE — **in•ob•ser•vant** \-vənt\ *adj*

in•oc•u•late \in-ˈäk-yə-ˌlāt\ *vt* **1 a** : to introduce a microorganism into ⟨beans *inoculated* with nitrogen-fixing bacteria⟩ **b** : to introduce (a microorganism) into a suitable situation for growth **c** : to introduce a serum, antibody, or antigen into in order to treat or prevent a disease **2** : to introduce something into the mind of [Latin *inoculare* "to insert a bud in a plant", from *in-* + *oculus* "eye, bud"] — **in•oc•u•la•tive** \-ˌlāt-iv\ *adj* — **in•oc•u•la•tor** \-ˌlāt-ər\ *n*

△ **origin** We often give to inanimate objects the names of parts of the body. We speak, for example, of the foot of a mountain, the leg of a table, the lip of a pitcher. And an undeveloped bud on a potato is an eye. In Latin, any bud of a plant may be called *oculus* "eye". And the verb *inoculare* means "to insert or graft a bud from one plant into another". When *inoculate* was first borrowed into English it had the same meaning as the Latin verb. Later, by extension, *inoculate* came to mean "to introduce a microorganism or serum into".

in•oc•u•la•tion \in-ˌäk-yə-ˈlā-shən\ *n* **1** : the act or process or an instance of inoculating **2** : INOCULUM

in•oc•u•lum \in-ˈäk-yə-ləm\ *n, pl* **-la** \-lə\ : material used for inoculation [New Latin]

in•of•fen•sive \ˌin-ə-ˈfen-siv\ *adj* : not offensive : HARMLESS — **in•of•fen•sive•ly** *adv* — **in•of•fen•sive•ness** *n*

in•op•er•a•ble \in-ˈäp-rə-bəl, ˈin-, -ə-rə-\ *adj* **1** : not suitable for surgery **2** : not being in working order

in•op•er•a•tive \-ˈäp-rət-iv, -ə-rət-; -ˈäp-ə-ˌrāt-\ *adj* : not operative: as **a** : not functioning ⟨an *inoperative* clock⟩ **b** : having no effect or force ⟨an *inoperative* law⟩ — **in•op•er•a•tive•ness** *n*

in•oper•cu•late \ˌin-ō-ˈpər-kyə-lət\ *adj* : lacking an operculum ⟨*inoperculate* snails⟩

in•op•por•tune \in-ˌäp-ər-ˈtün, ˌin-, -ˈtyün\ *adj* : INCONVENIENT ⟨happened at an *inopportune* time⟩ — **in•op•por•tune•ly** *adv* — **in•op•por•tune•ness** \-ˈtün-nəs, -ˈtyün-\ *n*

in order that *conj* : THAT

in•or•di•nate \in-ˈȯrd-n-ət, -ˈȯrd-nət\ *adj* : exceeding reasonable limits : IMMODERATE ⟨an *inordinate* curiosity⟩ [Latin *inordinatus* "disordered", from *in-* + *ordinare* "to arrange", from *ordin-, ordo* "order"] **syn** see EXCESSIVE — **in•or•di•nate•ly** *adv* — **in•or•di•nate•ness** *n*

in•or•gan•ic \ˌin-ȯr-ˈgan-ik\ *adj* **1** : being or composed of matter of other than plant or animal origin : MINERAL **2** : of or relating to a branch of chemistry concerned with substances not usually classed as organic — **in•or•gan•i•cal•ly** \-ˈgan-i-kə-lē, -klē\ *adv*

in•pa•tient \ˈin-ˌpā-shənt\ *n* : a hospital patient who receives lodging and food as well as treatment — compare OUTPATIENT

in•put \ˈin-ˌpu̇t\ *n* **1** : something that is put in; *esp* : power or energy put into a machine or system **2** : a point at which an input (as power, an electronic signal, or data) is made **3** : the act or process of putting in

in•quest \ˈin-ˌkwest\ *n* **1** : a judicial or official inquiry or investigation especially before a jury **2** : a body of men assembled to conduct an inquest **3** : the finding of an inquest [Old French *enqueste,* derived from Latin *inquirere* "to inquire"]

in•qui•line \ˈin-kwə-ˌlīn, ˈing-, -lən\ *n* : an animal that habitually lives in the nest or den of another kind of animal [Latin *inquilinus* "tenant, lodger", from *in-* + *colere* "to cultivate, dwell"] — **in•qui•lin•ism** \-ˌiz-əm\ *n* — **in•qui•li•nous** \ˌin-kwə-ˈlī-nəs, ˌing-\ *adj*

in•quire *also* **en•quire** \in-ˈkwīr\ *vb* **1** : to ask about **2** : to make an investigation or inquiry : INVESTIGATE **3** : to seek information by questioning [Old French *enquerre,* from Latin *inquirere,* from *in-* + *quaerere* "to seek"] — **in•quir•er** *n* — **in•quir•ing•ly** \-ing-lē\ *adv* — **inquire after** : to ask about the health of

in•qui•ry *also* **en•qui•ry** \ˈin-ˌkwīr-ē, in-ˈ; ˈin-kwə-rē, ˈing-\ *n, pl* **-ries 1 a** : the act of inquiring ⟨learn by *inquiry*⟩ **b** : a request for information ⟨make *inquiries* at the station⟩ **2** : a search for truth or knowledge **3** : a systematic examination : INVESTIGATION

in•qui•si•tion \ˌin-kwə-ˈzish-ən\ *n* **1** : the act of inquiring **2** : a judicial or official inquiry **3 a** *cap* : a former Roman Catholic tribunal for the discovery and punishment of heresy **b** : an investigation conducted with little regard for individual rights **c** : a severe questioning [Middle French, from Latin *inquisitio,* from *inquirere* "to inquire"] — **in•qui•si•tion•al** \-ˈzish-nəl, -ən-l\ *adj*

in•quis•i•tive \in-ˈkwiz-ət-iv\ *adj* **1** : given to examination or investigation **2** : given to asking questions; *esp* : too curious about other people's affairs **syn** see CURIOUS — **in•quis•i•tive•ly** *adv* — **in•quis•i•tive•ness** *n*

in•quis•i•tor \in-ˈkwiz-ət-ər\ *n* : one that inquires; *esp* : one that conducts an inquisition — **in•quis•i•to•ri•al** \-ˌkwiz-ə-ˈtōr-ē-əl, -ˈtȯr-\ *adj* — **in•quis•i•to•ri•al•ly** \-ē-ə-lē\ *adv*

in re \in-ˈrē, -ˈrā\ *prep* : in the matter of : CONCERNING, RE [Latin]

in•road \ˈin-ˌrōd\ *n* **1** : a sudden hostile entry : RAID **2** : a serious encroachment ⟨the children made *inroads* on the cookies⟩

in•rush \ˈin-ˌrəsh\ *n* : a crowding or flooding in : INFLUX

in•sa•lu•bri•ous \ˌin-sə-ˈlü-brē-əs\ *adj* : UNWHOLESOME, NOXIOUS — **in•sa•lu•bri•ty** \-brət-ē\ *n*

in•sane \in-ˈsān, ˈin-\ *adj* **1** : not sane : unsound in mind **2** : showing evidence of an unsound mind ⟨an *insane* look⟩ **3** : used by or for the insane ⟨an *insane* asylum⟩ **4** : utterly foolish or unreasonable — **in•sane•ly** *adv* — **in•sane•ness** \-ˈsān-nəs\ *n*

• **syn** MAD, CRAZY: INSANE technically means such unsoundness of mind that one is not responsible for one's actions; in general use it implies utter folly or irrationality ⟨an *insane* scheme⟩ MAD carries implications of wildness or rashness or lack of restraint ⟨*mad* pursuit of fortunes⟩ CRAZY suggests a distraught state of mind induced by intense emotion ⟨*crazy* with anxiety⟩

in•san•i•tary \in-ˈsan-ə-ˌter-ē, ˈin-\ *adj* : unclean enough to endanger health : CONTAMINATED

in•san•i•ty \in-ˈsan-ət-ē\ *n, pl* **-ties 1 a** : unsoundness or disorder of the mind **b** : a mental illness **2** : such unsoundness of mind as excuses one from criminal or civil responsibility **3 a** : extreme folly or unreasonableness **b** : something utterly foolish or unreasonable

• **syn** INSANITY, LUNACY, MANIA denote serious mental disorder. INSANITY implies unfitness to manage one's own affairs or to behave safely in a state of freedom; LUNACY may imply alternating periods of madness and lucidity and commonly stresses wildness of thought and behavior; MANIA is often used specifically of one of the spells of intense excitement characteristic of some mental disorders.

in•sa•tia•ble \in-'sā-shə-bəl, 'in-\ *adj* **:** incapable of being satisfied ⟨*insatiable* thirst⟩ ⟨an *insatiable* desire for knowledge⟩ — **in•sa•tia•bil•i•ty** \in-ˌsā-shə-'bil-ət-ē\ *n* — **in•sa•tia•ble•ness** \in-'sā-shə-bəl-nəs, 'in-\ *n* — **in•sa•tia•bly** \-blē\ *adv*

in•sa•tiate \-'sā-shət, -shē-ət\ *adj* **:** not satiated or satisfied; *also* **:** INSATIABLE ⟨*insatiate* desires⟩ — **in•sa•tiate•ly** *adv* — **in•sa•tiate•ness** *n*

in•scribe \in-'skrīb\ *vt* **1 a :** to write, engrave, or print as a lasting record **b :** to enter on a list **:** ENROLL **2 a :** to write, engrave, or print characters on **b :** to autograph or address as a gift **c :** to stamp deeply **:** IMPRESS ⟨a scene *inscribed* on their memories⟩ **3 :** to dedicate (as a poem) to someone **4 :** to draw within a figure so as to touch in as many places as possible [Latin *inscribere,* from *in-* + *scribere* "to write"] — **in•scrib•er** *n*

in•scrip•tion \in-'skrip-shən\ *n* **1 :** something that is inscribed **2 :** the wording on a coin, medal, or seal **:** LEGEND **3 :** the dedication of a book or work of art **4 :** the act of inscribing [Latin *inscriptio,* from *inscribere* "to inscribe"] — **in•scrip•tion•al** \-shnəl, -shən-l\ *adj*

in•scru•ta•ble \in-'skrüt-ə-bəl\ *adj* **:** not readily understood **:** ENIGMATIC ⟨an *inscrutable* mystery⟩ [Late Latin *inscrutabilis,* from Latin *in-* + *scrutari* "to search"] — **in•scru•ta•bil•i•ty** \-ˌskrüt-ə-'bil-ət-ē\ *n* — **in•scru•ta•ble•ness** \-'skrüt-ə-bəl-nəs\ *n* — **in•scru•ta•bly** \-blē\ *adv*

in•seam \'in-ˌsēm\ *n* **:** the seam on the inside of the leg of a pair of pants; *also* **:** the length of this seam

in•sect \'in-ˌsekt\ *n* **1 :** any of numerous small animals that are usually more or less obviously segmented **2 :** any of a class (Insecta) of arthropods (as bugs or bees) with well-defined head, thorax, and abdomen, three pairs of jointed legs, and typically one or two pairs of wings [Latin *insectum,* from *insecare* "to cut into", from *in-* + *secare* "to cut"]

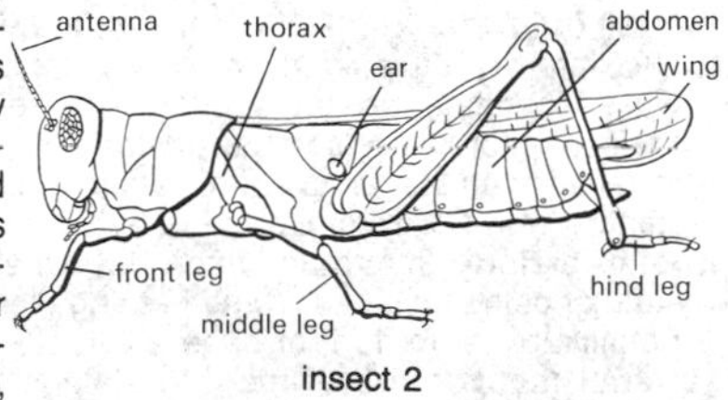

insect 2

△ **origin** The bodies of insects are segmented. This makes them look as if notches have been cut into them at intervals. For this reason the Greek philosopher Aristotle gave insects the name *entomon,* "a thing cut into", derived from the prefix *en-,* "in", and the verb *temnein,* "to cut". (From this Greek word we derive our name for the study of insects, *entomology.*) Later, when the Romans wanted a word for this kind of creature, they did not simply borrow the Greek word but translated it *insectum,* from the verb *insecare* "to cut into". The Latin word was borrowed into English.

in•sec•ta•ry \'in-ˌsek-tə-rē\ *also* **in•sec•tar•i•um** \ˌin-ˌsek-'ter-ē-əm\ *n, pl* **-taries** \-tə-rēz\ *also* **-tar•ia** \-'ter-ē-ə\ **:** a place for rearing or keeping live insects

in•sec•ti•cide \in-'sek-tə-ˌsīd\ *n* **:** an agent that destroys insects — **in•sec•ti•cid•al** \-ˌsek-tə-'sīd-l\ *adj*

in•sec•ti•vore \in-'sek-tə-ˌvōr, -ˌvȯr\ *n* **1 :** any of an order (Insectivora) of mammals comprising forms (as the moles, shrews, hedgehogs) that are mostly small, insectivorous, and nocturnal **2 :** an insectivorous plant or animal [derived from Latin *insectum* "insect" + *vorare* "to devour"]

in•sec•tiv•o•rous \ˌin-ˌsek-'tiv-rəs, -ə-rəs\ *adj* **:** depending on insects as food

in•se•cure \ˌin-si-'kyu̇r\ *adj* **1 :** not confident or sure **2 :** not well protected **3 :** not firmly fastened **4 :** not stable or well-adjusted — **in•se•cure•ly** *adv* — **in•se•cure•ness** *n* — **in•se•cu•ri•ty** \-'kyu̇r-ət-ē\ *n*

in•sem•i•nate \in-'sem-ə-ˌnāt\ *vt* **:** to introduce semen into the genital tract of (a female) — **in•sem•i•na•tion** \-ˌsem-ə-'nā-shən\ *n*

in•sen•sate \in-'sen-ˌsāt, 'in-\ *adj* **1 :** lacking awareness or sensation **:** INANIMATE **2 :** lacking sense or understanding; *also* **:** FOOLISH **3 :** lacking humane feeling **:** BRUTAL ⟨*insensate* hatred⟩ — **in•sen•sate•ly** *adv* — **in•sen•sate•ness** *n*

in•sen•si•ble \in-'sen-sə-bəl, 'in-\ *adj* **1 :** incapable or deprived of feeling or sensation: as **a :** INANIMATE 1a, INSENTIENT ⟨*insensible* earth⟩ **b :** UNCONSCIOUS 2b **c :** lacking or deprived of sensory perception **:** INSENSITIVE ⟨*insensible* to pain⟩ **2 a :** IMPERCEPTIBLE 1 **b :** SLIGHT, GRADUAL ⟨*insensible* motion⟩ **3 :** APATHETIC, INDIFFERENT ⟨*insensible* to fear⟩; *also* **:** UNAWARE ⟨*insensible* of their danger⟩ **4 :** not intelligible **:** MEANINGLESS **5 :** lacking delicacy or refinement — **in•sen•si•bil•i•ty** \in-ˌsen-sə-'bil-ət-ē\ *n* — **in•sen•si•ble•ness** \in-'sen-sə-bəl-nəs, 'in-\ *n* — **in•sen•si•bly** \-blē\ *adv*

in•sen•si•tive \in-'sen-sət-iv, 'in-, -'sen-stiv\ *adj* **:** not sensitive; *esp* **:** lacking feeling — **in•sen•si•tive•ly** *adv* — **in•sen•si•tive•ness** *n* — **in•sen•si•tiv•i•ty** \in-ˌsen-sə-'tiv-ət-ē\ *n*

in•sen•tient \in-'sen-chənt, 'in-, -chē-ənt\ *adj* **:** lacking perception, consciousness, or animation — **in•sen•tience** \-chəns, -chē-əns\ *n*

in•sep•a•ra•ble \in-'sep-rə-bəl, 'in-, -ə-rə-\ *adj* **:** incapable of being separated ⟨*inseparable* friends⟩ — **in•sep•a•ra•bil•i•ty** \in-ˌsep-rə-'bil-ət-ē, -ə-rə-\ *n* — **in•sep•a•ra•ble•ness** \in-'sep-rə-bəl-nəs, 'in-, -ə-rə-\ *n* — **in•sep•a•ra•bly** \-blē\ *adv*

[1]**in•sert** \in-'sərt\ *vb* **1 :** to put or place in ⟨*inserted* the key in the lock⟩ **2 :** to introduce into the body of something **:** INTERPOLATE ⟨*insert* an explanation into a text⟩ **3 :** to set in and make fast **4 :** to be in attachment to the part to be moved ⟨a muscle which *inserts* on the humerus⟩ [Latin *insertus,* past participle of *inserere* "to insert", from *in-* + *serere* "to join"] **syn** see INTRODUCE — **in•sert•er** *n*

[2]**in•sert** \'in-ˌsərt\ *n* **:** something that is inserted or is for insertion

in•ser•tion \in-'sər-shən\ *n* **1 :** the act or process of inserting **2 :** something that is inserted: as **a :** the part of a muscle that inserts on a part to be moved **b :** the mode or place of attachment of an organ or part **c :** embroidery or needlework inserted as ornament between two pieces of fabric — **in•ser•tion•al** \-shnəl, -shən-l\ *adj*

in•ses•so•ri•al \ˌin-ˌse-'sōr-ē-əl, -'sȯr-\ *adj* **:** adapted for perching **:** PERCHING ⟨*insessorial* birds⟩ [Latin *insessus,* past participle of *insidēre* "to sit on", from *in-* + *sedēre* "to sit"]

[1]**in•set** \'in-ˌset\ *n* **:** something that is inset: as **a :** a small graphic representation (as a map or picture) set within the compass of a larger one **b :** a piece of cloth set into a garment for decoration

[2]**in•set** \'in-ˌset, in-'\ *vt* **inset** *or* **in•set•ted; in•set•ting :** to set in **:** insert as an inset

[1]**in•shore** \'in-'shōr, -'shȯr\ *adj* **1 :** situated or carried on near shore ⟨*inshore* fishing⟩ **2 :** moving toward shore ⟨an *inshore* wind⟩

[2]**inshore** *adv* **:** to or toward shore ⟨debris drifting *inshore*⟩

[1]**in•side** \in-'sīd, 'in-ˌ\ *n* **1 :** an inner side or surface **2 a :** an interior or internal part **b :** inward nature, thoughts, or feeling **c :** VISCERA, ENTRAILS — usually used in pl. — **inside** *adj*

[2]**inside** *prep* **1 a :** in or into the interior of ⟨went *inside* the house⟩ **b :** on the inner side of ⟨put the dot *inside* the curve⟩ **2 :** before the end of **:** WITHIN ⟨*inside* an hour⟩

[3]**inside** *adv* **1 :** on the inner side ⟨cleaned the car *inside* and out⟩ **2 :** in or into the interior ⟨went *inside*⟩

inside of *prep* **:** INSIDE

in•sid•er \in-'sīd-ər, 'in-\ *n* **:** a person who has access to confidential information

inside track *n* **:** an advantageous competitive position [from the fact that the inner side of a curved racetrack is shorter than the outer]

in•sid•i•ous \in-'sid-ē-əs\ *adj* **1 a :** awaiting a chance to entrap **:** TREACHEROUS **b :** harmful but attractive **2 :** having a gradual and cumulative effect ⟨an *insidious* disease⟩ [Latin *insidiosus,* from *insidiae* "ambush", from *insidēre* "to sit in, sit on", from *in-* + *sedēre* "to sit"] — **in•sid•i•ous•ly** *adv* — **in•sid•i•ous•ness** *n*

in•sight \'in-ˌsīt\ *n* **1 :** the power or act of seeing into a situation **2 :** the act of understanding the inner nature of things or of seeing intuitively

in•sig•nia \in-ˈsig-nē-ə\ *or* **in•sig•ne** \-nē\ *n, pl* **-nia** *or* **-ni•as** : a distinguishing mark especially of authority, office, or honor : BADGE, EMBLEM [Latin *insignia,* pl. of *insigne* "mark, badge", from *in-* + *signum* "mark, sign"]

in•sig•nif•i•cant \ˌin-sig-ˈnif-i-kənt\ *adj* : not significant: as **a** : lacking meaning or importance : INCONSEQUENTIAL ⟨*insignificant* details⟩ **b** : lacking weight, position, or influence : CONTEMPTIBLE ⟨an *insignificant* hanger-on⟩ **c** : LITTLE, TRIVIAL ⟨an *insignificant* amount⟩ — **in•sig•nif•i•cance** \-kəns\ *n* — **in•sig•nif•i•cant•ly** *adv*

in•sin•cere \ˌin-sin-ˈsiər\ *adj* : lacking in sincerity — **in•sin•cere•ly** *adv* — **in•sin•cer•i•ty** \-ˈser-ət-ē, -ˈsir-\ *n*

in•sin•u•ate \in-ˈsin-yə-ˌwāt\ *vt* **1** : to introduce gradually or in a subtle, indirect, or artful way **2** : to imply in a subtle or devious way [Latin *insinuare,* from *in-* + *sinuare* "to bend, curve", from *sinus* "curve"] — **in•sin•u•a•tor** \-ˌwāt-ər\ *n*

in•sin•u•at•ing *adj* **1** : tending gradually to cause doubt, distrust, or change of outlook ⟨*insinuating* remarks⟩ **2** : intended to win favor and confidence by subtle or artful means ⟨an *insinuating* voice⟩ — **in•sin•u•at•ing•ly** \-ˌwāt-iŋ-lē\ *adv*

in•sin•u•a•tion \in-ˌsin-yə-ˈwā-shən\ *n* **1** : a subtle suggestion : INNUENDO **2** : the artful pursuit of favor : INGRATIATION

in•sip•id \in-ˈsip-əd\ *adj* **1** : lacking taste or savor : TASTELESS **2** : lacking in interest, stimulation, or challenge : DULL, FLAT ⟨*insipid* fiction⟩ [Late Latin *insipidus,* from Latin *in-* + *sapidus* "savory", from *sapere* "to taste"] — **in•si•pid•i•ty** \ˌin-sə-ˈpid-ət-ē\ *n* — **in•sip•id•ly** \in-ˈsip-əd-lē\ *adv*

• **syn** VAPID, BANAL, INANE: INSIPID implies a lack of sufficient taste or savor to please or interest ⟨over-cooked *insipid* cabbage⟩ ⟨*insipid* art and dull prose⟩ VAPID suggests lack of liveliness, force, or spirit ⟨exchange of *vapid* remarks⟩ BANAL stresses the complete absence of freshness, novelty, or immediacy ⟨a *banal* tale of unrequited love⟩ INANE implies lacking any significant or convincing quality ⟨a purposeless *inane* life⟩ ⟨*inane* criticism⟩

in•sist \in-ˈsist\ *vb* **1** : to place special emphasis or great importance ⟨*insists* on punctuality⟩ **2** : to request urgently ⟨*insisted* that I come⟩ **3** : to maintain in a persistent or positive manner ⟨*insisted* that their rights had been violated⟩ [Latin *insistere* "to stand upon, insist", from *in-* + *sistere* "to stand"]

in•sis•tence \in-ˈsis-təns\ *n* **1** : the act of insisting **2** : the quality or state of being insistent : URGENCY ⟨the *insistence* of a need⟩

in•sis•tent \-tənt\ *adj* : compelling attention : PERSISTENT ⟨*insistent* demands⟩ — **in•sist•ent•ly** *adv*

in situ \in-ˈsī-tü *also* -ˈsi-\ *adv or adj* : in the natural or original position [Latin, "in position"]

in•so•far as \ˌin-sə-ˌfär-əz\ *conj* : to the extent or degree that

in•so•la•tion \ˌin-ˌsō-ˈlā-shən\ *n* **1** : solar radiation that has been received **2** : the rate of delivery of all direct solar energy per unit of horizontal surface [Latin *insolatio* "exposure to the sun", from *insolare* "to expose to the sun", from *in-* + *sol* "sun"]

in•sole \ˈin-ˌsōl\ *n* **1** : an inside sole of a shoe **2** : a loose thin strip placed inside a shoe for warmth or comfort

in•so•lent \ˈin-sə-lənt\ *adj* **1** : arrogant or rude in speech or conduct ⟨an *insolent* child⟩ **2** : exhibiting boldness or rudeness ⟨an *insolent* act⟩ [Latin *insolens*] — **in•so•lence** \-ləns\ *n* — **in•so•lent•ly** *adv*

in•sol•u•ble \in-ˈsäl-yə-bəl, ˈin-\ *adj* : not soluble: as **a** : incapable of being solved or explained **b** : incapable of being dissolved in a liquid or soluble only with difficulty or to a slight degree — **in•sol•u•bil•i•ty** \in-ˌsäl-yə-ˈbil-ət-ē\ *n* — **insoluble** *n* — **in•sol•u•ble•ness** \in-ˈsäl-yə-bəl-nəs, ˈin-\ *n* — **in•sol•u•bly** \-blē\ *adv*

in•sol•vent \in-ˈsäl-vənt, ˈin-\ *adj* **1** : unable or having ceased to pay debts **2** : insufficient to pay all debts ⟨an *insolvent* estate⟩ — **in•sol•ven•cy** \-vən-sē\ *n* — **insolvent** *n*

in•som•nia \in-ˈsäm-nē-ə\ *n* : prolonged and usually abnormal inability to get enough sleep [Latin, from *insomnis* "sleepless", from *in-* + *somnus* "sleep"] — **in•som•ni•ac** \-nē-ˌak\ *adj or n*

in•so•much as \ˌin-sə-ˌməch-əz\ *conj* : inasmuch as

insomuch that \-t͟hət\ *conj* : to such a degree that : so that

in•sou•ci•ance \in-ˈsü-sē-əns\ *n* : a lighthearted unconcern : NONCHALANCE [French] — **in•sou•ci•ant** \-ənt\ *adj* — **in•sou•ci•ant•ly** *adv*

in•spect \in-ˈspekt\ *vb* **1** : to examine closely (as for judging quality or condition) ⟨*inspect* foodstuffs⟩ **2** : to view and examine (as troops) officially **3** : to make an examination [Latin *inspectus,* past participle of *inspicere* "to inspect", from *in-* + *specere* "to look"] — **in•spec•tive** \-ˈspek-tiv\ *adj*

in•spec•tion \in-ˈspek-shən\ *n* **1 a** : the act of inspecting : EXAMINATION **b** : the immediate solving of a mathematical problem by insight rather than by involved calculation **2** : a checking or testing of an individual against established standards

in•spec•tor \in-ˈspek-tər\ *n* **1** : a person employed to make inspections ⟨meat *inspector*⟩ **2** : a police officer ranking next below a superintendent or deputy superintendent — **in•spec•tor•ate** \-tə-rət, -trət\ *n* — **in•spec•tor•ship** \-tər-ˌship\ *n*

in•spi•ra•tion \ˌin-spə-ˈrā-shən\ *n* **1** : a divine influence on a person **2** : the drawing of air into the lungs in breathing : INHALATION **3** : the act or power of stimulating the intellect or emotions ⟨the *inspiration* of music⟩ **4 a** : the quality or state of being inspired ⟨the artist's *inspiration* came from many sources⟩ **b** : something that is inspired ⟨a scheme that was an *inspiration*⟩ **5** : one that inspires — **in•spi•ra•tion•al** \-shnəl, -shən-l\ *adj* — **in•spi•ra•tion•al•ly** \-ē\ *adv*

in•spire \in-ˈspīr\ *vb* **1 a** (1) : to move or guide by divine or supernatural influence ⟨prophets *inspired* by God⟩ (2) : to exert an animating, enlivening, or exalting influence on ⟨*inspired* by their mother⟩ **b** : to give inspiration **c** : to affect with a particular thought or feeling ⟨a childhood that *inspired* them with a desire for education⟩ **2** : INHALE **3 a** : to communicate to an agent supernaturally ⟨words *inspired* by God⟩ **b** : to infuse or introduce into the mind : AROUSE ⟨*inspire* trust in listeners⟩ **4** : to bring about : OCCASION ⟨studies that *inspired* several inventions⟩ [Latin *inspirare,* literally, "to breathe into", from *in-* + *spirare* "to breathe"] — **in•spir•er** *n*

in•spir•it \in-ˈspir-ət\ *vt* : to fill with spirit, courage, or energy

in•sta•bil•i•ty \ˌin-stə-ˈbil-ət-ē\ *n* : the quality or state of being unstable

in•stall *or* **in•stal** \in-ˈstȯl\ *vt* **in•stalled**; **in•stall•ing** **1** : to induct into an office, rank, or order **2** : to put in an indicated place, condition, or status ⟨*install* oneself in the best chair⟩ **3** : to set up for use or service ⟨*install* a furnace⟩ [Middle French *installer,* from Medieval Latin *installare,* from *in-* "in" + *stallum* "stall", from Old High German *stal*] — **in•stall•er** *n*

in•stal•la•tion \ˌin-stə-ˈlā-shən\ *n* **1** : the act of installing : the state of being installed **2** : something that is installed for use **3** : a military camp, fort, or base

¹in•stall•ment *or* **in•stal•ment** \in-ˈstȯl-mənt\ *n* : INSTALLATION 1

²installment *also* **instalment** *n* **1** : one of the parts into which a debt is divided when payment is made at intervals **2** : one of several parts (as of a publication) presented at intervals [earlier *estallment* "payment by parts", derived from Old French *estaler* "to place, fix", from *estal* "place", of Germanic origin] — **installment** *adj*

installment plan *n* : a system of paying for something in installments

¹in•stance \ˈin-stəns\ *n* **1** : SUGGESTION, REQUEST ⟨entered a contest at the *instance* of his teacher⟩ **2** : an individual illustrative of a category ⟨an *instance* of rare courage⟩ **3** : OCCASION, CASE ⟨in the first *instance*⟩ — **for instance** \fər-ˈin-stəns, ˈfrin-stəns\ : as an example

• **syn** INSTANCE, CASE, EXAMPLE mean something that exhibits the distinguishing characteristics of its category. INSTANCE applies to any individual person, act, or thing that may be offered to illustrate or explain ⟨a good *instance* of the power of suggestion⟩ CASE is used to direct attention to a real or assumed occurrence or situation that is to be considered, studied, or dealt with ⟨reported isolated *cases* of typhoid⟩ EXAMPLE applies to a typical or illustrative instance or case ⟨a fine *example* of Georgian architecture⟩

²instance *vt* **1** : to illustrate or demonstrate by an instance **2** : to mention as a case or example : CITE

¹in•stant \ˈin-stənt\ *n* : a very short period of time : MOMENT [Medieval Latin *instans,* from Latin, "present, urgent", from *instare* "to stand on, impend, urge", from *in-* + *stare* "to stand"]

²instant *adj* **1** : PRESSING 1, URGENT ⟨in *instant* need⟩ **2** : IMMEDIATE, DIRECT ⟨an *instant* response⟩ **3 a** : partially prepared by the manufacturer to make final preparation easy ⟨*instant* mashed potatoes⟩ **b** : immediately soluble in water ⟨*instant* coffee⟩ [Latin *instans,* from *instare* "to urge"] — **in•stant•ness** *n*

in•stan•ta•neous \ˌin-stən-ˈtā-nē-əs, -nyəs\ *adj* **1 :** done, occurring, or acting in an instant ⟨death was *instantaneous*⟩ **2 :** done without delay **3 :** occurring or present at a particular instant ⟨*instantaneous* velocity⟩ **[**Medieval Latin *instantaneus,* from *instans* "instant"**]** — **in•stan•ta•neous•ly** *adv* — **in•stan•ta•neous•ness** *n*

in•stan•ter \in-ˈstant-ər\ *adv* **:** at once **:** INSTANTLY **[**Medieval Latin, from *instans* "instant"**]**

in•stant•ly \ˈin-stənt-lē\ *adv* **1 :** IMPORTUNATELY, URGENTLY **2 :** without the least delay **:** IMMEDIATELY

in•star \ˈin-ˌstär\ *n* **:** a stage in the life of an insect between two successive molts **[**Latin, "equivalent, figure"**]**

in•stead \in-ˈsted\ *adv* **:** as a substitute or alternative ⟨was going to write but called *instead*⟩

instead of \in-ˌsted-əv, -ˌsted-ə, -ˌstid-\ *prep* **:** as a substitute for or alternative to ⟨called *instead of* writing⟩

in•step \ˈin-ˌstep\ *n* **1 :** the arched middle part of the human foot **2 :** the part of a shoe or stocking over the instep

in•sti•gate \ˈin-stə-ˌgāt\ *vt* **:** to goad or urge forward **[**Latin *instigare***]** **syn** see INCITE — **in•sti•ga•tion** \ˌin-stə-ˈgā-shən\ *n* — **in•sti•ga•tive** \ˈin-stə-ˌgāt-iv\ *adj* — **in•sti•ga•tor** \-ˌgāt-ər\ *n*

in•still *also* **in•stil** \in-ˈstil\ *vt* **in•stilled**; **in•still•ing** **1 :** to cause to enter drop by drop **2 :** to impart gradually ⟨*instill* a love of music⟩ **[**Latin *instillare,* from *in-* + *stillare* "to drip"**]** — **in•stil•la•tion** \ˌin-stə-ˈlā-shən\ *n* — **in•still•er** \in-ˈstil-ər\ *n* — **in•still•ment** \-ˈstil-mənt\ *n*

¹in•stinct \ˈin-ˌstingt, -ˌstingkt\ *n* **1 :** a natural aptitude, impulse, or capacity **2 a :** a complex pattern of response by an organism to environmental stimuli that is largely inborn and unalterable **b :** behavior based on reactions below the conscious level **[**Latin *instinctus* "impulse", from *instinguere* "to incite"**]** — **in•stinc•tu•al** \in-ˈsting-chə-wəl, -chəl\ *adj*

²in•stinct \in-ˈstingt, -ˈstingkt, ˈin-ˌ\ *adj* **:** entirely filled ⟨a heart *instinct* with faith⟩

in•stinc•tive \in-ˈsting-tiv, -ˈstingk-\ *adj* **:** of, relating to, or prompted by instinct **syn** see SPONTANEOUS — **in•stinc•tive•ly** *adv*

¹in•sti•tute \ˈin-stə-ˌtüt, -ˌtyüt\ *vt* **1 :** to set up **:** ESTABLISH, FOUND ⟨*institute* a society⟩ **2 :** to set going **:** BEGIN ⟨*institute* an investigation⟩ **[**Latin *institutus,* past participle of *instituere* "to institute", from *in-* + *statuere* "to set up", from *status* "condition, state"**]** — **in•sti•tut•er** *or* **in•sti•tu•tor** \-ˌtüt-ər, -ˌtyüt-\ *n*

²institute *n* **1 :** something that is instituted **2 a :** an organization for the promotion of a cause **:** ASSOCIATION ⟨an *institute* for mental health⟩ **b :** an educational institution **3 :** a brief course of instruction ⟨teachers' *institute*⟩

in•sti•tu•tion \ˌin-stə-ˈtü-shən, -ˈtyü-\ *n* **1 :** the act of instituting **:** ESTABLISHMENT **2 :** an established custom, practice, or law ⟨the turkey dinner is a Thanksgiving *institution*⟩ **3 a :** an established society or corporation; *esp* **:** a public one ⟨educational *institutions*⟩ **b :** the building used by such an organization — **in•sti•tu•tion•al** \-shnəl, -shən-l\ *adj* — **in•sti•tu•tion•al•ly** \-ē\ *adv*

in•sti•tu•tion•al•ize \-ˈtü-shnə-ˌlīz, -ˈtyü-, -shən-l-ˌīz\ *vt* **1 :** to make into or treat like an institution ⟨*institutionalized* graft⟩ **2 :** to put in the care of an institution ⟨*institutionalized* alcoholics⟩ — **in•sti•tu•tion•al•iza•tion** \-ˌtü-shnəl-ə-ˈzā-shən, -ˌtyü-, -shən-l-\ *n*

in•struct \in-ˈstrəkt\ *vt* **1 :** to impart knowledge to **:** TEACH **2 :** to give information to **:** INFORM **3 :** to give directions or commands to **[**Latin *instructus,* past participle of *instruere* "to construct, instruct", from *in-* + *struere* "to build"**]** **syn** see TEACH

in•struc•tion \in-ˈstrək-shən\ *n* **1 a :** LESSON **b :** COMMAND 2, ORDER **c** *pl* **:** an outline or manual of procedure to be followed **:** DIRECTIONS **2 :** the action or practice of an instructor or teacher — **in•struc•tion•al** \-shnəl, -shən-l\ *adj*

in•struc•tive \in-ˈstrək-tiv\ *adj* **:** giving knowledge **:** serving to instruct or inform ⟨an *instructive* experience⟩ — **in•struc•tive•ly** *adv* — **in•struc•tive•ness** *n*

in•struc•tor \-tər\ *n* **:** one that instructs **:** TEACHER; *esp* **:** a college teacher below professorial rank — **in•struc•tor•ship** \-ˌship\ *n*

in•struc•tress \-ˈstrək-trəs\ *n* **:** a woman who is an instructor

in•stru•ment \ˈin-strə-mənt\ *n* **1 :** a means whereby something is done **2 a :** IMPLEMENT; *esp* **:** one designed for precision work ⟨a surgical *instrument*⟩ **b :** a device used to produce music **3 :** a formal legal document (as a deed, bond, or agreement) **4 a :** a measuring device for determining the present value of a quantity under observation **b :** an electrical or mechanical device used in navigating an airplane; *esp* **:** such a device used as the sole means of navigating **[**Latin *instrumentum,* from *instruere* "to construct, instruct"**]** **syn** see IMPLEMENT

in•stru•men•tal \ˌin-strə-ˈment-l\ *adj* **1 :** acting as an instrument or means ⟨*instrumental* in sending a thief to jail⟩ **2 :** designed for or performed with or on an instrument and especially a musical instrument ⟨an unusual *instrumental* arrangement⟩ — **in•stru•men•tal•ly** \-l-ē\ *adv*

in•stru•men•tal•ist \-l-əst\ *n* **:** a player of a musical instrument

in•stru•men•tal•i•ty \ˌin-strə-mən-ˈtal-ət-ē, -ˌmen-\ *n, pl* **-ties** **1 :** the quality or state of being instrumental **2 :** AGENCY 2, MEANS

in•stru•men•ta•tion \ˌin-strə-mən-ˈtā-shən, -ˌmen-\ *n* **1 :** the use or application of instruments for observation, measurement, or control **2 :** the arrangement or composition of music for instruments **3 :** instruments for a particular purpose

instrument flying *n* **:** navigation of an airplane by instruments only

instrument landing *n* **:** a landing made with little or no external visibility by means of instruments within an airplane and by ground radio devices

instrument panel *n* **:** a panel on which instruments are mounted; *esp* **:** DASHBOARD 2

in•sub•or•di•nate \ˌin-sə-ˈbȯrd-n-ət, -ˈbȯrd-nət\ *adj* **:** unwilling to submit to authority **:** DISOBEDIENT — **in•sub•or•di•nate•ly** *adv* — **in•sub•or•di•na•tion** \ˌin-sə-ˌbȯrd-n-ˈā-shən\ *n*

in•sub•stan•tial \ˌin-səb-ˈstan-chəl\ *adj* **1 :** lacking substance or reality **:** IMAGINARY **2 :** lacking firmness or solidity — **in•sub•stan•ti•al•i•ty** \-ˌstan-chē-ˈal-ət-ē\ *n*

in•suf•fer•able \in-ˈsəf-rə-bəl, ˈin-, -ə-rə-\ *adj* **:** incapable of being endured **:** INTOLERABLE ⟨an *insufferable* bore⟩ ⟨*insufferable* wrongs⟩ — **in•suf•fer•able•ness** *n* — **in•suf•fer•ably** \-blē\ *adv*

in•suf•fi•cien•cy \ˌin-sə-ˈfish-ən-sē\ *n, pl* **-cies** **1 :** the quality or state of being insufficient: as **a :** lack of mental or moral fitness **b :** lack of adequate supply **c :** lack of physical or functional adequacy ⟨cardiac *insufficiency*⟩ **2 :** something insufficient ⟨aware of their own *insufficiencies*⟩

in•suf•fi•cient \-ˈfish-ənt\ *adj* **:** not sufficient **:** INADEQUATE; *also* **:** INCOMPETENT — **in•suf•fi•cient•ly** *adv*

in•su•lar \ˈins-ə-lər, -yə-; ˈin-shə-lər\ *adj* **1 :** of, relating to, or forming an island **2 :** ISOLATED, DETACHED ⟨an *insular* building⟩ **3 :** being isolated and illiberal **:** NARROW **[**Late Latin *insularis,* from Latin *insula* "island"**]** — **in•su•lar•ism** \-lə-ˌriz-əm\ *n* — **in•su•lar•i•ty** \ˌins-ə-ˈlar-ət-ē, -yə-; ˌin-shə-ˈlar-\ *n* — **in•su•lar•ly** *adv*

in•su•late \ˈin-sə-ˌlāt\ *vt* **:** to place in a detached situation **:** ISOLATE; *esp* **:** to separate from conducting bodies by means of nonconductors so as to prevent transfer of electricity, heat, or sound **[**Latin *insula* "island"**]**

in•su•la•tion \ˌin-sə-ˈlāshən\ *n* **1 :** the act of insulating **:** the state of being insulated **2 :** material used in insulating

in•su•la•tor \ˈin-sə-ˌlāt-ər\ *n* **:** one that insulates; *esp* **:** a material that is a poor conductor of electricity or a device made of such material

in•su•lin \ˈin-sə-lən, -slən\ *n* **:** a pancreatic hormone needed especially for the normal utilization of sugar by the body and used in the treatment and control of diabetes **[**New Latin *insula* "islet of Langerhans", from Latin, "island"**]**

insulin shock *n* **:** a condition of deficient blood sugar associated with excessive insulin in the system and marked by progressive development of coma

¹in•sult \in-ˈsəlt\ *vt* **1 :** to treat with insolence, indignity, or contempt **:** AFFRONT **2 :** to make little of **:** BELITTLE **[**Latin *insultare,* literally, "to spring upon", from *in-* + *saltare* "to leap"**]** **syn** see OFFEND — **in•sult•er** *n*

²in•sult \ˈin-ˌsəlt\ *n* **1 :** an act or speech showing disrespect or contempt **2 :** damage to the body or one of its parts; *also* **:** a cause of this ⟨thermal *insult*⟩ **syn** see AFFRONT

\ə\ **abut**	\au̇\ **out**	\i\ **tip**	\ȯ\ **saw**	\u̇\ **foot**
\ər\ **further**	\ch\ **chin**	\ī\ **life**	\ȯi\ **coin**	\y\ **yet**
\a\ **mat**	\e\ **pet**	\j\ **job**	\th\ **thin**	\yü\ **few**
\ā\ **take**	\ē\ **easy**	\ng\ **sing**	\t͟h\ **this**	\yu̇\ **cure**
\ä\ **cot, cart**	\g\ **go**	\ō\ **bone**	\ü\ **food**	\zh\ **vision**

in·su·per·a·ble \in-ˈsü-pə-rə-bəl, ˈin-, -prə-bəl\ *adj* **:** incapable of being surmounted or overcome ⟨*insuperable* difficulties⟩ [Latin *insuperabilis,* from *in-* + *superare* "to surmount", from *super* "over"] — **in·su·per·a·bly** \-blē\ *adv*

in·sup·port·able \ˌin-sə-ˈpōrt-ə-bəl, -ˈpȯrt-\ *adj* **:** not supportable: **a :** UNENDURABLE ⟨an *insupportable* burden⟩ **b :** UNJUSTIFIABLE ⟨*insupportable* charges⟩ — **in·sup·port·able·ness** *n* — **in·sup·port·ably** \-blē\ *adv*

in·sup·press·ible \ˌin-sə-ˈpres-ə-bəl\ *adj* **:** not suppressible — **in·sup·press·ibly** \-blē\ *adv*

in·sur·able \in-ˈshu̇r-ə-bəl\ *adj* **:** capable of being insured — **in·sur·abil·i·ty** \in-ˌshu̇r-ə-ˈbil-ət-ē\ *n*

in·sur·ance \in-ˈshu̇r-əns\ *n* **1 :** the act of insuring **:** the state of being insured **2 a :** the business of insuring persons or property **b :** coverage by contract whereby one party undertakes to guarantee another against loss by a specified event or peril **c :** the sum for which something is insured

in·sure \in-ˈshu̇r\ *vt* **1 :** to give or procure insurance on or for **2 :** to make certain **:** ENSURE

in·sured *n* **:** a person whose life or property is insured

in·sur·er \in-ˈshu̇r-ər\ *n* **:** one that insures

in·sur·gence \in-ˈsər-jəns\ *n* **:** UPRISING

in·sur·gen·cy \-jən-sē\ *n, pl* **-cies 1 :** the quality or state of being insurgent; *esp* **:** a state of revolt against a government that is less than an organized revolution **2 :** UPRISING

[1]**in·sur·gent** \in-ˈsər-jənt\ *n* **:** a person who revolts; *esp* **:** a rebel not recognized as a belligerent [Latin *insurgere* "to rise up", from *in-* + *surgere* "to rise"]

[2]**insurgent** *adj* **:** rising in opposition to authority **:** REBELLIOUS — **in·sur·gent·ly** *adv*

in·sur·rec·tion \ˌin-sə-ˈrek-shən\ *n* **:** an act or instance of revolting against civil authority or an established government [Middle French, from Late Latin *insurrectio,* from Latin *insurgere* "to rise up"] — **in·sur·rec·tion·ary** \-shə-ˌner-ē\ *adj or n* — **in·sur·rec·tion·ist** \-shə-nəst\ *n*

in·tact \in-ˈtakt\ *adj* **:** untouched especially by anything that harms or diminishes **:** ENTIRE, UNINJURED [Latin *intactus,* from *in-* + *tangere* "to touch"] — **in·tact·ness** \-ˈtakt-nəs, -ˈtak-nəs\ *n*

in·ta·glio \in-ˈtal-yō, -ˈtag-lē-ˌō\ *n, pl* **-glios 1 a :** an engraving or incised figure in a hard material (as stone) depressed below the surface of the material **b :** the process of making intaglios **c :** printing (as in photogravure) done from a plate in which the image is sunk below the surface **2 :** something (as a gem) carved in intaglio [Italian, from *intagliare* "to engrave", from Medieval Latin *intaliare,* from Latin *in-* + Late Latin *taliare* "to cut"]

intaglio

in·take \ˈin-ˌtāk\ *n* **1 :** a place where liquid or air is taken into something (as a pump) **2 :** the act of taking in **3 :** something taken in ⟨food *intake*⟩

[1]**in·tan·gi·ble** \in-ˈtan-jə-bəl, ˈin-\ *adj* **:** not tangible: as **a :** incapable of being touched ⟨light is *intangible*⟩ **b :** incapable of being thought of as matter or substance **:** ABSTRACT ⟨goodwill is an *intangible* asset⟩ — **in·tan·gi·bil·i·ty** \in-ˌtan-jə-ˈbil-ət-ē\ *n* — **in·tan·gi·ble·ness** \in-ˈtan-jə-bəl-nəs, ˈin-\ *n* — **in·tan·gi·bly** \-blē\ *adv*

[2]**intangible** *n* **:** something intangible; *esp* **:** an asset (as goodwill) that is not corporeal

in·te·ger \ˈint-i-jər\ *n* **1 :** a number that is a natural number (as 1, 2, or 3), the negative of a natural number, or 0 — called also *whole number* **2 :** a complete entity [Latin, "whole, entire"]

in·te·gral \ˈint-i-grəl (*usually so in mathematics*); in-ˈteg-rəl, -ˈtēg-\ *adj* **1 a :** essential to completeness **:** CONSTITUENT ⟨an *integral* part of the plan⟩ **b :** of, relating to, or being a mathematical integer ⟨9 is an *integral* factor of 72⟩ **c :** formed as a unit with another part **2 :** composed of integral parts **:** INTEGRATED **3 :** lacking nothing essential **:** ENTIRE — **in·te·gral·i·ty** \ˌint-ə-ˈgral-ət-ē\ *n* — **in·te·gral·ly** \ˈint-i-grə-lē; in-ˈteg-rə-, -ˈtēg-\ *adv*

integral calculus *n* **:** a branch of mathematics applying special advanced techniques especially to the determination of lengths, areas, and volumes — compare DIFFERENTIAL CALCULUS

in·te·grate \ˈint-ə-ˌgrāt\ *vb* **1 :** to form into a whole **:** UNITE ⟨*integrate* the countries' economies⟩ **2 a :** to unite with something else ⟨free enterprise *integrated* with some government controls⟩ **b :** to incorporate into a larger unit ⟨*integrate* migrant workers into the organized labor movement⟩ **3 a :** to end the segregation of and bring into common and equal membership in society or an organization **b :** DESEGREGATE ⟨*integrate* school districts⟩ **4 :** to become integrated [Latin *integrare,* from *integer* "whole, entire"]

integrated circuit *n* **:** a tiny complex of electronic components and their connections that is produced in or on a small slice of material (as silicon) — **integrated circuitry** *n*

in·te·gra·tion \ˌint-ə-ˈgrā-shən\ *n* **:** the act, the process, or an instance of integrating; *esp* **:** incorporation as equals into society or an organization of persons from different groups (as races)

in·te·gra·tion·ist \-shə-nəst, -shnəst\ *n* **:** a person who believes in, advocates, or practices social integration

in·teg·ri·ty \in-ˈteg-rət-ē\ *n* **1 :** an unimpaired condition **:** SOUNDNESS **2 :** adherence to a code of especially moral or artistic values **3 :** the quality or state of being complete or undivided **:** COMPLETENESS

in·teg·u·ment \in-ˈteg-yə-mənt\ *n* **:** something that covers or encloses; *esp* **:** an enclosing layer (as a skin, membrane, or husk) of an organism or one of its parts [Latin *integumentum,* from *integere* "to cover", from *in-* + *tegere* "to cover"] **in·teg·u·men·tal** \in-ˌteg-yə-ˈment-l\ *adj* — **in·teg·u·men·ta·ry** \-ˈment-ə-rē, -ˈmen-trē\ *adj*

in·tel·lect \ˈint-l-ˌekt\ *n* **1 a :** the power of knowing **b :** the capacity for thought especially when highly developed **2 :** a person of superior intellect [Latin *intellectus,* from *intellegere* "to understand"]

in·tel·lec·tion \ˌint-l-ˈek-shən\ *n* **1 :** exercise of the intellect **:** REASONING **2 :** a specific act of the intellect **:** THOUGHT — **in·tel·lec·tive** \-ˈek-tiv\ *adj* — **in·tel·lec·tive·ly** *adv*

[1]**in·tel·lec·tu·al** \ˌint-l-ˈek-chə-wəl, -chəl\ *adj* **1 a :** having to do with the intellect or understanding **b :** originating in or chiefly guided by intellect rather than by emotion or experience **c :** performed by the intellect ⟨*intellectual* processes⟩ **2 :** having intellect to a high degree **:** engaged in or given to learning and thinking ⟨an *intellectual* person⟩ **3 :** requiring study and thought ⟨*intellectual* work⟩ **syn** see INTELLIGENT, MENTAL — **in·tel·lec·tu·al·i·ty** \-ˌek-chə-ˈwal-ət-ē\ *n* — **in·tel·lec·tu·al·ly** \-ˈek-chə-wə-lē, -chə-lē\ *adv* — **in·tel·lec·tu·al·ness** \-chə-wəl-nəs, -chəl-\ *n*

[2]**intellectual** *n* **:** an intellectual person

in·tel·lec·tu·al·ism \ˌint-l-ˈek-chə-wə-ˌliz-əm, -chə-ˌliz-\ *n* **:** devotion to the exercise of intellect or to intellectual pursuits — **in·tel·lec·tu·al·ist** \-ləst\ *n* — **in·tel·lec·tu·al·is·tic** \-ˌek-chə-wə-ˈlis-tik, -chə-ˈlis-\ *adj*

in·tel·lec·tu·al·ize \ˌint-l-ˈek-chə-wə-ˌlīz, -chə-ˌlīz\ *vt* **:** to give rational form or content to

in·tel·li·gence \in-ˈtel-ə-jəns\ *n* **1 a :** the ability to learn and understand or to deal with new or challenging situations **:** REASON, INTELLECT **b :** mental acuteness **:** SHREWDNESS **2 :** an intelligent being **3 :** the act of understanding **:** COMPREHENSION **3 a :** information communicated **:** NEWS **b :** information concerning an enemy or possible enemy; *also* **:** a group or agency gathering such intelligence

intelligence quotient *n* **:** a number held to express the relative intelligence of a person and determined by dividing his mental age by his chronological age and multiplying by 100

intelligence test *n* **:** a test designed to measure the relative mental capacity of a person

in·tel·li·gent \in-ˈtel-ə-jənt\ *adj* **:** having or indicating a high or satisfactory degree of intelligence [Latin *intelligens,* from *intelligere, intellegere* "to understand", from *inter-* + *legere* "to select"] — **in·tel·li·gent·ly** *adv*

• **syn** INTELLECTUAL: INTELLIGENT implies having quickness of perception and understanding of any sort; INTELLECTUAL suggests having greater than average interest in things of the mind or in thinking abstractly and often implies a contrast with practical activity or capacity for simple emotional response to experience. **syn** see in addition CLEVER

in·tel·li·gen·tsia \in-ˌtel-ə-ˈjen-sē-ə, -ˈgen-\ *n* **:** intellectuals as a group [Russian *intelligentsiya,* from Latin *intelligentia* "intelligence"]

in•tel•li•gi•ble \in-'tel-ə-jə-bəl\ *adj* **:** capable of being understood **:** COMPREHENSIBLE — **in•tel•li•gi•bil•i•ty** \-ˌtel-ə-jə-'bil-ət-ē\ *n* — **in•tel•li•gi•ble•ness** \-'tel-ə-jə-bəl-nəs\ *n* — **in•tel•li•gi•bly** \-blē\ *adv*

in•tem•per•ance \in-'tem-pə-rəns, 'in-, -prəns\ *n* **:** lack of moderation; *esp* **:** habitual or excessive use of intoxicants

in•tem•per•ate \-pə-rət, -prət\ *adj* **:** not temperate: as **a :** not moderate or mild **:** EXTREME, SEVERE ⟨*intemperate* weather⟩ **b :** lacking or showing lack of restraint or self-control **c :** given to excessive use of intoxicants — **in•tem•per•ate•ly** *adv* — **in•tem•per•ate•ness** *n*

in•tend \in-'tend\ *vt* **:** to have in mind as a purpose or aim **:** PLAN [Middle French *entendre,* from Latin *intendere* "to stretch out, intend", from *in-* + *tendere* "to stretch"]

in•ten•dant \in-'ten-dənt\ *n* **:** an administrative official (as a governor) especially under the French, Spanish, or Portuguese monarchies [French, from Latin *intendere* "to intend, give attention to"]

[1]**in•tend•ed** \in-'ten-dəd\ *adj* **1 :** planned for the future ⟨one's *intended* career⟩ **2 :** INTENTIONAL ⟨an *intended* insult⟩

[2]**intended** *n* **:** an affianced person **:** BETROTHED

in•tense \in-'tens\ *adj* **1 a :** existing in an extreme degree ⟨an *intense* light⟩ **b :** having or showing a characteristic trait in extreme degree ⟨an *intense* sun shone down⟩ **c :** very large ⟨*intense* amounts of radiation⟩ **2 :** most energetic or concentrated ⟨*intense* study⟩ **3 a :** feeling deeply especially by nature or temperament ⟨an *intense* person⟩ **b :** deeply felt ⟨*intense* convictions⟩ [Middle French, from Latin *intensus,* from *intendere* "to stretch out, intend"] — **in•tense•ly** *adv* — **in•tense•ness** *n*

in•ten•si•fy \in-'ten-sə-ˌfī\ *vb* **-fied; -fy•ing 1 :** to make or become intense or more intensive **:** STRENGTHEN **2 :** to make or become more acute **:** SHARPEN — **in•ten•si•fi•ca•tion** \-ˌten-sə-fə-'kā-shən\ *n* — **in•ten•si•fi•er** \-'ten-sə-ˌfī-ər, -ˌfīr\ *n*

• syn INTENSIFY, HEIGHTEN, AGGRAVATE, ENHANCE mean to increase markedly in measure or degree. INTENSIFY implies a deepening or strengthening of a thing or its characteristics ⟨*intensify* efforts for peace⟩ ⟨colors were *intensified* by the clear atmosphere⟩ HEIGHTEN suggests a lifting above the ordinary or accustomed ⟨tried to *heighten* awareness of possible danger⟩ AGGRAVATE stresses the worsening of something already bad ⟨inflation *aggravated* the economic depression⟩ ENHANCE suggests a raising above normal in desirability or attractiveness ⟨shrubbery *enhances* a lawn⟩

in•ten•si•ty \in-'ten-sət-ē\ *n, pl* **-ties 1 :** the quality or state of being intense; *esp* **:** extreme degree of strength, force, or energy **2 a :** the degree or amount of a quality or condition **b :** the magnitude of force or energy per unit (as of surface, charge, or mass) ⟨the *intensity* of an electric or magnetic field⟩ **3 :** SATURATION 2

[1]**in•ten•sive** \in-'ten-siv\ *adj* **1 :** involving or marked by special effort **:** THOROUGH, EXHAUSTIVE ⟨an *intensive* campaign⟩ ⟨*intensive* agriculture⟩ **2 :** serving to give emphasis ⟨the *intensive* pronoun *myself* in the sentence "I myself was present"⟩ — **in•ten•sive•ly** *adv* — **in•ten•sive•ness** *n*

[2]**intensive** *n* **:** an intensive word

[1]**in•tent** \in-'tent\ *n* **1 :** the act, fact, or state of mind of intending ⟨with *intent* to kill⟩ **2 :** MEANING, SIGNIFICANCE ⟨understand the *intent* of the message⟩ [Old French *entent,* from Late Latin *intentus,* from Latin *intendere* "to intend"]

[2]**intent** *adj* **1 :** directed with strained or eager attention ⟨an *intent* gaze⟩ **2 a :** closely occupied ⟨*intent* upon their plans⟩ **b :** set on some end or purpose ⟨*intent* on going⟩ — **in•tent•ly** *adv* — **in•tent•ness** *n*

in•ten•tion \in-'ten-chən\ *n* **1 :** a determination to act in a certain way ⟨done without *intention*⟩ **2 :** an intended object **:** PURPOSE, END ⟨carry out one's *intention*⟩ **3 :** IMPORT, SIGNIFICANCE ⟨grasp the *intention* of a speaker⟩

• syn PURPOSE, DESIGN, AIM: INTENTION applies to what one has in mind to do or bring about; PURPOSE suggests a more settled determination; DESIGN implies a carefully calculated plan; AIM adds implications of definite purpose and effort to attain or accomplish an end.

in•ten•tion•al \in-'tench-nəl, -'ten-chən-l\ *adj* **:** done by intention or design **:** DELIBERATE ⟨*intentional* damage⟩ **syn** see VOLUNTARY — **in•ten•tion•al•i•ty** \-ˌten-chə-'nal-ət-ē\ *n* — **in•ten•tion•al•ly** \in-'tench-nə-lē, -'ten-chən-l-ē\ *adv*

in•ter \in-'tər\ *vt* **in•terred; in•ter•ring :** to deposit (a dead body) in the earth or in a tomb [Old French *enterrer,* from Latin *in-* + *terra* "earth"]

inter- *prefix* **1 :** between **:** among **:** in the midst ⟨*inter*penetrate⟩ ⟨*inter*stellar⟩ **2 :** reciprocal **:** reciprocally ⟨*inter*marry⟩ **3 :** located between ⟨*inter*face⟩ **4 :** carried on between ⟨*inter*national⟩ **5 :** occurring between **:** intervening ⟨*inter*glacial⟩ **6 :** shared by or derived from two or more ⟨*inter*faith⟩ [Latin, from *inter*]

See *inter-* and 2d element

interaccount
interagency
interallelic
interbank
interborough
interbranch
interbusiness
intercampus
interchannel
interchurch
intercity
interclan
interclass
interclub
intercoastal
intercolonial
intercommunal
intercommunity
intercompany
intercounty
interdialectal
interdivisional
interelectrode
interelectron
interelectronic
interenvironmental
interethnic
interfaculty
interfamily
interfarm
interfiber
interfraternity
intergang
intergeneration
intergenerational
intergovernmental
intergovernmentally
intergroup
interhemisphere
interhospital
interindividual
interindustry
interinstitutional
interisland
interlevel
interlibrary
intermountain
intermuseum
interoceanic
interparish
interparty
interpersonal
interpersonally
interpopulation
interprofessional
interprovincial
interpupil
interregional
interreligious
interrow
intersample
interschool
intersectional
intersegmental
intersocietal
intertemple
interterminal
interterritorial
intertribal
intertroop
intertropical
interunion
interunit
interuniversity
intervalley
intervillage
interwar
interzonal
interzone

in•ter•act \ˌint-ə-'rakt\ *vi* **:** to act upon one another ⟨students *interacting* with their teacher⟩ — **in•ter•ac•tion** \ˌint-ə-'rak-shən\ *n* — **in•ter•ac•tion•al** \-shnəl, -shən-l\ *adj* — **in•ter•ac•tive** \-'rak-tiv\ *adj*

in•ter alia \ˌint-ə-'rā-lē-ə, -'rä-\ *adv* **:** among other things [Latin]

in•ter•atom•ic \ˌint-ə-rə-'täm-ik\ *adj* **:** situated or acting between atoms

in•ter•breed \ˌint-ər-'brēd\ *vb* **-bred** \-'bred\; **-breed•ing :** to breed or cause to breed together; *esp* **:** CROSSBREED

in•ter•ca•lary \in-'tər-kə-ˌler-ē, ˌint-ər-'kal-ə-rē\ *adj* **:** inserted between other things or parts

in•ter•ca•late \in-'tər-kə-ˌlāt\ *vt* **1 :** to insert (as a day) in a calendar **2 :** to insert between or among existing elements or layers [Latin *intercalare,* from *inter-* + *calare* "to call, summon"] — **in•ter•ca•la•tion** \-ˌtər-kə-'lā-shən\ *n*

in•ter•cede \ˌint-ər-'sēd\ *vi* **1 :** to act as a go-between between unfriendly parties **2 :** to beg or plead in behalf of another ⟨*intercede* for a friend⟩ [Latin *intercedere,* from *inter-* + *cedere* "to go"] **syn** see INTERPOSE

in•ter•cel•lu•lar \ˌint-ər-'sel-yə-lər\ *adj* **:** lying or taking place between cells ⟨*intercellular* spaces⟩

[1]**in•ter•cept** \ˌint-ər-'sept\ *vt* **1 :** to stop or seize on the way to or before arrival at a destination ⟨*intercept* a letter⟩ ⟨*intercept* a pass in football⟩ **2 :** to include part of (a curve, surface, or solid) between two points, curves, or surfaces ⟨a line *intercepted* between points A and B⟩ [Latin *interceptus,* past participle of *intercipere* "to intercept", from *inter-* + *capere* "to take, seize"]

[2]**in•ter•cept** \'int-ər-ˌsept\ *n* **:** the distance from the origin to a point where a graph crosses a coordinate axis

in•ter•cep•tion \ˌint-ər-'sep-shən\ *n* **:** the act of intercepting **:** the state of being intercepted ⟨the *interception* of a message⟩

in•ter•cep•tor *or* **in•ter•cep•ter** \ˌint-ər-'sep-tər\ *n* **:** one that intercepts; *esp* **:** a light high-speed fast-climbing fighter plane designed for defense against raiding bombers

\ə\ abut	\au̇\ **out**	\i\ **tip**	\ȯ\ **saw**	\u̇\ **foot**
\ər\ **further**	\ch\ **chin**	\ī\ **life**	\ȯi\ **coin**	\y\ **yet**
\a\ **mat**	\e\ **pet**	\j\ **job**	\th\ **thin**	\yü\ **few**
\ā\ **take**	\ē\ **easy**	\ng\ **sing**	\t͟h\ **this**	\yu̇\ **cure**
\ä\ **cot, cart**	\g\ **go**	\ō\ **bone**	\ü\ **food**	\zh\ **vision**

in•ter•ces•sion \ˌint-ər-ˈsesh-ən\ *n* **:** the act of interceding **:** MEDIATION [Latin *intercessio,* from *intercedere* "to intercede"] — **in•ter•ces•sion•al** \-ˈsesh-nəl, -ən-l\ *adj* — **in•ter•ces•sor** \-ˈses-ər\ *n* — **in•ter•ces•so•ry** \-ˈses-rē, -ə-rē\ *adj*

[1]**in•ter•change** \ˌint-ər-ˈchānj\ *vb* **1 :** to put each of (two things) in the place of the other ⟨*interchange* two tires⟩ **2 :** EXCHANGE ⟨*interchange* ideas⟩ **3 :** to change places mutually — **in•ter•chang•er** *n*

[2]**in•ter•change** \ˈint-ər-ˌchānj\ *n* **1 :** the act, the process, or an instance of interchanging **:** EXCHANGE **2 :** a joining of two or more highways by a system of separate levels that permit traffic to pass from one to another without the crossing of traffic streams

in•ter•change•able \ˌint-ər-ˈchān-jə-bəl\ *adj* **:** capable of being interchanged; *esp* **:** permitting mutual substitution ⟨*interchangeable* parts⟩ — **in•ter•change•abil•i•ty** \-ˌchān-jə-ˈbil-ət-ē\ *n* — **in•ter•change•able•ness** \-ˈchān-je-bəl-nəs\ *n* — **in•ter•change•ably** \-blē\ *adv*

in•ter•col•le•giate \ˌint-ər-kə-ˈlē-jət, -jē-ət\ *adj* **:** existing or carried on between colleges ⟨*intercollegiate* athletics⟩

in•ter•com \ˈint-ər-ˌkäm\ *n* **:** INTERCOMMUNICATION SYSTEM

in•ter•com•mu•ni•cate \ˌint-ər-kə-ˈmyü-nə-ˌkāt\ *vi* **1 :** to exchange communication with one another **2 :** to afford passage from one to another ⟨the rooms *intercommunicate*⟩ — **in•ter•com•mu•ni•ca•tion** \-ˌmyü-nə-ˈkā-shən\ *n*

intercommunication system *n* **:** a two-way communication system with microphone and loudspeaker at each station for localized use

in•ter•com•mu•nion \ˌint-ər-kə-ˈmyü-nyən\ *n* **:** interdenominational participation in communion

in•ter•con•nect \ˌint-ər-kə-ˈnekt\ *vb* **:** to connect with one another ⟨the rooms *interconnect*⟩ ⟨*interconnected* switches⟩ — **in•ter•con•nec•tion** \-ˈnek-shən\ *n*

in•ter•con•ti•nen•tal \ˌint-ər-ˌkänt-n-ˈent-l\ *adj* **1 :** extending among or carried on between continents ⟨*intercontinental* trade⟩ **2 :** capable of traveling between continents ⟨an *intercontinental* missile⟩

in•ter•con•ver•sion \ˌint-ər-kən-ˈvər-zhən, -shən\ *n* **:** mutual conversion ⟨*interconversion* of chemical compounds⟩ — **in•ter•con•vert** \-ˈvərt\ *vt* — **in•ter•con•vert•ible** \-ˈvərt-ə-bəl\ *adj*

in•ter•cool•er \ˌint-ər-ˈkü-lər\ *n* **:** a device for cooling a fluid between successive heat-generating processes

in•ter•cos•tal \ˌint-ər-ˈkäs-tl\ *adj* **:** situated between the ribs; *also* **:** of or relating to an intercostal part [Latin *costa* "rib"] — **intercostal** *n* — **in•ter•cos•tal•ly** \-ˈkäs-tə-lē\ *adv*

in•ter•course \ˈint-ər-ˌkōrs, -ˌkȯrs\ *n* **1 :** connection or relations between persons or groups **:** COMMUNICATION ⟨*social* intercourse⟩ **2 :** SEXUAL INTERCOURSE [derived from Latin *intercursus* "act of running between", from *intercurrere* "to run between", from *inter-* + *currere* "to run"]

in•ter•crop \ˌint-ər-ˈkräp\ *vb* **:** to grow two or more crops at one time on the same piece of land ⟨*intercrop* corn and pumpkins⟩

in•ter•cross \ˈint-ər-ˌkrȯs\ *n* **:** an instance or a product of cross-breeding — **in•ter•cross** \ˌint-ər-ˈkrȯs\ *vb*

in•ter•cul•tur•al \ˌint-ər-ˈkəlch-rəl, -ə-rəl\ *adj* **:** occurring between or relating to two or more cultures

in•ter•de•nom•i•na•tion•al \ˌint-ər-di-ˌnäm-ə-ˈnā-shnəl, -shən-l\ *adj* **:** involving or occurring between different denominations — **in•ter•de•nom•i•na•tion•al•ism** \-ˌiz-əm\ *n*

in•ter•de•part•men•tal \ˌint-ər-di-ˌpärt-ˈment-l, -ˌdē-\ *adj* **:** carried on between or involving different departments (as of a college) — **in•ter•de•part•men•tal•ly** \-l-ē\ *adv*

in•ter•de•pend \ˌint-ər-di-ˈpend\ *vi* **:** to depend upon one another — **in•ter•de•pen•dence** \-ˈpen-dəns\ *n* — **in•ter•de•pen•den•cy** \-dən-sē\ *n* — **in•ter•de•pen•dent** \-dənt\ *adj* — **in•ter•de•pen•dent•ly** *adv*

[1]**in•ter•dict** \ˈint-ər-ˌdikt\ *n* **1 :** a Roman Catholic church censure withdrawing most sacraments and Christian burial from a person or district **2 :** PROHIBITION 2 [Old French *entredit,* from Latin *interdictum* "official prohibition", from *interdicere* "to interpose, forbid", from *inter-* + *dicere* "to say"]

[2]**in•ter•dict** \ˌint-ər-ˈdikt\ *vt* **:** to prohibit or forbid especially by an interdict — **in•ter•dic•tion** \ˌint-ər-ˈdik-shən\ *n* — **in•ter•dic•tor** \-ˈdik-tər\ *n* — **in•ter•dic•to•ry** \-ˈdik-tə-rē, -trē\ *adj*

in•ter•dig•i•tate \-ˈdij-ə-ˌtāt\ *vi* **:** to interlock like the fingers of folded hands [Latin *digitus* "finger"] — **in•ter•dig•i•ta•tion** \-ˌdij-ə-ˈtā-shən\ *n*

in•ter•dis•ci•pli•nary \ˌint-ər-ˈdis-ə-plə-ˌner-ē\ *adj* **:** involving two or more academic disciplines

[1]**in•ter•est** \ˈin-trəst; ˈint-ə-ˌrest, -ə-rəst, -ərst; ˈin-ˌtrest\ *n* **1 :** a right, title, or legal share in something **2 :** WELFARE, BENEFIT; *esp* **:** SELF-INTEREST **3 a :** a charge for borrowed money that is generally a percentage of the amount borrowed **b :** the return received by capital on its investments **4 :** a group financially interested in an industry or enterprise ⟨mining *interests*⟩ **5 a :** readiness to be concerned with or moved by something **b :** the quality in a thing that arouses interest ⟨your plans are of great *interest* to me⟩ [derived from Latin *interesse* "to make a difference, concern", from *inter-* + *esse* "to be"]

[2]**interest** *vt* **1 :** to engage (oneself) in advancing something ⟨*interest* oneself in a friend's welfare⟩ **2 :** to persuade to participate or take part **3 :** to arouse the interest of ⟨a market to *interest* any investor⟩

in•ter•est•ed *adj* **1 :** having the attention occupied ⟨*interested* listeners⟩ **2 :** being involved ⟨*interested* parties⟩ — **in•ter•est•ed•ly** *adv*

interest group *n* **:** a group of persons having a common interest that often provides a basis for action

in•ter•est•ing *adj* **:** holding the attention **:** arousing interest — **in•ter•est•ing•ly** \-ing-lē\ *adv*

in•ter•face \ˈint-ər-ˌfās\ *n* **1 :** a surface forming a common boundary of two bodies, spaces, or phases ⟨an *interface* between oil and water⟩ **2 :** a place at which two independent systems meet and act on or communicate with each other; *also* **:** a means of communication at an interface — **interface** *vb* — **in•ter•fa•cial** \ˌint-ər-ˈfā-shəl\ *adj*

in•ter•faith \ˈint-ər-ˌfāth\ *adj* **:** involving persons of different religious faiths ⟨*interfaith* conference⟩

in•ter•fere \ˌint-ər-ˈfiər, ˌint-ə-ˈfiər\ *vi* **1 :** to strike one foot against the opposite foot or ankle in walking or running **2 :** to come in collision or be in opposition **:** CLASH ⟨our neighbor's arrival *interfered* with our plan⟩ **3 :** to meddle in the affairs of others ⟨don't *interfere* with my business⟩ **4 :** to act so as to augment, diminish, or otherwise affect one another ⟨*interfering* light waves⟩ **5 :** to hinder illegally an attempt of a player to receive a pass or to play a ball or puck [Middle French *s'entreferir* "to strike one another", from Old French *entre-* "inter-" + *ferir* 'to strike", from Latin *ferire*] **syn** see INTERPOSE — **in•ter•fer•er** *n*

in•ter•fer•ence \ˌint-ər-ˈfir-əns, ˌint-ə-ˈfir-\ *n* **1 a :** the act or process of interfering **b :** something that interferes **:** OBSTRUCTION **2 :** the mutual effect on meeting of two waves (as of light or sound) whereby the resulting neutralization at some points and reinforcement at others produces in the case of light waves alternate light and dark bands or colored bands **3 a :** the legal blocking of an opponent in football **b :** the illegal hindering of an opponent (as in baseball) **4 a :** confusion of received radio signals due to undesired signals or electrical effects **b :** an electrical effect that produces such confusion — **in•ter•fer•en•tial** \-fə-ˈren-chəl, -ˌfir-ˈen-\ *adj*

in•ter•fer•tile \ˌint-ər-ˈfərt-l\ *adj* **:** capable of interbreeding — **in•ter•fer•til•i•ty** \-fər-ˈtil-ət-ē\ *n*

in•ter•fuse \ˌint-ər-ˈfyüz\ *vb* **1 :** to combine by or as if by fusing **:** INTERMINGLE **2 :** PERVADE, PERMEATE — **in•ter•fu•sion** \-ˈfyü-zhən\ *n*

in•ter•ga•lac•tic \ˌint-ər-gə-ˈlak-tik\ *adj* **:** situated or occurring in the spaces between galaxies

in•ter•ge•ner•ic \-jə-ˈner-ik\ *adj* **:** existing or occurring between genera ⟨*intergeneric* hybridization⟩

in•ter•gla•cial \ˌint-ər-ˈglā-shəl\ *adj* **:** occurring or relating to the time between successive glaciations

in•ter•grade \ˌint-ər-ˈgrād\ *vi* **:** to merge gradually one with another through a continuous series of intermediates — **in•ter•gra•da•tion** \-grā-ˈdā-shən, -grə-\ *n* — **in•ter•gra•da•tion•al** \-shnəl, -shən-l\ *adj*

in•ter•im \ˈint-ə-rəm\ *n* **:** an intervening time **:** INTERVAL [Latin, adv., "meanwhile", from *inter* "between"] — **interim** *adj*

[1]**in•te•ri•or** \in-ˈtir-ē-ər\ *adj* **1 :** being or acting within a limiting boundary **2 :** remote from the border or shore **:** INLAND [Latin] — **in•te•ri•or•ly** *adv*

[2]**interior** *n* **1 :** the internal part of something ⟨the *interior* of the body⟩ **2 :** the inland part (as of a country) **3 :** inner nature **:** CHARACTER **4 :** the internal affairs of a state or nation — **in•te•ri•or•i•ty** \in-ˌtir-ē-ˈȯr-ət-ē, -ˈär-\ *n*

interior angle *n* **1 :** the inner of the two angles formed where two sides of a polygon come together **2 :** any of the four angles formed in the area between a pair of parallel lines when a third line cuts them

interior decoration *n* **:** INTERIOR DESIGN

interior design *n* **:** the art of planning the layout and furnishings of the interior of a building

in•ter•ject \ˌint-ər-ˈjekt\ *vt* **:** to throw in between or among other things **:** INSERT ⟨*interject* a remark⟩ [Latin *interjectus,* past participle of *intericere* "to interject", from *inter-* + *jacere* "to throw"] **syn** see INTRODUCE — **in•ter•jec•tor** \-ˈjek-tər\ *n* — **in•ter•jec•to•ry** \-tə-rē, -trē\ *adj*

in•ter•jec•tion \ˌint-ər-ˈjek-shən\ *n* **1 :** an interjecting of something **2 :** something interjected ⟨the speaker was interrupted by *interjections* from the audience⟩ **3 :** a word or cry expressing sudden or strong feeling and usually lacking grammatical connection — **in•ter•jec•tion•al** \-shnəl, -shən-l\ *adj* — **in•ter•jec•tion•al•ly** \-ē\ *adv*

in•ter•lace \ˌint-ər-ˈlās\ *vb* **1 :** to unite by or as if by lacing together ⟨*interlaced* fibers⟩ **2 :** to vary by alternating **:** INTERSPERSE **3 :** to cross one another as if woven together ⟨*interlacing* boughs⟩ — **in•ter•lace•ment** \-ˈlā-smənt\ *n*

in•ter•lard \ˌint-ər-ˈlärd\ *vt* **:** to insert or introduce at intervals **:** INTERSPERSE ⟨a speech *interlarded* with quotations⟩

in•ter•lay•er \ˈint-ər-ˌlā-ər, -ˌle-ər, -ˌler\ *n* **:** a layer placed between other layers

¹in•ter•leaf \ˌint-ər-ˈlēf\ *vt* **:** INTERLEAVE

²in•ter•leaf \ˈint-ər-ˌlēf\ *n* **:** a usually blank leaf inserted between two leaves of a book

in•ter•leave \ˌint-ər-ˈlēv\ *vt* **-leaved**; **-leaving 1 :** to equip with an interleaf **2 :** to arrange in or as if in alternating layers

¹in•ter•line \ˌint-ər-ˈlīn\ *vt* **:** to insert between lines already written or printed — **in•ter•lin•ea•tion** \-ˌlin-ē-ˈā-shən\ *n*

²interline *vt* **:** to provide (a garment) with an interlining

in•ter•lin•ear \ˌint-ər-ˈlin-ē-ər\ *adj* **1 :** inserted between lines already written or printed **2 :** written or printed in different languages or texts in alternate lines — **in•ter•lin•ear•ly** *adv*

in•ter•lin•ing \ˈint-ər-ˌlī-ning\ *n* **:** a lining (as of a coat) between the ordinary lining and the outside fabric

in•ter•link \ˌint-ər-ˈlingk\ *vt* **:** to link together

in•ter•lock \ˌint-ər-ˈläk\ *vb* **:** to lock together **:** UNITE ⟨*interlocked* fingers⟩ ⟨a series of rings *interlocking* to form a chain⟩ — **in•ter•lock** \ˈint-ər-ˌläk\ *n* — **in•ter•lock•er** \ˌint-ər-ˈläk-ər\ *n*

in•ter•lo•cu•tion \ˌint-ər-lō-ˈkyü-shən\ *n* **:** interchange of speech **:** CONVERSATION

in•ter•loc•u•tor \ˌint-ər-ˈläk-yət-ər\ *n* **1 :** one who takes part in dialogue or conversation **2 :** a man in a minstrel show who questions the end men

in•ter•lop•er \ˌint-ər-ˈlō-pər, ˈint-ər-ˌ\ *n* **:** a person who intrudes or interferes wrongly **:** INTRUDER [probably derived from Dutch *loper* "runner", from *lopen* "to run"]

in•ter•lude \ˈint-ər-ˌlüd\ *n* **1 :** a performance or entertainment between the acts of a play **2 :** an intervening period, space, or event **:** INTERVAL ⟨an *interlude* of peace between wars⟩ **3 :** a musical composition inserted between the parts of a longer composition, a drama, or a religious service [Medieval Latin *interludium,* from Latin *inter-* + *ludus* "play"]

in•ter•mar•riage \ˌint-ər-ˈmar-ij\ *n* **:** marriage between members of different racial, social, or religious groups

in•ter•mar•ry \-ˈmar-ē\ *vi* **1 :** to marry each other **2 :** to become connected by intermarriage

in•ter•med•dle \ˌint-ər-ˈmed-l\ *vi* **:** to meddle officiously — **in•ter•med•dler** \-ˈmed-lər, -l-ər\ *n*

¹in•ter•me•di•ary \ˌint-ər-ˈmēd-ē-ˌer-ē\ *adj* **1 :** INTERMEDIATE ⟨an *intermediary* stage⟩ **2 :** acting as a mediator ⟨an *intermediary* agent⟩

²intermediary *n, pl* **-ar•ies :** MEDIATOR 1, GO-BETWEEN

¹in•ter•me•di•ate \ˌint-ər-ˈmēd-ē-ət\ *adj* **:** being or occurring at the middle place or degree or between extremes [Medieval Latin *intermediatus,* from Latin *intermedius,* from *inter-* + *medius* "middle"] — **in•ter•me•di•ate•ly** *adv* — **in•ter•me•di•ate•ness** *n*

²intermediate *n* **1 :** an intermediate term, thing, or class **2 :** MEDIATOR 1, GO-BETWEEN

in•ter•ment \in-ˈtər-mənt\ *n* **:** FUNERAL 1, BURIAL

in•ter•mez•zo \ˌint-ər-ˈmet-sō, -ˈmed-zō\ *n, pl* **-zi** \-sē, -zē\ *or* **-zos 1 :** a short light piece between the acts of a serious drama or opera **2 a :** a movement coming between the major sections of an extended musical work (as a symphony) **b :** a short independent instrumental composition [Italian, derived from Latin *intermedius* "intermediate"]

in•ter•mi•na•ble \in-ˈtərm-nə-bəl, ˈin-, -ə-nə-\ *adj* **:** ENDLESS; *esp* **:** wearisomely dragged out ⟨an *interminable* speech⟩ — **in•ter•mi•na•ble•ness** *n* — **in•ter•mi•na•bly** \-blē\ *adv*

in•ter•min•gle \ˌint-ər-ˈming-gəl\ *vb* **:** INTERMIX

in•ter•mis•sion \ˌint-ər-ˈmish-ən\ *n* **1 :** INTERRUPTION ⟨continuing without *intermission*⟩ **2 :** a pause or interval especially between the acts of a play [Latin *intermissio,* from *intermittere* "to intermit"]

in•ter•mit \-ˈmit\ *vb* **-mit•ted**; **-mit•ting :** to stop for a time or at intervals [Latin *intermittere,* from *inter-* + *mittere* "to send"] — **in•ter•mit•ter** *n*

in•ter•mit•tent \-ˈmit-nt\ *adj* **:** coming and going at intervals **:** not continuous ⟨*intermittent* rain⟩ — **in•ter•mit•tence** \-ˈmit-ns\ *n* — **in•ter•mit•tent•ly** *adv*

in•ter•mix \ˌint-ər-ˈmiks\ *vb* **:** to mix together — **in•ter•mix•ture** \-ˈmiks-chər\ *n*

in•ter•mo•lec•u•lar \ˌint-ər-mə-ˈlek-yə-lər\ *adj* **:** existing or acting between molecules — **in•ter•mo•lec•u•lar•ly** *adv*

¹in•tern \ˈin-ˌtərn, in-ˈ\ *vt* **:** to confine or impound especially during a war ⟨*intern* enemy aliens⟩ [French *interner,* from Latin *internus* "internal"]

²in•tern *or* **in•terne** \ˈin-ˌtərn\ *n* **:** an advanced student or graduate especially in medicine gaining supervised practical experience (as in a hospital) [French *interne,* from *interne* "internal", from Latin *internus*] — **in•tern•ship** \-ˌship\ *n*

³in•tern \ˈin-ˌtərn\ *vi* **:** to act as an intern

in•ter•nal \in-ˈtərn-l\ *adj* **1 a :** existing or situated within the limits or surface of something ⟨*internal* structure⟩ **b :** having to do with or situated in the inside of the body ⟨*internal* organs⟩ ⟨*internal* pain⟩ **2 :** relating or belonging to or existing within the mind **3 :** INTRINSIC, INHERENT ⟨*internal* evidence⟩ **4 :** of or relating to the domestic affairs of a state ⟨*internal* revenue⟩ [Latin *internus*] — **in•ter•nal•i•ty** \ˌin-ˌtər-ˈnal-ət-ē\ *n* — **in•ter•nal•ly** \in-ˈtərn-l-ē\ *adv*

internal–combustion engine *n* **:** an engine run by a fuel mixture ignited within the engine cylinder

internal medicine *n* **:** a branch of medicine that deals with nonsurgical diseases

internal respiration *n* **:** exchange of gases between the cells of the body and the blood — compare EXTERNAL RESPIRATION

internal rhyme *n* **:** rhyme between a word within a line and another at the end of the same line or within another line

internal secretion *n* **:** HORMONE

¹in•ter•na•tion•al \ˌint-ər-ˈnash-nəl, -ən-l\ *adj* **1 :** involving or affecting two or more nations ⟨*international* trade⟩ **2 :** of, relating to, or constituting a group having members in two or more nations ⟨an *international* union⟩ — **in•ter•na•tion•al•i•ty** \-ˌnash-ə-ˈnal-ət-ē\ *n* — **in•ter•na•tion•al•ly** \-ˈnash-nə-lē, -ən-l-ē\ *adv*

²in•ter•na•tion•al \-ˈnash-nəl, -ən-l, *in sense 1 often* -ˌnash-ə-ˈnal, -ˈnäl\ *n* **1 :** one of several socialist or communist organizations of international scope **2 :** a labor union having locals in more than one country

international date line *n* **:** DATE LINE

in•ter•na•tion•al•ism \ˌint-ər-ˈnash-nəl-ˌiz-əm, -ˈnash-ən-l-\ *n* **1 :** international character or outlook **2 a :** a policy of political and economic cooperation among nations **b :** an attitude favoring such a policy — **in•ter•na•tion•al•ist** \-əst\ *n or adj*

in•ter•na•tion•al•ize \-ˈnash-nəl-ˌīz, -ˈnash-ən-l-\ *vt* **:** to make international; *esp* **:** to place under international control — **in•ter•na•tion•al•iza•tion** \-ˌnash-nəl-ə-ˈzā-shən, -ˌnash-ən-l-\ *n*

international law *n* **:** a body of rules that control or affect the rights of nations in their relations with each other

international unit *n* **:** a quantity (as of a vitamin) that barely produces a particular biological effect agreed upon as an international standard of activity

in•ter•nec•ine \ˌint-ər-ˈnes-ˌēn, -ˈnē-ˌsīn; in-ˈtər-nə-ˌsēn\ *adj* **1 :** marked by slaughter **:** DEADLY **2 :** of, relating to, or involving conflict within a group ⟨bitter *internecine* feuds⟩ [Latin *in-*

ternecinus, from *internecare* "to slay", from *inter-* + *necare* "to kill", from *nex* "violent death"]

in•tern•ee \ˌin-ˌtər-ˈnē\ *n* : an interned person

in•ter•neu•ron \ˌint-ər-ˈnü-ˌrän, -ˈnyü-; -ˈnu̇r-ˌän, -ˈnyu̇r-\ *n* : a nerve cell that carries an impulse from one nerve cell to another

in•ter•nist \in-ˈtər-nəst\ *n* : a specialist in internal medicine [*internal* medicine]

in•tern•ment \in-ˈtərn-mənt\ *n* : the act of interning : the state of being interned

in•ter•node \ˈint-ər-ˌnōd\ *n* : a space or part between two nodes (as of a stem) : SEGMENT

in•ter•nu•cle•ar \ˌint-ər-ˈnü-klē-ər, -ˈnyü-\ *adj* : situated or occurring between nuclei

in•ter•nun•ci•al \ˌint-ər-ˈnən-sē-əl, -ˈnu̇n-\ *adj* **1** : of or relating to an internuncio **2** : serving to link sensory and motor neurons — **in•ter•nun•ci•al•ly** \-sē-ə-lē\ *adv*

in•ter•nun•cio \-sē-ˌō\ *n* : a papal legate of lower rank than a nuncio [Italian *internunzio,* literally, "messenger between two parties", from Latin *internuntius,* from *inter-* + *nuntius* "messenger"]

in•tero•cep•tive \ˌint-ə-rō-ˈsep-tiv\ *adj* : of, relating to, or being stimuli arising within the body and especially the viscera [*inter-* (as in *interior*) + *-o-* + *-ceptive* (as in *receptive*)] — **in•tero•cep•tor** \-ˈsep-tər\ *n*

in•ter•of•fice \ˌint-ə-ˈrȯf-əs, -ˈräf-\ *adj* : taking place or communicating between the offices of an organization ⟨an *interoffice* memo⟩

in•ter•pen•e•trate \ˌint-ər-ˈpen-ə-ˌtrāt\ *vb* **1** : to penetrate between, within, or throughout : PERMEATE **2** : to penetrate mutually — **in•ter•pen•e•tra•tion** \-ˌpen-ə-ˈtrā-shən\ *n*

in•ter•phase \ˈint-ər-ˌfāz\ *n* : the period between the end of one mitotic division and the beginning of the next

in•ter•plan•e•tary \ˌint-ər-ˈplan-ə-ˌter-ē\ *adj* : existing, carried on, or operating between planets ⟨*interplanetary* travel⟩

in•ter•plant \ˌint-ər-ˈplant\ *vt* : to plant (a crop) between plants of another kind

in•ter•play \ˈint-ər-ˌplā\ *n* : mutual action or influence : INTERACTION ⟨an *interplay* of thought and feeling⟩ — **in•ter•play** \ˌint-ər-ˈplā\ *vi*

in•ter•po•late \in-ˈtər-pə-ˌlāt\ *vb* **1 a** : to alter or corrupt (as a text) by inserting new matter **b** : to insert (words) into a text or into a conversation **2** : to insert between other things or parts **3** : to estimate values of (as a logarithm) between two known values **4** : to make insertions [Latin *interpolare*] **syn** see INTRODUCE — **in•ter•po•la•tion** \-ˌtər-pə-ˈlā-shən\ *n* — **in•ter•po•la•tive** \-ˈtər-pə-ˌlāt-iv\ *adj* — **in•ter•po•la•tor** \-ˌlāt-ər\ *n*

in•ter•pose \ˌint-ər-ˈpōz\ *vb* **1 a** : to place in an intervening position **b** : to put (oneself) between : INTRUDE **2** : to introduce or throw in between the parts of a conversation or argument **3** : to be or come between; *esp* : to step in between opposing parties [Middle French *interposer,* from Latin *interponere,* from *inter-* + *ponere* "to put"] — **in•ter•pos•er** *n* — **in•ter•po•si•tion** \-pə-ˈzish-ən\ *n*

• **syn** INTERPOSE, INTERFERE, INTERVENE, INTERCEDE mean to come or go between. INTERPOSE implies no more than this ⟨*interposed* in the argument⟩ INTERFERE implies a getting in the way or otherwise hindering ⟨strikes *interfere* with production plans⟩ INTERVENE may imply an occurring in space or time between two things or a stepping in to halt or settle a dispute ⟨years *intervening* between graduation and marriage⟩ INTERCEDE implies acting in behalf of an offender or between two parties needing reconciliation ⟨the United Nations *intercedes* in international disputes⟩

in•ter•pret \in-ˈtər-prət\ *vb* **1** : to explain or tell the meaning of ⟨*interpret* a dream⟩ **2** : to understand according to one's own belief, judgment, or interest ⟨*interpret* an action as unfriendly⟩ **3** : to bring out the meaning of by performing ⟨an actor *interprets* a role⟩ **4** : to translate orally for others [Latin *interpretari,* from *interpres* "agent, interpreter"] **syn** see EXPLAIN — **in•ter•pret•able** \-prət-ə-bəl\ *adj* — **in•ter•pret•er** *n* — **in•ter•pre•tive** \-prət-iv\ *adj* — **in•ter•pre•tive•ly** *adv*

in•ter•pre•ta•tion \in-ˌtər-prə-ˈtā-shən\ *n* **1** : the act or the result of interpreting : EXPLANATION **2** : an instance of artistic interpretation in performance — **in•ter•pre•ta•tion•al** \-shnəl, -shən-l\ *adj* — **in•ter•pre•ta•tive** \-ˈtər-prə-ˌtāt-iv\ *adj* — **in•ter•pre•ta•tive•ly** *adv*

in•ter•ra•cial \ˌint-ər-ˈrā-shəl, ˌint-ə-ˈrā-\ *adj* : of, involving, or designed for members of different races

in•ter•reg•num \ˌint-ə-ˈreg-nəm\ *n, pl* **-nums** *or* **-na** \-nə\ **1** : a period between two successive reigns or regimes **2** : a lapse or pause in a continuous series [Latin, from *inter-* + *regnum* "reign"]

in•ter•re•late \ˌint-ər-ri-ˈlāt, ˌint-ə-ri-\ *vb* : to bring into or have a mutual relationship — **in•ter•re•la•tion** \-ˈlā-shən\ *n* — **in•ter•re•la•tion•ship** \-ˌship\ *n*

in•ter•ro•gate \in-ˈter-ə-ˌgāt\ *vt* : to question usually formally and systematically ⟨*interrogate* a prisoner of war⟩ [Latin *interrogare,* from *inter-* + *rogare* "to ask"] — **in•ter•ro•ga•tion** \-ˌter-ə-ˈgā-shən\ *n* — **in•ter•ro•ga•tion•al** \-shnəl, -shən-l\ *adj* — **in•ter•ro•ga•tor** \-ˈter-ə-ˌgāt-ər\ *n*

interrogation point *n* : QUESTION MARK

¹in•ter•rog•a•tive \ˌint-ə-ˈräg-ət-iv\ *adj* **1** : having the form or force of a question ⟨an *interrogative* phrase⟩ **2** : used in a question ⟨an *interrogative* pronoun⟩ — **in•ter•rog•a•tive•ly** *adv*

²interrogative *n* : a word (as *who, what, which*) used in asking questions

in•ter•rog•a•to•ry \-ˈräg-ə-ˌtōr-ē, -ˌtȯr-\ *adj* : containing, expressing, or implying a question ⟨an *interrogatory* tone of voice⟩

in•ter•rupt \ˌint-ə-ˈrəpt\ *vb* **1** : to stop or hinder by breaking in ⟨*interrupt* a conversation⟩ **2** : to break the uniformity or continuity of ⟨*interrupt* a sequence⟩ **3** : to break in upon an action; *esp* : to break in with questions or remarks while another is speaking [Latin *interruptus,* past participle of *interrumpere* "to interrupt", from *inter-* + *rumpere* "to break"] — **in•ter•rupt•ible** \-ˈrəp-tə-bəl\ *adj* — **in•ter•rup•tion** \-ˈrəp-shən\ *n* — **in•ter•rup•tive** \-ˈrəp-tiv\ *adj*

in•ter•rupt•er \ˌint-ə-ˈrəp-tər\ *n* : one that interrupts; *esp* : a device for periodically and automatically interrupting an electric current

in•ter•scho•las•tic \ˌint-ər-skə-ˈlas-tik\ *adj* : existing or carried on between schools ⟨*interscholastic* athletics⟩

in•ter se \ˌint-ər-ˈsā, -ˈsē\ *adv or adj* : among or between themselves [Latin]

in•ter•sect \ˌint-ər-ˈsekt\ *vb* **1** : to pierce or divide by passing through or across : CROSS ⟨a line *intersects* a plane in a point⟩ **2** : to meet and cross at a point ⟨the streets *intersect* at right angles⟩ [Latin *intersectus,* past participle of *intersecare* "to intersect", from *inter-* + *secare* "to cut"]

in•ter•sec•tion \ˌint-ər-ˈsek-shən\ *n* **1** : the act or process of intersecting **2** : the place or point where two or more things and especially streets intersect ⟨a busy *intersection*⟩ **3** : the set of elements common to two sets; *esp* : the set of points common to two geometric figures

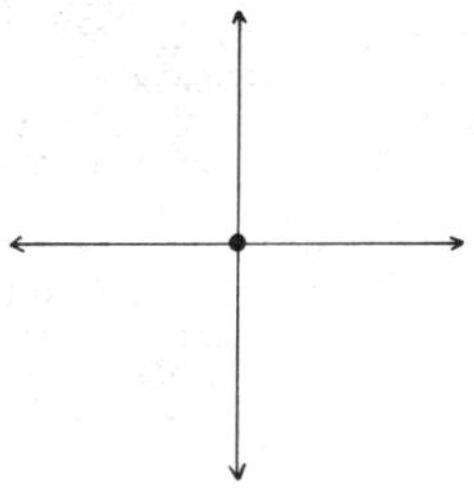

intersection 3

in•ter•sex \ˈint-ər-ˌseks\ *n* : an intersexual individual

in•ter•sex•u•al \ˌint-ər-ˈsek-shə-wəl, -shəl\ *adj* **1** : existing between sexes ⟨*intersexual* hostility⟩ **2** : intermediate in sexual characters between a typical male and a typical female — **in•ter•sex•u•al•i•ty** \-ˌsek-shə-ˈwal-ət-ē\ *n* — **in•ter•sex•u•al•ly** \-ˈseksh-wə-lē, -ə-wə-; -ˈseksh-lē, -ə-lē\ *adv*

¹in•ter•space \ˈint-ər-ˌspās\ *n* : an intervening space : INTERVAL

²in•ter•space \ˌint-ər-ˈspās\ *vt* : to separate by spaces

in•ter•spe•cif•ic \ˌint-ər-spi-ˈsif-ik\ *or* **in•ter•spe•cies** \-ˈspē-shēz, -sēz\ *adj* : existing or rising between species ⟨*interspecific* hybrids⟩

in•ter•sperse \ˌint-ər-ˈspərs\ *vt* **1** : to place here and there among others ⟨*intersperse* pictures in a book⟩ **2** : to vary with things inserted here and there ⟨a serious talk *interspersed* with jokes⟩ [Latin *interspersus* "interspersed", from *inter-* + *sparsus,* past participle of *spargere* "to scatter"] — **in•ter•sper•sion** \-ˈspər-zhən\ *n*

in•ter•state \ˌint-ər-ˈstāt\ *adj* : of, connecting, or existing between two or more states especially of the United States

in•ter•stel•lar \-ˈstel-ər\ *adj* : located or taking place among the stars ⟨*interstellar* space⟩

in•ter•stice \in-ˈtər-stəs\ *n, pl* **in•ter•stic•es** \-stə-ˌsēz, -stəsəz\ : a little space between two things : CHINK, CREVICE [French, from Late Latin *interstitium,* from Latin *intersistere* "to stand in the middle", from *inter-* + *sistere* "to stand"]

in·ter·sti·tial \ˌint-ər-ˈstish-əl\ *adj* **1** : relating to or situated in the interstices **2** : situated within organs or tissues ⟨*interstitial* connective tissue⟩; *also* : affecting the interstitial tissues of a body part — **in·ter·sti·tial·ly** \-ˈstish-ə-lē\ *adv*

in·ter·tid·al \-ˈtīd-l\ *adj* : of, relating to, or being the area that is above low-tide mark but exposed to tidal flooding

in·ter·twine \-ˈtwīn\ *vb* : to twine or cause to twine about one another : INTERLACE — **in·ter·twine·ment** \-mənt\ *n*

in·ter·twist \-ˈtwist\ *vb* : INTERTWINE — **intertwist** *n*

in·ter·ur·ban \ˌint-ər-ˈər-bən\ *adj* : connecting cities or towns ⟨an *interurban* bus line⟩

in·ter·val \ˈint-ər-vəl\ *n* **1** : a space of time between events or states ⟨the *interval* between elections⟩ ⟨an *interval* of three months⟩ **2 a** : a space between things ⟨the *interval* between two desks⟩ **b** : difference in pitch between tones **3** : a set of numbers between two numbers either including or excluding one or both of them; *also* : the set of real numbers greater or less than and including or excluding a real number [Middle French *intervalle,* from Latin *intervallum* "space between ramparts, interval", from *inter-* + *vallum* "rampart"]

in·ter·vene \ˌint-ər-ˈvēn\ *vi* **1** : to happen as an unrelated event ⟨rain *intervened* and we postponed the match⟩ **2** : to come between events or points of time ⟨a second *intervened* between the flash and the report⟩ **3** : to interpose in order to stop, settle, or change something ⟨*intervene* in a quarrel⟩ **4** : to be or lie between ⟨*intervening* hills⟩ [Latin *intervenire* "to come between", from *inter-* + *venire* "to come"] **syn** see INTERPOSE — **in·ter·ve·nor** \-ˈvē-nər, -ˌnȯr\ *also* **in·ter·ven·er** \-ˈvē-nər\ *n* — **in·ter·ven·tion** \-ˈven-chən\ *n*

in·ter·ven·tion·ism \-ˈven-chə-ˌniz-əm\ *n* : the theory or practice of intervening; *esp* : interference by one country in the political affairs of another — **in·ter·ven·tion·ist** \-ˈvench-nəst, -ə-nəst\ *n or adj*

in·ter·ver·te·bral \-ˈvərt-ə-brəl\ *adj* : situated between adjacent vertebrae ⟨*intervertebral* disks⟩

in·ter·view \ˈint-ər-ˌvyü\ *n* **1** : a face-to-face meeting especially for the purpose of talking or consulting **2** : a meeting at which information is obtained (as by a journalist) from a person; *also* : an account of such a meeting — **interview** *vt* — **in·ter·view·er** *n*

in·ter·vo·cal·ic \ˌint-ər-vō-ˈkal-ik\ *adj* : immediately preceded and immediately followed by a vowel

in·ter·weave \ˌint-ər-ˈwēv\ *vb* **-wove** \-ˈwōv\ *also* **-weaved**; **-wo·ven** \-ˈwō-vən\ *also* **-weaved**; **-weav·ing** **1** : to weave together **2** : to blend or cause to blend together

[1]**in·tes·tate** \in-ˈtes-ˌtāt, -ˈtes-tət\ *adj* **1** : not having made a will ⟨died *intestate*⟩ **2** : not disposed of by will — **in·tes·ta·cy** \-ˈtes-tə-sē\ *n*

[2]**intestate** *n* : one who dies intestate

in·tes·ti·nal \in-ˈtes-tən-l\ *adj* **1** : of or relating to the intestine **2** : affecting or occurring in the intestine — **in·tes·ti·nal·ly** \-l-ē\ *adv*

intestinal fortitude *n* : COURAGE, GRIT [euphemism for *guts*]

[1]**in·tes·tine** \in-ˈtes-tən\ *adj* : INTERNAL; *esp* : of or relating to the internal affairs of a state or country [Latin *intestinus* "internal", from *intus* "within"]

[2]**intestine** *n* : the tubular part of the alimentary canal that extends from the stomach to the anus [Middle French *intestin,* from Latin *intestinum,* from *intestinus* "internal", from *intus* "within"]

in·ti·ma·cy \ˈint-ə-mə-sē\ *n* : the state of being intimate

[1]**in·ti·mate** \ˈint-ə-ˌmāt\ *vt* **1** : to announce formally : DECLARE **2** : to communicate indirectly : HINT [Late Latin *intimare* "to put in, announce", from Latin *intimus* "innermost"] **syn** see SUGGEST — **in·ti·mat·er** *n* — **in·ti·ma·tion** \ˌint-ə-ˈmā-shən\ *n*

[2]**in·ti·mate** \ˈint-ə-mət\ *adj* **1** : belonging to or characterizing one's deepest nature ⟨*intimate* reflections⟩ **2** : marked by very close association or contact **3 a** : marked by a warm friendship developing through long association ⟨on *intimate* terms with a neighbor⟩ **b** : suggesting informal warmth or privacy ⟨*intimate* clubs⟩ **4** : of a very personal or private nature ⟨*intimate* family matters⟩ [derived from Latin *intimus* "innermost"] — **in·ti·mate·ly** *adv* — **in·ti·mate·ness** *n*

[3]**in·ti·mate** \ˈint-ə-mət\ *n* : an intimate friend : CONFIDANT

in·tim·i·date \in-ˈtim-ə-ˌdāt\ *vt* : to make timid or fearful; *esp* : to compel or deter by or as if by threats — **in·tim·i·da·tion** \-ˌtim-ə-ˈdā-shən\ *n* — **in·tim·i·da·tor** \-ˈtim-ə-ˌdāt-ər\ *n*

in·to \ˈin-tə, -tü\ *prep* **1 a** : to the inside of ⟨came *into* the room⟩ **b** — used as a function word to indicate entry, introduction, or inclusion ⟨enter *into* an alliance⟩ **2 a** : to the state, condition, or form of ⟨got *into* trouble⟩ **b** : to the occupation, action, or possession of ⟨go *into* farming⟩ **c** : involved with ⟨wasn't *into* drugs anymore⟩ **3** : to a position of contact with : AGAINST ⟨ran *into* a wall⟩

in·tol·er·able \in-ˈtäl-rə-bəl, -ˈtäl-ə-rə-bəl, -ˈtäl-ər-bəl, ˈin-\ *adj* **1** : not tolerable : UNBEARABLE **2** : EXTREME 1c, EXCESSIVE — **in·tol·er·abil·i·ty** \in-ˌtäl-rə-ˈbil-ət-ē, -ə-rə-\ *n* — **in·tol·er·able·ness** *n* — **in·tol·er·ably** \-blē\ *adv*

in·tol·er·ance \in-ˈtäl-ə-rəns, ˈin-\ *n* **1** : the quality or state of being intolerant **2** : exceptional sensitivity (as to a drug or food)

in·tol·er·ant \-rənt\ *adj* **1** : unable or unwilling to endure **2 a** : unwilling to grant equality or freedom especially in religious matters **b** : unwilling to grant or share social, political, or professional advantages — **in·tol·er·ant·ly** *adv*

in·to·nate \ˈin-tə-ˌnāt\ *vt* : UTTER 1, INTONE

in·to·na·tion \ˌin-tə-ˈnā-shən\ *n* **1** : the act of intoning; *also* : something intoned **2** : the act of producing tones on a musical instrument **3** : the rise and fall in pitch of the voice in speech — **in·to·na·tion·al** \-shnəl, -shən-l\ *adj*

in·tone \in-ˈtōn\ *vb* : to utter in musical or prolonged tones : CHANT — **in·ton·er** *n*

in to·to \in-ˈtōt-ō\ *adv* : TOTALLY, ENTIRELY ⟨accepted the plan *in toto*⟩ [Latin, "on the whole"]

in·tox·i·cant \in-ˈtäk-si-kənt\ *n* : something (as alcohol) that intoxicates — **intoxicant** *adj*

in·tox·i·cate \in-ˈtäk-sə-ˌkāt\ *vt* **1 a** : POISON 1a **b** : to affect by alcohol or a drug especially to the point where physical and mental control is greatly diminished **2** : to excite or elate to the point of enthusiasm or frenzy ⟨*intoxicated* with joy⟩

in·tox·i·ca·tion \in-ˌtäk-sə-ˈkā-shən\ *n* **1 a** : an abnormal state that is essentially a poisoning ⟨intestinal *intoxication*⟩ **b** : the condition of being drunk : INEBRIATION **2** : a strong excitement or elation

in·tra- \ˌin-trə, -trä, -ˌträ\ *prefix* **1** : within ⟨*intra*cellular⟩ **2** : in : into ⟨*intra*venous⟩ [Latin *intra*]

See *intra-* and 2d element

intra-abdominal	**intradepartmental**	**intranational**
intra-agency	**intradistrict**	**intranuclear**
intra-amniotic	**intradivisional**	**intraoceanic**
intra-atomic	**intraethnic**	**intraocular**
intraborough	**intraexperimental**	**intraoffice**
intrabranch	**intrafamilial**	**intraorgan**
intrabreed	**intragalactic**	**intraorganismic**
intracarotid	**intragastral**	**intraorganizational**
intracerebral	**intragenerational**	**intraparty**
intracerebrally	**intragenic**	**intrapituitary**
intrachromosomal	**intragovernmental**	**intraprofessional**
intracity	**intragroup**	**intraracial**
intraclass	**intrahospital**	**intraregional**
intraclassroom	**intraindividual**	**intrarenal**
intracloud	**intraindustry**	**intrasleep**
intracoastal	**intrainstitutional**	**intrasocietal**
intracompany	**intramembrane**	**intratheater**
intracontinental	**intramembranous**	**intrathoracic**
intracranial	**intramuscular**	**intratribal**
intracultural	**intramuscularly**	**intraunion**
intracytoplasmic	**intranasal**	**intrauniversity**
intraday	**intranasally**	**intraurban**

in·tra·cel·lu·lar \ˌin-trə-ˈsel-yə-lər\ *adj* : being or occurring within a protoplasmic cell — **in·tra·cel·lu·lar·ly** *adv*

in·trac·ta·ble \in-ˈtrak-tə-bəl, ˈin-\ *adj* **1** : not easily managed or controlled ⟨an *intractable* child⟩ **2** : not easily relieved or cured ⟨*intractable* pain⟩ — **in·trac·ta·bil·i·ty** \in-ˌtrak-tə-ˈbil-ət-ē\ *n* — **in·trac·ta·ble·ness** \in-ˈtrak-tə-bəl-nəs, ˈin-\ *n* — **in·trac·ta·bly** \-blē\ *adv*

in•tra•cu•ta•ne•ous \ˌin-trə-kyu̇-ˈtā-nē-əs\ *adj* : INTRADERMAL

in•tra•der•mal \-ˈdər-məl\ *adj* : situated or done within or between the layers of the skin — **in•tra•der•mal•ly** \-mə-lē\ *adv*

in•tra•dos \ˈin-trə-ˌdäs, -ˌdō; in-ˈtrā-ˌdäs\ *n, pl* **-dos** \-ˌdōz, -ˌdäs\ *or* **-dos•es** \-ˌdäs-əz\ : the interior curve of an arch [French, from Latin *intra* "within" + French *dos* "back", from Latin *dorsum*]

1 intrados

in•tra•mo•lec•u•lar \ˌin-trə-mə-ˈlek-yə-lər\ *adj* : situated, acting, or occurring within the molecule — **in•tra•mo•lec•u•lar•ly** *adv*

in•tra•mu•ral \-ˈmyu̇r-əl\ *adj* : being, occurring, or undertaken within the limits usually of a school ⟨*intramural* sports⟩ — **in•tra•mu•ral•ly** \-ˈmyu̇r-ə-lē\ *adv*

in•tran•si•geance \in-ˈtrans-ə-jəns, -ˈtranz-\ *n* : INTRANSIGENCE — **in•tran•si•geant** \-jənt\ *adj or n* — **in•tran•si•geant•ly** *adv*

in•tran•si•gence \-jəns\ *n* : the quality or state of being intransigent

in•tran•si•gent \-jənt\ *adj* **1 a** : refusing to compromise or to give up an extreme position or attitude : UNCOMPROMISING **b** : IRRECONCILABLE ⟨*intransigent* enemies⟩ **2** : characteristic of one that is uncompromising [Spanish *intransigente,* from *in-* + *transigir* "to compromise", from Latin *transigere* "to transact"] — **intransigent** *n* — **in•tran•si•gent•ly** *adv*

in•tran•si•tive \in-ˈtrans-ət-iv, -ˈtranz-, ˈin-\ *adj* : not transitive; *esp* : characterized by not having or containing a direct object ⟨an *intransitive* verb⟩ — **in•tran•si•tive•ly** *adv* — **in•tran•si•tive•ness** *n*

in•tra•spe•cif•ic \ˌin-trə-spi-ˈsif-ik\ *also* **in•tra•spe•cies** \-ˈspē-shēz, -sēz\ *adj* : occurring within a species or involving members of one species ⟨*intraspecific* variation⟩

in•tra•state \ˌin-trə-ˈstāt\ *adj* : existing or occurring within a state

in•tra•uter•ine \-ˈyüt-ə-rən, -ˌrīn\ *adj* : being or occurring within the uterus ⟨*intrauterine* growth⟩

in•tra•ve•nous \ˌin-trə-ˈvē-nəs\ *adj* : being within or entering by way of the veins ⟨*intravenous* feeding⟩ — **in•tra•ve•nous•ly** *adv*

in•tra•vi•tam \-ˈvī-ˌtam, -ˈwē-ˌtäm\ *adj* : done, acting on, or found in a living subject [New Latin *intra vitam* "during life"]

in•tra•zon•al \ˌin-trə-ˈzōn-l\ *adj* : of, relating to, or being a soil or a major soil group having relatively well-developed characteristics — compare AZONAL, ZONAL

intrench *variant of* ENTRENCH

in•trep•id \in-ˈtrep-əd\ *adj* : resolutely firm and fearless [Latin *intrepidus,* from *in-* + *trepidus* "alarmed"] — **in•tre•pid•i•ty** \ˌin-trə-ˈpid-ət-ē\ *n* — **in•trep•id•ly** \in-ˈtrep-əd-lē\ *adv* — **in•trep•id•ness** *n*

in•tri•ca•cy \ˈin-tri-kə-sē\ *n, pl* **-cies 1** : the quality or state of being intricate **2** : something intricate

in•tri•cate \ˈin-tri-kət\ *adj* : difficult to follow, understand, or analyze : COMPLICATED ⟨an *intricate* machine⟩ ⟨*intricate* problems⟩ [Latin *intricatus,* past participle of *intricare* "to entangle", from *in-* + *tricae* "trifles, impediments"] **syn** see COMPLEX — **in•tri•cate•ly** *adv* — **in•tri•cate•ness** *n*

¹in•trigue \in-ˈtrēg\ *vb* **1** : to make or accomplish by intrigue ⟨*intrigued* their way into power⟩ **2** : PLOT 3, SCHEME **3** : to arouse the interest or curiosity of ⟨was *intrigued* by the tale⟩ [French *intriguer,* from Italian *intrigare,* from Latin *intricare* "to entangle, perplex"] — **in•trigu•er** *n*

²in•trigue \ˈin-ˌtrēg, in-ˈ\ *n* **1** : a secret and involved scheme : PLOT **2** : a secret love affair **syn** see PLOT

in•trin•sic \in-ˈtrin-zik, -ˈtrin-sik\ *adj* : belonging to the essential nature or makeup of a thing : REAL [Middle French *intrinsèque* "internal", from Latin *intrinsicus* "inwardly"] — **in•trin•si•cal** \-zi-kəl, -si-\ *adj* — **in•trin•si•cal•ly** \-kə-lē, -klē\ *adv* — **in•trin•si•cal•ness** \-kəl-nəs\ *n*

intro- *prefix* **1** : in : into **2** : inward ⟨*introvert*⟩ [Latin, from *intro* "inside, to the inside"]

in•tro•duce \ˌin-trə-ˈdüs, -ˈdyüs\ *vt* **1** : to lead or bring in especially for the first time **2** : to bring into practice or use ⟨*introduce* a new fashion⟩ **3 a** : to cause to be acquainted ⟨*introduce* two strangers⟩ **b** : to present formally ⟨*introduce* a speaker to a group⟩ **4** : to present or bring forward for discussion ⟨*introduce* a topic⟩ **5** : to put in : INSERT ⟨*introduce* a probe into a cavity⟩ [Latin *introducere,* from *intro-* + *ducere* "to lead"] — **in•tro•duc•er** *n*

• **syn** INTRODUCE, INSERT, INTERPOLATE, INTERJECT mean to put among or between others. INTRODUCE is the general term for bringing or putting a thing or person into a body or thing already in existence; INSERT implies putting into an open, fixed, or prepared space between or among things; INTERPOLATE applies especially to the inserting of something extraneous or spurious; INTERJECT strongly implies an abrupt or forced introduction.

in•tro•duc•tion \ˌin-trə-ˈdək-shən\ *n* **1 a** : the action of introducing **b** : something introduced **2** : the part of a book that leads up to and explains what will be found in the main part : PREFACE **3** : a book for beginners in a subject ⟨an *introduction* to chemistry⟩

in•tro•duc•to•ry \ˌin-trə-ˈdək-tə-rē, -trē\ *adj* : serving to introduce : PRELIMINARY — **in•tro•duc•to•ri•ly** \-tə-rə-lē, -trə-\ *adv*

in•troit \ˈin-ˌtrō-ət, -ˌtrȯit, in-ˈ\ *n* **1** *often cap* : the first part of the proper of the Mass consisting of an antiphon, verse from a psalm, and the Gloria Patri **2** : a piece of music sung or played at the beginning of a worship service [Middle French *introite,* from Latin *introitus* "entrance", from *introire* "to go in", from *intro-* + *ire* "to go"]

in•tro•spec•tion \ˌin-trə-ˈspek-shən\ *n* : a reflective examination of one's own thoughts or feelings [Latin *introspectus,* past participle of *introspicere* "to look into", from *intro-* + *specere* "to look"] — **in•tro•spect** \-ˈspekt\ *vb* — **in•tro•spec•tion•al** \-ˈspek-shnəl, -shən-l\ *adj* — **in•tro•spec•tive** \-ˈspek-tiv\ *adj* — **in•tro•spec•tive•ly** *adv*

in•tro•ver•sion \ˌin-trə-ˈvər-zhən, -shən\ *n* : the state of an introvert

¹in•tro•vert \ˈin-trə-ˌvərt\ *n* : a person whose attention and interests are directed wholly or predominantly toward what is within the self [earlier *introvert* "to turn inward", from *intro-* + *-vert* (as in *divert*)]

²introvert *adj* : turning in upon itself; *esp* : INTROVERTED

in•tro•vert•ed \ˈin-trə-ˌvərt-əd\ *adj* : characteristic of or having the characteristics of an introvert ⟨an *introverted* voice⟩ ⟨*introverted* people⟩

in•trude \in-ˈtrüd\ *vb* **1** : to bring or force in unasked ⟨*intrude* one's views into a discussion⟩ **2** : to come or go in without invitation : TRESPASS ⟨*intrude* on another's property⟩ **3** : to enter or cause to enter as if by force [Latin *intrudere* "to thrust in", from *in-* + *trudere* "to thrust"] — **in•trud•er** *n*

• **syn** INTRUDE, OBTRUDE mean to thrust oneself or something in without invitation or authorization. INTRUDE implies rudeness, officiousness, or encroachment ⟨no wish to *intrude* on your privacy⟩ OBTRUDE suggests more strongly the impropriety, boldness, futility, or disagreeableness of an intrusion ⟨*obtrude* personal matters in a serious discussion⟩

in•tru•sion \in-ˈtrü-zhən\ *n* **1** : the act of intruding : the state of being intruded **2** : the forcible entry of magma into or between other rock formations; *also* : the intruded magma [Middle French, from Medieval Latin *intrusio,* from Latin *intrudere* "to thrust in"]

in•tru•sive \in-ˈtrü-siv, -ziv\ *adj* **1** : characterized by intrusion; *esp* : intruding where one is not welcome or invited **2** : having been forced while in a molten state into cavities or between layers ⟨*intrusive* rock⟩ — **in•tru•sive•ly** *adv* — **in•tru•sive•ness** *n*

intrust *variant of* ENTRUST

in•tu•i•tion \ˌin-tu̇-ˈish-ən, -tyu̇-\ *n* **1** : the power of knowing immediately and without conscious reasoning **2** : something known or understood at once and without an effort of the mind ⟨act upon an *intuition*⟩ [Late Latin *intuitio* "act of contemplating", from Latin *intueri* "to contemplate", from *in-* + *tueri* "to look at"] — **in•tu•i•tion•al** \-ˈish-nəl, -ən-l\ *adj*

in•tu•i•tive \in-ˈtü-ət-iv, -ˈtyü-\ *adj* **1** : knowing or understanding by intuition ⟨an *intuitive* person⟩ **2** : having or characterized by intuition ⟨an *intuitive* mind⟩ **3** : known or understood by intuition ⟨*intuitive* knowledge⟩ — **in•tu•i•tive•ly** *adv* — **in•tu•i•tive•ness** *n*

in•u•lin \ˈin-yə-lən\ *n* : a white polysaccharide that consists of fructose molecules and occurs as a storage carbohydrate especially in the roots or tubers of plants of the composite family [derived from Latin *inula,* a kind of composite plant]

in•un•date \ˈin-ən-ˌdāt\ *vt* **1** : to cover with a flood : OVERFLOW **2** : DELUGE 2 [Latin *inundare,* from *in-* + *unda* "wave"] — **in•un•da•tion** \ˌin-ən-ˈdā-shən\ *n* — **in•un•da•tor** \ˈin-ən-ˌdāt-ər\ *n* — **in•un•da•to•ry** \in-ˈən-də-ˌtōr-ē, -ˌtȯr-\ *adj*

in•ure \in-ˈu̇r, -ˈyu̇r\ *vb* **1** : to make less sensitive : HARDEN ⟨*inured* to cold⟩ **2** : to become advantageous ⟨profits that *inure* from education⟩ [Middle English *enuren,* from *en-* + *ure* "use, custom", from Middle French *uevre* "work", from Latin *opera*] — **in•ure•ment** \-mənt\ *n*

in vac•uo \in-ˈvak-yə-ˌwō\ *adv* : in a vacuum [New Latin]

in•vade \in-ˈvād\ *vt* **1** : to enter for conquest or plunder ⟨*invade* a country⟩ **2** : to encroach upon : INFRINGE ⟨*invaded* their privacy⟩ **3** : to spread progressively over or into and usually affect injuriously ⟨bacteria *invading* tissue⟩ ⟨stores *invading* a residential section⟩ [Latin *invadere,* from *in-* + *vadere* "to go"] — **in•vad•er** *n*

in•vag•i•nate \in-ˈvaj-ə-ˌnāt\ *vb* : to fold or cause to fold in so that an outer becomes an inner surface [Medieval Latin *invaginare* "to enclose, sheathe", from Latin *in-* + *vagina* "sheath"] — **in•vag•i•na•tion** \-ˌvaj-ə-ˈna-shən\ *n*

1in•val•id \in-ˈval-əd, ˈin-\ *adj* : having no force or effect : not valid ⟨an *invalid* license⟩ [Latin *invalidus* "weak", from *in-* + *validus* "strong"] — **in•va•lid•i•ty** \ˌin-və-ˈlid-ət-ē\ *n* — **in•val•id•ly** \in-ˈval-əd-lē, ˈin-\ *adv* — **in•val•id•ness** *n*

2in•va•lid \ˈin-və-ləd\ *adj* **1** : suffering from disease or disability : SICKLY **2** : of, relating to, or suited to one that is sick [French *invalide,* from Latin *invalidus* "weak"]

3invalid *like* 2\ *n* : one that is ill, sickly, or disabled — **in•va•lid•ism** \-ˌiz-əm\ *n*

4in•va•lid \ˈin-və-ləd, -ˌlid\ *vt* **1** : to make an invalid of ⟨*invalided* by heart disease⟩ **2** : to remove from active duty by reason of sickness or disability ⟨*invalided* home after the battle⟩

in•val•i•date \in-ˈval-ə-ˌdāt, ˈin-\ *vt* : to make invalid ⟨a petition *invalidated* by false signatures⟩; *esp* : to weaken or destroy the effect of **syn** see NULLIFY — **in•val•i•da•tion** \in-ˌval-ə-ˈdā-shən\ *n* — **in•val•i•da•tor** \in-ˈval-ə-ˌdāt-ər\ *n*

in•valu•able \in-ˈval-yə-wə-bəl, -yə-bəl\ *adj* : having value too great to be estimated : PRICELESS — **in•valu•able•ness** *n* — **in•valu•ably** \-blē\ *adv*

in•vari•able \in-ˈver-ē-ə-bəl, -ˈvar-, ˈin-\ *adj* : not changing or capable of change : CONSTANT ⟨an *invariable* daily routine⟩ — **in•vari•abil•i•ty** \in-ˌver-ē-ə-ˈbil-ət-ē, -ˌvar-\ *n* — **invariable** *n* — **in•vari•able•ness** *n* — **in•vari•ably** \in-ˈver-ē-ə-blē, -ˈvar-, ˈin-\ *adv*

in•vari•ant \in-ˈver-ē-ənt, -ˈvar-, ˈin-\ *adj* : CONSTANT, UNCHANGING ⟨an *invariant* factor⟩ — **in•vari•ance** \-əns\ *n* — **invariant** *n*

in•va•sion \in-ˈvā-zhən\ *n* **1** : an act of invading; *esp* : entrance of an army into a country for conquest **2** : the entry or spread of some usually harmful thing ⟨bacterial *invasion* of tissue⟩ [Middle French, from Late Latin *invasio,* from Latin *invadere* "to invade"] — **in•va•sive** \-ˈvā-siv, -ziv\ *adj* — **in•va•sive•ness** *n*

in•vec•tive \in-ˈvek-tiv\ *n* : condemnation expressed in a harsh or bitter tone ⟨attack the opposing candidate with *invective*⟩ [Middle French *invectif* "condemnatory", from Latin *invectivus,* from *invehere* "to carry in"] **syn** see ABUSE

in•veigh \in-ˈvā\ *vi* : to protest or complain bitterly : RAIL ⟨*inveigh* against high taxes⟩ [Latin *invehi* "to attack, inveigh", from *invehere* "to carry in", from *in-* + *vehere* "to carry"] — **in•veigh•er** *n*

in•vei•gle \in-ˈvā-gəl, -ˈvē-\ *vt* **in•vei•gled**; **in•vei•gling** \-gə-ling, -gling\ **1** : to bring or lead by flattery : ENTICE ⟨was *inveigled* into marriage⟩ **2** : to acquire by ingenuity or flattery ⟨*inveigled* a loan⟩ [Middle French *aveugler* "to blind, hoodwink", from Old French *avogle* "blind", from Medieval Latin *ab oculis,* literally, "lacking eyes"] — **in•vei•gle•ment** \-gəl-mənt\ *n* — **in•vei•gler** \-gə-lər, -glər\ *n*

△ **origin** When we permit ourselves to be inveigled we are blinded, figuratively speaking, by flattery. The ancestor of our word *inveigle* is a Medieval Latin phrase meaning "blind". Literally, *ab oculis* is "lacking (or away from) eyes" — the Latin preposition *ab* expresses separation. From *ab oculis* are derived the French adjective *aveugle* "blind" and the verb *aveugler* "to blind". French *aveugler,* like its English equivalent, *blind,* is often used figuratively. When English borrowed the French verb in the late Middle Ages, only the figurative use was taken. English *inveigle* originally meant "to blind or delude in judgment". This sense is now obsolete, but the present meaning is not far removed.

in•vent \in-ˈvent\ *vt* **1** : to think up : make up ⟨*invent* an excuse⟩ **2** : to create or produce for the first time [Latin *inventus,* past participle of *invenire* "to come upon, find", from *in-* + *venire* "to come"] **syn** see DISCOVER — **in•ven•tor** \-ˈvent-ər\ *n*

in•ven•tion \in-ˈven-chən\ *n* **1** : something invented: as **a** : an original device or process **b** : a product of the imagination; *esp* : FALSEHOOD **2** : the act, process, or power of inventing

in•ven•tive \in-ˈvent-iv\ *adj* : gifted with the skill and imagination to invent — **in•ven•tive•ly** *adv* — **in•ven•tive•ness** *n*

1in•ven•to•ry \ˈin-vən-ˌtōr-ē, -ˌtȯr-\ *n, pl* **-ries** **1** : an itemized list of assets or goods on hand **2** : the stock of goods on hand **3** : the act or process of making an inventory — **in•ven•to•ri•al** \ˌin-vən-ˈtōr-ē-əl, -ˈtȯr-\ *adj* — **in•ven•to•ri•al•ly** \-ē-ə-lē\ *adv*

2inventory *vt* **-ried**; **-ry•ing** : to make an inventory of : CATALOG

in•ver•ness \ˌin-vər-ˈnes\ *n* : a loose belted coat having a cape with a close round collar [*Inverness,* Scotland]

1in•verse \in-ˈvərs, ˈin-, ˈin-ˌ\ *adj* **1** : opposite in order, nature, or effect **2** : so relating two numbers that their product is a constant ⟨an *inverse* proportion⟩ [Latin *inversus,* from *invertere* "to invert"] — **in•verse•ly** *adv*

2in•verse \ˈin-ˌvərs, in-ˈvərs\ *n* : something inverse or resulting in or from inversion: as **a** : a statement formed by contradicting the hypothesis of a given statement but keeping the conclusion unchanged **b** : an inverse function or operation in mathematics ⟨addition is the *inverse* of subtraction⟩

inverse function *n* : a function that in relation to a given function of two variables has the two variables interchanged

inverse square law *n* : a statement in physics: a physical quantity (as illumination) varies with the distance from the source inversely as the square of the distance

in•ver•sion \in-ˈvər-zhən, -shən\ *n* **1** : the act or process of inverting **2** : a reversal of position, order, or relationship

in•ver•sive \in-ˈvər-siv, -ziv\ *adj* : marked by inversion

in•vert \in-ˈvərt\ *vt* **1 a** : to turn inside out or upside down **b** : to turn inward **2** : to reverse the position, order, or relationship of [Latin *invertere,* from *in-* + *vertere* "to turn"] **syn** see REVERSE — **in•vert•ible** \-ə-bəl\ *adj*

in•ver•tase \in-ˈvərt-ˌās, -ˌāz; ˈin-vər-ˌtās, -ˌtāz\ *n* : an enzyme that splits sucrose into glucose and fructose

in•ver•te•brate \in-ˈvərt-ə-brət, -ˌbrāt, ˈin-\ *adj* : lacking a spinal column; *also* : of or relating to invertebrate animals — **invertebrate** *n*

in•vert•er \in-ˈvərt-ər\ *n* : a device for converting direct current into alternating current

in•vert sugar \ˌin-ˌvərt-\ *n* : a mixture of dextrose and levulose found in fruits or produced artificially from sucrose

1in•vest \in-ˈvest\ *vt* **1 a** : INSTALL 1 **b** : to furnish with power or authority **2** : to cover completely : ENVELOP **3** : to surround with troops or ships : BESIEGE **4** : to endow with a quality or characteristic ⟨*invest* an incident with mystery⟩ [Latin *investire* "to clothe, surround", from *in-* + *vestis* "garment"]

2invest *vb* **1** : to lay out money in order to earn a financial return **2** : to expend for future benefits or advantages ⟨*invest* time and effort in a project⟩ [Italian *investire* "to clothe, invest money", from Latin, "to clothe"] — **in•vest•able** \-ˈves-tə-bəl\ *adj* — **in•ves•tor** \-tər\ *n*

in•ves•ti•gate \in-ˈves-tə-ˌgāt\ *vb* : to observe or study by close and systematic examination [Latin *investigare* "to track, investigate", from *in-* + *vestigium* "footprint"] — **in•ves•ti•ga•tion** \-ˌves-tə-ˈgā-shən\ *n* — **in•ves•ti•ga•tive** \-ˈves-tə-ˌgāt-iv\ *adj* — **in•ves•ti•ga•tor** \-ˌgāt-ər\ *n* — **in•ves•ti•ga•to•ry** \-ˈves-ti-gə-ˌtōr-ē, -ˌtȯr-\ *adj*

in•ves•ti•ture \in-ˈves-tə-ˌchu̇r, -chər\ *n* : the action of investing a person especially with the robes of office [Medieval Latin *investitura,* from Latin *investire* "to clothe"]

1in•vest•ment \in-ˈvest-mənt, -ˈves-\ *n* **1** : an outer layer of any kind : ENVELOPE, COATING **2** : INVESTITURE **3** : SIEGE 1, BLOCKADE

[2]investment *n* : an outlay of money for income or profit; *also* : the sum invested or the property purchased

in•vet•er•ate \in-ˈvet-ə-rət, -ˈve-trət\ *adj* **1** : firmly established by age or by being long continued **2** : HABITUAL ⟨an *inveterate* smoker⟩ [Latin *inveteratus,* from *inveterare* "to age", from *in-* + *veter-, vetus* "old"] — **in•vet•er•a•cy** \-ˈvet-ə-rə-sē, -ˈve-trə-sē\ *n* — **in•vet•er•ate•ly** *adv*

in•vi•a•ble \in-ˈvī-ə-bəl, ˈin-\ *adj* : incapable of surviving — **in•vi•a•bil•i•ty** \in-ˌvī-ə-ˈbil-ət-ē\ *n*

in•vid•i•ous \in-ˈvid-ē-əs\ *adj* : tending to cause dislike, ill will, or envy ⟨*invidious* criticism⟩ [Latin *invidiosus* "envious, invidious", from *invidia* "envy"] — **in•vid•i•ous•ly** *adv* — **in•vid•i•ous•ness** *n*

in•vig•o•rate \in-ˈvig-ə-ˌrāt\ *vt* : to give life and energy to : ANIMATE — **in•vig•o•ra•tion** \-ˌvig-ə-ˈrā-shən\ *n* — **in•vig•o•ra•tor** \-ˈvig-ə-ˌrāt-ər\ *n*

in•vin•ci•ble \in-ˈvin-sə-bəl, ˈin-\ *adj* : incapable of being defeated, overcome, or subdued ⟨an *invincible* army⟩ [Middle French, from Late Latin *invincibilis,* from Latin *in-* + *vincere* "to conquer"] **syn** see INDOMITABLE — **in•vin•ci•bil•i•ty** \in-ˌvin-sə-ˈbil-ət-ē\ *n* — **in•vin•ci•ble•ness** *n* — **in•vin•ci•bly** \in-ˈvin-sə-blē, ˈin-\ *adv*

in•vi•o•la•ble \in-ˈvī-ə-lə-bəl, ˈin-\ *adj* **1** : too sacred to be violated ⟨an *inviolable* oath⟩ **2** : incapable of being assaulted or destroyed — **in•vi•o•la•bil•i•ty** \in-ˌvī-ə-lə-ˈbil-ət-ē\ *n* — **in•vi•o•la•bly** \in-ˈvī-ə-lə-blē, ˈin-\ *adv*

in•vi•o•late \in-ˈvī-ə-lət, ˈin-\ *adj* **1** : not violated or profaned; *esp* : PURE **2** : INVIOLABLE 2 — **in•vi•o•late•ly** *adv* — **in•vi•o•late•ness** *n*

in•vis•i•ble \in-ˈviz-ə-bəl\ *adj* **1 a** : incapable of being seen ⟨sound is *invisible*⟩ **b** : inaccessible to view : HIDDEN ⟨the sun is *invisible* on a cloudy day⟩ **2** : IMPERCEPTIBLE, INCONSPICUOUS ⟨an *invisible* hair net⟩ — **in•vis•i•bil•i•ty** \in-ˌviz-ə-ˈbil-ət-ē\ *n* — **invisible** *n* — **in•vis•i•ble•ness** *n* — **in•vis•i•bly** \in-ˈviz-ə-blē, ˈin-\ *adv*

in•vi•ta•tion \ˌin-və-ˈtā-shən\ *n* **1** : the act of inviting **2** : the written, printed, or spoken expression by which a person is invited — **in•vi•ta•tion•al** \-shnəl, -shən-l\ *adj*

[1]in•vite \in-ˈvīt\ *vt* **1** : to increase the likelihood of : INDUCE ⟨*invite* disaster by speeding⟩ **2 a** : to request the presence or participation of **b** : to request formally or politely : ENCOURAGE ⟨*invite* suggestions⟩ [Latin *invitare*] — **in•vit•er** *n*

[2]in•vite \ˈin-ˌvīt\ *n, chiefly dialect* : INVITATION

in•vit•ing \in-ˈvīt-ing\ *adj* : ATTRACTIVE, TEMPTING ⟨a very *inviting* dinner⟩ — **in•vit•ing•ly** \-ing-lē\ *adv*

in vi•tro \in-ˈvē-ˌtrō\ *adv or adj* : outside the living body and in an artificial environment [New Latin, literally, "in glass"]

in vi•vo \in-ˈvē-vō\ *adv or adj* : in the living body of a plant or animal [New Latin, literally, "in the living"]

in•vo•ca•tion \ˌin-və-ˈkā-shən\ *n* **1** : the act or process of invoking **2** : a prayer for blessing or guidance especially at the beginning of a religious service **3** : a formula for conjuring : INCANTATION **4** : an act of legal or moral enforcement ⟨*invocation* of the law⟩ — **in•vo•ca•tion•al** \-shnəl, -shən-l\ *adj*

[1]in•voice \ˈin-ˌvȯis\ *n* : an itemized statement given to a buyer by a seller and usually specifying the price of goods or services and the terms of sale; *also* : a shipment of goods sent with such a statement [Middle French *envois,* pl. of *envoi* "message", from *envoier* "to send on one's way", from Latin *in* "in, on" + *via* "way"]

[2]invoice *vt* : to submit an invoice for : BILL

in•voke \in-ˈvōk\ *vt* **1 a** : to call on for aid or protection (as in prayer) ⟨*invoke* God's blessing⟩ **b** : to appeal to as an authority or for support ⟨*invoke* a law⟩ **2** : to call forth by magic : CONJURE ⟨*invoke* spirits⟩ [Middle French *invoquer,* from Latin *invocare,* from *in-* + *vocare* "to call"] — **in•vok•er** *n*

in•vo•lu•cre \ˈin-və-ˌlü-kər\ *n* : one or more whorls of bracts immediately below a flower, flower cluster, or fruit [French, from Latin *involucrum* "sheath", from *involvere* "to wrap, involve"] — **in•vo•lu•cral** \ˌin-və-ˈlü-krəl\ *adj*

in•vol•un•tary \in-ˈväl-ən-ˌter-ē, ˈin-\ *adj* **1** : not made or done willingly or from choice **2** : COMPULSORY ⟨*involuntary* servitude⟩ **3** : not subject to direct control by the will : REFLEX — **in•vol•un•tar•i•ly** \in-ˌväl-ən-ˈter-ə-lē\ *adv*

involuntary muscle *n* : SMOOTH MUSCLE

in•vo•lu•tion \ˌin-və-ˈlü-shən\ *n* **1 a** : the act or an instance of enfolding or entangling : INVOLVEMENT **b** : INTRICACY 1, COMPLEXITY **2** : the act or process of raising a quantity to any power **3** : an inward curving or penetration **4 a** : a shrinking or return to a former size **b** : the regressive changes that accompany aging and are marked by a decrease of bodily vigor [Latin *involutio,* from *involvere* "to wrap, involve"] — **in•vo•lu•tion•al** \-shnəl, -shən-l\ *adj* — **in•vo•lu•tion•ary** \-shə-ˌner-ē\ *adj*

involucre

in•volve \in-ˈvälv, -ˈvȯlv\ *vt* **1 a** : to draw in as a participant : ENGAGE ⟨many workers are *involved* in the job⟩ **b** : to oblige to take part ⟨was *involved* in a lawsuit⟩ **c** : to occupy (as oneself) absorbingly ⟨was *involved* in the hero's fate⟩ **2 a** : to have within or as part of itself : INCLUDE ⟨one problem *involves* others⟩ **b** : to require as a necessary accompaniment ⟨the road job *involved* building 10 bridges⟩ **c** : to have an effect on ⟨breathing *involves* the whole organism⟩ [Latin *involvere* "to roll up, wrap, involve", from *in-* + *volvere* "to roll"] **syn** see include — **in•volve•ment** \-mənt\ *n* — **in•volv•er** *n*

in•volved \-ˈvälvd, -ˈvȯlvd\ *adj* **1** : INTRICATE 1 ⟨an *involved* plot⟩ **2** : difficult to deal with because of confusion or disorder : TANGLED **syn** SEE COMPLEX — **in•volv•ed•ly** \-ˈväl-vəd-lē, -ˈvȯl-\ *adv*

in•vul•ner•a•ble \in-ˈvəln-rə-bəl, -ə-rə-; -ˈvəl-nər-bəl\ *adj* **1** : incapable of being wounded, injured, or damaged **2** : immune to or secure against attack : IMPREGNABLE — **in•vul•ner•a•bil•i•ty** \in-ˌvəln-rə-ˈbil-ət-ē, -ə-rə\ *n* — **in•vul•ner•a•ble•ness** \in-ˈvəln-rə-bəl-nəs, -ə-rə-; -ˈvəl-nər-bəl-\ *n* — **in•vul•ner•a•bly** \-blē\ *adv*

[1]in•ward \ˈin-wərd\ *adj* **1** : located on the inside : INNER **2** : of or relating to the mind or spirit **3** : directed toward the interior ⟨an *inward* flow⟩

[2]inward *or* **in•wards** \-wərdz\ *adv* **1** : toward the inside, center, or interior ⟨slope *inward*⟩ **2** : toward the inner being ⟨turned their thoughts *inward*⟩

[3]inward *n* : something that is inward

in•ward•ly \ˈin-wərd-lē\ *adv* **1** : in the mind or spirit **2 a** : on the inside ⟨bled *inwardly*⟩ **b** : to oneself : PRIVATELY ⟨cursed *inwardly*⟩

in•ward•ness *n* **1** : fundamental nature : ESSENCE **2** : absorption in one's own mental or spiritual life

in•weave \in-ˈwēv, ˈin-\ *vt* **-wove** \-ˈwōv\ *also* **-weaved**; **-woven** \-ˈwō-vən\ *also* **-weaved**; **-weav•ing** : to weave in or together : INTERLACE

in•wrought \in-ˈrȯt, ˈin-\ *adj* : having or being a decorative element worked or woven in

iod- *or* **iodo-** *combining form* : iodine ⟨iodize⟩ ⟨*iodo*form⟩ [French *iode*]

io•dide \ˈī-ə-ˌdīd\ *n* : a compound of iodine with another element or radical

io•dine \ˈī-ə-ˌdīn, -əd-n, -ə-ˌdēn\ *n* **1** : a nonmetallic usually univalent chemical element that occurs in seawater, seaweeds, and underground brines, is obtained usually as heavy shining blackish gray crystals, and is used especially in medicine, photography, and analysis — see ELEMENT table **2** : a solution of iodine in alcohol used as an antiseptic [French *iode,* from Greek *ioeidēs* "violet colored", from *ion* "violet"]

io•dize \ˈī-ə-ˌdīz\ *vt* : to treat with iodine or an iodide ⟨*iodized* salt⟩

io•do•form \ī-ˈōd-ə-ˌfȯrm, -ˈäd-\ *n* : a yellow crystalline volatile iodine compound that is used as an antiseptic dressing [*iod-* + *-form* (as in *chloroform*)]

io•dop•sin \ˌī-ə-ˈdäp-sən\ *n* : a violet light-sensitive pigment in the retinal cones that is formed from vitamin A and is important in daylight vision — compare RHODOPSIN [Greek *ioeidēs* "violet colored" + *opsis* "sight, vision"]

io moth \ˌī-ō-\ *n* : a large yellowish American moth with a large spot on each hind wing [Latin *Io,* a mythical maiden loved by Zeus, from Greek *Iō*]

ion \ˈī-ən, ˈī-ˌän\ *n* : an atom or group of atoms that carries a positive or negative electric charge as a result of having lost or gained one or more electrons [Greek *iōn,* present participle of *ienai* "to go"]

-ion *n suffix* **1 a :** act or process ⟨validat*ion*⟩ **b :** result of an act or process ⟨regulat*ion*⟩ **2 :** state or condition ⟨deflat*ion*⟩ [Latin *-ion-, -io*]

Io•ni•an \ī-'ō-nē-ən\ *n* **1 :** one of an ancient Greek people who settled in Attica, on the islands of the Aegean sea, and on the shore of Asia Minor **2 :** a native or inhabitant of Ionia — **Ionian** *adj*

ion•ic \ī-'än-ik\ *adj* **:** of, relating to, or existing in the form of ions

Ion•ic \ī-'än-ik\ *adj* **1 :** of or relating to Ionia or the Ionians **2 :** belonging to or resembling the Ionic order of architecture characterized especially by the spiral volutes of its capital

ionic bond *n* **:** a chemical bond formed between ions of opposite charge

io•ni•um \ī-'ō-nē-əm\ *n* **:** a natural radioactive isotope of thorium having a mass number of 230 [*ion*; from its ionizing action]

ion•ize \'ī-ə-,nīz\ *vb* **:** to convert or become converted wholly or partly into ions — **ion•iza•tion** \,ī-ə-nə-'zā-shən\ *n* — **ion•iz•er** \'ī-ə-,nī-zər\ *n*

iono•sphere \ī-'än-ə-,sfiər\ *n* **:** the part of the earth's atmosphere beginning at an altitude of about 40 kilometers and extending outward 400 kilometers or more and containing free electrically charged particles by means of which radio waves are transmitted to great distances around the earth — **iono•spher•ic** \ī-,än-ə-'sfiər-ik, -'sfer-\ *adj*

io•ta \ī-'ōt-ə\ *n* **1 :** the 9th letter of the Greek alphabet — Ι or ι **2 :** a tiny amount **:** JOT ⟨not one *iota* of truth⟩

IOU \,ī-ō-'yü\ *n* **:** a paper that has on it the letters IOU, a stated sum, and a signature and that is given as an acknowledgment of debt [from the pronunciation of *I owe you*]

-ious *adj suffix* **:** -ous ⟨capac*ious*⟩ [partly from Latin *-iosus*, from *-i-* + *-osus* "-ous"; partly from Latin *-ius*, adj. suffix]

IPA \,ī-,pē-'ā\ *n* **:** an alphabet designed to represent each human speech sound with a different character [*I*nternational *P*honetic *A*lphabet]

ip•e•cac \'ip-i-,kak\ *or* **ipe•ca•cu•a•nha** \ē-,pek-ə-kü-'an-yə\ *n* **:** a South American creeping plant of the madder family; *also* **:** its dried rhizome and roots or an extract of these used especially formerly as an emetic and purgative [Portuguese *ipecacuanha*, from Tupi *ipekaaguéne*]

ip•se dixit \,ip-sē-'dik-sət\ *n* **:** an assertion made but not proved **:** DICTUM [Latin, "he himself said it"]

ip•so facto \,ip-sō-'fak-tō\ *adv* **:** by the very nature of the case [New Latin, literally, "by the fact itself"]

IQ \'ī-'kyü\ *n* **:** INTELLIGENCE QUOTIENT

ir- — see IN-

Ira•ni•an \ir-'ā-nē-ən\ *n* **1 :** a native or inhabitant of Iran **2 :** a branch of the Indo-European family of languages that includes Persian — **Iranian** *adj*

iras•ci•ble \ir-'as-ə-bəl, ī-'ras-\ *adj* **:** marked by hot temper and easily aroused anger [Middle French, from Late Latin *irascibilis*, from Latin *irasci* "to become angry", from *ira* "ire"] — **iras•ci•bil•i•ty** \ir-,as-ə-'bil-ət-ē, ī-,ras-\ *n* — **iras•ci•ble•ness** \ir-'as-ə-bəl-nəs, ī-'ras-\ *n* — **iras•ci•bly** \-blē\ *adv*

• **syn** IRASCIBLE, CHOLERIC, TESTY, TOUCHY mean easily angered. IRASCIBLE implies a tendency to be fiery tempered; CHOLERIC may suggest impatient excitability and unreasonable irritability; TESTY implies a quick temper irritated by trivial annoyances; TOUCHY suggests oversensitive readiness to take offense or flare up at slight or implied criticism.

irate \ī-'rāt\ *adj* **:** ANGRY 1a, b ⟨*irate* taxpayers⟩ — **irate•ly** *adv* — **irate•ness** *n*

ire \'īr\ *n* **:** WRATH 1, ANGER [Old French, from Latin *ira*] — **ire** *vt* — **ire•ful** \-fəl\ *adj* — **ire•ful•ly** \-fə-lē\ *adv*

iren•ic \ī-'ren-ik\ *adj* **:** PACIFIC 1 [Greek *eirēnikos*, from *eirēnē* "peace"] — **iren•i•cal•ly** \-'ren-i-kə-lē, -klē\ *adv*

ir•i•des•cence \,ir-ə-'des-ns\ *n* **:** a play of colors producing rainbow effects (as in a soap bubble) [derived from Latin *irid-, iris* "rainbow"] — **ir•i•des•cent** \-nt\ *adj* — **ir•i•des•cent•ly** *adv*

irid•i•um \ir-'id-ē-əm\ *n* **:** a silver-white hard brittle very heavy metallic chemical element — see ELEMENT table [New Latin, from Latin *irid-, iris* "rainbow"; from the colors produced by its dissolving in hydrochloric acid]

iris \'ī-rəs\ *n, pl* **iris•es** *or* **iri•des** \'ī-rə-,dēz, 'ir-ə-\ **1 :** the colored part of the eye that surrounds the pupil and alters in size to control the amount of light entering the eye **2 :** any of a large genus of perennial herbaceous plants with sword-shaped basal leaves and large showy flowers [Latin, "rainbow, iris plant", from Greek, "rainbow, iris plant, iris of the eye"]

iris 2

iris diaphragm *n* **:** an adjustable diaphragm of thin opaque plates used for changing the diameter of a central opening to control the amount of light passing (as into a microscope or camera)

Irish \'ī-rish\ *n* **1** *pl in construction* **:** the natives or inhabitants of Ireland or their descendants **2 :** the Celtic language of Ireland — **Irish** *adj* — **Irish•man** \-mən\ *n* — **Irish•wom•an** \-,wu̇m-ən\ *n*

Irish Gaelic *n* **:** the Celtic language of Ireland especially as used since the end of the medieval period

Irish•ism \'ī-rish-,iz-əm\ *n* **:** a word, phrase, or expression characteristic of the Irish

Irish moss *n* **:** either of two red algae; *also* **:** the dried and bleached plants of these used especially in cooking and pharmacy

Irish potato *n* **:** POTATO 2b

Irish setter *n* **:** any of a breed of bird dogs similar to English setters but with a chestnut-brown or mahogany-red coat

irk \'ərk\ *vt* **:** to make weary, irritated, or bored **:** ANNOY [Middle English *irken*]

irk•some \'ərk-səm\ *adj* **:** tending to irk **:** TEDIOUS — **irk•some•ly** *adv* — **irk•some•ness** *n*

1**iron** \'ī-ərn, 'īrn\ *n* **1 :** a heavy malleable ductile magnetic silver-white metallic chemical element that readily rusts in moist air, occurs in meteorites and combined in rocks, and is vital to biological processes — see ELEMENT table **2 :** something made of iron: as **a :** something (as handcuffs or chains) used to bind or restrain — usually used in pl. **b :** a heated metal implement used for branding **c :** FLATIRON **d :** one of a set of golf clubs with flat metal heads **3 :** great strength or hardness ⟨muscles of *iron*⟩ [Old English *īsern, īren*]

2**iron** *adj* **1 :** of, relating to, or made of iron **2 :** resembling iron (as in hardness or strength) **3 a :** being strong and healthy **:** ROBUST ⟨an *iron* constitution⟩ **b :** INFLEXIBLE, UNRELENTING ⟨*iron* determination⟩

3**iron** *vb* **1 :** to furnish or cover with iron **2 :** to smooth or press with a heated flatiron ⟨*iron* a shirt⟩ **3 :** to iron clothes ⟨spent all day *ironing*⟩

Iron Age *n* **:** the period of human culture characterized by the first smelting and use of iron and beginning somewhat before 1000 B.C. in western Asia and Egypt

1**iron•clad** \-'klad\ *adj* **1 :** sheathed in iron armor **2 :** RIGOROUS, EXACTING ⟨*ironclad* laws⟩

2**iron•clad** \-,klad\ *n* **:** an armored naval vessel

iron curtain *n* **:** a political, military, and ideological barrier that cuts off and isolates an area; *esp* **:** one between an area under Soviet control and other areas

iron hand *n* **:** stern or rigorous control ⟨rule with an *iron hand*⟩

iron horse *n* **:** a locomotive engine

iron•ic \ī-'rän-ik\ *adj* **1 :** relating to, containing, or constituting irony ⟨an *ironic* turn of events⟩ **2 :** given to irony — **iron•i•cal** \-i-kəl\ *adj* — **iron•i•cal•ly** \-i-kə-lē, -klē\ *adv*

iron lung *n* **:** a device for artificial respiration in which rhythmic alternations in the air pressure in a chamber surrounding a patient's chest force air into and out of the lungs

iron oxide *n* **1 :** FERRIC OXIDE **2 :** FERROUS OXIDE **3 :** a black magnetic oxide of iron Fe_3O_4 used as a pigment and polishing material

iron pyrites *n* **:** PYRITE — called also *iron pyrite*

iron•stone \'ī-ərn-,stōn, 'īrn-\ *n* **1 :** a hard sedimentary rock rich in iron **2 :** a hard white pottery first made in England during the 18th century — called also *ironstone china*

\ə\ **abut**	\au̇\ **out**	\i\ **tip**	\ȯ\ **saw**	\u̇\ **foot**
\ər\ **further**	\ch\ **chin**	\ī\ **life**	\ȯi\ **coin**	\y\ **yet**
\a\ **mat**	\e\ **pet**	\j\ **job**	\th\ **thin**	\yü\ **few**
\ā\ **take**	\ē\ **easy**	\ng\ **sing**	\th\ **this**	\yu̇\ **cure**
\ä\ **cot, cart**	\g\ **go**	\ō\ **bone**	\ü\ **food**	\zh\ **vision**

iron•ware \-ˌwaər, -ˌweər\ *n* **:** articles made of iron
iron•wood \-ˌwu̇d\ *n* **1 :** any of numerous trees and shrubs with exceptionally tough or hard wood **2 :** the wood of an ironwood
iron•work \-ˌwərk\ *n* **1 :** work in iron **2** *pl* **:** a mill or building where iron or steel is smelted or heavy iron or steel products are made — **iron•work•er** \-ˌwər-kər\ *n*
iro•ny \ˈī-rə-nē\ *n, pl* **-nies 1 a :** the humorous or sardonic use of words to express the opposite of what one really means (as when words of praise are given but blame is intended) **b :** an ironic expression or utterance **2 a :** inconsistency between an actual and an expected result **b :** a result marked by such inconsistency **[**Latin *ironia,* from Greek *eirōnia,* from *eirōn* "dissembler"**]**
Ir•o•quoi•an \ˌir-ə-ˈkwȯi-ən\ *n* **1 :** a stock of Indian languages spoken from the St. Lawrence valley to the southern Appalachian mountains **2 :** a member of the Indian peoples speaking Iroquoian languages — **Iroquoian** *adj*
Ir•o•quois \ˈir-ə-ˌkwȯi\ *n, pl* **Iroquois** \-ˌkwȯi, -ˌkwȯiz\ **:** a member of an Indian confederacy consisting originally of the Cayugas, Mohawks, Oneidas, Onondagas, and Senecas and later including the Tuscaroras **[**French, of American Indian origin**]**
ir•ra•di•ant \ir-ˈād-ē-ənt\ *adj* **:** emitting rays of light — **ir•ra•di•an•cy** \-ən-sē\ *n*
ir•ra•di•ate \ir-ˈād-ē-ˌāt\ *vt* **1 a :** to cast rays of light on **:** ILLUMINATE **b :** to affect or treat by exposure to radiations (as of ultraviolet light, X rays, or gamma rays) **2 :** to emit like rays of light **:** RADIATE — **ir•ra•di•a•tion** \-ˌād-ē-ˈā-shən\ *n* — **ir•ra•di•a•tive** \-ˈād-ē-ˌāt-iv\ *adj*
ir•ra•tio•nal \ir-ˈash-nəl, ˈir-, -ən-l\ *adj* **1 a :** incapable of reasoning ⟨*irrational* beasts⟩ **b :** not governed by or according to reason ⟨an *irrational* hatred of strangers⟩ **2 :** of, relating to, or being an irrational number — **ir•ra•tio•nal•i•ty** \ir-ˌash-ə-ˈnal-ət-ē\ *n* — **ir•ra•tio•nal•ly** \ir-ˈash-nə-lē, ˈir-, -ˈash-ən-l-ē\ *adv* — **ir•ra•tio•nal•ness** \-nəl-nəs, -ən-l-nəs\ *n*
• **syn** IRRATIONAL, UNREASONABLE mean not guided by reason. IRRATIONAL may imply mental derangement but oftener suggests lack of control or guidance by reason ⟨*irrational* fears⟩ UNREASONABLE suggests control by some force other than reason (as greed or rage) which makes for a deficiency in good sense ⟨*unreasonable* demands⟩
irrational number *n* **:** a real number (as $\sqrt{2}$) that is not expressible as the quotient of two integers — called also *irrational*
ir•re•claim•able \ˌir-i-ˈklā-mə-bəl\ *adj* **:** incapable of being reclaimed — **ir•re•claim•ably** \-blē\ *adv*
ir•rec•on•cil•able \ir-ˌek-ən-ˈsī-lə-bəl; ir-ˈek-ən-, ˈir-\ *adj* **:** impossible to reconcile, adjust, or harmonize ⟨*irreconcilable* enemies⟩ — **ir•rec•on•cil•abil•i•ty** \ir-ˌek-ən-ˌsī-lə-ˈbil-ət-ē\ *n* — **ir•rec•on•cil•ably** \ir-ˌek-ən-ˈsī-lə-blē; ir-ˈek-ən-ˌ, ˈir-\ *adv*
ir•re•cov•er•able \ˌir-i-ˈkəv-rə-bəl, -ə-rə-\ *adj* **:** not capable of being recovered ⟨an *irrecoverable* debt⟩ — **ir•re•cov•er•ably** \-blē\ *adv*
ir•re•deem•able \ˌir-i-ˈdē-mə-bəl\ *adj* **1 :** not redeemable; *esp* **:** not convertible into gold or silver at the will of the holder **2 :** being beyond remedy **:** HOPELESS ⟨*irredeemable* mistakes⟩ — **ir•re•deem•ably** \-blē\ *adv*
ir•re•duc•ible \ˌir-i-ˈdü-sə-bəl, -ˈdyü-\ *adj* **:** not reducible — **ir•re•duc•ibil•i•ty** \-ˌdü-sə-ˈbil-ət-ē, -ˌdyü-\ *n* — **ir•re•duc•ibly** \-ˈdü-sə-blē, -ˈdyü-\ *adv*
ir•re•fut•able \ˌir-i-ˈfyüt-ə-bəl; ir-ˈef-yət-, ˈir-\ *adj* **:** not capable of being proved wrong **:** INDISPUTABLE — **ir•re•fut•abil•i•ty** \ˌir-i-ˌfyüt-ə-ˈbil-ət-ē, ir-ˌef-yət-ə-ˈbil-\ *n* — **ir•re•fut•ably** \ˌir-i-ˈfyüt-ə-blē; ir-ˈef-yət-, ˈir-\ *adv*
¹ir•reg•u•lar \ir-ˈeg-yə-lər, ˈir-\ *adj* **1 a :** not conforming to established laws, customs, or moral principles **b :** not belonging to a recognized or organized body ⟨*irregular* troops⟩ ⟨*irregular* Democrats⟩ **2 :** not conforming to the normal or usual manner of inflection ⟨the *irregular* verbs *sell* and *cast*⟩; *esp* **:** STRONG 13 ⟨the *irregular* verb *write*⟩ **3 :** lacking perfect symmetry or evenness **4 :** lacking continuity or regularity of occurrence ⟨*irregular* intervals⟩ ⟨*irregular* payments⟩ — **ir•reg•u•lar•ly** *adv*
²irregular *n* **:** a soldier (as a guerrilla) who is not a member of a regular military force
ir•reg•u•lar•i•ty \ir-ˌeg-yə-ˈlar-ət-ē\ *n, pl* **-ties 1 :** the quality or state of being irregular **2 :** something (as dishonest conduct) that is irregular
ir•rel•e•vant \ir-ˈel-ə-vənt, ˈir-\ *adj* **:** not relevant **:** not applicable or pertinent — **ir•rel•e•vance** \-vəns\ *or* **ir•rel•e•van•cy** \-vən-sē\ *n* — **ir•rel•e•vant•ly** *adv*
ir•re•li•gious \-ˈlij-əs\ *adj* **1 :** lacking religious emotions, doctrines, or practices **2 :** indicating lack of religion ⟨*irreligious* talk⟩ — **ir•re•li•gious•ly** *adv*
ir•re•me•di•a•ble \ˌir-i-ˈmēd-ē-ə-bəl\ *adj* **:** not remediable — **ir•re•me•di•a•ble•ness** *n* — **ir•re•me•di•a•bly** \-blē\ *adv*
ir•re•mov•able \ˌir-i-ˈmü-və-bəl\ *adj* **:** not removable — **ir•re•mov•abil•i•ty** \-ˌmü-və-ˈbil-ət-ē\ *n* — **ir•re•mov•ably** \-ˈmü-və-blē\ *adv*
ir•rep•a•ra•ble \ir-ˈep-rə-bəl, ˈir-, -ə-rə-\ *adj* **:** not capable of being repaired or made good ⟨an *irreparable* loss⟩ — **ir•rep•a•ra•ble•ness** *n* — **ir•rep•a•ra•bly** \-blē\ *adv*
ir•re•place•able \ˌir-i-ˈplā-sə-bəl\ *adj* **:** not replaceable
ir•re•press•ible \ˌir-i-ˈpres-ə-bəl\ *adj* **:** not capable of being checked or held back ⟨*irrepressible* laughter⟩ — **ir•re•press•ibil•i•ty** \-ˌpres-ə-ˈbil-ət-ē\ *n* — **ir•re•press•ibly** \-ˈpres-ə-blē\ *adv*
ir•re•proach•able \-ˈprō-chə-bəl\ *adj* **:** not reproachable **:** BLAMELESS — **ir•re•proach•able•ness** *n* — **ir•re•proach•ably** \-blē\ *adv*
ir•re•sist•ible \-ˈzis-tə-bəl\ *adj* **:** impossible to successfully resist or oppose ⟨an *irresistible* attraction⟩ — **ir•re•sist•ibil•i•ty** \-ˌzis-tə-ˈbil-ət-ē\ *adj* — **ir•re•sist•ible•ness** \-ˈzis-tə-bəl-nəs\ *n* — **ir•re•sist•ibly** \-blē\ *adv*
ir•res•o•lute \ir-ˈez-ə-ˌlüt, ˈir-, -lət\ *adj* **:** uncertain how to act or proceed **:** HESITANT — **ir•res•o•lute•ly** *adv* — **ir•res•o•lute•ness** *n* — **ir•res•o•lu•tion** \ir-ˌez-ə-ˈlü-shən\ *n*
irrespective of *prep* **:** without regard to **:** regardless of
ir•re•spon•si•ble \ˌir-i-ˈspän-sə-bəl\ *adj* **:** not responsible: as **a :** not answerable to higher authority **b :** said or done with no sense of responsibility ⟨*irresponsible* charges⟩ **c :** lacking a sense of responsibility **d :** unable especially mentally or financially to bear responsibility — **ir•re•spon•si•bil•i•ty** \-ˌspän-sə-ˈbil-ət-ē\ *n* — **ir•re•spon•si•bly** \-ˈspän-sə-blē\ *adv*
ir•re•triev•able \ˌir-i-ˈtrē-və-bəl\ *adj* **:** not capable of being regained or remedied ⟨an *irretrievable* mistake⟩ — **ir•re•triev•ably** \-blē\ *adv*
ir•rev•er•ence \ir-ˈev-rəns, ˈir-, -ˈev-ə-rəns, -ˈev-ərns\ *n* **1 :** lack of reverence **2 :** an irreverent act or utterance
ir•rev•er•ent \-ˈev-rənt, -ˈev-ə-rənt, -ˈev-ərnt\ *adj* **:** showing lack of reverence **:** DISRESPECTFUL — **ir•rev•er•ent•ly** *adv*
ir•re•vers•ible \ˌir-i-ˈvər-sə-bəl\ *adj* **:** incapable of being reversed — **ir•re•vers•ibil•i•ty** \-ˌvər-sə-ˈbil-ət-ē\ *n* — **ir•re•vers•ibly** \-ˈvər-sə-blē\ *adv*
ir•rev•o•ca•ble \ir-ˈev-ə-kə-bəl, ˈir-\ *adj* **:** not capable of being revoked ⟨an *irrevocable* decision⟩ — **ir•rev•o•ca•bil•i•ty** \ir-ˌev-ə-kə-ˈbil-ət-ē\ *n* — **ir•rev•o•ca•bly** \ir-ˈev-ə-kə-blē, ˈir-\ *adv*
ir•ri•gate \ˈir-ə-ˌgāt\ *vb* **1 :** WET, MOISTEN: as **a :** to supply (as land) with water by artificial means **b :** to flush with a liquid ⟨*irrigate* a wound⟩ **2 :** to practice irrigation **[**Latin *irrigare,* from *in-* + *rigare* "to water"**]** — **ir•ri•ga•tion** \ˌir-ə-ˈgā-shən\ *n* — **ir•ri•ga•tor** \ˈir-ə-ˌgāt-ər\ *n*
ir•ri•ta•bil•i•ty \ˌir-ət-ə-ˈbil-ət-ē\ *n, pl* **-ties :** the quality or state of being irritable: as **a :** quick excitability to annoyance, impatience, or anger **b :** the property of protoplasm and of living organisms that permits them to react to stimuli
ir•ri•ta•ble \ˈir-ət-ə-bəl\ *adj* **:** capable of being irritated; *esp* **:** readily or easily irritated — **ir•ri•ta•ble•ness** *n* — **ir•ri•ta•bly** \-blē\ *adv*
ir•ri•tant \ˈir-ə-tənt\ *adj* **:** IRRITATING; *esp* **:** tending to produce physical irritation — **irritant** *n*
ir•ri•tate \ˈir-ə-ˌtāt\ *vb* **1 :** to excite impatience, anger, or displeasure in **:** ANNOY **2 :** to make sore or inflamed **[**Latin *irritare***]** — **ir•ri•ta•tive** \-ˌtāt-iv\ *adj*
• **syn** AGGRAVATE, EXASPERATE, PROVOKE: IRRITATE implies arousing feelings that may range from impatience to rage; AGGRAVATE may apply to repeated action that intensifies anger or irritation; EXASPERATE suggests intense annoyance or patience strained beyond endurance; PROVOKE implies an often deliberate arousing of strong annoyance or vexation that may excite to action.
ir•ri•ta•tion \ˌir-ə-ˈtā-shən\ *n* **1 :** the act of irritating **2 :** something that irritates **3 :** the state of being irritated
ir•rupt \ir-ˈəpt, ˈir-\ *vi* **1 :** to rush in forcibly or violently **2 :** to increase suddenly in numbers ⟨rabbits *irrupt* in cycles⟩ **[**Latin *irruptus,* past participle of *irrumpere* "to break in, irrupt", from *in-* + *rumpere* "to break"**]** — **ir•rup•tion** \ir-ˈəp-shən, ˈir-\ *n*

— **ir•rup•tive** \-'əp-tiv\ *adj* — **ir•rup•tive•ly** \-'əp-tiv-lē\ *adv*

is *present 3d sing of* BE [Old English]

is- *or* **iso-** *combining form* **1** : equal : uniform ⟨*iso*bar⟩ **2** : isomeric ⟨*iso*leucine⟩ [Greek *isos*]

Isa•iah \ī-'zā-ə\ *n — see* BIBLE table

Isa•ias \-əs\ *n* — see BIBLE table

isch•emia \is-'kē-mē-ə\ *n* : local deficiency of blood due to decreased arterial inflow [Greek *ischaimos* "styptic", from *ischein* "to restrain" + *haima* "blood"] — **isch•emic** \-mik\ *adj*

is•chi•um \'is-kē-əm\ *n, pl* **-chia** \-kē-ə\ : the dorsal and posterior of the three principal bones composing either half of the pelvis [Latin, "hip joint", from Greek *ischion*] — **is•chi•al** \-kē-əl\ *adj*

-ise \,īz\ *vb suffix, chiefly British* : -IZE

-ish \ish\ *adj suffix* **1** : of, relating to, or being ⟨Finn*ish*⟩ **2 a** : characteristic of ⟨girl*ish*⟩ : having the undesirable qualities of ⟨mul*ish*⟩ **b** : inclined or liable to ⟨book*ish*⟩ ⟨qualm*ish*⟩ **c** (1) : somewhat ⟨small*ish*⟩ (2) : having the approximate age of ⟨forty*ish*⟩ (3) : being or occurring at the approximate time of ⟨eight*ish*⟩ [Old English *-isc*]

Ish•ma•el \'ish-mē-əl\ *n* : a social outcast [*Ishmael,* outcast son of Abraham and Hagar]

Ish•ma•el•ite \'ish-mē-ə-,līt\ *n* : a member of an ancient Semitic people of the deserts of southwestern Asia held to be descended from Ishmael and sometimes held to be ancestral to the modern Arabs

isin•glass \'īz-n-,glas, 'ī-zing-\ *n* **1** : a very pure gelatin prepared from the air bladders of fishes **2** : mica in thin sheets [probably by folk etymology from Dutch *huizenblas,* from *huus* "sturgeon" + *blase* "bladder"]

Is•lam \is-'läm, iz-, -'lam, 'is-,, 'iz-,\ *n* **1** : a religion dominant in much of Asia and northern Africa since the 7th century A.D. that is marked by belief in Allah as the sole deity, in Muhammad as his prophet, and in the Koran **2 a** : the civilization erected upon Islamic faith **b** : the group of modern nations in which Islam is the dominant religion [Arabic *islām* "submission (to the will of Allah)"] — **Is•lam•ic** \is-'läm-ik, iz-, -'lam-\ *adj* — **Is•lam•ize** \'iz-lə-,mīz\ *vt*

is•land \'ī-lənd\ *n* **1** : an area of land surrounded by water and smaller than a continent **2** : something (as a safety zone in a street) suggestive of an island [Middle English *iland,* from Old English *igland*]

△ **origin** The words *island* and *isle* are etymologically distinct. *Island* can be traced back to Old English *īgland*, composed of two elements *īg* and *land. Land*, as we might expect, means "land", but *īg* is also found in Old English as a word meaning "island". In a sense, then, *īgland* is "island-land". English *isle,* on the other hand, is derived through Old French from Latin *insula*. In the 16th century, under the influence of *isle,* the letter s was added to *iland,* the earlier form of *island*.

is•land•er \'ī-lən-dər\ *n* : a native or inhabitant of an island

island universe *n* : a galaxy other than the Milky Way

isle \'īl\ *n* : ISLAND 1; *esp* : a small island [Old French, from Latin *insula* — see ISLAND *origin*]

is•let \'ī-lət\ *n* : a little island

islet of Lang•er•hans \-'läng-ər-,häns, -,hänz\ : any of the groups of small granular endocrine cells that form interlacing strands in the pancreas and secrete insulin [Paul *Langerhans,* died 1888, German physician]

ism \'iz-əm\ *n* : a distinctive doctrine, cause, or theory [*-ism*]

-ism \,iz-əm\ *n suffix* **1 a** : act : practice : process ⟨plagiar*ism*⟩ **b** : manner of action or behavior characteristic of a (specified) person or thing ⟨animal*ism*⟩ **2 a** : state : condition : property ⟨barbarian*ism*⟩ **b** : abnormal state or condition resulting from excess of a (specified) thing ⟨alcohol*ism*⟩ or marked by resemblance to (such) a person or thing ⟨mongol*ism*⟩ **3 a** : doctrine : theory : cult ⟨Buddh*ism*⟩ **b** : adherence to a system or a class of principles ⟨stoic*ism*⟩ **4** : characteristic or peculiar feature or trait ⟨colloquial*ism*⟩ [Greek *-isma* and *-ismos,* from verbs in *-izein* "-ize"]

isn't \'iz-nt\ : is not

iso•bar \'ī-sə-,bär\ *n* : a line drawn on a map connecting places having the same atmospheric pressure at a given time or for a given period [*is-* + Greek *baros* "weight"] — **iso•bar•ic** \,ī-sə-'bär-ik, -'bar-\ *adj*

iso•ga•mete \,ī-sō-gə-'mēt, -'gam-,ēt\ *n* : a gamete indistinguishable from another gamete with which it can unite to form a zygote — **iso•ga•met•ic** \-gə-'met-ik\ *adj*

iso•gon•ic line \,ī-sə-,gän-ik-\ *n* : a line on a map joining points on the earth's surface at which the magnetic declination is the same [Greek *gōnia* "angle"]

iso•late \'ī-sə-,lāt *also* 'is-ə-\ *vb* **1** : to set apart from others; *also* : QUARANTINE **2** : to select from among others; *esp* : to separate from other substances so as to obtain pure or in a free state [back-formation from *isolated* "set apart", from French *isolé,* from Italian *isolato,* from *isola* "island", from Latin *insula*]

iso•la•tion \,ī-sə-'lā-shən, ,is-ə-\ *n* : the act of isolating : the condition of being isolated

iso•la•tion•ism \-shə-,niz-əm\ *n* : a national policy of avoiding international political and economic relations (as alliances) — **iso•la•tion•ist** \-shə-nəst, -shnəst\ *n or adj*

iso•leu•cine \,ī-sō-'lü-,sēn\ *n* : a crystalline essential amino acid isomeric with leucine

iso•mer \'ī-sə-mər\ *n* : a compound, radical, ion, or nuclide exhibiting isomerism with one or more others [back-formation from *isomeric,* from Greek *isomerēs* "equally divided", from *isos* "equal" + *meros* "part"]

isom•er•ism \ī-'säm-ə-,riz-əm\ *n* **1** : the relation of two or more chemical compounds, radicals, or ions that contain the same numbers of atoms of the same elements but differ in structural arrangement and properties **2** : the relation of two or more nuclides with the same mass numbers and atomic numbers but different energy states and rates of radioactive decay — **iso•mer•ic** \,ī-sə-'mer-ik\ *adj*

iso•met•ric \,ī-sə-'me-trik\ *adj* **1** : of, relating to, or characterized by equality of measure **2** : relating to or being a crystallographic system characterized by three equal axes at right angles — **iso•met•ri•cal•ly** \-tri-kə-lē, -klē\ *adv*

iso•met•rics \,ī-sə-'me-triks\ *n sing or pl* : a form of exercise in which the muscles strain against an unmoving resistance (as a wall or door frame)

iso•pod \'ī-sə-,päd\ *n* : any of a large order (Isopoda) of small sessile-eyed crustaceans with seven free thoracic segments each bearing a pair of legs — **isop•o•dan** \ī-'säp-əd-ən\ *adj or n*

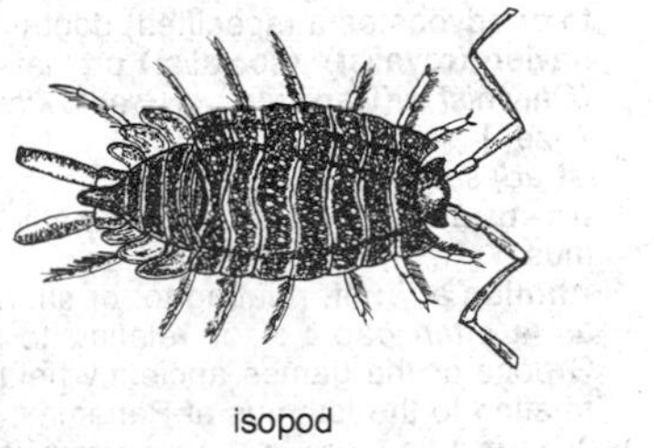

isopod

iso•pro•pyl alcohol \,ī-sə-'prō-pəl-\ *n* : a volatile flammable alcohol C_3H_8O used especially as a solvent and rubbing alcohol [*isopropyl* from *is-* + *prop-* (derived from *propionic acid)* + *-yl*]

isos•ce•les \ī-'säs-,lēz, -ə-,lēz\ *adj* **1** : being a triangle with two equal sides **2** : being a trapezoid whose two nonparallel sides are equal [Late Latin, from Greek *isoskelēs,* from *isos* "equal" + *skelos* "leg"]

isos•ta•sy \ī-'säs-tə-sē\ *n* : general equilibrium in vertical movement between segments of the earth's crust maintained by a yielding flow of rock material beneath the surface under the force of gravity [Greek *-stasia* "condition of standing", from *histanai* "to cause to stand"] — **iso•stat•ic** \,ī-sə-'stat-ik\ *adj*

iso•therm \'ī-sə-,thərm\ *n* : a line on a map connecting points having the same temperature at a given time or the same mean temperature for a given period [French *isotherme* "isothermal", from Greek *isos* "equal" + *thermē* "heat"]

iso•ther•mal \,ī-sə-'thər-məl\ *adj* : of, relating to, or marked by equality of temperature

iso•ton•ic \,ī-sə-'tän-ik\ *adj* : having the same or equal osmotic pressure ⟨a salt solution *isotonic* with red blood cells⟩ [Greek *tonos* "tension, tone"] — **iso•ton•i•cal•ly** \-'tän-i-kə-lē, -klē\ *adv* — **iso•to•nic•i•ty** \-tō-'nis-ət-ē\ *n*

iso•tope \'ī-sə-,tōp\ *n* : any of two or more species of atoms of a chemical element with the same atomic number and position

\ə\ **abut**	\au̇\ **out**	\i\ **tip**	\ȯ\ **saw**	\u̇\ **foot**
\ər\ **further**	\ch\ **chin**	\ī\ **life**	\ȯi\ **coin**	\y\ **yet**
\a\ **mat**	\e\ **pet**	\j\ **job**	\th\ **thin**	\yü\ **few**
\ā\ **take**	\ē\ **easy**	\ng\ **sing**	\t͟h\ **this**	\yu̇\ **cure**
\ä\ **cot, cart**	\g\ **go**	\ō\ **bone**	\ü\ **food**	\zh\ **vision**

in the periodic table and nearly identical chemical behavior but with differing atomic mass or mass number and different physical properties [Greek *topos* "place"] — **iso·top·ic** \ˌī-sə-ˈtäp-ik, -ˈtō-pik\ *adj* — **iso·top·i·cal·ly** \-ˈtäp-i-kə-lē, -ˈtō-pi-, -klē\ *adv*

Is·ra·el \ˈiz-rē-əl\ *n* **1 :** the Jewish people **2 :** a group of people held to be God's elect [derived from Hebrew *Yisrā'ēl*] — **Israel** *adj*

Is·rae·li \iz-ˈrā-lē\ *adj* of, relating to, or characteristic of the republic of Israel or its people — **Israeli** *n*

Is·ra·el·ite \ˈiz-rē-ə-ˌlīt\ *n* **:** a descendant of the Hebrew patriarch Jacob; *esp* **:** a native or inhabitant of the ancient northern kingdom of Israel — **Israelite** *or* **Is·ra·el·it·ish** \-ˌlīt-ish\ *adj*

is·su·ance \ˈish-ə-wəns\ *n* **:** the act of issuing especially officially

1is·sue \ˈish-ü\ *n* **1 :** the action of going, coming, or flowing out **2 :** a means or place of going out **:** EXIT, OUTLET **3 :** PROGENY 1 **4 :** final outcome **:** RESULT **5 a :** a matter in dispute **:** a point of debate or controversy **b :** a final result or conclusion **:** DECISION **6 :** something issued or issuing; *esp* **:** the copies of a periodical published at one time ⟨the latest *issue* of a magazine⟩ [Middle French, from *issir* "to come out, go out", from Latin *exire*, from *ex-* + *ire* "to go"]

2issue *vb* **1 :** to go, come, or flow out **:** DISCHARGE ⟨water *issuing* from a pipe⟩ **2 a :** to cause to come forth **:** EMIT **b :** to distribute officially ⟨*issue* a new stamp⟩ **c :** to send out for sale or circulation **:** PUBLISH **3 :** to come as an effect **:** RESULT — **is·su·er** *n*

1-ist \əst\ *n suffix* **1 a :** one that performs a (specified) action ⟨cycl*ist*⟩ **:** one that makes or produces ⟨novel*ist*⟩ **b :** one that plays a (specified) musical instrument ⟨harp*ist*⟩ **c :** one that operates a (specified) mechanical instrument or contrivance ⟨automobil*ist*⟩ **2 :** one that specializes in a (specified) art or science or skill ⟨geolog*ist*⟩ ⟨ventriloqu*ist*⟩ **3 :** one that adheres to or advocates a (specified) doctrine or system or code of behavior ⟨royal*ist*⟩ ⟨social*ist*⟩ or that of a (specified) individual ⟨Calvin*ist*⟩ ⟨Darwin*ist*⟩ [Greek *-istēs*, from verbs in *-izein* "-ize"]

2-ist *adj suffix* **:** -ISTIC

1isth·mi·an \ˈis-mē-ən\ *n* **:** a native or inhabitant of an isthmus

2isthmian *adj* **:** of, relating to, or situated in or near an isthmus: as **a** *often cap* **:** of or relating to the Isthmus of Corinth in Greece or the games anciently held there **b** *often cap* **:** of or relating to the Isthmus of Panama

isth·mus \ˈis-məs\ *n* **1 :** a narrow strip of land connecting two larger land areas **2 :** a narrow anatomical part or passage connecting two larger structures or cavities [Latin, from Greek *isthmos*]

-is·tic \ˈis-tik\ *also* **-is·ti·cal** \ˈis-ti-kəl\ *adj suffix* **:** of, relating to, or characteristic of ⟨altru*istic*⟩ [Greek *-istikos*, from *-istēs* "-ist" + *-ikos* "-ic"]

is·tle \ˈist-lē\ *n* **:** a strong fiber (as for cordage or basketry) from tropical American plants [American Spanish *ixtle*, from Nahuatl *ichtli*]

1it \it, ˈit, ət\ *pron* **1 :** that one — used usually in reference to a lifeless thing ⟨caught the ball and threw *it* back⟩, a plant, a person or animal whose sex is unknown or disregarded ⟨don't know who *it* is⟩, a group of individuals or things, or an abstract entity; compare HE, ITS, SHE, THEY **2** — used as subject of a verb that expresses a condition or action without reference to an agent ⟨*it* is raining⟩ **3 a** — used to mark the logical place of a noun, phrase, or clause that has been shifted to a later place in a sentence ⟨*it* is necessary to repeat the whole thing⟩; often used to shift emphasis to a part of a statement other than the subject ⟨*it* was in this city that the treaty was signed⟩ **b** — used with many verbs as a direct object with little or no meaning ⟨footed *it* back to camp⟩ **4 :** the general state of affairs or circumstances ⟨how is *it* going⟩ [Old English *hit*]

2it \ˈit\ *n* **:** the player in a game who performs the principal action of the game (as trying to catch others in a game of tag)

Ital·ian \ə-ˈtal-yən, i-\ *n* **1 a :** a native or inhabitant of Italy **b :** a person of Italian descent **2 :** the Romance language of the Italians — **Italian** *adj*

Italian sonnet *n* **:** a sonnet consisting of an octave rhyming *abba abba* and a sestet rhyming in any of several patterns (as *cde cde* or *cdc dcd*)

1ital·ic \ə-ˈtal-ik, i-, ī-\ *adj* **1** *cap* **:** of or relating to ancient Italy, its peoples, or their Indo-European languages **2 :** of or relating to a type style with characters that slant upward to the right (as in "*these words are italic*")

2italic *n* **:** an italic character or type

ital·i·cize \ə-ˈtal-ə-ˌsīz, i-, ī-\ *vt* **1 :** to print in italics **2 :** to underscore with a single line — **ital·i·ci·za·tion** \-ˌtal-ə-sə-ˈzā-shən\ *n*

1itch \ˈich\ *vb* **1 :** to have or produce an itch **2 :** to cause to itch **3 :** to have a strong persistent desire ⟨*itching* to get a new car⟩ [Middle English *icchen*, from Old English *giccan*]

2itch *n* **1 a :** an uneasy irritating sensation in the skin usually held to result from mild stimulation of pain receptors **b :** a skin disorder accompanied by an itch; *esp* **:** a contagious eruption caused by a mite **2 :** a constant restless desire ⟨an *itch* to travel⟩ — **itch·i·ness** \ˈich-ē-nəs\ *n* — **itchy** \-ē\ *adj*

it'd \ˌit-əd\ **:** it had **:** it would

1-ite \ˌīt\ *n suffix* **1 a :** native **:** resident ⟨Brooklyn*ite*⟩ **b :** descendant ⟨Ishmael*ite*⟩ **c :** adherent **:** follower ⟨Jacob*ite*⟩ **2 :** product ⟨metabol*ite*⟩ **3 :** fossil ⟨ammon*ite*⟩ **4 :** mineral ⟨hal*ite*⟩ **:** rock ⟨quartz*ite*⟩ **5 :** segment or constituent part ⟨som*ite*⟩ [Greek *-itēs*]

2-ite *n suffix* **:** salt or ester of an acid with a name ending in *-ous* ⟨nitr*ite*⟩ [French, alteration of *-ate* "1-ate"]

item \ˈīt-əm\ *n* **1 :** a separate thing in a list, account, group, or series **:** ARTICLE ⟨check each *item* before you pack it⟩ **2 :** a separate piece of news or information **:** a short news paragraph ⟨column of local *items*⟩ [Latin *item* "also", from *ita* "thus"]

item·ize \ˈīt-ə-ˌmīz\ *vt* **:** to set down in detail **:** LIST ⟨*itemize* expenditures⟩ — **item·iza·tion** \ˌīt-ə-mə-ˈzā-shən\ *n*

it·er·ate \ˈit-ə-ˌrāt\ *vt* **:** REITERATE, REPEAT [Latin *iterare*, from *iterum* "again"] — **it·er·a·tion** \ˌit-ə-ˈrā-shən\ *n* — **it·er·a·tive** \ˈit-ə-ˌrāt-iv, -rət-\ *adj*

itin·er·ant \ī-ˈtin-ə-rənt, ə-ˈtin-\ *adj* **:** traveling from place to place ⟨*itinerant* preachers⟩ [Late Latin *itinerari* "to journey", from Latin *itiner-, iter* "journey", from *ire* "to go"] — **itin·er·an·cy** \-rən-sē\ *or* **itin·er·a·cy** \-rə-sē\ *n* — **itinerant** *n* — **itin·er·ant·ly** *adv*

itin·er·ary \ī-ˈtin-ə-ˌrer-ē, ə-\ *n, pl* **-ar·ies 1 :** the route of a trip **2 :** a travel diary **3 :** a travel guidebook — **itinerary** *adj*

-i·tis \ˈīt-əs\ *n suffix, pl* **-i·tis·es** *also* **-it·i·des** \ˈit-ə-ˌdēz\ *or* **-i·tes** \ˈīt-ēz\ **1 :** disease or inflammation ⟨bronch*itis*⟩ **2 :** heated or excessive response (as of distress or enthusiasm) to [Greek]

it'll \ˌit-l\ **:** it shall **:** it will

its \its, ˌits, əts\ *adj* **:** of or relating to it or itself especially as possessor, agent, or object of an action ⟨going to *its* kennel⟩ ⟨a child proud of *its* first drawings⟩ ⟨*its* final enactment into law⟩

it's \its, ˌits, əts\ **:** it is **:** it has

it·self \it-ˈself, ət-\ *pron* **1 :** that identical one — used reflexively or for emphasis ⟨watched the cat giving *itself* a bath⟩ ⟨the letter *itself* was missing⟩; compare IT 1 **2 :** its normal, healthy, or sane condition or self

-ity \ət-ē\ *n suffix, pl* **-ities :** quality **:** state **:** degree ⟨asinin*ity*⟩ [Old French or Latin; Old French *-ité*, from Latin *-itat-, -itas*]

-ium *n suffix* **1 :** chemical element ⟨europ*ium*⟩ **2 :** chemical radical ⟨ammon*ium*⟩ [Latin, ending of some neuter nouns]

-ive \iv\ *adj suffix* **:** that performs or tends toward an (indicated) action ⟨regress*ive*⟩ [Latin *-ivus*]

I've \īv, ˌīv\ **:** I have

ivied \ˈī-vēd\ *adj* **:** overgrown with ivy

ivo·ry \ˈīv-rē, -ə-rē\ *n, pl* **-ries 1 :** the hard creamy-white modified dentine that composes the tusks of a tusked mammal (as an elephant) **2 :** a pale yellow **3 :** something (as piano keys) made of ivory or of a similar substance [Old French *ivoire*, from Latin *eboreus* "of ivory", from *ebur* "ivory", from Egyptian *ꜣb* "elephant, ivory"]

ivory black *n* **:** a fine black pigment made by calcining ivory

ivory tower *n* **1 :** a lack of concern with practical matters or urgent problems **2 :** a secluded place for meditation **:** RETREAT

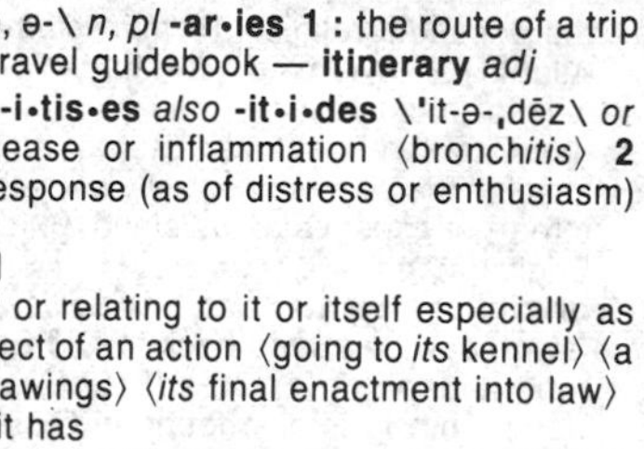

ivy 1

ivy \ˈī-vē\ *n, pl* **ivies 1 :** a climbing woody vine with glossy evergreen leaves, small yellowish flowers, and black berries **2 :** any of several plants resembling ivy [Old English *īfig*]

Ivy League *adj* : of, relating to, or characteristic of a group of long-established eastern United States colleges widely regarded as high in scholastic and social prestige [from the prevalence of ivy-covered buildings on the campuses of the older United States colleges]

-iza•tion \ə-'zā-shən *also especially when an unstressed syllable precedes* ī-'zā-\ *n suffix* : action, process, or result of making ⟨social*ization*⟩ ⟨union*ization*⟩ ⟨special*ization*⟩

-ize \ˌīz\ *vb suffix* **1 a** (1) : cause to be or conform to or resemble ⟨american*ize*⟩ : cause to be formed into ⟨union*ize*⟩ (2) : subject to a (specified) action ⟨satir*ize*⟩ (3) : impregnate or treat or combine with ⟨macadam*ize*⟩ **b** : treat like ⟨idol*ize*⟩ **2 a** : become : become like ⟨crystall*ize*⟩ **b** : be productive in or of ⟨hypothes*ize*⟩ : engage in a (specified) activity ⟨botan*ize*⟩ [Greek *-izein*]

J j—juxtapositional

j \'jā\ *n, pl* **j's** *or* **js** \ˌjāz\ *often cap* : the 10th letter of the English alphabet

jab \'jab\ *vb* **jabbed**; **jab•bing** : to thrust quickly or abruptly with or as if with something sharp : POKE [Middle English *jobben*] — **jab** *n*

jab•ber \'jab-ər\ *vb* **jab•bered**; **jab•ber•ing** \'jab-ring, -ə-ring\ : to utter or speak rapidly, indistinctly, or unintelligibly [Middle English *jaberen*] — **jabber** *n* — **jab•ber•er** \'jab-ər-ər\ *n*

jab•ber•wocky \'jab-ər-ˌwäk-ē\ *n* : meaningless speech or writing [*Jabberwocky,* nonsense poem by Lewis Carroll]

ja•bot \zha-'bō, 'jab-ˌō\ *n* : a ruffle of cloth or lace that falls from the collar down the front of a dress or shirt [French]

jac•a•ran•da \ˌjak-ə-'ran-də\ *n* : a tropical American tree often grown for its showy panicles of blue flowers [Portuguese]

ja•cinth \'jās-nth, 'jas-; zhä-'sant\ *n* : HYACINTH 1 [Old French *jacinthe,* from Latin *hyacinthus,* a flowering plant]

[1]**jack** \'jak\ *n* **1** *often cap* : SAILOR 1a **2 a** : a device for turning a spit (as in roasting meat) **b** : any of various portable mechanisms for exerting pressure or lifting a heavy body a short distance **3** : any of various animals: as **a** : a male ass **b** : JACKRABBIT **4 a** : a small target ball in lawn bowling **b** : a small national flag flown by a ship **c** (1) : a small 6-pointed metal object used in a game (2) *pl* : a game played with jacks **5** : a playing card bearing the stylized figure of a man **6** *slang* : MONEY 1 **7** : a socket in an electric circuit used with a plug to make a connection with another circuit [*Jack,* nickname for *John*]

[2]**jack** *vb* **1** : to hunt or fish for game at night with a jacklight **2** : to move or lift by or as if by a jack **3** : to raise the level or quality of ⟨*jack* up prices⟩ — **jack•er** *n*

jack•al \'jak-əl, -ˌȯl\ *n* **1** : any of several Old World wild dogs smaller than the related wolves **2** : a person who performs routine or menial tasks for another [Turkish *çakal,* from Persian *shagāl,* from Sanskrit *śṛgāla*]

jack•a•napes \'jak-ə-ˌnāps\ *n* **1** : MONKEY 1, APE **2** : an impudent or conceited person [Middle English *Jack Napis,* nickname for William de la Pole, died 1450, duke of Suffolk]

jack•ass \'jak-ˌas\ *n* **1** : a male ass; *also* : DONKEY **2** : ASS 2

jack•boot \'jak-ˌbüt\ *n* **1** : a heavy military boot reaching above the knee and worn especially in the 17th and 18th centuries **2** : a laceless military boot reaching to the calf

jack•daw \'jak-ˌdȯ\ *n* : a common black and gray Eurasian bird smaller than the related common crow

jack•et \'jak-ət\ *n* **1** : a short coat usually having a front opening, collar, and sleeves **2** : an outer covering or casing: as **a** : a tough metal covering on a bullet or projectile **b** : a coating or covering of a nonconducting material used to prevent heat radiation **c** : a detachable outer paper wrapper on a bound book [Middle French *jaquet,* from *jaque* "short jacket", from *jaques* "peasant", from the name *Jaques* "James"] — **jack•et•ed** \-ət-əd\ *adj*

Jack Frost *n* : frost or frosty weather personified

jack•ham•mer \'jak-ˌham-ər\ *n* : a pneumatic percussive tool for drilling or breaking up hard substances (as rock or pavement)

jack–in–the–box \'jak-ən-t͟hə-ˌbäks\ *n, pl* **jack–in–the–boxes** *or* **jacks–in–the–box** : a small box out of which a figure (as of a clown's head) springs when the lid is raised

jack–in–the–pul•pit \ˌjak-ən-t͟hə-'pu̇l-ˌpit\ *n, pl* **jack–in–the–pulpits** *or* **jacks–in–the–pulpit** : an American spring-flowering woodland herb with an upright club-shaped flower cluster arched over by a green and purple spathe

[1]**jack•knife** \'jak-ˌnīf\ *n* **1** : a large strong clasp knife for the pocket **2** : a dive in which the diver bends from the waist and touches the ankles before straightening out

[2]**jackknife** *vi* **1** : to double up like a jackknife **2** : to turn or rise and form an angle of 90 degrees or less with each other — used especially of a pair of connected vehicles

jack•leg \'jak-ˌleg\ *adj* **1** : lacking skill or training : AMATEUR ⟨a *jackleg* carpenter⟩ **2** : designed as a temporary expedient : MAKESHIFT

jack•light \'jak-ˌlīt\ *n* : a light used especially in hunting or fishing at night

jack–of–all–trades \ˌjak-ə-'vȯl-ˌtrādz\ *n, pl* **jacks–of–all–trades** : a person who can do a satisfactory job at varied kinds of work : a versatile person

jack–o'–lan•tern \'jak-ə-ˌlant-ərn\ *n* **1** : IGNIS FATUUS **2** : a lantern made of a pumpkin cut to look like a human face

jack pine *n* : a North American pine with paired twisted needles that is used for pulp and box lumber

jack•pot \'jak-ˌpät\ *n* **1 a** : a large pot (as in poker) formed by the accumulation of stakes from previous play **b** (1) : a combination on a slot machine that wins a top prize or all the coins in the machine (2) : the sum so won **2** : an impressive often unexpected success or reward

jack•rab•bit \-ˌrab-ət\ *n* : any of several large hares of western North America with long ears and long hind legs [*jackass* + *rabbit*; from its long ears]

jackrabbit

jack•screw \-ˌskrü\ *n* : a screw-operated jack for lifting or for exerting pressure

Jack•so•ni•an \jak-'sō-nē-ən\ *adj* : of, relating to, or characteristic of Andrew Jackson or his political principles or policies — **Jacksonian** *n*

jack•stone \'jak-ˌstōn\ *n* **1** : JACK 4c(1) **2** *pl* : JACK 4c(2)

jack•straw \-ˌstrȯ\ *n* **1** : one of the pieces used in the game jackstraws **2** *pl* : a game in which a set of straws or thin strips are dropped in a heap with each player in turn trying to remove one at a time without disturbing the rest

jack–tar \-'tär\ *n, often cap* : SAILOR 1a

Jac•o•be•an \ˌjak-ə-'bē-ən\ *adj* : of, relating to, or characteristic of James I of England or his age [New Latin *Jacobus* "James"] — **Jacobean** *n*

Jac•o•bin \'jak-ə-bən\ *n* : a member of a radical political group advocating egalitarian democracy and engaging in terrorist activities during the French Revolution of 1789 [French, from *Jacobin* "Dominican" (from Late Latin *Jacobus* "James"; from the location of the first Dominican convent in Paris in the street of Saint James — *Rue Saint Jacques*); from the group's having been founded in a former Dominican convent] — **Jac•o•bin•ism** \-bə-ˌniz-əm\ *n*

Jac•o•bite \ˈjak-ə-ˌbīt\ *n* **:** a partisan of James II of England or of the Stuarts after the revolution of 1688 — **Jac•o•bit•i•cal** \ˌjak-ə-ˈbit-i-kəl\ *adj* — **Jac•o•bit•ism** \ˈjak-ə-ˌbīt-ˌiz-əm\ *n*

Jacob's ladder *n* **:** a ship's ladder of rope or chain with wooden or iron steps [from the ladder seen in a dream by Jacob in Genesis 28:12]

jac•quard \ˈjak-ˌärd\ *n, often cap* **:** a fabric of intricate variegated weave or pattern [Joseph *Jacquard*, died 1834, French inventor]

[1]jade \ˈjād\ *n* **1 :** a broken-down, vicious, or worthless horse **2 :** a disreputable woman [Middle English]

△ **origin** The English word *jade* that is used for a horse or a woman is not related to the name of the green stone jade. The origin of the earlier *jade* is uncertain. It was first used in Middle English to mean "a broken-down horse". Later the word for a worthless horse was often applied to a woman (or, very rarely, to a man) considered worthless. Now a *jade* is more often a disreputable woman than a broken-down horse.

Jaded, meaning "worn out", is also derived from the equine *jade*. Originally, to *jade* a horse was to make a *jade* of it, to wear it out or break it down by overwork or abuse. It was not long before people, too, could be called *jaded*.

[2]jade *vb* **1 a :** to wear out by overwork or abuse **b :** to tire by tedious tasks **2 :** to become weary

[3]jade *n* **:** a tough dense usually green gemstone that takes a high polish [French, from obsolete Spanish (*piedra de la*) *ijada*, literally "loin stone"]

△ **origin** Gemstones were once believed to have magical and medicinal properties. Jade was supposed to be especially effective in combating kidney disorders. The 16th century Spanish, who brought jade home with them from the New World, named the powerful green stone *piedra de la ijada*, "loin stone". Not only in Spain but throughout western Europe jade became popular both as an ornament and as a cure or preventive for internal problems. In England jade was formerly called *spleen stone*, but this term has not survived. Our modern word *jade* was borrowed from the French, who had so transformed Spanish *ijada*.

jad•ed *adj* **1 :** very fatigued **2 :** dulled by overindulgence — **jad•ed•ly** *adv* — **jad•ed•ness** *n*

jade green *n* **:** a light bluish green

jae•ger \ˈyā-gər\ *n* **:** any of several large dark-colored birds of northern seas that harass weaker birds and steal their prey [German *jäger* "hunter"]

[1]jag \ˈjag\ *vb* **jagged** \ˈjagd\; **jag•ging :** to make ragged **:** NOTCH [Middle English *jaggen*]

[2]jag *n* **:** a sharp projecting part **:** BARB

[3]jag *n* **1 :** a small load (as of hay) **2 :** SPREE ⟨a crying *jag*⟩ ⟨drinking *jags*⟩ [origin unknown]

jag•ged \ˈjag-əd\ *adj* **:** sharply notched **:** ROUGH ⟨a *jagged* edge⟩ — **jag•ged•ly** *adv* — **jag•ged•ness** *n*

jag•uar \ˈjag-ˌwär, ˈjag-yə-ˌwär\ *n* **:** a large cat of tropical America that is larger and stockier than the leopard and is brownish yellow or buff with black spots [Spanish *yaguar* and Portuguese *jaguar*, from Tupi *jaguara*]

jaguar

jag•ua•run•di \ˌzhag-wə-ˈrən-dē\ *n* **:** a slender long-tailed short-legged grayish wildcat of Central and South America [American Spanish and Portuguese, from Tupi]

jai alai \ˈhī-ˌlī, ˌhī-ə-ˈlī\ **:** a court game played by two or four players in which the ball is caught and hurled against the front wall with a long curved wicker basket strapped to the hand [Spanish, from Basque, from *jai* "festival" + *alai* "merry"]

[1]jail \ˈjāl\ *n* **:** PRISON; *esp* **:** a building for the temporary custody of prisoners [Old French *jaiole*, from Late Latin *caveola* "little cage", from Latin *cavea* "cage"]

△ **origin** *Jail* and *cage*, similar in meaning but quite different in form, are actually etymologically related. Both are descendants of Latin *cavea*, which means "cavity" or "cage". In medieval France the direct descendant of Latin *cavea* appeared in a variety of forms. Among these variants were *gave, gage, cage*, and *jaie*. It was *cage* that survived into modern French, and it was *cage* that was borrowed into English. During the Late Latin period a diminutive of Latin *cavea* was formed. This diminutive, *caveola*, developed into Old French *jaole, jaiole*, and *geole*. This Old French word is the source of our British and American English variants *gaol* and *jail*.

[2]jail *vt* **:** to confine in or as if in a jail

jail•bird \ˈjāl-ˌbərd\ *n* **:** a person confined in jail; *esp* **:** an habitual criminal

jail•break \-ˌbrāk\ *n* **:** an escape from jail

jail•er *or* **jail•or** \ˈjā-lər\ *n* **:** the keeper of a jail

Jain \ˈjīn\ *or* **Jai•na** \ˈjī-nə\ *n* **:** an adherent of Jainism [Hindi *Jain*, from Sanskrit *jaina*]

Jain•ism \ˈjī-ˌniz-əm\ *n* **:** a religion of India originating in the 6th century B.C. and teaching liberation of the soul by right knowledge, right faith, and right conduct

jal•ap \ˈjal-əp, ˈjäl-\ *n* **:** a purgative tuberous root obtained especially from a Mexican plant related to the morning glory; *also* **:** a drug prepared from this [French, from Spanish *jalapa*, from *Jalapa*, Mexico]

ja•lopy \jə-ˈläp-ē\ *n, pl* **-lop•ies :** a dilapidated old automobile or airplane [origin unknown]

jal•ou•sie \ˈjal-ə-sē\ *n* **1 :** a blind with adjustable horizontal slats for admitting light and air while excluding sun and rain **2 :** a window made of adjustable glass louvers that control ventilation [French, literally, "jealousy"]

[1]jam \ˈjam\ *vb* **jammed; jam•ming 1 a :** to press into a close or tight position ⟨*jam* a hat on⟩ **b :** to cause to be wedged so as to be unworkable ⟨*jam* the typewriter keys⟩ **c :** to block passage of **:** OBSTRUCT **d :** to fill full or to excess **:** PACK **2 :** to push forcibly; *esp* **:** to apply the brakes suddenly with full force **3 :** to squeeze or crush painfully ⟨*jammed* a finger⟩ **4 :** to make unintelligible by sending out interfering signals or messages ⟨*jam* a radio program⟩ **5 :** to become unworkable through the jamming of a movable part ⟨the gun *jammed*⟩ **6 :** to force one's way into a restricted space [perhaps imitative] — **jam•mer** *n*

[2]jam *n* **1 a :** an act or instance of jamming **b :** a crowded mass that impedes or blocks ⟨a traffic *jam*⟩ **2 :** a difficult state of affairs

[3]jam *n* **:** a spread made by boiling fruit and sugar to a thick consistency [probably from [1]*jam*]

jamb \ˈjam\ *n* **:** an upright piece forming the side of an opening (as of a door) [Middle French *jambe*, literally, "leg", from Late Latin *gamba*]

jam•ba•laya \ˌjəm-bə-ˈlī-ə\ *n* **:** rice cooked with ham, sausage, chicken, shrimp, or oysters and seasoned with herbs [Louisiana French, from Provençal *jambalaia* "stew of rice and fowl"]

jam•bo•ree \ˌjam-bə-ˈrē\ *n* **1 :** a large festive gathering **2 :** a national or international camping assembly of boy scouts [origin unknown]

James \ˈjāmz\ *n* — see BIBLE table

jam session *n* **:** an informal performance by jazz musicians characterized by group improvisation [[2]*jam*]

[1]jan•gle \ˈjang-gəl\ *vb* **jan•gled; jan•gling** \-gə-ling, -gling\ **1 :** to quarrel verbally **2 :** to make or cause to make a harsh or discordant sound [Old French *jangler*, of Germanic origin] — **jan•gler** \-gə-lər, -glər\ *n*

[2]jangle *n* **1 :** noisy quarreling **2 :** discordant sound

jan•is•sary *or* **jan•i•zary** \ˈjan-ə-ˌser-ē, -ˌzer-\ *n, pl* **-sar•ies** *or* **-zar•ies** *often cap* **:** a soldier of a select corps of Turkish troops organized in the 14th century and abolished in 1826 [Italian *gianizzero*, from Turkish *yeniçeri*]

jan•i•tor \ˈjan-ət-ər\ *n* **1 :** DOORKEEPER **2 :** a person who has the care of a building [Latin, from *janua* "door", from *janus* "arch, gate"] — **jan•i•to•ri•al** \ˌjan-ə-ˈtōr-ē-əl, -ˈtȯr-\ *adj*

Jan•u•ary \ˈjan-yə-ˌwer-ē\ *n* **:** the 1st month of the year [Latin *Januarius*, from *Janus*, a Roman god]

[1]ja•pan \jə-ˈpan\ *n* **1 :** a varnish giving a hard brilliant surface coating **2 :** work varnished and figured in the Japanese manner [*Japan*, country of Asia]

[2]japan *vt* **ja•panned; ja•pan•ning :** to cover with or as if with a coat of japan

Jap•a•nese \ˌjap-ə-ˈnēz, -ˈnēs\ *n, pl* **Japanese 1 a :** a native or inhabitant of Japan **b :** a person of Japanese descent **2 :** the language of the Japanese — **Japanese** *adj*

Japanese beetle *n* **:** a small metallic green and brown scarab beetle introduced into America from Japan that as a grub feeds on roots and decaying vegetation and as an adult consumes foliage and fruits

Japanese iris *n* : any of various beardless garden irises with very large showy flowers

Japanese persimmon *n* : an Asian persimmon widely grown for its large edible fruits

Japanese quince *n* : a hardy Chinese ornamental shrub of the rose family with scarlet flowers

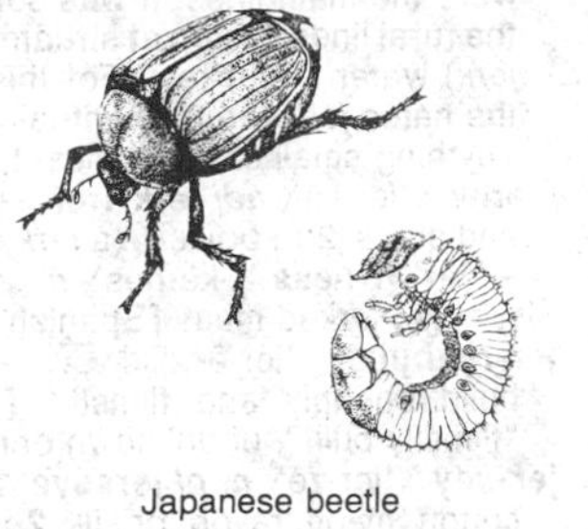
Japanese beetle

[1]**jape** \ˈjāp\ *vt* : to make mocking fun of [Middle English *japen*] — **jap•er** \ˈjā-pər\ *n* — **jap•ery** \ˈjā-pə-rē, -prē\ *n*

[2]**jape** *n* : JEST 2, GIBE

ja•pon•i•ca \jə-ˈpän-i-kə\ *n* : JAPANESE QUINCE [New Latin, from *Japonicus* "Japanese", from *Japonia* "Japan"]

[1]**jar** \ˈjär\ *vb* **jarred**; **jar•ring** **1 a** : to make a harsh or discordant sound **b** : to affect disagreeably **c** : to be out of harmony; *esp* : BICKER **d** : to have a harsh or disagreeable effect **2** : to undergo severe vibration **3** : to make unstable : SHAKE [probably imitative]

[2]**jar** *n* **1** : a harsh grating sound **2** : CONFLICT 2, DISCORD **3** : JOLT 1 **4** : an unsettling shock

[3]**jar** *n* **1** : a widemouthed container usually of earthenware or glass **2** : the quantity that a jar will hold [Middle French *jarre*, from Provençal *jarra*, from Arabic *jarrah* "earthen water vessel"] — **jar•ful** \-ˌfu̇l\ *n*

jar•di•niere \ˌjärd-n-ˈiər\ *n* : an ornamental stand or receptacle for potted plants or flowers [French *jardinière*, literally, "female gardener"]

jar•gon \ˈjär-gən, -ˌgän\ *n* **1 a** : confused unintelligible language : GIBBERISH **b** : a hybrid language or dialect used for communication between peoples of different speech **2** : the technical or specialized vocabulary of a particular profession or group **3** : obscure and often pretentiously wordy language [Middle French] **syn** see DIALECT

jas•mine \ˈjaz-mən\ *or* **jes•sa•mine** \ˈjes-mən, -ə-mən\ *n* : any of numerous often climbing shrubs of the olive family with extremely fragrant flowers; *also* : any of various plants noted for sweet-scented flowers — compare YELLOW JESSAMINE [French *jasmin*, from Arabic *yāsamīn*, from Persian]

jas•per \ˈjas-pər\ *n* : an opaque fine-grained usually red, yellow, or brown quartz; *esp* : green chalcedony [Middle French *jaspre*, from Latin *jaspis*, from Greek *iaspis*, of Semitic origin] — **jas•pery** \-pə-rē\ *adj*

ja•to unit \ˈjāt-ō-\ *n* : a special rocket engine to help an airplane take off [*j*et-*a*ssisted *t*ake*o*ff]

jaun•dice \ˈjȯn-dəs, ˈjän-\ *n* **1** : yellowish discoloration of the skin, tissues, and body fluids caused by the deposition of bile pigments; *also* : a disease or abnormal condition marked by jaundice **2** : a state or attitude marked by satiety, distaste, or hostility [Middle French *jaunisse*, from *jaune* "yellow", derived from Latin *galbus*]

jaun•diced \-dəst\ *adj* **1** : affected with or as if with jaundice **2** : showing or influenced by envy, distaste, or hostility

jaunt \ˈjȯnt, ˈjänt\ *n* : a short trip taken for pleasure [origin unknown] — **jaunt** *vi*

jaun•ty \ˈjȯnt-ē, ˈjänt-\ *adj* **jaun•ti•er**; **-est** : sprightly in manner or appearance : LIVELY [French *gentil* "genteel"] — **jaun•ti•ly** \ˈjȯnt-l-ē, ˈjänt-\ *adv* — **jaun•ti•ness** \ˈjȯnt-ē-nəs, ˈjänt-\ *n*

Ja•va man \ˌjäv-ə-, ˌjav-\ *n* : PITHECANTHROPUS

Ja•va•nese \ˌjav-ə-ˈnēz, ˌjäv-, -ˈnēs\ *n* **1** : a member of an Indonesian people inhabiting the island of Java **2** : an Austronesian language of the Javanese people — **Javanese** *adj*

jav•e•lin \ˈjav-lən, -ə-lən\ *n* **1** : a light spear **2** : a slender usually metal shaft thrown for distance in an athletic field event [Middle French *javeline*, of Celtic origin]

[1]**jaw** \ˈjȯ\ *n* **1 a** : either of two cartilaginous or bony structures that support the soft parts enclosing the mouth and usually bear teeth on their oral margin — compare MANDIBLE 1a, MAXILLA 1 **b** : the structures including the jaws and soft parts that make up the walls of the mouth and that serve to open and close it — usually used in pl. **c** : any of various organs of invertebrates that perform the function of the vertebrate jaws **2** : something resembling the jaw of an animal in form or action ⟨the *jaws* of a mountain pass⟩; *esp* : one of a set of opposing parts that open and close for holding or crushing something between them ⟨the *jaws* of a vise⟩ [Middle English] — **jawed** \ˈjȯd\ *adj*

[2]**jaw** *vi* : to talk in a scolding or boring way

jaw•bone \ˈjȯ-ˈbōn, -ˌbōn\ *n* : one of the bones of an animal's jaw; *esp* : MANDIBLE 1a

jaw•break•er \-ˌbrā-kər\ *n* **1** : a word difficult to pronounce **2** : a round hard candy

jaw•less fish \ˌjȯ-ləs-\ *n* : CYCLOSTOME

jaw•line \ˈjȯ-ˌlīn\ *n* : the outline of the lower jaw

jay \ˈjā\ *n* : any of several noisy birds of the crow family that are smaller and usually more brightly colored than a crow [Middle French *jai*, from Latin *gaius*]

Jay•cee \ˈjā-ˈsē\ *n* : a member of a junior chamber of commerce [*j*unior *c*hamber]

jay•vee \ˈjā-ˈvē\ *n* **1** : JUNIOR VARSITY **2** : a member of a junior varsity team [*j*unior *v*arsity]

jay•walk \ˈjā-ˌwȯk\ *vi* : to cross a street carelessly without heeding traffic regulations and signals — **jay•walk•er** *n*

[1]**jazz** \ˈjaz\ *vt* **1** : ENLIVEN — usually used with *up* **2** : to play in the manner of jazz [English slang *jazz* "to copulate with", of unknown origin]

[2]**jazz** *n* **1** : music of American origin developed mainly from blues and ragtime and marked especially by solo instrumental improvisation **2** : empty talk : HUMBUG **3** : STUFF 3b

jazzy \ˈjaz-ē\ *adj* **jazz•i•er**; **-est** **1** : having the characteristics of jazz **2** : marked by unrestraint, animation, or flashiness — **jazz•i•ly** \ˈjaz-ə-lē\ *adv* — **jazz•i•ness** \ˈjaz-ē-nəs\ *n*

jeal•ous \ˈjel-əs\ *adj* **1 a** : intolerant of rivalry or unfaithfulness **b** : suspicious that a person one loves is not faithful **2** : hostile toward a rival or one believed to enjoy an advantage : ENVIOUS **3** : careful in guarding a right or possession ⟨their *jealous* love of freedom⟩ [Old French *jelous*, from Late Latin *zelus* "zeal"] **syn** see ENVIOUS — **jeal•ous•ly** *adv*

jeal•ou•sy \ˈjel-ə-sē\ *n, pl* **-sies** **1** : a jealous disposition, attitude, or feeling **2** : zealous vigilance

jean \ˈjēn\ *n* **1** : a durable twilled cotton cloth used especially for sportswear and work clothes **2** *pl* : close-fitting pants made of jean, denim, or corduroy [short for *jean fustian*, from Middle English *Gene*, *Jene* "Genoa, Italy" + *fustian*]

jeep \ˈjēp\ *n* : a small general-purpose motor vehicle with ¼-ton capacity and four-wheel drive used by the United States Army in World War II [alteration of *gee pee*, from *g*eneral-*p*urpose]

△ **origin** In 1937 work was begun by several American manufacturers to develop an all-purpose vehicle for military use. When the vehicle was ready, it was apparently designated *g.p.* for *general purpose*. The pronunciation of the letters *g.p.* became shortened to one syllable and the spelling *jeep* was adopted. For a similar alteration, compare the spelling and pronunciation of *veep*, from *v.p.*, an abbreviation of *vice-president*.

Jeep *trademark* — used for a civilian automotive vehicle

jee•pers \ˈjē-pərz\ *interj* — used as a mild oath or to express surprise [euphemism for *Jesus*]

[1]**jeer** \ˈjiər\ *vb* **1** : to speak or cry out in derision or mockery **2** : DERIDE, MOCK ⟨the crowd *jeered* the speaker⟩ [origin unknown] **syn** see SCOFF — **jeer•er** \ˈjir-ər\ *n* — **jeer•ing•ly** \-ing-lē\ *adv*

[2]**jeer** *n* : a jeering remark or sound : TAUNT

Jef•fer•so•ni•an \ˌjef-ər-ˈsō-nē-ən\ *adj* : of, relating to, or characteristic of Thomas Jefferson or his political principles — **Jeffersonian** *n*

Je•ho•vah \ji-ˈhō-və\ *n* : GOD 1 [New Latin, from Hebrew *Yahweh*]

Jehovah's Witness *n* : a member of a group that by distributing literature and by personal evangelism witness to beliefs in the theocratic rule of God, the sinfulness of organized religions and governments, and an approaching millennium

je•june \ji-ˈjün\ *adj* **1** : lacking nutritive value ⟨*jejune* diets⟩ **2** : lacking interest or significance : DULL **3** : lacking maturity : CHILDISH ⟨*jejune* remarks⟩ [Latin *jejunus*] — **je•june•ly** *adv* — **je•june•ness** \-ˈjün-nəs\ *n*

je•ju•num \ji-ˈjü-nəm\ *n* : the section of the small intestine between the duodenum and the ileum [Latin, from *jejunus* "jejune"] — **je•ju•nal** \-ˈjün-l\ *adj*

\ə\ **abut**	\au̇\ **out**	\i\ **tip**	\ȯ\ **saw**	\u̇\ **foot**
\ər\ **further**	\ch\ **chin**	\ī\ **life**	\ȯi\ **coin**	\y\ **yet**
\a\ **mat**	\e\ **pet**	\j\ **job**	\th\ **thin**	\yü\ **few**
\ā\ **take**	\ē\ **easy**	\ng\ **sing**	\th\ **this**	\yu̇\ **cure**
\ä\ **cot, cart**	\g\ **go**	\ō\ **bone**	\ü\ **food**	\zh\ **vision**

jell \ˈjel\ *vb* **1 :** to make or become jelly **2 :** to take shape **:** FORM ⟨an idea began to *jell* in my mind⟩ [back-formation from *jelly*]

Jell–O \ˈjel-ō\ *trademark* — used for a fruit-flavored gelatin dessert

[1]**jel•ly** \ˈjel-ē\ *n, pl* **jellies 1 :** a food with a soft elastic consistency due usually to gelatin or pectin; *esp* **:** a fruit product made by boiling sugar and the juice of fruit **2 :** a substance resembling jelly in consistency [Middle French *gelee,* from *geler* "to freeze, congeal", from Latin *gelare*] — **jel•ly•like** \-ē-ˌlīk\ *adj*

[2]**jelly** *vb* **jel•lied; jel•ly•ing 1 :** JELL 1 **2 :** to set in jelly ⟨*jellied* salmon⟩

jelly bean *n* **:** a sugar-glazed bean-shaped candy

jel•ly•fish \ˈjel-ē-ˌfish\ *n* **1 :** a free-swimming sexually-reproducing coelenterate animal with a gelatinous, disk-shaped, and usually nearly transparent body; *also* **:** any of various somewhat similar sea animals (as a ctenophore) **2 :** a weak spineless person

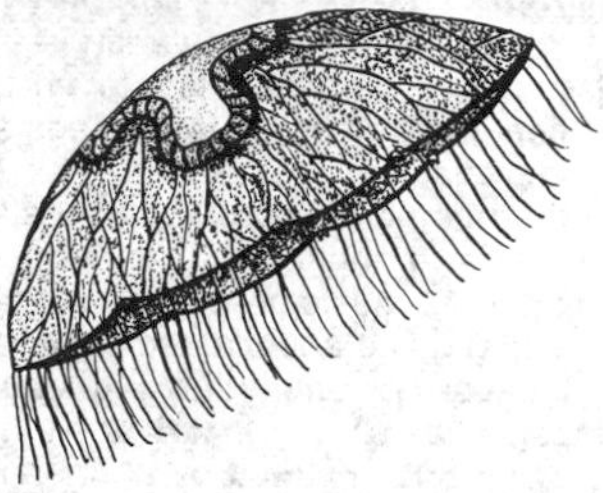

jellyfish 1

jelly roll *n* **:** a thin sheet of sponge cake spread with jelly and rolled up

jen•net \ˈjen-ət\ *n* **1 :** a small Spanish horse **2 :** a female donkey [Middle French *genet,* from Catalan]

jen•ny \ˈjen-ē\ *n, pl* **jennies 1 a :** a female bird ⟨*jenny* wren⟩ **b :** a female donkey **2 :** SPINNING JENNY [from the name *Jenny*]

jeop•ar•dize \ˈjep-ər-ˌdīz\ *vt* **:** to expose to danger **:** IMPERIL

jeop•ar•dy \ˈjep-ərd-ē\ *n* **1 :** exposure to death, loss, or injury **:** DANGER **2 :** the danger of conviction and punishment that an accused person is subjected to when on trial for a criminal offense [Old French *jeu parti* "alternative", literally, "divided game"]

△ **origin** In French *jeu parti* means literally "divided game". In Old French, the major criterion for a *jeu parti* was the involvement of alternative possibilities or opposed viewpoints. A *jeu parti* could be a poem in dialogue form representing the discussion of problems. Or it could be a situation in a game like chess in which the relative worth of alternative plays is uncertain. The word was borrowed into English in this sense. Any position that provides equal chances of success and of failure can be described in terms of a similar position in chess and called a *jeopardy.* But the word was early used in its present extended sense, "risk or danger, with a greater probability of losing than of winning".

jer•boa \jər-ˈbō-ə\ *n* **:** any of several social nocturnal Old World jumping rodents with long hind legs and long tail [Arabic *yarbū'*]

jerboa

Jer•e•mi•ah \ˌjer-ə-ˈmī-ə\ *n* — see BIBLE table

Jer•e•mi•as \-ˈmī-əs\ *n* — see BIBLE table

[1]**jerk** \ˈjərk\ *vb* **1 :** to give a sharp quick push, pull, or twist to **2 a :** to make or move in jerks **:** move with a jerk **3 :** to mix and dispense (as sodas) [probably from Middle English *yerken* "to bind tightly"] — **jerk•er** *n*

[2]**jerk** *n* **1 a :** a single quick motion **b :** a jolting, bouncing, or thrusting motion **2 a :** an involuntary muscular movement or spasm due to reflex action **b** *pl* **:** involuntary twitchings due to nervous excitement **3 :** FOOL 1

[3]**jerk** *vt* **:** to cut (meat) into long strips and dry in the sun [back-formation from [2]*jerky*]

jer•kin \ˈjər-kən\ *n* **:** a close-fitting hip-length sleeveless jacket [origin unknown]

jerk•wa•ter \ˈjər-ˌkwȯt-ər, -ˌkwät-\ *adj* **:** being small and remote ⟨*jerkwater* towns⟩ [earlier *jerkwater* "rural train"]

△ **origin** In the early days of the steam locomotive many rural railroad lines were not so well-provided with water tanks as were the main lines. It was sometimes necessary for trains on the rural lines to stop at streams while the crew went to fetch (or *jerk*) water in buckets. For this reason rural trains were given the name *jerkwater.* Eventually the term came to be applied to anything small or insignificant.

[1]**jerky** \ˈjər-kē\ *adj* **jerk•i•er; -est 1 :** moving by sudden starts and stops **2 :** FOOLISH ⟨a *jerky* idea⟩ — **jerk•i•ly** \-kə-lē\ *adv* — **jerk•i•ness** \-kē-nəs\ *n*

[2]**jerky** *n* **:** jerked meat [Spanish *charqui*]

jer•ry–build \ˈjer-ē-ˌbild\ *vt* **–built** \-ˌbilt\; **–build•ing :** to build cheaply and flimsily [back-formation from *jerry-built* "flimsily built", of unknown origin] — **jer•ry–build•er** *n*

jer•sey \ˈjər-zē\ *n, pl* **jerseys 1 :** a plain knitted fabric of wool, cotton, nylon, rayon, or silk **2 :** any of various close-fitting knitted garments for the upper body **3 :** any of a breed of small usually fawn-colored dairy cattle noted for their rich milk [*Jersey,* one of the Channel islands]

Je•ru•sa•lem artichoke \jə-ˌrü-sə-ləm-, -sləm-; -ˌrüz-ləm-, -ələm-\ *n* **:** a perennial American sunflower grown for its edible tubers [*Jerusalem* by folk etymology from Italian *girasole*]

Jerusalem cherry *n* **:** a plant of the potato family grown as a houseplant for its showy orange or red berries [*Jerusalem,* Israel]

jess \ˈjes\ *n* **:** a strap placed on a leg of a falcon or hawk for attachment of a leash [Middle French *gies,* derived from *jeter* "to throw"]

jes•sa•mine *variant of* JASMINE

[1]**jest** \ˈjest\ *n* **1 a :** an act intended to cause laughter **:** PRANK **b :** a comic incident **2 :** a witty remark **3 a :** a frivolous mood or manner ⟨spoken in *jest*⟩ **b :** a state of gaiety and merriment **4 :** [3]BUTT 2, LAUGHINGSTOCK [Old French *geste* "exploit, tale", from Latin *gesta* "exploits", from *gerere* "to carry, perform"]

• **syn** JEST, JOKE, QUIP, WISECRACK mean something said for the purpose of evoking laughter. JEST applies to an utterance not seriously intended whether sarcastic, ironic, witty, or merely playful; JOKE may apply to an act as well as an utterance and suggests no intent to hurt feelings; QUIP suggests a quick, light, neatly phrased remark; WISECRACK stresses cleverness of phrasing and may suggest unfeeling flippancy.

[2]**jest** *vi* **1 :** to utter taunts **:** GIBE **2 :** to speak or act without seriousness **3 :** JOKE 1

jest•er \ˈjes-tər\ *n* **1 :** FOOL 2a ⟨court *jester*⟩ **2 :** one given to jests

Je•su•it \ˈjezh-wət, -ə-wət, ˈjez-\ *n* **:** a member of the Roman Catholic Society of Jesus founded by Saint Ignatius of Loyola in 1534 and devoted to missionary and educational work — **je•su•it•ic** \ˌjezh-ə-ˈwit-ik, ˌjez-\ *adj, often cap* — **je•su•it•i•cal•ly** \-i-kə-lē, -klē\ *adv, often cap*

Je•sus \ˈjē-zəs, -zəz\ *n* **:** the founder of the Christian religion — called also *Jesus Christ* [Late Latin, from Greek *Iēsous,* from Hebrew *Yēshūa'*]

[1]**jet** \ˈjet\ *n* **1 :** a dense velvet-black coal that takes a good polish and is often used for jewelry **2 :** an intense black [Middle French *jaiet,* from Latin *gagates,* from Greek *gagatēs,* from *Gagas,* town and river in Asia Minor]

[2]**jet** *vb* **jet•ted; jet•ting :** to spout or emit in a stream **:** SPURT [Middle French *jeter,* literally, "to throw", from Latin *jactare,* from *jactus,* past participle of *jacere* "to throw"]

[3]**jet** *n* **1 a :** a forceful rush of liquid, gas, or vapor through a narrow opening or a nozzle **b :** a nozzle for a jet of fluid (as gas or water) **2 a :** JET ENGINE **b :** JET AIRPLANE

[4]**jet** *vi* **jet•ted; jet•ting :** to travel by jet airplane

jet airplane *n* **:** an airplane powered by a jet engine — called also *jet plane*

jet engine *n* **:** an engine that produces motion as a result of the rearward discharge of a jet of fluid; *esp* **:** an airplane engine having one or more exhaust nozzles for discharging a jet of heated air and exhaust gases

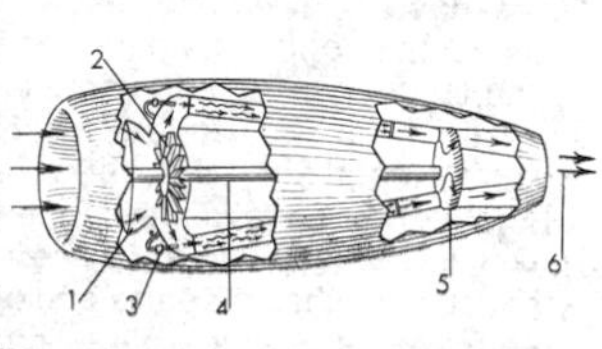

jet engine: *1* air intake, *2* compressor, *3* fuel injection, *4* drive shaft, *5* turbine, *6* exhaust

jet–pro•pelled \ˌjet-prə-ˈpeld\ *adj* **:** propelled by a jet engine

jet propulsion *n* **:** propulsion of a body in a forward direction as a result of the rearward discharge of a jet of fluid;

esp : propulsion of an airplane by jet engines

jet·sam \'jet-səm\ *n* : goods thrown overboard to lighten a ship in distress [alteration of *jettison*]

jet set *n* : an international social group of wealthy people who frequent fashionable resorts — **jet–set·ter** \'jet-ˌset-ər\ *n*

jet stream *n* : a long narrow meandering current of high-speed winds blowing from a generally westerly direction several miles above the earth's surface

1jet·ti·son \'jet-ə-sən\ *n* : a voluntary sacrifice of cargo to lighten a ship's load in time of distress [Old French *getaison* "act of throwing", from Latin *jactatio,* from *jactare* "to throw"]

2jettison *vt* **1 a :** to throw (goods) overboard to lighten a ship in distress **b :** to drop from an airplane or spacecraft in flight **2 :** to cast away or aside : DISCARD — **jet·ti·son·able** \-sə-nə-bəl\ *adj*

jet·ty \'jet-ē\ *n, pl* **jetties 1 :** a pier built out into the water to influence the current or to protect a harbor **2 :** a landing wharf [Middle French *jetee,* from *jeter* "to throw"]

Jew \'jü\ *n* **1 a :** a member of the tribe of Judah **b :** ISRAELITE **2 :** a member of a nation existing in Palestine from the 6th century B.C. to the 1st century A.D. **3 a :** a person of Jewish descent **b :** one whose religion is Judaism [Old French *gyu,* from Latin *Judaeus,* from Greek *Ioudaios,* from Hebrew *Yĕhūdī,* from *Yĕhūdāh,* "Judah, Jewish kingdom"]

1jew·el \'jü-əl\ *n* **1 :** an ornament of precious metal set with stones or finished with enamel and worn as an accessory of dress **2 :** one that is highly esteemed **3 :** a precious stone : GEM **4 :** a bearing for a pivot in a watch made of a crystal, precious stone, or glass [Old French *juel,* from *jeu* "game, play", from Latin *jocus* "joke, game"]

2jewel *vt* **-eled** *or* **-elled**; **-el·ing** *or* **-el·ling :** to adorn or equip with jewels

jew·el·er *or* **jew·el·ler** \'jü-ə-lər\ *n* : a maker or repairer of or dealer in jewelry

jew·el·ry \'jü-əl-rē\ *n* : JEWELS; *esp* : objects of precious metal set with gems and worn for personal adornment

jew·el·weed \'jü-əl-ˌwēd\ *n* : IMPATIENS

Jew·ess \'jü-əs\ *n* : a Jewish girl or woman

jew·fish \'jü-ˌfish\ *n* : any of various large groupers that are usually dusky green or blackish, thickheaded, and rough-scaled

Jew·ish \'jü-ish\ *adj* : of, relating to, or characteristic of the Jews — **Jew·ish·ly** *adv* — **Jew·ish·ness** *n*

Jewish calendar *n* : a calendar in use among Jewish peoples that is reckoned from the year 3761 B.C. and dates in its present form from about A.D. 360

Jew·ry \'jùr-ē, 'jü-rē\ *n* **1** *pl* **Jewries :** a community of Jews **2 :** the Jewish people

Jew's harp *or* **Jews' harp** \'jüz-ˌhärp\ *n* : a small lyre-shaped instrument that when placed between the teeth gives tones from a metal tongue struck by the finger

1jib \'jib\ *n* : a triangular sail set on a stay forward of the mast or foremast [origin unknown]

2jib *vb* **jibbed**; **jib·bing 1 :** to shift or swing from one side of a ship to the other **2 :** to cause (a sail) to jib

3jib *n* **1 :** the projecting arm of a crane **2 :** a derrick boom [probably from *gibbet*]

jib·boom \'jib-'büm, -'üm\ *n* : a spar that serves as an extension of the bowsprit

1jibe *or* **gybe** \'jīb\ *vb* **1 :** to shift suddenly from one side to the other **2 :** to change the course of a ship when sailing with the wind aft so that the sail jibes **3 :** to cause (a sail) to jibe [perhaps from Dutch *gijben*]

2jibe *variant of* GIBE

3jibe *vi* : to be in accord : AGREE [origin unknown]

jif·fy \'jif-ē\ *n* : MOMENT 1, INSTANT ⟨in a *jiffy*⟩ [origin unknown]

1jig \'jig\ *n* **1 :** a lively springy dance in triple rhythm **2 :** TRICK, GAMBIT ⟨the *jig* is up⟩ **3 a :** any of several fishing lures that are jerked up and down and drawn through the water **b :** a device used to maintain mechanically the correct position of a piece of work and a tool or of parts of work during assembly [probably from Middle French *giguer* "to dance", from *gigue* "fiddle", of Germanic origin]

2jig *vb* **jigged**; **jig·ging 1 :** to dance a jig **2 :** to jerk up and down or to and fro **3 :** to fish or catch with a jig **4 :** to machine by means of a jig-controlled tool operation

1jig·ger \'jig-ər\ *n* **1 :** one that jigs or operates a jig **2 :** JIG 3a **3 :** the mast nearest the stern of a 4-masted ship **4 a :** a mechanical device; *esp* : one operating with a jerky reciprocating motion **b :** CONTRIVANCE 2, GADGET **5 :** a measure used in mixing drinks that usually holds 1½ ounces (about 44 milliliters)

2jigger *n* : CHIGGER [of African origin]

jig·gle \'jig-əl\ *vb* **jig·gled**; **jig·gling** \'jig-ling, -ə-ling\ **:** to move or cause to move with quick little jerks [derived from 2*jig*] — **jiggle** *n*

jig·saw \'jig-ˌsȯ\ *n* **1 :** a machine saw with a narrow blade that moves up and down for cutting curved and irregular lines or openwork patterns **2 :** SCROLL SAW

jigsaw puzzle *n* : a puzzle consisting of small irregular pieces fitted together to form a picture

1jilt \'jilt\ *n* : a person who jilts a lover [from earlier *jillet* "flirtatious girl", from the name *Jill*]

2jilt *vt* : to drop (one's lover) capriciously or unfeelingly

jim crow \'jim-'krō\ *n, often cap J & C* : ethnic discrimination especially against blacks by legal enforcement or traditional sanctions [from *Jim Crow,* stereotype Negro in a 19th century song-and-dance act] — **jim·crow·ism** \-ˌiz-əm\ *n, often cap J & C*

jim–dan·dy \'jim-'dan-dē\ *n* : something excellent of its kind

1jim·my \'jim-ē\ *n, pl* **jimmies :** a short crowbar [from *Jimmy,* nickname for *James*]

2jimmy *vt* **jim·mied**; **jim·my·ing :** to force open with or as if with a jimmy ⟨*jimmy* a window⟩

jim·son·weed \'jim-sən-ˌwēd, 'jimp-\ *n, often cap* : a poisonous coarse annual weed of the potato family with rank-smelling foliage and large white or violet trumpet-shaped flowers [alteration of *Jamestown weed,* from *Jamestown,* Virginia]

1jin·gle \'jing-gəl\ *vb* **jin·gled**; **jin·gling** \-gə-ling, -gling\ **1 :** to make or cause to make a light clinking sound **2 :** to rhyme or sound in a catchy repetitious manner [Middle English *ginglen*] — **jin·gler** \-gə-lər, -glər\ *n*

2jingle *n* **1 :** a light clinking sound **2 a :** a catchy repetition of sounds in a poem **b :** a short verse or song with such repetition — **jin·gly** \-gə-lē, -glē\ *adj*

1jin·go \'jing-gō\ *interj* — used as a mild oath usually in the phrase *by jingo* [probably euphemism for *Jesus*]

2jingo *n, pl* **jingoes :** one characterized by jingoism [from the fact that the phrase *by jingo* appeared in the refrain of a chauvinistic song] — **jin·go·ish** \-ish\ *adj*

jin·go·ism \'jing-gō-ˌiz-əm\ *n* : extreme chauvinism or nationalism marked especially by a belligerent foreign policy — **jin·go·ist** \-əst\ *n* — **jin·go·is·tic** \ˌjing-gō-'is-tik\ *adj* — **jin·go·is·ti·cal·ly** \-'is-ti-kə-lē, -klē\ *adv*

jin·ni \jə-'nē, 'jin-ē\ *or* **jinn** \'jin\ *n, pl* **jinn** *or* **jinns :** one of a class of spirits held by the Muslims to inhabit the earth, to assume various forms, and to exercise supernatural power [Arabic *jinnīy* "demon"]

jin·rik·i·sha \jin-'rik-ˌshȯ\ *n* : RICKSHA [Japanese, from *jin* "man" + *-riki* "strength" + *sha* "vehicle"]

1jinx \'jings, 'jingks\ *n* **1 :** one that brings bad luck **2 :** the state or spell of bad luck brought on by a jinx [probably from *jynx,* a kind of woodpecker; from the use of woodpeckers in witchcraft]

2jinx *vt* : to bring bad luck to

jit·ney \'jit-nē\ *n, pl* **jitneys 1** *slang* : NICKEL 2a **2 :** BUS 1a; *esp* : a small bus that carries passengers over a regular route according to a flexible schedule [origin unknown; sense 2 from the original 5-cent fare]

jit·ter·bug \'jit-ər-ˌbəg\ *n* **1 :** a dance in which couples swing, balance, and twirl in standardized patterns often with vigorous acrobatics **2 :** one who dances the jitterbug [from earlier *jitter* "to be nervous", of unknown origin] — **jitterbug** *vi*

jit·ters \'jit-ərz\ *n pl* : extreme nervousness — **jit·tery** \-ə-rē\ *adj*

jiu·jit·su *or* **jiu·jut·su** *variant of* JUJITSU

1jive \'jīv\ *n* **1 :** swing music or dancing performed to it **2 a :** glib, deceptive, or silly talk **b :** the jargon of hipsters **c :** a special jargon of difficult or slang terms [origin unknown]

2jive *vb* **1 :** KID 1 **2 :** to dance to or play jive

1job \'jäb\ *n* **1 a :** a piece of work; *esp* : one undertaken at a stated rate **b :** something produced by or as if by work **2 a**

: something done for private advantage **b** : a criminal act; *esp* : ROBBERY **3 a** : TASK, DUTY ⟨your *job* is to mow the lawn⟩ **b** : a position at which one regularly works for pay ⟨lost their *jobs*⟩ [perhaps from obsolete *job* "lump"] **syn** see TASK — **job•less** \-ləs\ *adj* — **job•less•ness** *n*

²job *vb* **jobbed**; **job•bing 1** : to do occasional pieces of work for hire **2** : to hire or let by the job

Job \'jōb\ *n* — see BIBLE table

job action *n* : a temporary action (as a slowdown) by workers as a protest and means of enforcing demands

job•ber \'jäb-ər\ *n* **1** : one that buys goods and sells them to other dealers (as retailers) : MIDDLEMAN **2** : one that works by the job

job•hold•er \'jäb-ˌhōl-dər\ *n* : one having a regular job

job lot *n* **1** : a miscellaneous collection of goods for sale as a lot usually to a retailer **2** : a miscellaneous and often inferior collection or group

Job's tears \'jōbz-\ *n* : an Asian grass with large hard pearly white seeds often used as beads

¹jock \'jäk\ *n* **1** : JOCKEY 1 **2** : DISC JOCKEY

²jock *n* **1** : ATHLETIC SUPPORTER **2** : ATHLETE [short for earlier *jockstrap*]

¹jock•ey \'jäk-ē\ *n, pl* **jockeys 1** : one who rides a horse especially as a professional in a race **2** : OPERATOR 1a [*Jockey,* Scottish nickname for *John*]

²jockey *vb* **jock•eyed**; **jock•ey•ing 1** : to ride (a horse) as a jockey **2** : to move or maneuver skillfully ⟨*jockey* a truck into a lot⟩ ⟨*jockey* for power⟩ **3** : FINESSE 2a, OUTWIT

jo•cose \jō-'kōs\ *adj* **1** : given to joking : MERRY **2** : characterized by joking : HUMOROUS [Latin *jocosus,* from *jocus* "joke, sport"] — **jo•cose•ly** *adv* — **jo•cose•ness** *n*

joc•u•lar \'jäk-yə-lər\ *adj* **1** : JOCOSE 1 **2** : said or done in jest : PLAYFUL [Latin *jocularis,* from *joculus* "little jest", from *jocus* "joke"] — **joc•u•lar•i•ty** \ˌjäk-yə-'lar-ət-ē\ *n* — **joc•u•lar•ly** *adv*

joc•und \'jäk-ənd *also* 'jōk-ənd\ *adj* : GAY 1, MERRY [Late Latin *jocundus* "pleasant, agreeable", from Latin *jucundus,* from *juvare* "to help"] — **joc•und•ly** *adv*

jodh•pur \'jäd-pər\ *n* **1** *pl* : riding breeches cut full through the hips and close-fitting from knee to ankle **2** : an ankle-high boot fastened with a strap that is buckled at the side [*Jodhpur,* India]

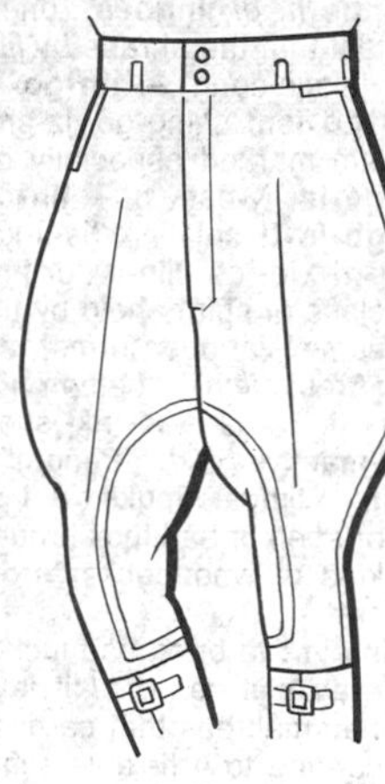

jodhpur 1

Jo•el \'jō-əl\ *n* — see BIBLE table

¹jog \'jäg\ *vb* **jogged**; **jog•ging 1** : to give a slight shake or push to : NUDGE **2** : STIR 5 ⟨*jog* one's memory⟩ **3** : to move up and down or about with a short heavy motion **4 a** : to go or cause to go at a jog **b** : to run at a slow pace especially for exercise **c** : to go at a slow or monotonous pace : TRUDGE [probably from Middle English *shoggen*] — **jog•ger** *n*

²jog *n* **1** : a slight shake : PUSH **2 a** : a jogging movement, pace, or trip **b** : a horse's slow gait with marked beats

³jog *n* **1** : a projecting or retreating part (as of a line or surface) **2** : a brief abrupt change in direction [probably alteration of ²*jag*]

¹jog•gle \'jäg-əl\ *vb* **jog•gled**; **jog•gling** \'jäg-ling, -ə-ling\ **1** : to shake slightly **2** : to move shakily or jerkily [derived from ¹*jog*] — **jog•gler** \'jäg-lər, -ə-lər\ *n*

²joggle *n* : ²JOG 2a

John \'jän\ *n* — see BIBLE table

john•boat \'jän-ˌbōt\ *n* : a narrow flat-bottomed square-ended boat propelled by a pole or paddle and used on inland waterways [from the name *John*]

John Bull \'jän-'bu̇l\ *n* **1** : the English nation personified : the English people **2** : a typical Englishman [*John Bull,* character typifying the English nation in *The History of John Bull* (1712) by John Arbuthnot, died 1735, Scottish physician and writer]

John Doe \-'dō\ *n* **1** : a party to legal proceedings whose true name is unknown **2** : MAN IN THE STREET

John Do•ry \-'dōr-ē, -'dȯr-\ *n, pl* **John Dories** : a yellow to olive marine food fish with a dark spot on each side [earlier *dory,* from Middle French *doree,* literally, "gilded one"]

John Han•cock \-'han-ˌkäk\ *n* : an autograph signature [from the prominence of John Hancock's signature on the Declaration of Independence]

john•ny \'jän-ē\ *n, pl* **johnnies** : a short gown opening in the back that is used by hospital bed patients [from *Johnny,* nickname for *John*]

john•ny•cake \'jän-ē-ˌkāk\ *n* : a bread made with cornmeal

John•ny–come–late•ly \ˌjän-ē-kəm-'lāt-lē\ *n, pl* **Johnny–come–latelies** *or* **Johnnies–come–lately 1** : a late or recent arrival **2** : UPSTART

John•ny–jump–up \ˌjän-ē-'jəm-ˌpəp\ *n* : WILD PANSY; *also* : any of various other small-flowered pansies or violets

John•ny–on–the–spot \ˌjän-ē-ˌȯn-t͟hə-'spät, -ē-ˌän-\ *n* : one that is on hand and ready to act whenever needed

Johnny Reb \-'reb\ *n* : a Confederate soldier [*reb,* short for *rebel*]

John•so•ni•an \jän-'sō-nē-ən\ *adj* : of, relating to, or characteristic of Samuel Johnson or his writings

joie de vi•vre \ˌzhwäd-ə-'vēvr\ *n* : keen enjoyment of life [French, literally, "joy of living"]

¹join \'jȯin\ *vb* **1 a** : to bring or fasten together in close physical contact ⟨*join* hands⟩ **b** : to connect (as points) by a line **2** : to come or bring into close associaton ⟨*join* a club⟩ ⟨*joined* them in marriage⟩ **3** : to come into the company of ⟨*join* friends for lunch⟩ **4 a** : to come together so as to be connected ⟨nouns *join* to form compounds⟩ **b** : ADJOIN ⟨the two estates *join*⟩ **5** : to take part in a collective activity ⟨*join* in singing⟩ [Old French *joindre,* from Latin *jungere*] — **join•able** \-ə-bəl\ *adj*

• **syn** JOIN, COMBINE, UNITE, CONNECT mean to bring or come together in some kind of union. JOIN suggests a physical contact or conjunction between two or more things ⟨*join* the ends with glue⟩ ⟨*joined* forces in a common purpose to win⟩ COMBINE implies some merging or mingling with corresponding loss of identity of each unit; UNITE implies a greater loss of separate identity; CONNECT suggests a loose or external attachment with little or no loss of separate identity.

²join *n* : a point of joining : JOINT

join•er \'jȯi-nər\ *n* : one that joins: as **a** : a person whose craft is to construct articles by joining pieces of wood **b** : a gregarious person who joins many organizations

join•ery \'jȯin-rē, -ə-rē\ *n* **1** : the craft or trade of a joiner **2** : articles made by a joiner

¹joint \'jȯint\ *n* **1 a** (1) : the point of contact between elements of an animal skeleton together with the parts that surround and support it (2) : a node of a plant stem **b** : a part or space included between two animal or plant joints **c** : a large piece of meat for roasting **2 a** : a place where two things or parts are joined ⟨a *joint* in a pipe⟩ **b** : a space between the adjacent surfaces of two bodies joined and held together by an adhesive material (as cement or mortar) ⟨a thin *joint*⟩ **c** : a fracture or crack in rock **3 a** : a shabby or disreputable place of entertainment **b** : PLACE 2b, ESTABLISHMENT **4** : a marijuana cigarette [Old French *jointe,* from *joindre* "to join"] — **joint•ed** \-əd\ *adj*

²joint *adj* **1** : UNITED 1 ⟨the *joint* effect of study and play⟩ **2** : common to two or more: as **a** : done or shared by two or more ⟨a *joint* report⟩ ⟨*joint* efforts⟩ **b** : sharing in something (as a right or duty ⟨*joint* owners⟩

³joint *vb* **1 a** : to unite by a joint **b** : to provide with a joint **2** : to separate the joints of — **joint•er** *n*

joint•ly *adv* : TOGETHER ⟨owned *jointly*⟩

joint–stock company *n* : a form of business organization intermediate in many respects between a partnership and a corporation

joist \'jȯist\ *n* : any of the small timbers or metal beams placed parallel from wall to wall in a building to support the floor or ceiling [Middle French *giste,* derived from Latin *jacēre* "to lie"]

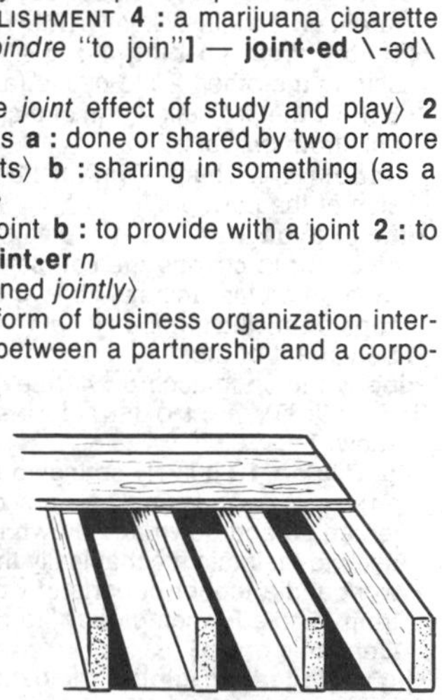

joist

¹joke \'jōk\ *n* **1 a** : something said or done to provoke laughter; *esp* : a brief oral narrative with a climactic humorous twist **b** (1) : the humorous or ridiculous element in something (2) : RAILLERY, KIDDING ⟨can't take a *joke*⟩ **c** : PRACTICAL JOKE **d** : LAUGHINGSTOCK **2 a** : something not to be taken seriously **b** : something presenting no difficulty [Latin *jocus*] **syn** see JEST

2joke *vb* **1** : to make jokes : JEST **2** : to make the object of a joke : KID — **jok•ing•ly** \ˈjō-king-lē\ *adv*

jok•er \ˈjō-kər\ *n* **1** : a person who jokes **2** : an extra card used in some card games **3** : a part (as of an agreement) meaning something quite different from what it seems to mean and changing the apparent intention of the whole

jol•li•fi•ca•tion \ˌjäl-i-fə-ˈkā-shən\ *n* : FESTIVITY 3, MERRYMAKING

jol•li•ty \ˈjäl-ət-ē\ *n, pl* **-ties** : the quality or state of being jolly **syn** see MIRTH

1jol•ly \ˈjäl-ē\ *adj* **jol•li•er**; **-est 1 a** (1) : full of high spirits : JOYOUS (2) : given to conviviality : JOVIAL **b** : expressing, suggesting, or inspiring gaiety : CHEERFUL **2** : extremely pleasant or agreeable : SPLENDID [Old French *joli*] **syn** see MERRY

2jolly *adv* : VERY ⟨had a *jolly* good time⟩

3jolly *vb* **jol•lied**; **jol•ly•ing 1** : to engage in good-natured banter **2** : to put in good humor especially in order to gain an end

jol•ly boat \ˈjäl-ē-\ *n* : a medium-sized ship's boat used for general rough or small work [origin unknown]

Jol•ly Rog•er \ˌjäl-ē-ˈräj-ər\ *n* : a black flag with a white skull and crossbones

1jolt \ˈjōlt\ *vb* **1** : to move or cause to move with a sudden jerky motion **2** : to give a knock or blow to : JAR **3** : to disturb the composure of **4** : to interfere with roughly, abruptly, and disconcertingly [probably blend of obsolete *joll* "to strike" and *jot* "to bump"] — **jolt•er** *n*

2jolt *n* **1** : an abrupt sharp jerky blow or movement **2** : a sudden shock, surprise, or disappointment

Jo•nah \ˈjō-nə\ *n* **1** — see BIBLE table **2** : JINX 1 [sense 2 from the fact that by disobeying God's command Jonah caused a storm to endanger the ship he was traveling in]

Jo•nas \ˈjō-nəs\ *n* — see BIBLE table

jon•gleur \zhō^{n}-ˈglər\ *n* : a wandering medieval minstrel [French, from Old French *jogleour*, derived from Latin *jocus* "joke"]

jon•quil \ˈjän-kwəl, ˈjäng-\ *n* : a Mediterranean perennial bulbous herb with long grassy leaves that is widely grown for its yellow or white fragrant short-tubed clustered flowers — compare DAFFODIL [French *jonquille*, from Spanish *junguillo*, from *junco* "reed", from Latin *juncus*]

Jor•dan almond \ˌjȯrd-n-\ *n* **1** : an almond imported from Málaga **2** : an almond coated with sugar [Middle English *jardin almande*, from Middle French *jardin* "garden" + Middle English *almande* "almond"]

jo•seph \ˈjō-zəf\ *n* : a long cloak worn especially by women in the 18th century [probably from *Joseph*, Old Testament patriarch; from his coat of many colors (Genesis 37:3)]

josh \ˈjäsh\ *vb* : to make fun of : TEASE, JOKE [origin unknown] — **josh•er** *n*

Josh•ua \ˈjäsh-wə, -ə-wə\ *n* — see BIBLE table

Joshua tree *n* : a tall branched yucca of the southwestern United States with short leaves and clustered greenish white flowers

Joshua tree

joss \ˈjäs, ˈjȯs\ *n* : a Chinese idol or cult image [Pidgin English, from Portuguese *deus* "god," from Latin]

joss house *n* : a Chinese temple or shrine

1jos•tle \ˈjäs-əl\ *vb* **jos•tled**; **jos•tling** \ˈjäs-ling, -ə-ling\ **1** : to move against so as to jar : push roughly ⟨*jostled* by a crowd⟩ **2** : to make one's way by pushing and shoving : ELBOW [earlier *justle*, derived from *joust*]

2jostle *n* **1** : a jostling encounter or experience **2** : the state of being jostled together

Jos•ue \ˈjäsh-ə-ˌwā\ *n* : JOSHUA

1jot \ˈjät\ *n* : the least bit : IOTA [Latin *iota, jota* "iota"]

△ **origin** "Till heaven and earth pass, one jot or one tittle shall in no wise pass from the law, till all be fulfilled." This is Christ's assurance (Matthew 5:18) that He was not "come to destroy the law or the prophets." Not the smallest letter, not a single stroke of a letter, we are told, will be lost. *Jot* is an anglicized form of Latin *jota* (or *iota*), itself simply a transliteration of the Greek name of the ninth letter of the Greek alphabet. The original Aramaic version must have referred to *yōdh*, the smallest letter in the Hebrew alphabet. The transfer across language boundaries was easily made because the Greek equivalent *iōta* was also the smallest letter in its alphabet. A *jot* now simply means "a very small part".

2jot *vt* **jot•ted**; **jot•ting** : to write briefly or hurriedly : set down in the form of a note ⟨*jot* this down⟩

jot•ting \ˈjät-ing\ *n* : a brief note : MEMORANDUM

joule \ˈjül, ˈjau̇l\ *n* : the mks unit of work equal to the work done by a force of one newton acting through a distance of one meter [James P. *Joule*, died 1889, English physicist]

jounce \ˈjau̇ns\ *vb* : to move or cause to move in an up-and-down manner [Middle English *jouncen*] — **jounce** *n*

jour•nal \ˈjərn-l\ **1 a** : a brief account of daily events **b** : a record of experiences, ideas, or reflections kept for private use **c** : a record of transactions kept by a deliberative or legislative body **2 a** : a daily newspaper **b** : a periodical that deals with current events **3** : the part of a rotating shaft, axle, roll, or spindle that turns in a bearing [Middle French, "service book containing the day hours", from *journal* "daily", from Latin *diurnalis*, from *diurnus* "of the day", from *dies* "day"]

jour•nal•ese \ˌjərn-l-ˈēz, -ˈēs\ *n* : a style of writing held to be characteristic of newspapers

jour•nal•ism \ˈjərn-l-ˌiz-əm\ *n* **1** : the collection and editing of material of current interest for presentation through news media (as newspapers or television) **2** : writing designed for or characteristic of newspapers or popular magazines

jour•nal•ist \-l-əst\ *n* : a person engaged in journalism

jour•nal•is•tic \ˌjərn-l-ˈis-tik\ *adj* : of, relating to, or characteristic of journalism or journalists — **jour•nal•is•ti•cal•ly** \-ti-kə-lē, -klē\ *adv*

jour•nal•ize \ˈjərn-l-ˌīz\ *vt* : to record in a journal — **jour•nal•iz•er** *n*

1jour•ney \ˈjər-nē\ *n, pl* **journeys** : travel or passage from one place to another [Old French *journee* "day's journey", from *jour* "day", from Late Latin *diurnum*, from Latin *diurnus* "of a day", from *dies* "day"]

2journey *vb* **jour•neyed**; **jour•ney•ing 1** : to go on a journey : TRAVEL **2** : to travel over or through : TRAVERSE — **jour•ney•er** *n*

jour•ney•man \ˈjər-nē-mən\ *n* **1** : a worker who has learned a trade and usually works for wages **2** : an experienced and reliable but not brilliant worker or performer [Middle English *journey* "journey, day's labor"]

1joust \ˈjau̇st\ *vi* : to engage in a joust : TILT [Old French *juster*, derived from Latin *juxta* "near"] — **joust•er** *n*

2joust *n* : a combat on horseback between two knights with lances especially as part of a tournament

jo•vi•al \ˈjō-vē-əl\ *adj* : markedly good-humored especially as shown by jollity and good-fellowship [Late Latin *jovialis* "of the god Jupiter", from Latin *Jov-, Juppiter* "Jupiter"; from the belief that those born under the astrological influence of the planet Jupiter are jolly] **syn** see MERRY — **jo•vi•al•i•ty** \ˌjō-vē-ˈal-ət-ē\ *n* — **jo•vi•al•ly** \ˈjō-vē-ə-lē\ *adv*

1jowl \ˈjau̇l\ *n* **1** : JAW; *esp* : the lower jaw **2** : CHEEK 1 [Old English *ceafl*]

2jowl *n* : loose flesh (as a wattle) hanging from the lower jaw or throat [Middle English *cholle*] — **jowly** \-ē\ *adj*

1joy \ˈjȯi\ *n* **1** : a feeling of great pleasure or happiness that comes from success, good fortune, or a sense of well-being : GLADNESS **2** : something that gives great pleasure or happiness ⟨a *joy* to behold⟩ [Old French *joie*, from Latin *gaudium*, from *gaudēre* "to rejoice"]

2joy *vi* : to experience great pleasure or delight : REJOICE

joy•ful \ˈjȯi-fəl\ *adj* : experiencing, causing, or showing joy : HAPPY — **joy•ful•ly** \-fə-lē\ *adv* — **joy•ful•ness** *n*

joy•less \ˈjȯi-ləs\ *adj* : not feeling or causing joy : CHEERLESS — **joy•less•ly** *adv* — **joy•less•ness** *n*

\ə\ **abut**	\au̇\ **out**	\i\ **tip**	\ȯ\ **saw**	\u̇\ **foot**
\ər\ **further**	\ch\ **chin**	\ī\ **life**	\ȯi\ **coin**	\y\ **yet**
\a\ **mat**	\e\ **pet**	\j\ **job**	\th\ **thin**	\yü\ **few**
\ā\ **take**	\ē\ **easy**	\ng\ **sing**	\th\ **this**	\yu̇\ **cure**
\ä\ **cot, cart**	\g\ **go**	\ō\ **bone**	\ü\ **food**	\zh\ **vision**

joy•ous \'jȯi-əs\ *adj* : JOYFUL — **joy•ous•ly** *adv* — **joy•ous•ness** *n*

joy•ride \'jȯi-ˌrīd\ *n* : a ride taken for pleasure and often marked by reckless driving — **joy•rid•er** *n* — **joy•rid•ing** *n*

ju•bi•lant \'jü-bə-lənt\ *adj* : feeling or expressing great joy : EXULTANT [Latin *jubilare* "to rejoice"] — **ju•bi•lant•ly** *adv*

ju•bi•la•tion \ˌjü-bə-'lā-shən\ *n* **1** : an act of rejoicing : the state of being jubilant **2** : an expression of great joy

ju•bi•lee \'jü-bə-ˌlē, ˌjü-bə-'lē\ *n* **1 a** : a special anniversary; *esp* : a 50th anniversary **b** : a celebration of such an anniversary **2 a** : a period of time proclaimed by the Roman Catholic pope ordinarily every 25 years as a time of special solemnity **b** : a special plenary indulgence granted during a year of jubilee to Roman Catholics who perform specified works of repentance and piety [Late Latin *jubilaeus* "year of emancipation and restoration provided by ancient Hebrew law", from Late Greek *iōbēlaios*, from Hebrew *yōbhēl*, literally, "ram's horn"]

△ **origin** Ancient Hebrew law established every 50th year as a year of emancipation and restoration. All Hebrew slaves were freed; lands were restored to their former owners; fields were left uncultivated. This year took its name, *yōbhēl*, from the ram's horn trumpets used to proclaim its coming. When the Old Testament was translated into Greek and later into Latin, the translators borrowed the Hebrew name. The Greek form *iōbēlaios* was borrowed into Latin as *jubilaeus*. Since *jubilee* came into English with the translation of the Bible from Latin, it has acquired new meanings. *Jubilee* is used for any 50th anniversary and even for other special anniversaries.

Ju•da•ic \jü-'dā-ik\ *adj* : of, relating to, or characteristic of Jews or Judaism [Latin *judaicus*, from Greek *ioudaikos*, from *Ioudaios* "Jew"] — **Ju•da•ical** \-'dā-ə-kəl\ *adj*

Ju•da•ism \'jüd-ə-ˌiz-əm, 'jüd-ē-\ *n* **1** : a religion developed among the ancient Hebrews and marked by belief in one God who is creator, ruler, and redeemer of the universe and by the moral and ceremonial laws of the Old Testament and the rabbinic tradition **2** : conformity to Jewish rites, ceremonies, and practices **3** : the cultural, social, and religious beliefs and practices of the Jews **4** : the whole body of Jews — **Ju•da•ist** \-ə-əst, -ē-əst\ *n* — **Ju•da•is•tic** \ˌjüd-ə-'is-tik, ˌjüd-ē-\ *adj*

Ju•da•ize \'jüd-ə-ˌīz, 'jüd-ē-\ *vb* **1** : to adopt the customs, beliefs, or character of a Jew **2** : to make Jewish — **Ju•da•iza•tion** \ˌjüd-ə-ə-'zā-shən, ˌjüd-ē-ə-\ *n* — **Ju•da•iz•er** *n*

Ju•das \'jüd-əs\ *n* : TRAITOR [*Judas* Iscariot, apostle who betrayed Jesus]

Judas tree *n* : a leguminous tree often grown for its showy usually rosy flowers borne before the leaves appear [from the belief that Judas Iscariot hanged himself from a tree of this kind]

Jude \'jüd\ *n* — see BIBLE table

¹judge \'jəj\ *vb* **1** : to form an authoritative opinion **2** : to decide as a judge : TRY **3** : to determine or pronounce after inquiry and deliberation : CONSIDER **4** : GOVERN, RULE — used of a Hebrew tribal leader **5** : to form an estimate, conclusion, or evaluation about something : THINK [Old French *jugier*, from Latin *judicare*, from *judic-*, *judex* "judge", from *jus* "right, law" + *dicere* "to say"] — **judg•er** *n*

²judge *n* **1** : a public official authorized to decide questions brought before a court **2** *often cap* : a tribal hero exercising authority over the Hebrews after the death of Joshua **3** : one who decides in a contest or competition : UMPIRE **4** : one who gives an authoritative opinion : CRITIC — **judge•ship** \-ˌship\ *n*

Judg•es \'jəj-əz\ *n* — see BIBLE table

judg•ment *or* **judge•ment** \'jəj-mənt\ *n* **1 a** : the act of judging **b** : a decision or opinion formed or given after judging **2 a** : a formal decision given by a court **b** : a court decree that a defendant has an obligation to the plaintiff for a specified amount **3** *cap* : the final judging of mankind by God — called also *Last Judgment* **4** : the process of forming an opinion by discerning and comparing **5** : the capacity for judging : DISCERNMENT — **judg•men•tal** \ˌjəj-'ment-l\ *adj*

Judgment Day *n* : the day of the Last Judgment

ju•di•ca•ture \'jüd-i-kə-ˌchu̇r\ *n* **1** : the administration of justice **2** : JUDICIARY 1 [Middle French, from Medieval Latin *judicatura*, from Latin *judicare* "to judge"]

ju•di•cial \jü-'dish-əl\ *adj* **1** : of or relating to a judgment, the function of judging, the administration of justice, or the judiciary **2** : pronounced, ordered, or enforced by a court ⟨a *judicial* decision⟩ **3** : of, characterized by, or expressing judgment : CRITICAL [Latin *judicialis*, from *judicium* "judgment", from *judex* "judge"] — **ju•di•cial•ly** \-'dish-lē, -ə-lē\ *adv*

ju•di•cia•ry \jü-'dish-ē-ˌer-ē, -'dish-ə-rē\ *n, pl* **-ries 1 a** : a system of law courts **b** : the judges of these courts **2** : a branch of government in which judicial power is vested — **judiciary** *adj*

ju•di•cious \jü-'dish-əs\ *adj* : having, exercising, or characterized by sound judgment : DISCREET — **ju•di•cious•ly** *adv* — **ju•di•cious•ness** *n*

Ju•dith \'jüd-əth\ *n* — see BIBLE table

ju•do \'jüd-ō\ *n, pl* **judos** : a form of wrestling developed in Japan from jujitsu [Japanese *jūdō*, from *jū* "weakness, gentleness" + *dō* "art"]

¹jug \'jəg\ *n* **1 a** : a large deep earthenware, glass, or plastic container with a narrow mouth and a handle **b** : JUGFUL **2** : JAIL [perhaps from *jug*, nickname for *Joan*]

²jug *vt* **jugged**; **jug•ging** : IMPRISON

jug•ful \'jəg-ˌfu̇l\ *n, pl* **jugfuls** \-ˌfu̇lz\ *or* **jugs•ful** \'jəgz-ˌfu̇l\ : the quantity held by a jug

jug•ger•naut \'jəg-ər-ˌnȯt\ *n* : a massive inexorable force or object that crushes whatever is in its path [Hindi *Jagannāth*, title of Vishnu, literally, "lord of the world"]

△ **origin** One of the titles of the Hindu god Vishnu is *Jagannāth*, which means "lord of the world". Every year the image of *Jagannāth* is taken from his temple at Puri, India, placed on an enormous car or carriage, and drawn through the streets in procession. In earlier times, some of the worshipers of *Jagannāth* would allow themselves to be crushed beneath the wheels of the car in sacrifice to their god. The English form of the god's name, *Juggernaut*, came to be used in the sense of a massive inexorable force or object that crushes everything in its path.

¹jug•gle \'jəg-əl\ *vb* **jug•gled**; **jug•gling** \'jəg-ling, -ə-ling\ **1** : to keep several objects in motion in the air at the same time **2** : to manipulate especially in order to achieve a desired and often fraudulent end ⟨*juggle* an account to hide a loss⟩ **3** : to hold or balance insecurely [Middle French *jogler* "to joke, sing", from Latin *joculari* "to joke", from *joculus* "little joke", from *jocus* "joke"] — **jug•gler** \'jəg-lər, -ə-lər\ *n*

²juggle *n* : an act or instance of juggling

jug•glery \'jəg-lə-rē\ *n, pl* **-gler•ies 1** : the art or practice of a juggler **2** : TRICKERY

¹jug•u•lar \'jəg-yə-lər\ *adj* **1** : of, relating to, or situated in or on the throat or neck **2** : of or relating to the jugular vein [Late Latin *jugularis*, from Latin *jugulum* "collarbone, throat"]

²jugular *n* : JUGULAR VEIN

jugular vein *n* : any of several veins of each side of the neck that return blood from the head

juice \'jüs\ *n* **1** : the fluid contents that can be separated from cells or tissues **2 a** : the natural fluids (as blood and lymph) of an animal body; *esp* : any of several chiefly digestive secretions **b** : the liquid or moisture contained in something **3** : a medium (as electricity or gasoline) that supplies power [Old French *jus* "broth, juice", from Latin] — **juiced** \'jüst\ *adj* — **juice•less** \'jüs-ləs\ *adj*

juic•er \'jü-sər\ *n* : an appliance for extracting juice from fruit or vegetables

juice up *vt* : to give life, energy, or spirit to

juicy \'jü-sē\ *adj* **juic•i•er**; **-est 1** : having much juice : SUCCULENT **2 a** : rich in interest : COLORFUL **b** : agreeably interesting or titillating ⟨a *juicy* scandal⟩ — **juic•i•ly** \-sə-lē\ *adv* — **juic•i•ness** \-sē-nəs\ *n*

ju•jit•su *or* **ju•jut•su** *or* **jiu•jit•su** *or* **jiu•jut•su** \jü-'jit-sü\ *n* : the Japanese art of unarmed fighting employing holds, throws, and paralyzing blows [Japanese *jūjutsu*, from *jū* "weakness" + *jutsu* "art, skill"]

ju•jube \'jü-ˌjüb, *2 is often* 'jü-jü-ˌbē\ *n* **1** : the edible fruit of a tree of the buckthorn family; *also* : this tree **2** : a fruit-flavored gumdrop or lozenge [Medieval Latin *jujuba*, from Latin *zizi-phum*, from Greek *zizyphon*]

juke•box \'jük-ˌbäks\ *n* : a coin-operated phonograph that automatically plays records selected from its list [Gullah (a dialect used by Negroes on sea islands of the southeastern United States) *juke* "disorderly", of African origin]

△ **origin** The Gullahs, descendants of slaves, live on sea islands and coastal districts of the southeastern United States. They speak a dialect of English that contains many words derived from various languages of Africa. One of these words is *juke*, which means "disorderly". A *juke house*, in Gullah, is a disorderly house or brothel. By the 1930's *juke*, or *juke house*, was more widely used in the southeast as a name for a small business providing cheap food and drink and music for dancing. Soon the name *jukebox* was given to the type of music machine found in such establishments.

juke joint *n* : a small inexpensive establishment for eating, drinking, or dancing to the music of a jukebox

ju•lep \ˈjü-ləp\ *n* : a drink of alcoholic liquor and sugar poured over crushed ice and garnished with mint — called also *mint julep* [Middle French, a drink made from syrup, from Arabic *julāb,* from Persian *gulāb,* from *gul* "rose" + *āb* "water"]

Ju•lian calendar \ˌjül-yən-\ *n* : a calendar introduced in Rome in 46 B.C. establishing the 12-month year of 365 days with each 4th year having 366 days and the months each having 31 or 30 days except for February which has 28 or in leap years 29 days — compare GREGORIAN CALENDAR [Gaius *Julius* Caesar, who introduced it]

Ju•ly \jü-ˈlī\ *n* : the 7th month of the year [Old English *Julius,* from Latin, from Gaius *Julius* Caesar]

¹jum•ble \ˈjəm-bəl\ *vb* **jum•bled**; **jum•bling** \-bə-ling, -bling\ : to move or mix in a confused mass [perhaps imitative]

²jumble *n* : a disorderly mass or pile

jum•bo \ˈjəm-bō\ *n, pl* **jumbos** : a very large specimen of its kind [*Jumbo,* a huge elephant exhibited by P.T. Barnum] — **jumbo** *adj*

¹jump \ˈjəmp\ *vb* **1 a** : to spring or cause to spring into the air : LEAP ⟨*jump* up⟩ ⟨*jump* a horse over a ditch⟩ **b** : to give a sudden movement : START **c** : to move over a position occupied by an opponent's piece in a board game **d** : SKIP ⟨this typewriter *jumps*⟩ **e** : to begin a forward movement — used with *off* **2 a** : to rise or cause to rise suddenly in rank or status **b** : to undergo or cause to undergo a sudden sharp increase ⟨prices *jumped*⟩ **3** : to pounce suddenly or unexpectedly : ATTACK **4** : to bustle with activity **5 a** : to leap over ⟨*jump* a hurdle⟩ **b** : BYPASS ⟨*jump* electrical connections⟩ **c** : ANTICIPATE ⟨*jump* the gun in starting the race⟩ **d** : to escape from usually in a hasty or furtive manner ⟨*jump* town without paying their bills⟩ **e** : to abscond while at liberty under (bail) **f** : to depart from (a normal course) ⟨*jump* the track⟩ **g** : to get aboard by jumping ⟨*jump* a train⟩ **h** : to occupy illegally ⟨*jump* a mining claim⟩ [probably related to Low German *gumpen* "to jump"]

²jump *n* **1 a** (1) : an act of jumping : LEAP (2) : a sports competition featuring a leap, spring, or bound (3) : a distance covered by a leap **b** : a sudden involuntary movement **c** : a move made in a board game by jumping **2 a** : a sharp sudden increase **b** : one in a series of moves **3** : an advantage at the start

jump ball *n* : a method of putting a basketball into play in which the referee tosses the ball up between two opposing players who jump and try to tap it to a teammate

¹jump•er \ˈjəm-pər\ *n* **1** : one that jumps **2** : any of various devices operating with a jumping motion **3** : a wire used to close a break or cut out part of a circuit

²jumper *n* **1** : a loose blouse or jacket worn by workmen **2** : a sleeveless one-piece dress worn usually with a blouse **3** *pl* : a child's coverall [probably from English dialect *jump* "jumper"]

jumping bean *n* : a seed of any of several Mexican shrubs of the spurge family that tumbles about because of the movements of the larva of a small moth inside it

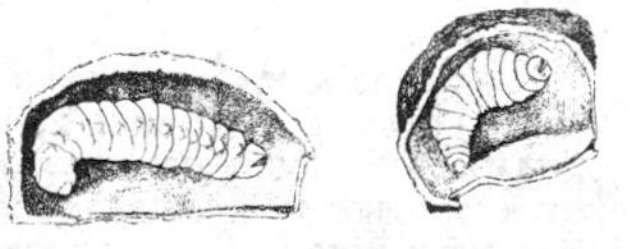

jumping bean

jumping jack *n* : a toy figure of a man jointed and made to jump or dance by means of strings or a sliding stick

jumping mouse *n* : any of several small hibernating North American rodents with long hind legs and tail and no cheek pouches

jump•ing–off place \ˌjəm-ping-ˈóf-\ *n* **1** : a remote or isolated place **2** : a place from which an enterprise is launched

jump seat *n* **1** : a movable carriage seat **2** : a folding seat between the front and rear seats of a passenger automobile

jump shot *n* : a shot made by a basketball player at the peak of a jump

jumpy \ˈjəm-pē\ *adj* **jump•i•er**; **-est** : very nervous : JITTERY — **jump•i•ness** *n*

jun•co \ˈjəng-kō\ *n, pl* **juncos** *or* **juncoes** : any of a genus of small American finches usually with a pink bill, ashy gray head and back, and conspicuous white lateral tail feathers [Spanish, "reed", from Latin *juncus*]

junc•tion \ˈjəng-shən, ˈjəngk-\ *n* **1** : an act of joining : the state of being joined **2** : a place or point of meeting ⟨a railroad *junction*⟩ **3** : something that joins [Latin *junctio,* from *jungere* "to join"] — **junc•tion•al** \-shnəl, -shən-l\ *adj*

junc•ture \ˈjəng-chər, ˈjəngk-\ *n* **1** : an instance of joining : UNION **2 a** : JOINT 2a, CONNECTION **b** : the manner of transition between two consecutive sounds in speech **3** : a point of time; *esp* : one made critical by a concurrence of circumstances — **junc•tur•al** \-chə-rəl, -shrəl\ *adj*

• **syn** JUNCTURE, EMERGENCY, CRISIS mean a critical or crucial time or state of affairs. JUNCTURE stresses the significant convergence of events or developments; EMERGENCY emphasizes the sudden unforeseen nature of a situation and the need for quick action; CRISIS applies to a juncture whose outcome will make a decisive difference.

June \ˈjün\ *n* : the 6th month of the year [Latin *Junius*]

june beetle *n, often cap J* : any of various large leaf-eating beetles that fly chiefly in late spring and have as larvae white grubs that live in soil and feed on roots — called also *june bug*

June•ber•ry \ˈjün-ˌber-ē\ *n* : SERVICEBERRY 2

jun•gle \ˈjəng-gəl\ *n* **1 a** : a thick tangled mass of tropical vegetation **b** : a tract overgrown with jungle or other rank vegetation **2** : a hobo camp **3** : a place of ruthless struggle for survival [Hindi *jaṅgal*] — **jun•gly** \-gə-lē, -glē\ *adj*

jungle fowl *n* : any of several Asian wild birds related to the pheasants; *esp* : one from which domestic fowls are held to have descended

jungle gym *n* : a structure of vertical and horizontal bars for use of children at play

¹ju•nior \ˈjün-yər\ *n* **1** : a person who is younger or of lower rank than another **2** : a student in the next-to-last year before graduating from an educational institution of secondary or higher level [Latin, from *junior,* comparative of *juvenis* "young"]

²junior *adj* **1 a** : YOUNGER — used chiefly to distinguish a son with the same given name or names as his father and usually placed in its abbreviated form after a surname ⟨John M. Doe, *Jr.*⟩ **b** : of more recent date **2** : lower in standing or rank ⟨*junior* partner⟩ **3** : of or relating to juniors in a school or college

ju•nior•ate \ˈjün-yə-ˌrāt, -rət\ *n* **1** : a course of high school or college study for candidates for the priesthood, brotherhood, or sisterhood; *esp* : one preparatory to the course in philosophy **2** : a seminary for the juniorate

junior college *n* : an educational institution that offers two years of studies corresponding to the first two years of a four-year college

junior high school *n* : a school usually including the 7th, 8th, and 9th grades

junior varsity *n* : a team composed of players lacking the experience or qualifications for the varsity

ju•ni•per \ˈjü-nə-pər\ *n* **1** : any of a genus of evergreen shrubs and trees of the pine family; *esp* : one of prostrate or shrubby habit **2** : any of various coniferous trees resembling true junipers [Latin *juniperus*]

¹junk \ˈjəngk\ *n* **1** : hard salted beef for use on shipboard **2 a** (1) : waste (as iron or glass) that may be used again in some form (2) : articles discarded as worthless **b** : a shoddy product : TRASH [Middle English *jonke* "piece of old rope or cable"] — **junk•man** \-ˌman\ *n* — **junky** *adj*

²junk *vt* : to get rid of as worthless : SCRAP

³junk *n* : a flat-bottomed sailing vessel of Chinese waters having an overhanging bow, high stern, high masts with lugsails, and a deep rudder [Portuguese *junco,* of Austronesian origin]

³junk

Jun•ker \ˈyu̇ng-kər\ *n* : a member of the Prussian landed aristocracy [German, from Old High German *junchēro,* literally, "young lord"]

¹jun•ket \ˈjəng-kət\ *n* **1** : a dessert of sweetened flavored milk

\ə\ **abut**	\au̇\ **out**	\i\ **tip**	\ȯ\ **saw**	\u̇\ **foot**
\ər\ **further**	\ch\ **chin**	\ī\ **life**	\ȯi\ **coin**	\y\ **yet**
\a\ **mat**	\e\ **pet**	\j\ **job**	\th\ **thin**	\yü\ **few**
\ā\ **take**	\ē\ **easy**	\ng\ **sing**	\t͟h\ **this**	\yu̇\ **cure**
\ä\ **cot, cart**	\g\ **go**	\ō\ **bone**	\ü\ **food**	\zh\ **vision**

with a jellylike consistency **2 a :** a festive social affair **b :** JOURNEY, TRIP; *esp* **:** a trip made by an official at public expense [probably from Italian *giuncata* "cream cheese", from Latin *juncus* "reed, rush"]

△ **origin** Long ago a type of cream cheese was prepared in baskets made of reeds or rushes. In Italy in the Middle Ages this cream cheese was called *giuncata,* a derivative of Latin *juncus,* which means "reed" or "rush". It was probably from this Italian source that English borrowed *junket. Junket* was first used for cream cheese and later for a dessert made of sweetened curdled milk. In the early modern period, indeed, *junket* was a popular term for any sweet dish. From this sense of *junket* developed the extended sense "a feast or banquet". *Junket* came to be used for large picnics and later for any pleasure outing or trip.

²junket *vi* **1 :** BANQUET, FEAST **2 :** to go on a junket

junk•ie *or* **junky** \'jəng-kē\ *n, pl* **junk•ies** *slang* **:** a narcotics peddler or addict [English slang *junk* "narcotics", from ¹*junk*]

jun•ta \'hùn-tə, 'jənt-ə, 'hən-tə\ *n* **1 :** a council or committee for political or governmental purposes; *esp* **:** a group of persons controlling a government after a revolutionary seizure of power **2 :** JUNTO [Spanish, from *junto* "joined", from Latin *jungere* "to join"]

jun•to \'jənt-ō\ *n, pl* **juntos :** a group of persons joined for a common purpose [probably alteration of *junta*]

Ju•pi•ter \'jü-pət-ər\ *n* **:** the largest of the planets and 5th in order of distance from the sun — see PLANET table [Latin *Jupiter,* chief Roman god]

Ju•ras•sic \jù-'ras-ik\ *n* **:** the period of the Mesozoic era between the Triassic and Cretaceous marked by the presence of dinosaurs and the first appearance of birds; *also* **:** the corresponding system of rocks — see GEOLOGIC TIME table [French *jurassique,* from *Jura* mountain range] — **Jurassic** *adj*

ju•rid•i•cal \jù-'rid-i-kəl\ *adj* **1 :** of or relating to the administration of justice or the office of a judge **2 :** of or relating to law or jurisprudence **:** LEGAL [Latin *juridicus,* from *jur-, jus* "right, law" + *dicere* "to say"] — **ju•rid•i•cal•ly** \-kə-lē, -klē\ *adv*

ju•ris•dic•tion \ˌjùr-əs-'dik-shən\ *n* **1 :** the power, right, or authority to interpret and apply the law **2 :** the authority of a sovereign power to govern or legislate **3 :** the limits or territory within which authority may be exercised [Latin *jurisdictio,* from *jur-, jus* "right, law" + *dictio* "act of saying", from *dicere* "to say"] — **ju•ris•dic•tion•al** \-shnəl, -shən-l\ *adj* — **ju•ris•dic•tion•al•ly** \-ē\ *adv*

ju•ris•pru•dence \ˌjùr-ə-'sprüd-ns\ *n* **1 :** a system of laws **2 :** the science or philosophy of law **3 :** a department of law ⟨medical *jurisprudence*⟩ [Late Latin *jurisprudentia,* from *jur-, jus* "right, law" + *prudens* "skilled, prudent"] — **ju•ris•pru•den•tial** \-sprü-'den-chəl\ *adj* — **ju•ris•pru•den•tial•ly** \-'dench-lē, -ə-lē\ *adv*

ju•rist \'jùr-əst\ *n* **:** one having a thorough knowledge of law [Middle French *juriste,* from Latin *jur-, jus* "law, right"]

ju•ris•tic \jù-'ris-tik\ *adj* **1 :** of or relating to a jurist or jurisprudence **2 :** of, relating to, or recognized in law — **ju•ris•ti•cal•ly** \-ti-kə-lē, -klē\ *adv*

ju•ror \'jùr-ər, 'jùr-ˌòr\ *n* **:** a member of or a person summoned to serve on a jury

¹ju•ry \'jùr-ē\ *n, pl* **juries 1 :** a body of persons sworn to hear evidence on a matter submitted to them and to give their verdict according to the evidence presented **2 :** a committee that judges and awards prizes at an exhibition or contest [Anglo-French *juree,* from Old French *jurer* "to swear", from Latin *jurare,* from *jur-, jus* "law"] — **ju•ry•man** \-mən\ *n* — **ju•ry•wom•an** \-ˌwù-mən\ *n*

²jury *adj* **:** improvised for temporary use especially in an emergency **:** MAKESHIFT ⟨a *jury* mast⟩ [origin unknown]

¹just \'jəst\ *adj* **1 a :** having a basis in or conforming to fact or reason **:** REASONABLE ⟨a *just* comment⟩ **b** *archaic* **:** faithful to an original **c :** conforming to a standard of correctness **:** PROPER ⟨*just* proportions⟩ **2 a** (1) **:** morally right or good **:** RIGHTEOUS ⟨a *just* war⟩ (2) **:** MERITED, DESERVED ⟨*just* punishment⟩ **b :** legally right ⟨a *just* title⟩ [Latin *justus,* from *jus* "right, law"] — **just•ly** *adv* — **just•ness** \'jəst-nəs, 'jəs-\ *n*

²just \jəst, ˌjəst, jist, ˌjist, jest, ˌjest\ *adv* **1 a :** EXACTLY, PRECISELY ⟨*just* right⟩ **b :** very recently ⟨the bell *just* rang⟩ **2 a :** by a very small margin **:** BARELY ⟨*just* over the line⟩ **b :** only a little ⟨*just* west of here⟩ **3 a :** no more than **:** MERELY ⟨*just* a note⟩ **b :** QUITE, VERY ⟨*just* wonderful⟩

jus•tice \'jəs-təs\ *n* **1 a :** the maintenance or administration of what is just **b :** JUDGE a **c :** the administration of law **2 a :** the quality of being just, impartial, or fair **b :** RIGHTEOUSNESS ⟨defend the *justice* of their cause⟩ **c :** the quality of conforming to law [Old French, from Latin *justitia,* from *justus* "just"] — **do justice 1 a :** to act justly **b :** to treat fairly or properly **c :** to consume in a manner showing due appreciation **2 :** to conduct in a way worthy of one's capabilities

justice of the peace : a local magistrate empowered chiefly to try minor cases, to administer oaths, and to perform marriages

jus•ti•fi•able \'jəs-tə-ˌfī-ə-bəl\ *adj* **:** capable of being justified **:** EXCUSABLE — **jus•ti•fi•ably** \-blē\ *adv*

jus•ti•fi•ca•tion \ˌjəs-tə-fə-'kā-shən\ *n* **1 :** the act, process, or state of being justified by God **2 a :** the act or an instance of justifying **:** VINDICATION **b :** something that justifies **:** DEFENSE

jus•ti•fy \'jəs-tə-ˌfī\ *vb* **-fied**; **-fy•ing 1 a :** to prove or show to be just, right, or reasonable **:** VINDICATE **b :** to show a sufficient lawful reason for an act done **2 :** to release from the guilt of sin and accept as righteous **3 :** to adjust or arrange exactly; *esp* **:** to cause (as lines of typewritten text) to come out even at the right margin **syn** see MAINTAIN — **jus•ti•fi•er** \-ˌfī-ər, -ˌfīr\ *n*

¹jut \'jət\ *vb* **jut•ted**; **jut•ting :** to shoot or cause to shoot out, up, or forward **:** PROJECT [perhaps from Middle English *jutteyen*]

²jut *n* **:** something that juts **:** PROJECTION

jute \'jüt\ *n* **:** a glossy fiber from either of two East Indian plants that is used chiefly for sacking and twine [Hindi and Bengali *jūṭ*]

Jute \'jüt\ *n* **:** a member of a Germanic people invading England from Jutland and settling in Kent in the 5th century A.D. — compare ANGLO-SAXON [Medieval Latin *Jutae* "Jutes"] — **Jut•ish** \'jüt-ish\ *adj*

¹ju•ve•nile \'jü-və-ˌnīl, -vən-l\ *adj* **1 a :** showing incomplete development **:** IMMATURE **b :** CHILDISH 2 ⟨*juvenile* conduct⟩ **2 :** derived from sources within the earth and coming to the surface for the first time ⟨*juvenile* water⟩ **3 :** of, relating to, or characteristic of children or young people [Latin *juvenilis,* from *juvenis* "young person", from *juvenis* "young"] — **ju•ve•nil•i•ty** \ˌjü-və-'nil-ət-ē\ *n*

²juvenile *n* **1 a :** a young person **:** YOUTH **b :** a book for young people **2 a :** a fledged bird not yet in adult plumage **b :** a 2-year-old racehorse **3 :** an actor or actress who plays youthful parts

juvenile delinquency *n* **:** violation of the law or antisocial behavior by a juvenile — **juvenile delinquent** *n*

jux•ta•pose \'jək-stə-ˌpōz\ *vt* **:** to place side by side [probably back-formation from *juxtaposition*]

jux•ta•po•si•tion \ˌjək-stə-pə-'zish-ən\ *n* **:** a placing or being placed side by side [Latin *juxta* "near" + English *position*] — **jux•ta•po•si•tion•al** \-'zish-nəl, -ən-l\ *adj*

K k—kyrie eleison

k \'kā\ *n, pl* **k's** *or* **ks** \'kāz\ *often cap* **:** the 11th letter of the English alphabet

kabbala *or* **kabbalah** *or* **kabala** *variant of* CABALA

ka•bob *or* **ke•bab** *also* **ke•bob** \'kā-,bāb, kə-'\ *n* **:** cubes of meat cooked with vegetables usually on a skewer [Arabic *kabāb,* from Turkish *kebap*]

Ka•bu•ki \kə-'bü-kē, 'käb-ü-,kē\ *n* **:** traditional Japanese popular drama with singing and dancing performed in a stylized manner [Japanese, literally, "art of singing and dancing"]

kad•dish \'käd-ish\ *n, often cap* **:** a Jewish prayer recited in the daily ritual of the synagogue and by mourners at public services after the death of a close relative [Aramaic *qaddīsh* "holy"]

kaf•fee•klatsch \'kōf-ē-,kläch, 'käf-, -,klach, -,kləch\ *n, often cap* **:** an informal social gathering for coffee and talk [German, from *kaffee* "coffee" + *klatsch* "gossip"]

Kaf•fir *or* **Kaf•ir** \'kaf-ər\ *n* **:** a member of a group of southern African Bantu-speaking peoples [Arabic *kāfir* "infidel"]

kaf•ir \'kaf-ər\ *n* **:** a stocky grain sorghum with erect heads

kaftan *variant of* CAFTAN

kai•ser \'kī-zər\ *n* **:** EMPEROR; *esp* **:** the ruler of Germany from 1871 to 1918 [Old Norse *keisari* and German *kaiser;* both from Latin *Caesar,* cognomen of the Emperor Augustus] — **kai•ser•dom** \-zərd-əm\ *n* — **kai•ser•ism** \-zə-,riz-əm\ *n*

△ **origin** Although Julius Caesar was never emperor, his name became synonymous with the office of emperor of the Roman empire. Caesar adopted his grandnephew Gaius Octavius, who, upon his adoption, took the name Gaius Julius Caesar Octavianus. This man, after the death of Julius Caesar, gained control in Italy and became the first Roman emperor, with the title *Augustus,* "exalted, august". Later Roman emperors adopted his name, Caesar, to indicate their right to the imperial title. Subsequently other European languages borrowed this name from Latin as a word for emperor.

ka•ka \'käk-ə\ *n* **:** a brownish New Zealand parrot with gray and red markings that is a good mimic and talker [Maori]

kal•an•choe \,kal-ən-'kō-ē, kə-'lang-kə-wē\ *n* **:** any of a genus of succulent tropical Old World plants including several grown as ornamentals [New Latin, genus name, probably of Chinese origin]

kale \'kāl\ *n* **:** a hardy cabbage with curled often finely cut leaves that do not form a dense head [Scottish, from Old English *cāl*]

ka•lei•do•scope \kə-'līd-ə-,skōp\ *n* **1 :** an instrument containing loose bits of colored glass between two flat plates and two plane mirrors so placed that changes of position of the bits of glass are reflected in an endless variety of symmetrical patterns **2 :** a changing pattern or scene [Greek *kalos* "beautiful" + *eidos* "shape, form" + English *-scope*] — **ka•lei•do•scop•ic** \-,līd-ə-'skäp-ik\ *adj* — **ka•lei•do•scop•i•cal•ly** \-'skäp-i-kə-lē, -klē\ *adv*

kalends *variant of* CALENDS

Kal•muck *or* **Kal•muk** \'kal-,mək, kal-'\ *n* **1 :** a member of a Buddhist Mongol people of northern Sinkiang, China **2 :** the language of the Kalmucks [Russian *Kalmyk*]

kal•so•mine *variant of* CALCIMINE

ka•ma•ai•na \,käm-ə-'ī-nə\ *n* **:** one who has lived in Hawaii for a long time [Hawaiian *kama'āina,* from *kama* "child" + *'āina* "land"]

kame \'kām\ *n* **:** a short ridge or mound of material deposited by water from a melting glacier [Scottish, literally, "comb", from Old English *camb*]

ka•mi•ka•ze \,käm-i-'käz-ē\ *n* **:** a member of a corps of Japanese pilots in World War II assigned to make a crash on a target; *also* **:** an airplane flown in such an attack [Japanese, literally, "divine wind"]

△ **origin** In 1281 Kublai Khan sent an immense fleet against Japan. Although Japan was prepared, the Mongol horde was not easy to resist. But after some weeks of fighting, a great and sudden storm arose and destroyed the Mongol fleet. To the Japanese this salvation was *kamikaze,* "divine wind". In the Second World War Japan sent out pilots willing to give up their lives to help save their country by destroying American ships. These were the members of a special corps named *kamikaze* after the storm that had saved Japan some seven centuries earlier.

kan•ga•roo \,kang-gə-'rü\ *n, pl* **-roos :** any of various plant-eating leaping marsupial mammals of Australia, New Guinea, and adjacent islands with a small head, long powerful hind legs, and a long thick tail used as a support and in balancing [probably native name in Australia]

kangaroo

kangaroo court *n* **1 :** a court whose status or procedures are irresponsible or irregular **2 :** judgment or punishment given outside of legal procedure

kangaroo rat *n* **:** a pouched burrowing rodent of dry regions of the western United States

Kant•ian \'kant-ē-ən, 'känt-\ *adj* **:** of, relating to, or characteristic of Kant or his philosophy

ka•o•lin *also* **ka•o•line** \'kā-ə-lən\ *n* **:** a fine usually white clay that is used in ceramics and refractories and as an adsorbent [French *kaolin,* from *Kao-ling,* hill in China]

ka•pok \'kā-,päk\ *n* **:** a mass of silky fibers that clothe the seeds of the ceiba tree and are used as a filling for mattresses, life preservers, and sleeping bags and as insulation [Malay]

kap•pa \'kap-ə\ *n* **:** the 10th letter of the Greek alphabet — Κ or κ

ka•put \kä-'pu̇t, kə-, -'püt\ *adj* **1 :** utterly defeated or destroyed **2 :** made useless or unable to function **3 :** hopelessly outmoded [German, from French *capot* "not having made a trick at piquet"]

△ **origin** To win all the tricks in the card game piquet is *faire capot,* "to make *capot*", in French, while *être capot,* "to be *capot*", is to have lost all the tricks in a game. In German *capot* was transliterated as *kaput,* and from the sense of having lost a game German *kaput* developed the senses "broken", "finished", "utterly destroyed". *Kaput* was borrowed into English from German early in the 20th century.

kar•a•kul \'kar-ə-kəl\ *n* **1 :** any of a breed of hardy fat-tailed Asian sheep with coarse wiry brown fur **2 :** the tightly curled glossy black coat of the newborn lamb of a karakul valued as fur [*Karakul,* village in Soviet Central Asia]

kar•at *or* **car•at** \'kar-ət\ *n* **:** a unit of fineness for gold equal to 1/24 part of pure gold in an alloy [probably from Middle French *carat,* from Medieval Latin *carratus* "²carat"]

ka•ra•te \kə-'rät-ē\ *n* **:** an oriental system of self-defense in which an attacker is disabled with kicks and punches [Japanese, literally, "empty hand"]

kar•ma \'kär-mə, 'kər-\ *n, often cap* **1 :** the force generated by one's actions that is held in Hinduism and Buddhism to sustain the cycle of deaths and rebirths and to determine destiny in one's next existence **2 :** a distinctive spirit or atmosphere that can be sensed [Sanskrit *karman,* literally, "work"] — **kar•mic** \-mik\ *adj, often cap*

kar•roo *or* **ka•roo** \kə-'rü\ *n* **:** a dry tableland of southern Africa [Afrikaans *karo*]

karst \'kärst\ *n* **:** an irregular limestone region with sinks, underground streams, and caverns [German]

kart•ing \'kärt-iŋ\ *n* **:** the sport of racing miniature automobiles [probably from *GoKart*, a trademark]

kary- *or* **karyo-** *combining form* **:** nucleus of a cell ⟨*karyo*kinesis⟩ [Greek *karyon* "nut"]

karyo•ki•ne•sis \,kar-ē-ō-kə-'nē-səs, -kī-'nē-\ *n* **:** MITOSIS — **karyo•ki•net•ic** \-'net-ik\ *adj*

[1]**karyo•type** \'kar-ē-ə-,tīp\ *n* **:** the set of characteristics that distinguish the chromosomes of a particular cell or group — **karyo•typ•ic** \,kar-ē-ə-'tip-ik\ *adj* — **karyo•typ•i•cal•ly** \-i-kə-lē, -klē\ *adv*

[2]**karyotype** *vt* **:** to determine the karyotype of

Kash•mir goat \,kash-,miər-, ,kazh-\ *n* **:** an Indian goat whose soft woolly undercoat forms cashmere wool [*Kashmir*, region in India]

kash•ruth *or* **kash•rut** \kä-'shrüt, -'shrüth\ *n* **1 :** the state of being kosher **2 :** the Jewish dietary laws [Hebrew *kashrūth*, literally, "fitness"]

Kas•site \'kas-,īt\ *n* **:** a member of a people from the Iranian plateau ruling Babylon between 1600 and 1200 B.C.

ka•ty•did \'kāt-ē-,did\ *n* **:** any of several large green American long-horned grasshoppers with stridulating organs on the fore wings of the males that produce a loud shrill sound [imitative]

kau•ri \'kaur-ē\ *n* **1 a :** any of several trees of the pine family; *esp* **:** a tall New Zealand timber tree **b :** the tough white straight-grained wood of a kauri **2 :** a recent or fossil resin from New Zealand kauris used especially in varnish and linoleum [Maori *kawri*]

kay•ak \'kī-,ak\ *n* **1 :** an Eskimo canoe made of a frame entirely covered with skins except for a small opening in the center where one or two paddlers sit **2 :** a covered canoe resembling a kayak [Eskimo *qajaq*]

kayak 1

ka•zoo \kə-'zü\ *n, pl* **kazoos :** a toy musical instrument containing a membrane which produces a buzzing tone when one hums or sings into the mouth hole [imitative]

kea \'kē-ə\ *n* **:** a New Zealand parrot that is normally insectivorous but sometimes attacks and kills sheep for their flesh [Maori]

ke•bab *or* **ke•bob** *variant of* KABOB

[1]**kedge** \'kej\ *vt* **:** to move (a ship) by hauling on a line attached to a small anchor dropped at the distance and in the direction desired [Middle English *caggen*]

[2]**kedge** *n* **:** a small anchor used especially in kedging

[1]**keel** \'kēl\ *n* **1 a :** a timber or plate running lengthwise along the center of the bottom of a ship and usually projecting from the bottom **b :** SHIP **2 a :** something (as the breastbone of a bird) like a ship's keel in form or use; *esp* **:** a ridged part **b :** the lower two petals of a pea flower [Old Norse *kjölr*]

[2]**keel** *vb* **1 a :** to turn over **b :** to fall in or as if in a faint — usually used with *over* **2 :** to provide with a keel

keel•boat \'kēl-,bōt\ *n* **:** a shallow covered riverboat with a keel that is usually rowed, poled, or towed and that is used for freight — **keel•boat•man** \-mən\ *n*

keel•haul \-,hȯl\ *vt* **1 :** to haul under the keel of a ship as punishment or torture **2 :** to rebuke severely

keel•son \'kel-sən, 'kēl-\ *n* **:** a structure running above and fastened to the keel of a ship in order to strengthen its framework [probably of Scandinavian origin]

[1]**keen** \'kēn\ *adj* **1 :** having a fine edge or point **:** SHARP ⟨a *keen* knife⟩ **2 :** CUTTING 2, STINGING ⟨a *keen* wind⟩ **3 :** EAGER, ENTHUSIASTIC ⟨*keen* about baseball⟩ **4 a :** very alert and perceptive ⟨a *keen* mind⟩ **b :** unusually sensitive ⟨*keen* eyesight⟩ [Old English *cēne* "brave, fierce"] **syn** see SHARP — **keen•ly** *adv* — **keen•ness** \'kēn-nəs\ *n*

[2]**keen** *vb* **:** to lament with a keen [Irish Gaelic *caoinim* "I lament"] — **keen•er** *n*

[3]**keen** *n* **:** a loud wailing lament for the dead

[1]**keep** \'kēp\ *vb* **kept** \'kept\; **keep•ing 1 a :** to perform as a duty **:** FULFILL ⟨*keep* a promise⟩ **b :** to observe in a fitting or customary manner **:** not neglect ⟨*keep* a holiday⟩ **2 a :** GUARD ⟨*keep* us from harm⟩ **b :** to take care of ⟨*keep* a war orphan⟩ ⟨*keep* house⟩ **3 :** to continue doing something **:** MAINTAIN ⟨*keep* silence⟩ ⟨*keep* on working⟩ **4 :** HOLD, DETAIN ⟨*keep* a prisoner in jail⟩ **5 a :** to cause to remain in a given place, situation, or condition ⟨*keep* someone waiting⟩ **b :** to remain unspoiled ⟨milk may not *keep* in hot weather⟩ **6 :** to hold back **:** WITHHOLD ⟨*keep* a secret⟩ **7 :** to possess permanently ⟨*keep* what you have earned⟩ **8 :** REFRAIN ⟨unable to *keep* from talking⟩ **9 :** to have in one's service or at one's disposal ⟨*keep* servants⟩ ⟨*keep* a car⟩ **10 :** to preserve a record in ⟨*keep* a diary⟩ **11 :** STAY, REMAIN ⟨*keep* off the grass⟩ **12 :** to have on hand regularly for sale ⟨*keep* neckties⟩ [Old English *cēpan*]
• syn KEEP, OBSERVE, CELEBRATE, COMMEMORATE mean to notice or honor a day, occasion, or deed. KEEP stresses the idea of not neglecting or violating ⟨*keep* the Sabbath⟩ OBSERVE is likely to imply marking by ceremonious performance ⟨not all holidays are *observed* nationally⟩ CELEBRATE suggests acknowledging an occasion by festivity ⟨*celebrate* Christmas by giving gifts⟩ COMMEMORATE implies remembrance and suggests observances that tend to call to mind what the occasion stands for ⟨*commemorate* Memorial Day with the laying of wreaths⟩ — **keep one's end up :** to do one's share or duty

[2]**keep** *n* **1 :** FORTRESS; *esp* **:** the strongest part of a medieval castle **2 :** the means by which one is kept; *esp* **:** one's food and lodging ⟨earned their *keep*⟩ — **for keeps 1 a :** with the provision that one keep one's winnings ⟨play marbles *for keeps*⟩ **b :** with deadly seriousness **2 :** PERMANENTLY ⟨came home *for keeps*⟩

keep•er \'kē-pər\ *n* **:** a person who watches, guards, maintains, or takes care of something ⟨the *keeper* of a bar⟩

keep•ing \'kē-piŋ\ *n* **1 :** OBSERVANCE ⟨the *keeping* of a holiday⟩ **2 :** CUSTODY 1, CARE **3 :** AGREEMENT, HARMONY ⟨in *keeping* with good taste⟩

keep•sake \'kēp-,sāk\ *n* **:** something kept or given to be kept as a memento [*keep* + *-sake* (as in *namesake*)]

keep up *vb* **1 :** MAINTAIN, SUSTAIN ⟨*keep* standards *up*⟩ **2 :** to keep informed ⟨*keep up* on politics⟩ **3 :** to continue without interruption ⟨rain *kept up* all night⟩ **4 :** to stay even with others (as in a race)

keet \'kēt\ *n* **:** a young guinea fowl [imitative]

keg \'keg, 'kag, 'kāg\ *n* **1 :** a small cask or barrel holding about 114 liters or less **2 :** the contents of a keg [Middle English *kag*, of Scandinavian origin]

kelp \'kelp\ *n* **1 :** any of various large brown seaweeds; *also* **:** a mass of these **2 :** the ashes of seaweed used as a fertilizer and a source of iodine [Middle English *culp*]

kel•pie \'kel-pē\ *n* **:** an Australian sheep dog of a breed developed by crossing the dingo with British sheep dogs [*Kelpie*, the name of an early dog of this breed]

kelpie

Kelt, Kelt•ic *variant of* CELT, CELTIC

kel•vin \'kel-vən\ *n* **:** a unit of temperature equal to 1/273.16 of the Kelvin scale temperature of the triple point of water

Kel•vin \'kel-vən\ *adj* **:** relating to, conforming to, or having a temperature scale on which the unit of measurement is the same size as the Celsius degree and according to which absolute zero is 0° or the equivalent of −273.15°C — abbreviation *K* [William Thomson, Lord *Kelvin*]

[1]**ken** \'ken\ *vb* **kenned**; **ken•ning** *chiefly Scottish* **:** KNOW [Old Norse *kenna* "to perceive"]

[2]**ken** *n* **1 :** range of vision **2 :** range of understanding

ke•naf \kə-'naf\ *n* **:** an East Indian hibiscus that yields a strong cordage fiber; *also* **:** its fiber [Persian]

ken•do \'ken-dō\ *n* **:** a traditional Japanese sport of fencing with bamboo staves [Japanese *kendō*, from *ken* "sword" + *dō* "art"]

[1]**ken•nel** \'ken-l\ *n* **1 :** a shelter for a dog **2 :** an establishment for the breeding or boarding of dogs [derived from Latin *canis* "dog"]

[2]**kennel** *vb* **-neled** *or* **-nelled**; **-nel•ing** *or* **-nel•ling** : to put, keep, or take shelter in or as if in a kennel

Ken•tucky coffee tree \kən-ˌtək-ē-\ *n* : a tall North American leguminous tree with large woody pods whose seeds have been used as a substitute for coffee

ke•pi \ˈkā-pē, ˈkep-ē\ *n* : a military cap with a round flat top sloping toward the front and a visor [French *képi*]

ker•a•tin \ˈker-ət-n\ *n* : any of various sulfur-containing fibrous proteins that form the chemical basis of hair and horny tissues [Greek *kerat-, keras* "horn"] — **ke•ra•ti•nous** \kə-ˈrat-n-əs, ˌker-ə-ˈtī-nəs\ *adj*

kerb \ˈkərb\ *n, British* : CURB 4

ker•chief \ˈkər-chəf, -ˌchēf\ *n, pl* **kerchiefs** \-chəfs, -ˌchēfs\ *also* **kerchieves** \-ˌchēvz\ **1** : a square of cloth worn especially by women as a head covering or around the neck **2** : HANDKERCHIEF 1 [Old French *cuevrechief,* from *covrir* "to cover" + *chief* "head", from Latin *caput*]

kerf \ˈkərf\ *n* : a slit or notch made by a saw or cutting torch [Old English *cyrf* "action of cutting"]

ker•mes \ˈkər-mēz\ *n* : the dried bodies of the females of various scale insects used as a red dyestuff [French *kermès,* from Arabic *qirmiz*]

ker•mis *or* **ker•mess** \ˈkər-məs\ *n* : an outdoor festival of the Low Countries [Dutch *kermis*]

kern *or* **kerne** \ˈkərn, ˈkeərn\ *n* : a lightly armed foot soldier of medieval Ireland or Scotland [Irish *cethern* "band of soldiers"]

ker•nel \ˈkərn-l\ *n* **1 a** : the inner softer part of a seed, fruit stone, or nut **b** : a whole seed of a cereal **2** : a central or essential part : CORE [Old English *cyrnel,* from *corn* "grain"]

kern•ite \ˈkər-ˌnīt\ *n* : a mineral $Na_2B_4O_7 \cdot 4H_2O$ that consists of sodium, boron, and water and is an important source of borax [*Kern* county, California]

ker•o•sene *or* **ker•o•sine** \ˈker-ə-ˌsēn, ˌker-ə-ˈ, ˈkar-, ˌkar-\ *n* : a thin oil consisting of a mixture of hydrocarbons usually obtained by distillation of petroleum and used for a fuel and as a solvent [Greek *kēros* "wax"]

ker•ria \ˈker-ē-ə\ *n* : any of a genus of yellow-flowered shrubs related to the roses [William *Kerr,* died 1814, English gardener]

Ker•ry blue terrier \ˌker-ē-\ *n* : any of an Irish breed of medium-sized terriers with a long head, deep chest, and silky bluish coat [County *Kerry,* Ireland]

ker•sey \ˈkər-zē\ *n* : a coarse ribbed woolen cloth for hose and work clothes [*Kersey,* England]

kes•trel \ˈkes-trəl\ *n* : a small European falcon that hovers in the air against a wind [Middle French *crecerelle*]

ketch \ˈkech\ *n* : a 2-masted fore-and-aft-rigged sailing vessel with the mizzenmast forward of the rudder [Middle English *cache*]

ketch

ketch•up *variant of* CATSUP

ke•tone \ˈkē-ˌtōn\ *n* : an organic compound with a carbonyl group attached to two carbon atoms [German *keton*] — **ke•ton•ic** \kē-ˈtän-ik\ *adj*

ket•tle \ˈket-l\ *n* : a metallic vessel for boiling liquids; *esp* : TEAKETTLE [Old Norse *ketill,* from Latin *catillus* "small bowl", from *catinus* "bowl"]

ket•tle•drum \-ˌdrəm\ *n* : a brass or copper kettle-shaped drum with parchment stretched across the top that can be tuned to definite pitches

[1]**key** \ˈkē\ *n, pl* **keys 1 a** : a usually metal instrument by which the bolt of a lock is turned **b** : a device having the form or function of a key ⟨a *key* for winding a clock⟩ **2 a** : a means of gaining or preventing entrance, possession, or control **b** : an instrumental or deciding factor **3 a** : something that gives an explanation or solution **b** : a list of words or phrases giving an explanation of symbols or abbreviations **c** : an arrangement of usually opposed characteristics of a group of plants or animals used for identification **d** : a map legend **4** : a small piece of wood or metal used as a wedge or for preventing motion between parts **5** : one of the levers with a flat surface that is pressed by a finger in operating or playing an instrument (as a typewriter, piano, or clarinet) **6** : SAMARA **7** : a system of seven tones based on their relationship to a tonic; *esp* : the tonality of a scale **8 a** : characteristic style or tone **b** : the tone or pitch of a voice **9** : a small switch for opening or closing an electric circuit [Old English *cǣg*]

[2]**key** *vb* **keyed** \ˈkēd\; **key•ing 1** : to lock or secure with a key **2** : to regulate the musical pitch of **3** : to make appropriate : ATTUNE **4** : to make nervous or tense — usually used with *up* ⟨was all *keyed* up about the examination⟩ **5** : to use a key

[3]**key** *adj* : of basic importance : FUNDAMENTAL

[4]**key** *n* : a low island or reef; *esp* : one of the coral islets off the southern coast of Florida [Spanish *cayo,* of American Indian origin]

[1]**key•board** \ˈkē-ˌbōrd, -ˌbȯrd\ *n* **1** : a bank of keys on a musical instrument (as a piano) **2** : an arrangement of keys by which a machine (as a typewriter) is operated

[2]**keyboard** *vb* **1** : to operate a machine with a keyboard **2** : to capture or set (as data or text) by means of a machine with a keyboard — **key•board•er** *n*

key•hole \ˈkē-ˌhōl\ *n* : a hole for receiving a key

[1]**key•note** \-ˌnōt\ *n* **1** : the first and fundamental tone of a scale **2** : the fundamental or central fact, idea, or mood ⟨humor is the *keynote* of the play⟩

[2]**keynote** *vt* **1** : to set the keynote of **2** : to deliver the keynote address at — **key•not•er** *n*

keynote address *n* : an address designed to present the issues of primary interest to a gathering (as a political convention) and often to arouse unity and enthusiasm — called also *keynote speech*

key•punch \ˈkē-ˌpənch\ *n* : a machine with a keyboard used to cut holes or notches in punch cards — **keypunch** *vt* — **key•punch•er** *n*

key signature *n* : the sharps or flats placed after a clef in music to indicate the key

key•stone \ˈkē-ˌstōn\ *n* **1** : the wedge-shaped piece at the crown of an arch that locks the other pieces in place **2** : something on which associated things depend for support

1 keystone 1

key•stroke \-ˌstrōk\ *n* : the act or an instance of pushing down a key on a keyboard — **keystroke** *vb*

key•way \-ˌwā\ *n* : a groove or channel for a key

kha•ki \ˈkak-ē, ˈkäk-, *Canadian often* ˈkärk-\ **1** : a light yellowish brown **2 a** : a khaki-colored cloth made usually of cotton or wool **b** : a military uniform of this cloth — usually used in pl. [Hindi *khākī* "dust-colored", from *khāk* "dust", from Persian]

Khal•kha \ˈkal-kə\ *n* **1** : a member of a Mongol people of Outer Mongolia **2** : the language of the Khalkha people used as the official language of the Mongolian People's Republic

[1]**khan** \ˈkän, ˈkan\ *n* **1** : a medieval sovereign of China and ruler over the Turkish, Tatar, and Mongol tribes **2** : a local chieftain or man of rank in some countries of central Asia [Middle French *caan,* of Turkic origin] — **khan•ate** \-ˌāt\ *n*

[2]**khan** *n* : an inn or rest house in some Asian countries : CARAVANSARY [Arabic *khān*]

khe•dive \kə-ˈdēv\ *n* : a Turkish governor of Egypt from 1867 to 1914 [French *khédive,* from Turkish *hidiv*]

Khmer \kə-ˈmeər\ *n* **1** : a member of an aboriginal people of Cambodia **2** : the official language of Cambodia — **Khmer•ian** \-ˈmer-ē-ən\ *adj*

kib•butz \kib-ˈu̇ts, -ˈüts\ *n, pl* **kib•but•zim** \-ˌu̇t-ˈsēm, -ˌüt-\ : a collective farm or settlement in Israel [Modern Hebrew *qibbūṣ*]

kibe \ˈkīb\ *n, archaic* : CHILBLAIN [Middle English]

kib•itz•er \ˈkib-ət-sər\ *n* : one who looks on and often offers unwanted advice or comment especially at a card game [Yiddish *kibitsen* "to kibitz", from German *kiebitzen,* from *kiebitz* "peewit, busybody"] — **kib•itz** \-əts\ *vb*

\ə\ **abut**	\au̇\ **out**	\i\ **tip**	\ȯ\ **saw**	\u̇\ **foot**
\ər\ **further**	\ch\ **chin**	\ī\ **life**	\ȯi\ **coin**	\y\ **yet**
\a\ **mat**	\e\ **pet**	\j\ **job**	\th\ **thin**	\yü\ **few**
\ā\ **take**	\ē\ **easy**	\ng\ **sing**	\t͟h\ **this**	\yu̇\ **cure**
\ä\ **cot, cart**	\g\ **go**	\ō\ **bone**	\ü\ **food**	\zh\ **vision**

△ **origin** Peewits, or lapwings, gather in flocks in fields and pastures, crying "pewit", or "kiebitz," or the like. (The variation is not in the birds' call, of course, but in human interpretations of it.) These creatures seem to show a general curiosity about the world, though they are really only looking for food. The peewit's German name, *kiebitz,* came to be applied to human busybodies as well as to the inquisitive birds. Later a verb was formed from the noun: a nosy onlooker at cards could be said to *kiebitzen.* The word passed from German into Yiddish as *kibitsen,* and thence to English as *kibitz.*

ki•bosh \ˈkī-ˌbäsh\ *n* : something that serves as a check or stop ⟨put the *kibosh* on⟩

[1]**kick** \ˈkik\ *vb* **1** : to strike out (as in defense or at a ball in games) with the foot or feet **2** : to strike, thrust, or hit violently with the foot **3** : to object strongly : PROTEST ⟨*kick* because prices were raised⟩ **4** : to recoil when fired **5** : to score by kicking a ball ⟨*kick* the point after touchdown⟩ [Middle English *kiken*] — **kick•er** *n*

[2]**kick** *n* **1 a** (1) : a blow with the foot (2) : a propelling of a ball with the foot **b** : the power to kick **c** : a rhythmic motion of the legs in swimming **2** : a forceful jolt or thrust suggesting a kick; *esp* : the recoil of a gun **3 a** : a feeling or expression of opposition or objection **b** : the grounds for objection **4** : a stimulating effect especially of pleasure

kick around *vt* **1** : to treat in an inconsiderate or high-handed fashion **2** : to consider, examine, or discuss from various angles ⟨*kicked* the idea *around* at the meeting⟩

kick•back \ˈkik-ˌbak\ *n* **1** : a sharp violent reaction **2** : a secret return of a part of a sum received

kick in *vb* : CONTRIBUTE 1

kick•off \ˈkik-ˌȯf\ *n* **1** : a kick that puts the ball into play in a football or soccer game **2** : COMMENCEMENT 1

kick off \kik-ˈȯf, ˈkik-\ *vb* **1** : to start or resume play in football or soccer by a placekick **2** : to begin or begin something : COMMENCE ⟨*kicked* the campaign *off* with a dinner⟩

kick out *vt* : to throw out ⟨*kicked* them *out* of the club for nonpayment of dues⟩

[1]**kid** \ˈkid\ *n* **1** : the young of a goat or of a related animal **2 a** : the flesh, fur, or skin of a kid **b** : something (as leather) made of kid **3** : CHILD 2a, YOUNGSTER [Middle English *kide,* of Scandinavian origin] — **kid•dish** \ˈkid-ish\ *adj*

[2]**kid** *vb* **kid•ded; kid•ding 1** : to deceive as a joke : FOOL **2** : to make fun of : TEASE [probably from [1]*kid*] — **kid•der** *n* — **kid•ding•ly** \ˈkid-ing-lē\ *adv*

kid glove *n* : a dress glove made of kidskin — **kid–gloved** \ˈkid-ˈgləvd\ *adj* — **with kid gloves** : with special consideration

kid•nap \ˈkid-ˌnap\ *vb* **kid•napped** *or* **kid•naped** \-ˌnapt\; **kid•nap•ping** *or* **kid•nap•ing** \-ˌnap-ing\ : to carry away a person by unlawful force or by fraud and against his or her will [probably back-formation from *kidnapper,* from [1]*kid* + obsolete *napper* "thief"] — **kid•nap•per** *or* **kid•nap•er** \-ˌnap-ər\ *n*

kid•ney \ˈkid-nē\ *n, pl* **kidneys 1** : either of a pair of oval to bean-shaped organs situated in the body cavity near the spinal column that excrete waste in the form of urine **2** : an excretory organ of an invertebrate animal [Middle English]

kidney bean *n* : a common garden bean grown especially for its nutritious seeds; *also* : a rather large dark red bean seed

kid•skin \ˈkid-ˌskin\ *n* : the skin of a young goat or leather made from or resembling this

kie•sel•guhr *or* **kie•sel•gur** \ˈkē-zəl-ˌgu̇r\ *n* : loose or porous diatomite [German *kieselgur*]

[1]**kill** \ˈkil\ *vb* **1** : to deprive of life : put to death **2** : DESTROY, RUIN ⟨*kill* all chance of success⟩ **3** : to use up ⟨*kill* time⟩ **4** : DEFEAT ⟨*kill* a proposed law⟩ **5** : to mark for omission ⟨*kill* a news story⟩ **6** : to hit so hard that a return is impossible [Middle English *killen*]

• syn KILL, SLAY, MURDER, ASSASSINATE mean to deprive of life. KILL simply states the fact of death by any agency in any manner; SLAY, chiefly literary, implies deliberateness and violence but not necessarily motive; MURDER implies motive and premeditation and usually secrecy and stresses full moral responsibility; ASSASSINATE applies to open or secret killing often for political motives.

[2]**kill** *n* **1** : an act of killing **2 a** : an animal killed in a hunt, season, or particular period of time **b** : an enemy airplane, submarine, or ship destroyed by military action

kill•deer \ˈkil-ˌdiər\ *n, pl* **killdeers** *or* **killdeer** : a North American plover with a plaintive penetrating cry [imitative]

kill•er \ˈkil-ər\ *n* **1** : one that kills **2** : KILLER WHALE

killer whale *n* : a gregarious largely black flesh-eating whale 5 to 10 meters long

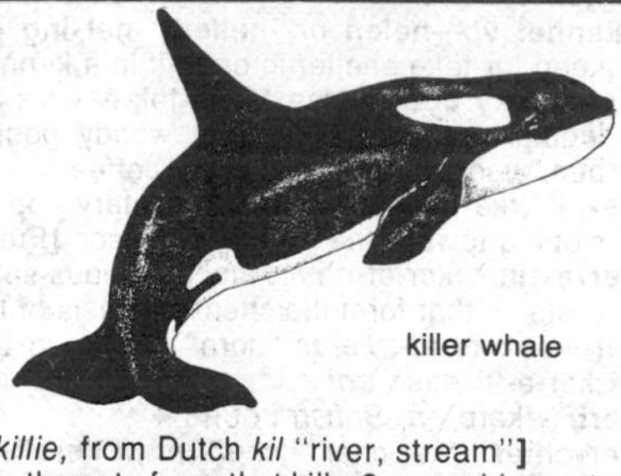

killer whale

kil•li•fish \ˈkil-ē-ˌfish\ *n* : any of numerous small fishes including some used as bait, in mosquito control, and as aquarium fishes [earlier *killie,* from Dutch *kil* "river, stream"]

kill•ing \ˈkil-ing\ *n* **1** : the act of one that kills **2** : a sudden notable gain or profit ⟨made a *killing* in the stock market⟩

kill•joy \ˈkil-ˌjȯi\ *n* : a person who spoils the pleasure of others

kiln \ˈkiln, ˈkil\ *n* : an oven, furnace, or heated enclosure for processing a substance by burning, firing, or drying [Old English *cyln,* from Latin *culina* "kitchen"] — **kiln** *vt*

ki•lo \ˈkē-lō\ *n, pl* **kilos 1** : KILOGRAM **2** : KILOMETER

kilo- *combining form* : thousand ⟨*kilo*ton⟩ [French, from Greek *chilioi*]

ki•lo•cal•o•rie \ˈkē-lə-ˌkal-rē, ˈkil-ə-, -ə-rē\ *n* : CALORIE 1b

kilo•cy•cle \ˈkil-ə-ˌsī-kəl\ *n* : 1000 cycles; *esp* : KILOHERTZ

ki•lo•gram \ˈkē-lə-ˌgram, ˈkil-ə-\ *n* : the basic metric unit of mass and weight equal to 1000 grams — see METRIC SYSTEM table

ki•lo•hertz \ˈkil-ə-ˌhərts, ˈkē-lə-, -ˌheərts\ *n* : 1000 hertz

kilo•li•ter \ˈkil-ə-ˌlēt-ər\ *n* — see METRIC SYSTEM table

ki•lo•me•ter \kil-ˈäm-ət-ər, ˈkil-ə-ˌmēt-\ *n* — see METRIC SYSTEM table

ki•lo•ton \ˈkē-lə-ˌtən, ˈkil-ə-\ *n* **1** : 1000 tons **2** : an explosive force equivalent to that of 1000 tons of TNT

ki•lo•volt \-ˌvōlt\ *n* : a unit of electromotive force equal to 1000 volts

kilo•watt \ˈkil-ə-ˌwät\ *n* : a unit of power equal to 1000 watts

kilowatt–hour *n* : a unit of work or energy (as electrical energy) equal to that expended in one hour at a rate of one kilowatt

kilt \ˈkilt\ *n* **1** : a knee-length pleated skirt usually of tartan worn by men in Scotland and by members of Scottish regiments in the British army **2** : a garment that resembles a Scottish kilt [Middle English *kilten* "to gather up (a skirt)", of Scandinavian origin] — **kilt•ed** \ˈkil-təd\ *adj*

kil•ter \ˈkil-tər\ *n* : proper condition : ORDER ⟨out of *kilter*⟩ [origin unknown]

ki•mo•no \kə-ˈmō-nə\ *n, pl* **-nos 1** : a loose robe with wide sleeves and a broad sash traditionally worn as an outer garment by the Japanese **2** : a loose dressing gown worn chiefly by women [Japanese, "clothes"]

kimono 1

[1]**kin** \ˈkin\ *n* **1** : a person's relatives : KINDRED **2** : KINSMAN [Old English *cyn*]

[2]**kin** *adj* : KINDRED, RELATED

-kin \kən\ *also* **-kins** \kənz\ *n suffix* : little ⟨nap*kin*⟩ [Dutch *-kin*]

[1]**kind** \ˈkīnd\ *n* **1 a** : a natural group : VARIETY ⟨different *kinds* of sharks⟩ **b** : a group united by common qualities, traits, or interests : CATEGORY **c** : a doubtful or barely admissible member of a category ⟨a *kind* of gray⟩ **2** : essential quality or character ⟨punishment different in *kind* rather than degree⟩ **3 a** : goods or commodities as distinguished from money **b** : the equivalent of what has been offered or received [Old English *cynd* "birth, nature"]

• syn SORT, TYPE: KIND and SORT are close synonyms and usually imply a group with less specific resemblances than TYPE; KIND may suggest natural or logical grouping; SORT sometimes suggests disparagement ⟨the flashier *sort* of holiday resorts⟩ TYPE may suggest clearly marked similarity throughout the items included so that each is typical of the group; TYPE, KIND, and SORT are usually interchangeable and are used most of the time without attention to special connotations.

[2]**kind** *adj* **1 :** having the will to do good and to bring happiness to others **2 :** showing or growing out of gentleness or goodness of heart ⟨a *kind* act⟩

kin•der•gar•ten \ˈkin-dər-ˌgärt-n, -də-, -ˌgärd-\ *n* **:** a school or class for children usually from four to six years old [German, from *kinder* "children" + *garten* "garden"]

kin•der•gart•ner \-ˌgärt-nər, -ˌgärd-\ *n* **1 :** a kindergarten pupil **2 :** a kindergarten teacher

kind•heart•ed \ˈkīnd-ˈhärt-əd\ *adj* **:** having or showing a kind and sympathetic nature — **kind•heart•ed•ly** *adv* — **kind-heart•ed•ness** *n*

kin•dle \ˈkin-dl\ *vb* **kin•dled; kin•dling** \-dling, -dl-ing\ **1 :** to set on fire or catch fire **:** start burning ⟨*kindle* a fire⟩ **2 :** to stir up **:** AROUSE ⟨*kindle* anger⟩ **3 :** to light up as if with flame **:** GLOW ⟨with *kindling* eyes⟩ [Old Norse *kynda*] — **kin•dler** \-dlər, -dl-ər\ *n*

kin•dling \ˈkin-dling\ *n* **:** material that burns easily for starting a fire

[1]**kind•ly** \ˈkīn-dlē\ *adj* **kind•li•er; -est 1 :** of an agreeable or beneficial nature **:** PLEASANT ⟨*kindly* climate⟩ **2 :** of a sympathetic or generous nature **:** FRIENDLY ⟨*kindly* people⟩ — **kind-li•ness** *n*

[2]**kindly** *adv* **1 :** READILY ⟨does not take *kindly* to criticism⟩ **2 a :** in a kind manner **b :** as a gesture of goodwill **c :** in a gracious manner **:** COURTEOUSLY

kind•ness \ˈkīnd-nəs, ˈkīn-\ *n* **1 :** a kind deed **:** FAVOR **2 :** the quality or state of being kind

[1]**kin•dred** \ˈkin-drəd\ *n* **1 :** a group of related individuals **2 :** a person's relatives [Middle English, from *kin* + Old English *rǣden* "condition", from *rǣdan* "to advise, read"]

[2]**kindred** *adj* **:** of like nature or character

kine \ˈkīn\ *archaic pl of* COW

ki•ne•mat•ics \ˌkin-ə-ˈmat-iks, ˌkī-nə-\ *n* **:** a science that deals with aspects of motion (as acceleration and velocity) apart from considerations of mass and force [French *cinématique,* from Greek *kinēma* "motion", from *kinein* "to move"] — **ki•ne•mat-ic** \-ˈmat-ik\ *adj*

ki•ne•scope \ˈkin-ə-ˌskōp, ˈkī-nə-\ *n* **1 :** PICTURE TUBE **2 :** a moving picture made from the image on a kinescope [*Kinescope,* a former trademark] — **kinescope** *vt*

ki•ne•si•ol•o•gy \kə-ˌnē-sē-ˈäl-ə-jē, kī-, -ˌnē-zē-\ *n* **:** the study of the mechanical and anatomical relations involved in human movement

-ki•ne•sis \kə-ˈnē-səs, kī-, ˌkī-\ *n combining form, pl* **-ki•ne-ses** \-ˌsēz\ **:** division ⟨karyo*kinesis*⟩ [Greek *kinēsis* "motion", from *kinein* "to move"]

kin•es•the•sia \ˌkin-əs-ˈthē-zhə, -zhē-ə\ *or* **kin•es•the•sis** \-ˈthē-səs\ *n, pl* **-the•sias** *or* **-the•ses** \-ˈthē-ˌsēz\ **:** the sensation of bodily position, movement, or effort arising from receptors in the joints, tendons, and muscles; *also* **:** the sense involved [Greek *kinein* "to move" + *aisthēsis* "perception"] — **kin•es•thet•ic** \-ˈthet-ik\ *adj* — **kin•es•thet•i•cal•ly** \-ˈthet-i-kə-lē, -klē\ *adv*

ki•net•ic \kə-ˈnet-ik, kī-\ *adj* **:** of or relating to the motion of material bodies and the forces and energy associated with them [Greek *kinētikos,* from *kinein* "to move"]

kinetic energy *n* **:** energy associated with motion

ki•net•ics \kə-ˈnet-iks, kī-\ *n sing or pl* **1 :** a science that deals with the effects of forces upon the motions of material bodies or with changes in a physical or chemical system **2 :** the means by which a physical or chemical change is effected

kinetic theory *n* **:** a theory that states that all matter is composed of particles in motion and that the rate of motion varies directly with the temperature

kin•folk \ˈkin-ˌfōk\ *n* **:** a person's relatives

king \ˈking\ *n* **1 :** a male ruler of a country; *esp* **:** one whose position is hereditary and who rules for life **2** *cap* (1) **:** GOD 1 (2) **:** CHRIST **3 :** one that holds a dominant position; *esp* **:** a chief among competitors **4 :** the principal piece in a set of chessmen that can move ordinarily one square in any direction and has the power to capture but may never enter or remain in exposure to capture **5 :** a playing card bearing the stylized figure of a king **6 :** a checker that has been crowned [Old English *cyning*]

king•bird \-ˌbərd\ *n* **:** an American tyrant flycatcher

king crab *n* **1 :** HORSESHOE CRAB **2 :** any of several large edible crabs

king•dom \ˈking-dəm\ *n* **1 :** a country whose ruler is a king or queen **2 :** a sphere in which something or someone is dominant **3 :** one of the three primary divisions into which natural objects are classified — compare ANIMAL KINGDOM, MINERAL KINGDOM, PLANT KINGDOM

king•fish \ˈking-ˌfish\ *n* **:** any of various sea fishes; *esp* **:** a large sport and food fish of the warm western Atlantic resembling the related Spanish mackerel

king•fish•er \-ˌfish-ər\ *n* **:** any of a family of usually crested and bright-colored birds with a short tail and a long stout sharp bill

kingfisher

king•let \ˈking-lət\ *n* **:** any of several small birds that resemble warblers but have some of the habits of titmice

king•ly \ˈking-lē\ *adj* **1 :** having royal rank **2 :** of, relating to, or befitting a king — **king•li•ness** *n* — **kingly** *adv*

king•pin \ˈking-ˌpin\ *n* **1 :** the number 5 bowling pin **2 :** the chief person in a group or undertaking **3 :** a vertical bolt by which the forward axle and wheels of a vehicle are connected with other parts

king post *n* **:** a vertical member connecting the apex of a triangular truss with the base

Kings \ˈkingz\ *n* — see BIBLE table

King's English *n* **:** standard or correct English speech or usage

king•ship \ˈking-ˌship\ *n* **1 :** the position, office, or dignity of a king **2 :** the personality of a king **3 :** government by a king

king–size \ˈking-ˌsīz\ *or* **king–sized** \-ˌsīzd\ *adj* **:** longer or larger than the usual or standard size

king snake *n* **:** any of numerous harmless brightly marked snakes of the southern and central United States that feed on rodents

[1]**kink** \ˈkingk\ *n* **1 :** a short tight twist or curl **2 :** a mental or physical peculiarity **:** QUIRK **3 :** a cramp or stiffness in some part of the body **:** CRICK **4 :** an imperfection (as in design) likely to cause difficulties in operation [Dutch] — **kinky** \ˈking-kē\ *adj*

[2]**kink** *vb* **:** to form a kink **:** make a kink in

kin•ka•jou \ˈking-kə-ˌjü\ *n* **:** a slender long-tailed mammal of Central and South America related to the raccoon [French, of American Indian origin]

-kins — see -KIN

kins•folk \ˈkinz-ˌfōk\ *n* **:** a person's relatives

kin•ship \ˈkin-ˌship\ *n* **:** the quality or state of being kin

kins•man \ˈkinz-mən\ *n* **:** RELATIVE 3; *esp* **:** a male relative

kins•wom•an \ˈkinz-ˌwu̇m-ən\ *n* **:** a female relative

ki•osk \ˈkē-ˌäsk, kē-ˈ\ *n* **1 :** an open summerhouse or pavilion **2 :** a small light structure with one or more open sides used especially as a newsstand or a telephone booth [Turkish *kösk,* from Persian *kūshk* "portico"]

[1]**kip•per** \ˈkip-ər\ *n* **:** a kippered herring or salmon [Old English *cypera* "spawning salmon"]

[2]**kipper** *vt* **kip•pered; kip•per•ing** \ˈkip-ring, -ə-ring\ **:** to cure by salting and smoking

Kir•ghiz \kiər-ˈgēz\ *n* **:** a member of a Mongolian people with some Caucasian intermixture inhabiting chiefly the Kirghiz Republic

kirk \ˈkiərk, ˈkərk\ *n* **1** *chiefly Scottish* **:** CHURCH 1 **2** *cap* **:** the national church of Scotland as distinguished from the Church of England or the Anglican Church in Scotland [Old Norse *kirkja,* from Old English *cirice*]

kir•tle \ˈkərt-l\ *n* **:** a woman's dress, skirt, or petticoat [Old English *cyrtel*]

[1]**kiss** \ˈkis\ *vb* **1 :** to touch with the lips as a mark of affection or greeting **2 :** to touch gently or lightly ⟨a soft wind *kissing* the trees⟩ [Old English *cyssan*] — **kiss•able** \-ə-bəl\ *adj*

[2]**kiss** *n* **1 :** a caress with the lips **2 :** a gentle touch or contact **3 :** a bite-size candy often wrapped in paper or foil

\ə\ **abut**	\au̇\ **out**	\i\ **tip**	\ȯ\ **saw**	\u̇\ **foot**
\ər\ **further**	\ch\ **chin**	\ī\ **life**	\ȯi\ **coin**	\y\ **yet**
\a\ **mat**	\e\ **pet**	\j\ **job**	\th\ **thin**	\yü\ **few**
\ā\ **take**	\ē\ **easy**	\ng\ **sing**	\t͟h\ **this**	\yu̇\ **cure**
\ä\ **cot, cart**	\g\ **go**	\ō\ **bone**	\ü\ **food**	\zh\ **vision**

kiss•er \'kis-ər\ *n* **1 :** one that kisses **2** *slang* **:** MOUTH 1a; *also* **:** FACE 1

[1]kit \'kit\ *n* **1 a :** a collection of articles for personal use ⟨a travel *kit*⟩ **b :** a set of tools or implements ⟨a carpenter's *kit*⟩ **c :** a set of parts to be assembled ⟨model-airplane *kit*⟩ **d :** a packaged collection of related material ⟨convention *kit*⟩ **2 :** a container (as a bag or case) for a kit [Middle English, "wooden tub"]

[2]kit *n* **1 :** KITTEN **2 :** a young or undersized fur-bearing animal; *also* **:** its pelt

kitch•en \'kich-ən\ *n* **:** a place (as a room) with cooking facilities [Old English *cycene,* from Late Latin *coquina,* from Latin *coquere* "to cook"]

kitchen cabinet *n* **1 :** a cupboard with drawers and shelves for use in a kitchen **2 :** an informal group of advisers to the head of a government

kitch•en•ette \ˌkich-ə-'net\ *n* **:** a small kitchen or an alcove containing cooking facilities

kitchen garden *n* **:** a plot in which vegetables are grown for domestic use

kitchen midden *n* **:** a refuse heap; *esp* **:** a mound marking the site of a primitive human habitation

kitchen police *n* **:** KP

kitch•en•ware \'kich-ən-ˌwaər, -ˌweər\ *n* **:** utensils and appliances for use in a kitchen

kite \'kīt\ *n* **1 :** any of various hawks with long narrow wings, a deeply forked tail, and feet adapted for taking insects and small reptiles as prey **2 :** a light frame covered with paper or cloth, often provided with a balancing tail, and designed to be flown in the air at the end of a long string [Old English *cȳta*]

kith \'kith\ *n* **:** familiar friends, neighbors, or relatives ⟨*kith* and kin⟩ [Old English *cȳthth,* from *cūth* "known"]

kitsch \'kich\ *n* **:** second-rate or trashy art or literature [German]

kit•ten \'kit-n\ *n* **:** the young of a small mammal and especially of a cat [Middle English *kitoun,* derived from Late Latin *cattus* "cat"]

kit•ten•ish \'kit-nish, -n-ish\ *adj* **:** resembling a kitten; *esp* **:** PLAYFUL — **kit•ten•ish•ly** *adv* — **kit•ten•ish•ness** *n*

kit•ti•wake \'kit-ē-ˌwāk\ *n* **:** any of various gulls having the hind toe short and the wing tips black [imitative]

[1]kit•ty \'kit-ē\ *n, pl* **kitties :** CAT 1a; *esp* **:** KITTEN

[2]kitty *n, pl* **kitties 1 :** a fund in a poker game made up of contributions from each pot **2 :** a sum of money or a collection of goods made up of small contributions **:** POOL [[1]*kit*]

kit•ty-cor•ner *or* **kit•ty-cor•nered** *variant of* CATERCORNER

ki•va \'kē-və\ *n* **:** a Pueblo Indian ceremonial structure that is usually round and partly underground [Hopi]

Ki•wa•ni•an \kə-'wän-ē-ən\ *n* **:** a member of one of the major service clubs

ki•wi \'kē-ˌwē\ *n* **:** a flightless New Zealand bird with rudimentary wings, stout legs, a long bill, and grayish brown hairlike plumage [Maori]

kiwi

Klan \'klan\ *n* **:** an organization of Ku Kluxers; *also* **:** a subordinate unit of such an organization — **Klans•man** \'klanz-mən\ *n*

Klee•nex \'klē-ˌneks\ *trademark* — used for a cleansing tissue

klep•to•ma•nia \ˌklep-tə-'mā-nē-ə, -nyə\ *n* **:** a persistent neurotic impulse to steal especially without economic motive [Greek *kleptein* "to steal"] — **klep•to•ma•ni•ac** \-nē-ˌak\ *adj or n*

klieg light *or* **kleig light** \'klēg-'līt\ *n* **:** an arc lamp used in taking motion pictures [John H. *Kliegl,* died 1959, and Anton T. *Kliegl,* died 1927, German-born American lighting experts]

knack \'nak\ *n* **1 :** a clever way of doing something **:** TRICK **2 :** a natural ability **:** TALENT ⟨has a *knack* for using tools⟩ [Middle English *knak*]

knack•er \'nak-ər\ *n, British* **:** a buyer or processor of worn-out animals or their carcasses especially for animal feed and fertilizer [probably from English dialect *knacker* "saddle maker"] — **knack•ery** \-ə-rē\ *n*

knap•sack \'nap-ˌsak\ *n* **:** a case strapped on the back to carry supplies while on a march or hike [Low German *knappsack,* from *knappen* "to eat" + *sack* "bag"]

knap•weed \'nap-ˌwēd\ *n* **:** any of several weedy plants related to the cornflower [Middle English *knopwed,* from *knop* "knob" + *wed* "weed"]

knave \'nāv\ *n* **1** *archaic* **a :** a male servant **b :** a person of humble birth or position **2 :** a tricky deceitful person **:** ROGUE **3 :** JACK 5 [Old English *cnafa* "boy, servant"]

knav•ery \'nāv-rē, -ə-rē\ *n, pl* **-er•ies 1 :** the practices of a knave **:** RASCALITY **2 :** a roguish or mischievous act

knav•ish \'nā-vish\ *adj* **:** of, relating to, or characteristic of a knave; *esp* **:** DISHONEST — **knav•ish•ly** *adv*

knead \'nēd\ *vt* **1 :** to work and press into a mass with or as if with the hands **2 a :** to form or shape as if by kneading **b :** to work on as if by kneading [Old English *cnedan*] — **knead•er** *n*

[1]knee \'nē\ *n* **1 :** the joint or middle part of the human leg in which the femur, tibia, and kneecap come together; *also* **:** a corresponding part of a four-footed animal **2 :** something resembling the human knee **3 :** the part of a garment covering the knee [Old English *cnēow*] — **kneed** \'nēd\ *adj* — **to one's knees :** into a state of submission or defeat

[2]knee *vt* **kneed; knee•ing :** to strike with the knee

knee•cap \'nē-ˌkap\ *n* **:** a thick flat triangular bone that forms the front part of the knee and protects the front of the joint — called also *patella*

knee–deep \-'dēp\ *adj* **:** sunk to the knees ⟨*knee-deep* in mud⟩

knee–high \-'hī\ *adj* **:** rising or reaching upward to the knees

knee•hole \-ˌhōl\ *n* **:** a space (as under a desk) for the knees

knee jerk *n* **:** an involuntary forward kick produced by a light blow on the tendon below the kneecap

kneel \'nēl\ *vi* **knelt** \'nelt\ *or* **kneeled** \'nēld\; **kneel•ing :** to bend the knee **:** fall or rest on the knees [Old English *cnēowlian*] — **kneel•er** *n*

[1]knell \'nel\ *vb* **1 :** to ring especially for a death, funeral, or disaster **:** TOLL **2 :** to sound as a knell **3 :** to summon, announce, or proclaim by or as if by a knell [Old English *cnyllan*]

[2]knell *n* **1 :** a stroke or sound of a bell especially when rung slowly for a death, funeral, or disaster **2 :** DEATH KNELL

knew *past of* KNOW

knick•er•bock•er \'nik-ər-ˌbäk-ər, 'nik-ə-ˌ\ *n* **1** *cap* **:** a native or resident of the city or state of New York; *esp* **:** a descendant of the early Dutch settlers of New York **2** *pl* **:** KNICKERS [Diedrich *Knickerbocker,* fictitious author of *History of New York* (1809) by Washington Irving]

knick•ers \'nik-ərz\ *n pl* **:** loose-fitting short pants gathered just below the knee [short for *knickerbockers*]

knick•knack *or* **nick•nack** \'nik-ˌnak\ *n* **:** a small article intended for ornament [reduplication of *knack*]

[1]knife \'nīf\ *n, pl* **knives** \'nīvz\ **1 a :** a cutting instrument consisting of a sharp blade fastened to a handle **b :** a weapon resembling a knife **2 :** a sharp cutting blade or tool in a machine [Old English *cnīf*]

[2]knife *vb* **1 :** to stab, slash, or wound with a knife **2 :** to move like a knife ⟨*knifed* through the water⟩

knife–edge \'nī-ˌfej\ *n* **:** a sharp wedge usually of steel used as a fulcrum for a lever beam in a precision instrument (as a balance)

knife pleat *n* **:** one of a series of narrow sharply pressed pleats all turned in one direction

[1]knight \'nīt\ *n* **1 a :** a mounted warrior of feudal times serving a superior (as a king); *esp* **:** one who after a period of early service has been awarded a special military rank and has sworn to obey certain rules of conduct **b :** a man honored by a sovereign for merit and in Great Britain ranking below a baronet **c :** a person of another age or area resembling a medieval knight in rank or way of life **d :** a member of any of various orders or societies **e :** a man devoted to the service of a lady as her attendant or champion **2 :** a chess piece that has an L-shaped move of two squares in any row and one square in a perpendicular row over squares that may be occupied [Old English *cniht* "boy, warrior"]

[2]knight *vt* **:** to make a knight of

knight bachelor *n, pl* **knights bachelor :** a knight of the most ancient and lowest order of English knights

knight–er•rant \'nīt-'er-ənt\ *n, pl* **knights–errant :** a knight traveling in search of adventures in which to exhibit his military skill and generosity — **knight–er•rant•ry** \ˈnīt-ˈer-ən-trē\ *n*

knight•hood \ˈnīt-ˌhu̇d\ *n* **1 :** the rank, dignity, or profession of a knight **2 :** the qualities befitting a knight **3 :** knights as a class or body

knight•ly \ˈnīt-lē\ *adj* **1 :** of, relating to, or characteristic of a knight **2 :** made up of knights — **knight•li•ness** *n* — **knightly** *adv*

Knight of Co•lum•bus \-kə-ˈləm-bəs\ *n, pl* **Knights of Columbus :** a member of a fraternal and benevolent society of Roman Catholic men [Christopher *Columbus*]

Knight Templar *n, pl* **Knights Templars** *or* **Knights Templar 1 :** TEMPLAR 1 **2 :** a member of an order of Freemasonry

knit \ˈnit\ *vb* **knit** *or* **knit•ted; knit•ting 1 :** to form a fabric or garment by interlacing yarn or thread in connected loops with needles ⟨*knit* a sweater⟩ **2 :** to draw or come together closely as if knitted **:** unite firmly ⟨wait for a broken bone to *knit*⟩ **3 :** WRINKLE ⟨*knit* one's brows⟩ **4 :** to bind by some tie ⟨*knit* by common interests⟩ [Old English *cnyttan*] — **knit•ter** *n*

knit stitch *n* **:** a basic knitting stitch usually made with the yarn at the back of the work by inserting the right needle into the front part of a loop on the left needle from the left side, catching the yarn with the point of the right needle, and bringing it through the first loop to form a new loop — compare PURL STITCH

knit•ting *n* **1 :** the action or method of one that knits **2 :** work done or being done by one that knits

knitting needle *n* **:** a slender rod with one or both ends pointed used for hand knitting and usually made of metal, bone, or plastic

knit•wear \ˈnit-ˌwaər, -ˌweər\ *n* **:** knitted clothing

knob \ˈnäb\ *n* **1 a :** a rounded bulge **:** LUMP **b :** a small rounded ornament or handle **2 :** a rounded usually isolated hill or mountain [Middle English *knobbe*] — **knobbed** \ˈnäbd\ *adj* — **knob•by** \ˈnäb-ē\ *adj*

1knock \ˈnäk\ *vb* **1 a :** to strike something with a sharp blow **b :** to drive, force, or make by so striking **2 :** to collide with something **3 a :** BUSTLE ⟨*knocked* around in the kitchen most of the afternoon⟩ **b :** WANDER ⟨*knocked* about the world for years⟩ **4 :** to make a pounding noise especially as a result of abnormal ignition ⟨an automobile engine that *knocks*⟩ **5 :** to find fault with [Old English *cnocian*] — **knock together :** to make or assemble especially hurriedly or in a makeshift way

2knock *n* **1 a :** a sharp blow **b :** a severe misfortune or hardship **2 a :** a pounding noise **b :** a sharp metallic noise in an automobile engine caused by abnormal ignition

1knock•about \ˈnäk-ə-ˌbau̇t\ *adj* **1 :** suitable for rough use **2 :** being noisy and rough ⟨*knockabout* games⟩

2knockabout *n* **:** a sloop with a simple rig and no bowsprit and topmast

1knock•down \ˈnäk-ˌdau̇n\ *n* **1 :** a knocking down of something or someone (as a boxer) **2 :** something that strikes down or overwhelms **3 :** something easily assembled or disassembled

2knockdown *adj* **1 :** having such force as to strike down or overwhelm **2 :** that can easily be assembled or disassembled

knock down \näk-ˈdau̇n, ˈnäk-\ *vt* **1 :** to dispose of to a bidder at an auction sale **2 :** to take apart **:** DISASSEMBLE

knock•er \ˈnäk-ər\ *n* **:** one that knocks; *esp* **:** a device hinged to a door for use in knocking

knock–knee \ˈnäk-ˈnē, -ˌnē\ *n* **:** a condition in which the legs curve inward at the knees — **knock–kneed** \-ˈnēd\ *adj*

knock off *vb* **:** to discontinue doing something **:** STOP

knock•out \ˈnäk-ˌau̇t\ *n* **1 a :** the act of knocking out **:** the condition of being knocked out **b :** a blow that knocks out an opponent **2 :** something or someone sensationally striking or attractive — **knockout** *adj*

knock out \näk-ˈau̇t, ˈnäk-\ *vt* **1 :** to knock (a boxing opponent) unconscious **2 :** to make inoperative, useless, or unconscious

knock over *vt* **:** STEAL**: a :** HIJACK 1 **b :** ROB 1

knoll \ˈnōl\ *n* **:** a small round hill **:** MOUND [Old English *cnoll*]

1knot \ˈnät\ *n* **1 :** an interlacing (as of string or ribbon) that forms a lump or knob **2 :** something hard to solve **:** PROBLEM **3 :** a bond of union; *esp* **:** the marriage bond **4 a :** a projecting lump or swelling in tissue **b :** the base of a woody branch enclosed in the stem from which it arises; *also* **:** its section in lumber **5 :** a cluster of persons or things **:** GROUP **6 :** an ornamental bow of ribbon **7 :** one nautical mile per hour [Old English *cnotta*]

2knot *vb* **knot•ted; knot•ting 1 :** to tie in or with a knot **:** form knots in **2 :** to unite closely or intricately **:** ENTANGLE

3knot *n* **:** any of several sandpipers that breed in the Arctic and winter in temperate or warm regions [Middle English *knott*]

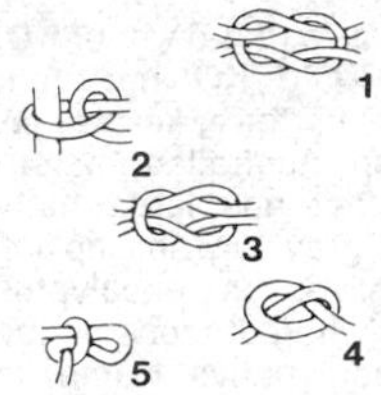

1knot 1: *1* granny, *2* half hitch, *3* square, *4* overhand, *5* slipknot

knot•grass \ˈnät-ˌgras\ *n* **:** a weed related to buckwheat with bluish gray grassy leaves and tiny flowers

knot•hole \-ˌhōl\ *n* **:** a hole in a board or tree trunk where a knot has come out

knot•ted *adj* **1 :** tied in or with a knot **2 :** full of knots **:** GNARLED **3 :** KNOTTY 2 **4 :** ornamented with knots or knobs

knot•ty \ˈnät-ē\ *adj* **knot•ti•er; -est 1 :** marked by or full of knots **2 :** puzzling because of intricacy **:** COMPLEX ⟨a *knotty* problem⟩

knotty pine *n* **:** pinewood with decorative distribution of knots used especially for interior finish

knout \ˈnau̇t, ˈnüt\ *n* **:** a whip for flogging criminals [Russian *knut,* of Scandinavian origin]

1know \ˈnō\ *vb* **knew** \ nü, ˈnyü\; **known** \ˈnōn\; **know•ing 1 a** (1) **:** to perceive directly **:** have direct awareness of (2) **:** to have understanding of ⟨*know* yourself⟩ **b**(1) **:** to perceive and remember the identity of **:** RECOGNIZE (2) **:** to be acquainted or familiar with **2 a :** to be able to declare truthfully ⟨*know* them to be honest⟩ **b :** to have a practical understanding of ⟨*knows* how to write⟩ **3 :** to have knowledge **4 :** to be or become aware ⟨*knew* about us⟩ [Old English *cnāwan*] — **know•able** \ˈnō-ə-bəl\ *adj* — **know•er** \ˈnō-ər, ˈnōr\ *n*

2know *n* **:** KNOWLEDGE — **in the know :** having confidential or exclusive information

know–how \ˈnō-ˌhau̇\ *n* **:** knowledge of how to do something smoothly and efficiently

1know•ing \ˈnō-ing\ *n* **:** ACQUAINTANCE 1, COGNIZANCE

2knowing *adj* **1 :** having or reflecting knowledge, information, or intelligence ⟨a *knowing* glance⟩ **2 :** shrewdly and keenly alert **3 :** INTENTIONAL — **know•ing•ly** \-ing-lē\ *adv*

knowl•edge \ˈnäl-ij\ *n* **1 :** understanding gained by actual experience ⟨a *knowledge* of carpentry⟩ **2 a :** the state of being aware of something or of having information **b :** range of information or awareness ⟨to the best of my *knowledge*⟩ **3 :** the act of understanding **:** clear perception of truth **4 :** something learned and kept in the mind **:** LEARNING ⟨a vast *knowledge* of history⟩ [Middle English *knowlege* "acknowledgment, cognizance", from *knowlechen* "to acknowledge", from *knowen* "to know"]

knowl•edge•able \ˈnäl-i-jə-bəl\ *adj* **:** having or exhibiting knowledge or intelligence **:** WISE — **knowl•edge•able•ness** *n* — **knowl•edge•ably** \-blē\ *adv*

know–noth•ing \ˈnō-ˌnəth-ing\ *n* **1 :** IGNORAMUS **2** *cap K&N* **:** a member of a 19th-century secret American political organization hostile to the political influence of recent immigrants and Roman Catholics

1knuck•le \ˈnək-əl\ *n* **1 :** the rounded lump formed by the ends of two bones where they come together in a joint; *esp* **:** such a lump at a finger joint **2 :** a cut of meat consisting of a tarsal or carpal joint with the adjoining flesh **3** *pl* **:** a set of joined metal finger rings worn over the front of the fist for use as a weapon — called also *brass knuckles* [Middle English *knokel*]

2knuckle *vi* **knuck•led; knuck•ling** \ˈnək-ling, -ə-ling\ **1 :** to place the knuckles on the ground in shooting a marble **2 :** to give in **:** SUBMIT — usually used with *under* **3 :** to apply oneself earnestly — usually used with *down*

knuck•le•bone \ˌnək-əl-ˈbōn, ˈnək-əl-ˌ\ *n* **:** a bone of a knuckle joint

knurl \ˈnərl\ *n* **1 :** a small protuberance or knob; *also* **:** a gnarl or twisted knot of wood **2 :** one of a series of small ridges or beads on a metal surface (as of a thumbscrew) to aid in gripping [probably blend of *knur* "gnarl" (from Middle English

\ə\ **abut**	\au̇\ **out**	\i\ **tip**	\ȯ\ **saw**	\u̇\ **foot**
\ər\ **further**	\ch\ **chin**	\ī\ **life**	\ȯi\ **coin**	\y\ **yet**
\a\ **mat**	\e\ **pet**	\j\ **job**	\th\ **thin**	\yü\ **few**
\ā\ **take**	\ē\ **easy**	\ng\ **sing**	\t͟h\ **this**	\yu̇\ **cure**
\ä\ **cot, cart**	\g\ **go**	\ō\ **bone**	\ü\ **food**	\zh\ **vision**

knorre) and *gnarl*] — **knurled** \ˈnərld\ *adj* — **knurly** \ˈnər-lē\ *adj*

1**KO** \kā-ˈō, ˈkā-ō\ *n, pl* **KO's** : a knockout in boxing [*k*nock *o*ut]

2**KO** *vt* **KO'd**; **KO'•ing** : to knock out in boxing

ko•ala \kō-ˈäl-ə, kə-ˈwäl-ə\ *n* : an Australian marsupial that has large hairy ears, gray fur, and no tail and lives in eucalyptus trees where it feeds on the leaves [native name in Australia]

koala

ko•bold \ˈkō-ˌbȯld\ *n* **1** : a gnome that in German folklore inhabits underground places **2** : an often mischievous spirit of German folklore [German]

Koch's postulates \ˈkȯks-\ *n pl* : a statement of the steps required to identify a microorganism as the cause of a disease [Robert *Koch,* died 1910, German bacteriologist]

kohl \ˈkōl\ *n* : a preparation used especially in Arabia and Egypt to darken the edges of the eyelids [Arabic *kuḥl*]

kohl•ra•bi \kōl-ˈrab-ē, -ˈräb-\ *n, pl* **-bies** : a cabbage that forms no head but has a swollen fleshy edible stem [German, from Italian *cavolo rapa,* from *cavolo* "cabbage" + *rapa* "turnip"]

ko•la nut \ˈkō-lə-\ *n* : the bitter seed of an African tree containing much caffeine and used in beverages and medicine for its stimulant effect [of African origin]

ko•lin•sky *or* **ko•lin•ski** \kə-ˈlin-skē\ *n, pl* **-skies** **1** : any of several Asian minks **2** : the fur or pelt of a kolinsky [Russian *kolinskiĭ* "of Kola", from *Kola,* town and peninsula in the Soviet Union]

kol•khoz \käl-ˈkȯz, -ˈkȯs\ *n, pl* **kol•kho•zy** \-ˈkȯ-zē\ *or* **kol•khoz•es** : a collective farm of the Soviet Union — compare SOVKHOZ [Russian, from *kol*lektivnoe *khoz*yaĭstvo "collective farm"]

Kol Nidre \kōl-ˈnid-rā\ *n* : an Aramaic prayer chanted in the synagogue on the eve of Yom Kippur [Aramaic *kol nidhrē* "all the vows"; from its opening phrase]

kook \ˈkük\ *n* : a person whose ideas or actions are eccentric or crazy [from *cuckoo*] — **kooky** \ˈkü-kē\ *adj*

kook•a•bur•ra \ˈku̇k-ə-ˌbər-ə, ˈku̇k-, -ˌbə-rə\ *n* : an Australian kingfisher that is about the size of a crow and has a call resembling loud laughter [native name in Australia]

ko•peck *or* **ko•pek** \ˈkō-ˌpek\ *n* **1** : a monetary unit equal to 1/100 ruble **2** : a coin representing one kopeck [Russian *kopeĭka*]

Ko•ran \kə-ˈran, -ˈrän, ˈkōr-ˌan, ˈkȯr-\ *n* : the book composed of writings accepted by Muslims as revelations made to Muhammad by Allah [Arabic *qur'ān*] — **Ko•ran•ic** \kə-ˈran-ik\ *adj*

Ko•re•an \kə-ˈrē-ən\ *n* **1** : a native or inhabitant of Korea **2** : the language of the Korean people — **Korean** *adj*

ko•ru•na \ˈkȯr-ə-ˌnä, ˈkär-\ *n, pl* **ko•ru•ny** \-ə-nē\ *or* **korunas** **1** : the basic monetary unit of Czechoslovakia **2** : a coin or note representing one koruna [Czech, literally, "crown", from Latin *corona*]

1**ko•sher** \ˈkō-shər\ *adj* **1 a** : accepted by Jewish law; *esp* : ritually fit for use **b** : selling or serving food ritually fit according to Jewish law **2** : PROPER 1 [Yiddish, from Hebrew *kāshēr* "fit, proper"]

2**kosher** *vt* **ko•shered**; **ko•sher•ing** \-shə-ring, -shring\ : to make kosher

kou•miss *or* **ku•miss** \kü-ˈmis, ˈkü-məs\ *n* : a fermented milk beverage made originally by the nomadic peoples of central Asia from mare's milk [Russian *kumys*]

1**kow•tow** \kau̇-ˈtau̇, ˈkau̇-ˌ\ *n* : an act of kowtowing [Chinese (Pekingese dialect) *k'o1 t'ou2*, from *k'o1* "to bump" + *t'ou2* "head"]

2**kowtow** *vi* **1** : to kneel and touch the forehead to the ground to show honor, worship, or deep respect **2** : to show slavish respect

KP \ˈkā-ˈpē\ *n, pl* **KPs** **1** : the military duty of helping to prepare, serve, and clean up after meals **2** : a person assigned to KP [*k*itchen *p*olice]

1**kraal** \ˈkrȯl, ˈkräl\ *n* **1** : a village of southern African natives **2** : an enclosure for domestic animals in southern Africa [Afrikaans, from Portuguese *curral* "enclosure, corral"]

2**kraal** *vt* : to pen in a kraal

kraft \ˈkraft\ *n* : a strong paper or board used especially for paper bags and corrugated boxes [German, literally, "strength"]

krait \ˈkrīt\ *n* : any of several brightly banded extremely venomous mostly Asian snakes [Hindi *karait*]

K ration \ˈkā-\ *n* : a lightweight packaged ration of emergency foods developed for the United States armed forces in World War II [A.B. *Keys,* born 1904, American physiologist]

kraut \ˈkrau̇t\ *n* : SAUERKRAUT

Krebs cycle \ˈkrebz-\ *n* : a sequence of reactions in the living organism in which oxidation of acetyl groups to carbon dioxide provides energy stored in ATP [H. A. *Krebs,* died 1900, German-born British biochemist]

krem•lin \ˈkrem-lən\ *n* **1** : the citadel of a Russian city **2** *cap* : the government of the Soviet Union [derived from Russian *kreml'*; sense 2 from the *Kremlin,* citadel of Moscow and governing center of the Soviet Union]

kreu•zer \ˈkrȯit-sər\ *n* : a small coin formerly used in Austria, Germany, and Hungary [German]

krill \ˈkril\ *n* : small planktonic organisms (as crustaceans and larvae) that form a major food of whales [Norwegian *kril* "recently hatched fishes"]

krim•mer \ˈkrim-ər\ *n* : a gray fur made from the pelts of young lambs of the Crimean peninsula region [German, from *Krim* "Crimea"]

kris \ˈkrēs\ *n* : a Malay or Indonesian dagger with a ridged and twisting blade [Malay *kĕris*]

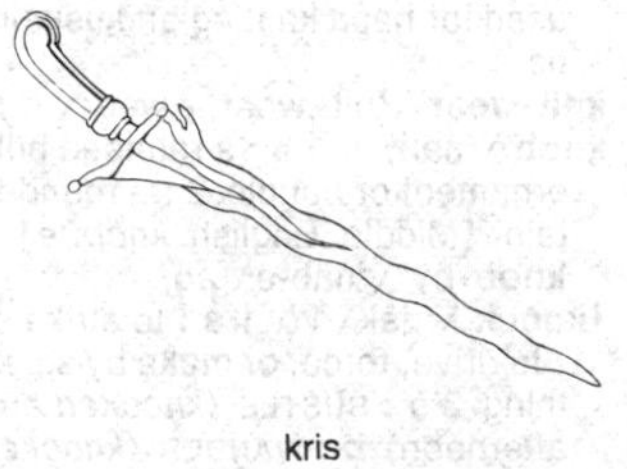
kris

1**kro•na** \ˈkrō-nə\ *n, pl* **kro•nur** \-nər\ **1** : the basic monetary unit of Iceland **2** : a coin representing one krona [Icelandic *krōna,* literally, "crown"]

2**kro•na** \ˈkrō-nə, ˈkrü-\ *n, pl* **kro•nor** \-ˌnȯr, -nər\ **1** : the basic monetary unit of Sweden **2** : a coin representing one krona [Swedish, literally, "crown"]

1**kro•ne** \ˈkrō-nə\ *n, pl* **kro•nen** \-nən\ **1** : the basic monetary unit of Austria from 1892 to 1925 **2** : a coin representing one krone [German, literally, "crown"]

2**kro•ne** \ˈkrō-nə\ *n, pl* **kro•ner** \-nər\ **1** : the basic monetary unit of Denmark and Norway **2** : a coin representing one krone [Danish, literally, "crown"]

kryp•ton \ˈkrip-ˌtän\ *n* : a colorless inert gaseous chemical element found in air and used especially in electric lamps — see ELEMENT table [Greek *kryptos* "hidden", from *kryptein* "to hide"]

ku•do \ˈkyüd-ō, ˈküd-\ *n, pl* **kudos** : AWARD, HONOR [back-formation from *kudos* (taken as a pl.)]

ku•dos \ˈkyü-ˌdäs, ˈkü-, -ˌdōs\ *n* : FAME, GLORY [Greek *kydos*]

ku•du *or* **koo•doo** \ˈküd-ü\ *n* : a large grayish brown African antelope with long ringed spirally twisted horns [Afrikaans *koedoe*]

kud•zu \ˈku̇d-zü\ *n* : a trailing Asian leguminous vine used widely for hay and forage and for erosion control [Japanese *kuzu*]

Ku Klux•er \ˈkü-ˌklək-sər, ˈkyü-\ *n* : a member of the Ku Klux Klan — **Ku Klux•ism** \-ˌklək-ˌsiz-əm\ *n*

Ku Klux Klan \ˌkü-ˌklək-ˈsklan, ˌkyü-, *also* ˌklü-\ *n* **1** : a post-Civil War secret society favoring white supremacy **2** : a 20th-century secret fraternal group held to confine its membership to American-born Protestant whites

ku•lak \kü-ˈlak, kyü-\ *n* : a prosperous peasant farmer in Czarist and early Soviet Russia [Russian, literally, "fist"]

kul•tur \ku̇l-ˈtu̇r\ *n, often cap* : German culture held to be superior especially by militant Nazi and Hohenzollern expansionists [German, "culture", from Latin *cultura*]

kum•quat \ˈkəm-ˌkwät\ *n* **1** : a small citrus fruit with sweet spongy rind and somewhat acid pulp used especially for preserves **2** : a tree or shrub that bears kumquats [Chinese (Cantonese dialect) *kam kwat,* from *kam* "gold" + *kwat* "orange"]

kung fu \ˌkəng-ˈfü, ˌku̇ng-\ *n* : a Chinese system of self-defense that resembles karate [Chinese dialect; related to Chinese (Pekingese dialect) *ch'üan2 fa3*, literally, "boxing principles"]

Kurd \'kùrd, 'kərd\ *n* : a member of a nomadic herding and agricultural people inhabiting a plateau region in bordering parts of Turkey, Iran, Iraq, Syria, and Soviet Armenia and Azerbaidzhan — **Kurd•ish** \-ish\ *adj*

Kurd•ish \'kùrd-ish, 'kərd-\ *n* : the Iranian language of the Kurds

kwash•i•or•kor \,kwäsh-ē-'òr-kər\ *n* : a disease of young children resulting from inadequate intake of protein [native name in Ghana, literally, "red boy"]

ky•mo•gram \'kī-mə-,gram\ *n* : a record made by a kymograph

ky•mo•graph \'kī-mə-,graf\ *n* : a device which graphically records motion or pressure (as of blood) [Greek *kyma* "wave"]

ky•pho•sis \kī-'fō-səs\ *n* : abnormal backward curvature of the spine — compare LORDOSIS, SCOLIOSIS [Greek *kyphōsis*, from *kyphos* "humpbacked"] — **ky•phot•ic** \-'fät-ik\ *adj*

ky•rie \'kir-ē-,ā\ *n, often cap* : a short liturgical prayer that begins with or consists of the words "Lord have mercy" [Late Latin *kyrie elei•son*, transliteration of Greek *kyrie eleēson* "Lord, have mercy"]

ky•rie elei•son \'kir-ē-,ā-ə-'lā-ə-,sän, -ə-sən\ *n, often cap K&E* : KYRIE

L l— -lyze

l \'el\ *n, pl* **l's** *or* **ls** \'elz\ *often cap* **1** : the 12th letter of the English alphabet **2** : fifty in Roman numerals

la \'lä\ *n* : the 6th note of the diatonic scale [Medieval Latin]

lab \'lab\ *n* : LABORATORY

¹la•bel \'lā-bəl\ *n* **1** : a slip (as of paper or cloth) with writing on it that is attached to something for identification or description **2** : a descriptive or identifying word or phrase: EPITHET [Middle French, "strip of cloth, ribbon"]

²label *vt* **la•beled** *or* **la•belled**; **la•bel•ing** *or* **la•bel•ling** \'lā-bə-ling, -bling\ **1 a** : to affix a label to ⟨*label* a medicine bottle⟩ **b** : to describe as : CALL ⟨*labeled* their opponents cheats⟩ **2** : to make (a chemical element) traceable (as through the steps of a biochemical process) by substitution of a detectable isotope — **la•bel•er** \-bə-lər, -blər\ *n*

la•bel•lum \lə-'bel-əm\ *n, pl* **-bel•la** \-'bel-ə\ : the median and often spurred petal of the corolla of an orchid [Latin, "little lip", from *labrum* "lip"] — **la•bel•late** \lə-'bel-ət\ *adj*

¹la•bi•al \'lā-bē-əl\ *adj* **1** : of or relating to the lips or labia **2** : uttered with the participation of one or both lips ⟨the *labial* sounds \f\, \p\, and \ü\⟩ [Latin *labium* "lip"] — **la•bi•al•ly** \-ə-lē\ *adv*

²labial *n* : a labial consonant

¹la•bi•ate \'lā-bē-ət, -bē-,āt\ *adj* **1** : LIPPED; *esp* : having a tubular corolla or calyx divided into two unequal parts projecting one over the other like lips **2** : of or relating to the mint family

²labiate *n* : a plant of the mint family

la•bile \'lā-,bīl, -bəl\ *adj* **1** : readily open to change : ADAPTABLE **2** : readily or continually undergoing chemical or physical change : UNSTABLE ⟨a *labile* mineral⟩ [French, from Late Latin *labilis* "fleeting, transient", from Latin *labi* "to slip"] — **la•bil•i•ty** \lā-'bil-ət-ē\ *n*

labio- *combining form* : labial and ⟨*labio*dental⟩

la•bio•den•tal \,lā-bē-ō-'dent-l\ *adj* : uttered with the participation of lip and teeth ⟨the *labiodental* sounds \f\ and \v\⟩ — **labiodental** *n*

la•bi•um \'lā-bē-əm\ *n, pl* **-bia** \-bē-ə\ **1** : any of the folds at the margin of the vulva **2** : the lower lip of a labiate corolla **3 a** : the lower lip of an insect **b** : a liplike part of various invertebrates [Latin, "lip"]

¹la•bor \'lā-bər\ *n* **1 a** : expenditure of physical or mental effort especially when difficult or compulsory **b** (1) : human activity that provides the goods or services in an economy (2) : the services performed by workers for wages as distinguished from those rendered by entrepreneurs for profits **c** (1) : the physical activities involved in childbirth (2) : the period of such labor **2** : TASK **3** . a product of labor **4 a** : those who do manual labor or work for wages **b** : labor unions or their officials **5** *usually* **Labour** \-bər\ : the Labour party of the United Kingdom or of another nation of the British Commonwealth [Old French, from Latin]

²labor *vb* **la•bored**; **la•bor•ing** \-bə-ring, -bring\ **1 a** : to exert one's body or mind : WORK **b** : to work for wages usually in actual production of goods **2** : to move with great effort **3** : to suffer from some disadvantage or distress ⟨*labor* under a delusion⟩ **4** : to pitch or roll heavily ⟨the ship *labored* in a rough sea⟩ **5** : to treat or work out in elaborate detail ⟨*labor* the obvious⟩ — **la•bor•er** \-bər-ər\ *n*

³labor *adj* **1** : of or relating to labor **2** *or* **Labour** *cap* : of, relating to, or constituting a political party held to represent the interests of workers or characterized by a membership in which organized labor groups predominate

lab•o•ra•to•ry \'lab-rə-,tōr-ē, -ə-rə-, -,tòr-\ *n, pl* **-ries** : a place equipped for experimental study in a science or for testing and analysis; *also* : a place providing opportunity for experimentation, observation, or practice in a field of study [Medieval Latin *laboratorium*, from Latin *laborare* "to labor", from *labor* "labor"] — **laboratory** *adj*

labor camp *n* **1** : a penal colony where forced labor is performed **2** : a camp for migratory laborers

Labor Day *n* : the 1st Monday in September observed in the United States and Canada as a legal holiday in recognition of the worker

la•bored *adj* **1** : produced or performed with labor; *esp* : not freely or easily done ⟨*labored* breathing⟩ **2** : lacking ease of expression ⟨a *labored* speech⟩

la•bo•ri•ous \lə-'bōr-ē-əs, -'bòr-\ *adj* **1** : INDUSTRIOUS **2** : requiring or characterized by hard or toilsome effort : LABORED — **la•bo•ri•ous•ly** *adv* — **la•bo•ri•ous•ness** *n*

La•bor•ite \'lā-bə-,rīt\ *n* **1** : a member of a political party devoted chiefly to the interests of labor **2** *usually* **La•bour•ite** \-bə-,rīt\ : a member of the British Labour party

la•bor•sav•ing \'lā-bər-,sā-ving\ *adj* : adapted to replace or decrease human labor and especially manual labor

labor union *n* : an organization of workers formed to advance its members' interests in respect to wages and working conditions

la•bour \'lā-bər\ *chiefly British variant of* LABOR

lab•ra•dor•ite \'lab-rə-,dòr-,īt\ *n* : a feldspar showing a play of several colors [*Labrador* peninsula, Canada]

Labrador retriever *n* : a retriever developed from stock originating in Newfoundland and characterized by a short dense usually black coat and broad head and chest [*Labrador*, Newfoundland]

la•brum \'lā-brəm\ *n* : the upper lip of an arthropod in front of or above the mandibles [Latin, "lip"]

la•bur•num \lə-'bər-nəm\ *n* : any of several poisonous Eurasian shrubs and trees of the pea family with pendulous racemes of bright yellow flowers [Latin]

lab•y•rinth \'lab-ə-,rinth, ,rintth\ *n* **1** : a place constructed of or full of passageways and blind alleys : MAZE **2** : something extremely complex or tortuous **3** : a tortuous anatomical structure; *esp* : the internal ear or its bony or membranous part [Latin *labyrinthus*, from Greek *labyrinthos*] — **lab•y•rin•thine** \,lab-ə-'rin-thən, -'rint-\ *adj*

lac \'lak\ *n* : a resinous substance secreted by a scale insect and used in the manufacture of shellac, lacquers, and sealing wax [Persian *lak* and Hindi *lākh*, from Sanskrit *lākṣā*]

lac•co•lith \'lak-ə-,lith\ *n* : a mass of igneous rock that intrudes between sedimentary layers and produces a dome-shaped bulge [Greek *lakkos* "cistern"]

[1]lace \ˈlās\ *n* **1 :** a cord or string used for drawing together two edges (as of a garment or a shoe) **2 :** an ornamental braid for trimming coats or uniforms **3 :** a fine openwork usually figured fabric made of thread and used chiefly for household coverings or for ornament of dress [Old French *laz,* from Latin *laqueus* "noose, snare"] — **laced** \ˈlāst\ *adj* — **lace•less** \ˈlā-sləs\ *adj* — **lace•like** \ˈlā-ˌslīk\ *adj*

[2]lace *vb* **1 :** to draw together the edges of with or as if with a lace passed through eyelets **2 a :** to adorn with or as if with lace **b :** INTERTWINE **3 :** BEAT 1a, b, LASH **4 a :** to add a dash especially of an alcoholic liquor to **b :** to give savor or zest to — **lac•er** *n*

[1]lac•er•ate \ˈlas-ə-rət\ *adj* **:** having the edges deeply and irregularly cut ⟨a flower with *lacerate* petals⟩

[2]lac•er•ate \ˈlas-ə-ˌrāt\ *vt* **1 :** to tear roughly **:** injure by tearing ⟨a *lacerated* knee⟩ **2 :** to cause sharp mental or emotional pain to **:** DISTRESS [Latin *lacerare*] — **lac•er•a•tive** \-ˌrāt-iv\ *adj*

lac•er•a•tion \ˌlas-ə-ˈrā-shən\ *n* **1 :** an act or instance of lacerating **2 :** a torn and ragged wound

lac•er•til•i•an \ˌlas-ər-ˈtil-ē-ən\ *adj* **:** of or relating to the lizards [derived from Latin *lacerta* "lizard"] — **lacertilian** *n*

lace•wing \ˈlā-ˌswing\ *n* **:** any of various neuropteran insects with delicate lacy wings, long antennae, and brilliant eyes

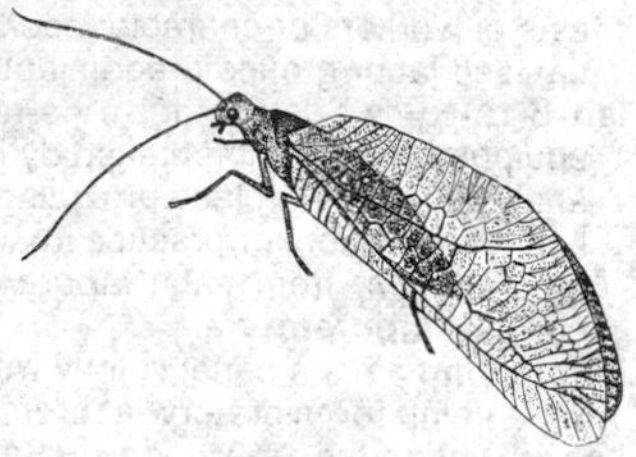

lacewing

lach•ry•mal *or* **lac•ri•mal** \ˈlak-rə-məl\ *adj* **:** of, relating to, or being the glands that produce tears [Latin *lacrima* "tear"]

lach•ry•mose \ˈlak-rə-ˌmōs\ *adj* **1 :** given to tears or weeping **:** TEARFUL **2 :** tending to cause tears **:** MOURNFUL ⟨*lacrymose* ballads⟩ — **lach•ry•mose•ly** *adv*

lac•ing \ˈlā-sing\ *n* **1 :** the action of one that laces **2 :** something that laces **:** LACE

la•cin•i•ate \lə-ˈsin-ē-ət, -ˌāt\ *adj* **:** bordered with a fringe [Latin *lacinia* "flap"] — **la•cin•i•a•tion** \lə-ˌsin-ē-ˈā-shən\ *n*

[1]lack \ˈlak\ *vb* **1 :** to be missing ⟨the will to win is *lacking*⟩ **2 :** to need, want, or be deficient in ⟨*lack* financial support⟩ [Dutch *laken*]

[2]lack *n* **1 :** the fact or state of being in short supply ⟨a *lack* of good manners⟩ **2 :** something that is lacking or is needed ⟨money is the club's biggest *lack*⟩

lack•a•dai•si•cal \ˌlak-ə-ˈdā-zi-kəl\ *adj* **:** lacking life, spirit or zest **:** LANGUID [derived from *lackaday,* interj. used to express regret, from *alack the day*] — **lack•a•dai•si•cal•ly** \-kə-lē, -klē\ *adv*

lack•ey \ˈlak-ē\ *n, pl* **lackeys 1 :** a liveried retainer **:** FOOTMAN **2 :** a servile follower [Middle French *laquais*]

lack•lus•ter \ˈlak-ˌləs-tər\ *adj* **:** lacking in sheen, radiance, or vitality **:** DULL — **lackluster** *n*

la•con•ic \lə-ˈkän-ik\ *adj* **:** sparing of words **:** TERSE [Latin *laconicus* "Spartan", from Greek *lakōnikos;* from the Spartan reputation for terseness of speech] — **la•con•i•cal•ly** \-ˈkän-i-kə-lē, -klē\ *adv*

lac•quer \ˈlak-ər\ *n* **1 :** any of various durable natural varnishes; *esp* **:** one from an Asian sumac **2 :** any of various clear or colored synthetic organic coatings that typically dry to form a film by evaporation of the solvent; *esp* **:** a solution of a cellulose derivative (as nitrocellulose) [Portuguese *lacré* "sealing wax", from *laca* "lac", from Arabic *lakk,* from Persian *lak*] — **lacquer** *vt*

lac•ri•ma•tion \ˌlak-rə-ˈmā-shən\ *n* **:** the secretion of tears especially when abnormal or excessive [Latin *lacrimatio,* from *lacrimare* "to weep", from *lacrima* "tear"]

lac•ri•ma•tor *or* **lach•ry•ma•tor** \ˈlak-rə-ˌmāt-ər\ *n* **:** TEAR GAS

la•crosse \lə-ˈkrȯs\ *n* **:** a game played on a field in which the players use a long-handled stick with a triangular head to catch, carry, or throw the ball [Canadian French *la crosse,* literally, "the crosier"]

lact- *or* **lacti-** *or* **lacto-** *combining form* **1 :** milk ⟨*lactogenic*⟩ **2 a :** lactic acid ⟨*lactate*⟩ **b :** lactose ⟨*lactase*⟩ [Latin *lact-, lac*]

lac•tase \ˈlak-ˌtās\ *n* **:** an enzyme that breaks down lactose and related compounds and occurs especially in the intestines of young mammals and in yeasts

[1]lac•tate \ˈlak-ˌtāt\ *n* **:** a salt or ester of lactic acid

[2]lactate *vi* **:** to secrete milk — **lac•ta•tion** \lak-ˈtā-shən\ *adj* — **lac•ta•tion•al** \-shnəl, -shən-l\ *adj* — **lac•ta•tion•al•ly** \-ē\ *adv*

[1]lac•te•al \ˈlak-tē-əl\ *adj* **1 :** consisting of, producing, or resembling milk **2 a :** conveying or containing a milky fluid **b :** of or relating to the lacteals [Latin *lacteus* "of milk", from *lact-, lac* "milk"]

[2]lacteal *n* **:** one of the lymphatic vessels beginning in the villi of the small intestine and carrying chyle to the thoracic duct

lac•tic \ˈlak-tik\ *adj* **:** relating to or producing lactic acid ⟨*lactic* fermentation⟩

lactic acid *n* **:** an organic acid $C_3H_6O_3$ present in cells and especially muscle, produced from carbohydrate usually by bacterial fermentation, and used mostly in food and medicine

lac•tif•er•ous \lak-ˈtif-rəs, -ə-rəs\ *adj* **1 :** secreting or conveying milk **2 :** yielding or containing a milky juice — **lac•tif•er•ous•ness** *n*

lac•to•ba•cil•lus \ˌlak-tō-bə-ˈsil-əs\ *n* **:** any of a genus of lactic-acid-forming bacteria

lac•to•gen•ic \ˌlak-tə-ˈjen-ik\ *adj* **:** inducing the secretion of milk

lac•tose \ˈlak-ˌtōs\ *n* **:** a sugar $C_{12}H_{22}O_{11}$ present in milk that breaks down into glucose and galactose and on fermentation yields especially lactic acid

la•cu•na \lə-ˈkü-nə, -ˈkyü-\ *n, pl* **-cu•nae** \-ˈkyü-nē, -ˈkü-ˌnī\ *or* **-cu•nas** \-ˈkü-nəz, -ˈkyü-\ **1 :** a blank space or a missing part **:** GAP **2 :** a small cavity or pit in an anatomical structure [Latin, "pool, pit, gap", from *lacus* "lake"] — **la•cu•nal** \-ˈkün-l, -ˈkyün-\ *adj* — **la•cu•nar** \-ˈkü-nər, -ˈkyü-\ *adj* — **la•cu•nate** \-nət\ *adj*

la•cus•trine \lə-ˈkəs-trən\ *adj* **:** of, relating to, or growing in lakes [derived from Latin *lacus* "lake"]

lacy \ˈlā-sē\ *adj* **lac•i•er; -est :** resembling or consisting of lace

lad \ˈlad\ *n* **1 :** BOY 1, YOUTH **2 :** FELLOW, CHAP [Middle English *ladde*]

lad•der \ˈlad-ər\ *n* **1 :** a structure for climbing that consists of two long parallel sidepieces joined at intervals by crosspieces on which one may step **2 :** something that suggests a ladder in form or use **3 :** a series of usually ascending steps or stages **:** SCALE [Old English *hlǣder*]

lad•die \ˈlad-ē\ *n* **:** a young lad

lade \ˈlād\ *vb* **lad•ed; lad•ed** *or* **lad•en** \ˈlād-n\; **lad•ing 1 a :** to put a load or burden on or in **:** LOAD ⟨*lade* a vessel⟩ **b :** SHIP 1a, STOW ⟨*lading* a rich cargo⟩ **2 :** to burden heavily **:** OPPRESS ⟨*laden* with cares⟩ **3 :** LADLE [Old English *hladan*]

la-di-da \ˌläd-ē-ˈdä\ *adj* **:** affectedly refined or polished [perhaps from earlier *lardy-dardy* "foppish"]

ladies' man *n* **:** a man who shows a marked liking for the company of women

lad•ing \ˈlād-ing\ *n* **1 :** the act of one that lades **2 :** CARGO, FREIGHT

la•di•no \lə-ˈdī-nō, -nə\ *n, pl* **-nos :** a large rapidly growing white clover widely planted for hay or silage [perhaps from *Lodi,* Italy]

[1]la•dle \ˈlād-l\ *n* **:** a deep-bowled long-handled spoon or dipper used especially for dipping up and moving liquids [Old English *hlædel,* from *hladan* "to lade"]

[2]ladle *vt* **la•dled; la•dling** \ˈlād-ling, -l-ing\ **:** to take up and move in or as if in a ladle ⟨*ladle* soup⟩

la•dy \ˈlād-ē\ *n, pl* **ladies 1 a :** a woman of property, rank, or authority; *esp* **:** one having a standing equivalent to that of a lord **b :** a woman receiving the homage or devotion of a knight or lover **2 a :** a woman of superior social position **b :** a woman of refinement and manners **c :** WOMAN — often used in a courteous reference ⟨show the *lady* to her seat⟩ **3 :** WIFE 2 **4 a** *cap* — used as a title of a woman of rank in Great Britain **b :** a woman who is a member of an order of knighthood — compare DAME 1c [Old English *hlǣfdīge,* from *hlāf* "loaf of bread" + *-dīge* "one that kneads"]

△ **origin** Over the centuries the meaning of *lady* has become more and more generalized, and it is now widely used as a courteous term for a woman. *Lady* was formerly used to refer primarily to women of superior social standing. The Old English form, *hlǣfdīge,* was originally used to mean "female head of a household" or "mistress of servants". This sense reflects something of the ultimate etymology, for *hlǣfdīge* is composed of Old English *hlāf,* "loaf", and *-dīge,* "kneader of bread", which is related to our modern English *dough.*

lady beetle *n* : LADYBUG

la•dy•bird \'lād-ē-ˌbərd\ *n* : LADYBUG

la•dy•bug \-ˌbəg\ *n* : any of numerous small, nearly hemispherical, and often brightly colored beetles that mostly feed both as larvae and adults on other insects [Our *Lady,* the Virgin Mary]

lady chapel *n, often cap L&C* : a chapel dedicated to the Virgin Mary

Lady Day *n* : the feast of the Annunciation

la•dy•fin•ger \'lād-ē-ˌfing-gər\ *n* : a small finger-shaped sponge cake

la•dy•fish \-ˌfish\ *n* : a large silvery food and sport fish that resembles a herring but is related to the tarpon — called also *bonefish, tenpounder*

la•dy-in-wait•ing \ˌlād-ē-in-'wāt-ing\ *n, pl* **ladies-in-waiting** : a lady appointed to attend a queen or princess

la•dy•like \'lād-ē-ˌlīk\ *adj* **1** : resembling a lady in appearance or manners **2** : suitable to a lady ⟨*ladylike* behavior⟩

la•dy•love \'lād-ē-ˌləv, lād-ē-'\ *n* : a beloved woman

la•dy•ship \'lād-ē-ˌship\ *n* **1** : the condition of being a lady **2** *often cap* : the rank or dignity of a lady — used as a form of address ⟨her *Ladyship*⟩ ⟨your *Ladyship*⟩ ⟨their *Ladyships*⟩

lady's slipper *or* **lady slipper** \'lād-ēz-ˌslip-ər, -ē-ˌslip-\ *n* : any of several North American temperate-zone orchids with flowers whose shape suggests a slipper

[1]lag \'lag\ *vi* **lagged**; **lag•ging** **1** : to stay or fall behind: as **a** : to hang back : LINGER ⟨*lagged* behind the other hikers⟩ **b** : to move, function, or develop with comparative slowness ⟨*lagged* behind the production schedule⟩ **2** : to slacken little by little : FLAG ⟨interest never *lagged* during the play⟩ **3** : to pitch or shoot something (as a marble) at a mark [probably of Scandinavian origin] — **lag•ger** *n*

[2]lag *n* **1 a** : the action or condition of lagging **b** : comparative slowness or retardation **2 a** : an amount of lagging or the time during which lagging continues **b** : INTERVAL 1

la•ger \'läg-ər\ *n* : a beer brewed by slow fermentation and stored in refrigerated cellars for maturing [German *lagerbier,* from *lager* "storehouse" + *bier* "beer"]

lag•gard \'lag-ərd\ *adj* : lagging or tending to lag : DILATORY ⟨moved at a *laggard* pace⟩ — **laggard** *n* — **lag•gard•ly** *adv or adj* — **lag•gard•ness** *n*

la•gniappe \'lan-ˌyap, lan-'\ *n* : something given free or by way of good measure [American French, from American Spanish *la ñapa* "the lagniappe"]

lago•morph \'lag-ə-ˌmȯrf\ *n* : any of an order (Lagomorpha) of gnawing mammals having two pairs of upper incisors one behind the other and comprising the rabbits, hares, and pikas — compare RODENT [derived from Greek *lagōs* "hare" + *morphē* "form"] — **lago•mor•phic** \ˌlag-ə-'mȯr-fik\ *adj* — **lago•mor•phous** \-fəs\ *adj*

la•goon \lə-'gün\ *n* : a shallow sound, channel, or pond near or connected with a larger body of water [French *lagune,* from Italian *laguna,* from Latin *lacuna* "pit, pool", from *lacus* "lake"]

la•ical \'lā-ə-kəl\ *or* **la•ic** \'lā-ik\ *adj* : of or relating to the laity : SECULAR — **laic** *n* — **la•ical•ly** \'lā-ə-kə-lē, -klē\ *adv*

la•icism \'lā-ə-ˌsiz-əm\ *n* : a political system characterized by the exclusion of church control and influence

la•icize \'lā-ə-ˌsīz\ *vt* **1** : to reduce to lay status **2** : to put under the direction of or throw open to the laity — **la•ici•za•tion** \ˌlā-ə-sə-'zā-shən\ *n*

laid *past of* LAY

lain *past participle of* LIE

lair \'laər, 'leər\ *n* **1** : the resting or living place of a wild animal : DEN **2** : REFUGE 1, HIDEAWAY [Old English *leger*]

laird \'laərd, 'leərd\ *n, Scottish* : a landed proprietor [Middle English *lard, lord,* "lord"]

lais•sez-faire \ˌle-ˌsā-'faər, ˌlā-, -ˌzā-, -'feər\ *n* : a doctrine opposing governmental interference in economic affairs beyond the minimum necessary for the maintenance of peace and property rights [French *laissez faire,* imperative of *laisser faire* "to let (people) do (as they choose)"] — **laissez-faire** *adj*

la•ity \'lā-ət-ē\ *n, pl* **-ities** **1** : the people of a religious faith as distinguished from its clergy **2** : the mass of the people as distinguished from those of a particular profession or skill [[5]*lay*]

[1]lake \'lāk\ *n* : a large inland body of standing water; *also* : a pool of liquid (as lava, oil, or pitch) [Old French *lac,* from Latin *lacus*]

[2]lake *n* **1** : any of numerous bright pigments composed of a soluble dye adsorbed on or combined with an inorganic substance **2** : a vivid red [French *laque* "lac", from Provençal *laca,* from Arabic *lakk,* from Persian *lak*]

lake dwelling *n* : a dwelling built on piles in a lake; *esp* : one built in prehistoric times — **lake dweller** *n*

lake herring *n* : any of several lake fish of commercial importance in the northern United States and Canada

lake trout *n* : any of several lake fishes: as **a** : BROWN TROUT **b** : a large dark American char that is an important sport and commerical fish in northern lakes

la•ma \'läm-ə\ *n* : a Lamaist monk [Tibetan *blama*]

La•ma•ism \'läm-ə-ˌiz-əm\ *n* : the form of Buddhism of Tibet and Mongolia marked by a dominant hierarchy of monks — **La•ma•ist** \'läm-ə-əst\ *n or adj* — **La•ma•is•tic** \ˌläm-ə-'is-tik\ *adj*

La•marck•ism \lə-'mär-ˌkiz-əm\ *n* : a theory of organic evolution asserting that environmental changes cause structural changes in animals and plants which are transmitted to offspring [J.B. de Monet *Lamarck*] — **La•marck•i•an** \-'mär-kē-ən\ *adj or n*

la•ma•sery \'läm-ə-ˌser-ē\ *n, pl* **-ser•ies** : a monastery of lamas [French *lamaserie,* from *lama* "lama + Persian *sarāī* "palace"]

[1]lamb \'lam\ *n* **1 a** : a young sheep; *esp* : one less than a year old or without permanent teeth **b** : the young of various animals (as the smaller antelopes) **2** : an innocent, weak, or gentle person **3** : the flesh of a lamb used as food [Old English]

[2]lamb *vb* **1** : to bring forth a lamb **2** : to tend (ewes) at lambing time — **lamb•er** \'lam-ər\ *n*

lam•baste *or* **lam•bast** \lam-'bāst, -'bast\ *vt* **1** : to assault violently : BEAT **2** : to attack verbally [probably of Scandinavian origin]

lamb•da \'lam-də\ *n* : the 11th letter of the Greek alphabet — Λ or λ

lam•bent \'lam-bənt\ *adj* **1** : playing lightly over a surface : FLICKERING ⟨a *lambent* flame⟩ **2** : softly radiant ⟨*lambent* eyes⟩ **3** : marked by lightness or brilliance ⟨*lambent* humor⟩ [Latin *lambens,* present participle of *lambere* "to lick"] — **lam•ben•cy** \-bən-sē\ *n*

lam•bre•quin \'lam-bər-kən, -bri-kən\ *n* : a short decorative drapery for a shelf edge or for the top of a window casing : VALANCE [French]

lamb•skin \'lam-ˌskin\ *n* : a lamb's skin or a small fine-grade sheepskin or the leather made from either

lamb's-quar•ters \'lamz-ˌkwȯrt-ərz, -ˌkwȯt-\ *n sing or pl* : a goosefoot with glaucous foliage that is sometimes used as a potherb

[1]lame \'lām\ *adj* **1 a** : physically disabled **b(1)** : having a part and especially a limb so disabled as to impair freedom of movement (2) : halting in movement : LIMPING **2** : lacking substance : WEAK ⟨a *lame* excuse⟩ [Old English *lama*] — **lame•ly** *adv* — **lame•ness** *n*

[2]lame *vt* **1** : to make lame : CRIPPLE **2** : to make weak or ineffective

la•mé \lä-'mā, la-\ *n* : a brocaded fabric woven with metallic filling threads often of gold or silver [French]

lame duck *n* : an elected official continuing to hold political office after being defeated and before a successor is inaugurated

la•mel•la \lə-'mel-ə\ *n, pl* **-mel•lae** \-'mel-ē, -ˌī\ *also* **-mellas** : a thin flat scale or part [Latin, "little plate", from *lamina* "thin plate"] — **la•mel•lar** \lə-'mel-ər\ *adj* — **la•mel•late** \-'mel-ət\ *adj* — **la•mel•late•ly** *adv*

lam•el•la•tion \ˌlam-ə-'lā-shən\ *n* **1** : formation or division into lamellae **2** : LAMELLA

la•mel•li•branch \lə-'mel-ə-ˌbrangk\ *n, pl* **-branchs** : any of a class (Lamellibranchia) of mollusks (as clams, oysters, or mussels) with a shell made up of right and left parts joined by a hinge [*lamella* + Latin *branchia* "gill"] — **lamellibranch** *adj* — **la•mel•li•bran•chi•ate** \lə-ˌmel-ə-'brang-kē-ət\ *adj or n*

[1]la•ment \lə-'ment\ *vb* **1** : to mourn aloud : WAIL **2** : to feel or express sorrow for : BEWAIL [Latin *lamentari,* from *lamentum* "lament"] — **lam•en•ta•tion** \ˌlam-ən-'tā-shən\ *n*

2lament *n* **1** : a crying out in grief : WAILING **2** : a mournful song or poem

lam•en•ta•ble \'lam-ən-tə-bəl, lə-'ment-ə-\ *adj* **1** : that is to be regretted : DEPLORABLE ⟨a *lamentable* error⟩ **2** : expressing grief : MOURNFUL — **lam•en•ta•ble•ness** *n* — **lam•en•ta•bly** \-blē\ *adv*

Lam•en•ta•tions \ˌlam-ən-'tā-shənz\ *n* — see BIBLE table

la•mia \'lā-mē-ə\ *n* : a man-eating she-demon [Latin, from Greek]

lam•i•na \'lam-ə-nə\ *n, pl* **-nae** \-ˌnē, -ˌnī\ *or* **-nas** **1** : a thin plate or scale **2** : BLADE 1b [Latin] — **lam•i•nar** \-nər\ *adj*

lam•i•nar•ia \ˌlam-ə-'ner-ē-ə, -'nar-\ *n* : any of various large kelps with an unbranched cylindrical or flattened stalk and a smooth or convoluted blade [derived from Latin *lamina* "lamina"] — **lam•i•nar•i•an** \-ē-ən\ *adj or n*

1lam•i•nate \'lam-ə-ˌnāt\ *vt* **1** : to roll or compress into a thin plate **2** : to make by uniting superposed layers of one or more materials — **lam•i•na•tor** \-ˌnāt-ər\ *n*

2lam•i•nate \-nət, -ˌnāt\ *adj* **1** : consisting of laminae **2** : bearing or covered with laminae

3lam•i•nate \-nət, -ˌnāt\ *n* : a product made by laminating

lam•i•nat•ed \-ˌnāt-əd\ *adj* : composed of layers of firmly united material; *esp* : made by bonding or impregnating superposed layers of paper, wood, or fabric with resin and compressing under heat

lam•i•na•tion \ˌlam-ə-'nā-shən\ *n* **1** : the process of laminating **2** : a laminate structure **3** : LAMINA

Lam•mas \'lam-əs\ *n* : August 1 originally celebrated in England as a harvest festival [Old English *hlāfmæsse,* from *hlāf,* "loaf" + *mæsse* "mass"]

lam•mer•gei•er *or* **lam•mer•gey•er** \'lam-ər-ˌgī-ər, -ˌgīr\ *n* : the largest Eurasian bird of prey found chiefly in mountainous regions [German *lämmergeier,* from *lämmer* "lambs" + *geier* "vulture"]

lammergeier

lamp \'lamp\ *n* : a device for producing light or heat: as **a** : a vessel with a wick for burning an inflammable liquid (as oil) **b** : an incandescent or fluorescent bulb together with its housing [Old French *lampe,* from Latin *lampas,* from Greek, from *lampein* "to shine"]

lamp•black \-ˌblak\ *n* : a finely powdered deep black soot made by incomplete burning of carbon-containing material and used chiefly as a pigment (as in paints and ink)

lamp•light•er \'lam-ˌplīt-ər\ *n* : one that lights a lamp; *esp* : a person employed to light gas street lights

1lam•poon \lam-'pün\ *n* **1** : a harsh satire usually aimed at an individual **2** : a light mocking satire [French *lampon*]

2lampoon *vt* : to make the subject of a lampoon : RIDICULE — **lam•poon•er** *n* — **lam•poon•ery** \-'pün-rē, -ə-rē\ *n*

lam•prey \'lam-prē\ *n, pl* **lampreys** : any of an order (Hyperoartia) of aquatic vertebrates that resemble eels but have a large sucking mouth with no jaws [Old French *lampreie,* from Medieval Latin *lampreda*]

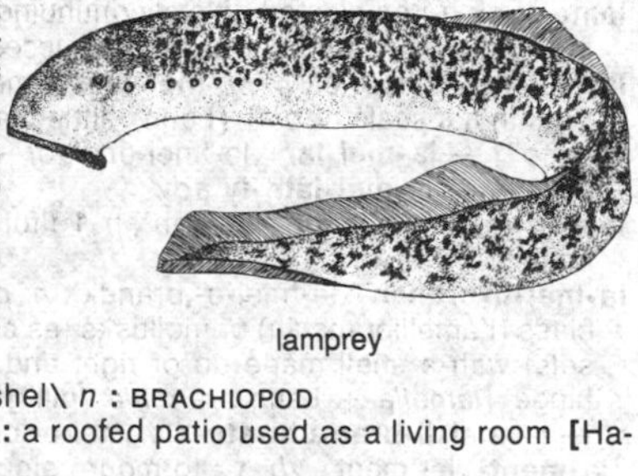

lamprey

lamp•shell \'lamp-ˌshel\ *n* : BRACHIOPOD

la•nai \lə-'nī, lä-\ *n* : a roofed patio used as a living room [Hawaiian]

la•nate \'lā-ˌnāt, 'lan-ˌāt\ *adj* : covered with fine hair or filaments : WOOLLY [Latin *lanatus,* from *lana* "wool"]

Lan•cas•tri•an \lan-'kas-trē-ən, lang-\ *adj* : of or relating to the English royal house that ruled from 1399 to 1461 — compare YORKIST [John of Gaunt, duke of *Lancaster,* died 1399] — **Lancastrian** *n*

1lance \'lans\ *n* **1** : a weapon consisting of a long shaft with a sharp head and carried by knights or light cavalry **2** : a sharp object suggestive of a lance; *esp* : LANCET **3** : LANCER 1b [Old French, from Latin *lancea*]

2lance *vt* **1** : to pierce with or as if with a lance **2** : to open with or as if with a lancet ⟨*lance* a boil⟩

lance corporal *n* : an enlisted rank in the Marine Corps above private first class and below corporal [*lance* (as in obsolete *lancepesade* "lance corporal", from Middle French *lancepessade*)]

lance•let \'lan-slət\ *n* : AMPHIOXUS

lan•ce•o•late \'lan-sē-ə-ˌlāt\ *also* **lan•ce•o•lat•ed** \-ˌlāt-əd\ *adj* : shaped like a lance head; *esp* : being narrow and tapering to a point at the tip ⟨*lanceolate* leaves⟩ [Late Latin *lanceolatus,* from Latin *lanceola* "small lance", from *lancea* "lance"]

lanc•er \'lan-sər\ *n* **1 a** : one that carries a lance **b** : a light cavalryman armed with a lance **2** *pl but sing in construction* **a** : a set of five quadrilles each in a different meter **b** : the music for such dances

lan•cet \'lan-sət\ *n* : a sharp-pointed and usually 2-edged surgical instrument

lancet arch *n* : an acutely pointed arch

1land \'land\ *n* **1** : the solid part of the surface of the earth **2** : a portion of the earth's solid surface distinguished by ownership boundaries: as **a** : COUNTRY 2 **b** : privately or publically owned territory ⟨buy some *land*⟩ **3** : REALM, DOMAIN ⟨in the *land* of dreams⟩ **4** : the people of a country : NATION [Old English] — **land•less** \'lan-dləs\ *adj*

2land *vb* **1 a** : to set or go ashore from a ship : DISEMBARK ⟨*land* troops⟩ ⟨troops *landed*⟩ **b** : to stop at or near a place on shore ⟨the boat *landed* at the dock⟩ **2** : to alight or cause to alight on a surface ⟨the plane *landed*⟩ ⟨*landed* the plane in a corn field⟩ **3** : to bring to or arrive at a specified destination, position, or condition ⟨*landed* downtown⟩ ⟨never *landed* a punch⟩ ⟨carelessness *landed* them in trouble⟩ **4 a** : to catch with a hook and bring in ⟨*land* a fish⟩ **b** : GAIN, SECURE ⟨*land* a job⟩

lan•dau \'lan-ˌdau̇, -dȯ\ *n* **1** : a four-wheeled carriage with a top divided into two sections that can be lowered, thrown back, or removed **2** : a closed automobile body with a folding top over the rear passenger compartment [*Landau,* Bavaria, Germany]

landau 1

land breeze *n* : a breeze blowing toward the sea

land•ed \'lan-dəd\ *adj* **1** : owning land ⟨*landed* proprietors⟩ **2** : consisting of real estate ⟨*landed* property⟩

land•fall \'land-ˌfȯl, 'lan-\ *n* : a sighting or reaching of land after a voyage or flight; *also* : the land first sighted

land•form \-ˌfȯrm\ *n* : a feature of the earth's surface attributable to natural causes

land grant *n* : a grant of land by a government especially for roads, railroads, or agricultural colleges

land•hold•er \'land-ˌhōl-dər\ *n* : one that holds or owns land — **land•hold•ing** \-ding\ *n*

land•ing \'lan-ding\ *n* **1** : the action of one that lands **2** : a place for discharging or taking on passengers and cargo **3** : a level part of a staircase (as at the end of a flight of stairs)

landing craft *n* : any of various naval craft designed for putting troops and equipment ashore

landing field *n* : a field where aircraft may land and take off

landing gear *n* : the part that supports an aircraft or spacecraft when on the ground

landing net *n* : a small net with a handle used to take a hooked fish from the water

landing strip *n* : AIRSTRIP

land•la•dy \'land-ˌlād-ē, 'lan-\ *n* : a female landlord

land•locked \-ˌläkt\ *adj* **1** : enclosed or nearly enclosed by land ⟨a *landlocked* country⟩ **2** : confined to fresh water by some barrier ⟨*landlocked* salmon⟩

land•lord \-ˌlȯrd\ *n* **1** : the owner of real estate which is leased or rented to another **2** : a person who runs an inn or rooming house : INNKEEPER

land•lub•ber \'lan-ˌdləb-ər, -ləb-\ *n* **1** : one whose life is spent on land **2 :** one who is unaquainted with the sea or seamanship — **land•lub•ber•ly** *adj*

land•mark \ˈland-ˌmärk, ˈlan-\ *n* **1 :** an object (as a stone or tree) that marks the boundary of land **2 a :** a conspicuous object on land that directs toward or identifies a place **b :** an anatomical structure used as a point of orientation in locating other structures **3 :** an event or development that marks a turning point or a stage ⟨the album was a musical *landmark*⟩ **4 :** a structure of unusual historic interest

land•mass \-ˌmas\ *n* **:** a large area of land

land–office business *n* **:** extensive and rapid business **[**from the fact that government land offices were swamped with would-be homesteaders when public lands were opened for homesteading**]**

land•own•er \ˈlan-ˌdō-nər\ *n* **:** an owner of land — **land•own•ing** \-ning\ *adj*

land–poor \ˈland-ˌpu̇r, ˈlan-\ *adj* **:** owning so much unprofitable or encumbered land as to lack funds to develop it or pay the charges due on it

land reform *n* **:** usually legislative measures intended to achieve a fairer distribution of agricultural land

¹land•scape \ˈland-ˌskāp, ˈlan-\ *n* **1 :** a picture of natural inland scenery **2 :** a portion of land that the eye can see in one glance **[**Dutch *landschap,* from *land* + *-schap* "-ship"**]**

²landscape *vt* **:** to modify or improve (a tract of land) by grading, clearing, or gardening

landscape gardener *n* **:** one skilled in the development and decorative planting of gardens and grounds

land•slide \ˈland-ˌslīd, ˈlan-\ *n* **1 :** the slipping down of a mass of rocks or earth on a steep slope; *also* **:** the mass of material that slides **2 :** an overwhelming victory especially in an election

lands•man \ˈlandz-mən, ˈlanz-\ *n* **:** LANDLUBBER

¹land•ward \ˈlan-dwərd\ *also* **land•wards** \-dwərdz\ *adv* **:** to or toward the land

²landward *adj* **:** lying or being toward the land or on the side toward the land

lane \ˈlān\ *n* **1 :** a narrow way between fences, hedges, or buildings **2 :** a relatively narrow way: as **a :** an ocean route for ships; *also* **:** AIR LANE **b :** a strip of roadway for a single line of vehicles **c :** a long hardwood surface with pins at one end for use in bowling **[**Old English *lanu***]**

Lan•go•bard \ˈlang-gə-ˌbärd\ *n* **:** LOMBARD **[**Latin *Langobardus***]**

lan•gouste \läⁿ-ˈgüst\ *n* **:** SPINY LOBSTER **[**French**]**

lang syne \lang-ˈzīn\ *n, chiefly Scottish* **:** times past **[**Middle English, from *lang* "long" + *syne* "since"**]** — **lang syne** *adv or adj, chiefly Scottish*

lan•guage \ˈlang-gwij\ *n* **1 a :** the words, their pronunciation, and the methods of combining them used and understood by a large group of people **b** (1) **:** audible, articulate, and meaningful sound as produced by the action of the vocal organs (2) **:** a systematic means of communicating ideas by signs or marks with understood meanings ⟨sign *language*⟩ **2 a :** form or manner of verbal expression; *esp* **:** STYLE ⟨forceful *language*⟩ **b :** the words and expressions of a particular group or field ⟨the *language* of medicine⟩ **3 :** the study of language especially as a school subject **[**Old French, from *langue* "tongue, language", from Latin *lingua***]**

lan•guid \ˈlang-gwəd\ *adj* **1 :** drooping or flagging from or as if from exhaustion **2 :** sluggish in character or disposition **:** LISTLESS **3 :** lacking force or quickness of movement **:** LAZY ⟨*languid* life in the tropics⟩ **[**Middle French *languide,* from Latin *languidus,* from *languēre* "to languish"**]** — **lan•guid•ly** *adv* — **lan•guid•ness** *n*

lan•guish \ˈlang-gwish\ *vi* **1 a :** to be or become languid **b :** to lose strength or force **:** DECLINE **2 :** to become depressed **:** PINE ⟨*languished* in prison⟩ **3 :** to assume a weary or sad look appealing for sympathy **[**Middle French *languiss-,* stem of *languir* "to languish", from Latin *languēre***]** — **lan•guish•er** *n* — **lan•guish•ing** *adj* — **lan•guish•ing•ly** \-ing-lē\ *adv* — **lan•guish•ment** \-gwish-mənt\ *n*

lan•guor \ˈlang-gər, -ər\ *n* **1 :** weakness or weariness of body or mind **2 :** a state of dreamy inactivity **[**Old French, from Latin, from *languēre* "to languish"**] syn** see LETHARGY — **lan•guor•ous** \-gə-rəs, -ə-rəs\ *adj* — **lan•guor•ous•ly** *adv*

lan•gur \läng-ˈgu̇r\ *n* **:** any of various slender long-tailed Asian monkeys **[**Hindi *lāgūr***]**

lank \ˈlangk\ *adj* **1 :** not well filled out **:** THIN ⟨*lank* cattle⟩ **2 :** hanging straight and limp without spring or curl ⟨*lank* hair⟩ **[**Old English *hlanc***]** — **lank•ly** *adv* — **lank•ness** *n*

langur

• syn LANKY, GAUNT, RAWBONED: LANK implies tallness as well as leanness of figure; LANKY suggests awkwardness and loose-jointedness as well as thinness; GAUNT implies marked thinness as from overwork, suffering, or undernourishment; RAWBONED suggests a large ungainly build without implying undernourishment.

lanky \ˈlang-kē\ *adj* **lank•i•er; -est :** being tall, thin, and usually loose-jointed **syn** see LANK — **lank•i•ly** \-kə-lē\ *adv* — **lank•i•ness** \-kē-nəs\ *n*

lan•ner \ˈlan-ər\ *n* **:** a widely distributed Old World falcon **[**Middle French *lanier***]**

lan•o•lin \ˈlan-l-ən\ *n* **:** the fatty coating of sheep's wool especially when refined for use in ointments and cosmetics **[**derived from Latin *lana* "wool" + *oleum* "oil"**]**

lan•ta•na \lan-ˈtän-ə\ *n* **:** any of a genus of tropical shrubs that are related to vervains and have showy heads of small bright flowers **[**Italian dialect, "viburnum"**]**

lan•tern \ˈlant-ərn\ *n* **1 :** a usually portable light that has a protective transparent or translucent covering **2 a :** the chamber in a lighthouse containing the light **b :** a structure with glazed or open sides above an opening in a roof for light, ventilation, or decoration **3 :** PROJECTOR 2b **[**Middle French *lanterne,* from Latin *lanterna,* from Greek *lamptēr,* from *lampein* "to shine"**]**

lantern jaw *n* **:** a long thin jaw — **lan•tern–jawed** \ˌlant-ərn-ˈjȯd\ *adj*

lan•tha•nide series \ˈlan-thə-ˌnīd-, ˈlant-\ *n* **:** a group of chemical elements consisting of the rare earth elements

lan•tha•num \ˈlan-thə-nəm, ˈlant-\ *n* **:** a white soft malleable metallic chemical element — see ELEMENT table **[**New Latin, from Greek *lanthanein* "to escape notice"**]**

lan•yard \ˈlan-yərd\ *n* **1 :** a piece of rope or line for fastening something in ships **2 a :** a cord worn around the neck to hold a knife or a whistle **b :** a cord worn on a uniform as a symbol of a military citation **3 :** a strong cord with a hook at one end used in firing cannon **[**Middle French *laniere* "thong, strap"**]**

Lao \ˈlau̇\ *or* **Lao•tian** \lā-ˈō-shən, ˈlau̇-shən\ *n* **1 :** a member of a Buddhist people living in Laos and northeastern Thailand and constituting a branch of the Tai race **2 :** the Thai language of the Lao people — **Lao** *or* **Laotian** *adj*

¹lap \ˈlap\ *n* **1 :** a loose panel in a garment **:** FLAP **2 a :** the clothing that lies on the knees and thighs of a seated person **b :** the front part of the lower trunk and thighs of a seated person **3 :** responsible custody **:** CONTROL ⟨dropped the problem into my *lap*⟩ **[**Old Englsih *læppa***]** — **lap•ful** \ˈlap-ˌfu̇l\ *n* — **the lap of luxury:** an environment of great comfort and wealth

²lap *vb* **lapped; lap•ping 1 :** ⁴WIND 6b, WRAP ⟨*lap* a bandage around the wrist⟩ **2 :** ENVELOP, SWATHE ⟨*lap* the child in a blanket⟩ **3 a :** to place or lay so that one covers part of another ⟨*lap* shingles on a roof⟩ **b :** to project or spread beyond a certain point **4 :** to smooth or polish (as a metal surface) to a fine finish or accurate fit — **lap•per** *n*

³lap *n* **1 a :** the amount by which one object overlaps or projects beyond another ⟨shingles with a 10-centimeter *lap*⟩ **b :** the part of an object that overlaps another **2 :** a smoothing and polishing tool **3 a :** one circuit around a racecourse **b :** one segment of a journey **c :** one complete turn (as of a rope around a drum)

⁴lap *vb* **lapped; lap•ping 1 :** to take in food or drink with the tongue; *also* **:** DEVOUR — usually used with *up* **2 :** to wash or splash gently ⟨waves *lapping* against the dock⟩ **[**Old English *lapian***]** — **lap•per** *n*

⁵lap *n* **1 a :** an act or instance of lapping **b :** the amount that can be carried to the mouth by one lick or scoop of the tongue **2 :** a gentle splashing sound

\ə\ **abut**	\au̇\ **out**	\i\ **tip**	\ȯ\ **saw**	\u̇\ **foot**
\ər\ **further**	\ch\ **chin**	\ī\ **life**	\ȯi\ **coin**	\y\ **yet**
\a\ **mat**	\e\ **pet**	\j\ **job**	\th\ **thin**	\yü\ **few**
\ā\ **take**	\ē\ **easy**	\ng\ **sing**	\t͟h\ **this**	\yu̇\ **cure**
\ä\ **cot, cart**	\g\ **go**	\ō\ **bone**	\ü\ **food**	\zh\ **vision**

lap•board \ˈlap-ˌbōrd, -ˌbȯrd\ *n* **:** a board used on the lap as a table or desk

lap•dog \-ˌdȯg\ *n* **:** a small dog that may be held in the lap

la•pel \lə-ˈpel\ *n* **:** the part of the front of a garment that is turned back and is usually a continuation of the collar [derived from [1]*lap*]

[1]**lap•i•dary** \ˈlap-ə-ˌder-ē\ *n, pl* **-dar•ies :** a person who cuts, polishes, and engraves precious stones [Latin *lapidarius,* from *lapid-, lapis* "stone"]

[2]**lapidary** *adj* **1 :** of or relating to precious stones or the art of cutting them **2 :** of, relating to, or suitable for engraved inscriptions

lap•in \ˈlap-ən\ *n* **:** rabbit fur usually sheared and dyed [French, "rabbit"]

la•pis la•zu•li \ˌlap-əs-ˈlazh-ə-lē, -ˈlaz-\ *n* **:** a deep blue semiprecious stone that is essentially a complex silicate often with spangles of iron pyrites [Medieval Latin, from Latin *lapis* "stone" + Medieval Latin *lazulum* "lapis lazuli", from Arabic *lāzaward*]

lap joint *n* **:** a joint made by overlapping two ends or edges and fastening them together — **lap–jointed** \ˈlap-ˈjȯint-əd\ *adj*

Lapp \ˈlap\ *n* **:** a member of a people of northern Scandinavia, Finland, and the Kola peninsula of Russia [Swedish]

lap•pet \ˈlap-ət\ *n* **1 :** a fold or flap on a garment or headdress **2 :** a flat overlapping or hanging piece

[1]**lapse** \ˈlaps\ *n* **1 a :** a slight error ⟨a *lapse* in manners⟩ **b :** a temporary deviation or fall especially from a higher to a lower state ⟨a *lapse* from grace⟩ **2 :** a becoming less **:** DECLINE **3 a :** the ending of a right or privilege by neglect to exercise it or failure to meet requirements **b :** DISUSE, DISCONTINUANCE ⟨*lapse* of a custom⟩ **4 :** a passage of time; *also* **:** INTERVAL [Latin *lapsus,* from *labi* "to slip"]

[2]**lapse** *vi* **1 a :** to fall from a better or higher state into a poorer or lower one ⟨*lapsed* into carelessness⟩ **b :** to sink or slip gradually ⟨*lapse* into silence⟩ **2 :** to fall into disuse **3 :** to come to an end **:** CEASE **4 :** to let something (as insurance or a legacy) come to an end or to pass to another by omission or negligence — **laps•er** *n*

lapse rate *n* **:** the rate of decrease in temperature of an air mass with increase in altitude

lap•wing \ˈlap-ˌwing\ *n* **:** a crested Old World plover with a slow irregular flapping flight and a shrill wailing cry [Old English *hlēapewince*]

lar•board \ˈlär-bərd\ *n* **:** [3]PORT — [Middle English *ladeborde*] — **lar•board** *adj*

lar•ce•ny \ˈlärs-nē, -n-ē\ *n, pl* **-nies :** the unlawful taking and carrying away of personal property with intent to deprive the owner of it permanently **:** THEFT [Middle French *larcin* "theft", from Latin *latrocinium* "robbery", from *latro* "mercenary soldier"] — **lar•ce•nous** \ˈlärs-nəs, -n-əs\ *adj*

larch \ˈlärch\ *n* **1 :** any of a genus of trees of the pine family with short deciduous needles; *also* **:** any of several related trees **2 :** the wood of a larch [probably from German *lärche,* from Latin *larix*]

[1]**lard** \ˈlärd\ *vt* **1 :** to insert strips of pork fat or bacon into (meat) before cooking **2 :** to smear with lard, fat, or grease **3 :** to add to; *esp* **:** ENRICH ⟨a book *larded* with illustrations⟩

[2]**lard** *n* **:** a soft white fat obtained from fatty tissue of the hog by heating [Old French, from Latin *lardum*] — **lardy** \ˈlärd-ē\ *adj*

lar•der \ˈlärd-ər\ *n* **:** a place where foods are kept [Middle French *lardier,* from *lard,* "lard"]

large \ˈlärj\ *adj* **:** exceeding most other things of like kind especially in quantity or size **:** BIG [Old French, "abundant, generous, broad", from Latin *largus* "abundant, generous"] — **large•ness** *n*

• **syn** LARGE, BIG, GREAT mean above average in magnitude. LARGE is likely to be chosen when the dimensions, extent, capacity, or quantity are being considered ⟨a *large* sum of money⟩ BIG suggests emphasis on bulk, weight, or volume ⟨*big* boxes⟩ GREAT may imply physical magnitude usually with connotations of wonder or awe but more often implies degree of intensity ⟨*great* kindness⟩ ⟨*great* fear⟩ LARGE figuratively implies breadth, comprehensiveness, or generosity; BIG suggests impressiveness often at the expense of solidity; GREAT implies eminence, distinction, or supremacy.

—**at large 1 :** at liberty **:** FREE ⟨an escaped prisoner still *at large*⟩ **2 :** as a whole **:** in general ⟨society *at large*⟩ **3 :** representing a whole area rather than one of its subdivisions — used in combination with a preceding noun ⟨a delagate-*at-large*⟩

large calorie *n* **:** CALORIE 1b

large•heart•ed \ˈlärj-ˈhärt-əd\ *adj* **:** GENEROUS 1, LIBERAL

large intestine *n* **:** the posterior division of the vertebrate intestine consisting of the cecum, colon, and rectum and functioning especially in the removal of water from digestive residues to form feces

large•ly \ˈlärj-lē\ *adv* **:** for the most part **:** CHIEFLY, MOSTLY

large–mind•ed \ˈlärj-ˈmīn-dəd\ *adj* **:** generous or comprehensive in outlook, range, or capacity — **large–mind•ed•ly** *adv* — **large–mind•ed•ness** *n*

large•mouth bass \ˌlärj-ˌmau̇th-\ *n* **:** a large bass of sluggish warm waters that is blackish green above and lighter below — called also *largemouth black bass*

large–scale \ˈlärj-ˈskāl\ *adj* **:** larger than others of its kind

lar•gess *or* **lar•gesse** \lär-ˈzhes, lär-ˈjes\ *n* **1 :** liberal giving **2 :** a generous gift [Old French *largesse,* from *large* "generous"]

[1]**lar•ghet•to** \lär-ˈget-ō\ *adv or adj* **:** slower than andante but not so slow as largo — used as a direction in music [Italian, "somewhat slow", from *largo* "slow"]

[2]**larghetto** *n, pl* **-tos :** a larghetto movement

[1]**lar•go** \ˈlär-gō\ *adv or adj* **:** in a very slow and broad manner — used as a direction in music [Italian, "slow, broad", from Latin *largus* "abundant"]

[2]**largo** *n, pl* **largos :** a largo movement

lar•i•at \ˈlar-ē-ət, ˈler-\ *n* **:** a long light rope used to catch livestock or to picket grazing animals [American Spanish *la reata* "the lasso"]

[1]**lark** \ˈlärk\ *n* **1 :** any of numerous Old World singing birds; *esp* **:** SKYLARK **2 :** any of various usually dull-colored ground-living birds (as the meadowlark) [Old English *lāwerce*]

[2]**lark** *n* **:** a merry adventure **:** FROLIC; *also* **:** PRANK [probably derived from Old Norse *leika* "to play, deceive, dance"] — **lark** *vi*

lark•spur \ˈlärk-ˌspər\ *n* **:** DELPHINIUM; *esp* **:** a cultivated annual delphinium grown for its flowers

lar•rup \ˈlar-əp\ *vt, dialect* **:** WHIP 2a, 4 [perhaps imitative]

lar•va \ˈlär-və\ *n, pl* **lar•vae** \-ˌvē, -ˌvī\ *also* **larvas 1 :** the immature, wingless, and often wormlike form that hatches from the egg of many insects **2 :** the early form of any animal that at birth or hatching is fundamentally unlike its parent ⟨the tadpole is the *larva* of the frog⟩ [Latin, "specter, mask"] — **lar•val** \-vəl\ *adj*

△ **origin** Many insects hatch from their eggs looking very different from their eventual adult forms. The caterpillar, although it is a young butterfly, seems to have very little in common with that winged creature. The immature insect appears to be in disguise, to be masked. Linnaeus, the great 18th-century Swedish naturalist, was struck by this and gave the immature insect form the name *larva,* from a Latin word that means "mask".

lar•vi•cide \ˈlär-və-ˌsīd\ *n* **:** an agent for killing larval pests — **lar•vi•cid•al** \ˌlär-və-ˈsīd-l\ *adj*

[1]**la•ryn•geal** \lə-ˈrin-jəl, -jē-əl, ˌlar-ən-ˈjē-əl\ *adj* **:** of, relating to, or used on the larynx [derived from Greek *laryng-, larynx* "larynx"] — **la•ryn•geal•ly** \-ē\ *adv*

[2]**laryngeal** *n* **:** a laryngeal part

lar•yn•gi•tis \ˌlar-ən-ˈjīt-əs\ *n* **:** inflammation of the larynx — **lar•yn•git•ic** \-ˈjit-ik\ *adj*

lar•ynx \ˈlar-ings, -ingks\ *n, pl* **la•ryn•ges** \lə-ˈrin-ˌjēz\ *or* **lar•ynx•es :** the modified upper part of the trachea that in humans and most mammals contains the vocal cords [Greek *laryng-, larynx*]

la•sa•gna \lə-ˈzän-yə\ *n* **:** broad flat noodles baked with a sauce usually of tomatoes, cheese, and meat [Italian *lasagna,* from Latin *lasanum* "cooking pot", from Greek *lasanon* "chamber pot"]

las•civ•i•ous \lə'siv-ē-əs\ *adj* **:** sexually loose **:** LEWD [Latin *lascivia* "wantonness", from *lascivus* "wanton"] — **las•civ•i•ous•ly** *adv* — **las•civ•i•ous•ness** *n*

la•ser \ˈlā-zər\ *n* **:** a device that utilizes the natural oscillations of atoms or molecules between energy levels for generating electromagnetic waves with a narrow frequency range [*l*ight *a*mplification by *s*timulated *e*mission of *r*adiation]

[1]**lash** \ˈlash\ *vb* **1 :** to move violently or suddenly ⟨a cat *lashing* its tail⟩ **2 :** to strike with or as if with a whip ⟨rain *lashing* the window⟩ **3 :** to attack or retort verbally — usually used with *out* [Middle English *lashen*] — **lash•er** *n*

[2]**lash** *n* **1 a** (1) **:** a stroke with or as if with a whip (2) **:** the flexible

part of a whip; *also* : WHIP **b** : a sudden swinging blow **2** : a verbal attack **3** : EYELASH

[3]**lash** *vt* : to bind with a rope, cord, or chain [Middle French *lacier* "to lace"] — **lash•er** *n*

lash•ing *n* : something used for binding, wrapping, or fastening

lass \ˈlas\ *n* **1** : young woman : GIRL **2** : SWEETHEART 2 [Middle English *las*]

lass•ie \ˈlas-ē\ *n* : LASS 1, GIRL

las•si•tude \ˈlas-ə-ˌtüd, -ˌtyüd\ *n* **1** : FATIGUE 1a, WEARINESS **2** : LANGUOR 2, LISTLESSNESS [Middle French, from Latin *lassitudo*, from *lassus* "weary"]

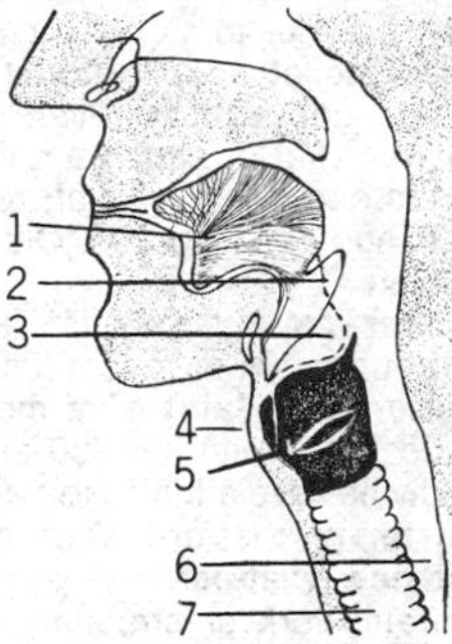

larynx: *1* tongue, *2* epiglottis opening larynx, *3* epiglottis closing larynx, *4* Adam's apple, *5* vocal cords, *6* esophagus, *7* trachea

las•so \ˈlas-ō, la-ˈsü\ *n, pl* **lassos** *or* **lassoes** : a rope or long thong of leather with a running noose that is used especially for catching livestock [Spanish *lazo*, from Latin *laqueus* "noose, snare"] — **lasso** *vt*

[1]**last** \ˈlast\ *vb* **1** : to continue in being or operation : go on ⟨the meeting *lasted* three hours⟩ **2 a** : to remain valid or important : ENDURE ⟨a book that will *last*⟩ **b** : to manage to continue ⟨won't *last* on that job⟩ **3** : to be enough for the needs of ⟨supplies to *last* you for a week⟩ [Old English *lǣstan* "to last, follow"] — **last•er** *n*

△ **origin** English *last* has several homonyms. The verb *last* means "to continue" or "to endure". In Old English, *lǣstan* was used like its modern decendant to mean "to continue", but it also meant "to follow". The original meaning was probably "to follow a track". Old English *lǣstan* is related to the Old English noun *lāst*, which means "footprint" or "track". This noun is the ancestor of the shoemaker's *last*, a form in the shape of a foot. The very common adjective and adverb *last*, which mean "after the others", are not related to this verb and noun. They come from Old English *latost*, superlative of *læt*, "late, slow."

[2]**last** *adj* **1 a** : following all the rest ⟨*last* on the list⟩ **b** : being the only remaining ⟨my *last* dollar⟩ **2 a** : belonging to the final stage ⟨the four *last* things⟩ **b** : administered to the dying ⟨*last* rites⟩ **3 a** : next before the present ⟨*last* week⟩ **b** : most up-to-date : LATEST **4** : least likely ⟨the *last* thing they'd want⟩ **5 a** : CONCLUSIVE, ULTIMATE ⟨no *last* answer to that problem⟩ **b** : highest in degree : SUPREME [Old English *latost*, superlative of *læt* "late"] — **last•ly** *adv*

• **syn** FINAL, ULTIMATE: LAST applies to something that comes at the end of a series but does not always imply that the series is completed or stopped ⟨the *last* stop on the bus line⟩ ⟨the *last* news bulletin I heard⟩ FINAL stresses a definite closing of a series, process, or stage of progress ⟨*final* exams⟩ ULTIMATE implies the last degree or stage of a long process beyond which further progress or change is impossible ⟨*ultimate* collapse of civilization⟩

[3]**last** *adv* **1** : after all others : at the end ⟨ran *last* in the race⟩ **2** : most lately ⟨saw them *last* in New York⟩ **3** : in conclusion ⟨and *last*, I'd like to talk about money⟩

[4]**last** *n* : something that is last

[5]**last** *n* : a wooden or metal form which is shaped like the human foot and on which a shoe is shaped or repaired [Old English *lǣste*, from *lāst* "footprint"]

[6]**last** *vt* : to shape with a last — **last•er** *n*

last•ing *adj* : existing or continuing a long while : ENDURING — **last•ing•ly** \ˈlas-ting-lē\ *adv* — **last•ing•ness** *n*

• **syn** LASTING, PERMANENT, DURABLE mean enduring for so long as to seem fixed or established. LASTING implies a capacity to continue indefinitely ⟨*lasting* friendships⟩ PERMANENT may add the implication of being designed to stand or continue indefinitely ⟨a *permanent* arrangement⟩ ⟨*permanent* buildings⟩ DURABLE implies power to resist destructive agencies ⟨*durable* fabrics⟩

Last Judgment *n* : JUDGMENT 3

Last Supper *n* : the supper eaten by Jesus and his disciples on the night of his betrayal

last straw *n* : the last of a series that brings one beyond the point of endurance [from the fable of the last straw that broke the camel's back when added to its burden]

last word *n* **1** : the final remark in a verbal exchange **2** : the power of final decision **3** : the most advanced, up-to-date, or fashionable one of its kind ⟨the *last word* in cars⟩

[1]**latch** \ˈlach\ *vi* **1** : to catch or get hold ⟨*latch* onto a pass⟩ **2** : to attach oneself [Old English *læccan*]

[2]**latch** *n* : a device that holds something in place by entering a notch or cavity; *esp* : a catch that holds a door or gate closed and that sometimes is operated by a key on one side and a knob on the other

[3]**latch** *vb* : to make fast with or as if with a latch : SHUT 1

latch•string \-ˌstring\ *n* : a string for raising a latch so as to release it

[1]**late** \ˈlāt\ *adj* **1 a** : coming or remaining after the due, usual, or proper time ⟨a *late* spring⟩ **b** : of or relating to an advanced stage in time or development ⟨the *late* Middle Ages⟩; *esp* : far advanced toward the close of the day or night ⟨*late* hours⟩ **2 a** : living comparatively recently ⟨the *late* president⟩ **b** : being something or holding a position or relationship recently but not now ⟨the *late* belligerents⟩ **c** : made, appearing, or happening in times close to the present ⟨a *late* discovery⟩ [Old English *læt*] **syn** see RECENT — **late•ness** *n*

[2]**late** *adv* **1 a** : after the usual or proper time **b** : at or to an advanced point of time ⟨stayed *late* at the party⟩ — often used with *on* ⟨see me *later* on⟩ **2** : not long ago : RECENTLY ⟨a person *late* of Chicago⟩ — **of late** : LATELY, RECENTLY

late•com•er \ˈlāt-ˌkəm-ər\ *n* : one that arrives late; *also* : a recent arrival

[1]**la•teen** \lə-ˈtēn\ *adj* : of, relating to, or being a sailing rig characterized by a triangular sail extended by a long spar crossing a low mast at an angle of about 45 degrees [French *voile latine* "lateen sail", derived from Latin *Latinus* "Latin"]

[2]**lateen** *n* **1** *also* **la•teen•er** \-ˈtē-nər\ : a lateen-rigged ship **2** : a lateen sail

[2]lateen 1

Late Greek *n* : the Greek language used in the 3d to 6th centuries

Late Latin *n* : the Latin language used by writers in the 3d to 6th centuries

late•ly \ˈlāt-lē\ *adv* : in recent time ⟨what have you done for me *lately*⟩

lat•en \ˈlāt-n\ *vb* : to grow or cause to grow late

la•ten•cy \ˈlāt-n-sē\ *n, pl* **-cies** : the quality or state of being latent : DORMANCY

la•tent \ˈlāt-nt\ *adj* : present but not visible or active ⟨*latent* abilities⟩⟨*latent* infection⟩ [Latin *latens*, from *latēre* "to lie hidden"] — **la•tent•ly** *adv*

• **syn** LATENT, DORMANT, QUIESCENT mean not now showing its presence or existence. LATENT applies to a power or quality that has not yet come forth but may emerge and develop ⟨talents which were *latent* in childhood⟩ DORMANT suggests inactivity as though sleeping ⟨a *dormant* volcano⟩ QUIESCENT suggests a temporary cessation of activity ⟨*quiescent* lung disease⟩

latent heat *n* : heat energy absorbed or evolved in a process (as fusion or vaporization)

latent period *n* : the interval (as the incubation period of a disease) between the introduction of a cause and the occurrence of its effect

lat•er•ad \ˈlat-ə-ˌrad\ *adv* : toward the side [Latin *later-*, *latus* "side"]

[1]**lat•er•al** \ˈlat-ə-rəl, ˈla-trəl\ *adj* **1** : of or relating to the side : situated on, directed toward, or coming from the side ⟨the *lateral* branches of a tree⟩ **2** : being a part of the outside of a geometric solid that is not a base or completely included in a base ⟨a *lateral* edge⟩ ⟨a *lateral* face⟩ [Latin *lateralis*, from *later-*, *latus* "side"] — **lat•er•al•ly** \-ē\ *adv*

[2]**lateral** *n* **1** : a lateral part or branch **2** : a pass in football thrown to the side or to the rear

lateral line *n* : a sense organ of the skin of most fishes that is sensitive to low vibrations and extends along each side of the body

lat•er•ite \'lat-ə-ˌrīt\ *n* : a residual product of rock decay that is red in color and rich in the oxides of iron and hydroxide of aluminum [Latin *later* "brick"] — **lat•er•it•ic** \ˌlat-ə-'rit-ik\ *adj*

la•tex \'lā-ˌteks\ *n pl* **lat•i•ces** \'lāt-ə-ˌsēz, 'lat-\ *or* **la•tex•es** **1** : a milky juice produced by plants especially of the milkweed family ⟨rubber is produced from a *latex*⟩ **2** : a water emulsion of a synthetic rubber or plastic used especially in paints and adhesives [Latin, "fluid"] — **lat•i•cif•er•ous** \ˌlāt-ə-'sif-rəs, ˌlat-, -ə-rəs\ *adj*

lath \'lath *also* 'lath\ *n, pl* **laths** **1** : a thin narrow strip of wood used especially as a base for plaster **2** : material (as wire cloth) used in sheets as a substitute for wooden laths **3** : a quantity of laths together [Old English *lætt*] — **lath** *vt*

lathe \'lāth\ *n* : a machine in which a piece of material is held and turned while being shaped by a tool [probably from Middle English *lath* "supporting stand"]

[1]lath•er \'lath-ər\ *n* **1** **a** : a thick foam or froth formed when a detergent is agitated in water **b** : foam or froth from profuse sweating (as on a horse) **2** : an overwrought state : DITHER [Old English *lēathor*] — **lath•ery** \'lath-rē, -ə-rē\ *adj*

[2]lather *vb* **lath•ered**; **lath•er•ing** \'lath-ring, -ə-ring\ **1** **a** : to spread lather over ⟨to *lather* one's face for shaving⟩ **b** : to form a lather or a froth like lather ⟨this soap *lathers* well⟩ **2** : to beat severely : FLOG — **lath•er•er** \'lath-ər-ər\ *n*

lath•ing \'lath-ing, 'lath-\ *n* **1** : the action or process of placing laths **2** : a quantity or an installation of laths

lat•i•me•ria \ˌlat-ə-'mir-ē-ə\ *n* : any of a genus of living coelacanth fishes of deep seas off southern Africa — compare LOBE-FIN [Marjorie E. D. Courtenay-*Latimer*, born 1907, South African museum director]

[1]Lat•in \'lat-n\ *adj* **1** **a** : of, relating to, or composed in Latin ⟨*Latin* grammar⟩ **b** : ROMANCE ⟨*Latin* languages⟩ **2** : of or relating to the part of the Catholic Church that until recently used a Latin rite **3** : of or relating to the peoples or countries using Romance languages; *esp* : of or relating to the peoples or countries of Latin America [Old English, from Latin *Latinus*, from *Latium*, ancient country of Italy]

[2]Latin *n* **1** : the Italic language of ancient Rome and until modern times the dominant language of school, church, and state in western Europe **2** : a Catholic of the Latin rite **3** : a member of one of the peoples speaking Romance languages; *esp* : a native or inhabitant of Latin America

Lat•in•ate \'lat-n-ˌāt\ *adj* : of, relating to, resembling, or derived from Latin

Latin cross *n* : a cross having a long upright shaft and a shorter crossbar above the middle

Lat•in•ism \'lat-n-ˌiz-əm\ *n* **1** : a word, idiom, or mode of speech derived from or modeled on Latin **2** : Latin quality, character, or mode of thought

Lat•in•ist \-n-əst\ *n* : a specialist in the Latin language or Roman culture

la•tin•i•ty \la-'tin-ət-e, lə-\ *n, often cap* **1** : a way of speaking or writing Latin **2** : LATINISM 2

lat•in•ize \'lat-n-ˌīz\ *vt, often cap* : to give Latin characteristics or forms to — **lat•in•iza•tion** \ˌlat-n-ə-'zā-shən\ *n*

lat•ish \'lāt-ish\ *adj* : somewhat late

lat•i•tude \'lat-ə-ˌtüd, -ˌtyüd\ *n* **1** **a** : angular distance north or south from the earth's equator measured in degrees **b** : angular distance of a celestial body from the ecliptic **c** : a region or locality as marked by its latitude **2** : the range of exposures within which a film or plate will produce a negative or positive of satisfactory quality **3** : freedom from narrow restrictions ⟨were allowed great *latitude* in their editorials⟩ [Latin *latitudin-*, *latitudo* "width", from *latus* "wide"] — **lat•i•tu•di•nal** \ˌlat-ə-'tüd-nəl, -'tyüd-, -n-əl\ *adj* — **lat•i•tu•di•nal•ly** \-ē\ *adv*

latitude 1a

lat•i•tu•di•nar•i•an \ˌlat-ə-ˌtüd-n-'er-ē-ən, -ˌtyüd-\ *n* : a person who is broad and liberal in standards of religious belief and conduct — **latitudinarian** *adj* — **lat•i•tu•di•nar•i•an•ism** \-ē-ə-ˌniz-əm\ *n*

la•trine \lə-'trēn\ *n* **1** : a receptacle (as a pit in the earth) for use as a toilet **2** : BATHROOM [French, from Latin *latrina* "bath, toilet", derived from *lavere* "to wash"]

lat•ter \'lat-ər\ *adj* **1** **a** : more recent : LATER **b** : of or relating to the end : FINAL **2** : of, relating to, or being the second of two things referred to [Old English *lætra*, comparative of *læt* "late"]

lat•ter–day \ˌlat-ər-ˌdā\ *adj* **1** : of a later or subsequent time **2** : of present or recent times

Latter–Day Saint *n* : a member of a religious body founded by Joseph Smith in 1830 and accepting the Book of Mormon as divine revelation : MORMON

lat•ter•ly \'lat-ər-lē\ *adv* : LATELY, RECENTLY

lat•tice \'lat-əs\ *n* **1** **a** : a framework or structure of crossed wood or metal strips **b** : a window, door, or gate having a lattice **2** : a regular geometrical arrangment of points or objects over an area or in space ⟨the *lattice* of atoms in a crystal⟩ [Middle French *lattis*] — **lattice** *vt* — **lat•ticed** \-əst\ *adj*

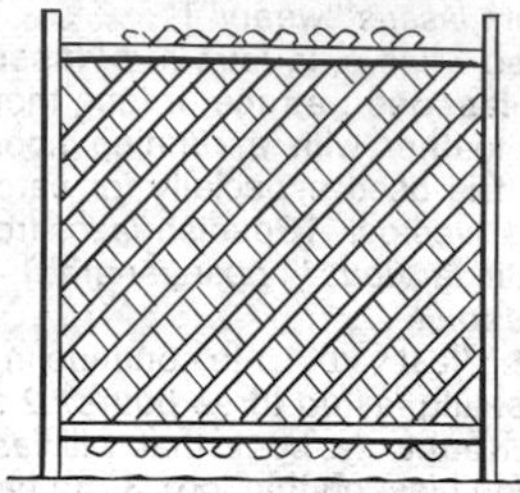
lattice 1a

lat•tice•work \'lat-ə-ˌswərk\ *n* : a lattice or work made of lattices

[1]Lat•vi•an \'lat-vē-ən\ *adj* : of, relating to, or characteristic of Latvia, the Latvians, or Latvian

[2]Latvian *n* **1** : a native or inhabitant of Latvia **2** : the Baltic language of the Latvian people

[1]laud \'lȯd\ *n* **1** *pl* : an office of solemn praise to God forming with matins the first of the canonical hours **2** : PRAISE 1, ACCLAIM [derived from Latin *laud-*, *laus* "praise"]

[2]laud *vt* : PRAISE 2, EXTOL

laud•able \'lȯd-ə-bəl\ *adj* : worthy of praise : COMMENDABLE — **laud•abil•i•ty** \ˌlȯd-ə-'bil-ət-ē\ *n* — **laud•able•ness** \'lȯd-ə-bəl-nəs\ *n* — **laud•ably** \-blē\ *adv*

lau•da•num \'lȯd-nəm, -n-əm\ *n* **1** : a formerly used preparation of opium **2** : a tincture of opium [New Latin]

lau•da•tion \lȯ-'dā-shən\ *n* : the act of praising : EULOGY

lau•da•to•ry \'lȯd-ə-ˌtōr-ē, -ˌtȯr-\ *adj* : of, relating to, or expressing praise

[1]laugh \'laf, 'láf\ *vb* **1** **a** : to show mirth, joy, or scorn with a smile and chuckle or explosive sound **b** : to become amused or derisive ⟨*laughed* at their early efforts⟩ **2** : to produce the sound or appearance of laughter **3** : to utter with a laugh ⟨to *laugh* one's consent⟩ [Old English *hliehhan*, *hlæhan*] — **laugh•er** *n*

[2]laugh *n* **1** : the act or sound of laughing **2** : a cause for derision or merriment

laugh•able \'laf-ə-bəl, 'láf-\ *adj* : of a kind to provoke laughter or derision : RIDICULOUS — **laugh•able•ness** *n* — **laugh•ably** \-blē\ *adv*

• **syn** LAUGHABLE, RISIBLE, LUDICROUS, RIDICULOUS mean provoking laughter or mirth. LAUGHABLE and RISIBLE may apply to anything that arouses laughter; LUDICROUS suggests obvious absurdity or preposterousness that excites both laughter and scorn or sometimes pity; RIDICULOUS implies extreme absurdity, foolishness, or ineptness.

laugh•ing *adj* : fit to be treated or accompanied with laughter : LAUGHABLE ⟨this is no *laughing* matter⟩

laughing gas *n* : NITROUS OXIDE

laughing jackass *n* : KOOKABURRA

laugh•ing•ly \'laf-ing-lē, 'láf-\ *adv* : with laughter

laugh•ing•stock \'laf-ing-ˌstäk, 'láf-\ *n* : an object of ridicule

laugh•ter \'laf-tər, 'láf-\ *n* : the action or sound of laughing [Old English *hleahtor*]

[1]launch \'lȯnch, 'länch\ *vb* **1** **a** : to throw forward : HURL ⟨*launch* a spear⟩ **b** : to send off (a self-propelled object) ⟨*launch* a rocket⟩ **2** : to set (a ship) afloat **3** **a** : to put in operation : BEGIN ⟨*launch* an attack⟩ **b** : to give (a person) a start ⟨*launched* their children in the family business⟩ **4** **a** : to make a start (as on a course of action) ⟨had *launched* on a difficult course of study⟩ **b** : to throw oneself energetically : PLUNGE ⟨*launched* into a dreary monologue⟩ [Old North French *lancher*, from Late Latin

lanceare "to wield a lance", from Latin *lancea* "lance"]
²**launch** *n* : an act of launching
³**launch** *n* : a small open or half-decked motorboat used for pleasure or short-distance transportation [Portuguese *lancha*]
launch•er \'lȯn-chər, 'län-\ *n* : one that launches: as **a** : a device for firing a grenade from a rifle **b** : a device for launching a rocket or rocket shell **c** : CATAPULT
launch pad *or* **launching pad** *n* : a nonflammable platform from which a rocket can be launched
laun•der \'lȯn-dər, 'län-\ *vb* **laun•dered**; **laun•der•ing** \-də-riŋ, -driŋ\ **1** : to wash (as clothes) in water; *also* : to wash and iron ⟨a freshly *laundered* shirt⟩ **2** : to wash or wash and iron clothing or household linens **3** : to undergo washing and ironing ⟨fabrics guaranteed to *launder* well⟩ [Middle English *launder* "launderer", from Middle French *lavandier*, from Medieval Latin *lavandarius*, from Latin *lavare* "to wash"] — **laun•der•er** \-dər-ər\ *n* — **laun•dress** \-drəs\ *n*
Laun•dro•mat \'lȯn-drə-ˌmat, 'län-\ *trademark* — used for a self-service laundry
laun•dry \'lȯn-drē, 'län-\ *n, pl* **-dries** **1** : clothes or linens that have been or are to be laundered **2** : a place where laundering is done
lau•re•ate \'lȯr-ē-ət, 'lär-\ *n* : a recipient of honor for achievement in an art or science; *esp* : POET LAUREATE [Latin *laureatus* "crowned with laurel", from *laurea* "laurel wreath", from *laurus* "laurel"] — **laureate** *adj* — **lau•re•ate•ship** \-ˌship\ *n*
lau•rel \'lȯr-əl, 'lär-\ *n* **1** : any of a genus of trees or shrubs related to the sassafras and cinnamon; *esp* : a small evergreen tree of southern Europe with foliage used by the ancient Greeks to crown victors in various contests **2** : a tree or shrub (as a mountain laurel) like the true laurel **3** : a crown of laurel : HONOR [derived from Latin *laurus*]
la•va \'läv-ə, 'lav-\ *n* : molten rock coming from a volcano; *also* : such rock that has cooled and hardened [Italian, from Latin *labes* "fall"]
la•va•bo \lə-'väb-ō\ *n, often cap* : a ceremony at Mass in which the celebrant after offering the oblations washes his hands and says Psalm 25:6–12 [Latin, "I shall wash", from *lavare* "to wash"]
la•vage \lə-'väzh\ *n* : a washing out (as of a wound or hollow organ) for medicinal reasons [French, from *laver* "to wash", from Latin *lavare*]
la•va•liere *or* **la•val•liere** \ˌläv-ə-'liər, ˌlav-\ *n* : a pendant on a fine chain that is worn as a necklace [French *lavallière* "necktie with a large bow"]
lav•a•to•ry \'lav-ə-ˌtōr-ē, -ˌtȯr-\ *n, pl* **-ries** **1** : a vessel for washing; *esp* : a fixed bowl or basin with running water and drainpipe **2** : a room with conveniences for washing and usually with one or more toilets **3** : WATER CLOSET [Medieval Latin *lavatorium*, from Latin *lavare* "to wash"]
lave \'lāv\ *vb* **1 a** : WASH 1 **b** *archaic* : to wash oneself : BATHE **2** : to flow along or against ⟨water *laving* the shore⟩ [Old English *lafian*, from Latin *lavare*]
lav•en•der \'lav-ən-dər\ **1** : a Mediterranean mint widely cultivated for its narrow aromatic leaves and spikes of lilac-purple flowers which are dried and used in sachets; *also* : any of several related plants used similarly **2** : a pale purple [Anglo-French *lavendre*, from Medieval Latin *lavandula*]
¹**la•ver** \'lā-vər\ *n* : a large basin used for ceremonial ablutions in ancient Judaism [Middle French *lavoir*, derived from Latin *lavare* "to wash"]
²**la•ver** \'lä-vər, 'lā-\ *n* : any of several mostly edible seaweeds [Latin, a water plant]
¹**lav•ish** \'lav-ish\ *adj* **1** : spending or giving more than is necessary : EXTRAVAGANT ⟨*lavish* with money⟩ ⟨*lavish* of praise⟩ **2** : produced or given freely or in abundance ⟨*lavish* hospitality⟩ [Middle English *lavas* "abundance", from Middle French *lavasse* "downpour of rain", from *laver* "to wash", from Latin *lavare*] — **lav•ish•ly** *adv* — **lav•ish•ness** *n*
²**lavish** *vt* : to spend or give freely ⟨*lavish* affection on a person⟩
law \'lȯ\ *n* **1 a** : a rule of conduct or action established by custom or laid down by the supreme governing authority of a community, state, or nation **b** : a body of such rules and customs **2 a** : the state of order brought about by observance and enforcement of laws ⟨preserve *law* and order⟩ **b** : an agent or agency for enforcing laws ⟨an officer of the *law*⟩ **c** : the action of laws and especially court action as a means of achieving justice or redressing wrongs **3** *cap* **a** : the revelation of the divine will set forth in the Old Testament **b** : the first part of the Jewish scriptures — compare HAGIOGRAPHA, PROPHETS **4 a** : the legal profession **b** : law as an area of knowledge ⟨study *law*⟩ **5** : a rule of construction or procedure (as in an art, craft, or game) **6** : something that has the force of authority and must be obeyed ⟨in the classroom the teacher's word is *law*⟩ **7** : a rule or principle stating something that always works in the same way under the same conditions ⟨the *law* of gravity⟩ [Old English *lagu*, of Scandinavian origin]
• **syn** LAW, REGULATION, STATUTE, ORDINANCE mean a principle that governs action or procedure. LAW implies imposition by a sovereign authority and obligation of obedience by all; REGULATION carries an implication of authority exercised in order to control an organization or system; STATUTE implies a law enacted by a legislative body often as distinguished from the common or unwritten law; ORDINANCE applies to an order governing some detail or procedure enforced by a limited authority such as a municipality ⟨city *ordinances* for traffic regulation⟩ **syn** see in addition HYPOTHESIS
law–abid•ing \'lȯ-ə-ˌbīd-iŋ\ *adj* : obedient to the law
law•break•er \'lȯ-ˌbrā-kər\ *n* : a person who breaks the law — **law•break•ing** \-kiŋ\ *adj or n*
law•ful \'lȯ-fəl\ *adj* **1** : permitted or not prohibited by law ⟨conduct a demonstration in a *lawful* manner⟩ **2** : established or recognized by law : RIGHTFUL ⟨the *lawful* owner⟩ — **law•ful•ly** \-'fə-lē, -flē\ *adv* — **law•ful•ness** \-fəl-nəs\ *n*
• **syn** LAWFUL, LEGAL, LEGITIMATE, LICIT mean being in accordance with law. LAWFUL stresses conformity to law of any kind; LEGAL implies reference to the law of courts; LEGITIMATE implies a legal right or one supported by tradition, custom, or accepted standards of authenticity ⟨the *legitimate* heir to the throne⟩ LICIT emphasizes strict conformity to law specifically regulating the way something is performed or carried on.
law•giv•er \'lȯ-ˌgiv-ər\ *n* **1** : one who gives a code of laws to a people **2** : LEGISLATOR
law•less \'lȯ-ləs\ *adj* **1** : having no laws : not based on or regulated by law ⟨the *lawless* frontier⟩ **2** : not controlled by law : UNRULY, DISORDERLY ⟨a *lawless* mob⟩ — **law•less•ly** *adv* — **law•less•ness** *n*
law•mak•er \'lȯ-ˌmā-kər\ *n* : a person who has a part in framing laws : LEGISLATOR — **law•mak•ing** *adj or n*
¹**lawn** \'lȯn, 'län\ *n* : a fine sheer linen or cotton fabric of plain weave that is thinner than cambric [*Laon*, France] — **lawny** \-ē\ *adj*
²**lawn** *n* : ground (as around a house) covered with grass that is kept mowed [Middle English *launde* "glade, pasture", from Middle French *lande* "heath", of Celtic origin]
lawn bowling *n* : a bowling game played on a green with wooden balls which are rolled at a jack
lawn mower *n* : a machine for cutting grass on lawns
lawn tennis *n* : TENNIS
law of cosines : a theorem in trigonometry: the square of a side of a plane triangle equals the sum of the squares of the remaining sides minus twice the product of those sides and the cosine of the angle included between them
law of definite proportions : a statement in chemistry: every definite compound always contains the same elements in the same proportions by weight
law of dominance : MENDEL'S LAW 3
law of independent assortment : MENDEL'S LAW 2
law of Mo•ses \-'mō-zəz, -zəs\ : PENTATEUCH
law of multiple proportions : a statement in chemistry: when two elements combine in more than one proportion to form two or more compounds the weights of one element that combine with a given weight of the other element are in the ratios of small whole numbers
law of segregation : MENDEL'S LAW 1
law of sines : a theorem in trigonometry: the ratio of the length of each side of a plane triangle to the sine of the opposite angle is the same for all three sides and angles
law•ren•ci•um \lȯ-'ren-sē-əm\ *n* : a short-lived radioactive ele-

ment produced from californium — see ELEMENT table [New Latin, from Ernest O. *Lawrence,* died 1958, American physicist]

law•suit \'lȯ-ˌsüt\ *n* : ACTION 1, SUIT

law•yer \'lȯ-yər, 'lȯi-ər\ *n* : one whose profession is to practice law and to advise clients on legal matters and represent them in court

lax \'laks\ *adj* **1** : lacking in restraint or the power to restrain ⟨*lax* bowels⟩ ⟨*lax* morals⟩ **2** : not strict or stringent ⟨*lax* discipline⟩ **3 a** : not firm or rigid **b** : having an open or loose texture ⟨a *lax* flower cluster⟩ **4** : produced with the speech muscles in a relatively relaxed state ⟨the *lax* vowels \i\ and \u̇\⟩ — compare TENSE [Latin *laxus* "loose"] — **lax•ly** \'lak-slē\ *adv* — **lax•ness** *n*

¹**lax•a•tive** \'lak-sət-iv\ *adj* : having a tendency to loosen or relax; *esp* : relieving constipation — **lax•a•tive•ly** *adv* — **lax•a•tive•ness** *n*

²**laxative** *n* : a usually mild laxative drug — compare PURGATIVE

lax•i•ty \'lak-sət-ē\ *n* : the quality or state of being lax ⟨*laxity* in discipline⟩

¹**lay** \'lā\ *vb* **laid** \'lād\; **lay•ing 1** : to beat or strike down ⟨wheat *laid* flat by a hailstorm⟩ **2 a** : to put or set on or against something ⟨*lay* the book on the table⟩ ⟨*lay* a watch to one's ear⟩ **b** : to place or put down in an orderly sequence ⟨*lay* a sewer⟩ **c** : to set in order for a meal ⟨*lay* the table⟩ ⟨three places were *laid*⟩ **3** : BURY 1 **4** : to produce and deposit eggs ⟨the hens won't *lay*⟩ **5 a** : to put forward for consideration : SUBMIT ⟨*laid* their case before the committee⟩ **b** : ASSERT, ALLEGE ⟨*lay* claim to the estate⟩ **c** : to place (as emphasis or importance) on something ⟨*lay* great stress on neatness⟩ **6** : SET, IMPOSE ⟨*lay* a tax on liquor⟩ **7 a** : CONTRIVE, DEVISE ⟨*lay* plans⟩ **b** : to make ready or put in operation ⟨*laid* a trap⟩ **8 a** : BET 1 ⟨*lay* $10 on the race⟩ **b** : BET 2 ⟨*lay* you ten to one⟩ **9** : to cause to settle or subside ⟨a shower *laid* the dust⟩; *also* : CALM, ALLAY ⟨*laid* their fears⟩ **10** : to assign as a burden of reproach ⟨*laid* the theft to the chauffeur⟩ **11** : to bring to a specified condition ⟨*lay* waste the land⟩ **12** : to place (as the action or a scene of a story) in a particular location ⟨the scene was *laid* in wartime London⟩ [Old English *lecgan*] — **lay aside 1** : DISCARD, ABANDON ⟨*lay aside* prejudices⟩ **2** : to put away for future or special use ⟨*lay* a few dollars *aside* each week⟩ — **lay bare** : to expose or make known : REVEAL — **lay eyes on** : to catch sight of : SEE — **lay for** : to lie in wait to attack — **lay hold of** : GRASP, SEIZE ⟨*lay hold of* a rope⟩ — **lay into** : ATTACK ⟨*laid into* the plan for reorganization⟩ — **lay one's finger on** : to discover and point out accurately

²**lay** *n* **1** : the way in which a thing lies or is laid in relation to something else ⟨*lay* of the land⟩ **2** : an egg-laying condition

³**lay** *past of* LIE

⁴**lay** *n* **1** : a simple narrative poem : BALLAD **2** : MELODY 2, SONG [Old French *lai*]

⁵**lay** *adj* **1** : of or relating to the laity : not ecclesiastical **2** : of or relating to members of a religious house occupied with domestic or manual work ⟨a *lay* brother⟩ **3** : not of or from a particular profession : UNPROFESSIONAL ⟨the *lay* public⟩ [Old French *lai,* from Late Latin *laicus,* from Greek *laikos* "of the people", from *laos* "people"]

lay away *vt* : to put aside for future use or delivery

lay by *vt* : to store for future use : SAVE

lay down *vt* **1** : to give up : SURRENDER ⟨*lay down* your arms⟩ **2 a** : ESTABLISH, PRESCRIBE ⟨*lays down* standards⟩ **b** : to assert or command dogmatically ⟨*lay down* the law⟩

¹**lay•er** \'lā-ər, 'le-ər, 'ler\ *n* **1** : one that lays ⟨the hens were poor *layers*⟩ **2** : one thickness, course, or fold laid or lying over or under another ⟨a *layer* of rock⟩ **3** : a shoot used in or a plant developed by layering — **lay•ered** \'lā-ərd, 'le-ərd, 'lerd\ *adj*

²**layer** *vt* : to propagate (a plant) by layering

lay•er•age \'lā-ə-rij, 'le-ə-\ *n* : the practice or art of layering plants

lay•er•ing \'lā-ə-ring, 'le-ər-ing, 'ler-ing\ *n* : the production of new plants by surrounding a stem which is often partly cut through with a rooting medium (as soil) until new roots have formed

lay•ette \lā-'et\ *n* : a complete outfit of clothing and equipment for a newborn infant [French, from Middle French *laye* "box", from Dutch *lade*]

lay figure \'lā-\ *n* **1** : a jointed model of the human body used by artists to show the disposition of drapery **2** : a person of no importance or individuality : DUMMY, PUPPET [obsolete *layman* "lay figure", from Dutch *ledeman, leeman,* from *lid* "limb" + *man* "man"]

lay in *vt* : to store up : lay by ⟨*lay in* a supply of groceries⟩

lay•man \ lā-mən\ *n* **1** : a person who is not a member of the clergy **2** : a person who is not a member of a particular profession

lay•off \'lā-ˌȯf\ *n* **1** : the act of laying off an employee or a work force **2** : a period of inactivity or idleness

lay off \lā-'ȯf, 'lā-\ *vb* **1** : to mark or measure off **2** : to cease to employ (a worker) usually temporarily **3 a** : to leave undisturbed ⟨*lay off* me, will you⟩ **b** : AVOID, QUIT ⟨*lay off* smoking⟩ **4** : to stop or rest from work

lay on *vi* : ATTACK ⟨grabbed clubs and *laid on* for all they were worth⟩

lay•out \'lā-ˌau̇t\ *n* **1** : ARRANGEMENT, PLAN ⟨the *layout* of a house⟩ **2** : something that is laid out ⟨a model train *layout*⟩ **3** : the way in which a piece of printed matter is arranged ⟨the *layout* of a page⟩; *also* : DUMMY 6 **4** : a set or outfit especially of tools

lay out \lā-'au̇t, 'lā-\ *vt* **1** : to prepare (a corpse) for burial **2** : to plan in detail ⟨*lay out* a campaign⟩ **3** : ARRANGE 1, DESIGN **4** : SPEND 1

lay•over \'lā-ˌō-vər\ *n* : STOPOVER 1

lay over \lā-'ō-vər, 'lā-\ *vi* : to make a temporary halt or stop ⟨*laid over* in New York for three days before flying back⟩

lay reader *n* **1** : an Anglican layman licensed to read sermons and conduct some religious services **2** : LECTOR

lay to \lā-'tü, 'lā-\ *vb* **1** : to bring (a ship) into the wind and hold stationary : lie to **2** : to apply or exert oneself

lay–up \'lā-ˌəp\ *n* **1** : the action of laying up or the condition of being laid up **2** : a jumping one-hand shot in basketball made from close under the basket by laying the ball over the rim or bouncing it off the backboard

lay up \lā-'əp, 'lā-\ *vt* **1** : to store up : lay by **2** : to disable or confine with illness or injury **3** : to take out of active service

lay•wom•an \-ˌwu̇m-ən\ *n* : a woman who is a member of the laity

la•zar \'laz-ər, 'lā-zər\ *n* : a person afflicted with a repulsive disease; *esp* : LEPER [Medieval Latin *lazarus,* from Late Latin *Lazarus,* beggar in parable in Luke 16:20–31]

laz•a•ret•to \ˌlaz-ə-'ret-ō\ *or* **laz•a•ret** \-'ret, -'rēt\ *n, pl* **-ret•tos** *or* **-rets 1** *usually lazaretto* : a hospital for contagious diseases **2** : a building or a ship used for detention in quarantine **3** *usually lazaret* : a space in a ship between decks used as a storeroom [Italian dialect *lazareto,* alteration of *nazareto,* from *Santa Maria di Nazaret,* church in Venice that maintained a hospital]

laze \'lāz\ *vb* : to pass time in idleness or relaxation : IDLE [back-formation from *lazy*]

la•zy \'lā-zē\ *adj* **la•zi•er**; **-est 1** : not willing to act or work : IDLE, INDOLENT **2** : SLOW, SLUGGISH ⟨a *lazy* stream⟩ [perhaps from Low German *lasich* "feeble"] — **la•zi•ly** \-zə-lē\ *adv* — **la•zi•ness** \-zē-nəs\ *n* — **la•zy•ish** \-zē-ish\ *adj*

la•zy•bones \'lā-zē-ˌbōnz\ *n sing or pl* : a lazy person

lazy Su•san \ˌlā-zē-'süz-n\ *n* : a revolving tray placed on a dining table for serving food, condiments, or relishes

lea *or* **ley** \'lē, 'lā\ *n* **1** : GRASSLAND, PASTURE **2** *usually ley* : arable land used temporarily for hay or grazing [Old English *lēah*]

leach \'lēch\ *vt* : to pass a liquid and especially water through to carry off the soluble components; *also* : to dissolve out by such means ⟨*leach* alkali from ashes⟩ [probably derived from Old English *leccan* "to wet, moisten"]

¹**lead** \'lēd\ *vb* **led** \'led\; **lead•ing** \'lēd-ing\ **1** : to force to go with one ⟨police *led* the prisoner to jail⟩ **2 a** : to guide on the way : show the way ⟨you *lead* and we will follow⟩ **b** : to serve as a route or passage ⟨this road *leads* straight into town⟩ **c** : to be an entrance or connection ⟨that door *leads* to the kitchen⟩ **3** : to serve as a channel for ⟨a pipe *leads* water to the house⟩ **4** : to pass one's days in : LIVE ⟨*lead* an active life⟩ **5 a** : to march or go at the head of ⟨*lead* a parade⟩ **b** : to have first place in ⟨*leads* the world in coffee exports⟩; *also* : to serve as an example — often used in the phrase *lead the way* ⟨*lead* the way on political reform⟩ **c** : to have a margin over ⟨*leading* by 20 points at halftime⟩ **d** : to direct the operations, activity, or performance of ⟨*lead* an orchestra⟩ ⟨*leads* a Bible-study group⟩ **e** : to serve as guide for by performing one's own part ⟨*led* the choir in singing⟩ **6 a** : to influence to come to a conclu-

sion ⟨you *led* me to believe you loved me⟩ **b :** to tempt or talk into going ⟨*led* them all astray⟩ **7 a :** to play as the first card or suit in a round ⟨*lead* trumps⟩ **b :** to be the first player of a round at cards ⟨*led* with an ace⟩ **8 :** to begin a series of blows in boxing ⟨*leading* with a right⟩ **9 :** to have as a definite aim or result ⟨study that *leads* to a degree⟩ [Old English *lǣdan*]

[2]lead *n* **1 a** (1) **:** position at the front **:** VANGUARD (2) **:** INITIATIVE 1 (3) **:** the act or privilege of leading in cards; *also* **:** the card or suit led **b :** EXAMPLE, PRECEDENT ⟨follow their *lead*⟩ **c :** a margin or measure of advantage or superiority or position in advance ⟨has a 2-length *lead*⟩ **2 :** one that leads: as **a :** INDICATION 2, CLUE **b :** a principal role in a dramatic production; *also* **:** one who plays such a role **c :** LEASH 1 **d :** an introductory section of a news story; *also* **:** a news story of chief importance **e :** the first in a series or exchange of blows in boxing **3 :** an insulated electrical conductor **4 :** a position taken by a base runner off a base toward the next

[3]lead *adj* **:** acting or serving as a lead or leader ⟨the *lead* article in this month's issue⟩

[4]lead \ˈled\ *n* **1 :** a heavy soft malleable bluish white metallic chemical element that is found mostly in combination and is used in pipes, cable sheaths, solder, and type metal — see ELEMENT table **2 a :** a mass of lead used on a line for finding the depth of water (as in the ocean) **b** *pl* **:** lead framing for panes in windows **c :** a thin strip of metal used to separate lines of type in printing **3 a :** a thin stick of marking substance (as graphite) in or for a pencil **b :** WHITE LEAD **4 :** bullets in quantity **5 :** TETRAETHYL LEAD [Old English *lēad*] — **lead•less** \-ləs\ *adj*

[5]lead \ˈled\ *vt* **1 :** to cover, line, or weight with lead **2 :** to fix (glass) in position with lead **3 :** to place lead or other spacing material between the lines of (type matter) **4 :** to treat or mix with lead or a lead compound ⟨*leaded* gasoline⟩

lead acetate *n* **:** a poisonous soluble salt of lead $PbC_4H_6O_4 \cdot 3H_2O$ used in dyeing and printing

lead arsenate *n* **:** an acid salt of lead $PbHAsO_4$ used as an insecticide

lead dioxide *n* **:** a poisonous compound PbO_2 that is used as an oxidizing agent and as an electrode in batteries — called also *lead peroxide*

lead•en \ˈled-ᵊn\ *adj* **1 a :** made of lead **b :** of the color of lead **:** dull gray **2 :** low in quality **:** POOR **3 a :** oppressively heavy **b :** SLUGGISH **c :** lacking spirit or animation **:** DULL ⟨*leaden* spirits⟩ — **lead•en•ly** *adv* — **lead•en•ness** \-n-nəs, -n-əs\ *n*

lead•er \ˈlēd-ər\ *n* **1 :** one that leads: as **a :** one that goes along to guide and show the way **b :** one that directs or has authority over others: (1) **:** COMMANDER 1 (2) **:** FOREMAN, STRAW BOSS **c :** one that is foremost or that sets an example ⟨a *leader* in fashion⟩ **d :** CONDUCTOR b **e :** an animal placed at the head of a team **f** *pl* **:** dots or hyphens used (as in an index) to lead the eye horizontally across the page; *also* **:** ELLIPSIS 2 **g :** a pipe for conducting fluid **h :** an article offered at an attractive special low price to stimulate business **2 a :** a main shoot of a plant **b :** TENDON, SINEW **3 :** a short length of material for attaching a lure or hook to the end of a fishing line — **lead•er•less** \-ləs\ *adj* — **lead•er•ship** \-ˌship\ *n*

lead–in \ˈlēdˌin\ *n* **:** something that leads in; *esp* **:** the part of a radio antenna that runs to the transmitting or receiving set — **lead–in** *adj*

lead•ing \ˈlēd-iŋ\ *adj* **1 :** coming or ranking first or among the first **:** FOREMOST **2 :** exercising leadership **3 :** serving to guide or direct ⟨a *leading* question⟩ **4 :** given most prominent display ⟨the *leading* story⟩

leading lady *n* **:** an actress who plays the leading feminine role in a play or movie

leading man *n* **:** an actor who plays the leading male role in a play or movie

leading tone *n* **:** the seventh musical degree of a major or minor scale — called also *subtonic* [from its leading harmonically to the tonic]

lead monoxide \ˈled-\ *n* **:** a yellow to brownish red poisonous compound PbO used in rubber manufacture and glassmaking

lead•off \ˈlēd-ˌȯf\ *n* **:** a beginning or leading action — **lead–off** *adj*

lead off \lēd-ˈȯf, ˈlēd-\ *vt* **:** to make a start on **:** BEGIN

lead on *vt* **:** to entice or induce to proceed in a course especially when unwise or mistaken ⟨*led on* by the promise of wealth⟩

lead pencil \ˈled-\ *n* **:** a pencil using graphite as the marking material

lead poisoning *n* **:** chronic intoxication produced by absorption of lead into the system and characterized by severe colicky pains, a dark line along the gums, and local muscular paralysis

lead up \lēd-ˈəp, ˈlēd-\ *vi* **1 :** to prepare the way — used with *to* ⟨events *leading up* to the war⟩ **2 :** to make a gradual or indirect approach to a topic — used with *to*

[1]leaf \ˈlēf\ *n, pl* **leaves** \ˈlēvz\ **1 a :** a usually flat lateral outgrowth from a plant stem that functions primarily in food manufacture by photosynthesis **b :** FOLIAGE **2 :** something suggestive of a leaf: as **a :** a part of a book or folded sheet containing a page on each side **b :** a part (as of window shutters, folding doors, or gates) that slides or is hinged **c :** a movable or removable part of a table top **d :** a thin sheet (as of metal) **:** LAMINA **e :** one of the plates of a leaf spring [Old English *lēaf*] — **leaf•less** \ˈlē-fləs\ *adj* — **leaf•like** \ˈlē-ˌflīk\ *adj*

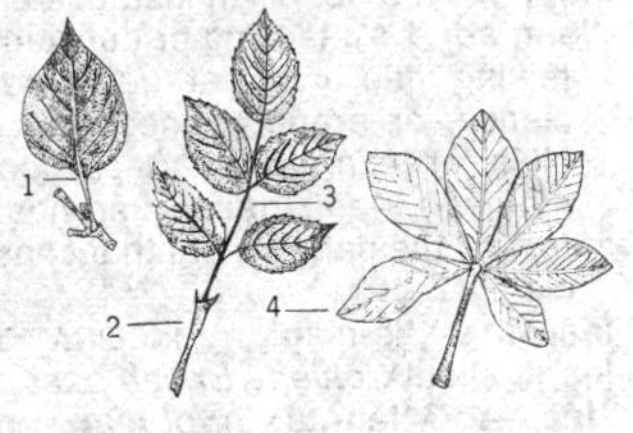

[1]leaf 1a: *1* petiole, *2* stipule, *3* rachis, *4* leaflet

[2]leaf *vi* **1 :** to produce leaves **2 :** to turn the pages of a book

leaf•age \ˈlē-fij\ *n* **:** FOLIAGE

leaf bud *n* **:** a bud that develops into a leafy shoot and does not produce flowers

leaf fat *n* **:** the fat that lines the abdominal cavity and encloses the kidneys; *esp* **:** such hog fat used in the manufacture of lard

leaf•hop•per \ˈlēf-ˌhäp-ər\ *n* **:** any of numerous small leaping insects that are related to the cicadas and suck the juices of plants

leaf lard *n* **:** high quality lard made from leaf fat

leaf•let \ˈlē-flət\ *n* **1 a :** one of the divisions of a compound leaf **b :** a small or young foliage leaf **2 a :** a single printed sheet of paper unfolded or folded but not trimmed at the fold **b :** a sheet of small pages folded but not stitched

leaf miner *n* **:** any of various small insects that as larvae burrow in and eat the tissue of leaves

leaf mold *n* **:** a compost or layer composed chiefly of decayed vegetable matter

leaf spring *n* **:** a usually crescent-shaped spring made of several strips of metal of unequal length stacked and fastened together and arranged in length from longest to shortest

leaf•stalk \ˈlēf-ˌstȯk\ *n* **:** PETIOLE 1

leafy \ˈlē-fē\ *adj* **leaf•i•er; -est 1 :** having or abounding in leaves ⟨*leafy* woodlands⟩ **2 :** consisting mostly of leaves ⟨*leafy* vegetables⟩

[1]league \ˈlēg\ *n* **:** any of various units of distance from about 2.4 to 4.6 statute miles (3.9 to 7.4 kilometers) [Late Latin *leuga,* of Gaulish origin]

[2]league *n* **1 a :** an association or alliance of nations for a common purpose **b :** an association of persons or groups united for common interests or goals; *esp* **:** an association of athletic teams **2 :** CLASS, CATEGORY ⟨a bit out of your *league*⟩ [Middle French *ligue,* from Italian *liga,* from *ligare* "to bind", from Latin] — **league** *vb*

leagu•er \ˈlē-gər\ *n* **:** a member of a league

[1]leak \ˈlēk\ *vb* **1 :** to enter or escape or permit to enter or escape through an opening usually by a fault or mistake ⟨fumes *leak* in⟩ **2 :** to become known despite efforts at concealment ⟨the secret *leaked* out⟩ **3 :** to give out (information) secretly ⟨*leaked* the story to the press⟩ [Old Norse *leka*]

[2]leak *n* **1 a :** a hole, crack, or flaw that lets something enter or escape **b :** a person who leaks information **2 :** LEAKAGE 1a — **leak•proof** \-ˌprüf\ *adj*

leak•age \ˈlē-kij\ *n* **1 a :** the act, process, or an instance of leaking **b :** loss of electricity due especially to faulty insulation **2 :** something or the amount that leaks in or out

leaky \ˈlē-kē\ *adj* **leak•i•er; -est :** permitting fluid to leak in or out — **leak•i•ness** *n*

\ə\ **abut**	\au̇\ **out**	\i\ **tip**	\ȯ\ **saw**	\u̇\ **foot**
\ər\ **further**	\ch\ **chin**	\ī\ **life**	\ȯi\ **coin**	\y\ **yet**
\a\ **mat**	\e\ **pet**	\j\ **job**	\th\ **thin**	\yü\ **few**
\ā\ **take**	\ē\ **easy**	\ŋ\ **sing**	\t͟h\ **this**	\yu̇\ **cure**
\ä\ **cot, cart**	\g\ **go**	\ō\ **bone**	\ü\ **food**	\zh\ **vision**

[1]**lean** \'lēn\ *vb* **leaned** \'lēnd, *chiefly British* 'lent\; **lean•ing** \'lē-ning\ **1 a :** to incline, deviate, or bend from a vertical position **b :** to shift one's weight to one side for support : rest against something ⟨*lean* on me⟩ **2 :** to rely for support or inspiration ⟨children who *lean* on their parents⟩ **3 :** to incline in opinion, taste, or desire ⟨*lean* toward simplicity⟩ [Old English *hleonian*]

[2]**lean** *n* **:** the act or an instance of leaning : INCLINATION

[3]**lean** *adj* **1 a :** lacking or deficient in flesh ⟨*lean* cattle⟩ **b :** containing little or no fat ⟨*lean* meat⟩ **2 :** lacking richness, sufficiency, or productiveness **3 :** characterized by economy of style or expression ⟨*lean,* compact writing⟩ [Old English *hlǣne*] — **lean•ness** \'lēn-nəs\ *n*

[4]**lean** *n* **:** the part of meat that consists principally of fat-free muscle

lean•ing \'lē-ning\ *n* **:** INCLINATION 2, TENDENCY

leant \'lent\ *chiefly British past of* LEAN

[1]**lean–to** \'lēn-,tü\ *n, pl* **lean–tos 1 :** a wing or extension of a building having a lean-to roof **2 :** a rough shed or shelter with a lean-to roof

[2]**lean–to** *adj* **:** having only one slope or pitch ⟨a *lean-to* roof⟩

[1]**leap** \'lēp\ *vb* **leaped** *or* **leapt** \'lēpt, 'lept\; **leap•ing** \'lē-ping\ **1 :** to spring or cause to spring free from or as if from the ground : JUMP ⟨*leap* over a fence⟩ ⟨*leap* a horse over a ditch⟩ **2 a :** to pass abruptly from one state or topic to another **b :** to act precipitately ⟨*leaped* at the chance⟩ [Old English *hlēapan*] — **leap•er** \'lē-pər\ *n*

[2]**leap** *n* **1 a :** an act of leaping : SPRING, BOUND **b (1) :** a place leaped over or from **(2) :** the distance covered by a leap **2 :** a sudden transition — **by leaps and bounds :** very rapidly ⟨improved *by leaps and bounds*⟩

leap•frog \'lēp-,frȯg, -,fräg\ *n* **:** a game in which one player vaults over another who has bent down

leap year *n* **:** a year in the Gregorian calendar containing 366 days with February 29 as the extra day

learn \'lərn\ *vb* **learned** \'lərnd, 'lərnt\ *also* **learnt** \'lərnt\; **learn•ing 1 a :** to gain knowledge or understanding of or skill in by study, instruction, or experience **b :** MEMORIZE ⟨*learn* the lines of a play⟩ **c :** to come to realize ⟨*learned* that honesty paid⟩ **2** *substandard* **:** to cause to learn : TEACH **3 :** to find out : ASCERTAIN **4 :** to acquire knowledge ⟨never too late to *learn*⟩ [Old English *leornian*] — **learn•able** \'lər-nə-bəl\ *adj* — **learn•er** *n*

• **syn** LEARN and TEACH are not synonyms; though LEARN has been used for TEACH this is not accepted usage. LEARN implies acquiring knowledge; TEACH implies imparting it.

learned *adj* **1** \'lər-nəd\ **:** characterized by or associated with learning ⟨*learned* professors⟩ **2** \'lərnd, 'lərnt\ **:** acquired by learning ⟨*learned* responses⟩ — **learn•ed•ly** \'lər-nəd-lē\ *adv* — **learn•ed•ness** \'lər-nəd-nəs\ *n*

learn•ing *n* **1 :** the act or experience of one that learns **2 :** knowledge or skill acquired by instruction or study

[1]**lease** \'lēs\ *n* **1 :** a contract by which one party grants the use of property or facilities to another for a fixed or open period of time usually for a specified rent; *also* **:** the act of making such a grant or the term for which it is made **2 :** a piece of land or property that is leased [Anglo-French *les,* from Old French *laissier* "to let go", from Latin laxare "to loosen", from *laxus* "loose"]

[2]**lease** *vt* **1 :** to grant by lease : LET **2 :** to hold or use under a lease **syn** see HIRE

lease•hold \'lēs-,hōld\ *n* **1 :** a tenure by lease **2 :** land held by lease — **lease•hold•er** \-,hōl-dər\ *n*

leash \'lēsh\ *n* **1 :** a line for leading or restraining an animal **2 :** a set of three animals (as dogs) [Old French *laisse,* from *laissier* "to let go", from Latin *laxare* "to loosen", from *laxus* "loose"] — **leash** *vt*

[1]**least** \'lēst\ *adj* **1 :** lowest in importance or position **2 a :** smallest in size or degree **b :** smallest possible : SLIGHTEST [Old English *lǣst,* superlative of *lǣssa* "less"]

[2]**least** *n* **:** one that is least (as in value, importance, or scope) ⟨I don't care in the *least*⟩ ⟨the *least* that can be said⟩ — **at least 1 :** at the minimum **2 :** in any case

[3]**least** *adv* **:** in the smallest or lowest degree

least common denominator *n* **:** the lowest common multiple of the denominators of two or more fractions

least common multiple *n* **:** the smallest common multiple of two or more numbers

least•wise \'lēst-,wīz\ *adv* **:** at least

[1]**leath•er** \'leth-ər\ *n* **1 :** animal skin dressed for use **2 :** something wholly or partly made of leather [Old English *lether-*] — **leather** *adj*

[2]**leather** *vt* **leath•ered**; **leath•er•ing** \'leth-ring, -ə-ring\ **1 :** to cover with leather **2 :** to beat with a strap : THRASH

leath•er•back \'leth-ər-,bak\ *n* **:** a very large sea turtle with a flexible carapace

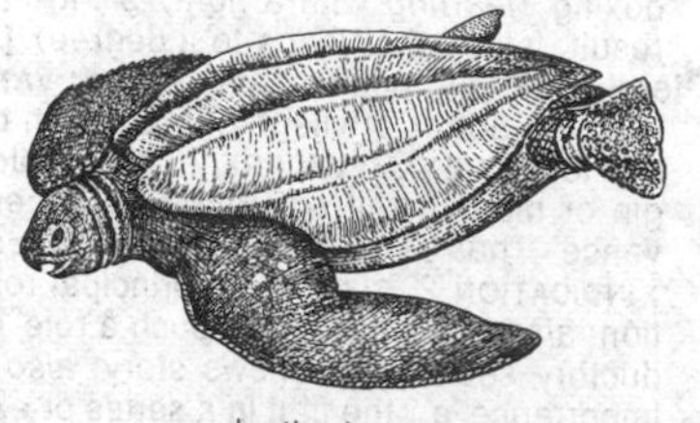
leatherback

Leath•er•ette \,leth-ə-'ret\ *trademark* — used for a product colored, finished, and embossed in imitation of leather grains

leath•ern \'leth-ərn\ *adj* **:** made of, consisting of, or resembling leather

leath•er•neck \'leth-ər-,nek\ *n* **:** a United States marine [from the leather collar formerly part of the uniform]

leath•ery \'leth-rē, -ə-rē\ *adj* **:** resembling leather in appearance or texture : TOUGH

[1]**leave** \'lēv\ *vb* **left** \'left\; **leav•ing 1 :** to allow or cause to remain behind ⟨*leave* your books at home⟩ **2 :** DELIVER ⟨*leave* a book at the library⟩ **3 :** to have remaining (as after death or subtraction) ⟨*leave* a widow and two children⟩ ⟨taking 7 from 10 *leaves* 3⟩ **4 :** to give by will : BEQUEATH **5 :** to let stay without interference ⟨*leave* someone alone⟩ **6 :** to go away : depart from ⟨*leave* the house⟩ [Old English *lǣfan*]

[2]**leave** *n* **1 a :** PERMISSION 2 **b :** authorized absence from duty or employment **2 :** an act of leaving : DEPARTURE [Old English *lēaf*]

[3]**leave** *vi* **leaved**; **leav•ing :** LEAF 1

leaved \'lēvd\ *adj* **:** having such or so many leaves ⟨broad-leaved⟩

[1]**leav•en** \'lev-ən\ *n* **1 a :** a substance (as yeast) used to produce gaseous fermentation (as in dough) **b :** a material (as baking powder) used to produce a gas that lightens dough or batter **2 :** something that modifies or lightens a mass or whole ⟨a *leaven* of common sense⟩ [Middle French *levain,* derived from Latin *levare* "to raise"]

[2]**leaven** *vt* **leav•ened**; **leav•en•ing** \'lev-ning, -ə-ning\ **1 :** to raise (dough) with a leaven **2 :** to lighten or improve with a leaven ⟨a speech *leavened* with wit⟩

leav•en•ing *n* **:** a leavening agent : LEAVEN

leave off *vb* **:** STOP 6, CEASE

leaves *pl of* LEAF

leave–tak•ing \'lēv-,tā-king\ *n* **:** DEPARTURE 1a, FAREWELL

leav•ings \'lē-vingz\ *n pl* **:** RESIDUE; *esp* **:** food leftovers

lech•ery \'lech-rē, -ə-rē\ *n, pl* **-er•ies :** excessive concern with or indulgence in sexual activity [Old French *lecherie* "gluttony, lechery", from *lechier* "to lick", of Germanic origin] — **lecher** *n* — **lech•er•ous** \-rəs\ *adj* — **lech•er•ous•ly** *adv* — **lech•er•ous•ness** *n*

lec•i•thin \'les-ə-thən\ *n* **:** any of several waxy phosphorus-containing substances that are common in animals and plants, form colloidal solutions in water, and have emulsifying, wetting, and antioxidant properties [Greek *lekithos* "egg yolk"]

lec•tern \'lek-tərn\ *n* **:** READING DESK; *esp* **:** one from which scripture lessons are read in a church service [Middle French *letrun,* from Medieval Latin *lectorinum,* from Latin *lector* "reader"]

lec•tor \'lek-tər\ *n* **:** one whose chief duty is to read the lessons in a church service [Latin, "reader", from *lectus,* past participle of *legere* "to read"]

[1]**lec•ture** \'lek-chər\ *n* **1 :** a discourse given before an audience especially for instruction **2 :** a dressing down : REPRIMAND [Late Latin *lectura* "act of reading", from Latin *legere* "to gather, read"]

[2]**lecture** *vb* **lec•tured**; **lec•tur•ing** \'lek-chə-ring, 'lek-shring\ **1 :** to give a lecture or a course of lectures **2 :** to instruct by lectures **3 :** to dress down : REPRIMAND — **lec•tur•er** \-chər-ər, -shrər\ *n*

led *past of* LEAD

le•der•ho•sen \'lād-ər-,hōz-n\ *n pl* **:** knee-length leather trousers worn especially in Bavaria [German, literally, "leather trousers"]

ledge \'lej\ *n* **1 :** a projecting ridge or raised edge along a surface : SHELF **2 :** an underwater ridge or reef especially near the shore **3 :** a narrow flat surface or shelf; *esp* **:** one that projects (as from a wall of rock) **4 :** LODE, VEIN [Middle English *legge* "bar of a gate"]

led•ger \ˈlej-ər\ *n* **:** a book containing accounts to which debits and credits are posted in final form [Middle English *legger*]

ledger line *n* **:** a short line added above or below a musical staff for notes that are too high or too low to be placed on the staff

¹lee \ˈlē\ *n* **1 :** protecting shelter **2 :** the side (as of a ship) that is sheltered from the wind [Old English *hlēo*]

²lee *adj* **:** of or relating to the lee — compare WEATHER

¹leech \ˈlēch\ *n* **1** *archaic* **:** PHYSICIAN, SURGEON **2 :** any of numerous flesh-eating or bloodsucking segmented usually flattened freshwater worms (class Hirudinea) having a sucker at each end **3 :** a hanger-on who seeks advantage or gain **:** PARASITE [Old English *lǣce;* sense 2 from the worm's former use by physicians for bleeding patients]

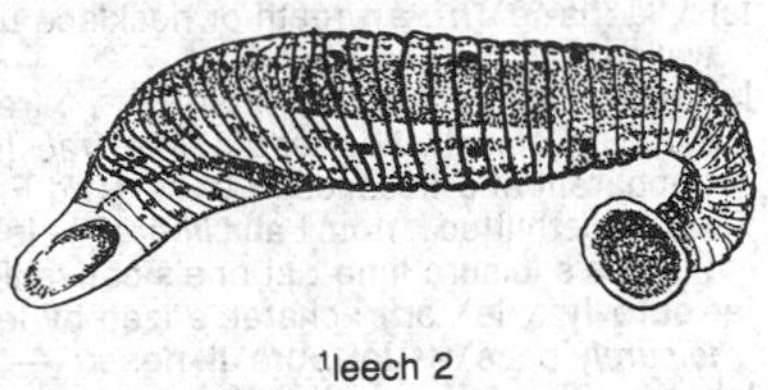

¹leech 2

²leech *vb* **1 :** to drain the substance of **:** EXHAUST **2 :** to attach oneself to a person as a leech

³leech *n* **1 :** either vertical edge of a square sail **2 :** the after edge of a fore-and-aft sail [Low German *līk* "rope stitched to the edges of a sail"]

leek \ˈlēk\ *n* **:** a garden herb closely related to the onion and grown for its mildly pungent leaves and thick stalk [Old English *lēac*]

¹leer \ˈliər\ *vi* **:** to cast a sidelong glance; *esp* **:** to give a suggestive, knowing, or malicious look [probably from obsolete *leer* "cheek", from Old English *hlēor*]

²leer *n* **:** suggestive, knowing, or malicious look

leery \ˈliər-ē\ *adj* **:** SUSPICIOUS 2, WARY

lees \ˈlēz\ *n pl* **:** the settlings of liquor during fermentation and aging **:** DREGS [Middle French *lie,* from Medieval Latin *lia*]

lee shore *n* **:** a shore lying off a ship's leeward side and toward which a ship could be driven by storm winds

¹lee•ward \ˈlē-wərd, *especially nautical* ˈlü-ərd\ *adj* **:** situated away from the wind **:** DOWNWIND — compare WINDWARD — **leeward** *adv*

²leeward *n* **:** the lee side

lee•way \ˈlē-ˌwā\ *n* **1 :** off-course lateral movement of a ship to leeward when under way **2 :** an allowable margin of freedom or variation **:** TOLERANCE ⟨allow enough *leeway* to arrive on time⟩

¹left \ˈleft\ *adj* **1 :** of, relating to, or being a bodily part on the side of the body in which the heart is mostly located **2 :** located nearer to the left side of the body than to the right ⟨the *left* arm of my chair⟩; *also* **:** lying in the direction that an observer's left hand would naturally extend ⟨the *left* fork of the road⟩ **3** *often cap* **:** of, adhering to, or constituted by the political Left [Old English, "weak"; from the left hand's being the weaker in most people] — **left** *adv*

²left *n* **1 a :** the left hand **b :** the location or direction of or part on the left side **2** *often cap* **a :** the part of a legislative chamber located to the left of the presiding officer **b :** the members of a continental European legislative body occupying the left and holding more radical political views than other members **3** *cap* **a :** those professing views usually characterized by desire to reform or overthrow the established order especially in politics and usually advocating greater freedom or well-being of the common man **b :** a liberal as distinguished from a conservative position

³left *past of* LEAVE

left field *n* **1 :** the part of the baseball outfield to the left looking out from the plate **2 :** the position of the player defending left field — **left fielder** *n*

left-hand \ˌleft-ˌhand\ *adj* **1 :** situated on the left **2 :** LEFT-HANDED 1, 2

left-hand•ed \ˈleft-ˈhan-dəd\ *adj* **1 :** using the left hand habitually or more easily than the right **2 :** relating to, designed for, or done with the left hand **3 a :** CLUMSY 1a, AWKWARD **b :** INSINCERE, DUBIOUS ⟨a *left-handed* compliment⟩ **4 a :** COUNTERCLOCKWISE **b :** having a structure involving a counterclockwise direction — **left-handed** *adv* — **left-hand•ed•ly** *adv* — **left-hand•ed•ness** *n* — **left-hand•er** \-ˈhan-dər\ *n*

left•ist \ˈlef-təst\ *n* **:** a liberal or radical in politics — **leftist** *adj*

left•over \ˈleft-ˌō-vər\ *n* **:** an unused or unconsumed residue; *esp* **:** food left over from one meal and served at another — **leftover** *adj*

left•ward \ˈleft-wərd\ *also* **left•wards** \-wərdz\ *adv* **:** toward or on the left — **leftward** *adj*

left wing *n* **1 :** the leftist division of a group **2 :** LEFT 3a — **left-wing** *adj* — **left-wing•er** \ˈleft-ˌwing-ər\ *n*

¹leg \ˈleg\ *n* **1 :** a limb of an animal used especially for supporting the body and for walking; *also* **:** the part of the vertebrate limb between the knee and foot **2 :** something resembling an animal leg in shape or use ⟨the *legs* of a table⟩ **3 :** the part of an article of clothing that covers the leg **4 :** a side of a triangle that is not a base or hypotenuse **5 :** BOOST 1, 3 — called also *leg up* **6 a :** the course and distance sailed by a boat on a single tack **b :** a portion of a trip **:** STAGE **c :** one section of a relay race **7 :** a branch or part of an object or system ⟨the *legs* of a pair of compasses⟩ [Old Norse *leggr*]

²leg *vi* **legged; leg•ging :** to use the legs in walking or especially in running

leg•a•cy \ˈleg-ə-sē\ *n, pl* **-cies 1 :** something left to a person by will **:** INHERITANCE, BEQUEST **2 :** something that has come from an ancestor or predecessor or the past ⟨a *legacy* of ill will⟩ [Medieval Latin *legatia* "office of a legate", from Latin *legatus* "legate"]

le•gal \ˈlē-gəl\ *adj* **1 :** of or relating to law or lawyers **2 a :** deriving authority from or founded on law **:** de jure **b :** established by law; *esp* **:** STATUTORY **3 :** conforming to or permitted by law or established rules **4 :** recognized or made effective at law rather than in equity [Middle French, from Latin *legalis,* from *leg-, lex* "law"] **syn** see LAWFUL — **le•gal•ly** \-gə-lē\ *adv*

legal age *n* **:** the age at which a person enters into full adult legal rights and responsibilities (as of making contracts or wills)

legal holiday *n* **:** a holiday established by legal authority and characterized by legal restrictions on work and transaction of official business

le•gal•ism \ˈlē-gə-ˌliz-əm\ *n* **:** strict, literal, or excessive conformity to the law or to a religious or moral code — **le•gal•ist** \-gə-ləst\ *n* — **le•gal•is•tic** \ˌlē-gə-ˈlis-tik\ *adj* — **le•gal•is•ti•cal•ly** \-ti-kə-lē, -klē\ *adv*

le•gal•i•ty \li-ˈgal-ət-ē\ *n, pl* **-ties :** the quality or state of being legal

le•gal•ize \ˈlē-gə-ˌlīz\ *vt* **:** to make legal; *esp* **:** to give legal validity to — **le•gal•iza•tion** \ˌlē-gə-lə-ˈzā-shən\ *n*

legal tender *n* **:** money that the law authorizes a debtor to pay with and requires a creditor to accept

leg•ate \ˈleg-ət\ *n* **:** an official representative (as an ambassador or envoy) [Latin *legatus* "deputy, emissary", from *legare* "to depute, bequeath", from *leg-, lex* "law"]

leg•a•tee \ˌleg-ə-ˈtē\ *n* **:** one to whom a legacy is bequeathed

le•ga•tion \li-ˈgā-shən\ *n* **1 :** a diplomatic mission; *esp* **:** one headed by a minister **2 :** the official residence and office of a diplomatic minister

le•ga•to \li-ˈgät-ō\ *adv or adj* **:** in a manner that is smooth and connected between successive tones — used as a direction in music [Italian, literally, "tied", from *legare* "to tie", from Latin *ligare*]

leg•end \ˈlej-ənd\ *n* **1 a :** a story coming down from the past whose truth is popularly accepted but cannot be checked **b :** a popular myth of recent origin **c :** a person or thing that inspires legends **2 a :** an inscription or title on an object (as a coin) **b :** CAPTION 2 **c :** an explanatory list of the symbols on a map or chart [Medieval Latin *legenda,* from Latin *legere* "to gather, read"] **syn** see MYTH

△ **origin** The Latin verb *legere* originally meant "to gather". In the course of time the verb came to be used in a figurative sense, "to gather with the eye, see", which led to the sense "to read". In Medieval Latin the word *legenda,* meaning literally "a thing to be read", was used specifically to mean "the story of the life of a saint". Many saints' lives that were written in the Middle Ages incorporated a generous measure of fanciful ma-

\ə\ **abut**	\au̇\ **out**	\i\ **tip**	\ȯ\ **saw**	\u̇\ **foot**
\ər\ **further**	\ch\ **chin**	\ī\ **life**	\ȯi\ **coin**	\y\ **yet**
\a\ **mat**	\e\ **pet**	\j\ **job**	\th\ **thin**	\yü\ **few**
\ā\ **take**	\ē\ **easy**	\ng\ **sing**	\t͟h\ **this**	\yu̇\ **cure**
\ä\ **cot, cart**	\g\ **go**	\ō\ **bone**	\ü\ **food**	\zh\ **vision**

terial along with solid fact. This accounts for the use of English *legend* to mean "a traditional story popularly believed to be historical though not entirely verifiable". We owe other senses of *legend,* "inscription", "caption", "explanatory list", to the literal meaning of Latin *legenda,* "a thing to be read".

leg·end·ary \ˈlej-ən-ˌder-ē\ *adj* **1 :** of or resembling a legend ⟨*legendary* heroes⟩ **2 :** consisting of legends ⟨*legendary* writings⟩ **syn** see FABULOUS

leg·er·de·main \ˌlej-ərd-ə-ˈmān\ *n* **1 :** SLEIGHT OF HAND, MAGIC **2 :** a display of skill or adroitness [Middle French *leger de main* "light of hand"]

legged \ˈleg-əd, ˈlegd\ *adj* **:** having (such or so many) legs ⟨four-*legged*⟩

leg·ging *or* **leg·gin** \ˈleg-ən, ˈleg-ing\ *n* **:** a covering for the leg

leg·gy \ˈleg-ē\ *adj* **leg·gi·er; -est 1 :** having disproportionately long legs **2 :** having attractive legs **3 :** SPINDLY ⟨a *leggy* plant⟩

leg·horn \ˈleg-ˌhȯrn, -ˌȯrn, ˈleg-ərn\ *n* **1 a :** a fine plaited straw made from an Italian wheat **b :** a hat of this straw **2 :** any of a Mediterranean breed of small hardy fowls noted for their large production of white eggs [*Leghorn,* Italy]

leg·i·ble \ˈlej-ə-bəl\ *adj* **:** capable of being read **:** PLAIN [Late Latin *legibilis,* from Latin *legere* "to read"] — **leg·i·bil·i·ty** \ˌlej-ə-ˈbil-ət-ē\ *n* — **leg·i·bly** \ˈlej-ə-blē\ *adv*

le·gion \ˈlē-jən\ *n* **1 :** the principal unit of the Roman army comprising 3000 to 6000 foot soldiers with cavalry **2 :** ARMY 1a **3 :** a very large number **:** MULTITUDE [Old French, from Latin *legio,* from *legere* "to gather, read"]

1le·gion·ary \ˈlē-jə-ˌner-ē\ *adj* **:** of, relating to, or constituting a legion

2legionary *n, pl* **-ar·ies :** LEGIONNAIRE

le·gion·naire \ˌlē-jə-ˈnaər, -ˈneər\ *n* **:** a member of a legion [French *légionnaire*]

leg·is·late \ˈlej-ə-ˌslāt\ *vb* **1 :** to make or enact laws **2 :** to cause, create, or bring about by legislation [back-formation from *legislator*]

leg·is·la·tion \ˌlej-ə-ˈslā-shən\ *n* **1 :** the action of making laws **2 :** the laws made by a legislator or legislative body

leg·is·la·tive \ˈlej-ə-ˌslāt-iv\ *adj* **1 :** having the power or performing the function of legislating ⟨the *legislative* branch⟩ **2 :** of or relating to a legislature or legislation — **leg·is·la·tive·ly** *adv*

legislative assembly *n, often cap L&A* **1 :** a bicameral legislature in an American state; *also* **:** its lower house **2 :** a unicameral legislature especially in a Canadian province

legislative council *n, often cap L&C* **:** a permanent committee from both houses of a state legislature that meets between sessions to study state problems and plan a legislative program

leg·is·la·tor \ˈlej-ə-ˌslāt-ər\ *n* **:** a person who makes laws for a state or community; *esp* **:** a member of a legislature [Latin *legis later,* literally, "proposer of a law"]

leg·is·la·ture \ˈlej-ə-ˌslā-chər\ *n* **:** an organized body of persons with authority to make laws for a political unit

le·git \li-ˈjit\ *adj, slang* **:** LEGITIMATE 2, 3

1le·git·i·mate \li-ˈjit-ə-mət\ *adj* **1 :** born of parents who are married to each other ⟨*legitimate* children⟩ **2 :** being in accordance with law or established requirements **:** LAWFUL ⟨a *legitimate* claim⟩ **3 :** being in keeping with what is right or in accordance with accepted standards ⟨a *legitimate* excuse for absence⟩ **4 :** relating to acted plays not including burlesque, revues, or some forms of musical comedy ⟨*legitimate* theater⟩ **syn** see LAWFUL — **le·git·i·ma·cy** \-mə-sē\ *n* — **le·git·i·mate·ly** *adv*

2le·git·i·mate \-ˌmāt\ *vt* **:** to make lawful or legal [Medieval Latin *legitimare,* from Latin *legitimus* "lawful", from *leg-, lex* "law"] — **le·git·i·ma·tion** \li-ˌjit-ə-ˈmā-shən\ *n*

le·git·i·ma·tize \li-ˈjit-ə-mə-ˌtīz\ *vt* **:** LEGITIMATE

le·git·i·mize \li-ˈjit-ə-ˌmīz\ *vt* **:** LEGITIMATE

leg·less \ˈleg-ləs\ *adj* **:** having no legs ⟨a *legless* insect⟩

leg·man \ˈleg-ˌman\ *n* **1 :** a newspaper employee assigned usually to gather information **2 :** an assistant who gathers information and runs errands

leg-of-mut·ton \ˌleg-əv-ˈmət-n, -ə-\ *adj* **:** having the sharply tapering shape or outline of a leg of mutton ⟨*leg-of-mutton* sleeves⟩

leg·ume \ˈleg-ˌyüm, li-ˈgyüm\ *n* **1 a :** any of a large family of herbs, shrubs, and trees that have fruits developing into dry single-celled pods and splitting into two valves when ripe, that bear nodules on the roots containing nitrogen-fixing bacteria, and that include important food and forage plants (as peas, beans, or clovers) **b :** the part (as seeds or pods) of a legume used as food; *also* **:** VEGETABLE 1b **2 :** the pod characteristic of a legume [French *légume,* from Latin *legumen,* from *legere* "to gather"] — **le·gu·mi·nous** \li-ˈgyü-mə-nəs, le-\ *adj*

leg·work \ˈleg-ˌwərk, ˈlāg-\ *n* **:** work (as gathering data) that involves physical activity and is the basis of more creative activity (as writing a book)

le·hua \lā-ˈhü-ə\ *n* **:** a showy tree of the myrtle family with bright red flowers and a hard wood; *also* **:** its flower [Hawaiian]

lei \ˈlā, ˈlā-ˌē\ *n* **:** a wreath or necklace usually of flowers [Hawaiian]

lei·sure \ˈlēzh-ər, ˈlezh-, ˈlāzh-\ *n* **1 :** freedom provided by the stopping of activities; *esp* **:** time free from work or duties **2 :** apparent effortlessness **:** EASE [Old French *leisir,* from *leisir* "to be permitted", from Latin *licēre*] — **leisure** *adj* — **at leisure :** in one's leisure time **:** at one's convenience

lei·sure·ly \-lē\ *adj* **:** characterized by leisure **:** UNHURRIED ⟨a *leisurely* pace⟩ — **lei·sure·li·ness** *n* — **leisurely** *adv*

leit·mo·tiv *or* **leit·mo·tif** \ˈlīt-mō-ˌtēf\ *n* **:** a dominant recurring theme (as in a musical or literary work) [German *leitmotiv,* from *leiten* "to lead" + *motiv* "motive"]

lem·ma \ˈlem-ə\ *n* **:** the lower of the two bracts enclosing the flower in the spikelet of grasses [Greek, "husk"]

lem·ming \ˈlem-ing\ *n* **:** any of several small short-tailed northern rodents with furry feet and small ears [Norwegian]

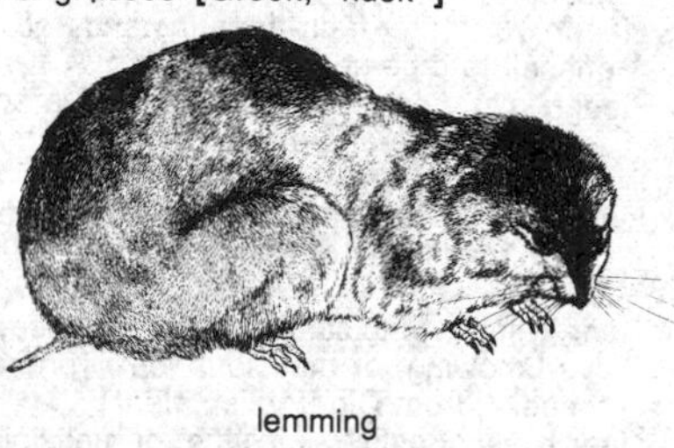

lemming

1lem·on \ˈlem-ən\ *n* **1 a :** an acid citrus fruit that is botanically a many-seeded pale yellow nearly oval berry **b :** the stout thorny tree that bears this fruit **2 :** DUD, FAILURE ⟨the new car proved to be a *lemon*⟩ [Middle French *limon,* from Medieval Latin *limo,* from Arabic *laymūn*]

2lemon *adj* **1 a :** containing lemon **b :** having the flavor or scent of lemon **2 :** of the color lemon yellow

lem·on·ade \ˌlem-ə-ˈnād\ *n* **:** a drink made of lemon juice, sugar, and water

lemon balm *n* **:** a perennial Old World mint often grown for its fragrant lemon-flavored leaves

lemon yellow *n* **:** a brilliant greenish yellow

lem·pi·ra \lem-ˈpir-ə\ *n* **1 :** the basic monetary unit of Honduras **2 :** a coin or note representing one lempira [American Spanish, from *Lempira,* 16th century Indian chief]

le·mur \ˈlē-mər\ *n* **:** any of numerous arboreal and mostly nocturnal mammals that are related to the monkeys and usually have a muzzle like a fox, large eyes, very soft woolly fur, and a long furry tail [Latin *lemures* "ghosts"]

△ **origin** The ancient Romans believed that if the dead were not buried their spirits would return by night to haunt the living. In Latin such ghosts were called *lemures.* In none of the Latin writings that have survived does the singular of this word appear, but the normal singular form would be *lemur.* In the trees of Madagascar lives a kind of small nocturnal mammal. Its large-eyed face, glimpsed through the trees at night, must look quite ghostly. 18th century naturalists, struck by the nocturnal habits and strange appearance of the creature, named it *lemur,* after the ancient Roman ghosts.

lend \ˈlend\ *vb* **lent** \ˈlent\; **lend·ing 1 :** to give or hand over as a loan ⟨lend a book⟩ ⟨*lend* money⟩ **2 :** to give temporarily ⟨*lend* assistance⟩ **3 :** to have the quality or nature that makes suitable ⟨a voice that *lends* itself to singing in opera⟩ [Old English *lǣnan,* from *lǣn* "loan"] — **lend·er** *n*

lending library *n* **:** RENTAL LIBRARY

lend-lease \ˈlen-ˈdlēs\ *n* **:** the transfer of goods and services to an ally to aid in a common cause with payment being made by a return of the original items or their use in the common cause or by a similar transfer of other goods and services [United States *Lend-Lease* Act (1941)] — **lend-lease** *vt*

length \ˈlength, ˈlengkth, ˈlenth\ *n* **1 a :** the longer or longest dimension of an object **b :** a measured distance or dimension ⟨a 2-meter *length*⟩ — see MEASURE table, METRIC SYSTEM table **c :** the quality or state of being long ⟨criticized the *length* of the story⟩ **2 a :** duration or extent in time ⟨the *length* of an interview⟩ **b :** relative duration or stress of a sound **3 :** the length of something taken as a unit of measure ⟨that horse led by a *length*⟩ **4 :** a piece constituting or usable as part of a whole or of a connected series **:** SECTION ⟨a *length* of pipe⟩ **5 :** a vertical dimension of an article of clothing [Old English *lengthu,* from *lang* "long"] — **at length 1 :** in full **:** FULLY **2 :** at last **:** FINALLY

length•en \'leng-thən, 'lengk-, 'len-\ *vb* **length•ened; length•en•ing** \'length-ning, 'lengkth-, 'lenth-, -ə-ning\ **:** to make or become longer **syn** see EXTEND — **length•en•er** \-nər\ *n*

length•ways \'length-,wāz, 'lengkth-, 'lenth-\ *adv* **:** LENGTHWISE

length•wise \-,wīz\ *adv* **:** in the direction of the length **:** LONGITUDINALLY — **lengthwise** *adj*

lengthy \'leng-thē, 'lengk-, 'len-\ *adj* **length•i•er; -est 1 :** excessively drawn out **:** OVERLONG ⟨a *lengthy* speech⟩ **2 :** LONG 1 ⟨a *lengthy* journey⟩ — **length•i•ly** \-thə-lē\ *adv* — **length•i•ness** \-thē-nəs\ *n*

le•ni•en•cy \'lē-nē-ən-sē\ *or* **le•ni•ence** \-əns\ *n* **:** the quality or state of being lenient **syn** see MERCY

le•ni•ent \'lē-nē-ənt\ *adj* **:** of mild and tolerant disposition or effect; *esp* **:** INDULGENT ⟨was *lenient* with the naughty child⟩ [Latin *leniens,* present participle of *lenire* "to soothe", from *lenis* "soft, mild"] — **le•ni•ent•ly** *adv*

Len•in•ism \'len-ə-,niz-əm\ *n* **:** the political, economic, and social principles and policies advocated by Lenin; *esp* **:** the theory and practice of communism developed by or associated with Lenin — **Len•in•ist** \-nəst\ *n or adj*

len•i•tive \'len-ət-iv\ *adj* **:** easing pain or acrimony **:** MITIGATING [Middle French *lenitif,* from Medieval Latin *lenitivus,* from Latin *lenire* "to soothe", from *lenis* "mild"] — **lenitive** *n*

lens \'lenz\ *n* **1 :** a piece of transparent substance (as glass) that has two opposite surfaces either both curved or one curved and the other plane and that is used either singly or combined in an optical instrument for forming an image by focusing rays of light **2 :** a device for directing or focusing radiation (as sound waves or electrons) other than light **3 :** something (as a geologic deposit) shaped like an optical lens **4 :** a transparent biconvex lens-shaped or nearly spherical body in the eye that focuses light rays (as upon the retina) [Latin, "lentil"; from its shape]

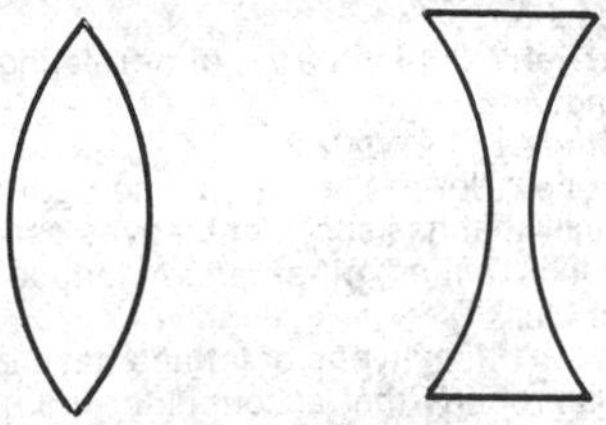
lens 1: *left* convex, *right* concave

Lent \'lent\ *n* **:** a period of penitence and fasting observed on the 40 weekdays from Ash Wednesday to Easter by many churches [Old English *lengten* "springtime"]

Lent•en \'lent-n\ *adj* **:** of, relating to, or suitable to Lent; *esp* **:** MEAGER ⟨*Lenten* fare⟩

len•ti•cel \'lent-ə-,sel\ *n* **:** a pore in a stem of a woody plant through which gases are exchanged between the atmosphere and the stem tissues [derived from Latin *lent-, lens* "lentil"]

len•tic•u•lar \len-'tik-yə-lər\ *adj* **:** shaped like a biconvex lens [Latin *lenticularis* "lentil-shaped", from *lenticula* "small lentil", from *lens* "lentil"]

len•til \'lent-l\ *n* **:** a Eurasian annual legume widely grown for its flattened edible seeds and leafy stalks used as fodder; *also* **:** its seed [Old French *lentille,* from Latin *lenticula,* from *lent-, lens*]

len•to \'len-,tō\ *adv or adj* **:** in a slow manner — used as a direction in music [Italian, from *lento,* adj., "slow", from Latin *lentus* "pliant, sluggish, slow"]

Leo \'lē-ō\ *n* **1 :** a zodiacal northern constellation east of Cancer **2 :** the 5th sign of the zodiac; *also* **:** one born under this sign [Latin, literally, "lion"]

le•o•nine \'lē-ə-,nīn\ *adj* **:** of, relating to, or resembling a lion [Latin *leoninus,* from *leo* "lion"]

leop•ard \'lep-ərd\ *n* **:** a large strong cat of southern Asia and Africa that is usually tawny or buff with black spots arranged in broken rings or rosettes — called also *panther* [Old French *leupart,* from Late Latin *leopardus,* from Greek *leopardos,* from *leōn* "lion" + *pardos* "leopard"] — **leop•ard•ess** \-əs\ *n*

leopard frog *n* **:** the common spotted frog of the eastern United States

le•o•tard \'lē-ə-,tärd\ *n* **:** a stretchable close-fitting one-piece garment typically covering the torso that is worn for practice or performance by dancers, acrobats, and aerialists [Jules Léotard, 19th century French aerial gymnast]

leopard

lep•er \'lep-ər\ *n* **1 :** a person affected with leprosy **2 :** PARIAH 2, OUTCAST [Old French *lepre* "leprosy", from Late Latin *lepra*]

lep•i•dop•tera \,lep-ə-'däp-tə-rə\ *n pl* **:** insects that are lepidopterans [New Latin, from Greek *lepid-, lepis* "scale" + *pteron* "wing"]

lep•i•dop•ter•an \,lep-ə-'däp-tə-rən\ *n* **:** any of a large order (Lepidoptera) of insects that comprise the butterflies and moths, as adults have four wings usually covered with minute overlapping often brightly colored scales, and as larvae are caterpillars — **lepidopteran** *adj* — **lep•i•dop•ter•ous** \-tə-rəs\ *adj*

lep•re•chaun \'lep-rə-,kän, -,kȯn\ *n* **:** a mischievous elf of Irish folklore usually believed to reveal the hiding place of treasure if caught [Irish Gaelic *leipreachān*]

lep•ro•sy \'lep-rə-sē\ *n* **:** a chronic bacterial disease marked by slow-growing spreading swellings accompanied by loss of sensation, wasting, and deformities — called also *Hansen's disease* [*leprous* + *-y*] — **lep•rot•ic** \le-'prät-ik\ *adj*

lep•rous \'lep-rəs\ *adj* **:** infected with, relating to, or resembling leprosy [Late Latin *leprosus,* from *lepra* "leprosy", from Greek, from *lepein* "to peel"] — **lep•rous•ly** *adv* — **lep•rous•ness** *n*

lep•to•ceph•a•lus \,lep-tə-'sef-ə-ləs\ *n, pl* **-li** \-,lī\ **:** the slender transparent first larva of an eel [New Latin, from Greek *leptos* "peeled, slender, small" + *kephalē* "head"]

les•bi•an \'lez-bē-ən\ *n, often cap* **:** a woman who is a homosexual [*Lesbos,* Greek island; from the reputed homosexual band associated with Sappho of Lesbos] — **lesbian** *adj, often cap* — **les•bi•an•ism** \-bē-ə-,niz-əm\ *n*

lese maj•es•ty *or* **lèse ma•jes•té** \'lēz-'maj-ə-stē\ *n* **1 a :** a crime committed against a sovereign power **b :** an offense violating the dignity of a ruler **2 :** a detraction from or affront to dignity or importance [Middle French *lese majesté,* from Latin *laesa majestas,* literally, "injured majesty"]

le•sion \'lē-zhən\ *n* **:** an abnormal structural change in an organ or part due to injury or disease [Middle French, "injury", from Latin *laesio,* from *laedere* "to injure"]

les•pe•de•za \,les-pə-'dē-zə\ *n* **:** any of a genus of herbaceous or shrubby plants of the pea family including some widely used for forage, soil improvement, and especially hay [derived from V. M. de *Zespedes,* 18th century Spanish governor of East Florida]

¹less \'les\ *adj* **1 :** of a smaller number **:** FEWER ⟨*less* than three⟩ **2 :** of lower rank, degree, or importance ⟨no *less* a person than the principal⟩ **3 a :** of reduced size or extent **b :** more limited in quantity ⟨in *less* time⟩ [Old English *lǣs,* adv. and n., and *lǣssa,* adj.] **syn** see FEWER

²less *adv* **:** to a lesser extent or degree ⟨*less* difficult⟩

³less *prep* **:** diminished by ⟨full price *less* the discount⟩

⁴less *n, pl* **less 1 :** a smaller portion or quantity ⟨spent *less* than usual⟩ **2 :** something of less importance ⟨could have killed them for *less*⟩

-less \-ləs\ *adj suffix* **1 :** destitute of **:** not having ⟨wit*less*⟩ **2 :** unable to be acted on or to act (in a specified way) ⟨daunt*less*⟩ ⟨fade*less*⟩ [Old English *-lēas,* from *lēas* "devoid, false"]

les•see \le-'sē\ *n* **:** a tenant under a lease [Anglo-French, from *lesser* "to lease"]

less•en \'les-n\ *vb* **less•ened; less•en•ing** \'les-ning, -n-ing\

\ə\ **abut**	\au̇\ **out**	\i\ **tip**	\ȯ\ **saw**	\u̇\ **foot**
\ər\ **further**	\ch\ **chin**	\ī\ **life**	\ȯi\ **coin**	\y\ **yet**
\a\ **mat**	\e\ **pet**	\j\ **job**	\th\ **thin**	\yü\ **few**
\ā\ **take**	\ē\ **easy**	\ng\ **sing**	\t͟h\ **this**	\yu̇\ **cure**
\ä\ **cot, cart**	\g\ **go**	\ō\ **bone**	\ü\ **food**	\zh\ **vision**

: to make or become less **syn** see DECREASE
[1]less•er \'les-ər\ *adj* : of less size, quality, or importance ⟨subtract the *lesser* number⟩ ⟨the *lesser* nobility⟩
[2]lesser *adv* : LESS ⟨*lesser*-known⟩
lesser celandine *n* : CELANDINE 2
[1]les•son \'les-n\ *n* **1** : a passage from sacred writings read in a worship service **2** : a piece of instruction ⟨the story carries a *lesson*⟩; *esp* : a reading or exercise to be studied by a pupil ⟨master each *lesson*⟩ **3 a** : something learned by study or experience ⟨the *lessons* of life⟩ **b** : a rebuke or punishment meant to forestall the repetition of an offense ⟨gave the naughty child a *lesson*⟩ [Old French *leçon,* from Latin *lectio* "act of reading", from *legere* "to read"]
[2]lesson *vt* **les•soned**; **les•son•ing** \'les-ning, -n-ing\ **1** : to give a lesson to **2** : REBUKE
les•sor \'les-,ȯr, le-'sȯr\ *n* : one that grants a lease [Anglo-French *lessour,* from *lesser* "to lease"]
lest \lest, ,lest\ *conj* : for fear that ⟨worried *lest* they be late⟩ [derived from Old English *lǣs* "less"]
[1]let \'let\ *vt* **let•ted**; **letted** *or* **let**; **let•ting** *archaic* : HINDER, PREVENT [Old English *lettan*]
[2]let \'let\ *n* **1** : something that impedes : OBSTRUCTION ⟨talk without *let* or hindrance⟩ **2** : a shot or rally (as in tennis) that is not counted and that must be played over because of interference with the play [Old English *lettan* "to delay, hinder"]
[3]let *vb* **let**; **let•ting** **1** : to cause to : MAKE ⟨*let* it be known⟩ **2 a** : to offer or grant for rent or lease ⟨*let* rooms⟩ **b** : to assign or award especially after bids ⟨*let* a contract⟩ **3 a** : to allow to ⟨live and *let* live⟩ ⟨*let* me go⟩ **b** : to allow to go or pass ⟨*let* them through⟩ **4** — used imperatively to introduce a request or proposal ⟨*let* us pray⟩ ⟨*let* *x* be any number⟩ **5** : to allow (sound) to issue or be uttered : RELEASE — used with *out* ⟨*let* out a whoop⟩ [Old English *lǣtan*]
• **syn** LET, ALLOW, PERMIT mean not to forbid or prevent. LET may imply a positive giving of permission but more often implies failure to prevent either through inadvertence and negligence or through lack of power or effective authority; ALLOW simply suggests a forbearing to prohibit; PERMIT implies willingness or acquiescence. **syn** see in addition HIRE
-let \lət\ *n suffix* **1** : small one ⟨book*let*⟩ **2** : article worn on ⟨wrist*let*⟩ [Middle French *-elet,* from *-el,* diminutive suffix (from Latin *-ellus*) + *-et*]
let alone *prep* : to say nothing of ⟨lacked the courage, *let alone* the skill⟩
let•down \'let-,dau̇n\ *n* **1** : DISAPPOINTMENT 2 **2** : a slackening of effort : RELAXATION
let down \let-'dau̇n, 'let-\ *vb* **1** : to fail to support : DESERT ⟨*let down* a friend in a crisis⟩ **2** : DISAPPOINT ⟨the end of the story *lets* the reader *down*⟩ **3** : to slacken effort : RELAX
[1]le•thal \'lē-thəl\ *adj* **1** : of, relating to, or causing death **2 a** : capable of causing death **b** : being or involving a gene that in some genetic conditions may prevent development or cause the death of an organism or its germ cells ⟨a *lethal* mutation⟩ [Latin *letalis, lethalis,* from *letum* "death"] **syn** see DEADLY — **le•thal•i•ty** \lē-'thal-ət-ē\ *n* — **le•thal•ly** \'lē-thə-lē\ *adv*
[2]lethal *n* : a lethal gene
le•thar•gic \li-'thär-jik, le-\ *adj* **1** : of, relating to, or characterized by lethargy : SLUGGISH **2** : APATHETIC — **le•thar•gi•cal•ly** \-ji-kə-lē, -klē\ *adv*
leth•ar•gy \'leth-ər-jē\ *n* **1** : abnormal drowsiness **2** : the quality or state of being lazy or indifferent [Late Latin *lethargia,* from Greek *lēthargia,* from *lēthargos* "forgetful, lethargic", from *lēthē* "forgetfulness" + *argos* "lazy", from *a-* + *ergon* "work"]
• **syn** LETHARGY, LANGUOR, STUPOR, TORPOR mean physical or mental inertness. LETHARGY implies drowsiness or apathy induced by disease, injury, or drugs; LANGUOR suggests inertia induced by enervating climate, illness, or amorous emotion; STUPOR implies a deadening of the mind and senses by shock, narcotics, or intoxicants; TORPOR implies a state of suspended animation or extreme sluggishness.
Le•the \'lē-thē\ *n* : OBLIVION, FORGETFULNESS ⟨the *Lethe* of sleep⟩ [Greek *Lēthē,* river of Hades whose water causes those who drink it to forget their past, from *lēthē* "forgetfulness"] — **Le•the•an** \'lē-thē-ən\ *adj*
let on *vb* **1** : ADMIT ⟨know more than they *let on*⟩ **2** : to make known ⟨don't *let on* that I told you⟩ **3** : PRETEND ⟨not so surprised as I *let on*⟩
let's \lets, ,lets, les, ,les\ : let us
Lett \'let\ *n* : a member of a people closely related to the Lithuanians and mainly inhabiting Latvia [German *Lette,* from Latvian *Latvi*]
[1]let•ter \'let-ər\ *n* **1** : a symbol in writing or print that stands for a speech sound and constitutes a unit of an alphabet **2** : a written or printed message addressed to a person or organization **3** *pl* **a** : LITERATURE 2a **b** : LEARNING 2 **4** : the strict meaning ⟨the *letter* of the law⟩ **5 a** : a single piece of type **b** : a style of type [Old French *lettre,* from Latin *littera* "letter of the alphabet" and *litterae,* pl., "epistle, literature"]
[2]letter *vt* **1** : to set down in letters : PRINT **2** : to mark with letters — **let•ter•er** \-ər-ər\ *n*
letter carrier *n* : a person who delivers mail or who collects mail from public mailboxes
let•tered \'let-ərd\ *adj* **1 a** : LEARNED, EDUCATED ⟨a *lettered* person⟩ **b** : of or relating to learning ⟨a *lettered* environment⟩ **2** : marked with or as if with letters ⟨a *lettered* sign⟩
let•ter•head \'let-ər-,hed\ *n* : stationery having a printed or engraved heading; *also* : the heading itself
let•ter•ing *n* : letters used in an inscription
let•ter–per•fect \,let-ər-'pər-fikt\ *adj* : correct in every detail; *esp* : VERBATIM
let•ter•press \'let-ər-,pres\ *n* : printing done directly by impressing the paper on an inked raised surface
letters of marque \-'märk\ : written authority granted to a private person by a government to seize the subjects of a foreign state or their goods; *esp* : a license granted to a private person to fit out an armed ship to plunder the enemy [obsolete *marque* "reprisal", from Middle French, from Provençal *marca,* from *marcar* "to mark, seize as pledge", of Germanic origin]
letters pat•ent \-'pat-nt\ *n pl* : a writing (as from a sovereign) that confers on a person a grant in a form open for public inspection
[1]Lett•ish \'let-ish\ *adj* : of or relating to the Letts or the Latvian language
[2]Lettish *n* : LATVIAN 2
let•tuce \'let-əs\ *n* : a common garden vegetable of the daisy family that has succulent leaves used especially in salads [Old French *laitues,* pl. of *laitue* "lettuce", from Latin *lactuca,* from *lac* "milk"]
△ **origin** Many types of lettuce have a milky white juice, and it is this property that accounts for the name of the vegetable. The English singular form, *lettuce,* comes from Old French *laitues,* the plural of *laitue.* The Old French word is derived in turn from Latin *lactuca,* which is still used as the scientific name of the lettuce. The root of *lactuca* is Latin *lac,* which means "milk".
let•up \'let-,əp\ *n* : a lessening of effort
let up \let-'əp, 'let-\ *vi* **1** : to lessen in force or intensity : ABATE **2** : STOP 6, CEASE **3** : to become less severe — used with *on* ⟨hope the principal *lets up* on me⟩
leu•cine \'lü-,sēn\ *n* : an essential amino acid obtained by the hydrolysis of most dietary proteins
leu•co•plast \'lü-kə-,plast\ *n* : a colorless plastid of a plant cell usually concerned with starch formation and storage [*leuk-* + *-plast* "granule", from Greek *plastos* "formed, molded"]
leuk- *or* **leuko-** *or* **leuc-** *or* **leuco-** *combining form* **1** : white : colorless : weakly colored ⟨*leuko*cyte⟩ **2** : leukocyte ⟨*leu*kemia⟩ [Greek *leukos*]
leu•ke•mia \lü-'kē-mē-ə\ *n* : a cancerous disease of warm-blooded animals (as human beings) in which leukocytes increase abnormally in the tissues and often in the blood — **leu•ke•mic** \-mik\ *adj*
leu•ko•cyte *also* **leu•co•cyte** \'lü-kə-,sīt\ *n* : any of the white or colorless blood cells having a nucleus — **leu•ko•cyt•ic** \,lü-kə-'sit-ik\ *adj*
leu•ko•cy•to•sis \,lü-kə-,sī-'tō-səs\ *n, pl* **-to•ses** \-'tō-,sēz\ : an increase in the number of leukocytes in the circulating blood — **leu•ko•cy•tot•ic** \-'tät-ik\ *adj*
leu•ko•pe•nia \,lü-kə-'pē-ne-ə\ *n* : a condition in which the number of leukocytes circulating in the blood is abnormally low [Greek *penia* "poverty, lack"] — **leu•ko•pe•nic** \-nik\ *adj*
leu•ko•sis \lü-'kō-səs\ *n, pl* **-ko•ses** \-,sēz\ : LEUKEMIA — **leu•kot•ic** \-'kät-ik\ *adj*
lev- *or* **levo-** *combining form* : turning the plane of polarization of light to the left ⟨*lev*ulose⟩ [Latin *laevus* "left"]
le•va•tor \li-'vāt-ər\ *n, pl* **lev•a•to•res** \,lev-ə-'tōr-ēz\ *or* **le•va•tors** \li-'vāt-ərz\ : a muscle that serves to raise a body part — compare DEPRESSOR [derived from Latin *levare* "to raise"]

[1]lev•ee \'lev-ē; lə-'vē, -'vā\ *n* **1 :** a reception held by a distinguished person originally on rising from bed **2 :** a reception usually in honor of a particular person [French *lever,* literally, "act of arising", from *se lever* "to raise oneself, rise"]
[2]levee \'lev-ē\ *n* **1 :** an embankment or dike to prevent flooding **2 :** a river landing place **:** PIER [French *levée,* from Old French, "act of raising", from *lever* "to raise", from Latin *levare*]
[1]lev•el \'lev-əl\ *n* **1 :** a device for establishing a horizontal line or plane ⟨a carpenter's *level*⟩ ⟨a surveyor's *level*⟩ **2 :** horizontal condition; *esp* **:** a condition of liquids marked by a horizontal surface of even altitude **3 :** a horizontal position, line, or surface often taken as an index of altitude ⟨placed at eye *level*⟩; *also* **:** a flat surface ⟨easier to walk on the *level*⟩ **4 :** a position in a scale or rank ⟨students at the same learning *level*⟩ [Middle French *livel,* from Latin *libella,* from *libra* "pound, balance"] — **on the level :** bona fide **:** HONEST
[2]level *vb* **lev•eled** *or* **lev•elled; lev•el•ing** *or* **lev•el•ling** \'lev-ling, -ə-ling\ **1 :** to make (a line or surface) horizontal **:** make flat or level ⟨*leveled* the ground for a road⟩ **2 :** DIRECT 3, AIM ⟨*leveled* a charge of fraud at them⟩ **3 :** to bring to a common level or plane **:** EQUALIZE **4 :** to lay level with the ground **:** RAZE ⟨the cyclone *leveled* the village⟩ **5 :** to attain or come to a level ⟨the jet *leveled* off at 10,000 meters⟩ — **lev•el•er** *or* **lev•el•ler** \'lev-lər, -ə-lər\ *n*
[3]level *adj* **1 :** having no part higher than another **2 :** being on a line with the horizon **:** HORIZONTAL **3 a :** of the same height or rank **:** being on a line **:** EVEN ⟨stood in water *level* with my shoulders⟩ **b** (1) **:** STEADY, UNWAVERING ⟨a *level* stare⟩ (2) **:** CALM, UNEXCITED ⟨spoke in *level* tones⟩ — **lev•el•ly** \'lev-əl-lē, 'lev-ə-lē\ *adv* — **lev•el•ness** \-əl-nəs\ *n* — **level best :** very best
lev•el•head•ed \,lev-əl-'hed-əd\ *adj* **:** having good judgment **:** SENSIBLE — **lev•el•head•ed•ness** *n*
[1]le•ver \'lev-ər, 'lē-vər\ *n* **1 a :** a bar used for prying or dislodging something **b :** an instrument or means used to achieve a purpose **:** TOOL ⟨used food distribution as a *lever* to gain votes⟩ **2 a :** a rigid bar that pivots on a fulcrum and that is used to exert a pressure or sustain a weight at one point of its length by the application of a force at a second **b :** a projecting piece by which a mechanism is operated or adjusted [Old French *levier,* from *lever* "to raise", from Latin *levare*]

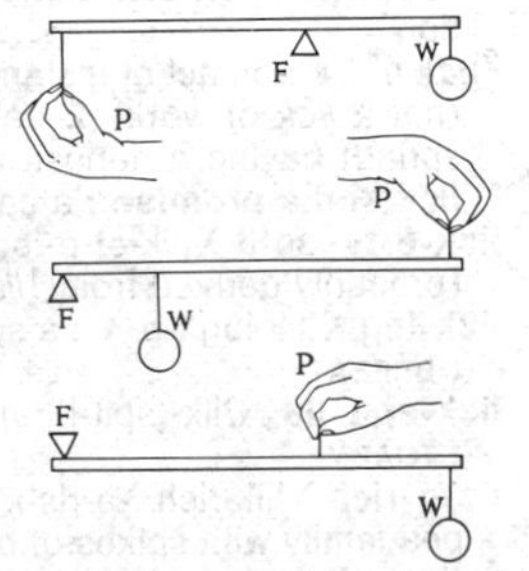

[1]lever 2a: *P* power, *F* fulcrum, *W* weight

[2]lever *vt* **le•vered; le•ver•ing** \'lev-ring, 'lēv-, -ə-ring\ **:** to pry, raise, or move with or as if with a lever
le•ver•age \'lev-rij, 'lēv-, -ə-rij\ *n* **1 :** the action of a lever or the mechanical advantage gained by it **2 :** power to influence or dominate ⟨the strike threat gave the union bargaining *leverage*⟩
lev•er•et \'lev-rət, -ə-rət\ *n* **:** a hare in its first year [Middle French *levre* "hare", from Latin *lepor-, lepus*]
le•vi•a•than \li-'vī-ə-thən\ *n* **1 a** *often cap* **:** a sea monster often symbolizing evil in the Old Testament and Christian literature **b :** a large sea animal **2 :** GIANT 3 [Late Latin, from Hebrew *liwyāthān*] — **leviathan** *adj*
Le•vi's \'lē-,vīz\ *trademark* — used for jeans
lev•i•tate \'lev-ə-,tāt\ *vb* **:** to rise or cause to rise in the air in seeming defiance of gravity [*levity*] — **lev•i•ta•tion** \,lev-ə-'tā-shən\ *n*
Le•vite \'lē-,vīt\ *n* **1 :** a member of the Hebrew tribe of Levi **2 :** a descendant of Levi assigned to assist the priests in the care of the temple — **Le•vit•i•cal** \li-'vit-i-kəl\ *adj*
Le•vit•i•cus \li-'vit-i-kəs\ *n* — *see* BIBLE table
lev•i•ty \'lev-ət-ē\ *n, pl* **-ties :** an often inappropriate lack of seriousness **:** FRIVOLITY [Latin *levitas,* from *levis* "light in weight"]
lev•u•lose \'lev-yə-,lōs\ *n* **:** FRUCTOSE [derived from *lev-* + *-ose*]
[1]levy \'lev-ē\ *n, pl* **lev•ies 1 a :** the imposition or collection of an assessment **b :** an amount levied **2 a :** the raising of men for military service **b :** troops raised by levy [Middle French *levee,* from Old French, "act of raising", from *lever* "to raise", from Latin *levare*]
[2]levy *vb* **lev•ied; lev•y•ing 1 a :** to impose or collect by legal authority ⟨*levy* a tax⟩ **b :** to require (as a service) by authority **2 :** to enlist or conscript for military service **3 :** to carry on (war) **:** WAGE **4 :** to seize property to satisfy a legal claim — **lev•i•er** *n*
lewd \'lüd\ *adj* **1 :** lacking in sexual restraint **:** LICENTIOUS **2 :** OBSCENE 2, SALACIOUS [Middle English *lewed* "vulgar", from Old English *lǣwede* "laical, ignorant"] — **lewd•ly** *adv* — **lewd•ness** *n*
lex•i•cal \'lek-si-kəl\ *adj* **1 :** of or relating to the vocabulary of a language **2 :** of or relating to a lexicon or to lexicography — **lex•i•cal•ly** \-si-kə-lē, -klē\ *adv*
lex•i•cog•ra•pher \,lek-sə-'käg-rə-fər\ *n* **:** a specialist in lexicography
lex•i•cog•ra•phy \-fē\ *n* **1 :** the editing or making of a dictionary **2 :** the principles and practices of dictionary making — **lex•i•co•graph•i•cal** \,lek-sə-kō-'graf-i-kəl\ *or* **lex•i•co•graph•ic** \-ik\ *adj* — **lex•i•co•graph•i•cal•ly** \-i-kə-lē, -klē\ *adv*
lex•i•con \'lek-sə-,kän, -si-kən\ *n, pl* **lex•i•ca** \-si-kə\ *or* **lexi•cons 1 :** DICTIONARY 1 **2 :** the vocabulary of a language, an individual speaker, or a subject [Late Greek *lexikon,* from *lexikos* "of words", from Greek *lexis* "speech, word", from *legein* "to say"]
ley *variant of* LEA
Ley•den jar \,līd-n-\ *n* **:** an electrical condenser consisting of a glass jar coated inside and outside with metal foil and having the inner coating connected to a conducting rod passed through the insulating stopper [*Leiden, Leyden,* Netherlands]
li•a•bil•i•ty \,lī-ə-'bil-ət-ē\ *n, pl* **-ties 1 :** the state of being liable ⟨*liability* for one's actions⟩ ⟨*liability* to disease⟩ **2** *pl* **:** that for which a person is liable **:** DEBTS **3 :** something that is a disadvantage **:** DRAWBACK
li•a•ble \'lī-ə-bəl, *especially in sense 2b also* 'lī-bəl\ *adj* **1 :** bound by law **:** RESPONSIBLE ⟨*liable* for damages⟩ **2 a :** SUSCEPTIBLE ⟨*liable* to disease⟩ **b :** exposed to or likely to experience something usually undesirable ⟨*liable* to get hurt⟩ [Old French *lier* "to bind", from Latin *ligare*] **syn** see APT
li•aise \lē-'āz\ *vi* **1 :** to establish liaison **2 :** to act as a liaison officer [back-formation from *liaison*]
li•ai•son \'lē-ə-,zän, lē-'ā-\ *n* **1 a :** a connecting link; *esp* **:** a linking or coordinating of activities **b :** AFFAIR 3a **2 :** the pronunciation of an otherwise absent consonant sound at the end of a word when immediately followed by a word beginning with a vowel sound **3 :** communication especially between parts of an armed force [French, from *lier* "to bind", from Latin *ligare*]
li•a•na \lē-'an-ə, -'an-ə\ *also* **li•ane** \-'än, -'an\ *n* **:** a climbing woody plant that roots in the ground especially in a tropical forest [French *liane*]
li•ar \'lī-ər, 'līr\ *n* **:** one that tells lies
li•ba•tion \lī-'bā-shən\ *n* **1 :** the act of pouring a liquid (as wine) in honor of a god; *also* **:** the liquid poured out **2 :** a drink usually of an alcoholic beverage [Latin *libatio,* from *libare* "to pour as an offering"] — **li•ba•tion•ary** \-shə-,ner-ē\ *adj*
[1]li•bel \'lī-bəl\ *n* **1 :** a written or spoken statement or a representation that gives an unjustly unfavorable impression of a person or thing **2 :** the act or crime of injuring a person's reputation by way of something printed or written or by a visible representation (as a picture) — compare SLANDER [Middle French, "written declaration", from Latin *libellus,* from *liber* "book"] — **li•bel•ous** \-bə-ləs\ *adj*
[2]libel *vt* **li•beled** *or* **li•belled; li•bel•ing** *or* **li•bel•ling** \-bə-ling, -bling\ **:** to make or publish a libel against — **li•bel•er** \-bə-lər\ *n* — **li•bel•ist** \-bə-list\ *n*
[1]lib•er•al \'lib-rəl, -ə-rəl\ *adj* **1 :** of, relating to, or based on the liberal arts ⟨a *liberal* education⟩ **2 a :** GENEROUS 1 ⟨a *liberal* giver⟩ **b :** AMPLE, BOUNTIFUL ⟨a *liberal* serving⟩ **3 :** not literal **:** LOOSE ⟨a *liberal* translation⟩ **4 :** BROAD-MINDED, TOLERANT; *esp* **:** not bound by orthodox or traditional forms or beliefs **5 a :** of, favoring, or based on the principles of liberalism **b** *cap* **:** of or making up a political party (as in the United Kingdom) advo-

\ə\ **abut**	\au̇\ **out**	\i\ **tip**	\ȯ\ **saw**	\u̇\ **foot**
\ər\ **further**	\ch\ **chin**	\ī\ **life**	\ȯi\ **coin**	\y\ **yet**
\a\ **mat**	\e\ **pet**	\j\ **job**	\th\ **thin**	\yü\ **few**
\ā\ **take**	\ē\ **easy**	\ng\ **sing**	\th\ **this**	\yu̇\ **cure**
\ä\ **cot, cart**	\g\ **go**	\ō\ **bone**	\ü\ **food**	\zh\ **vision**

cating or associated with the principles of political liberalism [Middle French, from Latin *liberalis* "suitable for a freeman, generous", from *liber* "free"] — **lib•er•al•ly** \-rə-lē\ *adv*
• **syn** RADICAL: LIBERAL suggests an independence of mind, a freedom from conventionality, tradition, or dogma, a practical tolerant recognition of changing conditions and the need to adapt to them, and readiness to experiment; RADICAL usually suggests extremeness in breaking with established order and in a political desire to uproot and destroy.

²liberal *n* **:** one who is liberal: as **a :** one who is open-minded or not strict in the observance of orthodox or traditional forms **b** *cap* **:** a member or supporter of a Liberal party **c :** an advocate of liberalism especially in individual rights

liberal arts *n pl* **:** the studies (as language, philosophy, history, literature, or abstract science) in a college or university intended to provide chiefly general knowledge and to develop the general intellectual capacities

lib•er•al•ism \'lib-rə-ˌliz-əm, -ə-rə-\ *n* **1 :** the quality or state of being liberal **2 a** *often cap* **:** a movement in modern Protestantism emphasizing intellectual liberty and the spiritual and ethical content of Christianity **b :** a theory in economics emphasizing individual freedom from restraint and usually based on free competition, the self-regulating market, and the gold standard **c :** a political philosophy based on belief in progress, the essential goodness of man, and the autonomy of the individual and standing for the protection of political and civil liberties **d** *cap* **:** the principles or policies of a Liberal party — **lib•er•al•ist** \-rə-ləst\ *n or adj* — **lib•er•al•is•tic** \ˌlib-rə-'lis-tik, -ə-rə-\ *adj*

lib•er•al•i•ty \ˌlib-ə-'ral-ət-ē\ *n, pl* **-ties :** the quality or state of being liberal; *also* **:** an instance of being liberal

lib•er•al•ize \'lib-rə-ˌlīz, -ə-rə-\ *vb* **:** to make or become liberal — **lib•er•al•iza•tion** \ˌlib-rə-lə-'zā-shən, -ə-rə-\ *n* — **lib•er•al•iz•er** \'lib-rə-ˌlī-zər, -ə-rə-\ *n*

lib•er•ate \'lib-ə-ˌrāt\ *vt* **1 :** to free from bondage or restraint **:** set at liberty ⟨*liberate* a prisoner⟩ ⟨*liberate* the mind from worry⟩ **2 :** to free (as a gas) from combination [Latin *liberare*, from *liber* "free"] **syn** see FREE — **lib•er•a•tion** \ˌlib-ə-'rā-shən\ *n* — **lib•er•a•tor** \'lib-ə-ˌrāt-ər\ *n*

lib•er•tar•i•an \ˌlib-ər-'ter-ē-ən\ *n* **1 :** an advocate of the doctrine of free will **2 :** one who upholds liberty of thought and action — **libertarian** *adj* — **lib•er•tar•i•an•ism** \-ē-ə-ˌniz-əm\ *n*

lib•er•tine \'lib-ər-ˌtēn\ *n* **:** a person who is unrestrained by convention or morality; *esp* **:** one leading a dissolute life [Latin *libertinus* "freedman", derived from *liber* "free"] — **libertine** *adj* — **lib•er•tin•ism** \-ˌtē-ˌniz-əm\ *n*

lib•er•ty \'lib-ərt-ē\ *n, pl* **-ties 1 :** the condition of being free and independent **:** FREEDOM **2 :** power to do what one pleases **:** freedom from restraint **3 a :** FAMILIARITY 4 **b :** an imprudent action **:** RISK ⟨don't take foolish *liberties* with your health⟩ **4 :** a short authorized absence from naval duty [Middle French *liberté*, from Latin *libertas*, from *liber* "free"] **syn** see FREEDOM — **at liberty 1 :** FREE 1a **2 :** at leisure **:** UNOCCUPIED

liberty cap *n* **:** a close-fitting conical cap used as a symbol of liberty by the French revolutionists and in the United States especially before 1800

li•bid•i•nous \lə-'bid-n-əs\ *adj* **1 :** having or marked by lustful desires **:** LASCIVIOUS **2 :** of or relating to the libido — **li•bid•i•nous•ly** *adv* — **li•bid•i•nous•ness** *n*

li•bi•do \lə-'bēd-ō, -'bīd-\ *n, pl* **-dos 1 :** emotion or psychic energy that in psychoanalytic theory is derived from primitive biological urges **2 :** sexual drive [Latin *libidin-, libido* "desire, lust"] — **li•bid•i•nal** \-'bid-n-əl, -'bid-nəl\ *adj* — **li•bid•i•nal•ly** \-ē\ *adv*

Li•bra \'lī-brə, 'lē-\ *n* **1 :** a southern zodiacal constellation between Virgo and Scorpio **2 :** the 7th sign of the zodiac; *also* **:** one born under this sign [Latin, literally, "scales, pound"]

li•brar•i•an \lī-'brer-ē-ən\ *n* **:** a specialist in the care or management of a library — **li•brar•i•an•ship** \-ˌship\ *n*

li•brary \'lī-ˌbrer-ē\ *n, pl* **-brar•ies 1 :** a place in which literary, reference, and artistic materials (as books, recordings, films) are kept for use but not for sale **2 :** a collection of literary or artistic materials (as books or prints) [Medieval Latin *librarium*, from Latin *liber* "book"]

li•bret•tist \lə-'bret-əst\ *n* **:** the writer of a libretto

li•bret•to \lə-'bret-ō\ *n, pl* **-tos** *or* **-ti** \-ē\ **:** the text of an opera or a musical; *also* **:** a book containing such a text [Italian, from *libro* "book", from Latin *liber*]

Lib•ri•um \'lib-rē-əm\ *trademark* — used for a tranquilizer containing chlordiazepoxide

lice *pl of* LOUSE

¹li•cense *or* **li•cence** \'līs-ns\ *n* **1 a :** permission to act **b :** freedom of action **2 a :** permission granted by competent authority to engage in a business, occupation, or activity otherwise unlawful **b :** a document, plate, or tag showing that a license has been granted **3 a :** freedom that is used irresponsibly **b :** licentious conduct **4 :** deviation from fact, form, or rule by an artist or writer for the sake of effect [Middle French *licence*, from Latin *licentia*, from *licēre* "to be permitted"] **syn** see FREEDOM

²license *also* **licence** *vt* **1 :** to issue a license to **2 :** to permit or authorize especially by formal license — **li•cens•able** \-ə-bəl\ *adj*

licensed practical nurse *n* **:** a trained person authorized by license (as from a state) to provide routine care for the sick

licensed vocational nurse *n* **:** a licensed practical nurse authorized by license to practice in the states of California or Texas

li•cens•ee \ˌlīs-n-'sē\ *n* **:** one that is licensed

li•cen•tious \lī-'sen-chəs\ *adj* **:** loose and lawless in behavior; *esp* **:** LEWD, LASCIVIOUS — **li•cen•tious•ly** *adv* — **li•cen•tious•ness** *n*

lichee *variant of* LITCHI

li•chen \'lī-kən\ *n* **:** any of numerous complex plants (group Lichenes) that are thallophytes and are made up of an alga and a fungus growing in symbiotic association on a solid surface (as a tree, a rock, or the ground) [Latin, from Greek *leichēn, lichēn*] — **li•chen•ous** \-kə-nəs\ *adj*

lic•it \'lis-ət\ *adj* **:** conforming to the requirements of the law **:** PERMISSIBLE [Middle French *licite*, from Latin *licitus*, from *licēre* "to be permitted"] — **lic•it•ly** *adv* **syn** see LAWFUL

¹lick \'lik\ *vb* **1 a :** to draw the tongue over **b :** to dart or dart at or over like a tongue ⟨flames *licked* the ceiling⟩ **2 :** to lap up **3 a :** to strike repeatedly **:** THRASH **b :** DEFEAT 2 [Old English *liccian*] — **lick into shape :** to put into proper form or condition

²lick *n* **1 a :** an act or instance of licking **b :** a small amount **:** BIT ⟨not a *lick* of work⟩ **2 :** a sharp hit **:** BLOW **3 :** a place (as a spring) having a deposit of salt that animals regularly lick — **lick and a promise :** a careless performance of a task

lick•e•ty–split \ˌlik-ət-ē-'split\ *adv* **:** at great speed **:** very fast [probably derived from ¹*lick* + *split*]

lick•ing \'lik-ing\ *n* **1 :** a sound thrashing **2 :** a severe setback **:** DEFEAT

lick•spit•tle \'lik-ˌspit-l\ *n* **:** a fawning or abject subordinate **:** TOADY

lic•o•rice \'lik-rish, -ə-rish, -rəs\ *n* **1 :** a European plant of the pea family with spikes of blue flowers **2 :** the dried root of licorice; *also* **:** an extract from it used especially in brewing, confectionery, and medicine [Old French, from Late Latin *liquiritia*, from Latin *glycyrrhiza*, from Greek *glykyrrhiza*, from *glykys* "sweet" + *rhiza* "root"]

lic•tor \'lik-tər\ *n* **:** a Roman officer carrying the fasces as the insignia of his office with duties that included attending the chief magistrates in public appearances [Latin]

lid \'lid\ *n* **1 :** a movable cover ⟨the *lid* of a box⟩ **2 :** EYELID **3** *slang* **:** CAP 1, HAT **4 :** RESTRAINT 2 ⟨put a *lid* on all news coverage⟩ [Old English *hlid*] — **lid•ded** \'lid-əd\ *adj* — **lid•less** \'lid-ləs\ *adj*

li•do \'lēd-ō\ *n, pl* **lidos :** a fashionable beach resort [*Lido*, Italy]

¹lie \'lī\ *vi* **lay** \'lā\; **lain** \'lān\; **ly•ing** \'lī-ing\ **1 a :** to be in, stay in, or take up a horizontal position ⟨decided to *lie* on the bed⟩ ⟨*lie* asleep⟩ **b** *archaic* **:** to have sexual intercourse — used with *with* **c :** to stay quietly (as in hiding) **2 :** to be in a helpless or defenseless state ⟨*lay* at the mercy of the invaders⟩ **3 :** to have direction **:** EXTEND ⟨the route *lay* to the west⟩ **4 a :** to occupy a specified relative place or position ⟨hills *lie* behind us⟩ **b :** to have an effect by mere presence, weight, or relative position ⟨guilt *lay* heavily on them⟩ **5 :** to have a place **:** EXIST ⟨the choice *lies* here⟩ **6 :** REMAIN ⟨machinery *lying* idle⟩ [Old English *licgan*] — **lie low 1 :** to stay in hiding **2 :** to bide one's time but remain ready for action

²lie *n* **1 :** the position in which something lies **2 :** the haunt of an animal **:** COVERT

³lie *vi* **lied**; **ly•ing** \'lī-ing\ **1 :** to make an untrue statement with intent to deceive ⟨*lie* about one's age⟩ **2 :** to create a false impression ⟨statistics sometimes *lie*⟩ [Old English *lēogan*]

[4]lie *n* **1 :** a deliberate telling of an untruth **2 :** something that misleads or deceives ⟨your show of innocence was a *lie*⟩
lie detector *n* **:** an apparatus for detecting bodily changes considered to accompany lying
lie down *vi* **1 :** to submit meekly to defeat, disappointment, or insult ⟨refused to take the setback *lying down*⟩ **2 :** to fail to do one's part ⟨*lying down* on the job⟩
lief \ˈlēv, ˈlēf\ *adv* **:** SOON, GLADLY ⟨I'd as *lief* go as not⟩ [Old English *lēof* "dear, agreeable"]
[1]liege \ˈlēj\ *adj* **1 :** having the right to receive service and allegiance ⟨*liege* lord⟩ **2 :** owing or giving service to a lord ⟨a *liege* subject⟩ [Old French, from Late Latin *laeticus,* from *laetus* "serf", of Germanic origin]
[2]liege *n* **1 :** VASSAL 1 **2 :** a feudal superior
liege man *n* **1 :** VASSAL 1 **2 :** a devoted follower
lie in *vi* **:** to be confined to give birth to a child
lien \ˈlēn, ˈlē-ən\ *n* **:** a legal claim on the property of a person until he or she has met a certain obligation (as a debt) [Middle French, "tie, band", from Latin *ligamen,* from *ligare* "to bind"]
lie to \lī-ˈtü, ˈlī-\ *vi* **:** to stay stationary with head to windward ⟨the ship had to *lie to* because of fog⟩
lieu \ˈlü\ *n, archaic* **:** PLACE, STEAD [Middle French, from Latin *locus*] — **in lieu of :** in the place of **:** instead of
lieu•ten•an•cy \lü-ˈten-ən-sē\ *n, pl* **-cies :** the office, rank, or commission of a lieutenant
lieu•ten•ant \lü-ˈten-ənt\ *n* **1 a :** an officer empowered to act for a higher official **b :** a representative of another in the performance of duty **:** ASSISTANT **2 a** (1) **:** FIRST LIEUTENANT (2) **:** SECOND LIEUTENANT **b :** an officer rank in the Navy and Coast Guard above lieutenant junior grade and below lieutenant commander **c :** a fire or police department officer ranking below a captain [Middle French, from *lieu* "place" + *tenant* "holding"]
lieutenant colonel *n* **:** an officer rank in the Army, Marine Corps, and Air Force above major and below colonel
lieutenant commander *n* **:** an officer rank in the Navy and Coast Guard above lieutenant and below commander
lieutenant general *n* **:** an officer rank in the Army, Marine Corps, and Air Force above major general and below general
lieutenant governor *n* **1 :** an elected official serving as deputy to the governor of an American state **2 :** the formal head of the government of a Canadian province appointed to represent the crown
lieutenant junior grade *n, pl* **lieutenants junior grade :** an officer rank in the Navy and Coast Guard above ensign and below lieutenant
[1]life \ˈlīf\ *n, pl* **lives** \ˈlīvz\ **1 a :** the quality that distinguishes a vital and functional being from a dead body or inanimate matter **b :** a state of an organism characterized especially by capacity for metabolism, growth, reaction to stimuli, and reproduction **2 :** the sequence of physical and mental experiences that make up the existence of an individual **3 :** BIOGRAPHY 1 **4 a :** the period during which an organism lives **b :** a specific phase or aspect of such a life ⟨adult *life*⟩ ⟨sex *life*⟩ **5 :** a way or manner of living **6 :** a vital or living being; *esp* **:** PERSON ⟨saving *lives*⟩ **7 :** ANIMATION, SPIRIT ⟨eyes full of *life*⟩ **8 :** the period of utility, duration, or existence of something ⟨*life* of a car⟩ **9 :** living beings (as of a kind or place) ⟨forest *life*⟩ **10 a :** human activities **b :** animate activity and movement ⟨stirrings of *life*⟩ **11 :** one providing interest and vigor ⟨the *life* of the party⟩ [Old English *līf*]
[2]life *adj* **1 :** of or relating to animate being ⟨the *life* force⟩ **2 :** LIFELONG ⟨*life* tenure⟩ **3 :** using a living model ⟨a *life* class⟩
life belt *n* **:** a life preserver in the form of a buoyant belt
life•blood \ˈlīf-ˈbləd\ *n* **:** something that gives strength and energy **:** the vital force or essence ⟨freedom of inquiry is the *lifeblood* of a university⟩
life•boat \-ˌbōt\ *n* **1 :** a strong buoyant boat especially designed for use in saving lives at sea **2 :** a boat carried by a ship for use in an emergency
life buoy *n* **:** a ring-shaped life preserver
life cycle *n* **1 :** the series of stages through which an organism passes from a particular first stage (as the egg) to the corresponding stage of its offspring **2 :** LIFE HISTORY 1a
life expectancy *n* **:** an expected number of years of life based on statistical probability
life•guard \ˈlīf-ˌgärd\ *n* **:** a usually expert swimmer employed to safeguard other swimmers
life history *n* **1 a :** a history of the changes through which an organism passes in its development from its first stage to its natural death **b :** LIFE CYCLE 1 **2 :** the history of an individual's development in a social environment
life insurance *n* **:** insurance providing for payment of a fixed sum to a specified individual upon death of the insured
life jacket *n* **:** a life preserver in the form of a sleeveless jacket or a collar which extends down the chest — called also *life vest*
life•less \ˈlīf-ləs\ *adj* **:** having no life: **a :** DEAD 1 **b :** INANIMATE ⟨*lifeless* as marble⟩ **c :** lacking qualities expressive of life and vigor **:** DULL ⟨*lifeless* voice⟩ **d :** destitute of living beings ⟨a *lifeless* desert⟩ — **life•less•ly** *adv* — **life•less•ness** *n*
life•like \ˈlīf-ˌlīk\ *adj* **:** accurately representing or imitating real life ⟨a *lifelike* portrait⟩ — **life•like•ness** *n*
life•line \ˈlīf-ˌlīn\ *n* **1 a :** a line to which persons may cling to save or protect their lives **b :** a line attached to a diver's helmet by which he is lowered and raised **c :** a rope line for lowering a person to safety **2 :** a land, sea, or air route regarded as indispensable
life•long \ˈlīf-ˌlȯng\ *adj* **:** continuing through life ⟨a *lifelong* friendship⟩
life plant *n* **:** BRYOPHYLLUM
life preserver *n* **:** a device designed to save a person from drowning by buoying up the body while in the water

life preserver

lif•er \ˈlī-fər\ *n* **:** a person sentenced to life imprisonment
life raft *n* **:** a raft usually made of wood or an inflatable material and designed for rescue use in an emergency at sea
life•sav•ing \ˈlīf-ˌsā-viŋ\ *n* **:** the skill or practice of saving or protecting lives especially of drowning persons — **life•sav•er** \-vər\ *n* — **lifesaving** *adj*
life science *n* **:** a branch of science (as biology, medicine, anthropology, or sociology) that deals with living organisms and life processes — **life scientist** *n*
life–size \ˈlīf-ˈsīz\ *or* **life–sized** \-ˈsīzd\ *adj* **:** of natural size **:** of the size of the original ⟨a *life-size* statue⟩
life span *n* **1 :** the duration of existence of an individual **2 :** the average length of life of a kind of organism or of a material object
life•time \-ˌtīm\ *n* **:** the duration of an individual's existence
life vest *n* **:** LIFE JACKET
life•work \ˈlīf-ˈwərk\ *n* **:** the entire or principal work of one's lifetime; *also* **:** a work extending over a lifetime
[1]lift \ˈlift\ *vb* **1 :** to raise from a lower to a higher position, rate, or amount **:** ELEVATE **2 :** REVOKE, REPEAL ⟨*lift* an embargo⟩ **3 a :** STEAL ⟨had their wallets *lifted*⟩ **b :** PLAGIARIZE **4 :** to move from one place to another **:** TRANSPORT **5 :** RISE, ASCEND ⟨the jet *lifted* from the airport⟩ **6 :** to disperse upward ⟨until the fog *lifts*⟩ [Old Norse *lypta*] — **lift•er** *n*
• **syn** LIFT, RAISE, HOIST, BOOST mean to move from a lower to a higher place or position. LIFT implies effort exerted to bring up from and especially clear of the ground and may apply to immaterial as well as material things; RAISE often suggests bringing something to a vertical or high position for which it is suited or intended; HOIST implies lifting something very heavy by mechanical means; BOOST suggests assisting to climb or advance by a push.
[2]lift *n* **1 :** the amount that may be lifted at one time **:** LOAD **2 :** the action or an instance of lifting **3 a :** ASSISTANCE, HELP **b :** a ride along one's way **4 :** the distance or extent to which something rises ⟨the *lift* of a canal lock⟩ **5 a** *chiefly British* **:** ELEVATOR 1b **b :** an apparatus for raising an automobile (as for repair) **c :** a conveyor for carrying people up or down a mountain slope **6 a :** an elevating influence **b :** an elevation of the spirits **7 :** the part of the total aerodynamic force acting on an airplane or airfoil that is upward and opposes the pull of gravity

\ə\ **abut**	\au̇\ **out**	\i\ **tip**	\ȯ\ **saw**	\u̇\ **foot**
\ər\ **further**	\ch\ **chin**	\ī\ **life**	\ȯi\ **coin**	\y\ **yet**
\a\ **mat**	\e\ **pet**	\j\ **job**	\th\ **thin**	\yü\ **few**
\ā\ **take**	\ē\ **easy**	\ng\ **sing**	\t͟h\ **this**	\yu̇\ **cure**
\ä\ **cot, cart**	\g\ **go**	\ō\ **bone**	\ü\ **food**	\zh\ **vision**

lift–off \'lift-ˌȯf\ *n* : a vertical takeoff by an aircraft, rocket, or missile

lig•a•ment \'lig-ə-mənt\ *n* : a tough band of tissue that holds bones together or keeps an organ in place in the body [Latin *ligamentum* "band, tie", from *ligare* "to bind"] — **lig•a•men•tous** \ˌlig-ə-'ment-əs\ *adj*

li•gate \'lī-ˌgāt, lī-'\ *vt* : to tie with a ligature — **li•ga•tion** \lī-'gā-shən\ *n*

lig•a•ture \'lig-ə-ˌchu̇r, -chər\ *n* **1** : a binding or tying of something **2** : something that binds or connects : BOND **3** : a thread or filament used in surgery especially for tying blood vessels **4** : a printed or written character consisting of two or more letters or characters united ⟨the *ligature* æ⟩ [Middle French, from Late Latin *ligatura*, from Latin *ligare* "to bind"]

[1]light \'līt\ *n* **1 a** : something that makes vision possible **b** : the sensation aroused by stimulation of the visual receptors **c** : an electromagnetic radiation in the wavelength range including infrared, visible, ultraviolet, and X rays and traveling in a vacuum with a speed of about 299,726 kilometers per second; *esp* : the part of this range that is visible to the human eye **2 a** : DAYLIGHT 1 **b** : DAWN 1 **3** : a source of light: as **a** : a celestial body **b** : CANDLE 1 **c** : an electric lamp ⟨turned on all the *lights*⟩ **4 a** : mental or spiritual insight **b** : TRUTH ⟨see the *light*⟩ **5 a** : public knowledge ⟨facts brought to *light*⟩ **b** : a particular aspect presented to view ⟨saw the matter in a false *light*⟩ **6** : a particular illumination ⟨by the *light* of the moon⟩ **7 a** : WINDOW 1 **b** : SKYLIGHT **8** *pl* : way of thinking : BELIEFS ⟨worship according to one's *lights*⟩ **9** : a noteworthy person : LUMINARY ⟨one of the leading *lights* in the organization⟩ **10** : a particular expression of the eye **11 a** : LIGHTHOUSE, BEACON **b** : TRAFFIC SIGNAL **12** : a source of heat for lighting something [Old English *lēoht*] — **light•less** \-ləs\ *adj*

[2]light *adj* **1** : having light : BRIGHT ⟨a *light* room⟩ **2 a** : not dark or swarthy in color ⟨a *light* skin⟩ **b** : medium in saturation and high in lightness ⟨*light* blue⟩

[3]light *vb* **light•ed** *or* **lit** \'lit\; **light•ing 1** : to make or become light : BRIGHTEN **2** : to burn or cause to burn : IGNITE **3 a** : to conduct with a light ⟨*light* them to their room⟩ **b** : ILLUMINATE ⟨rockets *lit* up the sky⟩

[4]light *adj* **1 a** : having little weight : not heavy ⟨*light* as a feather⟩ **b** : designed to carry a comparatively small load ⟨a *light* truck⟩ **c** : having relatively little weight in proportion to bulk ⟨aluminum is a *light* metal⟩ **2 a** : not important or serious : TRIVIAL **b** : not abundant : SCANTY ⟨*light* rain⟩ ⟨a *light* breakfast⟩ **3 a** : easily distrubed ⟨a *light* sleeper⟩ **b** : exerting little force or pressure : GENTLE ⟨a *light* touch⟩ **4** : requiring little effort ⟨*light* exercise⟩ **5** : capable of moving swiftly or nimbly ⟨the dancers were *light* on their feet⟩ **6** : FRIVOLOUS ⟨*light* conduct⟩ **7** : free from care : CHEERFUL **8** : intended chiefly to entertain ⟨*light* reading⟩ **9** : having a comparatively low alcoholic content ⟨*light* wines⟩ **10** : lightly armed or equipped ⟨*light* cavalry⟩ **11** : being coarse and sandy : easily reduced to dust ⟨*light* soil⟩ **12** : producing goods for direct consumption by the consumer ⟨*light* industry⟩ **13** : UNACCENTED ⟨*light* syllables⟩ **14** : having a clear soft quality ⟨a *light* voice⟩ [Old English *lēoht*]

[5]light *adv* **1** : LIGHTLY **2** : with little baggage ⟨travels *light*⟩

[6]light *vi* **light•ed** *or* **lit** \'lit\; **light•ing 1** : SETTLE, ALIGHT ⟨birds *lit* on the lawn⟩ **2 a** : to strike or fall unexpectedly ⟨bad luck *lighted* on the party⟩ **b** : to arrive by chance : HAPPEN ⟨*lit* upon a solution⟩ [Old English *līhtan* "to dismount, alight"]

light adaptation *n* : the process by which the eye adapts to seeing in strong light — **light–adap•ted** \'līt-ə-ˌdap-təd\ *adj*

[1]light•en \'līt-n\ *vb* **light•ened**; **light•en•ing** \'līt-ning, -n-ing\ **1** : to make or grow light or clear : BRIGHTEN **2** : to make or become lighter — **light•en•er** \'līt-nər, -n-ər\ *n*

[2]lighten *vb* **light•ened**; **light•en•ing** \'līt-ning, -n-ing\ **1** : to relieve of a burden in whole or in part ⟨*lighten* the plane⟩ ⟨*lighten* their duties⟩ **2** : GLADDEN **3** : to become lighter **syn** see RELIEVE — **light•en•er** \'līt-nər, -n-ər\ *n*

[1]ligh•ter \'līt-ər\ *n* : a large usually flat-bottomed barge used especially in unloading or loading ships [Dutch *lichten* "to unload"]

[2]lighter *vt* : to convey by a lighter

[3]light•er \'līt-ər\ *n* : one that lights; *esp* : a device for lighting ⟨a cigarette *lighter*⟩

lighter–than–air *adj* : of less weight than the air displaced

light•face \'līt-ˌfās\ *n* : a typeface having thin light lines — **light•faced** \-'fāst\ *adj*

light•fast \-'fast\ *adj* : resistant to light and especially to sunlight; *esp* : colorfast to light — **light•fast•ness** \-ˌfast-nəs, -ˌfas-\ *n*

light–fin•gered \-'fing-gərd\ *adj* **1** : adroit in stealing especially by picking pockets **2** : having a light and dexterous touch : NIMBLE — **light–fin•gered•ness** *n*

light–foot•ed \-'fu̇t-əd\ *adj* : having a light and springy step or movement

light–head•ed \-'hed-əd\ *adj* **1** : mentally disoriented : DIZZY **2** : lacking in maturity or seriousness : FRIVOLOUS — **light–head•ed•ly** *adv* — **light–head•ed•ness** *n*

light•heart•ed \-'härt-əd\ *adj* : free from care or anxiety : MERRY — **light•heart•ed•ly** *adv* — **light•heart•ed•ness** *n*

light heavyweight *n* : a boxer in a weight division having the approximate range of 75 to 81 kilograms

light•house \'līt-ˌhau̇s\ *n* : a structure (as a tower) with a powerful light signal for guiding navigators at night

light•ing \'līt-ing\ *n* **1 a** : ILLUMINATION 2 **b** : IGNITION 1 **2** : an artificial supply of light or the apparatus providing it

light•ly \'līt-lē\ *adv* **1** : with little weight or force : GENTLY **2** : in a small degree or amount ⟨sprinkle *lightly*⟩ **3** : with little difficulty : EASILY ⟨was let off *lightly* with a warning⟩ **4** : in an agile manner : NIMBLY **5** : with indifference or carelessness ⟨took the rebuff *lightly*⟩

light meter *n* **1** : a small portable device for measuring illumination **2** : a device for indicating correct photographic exposure under varying conditions of illumination

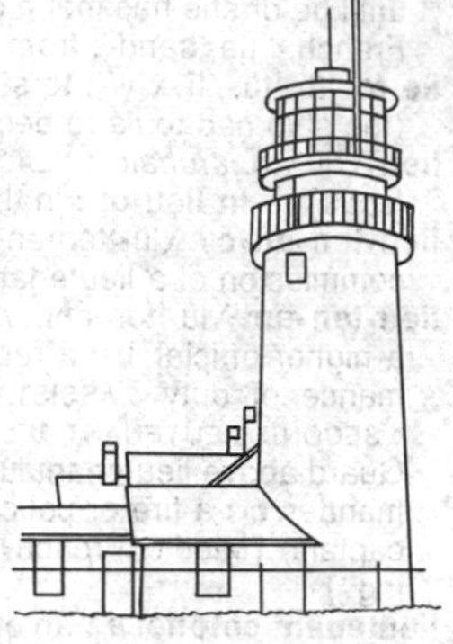
lighthouse

light microscope *n* : MICROSCOPE

light–mind•ed \'līt-'mīn-dəd\ *adj* : lacking in seriousness : FRIVOLOUS — **light•mind•ed•ly** *adv*

[1]light•ness \'līt-nəs\ *n* **1** : the quality or state of being light or lighted : ILLUMINATION **2** : the degree to which the achromatic element of a color is nearer white than black ⟨pink is high in *lightness*⟩

[2]lightness *n* **1** : the quality or state of being light in weight **2** : LEVITY **3 a** : physical agility **b** : cheery ease of style or manner **4** : DELICACY ⟨*lightness* of touch⟩

[1]light•ning \'līt-ning\ *n* : the flashing of light produced by a discharge of atmospheric electricity from one cloud to another or between a cloud and the earth; *also* : the discharge itself [Middle English, from *lightenen* "to lighten"]

[2]lightning *adj* : moving or accomplished with or as if with the speed of lightning ⟨a *lightning* attack⟩

lightning arrester *n* : a device for protecting an electrical apparatus from damage by lightning

lightning bug *n* : FIREFLY

lightning rod *n* : a metal rod set up on a building or a ship and connected with the earth or water below to decrease the chances of damage from lightning

light opera *n* : OPERETTA

light out *vi* : to leave in a hurry ⟨*lit out* for home when it began to rain⟩

light•plane \'līt-'plān\ *n* : a small and comparatively lightweight airplane; *esp* : a privately owned passenger airplane

light•proof \'līt-'prüf\ *adj* : impenetrable by light

lights \'līts\ *n pl* : the lungs especially of a slaughtered animal [Middle English *lightes*, from [4]*light*]

light•ship \'līt-ˌship\ *n* : a ship equipped with a powerful light signal and moored at a place dangerous to navigation

light•some \'līt-səm\ *adj* **1** : AIRY 3, NIMBLE **2** : free from care : CHEERFUL — **light•some•ly** *adv* — **light•some•ness** *n*

light–tight \'līt-ˌtīt\ *adj* : LIGHTPROOF

light trap *n* : a device for collecting or destroying insects by attracting them to a light and trapping or killing them

[1]light•weight \'līt-ˌwāt\ *n* **1** : one of less than average weight; *esp* : a boxer in a weight division having the approximate range of 57 to 60 kilograms **2** : an ineffectual or poorly qualified person

[2]lightweight *adj* **1** : of, relating to, or characteristic of a lightweight **2** : having less than average weight **3** : of no significance : UNIMPORTANT

light–year \'līt-,yiər\ *n* : a unit of length in astronomy equal to the distance that light travels in one year or 9,460,000,000,000 kilometers

lign- *or* **ligni-** *or* **ligno-** *combining form* : wood ⟨lignin⟩ [Latin *lignum*]

lig•ne•ous \'lig-nē-əs\ *adj* : of or resembling wood : WOODY [Latin *ligneus,* from *lignum* "firewood, wood", from *legere* "to gather"]

lig•ni•fy \'lig-nə-,fī\ *vb* **-fied**; **-fy•ing** : to convert into or become wood or woody tissue — **lig•ni•fi•ca•tion** \,lig-nə-fə-'kā-shən\ *n*

lig•nin \'lig-nən\ *n* : a substance related to cellulose that occurs in the woody cell walls of plants and in the cementing material between them

lig•nite \'lig-,nīt\ *n* : a usually brownish black coal intermediate between peat and bituminous coal; *esp* : one in which the texture of the original wood is distinct

lig•num vi•tae \,lig-nəm-'vīt-ē\ *n, pl* **lignum vitaes** : any of several tropical American trees or their very hard heavy wood [New Latin, literally, "wood of life"]

lig•u•late \'lig-yə-lət, -,lāt\ *also* **lig•u•lat•ed** \-,lāt-əd\ *adj* **1** : shaped like a strap ⟨*ligulate* ray flowers⟩ **2** : having ligules

lig•ule \'lig-yül\ *n* : an elongated flattened projection especially on a plant: as **a** : an appendage of a leaf and especially of the sheath of a blade of grass **b** : the limb of a ray flower [Latin *ligula* "small tongue, strap"]

lik•able *or* **like•able** \'lī-kə-bəl\ *adj* : easily liked : PLEASANT, AGREEABLE — **lik•able•ness** *n*

[1]**like** \'līk\ *vb* **1** : to feel attraction toward or take pleasure in : ENJOY ⟨*likes* baseball⟩ **2** : to feel toward : REGARD ⟨how do you *like* this plan⟩ **3** : to wish to have : WANT ⟨would *like* a vacation⟩ **4** : to feel inclined : CHOOSE ⟨allowed to do as they *liked*⟩ [Old English *līcian* "to be suitable, be pleasing"]

[2]**like** *n* : LIKING, PREFERENCE ⟨*likes* and dislikes⟩

[3]**like** *adj* **1 a** : the same or nearly the same (as in appearance, character, or quantity) ⟨suits of *like* design⟩ **b** : resembling or characteristic of something — used after the word modified and in combination ⟨dog*like*⟩ ⟨bell-*like*⟩ **2 a** : LIKELY 1 **3** : having the same unknowns raised to the same powers ⟨$9xy^4$ and $6xy^4$ are *like* terms⟩ [Old English *gelīc,* from *līc* "body"]

[4]**like** *prep* **1 a** : similar to ⟨their house is *like* a barn⟩ **b** : typical of ⟨was *like* them to do that⟩ **2** : in the manner of : similarly to ⟨acts *like* a fool⟩ **3** : inclined to ⟨looks *like* rain⟩ **4** : such as ⟨a subject *like* physics⟩

[5]**like** *n* : one that is like another : COUNTERPART ⟨may never see its *like* again⟩

[6]**like** *adv* **1** : LIKELY, PROBABLY ⟨*like* enough, you will⟩ **2** : to some extent : SEEMINGLY ⟨came in nonchalantly *like*⟩ **3** : close to ⟨the rate is more *like* 12 percent⟩

[7]**like** *conj* **1** : in the same way that : AS **2** : as if ⟨acted *like* they were scared⟩

like•li•hood \'lī-klē-,hu̇d\ *n* : PROBABILITY

[1]**like•ly** \'lī-klē\ *adj* **like•li•er**; **-est** **1** : being such as to make a certain happening or result probable ⟨the stronger team is *likely* to win⟩ **2** : seeming like the truth : BELIEVABLE ⟨a *likely* story⟩ **3** : PROMISING ⟨a *likely* place to fish⟩ [Old Norse *glīkligr,* from *glīkr* "like"]

[2]**likely** *adv* : in all probability : PROBABLY

like–mind•ed \'līk-'mīn-dəd\ *adj* : of the same mind or habit of thought — **like–mind•ed•ly** *adv* — **like–mind•ed•ness** *n*

lik•en \'lī-kən\ *vt* **lik•ened**; **lik•en•ing** \'līk-ning, -ə-ning\ : to represent as like something : COMPARE

like•ness \'līk-nəs\ *n* **1** : the quality or state of being like : RESEMBLANCE **2** : APPEARANCE, SEMBLANCE ⟨in the *likeness* of a clown⟩ **3** : COPY, PORTRAIT

• **syn** LIKENESS, SIMILARITY, RESEMBLANCE mean agreement or correspondence in details. LIKENESS implies a closer correspondence than SIMILARITY, which often implies that things are only somewhat alike; RESEMBLANCE implies similarity chiefly in appearance or external qualities.

like•wise \'līk-,wīz\ *adv* **1** : in like manner : SIMILARLY **2** : in addition : ALSO

lik•ing \'lī-king\ *n* : favorable regard : FONDNESS, TASTE

li•lac \'lī-lək, -,lak, -,läk\ *n* **1** : any of a genus of shrubs and trees of the olive family; *esp* : a European shrub widely grown for its showy clusters of fragrant pink, purple, or white flowers **2** : a moderate purple [obsolete French, from Arabic *līlak,* from Persian *nīlak* "bluish", from *nīl* "blue", from Sanskrit *nīla* "dark blue"]

lil•i•a•ceous \,lil-ē-'ā-shəs\ *adj* : of or relating to lilies

lil•li•pu•tian \,lil-ə-'pyü-shən\ *adj, often cap* **1** : extremely small : MINIATURE **2** : SMALL-MINDED, PETTY [*Lilliput,* island in Swift's *Gulliver's Travels* (1726) inhabited by people six inches high]

[1]**lilt** \'lilt\ *vi* **1** : to sing or speak rhythmically and with varying pitch **2** : to move in a lively springy manner [Middle English *lulten*] — **lilt•ing•ly** \'lil-ting-lē\ *adv*

[2]**lilt** *n* **1** : a lively and usually happy song or tune **2** : a rhythmical swing, flow, or cadence

[1]**lily** \'lil-ē\ *n, pl* **lil•ies** **1** : any of a genus of erect perennial leafy-stemmed bulbous herbs widely grown for their showy funnel-shaped flowers; *also* : any of various related plants **2** : any of varioius plants (as a water lily or a calla) with showy flowers [Old English *lilie,* from Latin *lilium*]

[2]**lily** *adj* : of, relating to, or resembling a lily

lily–liv•ered \,lil-ē-'liv-ərd\ *adj* : lacking courage : COWARDLY

△ **origin** White, the lily's color, is a color associated with fear. A badly frightened person may turn pale — "white as a sheet". But the sudden fright that drains the blood from one's face is quite different from the habitual cowardice of one who is lily-livered. Although the liver does not turn pale with fear, it was once believed that a deficiency of choler or yellow bile — the humor that governed anger, spirit, and courage — would leave the liver colorless. A person deficient in choler, and so white-livered, or lily-livered, would be spiritless and a coward.

lily of the valley : a low perennial herb of the lily family with usually two large oblong leaves and a stalk of fragrant nodding bell-shaped flowers

lily pad *n* : a floating leaf of a water lily

lily–white \,lil-ē-'hwīt, -'wīt\ *adj* **1** : white as a lily **2** : FAULTLESS, PURE

li•ma bean \,lī-mə-\ *n* : any of various bush or tall-growing beans widely grown for their flat edible usually pale green or whitish seeds; *also* : this seed [*Lima,* Peru]

[1]**limb** \'lim\ *n* **1** : one of the projecting paired appendages (as wings) of an animal body used especially for movement and grasping; *esp* : a leg or arm of a human being **2** : a large primary branch of a tree [Old English *lim*] — **limbed** \'limd\ *adj*

[2]**limb** *vt* : to cut off the limbs of (a felled tree)

[3]**limb** *n* **1** : the outer edge of the apparent disk of a celestial body ⟨the eastern *limb* of the sun⟩ **2** : the expanded portion of a bodily organ; *esp* : the spreading upper portion of a calyx or corolla that is not made up of separate parts [Latin *limbus* "border"]

[1]**lim•ber** \'lim-bər\ *adj* : bending easily : SUPPLE ⟨a *limber* willow twig⟩ ⟨a *limber* gymnast⟩ [origin unknown] — **lim•ber•ly** *adv* — **lim•ber•ness** *n*

[2]**limber** *vb* **lim•bered**; **lim•ber•ing** \'lim-bə-ring, -bring\ : to become or cause to become limber ⟨*limbered* up with calisthenics⟩

limbic system \,lim-bik-\ *n* : a group of structures below the cortex of the brain that are concerned especially with emotion and motivation [Latin *limbus* "border"]

limb•less \'lim-ləs\ *adj* : having no limbs

lim•bo \'lim-bō\ *n, pl* **limbos** **1** *often cap* : an abode of souls (as of unbaptized infants) barred from heaven through no fault of their own **2 a** : a place or state of restraint, confinement, or oblivion **b** : an intermediate or transitional place or state [Medieval Latin *in limbo* "on the border", from Latin *limbus* "border"]

Lim•burg•er \'lim-,bər-gər\ *n* : a creamy semisoft surface-ripened cheese with a pungent rind [*Limburg,* Belgium]

[1]**lime** \'līm\ *n* **1** : BIRDLIME **2 a** : a caustic highly infusible solid that consists of an oxide of calcium often together with magnesia, is obtained by calcining forms of calcium carbonate (as limestone or shells), and is used in mortar and plaster and in agriculture — called also *caustic lime* **b** : a dry white powder consisting essentially of an hydroxide of calcium that is made by treating lime with water **c** : CALCIUM ⟨carbonate of *lime*⟩ [Old English *līm*]

[2]lime *vt* : to treat or cover with lime
[3]lime *adj* : of, relating to, or containing lime or limestone
[4]lime *n* : a European linden tree [Old English *lind*]
[5]lime *n* : a citrus fruit like the lemon but smaller and with greenish yellow rind; *also* : the tree that bears it [French, from Provençal *limo,* from Arabic *līm*]
lime•ade \lī-ˈmād\ *n* : a drink made of lime juice, sugar, and water
lime•kiln \ˈlīm-ˌkiln, -ˌkil\ *n* : a furnace for reducing limestone or shells to lime by burning
lime•light \-ˌlīt\ *n* **1** : a device formerly used for lighting of the stage producing light by means of a flame directed on a cylinder of lime; *also* : the light produced by this device **2** : the center of public attention
lim•er•ick \ˈlim-rik, -ə-rik\ *n* : a light or humorous verse form of 5 lines of which the 1st, 2d, and 5th follow one rhyme and the 3d and 4th follow another [*Limerick,* Ireland]
lime•stone \ˈlīm-ˌstōn\ *n* : a rock that is formed chiefly by accumulation of organic remains (as shells or coral), consists mainly of calcium carbonate, is extensively used in building, and yields lime when burned
lime•wa•ter \ˈlīm-ˌwȯt-ər, -ˌwät-\ *n* : an alkaline water solution of calcium hydroxide often used in medicine as an antacid
[1]lim•it \ˈlim-ət\ *n* **1 a** : a geographical or political boundary **b** *pl* : [2]BOUND 3 **2 a** : something that bounds, restrains, or confines ⟨cooperate within *limits*⟩ **b** : the utmost extent ⟨reach the *limit* of one's tolerance⟩ **3** : LIMITATION 2 **4** : a prescribed maximum or minimum amount, quantity, or number **5** : a fixed number that is related to a variable in such a way that the difference between them as the variable approaches the number becomes and remains less than any positive value no matter how close to zero **6** : one that is exasperating or intolerable [Middle French *limite,* from Latin *limit-, limes* "boundary"]
[2]limit *vt* **1** : to set limits to **2** : to reduce in quantity or extent — **lim•it•able** \ˈlim-ət-ə-bəl\ *adj* — **lim•it•er** *n*
lim•i•ta•tion \ˌlim-ə-ˈtā-shən\ *n* **1** : an act or instance of limiting **2** : the quality or state of being limited **3** : something that limits : RESTRAINT — **lim•i•ta•tion•al** \-shnəl, -shən-l\ *adj*
lim•it•ed *adj* **1 a** : confined within limits : RESTRICTED **b** : having a limited number of passengers and offering superior and faster service and transportation ⟨a *limited* train⟩ **2** : relating to or being a government in which constitutional limitations are placed on the powers of one or more of its branches ⟨a *limited* monarchy⟩ — **lim•it•ed•ly** *adv* — **lim•it•ed•ness** *n*
limited war *n* : a war with an objective less than the total defeat of the enemy
lim•it•ing *adj* **1** : functioning as a limit : RESTRICTIVE ⟨*limiting* value⟩ **2** : serving to limit population size of organisms in an environment ⟨food is a *limiting* factor⟩
lim•it•less \ˈlim-ət-ləs\ *adj* : having no limits — **lim•it•less•ly** *adv* — **lim•it•less•ness** *n*
limn \ˈlim\ *vt* **limned; limn•ing** \ˈlim-ing, -ning\ **1** : to draw or paint on a surface **2 a** : to outline in clear sharp detail **b** : to describe or portray in symbols (as words or musical notes) [Middle English *luminen, limnen* "to illuminate", derived from Latin *illuminare*] — **limn•er** \ˈlim-ər, -nər\ *n*
lim•nol•o•gy \lim-ˈnäl-ə-jē\ *n* : the scientific study of fresh waters [Greek *limnē* "pool"] — **lim•no•log•i•cal** \ˌlim-nə-ˈläj-i-kəl\ *adj* — **lim•nol•o•gist** \lim-ˈnäl-ə-jəst\ *n*
li•mo•nite \ˈlī-mə-ˌnīt\ *n* : an ore of iron consisting of a hydrous ferric oxide or a mixture of oxides [German *limonit,* from Greek *leimōn* "meadow"] — **li•mo•nit•ic** \ˌlī-mə-ˈnit-ik\ *adj*
lim•ou•sine \ˈlim-ə-ˌzēn, ˌlim-ə-ˈ\ *n* **1** : a large luxurious often chauffeur-driven sedan **2** : a small bus with doors along the sides ⟨an airport *limousine*⟩ [French, literally, "cloak", from *Limousin,* France]
[1]limp \ˈlimp\ *vi* **1** : to walk lamely **2** : to proceed slowly or with difficulty ⟨the ship *limped* into port⟩ [probably from Middle English *lympen* "to fall short"] — **limp•er** *n*
[2]limp *n* : a limping movement or gait ⟨walked with a *limp*⟩
[3]limp *adj* **1** : lacking firm texture, substance, or structure ⟨*limp* curtains⟩ ⟨a *limp* bookbinding⟩ **2 a** : WEARY 1, EXHAUSTED **b** : lacking strength or firmness : SPIRITLESS [related to [1]*limp*] — **limp•ly** *adv* — **limp•ness** *n*
• **syn** LIMP, FLACCID, FLABBY mean lacking in firmness in texture or substance; LIMP implies a lack or loss of stiffness and a tendency to droop ⟨arms *limp* from exhaustion⟩ FLACCID implies a loss of power to keep or return to shape ⟨*flaccid* muscles⟩ FLABBY implies hanging or sagging by its own weight as through loss of muscular tone ⟨*flabby* cheeks⟩
lim•pet \ˈlim-pət\ *n* : any of numerous marine gastropod mollusks that have a low conical shell, browse over rocks or timbers, and cling very tightly when disturbed [Old English *lempedu,* from Medieval Latin *lampreda*]

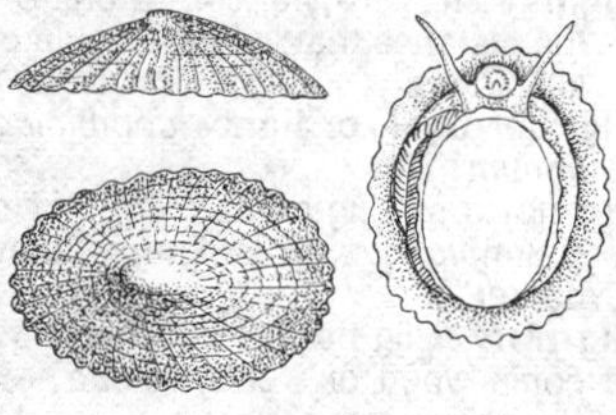
limpet

lim•pid \ˈlim-pəd\ *adj* **1** : completely free from cloudiness or other obstacles to the passage of light ⟨a *limpid* pool of water⟩ **2** : clear and simple in style ⟨*limpid* prose⟩ [Latin *limpidus,* from *lympha, limpa* "water"] — **lim•pid•i•ty** \lim-ˈpid-ət-ē\ *n* — **lim•pid•ly** \ˈlim-pəd-lē\ *adv* — **lim•pid•ness** *n*
• **syn** LIMPID, LUCID, PELLUCID mean clear and untroubled. LIMPID stresses freedom from murkiness or agitation and suggests the soft transparency of pure quiet water; LUCID, chiefly literary in this use, implies being both clear and full of light; PELLUCID suggests unusual transparency or shining clearness as of crystal.
limp•kin \ˈlim-kən, ˈlimp-\ *n* : a large brown wading bird resembling a bittern but having longer bill, neck, and legs and white stripes on head and neck [[1]*limp*]
lim•u•lus \ˈlim-yə-ləs\ *n, pl* **-li** \-ˌlī, -ˌlē\ : HORSESHOE CRAB [derived from Latin *limus* "sidelong"]
limy \ˈlī-mē\ *adj* **lim•i•er; -est** : containing lime or limestone
lin•age \ˈlī-nij\ *n* **1** : the number of lines of printed or written matter **2** : payment for literary matter based on the number of lines
linch•pin \ˈlinch-ˌpin\ *n* : a locking pin inserted crosswise (as through the end of an axle or shaft) [Old English *lynis* "linch pin"]
lin•dane \ˈlin-ˌdān\ *n* : an insecticide consisting of not less than 99 percent of an isomer of a chloride of benzene [T. van der *Linden,* 20th-century Dutch chemist]
lin•den \ˈlin-dən\ *n* **1** : any of a genus of trees with large heart-shaped leaves and clustered yellowish flowers rich in nectar **2** : the light fine-grained white wood of a linden; *esp* : BASSWOOD [Old English, "made of linden wood", from *lind* "linden tree"]
[1]line \ˈlīn\ *vt* **1** : to cover the inner surface of ⟨*line* a box with paper⟩ **2** : to put something in the inside of : FILL **3** : to serve as the lining of ⟨tapestries *lined* the walls⟩ [Middle English *linen,* from *line* "flax, linen", from Old English *līn*]
[2]line *n* **1** : THREAD, STRING, CORD, ROPE; *esp* : a comparatively strong slender cord ⟨a fishing *line*⟩ **2** : a cord, wire, or tape used in measuring and leveling **3 a** : piping for conveying a fluid (as steam or oil) **b** : wire connecting one telegraph or telephone station with another or a whole system of such wires **c** : the principal circuits of an electric power system ⟨a power *line*⟩ **4 a** : a horizontal row of written or printed characters **b** : a unit of verse formed by the grouping of metrical feet **c** : a short letter : NOTE ⟨drop me a *line*⟩ **d** : the words making up a part in a drama — usually used in pl. ⟨forgot my *lines*⟩ **5 a** : something (as a ridge, seam, or wrinkle) that is distinct, elongated, and narrow **b** : the course or direction of something in motion : ROUTE ⟨the *line* of flight of a bullet⟩ **c** : a boundary of an area ⟨the state *line*⟩ **d** : the track and roadbed of a railway **6** : a state of agreement ⟨bring ideas into *line*⟩ **7 a** : a course of conduct, action, or thought; *esp* : a publicly proclaimed policy ⟨a political *line*⟩ **b** : a field of activity or interest ⟨out of my *line*⟩ **c** : a glib persuasive way of talking **8 a** : LIMIT, RESTRAINT ⟨overstep the *line* of good taste⟩ **b** *archaic* : position in life : LOT **9** : any of various things arranged in or as if in a row or sequence: as **a** : LINEAGE ⟨a noble *line*⟩ **b** : a strain produced and maintained by selective breeding ⟨a high-fat *line* of cattle⟩ **c** (1) : the position of military forces in actual combat with the enemy at the front (2) : a military formation in which the different elements are abreast of each other (3) : naval ships arranged in a regular order (4) : fighting forces as distinguished from staff and supply personnel (5) : the force of a regular navy **d** : a set of objects of one general kind ⟨a *line* of merchandise⟩ **e** (1) : a group of public conveyances plying regularly under one management over a route (2) : a system of transportation; *also* : the company owning or operating it **f** : an arrangement of manufacturing processes in which each step is carried out sep-

arately and in proper order **g** : the football players who line up or within one foot of the line of scrimmage **10** : a long narrow mark: as **a** : a circle of latitude or longitude on a map **b** : EQUATOR 2 **c** : any of the horizontal parallel strokes on a music staff **d** : LINE OF SCRIMMAGE **11** : a geometric element that is generated by a moving point and that has length but no width or thickness; *esp* : a straight line **12 a** : a defining outline : CONTOUR ⟨a ship's *lines*⟩ **b** : a general plan ⟨thinking along these *lines*⟩ **13** : a source of information : INSIGHT ⟨got a *line* on their plans⟩ **14** : a complete game of 10 frames in bowling — called also *string* [partly from Old French *ligne,* from Latin *linea,* from *linum* "flax"; partly from Old English *līne*] — **between the lines 1** : in an indirect way **2** : by inference — **down the line** : all the way : FULLY — **in line for** : due or in a position to receive — **in the line of duty** : while on duty — **on the line 1** : in full view and at great risk **2** : on the border between two categories **3** : at once : IMMEDIATELY

^{3}line *vb* **1** : to mark or cover with a line **2** : to depict by lines : DRAW **3** : to place or form a line along ⟨pedestrians *line* the walks⟩

lin•e•age \ˈlin-ē-ij\ *n* **1** : lineal descent from a common progenitor **2** : a group of persons tracing descent from a common ancestor

lin•e•al \ˈlin-ē-əl\ *adj* **1** : LINEAR ⟨*lineal* measure⟩ **2 a** : consisting of or being in a direct line of ancestry or descent ⟨*lineal* descendants⟩ **b** : HEREDITARY 4 — **lin•e•al•ly** \-ē-ə-lē\ *adv*

lin•e•a•ment \ˈlin-ē-ə-mənt\ *n* : a feature or contour of a body or figure and especially of the face [Latin *lineamentum,* from *linea* "line"]

lin•ear \ˈlin-ē-ər\ *adj* **1 a** : relating to, consisting of, or resembling a line : STRAIGHT ⟨a direct *linear* approach⟩ **b** : involving a single dimension **c** : characterized by an emphasis on line ⟨*linear* art⟩ **d** (1) : containing variables and terms of the first degree only ⟨*linear* factors such as $x - 1$ and $x - 2$⟩ (2) : based on, involving, or expressed by linear functions or linear equations **2** : long and uniformly narrow ⟨the *linear* leaves of grasses⟩ — **lin•ear•i•ty** \ˌlin-ē-ˈar-ət-ē\ *n* — **lin•ear•ly** \ˈlin-ē-ər-lē\ *adv*

linear accelerator *n* : a device in which charged particles are accelerated in a straight line by successive impulses from a series of electric fields

linear combination *n* : a mathematical entity (as $4x + 5y + 6z$) composed of sums and differences of elements (as variables or equations) each multiplied by a constant coefficient

linear equation *n* : an equation in which each term is a monomial of degree one or a constant

linear function *n* : a polynomial function (as $f(x) = 2x - 3$) of degree one

linear interpolation *n* : estimation of a function (as a logarithm) by assuming that it is a straight line between known values

linear measure *n* **1** : a measure of length **2** : a system of measures of length

linear programming *n* : mathematical planning of industrial or military operations in terms of maximum or minimum values of linear functions in two or more variables subject to specific restrictions

line•back•er \ˈlīn-ˌbak-ər\ *n* : a defensive football player who lines up immediately behind the line of scrimmage

line•breed•ing \ˈlīn-ˈbrēd-ing\ *n* : the interbreeding of individuals within a particular line of descent usually to fix desirable characters — **line•breed** *vb*

line•cut \ˈlīn-ˌkət\ *n* : a letterpress printing plate made from a line drawing

line drawing *n* : a drawing made in solid lines especially as copy for a linecut

line drive *n* : a batted baseball hit in a nearly straight line not far off the ground — called also *liner*

line engraving *n* : a metal plate for use in intaglio printing made by hand-engraving lines of different widths and closeness; *also* : a process involving such plates or a print made with them

line graph *n* : a graph consisting of connected segments of straight lines which join points representing specific values

line•man \ˈlīn-mən\ *n* **1** : one who sets up or repairs electric wire communication or power lines — called also *linesman* **2** : a player in the line in football

lin•en \ˈlin-ən\ *n* **1 a** : cloth made of flax and noted for its strength, coolness, and luster **b** : thread or yarn spun from flax **2** : clothing or household articles made of linen cloth or a similar fabric **3** : paper made from linen fibers or with a linen finish [Old English *līnen* "of flax", from *līn* "flax, linen", from Latin *linum*] — **linen** *adj*

line of force : an imaginary line serving as a convenience in indicating the direction in space in which a force (as from an electric, magnetic, or gravitational field) acts

line of scrimmage : an imaginary line in football parallel to the goal lines that marks the position of the ball at the start of each down

line of sight 1 : a line from an observer's eye to a distant point toward which he is looking **2** : the straight path between a radio transmitting antenna and receiving antenna when unobstructed by the horizon — **line-of-sight** *adj*

line out *vb* **1** : to indicate with or as if with lines : OUTLINE ⟨*line out* a route⟩ **2 a** : to plant (young nursery stock) in rows **b** : to arrange in an extended line **3** : to move rapidly ⟨*lined out* for home⟩

^{1}lin•er \ˈlī-nər\ *n* **1** : one that makes, draws, or uses lines **2** : something with which lines are made **3 a** : a ship belonging to a regular line of ships **b** : an airplane belonging to an airline **4** : LINE DRIVE

^{2}liner *n* : one that lines or is used to line or back something

line segment *n* : SEGMENT 2b

lines•man \ˈlīnz-mən\ *n* **1** : LINEMAN 1 **2** : an official who assists a referee by determining whether a puck or ball or a player is beyond a boundary line

line•up \ˈlī-ˌnəp\ *n* **1** : a line of persons arranged especially for inspection or for identification by police **2 a** : a list of players taking part in a game (as of baseball); *also* : the players on such a list **b** : an alignment of persons or things having a common purpose or interest

line up \lī-ˈnəp, ˈlī-\ *vb* **1 a** : to assume an orderly linear arrangement ⟨*line up* for inspection⟩ **b** : to take one's position in a formation **2** : to put into alignment **3** : to organize and make available ⟨*line up* supporters⟩

^{1}ling \ˈling\ *n* **1** : any of various fishes (as a hake or burbot) of the cod family **2** : LINGCOD [Middle English]

^{2}ling *n* : a heath plant; *esp* : a common Old World heather [Old Norse *lyng*]

^{1}-ling \ling\ *n suffix* **1** : one connected with or having the quality of ⟨hire*ling*⟩ **2** : young, small, or inferior one ⟨duck*ling*⟩ [Old English]

^{2}-ling \ling\ *or* **-lings** \lingz\ *adv suffix* : in (such) a direction or manner ⟨side*ling*⟩ [Middle English *-ling, -linges*]

ling•cod \ˈling-ˌkäd\ *n* : a large greenish-fleshed food fish of the Pacific coast of North America related to the greenlings

lin•ger \ˈling-gər\ *vi* **lin•gered**; **lin•ger•ing** \-gə-ring, -gring\ **1** : to be slow in leaving a place or activity ⟨*lingered* in bed⟩ **2** : to remain alive although close to dying **3** : to be slow to act [Middle English *lengeren* "to dwell", from Old English *lengan* "to prolong"] **syn** see STAY — **lin•ger•er** \-gər-ər\ *n* — **lin•ger•ing•ly** \-gə-ring-lē, -gring-\ *adv*

lin•ge•rie \ˌlän-jə-ˈrā, ˌla^{n}-zhə-, -ˈrē\ *n* : women's intimate apparel [French, from *linge* "linen", from Latin *lineus* "made of linen", from *linum* "flax, linen"]

lin•go \ˈling-gō\ *n, pl* **lingoes 1** : strange or incomprehensible language or speech; *esp* : a foreign language **2** : JARGON 2 **3** : language characteristic of an individual [probably from Provençal, "tongue", from Latin *lingua*] **syn** see DIALECT

lin•gua fran•ca \ˌling-gwə-ˈfrang-kə\ *n, pl* **lingua francas** *or* **lin•guae fran•cae** \-ˌgwī-ˈfrang-ˌkī\ **1** : a common language that consists of Italian mixed with French, Spanish, Greek, and Arabic and is spoken in Mediterranean ports **2** : any of various languages used as common or commercial tongues among speakers of different languages [Italian, literally, "Frankish language"]

lin•gual \ˈling-gwəl, -gyə-wəl\ *adj* **1 a** : of, relating to, or resembling a tongue **b** : lying near or next to the tongue; *esp* : relating to or being the surface of a tooth next to the tongue **2** : produced by the tongue ⟨*lingual* sounds such as \t\ or \l\⟩ [Medieval Latin *lingualis,* from Latin *lingua* "tongue, language"] — **lin•gual•ly** \-ē\ *adv*

lin•guist \ˈling-gwəst\ *n* **1** : a person skilled in languages **2** : one who specializes in linguistics

\ə\ **abut**	\au̇\ **out**	\i\ **tip**	\ȯ\ **saw**	\u̇\ **foot**
\ər\ **further**	\ch\ **chin**	\ī\ **life**	\ȯi\ **coin**	\y\ **yet**
\a\ **mat**	\e\ **pet**	\j\ **job**	\th\ **thin**	\yü\ **few**
\ā\ **take**	\ē\ **easy**	\ng\ **sing**	\t͟h\ **this**	\yu̇\ **cure**
\ä\ **cot, cart**	\g\ **go**	\ō\ **bone**	\ü\ **food**	\zh\ **vision**

lin•guis•tic \liŋ-ˈgwis-tik\ *adj* : of or relating to language or linguistics — **lin•guis•ti•cal•ly** \-ti-kə-lē, -klē\ *adv*
linguistic form *n* : a meaningful unit of speech (as a morpheme, word, or sentence)
lin•guis•tics \liŋ-ˈgwis-tiks\ *n* : the study of human speech including the units, nature, structure, and modification of language
lin•i•ment \ˈlin-ə-mənt\ *n* : a preparation that is thinner in consistency than an ointment and is used on the skin especially to relieve pain [Late Latin *linimentum,* from Latin *linere* "to smear"]
lin•ing \ˈlī-niŋ\ *n* : material used to line something (as a garment)
[1]link \ˈliŋk\ *n* **1** : a connecting structure: as **a** : a single ring or division of a chain **b** : a division of a surveyor's chain that is 7.92 inches (about 20.12 centimeters) long and is used as a measure of length **c** : a usually ornamental device for fastening a cuff **d** : BOND 3b **e** : an intermediate rod or piece for transmitting force or motion **2** : something resembling a link of chain: as **a** : a segment of sausage in a chain **b** : a connecting element ⟨a *link* with the past⟩ [of Scandinavian origin]
[2]link *vb* : to join by or as if by a link : UNITE — **link•er** *n*
link•age \ˈliŋ-kij\ *n* **1** : the manner or style of being united: as **a** : the manner in which atoms or radicals are linked in a molecule **b** : BOND 3b **2** : the quality or state of being linked; *esp* : the occurrence of genes on the same chromosome so that they tend to be inherited and expressed together **3** : a system of links; *esp* : a system of links or bars jointed together by means of which lines or curves may be traced
linked \ˈliŋt, ˈliŋkt\ *adj* : marked by linkage and especially genetic linkage
linking verb *n* : a verb that connects the subject of a sentence with a word or phrase that tells how, what, or where the subject is ⟨the *feel* of "I feel bad," *seems* of "it seems a reasonable request" and *am* of "I am upstairs" are *linking verbs*⟩
links \ˈliŋs, ˈliŋks\ *n pl* : a golf course [Old English *hlinc* "ridge, hill"]
link•up \ˈliŋ-ˌkəp\ *n* **1** : establishment of contact : MEETING **2** : something that serves as a linking device or factor
Lin•nae•an *or* **Lin•ne•an** \lə-ˈnē-ən, -ˈnā-; ˈlin-ē-\ *adj* : of, relating to, or following the method of the Swedish botanist Linnaeus who established the system of binomial nomenclature [Carolus *Linnaeus* (Carl von Linné)]
lin•net \ˈlin-ət\ *n* : a common small Old World finch with variable plumage [Middle French *linette,* from *lin* "flax", from Latin *linum*]
lin•ole•ic acid \ˌlin-ə-ˌlē-ik-, -ˌlā-\ *n* : a liquid unsaturated fatty acid found in various oils and held to be essential in animal nutrition [Greek *linon* "flax" + English *oleic acid*]
lin•ole•nic acid \-ˌlē-nik-, -ˌlā-\ *n* : a liquid unsaturated fatty acid found especially in drying oils and held to be essential in animal nutrition [derived from *linoleic acid*]
li•no•leum \lə-ˈnō-lē-əm, -ˈnōl-yəm\ *n* : a floor covering with a canvas back and a surface of hardened linseed oil and a filler (as cork dust) [Latin *linum* "flax" + *oleum* "oil"]
Li•no•type \ˈlī-nə-ˌtīp\ *trademark* — used for a keyboard-operated typesetting machine that uses circulating matrices and produces each line of type in the form of a solid metal slug
lin•seed \ˈlin-ˌsēd\ *n* : FLAXSEED [Old English *līnsǣd,* from *līn* "flax" + *sǣd* "seed"]
linseed oil *n* : a yellowish drying oil obtained from flaxseed and used especially in paint, varnish, printing ink, and linoleum
lin•sey–wool•sey \ˌlin-zē-ˈwu̇l-zē\ *n* : a coarse sturdy fabric of wool and linen or cotton [Middle English *lynsy wolsye*]
lint \ˈlint\ *n* **1 a** : a soft fleecy material made from linen usually by scraping **b** : fuzz consisting of short fibers from yarn and fabric **2** : fibers forming a close thick coating about cotton seeds and constituting the staple of cotton [Middle English] — **linty** \-ē\ *adj*
lin•tel \ˈlint-l\ *n* : a horizontal piece across the top of an opening (as of a door) that carries the weight of the structure above it [Middle French, from Late Latin *limitaris* "threshold", from Latin *limit-, limes* "boundary"]
lint•er \ˈlint-ər\ *n* **1** : a machine for removing linters **2** *pl* : the fuzz of short fibers that adheres to cottonseed after ginning
li•on \ˈlī-ən\ *n, pl* **lion** *or* **lions 1 a** : a large tawny flesh-eating chiefly nocturnal cat of open or rocky areas of Africa and especially formerly southern Asia with a tufted tail and a shaggy mane in the male **b** : any of several large wildcats; *esp* : COUGAR **2 a** : a person held to resemble a lion (as in courage or ferocity) **b** : a person of outstanding interest or importance ⟨a literary *lion*⟩ **3** *cap* : a member of one of the major service clubs [Old French, from Latin *leo,* from Greek *leōn*] — **li•on•ess** \ˈlī-ə-nəs\ *n* — **li•on•like** \ˈlī-ən-ˌlīk\ *adj*

1 lintel

li•on•heart•ed \ˌlī-ən-ˈhärt-əd\ *adj* : BOLD 1, COURAGEOUS
li•on•ize \ˈlī-ə-ˌnīz\ *vt* : to treat as an object of great interest or importance — **li•on•iza•tion** \ˌlī-ə-nə-ˈzā-shən\ *n*
lion's share *n* : the largest portion
[1]lip \ˈlip\ *n* **1** : either of the two fleshy folds that surround the mouth **2** *slang* : BACK TALK **3 a** : a fleshy edge or margin ⟨*lips* of a wound⟩ **b** : LABIUM 2; *also* : the protruding part of an irregular corolla (as of an orchid) **4 a** : the edge of a hollow vessel especially where it flares slightly **b** : a projecting edge ⟨the *lip* of a cliff⟩ **c** : a short open spout (as on a pitcher) **5** : EMBOUCHURE 1 [Old English *lippa*] — **lip•less** \-ləs\ *adj* — **lip-like** \-ˌlīk\ *adj*
[2]lip *adj* **1** : spoken with the lips only : INSINCERE ⟨*lip* praise⟩ **2** : produced with the lips : LABIAL ⟨*lip* consonants⟩
[3]lip *vt* **lipped; lip•ping 1** : to touch with the lips; *esp* : KISS **2** : to speak usually softly
lip- *or* **lipo-** *combining form* : fat : fatty tissue : fatty ⟨*lipoma*⟩ [Greek *lipos*]
li•pase \ˈlī-ˌpās, -ˌpāz\ *n* : an enzyme that functions especially in the breakdown or digestion of fats
lip•id \ˈlip-əd\ *n* : any of various substances including fats, waxes, and phosphatides that with proteins and carbohydrates constitute the principal structural components of living cells
li•poid \ˈlī-ˌpȯid, ˈlip-ˌȯid\ *n* : LIPID — **lipoid** *or* **li•poi•dal** \lī-ˈpȯid-l, lip-ˈȯid-\ *adj*
li•po•ma \lī-ˈpō-mə, lip-ˈō-\ *n, pl* **-mas** *or* **-ma•ta** \-mət-ə\ : a tumor of fatty tissue — **li•po•ma•tous** \-mət-əs\ *adj*
li•po•pro•tein \ˌlī-pō-ˈprō-ˌtēn, ˌlip-ō-, -ˈprōt-ē-ən\ *n* : a protein containing a lipid group
lipped \ˈlipt\ *adj* : having lips or a lip : having such or so many lips ⟨tight-*lipped*⟩ ⟨a 2-*lipped* corolla⟩
lip•py \ˈlip-ē\ *adj* **lip•pi•er; -est** : given to back talk
lip•read•ing \ˈlip-ˌrēd-iŋ\ *n* : interpretation of speech by watching the speaker's lip and facial movements — **lip–read** *vb* — **lip–read•er** *n*
lip service *n* : a declaration of allegiance not matched by action
lip•stick \ˈlip-ˌstik\ *n* : a waxy solid usually colored cosmetic in stick form for the lips; *also* : this cosmetic with its case
liq•ue•fac•tion \ˌlik-wə-ˈfak-shən\ *n* **1** : the process of making or becoming liquid **2** : the state of being liquid [Late Latin *liquefactio,* from Latin *liquefacere* "to liquefy"]
liquefied petroleum gas *n* : a compressed gas consisting of flammable light hydrocarbons and used especially as fuel or as raw material for chemical synthesis
liq•ue•fy *also* **liq•ui•fy** \ˈlik-wə-ˌfī\ *vb* **-fied; -fy•ing** : to make or become liquid [Middle French *liquefier,* from Latin *liquefacere,* from *liquēre* "to be fluid" + *facere* "to make"] — **liq•ue•fi•able** \-ˌfī-ə-bəl\ *adj* — **liq•ue•fi•er** \-ˌfī-ər, -ˌfīr\ *n*
li•queur \li-ˈkər, -ˈkyu̇r, -ˈku̇r\ *n* : an alcoholic beverage flavored with aromatic substances and usually sweetened [French, literally, "liquor, liquid", from Latin *liquor*]
[1]liq•uid \ˈlik-wəd\ *adj* **1** : flowing freely like water **2** : neither solid nor gaseous : characterized by free movement of the constituent molecules among themselves but without the tendency to separate that characterizes gases ⟨*liquid* mercury⟩ **3 a** : shining clear ⟨large *liquid* eyes⟩ **b** : being musical and free of harshness in sound **c** : smooth and unconstrained in movement **d** : pronounced without friction and capable of being prolonged like a vowel ⟨the *liquid* consonant \l\⟩ **4** : consisting of or capable of ready conversion into cash ⟨*liquid* assets⟩ [Middle French *liquide,* from Latin *liquidus,* from *liquēre* "to be fluid"] — **li•quid•i•ty** \lik-ˈwid-ət-ē\ *n* — **liq•uid•ly** \ˈlik-wəd-lē\ *adv* — **liq•uid•ness** *n*
[2]liquid *n* **1** : a liquid substance **2** : a liquid consonant
liquid air *n* : air in the liquid state prepared by subjecting it to

great pressure and then cooling it by its own expansion and used chiefly as a refrigerant

liq·ui·date \ˈlik-wə-ˌdāt\ *vt* **1** : to pay off ⟨*liquidate* a debt⟩ **2** : to bring (as a business) to an end by selling off assets, paying debts, and dividing any remainder among the owners **3 a** : to dispose of ⟨*liquidate* doubt by explanation⟩ **b** : to get rid of by force or violence; *esp* : to murder as a political measure [Late Latin *liquidare* "to melt", from Latin *liquidus* "liquid"] — **liq·ui·da·tion** \ˌlik-wə-ˈdā-shən\ *n* — **liq·ui·da·tor** \ˈlik-wə-ˌdāt-ər\ *n*

liquid measure *n* **1** : a unit or series of units for measuring liquid capacity — see MEASURE table, METRIC SYSTEM table **2** : a measure for liquids

[1]**li·quor** \ˈlik-ər\ *n* : a liquid substance; *esp* : a distilled alcoholic beverage [Old French *licour,* from Latin *liquor,* from *liquēre* "to be fluid"]

[2]**liquor** *vb* **li·quored**; **li·quor·ing** \ˈlik-ring, -ə-ring\ : to make or become drunk with alcoholic liquor — usually used with *up*

li·quo·rice *chiefly British variant of* LICORICE

li·ra \ˈlir-ə, ˈlē-rə\ **1** *pl* **li·re** \ˈlē-rā\ *also* **liras** : the basic monetary unit of Italy **2** *pl* **liras** *also* **lire** : the basic monetary unit of Turkey **3** : a coin or note representing one lira [Italian, from Latin *libra* "pound"]

lisle \ˈlīl\ *n* : a smooth tightly twisted thread usually made of long-staple cotton [*Lisle* "Lille, France"]

[1]**lisp** \ˈlisp\ *vb* **1** : to pronounce \s\ and \z\ imperfectly especially by giving them the sound of \th\ and \t͟h\ **2** : to speak falteringly, childishly, or with a lisp [Old English *-wlyspian*] — **lisp·er** *n*

[2]**lisp** *n* **1** : a speech defect or mannerism marked by lisping **2** : a sound resembling a lisp

lis·some *also* **lis·som** \ˈlis-əm\ *adj* **1** : LITHE 1 **2** : NIMBLE 1 [alteration of *lithesome*] — **lis·some·ly** *adv* — **lis·some·ness** *n*

[1]**list** \ˈlist\ *vb* **1** : LISTEN **2** : to listen to : HEAR [Old English *hlystan,* from *hlyst* "hearing", from *hlysnan* "to listen"]

[2]**list** *n* **1** : a band or strip of material; *esp* : SELVAGE **2** *pl* **a** : an arena for jousting **b** : an arena for combat ⟨entered the *lists*⟩ **c** : a field of competition or controversy [Old English *līste* "border"]

[3]**list** *n* : a roll, record, or catalog of names or objects ⟨*guest* list⟩ ⟨*grocery* list⟩ [French *liste,* from Italian *lista,* of Germanic origin]

[4]**list** *vb* **1 a** : to make a list of : ENUMERATE **b** : to include on a list : REGISTER ⟨securities *listed* on the exchange⟩ **2 a** : to place (oneself) in a specified category **b** : to have a list price ⟨a coat that *lists* for $75⟩

[5]**list** *vb* : to lean or cause to lean to one side : TILT ⟨a ship *listing* to port⟩ [origin unknown]

[6]**list** *n* : a deviation from the vertical : TILT

lis·ten \ˈlis-n\ *vi* **lis·tened**; **lis·ten·ing** \ˈlis-ning, -n-ing\ **1** : to pay attention in order to hear ⟨*listen* for a signal⟩ ⟨*listen* to a record⟩ **2** : to give heed : follow advice ⟨*listen* to a warning⟩ [Old English *hlysnan* "to hear"] **syn** see HEAR — **lis·ten·er** \ˈlis-nər, -n-ər\ *n*

listen in *vi* **1** : to tune in to or monitor a broadcast **2** : to listen to a conversation without participating in it; *esp* : EAVESDROP — **lis·ten·er–in** \ˌlis-nər-ˈin, -n-ər-\ *n*

list·er \ˈlis-tər\ *n* : a double-moldboard plow that throws up ridges of earth on both sides of the furrow [derived from Old English *līste* "border"]

list·ing \ˈlis-ting\ *n* **1** : an act or instance of making or including in a list **2** : something listed

list·less \ˈlist-ləs\ *adj* : marked by lack of energy or willingness to exert oneself : LANGUID [Middle English *list* "desire, inclination"] — **list·less·ly** *adv* — **list·less·ness** *n*

list price *n* : a price of an item published (as in a catalog or advertisement) but subject to discounts

lit *past of* LIGHT

lit·a·ny \ˈlit-n-ē\ *n, pl* **-nies** **1** : a prayer consisting of a series of supplications and responses said alternately by a leader and a group **2** : a resonant or repetitive recital ⟨a *litany* of objections⟩ [Old French *letanie,* from Late Latin *litania,* from Greek *litaneia* "entreaty"]

li·tchi *also* **li·chee** \ˈlī-chē, ˈlē-\ *n* : the oval fruit of an Asian tree having a hard outer covering and a seed surrounded by sweetish edible flesh that when dried is firm and black; *also* : the tree bearing this fruit [Chinese (Pekingese dialect) *li*[4] *chih*[1]]

-lite \ˌlīt\ *n combining form* : mineral : rock : fossil ⟨cryo*lite*⟩ [French, from Greek *lithos* "stone"]

li·ter *or* **li·tre** \ˈlēt-ər\ *n* : a metric unit of capacity equal to one cubic decimeter — see METRIC SYSTEM table [French *litre,* from Medieval Latin *litra,* a measure, from Greek, a weight]

lit·er·a·cy \ˈlit-ə-rə-sē, ˈli-trə-sē\ *n* : the quality or state of being literate

lit·er·al \ˈlit-ə-rəl, ˈli-trəl\ *adj* **1 a** : according with the letter of the scriptures **b** : following the ordinary or usual meaning of a term or expression **c** : FACTUAL 2, ACCURATE **d** : concerned mainly with facts : PROSAIC ⟨a very *literal* person⟩ **e** : UNVARNISHED 1, PLAIN **2** : of, relating to, or expressed in letters **3** : reproduced word for word ⟨a *literal* translation⟩ [Middle French, from Latin *litteralis* "of a letter", from *littera* "letter"] — **lit·er·al·ly** \-ē\ *adv* — **lit·er·al·ness** *n*

lit·er·al·ism \ˈlit-ə-rə-ˌliz-əm, ˈli-trə-\ *n* **1** : adherence to the exact meaning of an idea or expression **2** : fidelity to fact : REALISM — **lit·er·al·ist** \-ləst\ *n* — **lit·er·al·is·tic** \ˌlit-ə-rə-ˈlis-tik, ˌli-trə-\ *adj*

lit·er·ary \ˈlit-ə-ˌrer-ē\ *adj* **1 a** : of, relating to, or having the characteristics of literature or humane learning **b** : BOOKISH 2 **2 a** : LITERATE 2a, WELL-READ **b** : of or relating to writers or writing as a profession — **lit·er·ar·i·ly** \ˌlit-ə-ˈrer-ə-lē\ *adv* — **lit·er·ar·i·ness** \ˈlit-ə-ˌrer-ē-nəs\ *n*

lit·er·ate \ˈlit-ə-rət, ˈli-trət\ *adj* **1 a** : characterized by education and culture **b** : able to read and write **2 a** : versed in literature or creative writing **b** : showing competence in execution ⟨a *literate* report⟩ — **literate** *n* — **lit·er·ate·ly** *adv*

li·te·ra·ti \ˌlit-ə-ˈrät-ē\ *n pl* **1** : INTELLIGENTSIA **2** : distinguished scholars and writers [obsolete Italian *litterati,* from Latin *litteratus* "literate", from *littera* "letter"]

lit·er·a·tim \ˌlit-ə-ˈrāt-əm, -ˈrät-\ *adv or adj* : letter for letter [Medieval Latin, from Latin *littera* "letter"]

lit·er·a·ture \ˈlit-ə-rə-ˌchu̇r, ˈli-trə-, -chər\ *n* **1** : the writing of literary work especially as an occupation **2 a** : writings in prose or verse; *esp* : writings that are excellent in form or expression and that set forth ideas of permanent or universal interest **b** : the body of writings on a particular subject ⟨medical *literature*⟩ **c** : printed matter (as leaflets or circulars) **3** : a whole body of musical compositions

lith- *or* **litho-** *combining form* : stone ⟨*litho*logy⟩ [Greek *lithos*]

-lith \ˌlith\ *n combining form* **1** : structure or implement of stone ⟨mega*lith*⟩ **2** : calculus ⟨oto*lith*⟩ **3** : -LITE ⟨rego*lith*⟩ [Greek *lithos* "stone"]

li·tharge \ˈlith-ˌärj, lith-ˈ\ *n* : LEAD MONOXIDE [Middle French, from Latin *lithargyrus,* from Greek *lithargyros,* from *lithos* "stone" + *argyros* "silver"]

lithe \ˈlīt͟h, ˈlīth\ *adj* **1** : easily bent : FLEXIBLE ⟨long *lithe* stems⟩ **2** : gracefully limber : SUPPLE ⟨*lithe* dancers⟩ [Old English *līthe* "gentle"] — **lithe·ly** *adv* — **lithe·ness** *n*

lithe·some \ˈlīt͟h-səm, ˈlīth-\ *adj* : LITHE 2

lith·ia \ˈlith-ē-ə\ *n* : an oxide of lithium occurring as a white crystalline substance [New Latin, from Greek *lithos* "stone"]

lith·ic \ˈlith-ik\ *adj* **1** : of, relating to, or made of stone **2** : of or relating to lithium — **lith·i·cal·ly** \ˈlith-i-kə-lē, -klē\ *adv*

-lithic \ˈlith-ik\ *adj combining form* : relating to or characteristic of a (specified) stage in the use of stone as a cultural tool by humans ⟨Neo*lithic*⟩

lith·i·um \ˈlith-ē-əm\ *n* : a soft silver-white univalent chemical element that is the lightest metal known and is used especially in nuclear reactions and metallurgy — see ELEMENT table [New Latin, from *lithia*]

[1]**litho·graph** \ˈlith-ə-ˌgraf\ *vt* : to produce, copy, or portray by lithography — **li·thog·ra·pher** \lith-ˈäg-rə-fər, ˈlith-ə-ˌgraf-ər\ *n*

[2]**lithograph** *n* : a print made by lithography — **litho·graph·ic** \ˌlith-ə-ˈgraf-ik\ *adj* — **litho·graph·i·cal·ly** \-ˈgraf-i-kə-lē, -klē\ *adv*

li·thog·ra·phy \lith-ˈäg-rə-fē\ *n* **1** : the process of printing from a flat surface (as a smooth stone or metal plate) on which the image to be printed is ink-receptive and the blank area ink-repellent **2** : PLANOGRAPHY

li·thol·o·gy \lith-ˈäl-ə-jē\ *n* **1** : the study of rocks **2** : the character of a rock formation — **lith·o·log·ic** \ˌlith-ə-ˈläj-ik\ *adj* —

\ə\ **abut**	\au̇\ **out**	\i\ **tip**	\ȯ\ **saw**	\u̇\ **foot**
\ər\ **further**	\ch\ **chin**	\ī\ **life**	\ȯi\ **coin**	\y\ **yet**
\a\ **mat**	\e\ **pet**	\j\ **job**	\th\ **thin**	\yü\ **few**
\ā\ **take**	\ē\ **easy**	\ng\ **sing**	\t͟h\ **this**	\yu̇\ **cure**
\ä\ **cot, cart**	\g\ **go**	\ō\ **bone**	\ü\ **food**	\zh\ **vision**

lith•o•log•i•cal•ly \-'läj-i-kə-lē, -klē\ *adv*
lith•o•pone \'lith-ə-ˌpōn\ *n* : a white pigment consisting essentially of zinc sulfide and barium sulfate [*lith-* + Greek *ponos* "work, artifact"]
litho•sphere \-ˌsfiər\ *n* : the outer part of the solid earth
Lith•u•a•ni•an \ˌlith-ə-'wā-nē-ən, -yə-'wā-, -nyən\ *n* **1** : a native or inhabitant of Lithuania **2** : the Baltic language of the Lithuanian people — **Lithuanian** *adj*
lit•i•gant \'lit-i-gənt\ *n* : a party to a lawsuit
lit•i•gate \'lit-ə-ˌgāt\ *vb* **1** : to carry on a legal contest by judicial process **2** : to contest in law [Latin *litigare,* from *lit-, lis* "lawsuit" + *agere* "to drive, act, do"] — **lit•i•ga•tion** \ˌlit-ə-'gā-shən\ *n*
li•ti•gious \lə-'tij-əs\ *adj* **1 a** : CONTROVERSIAL 2, ARGUMENTATIVE **b** : inclined to engage in lawsuits **2** : of or relating to lawsuits — **li•ti•gious•ly** *adv* — **li•ti•gious•ness** *n*
lit•mus \'lit-məs\ *n* : a coloring matter from lichens that turns red in acid solutions and blue in alkaline solutions and is used as an acid-base indicator [of Scandinavian origin]
litmus paper *n* : paper impregnated with litmus and used as a pH indicator
li•to•tes \'lī́t-ə-ˌtēz, lī-'tōt-ˌēz\ *n, pl* **litotes** : understatement in which an affirmative is expressed by the negative of the contrary (as in "not a bad singer") [Greek *litotēs,* from *litos* "simple"]
litre *variant of* LITER
[1]**lit•ter** \'lit-ər\ *n* **1 a** : a covered and curtained couch having shafts that is used for carrying a single passenger **b** : a device (as a stretcher) for carrying a sick or injured person **2 a** : material used as bedding for animals **b** : the uppermost layer of organic debris on the forest floor **3** : the offspring of an animal at one birth **4 a** : trash, wastepaper, or garbage lying about ⟨roadside *litter*⟩ **b** : an untidy accumulation of objects [Old French *litiere,* from *lit* "bed", from Latin *lectus*]
△ **origin** Latin *lectus,* "bed", is the ancestor of English *litter.* From *lectus* comes the French *lit,* "bed". *Litiere,* an Old French derivative of *lit,* was used not only for a bed but also for that type of vehicle we call a *litter.* English *litter,* borrowed from the French, originally meant "bed" or "litter (vehicle)". The first sense, "bed", did not survive, but before it became obsolete it gave rise to other senses of *litter.* The straw, hay, or like material laid down or strewn about to serve as bedding was called *litter.* So were the offspring of an animal born, or "bedded", at one time. Once *litter* had been applied to straw laid down for bedding, it was not farfetched to use the word for any odds and ends of rubbish lying scattered about.
[2]**litter** *vb* **1** : to give birth to young **2 a** : to strew with litter **b** : to scatter about in disorder
lit•ter•a•teur \ˌlit-ə-rə-'tər, ˌli-trə-\ *n* : a literary person; *esp* : a professional writer [French *littérateur*]
lit•ter•bag \'lit-ər-ˌbag\ *n* : a bag used (as in an automobile) for temporary disposal of refuse
lit•ter•bug \'lit-ər-ˌbəg\ *n* : one who litters a public area
[1]**lit•tle** \'lit-l\ *adj* **lit•tler** \'lit-l-ər, 'lit-lər\ *or* **less** \'les\ *or* **less•er** \'les-ər\; **lit•tlest** \'lit-l-əst, 'lit-ləst\ *or* **least** \'lēst\ **1 a** : small in size or extent : TINY **b** : small in comparison with related forms ⟨*little* blue heron⟩ **c** : small in number **d** : small in condition, distinction, or scope **e** : NARROW, MEAN ⟨the pettiness of *little* minds⟩ **f** : pleasingly small ⟨a cute *little* thing⟩ **2 a** : small in quantity or degree : not much ⟨have *little* money⟩ **b** : short in duration : BRIEF **3** : small in importance or interest : TRIVIAL [Old English *lȳtel*] **syn** see SMALL — **lit•tle•ness** \'lit-l-nəs\ *n*
[2]**little** *adv* **less** \'les\ *or* **les•ser** \'les-ər\; **least** \'lēst\ **1 a** : in only a small quantity or degree : SLIGHTLY ⟨*little* known facts⟩ **b** : not at all ⟨cared *little* for them⟩ **2** : INFREQUENTLY, RARELY ⟨saw them very *little*⟩
[3]**little** *n* **1** : a small amount or quantity **2** : a short time or distance — **a little** : [2]SOMEWHAT, RATHER — **in little** : on a small scale; *esp* : in miniature
Little Bear *n* : URSA MINOR
Little Dipper *n* : DIPPER 2b
Little Hours *n pl* : the offices of prime, terce, sext, and none forming part of the canonical hours
Little League *n* : a commercially sponsored baseball league for children from 8 to 12 years old — **Little Leaguer** *n*
little slam *n* : the winning of all tricks except one in bridge
little theater *n* : a small theater for low-cost dramatic productions designed for fairly limited audiences
[1]**lit•to•ral** \'lit-ə-rəl; ˌlit-ə-'ral, -'räl\ *adj* : of, relating to, or situated or growing on or near a shore especially of the sea [Latin *litoralis,* from *litor-, litus* "seashore"]
[2]**littoral** *n* : a coastal region
li•tur•gi•cal \lə-'tər-ji-kəl\ *adj* **1** : of, relating to, or having the characteristics of liturgy **2** : using or favoring the use of liturgy — **li•tur•gi•cal•ly** \-kə-lē, -klē\ *adv*
lit•ur•gist \'lit-ər-jəst\ *n* : one who adheres to, compiles, or leads a liturgy
lit•ur•gy \'lit-ər-jē\ *n, pl* **-gies 1** *often cap* : a communion rite **2** : a rite or body of rites prescribed for public worship [Late Latin *liturgia,* from Greek *leitourgia* "public service, divine service"]
liv•abil•i•ty \ˌliv-ə-'bil-ət-ē\ *n* **1** : survival expectancy : VIABILITY **2** : suitability for human living
liv•able *also* **live•able** \'liv-ə-bəl\ *adj* **1** : suitable for living in or with **2** : ENDURABLE — **liv•able•ness** *n*
[1]**live** \'liv\ *vb* **1** : to be or continue alive : have life **2** : to maintain oneself : SUBSIST ⟨*live* on fruits⟩ **3** : to conduct or pass one's life ⟨*lived* up to their principles⟩ **4** : to occupy a home : RESIDE **5** : to attain eternal life **6** : to remain in human memory or record **7** : to have a life rich in experience **8** : COHABIT **9** : to pass through or spend the duration of **10** : PRACTICE ⟨*live* what you preach⟩ **11** : to exhibit vigor, gusto, or enthusiasm in [Old English *libban*]
[2]**live** \'līv\ *adj* **1** : having life : LIVING **2** : abounding with life : VIVID **3** : exerting force or containing energy: as **a** : AFIRE, GLOWING ⟨*live* coals⟩ **b** : carrying an electric current ⟨a *live* wire⟩ **c** : charged with explosives and containing shot or a bullet ⟨*live* ammunition⟩; *also* : UNEXPLODED ⟨*live* bomb⟩ **d** : rotating or imparting motion ⟨a *live* spindle⟩ **e** : power-driven ⟨a *live* axle⟩ **4** : of continuing or current interest : UNCLOSED ⟨*live* issue⟩ **5** : being in the native uncut state ⟨*live* rock⟩ **6** : of bright vivid color **7** : being in play ⟨a *live* ball⟩ **8 a** : of or involving the actual presence of real people ⟨*live* audience⟩ **b** : broadcast directly at the time of production instead of from recorded or filmed material ⟨a *live* television program⟩ [short for *alive*]
live–bear•ing \'līv-'baər-ing, -'beər-\ *adj* : VIVIPAROUS — **live–bear•er** \-ˌbar-ər, -ˌber-\ *n*
lived \'līvd, 'livd\ *adj* : having a life of a specified kind or length ⟨long-*lived*⟩
live down *vt* : to live so as to wipe out the memory or effects of ⟨*live down* a mistake⟩
live–for•ev•er \'liv-fə-ˌrev-ər\ *n* : SEDUM
live•li•hood \'līv-lē-ˌhu̇d\ *n* : means of support or subsistence ⟨an honest *livelihood*⟩ [Old English *līflād* "course of life", from *līf* "life" + *lād* "course"]
live•long \ˌliv-ˌlȯng\ *adj* : WHOLE, ENTIRE ⟨the *livelong* day⟩ [Middle English *lef long,* from *lef* "dear" + *long* "long"]
live•ly \'līv-lē\ *adj* **live•li•er**; **-est 1** : full of life or vigor : ACTIVE, ALERT **2** : KEEN, INTENSE ⟨a *lively* interest in sports⟩ **3** : SPIRITED, BRILLIANT ⟨a *lively* wit⟩ **4** : quick to rebound : RESILIENT — **live•li•ly** \'līv-lə-lē\ *adv* — **live•li•ness** \'līv-lē-nəs\ *n* — **lively** *adv*
• **syn** LIVELY, ANIMATED, VIVACIOUS mean being keenly alive. LIVELY suggests briskness, alertness, or energy; ANIMATED applies to what is spirited, active, or vigorous ⟨an *animated* conversation⟩ VIVACIOUS suggests attractive gaiety and quickness of gesture and wit.
liv•en \'lī-vən\ *vb* **liv•ened**; **liv•en•ing** \'līv-ning, -ə-ning\ : to make or become lively
live oak \'līv-ˌōk\ *n* : any of several American evergreen oaks
[1]**liv•er** \'liv-ər\ *n* **1 a** : a large vascular glandular organ of vertebrates that secretes bile and regulates the concentration of various blood substances (as by converting sugars into glycogen) **b** : any of various large probably digestive glands of invertebrate animals **2** : the tissue of the liver (as of a calf or pig) eaten as food [Old English *lifer*] — **liv•ered** \-ərd\ *adj*
[2]**liv•er** \'liv-ər\ *n* : one that lives in a specified way ⟨a fast *liver*⟩
liver fluke *n* : any of various flatworms that invade the liver of mammals
liv•er•ied \'liv-rēd, -ə-rēd\ *adj* : wearing a livery ⟨a *liveried* chauffeur⟩
liv•er•ish \'liv-rish, -ə-rish\ *adj* **1** : suffering from liver disorder : BILIOUS **2** : CROSS 3, MELANCHOLY — **liv•er•ish•ness** *n*
liv•er•wort \'liv-ər-ˌwərt, -ˌwȯrt\ *n* : any of a class (Hepaticae) of bryophytes resembling the related mosses but differing especially in reproduction and development

liv•er•wurst \ˈliv-ər-ˌwərst, ˈliv-ə-, -ˌwu̇rst, -ˌwu̇st, -ˌwu̇sht\ *n* : sausage consisting chiefly of liver [German *leberwurst,* from *leber* "liver" + *wurst* "sausage"]

liv•ery \ˈliv-rē, -ə-rē\ *n, pl* **-er•ies** **1** : a special uniform worn by the servants of a wealthy household ⟨a footman in *livery*⟩ **2** : distinctive dress ⟨the *livery* of a school⟩ **3 a** : the feeding, care, and stabling of horses for pay; *also* : the keeping of horses and vehicles for hire **b** : LIVERY STABLE [Old French *livree* "delivery, allotment of provisions to servants", from *livrer* "to deliver", from Latin *liberare* "to liberate"]

liv•ery•man \-mən\ *n* : the keeper of a livery stable

livery stable *n* : a stable where horses and vehicles are kept for hire and where stabling is provided

lives *pl of* LIFE

live steam *n* : steam direct from a boiler and under full pressure

live•stock \ˈlīv-ˌstäk\ *n* : animals kept or raised for use or pleasure; *esp* : farm animals kept for use and profit

live wire *n* : an alert, active, and aggressive person

liv•id \ˈliv-əd\ *adj* **1** : discolored by bruising : BLACK-AND-BLUE **2** : ASHEN, PALLID ⟨*livid* with fear⟩ **3** : very angry [French *livide,* from Latin *lividus,* from *livēre* "to be blue"] — **li•vid•i•ty** \liv-ˈid-ət-ē\ *n* — **liv•id•ly** \ˈliv-əd-lē\ *adv* — **liv•id•ness** *n*

1**liv•ing** \ˈliv-iŋ\ *adj* **1 a** : having life **b** : ACTIVE ⟨a *living* language⟩ **2** : exhibiting the life or motion of nature : NATURAL **3 a** : full of life or vigor ⟨made mathematics a *living* subject⟩ **b** : true to life : VIVID **4** : VERY — used as an intensive

2**living** *n* **1** : the condition of being alive **2** : conduct or manner of life **3** : means of subsistence : LIVELIHOOD

living fossil *n* : an animal or plant (as the horseshoe crab or ginkgo tree) that has remained almost unchanged from earlier geologic times and whose near relatives are nearly all extinct

living room *n* : a room in a residence used for the common social activities of the occupants

living wage *n* : a wage sufficient to provide the necessities and comforts held to comprise an acceptable standard of living

liz•ard \ˈliz-ərd\ *n* : any of a group (Lacertilia) of reptiles distinguished from the related snakes by a fused inseparable lower jaw, external ears, eyes with movable lids, and usually two pairs of functional limbs [Middle French *laisarde,* from Latin *lacerta*]

'll \l, ᵊl, əl\ *vb* : WILL ⟨it'*ll* do for now⟩ : SHALL ⟨I'*ll* be there⟩

lla•ma \ˈläm-ə\ *n* : any of several wild and domesticated South American cud-chewing mammals related to the camels but smaller and without a hump; *esp* : one domesticated in the Andes and used as a beast of burden and a source of food [Spanish, from Quechua]

llama

lla•no \ˈlän-ō, ˈlan-\ *n, pl* **llanos** : an open grassy plain especially of Spanish America [Spanish, "plain", from Latin *planum*]

lo \ˈlō\ *interj* — used to call attention or to express wonder or surprise [Old English *lā*]

loach \ˈlōch\ *n* : any of a family of small Old World freshwater fishes related to the carps [Middle French *loche*]

1**load** \ˈlōd\ *n* **1 a** : whatever is put on a person or pack animal to be carried : PACK **b** : whatever is put in a ship or vehicle or airplane for conveyance : CARGO; *esp* : a quantity of material assembled or packed as a shipping unit **c** : the quantity that can be carried at one time by a specified means — often used in combination ⟨a boat*load* of tourists⟩ **2** : a mass or weight supported by something **3 a** : something that weighs down the mind or spirits ⟨a *load* of care⟩ **b** : a burdensome or laborious responsibility **4** : a large quantity : LOT — usually used in pl. **5 a** : a charge for a firearm **b** : the quantity of material loaded into a device at one time **6** : external resistance overcome by a machine **7 a** : power output (as of a power plant) **b** : a device to which power is delivered **8 a** : the amount of work that a person, department, or machine performs or is expected to perform **b** : the demand upon the operating resources of a system (as a telephone exchange or a refrigerating apparatus) **9** *slang* : EYEFUL ⟨get a *load* of that⟩ [Old English *lād* "way, course, act of carrying"]

2**load** *vb* **1 a** : to put a load in or on; *also* : to receive a load **b** : to place in or on a means of conveyance or in a container ⟨*load* freight⟩ ⟨*load* film in a camera⟩ **2 a** : to encumber or oppress with something heavy, laborious, or disheartening : BURDEN **b** : to place as a burden or obligation ⟨*load* more work on us⟩ **3 a** : to increase the weight of by adding something heavy **b** : BIAS ⟨*loaded* questions⟩ **c** : to weight (as a test) with factors influencing validity or outcome **4** : to supply in abundance or excess : HEAP **5** : to alter by adding an adulterant or drug — **load•er** *n*

load•ed *adj* **1** *slang* : DRUNK **2** : having a large amount of money

load line *n* : the line on a ship indicating the depth to which it sinks in the water when properly loaded

load•star *variant of* LODESTAR

load•stone *variant of* LODESTONE

1**loaf** \ˈlōf\ *n, pl* **loaves** \ˈlōvz\ **1** : a shaped or molded mass of bread **2** : a regularly molded often rectangular mass: as **a** : a conical mass of sugar **b** : a dish (as of meat or fish) baked in the form of a loaf [Old English *hlāf*]

2**loaf** *vb* **1** : to spend time in idleness : LOUNGE **2** : to pass idly ⟨*loaf* the time away⟩ [probably back-formation from *loafer*]

loaf•er \ˈlō-fər\ *n* : one that loafs : IDLER [perhaps from German *landläufer* "tramp", from *land* "land" + *läufer* "runner"]

Loaf•er \ˈlō-fər\ *trademark* — used for a low leather step-in shoe

loam \ˈlōm, ˈlüm\ *n* : SOIL; *esp* : a soil consisting of a crumbly mixture of varying proportions of clay, silt, and sand [Old English *lām*] — **loamy** \ˈlō-mē, ˈlü-\ *adj*

1**loan** \ˈlōn\ *n* **1 a** : money let out at interest **b** : something loaned for the borrower's temporary use **2** : the grant of temporary use [Old Norse *lān*]

2**loan** *vt* : to give for temporary possession or use

loan shark *n* : a person who lends money at excessive rates of interest

loan•word \ˈlōn-ˌwərd\ *n* : a word taken from another language and at least partly naturalized

loath *or* **loth** \ˈlōth, ˈlō*th*\ *adj* : very unwilling or reluctant ⟨was *loath* to run for office again⟩ [Old English *lāth* "hateful, hostile"]

loathe \ˈlō*th*\ *vt* : to dislike greatly and often with disgust or intolerance : DETEST ⟨*loathe* the smell of burning rubber⟩ [Old English *lāthian,* from *lāth* "hateful"] **syn** see HATE

loath•ing \ˈlō-*th*iŋ\ *n* : extreme disgust : DETESTATION

1**loath•ly** \ˈlō*th*-lē, ˈlōth-\ *adj* : LOATHSOME, REPULSIVE

2**loath•ly** \ˈlōth-lē, ˈlō*th*-\ *adv* : not willingly

loath•some \ˈlōth-səm, ˈlō*th*-\ *adj* : utterly disgusting — **loath•some•ly** *adv* — **loath•some•ness** *n*

1**lob** \ˈläb\ *vb* **lobbed; lob•bing** **1 a** : to throw, hit, or propel in a high arc **b** : to propel a ball gently especially in a high arc **2** : to move slowly and heavily [probably of Low German origin]

2**lob** *n* : a ball that is lobbed

1**lob•by** \ˈläb-ē\ *n, pl* **lobbies** **1** : a corridor or hall connected with a larger room or series of rooms and used as a passageway or waiting room: as **a** : an anteroom of a legislative chamber **b** : a large hall serving as a foyer (as of a hotel or theater) **2** : a group of persons engaged in lobbying especially as representatives of a particular interest group [Medieval Latin *lobium* "gallery", of Germanic origin]

2**lobby** *vb* **lob•bied; lob•by•ing** **1** : to try to influence public officials and especially members of a legislative body **2** : to promote or secure the passage of by influencing public officials — **lob•by•ist** \ˈläb-ē-əst\ *n*

lobe \ˈlōb\ *n* : a curved or rounded projection or division; *esp* : such a subdivision of a bodily organ or part [Middle French, from Late Latin *lobus,* from Greek *lobos*] — **lo•bar** \ˈlō-bər, -ˌbär\ *adj* — **lo•bate** \-ˌbāt\ *adj* — **lobed** \ˈlōbd\ *adj*

lobe–fin \ˈlōb-ˌfin\ *n* : any of a large group (Crossopterygii) of mostly extinct fishes that have paired fins suggesting limbs and may be ancestral to the land-dwelling vertebrates — compare LATIMERIA — **lobe–finned** \-ˈfind\ *adj*

lo•be•lia \lō-ˈbēl-yə\ *n* : any of a genus of widely distributed herbs often grown for their terminal clusters of showy lipped

\ə\ **abut**	\au̇\ **out**	\i\ **tip**	\ȯ\ **saw**	\u̇\ **foot**
\ər\ **further**	\ch\ **chin**	\ī\ **life**	\ȯi\ **coin**	\y\ **yet**
\a\ **mat**	\e\ **pet**	\j\ **job**	\th\ **thin**	\yü\ **few**
\ā\ **take**	\ē\ **easy**	\ŋ\ **sing**	*th*\ **this**	\yu̇\ **cure**
\ä\ **cot, cart**	\g\ **go**	\ō\ **bone**	\ü\ **food**	\zh\ **vision**

flowers [Matthias de *Lobel,* died 1616, Flemish botanist]

lob•lol•ly pine \ˌläb-ˌläl-ē-\ *n* : a pine of the southern United States with thick flaky bark, long needles in threes, and spiny-tipped cones; *also* : its coarse-grained wood — called also *loblolly* [English dialect *loblolly* "gruel, mire"]

lo•bot•o•my \lō-ˈbät-ə-mē\ *n, pl* **-mies** : surgical cutting of nerve fibers especially in the frontal lobes of the brain for the relief of some mental disorders

lob•ster \ˈläb-stər\ *n* : any of several large edible marine crustaceans with stalked eyes, a pair of large claws, and a long abdomen; *also* : SPINY LOBSTER [Old English *loppestre,* from *loppe* "spider"]

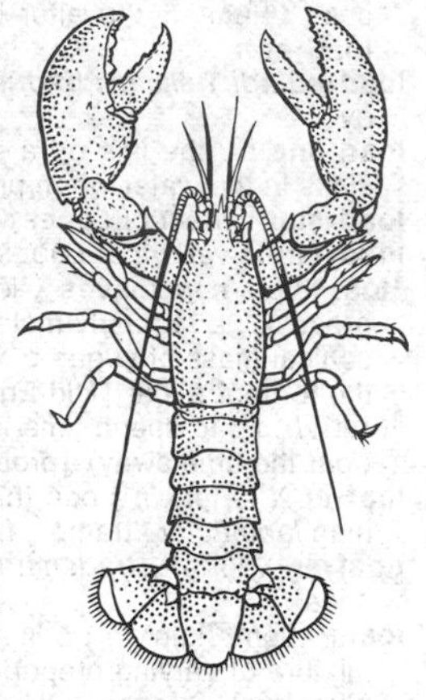

lobster

lobster pot *n* : a trap for catching lobsters

lob•ule \ˈläb-yül\ *n* : a small lobe; *also* : a subdivision of a lobe — **lob•u•lar** \ˈläb-yə-lər\ *adj* — **lob•u•late** \-ˌlāt\ *adj* — **lob•u•la•tion** \ˌläb-yə-ˈlā-shən\ *n*

[1]**lo•cal** \ˈlō-kəl\ *adj* **1** : characterized by or relating to position in space **2** : characterized by, relating to, being from, or occupying a particular place ⟨*local* news⟩ **3** : not broad or general; *esp* : involving or affecting only a small part of the body ⟨a *local* infection⟩ **4 a** : primarily serving the needs of a particular limited district ⟨*local* government⟩ **b** : making all the stops on a run ⟨a *local* train⟩ [Middle French, from Late Latin *localis,* from Latin *locus* "place"] — **lo•cal•ly** \-kə-lē\ *adv*

[2]**local** *n* : a local person or thing: as **a** : a local train or other public conveyance **b** : a local branch, lodge, or chapter (as of a labor union)

local color *n* : features and peculiarities used in a story or play that suggest a particular locality and its inhabitants

lo•cale \lō-ˈkal\ *n* **1** : a place or locality that is the setting for a particular event or characteristic **2** : SITE, SCENE ⟨the *locale* of a story⟩ [French *local,* from *local,* adj., "local"]

lo•cal•ism \ˈlō-kə-ˌliz-əm\ *n* **1** : often undue partiality for one's own locality : SECTIONALISM **2** : a local idiom or peculiarity of speech

lo•cal•i•ty \lō-ˈkal-ət-ē\ *n, pl* **-ties** : a particular spot, situation, or location

lo•cal•ize \ˈlō-kə-ˌlīz\ *vb* : to make or become local : fix in or assign or confine to a definite place or locality ⟨pain *localized* in a joint⟩ — **lo•cal•iza•tion** \ˌlō-kə-lə-ˈzā-shən\ *n*

local option *n* : the power granted by a legislature to a political subdivision to determine by popular vote whether a particular law is to apply locally

lo•cate \ˈlō-ˌkāt, lō-ˈ\ *vb* **1** : to establish oneself or one's business : set or establish in a particular spot **2 a** : to seek out and find the location of **b** : to find the position of (a point) by means of coordinates **3** : to find or fix the place of in a sequence [Latin *locare* "to place", from *locus* "place"] — **lo•cat•er** *n*

lo•ca•tion \lō-ˈkā-shən\ *n* **1** : the process of locating **2** : SITUATION, PLACE; *esp* : a locality of or for a building **3** : a tract of land (as a mining claim) whose boundaries and purpose have been designated **4** : a place outside a studio where a motion picture is filmed ⟨on *location* in the desert⟩ — **lo•ca•tion•al** \-shnəl, -shən-l\ *adj* — **lo•ca•tion•al•ly** \-ē\ *adv*

loc•a•tive \ˈläk-ət-iv\ *adj* : of or being a grammatical case that denotes place — **locative** *n*

loch \ˈläk, ˈläk\ *n* **1** *Scottish* : LAKE **2** *Scottish* : a bay or arm of the sea especially when nearly landlocked [Scottish Gaelic]

loci *pl of* LOCUS

[1]**lock** \ˈläk\ *n* : a strand or ringlet of hair; *also* : a lump of fibers (as of wool) [Old English *locc*]

[2]**lock** *n* **1 a** : a fastening (as for a door) in which a bolt is operated (as by a key) **b** : the mechanism for exploding the charge or cartridge of a firearm **2 a** : an enclosure (as in a canal) with gates at each end used in raising or lowering boats as they pass from level to level **b** : AIR LOCK **3** : a hold in wrestling that prevents movement of a part of the body ⟨a leg *lock*⟩ [Old English *loc*]

[3]**lock** *vb* **1 a** : to fasten the lock of **b** : to make or be made fast with or as if with a lock ⟨*lock* up the house⟩ **2 a** : to shut or keep or make secure or inaccessible by means of locks **b** : to hold fast or inactive : FIX **3 a** : to make fast by the interlacing or interlocking of parts **b** : to hold in a close embrace **c** : to grapple in conflict **4** : to move by raising or lowering in a lock : go or pass by means of a lock (as in a canal)

lock•age \ˈläk-ij\ *n* **1** : an act or the process of passing a ship through a lock **2** : a system of locks

lock•er \ˈläk-ər\ *n* **1 a** : a drawer, cabinet, compartment, or chest usually with a lock **b** : a storage chest or compartment on shipboard **2** : an insulated compartment for storing frozen food at a low temperature **3** : one that locks

locker room *n* : a room containing lockers for personal effects (as clothing); *esp* : a dressing room (as at a bathhouse, country club, or sports arena)

lock•et \ˈläk-ət\ *n* : a small case usually of precious metal that has space for a memento and that is usually worn suspended from a neck chain [Middle French *loquet* "latch", from Dutch *loke*]

lock•jaw \ˈläk-ˌjȯ\ *n* : a symptom of tetanus characterized by spasm of the jaw muscles and inability to open the jaws; *also* : TETANUS 1

lock•nut \ˈläk-ˌnət\ *n* **1** : a nut screwed down tightly on another to prevent it from loosening **2** : a nut constructed to remain fast when tightly screwed down

lock•out \ˈläk-ˌau̇t\ *n* : the suspension of work or closing of a plant by an employer during a labor dispute in order to make the employees accept terms

lock out \läk-ˈau̇t, ˈläk-\ *vt* : to subject (a body of employees) to a lockout

lock•smith \ˈläk-ˌsmith\ *n* : one who makes, repairs, or installs locks

lock•step \ˈläk-ˌstep\ *n* : a way of marching in step in which a body of marchers go one after another as closely as possible

lock•stitch \ˈläk-ˌstich\ *n* : a sewing machine stitch formed by the looping together of two threads one on each side of the material being sewn

lock, stock, and barrel *adv* : WHOLLY 1 ⟨sold out *lock, stock, and barrel*⟩ [from the principal parts of a flintlock]

lock•up \ˈläk-ˌəp\ *n* : JAIL; *esp* : one where persons are detained prior to court hearing

[1]**lo•co** \ˈlō-kō\ *n, pl* **locos** *or* **locoes** **1** : LOCOWEED **2** : LOCOISM [Mexican Spanish, from Spanish, "crazy"]

[2]**loco** *adj, slang* : out of one's mind : CRAZY [Spanish]

lo•co•ism \ˈlō-kō-ˌiz-əm\ *n* : a nervous disease of horses, cattle, and sheep caused by chronic poisoning with locoweeds

lo•co•mo•tion \ˌlō-kə-ˈmō-shən\ *n* : the act or power of moving from place to place [Latin *locus* "place" + English *motion*]

[1]**lo•co•mo•tive** \ˌlō-kə-ˈmōt-iv\ *adj* **1 a** : of, relating to, or functioning in locomotion **b** : having the ability to move independently from place to place **2** : of or relating to travel **3** : of, relating to, or being a machine that moves under its own power

[2]**locomotive** *n* : an engine that moves under its own power; *esp* : one that hauls cars on a railroad

lo•co•mo•tor \ˌlō-kə-ˈmōt-ər\ *adj* **1** : LOCOMOTIVE 1 **2** : affecting or involving the locomotive organs

locomotor ataxia *n* : a syphilitic disorder of the nervous system marked especially by disturbances of gait and difficulty in coordinating voluntary movements

lo•co•weed \ˈlō-kō-ˌwēd\ *n* : any of several plants of the pea family that are found in western North America and cause locoism in livestock

loc•ule \ˈläk-yül\ *n* : LOCULUS; *esp* : any of the cells of a compound ovary of a plant — **loc•uled** \-yüld\ *adj*

loc•u•lus \ˈläk-yə-ləs\ *n, pl* **-li** \-ˌlī, -ˌlē\ : a small chamber or cavity especially in a plant or animal body — compare LOCULE [Latin, "little place", from *locus* "place"]

lo•cum te•nens \ˌlō-kəm-ˈtē-ˌnenz\ *n, pl* **locum te•nen•tes** \-tə-ˈnen-ˌtēz\ : a person (as a doctor or clergyman) filling an office for a time or temporarily taking the place of another [Medieval Latin, literally, "one holding a place"]

lo•cus \ˈlō-kəs\ *n, pl* **lo•ci** \ˈlō-ˌsī, -ˌkī, -ˌkē\ **1** : PLACE 1b, LOCALITY **2** : the set of all points whose location is determined by stated conditions **3** : the position in a chromosome of a particular gene or allele [Latin]

lo•cus clas•si•cus \ˌlō-kəs-ˈklas-i-kəs\ *n, pl* **lo•ci clas•si•ci** \-ˌsī-ˈklas-ə-ˌsī, -ˌkī-ˈklas-ə-ˌkī, -ˌkē-ˈklas-ə-ˌkē\ : a standard passage important for the explanation of a word or subject [New Latin]

lo•cust \'lō-kəst\ *n* **1 a :** SHORT-HORNED GRASSHOPPER; *esp* **:** a migratory grasshopper often traveling in vast swarms and stripping the areas passed of vegetation **b :** CICADA — compare SEVENTEEN-YEAR LOCUST **2 a :** any of various hard-wooded trees of the pea family **b :** the wood of a locust [Latin *locusta*]

lo•cu•tion \lō-'kyü-shən\ *n* **1 :** a particular form of expression or phrasing ⟨involved *locutions*⟩ **2 :** style of discourse **:** PHRASEOLOGY [Latin *locutio,* from *loqui* "to speak"]

lode \'lōd\ *n* **:** an ore deposit [Old English *lād* "way, course, support"]

lode•star *or* **load•star** \-,stär\ *n* **1 :** a star that leads or guides; *esp* **:** NORTH STAR **2 :** one that is a guide or a focus of attention

lode•stone *or* **load•stone** \-,stōn\ *n* **1 :** magnetite having magnetic properties **2 :** something that strongly attracts

1lodge \'läj\ *vb* **1 a :** to provide temporary quarters for **b :** to establish or settle oneself in a place **c :** to rent lodgings to **2 :** to serve as a receptacle for **3 :** to bring or come to a rest and remain ⟨the bone *lodged* in the throat⟩ **4 :** to lay (as a complaint) before a proper authority **5 :** to fall or become beaten down ⟨the tall grass *lodged* in the storm⟩

2lodge *n* **1 a :** a house set apart for residence in a special season ⟨a hunting *lodge*⟩ **b :** a resort hotel **c :** a house for an employee on an estate ⟨a gamekeeper's *lodge*⟩ **2 :** a den or lair especially of a group of gregarious animals **3 :** the meeting place of a branch (as of a fraternal organization); *also* **:** the members of such a branch **4 a :** WIGWAM **b :** a family of North American Indians [Old French *loge* "hut, cabin", of Germanic origin]

lodge•pole pine \,läj-,pōl-\ *n* **:** either of two western North American pines with paired needles and short rough cones

lodg•er \'läj-ər\ *n* **:** one that lodges; *esp* **:** one that occupies a rented room in another's house

lodg•ing \'läj-ing\ *n* **1 :** DWELLING; *esp* **:** a temporary dwelling or sleeping place **2 :** a room or suite of rooms in the house of another person rented as a dwelling place — usually used in pl.

lodging house *n* **:** ROOMING HOUSE

loess \'les, 'lüs, 'lərs, 'lō-əs\ *n* **:** a usually yellowish brown loamy deposit believed to be deposited chiefly by the wind [German *löss*] — **loess•ial** \-ē-əl\ *adj*

1loft \'lȯft\ *n* **1 :** a room or floor above another **:** ATTIC **2 a :** a gallery in a church or hall ⟨an organ *loft*⟩ **b :** an upper floor of a warehouse or business building especially when not partitioned **c :** HAYLOFT **3 a :** the backward slant of the face of a golf-club head **b :** HEIGHT ⟨the ball had too much *loft* to reach the green⟩ [Old Norse *lopt* "air, sky, loft"]

2loft *vb* **1 :** to place, house, or store in a loft **2 :** to strike or throw a ball high into the air ⟨*lofted* a high fly to center field⟩

lofty \'lȯf-tē\ *adj* **loft•i•er; -est 1 :** marked by a haughty overbearing manner ⟨a *lofty* air⟩ **2 a :** elevated in character and spirit ⟨*lofty* ideals⟩ **b :** elevated in position **:** SUPERIOR **3 :** rising high in the air **:** TOWERING ⟨a *lofty* oak⟩ — **loft•i•ly** \-tə-lē\ *adv* — **loft•i•ness** \-tē-nəs\ *n*

1log \'lȯg, 'läg\ *n* **1 :** a bulky piece of unshaped timber; *esp* **:** a long piece of a tree trunk trimmed and ready for sawing **2 :** an apparatus for measuring the rate of a ship's motion through the water that consists of a block fastened to a line and run out from a reel **3 a :** the daily record of a ship's speed and progress **b :** the full record of a ship's voyage or of an aircraft's flight **4 :** a record of performance (as the operating history of an airplane or a piece of equipment, the flying time of a pilot, or a report on the construction of something) [Middle English *logge*] — **log** *adj*

2log *vb* **logged; log•ging 1 :** to cut trees for lumber or clear (land) of trees in lumbering **2 :** to enter details of or about in a log **3 a :** to move (an indicated distance) or attain (an indicated speed) as noted in a log **b** (1) **:** to sail a ship or fly an airplane for (an indicated distance or an indicated period of time) (2) **:** to have (an indicated record) to one's credit ⟨*logged* many hours on combat missions⟩

3log *n* **:** LOGARITHM

lo•gan•ber•ry \'lō-gən-,ber-ē\ *n* **:** a red-fruited upright-growing shrub related to the raspberry; *also* **:** its berry [James H. *Logan,* died 1928, American lawyer]

log•a•rithm \'lȯg-ə-,rit͟h-əm, 'läg-\ *n* **:** the exponent that indicates the power to which a number and especially 10 is raised to produce a given number ⟨the *logarithm* of 100 to the base 10 is 2⟩ [Greek *logos* "word, reckoning" + *arithmos* "number"]

log•a•rith•mic \,lȯg-ə-'rit͟h-mik, ,läg-\ *adj* **:** relating to, based on, or characteristic of logarithms ⟨a *logarithmic* table⟩

log•book \'lȯg-,bu̇k, 'läg-\ *n* **:** a book in which a log is kept; *also* **:** the log itself

loge \'lōzh\ *n* **1 a :** a small compartment **:** BOOTH **b :** a box in a theater **2 a :** a small partitioned area **b :** the forward section of a theater mezzanine [French, "hut, lodge, loge"]

log•ger \'lȯg-ər, 'läg-\ *n* **:** one engaged in logging

log•ger•head \'lȯg-ər-,hed, 'läg-\ *n* **:** any of various very large turtles; *esp* **:** a flesh-eating sea turtle of the warmer parts of the western Atlantic

log•gia \'läj-ē-ə, 'lō-jä\ *n* **:** a roofed gallery open on at least one side [Italian, from French *loge* "lodge, hut"]

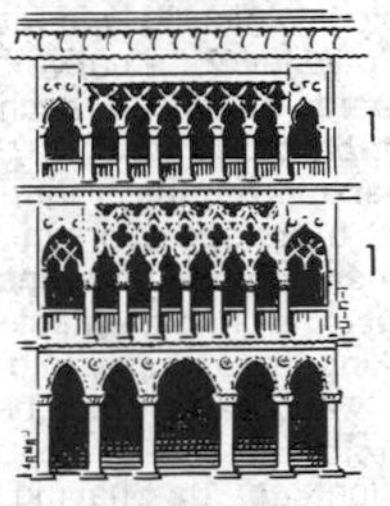

1 loggia

log•ic \'läj-ik\ *n* **1 :** a science that deals with the rules and tests of sound thinking and proof by reasoning **2 :** REASONING; *esp* **:** sound reasoning ⟨no *logic* in that remark⟩ **3 :** connection (as of facts or events) in a way that seems reasonable ⟨the *logic* of a situation⟩ **4 :** the principles of design of computer circuits for computation; *also* **:** the circuits themselves [Middle French *logique,* from Latin *logica,* from Greek *logikē,* from *logos* "speech, reason, word"] — **lo•gi•cian** \lō-'jish-ən\ *n*

log•i•cal \'läj-i-kəl\ *adj* **1 :** of or relating to logic **:** used in logic **2 :** conforming to or consistent with the rules of logic ⟨a *logical* argument⟩ **3 :** skilled in logic ⟨a *logical* thinker⟩ **4 :** being in agreement with what may be reasonably expected ⟨a *logical* result of an action⟩ — **log•i•cal•ly** \-kə-lē, -klē\ *adv* — **log•i•cal•ness** \-kəl-nəs\ *n*

lo•gis•tics \lō-'jis-tiks\ *n sing or pl* **1 :** a branch of military science that deals with the transportation, quartering, and supplying of troops in military operations **2 :** the handling of the details of an operation [French, literally, "art of calculating", from Greek *logistikē,* from *logizein* "to calculate", from *logos* "reason"] — **lo•gis•tic** \-tik\ *or* **lo•gis•ti•cal** \-ti-kəl\ *adj* — **lo•gis•ti•cal•ly** \-ti-kə-lē, -klē\ *adv*

log•jam \'lȯg-,jam, 'läg-\ *n* **1 :** a jumble of logs jammed together in a watercourse **2 :** IMPASSE 2

Lo•gos \'lō-,gäs, -,gōs\ *n* **:** the divine wisdom manifest in the creation, government, and redemption of the world and often identified with the second person of the Trinity [Greek, "speech, word, reason"]

log•roll•ing \'lȯg-,rō-ling, 'läg-\ *n* **1 :** the rolling of logs in water by treading; *also* **:** a sport in which individuals treading logs try to dislodge one another **2 :** the exchanging of assistance or favors; *esp* **:** the trading of votes by legislators to secure favorable action on projects of interest to each one — **log•roll•er** \-,rō-lər\ *n*

-logue *or* **-log** \,lȯg, ,läg\ *n combining form* **1 :** discourse **:** talk ⟨duo*logue*⟩ **2 :** student **:** specialist [Old French *-loque,* derived from Greek *-logos,* from *legein* "to speak"]

log•wood \'lȯg-,wu̇d, 'läg-\ *n* **:** a Central American and West Indian tree of the pea family; *also* **:** its hard brown or brownish red heartwood used in dyeing or an extract of this

lo•gy \'lō-gē\ *adj* **lo•gi•er; -est :** marked by sluggishness and lack of vitality [perhaps from Dutch *log* "heavy"] — **lo•gi•ly** \-gə-lē\ *adv* — **lo•gi•ness** \-gē-nəs\ *n*

-l•o•gy \l-ə-jē\ *n combining form* **1 :** oral or written expression ⟨phraseo*logy*⟩ **2 :** doctrine **:** theory **:** science ⟨ethno*logy*⟩ [Greek *-logia,* from *logos* "word, speech, reason"]

loin \'lȯin\ *n* **1 a :** the part of the body on each side of the spinal column and between the hip and the lower ribs **b :** a cut of meat comprising this part of one or both sides of a carcass with the adjoining half of the vertebrae included but without the flank **2** *pl* **a :** the pubic region **b :** the organs of reproduction [Middle French *loigne,* derived from Latin *lumbus*]

loin•cloth \\-ˌklȯth\\ *n* **:** a cloth worn about the loins often as the sole article of clothing in warm climates

loi•ter \\ˈlȯit-ər\\ *vi* **1 :** to interrupt or delay an activity with aimless idle stops and pauses **2 a :** to hang around idly **b :** to lag behind [Middle English *loiteren*] — **loi•ter•er** \\-ər-ər\\ *n*

loll \\ˈläl\\ *vb* **1 :** to hang or let hang loosely **:** DROOP **2 :** to act or move in a lax, lazy, or indolent manner **:** LOUNGE ⟨*loll* around in the sun⟩ [Middle English *lollen*]

lol•li•pop *or* **lol•ly•pop** \\ˈläl-ē-ˌpäp\\ *n* **:** a lump of hard candy on the end of a stick [probably from *loll* + *-i-* + *pop*]

Lom•bard \\ˈläm-ˌbärd, -bərd\\ *n* **1 :** a member of a Teutonic people invading Italy in A.D. 568 and establishing a kingdom in the Po valley **2 :** a native of Lombardy or of the Kingdom of the Lombards [Middle French, from Italian *Lombardo,* from Latin *Langobardus*]

Lom•bar•dy poplar \\ˌläm-ˌbärd-ē, -bərd-\\ *n* **:** a tall slender poplar of European origin that tapers at the top and has strongly ascending upright branches [*Lombardy,* Italy]

lo•ment \\ˈlō-ˌment, -mənt\\ *n* **:** a fruit resembling a pod but breaking transversely into segments at maturity [Latin *lomentum* "wash made from bean meal", derived from *lavare* "to wash"]

lone \\ˈlōn\\ *adj* **1 a :** having no company **:** SOLITARY ⟨a *lone* traveler⟩ **b :** preferring solitude **2 :** ONLY, SOLE ⟨the *lone* theater in town⟩ **3 :** situated by itself **:** ISOLATED [Middle English, short for *alone*] — **lone•ness** \\ˈlōn-nəs\\ *n*

lone•ly \\ˈlōn-lē\\ *adj* **lone•li•er; -est 1 :** being without company **:** LONE ⟨a *lonely* hiker⟩ **2 :** UNFREQUENTED, DESOLATE ⟨a *lonely* spot⟩ **3 :** LONESOME **syn** see ALONE — **lone•li•ness** *n*

lone•some \\ˈlōn-səm\\ *adj* **1 :** sad from lack of companionship or separation from others **2 a :** REMOTE, UNFREQUENTED ⟨a *lonesome* stretch of highway⟩ **b :** LONE **syn** see ALONE — **lone•some•ly** *adv* — **lone•some•ness** *n*

¹long \\ˈlȯng\\ *adj* **long•er** \\ˈlȯng-gər\\; **long•est** \\ˈlȯng-gəst\\ **1 :** of great or greater than usual extent from end to end **2 a :** having a specified length **b :** forming the chief linear dimension ⟨the *long* side⟩ **3 :** lasting for a considerable or a specified time **4 a :** containing many items in a series **b :** having a specified number of units ⟨300 pages *long*⟩ **5 a :** being a syllable or speech sound of relatively great duration **b :** being the member of a pair of similarly spelled vowel or vowel-containing sounds that is descended from a vowel long in duration ⟨*long a* in *fate*⟩ ⟨*long i* in *sign*⟩ **6 :** having the capacity to reach or extend a considerable distance **7 :** larger or longer than the standard **8 a :** extending far into the future **b :** extending beyond what is known **9 :** strong in or well furnished with something **10 :** of an unusual degree of difference between the amounts wagered on each side ⟨*long* odds⟩ [Old English *long, lang*] — **at long last :** after a long wait **:** FINALLY

²long *adv* **1 :** for or during a long time **2 :** for the duration of a specified period **3 :** at a distant point of time ⟨*long* before we arrived⟩ — **so long :** GOOD-BYE

³long *vi* **longed; long•ing** \\ˈlȯng-ing\\ **:** to feel a strong desire or wish **:** YEARN [Old English *langian*]

• **syn** LONG, YEARN, HANKER, PINE mean to have a strong desire for something. LONG implies wishing with one's whole heart and often striving to attain; YEARN suggests an eager, restless, or painful longing ⟨*yearned* to be understood⟩ HANKER suggests somewhat disparagingly an uneasiness due to an unsatisfied and often unreasonable appetite or desire ⟨*hankered* for complete approval⟩ PINE implies a languishing or fruitless longing.

long•boat \\ˈlȯng-ˌbōt\\ *n* **:** a large boat carried on a ship

long bone *n* **:** one of the bones supporting a vertebrate limb and consisting of a long nearly cylinder-shaped shaft that contains marrow and ends in enlarged heads that each form a joint with another bone

long•bow \\ˈlȯng-ˌbō\\ *n* **:** a wooden bow about 1¾ meters long that is drawn by hand

long-day *adj* **:** flowering or developing to maturity only in response to alternating long light and short dark periods — compare DAY-NEUTRAL, SHORT-DAY

¹long-dis•tance \\-ˈdis-təns\\ *adj* **:** of or relating to telephone communication with a distant point

²long-distance *adv* **:** by long-distance telephone

long distance *n* **1 :** communication by long-distance telephone **2 :** a telephone operator or exchange that gives long-distance connections

long division *n* **:** arithmetical division in which the several steps corresponding to the division of parts of the dividend by the divisor are indicated in detail

lon•gev•i•ty \\län-ˈjev-ət-ē, lȯn-\\ *n* **1 :** a long duration of individual life **2 :** length of life [Late Latin *longaevitas,* from Latin *longaevus* "long-lived", from *longus* "long" + *aevum* "age"]

long•hair \\ˈlȯng-ˌhaər, -ˌheər\\ *n* **1 :** a person of artistic gifts or interests; *esp* **:** a lover of classical music **2 :** an impractical intellectual **3 a :** a person having long hair **b :** HIPPIE — **long-hair** *or* **long-haired** \\-ˈhaərd, -ˈheərd\\ *adj*

long•hand \\ˈlȯng-ˌhand\\ *n* **:** the characters used in ordinary writing **:** HANDWRITING

long•head•ed \\-ˈhed-əd\\ *adj* **1 :** having unusual foresight or wisdom **2 :** having a head relatively long from front to back but narrow from side to side — **long•head•ed•ness** *n*

long•horn \\ˈlȯng-ˌhȯrn\\ *n* **:** any of the long-horned cattle of Spanish derivation formerly common in the southwestern United States

long-horned \\-ˈhȯrnd\\ *adj* **:** having long horns or antennae

long•house \\-ˌhau̇s\\ *n* **:** a communal dwelling of the Iroquois

longhouse

long hundredweight *n, British* **:** HUNDREDWEIGHT 2

lon•gi•corn \\ˈlän-jə-ˌkȯrn\\ *adj* **:** of, relating to, or being beetles with long antennae [Latin *longus* "long" + *cornu* "horn"]

long•ing \\ˈlȯng-ing\\ *n* **:** an eager desire often for the unattainable **:** CRAVING — **long•ing•ly** \\-ing-lē\\ *adv*

long•ish \\ˈlȯng-ish\\ *adj* **:** somewhat long

lon•gi•tude \\ˈlän-jə-ˌtüd, -ˌtyüd\\ *n* **:** distance measured by degrees or time east or west from the prime meridian ⟨the *longitude* of New York is 74 degrees or about five hours west of Greenwich⟩ [Latin *longitudin-, longitudo* "length", from *longus* "long"]

longitude

lon•gi•tu•di•nal \\ˌlän-jə-ˈtüd-nəl, -ˈtyüd-, -n-əl\\ *adj* **1 :** of or relating to length or the lengthwise dimension **2 :** placed or running lengthwise — **lon•gi•tu•di•nal•ly** \\-ē\\ *adv*

long jump *n* **:** a jump for distance in track-and-field sports — **long jumper** *n*

long•leaf pine \\ˌlȯng-ˌlēf-\\ *n* **:** a large pine of the southern United States that has long thin clustered needles and long cones and is a major timber tree; *also* **:** its tough coarse-grained durable wood

long-leaved pine \\ˌlȯng-ˌlēvd-\\ *n* **:** LONGLEAF PINE

long-lived \\ˈlȯng-ˈlīvd, -ˈlivd\\ *adj* **:** living or lasting a long time — **long-lived•ness** \\-ˈlīvd-nəs, -ˈlīv-, -ˈlivd-, -ˈliv-\\ *n*

long-play•ing \\ˈlȯng-ˈplā-ing\\ *adj* **:** of, relating to, or being a phonograph record designed to be played at 33⅓ revolutions per minute

long-range \\-ˈrānj\\ *adj* **1 :** capable of traveling or shooting over great distances ⟨a *long-range* gun⟩ **2 :** lasting over or taking into account a long period **:** LONG-TERM

long•shore•man \\ˈlȯng-ˈshōr-mən, -ˈshȯr-\\ *n* **:** a laborer who loads and unloads ships at a seaport [*longshore* "existing along the seacoast", short for *alongshore*]

long shot \\ˈlȯng-ˌshät\\ *n* **1 :** an entry (as in a horse race) given little chance of winning **2 :** a bet in which the chances of winning are slight but the possible winnings great **3 :** a venture involving great risk but promising a great reward if successful — **by a long shot :** at all **:** ANYWAY ⟨give up? Not *by a long shot*⟩

long•sight•ed \\-ˈsīt-əd\\ *adj* **:** FARSIGHTED — **long•sight•ed•ness** *n*

long–suf•fer•ing \-'səf-ring, -ə-ring\ *n* : long and patient endurance — **long–suffering** *adj* — **long–suf•fer•ing•ly** \-ring-lē\ *adv*

long suit *n* **1** : a suit containing the most cards in a hand **2** : the activity or quality in which a person excels

long–term \'lȯng-'tərm\ *adj* **1** : extending over or involving a long period of time **2** : constituting a financial obligation based on a term usually of more than 10 years ⟨a *long-term* mortgage⟩

long–wind•ed \'lȯng-'win-dəd\ *adj* **1** : not easily subject to loss of breath **2** : tediously long in speaking or writing — **long–wind•ed•ly** *adv* — **long–wind•ed•ness** *n*

loo \'lü\ *n* **1** : an old card game **2** : money staked at loo [short for obsolete *lanterloo*, from French *lanturelu* "piffle"]

1look \'lu̇k\ *vb* **1** : to exercise the power of vision upon : EXAMINE, SEE **2** : EXPECT ⟨we *look* to see you soon⟩ **3** : to express by the eyes or facial expression **4** : to have an appearance that suits or agrees with ⟨*look* my age⟩ **5** : to have the appearance of being : SEEM **6** : to direct one's attention or eyes ⟨*look* in the mirror⟩ **7** : to have a specified outlook : POINT ⟨the house *looks* east⟩ **8** : to gaze in wonder or surprise : STARE [Old English *lōcian*] — **look after** : to take care of : attend to — **look for 1** : to await with hope or anticipation : EXPECT **2** : to search for : SEEK — **look on** *or* **look upon** : CONSIDER, REGARD ⟨*looked upon* them as friends⟩

2look *n* **1 a** : the action of looking **b** : GLANCE 3b **2 a** : the expression of the face **b** : physical appearance; *esp* : attractive physical appearance — usually used in pl. **3** : the state or form in which something appears : ASPECT

look•er–on \,lu̇k-ər-'ȯn, -'än\ *n, pl* **lookers–on** : ONLOOKER, SPECTATOR

looking glass *n* : MIRROR 1

look•out \'lu̇k-,au̇t\ *n* **1** : a person engaged in watching; *esp* : one assigned to watch (as on a ship) **2** : an elevated place or structure offering a wide view for observation **3** : a careful looking or watching **4** : a probability for the future : OUTLOOK **5** : a matter of care or concern

1loom \'lüm\ *n* : a frame or machine for weaving together threads or yarns into cloth [Old English *gelōma* "tool"]

2loom *vi* **1** : to come into sight in an unnaturally large, indistinct, or distorted form ⟨*loomed* out of the fog⟩ **2** : to be about to happen ⟨trouble was *looming*⟩ [origin unknown]

loon \'lün\ *n* **1** : any of several fish-eating diving birds with webbed feet, black head, and white-spotted black back **2** : a person of dull or disordered mind : LUNATIC [of Scandinavian origin; sense 2 from the popular phrase *crazy as a loon*]

loon 1

loo•ny *or* **loo•ney** \'lü-nē\ *adj* **loo•ni•er; -est** : CRAZY 2, FOOLISH [derived from *lunatic*] — **loo•ny** *n*

1loop \'lüp\ *n* **1** : a fold or doubling of a line leaving an opening between the parts through which another line can be passed or into which a hook may be hooked **2** : a loop-shaped figure, bend, or course ⟨a *loop* in a river⟩ **3** : a circular airplane maneuver involving flying upside down **4 a** : the portion of a vibrating body between two nodes **b** : the middle point of such a portion **5** : a complete electric circuit **6** : a series of instructions for a computer that is repeated until a terminating condition is reached [Middle English *loupe*] — **for a loop** : into a state of amazement, confusion, or distress ⟨the news knocked us *for a loop*⟩

2loop *vb* **1** : to make or form a loop **2 a** : to make a loop in, on, or about **b** : to fasten with a loop **3** : to execute a loop in an airplane

loop•er \'lü-pər\ *n* **1** : any of numerous small hairless moth larvae that move with a looping movement **2** : one that loops

loop•hole \'lüp-,hōl\ *n* **1** : a small opening in a wall through which small firearms may be discharged **2** : a means of escape; *esp* : an ambiguity or omission (as in the wording of a law or contract) that makes evasion of one's obligation possible

loop of Hen•le \-'hen-lē\ : a part of the vertebrate nephron that lies in the midst of the convoluted portion and plays a part in water resorption [F. G. J. *Henle*, died 1885, German pathologist]

1loose \'lüs\ *adj* **1 a** : not rigidly fastened or securely attached **b** : having worked partly free from attachments **c** : not tight-fitting **2 a** : free from confinement, restraint, or obligation **b** : not brought together in a bundle, container, or binding **3** : not dense or compact in structure or arrangement ⟨*loose* soil⟩ **4** : lacking in restraint or power of restraint ⟨*loose* conduct⟩ **5 a** : not tightly drawn or stretched : SLACK **b** : having a flexible or relaxed character **6 a** : lacking in precision, exactness, or care **b** : permitting freedom of interpretation [Old Norse *lauss*] — **loose•ly** *adv* — **loose•ness** *n*

2loose *vb* **1 a** : to let loose : RELEASE **b** : to free from restraint **2** : to make loose : UNTIE ⟨*loose* a knot⟩ **3** : to let fly : DISCHARGE **4** : to make less rigid, tight, or strict : RELAX

loose constructionist *n* : one favoring a liberal interpretation of the United States Constitution as granting broad implied powers to the federal government

loose end *n* **1** : something left hanging loose **2** : a fragment of unfinished business

loose–joint•ed \'lüs-'jȯint-əd\ *adj* : having a flexibility or lack of rigidity suggesting the absence of rigid joints; *esp* : moving with unusual freedom or ease — **loose–joint•ed•ness** *n*

loos•en \'lüs-n\ *vb* **loos•ened; loos•en•ing** \'lüs-ning, -n-ing\ **1** : to release from restraint **2** : to make or become loose or looser **3** : to cause or permit to become less strict

loose•strife \'lüs-,strīf, 'lü-\ *n* **1** : any of a genus of plants of the primrose family with leafy stems and yellow or white flowers **2** : any of a genus of herbs including some with showy spikes of purple flowers [intended as translation of Greek *lysimacheios* "loosestrife" (as if from *lysis* "act of loosing" + *machesthai* "to fight"), from *Lysimachos*, 5th or 4th century B.C. Greek physician]

1loot \'lüt\ *n* **1** : goods taken in war : SPOIL **2** : something stolen or taken by force or violence **3** : the action of looting [Hindi *lūṭ*, from Sanskrit *luṇṭati* "he robs"]

2loot *vb* **1** : to plunder or sack in war **2** : to rob or steal especially on a large scale and by violence or corruption **3** : to seize and carry away by force especially in war — **loot•er** *n*

lop \'läp\ *vt* **lopped; lop•ping 1 a** : to cut branches or twigs from : TRIM ⟨*lop* a tree⟩ **b** : to cut or shear from a woody plant ⟨*lop* dead branches⟩ **c** : to cut (as a portion or part) from something **2** : to remove unnecessary or undesirable parts from — usually used with *off* [Middle English *loppe* "small branches and twigs cut from a tree"] — **lop•per** *n*

1lope \'lōp\ *n* **1** : an easy natural gait of a horse resembling a canter **2** : an easy bounding gait capable of being sustained for a long time [Old Norse *hlaup* "leap"]

2lope *vi* : to go, move, or ride at a lope — **lop•er** *n*

lop–eared \'läp-'iərd\ *adj* : having ears that droop [earlier *lop* "to droop"]

loph•o•phore \'läf-ə-,fōr, -,fȯr\ *n* : a circular or horseshoe-shaped organ about the mouth of a brachiopod or bryozoan that bears tentacles and functions especially in food-getting [Greek *lophos* "crest"]

lop•sid•ed \'läp-'sīd-əd\ *adj* **1** : leaning to one side **2** : lacking in balance, symmetry, or proportion — **lop•sid•ed•ly** *adv* — **lop•sid•ed•ness** *n*

lo•qua•cious \lō-'kwā-shəs\ *adj* : given to too much talking [Latin *loquac-, loquax*, from *loqui* "to speak"] — **lo•qua•cious•ly** *adv* — **lo•qua•cious•ness** *n* — **lo•quac•i•ty** \-'kwas-ət-ē\ *n*

lo•quat \'lō-,kwät\ *n* : a small Asian evergreen tree bearing a yellow plumlike fruit; *also* : its fruit used especially in preserves [Chinese (Cantonese dialect) *lō-kwat*]

1lord \'lȯrd\ *n* **1** : one having power and authority over others: **a** : a ruler to whom service and obedience are due **b** : a person from whom a feudal fee or estate is held **c** : HUSBAND **2** *cap* **a** : GOD 1 **b** : JESUS **3** : a man of rank or high position: as **a** : a feudal tenant whose right or title comes directly from the king **b** *often cap* : a British nobleman or a bishop in the Church of En-

\ə\ **abut**	\au̇\ **out**	\i\ **tip**	\ȯ\ **saw**	\u̇\ **foot**
\ər\ **further**	\ch\ **chin**	\ī\ **life**	\ȯi\ **coin**	\y\ **yet**
\a\ **mat**	\e\ **pet**	\j\ **job**	\th\ **thin**	\yü\ **few**
\ā\ **take**	\ē\ **easy**	\ng\ **sing**	\th̲\ **this**	\yu̇\ **cure**
\ä\ **cot, cart**	\g\ **go**	\ō\ **bone**	\ü\ **food**	\zh\ **vision**

gland entitled to sit in the House of Lords — used as a title **4** *pl, cap* : HOUSE OF LORDS [Old English *hlāford,* from *hlāf* "loaf" + *weard* "keeper, ward"]

△ **origin** *Lord* is etymologically similar to *lady.* A lady is, etymologically, a kneader of bread and a lord a keeper of bread. Old English *hlāford* is formed from *hlāf,* "loaf, bread", and *weard,* "keeper, guard", the Old English form of modern *ward.* The earliest known instances of *hlāford* show the sense of "head of household". Apparently the *hlāf-* element was to be taken no more literally than is the first element of the modern term *breadwinner.*

[2]lord *vi* : to act in an arrogant or domineering manner — used with *it*

lord chancellor *n, pl* **lords chancellor** : a British officer of state who presides over the House of Lords, serves as the head of the British judiciary, and is usually a leading member of the cabinet

lord•ly \ˈlȯrd-lē\ *adj* **lord•li•er**; **-est** **1 a** : of, relating to, or having the characteristics of a lord **b** : fit for a lord ⟨a *lordly* estate⟩ **2** : haughtily proud or superior — **lord•li•ness** *n* — **lordly** *adv*

lor•do•sis \lȯr-ˈdō-səs\ *n* : abnormal forward curvature of the spine — compare KYPHOSIS, SCOLIOSIS [Greek *lordōsis,* from *lordos* "curving forward"] — **lor•dot•ic** \-ˈdät-ik\ *adj*

Lord's day *n, often cap D* : SUNDAY

lord•ship \ˈlȯrd-ˌship\ *n* **1** *often cap* : the rank or dignity of a lord — used as a title ⟨his *Lordship* is not at home⟩ **2** : the authority, power, or territory of a lord

Lord's Prayer *n* : the prayer in Matthew 6:9–13 that Christ taught his disciples

Lord's Supper *n* : COMMUNION 1a

lore \ˈlōr, ˈlȯr\ *n* : KNOWLEDGE 4; *esp* : a particular body of knowledge or tradition ⟨forest *lore*⟩ [Old English *lār* "teaching"]

lor•gnette \lȯrn-ˈyet\ *n* : a pair of eyeglasses or opera glasses with a handle [French, from *lorgner* "to take a sidelong look at", from *lorgne* "cross-eyed"]

lo•ri•ca \lə-ˈrī-kə\ *n, pl* **-cae** \-ˌkē, -ˌsē\ *or* **-cas** \-kəz\ **1** : a Roman cuirass of leather or metal **2** : a hard protective case or shell (as of a rotifer) [Latin, from *lorum* "thong, rein"]

lor•i•keet \ˈlȯr-ə-ˌkēt, ˈlär-\ *n* : any of numerous small arboreal parrots of Australasia that feed chiefly on nectar [*lory,* a kind of parrot (from Malay *nuri, luri*) + *-keet* (as in *parakeet*)]

lo•ris \ˈlōr-əs, ˈlȯr-\ *n* : either of two small nocturnal slow-moving lemurs [French]

lorn \ ˈlȯrn\ *adj* : left alone : DESOLATE [Middle English, from *loren,* past participle of *lesen* "to lose", from Old English *lēosan*] — **lorn•ness** \ˈlȯrn-nəs\ *n*

lor•ry \ˈlȯr-ē, ˈlär-\ *n, pl* **lorries** **1** : a large low horse-drawn wagon without sides **2** *British* : a motor truck especially if open [origin unknown]

lose \ˈlüz\ *vb* **lost** \ˈlȯst\; **los•ing** \ˈlü-ziŋ\ **1** : to bring to destruction ⟨the ship was *lost* on the reef⟩ **2** : to be unable to find or have at hand ⟨*lose* a billfold⟩ **3** : to become deprived of especially accidentally or by death ⟨*lose* one's eyesight⟩ ⟨*lost* a child in the war⟩ **4** : to fail to keep control of or allegiance of ⟨*lose* votes⟩ **5 a** : to fail to use : let slip by : WASTE **b** (1) : to fail to win, gain, or obtain ⟨*lose* a prize⟩ ⟨*lose* a contest⟩ (2) : to undergo defeat ⟨*lose* with good grace⟩ **c** : to fail to catch with the senses or the mind ⟨*lost* part of what they said⟩ **6** : to cause the loss of ⟨one careless statement *lost* the election⟩ **7** : to fail to keep, sustain, or maintain ⟨*lose* one's balance⟩ **8 a** : to cause to miss one's way or bearings ⟨*lost* myself in the maze of streets⟩ **b** : to make (oneself) withdrawn from immediate reality ⟨*lost* myself in daydreaming⟩ **9 a** : to wander or go astray from ⟨*lost* my way⟩ **b** : to go faster than : shake off ⟨*lost* their pursuers⟩ **10** : to fail to keep in sight or in mind **11** : to free oneself from : get rid of ⟨dieting to *lose* some weight⟩ [Old English *losian* "to perish, lose", from *los* "destruction"] — **lose ground** : to suffer loss or disadvantage : fail to advance or improve — **lose one's heart** : to fall in love

lose out *vi* : to fail to win in competition : fail to receive an expected reward or gain

los•er \ˈlü-zər\ *n* **1** : one that loses **2** : one that does poorly : FAILURE

loss \ˈlȯs\ *n* **1 a** : the act of losing **b** : the harm or privation resulting from losing ⟨their death was a *loss* to the community⟩ **c** : an instance of losing **2 a** : a person or thing or an amount that is lost **b** *pl* : killed, wounded, or captured soldiers **3 a** : failure to gain, win, obtain, or utilize **b** : an amount by which the cost of an article or service exceeds the selling price **4** : decrease in amount, magnitude, or degree **5** : DESTRUCTION 2, RUIN [Middle English *loss*] — **at a loss** : unable to determine : PUZZLED, UNCERTAIN — **for a loss** : into a state of distress

loss leader *n* : an article sold at a loss in order to draw customers

lost \ˈlȯst\ *adj* **1** : not made use of, won, or claimed **2 a** : unable to find the way **b** : no longer visible **c** : lacking assurance or self-confidence **3** : ruined or destroyed physically or morally **4 a** : no longer possessed **b** : no longer known **5 a** : taken away or beyond reach or attainment ⟨regions *lost* to the faith⟩ **b** : become callous : INSENSIBLE ⟨*lost* to shame⟩ **6** : ABSORBED, RAPT ⟨*lost* in revery⟩ [past participle of *lose*] — **lost•ness** \ˈlȯst-nəs, ˈlȯs-\ *n*

[1]lot \ˈlät\ *n* **1** : an object used as a counter in determining a question by chance **2** : the use of lots as a means of deciding something ⟨choose by *lot*⟩; *also* : the resulting choice **3 a** : something that comes to one by or as if by lot : SHARE **b** : one's way of life or worldly fate : FORTUNE **4 a** : a portion of land ⟨a building *lot*⟩ **b** : a motion-picture studio and its adjoining property **5** : a number of units of an article or a parcel of articles offered as one item (as in an auction sale) **6** : a number of associated persons : SET **7** : a considerable quantity ⟨*lots* of money⟩ [Old English *hlot*] **syn** see FATE

[2]lot *vb* **lot•ted**; **lot•ting** **1** : to form or divide into lots **2** : ALLOT

loth \ˈlōth, ˈlō*th*\ *variant of* LOATH

lo•thar•io \lō-ˈthar-ē-ˌō, -ˈther-, -ˈthär-\ *n, pl* **-ios** *often cap* : SEDUCER [*Lothario,* seducer in the play *The Fair Penitent* (1703) by Nicholas Rowe]

lo•tion \ˈlō-shən\ *n* : a liquid preparation for cosmetic and medicinal use on the skin [Latin *lotio* "act of washing", from *lotus,* past participle of *lavare, lavere* "to wash"]

lots \ˈläts\ *adv* : MUCH 1a ⟨feeling *lots* better⟩ [pl. of [1]*lot*]

lot•tery \ˈlät-ə-rē, ˈlä-trē\ *n, pl* **-ter•ies** : a drawing of lots in which prizes are given to holders of the winning tickets

lot•to \ˈlät-ō\ *n* : a game of chance similar to bingo [Italian, "lottery, lotto", from French *lot* "lot", of Germanic origin]

lo•tus \ˈlōt-əs\ *n* **1** *also* **lo•tos** \ˈlōt-əs\ : a fruit held in Greek legend to cause indolence and forgetfulness; *also* : a tree bearing this fruit **2** : any of various water lilies including several represented in ancient Egyptian and Hindu art and religious symbolism **3** : any of various erect plants of the pea family including some used for hay and pasture [Latin, from Greek *lōtos,* from Hebrew *lōt* "myrrh"]

lotus 2

lotus–eater \ˈlōt-ə-ˌsēt-ər\ *n* **1** : one of a people in classical mythology who subsist on the lotus and live in its induced dreamy indolence **2** : DREAMER 2a, IDLER

loud \ˈlau̇d\ *adj* **1 a** : marked by intensity or volume of sound **b** : producing a loud sound **2** : CLAMOROUS, NOISY **3** : obtrusive or offensive in color or pattern ⟨a *loud* suit⟩ [Old English *hlūd*] — **loud** *adv* — **loud•ly** *adv* — **loud•ness** *n*

loud•en \ˈlau̇d-n\ *vb* **loud•ened**; **loud•en•ing** \ˈlau̇d-niŋ, -n-iŋ\ : to make or become loud or louder

loud•mouth \ˈlau̇d-ˌmau̇th\ *n* : a person given to loud offensive talk — **loud•mouthed** \-ˈmau̇*th*d, -ˌmau̇tht\ *adj*

loud•speak•er \ˈlau̇d-ˈspē-kər\ *n* : a device similar to a telephone receiver in operation but amplifying sound

lou•is d'or \ˌlü-ē-ˈdȯr\ *n, pl* **louis d'or** **1** : a French gold coin first struck in 1640 and issued up to the Revolution **2** : the French 20-franc gold piece issued after the Revolution [French, from *Louis* XIII of France + *d'or* "of gold"]

Lou•is Qua•torze \ˌlü-ē-kə-ˈtȯrz\ *adj* : of, relating to, or characteristic of the architecture or furniture of the reign of Louis XIV of France [French, "Louis XIV"]

Louis Quinze \-ˈkaⁿz\ *adj* : of, relating to, or characteristic of the architecture or furniture of the reign of Louis XV of France [French, "Louis XV"]

Louis Seize \-ˈsāz, -ˈsez\ *adj* : of, relating to, or characteristic of the architecture or furniture of the reign of Louis XVI of France [French, "Louis XVI"]

Louis Treize \-'trāz, -'trez\ *adj* : of, relating to, or characteristic of the architecture or furniture of the reign of Louis XIII of France [French, "Louis XIII"]

¹lounge \'lau̇nj\ *vb* **1** : to move or act idly or lazily : LOAF **2** : to stand, sit, or lie in a relaxed manner **3** : to pass (time) idly ⟨*lounged* away the day⟩ [origin unknown] — **loung•er** *n*

²lounge *n* **1** : a place for lounging: as **a** : LIVING ROOM **b** : LOBBY **c** : a room in a public building or vehicle often combining lounging, smoking, and toilet facilities **2** : a long couch

lounge car *n* : a railroad passenger car with seats for lounging and facilities for serving refreshments

loup–ga•rou \,lü-gə-'rü\ *n, pl* **loups–garous** \,lü-gə-'rü, -'rüz\ : WEREWOLF [Middle French]

lour \'lau̇-ər, 'lau̇r\ **lour•ing, loury** \'lau̇-rē, -ə-rē\ *variant of* LOWER, LOWERING, LOWERY

louse \'lau̇s\ *n* **1** *pl* **lice** \'līs\ **a** : any of various small wingless usually flat insects (orders Anoplura and Mallophaga) parasitic on warm-blooded animals **b** : any of several other small arthropods **2** *pl* **lous•es** \'lau̇-səz\ : a contemptible person [Old English *lūs*]

louse up *vb* : to make a mess of something : BUNGLE

lousy \'lau̇-zē\ *adj* **lous•i•er; -est 1** : infested with lice **2 a** : totally repulsive : CONTEMPTIBLE **b** : miserably poor or inferior **c** : amply supplied ⟨*lousy* with money⟩ — **lous•i•ly** \-zə-lē\ *adv* — **lous•i•ness** \-zē-nəs\ *n*

lout \'lau̇t\ *n* : a clownish awkward fellow [perhaps from Old Norse *lūtr* "bent down"] — **lout•ish** \-ish\ *adj* — **lout•ish•ly** *adv* — **lout•ish•ness** *n*

lou•ver *or* **lou•vre** \'lü-vər\ *n* **1** : an opening provided with one or more slanted fixed or movable strips (as of metal or wood) to allow flow of air but to exclude rain or sun or to provide privacy; *also* : a similar device with movable strips for controlling the passage of air or light **2** : one of the slanted strips of a louver [Middle French *lovier* "dormer window"] — **lou•vered** \-vərd\ *adj*

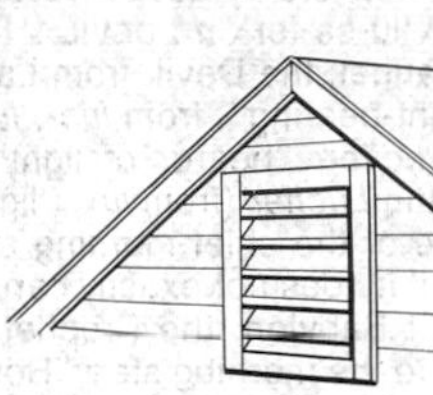
louver 1

lov•able *also* **love•able** \'ləv-ə-bəl\ *adj* : having qualities that win affection — **lov•able•ness** n — **lov•ably** \-blē\ *adv*

lov•age \'ləv-ij\ *n* : any of several aromatic perennial herbs of the carrot family [Anglo-French *lovache*]

¹love \'ləv\ *n* **1 a** : strong affection for another based on kinship ties ⟨maternal *love* for a child⟩ **b** : attraction based on sexual desire **c** : affection based on admiration or benevolence **2** : warm attachment, enthusiasm, or devotion ⟨*love* of the sea⟩ **3 a** : the object of attachment or devotion **b** : a beloved person : DARLING **4 a** : unselfish loyal concern for the good of another: (1) : the fatherly concern of God for man (2) : brotherly concern for others **b** : a person's adoration of God **5** : an amorous episode **6** : a score of zero in tennis [Old English *lufu*] — **in love** : feeling love for and devotion toward someone

²love *vb* **1** : to hold dear : CHERISH **2 a** : to feel a lover's passion, devotion, or tenderness for **b** : CARESS **3** : to like or desire actively : take pleasure in ⟨*loved* to play the violin⟩ **4** : to thrive in ⟨the rose *loves* sunlight⟩ **5** : to feel affection : experience desire

love•bird \'ləv-,bərd\ *n* : any of various small usually gray or green parrots that actively court their mates

love feast *n* **1** : a meal eaten in common by a Christian congregation in token of brotherly love **2** : a banquet or celebration held to reconcile differences or show someone honor

love–in–a–mist \'ləv-ə-nə-,mist\ *n* : a European garden plant of the buttercup family that has flowers enveloped in finely dissected bracts

love knot *n* : a stylized knot sometimes used as an emblem of love

love•less \'ləv-ləs\ *adj* **1** : marked by the absence of love ⟨a *loveless* marriage⟩ **2** : not feeling or showing love **3** : not loved — **love•less•ly** *adv* — **love•less•ness** *n*

love•lorn \'ləv-,lȯrn\ *adj* : deserted by one's love — **love•lorn•ness** \-,lȯrn-nəs\ *n*

love•ly \'ləv-lē\ *adj* **love•li•er; -est 1** : beautiful in moral or spiritual character : GRACIOUS **2** : delicately beautiful ⟨a *lovely* dress⟩ **3** : highly pleasing : FINE ⟨a *lovely* view⟩ **syn** see BEAUTIFUL— **love•li•ness** *n*

love•mak•ing \'ləv-,mā-king\ *n* **1** : COURTSHIP **2** : sexual activity

lov•er \'ləv-ər\ *n* **1 a** : a person in love; *esp* : a man in love **b** *pl* : two persons in love with each other **2** : the male partner in a sexual relationship other than that of husband and wife **3** : one who greatly enjoys something : DEVOTEE

lov•er•ly \-lē\ *adj* : befitting a lover

love seat *n* : a double chair, sofa, or settee for two persons

love–sick \'ləv-,sik\ *adj* **1** : languishing with love : YEARNING **2** : expressing a lover's longing — **love•sick•ness** *n*

lov•ing \'ləv-ing\ *adj* : feeling or showing love : AFFECTIONATE — **lov•ing•ly** \-ing-lē\ *adv*

loving cup *n* : a large ornamental drinking vessel with two or more handles; *esp* : one given as a prize or trophy

lov•ing–kind•ness \,ləv-ing-'kīnd-nəs, -'kīn-\ *n* : tender and benevolent affection

¹low \'lō\ *vi* : to utter a low or a similar sound [Old English *hlōwan*]

²low *n* : the characteristic deep sustained sound of a cow

³low \'lō\ *adj* **low•er** \'lō-ər, 'lōr\; **low•est** \'lō-əst\ **1 a** : not high or tall ⟨a *low* wall⟩ ⟨a *low* bridge⟩ **b** : having a low-cut neckline **2 a** : situated or passing below the normal level, surface, or base of measurement ⟨*low* ground⟩ **b** : marking a bottom ⟨the *low* point of a career⟩ **3** : PROSTRATE ⟨laid *low* by the flu⟩ **4** : not loud : SOFT; *also* : FLAT 10a **5 a** : being near the equator ⟨*low* latitudes⟩ **b** : being near the horizon ⟨the sun is *low*⟩ **6** : humble in status ⟨*low* birth⟩ **7 a** : lacking strength, health, or vitality **b** : lacking spirit or vivacity : DEPRESSED **8 a** : of lesser degree, size, or amount than average or ordinary ⟨*low* pressure⟩ **b** : less than usual in number, amount, or value ⟨a *low* price⟩ **9** : falling short of some standard: as **a** : lacking dignity or elevation ⟨a *low* style of writing⟩ **b** : morally reprehensible : BASE ⟨a *low* trick⟩ **c** : COARSE, VULGAR ⟨*low* language⟩ **10** : not advanced in complexity, development, or elaboration ⟨*low* organisms⟩ **11** : UNFAVORABLE a, DISPARAGING ⟨had a *low* opinion of it⟩ **12** : pronounced with a wide opening between the relatively flat tongue and the palate ⟨the *low* vowel \ä\⟩ [Old Norse *lāgr*] — **low** *adv* — **low•ness** *n*

⁴low *n* **1** : something that is low; *esp* : a region of low barometric pressure **2** : the arrangement of gears (as of an automobile) in a position to transmit the greatest power from the engine to the propeller shaft

low blood pressure *n* : blood pressure that is abnormally low especially in the arteries

low•born \'lō-'bȯrn\ *adj* : born in a low condition or rank

low•boy \'lō-,bȯi\ *n* : a chest of drawers about a meter high with long legs

low•bred \'lō-'bred\ *adj* : RUDE 2, VULGAR

low•brow \'lō-,brau̇\ *n* : an uncultivated person — **lowbrow** *adj*

Low Church *adj* : tending especially in Anglican worship to minimize the priesthood, sacraments, and formal rites and often to emphasize evangelical principles — compare HIGH CHURCH

lowboy

low comedy *n* : comedy based on burlesque, horseplay, or slapstick rather than wit or satire

low•down \-,dau̇n\ *n* : basic and usually private data

low–down \'lō-'dau̇n\ *adj* **1** : CONTEMPTIBLE, DESPICABLE **2** : deeply emotional ⟨*low-down* blues⟩

¹low•er *or* **lour** \'lau̇-ər, 'lau̇r\ *vi* **1** : to look sullen : FROWN **2** : to become dark, gloomy, and threatening [Middle English *louren*]

²lower *or* **lour** *n* : a lowering look : FROWN

³low•er \'lō-ər, 'lōr\ *adj* **1** : relatively low in position, rank, or order ⟨*lower* court⟩ **2 :** less advanced in the scale of evolutionary development ⟨*lower* animals⟩ **3 :** constituting the popular and more representative branch of a bicameral legislative body **4 a :** situated or held to be situated beneath the earth's surface **b** *cap* **:** of, relating to, or constituting an earlier geologic period or formation **5 :** SOUTHERN 2 ⟨*lower* New York State⟩

4low•er \'lō-ər, 'lōr\ *vb* **1 :** to move down **:** DROP; *also* **:** DIMINISH **2 a :** to let descend by its own weight **b :** to make the aim lower **c :** to reduce the height of **3 a :** to reduce in value or amount ⟨*lower* the price⟩ **b** (1) **:** to bring down **:** DEGRADE (2) **:** ABASE, HUMBLE **c :** to reduce the objective of — **lower the boom :** to crack down

low•er•case \ˌlō-ər-'kās, ˌlōr-\ *adj* **:** being a letter that belongs to or conforms to the series a, b, c, etc. rather than A, B, C, etc. [from the printer's practice of keeping such letters in the lower of a pair of type cases] — **lowercase** *n*

lower class *n* **:** a social class occupying a position below the middle class and having the lowest status in a society

low•er•ing *also* **lour•ing** \'laú-ring, -ə-ring\ *adj* **:** dark and threatening **:** GLOOMY

low•er•most \'lō-ər-ˌmōst, 'lōr-\ *adj* **:** LOWEST

low•ery *also* **loury** \'laú-rē, -ə-rē\ *adj* **:** GLOOMY, LOWERING ⟨a *lowery* sky⟩

lowest common denominator *n* **:** LEAST COMMON DENOMINATOR

lowest common multiple *n* **:** LEAST COMMON MULTIPLE

lowest terms *n pl* **:** the form of a fraction in which the numerator and denominator have no factor in common

low frequency *n* **:** a radio frequency in the range between 30 and 300 kilohertz — abbreviation *LF*

Low German *n* **1 :** the German dialects of northern Germany especially since the end of the medieval period **2 :** the West Germanic languages other than High German

low–grade \'lō-'grād\ *adj* **1 :** of inferior grade or quality **2 :** being nearer the lower or least favorable extreme of a range ⟨a *low-grade* fever⟩ ⟨a *low-grade* imbecile⟩

low–key \'lō-'kē\ *also* **low–keyed** \-'kēd\ *adj* **:** of low intensity **:** RESTRAINED

low•land \'lō-lənd, -ˌland\ *n* **:** low and usually level country — **lowland** *adj*

low•land•er \-lən-dər, -ˌlan-\ *n* **1 :** a native or inhabitant of a lowland region **2** *cap* **:** an inhabitant of the Lowlands of Scotland

1low•ly \'lō-lē\ *adv* **1 :** in a humble way **2 :** in a low position, manner, or degree **3 :** not loudly

2lowly *adj* **low•li•er; -est 1 :** HUMBLE 1, MEEK **2 :** of or relating to a low social or economic rank **3 :** LOW 10 ⟨*lowly* organisms like the amoeba⟩ **4 :** ranking low in some hierarchy — **low•li•ness** *n*

low mass *n, often cap L & M* **:** a mass that is said in the simplest ceremonial form — compare HIGH MASS

low–mind•ed \'lō-'mīn-dəd\ *adj* **:** inclined mentally to low or unworthy things — **low–mind•ed•ly** *adv* — **low–mind•ed•ness** *n*

low–pres•sure \'lō-'presh-ər\ *adj* **1 a :** having, exerting, or operating under a relatively small pressure **b :** having or resulting from a low atmospheric pressure **2 :** EASYGOING

low relief *n* **:** BAS-RELIEF

low–spir•it•ed \'lō-'spir-ət-əd\ *adj* **:** DEJECTED, DEPRESSED — **low–spir•it•ed•ly** *adv* — **low–spir•it•ed•ness** *n*

low tide *n* **:** the tide when the water is at its farthest ebb

1lox \'läks\ *n* **:** liquid oxygen [*l*iquid *ox*ygen]

2lox *n, pl* **lox** *or* **lox•es :** smoked salmon [Yiddish *laks,* from Middle High German *lahs* "salmon"]

loy•al \'lòi-əl, 'lòil\ *adj* **1 a :** faithful in allegiance to one's lawful government **b :** faithful to a private person to whom fidelity is due **2 :** faithful to a cause or ideal [Middle French, from Old French *leial,* from Latin *legalis* "legal"] **syn** see FAITHFUL — **loy•al•ly** \'lòi-ə-lē\ *adv*

loy•al•ist \'lòi-ə-ləst\ *n* **:** one who is loyal to a political cause, party, government, or sovereign; *esp* **:** TORY 2

loy•al•ty \'lòi-əl-tē, 'lòil-\ *n, pl* **-ties :** the quality or state of being loyal **syn** see FIDELITY

loz•enge \'läz-nj\ *n* **1 a :** a diamond-shaped figure **b :** something shaped like a lozenge **2 :** a small often medicated candy [Middle French *losange*]

LP \'el-'pē\ *trademark* — used for a long-playing phonograph record

LSD \ˌel-ˌes-'dē\ *n* **:** an organic compound that induces psychotic symptoms similar to those of schizophrenia [*lys*ergic acid *d*iethylamide]

lu•au \'lü-ˌaú\ *n* **:** an Hawaiian feast [Hawaiian *lu'au*]

lub•ber \'ləb-ər\ *n* **1 :** a big clumsy fellow **2 :** an unskilled seaman [Middle English *lobur*] — **lub•ber•li•ness** \-lē-nəs\ *n* — **lub•ber•ly** \-lē\ *adj or adv*

lube \'lüb\ *n* **:** LUBRICANT

lu•bri•cant \'lü-bri-kənt\ *n* **:** something (as a grease or oil) capable of reducing friction when applied between moving parts — **lubricant** *adj*

lu•bri•cate \'lü-brə-ˌkāt\ *vb* **1 :** to make smooth or slippery **2 :** to apply a lubricant to ⟨*lubricate* a car⟩ **3 :** to act as a lubricant [Latin *lubricare,* from *lubricus* "slippery"] — **lu•bri•ca•tion** \ˌlü-brə-'kā-shən\ *n* — **lu•bri•ca•tive** \'lü-brə-ˌkāt-iv\ *adj* — **lu•bri•ca•tor** \-ˌkāt-ər\ *n*

lu•bri•cious \lü-'brish-əs\ *or* **lu•bri•cous** \'lü-bri-kəs\ *adj* **1 :** LECHEROUS; *also* **:** SALACIOUS 1 **2 :** smooth or slippery in texture ⟨a *lubricious* skin⟩ [Latin *lubricus* "slippery, easily led astray"] — **lu•bri•cious•ly** *adv* — **lu•bric•i•ty** \lü-'bris-ət-ē\ *n*

lu•cent \'lüs-nt\ *adj* **1 :** glowing with light **:** LUMINOUS **2 :** marked by clearness or translucence [Latin *lucens,* present participle of *lucēre* "to shine"] — **lu•cent•ly** *adv*

lu•cerne *also* **lu•cern** \lü-'sərn\ *n, chiefly British* **:** ALFALFA [French *luzerne,* from Provençal *luserno*]

lu•cid \'lü-səd\ *adj* **1 a :** suffused with light **:** LUMINOUS **b :** penetrated with light **:** TRANSLUCENT **2 :** having full use of one's faculties **:** clear in mind **3 :** clear to the understanding **:** PLAIN [Latin *lucidus*] **syn** see LIMPID — **lu•cid•i•ty** \lü-'sid-ət-ē\ *n* — **lu•cid•ly** *adv* — **lu•cid•ness** *n*

Lu•ci•fer \'lü-sə-fər\ *n* **:** DEVIL 1 [Old English, the morning star, a fallen angel, the Devil, from Latin, the morning star, from *lucifer* "light-bearing", from *luc-, lux* "light" + *-fer* "-ferous"]

△ **origin** *Lucifer,* "bearer of light", is a strange name for the Devil. Latin *Lucifer* (from *lux,* "light", and *ferre,* "to carry") was the name of the chief morning star (the planet Venus), which heralds, if it does not exactly carry in, the dawn. In telling about the fall of Babylon, the Prophet Isaiah compares the king of Babylon to the morning star: "How art thou fallen from Heaven, O Lucifer, son of the morning!" (Isaiah 14:12). Later, Christians interpreted Isaiah's description of the downfall of Babylon as an allegory for the fall from heaven of the rebel archangel Satan. *Lucifer,* they concluded, must have been the Devil's original name.

lu•cif•er•ase \lü-'sif-ə-ˌrās\ *n* **:** an enzyme that catalyzes the oxidation of luciferin

lu•cif•er•in \lü-'sif-ə-rən\ *n* **:** a component of luminescent organisms that furnishes practically heatless light in undergoing oxidation [Latin *lucifer* "light-bearing"]

Lu•cite \'lü-ˌsīt\ *trademark* — used for an acrylic resin or plastic consisting essentially of methacrylate

luck \'lək\ *n* **1 :** whatever happens to a person apparently by chance **:** FORTUNE ⟨we had a run of good *luck*⟩ **2 :** the accidental way events occur ⟨happening by pure *luck*⟩ **3 :** good fortune **:** SUCCESS ⟨out of *luck*⟩ [Dutch *luc*] — **luck•less** \'lək-ləs\ *adj*

lucky \'lək-ē\ *adj* **luck•i•er; -est 1 :** favored by luck **:** FORTUNATE **2 :** producing or resulting in good by chance ⟨a *lucky* hit⟩ **3 :** seeming to bring good luck ⟨a *lucky* coin⟩ — **luck•i•ly** \'lək-ə-lē\ *adv* — **luck•i•ness** \'lək-ē-nəs\ *n*

• **syn** LUCKY, FORTUNATE mean meeting with unforeseen or unpredictable success. LUCKY stresses the operation of pure chance in producing a favorable result; FORTUNATE suggests being rewarded beyond what one strictly deserves or succeeding beyond reasonable expectation.

lu•cra•tive \'lü-krət-iv\ *adj* **:** producing wealth **:** PROFITABLE ⟨invested in a *lucrative* business⟩ — **lu•cra•tive•ly** *adv* — **lu•cra•tive•ness** *n*

lu•cre \'lü-kər\ *n* **:** monetary gain **:** PROFIT; *also* **:** MONEY 1 [Latin *lucrum*]

lu•cu•bra•tion \ˌlü-kyə-'brā-shən, -kə-\ *n* **1 :** laborious study **:** MEDITATION **2 :** studied or pretentious expression in speech or writing [Latin *lucubratio* "study by night", from *lucubrare* "to work by lamplight"]

lu•di•crous \'lüd-ə-krəs\ *adj* **1 :** amusing or laughable through obvious absurdity or incongruity **2 :** deserving scorn as absurdly inept, false, or foolish [Latin *ludicrus,* from *ludus* "play, sport"] **syn** see LAUGHABLE — **lu•di•crous•ly** *adv* — **lu•di•crous•ness** *n*

lu•es \'lü-,ēz\ *n, pl* **lues** : SYPHILIS [Latin, "plague"] — **lu•et•ic** \lü-'et-ik\ *adj*

[1]**luff** \'ləf\ *n* **1** : the act of turning a sailing vessel's head into the wind **2** : the forward edge of a fore-and-aft sail [Middle French *lof* "weather side of a ship"]

[2]**luff** *vi* : to turn the head of a sailing vessel into the wind

[1]**lug** \'ləg\ *vb* **lugged**; **lug•ging** **1** : DRAG 1a, PULL **2** : to carry laboriously **3** : to introduce in a forced manner ⟨*lug* a story into the conversation⟩ [Middle English *luggen*]

[2]**lug** *n* **1** : a part (as a handle) that projects like an ear **2** : a big loutish person [Middle English *lugge*]

lug•gage \'ləg-ij\ *n* **1** : a traveler's belongings : BAGGAGE **2** : containers (as suitcases) for carrying belongings

lug•ger \'ləg-ər\ *n* : a boat that carries one or more lugsails

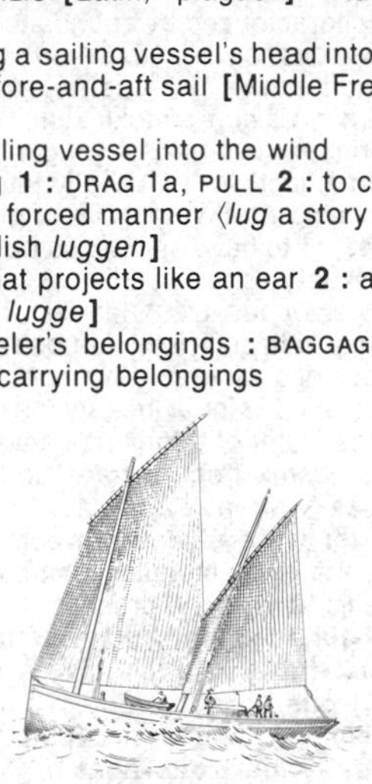

lugger

Lu•gol's solution \'lü-,gólz-, -,gälz-\ *n* : any of several deep brown solutions of iodine and potassium iodide in water or alcohol that are used in medicine and as microscopic stains — called also *Lugol's iodine solution* [J.G.A. *Lugol*, died 1851, French physician]

lug•sail \'ləg-,sāl, -səl\ *n* : a 4-sided sail fastened at the top to a yard that crosses the mast obliquely [perhaps from [2]*lug*]

lu•gu•bri•ous \lü-'gü-brē-əs, -'gyü-\ *adj* : MOURNFUL; *esp* : overly or affectedly mournful [Latin *lugubris*, from *lugēre* "to mourn"] — **lu•gu•bri•ous•ly** *adv* — **lu•gu•bri•ous•ness** *n*

lug•worm \'ləg-,wərm\ *n* : any of a genus of marine annelid worms that have a row of tufted gills along each side of the back and are used for bait [origin unknown]

Luke \'lük\ *n* — *see* BIBLE table

luke•warm \'lü-'kwórm\ *adj* **1** : neither hot nor cold : TEPID ⟨a *lukewarm* bath⟩ **2** : not enthusiastic : HALFHEARTED ⟨received a *lukewarm* reception⟩ [Middle English, from *luke* "lukewarm" + *warm*] — **luke•warm•ly** *adv* — **luke•warm•ness** *n*

[1]**lull** \'ləl\ *vt* **1** : to cause to sleep or rest : SOOTHE **2** : to cause to relax vigilance [Middle English *lullen*]

[2]**lull** *n* **1** : a temporary calm before or during a storm **2** : a temporary drop in activity

lul•la•by \'ləl-ə-,bī\ *n, pl* **-bies** : a song to quiet children or lull them to sleep [Middle English *lulla*, interj. used to lull a child + *by*, interj. used to lull a child]

lum•ba•go \,ləm-'bā-gō\ *n* : usually painful muscular rheumatism involving the lumbar region [Latin, from *lumbus* "loin"]

lum•bar \'ləm-bər, -,bär\ *adj* : of, relating to, or adjacent to the loins or the vertebrae between the thoracic vertebrae and sacrum ⟨*lumbar* region⟩ [Latin *lumbus* "loin"]

[1]**lum•ber** \'ləm-bər\ *vi* **lum•bered**; **lum•ber•ing** \-bə-ring, -bring\ **1** : to move heavily or clumsily **2** : RUMBLE 1 [Middle English *lomeren*]

[2]**lumber** *n* **1** : surplus or disused articles (as furniture) that are stored away **2** : timber or logs especially when sawed up for use [perhaps from earlier *Lombard* "moneylender" (from the prominence of Lombards as moneylenders); from the use of pawnshops as storehouses of disused property] — **lumber** *adj*

[3]**lumber** *vb* **lum•bered**; **lum•ber•ing** \-bə-ring, -bring\ **1** : to clutter with or as if with lumber : ENCUMBER **2** : to heap together in disorder **3** : to cut timber or saw logs into lumber — **lum•ber•er** \-bər-ər\ *n*

lum•ber•jack \'ləm-bər-,jak\ *n* : LOGGER

lum•ber•man \-mən\ *n* : one engaged in lumbering

lum•ber•yard \-,yärd\ *n* : a place where a stock of lumber is kept for sale

lu•men \'lü-mən\ *n, pl* **lu•mi•na** \-mə-nə\ *or* **lumens** **1** : the cavity or bore of a tube or tubular organ ⟨*lumen* of a blood vessel⟩ ⟨*lumen* of a catheter⟩ **2** : a unit of luminous flux equal to the light on a unit surface all points of which are at a unit distance from a uniform point source of one candle [Latin, "light, air shaft, opening"] — **lu•mi•nal** \'lü-mən-l\ *adj*

lumin- *or* **lumini-** *or* **lumino-** *combining form* : light ⟨*luminiferous*⟩ [Latin *lumin-*, *lumen*]

lu•mi•naire \,lü-mə-'naər, -'neər\ *n* : a complete lighting unit (as for a streetlight) [French, "lamp, lighting"]

lu•mi•nance \'lü-mə-nəns\ *n* : luminous intensity (as of a surface)

lu•mi•nary \'lü-mə-,ner-ē\ *n, pl* **-nar•ies** **1** : a source of light; *esp* : one of the celestial bodies **2** : a very famous and distinguished person — **luminary** *adj*

lu•mi•nes•cence \,lü-mə-'nes-ns\ *n* : emission of light at low temperatures as a by-product of a physiological, chemical, or electrical process; *also* : such light — **lu•mi•nesce** \-'nes\ *vi*

lu•mi•nes•cent \-'nes-nt\ *adj* : relating to, exhibiting, or adapted for the production of luminescence ⟨*luminescent* paint⟩ ⟨*luminescent* animals⟩

lu•mi•nif•er•ous \,lü-mə-'nif-rəs, -ə-rəs\ *adj* : transmitting, producing, or yielding light

lu•mi•nos•i•ty \,lü-mə-'näs-ət-ē\ *n, pl* **-ties** **1** : the quality or state of being luminous : BRIGHTNESS **2** : something luminous

lu•mi•nous \'lü-mə-nəs\ *adj* **1** : emitting light : SHINING **2** : bathed in or exposed to steady light ⟨a plaza *luminous* with sunlight⟩ **3** : CLEAR 3c, INTELLIGIBLE — **lu•mi•nous•ly** *adv* — **lu•mi•nous•ness** *n*

luminous flux *n* : radiant flux in the visible-wavelength range

lum•mox \'ləm-əks\ *n* : a clumsy person [origin unknown]

[1]**lump** \'ləmp\ *n* **1** : a piece or mass of indefinite size or shape **2** : AGGREGATE, TOTALITY ⟨taken in the *lump*⟩ **3** : an abnormal swelling or growth **4** : a thickset heavy person; *esp* : one who is stupid or dull **5** : [3]DESERT 2, COMEUPPANCE [Middle English]

[2]**lump** *vb* **1** : to group without discrimination **2** : to make into lumps **3** : to become formed into lumps

[3]**lump** *adj* : not divided into parts: ENTIRE ⟨a *lump* sum⟩

[4]**lump** *vt* : to put up with ⟨like it or *lump* it⟩ [origin unknown]

lump•ish \'ləm-pish\ *adj* **1** : DULL 3, SLUGGISH **2** : CLUMSY 1a, UNGAINLY — **lump•ish•ly** *adv* — **lump•ish•ness** *n*

lumpy \'ləm-pē\ *adj* **lump•i•er**; **-est** **1** : filled or covered with lumps **2** : having a thickset clumsy appearance — **lump•i•ly** \-pə-lē\ *adv* — **lump•i•ness** \-pē-nəs\ *n*

lu•na•cy \'lü-nə-sē\ *n, pl* **-cies** **1** : unsoundness of mind interrupted by lucid intervals **2** : wild foolishness : extreme folly [*lunatic*] **syn** see INSANITY

lu•na moth \,lü-nə-\ *n* : a large mostly pale green North American moth with long tails on the hind wings [Latin *luna* "moon"]

luna moth

lu•nar \'lü-nər\ *adj* **1** : of or relating to the moon **2** : measured by the moon's revolution ⟨*lunar* month⟩ [Latin *lunaris*, from *luna* "moon"]

lunar caustic *n* : silver nitrate fused and molded into sticks for use as a caustic

lunar eclipse *n* : an eclipse in which the moon passes partially or wholly through the umbra of the earth's shadow

lu•nate \'lü-,nāt\ *adj* : shaped like a crescent

lu•na•tic \'lü-nə-,tik\ *adj* **1 a** : affected with lunacy : INSANE **b** : designed for insane persons ⟨*lunatic* asylum⟩ **2** : wildly foolish or reckless [Late Latin *lunaticus*, from Latin *luna* "moon"; from the belief that lunacy fluctuated with the phases of the moon] — **lunatic** *n*

lunatic fringe *n* : the members of a political or social movement advocating eccentric or fanatical views

lunch \'lənch\ *n* **1** : a light meal; *esp* : one eaten in the middle of the day **2** : the food prepared for a lunch [probably short for *luncheon*] — **lunch** *vb* — **lunch•er** *n*

lun•cheon \'lən-chən\ *n* : a light meal at midday; *esp* : a formal lunch [perhaps alteration of *nuncheon* "light snack", from Middle English *noneschench*, literally, "noon drink", from *none* "noon" + *schench* "drink, cup"]

lun•cheon•ette \,lən-chə-'net\ *n* : a place where light lunches are sold

\ə\ abut	\aú\ **out**	\i\ **tip**	\ó\ **saw**	\ú\ **foot**
\ər\ **further**	\ch\ **chin**	\ī\ life	\ói\ **coin**	\y\ **yet**
\a\ mat	\e\ pet	\j\ **job**	\th\ **thin**	\yü\ **few**
\ā\ take	\ē\ **easy**	\ng\ **sing**	\th\ **this**	\yú\ cure
\ä\ cot, cart	\g\ **go**	\ō\ **bone**	\ü\ **food**	\zh\ vision

lunch•room \ˈlənch-ˌrüm, -ˌru̇m\ *n* **1** : LUNCHEONETTE **2** : a room (as in a school) where lunches supplied on the premises or brought from home may be eaten

lune \ˈlün\ *n* : a crescent-shaped figure on a plane surface or a sphere formed by two intersecting arcs of circles [Latin *luna* "moon"]

lung \ˈləŋ\ *n* **1 a** : one of the usually paired thoracic organs that form the special breathing apparatus of air-breathing vertebrates **b** : any of various other respiratory organs **2** : a device (as an iron lung) to promote and facilitate breathing [Old English *lungen*]

¹lunge \ˈlənj\ *vb* **1 a** : to stride forward and make a thrust with a sword **b** : to drive or thrust with or as if with a lunge **2** : to make a sudden forceful forward movement : RUSH [obsolete *allonge*, from French *allonger* "to extend (an arm), make long", derived from Latin *ad-* + *longus* "long"]

²lunge *n* **1** : a sudden stretching thrust or pass (as with a sword) **2** : the act of striding or leaping suddenly forward

¹lung•er \ˈlən-jər\ *n* : one that lunges

²lung•er \ˈləŋ-ər\ *n* : one suffering from a chronic disease of the lungs; *esp* : a tubercular person

lung•fish \ˈləŋ-ˌfish\ *n* : any of various fishes (order Dipneusti or Cladistia) that breathe by a modified air bladder as well as gills

lung•wort \ˈləŋ-ˌwərt, -ˌwȯrt\ *n* : a European herb that is related to the forget-me-not, has bristly leaves and bluish flowers, and was formerly used in the treatment of respiratory diseases

lunk•head \ˈləŋk-ˌhed\ *n* : a dull-witted person : DOLT [*lunk*, probably alteration of *lump*] — **lunk•head•ed** \-ˈhed-əd\ *adj*

lu•nule \ˈlü-nyül\ *n* : a crescent-shaped body part or marking; *esp* : the whitish mark at the base of a fingernail [Latin *lunula* "crescent-shaped ornament", from *luna* "moon"]

Lu•per•ca•lia \ˌlü-pər-ˈkā-lē-ə\ *n* : an ancient Roman festival celebrated February 15 to ensure fertility for the people, fields, and flocks [Latin, from *Lupercus*, god of flocks] — **Lu•per•ca•li•an** \-lē-ən\ *adj*

¹lu•pine \ˈlü-pən\ *n* : any of a genus of usually blue- or purple-flowered herbs of the pea family some of which are poisonous and others grown for green manure, fodder, or their edible seeds [Latin *lupinum*, from *lupinus* "of wolves", from *lupus* "wolf"]

²lu•pine \ˈlü-ˌpīn\ *adj* : of, relating to, or befitting or characteristic of wolves

lu•pus \ˈlü-pəs\ *n* : any of several diseases marked by skin lesions; *esp* : one of tuberculous origin [Medieval Latin, from Latin, "wolf"]

¹lurch \ˈlərch\ *n* : a decisive defeat (as in cribbage) in which an opponent wins a game by more than double the defeated player's score [Middle French *lourche* "defeated by a lurch, deceived"] — **in the lurch** : in a helpless or unsupported position ⟨left them *in the lurch*⟩

²lurch *n* : a sudden swaying or tipping movement ⟨the car gave a *lurch*⟩; *also* : a staggering gait [origin unknown]

³lurch *vi* : to roll or tip abruptly : PITCH; *also* : STAGGER

lurch•er \ˈlər-chər\ *n*, *British* : a mongrel dog; *esp* : one used by poachers [Middle English *lorchen* "to prowl, steal"]

¹lure \ˈlu̇r\ *n* **1 a** : an inducement to pleasure or gain : ENTICEMENT **b** : APPEAL 3, ATTRACTION **2** : a decoy for attracting animals to capture; *esp* : an artificial bait used for catching fish [Middle French *loire*, a device used by a falconer to recall a hawk, of Germanic origin]

²lure *vt* : to tempt with a promise of pleasure or gain : ENTICE — **lur•er** *n*

lu•rid \ˈlu̇r-əd\ *adj* **1** : ghastly pale : WAN, LIVID **2** : shining with the red glow of fire seen through smoke **3 a** : causing horror or revulsion : GRUESOME ⟨*lurid* tales of murder⟩ **b** : SENSATIONAL 2 [Latin *luridus* "pale yellow, sallow"] **syn** see GHASTLY — **lu•rid•ly** *adv* — **lu•rid•ness** *n*

lurk \ˈlərk\ *vi* **1 a** : to lie in ambush **b** : to move furtively or inconspicuously : SNEAK **c** : to persist in staying **2** : to be present but unseen or unrecognized ⟨a *lurking* danger⟩ [Middle English *lurken*] — **lurk•er** *n*

lus•cious \ˈləsh-əs\ *adj* **1** : having a delicious taste or smell ⟨*luscious* berries⟩ **2** : having sensual appeal : SEDUCTIVE **3** : richly luxurious or appealing to the senses; *also* : overly ornate [Middle English *lucius*] — **lus•cious•ly** *adv* — **lus•cious•ness** *n*

¹lush \ˈləsh\ *adj* **1** : producing or covered with luxuriant growth ⟨*lush* grass⟩ ⟨*lush* pastures⟩ **2 a** : doing well : VIGOROUS **b** : characterized by abundance : PLENTIFUL **3 a** : DELECTABLE 1, DELIGHTFUL **b** : LUXURIOUS 3, OPULENT [Middle English *lusch* "soft, tender"] — **lush•ly** *adv* — **lush•ness** *n*

²lush *n* **1** *slang* : intoxicating liquor : DRINK **2** : an habitual heavy drinker : DRUNKARD [origin unknown]

¹lust \ˈləst\ *n* **1** : usually intense sexual desire **2** : an intense longing : CRAVING [Old English, "pleasure, delight, lust"]

²lust *vi* : to have an intense desire or need : CRAVE; *esp* : to have sexual desire

lus•ter *or* **lus•tre** \ˈləs-tər\ *n* **1** : a shine or sheen especially from reflected light : GLOSS; *esp* : the appearance of the surface of a mineral with respect to its reflecting qualities ⟨a pearly *luster*⟩ **2** : inner beauty : RADIANCE **3** : GLORY 1a, SPLENDOR ⟨the *luster* of a famous name⟩ [Middle French *lustre*, from Italian *lustro*, from *lustrare* "to brighten", from Latin] — **lus•ter•less** \-tər-ləs\ *adj*

lus•ter•ware \-ˌwaər, -ˌweər\ *n* : pottery decorated by applying to the glaze metallic compounds which become iridescent metallic films in the process of firing

lust•ful \ˈləst-fəl\ *adj* : excited by lust; *esp* : LECHEROUS — **lust•ful•ly** \-fə-lē\ *adv* — **lust•ful•ness** n

lus•trous \ˈləs-trəs\ *adj* **1** : having a high gloss or shine **2** : radiant in character or reputation : ILLUSTRIOUS — **lus•trous•ly** *adv* — **lus•trous•ness** *n*

lus•trum \ˈləs-trəm\ *n, pl* **lustrums** *or* **lus•tra** \-trə\ **1 a** : a purification of the ancient Roman people made after the census every five years **b** : the Roman census **2** : a period of five years [Latin]

lusty \ˈləs-tē\ *adj* **lust•i•er**; **-est** : full of vitality : VIGOROUS — **lust•i•ly** \-tə-lē\ *adv* — **lust•i•ness** \-tē-nəs\ *n*

¹lute \ˈlüt\ *n* : a stringed instrument with a large pear-shaped body, a neck with a fretted fingerboard, and a head with pegs for tuning [Middle French *lut*, from Provençal *laut*, from Arabic *al-ʿūd*, literally, "the wood"]

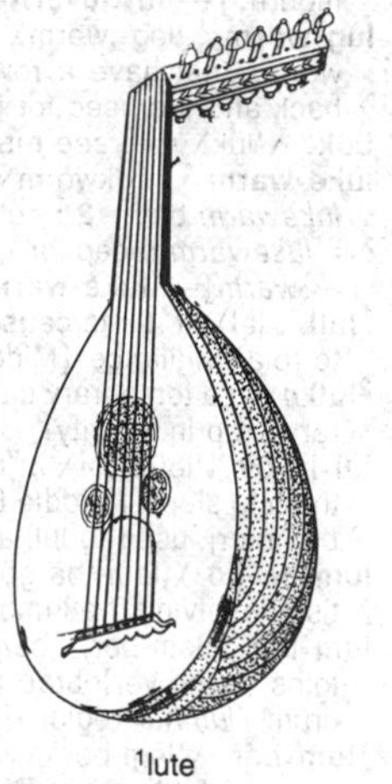

¹lute

²lute *n* : material (as cement or clay) for packing a joint or coating a porous surface to make it impervious to fluid [Latin *lutum* "mud"]

³lute *vt* : to seal or cover with lute ⟨*lute* a joint⟩

lu•te•al \ˈlüt-ē-əl\ *adj* : of, relating to, or involving the corpus luteum

lu•tein•iz•ing hormone \ˈlüt-ē-ə-ˌnīz-iŋ-, ˈlü-ˌtēn-ˌīz-\ *n* : a hormone of the pituitary gland that in the female stimulates especially the development of the corpora lutea

lu•te•nist *or* **lu•ta•nist** \ˈlüt-n-əst, ˈlüt-nəst\ *n* : one who plays the lute [Medieval Latin *lutanista*, from *lutana* "lute", probably from Middle French *lut*]

lu•teo•tro•phic hormone \ˌlüt-ē-ə-ˌtrō-fik-, -ˌträf-ik-\ *or* **lu•teo•tro•pic hormone** \-ˌtrō-pik-, -ˌträp-ik-\ *n* : PROLACTIN [*lute-* (as in *corpus luteum*) + Greek *trophē* "nourishment"]

lu•te•tium *or* **lu•te•cium** \lü-ˈtē-shē-əm, -shəm\ *n* : a soft ductile metallic chemical element — see ELEMENT table [New Latin, from Latin *Lutetia*, ancient name of Paris]

¹Lu•ther•an \ˈlü-thə-rən, -thrən\ *n* : a member of a Lutheran church

²Lutheran *adj* **1** : of or relating to Martin Luther or his religious doctrines **2** : of or relating to the Protestant churches adhering to Lutheran doctrines, liturgy, or polity — **Lu•ther•an•ism** \-ˌiz-əm\ *n*

lut•ing \ˈlüt-iŋ\ *n* : ²LUTE

lut•ist \ˈlüt-əst\ *n* : LUTENIST

lux \ˈləks\ *n, pl* **lux** *or* **lux•es** : a unit of illumination equal to one lumen per square meter [Latin, "light"]

lux•u•ri•ant \ləg-ˈzhu̇r-ē-ənt, ˌləg-; lək-ˈshu̇r-, ˌlək-\ *adj* **1 a** : yielding abundantly : PRODUCTIVE **b** : characterized by abundant growth : LUSH **2 a** : exuberantly rich and varied : PROFUSE **b** : excessively elaborate : FLORID **3** : LUXURIOUS 3 — **lux•u•ri•ance** \-əns\ *n* — **lux•u•ri•ant•ly** *adv*

• **syn** LUXURIOUS: LUXURIANT implies profuseness and rich abundance and suggests splendor of display ⟨a *luxuriant* bed of peonies⟩ ⟨a style decked with *luxuriant* imagery⟩ LUXURIOUS applies to what is choice and costly and suggests the satisfactions of sensuous comforts and pleasures ⟨a *luxurious* apartment⟩

lux•u•ri•ate \-ē-,āt\ *vi* **1** : to grow profusely : PROLIFERATE **2** : to indulge oneself luxuriously : REVEL ⟨spent the summer *luxuriating* at a seaside hotel⟩

lux•u•ri•ous \,ləg-'zhür-ē-əs, ,ləg-; lək-'shür-, ,lək-\ *adj* **1** : of or relating to unrestrained gratification of the senses : VOLUPTUOUS **2** : fond of luxury or self-indulgence **3 a** : characterized by opulence or rich abundance **b** : excessively ornate **syn** see LUXURIANT — **lux•u•ri•ous•ly** *adv* — **lux•u•ri•ous•ness** *n*

lux•u•ry \'ləksh-rē, 'ləgzh-, -ə-rē\ *n, pl* **-ries** **1** : sumptuous living or equipment : great ease or comfort : rich surroundings ⟨live in *luxury*⟩ **2 a** : something desirable but costly or hard to get ⟨a *luxury* few can afford⟩ **b** : something adding to pleasure but not absolutely necessary : FRILL [Middle French *luxurie,* from Latin *luxuria* "rankness, luxury, excess"] — **luxury** *adj*

[1]**-ly** \lē\ *adj suffix* **1** : like in appearance, manner, or nature : having the characteristics of ⟨king*ly*⟩ ⟨sister*ly*⟩ **2** : characterized by regular recurrence in (specified) units of time : every ⟨year*ly*⟩ [Old English *-līc, -lic,* from *līc* "body"]

[2]**-ly** *adv suffix* **1** : in a (specified) manner ⟨eas*ily*⟩ **2** : from a (specified) point of view ⟨theological*ly*⟩ **3** : with respect to ⟨part*ly*⟩ [Old English *-līce, -lice,* from *-līc,* adj. suffix]

ly•cée \lē-'sā\ *n* : a French public secondary school that prepares students for the university [French, from Middle French *lyceum,* from Latin *Lyceum*]

ly•ce•um \lī-'sē-əm, 'lī-sē-\ *n* **1** : a hall for public lectures or discussions **2** : an association providing public lectures, concerts, and entertainments [Latin *Lyceum,* gymnasium near Athens where Aristotle taught, from Greek *Lykeion,* from *lykeios,* epithet of Apollo]

lych–gate \'lich-,gāt\ *n* : a roofed gate in a churchyard under which a bier rests during the first part of a burial service [Middle English *lich, lych* "body, corpse", from Old English *līc*]

lych•nis \'lik-nəs\ *n* : any of a genus of often sticky-stemmed herbs of the pink family with usually red or white flowers [Latin, a kind of red flower, from Greek]

ly•co•pod \'lī-kə-,päd\ *n* : CLUB MOSS; *esp* : LYCOPODIUM 1

ly•co•po•di•um \,lī-kə-'pōd-ē-əm\ *n* **1** : any of a large genus of erect or creeping club mosses with evergreen leaves in four to many ranks **2** : a fine yellowish flammable powder of lycopodium spores used especially in pharmacy and in fireworks [Greek *lykos* "wolf" + *podion* "little foot", from *pod-, pous* "foot"]

Lyd•i•an \'lid-ē-ən\ *n* **1** : a native or inhabitant of Lydia **2** : an extinct Indo-European language of ancient Anatolia — **Lydian** *adj*

lye \'lī\ *n* **1** : a strong alkaline liquor rich in potassium carbonate leached from wood ashes and used especially in making soap and in washing **2** : any of various strong alkaline solutions; *also* : SODIUM HYDROXIDE **3** : a solid caustic [Old English *lēag*]

ly•gus bug \'lī-gəs-\ *n* : any of several small sucking bugs some of which transmit virus diseases to plants [New Latin *Lygus,* genus name]

ly•ing \'lī-ing\ *adj* : FALSE 2a, UNTRUTHFUL [present participle of [3]*lie*]

ly•ing–in \,lī-ing-'in\ *n, pl* **lyings–in** *or* **lying–ins** : the state during and immediately after childbirth — **lying–in** *adj*

lymph \'limf, 'limpf\ *n, pl* **lymphs** \'limfs, 'limpfs, 'lims, 'limps\ : a pale coagulable fluid that resembles blood plasma, contains white blood cells, circulates in lymphatic vessels, and bathes the cells of the body [Latin *lympha* "water goddess, water", from Greek *nymphē* "nymph"] — **lymph** *adj*

lymph•ad•e•ni•tis \,lim-,fad-n-'īt-əs\ *n* : inflammation of lymph glands [Greek *adēn* "gland"]

[1]**lym•phat•ic** \lim-'fat-ik\ *adj* **1 a** : of, relating to, or produced by lymph, lymphoid tissue, or lymphocytes **b** : conveying lymph **2** : lacking physical or mental energy — **lym•phat•i•cal•ly** \-'fat-i-kə-lē, -klē\ *adv*

[2]**lymphatic** *n* : a vessel that contains or conveys lymph

lymph node *n* : one of the masses of tissue occurring in association with the lymphatic vessels and giving rise to the lymphocytes — called also *lymph gland*

lym•pho•cyte \'lim-fə-,sīt, 'limp-\ *n* : a colorless weakly motile cell that is produced in lymphoid tissue, is the typical cellular element of lymph, and constitutes 20 to 30 percent of the leukocytes of normal human blood — **lym•pho•cyt•ic** \,lim-fə-'sit-ik, ,limp-\ *adj*

lym•phoid \'lim-,fȯid\ *adj* **1** : of, relating to, or resembling lymph **2** : of, relating to, or constituting the tissue characteristic of the lymph nodes

lynch \'linch\ *vt* : to put to death by mob action without due process of law [*lynch law*] — **lynch•er** *n*

lynch law *n* : the punishment of presumed crimes or offenses usually by death without due process of law [probably from Charles *Lynch,* died 1796, American justice of the peace; from his presiding over an irregular court to suppress Tory activity]

lynx \'lings, 'lingks\ *n, pl* **lynx** *or* **lynxes** : any of several wildcats with relatively long legs, a short stubby tail, mottled coat, and often tufted ears: as **a** : the common large wildcat of northern Europe and Asia **b** : BOBCAT **c** : a North American cat distinguished from the bobcat by its larger size, longer tufted ears, large padded paws, and wholly black tail tip — called also *Canadian lynx* [Latin, from Greek]

lynx c

lynx–eyed \'lings-'īd, 'lingks-\ *adj* : having keen sight

ly•on•naise \,lī-ə-'nāz\ *adj* : prepared with onions ⟨*lyonnaise* potatoes⟩ [French *à la lyonnaise* "in the manner of Lyons", from *Lyon* "Lyons, France"]

Ly•ra \'lī-rə\ *n* : a northern constellation containing Vega [Latin, literally, "lyre"]

lyre \'līr\ *n* : a stringed instrument of the harp class used by the ancient Greeks [Old French *lire,* from Latin *lyra,* from Greek]

lyre•bird \'līr-,bərd\ *n* : either of two Australian birds of which the males have very long tail feathers that are arranged during courtship in a way resembling a lyre

[1]**lyr•ic** \'lir-ik\ *adj* **1** : of or relating to a lyre **2 a** : resembling a song in form, feeling, or literary quality **b** : expressing a poet's own feeling : not narrative or dramatic **3** : having a light flexible quality ⟨a *lyric* soprano⟩

[2]**lyric** *n* **1** : a lyric poem or song **2** *pl* : the words of a song

lyr•i•cal \'lir-i-kəl\ *adj* **1** : resembling a song in mood or expression **2** : unrestrained in expressing enthusiasm, delight, or praise — **lyr•i•cal•ly** \-kə-lē, -klē\ *adv*

lyr•i•cism \'lir-ə-,siz-əm\ *n* **1** : the quality or state of being lyric **2** : an intense personal style or quality in an art (as poetry)

lyr•i•cist \'lir-ə-səst\ *n* : a writer of lyrics

lyr•ist \'līr-əst\ *n* : a lyre player

ly•ser•gic ac•id di•eth•yl•am•ide \lə-,sər-jik-'as-əd-,dī-,eth-ə-'lam-,īd, lī-\ *n* : LSD [*lysergic* from *lysis* + *ergot*]

ly•sin \'līs-n\ *n* : a substance capable of causing lysis; *esp* : an antibody capable of causing disintegration of red blood cells or microorganisms

ly•sine \'lī-,sēn\ *n* : a crystalline basic amino acid that is essential to animal nutrition

ly•sis \'lī-səs\ *n, pl* **ly•ses** \'lī-,sēz\ : a process of disintegration or dissolution; *esp* : disintegration of a bacterium following invasion by a bacteriophage [Greek, "act of loosening, breaking down", from *lyein* "to loosen"] — **lyt•ic** \'lit-ik\ *adj*

-ly•sis \l-ə-səs, 'lī-səs\ *n combining form, pl* **-l•y•ses** \l-ə-,sēz\ : decomposition ⟨electro*lysis*⟩ — **-lyt•ic** \'lit-ik\ *adj combining form*

ly•so•some \'lī-sə-,sōm\ *n* : a saclike cellular organelle that contains hydrolytic enzymes

ly•so•zyme \'lī-sə-,zīm\ *n* : any of various enzymes that destroy the capsules of certain bacteria and include some found in egg white and saliva

-lyze \,līz\ *vb combining form* : produce or undergo lytic disintegration or dissolution ⟨electro*lyze*⟩ [probably derived from *-lysis*]

\ə\ **abut**	\au̇\ **out**	\i\ **tip**	\ȯ\ **saw**	\u̇\ **foot**
\ər\ **further**	\ch\ **chin**	\ī\ **life**	\ȯi\ **coin**	\y\ **yet**
\a\ **mat**	\e\ **pet**	\j\ **job**	\th\ **thin**	\yü\ **few**
\ā\ **take**	\ē\ **easy**	\ng\ **sing**	\t͟h\ **this**	\yu̇\ **cure**
\ä\ **cot, cart**	\g\ **go**	\ō\ **bone**	\ü\ **food**	\zh\ **vision**

M m—myxomycete

m \'em\ *n, pl* **m's** *or* **ms** \'emz\ **1 :** the 13th letter of the English alphabet **2 :** one thousand in Roman numerals

'm \m\ *vb* **:** AM ⟨I'm going⟩

ma \'mä, 'mȯ\ *n, pl* **mas :** MOTHER [short for *mama*]

ma'am \'mam, *after "yes" often* əm\ *n* **:** MADAM

ma•ca•bre \mə-'käb, -'käb-rə, -'käb-ər, -'käbr\ *adj* **1 :** having death as a subject **:** including a representation of death personified **2 a :** dwelling on the gruesome **b :** tending to produce horror in a beholder ⟨a *macabre* procession of starving peasants⟩ [French, from *danse macabre* "dance of death", from Middle French *danse de Macabré*]

mac•ad•am \mə-'kad-əm\ *n* **:** macadamized roadway or pavement especially with a bituminous binder [John L. *McAdam,* died 1836, British engineer]

mac•a•da•mia nut \,mak-ə-'dā-mē-ə-\ *n* **:** a hard-shelled nut produced by an Australian evergreen tree [John *McAdam,* died 1865, Australian chemist]

mac•ad•am•ize \mə-'kad-ə-,mīz\ *vt* **:** to construct or surface (as a road) by packing a layer of small broken stone on a well-drained earth roadbed and using a binder for the mass

ma•caque \mə-'kak, -'käk\ *n* **:** any of several short-tailed monkeys of Asia and the East Indies; *esp* **:** RHESUS MONKEY [French, from Portuguese *macaco*]

mac•a•ro•ni \,mak-ə-'rō-nē\ *n, pl* **-nis** *or* **-nies :** a food made chiefly of semolina paste dried in the form of slender tubes [Italian *maccheroni,* pl. of *maccherone,* from Italian dialect *maccarone* "dumpling, macaroni"]

mac•a•roon \,mak-ə-'rün\ *n* **:** a cookie usually made of egg whites, sugar, and ground almonds or coconut [French *macaron,* from Italian dialect *maccarone* "dumpling, small cake, macaroni"]

ma•caw \mə-'kȯ\ *n* **:** any of numerous parrots of South and Central America including some of the largest and showiest [Portuguese *macau*]

macaw

Mac•ca•bees \'mak-ə-,bēz\ *n pl* **:** a priestly family who led a Jewish revolt against Hellenism and Syrian rule and governed Palestine from 142 B.C. to 63 B.C. — **Mac•ca•be•an** \,mak-ə-'bē-ən\ *adj*

Mc•Coy \mə-'kȯi\ *n* **:** something genuine ⟨the real *McCoy*⟩ [alteration of *Mackay* (in the phrase *the real Mackay* "the true chief of the Mackay clan", a position often disputed)]

¹mace \'mās\ *n* **1 :** a heavy spiked club used as a weapon in the Middle Ages **2 :** an ornamental staff borne as a symbol of authority [Middle French]

²mace *n* **:** a spice consisting of the dried outer fibrous covering of the nutmeg [Middle French *macis,* from Latin *macir,* a kind of spice, from Greek *makir*]

mac•er•ate \'mas-ə-,rāt\ *vb* **1 :** to waste away or cause to waste away **2 :** to cause to become soft or separated into constituent elements by or as if by steeping in fluid [Latin *macerare,* "to soften, steep"] — **mac•er•a•tion** \,mas-ə-'rā-shən\ *n*

Mach \'mäk\ *n* **:** MACH NUMBER

Mach•a•bees \'mak-ə-,bēz\ *n pl — see* BIBLE table

ma•chete \mə-'shet-ē, -'chet-ē; -'shet\ *n* **:** a large heavy knife used for cutting sugarcane and underbrush and as a weapon [Spanish]

Ma•chi•a•vel•lian \,mak-ē-ə-'vel-ē-ən, -'vel-yən\ *adj* **1 :** of or relating to Niccolò Machiavelli or Machiavellianism **2 :** characterized by cunning, deceitfulness, or bad faith — **Machiavellian** *n*

Ma•chi•a•vel•lian•ism \-,iz-əm\ *n* **:** the political theory of Machiavelli; *esp* **:** the view that any means however unscrupulous can justifiably be used in gaining and maintaining political power

mach•i•nate \'mak-ə-,nāt, 'mash-ə-\ *vb* **:** CONTRIVE, PLOT; *esp* **:** to plot or scheme to do harm [Latin *machinari,* from *machina* "machine, contrivance"] — **mach•i•na•tor** \-,nāt-ər\ *n*

mach•i•na•tion \,mak-ə-'nā-shən, ,mash-ə-\ *n* **:** a crafty scheme or plot usually intended to accomplish some evil end — usually used in pl.

¹ma•chine \mə-'shēn\ *n* **1 a :** VEHICLE, CONVEYANCE; *esp* **:** AUTOMOBILE **b :** a combination of parts that transmit forces, motion, and energy in a way that accomplishes some desired work ⟨a sewing *machine*⟩ **c :** an instrument (as a lever or pulley) designed to transmit or modify the application of power, force, or motion **2 a :** a person or organization that acts like a machine **b :** a combination of persons acting together for a common end together with the means they use; *esp* **:** a highly organized political group under the leadership of a boss or a small clique [Middle French, "structure, contrivance", from Latin *machina,* from Greek *mēchanē,* from *mēchos* "means, expedient"] — **ma•chine•like** \-,līk\ *adj*

²machine *vt* **:** to shape or finish by machine-operated tools — **ma•chin•able** *also* **ma•chine•able** \-'shē-nə-bəl\ *adj*

machine gun *n* **:** an automatic gun capable of continuous firing — **ma•chine–gun** \mə-'shēn-,gən\ *vb* — **machine gunner** *n*

ma•chin•ery \mə-'shēn-rē, -ə-rē\ *n* **1 :** MACHINES ⟨factory *machinery*⟩ **2 :** the working parts of a machine or instrument having moving parts ⟨the *machinery* of a watch⟩ **3 :** the organization or system by which something is done or carried on ⟨the *machinery* of government⟩

machine shop *n* **:** a workshop in which metal articles are machined and assembled

machine tool *n* **:** a machine (as a lathe or drill) that is operated by power and is partly or wholly automatic

ma•chin•ist \mə-'shē-nəst\ *n* **:** a person who makes or works on machines and engines

ma•chis•mo \mä-'chēz-mō, mə-, -'kēz-, -'kiz-, -'chiz-\ *n* **:** a strong sense of masculine pride **:** an exaggerated awareness and assertion of masculinity [Mexican Spanish, from Spanish *macho* "male"]

Mach number \'mäk-\ *n* **:** a number representing the ratio of the speed of a body to the speed of sound in the surrounding atmosphere ⟨a *Mach number* of 2 indicates a speed that is twice the speed of sound⟩ [Ernst *Mach,* died 1916, Austrian physicist]

¹ma•cho \'mä-,chō\ *adj* **:** aggressively virile [Spanish, "male", from Latin *masculus*]

²macho *n, pl* **machos 1 :** MACHISMO **2 :** one who exhibits machismo

mack•er•el \'mak-rəl, -ə-rəl\ *n, pl* **-el** *or* **-els :** a North Atlantic food fish that is green with blue bars above and silvery below; *also* **:** any of various usually small or medium-sized related fishes [Old French *makerel*]

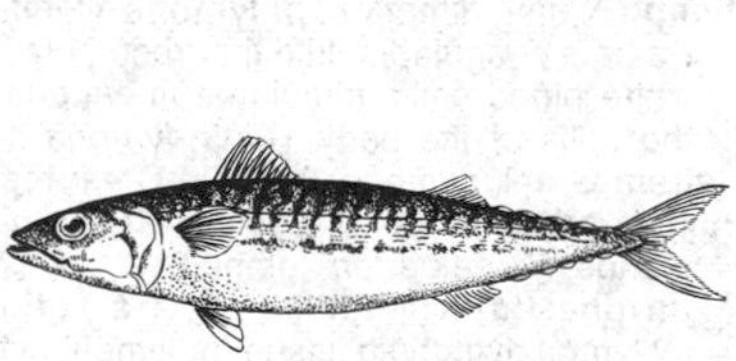
mackerel

mackerel sky *n* **:** a sky covered with rows of clouds resembling the patterns on a mackerel's back

mack•i•naw \'mak-ə-,nȯ\ *n* **1 :** a flat-bottomed boat with pointed prow and square stern formerly much used on the upper Great Lakes **2 :** a short heavy coat reaching to about mid-thigh [*Mackinaw* City, Michigan, formerly an Indian trading post]

mack•in•tosh *or* **mac•in•tosh** \'mak-ən-,täsh\ *n, chiefly British* : RAINCOAT [Charles *Macintosh,* died 1843, Scottish chemist and inventor]

macr- *or* **macro-** *combining form* : large ⟨*macro*nucleus⟩ [Greek *makros* "long"]

mac•ro•ceph•a•lous \,mak-rō-'sef-ə-ləs\ *or* **mac•ro•ce•phal•ic** \-sə-'fal-ik\ *adj* : having or being an exceptionally large head or cranium ⟨a *macrocephalic* idiot⟩ — **mac•ro•ceph•a•ly** \-'sef-ə-lē\ *n*

mac•ro•cosm \'mak-rə-,käz-əm\ *n* : the great world : UNIVERSE [French *macrocosme,* from Medieval Latin *macrocosmos,* from Greek *makros* "long, large" + *kosmos* "order, universe"] — **mac•ro•cos•mic** \,mak-rə-'käz-mik\ *adj* — **mac•ro•cos•mi•cal•ly** \-mi-kə-lē, -klē\ *adv*

mac•ro•eco•nom•ics \,mak-rō-,ek-ə-'näm-iks, -,ē-kə-\ *n* : a study of economics in terms of whole systems especially with reference to general levels of output and income and to the interrelations among sectors of the economy — compare MICROECONOMICS — **mac•ro•eco•nom•ic** \-ik\ *adj*

mac•ro•ga•mete \,mak-rō-gə-'mēt, -'gam-,ēt\ *n* : the larger and usually female gamete of an organism with two kinds of gametes — compare MICROGAMETE

mac•ro•mol•e•cule \,mak-rō-'mäl-i-,kyül\ *n* : a large molecule built up from smaller chemical structures — **mac•ro•mo•lec•u•lar** \,mak-rō-mə-'lek-yə-lər\ *adj*

ma•cron \'māk-,rän, 'mak-, -rən\ *n* : a mark ¯ placed over a vowel (as in \māk\) to show that the vowel is long [Greek *makron,* from *makros* "long"]

mac•ro•nu•cle•us \,mak-rō-'nü-klē-əs, -'nyü-\ *n* : a large densely staining nucleus held to exert a major influence over the nutritional activities of most ciliated protozoans

mac•ro•phage \'mak-rə-,fāj, -,fäzh\ *n* : a large phagocyte — **mac•ro•phag•ic** \,mak-rə-'faj-ik\ *adj*

mac•ro•scop•ic \,mak-rə-'skäp-ik\ *adj* **1** : large enough to be observed by the naked eye **2** : considered in terms of large units or elements [*macr-* + *-scopic* (as in *microscopic*)] — **mac•ro•scop•i•cal•ly** \-i-kə-lē, -klē\ *adv*

mac•u•la \'mak-yə-lə\ *n, pl* **-lae** \-,lē, -,lī\ *also* **-las** : an anatomical structure (as the macula lutea) having the form of a spot differentiated from surrounding tissues [Latin, "spot, stain"] — **mac•u•lar** \-lər\ *adj*

mac•u•la lu•tea \,mak-yə-lə-'lüt-ē-ə\ *n, pl* **mac•u•lae lu•te•ae** \-lē-'lüt-ē-,ē, -lī-'lüt-ē-,ī\ : a small yellowish area lying slightly lateral to the center of the retina that constitutes the region of most acute vision — called also *yellow spot* [New Latin, literally, "yellow spot"]

mac•u•la•tion \,mak-yə-'lā-shən\ *n* : the arrangement of spots and markings on an animal or plant

mac•ule \'mak-,yül\ *n* : a patch of skin altered in color but usually not elevated that is a characteristic feature of various diseases (as smallpox)

mad \'mad\ *adj* **mad•der; mad•dest 1** : disordered in mind : INSANE **2** : being rash and foolish ⟨a *mad* promise⟩ **3** : FURIOUS, ENRAGED ⟨a *mad* bull⟩ **4** : FRANTIC ⟨*mad* with pain⟩ **5** : carried away by enthusiasm ⟨*mad* about dancing⟩ **6** : wildly merry ⟨a *mad* party⟩ **7** : affected with rabies : RABID ⟨a *mad* dog⟩ [Old English *gemǣd*] **syn** see INSANE — **mad•ly** *adv*

mad•am \'mad-əm\ *n, pl* **madams 1** *pl* **mes•dames** \mə-'däm, -'dam\ — used as a form of respectful address to a high-ranking woman **2** *cap* — used as a title before the surname of a high-ranking woman and especially before a designation of her rank or office ⟨*Madam* President⟩ **3** : a woman who runs a house of prostitution [Old French *ma dame,* literally, "my lady"]

ma•dame \mə-'dam, ma-', *before a surname also,* ,mad-əm\ *n, pl* **mes•dames** \mā-'däm, -'dam\ — used as a courtesy title equivalent to *Mrs.* for a married woman not of English-speaking nationality [French, from Old French *ma dame* "my lady"]

mad•cap \'mad-,kap\ *adj* : being impulsive and rash ⟨a *madcap* scheme — **madcap** *n*

mad•den \'mad-n\ *vt* : to make mad

mad•den•ing \'mad-ning, -n-ing\ *adj* : that irritates or infuriates ⟨a *maddening* habit⟩ — **mad•den•ing•ly** \-ning-lē, -n-ing-lē\ *adv*

mad•der \'mad-ər\ *n* **1** : a Eurasian herb with spear-shaped leaves, small yellowish flowers followed by berries, and red fleshy roots used to make a dye; *also* : any of several related plants **2** : madder root or a dye prepared from it [Old English *mædere*]

mad•ding \'mad-ing\ *adj* **1** : acting as if mad : FRENZIED ⟨the *madding* crowd⟩ **2** : MADDENING

made *past of* MAKE

Ma•dei•ra \mə-'dir-ə, -'der-\ *n* : an amber-colored dessert wine of the Madeira islands; *also* : a similar wine made elsewhere

ma•de•moi•selle \,mad-mə-'zel, -ə-mə-, -mwə-'zel; mam-'zel\ *n, pl* **ma•de•moi•selles** \-'zelz\ *or* **mes•de•moi•selles** \,mād-mə-'zel, -ə-mə-, -mwə-'zel\ — used by or to French-speaking people as a courtesy title equivalent to *Miss* [French, from Old French *ma damoisele* "my young lady"]

made-up \'mād-'əp\ *adj* **1** : marked by the use of make-up ⟨*made-up* eyelids⟩ **2** : fancifully conceived or falsely devised ⟨a *made-up* story⟩ **3** : fully manufactured

mad•house \'mad-,haủs\ *n* **1** : a place where insane persons are detained and treated **2** : a place of bewildering uproar or confusion

mad•man \'mad-,man, -mən\ *n* : a man who is or acts as if insane

mad•ness \'mad-nəs\ *n* **1** : the quality or state of being mad : as **a** : INSANITY **b** : extreme folly **c** : FURY 1, RAGE **2** : any of several disorders of animals marked by frenzied behavior; *esp* : RABIES

Ma•don•na lily \mə-,dän-ə-\ *n* : a white-flowered lily often forced for spring bloom [*Madonna,* the Virgin Mary, from Italian *ma donna* "my lady"]

ma•dras \'mad-rəs; mə-'dras, -'dräs\ *n* : a fine usually corded or striped cotton fabric [*Madras,* India]

mad•ri•gal \'mad-ri-gəl\ *n* **1 a** : a short love poem suitable for a musical setting **b** : a musical setting for a madrigal **2** : a complex 16th century part-song [Italian *madrigale*] — **mad•ri•gal•ist** \-gə-ləst\ *n*

ma•dro•na \mə-'drō-nə\ *n* : an evergreen heath of western North America with shiny leaves and edible red berries [Spanish *madroño*]

mad•wom•an \'mad-,wủm-ən\ *n* : a woman who is or acts as if insane

Mae•ce•nas \mi-'sē-nəs\ *n* : a generous patron especially of literature or art [Latin, from Gaius *Maecenas,* died 8 B.C., Roman statesman and patron of literature]

mael•strom \'māl-strəm\ *n* **1** : a whirlpool of great force and violence **2** : something resembling a whirlpool especially in whirling confusion ⟨a *maelstrom* of emotions⟩ [obsolete Dutch, from *malen* "to grind" + *strom* "stream"]

mae•nad \'mē-,nad\ *n* **1** : BACCHANTE **2** : an excessively excited or distraught woman [Latin *maenad-, maenas,* from Greek *mained-, mainas,* from *mainesthai* "to be mad"] — **mae•nad•ic** \mē-'nad-ik\ *adj*

mae•sto•so \mī-'stō-sō, -zō\ *adv or adj* : so as to be majestic and stately — used as a direction in music [Italian, from Latin *majestosus,* from *majestas* "majesty"]

mae•stro \'mī-strō\ *n, pl* **mae•stros** \-strōz\ *or* **mae•stri** \-,strē\ : a master in an art; *esp* : an eminent composer, conductor, or teacher of music [Italian, literally, "master", from Latin *magister*]

Mae West \'mā-'west\ *n* : an inflatable life jacket in the form of a collar extending down the chest that was worn by fliers in World War II [*Mae West,* born 1892, American actress noted for her full figure]

Ma•fia \'mäf-ē-ə, 'maf-\ *n* **1** : a secret terrorist society **2** : a secret criminal organization held to control illicit activities (as racketeering) throughout the world [*Mafia, Maffia,* a Sicilian secret criminal society, from Italian]

ma•fi•o•so \,mäf-ē-'ō-sō ,maf-, -zō\ *n, pl* **-si** \-sē, -zē\ : a member of a Mafia [Italian, from *Mafia*]

mag•a•zine \'mag-ə-,zēn, ,mag-ə-'\ *n* **1** : STOREHOUSE 1, WAREHOUSE **2** : a place for keeping gunpowder in a fort or ship **3** : a periodical containing miscellaneous stories, articles, or poems **4** : a supply chamber: as **a** : a chamber in a gun for holding cartridges **b** : a chamber for film on a camera or motion-picture projector [Middle French *magazin,* from Provençal, from Arabic *makhāzin,* pl. of *makhzan* "storehouse"]

ma·gen·ta \mə-ˈjent-ə\ *n* **1 :** FUCHSINE **2 :** a deep purplish red [*Magenta,* Italy]

mag·got \ˈmag-ət\ *n* **1 :** a soft-bodied legless grub that is the larva of a two-winged fly (as the housefly) **2 :** an odd or fantastic idea **:** WHIM [of Scandinavian origin; sense 2 from the suggestion that a whim might be the result of a maggot in the brain] — **mag·goty** \-ət-ē\ *adj*

ma·gi \ˈmā-ˌjī\ *n pl, often cap* **:** the three wise men from the East who paid homage to the infant Jesus [Latin, pl. of *magus* "Persian wise man, magician", from Greek *magos*]

[1]**mag·ic** \ˈmaj-ik\ *n* **1 :** the art of persons who claim to be able to do things by the help of supernatural creatures or by their own knowledge of nature's secrets **2 a :** something that charms ⟨the *magic* of your smile⟩ **b :** seemingly hidden or secret power ⟨the *magic* of a great name⟩ **3 :** SLEIGHT OF HAND 1 [Middle French *magique,* from Latin *magice,* from Greek *magikos* "magical", from *magos* "Persian wise man, magician, sorcerer", of Iranian origin]

[2]**magic** *adj* **1 :** of or relating to magic **2 a :** having seemingly supernatural qualities or powers **b :** ENCHANTING — **mag·i·cal** \ˈmaj-i-kəl\ *adj* — **mag·i·cal·ly** \-kə-lē, -klē\ *adv*

ma·gi·cian \mə-ˈjish-ən\ *n* **1 :** a person skilled in magic; *esp* **:** SORCERER **2 :** a performer of sleight of hand

magic lantern *n* **:** an early type of slide projector

magic square *n* **:** a square containing a number of integers so arranged that the sum of the numbers in each row, column, and diagonal is always the same

4	9	2
3	5	7
8	1	6

6	3	10	15
9	16	5	4
7	2	11	14
12	13	8	1

magic square

mag·is·te·ri·al \ˌmaj-ə-ˈstir-ē-əl\ *adj* **1 :** AUTHORITATIVE 3 **2 :** of or relating to a magistrate or magistracy [Late Latin *magisterialis* "of authority", derived from Latin *magister* "master"] — **mag·is·te·ri·al·ly** \-ē-ə-lē\ *adv*

mag·is·tra·cy \ˈmaj-ə-strə-sē\ *n, pl* **-cies 1 :** the state of being a magistrate **2 :** the office, power, or dignity of a magistrate **3 :** a body of magistrates

ma·gis·tral \ˈmaj-ə-strəl, mə-ˈjis-trəl\ *adj* **:** MAGISTERIAL 1 — **ma·gis·tral·ly** \-ē\ *adv*

mag·is·trate \ˈmaj-ə-ˌstrāt, -strət\ *n* **:** an official entrusted with administration of the laws: as **a :** a principal official exercising executive powers over a major political unit **b :** a local official exercising administrative and often judicial functions **c :** a local judiciary official having jurisdiction in some criminal cases [Latin *magistratus* "magistracy, magistrate", from *magister* "master"]

mag·ma \ˈmag-mə\ *n* **:** molten rock material within the earth from which an igneous rock results by cooling [Latin *magmat-, magma* "dregs, sediment", from Greek, "pasty substance", from *massein* "to knead"] — **mag·mat·ic** \mag-ˈmat-ik\ *adj*

Mag·na Char·ta *or* **Mag·na Car·ta** \ˌmag-nə-ˈkärt-ə\ *n* **1 :** a charter of civil liberties to which the English barons forced King John to give his assent in June 1215 at Runnymede **2 :** a document constituting a fundamental guarantee of rights and privileges [Medieval Latin, literally, "great charter"]

mag·na cum lau·de \ˌmäg-nə-ˌkům-ˈlau̇d-ə, -ˈlau̇d-ē; ˌmag-nə-ˌkəm-ˈlȯd-ē\ *adv or adj* **:** with great academic distinction ⟨graduated *magna cum laude*⟩ [Latin, "with great praise"]

mag·na·nim·i·ty \ˌmag-nə-ˈnim-ət-ē\ *n, pl* **-ties 1 a :** nobility of character **:** HIGH-MINDEDNESS **b :** GENEROSITY 1 **2 :** a magnanimous act

mag·nan·i·mous \mag-ˈnan-ə-məs\ *adj* **1 :** showing or suggesting a lofty and courageous spirit **:** NOBLE **2 :** free of all meanness or pettiness [Latin *magnanimus,* from *magnus* "great" + *animus* "spirit"] — **mag·nan·i·mous·ly** adv — **mag·nan·i·mous·ness** *n*

mag·nate \ˈmag-ˌnāt, -nət\ *n* **:** a person of rank, power, influence, or distinction (as in an industry) [Late Latin *magnates,* pl., from Latin *magnus* "great"]

mag·ne·sia \mag-ˈnē-shə, -ˈnē-zhə\ *n* **1 :** a white highly infusible earthy solid MgO that consists of magnesium and oxygen and is used in refractories, fertilizers, and rubber and as an antacid and mild laxative **2 :** MAGNESIUM [New Latin, from *magnes carneus,* a white earth, literally, "flesh magnet"] — **mag·ne·sian** \-shən, -zhən\ *adj*

mag·ne·sium \mag-ˈnē-zē-əm, -zhəm\ *n* **:** a silver-white metallic element that is lighter than aluminum, is easily worked, burns with a dazzling light, and is used in making lightweight alloys — see ELEMENT table [New Latin, from *magnesia*]

magnesium chloride *n* **:** a bitter deliquescent salt $MgCl_2$ that consists of magnesium and chlorine, occurs in seawaters and underground brines, and is used in producing magnesium metal

magnesium sulfate *n* **:** any of several sulfates of magnesium; *esp* **:** EPSOM SALT

mag·net \ˈmag-nət\ *n* **1 :** a piece of some material (as the mineral iron oxide) that is able to attract iron; *esp* **:** a mass of iron or steel so treated that it has this property **2 :** something that attracts ⟨the *magnet* of fame⟩ [Middle French *magnete,* from Latin *magnes,* from Greek *magnēs lithos,* literally, "stone of Magnesia (ancient city in Asia Minor)"]

magnet- *or* **magneto-** *combining form* **:** magnetism **:** magnetic ⟨*magneto*electric⟩

mag·net·ic \mag-ˈnet-ik\ *adj* **1 :** of or relating to a magnet or magnetism **2 :** of or relating to the earth's magnetism ⟨the *magnetic* meridian⟩ **3 :** capable of being magnetized **4 :** working by magnetic attraction **5 :** gifted with great power to attract ⟨a *magnetic* personality⟩ — **mag·net·i·cal·ly** \-ˈnet-i-kə-lē, -klē\ *adv*

magnetic field *n* **:** the portion of space near a magnetic body or a body carrying an electric current within which magnetic forces due to the body or current can be detected

magnetic needle *n* **:** a narrow strip of magnetized steel that is free to swing horizontally or vertically to show the direction of the earth's magnetism and that is the essential part of a compass

magnetic north *n* **:** the northerly direction in the earth's magnetic field indicated by the north-seeking pole of a horizontal magnetic needle

magnetic pole *n* **1 :** either of the poles of a magnet **2 :** either of two small regions which are located respectively in the polar areas of the northern and southern hemispheres and toward which a compass needle points

magnetic recording *n* **:** the process of recording sound, data, or a television program by producing varying local magnetization of a moving tape, wire, or disc — **magnetic recorder** *n*

magnetic storm *n* **:** a marked temporary disturbance of the earth's magnetic field held to be related to sunspots

magnetic tape *n* **:** a thin ribbon (as of plastic) coated for use in magnetic recording

magnetic wire *n* **:** a thin wire used in magnetic recording

mag·ne·tism \ˈmag-nə-ˌtiz-əm\ *n* **1 a :** the property of attracting certain metals or producing a magnetic field as shown by a magnet, a magnetized material, or a conductor carrying an electric current **b :** the science that deals with magnetic occurrences or conditions **2 :** the power to attract or charm others

mag·ne·tite \ˈmag-nə-ˌtīt\ *n* **:** a black mineral Fe_3O_4 that is an oxide of iron, is strongly attracted by a magnet, and is an important iron ore

mag·ne·tize \ˈmag-nə-ˌtīz\ *vt* **1 :** to attract like a magnet **:** CHARM **2 :** to give magnetic properties to — **mag·ne·tiz·able** \-ˌtī-zə-bəl\ *adj* — **mag·ne·ti·za·tion** \ˌmag-nət-ə-ˈzā-shən\ *n* — **mag·ne·tiz·er** \ˈmag-nə-ˌtī-zər\ *n*

mag·ne·to \mag-ˈnēt-ō\ *n, pl* **-tos :** a small electric generator using permanent magnets; *esp* **:** one used to produce sparks in an internal-combustion engine [short for *magnetoelectric machine*]

mag·ne·to·elec·tric \mag-ˌnēt-ō-ə-ˈlek-trik\ *adj* **:** relating to electromotive forces developed by magnetic means ⟨*magnetoelectric* induction⟩

mag·ne·tom·e·ter \ˌmag-nə-ˈtäm-ət-ər\ *n* **:** an instrument for measuring magnetic intensity especially of the earth's magnetic field

mag·ne·to·sphere \mag-ˈnēt-ə-ˌsfiər, -ˈnet-\ *n* **:** a region of the upper atmosphere that extends out for thousands of kilometers and is dominated by the earth's magnetic field so that charged particles are trapped in it; *also* **:** a region surrounding a celestial body that is comparable to the earth's magnetosphere

mag·ne·to·stric·tion \mag-ˌnēt-ō-ˈstrik-shən, -ˌnet-\ *n* **:** the change in the dimensions of various magnetic bodies caused by a change in their state of magnetization [*magnet-* + *-striction* (as in *constriction*)] — **mag·ne·to·stric·tive** \-ˈstrik-tiv\ *adj*

magnet school *n* : a school with superior facilities and staff designed to attract pupils from all segments of the community

Mag•nif•i•cat \mag-'nif-i-,kat, -,kät; män-'yif-i-,kät\ *n* : the canticle of the Virgin Mary in Luke 1:46-55 [Latin, "magnifies", its first word]

mag•ni•fi•ca•tion \,mag-nə-fə-'kā-shən\ *n* **1** : the act of magnifying : the state of being magnified **2** : the apparent enlargement of an object by an optical instrument

mag•nif•i•cence \mag-'nif-ə-səns\ *n* : the quality or state of being magnificent : SPLENDOR, GRANDEUR [Middle French, from Latin *magnificentia,* from *magnificus* "noble, magnificent", from *magnus* "great" + *-ficus* "-fic"]

mag•nif•i•cent \-sənt\ *adj* **1** : having grandeur and beauty : SPLENDID ⟨*magnificent* palaces⟩ ⟨a *magnificent* view⟩ **2** : NOBLE 5 ⟨a *magnificent* character⟩ **syn** see GRAND — **mag•nif•i•cent•ly** *adv*

mag•nif•i•co \mag-'nif-i-,kō\ *n, pl* **-coes** *or* **-cos** **1** : a nobleman of Venice **2** : a person of high position or distinguished appearance [Italian, from *magnifico* "magnificent", from Latin *magnificus*]

mag•ni•fy \'mag-nə-,fī\ *vb* **-fied**; **-fy•ing** **1** : EXTOL, LAUD **2** : to enlarge in fact or appearance ⟨ a microscope *magnifies* an object seen through it⟩ **3** : to exaggerate in importance ⟨*magnify* a fault⟩ [Middle French *magnifier,* from Latin *magnificare,* from *magnificus* "great, magnificent"] — **mag•ni•fi•er** \-,fī-ər, -,fīr\ *n*

mag•ni•fy•ing glass *n* : a lens that magnifies an object seen through it

mag•ni•tude \'mag-nə-,tüd, -,tyüd\ *n* **1 a** : greatness especially in size or extent **b** : spatial quality : SIZE **2** : greatness in influence or effect **3** : degree of brightness; *esp* : a number representing the relative brightness of a star on a scale on which the lowest number represents the brightest star [Latin *magnitudo,* from *magnus* "large"]

mag•no•lia \mag-'nōl-yə\ *n* : any of a genus of North American and Asian shrubs and trees with usually showy white, yellow, rose, or purple flowers appearing in early spring [Pierre *Magnol,* died 1715, French botanist]

magnolia

mag•num opus \,mag-nə-'mō-pəs\ *n* : a great work; *esp* : a literary or artistic masterpiece [Latin]

mag•pie \'mag-,pī\ *n* **1** : any of numerous noisy birds related to the jays but having a long tapered tail and black-and-white plumage **2** : a person who chatters constantly [*Mag* (nickname for *Margaret*) + [1]*pie*]

ma•guey \mə-'gā\ *n, pl* **magueys** **1** : any of various fleshy-leaved agaves or closely related fiber-yielding plants **2** : any of several hard fibers derived from magueys [Spanish, of American Indian origin]

Mag•yar \'mag-,yär, 'mäg-; 'mäj-,är\ *n* **1** : a member of the dominant people of Hungary **2** : the language of the Magyars — called also *Hungarian* [Hungarian] — **Magyar** *adj*

ma•ha•ra•ja *or* **ma•ha•ra•jah** \,mä-hə-'räj-ə, -'räzh-ə\ *n* : a Hindu prince ranking above a raja [Sanskrit *mahārāja,* from *mahat* "great" + *rājan* "raja"]

ma•ha•ra•ni *or* **ma•ha•ra•nee** \-'rän-ē\ *n* **1** : the wife of a maharaja **2** : a Hindu princess ranking above a rani [Hindi *mahārānī,* from *mahā* "great" (from Sanskrit *mahat*) + *rānī* "rani"]

ma•hat•ma \mə-'hät-mə, -'hat-\ *n* : a person revered for high-mindedness, wisdom, and selflessness — used as a title of honor especially by Hindus [Sanskrit *mahātman,* from *mahat* "great" + *ātman* "soul"]

Ma•hi•can *variant of* MOHICAN

Mah–Jongg \mäzh-'äng, mäj-, -'ȯng\ *n* : a game of Chinese origin for 4 players that is played with usually 144 tiles in somewhat the same manner as rummy [from *Mah-Jongg,* a former trademark]

ma•hog•a•ny \mə-'häg-ə-nē\ *n, pl* **-nies** **1** : the wood of any of various chiefly tropical trees: as **a** : the durable usually reddish brown and moderately hard and heavy wood of a West Indian tree that is widely used for cabinetwork **b** : any of several African woods that vary in color from pinkish to deep reddish brown **2** : any of various woods resembling or substituted for true mahogany **3** : a tree that yields mahogany **4** : a moderate reddish brown [origin unknown]

ma•ho•nia \mə-'hō-nē-ə\ *n* : any of a genus of shrubs of the barberry family including one grown for its showy evergreen leaves that resemble holly [Bernard Mc*Mahon,* died 1816, American botanist]

ma•hout \mə-'hau̇t\ *n* : a keeper and driver of an elephant [Hindi *mahāut*]

maid \'mād\ *n* **1** : an unmarried girl or woman; *esp* : MAIDEN **2** : a female servant [Middle English *maide,* short for *maiden*]

[1]**maid•en** \'mād-n\ *n* : a young unmarried girl or woman [Old English *mægden, mǣden*] — **maid•en•hood** \-,hu̇d\ *n* — **maid•en•li•ness** \-lē-nəs\ *n* — **maid•en•ly** \-lē\ *adj*

[2]**maiden** *adj* **1 a** : not married ⟨my *maiden* aunt⟩ **b** : VIRGIN 1 **2** : of, relating to, or befitting a maiden **3** : FIRST, EARLIEST ⟨the ship's *maiden* voyage⟩ **4** : INTACT, FRESH

maid•en•hair \'mād-n-,haər, -,heər\ *n* : any of a genus of ferns with slender stems and delicate much-divided often feathery leaves — called also *maidenhair fern*

maidenhair tree *n* : GINKGO

maid•en•head \'mād-n-,hed\ *n* : HYMEN [Middle English *maidenhed* "maidenhood, virginity", from *maiden* + *-hed* "-hood"]

maiden name *n* : the surname of a woman before she is married

maid of honor **1** : an unmarried woman usually of noble birth who attends a queen or princess **2** : an unmarried woman serving as the principal female attendant of a bride at her wedding

maid•ser•vant \'mad-,sər-vənt\ *n* : a female servant

[1]**mail** \'māl\ *n* **1** : matter (as letters or parcels) sent under public authority from one person to another through the post office **2** : the whole system used in the public sending and delivery of letters and parcels ⟨do business by *mail*⟩ **3** : something that comes in the mail; *esp* : the contents of a single delivery **4** : a conveyance that transports mail [Middle English *male* "bag", from Old French, of Germanic origin]

[2]**mail** *vt* : to send by mail : POST — **mail•able** \'mā-lə-bəl\ *adj* — **mail•er** *n*

[3]**mail** *n* : a flexible network of small metal rings linked together for use as armor ⟨a coat of *mail*⟩ [Middle French *maille,* from Latin *macula* "spot, mesh"] — **mailed** \'māld\ *adj*

mail•box \'māl-,bäks\ *n* **1** : a public box for the collection of mail **2** : a private box for the delivery of mail

mail•man \'māl-,man\ *n* : LETTER CARRIER

mail order *n* : an order for goods that is received and filled by mail — **mail–order** \'māl-,ȯrd-ər\ *adj*

mail–order house *n* : a retail establishment whose business is conducted by mail

maim \'mām\ *vt* : to mutilate, disfigure, or wound seriously : CRIPPLE [Old French *maynier*] — **maim•er** *n*

[1]**main** \'mān\ *n* **1** : physical strength : FORCE — used in the phrase *with might and main* **2 a** : MAINLAND **b** : HIGH SEAS **3** : a principal pipe, duct, or circuit of a utility system ⟨gas *main*⟩ **4 a** : MAINMAST **b** : MAINSAIL [Old English *mægen*] — **in the main** : for the most part

[2]**main** *adj* **1** : CHIEF 2, PRINCIPAL **2** : fully exerted : SHEER ⟨by *main* force⟩ **3** : connected with or located near the mainmast or mainsail **4** : being a clause that is capable of standing alone as a simple sentence but actually is part of a larger sentence that includes also a subordinate clause or another main clause

main•land \'mān-,land, -lənd\ *n* : a continent or the main part of a continent as distinguished from an offshore island or sometimes from a cape or a peninsula — **main•land•er** \-ər\ *n*

main•line \'mān-'līn\ *vi, slang* : to inject a narcotic drug (as heroin) into a principal vein

main•ly \'mān-lē\ *adv* : for the most part : CHIEFLY

main•mast \'mān-,mast, -məst\ *n* : the principal mast of a sailing ship

main•sail \'mān-,sāl, 'mān-səl\ *n* : the principal sail on the mainmast

main•spring \-,spring\ *n* **1** : the principal spring in a mechanism especially of a watch or clock **2 :** the chief motive, cause, or force underlying or causing an action

main•stay \\-ˌstā\\ *n* **1 :** a forward stay which helps support the mainmast of a ship **2 :** a chief support ⟨the *mainstay* of the family⟩

main•stream \\ˈmān-ˌstrēm\\ *n* **:** a general movement or direction of activity or influence

main•tain \\mān-ˈtān, mən-\\ *vt* **1 :** to keep in an existing state; *esp* **:** to keep in good condition ⟨*maintain* one's health⟩ ⟨*maintain* machinery⟩ **2 :** to uphold and defend against opposition or danger ⟨*maintain* a position⟩ **3 :** to continue in **:** keep up ⟨*maintain* one's balance⟩ ⟨*maintain* one's composure⟩ **4 a :** to provide for **:** SUPPORT ⟨*maintain* their family by working⟩ **b :** SUSTAIN ⟨enough food to *maintain* life⟩ **5 :** to affirm in or as if in argument **:** ASSERT ⟨*maintained* that no child is really bad⟩ [Old French *maintenir,* from Latin *manu tenēre* "to hold in the hand"] — **main•tain•able** \\-ˈtā-nə-bəl\\ *adj* — **main•tain•er** *n*

• **syn** MAINTAIN, ASSERT, VINDICATE, JUSTIFY mean to uphold as true, right, or just. MAINTAIN stresses firmness of conviction; ASSERT suggests vigor of statement and determination to make others accept one's claim; VINDICATE implies successfully defending what was under question or attack; JUSTIFY implies showing to be true or valid especially by appeal to a standard or to precedent.

main•te•nance \\ˈmānt-nəns, -n-əns\\ *n* **1 :** the act of maintaining **:** the state of being maintained **2 :** something that maintains or supports; *esp* **:** a supply of necessities and conveniences **3 :** the upkeep of property or machinery ⟨workers in charge of *maintenance*⟩

maî•tre d'hô•tel \\ˌmā-trə-dō-ˈtel\\ *n, pl* **maîtres d'hôtel** *same*\\ **1 :** MAJORDOMO **2 :** HEADWAITER [French, literally, "master of house"]

maize \\ˈmāz\\ *n* **:** INDIAN CORN [Spanish *maíz,* of American Indian origin]

ma•jes•tic \\mə-ˈjes-tik\\ *adj* **:** being stately and dignified **:** NOBLE **syn** see GRAND — **ma•jes•ti•cal•ly** \\-ti-kə-lē, -klē\\ *adv*

maj•es•ty \\ˈmaj-ə-stē\\ *n, pl* **-ties 1 a :** sovereign power, authority, or dignity **b** *cap* — used as a form of address for reigning sovereigns and their consorts ⟨His *Majesty* King George⟩ ⟨Her *Majesty* Queen Elizabeth⟩ **2 a :** royal bearing or quality **:** GRANDEUR **b :** greatness of quality or character [Old French *majesté,* from Latin *majestas*]

¹ma•jor \\ˈmā-jər\\ *adj* **1 a :** greater in dignity, rank, or importance ⟨a *major* poet⟩ **b :** greater in number, quantity, or extent ⟨the *major* part of the blame⟩ **2 :** having attained majority **3 :** involving risk to life **:** SERIOUS ⟨a *major* illness⟩ **4 :** of or relating to an academic major **5 a :** having half steps between the 3d and 4th and the 7th and 8th degrees ⟨a *major* scale⟩ **b :** based on a major scale ⟨a *major* key⟩ ⟨a *major* chord⟩ [Latin, comparative of *magnus* "great, large"]

²major *n* **1 :** a major musical interval, scale, key, or mode **2 :** an officer rank in the Army, Marine Corps, and Air Force above captain and below lieutenant colonel **3 :** an academic subject chosen by a student as a field of specialization

³major *vi* **ma•jored; ma•jor•ing** \\ˈmāj-ring, -ə-ring\\ **:** to pursue an academic major

ma•jor•do•mo \\ˌmā-jər-ˈdō-mō\\ *n, pl* **-mos :** a man in charge of a great household and especially of a royal establishment [Spanish *mayordomo* or obsolete Italian *maiordomo,* from Medieval Latin *major domus,* literally, "chief of the house"]

majorette *n* **:** DRUM MAJORETTE

major general *n* **:** an officer rank in the Army, Marine Corps, and Air Force above brigadier general and below lieutenant general

ma•jor•i•ty \\mə-ˈjȯr-ət-ē, -ˈjär-\\ *n, pl* **-ties 1 a :** the age at which one is given full civil rights **b :** the status of one who has attained this age **2 a :** a number greater than half of a total **b :** the amount by which such a greater number exceeds the smaller number ⟨won by a *majority* of seven⟩ **c :** the greater part or share ⟨the *majority* of our fuel is imported⟩ **3 :** the group or party that makes up the greater part of a whole body of persons **4 :** the military office or rank of a major

• **syn** MAJORITY, PLURALITY mean a winning margin of votes. MAJORITY specifically refers to the number in excess of half of all the votes cast ⟨270 votes gave the winner a *majority* of 20 out of the total of 500 votes⟩ PLURALITY refers to the number that is in excess of those of the nearest rival but may not be more than half of the total votes cast.

majority rule *n* **:** a political principle providing that a majority of an organized group shall have the power to make decisions binding upon the whole group

major league *n* **:** a league in the highest class of United States professional baseball; *also* **:** a league of major importance in another sport (as hockey)

major order *n* **1 :** the order of priest or deacon in the Roman Catholic Church **2 :** the order of bishop, priest, or deacon in the Eastern or Anglican Church

major penalty *n* **:** a 5-minute suspension of a player in ice hockey

major suit *n* **:** hearts or spades in bridge

¹make \\ˈmāk\\ *vb* **made** \\ˈmād\\; **mak•ing 1 a :** to seem to begin an action ⟨*made* as if to go⟩ **b :** to act so as to appear ⟨*make* merry⟩ **2 a :** to cause to exist or occur **:** CREATE ⟨*make* a disturbance⟩ ⟨*made* trouble for us⟩ **b :** to create for some purpose or goal ⟨they were *made* for each other⟩ **3 a :** to form or shape out of material or parts **:** FASHION, BUILD ⟨*make* a dress⟩ ⟨*make* a table⟩ **b :** to comprise or become combined into a whole **:** CONSTITUTE ⟨a house *made* of stone⟩ **4 :** to frame or formulate in the mind ⟨*make* plans⟩ **5 a :** ESTIMATE 1, COMPUTE ⟨I *make* it an even $5⟩ **b :** UNDERSTAND ⟨unable to *make* anything of the story⟩ **6 :** to set in order **:** PREPARE ⟨*make* a bed⟩ **7 :** to cut and spread for drying ⟨*make* hay⟩ **8 :** to cause to be or become ⟨*make* oneself useful⟩ **9 a :** ENACT, ESTABLISH ⟨*make* laws⟩ **b :** to execute in an appropriate manner ⟨*make* a will⟩ **c :** SET, NAME ⟨*make* clubs trump⟩ **10 :** to complete an electric circuit **11 a :** to carry out a specific action ⟨*make* war⟩ ⟨*make* a curtsy⟩ **b :** FOLLOW, TRAVERSE ⟨*make* one's rounds⟩ **12 :** to produce by action or effort spent on something ⟨*made* a mess of the job⟩ **13 :** to cause to act in some manner **:** COMPEL ⟨*made* them return home⟩ **14 :** to cause or assure the success of ⟨the first case *makes* or breaks a lawyer⟩ **15 :** to amount to in significance ⟨it *makes* a great difference⟩ **16 :** REACH, ATTAIN ⟨the ship *makes* port tonight⟩ **17 a :** to gain by or as if by working ⟨*makes* good money at the foundry⟩ **b :** to acquire by effort ⟨*makes* friends easily⟩ **c :** to score in a game or sport ⟨*make* a point after a touchdown⟩ **18 a :** CATCH ⟨*make* the train⟩ **b :** to set out in pursuit ⟨*made* after the fox⟩ [Old English *macian* "to form, construct, do, act"] — **make a mountain out of a molehill :** to treat something unimportant as a matter of great importance — **make away with :** to carry off — **make believe :** FEIGN, PRETEND — **make do :** to get along with the means at hand — **make fun of :** to make an object of amusement or laughter — **make good 1 :** to make complete **:** FULFILL ⟨*make good* a promise⟩ **2 :** to make up for a deficiency ⟨*make good* the loss⟩ **3 :** SUCCEED ⟨*made good* as a photographer⟩ — **make it :** to be successful ⟨trying to *make it* as an actor⟩ — **make time 1 :** to travel fast **2 :** to gain time — **make way 1 :** to open or give room for passing or entering ⟨the crowd *made way* for the police⟩ **2 :** to make progress

²make *n* **1 :** the way in which a thing is made **:** manner of construction ⟨the *make* was so poor the chair fell apart⟩ **2 :** the type or process of making or manufacturing ⟨the latest *make* of car⟩

¹make–be•lieve \\ˈmāk-bə-ˌlēv\\ *n* **:** a pretending to believe (as in the play of children) **:** PRETENSE

²make–believe *adj* **:** PRETENDED, IMAGINARY ⟨a *make-believe* playmate⟩

make out *vb* **1 :** to draw up in writing ⟨*make out* a shopping list⟩ **2 :** to find or grasp the meaning of **:** UNDERSTAND ⟨couldn't *make out* what was going on⟩ **3 :** to represent as being ⟨*made* them *out* to be heroes⟩ **4 :** to see and identify with difficulty or effort⟨*make out* a form in the fog⟩ **5 :** SUCCEED, PROSPER ⟨*make out* well in business⟩ **6 :** to engage in kissing and petting

make over *vt* **1 :** to transfer the title of **:** CONVEY **2 :** REMAKE, REMODEL

mak•er \\ˈmā-kər\\ *n* **:** one that makes: as **a** *cap* **:** GOD 1 **b :** a person who makes a promissory note **c :** MANUFACTURER

make•ready \\ˈmā-ˌkred-ē\\ *n* **:** final preparation (as of a form on a printing press) for running

make•shift \\ˈmāk-ˌshift\\ *n* **:** a temporary replacement **:** SUBSTITUTE — **makeshift** *adj*

make•up \\ˈmā-ˌkəp\\ *n* **1 :** the way the parts or elements of somthing are put together **:** COMPOSITION ⟨last-minute changes in the *makeup* of the book⟩ **2 :** materials (as wigs or cosmetics) used in making up ⟨put on *makeup* for a play⟩

make up \\mā-ˈkəp, ˈmā-\\ *vb* **1 a :** INVENT, CONCOCT ⟨*make up* a story⟩ **b :** to combine to produce a whole **:** COMPRISE ⟨nine players *make up* a team⟩ **2 :** to form by fitting together or assembling **3 :** to compensate for a deficiency **4 :** to become reconciled ⟨they quarreled and *made up*⟩ **5 :** SETTLE, DECIDE ⟨*made up* their minds to sell the house⟩ **6 a :** to put on costumes or makeup (as for a play) **b :** to apply cosmetics

mak•ing \ˈmā-king\ *n* **1 :** the action of one that makes **2 :** a process or means of advancement or success ⟨misfortune is sometimes the *making* of a person⟩ **3 :** material from which something can be developed ⟨there is the *making* of a racehorse in this colt⟩ **4** *for cigarette materials usually* ˈmā-kənz\ *pl* **:** the materials from which something can be made ⟨roll a cigarette from the *makings*⟩

mal- *combining form* **1 :** bad **:** badly ⟨*mal*odorous⟩ ⟨*mal*practice⟩ **2 :** abnormal **:** abnormally ⟨*mal*formation⟩ [Middle French, from *mal* "bad", from Latin *malus*]

See *mal-* and 2d element

malabsorption	**malallocation**	**maleducation**
malabsorptive	**malapportion**	**malinvestment**
maladaptation	**malapportionment**	**maloccurrence**
maladapted	**malassignment**	**malorganization**
maladaptive	**malbehavior**	**malorientation**
maladaptively	**maldeveloped**	**malperception**
maladminister	**maldevelopment**	**malperformance**
maladministration	**maldigestion**	**malposition**
malaligned	**maldistributed**	**malutilization**
malalignment	**maldistribution**	

Mal•a•chi \ˈmal-ə-ˌkī\ *n* — see BIBLE table

Mal•a•chi•as \ˌmal-ə-ˈkī-əs\ *n* — see BIBLE table

mal•a•chite \ˈmal-ə-ˌkīt\ *n* **:** a green mineral $Cu_2CO_3(OH)_2$ that consists of copper, carbon, oxygen, and hydrogen and is used as an ore of copper and for ornamental objects [Latin *molochites,* from Greek *molochitēs,* from *molochē* "mallow"]

mal•a•col•o•gy \ˌmal-ə-ˈkäl-ə-jē\ *n* **:** a branch of zoology dealing with mollusks [French *malacologie,* derived from Greek *malakos* "soft"] — **mal•a•col•o•gist** \-jəst\ *n*

mal•ad•just•ed \ˌmal-ə-ˈjəs-təd\ *adj* **:** poorly or inadequately adjusted; *esp* **:** lacking harmony with one's environment — **mal•ad•just•ment** \-ˈjəst-mənt, -ˈjəs-\ *n*

mal•adroit \ˌmal-ə-ˈdrȯit\ *adj* **:** not adroit **:** AWKWARD, CLUMSY — **mal•adroit•ly** *adv* — **mal•adroit•ness** *n*

mal•a•dy \ˈmal-əd-ē\ *n, pl* **-dies :** a disease or disorder of the body or mind **:** AILMENT [Old French *maladie,* from *malade* "sick", from Latin *male habitus* "in bad condition"]

Mal•a•gasy \ˌmal-ə-ˈgas-ē\ *n* **1 :** a native or inhabitant of Madagascar or the Malagasy Republic **2 :** the language of the Malagasy people — **Malagasy** *adj*

mal•aise \mə-ˈlāz, ma-; ma-ˈlez\ *n* **:** a vague feeling of bodily or mental disorder [French, from *mal-* + *aise* "ease, comfort"]

mal•a•mute *or* **mal•e•mute** \ˈmal-ə-ˌmyüt\ *n* **:** a sled dog of northern North America; *esp* **:** ALASKAN MALAMUTE [*Malemute,* an Alaskan Eskimo people]

mal•a•pert \ˌmal-ə-ˈpərt\ *adj* **:** impudently bold **:** SAUCY [Middle French, "unskillful", from *mal-* + *apert* "skillful", from Latin *expertus* "expert"] — **mal•a•pert•ly** *adv* — **mal•a•pert•ness** *n*

mal•a•prop•ism \ˈmal-ə-ˌpräp-ˌiz-əm\ *n* **1 :** a usually humorous misuse of a word especially for one of similar sound by someone unaware of the error **2 :** an example of malapropism [Mrs. *Malaprop,* character in Sheridan's *The Rivals* (1775) given to misusing words] — **mal•a•prop** \-ˌpräp\ *or* **mal•a•prop•ian** \ˌmal-ə-ˈpräp-ē-ən\ *adj*

mal•ap•ro•pos \ˌmal-ˌap-rə-ˈpō\ *adv* **:** in an inappropriate or inopportune way [French *mal à propos*] — **malapropos** *adj*

ma•lar \ˈmā-lər, -ˌlär\ *adj* **:** of or relating to the cheek or the side of the head [Latin *mala* "jawbone, cheek"]

ma•lar•ia \mə-ˈler-ē-ə\ *n* **:** a disease caused by protozoan parasites in the red blood cells, transmitted by the bite of mosquitoes, and characterized by periodic attacks of chills and fever [Italian, from *mala aria* "bad air"] — **ma•lar•i•al** \-ē-əl\ *adj* — **ma•lar•i•ous** \-ē-əs\ *adj*

ma•lar•key \mə-ˈlär-kē\ *n* **:** insincere or foolish talk [origin unknown]

mal•a•thi•on \ˌmal-ə-ˈthī-ən, -ˌän\ *n* **:** a pesticide $C_{10}H_{19}O_6PS_2$ that is less toxic to mammals than parathion and is used against insects and mites [from *Malathion,* a former trademark]

Ma•lay \mə-ˈlā, ˈmā-ˌlā\ *n* **1 :** a member of a people of the Malay peninsula and adjacent islands **2 :** the language of the Malay people [obsolete Dutch *Malayo,* from Malay *Mĕlayu*] — **Malay** *adj* — **Ma•lay•an** \mə-ˈlā-ən, ˈmā-ˌlā-\ *adj or n*

mal•con•tent \ˌmal-kən-ˈtent\ *adj* **:** dissatisfied with the existing state of affairs — **malcontent** *n*

mal de mer \ˌmal-də-ˈmeər\ *n* **:** SEASICKNESS [French]

[1]**male** \ˈmāl\ *adj* **1 a :** of, relating to, or being the sex that fathers young **b :** STAMINATE; *esp* **:** having only staminate flowers and not producing fruit or seeds ⟨a *male* holly⟩ **2 a :** of, relating to, or characteristic of the male sex ⟨a deep *male* voice⟩ **b :** made up of males ⟨a *male* choir⟩ **3 :** designed for fitting into a corresponding hollow part [Middle French, from Latin *masculus,* from *mas* "male"] — **male•ness** *n*

[2]**male** *n* **:** a male plant or animal

mal•e•dic•tion \ˌmal-ə-ˈdik-shən\ *n* **:** a prayer for harm to befall someone **:** CURSE [Late Latin *maledictio,* from *maledicere* "to curse", from Latin, "to speak evil of", from *male* "badly" + *dicere* "to say"] — **mal•e•dic•to•ry** \-ˈdik-tə-rē, -trē\ *adj*

male•fac•tion \-ˈfak-shən\ *n* **:** an evil deed **:** CRIME

male•fac•tor \ˈmal-ə-ˌfak-tər\ *n* **1 :** one guilty of a crime or offense **2 :** EVILDOER [Latin, from *malefacere* "to do evil", from *male* "badly" + *facere* "to do"]

male fern *n* **:** a fern that yields a resinous substance used as a worm remedy

ma•lef•i•cent \mə-ˈlef-ə-sənt\ *adj* **:** doing or producing harm or evil **:** HARMFUL [back-formation from *maleficence,* from Italian *maleficenza,* from Latin *maleficentia,* from *maleficus* "baleful, harmful", from *male* "badly" + *-ficus* "-fic"] — **ma•lef•i•cence** \-səns\ *n*

ma•lev•o•lent \mə-ˈlev-ə-lənt\ *adj* **:** having or showing intense often vicious ill will toward others [Latin *malevolens,* from *male* "badly" + *volens,* present participle of *velle* "to wish"] **syn** see MALICE — **ma•lev•o•lence** \-ˈlev-ə-ləns\ *n* — **ma•lev•o•lent•ly** *adv*

mal•fea•sance \mal-ˈfēz-ns, ˈmal-\ *n* **:** wrongful conduct especially by a public official [*mal-* + obsolete *feasance* "doing", from Middle French *faisance,* from *faire* "to make, do"]

mal•for•ma•tion \ˌmal-fȯr-ˈmā-shən, -fər-\ *n* **:** an irregular or defective formation or structure

mal•formed \mal-ˈfȯrmd, ˈmal-\ *adj* **:** marked by malformation

mal•func•tion \mal-ˈfəng-shən, ˈmal-, -ˈfəngk-\ *vi* **:** to fail to operate in the normal or usual manner — **malfunction** *n*

ma•lic acid \ˌmal-ik-, ˌmā-lik-\ *n* **:** an acid $C_4H_6O_5$ found especially in various plant juices [French *acide malique,* from Latin *malum* "apple", from Greek *mēlon, malon*]

mal•ice \ˈmal-əs\ *n* **:** ILL WILL; *esp* **:** the deliberate intention of doing unjustified harm for the satisfaction of doing it [Old French, from Latin *malitia,* from *malus* "bad"]

• **syn** MALEVOLENCE, MALIGNITY: MALICE may range from a passing mischievous impulse to a deep-seated unreasoning dislike and desire to cause harm and suffering; MALEVOLENCE stresses evil intent or influence that is likely to lead to malicious action; MALIGNITY stresses the intensity and driving force of malevolence and suggests a quality that is part of one's nature.

ma•li•cious \mə-ˈlish-əs\ *adj* **1 :** feeling strong ill will **:** being mean and spiteful **2 :** done or carried on with malice or caused by malice ⟨*malicious* gossip⟩ — **ma•li•cious•ly** *adv* — **ma•li•cious•ness** *n*

[1]**ma•lign** \mə-ˈlīn\ *adj* **1 :** operating so as to injure or hurt ⟨hindered by *malign* influences⟩ **2 :** moved by ill will toward others **:** MALEVOLENT [Middle French *maligne,* from Latin *malignus,* from *male* "bad" + *gignere* "to beget"]

[2]**malign** *vt* **:** to utter injurious or false reports about **:** speak evil of **:** DEFAME **syn** see SLANDER

ma•lig•nan•cy \mə-ˈlig-nən-sē\ *n, pl* **-cies 1 :** the quality or state of being malignant **2 :** a malignant tumor

ma•lig•nant \-nənt\ *adj* **1 a :** evil in influence or effect **:** INJURIOUS **b :** passionately and relentlessly malevolent **2 :** tending or likely to produce death especially through being dispersed and growing throughout the body ⟨*malignant* tumor⟩ — **ma•lig•nant•ly** *adv*

\ə\ abut	\au̇\ out	\i\ tip	\ȯ\ saw	\u̇\ foot
\ər\ further	\ch\ chin	\ī\ life	\ȯi\ coin	\y\ yet
\a\ mat	\e\ pet	\j\ job	\th\ thin	\yü\ few
\ā\ take	\ē\ easy	\ng\ sing	\th\ this	\yu̇\ cure
\ä\ cot, cart	\g\ go	\ō\ bone	\ü\ food	\zh\ vision

ma•lig•ni•ty \mə-ˈlig-nət-ē\ *n, pl* **-ties 1 :** the quality or state of being malignant : MALIGNANCY **2 :** something (as an act or an event) that is malignant **syn** see MALICE

ma•li•hi•ni \ˌmäl-i-ˈhē-nē\ *n* : a newcomer to Hawaii [Hawaiian]

ma•lin•ger \mə-ˈliŋ-gər\ *vi* **ma•lin•gered; ma•lin•ger•ing** \-gə-riŋ, -griŋ\ : to pretend incapacity (as illness) so as to avoid duty or work [French *malingre* "sickly"] — **ma•lin•ger•er** \-gər-ər\ *n*

mall \ˈmȯl\ *n* **1 :** a shaded walk : PROMENADE **2 :** a grassy strip between two roadways **3 :** a group of stores and shops with associated passageways and parking space [The *Mall,* promenade in London, England]

mal•lard \ˈmal-ərd\ *n, pl* **mallard** *or* **mallards :** a common and widely distributed wild duck of the northern hemisphere that is the source of the domestic ducks [Middle French *mallart*]

mal•lea•ble \ˈmal-ē-ə-bəl, ˈmal-yə-bəl, ˈmal-ə-bəl\ *adj* **1 :** capable of being beaten out, extended, or shaped by hammer blows or by the pressure of rollers ⟨a *malleable* metal⟩ **2 :** ADAPTABLE, PLIABLE [Medieval Latin *malleabilis,* from *malleare* "to hammer", from Latin *malleus* "hammer"] — **mal•le•abil•i•ty** \ˌmal-ē-ə-ˈbil-ət-ē, ˌmal-yə-ˈbil, ˌmal-ə-ˈ\ *n*

mal•lee \ˈmal-ē\ *n* : a dense growth of shrubby eucalypts; *also* : Australian land covered with mallee [native name in Australia]

mal•let \ˈmal-ət\ *n* **1 :** a hammer usually having a barrel-shaped head of wood; *esp* : a tool with a short handle and a large head used for driving another tool (as a chisel) **2 :** a long-handled club with a cylindrical head used in playing croquet **3 :** a polo stick [Middle French *maillet,* from *mail* "hammer", from Latin *malleus*]

mal•le•us \ˈmal-ē-əs\ *n, pl* **mal•lei** \-ē-ˌī, -ē-ˌē\ : the outermost of the three small bones of the mammalian ear — compare INCUS, STAPES [Latin, "hammer"]

mal•low \ˈmal-ō\ *n* : any of a genus of herbs with lobed or dissected leaves, usually showy flowers, and a disk-shaped fruit [Old English *mealwe,* from Latin *malva*]

malm•sey \ˈmäm-zē, ˈmälm-\ *n, pl* **malmseys** *often cap* : a sweet aromatic wine originally produced in Greece [Medieval Latin *Malmasia* "Monemvasia", village in Greece]

mal•nour•ished \mal-ˈnər-isht, ˈmal-, -ˈnə-risht\ *adj* : marked by or affected with malnutrition

mal•nu•tri•tion \ˌmal-nu̇-ˈtrish-ən, -nyu̇-\ *n* : faulty and especially inadequate nutrition — **mal•nu•tri•tion•al** \-ˈtrish-nəl, -ən-l\ *adj*

mal•oc•clu•sion \ˌmal-ə-ˈklü-zhən\ *n* : faulty coming together of teeth in the upper and lower jaws when biting

mal•odor•ous \mal-ˈōd-ə-rəs, ˈmal-\ *adj* : bad-smelling — **mal•odor•ous•ly** *adv* — **mal•odor•ous•ness** *n*

Mal•pigh•i•an corpuscle \mal-ˌpig-ē-ən-, -ˌpē-gē-\ *n* : a kidney glomerulus with its membrane — called also *Malpighian body* [Marcello *Malpighi,* died 1694, Italian anatomist]

Malpighian tubule *n* : any of a group of long blind vessels opening into the intestine in various arthropods and functioning in excretion

mal•prac•tice \mal-ˈprak-təs, ˈmal-\ *n* **1 :** violation of professional standards especially by negligence or improper conduct **2 :** an injurious, negligent, or improper practice — **mal•prac•ti•tion•er** \ˌmal-ˌprak-ˈtish-(ə-)nər\ *n*

[1]malt \ˈmȯlt\ *n* **1 :** grain and especially barley softened by steeping in water, allowed to germinate, and used chiefly in brewing and distilling **2 :** MALTED MILK 2 [Old English *mealt*] — **malt** *adj* — **malty** \ˈmȯl-tē\ *adj*

[2]malt *vb* **1 :** to convert into malt **2 :** to make or treat with malt or malt extract **3 :** to become malt

malt•ase \ˈmȯl-ˌtās\ *n* : an enzyme that accelerates the hydrolysis of maltose to glucose

malted milk *n* **1 :** a soluble powder prepared from dried milk and malted cereals **2 :** a beverage made by dissolving malted milk in a liquid (as milk)

Mal•tese \mȯl-ˈtēz\ *n, pl* **Maltese 1 :** a native or inhabitant of Malta **2 :** the Semitic language of the Maltese people — **Maltese** *adj*

Maltese cat *n* : a bluish gray domestic short-haired cat

Maltese cross *n* : a cross with four arms of equal size that increase in width toward the outward ends

Mal•thu•sian \mal-ˈthü-zhən, mȯl-, -ˈthyü-\ *adj* : of or relating to Malthus or to his theory that population unless checked (as by war or disease) tends to increase at a faster rate than its means of subsistence — **Malthusian** *n* — **Mal•thu•sian•ism** \-zhə-ˌniz-əm\ *n*

malt•ose \ˈmȯl-ˌtōs\ *n* : a sugar formed especially from starch by the action of enzymes and used in brewing and distilling — called also *malt sugar*

mal•treat \mal-ˈtrēt, ˈmal-\ *vt* : to treat unkindly or roughly : ABUSE ⟨*maltreat* animals⟩ — **mal•treat•ment** \-mənt\ *n*

ma•ma *or* **mam•ma** \ˈmäm-ə\ *n* : MOTHER [baby talk]

mam•ba \ˈmäm-bə, ˈmam-\ *n* : any of several African venomous snakes related to the cobras but lacking a hood [Zulu *im=amba*]

mam•bo \ˈmäm-bō\ *n, pl* **mambos :** a dance of Haitian origin related to the rumba [American Spanish] — **mambo** *vi*

mam•ma \ˈmam-ə\ *n, pl* **mam•mae** \ˈmam-ˌē, -ˌī\ : a mammary gland and its accessory parts [Latin, "mother, breast"] — **mam•mate** \ˈmam-ˌāt\ *adj*

mam•mal \ˈmam-əl\ *n* : any of a class (Mammalia) of higher vertebrates comprising man and all other animals that nourish their young with milk secreted by mammary glands and have the skin usually more or less covered with hair — **mam•ma•li•an** \mə-ˈmā-lē-ən, ma-ˈmā-\ *adj or n*

mam•mal•o•gy \mə-ˈmal-ə-jē, ma-ˈmal-\ *n* : a branch of zoology dealing with mammals — **mam•mal•o•gist** \-jəst\ *n*

mam•ma•ry \ˈmam-ə-rē\ *adj* : of, relating to, lying near, or affecting the mammae

mammary gland *n* : one of the large compound sebaceous glands that in female mammals are modified to secrete milk and in males are usually rudimentary, are situated in pairs on the abdominal side of the organism, and usually end in a nipple

mam•mil•la•ry \ˈmam-ə-ˌler-ē, ma-ˈmil-ə-rē\ *adj* **1 :** of, relating to, or resembling a breast **2 :** studded with breast-shaped protuberances [Latin *mammilla* "breast, nipple", from *mamma* "mother, breast"]

mam•mil•lat•ed \ˈmam-ə-ˌlāt-əd\ *adj* : having or being small bluntly rounded protuberances

mam•mon \ˈmam-ən\ *n, often cap* : an often personified devotion to material possessions; *also* : WEALTH [Late Latin *mammona,* from Greek *mamōna,* from Aramaic *māmōnā* "riches"]

[1]mam•moth \ˈmam-əth\ *n* **1 :** any of numerous large hairy extinct elephants with very long upward-curving tusks **2 :** something immense of its kind : GIANT [Russian *mamont, mamot*]

[2]mammoth *adj* : of very great size : GIGANTIC

mam•my \ˈmam-ē\ *n, pl* **mammies 1 :** MAMA **2 :** a black woman serving as a nurse to white children especially formerly in the American South

[1]man \ˈman\ *n, pl* **men** \ˈmen\ **1 a :** HUMAN BEING; *esp* : an adult male human **b :** the human race : MANKIND **c :** any member of the natural family to which human beings belong including both human beings and extinct related forms known only from fossils **d :** one possessing in high degree the qualities considered distinctive of manhood **2 a :** VASSAL 1 **b :** an adult male servant **c** *pl* **:** the working force as distinguished from the employer **3 :** any person ⟨a *man* could easily be killed there⟩ **4 :** one of the pieces with which various games (as chess) are played [Old English]

[2]man *vt* **manned; man•ning 1 :** to supply with personnel (as for management or operation) ⟨*man* a business⟩ **2 :** to station members of a ship's crew at ⟨*man* the pumps⟩

man–about–town \ˌman-ə-ˌbau̇t-ˈtau̇n\ *n, pl* **men–about–town :** a worldly and socially active man

[1]man•a•cle \ˈman-i-kəl\ *n* **1 :** a shackle for the hand or wrist : HANDCUFF **2 :** something that restrains or restricts [Middle French *manicle,* from Latin *manicula* "little hand", from *manus* "hand"]

[2]manacle *vt* **-cled; -cling** \-kə-liŋ, -kliŋ\ **1 :** to put manacles on **2 :** SHACKLE 2 **syn** see HAMPER

man•age \ˈman-ij\ *vb* **1 :** to oversee and make decisions about : DIRECT ⟨*manage* a factory⟩ **2 :** to make responsive or submissive : HANDLE, MANIPULATE ⟨skill in *managing* problem children⟩ **3 :** to treat with care : use to best advantage ⟨there's enough food if it's *managed* well⟩ **4 :** to succeed in one's purpose : get along ⟨*manages* despite a handicap⟩ [Italian *maneggiare* "to handle", from *mano* "hand", from Latin *manus*] **syn** see CONDUCT

man•age•able \ˈman-ij-ə-bəl\ *adj* : capable of being managed — **man•age•abil•i•ty** \ˌman-ij-ə-ˈbil-ət-ē\ *n* — **man•age•able•ness** \ˈman-ij-ə-bəl-nəs\ *n* — **man•age•ably** \-blē\ *adv*

man·age·ment \ˈman-ij-mənt\ *n* **1** : the act or art of managing : CONTROL, DIRECTION **2** : skillfulness in managing **3** : those who manage an enterprise

man·ag·er \ˈman-ij-ər\ *n* : one that manages: as **a** : a person who conducts business or household affairs **b** : a person whose work or profession is management **c** : a person who directs a team or an athlete — **man·a·ge·ri·al** \ˌman-ə-ˈjir-ē-əl\ *adj* — **man·a·ge·ri·al·ly** \-ē-ə-lē\ *adv* — **man·ag·er·ship** \ˈman-ij-ər-ˌship\ *n*

ma·ña·na \mən-ˈyän-ə\ *n* : an indefinite time in the future [Spanish, literally, "tomorrow"] — **mañana** *adv*

man–at–arms \ˌman-ət-ˈärmz\ *n, pl* **men–at–arms** : SOLDIER; *esp* : a heavily armed mounted soldier

man·a·tee \ˈman-ə-ˌtē\ *n* : any of several chiefly tropical plant-eating aquatic mammals that differ from the related dugong especially in having the tail broad and rounded [Spanish *manatí*]

man·chi·neel \ˌman-chə-ˈnēl\ *n* : a tropical American tree with a blistering milky juice and poisonous apple-shaped fruits [French *mancenille*, from Spanish *manzanilla*, from *manzana* "apple"]

Man·chu \ˈman-chü, man-ˈ\ *n* **1** : a member of the native Mongolian race of Manchuria that conquered China and established a dynasty there in 1644 **2** : the language of the Manchu people — **Manchu** *adj*

man·ci·ple \ˈman-sə-pəl\ *n* : a person responsible for procuring and distributing food especially for a college or monastery [Medieval Latin *mancipium* "office of steward", from Latin *manceps* "purchaser", from *manus* "hand" + *capere* "to take"]

-man·cy \ˌman-sē\ *n combining form, pl* **-mancies** : divination [Greek *manteia*, from *mantis* "diviner, prophet"]

man·da·mus \man-ˈdā-məs\ *n* : a writ issued by a superior court commanding that a specified official act or duty be performed [Latin, "we enjoin", its first word]

[1]**man·da·rin** \ˈman-də-rən, -drən\ *n* **1** : a public official under the Chinese Empire of any of nine superior grades **2** *cap* **a** : the primarily northern dialect of China used by the court and the official classes under the Empire **b** : the chief dialect of China that is spoken in about four fifths of the country and has a standard variety centering about Peking **3** : a small spiny Chinese orange tree with yellow to reddish orange loose-skinned fruits; *also* : its fruit — compare TANGERINE [Portuguese *mandarim*, from Malay *mĕntĕri*, from Sanskrit *mantrin* "counselor"] — **man·da·rin·ate** \-ˌāt\ *n*

[2]**mandarin** *adj* : of, relating to, or typical of a mandarin

mandarin orange *n* : MANDARIN 3

man·da·tary \ˈman-də-ˌter-ē\ *n, pl* **-tar·ies** : MANDATORY

man·date \ˈman-ˌdāt\ *n* **1** : a formal order from a superior court or official to an inferior one **2 a** : an authoritative command, instruction, or direction **b** : authorization or approval given to a representative **3 a** : a commission granted by the former League of Nations to a member nation to administer a conquered territory as guardian on behalf of the League **b** : a mandated territory [Latin *mandatum* "command", from *mandare* "to entrust, enjoin"] — **mandate** *vt*

[1]**man·da·to·ry** \ˈman-də-ˌtōr-ē, -ˌtȯr-\ *adj* **1** : containing or constituting a command ⟨*mandatory* tasks⟩ **2** : of, relating to, or holding a League of Nations mandate ⟨a *mandatory* power⟩

[2]**mandatory** *n, pl* **-ries** : one given a mandate

man·di·ble \ˈman-də-bəl\ *n* **1 a** : a single bone or completely fused bones forming the lower jaw **b** : either the upper or lower segment of the bill of a bird **2** : an invertebrate mouthpart that holds or bites food; *esp* : either of the front pair of mouth appendages of an arthropod often forming strong biting jaws [Middle French, from Late Latin *mandibula*, from Latin *mandere* "to chew"] — **man·dib·u·lar** \man-ˈdib-yə-lər\ *adj*

man·do·lin \ˌman-də-ˈlin; ˈman-dl-ən\ *also* **man·do·line** \ˌman-də-ˈlēn, ˈman-dl-ən\ *n* : a musical instrument of the lute family that has a pear-shaped body and fretted neck and four to six pairs of strings [Italian *mandolino*] — **man·do·lin·ist** \ˌman-də-ˈlin-əst\ *n*

man·drag·o·ra \man-ˈdrag-ə-rə\ *n* : MANDRAKE 1

man·drake \ˈman-ˌdrāk\ *n* **1** : a Mediterranean herb of the potato family with a large forked root superstitiously credited with human and medicinal attributes **2** : MAYAPPLE [Old English *mandragora*, from Latin *mandragoras*, from Greek]

man·drel \ˈman-drəl\ *n* **1** : an axle or spindle inserted into a hole in a piece of work to support it during machining **2** : a metal bar used as a core around which material may be cast, shaped, or molded [probably from French *mandrin*]

mandolin

man·drill \ˈman-drəl\ *n* : a large gregarious baboon of western Africa with a red rump and in the male with blue ridges on each side of the red-bridged nose [probably from [1]*man* + [3]*drill*]

mane \ˈmān\ *n* **1** : long heavy hair growing about the neck of some mammals (as a horse) **2** : long heavy hair on a person's head [Old English *manu*] — **maned** \ˈmānd\ *adj*

man–eat·er \ˈman-ˌēt-ər\ *n* : one (as a cannibal, shark, or tiger) that has or is thought to have an appetite for human flesh — **man–eat·ing** \-ˌēt-ing\ *adj*

ma·nege *also* **ma·nège** \ma-ˈnezh\ *n* **1** : a school for teaching horsemanship **2** : the art of horsemanship or of training horses [French *manège*, from Italian *maneggio* "training of a horse", from *maneggiare* "to handle, manage"]

mandrake 1

ma·nes \ˈmän-ˌās, ˈmā-ˌnēz\ *n pl, often cap* : the deified spirits of the ancient Roman dead [Latin]

[1]**ma·neu·ver** *also* **ma·noeu·vre** *or* **ma·noeu·ver** \mə-ˈnü-vər, -ˈnyü-\ *n* **1 a** : a planned movement of military forces **b** : an armed forces training exercise; *esp* : an extensive exercise involving large-scale deployment of military forces **2 a** : a physical movement or procedure ⟨avoided a collision by a quick *maneuver*⟩ **b** : a variation from the straight and level flight path of an airplane **3** : a clever often evasive move or action : a shift of position to gain a tactical end ⟨tried by various *maneuvers* to win support from both sides⟩ [French *manœuvre*, from Medieval Latin *manuopera* "work done by hand", from Latin *manu operare* "to do work by hand"]

△**origin** We owe both *manure* and *maneuver* to the same source, Latin *manu operare* "to do work by hand". This Latin phrase is the ancestor of the Middle French verb *manouvrer*. The French verb originally meant "to work by hand" but later developed the more specific sense "to cultivate (land)". In the late Middle Ages the English borrowed the word as *manouren*, "to cultivate". From this verb we get the noun *manure* for the dung used to fertilize the land. Latin *manu operare* is also the source of French *manœuvre*, "maneuver". The original meaning of the French noun was "work done by hand", but the older sense gave way to a more general sense, "work". Still later the noun developed a new specific meaning, "military operation".

[2]**maneuver** *also* **manoeuvre** *or* **manoeuver** *vb* **1** : to move (as troops or ships) in a maneuver **2** : to perform a maneuver **3** : to guide with adroitness and design : HANDLE, MANIPULATE **4** : to use stratagems : SCHEME — **ma·neu·ver·abil·i·ty** \-ˌnüv-rə-ˈbil-ət-ē, -ˌnyüv-, -ə-rə-\ *n* — **ma·neu·ver·able** \-ˈnüv-rə-bəl, -ˈnyüv-, -ə-rə-\ *adj*

man Fri·day \ˈman-ˈfrīd-ē\ *n* : a valued efficient helper or employee [*Friday*, native servant in *Robinson Crusoe* (1719), novel by Daniel Defoe]

man·ful \ˈman-fəl\ *adj* : showing courage and resolution — **man·ful·ly** \-fə-lē\ *adv* — **man·ful·ness** *n*

man·ga·nese \ˈmang-gə-ˌnēz, -ˌnēs\ *n* : a grayish white usually hard and brittle metallic element that resembles iron but is not magnetic — see ELEMENT table [French *manganèse*, from

\ə\ **abut**	\au̇\ **out**	\i\ **tip**	\ȯ\ **saw**	\u̇\ **foot**
\ər\ **further**	\ch\ **chin**	\ī\ **life**	\ȯi\ **coin**	\y\ **yet**
\a\ **mat**	\e\ **pet**	\j\ **job**	\th\ **thin**	\yü\ **few**
\ā\ **take**	\ē\ **easy**	\ng\ **sing**	\t͟h\ **this**	\yu̇\ **cure**
\ä\ **cot, cart**	\g\ **go**	\ō\ **bone**	\ü\ **food**	\zh\ **vision**

Italian *manganese* "magnesia, manganese", from Medieval Latin *magnesia* "magnesia"]

manganese dioxide *n* **:** a brown or gray-black insoluble compound MnO_2 that consists of manganese and oxygen and is used as an oxidizing agent, in making glass, and in ceramics

man•gan•ic \man-'gan-ik, mang-\ *or* **man•ga•nous** \'mang-gə-nəs\ *adj* **:** of, relating to, or derived from manganese

mange \'mānj\ *n* **:** any of several persistent contagious skin diseases marked especially by itching and loss of hair in domestic animals and sometimes humans; *esp* **:** one caused by a minute parasitic mite **[**Middle French *mangene* "itching", from *mangier* "to eat"**]**

man•ger \'mān-jər\ *n* **:** a trough or open box for livestock feed or fodder **[**Middle French *maingeure,* from *mangier* "to eat", from Latin *manducare* "to chew, devour", from *manducus* "glutton", from *mandere* "to chew"**]**

¹man•gle \'mang-gəl\ *vt* **man•gled**; **man•gling** \-gə-ling, -gling\ **1 :** to cut, bruise, or hack with repeated blows or strokes **2 :** to spoil or injure in making or performing **:** BOTCH **[**Anglo-French *mangler,* from Old French *maynier* "to maim"**]** — **man•gler** \-gə-lər, -glər\ *n*

²mangle *n* **:** a machine for ironing laundry by passing it between heated rollers **[**Dutch *mangel***]**

³mangle *vt* **man•gled**; **man•gling** \-gə-ling, -gling\ **:** to press or smooth with a mangle — **man•gler** \-gə-lər, -glər\ *n*

man•go \'mang-gō\ *n, pl* **mangoes** *or* **mangos :** a yellowish red tropical fruit with a firm skin, hard central stone, and juicy aromatic mildly acid pulp; *also* **:** the evergreen tree of the sumac family that bears this fruit **[**Portuguese *manga,* from Tamil *mān-kāy***]**

man•go•steen \'mang-gə-ˌstēn\ *n* **:** a dark reddish brown fruit with thick rind and juicy flesh having a flavor suggestive of both peach and pineapple; *also* **:** an East Indian tree that bears this fruit **[**Malay *mangustan***]**

man•grove \'man-ˌgrōv, 'mang-\ *n* **:** any of various tropical trees or shrubs that throw out many prop roots and form dense masses in brackish marshes or shallow salt water **[**probably from Portuguese *mangue,* from Spanish *mangle,* of American Indian origin**]**

mangy \'mān-jē\ *adj* **mang•i•er**; **-est 1 :** affected with or resulting from mange **2 :** SHABBY 1, SEEDY — **mang•i•ness** \'mān-jē-nəs\ *n*

man•han•dle \'man-ˌhan-dl\ *vt* **1 :** to move or manage by human force **2 :** to handle roughly

man•hat•tan \man-'hat-n, mən-\ *n, often cap* **:** a cocktail consisting of vermouth and whiskey **[***Manhattan,* borough of New York City**]**

man•hole \'man-ˌhōl\ *n* **:** a hole through which a person may go especially to gain access to an underground or enclosed structure

man•hood \'man-ˌhu̇d\ *n* **1 :** qualities generally associated with a man **2 :** the condition of being an adult male **3 :** adult males **:** MEN ⟨the nation's *manhood*⟩

man–hour \'man-'au̇-ər, -'au̇r\ *n* **:** a unit of one hour's work by one person used especially as a basis for wages and in accounting

man•hunt \'man-ˌhənt\ *n* **:** an organized hunt for a person and especially for one charged with a crime

ma•nia \'mā-nē-ə, -nyə\ *n* **1 :** MADNESS 1; *esp* **:** insanity characterized by uncontrollable emotion or excitement **2 :** excessive or unreasonable enthusiasm **:** CRAZE **[**Late Latin, from Greek, from *mainesthai* "to be mad"**] syn** see INSANITY

¹ma•ni•ac \'mā-nē-ˌak\ *adj* **:** affected with or suggestive of madness — **ma•ni•a•cal** \mə-'nī-ə-kəl\ *adj* — **ma•ni•a•cal•ly** \-kə-lē, -klē\ *adv*

²maniac *n* **1 :** MADMAN, LUNATIC **2 :** a person wildly enthusiastic about something **:** FAN

man•ic \'man-ik\ *adj* **:** affected with, relating to, or resembling mania — **manic** *n*

man•ic–de•pres•sive \ˌman-ik-di-'pres-iv\ *adj* **:** characterized by alternating mania and depression — **manic–depressive** *n*

¹man•i•cure \'man-ə-ˌkyu̇r\ *n* **1 :** MANICURIST **2 :** a treatment for the care of the hands and nails **[**French, from Latin *manus* "hand" + French *-icure* (as in *pédicure* "pedicure")**]**

²manicure *vt* **1 :** to give a manicure to **2 :** to trim closely and evenly ⟨*manicure* the lawn⟩

man•i•cur•ist \-ˌkyu̇r-əst\ *n* **:** a person who gives manicures

¹man•i•fest \'man-ə-ˌfest\ *adj* **:** clear to the senses or mind **:** OBVIOUS ⟨heard the verdict with *manifest* relief⟩ **[**Latin *manifestus,* literally, "hit by the hand"**]** — **man•i•fest•ly** *adv*

²manifest *vt* **:** to show plainly **:** make evident **:** DISPLAY

³manifest *n* **:** a list (as of cargo or passengers) especially for a ship or plane

man•i•fes•ta•tion \ˌman-ə-fə-'stā-shən, -ˌfes-'tā-\ *n* **1 a :** the act, process, or an instance of manifesting **b :** an outward or visible expression **2 :** a public demonstration of power and purpose ⟨rallies, parades, and other *manifestations*⟩

manifest destiny *n, often cap M&D* **:** a future event accepted as inevitable ⟨in the 19th century expansion to the Pacific was regarded as the *manifest destiny* of the United States⟩

man•i•fes•to \ˌman-ə-'fes-tō\ *n, pl* **-tos** *or* **-toes :** a public declaration of policy, purpose, or views **[**Italian, derived from Latin *manifestus* "manifest"**]**

¹man•i•fold \'man-ə-ˌfōld\ *adj* **1 :** of many and various kinds ⟨*manifold* excuses⟩ **2 :** including or uniting various features ⟨a *manifold* personality⟩ — **man•i•fold•ly** *adv* — **man•i•fold•ness** \-ˌfōld-nəs, -ˌfōl-\ *n*

²manifold *n* **:** something that is manifold: as **a :** a whole consisting of many different elements **b :** a pipe fitting having several outlets for connecting one pipe with others **c :** a fitting on an internal-combustion engine that either receives exhaust gases or directs a fuel charge

³manifold *vb* **1 :** to make many or several copies ⟨*manifold* a manuscript⟩ **2 :** to make manifold

man•i•kin *or* **man•ni•kin** \'man-i-kən\ *n* **1 :** MANNEQUIN **2 :** a little man **:** DWARF, PYGMY

ma•nila *also* **ma•nil•la** \mə-'nil-ə\ *adj* **:** made of manila paper or from Manila hemp

Manila hemp *n* **:** a strong fiber obtained from the leafstalk of a Philippine banana — called also *abaca* **[***Manila,* Philippine islands**]**

manila paper *n, often cap M* **:** a tough brownish paper made originally from Manila hemp and used especially for wrapping

man in the street : a typical or ordinary person

man•i•oc \'man-ē-ˌäk\ *also* **man•i•o•ca** \ˌman-ē-'ō-kə\ *n* **:** CASSAVA **[**French *manioc* and Spanish and Portuguese *mandioca,* of American Indian origin**]**

man•i•ple \'man-ə-pəl\ *n* **1 :** a long narrow band worn at mass over the left arm by clerics of or above the order of subdeacon **2 :** a subdivision of a Roman legion consisting of either 120 or 60 men **[**Latin *manipulus* "handful", from *manus* "hand"**]**

ma•nip•u•late \mə-'nip-yə-ˌlāt\ *vt* **1 :** to treat or operate with the hands or by mechanical means especially with skill ⟨*manipulate* the TV dials ⟩ **2 a :** to manage or utilize skillfully ⟨*manipulate* masses of statistics⟩ **b :** to manage artfully, unfairly, or fraudulently ⟨*manipulate* accounts⟩ ⟨*manipulate* public opinion⟩ **c :** to influence (as prices) by artificial means **[**back-formation from *manipulation,* from French, derived from Latin *manipulus* "handful"**]** — **ma•nip•u•la•tion** \-ˌnip-yə-'lā-shən\ *n* — **ma•nip•u•la•tor** \-'nip-yə-ˌlāt-ər\ *n*

man•i•tou *or* **man•i•tu** \'man-ə-ˌtü\ *also* **man•i•to** \-ˌtō\ *n* **:** one of the Algonquian deities or spirits dominating the forces of nature **[**of American Indian origin**]**

man•kind *n sing or pl* **1** \'man-'kīnd, -ˌkīnd\ **:** HUMANITY 4 **2** \-'kīnd\ **:** men as distinguished from women

man•like \'man-ˌlīk\ *adj* **1 :** resembling human beings ⟨*manlike* apes⟩ **2 :** befitting or belonging to a man **:** MANLY

man•ly \'man-lē\ *adj* **man•li•er**; **-est 1 :** having desirable qualities held to be appropriate to a man **2 :** befitting a man ⟨*manly* sports⟩ — **man•li•ness** *n*

man–made \'man-'mād\ *adj* **:** made by humans rather than nature ⟨*man-made* systems⟩; *also* **:** SYNTHETIC ⟨*man-made* fibers⟩

man•na \'man-ə\ *n* **1 :** food miraculously supplied to the Israelites in the wilderness **2 :** something much needed and joyfully received **[**Old English, from Late Latin, from Greek, from Hebrew *mān***]**

manned \'mand\ *adj* **:** carrying or performed by a person ⟨*manned* spaceflight⟩

man•ne•quin \'man-i-kən\ *n* **1 :** an artist's, tailor's, or dressmaker's jointed figure of the human body; *also* **:** a form representing the human figure used especially for displaying clothes **2 :** a woman who models clothing **:** MODEL **[**French, from Dutch *mannekijn* "little man", from *man* "man"**]**

man•ner \'man-ər\ *n* **1 a :** KIND ⟨what *manner* of person are you⟩ **b :** SORTS ⟨all *manner* of information⟩ **2 a :** a way of acting or proceeding ⟨worked in a brisk *manner*⟩ **b :** HABIT, CUSTOM ⟨spoke bluntly as is my *manner*⟩ **c :** STYLE ⟨painted in the artist's early *manner*⟩ **3** *pl* **a :** social conduct or rules of conduct as shown in prevalent customs **b :** characteristic or habitual deportment **:** BEHAVIOR ⟨mind your *manners*⟩ **c :** pleasing or socially acceptable deportment ⟨teach children *manners*⟩ [Old French *maniere* "way of acting", from Latin *manuarius* "of the hand", from *manus* "hand"]

man•nered \'man-ərd\ *adj* **1 :** having manners of a specified kind ⟨well-*mannered*⟩ **2 :** having an artificial character ⟨a highly *mannered* style⟩

man•ner•ism \'man-ə-,riz-əm\ *n* **:** an often affected peculiarity of action, bearing, or treatment ⟨the *mannerism* of constantly smoothing one's hair⟩ **syn** see AFFECTATION

man•ner•ly \'man-ər-lē\ *adj* **:** showing good manners **:** POLITE — **man•ner•li•ness** \-lē-nəs\ *n* — **mannerly** *adv*

man•nish \'man-ish\ *adj* **:** resembling or suggesting, suitable to, or characteristic of a man rather than a woman ⟨a *mannish* voice⟩ ⟨often wore *mannish* clothes⟩ — **man•nish•ly** *adv* — **man•nish•ness** *n*

man•ni•tol \'man-ə-,tȯl, -,tōl\ *n* **:** a slightly sweet crystalline alcohol $C_6H_8(OH)_6$ found in many plants [derived from *manna*]

manoeuvre, manoeuver *variant of* MANEUVER

man–of–war \,man-əv-'wȯər, -ə-\ *n, pl* **men–of–war** \,men-\ **:** WARSHIP

ma•nom•e•ter \mə-'näm-ət-ər\ *n* **:** an instrument for measuring pressure (as of gases and vapors) [derived from Greek *manos* "sparse, loose, rare"]

man•or \'man-ər\ *n* **:** a usually large landed estate; *esp* **:** one granted by a sovereign to a feudal lord [Old French *manoir* "residence", from *manoir* "to dwell", from Latin *manēre* "to stay"] — **ma•no•ri•al** \mə-'nōr-ē-əl, -'nȯr-\ *adj* — **ma•no•ri•al•ism** \-ē-ə-,liz-əm\ *n*

manor house *n* **:** the house of the lord of a manor

man–o'–war bird \,man-ə-'wȯr-,bərd\ *n* **:** FRIGATE BIRD

man power *n* **1 :** power available from or supplied by the physical effort of humans **2** *usually* **man•pow•er** \'man-,pau̇-ər, -,pau̇r\ **:** the total supply of persons available and fitted for service (as in the armed forces or industry)

man•qué \mäⁿ-'kā\ *adj* **:** UNSUCCESSFUL — used after the word modified ⟨a poet *manqué*⟩ [French, from *manquer* "to lack, fall short"]

man•sard \'man-,särd, -sard\ *n* **:** a roof having two slopes on all sides with the lower slope much steeper than the upper [French *mansarde,* from François *Mansart,* died 1666, French architect]

manse \'mans\ *n* **:** the residence of a member of the clergy; *esp* **:** the house of a Presbyterian minister [Medieval Latin *mansa* "residence", from Latin *manēre* "to stay, dwell"]

man•ser•vant \'man-,sər-vənt\ *n, pl* **men•ser•vants** \'men-,sər-vəns\ **:** a male servant

man•sion \'man-chən\ *n* **:** a large imposing residence [Middle French, literally, "act of staying, lodging", from Latin *mansio,* from *manēre* "to stay"]

man–size \'man-,sīz\ *or* **man–sized** \-,sīzd\ *adj* **1 :** suitable for or felt to require a man ⟨a *man-size* job⟩ **2 :** LARGE-SCALE ⟨a *man-size* model⟩

man•slaugh•ter \'man-,slȯt-ər\ *n* **:** the unlawful killing of a person without intent to do so

man•slay•er \-,slā-ər\ *n* **:** one that slays a person

man•sue•tude \'man-swi-,tüd, man-'sü-ə-,tüd, -,tyüd\ *n* **:** the quality or state of being gentle **:** MEEKNESS, TAMENESS [Latin *mansuetudo,* from *mansuetus* "tame, mild", from *mansuescere* "to tame", from *manus* "hand" + *suescere* "to accustom"]

man•ta \'mant-ə\ *n* **1 :** a square piece of cloth or blanket used in southwestern United States and Latin America as a cloak or shawl **2 :** DEVILFISH 1 [Spanish; sense 2 from its being caught in traps resembling blankets]

man•teau \man-'tō\ *n* **:** a loose cloak, coat, or robe [French, from Old French *mantel*]

man•tel \'mant-l\ *n* **1 :** the beam, stone, arch, or shelf above a fireplace **2 :** the finish covering the chimney around a fireplace [Middle French, from Old French, "mantle"]

man•telet \'mant-lət\ *n* **:** a very short cape or cloak

man•tel•piece \'mant-l-,pēs\ *n* **1 :** a mantel with its side elements **2 :** the shelf of a mantel

man•ti•core \'mant-i-,kōr, -,kȯr\ *n* **:** a legendary animal with the head of a man, the body of a lion, and the tail of a dragon or scorpion [Latin *mantichora,* from Greek *mantichōras*]

man•til•la \man-'tē-ə, -'tē-yə, -'til-ə\ *n* **1 :** a light scarf worn over the head and shoulders especially by Spanish and Latin American women **2 :** a short light cape or cloak [Spanish, from *manta* "manta"]

man•tis \'mant-əs\ *n, pl* **man•tis•es** *or* **man•tes** \'man-,tēz\ **:** any of various insects related to the grasshoppers and roaches that feed upon insects and hold their prey in forelimbs raised as if in prayer [Greek, literally, "diviner, prophet"]

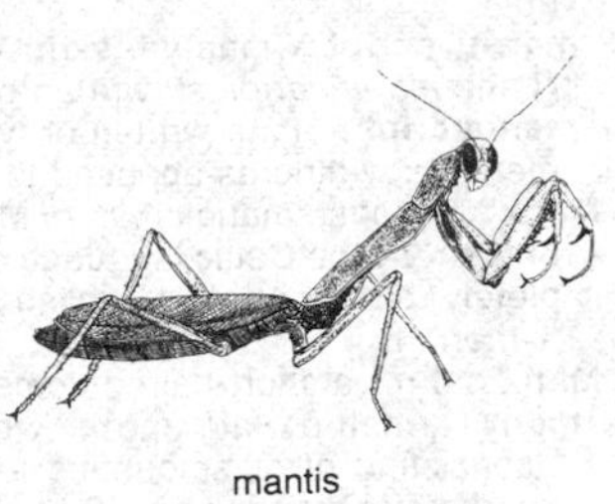

mantis

man•tis•sa \man-'tis-ə\ *n* **:** the decimal part of a logarithm [Latin *mantisa, mantissa* "something used to make up weight", from Etruscan]

1man•tle \'mant-l\ *n* **1 :** a loose sleeveless outer garment **:** CLOAK **2 a :** something that covers or envelops **b :** a fold or lobe or pair of lobes of the body wall of a mollusk or brachiopod lining and secreting the shell in shell-bearing forms **3 :** a lacy sheath that gives light by incandescence when placed over a flame [Old French *mantel,* from Latin *mantellum*]

2mantle *vt* **man•tled; man•tling** \'mant-ling, -l-ing\ **:** to cover or envelop with or as if with a mantle

man•tle•rock \'mant-l-,räk\ *n* **:** unconsolidated material that overlies the earth's solid rock

man•trap \'man-,trap\ *n* **:** a trap for catching men **:** SNARE

man•tua \'manch-wə, -ə-wə\ *n* **:** a usually loose-fitting gown worn especially in the 17th and 18th centuries [French *manteau*]

1man•u•al \'man-yə-wəl, -yəl\ *adj* **1 a :** of, relating to, or involving the hands ⟨*manual* dexterity⟩ **b :** worked by hand ⟨a *manual* choke⟩ **2 :** requiring or using physical skill and energy ⟨*manual* labor⟩ ⟨*manual* workers⟩ [Middle French *manuel,* from Latin *manualis,* from *manus* "hand"] — **man•u•al•ly** \-ē\ *adv*

2manual *n* **1 :** a small book; *esp* **:** HANDBOOK **2 :** the set movements in the handling of a weapon during a military drill or ceremony

manual alphabet *n* **:** an alphabet for deaf-mutes in which the letters are represented by finger positions

manual training *n* **:** a course of training to develop skill in using the hands (as in woodworking)

ma•nu•bri•um \mə-'nü-brē-əm, -'nyü-\ *n, pl* **-bria** \-brē-ə\ *also* **-briums :** an anatomical part (as the upper end of the sternum) suggesting a handle [Latin, "handle", from *manus* "hand"]

man•u•fac•to•ry \,man-yə-'fak-tə-rē, ,man-ə-, -trē\ *n, pl* **-ries :** FACTORY

1man•u•fac•ture \,man-yə-'fak-chər, ,man-ə-\ *n* **1 :** something made from raw materials **2 :** the process of making wares by hand or by machinery especially when carried on systematically with division of labor **3 :** the act or process of producing something ⟨the *manufacture* of blood by the body⟩ [Middle French, from Latin *manu factus* "made by hand"]

2manufacture *vt* **-fac•tured; -fac•tur•ing** \-'fak-chə-ring, -'fak-shring\ **1 :** to make into a product suitable for use **2 :** to make from raw materials by hand or by machinery especially systematically and with division of labor **3 :** FABRICATE 2, INVENT — **man•u•fac•tur•ing** *n*

man•u•fac•tur•er \-'fak-chər-ər, -'fak-shrər\ *n* **:** one that manufactures; *esp* **:** an employer of workers in manufacturing

man•u•mis•sion \,man-yə-'mish-ən\ *n* **:** emancipation from slavery [Middle French, from Latin *manumissio,* from *manumittere* "to manumit"]

man•u•mit \,man-yə-'mit\ *vt* **-mit•ted; -mit•ting :** to release from slavery [Middle French *manumitter,* from Latin *manumittere,* from *manus* "hand" + *mittere* "to let go, send"]

1ma•nure \mə-'nu̇r, -'nyu̇r\ *vt* **:** to enrich (land) by the application of manure [Middle English *manouren* "to cultivate", from Middle French *manouvrer,* literally, "to work by hand", from Latin *manu operare* — see MANEUVER *origin*]

2manure *n* **:** material that fertilizes land; *esp* **:** refuse of stables and barnyards consisting of bodily waste of birds and animals with or without litter — **ma•nu•ri•al** \mə-ˈnu̇r-ē-əl, -ˈnyu̇r-\ *adj*

[1]man•u•script \ˈman-yə-ˌskript\ *adj* : written by hand or typed [Latin *manu scriptus* "written by hand"]

[2]manuscript *n* **1** : a written or typewritten composition or document **2** : writing as opposed to print

Manx \ˈmaŋs, ˈmaŋks\ *n, pl* **Manx 1** *pl* : the people of the Isle of Man **2** : the Celtic language of the Manx people almost completely displaced by English — **Manx** *adj* — **Manx•man** \-mən\ *n*

Manx cat *n* : a short-haired domestic cat having no external tail

[1]many \ˈmen-ē\ *adj* **more** \ˈmōr, ˈmȯr\; **most** \ˈmōst\ **1** : consisting of or amounting to a large but indefinite number ⟨worked for *many* years⟩ **2** : being one of a large but indefinite number ⟨*many* a person⟩ [Old English *manig*] — **as many** : the same in number ⟨saw three plays in *as many* days⟩
• **syn** NUMEROUS, COUNTLESS: MANY implies a relatively large number usually of like things in contrast with a few or several or with an exact number; NUMEROUS implies very many and often suggests crowding, thronging, or clustering; COUNTLESS may imply a number too great to count or apparently without limit.

[2]many *pron, pl in construction* : a large number of persons or things ⟨*many* of them⟩

[3]many *n, pl in construction* : a large but indefinite number ⟨a good *many* went⟩

many•fold \ˌmen-ē-ˈfōld\ *adv* : by many times

many–sid•ed \ˌmen-ē-ˈsīd-əd\ *adj* **1** : having many sides or aspects **2** : having many interests or aptitudes : VERSATILE — **many•sid•ed•ness** *n*

man•za•ni•ta \ˌman-zə-ˈnēt-ə\ *n* : any of various western North American evergreen shrubs of the heath family [American Spanish, from Spanish *manzana* "apple"]

Mao•ism \ˈmau̇-ˌiz-əm\ *n* : the theory and practice of Marxism-Leninism developed in China chiefly by Mao Tse-tung — **Mao•ist** \ˈmau̇-əst\ *n or adj*

Mao•ri \ˈmau̇-rē\ *n, pl* **Maori** *or* **Maoris 1** : a member of a Polynesian people native to New Zealand **2** : the language of the Maori people — **Maori** *adj*

[1]map \ˈmap\ *n* **1 a** : a drawing or picture showing features of an area (as the surface of the earth) **b** : a drawing or picture of the sky showing the position of stars and planets **2** : the arrangement of genes on a chromosome as deduced from genetic experiments [Medieval Latin *mappa,* from Latin, "napkin"]

[2]map *vt* **mapped**; **map•ping 1 a** : to make a map of ⟨*map* the surface of the moon⟩ **b** : to assign to every element of (a mathematical set) an element of the same or another set **2** : to plan in detail ⟨*map* out a campaign⟩ — **map•per** *n*

ma•ple \ˈmā-pəl\ *n* : any of a genus of trees or shrubs with opposite leaves and a 2-winged dry fruit; *also* : the hard light-colored close-grained wood of a maple [Old English *mapul-*]

maple sugar *n* : a brown sugar made by boiling maple syrup

maple syrup *n* : syrup made by concentrating the sap of maples and especially the sugar maple

map•ping \ˈmap-iŋ\ *n* **1** : the act or process of making a map **2** : FUNCTION 5a ⟨a one-to-one *mapping* of the positive integers onto their squares⟩

ma•quette \ma-ˈket\ *n* : a usually small preliminary model (as of a sculpture) [French]

ma•quis \ma-ˈkē, mä-\ *n, pl* **ma•quis** \-ˈkē, -ˈkēz\ *often cap* : a guerrilla fighter in the French underground during World War II [French, literally, "underbrush"]

mar \ˈmär\ *vt* **marred**; **mar•ring 1** : to make a blemish on : DAMAGE, SPOIL **2** *archaic* **a** : [1]MANGLE 1, MUTILATE **b** : DESTROY 1 [Old English *mierran* "to waste"]

mar•a•bou *or* **mar•a•bout** \ˈmar-ə-ˌbü\ *n* **1 a** : a large Old World stork **b** : the long soft feathers from under the tail and wings of this bird used especially formerly in millinery **2 a** : a thrown raw silk **b** : a fabric (as a feathery trimming material) made of this silk [French *marabout,* literally, "marabout"]

mar•a•bout \ˈmar-ə-ˌbü\ *n, often cap* : a dervish in Muslim Africa held to have supernatural power [French, from Portuguese *marabuto,* from Arabic *marābiṭ*]

ma•ra•ca \mə-ˈräk-ə, -ˈrak-\ *n* : a dried gourd or a rattle like a gourd that contains dried seeds or pebbles and is used as a percussion instrument [Portuguese *maracá*]

mar•a•schi•no \ˌmar-ə-ˈskē-nō, -ˈshē-\ *n, often cap* **1** : a sweet liqueur distilled from the fermented juice of a bitter wild cherry **2** : a usually large cherry preserved in true or imitation maraschino [Italian, from *marasca* "bitter wild cherry"]

ma•ras•mus \mə-ˈraz-məs\ *n* : a progressive wasting away usually associated with faulty nutrition [Late Latin, from Greek *marasmos,* from *marainein* "to waste away"]

marabou 1a

Ma•ra•thi \mə-ˈrät-ē\ *n* : the chief Indic language of the state of Maharashtra in India [Marathi *marāṭhī*]

mar•a•thon \ˈmar-ə-ˌthän\ *n* **1** : a long-distance race; *esp* : a footrace run on an open course of 26 miles 385 yards (about 42 kilometers) **2** : an unusually long and exhausting contest or activity [*Marathon,* Greece, site of a victory of Greeks over Persians in 490 B.C., the news of which was carried to Athens by a long-distance runner] — **marathon** *adj*

ma•raud \mə-ˈrȯd\ *vb* : to roam about and raid in search of plunder [French *marauder*] — **ma•raud•er** *n*

[1]mar•ble \ˈmär-bəl\ *n* **1 a** : a usually crystalline metamorphosed limestone that is capable of taking a high polish and is used in architecture and sculpture **b** : something made from marble; *esp* : a piece of sculpture **2 a** : a little ball (as of glass) used in various games **b** *pl* : a children's game played with these little balls [Old French *marbre,* from Latin *marmor,* from Greek *marmaros*]

[2]marble *vt* **mar•bled**; **mar•bling** \ˈmar-bə-liŋ, -bliŋ\ : to give a mottled appearance to ⟨*marble* the edges of a book⟩

[3]marble *adj* : made of, resembling, or suggestive of marble

mar•ble•ize \ˈmär-bə-ˌlīz\ *vt* : MARBLE

mar•bling \ˈmär-bə-liŋ, -bliŋ\ *n* **1** : coloration or markings resembling or suggestive of marble **2** : an intermixture of fat through the lean of a cut of meat

mar•bly \ˈmär-bə-lē, -blē\ *adj* : MARBLE

mar•ca•site \ˈmär-kə-ˌsīt, -ˌzīt; ˌmär-kə-ˈzēt\ *n* : a mineral FeS_2 consisting of iron and sulfur and having a metallic luster [Medieval Latin *marcasita,* from Arabic *marqashīthā*]

[1]mar•cel \mär-ˈsel\ *n* : a deep soft wave made in the hair by the use of a heated curling iron [*Marcel* Grateau, died 1936, French hairdresser]

[2]marcel *vt* **mar•celled**; **mar•cel•ling** : to make a marcel in

[1]march \ˈmärch\ *n* : a border region : FRONTIER; *esp* : a district originally set up to defend a boundary ⟨the Welsh *marches*⟩ [Old French *marche,* of Germanic origin]

[2]march *vi* : to have common borders or frontiers

[3]march \ˈmärch, *imperatively often* härch *in the military*\ *vb* **1** : to move along usually with a steady regular stride in step with others **2 a** : to move in a direct purposeful manner : PROCEED **b** : to make steady progress : ADVANCE [Middle French *marchier*] — **march•er** *n*

[4]march \ˈmärch\ *n* **1 a** : the action of marching **b** : the distance covered within a specific period of time by marching **c** : a regular even step used in marching **2** : forward movement **3** : a musical composition in duple rhythm (as 4/4 time) with a strongly accentuated beat suitable to accompany marching

March \ˈmärch\ *n* : the 3d month of the year [Old French, from Latin *Martius,* from *Mart-, Mars,* the god Mars]

mär•chen \ˈmeər-kən\ *n, pl* **märchen** : TALE 1; *esp* : FOLKTALE [German]

mar•chio•ness \ˈmär-shə-nəs, -shnəs\ *n* **1** : the wife or widow of a marquess **2** : a woman who holds the rank of marquess in her own right [Medieval Latin *marchionissa,* from *marchio* "marquess", from *marca* "border region", of Germanic origin]

march•pane \ˈmärch-ˌpān\ *n* : MARZIPAN [Italian *marzapane*]

march–past \ˈmärch-ˌpast\ *n* : a marching by especially of troops in review

Mar•di Gras \ˌmärd-ē-ˈgrä\ *n* : Shrove Tuesday often observed with parades and festivities [French, literally, "fat Tuesday"]

[1]mare \ˈmaər, ˈmeər\ *n* : the female of a member of the horse family [Old English *mere*]

[2]ma•re \ˈmär-ˌā\ *n, pl* **ma•ria** \ˈmär-ē-ə\ : one of several large dark areas on the surface of the moon or Mars [Latin, "sea"]

ma•re clau•sum \ˌmär-ˌā-ˈklau̇-səm, -ˈklȯ-\ *n* : a navigable

body of water (as a sea) under the jurisdiction of one nation and closed to other nations [New Latin, literally, "closed sea"]
mare's nest *n, pl* **mare's nests** *or* **mares' nests 1 :** a false discovery or a deliberate hoax **2 :** a situation or condition of great confusion
mare's tail *n* **:** a cirrus cloud that has a long slender flowing appearance
mar·ga·rine \'mär-jən, -ə-rən, -ə-,rēn\ *n* **:** a food product made usually from vegetable oils and skim milk often with vitamins A and D added and used as a spread and a cooking fat [French, from Greek *margaron* "pearl"]
mar·gay \'mär-,gā\ *n* **:** a small American spotted wildcat [French, from Tupi *maracaja*]
marge \'märj\ *n* **:** MARGIN 2
[1]**mar·gin** \'mär-jən\ *n* **1 :** the part of a page outside the main body of printed or written matter **2 :** the outside limit and adjoining area of something **3 a :** an allowance (as of time or money) to meet unexpected demands **b :** the point (as of rising costs or shortage of raw material) at which an economic activity becomes impracticable **4 a :** the difference between cost and selling price **b :** cash or collateral deposited to secure a broker from loss on a contract **c :** an allowance above or below a certain figure within which a purchase or sale is to be made **5 :** measure or degree of difference ⟨won by a single vote *margin*⟩ [Latin *margin-, margo* "border"] **syn** see BORDER — **mar·gined** \-jənd\ *adj*
[2]**margin** *vt* **1 :** to provide with an edging or border **2 :** BORDER 2
mar·gin·al \'märj-nəl, -ən-l\ *adj* **1 :** written or printed in the margin of a page or sheet ⟨*marginal* notes⟩ **2 :** of, relating to, or situated at a margin or border **3 a :** close to the lower limit of qualification or acceptability ⟨*marginal* students⟩ **b :** yielding a supply of goods which when marketed at existing price levels will barely cover the cost of production ⟨*marginal* land⟩; *also* **:** relating to or derived from goods produced and marketed and with such result ⟨*marginal* profits⟩ — **mar·gin·al·i·ty** \,mär-jə-'nal-ət-ē\ *n* — **mar·gin·al·ly** \'märj-nə-lē, -ən-l-ē\ *adv*
mar·gi·na·lia \,mär-jə-'nā-lē-ə\ *n pl* **:** marginal notes
marginal utility *n* **:** the amount of additional utility to a consumer provided by an additional unit of an economic good or service
mar·grave \'mär-,grāv\ *n* **1 :** the military governor especially of a medieval German border province **2 :** a member of the German nobility corresponding in rank to a British marquess [Dutch *markgraaf*] — **mar·gra·vate** \-grə-,vāt\ *or* **mar·gra·vi·ate** \mär-'grā-vē-ət\ *n* — **mar·gra·vi·al** \-vē-əl\ *adj*
mar·gra·vine \'mär-grə-,vēn, ,mär-grə-'\ *n* **:** the wife of a margrave
mar·gue·rite \,mär-gyə-'rēt, -gə-\ *n* **1 :** DAISY 1a **2 :** any of various single-flowered chrysanthemums **3 :** any of several cultivated chamomiles [French, derived from Greek *margaron* "pearl"]
maria *pl of* [2]MARE
Mar·i·an \'mer-ē-ən, 'mar-ē-, 'mā-rē-\ *adj* **1 :** of or relating to Mary Tudor or her reign (1553-58) **2 :** of or relating to the Virgin Mary
Mar·i·an·ist \-ē-ə-nəst\ *n* **:** a member of the Roman Catholic Society of Mary of Paris devoted especially to education
mari·gold \'mar-ə-,gōld, 'mer-\ *n* **1 :** POT MARIGOLD **2 :** any of a genus of tropical American herbs of the daisy family that are grown for their showy variously colored yellow, orange, or maroon flower heads [Middle English, from *Mary,* mother of Jesus + *gold*]
mar·i·jua·na *or* **mar·i·hua·na** \,mar-ə-'wän-ə *also* -'hwän-\ *n* **1 :** HEMP **2 :** the dried leaves and flowering tops of the female hemp plant that are sometimes smoked for their intoxicating effect — compare BHANG, CANNABIS, HASHISH [Mexican Spanish *mariguana, marihuana*]
ma·rim·ba \mə-'rim-bə\ *n* **:** a primitive xylophone with resonators beneath each bar; *also* **:** a modern form of this instrument [of African origin]
ma·ri·na \mə-'rē-nə\ *n* **:** a dock or basin providing secure moorings for boats and yachts [Italian and Spanish, "seashore", from *marino,* adj., "marine", from Latin *marinus*]
[1]**mar·i·nade** \,mar-ə-'nād\ *vt* **:** MARINATE
[2]**marinade** *n* **:** a savory usually acid sauce in which food (as meat) is soaked to enrich its flavor
mar·i·nate \'mar-ə-,nāt\ *vt* **:** to soak in a marinade [probably from Italian *marinare,* from *marino* "marine"]
[1]**ma·rine** \mə-'rēn\ *adj* **1 a :** of or relating to the sea ⟨*marine* life⟩ **b :** of or relating to the navigation of the sea **:** NAUTICAL ⟨a *marine* chart⟩ **c :** of or relating to the commerce of the sea ⟨*marine* insurance⟩ **2 :** of or relating to marines ⟨*marine* barracks⟩ [Latin *marinus,* from *mare* "sea"]

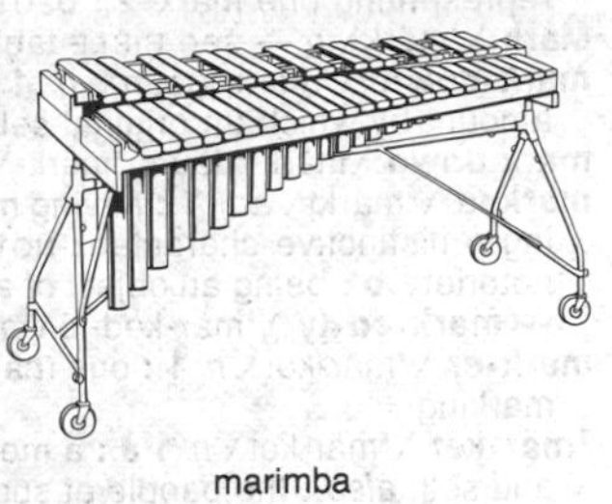
marimba

[2]**marine** *n* **1 :** the mercantile and naval shipping of a country **2 :** one of a class of soldiers serving on shipboard or in close association with a naval force; *esp* **:** a member of the United States Marine Corps
mar·i·ner \'mar-ə-nər\ *n* **:** one who navigates or assists in navigating a ship **:** SAILOR
Mar·i·ol·a·try \,mer-ē-'äl-ə-trē, ,mar-\ *n* **:** excessive veneration of the Virgin Mary [*Mary* + Greek *latreia* "worship"]
mar·i·o·nette \,mar-ē-ə-'net, ,mer-\ *n* **:** a small usually wooden figure with jointed limbs moved by strings or wires [French *marionnette,* from the name *Marion*]
Mar·i·po·sa lily \,mar-ə-,pō-zə-, -sə-\ *n* **:** any of a genus of western North American plants of the lily family with showily blotched flowers [probably from American Spanish *mariposa,* from Spanish, "butterfly"]
Mar·ist \'mar-əst, 'mer-\ *n* **:** a member of the Roman Catholic Society of Mary devoted to education
mar·i·tal \'mar-ət-l\ *adj* **1 :** of or relating to marriage **:** CONJUGAL **2 :** of or relating to a husband [Latin *maritalis,* from *maritus* "married"] **syn** see MATRIMONIAL — **mar·i·tal·ly** \-l-ē\ *adv*
mar·i·time \'mar-ə-,tīm\ *adj* **1 :** of or relating to navigation or commerce on the sea ⟨*maritime* law⟩ **2 :** of, relating to, or bordering on the sea ⟨a *maritime* province⟩ **3 :** having characteristics controlled primarily by oceanic winds and air masses ⟨a *maritime* climate⟩ [Latin *maritimus,* from *mare* "sea"]
mar·jo·ram \'märj-rəm, -ə-rəm\ *n* **:** any of various usually fragrant and aromatic mints sometimes used in cookery [Middle French *marjorane,* from Medieval Latin *marjorana*]
[1]**mark** \'märk\ *n* **1 :** [1]MARCH **2 a** (1) **:** a conspicuous object serving as a guide for travelers (2) **:** something (as a line, notch, or fixed object) designed to record position ⟨high-water *mark*⟩ **b :** something aimed at **:** TARGET **c :** the starting line or position **d** (1) **:** an object of ridicule or abuse **:** BUTT (2) **:** the point under discussion ⟨a comment beside the *mark*⟩ **e :** a standard of performance, quality, or condition **:** NORM **3 a** (1) **:** SIGN, INDICATION ⟨gave the necklace as a *mark* of esteem⟩ (2) **:** an impression (as a scratch, scar, or stain) made on something (3) **:** a distinguishing trait or quality **:** CHARACTERISTIC ⟨the *marks* of an educated person⟩ **b :** a symbol used for identification or indication of ownership **c :** a cross made in place of a signature **d :** a symbol (as a number or letter) representing an estimation of the quality of work or conduct; *esp* **:** GRADE 5 **4 a :** ATTENTION, NOTICE ⟨nothing worthy of *mark*⟩ **b :** IMPORTANCE, DISTINCTION ⟨a person of *mark*⟩ **c :** a lasting or strong impression ⟨make one's *mark* in the world⟩ [Old English *mearc* "boundary, march, sign"]
[2]**mark** *vt* **1 a** (1) **:** to fix or trace out the bounds of (2) **:** to plot the course of **:** CHART **b :** to set apart by a line or boundary ⟨*mark* off a mining claim⟩ **2 a :** to designate as if by a mark ⟨*marked* for greatness⟩ **b :** to make a mark on **c :** to furnish with natural marks ⟨wings *marked* with white⟩ **d :** to label so as to indicate price or quality **e :** to make note of in writing **:** JOT **f :** to indicate by a mark or symbol; *also* **:** RECORD **g :** to determine the quality or value of by means of marks or symbols **:** GRADE **h :** CHARACTERIZE, DISTINGUISH ⟨the flamboyance that *marks* their stage performance⟩ **3 :** to take notice of **:** OBSERVE ⟨*mark* my words⟩ — **mark time 1 :** to keep the time of a marching step by moving the feet alternately without advancing **2 :** to function or operate without making progress
[3]**mark** *n* **1 a :** the basic monetary unit of East Germany **b :** a coin

\ə\ **abut**	\au̇\ **out**	\i\ **tip**	\ȯ\ **saw**	\u̇\ **foot**
\ər\ **further**	\ch\ **chin**	\ī\ **life**	\ȯi\ **coin**	\y\ **yet**
\a\ **mat**	\e\ **pet**	\j\ **job**	\th\ **thin**	\yü\ **few**
\ā\ **take**	\ē\ **easy**	\ng\ **sing**	\t͟h\ **this**	\yu̇\ **cure**
\ä\ **cot, cart**	\g\ **go**	\ō\ **bone**	\ü\ **food**	\zh\ **vision**

representing one mark **2 :** DEUTSCHE MARK [German]
Mark \ˈmärk\ *n* — see BIBLE table
mark·down \ˈmärk-ˌdau̇n\ *n* **1 :** a lowering of price **2 :** the amount by which an original selling price is reduced
mark down \märk-ˈdau̇n, ˈmärk-\ *vt* **:** to put a lower price on
marked \ˈmärkt\ *adj* **1 :** having marks ⟨a *marked* card⟩ **2 :** having a distinctive character **:** NOTICEABLE **3 a :** having fame or notoriety **b :** being an object of attack, suspicion, or vengeance — **mark·ed·ly** \ˈmär-kəd-lē\ *adv*
mark·er \ˈmär-kər\ *n* **1 :** one that marks **2 :** something used for marking
1mar·ket \ˈmär-kət\ *n* **1 a :** a meeting together of people to buy and sell; *also* **:** the people at such a meeting **b :** a public place where a market is held; *esp* **:** a place where provisions are sold at wholesale **c :** a retail establishment usually of a specified kind ⟨a meat *market*⟩ **2 a :** a geographical area of demand for commodities ⟨our foreign *markets*⟩ **b :** the course of commercial activity by which the exchange of commodities is effected ⟨the *market* is dull⟩ **c :** an opportunity for selling ⟨a good *market* for used cars⟩ **3 :** the area of economic activity in which buyers and sellers come together and the forces of supply and demand affect prices [Old North French, from Latin *mercatus* "trade, marketplace", from *mercari* "to trade", from *merx* "merchandise"] — **in the market :** interested in buying ⟨*in the market* for a house⟩
2market *vb* **1 :** to deal in a market **2 :** to offer for sale in a market **:** SELL — **mar·ke·teer** \ˌmär-kə-ˈtiər\ *or* **mar·ket·er** \ˈmär-kət-ər\ *n* — **mar·ket·ing** \ˈmär-kət-iŋ\ *n*
mar·ket·able \ˈmär-kət-ə-bəl\ *adj* **1 :** fit for sale **2 :** wanted by purchasers **:** SALABLE — **mar·ket·abil·i·ty** \ˌmär-kət-ə-ˈbil-ət-ē\ *n*
market garden *n* **:** a plot in which vegetables are raised for market — **market gardener** *n* — **market gardening** *n*
mar·ket·place \ˈmär-kət-ˌplās\ *n* **1 :** an open square or place in a town where markets or public sales are held **2 :** the world of trade or economic activity
market price *n* **:** a price actually given in current market dealings
market research *n* **:** the gathering of factual information as to consumer preferences for goods and services
market value *n* **:** a price at which both buyers and sellers are willing to do business
mark·ing \ˈmär-kiŋ\ *n* **1 :** the act, process, or an instance of making or giving a mark **2 a :** a mark made **b :** arrangement, pattern, or disposition of marks (as on the coat of a mammal)
mark·ka \ˈmär-ˌkä\ *n, pl* **mark·kaa** \ˈmär-ˌkä\ *or* **mark·kas** \-ˌkäz\ **1 :** the basic monetary unit of Finland **2 :** a coin representing one markka [Finnish, from Swedish *mark,* a unit of value]
marks·man \ˈmärk-smən\ *n* **:** one that shoots at a mark; *esp* **:** a person skilled at target shooting — **marks·man·ship** \-ˌship\ *n*
mark·up \ˈmär-ˌkəp\ *n* **1 :** a raising of price **2 :** an amount added to the cost price of an article to determine the selling price
mark up \mär-ˈkəp, ˈmär-\ *vt* **:** to put a higher price on
1marl \ˈmärl\ *n* **:** a loose or crumbling earthy deposit that contains a substantial amount of calcium carbonate [Middle French *marle,* from Medieval Latin *margila,* from Latin *marga,* from Gaulish] — **marly** \ˈmär-lē\ *adj*
2marl *vt* **:** to dress (land) with marl
mar·lin \ˈmär-lən\ *n* **:** any of several large oceanic sport fishes related to sailfishes [short for *marlinespike;* from the appearance of its beak]

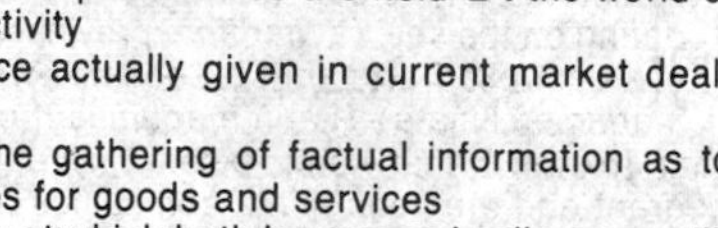
marlin

mar·line \ˈmär-lən\ *also* **mar·lin** *n* **:** a small loosely twisted line of two strands used for seizing and as a covering for wire rope [Dutch *marlijn*]
mar·line·spike *also* **mar·lin·spike** \ˈmär-lən-ˌspīk\ *n* **:** a pointed iron tool used to separate strands of rope or wire (as in splicing)
mar·ma·lade \ˈmär-mə-ˌlād\ *n* **:** a clear jelly in which pieces of fruit and fruit rind are suspended [Portuguese *marmelada* "quince conserve", from *marmelo* "quince", from Latin *melimelum,* a kind of sweet apple, from Greek *melimēlon,* from *meli* "honey" + *mēlon* "apple"]

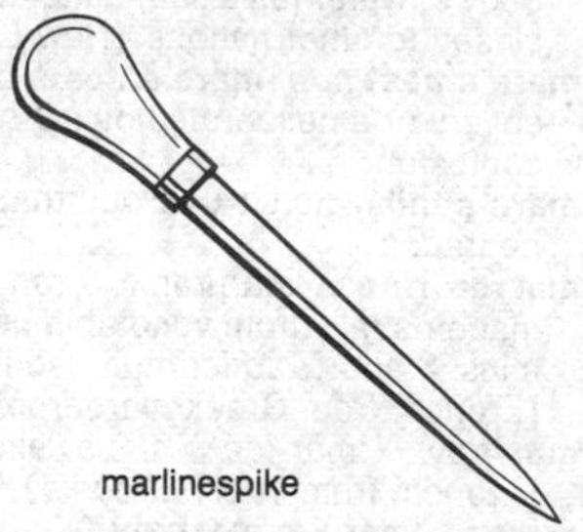
marlinespike

mar·mo·re·al \mär-ˈmōr-ē-əl, mär-ˈmȯr-\ *also* **mar·mo·re·an** \-ē-ən\ *adj* **:** of, relating to, or resembling marble or a marble statue [Latin *marmoreus,* from *marmor* "marble"] — **mar·mo·re·al·ly** \-ē-ə-lē\ *adv*
mar·mo·set \ˈmär-mə-ˌset, -mə-ˌzet\ *n* **:** any of numerous soft-furred bushy-tailed South and Central American monkeys with claws instead of nails except on the great toe [Middle French, "grotesque figure", from *marmouser* "to mumble"]
mar·mot \ˈmär-mət\ *n* **:** a stout-bodied short-legged burrowing rodent with coarse fur, a short bushy tail, and very small ears — compare WOODCHUCK [French *marmotte*]
1ma·roon \mə-ˈrün\ *vt* **1 :** to put ashore and abandon on a desolate island or coast **2 :** to leave isolated and helpless [American Spanish *cimarrón* "fugitive Negro slave", from *cimarrón* "wild, savage"]
2maroon *n* **:** a dark red [French *marron* "Spanish chestnut"]
mar·quee \mär-ˈkē\ *n* **1 :** a large tent set up for an outdoor party, reception, or exhibition **2 :** a canopy usually of metal and glass projecting over an entrance ⟨a theater *marquee*⟩ [French *marquise,* literally, "marchioness"]
mar·quess \ˈmär-kwəs\ *or* **mar·quis** \ˈmär-kwəs, mär-ˈkē\ *n, pl* **mar·quess·es** *or* **mar·quis·es** \-kwə-səz\ *or* **mar·quis** \-ˈkē, -ˈkēz\ **1 :** a nobleman of hereditary rank in Europe and Japan **2 :** a member of the British peerage ranking below a duke and above an earl [Middle French *marquis,* alteration of *marchis,* from *marche* "border region, march"] — **marquess·ate** \ˈmär-kwə-sət\ *or* **mar·quis·ate** \ˈmär-kwə-zət, -sət\ *n*
mar·que·try \ˈmär-kə-trē\ *n, pl* **-tries :** decoration in which elaborate patterns are formed by the insertion of pieces of wood, shell, or ivory into a wood veneer that is then applied to a piece of furniture [Middle French *marqueterie,* from *marqueter* "to checker, inlay", from *marque* "mark"]
mar·quise \mär-ˈkēz\ *n, pl* **mar·quises** \-ˈkēz, -ˈkēz-əz\ **:** MARCHIONESS [French, from *marquis* "marquess"]
mar·qui·sette \ˌmär-kwə-ˈzet, -kə-\ *n* **:** a sheer meshed fabric used for clothing, curtains, and mosquito nets
mar·riage \ˈmar-ij\ *n* **1 a :** the state of being married **b :** the mutual relation of husband and wife **:** WEDLOCK **c :** the institution whereby a man and a woman are joined in a special social and legal relationship for the purpose of making a home and raising a family **2 a :** an act of marrying **b :** WEDDING 1 **3 :** an intimate or close union ⟨a *marriage* of music and verse⟩ — **mar·riage·able** \-ə-bəl\ *adj*
marriage of convenience : a marriage contracted for social, political, or economic advantage
mar·ried \ˈmar-ēd\ *adj* **1 :** united in marriage **:** WEDDED ⟨a *married* couple⟩ **2 :** of or relating to marriage
mar·ron \ma-ˈrō^{n}\ *n* **1 :** a Mediterranean chestnut or its large sweet nut **2** *pl* **:** chestnuts preserved in vanilla-flavored syrup [French]
mar·row \ˈmar-ō\ *n* **1 a :** a soft vascular tissue that fills the cavities of most bones **b :** the substance of the spinal cord **2 :** HEART 5b, CORE [Old English *mearg*] — **mar·row·less** \-ō-ləs\ *adj* — **mar·rowy** \ˈmar-ə-wē\ *adj*
mar·row·bone \ˈmar-ə-ˌbōn\ *n* **1 :** a bone (as a shinbone) rich in marrow **2** *pl* **:** a person's knees
mar·row·fat \ˈmar-ō-ˌfat\ *n* **:** any of several wrinkled-seeded garden peas
1mar·ry \ˈmar-ē\ *vb* **mar·ried; mar·ry·ing 1 a :** to join as husband and wife according to law or custom ⟨were *married* yesterday⟩ **b :** to give in marriage ⟨*married* their daughter to a lawyer⟩ **c :** to take as husband or wife ⟨*married* my neighbor⟩ **d :** to take a spouse **:** WED **2 :** to unite in a close and usually permanent relation [Old French *marier,* from Latin *maritare,* from *maritus* "married"]
2marry *interj, archaic* — used to express amused or surprised

agreement [Middle English *mario,* from *Marie,* the virgin Mary]

Mars \'märz\ *n* **:** the planet 4th in order from the sun conspicuous for the redness of its light — see PLANET table [Latin, from *Mars,* god of war]

marsh \'märsh\ *n* **:** an area of soft wet land usually overgrown by grasses and sedges — compare SWAMP [Old English *mersc*]

¹mar•shal \'mär-shəl\ *n* **1 a :** a high official in a medieval royal household **b :** a person who arranges and directs ceremonies **2 :** an officer of the highest rank in some military forces **3 : a** federal official having duties similar to those of a sheriff; *also* **:** a city official having similar duties [Old French *mareschal,* of Germanic origin] — **mar•shal•cy** \-sē\ *n* — **mar•shal•ship** \-ˌship\ *n*

△ **origin** The Old French word *mareschal* was borrowed from a Germanic language. A *mareschal* is, etymologically, a "horse-servant"; the compound is related to Old English *mere* (modern English *mare*) and *scealc,* "servant". In addition to its original sense of "a groom or keeper of horses", Old French *mareschal* became the title of a high official in a royal court. In the Middle English period, the English borrowed French *mareschal,* "high official". The earlier sense, "keeper of horses", was borrowed a little later but is now obsolete.

²marshal *vt* **mar•shaled** *or* **mar•shalled; mar•shal•ing** *or* **mar•shal•ling** \'märsh-ling, -ə-ling\ **1 :** to arrange in proper position or order ⟨*marshal* troops⟩ ⟨*marshal* arguments⟩ **2 :** to lead ceremoniously or solicitously **:** USHER

marsh gas *n* **:** METHANE

marsh hawk *n* **:** a common North American hawk with a conspicuous white patch on the rump

marsh•mal•low \'märsh-ˌmel-ō, -ˌmal-\ *n* **1 :** a pink-flowered perennial herb of the mallow family that has a root sometimes used in confectionery and in medicine **2 :** a confection made from the root of the marshmallow or from corn syrup, sugar, albumen, and gelatin

marsh marigold *n* **:** a swamp herb having bright yellow flowers resembling those of the related buttercups — called also *cowslip*

marshy \'mär-shē\ *adj* **marsh•i•er; -est 1 :** resembling or constituting marsh **2 :** of or relating to marshes — **marsh•i•ness** \-shē-nəs\ *n*

¹mar•su•pi•al \mär-'sü-pē-əl\ *adj* **:** of, relating to, or being a marsupial

²marsupial *n* **:** any of an order (Marsupialia) of lowly mammals (as a kangaroo or opossum) that have a pouch on the abdomen of the female containing the teats and serving to carry the young

mar•su•pi•um \-pē-əm\ *n, pl* **-pia** \-pē-ə\ **1 :** the pouch of a female marsupial **2 :** a structure analogous to the marsupium in which an invertebrate animal carries eggs or young [Latin, "purse, pouch", from Greek *marsypion*]

mart \'märt\ *n* **:** MARKET 1b [Dutch *marct, mart,* probably from Old North French *market*]

mar•ten \'märt-n\ *n, pl* **marten** *or* **martens :** a slim flesh-eating mammal larger than the related weasels; *also* **:** its soft gray or brown fur [Middle French *martrine* "marten fur", from *martre* "marten", of Germanic origin]

mar•tial \'mär-shəl\ *adj* **1 :** of, relating to, or suited for war or a warrior ⟨a *martial* stride⟩ **2 :** of or relating to an army or to military life [Latin *martialis* "of Mars", from *Mart-, Mars* "Mars"] — **mar•tial•ly** \-shə-lē\ *adv*

• **syn** MARTIAL, WARLIKE, MILITARY mean relating to or characteristic of war. MARTIAL suggests especially the pomp and ceremony of war and preparation for war ⟨*martial* music⟩ WARLIKE implies the feeling or temper that leads to or accompanies war ⟨*warlike* mountain tribes⟩ MILITARY applies to anything pertaining to the art or conduct of organized warfare especially on land ⟨*military* campaigns⟩

martial law *n* **:** the law applied (as by military or police forces) in occupied territory or in an emergency

Mar•tian \'mär-shən\ *adj* **:** of or relating to the planet Mars or its hypothetical inhabitants — **Martian** *n*

mar•tin \'märt-n\ *n* **:** a small European swallow with a forked tail, bluish black head and back, and white rump and underparts; *also* **:** any of various other swallows and flycatchers [Middle French, from Saint *Martin*]

mar•ti•net \ˌmärt-n-'et\ *n* **:** a strict disciplinarian [Jean *Martinet,* 17th century French army officer]

mar•tin•gale \'märt-n-ˌgāl\ *n* **:** a strap connecting a horse's girth to the bit or reins so as to hold down its head [Middle French]

mar•ti•ni \mär-'tē-nē\ *n* **:** a cocktail consisting of gin or vodka and dry vermouth [probably from the name *Martini*]

Mar•tin•mas \'märt-n-məs, -ˌmas\ *n* **:** November 11 celebrated as the feast of Saint Martin [Middle English *martinmasse,* from Saint *Martin* + *masse* "mass"]

¹mar•tyr \'märt-ər\ *n* **1 :** a person who suffers death rather than give up his or her religion **2 :** one who sacrifices his or her life or something of great value for a principle or a cause **3 :** a great or constant sufferer [Old English, from Late Latin, from Greek *martys,* literally, "witness"] — **mar•tyr•iza•tion** \ˌmärt-ə-rə-'zā-shən\ *n* — **mar•tyr•ize** \'märt-ə-ˌrīz\ *vb*

²martyr *vt* **1 :** to put to death for adhering to a belief **2 :** TORTURE 1, 2

mar•tyr•dom \'märt-ər-dəm\ *n* **1 :** the sufferings and death of a martyr **2 :** TORMENT 1, 2, TORTURE

¹mar•vel \'mär-vəl\ *n* **:** something that causes wonder or astonishment [Old French *merveille,* from Late Latin *mirabilia* "marvels", from Latin *mirabilis* "wonderful", from *mirari* "to wonder"]

²marvel *vb* **mar•veled** *or* **mar•velled; mar•vel•ing** *or* **mar•vel•ling** \'marv-ling, -ə-ling\ **:** to become filled with surprise or astonishment ⟨*marveled* at the acrobat's feats⟩

mar•vel•ous *or* **mar•vel•lous** \'märv-ləs, -ə-ləs\ *adj* **1 :** causing wonder **:** ASTONISHING **2 :** MIRACULOUS 1 **3 :** of the highest quality **:** SPLENDID ⟨a *marvelous* party⟩ — **mar•vel•ous•ly** *adv* — **mar•vel•ous•ness** *n*

Marx•ian \'märk-sē-ən, 'märk-shən\ *adj* **:** of, developed by, or influenced by the doctrines of Karl Marx ⟨*Marxian* socialism⟩

Marx•ism \'märk-ˌsiz-əm\ *n* **:** the political, economic, and social doctrines developed by Karl Marx that provide the basis for Marxian socialism and much of modern Communism — **Marx•ist** \'märk-səst\ *n or adj*

Marx•ism–Len•in•ism \-'len-ə-ˌniz-əm\ *n* **:** a theory and practice of Communism developed by Lenin from Marxism primarily to fit Russian conditions — **Marx•ist–Len•in•ist** \-'len-ə-nəst\ *n or adj*

Mary Jane \'meər-ē-ˌjān, 'maər-ē-, 'mā-rē-\ *n, slang* **:** MARIJUANA [by folk etymology]

Mary•knoll•er \-ˌnō-lər\ **:** a member of the Catholic Foreign Mission Society of America founded at Maryknoll, N. Y., in 1911

mar•zi•pan \'märt-sə-ˌpän, -ˌpan; 'mär-zə-ˌpan\ *n* **:** a confection of almond paste, sugar, and egg white that is often shaped into forms [German, from Italian *marzapane,* a medieval coin, marzipan, from Arabic *mawthabān,* a medieval coin]

mas•cara \ma-'skar-ə\ *n* **:** a cosmetic for coloring the eyelashes and eyebrows [Italian *maschera* "mask"]

mas•con \'mas-ˌkän\ *n* **:** any of the large dense concentrations of mass under the surface of the maria of the moon [*mass* + *con*centration]

mas•cot \'mas-ˌkät *also* -kət\ *n* **:** a person, animal, or object adopted by a group as a symbol and supposed to bring good luck [French *mascotte,* from Provençal *mascoto* "charm, sorcery", from *masco* "witch", from Medieval Latin *masca*]

△ **origin** The Medieval Latin word *masca,* meaning "witch", was borrowed as *masco* into the Provençal language of southern France. *Mascoto,* a diminutive form of *masco,* was used to mean "charm" or "sorcery". This word was borrowed into French as *mascotte* and was popularized by the operetta *La Mascotte,* composed by Edmond Audran in 1880. In this operetta *"la mascotte"* is the beautiful maiden Bettina, whose influence brings victories to the army of the prince of Pisa. *Mascot* appeared in English soon afterward, used to mean "a person or thing held to bring good luck".

¹mas•cu•line \'mas-kyə-lən\ *adj* **1 :** of the male sex **2 :** characteristic of or belonging to men **:** MANLY **3 :** of, relating to, or constituting the class of words that ordinarily includes most of those referring to males ⟨a *masculine* noun⟩ ⟨*masculine* gender⟩ **4 :** having or occurring in a stressed final syllable ⟨*mascu-*

line rhyme⟩ [Middle French *masculin,* from Latin *masculinus,* from *masculus* "male", from *mas* "male"] — **mas•cu•line•ly** *adv* — **mas•cu•line•ness** \-lən-nəs\ *n* — **mas•cu•lin•i•ty** \ˌmas-kyə-ˈlin-ət-ē\ *n*

[2]masculine *n* **1 :** a word or form of the masculine gender **2 :** the masculine gender

ma•ser \ˈmā-zər\ *n* **:** a device that utilizes the natural oscillations of atoms or molecules between energy levels for generating monochromatic microwave radiation [*m*icrowave *a*mplification by *s*timulated *e*mission of *r*adiation]

[1]mash \ˈmash\ *n* **1 :** crushed malt or grain meal steeped and stirred in hot water to ferment (as in making whiskey) **2 :** a mixture of ground feeds for livestock **3 :** a soft pulpy mass [Old English *māx-*]

[2]mash *vt* **1 :** to reduce to a soft pulpy state by beating or pressure **2 :** to subject (as crushed malt) to the action of water with heating and stirring — **mash•er** *n*

[1]mask \ˈmask\ *n* **1 :** a cover for the face used for disguise or protection ⟨a Halloween *mask*⟩ ⟨a baseball catcher's *mask*⟩ **2 :** a device usually covering the mouth and nose either to aid in or prevent the inhaling of something (as a gas or spray) **3 :** a covering (as of gauze) for the mouth and nose to prevent infective droplets from being blown into the air **4 :** something that disguises or conceals **:** CLOAK, PRETENSE **5 :** one that wears a mask **:** MASKER **6 :** a sculptured face made by a mold in plaster or wax ⟨a death *mask*⟩ **7 :** the face of a mammal (as a fox or dog) **8 :** MASQUE 2 [Middle French *masque,* from Italian *maschera*] **syn** see DISGUISE

[1]mask 1

[2]mask *vb* **1 :** to take part in a masquerade **2 :** to put on or wear a mask **3 :** CONCEAL, DISGUISE ⟨*mask* one's real purpose⟩ **4 :** to cover for protection ⟨*mask* the glass before painting the windows⟩

masked \ˈmaskt\ *adj* **:** marked by the use of masks ⟨a *masked* ball⟩

mask•er \ˈmas-kər\ *n* **:** one that wears a mask; *esp* **:** a participant in a masquerade

mas•och•ism \ˈmas-ə-ˌkiz-əm, ˈmaz-\ *n* **1 :** a sexual perversion characterized by pleasure in being abused especially by a loved one **2 :** a taste for suffering [Leopold von Sacher-*Masoch,* died 1895, German novelist]

ma•son \ˈmās-n\ *n* **1 :** a skilled worker who builds with stone, brick, or cement **2** *cap* **:** FREEMASON [Old French *maçon*]

Ma•son•ic \mə-ˈsän-ik\ *adj* **:** of, relating to, or characteristic of Freemasons or Freemasonry

Ma•son•ite \ˈmās-n-ˌīt\ *trademark* — used for a fiberboard made from steam-treated wood fiber

ma•son jar \ˌmās-n-\ *n* **:** a widemouthed jar used for home canning [John L. *Mason,* 19th century American inventor]

ma•son•ry \ˈmās-n-rē\ *n, pl* **-ries 1 a :** something built of materials used by masons **b :** the art, trade, or occupation of a mason **c :** work done by a mason **2** *cap* **:** FREEMASONRY 1

mason wasp *n* **:** a solitary wasp that constructs nests of hardened mud

masque \ˈmask\ *n* **1 :** MASQUERADE 1 **2 :** a short allegorical dramatic entertainment of the 16th and 17th centuries performed by masked actors [Middle French]

masqu•er \ˈmas-kər\ *n* **:** MASKER

[1]mas•quer•ade \ˌmas-kə-ˈrād\ *n* **1 a :** a social gathering of persons wearing masks and often costumes **b :** a costume for wear at such a gathering **2 :** an action or appearance that is mere disguise or outward show [Middle French, from Italian dialect *mascarada,* from Italian *maschera* "mask"]

[2]masquerade *vi* **1 a :** to disguise oneself or go about disguised **b :** to take part in a masquerade **2 :** to assume the appearance of something one is not **:** POSE — **mas•quer•ad•er** *n*

[1]mass \ˈmas\ *n* **1** *cap* **:** a sequence of prayers and ceremonies forming the eucharistic service especially of the Roman Catholic Church **2** *often cap* **:** a celebration of the Eucharist **3 :** a musical setting for parts of the Mass [Old English *mæsse,* from Late Latin *missa* "dismissal after a religious service, mass", from Latin *mittere* "to send, let go"]

[2]mass *n* **1 a :** a quantity of matter or the form of matter that holds or clings together in one body ⟨a *mass* of metal⟩ **b :** greatness of size **:** BULK **c :** the principal part **:** main body **2 :** the property of a body that is a measure of its inertia and is commonly taken as a measure of the quantity of matter it contains **3 :** a large quantity, amount, or number **4 a :** a large body of persons in a compact group **b** *pl* **:** the body of common people as contrasted with the elite [Middle French *masse,* from Latin *massa,* from Greek *maza*] **syn** see BULK

[3]mass *vb* **:** to form or collect into a mass

[4]mass *adj* **1 a :** of, relating to, or designed for the mass of the people ⟨a *mass* market⟩ ⟨*mass* education⟩ **b :** participated in by or affecting a large number of individuals ⟨*mass* demonstrations⟩ **c :** occurring on a large scale ⟨*mass* production⟩ **2 :** viewed as a whole **:** TOTAL ⟨the *mass* effect of a design⟩

[1]mas•sa•cre \ˈmas-i-kər\ *vt* **-cred; -cring** \-kə-ring, -kring\ **:** to kill by massacre **:** SLAUGHTER — **mas•sa•crer** \-kər-ər, -i-krər\ *n*

[2]mas•sa•cre *n* **1 :** the violent, cruel, and indiscriminate killing of a number of people **2 :** a slaughter of animals in large numbers [Middle French]

[1]mas•sage \mə-ˈsäzh, -ˈsäj\ *n* **:** manipulation of bodily tissues (as by rubbing, stroking, kneading, or tapping) for relaxation or treatment especially with the hand or an instrument [French, from *masser* "to massage", from Arabic *massa* "to stroke"]

[2]massage *vt* **:** to subject to massage — **mas•sag•er** *n*

mas•sa•sau•ga \ˌmas-ə-ˈsȯ-gə\ *n* **:** any of several small rattlesnakes [*Missisauga* river, Ontario, Canada]

mass–energy equation *n* **:** an equation for the conversion of mass and energy into one another: $E = mc^2$ where *E* is energy in ergs, *m* is mass in grams, and *c* is the velocity of light in centimeters per second

mas•se•ter \mə-ˈsēt-ər, ma-\ *n* **:** a large muscle that raises the lower jaw and assists in chewing [Greek *masētēr,* from *masasthai* "to chew"] — **mas•se•ter•ic** \ˌmas-ə-ˈter-ik\ *adj*

mas•seur \ma-ˈsər, mə-\ *n* **:** a man who practices massage [French, from *masser* "to massage"]

mas•seuse \-ˈsu̇z, -ˈsərz, -ˈsüz\ *n* **:** a woman who practices massage [French, feminine of *masseur*]

mas•sif \ma-ˈsēf\ *n* **:** a principal mountain mass [French, from *massif* "massive"]

mas•sive \ˈmas-iv\ *adj* **1 :** forming or consisting of a large mass: **a :** WEIGHTY, HEAVY ⟨*massive* walls⟩ **b :** exceedingly large **:** GIGANTIC **c :** having no regular form but not necessarily lacking crystalline structure ⟨*massive* sandstone⟩ **2 a :** large, solid, or heavy in structure ⟨*massive* jaws⟩ **b :** large in scope or degree ⟨a *massive* effort⟩ ⟨*massive* retaliation⟩ — **mas•sive•ly** *adv* — **mas•sive•ness** *n*

mass medium *n, pl* **mass media :** a communications medium (as newspapers, radio, or television) that is designed to reach mass audiences — usually used in pl.

mass number *n* **:** an integer that expresses the mass of an isotope and designates the number of nucleons in the nucleus

mass–pro•duce \ˌmas-prə-ˈdüs, -ˈdyüs\ *vt* **:** to produce in quantity usually by machinery — **mass production** *n*

mass spectrograph *n* **:** an apparatus that separates a stream of charged particles into a spectrum according to their masses and records the data photographically

mass spectrometer *n* **:** an instrument similar to a mass spectrograph but usually adapted for the electrical measurement of the data

massy \ˈmas-ē\ *adj* **mass•i•er; -est :** MASSIVE 1b

[1]mast \ˈmast\ *n* **1 :** a long pole or spar that rises from the keel or deck of a ship or boat and supports the sails and rigging **2 :** a vertical or nearly vertical tall pole (as a post on a lifting crane) [Old English *mæst*] — **mast•ed** \ˈmas-təd\ *adj* — **before the mast :** as a common sailor

[2]mast *vt* **:** to furnish with a mast

[3]mast *n* **:** nuts accumulated on the forest floor and often serving as food for animals (as hogs) [Old English *mæst*]

mas•tec•to•my \ma-ˈstek-tə-mē\ *n, pl* **-mies :** surgical removal of a breast [Greek *mastos* "breast"]

[1]mas•ter \ˈmas-tər\ *n* **1 a :** a male teacher **b :** a person holding an academic degree higher than a bachelor's but lower than a doctor's **c** *often cap* **:** a revered religious leader **d :** an independent worker qualified to teach apprentices **e :** an artist or performer of great skill **2 a :** one having authority **:** RULER **b :** one that conquers or masters **:** SUPERIOR **c :** a person licensed to command a merchant ship **d** : an owner especially of a slave or animal **e** : the male head of a household **3 a** *archaic* : MISTER **b** *often cap* — used as a courtesy title before the name of a boy too young to be called *mister* **4** : a presiding officer in an institution or society [Old English *magister* and Old French *maistre,* both from Latin *magister*]

[2]master *vt* **mas•tered; mas•ter•ing** \'mas-tə-riŋ, -triŋ\ **1** : to get the better of : OVERCOME **2** : to become skilled or proficient in or in the use of ⟨*master* arithmetic⟩

[3]master *adj* **1** : being a master ⟨a *master* carpenter⟩ **2** : being the chief or guiding one ⟨a *master* plan⟩ **3** : controlling the operation of other mechanisms ⟨a *master* cylinder⟩ **4** : establishing a standard (as of dimension or weight) for reference ⟨a *master* gauge⟩

mas•ter–at–arms \,mas-tər-ət-'ärmz\ *n, pl* **masters–at–arms** : a petty officer charged with maintaining discipline aboard ship

master chief petty officer *n* : an enlisted rank in the Navy and Coast Guard above senior chief petty officer

mas•ter•ful \'mas-tər-fəl\ *adj* **1** : inclined to take control or dominate **2** : having or showing the technical or artistic skill of a master — **mas•ter•ful•ly** \-fə-lē\ *adv* — **mas•ter•ful•ness** *n*

• **syn** DOMINEERING, IMPERIOUS: MASTERFUL implies a strong forceful personality and the ability to deal authoritatively with people and affairs; DOMINEERING suggests an overbearing or tyrannical manner and an obstinate attempt to enforce one's will; IMPERIOUS applies to one who by position or nature is fitted to command and it often suggests arrogant assurance.

master gunnery sergeant *n* : an enlisted rank in the Marine Corps above master sergeant

master key *n* : a key designed to open several different locks

mas•ter•ly \'mas-tər-lē\ *adj* : suitable to or resembling a master; *esp* : showing superior knowledge or skill — **mas•ter•li•ness** *n* — **masterly** *adv*

mas•ter•mind \-,mīnd\ *n* : a person who invents or directs a project — **mastermind** *vt*

master of ceremonies **1** : a person who determines the forms to be observed on a public occasion **2** : a person who acts as host at a formal event **3** : a person who acts as host for an entertainment program (as on television)

mas•ter•piece \'mas-tər-,pēs\ *n* **1** : a piece of work presented to a medieval guild as evidence of qualification for the rank of master **2** : a work done with great skill; *esp* : a supreme intellectual or artistic achievement

master race *n* : a people held to be racially preeminent and hence fitted to rule or enslave other peoples

master sergeant *n* : an enlisted rank in the Army above sergeant first class and below staff sergeant major, in the Marine Corps above gunnery sergeant and below sergeant major, and in the Air Force above technical sergeant and below senior master sergeant

mas•ter•ship \'mas-tər-,ship\ *n* **1** : the authority or control of a master **2** : the office or position of a master **3** : the skill or ability of a master

mas•ter•stroke \-,strōk\ *n* : a masterly performance or move

mas•ter•work \-,wərk\ *n* : MASTERPIECE 2

mas•tery \'mas-tə-rē, -trē\ *n, pl* **-ter•ies** **1** : the position or authority of a master **2** : the upper hand in a contest or competition **3** : skill or knowledge that makes one master of something : COMMAND ⟨a *mastery* of French⟩

mast•head \'mast-,hed\ *n* **1** : the top of a mast **2 a** : the printed matter in a newspaper or periodical that gives the title and pertinent details of ownership, advertising rates, and subscription rates **b** : the name of a newspaper displayed on the top of the first page

mas•tic \'mas-tik\ *n* **1** : a yellowish to greenish resin of a small southern European tree used in varnish **2** : a pasty material (as a preparation of asphalt) used as protective coating or cement [Latin *mastiche,* from Greek *mastichē*]

mas•ti•cate \'mas-tə-,kāt\ *vb* **1** : to grind or crush with or as if with the teeth in preparation for swallowing : CHEW **2** : to soften or reduce to pulp by crushing or kneading [Late Latin *masticare,* from Greek *mastichan* "to gnash the teeth"] — **mas•ti•ca•tion** \mas-tə-'kā-shən\ *n* — **mas•ti•ca•tor** \'mas-tə-,kāt-ər\ *n* — **mas•ti•ca•to•ry** \'mas-ti-kə-,tōr-ē, -,tȯr-\ *adj*

mas•ti•ca•to•ry \'mas-ti-kə-,tōr-ē, -,tȯr-\ *n, pl* **-ries** : a substance chewed to increase saliva

mas•tiff \'mas-təf\ *n* : a large powerful smooth-coated dog used chiefly as a watchdog and guard dog [Middle French *mastin,* derived from Latin *mansuetus* "tame"]

mastiff

mas•ti•tis \mas-'tīt-əs\ *n, pl* **-tit•i•des** \-'tit-ə-,dēz\ : inflammation of the breast or udder usually caused by infection [Greek *mastos* "breast"]

mas•to•don \'mas-tə-,dän, -dən\ *also* **mas•to•dont** \'mas-tə-,dänt\ *n* : any of numerous huge extinct mammals related to the mammoths and existing elephants [Greek *mastos* "breast" + *odōn, odous* "tooth"] — **mas•to•don•ic** \,mas-tə-'dän-ik\ *adj*

[1]mas•toid \'mas-,tȯid\ *adj* : of, relating to, or occurring in the region of a somewhat conical process of the temporal bone behind the ear [Greek *mastoeidēs,* literally, "breast-shaped", from *mastos* "breast"]

[2]mastoid *n* **1** : a mastoid bone or process **2 a** : MASTOIDITIS **b** : an operation for the relief of mastoiditis

mas•toid•itis \,mas-,tȯid-'īt-əs\ *n* : inflammation of the mastoid process

mas•tur•ba•tion \,mas-tər-'bā-shən\ *n* : erotic stimulation of the genital organs apart from sexual intercourse and especially by use of the hand [Latin *masturbatus,* past participle of *masturbari* "to masturbate"] — **mas•tur•bate** \'mas-tər-,bāt\ *vb*

[1]mat \'mat\ *n* **1 a** : a piece of coarse fabric made of rushes, straw, or wool **b** : a piece of material in front of a door to wipe the shoes on **c** : a piece of material used under a dish or vase or as an ornament **d** : a paid or cushion for gynmastics or wrestling **2** : something made up of many intertwined or tangled strands ⟨a thick *mat* of vegetation⟩ [Old English *meatte,* from Late Latin *matta,* of Semitic origin]

[2]mat *vb* **mat•ted; mat•ting** **1** : to provide with a mat or matting **2** : to form into a tangled mass

[3]mat *or* **matt** *or* **matte** \'mat\ *vt* **mat•ted; mat•ting** **1** : to give a dull effect to **2** : to provide (a picture) with a mat

[4]mat *or* **matt** *or* **matte** *adj* : lacking luster or gloss [French *mat,* from Old French, "defeated", from Latin *mattus* "drunk"]

[5]mat *or* **matt** *or* **matte** *n* **1** : a border going around a picture between picture and frame or serving as the frame **2** : a dull finish or a roughened surface (as of gilt or paint) [French *mat* "dull color", from *mat* "mat, lacking luster"]

mat•a•dor \'mat-ə-,dȯr\ *n* : a bullfighter who has the principal role in the bullfight [Spanish, literally, "killer", from *matar* "to kill"]

[1]match \'mach\ *n* **1 a** : a person or thing equal or similar to another **b** : one able to cope with another ⟨a *match* for the enemy⟩ **c** : an exact counterpart **2** : a pair that go well together ⟨curtains and carpet are a *match*⟩ **3** : a contest between two or more parties ⟨a tennis *match*⟩ **4 a** : a marriage union **b** : a prospective marriage partner [Old English *mæcca*]

[2]match *vb* **1** : to meet successfully as a competitor **2 a** : to place in competition with or opposition to : PIT **b** : to provide with a worthy competitor **3** : to join or give in marriage **4 a** : to make or find the equal or the like of **b** : to cause to correspond **c** : to be the same as or suitable to one another ⟨these colors *match*⟩ **5 a** : to flip or toss (coins) and compare exposed faces **b** : to toss coins with — **match•er** *n*

[3]match *n* **1** : an evenly burning wick or cord formerly used for igniting a charge of powder **2** : a short slender piece of material (as wood) tipped with a mixture that ignites when subjected to friction [Middle French *meiche*]

match•board \'mach-,bōrd, -,bȯrd\ *n* : a board with a groove cut along one edge and a tongue along the other so as to fit snugly with the edges of similarly cut boards

match•book \'mach-,bu̇k\ *n* : a small folder containing rows of paper matches

match•less \'mach-ləs\ *adj* : having no equal : PEERLESS — **match•less•ly** *adv*

\ə\ abut	\au̇\ out	\i\ tip	\ȯ\ saw	\u̇\ foot
\ər\ further	\ch\ chin	\ī\ life	\ȯi\ coin	\y\ yet
\a\ mat	\e\ pet	\j\ job	\th\ thin	\yü\ few
\ā\ take	\ē\ easy	\ŋ\ sing	\t͟h\ this	\yu̇\ cure
\ä\ cot, cart	\g\ go	\ō\ bone	\ü\ food	\zh\ vision

match•lock \'mach-ˌläk\ *n* : an old form of gunlock in which the charge was lighted by a cord match; *also* : a gun equipped with such a lock

match•mak•er \-ˌmā-kər\ *n* : one that arranges a match and especially a marriage — **match•mak•ing** \-king\ *n*

match point *n* : the last point needed to win a match

match•wood \'mach-ˌwu̇d\ *n* : small bits of wood

[1]**mate** \'māt\ *vt* : CHECKMATE 2

[2]**mate** *n* : CHECKMATE 1

[3]**mate** *n* **1 a** : ASSOCIATE 1, COLLEAGUE **b** : an assistant to a more skilled worker : HELPER ⟨plumber's *mate*⟩ **2** : a deck officer on a merchant ship ranking below the captain **3** : one of a pair: as **a** : either member of a married couple **b** : either member of a breeding pair of animals ⟨a dove and its *mate*⟩ **c** : either of two matched objects ⟨a *mate* to a glove⟩ [Middle English]

[4]**mate** *vb* **1** : to join or fit together **2 a** : to bring together as mates **b** : to provide a mate for

ma•té *or* **ma•te** \'mä-ˌtā\ *n* : an aromatic beverage made from the leaves and shoots of a South American holly; *also* : these leaves and shoots [American Spanish *mate,* from Quechua]

[1]**ma•te•ri•al** \mə-'tir-ē-əl\ *adj* **1** : relating to, derived from, or consisting of matter; *esp* : PHYSICAL ⟨the *material* world⟩ ⟨*material* comforts⟩ **2** : having importance, relevance, or consequence ⟨facts *material* to the study⟩ **3** : relating to or concerned with physical rather than spiritual or intellectual things ⟨*material* progress⟩ **4** : of or relating to the production and distribution of economic goods and the social relationships of owners and laborers [Late Latin *materialis,* from Latin *materia* "matter"] — **ma•te•ri•al•i•ty** \-ˌtir-ē-'al-ət-ē\ *n* — **ma•te•ri•al•ly** \-'tir-ē-ə-lē\ *adv* — **ma•te•ri•al•ness** *n*

• **syn** MATERIAL, PHYSICAL, CORPOREAL mean of or belonging to actuality. MATERIAL implies formation out of tangible matter; used in contrast with *spiritual* or *ideal* it suggests what is mundane, ignoble, or grasping; PHYSICAL applies to whatever is perceived by the senses and may contrast with *mental, spiritual,* or *imaginary;* CORPOREAL stresses having such tangible qualities of a body as fixed shape and size and resistance to force.

[2]**material** *n* **1** : the elements, constituents, or substance of which something is composed or can be made ⟨building *materials*⟩ **2 a** : apparatus needed for doing or making something ⟨writing *materials*⟩ **b** : EQUIPMENT 2a(1)

ma•te•ri•al•ism \mə-'tir-ē-ə-ˌliz-əm\ *n* **1 a** : a theory that everything can be explained as being or coming from matter **b** : a doctrine that the only or the highest values lie in material well-being and material progress **c** : a doctrine that economic or social change is caused by material factors **2** : a preoccupation with material rather than intellectual or spiritual things — **ma•te•ri•al•ist** \-ē-ə-ləst\ *n or adj* — **ma•te•ri•al•is•tic** \-ˌtir-ē-ə-'lis-tik\ *adj* — **ma•te•ri•al•is•ti•cal•ly** \-'lis-ti-kə-lē, -klē\ *adv*

ma•te•ri•al•ize \mə-'tir-ē-ə-ˌlīz\ *vb* **1 a** : to give form and substance to ⟨*materialize* an idea in words⟩ **b** : to appear or cause to appear in bodily form ⟨*materialize* a spirit⟩ **2 a** : to come into existence **b** : to put in an appearance; *esp* : to appear suddenly — **ma•te•ri•al•iza•tion** \-ˌtir-ē-ə-lə-'zā-shən\ *n* — **ma•te•ri•al•iz•er** \-'tir-ē-ə-ˌlī-zər\ *n*

ma•te•ria med•i•ca \mə-ˌtir-ē-ə-'med-i-kə\ *n* **1** : material or substances used in medical remedies **2** : a branch of medical science that deals with the sources, nature, properties, and preparation of drugs [New Latin, literally, "medical matter"]

ma•té•ri•el *or* **ma•te•ri•el** \mə-ˌtir-ē-'el\ *n* : equipment, apparatus, and supplies used by an organization or institution [French *matériel* "material"]

ma•ter•nal \mə-'tərn-l\ *adj* **1** : of, relating to, or characteristic of a mother : MOTHERLY **2 a** : related through a mother ⟨*maternal* grandparents⟩ **b** : derived or received from a mother [Middle French *maternel,* from Latin *maternus,* from *mater* "mother"] — **ma•ter•nal•ly** \-l-ē\ *adv*

ma•ter•ni•ty \mə-'tər-nət-ē\ *n, pl* **-ties 1** : the state of being a mother : MOTHERHOOD **2** : the qualities of a mother : MOTHERLINESS

math \'math\ *n* : MATHEMATICS

math•e•mat•i•cal \ˌmath-ə-'mat-i-kəl, math-'mat-\ *adj* **1** : of, relating to, or according with mathematics **2** : very exact : PRECISE **3** : possible but highly improbable ⟨only a *mathematical* chance⟩ [Latin *mathematicus,* from Greek *mathēmatikos,* from *mathēma* "mathematics", from *manthanein* "to learn"] — **math•e•mat•i•cal•ly** \-i-kə-lē, -klē\ *adj*

mathematical induction *n* : INDUCTION 2b

math•e•ma•ti•cian \ˌmath-mə-'tish-ən, -ə-mə-\ *n* : a specialist or expert in mathematics

math•e•mat•ics \ˌmath-ə-'mat-iks, math-'mat-\ *n* : the science of numbers and sets and their operations, relations, and combinations and of space configurations and their structure, measurement, and transformations

mat•i•nee *or* **mat•i•née** \ˌmat-n-'ā\ *n* : a musical or dramatic performance held in the daytime and especially in the afternoon [French *matinée,* literally, "morning", from *matin* "morning", from Latin *matutinum,* from *matutinus* "of the morning", from *Matuta,* goddess of morning]

mat•ins \'mat-nz\ *n pl, often cap* **1** : the office of prayer forming with lauds the first of the canonical hours **2** : MORNING PRAYER [Old French *matines,* from Late Latin *matutinae,* from Latin *matutinus* "of the morning"]

matr- *or* **matri-** *or* **matro-** *combining form* : mother ⟨*matri*lineal⟩ [Latin *matr-, mater*]

ma•tri•arch \'mā-trē-ˌärk\ *n* : a woman who rules a group or state; *esp* : a mother who is the head of her family and descendants [*matr-* + Greek *archein* "to rule"] — **ma•tri•ar•chal** \ˌmā-trē-'är-kəl\ *adj*

ma•tri•ar•chate \'mā-trē-ˌär-kət, -ˌkāt\ *n* : MATRIARCHY 1

ma•tri•ar•chy \'mā-trē-ˌär-kē\ *n, pl* **-chies 1** : a family, group, or state governed or headed by a matriarch **2** : a system of social organization in which descent and inheritance are traced through the female line

ma•tri•cide \'ma-trə-ˌsīd, 'mā-\ *n* **1** : murder of a mother by her child **2** : one who murders his or her own mother — **ma•tri•cid•al** \ˌma-trə-'sīd-l, ˌmā-\ *adj*

ma•tric•u•late \mə-'trik-yə-ˌlāt\ *vb* : to enroll as a member of a body and especially of a college or university [Medieval Latin *matriculare,* from Late Latin *matricula* "public roll", from *matrix* "list", from Latin, "womb"] — **ma•tric•u•la•tion** \-ˌtrik-yə-'lā-shən\ *n*

ma•tri•lin•eal \ˌma-trə-'lin-ē-əl, ˌmā-\ *adj* : relating to, based on, or tracing descent through the maternal line ⟨a *matrilineal* society⟩ — **ma•tri•lin•eal•ly** \-ē-ə-lē\ *adv*

mat•ri•mo•ni•al \ˌma-trə-'mō-nē-əl, -nyəl\ *adj* : of or relating to matrimony — **mat•ri•mo•ni•al•ly** \-ē\ *adv*

• **syn** MARITAL, CONJUGAL, NUPTIAL: MATRIMONIAL may apply to whatever has to do with the married state or married persons; MARITAL may refer specifically to the husband's part in marriage but more often equals MATRIMONIAL; CONJUGAL refers especially to the relations and behavior of persons who are married; NUPTIAL applies to wedding rites and ceremonies.

mat•ri•mo•ny \'ma-trə-ˌmō-nē\ *n, pl* **-nies** : the union of man and woman as husband and wife : MARRIAGE [Middle French *matremoine,* from Latin *matrimonium,* from *mater* "mother, married woman"]

matrimony vine *n* : a shrub or vine of the potato family with often showy flowers and bright berries

ma•trix \'mā-triks\ *n, pl* **ma•tri•ces** \'mā-trə-ˌsēz, 'ma-\ *or* **ma•trix•es** \'mā-trik-səz\ **1 a** : intercellular substance (as of cartilage) **b** : the thickened tissue at the base of a fingernail or toenail from which the nail grows **2** : a place or a surrounding or enclosing substance (as a rock) within which something (as a mineral) originates or develops **3** : something (as a mold) that gives form, foundation, or origin to something else (as molten metal) enclosed in it or forced into it **4** : a rectangular array of mathematical elements that is subject to a special form of addition and multiplication [Latin, "womb", from *mater* "mother"]

ma•tron \'mā-trən\ *n* **1** : a usually mature and dignified or socially distinguished married woman **2 a** : a woman in charge of the household affairs of an institution **b** : a woman who supervises children or women (as in a school or a police station) [Middle French *matrone,* from Latin *matrona,* from *mater* "mother, married woman"]

ma•tron•ly \-lē\ *adj* : of, resembling, or suitable for a matron

matron of honor : a bride's principal married wedding attendant

matt *or* **matte** *variant of* MAT

[1]**mat•ter** \'mat-ər\ *n* **1 a** : a subject of interest or concern ⟨a *matter* of dispute⟩ **b** : something to be dealt with : AFFAIR, CONCERN ⟨a few personal *matters* to take care of⟩ **c** : a condition affecting a person or thing unfavorably ⟨what's the *matter* with me⟩ **2** : the material of thought or discourse especially as contrasted with its form **3 a** : the substance of which a physical

object is composed : something that occupies space and has weight **b** : material substance of a particular kind or function ⟨coloring *matter*⟩ ⟨the gray *matter* of the brain⟩ **c** : PUS **4** : a more or less definite amount or quantity ⟨a *matter* of 10 years or so⟩ **5** : something written or printed **6** : MAIL ⟨first-class *matter*⟩ [Old French *matere,* from Latin *materia* "physical substance, matter", from *mater* "mother"] — **for that matter** : so far as that is concerned — **no matter** : without regard to ⟨could remain cool *no matter* what the provocation⟩

[2]**matter** *vi* **1** : to be of importance : SIGNIFY **2** : to form or discharge pus : SUPPURATE ⟨a *mattering* wound⟩

matter of course : something that is to be expected as a natural or logical result of something else — **mat•ter–of–course** \ˌmat-ər-əv-ˈkōrs, -ər-ə-, -ˈkȯrs\ *adj*

mat•ter–of–fact \ˌmat-ər-ə-ˈfakt\ *adj* : sticking to or concerned with facts; *esp* : not fanciful or imaginative — **mat•ter–of–fact•ly** *adv* — **mat•ter–of–fact•ness** \-ˈfakt-nəs, -ˈfak-\ *n*

mat•tery \ˈmat-ə-rē\ *adj* : producing or containing pus or material resembling pus

Mat•thew \ˈmath-yü\ *n* — see BIBLE table — **Mat•the•an** *or* **Mat•thae•an** \ma-ˈthē-ən, mə-\ *adj*

mat•ting \ˈmat-ing\ *n* : material for mats; *also* : mats or stock of mats

mat•tock \ˈmat-ək\ *n* : an implement for digging consisting of a long wooden handle and a steel head one end of which comes to a blade and the other end to either a point or a cutting edge [Old English *mattuc*]

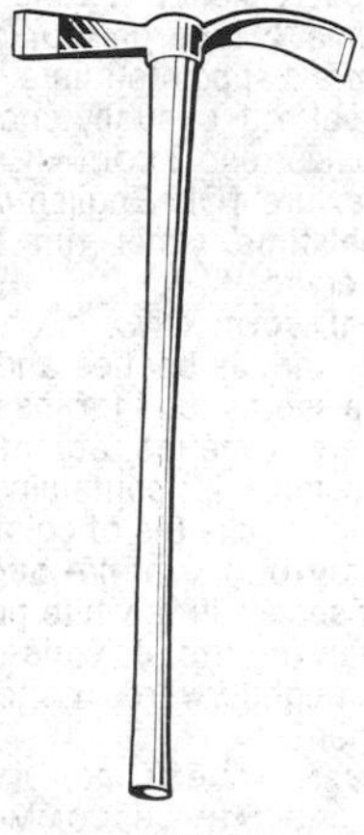

mattock

mat•tress \ˈma-trəs\ *n* **1** : a fabric case filled with springy material used either as a bed or on a bedstead **2** : an inflatable sack for use as a mattress — called also *air mattress* [Old French *materas,* from Arabic *maṭraḥ* "place where something is thrown"]

mat•u•ra•tion \ˌmach-ə-ˈrā-shən\ *n* **1** : the process of becoming mature **2** : the process by which diploid cells are transformed into haploid gametes — **mat•u•ra•tion•al** \-shnəl, -shən-l\ *adj*

[1]**ma•ture** \mə-ˈtu̇r, -ˈtyu̇r\ *adj* **1** : based on slow careful consideration ⟨a *mature* judgment⟩ **2 a** : fully grown and developed : ADULT, RIPE ⟨*mature* fruit⟩ ⟨a youth physically but not yet emotionally *mature*⟩ **b** : having attained a final or desired state ⟨*mature* wine⟩ **3** : characteristic of or suitable to a mature individual ⟨a *mature* outlook⟩ **4** : due for payment ⟨the note becomes *mature* in 90 days⟩ [Latin *maturus* "ripe"] — **ma•ture•ly** *adv* — **ma•ture•ness** *n*

[2]**mature** *vb* **1** : to bring to maturity or completion **2** : to become fully developed or ripe **3** : to become due ⟨when a bond *matures*⟩

ma•tu•ri•ty \mə-ˈtu̇r-ət-ē, -ˈtyu̇r-\ *n* **1** : the quality or state of being mature; *esp* : full development **2** : the date when an obligation (as a bond or note) becomes due

mat•zo \ˈmät-sə, ˌ-sō\ *n, pl* **mat•zoth** \-ˌsōth, -ˌsōt, -sōs\ *or* **mat•zos** \-səz, -səs, -ˌsōz\ **1** : unleavened bread eaten at the Passover **2** : a wafer of matzo [Yiddish *matse,* from Hebrew *maṣṣāh*]

maud•lin \ˈmȯd-lən\ *adj* **1** : weakly and excessively sentimental **2** : drunk enough to be emotionally silly [Mary *Magdalene;* from the practice of depicting her as a weeping, penitent sinner]

△ **origin** *Maudlin* is an alteration of *Magdalene,* the appellation of Mary, the woman mentioned in the Gospel of Luke (8.2): ". . . Mary, called Magdalene, out of whom went seven devils." Medieval representations of Mary Magdalene customarily showed her weeping, and by the 17th century *maudlin* had come to mean "tearful, weeping". Soon *maudlin* began to be used more generally to mean "tearfully or weakly emotional" and was used especially of anyone drunk enough to be emotionally silly, fuddled, or sentimental.

[1]**maul** \ˈmȯl\ *n* : a heavy hammer often with a wooden head used especially for driving wedges or posts [Old French *mail,* from Latin *malleus*]

[2]**maul** *vt* **1 a** : to beat severely **b** : to injure by beating : MANGLE **2** : to handle roughly — **maul•er** *n*

maun•der \ˈmȯn-dər, ˈmän-\ *vi* **maun•dered**; **maun•der•ing** \-də-ring, -dring\ **1** : WANDER 1 **2** : to speak in an incoherent rambling way [British dialect *maunder* "to grumble"] — **maun•der•er** \-dər-ər\ *n*

Maun•dy Thursday \ˌmȯn-dē-, ˌmän-\ *n* : the Thursday before Easter [Old French *mandé,* ceremony of washing the feet of the poor on Maundy Thursday, from Latin *mandatum* "command"]

mau•so•le•um \ˌmȯ-sə-ˈlē-əm, ˌmȯ-zə-\ *n, pl* **-le•ums** *or* **-lea** \-ˈlē-ə\ : a large tomb; *esp* : a usually stone building for entombing the dead above ground [Latin, from Greek *Mausōleion,* tomb of Mausolus, died 353 B.C., ruler of Caria]

mauve \ˈmōv, ˈmȯv\ *n* : a moderate purple, violet, or lilac color [French, "mallow", from Latin *malva*]

mav•er•ick \ˈmav-rik, -ə-rik\ *n* **1** : an unbranded range animal; *esp* : a motherless calf **2** : an independent individual who refuses to conform with the group [Samuel A. *Maverick,* died 1870, American pioneer who did not brand his calves]

△ **origin** In south Texas in the middle of the 19th century lived a lawyer, Samuel A. Maverick. A client once gave him 400 head of cattle instead of cash to settle a $1200 debt. Maverick had no use for the cattle, and so left them in the care of one of his men. The cattle were never branded and were left to roam at will. Eventually the term *maverick* came to be used to designate any unbranded cattle. Later *maverick* was applied to a member of a group who refused to accept one or more of the policies of that group or who refused to be "branded" with restrictive labels.

ma•vis \ˈmā-vəs\ *n* **1** : SONG THRUSH **2** : a European thrush with spotted underparts [Middle French *mauvis*]

maw \ˈmȯ\ *n* **1** : a receptacle (as a stomach or crop) into which food is taken by swallowing **2** : the throat, gullet, or jaws especially of a carnivore [Old English *maga*]

mawk•ish \ˈmȯ-kish\ *adj* **1** : having an insipid often unpleasant taste **2** : sickly sentimental [Middle English *mawke* "maggot", from Old Norse *mathkr*] — **mawk•ish•ly** *adv* — **mawk•ish•ness** *n*

maxi- *combining form* : extra-long : extra-large [*maximum*]

max•il•la \mak-ˈsil-ə\ *n, pl* **max•il•lae** \-ˈsil-ˌē, -ˈsil-ˌī\ *or* **max•il•las** **1 a** : an upper jaw especially of a mammal **b** : either of two bones of the upper jaw that bear the upper teeth **2** : one of the first or second pair of mouth appendages posterior to the mandibles in various arthropods [Latin] — **max•il•lary** \ˈmak-sə-ˌler-ē\ *adj or n*

max•il•li•ped \mak-ˈsil-ə-ˌped\ *n* : any of three pairs of appendages situated next behind the maxillae in a crustacean

max•im \ˈmak-səm\ *n* **1** : a general truth, fundamental principle, or rule of conduct **2** : a proverbial saying [Middle French *maxime,* from Medieval Latin *maxima,* from Latin *maximus,* superlative of *magnus* "great"]

max•i•mal \ˈmak-sə-məl, -sməl\ *adj* : MAXIMUM ⟨*maximal* growth⟩ ⟨a *maximal* dose⟩ — **max•i•mal•ly** \-ē\ *adv*

max•i•mize \ˈmak-sə-ˌmīz\ *vb* **1** : to increase to a maximum ⟨*maximize* profits⟩ **2** : to assign maximum importance to **3** : to find a maximum value of **4** : to interpret something in the broadest sense — **max•i•miz•er** *n*

max•i•mum \ˈmak-sə-məm, -sməm\ *n, pl* **max•i•ma** \-sə-mə\ *or* **max•i•mums** **1 a** : the greatest quantity or value attainable or attained **b** : the period of highest, greatest, or utmost development **2** : an upper limit allowed (as by a legal authority) [Latin, neuter of *maximus,* superlative of *magnus* "great"] — **maximum** *adj*

may \mā, ˈmā\ *auxiliary verb, past* **might** \mīt, ˈmīt\; *present sing & pl* **may** **1 a** : have permission to ⟨you *may* go now⟩ **b** : be in some degree likely to ⟨you *may* be right⟩ **2** — used to express a wish or desire ⟨long *may* you reign⟩ **3** — used to express purpose ⟨I laughed that I *might* not weep⟩, contingency ⟨I'll do my duty come what *may*⟩, or concession ⟨you *may* be slow but you are thorough⟩ [Old English *mæg* "can, may"] **syn** see CAN

May \ˈmā\ *n* : the 5th month of the year [Latin *Maius,* from *Maia,* a Roman goddess]

\ə\ **abut**	\au̇\ **out**	\i\ **tip**	\ȯ\ **saw**	\u̇\ **foot**
\ər\ **further**	\ch\ **chin**	\ī\ **life**	\ȯi\ **coin**	\y\ **yet**
\a\ **mat**	\e\ **pet**	\j\ **job**	\th\ **thin**	\yü\ **few**
\ā\ **take**	\ē\ **easy**	\ng\ **sing**	\t͟h\ **this**	\yu̇\ **cure**
\ä\ **cot, cart**	\g\ **go**	\ō\ **bone**	\ü\ **food**	\zh\ **vision**

Ma•ya \ˈmī-ə\ *n, pl* **Maya** *or* **Mayas** : a member of a group of Indian peoples of the Yucatán peninsula and adjacent areas [Spanish] — **Ma•yan** \ˈmī-ən\ *adj*

Ma•yan \ˈmī-ən\ *n* **1** : an extensive language stock of Central America and Mexico **2** : a member of any of the peoples speaking Mayan languages

may•ap•ple \ˈmā-ˌap-əl\ *n* : a North American woodland herb of the barberry family that has a poisonous rootstock, leaves up to one foot in diameter, and a single large waxy white flower followed by a yellow egg-shaped berry; *also* : its edible but insipid fruit

may•be \ˈmā-bē, ˈmeb-ē\ *adv* : PERHAPS

May•day \mā-ˈdā, ˈmā-ˌ\ — an international radio telephone signal word used as a distress call [French *m'aider* "help me"]

May Day \ˈmā-ˌdā\ *n* : May 1 celebrated as a springtime festival and in some countries as Labor Day

may•est *or* **mayst** \ˈmā-əst, māst, ˈmāst\ *archaic present 2d sing of* MAY

may•flow•er \ˈmā-ˌflau̇-ər, -ˌflau̇r\ *n* : any of various spring-blooming plants (as the trailing arbutus, hepatica, or several North American anemones)

may•fly \-ˌflī\ *n* : any of an order (Plectophora) of insects with an aquatic nymph and a short-lived fragile adult having membranous wings

may•hap \ˈmā-ˌhap, mā-ˈ\ *adv* : PERHAPS

may•hem \ˈmā-ˌhem, ˈmā-əm\ *n* **1** : willful and permanent crippling, mutilation, or disfigurement of any part of the body **2** : needless or willful damage **3** : wild disorderly activity or confusion [Anglo-French *mahaim,* from Old French *maynier* "to maim"]

may•ing \ˈmā-iŋ\ *n, often cap* : the celebrating of May Day

mayn't \ˈmā-ənt, mānt, ˈmānt\ : may not

may•on•naise \ˈmā-ə-ˌnāz, ˌmā-ə-ˈ\ *n* **1** : a dressing (as for salads) consisting chiefly of yolk of egg, vegetable oil, and vinegar or lemon juice [French]

may•or \ˈmā-ər, ˈme-ər, ˈmeər\ *n* : an official elected to act as chief executive or nominal head of a city or borough [Old French *maire,* from Latin *major,* comparative of *magnus* "great"] — **may•or•al** \ˈmā-ə-rəl, ˈme-ə-\ *adj*

may•or•al•ty \ˈmā-ə-rəl-tē, ˈme-; ˈmer-əl-\ *n, pl* **-ties** : the office or the term of office of a mayor

mayor–council *adj* : of, relating to, or being a method of municipal government in which a usually elective mayor and council exercise both policy-making and administrative powers

may•pole \ˈmā-ˌpōl\ *n, often cap* : a tall flower-wreathed pole forming a center for May Day sports and dances

may•pop \ˈmā-ˌpäp\ *n* : a climbing perennial passionflower of the southern United States; *also* : its ovoid yellow edible fruit [of American Indian origin]

May queen *n* : a girl chosen queen of a May Day festival

May•tide \ˈmā-ˌtīd\ *or* **May•time** \-ˌtīm\ *n* : the month of May

maze \ˈmāz\ *n* **1** : a confusingly intricate network of passages **2** *chiefly dialect* : a state of confusion or bewilderment [Middle English, from *mazen* "to confuse"]

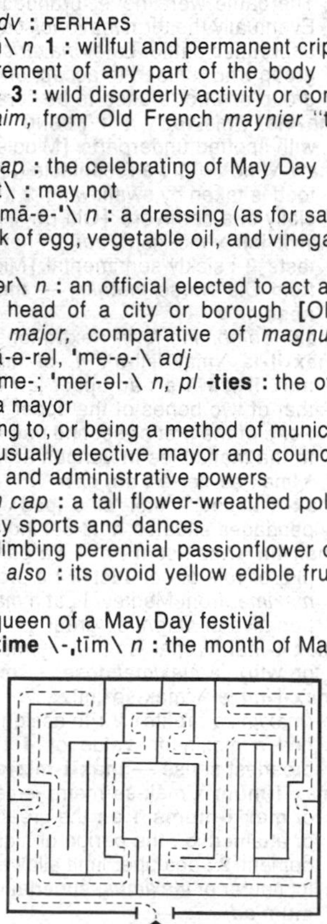
maze 1

ma•zur•ka \mə-ˈzər-kə, -ˈzu̇r-\ *n* **1** : a Polish dance in moderate triple measure **2** : music for the mazurka usually in moderate $3/4$ or $3/8$ time [Polish *mazurek*]

mazy \ˈmā-zē\ *adj* **maz•i•er; -est** : resembling a maze

maz•zard \ˈmaz-ərd\ *n* : SWEET CHERRY; *esp* : wild or seedling sweet cherry used as a rootstock for grafting [origin unknown]

MC \em-ˈsē, ˈem-ˈsē\ *n* : MASTER OF CEREMONIES

me \mē, ˈmē\ *pron, objective case of* I [Old English *mē*]

mead \ˈmēd\ *n* : a fermented drink made of water, honey, malt, and yeast [Old English *medu*]

mead•ow \ˈmed-ō\ *n* : land in or mainly in grass; *esp* : a tract of moist low-lying usually level grassland [Middle English *medwe,* from Old English *mǣd*] — **mead•ow•land** \-ˌland\ *n*

meadow beauty *n* : any of a genus of low perennial American herbs with showy flowers

meadow fescue *n* : a tall vigorous perennial fescue with broad flat leaves cultivated for pasture and hay

mead•ow•lark \ˈmed-ō-ˌlärk\ *n* : any of several North American songbirds largely brown and buff above with a yellow breast bearing a black crescent

meadow mushroom *n* : a common edible fungus that is the chief mushroom of commerce

meadow saffron *n* : a bulbous autumn-flowering herb of the lily family that bears white, lavender and white, or purple flowers and is a source of colchicine — called also *autumn crocus*

mead•ow•sweet \ˈmed-ō-ˌswēt\ *n* : any of several North American native or naturalized spireas with pink or white fragrant flowers

mea•ger *or* **mea•gre** \ˈmē-gər\ *adj* **1** : having little flesh : THIN **2** : deficient in quality or quantity ⟨a *meager* serving of meat⟩ [Middle French *maigre,* from Latin *macer*] — **mea•ger•ly** *adv* — **mea•ger•ness** *n*

• **syn** MEAGER, SCANTY, SPARSE mean falling short of what is normal, necessary, or desirable. MEAGER implies lack of fullness, richness, or plenty ⟨*meager* diets⟩ SCANTY stresses insufficiency in quantity, degree, or extent ⟨a *scanty* supply of fuel⟩ SPARSE implies a thin scattering of units ⟨a *sparse* population⟩

[1]**meal** \ˈmēl\ *n* **1** : the food eaten or prepared for eating at one time **2** : the time or occasion of eating a meal [Old English *mǣl* "appointed time, meal"]

[2]**meal** *n* **1** : usually coarsely ground seeds of a cereal grass or pulse; *esp* : CORNMEAL **2** : something like meal especially in texture [Old English *melu*] **syn** see FLOUR

meal•time \ˈmēl-ˌtīm\ *n* : the usual time at which a meal is served

meal•worm \-ˌwərm\ *n* : a small brownish worm that is the larva of various beetles and that lives in grain products and is often raised as food for insect-eating animals

mealy \ˈmē-lē\ *adj* **meal•i•er; -est** **1** : being soft, dry, and crumbly **2** : containing meal **3** : covered with fine granules or with flecks (as of color) **4** : MEALYMOUTHED

mealy•bug \ˈmē-lē-ˌbəg\ *n* : any of numerous destructive scale insects with a white powdery covering

mealy•mouthed \ˌmē-lē-ˈmau̇thd, -ˈmau̇tht\ *adj* : not plain or straightforward in speech : DEVIOUS ⟨a *mealymouthed* politician⟩

[1]**mean** \ˈmēn\ *adj* **1** : of low birth or station : HUMBLE **2** : ORDINARY 2a, COMMONPLACE ⟨a person of no *mean* ability⟩ **3** : POOR, SHABBY ⟨live in *mean* surroundings⟩ **4** : not honorable or worthy : UNKIND ⟨it is *mean* to take advantage of another's misfortunes⟩ **5** : STINGY 1, MISERLY **6** : SPITEFUL, MALICIOUS ⟨a *mean* remark⟩ **7** : of a vicious or troublesome disposition ⟨a *mean* horse⟩ **8** : UNWELL 1, INDISPOSED ⟨wake up feeling *mean*⟩ [Middle English *imene, mene,* from Old English *gemǣne*]

[2]**mean** \ˈmēn\ *vb* **meant** \ˈment\; **mean•ing** \ˈmē-niŋ\ **1 a** : to have as a purpose : INTEND ⟨I *mean* to go⟩ **b** : to intend for a particular purpose, use, or destination ⟨a book *meant* for children⟩ **2** : to serve to convey, show, or indicate : SIGNIFY ⟨what do these words *mean*⟩ ⟨those clouds *mean* rain⟩ **3** : to be of a specified degree of importance ⟨health *means* everything to me⟩ [Old English *mǣnan*] — **mean business** : to be in earnest

[3]**mean** *n* **1** : a middle point between extremes **2 a** : a value that lies within a range of values and is computed according to a prescribed rule; *esp* : ARITHMETIC MEAN **b** : the arithmetic mean of the two extremes of a range of values **c** : either of the middle two terms of a proportion **3** *pl* : something by the use or help of which a desired end is accomplished or furthered ⟨*means* of production⟩ ⟨ready to use any *means* at their disposal⟩ **4** *pl* : resources available for disposal; *esp* : WEALTH ⟨a person of *means*⟩ [Middle French *meien,* from *meien,* adj., "mean, median"] **syn** see AVERAGE — **by all means** : without fail : CERTAINLY — **by any means** : in any way : at all — **by means of** : through the use of — **by no means** : not at all : certainly not

[4]**mean** *adj* **1** : holding a middle position : INTERMEDIATE **2** : occupying a position about midway between extremes: as **a** : being near the average **b** : being the mean of a set of values ⟨*mean* temperature⟩ [Middle French *meien,* from Latin *medianus* "median"]

[1]**me•an•der** \mē-ˈan-dər\ *n* **1** : a turn or winding of a stream **2** : a winding path or course [Latin *maeander,* from Greek

maiandros, from *Maiandros* (now *Menderes*), river in Asia Minor]

²meander *vi* **-dered; -der•ing** \-dəring, -dring\ **1 :** to follow a winding or intricate course **2 :** to wander aimlessly **:** RAMBLE

¹mean•ing \ˈmē-ning\ *n* **1 a :** the sense one intends to convey especially by language **:** PURPORT ⟨do not mistake my *meaning*⟩ **b :** the sense that is conveyed ⟨the *meaning* of the poem is clear⟩ **2 :** INTENT 1, PURPOSE **3 :** intent to convey information **:** SIGNIFICANCE 1 ⟨a glance full of *meaning*⟩

• syn MEANING, SENSE, SIGNIFICATION, SIGNIFICANCE denote the idea conveyed to the mind by a word, sign, or symbol. MEANING is the general term used of anything (as a word, poem, action) requiring or allowing interpretation; SENSE applies especially to words or utterances and may denote one out of several meanings of any one word ⟨the word *charge* has many distinct *senses*⟩ SIGNIFICATION denotes the established meaning of a word, symbol, or written character; SIGNIFICANCE applies specifically to an underlying as distinguished from a surface meaning.

²meaning *adj* **:** SIGNIFICANT, EXPRESSIVE ⟨a *meaning* look⟩ — **mean•ing•ly** \-ning-lē\ *adv*

mean•ing•ful \-fəl\ *adj* **:** having a meaning or purpose; *esp* **:** SIGNIFICANT ⟨a *meaningful* experience⟩ — **mean•ing•ful•ly** \-fə-lē\ *adv* — **mean•ing•ful•ness** *n*

mean•ing•less \ˈmē-ning-ləs\ *adj* **1 :** lacking sense or significance **2 :** lacking motive — **mean•ing•less•ly** *adv* — **mean•ing•less•ness** *n*

mean•ly \ˈmēn-lē\ *adv* **1 :** in a poor, humble, or shabby manner ⟨*meanly* dressed⟩ **2 :** in an ungenerous or ignoble manner

mean•ness \ˈmēn-nəs\ *n* **1 :** the quality or state of being low in station or ignoble in conduct **2 :** a mean act

mean proportional *n* **1 :** GEOMETRIC MEAN 1 **2 :** MEAN 2c

means test \ˈmēnz-\ *n* **:** an examination of a person's financial state to determine his eligibility to receive public assistance

meant *past of* MEAN

¹mean•time \ˈmēn-ˌtīm\ *n* **:** the intervening time

²meantime *adv* **:** MEANWHILE

¹mean•while \ˈmēn-ˌhwīl, -ˌwīl\ *n* **:** MEANTIME

²meanwhile *adv* **:** during the intervening time

mea•sle \ˈmē-zəl\ *n* **1 :** infestation with or disease caused by larval tapeworms in the muscles and tissues **2 :** a tapeworm larva in the muscles of a domesticated mammal **[**Old French *mesel* "leprous, infested with tapeworms", from Medieval Latin *misellus* "leper", from Latin, "wretch", from *miser* "miserable"**]** — **mea•sled** \-zəld\ *adj*

mea•sles \ˈmē-zəlz\ *n sing or pl* **:** an acute contagious virus disease marked by fever and red spots on the skin; *also* **:** any of several similar diseases (as German measles) **[**Middle English *meseles*, pl. of *mesel* "measles, spot characteristic of measles"**]**

mea•sly \ˈmēz-lē, -ə-lē\ *adj* **mea•sli•er; -est 1 :** infected or infested with measles or with trichina worms **2 :** contemptibly small ⟨left a *measly* dime for a tip⟩

mea•sur•able \ˈmezh-rə-bəl, -ə-rə-; ˈmezh-ər-bəl; ˈmāzh-\ *adj* **:** capable of being measured — **mea•sur•abil•i•ty** \ˌmezh-rə-ˈbil-ət-ē, -ə-rə-, ˌmāzh-\ *n* — **mea•sur•able•ness** *n* — **mea•sur•ably** *adv*

¹mea•sure \ˈmezh-ər, ˈmāzh-\ *n* **1 a :** an adequate, fixed, or suitable limit or amount ⟨angry beyond *measure*⟩ ⟨all received their *measure* of praise or blame⟩ **b :** AMOUNT, EXTENT, DEGREE ⟨won themselves a *measure* of freedom⟩ **2 a :** the dimensions, capacity, or quantity of something as fixed by measuring ⟨give full *measure*⟩ **b :** something (as a yardstick or cup) used in measuring **c :** a unit used in measuring ⟨the foot is a *measure* of length⟩ **d :** a system of measuring ⟨metric *measure*⟩ **3 :** the act or process of measuring **4 a :** DANCE; *esp* **:** a stately dance **b :** rhythmic structure or movement in music or poetry **:** METER, CADENCE **c :** the part of a musical staff between two adjacent bars; *also* **:** the group or grouping of beats between these bars **5 :** a basis or standard of comparison **:** CRITERION **6 :** an action planned or taken as a means to an end; *esp* **:** a legislative bill or act **[**Old French *mesure*, from Latin *mensura*, from *mensus*, past participle of *metiri* "to measure**]**

²measure *vb* **mea•sured; mea•sur•ing** \ˈmezh-ring, ˈmāzh-, -ə-ring\ **1 :** to select or regulate with caution **:** GOVERN ⟨*measure one's* acts⟩ **2 a :** to mark or fix in multiples of a specific unit ⟨*measure* off three centimeters⟩ **b :** to allot or apportion in measured amounts ⟨ *measure* out two liters⟩ **3 :** to determine the dimensions, extent, or amount of ⟨*measure* the walk of the house⟩ **4 a :** ESTIMATE ⟨*measure* the distance by eye⟩ **b :** to bring into comparison ⟨*measure* one's skill against a rival⟩ **5 :** to serve as a measure of ⟨a thermometer *measures* temperature⟩ **6 :** to turn out to be of a certain measurement (as in length or breadth) ⟨the cloth *measures* 3 meters⟩ — **mea•sur•er** \-ər-ər\ *n*

mea•sured \-ərd\ *adj* **1 a :** marked by due proportion **b :** being slow and steady **:** EVEN ⟨walk with *measured* steps⟩ **2 :** DELIBERATE, CALCULATED ⟨speak with *measured* bluntness⟩ **3 :** METRICAL 1, RHYTHMICAL

mea•sure•less \-ər-ləs\ *adj* **:** being without measure **:** IMMEASURABLE

mea•sure•ment \ˈmezh-ər-mənt, ˈmāzh-\ *n* **1 :** the act or process of measuring **2 :** a figure, extent, or amount obtained by measuring **:** DIMENSION **3 :** a system of measures

measure up *vi* **1 :** to have necessary or fitting qualifications **2 :** to be the equal (as in ability) — used with *to*

measuring worm *n* **:** LOOPER 1

meat \ˈmēt\ *n* **1 a :** FOOD; *esp* **:** solid food as distinguished from drink **b :** the edible part of something as distinguished from the covering (as a shell or husk) **2 :** animal and especially mammal tissue used as food **[**Old English *mete***]**

meat•ball \-ˌbȯl\ *n* **:** a small ball of chopped or ground meat ⟨spaghetti and *meatballs*⟩

meat•man \-ˌman\ *n* **:** BUTCHER

me•a•tus \mē-ˈāt-əs\ *n, pl* **me•a•tus•es** *or* **me•a•tus** \-ˈāt-əs, -ˈā-ˌtüs\ **:** a natural body passage **[**Late Latin, from Latin *meare* "to go, pass"**]**

meaty \ˈmēt-ē\ *adj* **meat•i•er; -est 1 :** full of meat **:** FLESHY **2 :** rich in matter for thought **:** SUBSTANTIAL ⟨a *meaty* book⟩ — **meat•i•ness** \ˈmēt-ē-nəs\ *n*

mec•ca \ˈmek-ə\ *n, often cap* **:** a place considered extremely desirable especially by a particular group of people ⟨the university is a *mecca* for chemistry students⟩ **[***Mecca*, Saudi Arabia, birthplace of Muhammad and holy city of Islam**]**

¹me•chan•ic \mi-ˈkan-ik\ *adj* **:** of or relating to manual work or skill ⟨*mechanic* arts⟩ **[**derived from Greek *mēchanikos*, from *mēchanē* "machine"**]**

²mechanic *n* **1 :** a manual worker **:** ARTISAN **2 :** a repairer of machines

me•chan•i•cal \mi-ˈkan-i-kəl\ *adj* **1 a :** of or relating to machinery ⟨*mechanical* engineering⟩ **b :** made or operated by a machine or tool ⟨a *mechanical* concrete mixer⟩ ⟨a *mechanical* toy⟩ **2 :** of or relating to mechanics or artisans **3 :** done as if by machine **:** IMPERSONAL ⟨gave a *mechanical* reply⟩ **4 :** relating to or in accordance with the principles of mechanics **5 :** relating to a process that involves a purely physical change — **me•chan•i•cal•ly** \-i-kə-lē, -klē\ *adv*

mechanical advantage *n* **:** the ratio of the force that performs the useful work of a machine to the force that is applied to the machine

mechanical drawing *n* **:** a method of drawing that makes use of such instruments as compasses, squares, and triangles in order to insure mathematical precision; *also* **:** a drawing made by this method

me•chan•ics \mi-ˈkan-iks\ *n sing or pl* **1 :** a branch of physical science that deals with energy and forces and their effect on bodies **2 :** the practical application of mechanics to the making or operation of machines **3 :** mechanical or functional details ⟨the *mechanics* of running⟩ ⟨the *mechanics* of writing plays⟩

mech•a•nism \ˈmek-ə-ˌniz-əm\ *n* **1 :** a machine or mechanical device **2 a :** the parts by which a machine operates as a mechanical unit ⟨the *mechanism* of a watch⟩ **b :** the parts or steps that make up a process or activity ⟨the *mechanism* of democratic government⟩ **3 :** the doctrine that natural processes (as of life) are orderly and wholly subject to natural law — compare VITALISM **4 :** the fundamental physical or chemical processes involved in or responsible for a natural phenomenon (as an action or reaction) — **mech•a•nist** \-nəst\ *n*

mech•a•nis•tic \ˌmek-ə-ˈnis-tik\ *adj* **1 :** mechanically determined ⟨*mechanistic* universe⟩ **2 :** of or relating to the doctrine of mechanism — **mech•a•nis•ti•cal•ly** \-ti-kə-lē, -klē\ *adv*

MEASURES AND WEIGHTS[1]

UNIT	ABBREVIATION OR SYMBOL	EQUIVALENTS IN OTHER UNITS OF SAME SYSTEM	APPROXIMATE METRIC EQUIVALENT
		LENGTH	
mile	mi	5280 feet, 320 rods, 1760 yards	1.609 kilometers
rod	rd	5.5 yards, 16.5 feet	5.029 meters
yard	yd	3 feet, 36 inches	0.914 meter
foot	ft *or* ′	12 inches, 0.333 yard	30.480 centimeters
inch	in *or* ″	0.0833 foot, 0.0278 yard	2.540 centimeters
		AREA	
square mile	sq mi *or* mi^2	640 acres, 102,400 square rods	2.590 square kilometers
acre		4840 square yards, 43,560 square feet	4047 square meters
square rod	sq rd *or* rd^2	30.25 square yards, 0.00625 acre	25.293 square meters
square yard	sq yd *or* yd^2	1296 square inches, 9 square feet	0.836 square meter
square foot	sq ft *or* ft^2	144 square inches, 0.111 square yard	0.0929 square meter
square inch	sq in *or* in^2	0.00694 square foot, 0.000772 square yard	6.452 square centimeters
		VOLUME	
cubic yard	cu yd *or* yd^3	27 cubic feet, 46,656 cubic inches	0.765 cubic meter
cubic foot	cu ft *or* ft^3	1728 cubic inches, 0.037 cubic yard	0.0283 cubic meter
cubic inch	cu in *or* in^3	0.000579 cubic foot, 0.0000214 cubic yard	16.387 cubic centimeters
		WEIGHT *avoirdupois*	
ton			
short ton		20 short hundredweight, 2000 pounds	0.907 metric ton
long ton		20 long hundredweight, 2240 pounds	1.016 metric tons
hundredweight	cwt		
short hundredweight		100 pounds, 0.05 short ton	45.359 kilograms
long hundredweight		112 pounds, 0.05 long ton	50.802 kilograms
pound	lb *or* lb av *also* #	16 ounces, 7000 grains	0.454 kilogram
ounce	oz *or* oz av	16 drams, 437.5 grains	28.350 grams
dram	dr *or* dr av	27.343 grains, 0.0625 ounce	1.772 grams
grain	gr	0.0366 dram, 0.00229 ounce	0.0648 grams
		troy	
pound	lb t	12 ounces, 240 pennyweight, 5760 grains	0.373 kilogram
ounce	oz t	20 pennyweight, 480 grains	31.103 grams
pennyweight	dwt *also* pwt	24 grains, 0.05 ounce	1.555 grams
grain	gr	0.0417 pennyweight, 0.00208 ounce	0.0648 gram
		apothecaries'	
pound	lb ap	12 ounces, 5760 grains	0.373 kilogram
ounce	oz ap *or* ℥	8 drams, 480 grains	31.103 grams
dram	dr ap *or* ʒ	3 scruples, 60 grains	3.888 grams
scruple	s ap *or* ℈	20 grains, 0.333 dram	1.296 grams
grain	gr	0.05 scruple, 0.00208 ounce, 0.0166 dram	0.0648 grams
		CAPACITY *United States liquid measure*	
gallon	gal	4 quarts (231 cubic inches)	3.785 liters
quart	qt	2 pints (57.75 cubic inches)	0.946 liter
pint	pt	4 gills (28.875 cubic inches)	0.473 liter
gill	gi	4 fluidounces (7.218 cubic inches)	.118 liter
fluidounce	fl oz *or* f ℥	8 fluidrams (1.804 cubic inches)	29.574 milliliters
fluidram	fl dr *or* f ʒ	60 minims (0.225 cubic inch)	3.696 milliliters
minim	minim *or* ♏	1/60 fluidram (0.00376 cubic inch)	0.0616 milliliter
		United States dry measure	
bushel	bu	4 pecks (2150.42 cubic inches)	35.239 liters
peck	pk	8 quarts (537.605 cubic inches)	8.810 liters
quart	qt	2 pints (67.2 cubic inches)	1.101 liters
pint	pt	1/2 quart (33.6 cubic inches)	0.551 liter

[1]For United States equivalents of metric units see Metric System table

mech•a•nize \ˈmek-ə-ˌnīz\ *vt* **1 :** to make mechanical; *esp* **:** to make automatic **2 a :** to equip with machinery especially to replace human or animal labor **b :** to equip (a military force) with armed and armored motor-driven vehicles — **mech•a•ni•za•tion** \ˌmek-ə-nə-ˈzā-shən\ *n* — **mech•a•niz•er** \ˈmek-ə-ˌnī-zər\ *n*

me•co•ni•um \mi-ˈkō-nē-əm\ *n* **:** dark greenish matter in the bowel at birth [Latin, literally, "poppy juice", from Greek *mēkōnion,* from *mēkōn* "poppy"]

med•al \ˈmed-l\ *n* **1 :** a metal disk bearing a religious emblem or picture **2 :** a piece of metal often in the form of a coin issued to commemorate a person or event or as an award [Middle French *medaille,* from Italian *medaglia* "coin worth half a denarius, medal", from Late Latin *medialis* "medial"]

med•al•ist *or* **med•al•list** \-l-əst\ *n* **1 :** a designer or maker of medals **2 :** a recipient of a medal

me·dal·lion \mə-'dal-yən\ *n* **1** : a large medal **2** : something resembling a large medal; *esp* : a tablet or panel (as in a wall) bearing a figure in relief [French *médaillon,* from Italian *medaglione,* from *medaglia* "medal"]

med·dle \'med-l\ *vi* **med·dled** \-ld\; **med·dling** \'med-ling, -l-ing\ : to interest oneself in what is not one's concern ⟨*meddle* in another's business⟩ [Old French *mesler, medler* "to mix, meddle", derived from Latin *miscēre* "to mix"] — **med·dler** \'med-lər, -l-ər\ *n*

med·dle·some \'med-l-səm\ *adj* : given to meddling : INTRUSIVE — **med·dle·some·ness** *n*

Mede \'mēd\ *n* : a native or inhabitant of ancient Media in northwestern Iran

medi- *or* **medio-** *combining form* : middle ⟨*medi*eval⟩ [Latin, from *medius*]

media *pl of* MEDIUM

me·di·ae·val *variant of* MEDIEVAL

me·di·al \'mēd-ē-əl\ *adj* **1 a** : MEDIAN 1 **b** : extending toward the middle **2** : situated between the beginning and the end of a word **3** : ORDINARY 2a, AVERAGE [Late Latin *medialis,* from Latin *medius* "middle"] — **medial** *n* — **me·di·al·ly** \-ə-lē\ *adv*

[1]**me·di·an** \'mēd-ē-ən\ *n* **1** : a median part **2** : a value in a series below and above which there are an equal number of values or which is the average of the two middle values if there is no one middle number **3 a** : a line from a vertex of a triangle to the midpoint of the opposite side **b** : a line joining the midpoints of the nonparallel sides of a trapezoid **syn** see AVERAGE

median strip

[2]**median** *adj* **1** : being in the middle or in an intermediate position **2** : relating to or constituting a median

median strip *n* : a paved or planted strip separating the opposing lanes of a highway

me·di·ant \'mēd-ē-ənt\ *n* : the third tone above the tonic [Italian *mediante,* from Late Latin *mediare* "to be in the middle"]

me·di·as·ti·num \,mēd-ē-ə-'stī-nəm\ *n, pl* **-na** \-nə\ : an irregular median partition that divides the chest cavity into right and left halves, is formed of the opposing medial walls of the pleura, and encloses between these walls all the viscera of the chest except the lungs [New Latin, from Latin *mediastinus* "medial", from *medius* "middle"] — **me·di·as·ti·nal** \-'stīn-l\ *adj*

[1]**me·di·ate** \'mēd-ē-ət\ *adj* : acting through an intermediate agent or agency : not direct or immediate [Late Latin *mediatus* "intermediate", from *mediare* "to be in the middle", from Latin *medius* "middle"] — **me·di·ate·ly** *adv*

[2]**me·di·ate** \'mēd-ē-,āt\ *vb* **1** : to intervene between conflicting parties or viewpoints to promote reconciliation, settlement, or compromise **2 a** : to bring about by mediation ⟨*mediate* a settlement⟩ **b** : to bring accord out of by mediation ⟨*mediate* a dispute⟩ **3** : to transmit or act as an intermediate mechanism

me·di·a·tion \,mēd-ē-'ā-shən\ *n* : the act or process of mediating; *esp* : intervention by a third party in a dispute to promote reconciliation, settlement, or compromise between the conflicting parties

me·di·a·tor \'mēd-ē-,āt-ər\ *n* **1** : one that mediates; *esp* : an impartial third party (as a person, group, or country) that acts as a go-between in a dispute in order to arrange a peaceful settlement **2** : a mediating agent in a chemical or biological process — **me·di·a·to·ry** \'mēd-ē-ə-,tōr-ē, -,tȯr-\ *adj*

[1]**med·ic** \'med-ik\ *n* : any of a genus of herbs of the pea family resembling clovers and important for hay and forage [Latin *medica,* from Greek *mēdikē,* from *mēdikos* "of Media"]

[2]**medic** *n* : one (as a physician, a medical student, or a soldier or sailor assigned to the medical services) engaged in medical work [Latin *medicus* "physician"]

med·i·ca·ble \'med-i-kə-bəl\ *adj* : CURABLE, REMEDIABLE — **med·i·ca·bly** \-blē\ *adv*

med·ic·aid \'med-i-,kād\ *n* : a program of medical aid designed for those unable to afford regular medical service and financed jointly by the state and federal governments of the United States

med·i·cal \'med-i-kəl\ *adj* : of or relating to the science or practice of medicine or the treatment of disease [Late Latin *medicalis,* from Latin *medicus* "physician", from *mederi* "to heal"] — **med·i·cal·ly** \-kə-lē, -klē\ *adv*

me·dic·a·ment \mi-'dik-ə-mənt\ *n* : a medicine or healing application

medi·care \'med-i-,keər, -,kaər\ *n* : a government program of medical care especially for the aged

med·i·cate \'med-ə-,kāt\ *vt* **1** : to treat with medicine **2** : to add a medicinal substance to ⟨*medicate* a soap⟩

med·i·ca·tion \,med-ə-'kā-shən\ *n* **1** : the act or process of medicating **2** : a medicinal substance : MEDICAMENT

me·dic·i·nal \mə-'dis-nəl, -n-əl\ *adj* : tending or used to relieve or cure disease or pain — **me·dic·i·nal·ly** \-ē\ *adv*

medicinal leech *n* : a large European freshwater leech formerly used by physicians for bleeding patients

med·i·cine \'med-ə-sən\ *n* **1** : a substance or preparation used in treating disease **2 a** : the science and art dealing with the maintenance of health and the prevention, easing, and cure of disease **b** : the branch of medicine concerned with the nonsurgical treatment of disease **3** : an object held to give control over natural or magical forces; *also* : a magical power or rite [Old French, from Latin *medicina,* from *medicus* "physician", from *mederi* "to heal"]

medicine ball *n* : a large stuffed leather-covered ball used for conditioning exercises

medicine dropper *n* : DROPPER 2

medicine man *n* : a person among primitive peoples believed to be able to cure diseases by potions and charms

medicine show *n* : a traveling show using entertainers to attract a crowd that may buy remedies or nostrums

med·i·co \'med-i-,kō\ *n, pl* **-cos** : a medical practitioner : PHYSICIAN; *also* : a medical student [Italian *medico* or Spanish *médico,* both from Latin *medicus*]

me·di·eval *or* **me·di·ae·val** \,mēd-ē-'ē-vəl, ,med-, ,mid-; mē-'dē-vəl, med-'ē-, mid-'ē-\ *adj* : of, relating to, or characteristic of the Middle Ages [*medi-* + Latin *aevum* "age"] — **me·di·eval·ly** \-və-lē\ *adv*

me·di·eval·ism \-və-,liz-əm\ *n* **1** : medieval quality, character, or state **2** : devotion to the institutions, arts, and practices of the Middle Ages — **me·di·eval·ist** \-ləst\ *n*

Medieval Latin *n* : the Latin used especially for liturgical and literary purposes from the 7th to the 15th centuries inclusive

medio- — see MEDI-

me·di·o·cre \,mēd-ē-'ō-kər\ *adj* : of moderate or low quality : ORDINARY [Middle French, from Latin *mediocris,* literally, "halfway up a mountain", from *medi-* + *ocris* "stony mountain"]

me·di·oc·ri·ty \,mēd-ē-'äk-rət-ē\ *n, pl* **-ties** **1** : the quality or state of being mediocre **2** : a mediocre person

med·i·tate \'med-ə-,tāt\ *vb* **1 a** : to reflect on or muse over : CONTEMPLATE **b** : to engage in contemplation or reflection **2** : INTEND, PURPOSE [Latin *meditari*] — **med·i·ta·tor** \-,tāt-ər\ *n*

med·i·ta·tion \,med-ə-'tā-shən\ *n* : the act or process of meditating : serious contemplation or reflection

med·i·ta·tive \'med-ə-,tāt-iv\ *adj* : given to meditation — **med·i·ta·tive·ly** *adv* — **med·i·ta·tive·ness** *n*

Med·i·ter·ra·nean \,med-ə-tə-'rā-nē-ən, -'rā-nyən\ *adj* : of or relating to the Mediterranean sea or to the lands or peoples around it

Mediterranean fruit fly *n* : a widely distributed two-winged fly with black-and-white markings and a larva destructive to ripening fruit

[1]**me·di·um** \'mēd-ē-əm\ *n, pl* **me·di·ums** *or* **me·dia** \'mēd-ē-ə\ **1** : something that is between or in the middle; *also* : a middle condition or degree **2** : a means of effecting or conveying something; *esp* : a substance through which a force acts or through which something is transmitted ⟨air is the common *medium* of sound⟩ **3** *pl usually* **media** : a channel (as newspapers,

radio, or television) of communication **4 a :** GO-BETWEEN, INTERMEDIARY **b** *pl mediums* **:** a person through whom others seek to communicate with the spirits of the dead **5 a :** a surrounding substance **b :** a condition in which something may function or flourish ⟨slums are a good *medium* for delinquency⟩ **6 :** a nutrient system for the artificial cultivation of organisms (as bacteria) or cells [Latin, from *medius* "middle"]

[2]**medium** *adj* **:** intermediate in amount, quality, position, or degree

medium frequency *n* **:** a radio frequency in the range between 300 and 3000 kilohertz — abbreviation *MF*

medium of exchange : something commonly accepted in exchange for goods and services and recognized as representing a standard of value

med•lar \ˈmed-lər\ *n* **:** a small hairy-leaved Eurasian tree related to the apples; *also* **:** its fruit that resembles a crab apple and is used especially in preserves [Middle French *medlier,* from *medle* "medlar fruit", from Latin *mespilum,* from Greek *mespilon*]

med•ley \ˈmed-lē\ *n, pl* **medleys 1 :** MIXTURE 2; *esp* **:** a confused mixture **2 :** a musical composition made up of a series of songs or short musical pieces [Middle French *medlee,* from *mesler, medler* "to mix, meddle"]

me•dul•la \mə-ˈdəl-ə\ *n, pl* **-dul•las** *or* **-dul•lae** \-ˌē, -ˌī\ **1 a :** MARROW 1 **b :** MEDULLA OBLONGATA **2 :** the inner or deep part of an animal or plant structure (as the adrenal gland or the kidney) [Latin] — **med•ul•lary** \ˈmed-l-ˌer-ē, ˈmej-ə-ˌler-\ *adj*

medulla ob•lon•ga•ta \-ˌäb-ˌlȯng-ˈgät-ə\ *n* **:** the somewhat pyramid-shaped hind part of the vertebrate brain that is continuous with the spinal cord [New Latin, literally, "oblong medulla"]

medullary sheath *n* **:** a layer of myelin about a nerve fiber

med•ul•lat•ed \ˈmed-l-ˌāt-əd, ˈmej-ə-ˌlāt-\ *adj* **:** having a medullary sheath ⟨*medullated* nerve fibers⟩

me•du•sa \mi-ˈdü-sə, -ˈdyü-, -zə\ *n, pl* **-sae** \-ˌsē, -ˌzē\ *or* **-sas :** JELLYFISH [*Medusa,* one of the three Gorgons] — **me•du•san** \-ˈdüs-n, -ˈdüz-, -ˈdyüs-, -ˈdyüz-\ *adj or n*

meed \ˈmēd\ *n* **:** something deserved or earned **:** REWARD ⟨receive one's *meed* of praise⟩ [Old English *mēd*]

meek \ˈmēk\ *adj* **1 :** enduring injury with patience and without resentment **2 :** lacking self-assurance **:** HUMBLE ⟨they became *meek* when confronted with the evidence against them⟩ [of Scandinavian origin] — **meek•ly** *adv* — **meek•ness** *n*

meer•schaum \ˈmiər-shəm, -ˌshȯm\ *n* **1 :** a soft white lightweight mineral resembling a very fine clay used especially for tobacco pipes **2 :** a tobacco pipe made of meerschaum [German, from *meer* "sea" + *schaum* "foam"]

[1]**meet** \ˈmēt\ *vb* **met** \ˈmet\; **meet•ing 1 :** to come upon or across or into the presence of ⟨*met* an old friend by chance⟩ **2 :** to come close together or into contact and join or cross ⟨a fork where two roads *meet*⟩ **3 a :** to get together with **:** JOIN ⟨agreed to *meet* them at school⟩ **b :** to become acquainted ⟨the couple *met* at a dance⟩ **c :** to make the acquaintance of ⟨*met* interesting people there⟩ **4 a :** to come together as opponents ⟨the teams *met* in the finals⟩ **b :** to struggle against **:** OPPOSE ⟨was chosen to *meet* the champion⟩ **c :** to cope with **:** MATCH ⟨tries to *meet* the competitor's price⟩ **d :** ENDURE 2b, BEAR ⟨learned to *meet* defeat bravely⟩ **5 :** to come together for a common purpose **:** ASSEMBLE ⟨*meet* weekly for discussion⟩ **6 :** to become one **:** UNITE ⟨all the virtues *meet* in the child⟩ **7 :** to become noticed by ⟨sounds of revelry *meet* the ear⟩ **8 a :** to conform to or comply with **:** SATISFY ⟨*meets* all requirements⟩ **b :** to pay fully **:** DISCHARGE, FULFILL ⟨*meet* a financial obligation⟩ [Old English *mētan*]

[2]**meet** *n* **:** an assembly or meeting especially to engage in a competitive sport ⟨a track *meet*⟩

[3]**meet** *adj* **:** SUITABLE 2, PROPER [Old English *gemǣte*] — **meet•ly** *adv*

meet•ing \ˈmēt-ing\ *n* **1 :** the act of persons or things that meet ⟨a chance *meeting* with a friend⟩ **2 :** a coming together of a number of persons usually at a stated time and place and for a known purpose **:** ASSEMBLY, GATHERING ⟨the monthly club *meeting*⟩ **3 :** an assembly for religious worship ⟨a Quaker *meeting*⟩ **4 :** the place where two things come together **:** JUNCTION

meet•ing•house \-ˌhau̇s\ *n* **:** a building used for public assembly and especially for Protestant worship

mega- *or* **meg-** *combining form* **1 :** great **:** large ⟨*mega*spore⟩ **2 :** million **:** multiplied by one million ⟨*mega*cycle⟩ ⟨*meg*ohm⟩ [Greek *megas* "large"]

mega•cycle \ˈmeg-ə-ˌsī-kəl\ *n* **:** one million cycles; *esp* **:** MEGAHERTZ

mega•hertz \-ˌhərts, -ˌheərts\ *n* **:** one million hertz

mega•lith \ˈmeg-ə-ˌlith\ *n* **:** one of the huge stones used in various prehistoric monuments — **mega•lith•ic** \ˌmeg-ə-ˈlith-ik\ *adj*

meg•a•lo•ma•nia \ˌmeg-ə-lō-ˈmā-nē-ə, -nyə\ *n* **:** a disorder of mind marked by feelings of great personal power and importance [Greek *megal-, megas* "large"] — **meg•a•lo•ma•ni•ac** \-ˈmā-nē-ˌak\ *adj or n* — **meg•a•lo•ma•ni•a•cal** \-mə-ˈnī-ə-kəl\ *adj*

meg•a•lop•o•lis \ˌmeg-ə-ˈläp-ə-ləs\ *n* **1 :** a very large city **2 :** a thickly populated region centering in a metropolis or embracing several metropolises [Greek *megal-, megas* "large" + *polis* "city"] — **meg•a•lo•pol•i•tan** \meg-ə-lō-ˈpäl-ət-n\ *n or adj* — **meg•a•lo•pol•i•tan•ism** \-n-ˌiz-əm\ *n*

mega•phone \ˈmeg-ə-ˌfōn\ *n* **:** a cone-shaped device used to intensify or direct the voice — **mega•phon•ic** \ˌmeg-ə-ˈfän-ik\ *adj*

megaphone

mega•spore \ˈmeg-ə-ˌspōr, -ˌspȯr\ *n* **:** a plant spore that produces a female gametophyte

mega•ton \ˈmeg-ə-ˌtən\ *n* **:** an explosive force equal to that of one million tons of TNT

mega•watt \-ˌwät\ *n* **:** one million watts

meg•ohm \ˈmeg-ˌōm\ *n* **:** one million ohms

me•grim \ˈmē-grəm\ *n* **1 :** a dizzy disordered state; *esp* **:** MIGRAINE **2 a :** WHIM, FANCY **b** *pl* **:** low spirits **:** mental depression [Middle French *migraine*]

mei•o•sis \mī-ˈō-səs\ *n, pl* **-o•ses** \-ˈō-ˌsēz\ **:** a cellular process that includes two cell divisions but only one duplication of chromosomes and that results in the number of chromosomes in gamete-producing cells being reduced to one half [Greek *meiōsis* "diminution", from *meioun* "to diminish", from *meiōn* "less"] — **mei•ot•ic** \mī-ˈät-ik\ *adj* — **mei•ot•i•cal•ly** \-ˈät-i-kə-lē, -klē\ *adv*

Mei•ster•sing•er \ˈmī-stər-ˌsing-ər, -stər-ˌzing-\ *n, pl* **-sing•er** *or* **-sing•ers :** a member of any of various German guilds formed chiefly in the 15th and 16th centuries for the cultivation of poetry and music [German, literally, "master singer"]

mel•a•mine \ˈmel-ə-ˌmēn\ *n* **:** a synthetic resin composed of carbon, hydrogen, and nitrogen and used in molded products, adhesives, and coatings [German *melamin*]

mel•an•cho•lia \ˌmel-ən-ˈkō-lē-ə\ *n* **:** a morbid mental state characterized especially by depression [Late Latin, "melancholy"] — **mel•an•cho•li•ac** \-lē-ˌak\ *n*

mel•an•chol•ic \ˌmel-ən-ˈkäl-ik\ *adj* **1 :** inclined to or affected with melancholy **2 :** affected with or relating to melancholia **3 :** tending to depress the spirits — **mel•an•chol•i•cal•ly** \-ˈkäl-i-kə-lē, -klē\ *adv*

[1]**mel•an•choly** \ˈmel-ən-ˌkäl-ē\ *n, pl* **-chol•ies :** depression of spirits **:** DEJECTION, SADNESS [Middle French *melancolie,* from Late Latin *melancholia,* from Greek, from *melan-, melas* "black" + *cholē* "bile"; from the former belief that the condition was caused by an excess of black bile, a fluid once believed to be secreted by the spleen or kidneys]

• syn SADNESS, DEPRESSION, DEJECTION: MELANCHOLY suggests a sad and serious pensiveness often without evident cause; SADNESS usually suggests a mood of regret, longing, or disappointment without bitterness or anger; DEPRESSION suggests a condition in which one feels let down, disheartened, or enervated; DEJECTION implies a usually passing mood of discouragement or hopelessness.

[2]**melancholy** *adj* **1 a :** depressed in spirits **:** DEJECTED, SAD **b :** PENSIVE 2 **2 a :** suggestive or expressive of melancholy ⟨a *melancholy* voice⟩ **b :** causing sadness **:** DISMAL ⟨the *melancholy* conclusion that we were neither needed nor wanted⟩

Mel•a•ne•sian \ˌmel-ə-ˈnē-zhən, -shən\ *n* **:** a member of the dominant native group of Melanesia — **Melanesian** *adj*

mé•lange \mā-ˈlä^{n}zh, -ˈlänj\ *n* **:** a mixture often of incongruous elements ⟨a *mélange* of styles from all over the world⟩

[French, from Middle French *mesler, meler* "to mix"]
mel·a·nin \ˈmel-ə-nən\ *n* **:** a dark brown or black animal or plant pigment that in man makes some skins darker than others [Greek *melan-, melas* "black"]
mel·a·nism \ˈmel-ə-ˌniz-əm\ *n* **:** an exceptionally dark pigmentation (as of skin, feathers, or hair) of an individual or kind of organism — **mel·a·nis·tic** \ˌmel-ə-ˈnis-tik\ *adj*
mel·a·no·ma \ˌmel-ə-ˈnō-mə\ *n, pl* **-no·mas** *also* **-no·ma·ta** \-ˈnō-mət-ə\ **:** a usually malignant tumor containing dark pigment
mel·a·not·ic \-ˈnät-ik\ *adj* **:** having or characterized by black pigmentation ⟨*melanotic* tumors⟩
mel·ba toast \ˌmel-bə-\ *n* **:** very thin bread toasted till crisp [Nellie *Melba,* died 1931, Australian soprano]
Mel·chiz·e·dek \mel-ˈkiz-ə-ˌdek\ *adj* **:** of or relating to the higher order of the Mormon priesthood [*Melchizedek,* biblical priest-king]
1**meld** \ˈmeld\ *vb* **:** to show or lay down a combination of cards in a card game [German *melden* "to announce"]
2**meld** *n* **:** a card or combination of cards that is or can be melded
me·lee \ˈmā-ˌlā, mā-ˈlā\ *n* **:** a confused fight or struggle especially among several people [French *mêlée,* from Old French *meslee,* from *mesler* "to mix"]
me·lio·rate \ˈmēl-yə-ˌrāt, ˈmē-lē-ə-\ *vb* **:** to make or become better **:** IMPROVE [Late Latin *meliorare,* from Latin *melior* "better"] — **me·lio·ra·tion** \ˌmēl-yə-ˈrā-shən, ˌmē-lē-ə-\ *n* — **me·lio·ra·tive** \ˈmēl-yə-ˌrāt-iv, ˈmē-lē-ə-\ *adj* — **me·lio·ra·tor** \-ˌrāt-ər\ *n*
mel·lif·lu·ous \me-ˈlif-lə-wəs, mə-\ *adj* **:** smoothly or sweetly flowing ⟨*mellifluous* speech⟩ [Late Latin *mellifluus,* from Latin *mel* "honey" + *fluere* "to flow"] — **mel·lif·lu·ous·ly** *adv* — **mel·lif·lu·ous·ness** *n*
mel·lo·phone \ˈmel-ə-ˌfōn\ *n* **:** an althorn in circular form sometimes used as a substitute for the French horn [*mellow* + *-phone*]
1**mel·low** \ˈmel-ō\ *adj* **1 a :** tender and sweet because of ripeness ⟨*mellow* peaches⟩ **b :** well aged and pleasingly mild ⟨a *mellow* wine⟩ **2 :** made gentle by age or experience **3 :** of soft and loamy consistency ⟨*mellow* soil⟩ **4 :** being clear, full, and pure ⟨spoke in *mellow* tones⟩ [Middle English *melowe*] — **mel·low·ly** *adv* — **mel·low·ness** *n*
2**mellow** *vb* **:** to make or become mellow
me·lo·de·on \mə-ˈlōd-ē-ən\ *n* **:** a small reed organ in which a suction bellows draws air inward through the reeds [German *melodion,* from *melodie* "melody", from Old French]

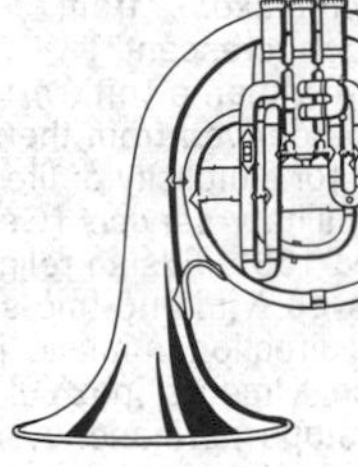
mellophone

me·lod·ic \mə-ˈläd-ik\ *adj* **:** of or relating to melody **:** MELODIOUS — **me·lod·i·cal·ly** \-ˈläd-i-kə-lē, -klē\ *adv*
me·lo·di·ous \mə-ˈlōd-ē-əs\ *adj* **1 :** pleasing to the ear because of a succession of sweet sounds **2 :** of, relating to, or producing melody ⟨*melodious* birds⟩ — **me·lo·di·ous·ly** *adv* — **me·lo·di·ous·ness** *n*
mel·o·dist \ˈmel-əd-əst\ *n* **:** a composer or singer of melodies
melo·dra·ma \ˈmel-ə-ˌdräm-ə, -ˌdram-\ *n* **1 a :** an extravagantly theatrical play in which action and plot predominate over characterization **b :** a dramatic category constituted by such plays **2 :** melodramatic events or behavior [French *mélodrame,* from Greek *melos* "song" + *drama* "drama"] — **melo·dram·a·tist** \ˈdram-ət-əst, -ˈdräm-\ *n*
melo·dra·mat·ic \-drə-ˈmat-ik\ *adj* **1 :** of or relating to melodrama ⟨*melodramatic* elements of suspense and surprise⟩ **2 :** resembling or suitable for melodrama **:** SENSATIONAL ⟨made a *melodramatic* announcement of the discovery⟩ **syn** see DRAMATIC — **melo·dra·mat·i·cal·ly** \-i-kə-lē, -klē\ *adv*
melo·dra·mat·ics \-ˈmat-iks\ *n sing or pl* **:** melodramatic conduct
mel·o·dy \ˈmel-əd-ē\ *n, pl* **-dies 1 :** pleasing succession of sounds **:** TUNEFULNESS **2 :** a rhythmical series of musical tones of a given key so arranged as to make a pleasing effect **3 :** the leading part in a harmonic composition [Old French *melodie,* from Late Latin *melodia,* from Greek *melōidia* "chanting, music", from *melos* "song, tune" + *aidein* "to sing"]
mel·on \ˈmel-ən\ *n* **:** any of several soft-fleshed sweet-flavored fruits (as a muskmelon or a watermelon) of the gourd family usually eaten raw [Middle French, from Late Latin *melo,* from Latin *melopepo,* from Greek *mēlopepōn,* from *mēlon* "apple" + *pepōn,* a kind of gourd]
1**melt** \ˈmelt\ *vb* **1 :** to change from a solid to a liquid state usually through the application of heat ⟨*melt* sugar⟩ ⟨snow *melts*⟩ **2 :** DISSOLVE ⟨sugar *melts* in the mouth⟩ **3 :** to grow less **:** disappear as if by dissolving ⟨their fears *melted*⟩ **4 :** to make or become gentle **:** SOFTEN ⟨a warm smile *melts* the heart⟩ **5 :** to lose distinct outline or shape **:** BLEND, MERGE ⟨sky *melting* into sea⟩ [Old English *meltan*] — **melt·abil·i·ty** \ˌmel-tə-ˈbil-ət-ē\ *n* — **melt·able** \ˈmel-tə-bəl\ *adj* — **melt·er** *n*
2**melt** *n* **:** a melted substance
3**melt** *n* **:** SPLEEN 1 [Old English *milte*]
melting point *n* **:** the temperature at which a solid melts
melting pot *n* **1 :** a container for melting something **:** CRUCIBLE **2 a :** a place (as a city or country) in which various nationalities or races live together and gradually blend into one community **b :** the population of such a place
mel·ton \ˈmelt-n\ *n* **:** a smooth heavy woolen cloth with a short nap used for overcoats [*Melton* Mowbray, England]
melt·wa·ter \ˈmelt-ˌwȯt-ər, -ˌwät-\ *n* **:** water derived from the melting of ice and snow
mem·ber \ˈmem-bər\ *n* **1 :** a part (as an arm, leg, leaf, or branch) of the body of a person, lower animal, or plant **2 :** one of the individuals or units belonging to or forming part of a group or organization ⟨a club *member*⟩ ⟨UN *members*⟩ **3 :** a part of a whole: as **a :** a part of a structure (as a building) ⟨a horizontal *member* in a bridge⟩ **b :** an element of a mathematical set **c :** the whole expression on one side or the other of a mathematical equation or inequality [Old French *membre,* from Latin *membrum*]
mem·ber·ship \-ˌship\ *n* **1 :** the state or status of being a member **2 :** all the members of an organization
mem·brane \ˈmem-ˌbrān\ *n* **:** a thin soft pliable sheet or layer especially of animal or plant origin [Latin *membrana* "skin, parchment", from *membrum* "member"] — **mem·bra·na·ceous** \ˌmem-brə-ˈnā-shəs\ — **mem·bra·nous** \ˈmem-brə-nəs\ *adj*
me·men·to \mi-ˈment-ō\ *n, pl* **-tos** *or* **-toes :** something that serves as a reminder **:** SOUVENIR ⟨*mementos* of a trip⟩ [Latin, "remember", from *meminisse* "to remember"]
me·men·to mo·ri \mi-ˌment-ō-ˈmōr-ē, -ˈmȯr-ē\ *n, pl* **memento mori :** a reminder (as a death's-head) of mortality [Latin, "remember that you must die"]
memo \ˈmem-ō\ *n, pl* **mem·os :** MEMORANDUM
mem·oir \ˈmem-ˌwär, -ˌwȯr\ *n* **1 a :** a story of a personal experience **b :** AUTOBIOGRAPHY — usually used in pl. **c :** BIOGRAPHY 1 **2 a :** REPORT 2 **b** *pl* **:** the proceedings of a learned society [French *mémoire,* literally, "memory", from Latin *memoria*]
mem·o·ra·bil·ia \ˌmem-ə-rə-ˈbil-ē-ə, -ˈbil-yə\ *n pl* **:** things worthy of remembrance; *also* **:** a record of such things [Latin, from *memorabilis* "memorable"]
mem·o·ra·ble \ˈmem-rə-bəl, -ə-rə-\ *adj* **:** worth remembering **:** NOTABLE [Latin *memorabilis,* from *memorare* "to remind", from *memor* "mindful"] — **mem·o·ra·ble·ness** *n* — **mem·o·ra·bly** \-blē\ *adv*
mem·o·ran·dum \ˌmem-ə-ˈran-dəm\ *n, pl* **-dums** *or* **-da** \-də\ **1 a :** an informal record or communication **b :** a written reminder **2 :** an informal written note of a transaction or proposed legal instrument [Latin, neuter of *memorandus* "to be remembered", from *memorare* "to remind"]
1**me·mo·ri·al** \mə-ˈmōr-ē-əl, -ˈmȯr-\ *adj* **:** serving to preserve the memory of a person or an event ⟨a *memorial* service⟩ — **me·mo·ri·al·ly** \-ē-ə-lē\ *adv*
2**memorial** *n* **1 :** something that keeps alive the memory of a person or event; *esp* **:** MONUMENT **2 a :** RECORD 2 **b :** a statement of facts accompanying a petition to a government official
Memorial Day *n* **1 :** May 30 formerly observed as a legal holiday in most states of the United States in remembrance of war dead

2 : the last Monday in May observed as a legal holiday in most states of the United States

me•mo•ri•al•ize \mə-ˈmōr-ē-ə-ˌlīz, -ˈmȯr-\ *vt* **1 :** to address or petition (as a government official) by a memorial **2 :** COMMEMORATE 1

mem•o•rize \ˈmem-ə-ˌrīz\ *vt* **:** to commit to memory **:** learn by heart — **mem•o•ri•za•tion** \ˌmem-rə-ˈzā-shən, -ə-rə-\ *n* — **mem•o•riz•er** \ˈmem-ə-ˌrī-zər\ *n*

mem•o•ry \ˈmem-rē, -ə-rē\ *n, pl* **-ries 1 a :** the power or process of recalling what has been learned and retained **b :** the store of things learned and retained ⟨recite from *memory*⟩ **2 :** commemorative remembrance ⟨a monument in *memory* of war dead⟩ **3 a :** something remembered ⟨has pleasant *memories* of the trip⟩ **b :** the time within which past events can be or are remembered **4 :** a device (as in a computer) in which information can be inserted and stored and from which it can be extracted when wanted **[**Middle French *memoire,* from Latin *memoria* from *memor* "mindful"**]**

• **syn** REMEMBRANCE, RECOLLECTION, REMINISCENCE: MEMORY applies both to the ability to recall mentally and to what is recalled; REMEMBRANCE stresses the act of remembering or the state of being remembered; RECOLLECTION adds an implication of deliberately recalling often with some effort; REMINISCENCE suggests the recalling of things, actions, and especially of people from one's remote past.

mem•sa•hib \ˈmem-ˌsä-ˌhib, -ˌib, -ˌsäb\ *n* **:** a white foreign woman of some social status living in India; *esp* **:** the wife of a British official — compare SAHIB **[**Hindi *memṣāḥib,* from English *ma'am* + Hindi *ṣāḥib* "sahib"**]**

men *pl of* MAN

[1]men•ace \ˈmen-əs\ *n* **1 :** a show of intention to inflict harm **:** THREAT **2 a :** someone or something that represents a threat **:** DANGER **b :** an annoying person **:** NUISANCE **[**Middle French, from Latin *minacia,* from *minax* "threatening", from *minari* "to threaten"**]**

[2]menace *vb* **1 :** to make a show of intention to harm ⟨*menaced* them with upraised arms⟩ **2 :** to appear likely to cause harm **:** ENDANGER **syn** see THREATEN — **men•ac•ing•ly** \ˈmen-ə-sing-lē\ *adv*

mé•nage \mā-ˈnäzh\ *n* **:** HOUSEHOLD **[**French, from Old French *mesnage* "dwelling", from Latin *mansio,* from *manēre* "to stay"**]**

me•nag•er•ie \mə-ˈnaj-ə-rē\ *n* **1 :** a place where animals are kept and trained especially for exhibition **2 :** a collection of wild or foreign animals kept especially for exhibition **[**French *ménagerie,* from *ménage* "household"**]**

[1]mend \ˈmend\ *vb* **1 a :** to improve in manners or morals **:** REFORM **b :** to put into good shape or working order again **:** REPAIR **2 :** to become corrected or improved **3 :** to improve in health; *also* **:** HEAL **[**Middle English *menden,* short for *amenden* "to amend"**]** — **mend•er** *n*

[2]mend *n* **1 :** an act of mending **:** REPAIR **2 :** a mended place — **on the mend :** getting better (as in health)

men•da•cious \men-ˈdā-shəs\ *adj* **:** given to or characterized by deception or falsehood **[**Latin *mendac-, mendax***]** — **men•da•cious•ly** *adv* — **men•da•cious•ness** *n*

men•dac•i•ty \men-ˈdas-ət-ē\ *n, pl* **-ties :** the quality or state of being mendacious; *also* **:** [4]LIE 1

men•de•le•vi•um \ˌmen-də-ˈlē-vē-əm\ *n* **:** a radioactive element artificially produced — see ELEMENT table **[**New Latin, from Dmitri *Mendeleev***]**

Men•de•lian \men-ˈdē-lē-ən, -ˈdēl-yən\ *adj* **:** of, relating to, or according with Mendel's laws or Mendelism — **Mendelian** *n*

Men•del•ism \ˈmen-dl-ˌiz-əm\ *n* **:** the principles or the operations of Mendel's laws

Men•del's law \ˌmen-dlz-\ *n* **1 :** a principle in genetics: genes occur in pairs that separate during gamete formation so that every gamete receives but one member of a pair — called also *law of segregation* **2 :** a principle in genetics: pairs of genes on different chromosomes are distributed to the gametes independently of each other, the gametes combine to form a zygote at random, and gene pairs on different chromosomes combine in the zygote in all their various possible combinations according to the laws of chance — called also *law of independent assortment* **3 :** a principle of genetics subject to many limitations and exceptions: because one of each pair of genes dominates the other in expression, characters are inherited alternatively on an all or nothing basis — called also *law of dominance* **[**Gregor *Mendel***]**

men•di•can•cy \ˈmen-di-kən-sē\ *n* **1 :** the condition of being a beggar **2 :** the act or practice of begging

men•di•cant \-kənt\ *n* **1 :** one who lives by begging **2 :** a member of a religious order (as the Franciscans) combining monastic life and outside religious activity and originally owning neither personal nor community property **:** FRIAR **[**Latin *mendicare* "to beg", from *mendicus* "beggar"**]** — **mendicant** *adj*

men•dic•i•ty \men-ˈdis-ət-ē\ *n* **:** MENDICANCY

men•folk \ˈmen-ˌfōk\ *or* **men•folks** \-ˌfōks\ *n pl* **1 :** men in general **2 :** the men of a family or community

men•ha•den \men-ˈhād-n, mən-\ *n, pl* **-den** *also* **-dens :** a fish of the herring family found along the Atlantic coast of the United States and used for bait or converted into oil and fertilizer **[**of American Indian origin**]**

men•hir \ˈmen-ˌhiər\ *n* **:** an upright monolith usually of prehistoric origin **[**French, from Breton, from *men* "stone" + *hir* "long"**]**

[1]me•nial \ˈmē-nē-əl, -nyəl\ *adj* **1 :** of, relating to, or suitable for servants **2 :** HUMBLE 2 **[**Middle English *meynie* "household, retinue", from Old French *mesnie,* from Latin *mansio* "dwelling"**]** — **me•nial•ly** \-ē\ *adv*

[2]menial *n* **:** a domestic servant

men•in•geal \ˌmen-ən-ˈjē-əl\ *adj* **:** of, relating to, or affecting the meninges

men•in•gi•tis \ˌmen-ən-ˈjīt-əs\ *n, pl* **-git•i•des** \-ˈjit-ə-ˌdēz\ **:** inflammation of the meninges; *also* **:** a usually bacterial disease in which this occurs — **men•in•git•ic** \-ˈjit-ik\ *adj*

me•ninx \ˈmē-nings, -ningks; ˈmen-ings, -ingks\ *n, pl* **me•nin•ges** \mə-ˈnin-ˌjēz\ **:** any of the three membranes that envelop the brain and spinal cord **[**Greek *mēninx* "membrane"**]**

me•nis•cus \mə-ˈnis-kəs\ *n, pl* **me•nis•ci** \-ˈnis-ˌkī, -ˌī, -ˌkē\ *also* **me•nis•cus•es 1 :** a crescent-shaped body **:** CRESCENT **2 :** a lens that is convex on one side and concave on the other **3 :** the curved upper surface of a liquid column that is concave when the containing walls are wetted by the liquid and convex when not **[**Greek *mēniskos,* from *mēnē* "moon, crescent"**]**

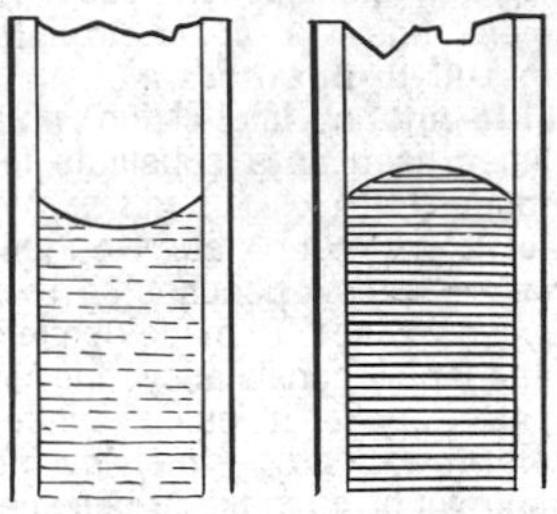

meniscus 3

Men•no•nite \ˈmen-ə-ˌnīt\ *n* **:** a member of one of the Protestant groups derived from the Anabaptist movement in Holland and noted for simplicity of life and rejection of oaths, public office, and military service **[**German *Mennonit,* from *Menno* Simons, died 1561, Frisian religious reformer**]**

me•no mos•so \ˌmā-nō-ˈmō-sō, -ˈmȯs-\ *adv* **:** less rapidly — used as a direction in music **[**Italian**]**

meno•pause \ˈmen-ə-ˌpȯz\ *n* **:** the period when menstruation naturally stops permanently usually between the ages of 45 and 50 **[**French *ménopause,* from *méno-* "menstruation" (from Greek *mēn* "month") + *pause* "pause"**]** — **meno•paus•al** \ˌmen-ə-ˈpȯ-zel\ *adj*

me•no•rah \mə-ˈnōr-ə, -ˈnȯr-\ *n* **:** a candelabrum used in Jewish worship **[**Hebrew *mĕnōrāh* "candlestick"**]**

menservants *pl of* MANSERVANT

men•ses \ˈmen-ˌsēz\ *n sing or pl* **:** the menstrual flow **[**Latin, from pl. of *mensis* "month"**]**

Men•she•vik \ˈmen-chə-ˌvik, -ˌvēk\ *n, pl* **Men•she•viks** *or* **Men•she•vi•ki** \ˌmen-chə-ˈvik-ē, -ˈvē-kē\ **:** a member of a wing of the Russian Social Democratic party before and during the Russian Revolution believing in the gradual achievement of socialism by parliamentary methods in opposition to the Bolsheviks **[**Russian *men'shevik,* from *men'she* "less"; from their forming the minority group of the party**]** — **Men•she•vism** \ˈmen-chə-ˌviz-əm\ *n* — **Men•she•vist** \-vest\ *n or adj*

men•stru•al \ˈmen-strə-wəl, -strəl\ *adj* **:** of or relating to menstruation

menstrual cycle *n* **:** the whole cycle of physiological changes from the beginning of one menstrual period to the beginning of the next

men•stru•ate \ˈmen-strə-ˌwāt, ˈmen-ˌstrāt\ *vi* **:** to undergo menstruation **[**Late Latin *menstruari,* from Latin *menstrua* "menses", from *menstruus* "monthly", from *mensis* "month"**]**

men•stru•a•tion \ˌmen-strə-ˈwā-shən, men-ˈstrā-shən\ *n* **:** a discharging of blood, secretions, and tissue debris from the uterus that recurs at approximately monthly intervals in breeding-age primate females that are not pregnant; *also* : PERIOD 5c

men•stru•um \'men-strə-wəm\ *n, pl* **men•stru•ums** *or* **men•strua** \-strə-wə\ : a substance that dissolves a solid or holds it in suspension : SOLVENT [Medieval Latin, literally, "menses", from Latin *menstrua*]

men•su•ra•ble \'men-sə-rə-bəl, 'men-chə-\ *adj* : MEASURABLE [Late Latin *mensurabilis,* from *mensurare* "to measure", from Latin *mensura* "measure"] — **men•su•ra•bil•i•ty** \ˌmen-sə-rə-'bil-ət-ē, ˌmen-chə-\ *n*

men•su•ra•tion \ˌmen-sə'rā-shən, ˌmen-chə-\ *n* **1** : the process or art of measuring **2** : the branch of mathematics that deals with the measurement of lengths, areas, and volumes

mens•wear \'menz-ˌwaər, -ˌweər\ *n* : clothing for men

-ment \mənt; *homographic verbs are* ˌment *also* mənt\ *n suffix* **1** : result, object, or means of a (specified) action ⟨embank*ment*⟩ ⟨entertain*ment*⟩ **2 a** : action : process ⟨develop*ment*⟩ **b** : place of a (specified) action ⟨encamp*ment*⟩ **3** : state : condition ⟨amaze*ment*⟩ [Latin *-mentum*]

men•tal \'ment-l\ *adj* **1 a** : of or relating to the mind ⟨*mental* powers⟩ **b** : carried on or experienced in the mind ⟨*mental* arithmetic⟩ **c** : relating to spirit or idea as opposed to matter **2 a** : of, relating to, or affected by a disorder of the mind ⟨a *mental* patient⟩ **b** : intended for the care or treatment of persons affected by mental disorders [Middle French, from Latin *ment-, mens* "mind"] — **men•tal•ly** \-l-ē\ *adv*

• **syn** INTELLECTUAL: MENTAL implies a contrast with what is physically or materially caused, expressed, or performed ⟨make a *mental* note⟩ ⟨form a *mental* picture⟩ INTELLECTUAL applies to the higher mental powers (as of generalizing or discriminating abstractions) and often implies a contrast with *moral, emotional,* or *practical* ⟨*intellectual* appreciation of music⟩ ⟨the *intellectual* value of scientific study⟩

mental age *n* : a measure used in psychological testing that expresses an individual's mental attainment in terms of the number of years it takes an average child to reach the same level

men•tal•i•ty \men-'tal-ət-ē\ *n, pl* **-ties** **1** : mental power or capacity : INTELLIGENCE **2** : way of thinking

men•thol \'men-ˌthȯl, -ˌthōl\ *n* : a white crystalline alcohol $C_{10}H_{20}O$ that occurs especially in mint oils and has the odor and cooling properties of peppermint [German, derived from Latin *mentha* "mint"]

men•tho•lat•ed \'men-thə-ˌlāt-əd\ *adj* : treated with or containing menthol

[1]**men•tion** \'men-chən\ *n* : a brief reference to something : a passing remark [Old French, from Latin *mentio,* from *ment-, mens* "mind"]

[2]**mention** *vt* **men•tioned**; **men•tion•ing** \'mench-ning, -ə-ning\ : to discuss or speak about briefly — **men•tion•able** \'mench-nə-bəl, -ə-nə-\ *adj* — **men•tion•er** \'mench-nər, -ə-nər\ *n*

men•tor \'men-ˌtȯr, 'ment-ər\ *n* : a wise and faithful adviser or teacher [*Mentor,* adviser of Telemachus in Homer's *Odyssey*]

menu \'men-yü, 'mān-\ *n* **1** : a list of dishes served at a meal or available to order (as in a restaurant) **2** : the dishes making up a meal [French, from *menu* "small, detailed", from Latin *minutus* "minute" (adj.)]

△ **origin** The French word *menu,* which means "a list of foods", comes from the adjective *menu,* which means "small", "slender", or "detailed". Presumably the last sense is the one that gave us the noun, since a menu is a detailed list. The French adjective *menu* is derived from the Latin *minutus,* "small", which is also the source of the English adjective *minute.*

[1]**me•ow** \mē-'au̇\ *n* : the characteristic cry of a cat [imitative]

[2]**meow** *vi* : to utter a meow or similar sound

me•phit•ic \mə-'fit-ik\ *adj* : foul-smelling [Latin *mephitis* "foul odor"]

mep•ro•bam•ate \ˌmep-rō-'bam-ˌāt\ *n* : a bitter drug $C_9H_{18}N_2O_4$ used as a tranquilizer [*methyl* + *prop-* (derived from *propionic acid*) + carbamate, a type of chemical, from *carb-* + *amide* + *-ate*]

mer•can•tile \'mər-kən-ˌtēl, -ˌtīl\ *adj* **1** : of or relating to merchants or trade **2** : of, relating to, or having the characteristics of mercantilism ⟨*mercantile* system⟩ [French, from Italian, from *mercante* "merchant", from Latin *mercans,* from *mercari* "to trade", from *merc-, merx* "merchandise"]

mer•can•til•ism \-ˌtēl-ˌiz-əm, -ˌtīl-\ *n* : an economic system developing during the 17th and 18th centuries to unify and increase the power and wealth of a nation by strict governmental regulation of the economy usually through policies designed to secure an accumulation of bullion, a favorable balance of trade, the development of agriculture and manufactures, and the establishment of foreign trading monopolies — **mer•can•til•ist** \-əst\ *n or adj* — **mer•can•til•is•tic** \ˌmər-kən-ˌtē-'lis-tik, -ˌtī-\ *adj*

Mer•ca•tor projection \mər-ˌkāt-ər-\ *n* : a map projection in which the meridians and parallels cross each other at right angles as they do on the globe providing accurate directional relations, but causing increasing distortion of shape and size with increasing distance from the equator [Gerhardus *Mercator*]

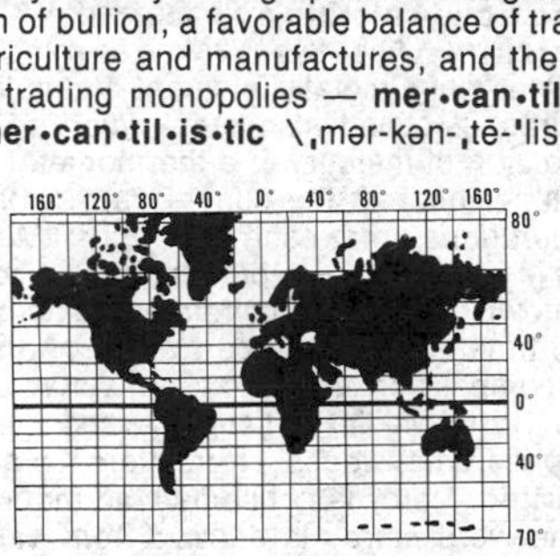

Mercator projection

[1]**mer•ce•nary** \'mərs-n-ˌer-ē\ *n, pl* **-nar•ies** : one that serves merely for wages; *esp* : a soldier hired by a foreign country to fight in its army [Latin *mercenarius,* from *merces* "wages", from *merc-, merx,* "merchandise"]

[2]**mercenary** *adj* **1** : serving only for pay or reward **2** : greedy for money — **mer•ce•nari•ly** \ˌmərs-n-'er-ə-lē\ *adv* — **mer•ce•nari•ness** \'mərs-n-ˌer-ē-nəs\ *n*

mer•cer \'mər-sər\ *n, British* : a dealer in textile fabrics [Old French *mercier* "merchant", from *mers* "merchandise", from Latin *merx*]

mer•cer•ize \'mər-sə-ˌrīz\ *vt* : to treat (cotton yarn or fabric) with a chemical so that the fibers are strengthened, take dyes better, and often acquire a sheen [John *Mercer,* died 1866, English calico printer]

[1]**mer•chan•dise** \'mər-chən-ˌdīz, -ˌdīs\ *n* : the goods that are bought and sold in trade [Old French *marcheandise,* from *marcheant* "merchant"]

[2]**merchandise** \-ˌdīz\ *vb* : to buy and sell : TRADE; *esp* : to try to further the sale of goods or use of services by attractive presentation and publicity — **mer•chan•dis•er** *n*

[1]**mer•chant** \'mər-chənt\ *n* **1** : a buyer and seller of goods for profit; *esp* : one who carries on trade on a large scale or with foreign countries **2** : the operator of a retail business : STOREKEEPER [Old French *marcheant,* derived from Latin *mercari* "to trade", from *merc-, merx* "merchandise"]

[2]**merchant** *adj* **1** : of, relating to, or used in trade ⟨a *merchant* ship⟩ **2** : of or relating to a merchant marine

mer•chant•able \-ə-bəl\ *adj* : of commercial quality : SALABLE ⟨*merchantable* goods⟩

mer•chant•man \-mən\ *n* : a ship used in commerce

merchant marine *n* **1** : the commercial ships of a nation **2** : the personnel of a merchant marine

mer•ci•ful \'mər-si-fəl\ *adj* : having, showing, or disposed to mercy : COMPASSIONATE — **mer•ci•ful•ly** \-fə-lē, -flē\ *adv* — **mer•ci•ful•ness** \-fəl-nəs\ *n*

mer•ci•less \'mər-si-ləs\ *adj* : having no mercy : PITILESS — **mer•ci•less•ly** *adv* — **mer•ci•less•ness** *n*

[1]**mer•cu•ri•al** \mər-'kyu̇r-ē-əl\ *adj* **1** : of or relating to the planet Mercury **2** : having qualities of eloquence, ingenuity, or thievishness **3** : marked by rapid and unpredictable change of mood ⟨a *mercurial* temperament⟩ **4** : of, relating to, or containing the element mercury ⟨*mercurial* medical preparations⟩ ⟨a *mercurial* thermometer⟩ — **mer•cu•ri•al•ly** \-ē-ə-lē\ *adv* — **mer•cu•ri•al•ness** *n*

[2]**mercurial** *n* : a drug or chemical containing mercury

mer•cu•ric \mər-'kyu̇r-ik\ *adj* : of, relating to, or containing mercury; *esp* : containing mercury that has a valence of two

mercuric chloride *n* : a heavy poisonous substance $HgCl_2$ used as a disinfectant and fungicide and in photography

Mer•cu•ro•chrome \mər-'kyu̇r-ə-ˌkrōm\ *trademark* — used for a red germicidal and antiseptic solution

\ə\ **abut**	\au̇\ **out**	\i\ **tip**	\ȯ\ **saw**	\u̇\ **foot**
\ər\ **further**	\ch\ **chin**	\ī\ **life**	\ȯi\ **coin**	\y\ **yet**
\a\ **mat**	\e\ **pet**	\j\ **job**	\th\ **thin**	\yü\ **few**
\ā\ **take**	\ē\ **easy**	\ng\ **sing**	\th\ **this**	\yu̇\ **cure**
\ä\ **cot, cart**	\g\ **go**	\ō\ **bone**	\ü\ **food**	\zh\ **vision**

mer•cu•rous \mər-'kyůr-əs, 'mər-kyə-rəs\ *adj* : of, relating to, or containing mercury; *esp* : containing mercury that has a valence of one

mercurous chloride *n* : CALOMEL

mer•cu•ry \'mər-kyə-rē, -kə-rē, -krē\ *n, pl* **-ries** **1 a** : a heavy silver-white metallic element that is liquid at ordinary temperatures — called also *quicksilver;* see ELEMENT table **b** : the column of mercury in a thermometer or barometer **2** *cap* : the planet nearest the sun — see PLANET table [Medieval Latin *mercurius,* from Latin *Mercurius* "Mercury (Roman god)"]

mer•cy \'mər-sē\ *n, pl* **mercies** **1** : compassion or forbearance shown to one (as an offender) having no claim to kindness **2** : a fortunate circumstance ⟨a *mercy* the weather cooled off⟩ **3** : compassion shown to victims of misfortune [Old French *merci,* from Medieval Latin *merces* "favor, mercy", from Latin, "price paid, wages", from *merc-, merx* "merchandise"]

△ **origin** Mercy is not something that can be bought or sold, but the word *mercy* is derived from Latin *merces,* which means "the price paid for something", "wages", "reward", or "recompense". The roots of what is now the primary sense of *mercy* are to be found in the Latin of Christian writers of the 6th century, who began to use *merces* for the spiritual reward that comes from kindness to those who do not necessarily have a claim to such mercy and from whom no recompense is to be expected.

• **syn** CLEMENCY, LENIENCY: MERCY implies kindness and compassion that withholds punishment even when justice demands it; CLEMENCY implies a mild or merciful disposition in one having the power or duty of punishing; LENIENCY suggests an easy or indulgent treatment of faults or misbehavior.

mercy killing *n* : the act or practice of killing (as an incurable invalid) for reasons of mercy — called also *euthanasia*

¹mere \'miər\ *n* : a sheet of standing water : POOL [Old English]

²mere *adj, superlative* **mer•est** : being only this and nothing else : nothing more than ⟨a *mere* whisper⟩ ⟨a *mere* child⟩ [Latin *merus* "pure, unmixed"] — **mere•ly** *adv*

-mere \,miər\ *n combining form* : part : segment ⟨meta*mere*⟩ [Greek *meros*]

mer•e•tri•cious \,mer-ə-'trish-əs\ *adj* : falsely attractive [Latin *meretricius* "of a prostitute", from *meretrix* "prostitute", from *merēre* "to earn"] — **mer•e•tri•cious•ly** *adv* — **mer•e•tri•cious•ness** *n*

mer•gan•ser \mər-'gan-sər\ *n, pl* **-sers** *or* **-ser** : any of various wild ducks with a slender hooked beak and a usually crested head [Latin *mergus,* a kind of waterfowl + *anser* "goose"]

merganser

merge \'mərj\ *vb* **1** : to be or cause to be swallowed up or absorbed in or within something else : MINGLE, BLEND ⟨*merging* traffic⟩ **2** : COMBINE, UNITE; *esp* : to undergo or cause to undergo a business merger [Latin *mergere* "to plunge"]

merg•er \'mər-jər\ *n* : the action or result of merging; *esp* : the combination of two or more business firms into one

me•rid•i•an \mə-'rid-ē-ən\ *n* **1** : the highest point attained **2 a** : an imaginary great circle on the earth's surface passing through the north and south poles and any given place between **b** : the half of such a circle included between the poles **c** : a representation of such a circle or half circle numbered for longitude on a globe or map [Middle French *meridien* "noon", from Latin *meridianus* "of noon", from *meridies* "noon", from *medius* "mid" + *dies* "day"] — **meridian** *adj*

me•rid•i•o•nal \mə-'rid-ē-ən-l\ *adj* **1** : of, relating to, or situated in the south : SOUTHERN **2** : of, relating to, or characteristic of people living in the south especially of France **3** : of or relating to a meridian [Middle French *meridionel,* derived from Latin *meridies* "noon, south"] — **me•rid•i•o•nal•ly** \-l-ē\ *adv*

me•ringue \mə-'rang\ *n* **1** : a mixture of beaten egg white and sugar put on pies or cakes and browned **2** : a shell of baked meringue filled with fruit or ice cream [French]

me•ri•no \mə-'rē-nō\ *n, pl* **-nos** **1** : any of a breed of fine-wooled white sheep producing a heavy fleece of exceptional quality **2** : a soft wool or wool and cotton fabric resembling cashmere **3** : a fine wool and cotton yarn [Spanish] — **merino** *adj*

mer•i•stem \'mer-ə-,stem\ *n* : a plant tissue made up of unspecialized cells capable of dividing indefinitely and of producing cells that differentiate into tissues and organs [Greek *meristos* "divided" + English *-em* (as in *system*)] — **mer•i•ste•mat•ic** \,mer-ə-stə-'mat-ik\ *adj*

¹mer•it \'mer-ət\ *n* **1** : the condition or fact of deserving well or ill **2** : a praiseworthy quality : VIRTUE ⟨an answer having the *merit* of honesty⟩ **3** : WORTH, EXCELLENCE ⟨an idea of great *merit*⟩ [Old French *merite,* from Latin *meritum,* from *merēre* "to deserve, earn"]

²merit *vb* : to earn by service or performance : DESERVE

mer•i•to•ri•ous \,mer-ə-'tōr-ē-əs, -'tȯr-\ *adj* : deserving reward or honor : PRAISEWORTHY — **mer•i•to•ri•ous•ly** *adv* — **mer•i•to•ri•ous•ness** *n*

merit system *n* : a system by which appointments and promotions in the civil service are based on competence rather than political favoritism

mer•lin \'mər-lən\ *n* : a small European falcon [Anglo-French *merilun*]

mer•maid \'mər-,mād\ *n* : an imaginary sea creature usually represented with a woman's body and a fish's tail [Old English *mere* "sea, mere"]

mer•man \-,man, -mən\ *n, pl* **mer•men** \-,men, -mən\ : an imaginary sea creature usually represented with a man's body and a fish's tail

-m•er•ous \m-ə-rəs\ *adj combining form* : having (such or so many) parts ⟨penta*merous*⟩ [Greek *meros* "part"]

mer•ri•ment \'mer-i-mənt\ *n* : MERRYMAKING 1, FUN

mer•ry \'mer-ē\ *adj* **mer•ri•er**; **-est** **1** : full of good humor and good spirits : MIRTHFUL **2** : marked by gaiety or festivity ⟨a *merry* Christmas⟩ [Old English *myrge, merge*] — **mer•ri•ly** \'mer-ə-lē\ *adv* — **mer•ri•ness** \'mer-ē-nəs\ *n*

• **syn** BLITHE, JOVIAL, JOLLY: MERRY suggests high spirits and unrestrained enjoyment of frolic or festivity; BLITHE implies lightheartedness and carefree gaiety; JOVIAL suggests behavior that stimulates conviviality and good-fellowship; JOLLY suggests often habitual good spirits expressed in laughing, bantering, and jesting.

mer•ry–an•drew \,mer-ē-'an-,drü\ *n, often cap M&A* : one that clowns publicly : BUFFOON [from the name *Andrew*]

mer•ry–go–round \'mer-ē-gō-,raůnd, -gə-\ *n* **1** : a circular revolving platform fitted with seats and figures of animals on which people sit for a ride **2** : a rapid round of activities : WHIRL ⟨a *merry-go-round* of parties⟩

mer•ry•mak•ing \-,mā-king\ *n* **1** : merry activity **2** : a merry occasion or party — **mer•ry•mak•er** \-kər\ *n*

mes- *or* **meso-** *combining form* **1** : mid : in the middle ⟨*meso*carp⟩ **2** : intermediate (as in size or type) ⟨*mes*on⟩ [Greek, from *mesos*]

me•sa \'mā-sə\ *n* : a flat-topped hill or small plateau with steep sides [Spanish, literally, "table", from Latin *mensa*]

més•al•liance \,mā-,zal-'yäⁿs, ,mā-zə-'lī-əns\ *n, pl* **-liances** \-'yäⁿs, -'yäⁿs-əz; -'lī-ən-səz\ : a marriage with a person of inferior social position [French, from *més-* "mis-" + *alliance* "alliance"]

mes•cal \me-'skal, mə-\ *n* **1** : a small cactus with rounded stems covered with jointed tubercles that are used as a stimulant and intoxicant especially among the Mexican Indians **2 a** : a usually colorless Mexican liquor distilled especially from the central leaves on maguey plants **b** : a plant from which mescal is produced [Spanish, from Nahuatl *mexcalli* "mescal liquor"]

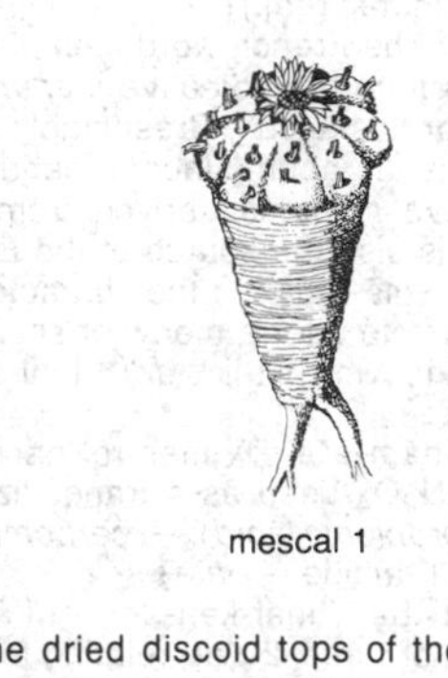
mescal 1

mescal button *n* : one of the dried discoid tops of the mescal cactus

mes•ca•line \'mes-kə-lən, -,lēn\ *n* : a hallucination-inducing alkaloid $C_{11}H_{17}NO_3$ found in mescal buttons

mesdames *pl of* MADAM *or of* MADAME *or of* MRS.

mesdemoiselles *pl of* MADEMOISELLE
me•seems \mi-ˈsēmz\ *vb impersonal, past* **me•seemed** \-ˈsēmd\ *archaic* : it seems to me
mes•en•ceph•a•lon \ˌmez-ˌen-ˈsef-ə-ˌlän, ˌmez-n-, ˌmēz-\ *n* : the middle division of the brain : MIDBRAIN — **mes•en•ce•phal•ic** \-ˌen-sə-ˈfal-ik, -n-sə-\ *adj*
mes•en•chyme \ˈmez-n-ˌkīm, ˈmēz-\ *n* : a loosely organized mesodermal tissue that produces connective tissues, blood, lymphatics, bone, and cartilage [German *mesenchym*] — **mes•en•chy•mal** \mə-ˈzeng-kə-məl, -ˈseng-; ˌmez-n-ˈkī-məl, ˌmēz-\ *adj*
mes•en•tery \ˈmez-n-ˌter-ē, ˈmes-\ *n, pl* **-ter•ies** : a membranous tissue or one of the membranes that envelop and support visceral organs (as the intestines) [Greek *mesenterion,* from *mes-* + *enteron* "intestine"] — **mes•en•ter•ic** \ˌmez-n-ˈter-ik, ˌmes-\ *adj*
[1]mesh \ˈmesh\ *n* **1** : one of the open spaces formed by the threads of a net or the wires of a sieve or screen **2 a** : a fabric of open texture with evenly spaced small holes **b** : NET 1a, NETWORK **3** : SNARE 2 — usually used in pl. ⟨caught in their own *meshes*⟩ **4** : the coming or fitting together of the teeth of two gears [probably from Dutch *maesche*] — **meshed** \ˈmesht\ *adj*
[2]mesh *vb* **1** : to catch in or as if in a mesh **2** : to fit together : INTERLOCK ⟨gears that *mesh*⟩
me•si•al \ˈmē-zē-əl, -sē-\ *adj* : of, relating to, or being the surface of a tooth that is next to the tooth in front of it or that is closest to the middle of the front of the jaw — **me•si•al•ly** \-ə-lē\ *adv*
mes•mer•ism \ˈmez-mə-ˌriz-əm\ *n* : HYPNOTISM [F. A. *Mesmer,* died 1815, Austrian physician] — **mes•mer•ic** \mez-ˈmer-ik\ *adj* — **mes•mer•ist** \ˈmez-mə-rəst\ *n*
mes•mer•ize \ˈmez-mə-ˌrīz\ *vt* **1** : HYPNOTIZE **2** : FASCINATE 1, SPELLBIND ⟨*mesmerized* by the sight of the burning building⟩ — **mes•mer•iz•er** *n*
me•so•carp \ˈmez-ə-ˌkärp, ˈmēz-, ˈmēs-, ˈmes-\ *n* : the often fleshy middle layer of the pericarp of a fruit — compare ENDOCARP, EPICARP
me•so•derm \-ˌdərm\ *n* : the middle of the three primary germ layers of an embryo from which most of the muscular, skeletal, and connective tissues develop; *also* : tissue derived from this layer — **me•so•der•mal** \ˌmez-ə-ˈdər-məl, mēz-, ˌmēs-, ˌmes-\ *adj*
me•so•glea *or* **me•so•gloea** \ˌmez-ə-ˈglē-ə, ˌmēz-, ˌmēs-, ˌmes-\ *n* : a jellylike substance between the endoderm and ectoderm of sponges or coelenterates [*mes-* + Late Greek *gloia, glia* "glue"]
Me•so•lith•ic \ˌmez-ə-ˈlith-ik, ˌmēz-, ˌmes-, ˌmēs-\ *adj* : of or relating to a period of the Stone Age that is transitional between the Paleolithic and the Neolithic
me•so•mor•phic \ˌmez-ə-ˈmȯr-fik, ˌmēz-, ˌmēs-, ˌmes-\ *adj* : of a muscular or athletic type of body-build — **me•so•morph** \ˈmez-ə-ˌmȯrf, ˈmēz-, ˈmēs-, ˈmes-\ *n*
me•son \ˈmez-ˌän, ˈmes-; ˈmā-ˌzän, ˈmē-, -ˌsän\ *n* : any of a group of elementary particles that have a mass between that of the electron and the proton and are either positively or negatively charged or neutral [*mes-* + *-on*]
me•so•pause \ˈmez-ə-ˌpȯz, ˈmēz-, ˈmēs-, ˈmes-\ *n* : the transition zone between the mesosphere and the exosphere
me•so•phyll \-ˌfil\ *n* : the tissue of a foliage leaf consisting of photosynthetic and storage cells that lie between the surface layers
me•so•phyte \-ˌfīt\ *n* : a plant that grows under medium conditions of moisture — **me•so•phyt•ic** \ˌmez-ə-ˈfit-ik, ˌmēz-, ˌmēs-, ˌmes-\ *adj*
me•so•sphere \ˈmez-ə-ˌsfiər, ˈmēz-, ˈmēs-, ˈmes-\ *n* : a layer of the atmosphere extending from the top of the stratosphere to an altitude of about 80 kilometers
me•so•the•li•um \ˌmez-ə-ˈthē-lē-əm, ˌmēz-, ˌmēs-, ˌmes-\ *n, pl* **-lia** \-lē-ə\ : epithelium derived from mesoderm — **me•so•the•li•al** \-lē-əl\ *adj*
me•so•tho•rax \-ˈthōr-ˌaks, -ˈthȯr-\ *n* : the middle of the three segments of the thorax of an insect
Me•so•zo•ic \-ˈzō-ik\ *n* **1** : the 4th of the five eras of geological history marked by the existence of dinosaurs, marine and flying reptiles, and evergreen trees — called also *Age of Reptiles;* see GEOLOGIC TIME table **2** : the system of rocks corresponding to the Mesozoic — **Mesozoic** *adj*
mes•quite \mə-ˈskēt, me-\ *n* : a spiny deep-rooted tree or shrub of the pea family that grows in the southwestern United States and in Mexico and bears pods rich in sugar and important as a livestock feed [Spanish, from Nahuatl *mizquitl*]

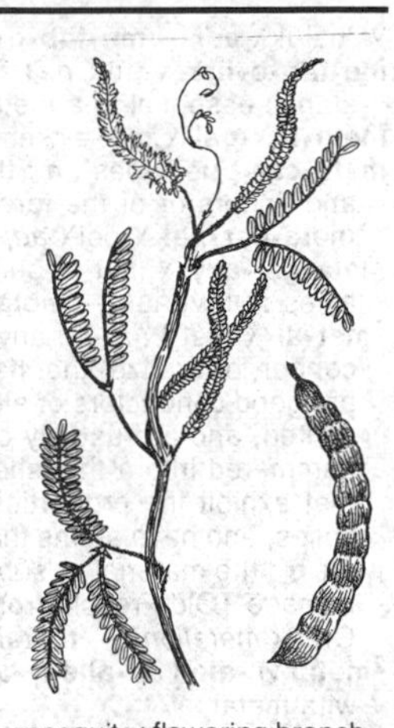
mesquite : flowering branch and pod

[1]mess \ˈmes\ *n* **1 a** : a quantity of food **b** : a dish of soft food ⟨a *mess* of porridge⟩ **2 a** : a group of people who regularly eat together; *also* : the meal they eat **b** : a place where meals are regularly served to a group ⟨an officers' *mess*⟩ **3 a** : a confused heap **b** : a state of confusion or disorder ⟨left things in a *mess*⟩ [Old French *mes,* from Late Latin *missus* "course at a meal", from *mittere* "to put", from Latin, "to send"]
[2]mess *vb* **1 a** : to supply with meals **b** : to take meals with a mess **2 a** : to make dirty or untidy **b** : BUNGLE ⟨*messed* up the job⟩ **3** : to interfere with **4** : PUTTER ⟨likes to *mess* around the garden⟩
mes•sage \ˈmes-ij\ *n* **1** : a communication in writing, in speech, or by signals **2** : a messenger's errand or function **3** : an underlying theme or idea [Old French, from Medieval Latin *missaticum,* from Latin *missus,* past participle of *mittere* "to send"]
messeigneurs *pl of* MONSEIGNEUR
mes•sen•ger \ˈmes-n-jər\ *n* : one that bears a message or does an errand [Old French *messagier,* from *message* "message"]
messenger RNA *n* : an RNA that carries the code for a particular protein from the nuclear DNA to the ribosome and acts as a template for the formation of that protein — compare TRANSFER RNA
mes•si•ah \mə-ˈsī-ə\ *n* **1** *cap* **a** : the expected king and deliverer of the Jews **b** : JESUS **2** : a professed or accepted leader of some hope or cause [Hebrew *māshīaḥ* and Aramaic *mĕshīḥā,* literally, "annointed"] — **mes•si•ah•ship** \-ˌship\ *n* — **mes•si•an•ic** \ˌmes-ē-ˈan-ik\ *adj* — **mes•si•a•nism** \ˈmes-ē-ə-ˌniz-əm, mə-ˈsī-ə-\ *n*
Mes•si•as \mə-ˈsī-əs\ *n* : MESSIAH 1 [Late Latin, from Greek, from Aramaic *mĕshīḥā*]
messieurs *pl of* MONSIEUR
mess jacket *n* : a man's short tight jacket
mess kit *n* : a kit consisting of cooking and eating utensils that fit together in a compact unit
mess•mate \ˈmes-ˌmāt\ *n* : a member of a mess (as on a ship)
Messrs. \ˌmes-ərz\ *pl of* MR.
messy \ˈmes-ē\ *adj* **mess•i•er; -est** : marked by confusion, disorder, or dirt : UNTIDY — **mess•i•ly** \ˈmes-ə-lē\ *adv* — **mess•i•ness** \ˈmes-ē-nəs\ *n*
mes•ti•za \me-ˈstē-zə\ *n* : a woman who is a mestizo [Spanish, feminine of *mestizo*]
mes•ti•zo \-zō\ *n, pl* **-zos** : a person of mixed blood; *esp* : one of mixed European and American Indian ancestry [Spanish, from *mestizo* "mixed", derived from Latin *miscēre* "to mix"]
met *past of* MEET
meta- *or* **met-** *combining form* **1 a** : occurring after **b** : situated behind or beyond ⟨*met*encephalon⟩ **2** : change : transformation [Greek, from *meta* "among, with, after"]
me•tab•o•lism \mə-ˈtab-ə-ˌliz-əm\ *n* **1 a** : the sum of the processes in the building up and destruction of protoplasm; *esp* : the chemical changes in living cells by which energy is provided for vital processes and activities and new material is assimilated **b** : the sum of the processes by which a particular substance is handled in the living body **2** : METAMORPHOSIS 3 [Greek *metabolē* "change", from *metaballein* "to change", from *meta-* + *ballein* "to throw"] — **met•a•bol•ic** \ˌmet-ə-

\ə\ **abut**	\au̇\ **out**	\i\ **tip**	\ȯ\ **saw**	\u̇\ **foot**
\ər\ **further**	\ch\ **chin**	\ī\ **life**	\ȯi\ **coin**	\y\ **yet**
\a\ **mat**	\e\ **pet**	\j\ **job**	\th\ **thin**	\yü\ **few**
\ā\ **take**	\ē\ **easy**	\ng\ **sing**	\t͟h\ **this**	\yu̇\ **cure**
\ä\ **cot, cart**	\g\ **go**	\ō\ **bone**	\ü\ **food**	\zh\ **vision**

'bäl-ik\ *adj* — **me•tab•o•lize** \me-'tab-ə-,līz\ *vb*

me•tab•o•lite \-,līt\ *n* **1** : a product of metabolism **2** : a substance essential to a metabolic process

meta•car•pal \,met-ə-'kär-pəl\ *n* : a bone of the metacarpus

meta•car•pus \-pəs\ *n* : the part of the hand between the wrist and fingers or of the forefoot between the ankle and toes — **meta•car•pal** \-pəl\ *adj*

meta•gal•axy \,met-ə-'gal-ək-sē\ *n* : the entire system of galaxies : UNIVERSE — **meta•ga•lac•tic** \-gə-'lak-tik\ *adj*

¹met•al \'met-l\ *n* **1** : any of various substances (as gold, tin, copper, or bronze) that have a more or less shiny appearance, are good conductors of electricity and heat, are opaque, can be melted, and are usually capable of being drawn into a wire or hammered into a thin sheet **2** : any of the chemical elements that exhibit the properties of a metal, typically are crystalline solids, and have atoms that readily lose electrons **3 a** : METTLE 2a **b** : the material or substance out of which a person or thing is made **[**Old French, from Latin *metallum* "mine, metal", from Greek *metallon***]** — **metal** *adj*

²metal *vt* **-aled** *or* **-alled**; **-al•ing** *or* **-al•ling** : to cover or furnish with metal

me•tal•lic \mə-'tal-ik\ *adj* **1** : of, relating to, or being a metal **2** : containing or made of metal **3** : having iridescent and reflective properties **4** : STRIDENT, HARSH ⟨a *metallic* voice⟩ — **me•tal•li•cal•ly** \-'tal-i-kə-lē, -klē\ *adv*

met•al•lif•er•ous \,met-l-'if-rəs, -ə-rəs\ *adj* : yielding or containing metal

met•al•lize \'met-l-,īz\ *vt* : to treat or combine with a metal

met•al•log•ra•phy \,met-l-'äg-rə-fē\ *n* : a study of the structure of metals especially with the microscope — **met•al•log•ra•pher** \-fər\ *n* — **me•tal•lo•graph•ic** \mə-,tal-ə-'graf-ik\ *adj*

met•al•loid \'met-l-,ȯid\ *n* : a chemical element intermediate in properties between the typical metals and other elements

met•al•lur•gy \'met-l-,ər-jē\ *n* : the science and technology of metals **[**Greek *metallon* "metal" + *ergon* "work"**]** — **met•al•lur•gi•cal** \,met-l-'ər-ji-kəl\ *adj* — **met•al•lur•gist** \'met-l-,ər-jəst\ *n*

met•al•ware \'met-l-,waər, -,weər\ *n* : metal utensils for household use

met•al•work \'met-l-,wərk\ *n* **1** : the process or occupation of making things from metal **2** : work and especially artistic work made of metal — **met•al•work•er** \,wər-kər\ *n* — **met•al•work•ing** \-king\ *n*

meta•mere \'met-ə-,miər\ *n* : any of the series of segments into which the body of a higher invertebrate or vertebrate is divisible — **me•tam•er•ism** \mə-'tam-ə-,riz-əm\ *n* — **meta•mer•ic** \,met-ə-'mer-ik, -'mir-\ *adj*

meta•mor•phism \,met-ə-'mȯr-,fiz-əm\ *n* : a change in the structure of rock; *esp* : a change to a more compact and more highly crystalline condition produced by such forces as pressure, heat, and water ⟨marble is produced by the *metamorphism* of limestone⟩ — **meta•mor•phic** \-'mȯr-fik\ *adj*

meta•mor•phose \-,fōz, -,fōs\ *vb* **1** : to change or cause to change in form : undergo metamorphosis **2** : to cause (a rock) to undergo metamorphism **syn** see TRANSFORM

meta•mor•pho•sis \,met-ə-'mȯr-fə-səs\ *n, pl* **-pho•ses** \-fə-,sēz\ **1 a** : a change of form, structure, or substance especially by witchcraft or magic **b** : a striking alteration in appearance, character, or circumstances **2** : a fundamental and usually rather abrupt change (as of an insect larva into an adult or a tadpole into a frog) in the form and often the habits of an animal **[**Latin, from Greek *metamorphōsis*, from *metamorphoun* "to transform", from *meta-* + *morphē* "form"**]**

meta•phase \'met-ə-,fāz\ *n* : the stage of mitosis and meiosis during which the chromosomes become arranged in the plane of the equator of the spindle

metaphase plate *n* : the plane at the equator of the spindle of a dividing cell in metaphase with the chromosomes arranged upon it — called also *equatorial plate*

met•a•phor \'met-ə-,fȯr *also* -fər\ *n* : a figure of speech in which a word or phrase denoting one kind of object or idea is used in place of another to suggest a similarity between them (as in *the ship plows the sea*) — compare SIMILE **[**Latin *metaphora*, from Greek, from *metapherein* "to transfer", from *meta-* + *pherein* "to carry"**]** — **met•a•phor•ic** \,met-ə-'fȯr-ik, -'fär-\ *or* **met•a•phor•i•cal** \-i-kəl\ *adj* — **met•a•phor•i•cal•ly** \-i-kə-lē, -klē\ *adv*

meta•phys•i•cal \,met-ə-'fiz-i-kəl\ *adj* **1** : of or relating to metaphysics **2** : SUPERNATURAL 1 **3** : highly abstract or difficult to understand **4** *often cap* : of or relating to poetry especially of the early 17th century that is marked by subtle and elaborate metaphors — **meta•phys•i•cal•ly** \-'fiz-i-kə-lē, -klē\ *adv*

meta•phy•si•cian \,met-ə-fə-'zish-ən\ *n* : a student of or specialist in metaphysics

meta•phys•ics \,met-ə-'fiz-iks\ *n* : the part of philosophy concerned with the ultimate causes and the underlying nature of things **[**Medieval Latin *Metaphysica*, title of Aristotle's treatise on the subject, from Greek *(ta) meta (ta) physika* "the (works) after the physical (works)"; from its position in his collected works**]**

meta•se•quoia \,met-ə-si-'kwȯi-ə\ *n* : any of a genus of fossil and living deciduous cone-bearing trees of the pine family

meta•sta•ble \,met-ə-'stā-bəl\ *adj* : marked by only a slight margin of stability ⟨a *metastable* chemical⟩

me•tas•ta•sis \mə-'tas-tə-səs\ *n, pl* **-ta•ses** \-,sēz\ : transfer of a disease-producing agency from its original site to another part of the body; *also* : a secondary growth of a malignant tumor **[**Late Latin, "transition", from Greek, from *methistanai* "to change", from *meta-* + *histanai* "to stand"**]** — **met•a•stat•ic** \,met-ə-'stat-ik\ *adj* — **met•a•stat•i•cal•ly** \-'stat-i-kə-lē, -klē\ *adv*

me•tas•ta•size \mə-'tas-tə-,sīz\ *vi* : to spread by metastasis

meta•tar•sal \,met-ə-'tär-səl\ *n* : a bone of the metatarsus

meta•tar•sus \-səs\ *n* : the part of the foot in a human being or of the hind foot in a four-footed animal between the toes and the joint between the foot and the leg — **meta•tar•sal** \-səl\ *adj*

me•tath•e•sis \mə-'tath-ə-səs\ *n, pl* **-e•ses** \-,sēz\ : a change of place or condition; *esp* : transposition of two sounds or letters in a word (as in Modern English *bird* from Old English *bridd*) **[**Greek, from *metatithenai* "to transpose", from *meta-* + *tithenai* "to place"**]**

meta•tho•rax \,met-ə-'thōr-,aks, -'thȯr-\ *n* : the hindmost of the three segments of the thorax of an insect

meta•zoa \,met-ə-'zō-ə\ *n pl* : animals that are metazoans

meta•zo•an \-'zō-ən\ *n* : any of a group (Metazoa) including all animals with a body composed of cells differentiated into tissues and organs — **metazoan** *adj*

mete \'mēt\ *vt* : to assign by measure ⟨*mete* out punishment⟩ **[**Old English *metan* "to measure"**]**

me•tem•psy•cho•sis \mə-,tem-si'kō-səs, -,temp-; ,met-əm-,sī-\ *n* : the passing of the soul at death into another body either human or animal **[**Greek *metempsychōsis*, dervied from *meta-* + *en-* + *psychē* "soul"**]**

met•en•ceph•a•lon \,met-,en-'sef-ə-,län\ *n* : the anterior segment of the rhombencephalon

me•te•or \'mēt-ē-ər, -ē-,ȯr\ *n* : one of the small bodies of matter in the solar system observable when it falls into the earth's atmosphere where the heat of friction may cause it to glow brightly for a short time; *also* : the streak of light produced by the passage of a meteor **[**Middle French *meteore*, from Medieval Latin *meteorum*, from Greek *meteōron* "phenomenon in the sky", from *meteōros* "high in the air"**]**

me•te•or•ic \,mēt-ē-'ȯr-ik, -'är-\ *adj* **1** : of or relating to a meteor ⟨a *meteoric* shower⟩ **2** : resembling a meteor in speed or in sudden and temporary brilliance ⟨a *meteoric* rise to fame⟩ — **me•te•or•i•cal•ly** \-i-kə-lē, -klē\ *adv*

me•te•or•ite \'mēt-ē-ə-,rīt\ *n* : a meteor that reaches the surface of the earth

me•te•or•oid \-,rȯid\ *n* : a meteor in interplanetary space

me•te•o•rol•o•gy \,mēt-ē-ə-'räl-ə-jē\ *n* : a science that deals with the atmosphere and its phenomena and especially with weather and weather forecasting — **me•te•o•ro•log•ic** \-rə-'läj-ik\ *or* **me•te•o•ro•log•i•cal** \-i-kəl\ *adj* — **me•te•o•rol•o•gist** \-'räl-ə-jəst\ *n*

¹me•ter *or* **me•tre** \'mēt-ər\ *n* : a systematic rhythm in verse and in music **[**Old English *mēter*, from Latin *metrum*, from Greek *metron* "measure, meter"**]**

²meter *n* : the basic metric unit of length — see METRIC SYSTEM table **[**French *mètre*, from Greek *metron* "measure"**]**

³meter *n* : an instrument for measuring and sometimes recording the amount of something ⟨a gas *meter*⟩

⁴meter *vt* **1** : to measure by means of a meter **2** : to supply in a measured or regulated amount

-me•ter \m-ət-ər, *in some words*, ,mēt-ər\ *n combining form* : instrument or means for measuring ⟨*barometer*⟩

meter-kilogram-second *adj* : of, relating to, or being a system of units based on the meter as the unit of length, the kilogram as the unit of mass, and the second as the unit of time — abbreviation *mks*

meth·ac·ry·late \meth-ˈak-rə-ˌlāt\ *n* **:** a light strong acrylic resin used especially as a substitute for glass **[***methyl* + *acrylic* + *-ate***]**

meth·a·done \ˈmeth-ə-ˌdōn\ *or* **meth·a·don** \-ˌdän\ *n* **:** a synthetic addictive narcotic drug used especially to replace heroin in the treatment of heroin addiction **[**derived from *methyl***]**

meth·am·phet·amine \ˌmeth-am-ˈfet-ə-ˌmēn, -əm-, -mən\ *n* **:** a derivative of amphetamine $C_{10}H_{15}N$ used as a stimulant of the central nervous system and in the treatment of obesity **[***methyl* + *amphetamine***]**

meth·ane \ˈmeth-ˌān\ *n* **:** an odorless flammable gas CH_4 consisting of carbon and hydrogen produced by decomposition of organic matter **[***methyl* + *-ane***]**

meth·a·nol \ˈmeth-ə-ˌnȯl, -ˌnōl\ *n* **:** a volatile flammable poisonous liquid CH_4O that consists of carbon, hydrogen, and oxygen and is used especially as a solvent and antifreeze

me·thinks \mi-ˈthiŋs, -ˈthiŋks\ *vb impersonal, past* **me·thought** \-ˈthȯt\ *archaic* **:** it seems to me

me·thi·o·nine \mə-ˈthī-ə-ˌnēn\ *n* **:** a crystalline sulfur-containing essential amino acid $C_5H_{11}NO_2S$ **[***methyl* + *thion-* (from Greek *theion* "sulfur") + *-ine***]**

meth·od \ˈmeth-əd\ *n* **1 :** a regular systematic plan for or way of doing something **2 a :** orderly arrangement **b :** habitual regularity and orderliness ⟨their work lacks *method*⟩ **[**Latin *methodus,* from Greek *methodos,* from *meta-* + *hodos* "way"**]**

me·thod·i·cal \mə-ˈthäd-i-kəl\ *adj* **1 :** arranged, characterized by, or performed with method or order **2 :** habitually following a method **:** SYSTEMATIC — **me·thod·i·cal·ly** \-i-kə-lē, -klē\ *adv* — **me·thod·i·cal·ness** \-kəl-nəs\ *n*

Meth·od·ist \ˈmeth-əd-əst\ *n* **:** a member of one of the denominations deriving from the Wesleyan revival, accepting the possibility of salvation for all and often a modified episcopal government, and stressing personal and social morality — **Meth·od·ism** \-ə-ˌdiz-əm\ *n* — **Methodist** *adj*

meth·od·ize \ˈmeth-ə-ˌdīz\ *vt* **:** to reduce to method **:** SYSTEMATIZE

meth·od·ol·o·gy \ˌmeth-ə-ˈdäl-ə-jē\ *n, pl* **-gies 1 :** a body of methods and rules followed in a science or discipline **2 :** the study of the principles or procedures of inquiry in a particular field — **meth·od·olog·i·cal** \ˌmeth-əd-l-ˈäj-i-kəl\ *adj* — **meth·od·ol·o·gist** \ˌmeth-ə-ˈdäl-ə-jəst\ *n*

meth·yl \ˈmeth-əl\ *n* **:** a chemical radical CH_3 consisting of carbon and hydrogen **[**back-formation from *methylene* "the radical CH_2" from French *méthylène,* from Greek *methy* "wine" + *hylē* "wood"**]**

methyl alcohol *n* **:** METHANOL

meth·y·lene blue \ˌmeth-ə-ˌlēn\ *n* **:** a basic dye used as a biological stain and as an antidote in cyanide poisoning

methyl orange *n* **:** a basic dye used as a chemical indicator that in dilute solution is yellow when neutral and pink when acid

me·tic·u·lous \mə-ˈtik-yə-ləs\ *adj* **:** extremely or excessively careful in small details **[**Latin *meticulosus* "timid", from *metus* "fear"**] syn** see CAREFUL — **me·tic·u·lous·ly** *adv* — **me·tic·u·lous·ness** *n*

mé·tier \mā-ˈtyā\ *n* **1 :** TRADE 2a **2 :** an area of activity in which one is expert or successful **:** FORTE **[**French, derived from Latin *ministerium* "work, service", from Latin *minister* "servant"**]**

mé·tis \mā-ˈtē, -ˈtēs\ *n, pl* **métis** \-ˈtē, -ˈtēs, -ˈtēz\ **:** one of mixed blood; *esp* **:** the offspring of an American Indian and a white person **[**French, derived from Latin *miscēre* "to mix"**]**

me·ton·y·my \mə-ˈtän-ə-mē\ *n, pl* **-mies :** a figure of speech in which the name of one thing is used for the name of another associated with or related to it (as in "lands belonging to the crown") **[**Latin *metonymia,* from Greek *metōnymia,* from *meta-* + *onyma* "name"**]** — **met·onym** \ˈmet-ə-ˌnim\ *n* — **met·onym·ic** \ˌmet-ə-ˈnim-ik\ *adj*

me–too \ˈmē-ˈtü\ *adj* **:** similar to or accepting successful or persuasive policies or practices of a political rival ⟨a *me-too* policy⟩ — **me–too·ism** \-ˌiz-əm\ *n*

metre *variant of* METER

met·ric \ˈme-trik\ *adj* **1 :** based on the meter as a standard of measurement ⟨the *metric* system⟩ **2 :** METRICAL 1

-met·ric \ˈme-trik\ *or* **-met·ri·cal** \-tri-kəl\ *adj combining form* **1 :** of, employing, or obtained by (such) a meter ⟨baro*metric*⟩ **2 :** of or relating to (such) an art, process, or science of measuring ⟨titri*metric*⟩

met·ri·cal \ˈme-tri-kəl\ *adj* **1 a :** of or relating to meter (as in poetry or music) **b :** arranged in meter ⟨*metrical* verse⟩ **2 :** of or relating to measurement — **met·ri·cal·ly** \-kə-lē, -klē\ *adv*

met·rics \ˈme-triks\ *n pl* **:** a part of prosody that deals with metrical structure

metric system *n* **:** a decimal system of weights and measures based on the meter as the unit of length and the kilogram as the unit of weight

metric ton *n* — see METRIC SYSTEM table

met·ro \ˈme-trō\ *n, pl* **metros :** SUBWAY **[**French *métro,* short for *chemin de fer métropolitain* "metropolitan railroad"**]**

me·trol·o·gy \me-ˈträl-ə-jē\ *n* **:** the science of weights and measures or of measurements — **met·ro·log·i·cal** \ˌme-trə-ˈläj-i-kəl\ *adj*

met·ro·nome \ˈme-trə-ˌnōm\ *n* **:** an instrument designed to mark exact musical time by a regularly repeated tick **[**Greek *metron* "meter" + *-nomos* "controlling", from *nomos* "law"**]** — **met·ro·nom·ic** \ˌme-trə-ˈnäm-ik\ *adj* — **met·ro·nom·i·cal·ly** \-ˈnäm-i-kə-lē, -klē\ *adv*

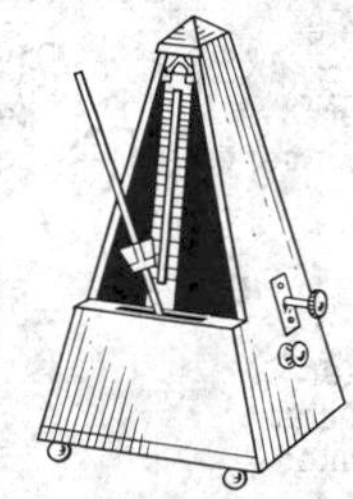
metronome

me·trop·o·lis \mə-ˈträp-ləs, -ə-ləs\ *n* **1 :** the mother city or state of a colony (as of ancient Greece) **2 :** the chief or capital city of a country, state, or region **3 a :** a principal seat or center of an activity **b :** a large important city **[**Late Latin, from Greek *mētropolis,* from *mētēr* "mother" + *polis* "city"**]**

[1]**met·ro·pol·i·tan** \ˌme-trə-ˈpäl-ət-n\ *n* **1 :** the head of an ecclesiastical see **2 :** one who lives in a metropolis or who exhibits metropolitan manners or customs

[2]**metropolitan** *adj* **1 :** of or constituting a metropolitan or his see **2 :** of, relating to, or characteristic of a metropolis

-m·e·try \m-ə-trē\ *n combining form* , *pl* **-metries :** art, process, or science of measuring (something specified) ⟨photo*metry*⟩

met·tle \ˈmet-l\ *n* **1 :** quality of temperament or disposition **2 a :** vigor and strength of spirit **:** ARDOR **b :** staying quality **:** STAMINA **[**alteration of *metal***]** — **on one's mettle :** eager and ready to do one's best

met·tle·some \-l-səm\ *adj* **:** full of mettle **:** SPIRITED

[1]**mew** \ˈmyü\ *n* **:** GULL; *esp* **:** the common European gull **[**Old English *mǣw***]**

[2]**mew** *vi* **:** MEOW **[**Middle English *mewen***]** — **mew** *n*

[3]**mew** *n* **1** *archaic* **:** a cage for hawks **2** *pl, chiefly British* **a :** stables usually with living quarters built around a court **b :** a back street **:** ALLEY **[**Middle French *mue,* from *muer* "to molt", from Latin *mutare* "to change"**]**

[4]**mew** *vt* **:** to shut up **:** CONFINE — often used with *up*

mewl \ˈmyül\ *vi* **:** to cry weakly **:** WHIMPER **[**imitative**]**

Mex·i·can \ˈmek-si-kən\ *n* **1 :** a native or inhabitant of Mexico **2 :** a person of Mexican descent — **Mexican** *adj*

Mexican bean beetle *n* **:** a spotted ladybug that is a garden pest feeding on bean plants

me·zu·zah *or* **me·zu·za** \mə-ˈzu̇z-ə\ *n* **:** a small parchment scroll inscribed with Deuteronomy 6:4–9 and 11:13–21 and the name *Shaddai* (the Almighty) and placed in a case fixed to the doorpost of some Jewish families as a sign and reminder of their faith **[**Hebrew *mĕzūzāh* "doorpost"**]**

mez·za·nine \ˈmez-n-ˌēn, ˌmez-n-ˈ\ **1 :** a low story between two main stories of a building often projecting as a balcony **2 :** the lowest balcony in a theater or its first few rows **[**French, from Italian *mezzanino,* from *mezzano* "middle", from Latin *medianus* "middle, median"**]**

mez·zo for·te \ˌmet-sō-ˈfȯr-ˌtā, ˌmed-zō-, -ˈfȯrt-ē\ *adj or adv* **:** moderately loud — used as a direction in music **[**Italian, from *mezzo* "half, medium, middle"**]**

mez·zo–so·pra·no \-sə-ˈpran-ō, -ˈprän-\ *n* **:** a woman's voice of

METRIC SYSTEM

LENGTH

unit	*abbreviation*	*number of meters*	*approximate United States equivalent*
kilometer	km	1,000	0.621 mile
hectometer	hm	100	109.361 yards
dekameter	dam	10	32.808 feet
meter	m	1	39.370 inches
decimeter	dm	0.1	3.937 inches
centimeter	cm	0.01	0.394 inch
millimeter	mm	0.001	0.039 inch

AREA

unit	*abbreviation*	*number of square meters*	*approximate United States equivalent*
square kilometer	sq km *or* km^2	1,000,000	0.386 square mile
hectare	ha	10,000	2.471 acres
are	a	100	119.599 square yards
centare	ca	1	10.764 square feet
square centimeter	sq cm *or* cm^2	0.0001	0.155 square inch

CAPACITY

unit	*abbreviation*	*number of liters*	*approximate United States equivalent*		
			cubic	*dry*	*liquid*
kiloliter	kl	1,000	1.308 cubic yards		
hectoliter	hl	100	3.532 cubic feet	2.838 bushels	
dekaliter	dal	10	0.353 cubic foot	1.135 pecks	2.642 gallons
liter	l	1	61.024 cubic inches	0.908 quart	1.0567 quarts
deciliter	dl	0.10	6.102 cubic inches	0.182 pint	0.211 pint
centiliter	cl	0.01	0.61 cubic inch		0.338 fluid-ounce
milliliter	ml	0.001	0.061 cubic inch		0.271 fluidram

MASS AND WEIGHT

unit	*abbreviation*	*number of grams*	*approximate United States equivalent*
metric ton	MT*or* t	1,000,000	1.102 tons
quintal	q	100,000	220.462 pounds
kilogram	kg	1,000	2.205 pounds
hectogram	hg	100	3.527 ounces
dekagram	dag	10	0.353 ounce
gram	g *or* gm	1	0.0353 ounce
decigram	dg	0.10	1.543 grains
centigram	cg	0.01	0.154 grain
milligram	mg	0.001	0.0154 grain

a full deep quality between that of the soprano and contralto; *also* : a singer having such a voice

mez•zo•tint \'met-sō-ˌtint, 'med-zō-\ *n* : a process of engraving on copper or steel by scraping or burnishing a roughened surface to produce light and shade; *also* : an engraving produced by this process [Italian *mezzatinta,* from *mezza* (feminine of *mezzo* "medium") + *tinta* "tint"]

mho \'mō\ *n, pl* **mhos** : the unit of conductance equal to the reciprocal of the ohm [backward spelling of *ohm*]

mi \'mē\ *n* : the 3d note of the diatonic scale [Medieval Latin]

mi•as•ma \mī-'az-mə, mē-\ *n, pl* **-mas** *or* **-ma•ta** \-mət-ə\ **1** : a vapor (as from a swamp) formerly believed to cause disease **2** : an unhealthy or harmful influence or atmosphere ⟨the *miasma* of poverty⟩ [Greek, "defilement", from *miainein* "to pollute"] — **mi•as•mal** \-məl\ *adj* — **mi•as•mat•ic** \ˌmī-əz-'mat-ik\ *or* **mi•as•mic** \mī-'az-mik, mē-\ *adj*

mi•ca \'mī-kə\ *n* : any of various silicon-containing minerals that may be separated easily into thin transparent sheets [Latin, "grain, crumb"] — **mi•ca•ceous** \mī-'kā-shəs\ *adj*

Mi•cah \'mī-kə\ *n* — *see* BIBLE table

mice *pl of* MOUSE

mi•celle \mī-'sel\ *n* **1** : an ordered region or structural unit in a fiber (as of cellulose) **2** : a molecular aggregate that constitutes a colloidal particle [New Latin *micella,* from Latin *mica* "crumb"] — **mi•cel•lar** \-'sel-ər\ *adj*

Mich•ael•mas \'mik-əl-məs\ *n* : September 29 celebrated as the feast of St. Michael the Archangel [Old English *Michaeles mæsse* "Michael's mass"]

Michaelmas daisy *n* : a wild aster; *esp* : one blooming about Michaelmas

Mi•che•as \'mī-kē-əs, mī-'\ *n* — see BIBLE table

Mick•ey Finn \ˌmik-ē-'fin\ : a drink of liquor doctored with a drug [probably from the name *Mickey Finn*]

Mickey Mouse \-'maùs\ *adj* : lacking importance : PETTY ⟨*Mickey Mouse* rules⟩ [*Mickey Mouse*, cartoon character created by Walt Disney]

The International System of Units (SI) as adopted by the General Conference of Weights and Measures

BASE UNITS

Quantity	*Name*	*Symbol*
length	metre	m
mass	kilogram	kg
time	second	S
electric current	ampere	A
thermodynamic temperature	kelvin	K
amount of substance	mole	mol
luminous intensity	candela	cd

PREFIXES

Factor	*Scientific Notation*	*Prefix*	*Symbol*
1,000,000,000,000	10^{12}	tera-	T
1,000,000,000	10^{9}	giga-	G
1,000,000	10^{6}	mega-	M
1,000	10^{3}	kilo-	k
100	10^{2}	hecto-	h
10	10^{1}	deka-	da
0.1	10^{-1}	deci-	d
0.01	10^{-2}	centi-	c
0.001	10^{-3}	milli-	m
0.000 001	10^{-6}	micro-	µ
0.000 000 001	10^{-9}	nano-	n
0.000 000 000 001	10^{-12}	pico-	p
0.000 000 000 000 001	10^{-15}	femto-	f
0.000 000 000 000 000 001	10^{-18}	atto-	a

Mic•mac \'mik-ˌmak\ *n, pl* **Micmac** *or* **Micmacs 1 :** a member of an Algonquian people of what is now eastern Canada **2 :** the language of the Micmac people [Micmac *Migmac,* literally, "allies"]

micr- *or* **micro-** *combining form* **1 a :** small : minute ⟨*micro*film⟩ **b :** used for or involving minute quantities or variations ⟨*micro*scope⟩ **2 :** millionth ⟨*micro*second⟩ **3 :** using or used in microscopy ⟨*micro*projector⟩ [Greek *mikros*]

mi•cro \'mī-krō\ *adj* : MICROSCOPIC

mi•cro•am•pere \ˌmī-krō-'am-ˌpiər\ *n* : one millionth of an ampere

mi•crobe \'mī-ˌkrōb\ *n* : MICROORGANISM, GERM [*micr-* + Greek *bios* "life"] — **mi•cro•bi•al** \mī-'krō-bē-əl\ *adj*

mi•cro•bi•ol•o•gy \ˌmī-krō-bī-'äl-ə-jē\ *n* : a branch of biology dealing especially with microscopic forms of life — **mi•cro•bi•o•log•i•cal** \-ˌbī-ə-'läj-i-kəl\ *adj* — **mi•cro•bi•o•log•i•cal•ly** \-i-kə-lē, -klē\ *adv* — **mi•cro•bi•ol•o•gist** \-bī-'äl-ə-jəst\ *n*

mi•cro•cap•sule \'mī-krō-ˌkap-səl, -sül\ *n* : a tiny capsule containing material (as a medicine) that is released when the capsule is broken, melted, or dissolved

mi•cro•cline \'mī-krō-ˌklīn\ *n* : a white to pale yellow, red, or green mineral $KAlSi_3O_8$ that is like orthoclase in composition [German *mikroklin,* from *mikr-* "micr-" + Greek *klinein* "to lean"]

mi•cro•coc•cus \ˌmī-krō-'käk-əs\ *n, pl* **-coc•ci** \-'käk-ˌsī, -ˌī\ : a small spherical bacterium

mi•cro•copy \'mī-krō-ˌkäp-ē\ *n* : a photographic copy in which graphic matter is reduced in size (as on microfilm) — **microcopy** *vb*

mi•cro•cosm \'mī-krə-ˌkäz-əm\ *n* : a little world; *esp* : an individual or a community that is a miniature universe or a world in itself [Medieval Latin *microcosmus,* from Greek *mikros kosmos*] — **mi•cro•cos•mic** \ˌmī-krə-'käz-mik\ *adj*

mi•cro•eco•nom•ics \ˌmī-krō-ˌek-ə-'näm-iks, -ˌē-kə-\ *n* : study of economics in terms of individual areas of activity (as a firm or a household)

mi•cro•el•e•ment \ˌmī-krō-'el-ə-mənt\ *n* : TRACE ELEMENT

mi•cro•en•cap•su•lat•ed \-in-'kap-sə-ˌlāt-əd\ *adj* : enclosed in a microcapsule ⟨*microencapsulated* aspirin⟩ — **mi•cro•en•cap•su•la•tion** \-in-ˌkap-sə-'lā-shən\ *n*

mi•cro•far•ad \ˌmī-krō-'far-ˌad, -'far-əd\ *n* : one millionth of a farad

mi•cro•fiche \'mī-krō-ˌfēsh, -ˌfish\ *n, pl* **-fiche** *or* **-fiches** \-ˌfēsh, -ˌfēsh-əz, -ˌfish, -ˌfish-əz\ : a sheet of microfilm containing rows of images usually of printed pages [French, from *micr-* "micr-" + *fiche* "peg, tag, slide", from *ficher* "to stick in"]

mi•cro•film \'mī-krə-ˌfilm\ *n* : a film bearing a photographic record on a greatly reduced scale of graphic matter (as printing) — **microfilm** *vb*

mi•cro•ga•mete \ˌmī-krō-gə-'mēt, -'gam-ˌēt\ *n* : the smaller and usually male gamete of an organism with two kinds of gametes — compare MACROGAMETE

mi•cro•gram \'mī-krə-ˌgram\ *n* : one millionth of a gram

mi•cro•graph \-ˌgraf\ *n* : a reproduction of the image of an object formed by a microscope

mi•cro•groove \'mī-krō-'grüv\ *n* : a minute closely spaced V-shaped groove used on long-playing phonograph records

¹mi•crom•e•ter \mī-'kräm-ət-ər\ *n* **1 :** an instrument used with a telescope or microscope for measuring very small distances **2 :** MICROMETER CALIPER — **mi•crom•e•try** \-ə-trē\ *n*

²mi•cro•me•ter \'mī-krō-ˌmēt-ər\ *n* : a unit of length equal to one millionth of a meter

mi•crom•e•ter cal•iper \mī-ˌkräm-ət-ər-\ *n* : a caliper having a spindle moved by a finely threaded screw for making precise measurements

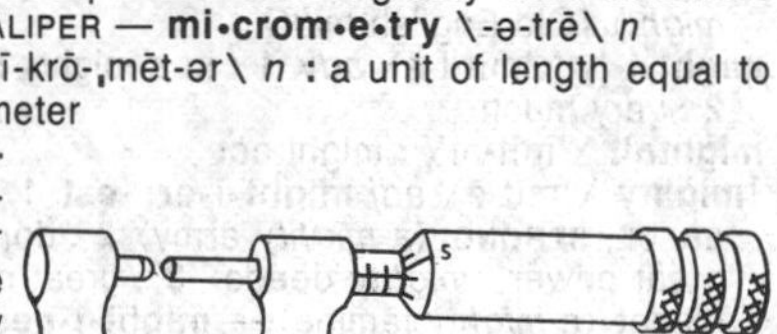
micrometer caliper

mi•cro•mi•cron \ˌmī-krō-'mī-ˌkrän\ *n* : one millionth of a micrometer

mi•cron \'mī-ˌkrän\ *n* : ²MICROMETER [Greek *mikron,* neuter of *mikros* "small"]

Mi•cro•ne•sian \ˌmī-krə-'nē-zhən, -shən\ *n* **1 :** a native or inhabitant of Micronesia **2 :** a group of Austronesian languages spoken in the Micronesian islands — **Micronesian** *adj*

mi•cro•nu•cle•us \ˌmī-krō-'nü-klē-əs, -'nyü-\ *n* : a minute nucleus held to be primarily concerned with reproductive and genetic functions in most ciliated protozoans

mi•cro•nu•tri•ent \-'nü-trē-ənt, -'nyü-\ *n* **1 :** TRACE ELEMENT **2 :** an organic compound (as a vitamin) essential in minute amounts to the growth and welfare of an animal

mi•cro•or•gan•ism \-'ȯr-gə-ˌniz-əm\ *n* : an organism (as a bacterium) of microscopic or less than microscopic size

mi•cro•phone \'mī-krə-ˌfōn\ *n* : an instrument used to amplify, record, or transmit sounds; *esp* : one used in radio and television to receive sound and convert it into electrical waves

mi•cro•pho•to•graph \ˌmī-krə-'fōt-ə-ˌgraf\ *n* **1 :** a small photograph that is normally magnified for viewing **2 :** PHOTOMICROGRAPH

mi•cro•print \'mī-krə-ˌprint\ *n* : a photographic copy of printed or drawn matter in reduced size — **microprint** *vb*

mi•cro•pro•jec•tor \ˌmī-krō-prə-'jek-tər\ *n* : a projector using a compound microscope to throw a greatly enlarged image of a microscopic object on a screen

mi•cro•pyle \'mī-krə-ˌpīl\ *n* : a tiny opening in an ovule of a seed plant through which the pollen tube penetrates to the embryo sac [*micr-* + Greek *pylē* "gate"] — **mi•cro•py•lar** \ˌmī-krə-'pī-lər\ *adj*

mi•cro•scope \'mī-krə-ˌskōp\ *n* **1 :** an optical instrument consisting of a lens or a combination of lenses for making enlarged images of minute objects — called also *light microscope* **2 :** an instrument using radiations other than light for making enlarged images of minute objects

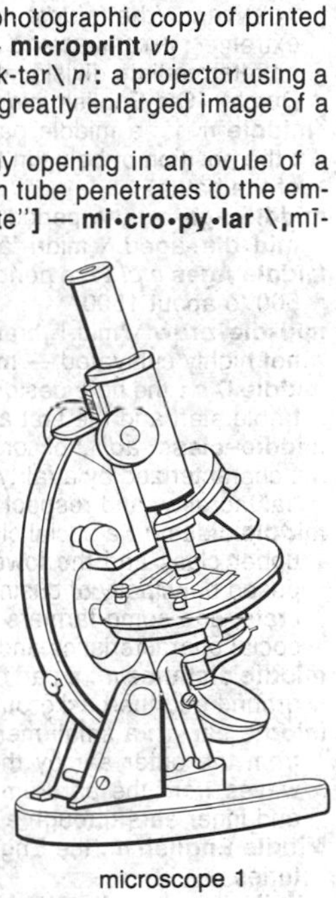
microscope 1

mi•cro•scop•ic \ˌmī-krə-'skäp-ik\ *or* **mi•cro•scop•i•cal** \-i-kəl\ *adj* **1 :** of, relating to, or conducted with the microscope or microscopy ⟨a *microscopic* examination⟩ **2 :** resembling a microscope especially in being able to see very tiny objects ⟨some insects have *microscopic* vision⟩ **3 :** able to be seen only through a microscope : very small ⟨a *microscopic* plant⟩ — **mi•cro•scop•i•cal•ly** \-'skäp-i-kə-lē, -klē\ *adv*

mi•cros•co•py \mī-'kräs-kə-pē\ *n* : the use of the microscope : investigation with the microscope — **mi•cros•co•pist** \-pəst\ *n*

mi•cro•sec•ond \ˌmī-krō-'sek-ənd, -ənt\ *n* : one millionth of a second

mi•cro•some \'mī-krə-ˌsōm\ *n* : a cellular particle that is obtained by centrifuging broken cells and that consists of various amounts of ribosomes, fragmented endoplasmic reticulum, and parts of mitochondria — **mi•cro•som•al** \ˌmī-krə-'sō-məl\ *adj*

mi•cro•sphere \'mī-krə-ˌsfiər\ *n* : a minute sphere ⟨a glass *microsphere* 30 micrometers in diameter⟩

mi•cro•spore \-ˌspōr, -ˌspȯr\ *n* : a plant spore that produces a male gametophyte

mi•cro•struc•ture \'mī-krō-ˌstrək-chər\ *n* : the microscopic structure of a material

mi•cro•sur•gery \ˌmī-krō-'sərj-rē, -ə-rē\ *n* : minute dissection or manipulation of living structures (as cells) for surgical or experimental purposes

mi•cro•tome \'mī-krə-ˌtōm\ *n* : an instrument for cutting sections (as of plant or animal tissues) for microscopic examination [*micr-* + Greek *tomos* "section", from *temnein* "to cut"]

mi•cro•wave \-ˌwāv\ *n* : a radio wave between 1 and 100 centimeters in wavelength

microwave oven *n* : an oven in which food is cooked by the heat produced as a result of penetration of the food by microwaves

mic•tu•rate \'mik-chə-,rāt, 'mik-tə-\ *vi* : URINATE [Latin *micturire*] — **mic•tu•ri•tion** \,mik-chə-'rish-ən, ,mik-tə-\ *n*
[1]**mid** \'mid\ *adj* **1** : being the part in the middle or midst ⟨in *mid* ocean⟩ ⟨*mid*-August⟩ **2** : occupying a middle position ⟨the *mid* finger⟩ **3** : uttered with the tongue midway between its highest and its lowest elevation ⟨the *mid* vowel \e\ in *pet*⟩ [Old English *midde*]
[2]**mid** \mid, ,mid\ *prep* : AMID
mid•brain \'mid-,brān\ *n* : the middle division of the embryonic vertebrate brain containing especially the optic lobes; *also* : the parts developed from it
mid•day \'mid-,dā, -'dā\ *n* : the middle part of the day : NOON — **midday** *adj*
mid•den \'mid-n\ *n* : a refuse heap; *esp* : KITCHEN MIDDEN [of Scandinavian origin]
[1]**mid•dle** \'mid-l\ *adj* **1** : equally distant from the extremes : CENTRAL ⟨the *middle* house in the row⟩ **2** : being at neither extreme : INTERMEDIATE ⟨of *middle* size⟩ **3** *cap* : constituting an intermediate division or period ⟨*Middle* Paleozoic⟩ ⟨*Middle* Dutch⟩ [Old English *middel*]
[2]**middle** *n* **1** : a middle part, point, or position **2** : WAIST 1a **3** : the position of being in the midst of something ⟨in the *middle* of the battle⟩
middle age *n* : the period of life from about 40 to about 60 — **mid•dle-aged** \,mid-l-'ājd\ *adj*
Middle Ages *n pl* : the period of European history from about A.D. 500 to about 1500
mid•dle•brow \'mid-l-,brau̇\ *n* : a person who is moderately but not highly cultivated — **middlebrow** *adj*
middle C *n* : the note designated by the first ledger line below the treble staff and the first above the bass staff
middle-class *adj* : of or relating to the middle class; *esp* : characterized by a fairly high material standard of living, sexual morality, and respect for property
middle class *n* : a social class occupying a position between the upper class and the lower class; *esp* : a fluid grouping composed principally of business and professional people, bureaucrats, and some farmers and skilled workers sharing common social characteristics and values
middle distance *n* : a part of a picture or scene between the foreground and the background
middle ear *n* : a small membrane-lined cavity that is separated from the outer ear by the eardrum and that transmits sound waves from the eardrum to the partition between the middle and inner ears through a chain of tiny bones
Middle English *n* : the English language of the 12th to 15th centuries
middle finger *n* : the third digit of the hand
Middle French *n* : the French language of the 14th to 16th centuries
Middle Greek *n* : the Greek language used in the 7th to 15th centuries
Middle High German *n* : the High German in use from about 1100 to 1500
middle lamella *n* : a layer of sticky material between adjacent plant cells that helps to hold them together
mid•dle•man \'mid-l-,man\ *n* : an agent between two parties; *esp* : a dealer or agent intermediate between the producer of goods and the retailer or the consumer
mid•dle-of-the-road \,mid-l-əv-t͟hə-'rōd, -ə-t͟hə-\ *adj* : standing for or following a course of action midway between extremes; *esp* : being neither liberal nor conservative in politics — **mid•dle-of-the-road•er** \-'rōd-ər\ *n*
middle school *n* : a school usually including grades 5–8 or 6–8
mid•dle•weight \'mid-l-,wāt\ *n* : one of average weight; *esp* : a boxer in a weight division having the approximate range of 67 to 75 kilograms
[1]**mid•dling** \'mid-ling, -lən\ *adj* **1** : of middle, medium, or moderate size, degree, or quality **2** : MEDIOCRE — **middling** *adv*
[2]**middling** *n* **1** : any of various commodities of medium quality or size **2** *pl* : a granular product of grain milling; *esp* : a wheat milling by-product used in animal feeds
mid•dy \'mid-ē\ *n, pl* **mid•dies** **1** : MIDSHIPMAN **2** : a loosely fitting blouse especially for children with a collar that is wide and square at the back
midge \'mij\ *n* : a very small fly : GNAT [Old English *mycg*]
midg•et \'mij-ət\ *n* : one that is much smaller than the usual or typical [*midge*] — **midget** *adj*
mid•gut \'mid-,gət\ *n* : the middle part of an alimentary canal
mid•land \'mid-lənd, -,land\ *n* **1** : the interior or central region of a country **2** *cap* : the dialect of English spoken in parts of New Jersey and Delaware, northern Maryland, central and southern Pennsylvania, Ohio, Indiana, Illinois, the Appalachian Mountain area, West Virginia, Kentucky, and most of Tennessee — **midland** *adj, often cap*
mid•line \-,līn\ *n* : a median line or plane
mid•most \'mid-,mōst\ *adj or adv* : in the exact middle — **midmost** *n*
mid•night \-,nīt\ *n* : the middle of the night; *esp* : 12 o'clock at night — **midnight** *adj* — **mid•night•ly** \-lē\ *adv or adj*
midnight sun *n* : the sun above the horizon at midnight in the arctic or antarctic summer
mid•point \'mid-,pȯint\ *n* : a point at or near the center or middle
mid•rib \-,rib\ *n* : the central vein of a leaf
mid•riff \-,rif\ *n* **1** : DIAPHRAGM 1 **2** : the middle region of the human torso [Old English *midhrif*, from *midde* "mid" + *hrif* "belly"]
mid•ship•man \'mid-,ship-mən, mid-'ship-\ *n* : one in training for a naval commission : a student naval officer
mid•ships \'mid-,ships\ *adv* : AMIDSHIPS
[1]**midst** \'midst\ *n* **1** : the interior or central part or point : MIDDLE ⟨in the *midst* of the forest⟩ **2** : a position among the members of a group ⟨a visitor in our *midst*⟩ **3** : the condition of being surrounded or beset ⟨in the *midst* of troubles⟩ [Middle English *middest*, alteration of *middes*, from *amiddes* "amid"]
[2]**midst** \midst, ,midst\ *prep* : AMID
mid•stream \'mid-'strēm\ *n* : the middle of a stream
mid•sum•mer \'mid-'səm-ər\ *n* **1** : the middle of summer **2** : the summer solstice
[1]**mid•way** \'mid-,wā, -'wā\ *adv or adj* : in the middle of the way or distance : HALFWAY
[2]**mid•way** \-,wā\ *n* : an avenue at a fair, carnival, or amusement park for concessions and light amusements [*Midway (Plaisance)*, Chicago, site of the amusement section of the Columbian Exposition of 1893]
mid•week \'mid-,wēk\ *n* : the middle of the week — **midweek** *adj* — **mid•week•ly** \-lē\ *adj or adv*
mid•wife \'mid-,wīf\ *n* : a woman who helps other women in childbirth [Middle English *midwif*, from *mid* "with" (from Old English) + *wif* "woman, wife"] — **mid•wife•ry** \mid-'wif-rē, -ə-rē; 'mid-,wīf-\ *n*
mid•win•ter \'mid-'wint-ər\ *n* **1** : the middle of winter **2** : the winter solstice
mid•year \-,yiər\ *n* **1** : the middle of an academic or a calendar year **2** : a midyear examination — **midyear** *adj*
mien \'mēn\ *n* : look, appearance, or bearing especially as showing mood or personality ⟨a kindly *mien*⟩ [derived from [1]*demean*]
[1]**miff** \'mif\ *n* **1** : a fit of ill humor **2** : a trivial quarrel [origin unknown]
[2]**miff** *vt* : to put into an ill humor : OFFEND ⟨was *miffed* by their behavior⟩
[1]**might** \mīt, 'mīt\ *past of* MAY — used as an auxiliary verb to express permission ⟨asked if they *might* leave⟩, probability ⟨I *might* go, if urged⟩, possibility in the past ⟨thought you *might* try⟩, or a present condition contrary to fact ⟨if you were older, you *might* understand⟩ [Old English *meahte, mihte*]
[2]**might** \'mīt\ *n* : power to do something : FORCE ⟨the nation's *might*⟩ [Old English *miht*]
might•i•ly \'mīt-l-ē\ *adv* **1** : in a mighty manner : VIGOROUSLY **2** : very much
mightn't \'mīt-nt\ : might not
[1]**mighty** \'mīt-ē\ *adj* **might•i•er**; **-est** **1** : having might : POWERFUL, STRONG ⟨a *mighty* army⟩ **2** : done by might : showing great power ⟨*mighty* deeds⟩ **3** : great or imposing in size or extent ⟨a *mighty* famine⟩ — **might•i•ness** *n*
[2]**mighty** *adv* : VERY, EXTREMELY ⟨a *mighty* strong smell⟩
mi•gnon•ette \,min-yə-'net\ *n* : a garden plant with long spikes of small fragrant greenish white flowers [French]
mi•graine \'mī-,grān\ *n* : a condition marked by recurrent severe headache often with nausea and vomiting [French, from Late Latin *hemicrania* "pain on one side of the head", from Greek *hēmikrania*, from *hēmi-* "hemi-" + *kranion* "cranium"] — **mi•grain•ous** \-,grā-nəs\ *adj*
mi•grant \'mī-grənt\ *n* : a person, animal, or plant that migrates — **migrant** *adj*
mi•grate \'mī-,grāt\ *vi* **1** : to move from one country, place, or

locality to another **2 :** to pass usually periodically from one region or climate to another for feeding or breeding **3 :** to change position in an organism or substance [Latin *migrare*] — **mi·gra·tion** \mī-ˈgrā-shən\ *n* — **mi·gra·tion·al** \-shnəl, -shən-l\ *adj*

mi·gra·to·ry \ˈmī-grə-ˌtōr-ē, -ˌtȯr-\ *adj* **:** of, relating to, or characterized by migration ⟨*migratory* birds⟩

mi·ka·do \mə-ˈkäd-ō\ *n, pl* **-dos :** an emperor of Japan [Japanese]

mike \ˈmīk\ *n* **:** MICROPHONE [by shortening and alteration]

mil \ˈmil\ *n* **:** a unit of length equal to 1/1000 inch (about .025 millimeter) used especially for the diameter of wire [Latin *mille* "thousand"]

mi·lady \mil-ˈād-ē, *in the United States also* mī-ˈlād-\ *n* **1 :** an Englishwoman of noble or gentle birth **2 :** a woman of fashion [French, from English *my lady*]

milch \ˈmilk, ˈmilch, ˈmilks\ *adj* **:** giving milk **:** kept for milk production ⟨a *milch* cow⟩ [Old English *-milce*]

mild \ˈmīld\ *adj* **1 :** gentle in nature or behavior **2 :** moderate in action or effect **:** not strong ⟨a *mild* drug⟩ **3 :** TEMPERATE ⟨*mild* weather⟩ [Old English *milde*] — **mild·ly** \ˈmīld-lē, ˈmīl-\ *adv* — **mild·ness** \ˈmīld-nəs, ˈmīl-\ *n*

[1]**mil·dew** \ˈmil-ˌdü, -ˌdyü\ *n* **:** a superficial usually whitish growth produced on organic matter or living plants by fungi; *also* **:** a fungus producing mildew [Old English *meledēaw* "honeydew"] — **mil·dewy** \-ē\ *adj*

[2]**mildew** *vb* **:** to affect with or become affected with mildew

mile \ˈmīl\ *n* **1 :** a unit of measure equal to 5280 feet (about 1609 meters) — called also *statute mile;* see MEASURE table **2 :** NAUTICAL MILE [Old English *mīl,* from Latin *milia* "miles", from *milia passuum,* literally, "thousands of paces"]

mile·age \ˈmī-lij\ *n* **1 :** an allowance for traveling expenses at a set rate per mile **2 :** distance or length in miles **3 a :** the number of miles that something (as a car or tire) will travel before wearing out **b :** the average number of miles a car will travel on a gallon of gas **4 :** USEFULNESS, PROFIT ⟨gets a lot of *mileage* out of that old joke⟩

mile·post \ˈmīl-ˌpōst\ *n* **:** a post indicating the distance in miles from or to a stated place

mil·er \ˈmī-lər\ *n* **:** a person or a horse that competes in mile races

mile·stone \ˈmīl-ˌstōn\ *n* **1 :** a stone serving as a milepost **2 :** an important point in progress or development

mil·foil \ˈmil-ˌfȯil\ *n* **:** YARROW [Old French, from Latin *millefolium,* from *mille* "thousand" + *folium* "leaf"]

mi·lieu \mēl-ˈyər, ˈmēl-ˌyü; mē-lyœ\ *n, pl* **milieus** *or* **mi·lieux** *same or* -ˈyərz, -ˌyüz, -lyœz\ **:** ENVIRONMENT 1 [French]

mil·i·tant \ˈmil-ə-tənt\ *adj* **1 :** engaged in warfare **2 :** aggressively active especially in a cause ⟨a *militant* conservationist⟩ — **mil·i·tan·cy** \-tən-sē\ *n* — **militant** *n* — **mil·i·tant·ly** *adv* — **mil·i·tant·ness** *n*

mil·i·ta·rism \ˈmil-ə-tə-ˌriz-əm\ *n* **1 a :** control or domination by a military class **b :** glorification of military virtues and ideals **2 :** a policy of aggressive military preparedness — **mil·i·ta·rist** \-rəst\ *n* — **mil·i·ta·ris·tic** \ˌmil-ə-tə-ˈris-tik\ *adj* — **mil·i·ta·ris·ti·cal·ly** \-ˈris-ti-kə-lē, -klē\ *adv*

mil·i·ta·rize \ˈmil-ə-tə-ˌrīz\ *vt* **1 :** to equip with military forces and defenses **2 :** to give a military character to — **mil·i·ta·ri·za·tion** \ˌmil-ə-tə-rə-ˈzā-shən, -trə-ˈzā-\ *n*

[1]**mil·i·tary** \ˈmil-ə-ˌter-ē\ *adj* **1 :** of, relating to, or characteristic of soldiers, arms, or war ⟨*military* drill⟩ **2 :** carried on or supported by armed force ⟨*military* dictatorship⟩ **3 :** of or relating to the army ⟨*military* and naval affairs⟩ [Middle French *militaire,* from Latin *militaris,* from *milit-, miles* "soldier"] **syn** see MARTIAL — **mil·i·tar·i·ly** \ˌmil-ə-ˈter-ə-lē\ *adv*

[2]**military** *n, pl* **military 1 :** ARMED FORCES **2 :** military persons; *esp* **:** army officers

military police *n* **:** a branch of an army that performs guard and police functions

mil·i·tate \ˈmil-ə-ˌtāt\ *vi* **:** to have an influence or effect ⟨factors *militating* against the success of an enterprise⟩ [Latin *militare* "to engage in warfare", from *milit-, miles* "soldier"]

mi·li·tia \mə-ˈlish-ə\ *n* **:** a body of citizens with military training who are called to active duty only in an emergency [Latin, "military service", from *milit-, miles* "soldier"] — **mi·li·tia·man** \-mən\ *n*

[1]**milk** \ˈmilk\ *n* **1 :** a fluid secreted by the mammary glands of females for the nourishment of their young **2 :** a liquid (as a plant juice) resembling milk [Old English *meolc, milc*]

[2]**milk** *vb* **1 :** to draw milk from the breasts or udder of **2 :** to draw or yield milk **3 :** to draw something from as if by milking; *esp* **:** to draw unreasonable or excessive profit or advantage from ⟨*milk* a business⟩ — **milk·er** *n*

milk–liv·ered \ˈmil-ˈkliv-ərd\ *adj, archaic* **:** COWARDLY 1

milk·maid \ˈmilk-ˌmād\ *n* **:** DAIRYMAID

milk·man \-ˌman, -mən\ *n* **:** a person who sells or delivers milk

milk of magnesia : a milk-white liquid preparation of magnesium in water used as a laxative and as a medicine to counteract acidity

milk shake *n* **:** a drink made of milk, a flavoring syrup, and often ice cream shaken or mixed thoroughly

milk snake *n* **:** a common harmless gray or tan snake with black-bordered blotches and an arrow-shaped spot on the head

milk·sop \ˈmilk-ˌsäp\ *n* **:** a timid unmanly man or boy

milk sugar *n* **:** LACTOSE

milk tooth *n* **:** one of the first temporary teeth of a young mammal that in human beings number 20

milk·weed \ˈmil-ˌkwēd\ *n* **:** any of a group of herbs and shrubs with milky juice and flowers usually in dense clusters

milkweed

milky \ˈmil-kē\ *adj* **milk·i·er; -est 1 :** resembling milk in color or consistency **2 :** TAME 3, TIMID **3 :** consisting of, containing, or full of milk — **milk·i·ness** *n*

milky disease *n* **:** a destructive bacterial disease of some beetle larvae used especially in the control of Japanese beetles

Milky Way *n* **1 :** a broad luminous irregular band of light that stretches across the sky and is caused by the light of a vast multitude of faint stars **2 :** MILKY WAY GALAXY **3 :** GALAXY 1b

Milky Way galaxy *n* **:** the galaxy of which the sun and the solar system are a part and which contains the myriads of stars that comprise the Milky Way

[1]**mill** \ˈmil\ *n* **1 :** a building with machinery for grinding grain into flour **2 :** a machine used in treating (as by grinding, crushing, stamping, cutting, or finishing) raw material **3 :** a building or group of buildings with machinery for manufacturing [Old English *mylen,* from Late Latin *molina,* from Latin *mola* "millstone, mill"] — **through the mill :** through a difficult experience

[2]**mill** *vb* **1 :** to subject to an operation or process in a mill: as **a :** to grind into flour, meal, or powder **b :** to shape or dress by means of a rotary cutter **c :** to mix and condition (as rubber) by passing between rotating rolls **2 :** to give a raised rim or a corrugated edge to (a coin) **3 :** to hit out hard with the fists **4 :** to move about in a disorderly mass ⟨rioters *milling* in the streets⟩ **5 :** to undergo milling

[3]**mill** *n* **:** one tenth of a cent [Latin *mille* "thousand"]

mill·dam \ˈmil-ˌdam\ *n* **:** a dam to make a millpond; *also* **:** MILLPOND

mil·le·nar·i·an \ˌmil-ə-ˈner-ē-ən\ *adj* **1 :** of or relating to 1000 years **2 :** of or relating to belief in the millennium — **millenarian** *n* — **mil·le·nar·i·an·ism** \-ē-ə-ˌniz-əm\ *n*

mil·le·nary \ˈmil-ə-ˌner-ē, mə-ˈlen-ə-rē\ *n, pl* **-nar·ies 1 :** a thousand units or things **2 :** 1000 years **:** MILLENNIUM [Late Latin *millenarium,* derived from Latin *mille* "thousand"] — **millenary** *adj*

mil·len·ni·um \mə-ˈlen-ē-əm\ *n, pl* **-nia** \-ē-ə\ *or* **-ni·ums 1 a :** a period of 1000 years **b :** a 1000th anniversary or its celebration **2 a :** the thousand years mentioned in Revelation 20 during which holiness is to prevail and Christ is to reign on earth **b :** a period of great happiness or of perfection in human existence [Latin *mille* "thousand" + *-ennium* (as in *biennium*)] — **mil·len·ni·al** \-ē-əl\ *adj*

\ə\ **abut**	\au̇\ **out**	\i\ **tip**	\ȯ\ **saw**	\u̇\ **foot**
\ər\ **further**	\ch\ **chin**	\ī\ **life**	\ȯi\ **coin**	\y\ **yet**
\a\ **mat**	\e\ **pet**	\j\ **job**	\th\ **thin**	\yü\ **few**
\ā\ **take**	\ē\ **easy**	\ng\ **sing**	\th\ **this**	\yu̇\ **cure**
\ä\ **cot, cart**	\g\ **go**	\ō\ **bone**	\ü\ **food**	\zh\ **vision**

mill•er \'mil-ər\ *n* **1** : one that operates a mill; *esp* : one that grinds grain into flour **2** : a moth whose wings are covered with powdery dust

mil•let \'mil-ət\ *n* **1** : any of several small-seeded annual cereal and forage grasses; *esp* : one with small shiny whitish seeds **2** : the seed of a millet [Middle French *milet,* from *mil* "millet", from Latin *milium*]

milli- *combining form* : thousandth ⟨*milli*ampere⟩ [Latin *mille* "thousand"]

mil•li•am•pere \ˌmil-ē-'am-ˌpiər\ *n* : one thousandth of an ampere

mil•liard \'mil-ˌyärd, 'mil-ē-ˌärd\ *n, British* : a thousand millions — see NUMBER table [French, derived from Latin *mille* "thousand"]

mil•li•bar \'mil-ə-ˌbär\ *n* : a unit used in measuring atmospheric pressure equal to a force of 1000 dynes per square centimeter [*bar,* unit of pressure equal to one million dynes per square centimeter, derived from Greek *baros* "weight"]

mil•li•gram \'mil-ə-ˌgram\ *n* — see METRIC SYSTEM table

mil•li•li•ter \'mil-ə-ˌlēt-ər\ *n* — see METRIC SYSTEM table

mil•li•me•ter \'mil-ə-ˌmēt-ər\ *n* — see METRIC SYSTEM table

mil•li•mi•cron \ˌmil-ə-'mī-ˌkrän\ *n* : a unit of length equal to 1/1000 micrometer

mil•li•ner \'mil-ə-nər\ *n* : a person who makes or sells women's hats [derived from *Milan,* Italy; from the importation of women's finery into England from Italy in the 16th century]

mil•li•nery \'mil-ə-ˌner-ē\ *n* **1** : women's hats **2** : the business or work of a milliner

mill•ing \'mil-ing\ *n* : a corrugated edge on a coin

milling machine *n* : a machine tool on which work usually of metal is secured to a carriage and shaped by being fed against rotating cutters

mil•lion \'mil-yən, 'mi-yən\ *n, pl* **millions** *or* **million** **1** : one thousand times one thousand; *also* : a symbol representing this — see NUMBER table **2** : a very large or indefinitely great number ⟨*millions* of mosquitoes⟩ [Middle French *milion,* from Italian *milione,* from *mille* "thousand", from Latin] — **million** *adj* — **mil•lionth** \-yənth, -yəntth\ *adj or n*

mil•lion•aire \ˌmil-yə-'naər, -'neər, 'mil-yə-ˌ, ˌmi-yə-', 'mi-yə-ˌ\ *n* : one whose wealth is estimated at a million or more (as of dollars) [French *millionnaire,* from *million* "million", from Middle French *milion*]

mil•li•pede *or* **mil•le•pede** \'mil-ə-ˌpēd\ *n* : any of a class (Diplopoda) of arthropods having a long segmented body with a hard covering, two pairs of legs on most apparent segments, and no poison fangs — compare CENTIPEDE [Latin *millipeda,* a small crawling animal, from *mille* "thousand" + *ped-, pes* "foot"]

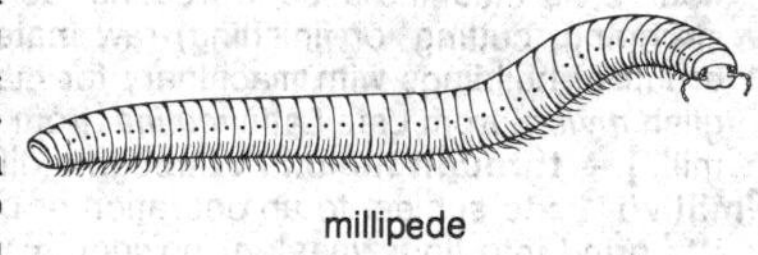
millipede

mil•li•sec•ond \'mil-ə-ˌsek-ənd\ *n* : one thousandth of a second

mil•li•volt \-ˌvōlt\ *n* : one thousandth of a volt

mill•pond \'mil-ˌpänd\ *n* : a pond produced by damming a stream to produce a head of water for operating a mill

mill•race \-ˌrās\ *n* : a canal in which water flows to and from a mill wheel; *also* : the current that drives the wheel

mill•stone \-ˌstōn\ *n* **1** : either of two circular stones used for grinding a substance (as grain) **2 a** : something that grinds or crushes **b** : a heavy burden

mill•stream \-ˌstrēm\ *n* **1** : a stream whose flow is utilized to run a mill **2** : the stream in a millrace

mill wheel *n* : a waterwheel that drives a mill

mill•wright \'mil-ˌrīt\ *n* : one whose occupation is planning and building mills or setting up their machinery

mi•lo \'mī-lō\ *n* : a small usually early and drought-resistant grain sorghum [of Bantu origin]

mi•lord \mil-'ȯr, -'ȯrd\ *n* : an Englishman of noble or gentle birth [French, from English *my lord*]

milt \'milt\ *n* : the sperm-containing fluid of fishes [probably from Dutch *milte*]

Mil•ton•ic \mil-'tän-ik\ *or* **Mil•to•ni•an** \mil-'tō-nē-ən\ *adj* : of, relating to, or characteristic of John Milton or his work

¹mime \'mīm, 'mēm\ *n* **1 a** : an actor of mime **b** : MIMIC 2 **2** : an ancient play or skit representing scenes from life usually in a ridiculous manner **3** : the art of portraying a character or of narration by body movement : PANTOMIME [Latin *mimus,* from Greek *mimos*]

²mime *vb* **1** : to act as a mime : play a part with gesture and action usually without words **2** : to imitate closely : MIMIC **3** : to act out in the manner of a mime

mim•eo•graph \'mim-ē-ə-ˌgraf\ *n* : a machine for making copies of typewritten or written matter by means of a stencil [from *Mimeograph,* a former trademark] — **mimeograph** *vb*

mi•me•sis \mə-'mē-səs, mī-\ *n* : IMITATION 1, MIMICRY [Late Latin, from Greek *mimēsis,* from *mimeisthai* "to imitate"]

mi•met•ic \-'met-ik\ *adj* **1** : IMITATIVE 2 **2** : relating to, characterized by, or exhibiting mimicry ⟨*mimetic* coloring of a butterfly⟩ [Late Latin *mimeticus,* from Greek *mimētikos,* from *mimeisthai* "to imitate"] — **mi•met•i•cal•ly** \-'met-i-kə-lē, -klē\ *adv*

¹mim•ic \'mim-ik\ *n* **1** : MIME 1a **2** : one that mimics

²mimic *adj* **1 a** : IMITATIVE 2 **b** : IMITATION, MOCK ⟨*mimic* battle⟩ **2** : of or relating to mime or mimicry [Latin *mimicus,* from Greek *mimikos,* from *mimos* "mime"]

³mimic *vt* **mim•icked** \'mim-ikt\; **mim•ick•ing** **1** : to imitate closely : APE **2** : to ridicule by imitation **3** : SIMULATE **4** : to resemble by biological mimicry **syn** see IMITATE

mim•ic•ry \'mim-i-krē\ *n, pl* **-ries** **1** : the action, art, or an instance of mimicking **2** : a superficial resemblance of one organism to another or to natural objects among which it lives that secures it a selective advantage (as protection from predators)

mi•mo•sa \mə-'mō-sə, mī-, -zə\ *n* : any of a genus of trees, shrubs, and herbs of the pea family that produce small white or pink flowers in ball-shaped heads [derived from Latin *mimus* "mime"]

mi•na \'mī-nə\ *n* : an ancient unit of weight and value equal to 1/60 talent (varying around 400 and 800 grams) [Latin, from Greek *mna,* of Semitic origin]

min•a•ret \ˌmin-ə-'ret, 'min-ə-ˌ\ *n* : a tall slender tower of a mosque from a balcony of which the people are called to prayer [French, from Turkish *minare,* from Arabic *manārah* "lighthouse"]

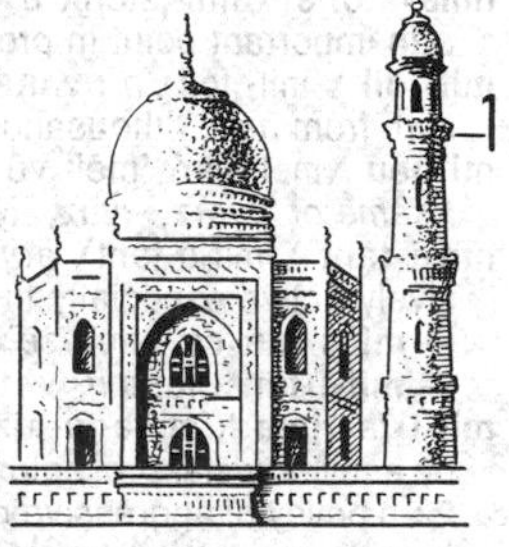
1 minaret

mi•na•to•ry \'min-ə-ˌtōr-ē, 'mī-nə-, -ˌtȯr-\ *adj* : having a menacing quality : THREATENING [Late Latin *minatorius,* from Latin *minari* "to threaten"]

¹mince \'mins\ *vb* **1** : to cut into very small pieces **2** : to utter with affectation **3** : to avoid being plainspoken in the use of (words) ⟨don't *mince* words with me⟩ **4** : to walk with short steps in a prim affected manner [Middle French *mincer,* from Latin *minutia* "smallness", from *minutus* "minute"] — **minc•er** *n*

²mince *n* : small bits into which something is chopped; *esp* : MINCEMEAT

mince•meat \'min-ˌsmēt\ *n* **1** : minced meat **2** : a finely chopped mixture of ingredients (as raisins, apples, or spices) with or without meat

mince pie *n* : a pie made of mincemeat

minc•ing \'min-sing\ *adj* : affectedly dainty or delicate — **minc•ing•ly** \-sing-lē\ *adv*

¹mind \'mīnd\ *n* **1** : MEMORY, RECOLLECTION ⟨keep it in *mind*⟩ **2 a** : the element or complex of elements in an individual that feels, perceives, thinks, wills, and especially reasons **b** : mental ability ⟨has the *mind* of a 5-year-old⟩ **3 a** : INTENTION, DESIRE ⟨that is not what I had in *mind*⟩ ⟨make up your *mind*⟩ **b** : OPINION, VIEW ⟨speak your *mind*⟩ **c** : CHOICE, LIKING ⟨to my *mind* it is satisfactory⟩ **d** : ATTENTION ⟨keep your *mind* on your work⟩ **4** : the normal or healthy condition of the mental faculties ⟨lose one's *mind*⟩ **5** : way of thinking or feeling : MOOD, DISPOSITION ⟨keep an open *mind* on the issue⟩ **6** : a person embodying mental qualities especially of a specified kind ⟨one of the greatest *minds* of the century⟩ **7** : IMAGINATION ⟨it's all in your *mind*⟩ **8** *dialect* : ATTENTION, HEED ⟨don't pay them any *mind*⟩ [Old English *gemynd*]

[2]**mind** *vb* **1** *chiefly dialect* : REMIND **2** *chiefly dialect* : REMEMBER 1 **3** : to attend to ⟨*mind* your own business⟩ **4** : to take notice of **5** : to give heed to ⟨*mind* your manners⟩; *also* : OBEY ⟨*mind* your parents⟩ **6 a** : to be concerned or troubled over ⟨never *mind* your mistake⟩ **b** : to have an objection : object to ⟨I don't *mind* if you go⟩ ⟨doesn't *mind* the cold⟩ **7 a** : to be careful : make sure ⟨*mind* you finish it⟩ **b** : to be cautious of : watch out for ⟨*mind* the broken glass⟩ **8** : to have charge of : TEND ⟨*mind* the store⟩

mind•ed \ˈmīn-dəd\ *adj* **1** : having a specified kind of mind — usually used in combination ⟨narrow-*minded*⟩ **2** : INCLINED 1, DISPOSED ⟨was *minded* to help⟩

mind–ex•pand•ing \ˈmīn-dik-ˌspan-diŋ\ *adj* : PSYCHEDELIC 1a

mind•ful \ˈmīnd-fəl, ˈmīn-\ *adj* : bearing in mind : AWARE ⟨*mindful* of the needs of others⟩ — **mind•ful•ly** \-fə-lē\ *adv* — **mind•ful•ness** *n*

mind•less \ˈmīn-dləs, -ləs\ *adj* **1** : lacking mind or consciousness; *esp* : UNINTELLIGENT **2** : HEEDLESS ⟨*mindless* of danger⟩ — **mind•less•ly** *adv* — **mind•less•ness** *n*

mind reader *n* : one who professes or is held to be able to perceive another's thought by telepathy — **mind reading** *n*

mind's eye *n* : the mental faculty of creating images or of recalling scenes previously seen

[1]**mine** \mīn, ˈmīn\ *adj, archaic* : MY — used before a word beginning with a vowel or *h* ⟨*mine* eyes⟩ ⟨*mine* host⟩ or sometimes as a modifier of a preceding noun ⟨mother *mine*⟩ [Old English *mīn*]

[2]**mine** \ˈmīn\ *pron, sing or pl in construction* : that which belongs to me : those which belong to me — used without a following noun as an equivalent in meaning to the adjective *my*

[3]**mine** \ˈmīn\ *n* **1** : a pit or tunnel from which mineral substances (as coal or gold) are taken **2** : a deposit of ore **3** : a subterranean passage under an enemy position **4 a** : a charge buried in the ground and set to explode when disturbed (as by an enemy) **b** : an explosive device placed underwater to sink enemy ships **5** : a rich source of supply ⟨a *mine* of information⟩ [Middle French]

[4]**mine** \ˈmīn\ *vb* **1** : to dig a mine **2** : to obtain from a mine ⟨*mine* coal⟩ **3** : to work in a mine **4 a** : to burrow in the earth : dig or form mines under a place **b** : to lay military mines in or under ⟨*mine* a harbor⟩

mine•lay•er \ˈmīn-ˌlā-ər\ *n* : a naval vessel for placing underwater mines

min•er \ˈmī-nər\ *n* : one that mines; *esp* : a person who works in a mine

[1]**min•er•al** \ˈmin-rəl, -ə-rəl\ *n* **1** : a naturally occurring crystalline element or compound (as diamond or quartz) that has a definite chemical composition and results from processes other than those of plants and animals ⟨most rocks are composed of more than one *mineral*⟩ **2** : any of various naturally occurring substances (as ore, coal, salt, sand, stone, petroleum, natural gas, or water) obtained for human use usually from the ground **3 a** : a natural substance that is neither plant nor animal **b** : an inorganic substance [Medieval Latin *minerale,* from *mineralis,* "of a mine", from *minera* "mine, ore", from Old French *miniere,* from *mine* "mine"]

[2]**mineral** *adj* **1** : of, relating to, or having the characteristics of a mineral : INORGANIC **2** : containing mineral salts or gases

min•er•al•ize \ˈmin-rə-ˌlīz, -ə-rə-\ *vb* **1** : to transform a metal into an ore **2** : PETRIFY ⟨*mineralized* bones⟩ **3 a** : to impregnate or supply with minerals **b** : to change into mineral form — **min•er•al•iza•tion** \ˌmin-rə-lə-ˈzā-shən, -ə-rə-\ *n*

mineral kingdom *n* : the one of the three basic groups of natural objects that includes inorganic objects — compare ANIMAL KINGDOM, PLANT KINGDOM

min•er•al•o•gy \ˌmin-ə-ˈräl-ə-jē, -ˈral-\ *n* : a science dealing with the properties and classification of minerals — **min•er•al•og•i•cal** \ˌmin-rə-ˈläj-i-kəl, -ə-rə-\ *adj* — **min•er•al•o•gist** \ˌmin-ə-ˈräl-ə-jəst, -ˈral-\ *n*

mineral oil *n* **1** : an oil (as petroleum) of mineral origin **2** : a refined petroleum oil having no color, odor, or taste that is used as a laxative

mineral water *n* : water naturally or artificially impregnated with mineral salts or gases

mineral wool *n* : any of various lightweight materials that resemble wool in texture, are made from slag, rock, or glass, and are used especially in heat and sound insulation

min•e•stro•ne \ˌmin-ə-ˈstrō-nē, -ˈstrōn\ *n* : a rich thick vegetable soup usually made with dried beans and pasta (as macaroni) [Italian, from *minestrare* "to serve", from Latin *ministrare,* from *minister* "servant"]

mine•sweep•er \ˈmīn-ˌswē-pər\ *n* : a warship designed for removing or neutralizing mines

Ming \ˈmiŋ\ *n* : a Chinese dynasty dated 1368–1644 and noted for restoration of earlier traditions and in the arts for perfection of established techniques [Chinese (Pekingese dialect) *ming*[2] "luminous"]

min•gle \ˈmiŋ-gəl\ *vb* **min•gled**; **min•gling** \-gə-liŋ, -gliŋ\ **1 a** : to bring or mix together or with something else usually without fundamental loss of identity **b** : to become mingled **2** : to come in contact : ASSOCIATE ⟨*mingles* with all sorts of people⟩ [Middle English *menglen,* from *mengen* "to mix", from Old English *mengan*] **syn** see MIX

ming tree \ˈmiŋ-\ *n* : a dwarfed usually evergreen tree grown in a pot; *also* : an artificial ming tree made from plant materials [perhaps from *Ming*]

mini- *combining form* : miniature : of small dimensions ⟨*mini*bike⟩ [*miniature*]

See *mini-* and 2d element

mini-airline	**minidrama**	**miniprice**
mini-album	**minidress**	**miniprincipality**
mini-ambulance	**mini-experiment**	**miniproblem**
mini-antenna	**mini-exposition**	**minipump**
mini-bag	**minifair**	**mini-rebellion**
mini-bank	**minifarm**	**minirecession**
mini-beard	**minifestival**	**mini-refrigerator**
mini-bet	**minifeud**	**minireview**
mini-bikini	**mini-filibuster**	**minirevolution**
minibiography	**miniflaw**	**mini-riot**
mini-bomb	**minigarden**	**mini-river**
minibonus	**minigolf**	**minirobot**
minibook	**minigovernment**	**minirose**
mini-boom	**minigown**	**mini-safari**
minibrain	**minigrant**	**miniscandal**
minibudget	**minigroup**	**mini-schism**
minibus	**miniguide**	**minischool**
minicab	**minihospital**	**mini-search**
minicalculator	**mini-kilt**	**minisedan**
minicamera	**minileague**	**mini-series**
minicar	**minilecture**	**miniski**
minicarnival	**mini-length**	**miniskyscraper**
mini-casino	**mini-market**	**mini-slump**
mini-castle	**mini-memo**	**minisociety**
mini-celebrity	**minimind**	**ministate**
minicircuit	**miniminded**	**mini-strike**
minicircus	**minimiracle**	**minisubmarine**
mini-city	**minimob**	**mini-survey**
mini-clock	**minimonument**	**minisystem**
minicoat	**minimountain**	**miniterritory**
minicollege	**minimuseum**	**minitheater**
minicommunity	**mini-nation**	**minitoga**
minicomponent	**mininetwork**	**minitornado**
minicomputer	**mininovel**	**minitrain**
mini-conglomerate	**mini-opera**	**minitunic**
mini-convention	**mini-panic**	**mini-vacation**
mini-course	**minipark**	**minivan**
minicrisis	**miniplan**	**mini-version**
minicruise	**mini-playground**	**miniwar**
miniculture	**minipool**	**mini-zoo**

[1]**min•ia•ture** \ˈmin-ē-ə-ˌchu̇r, ˈmin-i-ˌchu̇r, ˈmin-yə-, -chər\ *n* **1** : something much smaller than the usual size; *esp* : a copy on a much reduced scale **2** : a painting in an illuminated book or manuscript **3** : the art of painting miniatures **4** : a very small portrait or painting (as on ivory or metal) [Italian *miniatura* "art of illuminating a manuscript", from Medieval Latin, from Latin *miniare* "to color with red lead", from *minium* "red lead"] — **min•ia•tur•ist** \-ˌchu̇r-əst, -chər-\ *n*

\ə\ **abut**	\au̇\ **out**	\i\ **tip**	\ȯ\ **saw**	\u̇\ **foot**
\ər\ **further**	\ch\ **chin**	\ī\ **life**	\ȯi\ **coin**	\y\ **yet**
\a\ **mat**	\e\ **pet**	\j\ **job**	\th\ **thin**	\yü\ **few**
\ā\ **take**	\ē\ **easy**	\ŋ\ **sing**	\t͟h\ **this**	\yu̇\ **cure**
\ä\ **cot, cart**	\g\ **go**	\ō\ **bone**	\ü\ **food**	\zh\ **vision**

△ <u>**origin**</u> Before printing was introduced in Europe, books were written by hand; and titles and initials were often written in red to contrast with the black ink of the text. The red coloring often used for this purpose and for decorative drawings was called, in Latin, *minium.* The Italian word *miniatura,* derived from Latin *minium,* was used for the art of illuminating a manuscript and for a picture in a manuscript. Because manuscript illustrations are relatively small, the word *miniature,* borrowed into English from Italian, came to be used for anything very small.

2miniature *adj* **:** very small **:** represented on a small scale

miniature golf *n* **:** a novelty golf game played on a miniature course having such obstacles as bridges, tunnels, and windmills

min•ia•tur•ize \\-,chu̇r-,īz, -chər-\\ *vt* **:** to design or construct in small size — **min•ia•tur•iza•tion** \\,min-ē-ə-,chu̇r-ə-'zā-shən, ,min-i-,chu̇r-, ,min-yə-, -chər-\\ *n*

mini•bike \\'min-i-,bīk\\ *n* **:** a small one-passenger motorcycle having a low frame and elevated handlebars — **mini•bik•er** *n*

min•i•fy \\'min-ə-,fī\\ *vt* **-fied; -fy•ing :** to make small or smaller **:** LESSEN [Latin *minimus* "smallest" + English *-fy*]

min•im \\'min-əm\\ *n* **1 :** something very tiny **2 :** either of two units of liquid capacity equal to 1/60 fluidram (about .06 milliliter) — see MEASURE table [Latin *minimus* "least, smallest"]

min•i•mal \\'min-ə-məl\\ *adj* **:** relating to or being a minimum **:** LEAST — **min•i•mal•ly** \\-mə-lē\\ *adv*

min•i•mize \\'min-ə-,mīz\\ *vt* **1 :** to make as small as possible **:** reduce to a minimum ⟨*minimize* the chance of error⟩ **2 :** to place a low estimate or value on

min•i•mum \\'min-ə-məm\\ *n, pl* **-i•ma** \\-ə-mə\\ *or* **-i•mums 1 a :** the least quantity or value possible or permissible **b :** the least of a set of numbers; *esp* **:** the smallest value assumed by a function over a closed interval where its graph is an uninterrupted line or curve **2 :** the lowest degree or amount reached or recorded [Latin, neuter of *minimus* "smallest"] — **minimum** *adj*

minimum wage *n* **:** a wage fixed by legal authority or by contract as the least that may be paid either to employed persons generally or to a specific group of workers

min•ing \\'mī-ning\\ *n* **:** the process or business of working mines

min•ion \\'min-yən\\ *n* **1 :** a servile dependent **2 :** FAVORITE 1, IDOL **3 :** a subordinate official [Middle French *mignon* "darling"]

min•is•cule \\'min-əs-,kyül\\ *variant of* MINUSCULE

mini•skirt \\'min-i-,skərt\\ *n* **:** a woman's very short skirt — **mini•skirt•ed** \\-əd\\ *adj*

1min•is•ter \\'min-ə-stər\\ *n* **1 :** AGENT 3 **2 a :** one officiating or assisting at the administration of a sacrament **b :** a Protestant clergyman **c :** a person exercising the functions of a clergyman **3 :** a high government official entrusted with the management of a division of governmental activities **4 a :** a diplomatic representative (as an ambassador) sent to the seat of government of a foreign state **b :** a diplomatic representative ranking below an ambassador and usually sent to states of less importance [Old French *ministre,* from Latin *minister* "servant"]

2minister *vi* **min•is•tered; min•is•ter•ing** \\-stə-ring, -string\\ **:** to give aid or service ⟨*minister* to the sick⟩

min•is•te•ri•al \\,min-ə-'stir-ē-əl\\ *adj* **1 :** of or relating to a minister or ministry **2 a :** prescribed by law as part of the duties of an administrative office **b :** done in obedience to a legal order without exercise of personal judgment or discretion — **min•is•te•ri•al•ly** \\-ē-ə-lē\\ *adv*

min•is•trant \\'min-ə-strənt\\ *adj* **:** that ministers — **ministrant** *n*

min•is•tra•tion \\,min-ə-'strā-shən\\ *n* **:** the act or process of ministering

min•is•try \\'min-ə-strē\\ *n, pl* **-tries 1 :** MINISTRATION **2 :** the office, duties, or functions of a minister ⟨study for the *ministry*⟩ **3 :** the body of ministers of religion **:** CLERGY **4 :** AGENCY 2, INSTRUMENTALITY **5 :** the period of service or office of a minister or ministry **6** *often cap* **a :** the body of ministers governing a nation or state from which a smaller cabinet is sometimes selected **b :** the group of ministers constituting a cabinet **7 a :** a government department presided over by a minister ⟨*ministry* of foreign affairs⟩ **b :** the building in which the business of a ministry is transacted

min•i•ver \\'min-ə-vər\\ *n* **:** a white fur worn originally by medieval nobles and now used chiefly for robes of state [Old French *menu vair* "small fur"]

mink \\'mingk\\ *n, pl* **mink** *or* **minks** \\'mings, 'mingks\\ **:** any of several slender-bodied mammals resembling the related weasels, having partially webbed feet and a somewhat bushy tail, and living near water; *also* **:** the soft typically dark brown fur of a mink [Middle English]

mink

min•ne•sing•er \\'min-i-,sing-ər, 'min-ə-,zing-\\ *n* **:** one of a class of German lyric poets and musicians of the 12th to the 14th centuries [German, from *minne* "love" + *singer* "singer"]

min•now \\'min-ō\\ *n, pl* **minnows** *also* **minnow :** any of various small freshwater bottom-feeding fish (as the dace or shiner) related to the carps; *also* **:** any of various similar small fishes [Middle English *menawe*]

1Mi•no•an \\mə-'nō-ən, mī-\\ *adj* **:** of or relating to a Bronze Age culture centered in Crete (3000 B.C.–1100 B.C.) [Latin *minous* "of Minos (a legendary king of Crete)", from Greek *minōios,* from *Minōs* "Minos"]

2Minoan *n* **:** a native or inhabitant of ancient Crete

1mi•nor \\'mī-nər\\ *adj* **1 a :** inferior in dignity, rank, or importance ⟨a *minor* poet⟩ **b :** relatively small in number, quantity, or extent ⟨received a *minor* share of the blame⟩ **2 :** not having attained legal age **3 a :** having the 3d, 6th, and sometimes the 7th degrees lowered a half step ⟨a *minor* scale⟩ **b :** based on a minor scale ⟨*minor* keys⟩ **c :** less by a half step than the corresponding major interval ⟨*minor* third⟩ **4 :** not involving risk to life **:** not serious ⟨*minor* illness⟩ **5 :** of or relating to an academic minor [Latin, "smaller, inferior"]

2minor *n* **1 :** a person who has not attained legal age **2 :** a minor musical interval, scale, key, or mode **3 :** an academic subject chosen by a student as a secondary field of specialization

3minor *vi* **:** to pursue an academic minor

mi•nor•i•ty \\mə-'nȯr-ət-ē, mī-, -'när-\\ *n, pl* **-ties 1 a :** the period before attainment of legal age **b :** the state of being a legal minor **2 :** the smaller in number of two groups constituting a whole; *esp* **:** a group (as in a legislature) having less than the number of votes necessary for control **3 :** a part of a population differing from others (as in race) and often treated differently

minority leader *n* **:** the leader of the minority party in a legislative body

minor league *n* **:** a league of professional clubs in a sport (as baseball) other than the recognized major leagues

minor order *n* **:** one of the Roman Catholic or Eastern clerical orders that are lower in rank than major orders and involve minor liturgical duties — normally used in pl.

minor party *n* **:** a political party whose strength in elections is so small as to prevent its gaining control of a government except in rare and exceptional circumstances

minor penalty *n* **:** a two-minute suspension of a player in ice hockey

minor seminary *n* **:** a Roman Catholic seminary giving all or part of high school and junior college training

minor suit *n* **:** clubs or diamonds in bridge

min•ster \\'min-stər\\ *n* **1 :** a church attached or once attached to a monastery **2 :** a large or important church [Old English *mynster* "monastery, minster", from Late Latin *monasterium* "monastery"]

min•strel \\'min-strəl\\ *n* **1 :** a medieval musical entertainer; *esp* **:** a singer of verses to the accompaniment of a harp **2 a :** MUSICIAN **b :** POET 1 **3 a :** one of a troupe of performers typically giving a program of Negro melodies and jokes and usually blacked in imitation of Negroes **b :** a performance by a troupe of minstrels [Old French *menestrel* "servant, minstrel", derived from Latin *minister* "servant"]

min•strel•sy \\-sē\\ *n, pl* **-sies 1 :** the singing and playing of a minstrel **2 :** a body of minstrels **3 :** a collection of songs or verse [Middle French *menestralsie,* from *menestrel* "minstrel"]

1mint \\'mint\\ *n* **1 :** a place where coins, medals, or tokens are made **2 :** a huge amount ⟨caused a *mint* of trouble⟩ [Old English *mynet* "coin, money", from Latin *moneta* "mint, coin", from *Moneta,* epithet of the goddess Juno; from the fact that the Romans coined money in the temple of Juno Moneta]

2mint *vt* **1 :** to make (as coins) out of metal **2 :** CREATE 1, COIN — **mint•er** *n*

3mint *adj* **:** unmarred as if fresh from a mint ⟨*mint* coins⟩

4mint *n* **1 :** any of a family of herbs and shrubs (as basil and salvia) with square stems, opposite aromatic leaves, and commonly 2-lipped flowers; *esp* **:** one (as peppermint or spearmint) that is fragrant and yields a flavoring oil **2 :** a piece of candy flavored with mint [Old English *minte,* from Latin *mentha*]

mint•age \ˈmint-ij\ *n* **1 :** the action or process of minting coins **2 :** coins produced by minting

mint julep *n* **:** JULEP

min•u•end \ˈmin-yə-ˌwend\ *n* **:** a number from which another number is to be subtracted — compare SUBTRAHEND [Latin *minuendus* "to be lessened", from *minuere* "to lessen"]

min•u•et \ˌmin-yə-ˈwet\ *n* **1 :** a slow graceful dance consisting of forward balancing, bowing, and toe pointing **2 :** music for or in the rhythm of a minuet [French *menuet,* from Old French *menu* "small", from Latin *minutus*]

1mi•nus \ˈmī-nəs\ *prep* **1 :** diminished by ⟨seven *minus* four is three⟩ **2 :** deprived of **:** WITHOUT [Latin, "less", from *minor* "smaller"]

2minus *n* **1 :** a negative quantity **2 :** DEFECT, DEFICIENCY

3minus *adj* **1 :** mathematically negative ⟨a *minus* quantity⟩ **2 :** falling low in a specified range ⟨a grade of C *minus*⟩ **3 :** relating to or being a particular one of the two mating types that are required for successful fertilization in sexual reproduction in some lower plants (as a fungus)

mi•nus•cule \ˈmin-əs-ˌkyül, min-ˈəs-, ˈmin-yəs-, mī-ˈnəs\ *or* **min•is•cule** \ˈmin-əs-ˌkyül\ *adj* **:** very small [French *minuscule* "lowercase letter", from Latin *minusculus* "rather small", from *minor* "smaller"]

1min•ute \ˈmin-ət\ *n* **1 :** the 60th part of an hour of time or of a degree **2 :** the distance one can cover comfortably in a minute ⟨10 *minutes* from home to office⟩ **3 :** MOMENT 1 **4 a :** a brief note of instructions or recommendations written on a document **b :** an official memorandum authorizing or recommending some action **5** *pl* **:** a series of brief notes taken to provide a record of the proceedings of a meeting [Middle French, from Late Latin *minuta,* from Latin *minutus* "small, minute"]

2minute *vt* **1 a :** to write in or in the form of a minute ⟨*minuted* instructions⟩ **b :** to write a minute on ⟨*minute* a dispatch⟩ **2 :** to make notes or a brief summary of ⟨*minute* a meeting⟩

3mi•nute \mī-ˈnüt, mə-, -ˈnyüt\ *adj* **1 :** very small **:** INFINITESIMAL **2 :** of small importance **:** TRIFLING **3 :** marked by close attention to details ⟨*minute* description⟩ [Latin *minutus,* from *minuere* "to lessen, make small"] **syn** see CIRCUMSTANTIAL — **mi•nute•ness** *n*

mi•nute•ly \-lē\ *adv* **1 :** into very small pieces **2 :** in a minute manner or degree

min•ute•man \ˈmin-ət-ˌman\ *n* **:** a member of a militia ready to take up arms at a minute's notice during and immediately before the American Revolution

mi•nu•tia \mə-ˈnü-shē-ə, mī-, -ˈnyü-, -shə\ *n, pl* **-ti•ae** \-shē-ˌē, -shē-ˌī\ **:** a minute or minor detail — usually used in pl. [Latin, from *minutus* "minute"]

minx \ˈmiŋks, ˈmiŋgks\ *n* **1 :** a pert girl **2** *obsolete* **:** a wanton woman [origin unknown]

Mio•cene \ˈmī-ə-ˌsēn\ *n* **:** the epoch of the Tertiary between the Oligocene and Pliocene; *also* **:** the corresponding system of rocks [Greek *meiōn* "less"] — **Miocene** *adj*

mir \ˈmiər\ *n* **:** a village community common in czarist Russia in which the land was owned jointly by the peasants and cultivable land was redistributed among the individual families at regular intervals [Russian]

mi•ra•cid•i•um \ˌmir-ə-ˈsid-ē-əm, ˌmī-rə-\ *n, pl* **-cid•ia** \-ē-ə\ **:** the free-swimming ciliated first larva that is characteristic of a group (Digenea) of trematode worms and that seeks out and penetrates a suitable snail intermediate host [New Latin, from Greek *meirax* "youth, stripling"]

mir•a•cle \ˈmir-i-kəl\ *n* **1 :** an extraordinary event believed to manifest a supernatural work of God **2 :** an extremely outstanding or unusual event, thing, or accomplishment [Old French, from Latin *miraculum,* from *mirari* "to wonder at"]

miracle play *n* **1 :** MYSTERY PLAY **2 :** a medieval play based on the life of a saint or martyr

mi•rac•u•lous \mə-ˈrak-yə-ləs\ *adj* **1 :** of the nature of a miracle **:** SUPERNATURAL **2 :** resembling a miracle **:** MARVELOUS **3 :** working or able to work miracles — **mi•rac•u•lous•ly** *adv* — **mi•rac•u•lous•ness** *n*

mi•rage \mə-ˈräzh\ *n* **1 :** an optical effect that is sometimes seen at sea, in the desert, or over a hot pavement, that may have the appearance of a pool of water or a mirror in which distant objects are seen inverted, and that is caused by the bending or reflection of rays of light by a layer of heated air of varying density **2 :** something only seemingly real [French, from *mirer* "to look at", from Latin *mirari* "to wonder at"]

1mire \ˈmīr\ *n* **1 :** MARSH, BOG **2 :** heavy often deep mud, slush, or dirt [Old Norse *mȳrr*]

2mire *vb* **1 a :** to sink or stick fast in mire **b :** ENTANGLE, INVOLVE ⟨*mired* in detail⟩ **2 :** to soil with mud, slush, or dirt

mirk, mirky *variant of* MURK, MURKY

1mir•ror \ˈmir-ər\ *n* **1 :** a glass backed with a reflecting substance (as silver) **2 :** a smooth or polished surface that reflects an image **3 :** something that reflects a true likeness or gives a true description [Old French *mirour,* from *mirer* "to look at", from Latin *mirari* "to wonder at"]

2mirror *vt* **:** to reflect in or as if in a mirror

mirth \ˈmərth\ *n* **:** gladness or gaiety as shown by or accompanied with laughter [Old English *myrgth,* from *myrge* "merry"] • **syn** GLEE, JOLLITY, HILARITY: MIRTH implies generally lightness of heart and love of gaiety and specifically denotes laughter ⟨tried to suppress their *mirth*⟩ GLEE suggests an exulting sometimes malicious delight expressed in laughter or cries of joy; JOLLITY suggests exuberance or lack of restraint in mirth or glee; HILARITY implies loud or irrepressible laughter or boisterousness.

mirth•ful \-fəl\ *adj* **:** full of, expressing, or producing mirth — **mirth•ful•ly** \-fə-lē\ *adv* — **mirth•ful•ness** *n*

miry \ˈmīr-ē\ *adj* **mir•i•er; -est 1 :** MARSHY 1 **2 :** very muddy or slushy

mis- *prefix* **1 a :** badly **:** wrongly ⟨*mis*judge⟩ **b :** unfavorably **c :** in a suspicious manner ⟨*mis*doubt⟩ **2 :** bad **:** wrong ⟨*mis*deed⟩ **3 :** opposite or lack of ⟨*mis*trust⟩ **4 :** not ⟨*mis*fire⟩ [Old English]

See *mis-* and 2d element

misacquire
misaddress
misadjust
misadministration
misadvise
misaim
misalign
misalignment
misallocate
misallocation
misalphabetize
misanalysis
misanalyze
misapplication
misapply
misarrangement
misarticulate
misarticulation
misassemble
misassume
misassumption
misattribute
misattribution
misbind
misbook
misbuild
misbuttoned
miscaption
miscatalog
miscategorization
miscategorize
mischannel
mischaracterization
mischaracterize
mischoice
miscitation
misclassification
misclassify
miscommunicate
miscomputation
miscompute
misconnect
misconnection
miscopy
miscorrelate
miscorrelation
miscount
miscut
misdate
misdefine
misdescribe
misdescription
misdevelop
misdiagnose
misdiagnosis
misdial
miseducate
miseducation
miseducator
misemphasis
misemphasize
misemploy
misemployment
misestimate
misestimation
misevaluate
misevaluation
misfocus
misfunction
misgauge
misgrade
mishear
mishit
misidentification
misidentify
misimpression
misindex
miskick
mislabel
mislearn
mislocate
mislocation
mismake
mismeasure
mismotivate
misnumber
misorganize
mispair
misperceive
misperception
misplan
misplot
misposition
misprescribe
misquotation
misquote
misreckon
misregister
misregistration
misremember
misreport
misroute

\ə\ **abut**	\au̇\ **out**	\i\ **tip**	\ȯ\ **saw**	\u̇\ **foot**
\ər\ **further**	\ch\ **chin**	\ī\ **life**	\ȯi\ **coin**	\y\ **yet**
\a\ **mat**	\e\ **pet**	\j\ **job**	\th\ **thin**	\yü\ **few**
\ā\ **take**	\ē\ **easy**	\ng\ **sing**	\t͟h\ **this**	\yu̇\ **cure**
\ä\ **cot, cart**	\g\ **go**	\ō\ **bone**	\ü\ **food**	\zh\ **vision**

misserve	**mistitle**	**misutilization**
missort	**mistrack**	**misutilize**
misteach	**mistranslate**	**misvalue**
misthrow	**mistranslation**	**miswire**
mistime	**mistune**	**miswrite**

mis•ad•ven•ture \ˌmis-əd-ˈven-chər\ *n* : an unlucky adventure : MISHAP
mis•al•li•ance \ˌmis-ə-ˈlī-əns\ *n* : an improper or unsuitable alliance especially in marriage
mis•an•thrope \ˈmis-n-ˌthrōp\ *n* : a person who dislikes and distrusts other people [Greek *misanthrōpos* "hating mankind", from *misein* "to hate" + *anthrōpos* "man"]
mis•an•thro•py \mis-ˈan-thrə-pē, -ˈant-\ *n* : a dislike or hatred of other people — **mis•an•throp•ic** \ˌmis-n-ˈthräp-ik\ *adj* — **mis•an•throp•i•cal•ly** \-ˈthräp-i-kə-lē, -klē\ *adv*
mis•ap•pre•hend \ˌmis-ˌap-ri-ˈhend\ *vt* : MISUNDERSTAND — **mis•ap•pre•hen•sion** \-ˈhen-chən\ *n*
mis•ap•pro•pri•ate \ˌmis-ə-ˈprō-prē-ˌāt\ *vt* : to appropriate wrongly; *esp* : to take dishonestly for one's own use — **mis•ap•pro•pri•a•tion** \-ˌprō-prē-ˈā-shən\ *n*
mis•be•come \ˌmis-bi-ˈkəm\ *vt* : to be inappropriate or unbecoming to
mis•be•got•ten \ˌmis-bi-ˈgät-n\ *adj* **1** : ILLEGITIMATE 1 **2** : having or suggesting a disreputable or improper origin ⟨a *misbegotten* scheme⟩
mis•be•have \ˌmis-bi-ˈhāv\ *vi* : to behave in a wrong or improper manner — **mis•be•hav•ior** \-ˈhā-vyər\ *n*
mis•be•lief \ˌmis-bə-ˈlēf\ *n* : a mistaken or false belief
mis•be•liev•er \-ˈlē-vər\ *n* : one who is held to have false beliefs especially in religion
mis•brand \mis-ˈbrand, ˈmis-\ *vt* : to brand falsely or in a misleading way
mis•cal•cu•late \-ˈkal-kyə-ˌlāt\ *vb* : to calculate wrongly : make a mistake in calculation — **mis•cal•cu•la•tion** \ˌmis-ˌkal-kyə-ˈlā-shən\ *n*
mis•call \mis-ˈkȯl, ˈmis-\ *vt* : to call by a wrong name
mis•car•riage \mis-ˈkar-ij\ *n* **1** : a going astray: as **a** : a failure or blunder resulting usually from mismanagement ⟨a *miscarriage* of justice⟩ **b** : a failure (as of a letter) to arrive **c** : a failure of a purpose or plan **2** : the accidental separation and loss of an unborn child from the body of its mother before it is capable of living independently — compare ABORTION
mis•car•ry \mis-ˈkar-ē\ *vi* **1** : to have a miscarriage : give birth prematurely **2** : to fail of the intended purpose : go wrong ⟨the plan *miscarried*⟩
mis•cast \mis-ˈkast, ˈmis-\ *vt* : to cast in an unsuitable role
mis•ceg•e•na•tion \mis-ˌej-ə-ˈnā-shən, ˌmis-i-jə-ˈnā-\ *n* : a mixture of races; *esp* : marriage or cohabitation between a white person and a member of another race [Latin *miscēre* "to mix" + *genus* "kind, race"]
mis•cel•la•ne•ous \ˌmis-ə-ˈlā-nē-əs\ *adj* **1** : consisting of numerous things of different sorts **2 a** : marked by an interest in unrelated topics or subjects **b** : having the characteristics of a patchwork [Latin *miscellaneus*, from *miscellus* "mixed"] — **mis•cel•la•ne•ous•ly** *adv* — **mis•cel•la•ne•ous•ness** *n*
mis•cel•la•nist \ˈmis-ə-ˌlā-nəst\ *n* : a writer of miscellanies
mis•cel•la•ny \-nē\ *n, pl* **-nies 1** : a mixture of various things **2** *pl* : a collection of writings : ANTHOLOGY
mis•chance \mis-ˈchans, ˈmis-\ *n* **1** : bad luck **2** : a piece of bad luck **syn** see MISFORTUNE
mis•chief \ˈmis-chəf, ˈmish-\ *n* **1** : injury or damage caused by a human agency **2** : a source of mischief; *esp* : a person who causes mischief **3 a** : action that annoys ⟨that child always gets into *mischief*⟩ **b** : mischievous quality [Old French *meschief* "calamity", from *mes-* "mis-" (of Germanic origin) + *chief* "head, end", from Latin *caput*]
mis•chie•vous \ˈmis-chə-vəs, ˈmish-\ *adj* **1** : causing mischief : intended to do harm ⟨*mischievous* gossip⟩ **2 a** : causing or tending to cause petty injury or annoyance **b** : irresponsibly playful **3** : showing a spirit of mischief — **mis•chie•vous•ly** *adv* — **mis•chie•vous•ness** *n*
mis•ci•ble \ˈmis-ə-bəl\ *adj* : capable of being mixed; *esp* : soluble in each other ⟨alcohol and water are *miscible*⟩ [Medieval Latin *miscibilis*, from Latin *miscēre* "to mix"] — **mis•ci•bil•i•ty** \ˌmis-ə-ˈbil-ət-ē\ *n*
mis•con•ceive \ˌmis-kən-ˈsēv\ *vt* : to interpret incorrectly : MISJUDGE — **mis•con•ceiv•er** *n* — **mis•con•cep•tion** \-ˈsep-shən\ *n*
[1]**mis•con•duct** \mis-ˈkän-dəkt, ˈmis-, -ˌdəkt\ *n* **1** : bad management **2** : improper or unlawful behavior
[2]**mis•con•duct** \ˌmis-kən-ˈdəkt\ *vt* **1** : MISMANAGE **2** : to behave (oneself) badly
mis•con•struc•tion \ˌmis-kən-ˈstrək-shən\ *n* : the act, the process, or an instance of misconstruing
mis•con•strue \ˌmis-kən-ˈstrü\ *vt* : to construe wrongly : MISINTERPRET
mis•count \mis-ˈkau̇nt, ˈmis-\ *vb* : to count incorrectly — **miscount** *n*
mis•cre•ant \ˈmis-krē-ənt\ *n* : one that behaves badly : RASCAL [Middle English *miscreaunt* "infidel", from Middle French *mescreant*, present participle of *mescroire* "to disbelieve", from *mes-* "mis-" (of Germanic origin) + *croire* "to believe", from Latin *credere*] — **miscreant** *adj*
[1]**mis•cue** \mis-ˈkyü, ˈmis-\ *n* **1** : a faulty stroke (as in billiards) **2** : MISTAKE 2, SLIP
[2]**miscue** *vi* **1** : to make a miscue **2 a** : to miss a stage cue **b** : to answer a wrong cue
mis•deal \mis-ˈdēl, ˈmis-\ *vb* **-dealt** \-ˈdelt\; **-deal•ing** \-ˈdē-ling\ : to deal wrongly ⟨*misdeal* cards⟩ — **misdeal** *n*
mis•deed \mis-ˈdēd, ˈmis-\ *n* : a wrong deed; *esp* : an immoral or criminal action
mis•de•mean•or \ˌmis-di-ˈmē-nər\ *n* **1** : a crime less serious than a felony **2** : MISDEED
mis•di•rect \ˌmis-də-ˈrekt, -dī-\ *vt* : to direct incorrectly — **mis•di•rec•tion** \-ˈrek-shən\ *n*
mis•do \mis-ˈdü, ˈmis-\ *vt* **-did** \-ˈdid\; **-done** \-ˈdən\; **-do•ing** \-ˈdü-ing\; **-does** \-ˈdəz\ : to do wrongly or improperly — **mis•do•er** \-ˈdü-ər\ *n*
mis•do•ing \mis-ˈdü-ing, ˈmis-\ *n* **1** : wrong or improper behavior or action **2** : MISDEED
mis•doubt \mis-ˈdau̇t, ˈmis-\ *vt* **1** : to doubt the reality or truth of **2** : SUSPECT 1, FEAR — **misdoubt** *n*
mise–en–scène \ˌmē-ˌzäⁿ-ˈsen\ *n, pl* **mise–en–scènes** \-ˈsen, -ˈsenz\ **1** : the setting of a play **2** : physical setting : ENVIRONMENT [French *mise en scène* "putting onto the stage"]
mi•ser \ˈmī-zər\ *n* : a mean grasping person; *esp* : one who lives miserably in order to hoard wealth [Latin, "wretched, miserable"]
mis•er•a•ble \ˈmiz-ər-bəl, ˈmiz-rə-bəl, -ə-rə-\ *adj* **1 a** : wholly inadequate or scanty ⟨a *miserable* shanty⟩ **b** : causing great discomfort or unhappiness ⟨a *miserable* cold⟩ **2** : extremely poor or unhappy **3** : arousing pity **4** : SHAMEFUL ⟨played a *miserable* trick⟩ [Middle French, from Latin *miserabilis* "pitiable, wretched", from *miserari* "to pity", from *miser* "wretched"] — **miserable** *n* — **mis•er•a•ble•ness** *n* — **mis•er•a•bly** \-blē\ *adv*
Mi•se•re•re \ˌmiz-ə-ˈriər-ē, -ˈreər-, ˌmē-zə-ˈrā-rā\ *n* : the 50th Psalm in the Vulgate [Latin, "be merciful" (the first word of the Psalm), from *misereri* "to be merciful", from *miser* "wretched"]
mi•ser•ly \ˈmī-zər-lē\ *adj* : of, relating to, or characteristic of a miser **syn** see STINGY — **mi•ser•li•ness** *n*
mis•ery \ˈmiz-rē, -ə-rē\ *n, pl* **-er•ies 1** : a state of great suffering and want due to poverty or distress **2** : a source of suffering or discomfort ⟨the *miseries* of life in prison⟩ **3** : a state of great unhappiness and emotional distress **syn** see DISTRESS
mis•fea•sance \mis-ˈfēz-ns\ *n* : the performance of a lawful action in an illegal or improper manner [Middle French *mesfaisance*, from *mesfaire* "to do wrong", from *mes-* "mis-" (of Germanic origin) + *faire* "to do", from Latin *facere*]
mis•file \mis-ˈfīl, ˈmis-\ *vt* : to file in an inappropriate place
mis•fire \mis-ˈfīr, ˈmis-\ *vi* **1** : to have the explosive or propulsive charge fail to ignite at the proper time ⟨the engine *misfired*⟩ **2** : to fail to fire ⟨the gun *misfired*⟩ **3** : to miss an intended effect — **misfire** *n*
mis•fit \ˈmis-ˌfit, mis-ˈfit\ *n* **1** : something that fits badly **2** : a person poorly adjusted to his or her environment
mis•for•tune \mis-ˈfȯr-chən\ *n* **1** : bad fortune : ill luck **2** : an unfortunate condition or event : DISASTER
• **syn** MISFORTUNE, MISCHANCE, MISHAP mean adverse fortune or an instance of this. MISFORTUNE is a general term for bad luck; applied to a single instance it implies resulting distress usually of some considerable duration; MISCHANCE emphasizes the immediate practical inconvenience or disruption of plans resulting from a chance happening or fall of circumstances; MISHAP implies a trivial instance of bad luck.

mis•give \mis-'giv, 'mis-\ *vb* **-gave** \-'gāv\; **-giv•en** \-'giv-ən\; **-giv•ing 1 :** to suggest doubt or fear to **2 :** to be fearful
mis•giv•ing \-'giv-iŋ\ *n* **:** a feeling of doubt or suspicion especially concerning a future event
mis•gov•ern \-'gəv-ərn\ *vt* **:** to rule or govern badly — **mis•gov•ern•ment** \-ərn-mənt, -ər-mənt\ *n*
mis•guide \mis-'gīd, 'mis-\ *vt* **:** to lead astray **:** MISDIRECT — **mis•guid•ance** \-'gīd-ns\ *n* — **mis•guid•er** *n*
mis•guid•ed \-'gīd-əd\ *adj* **:** marked or directed by mistaken ideas, principles, or motives ⟨*misguided* philanthropists⟩ — **mis•guid•ed•ly** *adv* — **mis•guid•ed•ness** *n*
mis•han•dle \mis-'han-dl, 'mis-\ *vt* **1 :** to treat roughly **:** MALTREAT **2 :** to manage wrongly
mis•hap \'mis-,hap, mis-'\ *n* **1** *archaic* **:** bad luck **:** MISFORTUNE **2 :** an unfortunate accident **syn** see MISFORTUNE
mis•hear \mis-'hiər, 'mis-\ *vb* **1 :** to hear wrongly **2 :** to misunderstand what is heard
mish•mash \'mish-,mäsh, -,mash\ *n* **:** a disorderly mixture **:** JUMBLE [Middle High German *misch-masch,* reduplication of *mischen* "to mix"]
Mish•nah *or* **Mish•na** \'mish-nə\ *n* **:** the collection of Jewish halakic traditions compiled about A.D. 200 and made the basic half of the Talmud [Hebrew *mishnāh* "instruction"]
mis•in•form \,mis-n-'fȯrm\ *vt* **:** to give false or misleading information to — **mis•in•for•ma•tion** \,mis-,in-fər-'mā-shən\ *n*
mis•in•ter•pret \,mis-n-'tər-prət, *rapid* -pət\ *vt* **:** to understand or explain wrongly — **mis•in•ter•pre•ta•tion** \-,tər-prə-'tā-shən, *rapid* -pə-'tā-\ *n*
mis•judge \mis-'jəj, 'mis-\ *vb* **:** to judge wrongly or unjustly — **mis•judg•ment** \-'jəj-mənt\ *n*
mis•lay \mis-'lā, 'mis-\ *vt* **-laid** \-'lād\, **-lay•ing :** to put in a place later forgotten **:** LOSE
mis•lead \-'lēd\ *vt* **-led** \-'led\; **-lead•ing :** to lead in a wrong direction or into a mistaken action or belief **syn** see DECEIVE — **misleading** *adj*
mis•like \-'līk\ *vt* **:** DISLIKE — **mislike** *n*
mis•man•age \mis-'man-ij, 'mis-\ *vt* **:** to manage badly or improperly — **mis•man•age•ment** \-mənt\ *n*
mis•match \mis-'mach, 'mis-\ *vt* **:** to match (as in marriage) unsuitably or badly — **mismatch** *n*
mis•mate \-'māt\ *vt* **:** to mate unsuitably
mis•name \-'nām\ *vt* **:** to name incorrectly **:** MISCALL
mis•no•mer \mis-'nō-mər, 'mis-\ *n* **:** a wrong or unsuitable name [Middle French *mesnommer* "to misname", from *mes-* "mis-" (of Germanic origin) + *nommer* "to name", from Latin *nominare*]
mi•sog•a•mist \mə-'säg-ə-məst\ *n* **:** one who hates marriage [derived from Greek *misein* "to hate" + *gamos* "marriage"] — **mi•sog•a•my** \-'säg-ə-mē\ *n*
mi•sog•y•nist \mə-'säj-ə-nəst\ *n* **:** one who hates or distrusts women [from *mysogyny,* from Greek *misogynia,* from *misein* "to hate" and *gynē* "woman"] — **mis•o•gyn•ic** \,mis-ə-'jin-ik, -ə-'gī-nik\ *adj* — **mi•sog•y•ny** \mə-'säj-ə-nē\ *n*
mis•place \mis-'plās, 'mis-\ *vt* **1 :** to put in a wrong place **2 :** MISLAY — **mis•place•ment** \-mənt\ *n*
mis•play \'plā\ *n* **:** a wrong or unskillful play (as in a game or sport) — **misplay** *vt*
mis•print \mis-'print, 'mis-\ *vt* **:** to print incorrectly — **misprint** \'mis-,print, mis-', 'mis-'\ *n*
mis•prize \mis-'prīz, 'mis-\ *vt* **1 :** SCORN 1 **2 :** UNDERVALUE 1
mis•pro•nounce \,mis-prə-'nau̇ns\ *vt* **:** to pronounce incorrectly or in a way regarded as incorrect — **mis•pro•nun•ci•a•tion** \-,nən-sē-'ā-shən\ *n*
mis•read \mis-'rēd, 'mis-\ *vt* **-read** \-'red\; **-read•ing** \-'rēd-iŋ\ **1 :** to read incorrectly **2 :** to misinterpret in reading
mis•rep•re•sent \,mis-,rep-ri-'zent\ *vt* **:** to give a false or misleading representation of — **mis•rep•re•sen•ta•tion** \mis-,rep-ri-,zen-'tā-shən\ *n*
¹mis•rule \mis-'rül, 'mis-\ *vt* **:** to rule or govern badly
²misrule *n* **1 :** the action of misruling **:** the state of being misruled **2 :** public disorder **:** ANARCHY
¹miss \'mis\ *vb* **1 :** to fail to hit, catch, reach, or get ⟨*miss* a target⟩ **2 :** ESCAPE, AVOID ⟨just *missed* being hurt⟩ **3 :** to leave out **:** OMIT **4 :** to discover or feel the absence of ⟨*miss* an absent friend⟩ **5 :** to fail to understand, sense, or experience ⟨don't *miss* that movie⟩ **6 :** MISFIRE ⟨the engine *missed*⟩ [Old English *missan*] — **miss out on :** to lose a good opportunity for — **miss the boat :** to fail to take advantage of an opportunity
²miss *n* **1 :** a failure to reach a desired goal or result **2 :** an instance of misfiring
³miss *n* **1** *cap* **a** — used as a courtesy title before the name of an unmarried woman **b** — used before the name of a place, an activity, or an epithet to form a title for a woman representing the thing indicated ⟨*Miss* America⟩ **2 :** a woman whose marital status is unknown — used without a name as a conventional term of address [short for *mistress*]
mis•sal \'mis-əl\ *n* **:** a book containing the prayers to be said or sung in the Mass during the year [Medieval Latin *missale,* from Late Latin *missa* "mass"]
mis•send \mis-'send, 'mis-\ *vt* **-sent** \-'sent\; **-send•ing :** to send (as mail) to a wrong address
mis•shape \mis-'shāp, mish-, 'mis-, 'mish-\ *vt* **:** to shape badly **:** DEFORM — **mis•shap•en** \-'shā-pən\ *adj*
mis•sile \'mis-əl\ *n* **:** an object (as a stone, arrow, artillery shell, bullet, or rocket) that is thrown or projected usually so as to strike something at a distance; *esp* **:** GUIDED MISSILE [Latin, from *missilis* "capable of being thrown", from *mittere* "to let go, send"]
mis•sile•man \-mən\ *n* **:** one who helps to design, build, or operate guided missiles
mis•sile•ry \-rē\ *n* **1 :** MISSILES; *esp* **:** GUIDED MISSILES **2 :** the science dealing with the design, manufacture, and use of guided missiles
miss•ing \'mis-iŋ\ *adj* **:** ABSENT ⟨*missing* persons⟩; *also* **:** LOST ⟨a *missing* book⟩
missing link *n* **1 :** an absent member needed to complete a series **2 :** a hypothetical intermediate form between human beings and apes that has not been found as a fossil
mis•sion \'mish-ən\ *n* **1 a :** a ministry commisioned by a religious organization to spread its faith or carry on humanitarian work **b :** assignment to or work in missionary enterprise **c** (1) **:** a mission establishment (2) **:** a local church or parish dependent on a larger religious organization for direction or financial support **d** *pl* **:** organized missionary work **e :** a course of sermons and services given to convert to or quicken Christian faith **2 :** a group of persons sent to perform a service or carry on an activity: as **a :** a group sent to a foreign country to conduct negotiations **b :** a permanent embassy or legation **c :** a team of military or technical specialists or cultural leaders sent to a foreign country **3 :** a task or function assigned or undertaken; *esp* **:** an official assignment ⟨my *mission* is to recover the stolen plans⟩ [Latin *missio* "act of sending", from *missus,* past participle of *mittere* "to send"] — **mission** *adj*
¹mis•sion•ary \'mish-ə-,ner-ē\ *adj* **1 :** relating to, engaged in, or devoted to missions **2 :** characteristic of a missionary
²missionary *n, pl* **-ar•ies :** one sent to spread a religious faith among unbelievers
mis•sion•er \'mish-ə-nər\ *n* **:** MISSIONARY
Mis•sis•sip•pi•an \,mis-ə-'sip-ē-ən\ *adj* **1 :** of or relating to Mississippi, its people, or the Mississippi river **2 :** of, relating to, or being the period of the Paleozoic era between the Devonian and Pennsylvanian or the corresponding system of rocks — see GEOLOGIC TIME table — **Mississippian** *n*
mis•sive \'mis-iv\ *n* **:** a written communication **:** LETTER [Middle French *lettre missive,* literally, "letter intended to be sent"]
mis•spell \mis-'spel, 'mis-\ *vt* **:** to spell incorrectly
mis•spell•ing \-'spel-iŋ\ *n* **:** an incorrect spelling
mis•spend \mis-'spend, 'mis-\ *vt* **-spent** \-'spent\; **-spend•ing :** to spend unwisely ⟨a *misspent* youth⟩
mis•state \mis-'stāt, 'mis-\ *vt* **:** to give a false or inaccurate account of — **mis•state•ment** \-mənt\ *n*
mis•step \-'step\ *n* **1 :** a wrong step **2 :** a mistake in judgment or action **:** BLUNDER
missy \'mis-ē\ *n* **:** a young girl
¹mist \'mist\ *n* **1 :** water in the form of particles floating in the air or falling as fine rain **2 :** something (as a haze or film) that blurs or hinders vision **3 :** a cloud of small particles or objects resembling a mist [Old English] — **mist•like** \-,līk\ *adj*
²mist *vb* **1 :** to be or become misty **2 :** to become dim or blurred **3 :** to cover with mist

mis•tak•able \mə-ˈstā-kə-bəl\ *adj* : capable of being misunderstood or mistaken

¹mis•take \mə-ˈstāk\ *vb* **mis•took** \-ˈstu̇k\; **mis•tak•en** \-ˈstā-kən\; **mis•tak•ing 1** : to choose wrongly **2 a** : to understand wrongly : MISINTERPRET **b** : to estimate incorrectly ⟨*mistook* the strength of the enemy⟩ **3** : to identify wrongly — **mis•tak•en•ly** *adv* — **mis•tak•er** *n*

²mistake *n* **1** : a wrong judgment : MISUNDERSTANDING **2** : a wrong action or statement : BLUNDER **syn** see ERROR

mis•ter \ˈmis-tər, *for sense 1* ˌmis-tər\ *n* **1** *cap* **a** — used sometimes in writing instead of the usual *Mr.* before the name of a man **b** — used before the name of a place, an activity, or an epithet to form a title for a man representing the thing indicated ⟨*Mister* Conservative⟩ **2** : SIR — used without a name as a term of address for a man who is a stranger ⟨hey, *mister*, do you want to buy a paper?⟩ [alteration of *master*]

mistletoe

mis•tle•toe \ˈmis-əl-ˌtō\ *n* : a green plant with yellowish flowers and waxy white berries that grows on the branches and trunks of trees [Old English *misteltān*, from *mistel* "mistletoe" + *tān* "twig"]

mis•tral \ˈmis-trəl, mi-ˈsträl\ *n* : a strong cold dry northerly wind of the northwest Mediterranean [French, from Provençal, from *mistral* "masterful", from Latin *magistralis*, from *magister* "master"]

mis•treat \mis-ˈtrēt, ˈmis-\ *vt* : to treat badly : ABUSE — **mis•treat•ment** \-mənt\ *n*

mis•tress \ˈmis-trəs\ *n* **1** : a woman (as the head of a household or school) who has power, authority, or ownership **2** : something personified as female that rules or directs **3** : a woman with whom a man habitually fornicates **4** *cap* — used formerly as a courtesy title before the name of a woman [Middle French *maistresse*, feminine of *maistre* "master", from Latin *magister*]

mis•tri•al \mis-ˈtrī-əl, ˈmis-, -ˈtrīl\ *n* : a trial that is legally void because of some error in the proceedings

¹mis•trust \mis-ˈtrəst, ˈmis-\ *n* : a lack of confidence : DISTRUST — **mis•trust•ful** \-fəl\ *adj* — **mis•trust•ful•ly** \-fə-lē\ *adv* — **mis•trust•ful•ness** *n*

²mistrust *vt* **1** : SUSPECT ⟨I *mistrust* their motives⟩ **2** : to lack confidence in ⟨*mistrust* one's own ability⟩

misty \ˈmis-tē\ *adj* **mist•i•er**; **-est 1** : full of mist ⟨a *misty* valley⟩ **2** : blurred by or as if by mist ⟨*misty* eyes⟩ **3** : VAGUE, INDISTINCT ⟨a *misty* memory⟩ — **mist•i•ly** \-tə-lē\ *adv* — **mist•i•ness** \-tē-nəs\ *n*

mis•un•der•stand \mis-ˌən-dər-ˈstand, ˌmis-\ *vb* **-stood** \-ˈstu̇d\; **-stand•ing 1** : to fail to understand **2** : to interpret incorrectly

mis•un•der•stand•ing \-ˈstan-diŋ\ *n* **1** : a failure to understand **2** : QUARREL 2

mis•us•age \mish-ˈü-sij, mish-ˈyü-, mis-ˈyü-, -zij\ *n* **1** : bad treatment : ABUSE **2** : wrong or improper use

¹mis•use \mish-ˈüz, mish-ˈyüz, mis-ˈyüz\ *vt* **1** : to use incorrectly : MISAPPLY ⟨*misuse* words⟩ **2** : ABUSE 2, MISTREAT ⟨*misuse* one's talents⟩

²mis•use \mish-ˈüs, mish-ˈyüs, mis-ˈyüz\ *n* : incorrect or improper use : MISAPPLICATION ⟨*misuse* of public funds⟩

mite \ˈmīt\ *n* **1** : any of various tiny animals that are related to the ticks and spiders, often live on plants, animals, and stored foods, and include important carriers of disease **2** : a very small coin or sum of money **3** : a very small object or creature [Old English *mīte*]

¹mi•ter *or* **mi•tre** \ˈmīt-ər\ *n* **1** : a high pointed headdress worn by a bishop or abbot in church ceremonies **2 a** : the beveled surface of a piece where a miter joint is made **b** : MITER JOINT [Middle French *mitre*, from Latin *mitra* "headband, turban", from Greek]

²miter *or* **mitre** *vt* **mi•tered** *or* **mi•tred**; **mi•ter•ing** *or* **mi•tring** \ˈmīt-ə-riŋ\ **1** : to match or fit together in a miter joint **2** : to bevel the ends of for making a miter joint

miter box *n* : a device for guiding a handsaw at the proper angle in cutting wood for a miter joint

miter joint *n* : the joint or corner made by cutting the square edges of two boards at an angle and fitting them together

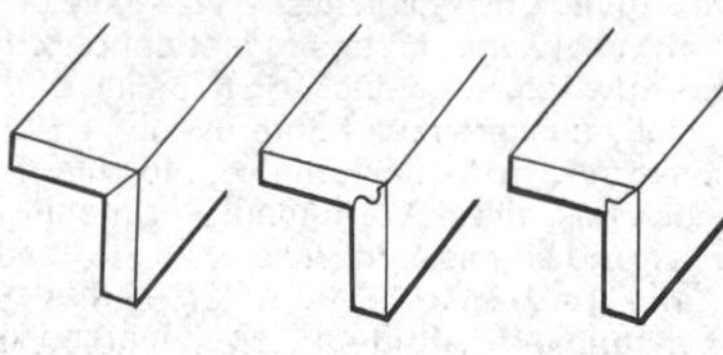
miter joint

mit•i•gate \ˈmit-ə-ˌgāt\ *vt* : to make less severe ⟨*mitigate* a punishment⟩ ⟨*mitigate* pain⟩ [Latin *mitigare* "to soften", from *mitis* "soft"] — **mit•i•ga•tion** \ˌmit-ə-ˈgā-shən\ *n* — **mit•i•ga•tive** \ˈmit-ə-ˌgāt-iv\ *adj* — **mit•i•ga•tor** \-ˌgāt-ər\ *n* — **mit•i•ga•to•ry** \ˈmit-i-gə-ˌtōr-ē, -ˌtȯr-\ *adj*

mi•to•chon•dri•on \ˌmīt-ə-ˈkän-drē-ən\ *n, pl* **-dria** \-drē-ə\ : any of various round or long cellular organelles that are located outside the nucleus, produce energy for the cell through cellular respiration, and are rich in fats, proteins, and enzymes [Greek *mitos* "thread" + *chondrion* "granule", from *chondros* "grain"] — **mi•to•chon•dri•al** \-drē-əl\ *adj*

mi•to•sis \mī-ˈtō-səs\ *n, pl* **-to•ses** \-ˌsēz\ **1** : a process that takes place in the nucleus of a dividing cell and results in the formation of two new nuclei each having the same number of chromosomes as the parent nucleus **2** : a cell division in which mitosis occurs [New Latin, from Greek *mitos* "thread"] — **mi•tot•ic** \-ˈtät-ik\ *adj* — **mi•tot•i•cal•ly** \-ˈtät-i-kə-lē, -klē\ *adv*

mi•tral valve \ˌmī-trəl-\ *n* : BICUSPID VALVE [from its resemblance in shape to a miter]

mitt \ˈmit\ *n* **1 a** : a woman's glove that leaves the fingers uncovered **b** : MITTEN **c** : a baseball catcher's or first baseman's glove in the style of a mitten **2** *slang* : HAND 1a [short for *mitten*]

mit•ten \ˈmit-n\ *n* : a covering for the hand and wrist having a separate section for the thumb only [Middle French *mitaine*]

mitz•vah \ˈmits-və\ *n, pl* **mitz•voth** \-ˌvōth, -ˌvōt, -ˌvōs\ *or* **mitz•vahs 1** : a commandment of the Jewish law **2** : a praiseworthy act [Hebrew *miṣwāh*]

¹mix \ˈmiks\ *vb* **1** : to combine or blend into one mass **2** : to make by blending different things ⟨*mix* a salad dressing⟩ **3** : to become one mass through blending ⟨oil will not *mix* with water⟩ **4** : to associate with others on friendly terms ⟨*mixes* well in any company⟩ **5** : CONFUSE ⟨*mix* up facts⟩ [Middle English *mixen*, back-formation from *mixte* "mixed", from Middle French, from Latin *mixtus*, past participle of *miscēre* "to mix"]

• **syn** MIX, MINGLE, BLEND, COALESCE mean to put or come together into a more or less uniform whole. MIX may or may not imply loss of each element's separate identity; MINGLE suggests that the elements are still somewhat distinguishable or separately active; BLEND implies that the elements lose some or all of their individuality; COALESCE stresses the action or process of like things growing into an organic unity.

²mix *n* : MIXTURE; *esp* : a commercially prepared mixture of food ingredients

mixed \ˈmikst\ *adj* **1** : combining features of more than one kind; *esp* : combining features of different systems ⟨a *mixed* economy⟩ **2** : involving individuals or items of more than one kind: as **a** : involving persons differing in race, national origin or religion ⟨a *mixed* marriage⟩ **b** : involving individuals of both sexes ⟨*mixed* company⟩ **c** : containing two or more kinds of organisms in abundance ⟨a *mixed* forest⟩ **3** : including or accompanied by inconsistent or incompatible elements ⟨*mixed* emotions⟩ **4** : deriving from two or more races or breeds ⟨a person of *mixed* blood⟩

mixed bud *n* : a plant that produces a branch and leaves as well as flowers

mixed nerve *n* : a nerve containing both sensory and motor fibers

mixed number *n* : a number (as 5⅔) composed of an integer and a fraction — called also *mixed numeral*

mix•er \ˈmik-sər\ *n* **1** : one that mixes: as **a** : something used in mixing **b** : ICEBREAKER 2 **2 a** : a sociable person **b** : a nonalcoholic beverage used in preparing an alcoholic drink

mix•ture \ˈmiks-chər\ *n* **1** : the act, the process, or an instance of mixing **2 a** : something mixed or being mixed ⟨add eggs to the *mixture*⟩ **b** : cloth made of thread of different colors **c** : a preparation consisting of two or more ingredients or kinds ⟨a smoking *mixture*⟩ **3** : the relative proportion of the elements in a mixture ⟨the choke controls the *mixture* of fuel and air in the carburetor⟩ **4 :** two or more substances mixed together but not chemically united and not necessarily present in definite proportions ⟨sand mixed with sugar forms a *mixture*⟩ [Middle French, from Latin *mixtura,* from *miscēre* "to mix"]

mix–up \ˈmik-ˌsəp\ *n* **1 :** a state or an instance of confusion ⟨a *mix-up* in plans⟩ **2 :** FIGHT 1a, MELEE

1**miz•zen** *or* **miz•en** \ˈmiz-n\ *n* **1 :** a fore-and-aft sail set on the mizzenmast **2 :** MIZZENMAST [Middle English *meson,* probably from Middle French *misaine,* derived from Arabic *mazzān* "mast"]

2**mizzen** *or* **mizen** *adj* **:** of or relating to the mizzenmast ⟨*mizzen* shrouds⟩

miz•zen•mast \-ˌmast, -məst\ *n* **:** the mast just behind the mainmast in a ship

mks system \ˌem-ˌkā-ˌes-\ *n* **:** a system of metric measure based on the meter, kilogram, and second as fundamental units

mne•mon•ic \ni-ˈmän-ik\ *adj* **1 :** assisting or intended to assist memory ⟨*mnemonic* devices⟩ **2 :** of or relating to memory [Greek *mnēmonikos,* from *mnēmōn* "mindful", from *mimnēskesthai* "to remember"] — **mne•mon•i•cal•ly** \-ˈmän-i-kə-lē, -klē\ *adv*

moa \ˈmō-ə\ *n* **:** any of various extinct flightless birds of New Zealand [Maori]

moa

Mo•ab•ite \ˈmō-ə-ˌbīt\ *n* **:** a member of an ancient Semitic people related to the Hebrews [*Moab,* ancient kingdom in Syria] — **Moabite** *or* **Mo•ab•it•ish** \-ˌbīt-ish\ *adj*

1**moan** \ˈmōn\ *n* **1 :** COMPLAINT 1, LAMENTATION **2 :** a low drawn-out sound usually indicative of pain or grief [Middle English *mone*]

2**moan** *vb* **1 :** LAMENT 1 **2 :** to utter with a moan or moans **3 :** COMPLAIN 1

moat \ˈmōt\ *n* **:** a deep wide trench around the walls of a castle or fortress usually filled with water [Middle English *mote*]

1**mob** \ˈmäb\ *n* **1 :** the lower classes of a community **:** RABBLE **2 :** a large disorderly crowd often tending to violent or destructive actions **3 :** an organized criminal group **:** GANG [Latin *mobile vulgus* "vacillating crowd"] **syn** see MULTITUDE

2**mob** *vt* **mobbed; mob•bing 1 :** to crowd about and attack or annoy **2 :** to crowd to capacity ⟨customers *mobbed* the store⟩

1**mo•bile** \ˈmō-bəl, -ˌbēl, -ˌbīl\ *adj* **1 :** MOVABLE 1 **2 :** changing quickly in expression ⟨a *mobile* face⟩ **3 :** readily moved ⟨*mobile* troops⟩ **4 :** characterized by movement from one class or group to another ⟨a *mobile* society⟩ [Middle French, from Latin *mobilis,* from *movēre* "to move"] — **mo•bil•i•ty** \mō-ˈbil-ət-ē\ *n*

2**mo•bile** \ˈmō-ˌbēl\ *n* **:** an artistic structure (as of sheet metal) with parts that can be moved by air currents especially when suspended

mo•bi•lize \ˈmō-bə-ˌlīz\ *vb* **1 :** to put into movement or circulation **2 :** to assemble and make ready for action ⟨*mobilize* army reserves⟩ — **mo•bi•li•za•tion** \ˌmō-bə-lə-ˈzā-shən, -blə-ˈzā-\

Mö•bi•us strip \ˌmœ̄b-ē-əs, ˌmərb-, ˌmōb-\ *n* **:** a continuous one-sided surface that is constructed from a rectangle by holding one end fixed, rotating the opposite end through 180 degrees, and applying it to the first end [August F. *Möbius,* died 1868, German mathematician]

mob•oc•ra•cy \mä-ˈbäk-rə-sē\ *n* **1 :** mob rule **2 :** the mob as a ruling class — **mob•o•crat** \ˈmäb-ə-ˌkrat\ *n* — **mob•o•crat•ic** \ˌmäb-ə-ˈkrat-ik\ *adj*

mob•ster \ˈmäb-stər\ *n* **:** a member of a criminal gang

moc•ca•sin \ˈmäk-ə-sən\ *n* **1 :** a soft leather shoe without a heel and with the sole and sides made of one piece joined on top by a seam to a U-shaped piece across the front; *also* **:** a shoe resembling a true moccasin **2 :** WATER MOCCASIN [of American Indian origin]

moccasin flower *n* **:** any of several lady's slippers; *esp* **:** a woodland orchid of eastern North America with usually pink flowers

mo•cha \ˈmō-kə\ *n* **1 a :** choice coffee grown in Arabia **b :** a flavoring made by mixing chocolate and coffee **2 :** a pliable suede-finished glove leather from African sheepskins [*Mocha,* seaport in Arabia]

1**mock** \ˈmäk, ˈmȯk\ *vt* **1 :** to laugh at scornfully **:** RIDICULE **2 :** to mimic in sport or derision [Middle French *mocquer*] **syn** see IMITATE, RIDICULE — **mock•er** *n* — **mock•ing•ly** \-ing-lē\ *adv*

2**mock** *n* **1 :** an act of mocking **:** JEER **2 :** an object of ridicule

3**mock** *adj* **:** not real **:** SHAM ⟨*mock* grief⟩ ⟨a *mock* diamond⟩

4**mock** *adv* **:** in an insincere or sham manner — usually used in combination ⟨*mock*-serious⟩

mock•ery \ˈmäk-rē, ˈmȯk-, -ə-rē\ *n, pl* **-er•ies 1 :** insulting or contemptuous action or speech **2 :** one that is laughed at **3 :** an insincere or a poor imitation ⟨the trial was a *mockery* of justice⟩ **4 :** something ridiculously unsuitable

mock–he•ro•ic \ˌmäk-hi-ˈrō-ik, ˌmȯk-\ *adj* **:** ridiculing or burlesquing heroic style, character, or action ⟨a *mock-heroic* poem⟩

mock•ing•bird \ˈmäk-ing-ˌbərd, ˈmȯk-\ *n* **:** a songbird of the southern United States that is related to the catbirds and thrashers and is noted for the sweetness of its song and for its imitations of the notes of other birds

mock orange *n* **:** a hardy white-flowered shrub; *esp* **:** PHILADELPHUS

mock turtle soup *n* **:** a soup made with meat (as calf's head or veal) in imitation of green turtle soup

mock–up \ˈmäk-ˌəp, ˈmȯk-\ *n* **:** a full-sized structural model built accurately to scale chiefly for study, testing, or display ⟨a *mock-up* of an airplane⟩

mod \ˈmäd\ *adj* **:** MODERN; *esp* **:** bold and free in style, behavior, or dress

mod•al \ˈmōd-l\ *adj* **1 :** of or relating to a mode or to form as opposed to substance **2 :** relating to or being a modal auxiliary — **mo•dal•i•ty** \mō-ˈdal-ət-ē\ *n* — **mo•dal•ly** \ˈmōd-l-ē\ *adv*

modal auxiliary *n* **:** a verb (as *can, must, might, should*) that is typically used with another verb to indicate that the state or action expressed is something other than a simple fact (as a possibility or a necessity) ⟨in "we may go tomorrow" *may* is a *modal auxiliary*⟩

1**mode** \ˈmōd\ *n* **1 :** an arrangement of the eight tones of an octave according to one of several fixed schemes of their intervals **2 :** 2MOOD **3 a :** a particular form or variety of something **b :** a form or manner of expression **:** STYLE **c :** a manner of doing something ⟨*mode* of travel⟩ **4 :** the most frequent value of a set of data [Latin *modus* "measure, manner, musical mode"]

2**mode** *n* **:** a prevailing fashion or style (as of dress or behavior) **syn** see FASHION [French, literally, "manner", from Latin *modus*]

1**mod•el** \ˈmäd-l\ *n* **1 a :** a small but exact copy of something ⟨a ship *model*⟩ **b :** a pattern or figure of something to be made ⟨clay *models* for a statue⟩ **2 :** a person who sets a good example ⟨a *model* of politeness⟩ **3 a :** a person or thing that serves as an artist's pattern; *esp* **:** a person who poses for an artist **b :** a person employed to display garments or other merchandise; *esp* **:** MANNEQUIN **4 :** a type of design of product (as a car or airplane) **5 a :** a description or analogy used to help visualize something (as an atom) that cannot be directly observed **b :** a system of assumptions, data, and inferences used to describe mathematically an object or state of affairs **6 :** a theoretical projection of a possible or imaginary system [Middle French *modelle,* from Italian *modello,* from Latin *modulus* "small measure", from *modus* "measure, mode"]

2**model** *vb* **mod•eled** *or* **mod•elled; mod•el•ing** *or* **mod•el•ling** \ˈmäd-ling, -l-ing\ **1 :** to plan or shape after a pattern ⟨a sports car *modeled* on a racing car⟩ **2 :** to make a model **:** MOLD ⟨*model* a dog in clay⟩ **3 :** to act or serve as a model ⟨*model* for an artist⟩ — **mod•el•er** *or* **mod•el•ler** \ˈmäd-lər, -l-ər\ *n*

3**model** *adj* **1 :** serving as or worthy of being a pattern ⟨a *model*

\ə\ **abut**	\au̇\ **out**	\i\ **tip**	\ȯ\ **saw**	\u̇\ **foot**
\ər\ **further**	\ch\ **chin**	\ī\ **life**	\ȯi\ **coin**	\y\ **yet**
\a\ **mat**	\e\ **pet**	\j\ **job**	\th\ **thin**	\yü\ **few**
\ā\ **take**	\ē\ **easy**	\ng\ **sing**	\t͟h\ **this**	\yu̇\ **cure**
\ä\ **cot, cart**	\g\ **go**	\ō\ **bone**	\ü\ **food**	\zh\ **vision**

student⟩ **2 :** being a miniature representation of something ⟨a *model* airplane⟩
¹mod•er•ate \ˈmäd-rət, -ə-rət\ *adj* **1 a :** avoiding extremes (as of behavior) ⟨a *moderate* smoker⟩ **b :** CALM, TEMPERATE ⟨were *moderate* in your protests⟩ **2 a :** tending toward the average ⟨a *moderate* rain⟩ **b :** neither very good nor very bad **:** MEDIOCRE ⟨*moderate* success⟩ **3 :** avoiding extreme political or social measures ⟨a *moderate* candidate⟩ **4 :** reasonable in price ⟨*moderate* rates⟩ **5 :** of medium lightness and medium chroma ⟨a *moderate* blue⟩ [Latin *moderatus,* from *moderare* "to moderate"] — **mod•er•ate•ly** *adv* — **mod•er•ate•ness** *n*
• syn MODERATE, TEMPERATE mean being neither very much nor very little. MODERATE implies absence or avoidance of excess ⟨*moderate* prices⟩ ⟨a *moderate* liking for candy⟩ TEMPERATE suggests the exercise of restraint ⟨*temperate* use of alcohol⟩
²mod•er•ate \ˈmäd-ə-ˌrāt\ *vb* **1 :** to make or become less violent, severe, or intense **2 :** to preside over a meeting
³mod•er•ate \ˈmäd-rət, -ə-rət\ *n* **:** one holding moderate views or belonging to a moderate group (as in politics)
mod•er•a•tion \ˌmäd-ə-ˈrā-shən\ *n* **1 :** the action of moderating **2 :** the quality or state of being moderate **:** an avoidance of extremes ⟨do everything in *moderation*⟩
mod•er•a•to \ˌmäd-ə-ˈrät-ō\ *adv or adj* **:** MODERATE 1a — used as a direction in music to indicate tempo [Italian, from Latin *moderatus*]
mod•er•a•tor \ˈmäd-ə-ˌrāt-ər\ *n* **1 :** one that moderates **2 :** a presiding officer (as of a Presbyterian governing body, a town meeting, or a discussion group) **3 :** a substance (as graphite) used for slowing down neutrons in a nuclear reactor — **mod•er•a•tor•ship** \-ˌship\ *n*
¹mod•ern \ˈmäd-ərn\ *adj* **1 :** of or relating to the period from about 1500 to the present ⟨*modern* history⟩ **2 :** of, relating to, or characteristic of the present or the immediate past **:** CONTEMPORARY **3 :** involving recent techniques, methods, and ideas **:** UP-TO-DATE [Late Latin *modernus,* from Latin *modo* "just now", from *modus* "measure, mode"] **syn** see RECENT — **mo•der•ni•ty** \mə-ˈdər-nət-ē, mä-\ *n* — **mod•ern•ly** \ˈmäd-ərn-lē\ *adv* — **mod•ern•ness** \-ərn-nəs\ *n*
²modern *n* **:** a modern person
Modern Greek *n* **:** Greek as used by the Greeks since the end of the Medieval period
Modern Hebrew *n* **:** Hebrew as used in present-day Israel
mod•ern•ism \ˈmäd-ər-ˌniz-əm\ *n* **1 :** a practice, usage, or expression peculiar to modern times **2** *often cap* **:** a movement to adapt religion to modern thought and especially to lessen traditional supernatural elements **3 :** the theory and practices of modern art; *esp* **:** an intentional break with the past and a search for new forms of expression — **mod•ern•ist** \-nəst\ *n or adj* — **mod•ern•is•tic** \ˌmäd-ər-ˈnis-tik\ *adj*
mod•ern•ize \ˈmäd-ər-ˌnīz\ *vb* **:** to make or become modern; *esp* **:** to adapt to present usage, style, or taste ⟨*modernize* an old house⟩ — **mod•ern•iza•tion** \ˌmäd-ər-nə-ˈzā-shən\ *n* — **mod•ern•iz•er** \ˈmäd-ər-ˌnī-zər\ *n*
mod•est \ˈmäd-əst\ *adj* **1 :** having a moderate opinion of one's own good qualities and abilities **:** not boastful ⟨a *modest* winner⟩ **2 :** showing moderation **:** not excessive ⟨a *modest* request⟩ ⟨a *modest* cottage⟩ **3 :** pure in thought, conduct, and dress **:** DECENT [Latin *modestus* "moderate"] **syn** see CHASTE, SHY — **mod•est•ly** *adv*
mod•es•ty \ˈmäd-ə-stē\ *n* **:** the quality of being modest; *esp* **:** freedom from conceit or impropriety
mo•di•cum \ˈmäd-i-kəm, ˈmōd-\ *n* **:** a limited quantity **:** a small amount ⟨a *modicum* of intelligence⟩ [Latin, neuter of *modicus* "moderate", from *modus* "measure, mode"]
mod•i•fi•ca•tion \ˌmäd-ə-fə-ˈkā-shən\ *n* **1 :** a limiting of the meaning or application (as of a statement) **2 :** partial alteration ⟨*modification* of plans⟩
mod•i•fi•er \ˈmäd-ə-ˌfī-ər, -ˌfīr\ *n* **:** a word (as an adjective or adverb) used with another word to limit or qualify its meaning
mod•i•fy \ˈmäd-ə-ˌfī\ *vb* **-fied; -fy•ing 1 a :** to make changes in **:** ALTER ⟨*modify* a plan⟩ **b :** to become modified **2 :** to lower or reduce in extent or degree **:** MODERATE ⟨*modify* a punishment⟩ **3 :** to limit in meaning **:** QUALIFY ⟨in the phrase "green gloves" "green" *modifies* "gloves"⟩ [Middle French *modifier,* from Latin *modificare* "to measure, moderate", from *modus* "measure"] **syn** see CHANGE — **mod•i•fi•able** \-ˌfī-ə-bəl\ *adj* — **mod•i•fi•able•ness** *n*
mod•ish \ˈmōd-ish\ *adj* **:** FASHIONABLE 1, STYLISH ⟨was a *modish* dresser⟩ — **mod•ish•ly** *adv* — **mod•ish•ness** *n*
mod•u•lar \ˈmäj-ə-lər\ *adj* **:** of, relating to, or based on a module or a modulus
modular arithmetic *n* **:** arithmetic that deals with whole numbers where the numbers are replaced by their remainders after division by a fixed number ⟨5 hours after 10 o'clock is 3 o'clock because clocks follow a *modular arithmetic* with modulus 12⟩
mod•u•late \ˈmäj-ə-ˌlāt\ *vb* **1 :** to tune to a key or pitch **2 :** to adjust or regulate to a certain proportion ⟨*modulated* the voice⟩ **3 :** to vary the frequency, amplitude, or phase of (a carrier wave or signal) in radio, television, telephony, or telegraphy **4 :** to pass from one musical key to another usually in a gradual movement [Latin *modulari* "to play, sing", from *modulus* "small measure, rhythm", from *modus* "measure, mode"] — **mod•u•la•tor** \-ˌlāt-ər\ *n* — **mod•u•la•to•ry** \-lə-ˌtōr-ē, -ˌtór-\ *adj*
mod•u•la•tion \ˌmäj-ə-ˈlā-shən\ *n* **1 :** an action of modulating **2 :** the extent or degree by which something is modulated **3 :** variation of some quality (as the frequency or amplitude) of the carrier wave in radio, television, telephony, or telegraphy in accordance with the signal that is to be transmitted
mod•ule \ˈmäj-ül\ *n* **1 :** a standard or unit of measurement **2 a :** any of a series of units intended for use together **b :** a usually packaged functional subassembly of parts (as for an electronic device) **3 :** an independent unit that is a part of the total structure of a space vehicle [Latin *modulus* "small measure", from *modus* "measure, mode"]
mod•u•lo \ˈmäj-ə-ˌlō\ *prep* **:** with respect to a modulus of [New Latin, from *modulus*]
mod•u•lus \ˈmäj-ə-ləs\ *n, pl* **-li** \-ˌlī, -ˌlē\ **1 :** a number that expresses the degree in which a property (as elasticity) is possessed by a substance or body **2 a :** ABSOLUTE VALUE 2 **b :** an integer that when divided into the difference of two numbers leaves no remainder **c :** the number of different numbers used in a system of modular arithmetic [New Latin, from Latin, "small measure"]
mo•dus ope•ran•di \ˌmōd-ə-ˌsäp-ə-ˈran-dē, -ˌdī\ *n, pl* **mo•di operandi** \ˌmō-ˌdē-ˌäp-, ˈmō-ˌdī-\ **:** a method of procedure [New Latin]
mo•dus vi•ven•di \ˌmō-dəs-vi-ˈven-dē, -ˌdī\ *n, pl* **mo•di vivendi** \ˈmō-ˌdē-vi-, ˈmō-ˌdī-\ **1 :** a feasible arrangement or practical compromise **2 :** a way of life [New Latin, "manner of living"]
¹mo•gul \ˈmō-gəl, ˈmō-ˌgəl, mō-ˈgəl\ *n* **1** *or* **mo•ghul** *often cap* **:** an Indian Muslim of or descended from one of several conquering groups of Mongol, Turkish, and Persian origin **2 :** a great personage **:** MAGNATE [Persian *Mughul,* from Mongolian *Mongol* "Mongol"] — **mogul** *adj, often cap*
²mogul \ˈmō-gəl\ *n* **:** a bump on a ski slope [probably of Scandinavian origin]
mo•hair \ˈmō-ˌhaər, -ˌheər\ *n* **:** a fabric or yarn made of or with the long silky hair of the Angora goat; *also* **:** hair of this goat [obsolete Italian *mocaiarro,* from Arabic *mukhayyar,* literally, "choice"]
Mo•ham•med•an *variant of* MUHAMMADAN
Mo•hawk \ˈmō-ˌhók\ *pl* **Mohawk** *or* **Mohawks :** a member of an Iroquoian people of what is now northeastern and east central New York
Mo•hi•can \mō-ˈhē-kən, mə-\ *or* **Ma•hi•can** \mə-\ *n, pl* **Mohican** *or* **Mohicans** *or* **Mahican** *or* **Mahicans 1 :** a member of an Algonquian people of the upper Hudson river valley **2 :** the language of the Mohican people
Mo•ho \ˈmō-ˌhō\ *n* **:** the transition zone between the earth's crust and mantle [short for *Mohorovicic discontinuity,* from Andrija *Mohorovičic,* died 1936, Yugoslav geologist]
Mo•ho•ro•vi•cic discontinuity \ˌmō-hə-ˈrō-və-ˌchich-\ *n* **:** MOHO
Mohs' scale \ˈmōz-, ˈmōs-, ˌmō-səz-\ *n* **:** a scale of hardness for minerals ranging from 1 for the softest to 10 for the hardest in which 1 represents the hardness of talc; 2, gypsum; 3, calcite; 4, fluorite; 5, apatite; 6, orthoclase; 7, quartz; 8, topaz; 9, corundum; and 10, diamond [Friedrich *Mohs,* died 1839, German mineralogist]
moi•ety \ˈmói-ət-ē\ *n, pl* **-ties :** one of two equal or approximately equal parts **:** HALF [Middle French *moité,* from Late Latin *medietas,* from Latin *medius* "middle"]
¹moil \ˈmóil\ *vi* **:** to work hard **:** DRUDGE [Middle English *moillen* "to wet, dirty", from Middle French *moillier* "to wet", derived from Latin *mollis* "soft"] — **moil•er** *n*

[2]**moil** *n* **1** : hard work : DRUDGERY **2** : CONFUSION 1

moi•ré \mȯ-'rā, mwä-\ *or* **moire** *same, or* 'mȯir, 'mȯr, 'mwär\ *n* : a fabric with a shimmering watery look; *also* : an appearance suggesting this [French *moiré,* from *moire* "watered mohair", from English *mohair*] — **moiré** *adj*

moist \'mȯist\ *adj* : slightly wet : not completely dry : DAMP ⟨*moist* earth⟩ [Middle French *moiste,* derived from Latin *mucidus* "slimy", from *mucus* "mucus"] — **moist•ly** *adv* — **moist•ness** \'mȯist-nəs, 'mȯis-\ *n*

moist•en \'mȯis-ⁿn\ *vb* **moist•ened**; **moist•en•ing** \-n-ing, 'mȯis-ning\ : to make or become moist — **moist•en•er** \'mȯis-n-ər, 'mȯis-nər\ *n*

mois•ture \'mȯis-chər\ *n* : the small amount of liquid that causes moistness : DAMPNESS

mol•al \'mō-ləl\ *adj* : of, relating to, or containing one mole of solute per 1000 grams of solvent — **mo•lal•i•ty** \mō-'lal-ət-ē\ *n*

[1]**mo•lar** \'mō-lər\ *n* : a tooth with a rounded or flattened surface adapted for grinding; *esp* : a grinding tooth of a mammal that is situated behind the premolars [Latin *molaris,* from *mola* "millstone"]

[2]**molar** *adj* **1** : able or fitted to grind **2** : of or relating to a molar

[3]**molar** *adj* **1** : of or relating to a molecule or mole **2** : of, relating to, or containing one mole of solute per liter of solution — **mo•lar•i•ty** \mō-'lar-ət-ē\ *n*

mo•las•ses \mə-'las-əz\ *n* : a thick brown syrup that is separated from raw sugar in sugar manufacture [Portuguese *melaço,* from Late Latin *mellaceum* "grape juice", from Latin *mel* "honey"]

[1]**mold** *or* **mould** \'mōld\ *n* : light rich crumbly earth containing decayed organic matter [Old English *molde*]

[2]**mold** *or* **mould** **1** : distinctive nature or character : TYPE ⟨a person of austere *mold*⟩ **2** : the frame on or around which an object is constructed **3 a** : a cavity in which something is shaped ⟨a *mold* for metal type⟩ **b** : something shaped in a mold ⟨a *mold* of ice cream⟩ [Old French *modle,* from Latin *modulus* "small measure", from *modus* "measure, mode"]

[3]**mold** *or* **mould** *vb* **1** : to knead into shape ⟨*mold* loaves of bread⟩ **2** : to form or become formed in or as if in a mold ⟨*mold* butter⟩ ⟨*mold* the character of a child⟩ — **mold•able** \'mōl-də-bəl\ *adj* — **mold•er** *n*

[4]**mold** *also* **mould** *n* : an often woolly surface growth of fungus especially on damp or decaying organic matter; *also* : a fungus that produces mold [Middle English *mowlde*]

[5]**mold** *also* **mould** *vi* : to become moldy

mold•board \'mōld-,bōrd, 'mōl-, -,bȯrd\ *n* : a curved iron plate attached above the plowshare of a plow to lift and turn the soil

mol•der \'mōl-dər\ *vi* **mol•dered**; **mol•der•ing** \-də-ring, -dring\ : to crumble into particles [derived from [5]*mold*]

mold•ing \'mōl-ding\ *n* **1** : the act or work of a person who molds **2** : an object produced by molding **3** : a strip of material having a shaped surface and used (as on a wall or the edge of a table) as a decoration or finish

moldy \'mōl-dē\ *adj* **mold•i•er**; **-est** **1** : of, resembling, or covered with a mold **2 a** : being old and moldering **b** : OUTMODED — **mold•i•ness** n

[1]**mole** \'mōl\ *n* : a small usually brown and sometimes protruding permanent spot on the skin [Old English *māl*]

[2]**mole** *n* : any of numerous burrowing insectivores with tiny eyes, concealed ears, and soft fur [Middle English]

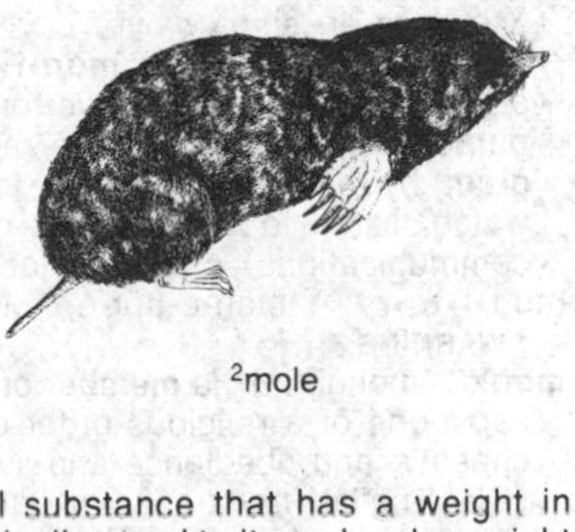

[2]mole

[3]**mole** *n* **1** : a heavy masonry structure built in the sea as a breakwater or pier **2** : the harbor formed by a mole [Middle French, from Italian *molo,* from Late Greek *mōlos,* from Latin *moles,* literally, "mass"]

[4]**mole** *also* **mol** \'mōl\ *n* : the quantity of a chemical substance that has a weight in mass units (as grams) numerically equal to its molecular weight [German *mol,* short for *molekulargewicht* "molecular weight"]

mo•lec•u•lar \mə-'lek-yə-lər\ *adj* : of, relating to, or produced by molecules

molecular biology *n* : a branch of biology dealing with the ultimate physical and chemical organization of living matter and with the molecular basis of inheritance and protein synthesis — **molecular biologist** *n*

molecular formula *n* : a chemical formula that gives the total number of atoms of each element present in a molecule

molecular weight *n* : the weight of a molecule equal to the sum of the weights of the atoms contained in it

mol•e•cule \'mäl-i-,kyül\ *n* **1** : the smallest portion of a substance that retains all the properties of the substance and is composed of one or more atoms **2** : a very small bit : PARTICLE [French *molécule,* derived from Latin *moles* "mass"]

mole•hill \'mōl-,hil\ *n* : a little ridge of earth thrown up by a mole

mole•skin \-,skin\ *n* **1** : the skin of the mole used as fur **2 a** : a heavy cotton fabric with a velvety nap on one side **b** *pl* : trousers of this fabric

mo•lest \mə-'lest\ *vt* **1** : to annoy, disturb, or persecute especially with hostile or injurious effect **2** : to take indecent liberties with [Middle French *molester,* from Latin *molestare,* from *molestus* "burdensome", from *moles* "mass, burden"] — **mo•les•ta•tion** \,mōl-,es-'tā-shən, ,mōl-əs-, mäl-\ *n* — **mo•lest•er** \mə-'les-tər\ *n*

moll \'mäl\ *n* : a gangster's girl friend [probably from *Moll,* nickname for *Mary*]

mol•lie \'mäl-ē\ *n* : any of several brightly colored topminnows often kept in a tropical aquarium [François N. *Mollien,* died 1850, French statesman]

mol•li•fy \'mäl-ə-,fī\ *vt* **-fied**; **-fy•ing** **1** : CALM 2, QUIET **2** : to soothe in temper or disposition [Middle French *mollifier,* from Late Latin *mollificare,* from Latin *mollis* "soft"] **syn** see PACIFY — **mol•li•fi•ca•tion** \,mäl-ə-fə-'kā-shən\ *n*

mol•lusk *or* **mol•lusc** \'mäl-əsk\ *n* : any of a large phylum (Mollusca) of invertebrate animals (as snails or clams) with a soft body lacking segments and usually enclosed in a calcareous shell [French *mollusque,* derived from Latin *molluscus* "soft", from *mollis*] — **mol•lus•can** \mə-'ləs-kən, mä-\ *adj*

[1]**mol•ly•cod•dle** \'mäl-ē-,käd-l\ *n* : a person who is used to being coddled or petted; *esp* : a pampered man or boy [from *Molly,* nickname for *Mary*]

[2]**mollycoddle** *vt* **cod•dled**; **-cod•dling** \-,käd-ling, -l-ing\ : CODDLE 2, PAMPER — **mol•ly•cod•dler** \-,käd-lər, -l-ər\ *n*

Mo•lo•tov cocktail \,mäl-ə-,tȯf-, ,mȯl-, ,mōl-, -,tȯv-\ *n* : a crude incendiary device made of a bottle filled with a flammable liquid (as gasoline) and fitted with a wick or saturated rag that is ignited at the moment of hurling [Vyacheslav M. *Molotov*]

[1]**molt** *or* **moult** \'mōlt\ *vb* : to shed hair, feathers, outer skin, or horns periodically with the cast-off parts being replaced by a new growth [Middle English *mouten,* derived from Latin *mutare* "to change"] — **molt•er** *n*

[2]**molt** *or* **moult** *n* : the act or process of molting

mol•ten \'mōlt-ⁿn\ *adj* **1** *obs* : made by melting and casting **2** : melted especially by intense heat ⟨*molten* rock⟩ [Middle English, from past participle of *melten* "to melt"]

mol•to \'mōl-tō, 'mȯl-\ *adv* : MUCH, VERY — used in music directions ⟨*molto* adagio⟩ [Italian, from Latin *multum,* from *multus,* adj., "much"]

mo•ly \'mō-lē\ *n* : a mythical herb with black root, white flowers, and magic powers [Latin, from Greek *mōly*]

mo•lyb•de•nite \mə-'lib-də-,nīt\ *n* : a soft bluish gray mineral MoS_2 consisting of molybdenum and sulfur and constituting a source of molybdenum

mo•lyb•de•num \-də-nəm\ *n* : a gray metallic element used in steel alloys to give greater strength and hardness — see ELEMENT table [New Latin, from Latin *molybdaena* "galena", from Greek *molybdaina,* from *molybdos* "lead"]

mom \'mäm, 'məm\ *n* : MOTHER 1a [short for *momma,* variant of *mama*]

mo•ment \'mō-mənt\ *n* **1** : a minute portion or point of time : INSTANT **2 a** : present time **b** : a time of importance or conspicuousness ⟨we have our *moments*⟩ **3** : IMPORTANCE, CONSEQUENCE ⟨a matter of great *moment*⟩ [Middle French, from Latin *momentum* "movement, particle sufficient to turn the scales, moment", from *movēre* "to move"]

\ə\ **abut**	\au̇\ **out**	\i\ **tip**	\ȯ\ **saw**	\u̇\ **foot**
\ər\ **further**	\ch\ **chin**	\ī\ **life**	\ȯi\ **coin**	\y\ **yet**
\a\ **mat**	\e\ **pet**	\j\ **job**	\th\ **thin**	\yü\ **few**
\ā\ **take**	\ē\ **easy**	\ng\ **sing**	\t͟h\ **this**	\yu̇\ **cure**
\ä\ **cot, cart**	\g\ **go**	\ō\ **bone**	\ü\ **food**	\zh\ **vision**

mo•men•tar•i•ly \ˌmō-mən-ˈter-ə-lē\ *adv* **1** : for a moment ⟨the pain eased *momentarily*⟩ **2** : INSTANTLY ⟨was stunned by the blow but recovered *momentarily*⟩ **3** : at any moment ⟨we expect them *momentarily*⟩

mo•men•tary \ˈmō-mən-ˌter-ē\ *adj* : lasting only a moment : SHORT-LIVED, TRANSITORY — **mo•men•tar•i•ness** *n*

mo•ment•ly \ˈmō-mənt-lē\ *adv* **1** : from moment to moment **2** : MOMENTARILY 1, 3

mo•men•tous \mō-ˈment-əs\ *adj* : very important : CONSEQUENTIAL ⟨a *momentous* decision⟩ — **mo•men•tous•ly** *adv* — **mo•men•tous•ness** *n*

mo•men•tum \mō-ˈment-əm\ *n, pl* **-men•ta** \-ˈment-ə\ *or* **-men•tums** **1** : property of a moving body that determines the length of time required to bring it to rest when under the action of a constant force or moment : the product of the mass of a body and its velocity **2** : IMPETUS 1 [Latin, "movement, moment"]

mon- *or* **mono-** *combining form* **1** : one : single : alone ⟨*mono*mania⟩ ⟨*mono*plane⟩ **2** : containing one (usually specified) atom or group ⟨*mon*oxide⟩ [Greek, from *monos* "alone, single"]

mo•nad•nock \mə-ˈnad-ˌnäk\ *n* : a hill or mountain of resistant rock surmounting a peneplain [Mount *Monadnock,* New Hampshire]

mon•arch \ˈmän-ərk, -ˌärk\ *n* **1** : a person who reigns over a kingdom or empire: **a** : a sovereign ruler ⟨an absolute *monarch*⟩ **b** : one acting primarily as chief of state and exercising only limited powers ⟨a constitutional *monarch*⟩ — compare CZAR, EMPEROR, KAISER, KING, QUEEN **2** : one holding preeminent position or power **3** : a large orange and black migratory American butterfly called also *monarch butterfly* [Late Latin *monarcha,* from Greek *monarchos,* from *mon-* + *archein* "to rule"] — **mo•nar•chal** \mə-ˈnär-kəl, mä-\ *or* **mo•nar•chi•al** \-kē-əl\ *adj*

mo•nar•chi•cal \mə-ˈnär-ki-kəl, mä-\ *or* **mo•nar•chic** \-ˈnär-kik\ *adj* : of, relating to, or characteristic of a monarch or monarchy — **mo•nar•chi•cal•ly** \-ki-kə-lē, -klē\ *adv*

mon•ar•chism \ˈmän-ər-ˌkiz-əm\ *n* : the principles of monarchical government; *also* : belief in such principles — **mon•ar•chist** \-kəst\ *n*

mon•ar•chy \ˈmän-ər-kē\ *n, pl* **-chies** **1** : undivided or absolute rule by one person **2** : a nation or country having a monarch as chief of state **3** : a government having a hereditary chief of state with life tenure and powers varying from nominal to absolute

mon•as•tery \ˈmän-ə-ˌster-ē\ *n, pl* **-ter•ies** : an establishment in which members of a religious community (as of monks) live and carry on their work [Late Latin *monasterium,* from Late Greek *monastērion,* from Greek, "hermit's cell", from *monazein* "to live alone", from *monos* "alone"]

mo•nas•tic \mə-ˈnas-tik\ *adj* **1** : of or relating to monks or monasteries **2** : separated from worldly affairs ⟨a *monastic* life⟩ — **monastic** *n* — **mo•nas•ti•cal•ly** \-ti-kə-lē, -klē\ — **mo•nas•ti•cism** \-tə-ˌsiz-əm\ *n*

mon•atom•ic \ˌmän-ə-täm-ik\ *adj* : consisting of one atom; *esp* : having one atom in the molecule

mon•au•ral \mä-ˈnȯr-əl, ˈmä-\ *adj* : MONOPHONIC 2 — **monau•ral•ly** \-rə-lē\ *adv*

Mon•day \ˈmən-dē\ *n* : the 2d day of the week [Old English *mōnandæg,* derived from a translation of Latin *dies Lunae* "day of the moon", translation of Greek *hēmera Selēnēs*]

mon•e•tary \ˈmän-ə-ˌter-ē, ˈmən-\ *adj* : of or relating to money **syn** see FINANCIAL [Late Latin *monetarius,* from Latin *moneta* "mint, money"]

monetary unit *n* : the standard unit of value of a currency

mon•e•tize \ˈmän-ə-ˌtīz, ˈmən-\ *vt* : to coin into money; *also* : to establish as legal tender — **mon•e•ti•za•tion** \ˌmän-ət-ə-ˈzā-shən, ˌmən-\ *n*

mon•ey \ˈmən-ē\ *n, pl* **mon•eys** *or* **mon•ies** \-ēz\ **1** : something generally accepted as a medium of exchange, a measure of value, or a means of payment: as **a** : officially coined or stamped metal currency **b** : PAPER MONEY **c** : an amount or a sum of money **2** : wealth reckoned in terms of money **3** : a form or denomination of coin or paper money **4** : the 1st, 2d, and 3d place in a horse or dog race ⟨finished in the *money*⟩ **5** : persons or interests possessing or controlling great wealth [Middle French *moneie,* from Latin *moneta* "mint, money"]

money changer *n* : one whose business is the exchanging of kinds or denominations of currency

mon•eyed *or* **mon•ied** \ˈmən-ēd\ *adj* **1** : having money : WEALTHY **2** : consisting of or derived from money

mon•ey•lend•er \ˈmən-ē-ˌlen-dər\ *n* : one whose business is lending money

mon•ey–mak•er \ˈmən-ē-ˌmā-kər\ *n* **1** : one who accumulates wealth **2** : a plan or product that produces profit — **mon•ey–mak•ing** \-king\ *adj or n*

money order *n* : an order for the payment of a specified amount of money to a named payee that can be purchased and cashed at issuing offices (as post offices or banks)

mon•ger \ˈməng-gər, ˈmäng-\ *n* **1** : a dealer in some commodity — usually used in combination ⟨fish*monger*⟩ **2** : one dealing in or promoting something petty or discreditable — usually used in combination ⟨hate*monger*⟩ [Old English *mangere,* from Latin *mango,* of Greek origin]

Mon•gol \ˈmäng-gəl, ˈmän-ˌgōl\ *n* **1 a** : a member of one of the chiefly pastoral Mongoloid peoples of Mongolia **b** : MONGOLOID **2** : MONGOLIAN 2 [Mongolian *Mongol*]

Mon•go•lian \män-ˈgōl-yən, mäng-\ *n* **1** : a native or inhabitant of Mongolia **2** : the Mongolic language of the Mongol people — **Mongolian** *adj*

Mon•gol•ic \män-ˈgäl-ik, mäng-\ *n* : a subfamily of Altaic languages including Mongolian and Kalmuck — **Mongolic** *adj*

mon•gol•ism \ˈmäng-gə-ˌliz-əm\ *n* : DOWN'S SYNDROME

mon•gol•oid \ˈmäng-gə-ˌlȯid\ *adj* **1** *cap* : of or relating to a major racial stock native to Asia and considered to comprise peoples of northern and eastern Asia, Malaysians, Eskimos, and often American Indians **2** : affected with Down's syndrome — **mongoloid** *n, often cap*

mon•goose \ˈmän-ˌgüs, ˈmäng-\ *n, pl* **mon•goos•es** : an agile Indian mammal that is related to the civets, is about the size of a ferret, and feeds on snakes and rodents; *also* : any of several related mammals [Hindi *māgūs*]

mongoose

mon•grel \ˈməng-grəl, ˈmäng-\ *n* **1** : the offspring of parents of different breeds (as of dogs); *esp* : one of uncertain ancestry **2** : a person or thing of mixed origin [probably from Middle English *mong* "mixture"] — **mongrel** *adj* — **mon•grel•iza•tion** \ˌməng-grə-lə-ˈzā-shən, ˌmäng-\ *n* — **mon•grel•ize** \ˈməng-grə-ˌlīz, ˈmäng-\ *vt*

mon•i•ker *or* **mon•ick•er** \ˈmän-i-kər\ *n, slang* : NAME 1, NICKNAME [origin unknown]

mo•nism \ˈmō-ˌniz-əm, ˈmän-ˌiz-\ *n* : a view that a complex entity (as the universe) is basically one — **mo•nist** \ˈmō-nəst, ˈmän-əst\ *n* — **mo•nis•tic** \mō-ˈnis-tik, mä-\ *or* **mo•nis•ti•cal** \-ti-kəl\ *adj*

[1]**mon•i•tor** \ˈmän-ət-ər\ *n* **1 a** : a student appointed to assist a teacher **b** : one that warns or instructs **c** : one that monitors or is used in monitoring; *esp* : a receiver used to view the picture being picked up by a television camera **2** : any of various large tropical Old World lizards closely related to the iguanas [Latin, "one that warns, overseer", from *monēre* "to warn"] — **mon•i•to•ri•al** \ˌmän-ə-ˈtōr-ē-əl, -ˈtȯr-\ *adj* — **mon•i•tor•ship** \ˈmän-ət-ər-ˌship\ *n*

[2]**monitor** *vt* **mon•i•tored**; **mon•i•tor•ing** \ˈmän-ət-ə-ring, ˈmän-ə-tring\ : to watch, observe, or check especially for a special purpose: as **a** : to check (a radio or television signal or program) by means of a receiver for quality of transmission **b** : to watch, listen to, or intercept often secretly ⟨*monitor* enemy communications⟩ **c** : to test for intensity of radioactivity

mon•i•to•ry \ˈmän-ə-ˌtōr-ē, -ˌtȯr-\ *adj* : giving admonition : WARNING

monk \ˈməngk\ *n* : a member of a religious community of men; *esp* : one of a religious order of men taking vows of poverty, chastity, and obedience and living in community under a rule [Old English *munuc,* from Late Latin *monachus,* from Late Greek *monachos,* from Greek *monos* "alone"] — **monk•hood** \-ˌhu̇d\ *n*

[1]**mon•key** \ˈməng-kē\ *n, pl* **monkeys** **1** : a primate mammal other than human beings or usually the lemurs and tarsiers; *esp* : any of the smaller longer-tailed primates as contrasted

with the apes **2 :** a ludicrous figure **:** DUPE [probably of Low German origin] — **mon•key•ish** \-kē-ish\ *adj*

²monkey *vi* **mon•keyed**; **mon•key•ing 1 :** to act in a grotesque or mischievous manner **2 :** FOOL 1b, TRIFLE

monkey business *n* **:** mischievous activity or behavior

mon•key•shine \ˈməng-kē-ˌshīn\ *n* **:** a mischievous trick

monkey wrench *n* **1 :** an adjustable wrench having jaws at right angles to a straight handle **2 :** something that disrupts ⟨the storm threw a *monkey wrench* into our plans⟩

monk•ish \ˈməng-kish\ *adj* **1 :** of or relating to monks **2 :** having features associated with monks or monasticism ⟨lived in *monkish* retirement⟩ — **monk•ish•ly** *adv* — **monk•ish•ness** *n*

monks•hood \ˈməngs-ˌhu̇d, ˈməngks-\ *n* **:** a poisonous Eurasian herb related to the buttercups and often cultivated for its showy hood-shaped white or purplish flowers

mono- — see MON-

See *mono-* and 2d element

monoatomic	**monocolor**	**monodisciplinary**
monoaxial	**monocrop**	**monofunctional**
monocausal	**monocropping**	**monoparental**
monocellular	**monodialectal**	**monopolar**
monocentric	**monodirectional**	

mono•ba•sic \ˌmän-ə-ˈbā-sik\ *adj* **:** having only one hydrogen atom replaceable by an atom or radical ⟨*monobasic* acid⟩

mono•chrome \ˈmän-ə-ˌkrōm\ *n* **:** a painting, drawing, or photograph in a single hue — **monochrome** *adj*

mon•o•cle \ˈmän-i-kəl\ *n* **:** an eyeglass for one eye [French, from Late Latin *monoculus* "one-eyed", from Latin *mon-* "mon-" + *oculus* "eye"] — **mon•o•cled** \-kəld\ *adj*

monocle

mono•clin•ic \ˌmän-ə-ˈklin-ik\ *adj* **:** being a crystal in which the three axes are of unequal length with two of them at right angles to each other and the third perpendicular to only one of the other two

mono•cli•nous \-ˈklī-nəs\ *adj* **:** having both stamens and pistils in the same flower — compare DICLINOUS [*mon-* + Greek *klinē* "bed", from *klinein* "to lean, recline"]

mon•o•cot \ˈmän-ə-ˌkät\ *n* **:** MONOCOTYLEDON — **monocot** *adj*

mono•cot•y•le•don \ˌmän-ə-ˌkät-l-ˈēd-n\ *n* **:** any of a group (Monocotyledoneae) of seed plants having an embryo with a single cotyledon and usually parallel-veined leaves and flower parts in groups of three — **mono•cot•y•le•don•ous** \-n-əs\ *adj*

mon•oc•u•lar \mä-ˈnäk-yə-lər, mə-\ *adj* **:** of, relating to, or suitable for use with only one eye

mono•cul•ture \ˈmän-ə-ˌkəl-chər\ *n* **:** the cultivation of a single crop to the exclusion of other uses of land

mono•cyte \ˈmän-ə-ˌsīt\ *n* **:** a large phagocytic white blood cell — **mono•cyt•ic** \ˌmän-ə-ˈsit-ik\ *adj*

mon•o•dy \ˈmän-əd-ē\ *n, pl* **-dies 1 :** ELEGY **2 :** a style of musical composition in which one voice part carries the melody; *also* **:** a composition in this style [Medieval Latin *monodia* "lyric sung by one voice", from Greek *monōidia,* from *mon-* + *aidein* "to sing"] — **mo•nod•ic** \mə-ˈnäd-ik\ *adj* — **mon•o•dist** \ˈmän-əd-əst\ *n*

mon•oe•cious \mə-ˈnē-shəs, män-ˈē-\ *adj* **:** having pistils and stamens in different flowers on the same plant [derived from Greek *mon-* + *oikos* "house"] — **mon•oe•cism** \mə-ˈnē-ˌsiz-əm, män-ˈē-\ *n*

mo•nog•a•mous \mə-ˈnäg-ə-məs\ *adj* **:** of, relating to, or practicing monogamy — **mo•nog•a•mous•ly** *adv* — **mo•nog•a•mous•ness** *n*

mo•nog•a•my \mə-ˈnäg-ə-mē\ *n* **:** marriage with only one person at a time — **mo•nog•a•mist** \-ˈnäg-ə-məst\ *n*

mono•gram \ˈmän-ə-ˌgram\ *n* **:** an identifying symbol or character usually made up of two or more letters — **monogram** *vt* — **mono•grammed** \-ˌgramd\ *adj*

mono•graph \ˈmän-ə-ˌgraf\ *n* **:** a learned treatise on a particular subject; *esp* **:** a scholarly or scientific paper printed in a journal or as a pamphlet

mono•hy•brid \ˌmän-ə-ˈhī-brəd\ *adj* **:** heterozygous in respect to a single gene pair — **monohybrid** *n*

mono•lay•er \ˈmän-ə-ˌlā-ər, -ˌle-ər, -ˌler\ *n* **:** a layer or film one cell or molecule in thickness

mono•lin•gual \ˌmän-ə-ˈling-gwəl\ *adj* **:** expressed in or knowing or using only one language

mon•o•lith \ˈmän-l-ˌith\ *n* **1 :** a single great stone often in the form of a monument or column **2 :** something (as a political organization) held to be a single massive whole exhibiting solid uniformity — **mon•o•lith•ic** \ˌmän-l-ˈith-ik\ *adj*

mon•o•logue *or* **mon•o•log** \ˈmän-l-ˌȯg, -ˌäg\ *n* **1 :** a dramatic scene in which one person speaks alone **2 :** a drama performed by one actor **3 :** a literary composition (as a poem) in the form of a soliloquy **4 :** a long speech monopolizing a conversation [French *monologue,* from *mon-* "mon-" + *-logue* (as in dialogue)] — **mon•o•logu•ist** \ˈmän-l-ˌȯg-əst, -ˌäg-\ *or* **mo•no•lo•gist** *same or* mə-ˈnäl-ə-jest\ *n*

mono•ma•nia \ˌmän-ə-ˈmā-nē-ə, -ˈmā-nyə\ *n* **:** excessive concentration on a single object or idea — **mono•ma•ni•ac** \-ˈmā-nē-ˌak\ *n or adj*

mon•o•mer \ˈmän-ə-mər\ *n* **:** one of the molecular units of a polymer [*mon-* + *-mer* (as in *polymer*)] — **mon•o•mer•ic** \ˌmän-ə-ˈmer-ik\ *adj*

mo•nom•e•ter \mə-ˈnäm-ət-ər, mä-\ *n* **:** a line of verse consisting of one metrical foot

mo•no•mi•al \mä-ˈnō-mē-əl, mə-ˈnō-\ *n* **:** a mathematical expression consisting of a single term [blend of *mon-* and *-nomial* (as in *binomial*)] — **monomial** *adj*

mono•mo•lec•u•lar \ˌmän-ō-mə-ˈlek-yə-lər\ *adj* **:** being only one molecule thick ⟨a *monomolecular* film⟩ — **mono•mo•lec•u•lar•ly** *adv*

mono•nu•cle•o•sis \ˌmän-ə-ˌnü-klē-ˈō-səs, -ˌnyü-\ *n* **:** an abnormal increase in the blood of leukocytes lacking cytoplasmic granules; *esp* **:** INFECTIOUS MONONUCLEOSIS

mono•phon•ic \ˌmän-ə-ˈfän-ik\ *adj* **1 :** having a single melodic line with little or no accompaniment **2 :** of or relating to sound transmission, recording, or reproduction involving a single transmission path — compare STEREOPHONIC

mon•oph•thong \ˈmän-əf-ˌthȯng, ˈmän-ə-ˌ\ *n* **:** a vowel sound that throughout its duration has a single constant articulatory position [Late Greek *monophthongos* "single vowel", from Greek *mon-* + *phthongos* "sound"] — **mon•oph•thon•gal** \ˌmän-əf-ˈthong-əl, män-ə-ˈ, -gəl\ *adj*

mono•plane \ˈmän-ə-ˌplān\ *n* **:** an airplane with only one pair of wings

mono•ploid \ˈmän-ə-ˌplȯid\ *adj* **:** having or being a chromosome set comprising a single genome [*mon-* + *-ploid* (as in *diploid*)] — **monoploid** *n*

mo•nop•o•list \mə-ˈnäp-ə-ləst\ *n* **:** one who has a monopoly or favors monopoly

mo•nop•o•lis•tic \mə-ˌnäp-ə-ˈlis-tik\ *adj* **:** tending toward or having the characteristics of monopoly — **mo•nop•o•lis•ti•cal•ly** \-ˈlis-ti-kə-lē, -klē\ *adv*

mo•nop•o•lize \mə-ˈnäp-ə-ˌlīz\ *vt* **:** to get or have a monopoly of — **mo•nop•o•li•za•tion** \-ˌnäp-ə-lə-ˈzā-shən\ *n* — **mo•nop•o•liz•er** \-ˈnäp-ə-ˌlī-zər\ *n*

mo•nop•o•ly \mə-ˈnäp-lē, -ə-lē\ *n, pl* **-lies 1 a :** exclusive ownership or control through legal privilege, command of supply, or group action **b :** exclusive possession **2 :** an instance of monopoly **3 :** a commodity controlled by one party **4 :** a person or group having a monopoly [Latin *monopolium,* from Greek *monopōlion,* from *mon-* + *pōlein* "to sell"]

• **syn** TRUST, SYNDICATE, CARTEL: MONOPOLY implies exclusive power to buy or sell in a specified market; TRUST applies specifically to a merger of corporations by which control is given to trustees and the individual owners are compensated by shares of stock; SYNDICATE applies to a group organized to carry out an enterprise or purchase a property requiring large capital outlay; CARTEL commonly implies an international combination of firms for controlling production and control of products in one field or division of industry.

mono•rail \'män-ə-,rāl\ *n* : a single rail serving as a track for cars that are balanced upon it or suspended from it; *also* : a vehicle or system using such a track

mono•sac•cha•ride \,män-ə-'sak-ə-,rīd\ *n* : a sugar (as glucose) not decomposable to simpler sugars by hydrolysis

mono•so•mic \,män-ə-'sō-mik\ *adj* : having one less than the diploid number of chromosomes — **monosomic** *n* — **mono•so•my** \'män-ə-,sō-mē\ *n*

mono•syl•la•ble \'män-ə-,sil-ə-bəl, ,män-ə-'\ *n* : a word of one syllable — **mono•syl•lab•ic** \,män-ə-sə-'lab-ik\ *adj* — **mono•syl•lab•i•cal•ly** \-'lab-i-kə-lē, -klē\ *adv*

mono•the•ism \'män-ə-,thē-,iz-əm\ *n* : a doctrine or belief that there is only one deity — **mono•the•ist** \-,thē-əst\ *n* — **mono•the•is•tic** \-thē-'is-tik\ *adj*

mono•tone \'män-ə-,tōn\ *n* **1** : a succession of syllables, words, or sentences in one unvaried key or pitch ⟨speak in a *monotone*⟩ **2** : a single unvaried musical tone **3** : tedious sameness or repetition ⟨a *monotone* of yellow fields⟩ **4** : a person unable to produce or distinguish between musical intervals — **monotone** *adj* — **mono•ton•ic** \,män-ə-'tän-ik\ *adj* — **mono•ton•i•cal•ly** \-'tän-i-kə-lē, -klē\ *adv*

mo•not•o•nous \mə-'nät-n-əs, -'nät-nəs\ *adj* **1** : uttered or sounded in one unvarying tone **2** : tediously uniform or unvarying ⟨*monotonous* scenery⟩ — **mo•not•o•nous•ly** *adv* — **mo•not•o•nous•ness** *n*

mo•not•o•ny \mə-'nät-n-ē, -'nät-nē\ *n, pl* **-nies** **1** : sameness of tone or sound **2** : lack of variety; *esp* : tiresome sameness ⟨the *monotony* of the empty landscape⟩

mono•treme \'män-ə-,trēm\ *n* : any of an order (Monotremata) of primitive mammals (as the echidna) that lay eggs [derived from Greek *mon-* + trēma "hole"]

mono•va•lent \,män-ə-'vā-lənt\ *adj* : UNIVALENT

mon•ovu•lar \män-'ō-vyə-lər, 'män-\ *adj* : MONOZYGOTIC

mon•ox•ide \mə-'näk-,sīd\ *n* : an oxide containing only one oxygen atom in the molecule

mono•zy•got•ic \,män-ə-zī-'gät-ik\ *adj* : derived from a single egg ⟨*monozygotic* twins⟩

Mon•roe Doctrine \mən-,rō-\ *n* : a statement of United States foreign policy proclaimed in 1823 by President James Monroe expressing opposition to extension of European control or influence in the western hemisphere

mon•sei•gneur \,mō^{n}-,sān-'yər\ *n, pl* **mes•sei•gneurs** \,mā-,sān-'yər, -'yərz\ : a French dignitary — used as a title before another title of office or rank ⟨*Monseigneur* the Archbishop⟩ [French, literally, "my lord"]

mon•sieur \məs-yə, məsh-; mə-'siər\ *n, pl* **mes•sieurs** \məs-yə, -yəz, məsh-, mās-; mə-'siər, -'siərz\ — used by or to French-speaking people as a courtesy title equivalent to *Mr.* [Middle French, literally, "my lord"]

mon•si•gnor \män-'sē-nyər, mən-\ *n, pl* **mon•si•gnors** *or* **mon•si•gno•ri** \,män-,sēn-'yōr-ē, -'yòr-\ : a Roman Catholic prelate — used as a title before the surname or before the given name and the surname ⟨*Monsignor* Smith⟩ ⟨*Monsignor* John Smith⟩ [Italian *monsignore,* from French *monseigneur*] — **mon•si•gno•ri•al** \,män-,sēn-'yōr-ē-əl, -'yòr\ *adj*

mon•soon \män-'sün\ *n* **1** : a wind in the Indian ocean and southern Asia that blows from the southwest from April to October and from the northeast from Ocotober to April **2** : the rainy season that accompanies the southwest monsoon in India and adjacent areas [obsolete Dutch *monssoen,* from Portuguese *monção,* from Arabic *mawsim* "time, season"]

[1]**mon•ster** \'män-stər\ *n* **1** : an animal or plant of abnormal form or structure **2** : a creature of strange or horrible form **3** : one unusually large for its kind **4** : an extremely wicked or cruel person [Middle French *monstre,* from Latin *monstrum* "omen, monster"]

[2]**monster** *adj* : very large : ENORMOUS

mon•strance \'män-strəns\ *n* : a vessel used for showing the Blessed Sacrament [Middle French, from Medieval Latin *monstrantia,* from Latin *monstrare* "to show"]

mon•stros•i•ty \män-'sträs-ət-ē\ *n, pl* **-ties** **1** : the condition of being monstrous **2** : something monstrous : MONSTER

mon•strous \'män-strəs\ *adj* **1** : being great or overwhelming in size : GIGANTIC **2** : having the qualities or appearance of a monster **3 a** : very ugly or vicious : HORRIBLE **b** : shockingly wrong or ridiculous **4** : very different from the usual, natural, or expected — **mon•strous•ly** *adv* — **mon•strous•ness** *n*

• **syn** MONSTROUS, PRODIGIOUS, TREMENDOUS, STUPENDOUS mean extremely impressive especially in size. MONSTROUS further implies ugliness or abnormality; PRODIGIOUS suggests a marvelousness that strains belief; TREMENDOUS implies an awe-inspiring or terrifying effect; STUPENDOUS suggests a power to stun or astound.

mon•tage \män-'täzh, mō^{n}-, -'täzh\ *n* **1** : an artistic composition made up of several different kinds of items (as strips of newspaper or bits of wood) arranged together **2** : PHOTOMONTAGE [French, from *monter* "to mount"]

mon•tane \män-'tān, 'män-,\ *adj* : of, relating to, growing in, or being the relatively moist cool upland slopes below timberline characterized by large evergreen trees as the dominant form of life [Latin *montanus* "of a mountain", from *mont-, mons* "mountain"]

month \'mənth, 'məntth\ *n, pl* **months** \'məns, 'mənths, 'məntths\ : one of the 12 portions into which the year is divided [Old English *mōnath*]

[1]**month•ly** \'mənth-lē, 'məntth-\ *adj* **1** : occurring, done, produced, or issued every month **2** : computed in terms of one month **3** : lasting a month — **monthly** *adv*

[2]**monthly** *n, pl* **monthlies** : a monthly periodical

mon•u•ment \'män-yə-mənt\ *n* **1** : something that serves as a memorial; *esp* : a building, pillar, stone, or statue erected in memory of a person or event **2** : a work, saying, or deed that lasts or that is worth preserving ⟨the book is a *monument* of scholarship⟩ **3** : a boundary marker (as a stone) **4** : a natural feature or historic site set aside and maintained by the government as public property [Latin *monumentum,* from *monēre* "to remind, warn"]

mon•u•men•tal \,män-yə-'ment-l\ *adj* **1** : serving as a monument **2** : OUTSTANDING ⟨a *monumental* achievement⟩ **3** : of, relating to, or suitable for a monument **4** : very great : COLOSSAL ⟨*monumental* stupidity⟩; *esp* : MASSIVE 1 — **mon•u•men•tal•ly** \-l-ē\ *adv*

moo \'mü\ *vi* : to make the natural throat noise of a cow : LOW [imitative] — **moo** *n*

[1]**mood** \'müd\ *n* : a state or frame of mind : HUMOR ⟨in a good *mood*⟩ [Old English *mōd* "mind, mood"]

• **syn** MOOD, HUMOR, TEMPER mean a state of mind in which one emotion or desire temporarily has control. MOOD implies a pervasiveness and compelling quality of the emotion ⟨you can really write when you are in the *mood*⟩ HUMOR implies a mood resulting from one's special temperament or present physical condition ⟨a good dinner put us in a better *humor*⟩ TEMPER suggests the domination of a single strong emotion such as anger ⟨was in a foul *temper* that night⟩

[2]**mood** *n* : a set of inflectional forms of a verb that show whether the action or state expressed is to be thought of as a fact, a command, or a wish or possibility — compare IMPERATIVE, INDICATIVE, SUBJUNCTIVE [alteration of [1]*mode*]

moody \'müd-ē\ *adj* **mood•i•er; -est** **1** : given to moods; *esp* : subject to fits of depression or temper **2** : showing a moody state of mind ⟨a *moody* face⟩ — **mood•i•ly** \'müd-l-ē\ *adv* — **mood•i•ness** \'müd-ē-nəs\ *n*

[1]**moon** \'mün\ *n* **1 a** : the earth's natural satellite shining by the sun's reflected light, revolving about the earth from west to east in about 29 1/2 days, and having a diameter of 3475 kilometers, a mean distance from the earth of about 384,321 kilometers, and a volume about one forty-ninth that of the earth **b** : SATELLITE 2 **2** : the average period of revolution of the moon about the earth **3** : MOONLIGHT [Old English *mōna*] — **moon•less** \-ləs\ *adj* — **moon•like** \-,līk\ *adj*

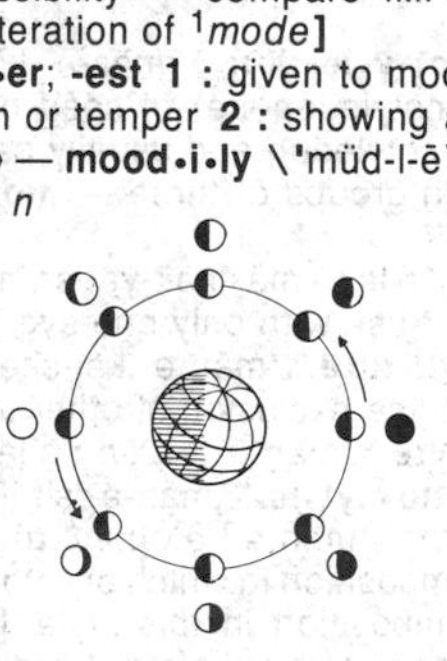

[1]moon 1a

[2]**moon** *vb* : to spend time in idle thought : DREAM

moon•beam \'mün-,bēm\ *n* : a ray of light from the moon

moon blindness *n* : a recurrent eye disorder of the horse — **moon–blind** \-,blīnd\ *adj*

moon•calf \-,kaf, -,käf\ *n* **1** : MONSTER 1 **2** : a foolish or absentminded person : SIMPLETON

moon•fish \-,fish\ *n* : any of various compressed often short deep-bodied silvery or yellowish marine fishes; *also* : PLATY

moon•flow•er \-,flau̇-ər, -,flau̇r\ *n* : a tropical American morning glory with fragrant night-blooming flowers; *also* : any of several related plants

moon·let \'mün-lət\ *n* : a small natural or artificial satellite

1moon·light \-,līt\ *n* : the light of the moon

2moonlight *vi* **-light·ed; -light·ing** : to hold a second usually nighttime job in addition to a regular one — **moon·light·er** *n*

moon·lit \'mün-,lit\ *adj* : lighted by the moon ⟨a *moonlit* night⟩

moon·scape \-,skāp\ *n* : the surface of the moon as seen or as pictured

moon·shine \-,shīn\ *n* **1** : MOONLIGHT **2** : empty talk : NONSENSE **3** : intoxicating liquor; *esp* : illegally distilled corn whiskey — **moon·shin·er** \-,shī-nər\ *n*

moon·stone \-,stōn\ *n* : a transparent or translucent mineral with a pearly greenish or bluish luster that is a variety of feldspar and is used in jewelry

moon·struck \-,strək\ *adj* **1** : mentally unbalanced **2** : romantically sentimental

1moor \'mu̇r\ *n* **1** *chiefly British* : an expanse of open rolling infertile land **2** : a boggy peaty area dominated by grasses and sedges [Old English *mōr*]

2moor *vb* : to secure (as a boat) with cables, lines, or anchors [Middle English *moren*] — **moor·age** \-ij\ *n*

Moor \'mu̇r\ *n* : one of a North African people of mixed Arab and Berber ancestry conquering Spain in the 8th century and ruling until 1492 [Middle French *More,* from Latin *Maurus* "inhabitant of Mauretania"] — **Moor·ish** \-ish\ *adj*

moor·hen \'mu̇r-,hen\ *n* : GALLINULE

moor·ing \'mu̇r-ing\ *n* **1 a** : a place where or an object to which a craft can be made fast **b** : a device (as a chain or line) by which an object is moored **2** : moral or spiritual resources — usually used in pl.

moor·land \'mu̇r-lənd, -,land\ *n* : land consisting of moors

moose \'müs\ *n, pl* **moose** **1** : a large ruminant mammal of the forested parts of Canada and the northern United States that has huge antlers in the male and is related to the typical deers **2** : ELK 1a [of American Indian origin]

1moot \'müt\ *vt* **1** : to bring up for discussion **2** : DISCUSS 1 [obsolete *moot* "discussion", from Old English *mōt* "assembly"]

2moot *adj* **1** : subject to argument or discussion : DEBATABLE ⟨a *moot* question⟩ **2** : ACADEMIC 4

moot court *n* : a mock court in which students of law argue hypothetical cases for practice

1mop \'mäp\ *n* **1** : an implement for cleaning made of a bundle of cloth or yarn or a sponge fastened to a handle **2** : something resembling a mop ⟨a *mop* of hair⟩ [Middle English *mappe*]

2mop *vb* **mopped; mop·ping** : to wipe or clean with or as if with a mop ⟨*mop* one's brow⟩ — **mop·per** *n*

1mope \'mōp\ *vi* **1** : to be in a dull and dispirited state **2** : to move slowly or aimlessly : DAWDLE [probably from obsolete *mop, mope* "fool"] — **mop·er** *n*

2mope *n* **1** : a dull listless person **2** *pl* : low spirits : BLUES ⟨a fit of the *mopes*⟩

mo·ped \'mō-,ped\ *n* : a lightweight low-powered motorbike that can be pedaled [Swedish, from *mo*tor "motor" + *ped*al "pedal"]

mop·pet \'mäp-ət\ *n* : a young child [obsolete *mop* "fool, child"]

mop-up \'mäp-,əp\ *n* : a final clearance or disposal : a concluding action

mop up \mäp-'əp, 'mäp-\ *vb* **1** : to clean up by or as if by mopping ⟨*mop up* spilt milk⟩ **2** : to eliminate remaining resistance ⟨*mop up* enemy forces⟩ **3** : to finish a task

mo·raine \mə-'rān\ *n* : an accumulation of earth and stones deposited by a glacier [French] — **mo·rain·al** \-'rān-l\ *adj* — **mo·rain·ic** \-'rā-nik\ *adj*

1mor·al \'mȯr-əl, 'mär-\ *adj* **1 a** : of or relating to principles of right and wrong in behavior : ETHICAL **b** : expressing or teaching a conception of right behavior ⟨a *moral* poem⟩ **c** : conforming to a standard of right behavior : VIRTUOUS, GOOD ⟨a *moral* life⟩ **d** : capable of right and wrong action **2** : probable but not proved : VIRTUAL ⟨a *moral* certainty⟩ [Middle French, from Latin *moralis,* from *mor-, mos* "custom"] — **mor·al·ly** \-ə-lē\ *adv*

• **syn** ETHICAL: MORAL and ETHICAL are both concerned with rightness or wrongness of actions and conduct, but MORAL is more often applied to the practice or acts of individuals, often specifically in sexual relations, ETHICAL more often to theoretical or general questions of rightness, fairness, or equity.

2moral *n* **1** : the moral significance or practical lesson (as of a story) **2** *pl* : moral conduct **3** *pl* : moral teachings or principles

mo·rale \mə-'ral\ *n* : the mental and emotional condition (as of enthusiasm, spirit, loyalty) of an individual or a group with regard to the function or tasks at hand [French *moral,* from *moral,* adj., "moral"]

mor·al·ist \'mȯr-ə-ləst, 'mär-\ *n* **1** : one who leads a moral life **2** : one who moralizes; *esp* : a person who teaches, studies, or points out morals

mor·al·is·tic \,mȯr-ə-'lis-tik, ,mär-\ *adj* **1** : teaching or pointing out morals ⟨a *moralistic* story⟩ **2** : narrowly conventional in morals ⟨*moralistic* attitudes⟩ — **mor·al·is·ti·cal·ly** \-'lis-ti-kə-lē, -klē\ *adv*

mo·ral·i·ty \mə-'ral-ət-ē\ *n, pl* **-ties** **1** : moral quality or character : VIRTUE ⟨judge the *morality* of an action⟩ **2** : moral conduct ⟨standards of *morality*⟩ **3** : a system of morals : principles of conduct

morality play *n* : an allegorical play especially of the 15th and 16th centuries in which the characters personify moral qualities or abstractions (as beauty or death)

mor·al·ize \'mȯr-ə-,līz, 'mär-\ *vb* **1** : to explain in moral terms **2** : to make moral or morally better **3** : to talk or write in a moralistic way — **mor·al·iza·tion** \,mȯr-ə-lə-'zā-shən, ,mär-\ *n* — **mor·al·iz·er** \'mȯr-ə-,lī-zər, 'mär-\ *n*

mo·rass \mə-'ras\ *n* : MARSH, SWAMP [Dutch *moeras*]

mor·a·to·ri·um \,mȯr-ə-'tōr-ē-əm, ,mär-, -'tȯr-\ *n, pl* **-ri·ums** *or* **-ria** \-ē-ə\ **1** : a legally authorized period of delay in the performance of an obligation (as the payment of a debt) ⟨a *moratorium* on war debt payments⟩ **2** : a temporary ban or suspension ⟨a *moratorium* on atomic testing⟩ [New Latin, derived from Latin *morari* "to delay", from *mora* "delay"]

Mo·ra·vi·an \mə-'rā-vē-ən\ *n* **1** : a member of a Christian denomination that traces its history back through the evangelical movement in Moravia and Bohemia to the doctrines of reformer John Huss **2 a** : a native or inhabitant of Moravia **b** : the group of Czech dialects spoken by the Moravian people — **Moravian** *adj*

mo·ray \mə-'rā, 'mȯr-,ā\ *n* : any of numerous often brightly colored eels of warm seas that have sharp teeth capable of inflicting severe bites and that include a Mediterranean eel valued for food [Portuguese *moréia,* from Latin *muraena,* from Greek *myraina*]

mor·bid \'mȯr-bəd\ *adj* **1 a** : of, relating to, or characteristic of disease ⟨*morbid* anatomy⟩ **b** : not healthful : DISEASED ⟨*morbid* conditions⟩ **2** : characterized by gloomy or unwholesome ideas or feelings ⟨takes a *morbid* interest in funerals⟩ [Latin *morbidus* "diseased", from *morbus* "disease"] — **mor·bid·ly** *adv* — **mor·bid·ness** *n*

mor·bid·i·ty \mȯr-'bid-ət-ē\ *n, pl* **-ties** **1** : the quality or state of being morbid **2** : the relative incidence of disease

1mor·dant \'mȯrd-nt\ *adj* : biting and caustic in thought, manner, or style : INCISIVE ⟨*mordant* criticism⟩ [Middle French, present participle of *mordre* "to bite", from Latin *mordēre*] — **mor·dan·cy** \-n-sē\ *n* — **mor·dant·ly** *adv*

2mordant *n* **1** : a chemical that fixes a dye in or on a substance by combining with the dye to form an insoluble compound **2** : a corroding substance used in etching

3mordant *vt* : to treat with a mordant

mor·dent \'mȯrd-nt, mȯr-'dent\ *n* : a musical ornament made by a quick alternation of a principal tone with the tone below [Italian *mordente,* from Latin *mordēre* "to bite"]

1more \'mōr, 'mȯr\ *adj* **1** : greater in amount or degree ⟨felt *more* pain⟩ **2** : ADDITIONAL, FURTHER ⟨bought *more* apples⟩ [Old English *māra*]

2more *adv* **1 a** : in addition **b** : MOREOVER **2** : to a greater or higher degree — often used with an adjective or adverb to form the comparative ⟨*more* active⟩ ⟨*more* actively⟩

3more *n* **1** : a greater amount or number ⟨got *more* than we expected⟩ **2 a** : an additional amount ⟨too full to eat *more*⟩ **b** : additional persons or things ⟨the *more* the merrier⟩

mo·rel \mə-'rel, mō-\ *n* : any of several large pitted edible fungi

[French *morille,* of Germanic origin]

mo•rel•lo \mə-'rel-ō\ *n* : a cultivated sour cherry with dark red fruit [probably from Flemish *amarelle, marelle*]

more•over \mōr-'ō-vər, mȯr-\ *adv* : in addition to what has been said : BESIDES

mo•res \'mȯr-ˌāz, 'mōr-, -ˌēz\ *n, pl* **1 :** the fixed morally binding customs of a particular group **2 :** habitual behavior [Latin, pl. of *mor-, mos* "custom"]

Mor•gan \'mȯr-gən\ *n* : any of an American breed of light horses originated in Vermont and noted for stamina, docility, beauty, courage, and especially longevity [Justin *Morgan,* died 1798, American teacher]

morel

mor•ga•nat•ic marriage \ˌmȯr-gə-ˌnat-ik-\ *n* : a marriage between a person of royal or noble rank and a commoner who does not assume the superior partner's rank and whose children do not succeed to the title or inheritance of the parent of superior rank [New Latin *matrimonium ad morganaticum,* literally, "marriage with morning gift (given by the husband to the wife on the morning after consummation of the marriage)"]

morgue \'mȯrg\ *n* **1 :** a place where the bodies of persons found dead are kept temporarily usually for identification **2 :** a department of a newspaper where reference material is filed [French]

mor•i•bund \'mȯr-ə-ˌbənd, 'mär-, -bənd\ *adj* : being in a dying state [Latin *moribundus,* from *mori* "to die"] — **mor•i•bun•di•ty** \ˌmȯr-ə-'bən-dət-ē, ˌmär-\ *n*

Mor•mon \'mȯr-mən\ *n* : LATTER-DAY SAINT; *esp* : a member of the Church of Jesus Christ of Latter-Day Saints [*Mormon,* ancient compiler of the Book of Mormon presented as divine revelation by Joseph Smith] — **Mormon** *adj* — **Mor•mon•ism** \'mȯr-mə-ˌniz-əm\ *n*

morn \'mȯrn\ *n* : MORNING [Old English *morgen*]

morn•ing \'mȯr-ning\ *n* **1 a :** DAWN 1 **b :** the time from sunrise to noon **c :** the time from midnight to noon **2 :** the first or early part ⟨the *morning* of life⟩ [Middle English, from *morn* + *-ing* (as in *evening*)]

morning glory *n* : any of various usually twining plants with showy trumpet-shaped flowers that usually close by noon; *also* : any of various related plants including herbs, vines, shrubs, or trees with alternate leaves and regular usually funnel-shaped flowers

morning glory

Morning Prayer *n* : a morning service of the Anglican communion

morn•ings \'mȯr-ningz\ *adv* : in the morning repeatedly ⟨we work *mornings*⟩

morning sickness *n* : nausea on arising usually associated with early pregnancy

morning star *n* : a bright planet (as Venus) seen in the eastern sky before sunrise

mo•roc•co \mə-'räk-ō\ *n* : a fine leather made of goat skins tanned with sumac [*Morocco,* Africa]

mo•ron \'mōr-ˌän, 'mȯr-\ *n* **1 :** a feebleminded person having a potential mental age of between 8 and 12 years and being capable of doing routine work under supervision **2 :** a very stupid person [Greek *mōros* "foolish, stupid"] **syn** see IDIOT — **mo•ron•ic** \mə-'rän-ik, mȯ-\ *adj* — **mo•ron•i•cal•ly** \-'rän-i-kə-lē, -klē\ *adv*

mo•rose \mə-'rōs, mȯ-\ *adj* **1 :** having a sullen and gloomy disposition **2 :** marked by or expressive of gloom [Latin *morosus,* literally, "capricious", from *mor-, mos* "custom, will"] — **mo•rose•ly** *adv* — **mo•rose•ness** *n*

mor•pheme \'mȯr-ˌfēm\ *n* : a word or part of a word (as an affix or a base) that contains no smaller meaningful parts [French *morphème,* from Greek *morphē* "form"]

mor•phia \'mȯr-fē-ə\ *n* : MORPHINE

-mor•phic \'mȯr-fik\ *adj combining form* : having (such) a form ⟨endo*morphic*⟩ [Greek *morphē* "form"]

mor•phine \'mȯr-ˌfēn\ *n* : a bitter white crystalline habit-forming drug made from opium and used to deaden pain and to induce sleep [French, from *Morpheus,* Greek god of dreams]

mor•phol•o•gy \mȯr-'fäl-ə-jē\ *n* **1 a :** a branch of biology that deals with the form and structure of animals and plants **b :** the form and structure of an organism or any of its parts **2 :** the part of grammar dealing with word formation and including inflection, derivation, and the formation of compounds **3 :** STRUCTURE, FORM ⟨the *morphology* of rocks⟩ [German *morphologie,* from Greek *morphē* "form"] — **mor•pho•log•i•cal** \ˌmȯr-fə-'läj-i-kəl\ *adj* — **mor•pho•log•i•cal•ly** \-i-kə-lē, -klē\ *adv* — **mor•phol•o•gist** \mȯr-'fäl-ə-jəst\ *n*

-mor•phous \'mȯr-fəs\ *adj combining form* : having (such) a form [Greek *-morphos,* from *morphē* "form"]

mor•ris \'mȯr-əs, 'mär-\ *n* : a vigorous English dance performed by men wearing costumes and bells [Middle English *moreys* "Moorish"]

mor•ris chair *n* : an easy chair with adjustable back and removable cushions [William *Morris,* died 1896, English poet and artist]

mor•row \'mär-ō, 'mȯr-\ *n* **1** *archaic* : MORNING **2 :** the next day [Middle English *morn, morwen,* from Old English *morgen*]

Morse code \'mȯrs-\ *n* : either of two codes consisting of dots and dashes or long and short sounds used for transmitting messages by audible or visual signals [Samuel F. B. *Morse*]

INTERNATIONAL MORSE CODE[1]

A	•–	N	–•	Á	•––•–	8	–––••
B	–•••	O	–––	Ä	•–•–	9	––––•
C	–•–•	P	•––•	É	••–••	0	–––––
D	–••	Q	––•–	Ñ	––•––	,	(comma) ––••––
E	•	R	•–•	Ö	–––•	.	•–•–•–
F	••–•	S	•••	Ü	••––	?	••––••
G	––•	T	–	1	•––––	;	–•–•–•
H	••••	U	••–	2	••–––	:	–––•••
I	••	V	•••–	3	•••––	'	(apostrophe) •––––•
J	•–––	W	•––	4	••••–	-	(hyphen) –••••–
K	–•–	X	–••–	5	•••••	/	–••–•
L	•–••	Y	–•––	6	–••••	parenthesis	–•––•–
M	––	Z	––••	7	––•••	underline	••––•–

[1]Often called the continental code; a modification of this code, with dots only, is used on ocean cables

mor•sel \'mȯr-səl\ *n* **1 :** a small piece of food : BITE **2 :** a small quantity or piece [Old French, from *mors* "bite", from Latin *morsus,* from *mordēre* "to bite"]

¹mor•tal \'mȯrt-l\ *adj* **1 :** capable of causing death : FATAL ⟨a *mortal* wound⟩ **2 :** subject to death ⟨*mortal* man⟩ **3 :** extremely hostile ⟨a *mortal* enemy⟩ **4 a :** too grave or wicked to leave room for forgiveness : UNPARDONABLE ⟨a *mortal* sin⟩ **b :** very great, intense, or severe ⟨in *mortal* fear⟩ **5 :** HUMAN ⟨*mortal* limitations⟩ **6 :** of, relating to, or connected with death ⟨*mortal* agony⟩ [Middle French, from Latin *mortalis,* from *mort-, mors* "death"] **syn** see DEADLY — **mor•tal•ly** \-l-ē\ *adv*

²mortal *n* : a human being

mor•tal•i•ty \mȯr-'tal-ət-ē\ *n, pl* **-ties 1 :** the quality or state of being mortal **2 :** the death of large numbers **3 :** the human race : MANKIND **4 a :** the number of deaths in a given time or place **b :** the ratio of deaths to total population

mortality table *n* : a table of mortality statistics over a number of years used chiefly by insurance companies in computing premiums

¹mor•tar \'mȯrt-ər\ *n* **1 :** a strong bowl-shaped container in which substances are pounded or rubbed with a pestle **2 :** a muzzle-loading cannon that has a tube short in relation to its caliber and is used to throw projectiles at high angles [Middle French *mortier,* from Latin *mortarium*]

²mortar *n* : a building material (as one made of lime and cement mixed with sand and water) that hardens and is spread between bricks or stones to hold them together — **mortar** *vt*

mor•tar•board \'mȯrt-ər-ˌbōrd, -ˌbȯrd\ *n* **1 :** a board for holding mortar while it is being applied **2 :** an academic cap with a

broad projecting square top

[1]mortar 1

[1]**mort·gage** \ˈmȯr-gij\ *n* **1 :** a transfer of rights to a piece of property usually as security for the payment of a loan or debt that becomes void when the debt is paid **2 :** the formal document by which a mortgage is made [Middle French, from *mort* "dead" + *gage* "pledge, gage"]

[2]**mortgage** *vt* **:** to subject to or as if to a mortgage

mort·gag·ee \ˌmȯr-gi-ˈjē\ *n* **:** a person to whom property is mortgaged

mort·ga·gor \ˌmȯr-gi-ˈjȯr\ *also* **mort·gag·er** \ˈmȯr-gi-jər\ *n* **:** a person who mortgages property

mor·ti·cian \mȯr-ˈtish-ən\ *n* **:** UNDERTAKER [Latin *mort-, mors* "death"]

mor·ti·fy \ˈmȯrt-ə-ˌfī\ *vb* **-fied; -fy·ing 1 :** to subdue bodily appetites through penance and self-denial **2 :** to subject to humiliation or shame **3 :** to become necrotic or gangrenous [Middle French *mortifier* "to mortify, put to death", from Late Latin *mortificare* "to put to death", from Latin *mort-, mors* "death"] — **mor·ti·fi·ca·tion** \ˌmȯrt-ə-fə-ˈkā-shən\ *n*

[1]**mor·tise** *also* **mor·tice** \ˈmȯrt-əs\ *n* **:** a hole cut in a piece of wood or other material into which a tenon fits so as to form a joint [Middle French *mortaise*]

[2]**mortise** *also* **mortice** *vt* **1 :** to join or fasten securely especially by a tenon and mortise **2 :** to cut a mortise in — **mor·tised** \-əst\ *adj*

[1]**mor·tu·ary** \ˈmȯr-chə-ˌwer-ē\ *n, pl* **-ar·ies :** a place in which dead bodies are kept until burial; *esp* **:** FUNERAL HOME [Medieval Latin *mortuarium,* from Latin *mortuus* "dead", from *mori* "to die"]

[2]**mortuary** *adj* **:** of or relating to death or the burial of the dead

mor·u·la \ˈmȯr-ə-lə, ˈmär-, -yə-lə\ *n, pl* **-lae** \-ˌlē, -ˌlī\ *or* **-las :** an early embryo that is a solid mass of cells and typically precedes the blastula [New Latin, from Latin *morum* "mulberry"]

mo·sa·ic \mō-ˈzā-ik\ *n* **1 :** a surface decoration made by inlaying small pieces of variously colored material to form pictures or patterns; *also* **:** the process of making it **2 :** a picture or design made in mosaic **3 :** something resembling a mosaic; *esp* **:** a virus disease of plants characterized by mottling of the foliage **4 :** the part of a television camera tube consisting of many minute particles that convert light to an electric charge [Middle French *mosaique,* from Italian *mosaico,* from Medieval Latin *musaicum,* derived from Latin *Musa* "Muse"] — **mosaic** *adj* — **mo·sa·i·cal·ly** \-ˈzā-i-kə-lē, -klē\ *adv*

Mos·lem \ˈmäz-ləm *also* ˈmäs-\ *variant of* MUSLIM

mosque \ˈmäsk\ *n* **:** a Muslim place of worship [Middle French *mosquee,* from Italian *moschea,* from Spanish *mezquita,* from Arabic *masjid,* from *sajada* "to prostrate oneself"]

mos·qui·to \mə-ˈskēt-ō\ *n, pl* **-toes** *also* **-tos :** any of numerous two-winged flies having females with a needlelike proboscis adapted to puncture the skin of animals and suck their blood [Spanish, from *mosca* "fly", from Latin *musca*] — **mos·qui·to·ey** \-ˈskēt-ə-wē\ *adj*

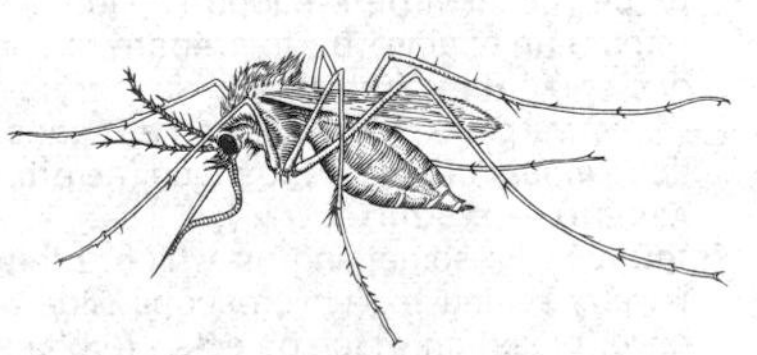

mosquito

mosquito net *n* **:** a net for keeping out mosquitoes

moss \ˈmȯs\ *n* **1 :** any of a class (Musci) of plants without flowers but with small leafy often tufted stems growing in patches and bearing sex organs at the tip **2 :** any of various plants (as lichens) resembling mosses [Old English *mōs* "bog, swamp"] — **moss·like** \-ˌlīk\ *adj*

moss animal *n* **:** BRYOZOAN

moss pink *n* **:** a low tufted perennial phlox widely cultivated for its abundant usually pink or white flowers

mossy \ˈmȯ-sē\ *adj* **moss·i·er; -est 1 :** covered with moss or something like moss ⟨a *mossy* grave⟩ **2 :** resembling moss

[1]**most** \ˈmōst\ *adj* **1 :** the majority of ⟨*most* people⟩ **2 :** greatest in quanitity, extent, or degree ⟨the *most* ability⟩ [Old English *mǣst*]

[2]**most** *adv* **1 :** to the greatest or highest degree — often used with an adjective or adverb to form the superlative ⟨*most* active⟩ ⟨*most* actively⟩ **2 :** to a very great degree ⟨a *most* careful driver⟩

[3]**most** *n* **:** the greatest amount, number, or part — **at most** *or* **at the most :** as an extreme limit ⟨takes an hour *at most*⟩

[4]**most** *adv* **:** ALMOST

-most \ˌmōst\ *adj suffix* **:** most ⟨inner*most*⟩ **:** most toward ⟨head*most*⟩ [Middle English, alteration of Old English *-mest* (as in *formest* "foremost")]

most·ly \ˈmōst-lē\ *adv* **:** for the greatest part **:** MAINLY

Most Reverend — used as a title for an archbishop or a Roman Catholic bishop

mot \ˈmō\ *n, pl* **mots** \ˈmō, ˈmōz\ **:** a pithy or witty saying [French, "word, saying", from Latin *muttum* "grunt", from *muttire* "to mutter"]

mote \ˈmōt\ *n* **:** a small particle **:** SPECK [Old English *mot*]

mo·tel \mō-ˈtel\ *n* **:** a building or group of buildings used as a hotel in which the rooms are directly accessible from an outdoor parking area for automobiles [blend of *motor* and *hotel*]

mo·tet \mō-ˈtet\ *n* **:** a polyphonic choral composition on a sacred text usually without accompaniment [Middle French, from *mot* "word"]

moth \ˈmȯth\ *n, pl* **moths** \ˈmȯthz, ˈmȯths\ **1 :** CLOTHES MOTH **2 :** a usually night-flying insect (order Lepidoptera) often with a stouter body, duller coloring, and proportionately smaller wings than the related butterflies [Old English *moththe*]

moth·ball \ˈmȯth-ˌbȯl\ *n* **1 :** a ball (as of naphthalene) used to keep moths out of clothing **2** *pl* **:** protective storage ⟨a fleet put in *mothballs* after the war⟩

moth–eat·en \ˈmȯth-ˌēt-n\ *adj* **1 :** eaten into by moth larvae **2 a :** RUN-DOWN 1 **b :** OLD-FASHIONED 1

[1]**moth·er** \ˈmət͟h-ər\ *n* **1 a :** a female parent **b :** a woman in authority; *esp* **:** the superior of a religious order — often used as a title **2 :** an old or elderly woman **3 :** SOURCE, ORIGIN ⟨necessity is the *mother* of invention⟩ [Old English *mōdor*] — **moth·er·hood** \-ˌhu̇d\ *n* — **moth·er·less** \-ləs\ *adj* — **moth·er·less·ness** *n*

[2]**mother** *adj* **1 a :** of, relating to, or being a mother **b :** being in the relation of a mother to others ⟨a *mother* church⟩ ⟨a *mother* country⟩ **2 :** derived from or as if from one's mother

[3]**mother** *vt* **moth·ered; moth·er·ing** \ˈmət͟h-ring, -ə-ring\ **:** to be or act as mother to

[4]**mother** *n* **:** a slimy mass of yeast cells and bacteria that forms on the surface of fermenting alcoholic liquids and is added to wine or cider to produce vinegar [related to Low German *mudde* "mud"]

Mother Car·ey's chicken \ˌmət͟h-ər-ˌkar-ēz-, -ˌker-\ *n* **:** any of several small petrels; *esp* **:** STORM PETREL [origin unknown]

mother cell *n* **:** a cell that gives rise to other cells usually of a different sort

moth·er·house \ˈmət͟h-ər-ˌhau̇s\ *n* **1 :** the convent in which the superior of a religious community resides **2 :** the original convent of a religious community

Mother Hubbard \ˌmət͟h-ər-ˈhəb-ərd\ *n* **:** a loose usually shapeless dress [probably from *Mother Hubbard,* character in a nursery rhyme]

moth·er-in-law \ˈmət͟h-ər-ən-ˌlȯ, ˈmət͟h-ərn-ˌlȯ\ *n, pl* **moth·ers-in-law** \-ər-zən-ˌlȯ\ **:** the mother of one's husband or wife

moth·er·land \ˈmət͟h-ər-ˌland\ *n* **1 :** the land of origin of something **2 :** FATHERLAND

moth·er·ly \ˈmət͟h-ər-lē\ *adj* **1 :** of, relating to, or characteristic of a mother ⟨*motherly* affection⟩ **2 :** resembling a mother **:** MATERNAL — **moth·er·li·ness** \-lē-nəs\ *n*

moth·er-of-pearl \ˌmət͟h-ər-əv-ˈpərl, -ər-ə-ˈpərl\ *n* **:** the hard pearly iridescent substance forming the inner layer of a mollusk shell

Mother's Day *n* **:** the 2d Sunday in May appointed for the honoring of mothers

\ə\ abut	\au̇\ out	\i\ tip	\ȯ\ saw	\u̇\ foot
\ər\ further	\ch\ chin	\ī\ life	\ȯi\ coin	\y\ yet
\a\ mat	\e\ pet	\j\ job	\th\ thin	\yü\ few
\ā\ take	\ē\ easy	\ng\ sing	\t͟h\ this	\yu̇\ cure
\ä\ cot, cart	\g\ go	\ō\ bone	\ü\ food	\zh\ vision

mother tongue *n* **1 :** one's native language **2 :** a language from which another language derives

mo·tif \mō-'tēf\ *n* **1 :** a recurring idea or theme **2 :** a feature in a decoration or design ⟨a flower *motif* in wallpaper⟩ [French, "motive, motif"]

mo·tile \'mōt-l, 'mō-ˌtīl\ *adj* **:** exhibiting or being capable of movement [Latin *motus*, past participle of *movēre* "to move"] — **mo·til·i·ty** \mō-'til-ət-ē\ *n*

[1]mo·tion \'mō-shən\ *n* **1 :** a formal proposal for action made in a deliberative assembly ⟨a *motion* to adjourn⟩ **2 :** an act, process, or instance of changing place **:** MOVEMENT [Middle French, from Latin *motio* "movement", from *movēre* "to move"] — **mo·tion·less** \-ləs\ *adj* — **mo·tion·less·ly** *adv* — **mo·tion·less·ness** *n*

[2]motion *vb* **mo·tioned**; **mo·tion·ing** \'mō-shə-ning, 'mōsh-ning\ **:** to direct or signal by a movement or gesture

motion picture *n* **1 :** a series of pictures projected on a screen in rapid succession so as to produce the optical effect of a continuous picture in which the objects move **2 :** MOVIE 2

motion sickness *n* **:** sickness induced by motion (as in travel by air, car, or ship) and characterized by nausea

mo·ti·vate \'mōt-ə-ˌvāt\ *vt* **:** to provide with a motive **:** INDUCE — **mo·ti·va·tion** \ˌmōt-ə-'vā-shən\ *n* — **mo·ti·va·tion·al** \-shnəl, -shən-l\ *adv* — **mo·ti·va·tive** \'mōt-ə-ˌvāt-iv\ *adj*

[1]mo·tive \'mōt-iv, *2 is also* mō-'tēv\ *n* **1 :** something (as a need or a state of mind) that leads or influences a person to do something ⟨their *motive* in running away was to avoid trouble⟩ **2 :** MOTIF 1 [Middle French *motif*, from *motif*, adj., "moving", derived from Latin *movēre* "to move"] — **mo·tive·less** \-ləs\ *adj*

• **syn** MOTIVE, IMPULSE mean a stimulus to action. MOTIVE implies a desire or emotion causing the will to act; IMPULSE suggests a driving power arising from personal temperament often without explainable cause

[2]motive *adj* **:** of or relating to motion or the causing of motion ⟨*motive* power⟩

[1]mot·ley \'mät-lē\ *adj* **1 :** having various colors **2 :** of various mixed kinds or parts ⟨a *motley* crowd⟩ [Middle English]

[2]motley *n* **1 :** an old English woolen fabric of mixed colors **2 a :** a garment of motley constituting the characteristic dress of a court jester **b :** FOOL 2a, JESTER **3 :** a mixture of diverse elements

mo·to·cross \'mōt-ō-ˌkrȯs\ *n* **:** a motorcycle race on a course laid out over natural terrain

mo·to·neu·ron \ˌmōt-ə-'nü-ˌrän, -'nyü-; -'nu̇r-ˌän, -'nyu̇r-\ *n* **:** a nerve cell with its processes that conducts an impulse to a muscle or gland — called also *motor neuron*

[1]mo·tor \'mōt-ər\ *n* **1 :** a small compact engine **2** INTERNAL-COMBUSTION ENGINE; *esp* **:** a gasoline engine **3 :** MOTOR VEHICLE; *esp* **:** AUTOMOBILE **4 :** a rotating machine that transforms electrical energy into mechanical energy [Latin, "one that moves", from *motus*, past participle of *movēre* "to move"]

[2]motor *adj* **1 :** causing or imparting motion ⟨*motor* power⟩ **2 a :** of, relating to, or being a nerve or nerve fiber that conducts an impulse to a muscle or gland which results in functional activity **b :** concerned with or involving muscular movement ⟨*motor* areas of the brain⟩ ⟨a *motor* reaction⟩ **3 a :** equipped with or driven by a motor **b :** of or relating to an automobile **c :** designed for motor vehicles or motorists

[3]motor *vi* **:** to travel by automobile

mo·tor·bike \'mōt-ər-ˌbīk\ *n* **:** a small usually lightweight motorcycle

mo·tor·boat \'mōt-ər-ˌbōt\ *n* **:** a boat propelled by a motor

motor bus *n* **:** BUS 1a

mo·tor·cade \'mōt-ər-ˌkād\ *n* **:** a procession of motor vehicles [*motor* + *-cade* (as in *cavalcade*)]

mo·tor·car \-ˌkär\ *n* **:** AUTOMOBILE

motor court *n* **:** MOTEL

mo·tor·cy·cle \'mōt-ər-ˌsī-kəl\ *n* **:** a 2-wheeled motor vehicle having one or two saddles — **motorcycle** *vi* — **mo·tor·cy·clist** \-ˌsī-kə-ləst, -kləst\ *n*

motor home *n* **:** an automotive vehicle built on a truck or bus chassis and equipped as a self-contained traveling home

motor inn *n* **:** a usually multistory urban motel — called also *motor hotel*

mo·tor·ist \'mōt-ə-rəst\ *n* **:** a person who travels by automobile; *esp* **:** one who drives an automobile

mo·tor·ize \'mōt-ə-ˌrīz\ *vt* **1 :** to equip with a motor **2 :** to equip with motor-driven vehicles for transportation ⟨*motorized* troops⟩ — **mo·tor·iza·tion** \ˌmōt-ə-rə-'zā-shən\ *n*

mo·tor·man \'mōt-ər-mən\ *n* **:** an operator of a motor-driven vehicle (as a streetcar or a subway train)

motor pool *n* **:** a group of motor vehicles centrally controlled (as by a government agency) and dispatched for use as needed

motor scooter *n* **:** a low 2- or 3-wheeled automotive vehicle resembling a child's scooter but having a seat

motor torpedo boat *n* **:** PT BOAT

mo·tor·truck \'mōt-ər-ˌtrək\ *n* **:** an automotive truck for transporting freight

motor vehicle *n* **:** an automotive vehicle not operated on rails; *esp* **:** one for use on highways

mot·tle \'mät-l\ *n* **1 :** a colored spot **2 :** a pattern of colored spots or blotches [probably back-formation from [1]*motley*] — **mottle** *vt* — **mot·tled** \-ld\ *adj* — **mot·tler** \'mät-lər, -l-ər\ *n*

mottled enamel *n* **:** spotted tooth enamel caused by drinking water containing excessive fluorides during the time calcium salts are being deposited in the teeth

mot·to \'mät-ō\ *n, pl* **mottoes** *also* **mottos 1 :** a sentence, phrase, or word inscribed on something as suitable to its character or use ⟨a *motto* on a sundial⟩ **2 :** a short expression of a guiding principle [Italian, from Latin *muttum* "grunt", from *muttire* "to mutter"]

moue \'mü\ *n* **:** a little grimace **:** POUT [French, of Germanic origin]

mou·flon *or* **mouf·flon** \mü-'flō^n\ *n* **:** a wild sheep of the mountains of Sardinia and Corsica with large curling horns in the male; *also* **:** a wild sheep with large horns [French *mouflon*, from Italian dialect *movrone*, from Late Latin *mufro*]

mouflon

mou·jik \mü-'zhēk, -'zhik\ *variant of* MUZHIK

mould *variant of* MOLD

moult *variant of* MOLT

[1]mound \'mau̇nd\ *vt* **:** to form into a mound [origin unknown]

[2]mound *n* **1 :** a small hill or heap of dirt **2 :** the slightly elevated ground on which a baseball pitcher stands [origin unknown]

Mound Builder *n* **:** a member of a prehistoric Amerindian people whose extensive earthworks are found from the Great Lakes down the Mississippi valley to the Gulf of Mexico

[1]mount \'mau̇nt\ *n* **:** a high hill **:** MOUNTAIN — used especially before a proper name ⟨*Mount* Everest⟩ [Old English *munt* and Old French *mont*; both from Latin *mont-*, *mons*]

[2]mount *vb* **1 a :** RISE 7a, ASCEND **b :** to go up **:** CLIMB ⟨*mount* a ladder⟩ **2 a :** to get up onto ⟨*mount* a platform⟩ **b :** to get astride a horse **3 :** to furnish with riding animals or vehicles ⟨*mounted* police⟩ **4 :** to increase rapidly in amount ⟨debts *mounting*⟩ **5 a :** to prepare for use or display by fastening in proper position on a support ⟨*mount* a picture on cardboard⟩ ⟨*mount* an engine⟩ **b :** to prepare (a specimen) for examination or display **6 :** to furnish with scenery, properties, and costumes ⟨*mount* a play⟩ **7 :** to post as a means of defense or observation ⟨*mount* guard⟩ **8 :** to place (as artillery) in position **syn** see ASCEND — **mount·er** *n*

[3]mount *n* **1 :** something on which a thing is mounted: as **a :** a jewelry setting **b :** a microscope slide with its accessories (as a cover glass) on which objects are placed for examination **2 :** a means of conveyance; *esp* **:** SADDLE HORSE — **mount·able** \'mau̇nt-ə-bəl\ *adj*

moun·tain \'mau̇nt-n\ *n* **1 :** a land mass that is higher than a hill **2 :** a great quantity or amount ⟨a *mountain* of mail⟩ [Old French *montaigne*, derived from Latin *mont-*, *mons*]

mountain ash *n* **:** any of various trees of the rose family with red fruits and compound leaves having numerous leaflets

moun·tain·eer \ˌmau̇nt-n-'iər\ *n* **1 :** a person who lives in the mountains **2 :** a mountain climber — **mountaineer** *vi*

mountain goat *n* **:** an antelope of the mountains of western North America that has a thick white hairy coat and slightly curved black horns and closely resembles a goat

mountain laurel *n* **:** a North American evergreen shrub of the heath family with glossy leaves and pink or white cup-shaped flowers

mountain lion *n* : COUGAR

moun•tain•ous \ˈmau̇nt-n-əs, ˈmau̇nt-nəs\ *adj* **1** : having many mountains ⟨*mountainous* country⟩ **2** : resembling a mountain especially in size : HUGE ⟨*mountainous* waves⟩ — **moun•tain•ous•ly** *adv* — **moun•tain•ous•ness** *n*

mountain range *n* : a series of mountains or mountain ridges closely related in direction and position

mountain sheep *n* : any of various wild sheep (as a bighorn) inhabiting high mountains

moun•tain•side \ˈmau̇nt-n-ˌsīd\ *n* : the side of a mountain

mountain goat

Mountain time *n* : the time of the 7th time zone west of Greenwich that includes the west central United States

moun•tain•top \ˈmau̇nt-n-ˌtäp\ *n* : the summit of a mountain

moun•te•bank \ˈmau̇nt-i-ˌbangk\ *n* **1** : a person who sells quack medicines : QUACK **2** : an unscrupulous impostor : SWINDLER [Italian *montimbanco*] — **moun•te•bank•ery** \-ˌbang-kə-rē, -krē\ *n*

Mount•ie \ˈmau̇nt-ē\ *n* : a member of the Royal Canadian Mounted Police

mount•ing \ˈmau̇nt-ing\ *n* **1** : the act of one that mounts **2** : something that serves as a mount : SUPPORT ⟨an engine *mounting*⟩ ⟨a *mounting* for a diamond⟩

mourn \ˈmōrn, ˈmȯrn\ *vb* : to feel or show grief or sorrow; *esp* : to grieve over someone's death [Old English *murnan*] — **mourn•er** *n* — **mourn•ing•ly** \-ing-lē\ *adv*

mourn•ful \ˈmōrn-fəl, ˈmȯrn-\ *adj* **1** : full of sorrow : SAD ⟨a *mournful* face⟩ **2** : causing sorrow : SADDENING ⟨*mournful* news⟩ **3** : of a melancholy nature ⟨took a *mournful* view of the future⟩ — **mourn•ful•ly** \-fə-lē\ *adv* — **mourn•ful•ness** *n*

mourn•ing \ˈmōr-ning, ˈmȯr-\ *n* **1** : an act of grieving **2** : an outward sign (as black clothes or a veil) of grief for a person's death ⟨wear *mourning*⟩ **3** : a period of time during which signs of grief are shown

mourning cloak *n* : a blackish brown butterfly of North America, Europe, and parts of Asia having a broad yellow border on the wings

mourning dove *n* : a wild dove of the United States with a mournful cry

1**mouse** \ˈmau̇s\ *n, pl* **mice** \ˈmīs\ **1** : any of numerous small rodents with a pointed snout, rather small ears, an elongated body, and a slender tail **2** : a timid or spiritless person **3** : a dark-colored swelling caused by a blow; *esp* : BLACK EYE [Old English *mūs*]

2**mouse** \ˈmau̇z, ˈmau̇s\ *vb* **1** : to hunt for mice **2** : to search or move stealthily or slowly **3** : to discover by careful searching ⟨*mouse* out a scandal⟩

mous•er \ˈmau̇-zər, -sər\ *n* : a catcher of mice and rats; *esp* : a cat proficient at mousing

mouse•trap \ˈmau̇-ˌstrap\ *n* : a trap for mice

mousse \ˈmüs\ *n* : a light spongy food; *esp* : a molded chilled dessert of sweetened and flavored whipped cream or egg whites and gelatin [French, literally, "froth", from Late Latin *mulsa* "mixture of honey and water"]

mous•tache *variant of* MUSTACHE

mous•ta•chio *variant of* MUSTACHIO

mousy *or* **mous•ey** \ˈmau̇-sē, -zē\ *adj* **mous•i•er**; **-est** : of, relating to, or resembling a mouse: as **a** : TIMID **b** : making no noise **c** : DRAB 1

1**mouth** \ˈmau̇th\ *n, pl* **mouths** \ˈmau̇t͟hz, ˈmau̇ths\ **1 a** : the opening through which food passes into the body of an animal **b** : the cavity that encloses in the typical vertebrate the tongue, gums, and teeth **2** : GRIMACE ⟨make a *mouth*⟩ **3** : something that resembles a mouth especially in affording entrance or exit ⟨the *mouth* of a cave⟩ **4** : the place where a stream enters a larger body of water [Old English *mūth*] — **mouthed** \ˈmau̇t͟hd, ˈmau̇tht\ *adj* — **mouth•like** \ˈmau̇th-ˌlīk\ *adj* — **down in the mouth** : DEPRESSED 1

2**mouth** \ˈmau̇t͟h\ *vb* **1 a** : UTTER 2, PRONOUNCE **b** : to utter loudly or pompously **c** : to repeat without understanding or sincerity ⟨*mouth* platitudes⟩ **2** : to take into the mouth; *esp* : EAT — **mouth•er** \ˈmau̇-t͟hər\ *n*

mouth•breed•er \ˈmau̇th-ˌbrēd-ər\ *n* : a fish that carries its eggs and young in its mouth

mouth•ful \ˈmau̇th-ˌfu̇l\ *n* **1** : as much as the mouth will hold; *also* : the amount put into the mouth at one time **2** : a word or phrase that is very long or difficult to say

mouth hook *n* : one of a pair of clawlike structures that occur on either side of the mouth opening of some fly larvae and function as jaws

mouth organ *n* : HARMONICA

mouth•part \ˈmau̇th-ˌpärt\ *n* : a structure or appendage near the mouth

mouth•piece \-ˌpēs\ *n* **1** : something placed at or held in the mouth **2** : a part (as of an instrument) to which the mouth is held ⟨a telephone *mouthpiece*⟩ **3 a** : one that expresses another's views : SPOKESPERSON **b** *slang* : a criminal lawyer

mouth–to–mouth *adj* : of, relating to, or being a method of artificial respiration in which the rescuer's mouth is placed tightly over the victim's mouth in order to force air into the lungs by blowing forcefully enough every few seconds to inflate them

mouth•wash \-ˌwȯsh, -ˌwäsh\ *n* : a usually antiseptic liquid preparation for cleaning the mouth and teeth or freshening the breath

mouthy \ˈmau̇-t͟hē, -thē\ *adj* **mouth•i•er**; **-est 1** : excessively talkative **2** : given to or marked by bombast

mou•ton \ˈmü-ˌtän\ *n* : processed sheepskin that has been sheared and dyed to resemble beaver or seal [French, "sheep, mutton"]

1**mov•able** *or* **move•able** \ˈmü-və-bəl\ *adj* **1** : capable of being moved ⟨*movable* property⟩ **2** : changing date from year to year ⟨Easter is a *movable* holiday⟩ — **mov•abil•i•ty** \ˌmü-və-ˈbil-ət-ē\ *n* — **mov•able•ness** *n* — **mov•ably** \ˈmü-və-blē\ *adv*

2**movable** *or* **moveable** *n* : a piece of property (as an article of furniture) that can be moved

1**move** \ˈmüv\ *vb* **1** : to change the place or position of : SHIFT ⟨*move* the chair closer⟩ **2** : to go from one place to another ⟨*move* into the shade⟩ **3** : to proceed in a given direction or toward a given condition ⟨*moved* ahead in business⟩ **4** : to set in motion ⟨*moved* their feet⟩ **5 a** : to cause a person to act or decide : PERSUADE ⟨*moved* me to change my mind⟩ **b** : to take action : ACT **6** : to affect the feelings of ⟨the sad story *moved* them to tears⟩ **7 a** : to propose something formally in a deliberative assembly ⟨*move* that the meeting adjourn⟩ **b** : to present a motion or make an appeal **8** : to change hands or cause to change hands through sale or rental ⟨the store's stock must be *moved*⟩ **9 a** : to change residence ⟨*move* to Iowa⟩ **b** : to change position or posture : STIR ⟨don't *move*⟩ **10** : to cause to operate or function : ACTUATE ⟨*move* the handle to increase pressure⟩ **11** : to live one's life in a specified environment ⟨*moves* in high circles⟩ **12** : to go away : DEPART ⟨made the crowd *move* on⟩ **13** : to transfer a piece in a game (as chess or checkers) from one place to another **14** : to evacuate or cause to evacuate ⟨the medicine *moves* the bowels⟩ [Middle French *movoir*, from Latin *movēre*]

• **syn** MOVE, ACTUATE, DRIVE, IMPEL mean to set or keep in motion. MOVE is very general and implies no more than the fact of changing position; ACTUATE stresses the transmission of power so as to work or set in motion; DRIVE implies imparting continuous forward motion and often stresses the effect rather than the impetus; IMPEL implies a greater impetus producing more headlong action.

2**move** *n* **1 a** : the act of moving a piece in a game **b** : the turn of a player to move **2 a** : a step taken to gain an objective : MANEUVER **b** : the action of moving : MOVEMENT **c** : a change of residence or location — **on the move 1** : in a state of moving from one place to another **2** : in a state of making progress

move•less \ˈmüv-ləs\ *adj* : not moving — **move•less•ly** *adv* — **move•less•ness** *n*

move•ment \ˈmüv-mənt\ *n* **1 a** : the act or process of moving **b** : an instance or manner of moving ⟨observe the *movement* of a star⟩ **c** : ACTION, ACTIVITY ⟨a lot of *movement* in the crowd⟩ **2** : TENDENCY, TREND ⟨a *movement* toward fairer pricing⟩ **3 a** : a series of actions taken by a group to achieve an objective ⟨a *movement* for reform⟩ **b :** the group taking part in such a series ⟨joined the *movement*⟩ **4 :** a mechanical arrangement (as of wheels) for causing a particular motion (as in a clock or watch) **5 a :** RHYTHM 2 **b :** CADENCE 1a, TEMPO **c :** a section of a longer piece of music ⟨a *movement* in a symphony⟩ **6 :** an emptying of the bowels or the matter emptied

mov•er \ˈmü-vər\ *n* **:** one that moves or sets in motion; *esp* **:** a person or company that moves the belongings of others from one home or place of business to another

mov•ie \ˈmü-vē\ *n* **1 :** MOTION PICTURE 1 **2 a :** a representation of a story or other subject matter by means of motion pictures **b :** a showing of a motion picture — often used in pl. with *the* **3** *pl* **:** the motion-picture industry [*moving picture*]

mov•ing \ˈmü-ving\ *adj* **1 a :** marked by or capable of moving ⟨a machine with *moving* parts⟩ **b :** of or relating to a change of residence ⟨a *moving* van⟩ **2 :** causing motion or action **3 :** having the power to affect feelings or sympathies — **mov•ing•ly** \-ving-lē\ *adv*

moving picture *n* **:** MOTION PICTURE 1

[1]mow \ˈmau̇\ *n* **1 :** a stack of hay or straw especially in a barn **2 :** the part of a barn where hay or straw is stored [Old English *mūga* "heap, stack"]

[2]mow \ˈmō\ *vb* **mowed; mowed** *or* **mown** \ˈmōn\; **mow•ing 1 :** to cut down with a scythe or machine ⟨*mow* hay⟩ **2 :** to cut the standing herbage from ⟨*mow* a lawn⟩ **3 :** to kill or destroy in great numbers ⟨machine guns *mowed* down the attackers⟩ **4 :** to overcome decisively [Old English *māwan*] — **mow•er** \ˈmō-ər, ˈmōr\ *n*

mowing machine *n* **:** an implement with blades for cutting standing grass or grain

mox•ie \ˈmäk-sē\ *n* **1 :** ENERGY 1, PEP **2 :** BRAVERY 2, COURAGE [from *Moxie*, a trademark for a soft drink]

moz•za•rel•la \ˌmät-sə-ˈrel-ə\ *n* **:** a moist white cheese with a mild flavor and smooth texture [Italian]

Mr. \ˌmis-tər\ *n, pl* **Messrs.** \ˌmes-ərz\ **1 —** used as a courtesy title before the name of a man **2 —** used as a form of respectful address to a high-ranking man and followed by a designation of his rank or office ⟨*Mr.* President⟩ **3 —** used before the name of a place, an activity, or an epithet to form a title for a man representing the thing indicated ⟨*Mr.* Baseball⟩ [*Mr.* from Middle English, abbreviation of *maister* "master"; *Messrs.* abbreviation of *Messieurs*, from French, pl. of *Monsieur*]

Mrs. \ˌmis-əz, -əs; *especially South* ˌmiz-əz, -əs, (*for sense 1*) miz, ˌmis, *before given names* mis, ˌmis\ *n, pl* **Mes•dames** \mā-ˈdäm, -ˈdam\ **1 —** used as a courtesy title before the name of a married woman **2 —** used before the name of a place, an activity, or an epithet to form a title for a married woman representing the thing indicated ⟨*Mrs.* America⟩ [*Mrs.* from abbreviation of *mistress*; *Mesdames* from French, pl. of *Madame*]

Ms. \miz, ˈmiz\ *n —* used instead of *Miss* or *Mrs.* as a courtesy title for a woman whose marital status is unknown or irrelevant ⟨*Ms.* Mary Smith⟩ [probably blend of *Miss* and *Mrs.*]

mu \ˈmyü, ˈmü\ *n* **:** the 12th letter of the Greek alphabet — Μ or μ

[1]much \ˈməch\ *adj* **more** \ˈmōr, ˈmȯr\; **most** \ˈmōst\ **:** great in quantity, amount, extent, or degree ⟨has *much* money⟩ ⟨takes too *much* time⟩ [Middle English *michel, muchel, muche* "large, much", from Old English *micel, mycel*]

[2]much *adv* **more; most 1 a :** to a great degree or extent **:** CONSIDERABLY ⟨*much* happier⟩ **b (1) :** many times **:** OFTEN (2) **:** LONG 1 **2 :** just about **:** NEARLY ⟨*much* the same⟩

[3]much *n* **1 :** a great quantity, amount, extent, or degree **2 :** something considerable or impressive

mu•ci•lage \ˈmyü-sə-lij, -slij\ *n* **1 :** a gelatinous substance especially from seaweeds that contains protein and carbohydrates and is similar to plant gums **2 :** an aqueous solution of a gum or similar substance used especially as an adhesive [Late Latin *mucilagin-, mucilago* "musty juice, mucus", from Latin *mucus*]

mu•ci•lag•i•nous \ˌmyü-sə-ˈlaj-ə-nəs\ *adj* **1 :** STICKY 1a, VISCID **2 :** producing or full of mucilage — **mu•ci•lag•i•nous•ly** *adv*

mu•cin \ˈmyüs-n\ *n* **:** any of various complex proteins found as viscid solutions in animal secretions and tissues [*mucus*] — **mu•cin•ous** \-əs\ *adj*

muck \ˈmək\ *n* **1 :** soft moist barnyard manure **2 :** DIRT 1a, FILTH **3 a :** dark highly organic soil **b :** MIRE 2, MUD [Middle English *muk*] — **mucky** \ˈmək-ē\ *adj*

muck•rake \ˈmək-ˌrāk\ *vi* **:** to search out and expose publicly real or seeming misconduct of prominent people [obsolete *muckrake*, n., "rake for dung"] — **muck•rak•er** *n*

mu•co•sa \myü-ˈkō-zə\ *n, pl* **-sae** \-ˌzē, -ˌzī\ *or* **-sas :** MUCOUS MEMBRANE [New Latin, from Latin *mucosus* "mucous"] — **mu•co•sal** \-zəl\ *adj*

mu•cous \ˈmyü-kəs\ *adj* **1 :** of, relating to, or resembling mucus ⟨*mucous* discharges⟩ **2 :** secreting or containing mucus ⟨a *mucous* gland⟩ [Latin *mucosus*, from *mucus* "mucus"]

mucous membrane *n* **:** a membrane rich in mucous glands; *esp* **:** one that lines body passages and cavities which communicate directly or indirectly with the exterior

mu•cro \ˈmyü-ˌkrō\ *n, pl* **mu•cro•nes** \myü-ˈkrō-ˌnēz\ **:** an abrupt sharp terminal point (as of a leaf) [Latin *mucron-, mucro* "point, edge"] — **mu•cro•nate** \ˈmyü-krə-ˌnāt\ *adj*

mu•cus \ˈmyü-kəs\ *n* **:** a slippery animal secretion produced especially by mucous membranes which it moistens and protects [Latin, "nasal mucus"] — **mu•coid** \-ˌkȯid\ *adj*

mud \ˈməd\ *n* **:** soft wet earth [Middle English *mudde*, probably from Low German]

mud dauber *n* **:** any of various wasps that construct mud cells in which the female places an egg with spiders or insects paralyzed by a sting to serve as food for the larva

[1]mud•dle \ˈməd-l\ *vb* **mud•dled; mud•dling** \ˈməd-ling, -l-ing\ **1 :** CONFUSE 1b, BEFUDDLE ⟨*muddled* by too much advice⟩ **2 :** to throw into disorder ⟨*muddle* the household accounts⟩ **3 :** to think or act in a confused aimless way ⟨*muddle* through a task⟩ [probably from obsolete Dutch *moddelen*, from *modde* "mud"] — **mud•dler** \ˈməd-lər, -l-ər\ *n*

[2]muddle *n* **1 :** a state of confusion **2 :** a confused mess

mud•dle•head•ed \ˌməd-l-ˈhed-əd\ *adj* **1 :** mentally confused **2 :** INEPT 4, BUNGLING — **mud•dle•head•ed•ness** *n*

[1]mud•dy \ˈməd-ē\ *adj* **mud•di•er; -est 1 :** filled or covered with mud **2 :** resembling or suggesting mud ⟨a *muddy* color⟩ ⟨a *muddy* flavor⟩ **3 :** not clear or bright **:** DULL, CLOUDY ⟨a *muddy* complexion⟩ **4 :** CONFUSED, MUDDLED ⟨*muddy* thinking⟩ — **mud•di•ly** \ˈməd-l-ē\ *adv* — **mud•di•ness** \ˈməd-ē-nəs\ *n*

[2]muddy *vt* **mud•died; mud•dy•ing 1 :** to soil or stain with or as if with mud **2 :** to make turbid **3 :** to make cloudy or dull **4 :** CONFUSE 2

mud•guard \ˈməd-ˌgärd\ *n* **1 :** FENDER d **2 :** SPLASH GUARD

mud puppy *n* **:** any of several large American salamanders; *esp* **:** HELLBENDER

mud•sling•er \ˈməd-ˌsling-ər\ *n* **:** one that uses abusive tactics (as invective or slander) especially against a political opponent — **mud•sling•ing** \-ˌsling-ing\ *n*

mud turtle

mud•stone \ˈməd-ˌstōn\ *n* **:** a hardened shale produced by the consolidation of mud

mud turtle *n* **:** a bottom-dwelling freshwater turtle (as a musk turtle)

Muen•ster \ˈmən-stər, ˈmün-, ˈmyün-, ˈmu̇n-\ *n* **:** a semisoft cheese whose flavor may be bland or sharp [*Münster, Munster*, France]

mu•ez•zin \mü-ˈez-n, myü-\ *n* **:** a Muslim crier who calls the hours of daily prayers [Arabic *mu'adhdhin*]

[1]muff \ˈməf\ *n* **:** a warm tube-shaped cover for the hands [Dutch *mof*, from Middle French *moufle* "mitten", from Medieval Latin *muffula*]

[2]muff *n* **:** a bungling performance; *esp* **:** a failure to hold a ball in attempting a catch — **muff** *vb*

muf•fin \ˈməf-ən\ *n* **:** a bread made of egg batter and baked in individual servings [probably from Low German *muffen*, pl. of *muffe* "cake"]

muf•fle \ˈməf-əl\ *vt* **muf•fled; muf•fling** \ˈməf-ling, -ə-ling\ **1 :** to wrap up so as to conceal or protect **2 :** to deaden the sound of **3 :** to keep down **:** SUPPRESS ⟨*muffled* the opposition⟩ [Middle English *muflen*]

muf•fler \ˈməf-lər\ *n* **1 :** a scarf for the neck **2 :** a device that deadens noises; *esp* **:** one forming part of the exhaust system of an automotive vehicle

1muf·ti \ˈməf-tē\ *n* : a professional jurist who interprets Muslim law [Arabic *muftī*]

2mufti *n* : civilian clothes

1mug \ˈməg\ *n* **1** : a usually large cylindrical drinking cup **2** : the face or mouth of a person **3** : a stupid or criminal person [origin unknown]

2mug *vb* **mugged**; **mug·ging** **1** : to make faces especially to attract attention **2** : PHOTOGRAPH; *esp* : to take a police photograph of

3mug *vt* **mugged**; **mug·ging** : to assault with intent to rob [back-formation from *2mugger*]

1mug·ger \ˈməg-ər\ *n* : a common usually harmless freshwater crocodile of southeastern Asia [Hindi *magar*, from Sanskrit *makara* "water monster"]

2mugger *n* : one that attacks with intent to rob [probably from obsolete *mug* "to punch in the face"]

mug·gy \ˈməg-ē\ *adj* **mug·gi·er**; **-est** : being warm, damp, and stifling [English dialect *mug* "drizzle"] — **mug·gi·ly** \ˈməg-ə-lē\ *adv* — **mug·gi·ness** \ˈməg-ē-nəs\ *n*

mu·gho pine \ˌmü-gō-, ˌmyü-\ *n* : a shrubby spreading pine widely grown as an ornamental [probably from French *mugho* "mugho pine", from Italian *mugo*]

mug·wump \ˈməg-ˌwəmp\ *n* **1** : a bolter from the Republican party in 1884 **2** : a person who is undecided or neutral in politics [obsolete slang, "chief, kingpin", from Natick (an American Indian language of Massachusetts) *mugwomp* "captain"]

△ **origin** When James G. Blaine received the Republican Party's nomination for the presidency in 1884, many Republicans refused to have anything to do with his candidacy, supporting instead the Democratic candidate, Grover Cleveland. Those Republicans who remained loyal to their party accused the bolters of a lofty and supercilious attitude and nicknamed them *mugwumps*. The word had previously been used as a jesting term for someone who considered himself a great man. *Mugwump* originally came from *mugwomp*, a word meaning "captain" in the American Indian language Natick.

Mu·ham·mad·an *or* **Mo·ham·med·an** \mō-ˈham-əd-ən, mü-\ *n* : MUSLIM — **Muhammadan** *adj* — **Mu·ham·mad·an·ism** \-əd-ə-ˌniz-əm\ *n*

muk·luk \ˈmək-ˌlək\ *n* **1** : an Eskimo boot of sealskin or reindeer skin **2** : a boot with a soft leather sole often worn over several pairs of socks [Eskimo *muklok* "large seal"]

mu·lat·to \mu̇-ˈlat-ō, myu̇-\ *n, pl* **-toes** *or* **-tos** **1** : a person with one Negro and one white parent **2** : a person of mixed white and Negro descent [Spanish *mulato*, from *mulo* "mule", from Latin *mulus*]

mul·ber·ry \ˈməl-ˌber-ē\ *n* **1** : any of a genus of trees with edible usually purple fruits; *also* : this fruit **2** : a dark purple or purplish black [Middle English *murberie, mulberie*, from Old French *moure* "mulberry", from Latin *morum*, from Greek *moron*]

mulch \ˈməlch\ *n* : a protective covering (as of straw, compost, or paper) used on the ground especially to reduce evaporation, prevent erosion, control weeds, or enrich the soil; *also* : the material used [perhaps from English dialect *melch* "soft, mild"] — **mulch** *vt*

1mulct \ˈməlkt\ *n* : a fine imposed as a punishment [Latin *multa, mulcta*]

2mulct *vt* **1** : to punish by a fine **2 a** : to defraud especially of money : SWINDLE **b** : to obtain (as money) by fraud, duress, or theft

1mule \ˈmyül\ *n* **1 a** : a hybrid between a horse and a donkey; *esp* : the offspring of a male donkey and a mare **b** : a usually sterile hybrid plant or animal **2** : a very stubborn person **3** : a machine for drawing and twisting fiber into yarn or thread and winding it onto spindles [Old French *mul*, from Latin *mulus*]

2mule *n* : a slipper whose upper does not extend around the heel of the foot [Middle French, a kind of slipper, from Latin *mulleus* "shoe worn by magistrates"]

mule deer *n* : a long-eared deer of western North America that is larger and more heavily built than the common white-tailed deer

mule skinner *n* : a driver of mules

mu·le·teer \ˌmyü-lə-ˈtiər\ *n* : a driver of mules [French *muletier*, from *mulet* "mule", from Old French *mul*]

mu·ley *also* **mul·ley** \ˈmyü-lē, ˈmu̇l-ē\ *adj* : having no horns; *esp* : naturally hornless ⟨a *muley* cow⟩ [of Celtic origin]

mul·ish \ˈmyü-lish\ *adj* : STUBBORN 1b, OBSTINATE — **mul·ish·ly** *adv* — **mul·ish·ness** *n*

1mull \ˈməl\ *vb* : to consider at length : PONDER ⟨*mull* over an idea⟩ [Middle English *mullen* "to grind, pulverize", from *mul* "dust"]

1mule 1a

2mull *vt* : to sweeten, spice, and heat ⟨*mulled* wine⟩ [origin unknown]

3mull *n* : granular forest humus with a layer of mixed organic matter and mineral soil merging gradually into the mineral soil beneath [German, from Danish *muld*, from Old Norse *mold* "dust, soil"]

mul·lah \ˈməl-ə, ˈmu̇l-ə\ *n* : a Muslim of a class trained in traditional law and doctrine; *esp* : one who is head of a mosque [Hindi *mulla*, from Arabic *mawlā*]

mul·lein *also* **mul·len** \ˈməl-ən\ *n* : a tall herb having coarse woolly leaves and spikes of usually yellow flowers [Anglo-French *moleine*]

mul·let \ˈməl-ət\ *n, pl* **mullet** *or* **mullets** **1** : any of a family of largely gray food fishes **2** : any of a family of moderate-sized usually red or golden fishes with two barbels on the chin [Middle French *mulet*, from Latin *mullus* "red mullet", from Greek *myllos*]

mul·li·gan \ˈməl-i-gən\ *n* : a stew basically of vegetables and meat or fish [probably from the name *Mulligan*]

mul·li·ga·taw·ny \ˌməl-i-gə-ˈtȯ-nē, -ˈtän-ē\ *n* : a soup usually of chicken stock seasoned with curry [Tamil *miḷakutaṇṇi*, a strongly seasoned soup, from *miḷaku* "pepper" + *taṇṇi* "water"]

mul·lion \ˈməl-yən\ *n* : a slender vertical bar between units of windows, doors, or screens [probably from earlier *monial* "mullion", from Middle French *moinel*] — **mullion** *vt*

multi- *combining form* **1 a** : many : multiple : much ⟨*multi*valent⟩ **b** : more than two ⟨*multi*lateral⟩ **c** : more than one ⟨*multi*stage⟩ **2** : many times over ⟨*multi*millionaire⟩ [Latin, from *multus* "much, many"]

See *multi-* and 2d element

multiage	**multidisciplinary**	**multimegaton**
multiagency	**multidiscipline**	**multimember**
multiapproach	**multidivisional**	**multimetallic**
multiarmed	**multidwelling**	**multimillennial**
multiaxial	**multielement**	**multimillion**
multibarreled	**multiengine**	**multimodal**
multibillion	**multienvironmental**	**multimolecular**
multibillionaire	**multiethnic**	**multimotor**
multibladed	**multifaceted**	**multinational**
multibranched	**multifactional**	**multiparameter**
multibuilding	**multifamily**	**multipart**
multicampus	**multifilament**	**multipartite**
multicar	**multifocal**	**multiparty**
multicausal	**multifunction**	**multiphasic**
multicelled	**multifunctional**	**multiplant**
multicenter	**multigenerational**	**multiplot**
multichambered	**multigenic**	**multipolar**
multichannel	**multigrade**	**multipole**
multicharacter	**multihandicapped**	**multipotential**
multicity	**multiheaded**	**multipower**
multicolor	**multihormonal**	**multiproblem**
multicolumn	**multihospital**	**multiproduct**
multicomponent	**multihued**	**multipronged**
multicounty	**multiindustry**	**multipurpose**
multicrested	**multiinstitutional**	**multiroomed**
multicultural	**multilane**	**multiseason**
multicurrency	**multilanguage**	**multiservice**
multidenominational	**multilayered**	**multisided**
multidialectal	**multilevel**	**multisite**
multidimensional	**multilobed**	**multisize**
multidirectional	**multimanned**	**multiskilled**

multisource	**multitalented**	**multiunion**
multispeed	**multitiered**	**multiunit**
multistep	**multiton**	**multiuse**
multistory	**multitone**	**multiwarhead**
multisyllabic	**multitowered**	**multiyear**
multisystem	**multitrack**	

mul•ti•cel•lu•lar \ˌməl-ti-ˈsel-yə-lər, -ˌtī-\ *adj* : having or consisting of many cells — **mul•ti•cel•lu•lar•i•ty** \-ˌsel-yə-ˈlar-ət-ē\ *n*

mul•ti•col•ored \ˌməl-ti-ˈkəl-ərd\ *adj* : having or including many colors

mul•ti•far•i•ous \ˌməl-tə-ˈfar-ē-əs, -ˈfer-\ *adj* : of various kinds : being many and varied ⟨the *multifarious* complexities of language⟩ [Latin *multifarius*] — **mul•ti•far•i•ous•ly** *adv* — **mul•ti•far•i•ous•ness** *n*

mul•ti•flo•ra rose \ˌməl-tə-ˌflōr-ə-, -ˌflȯr-\ *n* : a vigorous thorny rose that produces clusters of small flowers and is used for hedges

mul•ti•fold \ˈməl-ti-ˌfōld\ *adj* : MANIFOLD 1

mul•ti•form \ˈməl-ti-ˌfȯrm\ *adj* : having many forms, shapes, or appearances

mul•ti•lat•er•al \ˌməl-ti-ˈlat-ə-rəl, -ˌtī-, -ˈla-trəl\ *adj* **1** : having many sides **2** : involving more than two nations or parties ⟨a *multilateral* treaty⟩ — **mul•ti•lat•er•al•ly** \-ē\ *adv*

mul•ti•mil•lion•aire \-ˌmil-yə-ˈnaər, -ˈneər, -ˈmil-yə-ˌ\ *n* : a person whose wealth amounts to many millions (as of dollars)

mul•ti•nu•cle•ate \-ˈnü-klē-ət, -ˈnyü-\ *adj* : having more than two nuclei

mul•ti•par•tite \ˌməl-ti-ˈpär-ˌtīt\ *adj* : having numerous members or signatories ⟨a *multipartite* treaty⟩

1mul•ti•ple \ˈməl-tə-pəl\ *adj* : containing, involving, or consisting of more than one ⟨*multiple* copies⟩ [French, from Latin *multiplex*, from *multi-* + *-plex* "-fold"]

2multiple *n* : the product of a quantity by an integer ⟨35 is a *multiple* of 7⟩

multiple allele *n* : any of a group of more than two different alleles any two of which can make up a particular gene pair on homologous chromosomes

multiple–choice *adj* : having several answers given from which the correct one is to be chosen ⟨a *multiple-choice* question⟩

multiple fruit *n* : a fruit (as a mulberry) formed from a cluster of flowers

multiple sclerosis *n* : a disease marked by patches of hardened tissue in the brain or spinal cord resulting in partial or complete paralysis and muscular twitching

mul•ti•plex \ˈməl-tə-ˌpleks\ *adj* **1** : MULTIPLE **2** : being or relating to a system of transmitting several messages simultaneously on the same circuit or channel [Latin]

mul•ti•pli•cand \ˌməl-tə-pli-ˈkand\ *n* : the number that is to be multiplied by another [Latin *multiplicandus* "to be multiplied", from *multiplicare* "to multiply"]

mul•ti•pli•ca•tion \ˌməl-tə-plə-ˈkā-shən\ *n* **1** : the act or process of multiplying **2 a** : a mathematical operation that at its simplest is an abbreviated process of adding an integer to itself a specified number of times and that is extended to other numbers in accordance with laws that are valid for integers **b** : a similar mathematical operation defined for sets of mathematical elements (as matrices or complex numbers) other than the real numbers — **mul•ti•pli•ca•tive** \ˌməl-tə-ˈplik-ət-iv, ˈməl-tə-plə-ˌkāt-\ *adj* — **mul•ti•pli•ca•tive•ly** *adv*

multiplicative identity *n* : an identity element in a set that when multiplied by any element of the set leaves the element unchanged ⟨the integer 1 is a *multiplicative identity* element in the set of all real numbers⟩

multiplicative inverse *n* : an element of a mathematical set that when multiplied by a given element gives the identity element

mul•ti•plic•i•ty \ˌməl-tə-ˈplis-ət-ē\ *n, pl* **-ties 1** : the quality or state of being multiple or various **2** : a great number ⟨a *multiplicity* of ideas⟩

mul•ti•pli•er \ˈməl-tə-ˌplī-ər, -ˌplīr\ *n* : one that multiplies: as **a** : a number by which another is multiplied **b** : a device for multiplying or for intensifying some effect

mul•ti•ply \ˈməl-tə-ˌplī\ *vb* **-plied**; **-ply•ing 1 a** : to increase in number : make or become more numerous **b** : to produce offspring : BREED, PROPAGATE **2 a** : to find the product of by multiplication ⟨*multiply* 7 and 8⟩ **b** : to perform the operation of multiplication [Old French *multiplier*, from Latin *multiplicare*, from *multiplex* "multiple"]

mul•ti•ra•cial \ˌməl-ti-ˈrā-shəl, -ˌtī-\ *adj* : composed of, relating to, or representing various races

mul•ti•stage \-ˌstāj\ *adj* : operating in or involving two or more steps or stages ⟨a *multistage* rocket⟩

mul•ti•tude \ˈməl-tə-ˌtüd, -ˌtyüd\ *n* : a very great number of things or people : HOST [Latin *multitudin-*, *multitudo*, from *multus* "much"]

• **syn** CROWD, THRONG, MOB : MULTITUDE implies great numbers ⟨a *multitude* of stars⟩ CROWD stresses packing together and loss of individuality ⟨a *crowd* of onlookers⟩ THRONG suggests a crowd in motion ⟨people came to the fair in *throngs*⟩ MOB implies disorganization and agitation and in specific use the intent of violence ⟨police dispersed the *mob*⟩

mul•ti•tu•di•nous \ˌməl-tə-ˈtüd-nəs, -ˈtyüd-, -n-əs\ *adj* : consisting of a multitude ⟨a *multitudinous* gathering⟩ — **mul•ti•tu•di•nous•ly** *adv* — **mul•ti•tu•di•nous•ness** *n*

mul•ti•va•lent \ˌməl-ti-ˈvā-lənt, -ˌtī-\ *adj* : POLYVALENT

mul•ti•vi•ta•min \-ˈvīt-ə-mən\ *adj* : containing several vitamins and especially all known to be essential to health ⟨a *multivitamin* formula⟩

mul•ti•vol•ume \-ˈväl-yəm, -ˌyüm\ *or* **mul•ti•vol•umed** \-yəmd, -ˌyümd\ *adj* : composed of several volumes

1mum \ˈməm\ *adj* : SILENT ⟨keep *mum*⟩ [probably imitative of a sound made with closed lips]

2mum *n* : CHRYSANTHEMUM

mum•ble \ˈməm-bəl\ *vb* **mum•bled**; **mum•bling** \-bə-ling, -bling\ **1** : to speak indistinctly usually with lips partly closed ⟨*mumble* one's words⟩ **2** : to chew or bite with or as if with toothless gums ⟨a baby *mumbling* its food⟩ [Middle English *momelen*] — **mumble** *n* — **mum•bler** \-bə-lər, -blər\ *n* — **mum•bling•ly** \-bling-lē\ *adv*

mum•ble•ty–peg \ˈməm-bəl-tē-ˌpeg, -bəl-ˌpeg\ *n* : a game in which the players try to flip a knife from various positions so that the blade will stick into the ground [from the phrase *mumble the peg*; from the loser's originally having to pull out with his teeth a peg driven into the ground]

mum•bo jum•bo \ˌməm-bō-ˈjəm-bō\ *n* **1** : an object of superstitious homage and fear **2 a** : a complicated ritual with elaborate trappings **b** : complicated activity or language that obscures and confuses [*Mumbo Jumbo*, an idol or deity held to have been worshiped in Africa]

mum•mer \ˈməm-ər\ *n* **1** : an actor especially in a pantomime **2** : one who goes merrymaking in disguise during festivals [Middle French *momeur*, from *momer* "to go masked"]

mum•mery \ˈməm-ə-rē\ *n, pl* **-mer•ies 1** : a performance by mummers **2** : a ridiculous or pompous ceremony

mum•mi•fy \ˈməm-i-ˌfī\ *vb* **-fied**; **-fy•ing 1** : to embalm and dry as a mummy **2** : to dry up like the skin of a mummy : SHRIVEL — **mum•mi•fi•ca•tion** \ˌməm-i-fə-ˈkā-shən\ *n*

mum•my \ˈməm-ē\ *n, pl* **mummies 1** : a body embalmed for burial in the manner of the ancient Egyptians **2** : an unusually well-preserved body [Middle French *momie* "powdered parts of a mummy used as a drug", from Medieval Latin *mumia* "mummy, powdered mummy", from Arabic *mūmiyah* "bitumen, mummy", from Persian *mūm* "wax"]

mumps \ˈməmps\ *n sing or pl* : an acute contagious virus disease marked by fever and by swelling especially of salivary glands [obsolete *mump* "grimace"]

munch \ˈmənch\ *vb* : to chew with a crunching sound ⟨*munch* on celery⟩ [Middle English *monchen*] — **munch•er** *n*

mun•dane \ˌmən-ˈdān, ˈmən-ˌ\ *adj* **1** : of or relating to the world : WORLDLY **2** : concerned with the practical, immediate, and ordinary ⟨*mundane* problems of everyday life⟩ [Middle French *mondain*, from Late Latin *mondanus*, from Latin *mundus* "world"] **syn** see EARTHLY — **mun•dane•ly** *adv*

mu•nic•i•pal \myu̇-ˈnis-ə-pəl\ *adj* **1** : of or relating to the internal affairs of a nation **2** : of or relating to a municipality ⟨*municipal* government⟩ [Latin *municipalis* "of a municipality", from *municeps* "inhabitant of a municipality", from *munus* "duty" + *capere* "to take"] — **mu•nic•i•pal•ly** \-pə-lē, -plē\ *adv*

mu•nic•i•pal•i•ty \myu̇-ˌnis-ə-ˈpal-ət-ē\ *n, pl* **-ties** : a primarily urban political unit (as a city or town) having corporate status and usually powers of self-government

mu•nif•i•cent \myu̇-ˈnif-ə-sənt\ *adj* : extremely liberal in giving : very generous [derived from Latin *munificus* "generous", from *munus* "service, gift" + *-ficus* "-fic"] **syn** see GENEROUS — **mu•nif•i•cence** \-səns\ *n* — **mu•nif•i•cent•ly** *adv*

mu•ni•tions \myu̇-ˈnish-ənz\ *n pl* : military supplies, equipment, or provisions; *esp* : AMMUNITION [Middle French *muni-*

tion "rampart, defense", from Latin *munitio*, from *munire* "to fortify", from *moenia* "walls"] — **mu·ni·tion** \-ˈnish-ən\ *vt*

mun·tin \ˈmənt-n\ *or* **munt·ing** \-n, -iŋ\ *n* : a strip separating panes of glass in a sash [French *montant* "vertical dividing bar", from *monter* "to rise", derived from Latin *mont-, mons* "mount"]

[1]mu·ral \ˈmyu̇r-əl\ *adj* **1** : of or relating to a wall **2** : applied to and made a part of a wall surface ⟨a *mural* painting⟩ [Latin *muralis*, from *murus* "wall"]

[2]mural *n* : a mural painting — **mu·ral·ist** \-ə-ləst\ *n*

[1]mur·der \ˈmərd-ər\ *n* : the crime of unlawfully killing a person especially with deliberate intent or design [partly from Old English *morthor*; partly from Old French *murdre*, of Germanic origin]

[2]murder *vb* **mur·dered**; **mur·der·ing** \ˈmərd-riŋ, -ə-riŋ\ **1** : to kill a human being unlawfully and especially with deliberate intent or design : commit murder **2** : to spoil by performing in a wretched manner ⟨*murder* a song⟩ **syn** see KILL — **mur·der·er** \ˈmərd-ər-ər\ *n* — **mur·der·ess** \ˈmərd-ə-rəs\ *n*

mur·der·ous \ˈmərd-rəs, -ə-rəs\ *adj* **1 a** : characterized by or causing murder or bloodshed ⟨*murderous* machine-gun fire⟩ ⟨a *murderous* act⟩ **b** : having or appearing to have the purpose of murder ⟨with *murderous* intent⟩ ⟨a *murderous* glance⟩ **2** : dangerously severe ⟨the desert's *murderous* heat⟩ — **mur·der·ous·ly** *adv* — **mur·der·ous·ness** *n*

mu·rex \ˈmyu̇r-ˌeks\ *n, pl* **mu·ri·ces** \ˈmyu̇r-ə-ˌsēz\ *or* **mu·rex·es** : any of a genus of sea snails that yield a purple dye [Latin, a kind of mollusk]

mu·ri·ate \ˈmyu̇r-ē-ˌāt\ *n* : CHLORIDE [French, from (*acide*) *muriatique* "muriatic acid"]

mu·ri·at·ic acid \ˌmyu̇r-ē-ˌat-ik-\ *n* : HYDROCHLORIC ACID [French *muriatique*, derived from Latin *muria* "brine"]

mu·rine \ˈmyu̇r-ˌīn\ *adj* : of or relating to the common house mouse or closely related rodents ⟨*murine* typhus⟩ [derived from Latin *mur-, mus* "mouse"]

murk *also* **mirk** \ˈmərk\ *n* : intense darkness or gloom; *also* : FOG [Middle English *mirke*] — **murk·i·ly** \-kə-lē\ *adv* — **murk·i·ness** \-kē-nəs\ *n* — **murky** \ˈmər-kē\ *adj*

mur·mur \ˈmər-mər\ *n* **1** : a muttered complaint : GRUMBLE **2** : a low indistinct sound ⟨the *murmur* of the wind⟩ **3** : an abnormal heart sound occurring when the heart is disordered in function or structure [Middle French *murmure*, from Latin *murmur* "murmur, roar"] — **murmur** *vb* — **mur·mur·er** \ˈmər-mər-ər\ *n*

mur·mur·ous \ˈmərm-rəs, -ə-rəs\ *adj* : filled with or characterized by murmurs — **mur·mur·ous·ly** *adv*

mur·rain \ˈmər-ən, ˈmə-rən\ *n* : a pestilence or plague especially of domestic animals [Middle French *morine*, from *morir* "to die", from Latin *mori*]

murre \ˈmər\ *n* : any of several guillemots [origin unknown]

mus·ca·dine \ˈməs-kə-ˌdīn\ *n* : a grape of the southern United States with musky fruits in small clusters [probably alteration of *muscatel*]

mus·cat \ˈməs-ˌkat, -kət\ *n* : any of several cultivated grapes used in making wine and raisins [French, from Provencal, from *muscat* "musky", from *musc* "musk", from Latin *muscus*]

mus·ca·tel \ˌməs-kə-ˈtel\ *n* : a sweet wine made from muscat grapes [Middle French *muscadel*, from Provencal, from *muscat* "muscat"]

[1]mus·cle \ˈməs-əl\ *n* **1 a** : a body tissue consisting of long cells that contract when stimulated and produce motion **b** : an organ that is essentially a mass of muscle tissue attached at either end to a fixed point and that by contracting moves or checks the movement of a body part **2 a** : muscular strength : BRAWN **b** : effective strength : POWER [Middle French, from Latin *musculus* "muscle, little mouse", from *mus* "mouse"]

△ **origin** Diminutives like Latin *musculus*, "little mouse", are used not only to name small things but often to express such diverse feelings as endearment and ridicule as well. Some muscles, especially the major muscles of the arm and leg, look a little like stylized mice, their tendons playing the part of a mouse's tail. This fancied resemblance, which ignores the fact that muscles are often much larger than mice, accounts for the Latin word *musculus*, the ultimate source of English *muscle*.

[2]muscle *vi* **mus·cled**; **mus·cling** \ˈməs-liŋ, -ə-liŋ\ : to force one's way ⟨*muscle* in on a business⟩

mus·cle–bound \ˈməs-əl-ˌbau̇nd\ *adj* : having some of the muscles abnormally enlarged and lacking in elasticity (as from excessive athletic exercise)

mus·co·vite \ˈməs-kə-ˌvīt\ *n* **1** *cap* **a** : a native or resident of the ancient principality of Moscow or of the city of Moscow **b** : RUSSIAN 1 **2** : a mineral that consists of a colorless to pale brown potassium-containing mica [Medieval Latin *Muscovia* "Moscow"] — **Muscovite** *adj*

Mus·co·vy duck \ˌməs-ˌkō-vē-\ *n* : a large crested tropical American duck widely kept in domestication [*Muscovy*, principality of Moscow, Russia]

Muscovy duck

mus·cu·lar \ˈməs-kyə-lər\ *adj* **1 a** : of, relating to, or constituting muscle **b** : performed by the muscles **2 a** : having well-developed muscles **b** : of or relating to physical strength : STRONG — **mus·cu·lar·i·ty** \ˌməs-kyə-ˈlar-ət-ē\ *n* — **mus·cu·lar·ly** \ˈməs-kyə-lər-lē\ *adv*

muscular dystrophy *n* : a disease characterized by progressive wasting of muscles

mus·cu·la·ture \ˈməs-kyə-lə-ˌchu̇r\ *n* : the muscles of the body or of one of its parts

[1]muse \ˈmyüz\ *vb* : to consider carefully : PONDER, MEDITATE [Middle French *muser* "to gape, muse", from *muse* "mouth of an animal"] — **mus·er** *n*

[2]muse *n* **1** *cap* : any of nine sister goddesses in Greek mythology presiding over song and poetry and the arts and sciences **2** : a source of inspiration [Middle French, from Latin *Musa*, from Greek *Mousa*]

mu·sette \myü-ˈzet\ *n* : a small knapsack with a shoulder strap used especially by soldiers — called also *musette bag* [French, literally, "small bagpipe", derived from Middle French *muser* "to muse, play the bagpipe"]

mu·se·um \myü-ˈzē-əm\ *n* : a building or part of a building in which are displayed objects of permanent interest in one or more of the arts or sciences [Latin, "place for learned occupation", from Greek *Mouseion*, from *Mousa* "Muse"]

[1]mush \ˈməsh\ *n* **1** : cornmeal boiled in water **2** : something soft and spongy or shapeless **3** : insipid sentimentality or courting [probably alteration of *mash*]

[2]mush *vi* : to travel over snow with a sled drawn by dogs — sometimes used as a command to a dog team [probably from American French *moucher* "to go fast", from French *mouche* "fly", from Latin *musca*] — **mush·er** *n*

[3]mush *n* : a hike across snow with a dog team

[1]mush·room \ˈməsh-ˌrüm, -ˌru̇m\ *n* **1** : a fleshy aerial fruiting body of a fungus that consists typically of a stem bearing a flattened cap; *esp* : one that is edible **2** : FUNGUS 1 [Middle French *mousseron*, from Medieval Latin *mussirio*]

[1]mushroom 1

[2]mushroom *adj* **1** : springing up suddenly or multiplying rapidly ⟨*mushroom* growth of new agencies⟩ **2** : having the shape of a mushroom

[3]mushroom *vi* : to spring up suddenly or multiply rapidly

mushy \ˈməsh-ē\ *adj* **mush·i·er**; **-est** **1** : soft like mush **2** : weakly sentimental — **mush·i·ly** \ˈməsh-ə-lē\ *adv* — **mush·i·ness** \ˈməsh-ē-nəs\ *n*

mu·sic \ˈmyü-zik\ *n* **1 a** : the art of combining tones so that they are pleasing, expressive, or intelligible **b** : compositions made according to the rules of music **c** : the score of music compositions set down on paper ⟨did you bring your *music* with you⟩ **2** : sounds that have rhythm, harmony, and melody; *also* : an agreeable sound ⟨the *music* of a brook⟩ **3** : punishment for a

\ə\ **abut**	\au̇\ **out**	\i\ **tip**	\ȯ\ **saw**	\u̇\ **foot**
\ər\ **further**	\ch\ **chin**	\ī\ **life**	\ȯi\ **coin**	\y\ **yet**
\a\ **mat**	\e\ **pet**	\j\ **job**	\th\ **thin**	\yü\ **few**
\ā\ **take**	\ē\ **easy**	\ŋ\ **sing**	\th\ **this**	\yu̇\ **cure**
\ä\ **cot, cart**	\g\ **go**	\ō\ **bone**	\ü\ **food**	\zh\ **vision**

misdeed ⟨must face the *music*⟩ [Old French *musique*, from Latin *musica*, from Greek *mousikē* "art presided over by the Muses", from *Mousa* "Muse"]

[1]**mu•si•cal** \'myü-zi-kəl\ *adj* **1 a :** of or relating to music ⟨*musical* instruments⟩ **b :** having the pleasing harmonious qualities of music **:** MELODIOUS ⟨a *musical* voice⟩ **2 :** having an interest in or talent for music ⟨a *musical* family⟩ **3 :** set to or accompanied by music **4 :** of or relating to musicians or music lovers — **mu•si•cal•i•ty** \ˌmyü-zi-'kal-ət-ē\ *n* — **mu•si•cal•ly** \'myü-zi-kə-lē, -klē\ *adv*

[2]**musical** *n* **:** a film or theatrical production consisting of musical numbers and dialogue that develop a plot — called also *musical comedy*; compare REVUE

musical chairs *n pl* **:** a children's game in which players march to music around a group of chairs numbering one less than the number of players and scramble for a seat when the music stops

mu•si•cale \ˌmyü-zi-'kal\ *n* **:** a usually private social gathering featuring a concert of music [French *soirée musicale*, literally, "musical evening"]

music box *n* **:** a box or case enclosing an apparatus that reproduces music mechanically when activated by clockwork

music hall *n* **:** a vaudeville theater

mu•si•cian \myu̇-'zish-ən\ *n* **:** one skilled in music; *esp* **:** a composer or professional performer of music — **mu•si•cian•ly** \-lē\ *adj* — **mu•si•cian•ship** \-ˌship\ *n*

mu•si•col•o•gy \ˌmyü-zi-'käl-ə-jē\ *n* **:** a study of music as a branch of knowledge or field of research — **mu•si•co•log•i•cal** \-zi-kə-'läj-i-kəl\ *adj* — **mu•si•col•o•gist** \-zi-'käl-ə-jəst\ *n*

mus•ing \'myü-ziŋ\ *n* **:** MEDITATION ⟨considered it in their *musings*⟩ — **musing** *adj* — **mus•ing•ly** \-ziŋ-lē\ *adv*

musk \'məsk\ *n* **1 a :** a substance of penetrating persistent odor obtained usually from the male musk deer and used in perfume **b :** a substance (as from a skunk) of comparable odor **2 :** the odor of a musk [Middle French *musc*, from Late Latin *muscus*, from Greek *moschos*, from Persian *mushk*, from Sanskrit *muṣka* "testicle", from *mūṣ* "mouse"]

musk deer *n* **:** a small hornless deer about one meter long and ½ meter tall that lives in the high regions of central Asia

musk deer

mus•keg \'məs-ˌkeg\ *n* **:** BOG; *esp* **:** a dense sphagnum bog of northern North America [of American Indian origin]

mus•kel•lunge \'məs-kə-ˌlənj\ *n, pl* **muskellunge :** a large North American pike that may weigh 30 to 35 kilograms and is a valuable sport fish [of American Indian origin]

mus•ket \'məs-kət\ *n* **:** a large-caliber usually muzzle-loading military shoulder firearm with a smooth bore [Middle French *mousquet*, from Italian *moschetto* "arrow for a crossbow, musket", from *mosca* "fly", from Latin *musca*]

△ **origin** The musket was originally a Spanish weapon, first used by the Spanish army in the 16th century. The musket was introduced to France through her conflict with Spain, which was fought in Italy. Although the French borrowed the new weapon from their enemy, they took the name *mousquet* from the Italians. Italian *moschetto*, diminutive of *mosca*, "fly", was the word for the arrow of a crossbow. When the new weapon was introduced, the name of the old one was taken over for it. French *mousquet* was borrowed into English (as *musket*) late in the 16th century.

mus•ke•teer \ˌməs-kə-'tiər\ *n* **:** a soldier armed with a musket

mus•ket•ry \'məs-kə-trē\ *n, pl* **-ries :** small-arms fire

musk•mel•on \'məsk-ˌmel-ən\ *n* **:** a small round to oval and sometimes ridged melon that has usually sweet edible green or orange flesh; *also* **:** a vine bearing muskmelons — compare CANTALOUPE

Mus•ko•gee \məs-'kō-gē, ˌməs-\ *n* **:** a member of an Indian people of what is now Georgia, South Carolina, and eastern Alabama

musk–ox \'məs-ˌkäks\ *n* **:** a heavy-set shaggy-coated wild ox that is confined to Greenland and to the barren lands of northern North America

musk-ox

musk•rat \'məs-ˌkrat\ *n, pl* **muskrat** *or* **muskrats :** a North American aquatic rodent with a long scaly tail, webbed hind feet, and dark glossy brown fur; *also* **:** its fur or pelt [probably by folk etymology from a word of American Indian origin]

musk turtle *n* **:** any of several small American freshwater turtles with a strong musky odor

musky \'məs-kē\ *adj* **musk•i•er; -est :** having an odor of or resembling musk — **musk•i•ness** *n*

Mus•lim \'məz-ləm, 'mu̇s-, 'mu̇z-\ *or* **Mos•lem** \'mäz-ləm *also* 'mäs-\ *n* **:** an adherent of Islam [Arabic *muslim*, literally, "one who surrenders (to God)"] — **Muslim** *adj*

mus•lin \'məz-lən\ *n* **:** a cotton fabric of plain weave [French *mousseline*, from Italian *mussolina*, from Arabic *mawṣilīy* "of Mosul", from *al-Mawṣil* "Mosul, Iraq"]

mus•quash \'məs-ˌkwäsh, -ˌkwósh\ *n* **:** MUSKRAT [of American Indian origin]

[1]**muss** \'məs\ *n* **:** a state of disorder **:** MESS [origin unknown]

[2]**muss** *vt* **:** to make untidy **:** RUMPLE ⟨*mussed* my hair⟩

mus•sel \'məs-əl\ *n* **1 :** an edible saltwater 2-valved mollusk with a long dark shell **2 :** any of numerous 2-valved freshwater mollusks especially of the central United States having shells with pearly inner linings [Old English *muscelle*, derived from Latin *musculus* "muscle, mussel"]

mussy \'məs-ē\ *adj* **muss•i•er; -est :** MESSY, UNTIDY — **muss•i•ly** \'məs-ə-lē\ *adv* — **muss•i•ness** \'məs-ē-nəs\ *n*

[1]**must** \məst, məs, 'məst\ *auxiliary verb, present & past all persons* **must 1 a :** be commanded or requested to ⟨the train *must* stop⟩ **b :** be urged to ⟨you *must* read that book⟩ **2 a :** be compelled, required, or obliged to ⟨one *must* eat to live⟩ ⟨we *must* be quiet⟩ **b :** be determined to ⟨if you *must* go⟩ **3 :** be logically inferred or supposed to ⟨it *must* be time⟩ **4 :** be reasonably certain to ⟨I *must* have lost it⟩ [Old English *mōste* "was allowed to, had to", past of *mōtan* "to be allowed to, have to"]

[2]**must** \'məst\ *n* **:** something necessary, required, or indispensable ⟨new shoes are a *must*⟩

[3]**must** *n* **:** the juice of fruit (as grapes) before and during fermentation [Old English, from Latin *mustum*]

mus•tache *or* **mous•tache** \'məs-ˌtash, məs-'\ *n* **1 :** the hair growing on the human upper lip **2 :** hair or bristles about the mouth of a lower animal [Middle French *moustache*, from Italian *mustaccio*, derived from Greek *mystax* "upper lip, mustache"]

mus•ta•chio *or* **mous•ta•chio** \məs-'tash-ō, -'täsh-, -ē-ˌō\ *n, pl* **-chios :** MUSTACHE; *esp* **:** a large mustache [Italian *mustaccio*] — **mus•ta•chioed** \-ōd, -ē-ˌōd\ *adj*

mus•tang \'məs-ˌtaŋ\ *n* **:** the small hardy naturalized horse of the western plains directly descended from horses brought in by the Spaniards; *also* **:** BRONCO [American Spanish *mestengo*, from Spanish, "stray", from *mesta* "annual roundup of stray cattle", from Medieval Latin (*animalia*) *mixta* "mixed animals"]

mus•tard \'məs-tərd\ *n* **1 :** a pungent yellow powder of the seeds of a common mustard used as a seasoning or in medicine **2 :** any of several yellow-flowered herbs related to the turnips and cabbages [Old French *mostarde*, from *moust* "must", from Latin *mustum*]

mustard gas *n* **:** a poisonous oily liquid $C_4H_8Cl_2S$ consisting of carbon, hydrogen, chlorine, and sulfur and having violent irritating and especially blistering effects

mustard plaster *n* **:** a counterirritant medicinal plaster containing powdered mustard

[1]**mus•ter** \'məs-tər\ *vb* **mus•tered; mus•ter•ing** \-tə-riŋ, -triŋ\ **1 :** to enlist or enroll a person in military service **2 a :** to assemble (as troops or a ship's company) for roll call or inspection **b :** CONGREGATE, ASSEMBLE **3 :** to collect and display ⟨all the strength I could *muster*⟩ [Middle English *mustren* "to show, muster", from Old French *monstrer* "to show", from Latin *monstrare*, from *monstrum* "sign, portent, monster"]

[2]**muster** *n* **1 a :** an act of assembling; *esp* **:** a formal military inspection **b :** critical examination ⟨slipshod work that would

never pass *muster*⟩ **2 :** an assembled group
muster out *vt* **:** to discharge from service
mustn't \'məs-nt\ **:** must not
musty \'məs-tē\ *adj* **must•i•er; -est 1 a :** impaired by damp or mildew **:** MOLDY **b :** tasting or smelling of damp and decay **2 a :** TRITE, STALE ⟨a *musty* proverb⟩ **b :** OUTMODED 2 ⟨*musty* laws⟩ [earlier *must* "musk, mold", from Middle French, "musk", from *musc*] — **must•i•ly** \-tə-lē\ *adv* — **must•i•ness** \-tē-nəs\ *n*
mu•ta•ble \'myüt-ə-bəl\ *adj* **1 :** prone to change **:** INCONSTANT **2 a :** capable of change in form or nature **b :** capable of or liable to mutation ⟨*mutable* vowels⟩ ⟨a *mutable* bacterium⟩ [Latin *mutabilis*, from *mutare* "to change"] — **mu•ta•bil•i•ty** \ˌmyüt-ə-'bil-ət-ē\ *n*
mu•ta•gen \'myüt-ə-jən, -ˌjen\ *n* **:** an agent inducing mutation — **mu•ta•gen•ic** \ˌmyüt-ə-'jen-ik\ *adj* — **mu•ta•ge•nic•i•ty** \-jə-'nis-ət-ē\ *n*
mu•tant \'myüt-nt\ *adj* **:** of, relating to, or produced by mutation — **mutant** *n*
mu•tate \'myü-ˌtāt\ *vb* **:** to undergo or cause to undergo mutation [Latin *mutare* "to change"]
mu•ta•tion \myü-'tā-shən\ *n* **1 :** a basic alteration **:** CHANGE **2 a :** a relatively permanent change in hereditary material involving either a change in the position of the genes on the chromosomes or a fundamental change in the chemical structure of the genes themselves **b :** an individual or strain resulting from mutation — **mu•ta•tion•al** \-shnəl, -shən-l\ *adj* — **mu•ta•tive** \'myü-ˌtāt-iv, 'myüt-ət-iv\ *adj*
mu•ta•tis mu•tan•dis \mü-ˌtät-ə-smü-'tän-dəs\ *adv* **:** with the necessary changes having been made [New Latin]
[1]mute \'myüt\ *adj* **1 :** unable to speak **:** DUMB **2 :** marked by absence of speech ⟨a *mute* appeal for help⟩ **3 :** not pronounced **:** SILENT ⟨the *mute b* in *thumb*⟩ [Middle French *muet*, from Latin *mutus*] **syn** see DUMB — **mute•ly** *adv* — **mute•ness** *n* — **mut•ism** \'myüt-ˌiz-əm\ *n*
[2]mute *n* **1 a :** a person who cannot or does not speak **b :** a professional mourner formerly hired to take part in a funeral **2 :** a device on a musical instrument that deadens, softens, or muffles its tone **3 :** STOP 8
[3]mute *vt* **1 :** to muffle or reduce the sound of **2 :** to tone down ⟨*muted* their criticism⟩ ⟨*muted* the colors⟩
mu•ti•late \'myüt-l-ˌāt\ *vt* **1 a :** to deprive of an essential part ⟨*mutilated* refugees⟩ **b :** to cut off or permanently destroy the use of (as a limb) **2 :** to make imperfect by cutting or alteration ⟨*multilate* a document⟩ [Latin *mutilare*] — **mu•ti•la•tion** \ˌmyüt-l-'ā-shən\ *n* — **mu•ti•la•tor** \'myüt-l-ˌāt-ər\ *n*
mu•ti•neer \ˌmyüt-n-'iər\ *n* **:** one that mutinies
mu•ti•nous \'myüt-n-əs, 'myüt-nəs\ *adj* **1 :** disposed to or engaged in mutiny **:** REBELLIOUS ⟨a *mutinous* crew⟩ **2 :** of, relating to, or constituting mutiny ⟨*mutinous* acts⟩ — **mu•ti•nous•ly** *adv* — **mu•ti•nous•ness** *n*
mu•ti•ny \'myüt-n-ē, 'myüt-nē\ *n, pl* **-nies 1 :** willful refusal to obey constituted authority; *esp* **:** revolt by a military group against a superior officer **2 :** an act or instance of mutiny [obsolete *mutine* "to rebel", from Middle French *se mutiner*, from *meute* "revolt", derived from Latin *movēre* "to move"] — **mutiny** *vi*
mutt \'mət\ *n* **:** MONGREL 1, CUR [earlier *mutt* "fool", short for *muttonhead*]
mut•ter \'mət-ər\ *vb* **1 :** MUMBLE 1 **2 :** to murmur complainingly or angrily **:** GRUMBLE [Middle English *muteren*] — **mutter** *n* — **mut•ter•er** \'mət-ər-ər\ *n*
mut•ton \'mət-n\ *n* **:** the flesh of a mature sheep [Old French *moton* "sheep", of Celtic origin] — **mut•tony** \-ē\ *adj*
mut•ton•chops \-ˌchäps\ *n pl* **:** side-whiskers that are narrow at the temple and broad and round by the lower jaws — called also *muttonchop whiskers*
mu•tu•al \'myüch-wəl, -ə-wəl, 'myü-chəl\ *adj* **1 a :** given and received in equal amount ⟨*mutual* favors⟩ **b :** having the same feelings one for the other ⟨*mutual* enemies⟩ **2 :** participated in, shared, or enjoyed by two or more at the same time **:** JOINT ⟨our *mutual* friend⟩ ⟨*mutual* defense⟩ **3 :** organized so that the members share in the profits, benefits, expenses, and liabilities ⟨*mutual* savings bank⟩ ⟨*mutual* life insurance company⟩ [Middle French *mutuel*, from Latin *mutuus*] **syn** see RECIPROCAL — **mu•tu•al•i•ty** \ˌmyü-chə-'wal-ət-ē\ *n* — **mu•tu•al•ly** \'myü-chə-wə-lē, -chə-lē\ *adv*
mutual fund *n* **:** an investment company that invests money of its shareholders in a usually diversified group of securities
mu•tu•al•ism \'myüch-wə-ˌliz-əm, -ə-wə-, 'myü-chə-ˌliz-\ *n* **:** mutually beneficial association between different kinds of organisms — **mu•tu•al•is•tic** \ˌmyü-chə-wə-'lis-tik, -chə-'lis-\ *adj*
muu•muu \'mü-mü\ *n* **:** a loose dress of Hawaiian origin for informal wear [Hawaiian *mu'umu'u*]
mu•zhik *or* **mou•jik** \mü-'zhēk, -'zhik\ *n* **:** a Russian peasant [Russian]
[1]muz•zle \'məz-əl\ *n* **1 :** the projecting jaws and nose of an animal **:** SNOUT **2 :** a fastening or covering for the mouth of an animal used to prevent eating or biting **3 :** the open end of a weapon from which the missile is discharged [Middle French *musel*, from *muse* "mouth of an animal"]

[1]muzzle 1

[2]muzzle *vt* **muz•zled; muz•zling** \'məz-ling, -ə-ling\ **1 :** to fit with a muzzle **2 :** to prevent free or normal expression by **:** GAG ⟨*muzzle* the press⟩ — **muz•zler** \'məz-lər, -ə-lər\ *n*
muz•zle–load•er \ˌməz-əl-'lōd-ər, -ə-'\ *n* **:** a gun that is loaded through the muzzle — **muz•zle–load•ing** \-'lōd-ing\ *adj*
muz•zy \'məz-ē\ *adj* **muz•zi•er; -est 1 :** muddled or confused in mind **2 a :** not clear ⟨a *muzzy* photograph⟩ ⟨*muzzy* ideas⟩ **b :** DULL, GLOOMY ⟨a *muzzy* day⟩ [perhaps blend of *muddled* and *fuzzy*] — **muz•zi•ly** \'məz-ə-lē\ *adv* — **muz•zi•ness** \'məz-ē-nəs\ *n*
my \mī, 'mī, mə\ *adj* **1 :** of or relating to me or myself especially as possessor, agent, or object of an action ⟨*my* car⟩ ⟨*my* promise⟩ ⟨*my* injuries⟩ **2** — used interjectionally to express surprise ⟨oh *my*⟩ [Old English *mīn*]
my- *or* **myo-** *combining form* **:** muscle ⟨*myo*fibril⟩ **:** muscle and ⟨*myo*neural⟩ [Greek *mys* "mouse, muscle"]
my•as•the•nia gra•vis \ˌmī-əs-ˌthē-nē-ə-'grav-əs, -'gräv-\ *n* **:** a disease of the muscular system characterized by fatigue and weakness and progressive paralysis without wasting or sensory disturbance [New Latin *myasthenia* "muscular debility" (from *my-* + Greek *asthenia* "asthenia") + Latin *gravis* "grave"]
myc- *or* **myco-** *combining form* **:** fungus ⟨*myc*ology⟩ [Greek *mykēs*]
my•ce•li•um \mī-'sē-lē-əm\ *n, pl* **-lia** \-lē-ə\ *also* **-li•ums :** the vegetative part of the body of a fungus typically consisting of a mass of interwoven hyphae and often being submerged in another body (as of soil, organic matter, or the tissues of a plant or animal host) [derived from Greek *mykēs* "fungus" + *hēlos* "nail, wart, callus"] — **my•ce•li•al** \-lē-əl\ *adj*
My•ce•nae•an \ˌmī-sə-'nē-ən\ *adj* **:** of or relating to the Bronze Age culture of the eastern Mediterranean area centering in Mycenae especially from 1600 to 1100 B.C.
my•co•bac•te•ri•um \ˌmī-kō-bak-'tir-ē-əm\ *n* **:** any of a genus of bacteria that includes the causative agents of tuberculosis and of leprosy as well as harmless saprophytes
my•col•o•gy \mī-'käl-ə-jē\ *n* **1 :** a branch of botany dealing with fungi **2 :** fungal life — **my•co•log•i•cal** \ˌmī-kə-'läj-i-kəl\ *adj* — **my•col•o•gist** \mī-'käl-ə-jəst\ *n*
my•co•plas•ma \ˌmī-kō-'plaz-mə\ *n, pl* **-mas** *or* **-ma•ta** \-mət-ə\ **:** any of a genus of minute microorganisms without cell walls that are intermediate in some respects between viruses and bacteria and are parasitic usually in mammals
my•cor•rhi•za \ˌmī-kə-'rī-zə\ *n, pl* **-zae** \-ˌzē\ *or* **-zas :** a symbiotic association of the mycelium of a fungus with the roots of a seed plant [*myc-* + Greek *rhiza* "root"] — **my•cor•rhi•zal** \-zəl\ *adj*
my•co•sis \mī-'kō-səs\ *n, pl* **-co•ses** \-ˌsēz\ **:** infection with or disease caused by a fungus — **my•cot•ic** \-'kät-ik\ *adj*
my•e•lin \'mī-ə-lən\ *n* **:** a soft white somewhat fatty material that forms a thick sheath about certain nerve fibers [derived from Greek *myelos* "marrow", from *mys* "mouse, muscle"] —

\ə\ **abut**	\au̇\ **out**	\i\ **tip**	\ȯ\ **saw**	\u̇\ **foot**
\ər\ **further**	\ch\ **chin**	\ī\ **life**	\ȯi\ **coin**	\y\ **yet**
\a\ **mat**	\e\ **pet**	\j\ **job**	\th\ **thin**	\yü\ **few**
\ā\ **take**	\ē\ **easy**	\ng\ **sing**	\t͟h\ **this**	\yu̇\ **cure**
\ä\ **cot, cart**	\g\ **go**	\ō\ **bone**	\ü\ **food**	\zh\ **vision**

my•e•lin•at•ed \-lə-ˌnāt-əd\ *adj*

my•i•a•sis \mī-ˈī-ə-səs, mē-\ *n, pl* **-a•ses** \-ə-ˌsēz\ : infestation (as of tissue) with fly maggots [Greek *myia* "fly"]

my•na *or* **my•nah** \ˈmī-nə\ *n* : any of various Asian starlings; *esp* : a dark brown slightly crested bird of southeastern Asia with a white tail tip and wing markings and bright yellow bill and feet [Hindi *mainā,* from Sanskrit *madana*]

myna

myo- — see MY-

myo•car•di•um \ˌmī-ə-ˈkärd-ē-əm\ *n* : the middle muscular layer of the heart wall [New Latin, from *my-* + Greek *kardia* "heart"] — **myo•car•di•al** \-ē-əl\ *adj*

myo•fi•bril \ˌmī-ō-ˈfīb-rəl, -ˈfib-\ *n* : one of the long thin protein filaments of a muscle cell that are the contractile elements of muscle

myo•glo•bin \ˌmī-ə-ˈglō-bən, ˈmī-ə-ˌ\ *n* : a red iron-containing protein pigment in muscles that is similar to hemoglobin

myo•neu•ral junction \ˌmī-ə-ˌnu̇r-əl-, -ˌnyu̇r-\ *n* : the region of contact between a motor neuron and a muscle fiber

my•o•pia \mī-ˈō-pē-ə\ *n* : the condition of being nearsighted [Greek *myōpia,* from *myein* "to be closed" + *ōps* "eye, face"] — **my•o•pic** \-ˈōp-ik, -ˈäp-\ *adj* — **my•o•pi•cal•ly** \-i-kə-lē, -klē\ *adv*

my•o•sin \ˈmī-ə-sən\ *n* : a protein of muscle that with actin is active in muscular contraction [derived from Greek *mys* "mouse, muscle"]

¹myr•i•ad \ˈmir-ē-əd\ *n* **1** : ten thousand **2** : an indefinitely large number ⟨the *myriads* of stars⟩ [Greek *myriad-, myrias,* from *myrioi* "countless, ten thousand"]

²myriad *adj* : consisting of a very great but indefinite number ⟨the *myriad* grains of sand on a beach⟩

myr•ia•me•ter \ˈmir-ē-ə-ˌmēt-ər\ *n* : a metric unit of length equal to 10,000 meters

myri•io•pod *or* **myr•ia•pod** \ˈmir-ē-ə-ˌpäd\ *n* : any of a group (Myriopoda) of arthropods including the millipedes and centipedes [derived from Greek *myrioi* "countless, ten thousand" + *pod-, pous* "foot"] — **myriopod** *adj*

myr•mi•don \ˈmər-mə-ˌdän, ˈmər-məd-ən\ *n* **1** *cap* : any of a legendary Thessalian people following Achilles to the Trojan war **2 a** : a loyal follower or retainer **b** : a subordinate who executes orders without question or scruple [Greek *Myrmidōn*]

myrrh \ˈmər\ *n* : a brown slightly bitter aromatic gum resin obtained from African and Arabian trees and used especially in perfumes or formerly in incense [Old English *myrre,* from Latin *myrrha,* from Greek, of Semitic origin]

myr•tle \ˈmərt-l\ *n* **1** : a common evergreen bushy shrub of southern Europe with oval to lance-shaped shining leaves, fragrant white or rosy flowers, and black berries **2 a** : any of the family of chiefly tropical shrubs or trees to which the common myrtle of Europe belongs : ¹PERIWINKLE [Middle French *mirtille,* from Medieval Latin *myrtillus,* from Latin *myrtos,* from Greek *myrtos*]

my•self \mī-ˈself, mə-\ *pron* **1** : that identical one that is I — used reflexively or for emphasis ⟨I'm going to get *myself* a new suit⟩ ⟨I *myself* will go⟩ **2** : my normal, healthy, or sane condition or self ⟨didn't feel *myself* yesterday⟩

mys•te•ri•ous \mis-ˈtir-ē-əs\ *adj* : containing, suggesting, or implying a mystery ⟨the *mysterious* ways of nature⟩ — **mys•te•ri•ous•ly** *adv* — **mys•te•ri•ous•ness** *n*

mys•tery \ˈmis-tə-rē, -trē\ *n, pl* **-ter•ies** **1 a** : a religious truth that man can know by revelation alone and cannot fully understand **b** : any of the 15 events (as the Nativity, the Crucifixion, or the Assumption) serving as a subject for meditation during the saying of the rosary **2 a** : something that has not been or cannot be explained ⟨where they went is a *mystery*⟩ **b** : a deep secret ⟨kept our plans a *mystery*⟩ **3** : a piece of fiction dealing with a mysterious crime **4** : mysterious quality or character ⟨the *mystery* of that smile⟩ [Latin *mysterium,* from Greek *mystērion,* from *myein* "to be closed (of eyes or lips)"]

• **syn** ENIGMA, RIDDLE: MYSTERY applies to what is not or cannot be fully understood or explained ⟨the disappearance of the money remained a *mystery*⟩ ENIGMA applies to words or actions very difficult to interpret correctly; RIDDLE suggests especially a problem or enigma involving paradox or apparent contradiction.

mystery play *n* : a medieval play based on scriptural incidents (as the life, death, and resurrection of Christ)

¹mys•tic \ˈmis-tik\ *adj* **1** : MYSTICAL 1 **2** : of or relating to mysteries or magical rites : OCCULT **3** : of or relating to mysticism or mystics **4 a** : MYSTERIOUS **b** : AWESOME 2 **c** : MAGICAL [Latin *mysticus* "of mysteries", from Greek *mystikos,* from *myein* "to be closed"]

²mystic *n* : a person who seeks direct knowledge of God through contemplation and prayer

mys•ti•cal \ˈmis-ti-kəl\ *adj* **1** : having a spiritual meaning or reality that is neither apparent to the senses nor obvious to the intelligence **2** : of, relating to, or resulting from direct communion with God or ultimate reality **3** : MYSTIC 2 — **mys•ti•cal•ly** \-ti-kə-lē, -klē\ *adv*

mys•ti•cism \ˈmis-tə-ˌsiz-əm\ *n* **1** : the experience of mystical union or direct communion with ultimate reality **2** : the belief that direct knowledge of God or of spiritual truth can be achieved by personal insight and inspiration **3** : vague guessing or speculation

mys•ti•fy \ˈmis-tə-ˌfī\ *vb* **-fied; -fy•ing** **1** : to make obscure or difficult to understand **2** : to baffle and disturb the mind of : PERPLEX ⟨strange actions that *mystified* everyone⟩ **syn** see PUZZLE — **mys•ti•fi•ca•tion** \ˌmis-tə-fə-ˈkā-shən\ *n*

mys•tique \mi-ˈstēk\ *n* : a set of beliefs and attitudes developing around an object or associated with a particular group : CULT ⟨the *mystique* of mountain climbing⟩ [French, from *mystique* "mystic", from Latin *mysticus*]

myth \ˈmith\ *n* **1** : a usually legendary narrative that presents part of the beliefs of a people or explains a practice, belief, or natural phenomenon **2** : PARABLE, ALLEGORY **3 a** : a person or thing having only an imaginary existence ⟨the dragon is a *myth*⟩ **b** : a false or unsupported belief [Greek *mythos*]

• **syn** LEGEND, FABLE: in specific use a MYTH is a story dealing with gods or imaginary beings representing natural phenomena; a LEGEND may include supernatural incidents but deals with human beings or particular places; a FABLE is an invented story in which talking animals or things illustrate human follies and weaknesses.

myth•i•cal \ˈmith-i-kəl\ *also* **myth•ic** \-ik\ *adj* **1** : based on, described in, or being a myth ⟨Hercules is a *mythical* hero⟩ **2** : IMAGINARY, INVENTED ⟨the novelist created a *mythical* town⟩ **syn** see FABULOUS — **myth•i•cal•ly** \-i-kə-lē, -klē\ *adv*

my•thol•o•gy \mith-ˈäl-ə-jē\ *n, pl* **-gies** **1** : a body of myths; *esp* : the myths dealing with the gods and heroes of a people ⟨Greek *mythology*⟩ **2** : a branch of knowledge that deals with myth — **myth•o•log•i•cal** \ˌmith-ə-ˈläj-i-kəl\ *adj* — **myth•o•log•i•cal•ly** \-kə-lē, -klē\ *adv* — **my•thol•o•gist** \mith-ˈäl-ə-jəst\ *n*

myth•os \ˈmith-ˌōs, -ˌäs\ *n, pl* **myth•oi** \-ˌöi\ : a pattern of beliefs expressing often symbolically the characteristic or prevalent attitudes in a group or culture [Greek, "myth"]

myx•ede•ma \ˌmik-sə-ˈdē-mə\ *n* : a disorder caused by deficient thyroid secretion and marked by puffy swelling, dry skin and hair, and loss of mental and physical vigor [Greek *myxa* "lamp wick, nasal mucus" + New Latin *edema* "edema"] — **myx•ede•ma•tous** \-ˈdem-ət-əs, -ˈdē-mət-\ *adj*

myxo•my•cete \ˌmik-sō-ˈmī-ˌsēt, -mī-ˈsēt\ *n* : SLIME MOLD [derived from Greek *myxa* "mucus" + *mykēt-, mykēs* "fungus"]

N n—nystagmus

n \'en\ *n, pl* **n's** *or* **ns** \'enz\ *often cap* **1 :** the 14th letter of the English alphabet **2 :** an unspecified quantity ⟨sum the integers from one to *n*⟩ **3 :** the haploid number of chromosomes

-n — see -EN

nab \'nab\ *vt* **nabbed**; **nab•bing 1 :** to seize and take into custody **:** ARREST **2 :** to seize suddenly [perhaps from English dialect *nap* "to grab, nab"]

na•bob \'nā-,bäb\ *n* **1 :** a provincial governor of the Mogul empire in India **2 :** a man of great wealth or prominence [Hindi *nawwāb,* from Arabic *nuwwāb,* pl. of *nā'ib* "governor"]

na•celle \nə-'sel\ *n* **:** an enclosed shelter on an aircraft for an engine or sometimes for crew [French, literally, "small boat", from Late Latin *navicella,* from Latin *navis* "ship"]

na•cre \'nā-kər\ *n* **:** MOTHER-OF-PEARL [Middle French, from Italian *naccara* "drum, nacre", from Arabic *naqqārah* "drum"] — **na•cre•ous** \-krē-əs, -kə-rəs, -krəs\ *adj*

NAD \,en-,ā-'dē\ *n* **:** a coenzyme $C_{21}H_{27}N_7O_{14}P_2$ of numerous dehydrogenases that occurs in most cells and plays an important role in respiration and photosynthesis as an oxidizing agent or when in the reduced form as a reducing agent — called also *nicotinamide-adenine dinucleotide*

na•dir \'nā-,diər, 'nād-ər\ *n* **1 :** the point of the celestial sphere that is directly opposite the zenith and vertically downward from the observer **2 :** the lowest point ⟨our hopes had reached their *nadir*⟩ [Middle French, from Arabic *naẓīr* "opposite"]

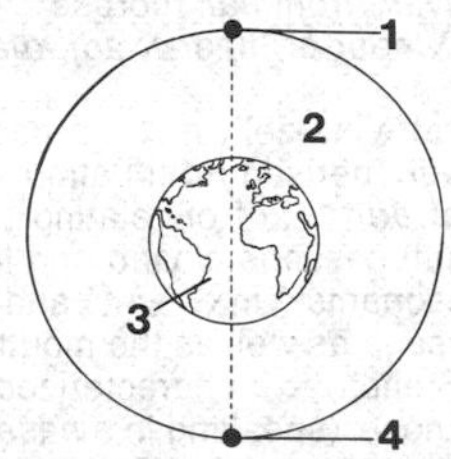

nadir 1: *1* zenith, *2* celestial sphere, *3* earth, *4* nadir

NADP \,en-,ā-,dē-'pē\ *n* **:** a coenzyme $C_{21}H_{28}N_7O_{17}P_3$ of numerous dehydrogenases that plays a role in respiration and photosynthesis similar to NAD — called also *nicotinamide-adenine diphosphate*

¹nag \'nag\ *n* **:** HORSE; *esp* **:** one that is old or in poor condition [Middle English *nagge*]

²nag *vb* **nagged**; **nag•ging 1 :** to find fault incessantly **:** COMPLAIN **2 :** to irritate by constant scolding or urging **3 :** to be a continuing source of annoyance ⟨a *nagging* toothache⟩ [probably of Scandinavian origin] — **nag•ger** *n*

Na•huatl \'nä-,wät-l\ *n* **1 :** a group of peoples of southern Mexico and Central America **2 :** the language of the Nahuatl people [Spanish, from Nahuatl] — **Na•huat•lan** \-,wät-lən\ *adj or n*

Na•hum \'nā-əm, -həm\ *n* — see BIBLE table

na•iad \'nā-əd, 'nī-, -,ad\ *n, pl* **na•iads** *or* **na•ia•des** \-ə-,dēz\ **1 :** one of the nymphs in classical mythology living in and giving life to lakes, rivers, springs, and fountains **2 :** the aquatic young of a mayfly, dragonfly, damselfly, or stone fly [Latin *naiad-, naias,* from Greek, from *nan* "to flow"]

¹nail \'nāl\ *n* **1 a :** a horny sheath protecting the end of each finger and toe in man and most other primates **b :** a corresponding structure (as a claw) terminating a digit in other vertebrates **2 :** a slender pointed piece of metal driven into or through something for fastening [Old English *nægl*]

²nail *vt* **1 :** to fasten with or as if with a nail **2 :** CATCH, TRAP ⟨*nail* a thief⟩ — **nail•er** *n*

nail•brush \'nāl-,brəsh\ *n* **:** a small firm-bristled brush for cleaning the hands and fingernails

nail down *vt* **:** to settle or establish clearly and unmistakably

na•ive *or* **na•ïve** \nä-'ēv\ *adj* **1 :** marked by unaffected simplicity **2 :** showing lack of informed judgment [French *naïve,* feminine of *naïf,* from Old French, "inborn, natural", from Latin *nativus* "native"] — **na•ive•ly** *adv* — **na•ive•ness** *n*

na•ive•té *or* **na•ïve•té** *or* **na•ive•te** \nä-,ē-və-'tā, nä-'ē-və-,\ *n* **1 :** the quality or state of being naive **2 :** a naive remark or action [French *naïveté,* from *naïf* "naive"]

na•ive•ty *also* **na•ïve•ty** \nä-'ē-vət-ē, -'ēv-tē\ *n* **:** NAIVETÉ

na•ked \'nā-kəd, *especially South* 'nek-əd\ *adj* **1 :** having no clothes on **:** NUDE **2 a :** lacking a usual or natural covering (as of foliage or feathers) ⟨*naked* hills⟩ **b :** not sheathed ⟨a *naked* sword⟩ **c :** lacking protective enveloping parts (as membranes, scales, or shells) ⟨a *naked* seed⟩ ⟨slugs and other *naked* mollusks⟩ **3 :** lacking embellishment of any kind **:** PLAIN ⟨the *naked* truth⟩ **4 :** not aided by artificial means ⟨seen by the *naked* eye⟩ [Old English *nacod*] — **na•ked•ly** *adv* — **na•ked•ness** *n*

nam•by-pam•by \,nam-bē-'pam-bē\ *adj* **1 :** lacking in character or substance **:** INSIPID **2 :** WEAK 1c, INDECISIVE [*Namby Pamby,* nickname given to Ambrose Phillips, died 1749, English poet, to ridicule the style of his poetry] — **namby-pamby** *n*

¹name \'nām\ *n* **1 :** a word or combination of words by which a person or thing is regularly known **2 :** a descriptive often disparaging term ⟨call someone *names*⟩ **3 :** REPUTATION; *esp* **:** a distinguished reputation ⟨make a *name* for oneself⟩ **4 :** FAMILY, CLAN ⟨was a disgrace to the *name*⟩ **5 :** appearance as opposed to fact ⟨a friend in *name* only⟩ [Old English *nama*]

²name *vt* **1 :** to give a name to **:** CALL **2 a :** to mention or identify by name **b :** to accuse by name **3 :** to nominate for office **:** APPOINT **4 :** to decide on **:** CHOOSE **5 :** to speak about **:** MENTION ⟨*name* a price⟩ — **name•able** *also* **nam•able** \'nā-mə-bəl\ *adj* — **nam•er** *n*

³name *adj* **1 :** of, relating to, or bearing a name ⟨a *name* tag⟩ **2 :** having an established reputation ⟨*name* brands⟩

name•less \'nām-ləs\ *adj* **1 :** having no name **2 :** not marked with a name ⟨a *nameless* grave⟩ **3 :** not known by name **:** ANONYMOUS ⟨a *nameless* author⟩ **4 :** not to be described ⟨*nameless* fears⟩ — **name•less•ly** *adv* — **name•less•ness** *n*

name•ly \'nām-lē\ *adv* **:** that is to say ⟨the cat family, *namely,* lions, tigers, and related animals⟩

name•plate \-,plāt\ *n* **:** a plate or plaque bearing a name

name•sake \'nām-,sāk\ *n* **:** one that has the same name as another; *esp* **:** one named after another

nan•keen \nan-'kēn, 'nan-\ *also* **nan•kin** \-'kēn, -'kin\ *n* **:** a durable brownish yellow cotton fabric originally woven by hand in China [*Nanking,* China]

nan•ny goat \'nan-ē-\ *n* **:** a female domestic goat [*Nanny,* nickname for *Anne*]

nano- \'nan-ō, -ə\ *combining form* **:** billionth [Greek *nanos* "dwarf"]

¹nap \'nap\ *vi* **napped**; **nap•ping 1 :** to sleep briefly especially during the day **:** DOZE **2 :** to be off guard ⟨was caught *napping*⟩ [Old English *hnappian*]

²nap *n* **:** a short sleep especially during the day **:** SNOOZE

³nap *n* **:** a hairy or downy surface (as on cloth) [Dutch *noppe* "tuft of wool, nap"] — **nap•less** \'nap-ləs\ *adj* — **napped** \'napt\ *adj* — **nap•py** \'nap-ē\ *adj*

⁴nap *vt* **napped**; **nap•ping :** to raise a nap on (as cloth)

na•palm \'nā-,päm, -,pälm\ *n* **1 :** a thickener used in jelling gasoline especially for incendiary bombs and flamethrowers **2 :** fuel jelled with napalm [derived from *naphtha* + *palmitic acid*]

nape \'nāp, 'nap\ *n* **:** the back of the neck [Middle English]

naph•tha \'naf-thə, 'nap-\ *n* **1 :** PETROLEUM **2 :** any of various volatile often flammable liquid hydrocarbon mixtures used chiefly as solvents and diluting agents [Latin, from Greek, of Iranian origin]

naph•tha•lene \-,lēn\ *n* **:** a crystalline hydrocarbon $C_{10}H_8$ usually obtained by distillation of coal tar and used in chemical

\ə\ **a**but	\aù\ **ou**t	\i\ t**i**p	\ò\ s**aw**	\ù\ f**oo**t
\ər\ f**ur**th**er**	\ch\ **ch**in	\ī\ l**i**fe	\òi\ c**oi**n	\y\ **y**et
\a\ m**a**t	\e\ p**e**t	\j\ **j**ob	\th\ **th**in	\yü\ f**ew**
\ā\ t**a**ke	\ē\ **ea**sy	\ng\ si**ng**	\t͟h\ **th**is	\yù\ c**u**re
\ä\ c**o**t, c**a**rt	\g\ **g**o	\ō\ b**o**ne	\ü\ f**oo**d	\zh\ vi**si**on

manufacture and as a moth repellent [derived from *naphtha*] — **naph·tha·le·nic** \ˌnaf-thə-ˈlēn-ik, ˌnap-, -ˈlen-\ *adj*

naph·thol \ˈnaf-ˌthȯl, ˈnap-, -ˌthōl\ *n* **:** either of two derivatives of napththalene found in coal tar or made synthetically and used as antiseptics and in the manufacture of dyes

Na·pier·ian logarithm \nə-ˌpir-ē-ən-, nā-\ *n* **:** NATURAL LOGARITHM [John *Napier,* died 1617, Scottish mathematician]

nap·kin \ˈnap-kən\ *n* **1 :** a piece of material (as cloth or paper) used at table to wipe the lips or fingers and protect the clothes **2 :** a small cloth or towel [Middle English *nappekin,* from *nappe* "tablecloth", from Middle French, from Latin *mappa* "napkin"]

na·po·leon \nə-ˈpōl-yən, -ˈpō-lē-ən\ *n* **1 :** a French 20-franc gold coin **2 :** an oblong pastry consisting of layers of puff paste with a filling of cream, custard, or jelly [French *napoléon,* from *Napoléon* "Napoleon I"]

nappe \ˈnap\ *n* **:** one of the two similar parts of a conical surface on either side of the vertex [French, "tablecloth, sheet", from Latin *mappa* "napkin"]

narc *or* **nark** \ˈnärk\ *n* **:** a person (as a government agent) who investigates narcotics violations

nar·cis·sism \ˈnär-sə-ˌsiz-əm\ *n* **:** undue dwelling on one's own self or attainments **:** SELF-LOVE [German *narzissismus,* from *Narziss* "Narcissus (mythological character)" — see NARCISSUS *origin*] — **nar·cis·sist** \ˈnär-sə-səst\ *n or adj* — **nar·cis·sis·tic** \ˌnär-sə-ˈsis-tik\ *adj*

nar·cis·sus \när-ˈsis-əs\ *n, pl* **-cissus** *or* **-cis·sus·es** \-ˈsis-ə-səz\ *or* **-cis·si** \-ˈsis-ˌī, -ˌē\ **:** DAFFODIL; *esp* **:** one whose flowers have a short corona and are usually borne separately [*Narcissus,* Greek mythological character, from Latin, from Greek *Narkissos*]

narcissus

△ **origin** Narcissus, according to Greek mythology, was an unusually beautiful young man. The nymph Echo loved him but was rebuffed and wasted away. To punish Narcissus for his indifference, the gods made him fall in love with his own image, which he saw reflected in a fountain. He sat admiring himself day after day and finally pined away and was transformed into the flower that we call *narcissus.* From the youth *Narcissus* we also get a word for self-love, *narcissism.*

nar·co·sis \när-ˈkō-səs\ *n, pl* **-co·ses** \-ˈkō-ˌsēz\ **:** a state of stupor, unconsciousness, or arrested activity produced by the influence of chemicals (as narcotics)

[1]**nar·cot·ic** \när-ˈkät-ik\ *n* **1 a :** a drug (as opium) that in moderate doses dulls the senses, relieves pain, and induces sleep but in excessive doses causes stupor, coma, or convulsions **b :** a drug (as marijuana or LSD) subject to restriction similar to that of addictive narcotics whether in fact physiologically addictive and narcotic or not **2 :** something that soothes, relieves, or lulls [Middle French *narcotique,* from *narcotique,* adj., from Medieval Latin *narcoticus,* from Greek *narkōtikos,* from *narkoun* "to benumb", from *narkē* "numbness"]

[2]**narcotic** *adj* **1 :** having the properties of or yielding a narcotic **2 :** of or relating to narcotics, to their use, or to addicts — **nar·cot·i·cal·ly** \-ˈkät-i-kə-lē, -klē\ *adv*

nar·co·tize \ˈnär-kə-ˌtīz\ *vt* **1 a :** to treat with or subject to a narcotic **b :** to put into a state of narcosis **2 :** to soothe to unconsciousness or unawareness

nard \ˈnärd\ *n* **:** SPIKENARD 1b [Latin *nardus,* from Greek *nardos,* of Semitic origin]

na·ris \ˈnar-əs, ˈner-\ *n, pl* **na·res** \ˈnaər-ˌēz, ˈneər-\ **:** any of the internal or external openings of the nose or nasal cavity of a vertebrate [Latin]

nar·rate \ˈnar-ˌāt, na-ˈrāt\ *vt* **:** to recite the details of (as a story) **:** RELATE, TELL [Latin *narrare,* from *gnarus* "knowing"] — **nar·ra·tor** \ˈnar-ˌāt-ər; na-ˈrāt-, nə-; ˈnar-ət-\ *n*

nar·ra·tion \na-ˈrā-shən, nə-\ *n* **1 :** the act or process or an instance of narrating **2 :** NARRATIVE 1, STORY — **nar·ra·tion·al** \-shnəl, -shən-l\ *adj*

nar·ra·tive \ˈnar-ət-iv\ *n* **1 :** something (as a story) that is narrated **2 :** the art or practice of narration — **narrative** *adj* — **nar·ra·tive·ly** *adv*

[1]**nar·row** \ˈnar-ō\ *adj* **1 a :** of slender width **b :** of less than standard width **2 :** limited in size or scope **:** RESTRICTED **3 a :** not liberal in views **:** PREJUDICED **b :** interpreted or interpreting strictly ⟨a *narrow* view⟩ **4 :** barely sufficient **:** CLOSE ⟨a *narrow* escape⟩ ⟨won by a *narrow* margin⟩ [Old English *nearu*] — **nar·row·ly** *adv* — **nar·row·ness** *n*

[2]**narrow** *n* **:** a narrow part or passage; *esp* **:** a strait connecting two bodies of water — usually used in pl.

[3]**narrow** *vb* **:** to lessen in width or extent **:** CONTRACT

nar·row–mind·ed \ˌnar-ō-ˈmīn-dəd\ *adj* **:** lacking in tolerance or breadth of vision — **nar·row–mind·ed·ly** *adv* — **nar·row–mind·ed·ness** *n*

nar·thex \ˈnär-ˌtheks\ *n* **1 :** the portico of an ancient church **2 :** a vestibule leading to the nave of a church [Late Greek *narthēx,* from Greek, "giant fennel, cane, casket"]

nar·whal \ˈnär-ˌhwäl, -ˌwäl, -ˌhwȯl, -ˌhwōl, -ˌwȯl, -hwäl, -ˌwäl, -wəl\ *n* **:** an arctic sea animal about 6 meters long that is related to the dolphin and in the male has a long twisted ivory tusk [Norwegian and Danish *narhval* and Swedish *narval,* derived from Old Norse *nāhvalr,* from *nār* "corpse" + *hvalr* "whale"]

narwhal

nary \ˈnaər-ē, ˈneər-\ *adj, dialect* **:** not one [alteration of *ne'er a*]

[1]**na·sal** \ˈnā-zəl\ *n* **1 :** a nasal part **2 :** a nasal consonant or vowel [derived from Latin *nasus* "nose"]

[2]**nasal** *adj* **1 :** of or relating to the nose **2 a :** uttered with the mouth passage closed and the nose passage open ⟨the *nasal* consonants \m\, \n\, and \ng\⟩ **b :** uttered with the nose passage as well as the mouth passage open ⟨the *nasal* vowels in French⟩ **c :** characterized by resonance produced through the nose ⟨speaking in a *nasal* tone⟩ — **na·sal·i·ty** \nā-ˈzal-ət-ē\ *n* — **na·sal·ly** \ˈnā-zə-lē\ *adv*

nasal cavity *n* **:** an incompletely divided chamber that lies between the floor of the skull and the roof of the mouth and functions in the warming and filtering of inhaled air and in the sensing of odors

nas·cent \ˈnas-nt, ˈnās-\ *adj* **:** coming into existence **:** beginning to develop [Latin *nascens,* from *nasci* "to be born"] — **nas·cence** \-ns\ *n*

na·so·phar·ynx \ˌnā-zō-ˈfar-ings, -ingks\ *n* **:** the upper part of the pharynx continuous with the nasal passages — **na·so·pha·ryn·geal** \ˌnā-zō-fə-ˈrin-jəl, -ˌfar-ən-ˈjē-əl\ *adj*

nas·tic \ˈnas-tik\ *adj* **:** of, relating to, or being a movement of a plant part caused by disproportionate growth or increase of turgor in one surface [Greek *nastos* "close-pressed", from *nassein* "to press"]

nas·tur·tium \nə-ˈstər-shəm, na-\ *n* **:** any of a genus of watery-stemmed herbs with showy spurred flowers and pungent 3-seeded fruits [Latin, a kind of cress]

nas·ty \ˈnas-tē\ *adj* **nas·ti·er; -est 1 :** very dirty or foul **:** FILTHY **2 :** morally offensive **:** VILE **3 :** DISAGREEABLE ⟨*nasty* weather⟩ **4 :** MEAN, ILL-NATURED ⟨a *nasty* temper⟩ **5 :** DISHONORABLE ⟨a *nasty* trick⟩ **6 :** HARMFUL, DANGEROUS ⟨a *nasty* fall on the ice⟩ [Middle English] **syn** see DIRTY — **nas·ti·ly** \-tə-lē\ *adv* — **nas·ti·ness** \-tē-nəs\ *n*

na·tal \ˈnāt-l\ *adj* **1 :** NATIVE **2 :** of, relating to, or present at birth [Latin *natalis,* from *natus,* past participle of *nasci* "to be born"]

na·tal·i·ty \nā-ˈtal-ət-ē, nə-\ *n, pl* **-ties :** BIRTHRATE

na·ta·tion \nā-ˈtā-shən, na-\ *n* **:** the action or art of swimming [Latin *natatio,* from *natare* "to swim"]

na·ta·to·ri·al \ˌnāt-ə-ˈtōr-ē-əl, ˌnat-, -ˈtȯr-\ *or* **na·ta·to·ry** \ˈnāt-ə-ˌtōr-ē, ˈnat-, -ˌtȯr-\ *adj* **:** of or relating to swimming

na·ta·to·ri·um \ˌnāt-ə-ˈtōr-ē-əm, ˌnat-, -ˈtȯr-\ *n* **:** an indoor swimming pool [Late Latin, from Latin *natare* "to swim"]

Natch·ez \ˈnach-əz\ *n* **:** a member of an Indian people of the region along the Mississippi river in what is now central Mississippi and Louisiana [French, of American Indian origin]

na•tion \'nā-shən\ *n* **1 a :** NATIONALITY 3a **b :** a community of people composed of one or more nationalities with its own territory and government **c :** the territory of a nation **2 :** a tribe or federation of tribes (as of American Indians) [Middle French, from Latin *natio* "birth, race, nation", from *nasci* "to be born"]

¹na•tion•al \'nash-nəl, -ən-l\ *adj* **1 :** of or relating to a nation **2 :** comprising or characteristic of a nationality **3 :** FEDERAL 1c — **na•tion•al•ly** \-ē\ *adv*

²national *n* **:** one who is under the protection of a nation without regard to the more formal status of citizen or subject **syn** see CITIZEN

national anthem *n* **:** a song or hymn officially adopted and played or sung on formal occasions as a mark of loyalty to the nation

national bank *n* **:** a commercial bank organized under laws passed by Congress and chartered and supervised by the national government

National Guard *n* **:** a militia force recruited by each state, equipped by the federal government, and subject to the call of either

national income *n* **:** the total earnings from a nation's current production including wages of employees, interest, rental income, and business profits after taxes

na•tion•al•ism \'nash-nəl-iz-əm, -ən-l-\ *n* **:** loyalty and devotion to a nation especially as expressed by praise of one nation above all others and intense concern with promotion of its culture and interests

na•tion•al•ist \-nəl-əst, -ən-l-əst\ *n* **1 :** an advocate of nationalism **2** *cap* **:** a member of a political party or group advocating national independence or strong national government — **nationalist** *adj, often cap* — **na•tion•al•is•tic** \ˌnash-nəl-'is-tik, -ən-l-'is-\ *adj*

na•tion•al•i•ty \ˌnash-'nal-ət-ē, -ə-'nal-\ *n, pl* **-ties 1 :** the fact or state of belonging to a nation ⟨a person of French *nationality*⟩ **2 :** political independence or existence as a separate nation **3 a :** a people having a common origin, tradition, and language and capable of forming or actually constituting a state **b :** an ethnic group within a larger unit (as a nation)

na•tion•al•ize \'nash-nəl-ˌīz, -ən-l-\ *vt* **1 :** to make national **:** make a nation of **2 :** to remove from private ownership and place under government control ⟨*nationalize* railroads⟩ — **na•tion•al•iza•tion** \ˌnash-nəl-ə-'zā-shən, ˌnash-ən-l-\ *n* — **na•tion•al•iz•er** *n*

national park *n* **:** an area of special scenic, historical, or scientific importance set aside and maintained by a national government especially for recreation or study

national socialism *n* **:** NAZISM — **national socialist** *adj*

na•tion•hood \'nā-shən-ˌhu̇d\ *n* **:** the quality or state of being a nation

na•tion•wide \ˌnā-shən-'wīd\ *adj* **:** extending throughout a nation

¹na•tive \'nāt-iv\ *adj* **1 :** INBORN, NATURAL ⟨*native* shrewdness⟩ **2 :** born in a particular place or country ⟨*native* Americans⟩ **3 :** belonging to a person because of the place or circumstances of birth ⟨one's *native* language⟩ **4 :** grown, produced, or having its origin in a particular region ⟨*native* art⟩ **5 :** occurring in nature **:** not artificially prepared ⟨*native* salt⟩ [Middle French *natif,* from Latin *nativus,* from *nasci* "to be born"] — **na•tive•ly** *adv* — **na•tive•ness** *n*

• **syn** NATIVE, INDIGENOUS, ENDEMIC, ABORIGINAL mean belonging to a locality. NATIVE implies birth or origin in a place or region and may suggest special compatibility with it; INDIGENOUS applies to species or races and adds an implication of not having been introduced from elsewhere; ENDEMIC stresses the notion that something is peculiar to a place; ABORIGINAL implies having no known predecessor in occupying a region.

²native *n* **1 :** one born or reared in a particular place **2 a :** an original inhabitant **b :** something (as an animal or plant) native to a particular locality **3 :** a local or lifelong resident

na•tiv•i•ty \nə-'tiv-ət-ē, nā-\ *n, pl* **-ties 1** *cap* **:** the birth of Christ **2** *cap* **:** CHRISTMAS 1 **3 :** the process or circumstances of being born **:** BIRTH

nat•ty \'nat-ē\ *adj* **nat•ti•er; -est :** trimly neat and tidy **:** SMART [perhaps from obsolete *net* "neat, clean"] — **nat•ti•ly** \'nat-l-ē\ *adv* — **nat•ti•ness** \'nat-ē-nəs\ *n*

¹nat•u•ral \'nach-rəl, -ə-rəl\ *adj* **1 :** born in or with one **:** INNATE ⟨*natural* ability⟩ **2 :** being such by nature **:** BORN ⟨a *natural* fool⟩ **3 :** born of unmarried parents **:** ILLEGITIMATE ⟨a *natural* child⟩ **4 :** existing or used in or produced by nature ⟨the *natural* woodland flora⟩ ⟨meat is the *natural* food of dogs⟩ **5 :** having or showing qualities held to be part of human nature ⟨it is not *natural* to hate your children⟩ **6 a :** of or relating to nature as an object of study and research **b :** conforming to the laws of nature or of the physical world ⟨*natural* causes⟩ ⟨*natural* history⟩ **7 :** not made or altered by humans ⟨a *natural* complexion⟩ **8 :** marked by simplicity and sincerity ⟨*natural* manners⟩ **9 :** closely resembling the object imitated **:** LIFELIKE ⟨the people in the picture look *natural*⟩ **10 :** having neither sharps nor flats in the key signature or having a sharp or a flat changed in pitch by a natural sign — **nat•u•ral•ness** *n*

²natural *n* **1 :** IDIOT **2 a :** a sign ♮ placed on a line or space of the musical staff to nullify the effect of a preceding sharp or flat **b :** a note or tone affected by the natural sign **3 a :** one having natural skills, talents, or abilities **b :** one obviously suitable for a specific purpose **4 :** AFRO

natural gas *n* **:** gas issuing from the earth's crust through natural openings or bored wells; *esp* **:** a combustible mixture of methane and higher hydrocarbons used chiefly as a fuel and raw material

natural history *n* **:** the study of natural objects especially in the field from an amateur or popular point of view

natural immunity *n* **:** inherent genetically determined immunity as distinguished from that acquired by vaccination or having a disease

nat•u•ral•ism \'nach-rə-ˌliz-əm, -ə-rə-\ *n* **1 :** a theory denying a supernatural explanation of the origin and development of the universe and holding that scientific laws account for everything in nature **2 :** realism in art or literature; *esp* **:** a theory in literature emphasizing realistic observation of life without idealization or the avoidance of the ugly

nat•u•ral•ist \-ləst\ *n* **1 :** one that advocates or practices naturalism **2 :** a student of natural history; *esp* **:** a field biologist — **naturalist** *adj*

nat•u•ral•is•tic \ˌnach-rə-'lis-tik, -ə-rə-\ *adj* **:** of, characterized by, or according with naturalism — **nat•u•ral•is•ti•cal•ly** \-ti-kə-lē, -klē\ *adv*

nat•u•ral•ize \'nach-rə-ˌlīz, -ə-rə-\ *vb* **1 :** to introduce into common use ⟨*naturalize* a foreign word⟩ **2 :** to become or cause to become established as if native ⟨*naturalized* weeds⟩ **3 :** to make less artificial or conventional **4 :** to confer the rights and privileges of citizenship on (an alien) — **nat•u•ral•iza•tion** \ˌnach-rə-lə-'zā-shən, -ə-rə-\ *n*

natural law *n* **:** a body of law or a specific principle held to be derived from nature and binding on human society in the absence of or in addition to positive law

natural logarithm *n* **:** a logarithm in a system that uses as a base the transcendental number *e* whose value is approximately 2.71828

nat•u•ral•ly \'nach-rə-lē, -ə-rə-; 'nach-ər-lē\ *adv* **1 :** by natural character or ability ⟨*naturally* timid⟩ **2 :** according to the usual course of things ⟨we *naturally* dislike being hurt⟩ **3 a :** without artificial aid ⟨hair that curls *naturally*⟩ **b :** without affectation ⟨speak *naturally*⟩ **4 :** in a lifelike manner ⟨paints flowers *naturally*⟩

natural number *n* **:** the number 1 or any number (as 3, 12, or 432) obtained by repeatedly adding 1 to this number

natural philosophy *n* **:** NATURAL SCIENCE; *esp* **:** PHYSICAL SCIENCE

natural resource *n* **:** something (as a mineral, waterpower source, forest, or kind of animal) that occurs in nature and is of value to human life

natural science *n* **:** a science (as physics, chemistry, or biology) that deals with matter, energy, and their interrelations and transformations or with objectively measurable phenomena — **natural scientist** *n*

natural selection *n* **:** a natural process that results in the survival of individuals or groups best adapted to the conditions under which they live and in the perpetuation of adaptive genetic traits and the elimination of those that are not adaptive

na•ture \'nā-chər\ *n* **1 :** the basic quality, character, or constitution of a person or thing ⟨the *nature* of steel⟩ **2 :** general character **:** KIND ⟨and things of that *nature*⟩ **3 :** DISPOSITION,

TEMPERAMENT ⟨behavior contrary to one's *nature*⟩ **4** *often cap* **:** a power or set of forces thought of as controlling the universe ⟨Mother *Nature*⟩ **5 :** natural feeling especially as shown in one's attitude toward others **6 :** humanity's native state **:** primitive life ⟨return to *nature*⟩ **7 :** the whole physical universe ⟨the study of *nature*⟩ **8 :** the physical workings or drives of an organism ⟨sex is a part of *nature*⟩ **9 :** natural scenery ⟨the beauties of *nature*⟩ [Middle French, from Latin *natura,* from *nasci* "to be born"]

¹naught *or* **nought** \ˈnȯt, ˈnät\ *pron* **:** NOTHING [Old English *nā-wiht,* from *nā* "no" + *wiht* "creature, thing"]

²naught *or* **nought** *n* **1 a :** NOTHING **b :** the quality or state of being nothing **2 :** ZERO 1 — see NUMBER table

³naught *or* **nought** *adj* **:** of no importance **:** INSIGNIFICANT

naugh•ty \ˈnȯt-ē, ˈnät-\ *adj* **naugh•ti•er; -est 1 :** guilty of disobedience or misbehavior **2 :** not moral or proper [²*naught*] — **naugh•ti•ly** \ˈnȯt-l-ē, ˈnät-\ *adv* — **naugh•ti•ness** \ˈnȯt-ē-nəs, ˈnät-\ *n*

nau•pli•us \ˈnȯ-plē-əs\ *n, pl* **-plii** \-plē-ˌī, -ˌē\ **:** an early crustacean larva with three pairs of appendages and a median eye [Latin, a kind of shellfish, from Greek *nauplios*]

nau•sea \ˈnȯ-zē-ə, -sē-ə; ˈnȯ-zhə, -shə\ *n* **1 :** a stomach distress with distaste for food and an urge to vomit **2 :** extreme disgust [Latin, "seasickness, nausea", from Greek *nautia, nausia,* from *nautēs* "sailor", from *naus* "ship"]

△ **origin** Nausea, stomach distress accompanied by an urge to vomit, is one of the most unpleasant symptoms of seasickness. Latin *nausea* and its Greek source *nausia* or *nautia* have the same meaning as English *nausea.* But these Greek and Latin words also have the specific sense of "seasickness". The Greek name for the illness is derived from the word *naus,* which means "ship".

nau•se•ate \ˈnȯ-zē-ˌāt, -sē-, -zhē-, -shē-\ *vb* **:** to affect or become affected with nausea — **nau•se•at•ing** \-ˌāt-ing\ *adj* — **nau•se•at•ing•ly** \-ing-lē\ *adv*

nau•seous \ˈnȯ-shəs, ˈnȯ-zē-əs\ *adj* **1 :** causing nausea ⟨*nauseous* odors⟩ **2 :** affected with nausea ⟨feel *nauseous*⟩ — **nau•seous•ly** *adv* — **nau•seous•ness** *n*

nau•ti•cal \ˈnȯt-i-kəl\ *adj* **:** of or relating to seamen, ships, or navigation on water [Latin *nauticus,* from Greek *nautikos,* from *nautēs* "sailor", from *naus* "ship"] — **nau•ti•cal•ly** \-kə-lē, -klē\ *adv*

nautical mile *n* **:** a unit of distance used for sea and air navigation equal to about 6076 feet (1852 meters)

nau•ti•loid \ˈnȯt-l-ˌȯid\ *n* **:** any of an ancient group (Nautiloidea) of cephalopods represented in the recent fauna by the nautiluses — **nautiloid** *adj*

nau•ti•lus \ˈnȯt-l-əs\ *n, pl* **-lus•es** *or* **-li** \-l-ˌī, -ˌē\ **1 :** any of a genus of cephalopod mollusks of the South Pacific and Indian oceans having a spiral chambered shell that is pearly on the inside **2 :** PAPER NAUTILUS [Latin, "paper nautilus", from Greek *nautilos,* literally, "sailor", from *naus* "ship"]

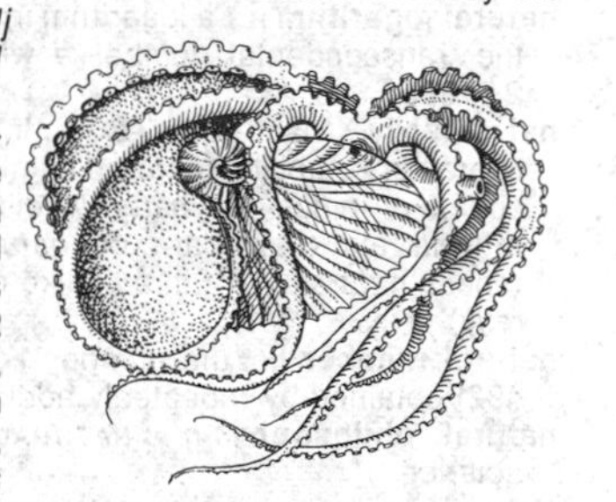
nautilus 1

Na•va•ho *or* **Na•va•jo** \ˈnav-ə-ˌhō, ˈnäv-\ *n, pl* **Navaho** *or* **Navahos** *or* **Navajo** *or* **Navajos 1 :** a member of an Amerindian people of what is now northwestern New Mexico and the adjacent part of Arizona **2 :** the language of the Navaho people [Spanish *Apache de Navajó,* literally, "Apache of Navajó", from *Navajó,* a pueblo]

na•val \ˈnā-vəl\ *adj* **1 :** of or relating to a navy or warships ⟨*naval* shipyards⟩ **2 :** possessing a navy ⟨a *naval* power⟩

naval stores *n pl* **:** products (as pitch, turpentine, or rosin) obtained from resinous conifers (as pines) [from their former use in the construction and maintenance of wooden sailing vessels]

¹nave \ˈnāv\ *n* **:** the hub of a wheel [Old English *nafu* — see AUGER *origin*]

²nave *n* **:** the main body of a church interior; *esp* **:** the long central hall in a cruciform church that rises higher than the aisles flanking it to form a clerestory [Medieval Latin *navis,* from Latin, "ship"]

na•vel \ˈnā-vəl\ *n* **1 :** a depression in the middle of the abdomen marking the point of attachment of the umbilical cord or yolk stalk **2 :** the central point **:** MIDDLE [Old English *nafela* — see AUGER *origin*]

navel orange *n* **:** a seedless orange having a pit at the apex where the fruit encloses a small secondary fruit

nav•i•ga•ble \ˈnav-i-gə-bəl\ *adj* **1 :** deep enough and wide enough to afford passage to ships **2 :** capable of being steered ⟨a *navigable* balloon⟩ — **nav•i•ga•bil•i•ty** \ˌnav-i-gə-ˈbil-ət-ē\ *n* — **nav•i•ga•ble•ness** \ˈnav-i-gə-bəl-nəs\ *n* — **nav•i•ga•bly** \-blē\ *adv*

nav•i•gate \ˈnav-ə-ˌgāt\ *vb* **1 a :** to travel by water **b :** to sail over, on, or through **2 a :** to direct one's course in a ship or aircraft **b :** to steer, direct, or control the course of (as a boat or aircraft) **3 a :** to get about; *esp* **:** WALK **b :** to make one's way over or through [Latin *navigare,* derived from *navis* "ship"]

nav•i•ga•tion \ˌnav-ə-ˈgā-shən\ *n* **1 :** the act or practice of navigating **2 :** the science of getting ships or airplanes from place to place; *esp* **:** the method of determining position, course, and distance traveled **3 :** ship traffic or commerce — **nav•i•ga•tion•al** \-shnəl, -shən-l\ *adj* — **nav•i•ga•tion•al•ly** \-ē\ *adv*

nav•i•ga•tor \ˈnav-ə-ˌgāt-ər\ *n* **:** a person who navigates or is qualified to navigate: as **a :** an officer on a ship or airplane responsible for its navigation **b :** a person who explores by ship

nav•vy \ˈnav-ē\ *n, pl* **navvies** *British* **:** an unskilled laborer [from *navigator* "construction worker on a canal, navvy"]

na•vy \ˈnā-vē\ *n, pl* **navies 1 :** a group of ships **:** FLEET **2 :** a nation's warships **3** *often cap* **:** a nation's complete naval establishment including yards, stations, ships, and personnel **4 :** a dark blue [Middle French *navie,* from Latin *navigia* "ships", from *navigare* "to navigate"]

navy bean *n* **:** a kidney bean grown especially for its small white nutritious seeds

navy yard *n* **:** a naval installation where naval vessels are built or repaired

na•wab \nə-ˈwäb\ *n* **1 :** NABOB 1 **2 :** a Muslim prince of India [Hindi *nawwāb*]

¹nay \ˈnā\ *adv* **1 :** NO 3 **2 :** not merely this but also **:** not only so but ⟨the letter made me happy, *nay,* ecstatic⟩ [Old Norse *nei,* from *ne* "not" + *ei* "ever"]

²nay *n* **1 :** REFUSAL 1, DENIAL **2 a :** a negative reply or vote **b :** one who votes no

Naz•a•rene \ˌnaz-ə-ˈrēn\ *n* **1 :** a native or resident of Nazareth **2 :** a member of the Church of the Nazarene which adheres to Wesleyan doctrine and church government — **Nazarene** *adj*

na•zi \ˈnät-sē, ˈnat-\ *n* **1** *often cap* **:** a member of a German fascist party controlling Germany from 1933 to 1945 under Adolf Hitler **2** *often cap* **:** one held to resemble a German Nazi [German, from *Nationalsozialist* "national socialist"] — **nazi** *adj, often cap* — **na•zi•fi•ca•tion** \ˌnät-si-fə-ˈkā-shən, ˌnat-\ *n, often cap* — **na•zi•fy** \ˈnät-si-ˌfī, ˈnat-\ *vt, often cap* — **Na•zism** \ˈnät-ˌsiz-əm, ˈnat-\ *or* **Na•zi•ism** \-sē-ˌiz-əm\ *n*

-nd *symbol* — used after the figure 2 to indicate that the number is an ordinal ⟨2*nd*⟩ ⟨32*nd*⟩

ne- *or* **neo-** *combining form* **:** new **:** recent ⟨*neo*-impressionism⟩ [Greek, from *neos* "new"]

Ne•an•der•thal \nē-ˈan-dər-ˌthȯl, -ˌtȯl; nā-ˈän-dər-ˌtäl\ *adj* **1 :** being, relating to, or resembling Neanderthal man **2 :** suggesting a caveman in appearance or behavior — **Neanderthal** *n*

Neanderthal man *n* **:** a prehistoric man known from skeletal remains and artifacts and intermediate in some respects between modern man and pithecanthropus [*Neanderthal,* valley in western Germany] — **Ne•an•der•thal•oid** \-ˌȯid\ *adj or n*

neap \ˈnēp\ *adj* **:** of, relating to, or constituting a neap tide [Old English *nēp* "being at the stage of neap tide"]

Ne•a•pol•i•tan ice cream \ˌnē-ə-ˌpäl-ət-n-\ *n* **:** a brick of from two to four layers of ice cream of different flavors [*Neapolitan* "of Naples, Italy", derived from Greek *Neapolis* "Naples"]

neap tide *n* **:** a tide of minimum range occurring at the first and the third quarters of the moon

¹near \ˈniər\ *adv* **1 :** at, within, or to a short distance or time **2 :** ALMOST, NEARLY ⟨*near* dead⟩ **3 :** CLOSELY ⟨*near* related⟩ [partly from Old English *nēar* "nearer", comparative of *nēah* "nigh"; partly from Old Norse *nær* "nearer, near", from comparative of *nā-* "nigh"]

²near *prep* **:** close to ⟨standing *near* the door⟩

³near *adj* **1 :** closely related or associated **2 a :** being little apart in time, place, value, or degree ⟨the *near* future⟩ **b** : barely avoided ⟨a *near* disaster⟩ **c** : failing or missing by very little ⟨a *near* miss⟩ **3 a** : being the closer of two ⟨the *near* side⟩ **b** : being the left-hand one of a pair ⟨the *near* wheel of a cart⟩ **4** : DIRECT, SHORT ⟨the *nearest* route⟩ **5** : STINGY 1 **6 a** : closely resembling a prototype **b** : approximating the genuine ⟨*near* silk⟩ — **near•ness** *n*

• **syn** NEAR, CLOSE mean not distant or not much removed in space, time, or resemblance. NEAR implies that the space, interval, or degree of difference though small is none the less distinct and real; CLOSE implies virtual or approximate contact, coincidence, or identity.

[4]**near** *vb* : to draw near : APPROACH

near•by \niər-'bī, 'niər-ˌ\ *adv or adj* : close at hand

near•ly \'niər-lē\ *adv* : ALMOST ⟨we *nearly* got hit⟩

near•sight•ed \'niər-'sīt-əd\ *adj* : able to see near things more clearly than distant ones : MYOPIC — **near•sight•ed•ly** *adv* — **near•sight•ed•ness** *n*

[1]**neat** \'nēt\ *n, pl* **neat** : the common domestic bovine (as a cow, bull, or ox) **[**Old English *nēat***]**

[2]**neat** *adj* **1** : not mixed or diluted ⟨*neat* brandy⟩ **2** : marked by tasteful simplicity **3 a** : PRECISE, SYSTEMATIC ⟨*neat* plans⟩ **b** : marked by skill or ingenuity : ADROIT **4** : being orderly and clean : TIDY **5** : CLEAR, NET ⟨a *neat* profit⟩ **6** *slang* : TERRIFIC 3 **[**Middle French *net,* from Latin *nitidus* "bright, neat", from *nitēre* "to shine"**]** — **neat•ly** *adv* — **neat•ness** *n*

neat's–foot oil \'nēts-ˌfu̇t-\ *n* : a pale yellow fatty oil made especially from the bones of cattle and used chiefly to condition leather

neb \'neb\ *n* **1 a** : the beak of a bird or tortoise : BILL **b** : NOSE 1, 3, SNOUT **2** : NIB 2b, 3 **[**Old English**]**

neb•u•la \'neb-yə-lə\ *n, pl* **-las** *or* **-lae** \-ˌlē, -ˌlī\ **1** : any of many immense bodies of highly rarefied gas or dust in interstellar space **2** : GALAXY 1b **[**Latin, "mist, cloud"**]** — **neb•u•lar** \-lər\ *adj*

nebular hypothesis *n* : a hypothesis in astronomy: the solar system has evolved from a hot gaseous nebula

neb•u•lize \'neb-yə-ˌlīz\ *vt* : to reduce to a fine spray — **neb•u•li•za•tion** \ˌneb-yə-lə-'zā-shən\ *n* — **neb•u•liz•er** \'neb-yə-ˌlī-zər\ *n*

neb•u•los•i•ty \ˌneb-yə-'läs-ət-ē\ *n, pl* **-ties 1** : the quality or state of being nebulous **2** : nebulous matter : NEBULA

neb•u•lous \'neb-yə-ləs\ *adj* **1** : VAGUE ⟨*nebulous* concepts⟩ **2** : of, relating to, or resembling a nebula : NEBULAR — **neb•u•lous•ly** *adv* — **neb•u•lous•ness** *n*

[1]**nec•es•sary** \'nes-ə-ˌser-ē\ *n, pl* **-sar•ies** : an indispensable item : ESSENTIAL ⟨*necessaries* of life⟩

[2]**necessary** *adj* **1 a** : bound to happen : INEVITABLE **b (1)** : being the only possible result of an argument **(2)** : logically required for a particular result **c** : COMPULSORY 1 **2** : absolutely needed : INDISPENSABLE **[**Latin *necessarius,* from *necesse* "necessary", from *ne-* "not" + *cedere* "to withdraw"**]** — **nec•es•sar•i•ly** \ˌnes-ə-'ser-ə-lē\ *adv*

• **syn** REQUISITE, ESSENTIAL: NECESSARY applies to what cannot be done without or avoided and may stress lack of choice or uselessness of wishing or resisting; REQUISITE implies being needful especially for fulfillment or attainment of a set purpose or standard; ESSENTIAL implies being absolutely or urgently necessary.

ne•ces•si•tate \ni-'ses-ə-ˌtāt\ *vt* : to make necessary or unavoidable : REQUIRE, COMPEL ⟨the attack *necessitated* a troop withdrawal⟩ — **ne•ces•si•ta•tion** \-ˌses-ə-'tā-shən\ *n*

ne•ces•si•tous \ni-'ses-ət-əs\ *adj* **1** : hard up : NEEDY **2** : forced by necessity : NECESSARY ⟨*necessitous* bargaining⟩ — **ne•ces•si•tous•ly** *adv* — **ne•ces•si•tous•ness** *n*

ne•ces•si•ty \ni-'ses-ət-ē, -'ses-tē\ *n, pl* **-ties 1** : very great need especially of help or relief **2** : conditions that cannot be changed ⟨compelled by *necessity*⟩ **3** : lack of necessary things : WANT, POVERTY **4** : something badly needed ⟨daily *necessities*⟩ **syn** see NEED

[1]**neck** \'nek\ *n* **1** : the part of the body connecting the head and the trunk **2** : the part of a garment covering or nearest to the neck **3** : something like a neck in shape or position ⟨the *neck* of a bottle⟩ ⟨a *neck* of land⟩ **4** : a narrow margin ⟨won by a *neck*⟩ **[**Old English *hnecca***]** — **necked** \'nekt\ *adj*

[2]**neck** *vb* : to kiss and caress amorously

neck•er•chief \'nek-ər-chəf, -ˌchif, -ˌchēf\ *n, pl* **-chiefs** *also* **-chieves** *see* HANDKERCHIEF *pl*\ : a kerchief for the neck

neck•lace \'nek-ləs\ *n* : an ornament for the neck

neck•line \-ˌlīn\ *n* : the line formed by the neck opening of a garment

neck•tie \-ˌtī\ *n* : a band or strip of material worn about the neck and tied in front; *esp* : FOUR-IN-HAND

necr- *or* **necro-** *combining form* **1** : those that are dead ⟨*necrology*⟩ **2** : dead body ⟨*necropsy*⟩ **[**Greek *nekros* "dead body"**]**

ne•crol•o•gy \nə-'kräl-ə-jē, ne-\ *n, pl* **-gies 1** : a list of the recently dead **2** : OBITUARY — **nec•ro•log•i•cal** \ˌnek-rə-'läj-i-kəl\ *adj* — **ne•crol•o•gist** \nə-'kräl-ə-jəst, ne-\ *n*

nec•ro•man•cy \'nek-rə-ˌman-sē\ *n* **1** : the practice of conjuring up the spirits of the dead for purposes of magically revealing the future or influencing the course of events **2** : MAGIC 1, SORCERY — **nec•ro•man•cer** \-sər\ *n* — **nec•ro•man•tic** \ˌnek-rə-'mant-ik\ *adj* — **nec•ro•man•ti•cal•ly** \-'mant-i-kə-lē, -klē\ *adv*

ne•crop•o•lis \nə-'kräp-ə-ləs, ne-\ *n, pl* **-lis•es** *or* **-les** \-ˌlēz\ : CEMETERY; *esp* : a large elaborate cemetery of an ancient city **[**Late Latin, "city of the dead", from Greek *nekropolis,* from *nekros* "dead body" + *polis* "city"**]**

nec•rop•sy \'nek-ˌräp-sē\ *n, pl* **-sies** : POSTMORTEM EXAMINATION

ne•cro•sis \nə-'krō-səs, ne-\ *n, pl* **-cro•ses** \-'krō-ˌsēz\ : usually local death of body tissue — **ne•crot•ic** \-'krät-ik\ *adj*

nec•tar \'nek-tər\ *n* **1 a** : the drink of the Greek and Roman gods **b** : a delicious drink **2** : a sweet liquid secreted by plants that is the chief raw material of honey **[**Latin, from Greek *nektar***]**

nec•tar•ine \ˌnek-tə-'rēn\ *n* : a smooth-skinned peach; *also* : a tree producing this fruit

nec•tary \'nek-tə-rē, -trē\ *n, pl* **-tar•ies** : a plant gland that secretes nectar

née *or* **nee** \'nā\ *adj* : BORN — used to identify a woman by her maiden family name ⟨Mrs. Jane Doe, *née* Roe⟩ **[**French *née,* feminine of *né* "born", from *naître* "to be born", from Latin *nasci***]**

[1]**need** \'nēd\ *n* **1** : necessary duty ⟨no *need* to go⟩ **2 a** : a lack of something necessary, desirable, or useful **b** : REQUIREMENT ⟨my *needs* are few and simple⟩ **3** : a condition requiring supply or relief **4** : POVERTY 1 **[**Old English *nīed, nēd***]**

• **syn** NEED, NECESSITY, EXIGENCY mean a pressing lack of something essential. NEED implies urgency and may suggest distress ⟨a critical *need* for medical supplies⟩ NECESSITY stresses imperative demand or compelling cause ⟨the great *necessity* for a new investigation⟩ EXIGENCY implies unusual or special difficulty ⟨deprivations caused by the *exigencies* of war⟩

[2]**need** *vb* **1** : to be in want **2** : to have cause or occasion for ⟨they *need* advice⟩ **3** : to be obligated to — used as an auxiliary verb ⟨you *need* not answer⟩

need•ful \'nēd-fəl\ *adj* : NECESSARY 2, REQUISITE — **need•ful•ly** \-fə-lē\ *adv* — **need•ful•ness** *n*

[1]**nee•dle** \'nēd-l\ *n* **1 a** : a slender usually steel instrument having an eye for thread and used for sewing **b** : a device for carrying thread and making stitches (as in suturing a wound) **c** : a slender hollow instrument for introducing material into or removing material from the body **2** : a slender usually sharp-pointed indicator on a dial; *esp* : MAGNETIC NEEDLE **3 a** : a slender pointed object resembling a needle (as a pointed crystal) **b** : OBELISK **c** : a needle-shaped leaf (as of a pine) **d** : a slender piece of jewel, steel, wood, or fiber with a rounded tip used in a phonograph to transmit vibrations from the record **e** : a slender pointed rod controlling a fine inlet or outlet (as in a valve) **[**Old English *nǣdl***]** — **nee•dle•like** \'nēd-l-ˌlīk, -ˌīk\ *adj*

[2]**needle** *vb* **nee•dled**; **nee•dling** \'nēd-ling, -l-ing\ **1** : to sew or pierce with or as if with a needle **2 a** : TEASE 2a, HARASS **b** : to incite to action by repeated gibes ⟨*needled* us into a fight⟩ — **nee•dler** \'nēd-lər, -l-ər\ *n* — **nee•dling** *n*

nee•dle•point \'nēd-l-ˌpȯint\ *n* **1** : lace worked with a needle in buttonhole stitch over a paper pattern **2** : embroidery done on canvas usually in simple even stitches across counted threads —**needlepoint** *adj*

\ə\ **abut**	\au̇\ **out**	\i\ **tip**	\ȯ\ **saw**	\u̇\ **foot**
\ər\ **further**	\ch\ **chin**	\ī\ **life**	\ȯi\ **coin**	\y\ **yet**
\a\ **mat**	\e\ **pet**	\j\ **job**	\th\ **thin**	\yü\ **few**
\ā\ **take**	\ē\ **easy**	\ng\ **sing**	\t͟h\ **this**	\yu̇\ **cure**
\ä\ **cot, cart**	\g\ **go**	\ō\ **bone**	\ü\ **food**	\zh\ **vision**

need·less \ˈnēd-ləs\ *adj* : UNNECESSARY ⟨*needless* expenses⟩ — **need·less·ly** *adv* — **need·less·ness** *n*
nee·dle·wom·an \ˈnēd-l-ˌwu̇m-ən\ *n* : a woman who does needlework; *esp* : SEAMSTRESS
nee·dle·work \-ˌwərk\ *n* : work done with a needle; *esp* : work (as embroidery) other than plain sewing — **nee·dle·work·er** *n*
needn't \ˈnēd-nt\ : need not
needs \ˈnēdz\ *adv* : of necessity : NECESSARILY ⟨must *needs* be recognized⟩ [Old English *nēdes,* from genitive of *nēd* "need"]
needy \ˈnēd-ē\ *adj* **need·i·er; -est** : being in want : very poor — **need·i·ness** *n*
ne'er \neər, ˈneər, naər, ˈnaər\ *adv* : NEVER
ne'er–do–well \ˈneər-du̇-ˌwel, ˈnaər-\ *n* : an idle worthless person — **ne'er–do–well** *adj*
ne·far·i·ous \ni-ˈfar-ē-əs, -ˈfer-\ *adj* : flagrantly wicked or impious : EVIL [Latin *nefarius,* from *nefas* "crime", from *ne-* "not" + *fas* "right, divine law"] — **ne·far·i·ous·ly** *adv* — **ne·far·i·ous·ness** *n*
ne·gate \ni-ˈgāt\ *vt* **1** : to deny the existence or truth of **2** : to cause to be ineffective or invalid [Latin *negare* "to say no, deny"] **syn** see NULLIFY — **ne·ga·tor** \-ˈgāt-ər\ *n*
ne·ga·tion \ni-ˈgā-shən\ *n* **1 a** : the action of negating : DENIAL **b** : a negative statement; *esp* : NEGATIVE 1a **2** : something considered the opposite of something positive — **ne·ga·tion·al** \-shnəl, -shən-l\ *adj*
[1]**neg·a·tive** \ˈneg-ət-iv\ *adj* **1** : marked by denial, prohibition, or refusal ⟨a *negative* reply⟩ **2** : not positive or constructive ⟨a *negative* attitude⟩ **3 a** : less than zero and opposite in sign to a positive number of like absolute value **b** : taken in a direction opposite to one chosen as positive ⟨a *negative* angle⟩ **4 a** : of, being, or relating to electricity of a kind of which the electron is the elementary unit ⟨a *negative* charge⟩ **b** : being the part toward which the electric current flows from the external circuit ⟨the *negative* pole of a discharging storage battery⟩ **c** : electron-emitting — used of an electrode in an electron tube **5 a** : not affirming the presence of what is sought or suspected ⟨a *negative* TB test⟩ **b** : directed or moving away from a source of stimulation ⟨a *negative* tropism⟩ **6** : having the light and dark parts in approximately inverse order to those of the original photographic subject ⟨a *negative* photographic image⟩ — **neg·a·tive·ly** *adv* — **neg·a·tive·ness** *n* — **neg·a·tiv·i·ty** \ˌneg-ə-ˈtiv-ət-ē\ *n*
[2]**negative** *n* **1 a** : a proposition by which something is denied or contradicted **b** : a reply that indicates the withholding of assent : REFUSAL **2** : NEGATION 2 **3 a** : an expression (as the word *no*) of negation or denial **b** : a negative number; *also* : ADDITIVE INVERSE **4** : the side that argues or votes against something in a debate **5** : a negative photographic image on transparent material used for printing positive pictures; *also* : the material that carries such an image
[3]**negative** *vt* **1** : to refuse to accept or approve : VETO **2** : DENY 4 **3** : NEGATE 2
neg·a·tiv·ism \ˈneg-ət-iv-ˌiz-əm\ *n* : an attitude of skepticism about nearly everything affirmed or suggested by others — **neg·a·tiv·ist** \-iv-əst\ *n* — **neg·a·tiv·is·tic** \ˌneg-ət-iv-ˈis-tik\ *adj*
[1]**ne·glect** \ni-ˈglekt\ *vt* **1** : to give little attention, respect, or care to : DISREGARD ⟨*neglect*ed their children⟩ **2** : to leave undone or unattended to especially through carelessness ⟨*neglect* one's duty⟩ **3** : FAIL ⟨*neglect*ed to mention a previous conviction⟩ [Latin *neglectus,* past participle of *neglegere* "to neglect", from *neg-* "not" + *legere* "to gather"] — **ne·glect·er** *n*
[2]**neglect** *n* **1** : an act or instance of neglecting **2** : the condition of being neglected
ne·glect·ful \ni-ˈglekt-fəl, -ˈglek-\ *adj* : given to neglecting : CARELESS **syn** see NEGLIGENT — **ne·glect·ful·ly** \-fə-lē\ *adv* — **ne·glect·ful·ness** *n*
neg·li·gee *also* **neg·li·gé** \ˌneg-lə-ˈzhā\ *n* **1** : a woman's long flowing dressing gown **2** : carelessly informal or incomplete attire [French *négligé,* from *négliger* "to neglect", from Latin *neglegere*]
neg·li·gence \ˈneg-li-jəns\ *n* **1 a** : the quality or state of being negligent **b** : failure to use the care that a prudent person exercises **2** : an act or instance of negligence
neg·li·gent \-jənt\ *adj* **1** : marked by or given to neglect **2** : marked by a carelessly easy manner [Latin *neglegens,* present participle of *neglegere* "to neglect"] — **neg·li·gent·ly** *adv*
• **syn** NEGLECTFUL, REMISS: NEGLIGENT implies inattention to one's duty or business; NEGLECTFUL adds a stronger implication of laziness or callousness; REMISS implies blameworthy carelessness or forgetfulness in performance of duty.
neg·li·gi·ble \ˈneg-li-jə-bəl\ *adj* : deserving neglect : TRIVIAL — **neg·li·gi·bil·i·ty** \ˌneg-li-jə-ˈbil-ət-ē\ *n* — **neg·li·gi·bly** \ˈneg-li-jə-blē\ *adv*
ne·go·tia·ble \ni-ˈgō-shə-bəl, -shē-ə-bəl\ *adj* : capable of being negotiated: as **a** : transferable from one person to another by being delivered with or without endorsement so that the title passes to the recipient ⟨*negotiable* bonds⟩ **b** : that can be traversed or accomplished ⟨a *negotiable* road⟩ **c** : that can be discussed or changed ⟨*negotiable* demands⟩ — **ne·go·tia·bil·i·ty** \-ˌgō-shə-ˈbil-ət-ē, -shē-ə-\ *n*
ne·go·tiant \ni-ˈgō-shē-ənt, -shənt\ *n* : one that negotiates
ne·go·ti·ate \ni-ˈgō-shē-ˌāt\ *vb* **1** : to discuss with another so as to arrive at a settlement or agreement; *also* : to arrange for or bring about by such conference ⟨*negotiate* a treaty⟩ **2** : to transfer to another in return for something of equal value ⟨*negotiate* a check⟩ **3** : to get through, around, or over successfully ⟨*negotiate* a turn⟩ [Latin *negotiari* "to transact business", from *negotium* "business", from *neg-* "not" + *otium* "leisure"] — **ne·go·ti·a·tion** \-ˌgō-shē-ˈā-shən, -sē-ˈā-\ *n* — **ne·go·ti·a·tor** \-ˈgō-shē-ˌāt-ər\ *n* — **ne·go·tia·to·ry** \-shə-ˌtōr-ē, -shē-ə-, -ˌtȯr-\ *adj*
Ne·gril·lo \ni-ˈgril-ō; -ˈgrē-ō, -yō\ *n, pl* **-los** *or* **-loes** : a member of a people (as the Pygmies) belonging to a group of African negroid peoples of small stature [Spanish, from *negro* "Negro"]
Ne·gri·to \nə-ˈgrēt-ō\ *n, pl* **-tos** *or* **-toes** : a member of a people (as the Andamanese) belonging to a group of negroid peoples of small stature that live in Oceania and southeastern Asia [Spanish, from *negro* "Negro"]
ne·gri·tude \ˈneg-rə-ˌtüd, ˈnē-grə-, -ˌtyüd\ *n* : a consciousness of and pride in black culture and history [French *négritude,* from *nègre* "Negro"]
Ne·gro \ˈnē-grō\ *n, pl* **Negroes** **1** : a member of the black race of mankind distinguished from members of other races by classification according to physical features but without regard to language or culture; *esp* : a member of a black people of Africa **2** : a person of Negro ancestry [Spanish or Portuguese, from *negro,* adj., "black", from Latin *niger*] — **Negro** *adj* — **ne·groid** \ˈnē-ˌgrȯid\ *n or adj, often cap*
ne·gus \ˈnē-gəs\ *n* : a beverage of wine, hot water, sugar, lemon juice, and nutmeg [Francis *Negus,* died 1732, English colonel]
Ne·he·mi·ah \ˌnē-ə-ˈmī-ə, ˌnē-hə-\ *n* — see BIBLE table
neigh \ˈnā\ *vi* : to utter the characteristic loud prolonged cry of a horse or a similar sound [Old English *hnǣgan*] — **neigh** *n*
[1]**neigh·bor** \ˈnā-bər\ *n* **1** : one living or located near another **2** : a fellow being [Old English *nēahgebūr,* from *nēah* "near" + *gebūr* "dweller"]
[2]**neighbor** *vt* **neigh·bored; neigh·bor·ing** \-bə-riŋ, -briŋ\ : to be next to or near to
neigh·bor·hood \ˈnā-bər-ˌhu̇d\ *n* **1** : the quality or state of being neighbors : NEARNESS **2 a** : a place or region near : VICINITY **b** : an approximate amount, extent, or degree ⟨cost in the *neighborhood* of $10⟩ **3 a** : the people living near one another **b** : a section lived in by neighbors and usually having distinguishing characteristics ⟨an older *neighborhood*⟩
neigh·bor·ly \ˈnā-bər-lē\ *adj* : of, relating to, or characteristic of neighbors; *esp* : FRIENDLY — **neigh·bor·li·ness** *n*
[1]**nei·ther** \ˈnē-t͟hər *also* ˈnī-\ *pron* : not the one and not the other ⟨*neither* of the two⟩ [Middle English, alteration of *nauther,* from Old English *nāhwæther,* from *nā* "not" + *hwæther* "which of two, whether"]
[2]**neither** *conj* **1** : not either ⟨*neither* black nor white⟩ **2** : also not ⟨*neither* did I⟩
[3]**neither** *adj* : not either ⟨*neither* hand⟩
nek·ton \ˈnek-tən, -ˌtän\ *n* : free-swimming aquatic animals whose distribution is essentially independent of wave and current action — compare PLANKTON [German, from Greek *nēktos* "swimming", from *nēchein* "to swim"] — **nek·ton·ic** \nek-ˈtän-ik\ *adj*
nel·son \ˈnel-sən\ *n* : a wrestling hold in which leverage is exerted against an opponent's arm, neck, and head [probably from the name *Nelson*]

ne•ma \'nē-mə\ *n* : NEMATODE

ne•ma•to•cide \'nem-ət-ə-,sīd, ni-'mat-ə-\ *n* : a substance or preparation used to destroy nematodes — **ne•ma•to•cid•al** \,nem-ət-ə-'sīd-l, ni-,mat-ə-\ *adj*

ne•ma•to•cyst \'nem-ət-ə-,sist, nə-'mat-ə-\ *n* : one of the minute stinging organs of various coelenterates [Greek *nēmat-, nēma* "thread"]

nem•a•tode \'nem-ə-,tōd\ *n* : any of a class or phylum (Nematoda) of elongated cylindrical worms parasitic in animals or plants or free-living in soil or water [derived from Greek *nēmat-, nēma* "thread"] — **nematode** *adj*

Nem•bu•tal \'nem-byə-,tòl\ *trademark* — used for the sodium salt of pentobarbital

ne•mer•te•an \ni-'mərt-ē-ən\ *n* : any of a class (Nemertea) of often vividly colored marine worms most of which burrow in the mud or sand along seacoasts [derived from Greek *Nēmertēs* "Nemertes (a sea nymph)"] — **nemertean** *adj* — **nem•er•tine** \'nem-ər-,tīn\ *adj or n*

nem•e•sis \'nem-ə-səs\ *n, pl* **-e•ses** \-ə-,sēz\ **1 a** : one that inflicts retribution or vengeance **b** : a formidable and usually victorious rival or opponent **2 a** : an act or instance of just punishment **b** : BANE 2 [*Nemesis,* Greek goddess of fate and punisher of pride]

ne•moph•i•la \ni-'mäf-ə-lə\ *n* : any of a genus of American herbs widely grown for their showy blue or white usually spotted flowers [Greek *nemos* "wooded pasture" + *philos* "loving"]

neo- — see NE-

neo•clas•sic \,nē-ō-'klas-ik\ *adj* : of or relating to a revival or adaptation of the classical style especially in literature, art, architecture, or music — **neo•clas•si•cal** \-'klas-i-kəl\ *adj* — **neo•clas•si•cism** \-'klas-ə-,siz-əm\ *n*

neo-Dar•win•ism \-'där-wə-,niz-əm\ *n* : a theory that explains evolution in terms of natural selection and the genetics of populations and specifically denies the possibility of inheriting acquired characters — **neo-Dar•win•i•an** \-där-'win-ē-ən\ *adj* — **neo-Dar•win•ist** \-'där-wə-nəst\ *n*

neo•dym•i•um \,nē-ō-'dim-ē-əm\ *n* : a yellow metallic chemical element — see ELEMENT table [*ne-* + *-dymium* (from *didymium,* a mixture of rare-earth elements, from Greek *didymos* "double", from *dyo* "two")]

neo-im•pres•sion•ism \-im-'presh-ə-,niz-əm\ *n, often cap N & I* : a late 19th century French art theory and practice marked by an attempt to make impressionism more precise in form and the use of a pointillist painting technique — **neo-im•pres•sion•ist** \-'presh-nəst, -ə-nəst\ *adj or n, often cap N & I*

neo•lith \'nē-ə-,lith\ *n* : a Neolithic stone implement

Ne•o•lith•ic \,nē-ə-'lith-ik\ *adj* : of or relating to the latest period of the Stone Age characterized by polished stone implements — compare EOLITHIC, PALEOLITHIC

ne•ol•o•gism \nē-'äl-ə-,jiz-əm\ *n* : a new word or expression — **ne•ol•o•gist** \-jəst\ *n* — **ne•ol•o•gis•tic** \-,äl-ə-'jis-tik\ *adj*

ne•ol•o•gy \-jē\ *n, pl* **-gies** : the use of a new word or expression or of an established word in a new or different sense

neo•my•cin \,nē-ə-'mīs-n\ *n* : a broad-spectrum antibiotic or mixture of antibiotics produced by a soil actinomycete

ne•on \'nē-,än\ *n* **1** : a colorless odorless inert gaseous chemical element found in minute amounts in air and used in electric lamps — see ELEMENT table **2 a** : a discharge lamp in which the gas contains a large amount of neon **b** : a sign composed of such lamps [Greek, neuter of *neos* "new"]

neo•na•tal \,nē-ō-'nāt-l\ *adj* : of, relating to, or affecting the newborn — **neo•na•tal•ly** \-l-ē\ *adv* — **neo•nate** \'nē-ə-,nāt\ *n*

neo•or•tho•dox \,nē-ō-'òr-thə-,däks\ *adj* : of or relating to a 20th century Protestant theological movement characterized by a reaction against liberalism and emphasis on Reformation doctrines — **neo•or•tho•doxy** \-,däk-sē\ *n*

neo•phyte \'nē-ə-,fīt\ *n* **1** : a new convert : PROSELYTE **2** : NOVICE 2 [Late Latin *neophytus,* from Greek *neophytos,* from *neophytos* "newly planted", from *neos* "new" + *phyein* "to bring forth"]

neo•plasm \'nē-ə-,plaz-əm\ *n* : a new growth of tissue serving no physiologic function : TUMOR — **neo•plas•tic** \,nē-ə-'plas-tik\ *adj*

neo•prene \'nē-ə-,prēn\ *n* : a synthetic rubber that is resistant to deterioration caused by oil, gasoline, oxygen, and ozone [*ne-* + *-prene* (as in *isoprene,* a flammable liquid used in synthetic rubber, probably from *is-* + *propyl* + *-ene*)]

ne•o•te•ny \nē-ə-,tē-nē, nē-'ät-n-ē\ *n* : attainment of sexual maturity during the larval stage; *also* : retention of immature characters in adulthood [*ne-* + Greek *teinein* "to stretch"] — **ne•o•ten•ic** \,nē-ə-'ten-ik\ *adj*

ne•pen•the \nə-'pen-thē, -'pent-\ *n* **1** : a potion used by the ancients to dull pain and sorrow **2** : something capable of making one forget grief or suffering [Latin *nepenthes,* from Greek *nēpenthēs* "banishing pain and sorrow", from *nē-* "not" + *penthos* "sorrow"] — **ne•pen•the•an** \-thē-ən\ *adj*

neph•e•line \'nef-ə-,lēn\ *also* **neph•e•lite** \-,līt\ *n* : a usually glassy silicate mineral common in igneous rocks [French *néphéline,* from Greek *nephelē* "cloud"]

neph•ew \'nef-yü\ *n* : a son of one's brother, sister, brother-in-law, or sister-in-law [Old Fench *neveu,* from Latin *nepos* "grandson, nephew"]

nepho•scope \'nef-ə-,skōp\ *n* : an instrument for observing the direction and velocity of cloud motion [Greek *nephos* "cloud"]

neph•ric \'nef-rik\ *adj* : RENAL

ne•phrid•i•um \ni-'frid-ē-əm\ *n, pl* **-ia** \-ē-ə\ : a tubular excretory organ of various invertebrates (as an earthworm) [New Latin, from Greek *nephros* "kidney"] — **ne•phrid•i•al** \-ē-əl\ *adj*

ne•phri•tis \ni-'frīt-əs\ *n, pl* **ne•phrit•i•des** \-'frit-ə-,dēz\ : inflammation of the kidneys — **ne•phrit•ic** \-'frit-ik\ *adj*

neph•ron \'nef-,rän\ *n* : a single excretory unit especially of the vertebrate kidney [German, from Greek *nephros* "kidney"]

ne plus ul•tra \,nā-,pləs-'əl-trə, ,nē-\ *n* : the highest point capable of being attained : ACME ⟨that hotel is the *ne plus ultra* of elegance⟩ [New Latin, "no more beyond"]

nep•o•tism \'nep-ə-,tiz-əm\ *n* : favoritism shown to a relative (as by giving an appointive job) [French *népotisme,* from Italian *nepotismo,* from *nepote* "nephew", from Latin *nepot-, nepos* "grandson, nephew"]

Nep•tune \'nep-,tün, -,tyün\ *n* : the planet 8th in order from the sun — see PLANET table [Latin *Neptunus,* Roman god of the sea] — **Nep•tu•ni•an** \nep-'tü-nē-ən, -'tyü-\ *adj*

nep•tu•ni•um \nep-'tü-nē-əm, -'tyü-\ *n* : a radioactive metallic chemical element that is similar to uranium and is obtained in nuclear reactors as a by-product in the production of plutonium — see ELEMENT table [New Latin, from *Neptunus,* the planet Neptune]

ne•re•is \'nir-ē-əs\ *n, pl* **ne•re•ides** \nə-'rē-ə-,dēz\ : any of a genus of usually large greenish marine annelid worms [Latin, a sea nymph]

ne•rit•ic \nə-'rit-ik\ *adj* : of, relating to, or being the shallow water adjoining the seacoast [perhaps from New Latin *Nerita,* a genus of marine snails]

ner•va•tion \,nər-'vā-shən\ *n* : an arrangement or system of nerves; *also* : VENATION

[1]nerve \'nərv\ *n* **1** : SINEW 1, TENDON ⟨strain every *nerve*⟩ **2** : one of the filamentous bands of nervous tissue connecting parts of the nervous system with the other organs and conducting nervous impulses **3 a** : power of endurance or control **b** (1) : venturesome boldness (2) : BRASS 3, GALL **4 a** : a sore or sensitive point **b** *pl* : nervous disorganization or collapse : HYSTERIA **5** : VEIN 2b, 2c **6** : the sensitive pulp of a tooth [Latin *nervus* "sinew, nerve"] — **nerve** *adj* — **nerved** \'nərvd\ *adj*

[2]nerve *vt* : to give strength or courage to

nerve cell *n* : NEURON; *also* : a nerve cell body exclusive of its processes

nerve center *n* **1** : CENTER 2b **2** : a source of leadership, control, or energy

nerve cord *n* **1** : the pair of closely united ventral longitudinal nerves with their segmental ganglia that is characteristic of many elongate invertebrates **2** : the dorsal tubular cord of nervous tissue that develops into the central nervous system in chordates

nerve ending *n* : a structure forming an end of a nerve axon that is distant from the cell body

nerve fiber *n* : AXON, DENDRITE

\ə\ abut	\aù\ out	\i\ tip	\ò\ saw	\ù\ foot
\ər\ further	\ch\ chin	\ī\ life	\òi\ coin	\y\ yet
\a\ mat	\e\ pet	\j\ job	\th\ thin	\yü\ few
\ā\ take	\ē\ easy	\ng\ sing	\t͟h\ this	\yù\ cure
\ä\ cot, cart	\g\ go	\ō\ bone	\ü\ food	\zh\ vision

nerve gas *n* : a war gas damaging especially to the nervous and respiratory systems

nerve impulse *n* : the progressive alteration along a nerve fiber that follows stimulation and serves to transmit a record of sensation from a receptor or an instruction to act to an effector — called also *nervous impulse*

nerve•less \'nərv-ləs\ *adj* **1** : lacking strength or courage : FEEBLE **2** : showing control or balance : POISED, COOL — **nerve•less•ly** *adv* — **nerve•less•ness** *n*

nerve net *n* : a network of nerve cells apparently continuous one with another and conducting impulses in all directions; *also* : a nervous system (as in a jellyfish) consisting of such a network

nerve-rack•ing *or* **nerve-wrack•ing** \'nərv-,rak-ing\ *adj* : extremely trying on the nerves

nerve tube *n* : NERVE CORD 2

nerv•ous \'nər-vəs\ *adj* **1** : marked by vigor of thought, feeling, or style : SPIRITED **2 a** : of, relating to, or composed of neurons **b** : of or relating to the nerves; *also* : originating in or affected by the nerves **3 a** : easily excited or irritated : JUMPY **b** : TIMID, APPREHENSIVE ⟨a *nervous* smile⟩ **4** : tending to cause nervousness or agitation : TRYING ⟨a *nervous* situation⟩ — **nerv•ous•ly** *adv* — **nerv•ous•ness** *n*

nervous breakdown *n* : a serious mental or emotional disorder; *esp* : one that incapacitates or requires hospital care

nervous system *n* : the bodily system that receives and interprets stimuli and transmits impulses to the effector organs and that in vertebrates is made up of brain and spinal cord, nerves, ganglia, and parts of the receptor organs

nervy \'nər-vē\ *adj* **nerv•i•er; -est 1 a** : showing calm courage : BOLD **b** : marked by impudence or presumption : BRASH ⟨a *nervy* salesperson⟩ **2** : NERVOUS 3a — **nerv•i•ness** *n*

ne•science \'nesh-əns, 'nēsh-, -ē-əns\ *n* : lack of knowledge or awareness : IGNORANCE [Late Latin *nescientia,* from Latin *nescire* "not to know", from *ne-* "not" + *scire* "to know"] — **nescient** \-ənt\ *adj*

ness \'nes\ *n* : [1]CAPE, PROMONTORY [Old English *næss*]

-ness \nəs\ *n suffix* : state : condition : quality : degree ⟨hard*ness*⟩ [Old English]

Nes•sel•rode \'nes-əl-,rōd\ *n* : a mixture of candied fruits, nuts, and maraschino used in puddings, pies, and ice cream [Count Karl R. *Nesselrode,* died 1862, Russian statesman]

[1]nest \'nest\ *n* **1 a** : a bed or shelter prepared by a bird for its eggs and young **b** : a place where eggs are laid and hatched **2 a** : a place of rest, retreat, or lodging **b** : DEN 2a, HANGOUT **3** : the occupants or frequenters of a nest **4 a** : a group of similar things : AGGREGATION **b** : HOTBED 2 **5** : a group of objects made to fit close together or one within another ⟨a *nest* of tables⟩ [Old English]

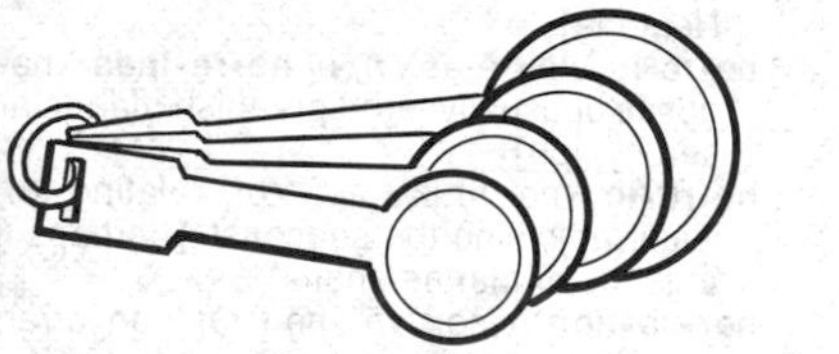

[1]nest 5

[2]nest *vb* **1** : to build or occupy a nest ⟨robins *nested* in the underbrush⟩ **2** : to fit compactly together or within one another

nest egg *n* **1** : a natural or artificial egg left in a nest to induce a fowl to continue to lay there **2** : a fund of money set aside as a reserve

nest•er \'nes-tər\ *n* **1** : one that nests **2** *West* : a homesteader or squatter who takes up open range for a farm

nes•tle \'nes-əl\ *vb* **nes•tled; nes•tling** \'nes-ling, -ə-ling\ **1** : to settle snugly or comfortably **2 a** : to settle, shelter, or house as if in a nest **b** : to press closely and affectionately : CUDDLE [Old English *nestlian* "to make a nest", from *nest*] — **nes•tler** \-lər\ *n*

nest•ling \'nest-ling\ *n* : a young bird not yet able to leave the nest

[1]net \'net\ *n* **1 a** : a meshed fabric twisted, knotted, or woven together at regular intervals **b** : something made of net: as (1) : a device for catching fish, birds, or insects (2) : a fabric barricade which divides a court in half (as for tennis) and over which a ball or shuttlecock must be hit in play **2** : an entrapping situation ⟨in a *net* of suspicion⟩ **3** : a network of lines, fibers, or figures [Old English *nett*] — **net•like** \-,līk\ *adj* — **net•ty** \'net-ē\ *adj*

[2]net *vt* **net•ted; net•ting 1** : to cover with or as if with a net **2** : to catch in or as if in a net — **net•ter** *n*

[3]net *adj* **1** : free from all charges or deductions ⟨a *net* profit⟩ ⟨*net* weight⟩ — compare GROSS 3b **2** : FINAL ⟨the *net* result⟩ [Middle French, "clean, neat"]

[4]net *vt* **net•ted; net•ting** : to gain or produce as profit : CLEAR

[5]net *n* : a net amount, profit, or price

neth•er \'neth-ər\ *adj* **1** : situated down or below : LOWER **2** : situated beneath the earth's surface ⟨the *nether* regions⟩ [Old English *nithera,* from *nither* "down"]

neth•er•most \-,mōst\ *adj* : farthest down : LOWEST

neth•er•world \-,wərld\ *n* **1** : the world of the dead **2** : UNDERWORLD 2, 3

net•ting \'net-ing\ *n* **1** : NETWORK 1 **2** : the act or process of making a net or network

[1]net•tle \'net-l\ *n* : any of various coarse herbs with stinging hairs [Old English *netel*]

[2]nettle *vt* **net•tled; net•tling** \'net-ling, -l-ing\ **1** : to strike or sting with or as if with nettles **2** : IRRITATE 1, PROVOKE

net•tle•some \'net-l-səm\ *adj* : causing annoyance

net-veined \'net-'vānd\ *adj* : having veins that branch and interlace to form a network ⟨dicotyledons have *net-veined* leaves⟩ — compare PARALLEL-VEINED

net•work \'net-,wərk\ *n* **1** : a fabric or structure of cords or wires that cross at regular intervals and are knotted or secured at the crossings **2** : a system of elements (as lines or channels) resembling a network **3 a** : an interconnected or interrelated chain, group, or system; *esp* : a group of radio or television stations linked by wire or radio relay **b** : a television or radio company that broadcasts over such a network

neur- *or* **neuro-** *combining form* : nerve ⟨*neur*al⟩ ⟨*neuro*logy⟩ [Greek *neuron* "sinew, nerve"]

neu•ral \'nu̇r-əl, 'nyu̇r-\ *adj* **1** : of, relating to or involving a nerve or the nervous system **2** : situated in the region of or on the same side of the body as the brain and spinal cord — **neu•ral•ly** \-ə-lē\ *adv*

neu•ral•gia \nu̇-'ral-jə, nyu̇-\ *n* : a condition marked by acute pain that follows the course of a nerve — **neu•ral•gic** \-jik\ *adj*

neural tube *n* : a hollow longitudinal tube produced from dorsal ectodermal folds and giving rise to the central nervous system of a vertebrate embryo

neu•ri•lem•ma \,nu̇r-ə-'lem-ə, ,nyu̇r-\ *n* : the outer sheath of a nerve fiber [*neur-* + Greek *eilēma* "covering, coil", from *eilein* "to wind"] — **neu•ri•lem•mal** \-'lem-əl\ *adj*

neu•ri•tis \nu̇-'rīt-əs, nyu̇-\ *n, pl* **-rit•i•des** \-'rit-ə-,dēz\ *or* **-ri•tis•es** : inflammation of a nerve — **neu•rit•ic** \-'rit-ik\ *adj or n*

neu•ro•fi•bril \,nu̇r-ō-'fīb-rəl, ,nyu̇r-, -'fib-\ *n* : a filament (as in a protozoan or a neuron) believed to be a conducting element

neu•rog•lia \nu̇-'räg-lē-ə, nyu̇-; ,nu̇r-ə-'glē-ə, ,nyu̇r-, -'glī-\ *n* : supporting tissue of the brain, spinal cord, and ganglia [*neur-* + Middle Greek *glia* "glue"] — **neu•rog•li•al** \-əl\ *adj*

neu•ro•hor•mone \,nu̇r-ō-'hȯr-,mōn, ,nyu̇r-\ *n* : a hormone (as acetylcholine or norepinephrine) produced by or acting on nervous tissue

neu•ro•hu•mor \,nu̇r-ō-'hyü-mər, ,nyu̇r-, -'yü-\ *n* : a substance released at a nerve ending that plays a part in transmitting a nerve impulse — **neu•ro•hu•mor•al** \-'hyüm-rəl, -'yüm-, -ə-rəl\ *adj*

neu•rol•o•gy \nu̇-'räl-ə-jē, nyu̇-\ *n* : the scientific study of the structure, functions, and disorders of the nervous system — **neu•ro•log•i•cal** \,nu̇r-ə-'läj-i-kəl, ,nyu̇r-\ *or* **neu•ro•log•ic** \-'läj-ik\ *adj* — **neu•rol•o•gist** \nu̇-'räl-ə-jəst, nyu̇-\ *n*

neu•ro•mo•tor \,nu̇r-ə-'mōt-ər, ,nyu̇r-\ *adj* : relating to efferent nervous impulses

neu•ro•mus•cu•lar \,nu̇r-ō-'məs-kyə-lər, ,nyu̇r-\ *adj* : of or relating to nerves and muscles; *esp* : jointly involving nervous and muscular elements ⟨a *neuromuscular* junction⟩

neu•ron \'nü-,rän, 'nyü-; 'nu̇r-,än, 'nyu̇r-\ *also* **neu•rone** \-,rōn, -,ōn\ *n* : a cell with specialized processes that is the fundamental functional unit of nervous tissue [Greek *neuron* "nerve, sinew"] — **neu•ro•nal** \'nu̇r-ən-l, 'nyu̇r-, nu̇-'rōn-l, nyu̇-\ *adj*

neu•rop•ter•an \nu̇-'räp-tə-rən, nyu̇-\ *n* : any of a family (order Neuroptera) of insects (as an ant lion) with a fine network of wing veins [derived from Greek *neuron* "sinew, nerve" + *pteron* "wing"] — **neuropteran** *adj*

neu•ro•sis \nu̇-'rō-səs, nyu̇-\ *n, pl* **-ro•ses** \-'rō-,sēz\ : a nervous disorder marked by anxiety and the use of defense mechanisms to escape from it and by the absence of obvious physical cause

neu·ros·po·ra \nu̇-ˈräs-pə-rə, nyu̇-\ *n* : any of a genus of often pink-spored ascomycetous fungi that are destructive in bakeries but important objects of genetic research [New Latin, from *neur-* + *spora* "spore"]

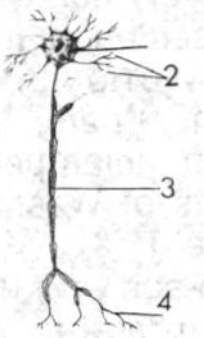

neuron: *1* cell body, *2* dendrite, *3* axon, *4* nerve ending

1**neu·rot·ic** \nu̇-ˈrät-ik, nyu̇-\ *adj* : of, relating to, constituting, or affected with neurosis — **neu·rot·i·cal·ly** \-ˈrät-i-kə-lē, -klē\ *adv*

2**neurotic** *n* : an emotionally unstable person or one affected with a neurosis

neu·ro·tox·ic \ˌnu̇r-ə-ˈtäk-sik, ˌnyu̇r-\ *adj* : poisonous to nervous tissue

neu·ro·tox·in \-ˈtäk-sən\ *n* : a poisonous protein that acts on the nervous system

1**neu·ter** \ˈnüt-ər, ˈnyüt-\ *adj* **1** : of, relating to, or constituting the class of words that ordinarily includes most of those referring to things that are neither male nor female ⟨a *neuter* noun⟩ ⟨the *neuter* gender⟩ **2** : lacking sex organs; *also* : having imperfectly developed sex organs [Latin, literally, "neither", from *ne-* "not" + *uter* "which of two"]

2**neuter** *n* **1 a** : a word or form of the neuter gender **b** : the neuter gender **2** : one that is neutral **3 a** : WORKER 2 **b** : a spayed or castrated animal

3**neuter** *vt* : ALTER 2, CASTRATE

1**neu·tral** \ˈnü-trəl, ˈnyü-\ *adj* **1** : not favoring either side in a quarrel, contest, or war **2** : of or relating to a neutral state or power **3 a** : neither one thing nor the other : INDIFFERENT **b** : ACHROMATIC **c** : neither acid nor basic **d** : not electrically charged **4** : produced with the tongue in the position it has when at rest ⟨the *neutral* vowels of \ə-ˈbəv\ *above*⟩ [Middle French, from Latin *neutralis* "of neuter gender", from *neuter* "neuter, neither"] — **neu·tral·ly** \-trə-lē\ *adv* — **neu·tral·ness** *n*

2**neutral** *n* **1** : one that is neutral **2** : a neutral color **3** : a position of disengagement (as of gears)

neu·tral·ism \ˈnü-trə-ˌliz-əm, ˈnyü-\ *n* : a policy or the advocacy of neutrality especially in international affairs — **neu·tral·ist** \-ləst\ *n* — **neu·tral·is·tic** \ˌnü-trə-ˈlis-tik, ˌnyü-\ *adj*

neu·tral·i·ty \nü-ˈtral-ət-ē, nyü-\ *n* **1** : the quality or state of being neutral **2** : immunity from invasion or from use by belligerents

neu·tral·ize \ˈnü-trə-ˌlīz, ˈnyü-\ *vt* **1** : to make chemically neutral **2** : to destroy the effectiveness of : NULLIFY ⟨*neutralize* an opponent's move⟩ **3** : to make electrically inert by combining equal positive and negative quantities **4** : to provide for the neutrality of under international law ⟨*neutralize* a country⟩ — **neu·tral·i·za·tion** \ˌnü-trə-lə-ˈzā-shən, ˌnyü-\ *n* — **neu·tral·iz·er** \ˈnü-trə-ˌlī-zər, ˈnyü-\ *n*

neutral spirits *n pl* : ethyl alcohol of 190 or higher proof used especially for blending alcoholic liquors

neu·tri·no \nü-ˈtrē-nō, nyü-\ *n, pl* **-nos** : an uncharged elementary particle having a mass less than 1/10 that of the electron [Italian, from *neutrone* "neutron"]

neu·tron \ˈnü-ˌträn, ˈnyü-\ *n* : an uncharged elementary particle that has a mass nearly equal to that of the proton and is present in all known atomic nuclei except the hydrogen nucleus [probably from *neutral* + *-on*]

neutron star *n* : any of various hypothetical dense celestial objects that consist of closely packed nuclear particles and result from the collapse of a much larger star [from the hypothesis that the cores of such stars are composed entirely of neutrons]

neu·tro·phil \ˈnü-trə-ˌfil, ˈnyü-\ *also* **neu·tro·phile** \-ˌfīl\ *n* : a finely granular cell that is the chief phagocytic white blood cell [Latin *neuter* "neither"; from its staining to the same degree with acid or basic dyes]

né·vé \nā-ˈvā\ *n* : the partially compacted granular snow that forms the surface part of the upper end of a glacier; *also* : a field of granular snow [French (Swiss dialect), from Latin *niv-, nix* "snow"]

nev·er \ˈnev-ər\ *adv* **1** : not ever : at no time ⟨*never* saw them before⟩ **2** : not in any degree, way, or condition ⟨*never* fear, we'll win⟩ [Old English *nǣfre*, from *ne* "not" + *ǣfre* "ever"]

nev·er·more \ˌnev-ər-ˈmōr, -ˈmȯr\ *adv* : never again

nev·er–nev·er land \ˌnev-ər-ˈnev-ər-\ *n* : an ideal or imaginary place

nev·er·the·less \ˌnev-ər-t͟hə-ˈles\ *adv* : in spite of that : HOWEVER

ne·vus \ˈnē-vəs\ *n, pl* **ne·vi** \-ˌvī\ : a congenital pigmented area on the skin : BIRTHMARK [Latin *naevus*]

1**new** \ˈnü, ˈnyü\ *adj* **1** : not old : RECENT, MODERN **2** : not the same as the former : taking the place of one that came before ⟨a *new* teacher⟩ **3** : recently discovered, recognized, or learned about ⟨*new* lands⟩ **4** : not formerly known or experienced ⟨*new* feelings⟩ **5** : not accustomed ⟨*new* to her work⟩ **6** : beginning as a repetition of some previous act or thing ⟨a *new* year⟩ ⟨make a *new* start⟩ **7** : renewed in strength and vigor **8** : being in a position or place for the first time ⟨a *new* member⟩ **9** *cap* : having been in use after medieval times : MODERN ⟨*New* Latin⟩ [Old English *nīwe*] — **new·ness** *n*

• **syn** NEW, NOVEL, FRESH mean having recently come into existence or use. NEW may apply to what is freshly made and unused ⟨*new* bricks⟩ or has not been known before ⟨a *new* design⟩ or not experienced before ⟨start on a *new* job⟩ NOVEL applies to what is not only new but strange and unprecedented ⟨*novel* hair styles⟩ FRESH applies to what has not yet had time to grow dim, soiled, or stale ⟨put on a *fresh* shirt⟩ ⟨offering *fresh* ideas⟩

2**new** *adv* : NEWLY, RECENTLY ⟨*new*-mown hay⟩

new·born \ˈnü-ˈbȯrn, ˈnyü-\ *adj* **1** : recently born **2** : born again

new·com·er \ˈnü-ˌkəm-ər, ˈnyü-\ *n* **1** : one recently arrived **2** : NOVICE 2, BEGINNER

New Deal *n* **1** : the legislative and administrative program of President Franklin D. Roosevelt designed to promote economic recovery and social reform during the 1930s **2** : the period of the New Deal — **New Deal·er** \-ˈdē-lər\ *n*

new·el \ˈnü-əl, ˈnyü-\ *n* **1** : an upright post about which the steps of a circular staircase wind **2** : a post at the foot of a straight stairway or one at a landing [Middle French *nouel* "stone of a fruit", from Late Latin *nucalis "like a nut", from Latin nuc-, nux* "nut"]

new·fan·gled \ˈnü-ˈfang-gəld, ˈnyü-\ *adj* : of the newest style : NOVEL ⟨*newfangled* ideas⟩ [Middle English, from *newefangel*, from *new* + Old English *fangen*, past participle of *fōn* "to take, seize"]

new–fash·ioned \-ˈfash-ənd\ *adj* **1** : made in a new fashion or form **2** : UP-TO-DATE 2

new·found \-ˈfau̇nd\ *adj* : newly found ⟨a *newfound* friend⟩

New·found·land \ˈnü-fən-dlənd, ˈnyü-, -lənd, -ˌdland, -ˌland; nü-ˈfau̇n-dlənd, nyü-, -lənd\ *n* : any of a breed of very large usually black dogs developed in Newfoundland

New Hamp·shire \nü-ˈham-shər, nyü-, -ˈhamp-, -ˌshiər\ *n* : any of a breed of single-combed domestic fowls developed chiefly in New Hampshire and noted for heavy winter egg production

new·ish \ˈnü-ish, ˈnyü-\ *adj* : rather new

New Latin *n* : Latin as used since the end of the medieval period especially in scientific description and classification

New Left *n* : a political movement beginning in the United States during the 1960s that is composed chiefly of students and extremist groups and advocates (as by demonstrations) radical changes in political, social, and educational practices — **New Leftist** *adj or n*

new·ly \ˈnü-lē, ˈnyü-\ *adv* **1** : LATELY, RECENTLY ⟨*newly* married⟩ **2** : ANEW, AFRESH ⟨a *newly* furnished house⟩

new·ly·wed \-ˌwed\ *n* : one recently married

new math *n* : mathematics that is based on set theory especially as taught in elementary and secondary school — called also *new mathematics*

new moon *n* **1** : the moon's phase when it is in conjunction with the sun so that its dark side is toward the earth; *also* : the thin crescent moon seen shortly after sunset a few days after the actual occurrence of the new moon phase **2** : the 1st day of the Jewish month

\ə\ **abut**	\au̇\ **out**	\i\ **tip**	\ȯ\ **saw**	\u̇\ **foot**
\ər\ **further**	\ch\ **chin**	\ī\ **life**	\ȯi\ **coin**	\y\ **yet**
\a\ **mat**	\e\ **pet**	\j\ **job**	\th\ **thin**	\yü\ **few**
\ā\ **take**	\ē\ **easy**	\ng\ **sing**	\t͟h\ **this**	\yu̇\ **cure**
\ä\ **cot, cart**	\g\ **go**	\ō\ **bone**	\ü\ **food**	\zh\ **vision**

new penny *n* : a British monetary unit equal to 1/100 pound; *also* : a coin representing this unit
news \ˈnüz, ˈnyüz\ *n* **1** : a report of recent events ⟨brought us the office *news*⟩ **2 a** : material reported in a newspaper or news periodical or on a newscast **b** : matter that is newsworthy
news agency *n* : an organization that supplies news to subscribing newspapers, periodicals, and newscasters — called also *news service*
news•boy \ˈnüz-ˌbȯi, ˈnyüz-\ *n* : a person who delivers or sells newspapers
news•cast \-ˌkast\ *n* : a radio or television news broadcast [*news* + broad*cast*] — **news•cast•er** \-ˌkas-tər\ *n*
news conference *n* : PRESS CONFERENCE
news•girl \ˈnüz-ˌgərl, ˈnyüz-\ *n* : a girl or woman who delivers or sells newspapers
news•let•ter \ˈnüz-ˌlet-ər, ˈnyüz-\ *n* : a newspaper containing news or information of interest chiefly to a special group
news•man \-mən, -ˌman\ *n* : one (as a reporter or correspondent) who gathers, reports, or comments on the news
news•mon•ger \-ˌməng-gər, -ˌmäng-\ *n* : GOSSIP 1
news•pa•per \ˈnüz-ˌpā-pər, ˈnyüz-, ˈnüs-, ˈnyüs-\ *n* **1** : a paper that is printed and distributed usually daily or weekly and contains news, articles of opinion, features, and advertising **2** : an organization publishing a newspaper **3** : the paper making up a newspaper
news•pa•per•man \-ˌman\ *n* : one who owns or is employed by a newspaper; *esp* : one who writes or edits copy for a newspaper
news•print \ˈnüz-ˌprint, ˈnyüz-\ *n* : a relatively cheap paper made from wood pulp and used mostly for newspapers
news•reel \-ˌrēl\ *n* : a short motion picture dealing with current events
news•stand \ˈnüz-ˌstand, ˈnyüz-\ *n* : a place where newspapers and periodicals are sold
New Style *adj* : using or according to the Gregorian calendar
news•wom•an \ˈnüz-ˌwu̇m-ən, ˈnyüz-\ *n* : a woman who works as a newsman
news•wor•thy \ˈnüz-ˌwər-t͟hē, ˈnyüz-\ *adj* : sufficiently interesting to the general public to warrant reporting
newsy \ˈnü-zē, ˈnyü-\ *adj* **news•i•er**; **-est** : filled with news; *esp* : CHATTY ⟨a *newsy* letter⟩
newt \ˈnüt, ˈnyüt\ *n* : any of various small salamanders that live mostly in water [Middle English *newte*, the phrase *an ewte* (from Old English *efete* "eft") being understood as *a newte*]

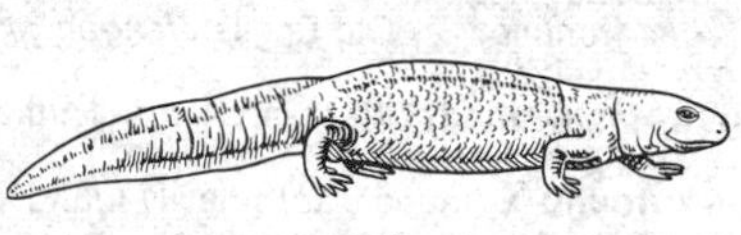
newt

New Testament *n* : the second of the two chief divisions of the Christian Bible consisting of the books dealing with Christ's life and death and the work done by his apostles after his death — see BIBLE table
new•ton \ˈnüt-ⁿn, ˈnyüt-ⁿn\ *n* : a unit of force in the mks system of such size that under its influence a body whose mass is one kilogram would experience an acceleration of one meter per second per second [Sir Isaac *Newton*]
New•to•ni•an \nü-ˈtō-nē-ən, nyü-\ *adj* : of, relating to, or characteristic of Sir Isaac Newton, his discoveries, or his doctrines
New World *n* : the western hemisphere; *esp* : the continental landmass of North and South America
New Year \ˈnü-ˌyiər, ˈnyü-\ *n* **1** : NEW YEAR'S DAY; *also* : the first days of the year **2** : ROSH HASHANAH
New Year's Day *n* : January 1 observed as a legal holiday
^{1}**next** \ˈnekst\ *adj* : immediately preceding or following : NEAREST ⟨the *next* page⟩ ⟨the *next* house was empty⟩ [Old English *nīehst*, superlative of *nēah* "nigh"]
^{2}**next** *adv* **1** : in the time, place, or order nearest or immediately succeeding ⟨open this package *next*⟩ **2** : on the first occasion to come ⟨when *next* we meet⟩
^{3}**next** *prep* : next to
next of kin : a person's nearest relation or relations
^{1}**next to** *prep* : immediately following : adjacent to ⟨*next to* the head of the class⟩
^{2}**next to** *adv* : very nearly : ALMOST ⟨*next to* impossible⟩
nex•us \ˈnek-səs\ *n, pl* **nex•us•es** \-sə-səz\ *or* **nex•us** \-səs, -ˌsüs\ : CONNECTION 2, LINK [Latin, from *nectere* "to bind"]
Nez Percé \ˈnez-ˈpərs, ˈnes-ˈpeərs, *French* nā-per-sā\ *n* : a member of an Indian people of what is now central Idaho and adjacent parts of Washington and Oregon [French, literally, "pierced nose"]
ni•a•cin \ˈnī-ə-sən\ *n* : NICOTINIC ACID [*ni*cotinic *a*cid + *-in*]
Ni•ag•a•ra \nī-ˈag-rə, -ə-rə\ *n* : an overwhelming flood : TORRENT ⟨a *Niagara* of protests⟩ [*Niagara* Falls, waterfall of the Niagara river]
nib \ˈnib\ *n* **1** : BEAK 1, BILL **2 a** : the sharpened point of a quill pen **b** : a pen point **3** : a small pointed or projecting part [probably alteration of *neb*]
^{1}**nib•ble** \ˈnib-əl\ *vb* **nib•bled**; **nib•bling** \ˈnib-ling, -ə-ling\ **1 a** : to bite or chew gently or bit by bit **b** : to take away gradually ⟨*nibbling* our freedom⟩ **2** : to deal with something cautiously [origin unknown] — **nib•bler** \ˈnib-lər, -ə-lər\ *n*
^{2}**nibble** *n* **1** : an act of nibbling; *esp* : a small bite or cautious approach **2 a** : a very small quantity **b** : a dainty morsel
Ni•be•lung \ˈnē-bə-ˌlu̇ng\ *n* **1** : a member of a race of dwarfs in Germanic legend from whom a hoard and ring were taken by Siegfried **2** : any of the followers of Siegfried **3** : any of the Burgundian kings in the medieval German epic *Nibelungenlied* [German]
nibs \ˈnibz\ *n* : an important or self-important person — used chiefly in the phrase *his* (or *her*) *nibs* [origin unknown]
nice \ˈnīs\ *adj* **1** : showing fastidious or finicky tastes **2** : marked by or demanding delicate discrimination or treatment ⟨a *nice* distinction⟩ **3 a** : PLEASING, AGREEABLE ⟨a *nice* time⟩ ⟨a *nice* person⟩ **b** : well-executed : GOOD ⟨a *nice* shot⟩ **4 a** : socially acceptable : WELL-BRED ⟨offensive to *nice* people⟩ **b** : VIRTUOUS, RESPECTABLE [Middle English, "foolish, wanton", from Old French, from Latin *nescius* "ignorant", from *nescire* "not to know", from *ne-* "not" + *scire* "to know"] — **nice•ly** *adv* — **nice•ness** *n*
△ **origin** While it is difficult to trace the precise development of the many senses of this word in English, a brief look at its history reveals that *nice* has come to have a number of meanings that are almost opposite to its earliest senses. *Nice* is derived from Latin *nescius*, "ignorant". It was earliest used in English, in the 13th and 14th centuries, to mean "foolish" or "stupid". Also in its early history in English *nice* had the sense of "wanton" or "dissolute". From these senses *nice* began in the 16th century to develop the meaning "coy" or "reserved", and then "fastidious" or "finicky". Not until the 18th century did *nice* come to be used in the variety of senses generally meaning "pleasurable" or "agreeable".
Ni•cene Creed \ˌnī-ˌsēn-\ *n* : a Christian creed issued by the first Council of Nicaea in A.D. 325 and later expanded that begins "I believe in one God" [Late Latin *nicaenus* "of Nicaea"]
nice–nel•ly \ˈnīs-ˈnel-ē\ *adj, often cap 2d N* **1** : PRUDISH **2** : EUPHEMISTIC [from the name *Nelly*] — **nice nelly** *n, often cap 2d N* — **nice–nel•ly•ism** \-ˌiz-əm\ *n, often cap 2d N*
ni•ce•ty \ˈnī-sət-ē, -stē\ *n, pl* **-ties** **1** : a dainty, delicate, or elegant thing ⟨the *niceties* of life⟩ **2** : a small point : a fine detail ⟨the *niceties* of manners⟩ **3** : careful attention to details ⟨the greatest *nicety* is needed in making watches⟩ **4** : the point at which a thing is at its best ⟨roasted to a *nicety*⟩
^{1}**niche** \ˈnich\ *n* **1 a** :a recess in a wall especially for a statue **b** : something that resembles a niche **2** : a place, use, or work for which a person is best fitted **3** : the ecological role of an organism in a community [French, from Middle French *nicher* "to nest", from Latin *nidus* "nest"]
^{2}**niche** *vt* : to place in a niche
^{1}**nick** \ˈnik\ *n* **1** : a small groove, notch, or cut **2** : CHIP ⟨a *nick* in a cup⟩ **3** : the final critical moment ⟨in the *nick* of time⟩ [Middle English *nyke*]
^{2}**nick** *vb* **1 a** : to make a nick in : NOTCH, CHIP **b** : to wound or cut slightly ⟨a bullet *nicked* my leg⟩ **2** : to make petty attacks : SNIPE **3** : to complement one another genetically and produce superior offspring
^{1}**nick•el** \ˈnik-əl\ *n* **1** : a silver-white hard malleable ductile metallic chemical element that is capable of a high polish, resistant to corrosion, and used chiefly in alloys and as a catalyst — see ELEMENT table **2 a** *also* **nick•le** : the United States 5-cent piece made of nickel and copper **b** : five cents [derived from German *kupfernickel* "a compound of nickel and arsenic",

probably from *kupfer* "copper" + *nickel* "goblin"; from the deceptive copper color of the ore]

[2]**nick•el** *vb* **-eled** *or* **-elled**; **-el•ing** *or* **-el•ling** \ˈnik-liŋ, -ə-liŋ\ : to plate with nickel

nic•kel•ic \nik-ˈel-ik\ *adj* : of, relating to, or containing nickel especially with a higher valence than two

nick•el•if•er•ous \ˌnik-ə-ˈlif-rəs, -ə-rəs\ *adj* : containing nickel

nick•el•ode•on \ˌnik-ə-ˈlōd-ē-ən\ *n* **1** : a theater presenting entertainment for an admission price of five cents **2** : JUKEBOX [probably from *nickel* + *-odeon* (as in archaic *melodeon* "music hall")]

nick•el•ous \ˈnik-ə-ləs\ *adj* : of, relating to, or containing nickel especially with a valence of two

nickel silver *n* : a silver-white alloy of copper, zinc, and nickel

nick•er \ˈnik-ər\ *vi* **nick•ered**; **nick•er•ing** \ˈnik-riŋ, -ə-riŋ\ : to neigh gently : WHINNY [perhaps alteration of *neigh*] — **nicker** *n*

nick•nack *variant of* KNICKKNACK

[1]**nick•name** \ˈnik-ˌnām\ *n* **1** : a usually descriptive name given instead of or in addition to the one belonging to an individual **2** : a familiar form of a proper name [Middle English *nekename* "additional name", the phrase *an ekename* (from *eke* "addition" + *name*) being understood as *a nekename*]

△ **origin** *Nickname* was earliest used for a descriptive name given to a person, or even a place, in addition to the proper name. Today it can also mean "a shortened or familiar form of a proper name". In Middle English the word expressed the first of these senses very explicitly. The noun *eke,* meaning "an addition or extension", was combined with *name,* and an *ekename* was an additional name. By the 15th century *an ekename* began to be *a nekename,* in modern spelling *a nickname.* The Middle English noun *eke* is related to the verb *eke,* as in "eke out a living".

[2]**nickname** *vt* **1** : MISCALL **2** : to give a nickname to — **nick•nam•er** *n*

ni•co•ti•ana \nik-ˌō-shē-ˈan-ə, -ˈän-ə, -ˈā-nə\ *n* : any of several tobaccos grown for their showy flowers [Jean *Nicot,* died 1600, French diplomat and scholar who introduced tobacco into France]

nic•o•tin•amide \ˌnik-ə-ˈtē-nə-ˌmīd, -ˈtin-ə-\ *n* : a compound of the vitamin B complex found especially as a constituent of coenzymes and used similarly to nicotinic acid

nic•o•tin•amide–ad•e•nine di•nu•cle•o•tide \ˌnik-ə-ˈtē-nə-ˌmīd-ˌad-n-ˌēn-dī-ˈnü-klē-ə-ˌtīd, -ˈnyü-\ *n* : NAD

nicotinamide–adenine dinucleotide phos•phate \-ˈfäs-ˌfāt\ *n* : NADP

nic•o•tine \ˈnik-ə-ˌtēn\ *n* : a poisonous alkaloid that is the chief active principle of tobacco and is used as an insecticide

nic•o•tin•ic \ˌnik-ə-ˈtē-nik, -ˈtin-ik\ *adj* : of or relating to nicotine or nicotinic acid

nicotinic acid *n* : an organic acid of the vitamin B complex found widely in animals and plants and used especially against pellagra — called also *niacin*

nic•ti•tat•ing membrane \ˌnik-tə-ˌtāt-iŋ-\ *n* : a thin membrane found in many animals at the inner angle or beneath the lower lid of the eye and capable of extending across the eyeball [derived from Latin *nictare* "to wink"]

niece \ˈnēs\ *n* : a daughter of one's brother, sister, brother-in-law, or sister-in-law [Old French, "granddaughter, niece", from Late Latin *neptia,* from Latin *neptis*]

nif•ty \ˈnif-tē\ *adj* **nif•ti•er**; **-est** : FINE, SWELL ⟨*nifty* new clothes⟩ [origin unknown] — **nifty** *n*

nig•gard \ˈnig-ərd\ *n* : a meanly covetous and stingy person [of Scandinavian origin] — **niggard** *adj*

nig•gard•ly \-lē\ *adj* **1** : grudgingly reluctant to spend or grant : STINGY **2** : provided in meanly limited supply : SCANTY — **nig•gard•li•ness** *n* — **niggardly** *adv*

nig•gling \ˈnig-liŋ, -ə-liŋ\ *adj* **1** : PETTY 2 **2** : demanding meticulous care [from earlier *niggle* "to carp", of unknown origin] — **niggling** *n* — **nig•gling•ly** \-lē\ *adv*

[1]**nigh** \ˈnī\ *adv* **1** : near in place, time, or relationship **2** : NEARLY, ALMOST [Old English *nēah*]

[2]**nigh** *adj* **1** : not far : NEAR **2** : being on the left side ⟨the *nigh* horse⟩

[3]**nigh** *prep* : NEAR

[4]**nigh** *vb* : to draw near : APPROACH

night \ˈnīt\ *n* **1** : the time between dusk and dawn when there is no sunlight **2** : the beginning of darkness : NIGHTFALL **3** : the darkness of night [Old English *niht*]

night blindness *n* : subnormal vision in faint light (as at night) — **night–blind** \ˈnīt-ˌblīnd\ *adj*

night–blooming cereus *n* : any of several night-blooming cacti; *esp* : a slender sprawling or climbing cactus often grown for its large showy fragrant white flowers

night•cap \ˈnīt-ˌkap\ *n* **1** : a cloth cap worn with nightclothes **2** : a usually alcoholic drink taken at bedtime **3** : the final race or contest of a day's sports; *esp* : the final game of a baseball doubleheader

night•clothes \-ˌklōz, -ˌklōt͟hz\ *n pl* : clothing worn in bed

night•club \-ˌkləb\ *n* : a place of entertainment open at night that usually serves food and liquor, has a floor show, and provides music and space for dancing

night crawler *n* : EARTHWORM; *esp* : a large earthworm that often occurs on the soil surface at night

night•dress \ˈnīt-ˌdres\ *n* **1** : NIGHTGOWN **2** : NIGHTCLOTHES

night•fall \-ˌfȯl\ *n* : the coming of night

night•gown \-ˌgau̇n\ *n* : a loose garment worn in bed

night•hawk \-ˌhȯk\ *n* **1** : any of several goatsuckers that resemble the related whippoorwill **2** : NIGHT OWL

night•ie \ˈnīt-ē\ *n* : a nightgown for a woman or a child [*nightgown* + *-ie*]

night•in•gale \ˈnīt-n-ˌgāl\ *n* : any of several Old World thrushes noted for the sweet usually nocturnal song of the male [Old English *nihtegale,* from *niht* "night" + *galan* "to sing"]

nightingale

night•jar \ˈnīt-ˌjär\ *n* : a common grayish brown European goatsucker; *also* : GOATSUCKER [from its harsh sound]

night latch *n* : a door lock having a spring bolt operated from the outside by a key and from the inside by a knob

night letter *n* : a telegram sent at night at a reduced rate for delivery the following morning — compare DAY LETTER

[1]**night•long** \ˈnīt-ˌlȯŋ\ *adj* : lasting the whole night

[2]**night•long** \-ˈlȯŋ\ *adv* : through the whole night

night•ly \ˈnīt-lē\ *adj* **1** : of or relating to the night or every night **2** : happening, done, or produced by night or every night — **nightly** *adv*

night•mare \-ˌmaər, -ˌmeər\ *n* **1** : a horribly frightening dream **2** : an experience, situation, or object having the monstrous character of a nightmare or producing a feeling of anxiety or terror [Middle English "evil spirit thought to oppress people during sleep", from *night* + *mare* "incubus", from Old English] — **night•mar•ish** \-ish\ *adj*

night owl *n* : a person who habitually stays up late

night rider *n* : a member of a secret band who ride masked at night doing acts of violence for the purpose of punishing or terrorizing

night–robe \ˈnīt-ˌrōb\ *n* : NIGHTGOWN

nights \ˈnīts\ *adv* : in the nighttime repeatedly ⟨getting a degree by going to school *nights*⟩

night•shade \ˈnīt-ˌshād\ *n* **1** : any of a genus of herbs, shrubs, and trees having alternate leaves, cymes of usually white, yellow, or purple flowers, and fruits that are berries and including many poisonous forms and important food plants (as the potato, tomato, and eggplant) **2** : BELLADONNA 1

night•shirt \-ˌshərt\ *n* : a nightgown resembling a shirt

night•stick \-ˌstik\ *n* : a police officer's club : BILLY

night•tide \ˈnīt-ˌtīd\ *n* : NIGHTTIME

night•time \ˈnīt-ˌtīm\ *n* : the time from dusk to dawn

night•walk•er \-ˌwȯ-kər\ *n* : a person who roves about at night especially with criminal or immoral intent

ni•gri•tude \ˈnī-grə-ˌtüd, ˈnig-rə-, -ˌtyüd\ *n* : intense darkness : BLACKNESS [Latin *nigritudo,* from *niger* "black"]

ni•hil•ism \ˈnī-ə-ˌliz-əm, ˈnē-\ *n* : a doctrine or belief that condi-

\ə\ **abut**	\au̇\ **out**	\i\ **tip**	\ȯ\ **saw**	\u̇\ **foot**
\ər\ **further**	\ch\ **chin**	\ī\ **life**	\ȯi\ **coin**	\y\ **yet**
\a\ **mat**	\e\ **pet**	\j\ **job**	\th\ **thin**	\yü\ **few**
\ā\ **take**	\ē\ **easy**	\ŋ\ **sing**	\t͟h\ **this**	\yu̇\ **cure**
\ä\ **cot, cart**	\g\ **go**	\ō\ **bone**	\ü\ **food**	\zh\ **vision**

tions in the social organization are so bad as to make destruction desirable for its own sake independent of any constructive program [German *nihilismus,* from Latin *nihil* "nothing"] — **ni•hil•ist** \-ə-ləst\ *n* — **nihilist** *or* **ni•hil•is•tic** \ˌnī-ə-'lis-tik, ˌnē-\ *adj*

ni•hil•i•ty \nī-'hil-ət-ē, nē-\ *n* : NOTHINGNESS

ni•hil ob•stat \ˌnī-ˌhil-'äb-ˌstät, ˌnē-ˌhil-, ˌnik-ˌil-, -ˌstat\ *n* : authoritative or official approval (as of a censor) [Latin, "nothing hinders"]

-nik \nik\ *n suffix* : one connected with or characterized by being ⟨beat*nik*⟩ [Yiddish, from Russian and Polish]

nil \'nil\ *n* : nothing at all : ZERO [Latin, "nothing", contraction of *nihil*] — **nil** *adj*

nile green \'nīl-\ *n, often cap N* : a pale yellow green [*Nile* river, Africa]

Ni•lot•ic \nī-'lät-ik\ *adj* : of or relating to the Nile or the peoples of the Nile basin

nim•ble \'nim-bəl\ *adj* **nim•bler** \-bə-lər, -blər\; **-blest** \-bə-ləst, -bləst\ **1** : quick and light in motion : AGILE ⟨a *nimble* dancer⟩ **2** : quick in understanding and learning : CLEVER ⟨a *nimble* mind⟩ [Old English *numol* "holding much", from *niman* "to take"] — **nim•ble•ness** \-bəl-nəs\ *n* — **nim•bly** \-blē\ *adv*

nim•bo•stra•tus \ˌnim-bō-'strāt-əs, -'strat-\ *n* : a low dark gray cloud layer that usually produces precipitation

nim•bus \'nim-bəs\ *n, pl* **nim•bi** \-ˌbī, -ˌbē\ *or* **nim•bus•es** **1** : a luminous vapor, cloud, or atmosphere about a god or goddess when on earth **2** : an indication (as a circle) of radiant light or glory about the head of a drawn or sculptured divinity, saint, or sovereign **3** : a rain cloud that is of uniform grayness and extends over the entire sky [Latin, "rainstorm, cloud"]

nimbus 2

nim•rod \'nim-ˌräd\ *n, often cap* : HUNTER 1a [*Nimrod,* grandson of Noah]

nin•com•poop \'nin-kəm-ˌpüp, 'ning-\ *n* : SIMPLETON, BOOBY [origin unknown]

nine \'nīn\ *n* **1** : one more than eight; *also* : a symbol representing this — see NUMBER table **2** : the ninth in a set or series **3** : something having nine units or members [Old English *nigon*] — **nine** *adj or pron*

nine days' wonder *n* : something that creates a short-lived sensation

nine•pin \'nīn-ˌpin\ *n* **1** : a pin used in ninepins **2** *pl* : a bowling game resembling tenpins played with nine pins in a diamond arrangement

nine•teen \nīn-'tēn, nīnt-, 'nīn-, 'nīnt-\ *n* : one more than 18; *also* : a symbol representing this — see NUMBER table [Old English *nigontēne*] — **nineteen** *adj or pron* — **nine•teenth** \-'tēnth, -'tēntth\ *adj or n*

nine•ty \'nīnt-ē\ *n, pl* **nineties** : ten more than 80; *also* : a symbol representing this — see NUMBER table [Old English *nigontig*] — **ninety** *adj or pron* — **nine•ti•eth** \-ē-əth\ *adj or n*

nin•ny \'nin-ē\ *n, pl* **ninnies** : FOOL 1, SIMPLETON [perhaps from *an innocent*]

nin•ny•ham•mer \'nin-ē-ˌham-ər\ *n* : NINNY

ninth \'nīnth, 'nīntth\ *n, pl* **ninths** \'nīns, 'nīnts, 'nīnths, 'nīntths\ **1** : number nine in a countable series — see NUMBER table **2 a** : a musical interval embracing an octave and a second **b** : a chord containing a ninth — **ninth** *adj or adv*

ni•o•bi•um \nī-'ō-bē-əm\ *n* : a lustrous platinum-gray ductile metallic chemical element that is used in alloys — see ELEMENT table [New Latin, from *Niobe,* a daughter of Tantalus; from its occurrence in ores with tantalum]

1nip \'nip\ *vb* **nipped**; **nip•ping** **1** : to catch hold of and squeeze tightly between two surfaces, edges, or points ⟨the dog *nipped* my ankle⟩ **2 a** : to sever by or as if by pinching sharply **b** : to destroy the growth, progress, maturing, or fulfillment of ⟨*nipped* the conspiracy in the bud⟩ **3** : to injure or make numb with cold : CHILL **4** : STEAL ⟨*nipped* the dessert⟩ **5** *chiefly British* : to move briskly, nimbly, or quickly [Middle English *nippen*]

2nip *n* **1** : something that nips: as **a** : a sharp stinging cold **b** : a biting or pungent flavor : TANG **2** : the act of nipping : PINCH, BITE **3** : a small portion : BIT

3nip *n* : a small quantity of liquor ⟨takes a *nip* now and then⟩ [probably from *nipperkin,* a liquor container, of unknown origin]

4nip *vi* **nipped**; **nip•ping** : to take liquor in nips : TIPPLE

ni•pa \'nē-pə\ *n* **1** : an alcoholic drink made from the juice of an Australasian creeping palm; *also* : this palm **2** : thatch made of nipa leaves [probably from Italian, from Malay *nipah* "nipa palm"]

nip and tuck \ˌnip-ən-'tək\ *adj or adv* : so close that the lead or advantage shifts rapidly from one contestant to another

nip•per \'nip-ər\ *n* **1** : a device (as pincers) for nipping — usually used in pl. **2** : CHELA **3** *chiefly British* : CHILD; *esp* : a small boy

nip•ple \'nip-əl\ *n* **1** : the protuberance of a mammary gland upon which the ducts open and from which milk is drawn **2** : something resembling a nipple; *esp* : the mouthpiece of a baby's nursing bottle [earlier *neble, nible,* probably from *neb, nib*]

Nip•pon•ese \ˌnip-ə-'nēz, -'nēs\ *adj* : JAPANESE 1 [*Nippon* (Japan)] — **Nipponese** *n*

nip•py \'nip-ē\ *adj* **nip•pi•er**; **-est** **1** : brisk, quick, or nimble in movement **2** : CHILLY, CHILLING ⟨a *nippy* day⟩

nir•va•na \niər-'vän-ə, nər-\ *n, often cap* **1** : the final beatitude that transcends suffering, karma, and samsara and is sought in Hinduism and Buddhism through the extinction of desire and individual consciousness **2** : a place or state of oblivion to care, pain, or external reality [Sanskrit *nirvāna,* literally, "act of extinguishing"]

ni•sei \nē-'sā, 'nē-\ *n, pl* **nisei** *also* **niseis** : a son or daughter of immigrant Japanese parents who is born and educated in America [Japanese, literally, "second generation"]

Nis•sen hut \ˌnis-n-\ *n* : a prefabricated shelter built of a semicircular arching roof of corrugated iron and a cement floor [Peter N. *Nissen,* died 1930, British mining engineer]

nit \'nit\ *n* : the egg of a louse or other parasitic insect; *also* : the insect itself when young [Old English *hnitu*]

ni•ter *also* **ni•tre** \'nīt-ər\ *n* **1** : POTASSIUM NITRATE **2** : SODIUM NITRATE [Middle French *nitre* "sodium carbonate", from Latin *nitrum,* from Greek *nitron,* from Egyptian *ntry*]

nit•pick \'nit-ˌpik\ *vi* : to engage in nit-picking — **nit•pick•er** *n*

nit–pick•ing \'nit-ˌpik-ing\ *n* : minute and usually unjustified criticism

nitr- *or* **nitro-** *combining form* **1** : niter : nitrate **2 a** : nitrogen ⟨*nitr*ide⟩ **b** *usually* **nitro-** : containing the univalent group $-NO_2$ composed of one nitrogen and two oxygen atoms ⟨*nitro*benzene⟩

1ni•trate \'nī-ˌtrāt, -trət\ *n* **1** : a salt or ester of nitric acid **2** : sodium nitrate or potassium nitrate used as a fertilizer

2ni•trate \-ˌtrāt\ *vt* : to treat or combine with nitric acid or a nitrate — **ni•tra•tion** \nī-'trā-shən\ *n* — **ni•tra•tor** \'nī-ˌtrāt-ər\ *n*

nitrate bacterium *n* : a bacterium functioning in the nitrogen cycle to convert nitrites to nitrates — compare NITRITE BACTERIUM

ni•tric \'nī-trik\ *adj* : of, relating to, or containing nitrogen especially with a higher valence than in corresponding nitrous compounds

nitric acid *n* : a corrosive liquid acid HNO_3 used especially as an oxidizing agent, in nitrations, and in making fertilizers, explosives, and dyes

nitric oxide *n* : a colorless poisonous gas NO obtained by oxidation of nitrogen or ammonia

ni•tride \'nī-ˌtrīd\ *n* : a compound of nitrogen with a more electropositive element

ni•tri•fi•ca•tion \ˌnī-trə-fə-'kā-shən\ *n* : the process of combining or impregnating with nitrogen or a nitrogen compound; *esp* : the oxidation (as by bacteria) of ammonium salts to nitrites and the further oxidation of nitrites to nitrates

ni•tri•fi•er \'nī-trə-ˌfī-ər, -ˌfīr\ *n* : any of various soil organisms capable of nitrification

ni•tri•fy•ing \-ˌfī-ing\ *adj* : active in nitrification

ni•trite \'nī-ˌtrīt\ *n* : a salt or ester of nitrous acid

nitrite bacterium *n* : a bacterium functioning in the nitrogen cycle to convert ammonium compounds to nitrites — compare NITRATE BACTERIUM

ni•tro \'nī-trō\ *n* **:** any of various nitrated products; *esp* **:** NITROGLYCERIN

ni•tro•ben•zene \ˌnī-trō-'ben-ˌzēn, -ˌben-'\ *n* **:** a poisonous insoluble oil made by nitration of benzene and used as a solvent, oxidizing agent, and source of aniline

ni•tro•cel•lu•lose \-'sel-yə-ˌlōs\ *n* **:** CELLULOSE NITRATE — **ni•tro•cel•lu•los•ic** \-ˌsel-yə-'lō-sik\ *adj*

ni•tro•gen \'nī-trə-jən\ *n* **:** a colorless tasteless odorless gaseous chemical element that constitutes 78 percent of the atmosphere by volume and is a constituent of all living tissues — see ELEMENT table [French *nitrogène,* from *nitre* "niter" + *-gène* "-gen"] — **ni•trog•e•nous** \nī-'träj-ə-nəs\ *adj*

nitrogen balance *n* **:** the ratio between nitrogen intake and nitrogen loss of the body or the soil

nitrogen cycle *n* **:** a continuous series of natural processes by which nitrogen passes successively from air to soil to organisms and back involving principally nitrogen fixation, nitrification, decay, and denitrification

nitrogen dioxide *n* **:** a brownish to yellowish poisonous gas NO_2 that is used especially in making nitric acid and in nitration and is an air pollutant formed in the oxidation of automobile exhausts

nitrogen fixation *n* **:** the conversion of free nitrogen into combined forms especially by microorganisms in soil and root nodules and its subsequent release in a form fit for plant use

nitrogen–fixing *adj* **:** capable of nitrogen fixation ⟨*nitrogen-fixing* bacteria⟩ — **nitrogen–fixer** *n*

nitrogen mustard *n* **:** any of various toxic blistering compounds that are analogous to mustard gas but with nitrogen replacing sulfur

ni•tro•glyc•er•in *or* **ni•tro•glyc•er•ine** \ˌnī-trō-'glis-rən, -ə-rən\ *n* **:** a heavy oily explosive poisonous liquid obtained by nitrating glycerol and used chiefly in making dynamites and in medicine to expand blood vessels

ni•trous \'nī-trəs\ *adj* **1 :** of, relating to, or containing niter **2 :** of, relating to, or containing nitrogen especially with a lower valence than in corresponding nitric compounds

nitrous acid *n* **:** an unstable acid HNO_2 known only in solution or in the form of its salts

nitrous oxide *n* **:** a colorless gas N_2O that when inhaled produces loss of sensibility to pain preceded by exhilaration and sometimes laughter and is often used as an anesthetic in dentistry — called also *laughing gas*

nit•ty–grit•ty \'nit-ē-ˌgrit-ē, ˌnit-ē-'grit-ē\ *n* **:** what is essential and basic **:** specific practical details [origin unknown] — **nitty–gritty** *adj*

nit•wit \'nit-ˌwit\ *n* **:** a scatterbrained or stupid person [probably from German dialect *nit* "not" + English *wit*]

1**nix** \'niks\ *n* **:** a water sprite of Germanic folklore [German]

2**nix** *adv* **:** NO — used to express disagreement or the withholding of permission [German *nichts* "nothing"]

3**nix** *vt* **:** VETO, FORBID ⟨the court *nixed* the merger⟩

nix•ie \'nik-sē\ *n* **:** NIX [German *nixe* "female nix"]

ni•zam \ni-'zäm, 'nī-ˌzam, nī-'\ *n* **:** one of a line of sovereigns of Hyderabad from 1713 to 1950 [Hindi *niẓām* "order, governor", from Arabic *niẓām*] — **ni•zam•ate** \-ˌāt\ *n*

1**no** \nō, 'nō\ *adv* **1 a :** *chiefly Scottish* **:** NOT **b —** used to express the negative of an alternative choice or possibility ⟨shall we continue or *no*⟩ **2 :** in no respect or degree — used in comparisons ⟨they are *no* better than they should be⟩ **3 :** not so — used to express negation, dissent, denial, or refusal ⟨*no,* I'm not hungry⟩ **4 —** used with a following adjective to imply a meaning expressed by the opposite positive statement ⟨*no* uncertain terms⟩ **5 —** used to introduce a word that is stronger or more emphatic than the preceding one ⟨has the right, *no,* the duty to continue⟩ **6 —** used as an interjection to express surprise, doubt, or incredulity ⟨*no* — you don't say⟩ [Old English *nā,* from *ne* "not" + *ā* "always"]

2**no** *adj* **1 a :** not any ⟨I've *no* money⟩ **b :** hardly any **:** very little ⟨finished in *no* time⟩ **2 :** not a **:** quite other than a ⟨I'm *no* expert⟩

3**no** \'nō\ *n, pl* **noes** *or* **nos** \'nōz\ **1 :** an act or instance of refusing or denying by the use of the word *no* **:** DENIAL **2 a :** a negative vote or decision **b** *pl* **:** persons voting in the negative

nob \'näb\ *n, chiefly British* **:** one in a superior position in life [perhaps from earlier *nob* "head", probably from *knob*]

nob•by \'näb-ē\ *adj* **nob•bi•er; -est :** of the first quality or style **:** SMART

no•bel•i•um \nō-'bel-ē-əm\ *n* **:** a radioactive chemical element produced artificially — see ELEMENT table [Alfred B. *Nobel*]

No•bel prize \nō-ˌbel-\ *n* **:** any of various annual prizes (as in peace, literature, medicine) established by the will of Alfred Nobel for the encouragement of persons who work for the interests of humanity

no•bil•i•ty \nō-'bil-ət-ē\ *n, pl* **-ties 1 :** the quality or state of being noble ⟨*nobility* of character⟩ **2 :** noble rank ⟨confer *nobility* on a person⟩ **3 :** a class or group of nobles ⟨the British *nobility*⟩ [Middle French *nobilité,* from Latin *nobilitas,* from *nobilis* "noble"]

1**no•ble** \'nō-bəl\ *adj* **no•bler** \-bə-lər, -blər\; **no•blest** \-bə-ləst, -bləst\ **1 a :** having outstanding qualities **:** ILLUSTRIOUS ⟨a *noble* warrior⟩ **b :** FAMOUS, NOTABLE ⟨*noble* deeds⟩ **2 :** of high birth or exalted rank **:** ARISTOCRATIC **3 :** having fine qualities ⟨a *noble* hawk⟩ **4 :** grand or impressive especially in appearance **:** IMPOSING ⟨a *noble* edifice⟩ **5 :** having or characterized by superiority of mind or character **:** LOFTY ⟨*noble* aims⟩ **6 :** chemically inert or inactive especially toward oxygen ⟨a *noble* metal⟩ [Old French, from Latin *nobilis* "knowable, well known, noble", from *noscere* "to come to know"] — **no•ble•ness** \-bəl-nəs\ *n* — **no•bly** \-blē\ *adv*

2**noble** *n* **:** a person of noble rank or birth

no•ble•man \'nō-bəl-mən\ *n* **:** a man of the nobility

no•blesse oblige \nō-ˌbles-ə-'blēzh\ *n* **:** the obligation to behave honorably that is associated with high rank or birth [French, literally, "nobility obligates"]

no•ble•wom•an \'nō-bəl-ˌwu̇m-ən\ *n* **:** a woman of the nobility

1**no•body** \'nō-ˌbäd-ē, -bəd-ē\ *pron* **:** no person **:** not anybody

2**nobody** *n, pl* **no•bod•ies :** a person of no influence or importance

1**nock** \'näk\ *n* **:** a notch on the end of a bow or in an arrow in which the bowstring fits [Middle English *nocke* "notch on the end of a bow"]

2**nock** *vt* **1 :** to make a nock in (a bow or an arrow) **2 :** to fit (an arrow) against the bowstring for shooting

noc•ti•lu•ca \ˌnäk-tə-'lü-kə\ *n* **:** any of a genus of marine luminescent flagellates that often cause phosphorescence of the sea [Latin, "something that shines by night", from *noct-, nox* "night" + *lucēre* "to shine"]

noc•tur•nal \näk-'tərn-l\ *adj* **1 :** of, relating to, or occurring in the night ⟨a *nocturnal* journey⟩ **2 :** active at night ⟨*nocturnal* insects⟩ [Late Latin *nocturnalis,* from Latin *nocturnus,* from *noct-, nox* "night"] — **noc•tur•nal•ly** \-l-ē\ *adv*

noc•turne \'näk-ˌtərn\ *n* **:** a work of art dealing with night; *esp* **:** a dreamy pensive composition for the piano [French, "nocturnal", from Latin *nocturnus*]

noc•u•ous \'näk-yə-wəs\ *adj* **:** likely to cause injury **:** HARMFUL [Latin *nocuus,* from *nocēre* "to harm"] — **noc•u•ous•ly** *adv*

1**nod** \'näd\ *vb* **nod•ded; nod•ding 1 :** to make a quick downward motion of the head (as in answering "yes" or in going to sleep); *also* **:** to cause (the head) to move in this way **2 :** to move up and down ⟨the tulips *nodded* in the breeze⟩ **3 :** to show by a nod of the head ⟨*nod* agreement⟩ **4 :** to make a slip or an error in a moment of inattention [Middle English *nodden*] — **nod•der** *n*

2**nod** *n* **:** the action of nodding

nod•dle \'näd-l\ *n* **:** HEAD 1 [Middle English *nodle* "back of the head or neck"]

nod•dy \'näd-ē\ *n, pl* **nod•dies 1 :** a stupid person **2 :** any of several stout-bodied terns of warm seas [probably from obsolete *noddypoll*]

node \'nōd\ *n* **1 :** an entangling complication (as in a drama) **2 a :** a thickened or swollen enlargement (as of a rheumatic joint) **b :** a discrete mass of one kind of tissue enclosed in tissue of a different kind **3**

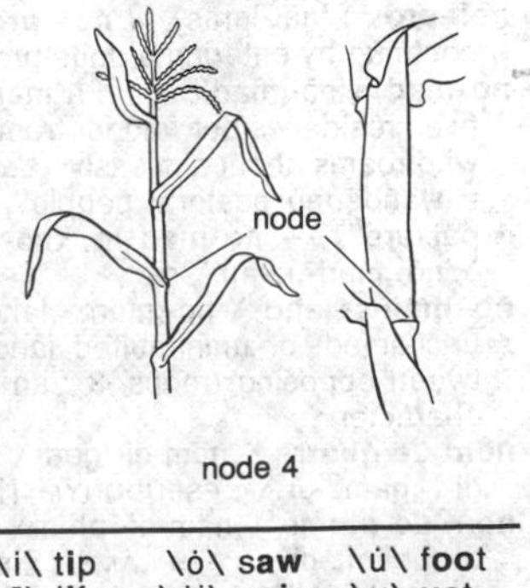

node 4

\ə\ **abut**	\au̇\ **out**	\i\ **tip**	\ȯ\ **saw**	\u̇\ **foot**
\ər\ **further**	\ch\ **chin**	\ī\ **life**	\ȯi\ **coin**	\y\ **yet**
\a\ **mat**	\e\ **pet**	\j\ **job**	\th\ **thin**	\yü\ **few**
\ā\ **take**	\ē\ **easy**	\ng\ **sing**	\t͟h\ **this**	\yu̇\ **cure**
\ä\ **cot, cart**	\g\ **go**	\ō\ **bone**	\ü\ **food**	\zh\ **vision**

: either of the two points where the orbit of a planet or comet intersects the ecliptic **4 :** a point on a stem at which a leaf is attached **5 :** a part of a vibrating body marked by absolute or relative freedom from vibratory motion [Latin *nodus* "knot, node"] — **nod•al** \ˈnōd-l\ *adj*

no•di•cal \ˈnōd-i-kəl, ˈnäd-\ *adj* **:** of or relating to astronomical nodes

nod•ule \ˈnäj-ül\ *n* **:** a small mass of rounded or irregular shape: as **a :** a small rounded lump of a mineral or mineral aggregate **b :** a swelling on the root of a legume that contains nitrogen-fixing bacteria — **nod•u•lar** \ˈnäj-ə-lər\ *adj*

no•el \nō-ˈel\ *n* **1 :** a Christmas carol **2** *cap* **:** the Christmas season [French *noël* "Christmas, carol", from Latin *natalis* "birthday", from *natalis* "natal"]

noes *pl of* NO

nog \ˈnäg\ *n* **1 :** a strong ale formerly brewed in Norfolk, England **2 :** EGGNOG [origin unknown]

nog•gin \ˈnäg-ən\ *n* **1 :** a small mug or cup **2 :** a small quantity of drink usually equivalent to a gill (about .1 liter) **3 :** HEAD 1 [origin unknown]

¹no–good \ˌnō-ˌgu̇d\ *adj* **:** having no worth, use, or chance of success

²no–good \ˈnō-ˌgu̇d\ *n* **:** a no-good person or thing

no•how \ˈnō-ˌhau̇\ *adv* **:** in no manner or way ⟨*nohow* up to the job⟩

¹noise \ˈnȯiz\ *n* **1 :** loud, confused, or senseless shouting or outcry **2 a :** SOUND; *esp* **:** one that lacks agreeable musical quality or is noticeably unpleasant **b :** an unwanted signal in an electronic communication system [Old French, "strife, quarrel, noise", from Latin *nausea* "seasickness, nausea"] — **noise•less** \-ləs\ *adj* — **noise•less•ly** *adv* — **noise•less•ness** *n*

△ **origin** The commotion and complaints so often associated with sufferers of seasickness have given us the word *noise*, a derivative of Latin *nausea*, which means "seasickness" or "nausea". The form *noise* developed in Old French, with the meanings "noisy strife", "quarrel", and "noise". Today in English *noise* may be used of sound in general, but it most often denotes disagreeable or undesirable sound.

²noise *vt* **:** to spread by rumor or report

noise•mak•er \-ˌmā-kər\ *n* **:** one that makes noise; *esp* **:** a device used to make noise at parties

noise pollution *n* **:** environmental pollution consisting of annoying or harmful noise (as of jet planes) — called also *sound pollution*

noi•some \ˈnȯi-səm\ *adj* **1 :** UNHEALTHY 1, NOXIOUS **2 :** offensive especially to the sense of smell [Middle English *noysome*, from *noy* "annoyance", from Old French *enui*, from *enuier* "to annoy"] — **noi•some•ly** *adv* — **noi•some•ness** *n*

noisy \ˈnȯi-zē\ *adj* **nois•i•er; -est 1 :** making noise **2 :** full of or characterized by noise — **nois•i•ly** \-zə-lē\ *adv* — **nois•i•ness** \-zē-nəs\ *n*

nol•le pro•se•qui \ˌnäl-ē-ˈpräs-ə-ˌkwī\ *n* **:** an entry on the record of a legal action that the prosecutor or plaintiff will proceed no further in an action or suit [Latin, "to be unwilling to pursue"]

no•lo con•ten•de•re \ˌnō-lō-kən-ˈten-də-rē\ *n* **:** a plea by the defendant in a criminal prosecution that without admitting guilt subjects him or her to conviction but does not preclude denial of the charges in another proceeding [Latin, "I do not wish to contend"]

nol–pros \ˈnäl-ˈpräs\ *vt* **nol–prossed; nol–pros•sing :** to discontinue by entering a nolle prosequi

no•mad \ˈnō-ˌmad\ *n* **1 :** a member of a people that have no fixed residence but wander from place to place **2 :** an individual who roams about aimlessly [Latin *nomad-*, *nomas* "member of a wandering pastoral people", from Greek, from *nemein* "to pasture"] — **no•mad•ic** \nō-ˈmad-ik\ *adj* — **no•mad•ism** \ˈnō-ˌmad-ˌiz-əm\ *n*

no–man's–land \ˈnō-ˌmanz-ˌland\ *n* **1 :** an area of unowned, unclaimed, or uninhabited land **2 :** an unoccupied area between opposing troops **3 :** an area of indefinite or uncertain character

nom de guerre \ˌnäm-di-ˈgeər\ *n, pl* **noms de guerre** \ˌnäm-di-, ˌnämz-di-\ **:** PSEUDONYM [French, literally, "war name"]

nom de plume \ˌnäm-di-ˈplüm\ *n, pl* **noms de plume** \ˌnäm-di-, ˌnämz-di-\ **:** PEN NAME [French *nom* "name" + *de* "of" + *plume* "pen"]

no•men \ˈnō-mən\ *n, pl* **no•mi•na** \ˈnäm-ə-nə, ˈnō-mə-\ **:** the second of the usual three names of an ancient Roman [Latin, literally, "name"]

no•men•cla•ture \ˈnō-mən-ˌklā-chər\ *n* **1 :** NAME 1, DESIGNATION **2 :** a system of terms used in a particular science, discipline, or art; *esp* **:** the standardized New Latin names used in biology for kinds and groups of kinds of plants and animals [Latin *nomenclatura* "calling by name, list of names", from *nomen* "name" + *calare* "to call"] — **no•men•cla•tur•al** \ˌnō-mən-ˈklāch-rəl, -ə-rəl\ *adj*

¹nom•i•nal \ˈnäm-ən-l, ˈnäm-nəl\ *adj* **1 :** of, relating to, or being a noun or a word or expression taking a noun construction **2 :** of, relating to, or being a name **3 a :** existing or being something in name or form only ⟨the *nominal* head of the party⟩ **b :** very small **:** TRIFLING ⟨a *nominal* price⟩ [Latin *nominalis* "of a name", from Latin *nomen* "name"] — **nom•i•nal•ly** \-ē\ *adv*

²nominal *n* **:** a word or word group functioning as a noun

nom•i•nate \ˈnäm-ə-ˌnāt\ *vt* **:** to choose as a candidate for election, appointment, or honor; *esp* **:** to propose for office ⟨was *nominated* for president⟩ [Latin *nominare* "to name", from *nomen* "name"] — **nom•i•na•tor** \-ˌnāt-ər\ *n*

nom•i•na•tion \ˌnäm-ə-ˈnā-shən\ *n* **1 :** the act, process, or an instance of nominating **2 :** the state of being nominated ⟨three names have been placed in *nomination*⟩

nom•i•na•tive \ˈnäm-nət-iv, -ə-nət-\ *adj* **:** relating to or being a grammatical case marking typically the subject of a verb — **nominative** *n*

nom•i•nee \ˌnäm-ə-ˈnē\ *n* **:** a person who has been nominated

non- *before syllables with primary stress* nän, ˈnän *also* ˌnən, ˈnən; *before syllables with secondary or weak stress* ˌnän *also* ˌnən\ *prefix* **:** not **:** reverse of **:** absence of ⟨*non*calcareous⟩ [Middle French, from Latin *non* "not"]

See *non-* and 2d element

nonabrasive
nonabrupt
nonabsorbable
nonabsorbent
nonabsorptive
nonabstemious
nonabstract
nonacademic
nonacceptable
nonacceptance
nonaccessible
nonaccountable
nonaccredited
nonacid
nonacidic
nonacquisitive
nonactinic
nonaction
nonactive
nonadaptive
nonaddicted
nonaddicting
nonaddictive
nonadditive
nonadherence
nonadherent
nonadhesion
nonadhesive
nonadjacent
nonadjustable
nonadministrative
nonadmission
nonadolescent
nonaffiliated
nonaffluent
nonaggression
nonaggressive
nonagreement
nonagricultural
nonalcoholic
nonallergenic
nonallergic
nonalphabetic
nonanalytic
nonanthropological
nonantigenic
nonappearance
nonaquatic
nonaqueous
nonarbitrary
nonaromatic
nonascetic
nonaspirated
nonassessable
nonassociative
nonathlete
nonathletic
nonattendance
nonattentive
nonattributive
nonauditory
nonauthoritative
nonautomatic
nonautomotive
nonbacterial
nonbasic
nonbearing
nonbeing
nonbeliever
nonbelieving
nonbelligerency
nonbelligerent
nonbetting
nonbinding
nonbiodegradable
nonbiological
nonbiologist
nonbiting
nonbonded
nonbonding
nonbreakable
nonburnable
noncaking
noncancerous
noncanonical
noncarbohydrate
noncarbonaceous
noncarbonated
noncarnivorous
noncash
noncatalytic
noncellular
noncertified
nonchallenging
nonchargeable
nonchauvinist
nonchosen
non-Christian
nonchurchgoer
noncitizen
nonclassical
nonclassified
nonclerical
nonclinical
nonclotting
noncoagulable
noncoated
noncoercive
noncognitive
noncoherent
noncohesive
noncollapsible
noncollectible
noncollinear
noncolloid
noncombat
noncombining
noncombustible
noncommercial
noncommunicable
noncommunicant
noncommunication
non-Communist
noncommutative
noncommutativity
noncompensating
noncompetent
noncompeting
noncompetition
noncompetitive
noncomplementary
noncompliance
noncomplying
noncompound
noncomprehension
noncompressible
nonconclusive
nonconcurrent
noncondensable
noncondensing
nonconditioned

nonconfidential
nonconflicting
nonconforming
noncongenital
noncongruent
nonconjugated
nonconscious
nonconsecutive
nonconservation
nonconserved
nonconsolidated
nonconstitutional
nonconstructive
nonconsumable
noncontact
noncontagious
noncontemporary
noncontentious
noncontiguous
noncontinuous
noncontraband
noncontradiction
noncontradictory
noncontributing
noncontributory
noncontrollable
noncontrolled
noncontrolling
noncontroversial
nonconventional
nonconvertible
noncoplanar
noncorporate
noncorrectable
noncorrodible
noncorroding
noncorrosive
noncovalent
noncovered
noncreative
noncriminal
noncritical
noncrystalline
noncultivated
noncultivation
noncumulative
noncurrent
noncyclic
noncyclical
nondeceptive
nondecreasing
nondeferrable
nondefining
nondegenerate
nondegenerated
nondegradable
nondelinquent
nondelivery
nondemocratic
nondepartmental
nonderivative
nondestructive
nondeteriorative
nondetonating
nondevelopable
nondevelopment
nondiabetic
nondifferentiation
nondiffusible
nondigestible
nondipolar
nondirectional
nondisclosure
nondiscrimination
nondiscriminatory
nondiscursive
nondisqualifying
nondisruptive
nondistribution
nondivided
nondoctrinaire
nondocumentary
nondogmatic
nondollar
nondomesticated
nondramatic
nondurable
nondynastic
nonecclesiastical
noneducational
noneffective
noneffervescent
nonelastic
nonelected
nonelectric
nonelectrical
nonelectronic
noneligible
nonelite
nonemergency
nonemotional
nonempirical
nonempty
nonencapsulated
nonenforceable
nonenforcement
nonentanglement
nonequal
nonequilateral
nonequilibrium
nonequivalence
nonequivalent
noneruptive
nonessential
nonesterified
nonethical
nonexchangeable
nonexclusive
nonexempt
nonexistence
nonexistent
nonexpendable
nonexperimental
nonexpert
nonexplosive
nonexposed
nonextant
nonfaculty
nonfading
nonfan
nonfarm
nonfarmer
nonfatal
nonfattening
nonfebrile
nonfederal
nonfederated
nonfeeding
nonferromagnetic
nonferrous
nonfilamentous
nonfilterable
nonfinancial
nonfissionable
nonflagellated
nonflammable
nonfluorescent
nonflying
nonforfeiture
nonfossiliferous
nonfraternal
nonfreezing
nonfulfillment
nonfunctional
nongaseous
nongeneric
nongenetic
nonghetto
nonglamorous
nongovernment
nongovernmental
nongraded
nongranular
nongregarious
nongrowing
nonhandicapped
nonhardy
nonharmonic
nonhazardous
nonhelical
nonhereditary
nonheritable
nonhistorical
nonhomogeneous
nonhormonal
nonhostile
nonideal
nonidentical
nonidentity
nonideological
nonimmigrant
nonimmune
nonimmunity
nonincreasing
nonindustrial
nonindustrialized
noninfectious
noninfective
noninfested
noninflammable
noninflammatory
noninflationary
noninflectional
noninformation
noninjurious
noninjury
noninsecticidal
noninstitutional
noninstitutionalized
noninstructional
nonintegral
nonintegrated
nonintellectual
noninterference
nonintersecting
nonintoxicant
nonintoxicating
noninvasive
noninvolvement
nonirradiated
nonirrigated
nonirritating
non-hermal
non-Jew
non-Jewish
nonleaded
nonlegal
nonleguminous
nonlethal
nonlexical
nonlife
nonlinguistic
nonliquid
nonliterary
nonliturgical
nonliving
nonlocal
nonlogical
nonluminous
nonmagnetic
nonmailable
nonmalicious
nonmalignant
nonmalleable
nonmammalian
nonmanagerial
nonmanufacturing
nonmarine
nonmarital
nonmarketable
nonmaterial
nonmaterialistic
nonmathematical
nonmathematician
nonmeaningful
nonmeasurable
nonmechanical
nonmechanistic
nonmedical
nonmember
nonmembership
nonmetered
nonmetric
nonmetrical
nonmetropolitan
nonmicrobial
nonmigratory
nonmilitary
nonmimetic
nonmolecular
nonmoney
nonmotile
nonmotility
nonmoving
nonmusical
nonmutant
nonnarcotic
nonnational
nonnative
nonnatural
nonnaturalism
nonnaturalist
nonnecessity
nonnegotiable
nonnitrogenous
nonnormative
nonnumerical
nonnutritious
nonnutritive
nonobese
nonobligatory
nonobscene
nonobservance
nonobvious
nonoccurrence
nonofficial
nonoily
nonopaque
nonoperating
nonoperational
nonorganic
nonoriented
nonoriginal
nonorthodox
nonorthogonal
nonoscillatory
nonoverlapping
nonpalatal
nonparallel
nonparalytic
nonparasitic
nonparticipant
nonparticipating
nonparticipation
nonparticipatory
nonparty
nonpathogenic
nonpaying
nonpayment
nonpeak
nonpecuniary
nonpenetrating
nonperformance
nonperishable
nonpermanent
nonpermissive
nonpersonal
nonphonemic
nonphonetic
nonphosphatic
nonphotosynthetic
nonphysical
nonphysiological
nonpigmented
nonplastic
nonplaying
nonpoisonous
nonpolarizable
nonpolitical
nonpolluting
nonpoor
nonporosity
nonporous
nonpossession
nonpractical
nonpredicative
nonpregnant
nonprinting
nonproducer
nonprofessional
nonprofessionally
nonprogressive
nonproportional
nonpropositional
nonproprietary
nonprotein
nonproven
nonpsychedelic
nonpublic
nonpungent
nonpunitive
nonquota
nonrabbinic
nonracial
nonracialism
nonracially
nonradiative
nonradical
nonradioactive
nonrandom
nonrandomness
nonrated
nonrational
nonreactive
nonreactivity
nonreactor
nonrealistic
nonreciprocal
nonrecognition
nonrecoverable
nonrecurrent
nonrecurring
nonreducing
nonredundant
nonrefillable
nonregistered
nonregulation
nonrelevant
nonreligious
nonremovable
nonrenewable
nonrepayable
nonrepresentative
nonresidential
nonresonant
nonrespondent
nonresponse
nonresponsive
nonrestraint
nonrestricted
nonretractile
nonretroactive
nonreusable
nonrevenue
nonreversible
nonrhetorical
nonrhombic
nonrioter
nonrioting
nonrotating
nonruminant
non-Russian
nonsalable
nonsaline
nonscientific
nonscientist
nonseasonal
nonsecret
nonsecretory
nonsecure
nonsegregated
nonsegregation
nonselected
nonselective
non-self-governing
nonsensitive
nonserious
nonsexist
nonsexual
nonshrinkable
nonsignificance
nonsignificant
nonsingular
nonsinkable
nonskier
nonslaveholding
nonsolar
nonsolid
nonspatial
nonspeaking
nonspecialist
nonspecialized
nonspecific
nonspecifically
nonspectacular
nonspectral
nonspeculative
nonspherical
nonspontaneous
nonstaining
nonstarchy
nonstationary
nonstatistical
nonstellar
nonstrategic
nonstriker
nonstriking
nonstructural
nonstructured
nonstudent
nonsubscriber
nonsuccess
nonsugar
nonsurfer
nonsurgical
nonsusceptible

\ə\ abut	\au̇\ out	\i\ tip	\ȯ\ saw	\u̇\ foot
\ər\ further	\ch\ chin	\ī\ life	\ȯi\ coin	\y\ yet
\a\ mat	\e\ pet	\j\ job	\th\ thin	\yü\ few
\ā\ take	\ē\ easy	\ng\ sing	\t͟h\ this	\yu̇\ cure
\ä\ cot, cart	\g\ go	\ō\ bone	\ü\ food	\zh\ vision

nonsymbiotic
nonsymbolic
nonsymmetric
nonsymmetrical
nonsynchronous
nonsyntactical
nonsystemic
nontarnishable
nontaxable
nontechnical
nontechnological
nonteleological
nontemporal
nontenured
nonterritorial
nontheatrical
nontheistic
nonthermal
nonthreatening
nontidal
nontobacco
nontoxic
nontoxicity
nontraditional
nontransferable
nontransparency
nontransparent
nontransposing
nontreated
nontrivial
nontropical
nontrump
nontuberculous
nontypical
nonunanimous
nonunderstandable
nonuniform
nonuniformity
nonurban
nonurgent
nonuse
nonuser
nonutilitarian
nonvariable
nonvariant
nonvegetative
nonvenomous
nonverbal
nonvertical
nonvibratory
nonviewer
nonvintage
nonviolation
nonviral
nonvirulent
nonviscous
nonvisual
nonvocal
nonvocational
nonvoluntary
nonvoter
nonvoting
nonwoody
nonworker
nonworking
nonyellowing

non•age \'nän-ij, 'nō-nij\ *n* **1** : MINORITY 1 **2 a** : a period of youth **b** : lack of maturity [Middle French, from *non-* + *age* "age"]

no•na•ge•nar•i•an \,nō-nə-jə-'ner-ē-ən, ,nän-ə-\ *n* : a person who is 90 or more but less than 100 years old [Latin *nonagenarius* "containing ninety", derived from *nonaginta* "ninety"] — **nonagenarian** *adj*

no•na•gon \'nō-nə-,gän\ *n* : a polygon of nine angles and nine sides [Latin *nonus* "ninth"]

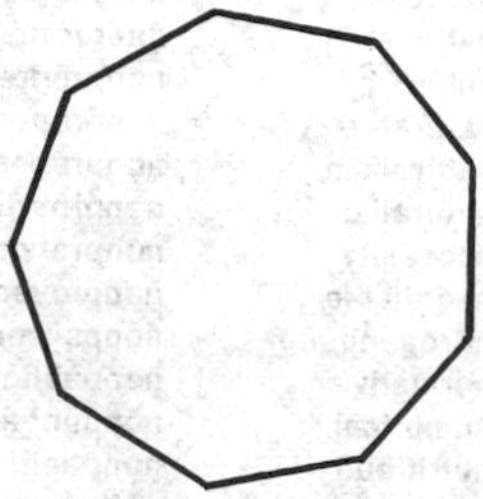
nonagon

non•aligned \,nän-l-'īnd\ *adj* : not allied with other nations

non•al•le•lic \,nän-ə-'lē-lik, -'lel-ik\ *adj* : not behaving as alleles toward one another ⟨*nonallelic* genes⟩

non•cal•car•e•ous \,nän-kal-'kar-ē-əs, -'ker-\ *adj* : lacking or deficient in lime ⟨*noncalcareous* soils⟩

[1]**nonce** \'näns\ *n* : the one, particular, or present occasion, purpose, or use ⟨for the *nonce*⟩ [Middle English *nanes*, from incorrect division of *then anes* in such phrases as *to then anes* "for the one purpose"]

[2]**nonce** *adj* : occurring, used, or made only once or for a special occasion ⟨a *nonce* word⟩

non•cha•lant \,nän-shə-'länt, 'nän-shə-,\ *adj* : giving an effect of easy unconcern or indifference ⟨face a crowd with *nonchalant* ease⟩ [French, from Old French *nonchaloir* "to disregard", from *non-* + *chaloir* "to concern", from Latin *calēre* "to be warm"] — **non•cha•lance** \-'läns, -,läns\ *n* — **non•cha•lant•ly** \,nän-shə-'länt-lē, 'nän-\ *adv*

non•com \'nän-,käm\ *n* : NONCOMMISSIONED OFFICER

non•com•bat•ant \,nän-kəm-'bat-nt; nän-'käm-bət-ənt, 'nän-\ *n* : a member (as a chaplain) of the armed forces whose duties exclude fighting; *also* : CIVILIAN — **noncombatant** *adj*

non•com•mis•sioned officer \,nän-kə-,mish-ənd-\ *n* : a subordinate officer (as a sergeant) in the armed forces appointed from enlisted personnel

non•com•mit•tal \,nän-kə-'mit-l\ *adj* : not telling or showing one's thoughts or decisions ⟨a *noncommittal* answer⟩ — **non•com•mit•tal•ly** \-l-ē\ *adv*

non com•pos men•tis \,nän-,käm-pə-'sment-əs, ,nōn-\ *adj* : not of sound mind [Latin, literally, "not having control of one's mind"]

non•con•duc•tor \,nän-kən-'dək-tər\ *n* : a substance that conducts heat, electricity, or sound only in very small degree

non•con•fi•dence \nän-'kän-fəd-əns, -fə-,dens\ *n* : lack of confidence especially of a parliamentary body in a government ⟨a vote of *nonconfidence*⟩

non•con•form•ist \,nän-kən-'fȯr-məst\ *n* **1** *often cap* : a person who does not conform to an established church and especially the Church of England **2** : a person who does not conform to a generally accepted pattern of thought or action — **nonconformist** *adj, often cap*

non•con•for•mi•ty \-'fȯr-mət-ē\ *n* **1 a** : failure or refusal to conform to an established church **b** *often cap* : the movement or principles of English Protestant dissent **c** *often cap* : the body of English Nonconformists **2** : refusal to conform to conventional rules or customs

non•co•op•er•a•tion \,nän-kō-,äp-ə-'rā-shən\ *n* : failure or refusal to cooperate especially with the government of a country — **non•co•op•er•a•tive** \-'äp-rət-iv, -ə-rət-, -ə-,rāt-\ *adj*

non•de•nom•i•na•tion•al \,nän-di-,näm-ə-'nā-shnəl, -shən-l\ *adj* : not restricted to a single religious denomination ⟨a *nondenominational* church⟩

non•de•script \,nän-di-'skript\ *adj* : belonging or seeming to belong to no particular class or kind [*non-* + Latin *descriptus*, past participle of *describere* "to describe"] — **nondescript** *n*

non•dis•junc•tion \,nän-dis-'jəng-shən, -'jəngk-\ *n* : the failure of two homologous chromosomes to separate during meiosis so that one daughter cell has both and the other neither of the chromosomes — **non•dis•junc•tion•al** \-shnəl, -shən-l\ *adj*

[1]**none** \'nən\ *pron, sing or pl in construction* **1** : not any ⟨*none* of them went⟩ ⟨*none* of it is needed⟩ **2** : not one ⟨*none* of the family⟩ **3** : not any such thing or person ⟨half a loaf is better than *none*⟩ [Old English *nān*, from *ne* "not" + *ān* "one"]

[2]**none** *adj, archaic* : not any : NO

[3]**none** *adv* **1** : by no means : not at all ⟨*none* too soon⟩ **2** : in no way : to no extent ⟨*none* the worse for wear⟩

[4]**none** \'nōn\ *n, often cap* : the fifth of the canonical hours [Late Latin *nona*, from Latin, "9th hour of the day (from sunrise)", from *nonus* "ninth"]

non•elec•tro•lyte \,nän-ə-'lek-trə-,līt\ *n* : a substance (as sugar) that does not ionize in water and is therefore a poor conductor of electricity

non•en•ti•ty \nä-'nent-ət-ē, -'nen-ət-\ *n* **1** : something that does not exist or exists only in the imagination **2** : one of no consequence or significance

nones \'nōnz\ *n pl* : the 9th day before the ides according to ancient Roman reckoning [Latin *nonae*, from *nonus* "ninth"]

none•such \'nən-,səch\ *or* **non•such** \'nən-,səch *also* 'nän-\ *n* : a person or thing without an equal — **nonesuch** *adj*

none•the•less \,nən-thə-'les\ *adv* : HOWEVER 2, NEVERTHELESS

non–eu•clid•e•an \,nän-yu̇-'klid-ē-ən\ *adj, often cap E* : not assuming or in accordance with all the postulates of Euclid's *Elements* ⟨*non-euclidean* geometry⟩

non•fat \'nän-'fat\ *adj* : having much or all of the fat removed ⟨*nonfat* milk⟩

non•fea•sance \nän-'fēz-ns, 'nän-\ *n* : omission to do especially what ought to be done [*non-* + obsolete *feasance* "performance, doing", from Middle French *faisance* "act", from *faire* "to do", from Latin *facere*]

non•fic•tion \'nän-'fik-shən\ *n* : literature that is not fictional — **non•fic•tion•al** \nän-'fik-shnəl, 'nän-, -shən-l\ *adj*

non•flow•er•ing \nän-'flau̇-ring, 'nän-, -ə-ring\ *adj* : lacking a flowering stage in the life cycle

non•green \'nän-'grēn\ *adj* : lacking chlorophyll ⟨*nongreen* plants such as fungi⟩

non•ho•mol•o•gous \,nän-hō-'mäl-ə-gəs, -hə-\ *adj* : of unlike genic constitution ⟨*nonhomologous* chromosomes⟩

non•hu•man \nän-'hyü-mən, 'nän-, 'yü-mən\ *adj* **1** : not belonging to the human race **2** : not befitting to, produced by, or involving human beings

no•nil•lion \nō-'nil-yən\ *n* — see NUMBER table [French, from Latin *nonus* "ninth" + French *-illion* (as in *million*)]

non•in•ter•ven•tion \,nän-,int-ər-'ven-chən\ *n* : the state or habit of not intervening ⟨*nonintervention* in the affairs of other countries⟩ — **non•in•ter•ven•tion•ist** \-'vench-nəst, -ə-nəst\ *n or adj*

non•ju•ror \nän-'jür-ər, 'nän-\ *n* : a person refusing to take an oath (as of allegiance) — **non•jur•ing** \-'jür-ing\ *adj*

non•lin•e•ar \nän-'lin-ē-ər, 'nän-\ *adj* : not linear; *esp* : not representing or being a curve that can be graphed as a straight line ⟨*nonlinear* equations⟩

non•man•u•al \-'man-yə-wəl, -'man-yəl\ *adj* : not involving or occupied with manual labor

non•met•al \-'met-l\ *n* : a chemical element (as carbon or nitrogen) that lacks metallic properties

non•me•tal•lic \,nän-mə-'tal-ik\ *adj* **1** : not metallic **2** : of, relating to, or being a nonmetal

non•neg•a•tive \nän-'neg-ət-iv, 'nän-\ *adj* : being either positive or zero ⟨*nonnegative* real numbers⟩
no–no \'nō-,nō\ *n, pl* **no-no's** *or* **no-nos** : something unacceptable or forbidden
non•ob•jec•tive \,nän-əb-'jek-tiv\ *adj* : representing or intended to represent no natural or actual object, figure, or scene ⟨*nonobjective* art⟩
[1]**non•pa•reil** \,nän-pə-'rel\ *adj* : having no equal [Middle French, from *non-* + *pareil* "equal", from Latin *par*]
[2]**nonpareil** *n* **1** : one of unequaled excellence : PARAGON **2 a** : a small flat chocolate disk covered with white sugar pellets **b** : small sugar pellets of various colors
non•par•ti•san \nän-'pärt-ə-zən, 'nän-\ *adj* : not partisan; *esp* : free from party affiliation, bias, or designation ⟨*nonpartisan* ballot⟩ ⟨a *nonpartisan* board⟩ — **non•par•ti•san•ship** \-,ship\ *n*
non•pas•ser•ine \nän-'pas-ə-,rīn, 'nän-\ *adj* : not passerine; *esp* : belonging to the order (Coraciiformes) that includes the kingfishers and related birds
non•per•sis•tent \,nän-pər-'sis-tənt, -'zis-\ *adj* : not persistent; *esp* : decomposed rapidly by environmental action ⟨*nonpersistent* insecticides⟩
[1]**non•plus** \nän-'pləs, 'nän-\ *n* : a state of bafflement or perplexity : QUANDARY [Latin *non plus* "no more"]
[2]**nonplus** *vt* **non•plussed** *also* **non•plused**; **non•plus•sing** *also* **non•plus•ing** : to cause to be at a loss as to what to say, think, or do : PERPLEX
non•po•lar \nän-'pō-lər, 'nän-\ *adj* **1** : lacking electrical poles ⟨a *nonpolar* molecule⟩ **2** : of or characterized by covalence ⟨a *nonpolar* liquid⟩
non•pos•i•tive \nän-'päz-ət-iv, 'nän-, -'päz-tiv\ *adj* : being either negative or zero ⟨*nonpositive* real numbers⟩
non•pro•duc•tive \,nän-prə-'dək-tiv\ *adj* **1** : failing to produce or yield : UNPRODUCTIVE ⟨*nonproductive* land⟩ **2** : not directly concerned with production ⟨*nonproductive* labor⟩ — **non•pro•duc•tive•ness** *n*
non•prof•it \nän-'präf-ət, 'nän-\ *adj* : not conducted or maintained for the purpose of profit ⟨a *nonprofit* organization⟩
non•re•peat•ing decimal \,nän-ri-'pēt-ing-\ *n* : a decimal that has an infinite number of digits but is not a repeating decimal
non•rep•re•sen•ta•tion•al \,nän-,rep-ri-,zen-'tā-shnəl, -shən-l\ *adj* : NONOBJECTIVE
non•res•i•dent \nän-'rez-əd-ənt, 'nän-, -'rez-dənt, -'rez-ə-,dent\ *adj* : not living in a specified or implied place — **non•res•i•dence** \-'rez-əd-əns, -'rez-dəns, -'rez-ə-,dens\ — **nonresident** *n*
non•re•sis•tance \,nän-ri-'zis-təns\ *n* : the principles or practice of passive submission to authority even when unjust or oppressive; *also* : the principle or practice of not resisting violence by force — **non•re•sis•tant** \-tənt\ *adj*
non•re•stric•tive \,nän-ri-'strik-tiv\ *adj* **1** : not restrictive **2** : not limiting the reference of a modified word or phrase ⟨a *nonrestrictive* clause⟩
non•rig•id \nän-'rij-əd, 'nän-\ *adj* : maintaining form by pressure of contained gas ⟨a *nonrigid* airship⟩
non•sched•uled \-'skej-üld, -əld\ *adj* : licensed to carry passengers or freight by air without a regular schedule ⟨*nonscheduled* airline⟩
non•sec•tar•i•an \,nän-sek-'ter-ē-ən\ *adj* : not having a sectarian character ⟨a *nonsectarian* school⟩
non•sense \'nän-,sens, 'nän-səns\ *n* **1** : foolish or meaningless words or actions **2** : things of no importance or value ⟨spent their money on *nonsense*⟩ — **non•sen•si•cal** \nän-'sen-si-kəl, 'nän-\ *adj* — **non•sen•si•cal•ly** \-kə-lē, -klē\ *adv* — **non•sen•si•cal•ness** \-kəl-nəs\ *n*
non se•qui•tur \nän-'sek-wət-ər, 'nän-\ *n* : a statement that does not follow logically from anything previously said [Latin, "it does not follow"]
non•sked \nän-'sked, 'nän-\ *n* : a nonscheduled airline or transport plane
non•skid \nän-'skid, 'nän-\ *adj* : designed or equipped to prevent skidding
non•smok•er \-'smō-kər\ *n* : a person who does not smoke tobacco — **non•smok•ing** \-'smō-king\ *n*
non•sport•ing \-'spōrt-ing, -'sport-\ *adj* : lacking the qualities characteristic of a hunting dog
non•stan•dard \-'stan-dərd\ *adj* **1** : not standard **2** : not conforming in pronunciation, grammatical construction, idiom, or word choice to the usage generally characteristic of educated native speakers of the language
non•stick \nän-'stik, 'nän-\ *adj* : allowing easy removal of cooked food particles ⟨a *nonstick* coating on a pan⟩
non•stop \-'stäp\ *adj* : done or made without a stop ⟨a *nonstop* flight⟩ — **nonstop** *adv*
non•stri•at•ed muscle \nän-,strī-,āt-əd-\ *n* : SMOOTH MUSCLE
non•such *variant of* NONESUCH
non•suit \nän-'süt, 'nän-\ *n* : a judgment against a plaintiff for failure to prosecute the case or inability to establish a prima facie case [Anglo-French *nounsuyte*, from *noun-* "non-" + Old French *siute* "following, pursuit"] — **nonsuit** *vt*
non•sup•port \,nän-sə-'pōrt, -'port\ *n* : failure to support; *esp* : failure (as of a parent) to honor an obligation to provide financial support to a dependent
non•syl•lab•ic \,nän-sə-'lab-ik\ *adj* : not constituting a syllable or the nucleus of a syllable
non•tast•er \nän-'tā-stər, 'nän-\ *n* : a person unable to taste the chemical phenylthiocarbamide
non trop•po \nän-'trò-pō, 'nän-, 'nōn-\ *adv or adj* : not too much so : without excess — used as a direction in music [Italian, literally, "not too much"]
non•union \nän-'yün-yən, 'nän-\ *adj* **1** : not belonging to a trade union ⟨*nonunion* carpenters⟩ **2** : not recognizing or favoring trade unions or their members
non•vas•cu•lar plant \,nän-,vas-kyə-lər-\ *n* : a plant (as an alga or a fungus) that has no vascular tissue
non•vi•a•ble \nän-'vī-ə-bəl, 'nän-\ *adj* : not capable of living, growing, or developing and functioning successfully
non•vi•o•lence \-'vī-ə-ləns\ *n* **1** : abstention on principle from violence; *also* : the principle of such abstention **2** : nonviolent demonstrations to secure political ends — **non•vi•o•lent** \-lənt\ *adj*
non•vol•a•tile \nän-'väl-ət-l\ *adj* : not volatile : not volatilizing readily
non•ze•ro \nän-'zē-rō, -'ziər-ō\ *adj* : either positive or negative but not zero
[1]**noo•dle** \'nüd-l\ *n* **1** : a stupid person : SIMPLETON **2** : HEAD 1 [perhaps alteration of *noddle*]
[2]**noodle** *n* : a food paste made with egg and shaped into long flat strips [German *nudel*]
nook \'nu̇k\ *n* **1** : an interior angle formed by two meeting walls : RECESS ⟨a chimney *nook*⟩ **2** : a secluded or sheltered place ⟨a shady *nook*⟩ [Middle English *noke, nok*]
noon \'nün\ *n* : the middle of the day : 12 o'clock in the daytime [Old English *nōn* "9th hour from sunrise", from Latin *nona*, from *nonus* "ninth"] — **noon** *adj*

△ **origin** *Noon* has not always indicated that time of day at which the sun is most nearly overhead. According to the Roman method of reckoning time, the hours of the day were counted from sunrise to sunset. English *noon* is derived from Latin *nona*, from *nonus*, which means "ninth". *Noon*, then, was the ninth hour of the day, or about three p.m. A church service which was held daily at this time is called *none*, and perhaps in anticipation of this service or possibly of a mealtime, the time denoted by *none* or *noon* shifted to the hour of midday.

noon•day \-,dā\ *n* : MIDDAY
no one *pron* : NOBODY
noon•ing \'nü-ning, -nən\ *n, chiefly dialect* : a midday meal; *also* : a period at noon for eating or resting
noon•tide \'nün-,tīd\ *n* **1** : NOONTIME **2** : the highest or culminating point
noon•time \-,tīm\ *n* : the time of noon : MIDDAY
[1]**noose** \'nüs\ *n* : a loop with a running knot that becomes tighter the more it is drawn [probably from Provençal *nous* "knot", from Latin *nodus*]
[2]**noose** *vt* : to catch or fasten with or as if with a noose
no–par *adj* : having no face value ⟨*no-par* stock⟩
nor \nər, nor, 'nor\ *conj* : and not ⟨the book is too long; *nor* is the style easy⟩ ⟨not for you *nor* for me⟩ — used especially to introduce and negate the second member and each later member of a series of items of which the first is preceded by *neither* ⟨neither here *nor* there⟩ [Middle English, contraction of *nother* "neither, nor"]

nor·adren·a·line \ˌnór-ə-ˈdren-l-ən\ *n* : NOREPINEPHRINE [*normal* + *adrenaline*]

¹Nor·dic \ˈnórd-ik\ *adj* **1** : of or relating to the Germanic peoples of northern Europe and especially of Scandinavia **2** : of or relating to a physical type characterized by tall stature, long head, light skin and hair, and blue eyes [French *nordique,* from *nord* "north", from Old English *north*]

²Nordic *n* **1** : a native of northern Europe **2** : a person of Nordic physical type or of a hypothetical Nordic division of the Caucasian race **3** : a member of any of the peoples of Scandinavia

nor·epi·neph·rine \ˈnór-ˌep-ə-ˈnef-rən\ *n* : a compound that causes blood vessels to contract and assists in the transmission of nerve impulses in the sympathetic nervous system [*normal* + *epinephrine*]

Nor·folk jacket \ˌnór-fək-, -ˌfók-\ *n* : a loose-fitting belted single-breasted jacket with box pleats [*Norfolk,* England]

norm \ˈnórm\ *n* **1** : an authoritative standard : MODEL **2** : AVERAGE; *esp* : a set standard of development or achievement usually derived from the average or median achievement of a large group [Latin *norma,* literally, "carpenter's square"]

¹nor·mal \ˈnór-məl\ *adj* **1** : forming a right angle; *esp* : perpendicular to a tangent at a point of tangency **2** : constituting or not deviating from a norm, rule, or principle : REGULAR **3 a** : of, relating to, or characterized by average intelligence or development **b** : free from disorder of body or mind : SOUND, SANE **4 a** : having a concentration of one gram equivalent of solute per liter ⟨a *normal* salt solution⟩ **b** : containing neither basic hydroxyl nor acid hydrogen ⟨a *normal* salt⟩ **c** : having a straight-chain structure ⟨a *normal* alcohol⟩ [Latin *normalis,* from *norma* "carpenter's square"] **syn** see REGULAR — **nor·mal·cy** \-sē\ *n* — **nor·mal·i·ty** \nór-ˈmal-ət-ē\ *n* — **nor·mal·ly** \ˈnór-mə-lē\ *adv*

△ **origin** Latin *norma* means "rule" or "pattern" as well as "carpenter's square", for a square provides a standard or rule which ensures that a carpenter can make corners and edges that are straight and that form right angles. The Latin adjective *normalis,* formed from *norma,* originally meant "forming a right angle" or "according to a square", and it is from this Latin sense that we get the earliest sense of *normal* in English, "perpendicular". Latin *normalis* was also used in more extended senses, however, and by the Late Latin period its usual meaning was "according to rule". Most of the senses of our word *normal* are derived from this Late Latin usage.

²normal *n* **1** : one (as a line or person) that is normal **2** : a form or state regarded as the norm : STANDARD

normal school *n* : a usually two-year school for training chiefly elementary teachers [translation of French *école normale*; from the fact that the first French school so named was intended to serve as a model]

Nor·man \ˈnór-mən\ *n* **1** : any of the Scandinavians who conquered Normandy in the 10th century **2** : any of the people of mixed Norman and French blood who conquered England in 1066 **3** : a native or inhabitant of the province of Normandy [Old French *Normant,* from Old Norse *Northmathr* "Norseman", from *northr* "north" + *mathr* "man"] — **Norman** *adj*

Norman–French *n* : the French language of the medieval Normans

nor·ma·tive \ˈnór-mət-iv\ *adj* : of, relating to, conforming to, or prescribing norms — **nor·ma·tive·ly** *adv* — **nor·ma·tive·ness** *n*

Norse \ˈnórs\ *n, pl* **Norse 1** *pl* **a** : the Scandinavian people **b** : the Norwegian people **2 a** : NORWEGIAN 2 **b** : any of the western Scandinavian dialects or languages **c** : the Scandinavian group of Germanic languages [probably from obsolete Dutch *noorsch,* adj., "Norwegian, Scandinavian", from *noordsch* "northern", from *noord* "north"] — **Norse** *adj*

Norse·man \ˈnór-smən\ *n* : any of the ancient Scandinavians

¹north \ˈnórth\ *adv* : to, toward, or in the north [Old English]

²north *adj* **1** : situated toward or at the north **2** : coming from the north

³north *n* **1 a** : the direction to the left of one facing east **b** : the compass point directly opposite to south **2** *cap* : regions or countries north of a specified or implied point

north·bound \ˈnórth-ˌbau̇nd\ *adj* : headed north

¹north·east \nór-ˈthēst, *nautical* nó-ˈrēst\ *adv* : to, toward, or in the northeast

²northeast *n* **1 a** : the general direction between north and east **b** : the compass point midway between north and east N 45° E **2** *cap* : regions or countries northeast of a specified or implied point

³northeast *adj* **1** : coming from the northeast **2** : situated toward or at the northeast

north·east·er \nór-ˈthē-stər, nó-ˈrē-\ *n* **1** : a strong northeast wind **2** : a storm with northeast winds

north·east·er·ly \nór-ˈthē-stər-lē\ *adv or adj* **1** : from the northeast **2** : toward the northeast

north·east·ern \-stərn\ *adj* **1** *often cap* : of, relating to, or characteristic of a region conventionally designated Northeast **2** : lying toward or coming from the northeast — **north·east·ern·most** \-stərn-ˌmōst\ *adj*

North·east·ern·er \-stər-nər, -stə-nər\ *n* : a native or inhabitant of a northeastern region (as of the United States)

¹north·east·ward \nór-ˈthēs-twərd\ *adv or adj* : toward the northeast — **north·east·wards** \-twərdz\ *adj*

²northeastward *n* : NORTHEAST

north·er \ˈnór-t͟hər\ *n* **1** : a strong north wind **2** : a storm with north winds

¹north·er·ly \-lē\ *adv or adj* **1** : from the north **2** : toward the north

²northerly *n, pl* **-lies** : a wind from the north

north·ern \ˈnór-t͟hərn, -t͟hən\ *adj* **1** *often cap* : of, relating to, or characteristic of a region conventionally designated North **2** : lying toward or coming from the north [Old English *northerne*] — **north·ern·most** \-ˌmōst\ *adj*

Northern Cross *n* : a cross formed by six stars in Cygnus

Northern Crown *n* : CORONA BOREALIS

North·ern·er \ˈnór-t͟hər-nər, -t͟hə-nər\ *n* : a native or inhabitant of the North (as of the United States)

northern hemisphere *n* : the half of the earth that lies north of the equator

northern lights *n pl* : AURORA BOREALIS

north·ing \ˈnór-thing, -t͟hing\ *n* **1** : difference in latitude to the north from the last preceding point of reckoning **2** : northerly progress

north·land \ˈnórth-ˌland, -lənd\ *n, often cap* : land in the north : the north of a country or region

North·man \-mən\ *n* : NORSEMAN

north–north·east \ˈnórth-ˌnór-ˈthēst, *nautical* -ˌnó-ˈrēst\ *n* : two points east of north : N 22° 30′ E

north–north·west \ˈnórth-ˌnórth-ˈwest, *nautical* -ˌnór-ˈwest\ *n* : two points west of north : N 22° 30′ W

north pole *n* **1** *often cap N&P* : the northernmost point of the earth : the northern end of the earth's axis **2** : the pole of a magnet that points toward the north

North Star *n* : the star toward which the northern end of the earth's axis very nearly points — called also *polestar*

¹north·ward \ˈnórth-wərd\ *adv or adj* : toward the north — **north·wards** \-wərdz\ *adv*

²northward *n* : northward direction or part

¹north·west \nórth-ˈwest, *nautical* nór-ˈwest\ *adv* : to, toward, or in the northwest

²northwest *n* **1 a** : the general direction between north and west **b** : the compass point midway between north and west : N 45° W **2** *cap* : regions or countries northwest of a specified or implied point

³northwest *adj* **1** : coming from the northwest **2** : situated toward or at the northwest

north·west·er \nórth-ˈwes-tər, nór-ˈwes-\ *n* **1** : a strong northwest wind **2** : a storm with northwest winds

north·west·er·ly \nórth-ˈwes-tər-lē\ *adv or adj* **1** : from the northwest **2** : toward the northwest

north·west·ern \nórth-ˈwes-tərn\ *adj* **1** *often cap* : of, relating to, or characteristic of a region conventionally designated Northwest **2** : lying toward or coming from the northwest — **north·west·ern·most** \-tərn-ˌmōst\ *adj*

North·west·ern·er \-tər-nər, -tə-nər\ *n* : a native or inhabitant of a northwestern region (as of the United States)

¹north·west·ward \nórth-ˈwes-twərd\ *adv or adj* : toward the northwest — **north·west·wards** \-twərdz\ *adv*

²northwestward *n* : NORTHWEST

Nor·way maple \ˌnór-ˌwā-\ *n* : a European maple with dark green or often reddish leaves that is much planted for shade in the United States

Norway pine *n* : a North American pine with reddish bark and hard but not durable wood; *also* : its wood

Nor·we·gian \nór-ˈwē-jən\ *n* **1 a** : a native or inhabitant of Norway **b** : a person of Norwegian descent **2** : the Germanic language of the Norwegian people [Medieval Latin *Norwegia* "Norway"] — **Norwegian** *adj*

nos *pl of* NO

[1]nose \'nōz\ *n* **1 a** : the part of the face that bears the nostrils and covers the forepart of the nasal cavity; *also* : this part together with the nasal cavity **b** : the vertebrate organ of smell **2** : the sense of smell : OLFACTION **3** : something (as a point, edge, or projecting front part) that resembles a nose ⟨the *nose* of a plane⟩ **4 a** : the nose as a symbol of prying curiosity **b** : a knack for discovery or understanding ⟨a good *nose* for news⟩ [Old English *nosu*] — **nosed** \'nōzd\ *adj*

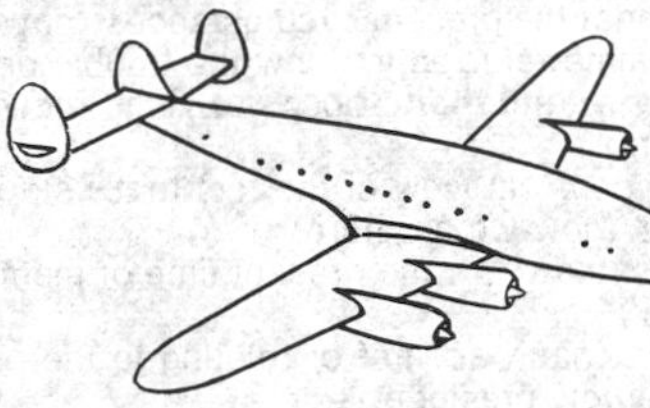

[1]nose 3

[2]nose *vb* **1** : to detect by or as if by smell : SCENT **2 a** : to push or move with the nose **b** : to touch or rub with the nose **3** : to search impertinently : PRY **4** : to move ahead slowly or cautiously ⟨the car *nosed* out into traffic⟩

nose•band \'nōz-ˌband\ *n* : the part of a bridle or halter that passes over a horse's nose

nose•bleed \-ˌblēd\ *n* : bleeding from the nose

nose cone *n* : a protective cone constituting the forward end of a rocket or missile

nose dive *n* **1** : the downward nose-first plunge of a flying object (as an airplane) **2** : a sudden extreme drop — **nose–dive** \'nōz-ˌdīv\ *vi*

nose•gay \'nōz-ˌgā\ *n* : a small bunch of flowers [*nose* + English dialect *gay* "ornament"]

nose•piece \-ˌpēs\ *n* **1** : a piece of armor for protecting the nose **2** : a fitting at the lower end of a microscope tube to which the objectives are attached

no–show \nō-'shō\ *n* : a person who reserves space especially on an airplane but neither uses nor cancels the reservation

nos•tal•gia \nä-'stal-jə, nə-\ *n* : a wistful sentimental yearning for something past or irrecoverable [New Latin, from Greek *nostos* "return home" + New Latin *-algia* "-algia"] — **nos•tal•gic** \-jik\ *adj* — **nos•tal•gi•cal•ly** \-ji-kə-lē, -klē\ *adv*

nos•toc \'näs-ˌtäk\ *n* : any of a genus of blue-green algae able to use atmospheric nitrogen [New Latin, genus name]

nos•tril \'näs-trəl\ *n* : either of the outer openings of the nose with its adjoining passage; *also* : either fleshy lateral wall of the nose [Old English *nosthyrl*, from *nosu* "nose" + *thyrel* "hole"]

nos•trum \'näs-trəm\ *n* **1** : a medicine of secret composition recommended especially by its preparer **2** : a questionable remedy or scheme : PANACEA [Latin, neuter of *noster* "our, ours", from *nos* "we"]

nosy *or* **nos•ey** \'nō-zē\ *adj* **nos•i•er; -est** : CURIOUS 2, SNOOPY — **nos•i•ly** \-zə-lē\ *adv* — **nos•i•ness** \-zē-nəs\ *n*

not \nät, 'nät\ *adv* **1** — used to make negative a group of words or a word ⟨the books are *not* here⟩ **2** — used to stand for the negative of a preceding group of words ⟨is sometimes hard to see and sometimes *not*⟩ [Middle English, alteration of *nought* "naught"]

no•ta•bil•i•ty \ˌnōt-ə-'bil-ət-ē\ *n, pl* **-ties 1** : the quality or state of being notable **2** : NOTABLE

[1]no•ta•ble \'nōt-ə-bəl\ *adj* **1** : worthy of note : REMARKABLE **2** : DISTINGUISHED 1, PROMINENT — **no•ta•bly** \-blē\ *adv*

[2]notable *n* : a person of note or of great reputation

no•ta•rize \'nōt-ə-ˌrīz\ *vt* : to make legally authentic through the use of the powers granted to a notary public — **no•ta•ri•za•tion** \ˌnōt-ə-rə-'zā-shən\ *n*

no•ta•ry public \ˌnōt-ə-rē-\ *n, pl* **notaries public** *or* **notary publics** : a public officer who attests or certifies writings (as deeds) as authentic and takes affidavits, depositions, and protests of negotiable paper — called also *notary* [Latin *notarius* "clerk, secretary", derived from *nota* "note"]

no•tate \'nō-ˌtāt\ *vt* : to put into notation

no•ta•tion \nō-'tā-shən\ *n* **1** : ANNOTATION, NOTE ⟨make *notations* for corrections on the margin⟩ **2** : the act, process, or method of representing data symbolically by marks, signs, figures, or characters; *also* : a system of symbols (as letters, numerals, or musical notes) used in such notation — **no•ta•tion•al** \-shnəl, -shən-l\ *adj*

[1]notch \'näch\ *n* **1** : a V-shaped or rounded indentation **2** : a narrow pass between mountains : GAP **3** : DEGREE, STEP ⟨the team moved up a *notch* in the standings⟩ [perhaps derived from Middle French *oche* "notch"] — **notched** \'nächt\ *adj*

[2]notch *vt* **1** : to cut or make notches in **2 a** : to mark or record with a notch **b** : ACHIEVE 2, SCORE ⟨*notched* another victory⟩

[1]note \'nōt\ *vt* **1 a** : to notice or observe with care **b** : to record in writing **2** : to make special mention of : REMARK [Old French *noter*, from Latin *notare* "to mark, note", from *nota* "note"] — **not•er** *n*

[2]note *n* **1 a** : a musical sound **b** : an animal's cry, call, or sound ⟨a bird's *note*⟩ **c** : a special tone of voice ⟨a *note* of fear⟩ **2 a** : MEMORANDUM 1b **b** : a brief and informal record **c** : a written or printed comment or explanation ⟨*notes* in the back of the book⟩ **d** : a short informal letter **e** : a formal diplomatic or official communication **3 a** : a written promise to pay — called also *promissory note* **b** : a piece of paper money **4** : a character in music that by its shape shows the length of time a tone is to be held and by its place on the staff shows the pitch of a tone **5** : MOOD, QUALITY ⟨a *note* of optimism⟩ **6 a** : REPUTATION, DISTINCTION ⟨a person of *note*⟩ **b** : NOTICE, HEED ⟨take *note* of the exact time⟩ [Latin *nota* "mark, character, written note"]

note•book \'nōt-ˌbu̇k\ *n* : a book for notes or memoranda

note•case \-ˌkās\ *n, British* : BILLFOLD, WALLET

not•ed \'nōt-əd\ *adj* : widely and favorably known ⟨a *noted* author⟩

• **syn** NOTORIOUS: NOTED implies being singled out for public attention for excellence of achievement; NOTORIOUS stresses being widely known for usually evil or questionable acts or qualities.

note•wor•thy \'nōt-ˌwər-t͟hē\ *adj* : worthy of note : REMARKABLE — **note•wor•thi•ly** \-t͟hə-lē\ *adv* — **note•wor•thi•ness** \-t͟hē-nəs\ *n*

[1]noth•ing \'nəth-iŋ\ *pron* **1** : not anything ⟨there's *nothing* in the box⟩ **2** : one of no interest, value, or consequence [Old English *nān thing, nāthing*, from *nān* "no, none" + *thing*] — **nothing doing** : by no means : definitely no

[2]nothing *adv* : not at all : in no degree

[3]nothing *n* **1 a** : something that does not exist **b** : absence of magnitude : ZERO **2** : something of little or no worth or importance — **noth•ing•ness** *n*

[1]no•tice \'nōt-əs\ *n* **1 a** : warning or indication of something : ANNOUNCEMENT **b** : notification of the ending of an agreement at a specified time **2** : ATTENTION, HEED ⟨sit up and take *notice*⟩ **3** : a written or printed announcement **4** : a short critical account [Middle French, "acquaintance", from Latin *notitia* "knowledge, acquaintance", from *notus* "known", from *noscere* to come to know"]

[2]notice *vt* **1** : to make mention of : remark on **2** : to take notice of : OBSERVE ⟨*notice* even the smallest details⟩

no•tice•able \'nōt-ə-sə-bəl\ *adj* **1** : worthy of notice ⟨*noticeable* for its fine coloring⟩ **2** : capable of being or likely to be noticed ⟨a slight but *noticeable* taste⟩ — **no•tice•ably** \-blē\ *adv*

no•ti•fi•ca•tion \ˌnōt-ə-fə-'kā-shən\ *n* **1** : the act or an instance of notifying **2** : written or printed matter that gives notice

no•ti•fy \'nōt-ə-ˌfī\ *vt* **-fied; -fy•ing 1** : to give notice of or report the occurrence of **2** : to give notice to [Middle French *notifier* "to make known", from Late Latin *notificare*, from Latin *notus* "known"] — **no•ti•fi•er** \-ˌfī-ər, -ˌfīr\ *n*

no•tion \'nō-shən\ *n* **1 a** : IDEA, CONCEPTION ⟨have a *notion* of a poem's meaning⟩ **b** : a belief held : OPINION **c** : WHIM, FANCY ⟨a sudden *notion* to go home⟩ **2** *pl* : small useful articles (as pins, needles, or thread) [Latin *notio*, from *noscere* "to come to know"]

no•tion•al \'nō-shnəl, -shən-l\ *adj* **1** : existing in idea only **2** : inclined to foolish or visionary fancies or moods

no•to•chord \'nōt-ə-ˌkȯrd\ *n* : a longitudinal flexible rod of cells that in the lowest chordates (as amphioxi and the lampreys) and in the embryos of the higher vertebrates forms the supporting axis of the body [Greek *nōton* "back" + Latin *chorda* "cord"] — **no·to·chord·al** \ˌnōt-ə-ˈkȯrd-l\ *adj*

no·to·ri·e·ty \ˌnōt-ə-ˈrī-ət-ē\ *n, pl* **-ties** : the quality or state of being notorious

no·to·ri·ous \nō-ˈtōr-ē-əs, -ˈtȯr-\ *adj* : generally known and talked of; *esp* : widely and unfavorably known [Medieval Latin *notorius,* derived from Latin *noscere* "to come to know"] **syn** see NOTED — **no·to·ri·ous·ly** *adv* — **no·to·ri·ous·ness** *n*

no–trump \ˈnō-ˈtrəmp\ *adj* : being a bid, contract, or hand suitable to play (as in bridge) without any suit being trumps — **no–trump** *n*

1**not·with·stand·ing** \ˌnät-with-ˈstan-diŋ, -wit͟h-\ *prep* : in spite of ⟨they failed *notwithstanding* their effort⟩

2**notwithstanding** *adv* : NEVERTHELESS, HOWEVER

3**notwithstanding** *conj* : ALTHOUGH

nou·gat \ˈnü-gət\ *n* : a candy of nuts or fruit pieces in a sugar paste [French, from Provençal, from *noga* "nut", from Latin *nuc-, nux*]

nought \ˈnȯt, ˈnät\ *variant of* NAUGHT

noun \ˈnau̇n\ *n* : a word that is the name of something (as a person, animal, plant, place, thing, substance, quality, idea, action, or state) and that is typically used in a sentence as subject or object of a verb or as object of a preposition [Anglo-French, "name, noun", from Old French *nom,* from Latin *nomen*]

nour·ish \ˈnər-ish, ˈnə-rish\ *vt* **1** : to promote the growth and development of **2** : to provide with food : FEED ⟨plants *nourished* by rain and soil⟩ **3** : SUPPORT, MAINTAIN ⟨a friendship *nourished* by trust⟩ [Old French *noriss-,* stem of *norrir* "to nourish", from Latin *nutrire*]

nour·ish·ing *adj* : giving nourishment : NUTRITIOUS ⟨*nourishing* food⟩

nour·ish·ment \ˈnər-ish-mənt, ˈnə-rish-\ *n* **1** : something that nourishes : NUTRIMENT **2** : the act of nourishing : the state of being nourished

nou·veau riche \ˌnü-ˌvō-ˈrēsh\ *n, pl* **nou·veaux riches** *same*\ : a person newly rich [French, literally, "new rich"]

no·va \ˈnō-və\ *n, pl* **novas** *or* **no·vae** \-ˌvē, -ˌvī\ : a star that suddenly increases greatly in brightness and then within a few months or years grows dim again [New Latin, from Latin *novus* "new"]

1**nov·el** \ˈnäv-əl\ *adj* : new or striking in conception, kind, or style : having no precedent [Middle French, "new", from Latin *novellus,* from *novus* "new"] **syn** see NEW

2**novel** *n* : a prose narrative longer than a short story that usually portrays imaginary characters and events [Italian *novella*] — **nov·el·is·tic** \ˌnäv-ə-ˈlis-tik\ *adj*

nov·el·ette \ˌnäv-ə-ˈlet\ *n* : a brief novel or long short story

nov·el·ist \ˈnäv-ləst, -ə-ləst\ *n* : a writer of novels

nov·el·ize \ˈnäv-ə-ˌlīz\ *vt* : to convert into the form of a novel — **nov·el·iza·tion** \ˌnäv-ə-lə-ˈzā-shən\ *n*

no·vel·la \nō-ˈvel-ə\ *n, pl* **no·vel·le** \-ˈvel-ē\ : a story with a compact and pointed plot [Italian, from *novello* "new", from Latin *novellus*]

nov·el·ty \ˈnäv-əl-tē\ *n, pl* **-ties** **1** : something new or unusual **2** : the quality or state of being novel **3** : a small manufactured article intended to amuse or for use as a plaything or an adornment — usually used in pl.

No·vem·ber \nō-ˈvem-bər\ *n* : the 11th month of the year [Old French *Novembre,* from Latin *November,* from *novem* "nine", from its having been originally the 9th month of the Roman calendar]

no·ve·na \nō-ˈvē-nə\ *n, pl* **-nas** *or* **-nae** \-ˌnē\ : a Roman Catholic devotion in which prayers are said for the same purpose on nine successive days [Medieval Latin, from Latin *novenus* "nine each", from *novem* "nine"]

nov·ice \ˈnäv-əs\ *n* **1** : a new member of a religious order who is preparing to take the vows of religion **2** : one who has no previous training or experience in a specific field or activity : BEGINNER [Middle French, from Medieval Latin *novicius,* from Latin, "new, inexperienced", from *novus* "new"]

no·vi·tiate \nō-ˈvish-ət\ *n* **1** : the period or state of being a novice **2** : NOVICE 1 **3** : a house where novices are trained [French *noviciat,* from Medieval Latin *noviciatus,* from *novicius* "novice"]

No·vo·cain \ˈnō-və-ˌkān\ *trademark* — used for the hydrochloride of procaine

1**now** \nau̇, ˈnau̇\ *adv* **1 a** : at the present time or moment ⟨I am busy *now*⟩ **b** : in the time immediately before the present ⟨they left just *now*⟩ **c** : in the time immediately to follow : FORTHWITH ⟨we will leave *now*⟩ **2** — used with the sense of present time weakened or lost to express command, request, or reproach ⟨*now* hear this⟩ **3** : SOMETIMES ⟨*now* one and *now* another⟩ **4** : under the present circumstances ⟨*now* what can we do⟩ **5** : at the time referred to ⟨*now* the trouble began⟩ [Old English *nū*] — **now and then** : OCCASIONALLY ⟨*now and then* we hear from them⟩

2**now** *conj* : in view of the fact that : SINCE — often followed by *that* ⟨*now* we are here⟩

3**now** \ˈnau̇\ *n* : the present time or moment ⟨had been ill up to *now*⟩

4**now** \ˈnau̇\ *adj* : of or relating to the present time : CURRENT ⟨the *now* president⟩

now·a·days \ˈnau̇-ə-ˌdāz, ˈnau̇-ˌdāz\ *adv* : at the present time [Middle English *now a dayes,* from *now* + *a dayes* "during the day"]

no·way \ˈnō-ˌwā\ *or* **no·ways** \-ˌwāz\ *adv* : NOWISE

no·where \ˈnō-ˌhweər, -ˌweər, -ˌhwaər, -ˌwaər, -hwər, -wər\ *adv* **1** : not in or at any place **2** : to no place — **nowhere** *n*

nowhere near *adv* : not nearly

no·wise \ˈnō-ˌwīz\ *adv* : in no way : not at all

nox·ious \ˈnäk-shəs\ *adj* : harmful or injurious especially to health or morals : UNWHOLESOME ⟨*noxious* fumes⟩ [Latin *noxius,* from *noxa* "harm"] — **nox·ious·ly** *adv* — **nox·ious·ness** *n*

noz·zle \ˈnäz-əl\ *n* : a projecting part with an opening that usually serves as an outlet ⟨the *nozzle* of a bellows⟩; *esp* : a short tube with a taper or constriction used on a hose or pipe to direct or speed up a flow of fluid [derived from *nose*]

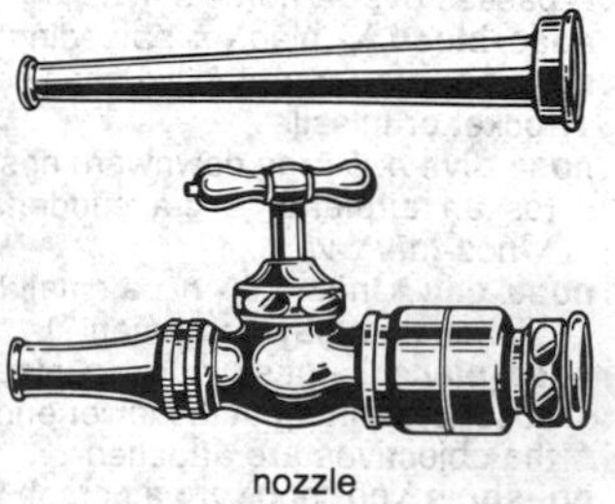
nozzle

n't \$^{ə}$nt, nt, ənt\ *adv* : not — used in combination ⟨*isn't*⟩ ⟨*doesn't*⟩

nth \ˈenth, ˈentth\ *adj* **1** : numbered with an indefinitely large or an unspecified ordinal number **2** : EXTREME, UTMOST ⟨to the *nth* degree⟩

nu \ˈnü, ˈnyü\ *n* : the 13th letter of the Greek alphabet — Ν or ν

nu·ance \ˈnü-ˌäns, ˈnyü-, -ˌä^{n}s, nü-ˈ, nyü-ˈ\ *n* : a slight shade or degree of difference : a delicate gradation or variation (as in color, tone, or meaning) [French, from *nuer* "to make shades of color", from *nue* "cloud", from Latin *nubes*]

nub \ˈnəb\ *n* **1** : KNOB 1a, LUMP **2** : GIST, POINT ⟨the *nub* of the story⟩ [English dialect *knub*]

nub·bin \ˈnəb-ən\ *n* **1** : a small or imperfect ear of Indian corn; *also* : any small shriveled or undeveloped fruit **2** : a small projecting part ⟨the horns were mere *nubbins*⟩ [perhaps from *nub*]

nub·ble \ˈnəb-əl\ *n* : a small knob or lump [derived from *nub*] — **nub·bly** \ˈnəb-lē, -ə-lē\ *adj*

nu·bile \ˈnü-bəl, ˈnyü-, -ˌbīl\ *adj* : of marriageable condition or age [French, from Latin *nubilis,* from *nubere* "to marry"] — **nu·bil·i·ty** \nü-ˈbil-ət-ē, nyü-\ *n*

nu·cel·lus \nü-ˈsel-əs, nyü-\ *n, pl* **-cel·li** \-ˈsel-ˌī\ : the central and chief part of a plant ovule containing the embryo sac [New Latin, from Latin *nucella* "small nut", from *nuc-, nux* "nut"] — **nu·cel·lar** \-ˈsel-ər\ *adj*

nu·chal \ˈnü-kəl, ˈnyü-\ *adj* : of, relating to, or lying in the region of the nape [Medieval Latin *nucha* "nape", from Arabic *nukhā* "spinal cord"] — **nuchal** *n*

nucle- *or* **nucleo-** *combining form* **1** : nucleus ⟨*nucle*on⟩ **2** : nucleic acid ⟨*nucleo*protein⟩

nu·cle·ar \ˈnü-klē-ər, ˈnyü-\ *adj* **1** : of, relating to, or constituting a nucleus (as of a cell) **2** : of, relating to, or utilizing the atomic nucleus, atomic energy, the atom bomb, or atomic power

nuclear energy *n* : ATOMIC ENERGY

nuclear membrane *n* : the boundary of a cell nucleus

nuclear reactor *n* : REACTOR 2b

nuclear sap *n* : the part of a cell nucleus that is relatively fluid and does not include the chromatin and nucleoli

nu·cle·ase \ˈnü-klē-ˌās, ˈnyü-\ *n* : an enzyme that promotes hydrolysis of nucleic acids

nu·cle·ate \ˈnü-klē-ˌāt, ˈnyü-\ *vb* **1** : to gather about or into a center; *also* **:** to act as a nucleus for or provide with a nucleus **2** **:** to form, act as, or have a nucleus — **nu•cle•ation** \ˌnü-klē-ˈā-shən, ˌnyü-\ *n*

nu•cle•at•ed \ˈnü-klē-ˌāt-əd, ˈnyü-\ *also* **nu•cle•ate** \-klē-ət\ *adj* **:** having a nucleus or nuclei ⟨*nucleated* cells⟩

nu•cle•ic acid \nü-ˌklē-ik-, nyü-, -ˌklā-\ *n* **:** any of various acids (as a DNA or an RNA) that are composed of a sugar or derivative of a sugar, phosphoric acid, and a base arranged in linked nucleotides and that are found especially in cell nuclei

nu•cle•o•lus \nü-ˈklē-ə-ləs, nyü-\ *n, pl* **-li** \-ˌlī\ **:** a spherical body in a cell nucleus that is associated with a specific part of a chromosome and contains much ribosomal RNA [New Latin, from Latin *nucleus* "kernel"] — **nu•cle•o•lar** \-lər\ *adj*

nu•cle•on \ˈnü-klē-ˌän, ˈnyü-\ *n* **:** a proton or a neutron especially in the atomic nucleus

nu•cle•on•ics \ˌnü-klē-ˈän-iks, ˌnyü-\ *n* **:** a branch of physical science that deals with nucleons or with all phenomena of the atomic nucleus

nu•cleo•plasm \ˈnü-klē-ə-ˌplaz-əm, ˈnyü-\ *n* **:** the protoplasm of a nucleus; *esp* **:** NUCLEAR SAP

nu•cleo•pro•tein \ˌnü-klē-ō-ˈprō-ˌtēn, ˌnyü-, -ˈprōt-ē-ən\ *n* **:** any of the proteins joined to nucleic acid that occur especially in the nuclei of living cells and are an essential constituent of genes and viruses

nu•cle•o•side \ˈnü-klē-ə-ˌsīd, ˈnyü-\ *n* **:** a compound that is formed by partial hydrolysis of a nucleic acid or a nucleotide and contains a purine or pyrimidine base combined with deoxyribose or ribose [*nucle-* + *-ose* + *-ide*]

nu•cle•o•tide \-ˌtīd\ *n* **:** any of several compounds that consist of a ribose or deoxyribose sugar joined to a purine or pyrimidine base and to a phosphate group and that are the basic structural groups of RNA and DNA [derived from *nucle-* + *-ide*]

nu•cle•us \ˈnü-klē-əs, ˈnyü-\ *n, pl* **-clei** \-klē-ˌī\ *also* **-cle•us•es :** a central point, group, or mass of something: as **a :** the small, brighter, and denser part of a galaxy or of the head of a comet **b :** a part of the cell that controls many cell functions (as reproduction and protein synthesis), contains the chromosomes, and is bounded by a nuclear membrane **c :** a mass of gray matter or group of nerve cells in the central nervous system **d :** a characteristic and stable complex of atoms or groups in a molecule **e :** the positively charged central part of an atom that comprises nearly all of the atomic mass and that consists of protons and neutrons except in hydrogen in which it consists of one proton only [Latin, "kernel", from *nuc-*, *nux* "nut"]

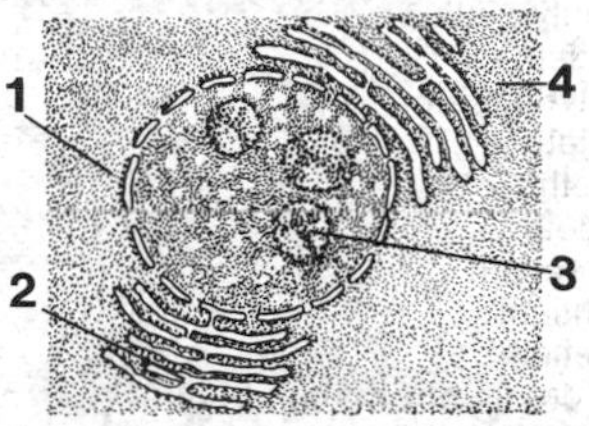

nucleus b: *1* nuclear membrane, *2* endoplasmic reticulum, *3* nucleolus, *4* cytoplasm

nu•clide \ˈnü-ˌklīd, ˈnyü-\ *n* **:** a species of atom characterized by the constitution of its nucleus [*nucleus* + Greek *eidos* "form, species"] — **nu•clid•ic** \nü-ˈklid-ik, nyü-\ *adj*

^{1}**nude** \ˈnüd, ˈnyüd\ *adj* **:** NAKED, BARE; *esp* **:** having no clothes on [Latin *nudus*] — **nude•ly** *adv* — **nude•ness** *n* — **nu•di•ty** \ˈnüd-ət-ē, ˈnyüd-\ *n*

^{2}**nude** *n* **1 :** a nude human figure especially as depicted in art **2 :** the condition of being nude ⟨in the *nude*⟩

nudge \ˈnəj\ *vt* **:** to touch or push gently; *esp* **:** to seek the attention of by a push with the elbow [perhaps of Scandinavian origin] — **nudge** *n* — **nudg•er** *n*

nu•di•branch \ˈnüd-ə-ˌbrangk, ˈnyüd-\ *n, pl* **-branchs :** any of a group (Nudibranchia) of marine mollusks without a shell as adults and without true gills [derived from Latin *nudus* "nude" + *branchia* "gill"] — **nudibranch** *adj*

nud•ism \ˈnü-ˌdiz-əm, ˈnyü-\ *n* **:** the practice of going nude especially in groups and during periods of time spent in secluded places — **nud•ist** \ˈnüd-əst, ˈnyüd-\ *n*

nug•get \ˈnəg-ət\ *n* **:** a solid lump usually of precious metal [origin unknown]

nui•sance \ˈnüs-ns, ˈnyüs-\ *n* **:** one that is annoying, unpleasant, or obnoxious [Anglo-French *nusaunce* "harm, injury", from Old French *nuisir* "to harm", from Latin *nocēre*]

^{1}**null** \ˈnəl\ *adj* **1 :** having no legal or binding force **:** INVALID **2 :** amounting to nothing **:** NIL **3 :** having no value **:** INSIGNIFICANT **4 :** containing no elements ⟨*null* set⟩ [Middle French *nul,* literally, "not any", from Latin *nullus,* from *ne-* "not" + *ullus* "any"]

^{2}**null** *n* **:** ZERO 2a

null and void *adj* **:** having no force, binding power, or validity

nul•li•fi•ca•tion \ˌnəl-ə-fə-ˈkā-shən\ *n* **1 :** the act of nullifying **:** the state of being nullified **2 :** the action of a state obstructing or attempting to prevent the operation and enforcement within its territory of a law of the United States — **nul•li•fi•ca•tion•ist** \-shə-nəst, -shnəst\ *n*

nul•li•fy \ˈnəl-ə-ˌfī\ *vt* **-fied**; **-fy•ing 1 :** to make null **:** VOID **2 :** to make of no value or consequence

• **syn** NULLIFY, NEGATE, ANNUL, INVALIDATE mean to deprive of effective or continued existence. NULLIFY implies counteracting completely the force, effectiveness, or value of something ⟨all our work *nullified* by one act of carelessness⟩ NEGATE implies the destruction or canceling out of each of two things by the other ⟨slavery *negates* freedom⟩ ANNUL suggests making ineffective by legal or official action ⟨the treaty *annuls* all previous agreements⟩ INVALIDATE implies a legal or moral flaw that makes something not acceptable or not valid ⟨the absence of a signature *invalidated* the will⟩

numb \ˈnəm\ *adj* **1 :** lacking in sensation especially as a result of cold or anesthesia **2 :** lacking in emotion **:** INDIFFERENT [Middle English *nomen,* from *nimen* "to take, seize", from Old English *niman*] — **numb** *vt* — **numb•ly** *adv* — **numb•ness** *n*

^{1}**num•ber** \ˈnəm-bər\ *n* **1 a :** the total of individual items taken together ⟨the *number* of people in the room⟩ **b :** an indefinite usually large total ⟨a *number* of accidents occur on wet roads⟩ **2 a :** the possibility of being counted ⟨mosquitoes in swarms beyond *number*⟩ **b :** the property involved in seeing things as units subject to separating ⟨observing the difference between few and many and calling it *number*⟩ **3 a :** a unit (as an integer or irrational number) belonging to a mathematical system and subject to its laws **b** *pl* **:** ARITHMETIC 1 **4 :** a distinction of word form to denote reference to one or more than one ⟨a verb agrees in *number* with its subject⟩; *also* **:** a form or group of forms so distinguished — compare PLURAL, SINGULAR **5 a :** a symbol (as a character, letter, or word) used to represent a mathematical number; *esp* **:** NUMERAL 1 **b :** a number used to identify or designate ⟨*number* one on the list⟩ ⟨a phone *number*⟩ **6** *pl* **:** regular count especially of syllables in poetry **:** METER; *also* **:** metrical verse **7 :** a member of a sequence or series ⟨the best *number* on the program⟩ ⟨lost the last *number* of the magazine⟩ **8** *pl* **:** a form of lottery in which bets are placed on numbers regularly published [Old French *nombre,* from Latin *numerus*] — **by the numbers 1 :** in unison to a specific count or cadence **2 :** in a systematic, routine, or mechanical manner

^{2}**number** *vb* **num•bered**; **num•ber•ing** \-bə-ring, -bring\ **1 :** COUNT 1, ENUMERATE **2 :** to claim as part of a total **:** INCLUDE **3 :** to restrict to a definite number ⟨their days are *numbered*⟩ **4 :** to assign a number to **5 :** to comprise in number ⟨our group *numbered* 10 in all⟩ **6 :** comprise a total number ⟨their fans *number* in the millions⟩ — **num•ber•able** \ˈnəm-bə-rə-bəl, -brə-bəl\ *adj* — **num•ber•er** \-bər-ər\ *n*

num•ber•less \ˈnəm-bər-ləs\ *adj* **:** too many to count

number line *n* **:** an infinite line whose points correspond to the real numbers according to their distance in a positive or negative direction from a point arbitrarily labeled zero

Num•bers \ˈnəm-bərz\ *n* — see BIBLE table

number theory *n* **:** the study of the properties of integers

numb•ing \ˈnəm-ing\ *adj* **:** causing numbness — **numb•ing•ly** \-ing-lē\ *adv*

numb•skull *variant of* NUMSKULL

nu•mer•a•ble \ˈnüm-rə-bəl, ˈnyüm-, -ə-rə-\ *adj* **:** that can be counted

nu•mer•al \ˈnüm-rəl, ˈnyüm-, -ə-rəl\ *n* **1 :** a symbol representing a number **2** *pl* **:** numbers designating by year a school or college class that are awarded for distinction especially in sports [Middle French, "of numbers", from Late Latin *numeralis,* from Latin *numerus* "number"]

nu•mer•ate \ˈnü-mə-ˌrāt, ˈnyü-\ *vt* **:** ENUMERATE [Latin *numerare* "to count", from *numerus* "number"]

\ə\ **abut**	\au̇\ **out**	\i\ **tip**	\ȯ\ **saw**	\u̇\ **foot**
\ər\ **further**	\ch\ **chin**	\ī\ **life**	\ȯi\ **coin**	\y\ **yet**
\a\ **mat**	\e\ **pet**	\j\ **job**	\th\ **thin**	\yü\ **few**
\ā\ **take**	\ē\ **easy**	\ng\ **sing**	\t͟h\ **this**	\yu̇\ **cure**
\ä\ **cot, cart**	\g\ **go**	\ō\ **bone**	\ü\ **food**	\zh\ **vision**

TABLE OF NUMBERS

CARDINAL NUMBERS[1]

NAME[2]	SYMBOL Arabic	SYMBOL Roman[3]
zero *or* naught *or* cipher	0	
one	1	I
two	2	II
three	3	III
four	4	IV
five	5	V
six	6	VI
seven	7	VII
eight	8	VIII
nine	9	IX
ten	10	X
eleven	11	XI
twelve	12	XII
thirteen	13	XIII
fourteen	14	XIV
fifteen	15	XV
sixteen	16	XVI
seventeen	17	XVII
eighteen	18	XVIII
nineteen	19	XIX
twenty	20	XX
twenty-one	21	XXI
twenty-two	22	XXII
twenty-three	23	XXIII
twenty-four	24	XXIV
twenty-five	25	XXV
twenty-six	26	XXVI
twenty-seven	27	XXVII
twenty-eight	28	XXVIII
twenty-nine	29	XXIX
thirty	30	XXX
thirty-one *etc*	31	XXXI
forty	40	XL
fifty	50	L
sixty	60	LX
seventy	70	LXX
eighty	80	LXXX
ninety	90	XC
one hundred	100	C
one hundred and one *or* one hundred one *etc*	101	CI
two hundred	200	CC
three hundred	300	CCC
four hundred	400	CD
five hundred	500	D
six hundred	600	DC
seven hundred	700	DCC
eight hundred	800	DCCC
nine hundred	900	CM
one thousand *or* ten hundred *etc*	1,000	M
two thousand *etc*	2,000	MM
five thousand	5,000	$\overline{V}$
ten thousand	10,000	$\overline{X}$
one hundred thousand	100,000	$\overline{C}$
one million	1,000,000	$\overline{M}$

ORDINAL NUMBERS[4]

NAME[5]	SYMBOL[6]
first	1st
second	2d *or* 2nd
third	3d *or* 3rd
fourth	4th
fifth	5th
sixth	6th
seventh	7th
eighth	8th
ninth	9th
tenth	10th
eleventh	11th
twelfth	12th
thirteenth	13th
fourteenth	14th
fifteenth	15th
sixteenth	16th
seventeenth	17th
eighteenth	18th
nineteenth	19th
twentieth	20th
twenty-first	21st
twenty-second	22d *or* 22nd
twenty-third	23d *or* 23rd
twenty-fourth	24th
twenty-fifth	25th
twenty-sixth	26th
twenty-seventh	27th
twenty-eighth	28th
twenty-ninth	29th
thirtieth	30th
thirty-first *etc*	31st
fortieth	40th
fiftieth	50th
sixtieth	60th
seventieth	70th
eightieth	80th
ninetieth	90th
hundredth *or* one hundredth	100th
hundred and first *or* one hundred and first *etc*	101st
two hundredth	200th
three hundredth	300th
four hundredth	400th
five hundredth	500th
six hundredth	600th
seven hundredth	700th
eight hundredth	800th
nine hundredth	900th
thousandth *or* one thousandth	1,000th
two thousandth *etc*	2,000th
five thousandth	5,000th
ten thousandth	10,000th
hundred thousandth *or* one hundred thousandth	100,000th
millionth *or* one millionth	1,000,000th

(continued on next page)

[1]The cardinal numbers are used in simple counting or in answer to "how many?" The words for these numbers may be used as nouns (I counted to *twelve*), as pronouns (*twelve* were found), or as adjectives (*twelve* cows).

[2]In formal contexts the numbers one to one hundred and in less formal contexts the numbers one to nine are commonly written out, while larger numbers are given in numerals. In nearly all contexts a number occuring at the beginning of a sentence is usually written out. Except in very formal contexts numerals are invariably used for dates. Arabic numerals from 1,000 to 9,999 are often written without commas (1000; 9999). Year numbers are always written without commas (1783).

[3]The Roman numerals are written either in capitals or in lowercase letters.

[4]The ordinal numbers are used to show the order of succession in which such items as names, objects, and periods of time are considered (the *twelfth* month; the *fourth* row of seats; the *18th* century).

[5]Each of the terms for the ordinal numbers excepting *first* and *second* is used in designating one of a number of parts into which a whole may be divided (a *fourth;* a *sixth;* a *tenth)* and used as the denominator in fractions designating the number of such parts constituting a certain portion of a whole (*one fourth; three fifths).* When used as nouns the fractions are usually written as two words, although they are regularly hyphenated as adjectives (a *two-thirds* majority). When fractions are written in numerals, the cardinal symbols are used ($1/4$, $3/5$, $5/6$).

[6]The Arabic symbols for the cardinal numbers may be read as ordinals in certain contexts (January 1 = January first; 2 Samuel = Second Samuel). The Roman numerals are sometimes read as ordinals (Henry IV = Henry the Fourth); sometimes they are written with the ordinal suffixes (XIXth Dynasty).

DENOMINATIONS ABOVE ONE MILLION

American system[1]

NAME	VALUE IN POWERS OF TEN	NUMBER OF ZEROS[2]	NUMBER OF GROUPS OF THREE 0'S AFTER 1,000
billion	10^{9}	9	2
trillion	10^{12}	12	3
quadrillion	10^{15}	15	4
quintillion	10^{18}	18	5
sextillion	10^{21}	21	6
septillion	10^{24}	24	7
octillion	10^{27}	27	8
nonillion	10^{30}	30	9
decillion	10^{33}	33	10

British system[1]

NAME	VALUE IN POWERS OF TEN	NUMBER OF ZEROS[2]	POWERS OF 1,000,000
milliard	10^{9}	9	—
billion	10^{12}	12	2
trillion	10^{18}	18	3
quadrillion	10^{24}	24	4
quintillion	10^{30}	30	5
sextillion	10^{36}	36	6
septillion	10^{42}	42	7
octillion	10^{48}	48	8
nonillion	10^{54}	54	9
decillion	10^{60}	60	10

[1]The American system of numeration for denominations above one million was modeled on the French system but more recently the French system has been changed to correspond to the British and German systems. In the American system each of the denominations above 1,000 millions (the American *billion)* is 1,000 times the one preceding (one trillion = 1,000 billions; one quadrillion = 1,000 trillions). In the British system the first denomination above 1,000 millions (the British *milliard)* is 1,000 times the preceding one, but each of the denominations above 1,000 milliards (the British *billion)* is 1,000,000 times the preceding one (one trillion = 1,000,000 billions; one quadrillion = 1,000,000 trillions).

[2]For convenience in reading large numerals the thousands, millions, etc., are usually separated by commas (21,530; 1,155,465) or by half spaces (1 155 465). Serial numbers (as social security number or the engine number of a car) are often written with hyphens (583-695-20).

nu•mer•a•tion \\ˌnü-mə-ˈrā-shən, ˌnyü-\\ *n* **:** the act or process or a system or instance of enumeration

nu•mer•a•tor \\ˈnü-mə-ˌrāt-ər, ˈnyü-\\ *n* **1 :** the part of a fraction written above or to the left of the line that signifies the number of parts of the denominator taken **2 :** one that counts something

nu•mer•i•cal \\nu̇-ˈmer-i-kəl, nyu̇-\\ *adj* **:** of, relating to, being, or expressed in numbers ⟨*numerical* calculations⟩ — **nu•mer•i•cal•ly** \\-kə-lē, -klē\\ *adv*

nu•mer•ol•o•gy \\ˌnü-mə-ˈräl-ə-jē, ˌnyü-\\ *n* **:** the study of the occult significance of numbers — **nu•mer•ol•o•gist** \\-jəst\\ *n*

nu•mer•ous \\ˈnüm-rəs, ˈnyüm-, -ə-rəs\\ *adj* **:** consisting of great numbers of units or individuals ⟨a *numerous* group of people⟩ ⟨*numerous* occasions⟩ **syn** see MANY — **nu•mer•ous•ly** *adv* — **nu•mer•ous•ness** *n*

nu•mis•mat•ic \\ˌnü-məz-ˈmat-ik, ˌnyü-, -məs-\\ *adj* **1 :** of or relating to numismatics **2 :** of or relating to coins **[**French *numismatique*, from Latin *nomisma* "coin", from Greek, "custom, coin"**]** — **nu•mis•mat•i•cal•ly** \\-ˈmat-i-kə-lē, -klē\\ *adv*

nu•mis•mat•ics \\-iks\\ *n* **:** the study or collection of coins, tokens, medals, or paper money — **nu•mis•ma•tist** \\nü-ˈmiz-mət-əst, nyü-\\ *n*

num•skull *or* **numb•skull** \\ˈnəm-ˌskəl\\ *n* **:** a stupid person **:** DUNCE **[***numb* + *skull***]**

nun \\ˈnən\\ *n* **:** a woman belonging to a religious order; *esp* **:** *one under solemn vows of poverty, chastity, and obedience* **[**Old English *nunne*, from Late Latin *nonna***]**

Nunc Di•mit•tis \\ˌnəngk-də-ˈmit-əs\\ *n* **:** the prayer of Simeon in Luke 2:29–32 used as a canticle **[**Latin, "now lettest thou depart"; from the first words of the canticle**]**

nun•ci•a•ture \\ˈnən-sē-ə-ˌchu̇r, ˈnu̇n-, -chər\\ *n* **1 :** the office or period of office of a nuncio **2 :** a papal delegation headed by a nuncio **[**Italian *nunciatura*, from *nuncio* "nuncio"**]**

nun•cio \\ˈnən-sē-ˌō, ˈnu̇n-\\ *n, pl* **-ci•os :** a papal representative of the highest rank permanently accredited to a civil government **[**Italian, from Latin *nuntius* "messenger, message"**]**

nun•cu•pa•tive \\ˈnən-kyu̇-ˌpāt-iv, ˌnən-ˈkyü-pət-\\ *adj* **:** not written **:** ORAL ⟨a *nuncupative* will⟩ **[**Medieval Latin *nuncupativus*, from Late Latin, "so-called", from Latin *nuncupare* "to name, call", from *nomen* "name" + *capere* "to take"**]**

nun•nery \\ˈnən-rē, -ə-rē\\ *n, pl* **-ner•ies :** a convent of nuns

[1]nup•tial \\ˈnəp-shəl, -chəl\\ *adj* **1 :** of or relating to marriage or the marriage ceremony **2 :** characteristic of mating or the breeding season **[**Latin *nuptialis*, from *nuptiae* "wedding", from *nubere* "to marry"**]** **syn** see MATRIMONIAL

[2]nuptial *n* **:** WEDDING 1 — usually used in pl.

[1]nurse \\ˈnərs\\ *n* **1 :** a woman who has the care of a young child **2 :** one skilled or trained in caring for the sick or infirm especially under the supervision of a physician **3 :** a worker of a social insect that cares for the young **[**Old French *nurice*, from Late Latin *nutricia*, from Latin *nutricius* "nourishing, nutritious"**]**

[2]nurse *vb* **1 :** to feed at the breast **:** SUCKLE **2 :** REAR 3b, EDUCATE **3 :** to manage with care or economy ⟨*nurse* one's funds⟩ **4 :** to care for as a nurse ⟨*nursed* them back to health⟩ **5 :** to hold in one's memory or consideration ⟨*nurse* a grudge⟩ **6 :** to treat with special care ⟨*nurse* a car over a rough road⟩ **7 :** to act or serve as a nurse **[**Middle English *nurshen* "to nourish", from *nurishen***]** **nurs•er** *n*

nurse•maid \\ˈnər-ˌsmād\\ *n* **:** a girl or woman employed to look after children

nurs•ery \\ˈnərs-rē, -ə-rē\\ *n, pl* **-er•ies 1 a :** a room or suite set apart in a house for the children **b :** a place where children are temporarily cared for in their parents' absence **c :** DAY NURSERY **2 :** something that fosters, develops, or promotes **3 :** a place where plants (as trees or shrubs) are grown for transplanting, for use as stocks in grafting, or for sale

nurs•ery•maid \\-ˌmād\\ *n* **:** NURSEMAID

nurs•ery•man \\-mən\\ *n* **:** a person whose occupation is the growing of plants (as trees and shrubs) especially for sale

nursery rhyme *n* **:** a short rhyme for children that often tells a story

nursery school *n* **:** a school for children usually under five years of age

nursing bottle *n* **:** a bottle with a nipple used for feeding a baby

nurs•ling \\ˈnərs-ling\\ *n* **1 :** one tended with special care **2 :** a nursing child

[1]nur•ture \\ˈnər-chər\\ *n* **1 :** TRAINING 1, UPBRINGING **2 :** something that nourishes **:** FOOD **3 :** the influences that modify the expression of the genes of an organism **[**Middle French *norriture*, from Late Latin *nutritura* "act of nursing", from Latin *nutrire* 'to nourish, nurse"**]**

[2]nurture *vt* **nur•tured; nur•tur•ing** \\ˈnərch-ring, -ə-ring\\ **1 :** to supply with nourishment **2 :** EDUCATE 2 **3 :** to further the development of **:** FOSTER — **nur•tur•er** \\ˈnər-chər-ər\\ *n*

[1]nut \\ˈnət\\ *n* **1 a :** a hard-shelled dry fruit or seed with a separable rind or shell and an inner kernel; *also* **:** this kernel **b :** a dry one-seeded fruit that has a woody outer layer and that does not split open when ripe **2 :** a small block usually of metal with a hole in it that has an internal screw thread and is used on a bolt or screw for tightening or holding something **3 :** the ridge in a stringed musical instrument over which the strings pass on the upper end of the fingerboard **4 a :** a foolish, eccentric, or crazy person **b :** ENTHUSIAST, FAN **[**Old English *hnutu***]** — **nut•like** \\-ˌlīk\\ *adj*

[2]nut *vi* **nut•ted; nut•ting :** to gather or seek nuts

nut•crack•er \\ˈnət-ˌkrak-ər\\ *n* **1 :** an instrument for cracking the shells of nuts **2 :** a bird related to the crows that lives largely on seeds from the cones of the pine tree

nut•hatch \\ˈnət-ˌhach\\ *n* **:** any of various small birds intermediate in appearance and habits between the titmice and creep-

\\ə\\ **abut**	\\au̇\\ **out**	\\i\\ **tip**	\\ȯ\\ **saw**	\\u̇\\ **foot**
\\ər\\ **further**	\\ch\\ **chin**	\\ī\\ **life**	\\ȯi\\ **coin**	\\y\\ **yet**
\\a\\ **mat**	\\e\\ **pet**	\\j\\ **job**	\\th\\ **thin**	\\yü\\ **few**
\\ā\\ **take**	\\ē\\ **easy**	\\ng\\ **sing**	\\t͟h\\ **this**	\\yu̇\\ **cure**
\\ä\\ **cot, cart**	\\g\\ **go**	\\ō\\ **bone**	\\ü\\ **food**	\\zh\\ **vision**

ers [Middle English *notehache,* from *note* "nut" + *hache* "ax", from Old French, "battle-ax"]

nut·let \'nət-lət\ *n* : a small fruit similar to a nut

nut·meg \'nət-,meg\ *n* **1** : the aromatic seed of a tree grown in the East and West Indies and Brazil; *also* : this tree **2** : a spice consisting of ground nutmeg seeds [Middle English *notemuge,* derived from Provencal *noz muscada,* from *noz* "nut" (from Latin *nux*) + *muscada,* feminine of *muscat* "musky"]

nuthatch

nut·pick \-,pik\ *n* : a small sharp-pointed table implement for extracting the kernels from nuts

nu·tria \'nü-trē-ə, 'nyü-\ *n* **1** : COYPU 1 **2** : the durable usually light brown fur of the coypu [Spanish, "otter", from Latin *lutra*]

[1]**nu·tri·ent** \'nü-trē-ənt, 'nyü-\ *adj* : furnishing nourishment [Latin *nutriens,* present participle of *nutrire* "to nourish"]

[2]**nutrient** *n* : a nutritive substance or ingredient

nu·tri·ment \'nü-trə-mənt, 'nyü-\ *n* : something that nourishes : FOOD

nu·tri·tion \nu̇-'trish-ən, nyu̇-\ *n* : the act or process of nourishing or being nourished; *esp* : the processes by which an animal or plant takes in and utilizes food substances [Middle French, from Late Latin *nutritio,* from Latin *nutrire* "to nourish"] — **nu·tri·tion·al** \-'trish-nəl, -ən-l\ *adj* — **nu·tri·tion·al·ly** \-ē\ *adv*

nu·tri·tion·ist \-'trish-nəst, -ə-nəst\ *n* : a specialist in the study of nutrition

nu·tri·tious \nu̇-'trish-əs, nyu̇-\ *adj* : NOURISHING [Latin *nutricius,* from *nutrix* "nurse"] — **nu·tri·tious·ly** *adv* — **nu·tri·tious·ness** *n*

nu·tri·tive \'nü-trət-iv, 'nyü-\ *adj* **1** : of or relating to nutrition **2** : NOURISHING — **nu·tri·tive·ly** *adv*

nuts \'nəts\ *adj* **1** : ENTHUSIASTIC, KEEN **2** : CRAZY 2a, DEMENTED

nut·shell \'nət-,shel\ *n* : the shell of a nut — **in a nutshell** : in a small space : in brief

nut·ty \'nət-ē\ *adj* **nut·tier; -est 1** : containing or suggesting nuts (as in flavor) **2** : ECCENTRIC 2 ⟨a *nutty* idea⟩; *also* : mentally unbalanced — **nut·ti·ness** *n*

nux vom·i·ca \'nəks-'väm-i-kə\ *n, pl* **nux vomica** : the poisonous seed of an Asian tree that contains strychnine; *also* : this tree [New Latin, literally, "emetic nut"]

nuz·zle \'nəz-əl\ *vb* **nuz·zled; nuz·zling** \'nəz-ling, -ə-ling\ **1** : to push or rub with the nose **2** : to lie close : NESTLE [Middle English *noselen* "to bring the nose toward the ground", from *nose*]

ny·lon \'nī-,län\ *n* **1** : any of numerous strong tough elastic synthetic materials used especially in textiles and plastics **2** *pl* : stockings made of nylon [coined word] — **nylon** *adj*

nymph \'nimf, 'nimpf\ *n, pl* **nymphs** \'nimfs, 'nimpfs, 'nims, 'nimps\ **1** : one of the minor divinities of nature in ancient mythology represented as beautiful maidens dwelling in the mountains, forests, meadows, and waters **2** : an immature insect (as a dragonfly or grasshopper) that differs from the adult especially in size and in its incompletely developed wings and sex organs [Middle French *nimphe,* from Latin *nympha* "bride, nymph", from Greek *nymphē*] — **nymph·al** \'nim-fəl, 'nimp-\ *adj*

nys·tag·mus \nis-'tag-məs\ *n* : a rapid involuntary oscillation (as from dizziness) of the eyeballs [Greek *nystagmos* "drowsiness", from *nystazein* "to doze"]

O o—ozonosphere

o \'ō\ *n, pl* **o's** *or* **os** \'ōz\ *often cap* **1** : the 15th letter of the English alphabet **2** : ZERO

O *variant of* OH

o- *or* **oo-** *combining form* : egg : ovum ⟨oocyte⟩ [Greek *ōion* "egg"]

-o- — used as a connective vowel originally to join word elements of Greek origin and now also to join word elements of Latin or other origin ⟨speedometer⟩ [Greek, stem vowel of many nouns and adjectives in combination]

o' *also* **o** \ə\ *prep* **1** *chiefly dialect* : ON **2** : OF ⟨one o'clock⟩

oaf \'ōf\ *n* : a stupid or awkward person [obsolete *oaf* "changeling", of Scandinavian origin] — **oaf·ish** \'ō-fish\ *adj* — **oaf·ish·ly** *adv* — **oaf·ish·ness** *n*

△ **origin** The elves, like the fairies, were believed to steal human children, leaving in their stead elf children, changelings. Such a changeling was called an *oaf;* the word is related to *elf.* The word *oaf* in its strictest sense should have been applied only to genuine changelings, but it was soon used for any deformed or retarded child. From the sense "idiot child" it was a short and easy step to the present meaning, "a stupid or awkward person".

oak \'ōk\ *n, pl* **oaks** *or* **oak 1** : any of various trees or shrubs closely related to the beech and chestnut and having a rounded one-seeded thin-shelled nut **2** : the usually tough hard durable wood of the oak much used for furniture and flooring [Old English *āc*] — **oak** *adj* — **oak·en** \'ō-kən\ *adj*

oak apple *n* : a large round gall produced on oak leaves by a small wasp

oa·kum \'ō-kəm\ *n* : hemp or jute fiber impregnated with tar or a tar derivative and used in caulking seams and packing joints [Old English *ācumba*]

oar \'ōr, 'ȯr\ *n* **1** : a long pole with a broad blade at one end used for propelling or steering a boat **2** : OARSMAN [Old English *ār*] — **oared** \'ōrd, 'ȯrd\ *adj*

oar·lock \'ōr-,läk, 'ȯr-\ *n* : a U-shaped device for holding an oar in place

oars·man \'ōrz-mən, 'ȯrz-\ *n* : a person who rows especially in a racing crew

oa·sis \ō-'ā-səs\ *n, pl* **oa·ses** \-'ā-,sēz\ : a fertile or green area in an arid region [Late Latin, from Greek]

oak 1

oat \'ōt\ *n* **1** : a cereal grass with long spikelets in loose clusters that is widely grown for its seed which is used for human food and livestock feed **2** *pl* : a crop or plot of the oat; *also* : oat seed [Old English *āte*]

oat·en \'ōt-n\ *adj* : of or relating to oats, oat straw, or oatmeal

oath \'ōth\ *n, pl* **oaths** \'ōthz, 'ōths\ **1** : a solemn appeal to God or to some revered person or thing to bear witness to the truth of one's word or the sacredness of a promise ⟨under *oath* to tell the truth⟩ **2** : a careless or profane use of a sacred name [Old English *āth*]

oat·meal \'ōt-,mēl, ōt-'\ *n* : oats husked and crushed into coarse meal or flattened into flakes; *also* : porridge made from such meal or flakes

ob- *prefix* : inversely ⟨obovate⟩ [Latin, "in the way, against, toward", from *ob* "in the way of, on account of"]

Oba·di·ah \,ō-bə-'dī-ə\ *n* — see BIBLE table

[1]**ob·bli·ga·to** \,äb-lə-'gät-ō\ *adj* : not to be omitted : OBLIGATORY —used as a direction in music [Italian, "obligatory", from *obbligare*

"to oblige", from Latin *obligare*]
[2]**obbligato** *n, pl* **-gatos** *also* **-ga•ti** \-'gät-ē\ **:** a prominent accompanying part usually played by a solo instrument ⟨a violin *obbligato*⟩; *also* **:** any accompanying part

oat 1

ob•du•ra•cy \'äb-də-rə-sē, -dyə-; äb-'du̇r-ə-, -'dyu̇r-\ *n, pl* **-cies** **:** the quality or state or an instance of being obdurate
ob•du•rate \'äb-də-rət, -dyə-; äb-'du̇r-ət, -'dyu̇r-\ *adj* **1 a :** hardened in feelings **b :** stubbornly persistent in wrongdoing **2 :** resisting change **:** UNYIELDING [Latin *obduratus,* past participle of *obdurare* "to harden", from *ob-* "against" + *durus* "hard"] — **ob•du•rate•ly** *adv* — **ob•du•rate•ness** *n*
obe•di•ence \ō-'bēd-ē-əns, ə-\ *n* **1 :** an act or instance of obeying **2 :** the quality or state of being obedient
obe•di•ent \-ənt\ *adj* **:** willing or inclined to obey [Old French, from Latin *oboediens,* from *oboedire* "to obey"] — **obe•di•ent•ly** *adv*
obei•sance \ō-'bās-ns, -'bēs-\ *n* **1 :** a movement of the body made as a sign of respect **:** BOW **2 :** DEFERENCE, HOMAGE [Middle French *obeissance* "obedience, obeisance", from *obeir* "to obey"] — **obei•sant** \-nt\ *adj*
obe•lia \ō-'bēl-yə\ *n* **:** any of a genus of small colonial marine hydroids that branch like trees [New Latin, genus name]
ob•e•lisk \'äb-ə-,lisk\ *n* **:** a 4-sided pillar that tapers toward the top and ends in a pyramid [Middle French *obelisque,* from Latin *obeliscus,* from Greek *obeliskos,* from *obelos* "spit, pointed pillar"]

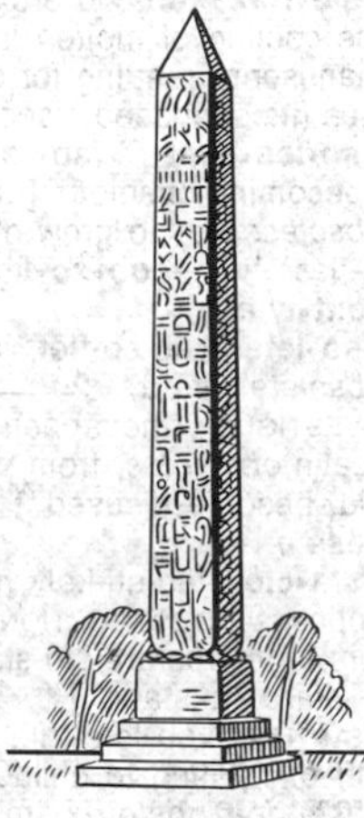
obelisk

obese \ō-'bēs\ *adj* **:** excessively fat [Latin *obesus,* from *obedere* "to eat up", from *ob-* "against" + *edere* "to eat"] — **obe•si•ty** \ō-'bē-sət-ē\ *n*
obey \ō-'bā, ə-\ *vb* **obeyed; obey•ing 1 :** to follow the commands or guidance of **2 :** to comply with **:** EXECUTE ⟨*obey* an order⟩ **3 :** to behave obediently [Old French *obeir,* from Latin *oboedire*] — **obey•er** *n*
ob•fus•cate \'äb-fə-,skāt, äb-'fəs-,kāt\ *vt* **1 :** to make dark or obscure **2 :** CONFUSE 2 [Late Latin *obfuscare,* from Latin *ob-* "in the way" + *fuscus* "dark brown"] — **ob•fus•ca•tion** \,äb-fəs-'kā-shən\ *n* — **ob•fus•ca•to•ry** \äb-'fəs-kə-,tōr-ē, -,tȯr-\ *adj*
obi \'ō-bē\ *n* **:** a broad sash worn with a Japanese kimono [Japanese]
obit \ō-'bit, 'ō-bət\ *n* **:** OBITUARY
obit•u•ary \ə-'bich-ə-,wer-ē\ *n, pl* **-ar•ies :** a notice of a person's death usually with a short biographical account [Medieval Latin *obituarium,* from Latin *obitus* "decease", from *obire* "to go to meet, die", from *ob-* "toward, against" + *ire* "to go"] — **obituary** *adj*
[1]**ob•ject** \'äb-jikt\ *n* **1 a :** something that may be seen or felt ⟨tables and chairs are *objects*⟩ **b :** something that may be thought about ⟨an *object* of study⟩ **2 :** something that arouses an emotional response (as of affection, hatred, or pity) ⟨an *object* of envy⟩ **3 :** AIM, PURPOSE ⟨the *object* is to raise money⟩ **4 a :** a word or phrase denoting someone or something that the action of a verb is directed toward **b :** the word or words in a prepositional phrase other than the preposition [Medieval Latin *objectum,* from Latin *obicere* "to throw in the way, present, hinder, object", from *ob-* "in the way" + *jacere* "to throw"] — **ob•ject•less** \'äb-jik-tləs\ *adj*
[2]**ob•ject** \əb-'jekt\ *vb* **1 :** to offer or cite as an objection ⟨*objected* that the price was too high⟩ **2 a :** to state one's opposition ⟨*objected* to the plan⟩ **b :** to be opposed ⟨I *object* to paying high prices for junk⟩ [Latin *objectus,* past participle of *obicere* "to throw in the way, object"] — **ob•jec•tor** \-'jek-tər\ *n*
object ball \'äb-jikt-, -jik-\ *n* **:** the ball struck by the cue ball in billiards and pool
ob•jec•tion \əb-'jek-shən\ *n* **1 :** an act of objecting **2 :** a reason for or feeling of disapproval
ob•jec•tion•able \-shə-nə-bəl, -shnə-bəl\ *adj* **:** DISPLEASING, OFFENSIVE ⟨was written in *objectionable* language⟩ — **ob•jec•tion•able•ness** *n* — **ob•jec•tion•ably** \-blē\ *adv*
[1]**ob•jec•tive** \əb-'jek-tiv\ *adj* **1 :** of or relating to an object or end ⟨reach our *objective* point⟩ **2 :** existing outside and independent of the mind ⟨dragons have no *objective* existence⟩ **3 :** treating facts without distortion by personal feelings or prejudices ⟨an *objective* study⟩ **4 :** of, relating to, or constituting a grammatical case marking typically the object of a verb or preposition — compare ACCUSATIVE — **ob•jec•tive•ly** *adv* — **ob•jec•tive•ness** *n* — **ob•jec•tiv•i•ty** \,äb-,jek-'tiv-ət-ē, əb-\ *n*
[2]**objective** *n* **1 :** an aim or end of action **:** GOAL **2 :** the objective case or a word in the objective case **3 :** a lens or system of lenses (as in a microscope) that forms an image of an object
objective complement *n* **:** a noun, adjective, or pronoun used in the predicate as complement to a verb and as qualifier of its direct object ⟨*green* in "paint the wall green" is an *objective complement*⟩
object lesson \'äb-jikt-\ *n* **:** a lesson taught by means of illustrative objects or concrete examples; *also* **:** something that teaches by a concrete example
ob•jet d'art \,ȯb-,zhā-'där\ *n, pl* **ob•jets d'art** *same*\ **:** an article of artistic value [French, literally, "art object"]
[1]**ob•late** \äb-'lāt, 'äb-,\ *adj* **:** flattened or depressed at the poles ⟨the *oblate* shape of the earth⟩ [New Latin *oblatus,* from *ob-* "ob-" + *-latus* (as in *prolatus* "elongated in the direction of the poles", from Latin, past participle of *proferre* "to extend", from *pro-* + *ferre* "to carry")]
[2]**ob•late** \'äb-,lāt\ *n* **1 :** a layman living in a monastery under a modified rule and without vows **2** *cap* **:** a member of one of several Roman Catholic communities of men or women [Medieval Latin *oblatus,* literally, "one offered up", from Latin, past participle of *offerre* "to offer"]
ob•la•tion \ə-'blā-shən, ō-\ *n* **:** a religious offering [Middle French, from Late Latin *oblatio,* from Latin *offerre* "to offer"]
[1]**ob•li•gate** \'äb-li-gət, -lə-,gāt\ *adj* **:** restricted to one particular mode of life ⟨an *obligate* parasite⟩ — **ob•li•gate•ly** *adv*
[2]**ob•li•gate** \'äb-lə-,gāt\ *vt* **:** to bring under obligation **:** bind legally or morally ⟨*obligated* to pay taxes⟩ [Latin *obligare,* from *ob-* "toward" + *ligare* "to bind"]
ob•li•ga•tion \,äb-lə-'gā-shən\ *n* **1 :** an act of binding oneself to a course of action **2 a :** something (as a promise or contract) that binds one to a course of action **b :** something one is bound to do **:** DUTY **3 :** indebtedness for an act of kindness
oblig•a•to•ry \ə-'blig-ə-,tōr-ē, ä-, -,tȯr-\ *adj* **:** legally or morally binding **:** REQUIRED ⟨a meeting at which attendance was *obligatory*⟩
oblige \ə-'blīj\ *vb* **1 :** FORCE, COMPEL ⟨laws *oblige* citizens to pay taxes⟩ **2 a :** to bind by a favor ⟨*oblige* an acquaintance with a loan⟩ **b :** to do something as a favor ⟨a person always willing to *oblige*⟩ [Old French *obliger,* from Latin *obligare* "to obligate"] — **oblig•er** *n*
oblig•ing \ə-'blī-jing\ *adj* **:** willing to do favors **:** ACCOMMODATING — **oblig•ing•ly** \-jing-lē\ *adv* — **oblig•ing•ness** *n*
[1]**oblique** \ō-'blēk, ə-, -'blīk\ *adj* **1 a :** neither perpendicular nor parallel **:** INCLINED **b :** having an axis or lateral edges that are not perpendicular to the plane of the base ⟨an *oblique* circular cone⟩ ⟨an *oblique* prism⟩ **2 :** not straightforward **:** INDIRECT ⟨*oblique* accusations⟩ [Latin *obliquus*] — **oblique•ly** *adv* — **oblique•ness** *n* — **obliq•ui•ty** \ō-'blik-wət-ē, ə-\ *n*
[2]**oblique** *n* **1 :** something that is oblique **2 :** any of several obliquely placed muscles; *esp* **:** one of the thin flat diagonal muscles of the abdominal wall
oblique angle *n* **:** an acute or obtuse angle
oblit•er•ate \ə-'blit-ə-,rāt, ō-\ *vt* **:** to remove or destroy completely **:** wipe out ⟨wind *obliterated* the tracks⟩ [Latin *oblitter-*

\ə\ **abut**	\au̇\ **out**	\i\ **tip**	\ȯ\ **saw**	\u̇\ **foot**
\ər\ **further**	\ch\ **chin**	\ī\ **life**	\ȯi\ **coin**	\y\ **yet**
\a\ **mat**	\e\ **pet**	\j\ **job**	\th\ **thin**	\yü\ **few**
\ā\ **take**	\ē\ **easy**	\ng\ **sing**	\t͟h\ **this**	\yu̇\ **cure**
\ä\ **cot, cart**	\g\ **go**	\ō\ **bone**	\ü\ **food**	\zh\ **vision**

are, from *ob* "in the way of", + *littera* "letter"] **syn** see ERASE — **ob·lit·er·a·tion** \-ˌblit-ə-ˈrā-shən\ *n* — **ob·lit·er·a·tive** \-ˈblit-ə-ˌrāt-iv\ *adj*

obliv·i·on \ə-ˈbliv-ē-ən, ō-, ä-\ *n* **1 :** an act or instance of forgetting **2 :** the quality or state of being forgotten [Middle French, from Latin *oblivio,* from *oblivisci* "to forget"]

obliv·i·ous \-ē-əs\ *adj* **1 :** lacking memory or mindful attention **:** FORGETFUL **2 :** lacking active conscious knowledge **:** UNAWARE ⟨*oblivious* to the risk of swimming alone⟩ — **obliv·i·ous·ly** *adv* — **obliv·i·ous·ness** *n*

ob·long \ˈäb-ˌlȯŋ\ *adj* **:** longer in one direction than in the other with opposite sides parallel **:** RECTANGULAR [Latin *oblongus,* from *ob-* "toward" + *longus* "long"] — **oblong** *n*

ob·lo·quy \ˈäb-lə-kwē\ *n, pl* **-quies 1 :** strongly condemnatory utterance or language **2 :** bad repute **:** DISGRACE [Late Latin *obloquium,* from *obloqui* "to speak against", from *ob-* "against" + *loqui* "to speak"]

ob·nox·ious \äb-ˈnäk-shəs, əb-\ *adj* **:** extremely disagreeable **:** OFFENSIVE [Latin *obnoxius,* from *ob* "in the way of, exposed to" + *noxa* "harm"] — **ob·nox·ious·ly** *adv* — **ob·nox·ious·ness** *n*

oboe \ˈō-bō\ *n* **:** a slender conical woodwind musical instrument with holes and keys that is played by blowing into a reed mouthpiece [Italian, from French *hautbois,* from *haut* "high" + *bois* "wood"] — **obo·ist** \ˈō-ˌbō-əst\ *n*

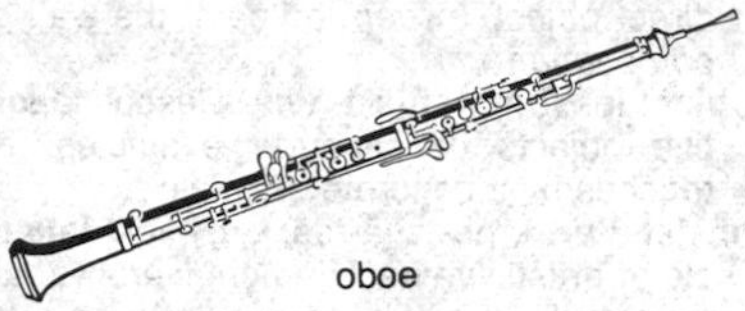

oboe

obol \ˈäb-əl, ˈō-bəl\ *n* **:** an ancient Greek coin or weight equal to 1/6 drachma (about .6 gram) [Latin *obolus,* from Greek *obolos*]

ob·ovate \äb-ˈō-ˌvāt, ˈäb-\ *adj* **:** ovate with the base narrower ⟨an *obovate* leaf⟩

ob·scene \äb-ˈsēn, əb-\ *adj* **1 :** disgusting to the senses **:** REPULSIVE **2 :** deeply offensive to morality or decency; *esp* **:** designed to incite to lust or depravity [Middle French "repulsive, disgusting", from Latin *obscenus*] **syn** see COARSE — **ob·scene·ly** *adv*

ob·scen·i·ty \-ˈsen-ət-ē\ *n, pl* **-ties 1 :** the quality or state of being obscene **2 :** something that is obscene

[1]**ob·scure** \äb-ˈskyu̇r, əb-\ *adj* **1 :** lacking or inadequately supplied with light **:** DIM, GLOOMY **2 a :** withdrawn from the centers of human activity **:** REMOTE ⟨an *obscure* country village⟩ **b :** not readily understood or not clearly expressed **c :** lacking showiness or prominence **:** HUMBLE ⟨an *obscure* poet⟩ **d :** not distinct **:** FAINT **3 :** constituting the unstressed vowel \ə\ or having unstressed \ə\ as its value [Middle French *obscur,* from Latin *obscurus*] — **ob·scure·ly** *adv* — **ob·scure·ness** *n* — **ob·scu·ri·ty** \äb-ˈskyu̇r-ət-ē, ab-\ *n*

• **syn** OBSCURE, DARK, VAGUE, CRYPTIC mean not clearly understandable. OBSCURE implies a veiling of meaning through defective expression or a withholding of full knowledge; DARK implies an imperfect revelation often with ominous or sinister suggestion ⟨*dark* prophecies⟩ VAGUE implies lacking clarity because imperfectly conceived, grasped, or thought out; CRYPTIC implies a purposely concealed meaning ⟨made *cryptic* remarks about future plans⟩

[2]**obscure** *vt* **1 :** to make dark, dim, or indistinct **2 :** to conceal or hide by or as if by covering **3 :** to use the unstressed vowel \ə\ as the sound of

ob·se·qui·ous \əb-ˈsē-kwē-əs, äb-\ *adj* **:** humbly or excessively attentive (as to a person in authority) **:** FAWNING, SERVILE [Latin *obsequiosus* "compliant", from *obsequi* "to comply", from *ob-* "toward" + *sequi* "to follow"] — **ob·se·qui·ous·ly** *adv* — **ob·se·qui·ous·ness** *n*

ob·se·quy \ˈäb-sə-kwē\ *n, pl* **-quies :** a funeral or burial rite — usually used in pl. [Middle French *obsequie,* from Medieval Latin *obsequiae,* pl., alteration of Latin *exsequiae,* from *exsequi* "to follow, perform", from *ex-* + *sequi* "to follow"]

ob·serv·ance \əb-ˈzər-vəns\ *n* **1 :** a customary practice or ceremony **2 :** an act or instance of following a custom, rule, or law **3 :** an act or instance of noticing **:** OBSERVATION

ob·serv·ant \-vənt\ *adj* **1 :** paying strict attention **:** WATCHFUL **2 :** careful in observing **:** MINDFUL **3 :** quick to observe **:** KEEN — **ob·serv·ant·ly** *adv*

ob·ser·va·tion \ˌäb-sər-ˈvā-shən, -zər-\ *n* **1 :** an act or the power of observing with the eyes or mind **2 :** the gathering of information (as for scientific studies) by noting facts or occurrences ⟨weather *observations*⟩ **3 a :** a conclusion drawn from observing **:** VIEW **b :** REMARK 3, COMMENT **4 :** the state of being observed — **observation** *adj* — **ob·ser·va·tion·al** \-shnəl, -shən-l\ *adj*

ob·ser·va·to·ry \əb-ˈzər-və-ˌtōr-ē, -ˌtȯr-\ *n, pl* **-ries 1 :** a place or institution given over to or equipped for observation of natural phenomena (as in astronomy) **2 :** a place or structure commanding a wide view

ob·serve \əb-ˈzərv\ *vb* **1 :** to conform one's action or practice to ⟨*observe* rules⟩ **2 :** to celebrate or solemnize (as an occasion) in a customary or accepted way **3 :** to pay attention to **:** WATCH **4 :** to discover by the senses or by considering mentally **:** NOTICE **5 :** to utter as a remark **6 :** to make a scientific observation of [Middle French *observer,* from Latin *observare* "to guard, watch, observe", from *ob-* "in the way, toward" + *servare* "to keep"] **syn** see KEEP — **ob·serv·able** \-ˈzər-və-bəl\ *adj* — **ob·serv·ably** \-ˈzər-və-blē\ *adv*

ob·serv·er \əb-ˈzər-vər\ *n* **:** one that observes; *esp* **:** a representative sent to observe but not participate officially

ob·sess \əb-ˈses, äb-\ *vt* **:** to occupy the mind of intensely or abnormally **:** HAUNT ⟨*obsessed* by fear⟩ [Latin *obsessus,* past participle of *obsidēre* "to besiege", from *ob-* "against" + *sedēre* "to sit"]

ob·ses·sion \äb-ˈsesh-ən, əb-\ *n* **:** a prolonged and disturbed concern with a thought, emotion, or impulse even when it is seen as unreasonable; *also* **:** such a thought, emotion, or impulse — **ob·ses·sive** \-ˈses-iv\ *adj* — **ob·ses·sive·ly** \-ˈses-iv-lē\ *adv*

ob·sid·i·an \əb-ˈsid-ē-ən\ *n* **:** a dark natural glass formed by the cooling of molten lava [Latin *obsidianus lapis,* mistaken manuscript reading for *obsianus lapis,* literally, "stone of Obsius (its supposed discoverer)"]

ob·so·les·cent \ˌäb-sə-ˈles-nt\ *adj* **:** going out of use **:** becoming obsolete [Latin *obsolescens,* present participle of *obsolescere* "to grow old, become disused"] — **ob·so·lesce** \-ˈles\ *vi* — **ob·so·les·cence** \-ˈles-ns\ *n* — **ob·so·les·cent·ly** *adv*

ob·so·lete \ˌäb-sə-ˈlēt, ˈäb-sə-ˌ\ *adj* **1 :** no longer in use ⟨an *obsolete* word⟩ **2 :** OUTMODED ⟨*obsolete* machinery⟩ **3 :** VESTIGIAL ⟨the appendix is an *obsolete* organ in humans⟩ [Latin *obsoletus,* from past participle of *obsolescere* "to grow old, become disused"] — **ob·so·lete·ly** *adv* — **ob·so·lete·ness** *n*

ob·sta·cle \ˈäb-sti-kəl\ *n* **:** something that stands in the way or opposes **:** OBSTRUCTION [Middle French, from Latin *obstaculum,* from *obstare* "to stand in the way", from *ob-* "in the way" + *stare* "to stand"]

ob·stet·ric \əb-ˈste-trik, äb-\ *or* **ob·stet·ri·cal** \-tri-kəl\ *adj* **:** of or relating to childbirth or obstetrics [derived from Latin *obstetric-, obstetrix* "midwife", from *obstare* "to stand in the way"] — **ob·stet·ri·cal·ly** \-tri-kə-lē, -klē\ *adv*

ob·ste·tri·cian \ˌäb-stə-ˈtrish-ən\ *n* **:** a physician specializing in obstetrics

ob·stet·rics \əb-ˈste-triks, äb-\ *n* **:** a branch of medical science that deals with childbirth and with the care of women before, during, and after this

ob·sti·na·cy \ˈäb-stə-nə-sē\ *n, pl* **-cies 1 :** the quality or state of being obstinate **2 :** an instance of being obstinate

ob·sti·nate \ˈäb-stə-nət\ *adj* **1 :** clinging to an opinion, purpose, or course in spite of reason, arguments, or persuasion **2 :** not easily subdued, remedied, or removed ⟨an *obstinate* fever⟩ [Latin *obstinatus,* past participle of *obstinare* "to be firm"] — **ob·sti·nate·ly** *adv* — **ob·sti·nate·ness** *n*

• **syn** OBSTINATE, DOGGED, STUBBORN, PERTINACIOUS mean fixed and unyielding in course or purpose. OBSTINATE implies a persistent adherence and suggests unreasonableness and perversity ⟨too *obstinate* to take advice⟩ DOGGED suggests a tenacious sometimes sullen persistence ⟨shoveled with a *dogged* regularity⟩ STUBBORN implies sturdiness in resisting attempts to change or abandon a course or opinion ⟨met persuasion with *stubborn* resistance⟩ PERTINACIOUS suggests an annoying persistence ⟨a *pertinacious* beggar⟩

ob·strep·er·ous \əb-ˈstrep-rəs, äb-, -ə-rəs\ *adj* **1 :** uncontrollably noisy **2 :** stubbornly defiant **:** UNRULY [Latin *obstreperus,* from *obstrepere* "to clamor against", from *ob-* "against" + *strepere* "to make a noise"] — **ob•strep•er•ous•ly** *adv* — **ob•strep•er•ous•ness** *n*

ob•struct \əb-ˈstrəkt, äb-\ *vt* **1 :** to block or close up by an obstacle **2 :** to hinder from passage, action, or operation **:** IMPEDE **3 :** to cut off from sight ⟨a wall *obstructing* the view⟩ [Latin *obstructus,* past participle of *obstruere* "to obstruct", from *ob-* "in the way" + *struere* "to build"] — **ob•struc•tive** \-ˈstrək-tiv\ *adj or n* — **ob•struc•tor** \-tər\ *n*

ob•struc•tion \əb-ˈstrək-shən, äb-\ *n* **1 :** an act of obstructing **:** the state of being obstructed **2 :** something that obstructs **:** HINDRANCE

ob•struc•tion•ist \-shə-nəst, -shnəst\ *n* **:** a person who hinders progress especially in a legislative body — **ob•struc•tion•ism** \-shə-ˌniz-əm\ *n* — **ob•struc•tion•is•tic** \-ˌstrək-shə-ˈnis-tik\ *adj*

ob•tain \əb-ˈtān, äb-\ *vb* **1 :** to gain, find, or attain usually by planning, calculation, or effort **2 :** to be generally recognized or established **:** PREVAIL [Middle French *obtenir,* from *obtinēre* "to hold on to, possess, obtain", from *ob-* "in the way" + *tenēre* to hold"] — **ob•tain•able** \-ˈtā-nə-bəl\ *adj* — **ob•tain•er** *n* — **ob•tain•ment** \-ˈtān-mənt\ *n*

ob•trude \əb-ˈtrüd, äb-\ *vb* **1 :** to thrust out **2 :** to thrust forward or call to notice without warrant or request **3 :** to thrust oneself upon attention [Latin *obtrudere* "to thrust out", from *ob-* "in the way" + *trudere* "to thrust"] **syn** see INTRUDE — **ob•trud•er** *n* — **ob•tru•sion** \-ˈtrü-zhən\ *n*

ob•tru•sive \əb-ˈtrü-siv, äb-, -ziv\ *adj* **:** inclined to obtrude **:** FORWARD, PUSHING [Latin *obtrusus,* past participle of *obtrudere* "to thrust at"] — **ob•tru•sive•ly** *adv* — **ob•tru•sive•ness** *n*

ob•tuse \äb-ˈtüs, -ˈtyüs\ *adj* **1 :** lacking sharpness or quickness of wit **:** DULL, INSENSITIVE **2 a** (1) **:** exceeding 90 degrees but less than 180 degrees ⟨*obtuse* angle⟩ (2) **:** having an obtuse angle ⟨an *obtuse* triangle⟩ **b :** not pointed or acute **:** BLUNT ⟨an *obtuse* leaf⟩ [Latin *obtusus* "blunt, dull", from *obtundere* "to beat against, blunt", from *ob-* "against" + *tundere* "to beat"] **syn** see BLUNT — **ob•tuse•ly** *adv* — **ob•tuse•ness** n

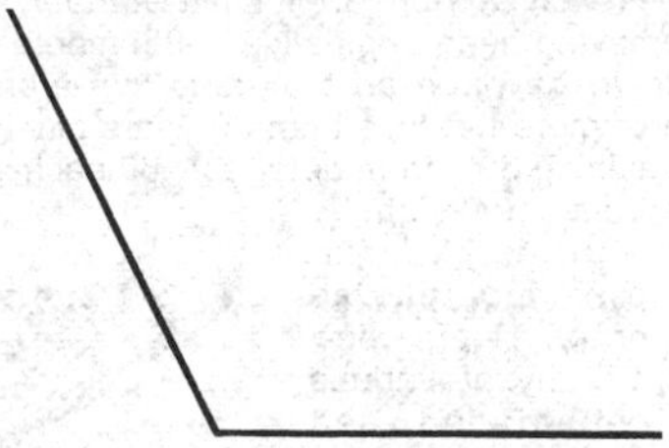
obtuse 2a(1)

[1]**ob•verse** \äb-ˈvərs, ˈäb-ˌ\ *adj* **1 :** facing the observer or opponent **2 :** being a counterpart or complement [Latin *obversus,* from *obvertere* "to turn toward", from *ob-* "toward" + *vertere* "to turn"] — **ob•verse•ly** *adv*

[2]**ob•verse** \ˈäb-ˌvərs, äb-ˈ\ *n* **1 :** the side of something (as a coin or medal) bearing the principal design or lettering **2 :** a front or principal surface **3 :** COUNTERPART 2

ob•vi•ate \ˈäb-vē-ˌāt\ *vt* **:** to anticipate and dispose of beforehand **:** make unnecessary ⟨*obviate* an objection⟩ [Late Latin *obviare* "to meet, withstand", from Latin *obviam* "in the way"] — **ob•vi•a•tion** \ˌäb-vē-ˈā-shən\ *n*

ob•vi•ous \ˈäb-vē-əs\ *adj* **:** easily discovered, seen, or understood **:** PLAIN ⟨an *obvious* mistake⟩ [Latin *obvius* "being in the way", from *obviam* "in the way", from *ob* "in the way of" + *via* "way"] — **ob•vi•ous•ly** *adv* — **ob•vi•ous•ness** *n*

oc•a•ri•na \ˌäk-ə-ˈrē-nə\ *n* **:** a wind instrument having an oval body with finger holes and giving soft flutelike tones — called also *sweet potato* [Italian, from *oca* "goose", from Late Latin *auca,* derived from Latin *avis* "bird"]

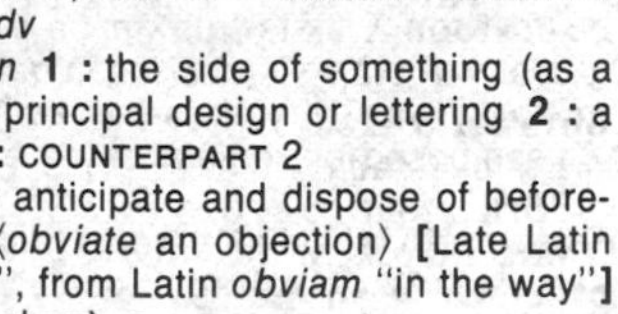

ocarina

[1]**oc•ca•sion** \ə-ˈkā-zhən\ *n* **1 :** a favorable opportunity or circumstance **2 :** a state of affairs that provides a ground or reason **3 :** an occurrence or condition that brings something about; *esp* **:** the immediate inciting circumstance as distinguished from fundamental cause **4 :** a time at which something happens **5 :** a need arising from a particular circumstance **:** EXIGENCY **6** *pl* **:** AFFAIR 1a, BUSINESS **7 :** a special event or ceremony **:** CELEBRATION [Latin *occasio,* from *occidere* "to fall, fall down", from *ob-* "toward" + *cadere* "to fall"] **syn** see CAUSE

[2]**occasion** *vt* **oc•ca•sioned; oc•ca•sion•ing** \-ˈkāzh-ning, -ə-ning\ **:** to give occasion to **:** CAUSE

oc•ca•sion•al \ə-ˈkāzh-nəl, -ən-l\ *adj* **1 :** happening or met with now and then ⟨made *occasional* references to the war⟩ **2 :** used or meant for a special occasion ⟨*occasional* verse⟩ — **oc•ca•sion•al•ly** \-ē\ *adv*

Oc•ci•dent \ˈäk-səd-ənt, -sə-ˌdent\ *n* **:** WEST 2 [Middle French, from Latin *occidens,* from *occidere* "to fall, set (of the sun)", from *ob-* "toward" + *cadere* "to fall"]

oc•ci•den•tal \ˌäk-sə-ˈdent-l\ *adj, often cap* **1 :** of, relating to, or situated in the Occident **:** WESTERN **2 :** of or relating to Occidentals — **oc•ci•den•tal•ly** \-l-ē\ *adv*

Occidental *n* **:** a member of one of the occidental peoples; *esp* **:** a person of European ancestry

oc•cip•i•tal \äk-ˈsip-ət-l\ *adj* **:** of or relating to the occiput or the occipital bone — **occipital** *n* — **oc•cip•i•tal•ly** \-l-ē\ *adv*

occipital bone *n* **:** a compound bone that forms the back part of the skull and articulates with the atlas

occipital lobe *n* **:** the back part of the cerebral hemisphere that contains the visual areas of the brain

oc•ci•put \ˈäk-sə-pət, -ˌpət\ *n, pl* **occiputs** *or* **oc•cip•i•ta** \äk-ˈsip-ət-ə\ **:** the back part of the head or skull [Latin *occipit-, occiput,* from *ob-* "against" + *capit-, caput* "head"]

oc•clude \ə-ˈklüd, ä-\ *vb* **1 :** to stop up **:** OBSTRUCT **2 :** to shut in or out **3 :** to take up and hold by absorption or adsorption **4 :** to come together with opposing surfaces in contact ⟨the teeth do not *occlude* properly⟩ [Latin *occludere* (past participle *occlusus*), from *ob-* "in the way" + *claudere* "to shut, close"] — **oc•clu•sive** \-ˈklü-siv, -ziv\ *adj*

occluded front *n* **:** OCCLUSION 2

oc•clu•sal \ə-ˈklü-səl, ä-, -zəl\ *adj* **:** of, relating to, or being the surface of a molar or premolar tooth that is used for crushing and grinding [Latin *occlusus,* past participle of *occludere* "to occlude"] — **oc•clu•sal•ly** \-ē\ *adv*

oc•clu•sion \ə-ˈklü-zhən\ *n* **1 :** the act of occluding **:** the state of being occluded **2 :** the front formed by a cold front overtaking a warm front and lifting the warm air over the cold air

oc•cult \ə-ˈkəlt, ä-\ *adj* **1 :** not revealed **:** SECRET, HIDDEN **2 :** ABSTRUSE, MYSTERIOUS **3 :** of or relating to supernatural agencies, their effects, or knowledge of them [Latin *occultus,* from *occulere* "to cover up, hide"] — **oc•cult•ly** *adv*

oc•cul•ta•tion \ˌäk-əl-ˈtā-shən, ˌäk-ˌəl-\ *n* **1 :** the state of being hidden from view or lost to notice **2 :** the shutting out of the light of one celestial body by the intervention of another; *esp* **:** an eclipse of a star or planet by the moon

oc•cult•ism \ə-ˈkəl-ˌtiz-əm, ä-\ *n* **:** a belief in or study of supernatural powers — **oc•cult•ist** \-təst\ *n*

oc•cu•pan•cy \ˈäk-yə-pən-sē\ *n, pl* **-cies :** the act of occupying **:** the state of being occupied

oc•cu•pant \ˈäk-yə-pənt\ *n* **:** one that occupies something or takes or has possession of it

oc•cu•pa•tion \ˌäk-yə-ˈpā-shən\ *n* **1 :** an activity in which one engages; *esp* **:** one's business or vocation **2 a :** the taking possession of property **:** OCCUPANCY **b :** the taking possession or holding and controlling of an area by a foreign military force; *also* **:** such a military force — **oc•cu•pa•tion•al** \-shnəl, -shən-l\ *adj* — **oc•cu•pa•tion•al•ly** \-ē\ *adv*

occupational therapy *n* **:** therapy by means of activity; *esp* **:** creative activity prescribed for its effect in promoting recovery or rehabilitation — **occupational therapist** *n*

oc•cu•py \ˈäk-yə-ˌpī\ *vt* **-pied; -py•ing 1 a :** to engage the attention or energies of ⟨*occupy* oneself with reading⟩ **b :** to fill up (an extent in space or time) ⟨sports *occupied* their spare time⟩ ⟨a liter of water *occupies* 1000 cubic centimeters of space⟩ **2 :** to take or hold possession of **3 :** to reside in as an owner or tenant [Middle French *occuper* "to take possession of", from Latin *occupare*] — **oc•cu•pi•er** \-ˌpī-ər, -ˌpīr\ *n*

oc•cur \ə-ˈkər\ *vi* **oc•curred; oc•cur•ring** \-ˈkər-ing\ **1 :** to be found or met with **:** APPEAR **2 :** to take place **3 :** to come to

\ə\ **abut**	\au̇\ **out**	\i\ **tip**	\ȯ\ **saw**	\u̇\ **foot**
\ər\ **further**	\ch\ **chin**	\ī\ **life**	\ȯi\ **coin**	\y\ **yet**
\a\ **mat**	\e\ **pet**	\j\ **job**	\th\ **thin**	\yü\ **few**
\ā\ **take**	\ē\ **easy**	\ng\ **sing**	\th\ **this**	\yu̇\ **cure**
\ä\ **cot, cart**	\g\ **go**	\ō\ **bone**	\ü\ **food**	\zh\ **vision**

mind : suggest itself [Latin *occurrere,* from *ob-* "in the way" + *currere* "to run"] **syn** see HAPPEN

oc•cur•rence \ə-ˈkər-əns, -ˈkə-rəns\ *n* **1 :** something that takes place; *esp* **:** something that happens unexpectedly **2 :** the action or process of taking place

• **syn** OCCURRENCE, EVENT, INCIDENT, EPISODE mean something that happens or takes place. OCCURRENCE suggests a happening without plan, intent, or volition; EVENT usually implies a significant occurrence and frequently one resulting from or giving rise to another ⟨Columbus' voyage was one of the great *events* of history⟩ INCIDENT suggests an occurrence of brief duration or secondary importance ⟨the plot of the play is strung with amusing *incidents*⟩ or a minor but unusual happening of consequence ⟨the death of the little-known general was one of those *incidents* that pass unnoticed⟩ EPISODE stresses the distinctiveness or apartness of an incident ⟨a memorable *episode* in their lives was their trip to Africa⟩

ocean \ˈō-shən\ *n* **1 :** the whole body of salt water that covers nearly three fourths of the surface of the earth **2 :** one of the large bodies of water into which the great ocean is divided **3 :** an immense space or quantity [Latin *oceanus,* from Greek *ōkeanos*] — **oce•an•ic** \ˌō-shē-ˈan-ik\ *adj*

ocean•ar•i•um \ˌō-shə-ˈnar-ē-əm, -ˈner-\ *n, pl* **-i•ums** *also* **-ia** \-ē-ə\ **:** a large marine aquarium

ocean•go•ing \ˈō-shən-ˌgō-ing\ *adj* **:** of, relating to, or suitable for travel on the ocean

Oce•anid \ō-ˈsē-ə-nəd\ *n* **:** any of the ocean nymphs in Greek mythology

ocean•og•ra•phy \ˌō-shə-ˈnäg-rə-fē\ *n* **:** a science that deals with the ocean and its phenomena — **ocean•og•ra•pher** \-fər\ *n* — **ocean•o•graph•ic** \ˌō-shə-nə-ˈgraf-ik\ *adj* — **ocean•o•graph•i•cal•ly** \-ˈgraf-i-kə-lē, -klē\ *adv*

ocel•lus \ō-ˈsel-əs\ *n, pl* **ocel•li** \-ˈsel-ˌī, -ˌē\ **1 :** a tiny simple eye or eyespot of an invertebrate **2 :** a spot of color encircled by a band of another color [Latin, "little eye", from *oculus* "eye"] — **ocel•lat•ed** \ˈō-sə-ˌlāt-əd\ *adj*

oc•e•lot \ˈäs-ə-ˌlät, ˈō-sə-\ *n* **:** a medium-sized American wildcat ranging from Texas to Patagonia and having a tawny yellow or grayish coat marked with black [French, from Nahuatl *ocelotl* "jaguar"]

ocelot

ocher *or* **ochre** \ˈō-kər\ *n* **1 :** an earthy usually red or yellow and often impure iron ore used as a pigment **2 :** the color of yellow ocher [Middle French *ocre,* from Latin *ochra,* from Greek *ōchra,* from *ōchros* "yellow"] — **ocher•ous** \ˈō-kə-rəs, -krəs\ *or* **ochre•ous** \ˈō-kə-rəs, -krəs, -krē-əs\ *adj*

-ock \ək, ik, ˌäk\ *n suffix* **:** small one ⟨hill*ock*⟩ [Old English *-oc*]

o'•clock \ə-ˈkläk\ *adv* **1 :** according to the clock ⟨the time is three *o'clock*⟩ **2 —** used for indicating position or direction as if on a clock dial ⟨an airplane approaching at eleven *o'clock*⟩ [contraction of *of the clock*]

oco•ti•llo \ˌō-kə-ˈtē-yō, -ˈtē-ō\ *n, pl* **-llos :** a thorny scarlet-flowered shrub of the southwestern United States and Mexico [Mexican Spanish]

octa- *or* **octo-** *also* **oct-** *combining form* **:** eight [Greek *oktō* and Latin *octo*]

oc•ta•gon \ˈäk-tə-ˌgän\ *n* **:** a polygon of eight angles and eight sides — **oc•tag•o•nal** \äk-ˈtag-ən-l\ *adj* — **oc•tag•o•nal•ly** \-l-ē\ *adv*

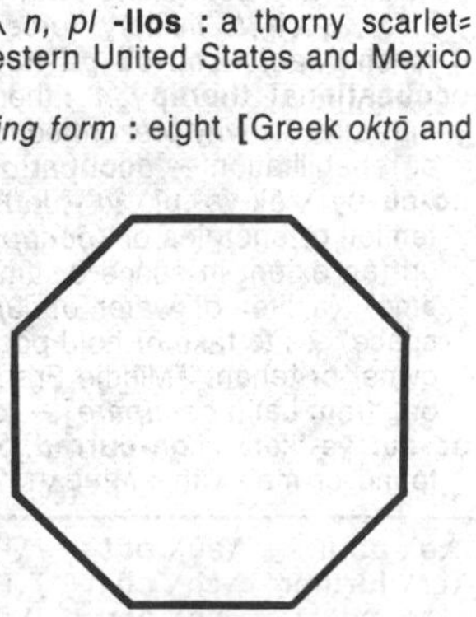

octagon

oc•ta•he•dron \ˌäk-tə-ˈhē-drən\ *n, pl* **-drons** *or* **-dra** \-drə\ **:** a solid bounded by eight plane faces — **oc•ta•he•dral** \-drəl\ *adj*

oc•tal \ˈäk-tl\ *adj* **:** of, relating to, or being a number system with a base of 8

oc•tam•e•ter \äk-ˈtam-ət-ər\ *n* **:** a line of verse consisting of eight metrical feet [Late Latin, "having eight feet", derived from Greek *oktō* "eight" + *metron* "measure"]

oc•tane \ˈäk-ˌtān\ *n* **1 :** any of several isomeric liquid hydrocarbons C_8H_{18} **2 :** OCTANE NUMBER

octane number *n* **:** a number that is used to measure or indicate the antiknock properties of a liquid motor fuel and that increases as the likelihood of knocking decreases — called also *octane rating*

oc•tant \ˈäk-tənt\ *n* **1 :** an instrument for observing altitudes of a celestial body from a moving ship or aircraft **2 :** any group of eight similar units or parts ⟨an *octant* of spores⟩ [Latin *octans* "eighth of a circle", from *octo* "eight"]

oc•tave \ˈäk-tiv, -təv, -ˌtāv\ *n* **1 :** an 8-day period of observances beginning with the festival day **2 :** a stanza or poem of eight lines; *esp* **:** the first eight lines of an Italian sonnet — compare SESTET **3 a :** a musical interval embracing eight degrees **b :** a tone or note at this interval **c :** the whole series of notes, tones, or keys within this interval **4 :** a group of eight [Medieval Latin *octava,* from Latin *octavus* "eighth", from *octo* "eight"]

oc•ta•vo \äk-ˈtā-vō, -ˈtäv-ō\ *n, pl* **-vos :** a book made of sheets of paper each folded 3 times to make 8 leaves or 16 pages [Latin ablative of *octavus* "eighth"]

oc•tet \äk-ˈtet\ *n* **1 :** a musical composition for eight voices or eight instruments; *also* **:** the performers of such a composition **2 :** a group or set of eight

oc•til•lion \äk-ˈtil-yən\ *n* — see NUMBER table [French, from *oct-* "octa-" + *-illion* (as in *million*)]

Oc•to•ber \äk-ˈtō-bər\ *n* **:** the 10th month of the year [Old French *Octobre,* from Latin *October,* from *octo* "eight"; from its having been originally the 8th month of the Roman calendar]

oc•to•ge•nar•i•an \ˌäk-tə-jə-ˈner-ē-ən\ *n* **:** a person who is 80 or more but less than 90 years old [Latin *octogenarius* "containing 80", from *octogeni* "80 each", from *octoginta* "eighty", from *octo* "eight"]

oc•to•pus \ˈäk-tə-pəs\ *n, pl* **-pus•es** *or* **-pi** \-ˌpī, -ˌpē\ **1 :** any of various cephalopod sea mollusks having eight muscular arms with two rows of suckers **2 :** something suggestive of an octopus; *esp* **:** a powerful grasping organization with many branches [Greek *oktōpous* "having 8 feet", from *oktō* "eight" + *pous* "foot"]

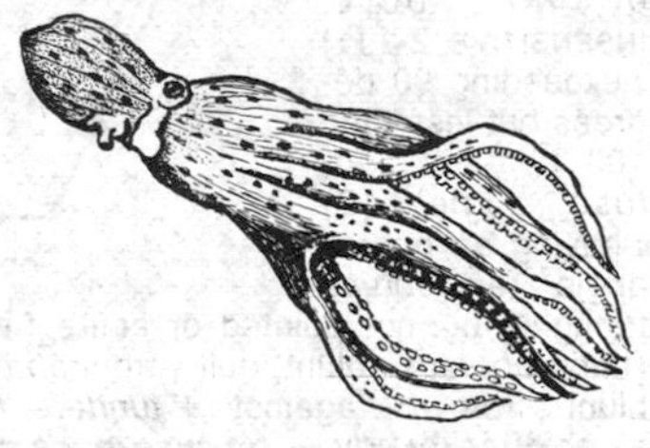

octopus 1

oc•to•roon \ˌäk-tə-ˈrün\ *n* **:** a person of one-eighth Negro ancestry [*octa-* + *-roon* (as in *quadroon*)]

oc•to•syl•lab•ic \ˌäk-tə-sə-ˈlab-ik\ *adj* **:** having eight syllables **:** composed of verses having eight syllables — **octosyllabic** *n*

¹oc•u•lar \ˈäk-yə-lər\ *adj* **1 :** of or relating to the eye or the eyesight **2 :** obtained or perceived by the sight **:** VISUAL ⟨*ocular* proof⟩ [Late Latin *ocularis* "of eyes", from Latin *oculus* "eye"]

²ocular *n* **:** EYEPIECE

oc•u•list \ˈäk-yə-ləst\ *n* **1 :** OPHTHALMOLOGIST **2 :** OPTOMETRIST

oc•u•lo•mo•tor \ˌäk-yə-lə-ˈmōt-ər\ *adj* **1 :** moving or acting to move the eyeball **2 :** of or relating to the oculomotor nerve

oculomotor nerve *n* **:** either of the 3d pair of cranial nerves that arise from the midbrain and supply most muscles of the eye — called also *oculomotor*

odd \ˈäd\ *adj* **1 :** being only one of a pair or set ⟨an *odd* shoe⟩ ⟨an *odd* chair⟩ **2 a :** being one of the sequence of natural numbers beginning with one and counting by twos that are divisible by two ⟨1, 3, 5, and 7 are *odd* numbers⟩ **b :** numbered with an odd number ⟨an *odd* year⟩ **c :** somewhat more than the number mentioned ⟨fifty *odd* years ago⟩ **3 :** additional to or apart from what is usual, planned on, or taken into account **:** RANDOM, CASUAL, OCCASIONAL ⟨*odd* jobs⟩ ⟨done at *odd* moments⟩ ⟨*odd* bits of material⟩ **4 :** not usual or conventional **:** STRANGE ⟨an *odd* way of behaving⟩ ⟨what an *odd* place to keep cereal⟩ [Old Norse *oddi* "point of land, triangle, odd number"] — **odd•ly** *adv* — **odd•ness** *n*

△ **origin** Although a triangle is a 3-angled figure, it is possible, by concentrating attention on the apex, to look at it as a point. An arrowhead, after all, is basically a triangle, and likewise a point of land reaching out into a body of water is roughly triangular in shape. The Old Norse word *oddi* was used both for a point of land and for a triangle. *Oddi* also developed the meaning "odd number", since the apex of a triangle is the unpaired angle and an odd number is a sum of pairs and one unpaired unit. English never called a triangle *odd*, but it did borrow the *odd* number from Old Norse *oddi*. Later anything singular or different came to be called *odd*.

odd•ball \'äd-ˌbȯl\ *n* : one whose behavior is eccentric

Odd Fellow *n* : a member of one of the major benevolent and fraternal orders [Independent Order of *Odd Fellows*]

odd•i•ty \'äd-ət-ē\ *n, pl* **-ties 1** : an odd person, thing, event, or trait **2** : the quality or state of being odd ⟨the *oddity* of your behavior⟩

odd•ment \'äd-mənt\ *n* : something left over : REMNANT

odds \'ädz\ *n pl* **1** *archaic* : unequal things or conditions **2** : DIFFERENCE ⟨made little *odds* whether they stayed⟩; *esp* : a difference by which one thing is favored over another ⟨the *odds* are in favor of our side⟩ **3 a** : the advantage of an unequal wager granted to a bettor believed to have a less than even chance of winning **b** : the ratio between the amount to be won and the amount wagered on a bet **4** : DISAGREEMENT, QUARRELING — used with *at* ⟨the children were at *odds*⟩

odds and ends *n pl* : miscellaneous things or matters

odds–on \'äd-'zȯn, -'zän\ *adj* : having or viewed as having a better than even chance to win

ode \'ōd\ *n* : a lyric poem characterized usually by elevated feeling and style, varied length of line, and complex stanza forms [Late Latin, from Greek *ōidē*, literally, "song", from *aidein* "to sing"]

-ode \ˌōd\ *n combining form* **1** : way : path ⟨electrode⟩ **2** : electrode ⟨diode⟩ [Greek *hodos*]

odi•ous \'ōd-ē-əs\ *adj* : causing or deserving hatred or repugnance — **odi•ous•ly** *adv* — **odi•ous•ness** *n*

odi•um \'ōd-ē-əm\ *n* **1** : the condition of being generally hated and condemned usually for shameful conduct : merited loathing **2** : the disgrace or shame attached to something considered hateful or low [Latin, "hatred", from *odisse* "to hate"]

odom•e•ter \ō-'däm-ət-ər\ *n* : an instrument for measuring the distance traveled (as by a vehicle) [French *odomètre*, from Greek *hodometron*, from *hodos* "way, road" + *metron* "measure"]

odon•tol•o•gy \ˌō-ˌdän-'täl-ə-jē\ *n* : a science dealing with the teeth, their structure and development, and their diseases [French *odontologie*, from Greek *odont-*, *odous* "tooth"] — **odon•tol•o•gist** \-jəst\ *n*

odor \'ōd-ər\ *n* **1** : something that stimulates the sense of smell : SCENT; *also* : the resulting sensation : SMELL **2 a** : a predominant quality : FLAVOR ⟨*odor* of sanctity⟩ **b** : REPUTE, ESTIMATION ⟨in bad *odor*⟩ [Old French *odour*, from Latin *odor*] **syn** see SMELL — **odored** \-ərd\ *adj* — **odor•less** \-ər-ləs\ *adj*

odor•ant \'ōd-ə-rənt\ *n* : an odorous substance

odor•if•er•ous \ˌōd-ə-'rif-rəs, -ə-rəs\ *adj* **1** : ODOROUS **2** : morally offensive — **odor•if•er•ous•ly** *adv* — **odor•if•er•ous•ness** *n*

odor•ous \'ōd-ə-rəs\ *adj* : having an odor — **odor•ous•ly** *adv* — **odor•ous•ness** *n*

odour \'ōd-ər\ *chiefly British variant of* ODOR

od•ys•sey \'äd-ə-sē\ *n, pl* **-seys** : a long wandering usually marked by many changes of fortune [the *Odyssey*, epic poem attributed to Homer recounting the long wanderings of Odysseus]

Oe•di•pus complex \'ed-ə-pəs, 'ēd-\ *n* : a sexual attraction of a child toward the parent of the opposite sex that may be a source of adult personality disorder if left unresolved [*Oedipus*, hero of ancient Greek legend who killed his father and married his mother] — **oe•di•pal** \'ed-ə-pəl, 'ēd-\ *adj*

oe•do•go•ni•um \ˌēd-ə-'gō-nē-əm\ *n* : any of a genus of threadlike green algae [New Latin, from Greek *oidos* "swelling" + *gonos* "offspring, seed"]

¹o'er \'ōr, 'ȯr\ *adv* : OVER

²o'er \ōr, ȯr, 'ōr, 'ȯr\ *prep* : OVER

oer•sted \'ər-stəd\ *n* : a unit of magnetic intensity equal to the intensity of a magnetic field in a vacuum in which a unit magnetic pole experiences a mechanical force of one dyne in the direction of the field [Hans Christian *Oersted*, died 1851, Danish physicist]

oe•soph•a•gus *variant of* ESOPHAGUS

oestr- *or* **oestro-** — see ESTR-

of \əv, 'əv, 'äv\ *prep* **1** : from as a point of reckoning ⟨north *of* the lake⟩ **2 a** : from by origin or derivation ⟨a person *of* noble birth⟩ **b** : from as a consequence ⟨died *of* flu⟩ **c** : by as author or doer ⟨plays *of* Shakespeare⟩ **d** : as experienced or performed by ⟨love *of* parents for their children⟩ **3** : having as its material, parts, or contents ⟨a throne *of* gold⟩ ⟨cups *of* water⟩ **4** — used as a function word to indicate the whole that includes the part denoted by the preceding word ⟨most *of* the army⟩ **5 a** : CONCERNING ⟨stories *of* their travels⟩ **b** : in respect to ⟨slow *of* speech⟩ **6** : possessed by : belonging to ⟨courage *of* the pioneers⟩ ⟨4 is the square *of* 2⟩ **7** — used as a function word to indicate separation ⟨eased *of* pain⟩ **8** : specified as : which is or are : BEING ⟨month *of* August⟩ ⟨crime *of* murder⟩ ⟨the city *of* Rome⟩ **9** : having as its object ⟨love *of* nature⟩ **10** : having as a distinctive quality or possession ⟨a person *of* courage⟩ [Old English, 'off, of']

¹off \'ȯf\ *adv* **1 a** (1) : from a place or position ⟨march *off*⟩ (2) : away from land ⟨the ship stood *off* to sea⟩ **b** : so as to prevent close approach ⟨drove the dogs *off*⟩ **c** (1) : from a course : ASIDE ⟨turned *off* into a bypath⟩ (2) : away from the wind **2** : into an unconscious state ⟨dozed *off*⟩ **3 a** : so as not to be supported ⟨rolled to the edge of the table and *off*⟩ or covering or enclosing ⟨blew the lid *off*⟩ or attached ⟨the handle came *off*⟩ **b** : so as to be divided ⟨surface marked *off* into squares⟩ **4** : to a state of discontinuance ⟨shut *off* an engine⟩ or exhaustion ⟨drink *off* a glass⟩ or completion ⟨paint to finish it *off*⟩ **5** : in absence from or suspension of regular work or service ⟨take time *off* for lunch⟩ [Old English *of*]

²off \ȯf, 'ȯf\ *prep* **1** : away from; *esp* : from a place or situation on ⟨take it *off* the table⟩ **2** : at the expense of ⟨lived *off* friends⟩ **3** : to seaward of ⟨two miles *off* the coast⟩ **4 a** : not now engaged in ⟨*off* duty⟩ **b** : below the usual standard or level of ⟨*off* my game⟩ ⟨a dollar *off* the list price⟩ **5 a** : diverging or opening from ⟨a path *off* the main walk⟩ **b** : being or occurring away or apart from ⟨a shop just *off* the main street⟩

³off \ȯf, 'ȯf\ *adj* **1 a** : more removed or distant ⟨the *off* side of the building⟩ **b** : SEAWARD **c** : RIGHT ⟨*off* horse in a team⟩ **2 a** : started on the way ⟨*off* on a spree⟩ **b** : CANCELED ⟨the picnic's *off*⟩ **c** : not operating ⟨current is *off*⟩ **d** : not placed so as to permit operation ⟨the switch is *off*⟩ **3 a** : not corresponding to fact : INCORRECT ⟨*off* in their reckoning⟩ **b** : not being at one's best : SUBNORMAL **c** : not entirely sane : ECCENTRIC **d** : REMOTE, SLIGHT ⟨an *off* chance⟩ **4 a** : spent off duty ⟨reading on our *off* days⟩ **b** : SLACK ⟨*off* season⟩ **5 a** : OFF-COLOR **b** : INFERIOR ⟨*off* grade of oil⟩ **c** : DOWN 1c ⟨stocks were *off*⟩ **6** : CIRCUMSTANCED ⟨comfortably *off*⟩

of•fal \'ȯ-fəl, 'äf-əl\ *n* **1** : the waste or by-product of a process: as **a** : trimmings of a hide **b** : the by-products of milling used especially for stock feeds **c** : the viscera and trimmings of a butchered animal removed in dressing **2** : RUBBISH [Middle English, from *of* "off" + *fall*]

¹off•beat \'ȯf-ˌbēt\ *n* : the unaccented part of a musical measure

²offbeat *adj* : ECCENTRIC, UNCONVENTIONAL ⟨offers *offbeat* entertainment⟩

off–col•or \'ȯf-'kəl-ər\ *or* **off–col•ored** \-ərd\ *adj* **1** : not having the right or standard color **2** : of doubtful propriety : RISQUÉ

of•fend \ə-'fend\ *vb* **1 a** : to transgress the moral or divine law : SIN **b** : to break a law or rule : do wrong **2 a** : to cause difficulty, discomfort, or injury **b** : to cause dislike, anger, or vexation **3** : to cause pain to **4** : to cause to feel vexed or resentful usually by hurting pride or self-respect [Middle French *offendre*, from Latin *offendere* "to strike against, offend"] — **of•fend•er** *n*

• **syn** OFFEND, OUTRAGE, INSULT, AFFRONT mean to cause hurt feelings or deep resentment. OFFEND may also suggest a violating of ideas of what is right or proper without implying intent ⟨such candor *offended* the diplomats⟩ OUTRAGE implies offend-

\ə\ **abut**	\au̇\ **out**	\i\ **tip**	\ȯ\ **saw**	\u̇\ **foot**
\ər\ **further**	\ch\ **chin**	\ī\ **life**	\ȯi\ **coin**	\y\ **yet**
\a\ **mat**	\e\ **pet**	\j\ **job**	\th\ **thin**	\yü\ **few**
\ā\ **take**	\ē\ **easy**	\ng\ **sing**	\t͟h\ **this**	\yu̇\ **cure**
\ä\ **cot, cart**	\g\ **go**	\ō\ **bone**	\ü\ **food**	\zh\ **vision**

ing beyond endurance and calling forth extreme feelings ⟨*outraged* by the vandalism⟩ INSULT suggests deliberately and insolently causing humiliation, hurt pride, or shame; AFFRONT implies treating with deliberate rudeness or contempt ⟨*affronted* by such arrogant neglect⟩

of•fense *or* **of•fence** \ə-ˈfens; *especially for 2* ˈäf-ˌens, ˈȯf-\ *n* **1** : something that outrages the moral or physical senses **2 a** : the act of attacking : ASSAULT **b** : the side that is attacking in a contest or battle **3 a** : the act of displeasing or affronting **b** : the state of being insulted or morally outraged **4 a** : a breach of moral or divine law **b** : an infraction of law : CRIME [Middle French, from Latin *offensa,* from *offendere* "to offend"] — **of•fense•less** \-ləs\ *adj*

[1]**of•fen•sive** \ə-ˈfen-siv\ *adj* **1 a** : of, relating to, or designed for attack ⟨*offensive* weapons⟩ **b** : being on the offense ⟨the *offensive* team⟩ **2** : giving unpleasant sensations ⟨*offensive* smells⟩ **3** : causing displeasure or resentment : INSULTING ⟨an *offensive* remark⟩ — **of•fen•sive•ly** *adv* — **of•fen•sive•ness** *n*

[2]**offensive** *n* **1** : the act of an attacking party ⟨on the *offensive*⟩ **2** : ATTACK ⟨launch an *offensive*⟩

[1]**of•fer** \ˈȯf-ər, ˈäf-\ *vb* **of•fered; of•fer•ing** \ˈȯf-ring, ˈäf-, -ə-ring\ **1** : to present as an act of worship : SACRIFICE **2** : to present for acceptance or rejection ⟨was *offered* a job⟩ **3 a** : PROPOSE, SUGGEST ⟨*offer* a solution to the problem⟩ **b** : to declare one's readiness or willingness ⟨*offered* to help me⟩ **4 a** : to put up ⟨*offered* stubborn resistance⟩ **b** : THREATEN ⟨*offered* to strike me with a cane⟩ **5** : to place (merchandise) on sale [derived from Latin *offerre* "to present, offer", from *ob-* "toward" + *ferre* "to carry"]

[2]**offer** *n* **1 a** : PROPOSAL **b** : an agreement to do or give something on condition that the party to whom the proposal is made do or give something specified in return **2** : a price named by one proposing to buy **3** : an action or movement indicating a purpose or intention

of•fer•ing *n* **1 a** : the act of one who offers **b** : something offered; *esp* : a sacrifice ceremonially offered as a part of worship **c** : a contribution to the support of a church **2** : something offered for sale

of•fer•to•ry \ˈȯf-ər-ˌtōr-ē, ˈȯf-ə-ˌ, ˈäf-, -ˌtȯr-\ *n, pl* **-ries 1** *often cap* **a** : the offering of the sacramental bread and wine to God before they are consecrated at Communion **b** : a verse from a psalm said or sung at the beginning of the offertory **2 a** : the presentation of the offerings of the congregation at public worship **b** : the music played or sung during an offertory [Medieval Latin *offertorium,* derived from Latin *offerre* "to offer"]

off•hand \ˈȯf-ˈhand\ *adv or adj* : without previous thought or preparation ⟨couldn't give the figures *offhand*⟩

off•hand•ed \-ˈhan-dəd\ *adj* : OFFHAND — **off•hand•ed•ly** *adv* — **off•hand•ed•ness** *n*

of•fice \ˈȯf-əs, ˈäf-\ *n* **1 a** : a special duty, charge, or position; *esp* : a position of authority in government ⟨hold public *office*⟩ **b** : a position of responsibility or some degree of executive authority ⟨the *office* of president⟩ **2** : a prescribed form or service of worship; *esp, cap* : DIVINE OFFICE **3** : RITE 1a, 2 **4 a** : an assigned or assumed duty, task, or role **b** : FUNCTION 2 **5** : a place where a business is transacted or a service is supplied ⟨ticket *office*⟩: as **a** : a place in which record keeping and clerical work are performed **b** : the directing headquarters of an enterprise or organization **c** : the place in which a professional person (as a physician) conducts business **6 a** : a major administrative unit in some governments ⟨British Foreign *Office*⟩ **b** : a subdivision of some government departments ⟨Patent *Office*⟩ [Old French, from Latin *officium* "service, duty, office", from *opus* "work" + *facere* "to do"]

office boy *n* : a boy employed for odd jobs in a business office

office girl *n* : a girl employed for odd jobs in a business office

of•fice•hold•er \-ˌhōl-dər\ *n* : one holding a public office

[1]**of•fi•cer** \ˈȯf-ə-sər, ˈäf-\ *n* **1** : POLICE OFFICER **2** : one who holds an office of trust, authority, or command **3 a** : one who holds a commission in the armed forces **b** : the master or a mate of a merchant or passenger ship

[2]**officer** *vt* **1** : to furnish with officers **2** : to command or direct as an officer

[1]**of•fi•cial** \ə-ˈfish-əl\ *n* **1** : one who holds an office : OFFICER **2** : REFEREE 2, UMPIRE

[2]**official** *adj* **1** : of or relating to an office, position, or trust ⟨*official* duties⟩ **2** : holding an office ⟨an *official* referee⟩ **3 a** : AUTHORITATIVE 1 ⟨*official* statement⟩ **b** : prescribed or recognized as authorized **4** : befitting or characteristic of a person in office : FORMAL ⟨an *official* greeting⟩ — **of•fi•cial•ly** \-ˈfish-lē, -ə-lē\ *adv*

of•fi•cial•dom \ə-ˈfish-əl-dəm\ *n* : officials as a class

of•fi•cial•ism \-ˈfish-ə-ˌliz-əm\ *n* : lack of flexibility and initiative combined with excessive adherence to regulations (as in the behavior of government officials)

of•fi•ci•ant \ə-ˈfish-ē-ənt\ *n* : an officiating clergyman

of•fi•ci•ate \ə-ˈfish-ē-ˌāt\ *vi* **1** : to perform a ceremony, function, or duty **2** : to act in an official capacity; *esp* : to serve as an officer or official — **of•fi•ci•a•tion** \-ˌfish-ē-ˈā-shən\ *n*

of•fi•cious \ə-ˈfish-əs\ *adj* : offering one's services where they are neither asked nor needed : MEDDLESOME [Latin *officiosus* "obliging, helpful", from *officium* "service, office"] — **of•fi•cious•ly** *adv* — **of•fi•cious•ness** *n*

off•ing \ˈȯf-ing, ˈäf-\ *n* **1** : the part of the deep sea seen from the shore **2** : the near or foreseeable future ⟨sees trouble in the *offing*⟩

off•ish \ˈȯf-ish\ *adj* : inclined to be aloof — **off•ish•ly** *adv* — **off•ish•ness** *n*

off•print \ˈȯf-ˌprint\ *n* : a separately printed excerpt (as from a magazine)

[1]**off•set** \ˈȯf-ˌset\ *n* **1 a** : a short prostrate shoot arising from the base of a plant **b** : OFFSHOOT 2b **2** : a horizontal ledge on the face of a wall formed by a decrease in its thickness above **3** : an abrupt bend in an object by which one part is turned aside out of line **4** : something that serves to counterbalance or to compensate for something else **5 a** : unintentional transfer of ink (as on a freshly printed sheet) **b** : a printing process in which an inked impression is first made on a rubber-blanketed cylinder and then transferred to the paper being printed

[2]**off•set** \ˈȯf-ˌset, *1 is also* ȯf-ˈ\ *vb* **-set; -set•ting 1 a** : BALANCE ⟨credits *offset* debits⟩ **b** : to compensate for **2** : to form an offset in ⟨*offset* a wall⟩ **syn** see COMPENSATE

off•shoot \ˈȯf-ˌshüt\ *n* **1** : a branch of a main stem especially of a plant **2 a** : a lateral branch (as of a mountain range) **b** : a collateral branch, descendant, or member

[1]**off•shore** \ˈȯf-ˈshōr, -ˈshȯr\ *adv* : from the shore : at a distance from the shore

[2]**off•shore** \ˈȯf-ˌ\ *adj* **1** : coming or moving away from the shore ⟨an *offshore* breeze⟩ **2 a** : situated off the shore but within waters under a country's control ⟨*offshore* fisheries⟩ **b** : distant from the shore

off•side \ˈȯf-ˈsīd\ *adv or adj* : illegally in advance of the ball or puck

off•spring \ˈȯf-ˌspring\ *n, pl* **offspring** *also* **offsprings** : the progeny of an animal or plant : YOUNG [Old English *ofspring,* from *of* "off" + *springan* "to spring"]

off•stage \ˈȯf-ˈstāj, -ˌstāj\ *adv or adj* : off or away from the stage

off-the-record *adj* : given or made in confidence and not for publication ⟨*off-the-record* remarks⟩

off-white \ˈȯf-ˈhwīt, -ˈwīt\ *n* : a yellowish or grayish white

off year *n* **1** : a year in which no major election is held **2** : a year of diminished activity or production

oft \ˈȯft\ *adv* : OFTEN ⟨an *oft* neglected factor⟩ [Old English]

of•ten \ˈȯ-fən, ˈȯf-tən\ *adv* : many times : FREQUENTLY [Middle English, from *oft,* from Old English]

of•ten•times \-ˌtīmz\ *or* **oft•times** \ˈȯf-ˌtīmz, ˈȯft-\ *adv* : OFTEN

ogee *also* **OG** \ˈō-ˌjē\ *n* **1** : a molding with an S-shaped profile **2** : a pointed arch having on each side a reversed curve near the apex [obsolete *ogee,* a kind of arch, from French *ogive*]

ogee 1

[1]**ogle** \ˈō-gəl\ *vb* **ogled; ogling** \-gə-ling, -gling\ : to glance in a flirtatious way : eye amorously [probably from Low German *oegeln,* from *oog* "eye"] — **ogler** \-gə-lər, -glər\ *n*

[2]**ogle** *n* : a flirtatious glance

ogre \ˈō-gər\ *n* **1** : a hideous man-eating giant of fairy tales and folklore **2** : a dreaded person or object [French] — **ogre•ish** \ˈō-gə-rish, -grish\ *adj*

[1]oh *or* **O** \ō, 'ō\ *interj* **1** — used to express an emotion (as astonishment, pain, or desire) **2** — used in direct address ⟨*oh* sir, you forgot your change⟩ **3** — used to express acknowledgment or understanding of a statement or explanation ⟨*oh*, that's how you do it⟩ [Middle English *o*]

[2]oh \'ō\ *n* : ZERO [*o;* from the similarity of the symbol for zero (0) to the letter *O*]

ohm \'ōm\ *n* : the mks unit of electric resistance equal to the resistance of a circuit in which a potential difference of one volt produces a current of one ampere [Georg Simon *Ohm*, died 1854, German physicist] — **ohm•age** \'ō-mij\ *n* — **ohm•ic** \'ō-mik\ *adj*

ohm•me•ter \'ōm-,mēt-ər, 'ō-\ *n* : an instrument for indicating resistance in ohms directly

[1]-oid \,ȯid\ *n suffix* : something resembling a (specified) object or having a (specified) quality ⟨planet*oid*⟩ [Latin *-oïdes*, from *-oïdes*, adj. suffix]

[2]-oid *adj suffix* : resembling : having the form or appearance of [Latin *-oïdes*, from Greek *-oeidēs*, from *-o-* + *eidos* "appearance, form"]

[1]oil \'ȯil\ *n* **1 a** : any of numerous greasy combustible and usually liquid substances from plant, animal, or mineral sources that are soluble in ether but not in water **b** : PETROLEUM **2** : a substance of oily consistency **3 a** : an oil color used by an artist **b** : a painting done in oil colors [Old French *oile*, from Latin *oleum* "olive oil", from Greek *elaion*, from *elaia* "olive"] — **oil** *adj*

[2]oil *vt* : to treat, furnish, or lubricate with oil

oil•cloth \'ȯil-,klȯth\ *n* : cloth treated with oil or paint and used for table and shelf coverings

oil color *n* : a pigment used for oil paint

oil•er \'ȯi-lər\ *n* : one that oils; *esp* : a receptacle or device for applying oil

oil field *n* : a region rich in petroleum deposits

oil gland *n* : a gland (as of the skin) that produces an oily secretion

oil–im•mer•sion \,ȯil-im-,ər-zhən, -shən\ *adj* : being an objective lens of short focal distance designed to work with a drop of oil connecting the lens and the cover glass of the slide

oil of vitriol : concentrated sulfuric acid

oil of wintergreen : the methyl ester of salicylic acid used as a flavoring

oil paint *n* : paint in which a drying oil is the vehicle

oil painting *n* **1 a** : the act or art of painting in oil colors **b** : a picture painted in oils **2** : painting that uses pigments ground in oil

oil•seed \'ȯil-,sēd\ *n* : a seed or crop (as flaxseed) grown largely for oil

oil•skin \-,skin\ *n* **1** : an oiled waterproof cloth used for coverings and garments **2** : an oilskin raincoat **3** *pl* : an oilskin suit of coat and trousers

oil slick *n* : a film of oil floating on water

oil•stone \'ȯil-,stōn\ *n* : a whetstone for use with oil

oil well *n* : a well from which petroleum is obtained

oily \'ȯi-lē\ *adj* **oil•i•er**; **-est** **1** : of, relating to, or consisting of oil **2** : covered or impregnated with oil : GREASY **3** : excessively smooth or suave in manner : UNCTUOUS — **oil•i•ness** *n*

oint•ment \'ȯint-mənt\ *n* : a semisolid usually greasy and medicated preparation for application to the skin [Old French *oignement*, from Latin *unguentum*, from *unguere* "to anoint"]

Ojib•wa *or* **Ojib•way** \ō-'jib-wā\ *n* : a member of an Algonquian people of the region around western Lake Superior [Ojibwa *ojib-ubway*, a kind of moccasin]

[1]OK *or* **okay** \ō-'kā\ *adv or adj* : all right [abbreviation of *oll korrect*, alteration of *all correct*]

△ **origin** In the late 1830s Boston newspapers were full of abbreviations. Apparently there was simply a fashion for abbreviation, and any expression might be abbreviated. The craze went so far as to produce abbreviations of intentional misspellings. Such popular expressions as *N.G.* (no go) and *A.R.* (all right) gave way to *K.G.* (know go) and *O.W.* (oll wright). *O.K.* (oll korrect) followed quite naturally. Several of these abbreviated misspellings gained some currency, but *OK* alone became widespread and survived.

[2]OK *or* **okay** *vt* **OK'd** *or* **okayed**; **OK'•ing** *or* **okay•ing** : APPROVE, AUTHORIZE

[3]OK *or* **okay** *n* : APPROVAL 1, ENDORSEMENT

oka•pi \ō-'käp-ē\ *n* : an African mammal closely related to the giraffe but lacking the long neck [native name in Africa]

okra \'ō-krə\ *n* : a tall annual plant related to the hollyhocks and grown for its edible green pods which are used especially in soups and stews; *also* : these pods [of African origin]

okapi

-ol \,ȯl, ,ōl\ *n suffix* : chemical compound (as an alcohol or phenol) containing hydroxyl ⟨glycer*ol*⟩ [*alcohol*]

[1]old \'ōld\ *adj* **1 a** : dating from the remote past : ANCIENT ⟨*old* traditions⟩ **b** : persisting from an earlier time : of long standing ⟨an *old* friend⟩ **2** *cap* : belonging to an early period in the development of a language ⟨*Old* Irish⟩ **3** : having existed for a specified period of time ⟨a child three years *old*⟩ **4** : of, relating to, or originating in a past era ⟨*old* chronicles record the event⟩ **5 a** : advanced in years or age ⟨an *old* person⟩ **b** : showing the characteristics or age ⟨looked *old* at 20⟩ **6** : FORMER ⟨my *old* students⟩ **7 a** : showing the effects of time or use ⟨*old* shoes⟩ **b** : no longer in use ⟨*old* rags⟩ **8** : long familiar ⟨the same *old* story⟩ [Old English *eald*]

• **syn** ANCIENT, ANTIQUE, ARCHAIC: OLD may imply actual or relative length of existence ⟨*old* castles⟩ ⟨*old* dogs⟩ ANCIENT implies occurrence, existence, or use in the distant past ⟨*ancient* history⟩ ANTIQUE is a close synonym of ANCIENT, though it suggests something old-fashioned that has acquired value through rarity and sentimental associations ⟨a collector of *antique* clocks⟩ ARCHAIC implies having the characteristics of an earlier period ⟨an *archaic* chivalry⟩ ⟨*methinks* is an *archaic* construction⟩

[2]old *n* : old or earlier time ⟨days of *old*⟩

Old Church Slavonic *n* : the Slavic language used in the Bible translation of Cyril and Methodius and as the liturgical language of several Eastern churches — called also *Old Church Slavic*

old country *n* : an emigrant's country of origin

old•en \'ōl-dən\ *adj* : of or relating to a bygone era

Old English *n* **1** : the language of the English people from the time of the earliest documents in the 7th century to about 1100 **2** : English of any period before Modern English

old–fash•ioned \'ōl-'fash-ənd, 'ōl-\ *adj* **1** : of, relating to, or characteristic of a past era **2** : adhering to customs of a past era : CONSERVATIVE **3** : OUTMODED

Old French *n* : the French language from the 9th to the 16th century; *esp* : French from the 9th to the 13th century

Old Glory *n* : the flag of the United States

old guard *n, often cap O&G* : the conservative or reactionary members especially of a political party

old hand *n* : VETERAN 1

Old High German *n* : High German exemplified in documents prior to the 12th century

old•ish \'ōl-dish\ *adj* : somewhat old : ELDERLY

old–line \'ōl-'dlīn, -'līn\ *adj* **1** : having an established reputation ⟨an *old-line* business⟩ **2** : adhering to traditional policies or practices

old maid *n* **1** : SPINSTER 2 **2** : a prim fussy person **3** : a simple card game in which players lay down matched pairs with the player holding the odd queen at the end being the loser — **old–maid•ish** \'ōld-'mād-ish, 'ōl-\ *adj*

old man *n* **1 a** : HUSBAND **b** : FATHER 1a **2** *cap* : one in authority; *esp* : COMMANDING OFFICER

old master *n* **1** : a superior artist or craftsman of established reputation; *esp* : a distinguished painter of the 16th, 17th, or early 18th century **2** : a work by an old master

Old Nick \'ōld-'nik, 'ōl-\ *n* : DEVIL 1

Old Norse *n* : the Germanic language of the Scandinavian peoples prior to about 1350

Old North French *n* : the northern dialects of Old French including especially those of Normandy and Picardy

old school *n* : adherents to traditional policies and practices
old–squaw \ˈōld-ˈskwȯ, ˈōl-\ *n* : a common sea duck of the more northern parts of the northern hemisphere
old•ster \ˈōld-stər, ˈōl-\ *n* : an old or elderly person
Old Style *n* : a style of reckoning time used before the adoption of the Gregorian calendar
Old Testament *n* : the first of the two chief divisions of the Bible consisting of the books dealing with the history of the Hebrews before the time of Christ — see BIBLE table
old–time \ˈōld-ˌtīm, ˈōl-\ *adj* : of, relating to, or characteristic of an earlier period
old–tim•er \-ˈtī-mər\ *n* **1 a** : VETERAN 1 **b** : OLDSTER **2** : something that is old-fashioned : ANTIQUE
old wives' tale *n* : a traditional tale or bit of lore (as a superstitious notion)
old–world \ˈōl-ˈdwərld, -ˈwərld\ *adj* : of, relating to, or having the qualities of the Old World; *esp* : PICTURESQUE ⟨narrow *old=world* streets⟩
Old World *n* : EASTERN HEMISPHERE; *esp* : Europe
ole•ag•i•nous \ˌō-lē-ˈaj-ə-nəs\ *adj* **1** : resembling or having the properties of oil; *also* : containing or producing oil **2** : UNCTUOUS 2 [Middle French *oleagineux,* from Latin *oleagineus* "of an olive tree", from *olea* "olive tree", from Greek *elaia*] — **ole•ag•i•nous•ly** *adv* — **ole•ag•i•nous•ness** *n*
ole•an•der \ˈō-lē-ˌan-dər\ *n* : a poisonous evergreen shrub of the dogbane family often grown for its showy fragrant white to red or purple flowers [Medieval Latin]
ole•as•ter \-ˌas-tər\ *n* : any of a genus of trees and shrubs with usually silvery foliage and fruits suggesting small olives [Latin, from *olea* "olive tree"]
ole•cra•non \ˌō-lə-ˈkrā-ˌnän\ *n* : a process of the ulna that projects behind the elbow joint [Greek *ōlekranon,* from *ōlenē* "elbow" + *kranion* "skull"]
ole•ic \ō-ˈlē-ik\ *adj* **1** : relating to, derived from, or contained in oil **2** : of or relating to oleic acid [Latin *oleum* "oil"]
oleic acid *n* : an unsaturated fatty acid $C_{18}H_{34}O_2$ found as glycerides in natural fats and oils
oleo \ˈō-lē-ˌō\ *n, pl* **ole•os** : MARGARINE
oleo•mar•ga•rine \ˌō-lē-ō-ˈmärj-rən, -ˈmärj-ə-rən, -ˈmärj-ə-ˌrēn\ *n* : MARGARINE [French *oléomargarine,* from Latin *oleum* "oil" + French *margarine*]
oleo•res•in \-ˈrez-n\ *n* : a plant product (as a turpentine) containing chiefly essential oil and resin — **oleo•res•in•ous** \-ˈrez-n-əs, -ˈrez-nəs\ *adj*
ole•um \ˈō-lē-əm\ *n, pl* **oleums** : a heavy oily fuming strongly corrosive solution of sulfur trioxide in anhydrous sulfuric acid [Latin, "oil"]
ol•fac•tion \äl-ˈfak-shən, ōl-\ *n* : the sense of smell : the act or process of smelling
ol•fac•to•ry \äl-ˈfak-tə-rē, ōl-, -trē\ *adj* : of, relating to, or concerned with the sense of smell [Latin *olfactorius,* from *olfacere* "to smell", from *olēre* "to have odor" + *facere* "to make, do"]
olfactory bulb *n* : a bulbous projection at the front of each olfactory lobe that is the place where the olfactory nerves terminate and is especially well developed in lower vertebrates (as fishes)
olfactory lobe *n* : a projection at the front of each cerebral hemisphere that is continuous with the olfactory nerve
olfactory nerve *n* : either of the 1st pair of cranial nerves that arise in the sensory membranes of the nose and conduct smell stimuli to the brain
ol•i•garch \ˈäl-ə-ˌgärk, ˈō-lə-\ *n* : a member of an oligarchy [Greek *oligarchēs,* from *oligos* "few" + *archein* "to rule"]
ol•i•gar•chy \-ˈgär-kē\ *n, pl* **-chies 1** : government by a few persons **2** : a government in which a small group exercises control usually for selfish purposes; *also* : the group of persons having such power — **ol•i•gar•chic** \ˌäl-ə-ˈgär-kik\ *or* **ol•i•gar•chi•cal** \-ki-kəl\ *adj*
Oli•go•cene \ˈäl-i-gō-ˌsēn, ˈō-li-, ə-ˈlig-ə-\ *n* : the epoch of the Tertiary between the Eocene and Miocene; *also* : the corresponding system of rocks [Greek *oligos* "few, little"] — **Oligocene** *adj*
oli•go•chaete \-ˌkēt\ *n* : any of a class or order (Oligochaeta) of annelid worms lacking a specialized head and including the earthworms [derived from Greek *oligos* "few, little" + *chaitē* "long hair"] — **oligochaete** *adj*
olio \ˈō-lē-ˌō\ *n, pl* **olio•os** : JUMBLE, MEDLEY [Spanish *olla,* a kind of stew, literally, "pot", from Latin]

[1]**ol•ive** \ˈäl-iv, -əv\ *n* **1** : an Old World evergreen tree grown for its fruit that is an important food and source of oil; *also* : this fruit **2** : a yellow to yellowish green color [Old French, from Latin *oliva,* from Greek *elaia*]

[1]olive 1

[2]**olive** *adj* **1** : of the color olive or olive green **2** : approaching olive in color or complexion
olive branch *n* **1** : a branch of the olive tree especially when used as a symbol of peace **2** : an offer or gesture of conciliation or goodwill
olive drab *n* **1** : a grayish olive color **2 a** : a wool or cotton fabric of an olive drab color **b** : a uniform of this fabric
olive green *n* : a color greener, lighter, and stronger than average olive color
olive oil *n* : a pale yellow to yellowish green oil obtained from the pulp of olives and used especially as a salad oil, in cooking, and in soaps
ol•iv•ine \ˈäl-i-ˌvēn\ *n* : a usually green mineral $(Mg,Fe)_2SiO_4$ that is a complex silicate of magnesium and iron [German *olivin,* from Latin *oliva* "olive"]
ol•la po•dri•da \ˌäl-ə-pə-ˈdrēd-ə\ *n, pl* **olla podridas** \-ˈdrēd-əz\ *also* **ollas podridas** \ˌäl-əz-pə-drēd-əz, ˌäl-ə-pə-\ : OLIO [Spanish, a kind of stew, literally, "rotten pot"]
olym•pi•ad \ə-ˈlim-pē-ˌad, ō-\ *n, often cap* **1** : one of the 4-year intervals between Olympic Games by which time was reckoned in ancient Greece **2** : a celebration of the modern Olympic Games [Middle French *Olympiade,* from Latin *Olympias,* from Greek, from *Olympia,* site of ancient Olympic Games]
[1]**Olym•pi•an** \-pē-ən\ *adj* **1** : of or relating to the ancient Greek region of Olympia **2** : of, relating to, or constituting the Olympic Games
[2]**Olympian** *n* : a participant in Olympic Games
[3]**Olympian** *adj* **1** : of or relating to Mount Olympus in Thessaly **2** : befitting or characteristic of the gods of Olympus : LOFTY ⟨*Olympian* ideals⟩
[4]**Olympian** *n* **1** : one of the 12 major gods in Greek mythology dwelling on Mount Olympus **2** : a being of lofty detachment or superior attainment
Olym•pic \ə-ˈlim-pik, ō-\ *adj* : [3]OLYMPIAN
Olympic Games *n pl* **1** : an ancient Panhellenic festival held at Olympia every 4th year and made up of contests in sports, music, and literature with the victor's prize being a crown of wild olive **2** : a modern revival of the Olympic Games held once every four years and made up of international athletic contests — called also *Olympics*
-o•ma \ˈō-mə\ *n suffix, pl* **-o•mas** \-məz\ *or* **-o•ma•ta** \-mət-ə\ : tumor ⟨lipoma⟩ [Greek *-ōmat-, -ōma,* ending of nouns denoting result formed from verbs in *-oun*]
Oma•ha \ˈō-mə-ˌhȯ, -ˌhä\ *n* : a member of a Siouan people of what is now northeastern Nebraska [Omaha, literally, "those going upstream or against the wind"]
oma•sum \ō-ˈmā-səm\ *n, pl* **-sa** \-sə\ : the division between the reticulum and the abomasum in the stomach of a ruminant [Latin, "tripe of a bullock"]
om•buds•man \ˈäm-ˌbu̇dz-mən, ˈȯm-ˌ-bədz-; äm-ˈbu̇dz-, ȯm-\ *n* **1** : a government appointee who receives and investigates complaints made by individuals against public officials **2** : one that investigates and helps settle reported complaints (as from students or consumers) [Swedish, literally, "representative", from Old Norse *umbothsmathr,* from *umboth* "commission" + *mathr* "man"]
ome•ga \ō-ˈmeg-ə, -ˈmē-gə, -ˈmā-gə\ *n* **1** : the 24th and last letter of the Greek alphabet — Ω or ω **2** : END
om•elet *also* **om•elette** \ˈäm-lət, -ə-lət\ : eggs beaten with milk or water, cooked usually without stirring until set, and folded over [French *omelette,* from Middle French *alumette,* alteration of *alumelle,* literally, "knife blade", from Latin *lamella* "small metal plate", from *lamina* "thin plate"]
△ **origin** The word *omelet* bears little resemblance to the Latin word *lamina,* but the shape of an omelet is rather like a thin plate, which is what *lamina,* the ancestor of *omelet,* means. The

Romans used *lamella,* a diminutive of *lamina,* to mean "a small metal plate". This became Middle French *alumelle,* which meant "knife blade". The word acquired the additional meaning "eggs beaten and cooked without stirring", because such a dish resembled a thin plate or blade. *Alumelle,* under the influence of the common suffix *-ette,* was altered to *alumette,* which became *omelette* in modern French.

omen \ˈō-mən\ *n* **:** an event or phenomenon believed to be a sign or warning of some future occurrence **:** PORTENT [Latin *omin-, omen*]

omen•tum \ō-ˈment-əm\ *n, pl* **-ta** \-ə\ *or* **-tums :** a free fold of peritoneum or one connecting or supporting abdominal structures (as the viscera) [Latin] — **omen•tal** \-ˈment-l\ *adj*

omer \ˈō-mər\ *n* **1 :** an ancient Hebrew unit of dry capacity equal to 1/10 ephah (about 3.5 liters) **2** *often cap* **:** a 7-week period in the Jewish year between Passover and Shabuoth [Hebrew *ʿōmer*]

omi•cron \ˈäm-ə-ˌkrän, ˈōm-\ *n* **:** the 15th letter of the Greek alphabet — Ο or ο

om•i•nous \ˈäm-ə-nəs\ *adj* **:** being or showing an omen; *esp* **:** foretelling evil ⟨*ominous* events leading to war⟩ — **om•i•nous•ly** *adv* — **om•i•nous•ness** *n*

omis•si•ble \ō-ˈmis-ə-bəl, ə-\ *adj* **:** that may be omitted

omis•sion \ō-ˈmish-ən, ə-\ *n* **1 :** something neglected or left undone **2 :** the act of omitting **:** the state of being omitted [Late Latin *omissio,* from Latin *omissus* past participle of *omittere* "to omit"]

omit \ō-ˈmit, ə-\ *vt* **omit•ted; omit•ting 1 :** to leave out or leave unmentioned ⟨*omitted* their names from the list⟩ **2 :** to fail to perform **:** leave undone **:** NEGLECT [Latin *omittere,* from *ob-* "toward" + *mittere* "to let go, send"]

om•ma•tid•i•um \ˌäm-ə-ˈtid-ē-əm\ *n, pl* **-ia** \-ē-ə\ **:** one of the elements corresponding to a small simple eye that make up the compound eye of an arthropod [New Latin, from Greek *omma* "eye"] — **om•ma•tid•i•al** \-ē-əl\ *adj*

omni- *combining form* **:** all **:** universally ⟨*omni*directional⟩ [Latin, from *omnis*]

[1]om•ni•bus \ˈäm-ni-ˌbəs, -bəs\ *n* **1 :** a usually automotive public vehicle designed to carry a comparatively large number of passengers **:** BUS **2 :** a book containing reprints of a number of works [French, from Latin, "for all", from *omnis* "all"]

[2]omnibus *adj* **:** of, relating to, or providing for many things or classes at once ⟨an *omnibus* legislative bill⟩

om•ni•di•rec•tion•al \ˌäm-ni-də-ˈrek-shnəl, -dī, -shən-l\ *adj* **:** receiving or sending radiations in all directions ⟨an *omnidirectional* antenna⟩

om•ni•far•i•ous \ˌäm-nə-ˈfar-ē-əs, -ˈfer-\ *adj* **:** of all varieties, forms, or kinds [Late Latin *omnifarius,* from Latin *omni-* + *-farius* (as in *multifarius* "having great diversity")]

om•nip•o•tence \äm-ˈnip-ət-əns\ *n* **:** the quality or state of being omnipotent

om•nip•o•tent \-ət-ənt\ *adj* **1** *often cap* **:** ALMIGHTY **2 :** having virtually unlimited authority or influence [Middle French, from Latin *omnipotens,* from *omni-* + *potens* "powerful, potent"] — **omnipotent** *n* — **om•nip•o•tent•ly** *adv*

om•ni•pres•ent \ˌäm-ni-ˈprez-nt\ *adj* **:** present in all places at all times — **om•ni•pres•ence** \-ns\ *n*

om•ni•range \ˈäm-ni-ˌrānj\ *n* **:** a system of radio navigation in which any bearing relative to a special radio transmitter on the ground may be chosen and flown by an airplane pilot

om•ni•scient \äm-ˈnish-ənt\ *adj* **1 :** having infinite awareness, understanding, and insight **2 :** possessed of universal or complete knowledge [derived from Medieval Latin *omniscientia* "omniscience", from Latin *omni-* + *scientia* "knowledge, science"] — **om•ni•science** \-əns\ *n* — **om•ni•scient•ly** *adv*

om•ni•um–gath•er•um \ˌäm-nē-əm-ˈgath-ə-rəm\ *n* **:** a miscellaneous collection of a variety of things or persons **:** HODGEPODGE [Latin *omnium* "of all" (from *omnis* "all") + English *gather* + Latin *-um,* n. ending]

om•ni•vore \ˈäm-ni-ˌvōr, -ˌvȯr\ *n* **:** one that is omnivorous

om•niv•o•rous \äm-ˈniv-rəs, -ə-rəs\ *adj* **1 :** feeding on both animal and vegetable substances **2 :** avidly taking in everything as if devouring or consuming [Latin *omnivorus,* from *omni-* + *vorare* "to devour"] — **om•niv•o•rous•ly** *adv* — **om•niv•o•rous•ness** *n*

[1]on \ȯn, ˈȯn, än, ˈän\ *prep* **1 a** (1) **:** over and in contact with or supported by ⟨the book *on* the table⟩ ⟨stand *on* one foot⟩ (2) **:** in contact or side by side with ⟨a fly *on* on the wall⟩ ⟨a town *on* the river⟩ (3) **:** in the area of ⟨*on* the right⟩ **b** (1) **:** to a position over and in contact with **:** ONTO ⟨jumped *on* the horse⟩ (2) **:** into contact with ⟨put the notice *on* the bulletin board⟩ **2** — used as a function word to indicate someone or something that action or feeling is directed against or toward ⟨crept up *on* them⟩ ⟨paid *on* account⟩ ⟨keen *on* sports⟩ **3** — used as a function word to indicate the basis or source (as of an action, opinion, or computation) ⟨know it *on* good authority⟩ ⟨ten cents *on* the dollar⟩ **4 :** with respect to ⟨agreed *on* a price⟩ **5 a :** in connection, association, or activity with or with regard to ⟨*on* a committee⟩ ⟨*on* tour⟩ **b :** in a state or process of ⟨*on* fire⟩ ⟨*on* the increase⟩ **6 :** during or at a specified time ⟨came *on* Monday⟩ ⟨every hour *on* the hour⟩ ⟨cash *on* delivery⟩ **7 :** through the means or agency of ⟨talking *on* the telephone⟩ **8 :** following in series **:** AFTER ⟨loss *on* loss⟩ [Old English *an, on*]

[2]on \ˈȯn, ˈän\ *adv* **1 a :** on a supporting surface ⟨put the plates *on*⟩ **b :** on one's person ⟨has new shoes *on*⟩ **2 a :** forward in space, time, or action **:** ONWARD ⟨let's go *on*⟩ ⟨went *on* home⟩ **b :** in continuance or succession ⟨and so *on*⟩ **3 :** into operation or a position permitting operation ⟨turn the light *on*⟩

[3]on \ˈȯn, ˈän\ *adj* **1 :** engaged in an activity or function (as a dramatic role) **2 a :** being in operation ⟨the radio is *on*⟩ **b :** placed so as to permit operation ⟨the switch is *on*⟩ **3 :** taking place or planned to take place ⟨the game is *on*⟩ ⟨has nothing *on* for tonight⟩

-on \ˌän\ *n suffix* **1 :** elementary particle ⟨nucle*on*⟩ **2 a :** unit **:** quantum ⟨phot*on*⟩ **b :** basic hereditary component ⟨oper*on*⟩ [*ion*]

on•a•ger \ˈän-i-jər\ *n* **1 :** an Asian wild ass **2 :** an ancient and medieval heavy catapult [Latin, "wild ass", from Greek *onagros,* from *onos* "ass" + *agros* "field"]

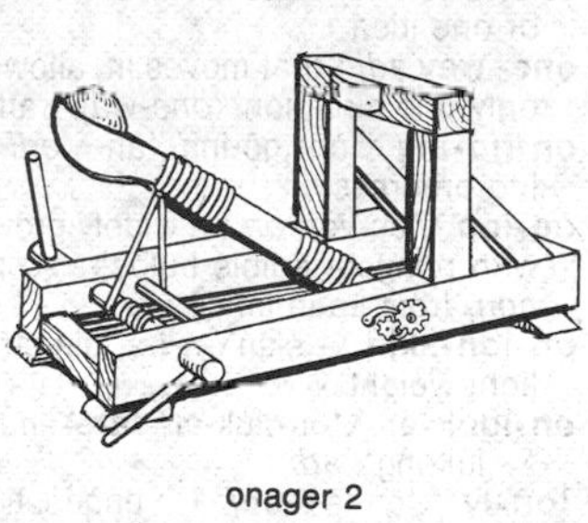

onager 2

[1]once \ˈwəns\ *adv* **1 :** one time and no more ⟨will repeat the question *once*⟩ **2 :** at any time **:** under any circumstances **:** EVER ⟨if you *once* hesitate, you are lost⟩ **3 :** at some indefinite time in the past **:** FORMERLY ⟨*once* lived in luxury⟩ **4 :** by one degree of relationship ⟨a cousin *once* removed⟩ [Middle English *ones,* from genitive of *on* "one"]

[2]once *n* **:** one single time **:** one time at least ⟨just this *once*⟩ — **at once 1 :** at the same time **:** SIMULTANEOUSLY **2 :** IMMEDIATELY

[3]once *conj* **:** at the moment when **:** as soon as ⟨*once* that's done, we can leave⟩

once–over \ˈwəns-ˌō-vər\ *n* **:** a swift examination or survey

on•col•o•gy \än-ˈkäl-ə-jē, äng-\ *n* **:** the study of tumors [Greek *onkos* "mass"]

on•com•ing \ˈȯn-ˌkəm-ing, ˈän-\ *adj* **:** coming on **:** APPROACHING ⟨*oncoming* traffic⟩ ⟨*oncoming* generations⟩

[1]one \ˈwən, ˌwən\ *adj* **1 :** being a single unit or thing ⟨*one* person left⟩ **2 a :** being one in particular ⟨early *one* morning⟩ **b :** being notably what is indicated ⟨*one* fine person⟩ **3 a :** being the same in kind or quality ⟨both of *one* race⟩ **b :** not divided **:** UNITED **4 :** existing or occurring as something not definitely fixed or placed ⟨will see you again *one* day⟩ **5 :** being the only individual of a stated or implied kind ⟨the *one* person they wanted to see⟩ [Middle English *on,* from Old English *ān*]

[2]one *pron* **1 a :** a single member or specimen of a usually specified class or group ⟨saw *one* of my friends⟩ **b :** a person in general **:** SOMEBODY ⟨*one* never knows⟩ **2** — used for *I* or *we* ⟨*one* hopes to see you there⟩

[3]one \ˈwən\ *n* **1 :** the number denoting unity; *also* **:** a symbol representing this — see NUMBER table **2 :** the first in a set or series **3 :** a single person or thing ⟨caught five big *ones*⟩

one another *pron* **:** EACH OTHER

one–horse *adj* **1 :** drawn or operated by one horse **2 :** small in scope or importance ⟨a *one-horse* town⟩

Onei•da \ō-ˈnīd-ə\ *n* : a member of an Iroquoian people originally of what is now central New York [Iroquois *Onē yóde'*, literally, "standing rock"]

onei•ric \ō-ˈnīr-ik\ *adj* : of or relating to dreams : DREAMY [Greek *oneiros* "dream"]

one•ness \ˈwən-nəs\ *n* **1** : the quality, state, or fact of being one (as in thought, spirit, or purpose) **2** : IDENTITY 1

oner•ous \ˈän-ə-rəs, ˈō-nə-\ *adj* : being difficult or burdensome ⟨an *onerous* task⟩ [Middle French *onereus*, from Latin *onerosus*, from *oner-*, *onus* "burden"] — **oner•ous•ly** *adv* — **oner•ous•ness** *n*

one•self \wən-ˈself, ˌwən-\ *also* **one's self** \wən-, ˌwən-, ˌwənz-\ *pron* **1** : a person's self : one's own self — used reflexively as object of a preposition or verb or for emphasis in various constructions **2** : one's normal, healthy, or sane condition or self

one–sid•ed \ˈwən-ˈsīd-əd\ *adj* **1** : lacking in objectivity : BIASED ⟨take a *one-sided* view of a problem⟩ **2** : decided or differing by a wide margin ⟨a *one-sided* game⟩ ⟨a *one-sided* score⟩

one–step \ˈwən-ˌstep\ *n* : a ballroom dance marked by quick walking steps backward and forward in 2/4 time — **one–step** *vi*

one•time \ˈwən-ˌtīm\ *adj* : FORMER ⟨a *onetime* teacher⟩

one–to–one \ˌwən-tə-ˈwən, -də-\ *adj* : pairing each element of a set with one and only one element of another set ⟨a *one-to-one* correspondence⟩

one–track *adj* : obsessed or seemingly obsessed with one thing or one idea

one–way *adj* : that moves in, allows movement in, or functions in only one direction ⟨*one-way* traffic⟩ ⟨a *one-way* ticket⟩

on•go•ing \ˈȯn-ˌgō-ing, ˈän-\ *adj* **1** : being in process **2** : making progress

on•ion \ˈən-yən\ *n* : a widely grown Asian herb of the lily family with pungent edible bulbs; *also* : its bulb [Middle French *oignon*, from Latin *unio*]

on•ion•skin \-ˌskin\ *n* : a thin strong translucent paper of very light weight

on•look•er \ˈȯn-ˌlu̇k-ər, ˈän-\ *n* : SPECTATOR — **on•look•ing** \-ˌlu̇k-ing\ *adj*

[1]**on•ly** \ˈōn-lē\ *adj* **1** : unquestionably best : PEERLESS ⟨the *only* dog for me⟩ **2** : alone in its class or kind : SOLE ⟨the *only* survivor⟩ [Old English *ānlīc*, from *ān* "one" + *-līc* "-ly"]

[2]**only** *adv* **1 a** : JUST, MERELY ⟨worked *only* in the morning⟩ **b** : EXCLUSIVELY, SOLELY ⟨known *only* to me⟩ **2** : at the very least ⟨it was *only* too true⟩ **3 a** : in the final outcome ⟨will *only* make you sick⟩ **b** : with nevertheless the final result being ⟨won the battles, *only* to lose the war⟩ **4 a** : as recently as ⟨*only* last week⟩ **b** : in the immediate past ⟨*only* just talked to them⟩

[3]**only** *conj* **1** : with this sole restriction ⟨you may go, *only* come back early⟩ **2** : were it not that ⟨would play tennis, *only* I'm too tired⟩

on•o•mat•o•poe•ia \ˌän-ə-ˌmat-ə-ˈpē-ə, -ˈpē-yə\ *n* **1** : formation of words in imitation of natural sounds (as *buzz* or *hiss*) **2** : the use of words whose sound suggests the sense [Late Latin, from Greek *onomatopoiia*, from *onoma* "name" + *poiein* "to make"] — **on•o•mat•o•poe•ic** \-ˈpē-ik\ *or* **on•o•mat•o•po•et•ic** \-pō-ˈet-ik\ *adj* — **on•o•mat•o•poe•i•cal•ly** \-ˈpē-ə-kə-lē, -klē\ *or* **on•o•mat•o•po•et•i•cal•ly** \-pō-ˈet-i-kə-lē, -klē\ *adv*

On•on•da•ga \ˌän-ən-ˈdȯ-gə, ˌän-ə-ˈdȯ-\ *n* : a member of an Iroquoian people of what is now central New York [Iroquois *Onōtáge'*, a village of the Onondaga people]

on•rush \ˈȯn-ˌrəsh, ˈän-\ *n* **1** : a rushing forward or onward **2** : ONSET ⟨the first *onrush* of grief⟩

on•set \-ˌset\ *n* **1** : ATTACK 1 **2** : BEGINNING 4a

on•shore \ˈȯn-ˌshōr, ˈän-, -ˌshȯr\ *adj* : moving toward the shore ⟨*onshore* winds⟩ — **on•shore** \ˈȯn-ˈ, ˈän-ˈ\ *adv*

on side *adv or adj* : in a position legally to play the ball or puck

on•slaught \ˈän-ˌslȯt, ˈȯn-\ *n* : an especially fierce attack [Dutch *aanslag* "act of striking"]

on•to \ˌȯn-tə, ˌän-; ˈȯn-tü, ˈän-\ *prep* **1** : to a position or point on ⟨climbed *onto* the roof⟩ **2** : in or into awareness of

on•tog•e•ny \än-ˈtäj-ə-nē\ *n, pl* **-nies** : the development or course of development of an individual organism — compare PHYLOGENY [Greek *ont-*, *ōn*, present participle of *einai* "to be"] — **on•to•ge•net•ic** \ˌän-tə-jə-ˈnet-ik\ *adj* — **on•to•ge•net•i•cal•ly** \-ˈnet-i-kə-lē, -klē\ *adv*

onus \ˈō-nəs\ *n* **1 a** : something (as a duty) that is burdensome or trying **b** : an obligation (as to do something) that is disagreeable **2** : BLAME 2 [Latin]

[1]**on•ward** \ˈȯn-wərd, ˈän-\ *also* **on•wards** \-wərdz\ *adv* : toward or at a point lying ahead in space or time : FORWARD ⟨kept moving *onward*⟩

[2]**onward** *adj* : directed or moving onward : FORWARD ⟨the *onward* march of time⟩

on•y•choph•o•ran \ˌän-i-ˈkäf-ə-rən\ *n* : PERIPATUS [derived from Greek *onych-*, *onyx* "claw" + *-phoros* "-phore"] — **onychophoran** *adj*

on•yx \ˈän-iks\ *n* : chalcedony with straight parallel layers of different colors [Latin *onych-*, *onyx*, from Greek, literally, "claw, nail"]

oo- — see O-

oo•cyte \ˈō-ə-ˌsīt\ *n* : an immature ovum

oo•dles \ˈüd-lz\ *n pl* : a great quantity [perhaps from [2]*huddle*]

oog•a•mous \ō-ˈäg-ə-məs\ *adj* : reproducing by egg and sperm : HETEROGAMETIC — **oog•a•my** \-mē\ *n*

oo•gen•e•sis \ˌō-ə-ˈjen-ə-səs\ *n, pl* **-gen•e•ses** \-ə-ˌsēz\ : formation and maturation of the egg — **oo•ge•net•ic** \-jə-ˈnet-ik\ *adj*

oo•go•ni•um \ˌō-ə-ˈgō-nē-əm\ *n, pl* **-nia** \-nē-ə\ **1** : a female sexual organ in various algae and fungi **2** : a cell that gives rise to oocytes [derived from Greek *ōion* "egg" + *gonos* "procreation, seed"] — **oo•go•ni•al** \-nē-əl\ *adj*

ooh \ˈü\ *interj* — used to express amazement, joy, or surprise [imitative]

oo•lite \ˈō-ə-ˌlīt\ *n* : a rock consisting of small round grains usually of calcium carbonate cemented together — **oo•lit•ic** \ˌō-ə-ˈlit-ik\ *adj*

oo•mi•ak *variant of* UMIAK

oomph \ˈu̇mf, ˈu̇mpf\ **1** : personal charm or magnetism : GLAMOUR **2** : SEX APPEAL **3** : VITALITY 2b, ENTHUSIASM

oops \ˈu̇ps, ˈwu̇ps\ *interj* — used to express mild apology, surprise, or dismay [imitative]

oo•spore \ˈō-ə-ˌspōr, -ˌspȯr\ *n* : ZYGOTE; *esp* : a spore that is produced by union of a large female cell with a small male cell and that yields a sporophyte — compare ZYGOSPORE

oo•tid \ˈō-ə-ˌtid\ *n* : an egg cell after meiosis [derived from Greek *ōion* "egg"]

[1]**ooze** \ˈüz\ *n* **1** : a soft deposit (as of mud, slime, or shells) especially on the bottom of a body of water **2** : soft wet ground : MUD [Old English *wāse* "mire"]

[2]**ooze** *n* **1** : the action of oozing **2** : something that oozes [Middle English *wose* "sap, juice", from Old English *wōs*]

[3]**ooze** *vb* **1** : to pass or flow slowly through or as if through small openings ⟨sap *oozed* from the tree⟩ **2** : to move slowly or imperceptibly **3** : to give off : EXUDE ⟨a manner that *oozed* confidence⟩

oozy \ˈü-zē\ *adj* **ooz•ier**; **-est** **1** : containing or composed of ooze **2** : exuding moisture : SLIMY

opac•i•ty \ō-ˈpas-ət-ē\ *n, pl* **-ties** **1** : the quality or state of being opaque to radiant energy (as light) **2** : obscurity of meaning **3** : mental dullness **4** : an opaque spot on an otherwise or normally transparent structure (as the lens of the eye) [French *opacité* "shadiness", from Latin *opacitas*, from *opacus* "shaded, dark"]

opal \ˈō-pəl\ *n* : a mineral that is a hydrated amorphous silica softer and less dense than quartz and typically with an irridescent play of colors [Latin *opalus*, from Sanskrit *upala* "stone, jewel"]

opal•es•cent \ˌō-pə-ˈles-nt\ *adj* : having a play of colors like an opal — **opal•esce** \-ˈles\ *vi* — **opal•es•cence** \-ˈles-ns\ *n*

opal•line \ˈō-pə-ˌlīn, -ˌlēn\ *adj* : resembling opal : OPALESCENT

[1]**opaque** \ō-ˈpāk\ *adj* **1** : exhibiting opacity : not transmitting radiant energy (as light) **2 a** : not easily understood : OBSCURE **b** : DULL 1, STUPID, OBTUSE [Latin *opacus* "shaded, dark"] — **opaque•ly** *adv* — **opaque•ness** *n*

[2]**opaque** *n* : something that is opaque

ope \ˈōp\ *vb, archaic* : OPEN

[1]**open** \ˈō-pən, ˈōp-m\ *adj* **1 a** : free or far from boundaries or restrictions ⟨*open* sea⟩ ⟨*open* range⟩ **b** : permitting passage or access : not shut or shut up : not stopped or clogged ⟨an *open* door⟩ ⟨*open* books⟩ ⟨*open* pores⟩ **c** : having openings or spaces ⟨an *open* soil⟩ ⟨*open* type⟩ **2 a** : not enclosed or covered : BARE ⟨an *open* boat⟩ ⟨an *open* fire⟩ ⟨*open* wounds⟩ **b** : not protected against something : LIABLE ⟨*open* to challenge⟩

⟨*open* to infection⟩ **c** (1) **:** not secret **:** exposed to general knowledge **:** PUBLIC ⟨*open* dislike⟩ (2) **:** candidly and often artlessly frank ⟨*open* about their plans⟩ **3 a :** free to the use, entry, or participation of all ⟨an *open* meeting⟩ ⟨*open* classes⟩ **b :** easy to enter, get through, or see ⟨*open* country⟩ ⟨an *open* woodland⟩; *also* **:** free from hampering restraints or controls ⟨an *open* economy⟩ ⟨*open* gambling⟩ **c :** available or ready for use or operation ⟨keep an hour *open* for our meeting⟩ ⟨the store was still *open*⟩ **4 :** not snowy or stormy ⟨an *open* winter⟩ **5 :** not drawn together **:** not folded or contracted **:** spread out ⟨an *open* flower⟩ ⟨*open* umbrellas⟩ **6 a :** not finally decided or settled ⟨an *open* question⟩ **b :** receptive to appeals or ideas **:** RESPONSIVE ⟨an *open* mind⟩ ⟨*open* to suggestion⟩ **7 :** not made up of a continuous closed system of vessels ⟨the insect circulatory system is *open*⟩ **8 :** not containing endpoints or boundary points ⟨an *open* interval⟩ [Old English] **syn** see FRANK — **open•ly** \'ō-pən-lē\ *adv* — **open•ness** \'ō-pən-nəs\ *n*

2open *vb* **opened** \'ō-pənd, 'ōp-md\; **open•ing** \'ōp-ning, -ə-ning\ **1 a :** to change or move from a shut condition **:** UNFASTEN, UNCLOSE ⟨*open* a book⟩ ⟨*open* a switch⟩ ⟨the door *opened* slowly⟩ **b :** to make or become open by or as if by clearing away obstacles ⟨*open* a road blocked with snow⟩ ⟨the clouds *opened*⟩ **c :** to make an opening or openings in ⟨*open* a boil⟩ **d :** to spread out **:** UNFOLD ⟨an *opening* flower⟩ ⟨*open* a napkin⟩ **2 :** to make or become functional ⟨*open* a new store⟩ ⟨the office *opens* early⟩ **3 :** to give access ⟨the rooms *open* onto a hall⟩ **4 :** to enter upon **:** BEGIN, START ⟨*open* fire⟩ ⟨*open* talks⟩ **5 :** to speak out — **open•able** \'ōp-nə-bəl, -ə-nə-\ *adj* — **open•er** \'ōp-nər, -ə-nər\ *n*

3open *n* **1 a :** open and unobstructed space or water **b :** OUTDOORS **2 :** an open contest, competition, or tournament

open–air *adj* **:** OUTDOOR ⟨pleasures of *open-air* life⟩ ⟨*open-air* theaters⟩

open air *n* **:** space where air is unconfined; *esp* **:** OUT-OF-DOORS

open–and–shut \,ōp-nən-'shət, -ə-nən-\ *adj* **:** perfectly simple **:** OBVIOUS

open door *n* **:** a policy giving opportunity for commercial relations with a country to all nations on equal terms — **open–door** *adj*

open–end *adj* **:** organized or formulated to allow for contingencies ⟨an *open-end* mortgage⟩

open–eyed \,ō-pə-'nīd\ *adj* **1 :** having the eyes open **2 a :** WATCHFUL **b :** DISCERNING

open•hand•ed \,ō-pən-'han-dəd\ *adj* **:** generous in giving **:** LIBERAL — **open•hand•ed•ly** *adv* — **open•hand•ed•ness** *n*

open•heart•ed \-'härt-əd\ *adj* **1 :** FRANK 1 **2 :** GENEROUS 1 — **open•heart•ed•ly** *adv* — **open•heart•ed•ness** *n*

open–hearth *adj* **:** being or relating to a process of making steel from pig iron in a furnace that reflects heat from the roof onto the material

open house *n* **:** ready and usually informal hospitality or entertainment for all comers

open•ing \'ōp-ning, -ə-ning\ *n* **1 :** an act or instance of making or becoming open **2 :** an open place or span **:** HOLE **3 :** something that constitutes a beginning: as **a :** a planned series of moves made at the start of a game of chess or checkers **b :** a first performance **4 a :** OCCASION 1, CHANCE **b :** an opportunity for employment

open letter *n* **:** a letter of protest or appeal intended for the general public and printed in a newspaper or periodical

open–mind•ed \,ō-pən-'mīn-dəd\ *adj* **:** willing to listen to arguments or ideas **:** not prejudiced — **open–mind•ed•ly** *adv* — **open–mind•ed•ness** *n*

open•mouthed \,ō-pən-'mau̇t͟hd, -'mau̇tht\ *adj* **1 :** having the mouth wide open **2 :** struck with amazement or wonder — **open•mouthed•ly** \-'mau̇-t͟həd-lē, -'mau̇th-tlē\ *adv* — **open–mouthed•ness** \-'mau̇-t͟həd-nəs, -'mau̇tht-nəs, -'mau̇th-nəs\ *n*

open–pol•li•nat•ed \,ō-pən-'päl-ə-,nāt-əd\ *adj* **:** pollinated by natural agencies without human interference

open secret *n* **:** something supposedly secret but in fact generally known

open sentence *n* **:** an equation or inequality that contains one or more unknown quantities and in itself is neither true nor false ⟨the *open sentence* $x + 3 = 5$⟩

open sesame \,ōpən-'ses-ə-mē\ *n* **:** something that unfailingly brings about a desired end [from *open sesame,* the magical command used by Ali Baba to open the door of the robbers' den in the story *Ali Baba and the Forty Thieves* in the *Arabian Nights' Entertainments*]

open shop *n* **:** an establishment that employs both members and nonmembers of a labor union

open•work \'ō-pən-,wərk\ *n* **:** work constructed so as to show openings through its substance — **openwork** *or* **open–worked** \,ō-pən-'wərkt\ *adj*

1opera *pl of* OPUS

2op•era \'äp-rə, -ə-rə\ *n* **1 :** a drama set to music and made up of vocal pieces with orchestral accompaniment and orchestral overtures and interludes **2 :** a performance of an opera; *also* **:** a building where operas are performed [Italian, "work, opera", from Latin "work, pains"] — **op•er•at•ic** \,äp-ə-'rat-ik\ *adj* — **op•er•at•i•cal•ly** \-i-kə-lē,-klē\ *adv*

op•er•a•ble \'äp-rə-bəl, -ə-rə-\ *adj* **1 :** fit, possible, or desirable to use **2 :** suitable for surgical treatment ⟨an *operable* cancer⟩

opé•ra bouffe \,äp-rə-'büf, -ə-rə-\ *n* **:** farcical comic opera [French, from Italian *opera buffa*]

opé•ra comique \,äp-rə-käm-'ēk, -ə-rə-, -kō-'mēk\ *n* **:** COMIC OPERA [French]

opera glasses *n pl* **:** small low-power binoculars or field glasses for use in a theater

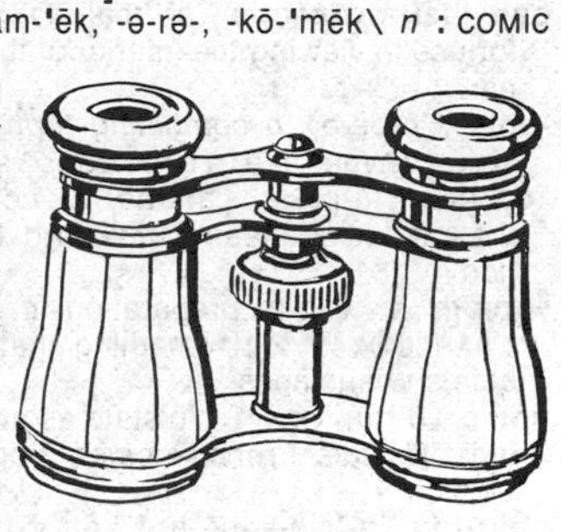

opera glasses

opera hat *n* **:** a collapsible top hat consisting usually of a dull silky fabric stretched over a steel frame

op•er•ate \'äp-,rāt, -ə-,rāt\ *vb* **1 :** to perform or cause to perform an appointed function ⟨the switch *operates* easily⟩ ⟨learn to *operate* a car safely⟩ **2 :** to produce an effect ⟨a drug that *operates* quickly⟩ **3 :** to carry on the activities of ⟨*operate* a farm⟩; *esp* **:** MANAGE ⟨*operate* a business⟩ **4 :** to perform surgery ⟨*operate* on a tumor⟩ [Latin *operari* "to work", from *oper-, opus* "work"]

op•er•a•tion \,äp-ə-'rā-shən\ *n* **1 :** a doing of a practical work **2 :** the quality or state of being functional or operative **3 :** a surgical procedure carried out on the living body **4 :** a process (as addition or multiplication) of deriving one mathematical expression from others according to a rule **5 a :** a usually military action, mission, or maneuver including its planning and execution **b** *pl* **:** the office of an airfield which controls flying from the field — **op•er•a•tion•al** \-shnəl, -shən-l\ *adj* — **op•er•a•tion•al•ly** \-ē\ *adv*

1op•er•a•tive \'äp-rət-iv, -ə-rət-; 'äp-ə-,rāt-\ *adj* **1 :** producing an appropriate or intended effect **2 :** exerting force or influence **:** OPERATING ⟨an *operative* motive⟩ **3 a :** having to do with physical operations ⟨*operative* costs⟩ **b :** engaged in work ⟨an *operative* craftsman⟩ **4 :** based on or consisting of operation ⟨*operative* dentistry⟩ — **op•er•a•tive•ly** *adv* — **op•er•a•tive•ness** *n*

2operative *n* **:** OPERATOR **:** as **a :** ARTISAN, MECHANIC **b** (1) **:** a secret agent (2) **:** DETECTIVE

op•er•a•tor \'äp-,rāt-ər, -ə-,rāt-\ *n* **1 :** one that operates: as **a :** one that operates a machine or device ⟨telephone *operator*⟩ **b :** one that operates a business **c :** one that deals in stocks or commodities **2 :** a shrewd person who knows how to get around restrictions or difficulties **3 :** a part of a chromosome that starts the formation of messenger RNA by one or more nearby structural genes and is itself subject to inhibition by a genetic repressor — called also *operator gene*; compare OPERON

oper•cu•lum \ō-'pər-kyə-ləm\ *n, pl* **-la** \-lə\ *also* **-lums 1 :** a lid or covering flap (as of a moss capsule) **2 :** a body part that suggests a lid: as **a :** a plate on the foot of a gastropod mollusk that closes the shell **b :** the covering of the gills of a fish [Latin, "cover", from *operire* "to shut, cover"] — **oper•cu•lar** \-lər\ *adj* — **oper•cu•late** \-lət\ *adj*

op•er•et•ta \ˌäp-ə-ˈret-ə\ *n* : a usually romantic comic opera that includes songs and dancing [Italian, from *opera* "opera"] — **op•er•et•tist** \-ˈret-əst\ *n*

op•er•on \ˈäp-ə-ˌrän\ *n* : the combination of an operator and the structural genes it regulates [*oper*ator + *-on*]

ophid•i•an \ō-ˈfid-ē-ən\ *adj* : of, relating to, or resembling snakes [derived from Greek *ophis* "snake"] — **ophidian** *n*

oph•thal•mia \äf-ˈthal-mē-ə, äp-\ *n* : inflammation of the conjunctiva or eyeball [Late Latin, from Greek, from *ophthalmos* "eye"]

oph•thal•mic \-mik\ *adj* : of, relating to, or situated near the eye : OCULAR

oph•thal•mol•o•gist \ˌäf-thə-ˈmäl-ə-jəst, ˌäp-, -thəl-, -ˌthal-\ *n* : a physician specializing in ophthalmology — compare OPTICIAN, OPTOMETRIST

oph•thal•mol•o•gy \-jē\ *n* : a branch of medical science dealing with the structure, functions, and diseases of the eye — **oph•thal•mo•log•i•cal•ly** \ˌäf-thə-mə-ˈläj-i-kə-lē, ˌäp-, -thəl-, -ˌthal-, -klē\ *adv*

oph•thal•mo•scope \äf-ˈthal-mə-ˌskōp, äp-\ *n* : an instrument for use in viewing the interior of the eye and especially the retina

-opia \ˈō-pē-ə\ *n combining form* : condition of having (such) vision ⟨hyper*opia*⟩ [Greek *ōps* "eye"]

[1]opi•ate \ˈō-pē-ət, -ˌāt\ *adj* **1** : containing or mixed with opium **2 a** : inducing sleep : NARCOTIC **b** : causing dullness or inaction

[2]opiate *n* **1** : a preparation or derivative of opium; *also* : NARCOTIC 1 **2** : something that induces rest or inaction or quiets uneasiness

opine \ō-ˈpīn\ *vb* **1** : to state as an opinion **2** : to express opinions [Middle French *opiner,* from Latin *opinari* "to have an opinion"]

opin•ion \ə-ˈpin-yən\ *n* **1** : a judgment about a person or thing ⟨has a high *opinion* of the doctor⟩ **2** : a belief stronger than an impression but less strong than positive knowledge **3** : a formal statement by an expert after careful study [Middle French, from Latin *opinio*]

• **syn** OPINION, BELIEF, CONVICTION mean a judgment one holds as true. OPINION implies a conclusion still open to dispute ⟨differing *opinions* on the safety of nuclear power⟩ BELIEF implies deliberate acceptance and intellectual assent ⟨a basic *belief* in a supreme being⟩ CONVICTION applies to a firm, unshakable belief ⟨a *conviction* that all life is sacred⟩

opin•ion•at•ed \-yə-ˌnāt-əd\ *adj* : adhering unduly to one's own opinions or preconceived notions — **opin•ion•at•ed•ly** *adv* — **opin•ion•at•ed•ness** *n*

opin•ion•ative \-ˌnāt-iv\ *adj* **1** : of, relating to, or consisting of opinion **2** : OPINIONATED

opi•um \ˈō-pē-əm\ *n* **1** : a bitter brownish addictive narcotic drug consisting of the dried juice from the unripe seed capsules of the opium poppy **2** : something having an effect like that of opium [Latin, from Greek *opion,* from *opos* "sap"]

opium poppy *n* : an annual Eurasian poppy grown since antiquity for opium, for its edible oily seeds, and for its showy flowers

opos•sum \ə-ˈpäs-əm, ˈpäs-əm\ *n, pl* **-sums** *also* **-sum** : any of various American marsupials; *esp* : a common largely nocturnal and arboreal mammal of the eastern United States [of American Indian origin]

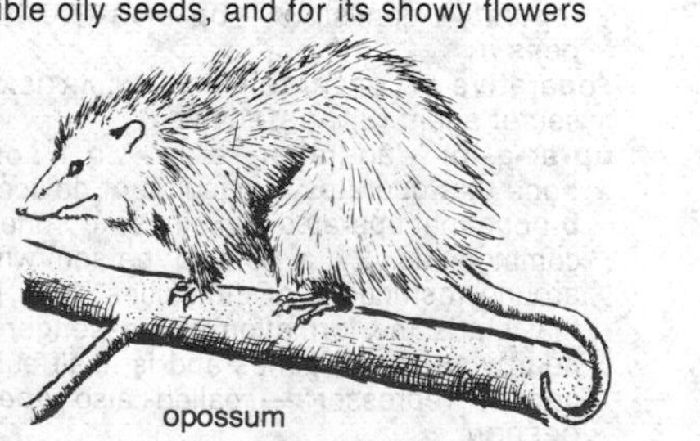

opossum

[1]op•po•nent \ə-ˈpō-nənt\ *n* **1** : a person or thing that opposes another person or thing **2** : a muscle that counteracts and resists the action of another [Latin *opponens,* present participle of *opponere* "to oppose"]

• **syn** ANTAGONIST, ADVERSARY: OPPONENT implies a position on the other side as in a debate, election, or conflict; ANTAGONIST implies sharper opposition in a struggle for supremacy; ADVERSARY suggests active hostility.

[2]opponent *adj* **1** : ANTAGONISTIC **2** : OPPOSITE 1

op•por•tune \ˌäp-ər-ˈtün, -ˈtyün\ *adj* : SUITABLE, TIMELY ⟨an *opportune* moment to act⟩ [Middle French *opportun,* from Latin *opportunus,* from *ob* "toward" + *portus* "port, harbor"] — **op•por•tune•ly** *adv* — **op•por•tune•ness** \-ˈtün-nəs, -ˈtyün-\ *n*

op•por•tun•ism \-ˈtü-ˌniz-əm, -ˈtyü-\ *n* : the art, policy, or practice of taking advantage of opportunities or circumstances especially with little regard for principles or ultimate consequences — **op•por•tun•ist** \-nəst\ *n or adj* — **op•por•tu•nis•tic** \-tü-ˈnis-tik, -tyü-\ *adj*

op•por•tu•ni•ty \ˌäp-ər-ˈtü-nət-ē, -ˈtyü-\ *n, pl* **-ties** **1** : a favorable juncture of circumstances, time and place **2** : a good chance for advancement or progress

op•pos•able \ə-ˈpō-zə-bəl\ *adj* **1** : capable of being resisted **2** : capable of being placed opposite something else ⟨the thumb is *opposable* to the forefinger⟩ — **op•pos•abil•i•ty** \ə-ˌpō-zə-ˈbil-ət-ē\ *n*

op•pose \ə-ˈpōz\ *vt* **1** : to place over against something for resistance, counterbalance, or contrast **2** : to offer resistance to [French *opposer,* from Latin *opponere,* from *ob-* "against" + *ponere* "to put, place"] — **op•pos•er** *n*

• **syn** RESIST, WITHSTAND: OPPOSE may apply to an act or attitude ranging from mild objection to bitter hostility or warfare; RESIST implies a recognition of a hostile or threatening force and a positive effort to counteract it ⟨*resist* temptation⟩ WITHSTAND usually suggests a successful resistance.

[1]op•po•site \ˈäp-ə-zət, ˈäp-sət\ *n* **1** : something that is opposed or contrary **2** : ADDITIVE INVERSE

[2]opposite *adj* **1 a** : set over against something that is at the other end or side ⟨*opposite* ends of a diameter⟩ **b** : attached to a stem or axis in exactly opposite pairs ⟨*opposite* leaves⟩ — compare ALTERNATE **2 a** : occupying an opposing and often hostile position ⟨*opposite* sides of the question⟩ **b** : as different as possible : CONTRADICTORY ⟨*opposite* meanings⟩ **3** : contrarily turned or moving ⟨go in *opposite* directions⟩ **4** : being the other of a matching or contrasting pair ⟨a member of the *opposite* sex⟩ [Middle French, from Latin *oppositus,* past participle of *opponere* "to oppose"] **syn** see CONTRARY — **op•po•site•ly** *adv* — **op•po•site•ness** *n*

[3]opposite *adv* : on or to an opposite side

[4]opposite *prep* : across from and usually facing

op•po•si•tion \ˌäp-ə-ˈzish-ən\ *n* **1** : a setting opposite or being set opposite; *also* : a configuration in which the difference in celestial longitude of two heavenly bodies is 180° **2** : resistant or contrary action or condition ⟨offer *opposition* to a plan⟩ ⟨the *opposition* of two forces⟩ **3 a** : something that opposes; *esp* : a body of persons opposing something **b** *often cap* : a political party opposing and prepared to replace the party in power — **op•po•si•tion•al** \-ˈzish-nəl, -ən-l\ *adj*

op•press \ə-ˈpres\ *vt* **1** : to crush or burden by harsh rule ⟨a country *oppressed* by a dictator's rule⟩ **2** : to burden in spirit as if with weight ⟨*oppressed* by debts⟩ [Middle French *oppresser,* from Latin *oppressus,* past participle of *opprimere* "to oppress", from *ob-* "against" + *premere* "to press"] **syn** see DEPRESS — **op•pres•sor** \-ˈpres-ər\ *n*

op•pres•sion \ə-ˈpresh-ən\ *n* **1 a** : unjust or cruel exercise of authority or power **b** : something that oppresses cruelly or unjustly **2** : a sense of being weighed down in body or mind : DEPRESSION

op•pres•sive \ə-ˈpres-iv\ *adj* **1** : unreasonably burdensome or severe ⟨*oppressive* laws⟩ **2** : TYRANNICAL ⟨*oppressive* rulers⟩ **3** : overpowering or depressing to the spirit or senses ⟨*oppressive* heat⟩ — **op•pres•sive•ly** *adv* — **op•pres•sive•ness** *n*

op•pro•bri•ous \ə-ˈprō-brē-əs\ *adj* **1** : expressing contemptuous distaste and usually reproach ⟨*opprobrious* language⟩ **2** : deserving of opprobrium : DESPICABLE — **op•pro•bri•ous•ly** *adv* — **op•pro•bri•ous•ness** *n*

op•pro•bri•um \-brē-əm\ *n* **1** : something that brings disgrace **2** : public disgrace or bad reputation that follows from conduct considered grossly wrong or vicious [Latin, from *opprobrare* "to reproach", from *ob* "in the way of" + *probrum* "reproach"]

op•so•nin \ˈäp-sə-nən\ *n* : a constituent of blood serum that makes foreign cells more susceptible to the action of the phagocytes [Latin *opsonium* "relish", from Greek *opsōnion* "victuals", from *opsōnein* "to purchase victuals"] — **op•son•ic** \äp-ˈsän-ik\ *adj*

-op•sy \ˌäp-sē, əp-\ *n combining form, pl* **-opsies** : examination ⟨necr*opsy*⟩ [Greek *opsis* "appearance"]

opt \ˈäpt\ *vi* : to make a choice : DECIDE [French *opter,* from Latin *optare*]

op•tic \'äp-tik\ *adj* : of or relating to vision or the eye [Middle French *optique,* from Medieval Latin *opticus,* from Greek *optikos,* from *opsesthai* "to be going to see"]

op•ti•cal \'äp-ti-kəl\ *adj* **1** : relating to optics **2** : OPTIC **3** : of, relating to, or using light ⟨an *optical* telescope⟩ — **op•ti•cal•ly** \-kə-lē, -klē\ *adv*

optical illusion *n* : ILLUSION 1c

op•ti•cian \äp-'tish-ən\ *n* **1** : a maker of or dealer in optical items and instruments **2** : one that grinds eyeglass lenses to prescription and sells glasses — compare OPHTHALMOLOGIST, OPTOMETRIST

optic lobe *n* : either of two prominences of the midbrain concerned with vision

optic nerve *n* : either of the 2d pair of cranial nerves that arise from the bottom part of the diencephalon, supply the eye, and conduct visual nerve impulses to the brain

op•tics \'äp-tiks\ *n* : a science that deals with the nature and properties of light and the effects that it undergoes and produces

op•ti•mal \'äp-tə-məl\ *adj* : most desirable or satisfactory : OPTIMUM — **op•ti•mal•ly** \-mə-lē\ *adv*

op•ti•mism \'äp-tə-,miz-əm\ *n* **1** : a doctrine that this world is the best possible world **2** : an inclination to put the most favorable construction upon actions and events or to anticipate the best possible outcome [French *optimisme,* from Latin *optimus* "best"] — **op•ti•mist** \-məst\ *n or adj* — **op•ti•mis•tic** \,äp-tə-'mis-tik\ *or* **op•ti•mis•ti•cal** \-ti-kəl\ *adj* — **op•ti•mis•ti•cal•ly** \-ti-kə-lē, -klē\ *adv*

op•ti•mum \'äp-tə-məm\ *n, pl* **-ma** \-mə\ *also* **-mums** **1** : the amount or degree of something that is most favorable to some end **2** : greatest degree attained under implied or specified conditions [Latin, from *optimus* "best"] — **optimum** *adj*

op•tion \'äp-shən\ *n* **1 a** : the power or right to choose **b** : a right to buy or sell something at a specified price during a specified period **c** : a right of an insured person to choose the form in which payments due him or her are to be made **2** : something offered for choice [French, from Latin *optio*] **syn** see CHOICE

op•tion•al \'äp-shnəl, -shən-l\ *adj* : permitting a choice : not compulsory — **op•tion•al•ly** \-ē\ *adv*

op•tom•e•trist \äp-'täm-ə-trəst\ *n* : a specialist in optometry — compare OPTICIAN, OPHTHALMOLOGIST

op•tom•e•try \-trē\ *n* : the art or profession of examining the eye for defects of vision and prescribing correctional glasses or exercises but not drugs or surgery [derived from Greek *opsesthai* "to be going to see"] — **op•to•met•ric** \,äp-tə-'me-trik\ *adj*

op•u•lence \'äp-yə-ləns\ *n* **1** : WEALTH 1, RICHES **2** : ABUNDANCE, PROFUSION

op•u•lent \-lənt\ *adj* : marked by opulence: as **a** : WEALTHY 1 **b** : richly abundant : PROFUSE ⟨*opulent* harvests⟩ ⟨*opulent* foliage⟩ **c** : amply fashioned [Latin *opulentus,* from *ops* "power, wealth, help"] — **op•u•lent•ly** *adv*

opun•tia \ō-'pən-chə, -chē-ə\ *n* : PRICKLY PEAR [Latin, a kind of plant, derived from *Opus,* ancient city in Greece]

opus \'ō-pəs\ *n, pl* **opera** \'ō-pə-rə, 'äp-ə-\ *also* **opus•es** \'ō-pə-səz\ : WORK 6; *esp* : a musical composition or set of compositions [Latin, "work"]

[1]or \ər, ȯr, ,ȯr\ *conj* — used as a function word to indicate an alternative ⟨coffee *or* tea⟩ ⟨sink *or* swim⟩ [Middle English *other, or,* from Old English *oththe*]

[2]or *prep, archaic* : BEFORE [Old Norse *ār,* adv., "early, before"]

[3]or *conj, archaic* : BEFORE

[4]or \'ȯr\ *n* : the heraldic color gold or yellow [Middle French, "gold", from Latin *aurum*]

-or \ər, ,ȯr, 'ȯr\ *n suffix* : one that does a (specified) thing ⟨elevator⟩ [Latin]

or•a•cle \'ȯr-ə-kəl, 'är-\ *n* **1 a** : a person (as a priestess of ancient Greece) through whom a deity is held to speak **b** : a shrine in which a deity so reveals hidden knowledge or the divine purpose **c** : an answer or revelation given by an oracle **2 a** : a person giving wise or authoritative decisions or opinions **b** : an authoritative or wise expression or answer [Middle French, from Latin *oraculum,* from *orare* "to speak"]

orac•u•lar \ȯ-'rak-yə-lər, ə-\ *adj* **1** : of, relating to, or being an oracle **2** : resembling an oracle in wisdom, solemnity, or obscurity — **orac•u•lar•i•ty** \-,rak-yə-'lar-ət-ē\ *n* — **orac•u•lar•ly** \-'rak-yə-lər-lē\ *adv*

oral \'ōr-əl, 'ȯr-, 'är-\ *adj* **1 a** : uttered by the mouth or in words : SPOKEN ⟨an *oral* agreement⟩ **b** : using speech or the lips ⟨*oral* reading⟩ **2** : of, relating to, given through, or situated near the mouth ⟨*oral* hygiene⟩ ⟨the *oral* surface of a starfish⟩ [Latin *or-, os* "mouth"] — **oral•ly** \-ə-lē\ *adv*

• **syn** VERBAL: ORAL applies to what is spoken rather than written ⟨an *oral* report⟩ VERBAL applies to words whether oral or written and stresses the use of words in contrast to other forms of communication or expression ⟨*verbal* communication was supplemented by signs and gestures⟩

or•ange \'ȯr-inj, 'är-, -ənj\ *n* **1 a** : a roundish citrus fruit with a reddish yellow rind and a sweet edible pulp **b** : any of various rather small evergreen citrus trees that bear oranges **2** : a color between red and yellow [Middle French, from Provençal *auranja,* from Arabic *nāranj,* from Persian *nārang,* from Sanskrit *nāraṅga,* of Dravidian origin] — **orange** *adj*

or•ange•ade \,ȯr-in-'jād, ,är-, -ən-\ *n* : a drink made of orange juice, sugar, and water

orange hawkweed *n* : a European plant of the daisy family that has bright orange-red flower heads and is a weed in northeastern North America — called also *Indian paintbrush*

Or•ange•man \'ȯr-inj-mən, 'är-\ *n* **1** : a member of a secret society organized in the north of Ireland in 1795 to defend the British sovereign and to support the Protestant religion **2** : a Protestant Irishman especially of Ulster [William III of England, prince of *Orange*]

or•ange•ry \'ȯr-inj-rē, 'är-, -ənj-, -ə-rē\ *n, pl* **-ries** : a protected place (as a greenhouse) for raising oranges in cool climates

or•ange•wood \-,wu̇d\ *n* : the wood of the orange tree used especially in turnery and carving

orang•u•tan *or* **orang•ou•tan** \ə-'rang-ə-,tang, -,tan\ *n* : a largely plant-eating and tree-dwelling anthropoid ape of Borneo and Sumatra about two thirds as large as the gorilla [Malay *orang hutan,* literally, "man of the forest"]

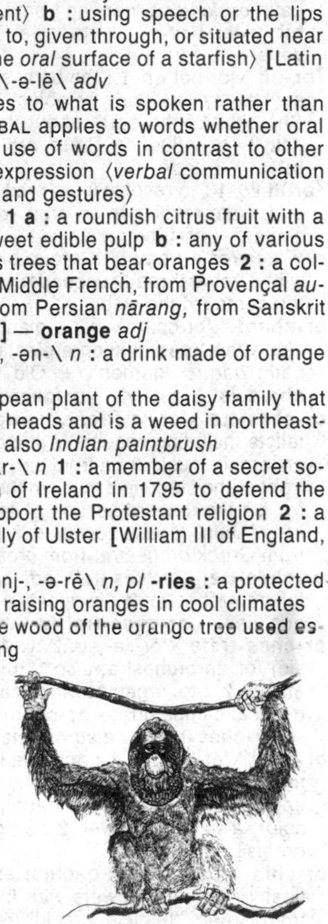

orangutan

orate \ȯ-'rāt\ *vi* : to speak in an elevated and often pompous manner [back-formation from *oration*]

ora•tion \ə-'rā-shən, ȯ-\ *n* : an elaborate discourse delivered in a formal and dignified manner [Latin *oratio,* from *orare* "to speak, pray"]

or•a•tor \'ȯr-ət-ər, 'är-\ *n* **1** : one that delivers an oration **2** : one noted for skill and power in public speaking

Or•a•to•ri•an \,ȯr-ə-'tōr-ē-ən, ,är-, -'tȯr-\ *n* : a member of the Congregation of the Oratory of St. Philip Neri founded in Rome in 1575 and comprising independent communities of secular priests under obedience but without vows — **Oratorian** *adj*

or•a•tor•i•cal \,ȯr-ə-'tȯr-i-kəl, ,är-ə-'tär-\ *adj* : of, relating to, or characteristic of an orator or oratory — **or•a•tor•i•cal•ly** \-kə-lē, -klē\ *adv*

or•a•to•rio \,ȯr-ə-'tōr-ē-,ō, ,är-, -'tȯr-\ *n, pl* **-ri•os** : a choral work usually on a scriptural subject consisting chiefly of recitatives, arias, and choruses without action or scenery [Italian, from the *Oratorio* di San Filippo Neri (Oratory of Saint Philip Neri) in Rome]

[1]or•a•to•ry \'ȯr-ə-,tōr-ē, 'är-, -,tȯr-\ *n, pl* **-ries** : a place of prayer; *esp* : a private or institutional chapel [Late Latin *oratorium,* from Latin *orare* "to speak, pray"]

[2]oratory *n* **1** : the art of speaking in public effectively **2** : public speaking that uses oratory [Latin *oratoria,* from *oratorius* "oratorical", from *orare* "to speak, pray"]

[1]orb \'ȯrb\ *n* : a spherical body: as **a** : a heavenly body (as a planet) **b** : EYE 1a **c** : a sphere surmounted by a cross symbolizing kingly power and justice [Middle French *orbe,* from Latin *orbis* "circle, disk, orbit"]

[2]orb *vt* **1** : to form into a disk or circle **2** *archaic* : ENCIRCLE 1, ENCLOSE

\ə\ **abut**	\au̇\ **out**	\i\ **tip**	\ȯ\ **saw**	\u̇\ **foot**
\ər\ **further**	\ch\ **chin**	\ī\ **life**	\ȯi\ **coin**	\y\ **yet**
\a\ **mat**	\e\ **pet**	\j\ **job**	\th\ **thin**	\yü\ **few**
\ā\ **take**	\ē\ **easy**	\ng\ **sing**	\t͟h\ **this**	\yu̇\ **cure**
\ä\ **cot, cart**	\g\ **go**	\ō\ **bone**	\ü\ **food**	\zh\ **vision**

or·bic·u·lar \ȯr-ˈbik-yə-lər\ *adj* **:** SPHERICAL, CIRCULAR [Late Latin *orbicularis,* derived from Latin *orbis* "circle, disk"] — **or·bic·u·lar·i·ty** \-ˌbik-yə-ˈlar-ət-ē\ *n* — **or·bic·u·lar·ly** \-ˈbik-yə-lər-lē\ *adv*

1or·bit \ˈȯr-bət\ *n* **1 :** the bony socket of the eye **2 :** a path described by one body or object in its revolution about another ⟨the *orbit* of the earth about the sun⟩ **3 :** range or sphere of activity or influence [Latin *orbita* "wheel track, orbit"] — **or·bit·al** \-l\ *adj*

2orbit *vb* **1 :** to revolve in an orbit around **:** CIRCLE **2 :** to send up and make revolve in an orbit ⟨*orbit* a satellite⟩ **3 :** to travel in circles — **or·bit·er** *n*

orb weaver *n* **:** any of a group of spiders that spin a large web with a spiral thread suspended on radial threads diverging from the center of the web

or·chard \ˈȯr-chərd\ *n* **:** a planting of fruit trees or nut trees; *also* **:** the trees of such a planting [Old English *ortgeard* from Latin *hortus* "garden" + Old English *geard* "yard"] — **or·chard·ist** \-əst\ *n* — **or·chard·man** \-mən, -ˌman\ *n*

or·ches·tra \ˈȯr-kə-strə, -ˌkes-trə\ *n* **1 :** a group of instrumentalists including especially string players organized to perform ensemble music **2 :** a front part of a theater: as **a :** the space in front of the stage in a modern theater that is used by an orchestra **b :** the forward section of seats on the main floor of a theater [Latin, "space occupied by the chorus in a Greek theater", from Greek *orchēstra,* from *orcheisthai* "to dance"]

or·ches·tral \ȯr-ˈkes-trəl\ *adj* **1 :** of, relating to, or composed for an orchestra **2 :** suggestive of an orchestra or its musical qualities — **or·ches·tral·ly** \-trə-lē\ *adv*

or·ches·trate \ˈȯr-kə-ˌstrāt\ *vt* **1 :** to compose or arrange (music) for an orchestra; *also* **:** to provide (as a ballet) with such music **2 :** to organize and manage skillfully ⟨*orchestrate* a political campaign⟩ — **or·ches·tra·tion** \ˌȯr-kə-ˈstrā-shən\ *n* — **or·ches·tra·tor** *also* **or·ches·trat·er** \ˈȯr-kə-ˌstrāt-ər\ *n*

or·chid \ˈȯr-kəd\ *n* **1 :** any of a large family of perennial plants that have usually showy 3-petaled flowers with the middle petal enlarged into a lip and differing from the others in shape and color; *also* **:** this flower **2 :** a light purple [derived from Latin *orchis*]

or·chis \ˈȯr-kəs\ *n* **:** ORCHID; *esp* **:** a woodland plant having fleshy roots and flowers with the lip spurred [Latin, "orchid", from Greek, "testicle, orchid"]

or·dain \ȯr-ˈdān\ *vb* **1 :** to admit to the Christian ministry or priesthood by the ritual of a church **:** confer holy orders upon **2 a :** to establish or order by appointment, decree, or law **b :** PREDESTINE, DESTINE [Old French *ordener,* from Latin *ordinare* "to put in order, appoint", from *ordin-, ordo* "order"] — **or·dain·er** *n* — **or·dain·ment** \-ˈdān-mənt\ *n*

or·deal \ȯr-ˈdēl\ *n* **1 :** a primitive method of deciding guilt or innocence by submitting the accused to dangerous or painful tests believed to be under supernatural control ⟨*ordeal* by fire⟩ **2 :** a severe trial or experience [Old English *ordāl*]

1or·der \ˈȯrd-ər\ *n* **1 a :** a group of people formally united in some way (as by living under the same religious rules, by having won the same distinction, or by loyalty to common interests and obligations) ⟨an *order* of monks⟩ ⟨an *order* of knighthood⟩ **b :** the badge or insignia of such an order **c :** a military decoration **2 a :** any of the several grades of the Christian ministry **b** *pl* **:** Christian ordination **3 a :** a rank, class, or special group in a community or society **b :** a class grouped according to quality, value, or natural characteristics; *esp* **:** a category of taxonomic classification ranking above the family and below the class **4 a :** RANK, KIND ⟨an artist of the first *order*⟩ ⟨emergencies of this *order*⟩ **b :** the arrangement or sequence of objects in position or of events in time **c :** the number of columns or rows in a matrix with the same number of rows and columns **d :** the prevailing mode or arrangement of things ⟨the old *order*⟩ **e :** regular or harmonious arrangement ⟨the *order* of nature⟩; *also* **:** a condition characterized by such an arrangement **5 a :** a customary or prescribed mode of procedure (as in debate or religious ritual) **b :** the rule of law or proper authority ⟨*order* was restored⟩ **c :** a specific rule, regulation, or authoritative direction **6 a :** a style of building **b :** an architectural column with its related structures forming the unit of a style **7 :** proper condition ⟨out of *order*⟩ **8 a :** a written direction to pay money to someone **b :** a commission to purchase, sell, or supply goods or to perform work **c :** goods or items bought or sold [Middle French *ordre,* from Latin *ordo* "arrangement, group, class, order"] — **in order to :** for the purpose of

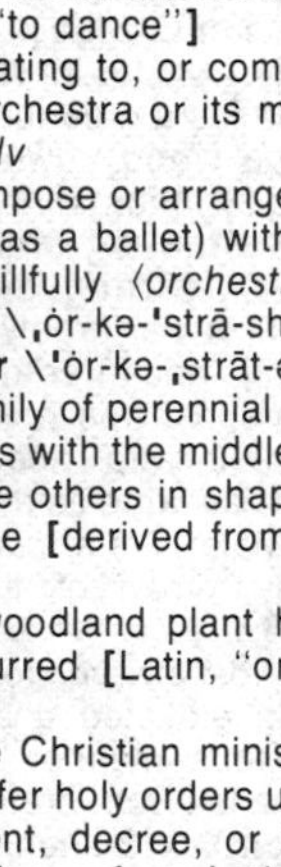

1order 6b

2order *vb* **1 :** to put in or bring about order **2 a :** to direct or command with an order ⟨*order* them to stop⟩ ⟨*order* troops forward⟩ **b :** to give an order for ⟨*order* breakfast⟩ **3 :** to place an order — **or·der·er** *n*

or·dered \ˈȯrd-ərd\ *adj* **:** having elements any two of which are related in such a way that one is greater than or less than the other ⟨the set of real numbers is *ordered*⟩

ordered pair *n* **:** a set with two elements in which one element is identified as the first and the other as the second

1or·der·ly \ˈȯrd-ər-lē\ *adj* **1 a :** arranged or disposed according to some order or pattern **:** REGULAR **b :** not marked by disorder **:** TIDY; *also* **:** METHODICAL **c :** governed by law or system ⟨an *orderly* universe⟩ **2 :** well behaved **:** PEACEFUL ⟨an *orderly* crowd⟩ — **or·der·li·ness** *n* — **orderly** *adv*

2orderly *n, pl* **-lies 1 :** a soldier who attends a superior officer to carry messages and perform services **2 :** a hospital attendant who does general work

1or·di·nal \ˈȯrd-nəl, -n-əl\ **1** *cap* **:** a collection of forms to be used in ordination **2 :** ORDINAL NUMBER [derived from Latin *ordin-, ordo* "order"]

2ordinal *adj* **:** of a specified order or rank (as sixth) in a series

ordinal number *n* **:** a number designating the place (as first, second, third) occupied by an item in an ordered sequence — see NUMBER table; compare CARDINAL NUMBER

or·di·nance \ˈȯrd-nəns, ˈȯrd-n-əns\ *n* **1 :** an authoritative decree or direction **:** ORDER **2 :** a law enacted by governmental authority; *esp* **:** a municipal regulation **3 :** a prescribed usage, practice, or ceremony [Middle French *ordenance,* literally, "art of arranging", from Medieval Latin *ordinantia,* from Latin *ordinare* "to put in order"] **syn** see LAW

or·di·nand \ˌȯrd-n-ˈand\ *n* **:** a person being ordained especially into holy orders [derived from Late Latin *ordinare* "to ordain", from Latin, "to put in order"]

or·di·nari·ly \ˌȯrd-n-ˈer-ə-lē\ *adv* **1 :** USUALLY ⟨would *ordinarily* be here by now⟩ **2 :** in an ordinary or commonplace way or manner

1or·di·nary \ˈȯrd-n-ˌer-ē\ *n, pl* **-nar·ies 1 :** a prelate (as the bishop of a diocese) exercising jurisdiction over a territory or group by virtue of the office **2** *often cap* **:** the parts of the Mass that do not vary from day to day **3 :** regular or customary condition or course of things ⟨nothing out of the *ordinary*⟩ **4 a** *British* **:** a meal served at a fixed price **b** *chiefly British* **:** a tavern or eating house serving regular meals [Medieval Latin *ordinarius,* from Latin *ordinarius,* adj., "ordinary"]

2ordinary *adj* **1 :** of a kind to be expected **:** ROUTINE, NORMAL **2 a :** of common quality, rank, or ability ⟨*ordinary* people⟩ **b :** POOR 4, INFERIOR [Latin *ordinarius,* from *ordin-, ordo* "order"] — **or·di·nar·i·ness** \ˈȯrd-n-ˌer-ē-nəs\ *n*

ordinary seaman *n* **:** a seaman with less experience than an able seaman

or·di·nate \ˈȯrd-nət, -n-ət, -n-ˌāt\ *n* **:** the vertical coordinate of a point in a plane Cartesian coordinate system obtained by measuring parallel to the y-axis — called also *y-coordinate;* compare ABSCISSA [New Latin *linea ordinate applicata,* literally, "line applied in an orderly manner"]

or·di·na·tion \ˌȯrd-n-ˈā-shən\ *n* **:** the act of ordaining **:** the state of being ordained

ord·nance \ˈȯrd-nəns\ *n* **1 a :** military supplies including weapons, ammunition, vehicles, and equipment **b :** a service of the army in charge of ordnance **2 :** ARTILLERY 1, CANNON [Middle French *ordenance,* literally, "act of arranging"]

Or·do·vi·cian \ˌȯrd-ə-ˈvish-ən\ *n* **:** the period of the Paleozoic era between the Cambrian and Silurian; *also* **:** the corresponding system of rocks — see GEOLOGIC TIME table [Latin *Ordovices,* ancient people in northern Wales] — **Ordovician** *adj*

or·dure \ˈȯr-jər\ *n* **1 :** EXCREMENT **2 :** something morally degrading or depraving [Middle French, from *ord* "filthy", from Latin *horridus* "horrid"]

ore \'ōr, 'ȯr\ *n* **:** a mineral containing a constituent for which it is mined and worked ⟨get iron from its *ore*⟩ [Old English *ār* "brass, copper, ore"]

öre \'ər-ə\ *n, pl* **öre** **1 :** a monetary unit equal to 1/100 krona or 1/100 krone **2 :** a coin representing one öre [Swedish *öre* and Danish and Norwegian *øre*]

ore•ad \'ōr-ē-ˌad, 'ȯr-, -ē-əd\ *n* **:** any of the nymphs of mountains and hills [Latin *oread-, oreas,* from Greek *oreiad-, oreias,* derived from *oros* "mountain"]

oreg•a•no \ə-'reg-ə-ˌnō\ *n, pl* **-nos :** a bushy perennial mint used as a seasoning and a source of aromatic oil — called also *wild marjoram* [Spanish *orégano,* from Latin *origanum*]

Or•e•gon grape \ˌȯr-i-gən-, ˌär-, -ˌgän-\ *n* **:** a yellow-flowered mahonia of the northwestern United States sometimes grown as an ornamental [*Oregon,* United States]

or•gan \'ȯr-gən\ *n* **1 a :** a wind instrument that consists of sets of pipes sounding by compressed air, controlled by keyboards, and producing a variety of musical effects — called also *pipe organ* **b :** REED ORGAN **c :** an instrument in which the sounds of the pipe organ are approximated by means of electronic devices **d :** any of various similar cruder instruments **2 :** a differentiated animal or plant structure (as a kidney or leaf) consisting of cells and tissues and performing some specific function — compare SYSTEM 1b(2) **3 :** a means of performing some function or accomplishing some end ⟨the courts and other *organs* of government⟩ **4 :** a publication (as a newspaper or magazine) expressing the opinions or serving the interests of a special group [Old English *organa* and Old French *organe,* both from Latin *organum,* from Greek *organon,* literally, "tool, instrument"]

organ- *or* **organo-** *combining form* **1 :** organ **2 :** organic

or•gan•dy *also* **or•gan•die** \'ȯr-gən-dē\ *n, pl* **-dies :** a very fine transparent muslin with a stiff finish [French *organdi*]

or•gan•elle \ˌȯr-gə-'nel\ *n* **:** a specialized part (as a mitochondrion) of a cell analogous to an organ [New Latin *organella,* from Latin *organum* "organ"]

organ-grind•er \'ȯr-gən-ˌgrīn-dər\ *n* **:** one that cranks a hand organ; *esp* **:** an itinerant street musician who grinds a barrel organ

or•gan•ic \ȯr-'gan-ik\ *adj* **1 a :** of, relating to, or arising in a bodily organ **b :** affecting the structure of the organism — compare FUNCTIONAL 1b **2 a** (1) **:** of, relating to, or derived from living organisms (2) **:** relating to or produced with the use of fertilizer of plant or animal origin and without chemically formulated fertilizers or pesticides ⟨*organic* foods⟩ **b** (1) **:** of, relating to, or containing carbon compounds (2) **:** of, relating to, or dealt with by a branch of chemistry concerned with carbon compounds **3 a :** forming an integral element of a whole **b :** having systematic coordination of parts **:** ORGANIZED ⟨an *organic* whole⟩ **c :** developing in the manner of a living plant or animal ⟨society is *organic*⟩ — **or•gan•i•cal•ly** \-i-kə-lē, -klē\ *adv*

or•gan•ism \'ȯr-gə-ˌniz-əm\ *n* **1 :** an individual constituted to carry on the activities of life by means of organs separate in function but mutually dependent **:** a living person, plant, or animal **2 :** a complex structure (as society) like a living organism in having many interdependent parts — **or•gan•is•mic** \-mik\ *adj* — **or•gan•is•mi•cal•ly** \-mi-kə-lē, -klē\ *adv*

or•gan•ist \'ȯr-gə-nəst\ *n* **:** one who plays an organ

or•ga•ni•za•tion \ˌȯrg-nə-'zā-shən, -ə-nə-\ *n* **1 :** the act or process of organizing or of being organized **2 :** the condition or manner of being organized **3 a :** ASSOCIATION 2 **b :** an administrative body or its personnel **c :** an administrative and functional unit (as a business or a political party) — **or•ga•ni•za•tion•al** \-shnəl, -shən-l\ *adj* — **or•ga•ni•za•tion•al•ly** \-ē\ *adv*

or•ga•nize \'ȯr-gə-ˌnīz\ *vb* **1 :** to develop an organic structure **:** undergo or cause to undergo organization **2 :** to arrange or form into a complete and functioning whole **3 a :** to set up an administrative structure for ⟨*organize* a business⟩ **b :** to enroll or associate in an organization (as a union) **4 :** to arrange by systematic planning and united effort ⟨*organize* a prom⟩

or•ga•niz•er \-ˌnī-zər\ *n* **1 :** one that organizes **2 :** something (as a kind of tissue) able to cause a specific type of development in undifferentiated tissue — called also *inductor*

or•gano•chlo•rine \ȯr-ˌgan-ə-'klōr-ˌēn, -'klȯr-, -ən\ *adj* **:** of, relating to, or belonging to the chlorinated hydrocarbon pesticides (as DDT) — **organochlorine** *n*

or•gano•phos•phate \-'fäs-ˌfāt\ *n* **:** an organophosphorus pesticide — **organophosphate** *adj*

or•gano•phos•pho•rus \-'fäs-fə-rəs, -frəs\ *adj* **:** of, relating to, or being a phosphorus-containing organic compound and especially a pesticide (as malathion) that acts by inhibiting cholinesterase — **organophosphorus** *n*

or•gan•za \ȯr-'gan-zə\ *n* **:** a sheer dress fabric resembling organdy and usually made of silk, rayon, or nylon [probably from *Lorganza,* a trademark]

or•gasm \'ȯr-ˌgaz-əm\ *n* **:** the climax of sexual excitement in coitus [Greek *orgasmos,* from *organ* "to grow ripe, be lustful"] — **or•gas•mic** \ȯr-'gaz-mik\ *or* **or•gas•tic** \-'gas-tik\ *adj*

or•gi•as•tic \ˌȯr-jē-'as-tik\ *adj* **:** of, relating to, or marked by orgies [Greek *orgiastikos,* from *orgiazein* "to celebrate orgies", from *orgia* "orgy"] — **or•gi•as•ti•cal•ly** \-ti-kə-lē, -klē\ *adv*

or•gu•lous \'ȯr-gyə-ləs\ *adj* **:** PROUD 1a, HAUGHTY [Old French *orgueilleus,* from *orgueil* "pride", of Germanic origin]

or•gy \'ȯr-jē\ *n, pl* **orgies 1 :** secret ceremonial rites held in honor of an ancient Greek or Roman deity and usually characterized by ecstatic singing and dancing **2 :** drunken revelry **3 :** any excessive indulgence ⟨an *orgy* of reading⟩ ⟨the riot was an *orgy* of senseless violence⟩ [Middle French *orgie,* from Latin *orgia,* pl., from Greek]

ori•el \'ōr-ē-əl, 'ȯr-\ *n* **:** a large bay window projecting from a wall and supported by a corbel or bracket [Middle English, "porch, oriel", from Middle French *oriol* "porch"]

oriel

[1]ori•ent \'ōr-ē-ənt, 'ȯr-, -ē-ˌent\ *adj* **1** *archaic* **:** ORIENTAL **2 :** being lustrous and sparkling ⟨*orient* gems⟩ **3** *archaic* **:** RISING

[2]ori•ent \-ˌent\ *vt* **1 a :** to cause to face or point toward the east; *esp* **:** to build (as a church) with the longitudinal axis pointing east and the chief altar at the eastern end **b :** to set or arrange in a definite position especially in relation to the points of the compass **2 a :** to set right by adjusting to facts or principles **b :** to acquaint with an existing situation or environment

Ori•ent \'ōr-ē-ənt, 'ȯr-, -ē-ˌent\ *n* **:** EAST 2; *esp* **:** the countries of eastern Asia [Middle French, from Latin *oriens,* from *oriri* "to rise"]

△ **origin** The noun *orient* is derived from the Latin adjective *oriens,* which comes from the present participle of the verb *oriri,* "to rise or come forth". The earliest English sense of *orient* is "the place on the horizon where the sun rises when it is near one of the equinoxes", that is, the east. *Orient* has come to be used today to refer to the Asian countries to the east of Europe. With the spread of Christianity into Europe it became customary to build churches with their longitudinal axes pointing eastward toward Jerusalem. This practice gave rise to the use of *orient* as a verb meaning "to cause to face or point to the east". This sense became generalized to yield the sense "to set or arrange in any determinate position, especially in relation to the points of the compass".

ori•en•tal \ˌōr-ē-'ent-l, ˌȯr-\ *adj, often cap* **:** of or relating to the Orient — **ori•en•tal•ly** \-lē\ *adv*

Oriental *n* **:** a member of one of the indigenous peoples of the Orient; *esp* **:** a Chinese, Japanese, or other Mongoloid

ori•en•tal•ism \-l-ˌiz-əm\ *n, often cap* **1 :** a trait, custom, or habit of expression characteristic of oriental peoples **2 :** learning in oriental subjects — **ori•en•tal•ist** \-l-əst\ *n, often cap*

ori•en•tal•ize \-l-ˌīz\ *vb* **:** to make or become oriental

Oriental poppy *n* **:** an Asian perennial poppy widely grown for its very large showy flowers

Oriental rug *n* **:** a handwoven or hand-knotted rug or carpet made in the Orient

ori•en•tate \'ōr-ē-ən-ˌtāt, 'ȯr-, -ˌen-\ *vb* **1 :** ORIENT 1b **2 :** to face east

ori•en•ta•tion \ˌōr-ē-ən-ˈtā-shən, ˌȯr-, -ˌen-\ *n* **1** : the act or process of orienting : the state of being oriented **2** : change of position by a cell, organelle, organ, or organism in response to external stimulus — **ori•en•ta•tion•al** \-shnəl, -shən-l\ *adj*

ori•en•teer•ing \ˌōr-ē-ən-ˈtiər-ing, ˌȯr-, -ˌen-\ *n* : cross-country racing in which participants must find their way over an unfamiliar course using a map and compass [Swedish *orientering,* from *orientera* "to orient"]

or•i•fice \ˈȯr-ə-fəs, ˈär-\ *n* : an opening (as a vent, mouth, hole, or aperture) through which something may pass [Middle French, from Late Latin *orificium,* from Latin *or-, os* "mouth"] — **or•i•fi•cial** \ˌȯr-ə-ˈfish-əl, ˌär-\ *adj*

ori•flamme \ˈȯr-ə-ˌflam, ˈär-\ *n* : a banner, symbol, or ideal inspiring devotion or courage [Middle French *oriflamble,* from Medieval Latin *aurea flamma,* literally, "golden flame"]

ori•ga•mi \ˌȯr-ə-ˈgäm-ē\ *n* : the art or process of Japanese paper folding [Japanese]

orig•a•num \ə-ˈrig-ə-nəm\ *n* : any of various fragrant aromatic plants of the mint or vervain families used as seasonings; *esp* : OREGANO [Latin, "wild marjoram", from Greek *origanon*]

or•i•gin \ˈȯr-ə-jən, ˈär-\ *n* **1** : ANCESTRY, PARENTAGE **2 a** : rise, beginning, or derivation from a source **b** : primary source or cause **3** : the more fixed, more central, or larger attachment of a muscle **4** : the intersection of the axes in a coordinate system [derived from Latin *origin-, origo,* from *oriri* "to rise"]

• **syn** ORIGIN, SOURCE, INCEPTION, ROOT mean the point at which something begins its course or existence. ORIGIN applies to the things or persons from which something is ultimately derived and often to the causes operating before the thing itself comes into being; SOURCE stresses the point from which something springs into being ⟨an insect bite was the *source* of the infection⟩ INCEPTION stresses the beginning point without implying causes ⟨a member from the *inception* of the club⟩ ROOT suggests a first, ultimate, or fundamental source not always discernible ⟨their quarrel had *roots* deep in the past⟩

¹orig•i•nal \ə-ˈrij-ən-l, -ˈrij-nəl\ *n* **1** *archaic* : the source or cause from which something arises **2 a** : that from which a copy, reproduction, or translation is made **b** : a work composed firsthand **3 a** : a person who is original in thought or action **b** *archaic* : an eccentric person

²original *adj* **1** : of or relating to a beginning : existing from the start : FIRST ⟨the *original* part of an old house⟩ ⟨*original* inhabitants⟩ **2 a** : not copied, reproduced, or translated ⟨*original* paintings⟩ ⟨an *original* idea⟩ **b** : being the one from which a copy, reproduction, or translation is made **3** : independent and creative in thought or action : INVENTIVE — **orig•i•nal•ly** \-ē\ *adv*

orig•i•nal•i•ty \ə-ˌrij-ə-ˈnal-ət-ē\ *n* **1** : the quality or state of being original : FRESHNESS, NOVELTY **2** : the power or ability to think, to act, or to do something in ways that are new ⟨an artist of great *originality*⟩

original sin *n* : the state of sin that according to Christian theology humans are born in as a result of the sin of Adam and Eve

orig•i•nate \ə-ˈrij-ə-ˌnāt\ *vb* **1** : to bring into existence : give rise to ⟨*originate* a plan⟩ **2** : to take or have origin : come into existence — **orig•i•na•tion** \ə-ˌrij-ə-ˈnā-shən\ *n* — **orig•i•na•tor** \ə-ˈrij-ə-ˌnāt-ər\ *n*

orig•i•na•tive \ə-ˈrij-ə-ˌnāt-iv\ *adj* : having ability to originate : CREATIVE — **orig•i•na•tive•ly** *adv*

ori•ole \ˈōr-ē-ˌōl, ˈȯr-, -ē-əl\ *n* **1** : any of a family of usually brightly colored Old World passerine birds related to the crows **2** : any of a family of New World passerine birds of which the males are usually black and yellow or orange and the females chiefly greenish or yellowish [French *oriol,* from Latin *aureolus* "golden", from *aureus* "golden", from *aurum* "gold"]

Ori•on \ə-ˈrī-ən, ō-\ *n* : a constellation on the equator east of Taurus [Latin, a hunter of Greek mythology, from Greek *Ōriōn*]

or•i•son \ˈȯr-ə-sən, ˈär-, -zən\ *n* : PRAYER [Old French, from Late Latin *oratio,* from Latin *orare* "to speak, pray"]

Or•lean•ist \ˈȯr-lē-ə-nəst; ȯr-ˈlē-nəst, -ə-nəst\ *n* : a supporter of the Orleans family in its claim to the throne of France by descent from a younger brother of Louis XIV

Or•lon \ˈȯr-ˌlän\ *trademark* — used for acrylic fiber

or•mo•lu \ˈȯr-mə-ˌlü\ *n* : a brass made to imitate gold and used for decorative purposes [French *or moulu,* literally, "ground gold"]

¹or•na•ment \ˈȯr-nə-mənt\ *n* **1** : something that adorns or adds beauty : DECORATION, EMBELLISHMENT **2** : the act of adorning : addition or inclusion of something that beautifies **3** : an embellishing note in music that does not belong to the essential harmony or melody [Old French *ornement,* from Latin *ornamentum,* from *ornare* "to adorn"]

²or•na•ment \-ˌment\ *vt* : to provide with ornament

¹or•na•men•tal \ˌȯr-nə-ˈment-l\ *adj* : of, relating to, or serving as ornament — **or•na•men•tal•ly** \-l-ē\ *adv*

²ornamental *n* : a decorative object; *esp* : a plant cultivated for its beauty rather than for use

or•na•men•ta•tion \ˌȯr-nə-mən-ˈtā-shən, -ˌmen-\ *n* **1** : the act or process of ornamenting : the state of being ornamented **2 a** : a decorative device **b** : the ornaments of something

or•nate \ȯr-ˈnāt\ *adj* **1** : marked by elaborate rhetoric or florid style **2** : elaborately or excessively decorated [Latin *ornatus,* past participle of *ornare* "to furnish, adorn"] — **or•nate•ly** *adv* — **or•nate•ness** *n*

or•nery \ˈȯrn-rē, ˈän-, -ə-rē\ *adj* **or•ner•i•er**; **-est** : having a touchy and self-willed disposition [alteration of *ordinary*] — **or•ner•i•ness** *n*

ornith- *or* **ornitho-** *combining form* : bird ⟨*ornitho*logy⟩ [Greek *ornith-, ornis*]

or•ni•thine \ˈȯr-nə-ˌthēn\ *n* : a crystalline amino acid $C_5H_{12}N_2O_2$ that functions in the body especially in urea production [*ornith*uric acid (an acid of which it is a component, found in the urine of birds) + *-ine*]

or•ni•thol•o•gy \ˌȯr-nə-ˈthäl-ə-jē\ *n* : a branch of zoology dealing with birds — **or•ni•tho•log•i•cal** \ˌȯr-ˌnith-ə-ˈläj-i-kəl\ *adj* — **or•ni•tho•log•i•cal•ly** \-i-kə-lē, -klē\ *adv* — **or•ni•thol•o•gist** \ˌȯr-nə-ˈthäl-ə-jəst\ *n*

or•ni•tho•sis \ˌȯr-nə-ˈthō-səs\ *n, pl* **-tho•ses** \-ˈthō-ˌsēz\ : PARROT FEVER

orog•e•ny \ȯ-ˈräj-ə-nē\ *n, pl* **-nies** : the process of mountain formation [Greek *oros* "mountain"] — **oro•gen•ic** \ˌōr-ə-ˈjen-ik, ˌȯr-\ *adj*

¹or•phan \ˈȯr-fən\ *n* **1** : a child whose parents are dead **2** : a motherless young animal [Late Latin *orphanus,* from Greek *orphanos*] — **or•phan•hood** \-ˌhu̇d\ *n*

²orphan *vt* **or•phaned**; **or•phan•ing** \ˈȯrf-ning, -ə-ning\ : to cause to become an orphan

or•phan•age \ˈȯrf-nij, -ə-nij\ *n* : an institution for the care of orphans

or•pi•ment \ˈȯr-pə-mənt\ *n* : a yellow to orange sulfide of arsenic used as a pigment [Middle French, from Latin *auripigmentum,* from *aurum* "gold" + *pigmentum* "pigment"]

or•pine \ˈȯr-pən\ *n* : a pink- or purple-flowered sedum formerly used in folk medicine [Middle French *orpin,* from *orpiment* "orpiment"]

or•ris \ˈȯr-əs, ˈär-\ *n* : a European iris with a fragrant rhizome used especially in perfume and sachet powder; *also* : its rootstock [probably derived from Latin *iris*]

or•ris•root \-ˌrüt, -ˌru̇t\ *n* : the rootstock of an orris

orth- *or* **ortho-** *combining form* **1** : straight : upright : vertical **2** : perpendicular ⟨*ortho*rhombic⟩ **3** : correct : corrective ⟨*ortho*dontics⟩ [Greek *orthos* "straight, right"]

or•tho•cen•ter \ˈȯr-thə-ˌsent-ər\ *n* : the common point of intersection of the altitudes of a triangle

or•tho•chro•mat•ic \ˌȯr-thə-krō-ˈmat-ik\ *adj* : sensitive to all colors except red ⟨an *orthochromatic* film⟩

or•tho•clase \ˈȯr-thə-ˌklās\ *n* : a mineral $KAlSi_3O_8$ consisting of common potassium feldspar often with sodium in place of some of the potassium [German *orthoklas,* from *orth-* "orth-" + Greek *klasis* "breaking", from *klan* "to break"]

orth•odon•tia \ˌȯr-thə-ˈdän-chē-ə, -chə\ *n* : ORTHODONTICS

orth•odon•tics \-ˈdänt-iks\ *n* : a branch of dentistry dealing with irregularities of the teeth and their correction [*orth-* + Greek *odont-, odous* "tooth"] — **orth•odon•tic** \-ˈdänt-ik\ *adj* — **orth•odon•tist** \-ˈdänt-əst\ *n*

or•tho•dox \ˈȯr-thə-ˌdäks\ *adj* **1** : holding established beliefs especially in religion ⟨an *orthodox* Christian⟩ **2** : approved as measuring up to some standard : CONVENTIONAL ⟨*orthodox* dress for a church wedding⟩ **3** : Eastern Orthodox [Late Latin *orthodoxus,* from Late Greek *orthodoxos,* from Greek *orthos* "right" + *doxa* "opinion"]

Orthodox Judaism *n* : Judaism that adheres to biblical law as interpreted in the authoritative rabbinic tradition and seeks to observe all the practices commanded in it

or•tho•doxy \ˈȯr-thə-ˌdäk-sē\ *n, pl* **-dox•ies** **1** : the quality or state of being orthodox **2** : an orthodox belief or practice

or•thog•o•nal \ȯr-ˈthäg-ən-l\ *adj* : mutually perpendicular

[Middle French, from Latin *orthogonius,* from Greek *orthogōnios,* from *orthos* "straight, upright" + *gōnia* "angle"] — **or·thog·o·nal·ly** \ȯr-ˈthäg-nə-lē, -ən-l-ē\ *adv*

or·thog·ra·phy \ȯr-ˈthäg-rə-fē\ *n, pl* **-phies** **1 a :** the writing of words with the proper letters according to standard usage **b :** a manner of representing the sounds of a language by written or printed symbols ⟨17th century *orthography*⟩ **2 :** a part of language study that deals with letters and spelling — **or·tho·graph·ic** \ˌȯr-thə-ˈgraf-ik\ *adj*

or·tho·pe·dic \ˌȯr-thə-ˈpēd-ik\ *adj* **1 :** of or relating to orthopedics **2 :** marked by deformities or crippling [French *orthopédique,* from *orthopédie* "orthopedics", from *orth-* "orth-" + Greek *paid-, pais* "child"] — **or·tho·pe·di·cal·ly** \-ˈpēd-i-kə-lē, -klē\ *adv*

or·tho·pe·dics \-ˈpēd-iks\ *n* **:** a medical specialty concerned with preserving and restoring the form and function of the skeletal system and associated structures (as tendons, muscles, and ligaments) — **or·tho·pe·dist** \-ˈpēd-əst\ *n*

or·thop·ter·an \ȯr-ˈthäp-tə-rən\ *n* **:** any of an order (Orthoptera) comprising insects with biting mouthparts, two pairs of wings or none, and an incomplete metamorphosis and usually including the grasshoppers, mantises, and crickets [Greek *pteron* "wing"] — **orthopteran** *adj*

or·tho·rhom·bic \ˌȯr-thə-ˈräm-bik\ *adj* **:** of, relating to, or constituting a system of crystallization characterized by three unequal axes at right angles to each other

¹-o·ry \ˌōr-ē, ˌȯr-ē, ə-rē, -rē\ *n suffix, pl* **-ories** **1 :** place of or for ⟨observat*ory*⟩ **2 :** something that serves for ⟨cremat*ory*⟩ [Latin *-orium,* from neuter of *-orius,* adj. suffix]

²-ory *adj suffix* **1 :** of, relating to, or characterized by ⟨gustat*ory*⟩ **2 :** serving for, producing, or maintaining ⟨classificat*ory*⟩ [Latin *-orius*]

oryx \ˈōr-iks, ˈȯr-, ˈär-\ *n, pl* **oryx·es** *or* **oryx :** a large straight-horned African antelope [Latin, a kind of gazelle, from Greek "pickax, antelope", from *oryssein* "to dig"]

os \ˈäs\ *n, pl* **os·sa** \ˈäs-ə\ **:** BONE [Latin]

Osage \ō-ˈsāj, ˈō-ˌ\ *n* **:** a member of a Siouan people of the area between the Missouri and Arkansas rivers in what is now Missouri and parts of Arkansas, Oklahoma, and Kansas

Osage orange *n* **:** an ornamental American tree of the mulberry family with shiny ovate leaves and hard bright orange wood; *also* **:** its yellowish fruit

Os·car \ˈäs-kər\ *n* **:** a golden statuette awarded annually for achievement in motion pictures [*Oscar* Pierce, 20th century American wheat and fruit grower]

△ **origin** The Academy of Motion Picture Arts and Sciences was founded in 1927 and presented its first awards in 1929. The Academy's award was simply spoken of as "the statuette". It was not until 1931 that it was given the name *Oscar,* by which it is now commonly known. In that year Mrs. Margaret Gledhill began work as librarian at the Academy. When she first saw the statuette she remarked, "He reminds me of my Uncle Oscar," and the name caught on. This "Uncle Oscar" was Oscar Pierce, who grew wheat and fruit in Texas and was not connected with the motion-picture industry at all.

os·cil·late \ˈäs-ə-ˌlāt\ *vi* **1 a :** to swing backward and forward like a pendulum **:** VIBRATE **b :** to move or travel back and forth between two points **2 :** to vary between opposing beliefs, feelings, or theories **3 :** to vary above and below a mean value **4 :** to exhibit or cause electrical oscillation [Latin *oscillare* "to swing" from *oscillum* "swing"] **syn** see SWAY — **os·cil·la·to·ry** \ä-ˈsil-ə-ˌtōr-ē, -ˌtȯr-\ *adj*

os·cil·la·tion \ˌäs-ə-ˈlā-shən\ *n* **1 :** the act or fact of oscillating **:** VIBRATION **2 :** VARIATION 1, FLUCTUATION **3 :** a flow of electricity changing periodically from a maximum to a minimum; *esp* **:** a flow periodically changing direction **4 :** a single swing or change (as of an oscillating body) from one extreme limit to the other — **os·cil·la·tion·al** \-shnəl, -shən-l\ *adj*

os·cil·la·tor \ˈäs-ə-ˌlāt-ər\ *n* **1 :** one that oscillates **2 :** a device for producing alternating current; *esp* **:** a radio-frequency or audio-frequency generator

os·cil·la·to·ria \ä-ˌsil-ə-ˈtōr-ē-ə,-ˈtȯr-\ *n* **:** any of a genus of blue-green algae growing in soil or water as filaments which have a gentle oscillatory movement

os·cil·lo·scope \ä-ˈsil-ə-ˌskōp, ə-\ *n* **:** an instrument in which the variations in a fluctuating electrical quantity appear temporarily as a visible wave form on the fluorescent screen of a cathode-ray tube

os·cu·lum \ˈäs-kyə-ləm\ *n, pl* **-la** \-lə\ **:** an opening of a sponge for the outflow of water [Latin, "little mouth, kiss", from *os* "mouth"]

¹-ose \ˌōs, ˈōs *sometimes* ˌōz, ˈōz\ *adj suffix* **:** full of **:** having **:** possessing the qualities of ⟨cym*ose*⟩ [Latin *-osus*]

²-ose \ˌōs, ˌōz\ *n suffix* **1 :** carbohydrate; *esp* **:** sugar ⟨pent*ose*⟩ **2 :** primary hydrolysis product ⟨prote*ose*⟩ [French, from *glucose*]

Osee \ˈō-ˌzē, ō-ˈzā-ə\ *n* — see BIBLE table

osier \ˈō-zhər\ *n* **1 :** any of various willows with pliable twigs used for furniture and basketry **2 :** a willow rod used in making baskets **3 :** any of several American dogwoods [Middle French, from Medieval Latin *auseria* "osier bed"]

-o·sis \ˈō-səs\ *n suffix, pl* **-o·ses** \-ˌsēz\ *or* **-o·sis·es** **1 :** action **:** process **:** condition ⟨hypn*osis*⟩ **2 :** abnormal or diseased condition ⟨leuk*osis*⟩ [Greek *-ōsis*]

os·mi·um \ˈäz-mē-əm\ *n* **:** a hard brittle blue-gray or blue-black metallic element with a high melting point that is the heaviest metal known and that is used especially as a catalyst and in hard alloys — see ELEMENT table [New Latin, from Greek *osmē* "odor"]

os·mom·e·ter \äz-ˈmäm-ət-ər, äs-\ *n* **:** an apparatus for measuring the pressure produced by osmosis

os·mose \ˈäz-ˌmōs, ˈäs-\ *vi* **:** to diffuse by osmosis [back-formation from *osmosis*]

os·mo·sis \äz-ˈmō-səs, äs-\ *n* **:** a diffusion through a semipermeable membrane typically separating a solvent and a solution that tends to equalize their concentrations; *esp* **:** the passage of solvent in distinction from the passage of solute [derived from Greek *ōsmos* "act of pushing", from *ōthein* "to push"] — **os·mot·ic** \-ˈmät-ik\ *adj* — **os·mot·i·cal·ly** \-ˈmät-i-kə-lē, -klē\ *adv*

os·prey \ˈäs-prē, -ˌprā\ *n, pl* **os·preys** **:** a large fish-eating brown and white hawk [derived from Latin *ossifraga* "sea eagle", literally, "bone breaker"]

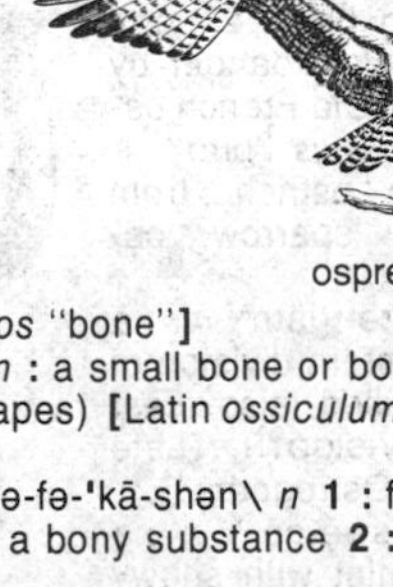

osprey

ossa *pl of* OS

os·se·ous \ˈäs-ē-əs\ *adj* **:** BONY 1 [Latin *osseus,* from *os* "bone"]

os·si·cle \ˈäs-i-kəl\ *n* **:** a small bone or bony structure (as the malleus, incus, or stapes) [Latin *ossiculum* "small bone", from *os* "bone"]

os·si·fi·ca·tion \ˌäs-ə-fə-ˈkā-shən\ *n* **1 :** formation of or conversion into bone or a bony substance **2 :** an area of ossified tissue

os·si·fy \ˈäs-ə-ˌfī\ *vb* **-fied; -fy·ing** **1 :** to become or change into bone or bony tissue **2 :** to become or make callous or set in one's ways

oste- *or* **osteo-** *combining form* **:** bone ⟨*osteo*pathy⟩ [Greek *osteon*]

os·ten·si·ble \ä-ˈsten-sə-bəl\ *adj* **:** shown outwardly **:** PROFESSED, APPARENT ⟨their *ostensible* and possibly real motive⟩ [French, from Latin *ostendere* "to show", from *obs-* "in front of" + *tendere* "to stretch"] — **os·ten·si·bly** \-blē\ *adv*

os·ten·ta·tion \ˌäs-tən-ˈtā-shən\ *n* **:** showy or excessive display [Middle French, from Latin *ostentatio,* from *ostentare* "to show off", from *ostendere* "to show"]

os·ten·ta·tious \-shəs\ *adj* **:** marked by or fond of ostentation — **os·ten·ta·tious·ly** *adv* — **os·ten·ta·tious·ness** *n*

os·teo·ar·thri·tis \ˌäs-tē-ō-ˌär-ˈthrīt-əs\ *n* **:** an arthritis marked by degeneration of the cartilage and bone of joints

os·teo·my·eli·tis \ˌäs-tē-ō-ˌmī-ə-ˈlīt-əs\ *n* **:** an infectious inflammatory disease of bone marked by local death and separation of nonliving from living tissue [*oste-* + Greek *myelos* "marrow" + English *-itis*]

os·teo·path \ˈäs-tē-ə-ˌpath\ *n* **:** a practitioner of osteopathy

os·te·op·a·thy \ˌäs-tē-ˈäp-ə-thē\ *n* **:** a system of treating diseases that places emphasis on manipulation especially of

\ə\ **abut**	\au̇\ **out**	\i\ **tip**	\ȯ\ **saw**	\u̇\ **foot**
\ər\ **further**	\ch\ **chin**	\ī\ **life**	\ȯi\ **coin**	\y\ **yet**
\a\ **mat**	\e\ **pet**	\j\ **job**	\th\ **thin**	\yü\ **few**
\ā\ **take**	\ē\ **easy**	\ng\ **sing**	\t͟h\ **this**	\yu̇\ **cure**
\ä\ **cot, cart**	\g\ **go**	\ō\ **bone**	\ü\ **food**	\zh\ **vision**

bones but does not exclude other treatment (as the use of medicine and surgery) — **os•teo•path•ic** \ˌäs-tē-ə-ˈpath-ik\ *adj* — **os•teo•path•i•cal•ly** \-ˈpath-i-kə-lē, -klē\ *adv*

os•ti•ole \ˈäs-tē-ˌōl\ *n* : a small opening [Latin *ostiolum* "little door", from *ostium* "door"]

os•ti•um \ˈäs-tē-əm\ *n, pl* **os•tia** \-tē-ə\ : an anatomical opening (as in the heart of a crayfish) [Latin, "door, mouth of a river"]

ostler *variant of* HOSTLER

os•tra•cism \ˈäs-trə-ˌsiz-əm\ *n* **1 :** a method of temporary banishment by popular vote without trial or special accusation practiced in ancient Greece **2 :** exclusion by general consent from common privileges or social acceptance

os•tra•cize \ˈäs-trə-ˌsīz\ *vt* **1 :** to exile by ostracism **2 :** to exclude from a group by common consent [Greek *ostrakizein* "to banish by voting with potsherds", from *ostrakon* "shell, potsherd"]

△ **origin** Greek *ostrakon* is a word for a shell or for an earthen vessel or a broken fragment of such a vessel. Such potsherds served ancient Athens as ballots in a particular kind of popular vote. Once a year the citizens would gather in the agora or marketplace of Athens to decide who, if anyone, should be banished temporarily for the good of the city. Each voter wrote a name on his *ostrakon.* If at least 6000 votes were cast and if a majority of them named one man, then that man was banished, or ostracized.

os•tra•cod \ˈäs-trə-ˌkäd\ *also* **os•tra•code** \-ˌkōd\ *n* : any of a group (Ostracoda) of small mostly freshwater crustaceans [derived from Greek *ostrakon* "shell"]

os•tra•co•derm \ˈäs-trə-kō-ˌdərm, äs-ˈtrak-ə-\ *n* : any of an order (Ostracodermi) of primitive fossil armored fishes [derived from Greek *ostrakon* "shell" + *derma* "skin"]

os•trich \ˈäs-trich, ˈōs-\ *n* **1 :** a swift-footed 2-toed flightless bird of Africa and Arabia with valuable wing and tail plumes that is the largest of existing birds **2 :** one that attempts to avoid danger by refusing to face it [Old French *ostrusce,* from Latin *avis* "bird" + Late Latin *struthio* "ostrich", from Greek *strouthos* "sparrow, ostrich"]

ostrich 1

Os•tro•goth \ˈäs-trə-ˌgäth\ *n* : a member of the eastern division of the Goths — called also *East Goth*; compare VISIGOTH [Late Latin *Ostrogothi* "Ostrogoths"]

Os•we•go tea \ä-ˌswē-gō-\ *n* : a North American mint with showy bright scarlet irregular flowers [*Oswego* river, New York]

ot- *or* **oto-** *combining form* : ear ⟨*otitis*⟩ [Greek *ōt-, ous*]

¹oth•er \ˈəth-ər\ *adj* **1 a :** being the one (as of two or more) left ⟨held my *other* arm straight⟩ **b :** being the ones distinct from those first mentioned ⟨thought the *other* members dull⟩ **c :** SECOND ⟨every *other* day⟩ **2 :** not the same : DIFFERENT ⟨*other* times and customs⟩ **3 :** ADDITIONAL ⟨some *other* guests are coming⟩ **4 :** recently past ⟨the *other* evening⟩ [Old English *ōther*]

²other *n* **1 a :** one that remains of two or more ⟨lift one foot and then the *other*⟩ **b :** a thing opposite to or excluded by something else ⟨from one side to the *other*⟩ **2 :** a different or additional one ⟨the *others* came later⟩

³other *pron, sometimes pl in construction* : a different or additional one ⟨something or *other* happened⟩

⁴other *adv* : OTHERWISE

oth•er•wise \ˈəth-ər-ˌwīz\ *adv* **1 :** in a different way : DIFFERENTLY ⟨could not do *otherwise*⟩ **2 :** in different circumstances ⟨*otherwise* we might have won⟩ **3 :** in other respects ⟨the *otherwise* busy street⟩ [Old English *on ōthre wīsan* "in another manner"] — **otherwise** *adj*

oth•er•world \ˈəth-ər-ˌwərld\ *n* : a world beyond death or beyond present reality — **oth•er•world•li•ness** \-ˌwərl-dlē-nəs, -lē-\ *n* — **oth•er•world•ly** \-ˌwərl-dlē, -lē\ *adj*

otic \ˈōt-ik\ *adj* : of, relating to, or located near the ear

-ot•ic \ˈät-ik\ *adj suffix* **1 :** of, relating to, or characterized by a (specified) action, process, or condition ⟨symbi*otic*⟩ **2 :** having an abnormal or diseased condition of a (specified) kind ⟨leuk*otic*⟩ [Greek *-ōtikos*]

oti•tis \ō-ˈtīt-əs\ *n* : inflammation of the ear

oto•lar•yn•gol•o•gy \ˈōt-ō-ˌlar-ən-ˈgäl-ə-jē\ *n* : a branch of medicine dealing with the ear, nose, and throat

oto•lith \ˈōt-l-ˌith\ *n* : a calcium-containing stony mass in the inner ear — **oto•lith•ic** \ˌōt-l-ˈith-ik\ *adj*

Ot•ta•wa \ˈät-ə-wə, -ˌwä, -ˌwȯ\ *n* : a member of an Algonquian people of what is now southern Ontario

ot•ter \ˈät-ər\ *n, pl* **otters** *also* **otter 1 :** any of several aquatic fish-eating mammals that are related to the weasels and minks and that have webbed and clawed feet and dark brown fur **2 :** the fur or pelt of an otter [Old English *otor*]

otter 1

ot•to•man \ˈät-ə-mən\ *n, pl* **-mans 1** *cap* : TURK 2 — called also *Ottoman Turk* **2 a :** an upholstered often overstuffed seat or couch usually without a back **b :** an overstuffed footstool [French, derived from Arabic *ʽothmānī,* from *ʽOthmān* "Othman (founder of the Ottoman Empire)"] — **Ottoman** *adj*

ouch \ˈau̇ch\ *interj* — used to express sudden pain [probably imitative]

ought \ˈȯt\ *auxiliary verb* — used to express obligation ⟨*ought* to pay our debts⟩, advisability ⟨*ought* to take care of yourself⟩, natural expectation ⟨*ought* to be here by now⟩, or logical consequence ⟨the result *ought* to be infinity⟩ [Middle English *oughte,* past of *owen* "to owe"]

oughtn't \ˈȯt-nt\ : ought not

¹ounce \ˈau̇ns\ *n* **1 a :** a unit of weight equal to 1/12 troy pound (about 31.1 grams) — see MEASURE table **b :** a unit of weight equal to 1/16 avoirdupois pound (about 28.3 grams) **c :** a small portion or quantity **2 :** FLUIDOUNCE [Middle French *unce,* from Latin *uncia* "twelfth part, ounce", from *unus* "one"]

△ **origin** The ancient Romans used a system of weights and measures based on units that were divided into 12 parts. The Latin *uncia,* meaning "a 12th part", was used for the 12th part of a *pes* or "foot". From this is derived Old English *ince* or *ynce,* which became modern English *inch.* The Roman pound, called *libra* in Latin, was also divided into 12 parts similarly designated by the word *uncia.* In this sense *uncia* followed a different path. It became Middle French *unce,* which was borrowed into Middle English as *unce* or *ounce.*

²ounce *n* : SNOW LEOPARD [Old French *once* "wildcat", from *lonce* (understood as *l'once* "the ounce"), from Latin *lynx* "lynx"]

our \är, au̇r, ˈau̇r\ *adj* : of or relating to us or ourselves or ourself especially as possessors or possessor, agents or agent, or objects or object of an action ⟨*our* throne⟩ ⟨*our* actions⟩ ⟨*our* being chosen⟩ [Old English *ūre*]

Our Father *n* : LORD'S PRAYER

ours \au̇rz, ˈau̇rz, ärz\ *pron, sing or pl in construction* : our one or our ones — used without a following noun as an equivalent in meaning to the adjective *our*

our•self \är-ˈself, au̇r-\ *pron* : MYSELF — used (as by a sovereign or writer) to refer to the single-person subject when *we* is used instead of *I*

our•selves \-ˈselvz\ *pron pl* **1 :** those identical ones that are we — used reflexively or for emphasis ⟨we're doing it solely for *ourselves*⟩ ⟨we *ourselves* will never go⟩; compare WE 1 **2 :** our normal, healthy, or sane condition or selves ⟨we weren't feeling *ourselves* that day⟩

-ous \əs\ *adj suffix* **1 :** full of : having : possessing the qualities of ⟨clamor*ous*⟩ ⟨poison*ous*⟩ **2 :** having a valence lower than in compounds or ions named with an adjective ending in *-ic* ⟨mercur*ous*⟩ [partly from Old French *-ous, -eus, -eux,* from Latin *-osus*; partly from Latin *-us,* nominative sing. masculine ending of many adjectives]

oust \ˈau̇st\ *vt* : to force or drive out (as from office or from possession of something) : EXPEL ⟨*oust* a corrupt official⟩ [Anglo-French *ouster,* from Old French *oster,* from Latin *obstare* "to stand against", from *ob-* "against" + *stare* "to stand"] **syn** see EJECT

oust•er \'au̇s-tər\ *n* : the act or an instance of ousting or being ousted : EXPULSION [Anglo-French, "to oust"]

[1]**out** \'au̇t\ *adv* **1 a** : in a direction away from the inside or the center ⟨look *out* of a window⟩ **b** : from among others ⟨picked *out* a hat⟩ **2** : away from home, business, or the usual or proper place ⟨*out* to lunch⟩ ⟨left a word *out*⟩ **3** : into a state of loss or deprivation ⟨vote the party *out* of office⟩ **4** : beyond control, possession, or occupation ⟨let a secret *out*⟩ ⟨lent *out* money⟩ **5** : into a state of disagreement ⟨friends fall *out*⟩ **6 a** : beyond the limits of existence, continuance, or supply ⟨the food ran *out*⟩ **b** : to extinction, exhaustion, or completion ⟨burn *out*⟩ **7 a** : in or into the open ⟨the sun came *out*⟩ **b** : ALOUD ⟨cried *out*⟩ **8** — used as an intensive with numerous verbs ⟨sketch *out* the plans⟩ **9 a** : so as to put out a batter or base runner ⟨the catcher threw *out* the runner trying to steal second base⟩ **b** : so as to be put out ⟨grounded *out* to the shortstop⟩ [Old English *ūt*]

[2]**out** *vi* : to become known ⟨the truth will *out*⟩

[3]**out** *adj* **1** : situated outside : EXTERNAL ⟨the *out* edge⟩ **2** : situated at a distance : OUTLYING ⟨the *out* islands⟩ **3 a** : not being in power ⟨the *out* party⟩ **b** : not successful in reaching base ⟨the batter was *out*⟩ **4** : directed outward or serving to direct something outward : OUTGOING ⟨put the letter in the *out* basket⟩ **5** : ABSENT ⟨a basket with its bottom *out*⟩ **6** : no longer in fashion

[4]**out** \au̇t, 'au̇t\ *prep* **1** : out through ⟨ran *out* the door⟩ **2** : outward along or on ⟨drive *out* the old road⟩

[5]**out** \'au̇t\ *n* **1** : one who is out of power **2 a** : the putting out of a batter or base runner in baseball **b** : a player put out **3** : a ball hit out of bounds in tennis or squash **4** : an item that is out of stock **5** : a way of escaping from an embarrassing situation or a difficulty

out- *prefix* : in a manner that goes beyond, surpasses, or excels ⟨*out*maneuver⟩ [[1]*out*]

See *out-* and 2d element

outaccelerate	**outeat**	**outrace**
outachieve	**outfight**	**outride**
outact	**outfish**	**outscheme**
outargue	**outfox**	**outscore**
outbellow	**outfumble**	**outscowl**
outbluff	**outglamorize**	**outscreech**
outboast	**outglitter**	**outshout**
outbox	**outgross**	**outsing**
outbrawl	**outhit**	**outsmile**
outbuy	**outhunt**	**outsparkle**
outcatch	**outhustle**	**outspeed**
outchallenge	**outjab**	**outspell**
outclimb	**outjump**	**outspend**
outcoach	**outkick**	**outsprint**
outcomment	**outleap**	**outstride**
outcompete	**outlearn**	**outswear**
outconnive	**outmarch**	**outswim**
outdance	**outmatch**	**outthink**
outdazzle	**outperform**	**outthrow**
outdebate	**outplay**	**outtotal**
outdesign	**outpoll**	**outvie**
outdress	**outpopulate**	**outwait**
outdrink	**outpray**	**outwalk**
outdrive	**outpreach**	**outwrite**
outearn	**outproduce**	**outyield**

out–and–out \ˌau̇t-n-'au̇t, -'dau̇t\ *adj* : being wholly what is stated ⟨an *out-and-out* crook⟩

out•bal•ance \au̇t-'bal-əns, 'au̇t-\ *vt* : OUTWEIGH

out•bid \-'bid\ *vt* **-bid**; **-bid•ding** : to make a higher bid than

[1]**out•board** \'au̇t-ˌbōrd, -ˌbȯrd\ *adj* **1** : situated outboard **2** : having or using an outboard motor

[2]**outboard** *adv* **1** : outside the line of a ship's bulwarks or hull : away from the center line of a ship **2** : in a position closer or closest to either of the wing tips of an airplane or of the sides of an automobile

outboard motor *n* : a small internal-combustion engine with propeller attached for mounting at the stern of a small boat

out•bound \'au̇t-ˌbau̇nd\ *adj* : outward bound ⟨*outbound* traffic⟩

out•brave \au̇t-'brāv, 'au̇t-\ *vt* **1** : to face or resist defiantly **2** : to exceed in courage

out•break \'au̇t-ˌbrāk\ *n* **1** : a sudden or violent breaking out : a sudden increase of activity or currency ⟨the *outbreak* of war⟩ **2** : something that breaks out: as **a** : EPIDEMIC ⟨an *outbreak* of measles⟩ **b** : INSURRECTION, REVOLT

out•breed *vt* **-bred** \-ˌbred, -'bred\; **-breed•ing 1** \'au̇t-ˌbrēd\ : to subject to outbreeding **2** \au̇t-', 'au̇t-'\ : to breed faster than

out•breed•ing \'au̇t-ˌbrēd-iŋ\ *n* : the interbreeding of relatively unrelated individuals

out•build•ing \'au̇t-ˌbil-diŋ\ *n* : a building separate from and smaller than the main one

out•burst \-ˌbərst\ *n* **1** : a violent expression of feeling **2** : a surge of activity or growth ⟨a new *outburst* of creative power⟩

out•cast \-ˌkast\ *n* : a person cast out by society : PARIAH — **outcast** *adj*

out•caste \-ˌkast\ *n* : one who has no caste

out•class \au̇t-'klas, 'au̇t-\ *vt* : to excel or surpass so decisively as to appear of a higher class

out•come \'au̇t-ˌkəm\ *n* : something that follows as a result

[1]**out•crop** \'au̇t-ˌkräp\ *n* : exposed bedrock or an unconsolidated deposit at the surface of the ground

[2]**out•crop** \'au̇t-'kräp\ *vi* : to come to the surface : APPEAR ⟨granite *outcropping* through softer rocks⟩

out•cross \'au̇t-ˌkrȯs\ *n* : a cross between relatively unrelated individuals or strains — **outcross** *vt*

out•cry \'au̇t-ˌkrī\ *n* **1** : a loud cry : CLAMOR **2** : a strong protest

out•dat•ed \au̇t-'dāt-əd, 'au̇t-\ *adj* : OUTMODED

out•dis•tance \au̇t-'dis-təns, 'au̇t-\ *vt* : to go far ahead of (as in a race) : OUTSTRIP

out•do \au̇t-'dü, 'au̇t-\ *vt* **-did** \-'did\; **-done** \-'dən\; **-do•ing** \-'dü-iŋ\ : to go beyond in action or performance : SURPASS

out•door \ˌau̇t-ˌdōr, -ˌdȯr\ *also* **out•doors** \-ˌdōrz, -ˌdȯrz\ *adj* **1** : of or relating to the outdoors ⟨an *outdoor* setting⟩ **2** : done outdoors ⟨*outdoor* games⟩ **3** : not roofed or enclosed ⟨an *outdoor* theater⟩ [*out (of) door, out (of) doors*]

[1]**out•doors** \au̇t-'dōrz, 'au̇t-, -'dȯrz\ *adv* : outside a building : in or into the open air

[2]**outdoors** *n* **1** : the open air **2** : the world away from human dwellings

out•draw \au̇t-'drȯ, 'au̇t-\ *vt* : to attract a larger audience or following than

out•er \'au̇t-ər\ *adj* **1** : EXTERNAL 1 ⟨*outer* appearance⟩ **2 a** : situated farther out ⟨the *outer* wall⟩ **b** : being away from a center ⟨the *outer* solar planets⟩

outer ear *n* : the outer visible portion of the ear that collects and directs sound waves toward the eardrum by way of a canal which extends inward through the temporal bone

out•er•most \'au̇t-ər-ˌmōst\ *adj* : farthest out

outer space *n* : SPACE 5; *esp* : the region beyond the solar system

out•face \au̇t-'fās, 'au̇t-\ *vt* **1** : to stare down **2** : to confront without fear or weakening : DEFY

out•fall \'au̇t-ˌfȯl\ *n* : the outlet of a river, stream, lake, drain, or sewer

out•field \-ˌfēld\ *n* : the part of a baseball field beyond the infield and between the foul lines — **out•field•er** \-ˌfēl-dər\ *n*

[1]**out•fit** \'au̇t-ˌfit\ *n* **1** : the equipment or apparel for some purpose or occasion ⟨a camping *outfit*⟩ ⟨a sports *outfit*⟩ **2** : a group of persons working together or associated in the same undertaking ⟨soldiers belonging to the same *outfit*⟩

[2]**outfit** *vt* **1** : to furnish with an outfit : EQUIP ⟨*outfit* an expedition⟩ **2** : SUPPLY 3 — **out•fit•ter** *n*

out•flank \au̇t-'flaŋk, 'au̇t-\ *vt* : to get around the flank of (an opposing force)

out•flow \'au̇t-ˌflō\ *n* **1** : a flowing out **2** : something that flows out

out•foot \au̇t-'fu̇t, 'au̇t-\ *vt* : to outdo in speed : OUTSTRIP

out•gen•er•al \-'jen-rəl, -ə-rəl\ *vt* **-gen•er•aled** *or* **-gen•er•alled**; **-gen•er•al•ing** *or* **-gen•er•al•ling** : to surpass in generalship : OUTMANEUVER

out•go \'au̇t-ˌgō\ *n*, *pl* **outgoes** : something (as goods or money) that goes out

out•go•ing \'au̇t-ˌgō-iŋ\ *adj* **1 a** : going out ⟨the *outgoing* tide⟩ **b :** retiring from a place or position ⟨the *outgoing* governor⟩ **2 :** FRIENDLY, RESPONSIVE ⟨an *outgoing* person⟩

out•grow \au̇t-ˈgrō, ˈau̇t-\ *vt* **-grew** \-ˈgrü\; **-grown** \-ˈgrōn\; **-grow•ing 1 :** to grow faster than **2 :** to grow too large or too mature for ⟨*outgrow* one's clothes⟩ ⟨children *outgrowing* fairy tales⟩

out•growth \ˈau̇t-ˌgrōth\ *n* **1 :** a product of growing out ⟨an *outgrowth* of hair⟩ **2 :** CONSEQUENCE, BY-PRODUCT ⟨crime is often an *outgrowth* of poverty⟩

out•guess \au̇t-ˈges, ˈau̇t-\ *vt* **:** to anticipate the intentions, plans, or actions of

out•house \ˈau̇t-ˌhau̇s\ *n* **:** OUTBUILDING; *esp* **:** PRIVY

out•ing \ˈau̇t-iŋ\ *n* **1 :** an excursion usually with a picnic ⟨the club *outing* at the seashore⟩ **2 :** a brief stay or trip in the open ⟨took the baby for an *outing*⟩

outing flannel *n* **:** a flannelette sometimes containing some wool

out•land•er \ˈau̇t-ˌlan-dər\ *n* **:** a person belonging to another culture or region

out•land•ish \au̇t-ˈlan-dish, ˈau̇t-\ *adj* **1 :** of or relating to another country **2 a :** of foreign or unfamiliar appearance or quality ⟨*outlandish* language⟩ **b :** strikingly out of the ordinary **:** BIZARRE **3 :** remote from civilization ⟨lived in *outlandish* places⟩ **syn** see STRANGE — **out•land•ish•ly** *adv* — **out•land•ish•ness** *n*

out•last \au̇t-ˈlast, ˈau̇t-\ *vt* **:** to last longer than

¹out•law \ˈau̇t-ˌlȯ\ *n* **1 :** a person excluded from the benefit or protection of the law **2 a :** a lawless person or a fugitive from the law **b :** one (as a person or organization) under a ban **[**Old English *ūtlaga,* from Old Norse *ūtlagi,* from *ūt* "out" + *lag-, lög* "law"**]** — **outlaw** *adj*

²outlaw *vt* **1 a :** to deprive of the benefit and protection of law **b :** to make illegal **2 :** to place under a ban — **out•law•ry** \ˈau̇t-ˌlȯ-rē\ *n*

out•lay \ˈau̇t-ˌlā\ *n* **1 :** the act of expending **2 :** EXPENDITURE 2

out•let \ˈau̇t-ˌlet, -lət\ *n* **1 :** a place or opening through which something is let out **2 :** a means of release or satisfaction for an emotion or impulse **3 :** a place (as in a wall) at which an electrical device can be plugged into the wiring system **4 a :** a market for a commodity **b :** a retail store or distributor

¹out•line \ˈau̇t-ˌlīn\ *n* **1 :** a line that traces or forms the outer limits of an object or figure and shows its shape **2 a :** a drawing or picture giving only the outlines of something **b :** this method of drawing **3 a :** a brief summary often in numbered divisions **b :** a preliminary account of a project **4 :** a brief treatment of a subject **:** DIGEST

²outline *vt* **1 :** to draw the outline of **2 :** to indicate the main features or parts of

out•live \au̇t-ˈliv, ˈau̇t-\ *vt* **:** to live longer than **:** OUTLAST

out•look \ˈau̇t-ˌlu̇k\ *n* **1 a :** a place offering a view **b :** a view from a particular place **2 :** POINT OF VIEW **3 :** the prospect for the future

out•ly•ing \ˈau̇t-ˌlī-iŋ\ *adj* **:** far from a center or main body ⟨an *outlying* suburb⟩

out•ma•neu•ver \ˌau̇t-mə-ˈnü-vər, -ˈnyü-\ *vt* **1 :** to get the better of by more skillful maneuvering **2 :** to be more maneuverable than

out•mod•ed \au̇t-ˈmōd-əd, ˈau̇t-\ *adj* **1 :** no longer in style ⟨an *outmoded* dress⟩ **2 :** no longer acceptable or usable ⟨*outmoded* beliefs⟩ ⟨*outmoded* equipment⟩

out•most \ˈau̇t-ˌmōst\ *adj* **:** farthest out **:** OUTERMOST

out•num•ber \au̇t-ˈnəm-bər, ˈau̇t-\ *vt* **:** to be greater in number than ⟨girls *outnumber* boys in the class⟩

out of *prep* **1 a** (1) **:** from within to the outside of ⟨walked *out of* the room⟩ (2) — used as a function word to indicate a change in quality, state, or form ⟨woke up *out of* a deep sleep⟩ **b**(1) **:** beyond the range or limits of ⟨*out of* sight⟩ (2) **:** from among ⟨one *out of* four survived⟩ **2 :** in or into a state of not having ⟨we were *out of* sugar⟩ ⟨cheat one *out of* a fortune⟩ **3 :** because of **:** FROM ⟨came *out of* curiosity⟩ **4** — used as a function word to indicate the constituent material, basis, or source ⟨built *out of* old lumber⟩

out–of–bounds \ˌau̇t-əv-ˈbau̇nz, -ə-\ *adv or adj* **:** outside the prescribed area of play

out–of–date \ˌau̇t-əv-ˈdāt, -ə-\ *adj* **:** OUTMODED ⟨*out-of-date* ideas⟩

out–of–door \ˌau̇t-əv-ˈdōr, -ə-, -ˈdȯr\ *or* **out–of–doors** \-ˈdōrz, -ˈdȯrz\ *adj* **:** OUTDOOR

out–of–doors *n* **:** OUTDOORS

out–of–the–way \ˌau̇t-əv-t͟hə-ˈwā, -ə-\ *adj* **1 :** not centrally or conveniently located ⟨an *out-of-the-way* restaurant⟩ **2 :** not commonly found or met **:** UNUSUAL ⟨the bookstore specializes in *out-of-the-way* titles⟩

out•pa•tient \ˈau̇t-ˌpā-shənt\ *n* **:** a person who receives diagnosis or treatment in a clinic or dispensary of a hospital — compare INPATIENT — **outpatient** *adj*

out•post \ˈau̇t-ˌpōst\ *n* **1 a :** a guard stationed at a distance from a military post **b :** the position occupied by an outpost **2 a :** an outlying settlement **b :** an outer limit **:** FRONTIER ⟨*outposts* of civilization⟩

out•pour \au̇t-ˈpōr, -ˈpȯr\ *vt* **:** to pour out — **out•pour** \ˈau̇t-ˌ\ *n*

out•pour•ing \ˈau̇t-ˌpōr-iŋ, -ˌpȯr-\ *n* **1 :** the act of pouring out **2 a :** something that pours out or is poured out **:** OUTFLOW **b :** an outburst of emotion

out•put \-ˌpu̇t\ *n* **1 :** the amount produced or able to be produced usually in a stated time by a man, machine, factory, or industry **2 a :** power or energy delivered by a machine or system **b :** a point at which something (as power, an electronic signal, or data) comes out

¹out•rage \ˈau̇t-ˌrāj\ *n* **1 :** a violent or brutal act **2 :** INJURY 1, INSULT **3 :** the resentment aroused by injury or insult **[**Old French, "excess, outrage", from *outre* "beyond, in excess" (from Latin *ultra*) + *-age***]**

△ **origin** The English word *outrage* is related neither to *out* nor to *rage.* It is ultimately derived from Latin *ultra,* "beyond". Latin *ultra* became *outre* in Old French. *Outre* was combined with the common suffix *-age* to produce the word *outrage,* which meant "excess, outrage", and the Old French word was borrowed into English in the Middle English period. Old French *outre* is also the ancestor of French *outré,* which was borrowed into English in modern times.

²outrage *vt* **1 a :** RAPE 2 **b :** to subject to violent injury or abuse **2 :** to arouse anger or great resentment in **syn** see OFFEND

out•ra•geous \au̇t-ˈrā-jəs\ *adj* **:** being beyond all bounds of decency or justice **:** extremely offensive, insulting, or shameful **:** SHOCKING — **out•ra•geous•ly** *adv* — **out•ra•geous•ness** *n*

• **syn** OUTRAGEOUS, ATROCIOUS, HEINOUS mean exceedingly bad or horrible. OUTRAGEOUS implies exceeding the limits of what is tolerable or decent ⟨*outrageous* manners⟩ ATROCIOUS implies merciless cruelty, savagery, or contempt of ordinary values ⟨*atrocious* killings by the invaders⟩ HEINOUS implies being so flagrantly evil as to induce hatred or horror ⟨the *heinous* torturing of prisoners⟩

out•rank \au̇t-ˈraŋk, ˈau̇t-\ *vt* **:** to rank higher than **:** be more important than

ou•tré \ü-ˈtrā\ *adj* **:** going beyond what is usual or proper **:** BIZARRE **[**French, from *outrer* "to carry to excess", from Old French *outre* "beyond" — see OUTRAGE *origin***]**

out•reach \au̇t-ˈrēch, ˈau̇t-\ *vb* **1 a :** to be greater in reach than **b :** to go beyond **:** EXCEED ⟨the demand *outreaches* the supply⟩ **2 :** to get the better of by trickery **:** OVERREACH **3 :** to go too far

out•rid•er \ˈau̇t-ˌrīd-ər\ *n* **1 :** a mounted attendant **2 :** FORERUNNER 1, HARBINGER

out•rig•ger \ˈau̇t-ˌrig-ər\ *n* **1 a :** a projecting frame on a float attached to the side of a canoe or boat to prevent upsetting **b :** a projecting beam run out from a ship's side to help secure the masts or from a mast to extend a rope or sail **c :** a craft fitted with an outrigger **2 :** a projecting frame to support the elevator or tail planes of an airplane or the rotor of a helicopter

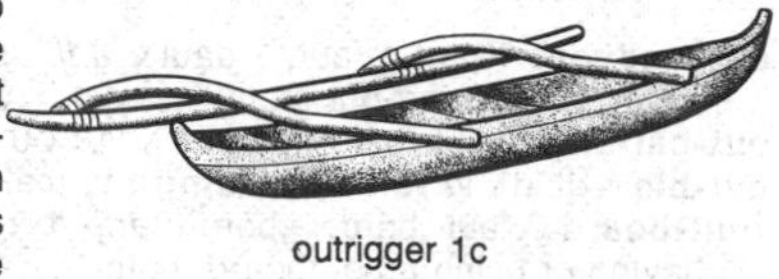
outrigger 1c

¹out•right \au̇t-ˈrīt, ˈau̇t-\ *adv* **1 a :** with nothing kept back **:** COMPLETELY ⟨repeal a law *outright*⟩ **b :** without restraint ⟨laughed *outright*⟩ **2 :** at once **:** INSTANTANEOUSLY ⟨killed *outright*⟩

²out•right \ˈau̇t-ˌrīt\ *adj* **1 :** being exactly what is stated ⟨*outright* persecution⟩ **2 :** given without reservation ⟨an *outright* gift⟩

out•run \au̇t-ˈrən, ˈau̇t-\ *vt* **-ran** \-ˈran\; **-run**; **-run•ning** : to run faster than; *also* : EXCEED ⟨their needs *outran* their funds⟩
out•sell \-ˈsel\ *vt* **-sold** \-ˈsōld\; **-sell•ing** **1** : to exceed in sales ⟨cigarettes far *outsold* cigars⟩ **2** : to surpass in selling
out•set \ˈau̇t-ˌset\ *n* : BEGINNING 1, START
out•shine \au̇t-ˈshīn, ˈau̇t-\ *vt* **-shone** \-ˈshōn\; **-shin•ing** **1 a** : to shine brighter than **b** : to exceed in splendor or showiness **2** : SURPASS ⟨*outshone* most of the competitors⟩
out•shoot \-ˈshüt\ *vt* **-shot** \-ˈshät\; **-shoot•ing** : to go beyond : SURPASS ⟨*outshoot* one's competitors⟩
¹out•side \au̇t-ˈsīd, ˈau̇t-ˌ\ *n* **1** : a place or region beyond an enclosure or boundary **2** : an outer side or surface **3** : the utmost limit or extent ⟨would sell 500 copies at the *outside*⟩
²outside *adj* **1** : of, relating to, or being on or toward the outside ⟨the *outside* edge⟩ **2 a** : situated or performed outside a particular place ⟨*outside* noises⟩ **b** : giving access to the outside ⟨the *outside* door⟩ **3** : MAXIMUM ⟨cost more than our *outside* estimate⟩ **4 a** : not included or originating in a particular group or organization ⟨*outside* influences⟩ **b** : not part of one's regular routine or duties ⟨*outside* activities⟩ ⟨*outside* reading⟩ **5** : barely possible : REMOTE ⟨an *outside* chance⟩
³outside *adv* : on or to the outside : OUTDOORS
⁴outside *prep* **1** : on or to the outside of ⟨*outside* the house⟩ **2** : beyond the limits of ⟨*outside* the law⟩ **3** : EXCEPT 1 ⟨nobody *outside* a few close friends⟩
outside of *prep* : OUTSIDE 2, 3
out•sid•er \au̇t-ˈsīd-ər, ˈau̇t-\ *n* **1** : a person who does not belong to a particular group **2** : a contender not expected to win
out•sit \-ˈsit\ *vt* **-sat** \-ˈsat\; **-sit•ting** : to remain sitting or in session longer than or beyond the time of
¹out•size \ˈau̇t-ˌsīz\ *n* : an unusual size; *esp* : a size larger than the standard
²outsize *also* **out•sized** \-ˌsīzd\ *adj* : unusually large or heavy
out•skirts \ˈau̇t-ˌskərts\ *n pl* : the outlying parts of a place or town
out•smart \au̇t-ˈsmärt, ˈau̇t-\ *vt* : to get the better of; *esp* : OUTWIT
out•soar \-ˈsōr, -ˈsȯr\ *vt* : to soar beyond or above
out•sole \ˈau̇t-ˌsōl\ *n* : the outside sole of a boot or shoe
out•spo•ken \au̇t-ˈspō-kən\ *adj* : direct and open in speech or expression : FRANK ⟨an *outspoken* person⟩ ⟨*outspoken* criticism⟩ — **out•spo•ken•ness** \-kən-nəs\ *n*
out•spread \au̇t-ˈspred\ *vt* **-spread**; **-spread•ing** : to spread out : EXTEND — **out•spread** \ˈau̇t-ˌspred\ *adj*
out•stand•ing \au̇t-ˈstan-diŋ\ *adj* **1** : standing out or projecting **2 a** : not paid ⟨*outstanding* bills⟩ **b** : remaining in existence ⟨among problems still *outstanding*⟩ **c** : publicly issued and sold ⟨20,000 shares *outstanding*⟩ **3 a** : standing out from a group : CONSPICUOUS ⟨*outstanding* talent⟩ **b** : DISTINGUISHED 1, EMINENT ⟨*outstanding* scholars⟩ — **out•stand•ing•ly** \au̇t-ˈstan-diŋ-lē\ *adv*
out•stay \au̇t-ˈstā, ˈau̇t-\ *vt* **1** : to stay beyond or longer than ⟨*outstay* one's welcome⟩ **2** : to surpass in staying power ⟨*outstayed* the early leaders to win at the finish⟩
out•stretch \au̇t-ˈstrech\ *vt* : to stretch out or beyond
out•strip \au̇t-ˈstrip\ *vt* **1** : to go faster or farther than ⟨*outstripped* the other runners⟩ **2 a** : EXCEL ⟨*outstripped* all rivals⟩ **b** : EXCEED ⟨demand *outstrips* supply⟩ [*out-* + obsolete *strip* "to move fast"]
¹out•ward \ˈau̇t-wərd\ *adj* **1** : moving or directed toward the outside or away from a center ⟨an *outward* flow⟩ **2** : exposed to view or notice : not private or inward ⟨*outward* optimism⟩
²outward *or* **out•wards** \-wərdz\ *adv* **1** : toward the outside ⟨the city stretches *outward* for miles⟩ ⟨fold it *outward*⟩ **2** *obs* : EXTERNALLY
out•ward•ly \ˈau̇t-wərd-lē\ *adv* : on the outside : in outward appearance ⟨*outwardly* calm⟩
out•wear \au̇t-ˈwaər, ˈau̇t-, -ˈweər\ *vt* **-wore** \-ˈwōr, -ˈwȯr\; **-worn** \-ˈwōrn, -ˈwȯrn\; **-wear•ing** : to wear or last longer than ⟨a fabric that *outwears* most others⟩
out•weigh \-ˈwā\ *vt* : to exceed in weight, value, or importance
out•wit \au̇t-ˈwit\ *vt* : to get the better of by superior cleverness : OUTSMART
¹out•work \au̇t-ˈwərk, ˈau̇t-\ *vt* : to outdo in working
²outwork \ˈau̇t-ˌwərk\ *n* : a minor defensive position constructed outside a fortified area
out•worn \au̇t-ˈwōrn, ˈau̇t-, -ˈwȯrn\ *adj* : no longer useful or accepted : OUT-OF-DATE ⟨an *outworn* system⟩
ou•zel \ˈü-zəl\ *n* **1** : a European blackbird or a related bird **2** : WATER OUZEL [Old English *ōsle*]
ov- *or* **ovi-** *or* **ovo-** *combining form* : egg ⟨*ovi*cidal⟩ [Latin *ovum*]
ova *pl of* OVUM
¹oval \ˈō-vəl\ *adj* : having the shape of an egg; *also* : broadly elliptical
²oval *n* : an oval figure or object

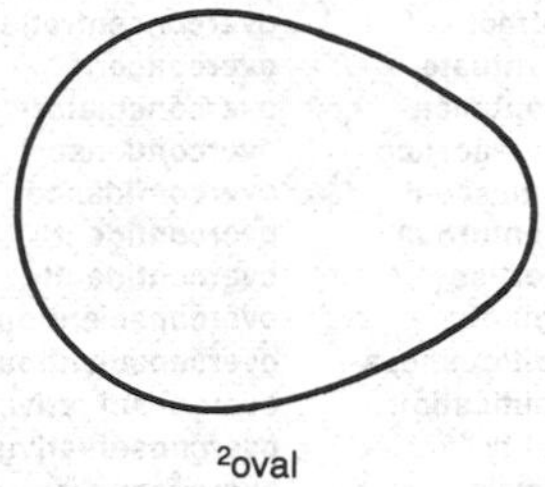

²oval

ova•ry \ˈōv-rē, -ə-rē\ *n, pl* **-ries** **1** : the typically paired female reproductive organ that produces eggs and in vertebrates female sex hormones **2** : the enlarged rounded part at the base of the pistil of a flowering plant in which seeds are produced [New Latin *ovarium*, from Latin *ovum* "egg"] — **ovar•i•an** \ō-ˈvar-ē-ən, -ˈver-\ *adj*
ovate \ˈō-ˌvāt\ *adj* : shaped like an egg especially with the basal end broader ⟨*ovate* leaves⟩
ova•tion \ō-ˈvā-shən\ *n* **1** : a ceremony honoring a Roman general who had won a victory less important than one for which a triumph was granted **2** : a public expression of praise : enthusiastic applause ⟨a standing *ovation*⟩ [Latin *ovatio*, from *ovare* "to exult"]
ov•en \ˈəv-ən\ *n* : a chamber used for baking, heating, or drying [Old English *ofen*]
ov•en•bird \-ˌbərd\ *n* : an American warbler that builds a dome-shaped nest on the ground [from the shape of its nest]

ovenbird

¹over \ˈō-vər\ *adv* **1 a** : across a barrier or intervening space ⟨fly *over* to London⟩ **b** : down or forward and down ⟨went too near the edge and fell *over*⟩ **c** : across the brim ⟨the soup boiled *over*⟩ **d** : so as to bring the underside up ⟨turned the cards *over*⟩ **e** : from a vertical to a prone or inclined position ⟨tripped and fell *over*⟩ ⟨knocked it *over*⟩ **f** : from one person or side to another ⟨hand it *over*⟩ **2 a** : ACROSS ⟨got their point *over*⟩ **b** : to agreement or concord ⟨won them *over*⟩ **3** : beyond a quantity, limit, or norm often by a specified amount or to a specified degree ⟨the show ran a minute *over*⟩; *also* : in or to excess **4** : so as to cover the whole surface ⟨windows boarded *over*⟩ **5 a** : at an end ⟨the day is *over*⟩ **b** — used on a two-way radio circuit to indicate that a message is complete and a reply is expected **6 a** (1) : THROUGH ⟨read it *over*⟩ (2) : in an intensive or comprehensive way **b** : once more ⟨do it *over*⟩ [Old English *ofer*]
²over *prep* **1** : higher than : ABOVE ⟨flew *over* the city⟩ **2 a** : having authority, power, or jurisdiction in regard to ⟨respected those *over* me⟩ **b** : having superiority, advantage, or preference in comparison to ⟨a big lead *over* the others⟩ **3** : more than ⟨cost *over* $5⟩ **4 a** : on or down on especially so as to cover ⟨laid a blanket *over* the child⟩ **b** : all through or throughout the area of ⟨went *over* my notes⟩ ⟨showed me *over* the house⟩ **c** : by or through the medium of ⟨heard it *over* TV⟩ **5 a** : moving above and across ⟨jump *over* a stream⟩ **b** : on the other side of ⟨lives *over* the way⟩ **6** : THROUGHOUT, DURING ⟨*over* the past 25 years⟩ **7** — used to indicate an object of solicitude or interest ⟨the Lord watches *over* his own⟩, an activity ⟨spent an hour *over* cards⟩, or concern ⟨trouble *over* money⟩ **8** : for values of the unknown from ⟨find the solution set of the

equation *over* the real numbers⟩ — **over one's head :** beyond one's comprehension or control

³over *adj* **1 :** being outside or above **2 a :** EXCESSIVE ⟨*over* imagination⟩ **b :** having or showing an excess or surplus ⟨the cash is $3 *over* in your books⟩

over- *prefix* **1 :** so as to exceed or surpass **2 :** excessive **3 :** excessively

See *over-* and 2d element

overabsorption
overabstract
overaccentuate
overacceptance
overacquiescence
overacquiescent
overadventurous
overadvertise
overambitious
overambitiousness
overamplification
overamplify
overanalysis
overanalyze
overanxiety
overanxious
overanxiously
overapologetic
overapplication
overapply
overargue
overarousal
overarouse
overarranged
overarticulate
overassert
overassertion
overassertive
overassertively
overassertiveness
overassess
overassessment
overassured
overattention
overattentive
overbake
overbill
overbleach
overboil
overbold
overbreed
overbreezy
overbright
overbroad
overbrowse
overbusy
overbusyness
overcapacity
overcareful
overcareless
overcaution
overcautious
overcelebrate
overcentralization
overcentralize
overcharitable
overcheerful
overchic
overchummy
overcivilized
overclean
overcommercialization
overcommercialize
overcommunicate
overcommunication
overcompetitive
overcomplacent
overcomplex
overcomplicate
overcompress
overcompression
overconcentrate
overconcentration
overconcern
overconciliatory
overcondense
overconfidence
overconfident
overconfidently
overconscientious
overconscientious
overconservative
overconservatively
overconsume
overconsumption
overcontented
overcontrol
overcook
overcorrect
overcorrection
overcritical
overcurious
overdainty
overdecorate
overdelicate
overdepend
overdependence
overdependency
overdependent
overdevoted
overdignify
overdiligent
overdiversify
overdogmatic
overdramatic
overdramatization
overdramatize
overdrink
overdrug
overeager
overeagerness
overearnest
overeat
overedit
overeducate
overeffective
overelaborate
overelaboration
overelusive
overemotional
overemphasis
overemphasize
overemphatic
overenergetic
overenthusiasm
overenthusiastic
overexaggerate
overexaggeration
overexcite
overexcitement
overexercise
overexert
overexertion
overexhaust
overexpand
overexpansion
overexpectation
overexplain
overexploit
overexploitation
overextraction
overextravagant
overexuberance
overexuberant
overfamiliar
overfamiliarity
overfastidious
overfat
overfatigued
overfearful
overfeed
overfertilization
overfertilize
overfond
overformal
overfry
overfull
overfussy
overgeneralization
overgeneralize
overgenerosity
overgenerous
overglamorize
overglib
overglorification
overharsh
overharvest
overhasty
overhunt
overidealize
overillustrate
overimaginative
overimbibe
overimpressed
overinclined
overinclusive
overindebted
overindividualize
overindulge
overindulgence
overindulgent
overindustrialization
overindustrialize
overinflate
overinflation
overinfluence
overinform
overingenious
overinsistent
overintellectualize
overintense
overintensity
overinvest
overinvestment
overinvolve
overinvolvement
overlabor
overladen
overlarge
overlavish
overlengthy
overliberal
overliteral
overlively
overlong
overloud
overloving
overlush
overmature
overmedicate
overmedication
overmodest
overmodestly
overmuscled
overnice
overnourish
overobvious
overoptimism
overoptimistic
overorganize
overornamented
overpamper
overparticular
overpatriotic
overpay
overpayment
overpedantic
overpermissive
overpermissiveness
overpessimism
overpessimistic
overplan
overpolite
overpoliteness
overpollute
overpopular
overpopularize
overpossessive
overpossessiveness
overpractice
overpraise
overprecise
overpreparation
overprepare
overprescribe
overprescription
overpressure
overprice
overprivileged
overproduce
overproduction
overpromise
overpromote
overpromotion
overpublicize
overpump
overqualification
overqualified
overquick
overreact
overreaction
overreactive
overreactiveness
overrealistic
overrefined
overregulate
overregulation
overreliance
overreliant
overreligious
overreport
overrepresent
overrepresentation
overrespond
overresponse
overresponsive
overrich
overromantic
oversanguine
oversaturate
oversaturation
oversceptical
overschedule
overscrupulous
oversensitive
oversensitivity
oversentimental
overserious
overseriously
oversimplification
oversimplify
overskilled
oversolicitous
oversophisticated
overspecialization
overspecialize
overspeculate
overstaff
overstimulate
overstimulation
overstrain
overstress
overstretch
overstrict
overstrictness
overstudious
oversubjective
oversusceptible
oversuspicious
overtalkative
overtax
overteach
overtense
overthin
overthrifty
overtight
overtighten
overtimid
overtimidity
overtip
overtired
overtolerance
overtolerant
overtrain
overtreat
overtreatment
overtruthful
overutilization
overutilize
overvaluation
overvalue
overventurous
overviolent
overvivid
overwithhold
overzealous
overzealousness

over•abun•dance \ˌō-və-rə-ˈbən-dəns\ *n* **:** EXCESS 1, SURFEIT — **over•abun•dant** \-dənt\ *adj*

over•achiev•er \ˌō-və-rə-ˈchē-vər\ *n* **:** one that achieves success above the standard level — **over•achieve•ment** \-ˈchēv-mənt\ *n*

over•act \ˌō-və-ˈrakt\ *vb* **:** to exaggerate or overdo in acting — **over•ac•tion** \-ˈrak-shən\ *n*

over•ac•tive \-ˈrak-tiv\ *adj* **:** excessively or abnormally active ⟨an *overactive* thyroid⟩ — **over•ac•tiv•i•ty** \-rak-ˈtiv-ət-ē\ *n*

over against *prep* **:** as opposed to **:** in contrast with

¹over•age \ˌō-və-ˈrāj\ *adj* **:** older than is normal for one's position, function, or grade ⟨*overage* students⟩ **[**²*over* + *age***]**

²over•age \ˈōv-rij, -ə-rij\ *n* **:** EXCESS 1, SURPLUS **[**³*over* + *-age***]**

¹over•all \ˌō-və-ˈrȯl\ *adv* **:** as a whole **:** GENERALLY ⟨we find your work satisfactory, *overall*⟩

²over•all \ˌō-və-ˈrȯl, ˈō-və-ˌ\ *adj* **:** including everything ⟨*overall* expenses⟩

over•alls \ˈō-və-ˌrȯlz\ *n pl* **:** trousers of strong material usually with a bib and shoulder straps

over and above *prep* **:** ²BESIDES

over and over *adv* **:** many times **:** OFTEN

over•arm \ˈō-və-ˌrärm\ *adj* **:** done with the arm raised above the shoulder ⟨swim with an *overarm* stroke⟩

over•awe \ˌō-və-ˈrȯ\ *vt* **:** to restrain or subdue by awe

over•bal•ance \ˌō-vər-ˈbal-əns\ *vb* **1 :** to have greater weight or importance than ⟨their good qualities more than *overbalanced* their shortcomings⟩ **2 :** to lose or cause to lose balance ⟨a boat *overbalanced* by shifting cargo⟩

over•bear \ˌō-vər-ˈbaər, -ˈbeər\ *vt* **-bore** \-ˈbōr, -ˈbȯr\; **-borne** \-ˈbōrn, -ˈbȯrn\ *also* **-born** \-ˈbȯrn\; **-bear•ing 1 :** to bear or carry down (as by too much weight) **:** OVERBURDEN **2 :** to domineer over

over•bear•ing \-ˈbaər-iŋ, -ˈbeər-\ *adj* **:** haughtily arrogant — **over•bear•ing•ly** \-iŋ-lē\ *adv*

over•bid \ˌō-vər-ˈbid\ *vb* **-bid; -bid•ding :** to bid too high; *esp*

: to bid more than the value of (as one's hand at cards) — **over·bid** \ˈō-vər-ˌbid\ *n*

1over·blown \ˌō-vər-ˈblōn\ *adj* **1** : excessively large in girth : FAT **2** : PRETENTIOUS ⟨*overblown* oratory⟩ [1*blow*]

2overblown *adj* : past the prime of bloom ⟨*overblown* roses⟩ [3*blow*]

over·board \ˈō-vər-ˌbōrd, -ˌbȯrd\ *adv* **1** : over the side of a ship into the water **2** : to extremes of enthusiasm ⟨go *overboard* for a new fad⟩ **3** : into discard : ASIDE ⟨threw the rules *overboard*⟩

over·build \ˌō-vər-ˈbild\ *vb* **-built** \-ˈbilt\; **-build·ing** : to build beyond need or demand

1over·bur·den \ˌō-vər-ˈbərd-n\ *vt* : to burden too heavily

2over·bur·den \ˈō-vər-ˌbərd-n\ *n* : material overlying a deposit of useful geological materials

over·buy \ˌō-vər-ˈbī\ *vb* **-bought** \-ˈbȯt\; **-buy·ing** : to buy beyond need or ability to pay

over·call \ˌō-vər-ˈkȯl\ *vb* **1** : to make a higher bridge bid than (the previous bid or player) **2** : to bid over an opponent's bid in bridge when one's partner has not bid or doubled — **over·call** \ˈō-vər-ˌkȯl\ *n*

over·cap·i·tal·ize \ˌō-vər-ˈkap-ət-l-ˌīz\ *vt* : to assign a value to (the capital of a business) greater than justified by assets or prospects — **over·cap·i·tal·iza·tion** \-ˌkap-ət-l-ə-ˈzā-shən\ *n*

1over·cast *vt* **-cast**; **-cast·ing** **1** \ˌō-vər-ˈkast, ˈō-vər-ˌ\ : DARKEN 1, OVERSHADOW **2** \ˈō-vər-ˌ\ : to sew (raw edges of a seam) with long slanting widely spaced stitches to prevent raveling

2over·cast \ˈō-vər-ˌkast, ˌō-vər-ˈ\ *adj* : clouded over : GLOOMY ⟨an *overcast* night⟩

3over·cast \ˈō-vər-ˌkast\ *n* : COVERING; *esp* : a covering of clouds over the sky

over·charge \ˌō-vər-ˈchärj\ *vb* **1** : to charge too much **2** : to load too full ⟨*overcharge* an old cannon⟩ **3** : EXAGGERATE 1 — **over·charge** \ˈō-vər-ˌchärj\ *n*

over·cloud \ˌō-vər-ˈklau̇d\ *vt* : to overspread with clouds

over·coat \ˈō-vər-ˌkōt\ *n* : a warm coat worn over indoor clothing

over·come \ˌō-vər-ˈkəm\ *vb* **-came** \-ˈkām\; **-come**; **-com·ing** **1** : to get the better of : CONQUER ⟨*overcome* an enemy⟩ ⟨*overcome* temptation⟩ **2** : to make helpless or exhausted ⟨*overcome* by gas⟩ **3** : to gain superiority : WIN ⟨we shall *overcome*⟩

over·com·pen·sa·tion \-ˌkäm-pən-ˈsā-shən, -ˌpen-\ *n* : excessive compensation; *esp* : excessive reaction to a feeling of inferiority, guilt, or inadequacy — **over·com·pen·sate** \-ˈkäm-pən-ˌsāt\ *vb* — **over·com·pen·sa·to·ry** \-kəm-ˈpen-sə-ˌtōr-ē, -ˌtȯr-\ *adj*

over·crowd \ˌō-vər-ˈkrau̇d\ *vb* : to be or cause to be too crowded

over·de·vel·op \ˌō-vər-di-ˈvel-əp\ *vt* : to develop excessively; *esp* : to subject (an exposed photographic plate or film) too long to the developing process — **over·de·vel·op·ment** \-mənt\ *n*

over·do \ˌō-vər-ˈdü\ *vb* **-did** \-ˈdid\; **-done** \-ˈdən\; **-do·ing** \-ˈdü-iŋ\ **1** : to do too much **2** : EXAGGERATE 1 **3** : to cook too long **4** : to tire oneself

1over·dose \ˈō-vər-ˌdōs\ *n* : too great a dose — **over·dos·age** \ˌō-vər-ˈdō-sij\ *n*

2over·dose \ˌō-vər-ˈdōs\ *vt* : to give an overdose or too many doses to

over·draft \ˈō-vər-ˌdraft, -ˌdráft\ *n* : an overdrawing of a bank account; *also* : the amount overdrawn

over·draw \ˌō-vər-ˈdrȯ\ *vb* **-drew** \-ˈdrü\; **-drawn** \-ˈdrȯn\; **-draw·ing** **1 a** : to draw checks on (a bank account) for more than the balance **b** : to make an overdraft **2** : EXAGGERATE, OVERSTATE ⟨*overdrew* the dangers in the task⟩

1over·dress \ˌō-vər-ˈdres\ *vb* : to dress too formally for an occasion

2over·dress \ˈō-vər-ˌdres\ *n* : a dress worn over another

over·drive \ˈō-vər-ˌdrīv\ *n* : an automotive gear mechanism so arranged as to provide a higher car speed for a specific engine speed than that provided by ordinary high gear

over·due \ˌō-vər-ˈdü, -ˈdyü\ *adj* **1 a** : unpaid when due ⟨*overdue* bills⟩ **b** : delayed beyond an appointed time ⟨an *overdue* train⟩ ⟨the flight is two hours *overdue*⟩ **2** : more than ready ⟨a country *overdue* for reform⟩

over·es·ti·mate \ˌō-və-ˈres-tə-ˌmāt\ *vt* : to estimate too highly — **over·es·ti·mate** \-mət\ *n* — **over·es·ti·ma·tion** \-ˌres-tə-ˈmā-shən\ *n*

over·ex·pose \ˌō-və-rik-ˈspōz\ *vt* : to expose excessively; *esp* : to expose (photographic material) for a longer time than is needed — **over·ex·po·sure** \-ˈspō-zhər\ *n*

over·ex·tend \-ˈstend\ *vt* : to extend or expand beyond a safe or reasonable point ⟨*overextend* credit⟩

over·fill \ˌō-vər-ˈfil\ *vb* : to fill to overflowing

over·fish \-ˈfish\ *vt* : to fish to the depletion of (a kind of fish) or to the detriment of (a fishing ground)

over·flight \ˈō-vər-ˌflīt\ *n* : a passage over an area in an airplane

1over·flow \ˌō-vər-ˈflō\ *vb* **1** : to cover with or as if with water : INUNDATE **2** : to flow over the top or edge of ⟨the stream *overflowed* its banks⟩ **3** : to flow over bounds ⟨the stream *overflows* every spring⟩

2over·flow \ˈō-vər-ˌflō\ *n* **1** : a flowing over : FLOOD **2** : SURPLUS, EXCESS **3** : an outlet or receptacle for surplus liquid

over·fly \ˌō-vər-ˈflī\ *vt* **-flew** \-ˈflü\; **-flown** \-ˈflōn\; **-fly·ing** : to fly over especially in an airplane

over·gar·ment \ˈō-vər-ˌgär-mənt\ *n* : an outer garment

over·glaze \-ˌglāz\ *adj* : applied or suitable for use over a fired glaze ⟨*overglaze* decoration on china⟩ — **overglaze** *n*

over·graze \ˌō-vər-ˈgrāz\ *vt* : to allow animals to graze (land) to the point of damaging the vegetation

over·grow \ˌō-vər-ˈgrō\ *vb* **-grew** \-ˈgrü\; **-grown** \-ˈgrōn\; **-grow·ing** **1** : to grow over so as to cover **2** : to grow beyond or rise above : OUTGROW **3** : to grow excessively **4** : to become grown over — **over·growth** \ˈō-vər-ˌgrōth\ *n*

over·grown \ˌō-vər-ˈgrōn\ *adj* : grown unusually or too big ⟨*overgrown* boys⟩ ⟨*overgrown* cities⟩

1over·hand \ˈō-vər-ˌhand\ *adj* : made with the hand brought down from above ⟨an *overhand* tennis stroke⟩ — **overhand** *adv* — **over·hand·ed** \ˌō-vər-ˈhan-dəd\ *adv*

2overhand *n* : an overhand stroke (as in tennis)

overhand knot \ˌō-vər-ˌhand-, -ˌhan-\ *n* : a small knot often used to prevent the end of a cord from fraying

1over·hang \ˈō-vər-ˌhaŋ, ˌō-vər-ˈ\ *vb* **-hung** \-ˌhəŋ, -ˈhəŋ\; **-hang·ing** \-ˌhaŋ-iŋ, -ˈhaŋ-\ **1** : to jut, project, or be suspended over **2** : to loom over threateningly

2over·hang \ˈō-vər-ˌhaŋ\ *n* : a part that overhangs ⟨the *overhang* of a roof⟩

over·haul \ˌō-vər-ˈhȯl\ *vt* **1** : to make a thorough examination of and the necessary repairs and adjustments on ⟨*overhaul* an engine⟩ **2** : OVERTAKE 1 — **over·haul** \ˈō-vər-ˌhȯl\ *n*

1over·head \ˌō-vər-ˈhed\ *adv* : above one's head : ALOFT

2over·head \ˈō-vər-ˌhed\ *adj* **1** : operating or lying above ⟨an *overhead* door⟩ **2** : of or relating to business overhead

3over·head \ˈō-vər-ˌhed\ *n* **1** : general business expenses (as rent or heating) **2** : a stroke (as in tennis) made above head height : SMASH

over·hear \ˌō-vər-ˈhiər\ *vb* **-heard** \-ˈhərd\; **-hear·ing** \-ˈhiər-iŋ\ : to hear without the speaker's knowledge or intention

over·heat \ˌō-vər-ˈhēt\ *vb* : to heat too much : become too hot

over·joy \ˌō-vər-ˈjȯi\ *vt* : to fill with great joy

1over·kill \ˌō-vər-ˈkil\ *vt* : to obliterate (a target) with more nuclear force than required

2over·kill \ˈō-vər-ˌkil\ *n* **1** : the capability of destroying a target with more nuclear force than required **2** : EXCESS 1 ⟨advertising *overkill*⟩

over·land \ˈō-vər-ˌland, -lənd\ *adv or adj* : by, on, or across land

over·lap \ˌō-vər-ˈlap\ *vb* **1** : to lap over **2** : to have something in common or in common with — **over·lap** \ˈō-vər-ˌlap\ *n*

1over·lay \ˌō-vər-ˈlā\ *vt* **-laid** \-ˈlād\; **-lay·ing** **1** : to lay or spread over or across : SUPERIMPOSE ⟨*overlay* silver on gold⟩ **2** : OVERLIE 1 ⟨silver *overlaying* gold⟩

2over·lay \ˈō-vər-ˌlā\ *n* : something (as a veneer on wood) that is overlaid

over·leap \ˌō-vər-ˈlēp\ *vt* **1** : to leap over or across ⟨*overleap* a ditch⟩ **2** : to defeat (oneself) by going too far

over·lie \ˌō-vər-ˈlī\ *vt* **-lay** \-ˈlā\; **-lain** \-ˈlān\; **-ly·ing** \-ˈlī-

\ə\ **abut**	\au̇\ **out**	\i\ **tip**	\ȯ\ **saw**	\u̇\ **foot**
\ər\ **further**	\ch\ **chin**	\ī\ **life**	\ȯi\ **coin**	\y\ **yet**
\a\ **mat**	\e\ **pet**	\j\ **job**	\th\ **thin**	\yü\ **few**
\ā\ **take**	\ē\ **easy**	\ŋ\ **sing**	\t͟h\ **this**	\yu̇\ **cure**
\ä\ **cot, cart**	\g\ **go**	\ō\ **bone**	\ü\ **food**	\zh\ **vision**

ing\ **1** : to lie over or on **2** : to kill by lying on
over•load \ˌō-vər-ˈlōd\ *vt* : to load to excess — **over•load** \ˈō-vər-ˌlōd\ *n*
over•look \ˌō-vər-ˈlu̇k\ *vt* **1** : to look over : INSPECT **2 a** : to look down on from above **b** : to provide a view of from above ⟨the hill *overlooks* a lake⟩ **3 a** : to fail to see : MISS **b** : to pass over : IGNORE **c** : EXCUSE ⟨*overlook* a beginner's mistakes⟩ **4** : to watch over : SUPERVISE
over•lord \ˈō-vər-ˌlȯrd\ *n* **1** : a lord who has supremacy over other lords **2** : an absolute ruler — **over•lord•ship** \-ˌship\ *n*
over•ly \ˈō-vər-lē\ *adv* : to an excessive degree
over•man \ˌō-vər-ˈman\ *vt* : to have or get too many workers for the needs of ⟨*overman* a ship⟩
over•mas•ter \ˌō-vər-ˈmas-tər\ *vt* : SUBDUE 1
over•match \ˌō-vər-ˈmach\ *vt* **1** : to be more than a match for : DEFEAT **2** : to match with a superior opponent ⟨a boxer who was badly *overmatched*⟩
¹over•much \ˌō-vər-ˈməch\ *adj or adv* : too much
²over•much \ˈō-vər-ˌməch, ˌō-vər-ˈ\ *n* : too great an amount
¹over•night \ˌō-vər-ˈnīt\ *adv* **1** : on or during the evening or night ⟨stayed away *overnight*⟩ **2** : SUDDENLY ⟨became famous *overnight*⟩
²overnight *adj* **1** : of, lasting, or staying the night ⟨an *overnight* trip⟩ ⟨*overnight* guests⟩ **2** : SUDDEN ⟨an *overnight* success⟩
¹over•pass \ˌō-vər-ˈpas\ *vt* **1** : SURPASS 1 **2** : to pass across, over, or beyond : CROSS ⟨*overpass* the bounds of politeness⟩ **3** : OVERLOOK 3b
²over•pass \ˈō-vər-ˌpas\ *n* : a crossing (as by means of a bridge) of two highways or of a highway and pedestrian path or railroad at different levels; *also* : the upper level of such a crossing
over•per•suade \ˌō-vər-pər-ˈswād\ *vt* : to persuade to act contrary to conviction or preference — **over•per•sua•sion** \-ˈswā-zhən\ *n*
over•play \ˌō-vər-ˈplā\ *vt* **1 a** : to present (as a dramatic role) extravagantly **b** : to give undue emphasis **2** : to rely too much on the strength of ⟨*overplayed* your hand⟩
over•plus \ˈō-vər-ˌpləs\ *n* : EXCESS 1, SURPLUS
over•pop•u•la•tion \ˌō-vər-ˌpäp-yə-ˈlā-shən\ *n* : the condition of having a population so dense as to cause environmental deterioration, a reduced quality of life, or a population crash — **over•pop•u•late** \-ˈpäp-yə-ˌlāt\ *vt*
over•pow•er \ˌō-vər-ˈpau̇-ər, -ˈpau̇r\ *vt* **1** : to overcome by superior force : DEFEAT **2** : OVERWHELM ⟨*overpowered* by hunger⟩
over•pow•er•ing \ˌō-vər-ˈpau̇r-ing\ *adj* : having great power or influence ⟨*overpowering* beauty⟩ — **over•pow•er•ing•ly** *adv*
¹over•print \ˌō-vər-ˈprint\ *vt* : to print over with something additional
²over•print \ˈō-vər-ˌprint\ *n* : something added by overprinting; *esp* : a printed marking added to a postage or revenue stamp (as to commemorate a special event)
over•pro•por•tion \ˌō-vər-prə-ˈpōr-shən, -ˈpȯr-\ *vt* : to make disproportionately large — **overproportion** *n* — **over•pro•por•tion•ate** \-shə-nət, -shnət\ *adj* — **over•pro•por•tionate•ly** *adv*
over•pro•tect \ˌō-vər-prə-ˈtekt\ *vt* : to protect beyond what is wholesome or desirable ⟨*overprotected* children⟩ — **over•pro•tec•tion** \-ˈtek-shən\ *n* — **over•pro•tec•tive** \-ˈtek-tiv\ *adj*
over•rate \ˌō-vər-ˈrāt, -və-\ *vt* : to rate too highly
over•reach \-ˈrēch\ *vb* **1** : to reach above or beyond **2** : to defeat (oneself) by seeking to do or gain too much **3** : to get the better of : OUTWIT **4** : to go to excess — **over•reach•er** *n*
over•ride \-ˈrīd\ *vt* **-rode** \-ˈrōd\; **-rid•den** \-ˈrid-ⁿn\; **-rid•ing** \-ˈrīd-ing\ **1** : to ride over or across : TRAMPLE **2** : to ride (as a horse) too much or too hard **3 a** : to prevail over : DOMINATE **b** : to set aside : ANNUL ⟨Congress *overrode* the president's veto⟩ **4** : to extend or pass over; *esp* : OVERLAP
over•ripe \-ˈrīp\ *adj* : passed beyond maturity or ripeness toward decay
over•rule \-ˈrül\ *vt* **1** : to rule against ⟨the judge *overruled* the objection⟩ **2** : to set aside : REVERSE ⟨a higher court *overruled* the judge's action⟩
¹over•run \-ˈrən\ *vt* **-ran** \-ˈran\; **-run**; **-run•ning** **1 a** : to defeat and occupy the positions of ⟨the enemy *overran* the outpost⟩ **b** : to spread or swarm over : INFEST ⟨a ship *overrun* with rats⟩ **2 a** : to run or go beyond ⟨the plane *overran* the runway⟩ **b** : EXCEED ⟨*overran* my allotted time⟩ **3** : to flow over
²over•run \ˈō-vər-ˌrən, -və-\ *n* : an act or instance of overrunning ⟨a cost *overrun*⟩; *also* : the amount by which something overruns
over•sea \ˌō-vər-ˈsē, ˈō-vər-ˌ\ *adj or adv* : OVERSEAS
over•seas \-ˈsēz, -ˌsēz\ *adv or adj* : beyond or across the sea
over•see \ˌō-vər-ˈsē\ *vt* **-saw** \-ˈsȯ\; **-seen** \-ˈsēn\; **-see•ing** **1** : to look down upon **2 a** : to look over : EXAMINE **b** : SUPERINTEND ⟨*oversee* a road crew⟩
over•seer \ˈō-vər-ˌsiər, -ˌsē-ər, ˌō-vər-ˈ, -və-\ *n* : one that oversees : SUPERINTENDENT
over•sell \ˌō-vər-ˈsel\ *vt* **-sold** \-ˈsōld\; **-sell•ing** **1 a** : to sell too much to **b** : to sell too much of **2** : to make excessive claims or claims for
over•set \ˌō-vər-ˈset\ *vt* **-set**; **-set•ting** : to turn or tip over : OVERTURN — **over•set** \ˈō-vər-ˌset\ *n*
over•sexed \ˌō-vər-ˈsekst\ *adj* : exhibiting an excessive sexual drive or interest
over•shad•ow \ˌō-vər-ˈshad-ō\ *vt* **1** : to cast a shadow over : DARKEN **2** : to exceed in importance : OUTWEIGH
over•shoe \ˈō-vər-ˌshü\ *n* : an outer shoe; *esp* : GALOSH
over•shoot \ˌō-vər-ˈshüt\ *vt* **-shot** \-ˈshät\; **-shoot•ing** : to pass swiftly beyond ⟨the train *overshot* the platform⟩; *also* : to miss by going beyond ⟨the plane *overshot* the runway⟩
over•shot \ˈō-vər-ˌshät\ *adj* **1** : having the upper jaw extending beyond the lower **2** : moved by water passing over and flowing from above ⟨an *overshot* waterwheel⟩
over•sight \ˈō-vər-ˌsīt\ *n* **1** : the act or duty of overseeing : SUPERVISION **2** : an unintentional omission or error
over•size \ˌō-vər-ˈsīz\ *or* **over•sized** \-ˈsīzd\ *adj* : being of more than ordinary size
over•skirt \ˈō-vər-ˌskərt\ *n* : a skirt worn over another skirt
over•sleep \ˌō-vər-ˈslēp\ *vi* **-slept** \-ˈslept\; **-sleep•ing** : to sleep beyond the time for waking
over•spend \-ˈspend\ *vb* **-spent** \-ˈspent\; **-spend•ing** **1** : to spend more than **2** : to spend beyond one's means or to excess
over•spread \ˌō-vər-ˈspred\ *vt* **-spread**; **-spread•ing** : to spread over or above ⟨branches *overspreading* a garden path⟩ — **over•spread** \ˈō-vər-ˌspred\ *n*
over•state \ˌō-vər-ˈstāt\ *vt* : to state in too strong terms : EXAGGERATE — **over•state•ment** \-mənt\ *n*
over•stay \ˌō-vər-ˈstā\ *vt* : to stay beyond the time or the limits of ⟨*overstay* one's welcome⟩
over•step \-ˈstep\ *vt* : to step over or go beyond : EXCEED ⟨*overstepped* their authority⟩
over•stock \ˌō-vər-ˈstäk\ *vb* : to stock beyond requirements or facilities — **over•stock** \ˈō-vər-ˌstäk\ *n*
over•strew \ˌō-vər-ˈstrü\ *vt* **-strewed**; **-strewed** *or* **-strewn** \-ˈstrün\; **-strew•ing** **1** : to scatter about **2** : to cover here and there
over•strung \ˌō-vər-ˈstrəng\ *adj* : too highly strung : too sensitive
over•stuffed \ˌō-vər-ˈstəft\ *adj* **1** : stuffed too full **2** : covered completely and deeply with upholstery ⟨an *overstuffed* chair⟩
over•sub•scribe \ˌō-vər-səb-ˈskrīb\ *vt* : to subscribe for more of than is available, asked for, or offered for sale — **over•sub•scrip•tion** \-ˈskrip-shən\ *n*
over•sub•tle \ˌō-vər-ˈsət-ᵊl\ *adj* : excessively or impracticably subtle
over•sup•ply \ˌō-vər-sə-ˈplī\ *n* : SURPLUS — **oversupply** *vt*
overt \ō-ˈvərt, ˈō-ˌvərt, ˈō-vərt\ *adj* : open to view : MANIFEST [Middle French *ouvert, overt,* from *ouvrir* "to open", derived from Latin *aperire*] — **overt•ly** *adv*
over•take \ˌō-vər-ˈtāk\ *vt* **-took** \-ˈtu̇k\; **-tak•en** \-ˈtā-kən\; **-tak•ing** **1 a** : to catch up with **b** : to catch up with and pass by **2** : to come upon suddenly ⟨a blizzard *overtook* the hunting party⟩
over–the–count•er *adj* **1** : not traded on an organized securities exchange **2** : sold lawfully without prescription
over•throw \ˌō-vər-ˈthrō\ *vt* **-threw** \-ˈthrü\; **-thrown** \-ˈthrōn\; **-throw•ing** **1** : OVERTURN 1, UPSET **2** : to bring down : DEFEAT ⟨a government *overthrown* by rebels⟩ — **over•throw** \ˈō-vər-ˌthrō\ *n*
over•time \ˈō-vər-ˌtīm\ *n* **1** : time exceeding a set limit; *esp* : working time exceeding a standard day or week **2** : the wage paid for overtime work — **overtime** *adv or adj*
over•tone \ˈō-vər-ˌtōn\ *n* **1** : one of the higher tones that with the fundamental comprise a musical tone : HARMONIC 1a **2** : a

secondary effect, quality, or meaning : SUGGESTION ⟨the words carried an unfriendly *overtone*⟩

over•top \ˌō-vər-ˈtäp\ *vt* **1** : to rise above the top of : surpass in height ⟨*overtopped* my cousin by 6 centimeters⟩ **2** : to stand above : OVERRIDE **3** : OVERSHADOW

over•trick \ˈō-vər-ˌtrik\ *n* : a card trick won in excess of the number bid

over•trump \ˌō-vər-ˈtrəmp\ *vb* : to trump with a higher trump card than the highest previously played to the same trick

over•ture \ˈō-vər-ˌchu̇r, -və-, -chər\ *n* **1** : an opening offer : a first proposal ⟨made *overtures* for peace⟩ **2** : an orchestral introduction to an oratorio, opera, or dramatic work; *also* : a composition in this style for concert performance [Middle English, literally, "opening", from Middle French *ouverture,* derived from Latin *apertura* "aperture"]

over•turn \ˌō-vər-ˈtərn\ *vb* **1** : to turn over : UPSET **2** : OVERTHROW 2, DESTROY — **over•turn** \ˈō-vər-ˌtərn\ *n*

over•use \ˌō-vər-ˈyüs\ *n* : excessive use — **over•use** \-ˈyüz\ *vt*

over•view \ˈō-vər-ˌvyü\ *n* : a general view : SURVEY

over•watch \ˌō-vər-ˈwäch\ *vt* : to watch over

over•ween•ing \ˌō-vər-ˈwē-ning\ *adj* **1** : unduly confident : PRESUMPTUOUS **2** : EXCESSIVE, IMMODERATE ⟨*overweening* greed⟩ [Middle English *overwening,* present participle of *overwenen* "to be arrogant", from *over* + *wenen* "to ween"] — **over•ween•ing•ly** \-ning-lē\ *adv*

over•weigh \ˌō-vər-ˈwā\ *vt* **1** : OUTWEIGH **2** : to weigh down : OPPRESS

¹over•weight \ˈō-vər-ˌwāt, *2 is usually* ˌō-vər-ˈ\ *n* **1** : weight above what is required or allowed **2** : excessive or burdensome weight; *esp* : bodily weight in excess of what is normal to one's age, height, and build — **over•weight** \ˌō-vər-ˈ\ *adj*

²over•weight \ˌō-vər-ˈwāt\ *vt* **1** : to give too much weight or consideration to ⟨you *overweight* their opinion⟩ **2** : to weight excessively ⟨*overweighted* prose⟩ **3** : OUTWEIGH

over•whelm \-ˈhwelm, -ˈwelm\ *vt* **1** : to cover completely : SUBMERGE ⟨a wave *overwhelmed* the boat⟩ **2** : WHIP 4 **3** : to overpower in thought or feeling : PROSTRATE ⟨*overwhelmed* by grief⟩ [Middle English *overwhelmen,* from *over* + *whelmen* "to turn over, cover up"] — **over•whelm•ing•ly** \-ˈhwel-ming-lē, -ˈwel-\ *adv*

over•wind \ˌō-vər-ˈwīnd\ *vt* **-wound** \-ˈwau̇nd\; **-wind•ing** : to wind too much

over•win•ter \ˌō-vər-ˈwint-ər\ *vi* : to spend or survive the winter

over•work \ˌō-vər-ˈwərk\ *vb* **1** : to work or cause to work too hard, too long, or to exhaustion **2** : to decorate all over ⟨a tombstone *overworked* with designs⟩ **3 a** : to work too much on : OVERDO **b** : to make excessive use of ⟨*overworked* phrases⟩ — **overwork** *n*

over•write \ˌō-vər-ˈrīt, -və-\ *vb* **-wrote** \-ˈrōt\; **-writ•ten** \-ˈrit-n\; **-writ•ing** \-ˈrīt-ing\ **1** : to write over the surface of **2** : to write in a too elaborate or pretentious style ⟨*overwritten* accounts of simple events⟩ **3** : to write too much

over•wrought \ˌō-vər-ˈrȯt, -və-\ *adj* **1** : extremely excited **2** : decorated to excess [past participle of *overwork*]

ovi- *or* **ovo-** — see OV-

ovi•cid•al \ˌō-və-ˈsīd-l\ *adj* : capable of killing eggs — **ovi•cide** \ˈō-və-ˌsīd\ *n*

ovi•duct \ˈō-və-ˌdəkt\ *n* : a tube for the passage of eggs from the ovary of an animal

ovine \ˈō-ˌvīn\ *adj* : of or relating to sheep [Late Latin *ovinus,* from Latin *ovis* "sheep"] — **ovine** *n*

ovip•a•rous \ō-ˈvip-rəs, -ə-rəs\ *adj* : producing eggs that develop and hatch outside the maternal body [Latin *oviparus,* from *ovum* "egg" + *parere* "to produce"] — **ovip•a•rous•ly** *adv*

ovi•pos•it \ˈō-və-ˌpäz-ət\ *vi* : to lay eggs — used especially of insects [probably back-formation from *ovipositor*] — **ovi•po•si•tion** \ˌō-və-pə-ˈzish-ən\ *n*

ovi•pos•i•tor \ˈō-və-ˌpäz-ət-ər\ *n* : a specialized organ (as of an insect) for depositing eggs [Latin *ovum* "egg" + *positor* "one that places", from *ponere* "to place"]

ovoid \ˈō-ˌvȯid\ *also* **ovoi•dal** \ō-ˈvȯid-l\ *adj* : shaped like an egg : OVATE — **ovoid** *n*

ovo•vi•vip•a•rous \ˌō-vō-ˌvī-ˈvip-rəs, -ə-rəs\ *adj* : producing eggs that develop within the maternal body and hatch within or immediately after leaving the parent — **ovo•vi•vip•a•rous•ly** *adv*

ovu•late \ˈäv-yə-ˌlāt, ˈōv-\ *vi* : to produce eggs or discharge them from an ovary — **ovu•la•tion** \ˌäv-yə-ˈlā-shən, ˌōv-\ *n*

ovule \ˈäv-ˌyül, ˈōv-\ *n* **1** : an outgrowth of the ovary of a seed plant that after fertilization develops into a seed **2** : a small egg; *esp* : one in an early stage of growth [New Latin *ovulum,* from Latin *ovum* "egg"] — **ovu•lar** \-yə-lər\ *adj*

ovum \ˈō-vəm\ *n, pl* **ova** \-və\ : a female gamete : MACROGAMETE — called also *egg, egg cell* [Latin, "egg"]

owe \ˈō\ *vb* **1** : to have (an emotion or attitude) to someone or something ⟨*owes* the seller a grudge⟩ **2 a** (1) : to be under obligation to pay or repay ⟨*owes* me $5⟩ (2) : to be obligated to render (as duty or a service) **b** : to be indebted to ⟨*owes* the grocer for supplies⟩ **c** : to be in debt ⟨*owes* for the house⟩ [Old English *āgan* "to possess, own, owe"]

owing to *prep* : because of ⟨delayed *owing to* a crash⟩

owl \ˈau̇l\ *n* : any of an order (Strigiformes) of birds of prey with large head and eyes, short hooked bill, strong talons, and more or less nocturnal habits [Old English *ūle*]

owl•et \ˈau̇-lət\ *n* : a young or small owl

owl•ish \ˈau̇-lish\ *adj* : resembling or suggesting an owl — **owl•ish•ly** *adv* — **owl•ish•ness** *n*

¹own \ˈōn\ *adj* : belonging to oneself or itself — usually used following a possessive case or possessive adjective ⟨wanted my *own* room⟩ [Old English *āgen*]

²own *vb* **1 a** : POSSESS 2a **b** : to have legal title to **2** : ACKNOWLEDGE, ADMIT ⟨*own* a debt⟩ **3** : CONFESS — used with *to* or *up* ⟨*owned* to being scared⟩ ⟨if you broke the window, *own* up⟩ — **own•er** \ˈō-nər\ *n* — **own•er•ship** \-ˌship\ *n*

³own *pron, sing or pl in construction* : one or ones belonging to oneself — used after a possessive and without a following noun as a pronoun equivalent in meaning to the adjective *own* ⟨want rooms of their *own*⟩ — **on one's own** : for or by oneself : INDEPENDENTLY

ox \ˈäks\ *n, pl* **ox•en** \ˈäk-sən\ *also* **ox** **1** : a common large domestic bovine mammal kept for milk, draft, and meat; *esp* : an adult castrated male **2** : any of the larger hollow-horned cud-chewing mammals (as a buffalo or yak) [Old English *oxa*]

ox- *or* **oxo-** *combining form* : oxygen [French, from *oxygène*]

ox•a•late \ˈäk-sə-ˌlāt\ *n* : a salt or ester of oxalic acid

ox•al•ic acid \äk-ˌsal-ik-\ *n* : a poisonous strong acid $C_2H_2O_4$ that occurs in various plants as oxalates and is used especially as a bleaching or cleaning agent and in making dyes [French *acide oxalique,* from Latin *oxalis* "wood sorrel"]

ox•al•is \äk-ˈsal-əs\ *n* : WOOD SORREL [Latin, from Greek, from *oxys* "sharp"]

ox•blood \ˈäks-ˌbləd\ *n* : a moderate reddish brown

ox•bow \ˈäks-ˌbō\ *n* **1** : a U-shaped collar worn by a draft ox **2 a** : a U-shaped bend in a river **b** : a U-shaped lake formed when such a bend becomes isolated when bypassed by the river channel — called also *oxbow lake* — **oxbow** *adj*

ox•eye \ˈäk-ˌsī\ *n* : any of several composite plants having heads with both disk and ray flowers; *esp* : DAISY 1b

oxeye daisy *n* : DAISY 1b

ox•ford \ˈäks-fərd\ *n* : a low shoe laced or tied over the instep [*Oxford,* England]

ox•heart \ˈäks-ˌhärt\ *n* : any of various large sweet cherries

ox•i•dant \ˈäk-səd-ənt\ *n* : OXIDIZING AGENT

ox•i•dase \ˈäk-sə-ˌdās, -ˌdāz\ *n* : any of various enzymes that catalyze oxidations

ox•i•da•tion \ˌäk-sə-ˈdā-shən\ *n* **1** : the process of oxidizing **2** : the state or result of being oxidized — **ox•i•da•tive** \ˈäk-sə-ˌdāt-iv\ *adj*

oxidation number *n* : the degree of oxidation of an atom (as in a compound) that is usually expressed as a positive or negative number representing the ionic charge or effective charge of the atom ⟨the usual *oxidation number* of hydrogen is +1 and of oxygen −2⟩ — called also *oxidation state*

oxidation–reduction *n* : a chemical reaction in which one or more electrons are transferred from one atom or molecule to another

ox•ide \ˈäk-ˌsīd\ *n* : a compound of oxygen with an element or radical [French, from *ox-* + *-ide* (from *acide* "acid")]

\ə\ abut	\au̇\ **out**	\i\ **tip**	\ȯ\ **saw**	\u̇\ **foot**
\ər\ further	\ch\ **chin**	\ī\ **life**	\ȯi\ **coin**	\y\ **yet**
\a\ mat	\e\ **pet**	\j\ **job**	\th\ **thin**	\yü\ **few**
\ā\ take	\ē\ **easy**	\ng\ **sing**	\t͟h\ **this**	\yu̇\ **cure**
\ä\ cot, cart	\g\ **go**	\ō\ **bone**	\ü\ **food**	\zh\ **vision**

ox•i•dize \ˈäk-sə-ˌdīz\ *vb* **1 :** to combine with oxygen **2 :** to dehydrogenate especially by the action of oxygen **3 :** to remove one or more electrons from (an atom, ion, or molecule) **4 :** to become oxidized — **ox•i•diz•er** *n*

oxidizing agent *n* **:** a substance (as oxygen or nitric acid) that oxidizes by taking up electrons

Ox•o•ni•an \äk-ˈsō-nē-ən\ *n* **:** a student or graduate of Oxford University [Medieval Latin *Oxonia* "Oxford"] — **Oxonian** *adj*

ox•tail \ˈäk-ˌstāl\ *n* **:** the tail of cattle; *esp* **:** the skinned tail for use as food

oxy \ˈäk-sē\ *adj* **:** OXYGENIC; *esp* **:** containing oxygen or additional oxygen — often used in combination ⟨*oxy*hemoglobin⟩ ⟨*oxy*hydrogen⟩ [French, from *oxygène* "oxygen"]

oxy•acet•y•lene \ˌäk-sē-ə-ˈset-l-ən, -l-ˌēn\ *adj* **:** of, relating to, or utilizing a mixture of oxygen and acetylene ⟨*oxyacetylene* torch⟩

ox•y•gen \ˈäk-si-jən\ *n* **:** a chemical element that is found free as a colorless tasteless odorless gas in the atmosphere of which it forms about 21 percent or combined in water, that is capable of combining with all elements except the inert gases, that is active in physiological processes, and that is involved in combustion processes — see ELEMENT table [French *oxygène,* from Greek *oxys* "sharp, acid" + French *-gène* "-gen"] — **ox•y•gen•ic** \ˌäk-si-ˈjen-ik\ *adj*

ox•y•gen•ate \ˈäk-si-jə-ˌnāt, äk-ˈsij-ə-\ *vt* **:** to impregnate, combine, or supply (as blood) with oxygen — **ox•y•gen•ation** \ˌäk-si-jə-ˈnā-shən, äk-ˌsij-ə-\ *n*

oxygen debt *n* **:** a cumulative oxygen deficit that develops during periods of intense bodily activity and must be made good when the body returns to rest

oxygen mask *n* **:** a device worn over the nose and mouth through which oxygen is supplied from a storage tank

oxygen tent *n* **:** a canopy which can be placed over a bedridden person and within which a flow of oxygen can be maintained

oxy•he•mo•glo•bin \ˌäk-si-ˈhē-mə-ˌglō-bən\ *n* **:** a compound of hemoglobin with oxygen that is the chief means of transportation of oxygen from the air (as in the lungs) by way of the blood to the tissues

oxy•hy•dro•gen \ˌäk-si-ˈhī-drə-jən\ *adj* **:** of, relating to, or utilizing a mixture of oxygen and hydrogen ⟨*oxyhydrogen* torch⟩

oxy•mo•ron \ˌäk-si-ˈmōr-ˌän, -ˈmȯr-\ *n, pl* **-mo•ra** \-ˈmōr-ə, -ˈmȯr-ə\ **:** a combination of contradictory or incongruous words (as *cruel kindness*) [Late Greek *oxymōron,* from *oxymōros* "pointedly foolish", from Greek *oxys* "sharp, keen" + *mōros* "foolish"]

oxy•to•cin \ˌäk-si-ˈtōs-n\ *n* **:** a pituitary hormone that helps to regulate blood pressure and stimulates the contraction of smooth muscle in the uterus [derived from Greek *oxys* "sharp, quick" + *tokos* "childbirth", from *tiktein* "to bear"]

oyez \ō-ˈyā, -ˈyes\ *imperative verb* — used by a court or public crier to gain attention before a proclamation [Anglo-French, "hear ye", from *oir* "to hear", from Latin *audire*]

oys•ter \ˈȯi-stər\ *n* **:** any of various marine bivalve mollusks having a rough irregular shell and including important edible shellfish [Middle French *oistre,* from Latin *ostrea,* from Greek *ostreon*]

oyster catcher

oyster bed *n* **:** a place where oysters grow or are cultivated

oyster catcher *n* **:** any of a genus of wading birds with stout legs, a heavy wedge-shaped bill, and often black and white plumage

oyster cracker *n* **:** a small salted cracker

oys•ter•man \ˈȯi-stər-mən\ *n* **:** a gatherer, opener, breeder, or seller of oysters

oyster plant *n* **:** SALSIFY

ozone \ˈō-ˌzōn\ *n* **1 :** a form O_3 of oxygen that has three atoms in the molecule, is a faintly blue irritating gas with a pungent odor, is generated usually in dilute form by a silent electric discharge in oxygen or air, and is used especially in disinfection and deodorization and in oxidation and bleaching **2 :** pure and refreshing air [German *ozon,* from Greek *ozōn,* present participle of *ozein* "to smell"] — **ozo•nic** \ō-ˈzō-nik\ *adj* — **ozo•nif•er•ous** \ˌō-ˌzō-ˈnif-rəs, -ə-rəs\ *adj*

ozo•no•sphere \ō-ˈzō-nə-ˌsfiər\ *n* **:** an atmospheric layer at heights of approximately 30 to 50 kilometers characterized by high ozone content

P p—pyx

p \ˈpē\ *n, pl* **p's** *or* **ps** \ˈpēz\ *often cap* **:** the 16th letter of the English alphabet

pa \ˈpä, ˈpȯ\ *n* **:** FATHER 1a [short for *papa*]

PABA \ˈpab-ə, ˌpē-ˌā-ˈbē-ˌā\ *n* **:** PARA-AMINOBENZOIC ACID [*p*ara-*a*mino*b*enzoic *a*cid]

pab•u•lum \ˈpab-yə-ləm\ *n* **:** FOOD; *esp* **:** a suspension or solution of nutrients suitable for absorption [Latin, "food, fodder"]

pa•ca \ˈpäk-ə, ˈpak-\ *n* **:** any of a genus of large South and Central American rodents [Portuguese and Spanish, from Tupi *páca*]

[1]**pace** \ˈpās\ *n* **1 :** rate of moving or progressing especially on foot **2 a :** a manner of walking **:** TREAD **b :** GAIT; *esp* **:** a fast 2-beat gait of a horse in which the legs on the same side move in pairs and support the animal alternately on the right and left **3 :** a single step or a measure based on the length of a human step [Old French *pas* "step", from Latin *passus,* from *pandere* "to spread"]

[2]**pace** *vb* **1 a :** to walk with slow measured steps **b :** to move along **:** PROCEED **2 :** to go or cover at a pace — used of a horse **3 :** to measure by paces — often used with *off* **4 a :** to set or regulate the pace of **b :** PRECEDE 2, LEAD — **pac•er** *n*

pace•mak•er \ˈpā-ˌsmā-kər\ *n* **1 :** one that sets the pace for another **2 a :** a bodily part (as of the heart) that serves to establish and maintain a rhythmic activity **b :** an electrical device for steadying or establishing the heartbeat

pa•chi•si \pə-ˈchē-zē\ *n* **:** an ancient board game played with dice and counters [Hindi *pacīsī*]

pachy•derm \ˈpak-i-ˌdərm\ *n* **:** any of various thick-skinned hoofed mammals (as an elephant or a rhinoceros) [French *pachyderme,* from Greek *pachydermos* "thick-skinned", from *pachys* "thick" + *derma* "skin"] — **pachy•der•ma•tous** \ˌpak-i-ˈdər-mət-əs\ *adj*

pach•ys•an•dra \ˌpak-ə-ˈsan-drə\ *n* **:** any of a genus of evergreen woody trailing plants of the box family often used as a ground cover [derived from Greek *pachys* "thick" + *andr-, anēr* "man"]

pa•cif•ic \pə-ˈsif-ik\ *adj* **1 :** making or promoting peace ⟨a *pacific* policy⟩ **2 :** having a mild and calm nature **:** PEACEABLE ⟨a quiet *pacific* people⟩ [Latin *pacificus,* from *pac-, pax* "peace"] — **pa•cif•i•cal•ly** \-ˈsif-i-kə-lē, -klē\ *adv*

pac•i•fi•ca•tion \ˌpas-ə-fə-ˈkā-shən\ *n* **:** the act or process of pacifying **:** the state of being pacified

Pacific time *n* **:** the time of the 8th time zone west of Greenwich that includes the Pacific coastal region of the United States

pac•i•fi•er \ˈpas-ə-ˌfī-ər, -ˌfīr\ *n* **1 :** one that pacifies **2 :** a usually nipple-shaped device for babies to suck on

pac•i•fism \ˈpas-ə-ˌfiz-əm\ *n* **:** opposition to war or violence as a means of settling disputes; *esp* **:** refusal to bear arms on moral or religious grounds — **pac•i•fist** \-fəst\ *n* — **pacifist** *or* **pac•i•fis•tic** \ˌpas-ə-ˈfis-tik\ *adj*

pac•i•fy \ˈpas-ə-ˌfī\ *vt* **-fied; -fy•ing 1 :** to ease the anger or agitation of **:** SOOTHE ⟨*pacify* a crying child⟩ **2 :** to restore to a peaceful state **:** SUBDUE ⟨*pacify* a country⟩ [Latin *pacificare,* from *pac-, pax* "peace"] — **pac•i•fi•able** \-ˌfī-ə-bəl\ *adj*

• **syn** APPEASE, PLACATE, MOLLIFY: PACIFY may imply a soothing or calming of anger or agitation or the forceful quelling of insurrection; APPEASE implies quieting anger or averting threats by making concessions to insistent demands; PLACATE suggests changing resentment or bitterness to goodwill; MOLLIFY stresses a soothing of feelings by concession or flattery.

1pack \ˈpak\ *n* **1 a :** a bundle arranged for carrying especially on the back **b :** a group or pile of related objects ⟨a *pack* of cards⟩ **2 :** a large amount or number **:** HEAP **3 :** an act, an instance, or a method of packing; *also* **:** arrangement in a pack **4 a :** a group of often predatory animals of the same kind **b :** a group of persons with a common interest ⟨a *pack* of thieves⟩ **c :** an organized troop (as of cub scouts) **5 :** a concentrated mass **6 :** absorbent material used medically (as for checking bleeding or applying medication or moisture) **7 a :** a cosmetic paste for the face **b :** an application or treatment of oils or creams for conditioning the scalp and hair [Middle English, of Low German or Dutch origin]

2pack *vb* **1 a :** to make into a compact bundle ⟨*pack* papers into an envelope⟩ **b :** to stow one's personal belongings in luggage ⟨I'll go home and *pack*⟩ **c :** to fill completely ⟨the stadium was *packed*⟩ **d :** to arrange closely and securely in a protective container ⟨glasses *packed* for shipment⟩ **2 a :** to crowd together so as to fill full **:** CRAM ⟨the crowd was *packed* into the hall⟩ **b :** to increase the density of **:** COMPRESS **3 :** to fill or cover so as to prevent passage (as of air or steam) ⟨*pack* a joint in a pipe⟩ **4 :** to send or go away without ceremony ⟨*pack* the children off to school⟩ **5 a :** to transport on foot or on the back of an animal ⟨*pack* water from a spring⟩ **b :** to be supplied or equipped with **:** POSSESS ⟨*pack* a gun⟩ **6 :** to assemble in a group **:** CONGREGATE **7 :** to process (foodstuffs) for use or storage usually on a wholesale scale — **pack•abil•i•ty** \ˌpak-ə-ˈbil-ət-ē\ *n* — **pack•able** \ˈpak-ə-bəl\ *adj*

3pack *vt* **:** to influence the makeup of (as a jury) improperly to gain a desired result [obsolete *pack* "to make a secret agreement"]

1pack•age \ˈpak-ij\ *n* **1 a :** a small or moderate-sized pack **:** PARCEL **b :** a unit of a product uniformly wrapped or sealed **2 :** a covering wrapper or container **3 :** something that suggests a package of merchandise; *esp* **:** PACKAGE DEAL

2package *vt* **:** to make into or enclose in a package — **pack•ager** *n*

package deal *n* **:** an offer or agreement involving more than one item or making acceptance of one item dependent on the acceptance of another

package store *n* **:** a store that sells alcoholic beverages only in containers that may not lawfully be opened on the premises

pack animal *n* **:** an animal (as a horse or donkey) used for carrying packs

pack•er \ˈpak-ər\ *n* **:** one that packs: as **a :** a dealer who prepares and packs foods for the market ⟨a meat *packer*⟩ **b :** 2PORTER 1 **c :** one that conveys goods on pack animals

pack•et \ˈpak-ət\ *n* **1 :** a small bundle or parcel **2 :** a passenger boat carrying mail and cargo on a regular schedule [Middle French *pacquet*, of Germanic origin]

pack•horse \ˈpak-ˌhȯrs\ *n* **:** a horse used as a pack animal

pack ice *n* **:** sea ice formed into a mass by the crushing together of fragments

pack•ing \ˈpak-ing\ *n* **:** material used to pack or caulk something

pack•ing•house \ˈpak-ing-ˌhau̇s\ *n* **:** an establishment for processing and packing foodstuffs and especially meat and its by-products — called also *packing plant*

pack rat *n* **1 :** WOOD RAT; *esp* **:** a large bushy-tailed rodent of the Rocky Mountain area that hoards food and miscellaneous objects **2 :** a person who hoards trivial or unneeded items

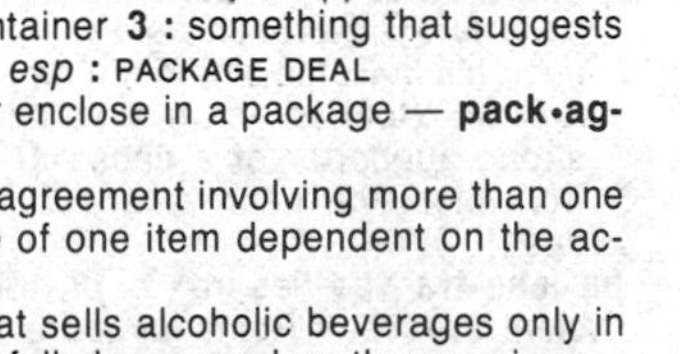

pack rat 1

pack•sack \ˈpak-ˌsak\ *n* **:** a case used to carry gear on the back when traveling on foot **:** BACKPACK

pack•sad•dle \ˈpak-ˌsad-l\ *n* **:** a saddle that supports the load on the back of a pack animal

pack•thread \-ˌthred\ *n* **:** strong thread or small twine used for sewing or tying packs or parcels

pact \ˈpakt\ *n* **:** 4COMPACT; *esp* **:** an international treaty [Middle French, from Latin *pactum*, from *pacisci* "to agree, contract"]

1pad \ˈpad\ *n* **1 a :** a cushioned part or thing **:** CUSHION **b :** a piece of material that holds ink for inking the surface of a rubber stamp **2 a :** the foot of some mammals **b :** the cushioned bottom of the toes of some mammals **3 :** a floating leaf of a water plant **4 :** TABLET 1b **5 :** LAUNCH PAD [origin unknown]

2pad *vt* **pad•ded; pad•ding 1 :** to furnish with a pad or padding **2 :** to expand with useless or trivial matter ⟨*pad* a short speech⟩

3pad *vb* **pad•ded; pad•ding 1 :** to go on foot **2 :** to move along with a muffled step [perhaps from Dutch *paden* "to follow a path", from *pad* "path"]

4pad *n* **:** a soft muffled or slapping sound [imitative]

pad•ding \ˈpad-ing\ *n* **:** material with which something is padded

1pad•dle \ˈpad-l\ *n* **1 a :** an implement with a flat blade to propel and steer a small craft (as a canoe) **b :** something (as the flipper of a seal) suggesting a paddle in appearance or action **2 :** an implement especially used for stirring, mixing, or beating **3 :** one of the broad boards at the circumference of a paddle wheel or waterwheel [Middle English *padell*]

2paddle *vb* **pad•dled; pad•dling** \ˈpad-ling, -l-ing\ **1 :** to go, propel, or carry by or as if by means of a paddle or paddle wheel **2 a :** to beat or stir with or as if with a paddle **b :** to punish with or as if with a paddle — **pad•dler** \ˈpad-lər, -l-ər\ *n*

3paddle *vi* **pad•dled; pad•dling** \ˈpad-ling, -l-ing\ **1 :** to move the hands or feet about in shallow water **2 :** TODDLE ⟨the small child *paddled* over to them⟩ [origin unknown]

pad•dle•fish \ˈpad-l-ˌfish\ *n* **:** a fish of the Mississippi valley about a meter long with a paddle-shaped snout

paddle wheel *n* **:** a wheel with paddles, floats, or boards around its circumference used to propel a vessel

pad•dock \ˈpad-ək, -ik\ *n* **:** a usually enclosed area used especially for pasturing or exercising animals; *esp* **:** an enclosure where racehorses are saddled and paraded before a race [alteration of Middle English *parrok*, from Old English *pearroc*]

pad•dy \ˈpad-ē\ *n, pl* **paddies 1 :** RICE; *esp* **:** threshed unmilled rice **2 :** wet land in which rice is grown [Malay *padi*]

pad•dy wagon \ˈpad-ē-\ *n* **:** PATROL WAGON [probably from English slang *Paddy* "Irishman, policeman", from *Paddy*, nickname for *Patrick*]

pad•lock \ˈpad-ˌläk\ *n* **:** a removable lock with a hinged bow-shaped piece attached at one end so that the other end can be passed through a staple (as on a hasp) and then snapped into a catch in the lock [Middle English *padlok*] — **padlock** *vt*

pa•dre \ˈpäd-rā, -rē\ *n* **1 :** a Christian clergyman; *esp* **:** PRIEST **2 :** a military chaplain [Spanish or Italian or Portuguese, literally, "father", from Latin *pater*]

pae•an \ˈpē-ən\ *n* **:** a joyous song of praise, tribute, thanksgiving, or triumph [Latin, "hymn of thanksgiving especially to Apollo", from Greek *paian*, from *Paian*, epithet of Apollo]

paed- *or* **paedo-** *or* **ped-** *or* **pedo-** *combining form* **:** child ⟨*pedi*atrics⟩ [Greek *paid-*, *pais* "child, boy"]

pa•gan \ˈpā-gən\ *n* **1 :** HEATHEN 1 **2 :** an irreligious person [Late Latin *paganus*, from Latin, "country dweller", from *pagus* "country district"] — **pagan** *adj* — **pa•gan•ish** \-gə-nish\ *adj* — **pa•gan•ism** \-gə-ˌniz-əm\ *n* — **pa•gan•ize** \-gə-ˌnīz\ *vt*

1page \ˈpāj\ *n* **1 :** a medieval youth being trained for knighthood in the service of a knight; *also* **:** a youth attending a person of rank **2 :** one employed (as by a hotel) especially to deliver messages or perform personal services for patrons [Old French, from Italian *paggio*]

2page *vt* **1 :** to serve in the capacity of a page **2 :** to summon by calling out the name of

3page *n* **1 a :** one side of a printed or written leaf; *also* **:** the entire leaf **b :** the matter printed or written on a page ⟨set several *pages* of type⟩ **2 a :** a written record ⟨the *pages* of history⟩ **b :** an event or circumstance worth recording ⟨an exciting *page* in one's life⟩ [Middle French, from Latin *pagina*]

4page *vt* **:** to number or mark the pages of

pag•eant \ˈpaj-ənt\ *n* **1 a :** a mere show **:** PRETENSE **b :** a

\ə\ **abut**	\au̇\ **out**	\i\ **tip**	\ȯ\ **saw**	\u̇\ **foot**
\ər\ **further**	\ch\ **chin**	\ī\ **life**	\ȯi\ **coin**	\y\ **yet**
\a\ **mat**	\e\ **pet**	\j\ **job**	\th\ **thin**	\yü\ **few**
\ā\ **take**	\ē\ **easy**	\ng\ **sing**	\t͟h\ **this**	\yu̇\ **cure**
\ä\ **cot, cart**	\g\ **go**	\ō\ **bone**	\ü\ **food**	\zh\ **vision**

showy display **2 :** a usually elaborate entertainment consisting of scenes based on history or legend ⟨a Christmas *pageant*⟩ [Middle English *padgeant,* literally, "scene of a play", from Medieval Latin *pagina,* from Latin, "page"]

pag•eant•ry \ˈpaj-ən-trē\ *n, pl* **-ries 1 :** pageants and the presentation of pageants **2 :** colorful, rich, or splendid display **:** SPECTACLE

page boy *n* **1 :** a boy serving as a page **2** *usually* **page•boy :** a woman's often shoulder-length haircut with the ends turned under in a smooth roll

pag•i•nal \ˈpaj-ən-l\ *adj* **:** of, relating to, or consisting of pages [Late Latin *paginalis,* from Latin *pagina* "page"]

pag•i•nate \ˈpaj-ə-ˌnāt\ *vt* **:** [4]PAGE

pag•i•na•tion \ˌpaj-ə-ˈnā-shən\ *n* **1 :** the paging of written or printed matter **2 :** the number and arrangement of pages (as of a book) or an indication of these

pa•go•da \pə-ˈgōd-ə\ *n* **:** a Far Eastern temple or memorial in the form of a tower usually with roofs curving upward at the division of each of several stories [Portuguese *pagode* "oriental idol, temple", derived from Sanskrit *bhagavatī,* epithet of Hindu goddesses, feminine of *bhagavat* "blessed"]

pagoda

paid *past of* PAY

pail \ˈpāl\ *n* **:** a usually cylindrical vessel that is open at the top and has a handle **:** BUCKET [Middle English *payle, paille*] — **pail•ful** \-ˌfu̇l\ *n*

[1]pain \ˈpān\ *n* **1** *pl* **:** PUNISHMENT ⟨prescribed *pains* and penalties⟩ **2 a (1) :** physical suffering associated with disease, injury, or other bodily disorder ⟨a *pain* in the back⟩ ⟨in constant *pain*⟩ **(2) :** a basic bodily sensation induced by a harmful stimulus, characterized by physical discomfort (as pricking, throbbing, or aching), and typically leading to attempts to escape its cause **b :** acute mental or emotional distress **:** GRIEF **3** *pl* **:** the throes of childbirth **4** *pl* **:** care or effort taken in accomplishing something ⟨took *pains* with their work⟩ **5 :** someone or something that annoys or is troublesome ⟨studying can be a real *pain*⟩ [Old French *peine,* from Latin *poena,* from Greek *poinē* "payment, penalty"] **syn** see EFFORT — **pain** *adj* — **pain•less** \-ləs\ *adj* — **pain•less•ly** *adv* — **pain•less•ness** *n* — **on pain of** *or* **under pain of :** subject to penalty or punishment by — **pain in the neck :** a source of annoyance **:** NUISANCE

[2]pain *vb* **1 :** to cause pain in or to **:** HURT **2 :** to give or experience pain

pain•ful \ˈpān-fəl\ *adj* **1 a :** feeling or giving pain **b :** that troubles or distresses ⟨a *painful* interview⟩ **2 :** requiring or involving effort or care ⟨a *painful* task⟩ — **pain•ful•ly** \-fə-lē\ *adv* — **pain•ful•ness** *n*

pain•kill•er \ˈpān-ˌkil-ər\ *n* **:** something (as a drug) that relieves pain — **pain•kill•ing** \-ing\ *adj*

pains•tak•ing \ˈpān-ˌstā-king\ *adj* **:** marked by diligent care and effort — **pains•tak•ing•ly** \-king-lē\ *adv*

[1]paint \ˈpānt\ *vb* **1 :** to apply paint or a comparable covering or coloring substance to ⟨*paint* a wall⟩ ⟨*paint* the wound with iodine⟩ **2 a :** to represent in lines and colors on a surface by applying pigments ⟨*paint* a picture⟩ **b :** to produce or evoke as if by painting ⟨*paints* glowing pictures of their vacation⟩ **3 :** to practice the art of painting **4 :** to use cosmetics [Old French *peint* "painted", from *peindre* "to paint", from Latin *pingere*]

[2]paint *n* **1 :** MAKEUP; *esp* **:** a cosmetic to add color **2 a :** a mixture of a pigment and a suitable liquid to form a closely adherent coating when spread on a surface in a thin coat **b :** an applied coating of paint ⟨scrape old *paint* from woodwork⟩

paint•brush \ˈpānt-ˌbrəsh\ *n* **1 :** a brush for applying paint **2 a :** INDIAN PAINTBRUSH 1 **b :** ORANGE HAWKWEED

painted bunting *n* **:** a brightly colored finch of the southern United States

painted turtle *n* **:** any of several common freshwater turtles that are found chiefly in the eastern United States and have a greenish black upper shell with yellow bands and red markings and a yellow lower shell

[1]paint•er \ˈpānt-ər\ *n* **:** one that paints: as **a :** an artist who paints **b :** a worker who applies paint as an occupation — **paint•er•ly** \-lē\ *adj*

[2]pain•ter \ˈpānt-ər\ *n* **:** a line used for securing or towing a boat [Middle English *paynter,* probably from Middle French *pendoir, pentoir* "line for hanging clothes to dry", from *pendre* "to hang"]

paint•ing \ˈpānt-ing\ *n* **1 :** a product of painting; *esp* **:** a painted work of art **2 :** the art or occupation of painting

[1]pair \ˈpaər, ˈpeər\ *n, pl* **pairs** *also* **pair 1 :** two corresponding things either naturally matched or intended to be used together ⟨a *pair* of hands⟩ ⟨a *pair* of gloves⟩ **2 :** a single unit made up of two corresponding pieces ⟨a *pair* of scissors⟩ **3 :** a set of two: as **a :** two mated animals **b :** a couple in love, engaged, or married **c :** two members of a deliberative body who hold opposing views and agree not to vote on a specific issue **4** *chiefly dialect* **:** a set or series of small objects (as beads) [Old French *paire,* from Latin *paria* "equal things", from *par* "equal"]

[2]pair *vb* **:** to join in a pair or in pairs ⟨*paired the guests*⟩

pair of compasses : COMPASS 2c

pais•ley \ˈpāz-lē\ *adj, often cap* **1 :** made typically of soft wool with colorful curved abstract figures ⟨a *paisley* shawl⟩ **2 :** having a pattern like that of a paisley fabric [*Paisley,* Scotland] — **paisley** *n*

Pai•ute \ˈpī-ˌüt, -ˌyüt\ *n* **:** a member of a group of Indian peoples of the Great Basin having an Aztec-related language

pa•ja•mas \pə-ˈjäm-əz, -ˈjam-\ *n pl* **:** a loose usually 2-piece lightweight suit designed especially for sleeping [Hindi *pājāma* "lightweight trousers", from Persian *pā* "leg" + *jāma* "garment"]

[1]pal \ˈpal\ *n* **:** a close friend [Romany *phral, phal* "brother, friend", from Sanskrit *bhrātṛ* "brother"]

[2]pal *vi* **palled; pal•ling :** to be or associate as pals

pal•ace \ˈpal-əs\ *n* **1 a :** the official residence of a sovereign **b** *chiefly British* **:** the official residence of an archbishop or bishop **2 a :** a large stately house **b :** a large public building **c :** a gaudy place for public amusement or refreshment ⟨a movie *palace*⟩ [Old French *palais,* from Latin *palatium,* from *Palatium,* hill in Rome where the emperors' residences were built]

pal•a•din \ˈpal-əd-ən\ *n* **1 :** a knightly hero or champion **2 :** a strong supporter of a cause [French, from Italian *paladino,* from Medieval Latin *palatinus* "courtier", from Latin, "palatine"]

pa•laes•tra \pə-ˈles-trə\ *n, pl* **-trae** \-ˌtrē\ **1 :** a school in ancient Greece or Rome for sports (as wrestling) **2 :** GYMNASIUM 1 [Latin, from Greek *palaistra,* from *palaiein* "to wrestle"]

pal•at•able \ˈpal-ət-ə-bəl\ *adj* **1 :** agreeable to the taste **:** SAVORY **2 :** agreeable to the mind **:** ACCEPTABLE — **pal•at•abil•i•ty** \ˌpal-ət-ə-ˈbil-ət-ē\ *n* — **pal•at•able•ness** \ˈpal-ət-ə-bəl-nəs\ *n* — **pal•at•ably** \-blē\ *adv*

pal•a•tal \ˈpal-ət-l\ *adj* **1 :** of or relating to the palate **2 :** pronounced with the front or blade of the tongue near or touching the hard palate ⟨the \y\ in *yeast* and the \sh\ in *she* are *palatal* sounds⟩ — **palatal** *n* — **pal•a•tal•ly** \-l-ē\ *adv*

pal•a•tal•ize \ˈpal-ət-l-ˌīz\ *vt* **:** to pronounce as or change into a palatal sound — **pal•a•tal•iza•tion** \ˌpal-ət-l-ə-ˈzā-shən\ *n*

pal•ate \ˈpal-ət\ *n* **1 :** the roof of the mouth separating the mouth from the nasal cavity **2 a :** intellectual relish or taste **b :** the sense of taste [Latin *palatum*]

pa•la•tial \pə-ˈlā-shəl\ *adj* **1 :** of, relating to, or being a palace **2 :** suitable to a palace **:** MAGNIFICENT — **pa•la•tial•ly** \-shə-lē\ *adv* — **pa•la•tial•ness** *n*

pa•lat•i•nate \pə-ˈlat-n-ət\ *n* **:** the territory of a palatine

[1]pal•a•tine \ˈpal-ə-ˌtīn\ *adj* **1 a :** of or relating to a palace especially of a Roman or Holy Roman emperor **b :** PALATIAL **2 a :** possessing royal privileges **b :** of or relating to a palatine or a palatinate [Latin *palatinus,* from *palatium* "palace"]

[2]palatine *n* **1 a :** a high officer of an imperial palace **b :** a feudal lord having sovereign power within his domains **2** *cap* **:** a native or inhabitant of the Palatinate

[3]palatine *adj* **:** of, relating to, or lying near the palate

[4]palatine *n* **:** a palatine bone

[1]pa•lav•er \pə-ˈlav-ər, -ˈläv-\ *n* **1 :** a long parley usually between persons of different cultural levels **2 a :** idle talk **b :** misleading or beguiling speech [Portuguese *palavra* "word, speech", from Late Latin *parabola* "parable, speech"]

[2]palaver *vi* **:** to talk at length or idly

[1]pale \ˈpāl\ *adj* **1 a :** lacking color or intensity of color **b :** not vivid in hue or luster; *esp* : low in saturation and high in lightness ⟨a *pale* pink⟩ **c** : not having the warm skin color of a person in good health **2** : not bright or brilliant : DIM ⟨a *pale* moon⟩ [Middle French, from Latin *pallidus* "pallid"] — **pale•ly** \'pāl-lē\ *adv* — **pale•ness** \'pāl-nəs\ *n* — **pal•ish** \'pā-lish\ *adj*

2pale *vb* : to make or become pale

3pale *vt* : to enclose with pales : FENCE [Middle French *paler*, from *pal* "stake", from Latin *palus*]

4pale *n* **1** : a stake or picket of a fence or palisade **2 a** : an enclosed place **b** : a territory within specified bounds or under a particular jurisdiction **3** : limits within which one is protected or privileged ⟨conduct beyond the *pale* of decency⟩

pale- *or* **paleo-** *or* **palae-** *or* **palaeo-** *combining form* **1** : involving or dealing with ancient forms or conditions ⟨*paleo*botany⟩ **2** : early : primitive : archaic ⟨*Paleo*lithic⟩ [Greek *palaios* "ancient", from *palai* "long ago"]

pa•lea \'pā-lē-ə\ *n, pl* **-le•as** *or* **-le•ae** \-lē-,ē\ : the upper bract of the flower of a grass [Latin, "chaff"]

pa•leo•bot•a•ny \,pā-lē-ō-'bät-n-ē, -'bät-nē\ *n* : a branch of botany dealing with fossil plants — **pa•leo•bot•a•nist** \-'bät-n-əst, -'bät-nəst\ *n*

Pa•leo•cene \'pā-lē-ə-,sēn\ *n* : the earliest epoch of the Tertiary; *also* : its system of rocks — **Paleocene** *adj*

pa•le•og•ra•phy \,pā-lē-'äg-rə-fē\ *n* **1 a** : an ancient manner of writing **b** : ancient writings **2** : the study of ancient writings and inscriptions — **pa•le•og•ra•pher** \-fər\ *n* — **pa•leo•graph•ic** \,pā-lē-ə-'graf-ik\ *adj* — **pa•leo•graph•i•cal•ly** \-'graf-i-kə-lē, -klē\ *adv*

pa•leo•lith \'pā-lē-ə-,lith\ *n* : a Paleolithic stone implement

Pa•leo•lith•ic \,pā-lē-ə-'lith-ik\ *adj* : of, relating to, or being the 2d period of the Stone Age which is characterized by rough or crudely chipped stone implements — compare EOLITHIC, NEOLITHIC

pa•le•on•tol•o•gy \,pā-lē-än-'täl-ə-jē\ *n* : a science dealing with the life of past geological periods as known especially from fossil remains [French *paléontologie*, from Greek *palaios* "ancient" + *onta* "existing things", from *ont-*, *ōn*, present participle of *cinai* "to be" + French *-logie* "-logy"] — **pa•le•on•to•log•i•cal** \-,änt-l-'äj-i-kəl\ *or* **pa•le•on•to•log•ic** \-'äj-ik\ *adj* — **pa•le•on•tol•o•gist** \-än-'täl-ə-jəst\ *n*

Pa•le•o•zo•ic \,pā-lē-ə-'zō-ik\ *n* : the 3d of the five eras of geological history which is the period of greatest development of nearly all classes of invertebrates except the insects and in the later epochs of which seed-bearing plants, amphibians, and reptiles first appeared; *also* : the corresponding system of rocks — see GEOLOGIC TIME table — **Paleozoic** *adj*

pal•ette \'pal-ət\ *n* **1** : a thin board or tablet on which a painter mixes pigments **2 a** : the set of colors put on the palette **b** : a particular range, quality, or use of color [French, from Middle French *pale* "spade, shovel", from Latin *pala*]

palette knife *n* : a knife with a flexible steel blade and no cutting edge used to mix or to apply colors

pal•frey \'pȯl-frē\ *n, pl* **palfreys** *archaic* : a saddle horse; *esp* : one suitable for a woman [Old French *palefrei*, from Medieval Latin *palafredus*, from Late Latin *paraveredus* "post-horse for secondary roads", from Greek *para-* "beside, subsidiary" + Latin *veredus* "post-horse", of Gaulish origin]

pal•imp•sest \'pal-əm-,sest, -əmp-\ *n* : writing material (as a parchment) used again after earlier writing has been erased [Latin *palimpsestus*, from Greek *palimpsēstos* "scraped again", from *palin* "back, again" + *psēn* "to scrape"]

pal•in•drome \'pal-ən-,drōm\ *n* : a word, verse, or sentence (as "Able was I ere I saw Elba") or a number (as 1881) that reads the same backward or forward [Greek *palindromos* "running back again", from *palin* "back, again" + *dramein* "to run"]

pal•ing \'pā-ling\ *n* **1** : 4PALE 1, PICKET **2 a** : material for pales **b** : a fence of pales

pal•in•ode \'pal-ə-,nōd\ *n* **1** : an ode or song recanting or retracting something in an earlier poem **2** : a formal retraction [Greek *palinōidia*, from *palin* "back" + *aeidein* "to sing"]

1pal•i•sade \,pal-ə-'sād\ *n* **1 a** : a stout high fence of stakes especially for defense **b** : a long strong stake pointed at the top and set close with others as a defense **2** : a line of steep cliffs **3** : PALISADE LAYER [French *palissade*, derived from Latin *palus* "stake"]

2palisade *vt* : to surround or fortify with palisades

palisade cell *n* : a cell of the palisade layer

palisade layer *n* : a layer of columnar or cylindrical chlorophyll-rich cells just under the upper epidermis of a leaf — called also *palisade parenchyma*; compare SPONGY PARENCHYMA

1pall \'pȯl\ *n* **1** : a chalice cover made of a square piece of stiffened linen **2** : a heavy cloth draped over a coffin **3** : something that covers, darkens, or produces a gloomy effect ⟨a *pall* of smoke⟩ [Old English *pæll* "cloak, mantle", from Latin *pallium*]

2pall *vi* : to become dull or uninteresting : lose the ability to give pleasure [Middle English *pallen*, from *appallen* "to become pale, make pale"]

1pal•la•di•um \pə-'lād-ē-əm\ *n, pl* **-dia** \-ē-ə\ : something that protects or defends : SAFEGUARD [Latin, a statue of Pallas Athene which was held to ensure the safety of Troy, from Greek *palladion*, from *Pallad-*, *Pallas* "Pallas"]

2palladium *n* : a silver-white ductile malleable metallic chemical element that is used especially as a catalyst and in alloys — see ELEMENT table [New Latin, from *Pallad-*, *Pallas*, an asteroid, from Latin, "Pallas, goddess of wisdom", from Greek]

pall•bear•er \'pȯl-,bar-ər, -,ber-\ *n* : a person who carries or escorts the coffin at a funeral

1pal•let \'pal-ət\ *n* **1** : a straw-filled tick or mattress **2** : a small, hard, or temporary bed [Middle English *pailet*, from Middle French *paille* "straw", from Latin *palea* "chaff, straw"]

2pallet *n* **1** : a flat-bladed tool for forming, beating, or rounding clay or glass **2** : PALETTE 1 **3** : a lever or surface in a timepiece that receives an impulse from the escapement wheel and imparts motion to a balance or pendulum [Middle French *palette* "small shovel", from *pale* "spade, shovel", from Latin *pala*]

pal•li•ate \'pal-ē-,āt\ *vt* **1** : to make (as a disease) less intense or severe **2** : to cover by excuses and apologies [Late Latin *palliare* "to cloak, conceal", from Latin *pallium* "cloak"] — **pal•li•a•tion** \,pal-ē-'ā-shən\ *n* — **pal•li•a•tor** \'pal-ē-,āt-ər\ *n*

pal•li•a•tive \'pal-ē-,āt-iv, 'pal-yət-\ *adj* : serving to palliate — **palliative** *n* — **pal•li•a•tive•ly** *adv*

pal•lid \'pal-əd\ *adj* : lacking color : WAN [Latin *pallidus*, from *pallēre* "to be pale"] — **pal•lid•i•ty** \pa-'lid-ət-ē\ *n* — **pal•lid•ly** \'pal-əd-lē\ *adv* — **pal•lid•ness** *n*

pal•li•um \'pal-ē-əm\ *n, pl* **-lia** \-ē-ə\ *or* **-li•mus 1 a** : a draped rectangular cloak worn by men of ancient Greece and Rome **b** : a white woolen band with pendants in front and back worn over the chasuble by a pope or archbishop [Latin]

pal•lor \'pal-ər\ *n* : lack of color especially of the face : PALENESS [Latin, from *pallēre* "to be pale"]

pal•ly \'pal-ē\ *adj* : sharing the relationship of pals : INTIMATE

1palm \'päm, 'pälm\ *n* **1** : any of a family of mostly tropical or subtropical trees, shrubs, or vines usually with a simple but often tall stem topped by a crown of huge feathery or fan-shaped leaves **2 a** : a palm leaf especially when carried as a symbol of victory or rejoicing **b** : a symbol of success; *also* : VICTORY, TRIUMPH [Old English, from Latin *palma*, literally, "palm of the hand"; from the resemblance of the tree's leaves to an outstretched hand] — **palm•like** \-,līk\ *adj*

1palm 1

2palm *n* **1** : the under part of the hand between the fingers and the wrist **2** : a unit of length based on the width or length of the hand [Middle French *paume*, from Latin *palma*]

3palm *vt* **1** : to conceal in or pick up stealthily with the hand ⟨*palm* a card⟩ **2** : to pass off by fraud ⟨trash was *palmed* off on the unwary⟩

pal•mar \'pal-mər, 'päm-ər, 'päl-mər\ *adj* : of, relating to, situated in, or involving the palm of the hand

pal•mate \'pal-,māt, 'päm-,āt, 'päl-,māt\ *adj* : resembling a hand with the fingers spread: **a** : having lobes or veins radiating from a common point ⟨a *palmate* leaf⟩ **b** : having the distal portion broad, flat, and lobed ⟨a *palmate* antler⟩ — **pal•mate-**

\ə\ **abut**	\au̇\ **out**	\i\ **tip**	\ȯ\ **saw**	\u̇\ **foot**
\ər\ **further**	\ch\ **chin**	\ī\ **life**	\ȯi\ **coin**	\y\ **yet**
\a\ **mat**	\e\ **pet**	\j\ **job**	\th\ **thin**	\yü\ **few**
\ā\ **take**	\ē\ **easy**	\ng\ **sing**	\t͟h\ **this**	\yu̇\ **cure**
\ä\ **cot, cart**	\g\ **go**	\ō\ **bone**	\ü\ **food**	\zh\ **vision**

ly *adv*

palm•er \'päm-ər, 'päl-mər\ *n* : a person wearing two crossed palm leaves as a sign of a pilgrimage to the Holy Land

pal•met•to \pal-'met-ō\ *n, pl* **-tos** *or* **-toes** : any of several usually low-growing palms with fan-shaped leaves [Spanish *palmito,* from *palma* "palm", from Latin]

palm•ist•ry \'päm-ə-strē, 'päl-mə-\ *n* : the art or practice of reading a person's character or future from markings on the palms [Middle English *pawmestry,* probably from *paume* "palm" + *maistrie* "mastery"] — **palm•ist** \'päm-əst, 'päl-məst\ *n*

pal•mit•ic acid \pal-,mit-ik-, pä-, päl-\ *n* : a waxy fatty acid occurring free or especially in the form of glycerides in most fats and fatty oils

pal•mi•tin \'pal-mət-ən, 'päm-ət-, 'päl-mət-\ *n* : an ester of glycerol and palmitic acid [French *palmitine,* derived from Latin *palma* "palm"]

palm oil *n* : an edible fat obtained from the fruit of several palms and used especially in soap, candles, and lubricating greases

Palm Sunday *n* : the Sunday before Easter celebrated in commemoration of Christ's triumphal entry into Jerusalem [from the palm branches strewn in Christ's way]

palmy \'päm-ē, 'päl-mē\ *adj* **palm•i•er; -est 1** : abounding in or bearing palms **2** : marked by prosperity : FLOURISHING

pal•o•mi•no \,pal-ə-'mē-nō\ *n, pl* **-nos** : a slender-legged short-bodied horse of a light tan or cream color with lighter mane and tail [American Spanish, from Spanish, "like a dove", from Latin *palumbinus,* from *palumbes,* a kind of pigeon]

palp \'palp\ *n* : PALPUS — **pal•pal** \'pal-pəl\ *adj*

pal•pa•ble \'pal-pə-bəl\ *adj* **1** : that can be touched or felt : TANGIBLE **2** : easily perceptible : NOTICEABLE **3** : easily understood : MANIFEST [Late Latin *palpabilis,* from Latin *palpare* "to stroke"] — **pal•pa•bil•i•ty** \,pal-pə-'bil-ət-ē\ *n* — **pal•pa•bly** \'pal-pə-blē\ *adv*

pal•pate \'pal-,pāt\ *vt* : to examine by touch especially medically [derived from Latin *palpare* "to stroke"] — **pal•pa•tion** \pal-'pā-shən\ *n*

pal•pi•tate \'pal-pə-,tāt\ *vi* : to beat rapidly and strongly : THROB, QUIVER ⟨*palpitating* with excitement⟩ [Latin *palpitare,* derived from *palpare* "to stroke"] — **pal•pi•tant** \'pal-pət-ənt\ *adj* — **pal•pi•ta•tion** \,pal-pə-'tā-shən\ *n*

pal•pus \'pal-pəs\ *n, pl* **pal•pi** \-,pī, -pē\ : a segmented sense organ on an arthropod mouthpart [Latin, "caress, soft palm of the hand"] — **pal•pate** \'pal-,pāt\ *adj*

pal•sy \'pȯl-zē\ *n, pl* **palsies 1** : PARALYSIS 1 **2** : a condition marked by uncontrollable tremor of the body or a part [Middle French *paralisie,* from Latin *paralysis*] — **palsy** *vt*

pal•ter \'pȯl-tər\ *vi* **pal•tered; pal•ter•ing** \-tə-ring, -tring\ **1** : to act insincerely : EQUIVOCATE **2** : HAGGLE 2, BARGAIN [origin unknown] — **pal•ter•er** \-tər-ər\ *n*

pal•try \'pȯl-trē\ *adj* **pal•tri•er; -est 1** : CHEAP 2, SHODDY **2** : contemptibly limited : MEAN, LITTLE ⟨*paltry* minds⟩ **3** : PETTY 2, TRIVIAL [obsolete *paltry* "trash"] — **pal•tri•ness** *n*

pal•y•nol•o•gy \,pal-ə-'näl-ə-jē\ *n* : a branch of science dealing with pollen and spores [Greek *palynein* "to sprinkle", from *pale* "fine meal"] — **pal•y•no•log•i•cal** \-nə-'läj-i-kəl\ *adj* — **pal•y•nol•o•gist** \-'näl-ə-jəst\ *n*

pam•pa \'pam-pə, 'päm-\ *n, pl* **pampas** \-pəz, -pəs\ : an extensive generally grass-covered plain of South America [American Spanish, from Quechua] — **pam•pe•an** \'pam-pē-ən, 'päm-, pam-', päm-'\ *adj*

pam•per \'pam-pər\ *vt* **pam•pered; pam•per•ing** \'pam-pə-ring, -pring\ : to treat with extreme or excessive care and attention [Middle English *pamperen*] — **pam•per•er** \-pər-ər\ *n*

pam•phlet \'pam-flət, 'pamp-\ *n* : an unbound printed publication with no cover or a paper cover [Middle English *pamflet* "unbound booklet", from *Pamphilus, seu De Amore* "Pamphilus, or About Love", popular Latin poem of the 12th century]

△ **origin** *Pamphilus, seu De Amore* ("Pamphilus, or About Love"), written in the late 12th century by an author now unknown, is a poem detailing a series of amusing amorous adventures. This poem was very popular in its day. In the late Middle Ages the names of short literary works were often given diminutive forms. *Pamphilus* became *Pamphilet* (at least in French — the name, although probably used, is not attested in English). And Middle English *pamflet* was soon the word for any written work too short to be called a book.

¹pam•phle•teer \,pam-flə-'tiər, ,pamp-\ *n* : a writer of pamphlets attacking something or urging a cause

²pamphleteer *vi* : to write and publish pamphlets

¹pan \'pan\ *n* **1 a** : a usually broad, shallow, and open container for household use **b** : a broad shallow open vessel: as (1) : either of the receptacles of a pair of scales (2) : a round shallow metal container used to wash waste from metal (as gold) **2** : a basin or depression in the earth ⟨a salt *pan*⟩ **3** : HARDPAN 1 [Old English *panne,* from Latin *patina,* from Greek *patanē*]

²pan *vb* **panned; pan•ning 1** : to wash earthy material in a pan to concentrate bits of native metal; *also* : to separate (metal) from debris by panning **2** : to yield precious metal in panning **3** : to criticize severely

pan- *combining form* **1** : all : completely ⟨*pan*chromatic⟩ **2** : involving all of a (specified) group ⟨*Pan*-American⟩ **3** : total : general ⟨*pan*leucopenia⟩ [Greek, from *pan,* neuter of *pas* "all, every"]

pan•a•cea \,pan-ə-'sē-ə\ *n* : a remedy for all ills or difficulties : CURE-ALL [Latin, from Greek *panakeia,* from *pan-* + *akeisthai* "to heal", from *akos* "remedy"] — **pan•a•ce•an** \-'sē-ən\ *adj*

pa•nache \pə-'nash, -'näsh\ *n* **1** : an ornamental tuft (as of feathers) especially on a helmet **2** : dash or colorfulness in style and action : VERVE [Middle French *pennache,* from Italian *pennachio,* from Latin *pinnaculum* "small wing", from *pinna* "feather, wing", alteration of *penna*]

pan•a•ma \'pan-ə-,mä, -,mȯ\ *n, often cap* : a lightweight hat made of narrow strips from the young leaves of a tropical American tree [American Spanish *panamá,* from *Panama,* Central America]

Pan–Amer•i•can \,pan-ə-'mer-ə-kən\ *adj* : of, relating to, or involving the independent republics of North America and South America

Pan American Day *n* : April 14 observed as the anniversary of the founding of the Pan American Union in 1890

Pan–Amer•i•can•ism \-kə-,niz-əm\ *n* : a movement for greater cooperation among the Pan-American nations especially in defense, commerce, and cultural relations

¹pan•cake \'pan-,kāk\ *n* : a flat cake made of thin batter and cooked on both sides (as on a griddle)

²pancake *vb* : to make or cause to make a pancake landing

pancake landing *n* : a landing in which an airplane is leveled off higher than for a normal landing causing it to stall and drop in an approximately horizontal position with little forward motion

pan•chro•mat•ic \,pan-krō-'mat-ik\ *adj* : sensitive to light of all colors in the visible spectrum ⟨*panchromatic* film⟩

pan•cre•as \'pang-krē-əs, 'pan-\ *n* : a large compound gland of vertebrates that lies near the stomach and secretes digestive enzymes and the hormone insulin [Greek *pankreat-, pankreas,* from *pan-* + *kreas* "flesh, meat"] **pan•cre•at•ic** \,pang-krē-'at-ik, ,pan-\ *adj*

pancreatic duct *n* : the duct leading from the pancreas and opening into the duodenum

pancreatic juice *n* : a clear alkaline secretion of pancreatic enzymes that is poured into the duodenum and acts on food already partly digested by the gastric juice and saliva

pan•da \'pan-də\ *n* **1** : a long-tailed flesh-eating reddish mammal of the Himalayas that resembles a raccoon **2** : a large black-and-white mammal of western China and Tibet that suggests a bear but is related to the raccoon — called also *giant panda* [French, from native name in Nepal]

panda 2

pan•da•nus \pan-'dā-nəs, -'dan-əs\ *n* : SCREW PINE [Malay *pandan*]

pan•dem•ic \pan-'dem-ik\ *n* : an outbreak of disease occurring over a wide area and affecting many people ⟨an influenza *pandemic*⟩ [derived from Greek *pan-* + *dēmos* "people"] — **pandemic** *adj*

pan•de•mo•ni•um \,pan-də-'mō-nē-əm\ *n* : a wild uproar : TUMULT [*Pandemonium,* capital of Hell, from *pan-* + Late Latin *daemonium* "evil spirit", from Greek *daimonion,* from *daimōn* "spirit, deity"]

[1]pan·der \ˈpan-dər\ *n* **1 a :** a go-between in love intrigues **b :** one who solicits clients for a prostitute **2 :** one who caters to or exploits the weaknesses of others [*Pandarus*]

[2]pander *vi* **pan·dered**; **pan·der·ing** \-də-riŋ, -driŋ\ **:** to act as a pander — **pan·der·er** \-dər-ər\ *n*

Pan·do·ra's box \pan-ˌdōr-əz-, -ˌdȯr-\ *n* **:** a source of many usually unforeseen troubles [from the box containing all the ills of mankind opened by the mythical Pandora against the command of Zeus]

pan·dow·dy \pan-ˈdau̇d-ē\ *n, pl* **-dies :** a deep-dish apple dessert spiced, sweetened, and covered with a rich crust [origin unknown]

pane \ˈpān\ *n* **1 a :** a section or side of something (as a facet of a gem) **b :** one of the sections into which a sheet of postage stamps is cut for distribution **2 :** a framed sheet of glass in a window or door [Middle French *pan* "strip of cloth, pane", from Latin *pannus* "cloth, rag"]

pan·e·gy·ric \ˌpan-ə-ˈjir-ik, -ˈjī-rik\ *n* **:** a formal speech or writing eulogizing someone or something; *also* **:** formal or elaborate praise [Latin *panegyricus,* from Greek *panēgyrikos,* from *panēgyris* "for a festival", from *panēgyris* "festival assembly", from *pan-* + *agyris* "assembly"] — **pan·e·gy·ri·cal** \-ˈjir-i-kəl, -ˈjī-ri-\ *adj* — **pan·e·gy·ri·cal·ly** \-kə-lē, -klē\ *adv* — **pan·e·gy·rist** \ˌpan-ə-ˈjir-əst, -ˈjī-rəst\ *n*

[1]pan·el \ˈpan-l\ *n* **1 a :** a schedule containing names of persons summoned as jurors; *also* **:** JURY 1 **b :** a group of persons who discuss a topic before an audience **c :** a group of entertainers or guests engaged as players in a quiz or guessing game on a radio or television program **2 :** a separate or distinct part of a surface: as **a :** a usually rectangular and sunken or raised section of a surface (as of a door, wall, or ceiling) set off by a margin **b :** a unit of construction material (as plywood) made to form part of a surface (as of a wall or an airplane wing) **c :** a vertical section (as a gore) of cloth **d :** a section of a switchboard; *also* **:** a mount for controls (as of an electrical device) **3 :** a thin flat piece of wood on which a picture is painted; *also* **:** a painting on such a surface [Middle English, "piece of cloth, slip of parchment, jury schedule", from Middle French, "piece of cloth", derived from Latin *pannus* "cloth"]

[2]panel *vt* **-eled** *or* **-elled**; **-el·ing** *or* **-el·ling :** to furnish or decorate with panels

panel heating *n* **:** space heating by means of wall, floor, baseboard, or ceiling panels with embedded electric conductors or hot-air or hot-water pipes

pan·el·ing \ˈpan-l-iŋ\ *n* **:** panels joined in a continuous surface; *esp* **:** decorative wood panels so combined

pan·el·ist \ˈpan-l-əst\ *n* **:** a member of a panel for discussion or entertainment

panel truck *n* **:** a small light motortruck with a fully enclosed body

pan·fish \ˈpan-ˌfish\ *n* **:** a small food fish (as a sunfish) usually caught with hook and line and not sold commercially

pang \ˈpaŋ\ *n* **:** a sudden sharp attack or spasm (as of pain or emotional distress) ⟨hunger *pangs*⟩ [origin unknown]

pan·go·lin \ˈpaŋ-gə-lən; pan-ˈgō-lən, paŋ-\ *n* **:** any of several Asian and African mammals having the body covered with large overlapping horny scales [Malay *pĕngguling*]

[1]pan·han·dle \ˈpan-ˌhan-dl\ *n* **:** a narrow projection of a larger territory (as a state)

[2]panhandle *vb* **-dled**; **-dling** \-dliŋ, -dl-iŋ\ **:** to beg for money or food on the street — **pan·han·dler** \-dlər\ *n*

Pan·hel·len·ic \ˌpan-hə-ˈlen-ik\ *adj* **1 :** of or relating to all Greece or all the Greeks **2 :** of or relating to the Greek-letter sororities or fraternities in American colleges and universities or to an association representing them

pan·ic \ˈpan-ik\ *n* **1 :** a sudden overpowering fright; *esp* **:** a sudden unreasoning terror often causing mass flight **2 :** a sudden widespread fright concerning financial affairs that causes hurried selling and a sharp fall in prices **3** *slang* **:** something very funny [*panic, adj.,* from French *panique,* from Greek *panikos,* literally, "of Pan", from *Pan* "Pan"] **syn** see FEAR — **panic** *adj* — **pan·icky** \ˈpan-i-kē\ *adj*

△ **origin** The Greek god Pan is often represented playing the panpipes, which he was believed to have invented. According to the story, Pan was once chasing a nymph named Syrinx. Unable to escape across a river, Syrinx asked the river nymphs for help, and they changed her into a bed of reeds. Pan cut pieces of those reeds and made a panpipe. Pan was also believed to have given a great shout which instilled fear into the giants in their battle against the gods. And in Athens Pan was worshiped because the citizens believed that it was he who had caused the Persians to flee in fear from the battle of Marathon. From this more awesome aspect of Pan's nature comes the word *panic.*

[2]panic *vb* **pan·icked** \-ikt\; **pan·ick·ing 1 :** to affect or be affected with panic **2 :** to produce demonstrative appreciation on the part of ⟨*panic* an audience with a gag⟩

pan·i·cle \ˈpan-i-kəl\ *n* **:** a branched flower cluster (as of a lilac or some grasses) in which each branch from the main axis bears more than one flower [Latin *panicula,* from *panus* "swelling"] — **pan·i·cled** \-kəld\ *adj* — **pa·nic·u·late** \pa-ˈnik-yə-lət\ *adj*

panicle

pan·ic–strick·en \ˈpan-ik-ˌstrik-ən\ *adj* **:** overcome with panic

Pan·ja·bi \ˌpən-ˈjäb-ē, -ˈjab-\ *n* **1 :** an Indic language of the Punjab region of the Indian subcontinent **2 :** PUNJABI 1 [Hindi *pañjābī,* from *pañjābī* "of Punjab"]

pan·jan·drum \pan-ˈjan-drəm\ *n* **:** a powerful personage or pretentious official [Grand *panjandrum,* title of an imaginary personage in nonsense lines by Samuel Foote, died 1777, English playwright]

pan·leu·co·pe·nia \ˌpan-ˌlü-kə-ˈpē-nē-ə\ *n* **:** an acute usually fatal viral disease of cats characterized by fever, diarrhea and dehydration, and extensive destruction of white blood cells

pan·nier \ˈpan-yər, ˈpan-ē-ər\ *n* **1 :** a large basket; *esp* **:** one of wicker carried on the back of an animal or the shoulder of a person **2 a :** either of a pair of hoops formerly used by women to expand their skirts at the hips **b :** an overskirt draped and puffed out at the sides [Middle French *panier,* from Latin *panarium,* from *panis* "bread"]

pan·ni·kin \ˈpan-i-kən\ *n, chiefly British* **:** a small pan or cup

pan·o·ply \ˈpan-ə-plē\ *n, pl* **-plies 1 a :** a full suit of armor **b :** ceremonial attire **2 :** something that covers or hides protectively **3 :** a magnificently impressive array or display [Greek *panoplia,* from *pan-* + *hopla* "arms, armor"] — **pan·o·plied** \-plēd\ *adj*

pan·ora·ma \ˌpan-ə-ˈram-ə, -ˈräm-\ *n* **1 a :** CYCLORAMA **b :** a picture exhibited a part at a time by being unrolled before the spectator **2 a :** a full and unobstructed view in every direction **b :** a comprehensive presentation of a subject **3 :** a mental picture of a series of images or events [*pan-* + Greek *horama* "sight", from *horan* "to see"] — **pan·oram·ic** \-ˈram-ik\ *adj*

pan out *vi* **:** to turn out; *esp* **:** SUCCEED [[2]*pan*]

pan·pipe \ˈpan-ˌpīp\ *n* **:** a primitive wind instrument consisting of a graduated series of short vertical pipes bound together with the mouthpieces in an even row — often used in pl. [*Pan,* its traditional inventor — see PANIC *origin*]

pan·sy \ˈpan-zē\ *n, pl* **pansies :** a garden plant originated by hybridization of various violets and violas; *also* **:** its showy velvety 5-petaled flower [Middle French *pensée,* from *pensée* "thought", from *penser* "to think", from Latin *pensare* "to ponder"]

[1]pant \ˈpant\ *vb* **1 a :** to take short rapid breaths **b :** to make a puffing sound **c :** to progress with panting ⟨the car *panted* up the hill⟩ **2 :** to long eagerly **:** YEARN **3 :** to utter with panting ⟨ran up and *panted* out the message⟩ [Middle English *panten,* from Middle French *pantaisier,* from Greek *phantasioun* "to have hallucinations", from *phantasia* "imagination"]

[2]pant *n* **1 :** a panting breath **2 :** a puffing sound

pan·ta·lets *or* **pan·ta·lettes** \ˌpant-l-ˈets\ *n pl* **:** long drawers with a ruffle at the bottom of each leg

pan·ta·loons \ˌpant-l-ˈünz\ *n pl* **:** close-fitting trousers usually with straps passing under the insteps [Italian *Pantaleone, Pantalone,* character in old Italian comedies]

pan·the·ism \ˈpan-thē-ˌiz-əm, ˈpant-\ *n* **:** a doctrine that

\ə\ **abut**	\au̇\ **out**	\i\ **tip**	\ȯ\ **saw**	\u̇\ **foot**
\ər\ **further**	\ch\ **chin**	\ī\ **life**	\ȯi\ **coin**	\y\ **yet**
\a\ **mat**	\e\ **pet**	\j\ **job**	\th\ **thin**	\yü\ **few**
\ā\ **take**	\ē\ **easy**	\ŋ\ **sing**	\t͟h\ **this**	\yu̇\ **cure**
\ä\ **cot, cart**	\g\ **go**	\ō\ **bone**	\ü\ **food**	\zh\ **vision**

equates God with the forces and laws of the universe — **pan·the·ist** \-thē-əst\ *n* — **pan·the·is·tic** \ˌpan-thē-ˈis-tik, ˌpant-\ *adj* — **pan·the·is·ti·cal** \-ti-kəl\ *adj* — **pan·the·is·ti·cal·ly** \-kə-lē, -klē\ *adv*

pan·the·on \ˈpan-thē-ˌän, ˈpant-\ *n* **1** : a temple dedicated to all the gods **2** : a building serving as the burial place of or containing memorials to famous dead **3** : the gods of a people; *esp* : the gods officially recognized [Latin, from Greek *pantheion,* from *pan-* + *theos* "god"]

pan·ther \ˈpan-thər, ˈpant-\ *n, pl* **panthers** *also* **panther 1**: LEOPARD **2** : COUGAR **3** : JAGUAR [Old French *pantere,* from Latin *panthera,* from Greek *panthēr*]

pant·ies \ˈpant-ēz\ *n pl* : a woman's or child's undergarment covering the lower trunk

pan·to·graph \ˈpant-ə-ˌgraf\ *n* : an instrument for manually copying a figure (as a map or plan) to scale [French *pantographe,* from Greek *pant-, pas* "all" + French *-graphe* "-graph"] — **pan·to·graph·ic** \ˌpant-ə-ˈgraf-ik\ *adj*

pan·to·mime \ˈpant-ə-ˌmīm\ *n* **1** : PANTOMIMIST **2** : a dramatic or dancing performance in which a story is told primarily by expressive bodily or facial movements of the performers **3** : conveyance of information by bodily or facial movements [Latin *pantomimus,* from Greek *pant-, pas* "all" + Latin *mimus* "mime"] — **pantomime** *vb* — **pan·to·mim·ic** \ˌpant-ə-ˈmim-ik\ *adj*

pan·to·mim·ist \ˈpant-ə-ˌmim-əst, -ˌmīm-\ *n* : an actor or dancer in or a composer of pantomimes

pan·to·then·ic acid \ˌpant-ə-ˌthen-ik-\ *n* : a viscous oily acid of the vitamin B complex found in all living tissues and necessary for growth [Greek *pantothen* "from all sides", from *pant-, pas* "all"]

pan·trop·ic \pan-ˈträp-ik, ˈpan-\ *or* **pan·trop·i·cal** \-ˈträp-i-kəl\ *adj* : occurring or growing throughout the tropics

pan·try \ˈpan-trē\ *n, pl* **pantries** : a small room in which food and dishes are kept or from which food is brought to the table [Middle French *paneterie,* from *panetier* "servant in charge of the pantry", from *pan* "bread", from Latin *panis*]

pants \ˈpans\ *n pl* **1** : an outer garment extending from the waist to the ankle and covering each leg separately **2** : UNDERPANTS; *esp* : PANTIES [short for *pantaloons*]

panty hose *n pl* : a one-piece undergarment for women that consists of hosiery combined with panties

panty·waist \ˈpant-ē-ˌwāst\ *n* **1** : a child's garment consisting of short pants buttoned to a waist **2** : SISSY

pan·zer \ˈpan-zər, ˈpänt-sər\ *adj* : of or relating to a panzer division or similar armored unit [German *panzer* "coat of mail, armor", from Old French *panciere,* from *pance* "belly, paunch", from Latin *pantex*]

panzer division *n* : a German armored division

¹pap \ˈpap\ *n* **1** *chiefly dialect* : NIPPLE 1, TEAT **2** : something shaped like a nipple [Middle English *pappe*]

²pap *n* : soft or bland food for infants or invalids [Middle English]

pa·pa \ˈpäp-ə\ *n* : FATHER 1a [French (baby talk)]

pa·pa·cy \ˈpā-pə-sē\ *n, pl* **-cies 1** : the office of pope **2** : a line of popes **3** : the term of a pope's reign **4** *cap* : the government of the Roman Catholic Church [Medieval Latin *papatia,* from Late Latin *papa* "pope"]

pa·pa·in \pə-ˈpā-ən, -ˈpī-ən\ *n* : a proteinase in papaya juice used especially as a meat tenderizer and in medicine

pa·pal \ˈpā-pəl\ *adj* : of or relating to the pope or the papacy [Middle French, from Medieval Latin *papalis,* from Late Latin *papa* "pope"] — **pa·pal·ly** \-pə-lē\ *adv*

pa·paw *or* **paw·paw** *n* **1** \pə-ˈpȯ\ : PAPAYA **2** \ˈpäp-ȯ, ˈpȯp-\ : a North American tree of the custard-apple family with purple flowers and a yellow edible fruit; *also* : its fruit [probably from Spanish *papaya*]

pa·pa·ya \pə-ˈpī-ə\ *n* : a tropical American tree with large lobed leaves and oblong yellow black-seeded edible fruit; *also* : its fruit [Spanish, of American Indian origin]

¹pa·per \ˈpā-pər\ *n* **1 a** : a felted sheet of usually vegetable fibers laid down on a fine screen from a water suspension **b** : a sheet or piece of paper **2 a** : a piece of paper containing a written or printed statement; *esp* : a document of identification or authorization **b** : a written composition (as a piece of schoolwork) **3** : a paper container or wrapper **4** : NEWSPAPER **5** : WALLPAPER [Middle French *papier,* from Latin *papyrus* "papyrus, paper"]

²paper *vb* **pa·pered**; **pa·per·ing** \ˈpā-pə-ring, -pring\ **1** : to cover or line with paper; *esp* : to apply wallpaper to **2** : to hang wallpaper — **pa·per·er** \-pər-ər\ *n*

³paper *adj* **1 a** : of, relating to, or made of paper or a related composition **b** : resembling paper : PAPERY **2** : NOMINAL 3a ⟨a *paper* blockade⟩

pa·per·back \ˈpā-pər-ˌbak\ *n* : a book with a flexible paper binding — **paperback** *adj*

pa·per·board \-ˌbōrd, -ˌbȯrd\ *n* : a material made from cellulose fiber (as wood pulp) like paper but usually thicker : CARDBOARD

paper boy *n* : NEWSBOY

paper cutter *n* : a machine or device for cutting or trimming sheets of paper

pa·per·hang·er \-ˌhang-ər\ *n* : one that applies wallpaper — **pa·per·hang·ing** \-ˌhang-ing\ *n*

paper money *n* : money consisting of government notes and bank notes

paper mulberry *n* : an Asian tree of the mulberry family widely grown as a shade tree

paper nautilus *n* : an 8-armed mollusk related to the octopus that in the female has two of the arms expanded at the tips to clasp the thin fragile shell — called also *nautilus*

paper profit *n* : a profit that can be realized only by selling something that has gone up in value

pa·per·weight \ˈpā-pər-ˌwāt\ *n* : an object used to hold down loose papers by its weight

paper work *n* : routine clerical or record-keeping work often incidental to a more important task

pa·pery \ˈpā-pə-rē, -prē\ *adj* : resembling paper in thinness or consistency — **pa·per·i·ness** *n*

pa·pier-mâ·ché \ˌpā-pər-mə-ˈshā, ˌpap-ˌyā-mə-, -ma-\ *n* : a light strong molding material of wastepaper pulped with glue and other additives [French, literally, "chewed paper"] — **papier-mâché** *adj*

pa·pil·la \pə-ˈpil-ə\ *n, pl* **-pil·lae** \-ˈpil-ē, -ˌī\ : a small projecting bodily structure (as one of those on the surface of the tongue) that suggests a nipple [Latin, "nipple"] — **pap·il·la·ry** \ˈpap-ə-ˌler-ē, pə-ˈpil-ə-rē\ *adj* — **pap·il·late** \ˈpap-ə-ˌlāt, pə-ˈpil-ət\ *adj*

pap·il·lo·ma \ˌpap-ə-ˈlō-mə\ *n, pl* **-mas** *or* **-ma·ta** \-mət-ə\ : a usually benign epithelial tumor

pa·pist \ˈpā-pəst\ *n, often cap* : ROMAN CATHOLIC — usually used disparagingly [Middle French *papiste,* from *pape* "pope", from Late Latin *papa*] — **papist** *adj* — **pa·pist·ry** \-pə-strē\ *n*

pa·poose \pa-ˈpüs, pə-\ *n* : a North American Indian infant [of American Indian origin]

pap·pus \ˈpap-əs\ *n, pl* **pap·pi** \ˈpap-ˌī, -ē\ : a downy or bristly appendage or tuft of appendages crowning the seed or fruit of some seed plants and functioning in its dispersal [Latin, from Greek *pappos*]

pa·pri·ka \pə-ˈprē-kə, pa-\ *n* : a mild red seasoning consisting of the dried finely ground pods of various cultivated sweet peppers; *also* : a sweet pepper used for making paprika [Hungarian, from Serbian, from *papar* "pepper", from Greek *peperi*]

Pap smear \ˈpap-\ *also* **Pap test** *n* : a method for the early detection of cancer using a special cell-staining technique to identify diseased tissue [George N. *Papanicolaou,* died 1962, American medical scientist]

pa·py·rus \pə-ˈpī-rəs\ *n, pl* **-rus·es** *or* **-ri** \-rē, -ˌrī\ **1** : a tall sedge of the Nile valley **2** : the pith of the papyrus plant especially when cut in strips and pressed to make a material to write on **3** : a writing on or written scroll of papyrus [Latin, from Greek *papyros*]

par \ˈpär\ *n* **1 a** : the established value of the monetary unit of one country expressed in terms of the monetary unit of another country using the same metal as the standard of value **b** : the face value of a security ⟨stocks that sell near *par*⟩ **2** : common level : EQUALITY ⟨their abilities are about on a *par*⟩ **3** : an accepted standard (as of health) ⟨not feeling up to *par*⟩ **4** : the score standard set for each hole of a golf course [Latin, "one that is equal", from *par* "equal"] — **par** *adj*

¹para- \ˌpar-ə, ˈpar-ə\ *or* **par-** *prefix* **1 a** : beside : alongside ⟨*para*thyroid⟩ **b** : beyond : outside of **2 a** : closely related to or resembling ⟨*para*typhoid⟩ **b** : associated in a subsidiary or accessory capacity ⟨*para*professional⟩ **3** : faulty : abnormal [Greek, from *para*]

²para- \ˈpar-ə\ *combining form* : parachute ⟨*para*troops⟩ [*parachute*]

para-ami•no•ben•zo•ic acid \ˌpar-ə-ə-ˌmē-ˌnō-ˌben-ˌzō-ik-, ˈpar-ə-ˌam-ə-ˌnō-\ *n* : a colorless organic acid that is a derivative of benzoic acid and is a growth factor of the vitamin B complex

par•a•ble \ˈpar-ə-bəl\ *n* : a short simple story illustrating a moral or spiritual truth [Middle French, from Late Latin *parabola,* from Greek *parabolē,* from *paraballein* to compare", from *para-* + *ballein* "to throw"]

pa•rab•o•la \pə-ˈrab-ə-lə\ *n* **1** : the curve formed by the intersection of a cone with a plane parallel to a straight line in its surface : a plane curve generated by a point moving so that its distance from a fixed point is equal to its distance from a fixed line **2** : something bowl-shaped [Greek *parabolē* "comparison, parable, parabola"] — **par•a•bol•ic** \ˌpar-ə-ˈbäl-ik\ *adj* — **par•a•bol•i•cal•ly** \-ˈbäl-i-kə-lē, -klē\ *adv*

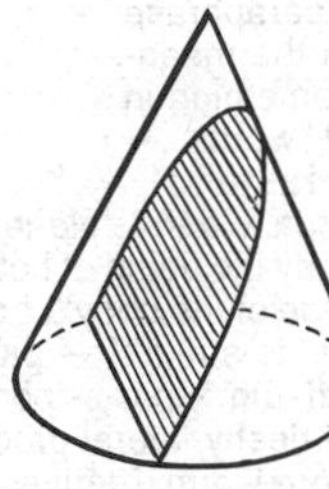

parabola 1

[1]para•chute \ˈpar-ə-ˌshüt\ *n* **1** : a folding umbrella-shaped device of light fabric used especially for making a safe descent after jumping from an airplane **2** : something (as the tuft of hairs on a dandelion seed) suggestive of a parachute in form, use, or operation [French, from *para-* (as in *parasol*) + *chute* "fall"]

[2]parachute *vb* : to convey or descend by means of a parachute

para•chut•ist \ˈpar-ə-ˌshüt-əst\ *n* : one that descends by parachute

Par•a•clete \ˈpar-ə-ˌklēt\ *n* : HOLY SPIRIT [Middle French *Paraclet,* from Late Latin *Paracletus,* from Greek *Paraklētos,* literally, "advocate, intercessor", from *parakalein* "to invoke", from *para-* + *kalein* "to call"]

[1]pa•rade \pə-ˈrād\ *n* **1** : pompous show or display **2** : a ceremonial formation of a body of troops before a superior officer **3** : a public procession (as of military units and bands) **4** : a place of promenade; *also* : those who promenade [French, from *parer* "to prepare", from Latin *parare*]

[2]parade *vb* **1 a** : to cause to maneuver or march **b** : to march in a procession **2** : PROMENADE **3** : to exhibit ostentatiously : show off — **pa•rad•er** *n*

para•di•chlo•ro•ben•zene \ˌpar-ə-ˌdī-ˌklōr-ə-ˈben-ˌzēn, -ˌklȯr-, -ˌben-ˈ\ *n* : a white crystalline chlorinated benzene used chiefly in mothballs

par•a•digm \ˈpar-ə-ˌdīm, -ˌdim\ *n* **1** : MODEL, PATTERN ⟨an essay that is a *paradigm* of clear writing⟩ **2** : an example of a conjugation or declension showing a word in all its inflectional forms [Late Latin *paradigma,* from Greek *paradeigma,* from *paradeiknynai* "to show side by side", from *para-* + *deiknynai* "to show"] — **par•a•dig•mat•ic** \ˌpar-ə-dig-ˈmat-ik\ *adj*

par•a•dise \ˈpar-ə-ˌdīs, -ˌdīz\ *n* **1** : the garden of Eden **2** : HEAVEN 2a **3** : a place or state of bliss [Old French *paradis,* from Late Latin *paradisus,* from Greek *paradeisos,* literally, "enclosed park", of Iranian origin]

par•a•di•si•a•cal \ˌpar-ə-də-ˈsī-ə-kəl, -ˌdī-, -ˈzī-\ *or* **par•a•dis•i•ac** \-ˈdiz-ē-ˌ-ak\ *adj* : of, relating to, or resembling paradise [Late Latin *paradisiacus,* from *paradisus* "paradise"] — **par•a•di•si•a•cal•ly** \-də-ˈsī-ə-kə-lē, -klē\ *adv*

par•a•dox \ˈpar-ə-ˌdäks\ *n* **1 a** : a statement that seems to contradict common sense and yet is perhaps true **b** : a self-contradictory statement that at first seems true **2** : something (as a person, condition, or act) with seemingly contradictory qualities or phases [Latin *paradoxum,* from Greek *paradoxon,* from *paradoxos* "contrary to expectation", from *para-* + *dokein* "to think"] — **par•a•dox•i•cal** \ˌpar-ə-ˈdäk-si-kəl\ *adj* — **par•a•dox•i•cal•ly** \-kə-lē, -klē\ *adv* — **par•a•dox•i•cal•ness** \-kəl-nəs\ *n*

[1]par•af•fin \ˈpar-ə-fən\ *n* **1** : a flammable waxy crystalline mixture of hydrocarbons obtained especially from distillates of wood, coal, or petroleum and used chiefly in coating and sealing, in candles, and in drugs and cosmetics **2** : a hydrocarbon of the methane series **3** *chiefly British* : KEROSENE [German, from Latin *parum* "too little" + *affinis* "bordering on, associated with"; from the small affinity it has for other bodies] — **par•af•fin•ic** \ˌpar-ə-ˈfin-ik\ *adj*

[2]paraffin *vt* : to coat or saturate with paraffin

par•a•gon \ˈpar-ə-ˌgän, -gən\ *n* : a model of excellence or perfection [Middle French, from Italian *paragone,* literally, "touchstone", from *paragonare* "to test on a touchstone", from Greek *parakonan* "to sharpen", from *para-* + *akonē* "whetstone", from *akē* "point"]

[1]para•graph \ˈpar-ə-ˌgraf\ *n* **1 a** : a subdivision of a piece of writing or a speech that consists of one or more sentences and develops in an organized manner one point of a subject or gives the words of one speaker **b** : a short written article (as in a newspaper) that is complete in one undivided section **2** : a character ¶ used as a reference mark or to indicate the beginning of a paragraph [Medieval Latin *paragraphus* "sign marking a paragraph", from Greek *paragraphos* "marginal sign used to mark change of speakers in a dialogue", from *para-* + *graphein* "to write"] — **para•graph•ic** \ˌpar-ə-ˈgraf-ik\ *adj*

[2]paragraph *vb* **1** : to divide into paragraphs **2** : to write paragraphs

para•graph•er \ˈpar-ə-ˌgraf-ər\ *n* : a writer of paragraphs especially for the editorial page of a newspaper

par•a•keet *or* **par•ra•keet** \ˈpar-ə-ˌkēt\ *n* : any of numerous small slender parrots with a long pointed tail [Spanish *periquito,* from Middle French *perroquet* "parrot"]

par•al•de•hyde \pa-ˈral-də-ˌhīd, pə-\ *n* : a liquid derivative of acetaldehyde used as a hypnotic

Par•a•li•pom•e•non \ˌpar-ə-lə-ˈpäm-ə-ˌnän, -lī-\ *n* — see BIBLE table [Late Latin, from Greek *Paraleipomenōn,* genitive of *Paraleipomena,* literally, "things left out", from *paraleipein* "to leave out", from *para-* + *leipein* "to leave"; from its forming a supplement to Samuel and Kings]

par•al•lax \ˈpar-ə-ˌlaks\ *n* : the apparent displacement or the difference in apparent direction of an object as seen from two different points not on a straight line with the object; *esp* : the difference in direction of a celestial body as measured from two points on the earth or from opposite points on the earth's orbit [Middle French *parallaxe,* from Greek *parallaxis,* from *parallassein* "to change", from *para-* + *allassein* "to change", from *allos* "other"] — **par•al•lac•tic** \ˌpar-ə-ˈlak-tik\ *adj*

[1]par•al•lel \ˈpar-ə-ˌlel\ *adj* **1 a** : extending in the same direction, everywhere equidistant, and not meeting ⟨*parallel* rows of trees⟩ **b** : everywhere equally distant ⟨concentric spheres are *parallel*⟩ **2 a** : marked by likeness or correspondence : SIMILAR, ANALOGOUS ⟨*parallel* situations⟩ **b** : having corresponding syntactical elements ⟨*parallel* clauses⟩ [Latin *parallelus,* from Greek *parallēlos,* from *para* "beside" + *allēlōn* "of one another", from *allos* "other"] **syn** see SIMILAR

[2]parallel *n* **1 a** : a parallel line, curve, or surface **b** (1) : one of the imaginary circles on the surface of the earth paralleling the equator and marking the latitude (2) : the corresponding line on a globe or map **c** : a character ‖ used as a reference mark **2 a** : something equal or similar in all essential particulars : COUNTERPART **b** : SIMILARITY 2, ANALOGUE **3** : a tracing of similarity ⟨draw a *parallel* between two eras⟩ **4 a** : the state of being physically parallel : PARALLELISM **b** : the arrangement of electrical devices in which all positive poles, electrodes, and terminals are joined to one conductor and all negative ones to another

[3]parallel *vt* **1** : to indicate similarity or analogy of : COMPARE **2 a** : to show something equal to : MATCH **b** : to correspond to **3** : to place so as to be parallel in direction with something **4** : to extend, run, or move in a direction parallel to ⟨the highway *parallels* the river⟩

[4]parallel *adv* : in a parallel manner — often used with *with* or *to*

parallel bars *n pl* : a pair of bars that are parallel to each other on an adjustable support and are used for swinging and balancing exercises in gymnastics

par•al•lel•epi•ped \ˌpar-ə-ˌlel-ə-ˈpī-pəd, -ˈpip-əd\ *n* : a 6-faced polyhedron all of whose faces are parallelograms lying in pairs of parallel planes [Greek *parallēlepipedon,* from *parallēlos* "parallel" + *epipedon* "plane surface", from *epipedos* "flat", from *epi-* + *pedon* "ground"]

parallel evolution *n* : CONVERGENT EVOLUTION

par•al•lel•ism \ˈpar-ə-ˌlel-ˌiz-əm\ *n* **1** : the quality or state of

\ə\ **abut**	\au̇\ **out**	\i\ **tip**	\ȯ\ **saw**	\u̇\ **foot**
\ər\ **further**	\ch\ **chin**	\ī\ **life**	\ȯi\ **coin**	\y\ **yet**
\a\ **mat**	\e\ **pet**	\j\ **job**	\th\ **thin**	\yü\ **few**
\ā\ **take**	\ē\ **easy**	\ng\ **sing**	\t͟h\ **this**	\yu̇\ **cure**
\ä\ **cot, cart**	\g\ **go**	\ō\ **bone**	\ü\ **food**	\zh\ **vision**

being parallel **2 :** RESEMBLANCE 1, CORRESPONDENCE **3 :** similarity of syntactical construction of adjacent word groups especially for rhetorical effect or rhythm

par•al•lel•o•gram \ˌpar-ə-ˈlel-ə-ˌgram\ *n* **:** a quadrilateral whose opposite sides are parallel and equal [Greek *parallēlogrammon,* derived from *parallēlos* "parallel" + *grammē* "line", from *graphein* "to write"]

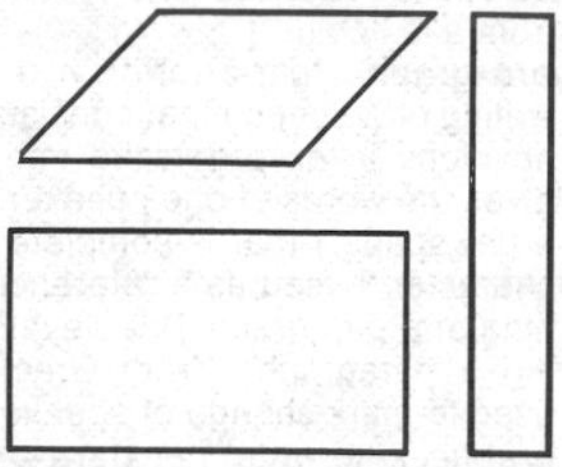
parallelogram

par•al•lel–veined \ˌpar-ə-ˌlel-ˈvānd, -ləl-\ *adj* **:** having linear veins that do not branch and interlace ⟨monocotyledons have *parallel-veined* leaves⟩ — compare NET-VEINED

pa•ral•y•sis \pə-ˈral-ə-səs\ *n, pl* **-y•ses** \-ə-ˌsēz\ **1 :** complete or partial loss of function especially when involving motion or sensation in a part of the body **2 :** loss of the ability to move or act ⟨*paralysis* of highway traffic⟩ [Latin, from Greek, from *paralyein* "to loosen, disable", from *para-* + *lyein* "to loosen"] — **par•a•lyt•ic** \ˌpar-ə-ˈlit-ik\ *adj or n*

par•a•lyze \ˈpar-ə-ˌlīz\ *vt* **1 :** to affect with paralysis **2 :** to make powerless, ineffective, or unable to act or function ⟨a labor dispute that *paralyzed* the industry⟩ [French *paralyser,* back-formation from *paralysie* "paralysis", from Latin *paralysis*] — **par•a•ly•za•tion** \ˌpar-ə-lə-ˈzā-shən\ *n*

para•mag•net•ic \ˌpar-ə-mag-ˈnet-ik\ *adj* **:** being or relating to a slightly magnetizable substance (as aluminum) — **para•mag•ne•tism** \-ˈmag-nə-ˌtiz-əm\ *n*

par•a•me•cium \ˌpar-ə-ˈmē-sē-əm, -shē-əm, -shəm\ *n, pl* **-cia** \-sē-ə, -shē-ə, -shə\ *also* **-ciums :** any of a genus of somewhat slipper-shaped protozoans that move by cilia [Greek *paramēkēs* "oblong", from *para-* + *mēkos* "length"]

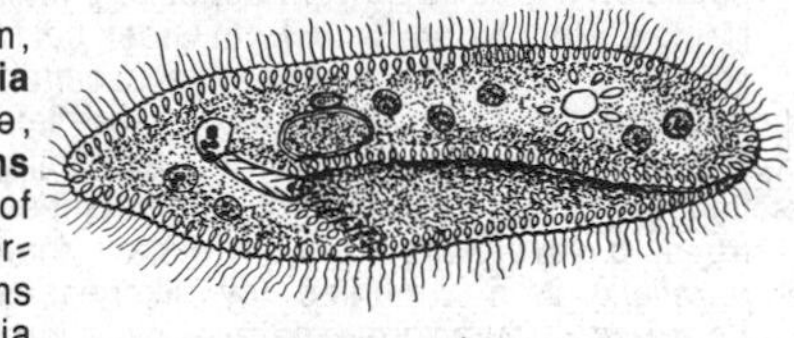
paramecium

para•med•ic \ˈpar-ə-ˌmed-ik\ *n* **:** one who assists a physician (as by giving injections and taking X rays)

pa•ram•e•ter \pə-ˈram-ət-ər\ *n* **1 :** an arbitrary constant each of whose values characterizes a member of a system (as a family of curves) **2 :** any set of physical properties whose values determine the characteristics or behavior of something **3 :** a characteristic element **:** CHARACTERISTIC, FACTOR ⟨political dissent as a *parameter* of modern life⟩ [*para-* + Greek *metron* "measure"] — **para•met•ric** \ˌpar-ə-ˈme-trik\ *adj*

par•a•mount \ˈpar-ə-ˌmau̇nt\ *adj* **:** superior to all others **:** SUPREME [Anglo-French *paramont,* from Old French *par* "by" (from Latin *per*) + *amont* "above", from *a* "to" (from Latin *ad*) + *mont* "mountain"]

par•amour \ˈpar-ə-ˌmu̇r\ *n* **:** an illicit lover [Old French *par amour* "by way of love"]

par•a•noia \ˌpar-ə-ˈnȯi-ə\ *n* **1 :** a serious mental disorder marked by feelings of persecution or distorted ideas of one's own importance usually without hallucinations **2 :** a tendency toward excessive or unreasonable feelings of suspicion or distrust of others [Greek, "madness", from *paranous* "demented", from *para-* + *nous* "mind"] — **par•a•noi•ac** \-ˈnȯi-ˌak, -ˈnȯi-ik\ *adj or n*

par•a•noid \ˈpar-ə-ˌnȯid\ *adj* **1 :** resembling paranoia **2 :** characterized by suspiciousness, feelings of persecution, or an exaggerated sense of one's own importance — **paranoid** *n*

par•a•pet \ˈpar-ə-pət, -ˌpet\ *n* **1 :** a wall of earth or stone to protect soldiers **2 :** a low wall or railing to protect the edge of a platform, roof, or bridge [Italian *parapetto,* from *parare* "to shield" (from Latin, "to prepare") + *petto* "breast, chest", from Latin *pectus*]

par•a•pher•na•lia \ˌpar-ə-fər-ˈnāl-yə, -fə-ˈnāl-\ *n sing or pl* **1 :** personal belongings **2 :** articles of equipment [Medieval Latin, derived from Greek *parapherna* "goods a bride brings over and above the dowry", from *para-* + *phernē* "dowry", from *pherein* "to bear"]

[1]**para•phrase** \ˈpar-ə-ˌfrāz\ *n* **:** a restatement of a text, passage, or work giving the meaning in another form

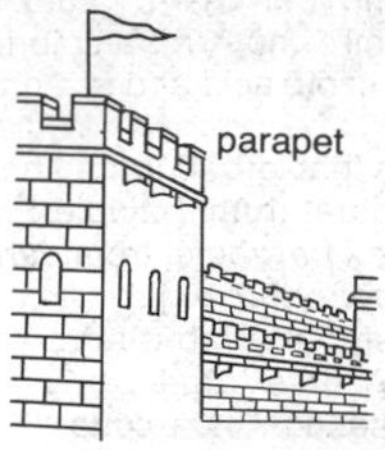

parapet 1

[2]**paraphrase** *vb* **:** to make a paraphrase of **:** give the meaning of something in different words — **para•phras•er** *n*

para•ple•gia \ˌpar-ə-ˈplē-jə, -jē-ə\ *n* **:** paralysis of the lower half of the body including of both legs [Greek *paraplēgiē* "paralysis of one side of the body", from *para-* + *-plēgia* "paralysis", from *plēssein* "to strike"] — **para•ple•gic** \-jik\ *adj or n*

para•po•di•um \ˌpar-ə-ˈpōd-ē-əm\ *n, pl* **-dia** \-ē-ə\ **:** either of a pair of fleshy lateral processes borne by most segments of a polychaete worm [derived from Greek *para-* + *podion* "small foot", from *pod-, pous* "foot"]

para•pro•fes•sion•al \-prə-ˈfesh-nəl, -ən-l\ *n* **:** a trained aide who assists a professional person

para•psy•chol•o•gy \ˌpar-ə-sī-ˈkäl-ə-jē\ *n* **:** a branch of study involving the investigation of telepathy, clairvoyance, and related psychological phenomena

par•a•site \ˈpar-ə-ˌsīt\ *n* **1 :** a person who lives at the expense of another **2 :** an organism living in or on another organism in parasitism **3 :** something that resembles a biological parasite in dependence on something else for existence or support without making a useful or adequate return [Middle French, "one habitually dining at the tables of others, sycophant", from Latin *parasitus,* from Greek *parasitos,* from *para-* + *sitos* "grain, food"] — **par•a•sit•ic** \ˌpar-ə-ˈsit-ik\ *also* **par•a•sit•i•cal** \-ˈsit-i-kəl\ *adj* — **par•a•sit•i•cal•ly** \-i-kə-lē, -klē\ *adv*

par•a•sit•ism \ˈpar-ə-ˌsīt-ˌiz-əm\ *n* **:** an intimate association between organisms of two or more kinds in which a parasite obtains benefits from a host which it usually injures

par•a•sit•ize \ˈpar-ə-sə-ˌtīz, -ˌsīt-ˌīz\ *vt* **:** to infest or live on or with as a parasite

par•a•si•tol•o•gy \ˌpar-ə-sə-ˈtäl-ə-jē, -ˌsīt-ˈäl-\ *n* **:** a branch of biology dealing with parasites and parasitism especially among animals — **par•a•si•tol•o•gist** \-jəst\ *n*

para•sol \ˈpar-ə-ˌsȯl\ *n* **:** a lightweight umbrella used as a protection against the sun [French, from Italian *parasole,* from *parare* "to shield" (from Latin, "to prepare") + *sole* "sun", from Latin *sol*]

para•sym•pa•thet•ic \ˌpar-ə-ˌsim-pə-ˈthet-ik\ *adj* **:** of, relating to, being, or acting on the parasympathetic nervous system — **parasympathetic** *n*

parasympathetic nervous system *n* **:** the part of the autonomic nervous system that tends to induce secretion, increase the tone of smooth muscle, and cause the dilatation of blood vessels — compare SYMPATHETIC NERVOUS SYSTEM

para•thi•on \ˌpar-ə-ˈthī-ən, -ˌän\ *n* **:** an extremely toxic insecticide that is a derivative of a sulfur-containing phosphoric acid [derived from *para-* + *thi-*]

par•a•thor•mone \ˌpar-ə-ˈthȯr-ˌmōn\ *n* **:** a hormone produced by the parathyroid glands and concerned with control of the use of calcium in the body

para•thy•roid \-ˈthī-ˌrȯid\ *adj* **:** of, relating to, or produced by the parathyroid glands — **parathyroid** *n*

parathyroid gland *n* **:** any of usually four small endocrine glands adjacent to or embedded in the thyroid gland that produce parathormone

para•troops \ˈpar-ə-ˌtrüps\ *n pl* **:** troops trained and equipped to parachute from an airplane — **para•troop** \-ˌtrüp\ *adj* — **para•troop•er** \-ˌtrü-pər\ *n*

[1]**para•ty•phoid** \ˌpar-ə-ˈtī-ˌfȯid, -tī-ˈ\ *adj* **1 :** resembling typhoid fever **2 :** of or relating to paratyphoid or its causative organisms ⟨*paratyphoid* infection⟩

[2]**paratyphoid** *n* **:** a disease caused by bacteria that resembles typhoid fever and occurs as a food poisoning

par•boil \ˈpär-ˌbȯil\ *vt* **:** to boil briefly usually before cooking in another manner [Middle French *parbouillir* "to boil thoroughly", from Late Latin *perbullire,* from Latin *per-* + *bullire* "to boil"]

[1]**par•cel** \ˈpär-səl\ *n* **1 :** a part of a whole **2 :** a plot of land **3 :** a group or collection of persons or things ⟨told a *parcel* of lies⟩ **4**

: a wrapped bundle : PACKAGE [Middle French, derived from Latin *particula* "small part, particle"]

[2]**parcel** *vt* **par•celed** *or* **par•celled**; **par•cel•ing** *or* **par•cel•ling** \ˈpär-sə-liŋ, -sliŋ\ **1** : to divide into parts : DISTRIBUTE **2** : to make up into a parcel

parcel post *n* **1** : a mail service handling parcels **2** : packages handled by parcel post

parch \ˈpärch\ *vb* **1** : to toast under dry heat **2** : to dry up : shrivel with heat [Middle English *parchen*]

parch•ment \ˈpärch-mənt\ *n* **1** : the skin of a sheep or goat prepared for use as a writing material **2** : a paper made to resemble parchment **3** : something (as a diploma) written on parchment [Old French *parchemin,* from Latin *pergamena,* from Greek *pergamēnē,* from *Pergamēnos* "of Pergamum", from *Pergamon* "Pergamum"]

[1]**pard** \ˈpärd\ *n, archaic* : LEOPARD [Old French *parde,* from Latin *pardus,* from Greek *pardos*]

[2]**pard** *n, chiefly dialect* : CHUM [short for *pardner,* alteration of *partner*]

[1]**par•don** \ˈpärd-n\ *n* **1 a** : the excusing of an offense without a penalty **b** : a release from the legal penalties of an offense **2** : excuse for a fault or discourtesy [Old French, from *pardonner* "to pardon", from Late Latin *perdonare* "to grant freely", from Latin *per-* + *donare* "to give"] — **par•don•able** \ˈpärd-nə-bəl, -n-ə-bəl\ *adj* — **par•don•ably** \-blē\ *adv*

[2]**pardon** *vt* **par•doned**; **par•don•ing** \ˈpärd-niŋ, -n-iŋ\ **1** : to free from penalty **2** : to allow (an offense) to pass without punishment : FORGIVE **syn** see EXCUSE

pare \ˈpaər, ˈpeər\ *vt* **1** : to cut or shave off the outside or the ends of ⟨*pare* an apple⟩ **2** : to reduce as if by paring ⟨*pare* expenses⟩ [Middle French *parer* "to prepare, trim", from Latin *parare* "to prepare, acquire"]

par•e•go•ric \ˌpar-ə-ˈgȯr-ik, -ˈgȯr-, -ˈgär-\ *n* : a solution of opium and camphor in alcohol used especially to relieve pain [French *parégorique* "alleviating pain", from Latin *paregoricus,* from Greek *parēgorikos,* from *parēgorein* "to talk over, soothe", from *para-* + *agora* "assembly"]

pa•ren•chy•ma \pə-ˈreŋ-kə-mə\ *n* **1** : a tissue of higher plants consisting of thin-walled living cells that remain capable of cell division even when mature, are agents of photosynthesis and storage, and make up much of the substance of leaves and roots and the pulp of fruits as well as parts of stems and supporting structures **2** : the distinctive functional tissue of an animal organ (as a gland) as distinguished from its supporting tissue or framework [Greek, "tissue of the viscera", from *parenchein* "to pour in beside", from *para-* + *en-* + *chein* "to pour"] — **par•en•chy•ma•tous** \ˌpar-ən-ˈkim-ət-əs, -ˈkīm-\ *also* **pa•ren•chy•mal** \pə-ˈreŋ-kə-məl\ *adj*

par•ent \ˈpar-ənt, ˈper-\ *n* **1 a** : a person who is a father or mother **b** : an animal or plant that produces offspring **2** : the source or originator of something [Middle French, from Latin *parens,* from *parere* "to give birth to"] — **parent** *adj*

par•ent•age \-ənt-ij\ *n* : descent from parents or ancestors : LINEAGE ⟨a person of noble *parentage*⟩

pa•ren•tal \pə-ˈrent-l\ *adj* : of, typical of, or being parents ⟨*parental* affection⟩ — **pa•ren•tal•ly** \-l-ē\ *adv*

pa•ren•the•sis \pə-ˈren-thə-səs\ *n, pl* **-the•ses** \-thə-ˌsēz\ **1 a** : a word, phrase, or sentence inserted in a passage to explain or comment on it **b** : DIGRESSION **2** : one of a pair of marks () used to enclose a parenthesis or to group a symbolic unit in a mathematical expression [Late Latin, from Greek, literally, "act of inserting", from *parentithenai* "to insert", from *para-* + *en-* + *tithenai* "to place"] — **par•en•thet•ic** \ˌpar-ən-ˈthet-ik\ *or* **par•en•thet•i•cal** \-ˈthet-i-kəl\ *adj* — **par•en•thet•i•cal•ly** \-i-kə-lē, -klē\ *adv*

pa•ren•the•size \pə-ˈren-thə-ˌsīz, -ˈrent-\ *vt* : to make a parenthesis of

par•ent•hood \ˈpar-ənt-ˌhu̇d, ˈper-\ *n* : the position, function, or standing of a parent

pa•re•sis \pə-ˈrē-səs, ˈpar-ə-\ *n, pl* **-re•ses** \-ˌsēz\ : GENERAL PARESIS [Greek, "paralysis, neglect", from *parienai* "to let fall", from *para-* + *hienai* "to let go, send"] — **pa•ret•ic** \pə-ˈret-ik\ *adj or n*

par excellence \ˌpär-ˌek-sə-ˈläⁿs\ *adv or adj* : in the highest degree [French, literally, "by excellence"]

par•fait \pär-ˈfā\ *n* **1** : a flavored custard containing whipped cream and syrup frozen without stirring **2** : a cold dessert made of layers of fruit, syrup, ice cream, and whipped cream [French, from *parfait* "perfect", from Latin *perfectus*]

par•he•lion \pär-ˈhēl-yən\ *n, pl* **-lia** \-yə\ : any one of several bright spots often tinged with color that often appear on both sides of the sun and at the same altitude as the sun [Latin *parelion,* from Greek *parēlion,* from *para-* + *hēlios* "sun"]

pa•ri•ah \pə-ˈrī-ə\ *n* **1** : a member of a former low caste of southern India and Burma **2** : a person despised or rejected by society : OUTCAST [Tamil *paraiyan,* literally, "drummer"]

pa•ri•e•tal \pə-ˈrī-ət-l\ *adj* : of, relating to, or forming the walls of a part or cavity and especially the upper back wall of the head [Middle French, from Latin *pariet-, paries* "wall"]

parietal bone *n* : either of a pair of bones of the roof of the skull between the frontal bones and the occipital bones

pari–mu•tu•el \ˌpar-i-ˈmyü-chə-wəl, -chəl\ *n* : a system of betting (as on a race) in which those who bet on the competitors finishing in the first three places share the total amount bet minus a percentage for the management [French *pari mutuel,* literally, "mutual stake"]

par•ing \ˈpaər-iŋ, ˈpeər-\ *n* **1** : the act of cutting away an edge or surface **2** : something pared off ⟨apple *parings*⟩

par•ish \ˈpar-ish\ *n* **1 a** : a section of a diocese in the charge of a priest or minister **b** : the persons who live in such a section and attend the parish church **2** : the members of any church **3** : a civil division of the state of Louisiana corresponding to a county in other states [Middle French *parroche,* from Late Latin *parochia,* from Late Greek *paroikia,* from *paroikos* "Christian", from Greek, "stranger", from *para-* + *oikos* "house"]

parish house *n* : a building for the educational and social activities of a church

pa•rish•io•ner \pə-ˈrish-nər, -ə-nər\ *n* : a member or resident of a parish

par•i•ty \ˈpar-ət-ē\ *n, pl* **-ties** : the quality or state of being equal or equivalent [Latin *paritas,* from *par* "equal"]

[1]**park** \ˈpärk\ *n* **1** : a tract of land attached to a country house and used for recreation **2 a** : a piece of ground in or near a city or town kept as a place of beauty and recreation **b** : an area maintained in its natural state as a public property **3 a** : a space occupied by military animals, vehicles, or materials **b** : PARKING LOT **4** : an enclosed arena or stadium used especially for ball games [Old French *parc* "enclosure"]

[2]**park** *vb* **1 a** : to leave a vehicle temporarily on a public way or in a parking lot or garage **b** : to land or leave an airplane **2** : to set and leave temporarily

parka

par•ka \ˈpär-kə\ *n* : a winter jacket with a hood [Aleut, "skin, outer garment", from Russian, "pelt", of Uralic origin]

parking lot *n* : an outdoor area for the parking of motor vehicles

park•way \ˈpär-ˌkwā\ *n* : a broad landscaped thoroughfare

par•lance \ˈpär-ləns\ *n* : choice of words : IDIOM [Middle French, from *parler* "to speak"]

par•lay \ˈpär-ˌlā, -lē\ *n* : a series of bets in which the original stake plus its winnings are risked on the successive wagers [French *paroli,* from Italian dialect, from *paro* "equal", from Latin *par*] — **parlay** *vt*

par•ley \ˈpär-lē\ *vi* **par•leyed**; **par•ley•ing** : to speak with another : CONFER; *esp* : to discuss terms with an enemy [Middle French *parler* "to speak", from Medieval Latin *parabolare,* from Late Latin *parabola* "speech, parable"] — **parley** *n*

par•lia•ment \ˈpär-lə-mənt *also* ˈpärl-yə-\ *n* **1** : a formal conference on public affairs; *esp* : a council of state in early medieval England **2 a** : an assemblage of the nobility, clergy, and commons called together by the British sovereign as the supreme legislative body in the United Kingdom **b** : a similar assemblage in another nation or state **3 a** : the supreme legislative body of a political unit comprising a series of successive parliaments **b :** the British House of Commons [Old French *parliament,* from *parler* "to speak"]

par•lia•men•tar•i•an \ˌpär-lə-ˌmen-ˈter-ē-ən, -mən- *also* ˌpärl-yə-\ *n* : an expert in parliamentary procedure

par•lia•men•ta•ry \-ˈment-ə-rē, -ˈmen-trē\ *adj* **1 :** of, relating to, or enacted by a parliament **2 :** of or relating to government by a cabinet whose members belong to and are responsible to the legislature **3 :** being in accordance with the rules and customs of a parliament or other deliberative body

par•lor \ˈpär-lər\ *n* **1 :** a room in a home, hotel, or club used for conversation or the reception of guests **2 :** any of various business places ⟨funeral *parlor*⟩ ⟨beauty *parlor*⟩ [Old French *parlour,* from *parler* "to speak"]

parlor car *n* : an extra-fare railroad passenger car equipped with individual chairs and formerly used for day travel

par•lous \ˈpär-ləs\ *adj* : full of uncertainty or risk ⟨*parlous* times⟩ [Middle English, alteration of *perilous*] — **par•lous•ly** *adv*

pa•ro•chi•al \pə-ˈrō-kē-əl\ *adj* **1 :** of or relating to a parish **2 :** limited in range or scope : NARROW ⟨a *parochial* attitude⟩ [Middle French, from Late Latin *parochialis,* from *parochia* "parish"] — **pa•ro•chi•al•ism** \-kē-ə-ˌliz-əm\ *n* — **pa•ro•chi•al•ly** \-kē-ə-lē\ *adv*

parochial school *n* : a school maintained by a religious body

par•o•dy \ˈpar-əd-ē\ *n, pl* **-dies 1 :** a literary or musical work in which the style of an author or work is closely imitated for comic effect or in ridicule **2 :** a feeble or ridiculous imitation [Latin *parodia,* from Greek *parōidia,* from *para-* + *aidein* "to sing"] **syn** see CARICATURE — **par•o•dist** \-əd-əst\ *n* — **parody** *vt*

1**pa•role** \pə-ˈrōl\ *n* **1 :** a promise confirmed by a pledge; *esp* **:** the promise of a prisoner of war to fulfill stated conditions in return for release **2 :** a conditional release of a prisoner before the sentence has expired [French, "speech, parole", from Late Latin *parabola* "speech, parable"]

2**parole** *vt* : to release (a prisoner) on parole — **pa•rol•ee** \pə-ˌrō-ˈlē, ˌpar-ə-ˈlē\ *n*

pa•rot•id \pə-ˈrät-əd\ *adj* : of or relating to the parotid gland [New Latin *parotis* "parotid gland", from Latin, "tumor near the ear", from Greek *parōtis,* from *para-* + *ōt-, ous* "ear"]

parotid gland *n* : either of a pair of large salivary glands situated below and in front of the ear

par•ox•ysm \ˈpar-ək-ˌsiz-əm\ *n* **1 :** a fit, attack, or sudden increase of violence of a disease that occurs at intervals ⟨a *paroxysm* of coughing⟩ **2 :** a sudden violent emotion or action ⟨*paroxysms* of rage⟩ [Medieval Latin *paroxysmus,* from Greek *paroxysmos,* from *paroxynein* "to stimulate", from *para-* + *oxynein* "to provoke", from *oxys* "sharp"] — **par•ox•ys•mal** \ˌpar-ək-ˈsiz-məl\ *adj*

par•quet \ˈpär-ˌkā, pär-ˈ\ *n* **1 :** a flooring of parquetry **2 :** the lower floor of a theater especially in front of the balcony [French, literally, "small enclosure", from *parc* "park"]

par•que•try \ˈpär-kə-trē\ *n, pl* **-tries :** a patterned wood inlay used especially for floors

parr \ˈpär\ *n, pl* **parr** *also* **parrs :** a young salmon actively feeding in fresh water [origin unknown]

par•ra•keet *variant of* PARAKEET

par•ri•cide \ˈpar-ə-ˌsīd\ *n* **1 :** one who murders one's father or mother or a close relative **2 :** the act of a parricide [Latin *parricida* "killer of a close relative"] — **par•ri•cid•al** \ˌpar-ə-ˈsīd-l\ *adj*

1**par•rot** \ˈpar-ət\ *n* **1 :** a bright-colored tropical bird of a family characterized by a strong hooked bill, by toes arranged in pairs with two in front and two behind, and often by the ability to mimic speech **2 :** a person who repeats words mechanically and without understanding [probably from Middle French *perroquet*]

2**parrot** *vt* : to repeat mechanically

parrot fever *n* : an infectious disease of birds caused by a rickettsia, marked by diarrhea and wasting, and communicable to man — called also *psittacosis*

parrot fish *n* : any of various sea fishes related to the perches that have the teeth fused into a cutting plate resembling a beak

par•ry \ˈpar-ē\ *vb* **par•ried; par•ry•ing 1 :** to ward off a weapon or blow : turn aside skillfully **2 :** to evade especially by a clever answer ⟨*parry* an embarrassing question⟩ [probably from French *parer,* from Provençal *parar,* from Latin *parare* "to prepare"] — **parry** *n*

parse \ˈpärs, ˈpärz\ *vb* **1 :** to analyze a sentence by naming its parts and their relations to each other **2 :** to give the part of speech of a word and explain its relation to other words in a sentence [Latin *pars orationis* "part of speech"]

parrot fish

par•sec \ˈpär-ˌsek\ *n* : a unit of measure for interstellar space equal to 19.2 trillion miles (about 30.8 trillion kilometers) [*par*allax + *sec*ond]

Par•si *also* **Par•see** \ˈpär-ˌsē\ *n* : a Zoroastrian descended from Persian refugees settled principally at Bombay [Persian *pārsi,* from *Pārs* "Persia"]

par•si•mo•ny \ˈpär-sə-ˌmō-nē\ *n* : extreme frugality : STINGINESS [Latin *parsimonia,* from *parcere* "to spare"] — **par•si•mo•ni•ous** \ˌpär-sə-ˈmō-nē-əs\ *adj* — **par•si•mo•ni•ous•ly** *adv*

pars•ley \ˈpär-slē\ *n, pl* **parsleys :** a southern European herb of the carrot family widely grown for its finely divided leaves which are used as a flavoring or garnish [Old English *petersilie,* from Latin *petroselinum,* from Greek *petroselinon,* from *petros* "stone" + *selinon* "celery"]

pars•nip \ˈpär-snəp\ *n* : a European biennial herb of the carrot family grown for its long white root used as a vegetable; *also* : this root [Middle English *pasnepe,* from Middle French *pasnaie,* from Latin *pastinaca*]

par•son \ˈpärs-n\ *n* **1 :** RECTOR 1 **2 :** CLERGYMAN; *esp* **:** a Protestant pastor [Old French *persone,* from Medieval Latin *persona,* literally, "person", from Latin]

par•son•age \ˈpär-snij, ˈpärs-n-ij\ *n* : the house provided by a church for its pastor

1**part** \ˈpärt\ *n* **1 a :** one of the portions into which something is divisible and which together constitute the whole **b :** one of several or many equal units of which something is composed ⟨a fifth *part* for each⟩ **c :** a portion of a plant or animal body : MEMBER, ORGAN ⟨wash the injured *part*⟩ **d :** a vocal or instrumental line or melody in music written in harmony; *also* : the score for it **e :** a constituent member of a machine or apparatus; *also* : a spare piece or member **2 :** something falling to one in a division or apportionment : SHARE **3 :** one's shared or allotted task ⟨one must do one's *part*⟩ **4 :** one of the sides in a conflict ⟨take someone's *part* in a quarrel⟩ **5 :** a portion of an unspecified territorial area — usually used in pl. ⟨took off for *parts* unknown⟩ **6 :** a function or course of action performed **7 a :** an actor's lines in a play **b :** the role of a character in a play **8 :** a constituent of character or capacity : TALENT ⟨a person of many *parts*⟩ **9 :** the line where the hair is divided in combing [Old French and Old English, both from Latin *part-, pars*]

• **syn** PART, PORTION, PIECE, SEGMENT mean something less than the whole. PART is the general term and is interchangeable with any of the others; PORTION suggests an assigned or allotted part ⟨a minor *portion* of the voting population⟩ ⟨each child received a *portion* of the cake⟩ PIECE applies to a separate or detached part ⟨a *piece* of pie⟩ SEGMENT applies to a part separated or marked out by natural lines of cleavage ⟨*segments* of an orange⟩

— **for the most part :** in general — **in part :** in some degree — **on the part of :** with regard to the one specified

2**part** *vb* **1 a :** to leave someone — used with *from* or *with* **b :** to take leave of one another ⟨the friends had to *part*⟩ **2 :** to become separated into parts **3 :** to go away : DEPART **4 :** to give up possession or control ⟨wouldn't *part* with the old car⟩ **5 a :** to divide into parts **b :** to separate by combing on each side of a line **6 a** to keep separate ⟨the channel that *parts* England and France⟩ **b :** to hold (as fighters) apart [Old French *partir,* from Latin *partire* "to divide", from *part-, pars* "part"]

3**part** *adv* : in a measure : PARTLY ⟨was only *part* right⟩

par•take \pär-ˈtāk, pər-\ *vi* **par•took** \-ˈtu̇k\; **par•tak•en** \-ˈtā-kən\; **par•tak•ing 1 a :** to take a share ⟨*partake* of a meal⟩ **b :** PARTICIPATE ⟨all may *partake* in the ceremony⟩ **2 :** to have some of the qualities or attributes of something ⟨their actions *partook* of rebellion⟩ [back-formation from *partaker,* from *part taker*] — **par•tak•er** *n*

part•ed \ˈpärt-əd\ *adj* : divided into parts

par•terre \pär-ˈteər\ *n* **1 :** an ornamental garden with paths between the beds **2 :** the part of the floor of a theater behind the orchestra [French, from *par terre* "on the ground"]

par•the•no•car•py \ˈpär-thə-nō-ˌkär-pē\ *n* **:** the production of fruits without fertilization [Greek *parthenos* "virgin" + *karpos* "fruit"] — **par•the•no•car•pic** \ˌpär-thə-nō-ˈkär-pik\ *adj*

par•the•no•gen•e•sis \ˌpär-thə-nō-ˈjen-ə-səs\ *n, pl* **-gen•e•ses** \-ə-ˌsēz\ **:** reproduction especially among lower plants and invertebrate animals in which an unfertilized gamete develops into a new individual [Greek *parthenos* "virgin"] — **par•the•no•ge•net•ic** \-jə-ˈnet-ik\ *adj* — **par•the•no•ge•net•i•cal•ly** \-ˈnet-i-kə-lē, -klē\ *adv*

par•tial \ˈpär-shəl\ *adj* **1 :** inclined to favor one side or party over another ⟨the judge was *partial*⟩ **2 :** markedly or overly fond of someone or something ⟨*partial* to milk shakes⟩ **3 :** of, relating to, or being a part rather than the whole ⟨a *partial* eclipse⟩ [Middle French, from Medieval Latin *partialis,* from Late Latin, "of a part", from Latin *part-, pars* "part"] — **par•tial•ly** \ˈpärsh-lē, -ə-lē\ *adv*

partial denture *n* **:** an often removable artificial replacement for one or more teeth

par•ti•al•i•ty \ˌpär-shē-ˈal-ət-ē, pär-ˈshal-\ *n, pl* **-ties 1 :** the quality or state of being partial **:** BIAS **2 :** a special taste or liking

partial product *n* **:** one of the products obtained by multiplying successively the multiplicand by each digit of the multiplier

par•ti•ble \ˈpärt-ə-bəl\ *adj* **:** DIVISIBLE

par•tic•i•pant \pər-ˈtis-ə-pənt, pär-\ *n* **:** one that participates

par•tic•i•pate \pər-tis-ə-ˌpāt, pär-\ *vi* **:** to engage or have a share in something in common with others [Latin *participare,* from *particeps* "participant", from *part-, pars* "part" + *capere* "to take"] — **par•tic•i•pa•tion** \-ˌtis-ə-ˈpā-shən\ *n* — **par•tic•i•pa•tor** \-ˈtis-ə-ˌpāt-ər\ *n* — **par•tic•i•pa•to•ry** \-ˈtis-ə-pə-ˌtōr-ē, -ˌtȯr-\ *adj*

par•ti•cip•i•al \ˌpärt-ə-ˈsip-ē-əl\ *adj* **:** of, relating to, or formed with or from a participle ⟨*participial* phrase⟩ — **par•ti•cip•i•al•ly** \-ē-ə-lē\ *adv*

par•ti•ci•ple \ˈpärt-ə-ˌsip-əl\ *n* **:** a verb form that sometimes can also be used like an adjective ⟨"burning" and "collapsed" are *participles* in "the burning building had collapsed"⟩ [Middle French, from Latin *participium,* from *particeps* "participant"]

par•ti•cle \ˈpärt-i-kəl\ *n* **1 :** one of the minute subdivisions of matter (as a molecule, atom, electron); *also* **:** ELEMENTARY PARTICLE **2 a :** a tiny amount or fragment **b :** the smallest possible part **3 :** a word (as an article, preposition, or conjunction) expressing a general meaning or a connective or limiting relation [Latin *particula,* from *part-, pars* "part"]

par•ti–col•ored \ˌpärt-ē-ˈkəl-ərd\ *adj* **:** showing different colors or tints [obsolete English *party* "parti-colored" (from Middle French *parti* "striped", from Old French *partir* "to divide, part") + English *colored*]

[1]**par•tic•u•lar** \pər-ˈtik-yə-lər, pə-, -ˈtik-ə-lər, -ˈtik-lər\ *adj* **1 :** of or relating to a single person or thing **2 :** of or relating to details **:** MINUTE **3 :** distinctive among others **:** SPECIAL **4 a :** attentive to details **:** EXACT **b :** hard to please **:** EXACTING [Middle French *particuler,* from Late Latin *particularis,* from Latin *particula* "small part, particle"] **syn** see CIRCUMSTANTIAL

[2]**particular** *n* **:** an individual fact, detail, or item — **in particular :** in distinction from others **:** SPECIFICALLY

par•tic•u•lar•i•ty \-ˌtik-yə-ˈlar-ət-ē\ *n, pl* **-ties 1 a :** a minute detail **b :** an individual characteristic **:** PECULIARITY **2 :** attentiveness to detail **:** EXACTNESS, CARE

par•tic•u•lar•ize \-ˈtik-yə-lə-ˌrīz, -ˈtik-lə-\ *vb* **:** to go into details **:** state in detail **:** SPECIFY — **par•tic•u•lar•iza•tion** \-ˌtik-yə-lə-rə-ˈzā-shən, -ˌtik-lə-\ *n*

par•tic•u•lar•ly \pər-ˈtik-yə-lē, pə-, -yə-lər-lē, -ˈtik-lē, -ˈtik-ə-lē\ *adv* **1 :** in detail **2 :** to an unusual degree

par•tic•u•late \pər-ˈtik-yə-lət, pär-, -ˌlāt\ *adj* **:** relating to or existing as minute separate particles — **particulate** *n*

particulate inheritance *n* **:** inheritance of characters specifically transmitted by genes in accord with Mendel's laws

[1]**part•ing** \ˈpärt-ing\ *n* **1 :** FAREWELL 2 **2 :** a place or point where a division or separation occurs — **parting of the ways 1 :** PARTING 2 **2 :** a place or time at which a choice must be made

[2]**parting** *adj* **:** involving, given, taken, or performed at parting ⟨a *parting* kiss⟩

par•ti•san \ˈpärt-ə-zən\ *n* **1 :** a person who supports the position of another; *esp* **:** a devoted adherent to the cause of another **2 :** an irregular soldier who operates behind enemy lines [Middle French *partisan,* from Italian *partigiano,* from *parte* "part", from Latin *part-, pars*] — **partisan** *adj* — **par•ti•san•ship** \-ˌship\ *n*

par•tite \ˈpär-ˌtīt\ *adj* **:** divided into a usually specified number of parts [Latin *partitus,* from *partire* "to divide", from *part-, pars* "part"]

par•ti•tion \pər-ˈtish-ən, pär-\ *n* **1 a :** the action of parting **:** DIVISION **b :** separation of a class or whole into components; *esp* **:** the division of a united territory among two or more governments **2 :** an interior dividing wall **3 :** PART 1a, SECTION — **partition** *vt* — **par•ti•tion•er** \-ˈtish-nər, -ə-nər\ *n*

par•ti•tive \ˈpärt-ət-iv\ *adj* **1 :** of, relating to, or denoting a part ⟨a *partitive* construction⟩ **2 :** serving to indicate the whole of which a part is specified ⟨*partitive* genitive⟩ — **partitive** *n* — **par•ti•tive•ly** *adv*

part•ly \ˈpärt-lē\ *adv* **:** in some measure or degree **:** PARTIALLY

[1]**part•ner** \ˈpärt-nər\ *n* **1 a :** one associated in action with another **:** COLLEAGUE **b :** either of a couple who dance together **c :** one of usually two persons who play together in a game against an opposing side **d :** SPOUSE **2 :** a member of a partnership [Middle English *partener* "sharer", alteration of *parcener,* from Old French *parçonier,* from *parçon* "division, share", from Latin *partitio,* from *partire* "to divide"]

[2]**partner** *vb* **:** to join as a partner **:** be or act as a partner

part•ner•ship \ˈpärt-nər-ˌship\ *n* **1 :** the state of being a partner **2 :** a business organization owned by two or more persons who agree to share the profits and usually are liable individually for losses

part of speech : a traditional class of words distinguished according to the kind of idea denoted and the function performed in a sentence — compare ADJECTIVE, ADVERB, CONJUNCTION, INTERJECTION, NOUN, PREPOSITION, PRONOUN, VERB

partook *past of* PARTAKE

par•tridge \ˈpär-trij\ *n, pl* **partridge** *or* **par•tridg•es :** any of several stout-bodied Old World game birds related to the common domestic fowl; *also* **:** any of various similar and related North American birds (as a bobwhite or ruffed grouse) [Old French *perdris,* from Latin *perdix,* from Greek]

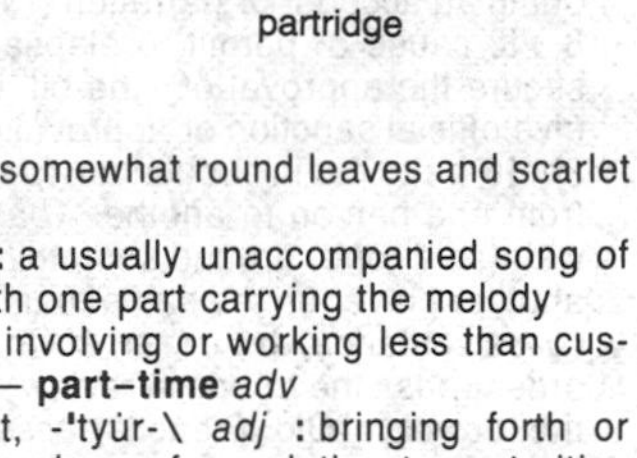

partridge

par•tridge•ber•ry \-ˌber-ē\ *n* **:** an American trailing evergreen plant with small somewhat round leaves and scarlet berries

part–song \ˈpärt-ˌsȯng\ *n* **:** a usually unaccompanied song of two or more voice parts with one part carrying the melody

part–time \ˈpärt-ˈtīm\ *adj* **:** involving or working less than customary or standard hours — **part–time** *adv*

par•tu•ri•ent \pär-ˈtu̇r-ē-ənt, -ˈtyu̇r-\ *adj* **:** bringing forth or about to bring forth young; *also* **:** of or relating to parturition [Latin *parturiens,* present participle of *parturire* "to be in labor", from *parere* "to bring forth"]

par•tu•ri•tion \ˌpärt-ə-ˈrish-ən, ˌpar-chə-\ *n* **:** the act or process of giving birth to offspring [Late Latin *parturitio,* from Latin *parturire* "to be in labor"]

[1]**par•ty** \ˈpärt-ē\ *n, pl* **parties 1 :** a side in a dispute or contest ⟨the *parties* to a lawsuit⟩ **2 :** a group of persons organized for the purpose of directing the policies of a government **3 :** a person or group participating in an activity **:** PARTICIPANT ⟨a *party* to the transaction⟩ **4 :** PERSON ⟨get the right *party* on the telephone⟩ **5 :** a small group engaged in a task ⟨a scouting *party*⟩ **6 :** a social gathering; *also* **:** the entertainment provided for it [Old French *partie* "part, party", from *partir* "to divide, part"] — **party** *adj*

[2]**par•ty** *vi* **par•tied; par•ty•ing :** to give or attend parties

party line *n* **1 :** a single telephone circuit connecting two or more subscribers with the exchange **2 :** the principles or policies of an individual or organization; *esp* **:** the official policies of a Communist party — **par•ty-lin•er** \ˌpärt-ē-ˈlī-nər\ *n*

par•ve•nu *also* **par•ve•nue** \ˈpär-və-ˌnü, -ˌnyü\ *n* **:** one who has recently or suddenly risen to wealth or power and has not yet secured the social position appropriate to it **:** UPSTART [French, from *parvenir* "to arrive", from Latin *pervenire,* from *per-* "through" + *venire* "to come"] — **parvenu** *also* **parvenue** *adj*

Pasch \ˈpask\ *n* **1 :** PASSOVER **2 :** EASTER [Old French *pasche,* from Late Latin *pascha,* from Greek, from Hebrew *pesah*] — **pas•chal** \ˈpas-kəl\ *adj*

Paschal Lamb *n* **:** AGNUS DEI 2

pas de deux \ˌpäd-ə-ˈdər, -ˈdü, -ˈdœ\ *n, pl* **pas de deux** \-ˈdər, -ˈdərz, -ˈdü, -ˈdüz, -ˈdœ, -ˈdœz\ **:** a dance or figure for two performers [French, literally, "step for two"]

pas de trois \-ˈtrwä, -trə-ˈwä\ *n, pl* **pas de trois** \-ˈtrwä, -ˈtrwäz, -trə-ˈwä, -trə-ˈwäz\ **:** a dance or figure for three performers [French, literally, "step for three"]

pa•sha \ˈpäsh-ə, ˈpash-ə, pə-ˈshä\ *n* **:** a high-ranking official (as in Turkey or northern Africa) [Turkish *paşa*]

Push•to \ˈpəsh-tō\ *also* **Push•tu** \-tü\ *n* **:** the Iranian language of the Pathan people which is the chief vernacular of eastern Afghanistan and adjacent parts of Pakistan [Persian *pashtu,* from Pashto]

pasque•flow•er \ˈpask-ˌflau̇-ər, -ˌflau̇r\ *n* **:** any of several low perennial herbs of the buttercup family that have compound leaves arranged like a hand with fingers spread and large usually white or purple flowers in early spring [Middle French *passefleur,* from *passer* 'to pass" + *fleur* "flower", from Latin *flor-, flos*]

¹pass \ˈpas\ *vb* **1 :** GO 1, PROCEED **2 a :** to go away **:** DEPART **b :** DIE 1 — often used with *on* or *away* **3 :** to go by **:** move past **4 a :** to go or cause or let go across, over, or through **b :** to go unchallenged ⟨let that remark *pass*⟩ **5 a :** to change or transfer ownership **b :** to go from the control or possession of one person or group to that of another ⟨the throne *passed* to the heir⟩ **6 a :** HAPPEN 2, OCCUR **b :** to take place as a mutual exchange or transaction ⟨words *passed*⟩ **7 a :** to become approved by a legislative body **b :** to go through or let go through an inspection, test, or course of study successfully **8 a :** to serve as a medium of exchange **b :** to be held or regarded ⟨*passed* for an honest person⟩ **9 :** to execute a pass in a game **10 :** to decline to bid, bet, or draw an additional card in a card game **11 :** to go beyond; *esp* **:** SURPASS ⟨*passes* all expectations⟩ **12 :** to leave out in an account or narration **13 a :** to live through **:** UNDERGO **b :** to cause or permit to elapse **:** SPEND ⟨*pass* time⟩ **14 :** to secure the approval of ⟨the bill *passed* the Senate⟩ **15 a :** to give official sanction or approval to ⟨*pass* a law⟩ **b :** OVERLOOK 3b **16 a :** to put in circulation ⟨*pass* bad checks⟩ **b :** to transfer from one person to another ⟨*pass* the salt⟩ **c :** to take a turn with (as a rope) around something **d :** to transfer (as a ball) to another player on the same team **17 a :** to pronounce judicially ⟨*pass* sentence⟩ **b :** UTTER 2 **18 :** to cause to march or go by in order ⟨*pass* the troops in review⟩ **19 :** to emit or discharge from the bowels [Old French *passer,* from Latin *passus* "step, pace"] — **pass•er** *n* — **in passing :** by the way **:** PARENTHETICALLY — **pass muster :** to pass an inspection or examination — **pass the buck :** to shift a responsibility to someone else — **pass the hat :** to take up a collection of money

²pass *n* **1 :** an opening or way for passing along or through **2 :** a gap in a mountain range

³pass *n* **1 :** the act or an instance of passing **:** PASSAGE **2 :** REALIZATION ⟨brought their dreams to *pass*⟩ **3 :** a usually difficult or disturbing state of affairs **4 a :** a written permission to enter or leave or to move about freely ⟨a soldier's 3-day *pass*⟩ **b :** a ticket allowing one free transportation or free admission **5 a :** a transference of objects by sleight of hand **b :** a moving of the hands over or along something **6 :** a transfer of a ball or a puck from one player to another on the same team **7 :** a refusal to bid, bet, or draw an additional card in a card game **8 :** EFFORT, TRY; *esp* **:** a sexually inviting approach

pass•able \ˈpas-ə-bəl\ *adj* **1 :** capable of being passed, crossed, or traveled on ⟨*passable* roads⟩ **2 :** barely good enough ⟨a *passable* meal⟩ — **pass•ably** \-blē\ *adv*

pas•sage \ˈpas-ij\ *n* **1 :** the action or process of passing from one place or condition to another **2 a :** a road, path, channel, or course by which something can pass ⟨nasal *passages*⟩ **b :** a corridor or lobby giving access to the different rooms or parts of a building or apartment **3 a :** a specific act of traveling especially by sea or air **b :** the right to travel as a passenger ⟨take *passage* on a freighter⟩ **4 :** the passing of a legislative measure **:** ENACTMENT **5 a :** INCIDENT 1a **b :** something that takes place between two persons mutually ⟨a *passage* of wit⟩ **6 a :** a usually brief portion of a written work or speech that concerns a point under discussion or is noteworthy for content or style **b :** a phrase or short section of a musical composition

pas•sage•way \-ˌwā\ *n* **:** a way that allows passage ⟨a *passageway* between two rooms⟩ ⟨a *passageway* between buildings⟩

pass•book \ˈpas-ˌbu̇k\ *n* **:** BANKBOOK

pas•sé \pa-ˈsā\ *adj* **1 :** no longer active or in use **:** OBSOLETE **2 :** OLD-FASHIONED 1 [French, from *passer* "to pass"]

passed ball *n* **:** a pitched ball that passes the catcher when he should have stopped it and that allows a base runner to advance

pas•sel \ˈpas-əl\ *n* **:** a large number ⟨a *passel* of worries⟩ [alteration of *parcel*]

pas•sen•ger \ˈpas-n-jər\ *n* **1 :** PASSERBY; *esp* **:** one passing on foot **2 :** a traveler in a public or private conveyance [Middle French *passager,* from *passage* "act of passing", from *passer* "to pass"]

passenger pigeon *n* **:** an extinct but formerly abundant North American migratory pigeon

passenger pigeon

passe–par•tout \ˌpas-pər-ˈtü\ *n* **1 :** something that passes or enables one to pass everywhere **2 :** strong paper gummed on one side and used especially for mounting pictures [French, from *passe partout* "pass everywhere"]

pass•er•by \ˌpas-ər-ˈbī\ *n, pl* **pass•ers•by** \-ərz-\ **:** one that passes by

pas•ser•ine \ˈpas-ə-ˌrīn\ *adj* **1 :** of or relating to the largest order (Passeriformes) of birds including more than half of all living birds and consisting chiefly of songbirds of perching habits **2 :** of or relating to the group (Passeres) comprising true songbirds with specialized vocal apparatus [Latin *passerinus* "of sparrows", from *passer* "sparrow"] — **passerine** *n*

pas seul \pä-ˈsərl, -ˈsəl, -ˈsœl\ *n* **:** a solo dance or dance figure [French, literally, "solo step"]

pas•sim \ˈpas-əm, -ˌim\ *adv* **:** here and there — used to indicate that something (as a phrase) is to be found at many places in the same book or work [Latin, from *passus* "scattered", from *pandere* "to spread"]

¹pass•ing \ˈpas-ing\ *n* **:** the act of one that passes or causes to pass; *esp* **:** DEATH

²passing *adj* **1 :** going by or past ⟨the *passing* crowd⟩ **2 :** having a brief duration ⟨a *passing* whim⟩ **3 :** marked by haste or inattention **:** SUPERFICIAL ⟨a *passing* glance⟩ **4 :** given on satisfactory completion of an examination or course of study ⟨a *passing* grade⟩

³passing *adv* **:** to a surpassing degee **:** EXCEEDINGLY ⟨*passing* fair⟩

pas•sion \ˈpash-ən\ *n* **1** *often cap* **:** the sufferings of Christ between the night of the Last Supper and his death **2 a** *pl* **:** the emotions as distinguished from reason **b :** violent, intense, or overmastering feeling **c :** an outbreak of anger **3 a :** ardent affection **:** LOVE **b :** a strong liking ⟨a *passion* for cars⟩ **c :** sexual desire **d :** an object of desire or deep interest ⟨bowling is their *passion*⟩ [Old French, from Late Latin *passio* "suffering", from Latin *pati* "to suffer"] — **pas•sion•al** \-ən-l\ *adj* — **pas•sion•less** \-ən-ləs\ *adj*

• **syn** PASSION, FERVOR, ARDOR mean intense emotion. PASSION implies an emotion that is deeply stirring or ungovernable ⟨stalked out of the room in a towering *passion*⟩ FERVOR implies a strong, steadily glowing emotion ⟨sang their hymns with deep *fervor*⟩ ARDOR suggests a warm excited feeling likely to be fitful or short-lived ⟨the cost of the project dampened their *ardor* for reform⟩ **syn** see in addition FEELING

pas•sion•ate \ˈpash-nət, -ə-nət\ *adj* **1 a :** easily aroused to anger **b :** filled with anger **:** ANGRY **2 :** capable of, affected by, or expressing intense feeling **3 :** strongly affected with sexual desire **syn** see IMPASSIONED — **pas•sion•ate•ly** *adv* — **pas•sion•ate•ness** *n*

pas•sion•flow•er \ˈpash-ən-ˌflau̇-ər, -ˌflau̇r\ *n* : any of a genus of chiefly tropical climbing vines or erect herbs having showy symmetrical flowers and pulpy often edible fruits [from the fancied resemblance of parts of the flower to the cross, nails, and crown of thorns used in Christ's crucifixion]

Pas•sion•ist \ˈpash-nəst, -ə-nəst\ *n* : a member of a Roman Catholic monastic order devoted chiefly to missionary work and retreats

passion play *n, often cap 1st P* : a play representing scenes connected with Christ's suffering and crucifixion

Passion Sunday *n* : the 5th Sunday in Lent

Pas•sion•tide \ˈpash-ən-ˌtīd\ *n* : the last two weeks of Lent

Passion Week *n* **1** : HOLY WEEK **2** : the 2d week before Easter

¹pas•sive \ˈpas-iv\ *adj* **1 a** : not active but acted on : receptive to or affected by outside force, agency, or influence ⟨*passive* spectators⟩ **b** : of, relating to, or being a verb form or voice indicating that the person or thing represented by the subject is subjected to the action represented by the verb ⟨"was bitten" in "I was bitten by a dog" is *passive*⟩ **2** : not involving expenditure of chemical energy ⟨*passive* transport across a cell membrane⟩ **3** : receiving or enduring without resistance : SUBMISSIVE ⟨*passive* surrender to fate⟩ [Latin *passivus*, from *pati* "to be acted upon, suffer"] — **pas•sive•ly** *adv* — **pas•sive•ness** *n* — **pas•siv•i•ty** \pa-ˈsiv-ət-ē\ *n*

²passive *n* **1** : a passive verb form **2** : the passive voice of a language

passive immunity *n* : immunity acquired by transfer (as by injection of serum from an individual with active immunity) of antibodies

passive resistance *n* : resistance especially to a government or an occupying power characterized mainly by failure to cooperate rather than by violent opposition

pass•key \ˈpas-ˌkē\ *n* **1** : MASTER KEY **2** : SKELETON KEY

pass off *vt* **1** : to make public or offer for sale with intent to deceive **2** : to give a false identity or character to

pass out *vi* **1** : to lose consciousness **2** : DIE 1

Pass•over \ˈpas-ˌō-vər\ *n* : a Jewish holiday celebrated in March or April in commemoration of the liberation of the Hebrews from slavery in Egypt [from the exemption of the Israelites from the slaughter of the firstborn of Egypt (Exodus 12:23-27)]

pass•port \ˈpas-ˌpōrt, -ˌpȯrt\ *n* **1 a** : an official document issued to a person that is usually necessary for exit from and reentry into the country, that allows the person to travel in foreign countries, and that requests protection for the person in foreign countries **b** : an identification document required by law to be carried by persons living or traveling in a country **2** : something that secures admission or acceptance ⟨education as a *passport* to success⟩ [Middle French *passeport*, from *passer* "to pass" + *port* "port"]

pass up *vt* : DECLINE 4b, c, REJECT

pass•word \ˈpas-ˌwərd\ *n* **1** : a word or phrase that a person must utter before being allowed to pass a guard **2** : WATCHWORD 1

¹past \ˈpast\ *adj* **1 a** : AGO ⟨10 years *past*⟩ **b** : just gone by ⟨for the *past* few days⟩ **2** : having existed or taken place in a period before the present : BYGONE ⟨*past* customs⟩ **3** : of, relating to, or being a verb tense that in English is usually formed by internal vowel change (as in *sang*) or by the addition of a suffix (as in *laughed*) and that expresses elapsed time **4** : no longer serving ⟨*past* president⟩ [Middle English, from past participle of *passen* "to pass"]

²past *prep* **1 a** : beyond the age for or of ⟨*past* playing with toys⟩ **b** : AFTER ⟨half *past* two⟩ **2 a** : at the farther side of : BEYOND **b** : in a course or direction going close to and then beyond ⟨drove *past* the house⟩ **3** : beyond the range, scope, or sphere of ⟨a situation *past* belief⟩

³past *n* **1 a** : time gone by **b** : something that happened or was done in the past **2 a** : PAST TENSE **b** : a verb form in the past tense **3** : a past life, history, or course of action; *esp* : a past life that is secret

⁴past *adv* : so as to reach and go beyond a point near at hand

pas•ta \ˈpäs-tə\ *n* **1** : a wheaten paste in processed form (as spaghetti) or in the form of fresh dough (as ravioli) **2** : pasta prepared for eating [Italian, from Late Latin "paste, dough"]

¹paste \ˈpāst\ *n* **1 a** : a dough rich in fat used for pastry **b** : a candy made by evaporating fruit with sugar or by flavoring a gelatin, starch, or gum arabic preparation **c** : a smooth food product made by evaporation or grinding ⟨almond *paste*⟩ **d** : a shaped dough (as spaghetti or ravioli) prepared from wheat products (as semolina, farina, or flour) **2** : a soft plastic mixture or composition: as **a** : a preparation of flour and water or starch and water used for sticking things together **b** : a clay mixture prepared for shaping into pottery or porcelain **3** : a very brilliant glass used for the manufacture of artificial gems [Middle French, from Late Latin *pasta* "dough, paste"]

²paste *vt* **1** : to cause to adhere by paste : STICK **2** : to cover with or as if with something pasted on ⟨*paste* a wall with notices⟩

³paste *vt* : to hit hard [alteration of *baste*]

paste•board \ˈpāst-ˌbōrd, ˈpās-, -ˌbȯrd\ *n* : paperboard with paper pasted to the outside to provide a smooth surface; *also* : CARDBOARD, PAPERBOARD

¹pas•tel \pas-ˈtel\ *n* **1 a** : a paste made of ground color and used for making crayons **b** : a crayon made of such paste **2** : a drawing in pastel **3** : any of various pale or light colors [French, from Italian *pastello*, from Late Latin *pastellus* "woad", from *pasta* "paste"]

²pastel *adj* **1 a** : of or relating to a pastel **b** : made with pastels **2** : pale and light in color

pas•tern \ˈpas-tərn\ *n* : the part of the foot of a horse between the fetlock and the joint at the hoof; *also* : the corresponding part of some other four-footed animals [Middle French *pasturon*, from *pasture* "pasture, tether attached to the foot of a horse at pasture"]

pas•teur•iza•tion \ˌpas-chə-rə-ˈzā-shən, ˌpas-tə-\ *n* : partial sterilization of a substance and especially a fluid (as milk) at a temperature and period of exposure that destroys objectionable organisms without major chemical alteration of the substance [Louis *Pasteur*] — **pas•teur•ize** \ˈpas-chə-ˌrīz, ˈpas-tə-\ *vt* — **pas•teur•iz•er** \-ˌrī-zər\ *n*

Pas•teur treatment \pas-ˈtər-\ *n* : a method of aborting rabies by stimulating antibody production through successive inoculations with attenuated virus of gradually increasing strength

pas•tiche \pas-ˈtēsh, päs-\ *n* : a composition (as in literature or music) made up of selections from different works : POTPOURRI [French, from Italian *pasticcio*, literally, "pasty", derived from Late Latin *pasta* "paste"]

pas•tille \pas-ˈtēl\ *n* **1** : a small mass of aromatic paste for fumigating or scenting the air of a room **2** : an aromatic or medicated lozenge : TROCHE [French *pastille*, from Latin *pastillus* "small loaf, lozenge"]

pas•time \ˈpas-ˌtīm\ *n* : something that helps to make time pass agreeably : DIVERSION

past master *n* **1** : one who has held the office of master (as in a guild, club, or lodge) **2** : one who is expert

past mistress *n* : a woman who is expert

pas•tor \ˈpas-tər\ *n* : a member of the clergy who is in charge of a church or parish [Old French *pastour*, from Latin *pastor* "herdsman", from *pascere* "to feed"] — **pas•tor•ship** \-ˌship\ *n*

¹pas•to•ral \ˈpas-tə-rəl, -trəl\ *adj* **1 a** : of or relating to shepherds or rural life **b** : devoted to or based on livestock raising **c** : RURAL **d** : depicting rural life and people especially in an idealistic way ⟨*pastoral* poetry⟩ **2** : of or relating to the pastor of a church — **pas•to•ral•ly** \-tə-rə-lē, -trə-lē\ *adv* — **pas•to•ral•ness** *n*

²pas•to•ral \ˈpas-tə-rəl, -trəl; *sense 2d is often* ˌpas-tə-ˈräl, -ˈral\ *n* **1** : a letter of a spiritual overseer; *esp* : one written by a bishop to his diocese **2 a** : a literary work dealing with shepherds or rural life in a usually artificial manner **b** : pastoral poetry or drama **c** : a rural picture or scene **d** : PASTORALE

pas•to•rale \ˌpas-tə-ˈräl, -ˈral\ *n* : an instrumental or vocal composition having a pastoral theme [Italian, from *pastorale* "pastoral"]

pas•tor•ate \ˈpas-tə-rət, -trət\ *n* **1** : the office, duties, or term of service of a pastor **2** : a body of pastors

past participle *n* : a participle that expresses completed action, that is traditionally one of the principal parts of the verb, and that is used in English in the formation of perfect tenses in the active voice and of all tenses in the passive voice ⟨*raised* in

"Many hands were raised" and *thrown* in "The ball has been thrown" are *past participles*⟩
past perfect *adj* **:** of, relating to, or being a verb tense formed in English with *had* and expressing an action or state completed at or before a past time spoken of — **past perfect** *n*
pas•tra•mi *also* **pas•tromi** \pə-ˈsträm-ē\ *n* **:** a highly seasoned smoked beef prepared especially from shoulder cuts [Yiddish, from Rumanian *pastramă*]
past•ry \ˈpā-strē\ *n, pl* **pastries 1 :** sweet baked goods made of dough or having a crust made of enriched dough **2 :** a piece of pastry [[1]*paste*]
past tense *n* **:** a verb tense expressing action or state in the past
pas•tur•age \ˈpas-chə-rij\ *n* **:** PASTURE
[1]**pas•ture** \ˈpas-chər\ *n* **1 :** plants (as grass) for the feeding especially of grazing animals **2 :** land or a plot of land used for grazing [Middle French, from Late Latin *pastura*, from Latin *pascere* "to feed"]
[2]**pasture** *vb* **1 :** to feed on or put (as cattle) to feed on pasture **:** GRAZE **2 :** to use as pasture
[1]**pas•ty** \ˈpas-tē\ *n, pl* **pasties :** [2]PIE 1; *esp* **:** a meat pie [Middle French *pasté*, from *paste* "dough, paste"]
[2]**pasty** \ˈpā-stē\ *adj* **past•i•er; -est :** resembling paste; *esp* **:** pallid and unhealthy in appearance — **past•i•ness** *n*
PA system \pē-ˈā-\ *n* **:** PUBLIC-ADDRESS SYSTEM
[1]**pat** \ˈpat\ *n* **1 :** a light blow especially with the hand or a flat instrument **2 :** a light tapping sound **3 :** something (as butter) provided in a small flat portion [Middle English *patte*]
[2]**pat** *vb* **pat•ted; pat•ting 1 :** to strike lightly with the hand or a flat instrument **:** strike or beat gently **2 :** to flatten, smooth, or shape with pats **3 :** to soothe, caress, or show approval with pats **4 :** [3]PATTER 2
[3]**pat** *adv* **:** in a pat manner **:** APTLY, PROMPTLY
[4]**pat** *adj* **1 a :** exactly suited to the purpose or occasion **:** APT ⟨a *pat* answer⟩ **b :** suspiciously suitable ⟨*pat* excuses⟩ **2 :** learned, mastered, or memorized exactly ⟨have a lesson down *pat*⟩
[5]**pat** *adv* **:** FAST 1, FIRMLY ⟨stand *pat* on the issue⟩
[1]**patch** \ˈpach\ *n* **1 :** a piece of material used to mend or cover a hole, a torn place, or a weak spot **2 :** a tiny piece of black silk or court plaster formerly worn on the face especially by women to cover a defect or to heighten beauty **3 :** a shield worn over the socket of an injured or missing eye **4 :** a small piece **:** SCRAP **5 a :** a small area or plot distinguished from its surroundings ⟨a *patch* of oats⟩ ⟨a *patch* of blistered skin⟩ **b :** a spot of color **:** BLOTCH ⟨a *patch* of white on a dog's head⟩ **6 :** a piece of cloth attached to a garment as an ornament or insignia [Middle English *pacche*]
[2]**patch** *vt* **1 :** to mend, cover, or fill up a hole or weak spot in **2 :** to provide with a patch **3 a :** to make out of patches **b :** to mend or put together especially hastily or clumsily **c :** SETTLE, ADJUST — usually used with *up* ⟨*patched* up their differences⟩
pa•tchou•li *or* **pa•tchou•ly** \ˈpach-ə-lē, pə-ˈchü-lē\ *n, pl* **-lis** *or* **-lies 1 :** an East Indian shrubby mint that yields a fragrant essential oil **2 :** a heavy perfume made from patchouli [Tamil *paccuii*]
patch pocket *n* **:** a flat pocket applied to the outside of a garment
patch test *n* **:** a test for determining allergy made by applying to the unbroken skin small pads soaked with the allergen in question
patch•work \ˈpach-ˌwərk\ *n* **1 :** something made up of various different parts **:** HODGEPODGE **2 :** pieces of cloth of various colors and shapes sewed together usually in a pattern — **patchwork** *adj*

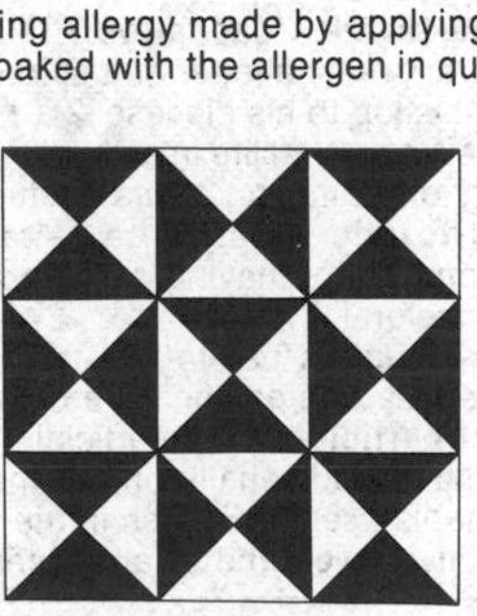
patchwork 2

patchy \ˈpach-ē\ *adj* **patch•i•er; -est :** consisting of or marked by patches; *also* **:** SPOTTY 2
pate \ˈpāt\ *n* **:** HEAD; *esp* **:** the crown of the head [Middle English] — **pat•ed** \ˈpāt-əd\ *adj*
pâ•té \pä-ˈtā, pa-\ *n* **1 :** a meat or fish pie or patty **2 :** a spread of finely mashed seasoned and spiced meat [French, from Old French *pasté*, from *paste* "dough, paste"]
pâ•té de foie gras \pä-ˌtād-ə-ˌfwä-ˈgrä, pa-\ *n, pl* **pâtés de foie gras** \-ˌtād-ə-, -ˌtāz-də-\ **:** a rich pâté of fat goose liver and truffles [French]
pa•tel•la \pə-ˈtel-ə\ *n, pl* **-tel•lae** \-ˈtel-ē, -ˌī\ *or* **-tellas :** KNEECAP [Latin, from *patina* "shallow dish, pan"] — **pa•tel•lar** \-ˈtel-ər\ *adj*
pat•en \ˈpat-n\ *n* **1 :** a plate of precious metal for holding the eucharistic bread **2 :** a shallow dish or plate **3 :** a thin metal disk [Old French *patene*, from Latin *patina* "shallow dish, pan"]
[1]**pa•tent** *1-4 are* ˈpat-nt, *5 is* ˈpāt-, *6 is* ˈpāt-, ˈpat-\ *adj* **1 :** open to public inspection — used chiefly in the phrase *letters patent* **2 :** protected by a patent ⟨*patent* locks⟩ **3 :** marketed as a proprietary commodity ⟨*patent* drugs⟩ **4 :** of, relating to, or concerned with the granting of patents especially for inventions ⟨a *patent* lawyer⟩ **5 :** offering free passage **:** UNOBSTRUCTED ⟨a *patent* opening⟩ **6 :** EVIDENT, OBVIOUS ⟨a *patent* lie⟩ [Middle French, from Latin *patens*, from *patēre* "to be open"] — **pa•ten•cy** \ˈpāt-n-sē\ *n* — **pa•tent•ly** \ˈpāt-n-tlē, ˈpat-, -lē\ *adv*
[2]**pat•ent** \ˈpat-nt\ *n* **1 :** an official document conferring a right or privilege **2 :** a writing securing to an inventor for a term of years the exclusive right to make, use, or sell his or her invention; *also* **:** the right so granted **3 :** something (as a privilege) resembling a patent
[3]**pat•ent** *vt* **1 :** to grant a privilege, right, or license to by patent **2 :** to obtain or secure by patent; *esp* **:** to secure by letters patent exclusive right to make, use, or sell **3 :** to obtain or grant a patent right to — **pat•ent•able** \ˈpat-n-tə-bəl\ *adj*
pat•en•tee \ˌpat-n-ˈtē\ *n* **:** one to whom a grant is made or a privilege secured by patent
pat•ent leather \ˌpat-n-, ˌpat-nt-\ *n* **:** a leather with a hard smooth glossy surface
patent medicine *n* **:** a packaged medicine made from a secret formula, often protected by a trademark, and sold without a prescription for use by the public with a label bearing the name of the medicine, the manufacturer's name, and directions for use
patent office *n* **:** a government office for examining claims to patents and granting patents
pat•en•tor \ˈpat-n-tər, ˌpat-n-ˈtȯr\ *n* **:** one that grants a patent
patent right *n* **:** a right granted by letters patent; *esp* **:** the exclusive right to an invention
pa•ter *n* **1** *often cap* \ˈpä-ˌteər\ **:** PATERNOSTER 1 **2** \ˈpāt-ər\ *chiefly British* **:** FATHER 1a [sense 2 from Latin *pater* "father"]
pa•ter•fa•mil•i•as \ˌpāt-ər-fə-ˈmil-ē-əs\ *n* **1 :** the male head of a household **2 :** the father of a family [Latin, from *pater* "father" + *familia* "family"]
pa•ter•nal \pə-ˈtərn-l\ *adj* **1 :** of or relating to a father **:** FATHERLY **2 :** received or inherited from one's father **3 :** related through the father ⟨a *paternal* grandfather⟩ [Latin *paternus*, from *pater* "father"] — **pa•ter•nal•ly** \-l-ē\ *adv*
pa•ter•nal•ism \-l-ˌiz-əm\ *n* **:** the principle or practice of governing or of exercising authority (as over employees) in a way suggesting that of a father over his children — **pa•ter•nal•ist** \-l-əst\ *adj or n* — **pa•ter•nal•is•tic** \-ˌtərn-l-ˈis-tik\ *adj*
pa•ter•ni•ty \pə-ˈtər-nət-ē\ *n* **1 :** the quality or state of being a father **2 :** origin or descent from a father
pat•er•nos•ter \ˌpät-ər-ˈnäs-tər, ˈpat-ər-ˌ, ˈpä-ˌteər-ˈ, -ˈnäs-ˌteər\ *n* **1** *often cap* **:** LORD'S PRAYER **2 :** a word formula repeated as a prayer or magical charm [Latin *pater noster* "our father"]
path \ˈpath, ˈpȧth\ *n, pl* **paths** \ˈpat͟hz, ˈpaths, ˈpȧt͟hz, ˈpȧths\ **1 :** a course or way formed by or as if by repeated footsteps **2 :** a track constructed for a particular use (as horseback riding) **3 a :** the way traversed by something **:** COURSE, ROUTE **b :** a way of life, conduct, or thought [Old English *pæth*] — **pathless** *adj*
path- *or* **patho-** *combining form* **:** pathological state **:** disease ⟨*pathogen*⟩ [Greek *pathos*, literally, "suffering"]
-path \ˌpath\ *n combining form* **1 :** practitioner of a (specified) system of medicine that emphasizes one aspect of disease or its treatment ⟨osteo*path*⟩ **2 :** one suffering from (such) an ailment ⟨psycho*path*⟩
Pa•than \pə-ˈtän\ *n* **:** a member of the principal ethnic group of Afghanistan [Hindi *Paṭhān*]
pa•thet•ic \pə-ˈthet-ik\ *adj* **1 :** arousing tenderness, pity, or

sorrow : PITIABLE **2** : marked by sorrow or melancholy : SAD ⟨a *pathetic* story⟩ [Late Latin *patheticus*, from Greek *pathētikos* "capable of feeling, pathetic", from *paschein* "to experience, suffer"] — **pa•thet•i•cal•ly** \-ˈthet-i-kə-lē, -klē\ *adv*

path•find•er \ˈpath-ˌfīn-dər, ˈpȧth-\ *n* : one that discovers a way and especially a new route for travelers in unexplored regions

patho•gen \ˈpath-ə-jən\ *n* : a specific cause (as a bacterium or virus) of disease — **patho•gen•ic** \ˌpath-ə-ˈjen-ik\ *adj* — **patho•gen•i•cal•ly** \-ˈjen-i-kə-lē, -klē\ *adv* — **patho•ge•nic•i•ty** \-jə-ˈnis-ət-ē\ *n*

pa•thol•o•gy \pə-ˈthäl-ə-jē, pa-\ *n, pl* **-gies 1** : the study of diseases and especially of the bodily changes produced by them **2** : something abnormal; *esp* : the disorders in structure and function that constitute disease or characterize a particular disease — **patho•log•i•cal** \ˌpath-ə-ˈläj-i-kəl\ *or* **patho•log•ic** \-ik\ *adj* — **patho•log•i•cal•ly** \-i-kə-lē, -klē\ *adv* — **pa•thol•o•gist** \pə-ˈthäl-ə-jəst, pa-\ *n*

pa•thos \ˈpā-ˌthäs, -ˌthȯs\ *n* **1** : an element in experience or in artistic representation arousing pity or compassion **2** : an emotion of sympathetic pity [Greek, "suffering, experience, emotion", from *paschein* "to experience, suffer"]

path•way \ˈpath-ˌwā, ˈpȧth-\ *n* : PATH 1, 3

-p•a•thy \p-ə-thē\ *n combining form, pl* **-pathies 1** : feeling : suffering ⟨em*pathy*⟩ : being acted upon ⟨tele*pathy*⟩ **2** : disease of (such) a part or kind **3** : system of medicine based on (such) a factor ⟨osteo*pathy*⟩

pa•tience \ˈpā-shəns\ *n* : the capacity, habit, or fact of being patient

¹pa•tient \ˈpā-shənt\ *adj* **1** : bearing pains or trials calmly or without complaint **2** : being kindly and tolerant **3** : not hasty or impetuous **4** : steadfast despite opposition, difficulty, or adversity ⟨years of *patient* labor⟩ [Middle French *pacient*, from Latin *patiens*, from *pati* "to suffer"] — **pa•tient•ly** *adv*

²patient *n* : an individual awaiting or under medical care and treatment

pat•i•na \ˈpat-ə-nə, pə-ˈtē-nə\ *n, pl* **patinas** *or* **pat•i•nae** \ˈpat-ə-ˌnē, -ˌnī\ **1** : a usually green film formed on copper and bronze by long exposure or by chemicals and often valued aesthetically **2** : a surface appearance (as a coloring or mellowing) of something grown beautiful especially with age or use [Latin, "shallow dish, pan"]

pa•tio \ˈpat-ē-ˌō *also* ˈpät-\ *n, pl* **pa•ti•os 1** : COURTYARD; *esp* : an inner court open to the sky **2** : an often paved recreation area that adjoins a dwelling [Spanish]

pa•tois \ˈpa-ˌtwä, ˈpä-\ *n, pl* **patois** \-ˌtwäz\ **1 a** : a dialect other than the standard or literary dialect **b** : illiterate or provincial speech **2** : JARGON 2 [French]

patr- *or* **patri-** *or* **patro-** *combining form* : father ⟨*patr*istic⟩ [Latin *pater* and Greek *patēr*]

pa•tri•arch \ˈpā-trē-ˌärk\ *n* **1 a** : one of the Old Testament fathers of the human race or of the Hebrew people **b** : a man who is father or founder **c** (1) : the oldest male member or representative of a group (2) : a venerable old man **2 a** : a bishop of the leading ancient sees of Constantinople, Alexandria, Antioch, Jerusalem, and Rome **b** : the head of any of various Eastern churches **c** : a Roman Catholic bishop next in rank to the pope [Old French *patriarche*, from Late Latin *patriarcha*, from Greek *patriarchēs*, from *patria* "lineage" (from *patēr* "father") + *-archēs* "-arch"] — **pa•tri•ar•chal** \ˌpā-trē-ˈär-kəl\ *adj*

pa•tri•arch•ate \ˈpā-trē-ˌär-kət, -ˌkāt\ *n* **1 a** : the office, jurisdiction, or time in office of a patriarch **b** : the residence or headquarters of a patriarch **2** : PATRIARCHY 2

pa•tri•ar•chy \-ˌär-kē\ *n, pl* **-chies 1** : social organization marked by the supremacy of the father in the clan or family and the reckoning of descent and inheritance in the male line **2** : a society organized according to the principles of patriarchy

pa•tri•cian \pə-ˈtrish-ən\ *n* **1** : a member of one of the original citizen families of ancient Rome **2** : a person of high birth and cultivation : ARISTOCRAT [Middle French *patricien*, from Latin *patricius*, from *patres* "senators", from pl. of *pater* "father"] — **patrician** *adj* — **pa•tri•ci•ate** \-ˈtrish-ē-ət, -ē-ˌāt\ *n*

pat•ri•cide \ˈpa-trə-ˌsīd\ *n* **1** : one who murders his or her own father **2** : the murder of one's own father — **pat•ri•cid•al** \ˌpa-trə-ˈsīd-l\ *adj*

pat•ri•mo•ny \ˈpa-trə-ˌmō-nē\ *n, pl* **-nies 1 a** : an estate inherited from one's father or ancestors **b** : something derived from one's father or ancestors : HERITAGE **2** : an estate or endowment belonging by ancient right to a church [Middle French *patrimonie*, from Latin *patrimonium*, from *pater* "father"] — **pat•ri•mo•ni•al** \ˌpa-trə-ˈmō-nē-əl\ *adj*

pa•tri•ot \ˈpā-trē-ət, -trē-ˌät\ *n* : a person who loves his or her country and zealously supports it [Middle French *patriote* "compatriot", from Late Latin *patriota*, from Greek *patriōtēs*, from *patrios* "of one's father", from *patēr* "father"]

pa•tri•ot•ic \ˌpā-trē-ˈät-ik\ *adj* **1** : inspired by patriotism **2** : suitable to or characteristic of a patriot — **pa•tri•ot•i•cal•ly** \-ˈät-i-kə-lē, -klē\ *adv*

pa•tri•o•tism \ˈpā-trē-ə-ˌtiz-əm\ *n* : love for or devotion to one's country

pa•tris•tic \pə-ˈtris-tik\ *adj* : of or relating to the church fathers or their writings — **pa•tris•ti•cal** \-ti-kəl\ *adj*

¹pa•trol \pə-ˈtrōl\ *n* **1 a** : the action or duty of going the rounds of an area for observation or guarding **b** : the person or group performing such an action **2** : a detachment of persons employed for reconnaissance, security, or combat **3 a** : a subdivision of a boy scout troop made up of two or more boys **b** : a subdivision of a girl scout troop usually made up of from six to eight girls [French *patrouille*, from *partouiller* "to patrol", from Middle French, 'to tramp around in the mud", from *patte* "paw"]

²patrol *vb* **pa•trolled**; **pa•trol•ling** : to be on patrol : carry out a patrol of — **pa•trol•ler** *n*

pa•trol•man \pə-ˈtrōl-mən\ *n* : one who patrols; *esp* : a police officer assigned to a beat

patrol wagon *n* : an enclosed motor vehicle used by police to carry prisoners

pa•tron \ˈpā-trən\ *n* **1** : a person chosen as a special guardian or supporter ⟨a *patron* of poets⟩ **2** : one who gives generous support or approval ⟨a *patron* of the arts⟩ **3** : a regular client or customer [Middle French, from Latin *patronus* "defender" from *pater* "father" — see PATTERN *origin*]

pat•ron•age \ˈpa-trə-nij, ˈpā-\ *n* **1** : the support or influence of a patron **2** : business or trade provided by customers **3 a** : the power to distribute government jobs on a basis other than merit alone **b** : the distribution of jobs on this basis **c** : the jobs so distributed

pa•tron•ess \ˈpā-trə-nəs\ *n* : a woman who is a patron

pa•tron•ize \ˈpā-trə-ˌnīz, ˈpa-\ *vt* **1** : to act as a patron to or of ⟨*patronize* the arts⟩ **2** : to treat with a superior air : be condescending toward **3** : to do business with ⟨*patronize* a neighborhood store⟩ — **pa•tron•iz•ing•ly** \-ˌnī-zing-lē\ *adv*

patron saint *n* : a saint to whose protection and intercession a person, a society, a church, or a place is dedicated

pat•ro•nym•ic \ˌpa-trə-ˈnim-ik\ *n* : a name derived from that of the father or a paternal ancestor [Late Latin *patronymicum*, derived from Greek *patronymia*, from *patēr* "father" + *onyma* "name"] — **patronymic** *adj*

pa•troon \pə-ˈtrün\ *n* : the proprietor of a manorial estate granted by the Dutch especially in New York or New Jersey [Dutch, literally, "boss, superior", from French *patron* "patron"]

pat•sy \ˈpat-sē\ *n, pl* **patsies** : one who is duped or victimized : SUCKER [perhaps from Italian *pazzo* "fool"]

¹pat•ter \ˈpat-ər\ *vb* **1** : to say or speak in a rapid or mechanical manner **2** : to talk glibly and volubly [Middle English *patren*, from *paternoster*] — **pat•ter•er** *n*

²patter *n* **1** : a specialized lingo : CANT; *esp* : the jargon of criminals (as thieves) **2** : the spiel of a street hawker or of a circus barker **3** : empty chatter **4 a** : the rapid-fire talk of a comedian **b** : the talk with which an entertainer accompanies a routine

³patter *vi* **1** : to strike or pat rapidly and repeatedly ⟨rain *pattering* on a roof⟩ **2** : to run with quick light-sounding steps [derived from ²*pat*]

⁴patter *n* : a quick succession of light sounds or pats ⟨the *patter* of little feet⟩

¹pat•tern \ˈpat-ərn\ *n* **1** : a form or model proposed for imitation : EXEMPLAR **2** : something designed or used as a model for making things ⟨a dress *pattern*⟩ **3** : a model for making a mold into which molten metal is poured to form a casting **4** : SPECIMEN 1, SAMPLE **5 a** : an artistic or mechanical design ⟨cloth with a small *pattern*⟩ **b** : form or style in literary or musical composition **6 :** a natural or chance configuration ⟨frost *patterns*⟩ **7 :** a complex of individual or group characteristics (as traits or behavior) ⟨behavior *patterns*⟩ ⟨the *pattern* of American industry⟩ [Middle English *patron,* from Middle French, "pattern, patron"]

△ **origin** Latin *patronus* is derived from *pater,* "father", and the duties of a Roman *patronus* were comparable to those of a father. He was a protector of his city or province; a defender in a court of law was his client's *patronus*; the man who freed his slave became that slave's *patronus.* The use of *patronus* in Medieval Latin shifted to suit the new requirements of the Christian era. Such a father figure as a patron saint or the patron of a benefice was called a *patronus,* as was anyone who served like a father as a model or pattern to be emulated. Middle English *patron* (borrowed from Middle French) had a range of meaning similar to that of its Medieval Latin ancestor. During the 16th century another pronunciation of *patron* appeared, represented by such spellings as *pattern.* By the beginning of the 18th century the two forms, *patron* and *pattern,* were identified with separate senses and became two distinct words.

2pattern *vt* **:** to make or fashion according to a pattern

pat•ty *also* **pat•tie** \ˈpat-ē\ *n, pl* **patties 1 :** a little pie **2 a :** a small flat cake of chopped food ⟨a hamburg *patty*⟩ **b :** a small flat candy ⟨mint *patties*⟩ [French *pâté*]

pau•ci•ty \ˈpȯ-sət-ē\ *n* **:** smallness of number or quantity ⟨a *paucity* of tenor voices⟩ ⟨*paucity* of experience⟩ [Latin *paucitas,* from *paucus* "little"]

Paul•ist \ˈpȯ-ləst\ *n* **:** a member of the Roman Catholic Congregation of the Missionary Priests of St. Paul the Apostle founded in the United States in 1858

pau•low•nia \pȯ-ˈlō-nē-ə\ *n* **:** a Chinese tree widely grown in warm regions for its showy clusters of fragrant violet flowers [Anna *Paulovna,* died 1865, Russian princess]

paunch \ˈpȯnch, ˈpänch\ *n* **1 a :** the belly together with its contents **b :** POTBELLY 1 **2 :** RUMEN [Middle French *panche,* from Latin *pantex*]

paunchy \ˈpȯn-chē, ˈpän-\ *adj* **:** having a potbelly — **paunch•i•ness** *n*

pau•per \ˈpȯ-pər\ *n* **:** a very poor person; *esp* **:** one supported by charity [Latin, "poor"] — **pau•per•ism** \-pə-ˌriz-əm\ *n* — **pau•per•ize** \-ˌrīz\ *vt*

1pause \ˈpȯz\ *n* **1 :** a temporary stop **2 a :** a break in a verse **b :** a brief suspension of the voice to indicate the limits and relations of sentences and their parts **3 :** temporary inaction often because of doubt or uncertainty **4 :** the sign denoting a musical hold **5 :** a reason or cause for pausing ⟨it was a thought to give one *pause*⟩ [Latin *pausa,* from Greek *pausis,* from *pauein* "to stop"]

2pause *vi* **1 :** to stop temporarily **2 :** to linger for a time ⟨*pause* on a high note⟩

pa•vane \pə-ˈvän, -ˈvan\ *also* **pa•van** *same or* ˈpav-ən\ *n* **1 :** a stately court dance by couples that was introduced from southern Europe into England in the 16th century **2 :** music for the pavane [Middle French *pavane,* from Spanish *pavana,* from Italian]

pave \ˈpāv\ *vt* **1 :** to lay or cover with material (as stone or concrete) that makes a firm level surface for travel **2 :** to cover firmly and solidly as if with paving material [Middle French *paver,* from Latin *pavire* "to strike, stamp"] — **pave the way :** to prepare a smooth easy way ⟨*pave the way* for those who come after⟩

pave•ment \ˈpāv-mənt\ *n* **1 :** a paved surface **2 :** the material with which something is paved

pa•vil•ion \pə-ˈvil-yən\ *n* **1 :** a usually large luxurious tent **2 :** a lightly constructed often ornamental building serving as a shelter in a park, garden, or athletic field **3 :** a part of a building projecting from the main body of the structure **4 :** a building either partly or completely detached from the main building or main group of buildings [Old French *paveillon,* from Latin *papilio* "butterfly"]

pav•ing \ˈpā-viŋ\ *n* **:** PAVEMENT

1paw \ˈpȯ\ *n* **1 :** the foot of a four-footed animal (as a lion or dog) that has claws; *also* **:** the foot of an animal **2 :** a human hand especially when large or clumsy [Middle French *poue*]

2paw *vb* **1 :** to feel or touch clumsily or rudely ⟨merchandise *pawed* by customers⟩ **2 :** to touch, strike, or scrape with a paw or hoof **3 :** to flail at or grab wildly ⟨hands *pawing* the air⟩

pawl \ˈpȯl\ *n* **:** a pivoted tongue or sliding bolt on one part of a machine that is adapted to fall into notches on another part (as a ratchet wheel) so as to permit motion in only one direction [perhaps from Dutch *pal*]

1pawn \ˈpȯn, ˈpän\ *n* **1 :** something deposited with another as security for a loan **:** PLEDGE **2 :** the state of being pledged ⟨the watch was in *pawn*⟩ [Middle French *pan*]

2pawn *vt* **:** to give temporarily as security ⟨*pawned* the silverware⟩ — **pawn•er** \ˈpȯ-nər, ˈpän-ər\ *n*

3pawn *n* **1 :** a piece in chess of least value that can move only one square forward at a time after its first move and can capture only diagonally forward **2 :** one used or exploited to further the purposes of another [Middle French *poon,* from Medieval Latin *pedon-, pedo* "foot soldier", from Latin *ped-, pes* "foot"]

pawn•bro•ker \ˈpȯn-ˌbrō-kər, ˈpän-\ *n* **:** one who lends money to customers who have pledged personal property as security — **pawn•bro•king** \-kiŋ\ *n*

Paw•nee \pȯ-ˈnē, pä-\ *n* **:** a member of an Amerindian people of what is now Nebraska and Kansas

pawn•shop \ˈpȯn-ˌshäp, ˈpän-\ *n* **:** a pawnbroker's shop

paw•paw *variant of* PAPAW

1pay \ˈpā\ *vb* **paid** \ˈpād\ *also in sense 7* **payed**; **paid**; **pay•ing 1 :** to give money especially in return for services received or for something bought ⟨*pay* the taxi driver⟩ ⟨*pay* for a ticket⟩ **2 :** to pay what is indicated or required by ⟨*pay* a bill⟩ ⟨*pay* a tax⟩ **3 :** to get even with ⟨*pay* someone back for an injury⟩ **4 :** to give or offer freely ⟨*pay* a compliment⟩ ⟨*pay* attention⟩ **5 :** to return as profit ⟨an investment *paying* 5 percent⟩ **6 :** to make or secure suitable return for expense or trouble **:** be worth the effort or pains required ⟨it *pays* to drive carefully⟩ **7 :** to make (as a rope) slack and allow to run out — usually used with *out* [Old French *paier,* from Latin *pacare* "to pacify", from *pac-, pax* "peace"]

△ **origin** Etymologically, to *pay* is "to pacify". The Latin verb *pacare,* "to pacify", is derived from *pax,* "peace". In the Middle Ages, *pacare* was used specifically to mean "to pacify a creditor by paying a debt" and eventually, more generally, "to pay". Old French *paier* had both the original sense "to pacify or appease" and the later, "to pay". Middle English *payen,* too, borrowed from the French in the late 12th or early 13th century, was used in both senses. But the original sense of *pay* is now long obsolete.

• **syn** PAY, COMPENSATE, REMUNERATE mean to give money or its equivalent in return for something. PAY implies the discharge of an obligation incurred ⟨*pay* the worker's wages⟩ COMPENSATE implies making up for services rendered or help given or loss suffered ⟨gave $10 more to *compensate* us for our trouble⟩ REMUNERATE suggests paying for services rendered rather than for material goods.

2pay *n* **1 a :** the act or fact of paying or being paid **:** PAYMENT **b :** the status of being paid by an employer **:** EMPLOY **2 :** something paid; *esp* **:** WAGES, SALARY

3pay *adj* **1 :** containing or leading to something precious or valuable (as gold or oil) ⟨*pay* rock⟩ **2 :** equipped with a coin slot for receiving a fee for use ⟨a *pay* phone⟩ **3 :** requiring payment ⟨*pay* TV⟩

pay•able \ˈpā-ə-bəl\ *adj* **:** that may, can, or must be paid; *esp* **:** DUE ⟨accounts *payable*⟩

pay•check \ˈpā-ˌchek\ *n* **1 :** a check in payment of wages or salary **2 :** WAGES, SALARY

pay dirt *n* **1 :** earth or ore that yields a profit to a miner **2 :** a useful or remunerative discovery or object ⟨really hit *pay dirt* with that invention⟩

pay•ee \pā-ˈē\ *n* **:** one to whom money is or is to be paid

pay•er \ˈpā-ər\ *also* **pay•or** \ˈpā-ər, pā-ˈȯr\ *n* **:** one that pays

pay•load \ˈpā-ˌlōd\ *n* **:** something (as cargo, passengers, instruments, or explosives) carried by a vehicle, missile, rocket, or spacecraft in addition to what is necessary for its operation

pay•mas•ter \-ˌmas-tər\ *n* **:** an officer or agent of an employer whose duty it is to pay salaries or wages

pay•ment \ˈpā-mənt\ *n* **1 :** the act of paying **2 :** money given to pay for something ⟨*payments* on a car⟩ ⟨*payment* for a day's work⟩

pay•off \ˈpā-ˌȯf\ *n* **1 :** payment at the outcome of an enterprise ⟨a big *payoff* from an investment⟩ **2 :** the climax of an incident or enterprise ⟨the *payoff* of a story⟩

pay off \pā-ˈȯf, ˈpā-\ *vt* **1 :** to pay in full often through small payments made at intervals ⟨*pay off* a mortgage⟩ **2 :** to take revenge on ⟨*pay off* an enemy⟩

pay•ola \pā-ˈō-lə\ *n* **:** secret or indirect payment for a commer-

cial favor [probably alteration of *payoff*]
pay•roll \'pā-ˌrōl\ *n* : a list of persons entitled to receive pay with the amounts due to each; *also* : the amount of money necessary to pay those on such a list
pay station *n* : a pay telephone or a booth containing a pay telephone
pay up *vb* : to pay (as an overdue debt) in full
PCB \ˌpē-ˌsē-'bē\ *n* : POLYCHLORINATED BIPHENYL
PDQ \ˌpē-ˌdē-'kyü\ *adv, often not cap* : IMMEDIATELY 2 [abbreviation of *pretty damned quick*]
pea \'pē\ *n, pl* **peas** *also* **pease** \'pēz\ **1 a** : a variable annual leguminous vine grown for its rounded smooth or wrinkled edible protein-rich seeds **b** : the seed of the pea **c** *pl* : the immature pods of the pea with their included seeds **2** : any of various plants of the same family as the pea [back-formation from Middle English *pease* (taken as a pl.), from Old English *pise*, from Late Latin *pisa*, pl. of *pisum*, from Greek *pison*]
peace \'pēs\ *n* **1** : a state of tranquillity or quiet: as **a** : freedom from civil disturbance or foreign war **b** : a state of security or order within a community protected by law or custom ⟨breach of the *peace*⟩ **2** : freedom from disquieting or oppressive thoughts or emotions **3** : harmony in personal relations **4 a** : a state or period of agreement between governments **b** : a pact or agreement between combatants to end hostilities [Old French *pais*, from Latin *pax*]
peace•able \'pē-sə-bəl\ *adj* **1** : inclined toward peace : not quarrelsome **2** : free from strife or disorder — **peace•ably** \-blē\ *adv*
peace•ful \'pēs-fəl\ *adj* **1** : PEACEABLE 1 ⟨a *peaceful* person⟩ **2** : untroubled by conflict, agitation, or commotion : QUIET, TRANQUIL ⟨a *peaceful* countryside⟩ **3** : free from violence or force ⟨settled the conflict by *peaceful* means⟩ — **peace•ful•ly** \-fə-lē\ *adv* — **peace•ful•ness** *n*
peace•mak•er \'pē-ˌsmā-kər\ *n* : a person who arranges a peace : one who settles an argument or stops a fight — **peace•mak•ing** \-king\ *n or adj*
peace offering *n* : a gift or service to procure peace or reconciliation
peace officer *n* : a civil officer (as a policeman or sheriff) whose duty it is to preserve the public peace
peace pipe *n* : an ornamented ceremonial pipe of the Amerindians — compare CALUMET
peace•time \'pē-ˌstīm\ *n* : a time when a nation is not at war
1peach \'pēch\ *n* **1** : a low spreading Chinese tree related to the plums and cherries that is grown in most temperate areas for its sweet juicy fruit with pulpy white or yellow flesh, thin downy skin, and single rough hard stone; *also* : its fruit **2** : a moderate yellowish pink **3** : one likened to a peach (as in beauty, or excellence) [Middle French *peche* "peach fruit", from Late Latin *persica*, from Latin *persicum*, from *persicus* "Persian", from *Persia*]
2peach *vi* : to turn informer : BLAB [Middle English *pechen*, short for *apechen* "to accuse, impeach", derived from Late Latin *impedicare* "to entangle"]
peachy \'pē-chē\ *adj* **peach•i•er**; **-est 1** : resembling a peach **2** : unusually fine : DANDY
1pea•cock \'pē-ˌkäk\ *n* **1** : a male peafowl distinguished by a small upright tuft on the head and by greatly elongated feathers in the tail mostly tipped with eyelike spots and erected and spread at will in a fan shimmering with iridescent color; *also* : PEAFOWL **2** : one showing off personal attributes or possessions (as clothing) [Middle English *pecok*, from *pe-* (from Old English *pēa* "peafowl", from Latin *pavo* "peacock") + *cok* "cock"]

1peacock 1

2peacock *vi* : to make a proud self-important display
peacock blue *n* : a moderate greenish blue
pea•fowl \'pē-ˌfaul\ *n* : a very large pheasant of southeastern Asia and the East Indies that is often kept in captivity for its beauty [*pea-* (as in *peacock*) + *fowl*]
pea green *n* : a moderate yellow-green
pea•hen \'pē-ˌhen, -'hen\ *n* : a female peafowl
pea jacket \'pē-\ *n* : a heavy woolen double-breasted jacket worn chiefly by sailors [by folk etymology from Dutch *pijjekker*, from *pij*, a kind of cloth + *jekker* "jacket"]
1peak \'pēk\ *n* **1** : a pointed or projecting part; *esp* : the visor of a cap or hat **2** : PROMONTORY **3** : a sharp or pointed ridge or end ⟨the *peak* of a roof⟩ **4 a** : the top of a hill or mountain ending in a point **b** : a whole hill or mountain especially when isolated **5** : the narrow part of a ship's bow or stern **6** : the highest level or value or greatest degree of development ⟨the *peak* of perfection⟩ [perhaps alteration of *pike*] **syn** see SUMMIT
2peak *vb* : to come or cause to come to a peak, point, or maximum
3peak *adj* : being at or reaching the maximum ⟨an athlete in *peak* condition⟩ ⟨a *peak* year for sales⟩
1peaked *adj* \'pēkt, 'pē-kəd\ : having a peak : POINTED — **peaked•ness** \'pēkt-nəs, 'pēk-nəs, 'pē-kəd-nəs\ *n*
2peak•ed \'pē-kəd\ *adj* : being pale and wan : SICKLY [from *peak* "to look sickly", of unknown origin]
1peal \'pēl\ *n* **1** : a loud ringing of bells **2** : a loud sound or succession of sounds ⟨a *peal* of laughter⟩ ⟨a *peal* of thunder⟩ [Middle English, "appeal, summons to church", short for *appel* "appeal", from *appelen* "to appeal"]
2peal *vb* : to sound in peals ⟨bells *pealing* in the distance⟩
pea•like \'pē-ˌlīk\ *adj* **1** : resembling a garden pea (as in firmness or shape) **2** : being showy and resembling a butterfly in shape ⟨*pealike* flowers⟩
pea•nut \'pē-nət, -ˌnət\ *n* **1** : a low-branching widely cultivated annual herb of the pea family with showy yellow flowers and pods that ripen underground; *also* : this pod or one of the oily edible seeds it contains **2** : an insignificant or tiny person **3** *pl* : a trifling amount

peanut 1

peanut butter *n* : a paste made by grinding roasted skinned peanuts
peanut oil *n* : a colorless to yellow fatty oil from peanuts that is used chiefly as a salad oil, in margarine, in soap, and as an inert medium in medicinal preparations and cosmetics
pear \'paər, 'peər\ *n* : a fleshy pome fruit that usually tapers toward the stem end; *also* : a tree that bears pears and is related to the apple [Old English *peru*, from Latin *pirum*]
1pearl \'pərl\ *n* **1 a** : a dense usually lustrous body formed of layers of nacre as an abnormal growth within the shell of some mollusks and used as a gem **b** : MOTHER-OF-PEARL **2** : something resembling a pearl (as in shape, color, or value) **3** : a slightly bluish medium gray [Middle French *perle*, derived from Latin *perna* "mussel"]
2pearl *vb* **1** : to set or adorn with pearls **2** : to sprinkle or bead with pearly drops **3** : to form into drops or beads like pearls or into small round grains **4** : to give a pearly color or luster to **5** : to fish or search for pearls — **pearl•er** *n*
3pearl *adj* **1 a** : of, relating to, or resembling pearl **b** : made of or adorned with pearls **2** : having grains of medium size ⟨*pearl* barley⟩
pearl gray *n* **1** : a yellowish to light gray **2** : a pale blue
pearly \'pər-lē\ *adj* **pearl•i•er**; **-est** : resembling, containing, or adorned with pearls or mother-of-pearl
peart \'piərt\ *adj, chiefly South & Midland* : in good spirits : LIVELY [alteration of *pert*]
peas•ant \'pez-nt\ *n* **1** : a European small farmer or farm laborer; *also* : one of similar agricultural status elsewhere **2** : an uncouth person or one of low social status [Middle French *paisant*, from *païs* "country", from Late Latin *pagensis* "inhabitant of a district", from Latin *pagus* "district"]
peas•ant•ry \'pez-n-trē\ *n* : peasants as a group ⟨a nation's *peasantry*⟩ ⟨the local *peasantry*⟩
pease *pl of* PEA

\ə\ abut	\au̇\ out	\i\ tip	\ȯ\ saw	\u̇\ foot
\ər\ further	\ch\ chin	\ī\ life	\ȯi\ coin	\y\ yet
\a\ mat	\e\ pet	\j\ job	\th\ thin	\yü\ few
\ā\ take	\ē\ easy	\ng\ sing	\th\ this	\yu̇\ cure
\ä\ cot, cart	\g\ go	\ō\ bone	\ü\ food	\zh\ vision

pea•shoot•er \'pē-'shüt-ər\ *n* : a toy blowgun for shooting peas

pea soup *n* **1** : a thick soup made of dried peas **2** : a heavy fog

peat \'pēt\ *n* **1** : TURF 2b **2** : a dark brown or black vegetable substance formed when some plants (as sphagnum moss) partly decay under water [Medieval Latin *peta*] — **peaty** \'pēt-ē\ *adj*

peat moss *n* : SPHAGNUM

pea•vey *or* **pea•vy** \'pē-vē\ *n, pl* **peaveys** *or* **peavies** : a lever like a cant hook but with the end armed with a strong sharp spike used in handling logs [probably from the name *Peavey*]

[1]**peb•ble** \'peb-əl\ *n* **1** : a small usually round stone especially when worn by the action of water **2** : an irregular, crinkled, or grainy surface [Middle English *pobble,* from Old English *papolstān*] — **peb•bly** \'peb-lē, -ə-lē\ *adj*

[2]**pebble** *vt* **peb•bled**; **peb•bling** \'peb-ling, -ə-ling\ : to treat (as leather) so as to produce a rough and irregularly indented surface

pe•can \pi-'kän, -'kan\ *n* : a large hickory of the south central United States; *also* : its edible oblong nut [of American Indian origin]

pec•ca•dil•lo \,pek-ə-'dil-ō\ *n, pl* **-loes** *or* **-los** : a slight offense or fault [Spanish *pecadillo,* from *pecado* "sin", from Latin *peccatum,* from *peccare* "to sin"]

pec•ca•ry \'pek-ə-rē\ *n, pl* **-ries** : either of two American chiefly tropical mammals resembling but smaller than the related pigs [of American Indian origin]

[1]**peck** \'pek\ *n* **1** — see MEASURE table **2** : a large quantity : great deal ⟨a *peck* of trouble⟩ [Old French *pek*]

[2]**peck** *vb* **1 a** (1) : to strike, pick up, or move with a pointed bill or tool ⟨chickens *pecking* corn⟩ (2) : to make by pecking ⟨*peck* a hole⟩ **b** : to strike at or pick up something with or as if with a bill **2** : to eat daintily : NIBBLE, PICK [Middle English *pecken,* from *piken* "to pierce, pick"] — **peck•er** *n*

[3]**peck** *n* **1** : an impression or hole made by pecking **2** : a quick sharp stroke

pecking order *or* **peck order** *n* **1** : a basic pattern of social organization within a flock of poultry in which each bird pecks another lower in the scale without being pecked in return and submits to pecking by one of higher rank **2** : a social order with ranks or classes

pec•ten \'pek-tən\ *n* : SCALLOP 1a [Latin, "comb, scallop"]

pec•tin \'pek-tən\ *n* : any of various water-soluble substances in plant tissues that yield a gel which is the basis of fruit jellies; *also* : a commercial product rich in pectins [French *pectine,* derived from Greek *pēktikos* "coagulating", from *pēgnynai* "to fix, coagulate"] — **pec•tin•ous** \-tə-nəs\ *adj*

pec•ti•nate \'pek-tə-,nāt\ *adj* : having narrow parallel projections or divisions resembling the teeth of a comb [Latin *pectinatus,* from *pecten* "comb"] — **pec•ti•na•tion** \,pek-tə-'nā-shən\ *n*

[1]**pec•to•ral** \'pek-tə-rəl, -trəl\ *adj* **1** : of, relating to, or situated in, near, or on the chest **2** : coming from the breast or heart as the seat of emotion : SUBJECTIVE [Latin *pectoralis,* from *pector-, pectus* "breast"]

[2]**pectoral** *n* **1** : PECTORAL FIN **2** : PECTORAL MUSCLE

pectoral cross *n* : a cross worn on the breast especially by a prelate

pectoral fin *n* : either of a pair of fins that correspond in a fish to the forelimbs of a four-footed animal — compare PELVIC FIN

pectoral girdle *n* : an arch of bone or cartilage supporting the forelimbs of a vertebrate

pectoral muscle *n* : one of the muscles which connect the ventral walls of the chest with the bones of the upper arm and shoulder and of which there are two on each side in humans

pec•u•late \'pek-yə-,lāt\ *vt* : EMBEZZLE [Latin *peculari,* from *peculium* "private property"] — **pec•u•la•tion** \,pek-yə-'lā-shən\ *n* — **pec•u•la•tor** \'pek-yə-,lāt-ər\ *n*

pe•cu•liar \pi-'kyül-yər\ *adj* **1** : belonging exclusively to one person or group **2** : characteristic of one only : DISTINCTIVE **3** : different from the usual or normal: **a** : SPECIAL 1a, PARTICULAR **b** : distinctly odd or eccentric [Latin *peculiaris* "of private property, special", from *peculium* "private property", from *pecu* "cattle"] **syn** see STRANGE, CHARACTERISTIC — **pe•cu•liar•ly** *adv*

pe•cu•liar•i•ty \pi-,kyül-'yar-ət-ē, -,kyü-lē-'ar-\ *n, pl* **-ties** **1** : the quality or state of being peculiar **2** : a distinguishing characteristic **3** : an odd trait or habit : QUIRK

pe•cu•ni•ary \pi-'kyü-nē-,er-ē\ *adj* : of, relating to, or consisting of money ⟨*pecuniary* aid⟩ ⟨*pecuniary* policies⟩ [Latin *pecuniarius,* from *pecunia* "money"] **syn** see FINANCIAL

ped- — see PAED-

-ped \,ped *also* pəd\ *or* **-pede** \,pēd\ *n combining form* : foot ⟨maxilli*ped*⟩ [Latin *ped-, pes*]

ped•a•gog•ics \,ped-ə-'gäj-iks, -'gōj-\ *n* : PEDAGOGY

ped•a•gogue *also* **ped•a•gog** \'ped-ə-,gäg\ *n* : TEACHER, SCHOOLMASTER; *esp* : a dull, formal, and pedantic teacher [Middle French *pedagoge,* from Latin *paedagogus,* from Greek *paidagōgos,* slave who escorted children to school, from *paid-* "paed-" + *agōgos* 'leader", from *agein* "to lead"]

ped•a•go•gy \'ped-ə-,gō-jē *also* -,gäj-ē\ *n* : the art, science, or profession of teaching; *esp* : EDUCATION 2 — **ped•a•gog•ic** \,ped-ə-'gäj-ik\ *or* **ped•a•gog•i•cal** \-'gäj-i-kəl\ *adj* — **ped•a•gog•i•cal•ly** \-i-kə-lē, -klē\ *adv*

[1]**ped•al** \'ped-l\ *n* **1** : a lever acted on by the foot in the playing of musical instruments **2** : a foot lever or treadle by which a part is activated in a mechanism

[2]**pedal** *adj* : of or relating to the foot [Latin *pedalis,* from *ped-, pes* "foot"]

[3]**pedal** *vb* **ped•aled** *also* **ped•alled**; **ped•al•ing** *also* **ped•al•ling** \'ped-l-ing, 'ped-ling\ **1 a** : to use or work the pedals of something **b** : to work the pedals of ⟨*pedal* a bike⟩ **2** : to ride a bicycle ⟨*pedal* down the street⟩

pedal point *n* : a single tone that is normally sustained in the bass and sounds against changing harmonies in the other parts

pedal pushers *n pl* : women's and girls' calf-length pants

ped•ant \'ped-nt\ *n* **1** : a person who shows off his or her learning **2** : a dull formal teacher who emphasizes petty details [Middle French, from Italian *pedante*] — **pe•dan•tic** \pə-'dant-ik\ *adj* — **pe•dan•ti•cal•ly** \-'dant-i-kə-lē, -klē\ *adv*

ped•ant•ry \'ped-n-trē\ *n, pl* **-ries** **1** : pedantic presentation or application of knowledge or learning **2** : an instance of pedantry

ped•dle \'ped-l\ *vb* **ped•dled**; **ped•dling** \'ped-ling, -l-ing\ **1** : to travel about especially from house to house with wares for sale **2** : to sell or offer for sale from place to place usually in small quantities : HAWK [back-formation from *peddler,* from Middle English *pedlere*] — **ped•dler** *or* **ped•lar** \'ped-lər\ *n*

ped•es•tal \'ped-əst-l\ *n* **1** : the support or foot of a column; *also* : the base of any upright structure (as a vase, lamp, or statue) **2** : a position of high regard or esteem ⟨placed on a *pedestal* by one's children⟩ [Middle French *piedestal,* from Italian *piedestallo,* from *pie di stallo* "foot of a stall"]

[1]**pe•des•tri•an** \pə-'des-trē-ən\ *adj* **1** : lacking imagination or originality : COMMONPLACE ⟨*pedestrian* writing⟩ **2 a** : going or performed on foot **b** : of or relating to walking **3** : of or designed for pedestrians [Latin *pedester,* literally, "going on foot", derived from *ped-, pes* "foot"]

[2]**pedestrian** *n* : a person going on foot

pe•des•tri•an•ism \-,iz-əm\ *n* **1 a** : the practice of walking **b** : fondness for walking **2** : the quality or state of being unimaginative or commonplace

pe•di•a•tri•cian \,pēd-ē-ə-'trish-ən\ *n* : a specialist in pediatrics

pe•di•at•rics \,pēd-ē-'a-triks\ *n* : a branch of medicine dealing with the development, care, and diseases of children [*paed-* + Greek *iatros* "physician"] — **pe•di•at•ric** \-trik\ *adj*

pe•di•a•trist \,pēd-ē-'a-trəst, pē-'dī-ə-\ *n* : PEDIATRICIAN

pedi•cab \'ped-i-,kab\ *n* : a small 3-wheeled hooded passenger vehicle that is pedaled [Latin *ped-, pes* "foot" + English *cab*]

ped•i•cel \'ped-ə-,sel\ *n* : a slender basal part of an organism; *esp* : a stalk that supports a single flower — compare PEDUNCLE [New Latin *pedicellus,* from Latin *pediculus* "little foot, pedicel", from *ped-, pes* "foot"]

pe•dic•u•lo•sis \pi-,dik-yə-'lō-səs\ *n* : infestation with lice [Latin *pediculus* "louse", from *pedis* "louse"] — **pe•dic•u•lous** \-'dik-yə-ləs\ *adj*

ped•i•cure \'ped-i-,kyu̇r\ *n* **1** : a specialist in chiropody **2 a** : care of the feet, toes, and toenails **b** : a single treatment of these parts [French *pédicure,* from Latin *ped-, pes* "foot" + *curare* "to take care", from *cura* "care"] — **ped•i•cur•ist** \-,kyu̇r-əst\ *n*

ped•i•gree \'ped-ə-,grē\ *n* **1** : a table or list showing the line of ancestors of an animal or person **2 a** : an ancestral line : LINEAGE **b** : the origin and history of something (as a document or a collector's coin or stamp) **3 a :** distinguished ancestry **b :** purity of a breed of an individual or strain recorded by a pedigree [Middle English *pedegru,* from Middle French *pie de grue* "crane's foot"; from the shape made by the lines of a genealogical chart] — **ped•i•greed** \-ˌgrēd\ *adj*

ped•i•ment \ˈped-ə-mənt\ *n* **:** a triangular space forming the gable of a 2-pitched roof in classic architecture; *also* **:** a similar form used as a decoration (as over a door or a window) [obsolete *periment,* probably alteration of *pyramid*] — **ped•i•men•tal** \ˌped-ə-ˈment-l\ *adj*

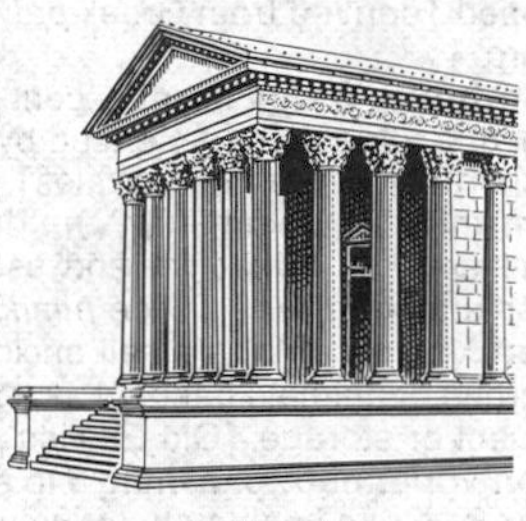

pediment

pedi•palp \ˈped-ə-ˌpalp\ *n* **:** either of the second pair of head appendages of an arachnid (as a spider) borne near the mouth and often modified for a special (as sensory) function [New Latin *pedipalpus,* from *ped-, pes* "foot" + *palpus* "palpus"]

pedo- — see PAED-

pe•dom•e•ter \pi-ˈdäm-ət-ər\ *n* **:** an instrument that measures the distance a walker covers by responding to body motion at each step [French *pédomètre,* from Latin *ped-, pes* "foot" + French *-mètre* "-meter"]

pe•dun•cle \ˈpē-ˌdəng-kəl, pi-ˈ\ *n* **:** a narrow part by which some larger part or the body of an organism is attached; *esp* **:** a stalk that supports a flower cluster — compare PEDICEL [New Latin *pedunculus,* from Latin *ped-, pes* "foot"] — **pe•dun•cu•late** \pi-ˈdəng-kyə-lət\ *or* **pe•dun•cu•lat•ed** \-ˌlāt-əd\ *adj*

[1]peek \ˈpēk\ *vi* **1 a :** to look slyly or stealthily **b :** to peer through a crack or hole or from a place of concealment **2 :** to take a brief look **:** GLANCE [Middle English *piken*]

[2]peek *n* **:** a brief or stealthy look

[1]peel \ˈpēl\ *vb* **1 :** to strip off the skin, bark, or rind of ⟨*peel* an apple⟩ **2 :** to remove as if by stripping or tearing ⟨*peeled* off my coat⟩ **3 a :** to come off in strips or patches ⟨the paint is *peeling*⟩ **b :** to lose the skin, bark, or rind ⟨your face is *peeling*⟩ [Middle French *peler,* from Latin *pilare* "to remove the hair from", from *pilus* "hair"] — **peel•er** *n*

[2]peel *n* **:** a skin or rind especially of a fruit

[3]peel *n* **:** a usually long-handled spade-shaped utensil used chiefly by bakers for getting something into or out of an oven [Middle French *pele,* from Latin *pala*]

peel•ing \ˈpē-ling\ *n* **:** a peeled-off piece or strip (as of skin)

peel off *vi* **:** to veer away from an airplane formation especially for diving or landing

peen \ˈpēn\ *n* **:** the usually hemispherical or wedge-shaped end of the head of some hammers opposite the face that is used for cutting and shaping [probably of Scandinavian origin]

[1]peep \ˈpēp\ *vi* **1 :** to utter the characteristic feeble shrill cry of a newly hatched bird or a similar sound **2 :** to speak with a small weak voice **:** utter the slightest sound [Middle English *pepen,* of imitative origin]

[2]peep *n* **1 :** a feeble shrill sound **2 :** a slight utterance especially of complaint or protest ⟨not another *peep* out of you⟩

[3]peep *vb* **1 a :** to peer through a crevice **b :** to look cautiously or slyly **2 :** to begin to emerge from concealment **:** show slightly **3 :** to cause (as the head of one peeping) to protrude slightly [Middle English *pepen,* perhaps alteration of *piken* "to peek"]

[4]peep *n* **1 :** the first glimpse or faint appearance ⟨at the *peep* of dawn⟩ **2 :** a brief or furtive look

[1]peep•er \ˈpē-pər\ *n* **:** any of various small tailless amphibians (as a spring peeper) that peep shrilly in spring

[2]peeper *n* **1 :** one that peeps; *esp* **:** PEEPING TOM **2 :** EYE 1a

peep•hole \ˈpēp-ˌhōl\ *n* **:** a hole or crevice to peep through

peeping tom \-ˈtäm\ *n, often cap* **:** a person who spies into the windows of private dwellings **:** one who furtively watches others [*Peeping Tom,* legendary 11th century tailor of Coventry supposed to have been struck blind for peeping at Lady Godiva]

peep show *n* **:** a display of objects or pictures viewed through a small hole usually fitted with a lens

peep sight *n* **:** a rear sight for a gun having an adjustable metal piece pierced with a small hole to look through in aiming

[1]peer \ˈpiər\ *n* **1 :** one that is of equal standing with another **:** EQUAL **2** *archaic* **:** COMPANION, FELLOW **3 a :** a member (as a duke, marquess, earl, viscount, or baron) of one of the five ranks of the British peerage **b :** NOBLE [Old French *per,* from *per,* adj., "equal", from Latin *par*]

[2]peer *vi* **1 :** to look narrowly or curiously; *esp* **:** to look searchingly at something difficult to discern **2 :** to come slightly into view [perhaps from *appear*]

peer•age \ˈpiər-ij\ *n* **1 :** the body of peers **2 :** the rank or dignity of a peer **3 :** a book containing a list of peers

peer•ess \ˈpir-əs\ *n* **1 :** the wife or widow of a peer **2 :** a woman who holds the rank of a peer in her own right

peer•less \ˈpiər-ləs\ *adj* **:** having no equal **:** MATCHLESS, INCOMPARABLE — **peer•less•ly** *adv* — **peer•less•ness** *n*

[1]peeve \ˈpēv\ *vt* **:** to make peevish or resentful **:** ANNOY, IRRITATE [back-formation from *peevish*]

[2]peeve *n* **1 :** a peevish mood **:** a feeling of resentment **2 :** a particular grievance **:** GRUDGE

pee•vish \ˈpē-vish\ *adj* **1 :** cross and complaining in temperament or mood **2 :** unreasonably stubborn **:** OBSTINATE **3 :** marked by ill temper [Middle English *pevish* "spiteful"] — **pee•vish•ly** *adv* — **pee•vish•ness** *n*

pee•wee \ˈpē-ˌwē\ *n* **:** something or someone diminutive or tiny [earlier *peewee* "pewee", of imitative origin] — **peewee** *adj*

pee•wit \ˈpē-ˌwit, ˈpyü-ət\ *n* **:** any of several birds: as **a :** LAPWING **b :** a small black-headed European gull **c :** PEWEE [imitative]

[1]peg \ˈpeg\ *n* **1 :** a small usually cylindrical pointed or tapered piece (as of wood) used especially to pin down or fasten things or to fit into or close holes ⟨a tent *peg*⟩ **2 :** a projecting piece used as a support or boundary marker **3 a :** any of the pins of a stringed musical instrument that are turned to regulate the pitch of the strings **b :** a step or degree especially in estimation ⟨took you down a *peg*⟩ **4 :** a pointed prong or claw for catching or tearing **5** *British* **:** a small drink (as of whiskey) **6 :** THROW ⟨a quick *peg* to first base⟩ [Middle English *pegge*]

[2]peg *vb* **pegged; peg•ging 1 a :** to fasten or mark with pegs **b :** to pin down **:** RESTRICT **c :** to fix or hold (as prices) at a planned level **d :** to place in a definite category **2 :** THROW 2 **3 :** to work steadily and diligently **4 :** to move along vigorously or hastily **:** HUSTLE

Peg•a•sus \ˈpeg-ə-səs\ *n* **:** a northern constellation near the vernal equinoctial point [*Pegasus,* winged horse in Greek mythology]

Peg–Board \ˈpeg-ˌbōrd, -ˌbȯrd\ *trademark* — used for material (as fiberboard) with regularly spaced perforations into which hooks may be inserted for the storage and display of articles

peg leg *n* **:** an artificial leg; *esp* **:** one fitted at the knee

peg•ma•tite \ˈpeg-mə-ˌtīt\ *n* **:** a coarse variety of granite occurring in dikes or veins [French, from Greek *pēgma* "something fastened together", from *pēgnynai* "to fasten together"]

peg–top \ˈpeg-ˈtäp\ *or* **peg–topped** \-ˈtäpt\ *adj* **:** wide at the top and narrow at the bottom ⟨*peg-top* trousers⟩

peg top *n* **1 :** a pear-shaped top with a sharp metal peg spun by a string as it is thrown from the hand **2** *pl* **:** peg-top trousers

pei•gnoir \pān-ˈwär, pen-\ *n* **:** a woman's loose negligee or dressing gown [French, from *peigner* "to comb the hair", from Latin *pectinare,* from *pecten* "comb"]

pe•jor•a•tive \pi-ˈjȯr-ət-iv, -ˈjär-; ˈpej-rət-, -ə-rət-\ *adj* **:** tending to disparage or belittle **:** DEPRECIATORY ⟨*pejorative* language⟩ [Late Latin *pejoratus,* past participle of *pejorare* "to make or become worse", from Latin *pejor* "worse"] — **pe•jor•a•tive•ly** *adv*

Pe•kin \pi-ˈkin, ˈpē-ˌ\ *n* **:** any of a breed of large white ducks of Chinese origin used for meat production [*Peking, Pekin,* China]

Pe•king•ese *or* **Pe•kin•ese** \ˌpē-kən-ˈēz, -king-, -ˈēs\ *n, pl* **Pekingese** *or* **Pekinese 1 a :** a native or resident of Peking **b :** the Chinese dialect of Peking **2 :** any of a Chinese breed of small short-legged dogs with a broad flat face and a profuse long soft coat

Pe•king man \ˌpē-ˌking-\ *n* **:** an extinct Pleistocene hominid known from skeletal and cultural remains found in cave deposits in northeastern China and now classified in the same genus (*Homo*) as modern man and as the same species as Java man

\ə\ abut	\au̇\ out	\i\ tip	\ȯ\ saw	\u̇\ foot
\ər\ further	\ch\ chin	\ī\ life	\ȯi\ coin	\y\ yet
\a\ mat	\e\ pet	\j\ job	\th\ thin	\yü\ few
\ā\ take	\ē\ easy	\ng\ sing	\th\ this	\yu̇\ cure
\ä\ cot, cart	\g\ go	\ō\ bone	\ü\ food	\zh\ vision

pel•age \'pel-ij\ *n* **:** the hairy covering of a mammal [French, from *poil* 'hair", from Latin *pilus*]

pe•lag•ic \pə-'laj-ik\ *adj* **:** of, relating to, living, or occurring in the open sea **:** OCEANIC [Latin *pelagicus,* from Greek *pelagikos,* from *pelagos* "sea"]

pel•ar•go•ni•um \ˌpel-är-'gō-nē-əm, ˌpel-ər-\ *n* **:** any of a genus of southern African herbs of the geranium family that includes the garden geraniums [derived from Greek *pelargos* "stork"]

Pe•las•gian \pə-'laz-jē-ən, -jən; -'laz-gē-ən\ *n* **:** any of an ancient people mentioned by classical writers as early inhabitants of Greece and the eastern islands of the Mediterranean [Greek *Pelasgoi* "Pelasgians"] — **Pelasgian** *adj*

pe•lecy•pod \pə-'les-ə-ˌpäd\ *adj or n* **:** LAMELLIBRANCH [derived from Greek *pelekys* "ax" + *pod-, pous* "foot"]

pelf \'pelf\ *n* **:** MONEY 2, RICHES [Middle French *pelfre* "booty"]

pel•i•can \'pel-i-kən\ *n* **:** any of a genus of large web-footed birds with a very large pouched bill in which fish are caught [Old English *pellican,* from Late Latin *pelecanus,* from Greek *pelekan*]

pelican

pel•la•gra \pə-'lag-rə, -'lāg-, -'läg-\ *n* **:** a disease associated with a diet deficient in niacin and protein and marked by skin rash, digestive disorders, and nervous and mental symptoms [Italian, derived from Latin *pellis* "skin" + *agra* "hunt, catch"] — **pel•la•grous** \-rəs\ *adj*

[1]**pel•let** \'pel-ət\ *n* **1 :** a little ball (as of food, medicine, or debris) **2 a :** a usually stone ball used as a missile in medieval times **b :** BULLET 1 **c :** a piece of small shot [Middle French *pelote,* derived from Latin *pila* "ball"]

[2]**pellet** *vt* **1 :** to form into pellets **2 :** to strike with pellets

pel•let•ize \'pel-ət-ˌīz\ *vt* **-ized; iz•ing :** to make or compact into pellets ⟨*pelletize* ore⟩ — **pel•let•iza•tion** \ˌpel-ət-ə-'zā-shən\ *n* — **pel•let•iz•er** \'pel-ət-ˌī-zər\ *n*

pel•li•cle \'pel-i-kəl\ *n* **:** a thin skin or film [Middle French *pellicule,* from Medieval Latin *pellicula,* from Latin *pellis* "skin"] — **pel•lic•u•lar** \pə-'lik-yə-lər\ *adj*

pell-mell \'pel-'mel\ *adv* **1 :** in confusion or disorder **2 :** in confused or headlong haste [Middle French *pelemele*] — **pell-mell** *adj or n*

pel•lu•cid \pə-'lü-səd\ *adj* **1 :** extremely clear or transparent **2 :** reflecting light evenly from all surfaces **3 :** very easy to understand [Latin *pellucidus,* from *per* "through" + *lucidus* "lucid"] **syn** see LIMPID — **pel•lu•cid•i•ty** \ˌpel-yü-'sid-ət-ē\ *n* — **pel•lu•cid•ly** \pə-'lü-səd-lē\ *adv* — **pel•lu•cid•ness** *n*

pe•lo•rus \pə-'lōr-əs, -'lȯr-\ *n* **:** a navigational instrument having a disk marked in degrees and two sights by which bearings are taken [origin unknown]

[1]**pelt** \'pelt\ *n* **:** a usually undressed skin with its hair, wool, or fur [Middle English]

[2]**pelt** *vb* **1 a :** to strike with or deliver a succession of blows or missiles ⟨*pelted* them with snowballs⟩ **b :** BOMBARD 2 ⟨was *pelted* with questions by the reporters⟩ **2 :** HURL, THROW **3 :** to beat or dash repeatedly ⟨hail *pelting* against a window⟩ **4 :** to move rapidly and vigorously or with pounding blows or thuds ⟨turned and *pelted* for home⟩ [Middle English *pelten*] — **pelter** *n*

[3]**pelt** *n* **1 :** a persistent falling or beating (as of rain, hail, or sleet) **2 :** a rapid pace or speed — used especially in the phrase *full pelt*

pelt•ry \'pel-trē\ *n, pl* **peltries :** animal pelts; *esp* **:** raw undressed skins

pel•vic \'pel-vik\ *adj* **:** of, relating to, or located in or near the pelvis — **pelvic** *n*

pelvic fin *n* **:** either of a pair of fins that correspond in a fish to the hind limbs of a four-footed animal — compare PECTORAL FIN

pelvic girdle *n* **:** an arch of bone or cartilage that supports the hind limbs of a vertebrate

pel•vis \'pel-vəs\ *n, pl* **pel•vis•es** *or* **pel•ves** \'pel-ˌvēz\ **1 :** a basin-shaped structure in the skeleton of many vertebrates formed by the pelvic girdle and adjoining bones of the spine; *also* **:** its cavity **2 :** the funnel-shaped cavity of the kidney into which urine is discharged [Latin, "basin"]

pel•y•co•saur \'pel-i-kə-ˌsȯər\ *n* **:** any of an order (Pelycosauria) of primitive Permian reptiles that resemble mammals and often have the back processes on the vertebrae greatly developed [derived from Greek *pelyx* "wooden bowl" + *sauros* "lizard"]

Pem•broke Welsh corgi \'pem-ˌbrōk-, -ˌbrůk-\ *n* **:** a Welsh corgi of a variety characterized by pointed ears, straight legs, and short tail [*Pembroke,* Wales] — called also *Pembroke*

pem•mi•can \'pem-i-kən\ *n* **:** dried lean meat pounded fine and mixed with melted fat and used for food especially by North American Indians [Cree *pimikân*]

[1]**pen** \'pen\ *n* **1 :** a small enclosure for animals; *also* **:** a small group of animals handled as a unit **2 :** a small place of confinement or storage [Old English *penn*]

[2]**pen** *vt* **penned; pen•ning :** to shut in a pen

[3]**pen** *n* **1 :** an implement for writing or drawing with ink or a similar fluid: as **a :** QUILL **b :** a small thin convex metal device tapering to a split point and fitting into a holder **c :** a penholder containing a pen **d :** FOUNTAIN PEN **e :** BALL-POINT PEN **2 a :** a writing instrument regarded as a means of expression **b :** WRITER **3 :** the internal horny feather-shaped shell of a squid [Middle French *penne* "feather, pen", from Latin *penna, pinna* "feather"]

[4]**pen** *vt* **penned; pen•ning :** to write especially with a pen

[5]**pen** *n* **:** a female swan [origin unknown]

[6]**pen** *n, slang* **:** PENITENTIARY

pe•nal \'pēn-l\ *adj* **:** of, relating to, or involving punishment, penalties, or punitive institutions ⟨*penal* laws⟩ ⟨a *penal* colony⟩ [Middle French, from Latin *poenalis,* from *poena* "punishment", from Greek *poinē* "payment, penalty"] — **pe•nal•ly** \-l-ē\ *adv*

penal code *n* **:** a code of laws concerning crimes and offenses and their punishment

pe•nal•ize \'pēn-l-ˌīz, 'pen-\ *vt* **1 :** to subject to a penalty ⟨*penalize* an athlete for a foul⟩ **2 :** to place at a disadvantage **:** HANDICAP ⟨the system *penalized* slow learners⟩ — **pe•nal•iza•tion** \ˌpēn-l-ə-'zā-shən, ˌpen-\ *n*

pen•al•ty \'pen-l-tē\ *n, pl* **-ties 1 :** punishment for a crime or offense **2 :** something forfeited when a person fails to do what he agreed to do **3 :** disadvantage, loss, or hardship due to some action or condition **4 :** a punishment or handicap imposed for breaking a rule in a sport or game

pen•ance \'pen-əns\ *n* **1 :** an act of self-abasement, mortification, or devotion performed to show sorrow or repentance for sin **2 :** a sacrament in the Roman Catholic and Eastern churches consisting in sorrow for sin, confession to a priest, a penance imposed by the confessor, and absolution [Old French, from Medieval Latin *poenitentia* "penitence"]

pence \'pens\ *pl of* PENNY

pen•chant \'pen-chənt\ *n* **:** a strong leaning **:** LIKING [French, from *pencher* "to lean, incline", derived from Latin *pendere* "to weigh"]

• **syn** FLAIR: PENCHANT may imply a decided taste and strong inclination for ⟨a *penchant* for gardening⟩ FLAIR implies instinctive ability or perception and acumen ⟨a real *flair* for cooking⟩

[1]**pen•cil** \'pen-səl\ *n* **1 a :** an implement for writing, drawing, or marking consisting of or containing a slender cylinder or strip of a solid marking substance **b :** a small medicated or cosmetic roll or stick **2 :** an aggregate of rays of light especially when diverging from or converging to a point **3 :** something long and thin like a pencil [Middle French *pincel* "artist's brush", from Latin *penicillus,* literally, "little tail", from *penis* "tail, penis"]

[2]**pencil** *vt* **-ciled** *or* **-cilled; -cil•ing** *or* **-cil•ling** \-sə-ling, -sling\ **:** to mark, draw, or write with or as if with a pencil — **pen•cil•ler** \-sə-lər, -slər\ *n*

pen•dant *also* **pen•dent** \'pen-dənt\ *n* **:** something that hangs down especially as an ornament [Middle French *pendant,* from *pendre* "to hang", from Latin *pendēre*]

pen•den•cy \'pen-dən-sē\ *n* **:** the state of being pending

pen•dent *or* **pen•dant** \'pen-dənt\ *adj* **1 :** supported from above **:** SUSPENDED **2 :** jutting or leaning over **:** OVERHANGING **3 :** remaining undetermined **:** PENDING — **pen•dent•ly** *adv*

[1]**pend•ing** \'pen-ding\ *prep* **1 :** DURING **2 :** while awaiting ⟨*pending* a reply⟩ [French *pendant,* from *pendre* "to hang"]

[2]**pending** *adj* **:** not yet decided ⟨cases *pending* before the court⟩

pen•du•lar \'pen-jə-lər, -dyə-lər, -dl-ər\ *adj* **:** being or resembling the movement of a pendulum

pen•du•lous \ˈpen-jə-ləs\ *adj* **1** : suspended so as to swing freely ⟨*pendulous* vines⟩ **2** : inclined or hanging downward ⟨flabby *pendulous* jowls⟩ [Latin *pendulus,* from *pendēre* "to hang"] — **pen•du•lous•ly** *adv*

pen•du•lum \ˈpen-jə-ləm, -dyə-ləm, -dl-əm\ *n* : a body suspended from a fixed point so as to swing freely to and fro under the action of gravity ⟨the *pendulum* of a clock⟩ [Latin, neuter of *pendulus* "pendulous"]

pe•ne•plain *also* **pe•ne•plane** \ˈpē-ni-ˌplān, ˈpen-\ *n* : a land surface of considerable area and slight relief shaped by erosion [Latin *paene, pene* "almost" + English *plain* or *plane*]

pen•e•tra•ble \ˈpen-ə-trə-bəl\ *adj* : capable of being penetrated — **pen•e•tra•bil•i•ty** \ˌpen-ə-trə-ˈbil-ət-ē\ *n* — **pen•e•tra•ble•ness** \ˈpen-ə-trə-bəl-nəs\ *n* — **pen•e•tra•bly** \-blē\ *adv*

pen•e•trate \ˈpen-ə-ˌtrāt\ *vb* **1 a** : to pass into or through **b** : to enter by overcoming resistance : PIERCE **2** : to come to understand **3** : to move deeply **4** : to seep through : PERMEATE [Latin *penetrare*] **syn** see ENTER

pen•e•trat•ing *adj* **1** : SHARP, BITING ⟨*penetrating* cold⟩ **2** : ACUTE, DISCERNING ⟨a *penetrating* mind⟩ — **pen•e•trat•ing•ly** \-ˌtrāt-ing-lē\ *adv*

pen•e•tra•tion \ˌpen-ə-ˈtrā-shən\ *n* **1** : the act or process of penetrating **2 a** : the depth to which something penetrates **b** : the power to penetrate; *esp* : the ability to discern deeply and acutely

pen•e•tra•tive \ˈpen-ə-ˌtrāt-iv\ *adj* : tending or able to penetrate — **pen•e•tra•tive•ly** *adv* — **pen•e•tra•tive•ness** *n*

pen•guin \ˈpen-gwən, ˈpeng-\ *n* : any of various erect short-legged flightless aquatic birds of the southern hemisphere with the wings reduced to flippers and used in swimming [origin unknown]

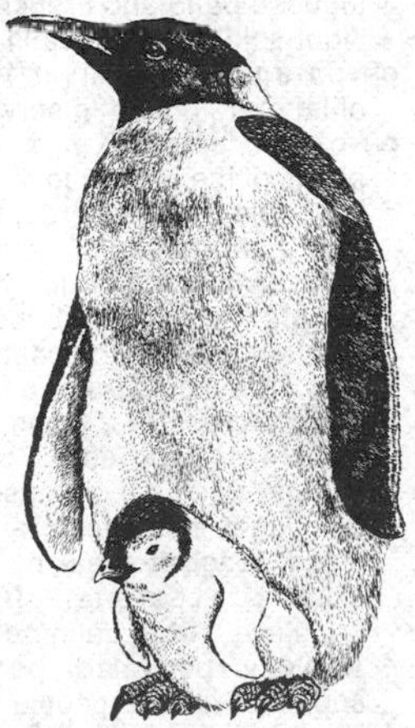
penguin

pen•hold•er \ˈpen-ˌhōl-dər\ *n* : a holder or handle for a pen

pen•i•cil•lin \ˌpen-ə-ˈsil-ən\ *n* : any of several antibiotics or a mixture of these produced by penicillia or synthetically and used especially against cocci

pen•i•cil•lin•ase \-ˈsil-ə-ˌnās, -ˌnāz\ *n* : an enzyme that inactivates the penicillins by hydrolyzing them and that is found especially in bacteria

pen•i•cil•li•um \-ˈsil-ē-əm\ *n, pl* **-lia** \-ē-ə\ : any of a genus of fungi comprising mostly blue molds found chiefly on moist nonliving organic matter — compare PENICILLIN [New Latin, from Latin *penicillus* "brush, little tail"]

pen•in•su•la \pə-ˈnin-sə-lə, -ˈnin-slə, -ˈnin-chə-lə\ *n* : a portion of land nearly surrounded by water; *also* : a piece of land jutting out into the water [Latin *paeninsula,* from *paene* "almost" + *insula* "island"] — **pen•in•su•lar** \-lər\ *adj*

pe•nis \ˈpē-nəs\ *n, pl* **pe•nes** \ˈpē-ˌnēz\ *or* **pe•nis•es** : a male organ of copulation [Latin, "penis, tail"] — **pe•nile** \-ˌnīl\ *adj*

pen•i•tence \ˈpen-ə-təns\ *n* : sorrow for one's sins or faults : REPENTANCE

• **syn** PENITENCE, REPENTANCE, CONTRITION mean regret for sin or wrongdoing. PENITENCE implies humble realization of and regret for one's faults; REPENTANCE emphasizes the change of mind of one who not only regrets errors but abandons them for a new standard; CONTRITION suggests penitence shown by signs of grief or pain.

[1]**pen•i•tent** \-tənt\ *adj* : feeling or expressing pain or sorrow for sins or offenses : REPENTANT [Middle French, from Latin *paenitens,* from *paenitēre* "to be sorry"] — **pen•i•tent•ly** *adv*

[2]**penitent** *n* **1** : a person who repents of sin **2** : a person under church censure but admitted to penance especially under the direction of a confessor

pen•i•ten•tial \ˌpen-ə-ˈten-chəl\ *adj* : of or relating to penitence or penance — **pen•i•ten•tial•ly** \-ˈtench-lē, -ə-lē\ *adv*

[1]**pen•i•ten•tia•ry** \ˌpen-ə-ˈtench-rē, -ə-rē\ *n, pl* **-ries** : a public institution in which criminals are confined; *esp* : a state or federal prison in the United States

[2]**penitentiary** *adj* : of, relating to, or incurring confinement in a penitentiary

pen•knife \ˈpen-ˌnīf\ *n* : a small pocketknife [from its original use for mending quill pens]

pen•man \ˈpen-mən\ *n* **1 a** : COPYIST 1, SCRIBE **b** : one who is expert in penmanship **2** : AUTHOR 1

pen•man•ship \ˈpen-mən-ˌship\ *n* **1** : the art or practice of writing with the pen **2** : quality or style of handwriting

pen name *n* : an author's pseudonym

pen•nant \ˈpen-ənt\ *n* **1 a** : a nautical flag tapering to a point or swallowtail and used for identification or signaling **b** : a long narrow flag or banner that tapers to a point **2** : a flag emblematic of championship [alteration of *pendant*]

pen•ner \ˈpen-ər\ *n* : one that pens a document : WRITER

pen•ni•less \ˈpen-i-ləs, ˈpen-l-əs\ *adj* : having no money at all : very poor

pen•non \ˈpen-ən\ *n* **1** : a long usually triangular or swallow-tailed streamer typically attached to the head of a lance as an ensign **2** : PENNANT 1a [Middle French *penon,* from *penne* "feather, pen"]

Penn•syl•va•nia Dutch \ˌpen-səl-ˌvā-nyə-\ *n* **1** : a people living mostly in eastern Pennsylvania whose characteristic cultural traditions go back to the German migrations of the 18th century **2** : a German dialect spoken by the Pennsylvania Dutch — **Pennsylvania Dutchman** *n*

Penn•syl•va•nian \-ˈvā-nyən\ *adj* **1** : of or relating to Pennsylvania or its people **2** : of, relating to, or being the period of the Paleozoic era between the Mississippian and Permian or the corresponding system of rocks — see GEOLOGIC TIME table — **Pennsylvanian** *n*

pen•ny \ˈpen-ē\ *n, pl* **pen•nies** \-ēz\ *or* **pence** \ˈpens\ **1 a** : a former British monetary unit equal to 1/240 pound or 1/12 shilling **b** : a similar monetary unit of any of various other countries in or formerly in the British Commonwealth **c** : a coin representing this unit **d** : NEW PENNY **2** : DENARIUS **3** *pl pennies* : a cent of the United States or Canada **4** : a piece or sum of money ⟨earn an honest *penny*⟩ [Old English *penning*]

penny ante *n* : poker played for very low stakes

penny arcade *n* : an amusement center where each device for entertainment may be operated for a small sum and originally for a penny

penny dreadful *n* : a novel of violent adventure or crime originally costing one penny

pen•ny pinch•er \ˈpen-ē-ˌpin-chər\ *n* : a stingy person — **pen•ny–pinch•ing** \-ching\ *adj or n*

pen•ny•roy•al \ˌpen-ē-ˈrȯi-əl, -ˈrȯil; ˈpen-i-ˌrīl\ *n* : a European perennial mint with small aromatic leaves; *also* : a similar American mint that yields an oil used in folk medicine and as a mosquito repellent [probably by folk etymology from Middle French *poullieul,* from Latin *pulegium*]

pen•ny•weight \ˈpen-ē-ˌwāt\ *n* — see MEASURE table

pen•ny–wise \-ˌwīz\ *adj* : wise or prudent only in small matters

pen•ny•worth \ˈpen-ē-ˌwərth\ *n, pl* **-worth** *or* **-worths** : a penny's worth : as much as a penny will buy

Pe•nob•scot \pə-ˈnäb-skət, -ˌskät\ *n, pl* **Penobscot** *or* **Penobscots** : a member of an Algonquian people of the Penobscot river valley and the Penobscot Bay region

pe•nol•o•gy \pi-ˈnäl-ə-jē\ *n* : a branch of criminology dealing with prison management and the treatment of offenders [Greek *poinē* "penalty"] — **pe•no•log•i•cal** \ˌpēn-l-ˈäj-i-kəl\ *adj* — **pe•nol•o•gist** \pi-ˈnäl-ə-jəst\ *n*

pen pal *n* : a friend made and kept through correspondence often without any face-to-face acquaintance

pen•sile \ˈpen-ˌsīl\ *adj* : suspended from above [Latin *pensilis,* from *pensus,* past participle of *pendēre* "to hang"]

[1]**pen•sion** *n* **1** \ˈpen-chən\ : a fixed sum paid regularly to a person; *esp* : one paid to a person following retirement or to surviving dependents **2** \pä^{n}s-yō^n\ : a boardinghouse especially in continental Europe [Middle French, from Latin *pensio,* from *pensus,* past participle of *pendere* "to weigh, pay"] — **pen•sion•less** \ˈpen-chən-ləs\ *adj*

\ə\ abut	\au̇\ out	\i\ tip	\ȯ\ saw	\u̇\ foot
\ər\ further	\ch\ chin	\ī\ life	\ȯi\ coin	\y\ yet
\a\ mat	\e\ pet	\j\ job	\th\ thin	\yü\ few
\ā\ take	\ē\ easy	\ng\ sing	\th\ this	\yu̇\ cure
\ä\ cot, cart	\g\ go	\ō\ bone	\ü\ food	\zh\ vision

[2]**pen•sion** \'pen-chən\ *vt* **pen•sioned**; **pen•sion•ing** \'pench-ning, -ə-ning\ **:** to grant or pay a pension to

pen•sion•er \'pench-nər, -ə-nər\ *n* **1 :** a person who receives or lives on a pension **2 :** a mercenary dependent **:** HIRELING

pen•sive \'pen-siv\ *adj* **1 :** musingly or dreamily thoughtful **2 :** suggestive of sad thoughtfulness **:** MELANCHOLY [Middle French *pensif,* from *penser* "to think", from Latin *pensare* "to ponder", from *pendere* "to weigh"] — **pen•sive•ly** *adv* — **pen•sive•ness** *n*

pen•stock \'pen-,stäk\ *n* **1 :** a sluice or gate for regulating a flow (as of water) **2 :** a conduit or pipe for conducting water

pent \'pent\ *adj* **:** shut up **:** held back ⟨*pent*-up feelings⟩ [probably from past participle of obsolete *pend* "to confine"]

penta- *or* **pent-** *combining form* **:** five ⟨*pent*ode⟩ [Greek, from *pente*]

pen•ta•gon \'pent-i-,gän\ *n* **:** a polygon of five angles and five sides — **pen•tag•o•nal** \pen-'tag-ən-l\ *adj*

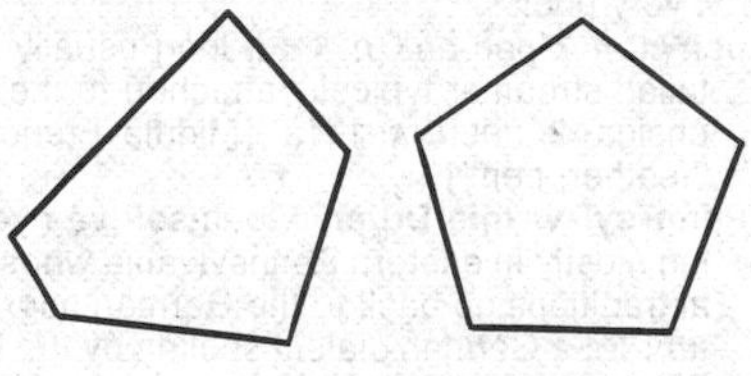
pentagon

Pentagon *n* **:** the American military establishment [the *Pentagon* building, headquarters of the United States Department of Defense]

pen•tam•e•ter \pen-'tam-ət-ər\ *n* **:** a line consisting of five metrical feet [Latin, derived from Greek *penta-* + *metron* "measure"]

pen•tane \'pen-,tān\ *n* **:** any of three isomeric hydrocarbons C_5H_{12} occurring in petroleum and natural gas

Pen•ta•teuch \'pent-ə-,tük, -,tyük\ *n* **:** the first five books of the Old Testament [Late Latin *Pentateuchus,* from Greek *Pentateuchos,* from *penta-* + *teuchos* "tool, vessel, book"]

pen•tath•lon \pen-'tath-lən, -,län\ *n* **:** an athletic contest in which each contestant participates in five different events [Greek, from *penta-* + *athlon* "contest"]

Pen•te•cost \'pent-i-,kȯst, -,käst\ *n* **1 :** SHABUOTH **2 :** the 7th Sunday after Easter observed as a church festival in commemoration of the descent of the Holy Spirit on the apostles [Old English *pentecosten,* from Late Latin *pentecoste,* from Greek *pentēkostē,* literally, "50th (day)", from *pentēkonta* "fifty"]

Pen•te•cos•tal \,pent-i-'käs-tl, -'kȯs-\ *adj* **1 :** of, relating to, or suggesting Pentecost **2 :** of, relating to, or constituting any of various usually fundamentalist sects that stress religious revivals — **Pentecostal** *n* — **Pen•te•cos•tal•ism** \-tə-,liz-əm\ *n*

pent•house \'pent-,hau̇s\ *n* **1 :** a roof or a shed attached to and sloping from a wall or building **2 :** a structure (as an apartment) built on the roof of a building [Middle English *pentis,* from Middle French *appentis,* probably from Medieval Latin *appenticium* "appendage", from Latin *appendix*]

△ **origin** In Middle English *pentis* meant primarily "a shed or roof attached to a wall or building". *Pentis,* borrowed from Middle French *appentis,* is probably derived from Latin *appendix,* which means "appendage" or "supplement". (A direct borrowing from Latin gives English *appendix* in its various senses.) A *pentis,* then, was a smaller building or structure attached to a larger one. It was widely though mistakenly believed that *pentis* was related to Middle French *pente* "slope", and this belief was likely encouraged by the fact that many such structures did have sloping roofs. The second syllable of the word was altered by folk etymology to *-house.*

pent•land•ite \'pent-lən-,dīt\ *n* **:** a bronzy yellow mineral $(Fe,Ni)_9S_8$ that is a nickel iron sulfide and the principal ore of nickel [Joseph *Pentland,* died 1873, Irish scientist]

pen•to•bar•bi•tal \,pent-ə-'bär-bə-,tȯl\ *n* **:** a barbiturate used especially in the form of its sodium or calcium salt chiefly as a sedative and hypnotic [*penta-* + *-o-* + *barbital*]

pen•tode \'pen-,tōd\ *n* **:** a vacuum tube with five electrodes

pen•tom•ic \pen-'täm-ik\ *adj* **1 :** made up of five battle groups ⟨a *pentomic* division⟩ **2 :** organized into pentomic divisions ⟨*pentomic* armies⟩ [blend of *penta-* and *atomic*]

pen•tose \'pen-,tōs\ *n* **:** any of various sugars $C_5H_{10}O_5$ containing five carbon atoms in the molecule

Pen•to•thal \'pent-ə-,thȯl\ *trademark* — used for a substance that is used as an intravenous anesthetic of short duration and as a hypnotic

pent•ox•ide \pent-'äk-,sīd\ *n* **:** an oxide containing five atoms of oxygen in the molecule

pent•ste•mon *or* **pen•ste•mon** \pen-'stē-mən, 'pen-stə-\ *n* **:** any of a genus of chiefly American herbs of the snapdragon family with showy blue, purple, red, yellow, or white flowers [derived from Greek *penta-* + *stēmōn* "thread"]

pe•nu•che \pə-'nü-chē\ *n* **:** fudge made usually of brown sugar, butter, cream or milk, and nuts [Mexican Spanish *panocha* "raw sugar", from Spanish *pan* "bread", from Latin *panis*]

pe•nult \'pē-,nəlt, pi-'\ *n* **:** the next to the last syllable of a word [Latin *paenultima,* from *paenultimus* "almost last", from *paene* "almost" + *ultimus* "last"]

pen•ul•ti•mate \pi-'nəl-tə-mət\ *adj* **1 :** next to the last **2 :** of or relating to a penult — **penultimate** *n* — **pen•ul•ti•mate•ly** *adv*

pen•um•bra \pə-'nəm-brə\ *n, pl* **-brae** \-,brē, -,brī\ *or* **-bras 1 :** the partial shadow surrounding a perfect shadow (as in an eclipse) **2 :** the shaded region around the dark central portion of a sunspot [Latin *paene* "almost" + *umbra* "shadow"] — **pen•um•bral** \-brəl\ *adj*

pe•nu•ri•ous \pə-'nu̇r-ē-əs, -'nyu̇r-\ *adj* **1 :** marked by or suffering from penury **2 :** given to or marked by extreme frugality **syn** see STINGY — **pe•nu•ri•ous•ly** *adv* — **pe•nu•ri•ous•ness** *n*

pen•u•ry \'pen-yə-rē\ *n* **1 :** extreme poverty **:** PRIVATION **2 :** absence of resources **:** SCANTINESS [Latin *penuria* "want"]

pe•on \'pē-,än, -ən\ *n* **1 :** a member of the landless laboring class in Spanish America **2 :** a person held in compulsory servitude to work out an indebtedness **3 :** DRUDGE, MENIAL [Portuguese *peão* and French *pion,* both from Medieval Latin *pedo* "foot soldier", from Latin *ped-, pes* "foot"]

pe•on•age \'pē-ə-nij\ *n* **1 :** the condition of a peon **2 :** the use of laborers bound in servitude because of debt

pe•o•ny \'pē-ə-nē\ *n, pl* **-nies :** any of a genus of perennial plants of the buttercup family widely grown for their large usually double flowers of red, pink, or white [Middle French *pioine,* from Latin *paeonia,* from Greek *paiōnia,* from *Paiōn* "Paeon (physician of the gods)"]

[1]**peo•ple** \'pē-pəl\ *n, pl* **people 1** *pl* **:** HUMAN BEINGS, PERSONS — often used in compounds instead of *persons* ⟨sales*people*⟩ **2** *pl* **:** the members of a family **:** KINDRED; *also* **:** ANCESTORS **3** *pl* **:** the mass of a community as distinguished from a special class **4** *pl* **peoples :** a body of persons united by a common culture, tradition, or sense of kinship, typically having common language, institutions, and beliefs, and often politically organized ⟨English-speaking *peoples*⟩ **5 :** a body of enfranchised citizens **:** ELECTORATE [Old French *peuple* "body of citizens, populace", from Latin *populus*]

[2]**people** *vt* **peo•pled**; **peo•pling** \'pē-pə-ling, -pling\ **1 :** to supply or fill with people **2 :** to dwell in **:** INHABIT

[1]**pep** \'pep\ *n* **:** brisk energy or initiative and high spirits **:** LIVELINESS [short for *pepper*]

[2]**pep** *vt* **pepped**; **pep•ping :** to inject pep into **:** STIMULATE ⟨*pep* them up⟩

pep•lum \'pep-ləm\ *n* **:** a short section attached to the waistline of a blouse, jacket, or dress [Latin, a kind of upper garment for women, from Greek *peplos*]

pe•po \'pē-pō\ *n* **:** a fleshy many-seeded fruit (as a pumpkin, squash, melon, or cucumber) of the gourd family that has a hard rind and is technically classed as a berry [Latin, a kind of melon]

[1]**pep•per** \'pep-ər\ *n* **1 a :** either of two pungent products from the fruit of an East Indian vine used as seasoning and in medicine: (1) **:** BLACK PEPPER (2) **:** WHITE PEPPER **b :** a woody vine with rounded leaves and flowers arranged in a spike that is widely cultivated in the tropics for its red berries from which pepper is prepared **c :** any of several somewhat similar products obtained from other plants **2 :** CAPSICUM; *esp* **:** a New World capsicum whose fruits are hot peppers or sweet peppers [Old English *pipor,* from Latin *piper,* from Greek *peperi*] — **pepper** *adj*

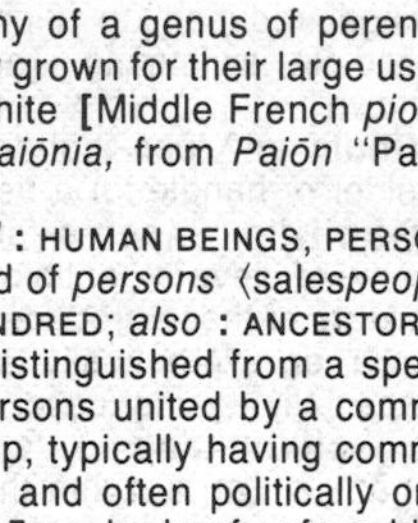
[1]pepper 1b

²pepper *vt* **pep·pered; pep·per·ing** \'pep-riŋ, -ə-riŋ\ **1 a :** to sprinkle or season with or as if with pepper **b :** to shower with missiles (as shot) **2 :** to hit with rapid repeated blows **3 :** to sprinkle as pepper is sprinkled

pep·per–and–salt \ˌpep-ər-ən-'sȯlt, ˌpep-ərn-'sȯlt\ *adj* **:** having black and white or dark and light color intermingled in small flecks ⟨a *pepper-and-salt* overcoat⟩

pep·per·corn \'pep-ər-ˌkȯrn\ *n* **:** a dried berry of the East Indian pepper

peppered moth *n* **:** a European moth that typically has white wings with small black specks but often has black wings in areas with heavy air pollution

pep·per·grass \'pep-ər-ˌgras\ *n* **:** any of a genus of herbs of the mustard family having a rounded fruit with a notch or depression at the top

pepper mill *n* **:** a hand mill for grinding peppercorns

pep·per·mint \-ˌmint, -mənt\ *n* **1 :** a pungent and aromatic mint with dark green leaves and whorls of small purple or white flowers in spikes **2 :** candy flavored with peppermint

pep·per·o·ni \ˌpep-ə-'rō-nē\ *n* **:** a highly seasoned beef and pork sausage [Italian *peperoni* "chilies", pl. of *peperone* "chili", from *pepe* "pepper", from Latin *piper*]

pep·per·pot \'pep-ər-ˌpät\ *n* **1 :** PEPPER SHAKER **2 :** a thick highly seasoned soup of tripe, meat, dumplings, and vegetables

pepper shaker *n* **:** a container with a perforated top for sprinkling pepper on food

pep·pery \'pep-rē, -ə-rē\ *adj* **1 :** of, relating to, or having the qualities of pepper **:** HOT, PUNGENT **2 :** having a hot temper **:** TOUCHY **3 :** FIERY, STINGING ⟨*peppery* words⟩

pep pill *n* **:** any of various stimulant drugs (as an amphetamine) in pill or tablet form

pep·py \'pep-ē\ *adj* **pep·pi·er; -est :** full of pep — **pep·pi·ness** *n*

pep·sin \'pep-sən\ *n* **1 :** a proteinase of the stomach that begins the digestion of most proteins **2 :** a preparation of pepsin obtained especially from the stomach of the hog and used medicinally [German, from Greek *pepsis* "digestion", from *pessein* "to cook, digest"]

pep·sin·o·gen \pep-'sin-ə-jən\ *n* **:** a product of the gastric glands that is converted into pepsin in the acid medium of the stomach

pep talk *n* **:** a usually brief, high-pressure, and emotional utterance designed to influence or encourage an audience

pep·tic \'pep-tik\ *adj* **1 :** relating to or promoting digestion **2 :** of, relating to, producing, or caused by pepsin ⟨*peptic* digestion⟩ **3 :** resulting from the action of digestive juices ⟨a *peptic* ulcer⟩ [Latin *pepticus,* from Greek *peptikos,* from *peptos* "cooked", from *peptein, pessein* "to cook, digest"]

pep·ti·dase \'pep-tə-ˌdās, -ˌdāz\ *n* **:** an enzyme that hydrolyzes simple peptides or their derivatives

pep·tide \'pep-ˌtīd\ *n* **:** any of various amides derived from two or more amino acids by combination of the amino group of one acid with the carboxyl group of another and usually obtained by partial hydrolysis of proteins [*peptone* + *-ide*]

peptide bond *n* **:** the chemical bond between carbon and nitrogen in the CO-NH group that unites the amino acid residues in a peptide

pep·tone \'pep-ˌtōn\ *n* **:** any of various water-soluble products of partial hydrolysis of proteins [German *pepton,* from Greek *peptos* "cooked", from *pessein* "to cook, digest"]

Pe·quot \'pē-ˌkwät\ *n* **:** a member of an Algonquian people of what is now southeastern Connecticut

per \pər, 'pər\ *prep* **1 :** by the means or agency of ⟨*per* bearer⟩ **2 :** to or for each ⟨$10 *per* day⟩ **3 :** as indicated by **:** according to ⟨*per* list price⟩ [Latin, "through, by"]

per- *prefix* **1 :** throughout **:** thoroughly **2 a :** containing the largest possible or a relatively large proportion of a (specified) chemical element ⟨*per*oxide⟩ **b :** containing an element in its highest or a high oxidation state ⟨*per*chloric acid⟩ [Latin, "through, throughout, thoroughly, to destruction", from *per*]

¹per·ad·ven·ture \'pər-əd-ˌven-chər, 'per-; ˌpər-əd-', ˌper-\ *adv, archaic* **:** PERHAPS, POSSIBLY [Old French *per aventure* "by chance"]

²peradventure *n* **:** a possibility of error or uncertainty

per·am·bu·late \pə-'ram-byə-ˌlāt\ *vb* **1 :** to travel over or through especially on foot **:** TRAVERSE **2 :** STROLL, RAMBLE [Latin *perambulare,* from *per-* + *ambulare* "to walk"] — **per·am·bu·la·tion** \-ˌram-byə-'lā-shən\ *n*

per·am·bu·la·tor \pə-'ram-byə-ˌlāt-ər\ *n* **1 :** one that perambulates **2** *chiefly British* **:** a baby carriage — **per·am·bu·la·to·ry** \-lə-ˌtōr-ē, -ˌtȯr-\ *adj*

per an·num \ˌpər-'an-əm\ *adv* **:** in or for each year **:** ANNUALLY [Medieval Latin]

per·cale \pər-'kāl, ˌpər-, -'kal\ *n* **:** a fine closely woven cotton cloth [Persian *pargālah*]

per cap·i·ta \ˌpər-'kap-ət-ə\ *adv or adj* **:** per unit of population **:** by or for each person ⟨*per capita* income⟩ [Medieval Latin, "by heads"]

per·ceiv·able \pər-'sē-və-bəl\ *adj* **:** that can be perceived — **per·ceiv·ably** \-blē\ *adv*

per·ceive \pər-'sēv\ *vt* **1 :** to attain awareness or understanding of **2 :** to become aware of through the senses and especially through sight [Old French *perceivre,* from Latin *percipere,* from *per-* "thoroughly" + *capere* "to take"] — **per·ceiv·er** *n*

¹per·cent \pər-'sent\ *adv* **:** in the hundred **:** of each hundred [*per* + Latin *centum* "hundred"]

²percent *n, pl* **percent 1 :** one part in a hundred **:** HUNDREDTH **2 :** PERCENTAGE

³percent *adj* **1 :** reckoned on the basis of a whole divided into one hundred parts **2 :** paying interest at a specified percent ⟨a 7 *percent* bond⟩

per·cent·age \pər-'sent-ij\ *n* **1 a :** a part of a whole expressed in hundredths **b :** the result obtained by multiplying a number by a percent **2 a :** a share of winnings or profits ⟨my agent collects a *percentage*⟩ **b :** ADVANTAGE, PROFIT ⟨no *percentage* in going it alone⟩ **3 :** an indeterminate part **:** PROPORTION **4 a :** PROBABILITY 3 ⟨a gambler who plays the *percentages*⟩ **b :** favorable odds

per·cen·tile \pər-'sen-ˌtīl\ *n* **:** a measure widely used in educational testing that expresses the standing of a score or grade in terms of the percentage of scores or grades falling with or below it ⟨a person in the 75th *percentile* has done as well as or better than 75 percent of the people with whom he or she is being compared⟩

per cen·tum \pər-'sent-əm\ *n* **:** PERCENT

per·cep·ti·ble \pər-'sep-tə-bəl\ *adj* **:** capable of being perceived ⟨a *perceptible* change⟩ — **per·cep·ti·bil·i·ty** \-ˌsep-tə-'bil-ət-ē\ *n* — **per·cep·ti·bly** \-'sep-tə-blē\ *adv*

per·cep·tion \pər-'sep-shən\ *n* **1 a :** a result of perceiving **:** OBSERVATION, DISCERNMENT **b :** a mental image **:** CONCEPT **2 :** awareness of the elements of environment through physical sensation ⟨color *perception*⟩ **3 a :** INSIGHT 2 **b :** a capacity for comprehension [Latin *perceptio* "act of perceiving", from *percipere* "to perceive"] — **per·cep·tion·al** \-shnəl, -shən-l\ *adj*

per·cep·tive \pər-'sep-tiv\ *adj* **1 :** responsive to sensory stimulus **:** DISCERNING **2 a :** capable of or exhibiting keen perception **:** OBSERVANT **b :** characterized by sympathetic understanding or insight — **per·cep·tive·ly** *adv* — **per·cep·tive·ness** *n* — **per·cep·tiv·i·ty** \pər-ˌsep-'tiv-ət-ē\ *n*

per·cep·tu·al \pər-'sep-chə-wəl\ *adj* **:** of, relating to, or involving stimulation of the senses as opposed to abstract concept — **per·cep·tu·al·ly** \-wə-lē\ *adv*

¹perch \'pərch\ *n* **1 :** a bar or peg on which something is hung **2 a :** a roost for a bird **b :** a resting place or vantage point **:** SEAT **c :** a prominent position **3** *chiefly British* **:** ROD 2 [Old French *perche,* from Latin *pertica* "pole"]

²perch *vb* **1 :** to place on a perch, a height, or precarious spot ⟨*perched* itself on the table⟩ **2 :** to alight, settle, or rest on or as if on a perch

³perch *n, pl* **perch** *or* **perch·es 1 :** a small largely olive-green and yellow European freshwater spiny-finned fish; *also* **:** YELLOW PERCH **2 :** any of numerous fishes related to or resembling the true perches [Middle French *perche,* from Latin *perca,* from Greek *perkē*]

per·chance \pər-'chans\ *adv* **:** PERHAPS, POSSIBLY

Per·che·ron \'pər-chə-ˌrän, -shə-\ *n* **:** any of a breed of powerful rugged draft horses that originated in France [French, from *Perche,* region in northern France]

per·chlo·rate \pər-'klōr-ˌāt, ˌpər-, -'klȯr-\ *n* **:** a salt or ester of perchloric acid

per•chlo•ric acid \pər-ˌklōr-ik-, ˌpər-, -ˌklȯr-\ *n* : a fuming corrosive strong acid $HClO_4$ that is a powerful oxidizing agent when heated

per•cip•i•ent \pər-ˈsip-ē-ənt\ *adj* : capable of or characterized by perception : DISCERNING [Latin *percipiens*, present participle of *percipiens* "to perceive"] — **per•cip•i•ence** \-ē-əns\ *n* — **percipient** *n*

per•coid \ˈpər-ˌkȯid\ *adj* : of or relating to a very large suborder (Percoidea) of spiny-finned fishes including the true perches, sunfishes, sea basses, and sea breams [derived from Latin *perca* "perch"] — **percoid** *n*

per•co•late \ˈpər-kə-ˌlāt\ *vb* **1 a** : to pass or cause to pass through a permeable substance (as a powdered drug) especially for extracting a soluble constituent : FILTER, SEEP **b** : to prepare (coffee) in a percolator **2** : to be or become diffused through : PENETRATE **3 a** : to become percolated **b** : to become lively or effervescent [Latin *percolare*, from *per-* "through" + *colare* "to sieve"] — **per•co•la•tion** \ˌpər-kə-ˈlā-shən\ *n*

per•co•la•tor \ˈpər-kə-ˌlāt-ər\ *n* : one that percolates; *esp* : a coffeepot in which boiling water rising through a tube is repeatedly deflected downward through a perforated basket containing the ground coffee beans

per•cuss \pər-ˈkəs\ *vt* : to tap sharply; *esp* : to practice percussion on

per•cus•sion \pər-ˈkəsh-ən\ *n* **1** : the act of tapping sharply: as **a** : the striking of a percussion cap so as to set off the charge in a firearm **b** : the beating or striking of a musical instrument **c** : the act or technique of tapping the surface of a body part to learn the condition of the parts beneath by the resultant sound **2** : the striking of sound sharply on the ear **3** : percussion instruments especially as forming a section of a band or orchestra [Latin *percussio*, from *percussus*, past participle of *percutere* "to beat", from *per-* "thoroughly" + *quatere* "to shake"] — **percussion** *adj*

percussion cap *n* : CAP 4

percussion instrument *n* : a musical instrument (as a drum) sounded by striking

per•cus•sion•ist \pər-ˈkəsh-nəst, -ə-nəst\ *n* : one skilled in the playing of percussion instruments

per•cus•sive \pər-ˈkəs-iv\ *adj* : of or relating to percussion; *esp* : operative or operated by striking — **per•cus•sive•ly** *adv* — **per•cus•sive•ness** *n*

per•cu•ta•ne•ous \ˌpər-kyü-ˈtā-nē-əs\ *adj* : effected or performed through the skin — **per•cu•ta•ne•ous•ly** *adv*

[1]per di•em \ˌpər-ˈdē-əm, -ˈdī-\ *adv* : by the day : for each day [Medieval Latin] — **per diem** *adj*

[2]per diem *n* **1** : a daily allowance (as for traveling expenses) **2** : a daily fee

per•di•tion \pər-ˈdish-ən\ *n* **1** *archaic* : utter destruction **2 a** : eternal damnation **b** : HELL [Late Latin *perditio*, from Latin *perdere* "to destroy", from *per-* "to destruction" + *dare* "to give"]

per•du•ra•ble \pər-ˈdu̇r-ə-bəl, -ˈdyu̇r-\ *adj* : very durable — **per•du•ra•bly** \-blē\ *adv*

per•e•gri•nate \ˈper-ə-grə-ˌnāt\ *vb* : to travel especially on foot : WALK, TRAVERSE — **per•e•gri•na•tion** \ˌper-ə-grə-ˈnā-shən\ *n*

per•e•grine \ˈper-ə-grən, -ˌgrēn\ *adj* : having a tendency to wander [Latin *peregrinus* "foreign"]

peregrine falcon *n* : a swift nearly cosmopolitan falcon much used in falconry — called also *peregrine*

pe•remp•to•ry \pə-ˈrem-tə-rē, -ˈremp-, -trē\ *adj* **1 a** : putting an end to or making impossible a right of action, debate, or delay **b** : not contradictable **2** : expressive of urgency or command : IMPERATIVE ⟨*peremptory* tone⟩ **3 a** : marked by self-assurance : POSITIVE **b** : HAUGHTY, DICTATORIAL [Latin *peremptorius* "destructive", from *perimere* "to take entirely, destroy", from *per-* + *emere* "to take"] — **pe•remp•to•ri•ly** \-tə-rə-lē, -trə-lē\ *adv* — **pe•remp•to•ri•ness** \-tə-rē-nəs, -trē-nəs\ *n*

pe•ren•ni•al \pə-ˈren-ē-əl\ *adj* **1** : present at all seasons of the year **2** : persisting for several years usually with new herbaceous growth from a basal crown ⟨*perennial* asters⟩ **3 a** : lasting indefinitely **b** : continuing without interruption : CONSTANT **c** : regularly repeated : RECURRENT [Latin *perennis*, from *per-* "throughout" + *annus* "year"] — **perennial** *n* — **pe•ren•ni•al•ly** \-ē-ə-lē\ *adv*

[1]per•fect \ˈpər-fikt\ *adj* **1 a** : being entirely without fault or defect **b** : satisfying all requirements **c** : corresponding to an ideal standard **2** : faithfully reproducing the original **3 a** : being exactly as stated ⟨*perfect* stillness⟩ **b** : lacking in no essential detail : COMPLETE **c** : of an extreme kind ⟨a *perfect* fool⟩ **4** : of, relating to, or constituting a verb form or verbal that expresses an action or state completed at the time of speaking or at a time spoken of **5** : belonging to the musical consonances unison, fourth, fifth, and octave **6** : MONOCLINOUS ⟨a *perfect* flower⟩ [Old French *parfit*, from Latin *perfectus*, from *perficere* "to carry out, perfect", from *per-* "thoroughly" + *facere* "to make, do"] **syn** see WHOLE — **per•fect•ness** \-fikt-nəs, -fik-nəs\ *n*

peregrine falcon

[2]per•fect \pər-ˈfekt, *also* ˈpər-fikt\ *vt* **1** : to make perfect : IMPROVE, REFINE **2** : to bring to final form — **per•fect•er** *n*

[3]per•fect \ˈpər-fikt\ *n* : the perfect tense of a language; *also* : a verb form in the perfect tense

per•fect•ible \pər-ˈfek-tə-bəl, *also* ˈpər-fik-\ *adj* : capable of improvement or perfection — **per•fect•ibil•i•ty** \pər-ˌfek-tə-ˈbil-ət-ē *also* ˌpər-fik-\ *n*

per•fec•tion \pər-ˈfek-shən\ *n* **1** : the quality or state of being perfect: as **a** : freedom from fault or defect : FLAWLESSNESS **b** : MATURITY 1 **c** : saintly quality or state **2 a** : an exemplification of supreme excellence **b** : an unsurpassable degree of accuracy or excellence **3** : the act or process of perfecting

per•fec•tion•ist \pər-ˈfek-shə-nəst, -shnəst\ *n* : a person who will not accept or be content with anything less than perfection — **perfectionist** *adj*

per•fect•ly \ˈpər-fik-tlē, -fik-lē\ *adv* **1** : in a perfect manner ⟨understand *perfectly*⟩ **2** : to an adequate extent : QUITE ⟨*perfectly* willing to go⟩

perfect number *n* : an integer that is equal to the sum of all its divisors except itself ⟨28 is a *perfect number* because it is the sum of 1 + 2 + 4 + 7 + 14⟩

perfect participle *n* : PAST PARTICIPLE

perfect square *n* : an integer whose square root is an integer ⟨9 is a *perfect square* because it is the square of 3⟩

perfect year *n* : a common year of 355 days or a leap year of 385 days in the Jewish calendar

per•fer•vid \ˌpər-ˈfər-vəd\ *adj* : extremely fervent

per•fid•i•ous \pər-ˈfid-ē-əs\ *adj* : of, relating to, or characterized by perfidy **syn** see FAITHLESS — **per•fid•i•ous•ly** *adv* — **per•fid•i•ous•ness** *n*

per•fi•dy \ˈpər-fəd-ē\ *n* : the quality or state of being faithless or disloyal : TREACHERY [Latin *perfidia*, from *perfidus* "faithless", from *per fidem decipere* "to betray", literally, "to deceive by trust"]

per•fo•rate \ˈpər-fə-ˌrāt\ *vb* **1** : to make a hole through or through something; *esp* : to make perforations in (as sheets of postage stamps) **2** : to pass through or into by or as if by making a hole [Latin *perforare* "to bore through", from *per-* "through" + *forare* "to bore"] — **per•fo•rate** \ˈpər-fə-rət, -frət, -fə-ˌrāt\ *adj* — **per•fo•ra•tor** \-fə-ˌrāt-ər\ *n*

per•fo•ra•tion \ˌpər-fə-ˈrā-shən\ *n* **1** : the act or process of perforating **2 a** : a hole or pattern made by or as if by piercing or boring **b** : any of the series of holes made between rows of postage stamps in a sheet

per•force \pər-ˈfōrs, -ˈfȯrs\ *adv* : by force of circumstances or necessity ⟨we went *perforce*⟩ [Middle French *par force* "by force"]

per•form \pər-ˈfȯrm\ *vb* **1** : to stick to the terms of : FULFILL ⟨*perform* a contract⟩ **2 a** : to carry out : DO ⟨*perform* miracles⟩ **b** : ACT, FUNCTION ⟨the car *performed* well⟩ **3 a** : to do in a formal manner or according to prescribed ritual **b** : to give a performance of : PRESENT ⟨the first time they had *performed* Hamlet⟩ [Anglo-French *performer*, from Old French *perfournir*, from *per-* "thoroughly" + *fournir* "to complete"] — **per•form•able** \-ˈfȯr-mə-bəl\ *adj* — **per•form•er** *n*

per•for•mance \pər-ˈfȯr-məns\ *n* **1 a** : the execution of an action **b** : something accomplished : DEED, FEAT **2** : the fulfillment of a claim, promise, or request **3 a** : the action of representing a character in a play **b** : a public presentation or exhibition ⟨a benefit *performance*⟩ **4 a** : the ability to perform : EFFICIENCY **b** : the manner in which a mechanism performs — **per•for•ma•to•ry** \-mə-ˌtōr-ē, -ˌtȯr-\ *adj*

per•form•ing *adj* : of, relating to, or constituting an art (as drama) that involves public performance

¹per•fume \ˈpər-ˌfyüm, pər-ˈ, ˌpər-ˈ\ *n* **1** : the scent of something sweet-smelling **2** : a substance that emits a pleasant odor; *esp* : a fluid preparation of floral essences or synthetics and a fixative used for scenting [Middle French *perfum*]

²per•fume \pər-ˈfyüm, ˌpər-ˈ, ˈpər-ˌ\ *vt* : to fill with an odor (as of something pleasant) ⟨a kitchen *perfumed* with spices⟩

per•fum•er \pər-ˈfyü-mər, pə-ˈfyü-\ *n* : one that makes or sells perfumes

per•fum•ery \pər-ˈfyüm-rē, pə-ˈfyüm-, -ə-rē\ *n, pl* **-er•ies** **1** : the art or process of making perfume **2** : the products made by a perfumer

per•func•to•ry \pər-ˈfəng-tə-rē, -ˈfəngk-, -trē\ *adj* **1** : characterized by routine or superficiality : MECHANICAL **2** : lacking in interest or enthusiasm : INDIFFERENT [Late Latin *perfunctorius,* from Latin *perfungi* "to accomplish, get through with", from *per-* "through" + *fungi* "to perform"] — **per•func•to•ri•ly** \-tə-rə-lē, -trə-lē\ *adv* — **per•func•to•ri•ness** \-tə-rē-nəs, -trē-nəs\ *n*

per•fuse \pər-ˈfyüz\ *vt* **1** : SUFFUSE **2 a** : to cause to flow or spread : DIFFUSE **b** : to force a fluid through (an organ or tissue) especially by way of the blood vessels [Latin *perfusus,* past participle of *perfundere* "to pour over", from *per-* "through" + *fundere* "to pour"] — **per•fu•sion** \-ˈfyü-zhən\ *n*

per•go•la \ˈpər-gə-lə, pər-ˈgō-\ *n* : a structure consisting of posts supporting an open roof in the form of a trellis [Italian, from Latin *pergula* "projecting roof"]

per•haps \pər-ˈhaps, pər-ˈaps, ˈpraps\ *adv* : possibly but not certainly : MAYBE [*per* + *hap*]

pe•ri \ˈpiər-ē\ *n, pl* **peris** : a supernatural being in Persian folklore descended from fallen angels and excluded from paradise until penance is accomplished [Persian *perī*]

peri- *prefix* **1** : all around : about ⟨*peri*scope⟩ **2** : near ⟨*peri*helion⟩ **3** : enclosing : surrounding ⟨*peri*odontal⟩ [Greek, "around, in excess", from *peri* "around"]

peri•anth \ˈper-ē-ˌanth, -ˌantth\ *n* : the outer part of a flower especially when consisting of a combined calyx and corolla [*peri-* + Greek *anthos* "flower"]

peri•car•di•um \ˌper-ə-ˈkärd-ē-əm\ *n, pl* **-dia** \-ē-ə\ : the cone-shaped sac of membrane that encloses the heart and the roots of the great blood vessels of vertebrates [New Latin, from Greek *perikardios* "around the heart", from *peri-* + *kardia* "heart"] — **peri•car•di•al** \-ē-əl\ *adj*

peri•carp \ˈper-ə-ˌkärp\ *n* : the ripened and variously modified walls of a plant ovary that form the substance of a fruit and enclose the seeds — compare ENDOCARP, EPICARP, MESOCARP

peri•cy•cle \ˈper-ə-ˌsī-kəl\ *n* : a thin layer of cells at the outer edge of a vascular cylinder in vascular plants [French *péricycle,* from Greek *perikyklos* "spherical", from *peri-* + *kyklos* "circle"]

peri•derm \ˈper-ə-ˌdərm\ *n* : an outer layer of tissue; *esp* : a cortical protective layer of many roots and stems — **peri•der•mal** \ˌper-ə-ˈdər-məl\ *adj*

peri•gee \ˈper-ə-ˌjē\ *n* : the point nearest the center of a celestial body (as the earth or moon) reached by an object (as a satellite) orbiting it — compare APOGEE [Greek *gē* "earth"]

pe•rig•y•nous \pə-ˈrij-ə-nəs\ *adj* **1** : growing from a ring or cup of the receptacle surrounding a pistil ⟨*perigynous* petals⟩ **2** : having perigynous flower parts — **pe•rig•y•ny** \-nē\ *n*

per•i•he•lion \ˌper-ə-ˈhēl-yən\ *n, pl* **-he•lia** \-ˈhēl-yə\ : the point in the path of a celestial body (as a planet) that is nearest to the sun — compare APHELION [New Latin, from *peri-* + Greek *hēlios* "sun"]

¹per•il \ˈper-əl\ *n* **1** : exposure to the risk of being injured, destroyed, or lost ⟨fire put the city in *peril*⟩ **2** : something that imperils : RISK ⟨*perils* of the highway⟩ [Old French, from Latin *periculum*] **syn** see DANGER

²peril *vt* **-iled** *also* **-illed**; **-il•ing** *also* **-il•ling** : to expose to danger : HAZARD, RISK

per•il•ous \ˈper-ə-ləs\ *adj* : full of or involving peril : HAZARDOUS — **per•il•ous•ly** *adv* — **per•il•ous•ness** *n*

pe•rim•e•ter \pə-ˈrim-ət-ər\ *n* **1** : the boundary of a closed plane figure; *also* : the length of this boundary **2** : a line or strip bounding or protecting an area **3** : outer limits [French *périmètre,* from Latin *perimetros,* from Greek, from *peri-* + *metron* "measure"]

per•i•ne•um \ˌper-ə-ˈnē-əm\ *n, pl* **-nea** \-ˈnē-ə\ : an area between the thighs which marks the approximate lower boundary of the pelvis and through which the urinary and genital ducts and rectum pass [Late Latin *perinaion,* from Greek, from *peri-* + *inein* "to empty out"] — **per•i•ne•al** \-ˈnē-əl\ *adj*

¹pe•ri•od \ˈpir-ē-əd\ *n* **1 a** : an utterance from one full stop to another : SENTENCE **b** : PERIODIC SENTENCE **2 a** : the full pause with which a sentence closes **b** : END 2a, STOP **3** : a punctuation mark . used chiefly to mark the end of a declarative sentence or an abbreviation **4** : the completion of a cycle, a series of events, or a single action : CONCLUSION **5 a** : a portion of time determined by some recurring phenomenon **b** : the interval of time required for a motion or phenomenon to complete a cycle and begin to repeat itself ⟨the *period* of a pendulum⟩ **c** : a single cyclic occurrence of menstruation **6 a** : a chronological division : STAGE **b** : a division of geologic time longer than an epoch and shorter than an era **c** : a stage of culture having a definable place in time and space ⟨the colonial *period*⟩ **7 a** : one of the divisions of the academic day **b** : one of the divisions of the playing time of a game **8** : the length of the shortest interval required on the x-axis for a periodic function to repeat itself **9** : a series of elements of increasing atomic number as listed in horizontal rows in the periodic table [Middle French *periode,* from Greek *periodos* "circuit, period of time, rhetorical period", from *peri-* + *hodos* "way"]

• **syn** PERIOD, EPOCH, ERA, AGE mean a division of time. PERIOD may designate any extent of time; EPOCH applies to a period begun by some striking or significant event ⟨the steam engine marked a new *epoch* in industry⟩ ERA suggests a period in history marked by a new or distinct order ⟨the *era* of exploration⟩ AGE is applied to a fairly definite period strongly dominated by a central figure ⟨the *age* of Jackson⟩ or by a prominent feature ⟨the nuclear *age*⟩

²period *adj* : of, relating to, or representing a particular historical period ⟨*period* furniture⟩

pe•ri•od•ic \ˌpir-ē-ˈäd-ik\ *adj* **1** : occurring or recurring at regular intervals **2** : consisting of or containing stages or values repeated at equal intervals : CYCLIC ⟨*periodic* vibrations⟩ ⟨the sine is a *periodic* function⟩ **3** : of or relating to a period — **pe•ri•od•ic•i•ty** \ˌpir-ē-ə-ˈdis-ət-ē\ *n*

¹pe•ri•od•i•cal \ˌpir-ē-ˈäd-i-kəl\ *adj* **1** : PERIODIC 1 **2 a** : published with a fixed interval between the issues or numbers **b** : published in, characteristic of, or connected with a periodical — **pe•ri•od•i•cal•ly** \-kə-lē, -klē\ *adv*

²periodical *n* : a periodical publication

periodic decimal *n* : REPEATING DECIMAL

periodic law *n* : a law in chemistry: the elements when arranged in the order of their atomic numbers show a periodic variation in most of their properties

periodic sentence *n* : a usually complex sentence that has no subordinate or trailing elements following its principal clause (as in "yesterday, while I was walking down the street, I saw them")

periodic table *n* : an arrangement of chemical elements based on the periodic law

peri•odon•tal \ˌper-ē-ō-ˈdänt-l\ *adj* **1** : surrounding or occurring about the teeth **2** : affecting periodontal tissues ⟨*periodontal* disease⟩ [*peri-* + Greek *odont-, odous* "tooth"]

periodontal membrane *n* : the fibrous connective-tissue layer covering the cement layer of a tooth

peri•os•te•um \ˌper-ē-ˈäs-tē-əm\ *n, pl* **-tea** \-tē-ə\ : the membrane of connective tissue that covers all bones except at the surfaces in a joint [Late Latin *periosteon,* from Greek *periosteos* "around the bone", from *peri-* + *osteon* "bone"] — **peri•os•te•al** \-tē-əl\ *adj*

peri•pa•tet•ic \ˌper-ə-pə-ˈtet-ik\ *adj* : moving about from place to place : ITINERANT ⟨a *peripatetic* preacher⟩ [Latin *peripateti-*

cus, from Greek *peripatētikos,* from *peripatein* "to walk about", from *peri-* + *patein* "to walk"] — **peri•pa•tet•i•cal•ly** \-'tet-i-kə-lē, -klē\ *adv*

pe•rip•a•tus \pə-'rip-ət-əs\ *n* **:** any of a class (Onychophora) of primitive tropical arthropods in some respects intermediate between annelid worms and typical arthropods [Greek *peripatos* "act of walking", from *peri-* + *patein* "to walk"]

pe•riph•er•al \pə-'rif-rəl, -ə-rəl\ *adj* **1 :** of, relating to, located in, or forming a periphery ⟨*peripheral* vision⟩ **2 :** of, relating to, or being part of the peripheral nervous system **3 :** having an auxiliary function ⟨*peripheral* equipment for a computer⟩ — **pe•riph•er•al•ly** \-ē\ *adv*

peripheral nervous system *n* **:** the part of the nervous system that is outside the central nervous system and consists of the cranial nerves, spinal nerves, and autonomic nervous system

pe•riph•ery \pə-'rif-rē, -ə-rē\ *n, pl* **-er•ies 1 :** the perimeter of a closed curve; *also* **:** the perimeter of a polygon **2 :** the external boundary or surface of a body **3 a :** the outward bounds of something as distinguished from its more internal regions or center **b :** an area lying beyond the strict limits of a thing [Middle French *peripherie,* from Late Latin *peripheria,* from Greek *periphereia,* from *peripherein* "to carry around", from *peri-* + *pherein* "to carry"]

pe•riph•ra•sis \pə-'rif-rə-səs\ *n, pl* **-ra•ses** \-rə-,sēz\ **:** use of a longer phrasing in place of a possible shorter and usually plainer form of expression **:** CIRCUMLOCUTION [Latin, from Greek, from *periphrazein* "to express periphrastically", from *peri-* + *phrazein* "to point out"]

per•i•phras•tic \,per-ə-'fras-tik\ *adj* **1 :** of, relating to, or characterized by periphrasis **2 :** formed by the use of function words or auxiliaries instead of by inflection ⟨*more fair* is a *periphrastic* comparative⟩ — **per•i•phras•ti•cal•ly** \-ti-kə-lē, -klē\ *adv*

peri•scope \'per-ə-,skōp\ *n* **:** a tubular optical instrument containing lenses and mirrors by which an observer (as on a submerged submarine) obtains an otherwise obstructed field of view — **peri•scop•ic** \,per-ə-'skäp-ik\ *adj*

periscope

per•ish \'per-ish\ *vi* **:** to pass away completely **:** become destroyed or ruined **:** DIE [Old French *periss-,* stem of *perir* "to perish", from Latin *perire,* from *per-* "to destruction" + *ire* "to go"]

per•ish•able \'per-ish-ə-bəl\ *adj* **:** liable to spoil or decay ⟨*perishable* products such as fruit⟩ — **per•ish•abil•i•ty** \,per-ish-ə-'bil-ət-ē\ *n* — **perishable** *n*

pe•ris•so•dac•tyl \pə-,ris-ə-'dak-tl\ *n* **:** any of an order (Perissodactyla) of hoofed mammals (as the horse or rhinoceros) with an odd number of functional toes on each foot [Greek *perissos* "excessive, odd" + *daktylos* "finger, toe"] — **perissodactyl** *adj*

peri•stal•sis \,per-ə-'stȯl-səs, -'stäl-, -'stal-\ *n, pl* **-stal•ses** \-,sēz\ **:** successive waves of involuntary contraction passing along the walls of a hollow muscular structure (as the intestine) and forcing the contents onward [derived from Greek *peristellein* "to wrap around", from *peri-* + *stellein* "to place"] — **peri•stal•tic** \-'stȯl-tik, -'stal-\ *adj* — **peri•stal•ti•cal•ly** \-ti-kə-lē, -klē\ *adv*

peri•style \'per-ə-,stīl\ *n* **1 :** a colonnade surrounding a building or court **2 :** an open space enclosed by a row of columns [French *péristyle,* from Latin *peristylum,* from Greek *peristylon,* derived from *peri-* + *stylos* "pillar"]

peri•to•ne•um \,per-ət-n-'ē-əm\ *n, pl* **-ne•ums** *or* **-nea** \-'ē-ə\ **:** the smooth transparent membrane that lines the cavity of the abdomen and encloses the abdominal and pelvic viscera [Late Latin, from Greek *peritonaios* "stretched around", from *peri-* + *teinein* "to stretch"] — **peri•to•ne•al** \-'ē-əl\ *adj*

peri•to•ni•tis \,per-ət-n-'īt-əs\ *n* **:** inflammation of the peritoneum

peri•wig \'per-i-,wig\ *n* **:** WIG [French *perruque*]

[1]**per•i•win•kle** \'per-i-,wing-kəl\ *n* **:** a European creeper widely grown as a ground cover and for its blue or white flowers — called also *myrtle* [Old English *perwince,* from Latin *pervinca*]

[2]**periwinkle** *n* **:** any of numerous small edible marine snails of coastal regions; *also* **:** the shell of a periwinkle [Old English *pīnewincle*]

per•jure \'pər-jər\ *vt* **per•jured**; **per•jur•ing** \'pərj-ring, -ə-ring\ **:** to make (oneself) guilty of perjury [Middle French *perjurer,* from Latin *perjurare,* from *per-* "to destruction, to the bad" + *jurare* "to swear"]

per•jur•er \'pər-jər-ər\ *n* **:** a person guilty of perjury

per•ju•ri•ous \pər-'jůr-ē-əs\ *adj* **:** marked by perjury — **per•ju•ri•ous•ly** *adv*

per•ju•ry \'pərj-rē, -ə-rē\ *n, pl* **-ries :** violation of an oath by knowingly swearing to what is untrue **:** false swearing

perk \'pərk\ *vb* **1 :** to stick up or out jauntily ⟨a dog *perking* its ears⟩ **2 :** to regain vigor or cheerfulness ⟨*perked* up as the cold got better⟩ **3 :** to smarten the appearance of ⟨*perked* the room up with new curtains⟩ [Middle English *perken* "to be jaunty"]

perky \'pər-kē\ *adj* **perk•i•er**; **-est :** JAUNTY, LIVELY — **perk•i•ly** \-kə-lē\ *adv* — **perk•i•ness** \-kē-nəs\ *n*

per•lite \'pər-,līt\ *n* **:** glassy cooled volcanic lava of shelly structure that when expanded by heat forms a lightweight water-absorbent material [French, from *perle* "pearl"]

per•ma•frost \'pər-mə-,frȯst\ *n* **:** a permanently frozen layer at variable depth below the earth's surface in frigid regions [*per*manent *frost*]

per•ma•nence \'pər-mə-nəns\ *n* **:** the quality or state of being permanent

per•ma•nen•cy \-nən-sē\ *n, pl* **-cies :** PERMANENCE

[1]**per•ma•nent** \'pər-mə-nənt\ *adj* **:** lasting or intended to last for a very long time without fundamental or marked change [Middle French, from Latin *permanēre,* from *per-* "throughout" + *manēre* "to remain"] **syn** see LASTING — **per•ma•nent•ly** *adv* — **per•ma•nent•ness** *n*

[2]**permanent** *n* **:** a long-lasting hair wave produced by mechanical and chemical means

permanent magnet *n* **:** a magnet that retains its magnetism after removal of the magnetizing force

permanent press *adj* **:** of, relating to, or made from a fabric chemically treated to resist wrinkling

permanent tooth *n* **:** one of the second set of teeth of a mammal that follow the milk teeth, typically persist into old age, and in humans are 32 in number

per•man•ga•nate \pər-'mang-gə-,nāt\ *n* **:** POTASSIUM PERMANGANATE

per•me•abil•i•ty \,pər-mē-ə-'bil-ət-ē\ *n, pl* **-ties 1 :** the quality or state of being permeable **2 :** the property of a substance that determines the degree to which it is magnetizable

per•me•able \'pər-mē-ə-bəl\ *adj* **:** having pores or openings that permit liquids or gases to pass through ⟨a *permeable* membrane⟩ ⟨*permeable* limestone⟩ — **per•me•able•ness** *n* — **per•me•ably** \-blē\ *adv*

per•me•ance \'pər-mē-əns\ *n* **:** PERMEATION

per•me•ate \'pər-mē-,āt\ *vb* **1 :** to pass through the pores or small openings of ⟨water *permeates* sand⟩ **2 :** to spread throughout **:** PERVADE ⟨a room *permeated* with the odor of tobacco⟩ [Latin *permeare,* from *per-* "through" + *meare* "to go, pass"] — **per•me•a•tion** \,pər-mē-'ā-shən\ *n* — **per•me•a•tive** \'pər-mē-,āt-iv\ *adj*

Perm•ian \'pər-mē-ən\ *n* **:** the most recent period of the Paleozoic era; *also* **:** the corresponding system of rocks — see GEOLOGIC TIME table [*Perm,* region in eastern Russia] — **Permian** *adj*

per•mis•si•ble \pər-'mis-ə-bəl\ *adj* **:** that may be permitted **:** ALLOWABLE — **per•mis•si•bil•i•ty** \-,mis-ə-'bil-ət-ē\ *n* — **per•mis•si•ble•ness** \-'mis-ə-bəl-nəs\ *n* — **per•mis•si•bly** \-blē\ *adv*

per•mis•sion \pər-'mish-ən\ *n* **1 :** the act of permitting **2 :** the consent of a person in authority **:** AUTHORIZATION [Middle French, from Latin *permissio,* from *permissus,* past participle of *permittere* "to permit"]

per•mis•sive \pər-'mis-iv\ *adj* **1 a :** granting or tending to grant permission **b :** allowing freedom (as of choice or behavior) **:** INDULGENT ⟨*permissive* parents⟩ **2 :** not forbidden **:** ALLOWABLE — **per•mis•sive•ly** *adv* — **per•mis•sive•ness** *n*

[1]**per•mit** \pər-'mit\ *vb* **per•mit•ted**; **per•mit•ting 1 :** to consent to expressly or formally **:** give permission **2 :** to make possible **:** give an opportunity **:** ALLOW ⟨if time *permits*⟩ [Latin *per-*

mittere "to let through, permit", from *per-* "through" + *mittere* "to let go, send"] **syn** see LET — **per•mit•ter** *n*

[2]**per•mit** \'pər-ˌmit, pər-'\ *n* : a written statement of permission given by one having authority ⟨a *permit* to learn to drive⟩

per•mu•ta•tion \ˌpər-myü-'tā-shən\ *n* **1** : a thorough change in character or condition : TRANSFORMATION **2 a** : the act or process of changing the order of a set of objects **b** : an ordered arrangement of a set of objects — **per•mu•ta•tion•al** \-shnəl, -shən-l\ *adj*

per•mute \pər-'myüt\ *vt* : to change the order or arrangement of; *esp* : to arrange in all possible ways [Latin *permutare,* from *per-* + *mutare* "to change"]

per•ni•cious \pər-'nish-əs\ *adj* : very destructive or injurious ⟨a *pernicious* disease⟩ ⟨a *pernicious* habit⟩ [Middle French *pernicieus,* from Latin *perniciosus,* from *pernicies* "destruction", from *per-* + *nec-*, *nex* "violent death"] — **per•ni•cious•ly** *adv* — **per•ni•cious•ness** *n*

pernicious anemia *n* : a severe anemia in which the red blood cells progressively decrease in number and increase in size and which is associated with a deficiency of vitamin B_{12}

per•nick•e•ty \pər-'nik-ət-ē\ *adj* : PERSNICKETY [perhaps alteration of *particular*]

per•ora•tion \ˌper-ər-'ā-shən, ˌpər-\ *n* **1** : the concluding part of a speech and especially an oration **2** : a very rhetorical speech — **per•orate** \'per-ər-ˌāt\ *vi* — **per•ora•tion•al** \ˌper-ər-'ā-shnəl, ˌpər-, -shən-l\ *adj*

[1]**per•ox•ide** \pə-'räk-ˌsīd\ *n* **1** : an oxide containing a high proportion of oxygen; *esp* : a compound (as hydrogen peroxide) in which oxygen is joined to oxygen **2** : HYDROGEN PEROXIDE

[2]**peroxide** *vt* : to bleach (hair) with hydrogen peroxide

[1]**per•pen•dic•u•lar** \ˌpər-pən-'dik-yə-lər\ *adj* **1 a** : exactly vertical or upright **b** : being at right angles to a given line or plane **2** : extremely steep : PRECIPITOUS [Middle French *perpendiculer,* from Latin *perpendicularis,* from *perpendiculum* "plumb line", from *per-* + *pendēre* "to hang"] **syn** see VERTICAL — **per•pen•dic•u•lar•i•ty** \-ˌdik-yə-'lar-ət-ē\ *n* — **per•pen•dic•u•lar•ly** \-'dik-yə-lər-lē\ *adv*

[2]**perpendicular** *n* : a line at right angles to the plane of the horizon or to another line or surface

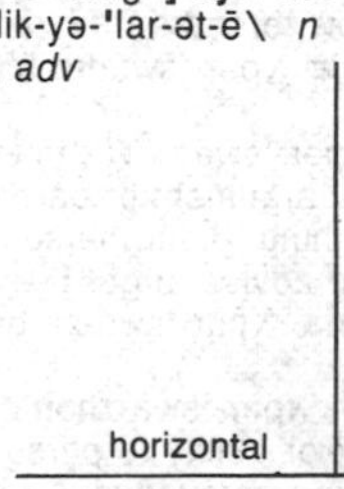

[2]perpendicular

per•pe•trate \'pər-pə-ˌtrāt\ *vt* : to be guilty of doing or performing : COMMIT ⟨*perpetrate* a crime⟩ [Latin *perpetrare,* from *per-* + *patrare* "to accomplish"] — **per•pe•tra•tion** \ˌpər-pə-'trā-shən\ *n* — **per•pe•tra•tor** \'pər-pə-ˌtrāt-ər\ *n*

per•pet•u•al \pər-'pech-ə-wəl, -'pech-əl\ *adj* **1 a** : continuing forever : EVERLASTING **b** (1) : valid for all time ⟨a *perpetual* right-of-way⟩ (2) : holding (as an office) for life or for an unlimited time **2** : going on and on without interruption : CONSTANT **3** : blooming continuously throughout the season [Middle French *perpetuel,* from Latin *perpetuus,* from *per-* + *petere* "to go to"] — **per•pet•u•al•ly** \-ē\ *adv*

perpetual calendar *n* : a table for finding the day of the week for any one of a wide range of dates

per•pet•u•ate \pər-'pech-ə-ˌwāt\ *vt* : to make perpetual or cause to last indefinitely ⟨*perpetuate* a tradition⟩ — **per•pet•u•a•tion** \-ˌpech-ə-'wā-shən\ *n* — **per•pet•u•a•tor** \-'pech-ə-ˌwāt-ər\ *n*

per•pe•tu•i•ty \ˌpər-pə-'tü-ət-ē, -'tyü-\ *n, pl* **-ties** **1** : perpetual existence or duration ⟨the *perpetuity* of their fame⟩ **2** : endless time : ETERNITY

per•plex \pər-'pleks\ *vt* **1** : to make mentally uncertain : BEWILDER, NONPLUS **2** : to make intricate or involved : COMPLICATE [Latin *perplexus* "involved, perplexed", from *per-* "thoroughly" + *plexus* "involved", from *plectere* "to braid, twine"] **syn** see PUZZLE

per•plexed \-'plekst\ *adj* **1** : filled with uncertainty **2** : full of difficulty : COMPLICATED — **per•plexed•ly** \-'plek-səd-lē, -'pleks-tlē\ *adv*

per•plex•i•ty \pər-'plek-sət-ē\ *n, pl* **-ties** **1** : the state of being perplexed : BEWILDERMENT **2** : something that perplexes

per•qui•site \'pər-kwə-zət\ *n* **1** : a profit made from one's employment in addition to one's regular pay; *esp* : such a profit when expected or promised **2** : [8]TIP [Medieval Latin *perquisitum* "property acquired by other means than inheritance", from *perquirere* "to purchase, acquire", from Latin, "to search out", from *per-* + *quaerere* "to seek"]

per•ry \'per-ē\ *n* : pear cider [Middle French *peré,* from Latin *pirum* "pear"]

per se \ˌpər-'sā\ *adv* : by, of, or in itself or oneself or themselves : as such : INTRINSICALLY [Latin]

per second per second *adv* : per second every second — used of acceleration

per•se•cute \'pər-si-ˌkyüt\ *vt* **1** : to harass in a manner to injure, grieve, or afflict; *esp* : to cause to suffer because of belief **2** : to annoy with persistent or urgent approaches : PESTER [Middle French *persecuter,* derived from Late Latin *persequi,* from Latin, "to pursue", from *per-* "through" + *sequi* "to follow"] — **per•se•cu•tor** \-ˌkyüt-ər\ *n* — **per•se•cu•to•ry** \-kyü-ˌtōr-ē, -ˌtòr-\ *adj*

per•se•cu•tion \ˌpər-si-'kyü-shən\ *n* **1** : the act or practice of persecuting especially those who differ in origin, religion, or social outlook **2** : the condition of being persecuted, harassed, or annoyed

Per•seus \'pər-ˌsüs, -sē-əs\ *n* : a northern constellation between Taurus and Cassiopeia [Latin *Perseus,* son of Zeus, from Greek]

per•se•ver•ance \ˌpər-sə-'vir-əns\ *n* : the action, condition, or an instance of persevering : STEADFASTNESS

per•se•vere \ˌpər-sə-'viər\ *vi* : to keep at something in spite of difficulties, opposition, or discouragement [Middle French *perseverer,* from Latin *perseverare,* from *per-* "through" + *severus* "severe"]

per•se•ver•ing \-'viər-ing\ *adj* : showing perseverance : PERSISTENT — **per•se•ver•ing•ly** \-ing-lē\ *adv*

Per•sian \'pər-zhən\ *n* **1** : one of the people of Persia: as **a** : one of the ancient Iranian Caucasians who under Cyrus and his successors dominated western Asia **b** : a member of one of the peoples forming the modern Iranian nation **2** : the modern language of Iran and western Afghanistan used also in Pakistan and by Indian Muslims as a literary language **3** : a thin soft silk formerly used especially for linings — **Persian** *adj*

Persian cat *n* : a stocky round-headed domestic cat with long silky fur

Persian lamb *n* : a pelt obtained from karakul lambs older than those yielding broadtail and characterized by very silky tightly curled fur

per•si•flage \'pər-sə-ˌfläzh, 'per-\ *n* : frivolous or lightly jesting talk : BANTER [French, from *persifler* "to banter", from *per-* "thoroughly" + *siffler* "to whistle, hiss, boo", from Latin *sibilare*]

per•sim•mon \pər-'sim-ən\ *n* **1** : any of a genus of trees with hard fine wood, oblong leaves, and small bell-shaped white flowers **2** : the usually orange several-seeded fruit of a persimmon that resembles a plum, is edible when fully ripe, and is technically a berry [of American Indian origin]

Persian cat

per•sist \pər-'sist, -'zist\ *vi* **1** : to go on resolutely in spite of opposition, warnings, or pleas : PERSEVERE **2** : to last on and on : continue to exist ⟨rain *persisting* for days⟩ [Middle French *persister,* from Latin *persistere,* from *per-* + *sistere* "to take a stand, stand firm"] — **per•sist•er** *n*

per•sis•tence \pər-'sis-təns, -'zis-\ *n* **1** : the act or fact of persisting **2** : the quality or state of being persistent; *esp* : PERSEVERANCE

per•sis•ten•cy \-tən-sē\ *n* : PERSISTENCE 2

per•sis•tent \-tənt\ *adj* **1** : continuing, existing, or acting for a long or longer than usual time ⟨a *persistent* cough⟩ ⟨*persistent*

\ə\ **abut**	\au̇\ **out**	\i\ **tip**	\ȯ\ **saw**	\u̇\ **foot**
\ər\ **further**	\ch\ **chin**	\ī\ **life**	\ȯi\ **coin**	\y\ **yet**
\a\ **mat**	\e\ **pet**	\j\ **job**	\th\ **thin**	\yü\ **few**
\ā\ **take**	\ē\ **easy**	\ng\ **sing**	\t͟h\ **this**	\yu̇\ **cure**
\ä\ **cot, cart**	\g\ **go**	\ō\ **bone**	\ü\ **food**	\zh\ **vision**

gills⟩ **2 :** DOGGED, TENACIOUS ⟨a *persistent* salesman⟩ [Latin *persistens,* present participle of *persistere* "to persist"] — **per•sis•tent•ly** *adv*

per•snick•e•ty \pər-ˈsnik-ət-ē\ *adj* **:** fussy about small details **:** FASTIDIOUS [alteration of *pernickety*]

per•son \ˈpərs-n\ *n* **1 :** HUMAN BEING, INDIVIDUAL — used in combination especially by those who prefer to avoid *man* in compounds applicable to both sexes ⟨chair*person*⟩ **2 :** a character or part in or as if in a play **:** GUISE **3 a :** bodily appearance **b :** the body of a human being **4 a :** the individual personality of a human being **:** SELF **b :** bodily presence ⟨appear in *person*⟩ **5 :** an entity (as a human being or corporation) recognized by law as having rights and duties **6 :** reference to the speaker, to one spoken to, or to one spoken of as indicated especially by means of certain pronouns [Old French *persone,* from Latin *persona* "actor's mask, character in a play, person"]

per•son•able \ˈpərs-nə-bəl, -n-ə-bəl\ *adj* **:** attractive in looks and manner **:** PLEASING — **per•son•able•ness** *n*

per•son•age \ˈpərs-nij, -n-ij\ *n* **1 :** a person of rank or distinction **2 :** a character in a book or play

[1]**per•son•al** \ˈpərs-nəl, -n-əl\ *adj* **1 :** of, relating to, or belonging to a person **:** PRIVATE **2 a :** done in person or proceeding from a single person **b :** carried on between individuals directly **3 :** relating to the person or body ⟨*personal* hygiene⟩ **4 :** closely related to an individual **:** INTIMATE **5 :** denoting grammatical person

[2]**personal** *n* **:** a short newspaper paragraph relating to a person or group or to personal matters

personal effects *n pl* **:** personal property (as clothing and toilet articles) normally worn or carried on the person

personal equation *n* **:** variation (as in scientific observation) due to the personal peculiarities of an individual; *also* **:** a correction or allowance made for such variation

personal foul *n* **:** a foul (as in basketball or lacrosse) which involves unnecessary roughness or illegal obstruction of an opponent

per•son•al•i•ty \ˌpərs-n-ˈal-ət-ē, ˌpər-ˈsnal-\ *n, pl* **-ties 1 :** the state of being a person **2 :** the emotional and behavioral characteristics of a person **:** INDIVIDUALITY **3 :** pleasing qualities of character ⟨lack *personality*⟩ **4 :** a person who has strongly marked qualities ⟨a great stage *personality*⟩ **5 :** a personal remark **:** a slighting reference to a person ⟨use *personalities* in an argument⟩

per•son•al•ize \ˈpərs-nə-ˌlīz, -n-ə-\ *vt* **1 :** PERSONIFY 1 **2 :** to make personal or individual; *esp* **:** to mark as belonging to a particular person ⟨*personalized* stationery⟩

per•son•al•ly \ˈpərs-nə-lē, -n-ə-\ *adv* **1 :** in person ⟨attend to the matter *personally*⟩ **2 :** as a person **:** in personality ⟨*personally* attractive but not very trustworthy⟩ **3 :** for oneself **:** as far as oneself is concerned ⟨*personally,* I am against it⟩

personal pronoun *n* **:** a pronoun (as *I, you,* or *they*) expressing a distinction of person

personal property *n* **:** movable property (as money, clothing, or furnishings) **:** CHATTELS — compare REAL PROPERTY

per•son•al•ty \ˈpərs-nəl-tē, -n-əl-\ *n, pl* **-ties :** PERSONAL PROPERTY

per•so•na non gra•ta \pər-ˌsō-nə-ˌnän-ˈgrat-ə, -ˈgrät-\ *adj* **:** personally unacceptable or unwelcome [New Latin, "person not acceptable"]

per•son•ate \ˈpərs-n-āt\ *vt* **1 :** IMPERSONATE, REPRESENT **2 :** to invest with personality or personal characteristics — **per•son•ation** \ˌpərs-n-ˈā-shən\ *n* — **per•son•ative** \ˈpərs-n-ˌāt-iv\ *adj* — **per•son•ator** \-ˌāt-ər\ *n*

per•son•i•fi•ca•tion \pər-ˌsän-ə-fə-ˈkā-shən\ *n* **1 :** the act of personifying **2 :** an imaginary being thought of as representing a thing or an idea **3 :** EMBODIMENT 1, INCARNATION ⟨you are the *personification* of generosity⟩ **4 :** a figure of speech in which a lifeless object or abstract quality is spoken of as if alive

per•son•i•fy \pər-ˈsän-ə-ˌfī\ *vt* **-fied; -fy•ing 1 :** to think of or represent as a person ⟨*personify* the forces of nature⟩ **2 :** to represent in a physical form ⟨the law was *personified* in the sheriff⟩ **3 :** to serve as the perfect type or example of ⟨a saint who *personified* kindness⟩ — **per•son•i•fi•er** \-ˌfī-ər, -ˌfīr\ *n*

per•son•nel \ˌpərs-n-ˈel\ *n* **:** a group of persons employed (as in a public service, a factory, or an office) [French]

[1]**per•spec•tive** \pər-ˈspek-tiv\ *n* **1 :** the art or technique of painting or drawing a scene so that objects in it have apparent depth and distance **2 :** the power to see or think of things in their true relationship to each other ⟨lose one's *perspective*⟩ **3 :** the true relationship of objects or events to one another ⟨view events in proper *perspective*⟩ **4 a :** a visible scene; *esp* **:** one giving a definite impression of distance **b :** a mental view or prospect **5 :** the appearance to the eye of objects in respect to their relative distance and positions [Middle French, probably from Italian *prospettiva,* from *prospetto* "view, prospect", from Latin *prospectus*]

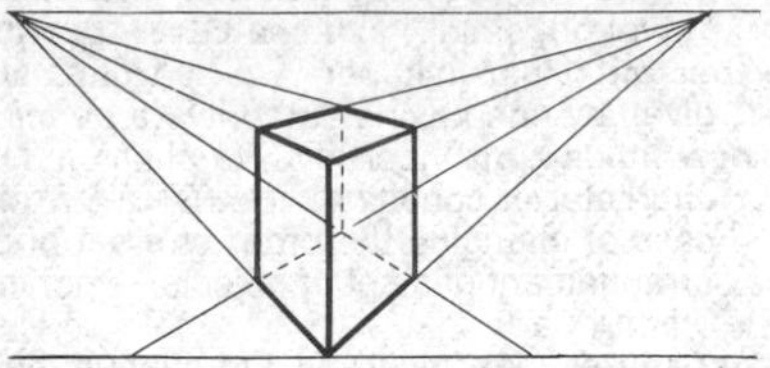
[1]perspective 1

[2]**perspective** *adj* **:** of, relating to, or seen in perspective — **perspec•tive•ly** *adv*

per•spi•ca•cious \ˌpər-spə-ˈkā-shəs\ *adj* **:** having or showing keen understanding or discernment [Latin *perspicax,* from *perspicere* "to look through, see clearly", from *per-* "through" + *specere* "to look"] — **per•spi•ca•cious•ly** *adv* — **per•spi•ca•cious•ness** *n*

per•spi•cac•i•ty \ˌpər-spə-ˈkas-ət-ē\ *n* **:** the quality or state of being perspicacious

per•spic•u•ous \pər-ˈspik-yə-wəs\ *adj* **:** plain to the understanding **:** CLEAR [Latin *perspicuus* "transparent, perspicuous", from *perspicere* "to look through"] — **per•spi•cu•ity** \ˌpər-spə-ˈkyü-ət-ē\ *n* — **per•spic•u•ous•ly** \pər-ˈspik-yə-wə-slē\ *adv* — **per•spic•u•ous•ness** *n*

per•spi•ra•tion \ˌpər-spə-ˈrā-shən\ *n* **1 :** the act or process of perspiring **2 :** a saline fluid secreted by the sweat glands **:** SWEAT

per•spire \pər-ˈspīr\ *vi* **:** to secrete and emit perspiration **:** SWEAT [French *perspirer,* from Latin *per-* "through" + *spirare* "to blow, breathe"]

per•suad•able \pər-ˈswād-ə-bəl\ *adj* **:** capable of being persuaded

per•suade \pər-ˈswād\ *vt* **:** to win over to a belief or to a course of action by argument or earnest request **:** induce to do or believe something [Latin *persuadēre,* from *per-* "thoroughly" + *suadēre* "to advise, urge"] — **per•suad•er** *n*

per•sua•si•ble \pər-ˈswā-zə-bəl, -ˈswā-sə-\ *adj* **:** PERSUADABLE

per•sua•sion \pər-ˈswā-zhən\ *n* **1 :** the act of persuading **2 :** the power or ability to persuade **:** persuasive quality **3 :** the state of being persuaded **4 :** a way of believing **:** BELIEF; *esp* **:** a system of religious beliefs **5 :** a group having the same religious beliefs [Latin *persuasio,* from *persuadēre* "to persuade"]

per•sua•sive \pər-ˈswā-siv, -ziv\ *adj* **:** tending to persuade **:** having the power or effect of persuading ⟨a *persuasive* speech⟩ — **per•sua•sive•ly** *adv* — **per•sua•sive•ness** *n*

pert \ˈpərt\ *adj* **1 a :** saucily free and forward **:** IMPUDENT **b :** being trim and chic **:** JAUNTY **c :** piquantly stimulating **2 :** VIVACIOUS, LIVELY [Middle English, "open, bold, pert", from Old French *apert,* from Latin *apertus* "open", from *aperire* "to open"] — **pert•ly** *adv* — **pert•ness** *n*

per•tain \pər-ˈtān\ *vi* **1 :** to belong as a part, quality, or function ⟨duties that *pertain* to an office⟩ **2 :** to have reference ⟨books *pertaining* to birds⟩ [Middle French *partenir,* from Latin *pertinēre* "to hold out, reach to, pertain", from *per-* "through" + *tenēre* "to hold"]

per•ti•na•cious \ˌpərt-n-ˈā-shəs\ *adj* **1 :** holding strongly to an opinion, purpose, or course of action **2 :** stubbornly or annoyingly persistent [Latin *pertinax,* from *per-* "thoroughly" + *tenax* "tenacious"] **syn** see OBSTINATE — **per•ti•na•cious•ly** *adv* — **per•ti•na•cious•ness** *n* — **per•ti•nac•i•ty** \ˌpərt-n-ˈas-ət-ē\ *n*

per•ti•nent \ˈpərt-n-ənt\ *adj* **:** having to do with the subject or matter that is being considered **:** being to the point ⟨a *pertinent* suggestion⟩ [Middle French, from Latin *pertinēre* "to pertain"] — **per•ti•nence** \-n-əns\ *or* **per•ti•nen•cy** \-n-ən-sē\ *n* — **per•ti•nent•ly** *adv*

per•turb \pər-ˈtərb\ *vt* **1 :** to disturb greatly in mind **:** DISQUIET **2 :** to throw into confusion **:** AGITATE [Middle French *perturber,* from Latin *perturbare* "to throw into confusion", from *per-* + *turbare* "to disturb"] **syn** see DISTURB — **per•turb•able** \-ˈtər-bə-bəl\ *adj*

per•tur•ba•tion \ˌpərt-ər-ˈbā-shən, ˌpər-ˌtər-\ *n* **1 :** the action of perturbing **:** the state of being perturbed **2 :** a cause of worry or disquiet **3 :** a disturbance of the regular motion of a celestial body produced by some force additional to that which causes its regular motion — **per•tur•ba•tion•al** \-shnəl, -shən-l\ *adj*

per•tus•sis \pər-ˈtəs-əs\ *n* **:** WHOOPING COUGH [Latin *per-* + *tussis* "cough"]

pe•ruke \pə-ˈrük\ *n* **:** WIG [Middle French *perruque,* from Italian *parrucca*]

pe•ruse \pə-ˈrüz\ *vt* **1 :** to examine or study attentively and in detail **2 :** READ 1a(1) [Middle English *perusen*] — **pe•rus•al** \-ˈrü-zəl\ *n* — **pe•rus•er** *n*

Pe•ru•vi•an bark \pə-ˌrü-vē-ən-\ *n* **:** CINCHONA 2

per•vade \pər-ˈvād\ *vt* **:** to spread or become diffused throughout every part of [Latin *pervadere* (past participle *pervasus*) "to go through, pervade", from *per-* "through" + *vadere* "to go"] — **per•va•sion** \-ˈvā-zhən\ *n* — **per•va•sive** \-ˈvā-siv, -ziv\ *adj* — **per•va•sive•ly** *adv* — **per•va•sive•ness** *n*

per•verse \pər-ˈvərs, ˈpər-ˌ\ *adj* **1 :** turned away from what is right or good **:** CORRUPT **2 a :** obstinate in opposing what is right, reasonable, or accepted **:** WRONGHEADED **b :** arising from or showing stubbornness or obstinacy **3 :** marked by peevishness or petulance **:** CRANKY [Latin *perversus,* from *pervertere* "to pervert"] — **per•verse•ly** *adv* — **per•verse•ness** *n* — **per•ver•si•ty** \pər-ˈvər-sət-ē, -stē\ *n*

per•ver•sion \pər-ˈvər-zhən\ *n* **1 :** the action of perverting **:** the condition of being perverted **2 :** a perverted form of something; *esp* **:** atypical sexual behavior

[1]**per•vert** \pər-ˈvərt\ *vt* **1 a :** to cause to turn aside or away from what is good or true or morally right **:** CORRUPT **b :** to cause to turn aside or away from what is generally done or accepted **:** MISDIRECT **2 a :** to divert to a wrong end or purpose **:** MISUSE **b :** to twist the meaning or sense of **:** MISINTERPRET [Middle French *pervertir,* from Latin *pervertere* "to overturn, corrupt, pervert", from *per-* + *vertere* "to turn"] — **per•ver•sive** \-ˈvər-siv, -ziv\ *adj* — **per•vert•er** *n*

[2]**per•vert** \ˈpər-ˌvərt\ *n* **:** one that is perverted; *esp* **:** one given to some form of sexual perversion

per•vert•ed \pər-ˈvərt-əd\ *adj* **1 :** CORRUPT 1, TWISTED **2 :** marked by perversion — **per•vert•ed•ly** *adv* — **per•vert•ed•ness** *n*

per•vi•ous \ˈpər-vē-əs\ *adj* **:** allowing entrance or passage **:** PERMEABLE ⟨*pervious* rock⟩ [Latin *pervius,* from *per-* "through" + *via* "way"] — **per•vi•ous•ness** *n*

Pe•sach \ˈpā-ˌsäk\ *n* **:** PASSOVER [Hebrew *pesaḥ*]

pe•se•ta \pə-ˈsāt-ə\ *n* **1 :** the basic monetary unit of Spain **2 :** a coin or note representing one peseta [Spanish, from *peso* "peso"]

pes•ky \ˈpes-kē\ *adj* **pes•ki•er; -est :** TROUBLESOME, VEXATIOUS [probably derived from *pest*] — **pes•ki•ly** \-kə-lē\ *adv* — **pes•ki•ness** \-kē-nəs\ *n*

pe•so \ˈpā-sō\ *n, pl* **pesos 1 :** an old silver coin of Spain and Spanish America equal to eight reals **2 a :** the basic monetary unit of Argentina, Bolivia, Colombia, Cuba, Dominican Republic, Mexico, Philippines, and Uruguay **b :** a coin or note representing one peso [Spanish, literally, "weight", from Latin *pensum,* from *pendere* "to weigh"]

pes•si•mism \ˈpes-ə-ˌmiz-əm\ *n* **1 :** an inclination to emphasize bad, disagreeable, or unpleasant aspects, conditions, and possibilities or to expect the worst **2 :** a belief that evil is more common or powerful than good [French *pessimisme,* from Latin *pessimus* "worst"] — **pes•si•mist** \-məst\ *n*

pes•si•mis•tic \ˌpes-ə-ˈmis-tik\ *adj* **:** marked by, given to, or exhibiting pessimism ⟨a *pessimistic* report on the economy⟩ ⟨*pessimistic* about our chances of winning⟩ — **pes•si•mis•ti•cal•ly** \-ti-kə-lē, -klē\ *adv*

pest \ˈpest\ *n* **1 :** an epidemic disease with a high mortality; *esp* **:** PLAGUE **2 :** something resembling a pest in destructiveness; *esp* **:** a plant or animal harmful to humans **3 :** one that pesters or annoys **:** NUISANCE [Middle French *peste,* from Latin *pestis*]

pes•ter \ˈpes-tər\ *vt* **pes•tered; pes•ter•ing** \-tə-ring, -tring\ **:** ANNOY, BOTHER [Middle French *empestrer* "to hobble (a horse), embarrass", derived from Latin *pastor* "herdsman"]

pest•hole \ˈpest-ˌhōl\ *n* **:** a place in which pestilences are common

pest•house \-ˌhau̇s\ *n* **:** a shelter or hospital for those infected with a contagious or epidemic disease

pes•ti•cide \ˈpes-tə-ˌsīd\ *n* **:** an agent used to destroy pests — **pes•ti•cid•al** \ˌpes-tə-ˈsīd-l\ *adj*

pes•tif•er•ous \pe-ˈstif-rəs, -ə-rəs\ *adj* **1 :** dangerous to society **:** PERNICIOUS **2 :** carrying or causing infection **3 :** causing annoyance **:** TROUBLESOME — **pes•tif•er•ous•ly** *adv* — **pes•tif•er•ous•ness** *n*

pes•ti•lence \ˈpes-tə-ləns\ *n* **:** a contagious or infectious epidemic disease that spreads quickly and has devastating effects; *esp* **:** BUBONIC PLAGUE

pes•ti•lent \-lənt\ *adj* **1 :** dangerous or destructive to life **:** DEADLY ⟨a *pestilent* drug⟩; *also* **:** being or conveying a pestilence ⟨a *pestilent* disease⟩ ⟨*pestilent* infections⟩ **2 :** harmful or dangerous to society **:** PERNICIOUS ⟨the *pestilent* influence of the slums⟩ **3 :** that is a pest ⟨a *pestilent* child⟩ [Latin *pestilens* "pestilential", from *pestis* "plague"] — **pes•ti•lent•ly** *adv*

pes•ti•len•tial \ˌpes-tə-ˈlen-chəl\ *adj* **:** causing or likely to cause pestilence **:** PESTILENT — **pes•ti•len•tial•ly** \-lench-lē, -ə-lē\ *adv*

pes•tle \ˈpes-əl, ˈpes-tl\ *n* **:** a usually club-shaped implement for pounding or grinding substances in a mortar [Middle French *pestel,* from Latin *pistillum*] — **pestle** *vb*

[1]**pet** \ˈpet\ *n* **1 :** a domesticated animal kept for pleasure rather than utility **2 a :** a pampered and usually spoiled child **b :** a person who is treated with unusual kindness or consideration **:** DARLING [perhaps from Middle English *pety* "small"]

[2]**pet** *adj* **1 :** kept or treated as a pet ⟨a *pet* dog⟩ **2 :** expressing fondness or endearment ⟨a *pet* name⟩ **3 :** FAVORITE ⟨a *pet* project⟩ ⟨my *pet* peeve⟩

[3]**pet** *vb* **pet•ted; pet•ting 1 :** to stroke in a gentle or loving manner **2 :** to treat with unusual kindness and consideration **:** PAMPER **3 :** to engage in amorous embracing, caressing, and kissing — **pet•ter** *n*

[4]**pet** *n* **:** a fit of peevishness, sulkiness, or anger [origin unknown]

pet•al \ˈpet-l\ *n* **:** one of the often brightly colored modified leaves making up the corolla of a flower [Greek *petalon*] — **pet•aled** *or* **pet•alled** \-ld\ *adj* — **pet•al•like** \-l-ˌlīk, -l-ˌīk\ *adj*

pe•tard \pə-ˈtärd, -ˈtär\ *n* **:** a case containing an explosive to break down a door or gate or breach a wall [Middle French, from *peter* "to break wind", from *pet* "expulsion of intestinal gas", from Latin *peditum,* from *pedere* "to break wind"]

pet•cock \ˈpet-ˌkäk\ *n* **:** a small cock, faucet, or valve for letting out air, releasing compression, or draining [*pet-* (perhaps from *petty*) + *cock*]

pe•ter \ˈpēt-ər\ *vi* **:** to diminish gradually and come to an end **:** give out ⟨the stream *peters* out⟩ [origin unknown]

Pe•ter \ˈpēt-ər\ *n* — see BIBLE table

Pe•ter's pence *n* **1 :** an annual tribute of a penny formerly paid by each householder in England to the papal see **2 :** a voluntary annual contribution made by Roman Catholics to the pope [from the tradition that Saint Peter founded the papal see]

pet•i•ole \ˈpet-ē-ˌōl\ *n* **1 :** the stem of a leaf **2 :** STALK; *esp* **:** a narrow segment joining the abdomen and thorax in some insects (as wasps) [Latin *petiolus* "small foot, fruit stalk", derived from *pes* "foot"] — **pet•i•o•late** \ˈpet-ē-ə-ˌlāt, ˌpet-ē-ˈō-lət\ *adj* — **pet•i•oled** \ˈpet-ē-ˌōld\ *adj*

pet•it \ˈpet-ē, ˈpet-ət\ *adj* **:** PETTY 1 — chiefly in legal compounds [Middle French, "small"]

pe•tite \pə-ˈtēt\ *adj* **:** having a small trim figure — usually used of a woman [French, feminine of *petit* "small"] — **pe•tite•ness** *n*

pe•tit four \ˌpet-ē-ˈfōr, -ˈfȯr\ *n, pl* **petits fours** *or* **petit fours** \-ē-ˈfōrz, -ˈfȯrz\ **:** a small frosted and ornamented cake cut from pound or sponge cake [French, literally, "small oven"]

[1]**pe•ti•tion** \pə-ˈtish-ən\ *n* **1 :** an earnest request **:** ENTREATY **2 :** a formal written request made to a superior or authority **3 :** something asked or requested [Middle French, from Latin *petitio,* from *petere* "to seek, request"] — **pe•ti•tion•ary** \-ˈtish-ə-ˌner-ē\ *adj*

[2]**petition** *vb* **pe•ti•tioned; pe•ti•tion•ing** \-ˈtish-ning, -ə-ning\ **:** to make a request to or for **:** SOLICIT; *esp* **:** to make a formal written request — **pe•ti•tion•er** \-ˈtish-nər, -ə-nər\ *n*

\ə\ **abut**	\au̇\ **out**	\i\ **tip**	\ȯ\ **saw**	\u̇\ **foot**
\ər\ **further**	\ch\ **chin**	\ī\ **life**	\ȯi\ **coin**	\y\ **yet**
\a\ **mat**	\e\ **pet**	\j\ **job**	\th\ **thin**	\yü\ **few**
\ā\ **take**	\ē\ **easy**	\ng\ **sing**	\t͟h\ **this**	\yu̇\ **cure**
\ä\ **cot, cart**	\g\ **go**	\ō\ **bone**	\ü\ **food**	\zh\ **vision**

pet•it jury \'pet-ē-\ *n* : a jury of 12 persons who listen to the testimony in a trial and try to determine which side is in the right

pe•tit mal \pə-ˌtē-'mal, -'mäl\ *n* : a mild form of epilepsy [French, literally, "small illness"]

pet•it point \'pet-ē-ˌpȯint\ *n* : TENT STITCH; *also* : embroidery made with this stitch [French, literally, "small point"]

petr- *or* **petri-** *or* **petro-** *combining form* : stone : rock ⟨*petro*logy⟩ [Greek *petros* "stone" and *petra* "rock"]

pe•trel \'pe-trəl, 'pē-\ *n* : any of various small long-winged seabirds (as the storm petrel) that fly far from land [alteration of earlier *pitteral*]

Pe•tri dish \ˌpē-trē-\ *n* : a small shallow dish of thin glass with a loose cover used especially for cultures in bacteriology [Julius R. *Petri,* died 1921, German bacteriologist]

pet•ri•fac•tion \ˌpe-trə-'fak-shən\ *n* **1** : the process of petrifying or state of being petrified **2** : something that is petrified — **pet•ri•fac•tive** \-'fak-tiv\ *adj*

pet•ri•fi•ca•tion \ˌpe-trə-fə-'kā-shən\ *n* : PETRIFACTION

pet•ri•fy \'pe-trə-ˌfī\ *vb* **-fied**; **-fy•ing** **1** : to convert (an organic object) into stony material **2** : to make or become rigid or inert like stone: **a** : to make lifeless or inactive : DEADEN **b** : to confound with fear, amazement, or awe : PARALYZE

Pe•trine \'pē-ˌtrīn\ *adj* : of, relating to, or characteristic of the apostle Peter or the doctrines associated with his name [Late Latin *Petrus* "Peter"]

pet•ro•chem•i•cal \ˌpe-trō-'kem-i-kəl\ *n* : a chemical isolated or derived from petroleum or natural gas

pe•trog•ra•phy \pə-'träg-rə-fē\ *n* : the description and systematic classification of rocks — compare PETROLOGY — **pe•trog•ra•pher** \-fər\ *n* — **pet•ro•graph•ic** \ˌpe-trə-'graf-ik\ *or* **pet•ro•graph•i•cal** \-'graf-i-kəl\ *adj*

pet•rol \'pe-trəl, -ˌträl\ *n, British* : GASOLINE [French *essence de pétrole,* literally, "essence of petroleum"]

pet•ro•la•tum \ˌpe-trə-'lāt-əm\ *n* : a tasteless, odorless, and oily or greasy substance from petroleum that is used especially in ointments and dressings [New Latin, from Medieval Latin *petroleum*]

pe•tro•leum \pə-'trō-lē-əm, -'trōl-yəm\ *n* : an oily flammable liquid widely distributed in the upper strata of the earth that is a complex mixture mostly of hydrocarbons and is the source of gasoline and lubricants and a major industrial raw material [Medieval Latin, from Latin *petr-* "petr-" + *oleum* "oil"]

petroleum jelly *n* : PETROLATUM

pe•trol•o•gy \pə-'träl-ə-jē\ *n* : a science that deals with the origin, history, occurrence, structure, chemical composition, and classification of rocks — compare PETROGRAPHY — **pet•ro•log•ic** \ˌpe-trə-'läj-ik\ *or* **pet•ro•log•i•cal** \-'läj-i-kəl\ *adj* — **pet•ro•log•i•cal•ly** \-i-kə-lē, -klē\ *adv* — **pe•trol•o•gist** \pə-'träl-ə-jəst\ *n*

[1]pet•ti•coat \'pet-ē-ˌkōt\ *n* **1 a** : an outer skirt formerly worn by women and small children **b** : a skirt worn under a dress or outer skirt **2** : something (as a valance) resembling a petticoat [Middle English *petycote* "short tunic, petticoat", from *pety* "small" + *cote* "coat"]

[2]petticoat *adj* : exercised by women ⟨*petticoat* rule⟩

pet•ti•fog \'pet-ē-ˌfȯg, -ˌfäg\ *vi* **-fogged**; **-fog•ging** **1** : to engage in legal trickery **2** : to quibble over insignificant details : CAVIL [back-formation from *pettifogger,* probably from *petty* + obsolete *fogger* "pettifogger"] — **pet•ti•fog•ger** *n* — **pet•ti•fog•gery** \-ˌfȯg-rē, -ˌfäg-, -ə-rē\ *n*

pet•tish \'pet-ish\ *adj* : FRETFUL 1, PEEVISH — **pet•tish•ly** *adv* — **pet•tish•ness** *n*

pet•ty \'pet-ē\ *adj* **pet•ti•er**; **-est** **1** : having secondary rank or importance : MINOR, SUBORDINATE ⟨a *petty* prince⟩ **2** : having little or no importance or significance **3** : marked by or reflective of narrow interests and sympathies [Middle English *pety* "small, minor", from Middle French *petit* "small"] — **pet•ti•ly** \'pet-l-ē\ *adv* — **pet•ti•ness** \'pet-ē-nəs\ *n*

petty cash *n* : cash kept on hand for payment of minor items

petty officer *n* : an officer in the Navy or Coast Guard appointed from among the enlisted ranks that is comparable to a noncommissioned officer in the Army

petty officer first class *n* : an enlisted rank in the Navy and Coast Guard above petty officer second class and below chief petty officer

petty officer second class *n* : an enlisted rank in the Navy and Coast Guard above petty officer third class and below petty officer first class

petty officer third class *n* : an enlisted rank in the Navy and Coast Guard above seaman and below petty officer second class

pet•u•lant \'pech-ə-lənt\ *adj* : characterized by temporary or capricious ill humor : PEEVISH [Latin *petulans*] — **pet•u•lance** \-ləns\ *n* — **pet•u•lant•ly** *adv*

petunia

pe•tu•nia \pə-'tü-nyə, -'tyü-\ *n* : any of a genus of tropical American herbs of the potato family widely grown for their showy funnel-shaped flowers [obsolete French *petun* "tobacco", from Tupi *petyn*]

pew \'pyü\ *n* **1** : a compartment in the auditorium of a church providing seats for several persons **2** : one of the benches with backs and sometimes doors fixed in rows in a church [Middle French *puie* "balustrade", from Latin *podium* "parapet, podium"]

pe•wee \'pē-wē, -ˌwē\ *n* : any of various small olive green flycatchers [imitative]

pew•ter \'pyüt-ər\ *n* **1** : any of various tin-based alloys; *esp* : a dull alloy with lead formerly used for domestic utensils **2** : wares (as table utensils) of pewter [Middle French *peutre*] — **pewter** *adj*

pew•ter•er \'pyüt-ər-ər\ *n* : one that makes pewter wares

pey•o•te \pā-'ōt-ē\ *also* **pey•otl** \-'ōt-l\ *n* : any of a genus of American cacti including the mescal; *also* : a drug obtained from mescal tops [Mexican Spanish *peyote,* from Nahuatl *peyotl*]

pfen•nig \'fen-ig, -ik\ *n, pl* **pfennigs** *or* **pfen•ni•ge** \'fen-i-gə\ **1** : a monetary unit equal to $1/100$ mark **2** : a coin representing one pfennig [German]

pH \pē-'āch, 'pē-\ *n* : a number used in expressing acidity or alkalinity that is the negative logarithm of the effective hydrogen-ion concentration on a scale whose values run from 0 to 14 with 7 representing neutrality, numbers less than 7 increasing acidity, and numbers greater than 7 increasing alkalinity; *also* : the condition with respect to acidity or alkalinity

△**origin** In 1909 the Danish chemist Søren Peter Lauritz Sørensen developed the concept of pH. He suggested that the concentration of hydrogen ions in a solution should be expressed in terms of the negative logarithm (the power to which 10 is raised). Sørensen's *p* stood for *Potenz,* the German word for "power", and his *H* for hydrogen.

phage \'fāj *also* 'fäzh\ *n* : BACTERIOPHAGE

-phage \ˌfāj *also* ˌfäzh\ *n combining form* : one that eats ⟨bacterio*phage*⟩ [Greek *phagein* "to eat"]

phago•cyte \'fag-ə-ˌsīt\ *n* : a cell (as a white blood cell) that takes in and consumes debris and foreign bodies [Greek *phagein* "to eat"] — **phago•cyt•ic** \ˌfag-ə-'sit-ik\ *adj*

phago•cy•to•sis \ˌfag-ə-sī-'tō-səs\ *n* : the taking and usually the destruction of particulate matter by phagocytes — **phago•cy•tot•ic** \-'tät-ik\ *adj*

-ph•a•gous \f-ə-gəs\ *adj combining form* : eating [Greek *phagein* "to eat"]

pha•lan•ger \fə-'lan-jər\ *n* : any of various marsupial mammals of the Australian region ranging in size from a mouse to a large cat [derived from Greek *phalanx* "log, line of battle, bone of the finger or toe"]

pha•lanx \'fā-ˌlangs, -ˌlangks\ *n, pl* **pha•lanx•es** *or* **pha•lan•ges** \fə-'lan-ˌjēz, fā-\ **1** : a body of heavily armed infantry formed in close deep ranks and files; *also* : a body of troops in close array **2** *pl phalanges* : one of the bones of a finger or toe **3** *pl usu phalanxes* **a** : a massed arrangement of persons, animals, or things **b** : an organized body of persons [Latin, from Greek, literally, "log"] — **pha•lan•geal** \fə-'lan-jē-əl, -jəl\ *adj*

phal•a•rope \'fal-ə-ˌrōp\ *n* : any of various small shorebirds that resemble sandpipers but have lobed toes and are good swimmers [French, derived from Greek *phalaris* "coot" + *pod-, pous* "foot"]

phal•lus \'fal-əs\ *n, pl* **phal•li** \'fal-ˌī, -ˌē\ *or* **phal•lus•es** **1** : a symbol or representation of the human penis **2** : PENIS [Latin, from Greek *phallos*] — **phal•lic** \'fal-ik\ *adj*

phan•tasm \'fan-ˌtaz-əm\ *n* **1** : a product of fantasy: as **a** : delusive appearance : ILLUSION **b** : GHOST 2, SPECTER **c** : a figment of the imagination : FANTASY **2** : a deceptive or illusory appearance of a thing [Old French *fantasme,* from Latin *phantasma,* from Greek, from *phantazein* "to present to the mind", from *phainein* "to show"] — **phan•tas•mal** \fan-'taz-məl\ *adj* — **phan•tas•mic** \-'taz-mik\ *adj*

phan•tas•ma•go•ria \fan-ˌtaz-mə-'gōr-ē-ə, -'gȯr-\ *n* **1** : an optical effect by which figures on a screen appear to dwindle into the distance or to rush toward the observer with enormous increase of size **2 a** : a constantly shifting complex succession of things seen or imagined **b** : a scene that constantly changes or fluctuates [French *phantasmagorie,* derived from *phantasme* "phantasm", from Old French *fantasme*] — **phan•tas•ma•go•ric** \-'gōr-ik, -'gȯr-, -'gär-\ *adj*

phantasy *variant of* FANTASY

[1]**phan•tom** \'fant-əm\ *n* **1 a** : something (as a specter) apparent to sense but with no substantial existence **b** : something elusive or visionary : WILL-O'-THE-WISP **c** : an object of continual dread or abhorrence : BUGBEAR **2** : something existing in appearance only **3** : a representation of something abstract, ideal, or incorporeal [Middle French *fantosme,* from Latin *phantasma* "phantasm"]

[2]**phantom** *adj* **1** : of the nature of, suggesting, or being a phantom **2** : FICTITIOUS, DUMMY ⟨*phantom* voters⟩

phar•aoh \'feər-ō, 'faər-ō, 'fā-rō\ *n, often cap* : a ruler of ancient Egypt [Late Latin *pharaon-, pharao,* from Greek *pharaō,* from Hebrew *par'ōh,* from Egyptian *pr-'*;] — **phar•a•on•ic** \ˌfer-ā-'än-ik, ˌfar-\ *adj, often cap*

phar•i•sa•ic \ˌfar-ə-'sā-ik\ *adj* **1** *cap* : of or relating to the Pharisees **2** : PHARISAICAL

phar•i•sa•i•cal \-'sā-ə-kəl\ *adj* : marked by hypocritical censorious self-righteousness — **phar•i•sa•i•cal•ly** \-kə-lē, -klē\ *adv* — **phar•i•sa•i•cal•ness** \-kəl-nəs\ *n*

phar•i•sa•ism \'far-ə-sā-ˌiz-əm, -ˌsā-\ *n* **1** *cap* : the doctrines or practices of the Pharisees **2** *often cap* : pharisaical character, spirit, or attitude

phar•i•see \'far-ə-ˌsē\ *n* **1** *cap* : a member of a Jewish sect of New Testament times noted for strict observance of rites and ceremonies of the written law and for insistence on the validity of the oral tradition **2** : a pharisaical person [Old French *farise,* from Late Latin *pharisaeus,* from Greek *pharisaios,* from Aramaic *pĕrīshayyā,* pl. of *pĕrīshā,* literally, "separated"]

[1]**phar•ma•ceu•ti•cal** \ˌfär-mə-'süt-i-kəl\ *or* **phar•ma•ceu•tic** \-'süt-ik\ *adj* : of or relating to pharmacy or pharmacists [Late Latin *pharmaceuticus,* from Greek *pharmakeutikos,* from *pharmakeuein* "to administer drugs"] — **phar•ma•ceu•ti•cal•ly** \-i-kə-lē, -klē\ *adv*

[2]**pharmaceutical** *n* : a medicinal drug

phar•ma•cist \'fär-mə-səst\ *n* : a specialist in pharmacy

pharmaco- *combining form* : medicine : drug ⟨*pharmaco*logy⟩ [Greek *pharmakon*]

phar•ma•col•o•gy \ˌfär-mə-'käl-ə-jē\ *n* **1** : the science of drugs especially as related to their use in medicine **2** : the properties and reactions of drugs especially with relation to their medicinal value — **phar•ma•co•log•i•cal** \-kə-'läj-i-kəl\ *or* **phar•ma•co•log•ic** \-'läj-ik\ *adj* — **phar•ma•co•log•i•cal•ly** \-i-kə-lē, -klē\ *adv* — **phar•ma•col•o•gist** \-'käl-ə-jəst\ *n*

phar•ma•co•poe•ia *also* **phar•ma•co•pe•ia** \ˌfär-mə-kə-'pē-ə\ *n* **1** : a book describing drugs, chemicals, and medicinal preparations **2** : a collection or stock of drugs [Late Greek *pharmakopoiia* "preparation of drugs", from Greek *pharmakon* "drug" + *poiein* "to make"] — **phar•ma•co•poe•ial** \-əl\ *adj*

phar•ma•cy \'fär-mə-sē\ *n, pl* **-cies** **1** : the art, practice, or profession of preparing, preserving, compounding, and dispensing drugs; *esp* : the profession of mixing drugs according to a doctor's prescription **2 a** : a place where medicines are compounded or dispensed **b** : DRUGSTORE **3** : PHARMACOPOEIA 2 [Late Latin *pharmacia* "administration of drugs", from Greek *pharmakeia,* from *pharmakeuein* "to administer drugs", from *pharmakon* "magic charm, poison, drug"]

phar•yn•gi•tis \ˌfar-ən-'jīt-əs\ *n* : inflammation of the pharynx

phar•ynx \'far-ings, -ingks\ *n, pl* **pha•ryn•ges** \fə-'rin-ˌjēz\ *also* **phar•ynx•es** : the space in a vertebrate just behind the cavity of the mouth into which the nostrils, eustachian tubes, esophagus, and trachea open; *also* : a corresponding part of an invertebrate [Greek, "throat, pharynx"] — **pha•ryn•geal** \fə-'rin-jē-əl, -jəl; ˌfar-ən-'jē-əl\ *adj*

phase \'fāz\ *n* **1** : the apparent shape of the moon or a planet at any time in its series of changes with respect to illumination ⟨the new moon and the full moon are *phases* of the moon⟩ **2 a** : a stage or interval in a development or cycle **b** : an aspect or part under consideration **3** : the stage of progress in a regularly recurring motion or a cyclic process (as a wave or vibration) in relation to a reference point **4 a** : a homogeneous physically distinct portion of matter present in a nonhomogeneous system **b** : one of the fundamental states of matter usually considered to include the solid, liquid, and gaseous forms [Greek *phasis* "appearance of a star, phase of the moon", from *phainein* "to show"] — **pha•sic** \'fā-zik\ *adj*

phase microscope *n* : a microscope that translates differences in phase of the light transmitted through or reflected by the object into differences of intensity in the image — called also *phase-contrast microscope*

pheas•ant \'fez-nt\ *n, pl* **pheasant** *or* **pheasants** : any of numerous large long-tailed brilliantly colored Old World birds related to the domestic fowl many of which are reared as ornamental or game birds [Old French *fesan,* from Latin *phasianus,* from Greek *phasianos,* from *Phasis,* river in Colchis]

pheasant

phel•lem \'fel-ˌem\ *n* : CORK 1b [Greek *phellos* "cork" + English *-em* (as in *phloem*)]

phel•lo•gen \'fel-ə-jən\ *n* : an outer layer of meristem that produces cells inwardly and outwardly in many roots and stems [Greek *phellos* "cork"]

phen- *or* **pheno-** *combining form* : related to or derived from benzene ⟨*phen*ol⟩ : containing phenyl ⟨*pheno*barbital⟩ [French *phène* "benzene", from Greek *phainein* "to show"; from its occurrence in illuminating gas]

phe•no•bar•bi•tal \ˌfē-nō-'bär-bə-ˌtȯl\ *n* : a crystalline barbiturate drug used as a hypnotic and sedative

phe•nol \'fē-ˌnōl, -ˌnȯl, fi-'\ *n* **1** : a caustic poisonous crystalline acidic compound C_6H_5OH present in coal tar and wood tar that in dilute solution is used as a disinfectant **2** : any of various acidic compounds analogous to phenol and regarded as hydroxyl derivatives of aromatic hydrocarbons — **phe•no•lic** \fi-'nō-lik, -'näl-ik\ *adj*

phe•no•lic \fi-'nō-lik, -'näl-ik\ *n* : a resin or plastic made by condensation of a phenol with an aldehyde and used especially for molding and electrical insulation and in coatings and adhesives

phe•nol•phtha•lein \ˌfē-ˌnōl-'thal-ē-ən, -'thal-ˌēn, -'thāl-\ *n* : a white or yellowish white crystalline compound used as a laxative and as an acid-base indicator because its solution is red in alkalies and is decolorized by acids [*phenol* + *phthalein,* a kind of dye, from *phthalic acid,* an acid, short for obsolete *naphthalic acid,* from *naphthalene*]

phe•nom•e•nal \fi-'näm-ən-l\ *adj* **1** : of, relating to, or being a phenomenon **2** : EXTRAORDINARY 1, REMARKABLE ⟨a *phenomenal* memory⟩ — **phe•nom•e•nal•ly** \-l-ē\ *adv*

phe•nom•e•non \fi-'näm-ə-ˌnän, -nən\ *n, pl* **-na** \-nə, -ˌnä\ *or* **-nons** **1** : an observable fact or event **2** : a fact or event that can be scientifically described and explained **3 a** : a rare or significant fact or event **b** *pl phenomenons* : an exceptional person, thing, or event : PRODIGY [Late Latin *phaenomenon,* from Greek *phainomenon,* from *phainesthai* "to appear", from *phainein* "to show"]

phe•no•thi•azine \ˌfē-nō-'thī-ə-ˌzēn\ *n* : any of various tranquilizing drugs (as chlorpromazine) used especially in the treatment of schizophrenia [*phen-* + *thi-* + *azine,* a type of nitrogen compound, derived from French *azote* "nitrogen", derived from Greek *a-* + *zōē* "life"]

\ə\ **abut**	\au̇\ **out**	\i\ **tip**	\ȯ\ **saw**	\u̇\ **foot**
\ər\ **further**	\ch\ **chin**	\ī\ **life**	\ȯi\ **coin**	\y\ **yet**
\a\ **mat**	\e\ **pet**	\j\ **job**	\th\ **thin**	\yü\ **few**
\ā\ **take**	\ē\ **easy**	\ng\ **sing**	\th\ **this**	\yu̇\ **cure**
\ä\ **cot, cart**	\g\ **go**	\ō\ **bone**	\ü\ **food**	\zh\ **vision**

phe•no•type \'fē-nə-ˌtīp\ *n* **:** the visible characters of an organism resulting from the interaction of genotype and environment [German *phänotypus,* from Greek *phainein* "to show" + *typos* "type"] — **phe•no•typ•ic** \ˌfē-nə-'tip-ik\ *adj* — **phe•no•typ•i•cal•ly** \-i-kə-lē, -klē\ *adv*

phe•nyl \'fen-l, 'fēn-\ *n* **:** a univalent radical C_6H_5 derived from benzene by removal of one hydrogen atom — **phe•nyl•ic** \fi-'nil-ik\ *adj*

phe•nyl•al•a•nine \ˌfen-l-'al-ə-ˌnēn, ˌfēn-\ *n* **:** an essential amino acid $C_9H_{11}NO_2$ obtained by the hydrolysis of proteins

phe•nyl•ke•ton•uria \-ˌkēt-n-'ůr-ē-ə, -'yůr-\ *n* **:** an inherited disorder of metabolism that is characterized by inability to oxidize a metabolic product of phenylalanine and by severe mental deficiency [*phenyl* + *ketone* + *-uria* (from Greek *ouron* "urine")]

phen•yl•thio•car•ba•mide \ˌfen-l-ˌthī-ō-'kär-bə-ˌmīd\ *n* **:** a crystalline compound $C_7H_8N_2S$ that is extremely bitter or tasteless depending on the presence or absence of a single dominant gene in the taster

pher•o•mone \'fer-ə-ˌmōn\ *n* **:** a chemical substance (as a scent) that is produced by an animal and serves to stimulate behavior of other individuals of the same species [*phero-* (from Greek *pherein* "to carry") + *-mone* (as in *hormone*)]

phi \'fī\ *n* **:** the 21st letter of the Greek alphabet — Φ or φ

phi•al \'fī-əl, 'fīl\ *n* **:** VIAL [Latin *phiala,* from Greek *phialē*]

phil- *or* **philo-** *combining form* **:** loving **:** having an affinity for [Greek, from *philos* "dear, friendly"]

-phil \ˌfil\ *or* **-phile** \ˌfīl\ *n combining form* **:** lover **:** one having an affinity for ⟨Franco*phile*⟩ [Greek *philos*] — **-phil** *or* **-phile** *adj combining form*

phil•a•del•phus \ˌfil-ə-'del-fəs\ *n* **:** any of a genus of shrubs of the saxifrage family including several widely grown for their showy white flowers — called also *mock orange, syringa* [Greek *philadelphos* "brotherly", from *phil-* + *adelphos* "brother"]

phi•lan•der \fə-'lan-dər\ *vi* **phi•lan•dered; phi•lan•der•ing** \-də-ring, -dring\ **:** to make love without serious intent [from obsolete *philander* "lover, philanderer", probably from the name *Philander*] — **phi•lan•der•er** \-dər-ər\ *n*

phil•an•throp•ic \ˌfil-ən-'thräp-ik\ *also* **phil•an•throp•i•cal** \-'thräp-i-kəl\ *adj* **:** of, relating to, or characterized by philanthropy **:** BENEVOLENT, CHARITABLE — **phil•an•throp•i•cal•ly** \-i-kə-lē, -klē\ *adv*

phi•lan•thro•pist \fə-'lan-thrə-pəst, -'lant-\ *n* **:** one who practices philanthropy

phi•lan•thro•py \-pē\ *n, pl* **-pies 1 :** goodwill to all people; *esp* **:** active effort to promote human welfare **2 a :** a philanthropic act or gift **b :** an organization distributing or supported by philanthropic funds

phi•lat•e•ly \fə-'lat-l-ē\ *n* **:** the collection and study of postage and imprinted stamps [French *philatélie,* from Greek *phil-* + *atelia* "tax exemption", derived from *a-* + *telos* "tax"; from the fact that a stamped letter frees the recipient from paying the mailing charges] — **phil•a•tel•ic** \ˌfil-ə-'tel-ik\ *adj* — **phi•lat•e•list** \fə-'lat-l-əst\ *n*

Phi•le•mon \fə-'lē-mən, fī-\ *n* — see BIBLE table

Phi•lip•pi•ans \fə-'lip-ē-ənz\ *n* — see BIBLE table

phi•lip•pic \fə-'lip-ik\ *n* **:** TIRADE [Middle French *philippique,* from Greek *philippikoi logoi,* speeches of Demosthenes against Philip II of Macedon, literally, "speeches relating to Philip"]

Phil•ip•pine mahogany \ˌfil-ə-ˌpēn-\ *n* **:** any of several Philippine timber trees with wood resembling that of the true mahoganies; *also* **:** this wood

phi•lis•tine \'fil-ə-ˌstēn; fə-'lis-tən, -ˌtēn\ *n* **1** *cap* **:** a native or inhabitant of ancient Philistia **2** *often cap* **a :** an individual guided by material rather than intellectual or artistic values **b :** one uninformed in a special area of knowledge

phil•o•den•dron \ˌfil-ə-'den-drən\ *n, pl* **-drons** *or* **-dra** \-drə\ **:** any of various arums grown for their showy often variegated foliage [Greek *philodendros* "loving trees", from *phil-* + *dendron* "tree"]

phi•lol•o•gy \fə-'läl-ə-jē\ *n* **1 :** the study of literature and of relevant fields **2 :** LINGUISTICS; *esp* **:** historical and comparative linguistics [French *philologie,* from Latin *philologia* "love of learning and literature", from Greek, from *phil-* + *logos* "word, speech"] — **phil•o•log•i•cal** \ˌfil-ə-'läj-i-kəl\ *adj* — **phil•o•log•i•cal•ly** \-'läj-i-kə-lē, -klē\ *adv* — **phi•lol•o•gist** \fə-'läl-ə-jəst\ *n*

phi•los•o•pher \fə-'läs-ə-fər\ *n* **1 a :** one that seeks wisdom or enlightenment **b :** a student of philosophy **2 :** a person who takes misfortunes with wisdom, calmness, and courage

philosophers' stone *n* **:** an imaginary stone, substance, or chemical preparation believed to have the power of transmuting base metals into gold and sought for by alchemists

phil•o•soph•ic \ˌfil-ə-'säf-ik\ *or* **phil•o•soph•i•cal** \-i-kəl\ *adj* **1 :** of, relating to, or based on philosophy **2 :** characterized by the attitude of a philosopher; *esp* **:** calm in the face of trouble — **phil•o•soph•i•cal•ly** \-i-kə-lē, -klē\ *adv*

phi•los•o•phize \fə-'läs-ə-ˌfīz\ *vi* **1 :** to reason in the manner of a philosopher **2 :** to expound a philosophy **:** MORALIZE — **phi•los•o•phiz•er** *n*

phi•los•o•phy \fə-'läs-ə-fē\ *n, pl* **-phies 1 :** the study of the nature of knowledge and existence and the principles of moral and esthetic value **2 :** the philosophical teachings or principles of a person or group ⟨Greek *philosophy*⟩ **3 :** the general principles of a field of study ⟨*philosophy* of history⟩ **4 :** the most general beliefs, concepts, and attitudes of an individual or group [Old French *philosophie,* from Latin *philosophia,* from Greek, from *philosophos* "philosopher", from *phil-* + *sophia* "wisdom", from *sophos* "wise"]

phil•ter *or* **phil•tre** \'fil-tər\ *n* **1 :** a potion, drug, or charm held to have the power to excite sexual passion **2 :** a magic potion [Middle French *philtre,* from Latin *philtrum,* from Greek *philtron*]

phle•bi•tis \fli-'bīt-əs\ *n* **:** inflammation of a vein [Greek *phleb-, phleps* "vein"]

phlegm \'flem\ *n* **1 :** viscid mucus secreted in abnormal quantity in the respiratory passages **2 a :** dull or apathetic coldness or indifference **b :** intrepid coolness **:** CALMNESS [Middle French *fleume,* from Late Latin *phlegmat-, phlegma,* from Greek, "flame, inflammation, phlegm", from *phlegein* "to burn"] — **phlegmy** \'flem-ē\ *adj*

phleg•mat•ic \fleg-'mat-ik\ *adj* **:** having or showing a slow and stolid temperament **syn** see IMPASSIVE — **phleg•mat•i•cal•ly** \-i-kə-lē, -klē\ *adv*

phlo•em \'flō-ˌem\ *n* **:** a vascular tissue of higher plants that transports dissolved food material, contains sieve tubes, and lies mostly external to the cambium — compare XYLEM [German, from Greek *phloios* "bark"]

phloem ray *n* **:** a vascular ray or part of a vascular ray that is located in phloem — compare XYLEM RAY

phlo•gis•ton \flō-'jis-tən\ *n* **:** the hypothetical principle of fire regarded formerly as a material substance [Greek *phlogistos* "inflammable", from *phlogizein* "to set on fire", from *phlog-, phlox* "flame", from *phlegein* "to burn"]

phlox \'fläks\ *n, pl* **phlox** *or* **phlox•es :** any of a genus of American annual or perennial herbs with showy red, purple, white, or variegated flowers [Greek, "flame, wallflower"]

-phobe \ˌfōb\ *n combining form* **:** one fearing or averse to (something specified) ⟨anglo*phobe*⟩ [Greek *phobos* "fear"] — **-pho•bic** \'fō-bik\ *adj combining form*

pho•bia \'fō-bē-ə\ *n* **:** an unreasonable persistent fear of a particular thing [Greek *-phobia,* from *phobos* "fear"] — **pho•bic** \'fō-bik\ *adj*

phoe•be \'fē-bē\ *n* **:** any of several American flycatchers; *esp* **:** one of the eastern United States that has a slight crest and is plain grayish brown above and yellowish white below [alteration of *pewee*]

phoebe

Phoe•ni•cian \fi-'nēsh-ən\ *n* **1 :** a native or inhabitant of ancient Phoenicia **2 :** the Semitic language of ancient Phoenicia — **Phoenician** *adj*

phoe•nix \'fē-niks\ *n* **:** a legendary bird that according to one account lived 500 years, burned itself to death, and rose youthfully alive from its own ashes [Old English *fenix,* from Latin *phoenix,* from Greek *phoinix*]

phon- *or* **phono-** *combining form* **:** sound **:** voice **:** speech ⟨*phon*ation⟩ ⟨*phono*graph⟩ [Greek *phōnē* "voice, sound"]

pho•na•tion \fō-'nā-shən\ *n* **:** the act or process of producing speech sounds ⟨organs of *phonation*⟩ — **pho•nate** \'fō-ˌnāt\ *vi*

[1]phone \'fōn\ *n* **1 :** EARPHONE **2 :** TELEPHONE
[2]phone *vb* **:** TELEPHONE
[3]phone *n* **:** a speech sound considered as a physical event without regard to its status in the structure of a language [Greek *phōnē*]
-phone \ˌfōn\ *n combining form* **:** sound ⟨homo*phone*⟩ — often in names of musical instruments and sound-transmitting and sound-receiving devices ⟨tele*phone*⟩ ⟨xylo*phone*⟩ [Greek *phōnē* "voice, sound"]
pho•neme \'fō-ˌnēm\ *n* **:** a member of the set of the smallest units of speech that serve to distinguish one utterance from another in a language or dialect ⟨\n\ and \t\ in *pin* and *pit* are different *phonemes*⟩ — compare ALLOPHONE [French *phonème*, from Greek *phōnēma* "speech sound", from *phōnein* "to sound"]
pho•ne•mic \fə-'nē-mik\ *adj* **1 :** of, relating to, or having the characteristics of a phoneme **2 :** being different phonemes ⟨in English \n\ and \ng\ are *phonemic*⟩ — **pho•ne•mi•cal•ly** \-mi-kə-lē, -klē\ *adv*
pho•net•ic \fə-'net-ik\ *adj* **1 a :** of or relating to spoken language or speech sounds **b :** of or relating to phonetics **2 :** representing speech sounds [Greek *phōnētikos, from phōnein* "to sound", from *phōnē* "voice"] — **pho•net•i•cal** \-'net-i-kəl\ *adj* — **pho•net•i•cal•ly** \-i-kə-lē, -klē\ *adv*
phonetic alphabet *n* **:** a set of symbols used for phonetic transcription
pho•ne•ti•cian \ˌfō-nə-'tish-ən\ *n* **:** a specialist in phonetics
pho•net•ics \fə-'net-iks\ *n* **1 :** the study and classification of speech sounds **2 :** the system of speech sounds of a language or group of languages
phon•ic \'fän-ik\ *adj* **1 :** of, relating to, or producing sound **2 :** of or relating to the sounds of speech or to phonics — **phon•i•cal•ly** \-i-kə-lē, -klē\ *adv*
phon•ics \'fän-iks\ *n* **:** a method of teaching beginners to read and pronounce words by learning the phonetic value of letters, letter groups, and especially syllables
pho•no•gram \'fō-nə-ˌgram\ *n* **:** a character or symbol used to represent a word, syllable, or phoneme
pho•no•graph \'fō-nə-ˌgraf\ *n* **:** an instrument for reproducing sounds by means of the vibration of a needle following a spiral groove on a revolving disc
pho•no•graph•ic \ˌfō-nə-'graf-ik\ *adj* **1 :** of or relating to phonography **2 :** of or relating to a phonograph — **pho•no•graph•i•cal•ly** \-i-kə-lē, -klē\ *adv*
pho•nog•ra•phy \fō-'näg-rə-fē\ *n* **:** spelling based on pronunciation
pho•nol•o•gy \fə-'näl-ə-jē, fō-\ *n* **:** the science of speech sounds including especially the history and theory of sound changes in a language or in two or more related languages — **pho•no•log•i•cal** \ˌfōn-l-'äj-i-kəl *also* ˌfän-l-\ *adj* — **pho•no•log•i•cal•ly** \-kə-lē, -klē\ *adv* — **pho•nol•o•gist** \fə-'näl-ə-jəst, fō-\ *n*
[1]pho•ny *or* **pho•ney** \'fō-nē\ *adj* **pho•ni•er**; **-est :** not genuine or real: as **a :** COUNTERFEIT ⟨a *phony* $10 bill⟩ **b :** probably dishonest ⟨a *phony* alibi⟩ **c :** FICTITIOUS ⟨*phony* publicity stories⟩ **d :** FALSE ⟨*phony* pearls⟩ [origin unknown] — **pho•ni•ly** \'fōn-l-ē\ *adv* — **pho•ni•ness** \'fō-nē-nəs\ *n*
[2]phony *or* **phoney** *n, pl* **phonies** *or* **phoneys :** one that is phony
phoo•ey \'fü-ē\ *interj* — used to express repudiation or disgust
-phore \ˌfōr, ˌfȯr\ *n combining form* **:** carrier ⟨sema*phore*⟩ [Greek *-phoros, from pherein* "to carry"]
phos•gene \'fäz-ˌjēn\ *n* **:** a colorless gas of unpleasant odor that is a severe irritant of the respiratory system and is used as a war gas [Greek *phōs* "light"; from its originally having been obtained by the action of sunlight]
phosph- *or* **phospho-** *combining form* **:** phosphorus ⟨*phos*phide⟩ ⟨*phospho*lipid⟩
phos•pha•tase \'fäs-fə-ˌtās, -ˌtāz\ *n* **:** any of various enzymes that accelerate the hydrolysis and synthesis of organic phosphates or the transfer of phosphate groups
phos•phate \'fäs-ˌfāt\ *n* **1 :** a salt or ester of a phosphoric acid **2 :** an effervescent drink of carbonated water with a small amount of phosphoric acid or an acid phosphate flavored with fruit syrup **3 :** a phosphatic material used for fertilizers
phos•phat•ic \fäs-'fat-ik, -'fāt-\ *adj* **:** of, relating to, or containing phosphoric acid or phosphates
phos•pha•tide \'fäs-fə-ˌtīd\ *n* **:** PHOSPHOLIPID — **phos•pha•tid•ic** \ˌfäs-fə-'tid-ik\ *adj*
phos•phide \'fäs-ˌfīd\ *n* **:** a compound of phosphorus usually with a more electropositive element or radical
phos•phite \-ˌfīt\ *n* **:** a salt or ester of phosphorous acid
phos•pho•glyc•er•al•de•hyde \ˌfäs-fō-ˌglis-ə-'ral-də-ˌhīd\ *n* **:** a phosphate of glyceraldehyde $C_3H_7PO_6$ formed especially in the anaerobic metabolism of carbohydrates by the splitting of a phosphate of fructose containing two phosphate groups
phos•pho•gly•cer•ic acid \-glis-ˌer-ik-\ *n* **:** either of two isomeric phosphates $C_3H_7PO_7$ of glyceric acid that are formed as intermediates in photosynthesis and in carbohydrate metabolism
phos•pho•lip•id \ˌfäs-fō-'lip-əd\ *n* **:** a complex phosphoric ester lipid found in all living cells in association with stored fats — called also *phosphatide*
phos•phor \'fäs-fər, -ˌfȯr\ *n* **:** a phosphorescent substance; *esp* **:** one that emits light when excited by radiation [derived from Greek *phōsphoros* "light-bearing", from *phōs* "light" + *pherein* "to carry, bring"]
phosphor bronze *n* **:** a bronze of great hardness, elasticity, and toughness that contains a small amount of phosphorous
phos•pho•res•cence \ˌfäs-fə-'res-ns\ *n* **1 :** the property of emitting light without easily perceptible heat shown by phosphorus or living organisms (as various bacteria and fungi); *also* **:** the light so produced **2 :** luminescence caused by the absorption of radiations (as X rays or ultraviolet light) and continuing for a noticeable time after these radiations have stopped — **phos•pho•resce** \ˌfäs-fə-'res\ *vi* — **phos•pho•res•cent** \-nt\ *adj*
phos•phor•ic \fäs-'fȯr-ik, -'fär-\ *adj* **:** of, relating to, or containing phosphorus especially with a valence higher than in phosphorous compounds
phosphoric acid *n* **:** an oxygen-containing acid of phosphorus; *esp* **:** a syrupy or crystalline acid H_3PO_4 used in making fertilizers and as a flavoring in soft drinks
phos•pho•rous \'fäs-fə-rəs, -frəs; fäs-'fōr-əs, -'fȯr-\ *adj* **:** of, relating to, or containing phosphorus especially with a valence lower than in phosphoric compounds
phosphorous acid *n* **:** a deliquescent crystalline acid H_3PO_3 used especially as a reducing agent and in making phosphites
phos•pho•rus \'fäs-fə-rəs, -frəs\ *n* **1 :** a phosphorescent substance; *esp* **:** one that glows in the dark **2 :** a poisonous active chemical element usually obtained in the form of waxy crystals that glow in moist air — see ELEMENT table [New Latin, from Greek *phōsphoros* "light-bearing", from *phōs* "light" + *pherein* "to carry"] — **phosphorus** *adj*
phos•phor•y•late \fäs-'fȯr-ə-ˌlāt\ *vt* **:** to cause (an organic compound) to take up or combine with phosphoric acid or a phosphorus-containing group — **phos•phor•y•la•tion** \ˌfäs-ˌfȯr-ə-'lā-shən\ *n* — **phos•phor•y•la•tive** \fäs-'fȯr-ə-ˌlāt-iv\ *adj*
phot- *or* **photo-** *combining form* **1 :** light ⟨*photo*graph⟩ ⟨*photo*n⟩ **2 :** photograph **:** photographic ⟨*photo*engraving⟩ **3 :** photoelectric ⟨*photo*cell⟩ [Greek *phōt-, phōs*]
pho•tic \'fōt-ik\ *adj* **1 :** of, relating to, or involving light especially in relation to organisms ⟨a *photic* response⟩ **2 :** penetrated by light especially of the sun ⟨*photic* layers of the sea⟩
pho•to \'fōt-ō\ *n, pl* **photos :** PHOTOGRAPH — **photo** *vb* — **photo** *adj*
pho•to•cell \'fōt-ə-ˌsel\ *n* **:** PHOTOELECTRIC CELL
pho•to•chem•is•try \ˌfōt-ō-'kem-ə-strē\ *n* **1 :** a branch of chemistry that deals with the effect of radiant energy in producing chemical changes **2 :** photochemical properties or processes — **pho•to•chem•i•cal** \-'kem-i-kəl\ *adj*
pho•to•com•pose \-kəm-'pōz\ *vt* **:** to set (as reading matter) by photocomposition — **pho•to•com•pos•er** *n*
pho•to•com•po•si•tion \-ˌkäm-pə-'zish-ən\ *n* **:** composition of reading matter directly on film or photosensitive paper for reproduction
pho•to•copy \'fōt-ə-ˌkäp-ē\ *n* **:** a photographic reproduction of graphic matter — **photocopy** *vb*
pho•to•du•pli•cate \ˌfōt-ō-'dü-plə-ˌkāt, -'dyü-\ *vb* **:** PHOTOCOPY — **pho•to•du•pli•cate** \-pli-kət\ *n*

pho•to•elec•tric \ˌfōt-ō-i-ˈlek-trik\ *adj* **:** relating to or utilizing electrical effects due to the interaction of light with matter — **pho•to•elec•tri•cal•ly** \-tri-kə-lē,-klē\ *adv*

photoelectric cell *n* **:** a cell in which variations of light are converted into corresponding variations in an electric current used especially in detection devices and light meters

photoelectric effect *n* **:** the emission of free electrons from a metal surface when light strikes it

pho•to•elec•tron \ˌfōt-ō-i-ˈlek-ˌträn\ *n* **:** an electron released in the photoelectric effect

pho•to•emis•sive \-i-ˈmis-iv\ *adj* **:** emitting electrons when exposed to radiation (as light)

pho•to•en•grave \-in-ˈgrāv\ *vt* **:** to make a photoengraving of — **pho•to•en•grav•er** *n*

pho•to•en•grav•ing \-ˈgrā-ving\ *n* **1 :** a process for making linecuts and halftone cuts by photographing an image on a metal plate and then etching **2 a :** a plate made by photoengraving **b :** a print made from such a plate

photo finish *n* **1 :** a race finish in which contestants are so close that a photograph of them as they cross the finish line has to be examined to determine the winner **2 :** a close contest

pho•to•flash \ˈfōt-ə-flash\ *n* **:** FLASHBULB

pho•to•flood \-ˌfləd\ *n* **:** a high-intensity electric lamp used in taking photographs

pho•to•ge•nic \ˌfōt-ə-ˈjen-ik, -ˈjēn-\ *adj* **:** suitable for being photographed **:** likely to photograph well ⟨a *photogenic* child⟩ — **pho•to•ge•ni•cal•ly** \-i-kə-lē, -klē\ *adv*

pho•to•gram•me•try \ˌfōt-ə-ˈgram-ə-trē\ *n* **:** the science of making reliable measurements by the use of usually aerial photographs in surveying and map making

[1]**pho•to•graph** \ˈfōt-ə-ˌgraf\ *n* **:** a picture or likeness obtained by photography

[2]**photograph** *vb* **1 :** to take a photograph of **2 :** to take photographs **3 :** to be photographed

pho•tog•ra•pher \fə-ˈtäg-rə-fər\ *n* **:** one that practices or is skilled in photography; *esp* **:** one who takes photographs as a business

pho•to•graph•ic \ˌfōt-ə-ˈgraf-ik\ *adj* **1 :** relating to, obtained by, or used in photography ⟨*photographic* supplies⟩ **2 :** representing nature and humans with the exactness of a photograph **3 :** capable of retaining vivid impressions ⟨a *photographic mind*⟩ — **pho•to•graph•i•cal•ly** \-i-kə-lē, -klē\ *adv*

pho•tog•ra•phy \fə-ˈtäg-rə-fē\ *n* **:** the art or process of producing images on a sensitized surface (as a film or plate) by the action of light or other radiant energy

pho•to•gra•vure \ˌfōt-ə-grə-ˈvyu̇r\ *n* **:** a process for making prints from an engraved plate prepared by photographic methods; *also* **:** a print produced by photogravure — **photogravure** *vt*

pho•to•li•thog•ra•phy \ˌfōt-ō-lith-ˈäg-rə-fē\ *n* **:** lithography in which photographically prepared plates are used — **pho•to•litho•graph•ic** \-ˌlith-ə-ˈgraf-ik\ *adj*

pho•tol•y•sis \fō-ˈtäl-ə-səs\ *n* **:** chemical decomposition by the action of radiant energy and especially light

pho•to•me•chan•i•cal \ˌfōt-ō-mi-ˈkan-i-kəl\ *adj* **:** relating to or involving any of various processes for producing printed matter from photographically prepared plates

pho•tom•e•ter \fō-ˈtäm-ət-ər\ *n* **:** an instrument for measuring luminous intensity, illumination, or brightness

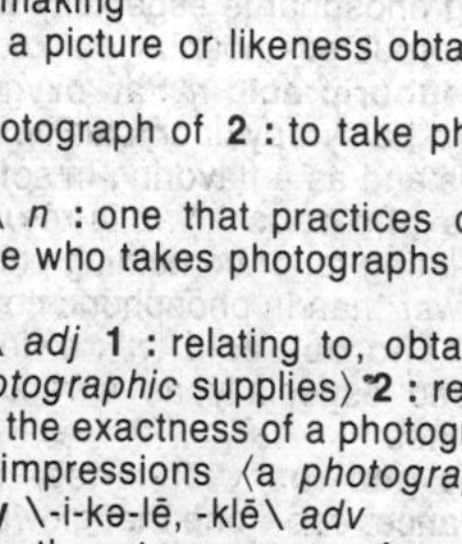

photometer

pho•to•met•ric \ˌfōt-ə-ˈme-trik\ *adj* **:** of or relating to photometry or the photometer — **pho•to•met•ri•cal•ly** \-tri-kə-lē, -klē\ *adv*

pho•tom•e•try \fō-ˈtäm-ə-trē\ *n* **:** a branch of science that deals with measurement of the intensity of light

pho•to•mi•cro•graph \ˌfōt-ə-ˈmī-krə-ˌgraf\ *n* **:** a photograph of a magnified image of a small object — **pho•to•mi•cro•graph•ic** \-ˌmī-krə-ˈgraf-ik\ *adj* — **pho•to•mi•crog•ra•phy** \-mī-ˈkräg-rə-fē\ *n*

pho•to•mon•tage \-män-ˈtäzh, -mōⁿ-, -ˈtäzh\ *n* **:** montage using photographic images; *also* **:** a picture made by photomontage

pho•to•mu•ral \ˌfōt-ō-ˈmyu̇r-əl\ *n* **:** a greatly enlarged photograph used on walls especially as decoration

pho•ton \ˈfō-ˌtän\ *n* **:** a quantum of radiant energy

pho•to–off•set \ˌfōt-ō-ˈóf-ˌset\ *n* **:** offset printing from photolithographic printing plates

pho•to•pe•ri•od \ˌfōt-ə-ˈpir-ē-əd\ *n* **:** the relative lengths of alternating periods of lightness and darkness as they affect the growth and maturity of an organism — **pho•to•pe•ri•od•ic** \-ˌpir-ē-ˈäd-ik\ *adj* — **pho•to•pe•ri•od•i•cal•ly** \-i-kə-lē, -klē\ *adv* — **pho•to•pe•ri•od•ism** \-ˈpir-ē-ə-ˌdiz-əm\ *n*

pho•to•phos•phor•y•la•tion \ˈfōt-ō-ˌfäs-ˌfór-ə-ˈlā-shən\ *n* **:** the formation of ATP in photosynthesis using radiant energy

pho•to•play \ˈfōt-ō-ˌplā\ *n* **:** MOVIE 2

pho•to•poly•mer \ˌfōt-ō-ˈpäl-ə-mər\ *n* **:** a photosensitive plastic used to make printing plates

pho•to•print \ˈfōt-ō-ˌprint\ *n* **:** a reproduction of graphic matter on photographic paper

pho•to•re•cep•tor \ˌfōt-ō-ri-ˈsep-tər\ *n* **:** a receptor for light stimuli — **pho•to•re•cep•tion** \-ˈsep-shən\ *n* — **pho•to•re•cep•tive** \-ˈsep-tiv\ *adj*

pho•to•sen•si•tive \-ˈsen-sət-iv, -ˈsen-stiv\ *adj* **:** sensitive or sensitized to the action of radiant energy and especially light — **pho•to•sen•si•tiv•i•ty** \-ˌsen-sə-ˈtiv-ət-ē\ *n* — **pho•to•sen•si•ti•za•tion** \-ˌsen-sət-ə-ˈzā-shən\ *n* — **pho•to•sen•si•tize** \-ˈsen-sə-ˌtīz\ *vt*

pho•to•sphere \ˈfōt-ə-ˌsfiər\ *n* **:** the luminous surface of the sun or a star — **pho•to•spher•ic** \ˌfōt-ə-ˈsfiər-ik, -ˈsfer-\ *adj*

pho•to•stat \ˈfōt-ə-ˌstat\ *vb* **:** to copy by a Photostat device — **pho•to•stat•ic** \ˌfōt-ə-ˈstat-ik\ *adj*

Pho•to•stat \ˈfōt-ə-ˌstat\ *trademark* — used for a device for making a photographic copy of graphic matter

pho•to•syn•the•sis \ˌfōt-ə-ˈsin-thə-səs, -ˈsint-\ *n* **:** synthesis of chemical compounds with the aid of radiant energy; *esp* **:** formation of carbohydrates from carbon dioxide and water by the chlorophyll-containing tissues of plants exposed to light — **pho•to•syn•the•size** \-ˌsīz\ *vb* — **pho•to•syn•thet•ic** \-sin-ˈthet-ik\ *adj* — **pho•to•syn•thet•i•cal•ly** \-ˈthet-i-kə-lē, -klē\ *adv*

pho•to•tax•is \ˌfōt-ə-ˈtak-səs\ *n* **:** a taxis in which light is the directive factor — **pho•to•tac•tic** \-ˈtak-tik\ *adj*

pho•tot•ro•pism \fō-ˈtä-trə-ˌpiz-əm\ *n* **:** a tropism in which light is the orienting stimulus — **pho•to•trop•ic** \ˌfōt-ə-ˈträp-ik\ *adj*

phras•al \ˈfrā-zəl\ *adj* **:** of, relating to, or consisting of a phrase ⟨*phrasal* prepositions⟩ — **phras•al•ly** \-zə-lē\ *adv*

[1]**phrase** \ˈfrāz\ *n* **1 :** a manner of expression **:** DICTION **2 :** a brief expression; *esp* **:** one commonly used **3 :** a musical unit typically two to four measures long and closing with a cadence **4 :** a group of two or more words that form a sense unit but that do not by themselves make up a complete sentence ⟨"over the fence" in "hit it over the fence" is an adverbial *phrase*⟩ [Latin *phrasis,* from Greek, from *phrazein* "to point out, explain, tell"]

[2]**phrase** *vt* **1 a :** to express in words **:** WORD ⟨*phrase* a reply⟩ **b :** to designate by a descriptive word or phrase **:** TERM **2 :** to divide into melodic phrases

phrase•ol•o•gy \ˌfrā-zē-ˈäl-ə-jē\ *n* **1 :** manner of organizing words and phrases into longer elements **:** STYLE **2 :** choice of words

phras•ing \ˈfrā-zing\ *n* **1 :** PHRASEOLOGY 1 **2 :** the act, method, or result of grouping notes into musical phrases

phre•net•ic \fri-ˈnet-ik\ *adj* **:** FRENETIC [Latin *phreneticus*]

phre•nol•o•gy \fri-ˈnäl-ə-jē\ *n* **:** the study of the conformation of the skull as indicative of mental faculties and character [Greek *phrēn* "diaphragm, mind"] — **phre•no•log•i•cal** \ˌfren-l-ˈäj-i-kəl, ˌfrēn-\ *adj* — **phre•nol•o•gist** \fri-ˈnäl-ə-jəst\ *n*

phy•co•cy•a•nin \ˌfī-kō-ˈsī-ə-nən\ *n* **:** any of the bluish green protein pigments of blue-green algae [Greek *phykos* "seaweed"]

phy•co•er•y•thrin \-ˈer-ə-thrən\ *n* **:** any of the red protein pigments of red algae [derived from Greek *phykos* "seaweed" + *erythros* "red"]

phy•co•my•cete \-ˈmī-ˌsēt, -mī-ˈsēt\ *n* **:** any of a large class (Phycomycetes) of highly variable lower fungi in many respects similar to algae [derived from Greek *phykos* "seaweed" + *mykēs* "fungus"] — **phy•co•my•ce•tous** \-mī-ˈsēt-əs\ *adj*

phyl- *or* **phylo-** *combining form* **:** tribe **:** race **:** phylum ⟨*phylogeny*⟩ [Greek *phylē, phylon* "race, tribe"]

phy•lac•tery \fə-ˈlak-tə-rē, -trē\ *n, pl* **-ter•ies 1 :** one of two small square leather boxes containing slips inscribed with scripture passages and worn by Jewish men during morning weekday prayers **2 :** CHARM 2, AMULET [derived from Greek *phylaktērion* "amulet, phylactery", from *phylassein* "to guard", from *phylax* "guard"]

phy·let·ic \fī-ˈlet-ik\ *adj* **:** of or relating to the course of evolutionary or phylogenetic development [derived from *phyl-*] — **phy·let·i·cal·ly** \-ˈlet-i-kə-lē, -klē\ *adv*

-phyll \ˌfil\ *n combining form* **:** leaf ⟨sporo*phyll*⟩ [Greek *phyllon* "leaf"]

phyl·lo·taxy \ˈfil-ə-ˌtak-sē\ *also* **phyl·lo·tax·is** \ˌfil-ə-ˈtak-səs\ *n* **:** the arrangement of leaves on a stem and in relation to one another [*phyll-* + Greek *taxis* "arrangement, order", from *tassein* "to arrange"]

phyl·lox·e·ra \ˌfil-ˌäk-ˈsir-ə, fə-ˈläk-sə-rə\ *n* **:** any of various wholly oviparous plant lice; *esp* **:** one destructive to grapevines [derived from Greek *phyllon* "leaf" + *xēros* "dry"] — **phyl·lox·e·ran** \-ˈsir-ən, -sə-rən\ *adj or n*

phy·log·e·ny \fī-ˈläj-ə-nē\ *n, pl* **-nies :** the evolutionary development of a group as distinguished from the individual development of an organism — compare ONTOGENY — **phy·lo·ge·net·ic** \-fī-lə-jə-ˈnet-ik\ *adj* — **phy·lo·ge·net·i·cal·ly** \-i-kə-lē, -klē\ *adv*

phy·lum \ˈfī-ləm\ *n, pl* **phy·la** \-lə\ **:** a group of animals or in some classifications plants sharing one or more fundamental characteristics that set them apart from all other animals and plants and forming a primary division of the animal or plant kingdom [New Latin, from Greek *phylon* "tribe, race"]

physi- *or* **physio-** *combining form* **1 :** nature ⟨*physio*graphy⟩ **2 :** physical ⟨*physio*therapy⟩ [Greek *physis*]

[1]**phys·ic** \ˈfiz-ik\ *n* **1 :** the practice or profession of medicine **2 :** a medicinal agent or preparation; *esp* **:** PURGATIVE

[2]**physic** *vt* **phys·icked** \-ikt\; **phys·ick·ing** \-i-king\; **physics** *or* **phys·icks :** to treat with or administer medicine to; *esp* **:** PURGE

phys·i·cal \ˈfiz-i-kəl\ *adj* **1 :** of or relating to nature or the laws of nature **2 :** of or relating to material things **:** not mental or spiritual **3 :** of or relating to natural science **4 :** of or relating to physics **5 :** of or relating to the body **:** BODILY; *also* **:** preoccupied with the body or its needs **syn** see MATERIAL — **phys·i·cal·ly** \-kə-lē, -klē\ *adv*

physical education *n* **:** instruction in the care and development of the body including training in hygiene, exercises, and athletic games

physical examination *n* **:** an examination of the bodily functions and condition of a person

physical geography *n* **:** a branch of geography that deals with the physical features of the earth and their interaction with human beings

physical science *n* **:** the natural sciences (as mineralogy or astronomy) that deal primarily with nonliving materials

physical therapy *n* **:** the treatment of disease by physical and mechanical means (as massage, exercise, water, or heat) — called also *physiotherapy* — **physical therapist** *n*

phy·si·cian \fə-ˈzish-ən\ *n* **:** a person skilled in the art of healing; *esp* **:** a doctor of medicine

phys·i·cist \ˈfiz-ə-səst\ *n* **:** a specialist in the science of physics

phys·ics \ˈfiz-iks\ *n* **1 :** a science that deals with matter and energy and their interactions in the fields of mechanics, heat, light, electricity, sound, and nuclear phenomena **2 :** physical composition, properties, or processes ⟨the *physics* of sound⟩ [Latin *physica*, pl., "natural science", from Greek *physika*, from *physikos* "of nature", from *physis* "growth, nature", from *phyein* "to bring forth"]

phys·i·og·no·my \ˌfiz-ē-ˈäg-nə-mē, -ˈä-nə-\ *n, pl* **-mies 1 :** the art of discovering temperament and character from outward appearance **2 :** the facial features held to show qualities of mind or character **3 :** external aspect; *also* **:** inner character or quality revealed outwardly [Middle French *physiognomie*, from Late Latin *physiognomonia, physiognomia*, from Greek *physiognōmonia*, derived from *physis* "nature, physique, appearance" + *gnōmōn* "interpreter", from *gignōskein* "to know"] — **phys·i·og·nom·ic** \-ē-əg-ˈnäm-ik, -ə-ˈnäm-\ *adj* — **phys·i·og·nom·i·cal·ly** \-i-kə-lē, -klē\ *adv*

phys·i·og·ra·phy \ˌfiz-ē-ˈäg-rə-fē\ *n* **:** the study of landforms **:** PHYSICAL GEOGRAPHY — **phys·i·og·ra·pher** \-rə-fər\ *n* — **phys·io·graph·ic** \ˌfiz-ē-ə-ˈgraf-ik\ *adj*

physiological saline *n* **:** a solution of a salt or salts with essentially the same concentration of ions as tissue fluids or blood

phys·i·ol·o·gy \ˌfiz-ē-ˈäl-ə-jē\ *n* **1 :** a branch of biology dealing with the functions and activities of life or of living matter — compare ANATOMY **2 :** the organic functions and activities of an organism or any of its parts or of a particular bodily process — **phys·i·o·log·i·cal** \ˌfiz-ē-ə-ˈläj-i-kəl\ *or* **phys·i·o·log·ic** \-ˈläj-ik\ *adj* — **phys·i·o·log·i·cal·ly** \-i-kə-lē, -klē\ *adv* — **phys·i·ol·o·gist** \ˌfiz-ē-ˈäl-ə-jəst\ *n*

phys·io·ther·a·py \ˌfiz-ē-ō-ˈther-ə-pē\ *n* **:** PHYSICAL THERAPY

phy·sique \fə-ˈzēk\ *n* **:** the build of a person's body **:** physical constitution [French, from *physique* "physical"]

phyt- *or* **phyto-** *combining form* **:** plant ⟨*phyto*plankton⟩ [Greek *phyton*, from *phyein* "to bring forth"]

-phyte \ˌfīt\ *n combining form* **1 :** plant having a (specified) characteristic or habitat ⟨xero*phyte*⟩ **2 :** pathological growth

phy·to·plank·ton \ˌfīt-ō-ˈplang-tən,-ˈplangk-,-ˌtän\ *n* **:** planktonic plant life — **phy·to·plank·ton·ic** \-plang-ˈtän-ik, -plangk-\ *adj*

[1]**pi** \ˈpī\ *n, pl* **pis** \ˈpīz\ **1 :** the 16th letter of the Greek alphabet — Π or π **2 a :** the symbol π denoting the ratio of the circumference of a circle to its diameter **b :** the ratio itself having a value to eight decimal places of 3.14159265

[2]**pi** *vb* **pied; pi·ing 1 :** to spill or throw (type or type matter) into disorder **2 :** to become pied [origin unknown]

pia ma·ter \ˈpī-ə-ˌmāt-ər, ˈpē-ə-ˌmät-\ *n* **:** the innermost and thin vascular membrane investing the brain and spinal cord [Latin, "tender mother"] — **pi·al** \ˈpī-əl\ *adj*

pi·a·nis·si·mo \ˌpē-ə-ˈnis-ə-ˌmō\ *adv or adj* **:** very softly — used as a direction in music [Italian, from *piano* "softly"]

pi·an·ist \pē-ˈan-əst,ˈpē-ə-nəst\ *n* **:** a person who plays the piano

[1]**pi·a·no** \pē-ˈän-ō\ *adv or adj* **:** in a soft or quiet manner — used as a direction in music [Italian, from Late Latin *planus* "smooth", from Latin, "level"]

[2]**pi·ano** \pē-ˈan-ō\ *n, pl* **-an·os :** a stringed percussion instrument having steel-wire strings that sound when struck by felt-covered hammers operated from a keyboard [Italian, short for *pianoforte*, from *piano e forte* "soft and loud"; from the fact that its tones could be varied in loudness]

△ **origin** A harpsichord is played by means of a mechanism that plucks the strings, so it is not possible to achieve fine gradations of loudness. Feeling the need to overcome this drawback in the harpsichord, a Florentine named Bartolommeo Cristofori around the year 1709 invented a mechanism by means of which the strings of the instrument are struck by felt-covered hammers. This device allows the player more control over the loudness of his playing. Cristofori called his new instrument a *gravicembalo col piano e forte*, that is "a harpsichord with soft and loud". The instrument came to be designated by the term *piano e forte* or by contraction *pianoforte*, which was subsequently shortened to *piano*.

pi·ano·forte \pē-ˈan-ə-ˌfōrt, -ˌfȯrt, -ˌfōrt-ē\ *n* **:** PIANO [Italian]

pi·as·ter *or* **pi·as·tre** \pē-ˈas-tər, -ˈäs-\ *n* **1 :** PIECE OF EIGHT **2 a :** a monetary unit of Egypt, Lebanon, Sudan, and Syria equal to 1/100 pound **b :** a coin representing one piaster [French *piastre*]

pi·az·za \pē-ˈaz-ə, *1 is usually* -ˈat-sə, -ˈät-\ *n, pl* **piazzas** *or* **pi·az·ze** \-ˈat-sā, -ˈät-\ **1 :** an open square especially in an Italian town **2 a :** an arcaded and roofed gallery **b** *dialect* **:** VERANDA, PORCH [Italian, from Latin *platea* "broad street", from Greek *plateia*, from *platys* "broad, flat"]

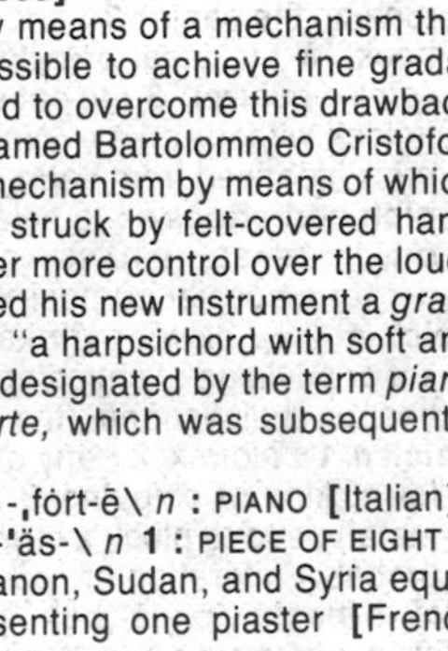

[2]piano

pi·broch \ˈpē-ˌbräk, -ˌbräk\ *n* **:** a set of martial or mournful variations for the Scottish bagpipe [Scottish Gaelic *piobaireachd* "pipe music"]

pi·ca \ˈpī-kə\ *n* **1 :** 12-point type **2 :** a unit of about 1/6 inch (about 4.2 millimeters) used in measuring typographical materi-

\ə\ **abut**	\au̇\ **out**	\i\ **tip**	\ȯ\ **saw**	\u̇\ **foot**
\ər\ **further**	\ch\ **chin**	\ī\ **life**	\ȯi\ **coin**	\y\ **yet**
\a\ **mat**	\e\ **pet**	\j\ **job**	\th\ **thin**	\yü\ **few**
\ā\ **take**	\ē\ **easy**	\ng\ **sing**	\t͟h\ **this**	\yu̇\ **cure**
\ä\ **cot, cart**	\g\ **go**	\ō\ **bone**	\ü\ **food**	\zh\ **vision**

al **3** : a typewriter type providing 10 characters to the inch [probably from Medieval Latin, "collection of church rules"]

pic·a·dor \ˈpik-ə-ˌdȯr, ˌpik-ə-ˈ\ *n, pl* **picadors** \-ˌdȯrz, -ˈdȯrz\ *or* **pic·a·do·res** \ˌpik-ə-ˈdōr-ēz, -ˈdȯr-\ : a horseman in a bullfight who prods the bull with a lance to weaken its neck and shoulder muscles [Spanish, from *picar* "to prick", derived from Latin *picus* "woodpecker"]

pi·ca·resque \ˌpik-ə-ˈresk, ˌpē-kə-\ *adj* : of or relating to rogues or rascals; *also* : of or relating to a type of fiction of Spanish origin dealing with rogues and vagabonds [Spanish *picaresco,* from *pícaro* "rogue"]

[1]**pic·a·yune** \ˌpik-ē-ˈün, -ˈyün\ *n* **1** : a small coin of Spanish origin formerly circulated in the southern United States **2** : something trivial [French *picaillon* "halfpenny", from Provençal *picaion,* from *picaio* "money", from *pica* "to strike, prick, jingle", derived from Latin *picus* "woodpecker"]

△ **origin** The eating habits of the woodpecker, which drills holes in trees in its search for insects, are responsible for the derivation from *picus,* its Latin name, of a verb meaning "to pierce or prick". The Provençal verb *pica* developed a wide range of senses including "to jingle" as well as "to prick". Before the widespread use of paper currency, *picaio* was an appropriate name for money, which was likely to jingle. A small copper coin came to be called *picaioun,* and this was borrowed into French as *picaillon.* In 19th century Louisiana the French name, respelled in English as *picayune,* was transferred to a Spanish coin then in common use in some states of the American South. The picayune went the way of other small sums of money, and the word came to be used for anything trivial or of little value.

[2]**picayune** *adj* : of little value : PALTRY; *also* : PETTY 3

pic·ca·lil·li \ˌpik-ə-ˈlil-ē\ *n* : a pungent relish of chopped vegetables and spices [probably alteration of *pickle*]

pic·co·lo \ˈpik-ə-ˌlō\ *n, pl* **-los** : a small shrill flute pitched an octave higher than an ordinary flute [Italian, short for *piccolo flauto* "small flute"] — **pic·co·lo·ist** \-əst\ *n*

[1]**pick** \ˈpik\ *vb* **1** : to pierce, penetrate, or break up with a pointed tool **2 a** : to clear or free from something by or as if by plucking ⟨*pick* meat from a bone⟩ **b** : to gather by plucking ⟨*pick* berries⟩ **c** : to play by plucking ⟨*pick* a guitar⟩ ⟨*pick* a tune on the banjo⟩ **3** : CHOOSE, SELECT ⟨*pick* out a suit⟩ ⟨*pick* a book⟩ **4** : to steal or pilfer from ⟨*pick* pockets⟩ **5** : PROVOKE ⟨*pick* a quarrel⟩ **6** : to eat sparingly or in a finicky manner **7** : to unlock without a key ⟨*pick* a lock⟩ [Middle French *piquer* "to prick", derived from Latin *picus* "woodpecker"] — **pick·er** *n* — **pick and choose** : to select carefully and deliberately — **pick on 1** : TEASE, HARASS ⟨*pick on* a smaller child⟩ **2** : to single out for a special purpose or for particular attention

[2]**pick** *n* **1** : a blow or stroke with a pointed instrument **2 a** : the act or privilege of choosing or selecting ⟨take your *pick*⟩ **b** : the best or choicest one ⟨the *pick* of the crop⟩

[3]**pick** *n* **1** : PICKAX **2** : any of several slender pointed implements for picking or chipping **3** : a small thin piece (as of plastic or metal) used to pluck a stringed instrument [Middle English *pik,* probably alteration of [1]*pike*]

pick·a·back \ˈpig-ē-ˌbak, ˈpik-ə-\ *variant of* PIGGYBACK

pick·a·nin·ny *or* **pic·a·nin·ny** \ˈpik-ə-ˌnin-ē, ˌpik-ə-ˈ\ *n, pl* **-nies** : a Negro child — often taken to be offensive [probably from Portuguese *pequenino* "very little"]

pick·ax \ˈpik-ˌaks\ *n* : a heavy tool with a wooden handle and a curved or straight blade pointed at one or both ends that is used especially in loosening or breaking up soil or rock [Old French *picois,* from *pic* "pick", from Latin *picus* "woodpecker"]

pick·er·el \ˈpik-rəl, -ə-rəl\ *n, pl* **pickerel** *or* **pickerels 1** : any of several comparatively small pikes or related fishes **2** : WALLEYE 2 [Middle English *pikerel,* from *pike*]

pick·er·el·weed \-ˌwēd\ *n* : any of various aquatic plants; *esp* : a blue-flowered American shallow-water herb

[1]**pick·et** \ˈpik-ət\ *n* **1** : a pointed stake or post (as for a fence) **2** : a soldier or a detachment of soldiers posted as a guard against surprise attack **3 a** : a striker or strike sympathizer who protests or demonstrates at the struck work site **b** : a person posted for a demonstration or protest [French *piquet,* from *piquer* "to prick"]

[2]**picket** *vb* **1** : to enclose, fence, or fortify with pickets **2** : to guard with or post as a picket **3** : TETHER **4 a** : to post pickets or act as a picket at ⟨*picket* a factory⟩ **b** : to serve as a picket — **pick·et·er** *n*

picket line *n* : a line of persons picketing a business, organization, or institution

pick·ings \ˈpik-ingz, -ənz\ *n pl* **1** : something available or left over; *esp* : eatable remains **2** : yield or return for effort expended

[1]**pick·le** \ˈpik-əl\ *n* **1** : a bath for preserving or cleaning; *esp* : a brine or vinegar solution in which foods are preserved **2** : a difficult situation : PLIGHT **3** : a food item (as a cucumber) preserved in brine or vinegar [Middle English *pekille*]

[2]**pickle** *vt* **pick·led**; **pick·ling** \ˈpik-ling, -ə-ling\ : to treat, preserve, or clean in or with a pickle

pick·lock \ˈpik-ˌläk\ *n* **1** : a tool for picking locks **2** : BURGLAR

pick off *vt* **1** : to shoot or bring down one by one **2** : to catch (a base runner) off base with a quick throw by the pitcher or catcher

pick out *vt* **1** : to make out : DISTINGUISH **2** : to play the notes of by ear or one by one

pick over *vt* : to examine in order to select the best or remove the unwanted

pick·pock·et \ˈpik-ˌpäk-ət\ *n* : a person who steals from pockets

pick·up \ˈpik-ˌəp\ *n* **1 a** : a revival of activity ⟨a business *pickup*⟩ **b** : ACCELERATION **2** : a temporary chance acquaintance **3** : the conversion of mechanical movements into electrical impulses in the reproduction of sound; *also* : a device (as on a phonograph) for making such conversion **4 a** : the reception of sound or an image into a radio or television transmitting apparatus for conversion into electrical signals **b** : a device (as a microphone or a television camera) for converting sound or the image of a scene into electrical signals **c** : the place where a broadcast originates **5** : a light truck having an open body with low sides

pick up \pik-ˈəp, ˈpik-\ *vb* **1 a** : to take hold of and lift ⟨*pick up* sticks⟩ **b** : to clean up : TIDY **2** : to take into a vehicle ⟨the bus *picked up* passengers⟩ **3 a** : to acquire casually, irregularly, or at a bargain ⟨*pick up* a bad habit⟩ ⟨*picked up* two shirts at the sale⟩ **b** : to strike up a casual acquaintance with (a previously unknown person) **4** : to take into custody ⟨was *picked up* by the police⟩ **5** : to bring within range of sight or hearing **6** : to gather or regain speed, vigor, or activity ⟨failed to *pick up* after the illness⟩

picky \ˈpik-ē\ *adj* **pick·i·er**; **-est** : FUSSY 2b, FINICKY

[1]**pic·nic** \ˈpik-nik, -ˌnik\ *n* **1** : an excursion or outing with food usually taken along and eaten in the open **2** : something pleasant or easy [French *pique-nique*]

[2]**picnic** *vi* **pic·nicked**; **pic·nick·ing** : to go on a picnic : eat in picnic fashion — **pic·nick·er** *n*

pi·co- \ˈpē-kō, -kə\ *combining form* : one trillionth part of [perhaps from Italian *piccolo* "small"]

[1]**pi·cot** \ˈpē-kō, pē-ˈ\ *n* : one of a series of small ornamental loops forming an edging on ribbon or lace [French, literally, "small point", from Middle French *pic* "prick", from *piquer* "to prick"]

[2]**picot** *vt* **pi·coted** \-kōd, -ˈkōd\; **pi·cot·ing** \-kō-ing, -ˈkō-\ : to finish with a picot

pic·ric acid \ˌpik-rik-\ *n* : a bitter toxic explosive yellow crystalline strong acid used especially in high explosives, as a dye, or in medicine [Greek *pikros* "bitter"]

Pict \ˈpikt\ *n* : any of a possibly non-Celtic people who once occupied Great Britain, were in many places displaced by the Britons, carried on continual border wars with the Romans, and about the 9th century became amalgamated with the Scots [Late Latin *Picti* "Picts"] — **Pict·ish** \ˈpik-tish\ *adj or n*

pic·to·gram \ˈpik-tə-ˌgram\ *n* : PICTOGRAPH

pic·to·graph \-ˌgraf\ *n* **1** : an ancient or prehistoric drawing or painting on a rock wall **2** : one of the symbols belonging to a system of picture writing **3** : a diagram representing statistical data by pictorial forms [Latin *pictus,* past participle of *pingere* "to paint" + English *-o-* + *-graph*] — **pic·to·graph·ic** \ˌpik-tə-ˈgraf-ik\ *adj*

pictograph 1

pic·tog·ra·phy \pik-ˈtäg-rə-fē\ *n* : PICTURE WRITING 1

pic·to·ri·al \pik-ˈtōr-ē-əl, -ˈtȯr-\ *adj* **1** : of or relating to painting or drawing ⟨*pictorial* art⟩ **2 a** : consisting of pictures ⟨*pictorial* records⟩ **b** : illustrated by pictures ⟨*pictorial* magazines⟩ **3** : having the qualities of a picture ⟨*pictorial* reporting⟩ [Late Latin *pictorius,* from Latin *pictor* "painter", from *pingere* "to paint"] — **pic·to·ri·al·ly** \-ē-ə-lē\ *adv*

[1]pic·ture \'pik-chər\ *n* **1** : a representation made on a surface (as by painting, drawing, or photography) **2** : a very vivid description **3 a** : an exact likeness : COPY **b** : a tangible or visible representation : EMBODIMENT ⟨the *picture* of health⟩ **4 a** : a transitory visible image (as on a television screen) **b** : MOTION PICTURE 1 **5** : a state of affairs : SITUATION ⟨the bleak economic *picture*⟩ [Latin *pictura,* from *pictus,* past participle of *pingere* "to paint"]

[2]picture *vt* **pic·tured; pic·tur·ing** \'pik-chə-ring, 'pik-shring\ **1** : to make a picture of (as by drawing) : DEPICT **2** : to describe vividly **3** : to form a mental image of : IMAGINE

picture hat *n* : a woman's dressy hat with a broad brim

pic·tur·esque \,pik-chə-'resk\ *adj* **1** : resembling a picture : suggesting a painted scene **2** : CHARMING, QUAINT ⟨a *picturesque* village⟩ **3** : evoking striking mental images **syn** see GRAPHIC — **pic·tur·esque·ly** *adv* — **pic·tur·esque·ness** *n*

picture tube *n* : a cathode-ray tube on which the picture appears in a television receiver

picture window *n* : an outsize window designed to frame a desirable exterior view

picture writing *n* **1** : the recording of events or messages by pictures representing actions or facts **2** : the record or message represented by picture writing

pid·dle \'pid-l\ *vi* **pid·dled; pid·dling** \'pid-ling, -l-ing\ : DAWDLE 1 [origin unknown]

pid·dling \'pid-lən, -l-ən, -ling, -l-ing\ *adj* : TRIVIAL 2, PALTRY

pid·dock \'pid-ək\ *n* : a marine bivalve mollusk that bores in stone, wood, or clay [origin unknown]

pid·gin \'pij-ən\ *n* : a simplified speech used for communication between people with different languages; *esp* : an English-based pidgin used in the Orient [short for *Pidgin English,* an English-based pidgin, from Pidgin English *pidgin* "business", from English *business*]

[1]pie \'pī\ *n* : MAGPIE [Old French, from Latin *pica*]

[2]pie *n* **1** : a dish consisting of a pastry crust and a filling (as of fruit or meat) **2** : a layer cake with a thick filling (as of custard) [Middle English]

[1]pie·bald \'pī-,bȯld\ *adj* : of two colors; *esp* : spotted or blotched with black and white ⟨a *piebald* horse⟩ [[1]*pie* + *bald*]

[2]piebald *n* : a piebald animal (as a horse)

[1]piece \'pēs\ *n* **1** : a usually separated part of a whole ⟨a *piece* of the pie⟩ **2** : one of a group, set, or class of things ⟨a 3-*piece* suite of furniture⟩ ⟨a chess *piece*⟩ ⟨a *piece* of mail⟩ **3** : a portion marked off ⟨a *piece* of land⟩ **4** : a single item, example, instance, or unit ⟨a *piece* of news⟩ ⟨buy lumber by the *piece*⟩ **5** : a literary, artistic, or musical composition **6** : FIREARM **7** : COIN ⟨a gold *piece*⟩ [Old French, of Gaulish origin] **syn** see PART — **of a piece:** of the same sort : ALIKE

[2]piece *vt* **1** : to repair, renew, or complete by adding pieces : PATCH **2** : to join into a whole ⟨*pieced* their stories together⟩ — **piec·er** *n*

pièce de ré·sis·tance \pē-,es-də-rə-,zē-'stäns\ *n, pl* **pièces de ré·sis·tance** *same*\ **1** : the chief dish of a meal **2** : an outstanding item [French, literally, "piece of resistance"]

piece goods *n pl* : cloth fabrics sold from the bolt at retail in lengths specified by the customer

[1]piece·meal \'pē-,smēl\ *adv* **1** : one piece at a time : GRADUALLY **2** : in pieces or fragments : APART [Middle English *pecemele,* from *pece* "piece" + *-mele* (from Old English *mǣl* "appointed time")]

[2]piecemeal *adj* : done, made, or accomplished piece by piece or in a fragmentary way : GRADUAL

piece of eight : an old Spanish peso of eight reals

piece·work \'pē-,swərk\ *n* : work done by the piece and paid for at a set rate per unit — **piece·work·er** \-,swər-kər\ *n*

pie chart *n* : a circular chart that illustrates quantities or frequencies by wedge-shaped segments

pied \'pīd\ *adj* : of two or more colors in blotches [[1]*pie*]

pied–à–terre \pē-,ād-ə-'teər\ *n, pl* **pieds–à–terre** *same*\ : a temporary or second lodging [French, literally, "foot to the ground"]

pied·mont \'pēd-,mänt\ *adj* : lying or formed at the base of mountains [*Piedmont,* region of Italy] — **piedmont** *n*

pie·plant \'pī-,plant\ *n* : garden rhubarb

pier \'piər\ *n* **1** : a support for a bridge span **2** : a structure built out into the water for use as a landing place or walk or to protect or form a harbor **3** : a single pillar or a structure used to support something **4** : a mass of masonry (as a buttress) used to strengthen a wall [Old English *per,* from Medieval Latin *pera*]

pierce \'piərs\ *vb* **1** : to run into or through as a pointed weapon does : STAB **2** : to make a hole through : PERFORATE **3** : to force or make a way into or through something **4** : to penetrate with the eye or mind : DISCERN **5** : to penetrate so as to move or touch the emotions of [Old French *percer*] **syn** see ENTER — **pierc·ing·ly** \'pir-sing-lē\ *adv*

pier glass *n* : a tall mirror; *esp* : one designed to occupy the wall space between windows

Pier·rot \'pē-ə-,rō\ *n* : a standard comic character of Old French pantomime usually with whitened face and loose white clothes

pier table *n* : a table to be placed under a pier glass

pies *pl of* PI *or of* PIE

pie·tà \,pē-ā-'tä, pyā-\ *n, often cap* : a representation of the Virgin Mary mourning over the dead body of Christ [Italian, literally, "pity", from Latin *pietas*]

pi·etism \'pī-ə-,tiz-əm\ *n* **1** : emphasis in religion on devotional experience and practices **2** : affected piety — **pi·etist** \'pī-ət-əst\ *n, often cap* — **pi·etis·tic** \,pī-ə-'tis-tik\ *adj* — **pi·etis·ti·cal·ly** \-'tis-ti-kə-lē, -klē\ *adv*

pi·ety \'pī-ət-ē\ *n, pl* **-eties** **1** : the quality or state of being pious: as **a** : loyalty to natural obligations (as to one's parents) **b** : dutifulness in religion : DEVOUTNESS **2** : an act inspired by piety [French *pieté* "piety, pity", from Latin *pietas,* from *pius* "dutiful, pious"]

pi·ezo·elec·tric·i·ty \pē-,ā-zō-ə-,lek-'tris-ət-ē, -,āt-sō-, -'tris-tē\ *n* : electricity or electric polarity resulting from the application of mechanical force to certain crystals (as quartz) [Greek *piezein* "to press"] — **pi·ezo·elec·tric** \-'lek-trik\ *adj* — **pi·ezo·elec·tri·cal·ly** \-'lek-tri-kə-lē, -klē\ *adv*

[1]pif·fle \'pif-əl\ *vi* **pif·fled; pif·fling** \'pif-ling, -ə-ling\ : to talk or act in a trivial, inept, or ineffective way : TRIFLE [perhaps blend of *piddle* and *trifle*]

[2]piffle *n* : NONSENSE 1

[1]pig \'pig\ *n* **1 a** : a young swine not yet sexually mature **b** : a wild or domestic swine **2 a** : PORK **b** : the dressed carcass of a young swine weighing less than 130 pounds **c** : PIGSKIN **3** : one held to resemble a pig **4** : a crude casting of metal (as iron or lead) [Middle English *pigge*] — **pig** *adj*

[2]pig *vb* **pigged; pig·ging** **1** : FARROW **2** : to live like a pig ⟨*pig* it⟩

pi·geon \'pij-ən\ *n* **1** : any of numerous birds (order Columbiformes) with a stout body, usually short legs, and smooth and compact plumage; *esp* : a domesticated bird derived from the rock pigeon **2** : an easy mark : DUPE [Middle French *pijon,* from Late Latin *pipio* "young bird", from Latin *pipere* "to chirp"]

pi·geon·heart·ed \,pij-ən-'härt-əd\ *adj* : COWARDLY 1

[1]pi·geon·hole \'pij-ən-,hōl\ *n* **1** : a hole or small place for pigeons to nest **2** : a small open compartment (as in a desk) for keeping letters or papers

[2]pigeonhole *vt* : to place in or as if in the pigeonhole of a desk: as **a** : to lay aside : SHELVE **b** : to assign to a category : CLASSIFY

pi·geon–toed \,pij-ən-'tōd\ *adj* : having the toes turned in

pig·gery \'pig-rē, -ə-rē\ *n, pl* **-ger·ies** : a place where pigs are kept

pig·gish \'pig-ish\ *adj* : suggesting a pig (as in greed, dirtiness, or stubbornness) — **pig·gish·ly** *adv*

pig·gy·back \'pig-ē-,bak\ *or* **pick·a·back** \'pig-ē-, 'pik-ə-\ *adv or adj* **1** : on the back or shoulders **2** : on a railroad flatcar [alteration of earlier *a pick pack,* of unknown origin]

piggy bank *n* : a coin bank often in the shape of a pig

pig·head·ed \'pig-'hed-əd\ *adj* : STUBBORN 1b, OBSTINATE

pig iron *n* : iron that is the direct product of the blast furnace and is refined to produce steel, wrought iron, or ingot iron

pig latin *n, often cap L* : a jargon that is made by systematic

\ə\ **abut**	\au̇\ **out**	\i\ **tip**	\ȯ\ **saw**	\u̇\ **foot**
\ər\ **further**	\ch\ **chin**	\ī\ **life**	\ȯi\ **coin**	\y\ **yet**
\a\ **mat**	\e\ **pet**	\j\ **job**	\th\ **thin**	\yü\ **few**
\ā\ **take**	\ē\ **easy**	\ng\ **sing**	\t͟h\ **this**	\yu̇\ **cure**
\ä\ **cot, cart**	\g\ **go**	\ō\ **bone**	\ü\ **food**	\zh\ **vision**

mutilation of English (as "ipskay the ointjay" for "skip the joint")

1pig•ment \'pig-mənt\ *n* **1 :** a substance that imparts black or white or a color to other materials; *esp* **:** a powdered substance mixed with a liquid in which it is relatively insoluble to impart color **2 :** a natural coloring matter in animals and plants; *also* **:** any of various related colorless substances [Latin *pigmentum,* from *pingere* "to paint"] — **pig•men•tary** \-mən-ˌter-ē\ *adj*

2pig•ment \-mənt, -ˌment\ *vt* **:** to color with or as if with pigment

pig•men•ta•tion \ˌpig-mən-'tā-shən, -ˌmen-\ *n* **:** coloration with or deposition of pigment; *esp* **:** excessive pigment in bodily cells or tissues

pigmy *variant of* PYGMY

pig•nut \'pig-ˌnət\ *n* **:** any of several bitter-flavored hickory nuts; *also* **:** a tree bearing these

pig•pen \-ˌpen\ *n* **1 :** PIGSTY 1 **2 :** a filthy or messy place

pig•skin \-ˌskin\ *n* **:** the skin of a swine or leather made of it

pig•sty \'pig-ˌstī\ *n* **1 :** a pen for pigs **2 :** PIGPEN 2

pig•tail \-ˌtāl\ *n* **1 :** tobacco in small twisted strands or rolls **2 :** a tight braid of hair

pig–tailed \-ˌtāld\ *adj* **:** wearing a pigtail or pigtails

pig•weed \-ˌwēd\ *n* **:** any of various weedy plants especially of the goosefoot or amaranth families

pi•ka \'pē-kə\ *n* **:** any of various small short-eared mammals of rocky areas in the mountains of Asia and western North America that are related to the rabbits — called also *coney* [Tungusic *piika*]

pigtail 2

1pike \'pīk\ *n* **1 :** PIKESTAFF 1 **2 :** a sharp point or spike; *also* **:** the tip of a spear [Old English *pīc* "pickax"] — **piked** \'pīkt\ *adj*

2pike *n, pl* **pike** *or* **pikes :** a large long-bodied and long-snouted freshwater fish valued for food and sport and widely distributed in cool northern waters; *also* **:** any of various related or similar fishes [Middle English, from 1*pike*]

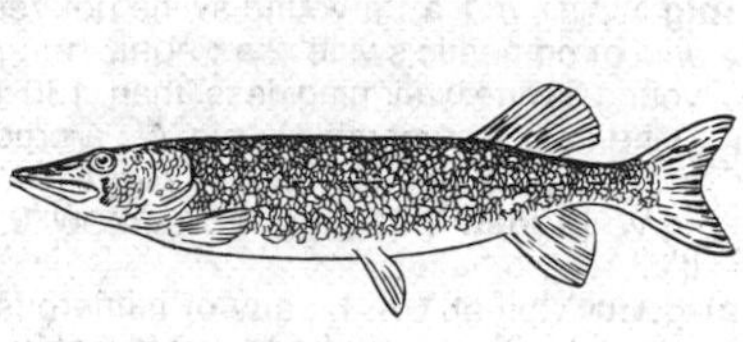

2pike

3pike *n* **:** a long wooden shaft with a pointed steel head formerly used as a weapon by infantry [Middle French *pique,* from *piquer* "to prick", derived from Latin *picus* "woodpecker"]

4pike *n* **:** TURNPIKE 2

5pike *n* **:** a body position (as in diving or gymnastics) in which the body is bent at the waist in the shape of a V [probably from 2*pike*]

pike perch *n* **:** a fish (as a walleye) of the perch group that resembles the pike

pik•er \'pī-kər\ *n* **1 :** one who gambles or speculates with small amounts of money **2 :** one who does things in a small way; *also* **:** TIGHTWAD, CHEAPSKATE [*Pike* county, Missouri, once thought to be the home of many shiftless gamblers]

pike•staff \'pīk-ˌstaf\ *n* **1 :** a spiked staff for use on slippery ground **2 :** the shaft of a soldier's pike

pi•laf *or* **pi•laff** \pi-'läf, 'pē-ˌ\ *or* **pi•lau** \pi-'lō, -'lȯ, 'pē-ˌ, *South often* 'pər-lü, -lō\ *n* **:** a dish made of seasoned rice and often meat [Persian and Turkish *pilāu*]

pi•las•ter \'pī-ˌlas-tər\ *n* **:** a rectangular slightly projecting column that ornaments or helps to support a wall [Middle French *pilastre,* from Italian *pilastro*]

pil•chard \'pil-chərd\ *n* **:** a fish resembling the related herring and occurring in great schools along the coasts of Europe; *also* **:** any of several related fishes — compare SARDINE [origin unknown]

1pile \'pīl\ *n* **:** a long slender column usually of timber, steel, or reinforced concrete driven into the ground to carry a vertical load [Old English *pīl* "dart, stake", from Latin *pilum* "javelin"]

2pile *vt* **:** to equip or support with piles

3pile *n* **1 a :** a quantity of things heaped together **b :** a heap of wood for burning a corpse or a sacrifice **:** PYRE **2 :** a great amount (as of money) **3 a :** a vertical series of alternate disks of two dissimilar metals (as copper and zinc) with disks of cloth or paper moistened with an electrolyte between them for producing a current of electricity **b :** a battery made up of cells similarly constructed **4 :** REACTOR 2b [Middle French, from Latin *pila* "pillar"]

4pile *vb* **1 :** to lay or place in a pile **:** STACK **2 :** to heap in abundance **:** LOAD **3 :** to move or press forward in or as if in a mass **:** CROWD ⟨*pile* into the car⟩

5pile *n* **1 :** a coat or surface of usually short close fine furry hairs **2 :** a velvety surface produced on textile by an extra set of filling yarns that form raised loops which are cut and sheared [Latin *pilus* "hair"] — **piled** \'pīld\ *adj*

pi•le•at•ed woodpecker \ˌpī-lē-ˌāt-əd-\ *n* **:** a North American woodpecker that is black with a red crest and white on the wings and sides of the neck [derived from Latin *pileus, pileum* "felt cap"]

pile driver *n* **:** a machine for driving or hammering piles into place

piles \'pīlz\ *n pl* **:** HEMORRHOIDS; *also* **:** the condition of one affected with hemorrhoids [Latin *pila* "ball"]

pi•le•us \'pī-lē-əs\ *n, pl* **-lei** \-lē-ˌī\ **:** CAP 3a [Latin, "felt cap"]

pil•fer \'pil-fər\ *vb* **pil•fered; pil•fer•ing** \-fə-ring, -fring\ **:** to steal articles of small value or in small amounts [Middle English *pelfrer,* from *pelfre* "booty"] — **pil•fer•age** \-fə-rij, 'frij\ *n* — **pil•fer•er** \-fər-ər\ *n*

pil•grim \'pil-grəm\ *n* **1 :** one who travels in foreign lands **:** WANDERER **2 :** one who travels to a shrine or holy place as a devotee **3** *cap* **:** one of the English colonists founding the first permanent settlement in New England at Plymouth in 1620 [Old French *peligrin,* from Late Latin *pelegrinus,* from Latin *peregrinus* "foreigner", from *pereger* "being abroad", from *per* "through" + *ager* "land"]

pil•grim•age \'pil-grə-mij\ *n* **:** a journey of a pilgrim — **pilgrimage** *vi*

pil•ing \'pī-ling\ *n* **:** a structure or collection of piles

Pi•li•pi•no \ˌpil-ə-'pē-nō, ˌpēl-\ *n* **:** the Tagalog-based official language of the Republic of the Philippines [Pilipino, from Spanish *Filipino* "Philippine"]

pill \'pil\ *n* **1 a :** medicine in a small rounded mass to be swallowed whole **b :** an oral contraceptive — usually used with *the* **2 :** something resembling a pill (as in distasteful quality or globular form) **3 :** a disagreeably tiresome person [Latin *pilula,* from *pila* "ball"]

1pil•lage \'pil-ij\ *n* **1 :** the act of looting or plundering especially in war **2 :** BOOTY 1 [Middle French, from *piller* "to plunder", from *peille* "rag", from Latin *pilleus, pileus* "felt cap"]

2pillage *vb* **:** to take booty **:** PLUNDER, LOOT — **pil•lag•er** *n*

pil•lar \'pil-ər\ *n* **1 :** a comparatively slender upright support (as for a roof) **2 :** a column or shaft standing alone (as for a monument) **3 :** one that suggests a pillar **:** a main support ⟨a *pillar* of society⟩ [Old French *piler,* from Medieval Latin *pilare,* from Latin *pila* "pillar"] — **pil•lared** \-ərd\ *adj* — **from pillar to post :** from one place or situation to another

pill•box \'pil-ˌbäks\ *n* **1 :** a small usually shallow round box for pills **2 :** a small low concrete emplacement for machine guns and antitank weapons **3 :** a small round hat without a brim

pill bug *n* **:** WOOD LOUSE [from its rolling into a ball when disturbed]

1pil•lion \'pil-yən\ *n* **1 :** a cushion or pad placed behind a saddle for an extra rider **2 :** a passenger's saddle (as on a motorcycle) [Scottish Gaelic *pillean* or Irish Gaelic *pillin*]

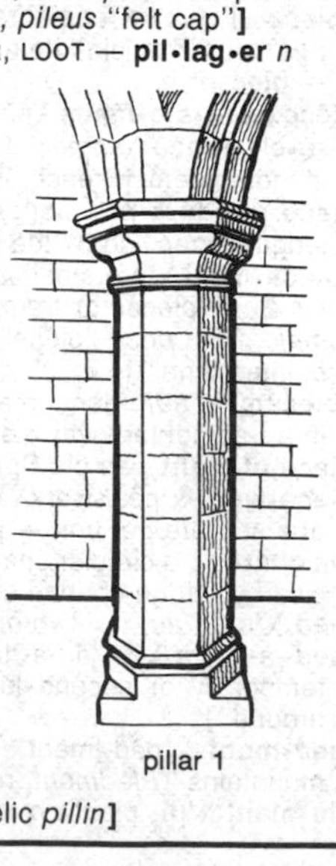

pillar 1

2**pillion** *adv* : on or as if on a pillion ⟨ride *pillion*⟩

pil•lo•ry \'pil-rē, -ə-rē\ *n, pl* **-ries** **1** : a device for publicly punishing offenders that consists of a wooden frame with holes in which the head and hands can be locked — compare STOCK **2** : a means for exposing to public scorn or ridicule [Old French *pilori*] — **pillory** *vt*

1**pil•low** \'pil-ō\ *n* : a support for the head of a person that consists usually of a bag filled with resilient material (as feathers or sponge rubber) [Old English *pyle, pylu,* from Latin *pulvinus*]

2**pillow** *vt* **1** : to place on or as if on a pillow **2** : to serve as a pillow for

pil•low•case \-,kās\ *n* : a removable covering for a pillow — called also *pillow slip*

1**pi•lot** \'pī-lət\ *n* **1 a** : one employed to steer a ship **b** : a person qualified and usually licensed to conduct a ship into and out of a port or in specified waters **2** : GUIDE 1a, d, LEADER **3** : COWCATCHER **4** : one who flies or is qualified to fly an airplane **5** : a piece that guides a tool or machine part **6** : a television show produced as a sample of a proposed series **7** : PILOT LIGHT 2 [Middle French *pilote,* from Italian *pilota,* alteration of *pedota,* derived from Greek *pēdon* "oar"] — **pi•lot•less** \-ləs\ *adj*

2**pilot** *vt* **1** : GUIDE 1, CONDUCT **2 a** : to direct the navigation of : STEER ⟨*pilot* the ship through the canal⟩ **b** : to act as pilot of : FLY ⟨*pilot* the plane to the west coast⟩

3**pilot** *adj* : serving as a guiding or tracing device, an activating or auxiliary unit, or a trial apparatus or operation ⟨a *pilot* study⟩ ⟨a *pilot* plant⟩

pi•lot•age \'pī-lət-ij\ *n* **1** : the act or business of piloting **2** : the compensation paid to a pilot

pilot balloon *n* : a small unmanned balloon sent up to show the direction and speed of the wind

pilot biscuit *n* : HARDTACK — called also *pilot bread*

pilot engine *n* : a locomotive going in advance of a train to make sure that the way is clear

pilot fish *n* : a spiny-finned fish with narrow body and widely forked tail that often accompanies a shark

pi•lot•house \'pī-lət-,haủs\ *n* : an enclosed area on the upper deck of a ship that contains the steering and navigating equipment

pilot light *n* **1** : a light indicating location (as of a switch) or operational state (as of a motor) **2** : a small permanent flame used to ignite gas at a burner

Pilt•down man \,pilt-,daủn-\ *n* : a supposedly very early primitive modern human based on skull fragments uncovered in a gravel pit at Piltdown, England, and used in combination with comparatively recent skeletal remains of various animals in the development of an elaborate fraud

Pi•ma \'pē-mə\ : a member of an Indian people of what is now southern Arizona having an Aztec-related language

Pi•ma cotton \,pē-mə-, ,pim-ə-\ *n* : an American cotton with fiber of exceptional strength and firmness derived from Egyptian cottons [*Pima* county, Arizona]

pi•men•to \pə-'ment-ō\ *n, pl* **-tos** *or* **-to** **1** : PIMIENTO **2** : ALLSPICE [Spanish *pimiento,* from *pimienta* "allspice, pepper", from Late Latin *pigmentum* "plant juice", from Latin, "pigment"]

pi•mien•to \pə-'ment-ō, pəm-'yent-\ *n, pl* **-tos** : any of various thick-fleshed sweet peppers of mild flavor used especially as a source of paprika [Spanish]

1**pimp** \'pimp\ *n* : PANDER 1b, PROCURER [origin unknown]

2**pimp** *vi* : to act as a pimp

pim•per•nel \'pim-pər-,nel\ *n* : any of a genus of herbs of the primrose family; *esp* : SCARLET PIMPERNEL [Middle French *pimprenelle,* from Late Latin *pimpinella,* a medicinal herb]

pim•ple \'pim-pəl\ *n* : a small inflamed swelling of the skin often containing pus : PUSTULE [Middle English *pinple*] — **pim•pled** \-pəld\ *adj* — **pim•ply** \-pə-lē, -plē\ *adj*

1**pin** \'pin\ *n* **1 a** : a piece of wood, metal, or plastic used especially for fastening separate articles together or for hanging one article from another **b** : one of the pieces constituting the target in various games (as bowling) **c** : the staff of the flag marking a hole on a golf course **d** : a peg for regulating the tension of the strings of a musical instrument **2 a** : a small pointed piece of wire with a head used especially for fastening cloth or paper **b** : an ornament or emblem fastened to clothing with a pin **c** : a device (as a hairpin or a safety pin) used for fastening **3** : LEG 1 **4** : something of small value : TRIFLE ⟨doesn't care a *pin* for it⟩ [Old English *pinn*]

2**pin** *vt* **pinned**; **pin•ning** **1** : to fasten, join, or pierce with or as if with a pin **2 a** : ATTACH, HANG ⟨*pinned* their hopes on a miracle⟩ **b** : to assign the blame or responsibility for ⟨*pinned* the robbery on the butler⟩ **3** : to hold (a wrestling opponent) down on the mat in a required position for a required length of time to win a match

pin•a•fore \'pin-ə-,fōr, -,fȯr\ *n* : a low-necked sleeveless garment worn by women and girls [2*pin* + *afore*]

pi•ña•ta *or* **pi•na•ta** \pēn-'yät-ə\ *n* : a decorated pottery jar filled with candies, fruits, and gifts and hung from the ceiling to be broken as part of Mexican Christmas festivities [Spanish, literally, "pot"]

pin•ball machine \'pin-,bȯl-\ *n* : an amusement device in which a ball propelled by a plunger scores points as it rolls down a slanting surface among pins and targets

pince–nez \pa^n-'snā, pan-\ *n, pl* **pince–nez** \-'snā, -'snāz\ : eyeglasses clipped to the nose by a spring [French, from *pincer* "to pinch" + *nez* "nose"]

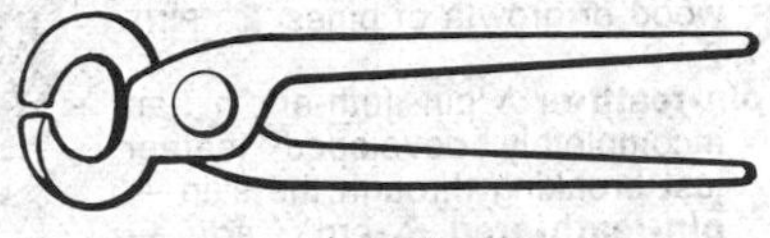

pincer 1a

pin•cer \'pin-chər, 'pin-sər\ *n* **1 a** *pl* : an instrument with two short handles and two pivoting jaws that is used for gripping things **b** : CHELA **2** : one of two attacking forces advancing one on each side of an enemy position so as to surround it [Middle English *pinceour*] — **pin•cer•like** \-,līk\ *adj*

1**pinch** \'pinch\ *vb* **1 a** : to squeeze between the finger and thumb or between the jaws of an instrument **b** : to squeeze painfully **c** : to cause to appear thin or shrunken ⟨a face *pinched* with hunger⟩ **2** : to subject to or practice strict economy **3 a** : STEAL 2a **b** : ARREST 2 [Middle English *pinchen*]

2**pinch** *n* **1 a** : a critical point : EMERGENCY **b** : a hurtful pressure or stress : HARDSHIP ⟨the *pinch* of hunger⟩ **2 a** : an act of pinching **b** : as much as may be taken between the finger and thumb ⟨a *pinch* of snuff⟩ **3 a** : the act of stealing : THEFT **b** : a police raid; *also* : ARREST

pinch bar *n* : a lever with a wedge-shaped end that is used especially to roll heavy wheels

pinch•beck \'pinch-,bek\ *n* **1** : an alloy of copper and zinc used especially to imitate gold in cheap jewelry **2** : something counterfeit or unauthentic [Christopher *Pinchbeck,* died 1732, English watchmaker] — **pinchbeck** *adj*

pinch•cock \-,käk\ *n* : a clamp used on a flexible tube to regulate the flow of a fluid through the tube

pinch•er \'pin-chər\ *n* **1** : one that pinches **2** : PINCER 1 — usually used in pl.

pinch hitter *n* **1** : a baseball player sent in to bat for another **2** : a person called on to do another's work in an emergency — **pinch–hit** \'pinch-'hit\ *vi*

pin curl *n* : a curl made usually by dampening a strand of hair, coiling it, and securing it with a hairpin or clip

pin•cush•ion \'pin-,kủsh-ən\ *n* : a small cushion in which pins may be stuck

Pin•dar•ic \pin-'dar-ik\ *adj* : of, relating to, or written in a manner or style characteristic of the poet Pindar

1**pine** \'pīn\ *vi* **1** : to lose vigor, health, or weight through grief, worry, or distress ⟨*pine* away⟩ **2** : to have a continuing fruitless desire : YEARN ⟨*pine* for home⟩ [Old English *pīnian,* derived from Latin *poena* "punishment, pain"] **syn** see LONG

2**pine** *n* **1** : any of a genus of cone-bearing evergreen trees having slender elongated needles and including valuable timber trees as well as many ornamentals **2** : the straight-grained white or yellow usually durable and resinous wood of a pine **3** : any of various Australian cone-bearing trees [Old English *pin,* from Latin *pinus*] — **piny** *or* **pin•ey** \'pī-nē\ *adj*

pi•ne•al \'pin-ē-əl, 'pī-nē-\ *adj* : of, relating to, or being the pineal body [French *pinéal,* from Latin *pinea* "pine cone", from *pinus* "pine"]

pineal body *n* **:** a small usually conical appendage of the brain of most vertebrates that has an eyelike structure in reptiles and functions in time measurement in some birds

pine·ap·ple \'pī-ˌnap-əl\ *n* **:** a tropical plant with stiff spiny sword-shaped leaves and a short flowering stalk that develops into a fleshy edible fruit; *also* **:** this fruit

pineapple

pine nut *n* **:** the edible seed of any of several chiefly western North American pines

pine tar *n* **:** tar obtained by distillation of pinewood and used especially in roofing and soaps and in the treatment of skin diseases

pine·wood \'pīn-ˌwu̇d\ *n* **1 :** a wood or growth of pines **2 :** PINE 2

pin·feath·er \'pin-ˌfe*th*-ər\ *n* **:** an incompletely developed feather just breaking through the skin — **pin·feath·ered** \-ərd\ *adj* — **pin·feath·ery** \-ˌfe*th*-rē, -ə-rē\ *adj*

ping \'ping\ *n* **1 :** a sharp sound like that of a bullet striking **2 :** ignition knock ⟨kept hearing a *ping* in the car engine⟩ **[**imitative**]** — **ping** *vi*

Ping–Pong \'ping-ˌpäng, -ˌpȯng\ *trademark* — used for table tennis

pin·head·ed \'pin-'hed-əd\ *adj* **:** lacking intelligence or understanding **:** STUPID — **pin·head·ed·ness** *n*

pin·hole \-ˌhōl\ *n* **:** a small hole made by, for, or as if by a pin

[1]**pin·ion** \'pin-yən\ *n* **1 :** the end part of a bird's wing; *also* **:** a bird's wing **2 :** a feather of a bird's pinion **[**Middle French *pignon***]** — **pinioned** \-yənd\ *adj*

[2]**pinion** *vt* **1 :** to restrain (a bird) from flight especially by cutting off the pinion of one wing **2 a :** to disable or restrain by binding the arms **b :** to bind fast **:** SHACKLE

[3]**pinion** *n* **1 :** a gear with a small number of teeth designed to mesh with a larger wheel or rack **2 :** the smallest of a train or set of gear wheels **[**French *pignon,* from Middle French *peignon,* from *peigne* "comb", from Latin *pecten***]**

[1]**pink** \'pingk\ *vt* **1 :** PIERCE 1, STAB **2 a :** to perforate in an ornamental pattern **b :** to cut a saw-toothed edge on **[**Middle English *pinken***]**

[2]**pink** *n* **1 :** any of a genus of annual or perennial herbs that have stems with thick nodes and are often grown for their showy flowers borne singly or in clusters **2 :** the highest degree ⟨the *pink* of condition⟩ **[**origin unknown**]** — **in the pink :** in the best of health

[3]**pink** *adj* **1 :** of the color pink **2 :** holding moderately radical and usually socialistic political or economic views **[**[2]*pink***]** — **pink·ly** *adv* — **pink·ness** *n*

[4]**pink** *n* **1 :** a pale red **2 a :** the scarlet color of a fox hunter's coat; *also* **:** a coat of this color **b** *pl* **:** light-colored trousers formerly worn by army officers **3 :** a person who holds moderately radical political or economic views **[**sense 3 from the viewing of pink as a weak form of red**]**

pink·eye \'ping-ˌkī\ *n* **:** a painful and infectious disease in which the inner surface of the eyelid and part of the eyeball become pinkish and sore

pin·kie *or* **pin·ky** \'ping-kē\ *n, pl* **pinkies :** a little finger **[**probably from Dutch *pinkje,* from *pink* "little finger"**]**

pinking shears *n pl* **:** shears with a saw-toothed inner edge on the blades for making a zigzag cut

pink·ish \'ping-kish\ *adj* **:** somewhat pink; *esp* **:** tending to be pink in politics — **pink·ish·ness** *n*

pinko \'ping-kō\ *n, pl* **pink·os** *or* **pink·oes :** [4]PINK 3

pin money *n* **:** money for incidental expenses

pin·na \'pin-ə\ *n, pl* **pin·nae** \'pin-ˌē, -ˌī\ *or* **pinnas 1 :** a primary division of a pinnate leaf or frond **2 :** the largely cartilaginous projecting portion of the external ear **[**Latin, "feather, wing"**]**

pin·nace \'pin-əs\ *n* **1 :** a light sailing ship used largely as a tender **2 :** any of various ship's boats **[**Middle French *pinace***]**

pin·na·cle \'pin-i-kəl\ *n* **1 :** an upright structure (as on a tower) generally ending in a small spire **2 :** a lofty peak **3 :** the highest point of achievement or development **[**Middle French *pinacle,* from Late Latin *pinnaculum* "gable", from Latin *pinna* "wing, battlement"**] syn** see SUMMIT

pin·nate \'pin-ˌāt\ *adj* **:** resembling a feather especially in having similar parts arranged on opposite sides of an axis ⟨a *pinnate* leaf⟩ **[**Latin *pinnatus* "feathered", from *pinna* "feather"**]** — **pin·nate·ly** *adv* — **pin·na·tion** \pin-'ā-shən\ *n*

pi·noch·le \'pē-ˌnək-əl\ *n* **:** a card game played with a 48-card pack containing two of each suit of A, K, Q, J, 10, 9; *also* **:** the combination of queen of spades and jack of diamonds which scores 40 points in this game **[**probably from German dialect *binokel,* a card game, from French dialect *binocle***]**

pi·no·cy·to·sis \ˌpin-ə-sə-'tō-səs, ˌpīn-, -ˌsī-\ *n, pl* **-to·ses** \-ˌsēz\ **:** the uptake of fluid by a cell by infolding and pinching off of the cell membrane **[**Greek *pinein* "to drink"**]**

pi·ñon *or* **pin·yon** \'pin-yōn, -ˌyän, -yən; pin-'yōn\ *n, pl* **piñons** *or* **pi·ño·nes** \pin-'yō-nēz\ *or* **pin·yons :** any of various low-growing pines of western North America with seeds that are pine nuts — called also *piñon pine* **[**American Spanish *piñón,* from Spanish, "pine nut", from *piña* "pine cone", from Latin *pinea,* from *pinus* "pine"**]**

[1]**pin·point** \'pin-ˌpȯint\ *vt* **1 :** to locate or determine with precision **2 :** to cause to stand out clearly **:** HIGHLIGHT

[2]**pinpoint** *adj* **1 :** extremely fine or precise **2 :** located, fixed, or directed with extreme precision

pin·prick \'pin-ˌprik\ *n* **1 :** a small puncture made by or as if by a pin **2 :** a petty irritation or annoyance — **pinprick** *vb*

pins and needles *n pl* **:** a pricking tingling sensation in a limb recovering from numbness — **on pins and needles :** in a nervous or jumpy state of anticipation

pin·set·ter \'pin-ˌset-ər\ *n* **:** one that sets up pins in a bowling alley

pin·spot·ter \-ˌspät-ər\ *n* **:** PINSETTER

pin·stripe \-ˌstrīp\ *n* **:** a very narrow stripe on a fabric — **pin–striped** \-ˌstrīpt\ *adj*

pint \'pīnt\ *n* **1 :** a unit of capacity equal to ½ quart (about .47 liter) — see MEASURE table **2 :** a pint vessel **[**Middle French *pinte,* from Medieval Latin *pincta,* derived from Latin *pingere* "to paint"**]**

pin·tail \'pin-ˌtāl\ *n, pl* **pintail** *or* **pintails :** a bird (as a duck or grouse) with long central tail feathers

pin·tailed \-ˌtāld\ *adj* **1 :** having a tapered tail with the middle feathers longest **2 :** having the tail feathers spiny

[1]**pin·to** \'pin-tō\ *n, pl* **pintos** *also* **pintoes :** a spotted horse or pony **[**American Spanish, from obsolete Spanish *pinto* "spotted", derived from Latin *pingere* "to paint"**]**

[2]**pinto** *adj* **:** PIED, MOTTLED

pinto bean *also* **pinto** *n* **:** a kidney bean grown extensively in Colorado and the southwestern United States where its mottled seed is used for food and its herbage for forage

pint–size \'pīnt-ˌsīz\ *or* **pint–sized** \-ˌsīzd\ *adj* **:** DIMINUTIVE 2

pin·up \'pin-ˌəp\ *n* **:** an accessory (as a lamp) attached to a wall

pin·wale \'pin-ˌwāl\ *adj* **:** made with narrow wales ⟨*pinwale* corduroy⟩

pin·wheel \-ˌhwēl, -ˌwēl\ *n* **1 :** a toy consisting of lightweight vanes that revolve at the end of a stick **2 :** a fireworks device in the form of a revolving wheel of colored fire

pin·worm \-ˌwərm\ *n* **:** any of numerous small nematode worms that infest the intestines and usually the cecum of various vertebrates; *esp* **:** one parasitic in humans

pinyon *variant of* PIÑON

[1]**pi·o·neer** \ˌpī-ə-'niər\ *n* **1 :** a person who goes before opening up new ways (as of thought or activity) ⟨*pioneers* of American medicine⟩ **2 :** one of the first to settle in an area **:** COLONIST **3 :** a plant or animal capable of establishing itself in a bare or barren area **[**Middle French *pionier* "member of a unit of military engineers, pioneer", from Old French *peonier* "foot soldier", from *peon* "foot soldier", from Medieval Latin *pedo,* from Latin *ped-, pes* "foot"**]** — **pioneer** *adj*

△ **origin** The pioneers Americans are most familiar with are people like Daniel Boone who opened up the American West. But a pioneer was originally a foot soldier. Old French *peonier* (derived from Latin *pes,* "foot") was used at first for any foot soldier, but by the Middle French period the word (now spelled *pionier*) had come to designate a particular type of foot soldier, a member of a unit that marched ahead of the army preparing the way by excavation and construction. Because of the *pio-*

nier's position in advance of the main body of the army, anyone who helps to develop something new, to prepare a way for others to follow, came to be called a *pionier*.

[2]**pioneer** *vb* **1 :** to act as a pioneer **2 :** to open or prepare for others to follow; *esp* **:** SETTLE **3 :** to originate or take part in the development of

pi•ous \ˈpī-əs\ *adj* **1 :** having or showing reverence to God **:** DEVOUT **2 :** marked by sham or hypocrisy ⟨a *pious* fraud⟩ [Latin *pius*] **syn** see DEVOUT — **pi•ous•ly** *adv* — **pi•ous•ness** *n*

[1]**pip** \ˈpip\ *n* **:** a disorder of a bird marked by formation of a scale or crust on the tongue; *also* **:** this scale or crust [Dutch *pippe*, derived from Latin *pituita* "phlegm, pip"]

[2]**pip** *n* **:** a dot or spot (as on dice or playing cards) to indicate numerical value [origin unknown]

[3]**pip** *n* **1 :** a small fruit seed ⟨orange *pips*⟩ **2** *slang* **:** something very good of its kind [short for *pippin*]

[4]**pip** *vi* **pipped; pip•ping 1 :** [1]peep 1 **2 a :** to break the shell of the egg in hatching **b :** to be broken by a pipping bird ⟨eggs starting to *pip*⟩ [imitative]

[5]**pip** *n* **:** a short high-pitched tone ⟨broadcast six *pips* as a time signal⟩ [imitative]

[1]**pipe** \ˈpīp\ *n* **1 a :** a musical instrument consisting of a tube of reed, wood, or metal that is played by blowing **b :** a tube producing a musical sound ⟨an organ *pipe*⟩ **c :** BAGPIPE — usually used in pl. **d :** the whistle, call, or note especially of a bird or an insect **2 a :** a long tube or hollow body used especially to conduct a substance (as water, steam, or gas) **b :** a cylindrical object, part, or passage **3 a :** a tube with a small bowl at one end used for smoking tobacco **b :** a toy pipe for blowing bubbles **4 a :** a large cask used especially for wine and oil **b :** any of various units of liquid capacity based on the size of a pipe; *esp* **:** a unit of liquid capacity equal to 2 hogsheads (about 477 liters) [Old English *pīpa*, derived from Latin *pipare* "to peep"] — **pipe•less** \ˈpī-pləs\ *adj*

[2]**pipe** *vb* **1 a :** to play on a pipe **b :** to convey orders or direct by signals on a boatswain's whistle **2 :** to speak in or have a high shrill tone **3 :** to furnish or trim with piping **4 :** to convey by or as if by pipes — **pip•er** *n*

pipe cleaner *n* **:** a piece of flexible wire in which tufted fabric is twisted and which is used to clean the stem of a tobacco pipe

pipe down *vi* **:** to become quiet **:** stop talking

pipe dream *n* **:** an unreal or fantastic plan, hope, or story [from the fantasies brought about by the smoking of opium]

pipe•fish \ˈpīp-ˌfish\ *n* **:** any of various long slender fishes that are related to the sea horses and have a tube-shaped snout and an angular body covered with bony plates

pipe fitter *n* **:** one who installs and repairs piping

pipe fitting *n* **1 :** a piece (as a coupling or elbow) used to connect pipe or as accessory to a pipe **2 :** the work of a pipe fitter

pipe•ful \ˈpīp-ˌfu̇l\ *n* **:** a quantity of tobacco smoked in a pipe at one time

pipe•line \ˈpī-ˌplīn\ *n* **1 :** a line of pipe with pumps, valves, and control devices for conveying liquids, gases, or finely divided solids **2 :** a direct channel for information or goods

pipe organ *n* **:** ORGAN 1a

pi•pette *or* **pi•pet** \pī-ˈpet\ *n* **:** a device for measuring and transferring small volumes of liquid that typically consists of a narrow glass tube into which the liquid is drawn by suction and retained by closing the upper end [French *pipette*, from *pipe* "pipe, cask"]

pipe up *vi* **:** to begin to play, sing, or speak

pip•ing \ˈpī-ping\ *n* **1 a :** the music of a pipe **b :** the producing of or a calling in shrill pipes ⟨the *piping* of frogs⟩ **2 :** a quantity or system of pipes **3 :** a narrow decorative fold stitched in seams or along edges (as of clothing or slipcovers)

piping hot *adj* **:** very hot

pip•it \ˈpip-ət\ *n* **:** any of various small singing birds resembling the lark [imitative]

pip•kin \ˈpip-kən\ *n* **:** a small earthenware or metal pot usually with a horizontal handle [perhaps from *pipe*]

pip•pin \ˈpip-ən\ *n* **1 :** any of numerous apples with usually yellow or greenish yellow skins strongly flushed with red **2 :** someone or something greatly admired [Old French *pepin*]

pip•sis•se•wa \pip-ˈsis-ə-ˌwȯ\ *n* **:** a low evergreen herb related to the wintergreens that has astringent leaves used medicinally [Cree *pipisisikweu*]

pip–squeak \ˈpip-ˌskwēk\ *n* **:** a small or insignificant person

pi•quant \ˈpē-kənt, -ˌkänt\ *adj* **1 :** agreeably stimulating to the sense of taste **2 :** pleasingly exciting ⟨a *piquant* bit of gossip⟩ **3 :** having a lively roguish charm ⟨a *piquant* face⟩ [Middle French, from *piquer* "to prick"] — **pi•quan•cy** \-kən-sē\ *n* — **pi•quant•ly** *adv* — **pi•quant•ness** *n*

[1]**pique** \ˈpēk\ *n* **1 :** offense taken by one slighted **2 :** a fit of resentment

[2]**pique** *vt* **1 :** to arouse anger or resentment in **:** IRRITATE; *esp* **:** to offend by slighting **2 :** EXCITE 1b, AROUSE ⟨the package *piqued* my curiosity⟩ [French *piquer*, literally, "to prick"]

pi•qué *or* **pi•que** \pi-ˈkā, ˈpē-ˌ\ *n* **:** a durable ribbed fabric [French *piqué*, from *piquer* "to prick, quilt"]

pi•quet \pi-ˈkā, pik-ˈet\ *n* **:** a two-handed card game played with 32 cards in which players score points for certain combinations and for winning tricks [French]

pi•ra•cy \ˈpī-rə-sē\ *n, pl* **-cies 1 :** robbery on the high seas **2 :** the unauthorized use of another's production or invention especially in violation of a copyright

pi•ra•nha \pə-ˈran-yə; -ˈrän-ə, -yə\ *n* **:** a small South American fish that often attacks and inflicts dangerous wounds upon men and large animals — called also *caribe* [Portuguese, from Tupi]

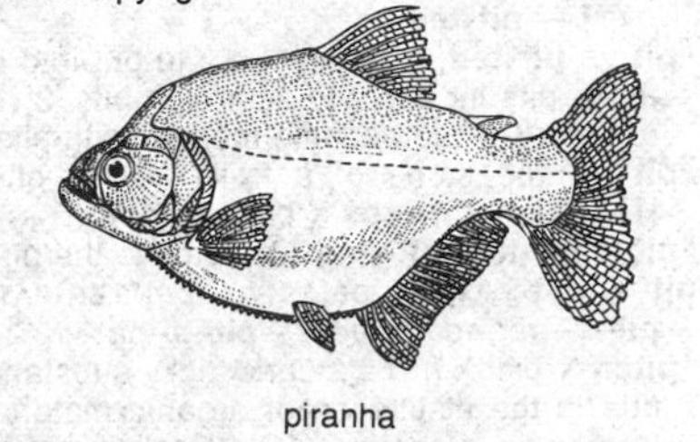

piranha

[1]**pi•rate** \ˈpī-rət\ *n* **:** a person who commits or practices piracy [Latin *pirata*, from Greek *peiratēs*, from *peiran* "to attempt"] — **pi•rat•i•cal** \pə-ˈrat-i-kəl, pī-\ *adj* — **pi•rat•i•cal•ly** \-ˈrat-i-kə-lē, -klē\ *adv*

[2]**pirate** *vt* **:** to take or make use of by piracy ⟨*pirate* an invention⟩

pi•rogue \ˈpē-ˌrōg\ *n* **1 :** DUGOUT 1 **2 :** a boat like a canoe [French, from Spanish *piragua*, of American Indian origin]

pir•ou•ette \ˌpir-ə-ˈwet\ *n* **:** a rapid whirling about of the body; *esp* **:** a full turn on the toe or ball of one foot in ballet [French] — **pirouette** *vi*

pis *pl of* PI

Pi•sces \ˈpī-ˌsēz, ˈpis-ˌēz\ *n* **1 :** a zodiacal constellation directly south of Andromeda **2 :** the 12th sign of the zodiac; *also* **:** one born under this sign [Latin, from pl. of *piscis* "fish"]

pi•scine \ˈpī-ˌsēn; ˈpis-ˌīn, -ˌkīn\ *adj* **:** of, relating to, or characteristic of fish [Latin *piscinus*, from *piscis* "fish"]

pis•mire \ˈpis-ˌmīr, ˈpiz-\ *n* **:** ANT [Middle English *pissemire*, from *pisse* "urine" + *mire* "ant", of Scandinavian origin]

pis•tach•io \pə-ˈstash-ē-ˌō, -ˈstash-ō, -ˈstäsh-\ *n, pl* **-chios :** a small tree of the sumac family whose fruit contains a greenish edible seed; *also* **:** its seed [Italian *pistacchio*, from Latin *pistacium* "pistachio nut", from Greek *pistakion*, from *pistakē* "*pistachio* tree", from Persian *pistah*]

pis•til \ˈpis-tl\ *n* **:** the seed-producing part and female reproductive organ of a flower consisting usually of stigma, style, and ovary [Latin *pistillum* "pestle"]

pis•til•late \ˈpis-tə-ˌlāt\ *adj* **:** having pistils; *esp* **:** having pistils but no stamens

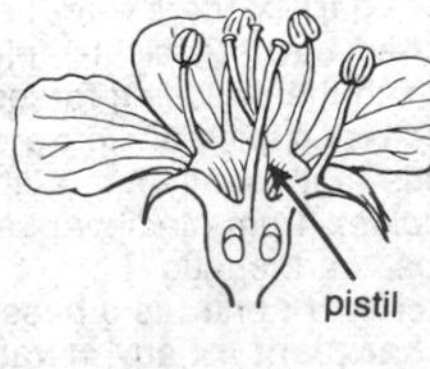

pistil

pis•tol \ˈpis-tl\ *n* **:** a short firearm intended to be aimed and fired with one hand [Middle French *pistole*, *from* German, from Czech *pišťal*, *literally*, "pipe"] — **pistol** *vt*

pis•tol–whip \-ˌhwip, -ˌwip\ *vt* **:** to beat with a pistol

pis•ton \ˈpis-tən\ *n* **1 :** a sliding piece moved by or moving against fluid pressure that usually consists of a short cylinder fitting

\ə\ **abut**	\au̇\ **out**	\i\ **tip**	\ȯ\ **saw**	\u̇\ **foot**
\ər\ **further**	\ch\ **chin**	\ī\ **life**	\ȯi\ **coin**	\y\ **yet**
\a\ **mat**	\e\ **pet**	\j\ **job**	\th\ **thin**	\yü\ **few**
\ā\ **take**	\ē\ **easy**	\ng\ **sing**	\t͟h\ **this**	\yu̇\ **cure**
\ä\ **cot, cart**	\g\ **go**	\ō\ **bone**	\ü\ **food**	\zh\ **vision**

within a cylindrical vessel along which it moves back and forth **2 :** a sliding valve in a brass wind instrument serving when pressed down to lower its pitch [French, from Italian *pistone,* from *pistare* "to pound", from Medieval Latin, from Latin *pistus,* past participle of *pinsere* "to crush"]

piston ring *n* **:** a springy split metal ring around a piston for making a tight fit

piston rod *n* **:** a rod by which a piston is moved or by which it transmits motion

¹pit \'pit\ *n* **1 :** a hole, shaft, or cavity in the ground ⟨a gravel *pit*⟩ **2 :** an area set off from and often lower than adjacent areas: as **a :** an enclosure where animals (as cocks) are set to fight **b :** the space occupied by an orchestra in a theater **3 a :** a hollowed or indented area especially in the surface of the body ⟨the *pit* of the stomach⟩ **b :** an indented scar (as from a boil) **c :** a thin area in a plant cell wall through which dissolved materials can pass [Old English *pytt*] — **pit•ted** *adj*

²pit *vb* **pit•ted; pit•ting 1 a :** to put into or store in a pit **b :** to make pits in; *esp* **:** to scar with pits **2 :** to place in opposition or rivalry **3 :** to become marked with pits

³pit *n* **:** the stone of a fruit (as the cherry) that is a drupe [Dutch] — **pit•less** \'pit-ləs\ *adj*

⁴pit *vt* **pit•ted; pit•ting :** to remove the pit from

pit–a–pat \,pit-i-'pat\ *n* **:** PITTER-PATTER [imitative] — **pit–a–pat** *adv or adj* — **pit–a–pat** *vi*

¹pitch \'pich\ *n* **1 :** a dark sticky substance obtained as a residue in the distillation of organic materials (as tars) **2 :** resin from various conifers [Old English *pic,* from Latin *pix*]

²pitch *vt* **:** to cover, smear, or treat with or as if with pitch

³pitch *vb* **1 :** to erect and fix firmly in place ⟨*pitch* a tent⟩ **2 :** THROW, TOSS ⟨*pitch* hay⟩; *also* **:** to deliver a baseball to a batter **3 a :** to cause to be at a particular pitch or level ⟨*pitch* a tune too high⟩ **b :** to incline or cause to incline at a particular angle **4 a :** to fall headlong **b :** to have the bow alternately plunge and rise abruptly ⟨a ship *pitching* in heavy seas⟩ **c :** BUCK 1a ⟨a *pitching* horse⟩ [Middle English *pichen*]

⁴pitch *n* **1 :** the action or a manner of pitching; *esp* **:** an up and down movement **2 a :** SLOPE 2; *also* **:** degree of slope **b** (1) **:** distance between one point on a gear tooth and the corresponding point on the next tooth (2) **:** distance from any point on the thread of a screw to the corresponding point on an adjacent thread measured parallel to the axis **c :** the distance advanced by an aircraft with one revolution of its propeller **3 :** a high point **:** ZENITH **4 a :** the property of a tone that is determined by the frequency of the sound waves producing it **:** highness or lowness of sound **b :** a standard frequency for tuning instruments **c :** the phonemic change of vibrational frequency in human speech ⟨in speech "yes!" and "yes?" have different *pitch*⟩ **5 :** a high-pressure sales talk **6 a :** the delivery of a baseball by a pitcher to a batter **b :** a baseball so thrown — **pitched** \'picht\ *adj*

pitch–black \'pich-'blak\ *adj* **:** extremely dark or black

pitch•blende \'pich-,blend\ *n* **:** a brown to black mineral that consists essentially of an oxide of uranium, often contains radium, and is a source of uranium [German *pechblende,* from *pech* "pitch" + *blende* "sphalerite"]

pitch–dark \-'därk\ *adj* **:** extremely dark

pitched battle \'picht-, 'pich-\ *n* **:** an intensely fought battle in which the opposing forces are locked in close combat

¹pitch•er \'pich-ər\ *n* **:** a container for holding and pouring liquids that usually has a lip or spout and a handle [Old French *pichier,* from Medieval Latin *bicarius* "goblet", from Greek *bikos* "earthen jug"]

²pitcher *n* **:** one (as a baseball player) that pitches

pitcher plant *n* **:** any of various plants with leaves modified into pitchers in which insects are trapped and digested by the plant

pitch•fork \'pich-,fȯrk\ *n* **:** a usually long-handled fork used in pitching hay or straw [Middle English *pikfork,* from *pik* "pick" + *fork*] — **pitchfork** *vt*

pitch in *vi* **1 :** to begin to work energetically **2 :** to contribute to a common activity

pitch•out \'pich-,au̇t\ *n* **1 :** a pitch in baseball deliberately out of reach of the batter to enable the catcher to check or put out a base runner **2 :** a lateral pass in football between two backs behind the line of scrimmage

pitch pipe *n* **:** a small pipe blown to indicate musical pitch especially for singers or for tuning an instrument

pitchy \'pich-ē\ *adj* **pitch•i•er; -est 1 :** full of pitch **:** TARRY **2 :** of, relating to, or having the qualities of pitch

pit•e•ous \'pit-ē-əs\ *adj* **:** PITIFUL 1 — **pit•e•ous•ly** *adv* — **pit•e•ous•ness** *n*

pit•fall \'pit-,fȯl\ *n* **1 :** TRAP 1, SNARE; *esp* **:** a covered or camouflaged pit used to capture and hold an animal or person **2 :** a hidden or not easily recognized danger or difficulty

¹pith \'pith\ *n* **1 a :** a central strand of spongy tissue in the stems of most vascular plants that probably functions chiefly in storage **b :** any of various loose spongy internal tissues or parts ⟨the *pith* of a feather⟩ **2 :** the essential part **:** CORE [Old English *pitha*] — **pith** *adj*

²pith *vt* **:** to destroy the spinal cord or central nervous system of (as a frog) by passing a wire or needle up and down the vertebral canal

pith•e•can•thro•pus \,pith-i-'kan-thrə-pəs, -'kant-; -kan-'thrō-\ *n, pl* **-thro•pi** \-,pī, -,pē\ **:** any of several primitive extinct humans from the Pliocene gravels of Java now usually classified in the same genus as modern human beings *(Homo)* and in the same species as Peking man [New Latin, from Greek *pithēkos* "ape" + *anthrōpos* "human being"]

pithy \'pith-ē\ *adj* **pith•i•er; -est 1 :** consisting of or filled with pith **2 :** being short and to the point ⟨a *pithy* comment⟩ — **pith•i•ly** \'pith-ə-lē\ *adv* — **pith•i•ness** \'pith-ē-nəs\ *n*

piti•able \'pit-ē-ə-bəl\ *adj* **1 :** deserving or exciting pity **:** LAMENTABLE **2 :** pitifully insignificant or scanty — **piti•able•ness** *n* — **piti•ably** \-blē\ *adv*

piti•ful \'pit-i-fəl\ *adj* **1 :** arousing pity or sympathy ⟨a *pitiful* orphan⟩ **2 :** deserving pitying contempt ⟨a *pitiful* excuse⟩ — **piti•ful•ly** \-fə-lē, -flē\ *adv*

piti•less \'pit-i-ləs, 'pit-l-əs\ *adj* **:** having no pity **:** MERCILESS — **piti•less•ly** *adv* — **piti•less•ness** *n*

pi•ton \'pē-,tän\ *n* **:** a spike, wedge, or peg that can be driven into a rock or ice surface as a support (as for a mountain climber) [French]

pit•tance \'pit-ns\ *n* **:** a small portion, amount, or allowance [Old French *pitance* "piety, pity, allowance of food given a member of a religious house", from Medieval Latin *pietantia,* from *pietare* "to be charitable", from Latin *pietas* "piety, pity"]

pit•ter–pat•ter \'pit-ər-,pat-ər, 'pit-ē-,pat-\ *n* **:** a rapid succession of light sounds or beats [imitative] — **pit•ter–pat•ter** \,pit-ər-', ,pit-ē-'\ *adv or adj* — **pit•ter–pat•ter** \,pit-ər-', ,pit-ē-'\ *vi*

pi•tu•i•tary \pə-'tü-ə-,ter-ē, -'tyü-\ *adj* **:** of, relating to, or being the pituitary gland [Latin *pituita* "phlegm"; from the former belief that the pituitary gland secreted phlegm]

pituitary gland *n* **:** a small oval endocrine organ attached to the base of the brain that produces various internal secretions with a direct or indirect regulatory action on most basic body functions and especially on growth and reproduction — called also *pituitary, pituitary body*

pit viper *n* **:** any of a family of mostly New World venomous snakes with a sensory pit on each side of the head and hollow perforated fangs

¹pity \'pit-ē\ *n, pl* **pit•ies 1 :** sympathetic sorrow for one suffering, distressed, or unhappy **:** COMPASSION **2 :** something to be regretted [Old French *pité,* from Latin *pietas* "piety, pity", from *pius* "pious"]

²pity *vb* **pit•ied; pity•ing :** to feel pity or pity for — **piti•er** *n*

pity•ing *adj* **:** expressing or feeling pity ⟨a *pitying* glance⟩ — **pity•ing•ly** \-ing-lē\ *adv*

¹piv•ot \'piv-ət\ *n* **1 :** a shaft or pin on which something turns **2 :** something upon which something else turns or depends **:** a central member, part, or point [French]

²pivot *vb* **1 :** to turn on or as if on a pivot **2 :** to provide with, mount on, or attach by a pivot **3 :** to cause to pivot

piv•ot•al \'piv-ət-l\ *adj* **1 :** of, relating to, or functioning as a pivot **2 :** vitally important **:** CRUCIAL — **piv•ot•al•ly** \-l-ē\ *adv*

pivot joint *n* **:** an anatomical joint (as that of the head and spine) that consists of a bony pivot in a ring of bone and cartilage and that permits rotatory movement only

pix•ie *or* **pixy** \'pik-sē\ *n, pl* **pix•ies :** a mischievous sprite or fairy [origin unknown] — **pix•ie•ish** \-sē-ish\ *adj*

piz•za \'pēt-sə\ *n* **:** an open pie made typically of thinly rolled bread dough spread with a spiced mixture (as of tomatoes, cheese, and ground meat) and baked [Italian, derived from Latin *pix* "pitch"]

piz•ze•ria \ˌpēt-sə-ˈrē-ə\ *n* : an establishment where pizzas are made or sold [Italian, from *pizza*]

piz•zi•ca•to \ˌpit-si-ˈkät-ō\ *adv or adj* : by means of plucking by the fingers instead of bowing — used as a direction in music [Italian]

pla•ca•ble \ˈplak-ə-bəl, ˈplā-kə-\ *adj* : easily placated — **pla•ca•bil•i•ty** \ˌplak-ə-ˈbil-ət-ē, ˌplā-kə-\ *n* — **pla•ca•bly** \ˈplak-ə-blē, ˈplā-kə-\ *adv*

[1]**plac•ard** \ˈplak-ərd, -ˌärd\ *n* : a notice posted or carried in a public place : POSTER [Middle French *placquart,* from *plaquier* "to plate, plaster"]

[2]**plac•ard** \ˈplak-ˌärd, -ərd\ *vt* **1** : to post placards on or in **2** : to anounce by or as if by posting

pla•cate \ˈplāk-ˌāt, ˈplak-\ *vt* : to calm the anger of especially by concessions : SOOTHE [Latin *placare*] **syn** see PACIFY — **pla•ca•tion** \plā-ˈkā-shən, pla-\ *n* — **pla•ca•tive** \ˈplāk-ˌāt-iv, ˈplak-\ *adj* — **pla•ca•to•ry** \ˈplāk-ə-ˌtōr-ē, ˈplak-, -ˌtȯr-\ *adj*

[1]**place** \ˈplās\ *n* **1 a** : physical extension : SPACE ⟨considerations of time and *place*⟩ **b** : a particular but often unspecified location : LOCALITY ⟨stopped several days at each *place*⟩ **2 a** : DWELLING **b** : a building or locality used for a particular purpose ⟨a *place* of resort⟩ ⟨a *place* of worship⟩ **3** : a particular part of a surface or body : SPOT ⟨a sore *place* on the shoulder⟩ ⟨lost my *place* in the book⟩ **4 a** : position in an ordering ⟨in the first *place*⟩ **b** : the position next after the winner in a race or contest **c** : the position of a figure in a numeral ⟨three *places* beyond the decimal point⟩ **5 a** : suitable or assigned location or situation ⟨not the *place* for an active person⟩ **b** : an accommodation occupied by or available for one person ⟨set 12 *places* at table⟩ **c** : space or situation customarily or formerly occupied ⟨paper towels taking the *place* of linen⟩ **d** : JOB 3b, POSITION ⟨lose one's *place* at the office⟩ [Middle French, "open space", from Latin *platea* "broad street", from Greek *plateia,* from *platys* "broad"] — **place•less** \ˈplā-sləs\ *adj*

[2]**place** *vb* **1** : to distribute in an orderly manner : ARRANGE **2 a** : to put in or direct to a particular place **b** : to present for consideration ⟨a question *placed* before the group⟩ **c** : to put in a particular state **3 a** : to appoint to a position **b** : to find employment or a home for **4 a** : to assign to or hold a position in a series : RANK **b** : ESTIMATE ⟨*placed* the value of the estate too high⟩ **c** : to identify by association ⟨could not *place* them although they looked familiar⟩ **5** : to give an order for ⟨*place* a bet⟩ **6** : to come in second in a horse race — **place•able** \ˈplā-sə-bəl\ *adj*

pla•ce•bo \plə-ˈsē-bō\ *n, pl* **-bos** : an inert medication used for psychological reasons or as a control in an experiment [Latin, "I shall please", from *placēre* "to please"]

place•hold•er \ˈplās-ˌhōl-dər\ *n* : a symbol used in a mathematical or logical expression that may be replaced by the name of any element of a given set

place•kick \ˈplā-ˌskik\ *n* : the kicking of a ball placed or held in a stationary position on the ground — **placekick** *vb*

place•ment \ˈplā-smənt\ *n* : an act or instance of placing; *esp* : the assignment of a person to a suitable place (as a class in school or a job)

pla•cen•ta \plə-ˈsent-ə\ *n, pl* **-centas** *or* **-cen•tae** \-ˈsent-ē\ **1** : the vascular organ in most mammals by which the fetus is joined to the maternal uterus and nourished; *also* : an analogous organ in another animal **2** : a part of a plant ovary that bears ovules [Latin, "flat cake", from Greek *plakount-, plakous,* from *plak-, plax* "flat surface"] — **pla•cen•tal** \-ˈsent-l\ *adj or n* — **pla•cen•ta•tion** \ˌplas-n-ˈtā-shən, plə-ˌsen-\ *n*

plac•er \ˈplas-ər\ *n* : an alluvial or glacial deposit containing particles of valuable mineral (as gold) [Spanish, from Catalan, "submarine plain", from *plaza* "place", from Latin *platea* "broad street"]

place value *n* : the value of the location of a digit in a numeral ⟨in 425 the location of the digit 2 has a *place value* of ten while the digit itself indicates that there are two tens⟩

plac•id \ˈplas-əd\ *adj* : peacefully free of interruption or disturbance : QUIET [Latin *placidus,* from *placēre* "to please"] **syn** see CALM — **pla•cid•i•ty** \pla-ˈsid-ət-ē, plə-\ *n* — **plac•id•ly** \ˈplas-əd-lē\ *adv* — **plac•id•ness** *n*

plack•et \ˈplak-ət\ *n* : a slit or opening in a garment (as a skirt) often forming the closure [origin unknown]

plac•o•derm \ˈplak-ə-ˌdərm\ *n* : any of a class (Placodermi) of extinct Paleozoic armored and jawed fishes [Greek *plak-, plax* "flat surface"]

plac•oid \ˈplak-ˌȯid\ *adj* : of, relating to, or being a fish scale (as of a shark) of dermal origin with an enamel-tipped spine [Greek *plak-, plax* "flat surface"]

pla•gia•rism \ˈplā-jə-ˌriz-əm\ *n* **1** : an act of plagiarizing **2** : something plagiarized [derived from Latin *plagiarius* "plunderer, plagiarist", from *plagium* "hunting net", from *plaga* "net"] — **pla•gia•rist** \-rəst\ *n* — **pla•gia•ris•tic** \ˌplā-jə-ˈris-tik\ *adj*

pla•gia•rize \ˈplā-jə-ˌrīz\ *vb* : to steal and pass off as one's own (the ideas or work of another) : commit literary theft — **pla•gia•riz•er** *n*

pla•gio•clase \ˈplā-jē-ə-ˌklās, ˈplā-jə-; ˈplaj-ē-ə-, ˈplaj-ə-; -ˌklāz\ *n* : a feldspar having calcium or sodium in its composition [Greek *plagios* "oblique" + *klasis* "breaking", from *klan* "to break"]

[1]**plague** \ˈplāg\ *n* **1** : a disastrous evil or destructively numerous influx ⟨a *plague* of locusts⟩; *also* : a cause or occasion of annoyance **2** : an epidemic disease causing a high rate of mortality : PESTILENCE; *esp* : BUBONIC PLAGUE [Middle French *plage,* from Late Latin *plaga,* from Latin, "blow"]

[2]**plague** *vt* **1** : to strike or afflict with or as if with disease, calamity, or natural evil **2** : TEASE 2a, TORMENT — **plagu•er** *n*

plagu•ey *or* **plaguy** \ˈplā-gē, ˈpleg-ē\ *adj, chiefly dialect* : causing irritation or annoyance : TROUBLESOME — **plaguey** *adv* — **plagu•i•ly** \ˈplā-gə-lē, ˈpleg-ə-\ *adv*

plaid \ˈplad\ *n* **1** : a rectangular length of tartan worn over the left shoulder by men and women as part of the Scottish national costume **2 a** : TARTAN 2 **b** : a fabric with a pattern of tartan or imitative of tartan **3 a** : TARTAN 1 **b** : a pattern of unevenly spaced repeated stripes crossing at right angles [Scottish Gaelic *plaide*] — **plaid** *adj* — **plaid•ed** \-əd\ *adj*

[1]**plain** \ˈplān\ *n* : an extensive area of level or rolling treeless country; *also* : a broad unbroken expanse [Old French, from Latin *planum,* from *planus* "flat, level"]

[2]**plain** *adj* **1** : lacking ornament or pattern ⟨the dress was *plain*⟩ ⟨*plain* fabrics⟩ **2** : free of added or extraneous matter : PURE ⟨a glass of *plain* water⟩ **3** : free of impediments to view ⟨in *plain* sight⟩ **4 a** : clear to the mind or senses ⟨the trouble was *plain* to the mechanic⟩ **b** : marked by candor : BLUNT ⟨*plain* speaking⟩ **5 a** : of common or average attainments or status : neither notable nor lowly : ORDINARY ⟨*plain* people⟩ **b** : free from complexity : SIMPLE ⟨a *plain* explanation⟩; *also* : containing or using only simple wholesome ingredients ⟨*plain* food⟩ ⟨*plain* cooking⟩ **c** : lacking beauty or ugliness : HOMELY [Middle French, "level", from Latin *planus*] **syn** see FRANK — **plain•ly** *adv* — **plain•ness** \ˈplān-nəs\ *n*

[3]**plain** *adv* : in a plain manner ⟨if I may speak *plain*⟩

plain•clothes•man \ˈplān-ˈklōz-mən, -ˈklō*th*z-, -ˌman\ *n* : a police officer who does not wear a uniform while on duty : DETECTIVE

plain sailing *n* : easy progress over an unobstructed course

plains•man \ˈplānz-mən\ *n* : an inhabitant of plains

plain•song \ˈplān-ˌsȯng\ *n* : rhythmic but not metrical liturgical chant sung in unison in various Christian rites; *esp* : GREGORIAN CHANT

plain•spo•ken \ˈplān-ˈspō-kən\ *adj* : speaking or spoken plainly and especially bluntly ⟨a *plainspoken* teacher⟩ — **plain•spo•ken•ness** \-kən-nəs\ *n*

plaint \ˈplānt\ *n* **1** : LAMENTATION, WAIL **2** : PROTEST 3, COMPLAINT [Middle French, from Latin *planctus,* from *plangere* "to strike, beat one's breast, lament"]

plain•tiff \ˈplānt-əf\ *n* : a person who begins a lawsuit to enforce a claim — compare DEFENDANT [Middle French *plaintif,* from *plaintif* "complaining, plaintive"]

plain•tive \ˈplānt-iv\ *adj* : expressive of suffering or woe : MELANCHOLY [Middle French *plaintif,* from *plaint* "plaint"] — **plain•tive•ly** *adv* — **plain•tive•ness** *n*

plain weave *n* : a weave in which the threads interlace alternately — **plain–wo•ven** \ˌplān-ˈwō-vən\ *adj*

[1]**plait** \ˈplāt, ˈplat\ *n* **1** : PLEAT **2** : a braid of material (as hair or straw) [Middle French *pleit,* derived from Latin *plicare* "to fold"]

[2]**plait** *vt* **1** : PLEAT 1 **2 a** : to interweave the strands or locks of : BRAID **b** : to make by plaiting — **plait•er** *n*

[1]**plan** \ˈplan\ *n* **1 :** a drawing or diagram showing the parts or outline of something **2 :** a method or scheme of acting, doing, or arranging ⟨a civil defense *plan*⟩ ⟨vacation *plans*⟩ **3 :** INTENT 1, AIM ⟨the *plan* was to stop them at the bridge⟩ **[**French, "plane, foundation, ground plan"; partly from Latin *planum* "plain, plane"; partly from French *planter* "to plant, fix in place", from Late Latin *plantare***]** — **plan•less** \-ləs\ *adj* — **plan•less•ly** *adv* — **plan•less•ness** *n*

• **syn** PLAN, DESIGN, PLOT, SCHEME mean a method of making or doing something or achieving an end. PLAN implies mental formulation and often graphic representation ⟨studied the *plans* for the stage sets⟩ DESIGN suggests a pattern and a degree of order or harmony ⟨*designs* for three new gowns⟩ PLOT implies a laying out in clearly distinguished sections with attention to their relations and proportions ⟨outlined the *plot* of the new play⟩ SCHEME stresses systematic choice and ordering of detail for the end in view and may suggest a plan motivated by craftiness and self-seeking ⟨a *scheme* to swindle a neighbor⟩

[2]**plan** *vb* **planned; plan•ning 1 :** to form a plan of or for **:** arrange the parts or details of in advance ⟨*plan* a church⟩ ⟨*plan* a party⟩ **2 :** to have in mind **:** INTEND; *also* **:** to make plans — **plan•ner** *n*

plan- *or* **plano-** *combining form* **:** flat **:** flat and ⟨*plano*-convex⟩ **[**Latin *planus* "flat, level"**]**

pla•nar \ˈplā-nər, -ˌnär\ *adj* **:** of, relating to, or lying in a plane

pla•nar•ia \plə-ˈnar-ē-ə, -ˈner-\ *n* **:** PLANARIAN; *esp* **:** one of a common freshwater genus **[**derived from Late Latin *planarius* "lying on a plane", from Latin *planum* "plane"**]**

pla•nar•i•an \-ē-ən\ *n* **:** any of an order (Tricladida) of small soft-bodied ciliated mostly aquatic flatworms — **planarian** *adj*

[1]**plane** \ˈplān\ *vt* **:** to make smooth or even especially with a plane; *also* **:** to remove by planing **[**Middle French *planer*, from Late Latin *planare*, from Latin *planus* "level"**]** — **plan•er** *n*

[2]**plane** *n* **:** PLANE TREE **[**Middle French, from Latin *platanus*, from Greek *platanos***]**

[3]**plane** *n* **:** a tool for smoothing or shaping a wood surface

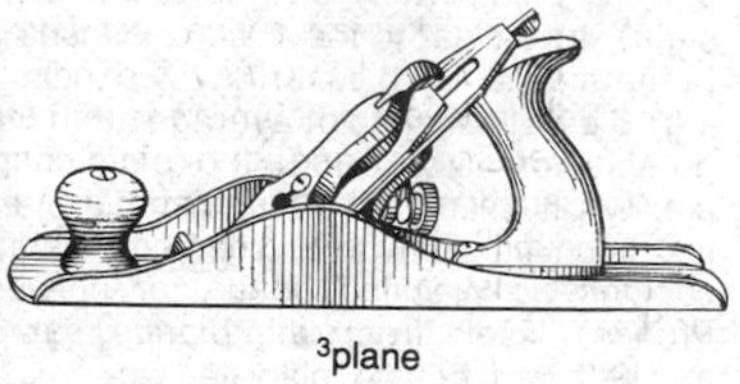

[3]plane

[4]**plane** *n* **1 a :** a surface such that any two of its points can be joined by a straight line lying wholly within the surface **b :** a flat or level material surface **2 :** a level of existence, consciousness, or development **3 a :** one of the main supporting surfaces of an airplane **b :** AIRPLANE **[**Latin *planum*, from *planus* "level"**]**

[5]**plane** *adj* **1 :** lacking elevations or depressions **:** FLAT, LEVEL **2 :** of, relating to, or lying in a plane ⟨*plane* curves⟩ **[**Latin *planus***]**

plane angle *n* **:** an angle formed by two intersecting lines each of which lies on a face of a dihedral angle and is perpendicular to the edge of the face

plane geometry *n* **:** a branch of elementary geometry that deals with plane figures — compare SOLID GEOMETRY

plan•et \ˈplan-ət\ *n* **:** a celestial body except a comet or meteor that revolves about the sun; *also* **:** such a body revolving about the sun of another solar system **[**Old French *planete*, from Late Latin *planeta*, from Greek *planēt-*, *planēs*, literally, "wanderer", from *planasthai* "to wander"**]**

△ origin In studying the sky ancient astronomers observed that while most of the stars maintain fixed relative positions there are a few celestial bodies that quite obviously change their positions in relation to each other and to the greater number of fixed stars. The most notable of these, of course, were the sun and moon, but five others were also observed — Mercury, Venus, Mars, Jupiter, and Saturn. The Greek name for these was *planēs*, whose literal meaning is "wanderer". This is the ancestor of English *planet*. Since ancient times three more planets have been discovered, Uranus in the 18th century, Neptune in the 19th, and Pluto in the 20th.

PLANETS

SYMBOL	NAME	MEAN DISTANCE FROM THE SUN		PERIOD OF REVOLUTION IN DAYS OR YEARS		EQUATORIAL DIAMETER IN KILOMETERS
		astronomical units	million kilometers			
☿	Mercury	0.387	57.9	87.969	d.	4840
♀	Venus	0.723	108.1	224.7	d.	12300
⊕	Earth	1.000	149.6	365.26	d.	12755
♂	Mars	1.524	227.8	687.0	d.	6790
♃	Jupiter	5.203	778.1	11.86	y.	142820
♄	Saturn	9.539	1426.7	29.46	y.	119320
♅	Uranus	19.182	2867	84.01	y.	47150
♆	Neptune	30.058	4496	164.8	y.	44700
♇	Pluto	39.44	5900	248.4	y.	5950

plan•e•tar•i•um \ˌplan-ə-ˈter-ē-əm\ *n, pl* **-i•ums** *or* **-ia** \-ē-ə\ **1 :** a model or representation of the solar system **2 a :** an optical device to project various celestial images and effects **b :** a building or room housing such a device

plan•e•tary \ˈplan-ə-ˌter-ē\ *adj* **1 a :** of or relating to a planet **b :** having a motion like that of a planet ⟨*planetary* electrons of the atomic nucleus⟩ **2 :** WORLDWIDE ⟨a matter of *planetary* concern⟩

plan•e•tes•i•mal \ˌplan-ə-ˈtes-ə-məl, -ˈtez-\ *n* **:** any of numerous small solid celestial bodies which may have existed at an early stage of the development of the solar system and from which the planets may have been formed **[***planet* + *-esimal* (as in *infinitesimal*)**]**

plan•e•toid \ˈplan-ə-ˌtȯid\ *n* **1 :** a body resembling a planet **2 :** ASTEROID

plane tree *n* **:** any of a genus of trees (as the sycamore) with large lobed leaves and flowers in globe-shaped heads — called also *plane*

plan•gent \ˈplan-jənt\ *adj* **1 :** having a loud reverberating sound **2 :** having an expressive especially plaintive quality **[**Latin *plangens*, present participle of *plangere* "to strike, lament"**]** — **plan•gen•cy** *n* — **plan•gent•ly** *adv*

[1]**plank** \ˈplaŋk\ *n* **1 :** a heavy thick board usually 5 to 10 centimeters thick and at least 20 centimeters wide **2 :** an article in the platform of a political party **[**Old North French *planke*, from Latin *planca***]**

[2]**plank** *vt* **1 :** to cover or floor with planks **2 :** to set down forcefully ⟨*planked* the book onto the shelf⟩ **3 :** to cook and serve on a board usually with an elaborate garnish

plank•ing *n* **:** a quantity or covering of planks ⟨deck *planking*⟩

plank•ter \ˈplaŋ-tər, ˈplaŋk-\ *n* **:** a planktonic organism **[**Greek *planktēr* "wanderer", from *plazesthai* "to wander"**]**

plank•ton \ˈplaŋ-tən, ˈplaŋk-, -ˌtän\ *n* **:** the passively floating or weakly swimming usually minute animal and plant life of a body of water — compare NEKTON **[**German, from Greek *planktos* "drifting", from *plazesthai* "to wander, drift"**]** — **plank•ton•ic** \plaŋ-ˈtän-ik, plaŋk-\ *adj*

plano- — see PLAN-

pla•no–con•cave \ˌplā-nō-kän-ˈkāv, -ˈkän-ˌ\ *adj* **:** flat on one side and concave on the other

pla•no–con•vex \-kän-ˈveks, -ˈkän-ˌ, -kən-ˈ\ *adj* **:** flat on one side and convex on the other

pla•nog•ra•phy \plā-ˈnäg-rə-fē, plə-\ *n* **:** a process (as lithography) for printing from a plane surface — **pla•no•graph•ic** \ˌplā-nə-ˈgraf-ik\ *adj*

[1]**plant** \ˈplant\ *vb* **1 a :** to put or set in the ground to grow ⟨*plant* seeds⟩ **b :** IMPLANT ⟨*plant* good habits⟩ **2 a :** to cause to become established ⟨*plant* colonies⟩ **b :** to stock, set, or sow with something usually to grow or increase ⟨*plant* fields to corn⟩ ⟨*plant* a stream with trout⟩ **3 a :** to place or fix in the ground ⟨*planted* stakes to hold the vines⟩ **b :** to place firmly or forcibly ⟨*plant* a blow on an opponent's nose⟩ ⟨*planted* the book with a thud⟩ ⟨*planting* themselves in our path⟩ **4 :** to hide, place secretly, or prearrange with intent to mislead ⟨*planted* nuggets in a worthless mine⟩ ⟨*plant* a spy in an office⟩ ⟨*plant* a rumor⟩ **5 :** to plant something **[**Old English *plantian*, from Late Latin *plantare* "to plant, fix in place", from Latin, "to plant", from *planta* "plant"**]** — **plant•able** \-ə-bəl\ *adj*

[2]**plant** *n* **1 :** any of a kingdom (Plantae) of living beings typically lacking the ability to move from place to place under their own power, having no obvious nervous or sensory organs, and possessing cellulose cell walls and capacity for indefinite growth — compare ANIMAL **2 a :** land, buildings, and equipment of a business, institution, or organization ⟨the college *plant*⟩ **b :** a factory or workshop for the manufacture of a product ⟨an automobile *plant*⟩ **3 :** something or someone planted ⟨the new clerk was a

police *plant*⟩ [Old English *plante,* from Latin *planta*] — **plant·like** \-ˌlīk\ *adj*

Plan·tag·e·net \plan-ˈtaj-nət, -ə-nət\ *adj* **:** of or relating to an English royal house furnishing sovereigns from 1154 to 1399 [*Plantagenet,* nickname of the family adopted as a surname] — **Plantagenet** *n*

[1]**plan·tain** \ˈplant-n\ *n* **:** any of several common short-stemmed or stemless weedy herbs with parallel-veined leaves and a long spike of tiny greenish flowers [Old French, from Latin *plantago,* from *planta* "sole of the foot", from its broad leaves]

[2]**plantain** *n* **:** a banana plant with large greenish starchy fruit that is eaten cooked and is a staple food in the tropics; *also* **:** this fruit [Spanish *plántano* "plane tree, banana tree", from Medieval Latin *plantanus* "plane tree", from Latin *platanus*]

plantain lily *n* **:** a plant of the lily family with ribbed basal leaves and racemes of white or lilac flowers

plan·tar \ˈplant-ər, ˈplan-ˌtär\ *adj* **:** of or relating to the sole of the foot [Latin *plantaris,* from *planta* "sole"]

plan·ta·tion \plan-ˈtā-shən\ *n* **1 :** a usually large group of plants and especially trees under cultivation **2 :** a settlement in a new country or region **:** COLONY **3 :** a planted area; *esp* **:** an agricultural estate worked by resident labor

plant·er \ˈplant-ər\ *n* **1 :** one that plants or cultivates ⟨a mechanical *planter*⟩; *esp* **:** an owner or operator of a plantation **2 :** one who settles or founds a colony **3 :** a container in which ornamental plants are grown

plant food *n* **1 :** FOOD 1b **2 :** soil fertilizer

plant hormone *n* **:** an organic substance that is not a nutrient, that in minute amounts modifies a plant physiological process, and that is active elsewhere than at the site of production

plan·ti·grade \ˈplant-ə-ˌgrād\ *adj* **:** walking on the sole with the heel touching the ground ⟨humans are *plantigrade* animals⟩ [French, from Latin *planta* "sole" + *gradi* "to step"] — **plantigrade** *n*

plant·ing *n* **:** an area where plants are grown for commercial or decorative purposes

plant kingdom *n* **:** the one of the three basic groups of natural objects that includes all living and extinct plants — compare ANIMAL KINGDOM, MINERAL KINGDOM

plant louse *n* **:** APHID; *also* **:** a related insect

plan·u·la \ˈplan-yə-lə\ *n, pl* **-lae** \-ˌlē, -ˌlī\ **:** the young usually flattened oval or oblong free-swimming ciliated larva of some coelenterates [New Latin, from Latin *planus* "level, flat"]

plaque \ˈplak\ *n* **1 :** an ornamental brooch; *esp* **:** the badge of an honorary order **2 :** a flat thin piece (as of metal) used for decoration; *also* **:** a commemorative or identifying inscribed tablet **3 :** a film of mucus harboring bacteria on a tooth **4 :** a clear area in a bacterial culture produced by destruction of cells by a virus [French, from Middle French, "metal sheet", from *plaquier* "to plate", from Dutch *placken* "to piece, patch"]

plash \ˈplash\ *n* **:** SPLASH [probably imitative] — **plash** *vb*

-pla·sia \ˈplā-zhə\ *n combining form* **:** development **:** formation ⟨hyper*plasia*⟩ [Greek *plasis* "molding", from *plassein* "to mold"]

-plasm \ˌplaz-əm\ *n combining form* **:** formative or formed material (as of a cell or tissue) ⟨endo*plasm*⟩ [Greek *plasma* "something molded", from *plassein* "to mold"]

plas·ma \ˈplaz-mə\ *n* **1 :** the fluid part of blood, lymph, or milk as distinguished from suspended material; *esp* **:** BLOOD PLASMA **2 :** a gas in a highly ionized condition [German, from Late Latin, "something molded", from Greek, from *plassein* "to mold"] — **plas·mat·ic** \plaz-ˈmat-ik\ *adj*

plas·ma·lem·ma \ˌplaz-mə-ˈlem-ə\ *n* **:** PLASMA MEMBRANE [*plasma* + Greek *lemma* "husk"]

plasma membrane *n* **:** a semipermeable outer covering of cell protoplasm that consists of a double layer of fat molecules sandwiched between an inner and outer layer of protein molecules

plas·mo·di·um \plaz-ˈmōd-ē-əm\ *n, pl* **-dia** \-ē-ə\ **1 :** a motile mass of protoplasm that is the nonreproductive stage of a slime mold and contains many nuclei without dividing cell walls **2 :** an individual malaria parasite [New Latin, from *plasma*] — **plas·mo·di·al** \-ē-əl\ *adj*

plas·mol·y·sis \plaz-ˈmäl-ə-səs\ *n* **:** shrinking of the cytoplasm away from the wall of a living cell — **plas·mo·lyt·ic** \ˌplaz-mə-ˈlit-ik\ *adj* — **plas·mo·lyze** \ˈplaz-mə-ˌlīz\ *vb*

[1]**plas·ter** \ˈplas-tər\ *n* **1 :** a medicated or protective dressing consisting of a film (as of cloth or plastic) spread with an often medicated substance ⟨adhesive *plaster*⟩ **2 :** a pasty composition (as of lime, water, and sand) that hardens on drying and is used for coating walls, ceilings, and partitions **3 :** PLASTER OF PARIS [Old English, from Latin *emplastrum,* from Greek *emplastron,* from *emplassein* "to plaster on", from *en-* + *plassein* "to mold, plaster"] — **plas·tery** \-tə-rē, -trē\ *adj*

[2]**plaster** *vb* **plas·tered; plas·ter·ing** \-tə-ring, -tring\ **1 :** to apply plaster **:** overlay or cover with plaster **2 :** to apply a plaster to **3 :** to cover over or conceal as if with a coat of plaster **4 :** to fasten or apply to another surface **:** stick tightly ⟨rain *plastered* the clothes to our backs⟩ **5 :** to cover or alter the surface of in a way suggestive of plastering ⟨*plaster* a wall with signs⟩ — **plas·ter·er** \-tər-ər\ *n*

plas·ter·board \ˈplas-tər-ˌbōrd, -ˌbȯrd\ *n* **:** a board used in large sheets as a backing or as a substitute for plaster in walls and consisting of several plies of fiberboard, paper, or felt usually bonded to a hardened gypsum plaster core

plaster cast *n* **:** a rigid dressing of gauze impregnated with plaster of paris

plaster of par·is \-ˈpar-əs\ *often cap 2d P* **:** a white powdery slightly hydrated calcium sulfate made by calcining gypsum and used chiefly for casts and molds in the form of a quick-setting paste with water [*Paris,* France]

[1]**plas·tic** \ˈplas-tik\ *adj* **1 :** FORMATIVE, CREATIVE ⟨*plastic* forces in nature⟩ **2 a :** capable of being molded or modeled ⟨*plastic* clay⟩ **b :** capable of adapting to varying conditions ⟨*plastic* species⟩ ⟨a *plastic* tissue⟩ **3 :** SCULPTURAL **4 :** made or consisting of a plastic **5 :** capable of being deformed continuously and permanently in any direction without rupture **6 :** of, relating to, or involving plastic surgery [Latin *plasticus* "of molding", from Greek *plastikos,* from *plassein* "to mold, form"] — **plas·ti·cal·ly** \-ti-kə-lē, -klē\ *adv* — **plas·tic·i·ty** \plas-ˈtis-ət-ē\ *n*

• **syn** PLASTIC, PLIABLE, PLIANT mean subject to being modified in form or nature and are applied to materials or to persons perceived as workable material. PLASTIC applies to substances soft enough to mold into any desired form or to beings that readily adapt to circumstance; PLIABLE implies lack of resistance to bending, folding, or manipulating and when applied to persons suggests obedience to another's will; PLIANT may stress flexibility and springiness and so suggest ready responsiveness either in material or individuals.

[2]**plastic** *n* **:** a plastic substance; *esp* **:** any of numerous organic synthetic or processed materials that can be formed into objects, films, or filaments

plas·ti·ciz·er \ˈplas-tə-ˌsī-zər\ *n* **:** a chemical added to rubbers and resins to impart flexibility, workability, or stretchability

plastic surgery *n* **:** surgery concerned with the repair or restoration of lost, injured, or deformed parts of the body — **plastic surgeon** *n*

plas·tid \ˈplas-təd\ *n* **:** any of various cytoplasmic organelles of photosynthetic cells [German, from Greek *plastos* "molded"]

plas·tron \ˈplas-trən\ *n* **1 :** a metal breastplate **2 :** the ventral part of the shell of a turtle **3 :** a trimming like a bib for a woman's dress [Middle French, from Italian *piastrone,* from *piastra,* "thin metal plate", from Latin *emplastra, emplastrum* "plaster"] — **plas·tral** \-trəl\ *adj*

-plas·ty \ˌplas-tē\ *n combining form, pl* **-plasties :** plastic surgery

[1]**plat** \ˈplat\ *n* **1 :** a small piece of ground **:** PLOT **2 :** a plan or map of a piece of land (as a town) with lots and landmarks marked out [probably alteration of *plot*]

[2]**plat** *vt* **plat·ted; plat·ting :** to make a plat of

[1]**plate** \ˈplāt\ *n* **1 :** a flat, thin, and usually smooth piece of material ⟨mica splits easily into *plates*⟩: as **a :** metal in sheets usually thicker than about 6 millimeters ⟨steel *plate*⟩ **b :** a thin layer of one metal deposited on another usually by electrical means **c :** one of the broad metal pieces used in medieval armor; *also* **:** armor made of plates **d :** a usually flat bony or horny outgrowth forming part of a covering of an animal (as some fishes or reptiles) **e :** HOME PLATE **f :** the thin fatty underpart of a forequarter of beef or the back part of this cut **g :** any of the large movable segments into which the earth's crust is held to be divided **2 :** precious metal; *esp* **:** silver bullion **3 a**

: domestic hollow-ware usually of or plated with precious metal (as silver) **b** : a shallow usually circular dish **c** (1) : a main course served on a plate; *also* : food and service for one person ⟨ten dollars a *plate*⟩ (2) : PLATEFUL **d** : a dish or pouch used in taking a collection (as in a church) **e** : a flat glass dish used chiefly for culturing microorganisms **4 a** : a flat piece or surface on which something (as letters or a design) is or is to be embossed or incised ⟨license *plates*⟩ **b** : a sheet of material (as metal or plastic) with a specially prepared surface for printing **c** : a sheet of material (as glass) coated with a light-sensitive photographic emulsion **5** : a horizontal truss that supports the roof trusses or rafters of a building **6 a** : the electrode to which the electrons flow in an electron tube **b** : a metallic grid with its interstices filled with active material that forms one of the structural units of a storage cell or battery **7** : the part of a denture that bears the teeth and fits to the mouth; *also* : DENTURE 2 **8** : a full-page illustration often on special paper ⟨a book with color *plates*⟩ [Old French, from *plat* "flat"] — **plate-like** \\-ˌlīk\\ *adj*

[2]**plate** *vt* **1** : to cover or equip with plate: as **a** : to arm with armor plate **b** : to cover with an adherent layer (as of metal) ⟨had the teapot *plated* with silver⟩ **c** : to deposit (as a layer of metal) on a surface ⟨*plate* silver onto copper⟩ **2** : to make a printing surface from or for

pla•teau \\pla-ˈtō, ˈpla-ˌ\\ *n, pl* **plateaus** *or* **plateaux** \\-ˈtōz, -ˌtōz\\ **1** : a usually large relatively level land area raised above adjacent land on at least one side : TABLELAND **2** : a relatively stable level, period, or condition [French, from Middle French, "platter", from *plat* "flat"]

plate•ful \\ˈplāt-ˌfu̇l\\ *n, pl* **platefuls** \\-ˌfu̇lz\\ *also* **plates•ful** \\ˈplāts-ˌfu̇l\\ : the amount a plate will hold

plate glass *n* : fine rolled, ground, and polished sheet glass

plate•let \\ˈplāt-lət\\ *n* : BLOOD PLATELET

plat•en \\ˈplat-n\\ *n* **1** : a flat plate of metal that exerts or receives pressure; *esp* : one in some printing presses that presses the paper against the type **2** : the roller of a typewriter [Middle French *plateine,* from *plate* "plate"]

plat•er \\ˈplāt-ər\\ *n* : one that plates

plate tec•ton•ics \\-tek-ˈtän-iks\\ *n* **1** : a theory that the lithosphere of the earth is divided into a small number of movable plates whose movement causes seismic activity **2** : the process and dynamics of plate movement [*tectonics* "science or art of construction, branch of geology concerned with structure", derived from Greek *tektonikos* "of a builder", from *tektōn* "builder"]

plat•form \\ˈplat-ˌfȯrm\\ *n* **1** : a declaration of principles; *esp* : a declaration of principles and policies adopted by a political party or a candidate **2** : a horizontal flat surface usually higher than the adjoining area; *esp* : a raised flooring (as for speakers or performers) **3** : a thick layered sole for a shoe; *also* : a shoe with such a sole [Middle French *plate-forme* "diagram, map", literally, "flat form"]

platform rocker *n* : a chair that rocks on a stable platform

platform scale *n* : a weighing machine with a flat platform on which objects are weighed

platform tennis *n* : a variation of paddle tennis played on a wooden platform enclosed by a wire fence

plat•ing \\ˈplāt-ing\\ *n* **1** : the act or process of covering especially with metal plate **2** : a coating of metal plates or plate ⟨the *plating* of a ship⟩ ⟨the *plating* wore off the spoons⟩

pla•tin•ic \\plə-ˈtin-ik\\ *adj* : of, relating to, or containing platinum especially with a valence of four

plat•i•nous \\ˈplat-nəs, -n-əs\\ *adj* : of, relating to, or containing platinum especially with a valence of two

plat•i•num \\ˈplat-nəm, -n-əm\\ *n* : a heavy precious grayish white ductile malleable metallic element that is used especially in chemical ware and apparatus, as a catalyst, and in jewelry — see ELEMENT table [New Latin, from Spanish *platina,* from *plata* "silver"]

platinum blonde *n* : a pale silvery blonde color usually produced in human hair by bleach and a bluish rinse; *also* : a person with such hair

plat•i•tude \\ˈplat-ə-ˌtüd, -ˌtyüd\\ *n* **1** : the quality or state of being dull or trite **2** : a flat or trite remark [French, from *plat* "flat, dull"] — **plat•i•tu•di•nous** \\ˌplat-ə-ˈtüd-nəs, -ˈtyüd-, -n-əs\\ *adj*

pla•ton•ic \\plə-ˈtän-ik, plā-\\ *adj* **1** *cap* : of, relating to, or characteristic of Plato or Platonism **2** : of or relating to love freed from sexual desire [Latin, *platonicus* "of Plato", from Greek *platōnikos,* from *Platōn* "Plato"] — **pla•ton•i•cal•ly** \\-ˈtän-i-kə-lē, klē\\ *adv*

Pla•to•nism \\ˈplāt-n-ˌiz-əm\\ *n* : the philosophy of Plato stressing especially that actual things and ideas (as of truth or beauty) are only copies of transcendent ideas which are the objects of true knowledge — **Pla•to•nist** \\-n-əst\\ *n*

pla•toon \\plə-ˈtün, pla-\\ *n* : a subdivision of a military company normally consisting of a headquarters and two or more squads [French *peloton* "small detachment", literally, "ball", from *pelote* "little ball, pellet"]

platoon sergeant *n* : an enlisted rank in the Army above staff sergeant and below first sergeant

plat•ter \\ˈplat-ər\\ *n* **1** : a large plate used especially for serving meat **2** : a phonograpoh record [Anglo-French *plater,* from Middle French *plat* "plate, dish"]

platy \\ˈplat-ē\\ *n, pl* **platy** *or* **plat•ys** *or* **plat•ies** : any of various small variably but brightly colored Mexican topminnows highly favored for the tropical aquarium [New Latin *Platypoecilus,* genus name, from Greek *platys* "broad, flat" + *poikilos* "many-colored"]

plat•y•pus \\ˈplat-i-pəs, -ˌpu̇s\\ *n* : a small aquatic egg-laying mammal of southern and eastern Australia and Tasmania with a fleshy bill resembling that of a duck, webbed feet, and a broad flattened tail [Greek *platypous* "flat-footed", from *platys* "broad, flat" + *pous* "foot"]

platypus

plau•dit \\ˈplȯd-ət\\ *n* **1** : APPLAUSE **2** : enthusiastic approval [Latin, *plaudite* "applaud", pl. imperative of *plaudere* "to applaud"]

plau•si•bil•i•ty \\ˌplȯ-zə-ˈbil-ət-ē\\ *n, pl* **-ties** **1** : the quality or state of being plausible **2** : something plausible

plau•si•ble \\ˈplȯ-zə-bəl\\ *adj* **1** : apparently reasonable or worthy of belief ⟨a *plausible* explanation⟩ **2** : apparently trustworthy or fair ⟨a very *plausible* liar⟩ [Latin *plausibilis* "worthy of applause", from *plaudere* "to applaud"] — **plau•si•ble•ness** *n* — **plau•si•bly** \\ˈplȯ-zə-blē\\ *adv*

• **syn** PLAUSIBLE, CREDIBLE, SPECIOUS mean outwardly acceptable as true or genuine. PLAUSIBLE implies reasonableness at first sight or hearing usually with a hint of a possibility of being deceived ⟨a *plausible* excuse⟩ CREDIBLE stresses worthiness of belief ⟨testimony given by a *credible* witness⟩ SPECIOUS stresses surface plausibility clearly with the implication of deceit or fraud ⟨*specious* reasoning⟩ ⟨*specious* claims for damage⟩

[1]**play** \\ˈplā\\ *n* **1 a** : a brisk handling or using (as of a weapon) **b** : the conduct, course, or action of or a particular act or maneuver in a game; *also* : one's turn to participate in a game **2 a** : recreational activity; *esp* : the spontaneous activity of children **b** : JEST ⟨said it in *play*⟩ **c** : PUN ⟨a *play* on words⟩ **3 a** : a way or manner of acting or proceeding ⟨fair *play*⟩ **b** : OPERATION, ACTIVITY ⟨the normal *play* of economic pressures⟩ **c** : brisk, fitful, or light movement ⟨the light *play* of a breeze⟩ **d** : free or unhindered motion ⟨a jacket that gave *play* in the shoulders⟩ **e** : scope or opportunity for action ⟨the new job gave *play* to their talents⟩ **4 a** : the stage representation of an action or story **b** : a dramatic composition : DRAMA [Old English *plega*] — **in play** : in condition or position to be legitimately played

[2]**play** *vb* **1 a** : to move swiftly, aimlessly, or lightly ⟨shadows *playing* on the wall⟩ **b** : to move freely within limits **c** : to treat or behave frivolously or lightly ⟨*played* with the idea of getting a job⟩ ⟨*play* a person for a fool⟩ **d** : to make use of double meaning or of the similarity of sound of two words usually for humorous effect **2 a** : to take advantage ⟨were *playing* upon fears⟩ **b** : to finger or trifle with something ⟨*played* with the pencil⟩ **c** : to discharge in a stream ⟨hoses *playing* on the fire⟩ **3 a** : to engage in sport or recreation and especially in spontaneous activity for amusement **b** : to imitate in playing ⟨*play* house⟩ **c** : to take part or engage in (as a game) ⟨*play* cards⟩ ⟨*play* ball⟩ **d** : to compete against in a game ⟨Pittsburgh *plays* Chicago today⟩ **e** : to bet on : WAGER ⟨*play* the horses⟩ **4 a** : to perform on a musical instrument ⟨*play* the piano⟩ **b** : to pro-

duce music ⟨listen to an organ *playing*⟩ **5** : to be performed ⟨a new show *playing* for one week⟩ **6 a** : ACT, BEHAVE; *esp* : to conduct oneself in a particular way ⟨*play* safe⟩ **b** : to perform on or as if on the stage ⟨*play* a part⟩; *also* : to act the part of ⟨*play* the fool⟩ **c** : to put or keep in action ⟨*play* a card in a game⟩ **d** : to do for amusement or from mischief ⟨*play* a trick on someone⟩; *also* : to bring about : WREAK ⟨the wind *played* havoc with the garden⟩ — **play•able** \-ə-bəl\ *adj* — **play ball** : COOPERATE — **play second fiddle** : to take a subordinate position

pla•ya \'plī-ə\ *n* : the flat-floored bottom of an undrained desert basin that becomes a shallow lake [Spanish, literally, "beach"]

play•act•ing \'plā-,ak-ting\ *n* **1** : performance in theatrical productions **2** : insincere or artificial behavior

play•back \plā-,bak\ *n* : an act of reproducing recorded sound or pictures often immediately after recording

play back \plā-'bak, 'plā-\ *vt* : to perform a playback of (a disc or tape)

play•bill \'plā-,bil\ *n* **1** : a poster advertising a play **2** : a theater program

play•boy \-,bȯi\ *n* : a man whose chief interest is the pursuit of pleasure

play–by–play \,plā-bə-,plā, -bī-\ *adj* **1** : being a running commentary on a sports event **2** : relating each event as it occurs

play down *vt* : to refrain from emphasizing

play•er \'plā-ər\ *n* : one that plays: as **a** : a person who plays a game **b** : MUSICIAN **c** : ACTOR 1b **d** : a mechanical device for producing or reproducing music ⟨a tape *player*⟩

player piano *n* : a piano containing a mechanical player

play•ful \-fəl\ *adj* **1** : full of play : SPORTIVE **2** : HUMOROUS, JOCULAR — **play•ful•ly** \-fə-lē\ *adv* — **play•ful•ness** *n*

play•girl \-,gərl\ *n* : a woman whose chief interest is the pursuit of pleasure

play•go•er \-,gō-ər, -,gȯr\ *n* : a person who frequently attends plays

play•ground \-,graůnd\ *n* : a piece of land used for games and recreation especially by children

play•house \-,haůs\ *n* **1** : THEATER 1 **2** : a small house for children to play in

playing card *n* : one of a set of usually 32, 48, or 52 thin rectangular pieces of paperboard or plastic marked on one side to show rank and suit (as spades, hearts, diamonds, or clubs) and used in playing various games

playing field *n* : a field for various games; *esp* : the part of a field officially marked off for play

play•let \'plā-lət\ *n* : a short play

play•mate \-,māt\ *n* : a companion in play

play–off \'plā-,ȯf\ *n* **1** : a final contest or series of contests to determine the winner between contestants or teams that have tied **2** : a series of contests played after the end of the regular season to determine a championship

play off \plā-'ȯf, 'plā-\ *vt* **1** : to complete the playing of (an interrupted contest) **2** : to break (a tie) by a play-off

play out *vb* **1** : to perform to the end **2 a** : to use up or become used up **b** : to become spent or exhausted **3** : UNREEL, UNFOLD

play•pen \'plā-,pen\ *n* : a portable enclosure in which a baby or young child may play

play•thing \-,thing\ *n* : TOY 2

play•time \-,tīm\ *n* : a time for play or diversion

play up *vt* : to give emphasis or prominence to — **play up to** \plā-'əp-tü\ : to support or flatter by eager agreement

play•wright \'plā-,rīt\ *n* : a person who writes plays [obsolete *wright* "maker", from Old English *wryhta*]

pla•za \'plaz-ə, 'pläz-\ *n* **1** : a public square in a city or town **2** : SHOPPING CENTER [Spanish, from Latin *platea* "broad street", from Greek *plateia,* from *platys* "broad"]

plea \'plē\ *n* **1** : a defendant's answer to a lawsuit or a criminal charge ⟨a *plea* of guilty⟩ **2** : something offered as an excuse **3** : an earnest request : APPEAL [Old French *plait, plaid* "lawsuit", from Medieval Latin *placitum,* from Latin, "decision, decree", from *placēre* "to please, be decided"]

plead \'plēd\ *vb* **plead•ed** \'plēd-əd\ *or* **pled** \'pled\; **plead•ing 1** : to argue a case in a court of law **2** : to make a plea of a specified nature ⟨*plead* not guilty⟩ **3 a** : to argue for or against a claim **b** : to appeal earnestly : IMPLORE **4** : to offer in defense, apology, or excuse [Old French *plaidier,* from *plaid* "lawsuit"] — **plead•able** \'plēd-ə-bəl\ *adj* — **plead•er** *n*

pleas•ant \'plez-nt\ *adj* **1** : giving pleasure : AGREEABLE **2** : having or characterized by pleasing manners, behavior, or appearance — **pleas•ant•ly** *adv* — **pleas•ant•ness** *n*

pleas•ant•ry \-n-trē\ *n, pl* **-ries 1** : agreeable playfulness especially in conversation **2** : a humorous act or speech : JEST

[1]**please** \'plēz\ *vb* **1** : to give pleasure or satisfaction : GRATIFY **2** : to feel the desire or inclination : LIKE ⟨do as you *please*⟩ [Middle French *plaisir,* from Latin *placēre*]

[2]**please** *adv* **1** — used as a function word to express politeness or emphasis in a request ⟨*please* come in⟩ **2** — used as a function word to express polite affirmation ⟨Have some tea? *Please.*⟩

pleas•ing \'plē-zing\ *adj* : giving pleasure : AGREEABLE — **pleas•ing•ly** \-zing-lē\ *adv* — **pleas•ing•ness** *n*

plea•sur•able \'plezh-rə-bəl, 'plāzh-, -ə-rə-\ *adj* : PLEASANT 1, GRATIFYING — **plea•sur•able•ness** \'plezh-rə-bəl-nəs, 'plāzh-, -ə-rə-\ *n* — **plea•sur•ably** \-blē\ *adv*

plea•sure \'plezh-ər, 'plāzh-\ *n* **1** : DESIRE, INCLINATION ⟨what's your *pleasure*⟩ **2** : a state of gratification : ENJOYMENT **3** : a source of delight or joy

[1]**pleat** \'plēt\ *vt* **1** : FOLD 1; *esp* : to arrange in pleats **2** : PLAIT 2 [Middle English *pleten,* from *plete, pleit* "plait"] — **pleat•er** *n*

[2]**pleat** *n* : a fold (as in cloth) made by doubling material over on itself — **pleat•ed** *adj*

plebe \'plēb\ *n* : a freshman at a military or naval academy [obsolete *plebe* "common people", from French *plèbe,* from Latin *plebs*]

[1]**ple•be•ian** \pli-'bē-ən, -yən\ *n* **1** : a member of the Roman plebs **2** : one of the common people [Latin *plebeius* "of the common people", from *plebs* "common people"] — **ple•be•ian•ism** \-ə-,niz-əm, -yə-\ *n*

[2]**plebeian** *adj* **1** : of or relating to plebeians **2** : crude or coarse in manner or style : COMMON — **ple•be•ian•ly** *adv*

pleb•i•scite \'pleb-ə-,sīt, -sət\ *n* : a popular vote by which the people indicate their wishes on a measure officially submitted to them [Latin *plebis scitum* "decree of the common people"]

plebs \'plebz\ *n* **1** : the common people of ancient Rome **2** : the general populace [Latin]

plec•trum \'plek-trəm\ *n, pl* **plec•tra** \-trə\ *or* **plectrums** : [3]PICK 3 [Latin, from Greek *plēktron,* from *plēssein* "to strike"]

[1]**pledge** \'plej\ *n* **1 a** : the handing over of a chattel to another as security for an obligation without transfer of title; *also* : the chattel so delivered **b** : the state of being held as a security ⟨given in *pledge*⟩ **2 a** : something given as security for the performance of an act **b** : a token, sign, or evidence of something else ⟨shake hands as a *pledge* of friendship⟩ **3 a** : TOAST 3 **b** : a binding promise or agreement **4 a** : a person pledged to join an organization (as a fraternity) **b** : a gift promised (as to a charity) [Middle French *plege* "security", from Late Latin *plebium*]

[2]**pledge** *vt* **1** : to deposit as a pledge **2** : to drink the health of : TOAST **3** : to bind by a pledge ⟨*pledge* oneself⟩ **4** : to promise by a pledge ⟨*pledge* money to charity⟩ — **pledg•ee** \ple-'jē\ *n* — **pledg•er** \'plej-ər\ *n* — **pled•gor** \'plej-ər, ple-'jȯr\ *n*

Ple•ia•des \'plē-ə-,dēz\ *n pl* **1** : a conspicuous loose cluster of stars in the constellation Taurus consisting of six stars visible to the average eye [Latin, the seven daughters of Atlas, who were transformed into a group of stars, from Greek]

pleio•tro•pic \,plī-ə-'trōp-ik, -'träp-\ *adj* : affecting the phenotype in more than one way ⟨*pleiotropic* genes⟩ [Greek *pleiōn* "more" + *tropos* "turn, way"] — **pleio•trop•ism** \-'trōp-,iz-əm, -'träp-\ *n*

Pleis•to•cene \'plī-stə-,sēn\ *n* : the earlier epoch of the Quaternary; *also* : the corresponding system of rocks [Greek *pleistos* "most"] — **Pleistocene** *adj*

ple•na•ry \'plē-nə-rē, 'plen-ə-\ *adj* **1** : COMPLETE, FULL ⟨*plenary* powers⟩ **2** : including all entitled to attend ⟨a *plenary* session of an assembly⟩ [Late Latin *plenarius,* from Latin *plenus* "full"]

plen•i•po•ten•tia•ry \,plen-ə-pə-'tench-rē, -ə-rē; -'ten-chē-,er-ē\ *n, pl* **-ries :** a person and especially a diplomatic agent having full power to transact any business [Medieval Latin *plenipotentiarius,* derived from Latin *plenus* "full" + *potens* "powerful, potent"] — **plenipotentiary** *adj*

plen•i•tude \'plen-ə-,tüd, -,tyüd\ *or* **plent•i•tude** \'plen-ə-, 'plent-ə-\ *n* **:** the quality or state of being full or plentiful **:** ABUNDANCE [Latin *plenitudo,* from *plenus* "full"]

plen•te•ous \'plent-ē-əs\ *adj* **:** PLENTIFUL — **plen•te•ous•ly** *adv* — **plen•te•ous•ness** *n*

plen•ti•ful \'plent-i-fəl\ *adj* **1 :** containing or yielding plenty **:** FRUITFUL **2 :** characterized by, constituting, or existing in plenty — **plen•ti•ful•ly** \-fə-lē\ *adv* — **plen•ti•ful•ness** *n*
• syn PLENTIFUL, AMPLE, ABUNDANT, COPIOUS mean more than sufficient yet not in excess. PLENTIFUL suggests a great or rich supply ⟨eggs are cheap when *plentiful*⟩ AMPLE implies a generous sufficiency to satisfy a particular requirement ⟨an income *ample* for one's needs⟩ ABUNDANT suggests an even greater or richer supply than does PLENTIFUL ⟨*abundant* harvests⟩ COPIOUS stresses largeness in quantity or number rather than fullness or richness ⟨shed *copious* tears⟩ ⟨took *copious* notes at the lecture⟩

[1]plen•ty \'plent-ē\ *n* **1 :** a full or abundant supply **:** a sufficient number or amount ⟨*plenty* to choose from⟩ ⟨got there in *plenty* of time⟩ **2 :** ABUNDANCE ⟨in times of *plenty*⟩ [Old French *plenté,* from Late Latin *plenitas,* from Latin, "fullness", from *plenus* "full"]

[2]plenty *adj* **:** PLENTIFUL, ABUNDANT ⟨had *plenty* help⟩

[3]plenty *adv* **:** ABUNDANTLY, QUITE ⟨a *plenty* exciting trip⟩

ple•num \'plen-əm, 'plēn-əm\ *n, pl* **-nums** *or* **-na** \-ə\ **:** a general assembly of all members of a public body [New Latin, from Latin *plenus* "full"]

ple•sio•saur \'plē-sē-ə-,sȯr, 'plē-zē-\ *n* **:** any of a group (Plesiosauria) of Mesozoic marine reptiles with flattened bodies and limbs modified into paddles [derived from Greek *plēsios* "close" + *sauros* "lizard"]

pleth•o•ra \'pleth-ə-rə\ *n* **:** an excessive quantity or fullness [Medieval Latin, from Greek *plēthōra,* from *plēthein* "to be full"] — **ple•tho•ric** \plə-'thȯr-ik, -'thär-; 'pleth-ə-rik\ *adj*

pleu•ra \'plu̇r-ə\ *n, pl* **pleu•rae** \'plu̇r-,ē, -,ī\ *or* **pleuras :** either of two separate membranous sacs each of which encloses a single lung of a mammal and consists of two layers of membrane with the outer layer lining half of the chest and the inner layer folded back over the surface of a lung [Greek, "rib, side"] — **pleu•ral** \'plu̇r-əl\ *adj*

pleu•ri•sy \'plu̇r-ə-sē\ *n* **:** inflammation of the pleura usually with fever, painful breathing, and coughing [Middle French *pleuresie,* derived from Greek *pleura* "side"] — **pleu•rit•ic** \plü-'rit-ic\ *adj*

pleu•ro•coc•cus \,plu̇r-ə-'käk-əs\ *n, pl* **-coc•cus•es** *or* **-coc•ci** \-'käk-,ī, -,sī; -'käk-,ē, -,sē\ **:** PROTOCOCCUS

pleu•ro•pneu•mo•nia \,plu̇r-ō-nu̇-'mō-nyə, -nyu̇-\ *n* **:** combined inflammation of the lungs and pleura; *also* **:** a disease (as of cattle) marked by this

Plexi•glas \'plek-si-,glas\ *trademark* — used for acrylic plastic sheets and molding powders

plex•us \'plek-səs\ *n* **:** an interlacing network especially of blood vessels or nerves [Latin, "braid, network", from *plectere* "to braid"]

pli•able \'plī-ə-bəl\ *adj* **1 :** capable of being bent or folded without damage **:** FLEXIBLE **2 :** easily influenced [Middle French, from *plier* "to bend, fold", from Latin *plicare* "to fold"] **syn** see PLASTIC — **pli•abil•i•ty** \,plī-ə-'bil-ət-ē\ *n* — **pli•able•ness** \'plī-ə-bəl-nəs\ *n* — **pli•ably** \-blē\ *adv*

pli•an•cy \'plī-ən-sē\ *n* **:** the quality or state of being pliant

pli•ant \'plī-ənt\ *adj* **1 :** readily yielding without breaking **:** FLEXIBLE ⟨*pliant* willow twigs⟩ **2 :** PLIABLE 2 **3 :** suitable for varied uses **:** ADAPTABLE **syn** see PLASTIC — **pli•ant•ly** *adv*

pli•cate \'plī-,kāt\ *adj* **:** having lengthwise folds or ridges ⟨a *plicate* leaf⟩ [Latin *plicatus,* past participle of *plicare* "to fold"] — **pli•cate•ly** *adv*

pli•ers \'plī-ərz, 'plīrz\ *n pl* **:** a small pincers with long jaws for holding small objects or for bending and cutting wire

[1]plight \'plīt\ *vt* **:** to put or give in pledge **:** ENGAGE [Old English *plihtan* "to endanger", from *pliht* "danger"] — **plight•er** *n*

[2]plight *n* **:** CONDITION 4a, STATE; *esp* **:** bad state or condition ⟨the *plight* of the unemployed⟩ [Anglo-French *plit,* derived from Latin *plicare* "to fold"]

Plim•soll mark \,plim-səl-, ,plimp-, -,sȯl-\ *n* **:** a load line or a set of load-line markings on an oceangoing cargo ship — called also *Plimsoll line* [Samuel *Plimsoll,* died 1898, English shipping reformer]

plink \'plingk\ *vb* **1 :** to make or cause to make a tinkling sound **2 :** to shoot at especially in a casual manner [imitative] — **plink** *n*

plinth \'plinth, 'plintth\ *n* **1 :** the lowest part of the base of an architectural column **2 :** a block used as a base (as for a statue or vase) [Latin *plinthus,* from Greek *plinthos*]

Plio•cene \'plī-ə-,sēn\ *n* **:** the latest epoch of the Tertiary; *also* **:** the corresponding system of rocks [Greek *pleiōn* "more"] — **Pliocene** *adj*

Plio•film \'plī-ə-,film\ *trademark* — used for a glossy membrane used especially for raincoats and packaging material

plod \'pläd\ *vi* **plod•ded; plod•ding 1 :** to walk heavily or slowly **:** TRUDGE **2 :** to work or study laboriously **:** DRUDGE [imitative] — **plod** *n* — **plod•der** *n* — **plod•ding•ly** \-ing-lē\ *adv*

ploi•dy \'plȯid-ē\ *n* **:** degree of repetition of the basic number of chromosomes [from such words as *diploidy, triploidy*]

plop \'pläp\ *vb* **plopped; plop•ping 1 :** to make or move with a sound like that of something dropping into water **2 :** to allow the body to drop heavily **3 :** to set, drop, or throw heavily [imitative] — **plop** *n*

[1]plot \'plät\ *n* **1 :** a small area of land **:** LOT **2 :** GROUND PLAN 1 **3 :** the main story of a literary work **4 :** a secret plan for accomplishing a usually evil or unlawful end **5 :** a graphic representation **:** CHART, DIAGRAM [Old English]
• syn PLOT, INTRIGUE, CONSPIRACY mean a plan secretly devised to accomplish an evil purpose. PLOT implies careful foresight in planning positive action ⟨an elaborate kidnapping *plot*⟩ INTRIGUE suggests secret maneuvering ⟨the court thrived on *intrigues*⟩ CONSPIRACY implies a secret agreement among a number of persons not necessarily for positive action ⟨*conspiracy* in restraint of trade⟩ **syn** see in addition PLAN

[2]plot *vb* **plot•ted; plot•ting 1 a :** to make a plot, map, or plan of **b :** to mark or note on or as if on a map or chart **2 a :** to locate (a point) by means of coordinates **b :** to locate (a curve) by plotted points **3 :** to plan or contrive especially secretly **:** CONSPIRE, SCHEME — **plot•ter** *n*

plo•ver \'pləv-ər, 'plō-vər\ *n, pl* **plover** *or* **plovers :** any of numerous shorebirds differing from the related sandpipers in having shorter and stouter bills [Middle French, derived from Latin *pluvia* "rain"]

[1]plow *or* **plough** \'plau̇\ *n* **1 :** an implement used to cut, lift, and turn over soil especially in preparing a seedbed **2 :** any of various devices (as for spreading or opening something) that operate like a plow; *esp* **:** SNOWPLOW [Old English *plōh* "land a yoke of oxen could plow in one day"]

[2]plow *or* **plough** *vb* **1 :** to open, break up, or work with a plow ⟨*plow* a straight furrow⟩ ⟨*plow* the soil⟩ ⟨*plow* a road out with a snowplow⟩ **2 a :** to move through like a plow cutting the soil ⟨a ship *plowing* the waves⟩ **b :** to proceed steadily and laboriously **:** PLOD ⟨*plow* through a report⟩ — **plow•able** \-ə-bəl\ *adj* — **plow•er** \'plau̇-ər, 'plau̇r\ *n*

plow back *vt* **:** to reinvest (profits) in a business

plow•boy \'plau̇-,bȯi\ *n* **:** a boy who guides a plow or leads the horse drawing it

plow•man \-mən\ *n* **1 :** one that plows **2 :** a farm laborer

plow•share \-,sheər, -,shaər\ *n* **:** the part of a plow that cuts the earth

plow sole *n* **:** a layer of earth at the bottom of the furrow compacted by repeated plowing at the same depth

ploy \'plȯi\ *n* **:** a tactic intended to embarrass or baffle an opponent [probably from *employ*]

[1]pluck \'plək\ *vb* **1 a :** to pull or pick off or out ⟨*pluck* a flower⟩ **b :** to remove something and especially hair or feathers from by or as if by plucking ⟨*pluck* a fowl⟩ **2 :** ROB 1, FLEECE **3 :** to move or separate forcibly **:** TUG, SNATCH ⟨*plucked* the child from danger⟩ **4 a :** to pick, pull, or grasp at **b :** to play by sounding the strings with the fingers or a pick ⟨*pluck* a guitar⟩ **5 :** to make a sharp pull or twitch ⟨a briar *plucked* at my sleeve⟩ [Old English *pluccian*] — **pluck•er** *n*

[2]pluck *n* **1 :** a sharp pull **:** TUG **2 :** the heart, liver, lungs, and windpipe of a slaughtered animal **3 :** courageous readiness to fight or continue against odds **:** SPIRIT

plucky \'plək-ē\ *adj* **pluck•i•er; -est :** COURAGEOUS — **pluck•i•ly** \'plək-ə-lē\ *adv* — **pluck•i•ness** \'plək-ē-nəs\ *n*

[1]plug \'pləg\ *n* **1 a :** a piece (as of wood or metal) used to stop or fill a hole **:** STOPPER **b :** an obtruding or obstructing mass of material (as in rock or tissue) resembling a stopper **2 :** a worn-out horse **3 a :** FIREPLUG **b :** SPARK PLUG 1 **4 :** a device for making an electrical connection by insertion into a receptacle **5 :** a flat cake of tightly pressed tobacco leaves **6 :** a fishing lure with two or more hooks **7 :** a piece of favorable publicity usually placed in general material **[**Dutch**]**

2plug *vb* **plugged**; **plug•ging 1 :** to stop, make tight, or secure with or as if with a plug **2 :** to hit with a bullet **3 :** to advertise or publicize insistently **4 :** to become plugged — usually used with *up* — **plug•ger** *n*

plug hat *n* **:** a man's stiff hat (as a bowler or top hat)

plug in *vb* **:** to establish or connect to an electric circuit by inserting a plug

plug–ugly \ˈpləg-ˌəg-lē\ *n, pl* **-ug•lies :** THUG, TOUGH

plum \ˈpləm\ *n* **1 a :** any of numerous trees and shrubs related to the peach and cherries and having round to oval smooth-skinned fruits with oblong pits **b :** the edible fruit of a plum **2 a :** a raisin for use in cooking **b :** SUGARPLUM **3 :** something excellent or superior; *esp* **:** something given as recompense for service **4 :** a dark reddish purple **[**Old English *plūme,* from Latin *prunum* "plum fruit", from Greek *proumnon***]** — **plum•like** \-ˌlīk\ *adj*

plum•age \ˈplü-mij\ *n* **:** the entire clothing of feathers of a bird

1plumb \ˈpləm\ *n* **:** a weight often of lead used on a line especially to determine a vertical direction or distance **[**derived from Latin *plumbum* "lead"**]** — **out of plumb** *or* **off plumb :** out of vertical or true

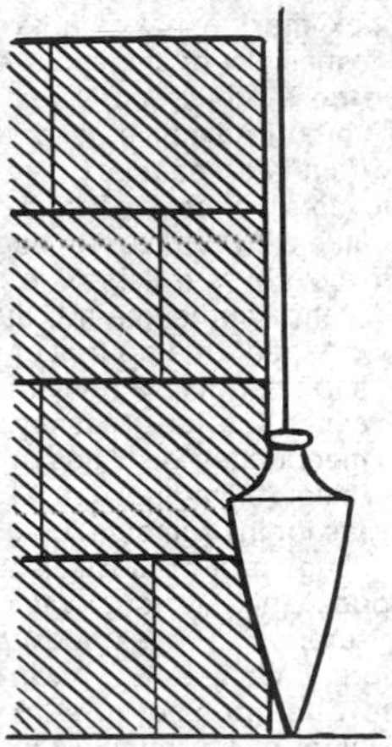
1plumb

2plumb *adv* **1 :** straight down or up **:** VERTICALLY **2** *chiefly dialect* **:** WHOLLY 1, ABSOLUTELY

3plumb *vb* **1 :** to sound, adjust, or test with a plumb ⟨*plumb* a wall⟩ ⟨*plumb* the depth of the well⟩ **2 :** to examine and determine hidden aspects of ⟨*plumbed* their motives⟩ **3 :** to supply with or install as plumbing; *also* **:** to work as a plumber

4plumb *also* **plum** *adj* **1 :** exactly vertical or true **2 :** ABSOLUTE 4, COMPLETE **syn** see VERTICAL

plum•ba•go \ˌpləm-ˈbā-gō\ *n* **:** GRAPHITE **[**Latin, "galena", from *plumbum* "lead"**]**

plumb bob *n* **:** the metal bob of a plumb line

plumb•er \ˈpləm-ər\ *n* **:** one that installs, repairs, and maintains piping, fittings, and fixtures involved in the distribution and use of water in a building **[**derived from Latin *plumbum* "lead"**]**

plum•bic \ˈpləm-bik\ *adj* **:** of, relating to, or containing lead especially with a valence of four

plumb•ing \ˈpləm-ing\ *n* **1 :** a plumber's occupation or trade **2 :** the apparatus (as pipes and fixtures) concerned in the distribution and use of water in a building

plumb line *n* **:** a line or cord having at one end a weight (as a plumb bob) and serving especially to determine whether something is vertical or to measure depth

plum•bous \ˈpləm-bəs\ *adj* **:** of, relating to, or containing lead especially with a valence of two

1plume \ˈplüm\ *n* **1 :** a feather of a bird; *esp* **:** a large conspicuous or showy feather **2 a :** a feather, cluster of feathers, tuft of hair, or similar object worn as an ornament **b :** a token of honor or victory **:** PRIZE **3 :** something (as a trail of smoke or a bushy tail of a dog) that resembles a plume **[**Middle French, from Latin *pluma* "small soft feather, down"**]** — **plumed** \ˈplümd\ *adj* — **plumy** \ˈplü-mē\ *adj*

2plume *vt* **1 :** to provide or deck with plumes ⟨*plume* a hat⟩ **2 :** to pride (oneself) on something **3 :** PREEN 1 ⟨a bird *pluming* itself⟩

1plum•met \ˈpləm-ət\ *n* **:** PLUMB BOB; *also* **:** PLUMB LINE **[**Middle French *plombet* "ball of lead", from *plomb* "lead", derived from Latin *plumbum***]**

2plummet *vi* **:** to drop straight down or sharply and abruptly

plu•mose \ˈplü-ˌmōs\ *adj* **:** FEATHERY, FEATHERED

1plump \ˈpləmp\ *vb* **1 :** to drop, sink, or come in contact suddenly or heavily ⟨*plumped* down into the chair⟩ **2 :** to favor someone or something strongly — used with *for* **[**Middle English *plumpen***]**

2plump *adv* **1 :** with a sudden or heavy drop **2 :** STRAIGHT, DIRECTLY ⟨ran *plump* into the wall⟩

3plump *n* **:** a sudden plunge, fall, or blow; *also* **:** the sound accompanying such an act

4plump *adj* **:** having a full rounded usually pleasing form **[**Middle English, "dull, blunt"**]** — **plump•ness** *n*

5plump *vb* **:** to make or become plump

plum pudding *n* **:** a boiled or steamed pudding containing fruits (as raisins) and usually rich in fat

plu•mule \ˈplü-myül\ *n* **1 :** EPICOTYL **2 :** a down feather **[**Latin *plumula* "small feather", from *pluma* "feather, down"**]**

1plun•der \ˈplən-dər\ *vb* **plun•dered**; **plun•der•ing** \-də-ring, -dring\ **:** to rob especially openly and by force (as in a raid) **[**German *plündern***]** — **plun•der•er** \-dər-ər\ *n*

2plunder *n* **1 :** an act of plundering **2 :** something taken by force or theft **:** LOOT

1plunge \ˈplənj\ *vb* **1 :** to thrust or force quickly and forcibly ⟨*plunging* a knife into the roast⟩ **2 :** to thrust or cast oneself into or as if into water **:** DIVE **3 a :** to throw oneself or move suddenly and sharply forward and downward ⟨the horse reared and *plunged*⟩ **b :** to move rapidly or suddenly downward ⟨the market *plunged* after war was declared⟩ **4 a :** to rush or act with reckless haste ⟨*plunged* into debt⟩; *also* **:** to bring to a usually unpleasant state or course of action suddenly or unexpectedly ⟨the president's illness *plunged* the nation into gloom⟩ **b :** to speculate or gamble recklessly **[**Middle French *plonger,* derived from Latin *plumbum* "lead"**]**

2plunge *n* **:** a sudden dive, leap, or rush — **take the plunge :** to get married

plung•er \ˈplən-jər\ *n* **1 :** a person (as a diver or a reckless gambler) that plunges **2 a :** a device (as a piston in a pump) that acts with a plunging motion **b :** a device consisting of a rubber suction cup on a handle used to free plumbing traps and waste outlets of obstructions

plunk \ˈpləngk\ *vb* **1 :** to make or cause to make a hollow metallic sound ⟨*plunk* the strings of a banjo⟩ **2 :** to drop heavily or suddenly ⟨*plunked* the money down⟩ **3 :** to publicly favor someone or something — used with *for* **[**imitative**]** — **plunk** *n*

plu•per•fect \plü-ˈpər-fikt, ˈplü-\ *adj* **:** PAST PERFECT **[**Late Latin *plusquamperfectus,* literally, "more than perfect"**]** — **pluperfect** *n*

plu•ral \ˈplu̇r-əl\ *adj* **1 :** belonging to a class of grammatical forms used to denote more than one ⟨a *plural* suffix⟩ **2 :** relating to, consisting of, or containing more than one **[**Latin *pluralis,* from *plur-, plus* "more"**]** — **plural** *n* — **plu•ral•ly** \-ə-lē\ *adv*

plu•ral•ism \ˈplu̇r-ə-ˌliz-əm\ **:** a state of society in which different (as ethnic or social) groups maintain their traditional cultures or special interests within the confines of a common civilization

plu•ral•i•ty \plu̇-ˈral-ət-ē\ *n, pl* **-ties 1 :** the state of being plural or numerous **2 :** the greater number or part ⟨a *plurality* of the nations want peace⟩ **3 a :** the fact of being chosen by the voters out of three or more candidates or measures when no one of them obtains more than half the total vote **b :** the excess of the number of votes received by one candidate over another; *esp* **:** that of the highest over the next highest **syn** see MAJORITY

plu•ral•ize \ˈplu̇r-ə-ˌlīz\ *vt* **:** to make plural or express in the plural form — **plu•ral•iza•tion** \ˌplu̇r-ə-lə-ˈzā-shən\ *n*

1plus \ˈpləs\ *prep* **1 :** increased by ⟨four *plus* five is nine⟩ ⟨the debt *plus* interest⟩ **2 :** WITH 8a **[**Latin, "more"**]**

2plus *n* **1 :** an added quantity **2 :** a positive quality **:** ADVANTAGE **3 :** the amount that remains when use or need is satisfied

3plus *adj* **1 a :** requiring addition ⟨the *plus* sign⟩ **b :** algebraically positive **2 :** having, receiving, or being in addition **3 a :** falling high in a specified range ⟨a grade of C *plus*⟩ **b :** greater than that specified **4 :** electrically positive **5 :** relating to or being a particular one of the two mating types that are required for successful fertilization in sexual reproduction in some lower plants (as fungus)

1plush \ˈpləsh\ *n* **:** a fabric with pile longer and less dense than that of velvet **[**Middle French *peluche***]** — **plushy** \-ē\ *adj*

²plush *adj* **1 :** relating to, resembling, or made of plush **2 :** very luxurious or satisfactory

Plu•to \'plüt-ō\ *n* **:** the planet farthest from the sun — see PLANET table [*Pluto,* Greek god of the dead]

plu•toc•ra•cy \plü-'täk-rə-sē\ *n, pl* **-cies 1 :** government by the wealthy **2 :** a controlling class of rich people [Greek *ploutokratia,* from *ploutos* "wealth"] — **plu•to•crat** \'plüt-ə-,krat\ *n* — **plu•to•crat•ic** \,plüt-ə-'krat-ik\ *adj* — **plu•to•crat•i•cal•ly** \-'krat-i-kə-lē, -klē\ *adv*

plu•ton•ic \plü-'tän-ik\ *adj* **:** formed by solidification of magma deep within the earth and crystalline throughout ⟨*plutonic* rock⟩ [Latin *Pluton-, Pluto,* god of the dead, from Greek *Ploutōn*]

plu•to•ni•um \plü-'tō-nē-əm\ *n* **:** a radioactive metallic chemical element that is formed by decay of neptunium and found in minute quantities in pitchblende and that is fissionable to yield atomic energy — see ELEMENT table [New Latin, from *Pluton-, Pluto,* the planet Pluto]

plu•vi•al \'plü-vē-əl\ *adj* **1 :** of or relating to rain **2 :** characterized by or resulting from the action of abundant rain ⟨a *pluvial* period⟩ [Latin *pluvialis,* from *pluvia* "rain", from *pluere* "to rain"]

¹ply \'plī\ *vt* **plied; ply•ing :** to twist together ⟨*ply* yarns⟩ [Middle French *plier* "to fold", from Latin *plicare*]

²ply *n, pl* **plies :** one of the folds, thicknesses, layers, or strands of which something (as yarn or plywood) is made up

³ply *vb* **plied; ply•ing 1 a :** to use or wield diligently ⟨*ply* an ax⟩ **b :** to practice or perform diligently ⟨*ply* a trade⟩ **2 a :** to keep supplying ⟨*ply* a guest with delicacies⟩ **b :** to press or harass with something ⟨*plied* them with questions⟩ **3 :** to go or travel regularly [Middle English *plien,* short for *applien* "to apply"]

Plym•outh Rock \,plim-əth-\ *n* **:** a bird of an American breed of medium-sized single-combed domestic fowl raised for meat and eggs [from *Plymouth Rock,* on which the Pilgrims are supposed to have landed in 1620]

ply•wood \'plī-,wu̇d\ *n* **:** a structural material consisting of thin sheets of wood glued or cemented together under heat and pressure with the grains of adjacent layers arranged at right angles or at a wide angle

pneu•mat•ic \nu̇-'mat-ik, nyu̇-\ *adj* **1 :** of, relating to, or using air, wind, or other gas **2 :** moved or worked by air pressure ⟨a *pneumatic* drill⟩ **3 :** adapted for holding or inflated with compressed air ⟨*pneumatic* tires⟩ [Latin *pneumaticus,* from Greek *pneumatikos,* from *pneuma* "air, breath, spirit", from *pnein* "to breathe"] — **pneu•mat•i•cal•ly** \-'mat-i-kə-lē, -klē\ *adv*

pneu•mat•ics \nu̇-'mat-iks, nyu̇-\ *n* **:** a branch of physics that deals with the mechanical properties of gases

pneu•mo•coc•cus \,nü-mə-'käk-əs, ,nyü-\ *n, pl* **-coc•ci** \-'käk-,ī, -,sī, -,ē, -,sē\ **:** a bacterium that causes pneumonia [Greek *pneuma* "air, breath, spirit" + *kokkos* "grain, seed"] — **pneu•mo•coc•cal** \-'käk-əl\ *or* **pneu•mo•coc•cic** \-'käk-ik, -sik\ *adj*

pneu•mo•nia \nu̇-'mō-nyə, nyu̇-\ *n* **:** a disease of the lungs characterized by inflammation and congestion and caused especially by infection [Greek, from *pneumōn* "lung", alteration of *pleumōn*]

pneu•mon•ic \nu̇-'män-ik, nyu̇-\ *adj* **1 :** of or relating to the lungs **2 :** of, relating to, or affected with pneumonia

pneu•mo•tho•rax \,nü-mə-'thōr-,aks, ,nyü-, -'thȯr-\ *n* **:** a state in which gas is present in the pleural cavity and which may occur in disease or injury or be induced surgically to collapse a lung for therapeutic reasons [Greek *pneuma* "air, breath"]

¹poach \'pōch\ *vt* **:** to cook in simmering liquid ⟨*poach* an egg⟩ [Middle French *pocher,* literally, "to put into a bag", from *poche* "bag, pocket", of Germanic origin]

²poach *vb* **:** to hunt or fish unlawfully [Middle French *pocher* "to push, poke", of Germanic origin] — **poach•er** *n*

po•chard \'pō-chərd\ *n* **:** any of several large-bodied large-headed diving ducks [origin unknown]

pock \'päk\ *n* **:** a small swelling on the skin (as in chicken pox or smallpox) similar to a pimple; *also* **:** the scar it leaves [Old English *pocc*] — **pock** *vt* — **pocky** \-ē\ *adj*

¹pock•et \'päk-ət\ *n* **1 a :** a small bag carried by a person **:** PURSE **b :** a small bag open at the top or side inserted in a garment **2 :** supply of money **:** MEANS ⟨out of *pocket*⟩ **3 a :** CONTAINER **b :** a hole at the corner or side of a billiard table **4 :** a small isolated area or group: **a :** a cavity containing a deposit (as of gold or water) **b :** a small body of ore **c :** AIR POCKET [Old North French *pokete,* from *poke* "bag", of Germanic origin]

²pocket *vt* **1 a :** to put or enclose in or as if in one's pocket ⟨*pocketed* the change⟩ **b :** to take for one's own use especially dishonestly ⟨*pocket* the profits⟩ **2 :** to put up with ⟨*pocket* an insult⟩ **3 :** to set aside **:** forget about ⟨*pocket* one's pride⟩ **4 a :** to hem in **b :** to drive (a ball) into a pocket of a pool table **5 :** to cover or supply with pockets

³pocket *adj* **1 a :** small enough to be carried in the pocket ⟨a *pocket* dictionary⟩ **b :** SMALL, MINIATURE ⟨a *pocket* submarine⟩ **2 :** of or relating to money **3 a :** carried in one's pocket **b :** used for small cash outlays ⟨*pocket* money⟩

pocket billiards *n* **:** POOL 2

pock•et•book \'päk-ət-,bu̇k\ *n* **1 a :** BILLFOLD, WALLET **b :** PURSE 1 **c :** HANDBAG 2 **2 a :** financial resources **b :** economic interests

pocket edition *n* **:** a miniature form of something

pock•et•ful \'päk-ət-,fu̇l\ *n, pl* **pocketfuls** \-,fu̇lz\ *or* **pock•ets•ful** \-əts-,fu̇l\ **:** as much or as many as the pocket will contain

pocket gopher *n* **:** GOPHER 2a

pock•et•knife \'päk-ət-,nīf\ *n* **:** a knife with a folding blade to be carried in the pocket

pocket veto *n* **:** an indirect veto of a legislative bill by an executive by failing to sign it before adjournment of the legislature

pock•mark \'päk-,märk\ *n* **:** the depressed scar left by a pock especially of smallpox — **pockmark** *vt*

po•co \,pō-kō, ,pȯ-\ *adv* **:** SOMEWHAT — used to qualify an adverb or adjective used as a direction in music [Italian, "little", from Latin *paucus*]

po•co a po•co \,pō-kō-ä-'pō-kō, ,pȯ-kō-ä-'pȯ-kō\ *adv* **:** little by little **:** GRADUALLY — used as a direction in music [Italian]

po•co•sin \pə-'kōs-n\ *n* **:** an upland swamp of the coastal plain of the southeastern United States [Delaware *pâkwesen*]

pod \'päd\ *n* **1 :** a fruit or seed vessel that splits open when ripe; *esp* **:** LEGUME **2 :** any of various natural protective coverings or cases (as for grasshopper eggs) **3 :** a streamlined compartment under the wings or fuselage of an airplane used as a container (as for fuel or a jet engine) **4 :** a detachable compartment (as for instruments) on a spacecraft [probably alteration of *cod* "bag", from Old English *codd*]

-pod \,päd\ *n combining form* **:** foot **:** part resembling a foot ⟨uro*pod*⟩ [Greek *pod-, pous* "foot"]

podgy \'päj-ē\ *adj* **podg•i•er; -est :** PUDGY

po•di•a•try \pə-'dī-ə-trē\ *n* **:** the professional care and treatment of the human foot in health and disease — called also *chiropody* [Greek *pod-, pous* "foot" + English *-iatry*] — **po•di•a•trist** \-trəst\ *n*

po•di•um \'pōd-ē-əm\ *n, pl* **-di•ums** *or* **-dia** \-ē-ə\ **1 :** a low wall serving as a foundation or terrace wall: as **a :** one around the arena of an ancient amphitheater serving as a base for the tiers of seats **b :** the masonry under the stylobate of a temple **2 a :** a dais especially for an orchestral conductor **b :** LECTERN [Latin, from Greek *podion* "base", from *pod-, pous* "foot"]

Po•dunk \'pō-,dəngk\ *n* **:** a small, unimportant, and isolated town [*Podunk,* village in Massachusetts or locality in Connecticut]

po•em \'pō-əm, -im, 'pōm *also* 'pō-,em\ *n* **1 :** a composition in verse **2 :** a creation, experience, or object likened to a poem [Middle French *poeme,* from Latin *poema,* from Greek *poiēma,* from *poiein* "to make, create"]

po•e•sy \'pō-ə-zē, -sē\ *n, pl* **-sies 1 a :** a body of poems **b :** poetic form or composition **2 :** poetic inspiration [Middle French *poesie,* from Latin *poesis,* from Greek *poiēsis,* literally, "creation", from *poiein* "to make, create"]

po•et \'pō-ət\ *n* **1 :** a writer of poetry **2 :** a creative artist of great imaginative and expressive gifts and special sensitivity to the medium [Old French *poete,* from Latin *poeta,* from Greek *poiētēs* "maker, poet", from *poiein* "to make, create"]

po•et•as•ter \'pō-ət-,as-tər\ *n* **:** an inferior poet [Latin *poeta* "poet" + *-aster,* suffix denoting partial resemblance]

po•et•ess \'pō-ət-əs\ *n* **:** a woman who is a poet

po•et•ic \pō-'et-ik\ *adj* **1 a :** of, relating to, or characteristic of poets or poetry ⟨*poetic* words⟩ **b :** given to writing poetry **2 :** written in verse

po•et•i•cal \pō-'et-i-kəl\ *adj* **1 :** POETIC 1 **2 :** highly and usually splendidly imaginative **:** IDEALIZED — **po•et•i•cal•ly** \-kə-lē, -klē\ *adv* — **po•et•i•cal•ness** \-kəl-nəs\ *n*

poetic justice *n* **:** an outcome in which vice is punished and virtue rewarded usually in a manner peculiarly or ironically appropriate

poetic license *n* : LICENSE 4

po•et•ics \pō-ˈet-iks\ *n sing or pl* **1 a** : a treatise on poetry or aesthetics **b** : poetic theory or practice **2** : poetic feelings or expression

poet laureate *n, pl* **poets laureate** *or* **poet laureates 1** : a poet honored for achievement **2** : a poet appointed by a British sovereign as a member of the royal household to write poems for state occasions **3** : one regarded by a country or region as its most eminent or representative poet

po•et•ry \ˈpō-ə-trē\ *n* **1 a** : metrical writing : VERSE **b** : the productions of a poet : POEMS **2** : writing in language chosen and arranged to create a particular emotional response through meaning, sound, and rhythm **3 a** : a quality that stirs the imagination **b** : a quality of ease and grace

po•go stick \ˈpō-gō\ *n* : a pole with a strong spring at the bottom and two footrests on which a person stands and moves along the ground by jumping [from *Pogo,* a former trademark]

po•grom \ˈpō-grəm; pō-ˈgräm, pə-\ *n* : an organized slaughter of helpless people and especially of Jews [Yiddish, from Russian, literally, "devastation"]

po•gy \ˈpō-gē\ *n, pl* **pogies** : MENHADEN [of American Indian origin]

poi \ˈpȯi\ *n, pl* **poi** *or* **pois** : a Hawaiian food made of cooked taro root pounded to a paste and often fermented [Hawaiian]

poi•gnant \ˈpȯi-nyənt\ *adj* **1** : PUNGENT **2 a** (1) : painfully affecting the feelings : PIERCING ⟨*poignant* grief⟩ (2) : deeply affecting : TOUCHING **b** : SARCASTIC, INCISIVE ⟨*poignant* satire⟩ **3 a** : pleasurably exciting **b** : being to the point : APT ⟨*poignant* remarks⟩ [Middle French *poignant,* present participle of *poindre* "to prick, sting", from Latin *pungere*] — **poi•gnan•cy** \-nyən-sē\ *n* — **poi•gnant•ly** *adv*

poi•ki•lo•therm \pȯi-ˈkē-lə-ˌthərm, -ˈkil-ə-\ *n* : a cold-blooded organism [Greek *poikilos* "variegated" + *thermē* "heat"] — **poi•ki•lo•ther•mic** \ˌpȯi-kə-lō-ˈthər-mik\ *adj* — **poi•ki•lo•ther•mism** \-ˈthər-ˌmiz-əm\ *n*

poin•ci•ana \ˌpȯin-sē-ˈan-ə, ˌpwän-\ *n* : any of several showy tropical trees or shrubs of the pea family with bright orange or red flowers [De *Poinci,* 17th century governor of part of the French West Indies]

poin•set•tia \pȯin-ˈset-ē-ə, -ˈset-ə\ *n* : a showy Mexican and South American plant of the spurge family with tapering scarlet bracts that grow like petals about its small yellow flowers [Joel R. *Poinsett,* died 1851, American diplomat]

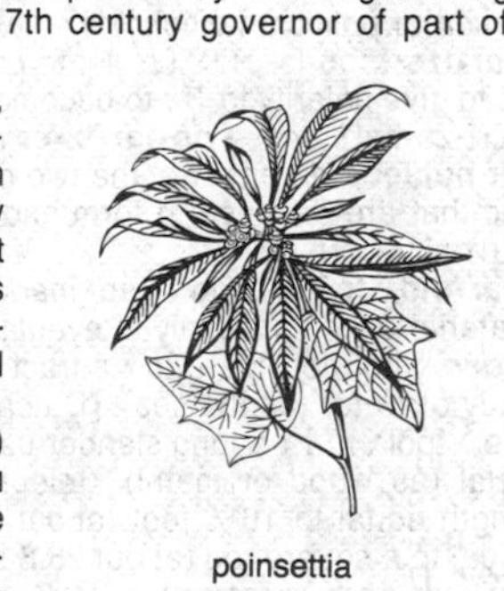

poinsettia

1point \ˈpȯint\ *n* **1 a** (1) : an individual detail : ITEM ⟨interesting *points* in the proposal⟩ (2) : a distinguishing detail : CHARACTERISTIC ⟨tact isn't my strong *point*⟩ **b** : the most important essential in a discussion or matter ⟨the *point* of the joke⟩ **c** : FORCE 1e, COGENCY **2** : an end or object to be achieved : PURPOSE ⟨there's no *point* in continuing⟩ **3 a** (1) : a geometric element of which it is postulated that at least two exist and that two suffice to determine a line (2) : a geometric element determined by an ordered set of coordinates **b** (1) : a narrowly localized place having a precisely indicated position ⟨a *point* 50 feet north of the tree⟩ (2) : a particular place : LOCALITY ⟨visited many *points* of interest⟩ **c** (1) : an exact moment ⟨at this *point* in time⟩ (2) : a time interval immediately before something indicated : VERGE ⟨at the *point* of death⟩ **d** (1) : a particular step, stage, or degree in development ⟨at the *point* where I no longer cared⟩ (2) : a definite position in a scale **4 a** : the terminal usually sharp or narrowly rounded part of something (as a fin, sword, or pencil) : TIP **b** : a weapon or tool having such a part and used for stabbing or piercing **c** : either of two metal pieces in a distributor through which the circuit is made or broken **5 a** : a projecting usually tapering piece of land or a sharp prominence **b** (1) : the tip of a projecting body part (2) *pl* : terminal bodily projections or their markings especially when differing from the rest of the body in color **6** : a short musical phrase; *esp* : a phrase in contrapuntal music **7 a** : a very small mark **b** (1) : PUNCTUATION MARK; *esp* : PERIOD (2) : DECIMAL POINT **8 a** : one of the 32 pointed marks indicating direction on a mariner's compass **b** : the difference of 11 1/4 degrees between two such adjacent points **9 a** : NEEDLEPOINT 1 **b** : lace made with a bobbin **10** : one of 12 spaces marked off on each side of a backgammon board **11** : a unit in a scale of measurement: as **a** : a unit of counting in the scoring of a game or contest **b** : a unit of academic credit **c** : a unit of about 1/72 inch (about .35 millimeters) used to measure the size of printing type **12** : the action of pointing; *esp* : the action in dancing of extending one leg so that only the tips of the toes touch the floor [Old French, "puncture, small spot, point in time or space", from Latin *punctum,* from *pungere* "to prick"] — **in point** : RELEVANT, PERTINENT ⟨a case *in point*⟩ — **to the point** : RELEVANT, PERTINENT, APT ⟨a remark that was quite *to the point*⟩

2point *vb* **1 a** : to furnish with a point **b** : to give added force, emphasis, or piquancy to ⟨*point* up a remark⟩ **2** : to scratch out the old mortar from the joints of (as a brick wall) and fill in with new material **3 a** (1) : PUNCTUATE 1 (2) : to separate (a decimal fraction) from an integer by a decimal point ⟨*point* off three decimal places⟩ **b** : to mark the vowels in (as Hebrew words) **4 a** (1) : to indicate the existence of ⟨*point* out a mistake⟩ (2) : to indicate the location of ⟨*point* a game bird⟩ **b** : to indicate the route or direction ⟨*point* to the West⟩ ⟨*point* to a house⟩ **5 a** : to turn, face, or cause to be turned in a particular direction : AIM ⟨*point* a gun⟩ **b** : to extend (a leg) in executing a point in dancing **6** : to indicate the fact or probability of something specified ⟨everything *points* to a bright future for them⟩ ⟨the evidence *points* to murder⟩

point–blank \ˈpȯint-ˈblangk\ *adj* **1 a** : marked by no noticeable drop below initial horizontal line of flight **b** : so close to a target that a missile fired will travel in a straight line to the mark ⟨fired from *point-blank* range⟩ **2** : DIRECT, BLUNT ⟨a *point-blank* refusal⟩ — **point–blank** *adv*

pointe \ˈpwa^{n}t, ˈpwa^{n}nt\ *n* : a position of balance in ballet on the extreme tip of the toe [French, literally, "point"]

point•ed \ˈpȯint-əd\ *adj* **1 a** : having a point **b** : having a crown tapering to a point ⟨the *pointed* arch of Gothic architecture⟩ **2 a** : being to the point : TERSE **b** : aimed at a particular person or group ⟨*pointed* remarks⟩ **3** : CONSPICUOUS 1, MARKED ⟨*pointed* indifference⟩ — **point•ed•ly** *adv* — **point•ed•ness** *n*

point•er \ˈpȯint-ər\ *n* **1 a** : one that points out; *esp* : a rod used to direct attention **b** *pl, cap* : the two stars in Ursa Major a line through which points to the North Star **2** : a large strong slender smooth-haired hunting dog that hunts by scent and indicates the presence of game by pointing **3** : a useful suggestion or hint : TIP ⟨gave a few *pointers* on how to study⟩

poin•til•lism \ˈpwa^n-tē-ˌiz-əm, ˈpwa^{n}n-\ *n* : the practice or technique of applying dots of color to a surface so that from a distance they blend together [French *pointillisme,* from *pointiller* "to stipple", from *point* "spot, point"] — **poin•til•list** \-tē-əst\ *n* — **poin•til•lis•tic** \ˌpwa^n-tē-ˈis-tik, ˌpwa^{n}n-\ *adj*

point•less \ˈpȯint-ləs\ *adj* **1** : having no point **2** : lacking meaning : SENSELESS ⟨a *pointless* remark⟩ **3** : INEFFECTIVE ⟨a *pointless* effort to help⟩ — **point•less•ly** *adv* — **point•less•ness** *n*

point of honor : a matter seriously affecting one's honor

point of view : a way of thinking about or looking at things : STANDPOINT

1poise \ˈpȯiz\ *vb* **1 a** : BALANCE; *esp* : to hold or carry in equilibrium **b** : to hold or be supported or suspended without motion in a steady position ⟨a bird *poised* in the air⟩ **2** : to hold or carry (the head) in a particular way **3** : to put into readiness : BRACE ⟨*poised* for action⟩ [Middle French *pois-,* stem of *peser* "to ponder", from Latin *pensare,* from *pensus,* past participle of *pendere* "to weigh"]

2poise *n* **1** : BALANCE 4a, EQUILIBRIUM **2 a** (1) : self-possessed composure, assurance, and dignity (2) : peaceful state : CALM **b** : a particular way of carrying oneself : BEARING

poised \ˈpȯizd\ *adj* : showing an easy composure in bearing and manner

1poi•son \ˈpȯiz-n\ *n* **1 a** : a substance that through its chemical action is able to kill, injure, or impair an organism **b** (1) : something destructive or harmful (2) : an object of aversion or abhorrence **2** : a substance that inhibits the activity of another

\ə\ **abut**	\au̇\ **out**	\i\ **tip**	\ȯ\ **saw**	\u̇\ **foot**
\ər\ **further**	\ch\ **chin**	\ī\ **life**	\ȯi\ **coin**	\y\ **yet**
\a\ **mat**	\e\ **pet**	\j\ **job**	\th\ **thin**	\yü\ **few**
\ā\ **take**	\ē\ **easy**	\ng\ **sing**	\t͟h\ **this**	\yu̇\ **cure**
\ä\ **cot, cart**	\g\ **go**	\ō\ **bone**	\ü\ **food**	\zh\ **vision**

substance or the course of a reaction or process ⟨a catalyst *poison*⟩ [Old French, "drink, poisonous drink, poison", from Latin *potio* "drink, potion"]

²poison *vb* **poi•soned**; **poi•son•ing** \ˈpȯiz-ning, -n-ing\ **1 a** : to injure or kill with poison **b** : to treat, taint, or impregnate with poison ⟨*poisoned* the air with its fumes⟩ **2** : to exert a baneful influence on : CORRUPT ⟨*poisoned* their minds⟩ **3** : to inhibit the activity, course, or occurrence of — **poi•son•er** \ˈpȯiz-nər, -n-ər\ *n*

³poison *adj* **1** : POISONOUS, VENOMOUS ⟨a *poison* plant⟩ ⟨a *poison* tongue⟩ **2** : impregnated with poison ⟨a *poison* arrow⟩

poison gas *n* : a poisonous gas or a liquid or a solid giving off poisonous vapors designed (as in chemical warfare) to kill, injure, or disable by inhalation or contact

poison hemlock *n* : a biennial poisonous herb of the carrot family with finely divided leaves and white flowers

poison ivy *n* **1** : a usually climbing plant of the sumac family mostly with three leaflets, greenish flowers and berries, and foliage and stems that when bruised and touched may cause an itching rash on the skin **2** : a rash caused by poison ivy

poison ivy 1

poison oak *n* : a slender woody plant of the sumac family closely resembling poison ivy and causing a similar rash but differing in not climbing or producing aerial roots

poi•son•ous \ˈpȯiz-nəs, -n-əs\ *adj* : having the properties or effects of poison : VENOMOUS — **poi•son•ous•ly** *adv*

poison sumac *n* : a swamp shrub of the sumac family that is related to poison ivy and causes a similar rash but has compound leaves with 7 to 13 leaflets

¹poke \ˈpōk\ *n, chiefly Midland* : BAG 1a, SACK [Old North French, of Germanic origin]

²poke *vb* **1 a** (1) : PROD, JAB ⟨*poked* me in the ribs⟩ (2) : to urge or stir by prodding or jabbing ⟨*poke* up the fire⟩ **b** (1) : PIERCE 1 (2) : to produce by piercing or jabbing ⟨*poke* a hole⟩ **c** : HIT 1a, PUNCH **2 a** : to cause to project ⟨*poked* its head out of the hole⟩ **b** (1) : to thrust forward so as to intrude or meddle ⟨don't *poke* your nose into our affairs⟩ (2) : MEDDLE ⟨*poking* about in other people's business⟩ **3** : to look about or through something without system : RUMMAGE **4** : to move or act slowly or aimlessly : DAWDLE ⟨*poke* along⟩ [Middle English *poken*] — **poke fun at** : RIDICULE, MOCK

³poke *n* **1 a** : a quick thrust : JAB **b** : a blow with the fist : PUNCH **2** : a projecting brim on the front of a woman's bonnet

poke•ber•ry \ˈpōk-ˌber-ē\ *n* : the berry of the pokeweed; *also* : POKEWEED

poke bonnet *n* : a woman's bonnet with a projecting brim at the front

¹pok•er \ˈpō-kər\ *n* : one that pokes; *esp* : a metal rod for stirring a fire

²po•ker \ˈpō-kər\ *n* : any of several card games in which players bet on the value of their hands [probably from French *poque,* a card game similar to poker]

poker face *n* : a face that does not reveal what a person thinks or feels [from the need of poker players to conceal the quality of their hands] — **po•ker–faced** \ˌpō-kər-ˈfāst\ *adj*

poke•weed \ˈpō-ˌkwēd\ *n* : an American perennial herb with spikes of white flowers, dark purple juicy berries, a poisonous root, and young shoots sometimes used as potherbs [*poke,* of American Indian origin]

poky *or* **pok•ey** \ˈpō-kē\ *adj* **pok•i•er**; **-est** **1** : being small and cramped ⟨a *poky* room⟩ **2** : SHABBY, DULL ⟨a *poky* way of writing⟩ **3** : annoyingly slow ⟨a *poky* horse⟩ [²*poke*] — **pok•i•ly** \-kə-lē\ *adv* — **pok•i•ness** \-kē-nəs\ *n*

Po•land Chi•na \ˌpō-lənd-ˈchī-nə, -lən-\ *n* : any of a breed of large white-marked black swine adapted to converting feed into fat [*Poland,* Europe + *China,* Asia]

po•lar \ˈpō-lər\ *adj* **1** : of or relating to a geographical pole or the region around it; *also* : coming from or having the characteristics of such a region **2 a** : of or relating to one or more poles (as of a magnet) **b** : having a dipole or characterized by molecules having dipoles ⟨a *polar* molecule⟩ **3** : serving as a guide ⟨a *polar* idea⟩ **4** : diametrically opposite **5** : PIVOTAL 2, CRUCIAL ⟨*polar* events⟩

polar bear *n* : a large creamy-white bear of arctic regions

polar bear

polar body *n* : a cell that separates from an oocyte during meiosis and that contains a nucleus produced in the first or second meiotic division but little cytoplasm

polar circle *n* : one of the two parallels of latitude each at a distance from a pole of the earth equal to about 23 degrees 27 minutes

polar coordinate *n* : either of two numbers that locate a point in a plane by its distance from a fixed point and the angle a line joining the two points makes with a fixed line

Po•lar•is \pə-ˈlar-əs, -ˈlär-\ *n* : NORTH STAR [New Latin, from *polaris* "polar"]

po•lari•scope \pō-ˈlar-ə-ˌskōp\ *n* : an instrument for studying the properties of substances in polarized light

po•lar•i•ty \pō-ˈlar-ət-ē, pə-\ *n, pl* **-ties** **1** : the quality or condition of being polar : having poles **2** : attraction toward a particular object or in a specific direction **3** : the particular state either positive or negative with reference to magnetic or electrical poles **4 a** : diametrical opposition **b** : an instance of diametrical opposition

po•lar•iza•tion \ˌpō-lə-rə-ˈzā-shən\ *n* **1** : the action of polarizing or state of being polarized: as **a** : the action of affecting radiation (as light) so that the vibrations of the wave assume a definite direction (as in one plane) **b** : the deposition of gas on one or both electrodes of an electrolytic cell increasing the resistance and setting up a counter electromotive force **c** : MAGNETIZATION **2 a** : division into two opposites ⟨*polarization* of views⟩ **b** : concentration about opposing extremes ⟨*polarization* of political factions⟩

po•lar•ize \ˈpō-lə-ˌrīz\ *vb* **1** : to cause to undergo polarization **2** : to give polarity to **3** : to become polarized — **po•lar•iz•able** \-ˌrī-zə-bəl\ *adj* — **po•lar•iz•er** *n*

polar nucleus *n* : either of the two nuclei of a seed plant embryo sac that are destined to form endosperm — compare DOUBLE FERTILIZATION

Po•lar•oid \ˈpō-lə-ˌrȯid\ *trademark* — used for a light-polarizing material used especially in eyeglasses to prevent glare

pol•der \ˈpōl-dər, ˈpäl-\ *n* : a tract of low land reclaimed from a body of water (as the sea) [Dutch]

¹pole \ˈpōl\ *n* **1** : a long slender usually cylindrical piece of material (as wood or metal) ⟨telephone *poles*⟩ **2 a** : a unit of length equal to 16½ feet (about 5 meters) **b** : a unit of area equal to a square rod (about 25.3 square meters) **3** : the inside position on a racetrack [Old English *pāl* "stake, pole", from Latin *palus* "stake"]

²pole *vb* **1** : to act upon, impel, or push with a pole **2 a** : to propel a boat with a pole **b** : to use ski poles to gain speed — **pol•er** *n*

³pole *n* **1** : either end of an axis of a sphere and especially of the earth's axis **2 a** : either of two related opposites **b** : a point of guidance or attraction **3 a** : one of the two terminals of an electric cell, battery, or dynamo **b** : one of two or more regions in a magnetized body at which the magnetism is concentrated **4** : either end of the spindle-shaped structure formed in dividing cells and toward which the chromosomes move [Latin *polus,* from Greek *polos* "pivot, pole"]

Pole \ˈpōl\ *n* **1** : a native or inhabitant of Poland **2** : a person of Polish descent [German, of Slavic origin]

pole•ax \ˈpō-ˌlaks\ *n* : a battle-ax with a short handle and often with a hook or point opposite the blade [Middle English *pollax,* from *polle* "poll" + *ax*]

pole bean *n* : a cultivated bean having long internodes and twining stems and usually trained to grow upright on supports

pole•cat \ˈpōl-ˌkat\ *n, pl* **polecats** *or* **polecat** **1** : a European flesh-eating mammal of which the ferret is considered a domesticated variety **2** : SKUNK [Middle English *polcat,* probably from Middle French *poul, pol* "cock" + Middle English *cat;* probably from its preying on poultry]

po•lem•ic \pə-ˈlem-ik\ *n* **1 a** : an aggressive attack on or refutation of the opinions or principles of another **b :** the art or practice of disputation or controversy — usually used in pl. **2 :** an aggressive controversialist **:** DISPUTANT **3** *pl* **:** the branch of Christian theology devoted to the refutation of errors [French *polémique,* derived from Greek *polemikos* "warlike, hostile", from *polemos* "war" — **polemic** *or* **po•lem•i•cal** \-'lem-i-kəl\ *adj* — **po•lem•i•cal•ly** \-i-kə-lē, -klē\ *adv* — **po•lem•i•cist** \-'lem-ə-səst\ *n*

pole•star \'pōl-ˌstär\ *n* **1 :** NORTH STAR **2 a :** a directing principle **:** GUIDE **b :** a center of attraction

pole vault *n* **:** a field event consisting of a vault for height over a crossbar with the aid of a pole — **pole-vault** \'pōl-ˌvȯlt\ *vi* — **pole-vault•er** *n*

1po•lice \pə-'lēs\ *n, pl* **police 1 :** the department of government the members of which constitute the police force **2 :** POLICE FORCE **3 :** a private organization resembling a police force ⟨railroad *police*⟩ [Middle French, "government", from Late Latin *politia,* from Greek *politeia,* from *politeuein* "to be a citizen, engage in political activity", from *politēs* "citizen", from *polis* "city, state"]

2police *vt* **1 :** to control, regulate, or keep in order by use or as if by use of police **2 :** to make clean and put in order **:** clean up ⟨*police* an area⟩ **3 :** to supervise the operation, execution, or administration of

police action *n* **:** a military action undertaken without formal declaration of war by regular forces against persons held to be violators of international peace and order

police court *n* **:** a court having jurisdiction over various minor offenses and authority to send cases involving serious offenses to a superior court

police dog *n* **1 :** a dog trained to assist police **2 :** GERMAN SHEPHERD

police force *n* **:** a body of trained officers entrusted by a government with maintenance of public peace and order, enforcement of laws, and prevention and detection of crime

po•lice•man \pə-'lē-smən\ *n* **:** a male police officer

police officer *n* **:** a member of a police force

police power *n* **:** the inherent power of a government to exercise reasonable control over persons and property within its jurisdiction in the interest of the general security, health, safety, morals, and welfare

police reporter *n* **:** a reporter assigned to cover police news (as crimes, accidents, and arrests)

police state *n* **:** a state in which the social, economic, and political activities of the people are under the arbitrary power of the government often acting through a secret police force

police station *n* **:** the headquarters of the police for a particular locality

po•lice•wom•an \pə-'lē-ˌswu̇m-ən\ *n* **:** a female police officer

1pol•i•cy \'päl-ə-sē\ *n, pl* **-cies 1 a :** prudence or wisdom in the management of affairs **:** SAGACITY **b :** management or procedure based primarily on material interest **2 :** a frame of reference or a set of principles or rules determining what and how things are done by a person or group ⟨it's our *policy* not to give refunds⟩ [Middle French *policie* "government, regulation", from Late Latin *politia*]

2policy *n, pl* **-cies 1 :** a writing embodying a contract of insurance **2 a :** a daily lottery in which participants bet that certain numbers will be drawn **b :** NUMBER 8 [Middle French *police* "certificate", from Italian *polizza,* from Medieval Latin *apodixa* "receipt", from Greek *apodeixis* "proof", from *apodeiknynai* "to demonstrate"]

pol•i•cy•hold•er \-ˌhōl-dər\ *n* **:** one granted an insurance policy

po•lio \'pō-lē-ˌō\ *n* **:** POLIOMYELITIS — **polio** *adj*

po•lio•my•e•li•tis \ˌpō-lē-ˌō-ˌmī-ə-'līt-əs\ *n* **:** an acute infectious virus disease marked by inflammation of nerve cells in the spinal cord accompanied by fever and often paralysis and wasting of muscles — called also *infantile paralysis* [Greek *polios* "gray" + *myelos* "marrow"] — **po•lio•my•e•lit•ic** \-'lit-ik\ *adj*

po•lio•vi•rus \'pō-lē-ō-ˌvī-rəs\ *n* **:** a virus that causes human poliomyelitis and occurs in several distinct forms

1pol•ish \'päl-ish\ *vb* **1 :** to make smooth and glossy usually by friction ⟨*polish* furniture⟩ **2 :** to smooth or refine in manners or condition **3 :** to bring to a highly developed, finished, or refined state **:** PERFECT ⟨*polish* a technique⟩ [Old French *poliss-,* stem of *polir* "to polish", from Latin *polire*] **syn** see BURNISH — **pol•ish•er** *n*

2polish *n* **1 a :** a smooth glossy surface **:** LUSTER **b :** REFINEMENT 2, CULTURE **c :** a state of high development or refinement **2 :** the action or process of polishing **3 :** a preparation used in polishing

1Pol•ish \'pō-lish\ *adj* **:** of, relating to, or characteristic of Poland, the Poles, or Polish

2Polish *n* **:** the Slavic language of the Poles

polish off *vt* **:** to dispose of rapidly or completely

po•lit•bu•ro \'päl-ət-ˌbyu̇r-ō, 'pō-lət-, pə-'lit-\ *n* **:** the principal policy-making body of a Communist party [Russian *politbyuro,* from *politicheskoe byuro* "political bureau"]

po•lite \pə-'līt\ *adj* **1 :** of, relating to, or having the characteristics of advanced culture ⟨customs of *polite* society⟩ **2 a :** showing or characterized by correct social usage ⟨*polite* forms of address⟩ **b :** marked by consideration, tact, deference, or courtesy **:** COURTEOUS [Latin *politus,* from *polire* "to polish"] **syn** see CIVIL — **po•lite•ly** *adv* — **po•lite•ness** *n*

po•li•tesse \ˌpäl-ē-'tes, ˌpȯ-li-\ *n* **:** formal politeness [French]

pol•i•tic \'päl-ə-ˌtik\ *adj* **1 :** characterized by shrewdness in managing, contriving, or dealing **2 :** sagacious in promoting a policy **3 :** shrewdly tactful ⟨a *politic* answer⟩ [Middle French *politique* "political", from Latin *politicus,* from Greek *politikos,* from *politēs* "citizen", from *polis* "citizen"] **syn** see EXPEDIENT

po•lit•i•cal \pə-'lit-i-kəl\ *adj* **1 :** of or relating to government, a government, or the conduct of government **2 :** of or relating to politics **3 :** organized in governmental terms ⟨*political* units⟩ **4 :** involving or concerned with acts against a government or political system ⟨*political* crimes⟩ ⟨*political* police⟩ — **po•lit•i•cal•ly** \-kə-lē, -klē\ *adv*

political economy *n* **:** a modern social science dealing with the interrelationship of political and economic processes — **political economist** *n*

political science *n* **:** a social science concerned chiefly with the description and analysis of political institutions and processes — **political scientist** *n*

pol•i•ti•cian \ˌpäl-ə-'tish-ən\ *n* **1 :** one experienced in the art or science of government; *esp* **:** one actively conducting governmental affairs **2 :** one engaged in party politics as a profession

pol•i•tick \'päl-ə-ˌtik\ *vi* **:** to engage in political discussion or activity — **pol•i•tick•er** *n*

po•lit•i•co \pə-'lit-i-ˌkō\ *n, pl* **-cos** *also* **-coes :** POLITICIAN 2 [Italian *politico* or Spanish *político,* derived from Latin *politicus* "political"]

pol•i•tics \'päl-ə-ˌtiks\ *n sing or pl* **1 a :** the art or science of government **b :** the art or science of guiding or influencing governmental policy **c :** the art or science of winning and holding control over a government **2 a :** political affairs or business; *esp* **:** competition between groups or individuals for power and leadership **b :** political life especially as a profession **3 :** political opinions

pol•i•ty \'päl-ət-ē\ *n, pl* **-ties 1 :** political organization **2 :** a form of political organization ⟨a republican *polity*⟩ **3 :** a politically organized unit **4 :** the form of government of a religious denomination

pol•ka \'pōl-kə\ *n* **1 :** a vivacious couple dance of Bohemian origin with three steps and a hop in duple time **2 :** a lively Bohemian dance tune in 2/4 time [Czech, from Polish *Polka* "Polish woman"] — **polka** *vi*

pol•ka dot \'pō-kə-ˌdät\ *n* **:** a dot in a pattern of regularly distributed dots in textile design — **polka-dot** *or* **polka-dot•ted** \-dät-əd\ *adj*

1poll \'pōl\ *n* **1 a :** HEAD 1 **b :** the prominent hairy top or back of the head **c :** NAPE **2 :** the broad or flat end of a hammer or similar tool **3 a :** a casting or recording of votes **b :** a place where votes are cast or recorded — usually used in pl. **4 a :** a questioning of persons to obtain information or opinions **b :** the information so obtained [Low German *polle*]

2poll *vb* **1 a :** to cut off or cut short the hair or wool of **:** CROP, SHEAR **b :** to cut off or cut short (as wool) **2 a :** to receive and record the votes of **b :** to request each member of to declare his or her vote individually ⟨*poll* a jury⟩ **3 :** to receive (as votes) in an election **4 :** to question or canvass in a poll **5 :** to cast one's vote at a poll — **poll•ee** \pō-ˈlē\ *n* — **poll•er** \ˈpō-lər\ *n*

pol•lack *or* **pol•lock** \ˈpäl-ək\ *n, pl* **pollack** *or* **pollock :** a commercially important north Atlantic food fish resembling the related cods but darker [Scottish *podlok*]

polled \ˈpōld\ *adj* **:** having no horns

pol•len \ˈpäl-ən\ *n* **:** a mass of microspores in a seed plant that usually appears as a fine yellow dust — compare POLLEN GRAIN, POLLEN TUBE [Latin *pollin-, pollen* "fine flour"]

pollen basket *n* **:** a flat or hollow area bordered with stiff hairs on the hind leg of a bee in which it carries pollen

pollen grain *n* **:** one of the granular microspores in pollen that give rise to the male gametophyte of a seed plant

pol•len•iz•er \ˈpäl-ə-ˌnī-zər\ *n* **1 :** a plant that is a source of pollen **2 :** POLLINATOR 1

pollen sac *n* **:** one of the pouches of a seed plant anther in which pollen is formed

pollen tube *n* **:** a tube formed by the pollen grain that passes down the style and conveys the sperm nuclei to the embryo sac of a flower

pol•lex \ˈpäl-ˌeks\ *n, pl* **pol•li•ces** \ˈpäl-ə-ˌsēz\ **:** THUMB 1 [Latin, "thumb, big toe"]

pol•li•nate \ˈpäl-ə-ˌnāt\ *vt* **:** to place pollen on the stigma of — **pol•li•na•tion** \ˌpäl-ə-ˈnā-shən\ *n*

pol•li•na•tor \ˈpäl-ə-ˌnāt-ər\ *n* **1 :** an agent that pollinates flowers **2 :** POLLENIZER 1

pol•li•no•sis *also* **pol•len•osis** \ˌpäl-ə-ˈnō-səs\ *n* **:** an acute recurrent allergic respiratory disorder caused by sensitivity to particular pollens

pol•li•wog *or* **pol•ly•wog** \ˈpäl-ē-ˌwäg, -ˌwȯg\ *n* **:** TADPOLE [Middle English *polwygle*, probably from *pol* "poll" + *wiglen* "to wiggle"]

poll•ster \ˈpōl-stər\ *n* **:** one that conducts a poll or compiles data obtained by a poll

poll tax *n* **:** a tax of a fixed amount per person sometimes levied as a requirement for voting

pol•lu•tant \pə-ˈlüt-nt\ *n* **:** something that pollutes

pol•lute \pə-ˈlüt\ *vt* **:** to make impure; *esp* **:** to contaminate (as a natural resource) with man-made waste ⟨industrial wastes *polluted* the river⟩ [Latin *pollutus*, past participle of *polluere* "to pollute"] — **pol•lut•er** *n* — **pol•lu•tion** \pə-ˈlü-shən\ *n*

Pol•lux \ˈpäl-əks\ *n* **:** a first-magnitude star in the constellation Gemini [*Pollux*, twin of Castor]

Pol•ly•an•na \ˌpäl-ē-ˈan-ə\ **:** one characterized by unshakable optimism and a tendency to find good in everything [*Pollyanna*, heroine of the novel *Pollyanna* (1913) by Eleanor Porter]

po•lo \ˈpō-lō\ *n* **1 :** a game played by teams of players on horseback using mallets with long flexible handles to drive a wooden ball **2 :** WATER POLO [of Tibetan origin] — **po•lo•ist** \ˈpō-lə-wəst\ *n*

polo coat *n* **:** a tailored casual overcoat made especially of camel's hair

po•lo•naise \ˌpäl-ə-ˈnāz, ˌpō-lə-\ *n* **1 :** an elaborate 18th century overdress with short-sleeved fitted waist and draped cutaway overskirt **2 a :** a stately 19th century Polish processional dance **b :** music for this dance in moderate 3/4 time [French, from *polonais* "Polish"]

po•lo•ni•um \pə-ˈlō-nē-əm\ *n* **:** a radioactive metallic chemical element that emits a helium nucleus to form an isotope of lead — see ELEMENT table [New Latin, from Medieval Latin *Polonia* "Poland"]

polo shirt *n* **:** a close-fitting knitted cotton pullover shirt with a turnover collar or round banded neck

pol•ter•geist \ˈpōl-tər-ˌgīst\ *n* **:** a noisy usually mischievous ghost held to be responsible for unexplained noises (as rappings) [German, from *poltern* "to knock" + *geist* "spirit"]

1pol•troon \päl-ˈtrün\ *n* **:** a spiritless coward **:** CRAVEN [Middle French *poultron*, from Italian *poltrone*, from *poltro* "colt", derived from Latin *pullus* "young of an animal"]

2poltroon *adj* **:** characterized by complete cowardice

poly- *combining form* **1 a :** many **:** several **:** much **:** MULTI- ⟨*polygyny*⟩ **b :** excessive **:** HYPER- **2 a :** containing more than one of a (specified) substance ⟨*poly*nucleotide⟩ **b :** polymeric ⟨*poly*ethylene⟩ [Greek, from *polys*]

See *poly-* and 2d element

polyatomic	**polycultural**	**polydirectional**
polycentric	**polydimensional**	**polydrug**
polyethnic	**polymetallic**	**polyrhythmic**
polyfunctional	**polymodal**	**polysemantic**
polygrooved	**polyracial**	**polysensory**

poly•an•dry \ˈpäl-ē-ˌan-drē\ *n* **:** the practice of having more than one husband or male mate at one time — compare POLYGYNY [Greek *polyandros* "having many husbands", from *poly-* + *andr-, anēr* "man, husband"] — **poly•an•drous** \ˌpäl-ē-ˈan-drəs\ *adj*

poly•chaete \ˈpäl-i-ˌkēt\ *n* **:** any of a class (Polychaeta) of chiefly marine annelid worms that usually have paired segmental appendages [derived from Greek *polychaitēs* "having much hair", from *poly-* + *chaitē* "long hair"] — **polychaete** *adj*

poly•chlo•ri•nat•ed biphenyl \ˌpäl-i-ˈklōr-ə-ˌnāt-əd-, -ˈklȯr-\ *n* **:** any of several compounds that have various industrial applications and are poisonous environmental pollutants which tend to accumulate in animal tissues

poly•chro•mat•ic \ˌpäl-i-krō-ˈmat-ik\ *adj* **:** showing a variety or a change of colors **:** MULTICOLORED

poly•chrome \ˈpäl-i-ˌkrōm\ *adj* **:** relating to, made with, or decorated in several colors ⟨*polychrome* pottery⟩

poly•clin•ic \ˌpäl-i-ˈklin-ik\ *n* **:** a clinic or hospital treating diseases of many sorts

poly•dac•ty•ly \ˌpäl-i-ˈdak-tə-lē\ *n* **:** the condition of having several to many and especially abnormally many toes or fingers [*poly-* + Greek *daktylos* "finger, toe"] — **poly•dac•tyl** \-ˈdak-tl\ *adj or n* — **poly•dac•ty•lous** \-tə-ləs\ *adj*

poly•es•ter \ˈpäl-ē-ˌes-tər\ *n* **:** a complex ester formed by polymerization or condensation and used especially in making fibers or plastics

poly•eth•yl•ene \ˌpäl-ē-ˈeth-ə-ˌlēn\ *n* **:** one of various lightweight plastics resistant to chemicals and moisture that are used especially in packaging and electrical insulation

po•lyg•a•mous \pə-ˈlig-ə-məs\ *adj* **1 :** of, relating to, or being a marriage form in which a spouse of either sex has more than one mate at one time **2 :** having more than one spouse or mate at one time — **po•lyg•a•mist** \-məst\ *n* — **po•lyg•a•mous•ly** *adv* — **po•lyg•a•my** \-mē\ *n*

poly•gene \ˈpäl-i-ˌjēn\ *n* **:** any of a group of genes that collectively control or modify the expression of a particular character — **poly•gen•ic** \ˌpäl-i-ˈjē-nik\ *adj*

poly•glot \ˈpäl-i-ˌglät\ *adj* **1 :** speaking or writing several languages **2 :** containing matter in or derived from several languages [Greek *polyglōttos*, from *poly-* + *glōtta* "language"] — **polyglot** *n*

poly•gon \ˈpäl-i-ˌgän\ *n* **:** a closed plane figure bounded by straight lines — **po•lyg•o•nal** \pə-ˈlig-ən-l\ *adj*

poly•graph \ˈpäl-i-ˌgraf\ *n* **:** an instrument for recording tracings of several different pulsations simultaneously; *also* **:** LIE DETECTOR — **poly•graph•ic** \ˌpäl-i-ˈgraf-ik\ *adj*

po•lyg•y•ny \pə-ˈlij-ə-nē\ *n* **:** the practice of having more than one wife or female mate at one time — compare POLYANDRY [*poly-* + Greek *gynē* "woman, wife"] — **po•lyg•y•nous** \-nəs\ *adj*

poly•he•dron \ˌpäl-i-ˈhē-drən\ *n, pl* **-drons** *or* **-dra** \-drə\ **:** a solid formed by plane faces — **poly•he•dral** \-drəl\ *adj*

poly•math \ˈpäl-i-ˌmath\ *n* **:** one of encyclopedic learning [Greek *polymathēs* "very learned", from *poly-* + *manthanein* "to learn"]

poly•mer \ˈpäl-ə-mər\ *n* **:** a chemical compound or mixture of compounds that is formed by polymerization and consists essentially of repeating structural units [back-formation from *polymeric*, from Greek *polymerēs* "having many parts", from *poly-* + *meros* "part"] — **poly•mer•ic** \ˌpäl-ə-ˈmer-ik\ *adj*

po•ly•mer•iza•tion \pə-ˌlim-ə-rə-ˈzā-shən, ˌpäl-ə-mə-rə-\ *n* **:** a chemical reaction in which two or more small molecules combine to form larger molecules — **po•ly•mer•ize** \pə-ˈlim-ə-ˌrīz, ˈpäl-ə-mə-\ *vb*

poly•morph \ˈpäl-i-ˌmȯrf\ *n* **:** a polymorphic organism; *also* **:** one of the several forms of such an organism

poly•mor•phic \ˌpäl-i-ˈmȯr-fik\ *or* **poly•mor•phous** \-fəs\ *adj* **:** having, assuming, or occurring in various forms, characters, or styles ⟨a *polymorphic* butterfly⟩ — **poly•mor•phism** \-ˌfiz-əm\ *n*

poly•mor•pho•nu•cle•ar \-ˌmȯr-fə-ˈnü-klē-ər, -ˈnyü-\ *adj* **:** having the nucleus complexly lobed ⟨*polymorphonuclear* leukocytes⟩ — **polymorphonuclear** *n*

Poly•ne•sian \ˌpäl-ə-ˈnē-zhən, -shən\ *n* **1 :** a member of any of the native peoples of Polynesia **2 :** a group of Austronesian languages spoken in Polynesia — **Polynesian** *adj*

poly•no•mi•al \ˌpäl-i-ˈnō-mē-əl\ *n* **:** a sum of two or more algebraic terms each of which consists of a constant multiplied by one or more variables raised to a nonnegative integral power ⟨$6 + 3x + 5x^2$ is a *polynomial*⟩ **[***poly-* + *-nomial* (as in *binomial*)**]** — **polynomial** *adj*

polynomial equation *n* **:** an equation in which one side is a polynomial and the other side is a constant, monomial, or polynomial

poly•nu•cle•o•tide \ˌpäl-i-ˈnü-klē-ə-ˌtīd, -ˈnyü-\ *n* **:** a polymeric chain of nucleotides

pol•yp \ˈpäl-əp\ *n* **1 :** a coelenterate (as a sea anemone) having a hollow cylindrical body closed and attached at one end and opening at the other by a central mouth surrounded by tentacles armed with minute stinging organs **2 :** a tumor that often has a stalk and occurs especially in the lower intestine **[**Middle French *polype* "octopus, nasal tumor", from Latin *polypus,* from Greek *polypous,* from *poly-* + *pous* "foot"**]** — **pol•yp•oid** \ˈpäl-ə-ˌpȯid\ *adj*

poly•pep•tide \ˌpäl-i-ˈpep-ˌtīd\ *n* **:** a chain of amino acids that contributes to the structure of a protein

poly•phase \ˈpäl-i-ˌfāz\ *or* **poly•pha•sic** \ˌpäl-i-ˈfā-zik\ *adj* **:** having or producing two or more phases ⟨a *polyphase* machine⟩ ⟨a *polyphase* current⟩

po•lyph•o•ny \pə-ˈlif-ə-nē\ *n* **:** music consisting of two or more independent but harmonious melodies **[**Greek *polyphōnia* "variety of tones", derived from *poly-* + *phōnē* "voice"**]** — **poly•phon•ic** \ˌpäl-i-ˈfän-ik\ *adj* — **poly•phon•i•cal•ly** \-i-kə-lē, -klē\ *adv*

poly•ploid \ˈpäl-i-ˌplȯid\ *adj* **:** having or being a chromosome number that is a multiple greater than two of the basic haploid chromosome number **[***poly-* + *-ploid* (as in *diploid*)**]** — **polyploid** *n* — **poly•ploi•dy** \-ˌplȯid-ē\ *n*

poly•po•dy \ˈpäl-ə-ˌpōd-ē\ *n, pl* **-dies :** a widely distributed fern with creeping rhizomes and usually deeply cleft fronds **[**Latin *polypodium,* from Greek *polypodion,* from *poly-* + *pod-, pous* "foot"**]**

poly•sac•cha•ride \ˌpäl-i-ˈsak-ə-ˌrīd\ *n* **:** a carbohydrate that can be decomposed by hydrolysis into two or more molecules of monosaccharides; *esp* **:** one of the more complex carbohydrates (as cellulose, starch, or glycogen)

poly•sty•rene \-ˈstīr-ˌēn\ *n* **:** a clear rigid plastic of good physical and electrical insulating properties

poly•syl•lab•ic \ˌpäl-i-sə-ˈlab-ik\ *adj* **1 :** having more than three syllables **2 :** using polysyllabic words — **poly•syl•lab•i•cal•ly** \-ˈlab-i-kə-lē, -klē\ *adv* — **poly•syl•la•ble** \ˈpäl-i-ˌsil-ə-bəl, ˌpäl-i-ˈ\ *n*

poly•syn•de•ton \ˌpäl-i-ˈsin-də-ˌtän\ *n* **:** repetition of conjunctions in close succession (as in "paper and pencils and books") **[**Late Greek, neuter of *polysyndetos* "using many conjunctions", from Greek *poly-* + *syndetos* "bound together"**]**

poly•tech•nic \ˌpäl-i-ˈtek-nik\ *adj* **:** relating to or devoted to instruction in many technical arts or applied sciences ⟨a *polytechnic* school⟩ **[**French *polytechnique,* from Greek polytechnos "skilled in many arts", from *poly-* + *technē* "art"**]** — **polytechnic** *n*

poly•the•ism \ˈpäl-i-ˌthē-ˌiz-əm\ *n* **:** belief in or worship of more than one god — **poly•the•ist** \-ˌthē-əst\ *adj or n* — **poly•the•is•tic** \ˌpäl-i-thē-ˈis-tik\ *adj*

poly•to•nal•i•ty \ˌpäl-i-tō-ˈnal-ət-ē\ *n* **:** the simultaneous use of two or more musical keys — **poly•ton•al** \-ˈtōn-l\ *adj*

poly•un•sat•u•rat•ed \ˌpäl-ē-ˌən-ˈsach-ə-ˌrāt-əd\ *adj* **:** rich in unsaturated chemical bonds ⟨a *polyunsaturated* oil⟩ ⟨*polyunsaturated* fats⟩

poly•va•lent \ˌpäl-i-ˈvā-lənt\ *adj* **1 a :** having a valence greater usually than two **b :** having variable valence **2 :** effective against or sensitive toward more than one exciting agent (as a toxin or antigen) — **poly•va•lence** \-ləns\ *n*

pom•ace \ˈpəm-əs, ˈpäm-\ *n* **:** the dry or pulpy residue of plant material (as apples, olives, or sugarcane) from which a liquid (as a juice) has been pressed or extracted **[**probably from Medieval Latin *pomacium* "cider", from Late Latin *pomum* "apple", from Latin, "fruit"**]**

po•made \pō-ˈmād, -ˈmäd\ *n* **:** a perfumed ointment especially for the hair or scalp **[**Middle French *pommade* "ointment formerly made from apples", from Italian *pomata,* from *pomo* "apple", from Late Latin *pomum***]** — **pomade** *vt*

po•man•der \ˈpō-ˌman-dər, pō-ˈ\ *n* **:** a mixture of aromatic substances enclosed in a perforated bag or box and formerly carried as a guard against infection **[**Middle French *pome d'ambre,* literally, "apple or ball of amber"**]**

pome \ˈpōm\ *n* **:** a fleshy fruit (as an apple) consisting of a central core with usually five seeds enclosed in a capsule and surrounded by a thick fleshy outer layer **[**Middle French *pome, pomme* "apple, pome, ball", from Late Latin *pomum* "apple", from Latin, "fruit"**]**

pome•gran•ate \ˈpäm-ˌgran-ət, ˈpäm-ə-ˌgran-, ˈpəm-ˌgran-\ *n* **:** a thick-skinned reddish fruit about the size of an orange having many seeds in a tangy crimson pulp; *also* **:** a tropical Old World tree bearing pomegranates **[**Middle French *pomme grenate,* literally, "seedy apple"**]**

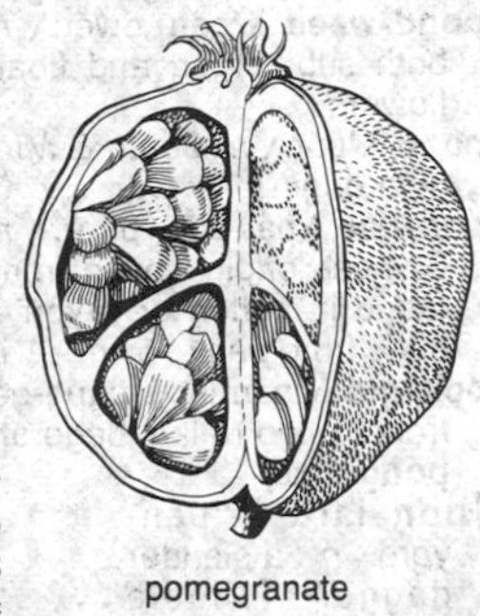

pomegranate

Pom•er•a•nian \ˌpäm-ə-ˈrā-nē-ən, -nyən\ *n* **1 :** a native or inhabitant of Pomerania **2 :** any of a breed of very small compact long-haired dogs — **Pomeranian** *adj*

[1]pom•mel \ˈpəm-əl, ˈpäm-\ *n* **1 :** the knob on the hilt of a sword or saber **2 :** the projection at the front and top of a saddlebow **3 :** either of a pair of rounded or U-shaped handles on a pommel horse **[**Middle French *pomel,* derived from Late Latin *pomum* "apple"**]**

[2]pom•mel \ˈpəm-əl\ *vt* **-meled** *or* **-melled; -mel•ing** *or* **-mel•ling** \ˈpəm-ling, -ə-ling\ **:** POUND 2a, PUMMEL **[***[1]pommel***]**

pommel horse *n* **:** a leather-covered rectangular or cylindrical form with two pommels on the top that is used for swinging and balancing feats in gymnastics

pomp \ˈpämp\ *n* **1 :** a show of magnificence **:** SPLENDOR ⟨the *pomp* of a coronation ceremony⟩ **2 :** a showy display ⟨a person who loves *pomp*⟩ **[**Middle French *pompe,* from Latin *pompa* "procession, pomp", from Greek *pompē***]**

pom•pa•dour \ˈpäm-pə-ˌdōr, -ˌdȯr\ *n* **:** a style of dressing the hair high over the forehead; *also* **:** hair dressed in this style **[**Marquise de *Pompadour***]**

pom•pa•no \ˈpäm-pə-ˌnō, ˈpəm-\ *n, pl* **-nos :** a spiny-finned food fish of the southern Atlantic and Gulf coasts having a narrow body and forked tail; *also* **:** any of several related or similar fishes **[**Spanish *pámpano,* a kind of fish**]**

[1]pom–pom \ˈpäm-ˌpäm\ *n* **:** an automatic gun of 20 to 40 millimeters mounted on ships in pairs, fours, or eights **[**imitative**]**

[2]pom–pom *n* **:** an ornamental ball or tuft used on clothing, caps, and costumes **[**alteration of *pompon***]**

pom•pon \ˈpäm-ˌpän\ *n* **1 :** [2]POM-POM **2 :** a chrysanthemum or dahlia with small rounded flower heads **[**French**]**

pom•pos•i•ty \päm-ˈpäs-ət-ē\ *n, pl* **-ties 1 :** the quality or state of being pompous **2 :** a pompous gesture or act

pomp•ous \ˈpäm-pəs\ *adj* **1 :** marked by stately show ⟨a *pompous* procession⟩ **2 :** SELF-IMPORTANT ⟨a very *pompous* person⟩ **3 :** too elevated or ornate ⟨*pompous* prose⟩ — **pomp•ous•ly** *adv* — **pomp•ous•ness** *n*

pon•cho \ˈpän-chō\ *n, pl* **ponchos :** a cloak resembling a blanket with a slit in the middle for the head; *also* **:** a waterproof garment of similar style worn chiefly as a raincoat **[**American Spanish, from Araucanian *pontho* "woolen fabric"**]**

pond \ˈpänd\ *n* **:** a body of standing water usually smaller than a lake **[**Middle English, "artificially confined body of water", alteration of *pounde* "enclosure"**]**

pon•der \ˈpän-dər\ *vb* **pon•dered; pon•der•ing** \ˈpän-dring, -də-ring\ **:** to consider carefully **[**Middle French *ponderer,* from Latin *ponderare* "to weigh, ponder", from *ponder-, pondus* "weight"**]** — **pon•der•er** \-dər-ər\ *n*

pon•der•a•ble \ˈpän-də-rə-bəl, -drə-bəl\ *adj* **:** capable of being weighed or appraised **:** APPRECIABLE **[**Late Latin *ponderabilis,* from Latin *ponderare* "to weigh, ponder"**]**

pon•der•o•sa pine \ˌpän-də-ˌrō-sə, -zə-\ *n* **:** a tall timber pine of western North America with long needles in bundles of 2 to 5;

also : its strong straight-grained wood [Latin *ponderosa*, feminine of *ponderosus* "ponderous"]

pon·der·ous \ˈpän-də-rəs, -drəs\ *adj* **1** : very heavy **2** : UNWIELDY **3** : unpleasantly or oppressively dull ⟨*ponderous* prose⟩ [Middle French *pondereux*, from Latin *ponderosus*, from *ponder-*, *pondus* "weight"] — **pon·der·ous·ly** *adv* — **pon·der·ous·ness** *n*

pond lily *n* : WATER LILY

pond scum *n* **1** : SPIROGYRA; *also* : any of various related algae **2** : a mass of tangled algal filaments in stagnant water

pond·weed \ˈpän-ˌdwēd\ *n* : any of several water plants with both submerged and floating leaves and spikes of greenish flowers

pone \ˈpōn\ *n, South & Midland* : CORN PONE [of American Indian origin]

pon·gee \pän-ˈjē, ˈpän-ˌ\ *n* : a thin soft beige or tan fabric of Chinese origin woven from raw silk; *also* : an imitation of this fabric in cotton or rayon [Chinese (Pekingese dialect) *pen*^{3} *chi*^{1}, from *pen*^{3} "own" + *chi*^{1} "loom"]

pon·gid \ˈpän-jəd, ˈpäng-gəd\ *n* : an anthropoid ape [derived from Kongo (a language of western Africa) *mpungu* "ape"] — **pongid** *adj*

[1]**pon·iard** \ˈpän-yərd\ *n* : a slender dagger [Middle French *poignard*, from *poing* "fist", from Latin *pugnus*]

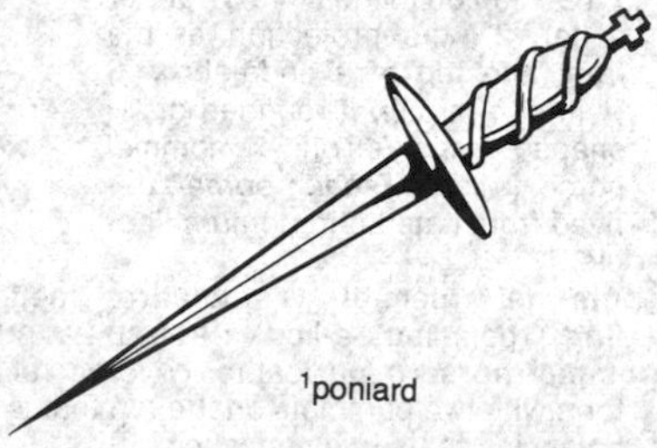
[1]poniard

[2]**poniard** *vt* : to stab with a poniard

pons \ˈpänz\ *n, pl* **pon·tes** \ˈpän-ˌtēz\ : a broad mass of nerve fibers on the ventral surface of the brain at the anterior end of the medulla oblongata [New Latin *pons Varoli*, literally, "bridge of Varoli", from Costanzo *Varoli*, died 1575, Italian surgeon and anatomist]

pon·ti·fex \ˈpänt-ə-ˌfeks\ *n, pl* **pon·tif·i·ces** \pän-ˈtif-ə-ˌsēz\ : a member of the ancient Roman council of priests [Latin *pontific-*, *pontifex*, literally, "bridge maker", from *pont-*, *pons* "bridge" + *facere* "to make"]

pon·tiff \ˈpänt-əf\ *n* **1** : PONTIFEX **2** : BISHOP 1; *esp* : POPE [French *pontif*, from Latin *pontifex*]

[1]**pon·tif·i·cal** \pän-ˈtif-i-kəl\ *adj* **1** : of or relating to a pontiff or pontifex **2** : celebrated by a prelate of episcopal rank with distinctive ceremonies ⟨a *pontifical* mass⟩ **3** : POMPOUS 2, 3 — **pon·tif·i·cal·ly** \-kə-lē, -klē\ *adv*

[2]**pontifical** *n* **1** : episcopal attire; *esp* : the insignia of the episcopal order worn by a prelate when celebrating a pontifical service — usually used in pl. **2** : a book containing the forms for sacraments and rites performed by a bishop

[1]**pon·tif·i·cate** \pän-ˈtif-i-kət, -ˈtif-ə-ˌkāt\ *n* : the office or term of office of a pontiff

[2]**pon·tif·i·cate** \-ˈtif-ə-ˌkāt\ *vi* **1** : to officiate as a pontiff **2** : to speak pompously ⟨*pontificating* on the subject⟩ — **pon·tif·i·ca·tor** \-ˌkāt-ər\ *n*

pon·toon \pän-ˈtün\ *n* **1** : a flat-bottomed boat; *esp* : a flat-bottomed boat or portable float used in building a floating temporary bridge **2** : a float of a seaplane [French *ponton* "floating bridge, punt", from Latin *ponto*, from *pont-*, *pons* "bridge"]

pontoon bridge *n* : a bridge whose deck is supported on pontoons

po·ny \ˈpō-nē\ *n, pl* **ponies** **1** : a small horse; *esp* : one of any of several breeds of very small stocky animals **2** : a small glass for an alcoholic drink or the amount it will hold **3** : a literal translation of a foreign language text [probably from obsolete French *poulenet*, from French *poulain* "colt", derived from Latin *pullus* "young of an animal, foal"]

Pony Express *n* : a rapid postal and express system across the western United States in 1860-61 operating by relays of horses

po·ny·tail \ˈpō-nē-ˌtāl\ *n* : hair arranged to resemble the tail of a pony

po·ny up \ˌpō-nē-ˈəp\ *vb* : to pay especially in settlement of an account [origin unknown]

pooch \ˈpüch\ *n* : DOG 1 [origin unknown]

poo·dle \ˈpüd-l\ *n* : any of an old breed of lively intelligent heavy-coated solid-colored dogs [German *pudel*, short for *pudelhund*, from *pudeln* "to splash" (from *pudel* "puddle") + *hund* "dog"]

pooh \ˈpü, ˈpu̇\ *interj* — used to express contempt or disapproval [imitative]

pooh–pooh \ˈpü-pü, pü-ˈpü\ *also* **pooh** \ˈpü\ *vb* **1** : to express contempt or impatience **2** : to make fun of : SCORN ⟨*pooh-poohed* the idea that the house is haunted⟩

[1]**pool** \ˈpül\ *n* **1** : a small and rather deep natural or artificial body of usually fresh water **2** : a small body of standing liquid : PUDDLE **3** : SWIMMING POOL [Old English *pōl*]

[2]**pool** *n* **1 a** : a stake to which each player of a game has contributed **b** : all the money bet by a number of persons on an event **2** : a game of billiards played with usually 15 object balls on a table having 6 pockets **3 a** : a common fund for buying or selling especially securities or commodities **b** : a combination between competing firms for the control of business by removing competition **4 a** : a group of people whose services or skills are available for use ⟨a typing *pool*⟩ ⟨a *pool* of talent⟩ **b** : a group whose members share or take turns providing a facility ⟨car *pool*⟩ [French *poule*, literally, "hen"]

[3]**pool** *vt* : to combine in a common fund, sample, or effort

pool·room \ˈpül-ˌrüm, -ˌru̇m\ *n* : a room for the playing of pool

[1]**poop** \ˈpüp\ *n* **1** *obs* : STERN 1 **2** : an enclosed superstructure at the stern of a ship above the main deck [Middle French *poupe* "stern", from Latin *puppis*]

[2]**poop** *vt* **1** : to break over the stern of **2** : to ship (a sea or wave) over the stern

[3]**poop** *vb* : to become or cause to become exhausted or worn out — often used with *out* [origin unknown]

poop deck *n* : a partial deck above the main deck at the stern of a ship

[1]**poor** \ˈpu̇r, ˈpōr\ *adj* **1** : lacking riches : NEEDY **2** : SCANTY, INSUFFICIENT ⟨a *poor* crop⟩ **3** : meriting pity ⟨the *poor* soul is lost⟩ **4** : not good of its kind ⟨*poor* workmanship⟩ ⟨in *poor* health⟩ **5** : lacking fertility ⟨*poor* land⟩ **6** : not good : UNFAVORABLE ⟨had a *poor* opinion of the child⟩ **7** : lacking in signs of wealth or good taste ⟨*poor* furnishings⟩ **8** : not efficient or capable ⟨a *poor* carpenter⟩ [Old French *povre*, from Latin *pauper*] — **poor·ly** *adv* — **poor·ness** *n*

[2]**poor** *n pl* : people who lack money or material riches

poor box *n* : a box for alms for the poor; *esp* : one placed near the door of a church

poor farm \ˈpu̇r-ˌfärm, ˈpōr-\ *n* : a farm formerly maintained at public expense for the support and employment of needy or dependent persons

poor·house \-ˌhau̇s\ *n* : a place formerly maintained at public expense to house needy or dependent persons

poor·ly \-lē\ *adj* : somewhat ill : INDISPOSED

poor–spir·it·ed \-ˈspir-ət-əd\ *adj* : lacking confidence or courage — **poor–spir·it·ed·ly** *adv* — **poor–spir·it·ed·ness** *n*

[1]**pop** \ˈpäp\ *vb* **popped**; **pop·ping** **1** : to burst or cause to burst with a pop ⟨the balloon *popped*⟩ **2** : to go, come, push, or enter quickly or unexpectedly **3** : to shoot with a gun **4** : to stick out ⟨eyes *popping* with surprise⟩ **5** : to cause to burst open ⟨*pop* corn⟩ **6** : to hit a pop fly [Middle English *poppen*] — **pop the question** : to propose marriage

[2]**pop** *n* **1** : a sharp explosive sound **2** : a shot from a gun **3** : a flavored carbonated beverage

[3]**pop** *adv* : like or with a pop : SUDDENLY

[4]**pop** *adj* **1** : POPULAR ⟨*pop* music⟩ **2** : of or relating to pop music ⟨*pop* singer⟩ **3** : of or relating to pop art

pop art *n* : art in which commonplace objects are used as subject matter

pop·corn \ˈpäp-ˌkȯrn\ *n* : an Indian corn with kernels that burst open to form a white starchy mass when heated; *also* : the popped kernels

pope \ˈpōp\ *n, often cap* : the head of the Roman Catholic Church [Old English *pāpa*, from Late Latin *papa*, from Greek *pappas*, title of bishops, literally, "papa"]

pop·ery \ˈpō-pə-rē, ˈpō-prē\ *n* : ROMAN CATHOLICISM — usually used disparagingly

pop·eyed \ˈpäp-ˈīd\ *adj* : having eyes that bulge (as from disease or excitement)

pop fly *n* : a short high fly in baseball

pop·gun \ˈpäp-ˌgən\ *n* : a toy gun that usually shoots a cork and makes a popping sound

pop·in·jay \ˈpäp-ən-ˌjā\ *n* : a vain talkative thoughtless person [Middle English *papejay* "parrot" from Middle French *papegai*, from Arabic *babghā'*]

pop•ish \ˈpō-pish\ *adj* **:** Roman Catholic — often used disparagingly — **pop•ish•ly** *adv*

pop•lar \ˈpäp-lər\ *n* **1 :** any of a genus of slender quick growing trees (as an aspen or cottonwood) of the willow family **2 :** the wood of a poplar [Middle French *pouplier,* from *pouple* "poplar", from Latin *populus*]

pop•lin \ˈpäp-lən\ *n* **:** a strong ribbed fabric in plain weave [French *papeline*]

pop•over \ˈpäp-ˌō-vər\ *n* **:** a quick bread that is made from a thin batter of eggs, milk, and flour which bakes into a hollow shell

pop•per \ˈpäp-ər\ *n* **:** one that pops; *esp* **:** a utensil for popping corn

pop•ple \ˈpäp-əl\ *n, chiefly dialect* **:** POPLAR 1 [Old English *popul,* from Latin *populus*]

pop•py \ˈpäp-ē\ *n, pl* **poppies :** any of a genus of chiefly annual or perennial herbs with milky juice, showy regular flowers, and capsular fruits including one that is the source of opium and several that are grown as ornamentals [Old English *popæg, popig,* from Latin *papaver*]

pop•py•cock \ˈpäp-ē-ˌkäk\ *n* **:** empty talk **:** NONSENSE [Dutch dialect *pappekak,* literally, "soft dung", from Dutch *pap* "pap" + *kak* "dung"]

pop•u•lace \ˈpäp-yə-ləs\ *n* **1 :** the common people **2 :** POPULATION 1 [Middle French, from Italian *popolaccio* "rabble", from *popolo* "the people", from Latin *populus*]

pop•u•lar \ˈpäp-yə-lər\ *adj* **1 :** of, relating to, or coming from the whole body of people ⟨*popular* government⟩ **2 :** suitable to the majority: as **a :** easy to understand ⟨*popular* science⟩ **b :** suited to the means of the majority **:** INEXPENSIVE ⟨*popular* prices⟩ **3 :** generally current **:** PREVALENT ⟨*popular* opinion⟩ **4 :** commonly liked or approved ⟨voted the most *popular* person in the class⟩ [Latin *popularis,* from *populus* "the people, a people"] — **pop•u•lar•ly** *adv*

pop•u•lar•i•ty \ˌpäp-yə-ˈlar-ət-ē\ *n* **:** the quality or state of being popular

pop•u•lar•ize \ˈpäp-yə-lə-ˌrīz\ *vt* **:** to make popular — **pop•u•lar•iza•tion** \ˌpäp-yə-lə-rə-ˈzā-shən\ *n* — **pop•u•lar•iz•er** \ˈpäp-yə-lə-ˌrī-zər\ *n*

pop•u•late \ˈpäp-yə-ˌlāt\ *vt* **:** to provide with inhabitants **:** PEOPLE

pop•u•la•tion \ˌpäp-yə-ˈlā-shən\ *n* **1 :** the whole number of people or inhabitants in a country or region **2 :** the act or process of populating **3 :** the organisms inhabiting a particular area or habitat **4 :** a group of persons or objects from which samples are taken for statistical measurement

population explosion *n* **:** the recent great increase in human numbers that is usually related to both increased survival and increased reproduction

pop•u•list \ˈpäp-yə-ləst\ *n* **1** *cap* **:** a member of a United States political party formed in 1891 primarily to represent agrarian interests and to advocate the free coinage of silver and government control of monopolies **2 :** a member of any of various popular or agrarian political parties — **pop•u•lism** \-ˌliz-əm\ *n, often cap* — **populist** *adj, often cap*

pop•u•lous \ˈpäp-yə-ləs\ *adj* **:** densely populated — **pop•u•lous•ly** *adv* — **pop•u•lous•ness** *n*

pop–up \ˈpäp-ˌəp\ *n* **:** POP FLY

por•bea•gle \ˈpȯr-ˌbē-gəl\ *n* **:** a small viviparous shark of northern seas with a pointed nose and crescent-shaped tail [Cornish *porgh-bugel*]

por•ce•lain \ˈpōr-sə-lən, ˈpȯr-, -slən\ *n* **:** a hard, fine-grained, nonporous, and usually translucent and white ceramic ware that consists essentially of kaolin, quartz, and feldspar and is used for dishes and chemical utensils [Middle French *porcelaine* "cowrie shell, porcelain", from Italian *porcellana,* from *porcello* "little pig, vulva", from Latin *porcellus,* from *porcus* "pig, vulva"] — **por•ce•lain•like** \-ˌlīk\ *adj*

porch \ˈpōrch, ˈpȯrch\ *n* **1 :** a covered entrance to a building usually with a separate roof **2 :** VERANDA [Old French *porche,* from Latin *porticus* "portico", from *porta* "gate"]

por•cine \ˈpȯr-ˌsīn\ *adj* **:** of, relating to, or suggesting swine [Latin *porcinus,* from *porcus* "pig"]

por•cu•pine \ˈpȯr-kyə-ˌpīn\ *n* **:** any of various rather large rodents with stiff sharp quills mingled with the hair [Middle French *porc espin,* from Italian *porcospino,* from Latin *porcus* "pig" + *spina* "spine, prickle"]

¹pore \ˈpōr, ˈpȯr\ *vi* **:** to gaze, study, or think long or earnestly ⟨*pore* over a book⟩ [Middle English *pouren*]

²pore *n* **:** a tiny opening or space (as in the skin or the soil) often giving passage to a fluid [Middle French, from Latin *porus,* from Greek *poros* "passage, pore"] — **pored** \ˈpōrd, ˈpȯrd\ *adj*

porcupine

por•gy \ˈpȯr-gē\ *n, pl* **porgies** *also* **porgy :** a blue-spotted crimson food fish of the coasts of Europe and America; *also* **:** any of various other fishes [partly from earlier *pargo* "porgy", derived from Latin *pagarus,* a kind of fish, from Greek *phagros;* partly from earlier *scuppaug* "porgy", of American Indian origin]

pork \ˈpōrk, ˈpȯrk\ *n* **:** the fresh or salted flesh of swine dressed for food [Old French *porc* "pig", from Latin *porcus*]

pork barrel *n* **:** a government project or appropriation yielding rich patronage benefits

pork•er \ˈpōr-kər, ˈpȯr-\ *n* **:** a domestic swine and especially a young pig suitable for use as fresh pork

por•nog•ra•phy \pȯr-ˈnäg-rə-fē\ *n* **:** pictures or writings describing erotic behavior and intended to cause sexual excitement [Greek *pornographos,* adj., "writing of harlots", from *pornē* "harlot" + *graphein* "to write"] — **por•nog•ra•pher** \-fər\ *n* — **por•no•graph•ic** \ˌpȯr-nə-ˈgraf-ik\ *adj* — **por•no•graph•i•cal•ly** \-ˈgraf-i-kə-lē, -klē\ *adv*

po•ros•i•ty \pə-ˈräs-ət-ē, pōr-ˈäs-, pȯ-ˈräs-\ *n, pl* **-ties 1 :** the quality or state of being porous **2 :** PORE

po•rous \ˈpōr-əs, ˈpȯr-\ *adj* **1 :** full of pores **2 :** capable of absorbing liquids **:** permeable to fluids — **po•rous•ly** *adv* — **po•rous•ness** *n*

por•phy•ry \ˈpȯr-fə-rē, -frē\ *n, pl* **-ries 1 :** a rock consisting of feldspar crystals embedded in a compact dark red or purple groundmass **2 :** an igneous rock having distinct crystals in a relatively fine-grained base [Medieval Latin *porphyrium,* from Latin *porphyrites,* from Greek *porphyritēs lithos,* literally, "purple-colored stone", from *porphyra* "purple"] — **por•phy•rit•ic** \ˌpȯr-fə-ˈrit-ik\ *adj*

por•poise \ˈpȯr-pəs\ *n* **1 :** any of several small blunt-snouted toothed whales that live and travel in groups **2 :** DOLPHIN 1a [Middle French *porpois,* from Medieval Latin *porcopiscis,* from Latin *porcus* "pig" + *piscis* "fish"]

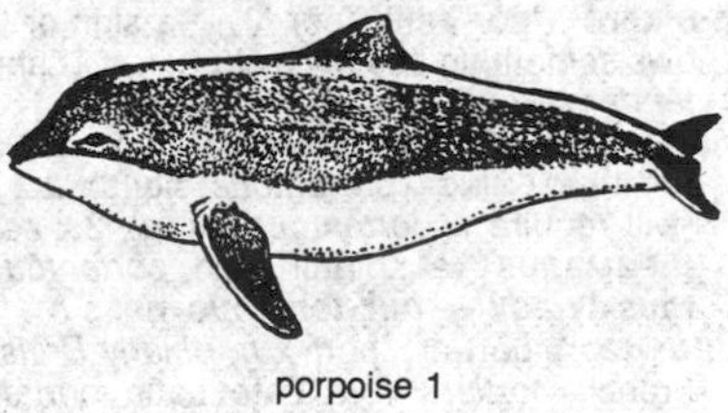
porpoise 1

por•ridge \ˈpȯr-ij, ˈpär-\ *n* **:** a soft food made by boiling meal in milk or water until thick [alteration of *pottage*]

por•rin•ger \ˈpȯr-ən-jər, ˈpär-\ *n* **:** a low one-handled metal bowl or cup [alteration of Middle English *poteger, potinger,* from Middle French *potager* "of pottage", from *potage* "pottage"]

¹port \ˈpōrt, ˈpȯrt\ *n* **1 :** a place where ships may ride secure from storms **2 a :** a harbor town or city where ships may take on or discharge cargo **b :** AIRPORT [Old English and Old French, both from Latin *portus* "house, door, port"]

²port *n* **1 :** an opening (as in machinery) for intake or exhaust of a fluid **2 :** PORTHOLE [Middle French *porte* "gate, door", from Latin *porta* "passage, gate"]

³port *n* **:** the left side of a ship or airplane looking forward — called also *larboard;* compare STARBOARD [probably from ¹*port* or ²*port*] — **port** *adj*

⁴port *vt* **:** to turn or put (the helm) to the left — used chiefly as a command

⁵port *n* **:** a rich sweet wine [*Oporto,* Portugal]

por·ta·ble \'pōrt-ə-bəl, 'pȯrt-\ *adj* : capable of being carried : easily moved from place to place [Middle French, from Late Latin *portabilis,* from Latin *portare* "to carry"] — **por·ta·bil·i·ty** \ˌpōrt-ə-'bil-ət-ē, ˌpȯrt-\ *n*

[1]por·tage \'pōrt-ij, 'pȯrt-, *2 is also* pȯr-'täzh\ *n* **1** : the labor of carrying or transporting **2** : the carrying of boats or goods overland from one body of water to another; *also* : a regular route for such carrying [Middle French, from *porter* "to carry", from Latin *portare*]

[2]portage \'pōrt-ij, 'pȯrt-; pȯr-'täzh\ *vb* **1** : to carry over a portage ⟨a canoe light enough to *portage*⟩ **2** : to move gear over a portage ⟨we *portaged* around the falls⟩

[1]por·tal \'pōrt-l, 'pȯrt-\ *n* **1** : DOOR 1a, ENTRANCE; *esp* : a grand or imposing one **2** : the point at which something enters the body of an organism ⟨infection *portals*⟩ [Middle French, from Medieval Latin *portale* "city gate, porch", derived from Latin *porta* "gate"]

[2]portal *adj* : of, relating to, or being a portal vein [derived from Latin *porta* "gate"]

portal–to–portal *adj* : of or relating to the time spent by a worker in traveling from the entrance to the employer's property to the actual working place (as in a mine) and in returning after the work shift

portal vein *n* : a vein that collects blood from one part of the body and distributes it in another through capillaries; *esp* : one carrying blood from the digestive organs and spleen to the liver

por·ta·men·to \ˌpōrt-ə-'men-tō, ˌpȯrt-\ *n, pl* **-ti** \-tē\ : a continuous glide effected by the voice, a trombone, or a bowed stringed musical instrument in passing from one tone to another [Italian, literally, "act of carrying", from *portare* "to carry", from Latin]

port·cul·lis \pōrt-'kəl-əs, pȯrt-\ *n* : a grating at the gateway of a castle or fortress that can be lowered to prevent entrance [Middle French *porte coleïce,* literally, "sliding door"]

porte co·chere \ˌpōrt-kō-'sheər, ˌpȯrt-\ *n* : a roofed structure extending from the entrance fo a building over an adjacent driveway and sheltering those getting in or out of vehicles [French *porte cochère,* literally, "coach door"]

por·tend \pȯr-'tend, pōr-\ *vt* : to give a sign or warning of beforehand ⟨the distant thunder *portended* a storm⟩ [Latin *portendere,* from *por-* "forward" + *tendere* "to stretch"]

por·tent \'pȯr-ˌtent, 'pōr-\ *n* : a sign or warning that foreshadows something usually evil : OMEN [Latin *portentum,* from *portendere* "to portend"]

por·ten·tous \pȯr-'tent-əs, pōr-\ *adj* **1** : being a portent : THREATENING ⟨*portentous* signs⟩ **2** : AMAZING, MARVELOUS ⟨will require a *portentous* effort⟩ **3** : self-consciously weighty : POMPOUS ⟨a solemn and *portentous* voice⟩ — **por·ten·tous·ly** *adv* — **por·ten·tous·ness** *n*

[1]por·ter \'pōrt-ər, 'pȯrt-\ *n, chiefly British* : DOORKEEPER [Old French *portier,* from Late Latin *portarius,* from Latin *porta* "gate"]

[2]porter *n* **1** : one that carries burdens; *esp* : one employed to carry baggage for patrons at a hotel or transportation terminal **2** : a parlor-car or sleeping-car attendant **3** : a dark heavy ale [Middle French *porteour,* from Late Latin *portator,* from Latin *portare* "to carry"; sense 3 short for *porter's beer*]

por·ter·house \-ˌhaüs\ *n* : a beefsteak with a large piece of tenderloin on a T-shaped bone [earlier *porterhouse* "house where porter is sold"]

port·fo·lio \pōrt-'fō-lē-ˌō, pȯrt-\ *n, pl* **-lios** **1** : a case for carrying papers or drawings **2** : the office and functions of a minister of state or member of a cabinet **3** : the securities held by an investor or a financial house [Italian *portafoglio,* from *portare* "to carry" (from Latin) + *foglio* "leaf, sheet", from Latin *folium;* sense 2 from the use of such a case to carry documents of state]

port·hole \'pōrt-ˌhōl, 'pȯrt-\ *n* **1** : an opening (as a window) in the side of a ship or airplane **2** : an opening (as in a wall) to shoot through **3** : [2]PORT 1

por·ti·co \'pōrt-i-ˌkō, 'pȯrt-\ *n, pl* **-coes** *or* **-cos** : a colonnade or covered walkway around or at the entrance of a building [Italian, from Latin *porticus,* from *porta* "gate"]

[1]por·tion \'pōr-shən, 'pȯr-\ *n* **1** : an individual's share of something ⟨a *portion* of food⟩ **2** : one's lot, fate, or fortune **3** : an element, section, or division of a whole [Old French, from Latin *portio*] **syn** see PART

[2]portion *vt* **por·tioned**; **por·tion·ing** \'pōr-shə-ning, 'pȯr-shning\ **1** : to divide into portions **2** : to give as a portion

port·land cement \ˌpōrt-lənd-, ˌpȯrt-, -lən-\ *n* : a cement made by burning and grinding a mixture of clay and limestone or a mixture of similar materials [Isle of *Portland,* England; from its resemblance to a limestone found there]

port·ly \'pōrt-lē, 'pȯrt-\ *adj* **port·li·er**; **-est** : heavy of body : STOUT [derived from Latin *portare* "to carry"] — **port·li·ness** *n*

port·man·teau \pōrt-'man-tō, pȯrt\ *n, pl* **-teaus** *or* **-teaux** \-tōz\ : a large traveling bag [Middle French *portemanteau,* from *porter* "to carry" + *manteau* "mantle", from Latin *mantellum*]

port of call : an intermediate port where ships customarily stop for supplies, repairs, or transferring of cargo

port of entry **1** : a place where foreign goods may be cleared through a customhouse **2** : a place where an alien may enter a country

por·trait \'pōr-trət, 'pȯr-, -ˌtrāt\ *n* **1** : a pictorial representation (as a painting) of a person usually showing the face **2** : a portrayal in words [Middle French, from *portraire* "to portray"]

por·trait·ist \-əst\ *n* : a maker of portraits

por·trai·ture \'pōr-trə-ˌchür, 'pȯr-, -chər\ *n* **1** : the making of portraits : PORTRAYAL **2** : PORTRAIT

por·tray \pōr-'trā, pȯr-\ *vt* **1** : to make a picture of **2 a** : to describe in words **b** : to play the role of : ENACT [Middle French *portraire,* from Latin *protrahere* "to draw forth, reveal", from *pro-* "forth" + *trahere* "to draw, drag"] — **por·tray·er** *n*

por·tray·al \-'trā-əl, -'trāl\ *n* **1** : the act or process of portraying : REPRESENTATION **2** : PORTRAIT

Por·tu·guese \ˌpōr-chə-'gēz, ˌpȯr-, -'gēs\ *n, pl* **Portuguese** **1 a** : a native or inhabitant of Portugal **b** : a person of Portuguese descent **2** : the Romance language of Portugal and Brazil — **Portuguese** *adj*

Portuguese man–of–war *n* : any of several large colonial coelenterates having a large crested bladder by means of which the colony floats at the surface of the sea

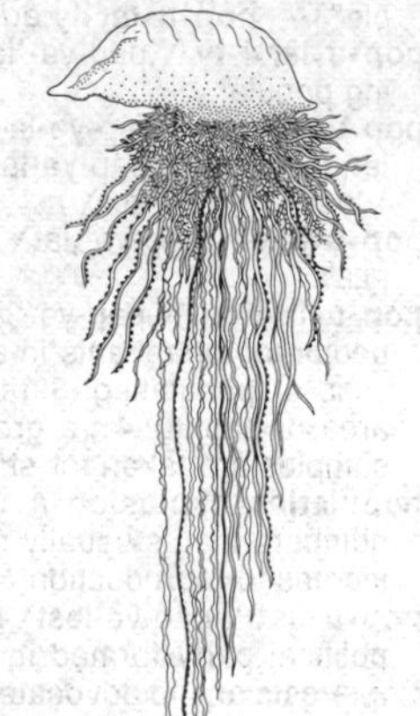

Portuguese man-of-war

por·tu·laca \ˌpōr-chə-'lak-ə, ˌpȯr-\ *n* : any of a genus of mostly tropical succulent herbs of the purslane family; *esp* : one cultivated for its showy flowers [Latin, "purslane", derived from *porta* "gate"; from the lid of its capsule]

[1]pose \'pōz\ *vb* **1 a** : to hold or cause to hold a special posture ⟨*posed* for fashion photographers⟩ **b** : to pretend to be what one is not ⟨*pose* as a hero⟩ **2** : to put forth : PROPOUND ⟨*pose* a question⟩ [Middle French *poser* "to put, place", from Late Latin *pausare* "to stop, rest, pause", from Latin *pausa* "pause"]

[2]pose *n* **1** : a sustained posture; *esp* : one assumed for artistic effect **2** : an assumed attitude ⟨that wide-eyed innocence is just a *pose*⟩ **syn** see AFFECTATION

[1]po·ser \'pō-zer\ *n* : a puzzling or baffling question [from earlier *pose* "to puzzle", derived from Middle English *opposen* "to oppose"]

[2]pos·er \'pō-zər\ *n* : a person who poses

po·seur \pō-'zər\ *n* : an affected person insincere in bearing or actions [French, from *poser* "to put, pose"]

posh \'päsh\ *adj* : ELEGANT 1, FASHIONABLE [origin unknown]

pos·it \'päz-ət\ *vt* : to assume the existence of : POSTULATE [Latin *positus,* past participle of *ponere* "to put, place, assume"]

[1]po·si·tion \pə-'zish-ən\ *n* **1** : the manner in which something is placed or arranged **2** : the stand taken on a question **3** : the point or area occupied by something ⟨the *position* of the heart⟩ **4 a** : social or official rank or status **b** : EMPLOYMENT 2b, JOB **c** : a situation that confers advantage or preference ⟨jockeyed for *position* in the race⟩ [Middle French, from Latin *positio,* from *positus,* past participle of *ponere* "to lay down, put, place"] — **po·si·tion·al** \-'zish-nəl, -ən-l\ *adj*

[2]position *vt* **po·si·tioned**; **po·si·tion·ing** \-'zish-ning, -ə-ning\ : to put in proper position

positional notation *n* : a system of expressing numbers in which the digits are arranged in succession, the position of each digit has a place value, and the number is equal to the sum of the products of each digit by its place value

[1]**pos•i•tive** \ˈpäz-ət-iv, ˈpäz-tiv\ *adj* **1 a** : formally laid down or imposed ⟨*positive* laws⟩ **b** : clearly or definitely stated ⟨*positive* orders⟩ **c** : fully assured : CONFIDENT ⟨were *positive* they'd win⟩ **2 a** : of the degree of comparison expressed by the unmodified and uninflected form of an adjective or adverb **b** : definite, accurate, or certain in its action ⟨*positive* traction of a sprocket chain⟩ **c** : UNQUALIFIED 2 ⟨a *positive* disgrace⟩ **3 a** : not fictitious : REAL ⟨a *positive* influence for good⟩ **b** : active in the social or economic sphere ⟨a *positive* government⟩ **4 a** : having or expressing actual existence or quality as distinguished from deprivation or deficiency ⟨a *positive* change in temperature⟩ **b** : capable of being logically applied ⟨*positive* suggestions for improvement⟩ **c** : showing light and shade similar in tone to the tones of the original subject ⟨a *positive* photographic image⟩ **d** : being a real number numerically greater than zero ⟨+2 is a *positive* integer⟩ **e (1)** : reckoned or proceeding in a direction taken as that of increase or progression **(2)** : directed or moving toward a source of stimulation ⟨a *positive* taxis⟩ **5 a** : of, being, or relating to electricity of a kind that predominates in a glass rod after being rubbed with silk ⟨a *positive* charge⟩ **b** : charged with positive electricity : having a deficiency of electrons ⟨a *positive* particle⟩ **c** : being the part from which the current flows to the external circuit ⟨the *positive* pole of a discharging storage battery⟩ **d** : electron-collecting — used of an electrode in an electron tube **6 a** : marked by or indicating agreement or affirmation ⟨a *positive* response⟩ **b** : affirming the presence of what is sought or suspected to be present ⟨a *positive* test for blood⟩ **[**Old French *positif,* from Latin *positivus,* from *positus,* past participle of *ponere* "to lay down, put, place"**]** **syn** see SURE — **pos•i•tive•ly** \-lē, *for emphasis often* ˌpäz-ə-ˈtiv-lē\ *adv* — **pos•i•tive•ness** *n*

[2]**positive** *n* : something positive: as **a** : the positive degree or a positive form in a language **b** : a positive photograph or a print from a negative

pos•i•tron \ˈpäz-ə-ˌträn\ *n* : a positively charged particle having the same mass and magnitude of charge as the electron **[***posi*tive + *-tron* (as in *electron*)**]**

pos•se \ˈpäs-ē\ *n* **1** : a group of people called upon by a sheriff to aid in law enforcement ⟨a *posse* pursued the robber⟩ **2** : a number of people organized to make a search (as for a lost child) **[**Medieval Latin *posse comitatus,* literally, "power of the county"**]**

pos•sess \pə-ˈzes\ *vt* **1 a** : to make (as a person) the owner or holder (as of property or power) **b** : to have possession of **2 a** : to have and hold as property : OWN **b** : to have as an attribute, knowledge, or skill ⟨*possesses* a keen wit⟩ **3 a** : to make one's own **b** : to enter into and control firmly : DOMINATE ⟨what *possessed* you to do that⟩ **[**Middle French *possesser* "to have or take possession of", from Latin *possidēre,* from *potis* "able, in power" + *sedēre* "to sit"**]** — **pos•sess•or** \-ər\ *n*

pos•ses•sion \pə-ˈzesh-ən\ *n* **1 a** : the act of possessing or holding as one's own : OWNERSHIP **b** : physical control of property without regard to ownership **2 a** : something held as one's own : PROPERTY **b** : an area under the control of but not formally part of a nation ⟨island *possessions* of the United States⟩ **3 a** : domination by something (as an evil spirit, an idea, or a passion) **b** : the fact or condition of being self-controlled — **pos•ses•sion•al** \-ˈzesh-nəl, -ən-l\ *adj*

[1]**pos•ses•sive** \pə-ˈzes-iv\ *adj* **1** : of, relating to, or being a grammatical case that denotes ownership or a similar relation — compare GENITIVE **2** : showing the desire to possess or keep ⟨a *possessive* attitude⟩ — **pos•ses•sive•ly** *adv* — **pos•ses•sive•ness** *n*

[2]**possessive** *n* **1** : the possessive case **2** : a word in the possessive case

possessive adjective *n* : a pronominal adjective expressing possession

possessive pronoun *n* : a pronoun that derives from a personal pronoun and expresses possession

pos•set \ˈpäs-ət\ *n* : a hot drink of sweetened and spiced milk curdled with ale or wine **[**Middle English *poshet, possot***]**

pos•si•bil•i•ty \ˌpäs-ə-ˈbil-ət-ē\ *n, pl* **-ties 1** : the condition or fact of being possible **2** : something possible

pos•si•ble \ˈpäs-ə-bəl\ *adj* **1** : being something that can be done or brought about **2** : being something that may or may not occur ⟨*possible* dangers⟩ **3** : able or fitted to be or to become ⟨a *possible* camp site⟩ **[**Middle French, from Latin *possibilis,* from *posse* "to be able", from *potis* "able" + *esse* "to be"**]** — **pos•si•bly** \-blē\ *adv*

• **syn** POSSIBLE, PRACTICABLE, FEASIBLE mean capable of being realized. POSSIBLE implies that a thing may exist or occur given the proper conditions; PRACTICABLE implies that something may be easily or readily put into operation by current available means ⟨when television became *practicable*⟩ FEASIBLE applies to what is likely to work or be useful in attaining an end ⟨commercially *feasible* for mass production⟩ **syn** see in addition PROBABLE

pos•sum \ˈpäs-əm\ *n* : OPOSSUM

[1]**post** \ˈpōst\ *n* **1** : a piece of timber or metal fixed firmly in an upright position especially as a stay or support : PILLAR, COLUMN **2** : a pole or stake set up to mark or indicate something ⟨starting *post*⟩ **[**Old English, from Latin *postis***]**

[2]**post** *vt* **1** : to fasten to a place (as a wall) for public notices **2 a** : to publish or announce by or as if by a placard **b** : to enter on a public listing ⟨*post* all daily flights⟩ **3** : to forbid persons from entering or using by putting up warning notices ⟨*post* a trout stream⟩

[3]**post** *n* **1** *obsolete* : one that carries messages : COURIER **2** *archaic* : one of a series of stations for keeping horses for relays **3** *chiefly British* **a** : a nation's organization for handling mail; *also* : the mail handled **b** : a single dispatch of mail **[**Middle French *poste* "relay station, courier", from Italian *posta* "relay station", from *posto,* past participle of *porre* "to place", from Latin *ponere***]**

[4]**post** *vb* **1** : to ride or travel with haste : HURRY **2** : MAIL ⟨*post* a letter⟩ **3 a** : to transfer (a bookkeeping item) from a book of original entry to a ledger **b** : to make transfer entries in **4** : to make familiar with a subject : INFORM ⟨kept *posted* on the latest news⟩ **[**earlier *post* "to travel with post-horses"**]**

[5]**post** *adv* : with post-horses : EXPRESS

[6]**post** *n* **1 a** : the place at which a soldier is stationed; *esp* : a sentry's beat or station **b** : a station or task to which one is assigned **c** : a place to which troops are assigned **d** : a local subdivision of a veterans' organization **2** : an office or position to which a person is appointed **3** : TRADING POST; *also* : SETTLEMENT 3a ⟨sent supplies to the frontier *posts*⟩ **[**Middle French, from Italian *posto,* from *porre* "to place"**]**

[7]**post** *vt* **1 a** : to station in a given place ⟨*post* a guard⟩ **b** : to carry ceremoniously to a position ⟨*posting* the colors⟩ **2** : to put up as security ⟨*post* bond⟩

post- *prefix* **1 a** : after : subsequent : later ⟨*post*date⟩ **b** : behind : posterior : following after ⟨*post*consonantal⟩ **2 a** : subsequent to : later than ⟨*post*operative⟩ **b** : posterior to **[**Latin, from *post***]**

See *post-* and 2d element

postaccident	**postflight**	**postpuberty**
postadolescence	**postgame**	**postpubescent**
postadolescent	**postgraduation**	**postradiation**
postattack	**postharvest**	**postrecession**
postbaccalaureate	**posthospital**	**postretirement**
postbiblical	**postimperial**	**postrevolutionary**
postcollege	**postinaugural**	**postseason**
postcolonial	**postindustrial**	**postsecondary**
postdrug	**postinjection**	**postsurgical**
postediting	**postinoculation**	**posttransfusion**
postelection	**postmarital**	**posttreatment**
postexercise	**postnuptial**	**posttrial**
postexperimental	**postoperative**	**postvaccination**
postfertilization	**postpubertal**	**postwar**

post•age \ˈpō-stij\ *n* : the charge imposed for carrying an article by mail

postage meter *n* : a machine that prints postal markings on pieces of mail, records the amount of postage given in the markings, and subtracts it from a total amount which has been paid at the post office and for which the machine has been set

\ə\ **abut**	\au̇\ **out**	\i\ **tip**	\ȯ\ **saw**	\u̇\ **foot**
\ər\ **further**	\ch\ **chin**	\ī\ **life**	\ȯi\ **coin**	\y\ **yet**
\a\ **mat**	\e\ **pet**	\j\ **job**	\th\ **thin**	\yü\ **few**
\ā\ **take**	\ē\ **easy**	\ng\ **sing**	\t͟h\ **this**	\yu̇\ **cure**
\ä\ **cot, cart**	\g\ **go**	\ō\ **bone**	\ü\ **food**	\zh\ **vision**

postage stamp *n* : a government stamp used on mail to show that postage has been paid
post•al \'pōst-l\ *adj* : of or relating to mail or to the post office
postal card *n* : POSTCARD; *esp* : one bearing a government imprinted stamp and sold by a post office
postal service *n* : POST OFFICE 1
postal union *n* : an association of governments setting up uniform regulations and practices for international mail
post•card \'pōst-,kärd, 'pōs-\ *n* : a card on which a message may be written for mailing without an envelope
post chaise *n* : a carriage usually having a closed body on four wheels and seating two or four persons [[3]*post*]
post•clas•si•cal \pōst-'klas-i-kəl, 'pōst-, pōs-, 'pōs-\ *adj* : of or relating to a period following the classical
post–com•mu•nion \,pōst-kə-'myü-nyən, ,pōs-\ *n, often cap P&C* : a prayer formerly following the communion at Mass
post•con•so•nan•tal \,pōst-,kän-sə-'nant-l, ,pōs-\ *adj* : immediately following a consonant
post•date \pōst-'dāt, 'pōst-, pōs-, 'pōs-\ *vt* **1** : to date with a date later than that of execution ⟨*postdate* a check⟩ **2** : to follow in time ⟨the text changes *postdated* the first printing⟩
post•doc•tor•al \-'däk-tə-rəl, -trəl\ *adj* : of, relating to, or engaged in advanced academic or professional work beyond a doctor's degree
post•er \'pō-stər\ *n* : a notice or advertisement to be posted in a public place
[1]**pos•te•ri•or** \pō-'stir-ē-ər, pä-\ *adj* **1** : later in time : SUBSEQUENT **2** : situated behind : situated toward or on the back [Latin, comparative of *posterus* "coming after", from *post* "after"] — **pos•te•ri•or•ly** *adv*
[2]**pos•te•ri•or** \pä-'stir-ē-ər, pō-\ *n* : the hinder parts of the body; *esp* : BUTTOCKS
pos•ter•i•ty \pä-'ster-ət-ē\ *n* **1** : offspring to the furthest generation **2** : those who come after in time ⟨leave a record for *posterity*⟩ [Middle French *posterité,* from Latin *posteritas,* from *posterus* "coming after"]
pos•tern \'pōs-tərn, 'päs-\ *n* **1** : a back door or gate **2** : a private or side entrance or way [Old French *posterne,* alteration of *posterle,* from Late Latin *posterula,* from *postera* "back door", from Latin *posterus* "coming after"] — **postern** *adj*
post exchange *n* : a store at a military post that sells to military personnel and authorized civilians
post•gan•gli•on•ic \,pōst-,gang-glē-'än-ik, ,pōs-\ *adj* : distal to a ganglion; *also* : of, relating to, or being an axon arising from a cell body within an autonomic ganglion
post•gla•cial \pōst-'glā-shəl, 'pōst-, pōs-, 'pōs-\ *adj* : coming or occurring after a period of glaciation
[1]**post•grad•u•ate** \-'graj-wət, -ə-wət, -ə-,wāt\ *adj* : GRADUATE 2
[2]**postgraduate** *n* : a student continuing his or her education after graduation from high school or college
post•haste \'pōst-'hāst\ *adv* : with all possible speed ⟨sent *posthaste* for the doctor⟩ [[3]*post*]
post•hole \'pōst-,hōl\ *n* : a hole for a post and especially a fence post
post–horse \-,hȯrs\ *n* : a horse for use especially by couriers or mail carriers [[3]*post*]
post•hu•mous \'päs-chə-məs\ *adj* **1** : born after the death of the father ⟨*posthumous* twins⟩ **2** : published after the death of the author ⟨a *posthumous* novel⟩ **3** : following or occurring after one's death ⟨*posthumous* fame⟩ ⟨a *posthumous* award⟩ [Latin *posthumus,* alteration of *postumus* "late-born, posthumous", from *posterus* "coming after"] — **post•hu•mous•ly** *adv*
post•hyp•not•ic \,pōst-hip-'nät-ik, ,pōst-ip-\ *adj* : of, relating to, or characteristic of the period following a hypnotic trance
pos•til•ion *or* **pos•til•lion** \pō-'stil-yən, pə-\ *n* : a person who rides as a guide on the left-hand horse of a pair drawing a coach [Middle French *postillon* "mail carrier using post-horses", from Italian *postiglione,* from *posta* "post"]
Post•im•pres•sion•ism \,pō-stim-'presh-ə-,niz-əm\ *n* : a theory or practice of art originating in France in the last quarter of the 19th century that in revolt against impressionism stresses variously volume, picture structure, or expressionism
post•lude \'pōst-,lüd\ *n* : a closing piece of music; *esp* : an organ voluntary at the end of a church service [*post-* + *-lude* (as in *prelude*)]
post•man \'pōst-mən, 'pōs-, -,man\ *n* : LETTER CARRIER
post•mark \-,märk\ *n* : an official postal marking on a piece of mail; *esp* : a cancellation of the postage stamp that gives the date and place of mailing — **postmark** *vt*
post•mas•ter \-,mas-tər\ *n* : an official in charge of a post office
postmaster general *n, pl* **postmasters general** : an official in charge of a national post office department
post me•ri•di•em \'pōst-mə-'rid-ē-əm, 'pōs-, -ē-,em\ *adj* : being after noon — abbreviation *p.m.* [Latin]
post•mis•tress \-,mis-trəs\ *n* : a woman in charge of a post office
post•mor•tem \pōst-'mȯrt-əm, pōs-\ *adj* **1 a** : occurring after death **b** : of or relating to a postmortem examination **2** : following the event ⟨a *postmortem* analysis of the game⟩ [Latin *post mortem* "after death"] — **postmortem** *n*
postmortem examination *n* : an examination of a dead body especially to determine the cause of death
post•na•sal drip \pōst-'nā-zəl-, 'pōst-, pōs-, 'pōs-\ *n* : a flow of mucous secretion from the back of the nasal cavity onto the wall of the pharynx that occurs in some allergic states (as hay fever)
post•na•tal \-'nāt-l\ *adj* : subsequent to birth; *also* : of or relating to a newborn child ⟨*postnatal* care⟩ — **post•na•tal•ly** \-l-ē\ *adv*
post office *n* **1** : a government department handling the transmission of mail **2** : a local branch of a post office department handling the mail for a particular place **3** : a kissing game in which the one pretending to deliver a letter may demand a kiss as payment
post•op•er•a•tive \pōst-'äp-rət-iv, 'pōst-, -ə-rət-, -ə-,rāt-\ *adj* : following a surgical operation ⟨*postoperative* care⟩ — **post•op•er•a•tive•ly** *adv*
post•paid \'pōst-'pād, 'pōs-\ *adv* : with postage paid by the sender and not chargeable to the receiver [[3]*post*]
post•par•tum \pōst-'pärt-əm, pōs-\ *adj* : following parturition [New Latin *post partum* "after birth"]
post•pone \-'pōn\ *vt* : to hold back to a later time : put off [Latin *postponere* "to place after, postpone", from *post-* + *ponere* "to place"] **syn** see DEFER — **post•pone•ment** \-mənt\ *n* — **post•pon•er** *n*
post•pran•di•al \-'pran-dē-əl\ *adj* : following a meal ⟨taking a *postprandial* nap⟩
post•script \'pōs-,skript, 'pō-\ *n* : a note or series of notes added at the end of a letter, article, or book [Latin *postscriptus,* past participle of *postscribere* "to write after", from *post-* + *scribere* "to write"]
pos•tu•lant \'päs-chə-lənt\ *n* **1** : a person admitted to a religious community as a probationary candidate for membership **2** : a person on probation before being admitted as a candidate for holy orders in the Episcopal Church [French, "petitioner, candidate, postulant", from *postuler* "to demand, solicit", from Latin *postulare*] — **pos•tu•lan•cy** \-lən-sē\ *n*
[1]**pos•tu•late** \'päs-chə-,lāt\ *vt* : to claim as true : assume as a postulate [Latin *postulare* "to demand", from *poscere* "to ask"] — **pos•tu•la•tion** \,päs-chə-'lā-shən\ *n*
[2]**pos•tu•late** \'päs-chə-lət, -,lāt\ *n* **1** : a hypothesis advanced as an essential basis of a system of thought or premise of a train of reasoning **2** : a statement (as in logic or mathematics) that often cannot be proved to be true or false but that is assumed to be true without proof; *also* : AXIOM 2a
[1]**pos•ture** \'päs-chər\ *n* **1** : the position or bearing of the body or of a body part ⟨an erect *posture*⟩ **2** : relative place or position : SITUATION **3** : a particular state with reference to something else ⟨a country's defense *posture*⟩ **4** : frame of mind : ATTITUDE ⟨a *posture* of arrogance⟩ [French, from Italian *postura,* from Latin *positura,* from *positus,* past participle of *ponere* "to place"] — **pos•tur•al** \-chə-rəl\ *adj*
[2]**posture** *vb* : to assume or cause to assume a given posture; *esp* : to strike a pose for effect — **pos•tur•er** *n*
post•vo•cal•ic \,pōst-vō-'kal-ik\ *adj* : immediately following a vowel
post•war \'pōst-'wȯr\ *adj* : of, relating to, or being a period after a war
po•sy \'pō-zē\ *n, pl* **posies 1** : a brief motto **2 a** : FLOWER 1c **b** : a bunch of flowers : BOUQUET [alteration of *poesy*]
[1]**pot** \'pät\ *n* **1 a** : a rounded metal or earthen container used chiefly for domestic purposes **b** : the quantity held by a pot **2** : an enclosed framework for catching fish or lobsters **3 a** : a large quantity or sum **b** : the total of the bets at stake at one

time **4** : RUIN 1, DETERIORATION ⟨their business went to *pot*⟩ **5** : MARIJUANA [Old English *pott*] — **pot·ful** *n*

²pot *vt* **pot·ted; pot·ting 1** : to preserve in a sealed pot, jar, or can ⟨*potted* chicken⟩ **2** : to plant or grow in a pot ⟨*potted* plants⟩ **3** : to shoot with a potshot ⟨*pot* a rabbit⟩

po·ta·ble \'pōt-ə-bəl\ *adj* : suitable for drinking [Late Latin *potabilis*, from Latin *potare* "to drink"] — **po·ta·bil·i·ty** \,pōt-ə-'bil-ət-ē\ *n* — **po·ta·ble·ness** \'pōt-ə-bəl-nəs\ *n*

po·tage \pó-'täzh\ *n* : a thick soup [Middle French, from Old French, "pottage"]

pot·ash \'pät-,ash\ *n* **1 a** : potassium carbonate especially from wood ashes **b** : POTASSIUM HYDROXIDE **2** : potassium or a potassium compound especially as used in agriculture or industry [¹*pot* + *ash*]

po·tas·si·um \pə-'tas-ē-əm\ *n* : a silver-white soft light low-melting univalent metallic chemical element that occurs abundantly in nature especially combined in minerals — see ELEMENT table [New Latin, from *potassa* "potash", from English *potash*]

potassium bromide *n* : a crystalline salt KBr with a saline taste used as a sedative and in photography

potassium carbonate *n* : a white salt K_2CO_3 that forms a strongly alkaline solution and is used in making glass and soap

potassium chlorate *n* : a crystalline salt $KClO_3$ that is used as an oxidizing agent in matches, fireworks, and explosives

potassium chloride *n* : a crystalline salt KCl that occurs as a mineral and in natural waters and is used as a fertilizer

potassium cyanide *n* : a very poisonous crystalline salt KCN used in electroplating

potassium dichromate *n* : a soluble salt $K_2Cr_2O_7$ forming large orange-red crystals used in dyeing, in photography, and as an oxidizing agent

potassium hydroxide *n* : a white deliquescent solid KOH that dissolves in water with much heat to form a strongly alkaline and caustic liquid and is used in making soap and as a reagent

potassium iodide *n* : a crystalline salt KI that is soluble in water and used in photographic emulsions and in medicine

potassium nitrate *n* : a crystalline salt KNO_3 that occurs as a product of nitrification in soil, is a strong oxidizer, and is used in making gunpowder, in preserving meat, and in medicine — called also *saltpeter*

potassium permanganate *n* : a dark purple salt $KMnO_4$ used as an oxidizer and disinfectant

po·ta·tion \pō-'tā-shən\ *n* **1** : a usually alcoholic drink or brew **2 a** : the act of drinking **b** : DRAFT 4a [Middle French, from Latin *potatio* "act of drinking", from *potare* "to drink"]

po·ta·to \pə-'tāt-ō, pət-'āt-\ *n, pl* **-toes 1** : SWEET POTATO **2 a** : an erect American herb of the nightshade family widely cultivated as a vegetable crop **b** : its edible starchy tuber — called also *white potato* [Spanish *batata*, of American Indian origin]

potato beetle *n* : COLORADO POTATO BEETLE

potato blight *n* : any of several destructive fungus diseases of the potato

potato bug *n* : COLORADO POTATO BEETLE

potato chip *n* : a thin slice of potato fried crisp and salted

pot·bel·ly \'pät-,bel-ē\ *n* **1** : an enlarged, swollen, or protruding abdomen **2** : a stove with a bulging body — called also *potbellied stove* — **pot·bel·lied** \-ēd\ *adj*

pot·boil·er \-,bȯi-lər\ *n* : a usually inferior work of art or literature produced only to earn money

pot cheese *n* : COTTAGE CHEESE

po·teen \pə-'tēn\ *n* : illicitly distilled whiskey of Ireland [Irish Gaelic *poitín*]

po·ten·cy \'pōt-n-sē\ *n, pl* **-cies** : the quality or condition of being potent; *esp* : power to bring about a given result

po·tent \'pōt-nt\ *adj* **1** : having or exercising force, authority, or influence : POWERFUL **2** : producing a given effect **3 a** : chemically or medicinally effective ⟨a *potent* vaccine⟩ **b** : rich in a constituent : STRONG ⟨*potent* tea⟩ **4** : able to copulate [Latin *potens*, derived from *potis*, *pote* "able"] — **po·tent·ly** *adv*

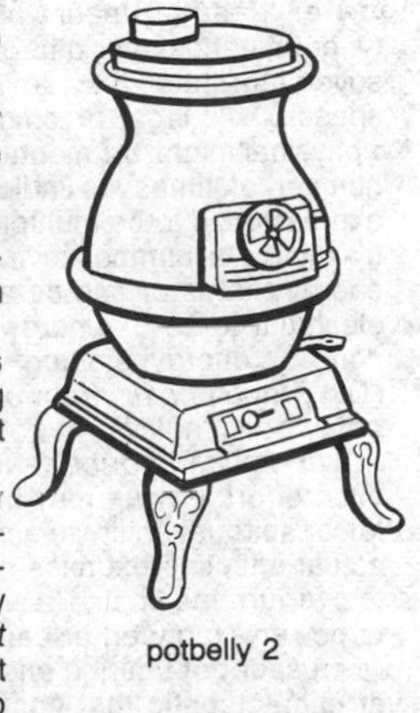

potbelly 2

po·ten·tate \'pōt-n-,tāt\ *n* : one who exercises controlling power

¹po·ten·tial \pə-'ten-chəl\ *adj* : capable of becoming real : POSSIBLE ⟨the *potential* dangers in the scheme⟩ [Late Latin *potentialis*, from Latin *potentia* "power", from *potens* "potent"] — **po·ten·tial·ly** \-'tench-lē, -ə-lē\ *adv*

²potential *n* **1** : something that can develop or become actual : POSSIBILITY **2** : the degree of electrification with reference to a standard

potential difference *n* : the difference in electrical potential between two points that represents the work involved or the energy released in the transfer of a unit quantity of electricity from one point to the other

potential energy *n* : the amount of energy a thing (as a weight raised to a height or a coiled spring) has because of its position or because of the arrangement of its parts

po·ten·ti·al·i·ty \pə-,ten-chē-'al-ət-ē\ *n, pl* **-ties 1** : the ability to develop or to come into existence **2** : POTENTIAL 1

po·ten·ti·ate \pə-'ten-chē-,āt\ *vt* : to make potent; *esp* : to increase (the effect of a drug or treatment) synergistically — **po·ten·ti·a·tion** \-,ten-chē-'ā-shən\ *n* — **po·ten·ti·a·tor** \-'ten-chē-,āt-ər\ *n*

po·ten·ti·om·e·ter \pə-,ten-chē-'äm-ət-ər\ *n* **1** : an instrument for measuring electromotive forces **2** : VOLTAGE DIVIDER [*potential* + *-o-* + *-meter*]

¹poth·er \'päth-ər\ *n* **1 a** : FLURRY 2, COMMOTION **b** : FUSS 2 **2** : a choking cloud of dust or smoke **3** : mental turmoil [origin unknown]

²pother *vb* **poth·ered; poth·er·ing** \'päth-ring, -ə-ring\ : to put into or be in a pother

pot·herb \'pät-,ərb, -,hərb\ *n* : an herb whose leaves or stems are cooked for use as greens; *also* : one (as mint) used to season food

pot·hole \-,hōl\ *n* : a large pit or hole (as in the bed of a river or in a road surface)

pot·hook \-,hu̇k\ *n* **1** : an S-shaped hook for hanging pots and kettles over an open fire **2** : an S-shaped stroke in writing

pot·hunt·er \-,hənt-ər\ *n* : one who hunts game for food — **pot-hunt·ing** \-,hənt-ing\ *n*

po·tion \'pō-shən\ *n* : a mixed drink (as of liquor) or dose (as of medicine) [Middle French, from Latin *potio* "drink, potion", from *potare* "to drink"]

pot·latch \'pät-,lach\ *n* **1** : a ceremonial feast of northwest coast Indians in which the host distributes gifts lavishly and the guests must reciprocate **2** *Northwest* : a social event or celebration [of American Indian origin]

pot liquor *n* : the liquid left in a pot after cooking

pot·luck \'pät-'lək\ *n* : the regular meal available to a guest for whom no special preparations have been made

pot marigold *n* : a variable hardy calendula widely grown especially for ornament

pot·pie \'pät-'pī\ *n* : a stew of meat or poultry usually with vegetables and served with a crust or dumplings

pot·pour·ri \,pō-pu̇-'rē\ *n* **1** : a jar of flower petals and spices used for scent **2** : a miscellaneous collection : MEDLEY [French *pot pourri*, literally, "rotten pot"]

pot roast *n* : a piece of beef cooked by braising usually on top of the stove

pot·sherd \'pät-,shərd\ *n* : a pottery fragment

pot·shot \-,shät\ *n* **1** : a shot taken in a casual manner or at an easy target **2** : a critical remark made in a random or sporadic way [from the sportsman's feeling that such shots were worthy only of pothunters] — **pot·shot** *vb*

pot·tage \'pät-ij\ *n* : a thick soup of vegetables or vegetables and meat [Old French *potage*, from *pot* "pot", of Germanic origin]

¹pot·ter \'pät-ər\ *n* : one that makes pottery

²potter *vi* : FIDDLE 2b, PUTTER [probably from English dialect *pote* "to poke"] — **pot·ter·er** *n*

potter's clay *n* : a plastic clay suitable for making pottery — called also *potter's earth*

\ə\ **abut**	\au̇\ **out**	\i\ **tip**	\ȯ\ **saw**	\u̇\ **foot**
\ər\ **further**	\ch\ **chin**	\ī\ **life**	\ȯi\ **coin**	\y\ **yet**
\a\ **mat**	\e\ **pet**	\j\ **job**	\th\ **thin**	\yü\ **few**
\ā\ **take**	\ē\ **easy**	\ng\ **sing**	\th\ **this**	\yu̇\ **cure**
\ä\ **cot, cart**	\g\ **go**	\ō\ **bone**	\ü\ **food**	\zh\ **vision**

potter's field *n* : a public burial place for paupers, unknown persons, and criminals [from the mention in Matthew 27:7 of the purchase of a potter's field for use as a graveyard]

potter's wheel *n* : a horizontal disk revolving on a spindle and carrying the clay being shaped by a potter

potter's wheel

pot•tery \'pät-ə-rē\ *n, pl* **-ter•ies** **1** : a place where earthen vessels are made **2** : the art of the potter : CERAMICS **3** : ware made usually from clay that is shaped while moist and soft and hardened by heat; *esp* : coarser ware so made

pot•to \'pät-ō\ *n, pl* **pottos** : one of several African primates; *esp* : a West African primate that has a vestigial index finger and tail [of African origin]

[1]**pot•ty** \'pät-ē\ *adj, chiefly British* : slightly crazy [probably from [1]*pot*]

[2]**potty** *n, pl* **potties** : a small child's pot for urinating or defecating

pot•ty–chair \-ˌcheər, -ˌchaər\ *n* : a child's chair having an open seat under which a pot is placed for toilet training

[1]**pouch** \'pau̇ch\ *n* **1** : a small drawstring bag carried on the person **2** : a bag of small or moderate size for storing or carrying goods; *esp* : a bag with a lock for first class mail or diplomatic dispatches **3** : an anatomical structure in the form of a bag or sac; *esp* : one for carrying the young on the abdomen of a female marsupial (as a kangaroo or opossum) [Middle French *pouche,* of Germanic origin] — **pouched** \'pau̇cht\ *adj*

[2]**pouch** *vb* : to put or form into or as if into a pouch

pouchy \'pau̇-chē\ *adj* **pouch•i•er**; **-est** : having, tending to have, or resembling a pouch

poult \'pōlt\ *n* : a young fowl; *esp* : a young turkey [Middle English *polet, pulte* "young fowl, pullet"]

poul•ter•er \'pōl-tər-ər\ *n* : one that deals in poultry [Middle French *pouletier*]

poul•tice \'pōl-təs\ *n* : a soft usually heated and often medicated mass spread on cloth and applied to lesions (as sores) [Medieval Latin *pultes* "pap", from Latin *pult-, puls* "porridge"] — **poultice** *vt*

poul•try \'pōl-trē\ *n* : domesticated birds kept for eggs or meat [Middle French *pouleterie,* from *pouletier* "poulterer", from *poulet* "young fowl, pullet"]

poul•try•man \-mən\ *n* **1** : one that raises domestic fowls especially on a commercial scale **2** : a dealer in poultry or poultry products

[1]**pounce** \'pau̇ns\ *vi* **1** : to swoop upon and seize something with or as if with talons ⟨the cat *pounced*⟩ **2** : to make an abrupt assault or approach [Middle English *pounce* "talon"]

[2]**pounce** *n* : the act of pouncing

[3]**pounce** *vt* : to dust, rub, finish, or stencil with pounce

[4]**pounce** *n* **1** : a fine powder formerly used to prevent ink from spreading **2** : a fine powder for making stenciled patterns [French *ponce* "pumice", from Latin *pumex*]

[1]**pound** \'pau̇nd\ *n, pl* **pounds** *also* **pound** **1** : any of various units of mass and weight; *esp* : a unit in general use among English-speaking peoples equal to 16 ounces (about 4.54 kilograms) — see MEASURE table **2 a** : the basic monetary unit of the United Kingdom — called also *pound sterling* **b** : the basic monetary unit of Cyprus, Egypt, Ireland, Israel, Lebanon, Malta, Sudan, and Syria **c** : a coin or note representing one pound [Old English *pund,* from Latin *pondo*]

[2]**pound** *vb* **1** : to reduce to powder or pulp by beating **2 a** : to strike heavily or repeatedly ⟨*pound* the piano⟩ **b** : to produce by means of repeated vigorous strokes ⟨*pound* out a story on the typewriter⟩ **c** : DRIVE 5b **3** : to move heavily or persistently ⟨the horses *pounded* along the lane⟩ [Old English *pūnian*]

[3]**pound** *n* : an act or sound of pounding

[4]**pound** *n* **1** : an enclosure for animals; *esp* : a public enclosure for stray or unlicensed animals **2 a** : an enclosure within which fish or crustaceans (as lobsters) are kept or caught; *esp* : the inner compartment of a fish trap **b** : an establishment selling live lobsters [Middle English, "enclosure", from Old English *pund-*]

pound•al \'pau̇n-dᵊl\ *n* : a unit of force equal to the force that would give a free mass of one pound an acceleration of one foot per second per second that is equal to .138 newton [*pound* + *-al* (as in *quintal*)]

pound cake *n* : a rich butter cake made with a large amount of eggs and shortening [from the original recipe calling for a pound of each of the principal ingredients]

[1]**pound•er** \'pau̇n-dər\ *n* : one that pounds

[2]**pounder** *n* **1** : one having a specified weight or value in pounds **2** : a gun throwing a projectile of a specified weight in pounds

pound–fool•ish \'pau̇nd-'fü-lish, 'pau̇n-\ *adj* : imprudent in dealing with large sums or weighty matters [from the phrase *penny-wise and pound-foolish*]

[1]**pour** \'pōr, 'pȯr\ *vb* **1** : to flow or to cause to flow in a stream ⟨*pour* the tea⟩ ⟨tears *pouring* down my cheeks⟩ **2** : to supply or produce copiously **3** : to rain hard [Middle English *pouren*] — **pour•able** \-ə-bəl\ *adj* — **pour•er** *n*

[2]**pour** *n* : the action of pouring: *esp* : a heavy rainfall

[1]**pout** \'pau̇t\ *n, pl* **pout** *or* **pouts** : any of several large-headed fishes (as a bullhead) [Old English *-pūte*]

[2]**pout** *vb* **1 a** : to show displeasure by thrusting out the lips **b** : SULK **2** : to protrude or cause to protrude [Middle English *pouten*]

[3]**pout** *n* **1** : a thrusting out of the lips expressing displeasure **2** *pl* : a fit of bad humor

pout•er \'pau̇t-ər\ *n* **1** : one that pouts **2** : a domestic pigeon of erect carriage with an inflatable crop

pouty \'pau̇t-ē\ *adj* : SULKY 1

pov•er•ty \'päv-ərt-ē\ *n* **1** : the state of being poor : lack of money or material possessions : WANT **2** : an inadequate supply : SCARCITY **3** : lack of fertility ⟨*poverty* of the soil⟩ [Old French *poverté,* from Latin *paupertas,* from *pauper* "poor"]

pov•er•ty–strick•en \-ˌstrik-ən\ *adj* : very poor : DESTITUTE

[1]**pow•der** \'pau̇d-ər\ *n* **1** : dry material made up of fine particles; *also* : a medicinal or cosmetic preparation in this form **2** : any of various solid explosives used chiefly in gunnery and blasting [Old French *poudre* "dust, powder", from Latin *pulver-, pulvis*]

[2]**powder** *vb* **1** : to sprinkle or cover with or as if with powder **2** : to reduce to or become powder — **pow•der•er** \-ər-ər\ *n*

powder blue *n* : a pale blue

powder horn *n* : a flask for carrying gunpowder; *esp* : one made of the horn of an ox or cow

powder keg *n* **1** : a small usually metal cask for holding gunpowder or blasting powder **2** : something (as an unstable political situation) liable to explode

powder puff *n* : a soft pad for applying cosmetic powder

powder room *n* : a rest room for women

pow•dery \'pau̇d-ə-rē\ *adj* **1 a** : resembling or consisting of powder **b** : easily reduced to powder : CRUMBLY **2** : covered with or as if with powder

powdery mildew *n* : a parasitic fungus producing abundant powdery conidia on the host; *also* : a plant disease caused by such a fungus

[1]**pow•er** \'pau̇-ər, 'pau̇r\ *n* **1 a** : possession of control, authority, or influence over others **b** : one having such power; *esp* : a sovereign state **2 a** : ability to act or do ⟨lose the *power* of speech⟩ **b** : legal or official authority, capacity, or right **3 a** : physical might **b** : mental strength and effectiveness **4 a** : the number of times as indicated by an exponent a number or expression is to be multiplied by itself **b** : the product obtained by raising a number or expression to a power **5 a** : force or energy that is or can be applied to work; *esp* : mechanical or electrical force or energy **b** : the time rate at which work is done or energy emitted or transferred **6** : MAGNIFICATION 2 [Old French *poeir,* from *poeir* "to be able", derived from Latin *potis, pote* "able"]

• **syn** POWER, FORCE, ENERGY, STRENGTH mean the ability to exert effort. POWER may imply latent or exerted physical, mental, or spiritual ability to act or be acted upon; FORCE implies the actual effective exercise of power ⟨pushed with enough *force* to overturn the chair⟩ ⟨a wind of intense *force*⟩ ENERGY applies to power expended or capable of being transformed into work ⟨a crusader of untiring *energy*⟩ STRENGTH applies to the quality or characteristic that enables one to exert force or withstand pressure or attack ⟨a mind of *strength* and decisiveness⟩

²power *adj* **:** relating to, supplying, or utilizing power; *esp* **:** utilizing mechanical or electrical energy ⟨a *power* drill⟩ ⟨*power* steering⟩

³power *vt* **:** to supply with power

pow•er•boat \-ˌbōt\ *n* **:** MOTORBOAT

power dive *n* **:** a dive of an airplane accelerated by the power of the engine — **power–dive** *vb*

pow•er•ful \ˈpau̇-ər-fəl, ˈpau̇r-\ *adj* **:** having great power, strength, or influence — **pow•er•ful•ly** \-fə-lē, -flē\ *adv*

pow•er•house \-ˌhau̇s\ *n* **1 a :** POWER PLANT 1 **b :** a source of influence or inspiration **2 :** one that has great power or unusual energy or strength

pow•er•less \-ləs\ *adj* **1 :** lacking power, force, or energy **:** unable to produce an effect **2 :** lacking authority to act — **pow•er•less•ly** *adv* — **pow•er•less•ness** *n*

power of attorney : a legal instrument authorizing a person to act as the attorney or agent of another

power pack *n* **:** a unit for converting a power supply to a voltage suitable for an electronic device

power plant *n* **1 :** an electric utility generating station **2 :** an engine and related parts supplying the motive power of a self-propelled vehicle

power play *n* **:** a situation in ice hockey in which the players on the ice for one team outnumber those for the other team because of a penalty

power politics *n sing or pl* **:** politics characterized by attempts to advance national interests through military and economic coercion

power shovel *n* **:** a power-operated excavating machine consisting of a boom or crane that supports a dipper handle with a dipper at the end of it

¹pow•wow \ˈpau̇-ˌwau̇\ *n* **1 :** an American Indian medicine man **2 a :** an American Indian ceremony (as for victory in war) **b :** a conference of or with American Indians **3 a :** a noisy gathering **b :** a meeting for discussion **[**of American Indian origin**]**

²powwow *vi* **:** to hold a powwow

pox \ˈpäks\ *n* **:** a disease (as smallpox, chicken pox, or syphilis) that causes a rash on the skin **[**alteration of *pocks,* pl. of *pock***]**

prac•ti•ca•ble \ˈprak-ti-kə-bəl\ *adj* **1 :** capable of being done, put into practice, or accomplished **:** FEASIBLE ⟨the idea was not *practicable*⟩ **2 :** USABLE ⟨a *practicable* substitute⟩ — **prac•ti•ca•bil•i•ty** \ˌprak-ti-kə-ˈbil-ət-ē\ *n* — **prac•ti•ca•ble•ness** \ˈprak-ti-kə-bəl-nəs\ *n* — **prac•ti•ca•bly** \-blē\ *adv*

• syn PRACTICABLE, PRACTICAL both mean relating to practice or use but they are not interchangeable. PRACTICABLE applies to what seems feasible but has not been tested in use; PRACTICAL applies to things and to persons and implies success in meeting the demands made by actual use of living **syn** see in addition POSSIBLE

prac•ti•cal \ˈprak-ti-kəl\ *adj* **1 :** actively engaged in an action or occupation ⟨a *practical* farmer⟩ **2 a :** of, relating to, or manifested in practice or action ⟨for *practical* purposes⟩ **b :** being such in practice or effect **:** VIRTUAL ⟨a *practical* failure⟩ **3 :** capable of being put to use or account **:** USEFUL **4 a :** inclined to action rather than planning or theorizing ⟨a *practical* person⟩ **b** (1) **:** qualified by practice or practical training (2) **:** designed to supplement theoretical training by experience **[**Latin *practicus,* from Greek *praktikos,* from *prassein* "to pass over, act, do"**]** **syn** see PRACTICABLE — **prac•ti•cal•i•ty** \ˌprak-ti-ˈkal-ət-ē\ *n* — **prac•ti•cal•ness** \ˈprak-ti-kəl-nəs\ *n*

practical joke *n* **:** a joke that depends on the tricking or abuse of a person at a disadvantage — **practical joker** *n*

prac•ti•cal•ly \ˈprak-ti-kə-lē, -klē\ *adv* **1 :** in a practical manner ⟨talked *practically* about the problem⟩ **2 :** NEARLY, ALMOST ⟨*practically* everyone was there⟩

practical nurse *n* **:** a nurse that cares for the sick professionally without having the training or experience required of a registered nurse; *esp* **:** LICENSED PRACTICAL NURSE

¹prac•tice *or* **prac•tise** \ˈprak-təs\ *vb* **1 a :** to perform or work at repeatedly so as to become skilled ⟨*practiced* their act⟩ **b :** to train by repeated exercises ⟨*practice* pupils in writing⟩ **2 a :** to carry out **:** APPLY ⟨*practice* what you preach⟩ **b :** to do or perform often, customarily, or habitually ⟨*practice* politeness⟩ **c :** to be professionally engaged in ⟨*practice* law⟩ **[**Middle French *practiser,* from *practique,* n., "practice", from Late Latin *practice,* from Greek *praktikē,* from *practikos* "practical"**]** — **prac•tic•er** *n*

²practice *also* **practise** *n* **1 a :** actual performance or application **b :** a repeated or customary action **c :** the usual way of doing something ⟨local *practices*⟩ **d :** an established manner of conducting legal proceedings **2 a :** systematic exercise for gaining skill ⟨*practice* makes perfect⟩ **b** *archaic* **:** skill acquired by practice **3 a :** the exercise of a profession ⟨the *practice* of law⟩ **b :** a professional business **syn** see HABIT — **in practice 1 :** in actual or accepted usage **2 :** in good or superior condition as a result of practice ⟨athletes must keep *in practice*⟩

prac•ticed *or* **prac•tised** \ˈprak-təst\ *adj* **1 :** EXPERIENCED, SKILLED ⟨a *practiced* welder⟩ **2 :** learned by practice

prac•tice–teach \ˌprak-təs-ˈtēch\ *vi* **:** to engage in practice teaching — **practice teacher** *n*

practice teaching *n* **:** teaching in which a student practices educational skills and methods under the supervision of an experienced teacher in preparation for professional teaching

prac•ti•tio•ner \prak-ˈtish-nər, -ə-nər\ *n* **1 :** a person who practices a profession and especially law or medicine **2 :** a Christian Scientist who is an authorized healer **[**from earlier *practician,* from Middle French *praticien,* from *pratique, practique* "practice"**]**

prae•no•men \prē-ˈnō-mən\ *n, pl* **-nomens** *or* **-no•mi•na** \-ˈnäm-ə-nə, -ˈnō-mə-\ **:** the first of the usual three names of an ancient Roman **[**Latin, from *prae-* "pre" + *nomen* "name"**]**

prae•tor \ˈprēt-ər\ *n* **:** an ancient Roman magistrate ranking below a consul and having chiefly judicial duties **[**Latin**]**

prae•to•ri•an \prē-ˈtōr-ē-ən, -ˈtȯr-\ *adj* **1 :** of or relating to a praetor **2** *often cap* **:** of, forming, or resembling the Roman imperial bodyguard — **praetorian** *n, often cap*

prag•mat•ic \prag-ˈmat-ik\ *also* **prag•mat•i•cal** \-ˈmat-i-kəl\ *adj* **1 a :** concerned with practical rather than intellectual or artistic matters **b :** practical as opposed to idealistic **2 :** relating to or in accordance with pragmatism **[**Latin *pragmaticus* "skilled in law or business", from Greek *pragmatikos,* from *pragma* "deed, action", from *prassein* "to do"**]** — **prag•mat•i•cal•ly** \-i-kə-lē, -klē\ *adv*

pragmatic sanction *n* **:** a solemn decree of a sovereign on a matter of primary importance and with the force of fundamental law

prag•ma•tism \ˈprag-mə-ˌtiz-əm\ *n* **1 :** a practical approach to problems and affairs **2 :** philosophical doctrine holding that the meaning of an idea is to be sought in its practical bearings, that the function of thought is to guide action, and that truth is to be tested by the practical consequences of belief — **prag•ma•tist** \-mət-əst\ *adj or n* — **prag•ma•tis•tic** \ˌprag-mə-ˈtis-tik\ *adj*

prai•rie \ˈpreər-ē\ *n* **:** a tract of grassland; *esp* **:** a large area of level or rolling land (as in the central United States) with deep fertile soil, a cover of tall coarse grasses, and few trees **[**French, derived from Latin *pratum* "meadow"**]**

prairie chicken *n* **:** a grouse of the Mississippi valley with a patch of bare inflatable skin on the neck

prairie dog *n* **:** a colonial buff or grayish American burrowing rodent related to the marmots

prairie dog

prairie schooner *n* **:** a covered wagon used by pioneers in cross-country travel — called also *prairie wagon*

prairie wolf *n* **:** COYOTE

¹praise \ˈprāz\ *vb* **1 :** to express approval **:** COMMEND **2 :** to glorify especially in song **:** EXTOL **[**Middle French *preisier* "to prize, praise", from Late Latin *pretiare* "to prize", from Latin *pretium* "price"**]** — **prais•er** *n*

²praise *n* **1 :** an act of praising **:** COMMENDATION **2 :** WORSHIP ⟨in *praise* of the Lord⟩

praise•wor•thy \-ˌwər-t͟hē\ *adj* **:** worthy of praise **:** LAUDABLE —

praise•wor•thi•ly \-thə-lē\ *adv* — **praise•wor•thi•ness** \-thē-nəs\ *n*

Pra•krit \ˈpräk-ˌrit, -rət\ *n* **1 :** any or all of the ancient Indic languages or dialects other than Sanskrit **2 :** any of the modern Indic languages [Sanskrit *prākṛta,* from *prākṛta* "natural, vulgar"]

pra•line \ˈprä-ˌlēn, ˈprā-\ *n* **:** a candy of nut kernels embedded in boiled brown sugar or maple sugar [French, from Count Plessy-*Praslin,* died 1675, French soldier]

pram \ˈpram\ *n, chiefly British* **:** a baby carriage [short for *perambulator*]

prance \ˈprans\ *vi* **1 :** to spring from the hind legs or move by so doing **2 :** to ride on a prancing horse **3 :** to move in a spirited manner **:** STRUT; *also* **:** CAPER [Middle English *prauncen*] — **prance** *n* — **pranc•er** \ˈpran-sər\ *n* — **pranc•ing•ly** \-sing-lē\ *adv*

pran•di•al \ˈpran-dē-əl\ *adj* **:** of or relating to a meal [Latin *prandium* "late breakfast, luncheon"]

[1]prank \ˈprangk\ *n* **:** a playful or mischievous act: as **a :** PRACTICAL JOKE ⟨Halloween *pranks*⟩ **b :** a ludicrous act [obsolete *prank* "to play tricks"] — **prank•ish** \ˈprang-kish\ *adj* — **prank•ish•ly** *adv* — **prank•ish•ness** *n*

[2]prank *vt* **:** to dress or adorn (as oneself) gaily or showily [probably from Dutch *pranken* "to strut"]

prank•ster \ˈprang-stər, ˈprangk-\ *n* **:** one that plays pranks

pra•seo•dym•i•um \ˌprā-zē-ō-ˈdim-ē-əm\ *n* **:** a yellowish white metallic chemical element used chiefly in the form of its salts as a coloring agent — see ELEMENT table [derived from Greek *prasios* "light green" + New Latin *didymium,* a mixture of rare earth elements, from Greek *didymos* "double"]

[1]prate \ˈprāt\ *vb* **:** to talk long and idly or foolishly [Dutch *praten*] — **prat•er** *n* — **prat•ing•ly** \ˈprāt-ing-lē\ *adv*

[2]prate *n* **:** idle or foolish talk

prat•fall \ˈprat-ˌfȯl\ *n* **1 :** a fall on the buttocks **2 :** a humiliating mishap or blunder [earlier *prat* "buttocks"]

pra•tique \pra-ˈtēk\ *n* **:** clearance given an incoming ship by the health authority of a port [French, literally, "practice"]

[1]prat•tle \ˈprat-l\ *vb* **prat•tled; prat•tling** \ˈprat-ling, -l-ing\ **1 :** PRATE **2 :** to utter meaningless sounds suggestive of the chatter of children [Low German *pratelen*] — **prat•tler** \ˈprat-lər, -l-ər\ *n* — **prat•tling•ly** \ˈprat-ling-lē\ *adv*

[2]prattle *n* **1 :** PRATE **2 :** a sound that is meaningless, repetitive, and suggestive of the chatter of children

prau \ˈprau̇\ *n* **:** any of several usually undecked Indonesian boats propelled by sails, oars, or paddles [Malay *pĕrahu*]

prawn \ˈprȯn, ˈprän\ *n* **:** any of numerous widely distributed edible decapod crustaceans resembling shrimps with large compressed abdomens; *also* **:** SHRIMP [Middle English *prane*]

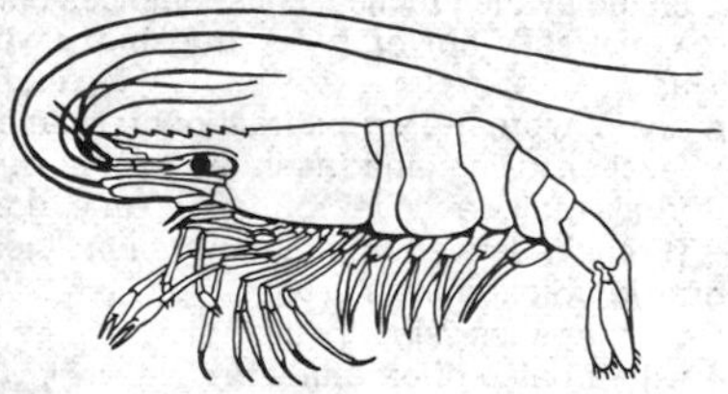
prawn

pray \ˈprā\ *vb* **1 :** ENTREAT, IMPLORE ⟨*pray* tell me the time⟩ **2 :** to get or bring by praying **3 :** to make entreaty or supplication **:** PLEAD **4 :** to address God with adoration, confession, supplication, or thanksgiving [Old French *preier,* from Latin *precari,* from *prec-, prex* "request, prayer"]

[1]prayer \ˈpraər, ˈpreər\ *n* **1 :** the act or practice of praying to God ⟨a moment of silent *prayer*⟩ **2 a :** a supplication or expression addressed to God ⟨a *prayer* of thanksgiving⟩ **b :** an earnest request or wish **:** PLEA **3 :** a religious service consisting chiefly of prayers ⟨had regular family *prayers*⟩ **4 :** a set form of words used in praying ⟨a book of *prayers*⟩ [Old French *preiere,* from Medieval Latin *precaria,* from Latin *precarius* "obtained by entreaty", from *prec-, prex* "request, entreaty"]

[2]pray•er \ˈprā-ər\ *n* **:** one that prays **:** SUPPLIANT

prayer book *n* **:** a book containing prayers and often other forms and directions for worship

prayer•ful \ˈpraər-fəl, -ˈpreər-\ *adj* **1 :** given to or characterized by prayer **:** DEVOUT **2 :** EARNEST 1 — **prayer•ful•ly** \-fə-lē\ *adv* — **prayer•ful•ness** *n*

prayer meeting *n* **:** a Protestant Christian service of evangelical worship usually held regularly on a weeknight — called also *prayer service*

prayer plant *n* **:** a Brazilian plant with oval leaves folding upward at night as if in prayer that is widely grown as an ornamental foliage plant

praying mantis *n* **:** MANTIS

pre- *prefix* **1 a** (1) **:** earlier than **:** prior to **:** before ⟨*pre*historic⟩ (2) preparatory or prerequisite to ⟨*pre*medical⟩ **b :** in advance **:** beforehand ⟨*pre*cancel⟩ **2 a :** in front of **:** anterior to ⟨*pre*molar⟩ **b :** front **:** anterior [Latin *prae-,* from *prae* "in front of, before"]

See *pre-* and 2d element

preaddiction
preaddress
preadmission
preadult
preagricultural
preaim
prealert
prealign
preallocate
preanesthetic
preannounce
prearraignment
prearrange
prearrangement
preattack
preaudit
preauthorization
preauthorize
preautomation
preautomobile
prebattle
prebiblical
prebirth
prebleach
preblend
preboom
prebound
prebreakfast
prebuilt
precalculate
precampaign
precensorship
precheck
prechosen
precivilization
preclean
preclear
preclearance
precode
precollege
precolonial
precombat
precombustion
precommitment
precompute
preconvention
precool
precoordinate
precoordination
precrash
predawn
predefine
predelinquency
predelinquent
predelivery
predeparture
predesignate
predesignation
predevelopment
predischarge
prediscovery
predrill
predug
predusk
preedit
preelection
preelectric
preelectronic
preemployment
preestablish
preexamination
prefestival
prefight
prefile
prefilter
prefire
prefuneral
pregame
preheat
prehung
preimmunization
preimmunize
preimpact
preinaugural
preindustrial
preinoculate
preinoculation
preinterview
preinvasion
prelaunch
prelaunder
prelife
preload
premarriage
premigration
premigrational
premigratory
premix
premodern
premodify
premoisten
premold
prenoon
prenotification
prenotify
preopening
peroperational
prepack
preplace
preplan
preplant
preproduction
preprofessional
preprogram
prepublication
prepunch
prepurchase
prequalification
prequalify
prerace
preregister
preregistration
prerehearsal
prerelease
preretirement
prerevolutionary
preriot
presale
preseason
preselect
preselection
preset
presoak
presort
prestamp
presterilize
prestrike
prestyle
presurgical
presweeten
pretape
pretelevision
pretournament
pretreat
pretreatment
pretrial
pretrip
preuniversity
prewar
prewash
preweigh
prewrap

preach \ˈprēch\ *vb* **1 a :** to deliver a sermon **:** utter publicly **b :** to set forth in a sermon ⟨*preach* the gospel⟩ **2 :** to urge acceptance or abandonment of an idea or course of action **:** ADVOCATE ⟨*preach* patience⟩; *esp* **:** to exhort in an officious or tiresome manner **3 :** to bring, put, or affect by preaching [Old French *prechier,* from Late Latin *praedicare,* from Latin, "to proclaim publicly", from *prae-* "pre-" + *dicare* "to proclaim"] — **preach•er** *n* — **preach•ing•ly** \ˈprē-ching-lē\ *adv*

preach•ify \ˈprē-chə-ˌfī\ *vi* **-fied; -fy•ing :** to preach ineptly or tediously

preach•ment \ˈprēch-mənt\ *n* **1 :** the act or practice of preaching **2 :** SERMON, EXHORTATION; *esp* **:** a tedious or unwelcome exhortation

preachy \ˈprē-chē\ *adj* **preach•i•er; -est :** marked by obvious moral exhortation — **preach•i•ly** \-chə-lē\ *adv* — **preach•i•ness** \-chē-nəs\ *n*

pre•ad•o•les•cence \ˌprē-ˌad-l-ˈes-ns\ *n* : the period of human development just preceding adolescence — **pre•ad•o•les•cent** \-nt\ *adj or n*

pre•am•ble \ˈprē-ˌam-bəl, prē-ˈ\ *n* **1** : an introductory statement; *esp* : the usually explanatory introductory part of a constitution or statute **2** : an introductory fact or circumstance : PRELIMINARY; *esp* : one indicating what is to follow [Middle French *preambule,* from Medieval Latin *praeambulum,* from Late Latin *praeambulus* "walking in front", from Latin *prae-* "pre-" + *ambulare* "to walk"]

pre•as•signed \ˌprē-ə-ˈsīnd\ *adj* : assigned beforehand

preb•end \ˈpreb-ənd\ *n* **1 a** : an endowment held by a cathedral or collegiate church for the maintenance of a prebendary **b** : the stipend paid from this endowment **2** : PREBENDARY [Middle French *prebende,* from Medieval Latin *praebenda,* from Late Latin, "subsistence allowance granted by the state", from Latin *praebēre* "to offer", from *prae-* "pre-" + *habēre* "to have, hold"]

preb•en•dary \ˈpreb-ən-ˌder-ē\ *n, pl* **-dar•ies** **1** : a clergyman receiving a prebend for officiating at stated times in the church **2** : an honorary canon

Pre•cam•bri•an \prē-ˈkam-brē-ən, ˈprē-\ *n* : the earliest era of geological history equivalent to the Archeozoic and Proterozoic; *also* : the corresponding system of rocks — **Precambrian** *adj*

pre•can•cel \prē-ˈkan-səl, ˈprē-\ *vt* : to cancel (a postage stamp) in advance of use — **pre•can•cel•la•tion** \ˌprē-ˌkan-sə-ˈlā-shən\ *n*

pre•can•cer•ous \prē-ˈkans-rəs, ˈprē-, -ə-rəs\ *adj* : likely to become cancerous ⟨a *precancerous* lesion⟩

pre•car•i•ous \pri-ˈkar-ē-əs, -ˈker-\ *adj* **1** : dependent upon uncertain premises ⟨*precarious* theories⟩ **2 a** : dependent on chance circumstances, unknown conditions, or uncertain developments **b** : characterized by a lack of security or stability that threatens with danger ⟨a *precarious* state of health⟩ [Latin *precarius* "obtained by entreaty, uncertain", from *prec-, prex* "request, entreaty"] — **pre•car•i•ous•ly** *adv* — **pre•car•i•ous•ness** *n*

pre•cau•tion \pri-ˈkȯ-shən\ *n* **1** : care taken in advance : FORESIGHT **2** : a measure taken beforehand to prevent harm or secure good : SAFEGUARD ⟨*precautions* against fire⟩ — **pre•cau•tion•ary** \-shə-ˌner-ē\ *adj*

pre•cede \pri-ˈsēd\ *vb* **1** : to surpass in rank, dignity, or importance **2** : to be, go, or come before or in front of in position or time **3** : to cause to be preceded : PREFACE ⟨*preceded* the speech with a welcome to the visitors⟩ [Middle French *preceder,* from *praecedere,* from *prae-* "pre-" + *cedere* "to go"]

pre•ce•dence \ˈpres-əd-əns, pri-ˈsēd-ns\ *n* **1** : the act or fact of preceding (as in time, importance, or position) **2** : PREFERENCE 1, PRIORITY

pre•ce•den•cy \-ən-sē, -n-sē\ *n* : PRECEDENCE

[1]**pre•ce•dent** \pri-ˈsēd-nt, ˈpres-əd-ənt\ *adj* : prior in time, order, arrangement, or significance [Middle French, from Latin *praecedens,* present participle of *praecedere* "to precede"]

[2]**prec•e•dent** \ˈpres-əd-ənt\ *n* **1** : an earlier occurrence of something similar **2** : something that may serve as an example or rule to authorize or justify a similar future act or statement ⟨this decision will set a *precedent*⟩

pre•ced•ing \pri-ˈsēd-ing\ *adj* : going before in time or place • **syn** PRECEDING, ANTECEDENT, FOREGOING mean being before. PRECEDING implies being immediately before in time or place ⟨on the *preceding* day⟩ ⟨the last line in the *preceding* stanza⟩ ANTECEDENT applies to order in time and may suggest a causal relation ⟨study the revolution and *antecedent* economic distress⟩ FOREGOING applies to what has preceded especially in a discourse ⟨the *foregoing* phrase⟩

pre•cen•tor \pri-ˈsent-ər\ *n* : a leader of the singing of a choir or congregation [Late Latin *praecentor,* from Latin *praecentus,* past participle of *praecinere* "to sing before", from *prae-* "pre-" + *canere* "to sing"] — **pre•cen•to•ri•al** \ˌprē-ˌsen-ˈtōr-ē-əl, -ˈtȯr-\ *adj* — **pre•cen•tor•ship** \pri-ˈsent-ər-ˌship\ *n*

pre•cept \ˈprē-ˌsept\ *n* : a command or principle intended as a general rule of action [Latin *praeceptum,* from *praeceptus,* past participle of *praecipere* "to take beforehand, instruct", from *prae-* "pre-" + *capere* "to take"]

pre•cep•tor \pri-ˈsep-tər, ˈprē-ˌ\ *n* **1** : TEACHER, TUTOR **2** : the principal of a school — **pre•cep•to•ri•al** \pri-ˌsep-ˈtōr-ē-əl, ˌprē-, -ˈtȯr-\ *adj* — **pre•cep•tor•ship** \pri-ˈsep-tər-ˌship, ˈprē-ˌ\ *n*

pre•ces•sion \prē-ˈsesh-ən\ *n* : a comparatively slow circling of the rotation axis of a spinning body about another line intersecting the axis [Medieval Latin *praecessio* "act of preceding", from Latin *praecessus,* past participle of *praecedere* "to precede"]

pre•cinct \ˈprē-ˌsingt, -ˌsingkt\ *n* **1** : an administrative subdivision of a territory: as **a** : a subdivision of a county, town, city, or ward for election purposes **b** : a division of a city for police control **2** : the enclosure bounded by the walls or limits of a building or place ⟨within the *precincts* of the college⟩ **3** *pl* : the region immediately surrounding a place : ENVIRONS ⟨the *precincts* of the city⟩ [Medieval Latin *praecinctum* "bounded district", from Latin *praecinctus,* past participle of *praecingere* "to gird about", from *prae-* "pre-" + *cingere* "to gird"]

pre•ci•os•i•ty \ˌpresh-ē-ˈäs-ət-ē, ˌpres-\ *n, pl* **-ties** : often excessive fastidious refinement (as in language)

[1]**pre•cious** \ˈpresh-əs\ *adj* **1** : of great value or high price ⟨diamonds, emeralds, and other *precious* stones⟩ **2** : highly esteemed or cherished ⟨*precious* memories⟩ **3** : excessively refined : AFFECTED ⟨*precious* language⟩ **4** : THOROUGHGOING, UTTER ⟨a *precious* scoundrel⟩ [Old French *precios,* from Latin *pretiosus,* from *pretium* "price"] — **pre•cious•ly** *adv* — **pre•cious•ness** *n*

[2]**precious** *adv* : EXTREMELY, VERY ⟨they had *precious* little to say⟩

prec•i•pice \ˈpres-ə-pəs\ *n* **1** : a very steep or overhanging place (as the face of a cliff) **2** : the brink of disaster [Middle French, from Latin *praecipitium,* from *praecipit-, praeceps* "headlong", from *prae-* "pre-" + *caput* "head"]

pre•cip•i•tance \pri-ˈsip-ət-əns\ *n* : rash haste

pre•cip•i•tan•cy \-ən-sē\ *n, pl* **-cies** : PRECIPITANCE

pre•cip•i•tant \-ənt\ *adj* : PRECIPITATE — **pre•cip•i•tant•ly** *adv* — **pre•cip•i•tant•ness** *n*

[1]**pre•cip•i•tate** \pri-ˈsip-ə-ˌtāt\ *vb* **1 a** : to throw violently :HURL **b** : to fall headlong **c** : to fall or come suddenly into some condition **2 a** : to move, urge, or press on with haste or violence **b** : to bring on abruptly ⟨the tactless remark *precipitated* a long, bitter quarrel⟩ **3 a** : to separate or cause to separate from solution or suspension **b** : to condense from a vapor and fall as rain or snow [Latin *praecipitare,* from *praecipit-, praeceps* "headlong"] — **pre•cip•i•ta•tor** \-ˌtāt-ər\ *n*

[2]**pre•cip•i•tate** \pri-ˈsip-ət-ət, -ə-ˌtāt\ *n* : a usually solid substance separated from a solution or suspension by chemical or physical change

[3]**pre•cip•i•tate** \pri-ˈsip-ət-ət\ *adj* **1** : exhibiting violent or unwise speed ⟨a *precipitate* attack⟩ **2** : falling, flowing, or rushing with steep descent — **pre•cip•i•tate•ly** *adv* — **pre•cip•i•tate•ness** *n*

pre•cip•i•ta•tion \pri-ˌsip-ə-ˈtā-shən\ *n* **1** : the quality or state of being precipitate : HASTE **2** : the process of precipitating or of forming a precipitate **3 a** : a deposit on the earth of hail, mist, rain, sleet, or snow; *also* : the quantity of water deposited **b** : PRECIPITATE

pre•cip•i•tin \pri-ˈsip-ət-ən\ *n* : an antibody that forms an insoluble precipitate when it unites with its antigen

pre•cip•i•tous \pri-ˈsip-ət-əs\ *adj* **1 a** : very steep, perpendicular, or overhanging **b** : having precipices ⟨a *precipitous* ledge⟩ **2** : falling very quickly : very rapid ⟨*precipitous* rush of water⟩ **3** : SUDDEN 2, RASH ⟨a *precipitous* act⟩ **syn** see STEEP — **pre•cip•i•tous•ly** *adv* — **pre•cip•i•tous•ness** *n*

pré•cis \prā-ˈsē, ˈprā-ˌsē\ *n, pl* **pré•cis** \-ˈsēz, -ˌsēz\ : a concise summary of essential points, statements, or facts [French, from *précis* "precise"]

pre•cise \pri-ˈsīs\ *adj* **1** : free from vagueness or inaccuracy **2** : very exact : ACCURATE ⟨*precise* scales⟩ ⟨*precise* time of arrival⟩ **3** : clear and sharp in enunciation : DISTINCT ⟨a low *precise* voice⟩ **4** : strictly conforming to rule or convention ⟨*precise* habits⟩ **5** : distinguished from every other ⟨at that *precise* moment⟩ [Middle French *precis;* from Latin *praecisus,* past participle of *praecidere* "to cut off", from *prae-* "pre-" + *caedere* "to cut"] **syn** see CORRECT — **pre•cise•ly** *adv* — **pre•cise•ness** *n*

pre•ci•sian \pri-ˈsizh-ən\ *n* : a person who stresses or practices scrupulous adherence to a strict standard especially of religious observance or morality

[1]**pre•ci•sion** \pri-'sizh-ən\ *n* **:** the quality or state of being precise; *esp* **:** the degree of refinement with which an operation is performed or a measurement stated — **pre•ci•sion•ist** \-'sizh-nəst, -ə-nəst\ *n*

[2]**precision** *adj* **1 :** adapted for extremely accurate measurement or operation ⟨a *precision* gauge⟩ **2 :** marked by precision of execution ⟨a *precision* drill team⟩

pre•clin•i•cal \prē-'klin-i-kəl, 'prē-\ *adj* **:** of or relating to the period preceding clinical manifestations ⟨*preclinical* infection⟩

pre•clude \pri-'klüd\ *vt* **:** to prevent or make impossible by acting, existing, or occurring beforehand [Latin *praecludere* (past participle *praeclusus*), literally, "to shut out", from *prae-* "pre-" + *claudere* "to close"] — **pre•clu•sion** \-'klü-zhən\ *n* — **pre•clu•sive** \-'klü-siv, -ziv\ *adj* — **pre•clu•sive•ly** *adv*

pre•co•cial \pri-'kō-shəl\ *adj* **:** capable of a high degree of independent activity from birth ⟨*precocial* birds⟩ — compare ALTRICIAL

pre•co•cious \pri-'kō-shəs\ *adj* **1 :** exceptionally early in development or occurrence ⟨*precocious* behavior⟩ **2 :** exhibiting mature qualities at an unusually early age ⟨a *precocious* child⟩ [Latin *praecoc-*, *praecox* "early ripening, precocious", from *prae-* "pre-" + *coquere* "to cook"] — **pre•co•cious•ly** *adv* — **pre•co•cious•ness** *n* — **pre•coc•i•ty** \pri-'käs-ət-ē\ *n*

pre•cog•ni•tion \ˌprē-käg-'nish-ən\ *n* **:** clairvoyance concerning something not yet experienced

pre•con•ceive \ˌprē-kən-'sēv\ *vt* **:** to form an opinion of prior to knowledge or experience ⟨*preconceived* ideas about foreigners⟩ — **pre•con•cep•tion** \-'sep-shən\ *n*

pre•con•cert•ed \ˌprē-kən-'sərt-əd\ *adj* **:** arranged or agreed upon in advance ⟨a *preconcerted* plan of attack⟩

pre•con•di•tion \ˌprē-kən-'dish-ən\ *vt* **:** to put in proper or desired condition or frame of mind in advance

pre•con•scious \prē-'kän-chəs, 'prē-\ *adj* **:** not present in consciousness but capable of being readily recalled — **pre•con•scious•ly** *adv*

pre•cook \prē-'kuk, 'prē-\ *vt* **:** to cook partially or entirely in advance

pre•cur•sor \pri-'kər-sər, 'prē-ˌ\ *n* **1 a :** one that precedes and indicates the approach of another **:** FORERUNNER **b :** PREDECESSOR 1 **2 :** a substance from which another substance is formed [Latin *praecursor,* from *praecurrere* "to run before", from *prae-* "pre-" + *currere* "to run"]

pre•cur•so•ry \pri-'kərs-rē, -ə-rē\ *adj* **:** having the character of a precursor **:** PRELIMINARY, PREMONITORY ⟨*precursory* symptoms of a fever⟩

pre•da•ceous *or* **pre•da•cious** \pri-'dā-shəs\ *adj* **:** living by preying on others **:** PREDATORY — **pre•da•ceous•ness** *n* — **pre•dac•i•ty** \-'das-ət-ē\ *n*

pre•date \prē-'dāt, 'prē-\ *vt* **:** ANTEDATE

pre•da•tion \pri-'dā-shən\ *n* **1 :** the act of preying or plundering **:** DEPREDATION **2 :** a mode of life in which food is primarily obtained by killing and consuming animals [Latin *praedatio,* from *praedatus,* past participle of *praedari* "to prey upon", from *praeda* "prey"] — **pred•a•tor** \'pred-ət-ər\ *n*

pred•a•to•ry \'pred-ə-ˌtōr-ē, -ˌtór-\ *adj* **1 :** of, relating to, or marked by plundering ⟨*predatory* raids⟩ **2 :** living by predation **:** PREDACEOUS; *also* **:** adapted to predation — **pred•a•to•ri•ly** \ˌpred-ə-'tōr-ə-lē, -'tór-\ *adv*

pre•de•cease \ˌprēd-i-sēs\ *vb* **:** to die before another person

pre•de•ces•sor \'pred-ə-ˌses-ər, 'prēd-\ *n* **1 :** one that precedes; *esp* **:** a person who has held a position or office before another **2** *archaic* **:** ANCESTOR 1 [Middle French *predecesseur,* from Late Latin *praedecessor,* from Latin *prae-* "pre-" + *decessor* "retiring governor", from *decessus,* past participle of *decedere* "to depart, retire from office", from *de-* + *cedere* "to go"]

pre•des•ti•nate \prē-'des-tə-ˌnāt\ *vt* **1 :** to foreordain to an earthly or eternal destiny by divine decree **2** *archaic* **:** PREDETERMINE 1b

pre•des•ti•na•tion \ˌprē-ˌdes-tə-'nā-shən\ *n* **:** the act of predestinating **:** the state of being predestinated

pre•des•tine \prē-'des-tən, 'prē-\ *vt* **:** to destine, decree, determine, appoint, or settle beforehand; *esp* **:** PREDESTINATE 1

pre•de•ter•mine \ˌprēd-i-'tər-mən\ *vt* **1 a :** FOREORDAIN, PREDESTINE **b :** to determine or settle beforehand ⟨meet at a *predetermined* place⟩ **2 :** to impose a direction or tendency on beforehand — **pre•de•ter•mi•na•tion** \-ˌtər-mə-'nā-shən\ *n*

pred•i•ca•ble \'pred-i-kə-bəl\ *adj* **:** capable of being predicated or affirmed

pre•dic•a•ment \pri-'dik-ə-mənt\ *n* **:** a difficult, perplexing, or trying situation **:** FIX [Late Latin *praedicamentum* "that which is predicated, category", from *praedicare* "to predicate"]

• syn DILEMMA, QUANDARY: PREDICAMENT suggests a difficult situation offering no satisfactory solution ⟨increased population poses a *predicament* for our society⟩ DILEMMA implies the need to choose between two alternatives offering essentially equal advantages or disadvantages ⟨in a *dilemma* about a choice of careers⟩ QUANDARY stresses puzzlement and perplexity ⟨in a *quandary* as to what excuse to make⟩

[1]**pred•i•cate** \'pred-i-kət\ *n* **1 :** something that is affirmed or denied of the subject in a proposition in logic ⟨in "paper is white", whiteness is the *predicate*⟩ **2 :** the part of a sentence or clause that expresses what is said of the subject and that usually consists of a verb with or without objects, complements, or adverbial modifiers [Late Latin *praedicatum,* from *praedicare* "to assert, predicate"] — **pred•i•ca•tive** \'pred-i-kət-iv, 'pred-ə-ˌkāt-\ *adj* — **pred•i•ca•tive•ly** *adv*

[2]**predicate** *adj* **:** belonging to the predicate; *esp* **:** completing the meaning of a linking verb ⟨*hot* in "the sun is hot" is a *predicate* adjective⟩ — compare ATTRIBUTIVE

[3]**pred•i•cate** \'pred-ə-ˌkāt\ *vt* **1 :** AFFIRM 1b, DECLARE **2 a :** to assert as a predicate in a proposition **b :** to assert to be a quality or property ⟨*predicate* sweetness of sugar⟩ **3 :** BASE, FOUND ⟨a proposal *predicated* upon the belief that sufficient support could be obtained⟩ [Late Latin *praedicare* "to assert, predicate, preach"]

predicate nominative *n* **:** a noun or pronoun in the nominative case completing the meaning of a linking verb

pred•i•ca•tion \ˌpred-ə-'kā-shən\ *n* **:** an act or instance of predicating; *esp* **:** the expression of action, state, or quality by a grammatical predicate

pre•dict \pri-'dikt\ *vt* **:** to declare in advance **:** foretell on the basis of observation, experience, or scientific reasoning [Latin *praedictus,* past participle of *praedicere* "to predict", from *prae-* "pre-" + *dicere* "to say"] **syn** see FORETELL — **pre•dict•able** \-'dik-tə-bəl\ *adj* — **pre•dict•ably** \-blē\ *adv*

pre•dic•tion \pri-'dik-shən\ *n* **1 :** an act of predicting **2 :** something that is predicted **:** FORECAST — **pre•dic•tive** \-'dik-tiv\ *adj* — **pre•dic•tive•ly** *adv*

pre•di•gest \ˌprēd-ī-'jest, ˌprēd-ə-\ *vt* **:** to subject to predigestion

pre•di•ges•tion \-'jes-chən, -'jesh-chən\ *n* **:** artificial partial digestion of food for use in illness or impaired digestion

pre•di•lec•tion \ˌpred-l-'ek-shən-, ˌprēd-\ *n* **:** an inclination in favor of something **:** PREFERENCE, PARTIALITY [French *prédilection,* from Medieval Latin *praedilectus,* past participle of *praediligere* "to prefer", from Latin *prae-* "pre-" + *diligere* "to love", from *dis-* "apart" + *legere* "to pick, choose"]

pre•dis•pose \ˌprēd-is-'pōz\ *vt* **:** to dispose in advance **:** make susceptible **:** INCLINE ⟨an inherited weakness *predisposing* one to certain diseases⟩

pre•dis•po•si•tion \ˌprē-ˌdis-pə-'zish-ən\ *n* **:** a condition of being predisposed **:** INCLINATION

pre•dom•i•nance \pri-'däm-ə-nəns\ *also* **pre•dom•i•nan•cy** \-nən-sē\ *n* **:** the quality or state of being predominant

pre•dom•i•nant \-nənt\ *adj* **:** having superior strength, influence, or authority ⟨the *predominant* color in a painting⟩ — **pre•dom•i•nant•ly** *adv*

pre•dom•i•nate \pri-'däm-ə-ˌnāt\ *vb* **1 :** to exert controlling power or influence **:** PREVAIL **2 :** to hold advantage in numbers or quantity **:** PREPONDERATE — **pre•dom•i•na•tion** \-ˌdäm-ə-'nā-shən\ *n*

pre•em•i•nence \prē-'em-ə-nəns\ *n* **:** the quality or state of being preeminent **:** SUPERIORITY

pre•em•i•nent \-nənt\ *adj* **:** of the highest rank, dignity, or importance **:** OUTSTANDING — **pre•em•i•nent•ly** *adv*

pre•empt \prē-'emt, -'empt\ *vt* **1 :** to settle upon (as public land) with the right to purchase before others; *also* **:** to take by such a right **2 :** to take before someone else can ⟨*preempt* a seat at the stadium⟩ [back-formation from *preemption,* from Medieval Latin *praeemptus,* past participle of *praeemere* "to buy before", from Latin *prae-* "pre-" + *emere* "to buy"] — **pre•emp•tion** \-'em-shən, -'emp-\ *n* — **pre•emp•tive** \-'em-tiv, -'emp-\ *adj* — **pre•emp•tive•ly** *adv* — **pre•emp•tor** \-tər\ *n*

preen \'prēn\ *vb* **1 :** to trim or dress with the bill **2 :** to dress or smooth oneself up : PRIMP **3** : to indulge oneself in pride : congratulate oneself : GLOAT [Middle English *preinen*] — **preen•er** *n*

pre•ex•ist \ˌprē-ig-ˈzist\ *vb* : to exist earlier or before something

pre•ex•ist•ence \-ˈzis-təns\ *n* : existence in a former state or previous to something else; *esp* : existence of the soul before its union with the body — **pre•ex•ist•ent** \-tənt\ *adj*

pre•fab \prē-ˈfab, ˈprē-ˌ\ *n* : a prefabricated structure — **prefab** *adj*

pre•fab•ri•cate \prē-ˈfab-ri-ˌkāt, ˈprē-\ *vt* **1** : to make the parts of at a factory so that construction consists mainly of assembling and uniting standardized parts **2** : to give a synthetic or artificial quality to — **pre•fab•ri•ca•tion** \ˌprē-ˌfab-ri-ˈkā-shən\ *n*

[1]pref•ace \ˈpref-əs\ *n* **1** *often cap* : a prayer introducing the central part of the eucharistic service **2** : the introductory remarks of a speaker or author : PROLOGUE [Middle French, from Latin *prefatio* "foreword", from *praefari* "to say beforehand", from *prae-* "pre-" + *fari* "to say"]

[2]preface *vb* **1** : to say or write as a preface ⟨a note *prefaced* to the manuscript⟩ **2** : PRECEDE 2, HERALD **3** : to introduce by or begin with a preface **4** : to locate in front of **5** : to be a preliminary to — **pref•ac•er** *n*

pref•a•to•ri•al \ˌpref-ə-ˈtōr-ē-əl, -ˈtȯr-\ *adj* : PREFATORY — **pref•a•to•ri•al•ly** \-ē-ə-lē\ *adv*

pref•a•to•ry \ˈpref-ə-ˌtōr-ē, -ˌtȯr-\ *adj* : of, relating to, or constituting a preface ⟨*prefatory* remarks⟩

pre•fect \ˈprē-ˌfekt\ *n* **1** : a high official or magistrate (as of ancient Rome or France) **2** : a presiding or chief officer or magistrate **3** : a student monitor in a private school [Middle French, from Latin *praefectus*, from *praeficere* "to place at the head of", from *prae-* "pre-" + *facere* "to make"]

prefect apostolic *n* : a Roman Catholic priest functioning like a bishop over a district of a missionary territory

pre•fec•ture \ˈprē-ˌfek-chər\ *n* **1** : the office or term of office of a prefect **2** : the district governed by a prefect — **pre•fec•tur•al** \prē-ˈfek-chə-rəl\ *adj*

pre•fer \pri-ˈfər\ *vt* **pre•ferred**; **pre•fer•ring** **1** : to choose or like above another ⟨*prefer* dark clothes⟩ **2** *archaic* : to put or set forward or before someone : RECOMMEND **3** : to present for action or consideration ⟨*prefer* charges against a person⟩ [Middle French *preferer*, from Latin *praeferre* "to put before, prefer", from *prae-* "pre-" + *ferre* "to carry"] — **pre•fer•rer** *n*

pref•er•a•ble \ˈpref-rə-bəl, -ə-rə-; ˈpref-ər-bəl\ *adj* : worthy to be preferred : more desirable — **pref•er•a•bil•i•ty** \ˌpref-rə-ˈbil-ət-ē, -ə-rə-\ *n* — **pref•er•a•ble•ness** \ˈpref-rə-bəl-nəs, -ə-rə-; -ər-bəl-nəs\ *n* — **pref•er•a•bly** \-blē\ *adv*

pref•er•ence \ˈpref-ərns; ˈpref-rəns, -ə-rəns\ *n* **1 a** : the act of preferring : the state of being preferred **b** : the power or opportunity of choosing ⟨gave us our *preference*⟩ **2** : one that is preferred : FAVORITE, CHOICE **3** : the act, fact, or principle of giving advantages to some over others ⟨show *preference*⟩ [French *préférence*, from Medieval Latin *praeferentia*, from Latin *praeferre* "to prefer"] **syn** see CHOICE

pref•er•en•tial \ˌpref-ə-ˈren-chəl\ *adj* **1** : showing preference ⟨*preferential* treatment⟩ **2** : creating or using preference ⟨a *preferential* tariff⟩ **3** : permitting the showing of preference or order of choice (as of candidates in an election) ⟨a *preferential* ballot⟩ **4** : giving preference in hiring to union members ⟨a *preferential* shop⟩ — **pref•er•en•tial•ly** \-ˈrench-lē, -ə-lē\ *adv*

pre•fer•ment \pri-ˈfər-mənt\ *n* **1 a** : advancement or promotion in dignity, office, or station **b** : a position or office of honor or profit **2** : the act of bringing forward (as charges)

preferred stock *n* : stock guaranteed priority by a corporation's charter over common stock in the payment of dividends and usually in the distribution of assets

pre•fig•ure \prē-ˈfig-yər, ˈprē-, *especially British* -ˈfig-ər\ *vt* **1** : to show, suggest, or announce by an earlier type, image, or likeness : FORESHOW ⟨other religions *prefigured* the Christian Easter⟩ **2** : to picture or imagine beforehand : FORESEE ⟨*prefigure* the outcome of a ball game⟩ — **pre•fig•u•ra•tion** \prē-ˌfig-yə-ˈrā-shən, -ˌfig-ə-\ *n* — **pre•fig•u•ra•tive** \prē-ˈfig-yə-rət-iv, ˈprē-, -ˈfig-ə-; -ˈfig-yərt-iv, -ərt-\ *adj* — **pre•fig•u•ra•tive•ly** *adv* — **pre•fig•u•ra•tive•ness** *n* — **pre•fig•ure•ment** \prē-ˈfig-yər-mənt, ˈprē-, *especially British* -ˈfig-ər-\ *n*

[1]pre•fix *vt* **1** \prē-ˈfiks, ˈprē-\ *archaic* : to fix or appoint beforehand **2** \ˈprē-ˌ, prē-ˈ\ : to place in front : add as a prefix ⟨*prefix* a syllable to a word⟩

[2]pre•fix \ˈprē-ˌfiks\ *n* : a sound or sequence of sounds or a letter or sequence of letters occurring as a bound form attached to the beginning of a word and serving to produce a derivative word [New Latin *praefixum*, from Latin *praefixus*, past participle of *praefigere* "to fasten before", from *prae-* "pre-" + *figere* "to fasten"] — **pre•fix•al** \ˈprē-ˌfik-səl, prē-ˈ\ *adj* — **pre•fix•al•ly** \-sə-lē\ *adv*

pre•flight \ˈprē-ˈflīt\ *adj* : preparing for or preliminary to flight ⟨*preflight* training⟩

pre•form \ˈprē-ˈfȯrm\ *vt* : to form or shape beforehand

pre•for•ma•tion \ˌprē-fȯr-ˈmā-shən\ *n* **1** : previous formation **2** : a discredited biological theory holding that every germ cell contains the organism of its kind fully formed and that development consists merely in increase in size — **pre•for•ma•tion•ist** \-shə-nəst\ *n*

pre•fron•tal \prē-ˈfrənt-l, ˈprē-\ *adj* : anterior to or involving the anterior part of a frontal structure ⟨a *prefrontal* bone⟩

pre•gan•gli•on•ic \ˌprē-ˌgang-glē-ˈän-ik\ *adj* : situated proximal to or preceding a ganglion; *also* : of, relating to, or being an axon passing from the central nervous system into an autonomic ganglion

preg•na•ble \ˈpreg-nə-bəl\ *adj* : capable of being taken or captured : VULNERABLE ⟨a *pregnable* fort⟩ [Middle French *prenable*, from *prendre* "to take", from Latin *prehendere*] — **preg•na•bil•i•ty** \ˌpreg-nə-ˈbil-ət-ē\ *n*

preg•nan•cy \ˈpreg-nən-sē\ *n*, *pl* **-cies** : the condition or quality of being pregnant : GESTATION

preg•nant \ˈpreg-nənt\ *adj* **1 a** : containing unborn young within the uterus **b** : capable of producing **2** : abounding in fancy, wit, or resourcefulness : INVENTIVE ⟨a *pregnant* mind⟩ **3** : rich in significance or implication : MEANINGFUL ⟨*pregnant* ideas⟩ **4** : containing the germ or shape of future events ⟨*pregnant* years⟩ **5** : exhibiting fertility ⟨nature was *pregnant* with life⟩ [Latin *praegnans*, alteration of *praegnas*] — **preg•nant•ly** *adv*

pre•hen•sile \prē-ˈhen-səl\ *adj* : adapted for grasping especially by wrapping around ⟨a *prehensile* tail⟩ [French *préhensile*, from Latin *prehensus*, past participle of *prehendere* "to grasp, take"]

pre•hen•sion \-ˈhen-chən\ *n* : the act of taking hold, seizing, or grasping

pre•his•tor•ic \ˌprē-is-ˈtȯr-ik, -his-, -ˈtär-\ *adj* : of, relating to, or existing in times before written history — **pre•his•tor•i•cal** \-i-kəl\ *adj* — **pre•his•tor•i•cal•ly** \-i-kə-lē, -klē\ *adv*

pre•his•to•ry \prē-ˈhis-tə-rē, ˈprē-, -trē\ *n* **1** : the study of prehistoric man **2** : a history of what leads up to an event or situation — **pre•his•to•ri•an** \ˌprē-is-ˈtōr-ē-ən, -his-, -ˈtȯr-\ *n*

pre•hu•man \ˈprē-ˈhyü-mən, -ˈyü-\ *adj* : being or relating to an animal in some respects like an ape but regarded as an ancestor of human beings — **prehuman** *n*

pre•judge \prē-ˈjəj, ˈprē-\ *vt* : to judge before hearing or before full and sufficient examination — **pre•judg•ment** \-ˈjəj-mənt\ *n*

[1]prej•u•dice \ˈprej-əd-əs\ *n* **1** : injury resulting from an unfair judgment or action of another; *esp* : an infringing of one's legal rights **2 a** (1) : a judgment or opinion formed before considering or without knowing the facts (2) : a favoring or dislike of something without grounds or before sufficient knowledge **b** : an irrational attitude of hostility directed against an individual, a group, or a race [Old French, from Latrin *praejudicium* "previous judgment, damage", from *prae-* "pre-" + *judicium* "judgment"]

• **syn** BIAS: PREJUDICE implies usually but not always an unfavorable view or fixed dislike and suggests a feeling rooted in suspicion, fear, or intolerance; BIAS implies partiality or distortion of individual judgments owing to a consistent mental leaning in favor of or against persons or things of a particular kind or class.

[2]prejudice *vt* **1** : to injure by an unfair judgment or action **2** : to cause to have predjudice : BIAS ⟨the incident *prejudiced* them against me⟩

\ə\ **abut**	\aù\ **out**	\i\ **tip**	\ȯ\ **saw**	\ù\ **foot**
\ər\ **further**	\ch\ **chin**	\ī\ **life**	\ȯi\ **coin**	\y\ **yet**
\a\ **mat**	\e\ **pet**	\j\ **job**	\th\ **thin**	\yü\ **few**
\ā\ **take**	\ē\ **easy**	\ng\ **sing**	\t͟h\ **this**	\yù\ **cure**
\ä\ **cot, cart**	\g\ **go**	\ō\ **bone**	\ü\ **food**	\zh\ **vision**

prej•u•di•cial \ˌprej-ə-ˈdish-əl\ *adj* **1 :** tending to injure or impair : DETRIMENTAL **2 :** leading to premature judgment or unwarranted opinion — **prej•u•di•cial•ly** \-ˈdish-lē, -ə-lē\ *adv* — **prej•u•di•cial•ness** \-ˈdish-əl-nəs\ *n*

prej•u•di•cious \ˌprej-ə-ˈdish-əs\ *adj* : PREJUDICIAL — **prej•u•di•cious•ly** *adv*

prel•a•cy \ˈprel-ə-sē\ *n, pl* **-cies 1 :** the office or dignity of a prelate **2 :** church government by prelates

prel•ate \ˈprel-ət\ *n* **:** a high-ranking clergyman (as a bishop) [Old French *prelat,* from Medieval Latin *praelatus,* literally, "one receiving preferment", from Latin, past participle of *praeferre* "to prefer"]

prelate nul•li•us \-nü-ˈlē-əs\ *n* **:** a Roman Catholic prelate usually a titular bishop with ordinary jurisdiction over a district independent of any diocese [*nullius* from New Latin *nullius dioecesis* "of no diocese"]

pre•lim \ˈprē-ˌlim, pri-ˈ\ *n or adj* : PRELIMINARY

[1]pre•lim•i•nary \pri-ˈlim-ə-ˌner-ē\ *n, pl* **-nar•ies :** something that precedes or is introductory or preparatory: as **a :** a preliminary scholastic examination ⟨pass the *preliminaries*⟩ **b :** a minor match preceding the main event [French *préliminaires,* pl., from Medieval Latin *praeliminaris,* adj., "preliminary", from Latin *prae-* "pre-" + *limin-, limen* "threshold"]

[2]preliminary *adj* **:** coming before the main part : INTRODUCTORY — **pre•lim•i•nar•i•ly** \-ˌlim-ə-ˈner-ə-lē\ *adv*

[1]pre•lude \ˈprel-ˌyüd, ˈprā-ˌlüd\ *n* **1 :** an introductory performance, action, or event preceding and preparing for a principal matter : INTRODUCTION ⟨the wind was a *prelude* to the storm⟩ **2 a :** a musical movement introducing the chief subject (as of a fugue) or serving as an introduction to an opera or oratorio **b :** a short musical piece (as an organ solo) played at the beginning of a church service **c :** a separate concert piece usually for piano or orchestra and based entirely on a short motif [Middle French, from Medieval Latin *praeludium,* from Latin *praeludere* "to play beforehand", from *prae-* "pre-" + *ludere* "to play"]

[2]prelude *vb* **1 :** to give, play, or serve as a prelude; *esp* **:** to play a musical introduction **2 :** FORESHADOW ⟨the gray dawn *preluded* a gloomy day⟩ — **pre•lud•er** *n*

pre•man \ˈprē-ˈman\ *n* **:** a hypothetical ancient primate immediately ancestral to human beings

pre•ma•ture \ˌprē-mə-ˈtu̇r, -ˈtyu̇r, -ˈchu̇r\ *adj* **:** happening, arriving, existing, or performed before the proper or usual time; *esp* **:** born after a gestation period of less than 37 weeks ⟨*premature* babies⟩ — **premature** *n* — **pre•ma•ture•ly** *adv* — **pre•ma•tu•ri•ty** \-ˈtu̇r-ət-ē, -ˈtyu̇r-, -ˈchu̇r-\ *n*

[1]pre•med \ˈprē-ˈmed\ *adj* : PREMEDICAL

[2]premed *n* **:** a premedical student or course of study

pre•med•i•cal \prē-ˈmed-i-kəl, ˈprē-\ *adj* **:** preceding and preparing for the professional study of medicine

pre•med•i•tate \pri-ˈmed-ə-ˌtāt, ˈprē-\ *vt* **:** to think about and plan beforehand ⟨*premeditate* murder⟩ — **pre•med•i•tat•ed•ly** \-ˌtāt-əd-lē\ *adv* — **pre•med•i•ta•tion** \pri-ˌmed-ə-ˈtā-shən, ˌprē-\ *n*

[1]pre•mier \pri-ˈmiər, -ˈmyiər; ˈprē-mē-ər, ˈprem-ē-\ *adj* **1 :** first in position, rank, or importance : PRINCIPAL **2 :** first in time : EARLIEST [Middle French, from Latin *primarius* "of the first rank", from *primus* "first"]

[2]premier *n* **:** the chief minister and head of government : PRIME MINISTER — **pre•mier•ship** \-ˌship\ *n*

[1]pre•miere \pri-ˈmyeər, -ˈmiər\ *n* **:** a first performance or exhibition ⟨the *premiere* of a play⟩ [French *première,* from *premier* "first"]

[2]premiere *vb* **:** to present or appear in a first public performance

[3]premiere *adj* **:** most eminent ⟨the nation's *premiere* author⟩ [alteration of [1]*premier*]

[1]prem•ise \ˈprem-əs\ *n* **1 :** a proposition assumed as a basis of argument or inference; *esp* **:** either of the first two propositions of a syllogism from which the conclusion is drawn **2** *pl* **:** matters previously stated **3** *pl* **a :** a tract of land with the buildings thereon **b :** a building or part of a building usually with its grounds [Medieval Latin *praemissa,* from Latin *praemittere* "to place ahead", from *prae-* "pre-" + *mittere* "to send"; sense 3 from its being identified in the premises of the deed]

[2]premise *vt* **1 :** to set forth beforehand as introductory or as postulated : POSTULATE **2 :** to offer as a premise in an argument

[1]pre•mi•um \ˈprē-mē-əm\ *n* **1 a :** a reward or recompense for a particular act **b :** a sum over and above a regular price or a face or par value **c :** something given free or at a reduced price with a purchase **2 :** the amount paid for a contract of insurance **3 :** a high value or a value in excess of that normally or usually expected ⟨put a *premium* on accuracy⟩ [Latin *praemium* "booty, profit, reward", from *prae-* "pre-" + *emere* "to take, buy"] — **at a premium :** usually valuable because of demand ⟨housing was *at a premium*⟩

[2]premium *adj* **:** of exceptional quality, value, or price

pre•mo•lar \prē-ˈmō-lər, ˈprē-\ *n* **:** any of the double-pointed grinding teeth which occur between the true molars and the canines and of which in man there are two on each side of each jaw — **premolar** *adj*

pre•mo•ni•tion \ˌprē-mə-ˈnish-ən, ˌprem-ə-\ *n* **1 :** previous warning or notice **2 :** anticipation of an event without conscious reason : PRESENTIMENT [Middle French, from Late Latin *praemonitio,* from Latin *praemonēre* "to warn in advance", from *prae-* "pre-" + *monēre* "to warn"] — **pre•mon•i•to•ry** \prē-ˈmän-ə-ˌtōr-ē, -ˌtȯr-\ *adj*

pre•name \ˈprē-ˌnām\ *n* : FORENAME

pre•na•tal \prē-ˈnāt-l, ˈprē-\ *adj* **:** occurring or existing before birth ⟨*prenatal* care⟩ — **pre•na•tal•ly** \-l-ē\ *adv*

pren•tice \ˈprent-əs\ *n* : APPRENTICE 1, LEARNER — **prentice** *adj*

pre•oc•cu•pied \prē-ˈäk-yə-ˌpīd\ *adj* **1 :** lost in thought ⟨too much *preoccupied* to notice⟩ **2 :** already occupied

pre•oc•cu•py *vt* **-pied; -py•ing 1** \prē-ˈäk-yə-ˌpī\ **:** to engage or absorb the attention of beforehand **2** \prē-, ˈprē-\ **:** to take possession of or fill beforehand or before another — **pre•oc•cu•pa•tion** \prē-ˌäk-yə-ˈpā-shən\ *n*

pre•op•er•a•tive \prē-ˈäp-rət-iv, ˈprē-, -ˈäp-ə-rət-, -ˈäp-ə-ˌrāt-\ *adj* **:** occurring before a surgical operation — **pre•op•er•a•tive•ly** *adv*

pre•or•dain \ˌprē-ȯr-ˈdān\ *vt* **:** to decree in advance : FOREORDAIN — **pre•or•di•na•tion** \prē-ˌȯrd-n-ˈā-shən\ *n*

[1]prep \ˈprep\ *n* : PREPARATORY SCHOOL

[2]prep *vb* **prepped; prep•ping 1 :** to engage in preparatory study or training **2 :** to get ready : PREPARE ⟨*prepped* the patient for the operation⟩

prep•a•ra•tion \ˌprep-ə-ˈrā-shən\ *n* **1 :** the action or process of getting something ready (as for use or service) or of getting ready for some occasion, test, or duty **2 :** a state of being prepared **3 :** a preparatory act or measure **4 :** something that is prepared; *esp* **:** a medicinal material made ready for use

pre•par•a•to•ry \pri-ˈpar-ə-ˌtōr-ē, -ˌtȯr-\ *adj* **:** preparing or serving to prepare for something : INTRODUCTORY — **pre•par•a•to•ri•ly** \-ˌpar-ə-ˈtōr-ə-lē, -ˈtȯr-\ *adv*

preparatory school *n* **1 :** a usually private school preparing students primarily for college **2** *British* **:** a private elementary school preparing students primarily for public schools

pre•pare \pri-ˈpaər, -ˈpeər\ *vb* **1 :** to make or get ready ⟨*prepared* them for the shocking news⟩ ⟨*prepare* for a test⟩ **2 :** to put together : COMPOUND ⟨*prepare* a vaccine⟩ ⟨*prepare* a prescription⟩ [Middle French *preparer,* from Latin *praeparare,* from *prae-* "pre-" + *parare* "to procure, prepare"] — **pre•par•er** *n*

pre•par•ed•ness \pri-ˈpar-əd-nəs, -ˈper-; -ˈpaərd-nəs, -ˈpeərd-\ *n* **:** the quality or state of being prepared

pre•pay \prē-ˈpā, ˈprē-\ *vt* **pre•paid;** \-ˈpād\ **pre•pay•ing :** to pay or pay for in advance — **pre•pay•ment** \-ˈpā-mənt\ *n*

pre•pon•der•ance \pri-ˈpän-də-rəns, -drəns\ *n* **1 :** a superiority in weight or in power, importance, or strength ⟨the *preponderance* of the evidence⟩ **2 :** a superiority or excess in number or quantity ⟨the *preponderance* of lawyers in the legislature⟩

pre•pon•der•ant \pri-ˈpän-də-rənt, -drənt\ *adj* **1 :** outweighing others : PREDOMINANT **2 :** having greater frequency or prevalence — **pre•pon•der•ant•ly** *adv*

pre•pon•der•ate \pri-ˈpän-də-ˌrāt\ *vi* **1 :** to exceed in weight, power, or importance : PREDOMINATE **2 :** to exceed in numbers [Latin *praeponderare,* literally, "to outweigh", from *prae-* "pre-" + *ponder-, pondus* "weight"] — **pre•pon•der•a•tion** \-ˌpän-də-ˈrā-shən\ *n*

prep•o•si•tion \ˌprep-ə-ˈzish-ən\ *n* **:** a linguistic form that combines with a noun, pronoun, or nominal to form a phrase that typically has an adverbial, adjectival, or substantival relation to some other word [Latin *praepositio,* from *praeponere* "to put in front", from *prae-* "pre-" + *ponere* "to put, place"] — **prep•o•si•tion•al** \-ˈzish-nəl, -ən-l\ *adj* — **prep•o•si•tion•al•ly** \-ē\ *adv*

pre•pos•sess \ˌprē-pə-ˈzes\ *vt* **1 :** to cause to be preoccupied

(as with an idea or belief) **2 :** to influence beforehand; *esp* **:** to move to a favorable opinion beforehand
pre•pos•sess•ing *adj* **:** tending to create a favorable impression **:** ATTRACTIVE ⟨a *prepossessing* appearance⟩ — **pre•pos•sess•ing•ly** \-iŋ-lē\ *adv* — **pre•pos•sess•ing•ness** *n*
pre•pos•ses•sion \ˌprē-pə-ˈzesh-ən\ *n* **1 :** an attitude, belief, or impression formed beforehand **:** PREJUDICE **2 :** an exclusive concern with one idea or object
pre•pos•ter•ous \pri-ˈpäs-tə-rəs, -trəs\ *adj* **:** contrary to nature, reason, or common sense **:** ABSURD **[**Latin *praeposterus,* literally, "with the back part in front", from *prae-* "pre-" + *posterus* "hinder, posterior"**]** — **pre•pos•ter•ous•ly** *adv* — **pre•pos•ter•ous•ness** *n*
pre•po•tent \prē-ˈpōt-nt, ˈprē-\ *adj* **:** having an unusual ability to transmit characters to offspring ⟨a *prepotent* sire⟩ — **pre•po•ten•cy** \-n-sē\ *n*
pre•pu•ber•ty \-ˈpyü-bərt-ē\ *n* **:** the period immediately preceding puberty — **pre•pu•ber•tal** \-bərt-l\ *adj*
pre•puce \ˈprē-ˌpyüs\ *n* **:** FORESKIN; *also* **:** a similar fold investing the clitoris **[**Middle French, from Latin *praeputium***]** — **pre•pu•tial** \prē-ˈpyü-shəl\ *n*
pre•re•cord \ˌprē-ri-ˈkȯrd\ *vt* **:** to record (as a radio or television program) in advance of presentation or use
pre•req•ui•site \prē-ˈrek-wə-zət, ˈprē-\ *n* **:** something that is required beforehand or is necessary as a preliminary to something else ⟨the course is a *prerequisite* for more advanced study⟩ — **prerequisite** *adj*
pre•rog•a•tive \pri-ˈräg-ət-iv\ *n* **:** a special privilege or advantage; *esp* **:** a right attached to an office, rank, or status ⟨a royal *prerogative*⟩ **[**Latin *praerogativa* "Roman century voting first in the assembly, privilege", from *praerogativus* "voting first", from *praerogare* "to ask for an opinion before another", from *prae-* "pre-" + *rogare* "to ask"**]**
¹pres•age \ˈpres-ij\ *n* **1 :** something that foreshadows or portends a future event **:** OMEN **2 :** FOREBODING, PRESENTIMENT **[**Latin *praesagium,* from *praesagire* "to forebode", from *prae-* "pre-" + *sagire* "to perceive keenly"**]** — **pre•sage•ful** \pri-ˈsāj-fəl\ *adj*
²pre•sage \ˈpres-ij, pri-ˈsāj\ *vt* **1 :** to give an omen or warning of **:** FORESHADOW, PORTEND **2 :** FORETELL, PREDICT
pre•sanc•ti•fied \prē-ˈsaŋ-ti-ˌfīd, ˈprē-, -ˈsaŋk-\ *adj* **:** consecrated at a previous service — used of eucharistic elements
pres•by•o•pia \ˌprez-bē-ˈō-pē-ə, ˌpres-\ *n* **:** a visual condition of old age in which loss of elasticity of the lens of the eye causes defective accommodation and inability to focus sharply for near vision **[**Greek *presbys* "old man"**]** — **pres•by•opic** \-ˈō-pik, -ˈäp-ik\ *adj or n*
pres•by•ter \ˈprez-bət-ər, ˈpres-\ *n* **1 :** a member of the governing body of an early Christian church **2 :** a Christian priest **[**Late Latin, "elder, priest", from Greek *presbyteros,* from *presbys* "old man"**]** — **pres•byt•er•ate** \prez-ˈbit-ə-rət, pres-\ *n*
Pres•by•te•ri•an \ˌprez-bə-ˈtir-ē-ən, ˌpres-\ *adj* **1** *often not cap* **:** characterized by a system of representative governing councils of ministers and elders **2 :** of, relating to, or constituting a Protestant Christian church that is presbyterian in government and traditionally Calvinistic in doctrine — **Presbyterian** *n* — **Pres•by•te•ri•an•ism** \-ē-ə-ˌniz-əm\ *n*
pres•by•tery \ˈprez-bə-ˌter-ē, ˈpres-\ *n, pl* **-ter•ies 1 :** the part of a church reserved for the officiating clergy **2 :** a ruling body in presbyterian churches consisting of the ministers and representative elders from congregations within a district **3 :** the territorial jurisdiction of a presbytery
pre•school \ˈprē-ˈskül\ *adj* **:** of, relating to, or being the period in a child's life from infancy to the age of five or six
pre•science \ˈprēsh-əns, ˈpresh-, -ē-əns\ **:** foreknowledge of events: **a :** omniscience with regard to the future **b :** FORESIGHT 1 **[**Late Latin *praescientia,* from Latin *praescire* "to know beforehand", from *prae-* "pre"- + *scire* "to know"**]** — **prescient** \-ənt\ *adj* — **pre•scient•ly** *adv*
pre•scribe \pri-ˈskrīb\ *vb* **1 a :** to lay down as a guide, direction, or rule of action **:** ORDAIN ⟨*prescribe* a way of life⟩ **b :** to specify with authority ⟨*prescribed* the courses for freshmen⟩ **2 :** to order or direct the use of something as a remedy ⟨the doctor *prescribed* rest⟩ **[**Latin *praescribere* "to write at the beginning, dictate, order", from *prae-* "pre-" + *scribere* "to write"**]** — **pre•scrib•er** *n*
pre•script \ˈprē-ˌskript\ *n* **:** something prescribed — **prescript** *adj*
pre•scrip•tion \pri-ˈskrip-shən\ *n* **1 a :** the establishment of a claim of title to something usually by use and enjoyment for a fixed period **b :** the right or title acquired by possession **2 :** the action of laying down authoritative rules or directions **3 a :** a written direction or order for the preparation and use of a medicine **b :** a medicine prescribed **[**Latin *praescriptio* "writing at the beginning, order", from *praescriptus,* past participle of *praescribere* "to write at the beginning, order"**]** — **pre•scrip•tive** \-ˈskrip-tiv\ *adj* — **pre•scrip•tive•ly** *adv*
pres•ence \ˈprez-ns\ *n* **1 :** the fact or condition of being present ⟨no one noticed my *presence*⟩ **2 a :** the part of space within one's immediate vicinity ⟨felt awkward in their *presence*⟩ **b :** the neighborhood of one of superior and especially royal rank **3 :** one that is present ⟨influential as an impressive *presence* in the group⟩ **4 :** the bearing or air of a person; *esp* **:** stately or distinguished bearing **5 :** something (as a spirit) felt to be present ⟨as eerie sense of some *presence* guiding us⟩
presence chamber *n* **:** the room where a dignitary receives those entitled to come into his or her presence
presence of mind : self-control in an emergency such that one can say and do the right thing
¹pres•ent \ˈprez-nt\ *n* **:** something presented **:** GIFT **[**Old French, from *presenter* "to present"**]**
²pre•sent \pri-ˈzent\ *vt* **1 a :** to bring or introduce into the presence of someone; *esp* **:** to introduce socially **b :** to bring (as a play) before the public **2 :** to make a gift to **3 :** to give or bestow formally **4 :** to lay (a charge) against a person **5 :** to offer to view **:** DISPLAY, SHOW **6 :** to aim, point, or direct (as a weapon) so as to face something or in a particular direction **[**Old French *presenter,* from Latin *praesentare,* from *praesens,* adj., "present"**]** **syn** see GIVE — **pre•sent•er** *n*
³pres•ent \ˈprez-nt\ *adj* **1 :** now existing or in progress **2 a :** being in view or at hand **b :** existing in something mentioned or under consideration **3 :** of, relating to, or being a verb tense that expresses present time or the time of speaking **[**Old French, from Latin *praesens,* from *praeesse* "to be before one", from *prae-* "pre-" + *esse* "to be"**]**
⁴pres•ent \ˈprez-nt\ *n* **1** *pl* **:** the present words or statements; *also* **:** the document in which these words are used ⟨know all men by these *presents*⟩ **2 a :** PRESENT TENSE **b :** a verb form in the present tense **3 :** the present time
pre•sent•able \pri-ˈzent-ə-bəl\ *adj* **1 :** capable of being presented ⟨whipped the speech into *presentable* form⟩ **2 :** being in condition to be seen or inspected especially by the critical ⟨made the room *presentable*⟩ — **pre•sent•abil•i•ty** \-ˌzent-ə-ˈbil-ət-ē\ *n* — **pre•sent•able•ness** \-ˈzent-ə-bəl-nəs\ *n* — **pre•sent•ably** \-blē\ *adv*
pre•sen•ta•tion \ˌprē-ˌzen-ˈtā-shən, ˌprez-n-\ *n* **1 :** the act of presenting **2 :** something presented: as **a :** something offered or given **:** GIFT **b :** something set forth for the attention of the mind — **pre•sen•ta•tion•al** \-shnəl, -shən-l\ *adj*
pres•ent-day \ˌprez-nt-ˌdā\ *adj* **:** now existing or occurring **:** CURRENT
pre•sen•ti•ment \pri-ˈzent-ə-mənt\ *n* **:** a feeling that something will or is about to happen **:** PREMONITION **[**French *pressentiment,* from *pressentir* "to have a presentiment", from Latin *praesentire* "to feel beforehand", from *prae-* "pre-" + *sentire* "to feel"**]**
pres•ent•ly \ˈprez-nt-lē\ *adv* **1** *archaic* **:** at once **2 :** before long **:** SOON ⟨*presently* they arrived⟩ **3 :** at the present time **:** NOW ⟨*presently* we have none⟩
pre•sent•ment \pri-ˈzent-mənt\ *n* **1 :** the act of presenting; *esp* **:** the act of offering a draft or a promissory note at the proper time and place to be paid by another **2 a :** the act of presenting to view or consciousness **b :** something set forth, presented, or exhibited
present participle *n* **:** a participle that expresses present action in relation to the time expressed by the finite verb in its clause and that in English is formed with the suffix *-ing* and is used in the formation of the progressive tenses
present perfect *adj* **:** of, relating to, or constituting a verb tense formed in English with *have* and expressing action or state completed at the time of speaking — **present perfect** *n*

\ə\ **a**but	\au̇\ **ou**t	\i\ t**i**p	\ȯ\ s**aw**	\u̇\ f**oo**t
\ər\ f**ur**ther	\ch\ **ch**in	\ī\ l**i**fe	\ȯi\ c**oi**n	\y\ **y**et
\a\ m**a**t	\e\ p**e**t	\j\ **j**ob	\th\ **th**in	\yü\ f**ew**
\ā\ t**a**ke	\ē\ **ea**sy	\ng\ si**ng**	\t͟h\ **th**is	\yu̇\ c**u**re
\ä\ c**o**t, c**a**rt	\g\ **g**o	\ō\ b**o**ne	\ü\ f**oo**d	\zh\ vi**si**on

present tense *n* : the tense of a verb that expresses action or state in the present time and is used of what occurs or is true at the time of speaking and of what is habitual or characteristic or is always or necessarily true, that is sometimes used to refer to action in the past (as in the historical present), and that is sometimes used for future events

1pre·ser·va·tive \pri-ˈzər-vət-iv\ *adj* : having the power of preserving

2preservative *n* : something that preserves; *esp* : an additive used to protect against decay, discoloration, or spoilage

1pre·serve \pri-ˈzərv\ *vt* **1** : to keep safe from harm or destruction : PROTECT ⟨*preserve* the republic⟩ **2 a** : to keep alive, intact, or free from decay ⟨*preserve* laboratory specimens⟩ **b** : to keep up : MAINTAIN **3 a** : to keep from decomposition **b** : to prepare (as by canning or pickling) for future use ⟨*preserve* beets⟩ [Middle French *preserver,* from Medieval Latin *praeservare,* from Latin *prae-* "pre-" + *servare* "to keep, guard"] — **pre·serv·able** \pri-ˈzər-və-bəl\ *adj* — **pres·er·va·tion** \ˌprez-ər-ˈvā-shən\ *n* — **pre·serv·er** *n*

2preserve *n* **1** : fruit canned or made into jams or jellies or cooked whole or in large pieces in a syrup so as to keep its shape — often used in pl. ⟨strawberry *preserves*⟩ **2** : an area restricted for the protection and preservation of natural resources (as animals and trees); *esp* : one used primarily for regulated hunting or fishing **3** : something regarded as reserved for certain persons

pre·shrunk \ˈprē-ˈshrəngk\ *adj* : of, relating to, or constituting a fabric subjected to a shrinking process during manufacture usually to reduce later shrinking

pre·side \pri-ˈzīd\ *vi* **1 a** : to occupy the place of authority : act as chairman **b** : to occupy a position similar to that of a president or chairman ⟨*preside* over a ceremony⟩ **2** : to exercise guidance or control ⟨*presided* over the destinies of the empire⟩ **3** : to occupy a position of featured instrumental performer ⟨*presided* at the organ⟩ [Latin *praesidēre,* literally, "to sit at the head of", from *prae-* "pre-" + *sedēre* "to sit"] — **pre·sid·er** *n*

pres·i·den·cy \ˈprez-əd-ən-sē, ˈprez-dən-; ˈprez-ə-ˌden-sē\ *n, pl* **-cies** **1** : the office or term of a president **2** : an executive council in the Mormon Church

pres·i·dent \ˈprez-əd-ənt, ˈprez-dənt, ˈprez-ə-ˌdent\ *n* **1** : one who presides over a meeting or assembly **2** : an appointed governor of a subordinate political unit **3** : the chief officer of an organization (as a corporation) **4** : the presiding officer of a governmental body **5 a** : an elected official serving as both chief of state and chief political executive in a republic having a presidential government **b** : an elected official having the position of chief of state but usually only minimal political powers in a republic having a parliamentary government [Middle French, from Latin *praesidens,* from *praesidēre* "to preside"] — **pres·i·den·tial** \ˌprez-ə-ˈden-chəl\ *adj*

Presidents' Day *n* : WASHINGTON'S BIRTHDAY 2 [from the fact that it falls between the birthdays of Presidents Lincoln and Washington]

pre·si·dio \pri-ˈsēd-ē-ˌō, -ˈsid-, -ˈzēd-, -ˈzid-\ *n, pl* **-di·os** : a garrisoned place; *esp* : a military post or fortified settlement in areas currently or originally under Spanish control [Spanish, from Latin *praesidium*]

pre·sid·i·um \pri-ˈsid-ē-əm, -ˈzid-\ *n, pl* **-ia** \-ē-ə\ *or* **-i·ums** : a permanent executive committee selected especially in Communist countries to act for a larger body [Russian *prezidium,* from Latin *praesidium* "garrison", from *praesid-, praeses* "guard, governor", from *praesidēre* "to guard, preside"]

1press \ˈpres\ *n* **1** : a crowd or a crowded condition **2** : an apparatus or machine for exerting pressure (as for shaping material, extracting liquid, drilling, or preventing something from warping) **3** : CLOSET 2 **4** : an act of pressing or pushing : PRESSURE **5** : the properly smoothed and creased condition of a freshly pressed garment **6 a** : PRINTING PRESS **b** : the act or the process of printing **c** : a printing or publishing establishment **7 a** : the gathering and publishing of news : JOURNALISM **b** : newspapers, periodicals, and often radio and television news broadcasting **c** : comment or notice in newspapers and periodicals ⟨is getting good *press*⟩ [Old French *presse,* from *presser* "to press"]

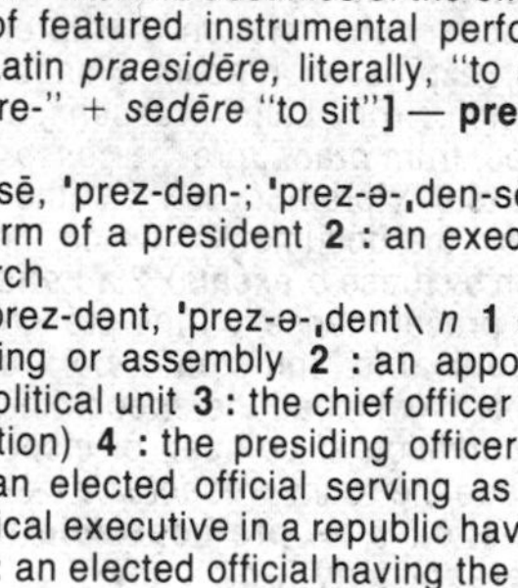

1press 6a

2press *vb* **1** : to act upon through steady pushing or thrusting force exerted in contact : SQUEEZE **2 a** : ASSAIL **b** : OPPRESS 1 **3 a** : to squeeze out the juice or contents of ⟨*press* grapes⟩ **b** : to squeeze out ⟨*press* juice from grapes⟩ **4 a** : to shape by pressure (as with an apparatus) **b** : to smooth by pressure and especially by ironing **5** : to urge strongly or forcefully : CONSTRAIN ⟨*pressed* them to attend⟩ **6 a** : to present earnestly or insistently ⟨*press* a claim⟩ **b** : to follow through (a course of action) **7** : to clasp in affection or courtesy : EMBRACE **8 a** : to crowd closely : MASS ⟨reporters *pressed* around the celebrity⟩ **b** : to force or push one's way ⟨*pressed* forward through the throng⟩ **9** : to seek urgently : CONTEND ⟨*pressed* for higher salaries⟩ [Middle French *presser,* from Latin *pressare,* from *pressus,* past participle of *premere* "to press"] — **press·er** *n*

3press *vt* : to force into service especially in an army or navy : IMPRESS [obsolete *prest* "to enlist by giving pay in advance", derived from Latin *praestare* "to be responsible for, perform, pay"]

press agent *n* : an agent employed to establish and maintain good public relations through publicity

press box *n* : a space reserved for reporters (as at a baseball or football game)

press conference *n* : an interview given by a public figure to newsmen by appointment

press–gang \ˈpres-ˌgang\ *n* : a detachment of men formerly empowered to force men into military or naval service [3*press*]

press·ing *adj* **1** : urgently important : CRITICAL ⟨the *pressing* national interest⟩ **2** : EARNEST, WARM ⟨a *pressing* invitation⟩ — **press·ing·ly** \-ing-lē\ *adv*

press·man \ˈpres-mən, -ˌman\ *n* **1** : an operator of a press; *esp* : the operator of a printing press **2** *British* : NEWSPAPERMAN

pres·sor \ˈpres-ˌȯr, -ər\ *adj* : raising or tending to raise blood pressure [Late Latin, "one that presses", from Latin *pressus,* past participle of *premere* "to press"]

press release *n* : material given in advance to a newspaper for publication at a future date

press·room \ˈpres-ˌrüm, -ˌru̇m\ *n* : a room in a printing plant containing the printing presses

press·run \-ˌrən\ *n* : a continuous operation of a printing press producing a specified number of copies; *also* : the number of copies printed

1pres·sure \ˈpresh-ər\ *n* **1 a** : a painful feeling of weight or burden : OPPRESSION, DISTRESS **b** : a burdensome or restricting force or influence ⟨the *pressure* of taxes⟩ ⟨the constant *pressures* of modern life⟩ **2 a** : the action of pressing ⟨use steady *pressure*⟩ **b** : the condition of being pressed ⟨kept under *pressure*⟩ **3 a** : the action of a force against an opposing force **b** : the force exerted over a surface divided by its area **c** : ELECTROMOTIVE FORCE **4** : the stress of matters demanding attention : URGENCY **5** : the force exerted by the weight of the atmosphere

2pressure *vt* **pres·sured**; **pres·sur·ing** \ˈpresh-ring, -ə-ring\ **1** : to apply pressure to : CONSTRAIN **2** : PRESSURIZE **3** : to cook in a pressure cooker

pressure cooker *n* : an airtight utensil for quick cooking or preserving of foods by means of steam under pressure — **pressure–cook** \ˌpresh-ər-ˈku̇k\ *vb*

pressure group *n* : an interest group that seeks to influence governmental policy but not to elect candidates to office

pressure point *n* : a point where a blood vessel runs near a bone and can be compressed (as to check bleeding) by pressure against the bone

pressure suit *n* : an inflatable suit for high-altitude or space flight to protect the body from low pressure

pres·sur·ize \ˈpresh-ə-ˌrīz\ *vt* **1** : to maintain near-normal atmospheric pressure in (as an airplane cabin) during high-altitude or space flight **2** : to apply pressure to — **pres·sur·iza·tion** \ˌpresh-ə-rə-ˈzā-shən\ *n* — **pres·sur·iz·er** *n*

pres·ti·dig·i·ta·tion \ˌpres-tə-ˌdij-ə-ˈtā-shən\ *n* : SLEIGHT OF HAND 1, LEGERDEMAIN [French, from *prestidigitateur* "prestidigitator", from *preste* "nimble, quick", (from Italian *presto*) + Latin *digitus* "finger"] — **pres·ti·dig·i·ta·tor** \-ˈdij-ə-ˌtāt-ər\ *n*

pres·tige \pre-ˈstēzh, -ˈstēj\ *n* : usually high standing or fine reputation based on past performance or merit [French, from Middle French, "conjuror's trick, illusion", from Latin *praestigiae*, pl., "conjuror's tricks", from *praestringere* "to blindfold", from *prae-* "pre-" + *stringere* "to bind tight"] — **pres·ti·gious** \-'stij-əs\ *adj* — **pres·ti·gious·ly** *adv* — **pres·ti·gious·ness** *n*

pres·to \'pres-tō\ *adv or adj* **1** : at once : QUICKLY ⟨a wave of the hand and, *presto,* it's gone⟩ **2** : at a rapid tempo — used as a direction in music [Italian, "quick, quickly", from Latin *praestus* "ready", from *praesto,* adv., "on hand"]

pre·sume \pri-'züm\ *vb* **1** : to undertake without leave or clear justification : DARE ⟨*presume* to question the authority of a superior⟩ **2** : to suppose to be true without proof ⟨our law *presumes* all persons charged with crime to be innocent until they are proved guilty⟩ **3** : to act or behave boldly without reason for doing so; *esp* : to take liberties ⟨*presume* upon a brief acquaintance to ask favors⟩ [Late Latin *praesumere* "to dare", from Latin, "to anticipate, assume", from *prae-* "pre-" + *sumere* "to take"] **syn** see ASSUME — **pre·sum·able** \-'zü-mə-bəl\ *adj* — **pre·sum·ably** \-blē\ *adv* — **pre·sum·er** *n*

pre·sum·ing *adj* : PRESUMPTUOUS — **pre·sum·ing·ly** \-'zü-ming-lē\ *adv*

pre·sump·tion \pri-'zəm-shən, -'zəmp-\ *n* **1** : presumptuous attitude or conduct : AUDACITY **2 a** : a conclusion reached on strong grounds of belief : something believed to be so but not proved **b** : the grounds or evidence leading one to believe something [Old French, from Latin *praesumptio* "assumption", from *praesumere* "to assume"]

pre·sump·tive \-'zəm-tiv, -'zəmp-\ *adj* **1** : giving grounds for reasonable opinion or belief ⟨*presumptive* evidence⟩ **2** : based on probability or presumption ⟨the *presumptive* heir⟩ — **pre·sump·tive·ly** *adv*

pre·sump·tu·ous \pri-'zəm-chə-wəs, -'zəmp-, -chəs, -shəs\ *adj* : overstepping due bounds : taking liberties — **pre·sump·tu·ous·ly** *adv* — **pre·sump·tu·ous·ness** *n*

pre·sup·pose \ˌprē-sə-'pōz\ *vt* : to suppose beforehand ⟨a book that *presupposes* wide knowledge in its readers⟩ — **pre·sup·po·si·tion** \prē-ˌsəp-ə-'zish-ən\ *n*

pre·tend \pri-'tend\ *vb* **1** : to give a false appearance of being, possessing, or performing : PROFESS **2 a** : to make believe : FEIGN **b** : to claim, represent, or assert falsely **3** : to put in a claim (as to a throne or title) [Latin *praetendere* "to allege as an excuse", literally, "to stretch in front of like a curtain", from *prae-* "pre-" + *tendere* "to stretch"]

pre·tend·ed *adj* : professed or avowed but not genuine ⟨*pretended* affection⟩ — **pre·tend·ed·ly** *adv*

pre·tend·er \pri-'ten-dər\ *n* : one that pretends; *esp* : a claimant to a throne who has no just title

pre·tense *or* **pre·tence** \'prē-ˌtens, pri-'\ *n* **1** : a claim made or implied and usually not supported by fact **2 a** : mere show : OSTENTATION **b** : a pretentious act or assertion **3** : an insincere attempt to attain a condition or quality **4** : professed rather than real intention or purpose : PRETEXT **5** : MAKE-BELIEVE, FICTION **6** : false show : SIMULATION ⟨saw through your *pretense* of indifference⟩ [Middle French *pretensse,* derived from Latin *praetendere* "to allege as an excuse"]

pre·ten·sion \pri-'ten-chən\ *n* **1** : PRETEXT **2** : an effort to establish a claim **3** : a claim or right to attention or honor because of merit **4** : VANITY 2c — **pre·ten·sion·less** \-ləs\ *adj*

pre·ten·tious \-chəs\ *adj* **1** : making or having claims especially as to excellence or worth : SHOWY ⟨living in a *pretentious* style⟩ **2** : making demands on one's skill, ability, or means : AMBITIOUS ⟨*pretentious* plans⟩ [French *prétentieux,* derived from Latin *praetendere* "to allege as an excuse"] — **pre·ten·tious·ly** *adv* — **pre·ten·tious·ness** *n*

pret·er·it *or* **pret·er·ite** \'pret-ə-rət\ *adj* : of, relating to, or constituting a verb tense that indicates action in the past without reference to duration, continuance, or repetition [Middle French *preterit,* from Latin *praeteritus,* from *praeterire* "to go by, pass", from *praeter* "beyond, past", + *ire* "to go"] — **preterit** *n*

pre·ter·nat·u·ral \ˌprēt-ər-'nach-rəl, -ə-rəl\ *adj* **1** : not conforming to what is natural or regular in nature : ABNORMAL **2** : inexplicable by ordinary means; *esp* : PSYCHIC [Medieval Latin *praeternaturalis,* from Latin *praeter naturam* "beyond nature"] — **pre·ter·nat·u·ral·ly** \-'nach-rə-lē, -ə-rə-; -'nach-ər-lē\ *adv* — **pre·ter·nat·u·ral·ness** \-'nach-rəl-nəs, -ə-rəl-\ *n*

pre·test \'prē-ˌtest, prē-'\ *n* : a preliminary test serving for exploration rather than evaluation — **pretest** *vt*

pre·text \'prē-ˌtekst\ *n* : a purpose or motive put forward in order to conceal a real intention or state of affairs [Latin *praetextus,* from *praetexere* "to assign as a pretext", literally, "to weave in front", from *prae-* "pre-" + *texere* "to weave"]

pret·ti·fy \'prit-i-ˌfī, 'pu̇rt-\ *vt* **-fied**; **-fy·ing** : to make pretty — **pret·ti·fi·ca·tion** \ˌprit-i-fə-'kā-shən, ˌpu̇rt-\ *n*

[1]pret·ty \'prit-ē, 'pu̇rt-\ *adj* **pret·ti·er**; **-est** **1 a** : ARTFUL 1, CLEVER **b** : PAT 1a, APT **2** : pleasing by delicacy or grace especially of appearance or sound : conventionally attractive but without elements of grandeur, stateliness, and excellence usually associated with true beauty ⟨a *pretty* face⟩ ⟨light *pretty* tunes⟩ ⟨a *pretty* manner⟩ **3** : MISERABLE ⟨a *pretty* mess we're in⟩ **4** : moderately large : CONSIDERABLE ⟨a very *pretty* profit⟩ [Old English *prættig* "tricky", from *prætt* "trick"] **syn** see BEAUTIFUL — **pret·ti·ly** \'prit-l-ē, 'pu̇rt-\ *adv* — **pret·ti·ness** \'prit-ē-nəs, 'pu̇rt-\ *n* — **pret·ty·ish** \-ē-ish\ *adj*

[2]pret·ty \ˌpu̇rt-ē, pərt-ē (*unstressed* pərt-), ˌprit-ē\ *adv* : in some degree : MODERATELY ⟨*pretty* cold weather⟩

[3]pretty *like*[1]\ *n, pl* **pretties** **1** : a pretty person or thing **2** *pl* : dainty clothes

pret·zel \'pret-səl\ *n* : a brittle glazed and salted cracker typically shaped like a loose knot [German *brezel,* derived from Latin *brachiatus* "having branches like arms", from *brachium* "arm"]

△ **origin** Pretzels were most likely introduced into the United States during the 19th century by German immigrants. Our word *pretzel* comes from the German *brezel.* The familiar knot-shaped pretzel has been known, at least in Germanic countries, for centuries. Its name is derived from Latin *brachiatus,* which means "having branches like arms". Apparently the pretzel is so called because of the similarity between its knot shape and a pair of folded arms.

pre·vail \pri-'vāl\ *vi* **1** : to gain ascendancy through strength or superiority : TRIUMPH **2** : to be or become effective or effectual **3** : to urge successfully ⟨was *prevailed* upon to sing⟩ **4** : to be frequent : PREDOMINATE ⟨the west winds that *prevail* in the mountains⟩ **5** : to be or continue in use or fashion : PERSIST ⟨a custom that still *prevails*⟩ [Latin *praevalēre,* from *prae-* "pre-" + *valēre* "to be strong"]

pre·vail·ing *adj* **1** : having superior force or influence **2 a** : most frequent ⟨*prevailing* winds⟩ **b** : generally current : COMMON — **pre·vail·ing·ly** \-'vā-ling-lē\ *adv*

• **syn** PREVAILING, PREVALENT, CURRENT mean generally circulated, accepted, or used in a certain time or place. PREVAILING applies especially to something that is predominant ⟨*prevailing* opinion⟩ PREVALENT implies widespread frequency ⟨a *prevalent* custom⟩ ⟨a disease that is *prevalent* in many countries⟩ CURRENT applies to things subject to change and implies prevalence at the present time ⟨*current* fashions⟩ ⟨*current* scientific trends⟩

prev·a·lent \'prev-lənt, -ə-lənt\ *adj* **1** *archaic* : being in ascendancy : DOMINANT **2** : generally or widely accepted, practiced, or favored : WIDESPREAD [Latin *praevalens* "very powerful", from *praevalēre* "to prevail"] **syn** see PREVAILING — **prev·a·lence** \-ləns\ *n* — **prev·a·lent·ly** *adv*

pre·var·i·cate \pri-'var-ə-ˌkāt\ *vi* : to avoid telling the truth [Latin *praevaricari* "to walk crookedly", from *prae-* "pre-" + *varicus* "having the feet spread apart", from *varus* "bent, knock-kneed"] — **pre·var·i·ca·tion** \-ˌvar-ə-'kā-shən\ *n* — **pre·var·i·ca·tor** \-'var-ə-ˌkāt-ər\ *n*

pre·vent \pri-'vent\ *vt* **1** : to keep from happening or existing ⟨steps to *prevent* war⟩ **2** : to hold or keep back : STOP, HINDER ⟨there's nothing to *prevent* us from going⟩ [Latin *praeventus,* past participle of *praevenire* "to come before, anticipate, forestall", from *prae-* "pre-" + *venire* "to come"] — **pre·vent·able** *also* **pre·vent·ible** \-ə-bəl\ *adj* — **pre·vent·er** *n*

• **syn** PREVENT, AVERT, FORESTALL mean to stop something from coming or occurring. PREVENT implies placing an insurmountable obstacle or impediment ⟨took measures to *prevent* an epidemic⟩ AVERT implies taking immediate or effective measures to force back, avoid, or counteract a threatening evil ⟨efforts to *avert* a revolution⟩ FORESTALL implies forehanded ac-

\ə\ **abut**	\au̇\ **out**	\i\ **tip**	\ȯ\ **saw**	\u̇\ **foot**
\ər\ **further**	\ch\ **chin**	\ī\ **life**	\ȯi\ **coin**	\y\ **yet**
\a\ **mat**	\e\ **pet**	\j\ **job**	\th\ **thin**	\yü\ **few**
\ā\ **take**	\ē\ **easy**	\ng\ **sing**	\t͟h\ **this**	\yu̇\ **cure**
\ä\ **cot, cart**	\g\ **go**	\ō\ **bone**	\ü\ **food**	\zh\ **vision**

tion to stop or interrupt something in its course ⟨radar helped *forestall* surprise attacks⟩

pre•ven•ta•tive \-'vent-ət-iv\ *adj or n* : PREVENTIVE

pre•ven•tion \pri-'ven-chən\ *n* : the act of preventing

¹pre•ven•tive \-'vent-iv\ *n* : something that prevents; *esp* : something used to prevent disease

²preventive *adj* : devoted to, concerned with, or undertaken for prevention — **pre•ven•tive•ly** *adv* — **pre•ven•tive•ness** *n*

¹pre•view \'prē-,vyü\ *vt* : to view or to show in advance

²preview *n* : an advance showing or viewing ⟨invited to a *preview* of the art exhibition⟩:as **a** *also* **pre•vue** \-,vyü\ : a showing of snatches from a motion picture advertised for appearance in the near future **b** : a statement giving advance information **c** : a preliminary survey

pre•vi•ous \'prē-vē-əs\ *adj* **1** : going before in time or order ⟨the *previous* lesson⟩ **2** : acting too soon : PREMATURE ⟨was a bit *previous* with the answer⟩ [Latin *praevius* "leading the way", from *prae-* "pre-" + *via* "way"] — **pre•vi•ous•ly** *adv* — **pre•vi•ous•ness** *n*

previous question *n* : a parliamentary motion that the pending question be put to an immediate vote without further debate or amendment

previous to *prep* : prior to : BEFORE

¹pre•vi•sion \prē-'vizh-ən\ *n* **1** : FORESIGHT 1, PRESCIENCE **2** : FORECAST, PREDICTION — **pre•vi•sion•al** \-'vizh-nəl, -ən-l\ *adj* — **pre•vi•sion•ary** \-'vizh-ə-,ner-ē\ *adj*

²prevision *vt* : FORESEE

pre•vo•cal•ic \,prē-vō-'kal-ik\ *adj* : immediately preceding a vowel

¹prey \'prā\ *n* **1 a** : an animal taken by a predator as food **b** : one that is helpless or unable to resist attack : VICTIM **2** : the act or habit of preying [Old French *preie* "booty, prey", from Latin *praeda*]

²prey *vi* **1** : to raid for booty **2** : to seize and devour something as prey **3** : to have an injurious, destructive, or wasting effect ⟨fears that *prey* on the mind⟩ — **prey•er** *n*

¹price \'prīs\ *n* **1 a** : the quantity of one thing that is exchanged or sought in barter or sale for another **b** : the amount of money given or asked for a specified thing **2** : the terms for the sake of which something is done or undertaken: as **a** : an amount sufficient to bribe one **b** : a reward for the apprehension or death of a person **3** : the cost at which something is obtainable ⟨the *price* of freedom⟩ [Old French *pris,* from Latin *pretium* "price, money"] **syn** see WORTH

²price *vt* **1** : to set a price on **2** : to ask the price of **3** : to drive by raising prices excessively ⟨*priced* themselves out of the market⟩ — **pric•er** *n*

price–cut•ter \'prī-,skət-ər\ *n* : one that reduces prices especially to a level designed to cripple competition

price•less \'pri-sləs\ *adj* **1** : having a value beyond any price : INVALUABLE **2** : surprisingly amusing, odd, or absurd

price support *n* : artificial maintenance of prices of a commodity at a level usually fixed through government action

price tag *n* **1** : a tag on merchandise showing the price at which it is offered for sale **2** : PRICE 1b, COST

price war *n* : a period of commercial competition in which prices are repeatedly cut below those of competitors

¹prick \'prik\ *n* **1** : a mark or shallow hole made by a pointed instrument **2** : a pointed instrument or part **3** : an instance of pricking or the sensation of being pricked [Old English *prica*]

²prick *vb* **1 a** : to pierce slightly with a sharp point **b** : to have or cause a pricking sensation **2** : to cause to feel anguish, grief, or remorse ⟨if your conscience *pricks* you⟩ **3** : to urge a horse with spurs **4** : to mark or outline with or as if with pricks ⟨*prick* a design on paper⟩ **5** : to make or become erect ⟨the dog *pricked* its ears⟩ — **prick up one's ears** : to listen intently

prick•er \'prik-ər\ *n* **1** : one that pricks **2** : PRICKLE 1, THORN

¹prick•le \'prik-əl\ *n* **1** : a fine sharp projection; *esp* : a sharp pointed process of the epidermis or bark of a plant **2** : a prickling sensation [Old English *pricle*]

²prickle *vb* **prickled; prick•ling** \'prik-ling, -ə-ling\ **1** : to prick slightly **2** : TINGLE

prick•ly \'prik-lē\ *adj* **prick•li•er; -est** **1** : full of or covered with prickles ⟨*prickly* plants⟩ **2** : marked by prickling ⟨a *prickly* sensation⟩ — **prick•li•ness** *n*

prickly heat *n* : a skin eruption of red pimples with intense itching and tingling caused by inflammation around the sweat ducts

prickly pear *n* **1** : any of numerous flat-jointed often prickly cacti **2** : the pear-shaped edible pulpy fruit of a prickly pear

¹pride \'prīd\ *n* **1** : the quality or state of being proud: as **a** : excessive self-esteem : CONCEIT **b** : a reasonable or justifiable self-respect **c** : pleasure or satisfaction taken in some act, accomplishment, or possession **2** : proud or disdainful behavior or treatment : DISDAIN **3** : something that is or is fit to be a source of pride ⟨this pup is the *pride* of the litter⟩ **4** : a company of lions [Old English *prȳde,* from *prūd* "proud"]

prickly pear 1

²pride *vt* : to indulge in pride : PLUME ⟨*pride* oneself on one's skill⟩

pride•ful \'prīd-fəl\ *adj* : full of pride: as **a** : HAUGHTY **b** : ELATED — **pride•ful•ly** \-fə-lē\ *adv* — **pride•ful•ness** *n*

prie–dieu \prēd-'yər, -'yü, -'yœ\ *n, pl* **prie–dieux** *same or* -'yərz, -'yüz, -'yœz\ : a small kneeling bench designed for use by a person at prayer and fitted with a raised shelf on which the elbows or a book may be rested [French, literally, "pray God"]

priest \'prēst\ *n* : a person who has the authority to conduct religious rites [Old English *prēost,* from Late Latin *presbyter* "elder, priest", from Greek *presbyteros,* from *presbys* "old man"]

priest•ess \'prē-stəs\ *n* : a woman who is a priest ⟨ancient Roman *priestesses*⟩

priest•hood \'prēst-,hüd, 'prē-,stüd\ *n* **1** : the office, dignity, or status of a priest **2** : the whole group of priests

priest•ly \'prēst-lē\ *adj* **priest•li•er; -est** **1** : of or relating to a priest or the priesthood **2** : characteristic of or befitting a priest — **priest•li•ness** *n*

prig \'prig\ *n* : a person who annoys others by a too careful or rigid observance of niceties and proprieties (as of speech or manners) [from earlier *prig* "fellow, person", probably from *prig* "to steal"] — **prig•gery** \'prig-ə-rē\ *n* — **prig•gish** \'prig-ish\ *adj* — **prig•gish•ly** *adv* — **prig•gish•ness** *n*

prim \'prim\ *adj* **prim•mer; prim•mest** : very or excessively formal and precise (as in conduct or dress) ⟨a *prim* scholar⟩ ⟨*prim* remarks⟩ [from earlier *prim* "to give a prim expression to", of unknown origin] — **prim•ly** *adv* — **prim•ness** *n*

pri•ma ballerina \,prē-mə-\ *n* : the principal female dancer in a ballet company [Italian, "leading ballerina"]

pri•ma•cy \'prī-mə-sē\ *n* **1** : the condition of being first (as in time, place, or rank) **2** : the office, status, or dignity of a bishop of the highest rank

pri•ma don•na \,prim-ə-'dän-ə, ,prē-mə-\ *n, pl* **prima donnas** **1** : a principal female singer (as in an opera) **2** : an extremely sensitive, vain, or undisciplined person [Italian, literally, "first lady"]

¹pri•ma fa•cie \,prī-mə-'fā-shə, -shē, -sē\ *adv* : at first view : on the first appearance [Latin]

²prima facie *adj* **1** : APPARENT, SEEMING ⟨a *prima facie* solution to a problem⟩ **2** : adequate to legally establish a fact or case unless disproved ⟨*prima facie* evidence⟩

pri•mal \'prī-məl\ *adj* **1** : ORIGINAL 1, PRIMITIVE **2** : first in importance : CHIEF [Medieval Latin *primalis,* from Latin *primus* "first"]

pri•mar•i•ly \prī-'mer-ə-lē\ *adv* **1** : for the most part : CHIEFLY **2** : in the first place : ORIGINALLY

¹pri•mary \'prī-,mer-ē; 'prīm-rē, -ə-rē\ *adj* **1 a** : first in order of time or development : INITIAL, PRIMITIVE ⟨the *primary* stages of a process⟩ **b** : not derived from or dependent on something else ⟨a *primary* source of information⟩ **c** : coming before and usually preparatory to something else ⟨*primary* school⟩ **2 a** : of first rank, importance, or value : CHIEF ⟨the *primary* elective officer is the president⟩ **b** : BASIC, FUNDAMENTAL ⟨our *primary* duty⟩ **c** : of, relating to, or constituting the strongest of the three or four degrees of stress ⟨the first syllable of *basketball* carries *primary* stress⟩ **d** : not derivable from other colors ⟨*primary* colors⟩ **e** : of, relating to, or being one of the principal quills of a bird's wing borne on the outer joint **3** : expressive of present or future time ⟨*primary* tenses⟩ **4** : of, relating to, or being the inducing current or its circuit in an induction coil or transformer **5 :** of, relating to, or being meristem **6 :** of, relating to, or involved in the production of organic substances by green plants [Late Latin *primarius* "basic, primary", from Latin, "principal", from *primus* "first"]

2**primary** *n, pl* **-mar•ies 1 :** something that is primary: as **a :** a planet as distinguished from its satellites **b :** a primary quill or feather **c :** any of a set of colors (as red, yellow, or blue) from which all other colors may be derived **2 :** an election in which voters select party candidates for political office, choose party officials, or select delegates for a party convention **3 :** PRIMARY COIL

primary cell *n* **:** a cell that converts chemical energy into electrical energy by irreversible chemical reactions

primary coil *n* **:** the coil through which the inducing current passes in an induction coil or transformer

primary germ layer *n* **:** GERM LAYER

primary root *n* **:** the root of a plant that develops first

pri•mate \'prī-ˌmāt *or especially for 1* -mət\ *n* **1 :** a bishop or archbishop governing or having highest status in a district, nation, or church **2 :** any of an order (Primates) of mammals comprising especially human beings, apes, monkeys, lemurs, and tarsiers [Old French *primat,* from Medieval Latin *primat-, primas* "archbishop", from Latin, "leader", from *primus* "first"]

1**prime** \'prīm\ *n* **1** *often cap* **:** the second of the canonical hours **2 :** the first part **:** earliest stage **3 :** the most active, thriving, or successful stage or period (as of one's life) **4 :** the chief or best individual or part **:** PICK ⟨the *prime* of the flock⟩ **5 :** PRIME NUMBER **6 :** the symbol ′ [Old English *prīm,* from Latin *prima hora* "first hour"]

2**prime** *adj* **1 :** first in time **:** ORIGINAL **2 a :** of, relating to, or being a prime number **b :** having no polynomial factors other than itself and no monomial factors other than 1 ⟨a *prime* polynomial⟩ **c :** expressed as a product of prime factors (as prime numbers and prime polynomials) ⟨a *prime* factorization⟩ **3 a :** first in rank, authority, or significance **:** PRINCIPAL **b :** first in excellence, quality, or value **c :** of the highest grade regularly marketed — used of meat and especially beef [Middle French, feminine of *prin* "first", from Latin *primus*] — **prime•ly** *adv* — **prime•ness** *n*

3**prime** *vt* **1 :** to prepare for firing by supplying with priming or a primer **2 :** to apply (as in painting) a first color, coating, or preparation to **3 :** to put into working order by filling or charging with something ⟨*prime* a pump with water⟩ **4 :** to instruct beforehand **:** COACH [probably from 1*prime*]

prime meridian *n* **:** the meridian of 0° longitude which runs through the original site of the Royal Observatory at Greenwich, England, and from which other longitudes are reckoned east and west

prime minister *n* **1 :** the chief minister of a ruler or state **2 :** the head of a cabinet or ministry; *esp* **:** the chief executive of a parliamentary government — **prime ministry** *n*

prime number *n* **:** an integer other than 0 or ±1 that is not divisible by any other integers except ±1 and ± the integer itself

1**prim•er** \'prim-ər, *especially British* 'prī-mər\ *n* **1 :** a small book for teaching children to read **2 :** a small introductory book on a subject [Medieval Latin *primarium,* from Late Latin *primarius* "primary"]

2**prim•er** \'prī-mər\ *n* **1 :** a device (as a cap, tube, or wafer) containing a substance that ignites an explosive charge **2 :** material used in priming a surface [3*prime*]

pri•me•val \prī-'mē-vəl\ *adj* **:** of or relating to the earliest ages **:** PRIMITIVE [Latin *primaevus,* from *primus* "first" + *aevum* "age"] — **pri•me•val•ly** \-və-lē\ *adv*

prim•ing *n* **1 :** the explosive used in priming a charge **2 :** 2PRIMER 2

1**prim•i•tive** \'prim-ət-iv\ *adj* **1 :** not derived **:** ORIGINAL, PRIMARY ⟨nature, the *primitive* source of art⟩ **2 a :** of or relating to the earliest age or period **:** PRIMEVAL ⟨*primitive* forests⟩ ⟨the *primitive* church⟩ **b :** little evolved and closely approximating an early ancestral type ⟨a *primitive* fish⟩ **3 a :** of or relating to a relatively simple people or culture ⟨*primitive* society⟩ **b :** marked by the style, simplicity, or crudity held to characterize simple people ⟨*primitive* building techniques⟩ **c :** lacking formal or technical training **:** SELF-TAUGHT ⟨a *primitive* artisan⟩; *also* **:** produced by a self-taught artist [Latin *primitivus,* from *primitus* "originally", from *primus* "first"] — **prim•i•tive•ly** *adv* — **prim•i•tive•ness** *n*

2**primitive** *n* **1 a :** something primitive; *esp* **:** a primitive idea, term, or proposition **b :** a root word **2 a** (1) **:** an artist of an early period of a culture or artistic movement (2) **:** a later imitator or follower of such an artist **b :** a work of art produced by a primitive artist **3 :** a member of a primitive people

pri•mo•gen•i•tor \ˌprī-mō-'jen-ət-ər\ *n* **:** ANCESTOR 1, FOREFATHER [Late Latin, from Latin *primus* "first" + *genitor* "begetter", from *genitus,* past participle of *gignere* "to beget"]

pri•mo•gen•i•ture \-'jen-ə-ˌchu̇r, -'jen-i-chər\ *n* **1 :** the state of being the firstborn of the children of the same parents **2 :** an exclusive right of inheritance belonging to the eldest son [Late Latin *primogenitura,* from Latin *primus* "first" + *genitura* "birth", from *genitus,* past participle of *gignere* "to beget"]

pri•mor•di•al \prī-'mȯrd-ē-əl\ *adj* **1 a :** first created or developed **:** PRIMEVAL **b :** earliest formed in the growth of an individual or organ **:** PRIMITIVE ⟨*primordial* germ cells⟩ **2 :** FUNDAMENTAL 1, PRIMARY [Late Latin *primordialis,* from Latin *primordium* "origin", from *primordius* "original", from *primus* "first" + *ordiri* "to begin"] — **pri•mor•di•al•ly** \-ē-ə-lē\ *adv*

pri•mor•di•um \-ē-əm\ *n, pl* **-dia** \-ē-ə\ **:** the first-formed rudiment of a part or organ [Latin, "origin"]

primp \'primp\ *vb* **:** to dress, adorn, or arrange in a careful or finicky manner [perhaps alteration of *prim* "to give a prim expression to, dress primly"]

prim•rose \'prim-ˌrōz\ *n* **:** any of a genus of perennial herbs with large tufted basal leaves and showy variously colored flowers borne in clusters on leafless stalks [Middle French *primerose*]

primrose

primrose path *n* **:** a path of ease or pleasure and especially sensual pleasure

primrose yellow *n* **:** a light to moderate yellow

prim•u•la \'prim-yə-lə\ *n* **:** PRIMROSE [Medieval Latin]

prince \'prins\ *n* **1 a :** MONARCH 1, SOVEREIGN **b :** the ruler of a principality or state **2 :** a male member of a royal family; *esp* **:** a son of a king **3 :** a nobleman of varying rank **4 :** a person of high standing in a class or profession [Old French, from Latin *princeps,* literally, "one who takes the first part", from *primus* "first"+*capere* "to take"] — **prince•dom** \-dəm\ *n* — **prince•ship** \-ˌship\ *n*

Prince Al•bert \prin-'sal-bərt\ *n* **:** a long double-breasted frock coat [Prince *Albert* Edward (later Edward VII, king of England), died 1910]

prince charming *n* **:** a suitor who fulfills the dreams of his beloved; *also* **:** a man deceptively charming and attractive to women [*Prince Charming,* hero of the fairy tale *Cinderella* by Charles Perrault, died 1703, French writer]

prince consort *n, pl* **princes consort :** the husband of a reigning female sovereign

prince•ling \'prins-ling\ *n* **:** a petty or insignificant prince

prince•ly \'prins-lē\ *adj* **prince•li•er; -li•est 1 :** of or relating to a prince **:** ROYAL **2 :** befitting a prince **:** REGAL, MAGNIFICENT ⟨*princely* manners⟩ ⟨a *princely* sum⟩ — **prince•li•ness** *n*

Prince of Wales \-'wālz\ **:** the male heir apparent to the British throne — used as a title only after it has been specifically conferred by the sovereign

prince's–feath•er \'prin-səz-ˌfeth-ər\ *n* **:** a showy annual amaranth often grown for its dense usually red spikes of bloom

1**prin•cess** \'prin-səs, 'prin-ˌses, prin-'ses\ *n* **1** *archaic* **:** a woman having sovereign power **2 :** a female member of a royal family; *esp* **:** a daughter or granddaughter of a sovereign **3 :** the wife of a prince **4 :** a woman of outstanding merit

2**princess** *like* 1\ *or* **prin•cesse** \prin-'ses\ *adj* **:** close-fitting and usually with gores from neck to flaring hemline ⟨a *princess* gown⟩

princess royal *n, pl* **princesses royal :** the eldest daughter of a sovereign

1**prin•ci•pal** \'prin-sə-pəl, -sə-bəl\ *adj* **1 :** most important or influential **:** CHIEF **2 :** of, relating to, or being principal or a princi-

\ə\ **abut**	\au̇\ **out**	\i\ **tip**	\ȯ\ **saw**	\u̇\ **foot**
\ər\ **further**	\ch\ **chin**	\ī\ **life**	\ȯi\ **coin**	\y\ **yet**
\a\ **mat**	\e\ **pet**	\j\ **job**	\th\ **thin**	\yü\ **few**
\ā\ **take**	\ē\ **easy**	\ng\ **sing**	\th\ **this**	\yu̇\ **cure**
\ä\ **cot, cart**	\g\ **go**	\ō\ **bone**	\ü\ **food**	\zh\ **vision**

pal [Old French, from Latin *principalis,* from *princip-, princeps* "one who takes the first part"] — **prin•ci•pal•ly** \-ē, ˈprin-splē\ *adv*

2principal *n* **1 a :** a person (as a ruler or employer) who exercises authority : HEAD, CHIEF **b :** the chief executive officer of a school **c :** one who engages another to act as his or her agent **d :** an actual participant in a crime **e :** the person primarily liable on a legal obligation **f :** a leading performer : STAR **2 a :** a capital sum placed at interest, due as a debt, or used as a fund **b :** the main body of an estate or bequest left by will — **prin•ci•pal•ship** \-,ship\ *n*

prin•ci•pal•i•ty \,prin-sə-ˈpal-ət-ē\ *n, pl* **-ties 1 :** the office or position of a prince or principal **2 :** the territory or jurisdiction of a prince

principal parts *n pl* **:** a series of verb forms from which all the other forms of a verb can be derived including in English the present infinitive, the past tense, the past participle, and sometimes the present participle

prin•ci•ple \ˈprin-sə-pəl, -sə-bəl\ *n* **1 a :** a fundamental law or doctrine **b :** a rule or code of conduct **c :** devotion to right principles **d :** the laws or facts of nature underlying the working of an artificial device ⟨trying to grasp the *principles* of radar⟩ **2 a :** a primary source : ORIGIN **b :** an underlying faculty or endowment ⟨such *principles* of human nature as greed and curiosity⟩ **3 :** a constituent that exhibits or imparts a characteristic quality ⟨quinine is the active *principle* of cinchona bark⟩ [Middle French *principe,* from Latin *principium* "beginning", from *princip-, princeps* "one taking the first part"]

prin•ci•pled \-sə-pəld, -sə-bəld, -spəld\ *adj* **:** exhibiting, based on, or characterized by principle ⟨high-*principled*⟩

prink \ˈpringk\ *vb* **:** PRIMP [probably alteration of *2prank*] — **prink•er** *n*

1print \ˈprint\ *n* **1 a :** a mark made by pressure : IMPRESSION **b :** something impressed with a print or formed in a mold **2 :** a device or instrument for impressing or forming a print **3 a :** printed state or form ⟨put a manuscript into *print*⟩ **b :** printed matter **c :** printed letters : TYPE **4 a :** a copy made by printing (as from a photographic negative) **b :** cloth with a pattern applied by printing; *also* **:** an article of such cloth [Old French *preinte,* from *preindre* "to press", from Latin *premere*] — **in print :** available from the publisher — **out of print :** not available from the publisher

2print *vb* **1 a :** to make an impression in or on **b :** to cause (as a mark) to be stamped **2 a :** to make a copy of especially by pressing paper against an inked surface **b :** to impress (a surface) with a design by pressure ⟨*print* wallpaper⟩ **c :** to publish in printed form **3 :** to write in unconnected letters like those made by a printing press **4 :** to make (a positive picture) on a sensitized photographic surface **5 :** to reproduce by printing ⟨a negative that *prints* well⟩

print•able \ˈprint-ə-bəl\ *adj* **1 :** capable of being printed or of being printed from **2 :** worthy or fit to be published — **print•abil•i•ty** \,print-ə-ˈbil-ət-ē\ *n*

printed circuit *n* **:** a circuit for electronic apparatus made by depositing conductive material on an insulating surface

printed matter *n* **:** matter mechanically printed that is eligible for mailing at a special rate

print•er \ˈprint-ər\ *n* **:** one that prints: as **a :** a person whose business or occupation is printing **b :** a device used for printing

printer's devil *n* **:** an apprentice in a printing office

print•ery \ˈprint-ə-rē\ *n, pl* **-er•ies :** an establishment where printing is done

print•ing *n* **1 :** reproduction in printed form **2 :** the art, practice, or business of a printer **3 :** IMPRESSION 4b

printing press *n* **:** a machine that produces printed copies; *esp* **:** one that is power driven

print•out \ˈprint-,au̇t\ *n* **:** a printed record produced by a computer

1pri•or \ˈprī-ər, ˈprīr\ *n* **1 :** the deputy head of an abbey **2 :** the head of a monastic house, province, or order [Old English and Middle French, both from Medieval Latin, from Latin, "former, superior"] — **pri•or•ate** \ˈprī-ə-rət\ *n* — **pri•or•ship** \ˈprī-ər-,ship\ *n*

2prior *adj* **1 :** earlier in time or order **2 :** taking precedence logically or in importance or value ⟨a *prior* responsibility⟩ [Latin, "former, superior"] — **pri•or•ly** *adv*

pri•or•ess \ˈprī-ə-rəs\ *n* **:** a nun who is the head of a religious house or order

pri•or•i•ty \prī-ˈȯr-ət-ē, -ˈär-\ *n, pl* **-ties 1 :** the quality or state of coming before another in time or importance: as **a :** superiority in rank, position, or privilege **b :** order of preference based on urgency, importance, or merit **2 :** something deserving or requiring attention before others of its kind ⟨it's high on our list of *priorities*⟩

prior to *prep* **:** in advance of : BEFORE

pri•o•ry \ˈprī-rē, -ə-rē\ *n, pl* **-ries :** a religious house under a prioress or prior

prise \ˈprīz\ *chiefly British variant of* 5PRIZE

prism \ˈpriz-əm\ *n* **1 :** a solid whose ends are similar, equal, and parallel polygons and whose faces are parallelograms **2 a :** a transparent body bounded in part by two plane faces that are not parallel used to deviate or disperse a beam of light **b :** a prism-shaped decorative glass pendant [Late Latin *prismat-, prisma,* literally, "anything sawn", from *priein* "to saw"]

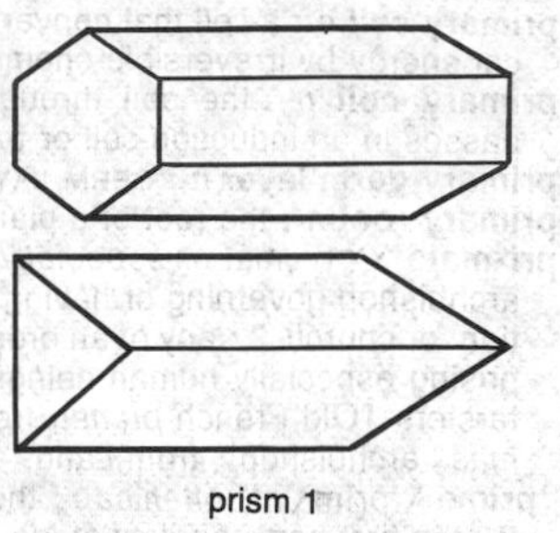

prism 1

pris•mat•ic \priz-ˈmat-ik\ *adj* **1 :** relating to, resembling, or being a prism **2 :** formed by refraction of light through a transparent prism ⟨*prismatic* colors⟩ **3 :** highly colored : BRILLIANT — **pris•mat•i•cal•ly** \-ˈmat-i-kə-lē, -klē\ *adv*

pris•ma•toid \ˈpriz-mə-,tȯid\ *n* **:** a polyhedron in which every vertex lies in one or the other of two parallel planes

pris•on \ˈpriz-n\ *n* **1 :** a state of confinement for criminals ⟨sentenced to *prison*⟩ **2 :** a place in which persons are locked up while awaiting or on trial or as punishment after conviction; *esp* **:** PENITENTIARY [Old French, from Latin *prehension-, prehensio* "act of seizing", from *prehensus,* past participle of *prehendere* "to seize"]

pris•on•er \ˈpriz-nər, -n-ər\ *n* **:** a person kept under involuntary restraint, confinement, or custody; *esp* **:** one in prison

prisoner of war : a person captured in war; *esp* **:** a member of the armed forces of a nation taken by the enemy during combat

prisoner's base *n* **:** a children's game in which players of one team seek to tag and imprison players of the other team who have ventured out of their home territory

pris•sy \ˈpris-ē\ *adj* **pris•si•er; -est :** being prim and finicky [probably blend of *prim* and *sissy*] — **pris•si•ly** \ˈpris-ə-lē\ *adv* — **pris•si•ness** \ˈpris-ē-nəs\ *n*

pris•tine \ˈpris-,tēn\ *adj* **:** of or relating to the earliest period or condition : ORIGINAL, PRIMITIVE; *esp* **:** having the purity or freshness of an original state [Latin *pristinus* — **pris•tine•ly** *adv*

prith•ee \ˈprith-ē, ˈprith-\ *interj, archaic* — used to express a wish or request [alteration of *(I) pray thee*]

pri•va•cy \ˈprī-və-sē\ *n, pl* **-cies 1 :** the condition of being apart from company or observation : SECLUSION ⟨a yard with lots of *privacy*⟩ **2 :** freedom from unauthorized intrusion ⟨a person's right to *privacy*⟩

1pri•vate \ˈprī-vət\ *adj* **1 a :** belonging to, concerning, or reserved for the use of a particular person or group : not public ⟨*private* property⟩ ⟨a *private* beach⟩ **b :** not under public control ⟨a *private* school⟩ **2 :** not holding public office or employment ⟨a *private* citizen⟩ **3 a :** offering privacy : SECLUDED ⟨a *private* office⟩ **b :** not publicly known : SECRET ⟨*private* agreements⟩ [Latin *privatus* "not holding public office, private", from *privare* "to deprive", from *privus* "private, set apart"] — **pri•vate•ly** *adv* — **pri•vate•ness** *n*

2private *n* **1 :** a person of low or lowest rank in an organized group (as a police or fire department) **2 :** the lowest enlisted rank in the Marine Corps and either of the two lowest enlisted ranks in the Army — **in private :** PRIVATELY, SECRETLY

private enterprise *n* **:** FREE ENTERPRISE

1pri•va•teer \,prī-və-ˈtiər\ *n* **1 :** an armed private ship commissioned to cruise against the commerce or warships of an enemy **2 :** the commander or one of the crew of a privateer

2privateer *vi* **:** to cruise in or as a privateer

private first class *n* **:** an enlisted rank in the Army above private and below corporal and in the Marine Corps above private and below lance corporal

pri·va·tion \prī-ˈvā-shən\ *n* **1 :** an act or instance of depriving **:** DEPRIVATION **2 :** the state of being deprived especially of what is needed for existence **:** WANT [Middle French, from Latin *privatio*, from *privare* "to deprive"]

[1]priv·a·tive \ˈpriv-ət-iv\ *n* **:** a privative prefix or suffix

[2]privative *adj* **:** constituting or predicating privation or absence of a quality ⟨*a-*, *un-*, *non-* are *privative* prefixes⟩ — **priv·a·tive·ly** *adv*

priv·et \ˈpriv-ət\ *n* **:** a shrub of the olive family with small white flowers that is widely used for hedges [origin unknown]

privet

priv·i·lege \ˈpriv-lij, -ə-lij\ *n* **:** something special one is allowed to have, be, or do [Old French, from Latin *privilegium* "law for or against a private person", from *privus* "private" + *leg-*, *lex* "law"]

priv·i·leged \-lijd\ *adj* **1 :** having or enjoying one or more privileges ⟨*privileged* classes⟩ **2 :** that need not be disclosed in a court of law ⟨a *privileged* communication⟩

priv·i·ly \ˈpriv-ə-lē\ *adv* **:** PRIVATELY, SECRETLY

[1]privy \ˈpriv-ē\ *adj* **1 :** belonging or relating to a person in his individual rather than his official capacity **2 :** PRIVATE 3a ⟨a *privy* place⟩ **3 :** sharing in a secret ⟨*privy* to the conspiracy⟩ [Old French *privé*, from Latin *privatus* "private"]

[2]privy *n, pl* **priv·ies :** a small building without plumbing that is used as a toilet; *also* **:** TOILET 2b

privy council *n* **1** *cap P & C* **:** an advisory council to the British crown usually functioning through its committees **2 :** a usually appointive advisory council to an executive — **privy councillor** *n*

privy purse *n, often cap both Ps* **:** an allowance for the private expenses of the British sovereign

[1]prize \ˈprīz\ *n* **1 :** something won or to be won in competition or in contests of chance; *also* **:** a premium given as an inducement to buy **2 :** something exceptionally desirable [Middle English *pris* "prize, price", from Old French, "price"]

[2]prize *adj* **1 a :** awarded a prize ⟨a *prize* essay⟩ **b :** awarded as a prize ⟨*prize* money⟩ **2 :** outstanding of its kind ⟨*prize* hogs⟩

[3]prize *vt* **1 :** to estimate the value of **:** RATE **2 :** to value highly **:** ESTEEM [Middle French *prisier*, from Late Latin *pretiare*, from Latin *pretium* "price, value"]

[4]prize *n* **1 :** something taken by force, stratagem, or threat; *esp* **:** property lawfully captured in time of war **2 :** an act of capturing or taking; *esp* **:** the wartime capture of a ship and its cargo at sea [Old French *prise* "act of taking", from *prendre* "to take", from Latin *prehendere*]

[5]prize *vb* **:** to press, force, or move with or as if with a lever **:** PRY [from earlier *prize* "lever", from [4]*prize*]

prize·fight \ˈprīz-ˌfīt\ *n* **:** a professional boxing match — **prize·fight·er** \-ər\ *n* — **prize·fight·ing** \-ing\ *n*

prize ring *n* **:** a boxing ring

prize·win·ner \-ˌwin-ər\ *n* **:** a winner of a prize — **prize·win·ning** \-ˌwin-ing\ *adj*

[1]pro \ˈprō\ *n, pl* **pros** \ˈprōz\ **1 :** a favorable argument or piece of evidence ⟨*pros* and cons⟩ **2 :** the affirmative position or one holding it [Latin, prep., "for"]

[2]pro *adv* **:** on the affirmative side

[3]pro *n or adj* **:** PROFESSIONAL

[1]pro- *prefix* **1 a :** prior to **:** prior ⟨*pro*gestational⟩ **b :** rudimentary **:** PROT- 2 **2 :** located in front of or at the front of ⟨*pro*thorax⟩ **3 :** projecting ⟨*pro*gnathous⟩ [Latin, from Greek, from *pro* "before, forward, forth, for"]

[2]pro- *prefix* **1 :** taking the place of **:** substituting for ⟨*pro*cathedral⟩ **2 :** favoring **:** supporting **:** championing ⟨*pro*-American⟩ [Latin *pro* "in front of, before, for"]

prob·a·bil·i·ty \ˌpräb-ə-ˈbil-ət-ē\ *n, pl* **-ties 1 :** the quality, state, or degree of being probable ⟨some *probability* of war⟩ **2 :** something probable **3 :** a measure of the likelihood of an outcome or event expressed as the frequency with which it is theoretically expected to occur or as the ratio of the number of times it occurs in a test series to the total number of trials in the series

prob·a·ble \ˈpräb-ə-bəl, ˈpräb-bəl\ *adj* **1 :** supported by evidence strong enough to make it likely though not certain to be true ⟨a *probable* explanation⟩ **2 :** likely to happen or to have happened ⟨the *probable* outcome of the game⟩ [Middle French, from Latin *probabilis*, from *probare* "to test, approve, prove", from *probus* "good, honest", from *pro* "for, in favor of"] — **prob·a·bly** \ˈpräb-ə-blē, ˈpräb-lē\ *adv*

• syn PROBABLE, POSSIBLE mean such as may be or may become true or actual. PROBABLE applies to what is supported by strong but not necessarily conclusive evidence ⟨the *probable* cause of the accident⟩ POSSIBLE refers to something which is within the limit of what may happen or of what a person or thing may do regardless of the chances for or against its actuality.

probable cause *n* **:** a reasonable ground for supposing that a criminal charge is well-founded

[1]pro·bate \ˈprō-ˌbāt\ *n* **1 :** proof before a probate court that the last will and testament of a deceased person is genuine **2 :** judicial determination of the validity of a will [Latin *probatus*, past participle of *probare* "to test, prove, approve"]

[2]probate *vt* **:** to establish (a will) by probate as valid

probate court *n* **:** a court having jurisdiction chiefly over the probate of wills and the administration of estates of deceased persons

pro·ba·tion \prō-ˈbā-shən\ *n* **1 :** critical examination and evaluation or subjection to such examination and evaluation **2 a :** subjection of an individual to a period of testing and trial to ascertain fitness (as for a job or school) **b :** the suspending of a convicted offender's sentence during good behavior under the supervision of a probation officer **c :** the state or a period of being subject to probation — **pro·ba·tion·al** \-shnəl, -shən-l\ *adj* — **pro·ba·tion·al·ly** \-ē\ *adv* — **pro·ba·tion·ary** \-shə-ˌner-ē\ *adj*

pro·ba·tion·er \prō-ˈbā-shə-nər, -shnər\ *n* **:** a person (as a new student nurse or a convict on a suspended sentence) who is undergoing probation

probation officer *n* **:** an officer appointed to investigate, report on, and supervise the conduct of convicted offenders on probation

pro·ba·tive \ˈprō-bət-iv\ *adj* **1 :** serving to test or try **2 :** serving to prove

pro·ba·to·ry \ˈprō-bə-ˌtōr-ē\ *adj* **:** PROBATIVE

[1]probe \ˈprōb\ *n* **1 :** a slender instrument for examining a cavity (as a wound) **2 a :** a pointed metal tip for making electrical contact with a circuit element being checked **b :** a device used to penetrate or send back information from outer space **3 :** a searching examination; *esp* **:** an inquiry to discover evidence of wrongdoing ⟨a legislative *probe*⟩ [Medieval Latin *proba* "examination", from Latin *probare* "to test, prove"]

[2]probe *vb* **1 :** to examine with or as if with a probe **2 :** to investigate thoroughly **3 :** to make an exploratory investigation — **prob·er** *n*

pro·bi·ty \ˈprō-bət-ē\ *n* **:** adherence to the highest principles and ideals **:** UPRIGHTNESS [Middle French *probité*, from Latin *probitas*, from *probus* "honest"]

[1]prob·lem \ˈpräb-ləm\ *n* **1 a :** a question raised for inquiry, consideration, or solution **b :** a proposition in mathematics or physics stating something to be done **2 a :** an intricate unsettled question **b :** a source of perplexity or vexation [Middle French *probleme*, from Latin *problema*, from Greek *problēma*, literally, "something thrown forward", from *proballein* "to throw forward", from *pro-* "forward" + *ballein* "to throw"]

[2]problem *adj* **1 :** dealing with a problem of human conduct or social relationship ⟨a *problem* play⟩ **2 :** difficult to deal with ⟨a *problem* child⟩

prob·lem·at·ic \ˌpräb-lə-ˈmat-ik\ *or* **prob·lem·at·i·cal** \-ˈmat-i-kəl\ *adj* **:** having the nature of a problem **:** difficult and uncertain **:** PUZZLING — **prob·lem·at·i·cal·ly** \-i-kə-lē, -klē\ *adv*

pro·bos·ci·de·an \prə-ˌbäs-ə-ˈdē-ən\ *or* **pro·bos·cid·i·an** \prə-ˌbäs-ˈid-ē-ən\ *n* **:** any of an order (Proboscidea) of large mammals comprising the elephants and extinct related forms [derived from Latin *proboscid-*, *proboscis* "proboscis"] — **proboscidean** *adj*

pro·bos·cis \prə-ˈbäs-əs, -kəs\ *n, pl* **-bos·cis·es** *also* **-bos·ci·des** \-ˈbäs-ə-ˌdēz\ **1 :** the trunk of an elephant; *also* **:** a

\ə\ **abut**	\aù\ **out**	\i\ **tip**	\ȯ\ **saw**	\ù\ **foot**
\ər\ **further**	\ch\ **chin**	\ī\ **life**	\ȯi\ **coin**	\y\ **yet**
\a\ **mat**	\e\ **pet**	\j\ **job**	\th\ **thin**	\yü\ **few**
\ā\ **take**	\ē\ **easy**	\ng\ **sing**	\t͟h\ **this**	\yù\ **cure**
\ä\ **cot, cart**	\g\ **go**	\ō\ **bone**	\ü\ **food**	\zh\ **vision**

long, flexible, or prominent snout or nose **2 :** an elongated sometimes extensible tubular process of the mouth region of an invertebrate (as a mosquito or butterfly) [Latin, from Greek *proboskis,* from *pro-* + *boskein* "to feed"]

pro•caine \'prō-ˌkān\ *n* **:** a drug resembling cocaine and used as a local anesthetic [[2]*pro-* + *cocaine*]

pro•cam•bi•um \prō-'kam-bē-əm, 'prō-\ *n* **:** the part of a plant meristem that forms cambium and primary vascular tissues — **pro•cam•bi•al** \-bē-əl\ *adj*

procaryote *variant of* PROKARYOTE

pro•ca•the•dral \ˌprō-kə-'thē-drəl\ *n* **:** a parish church used as a cathedral

pro•ce•dure \prə-'sē-jər\ *n* **1 :** a manner or method of proceeding in a process or a course of action ⟨legal *procedure*⟩ **2 :** an action or series of actions **:** the continuance or progress of a process or action ⟨making bread is a slow *procedure*⟩ — **pro•ce•dur•al** \prə-'sēj-rəl, -ə-rəl\ *adj* — **pro•ce•dur•al•ly** \-ē\ *adv*

pro•ceed \prō-'sēd, prə-\ *vi* **1 :** to come forth from a source **:** ISSUE **2 a :** to continue after a pause or interruption **b :** to go on in an orderly regulated way **3 a :** to begin and carry on an action, process, or movement ⟨*proceed* to tell them off⟩ **b :** to be in the process of being accomplished ⟨the work's *proceeding* well⟩ **4 :** to move along a course ⟨we *proceeded* south⟩ [Middle French *proceder,* from Latin *procedere,* from *pro-* "forward" + *cedere* "to go"]

pro•ceed•ing *n* **1 :** PROCEDURE 2 **2** *pl* **:** things that take place ⟨talked over the day's *proceedings*⟩ **3 a** *pl* **:** legal action **:** LITIGATION ⟨divorce *proceedings*⟩ **b :** a suit or action at law **4 :** a thing done ⟨a questionable *proceeding*⟩ **5** *pl* **:** an official record of things said or done

pro•ceeds \'prō-ˌsēdz\ *n pl* **:** the total amount or the profit arising (as from a business or tax) **:** RETURN

[1]**pro•cess** \'präs-ˌes, 'prōs-, -əs\ *n, pl* **pro•cess•es** \-ˌes-əz, -ə-səz, -ə-ˌsēz\ **1 a :** PROGRESS, ADVANCE ⟨things will come right in the *process* of time⟩ **b :** something going on **2 a :** a natural phenomenon marked by gradual changes that lead toward a particular result ⟨the *process* of growth⟩ **b :** a series of actions, operations, or changes leading to an end ⟨education is a long *process*⟩ **3 a :** the proceedings or manner of proceeding in a legal action ⟨due *process* of law⟩ **b :** a legal summons or writ used by a court to compel the appearance of the defendant or obedience to its orders **4 :** a prominent or projecting bodily part **:** OUTGROWTH ⟨a bony *process*⟩ [Middle French *proces,* from Latin *processus,* from *processus,* past participle of *procedere* "to proceed"]

[2]**process** *vt* **:** to subject to a process or treatment ⟨*process* metal⟩ ⟨*process* new troops⟩ — **pro•ces•sor** \-ˌes-ər, -ə-sər, -ə-ˌsȯr\ *n*

[3]**process** *adj* **:** treated or made by a special process especially when involving synthesis or artificial modification ⟨*process* cheese⟩

pro•ces•sion \prə-'sesh-ən\ *n* **1 :** continuous forward movement **:** PROGRESSION **2 :** a group of individuals moving along in an orderly often ceremonial way ⟨a funeral *procession*⟩

[1]**pro•ces•sion•al** \prə-'sesh-nəl, -ən-l\ *n* **:** a hymn sung during a procession (as of a choir entering the church at the beginning of a service); *also* **:** a ceremonial procession

[2]**processional** *adj* **:** of, relating to, or moving in a procession — **pro•ces•sion•al•ly** \-ē\ *adv*

pro•claim \prō-'klām\ *vt* **:** to announce publicly ⟨*proclaim* a holiday⟩ ⟨the prince was *proclaimed* king⟩ [Latin *proclamare,* from *pro-* "before" + *clamare* "to cry out"] **syn** see DECLARE — **pro•claim•er** *n*

proc•la•ma•tion \ˌpräk-lə-'mā-shən\ *n* **1 :** the action of proclaiming **:** an official publication ⟨*proclamation* of a new law⟩ **2 :** something proclaimed [Middle French, from Latin *proclamatio,* from *proclamare* "to proclaim"]

pro•cliv•i•ty \prō-'kliv-ət-ē\ *n, pl* **-ties :** a tendency or inclination of the mind or temperament **:** DISPOSITION ⟨a child with a marked *proclivity* toward laziness⟩ [Latin *proclivitas,* from *proclivis* "sloping, prone", from *pro-* "forward" + *clivus* "hill"]

[1]**pro•con•sul** \prō-'kän-səl, 'prō-\ *n* **1 :** a governor or military commander of an ancient Roman province **2 :** an administrator in a modern colony, dependency, or occupied area [Latin, from *pro consule* "for a consul"] — **pro•con•sul•ar** \-sə-lər, -slər\ *adj* — **pro•con•sul•ate** \-sə-lət, -slət\ *n* -- **pro•con•sul•ship** \-səl-ˌship\ *n*

[2]**proconsul** *n* **:** an African Miocene fossil ape possibly ancestral to the anthropoid apes and man [[1]*pro-* + *Consul,* a chimpanzee in the London Zoo]

pro•cras•ti•nate \prə-'kras-tə-ˌnāt\ *vb* **1 :** to put off repeatedly **2 :** to keep postponing something supposed to be done [Latin *procrastinare,* from *pro-* "forward" + *crastinus* "of tomorrow", from *cras* "tomorrow"] — **pro•cras•ti•na•tion** \-ˌkras-tə-'nā-shən\ *n* — **pro•cras•ti•na•tor** \-'kras-tə-ˌnāt-ər\ *n*

pro•cre•ate \'prō-krē-ˌāt\ *vb* **:** to beget or bring forth offspring **:** REPRODUCE [Latin *procreare,* from *pro-* "forth" + *creare* "to create"] — **pro•cre•a•tion** \ˌprō-krē-'ā-shən\ *n* — **pro•cre•a•tive** \'prō-krē-ˌāt-iv\ *adj* — **pro•cre•a•tor** \-ˌāt-ər\ *n*

pro•crus•te•an \prə-'krəs-tē-ən\ *adj, often cap* **:** marked by arbitrary often ruthless disregard of individual differences or special circumstances [*Procrustes,* legendary Greek robber who made his victims fit a certain bed by stretching or lopping off their legs]

procrustean bed *n, often cap P* **:** a scheme or pattern into which someone or something is arbitrarily forced

proc•tor \'präk-tər\ *n* **:** SUPERVISOR, MONITOR; *esp* **:** one appointed to supervise students (as at an examination) [Middle English *procutour* "procurator, proctor", alteration of *procuratour*] — **proctor** *vb* — **proc•to•ri•al** \präk-'tōr-ē-əl, -'tȯr-\ *adj* — **proc•tor•ship** \'präk-tər-ˌship\ *n*

pro•cum•bent \prō-'kəm-bənt\ *adj* **:** lying face down [Latin *procumbens,* present participle of *procumbere* "to fall or lean forward"]

proc•u•ra•tor \'präk-yə-ˌrāt-ər\ *n* **1 :** one that manages another's affairs **:** AGENT **2 :** a Roman provincial administrator and financial manager **3 :** a criminal prosecutor in various countries [Old French *procuratour,* from Latin *procurator,* from *procurare* "to take care of"] — **proc•u•ra•to•ri•al** \ˌpräk-yə-rə-'tōr-ē-əl, -'tȯr-\ *adj*

pro•cure \prə-'kyu̇r\ *vb* **1 a :** to get possession of **:** OBTAIN **b :** to make women available for promiscuous sexual intercourse **2 :** to bring about **:** ACHIEVE [Late Latin *procurare,* from Latin, "to take care of", from *pro-* "for" + *cura* "care"] — **pro•cur•able** \-'kyu̇r-ə-bəl\ *adj* — **pro•cure•ment** \-'kyu̇r-mənt\ *n*

pro•cur•er \-'kyu̇r-ər\ *n* **:** one that procures; *esp* **:** PANDER 1b

Pro•cy•on \'prō-sē-ˌän, 'präs-ē-\ *n* **:** a bright star in Canis Minor [Latin, from Greek *Prokyōn,* literally, "fore-dog"; from its rising before the Dog Star]

[1]**prod** \'präd\ *vt* **prod•ded; prod•ding 1 a :** to thrust a pointed instrument into **b :** to move to action **:** STIR **2 :** to poke or stir as if with a prod [origin unknown] — **prod•der** *n*

[2]**prod** *n* **1 :** a pointed instrument used to prod **2 :** something that moves one to act

[1]**prod•i•gal** \'präd-i-gəl\ *adj* **1 :** recklessly extravagant ⟨a *prodigal* spender⟩ **2 :** wastefully lavish ⟨*prodigal* entertainment⟩ [Latin *prodigus,* from *prodigere* "to drive away, squander", from *pro-, prod-* "forth" + *agere* "to drive"] — **prod•i•gal•i•ty** \ˌpräd-ə-'gal-ət-ē\ *n* — **prod•i•gal•ly** \'präd-i-gə-lē, -glē\ *adv*

[2]**prodigal** *n* **:** a person who spends prodigally **:** SPENDTHRIFT

pro•di•gious \prə-'dij-əs\ *adj* **1 :** exciting amazement or wonder **2 :** extraordinary in bulk, quantity, or degree **:** ENORMOUS **syn** see MONSTROUS — **pro•di•gious•ly** *adv* — **pro•di•gious•ness** *n*

prod•i•gy \'präd-ə-jē\ *n, pl* **-gies 1 :** something extraordinary or unexplainable **2 :** an amazing instance, deed, or performance ⟨a *prodigy* of strength and skill⟩ **3 :** a highly talented child [Latin *prodigium* "omen, monster"]

[1]**pro•duce** \prə-'düs, -'dyüs\ *vb* **1 :** to offer to view or notice **:** EXHIBIT ⟨*produce* evidence⟩ **2 :** to give birth or rise to ⟨a tree *producing* good fruit⟩ **3 :** to extend in length, area, or volume ⟨*produce* a side of a triangle⟩ **4 :** to present to the public on the stage or screen or over radio or television ⟨*produce* a play⟩ **5 :** to give being, form, or shape to **:** MAKE; *esp* **:** MANUFACTURE **6 :** to bring or cause to bring in a profit ⟨income-*producing* investments⟩ **7 :** to produce something [Latin *producere,* from *pro-* "foward" + *ducere* "to lead"]

[2]**pro•duce** \'präd-ˌüs, 'prōd- *also* -ˌyüs\ *n* **1 :** something produced **2 :** agricultural products; *esp* **:** fresh fruits and vegetables as distinguished from staple crops (as grain)

pro•duc•er \prə-'dü-sər, -'dyü-\ *n* **1 :** one that produces; *esp* **:** one that grows agricultural products or manufactures articles **2 :** a person who supervises or finances a stage or screen production or radio or television program **3 :** an organism (as a green plant) which produces its own organic compounds from simple precursors (as carbon dioxide and inorganic nitrogen) and many of which are food sources for other organisms — compare CONSUMER b

producer gas *n* : a manufactured fuel gas consisting chiefly of carbon monoxide, hydrogen, and nitrogen

producer goods *n pl* : goods (as tools) that are used to produce other goods

pro•duc•ible \prə-ˈdü-sə-bəl, -ˈdyü-\ *adj* : capable of being produced

prod•uct \ˈpräd-əkt, -ˌəkt\ *n* **1** : the number or expression resulting from the multiplication of two or more numbers or expressions **2** : something produced **3** : the amount, quantity, or total produced [Latin *productum* "something produced", from *productus,* past participle of *producere* "to produce"]

pro•duc•tion \prə-ˈdək-shən\ *n* **1 a** : something produced : PRODUCT **b** (1) : a literary or artistic work (2) : a work presented on the stage or screen or over the air **2 a** : the act or process of producing **b** : the making of goods available for human wants **3** : total output

pro•duc•tive \prə-ˈdək-tiv\ *adj* **1** : having the power to produce especially in abundance ⟨*productive* fishing waters⟩ **2** : effective in or bringing about a production ⟨an age *productive* of great men⟩ **3** : yielding or furnishing results, benefits, or profits ⟨a *productive* training program⟩ **4 a** : effecting or helping to effect production **b** : yielding or devoted to the satisfaction of wants or the creation of utilities **5** : continuing to be used in the formation of new words or constructions ⟨*un-* is a *productive* English prefix⟩ — **pro•duc•tive•ly** *adv* — **pro•duc•tive•ness** *n*

pro•duc•tiv•i•ty \ˌprō-ˌdək-ˈtiv-ət-ē, ˌpräd-ək-, prə-ˌdək-\ *n* **1** : the quality or state of being productive **2** : rate of production especially of food by fixation of the sun's energy by producer organisms

pro•em \ˈprō-ˌem\ *n* **1** : PREFACE 2 **2** : PRELUDE 1 [Middle French *proheme,* from Latin *prooemium,* from Greek *prooimion,* from *pro-* + *oimē* "song"]

prof \ˈpräf\ *n, slang* : PROFESSOR 2

pro•fa•na•tion \ˌpräf-ə-ˈnā-shən, ˌprō-fə-\ *n* : the act of profaning

pro•fa•na•to•ry \prō-ˈfan-ə-ˌtōr-ē, -ˈfā-nə-, -ˌtór-\ *adj* : tending to profane

[1]**pro•fane** \prō-ˈfān, prə-\ *vt* **1** : to violate or treat with irreverence, abuse, or contempt **2** : to put to a wrong, unworthy, or vulgar use — **pro•fan•er** *n*

[2]**profane** *adj* **1** : not concerned with religion or religious purposes **2** : not holy : not fit for religious uses **3** : serving to debase or defile what is holy : IRREVERENT [Middle French *prophane,* from Latin *profanus,* from *pro-* "before" + *fanum* "temple"] — **pro•fane•ly** *adv* — **pro•fane•ness** \-ˈfān-nəs\ *n*

pro•fan•i•ty \prō-ˈfan-ət-ē\ *n, pl* **-ties** **1 a** : the quality or state of being profane **b** : the use of profane language **2** : profane language **syn** see BLASPHEMY

pro•fess \prə-ˈfes\ *vt* **1 a** : to receive formally into a religious community following a novitiate by acceptance of the required vows **b** : to take (vows) as a member of a religious community or order **2 a** : to declare openly or freely ⟨*profess* confidence in a friend's honesty⟩ **b** : PRETEND, CLAIM ⟨*professed* to be a friend of mine⟩ **3** : to confess one's faith in or allegiance to ⟨*profess* Christianity⟩ **4** : to practice or claim to be versed in (a calling or profession) [derived from Latin *professus,* past participle of *profiteri* "to profess, confess", from *pro-* "before" + *fateri* "to acknowledge"]

pro•fessed \-ˈfest\ *adj* **1** : openly declared whether truly or falsely **2** : having taken the vows of a religious order

pro•fessed•ly \prə-ˈfes-əd-lē, -ˈfest-lē\ *adv* **1** : by one's own account **2** : supposedly but not really

pro•fes•sion \prə-ˈfesh-ən \ *n* **1** : the act of taking the vows of a religious community **2** : an act of openly declaring or publicly claiming a belief, faith, or opinion **3** : an avowed religious faith **4 a** : a calling requiring specialized knowledge and academic preparation **b** : a principal employment **c** : the whole body of persons engaged in a calling

[1]**pro•fes•sion•al** \prə-ˈfesh-nəl, -ən-l\ *adj* **1 a** : of, relating to, or characteristic of a profession **b** : engaged in one of the learned professions **2 a** : participating for gain or livelihood in an activity often engaged in by amateurs ⟨a *professional* golfer⟩ **b** : engaged in by persons receiving financial return ⟨*professional* football⟩ **3** : following a line of conduct as though it were a profession ⟨a *professional* patriot⟩ — **pro•fes•sion•al•ly** \-ē\ *adv*

[2]**professional** *n* : one that engages in an activity professionally

pro•fes•sion•al•ism \-ˌiz-əm\ *n* **1** : the conduct, aims, or qualities that mark a profession or a professional person **2** : the following of a profession (as athletics) for gain or livelihood

pro•fes•sion•al•ize \-ˌīz\ *vt* : to give a professional character to

pro•fes•sor \prə-ˈfes-ər\ *n* **1** : one that professes, avows, or declares **2 a** : a faculty member of the highest academic rank at an institution of higher education **b** : a teacher at a university, college, or sometimes secondary school — **pro•fes•so•ri•al** \ˌprō-fə-ˈsōr-ē-əl, ˌpräf-ə-, -ˈsór-\ *adj* — **pro•fes•so•ri•al•ly** \-ē-ə-lē\ *adv*

pro•fes•sor•ship \prə-ˈfes-ər-ˌship\ *n* : the office, duties, or position of an academic professor

[1]**prof•fer** \ˈpräf-ər\ *vt* **prof•fered**; **prof•fer•ing** \ˈpräf-ring, -ə-ring\ : to present for acceptance : TENDER, OFFER [Anglo-French *profrer,* from Old French *poroffrir,* from *por-* "forth" (from Latin *pro-*) + *offrir* "to offer"]

[2]**proffer** *n* : something proffered : OFFER

pro•fi•cien•cy \prə-ˈfish-ən-sē\ *n, pl* **-cies** **1** : advancement in knowledge or skill **2** : the quality or state of being proficient

pro•fi•cient \prə-ˈfish-ənt\ *adj* : well advanced in an art, occupation, or branch of knowledge [Latin *proficiens,* present participle of *proficere* "to go forward, accomplish", from *pro-* "forward" + *facere* "to make"] — **pro•fi•cient•ly** *adv*

• **syn** PROFICIENT, ADEPT, SKILLFUL, EXPERT mean having great knowledge and experience in a trade or profession. PROFICIENT stresses competence derived from training and practice ⟨a *proficient* typist⟩ ADEPT adds to proficiency the implication of aptitude or cleverness ⟨an *adept* writer of dialogue⟩ SKILLFUL stresses dexterity in execution or performance ⟨*skillful* jugglers⟩ EXPERT implies extraordinary proficiency and often connotes knowledge and technical skill ⟨*expert* in accountancy⟩ ⟨*expert* mimicry⟩

[1]**pro•file** \ˈprō-ˌfīl\ *n* **1** : a representation of something in outline; *esp* : a human head or face represented or seen in a side view **2** : an outline seen or represented in sharp relief **3** : a brief biographical sketch **4** : a vertical section of soil that shows the various zones — called also *soil profile* [Italian *profilo,* from *profilare* "to draw in outline", from *pro-* "forward" + *filare* "to spin"]

[1]profile 1

[2]**profile** *vt* **1** : to represent in profile : draw or write a profile of **2** : to shape the outline of by passing a cutter around

[1]**prof•it** \ˈpräf-ət\ *n* **1** : a valuable return : GAIN **2** : the gain after all expenses are subtracted from the total amount received **3** : the return coming to those who assume the risks of a business as distinguished from wages or rent [Middle French, from Latin *profectus* "advance, profit", from *proficere* "to go forward"] — **prof•it•less** \-ləs\ *adj*

[2]**profit** *vb* **1** : to be of service or advantage **2** : to derive benefit : GAIN ⟨*profit* by experience⟩ **3** : BENEFIT ⟨a business deal that *profited* no one⟩

prof•it•able \ˈpräf-ət-ə-bəl, ˈpräf-tə-bəl\ *adj* : yielding profits : PRODUCTIVE **syn** see BENEFICIAL — **prof•it•abil•i•ty** \ˌpräf-ət-ə-ˈbil-ət-ē, ˌpräf-tə-ˈbil-\ *n* — **prof•it•able•ness** \ˈpräf-ət-ə-bəl-nəs, ˈpräf-tə-bəl-\ *n* — **prof•it•ably** \-blē\ *adv*

prof•i•teer \ˌpräf-ə-ˈtiər\ *n* : one who makes an unreasonable profit especially on the sale of essential goods during an emergency — **profiteer** *vi*

profit sharing *n* : the sharing with employees of a part of the profits of an enterprise

prof•li•ga•cy \ˈpräf-li-gə-sē\ *n* : the quality or state of being profligate

prof•li•gate \ˈpräf-li-gət\ *adj* **1** : loose in character or morals **2**

: extremely wasteful [Latin *profligatus,* from *profligare* "to strike down, destroy, ruin"] — **profligate** *n* — **prof•li•gate•ly** *adv*

pro for•ma \prō-ˈfȯr-mə, ˈprō-\ *adj* : for the sake of or as a matter of form [Latin]

pro•found \prə-ˈfau̇nd\ *adj* **1 a :** having intellectual depth and insight ⟨a *profound* scholar⟩ **b :** difficult to understand ⟨a *profound* work⟩ **2 a :** extending far below the surface **b :** coming from, reaching to, or situated at a depth ⟨a *profound* sigh⟩ **3 a :** deeply felt : INTENSE ⟨*profound* regret⟩ **b :** COMPLETE ⟨*profound* sleep⟩ [Middle French *profond* "deep", from Latin *profundus,* from *pro-* "before" + *fundus* "bottom"] — **pro•found•ly** *adv* — **pro•found•ness** \-ˈfau̇nd-nəs, -ˈfau̇n-\ *n*

pro•fun•di•ty \prə-ˈfən-dət-ē\ *n, pl* **-ties 1 a :** intellectual depth **b :** something profound or hard to understand **2 :** the quality or state of being very profound or deep [Middle French *profundité,* from Latin *profunditas* "depth", from *profundus* "deep"]

pro•fuse \prə-ˈfyüs\ *adj* **1 :** very or too generous ⟨*profuse* in their thanks⟩ ⟨*profuse* spending⟩ **2 :** exhibiting great abundance [Latin *profusus,* past participle of *profundere* "to pour forth", from *pro-* "forth" + *fundere* "to pour"] — **pro•fuse•ly** *adv* — **pro•fuse•ness** *n*

pro•fu•sion \prə-ˈfyü-zhən\ *n* **1 :** profuse expenditure **2 :** lavish display ⟨*profusion* of flowers⟩

pro•gen•i•tor \prō-ˈjen-ət-ər\ *n* **1 a :** a direct ancestor : FOREFATHER **b :** a biologically ancestral form **2 :** one that originates or precedes [Middle French *progeniteur,* from Latin *progenitor,* from *progenitus,* past participle of *progignere* "to beget"]

prog•e•ny \ˈpräj-ə-nē\ *n, pl* **-nies :** offspring of animals or plants [Old French *progenie,* from Latin *progenies,* from *progignere* "to beget", from *pro-* "forth" + *gignere* "to beget"]

pro•ges•ta•tion•al \ˌprō-ˌjes-ˈtā-shnəl, -shən-l\ *adj* : preceding pregnancy or gestation; *esp* : of, relating to, inducing, or being the changes in a female mammal associated with ovulation and corpus luteum formation ⟨*progestational* hormones⟩

pro•ges•ter•one \prō-ˈjes-tə-ˌrōn\ *n* : a steroid progestational hormone $C_{21}H_{30}O_2$ that is produced by the corpus luteum and induces and maintains changes in the uterus to provide a suitable environment for a fertilized egg [*pro-* + *gestation* + *sterol* + *-one,* alteration of *-ene*]

pro•glot•tid \prō-ˈglät-əd, ˈprō-\ *n* : a segment of a tapeworm containing both male and female reproductive organs [New Latin *proglottid-, proglottis,* from Greek *proglōttis,* "tip of the tongue", from *pro-* + *glōtta* "tongue"]

pro•glot•tis \-ˈglät-əs\ *n, pl* **-glot•ti•des** \-ˈglät-ə-ˌdēz\ : PROGLOTTID

prog•na•thous \ˈpräg-nə-thəs, präg-ˈnā-\ *adj* : having the jaws projecting beyond the upper part of the face [*pro-* + Greek *gnathos* "jaw"] — **prog•na•thism** \-ˌthiz-əm\ *n*

prog•no•sis \präg-ˈnō-səs\ *n, pl* **-no•ses** \-ˈnō-ˌsēz\ **1 :** a forecast of the course of a disease; *also* : the outlook given by such a forecast **2 :** FORECAST [Late Latin, from Greek *prognōsis,* literally, "foreknowledge", from *progignōskein* "to know before", from *pro-* + gignōskein "to know"]

prog•nos•tic \präg-ˈnäs-tik\ *n* **1 :** something that foretells **2 :** PROPHECY 2 [Middle French *pronostique,* from Latin *prognosticum,* from Greek *prognōstikon,* from *prognōstikos* "foretelling", from *progignōskein* "to know before"] — **prognostic** *adj*

prog•nos•ti•cate \präg-ˈnäs-tə-ˌkāt\ *vt* **1 :** to foretell from signs or symptoms : PREDICT **2 :** to give an indication of in advance : FORESHOW — **prog•nos•ti•ca•tive** \-ˌkāt-iv\ *adj* — **prog•nos•ti•ca•tor** \-ˌkāt-ər\ *n*

prog•nos•ti•ca•tion \präg-ˌnäs-tə-ˈkā-shən\ *n* **1 :** an indication in advance : FORETOKEN **2 :** FORECAST

[1]**pro•gram** *or* **pro•gramme** \ˈprō-ˌgram, -grəm\ *n* **1 :** a brief statement or written outline of something (as a concert or play) **2 :** PERFORMANCE ⟨a television *program*⟩ **3 :** a plan of action **4 :** a sequence of coded instructions for a computer [French *programme* "agenda, public notice", from Greek *programma,* from *prographein* "to write before", from *pro-* + *graphein* "to write"]

[2]**program** *vt* **pro•grammed** *or* **pro•gramed** \-ˌgramd, -grəmd\; **pro•gram•ming** *or* **pro•gram•ing 1 a :** to arrange or furnish a program of or for **b :** to enter in a program **2 :** to provide (as a computer) with a program — **pro•gram•mer** *n*

programmed instruction *n* : instruction through information given in small steps with each step requiring a correct response before the learner can go on to the next

[1]**prog•ress** \ˈpräg-rəs, -ˌres, *chiefly British* ˈprō-ˌgres\ *n* **1 a :** a royal journey or tour **b :** an official journey **c :** a journeying forward **2 :** a forward movement : ADVANCE **3 :** gradual improvement; *esp* : the progressive development of mankind [Latin *progressus* "advance", from *progressus,* past participle of *progredi* "to go forth", from *pro-* "forward" + *gradi* "to go"]

[2]**pro•gress** \prə-ˈgres\ *vi* **1 :** to move forward : PROCEED **2 :** to develop to a higher, better, or more advanced stage

pro•gres•sion \prə-ˈgresh-ən\ *n* **1 :** a sequence of numbers in which each term is related to its predecessor by a uniform law: **a :** ARITHMETIC PROGRESSION **b :** GEOMETRIC PROGRESSION **2 a :** the action of progressing **b :** a connected series ⟨the rapid *progression* of incidents in a play⟩ **3 a :** series of musical chords **b :** the movement of voice parts in harmony — **pro•gres•sion•al** \-ˈgresh-nəl, -ən-l\ *adj*

[1]**pro•gres•sive** \prə-ˈgres-iv\ *adj* **1 a :** of, relating to, or characterized by progress or progression **b :** gradually increasing ⟨*progressive* income tax⟩ **2 :** of, relating to, or constituting an educational theory marked by emphasis on the individual child, informal classroom procedure, and encouragement of self-expression **3 :** moving forward or onward ⟨the *progressive* movements of the hands of a clock⟩ **4 :** increasing in extent or severity ⟨a *progressive* disease⟩ **5** *often cap* **:** of or relating to political Progressives **6 :** of, relating to, or constituting a verb form that expresses action or state in progress at the time of speaking or a time spoken of — **pro•gres•sive•ly** *adv* — **pro•gres•sive•ness** *n*

[2]**progressive** *n* **1 a :** one that is progressive **b :** one believing in moderate political change and social improvement by governmental action **2** *cap* **a :** a member of a minor United States political party split off from the Republicans about 1912 : BULL MOOSE **b :** a follower of Robert M. La Follette in the presidential campaign of 1924 **c :** a follower of Henry A. Wallace in the presidential campaign of 1948

pro•gres•siv•ism \prə-ˈgres-iv-ˌiz-əm\ *n* **1** *often cap* **:** the principles or beliefs of progressives or of Progressives **2 :** the theories of progressive education — **pro•gres•siv•ist** \-i-vəst\ *n or adj*

pro•hib•it \prō-ˈhib-ət\ *vt* **1 :** to forbid by authority ⟨*prohibit* all-day parking⟩ **2 a :** to prevent from doing something **b :** to make impossible ⟨the high walls *prohibit* escape⟩ [Latin *prohibitus,* past participle of *prohibēre* "to hold away", from *pro-* "forward" + *habēre* "to hold"] **syn** see FORBID

pro•hi•bi•tion \ˌprō-ə-ˈbish-ən\ *n* **1 :** the act of prohibiting **2 :** an order forbidding something **3 :** the forbidding by law of the sale and sometimes the manufacture and transportation of alcoholic liquors as beverages

pro•hi•bi•tion•ist \-ˈbish-nəst, -ə-nəst\ *n* : a person who is in favor of prohibiting the manufacture and sale of alcoholic liquors as beverages

pro•hib•i•tive \prō-ˈhib-ət-iv\ *adj* : serving or tending to prohibit ⟨*prohibitive* prices⟩ — **pro•hib•i•tive•ly** *adv*

pro•hib•i•to•ry \prō-ˈhib-ə-ˌtōr-ē, -ˌtȯr-\ *adj* : PROHIBITIVE

[1]**proj•ect** \ˈpräj-ˌekt, -ikt\ *n* **1 :** a particular plan or design : SCHEME **2 :** a planned undertaking: as **a :** a definitely formulated piece of research **b :** a large usually government-supported undertaking **c :** a task or problem engaged in usually by a group of students to supplement and apply classroom studies **3 :** a group of houses or apartment buildings constructed and arranged according to a single plan; *esp* : one built with government help to provide low-cost housing [Middle French *pourjet,* from *pourjeter* "to throw out, spy, plan", from *pour-* (from Latin *porro* "forward") + *jeter* "to throw"]

[2]**pro•ject** \prə-ˈjekt\ *vb* **1 :** to devise in the mind : DESIGN ⟨*project* civic improvements⟩ **2 :** to throw forward, upward, or outward **3 :** to stick out ⟨a stone jetty *projecting* into the bay⟩ **4 :** to cause (light or shadow) to fall into space or (an image) to fall on a surface ⟨*project* a beam of light⟩ ⟨*project* motion pictures on a screen⟩ **5 :** to reproduce (as a point, line, or area) on a line, plane, or surface in a prescribed manner [partly from Middle French *pourjeter* "to throw out, plan"; partly from Latin *projectus,* past participle of *proicere* "to throw forward", from *pro-* + *jacere* "to throw"] — **pro•ject•able** \-ˈjek-tə-bəl\ *adj*

[1]**pro•jec•tile** \prə-ˈjek-tl\ *n* **1 :** a body projected by external force and continuing in motion by its own inertia; *esp* : a missile for a weapon (as a firearm or cannon) **2 :** a self-propelling weapon (as a guided missile)

[2]**projectile** *adj* **1 :** projecting or impelling forward ⟨a *projectile*

force⟩ **2 :** capable of being thrust forward

pro•jec•tion \prə-ˈjek-shən\ *n* **1 a :** a method of projecting the curved surface of the earth or the celestial sphere on a flat surface map based on a systematic presentation of intersecting coordinate lines **b** (1) **:** the process of reproducing a spatial object upon a surface by projecting its points; *also* **:** the graphic reproduction so formed (2) **:** a set of points obtained by projecting another set of points onto a line, plane, or surface **2 :** the act of throwing or shooting forward **:** EJECTION **3 :** the forming of a plan **4 a :** a jutting out **b :** a part that juts out **5 :** the making objective of what is primarily subjective **6 :** the display of motion pictures by projecting an image from them upon a screen **7 :** an estimate of future possibilities based on a current trend — **pro•jec•tion•al** \-shnəl, -shən-ᵊl\ *adj*

• **syn** PROJECTION, PROTRUSION mean extension beyond a normal line or surface. PROJECTION implies a jutting out especially at a sharp angle; PROTRUSION suggests a thrusting or bulging out so as to seem a deformity.

pro•jec•tion•ist \-shə-nəst, -shnəst\ *n* **:** one that makes projections; *esp* **:** one that operates a motion-picture projector or television equipment

pro•jec•tive \prə-ˈjek-tiv\ *adj* **1 :** of, relating to, or involving geometric projection or projective geometry **2 :** jutting out

projective geometry *n* **:** a branch of mathematics concerned with the properties of geometric figures that remain unchanged by projection

pro•jec•tor \prə-ˈjek-tər\ *n* **1 :** one that plans a project; *esp* **:** PROMOTER **2 :** one that projects: as **a :** a device for projecting a beam of light **b :** an optical instrument or machine for projecting an image or pictures upon a surface

pro•kary•otc *or* **pro•cary•ote** \prō-ˈkar-ē-ˌōt, ˈprō-\ *n* **:** a cellular organism (as a bacterium or a blue-green alga) that does not have a distinct nucleus — compare EUKARYOTE **[***pro-* + *kary-* "cell nucleus" (from Greek *karyon* "nut, kernel") + *-ote* (as in *zygote*)**]** — **pro•kary•ot•ic** \ˌprō-ˌkar-ē-ˈät-ik\ *adj*

pro•lac•tin \prō-ˈlak-tən\ *n* **:** a protein hormone of the pituitary gland that induces lactation — called also *luteotrophic hormone*

pro•lapse \prō-ˈlaps\ *n* **:** the slipping of a body part from its usual position or relations **[**Late Latin *prolapsus* "fall", from Latin *prolabi* "to fall or slide forward", from *pro-* "forward" + *labi* "to slide"**]** — **prolapse** *vi*

pro•leg \ˈprō-ˌleg\ *n* **:** a fleshy leg on an abdominal segment of some insect larvae

pro•le•gom•e•non \ˌprō-li-ˈgäm-ə-ˌnän\ *n, pl* **-na** \-nə\ **:** introductory remarks; *esp* **:** a formal essay or critical discussion serving to introduce and interpret an extended work **[**Greek, neuter present passive participle of *prolegein* "to say beforehand", from *pro-* + *legein* "to say"**]** — **pro•le•gom•e•nous** \-nəs\ *adj*

[1]**pro•le•tar•i•an** \ˌprō-lə-ˈter-ē-ən\ *n* **:** a member of the proletariat **[**Latin *proletarius*, from *proles* "progeny"; from the fact that their chief contribution to the state was progeny rather than property**]**

[2]**proletarian** *adj* **:** of, relating to, or representative of the proletariat

pro•le•tar•i•at \ˌprō-lə-ˈter-ē-ət, -ˈtar-, -ē-ˌat\ *n* **1 :** the lowest social or economic class of a community **2 :** industrial workers who sell their labor to live **[**French *prolétariat*, from Latin *proletarius* "proletarian"**]**

pro•lif•er•ate \prə-ˈlif-ə-ˌrāt\ *vi* **:** to grow or increase by rapid production of new units (as cells or offspring) **[**back-formation from *proliferation*, from French *prolifération*, from *proliférer* "to proliferate", from *prolifère* "proliferative", from Latin *proles* "progeny" + *-fer* "-ferous"**]** — **pro•lif•er•a•tion** \-ˌlif-ə-ˈrā-shən\ *n* — **pro•lif•er•a•tive** \-ˈlif-ə-ˌrāt-iv\ *adj*

pro•lif•ic \prə-ˈlif-ik\ *adj* **1 :** producing young or fruit abundantly ⟨*prolific* orchard⟩ **2 :** highly inventive **:** PRODUCTIVE ⟨a *prolific* mind⟩ **3 :** causing or characterized by fruitfulness ⟨*prolific* growing season⟩ **[**French *prolifique*, from Latin *proles* "progeny"**]** **syn** see FERTILE — **pro•lif•i•cal•ly** \-ˈlif-i-kə-lē, -klē\ *adv* — **pro•lif•ic•ness** *n*

pro•line \ˈprō-ˌlēn\ *n* **:** an amino acid $C_5H_9NO_2$ that can be synthesized by animals from glutamate **[**German *prolin***]**

pro•lix \prō-ˈliks, ˈprō-ˌliks\ *adj* **:** using or containing too many words **:** WORDY, LONG-WINDED **[**Latin *prolixus* "extended", from *pro-* "forward" + *liquēre* "to be fluid"**]** — **pro•lix•i•ty** \prō-ˈlik-sət-ē\ *n* — **pro•lix•ly** \prō-ˈliks-lē, ˈprō-ˌ\ *adv*

pro•logue \ˈprō-ˌlȯg\ *n* **1 :** the preface or introduction to a literary work **2 a :** a speech often in verse addressed to the audience by an actor at the beginning of a play **b :** the actor speaking such a prologue **3 :** an introductory or preceding event or development **[**Old French, from Latin *prologus* "preface to a play", from Greek *prologos*, from *pro-* + *legein* "to speak"**]**

pro•long \prə-ˈlȯng\ *vt* **1 :** to make longer than usual **:** continue or lengthen in time ⟨a *prolonged* stay in the hospital⟩ **2 :** to lengthen in extent or range ⟨*prolong* a boundary line⟩ **[**Middle French *prolonguer*, from Late Latin *prolongare*, from Latin *pro-* "forward" + *longus* "long"**]** **syn** see EXTEND

pro•lon•ga•tion \prō-ˌlȯng-ˈgā-shən\ *n* **1 :** a lengthening in space or time **2 :** something that prolongs or is prolonged

prom \ˈpräm\ *n* **:** an often formal dance given by a high school or college class **[**short for *promenade***]**

[1]**prom•e•nade** \ˌpräm-ə-ˈnād, -ˈnäd\ *n* **1 :** a leisurely walk or ride especially in a public place for pleasure or display **2 :** a place for strolling **3 :** a ceremonious opening of a formal ball consisting of a grand march of all the guests **[**French, from *promener* "to take for a walk", from Latin *prominare* "to drive forward", from *pro-* "forward" + *minare* "to drive"**]**

[2]**promenade** *vb* **1 :** to take or go on a promenade **2 :** to walk about in or on ⟨*promenading* the sun deck⟩ — **prom•e•nad•er** *n*

promenade deck *n* **:** an upper deck of a passenger ship where passengers stroll

Pro•me•the•an \prə-ˈmē-thē-ən\ *adj* **:** of, relating to, or resembling Prometheus; *esp* **:** daringly original or creative

pro•me•thi•um \-thē-əm\ *n* **:** a metallic chemical element obtained as a fission product of uranium or from neutron-irradiated neodymium — see ELEMENT table **[**New Latin, from *Prometheus*, a Titan**]**

prom•i•nence \ˈpräm-ə-nəns\ *n* **1 :** the quality, state, or fact of being prominent or conspicuous ⟨a person of *prominence*⟩ **2 :** PROJECTION 4b **3 :** a mass or stream of gas resembling a cloud that arises from the chromosphere of the sun

prom•i•nent \-nənt\ *adj* **1 :** standing out or projecting beyond a surface or line **:** PROTUBERANT **2 :** readily noticeable **:** CONSPICUOUS **3 :** EMINENT, NOTABLE **[**Latin *prominens*, from *prominēre* "to jut forward"**]** — **prom•i•nent•ly** *adv*

prom•is•cu•i•ty \ˌpräm-əs-ˈkyü-ət-ē, prə-ˌmis-\ *n, pl* **-ties 1 :** a miscellaneous mingling of persons or things **2 :** promiscuous sexual behavior

pro•mis•cu•ous \prə-ˈmis-kyə-wəs\ *adj* **1 :** composed of all sorts of persons or things ⟨a *promiscuous* crowd of onlookers⟩ **2 :** not restricted to one person or class ⟨give *promiscuous* praise⟩; *esp* **:** not restricted to one sexual partner **3 :** HAPHAZARD, IRREGULAR ⟨*promiscuous* eating habits⟩ **[**Latin *promiscuus*, from *pro-* "forth" + *miscēre* "to mix"**]** — **pro•mis•cu•ous•ly** *adv* — **pro•mis•cu•ous•ness** *n*

[1]**prom•ise** \ˈpräm-əs\ *n* **1 :** a statement assuring someone that the person making the statement will do or not do something **:** PLEDGE ⟨a *promise* to pay⟩ **2 :** a cause or ground for hope or expectation especially of success or distinction ⟨the child shows *promise*⟩ **3 :** something promised **[**Latin *promissum*, from *promissus*, past participle of *promittere* "to send forth, promise", from *pro-* "forth" + *mittere* "to send"**]**

[2]**promise** *vb* **1 a :** to pledge onself to do, bring about, or provide ⟨*promise* aid⟩ **b :** to tell as a promise ⟨*promised* them we'd wait⟩ **c :** to make a promise **2 :** to suggest beforehand **:** FORETOKEN ⟨dark clouds *promising* rain⟩ — **prom•is•er** \ˈpräm-ə-sər\ *or* **prom•i•sor** \ˌpräm-ə-ˈsȯr\ *n*

promised land *n* **1 :** the land of Canaan that God promised to Abraham and his descendants **2 :** a better place that one hopes to reach or a better condition that one hopes to attain

prom•is•ing *adj* **:** full of promise **:** giving hope or assurance (as of success) ⟨a very *promising* pupil⟩ — **prom•is•ing•ly** \ˈpräm-ə-sing-lē\ *adv*

prom•is•so•ry \ˈpräm-ə-ˌsōr-ē, -ˌsȯr-\ *adj* **:** containing or conveying a promise or assurance ⟨a *promissory* note⟩

prom•on•to•ry \ˈpräm-ən-ˌtōr-ē, -ˌtȯr-\ *n, pl* **-ries :** a high point of land or rock jutting out into a body of water **:** HEADLAND **[**Latin *promunturium***]**

\ə\ **abut**	\au̇\ **out**	\i\ **tip**	\ȯ\ **saw**	\u̇\ **foot**
\ər\ **further**	\ch\ **chin**	\ī\ **life**	\ȯi\ **coin**	\y\ **yet**
\a\ **mat**	\e\ **pet**	\j\ **job**	\th\ **thin**	\yü\ **few**
\ā\ **take**	\ē\ **easy**	\ng\ **sing**	\t͟h\ **this**	\yu̇\ **cure**
\ä\ **cot, cart**	\g\ **go**	\ō\ **bone**	\ü\ **food**	\zh\ **vision**

pro•mot•able \prə-'mōt-ə-bəl\ *adj* : likely or deserving to be promoted

pro•mote \prə-'mōt\ *vt* **1** : to advance in position, rank, or honor : ELEVATE ⟨*promote* pupils to a higher grade⟩ **2** : to contribute to the growth, success, or development of : FURTHER ⟨good food *promotes* health⟩ **3** : to take the first steps in organizing (as a business) [Latin *promotus,* past participle of *promovēre,* literally, "to move forward", from *pro-* "forward" + *movēre* "to move"]

pro•mot•er \prə-'mōt-ər\ *n* : one that promotes; *esp* : one taking on the financial responsibilities of a sporting event

pro•mo•tion \prə-'mō-shən\ *n* **1** : the act or fact of being raised in position or rank **2** : the act of furthering the growth or development of something — **pro•mo•tion•al** \-shnəl, -shən-l\ *adj*

[1]**prompt** \'prämt, 'prämpt\ *vt* **1** : to move to action : CAUSE ⟨curiosity *prompted* me to ask the question⟩ **2** : to remind of something forgotten or poorly learned (as by suggesting the next few words in a speech) ⟨*prompt* an actor⟩ **3** : SUGGEST, INSPIRE ⟨pride *prompted* the act⟩ [Medieval Latin *promptare,* from Latin *promptus* "ready, prompt"]

[2]**prompt** *adj* **1 a** : being ready and quick as occasion demands ⟨*prompt* to answer⟩ **b** : PUNCTUAL ⟨*prompt* in arriving⟩ **2** : performed readily or immediately ⟨*prompt* assistance⟩ [Latin *promptus* "ready, prompt", from *promere* "to bring forth", from *pro-* "forth" + *emere* "to take"] — **prompt•ly** *adv* — **prompt•ness** *n*

prompt•book \'prämt-,bu̇k, 'prämp-\ *n* : a copy of a play with directions for performance used by a theater prompter

prompt•er \'präm-tər, 'prämp-\ *n* : a person who reminds another of the words to be spoken next (as in a play)

promp•ti•tude \'präm-tə-,tüd, 'prämp-, -,tyüd\ *n* : the quality or habit of being prompt : PROMPTNESS

prom•ul•gate \'präm-əl-,gāt; prō-'məl-\ *vt* **1** : to make known by open declaration : PROCLAIM **2 a** : to make public the terms of (a proposed law) **b** : to issue or give out (a law) by way of putting into execution [Latin *promulgare*] — **prom•ul•ga•tion** \,präm-əl-'gā-shən, ,prō-məl-\ *n* — **prom•ul•ga•tor** \'präm-əl-,gāt-ər, prō-'məl-\ *n*

pro•na•tion \prō-'nā-shən\ *n* : rotation of the hand or forearm so as to bring the palm facing downward or backward; *also* : rotation of a joint or part forward and toward the midline of the body [from *pronate,* from Late Latin *pronatus,* past participle of *pronare* "to bend forward", from Latin *pronus* "bent forward"] — **pro•nate** \'prō-,nāt\ *vt*

pro•na•tor \'prō-,nāt-ər\ *n* : a muscle that produces pronation

prone \'prōn\ *adj* **1** : having a tendency or inclination ⟨*prone* to laziness⟩ **2 a** : lying belly or face downward ⟨shoot from a *prone* position⟩ **b** : not erect : lying flat or prostrate ⟨the wind blew the trees *prone*⟩ [Latin *pronus* "bent forward, tending"] — **prone•ness** \'prōn-nəs\ *n*

• **syn** PRONE, PROSTRATE, SUPINE mean lying down. PRONE implies a position with the front of the body turned toward the supporting surface ⟨lying *prone* on the deck⟩ PROSTRATE implies lying at full length as in submission or physical collapse ⟨found the body *prostrate* on the floor⟩ SUPINE implies lying on one's back and may connote laziness or inertness.

[1]**prong** \'pro̊ng, 'präng\ *n* **1** : a tine of a fork **2** : a slender pointed or projecting part (as of a tooth or an antler) [Middle English *pronge*] — **pronged** \'pro̊ngd, 'prängd\ *adj*

[2]**prong** *vt* : to stab, pierce, or break up with a pronged device

prong•horn \'pro̊ng-,ho̊rn, 'präng-\ *n, pl* **pronghorn** *also* **pronghorns** : a cud-chewing mammal of treeless parts of western North America that resembles an antelope

pronghorn

pro•nom•i•nal \prō-'näm-ən-l\ *adj* **1** : of, relating to, or being a pronoun **2** : resembling a pronoun in identifying or specifying without describing ⟨the *pronominal* adjective *this* in "this dog"⟩ [Late Latin *pronominalis,* from Latin *pronomen* "pronoun"] — **pro•nom•i•nal•ly** \-l-ē\ *adv*

pro•noun \'prō-,nau̇n\ *n* : a word that is used as a substitute for a noun or a noun phrase, takes noun constructions, and refers to persons or things named or understood in the context [Latin *pronomen,* from *pro-* "for" + *nomen* "name"]

pro•nounce \prə-'nau̇ns\ *vt* **1** : to declare officially or solemnly ⟨the minister *pronounced* them man and wife⟩ ⟨the judge *pronounced* sentence⟩ **2** : to assert as an opinion ⟨*pronounce* the book a success⟩ **3** : to utter the sounds of : speak aloud ⟨practice *pronouncing* foreign words⟩; *esp* : to say or speak correctly ⟨can't *pronounce* your name⟩ [Middle French *prononcier,* from Latin *pronuntiare,* from *pro-* "forth" + *nuntiare* "to report", from *nuntius* "messenger"] — **pro•nounce•able** \-'nau̇n-sə-bəl\ *adj* — **pro•nounc•er** *n*

pro•nounced \-'nau̇nst\ *adj* : strongly marked : DECIDED ⟨a *pronounced* change for the better⟩ — **pro•nounc•ed•ly** \-'nau̇n-səd-lē\ *adv*

pro•nounce•ment \prə-'nau̇ns-mənt\ *n* **1** : a formal declaration of opinion **2** : an authoritative announcement

pron•to \'prän-,tō\ *adv* : right away : QUICKLY, PROMPTLY [Spanish, from Latin *promptus* "prompt"]

pro•nun•ci•a•men•to \prō-,nən-sē-ə-'ment-ō\ *n, pl* **-tos** *or* **-toes** : PROCLAMATION 1, PRONOUNCEMENT [Spanish *pronunciamiento,* from *pronunciar* "to pronounce", from Latin *pronuntiare*]

pro•nun•ci•a•tion \prə-,nən-sē-'ā-shən\ *n* : the act or manner of pronouncing something [Middle French *prononciation,* from Latin *pronuntiatio,* from *pronuntiare* "to pronounce"] — **pro•nun•ci•a•tion•al** \-shnəl, -shən-l\ *adj*

[1]**proof** \'prüf\ *n* **1 a** (1) : evidence of truth or correctness ⟨gave *proof* of their statement⟩ (2) : the process of or an instance of establishing the validity of a statement (as a mathematical theorem) especially by derivation from other statements by accepted rules of reasoning **b** : a test to find out or show the essential facts or truth ⟨put the theory to the *proof*⟩ ⟨the *proof* of the pudding is in the eating⟩ **2 a** : a copy (as of composed text) made for correction or examination **b** : a test photographic print made from a negative **3** : alcoholic content (as of a beverage) indicated by a number that is twice the percent by volume of alcohol present ⟨whiskey of 90 *proof* is 45% alcohol⟩ [Old French *preuve,* from Late Latin *proba,* from Latin *probare* "to prove"]

[2]**proof** *adj* **1** : designed for or successful in repelling, resisting, or withstanding ⟨*proof* against tampering⟩ — usually used in combination ⟨bomb*proof*⟩ ⟨water*proof*⟩ **2** : used in proving or testing or as a standard of comparison ⟨use only *proof* loads in a gun⟩

proof•read \'prü-,frēd\ *vb* : to read and make corrections (as in printer's proof) ⟨*proofread* a composition⟩

proof•read•er \-,frēd-ər\ *n* : a person who reads and makes corrections in printer's proof

[1]**prop** \'präp\ *n* : something that props or sustains : SUPPORT [Dutch *proppe* "stopper"]

[2]**prop** *vt* **propped; prop•ping 1 a** : to hold up or keep from falling or slipping by placing something under or against ⟨*prop* the limb up⟩ **b** : to support by placing against something ⟨*prop* a rake against the tree⟩ **2** : SUSTAIN, STRENGTHEN ⟨*propped* up by faith in times of crisis⟩

[3]**prop** *n* : PROPERTY 5

[4]**prop** *n* : PROPELLER

pro•pa•gan•da \,präp-ə-'gan-də, ,prō-pə-\ *n* **1** *cap* : a congregation of the Roman Catholic curia having jurisdiction over missionary territories and related institutions **2** : the spreading of ideas, information, or rumor for the purpose of helping or injuring a cause; *also* : the ideas, facts, or allegations so spread [New Latin, from *Congregatio de propaganda fide* "congregation for propagating the faith", organization established by Pope Gregory XV] — **pro•pa•gan•dist** \-dəst\ *n* — **pro•pa•gan•dis•tic** \-,gan-'dis-tik\ *adj* — **pro•pa•gan•dis•ti•cal•ly** \-ti-kə-lē, -klē\ *adv*

pro•pa•gan•dize \-'gan-,dīz\ *vb* **1** : to spread propaganda **2** : to influence or attempt to influence by propaganda

prop•a•gate \'präp-ə-,gāt\ *vb* **1** : to reproduce or increase by sexual or asexual means : MULTIPLY ⟨*propagate* an apple by grafting⟩ **2** : to pass along to offspring **3 a** : to cause to spread out and affect a greater number or greater area **b** : PUBLICIZE **c** : TRANSMIT 2 **4** : to increase in extent, number, or influence : EXTEND [Latin *propagare* "to set slips, propagate", from *propages* "slip, offspring", from *pro-* "before" + *pangere* "to fasten"] — **prop•a•ga•tive** \-,gāt-iv\ *adj* — **prop•a•ga•tor** \-,gāt-ər\ *n*

prop·a·ga·tion \ˌpräp-ə-ˈgā-shən\ *n* **:** the act or process of propagating: as **a :** multiplication (as of a kind of organism) in number of individuals **b :** the spreading of something (as a belief) abroad or into new regions **:** DISSEMINATION ⟨*propagation* of a faith⟩ — **prop·a·ga·tion·al** \-shnəl, -shən-l\ *adj*

pro·pane \ˈprō-ˌpān\ *n* **:** a heavy flammable gaseous hydrocarbon C_3H_8 found in crude petroleum and natural gas and used especially as fuel and in chemical synthesis [*prop*ionic acid + *-ane*]

pro·pel \prə-ˈpel\ *vt* **pro·pelled; pro·pel·ling 1 :** to push or drive usually forward or onward ⟨a bicycle is *propelled* by pedals⟩ **2 :** to give an impelling motive to **:** urge ahead ⟨people *propelled* by ambition⟩ [Latin *propellere,* from *pro-* "before" + *pellere* "to drive"] **syn** see PUSH

[1]**pro·pel·lant** *or* **pro·pel·lent** \-ˈpel-ənt\ *adj* **:** capable of propelling

[2]**propellant** *also* **propellent** *n* **:** something that propels: as **a :** an explosive for propelling projectiles **b :** fuel plus oxidizer used by a rocket engine **c :** a gas in a specially made container for expelling the contents when the pressure is released

pro·pel·ler *also* **pro·pel·lor** \prə-ˈpel-ər\ *n* **:** one that propels; *esp* **:** a device consisting of a hub with radiating blades that is used for propelling aircraft and boats

pro·pen·si·ty \prə-ˈpen-sət-ē\ *n, pl* **-ties :** a natural inclination or liking **:** BENT ⟨a *propensity* for drawing⟩ [derived from Latin *propensus,* past participle of *propendēre* "to incline", from *pro-* "before" + *pendēre* "to hang"]

[1]**prop·er** \ˈpräp-ər\ *adj* **1 :** suitable by reason of essential nature or condition **2 a :** appointed for the liturgy of a particular day **b :** belonging to one **:** OWN **3 :** belonging characteristically to a species or individual **:** PECULIAR **4 :** strictly limited to a specified thing, place, or idea ⟨outside the city *proper*⟩ **5 a :** strictly accurate **:** CORRECT **b :** strictly decorous **:** GENTEEL [Old French *propre* "proper, own", from Latin *proprius* "own"] **syn** see FIT

[2]**proper** *n, often cap* **:** the parts of the Mass or Divine Office that vary according to the day or feast

proper adjective *n* **:** an adjective formed from a proper noun

proper fraction *n* **:** a fraction in which the numerator is less in absolute value than the denominator

prop·er·ly \ˈpräp-ər-lē\ *adv* **1 :** in a suitable or fit manner ⟨behave *properly* in church⟩ **2 :** strictly in accordance with fact **:** CORRECTLY ⟨goods not *properly* labeled⟩ ⟨*properly* speaking, whales are not fish⟩

proper noun *n* **:** a noun that designates a particular being or thing and in English is usually capitalized — called also *proper name*

proper subset *n* **:** a subset containing fewer elements than the set to which it belongs

prop·er·tied \ˈpräp-ərt-ēd\ *adj* **:** owning property and especially much property

prop·er·ty \ˈpräp-ərt-ē\ *n, pl* **-ties 1 :** a special quality or characteristic of a thing **:** a quality or attribute common to all things called by the same name ⟨sweetness is a *property* of sugar⟩ **2 :** anything that is owned (as land, goods, or money) **3 :** a piece of real estate with or without a structure on it ⟨a business *property*⟩ **4 :** the legal right to property **:** OWNERSHIP **5 :** an article to be used on the stage during a play or on the set of a motion picture except artificial scenery or actors' costumes [Middle French *propreté,* from Latin *proprietas,* from *proprius* "own"] **syn** see QUALITY

prop·er·ty·less \-ləs\ *adj* **:** lacking property

property man *n* **:** one who is in charge of theater or motion-picture stage properties

pro·phage \ˈprō-ˌfāj, -ˌfäzh\ *n* **:** a form of a bacteriophage in which it is harmless to the host, is usually integrated into the hereditary material of the host, and reproduces when the host does

pro·phase \ˈprō-ˌfāz\ *n* **1 :** the initial phase of mitosis in which chromosomes are condensed from the resting form and split into paired chromatids **2 :** the initial stage of meiosis in which the chromosomes become visible, pairs of homologous chromosomes are associated and become shortened and thickened, individual chromosomes become visibly double as paired chromatids, cytological evidence of crossing-over appears, and the nuclear membrane disappears

proph·e·cy \ˈpräf-ə-sē\ *n, pl* **-cies 1 :** the work or revelation of a prophet inspired by God **2 :** the foretelling of the future ⟨the gift of *prophecy*⟩ **3 :** something foretold of the future **:** PREDICTION [Old French *prophecie,* from Late Latin *prophetia,* from Greek *prophēteia,* from *prophētēs* "prophet"]

proph·e·sy \ˈpräf-ə-ˌsī\ *vb* **-sied; -sy·ing 1 a :** to speak or write as a prophet **b :** to utter by divine inspiration **2 :** to predict on or as if on the basis of mystic knowledge ⟨*prophesy* bad weather⟩ [Middle French *prophesier,* from *prophecie* "prophecy"] **syn** see FORETELL — **proph·e·si·er** \-ˌsī-ər, -ˌsīr\ *n*

proph·et \ˈpräf-ət\ *n* **1 :** a person who declares publicly a message that he or she believes has been divinely inspired; *esp, often cap* **:** the writer of one of the prophetic books of the Old Testament **2 :** one gifted with more than ordinary spiritual and moral insight; *esp* **:** an inspired poet **3 :** one who foretells future events **4 :** an effective or leading spokesman for a cause, doctrine, or group ⟨a *prophet* of the revolution⟩ [Old French *prophete,* from Latin *propheta,* from Greek *prophētēs,* from *pro* "for" + *phanai* "to speak"]

proph·et·ess \-ət-əs\ *n* **:** a woman who is a prophet

pro·phet·ic \prə-ˈfet-ik\ *adj* **1 :** of, relating to, or characteristic of a prophet or prophecy ⟨*prophetic* insight⟩ **2 :** foretelling events **:** PREDICTIVE ⟨a *prophetic* statement⟩ — **pro·phet·i·cal** \-ˈfet-i-kəl\ *adj* — **pro·phet·i·cal·ly** \-i-kə-lē, -klē\ *adv*

Proph·ets \ˈpräf-əts\ *n pl* **:** the second part of the Jewish scriptures — compare HAGIOGRAPHA, LAW 3b

pro·phy·lac·tic \ˌprō-fə-ˈlak-tik\ *adj* **1 :** guarding from or preventing disease **2 :** tending to prevent or ward off **:** PREVENTIVE [Greek *prophylaktikos,* from *prophylassein* "to keep guard before", from *pro-* "before" + *phylassein* "to guard", from *phylax* "guard"] — **prophylactic** *n* — **pro·phy·lac·ti·cal·ly** \-ti-kə-lē, -klē\ *adv*

pro·phy·lax·is \-ˈlak-səs\ *n, pl* **-lax·es** \-ˈlak-ˌsēz\ **:** measures designed to preserve health and prevent the spread of disease [New Latin, from Greek *prophylaktikos* "prophylactic"]

pro·pin·qui·ty \prō-ˈping-kwət-ē\ *n* **1 :** nearness of blood **:** KINSHIP **2 :** nearness in place or time [Latin *propinquitas* "kinship, proximity", from *propinquus* "near, akin", from *prope* "near"]

pro·pi·on·ic acid \ˌprō-pē-ˌän-ik-\ *n* **:** a liquid sharp-odored fatty acid $C_3H_6O_2$ found in milk and distillates of wood, coal, and petroleum [*pro-* + Greek *piōn* "fat"]

pro·pi·ti·ate \prō-ˈpish-ē-ˌāt\ *vt* **:** to gain or regain the favor or goodwill of **:** APPEASE, CONCILIATE ⟨*propitiate* the angry gods with sacrifices⟩ [Latin *propitiare,* from *propitius* "propitious"] — **pro·pi·ti·a·tion** \-ˌpish-ē-ˈā-shən\ *n* — **pro·pi·ti·ator** \-ˈpish-ē-ˌāt-ər\ *n* — **pro·pi·tia·to·ry** \-ˈpish-ē-ə-ˌtōr-ē, -ˈpish-ə-, -ˌtȯr-\ *adj*

pro·pi·tious \prə-ˈpish-əs\ *adj* **1 :** favorably disposed ⟨the fates are *propitious*⟩ **2 :** of good omen **:** PROMISING ⟨*propitious* signs⟩ **3 :** likely to produce good results **:** OPPORTUNE ⟨the *propitious* moment for asking a favor⟩ [Latin *propitius,* from *pro-* "for" + *petere* "to seek"] — **pro·pi·tious·ly** *adv* — **pro·pi·tious·ness** *n*

prop·jet engine \ˌpräp-ˌjet-\ *n* **:** TURBO-PROPELLER ENGINE

prop·man \ˈpräp-ˌman\ *n* **:** PROPERTY MAN

prop·o·lis \ˈpräp-ə-ləs\ *n* **:** a brownish waxy resinous material collected by bees from the buds of trees and used as a cement [Latin, from Greek, from *pro-* "for" + *polis* "city"]

pro·po·nent \prə-ˈpō-nənt, ˈprō-ˌ\ *n* **:** one who argues in favor of something **:** ADVOCATE [Latin *proponens,* present participle of *proponere* "to propound"]

[1]**pro·por·tion** \prə-ˈpōr-shən, pə-, -ˈpȯr-\ *n* **1 :** the relation of one part to another or to the whole with respect to magnitude, quantity, or degree **:** RATIO **2 :** balanced or pleasing arrangement **3 :** a statement of the equality of two ratios (as $4/2 = 10/5$) **4 a :** fair or equal share **b :** QUOTA 1, PERCENTAGE **5 :** relative dimensions **:** SIZE ⟨a room of good *proportions*⟩ [Middle French, from Latin *proportio,* from *pro* "for" + *portio* "portion"] — **pro·por·tioned** \-shənd\ *adj*

[2]**proportion** *vt* **-tioned; -tion·ing** \-shə-ning, -shning\ **1 :** to adjust (a part or thing) in size relative to other parts or things **2 :** to make the parts of harmonious or symmetrical

[1]**pro·por·tion·al** \prə-ˈpōr-shnəl, pə-, -ˈpȯr-, -shən-l\ *adj* **1 a :** being in proportion **:** PROPORTIONATE ⟨wages *proportional* to

ability⟩ **b :** having the same or a constant ratio **2 :** regulated or determined in size or degree with reference to proportions — **pro·por·tion·al·i·ty** \-ˌpōr-shə-ˈnal-ət-ē, -ˌpȯr-\ *n* — **pro·por·tion·al·ly** \-ˈpōr-shnə-lē, -ˈpȯr-,-shən-l-ē\ *adv*

2proportional *n* **:** a number or quantity in a proportion

proportional parts *n pl* **:** fractional parts of the difference between successive entries in a table for use in linear interpolation

proportional representation *n* **:** an electoral system designed to represent in a legislative body each political group or party in proportion to its actual voting strength in the electorate

1pro·por·tion·ate \prə-ˈpōr-shə-nət, pə-, -ˈpȯr-, -shnət\ *adj* **:** being in proportion — **pro·por·tion·ate·ly** *adv*

2pro·por·tion·ate \-shə-ˌnāt\ *vt* **:** to make proportionate **:** PROPORTION

pro·pos·al \prə-ˈpō-zəl\ *n* **1 :** an act of offering something for consideration **2 a :** something proposed **:** SUGGESTION **b :** OFFER 1b; *esp* **:** an offer of marriage

pro·pose \prə-ˈpōz\ *vb* **1 :** to offer for consideration or discussion **:** SUGGEST ⟨*propose* terms of peace⟩ **2 :** to make plans **:** INTEND ⟨*propose* to buy a new house⟩ **3 :** to offer as a toast **:** suggest drinking to ⟨*propose* the health of a friend⟩ **4 :** NAME, NOMINATE ⟨*propose* one for membership⟩ **5 :** to make an offer of marriage **[**Middle French *proposer,* from Latin *proponere* "to propound"**]** — **pro·pos·er** *n*

prop·o·si·tion \ˌpräp-ə-ˈzish-ən\ *n* **1 a :** something offered for consideration or acceptance **:** PROPOSAL **b :** a theorem or problem to be demonstrated or performed **2 :** an expression in language or signs of something that can be either true or false **3 :** a project or situation requiring action **:** UNDERTAKING — **prop·o·si·tion·al** \-ˈzish-nəl, -ən-l\ *adj*

pro·pound \prə-ˈpau̇nd\ *vt* **:** to offer for consideration **:** PROPOSE **[**alteration of earlier *propone,* from Latin *proponere* "to display, propound", from *pro-* "before" + *ponere* "to put, place"**]** — **pro·pound·er** *n*

1pro·pri·etary \prə-ˈprī-ə-ˌter-ē\ *n, pl* **-tar·ies 1 :** one to whom a proprietary colony is granted **2 :** a body of proprietors **3 :** a drug whose name, composition, or process of manufacture is protected by secrecy, patent, or copyright against free competition **:** PATENT MEDICINE

2proprietary *adj* **1 :** of, relating to, or characteristic of a proprietor ⟨*proprietary* rights⟩ **2 :** made and marketed by one having the exclusive right to manufacture and sell **3 :** privately owned and managed ⟨a *proprietary* clinic⟩ **[**Late Latin *proprietarius,* from Latin *proprietas* "property"**]**

proprietary colony *n* **:** a colony granted to a proprietary with full prerogatives of government

pro·pri·etor \prə-ˈprī-ət-ər\ *n* **1 :** PROPRIETARY 1 **2 :** one who holds something as property or a possession **:** OWNER — **pro·pri·etor·ship** \-ˌship\ *n*

pro·pri·etress \-ˈprī-ə-trəs\ *n* **:** a woman who is a proprietor

pro·pri·ety \prə-ˈprī-ət-ē\ *n, pl* **-ties 1 :** the quality or state of being proper **2 :** correctness in manners or behavior **:** POLITENESS **3** *pl* **:** the rules and customs of polite society **[**Middle French *proprieté, propreté* "property"**] syn** see DECORUM

pro·prio·cep·tor \ˌprō-prē-ō-ˈsep-tər\ *n* **:** a sensory receptor excited by stimuli arising within the organism **[**Latin *proprius* "own" + English *-ceptor* (as in *receptor*)**]** — **pro·prio·cep·tive** \-tiv\ *adj*

prop root *n* **:** a root that braces or supports a plant

pro·pul·sion \prə-ˈpəl-shən\ *n* **1 :** the action or process of propelling **2 :** something that propels **[**Latin *propulsus,* past participle of *propellere* "to propel"**]**

pro·pul·sive \-ˈpəl-siv\ *adj* **:** tending or having power to propel

pro·pyl·ene gly·col \ˌprō-pə-ˌlēn-ˈglī-ˌkȯl, -ˌkōl\ *n* **:** a sweet viscous liquid $C_3H_8O_2$ used as an antifreeze, solvent, and preservative **[***propylene* from *pro*pionic acid + *-yl* + *-ene; glycol* from Greek *glykys* "sweet" + English *-ol***]**

pro ra·ta \prō-ˈrāt-ə, ˈprō-, -ˈrät-ə\ *adv* **:** according to share or liability **:** PROPORTIONATELY **[**Latin**]** — **pro rata** *adj*

pro·rate \prō-ˈrāt, ˈprō-\ *vb* **:** to divide, distribute, or assess proportionately **[***pro rata***]** — **pro·ra·tion** \prō-ˈrā-shən\ *n*

pro·rogue \prə-ˈrōg, pə-ˈrōg\ *vb* **1 :** DEFER, POSTPONE **2 :** to suspend or end a legislative session **[**Middle French *proroguer* "to prolong, defer", from Latin *prorogare,* from *pro-* "before" + *rogare* "to ask"**]** — **pro·ro·ga·tion** \ˌprōr-ō-ˈgā-shən, ˌprȯr-\ *n*

pros *pl of* PRO

pro·sa·ic \prō-ˈzā-ik\ *adj* **1 a :** characteristic of prose as distinguished from poetry **b :** unimaginative in style or expression **2 :** belonging to the everyday world **:** COMMONPLACE **[**Late Latin *prosaicus,* from Latin *prosa* "prose"**]** — **pro·sa·i·cal·ly** \-ˈzā-ə-kə-lē, -klē\ *adv*

pro·sce·ni·um \prō-ˈsē-nē-əm\ *n* **1 :** the stage of an ancient theater **2 :** the part of a modern stage in front of the curtain **3 :** the wall that separates the stage from the auditorium and provides the arch that frames it **[**Latin, from Greek *proskēnion* "front of the building forming the background for a dramatic performance, stage", from *pro-* + *skēnē* "building forming the background for a dramatic performance"**]**

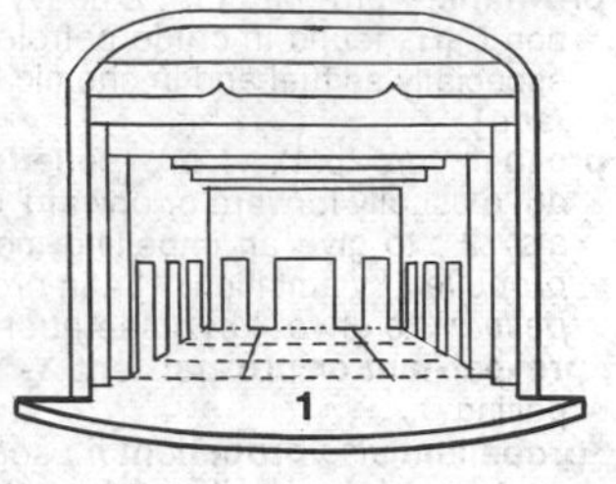

1 proscenium 2

pro·scribe \prō-ˈskrīb\ *vt* **1 :** to put outside the protection of the law **:** OUTLAW **2 :** to condemn or forbid as harmful **:** PROHIBIT **[**Latin *proscribere* (past participle *proscriptus*) "to publish, proscribe", from *pro-* "before" + *scribere* "to write"**]** — **pro·scrib·er** *n* — **pro·scrip·tion** \-ˈskrip-shən\ *n* — **pro·scrip·tive** \-ˈskrip-tiv\ *adj* — **pro·scrip·tive·ly** *adv*

1prose \ˈprōz\ *n* **1 a :** the ordinary language people use in speaking or writing **b :** a literary medium distinguished from poetry especially by its greater irregularity and variety of rhythm and its closer correspondence to the patterns of everyday speech **2 :** a prosaic style, quality, character, or condition ⟨the *prose* of everyday life⟩ **[**Middle French, from Latin *prosa,* from *prorsus, prosus* "straightforward", from *proversus,* past participle of *provertere* "to turn forward", from *pro-* "forward" + *vertere* "to turn"**]** — **prose** *adj*

2prose *vi* **1 :** to write prose **2 :** to write or speak in a dull prosaic manner

pros·e·cute \ˈpräs-i-ˌkyüt\ *vb* **1 :** to press on with **:** carry on ⟨*prosecute* a war⟩ **2 a :** to carry on a legal action against (an accused person) in order to prove guilt **b :** to start legal proceedings with respect to ⟨*prosecute* a crime⟩ **c :** to start and carry on a legal suit or prosecution **[**Latin *prosecutus,* past participle of *prosequi* "to pursue"**]** — **pros·e·cut·able** \-ˌkyüt-ə-bəl\ *adj*

pros·e·cu·tion \ˌpräs-i-ˈkyü-shən\ *n* **1 :** the act or process of prosecuting; *esp* **:** the starting and continuing of a criminal suit in court **2 :** the party by whom criminal proceedings are begun or conducted

pros·e·cu·tor \ˈpräs-i-ˌkyüt-ər\ *n* **1 :** a person who institutes an official prosecution before a court **2 :** an attorney who conducts proceedings in a court on behalf of the government **:** DISTRICT ATTORNEY

1pros·e·lyte \ˈpräs-ə-ˌlīt\ *n* **:** a new convert **[**Late Latin *proselytus* "proselyte, alien resident", from Greek *prosēlytos***]**

2proselyte *vb* **1 :** to convert from one religion, belief, or party to another **2 :** to recruit members especially by the offer of special inducements — **pros·e·ly·tism** \-ˌlīt-ˌiz-əm, -lə-ˌtiz-\ *n*

pros·e·ly·tize \-lə-ˌtīz\ *vb* **:** PROSELYTE

pro·sim·i·an \prō-ˈsim-ē-ən, ˈprō-\ *n* **:** a lower primate (as a lemur) — **prosimian** *adj*

pros·i·ness \ˈprō-zē-nəs\ *n* **:** the quality or state of being prosy

pro·sit \ˈprō-zət, -sət\ *or* **prost** \ˈprōst\ *interj* — used to wish good health especially before drinking **[**German, from Latin *prosit* "may it be beneficial", from *prodesse* "to be useful"**]**

pros·o·dist \ˈpräs-əd-əst\ *n* **:** a specialist in prosody

pros·o·dy \ˈpräs-əd-ē\ *n, pl* **-dies 1 :** the study of versification; *esp* **:** METRICS **2 :** a particular system, theory, or style of versification **[**Latin *prosodia* "accent of a syllable", from Greek *prosōidia* "song sung to instrumental music, accent", from *pros* "in addition to" + *ōidē* "song"**]** — **pro·sod·ic** \prə-ˈsäd-ik\ *adj* — **pro·sod·i·cal·ly** \-i-kə-lē, -klē\ *adv*

1pros·pect \ˈpräs-ˌpekt\ *n* **1 a :** a wide view **b :** a viewing with the mind **2 :** something extended to the view **:** SCENE **3 a :** act of looking forward **:** ANTICIPATION **b :** a mental picture of something to come **:** VISION **c :** something that is awaited or expected **:** POSSIBILITY **4 a :** a potential buyer or customer **b :** a candidate or a person likely to become a candidate ⟨presidential *prospects*⟩ **[**Latin *prospectus* "view, prospect", from *pros-*

picere "to look forward", from *pro-* "forward" + *specere* "to look"]

[2]**prospect** *vb* : to explore an area especially for mineral deposits — **pros•pec•tor** \-ˌpek-tər\ *n*

pro•spec•tive \prə-ˈspek-tiv *also* ˈprä-ˌ, prō-ˈ, prä-ˈ\ *adj* **1** : likely to come about : EXPECTED ⟨the *prospective* benefits of a law⟩ **2** : likely to be or become ⟨a *prospective* athlete⟩ — **pro•spec•tive•ly** *adv*

pro•spec•tus \prə-ˈspek-təs, prä-\ *n, pl* **-tus•es** : a printed statement describing an enterprise and distributed to prospective investors [Latin, "prospect"]

pros•per \ˈpräs-pər\ *vb* **pros•pered**; **pros•per•ing** \-pə-ring, -pring\ **1** : SUCCEED; *esp* : to succeed financially **2** : FLOURISH 1, THRIVE **3** : to cause to succeed or thrive [Middle French *prosperer,* from Latin *prosperare* "to cause to succeed", from *prosperus* "favorable"]

pros•per•i•ty \prä-ˈsper-ət-ē\ *n* : the condition of being successful or thriving; *esp* : economic well-being

pros•per•ous \ˈpräs-pə-rəs, -prəs\ *adj* **1** : AUSPICIOUS 1 **2** : marked by success or economic well-being — **pros•per•ous•ly** *adv* — **pros•per•ous•ness** *n*

pros•ta•glan•din \ˌpräs-tə-ˈglan-dən\ *n* : any of various fatty acids of animals that may perform a variety of physiological actions (as controlling blood pressure or smooth muscle contraction) [*prostate gland* + *-in;* from its occurrence in the sexual glands of animals]

pros•tate \ˈpräs-ˌtāt\ *also* **pros•tat•ic** \prä-ˈstat-ik\ *adj* : of, relating to, or being the prostate gland [Greek *prostatēs* "prostate gland", from *proïstanai* "to put in front", from *pro-* + *histanai* "to cause to stand"]

prostate gland *n* : a firm partly muscular partly glandular body about the base of the mammalian male urethra

pros•the•sis \präs-ˈthē-səs, ˈpräs-thə-\ *n, pl* **-the•ses** \-ˌsēz\ : an artificial device to replace a missing part of the body [Greek, "addition", from *prostithenai* "to add to", from *pros-* "in addition to" + *tithenai* "to put"] — **pros•thet•ic** \präs-ˈthet-ik\ *adj* — **pros•thet•i•cal•ly** \-ˈthet-i-kə-lē, -klē\ *adv*

prosthetic group *n* : a nonprotein group of a conjugated protein

[1]**pros•ti•tute** \ˈpräs-tə-ˌtüt, -ˌtyüt\ *vt* : to devote to corrupt or unworthy purposes : DEBASE ⟨*prostitute* one's talents⟩ [Latin *prostitutus,* past participle of *prostituere* "to offer for prostitution", from *pro-* "before" + *statuere* "to set up, station", from *status* "position, state"]

[2]**prostitute** *n* : a person who engages in sexual activities for money

pros•ti•tu•tion \ˌpräs-tə-ˈtü-shən, -ˈtyü-\ *n* **1** : the acts or practices of a prostitute **2** : the state of being prostituted

pro•sto•mi•um \prō-ˈstō-mē-əm\ *n, pl* **-mia** \-mē-ə\ : the portion of the head of various worms and mollusks situated in front of the mouth and usually held not to be a true segment [New Latin, from Greek *pro-* + *stoma* "mouth"] — **pro•sto•mi•al** \-mē-əl\ *adj*

[1]**pros•trate** \ˈpräs-ˌtrāt\ *adj* **1 a** : stretched out with face on the ground (as in adoration or submission) **b** : lying flat and stretched out **2** : lacking in vitality or will : OVERCOME **3** : trailing on the ground ⟨a *prostrate* shrub⟩ [Latin *prostratus,* past participle of *prosternere* "to prostrate", from *pro-* "before" + *sternere* "to spread out, throw down"] **syn** see PRONE

[2]**prostrate** *vt* **1** : to throw or put into a prostrate position **2** : to make helpless or exhausted : OVERCOME

pros•tra•tion \prä-ˈstrā-shən\ *n* **1** : the act of assuming or state of being in a prostrate position **2** : complete physical or mental exhaustion : COLLAPSE

prosy \ˈprō-zē\ *adj* **pros•i•er**; **-est** **1** : PROSAIC 1 **2** : TEDIOUS

prot- *or* **proto-** *combining form* **1** : first in time ⟨*proto*history⟩ **2** : first formed : primary ⟨*proto*nema⟩ **3** *cap* : relating to or constituting the recorded or assumed language that is ancestral to a language or to a group of related languages or dialects [Greek *prōtos* "foremost, first"]

prot•ac•tin•i•um \ˌprōt-ˌak-ˈtin-ē-əm\ *n* : a shiny metallic radioactive chemical element of relatively short life — see ELEMENT table

pro•tag•o•nist \prō-ˈtag-ə-nəst\ *n* **1** : one who takes the leading part in a drama, novel, or story **2** : the leader of a cause : CHAMPION **3** : a muscle that by its contraction actually causes a particular movement [Greek *prōtagōnistēs,* from *prōtos* "first" + *agōnistēs* "competitor at games, actor", derived from *agōn* "contest"]

prot•amine \ˈprōt-ə-ˌmēn\ *n* : any of various simple strongly basic proteins that are not coagulable by heat but are soluble in water and dilute ammonia

pro•te•an \ˈprōt-ē-ən\ *adj* : readily assuming different shapes or roles ⟨the *protean* amoeba⟩ ⟨a *protean* actor⟩ [*Proteus,* Greek sea god]

pro•te•ase \ˈprōt-ē-ˌās\ *n* : PROTEINASE, PEPTIDASE

pro•tect \prə-ˈtekt\ *vt* **1** : to cover or shield from injury or destruction : GUARD **2** : to shield or foster (an industry) by trade controls [Latin *protectus,* past participle of *protegere* "to protect", from *pro-* "in front" + *tegere* "to cover"] **syn** see DEFEND

pro•tec•tion \prə-ˈtek-shən\ *n* **1** : the act of protecting : the state of being protected **2 a** : one that protects **b** : the oversight or support of one that is smaller and weaker **3** : the freeing of the producers of a country from foreign competition especially by high duties on foreign goods **4** : money extorted by racketeers threatening violence **5** : COVERAGE 2b — **pro•tec•tive** \-ˈtek-tiv\ *adj* — **pro•tec•tive•ly** *adv*

pro•tec•tion•ist \-shə-nəst, -shnəst\ *n* : an advocate of government economic protection for domestic producers through restrictions on foreign competitors — **pro•tec•tion•ism** \-shə-ˌniz-əm\ *n* — **protectionist** *adj*

protective coloration *n* : coloration that makes an organism appear less visible or less attractive to predators

protective tariff *n* : a tariff intended primarily to protect domestic producers rather than to yield revenue

pro•tec•tor \prə-ˈtek-tər\ *n* **1 a** : one that protects : GUARDIAN **b** : a device used to prevent injury : GUARD **2** : one having the care of a kingdom (as during a king's minority) : REGENT — **pro•tec•tor•ship** \-ˌship\ *n*

pro•tec•tor•ate \prə-ˈtek-tə-rət, -trət\ *n* **1 a** : government by a protector; *esp* : the government of England (1653–59) under the Cromwells **b** : the rank, office, or period of rule of a protector **2 a** : the relationship of superior authority assumed by one state over a dependent one **b** : the dependent state in such a relationship

pro•té•gé \ˈprōt-ə-ˌzhā\ *n* : one under the care and protection of someone influential especially for the furthering of his or her career [French, from *protéger* "to protect", from Latin *protegere*]

pro•té•gée \-ˌzhā\ *n* : a girl or woman who is a protégé [French, feminine of *protégé*]

pro•tein \ˈprō-ˌtēn, ˈprōt-ē-ən\ *n* **1** : any of numerous naturally occurring nitrogen-containing substances that consist of chains of amino acids and are essential constituents of all living cells **2** : the total nitrogenous material in plant or animal substances [French *protéine,* derived from Greek *prōtos* "first"] — **pro•tein•aceous** \ˌprō-ˌtē-ˈnā-shəs, ˌprōt-ē-ə-ˈnā-\ *adj*

pro•tein•ase \ˈprō-ˌtē-ˌnās, ˈprōt-ē-ə-\ *n* : an enzyme that hydrolyzes proteins especially to peptides

pro tem \prō-ˈtem\ *adv* : pro tempore

pro tem•po•re \prō-ˈtem-pə-rē\ *adv* : for the present : TEMPORARILY [Latin]

pro•teo•lyt•ic \ˌprōt-ē-ə-ˈlit-ik\ *adj* : of, relating to, or producing the hydrolysis of proteins or peptides to simpler and soluble products ⟨*proteolytic* enzymes⟩ — **pro•te•ol•y•sis** \ˌprōt-ē-ˈäl-ə-səs\ *n*

pro•te•ose \ˈprōt-ē-ˌōs, -ˌōz\ *n* : any of various water-soluble protein derivatives formed by partial hydrolysis

Prot•ero•zo•ic \ˌprät-ə-rə-ˈzō-ik, ˌprōt-\ *n* : the 2d of the five eras of geological history that perhaps exceeds in length all of subsequent geological time and is marked by rocks that contain a few fossils indicating the existence of annelid worms and algae; *also* : the corresponding system of rocks — see GEOLOGIC TIME table [Greek *proteros* "former, earlier", from *pro* "before"] — **Proterozoic** *adj*

[1]**pro•test** \ˈprō-ˌtest\ *n* **1** : a formal declaration of opinion and usually of objection or complaint **2** : a declaration that payment of a note or bill has been refused and that all endorsers are liable for damages **3** : a complaint, objection, or display of unwillingness or disapproval

[2]**pro•test** \prə-ˈtest, ˈprō-ˌtest, prō-ˈ\ *vb* **1 a** : to make solemn

declaration of : ASSERT ⟨*protest* one's innocence⟩ **b** : to make a protestation **2 a** : to make a protest against ⟨*protested* the higher tax rate⟩ **b** : to object strongly ⟨*protest* against an arbitrary ruling⟩ [Middle French *protester,* from Latin *protestari,* from *pro-* "forth" + *testari* "to call to witness"] — **pro•test•er** *or* **pro•tes•tor** \-ˈtes-tər, -ˌtes-\ *n*

prot•es•tant \ˈprät-əs-tənt, *2 is also* prə-ˈtes-\ *n* **1** *cap* **a** : one of a group of German princes and cities presenting a defense of freedom of conscience against an edict of the Diet of Spires in 1529 intended to suppress the Lutheran movement **b** : a Christian denying the universal authority of the Pope and affirming the Reformation principles of justification by faith, the priesthood of all believers, and the primacy of the Bible **c** : a Christian not of a Catholic or Eastern church **2** : one who makes or enters a protest — **protestant** *adj, often cap* — **Prot•es•tant•ism** \ˈprät-əs-tənt-ˌiz-əm\ *n*

prot•es•ta•tion \ˌprät-əs-ˈtā-shən, ˌprō-ˌtes-\ *n* : the act of protesting : a solemn declaration or avowal

pro•thal•li•um \prō-ˈthal-ē-əm, ˈprō-\ *or* **pro•thal•lus** \-ˈthal-əs\ *n, pl* **-lia** \-ē-ə\ *or* **-li** \-ˌī, -ˌē\ : a small flat green thallus attached to the soil by rhizoids that is the gametophyte of a pteridophyte (as a fern) [New Latin, from *pro-* + *thallus*] — **pro•thal•li•al** \-ē-əl\ *adj*

pro•tho•rax \prō-ˈthōr-ˌaks, ˈprō-, -ˈthȯr-\ *n* : the first segment of the thorax of an insect — **pro•tho•rac•ic** \ˌprō-thə-ˈras-ik\ *adj*

pro•throm•bin \prō-ˈthräm-bən, ˈprō-\ *n* : a plasma protein produced in the liver in the presence of vitamin K and converted into thrombin in the clotting of blood

pro•tist \ˈprōt-əst\ *n* : any of a kingdom or group (Protista) of unicellular or noncellular organisms comprising bacteria, protozoans, various algae and fungi, and sometimes viruses [derived from Greek *prōtistos* "very first, primal", from *prōtos* "first"] — **pro•tis•tan** \prō-ˈtis-tən\ *adj or n*

pro•ti•um \ˈprōt-ē-əm, ˈprō-shē-\ *n* : the ordinary light hydrogen isotope of atomic mass 1 [New Latin, from Greek *prōtos* "first"]

proto- — see PROT-

pro•to•coc•cus \ˌprōt-ə-ˈkäk-əs\ *n* : any of a genus of globe-shaped and mostly terrestrial green algae [*prot-* + Greek *kokkos* "grain, seed"]

pro•to•col \ˈprōt-ə-ˌkȯl\ *n* **1** : an original draft, minute, or record of a document or transaction : MEMORANDUM **2** : a code of diplomatic or military etiquette and precedence [Middle French *prothocole,* from Medieval Latin *protocollum,* from Late Greek *prōtokollon* "first sheet of a papyrus roll bearing data of manufacture", from Greek *prōtos* "first" + *kollan* "to glue, from *kolla* "glue"]

pro•to•his•to•ry \ˌprōt-ō-ˈhis-tə-rē, -trē\ *n* : the study of humanity of the period that just antedates recorded history — **pro•to•his•tor•ic** \-his-ˈtȯr-ik, -ˈtär-\ *adj*

pro•ton \ˈprō-ˌtän\ *n* : an elementary particle identical with the nucleus of the hydrogen atom that along with the neutron is a constituent of all other atomic nuclei and carries a positive charge numerically equal to the negative charge of an electron [Greek *prōton,* neuter of *prōtos* "first"] — **pro•ton•ic** \prō-ˈtän-ik\ *adj*

pro•to•ne•ma \ˌprōt-ə-ˈnē-mə\ *n, pl* **-ne•ma•ta** \-ˈnē-mət-ə, -ˈnem-ət-\ : the primary usually filamentous stage of the gametophyte in mosses and some liverworts that is comparable to the fern prothallium [*prot-* + Greek *nēmat-, nēma* "thread"] — **pro•to•ne•mal** \-ˈnē-məl\ *adj* — **pro•to•ne•ma•tal** \-ˈnē-mət-l, -ˈnem-ət-\ *adj*

pro•to•plan•et \ˈprōt-ō-ˌplan-ət\ *n* : a whirling mass of gas and dust that rotates around a star and that is held to be the source of a planet

pro•to•plasm \ˈprōt-ə-ˌplaz-əm\ *n* **1** : a colloidal complex of protein, various organic and inorganic substances, and water that constitutes the living nucleus, cytoplasm, plastids, and mitochondria of the cell and is held to be the physical basis of life **2** : CYTOPLASM [German *protoplasma,* from *prot-* "prot-" + *plasma* "plasma"] — **pro•to•plas•mic** \ˌprōt-ə-ˈplaz-mik\ *adj*

pro•to•plast \ˈprōt-ə-ˌplast\ *n* : the nucleus, cytoplasm, and plasma membrane of a cell constituting a living unit distinct from inert walls and inclusions [Middle French *protoplaste* "prototype, something formed first", from Late Latin *protoplastos* "first man", from Greek *prōtoplastos* "first formed", from *prōtos* "first" + *plastos* "formed", from *plassein* "to mold"]

pro•to•type \ˈprōt-ə-ˌtīp\ *n* **1** : an original model on which something is patterned **2** : an individual that exhibits the essential features of a later type — **pro•to•typ•al** \ˌprōt-ə-ˈtī-pəl\ *adj* — **pro•to•typ•i•cal** \-ˈtip-i-kəl\ *adj*

pro•to•zo•an \ˌprōt-ə-ˈzō-ən\ *n* : any of a phylum or group (Protozoa) of minute animals that are either single-celled or not obviously divided into cells, have varied structure and physiology and often complex life cycles, are represented in almost every kind of habitat, and include some which are serious parasites of man and domestic animals [*prot-* + Greek *zōion* "animal"] — **protozoan** *adj*

pro•to•zo•ol•o•gy \-zō-ˈäl-ə-jē, -zə-ˈwäl-\ *n* : a branch of zoology dealing with protozoans — **pro•to•zo•ol•o•gist** \-jəst\ *n*

pro•to•zo•on \-ˈzō-ˌän\ *n, pl* **-zoa** \-ˈzō-ə\ : PROTOZOAN

pro•tract \prō-ˈtrakt\ *vt* **1** : to prolong in time or space **2** : PLOT 1a [Latin *protractus,* past participle of *protrahere* "to protract", literally, "to draw forward", from *pro-* "forward" + *trahere* "to draw"] **syn** see EXTEND — **pro•trac•tion** \-ˈtrak-shən\ *n*

pro•trac•tor \prō-ˈtrak-tər, ˈprō-ˌ\ *n* **1 a** : one that protracts, prolongs, or delays **b** : a muscle that extends a part — compare RETRACTOR **2** : an instrument for laying down and measuring angles that is used in drawing and plotting

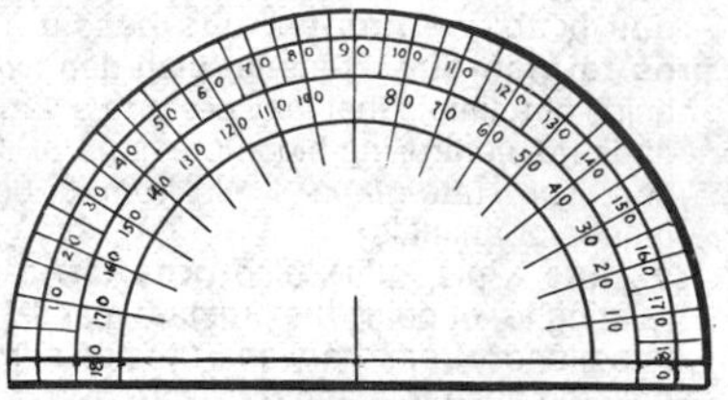

protractor 2

pro•trude \prō-ˈtrüd\ *vb* **1** : to cause to stick out : PROJECT **2** : to jut out from the surroundings [Latin *protrudere* (past participle *protrusus*) "to thrust forward", from *pro-* "forward" + *trudere* "to thrust"] — **pro•tru•si•ble** \-ˈtrü-sə-bəl, -zə-\ *adj*

pro•tru•sion \prō-ˈtrü-zhən\ *n* **1** : the act of protruding : the state of being protruded **2** : something that protrudes **syn** see PROJECTION

pro•tu•ber•ance \prō-ˈtü-bə-rəns, -ˈtyü-, -brəns\ *n* **1** : the quality or state of being protuberant **2** : something that is protuberant : BULGE

pro•tu•ber•ant \-bə-rənt, -brənt\ *adj* : bulging beyond the surrounding surface : PROMINENT [Late Latin *protuberans,* present participle of *protuberare* "to bulge out", from Latin *pro-* "forward" + *tuber* "hump, swelling"] — **pro•tu•ber•ant•ly** *adv*

proud \ˈpraud\ *adj* **1** : feeling or showing pride: as **a** : having or displaying excessive self-esteem **b** : much pleased : EXULTANT ⟨*proud* parents of the valedictorian⟩ **c** : having proper self-respect ⟨too *proud* to beg⟩ **2** : MAGNIFICENT 1, STATELY **3** : VIGOROUS, SPIRITED ⟨a *proud* steed⟩ [Old English *prūd*] — **proud•ly** *adv*

prove \ˈprüv\ *vb* **proved**; **proved** *or* **prov•en** \ˈprü-vən\; **prov•ing** **1** : to test by an experiment or a standard — often used with *up* **2 a** : to establish the truth or validity of by evidence or demonstration **b** : to check the correctness of (as an arithmetic operation) **3 a** : to ascertain the genuineness of : VERIFY **b** : to obtain probate of (a will) **4** : to turn out especially after trial or test ⟨the new drug *proved* effective⟩ [Old French *prover,* from Latin *probare* "to test, approve, demonstrate", from *probus* "good, honest"] — **prov•able** \ˈprü-və-bəl\ *adj*

prov•e•nance \ˈpräv-nəns, -ə-nəns\ *n* : ORIGIN 2b, SOURCE [French, from *provenir* "to come forth, originate", from Latin *provenire,* from *pro-* "forth" + *venire* "to come"]

Pro•ven•çal \ˌpräv-ən-ˈsäl, ˌprōv-, -ˌäⁿ-\ *n* **1** : a native or inhabitant of Provence **2** : a Romance language spoken in southeastern France [Middle French, from *provençal* "of Provence", from *Provence*] — **Provençal** *adj*

prov•en•der \ˈpräv-ən-dər\ *n* **1** : dry food for domestic animals : FEED **2** : FOOD 2, VICTUALS [Middle French *provende, provendre,* from Medieval Latin *provenda,* alteration of *praebenda* "prebend"]

pro•ve•nience \prə-ˈvē-nyəns\ *n* : ORIGIN 2b, SOURCE [alteration of *provenance*]

pro•ven•tric•u•lus \ˌprō-ven-ˈtrik-yə-ləs\ *n, pl* **-li** \-ˌlī, -ˌlē\ : a pouch of the digestive tract (as of an insect or earthworm); *esp* : the glandular stomach of a bird situated between the crop and gizzard [[1]*pro-* + Latin *ventriculus* "stomach, ventricle"]

prov•erb \'präv-,ərb\ *n* **:** a brief popular saying or maxim **:** ADAGE [Middle French *proverbe,* from Latin *proverbium,* from *pro-* + *verbum* "word"]

pro•ver•bi•al \prə-'vər-bē-əl\ *adj* **1 :** of, relating to, or resembling a proverb ⟨*proverbial* wisdom⟩ **2 :** commonly spoken of ⟨the *proverbial* beginner's luck⟩ — **pro•ver•bi•al•ly** \-bē-ə-lē\ *adv*

Prov•erbs \'präv-,ərbz\ *n* — see BIBLE table

pro•vide \prə-'vīd\ *vb* **1 :** to take precautionary measures ⟨*provide* against a possible shortage⟩ **2 :** to include as a condition **:** STIPULATE ⟨the contract *provided* for 10 paid holidays⟩ **3 :** to supply what is needed for sustenance or support ⟨*provides* for a large family⟩ **4 a :** OUTFIT, EQUIP ⟨*provide* the children with new shoes⟩ **b :** to supply for use **:** YIELD ⟨cows *provide* milk⟩ [Latin *providēre,* literally, "to see ahead", from *pro-* "forward" + *vidēre* "to see"] — **pro•vid•er** *n*

pro•vid•ed *conj* **:** on condition **:** IF — sometimes followed by *that*

prov•i•dence \'präv-əd-əns, -ə-,dens\ *n* **1 a** *often cap* **:** divine guidance or care **b** *cap* **:** God conceived as the power sustaining and guiding human destiny **2 :** the quality or state of being provident **:** PRUDENCE [Middle French, from Latin *providentia,* from *providens* "provident"]

prov•i•dent \-əd-ənt, -ə-,dent\ *adj* **1 :** making provision for the future **:** PRUDENT **2 :** FRUGAL, THRIFTY [Latin *providens,* from *providēre* "to provide"] — **prov•i•dent•ly** *adv*

prov•i•den•tial \,präv-ə-'den-chəl\ *adj* **1 :** of, relating to, or determined by Providence ⟨a *providential* plan⟩ **2 :** occurring by or as if by an intervention of Providence **:** FORTUNATE ⟨a *providential* escape⟩ — **prov•i•den•tial•ly** \-'dench-lē, -ə-lē\ *adv*

pro•vid•ing \prə-'vīd-ing\ *conj* **:** PROVIDED

prov•ince \'präv-əns\ *n* **1 a :** a country or region brought under the control of the ancient Roman government **b :** an administrative district or division of a country **c** *pl* **:** all of a country except the metropolis **2 :** a division of a country forming the jurisdiction of an archbishop or metropolitan **3 :** proper or appropriate business or scope **:** SPHERE ⟨a legal question outside the physician's *province*⟩ [French, from Latin *provincia*]

[1]**pro•vin•cial** \prə-'vin-chəl\ *n* **1 :** the superior of a province of a religious order **2 :** one living in or coming from a province **3 a :** a person of local or restricted outlook **b :** a person lacking urban polish or refinement

[2]**provincial** *adj* **1 :** of, relating to, or coming from a province **2 a :** limited in outlook **:** NARROW **b :** lacking the polish of urban society **:** UNSOPHISTICATED **3 :** of or relating to a decorative style (as in furniture) marked by simplicity and relative plainness — **pro•vin•ci•al•i•ty** \-,vin-chē-'al-ət-ē\ *n* — **pro•vin•cial•ly** \-'vinch-lē, -ə-lē\ *adv*

pro•vin•cial•ism \prə-'vin-chə-,liz-əm\ *n* **1 :** a dialectal or local word, phrase, or idiom **2 :** the quality or state of being provincial

proving ground *n* **1 :** a place for scientific experimentation or testing **2 :** a place where something new is tried out

[1]**pro•vi•sion** \prə-'vizh-ən\ *n* **1 a :** the act or process of providing ⟨*provision* of transportation for the trip⟩ **b :** a measure taken beforehand **:** PREPARATION ⟨make *provision* for emergencies⟩ **2 :** a stock of needed materials or supplies; *esp* **:** a stock of food — usually used in pl. **3 :** PROVISO 2, STIPULATION [Middle French, from Latin *provisio* "foresight", from *provisus,* past participle of *providēre* "to see ahead, provide"]

[2]**provision** *vt* **pro•vi•sioned; pro•vi•sion•ing** \-'vizh-ning, -ə-ning\ **:** to supply with provisions ⟨*provision* a military garrison⟩

pro•vi•sion•al \prə-'vizh-nəl, -ən-l\ *adj* **:** serving for the time being **:** TEMPORARY ⟨a *provisional* government⟩ — **pro•vi•sion•al•ly** \-ē\ *adv*

pro•vi•so \prə-'vī-zō\ *n, pl* **-sos** *or* **-soes 1 :** a part of a legal document that states a condition **2 :** a requirement that is a condition ⟨given a bicycle with the *proviso* that it be kept in good repair⟩ [Medieval Latin *proviso quod* "provided that"]

pro•vi•ta•min \prō-'vīt-ə-mən, 'prō-\ *n* **:** a precursor of a vitamin convertible into the vitamin in an organism

prov•o•ca•tion \,präv-ə-'kā-shən\ *n* **1 :** the act of provoking **:** INCITEMENT **2 :** something that provokes, arouses, or stimulates [Middle French, from Latin *provocatio,* from *provocare* "to provoke"]

pro•voc•a•tive \prə-'väk-ət-iv\ *adj* **:** serving as a provocation ⟨*provocative* comments⟩ — **pro•voc•a•tive•ly** *adv* — **pro•voc•a•tive•ness** *n*

pro•voke \prə-'vōk\ *vt* **1 :** to arouse to action or feeling; *esp* **:** to excite to anger **2 a :** to call forth **:** EVOKE **b :** to stir up purposely **c :** to provide the needed stimulus for ⟨*provoke* a response from a nerve⟩ [Middle French *provoquer,* from Latin *provocare,* from *pro-* "forth" + *vocare* "to call"]

• syn PROVOKE, EXCITE, STIMULATE mean to arouse as if by pricking. PROVOKE directs attention to the response called forth ⟨a joke that failed to *provoke* laughter⟩ ⟨such diplomatic moves as *provoke* nations to war⟩ EXCITE implies a stirring up or moving profoundly ⟨a performance that *excited* admiration⟩ STIMULATE suggests a rousing out of lethargy, inactivity, or indifference ⟨the need to *stimulate* the economy⟩

pro•vok•ing \-'vō-king\ *adj* **:** causing mild anger ⟨a *provoking* delay⟩ — **pro•vok•ing•ly** \-king-lē\ *adv*

pro•vost \'prō-,vōst, 'präv-əst, *before "marshal" often* ,prō-vō\ *n* **1 :** the chief dignitary of a collegiate or cathedral chapter **2 :** a chief magistrate or a high-ranking administrative officer (as in a university) [Old English *profost* and Old French *provost,* both from Medieval Latin *propositus,* from Latin *praepositus* "one in charge", from *praeponere* "to place at the head"]

provost marshal *n* **:** the head of the military police of a command

prow \'praů\ *n* **1 :** the bow of a ship **:** STEM **2 :** a pointed projecting front part [Middle French *proue,* probably from Italian dialect *prua,* from Latin *prora,* from Greek *prōira*]

prow•ess \'praů-əs\ *n* **1 :** distinguished bravery; *esp* **:** military valor and skill **2 :** extraordinary ability [Old French *proesse,* from *prou* "valiant", from Late Latin *prode* "advantageous", from Latin *prodesse* "to be advantageous"]

prowl \'praůl\ *vb* **1 :** to move about or wander stealthily in the manner of a wild beast seeking prey **2 :** to roam over in a predatory manner ⟨*prowled* the streets⟩ [Middle English *prollen*] — **prowl** *n* — **prowl•er** *n*

prowl car *n* **:** SQUAD CAR

prox•i•mal \'präk-sə-məl\ *adj* **1 :** being nearest **:** PROXIMATE **2 :** near or next to the point of attachment or origin (as of a bone or a limb) — compare DISTAL **3 :** of, relating to, or being the mesial and distal surfaces of a tooth [Latin *proximus*] — **prox•i•mal•ly** \-mə-lē\ *adv*

proximal convoluted tubule *n* **:** the convoluted portion of the vertebrate nephron that lies between Bowman's capsule and the loop of Henle and is held to be concerned especially with resorption of sugar, sodium and chloride ions, and water — called also *proximal tubule*

prox•i•mate \-mət\ *adj* **1 a :** very near **:** CLOSE **b :** soon forthcoming **2 :** next preceding or following **:** DIRECT ⟨the *proximate* cause⟩ [Latin *proximatus,* past participle of *proximare* "to approach", from *proximus* "nearest, next", superlative of *prope* "near"] — **prox•i•mate•ly** *adv* — **prox•i•mate•ness** *n*

prox•im•i•ty \präk-'sim-ət-ē\ *n* **:** the quality or state of being proximate

prox•i•mo \'präk-sə-,mō\ *adj* **:** of or occurring in the next month after the present [Latin *proximo mense* "in the next month"]

proxy \'präk-sē\ *n, pl* **prox•ies 1 a :** authority to act for another (as in voting) **b :** a document giving such authority **2 :** a person authorized to act for another [Middle English *procucie,* from Anglo-French *procuracie,* from Medieval Latin *procuratia,* from Latin *procuratio* "management, act of taking charge", from *procurare* "to take care of"] — **proxy** *adj*

prude \'prüd\ *n* **:** a person overly or priggishly concerned with modesty and decorum [French, "good woman, prudish woman", short for *prudefemme* "good woman"] — **prud•ish** \'prüd-ish\ *adj* — **prud•ish•ly** *adv* — **prud•ish•ness** *n*

pru•dence \'prüd-ns\ *n* **1 :** the ability to govern and discipline oneself by the use of reason **2 :** discretion and shrewdness in the management of affairs **3 :** skill and good judgment in the use of resources **4 :** CAUTION 2, CIRCUMSPECTION

pru•dent \-nt\ *adj* **1 :** marked by wisdom **2 :** shrewdly practical **3 :** CIRCUMSPECT, DISCREET **4 :** FRUGAL, PROVIDENT [Middle French, from Latin *prudens,* from *providens* "provident"] — **pru•dent•ly** *adv*

pru•den•tial \prü-'den-chəl\ *adj* **1 :** of, relating to, or resulting from prudence **2 :** using prudence — **pru•den•tial•ly** \-chə-lē\ *adv*

prud•ery \'prüd-rē, -ə-rē\ *n, pl* **-er•ies 1 :** the quality or state of being prudish : exaggerated or priggish modesty **2 :** a prudish remark or act

[1]prune \'prün\ *n* : a plum dried or capable of drying without fermentation [Middle French, "plum", from Latin *prunum*]

[2]prune *vt* **1 :** to cut off the dead or unwanted parts of (a woody plant) ⟨*prune* the hedge⟩ **2 a :** to reduce by eliminating superfluous matter ⟨*prune* an essay⟩ ⟨*prune* a budget⟩ **b :** to remove as superfluous [Middle French *proignier*] — **prun•er** *n*

pru•ri•ent \'pru̇r-ē-ənt\ *adj* **1 :** having indecent desires or thoughts : LEWD **2 :** inclined to or characterized by lasciviousness [Latin *pruriens,* present participle of *prurire* "to itch, crave, be wanton"] — **pru•ri•ence** \-ē-əns\ *n* — **pru•ri•ent•ly** *adv*

pru•ri•tus \prü-'rīt-əs, -'rēt-\ *n* : ITCH 1a [Latin, from *prurire* "to itch"] — **pru•rit•ic** \-'rit-ik\ *adj*

prus•sic acid \,prəs-ik-\ *n* : HYDROCYANIC ACID [French *acide prussique*]

[1]pry \'prī\ *vi* **pried; pry•ing :** to look closely or inquisitively; *esp* : to invade another's privacy ⟨*pry* into other people's affairs⟩ [Middle English *prien*]

[2]pry *vt* **pried; pry•ing 1 :** to raise, move, or pull apart with a pry or lever **2 :** to extract, detach, or open with difficulty ⟨*pry* a secret out of a person⟩ [alteration of [5]*prize*]

pry•ing *adj* : impertinently or officiously inquisitive or interrogatory **syn** see CURIOUS — **pry•ing•ly** \-iŋ-lē\ *adv*

psalm \'säm, 'sälm\ *n* : a sacred song or poem; *esp* : one of the hymns that make up the Old Testament Book of Psalms [Old English *psealm,* from Late Latin *psalmus,* from Greek *psalmos,* literally, "twanging of a harp", from *psallein* "to pluck"]

psalm•ist \-əst\ *n* : a writer or composer of psalms

psalm•o•dy \-əd-ē\ *n, pl* **-dies 1 :** the art or practice of singing psalms in worship **2 :** a collection of psalms [Late Latin *psalmodia,* from Late Greek *psalmōidia,* literally, "singing to the harp", from Greek *psalmos* "psalm, twanging of a harp" + *aidein* "to sing"]

Psalms \'sämz, 'sälmz\ *n* — see BIBLE table

Psal•ter \'sȯl-tər\ *n* : the Book of Psalms; *also* : a collection of Psalms for liturgical or devotional use [Old English *psalter,* from Late Latin *psalterium,* from Late Greek *psaltērion,* from Greek, "psaltery"]

psal•tery *also* **psal•try** \'sȯl-tə-rē, -trē\ *n, pl* **-ter•ies** *also* **-tries** : an ancient stringed musical instrument resembling the zither [Middle French *psalterie,* from Latin *psalterium,* from Greek *psaltērion,* from *psallein* "to pluck, play on a stringed instrument"]

pseud- *or* **pseudo-** *combining form* : false : sham : spurious ⟨*pseudo*coel⟩ [Greek, from *pseudēs*]

pseu•do \'süd-ō\ *adj* : SHAM 1, FALSE [*pseudo-*]

pseu•do•coel \'süd-ə-,sēl\ *also* **pseu•do•coe•lom** \-,sē-ləm\ *n* : a body cavity of an invertebrate that is not structurally or in origin a true coelom — **pseu•do•coe•lo•mate** \,süd-ə-'sē-lə-,māt\ *adj or n*

pseu•do•nym \'süd-n-,im\ *n* : a fictitious name; *esp* : PEN NAME [French *pseudonyme,* from Greek *pseudōnymos* "bearing a false name", from *pseud-* + *onyma, onoma* "name"]

pseu•do•pod \'süd-ə-,päd\ *n* : PSEUDOPODIUM — **pseu•dop•o•dal** \sü-'däp-əd-l\ or **pseu•do•po•di•al** \,süd-ə-'pōd-ē-əl\ *adj*

pseu•do•po•di•um \,süd-ə-'pōd-ē-əm\ *n, pl* **pseu•do•po•dia** \-ē-ə\ : a part of a cell that is temporarily protruded by moving cytoplasm (as in the amoeba) and that helps to move the cell and to take in its food [New Latin, from Greek *pseud-* + *podion* "little foot", from *pod-, pous* "foot"]

pshaw \'shȯ\ *interj* — used to express irritation, disapproval, contempt, or disbelief [imitative]

psi \'sī, 'psī\ *n* : the 23d letter of the Greek alphabet — Ψ or ψ

psi•lo•cy•bin \,sī-lə-'sī-bən\ *n* : a hallucinogenic organic compound $C_{12}H_{17}N_2O_4P$ obtained from a fungus [New Latin *Psilocybe,* genus name]

psi•lop•sid \sī-'läp-səd\ *n* : any of a major group (Psilopsida) of primitive rootless and often leafless vascular plants [derived from Greek *psilos* "bare" + *lykopsis,* a kind of plant] — **psilopsid** *adj*

psit•ta•cine \'sit-ə-,sīn\ *adj* : of or relating to the parrots [Latin *psittacinus,* from *psittacus* "parrot", from Greek *psittakos*] — **psittacine** *n*

psit•ta•co•sis \,sit-ə-'kō-səs\ *n* : PARROT FEVER

pso•ri•a•sis \sə-'rī-ə-səs\ *n* : a chronic skin disease characterized by circumscribed red patches covered with white scales [Greek *psōriasis,* from *psōrian* "to have the itch", from *psōra* "itch"] — **pso•ri•at•ic** \,sōr-ē-'at-ik, ,sȯr-\ *adj or n*

psych- *or* **psycho-** *combining form* **1 :** mind : mental processes and activities ⟨*psycho*logy⟩ **2 :** psychological methods ⟨*psycho*therapy⟩ **3 :** brain ⟨*psycho*surgery⟩ **4 :** mental and ⟨*psycho*somatic⟩ [Greek, from *psychē* "breath, principle of life, soul"]

psy•che \'sī-kē\ *n* : SOUL 1, SELF; *also* : MIND 2a [Greek *psychē*]

[1]psy•che•del•ic \,sī-kə-'del-ik\ *adj* **1 a :** of, relating to, or being a drug (as LSD) that radically alters the mind or mental processes usually only temporarily **b :** relating to the taking of psychedelic drugs ⟨a *psychedelic* experience⟩ **2 a :** imitating the effect of psychedelic drugs ⟨*psychedelic* art⟩ **b :** bright and glowing as a result of fluorescence ⟨*psychedelic* colors⟩ [Greek *psychē* "soul" + *dēloun* "to show"]

[2]psychedelic *n* : a psychedelic drug

psy•chi•a•try \sə-'kī-ə-trē, sī-\ *n* : a branch of medicine that deals with mental, emotional, or behavioral disorders — **psy•chi•at•ric** \,sī-kē-'a-trik\ *adj* — **psy•chi•at•ri•cal•ly** \-tri-kə-lē, -klē\ *adv* — **psy•chi•a•trist** \sə-'kī-ə-trəst, sī-\ *n*

[1]psy•chic \'sī-kik\ *adj* **1 :** of, relating to, affecting, or originating in the mind **2 :** not physical; *esp* : not to be explained by knowledge of natural laws **3 :** sensitive to influences or forces supposedly exerted from beyond the natural world — **psy•chi•cal** \-ki-kəl\ *adj* — **psy•chi•cal•ly** \-ki-kə-lē, -klē\ *adv*

[2]psychic *n* : a person (as a medium) apparently sensitive to nonphysical forces

psy•cho•anal•y•sis \,sī-kō-ə-'nal-ə-səs\ *n, pl* **-y•ses** \-,sēz\ : a method of explaining and treating psychic and especially emotional disorders that emphasizes the importance of the patient's talking freely about himself or herself while under treatment and especially about dreams and early childhood memories and experiences — **psy•cho•an•a•lyst** \-'an-l-əst\ *n* — **psy•cho•an•a•lyt•ic** \-,an-l-'it-ik\ *or* **psy•cho•an•a•lyt•i•cal** \-'it-i-kəl\ *adj* — **psy•cho•an•a•lyt•i•cal•ly** \-'it-i-kə-lē, -klē\ *adv* — **psy•cho•an•a•lyze** \-'an-l-,īz\ *vb*

psy•cho•gen•ic \,sī-kə-'jen-ik\ *adj* : originating in the mind or in mental or emotional conflict

psy•cho•log•i•cal \,sī-kə-'läj-i-kəl\ *also* **psy•cho•log•ic** \-'läj-ik\ *adj* **1 a :** of or relating to psychology **b :** relating to, characteristic of, arising in, or acting through the mind : MENTAL **2 :** intended to influence the will or mind ⟨*psychological* warfare⟩ — **psy•cho•log•i•cal•ly** \-i-kə-lē, -klē\ *adv*

psy•chol•o•gy \sī-'käl-ə-jē\ *n, pl* **-gies 1 :** the science or study of mind and behavior **2 :** the mental or behavioral characteristics of an individual or group — **psy•chol•o•gist** \-jəst\ *n*

psy•cho•neu•ro•sis \,sī-kō-nu̇-'rō-səs, -nyu̇-\ *n* : NEUROSIS — **psy•cho•neu•rot•ic** \-'rät-ik\ *adj or n*

psy•cho•path \'sī-kə-,path\ *n* : a person with a clear perception of reality but lacking a sense of social and moral obligation so that personal gain is sought by criminal acts, drug addiction, or sexual perversion without marked feelings of guilt; *also* : a mentally ill person — **psy•cho•path•ic** \,sī-kə-'path-ik\ *adj* — **psy•cho•path•i•cal•ly** \-i-kə-lē, -klē\ *adv*

psy•cho•pa•thol•o•gy \,sī-kō-pə-'thäl-ə-jē\ *n* : the study of mental disorders and of the associated psychologic and behavioral alterations and anomalies; *also* : such disordered state — **psy•cho•path•o•log•i•cal** \-,path-ə-'läj-i-kəl\ *adj* — **psy•cho•path•o•log•i•cal•ly** \-i-kə-lē, -klē\ *adv* — **psy•cho•pa•thol•o•gist** \-pə-'thäl-ə-jəst\ *n*

psy•cho•sis \sī-'kō-səs\ *n, pl* **-cho•ses** \-'kō-,sēz\ : fundamental or severe personality disorder characterized by defective or lost contact with reality and often by delusions and hallucinations — **psy•chot•ic** \-'kät-ik\ *adj or n* — **psy•chot•i•cal•ly** \-'kät-i-kə-lē, -klē\ *adv*

psy•cho•so•mat•ic \,sī-kə-sə-'mat-ik\ *adj* : of, relating to, or being bodily symptoms or bodily and mental symptoms resulting from conflict and anxiety — **psy•cho•so•mat•i•cal•ly** \-i-kə-lē, -klē\ *adv*

psy•cho•sur•gery \,sī-kō-'sərj-rē, -ə-rē\ *n* : brain surgery employed in treating the symptoms of mental illness — **psy•cho•sur•geon** \-'sər-jən\ *n* — **psy•cho•sur•gi•cal** \-'sər-ji-kəl\ *adj*

psy•cho•ther•a•py \ˌsī-kō-ˈther-ə-pē\ *n* : treatment of mental or emotional disorder or of related bodily ills by psychological means — **psy•cho•ther•a•pist** \-pəst\ *n*
Psy•cho•zo•ic \ˌsī-kə-ˈzō-ik\ *adj* : QUATERNARY
psy•chrom•e•ter \sī-ˈkräm-ət-ər\ *n* : an instrument for measuring the water vapor in the atmosphere by means of the difference in the readings of two thermometers when one of them is kept wet so that it is cooled by evaporation [Greek *psychros* "cold"] — **psy•chro•met•ric** \ˌsī-krō-ˈme-trik\ *adj*
psyl•la \ˈsil-ə\ *n* : any of a family of plant lice including many economic pests [Greek, "flea"] — **psyl•lid** \-əd\ *adj or n*
ptar•mi•gan \ˈtär-mi-gən\ *n, pl* **ptarmigans** *or* **ptarmigan** : any of various grouse of northern regions with completely feathered feet [Scottish Gaelic *tàrmachan*]
P T boat \ˈpē-ˈtē-\ *n* : a high-speed motorboat usually equipped with torpedoes, machine guns, and depth charges [patrol torpedo]
PTC \ˌpē-ˌtē-ˈsē\ *n* : PHENYLTHIOCARBAMIDE
pter•an•odon \tə-ˈran-ə-ˌdän\ *n* : any of a genus of Cretaceous flying reptiles with a wingspread of 25 feet [Greek *pteron* "wing, feather" + *anodōn* "toothless", from *an-* + *odōn* "tooth"]
pte•rid•o•phyte \tə-ˈrid-ə-ˌfīt\ *n* : any of a division (Pteridophyta) of vascular plants that have roots, stems, and leaves, lack flowers or seeds, and comprise the ferns and related forms [derived from Greek *pterid-*, *pteris* "fern" + *phyton* "plant"] — **pte•rid•o•phyt•ic** \tə-ˌrid-ə-ˈfit-ik\ *adj*
ptero•dac•tyl \ˌter-ə-ˈdak-tl\ *n* : any of several extinct flying reptiles with a featherless membrane extending from the body along the arms and forming the supporting surface of the wings [Greek *pteron* "wing" + *daktylos* "finger"]

ptarmigan

ptero•saur \ˈter-ə-ˌsȯr\ *n* : PTERODACTYL [derived from Greek *pteron* "wing" + *sauros* "lizard"]
Ptol•e•ma•ic \ˌtäl-ə-ˈmā-ik\ *adj* : of, relating to, or characteristic of Ptolemy [Greek *Ptolemaikos*, from *Ptolemaios* "Ptolemy"]
Ptolemaic system *n* : the system of planetary motions according to which the earth is at the center with the sun, moon, and planets revolving around it [*Ptolemy*, 2d century A.D. Alexandrian astronomer]
pto•maine \ˈtō-ˌmān, tō-ˈ\ *n* : any of various often poisonous organic compounds formed by bacteria-induced rotting of nitrogenous matter (as proteins) [Italian *ptomaina*, from Greek *ptōma* "fall, fallen body, corpse", from *piptein* "to fall"]
ptomaine poisoning *n* : food poisoning caused usually by bacteria or bacterial products
pty•a•lin \ˈtī-ə-lən\ *n* : an amylase found in the saliva of many animals [Greek *ptyalon* "saliva", from *ptyein* "to spit"]
pub \ˈpəb\ *n, chiefly British* : PUBLIC HOUSE
pub crawler *n* : one that goes from bar to bar
pu•ber•ty \ˈpyü-bərt-ē\ *n* **1** : the condition of being or the period of becoming first capable of reproducing sexually **2** : the age at which puberty occurs often construed legally as 14 in boys and 12 in girls [Latin *pubertas*, from *puber* "pubescent"] — **pu•ber•tal** \-bərt-l\ *adj*
pu•bes•cent \pyü-ˈbes-nt\ *adj* **1** : arriving at or having reached puberty **2** : covered with fine soft short hairs — **pu•bes•cence** \-ns\ *n*
pu•bic \ˈpyü-bik\ *adj* : of, relating to, or situated near the pubis [Latin *pubes* "pubic hair, pubic region"]
pu•bis \ˈpyü-bəs\ *n, pl* **pu•bes** \-ˌbēz\ : the ventral and anterior of the three principal bones composing each hipbone — called also *pubic bone* [New Latin *os pubis*, literally, "bone of the pubic region"]
[1]**pub•lic** \ˈpəb-lik\ *adj* **1 a** : of, relating to, or affecting all the people ⟨*public* law⟩ **b** : of or relating to government **c** : relating to or engaged in the service of the community or nation ⟨*public* life⟩ **2** : of or relating to mankind in general : UNIVERSAL **3** : of or relating to business or community interests as opposed to private affairs **4** : devoted to the general welfare : HUMANITARIAN ⟨*public* spirit⟩ **5** : accessible to or shared by all members of the community **6 a** : exposed to general view : OPEN **b** : WELL-KNOWN, PROMINENT ⟨a *public* figure⟩ [Middle French *publique*, from Latin *publicus*] — **pub•lic•ly** *adv* — **pub•lic•ness** *n*
[2]**public** *n* **1** : a place accessible or visible to the public ⟨seen together in *public*⟩ **2** : the people as a whole : POPULACE ⟨a lecture open to the *public*⟩ **3** : a particular group of people ⟨a writer's *public*⟩
public address system *n* : an apparatus including one or more loudspeakers for reproducing sound so that it may be heard by a large audience in an auditorium or outdoors
pub•li•can \ˈpəb-li-kən\ *n* **1** : a provincial tax collector for the ancient Romans **2** *chiefly British* : a keeper of a public house [Middle French, from Latin *publicanus*, from *publicum* "public revenue", from *publicus* "public"]
pub•li•ca•tion \ˌpəb-lə-ˈkā-shen\ *n* **1** : the act or process or an instance of publishing **2** : a published work [Middle French, from Late Latin *publicatio*, from Latin *publicare* "to publish"]
public domain *n* **1** : land owned directly by the government **2** : property rights that belong to the community at large, are unprotected by copyright or patent, and may be used by anyone
public house *n* **1** : INN 1, HOSTELRY **2** *chiefly British* : a licensed saloon or bar
pub•li•cist \ˈpəb-lə-səst\ *n* **1 a** : an expert in international law **b** : an expert or commentator on public affairs **2** : one that publicizes; *esp* : PRESS AGENT
pub•lic•i•ty \pə-ˈblis-ət-ē, ˌpə-\ *n* **1** : the condition of being public or publicly known **2** : something meant to attract attention; *esp* : information with a news value designed to further the interests of a place, person, or cause **3** : attention from the public and especially the communications media
pub•li•cize \ˈpəb-lə-ˌsīz\ *vt* : to give publicity to : ADVERTISE, PROMOTE
public opinion *n* : the general attitude of the public on some issue or the expression of this attitude ⟨*public opinion* favored the government's policy⟩
public relations *n* : the business of inducing the public to have understanding and goodwill for a person, firm, or institution; *also* : the degree of understanding and goodwill achieved
public school *n* **1** : any of various select endowed British schools that give a liberal education and prepare students for the universities **2** : an elementary or secondary school maintained by a local government
public servant *n* : a governmental official or employee
public service *n* **1** : the business of supplying a commodity (as electricity or gas) or service (as transportation) to any or all members of a community **2** : governmental employment; *esp* : CIVIL SERVICE
public speaking *n* **1** : the act or process of making speeches in public **2** : the art or science of effective oral communication with an audience
pub•lic-spir•it•ed \ˌpəb-lik-ˈspir-ət-əd\ *adj* : motivated by devotion to the general or national welfare — **pub•lic-spir•it•ed•ness** *n*
public utility *n* : a business organization (as a gas company) performing a public service and subject to special governmental regulation
public works *n pl* : works (as schools or highways) constructed for public use or enjoyment and financed and owned by the government
pub•lish \ˈpəb-lish\ *vb* **1** : to make generally known : make public announcement of ⟨*publish* a libel⟩ **2 a** : to produce or release for publication; *esp* : PRINT **b** : to issue the work of (an author) **3** : to have one's work accepted for publication ⟨a *publishing* scholar⟩ [Middle English *publishen*, from Middle French *publier*, from Latin *publicare*, from *publicus* "public"] **syn** see DECLARE — **pub•lish•able** \-ə-bəl\ *adj*
pub•lish•er \-ər\ *n* : one that publishes; *esp* : one that issues and offers for sale printed matter (as books, periodicals, or newspapers)
puc•coon \pə-ˈkün\ *n* : any of several American plants (as the bloodroot) that yield a red or yellow pigment [of American Indian origin]

\ə\ abut	\au̇\ out	\i\ tip	\ȯ\ saw	\u̇\ foot
\ər\ further	\ch\ chin	\ī\ life	\ȯi\ coin	\y\ yet
\a\ mat	\e\ pet	\j\ job	\th\ thin	\yü\ few
\ā\ take	\ē\ easy	\ng\ sing	\t͟h\ this	\yu̇\ cure
\ä\ cot, cart	\g\ go	\ō\ bone	\ü\ food	\zh\ vision

[1]**puck** \'pək\ *n* **1** *archaic* **:** an evil spirit **:** DEMON **2 :** a mischievous sprite **:** HOBGOBLIN 1 [Old English *pūca*]

[2]**puck** *n* **:** a hard rubber disk used in ice hockey [English dialect *puck* "to poke", alteration of English [2]*poke*]

pucka *variant of* PUKKA

[1]**puck•er** \'pək-ər\ *vb* **puck•ered**; **puck•er•ing** \'pək-ring, -ə-ring\ **:** to contract into folds or wrinkles ⟨the cloth *puckered* in shrinking⟩ [probably derived from [1]*poke*]

[2]**pucker** *n* **:** a fold or wrinkle in a normally even surface — **puck•ered** \'pək-ərd\ *adj* — **puck•ery** \'pək-rē, -ə-rē\ *adj*

puck•ish \'pək-ish\ *adj* **:** IMPISH, MISCHIEVOUS ⟨*puckish* humor⟩ [[1]*puck*] — **puck•ish•ly** *adv* — **puck•ish•ness** *n*

pud•ding \'pu̇d-ing\ *n* **1 :** a boiled or baked soft food usually with a cereal base ⟨corn *pudding*⟩ **2 :** a dessert of a soft, spongy, or thick creamy consistency ⟨bread *pudding*⟩ **3 :** a dish often containing suet or having a suet crust ⟨kidney *pudding*⟩ ⟨fig *pudding* ⟩[Middle English]

pudding stone *n* **:** conglomerate rock

[1]**pud•dle** \'pəd-l\ *n* **1 :** a very small pool of usually dirty or muddy water **2 :** an earthy mixture (as of clay, sand, and gravel) worked while wet into a compact mass that becomes impervious to water when dry [Middle English *podel*]

[2]**puddle** *vt* **pud•dled**; **pud•dling** \'pəd-ling, -l-ing\ **1 :** to make muddy or turbid **2 a :** to make a puddle of (as clay) **b :** to convert (melted pig iron) into wrought iron by stirring in the presence of an oxidizer **3 :** to strew with puddles — **pud•dler** \-lər, -l-ər\ *n*

pu•den•cy \'pyüd-n-sē\ *n* **:** MODESTY [Latin *pudentia,* from *pudēre* "to be ashamed"]

pu•den•dum \pyu̇-'den-dəm\ *n, pl* **-den•da** \-'den-də\ **:** the external genital organs especially of a woman [New Latin, sing. of Latin *pudenda,* from *pudendus* "shameful", from *pudēre* "to be ashamed"] — **pu•den•dal** \-'den-dl\ *adj*

pudgy \'pəj-ē\ *adj* **pudg•i•er**; **-est :** short and plump **:** CHUBBY [origin unknown] — **pudg•i•ness** *n*

pu•eb•lo \pü-'eb-lō, 'pweb-, pyü-'eb-\ *n, pl* **-los 1 :** an Amerindian village of Arizona or New Mexico consisting of flat-roofed stone or adobe houses joined in groups sometimes several stories high **2** *cap* **:** a member of any of several Amerindian peoples of the Southwest [Spanish, "village", literally, "people", from Latin *populus*]

pu•er•ile \'pyu̇-ər-əl, 'pyu̇r-, -,īl\ *adj* **1 :** JUVENILE 3 **2 :** CHILDISH, SILLY ⟨*puerile* remarks⟩ [Latin *puerilis,* from *puer* "boy, child"] — **pu•er•il•i•ty** \,pyu̇-ər-'il-ət-ē, ,pyu̇r-\ *n*

pu•er•per•al \pyü-'ər-pə-rəl, -prəl\ *adj* **:** of or relating to parturition ⟨*puerperal* infection⟩ [Latin *puerpera* "woman in childbirth", from *puer* "child", + *parere* "to give birth to"]

puerperal fever *n* **:** an abnormal condition that results from infection of the placental site following delivery or abortion and is characterized in mild form by fever but in serious cases may spread through the wall of the uterus or into the bloodstream — called also *childbed fever*

[1]**puff** \'pəf\ *vb* **1 a** (1) **:** to blow in short gusts (2) **:** to exhale forcibly **b :** to breathe hard **:** PANT ⟨*puffed* as we climbed the hill⟩ **c :** to emit, propel, blow, or expel by or as if by small whiffs or clouds (as of smoke) ⟨*puff* at a pipe⟩ ⟨a brisk breeze *puffed* the clouds away⟩ **2 a :** to speak or act in a scornful, conceited, or affected manner **b :** to make proud or conceited **:** ELATE **c :** to praise extravagantly (as in advertising) **3 a :** to distend or become distended with or as if with gas **:** SWELL ⟨the sprained ankle *puffed* up⟩ **b :** to open or appear in or as if in a puff [Old English *pyffan*]

[2]**puff** *n* **1 a :** an act or instance of puffing **:** WHIFF, GUST **b :** a slight explosive sound accompanying a puff **c :** a perceptible cloud (as of smoke or steam) emitted in a puff **2 :** a light pastry that rises high in baking **3 a :** a slight swelling **:** PROTUBERANCE **b :** a fluffy mass: as (1) **:** a small fluffy pad for applying cosmetic powder (2) **:** a soft loose roll of hair (3) **:** a quilted bed covering **4 :** a commendatory notice or review — **puff•i•ness** \'pəf-ē-nəs\ *n* — **puffy** \'pəf-ē\ *adj*

puff adder *n* **:** HOGNOSE SNAKE

puff•ball \'pəf-,bȯl\ *n* **:** any of various mostly edible globe-shaped fungi that discharge ripe spores in a cloud resembling smoke when they are disturbed

puff•er \'pəf-ər\ *n* **1 :** one that puffs **2 :** any of various fishes that can inflate their bodies with air — called also *globefish*

puf•fin \'pəf-ən\ *n* **:** any of several short-necked northern seabirds that are related to the auks and have a deep grooved bill marked with different colors [Middle English *pophyn*]

puff paste *n* **:** dough used in making light flaky pastries

puffin

pug \'pəg\ *n* **1 :** a small sturdy compact dog of Asian origin with a close coat, tightly curled tail, and broad wrinkled face **2 a :** PUG NOSE **b :** a close knot or coil of hair **:** BUN [obsolete *pug* "hobgoblin, monkey"]

pu•gi•list \'pyü-jə-ləst\ *n* **:** [1]BOXER [Latin *pugil* "boxer"] — **pu•gi•lism** \-,liz-əm\ *n* — **pu•gi•lis•tic** \,pyü-jə-'lis-tik\ *adj*

pug•na•cious \,pəg-'nā-shəs\ *adj* **:** having a quarrelsome or belligerent nature **:** TRUCULENT, COMBATIVE [Latin *pugnac-, pugnax,* from *pugnare* "to fight"] — **pug•na•cious•ly** *adv* — **pug•na•cious•ness** *n* — **pug•nac•i•ty** \-'nas-ət-ē\ *n*

pug nose *n* **:** a nose having a slightly concave bridge and flattened nostrils — **pug–nosed** \'pəg-'nōzd\ *adj*

puis•ne \'pyü-nē\ *adj, chiefly British* **:** inferior in rank ⟨a *puisne* judge⟩ [Middle French *puisné* "younger", literally, "born afterward"]

puis•sance \'pwis-ns, 'pyü-ə-səns\ *n* **:** ability to dominate or sway **:** MIGHT [Middle French, from *puissant* "powerful", from *poeir* "to be able, be powerful"] — **puis•sant** \-nt, -sənt\ *adj* — **puis•sant•ly** *adv*

puke \'pyük\ *vb* **:** VOMIT 1 [perhaps imitative]

puk•ka *or* **puc•ka** \'pək-ə\ *adj* **:** being genuine and authentic; *also* **:** FIRST-CLASS [Hindi *pakkā* "cooked, ripe, solid", from Sanskrit *pakva*]

pul•chri•tude \'pəl-krə-,tüd, -,tyüd\ *n* **:** physical comeliness **:** BEAUTY [Latin *pulchritudin-, pulchritudo,* from *pulcher* "beautiful"] — **pul•chri•tu•di•nous** \,pəl-krə-'tüd-n-əs, -'tyüd-\ *adj*

pule \'pyül\ *vi* **:** WHINE 1, WHIMPER ⟨a *puling* infant⟩ [probably imitative]

[1]**pull** \'pu̇l\ *vb* **1 :** to separate forcibly from a natural or firm attachment **:** PLUCK, EXTRACT ⟨*pull* a tooth⟩; *also* **:** to admit of being pulled ⟨the stump *pulled* hard⟩ **2 a :** to exert force upon so as to cause or tend to cause motion toward the force ⟨*pull* a wagon⟩ **b :** to stretch (cooling candy) repeatedly **c :** to strain by stretching abnormally ⟨*pull* a tendon⟩ **d** (1) **:** to use force in drawing, dragging, or tugging ⟨*pull* on that rope⟩ (2) **:** MOVE ⟨the car *pulled* away from the curb⟩ (3) **:** to take a drink (4) **:** to draw hard in smoking ⟨*pulled* at my pipe⟩ **e :** to work (an oar) by drawing back strongly **3 :** to hit (a ball) to the left side of the field from a right-handed stance or to the right side from a left-handed stance **4 :** to draw apart **:** REND, TEAR **5 :** to print (as a proof) by impression **6 :** REMOVE ⟨*pull* a crankshaft⟩ ⟨*pulled* the pitcher in the third inning⟩ **7 :** to bring (a weapon) into the open ⟨*pulled* a knife⟩ **8 :** to carry out with skill or daring **:** COMMIT ⟨*pull* a robbery⟩ **9 :** ATTRACT ⟨*pull* votes⟩ **10 :** to feel or express strong sympathy **:** ROOT ⟨*pulling* for their team to win⟩ [Old English *pullian*] — **pull•er** *n* — **pull oneself together :** to regain one's self-possession — **pull one's leg :** to deceive someone playfully **:** HOAX — **pull stakes** *or* **pull up stakes :** to move out **:** LEAVE — **pull strings** *or* **pull wires :** to exert secret influence or control — **pull together :** to work in harmony **:** COOPERATE

[2]**pull** *n* **1 a :** the act or an instance of pulling **b** (1) **:** a draft of liquid (2) **:** an inhalation of smoke **c :** a route, journey, or climb requiring effort ⟨a long *pull* uphill⟩ **d :** force required to overcome resistance to pulling **2 a :** ADVANTAGE ⟨the *pull* of a good family name⟩ **b :** special influence ⟨got a job through *pull*⟩ **3 :** PROOF 2a **4 :** a device for pulling something or for operating by pulling ⟨a bell *pull*⟩ **5 :** a force that attracts, compels, or influences **:** ATTRACTION ⟨the *pull* of gravity⟩

pull away *vi* **:** to draw oneself back or away **:** WITHDRAW

pull•back \'pu̇l-,bak\ *n* **:** a pulling back; *esp* **:** an orderly withdrawal of troops from a position

pull down *vt* **1 :** to tear down **:** WRECK **2 a :** to bring to a lower level **:** REDUCE **b :** to depress in health, strength, or spirits **3 :** to draw as wages or salary

pul•let \'pu̇l-ət\ *n* **:** a young hen; *esp* **:** a hen of the common fowl less than a year old [Middle English *polet* "young fowl", from Middle French *poulet,* from *poul* "fowl", from Late Latin *pullus,* from Latin, "young of an animal, chicken, sprout"]

pul•ley \ˈpu̇l-ē\ *n, pl* **pul-leys** **1 :** a small wheel with a grooved rim used singly with a rope or chain to change the direction and point of application of a pulling force and in combinations to increase the applied force especially for lifting weights; *also* **:** the simple machine constituted by such a pulley with ropes **2 :** a wheel used to transmit power by means of a band, belt, cord, rope, or chain [Middle French *poulie*]

pulley 1

pull in *vb* **1 :** CHECK, RESTRAIN ⟨*pull* a horse *in*⟩ **2 :** ARREST ⟨*pull in* a suspect⟩ **3 :** to arrive at a destination ⟨the train *pulled in* on time⟩

Pull•man \ˈpu̇l-mən\ *n* **:** a railroad passenger car with specially comfortable furnishings; *esp* **:** SLEEPING CAR [George M. *Pullman,* died 1897, American inventor]

pull off *vt* **:** to accomplish successfully especially against odds

pull•out \ˈpu̇l-ˌau̇t\ *n* **1 :** something that can be pulled out **2 :** the action in which an airplane goes from a dive to horizontal flight **3 :** PULLBACK

pull out \pu̇l-ˈau̇t, ˈpu̇l-\ *vi* **1 :** LEAVE, DEPART ⟨the ship finally *pulled out*⟩ **2 :** WITHDRAW ⟨*pulled out* at the last minute and left us a player short⟩

[1]**pull•over** \ˌpu̇l-ˌō-vər\ *adj* **:** put on by being pulled over the head

[2]**pullover** \ˈpu̇l-ˌō-vər\ *n* **:** a pullover garment

pull over \pu̇l-ˈō-vər, ˈpu̇l-\ *vi* **:** to steer one's vehicle to the side of the road

pull through *vb* **:** to survive or help through a dangerous or difficult period or situation

pull up *vb* **1 :** CHECK, REBUKE ⟨was *pulled up* for my bad manners⟩ **2 :** to bring or come to a stop **:** HALT ⟨*pulled* the car *up* in front of the hotel⟩ **3 :** to draw even with others in a race

pul•mo•nary \ˈpu̇l-mə-ˌner-ē, ˈpəl-\ *adj* **1 :** relating to or associated with the lungs **2 :** carried on by the lungs [Latin *pulmonarius,* from *pulmon-, pulmo* "lung"]

pulmonary artery *n* **:** an artery that conveys venous blood from the heart to the lungs

pulmonary circulation *n* **:** the passage of blood from the right side of the heart through arteries to the lungs where it picks up oxygen and is returned to the left side of the heart by veins

pulmonary vein *n* **:** a vein that returns oxygenated blood from the lungs to the heart

pul•mo•nate \ˈpu̇l-mə-nāt, ˈpəl-\ *adj* **:** having lungs or organs resembling lungs; *also* **:** air-breathing ⟨*pulmonate* snails⟩

pul•mo•tor \ˈpu̇l-ˌmōt-ər, ˈpəl-\ *n* **:** a respiratory apparatus for pumping oxygen or air into and out of the lungs (as of an asphyxiated person) [from *Pulmotor,* a former trademark]

[1]**pulp** \ˈpəlp\ *n* **1 a :** the soft juicy or fleshy part of a fruit or vegetable ⟨the *pulp* of an apple⟩ **b :** a mass of vegetable matter from which the juice has been pressed **2 :** the soft sensitive tissue that fills the central cavity of a tooth **3 :** a material prepared by chemical or mechanical means chiefly from wood and used in making paper and cellulose products **4 a :** pulpy condition **b :** something in a pulpy condition **5 :** a magazine or book using rough-surfaced paper made of wood pulp and often dealing with sensational material [Middle French *poulpe,* from Latin *pulpa* "flesh, pulp"] — **pulp•i•ness** \ˈpəl-pē-nəs\ *n* — **pulpy** \ˈpəl-pē\ *adj*

[2]**pulp** *vb* **:** to reduce to pulp **:** make or become pulpy — **pulp•er** *n*

pul•pit \ˈpu̇l-ˌpit, ˈpəl-, -pət\ *n* **1 :** an elevated platform or high reading desk used in preaching or conducting a worship service **2 a :** the preaching profession **b :** a position as a preacher [Late Latin *pulpitum,* from Latin, "staging, platform"]

pulp•wood \ˈpəlp-ˌwu̇d\ *n* **:** a wood (as aspen, hemlock, pine, or spruce) used in making pulp for paper

pul•que \ˈpu̇l-ˌkā\ *n* **:** a fermented drink made in Mexico from the juice of various magueys [Mexican Spanish]

pul•sar \ˈpəl-ˌsär\ *n* **:** a celestial source of pulsating radio waves characterized by a short nearly constant interval (as .033 second) between pulses that is held to be a rotating neutron star [*pulse* + *-ar* (as in *quasar*)]

pul•sate \ˈpəl-ˌsāt\ *vi* **1 :** PULSE 1 ⟨a *pulsating* artery⟩ ⟨*pulsating* drums⟩ **2 :** to be vibrant (as with life, activity, or feeling) ⟨a busy *pulsating* city⟩ [Latin *pulsare,* from *pulsus,* past participle of *pellere* "to drive, beat"]

pul•sa•tile \ˈpəl-sət-l, -sə-ˌtīl\ *adj* **:** that pulsates

pul•sa•tion \ˌpəl-ˈsā-shən\ *n* **:** pulsing movement or action (as of an artery); *also* **:** a single throb of such movement

[1]**pulse** \ˈpəls\ *n* **:** the edible seeds of several crops (as peas, beans, or lentils) of the pea family; *also* **:** a plant yielding pulse [Old French *pouls* "porridge", from Latin *puls*]

[2]**pulse** *n* **1 :** a regular throbbing caused in the arteries by the contractions of the heart **2 a :** rhythmical beating, vibrating, or sounding **b :** BEAT 1c, THROB **3 a :** a transient variation of a quantity (as electrical current or voltage) whose value is normally constant **b :** an electromagnetic wave or a sound wave of brief duration [Middle French *pouls,* from Latin *pulsus,* literally, "beating", from *pulsus,* past participle of *pellere* "to drive, beat"]

[3]**pulse** *vb* **1 :** to exhibit a pulse or pulsation **:** THROB **2 :** to drive by or as if by a pulsation **3 :** to cause to pulsate **4 :** to produce or modulate (as electromagnetic waves) in the form of pulses ⟨*pulsed* waves⟩

pul•ver•ize \ˈpəl-və-ˌrīz\ *vb* **1 :** to reduce or become reduced (as by beating or grinding) into a powder **2 :** to demolish as if by pulverizing **:** SMASH, ANNIHILATE [Middle French *pulveriser,* from Late Latin *pulverizare,* from Latin *pulver-, pulvis* "dust, powder"] — **pul•ver•iz•er** *n*

pu•ma \ˈpü-mə, ˈpyü-\ *n, pl* **pumas** *also* **puma** **:** COUGAR [Spanish, from Quechua]

pum•ice \ˈpəm-əs\ *n* **:** a volcanic glass full of cavities and very light in weight used especially in powder form for smoothing and polishing — called also *pumice stone* [Middle French *pomis,* from Latin *pumic-, pumex*]

pum•mel \ˈpəm-əl\ *vb* **-meled** *or* **-melled**; **-mel•ing** *or* **-mel•ling** **:** POUND 2a, BEAT [alteration of *pommel*]

[1]**pump** \ˈpəmp\ *n* **:** a device that raises, transfers, or compresses fluids especially by suction or pressure or both ⟨a water *pump*⟩ [Low German *pumpe* or Dutch *pompe*]

[2]**pump** *vb* **1 :** to raise, transfer, or compress by means of a pump ⟨*pump* water⟩ **2 :** to draw fluid from by the use of a pump ⟨*pump* a boat dry⟩ **3 :** to draw, force, or drive onward in the manner of a pump ⟨the heart *pumps* blood into the arteries⟩ **4 a :** to question persistently **b :** to draw out by persistent questioning **5 :** to move up and down like a pump handle ⟨*pump* the hand of a friend⟩ **6 :** to fill by means of a pump ⟨*pump* up a tire⟩ **7 :** to spurt out intermittently — **pump•er** *n*

[3]**pump** *n* **:** a low shoe without a fastening that grips the foot chiefly at the toe and heel [origin unknown]

pum•per•nick•el \ˈpəm-pər-ˌnik-əl\ *n* **:** a dark coarse sourdough rye bread [German]

pump•kin \ˈpəng-kən, ˈpəm-, ˈpəmp-\ *n* **1 :** the usually round deep yellow fruit of a vine of the gourd family widely used as food; *also* **:** a fruit (as a crookneck squash) of a closely related vine **2 :** a usually hairy prickly vine that produces pumpkins [French *popon, pompon* "melon, pumpkin", from Latin *pepon-, pepo,* from Greek *pepōn,* from *pepōn* "ripened"]

pump•kin•seed \-ˌsēd\ *n* **:** a small brilliantly colored North American freshwater sunfish

[1]**pun** \ˈpən\ *n* **:** the humorous use of a word in such a way as to suggest different meanings or applications or of words having the same or nearly the same sound but different meanings [perhaps from Italian *puntiglio* "fine point, quibble, scruple"]

[2]**pun** *vi* **punned**; **pun•ning** **:** to make puns

[1]**punch** \ˈpənch\ *vb* **1 a :** PROD 2, POKE **b :** to act as herdsman of (range cattle) **2 a :** to strike with a forward thrust of the fist **b :** to drive or push forcibly by or as if by a punch **3 :** to emboss, cut, perforate, or make with a punch **4 :** to strike or press sharply the operating mechanism of [Middle French *poinçonner* "to prick, stamp", from *poinçon* "puncheon"] — **punch•er** *n*

[2]**punch** *n* **1 :** the action of punching **2 :** a quick blow with or as if with the fist **3 :** energy or vigor that commands attention ⟨they lacked political *punch*⟩

[3]**punch** *n* **1 :** a tool or machine for piercing, cutting (as a hole or

notch), forming, driving the head of a nail below a surface or a bolt out of a hole, or impressing a design in a softer material **2** : a hole or notch resulting from a perforating operation [probably short for *puncheon*]

⁴punch *n* : a drink made of several ingredients (as fruit juices and spices) and often flavored with wine or distilled liquor [perhaps from Hindi *pā̃c* "five", from Sanskrit *pañca;* from the number of ingredients]

Punch-and-Judy show \ˌpən-chən-ˈjüd-ē-\ *n* : a traditional puppet show in which the hook-nosed humpback Punch fights comically with his wife Judy

punch bowl *n* : a large bowl from which a beverage (as punch) is served

punch card *n* : a card with holes punched in particular positions each with its own signification for use in data processing — called also *punched card*

punch-drunk \ˈpənch-ˌdrəngk\ *adj* **1** : suffering from brain injury received in prizefighting **2** : GROGGY ⟨*punch-drunk* with fatigue⟩ [²*punch*]

¹pun•cheon \ˈpən-chən\ *n* **1** : a pointed tool for piercing **2 a** : a short upright framing timber **b** : a split log or slab with the face smoothed **3** : a figured stamp die or punch used especially by goldsmiths and engravers [Middle French *poinçon,* derived from Latin *pungere* "to prick"]

²puncheon *n* **1** : a large cask of varying capacity **2** : any of various units of liquid capacity [Middle French *ponchon*]

punch in *vi* : to record the time of one's arrival or beginning work by punching a time clock

pun•chi•nel•lo \ˌpən-chə-ˈnel-ō\ *n* **1** *cap* : a fat short humpbacked clown or buffoon in Italian puppet shows **2** *pl* **-los** : a squat grotesque person [Italian dialect *polecenella*]

punching bag *n* : a usually suspended stuffed or inflated bag to be punched for exercise or for training in boxing

punch line *n* : the sentence, statement, or phrase (as in a joke) that makes the point

punch out *vi* : to record the time of one's stopping work or departure by punching a time clock

punch press *n* : a press for working on material (as metal) by the use of cutting, shaping, or combination dies

punchy \ˈpən-chē\ *adj* **punch•i•er; -est** : PUNCH-DRUNK

punc•tate \ˈpəng-ˌtāt, ˈpəngk-\ *adj* **1** : ending in or resembling a point **2** : marked with minute spots or depressions ⟨a *punctate* leaf⟩ [Latin *punctum* "point"] — **punc•ta•tion** \ˌpəng-ˈtā-shən, ˌpəngk-\ *n*

punc•til•io \ˌpəng-ˈtil-ē-ˌō, ˌpəngk-\ *n, pl* **-i•os** **1** : a minute detail of conduct in a ceremony or in observance of a code **2** : careful observance of forms (as in social conduct) [Italian *puntiglio* "point of honor, scruple, quibble", from Spanish *puntillo,* from *punto* "point", from Latin *punctum*]

punc•til•i•ous \-ē-əs\ *adj* : marked by precise exact accordance with the details of codes or conventions **syn** see CAREFUL — **punc•til•i•ous•ly** *adv* — **punc•til•i•ous•ness** *n*

punc•tu•al \ˈpəng-chə-wəl, ˈpəngk-\ *adj* **1** : PUNCTILIOUS **2 a** : being on time : PROMPT **b** : characterized by regular occurrence [Medieval Latin *punctualis,* from Latin *punctus* "pricking, point", from *pungere* "to prick"] — **punc•tu•al•i•ty** \ˌpəng-chə-ˈwal-ət-ē, ˌpəngk-\ *n* — **punc•tu•al•ly** \ˈpəng-chə-wə-lē, ˈpəngk-\ *adv* — **punc•tu•al•ness** \-wəl-nəs\ *n*

punc•tu•ate \ˈpəng-chə-ˌwāt, ˈpəngk-\ *vt* **1** : to mark or divide with punctuation marks **2** : to break into or interrupt at intervals ⟨a speech *punctuated* by coughs⟩ [Medieval Latin *punctuare,* from Latin *punctus* "point"] — **punc•tu•a•tor** \-ˌwāt-ər\ *n*

punc•tu•a•tion \ˌpəng-chə-ˈwā-shən, ˌpəngk-\ *n* : the act, practice, or system of inserting standardized marks or signs in written matter to clarify the meaning and separate structural units

punctuation mark *n* : any of the standardized marks or signs used in punctuation

¹punc•ture \ˈpəng-chər, ˈpəngk-\ *n* **1** : the act of puncturing **2** : a hole or a narrow wound resulting from puncturing ⟨a *puncture* of the abdomen⟩ ⟨a tire with a *puncture*⟩ [Latin *punctura,* from *punctus,* past participle of *pungere* "to prick"]

²puncture *vb* **punc•tured; punc•tur•ing** \ˈpəng-chə-ring, ˈpəng-shring, ˈpəngk-\ **1** : to pierce with a pointed instrument or object **2** : to suffer a puncture of **3** : to become punctured **4** : to make useless or absurd as if by a puncture ⟨*puncture* an argument⟩

pun•dit \ˈpən-dət\ *n* : a wise or learned person : AUTHORITY [Hindi *paṇḍit,* from Sanskrit *paṇḍita,* from *paṇḍita* "learned"]

pun•gen•cy \ˈpən-jən-sē\ *n* : the quality or state of being pungent

pun•gent \ˈpən-jənt\ *adj* **1** : sharply stimulating to the mind ⟨*pungent* criticism⟩ ⟨*pungent* wit⟩ **2** : causing a sharp or irritating sensation; *esp* : ACRID [Latin *pungens,* present participle of *pungere* "to prick, sting"] — **pun•gent•ly** *adv*

Pu•nic \ˈpyü-nik\ *adj* : of or relating to Carthage or the Carthaginians [Latin *punicus,* from *Poenus* "inhabitant of Carthage", from Greek *Phoinix* "Phoenician"]

pun•ish \ˈpən-ish\ *vb* **1** : impose punishment on for a fault or offense ⟨*punish* the children for disobeying⟩ **2** : to inflict punishment for (as a crime) ⟨*punish* treason with death⟩ **3** : to deal with severely or roughly ⟨badly *punished* by my opponent⟩ **4** : to inflict punishment [Middle French *puniss-,* stem of *punir* "to punish", from Latin *punire,* from *poena* "penalty, pain"] — **pun•ish•abil•i•ty** \ˌpən-ish-ə-ˈbil-ət-ē\ *n* — **pun•ish•able** \ˈpən-ish-ə-bəl\ *adj* — **pun•ish•er** *n*

• **syn** CHASTISE, DISCIPLINE: PUNISH implies subjection to penalty for wrongdoing; CHASTISE often implies corporal punishment but may suggest stern or painful verbal censure; DISCIPLINE may involve punishment but suggests action with the intent of bringing under control ⟨parents must *discipline* their children⟩

pun•ish•ing \ˈpən-ish-ing\ *adj* : very arduous, demanding, or painful ⟨a *punishing* race⟩ — **pun•ish•ing•ly** *adv*

pun•ish•ment \ˈpən-ish-mənt\ *n* **1** : the act of punishing **2 a** : suffering or pain that serves as retribution **b** : the penalty for a fault or crime ⟨the *punishment* for speeding⟩ **3** : severe, rough, or disastrous treatment ⟨trees showing the effects of *punishment* by a heavy storm⟩

pu•ni•tive \ˈpyü-nət-iv\ *adj* : inflicting, involving, or aiming at punishment [French *punitif,* from Medieval Latin *punitivus,* from Latin *punitus,* past participle of *punire* "to punish"] — **pu•ni•tive•ly** *adv* — **pu•ni•tive•ness** *n*

Pun•jabi \ˌpən-ˈjäb-ē, -ˈjab-\ *n* **1** : a native or inhabitant of the Punjab region of the Indian subcontinent **2** : PANJABI 1 — **Punjabi** *adj*

¹punk \ˈpəngk\ *n* **1** : a young inexperienced man **2** : a petty hoodlum [origin unknown]

²punk *adj* : very poor in quality : BAD, MISERABLE

³punk *n* **1** : wood so decayed as to be dry, crumbly, and useful for tinder **2** : a dry spongy substance prepared from fungi and used to ignite fuses especially of fireworks [perhaps alteration of *spunk* "tinder"]

pun•kah \ˈpəng-kə\ *n* : a large fan or a canvas-covered frame suspended from the ceiling and used especially in India for fanning a room [Hindi *pākhā*]

pun•kie *also* **pun•ky** \ˈpəng-kē\ *n, pl* **punkies** : a tiny biting fly : MIDGE [Dutch dialect *punki,* from Delaware *punk,* literally, "fine ashes, powder"]

pun•ster \ˈpən-stər\ *n* : one given to making puns

¹punt \ˈpənt\ *n* : a long narrow flat-bottomed square-ended boat usually propelled with a pole [Old English, from Latin *ponto,* from *pont-, pons* "bridge"]

²punt *vb* **1** : to propel (a boat) by pushing with a pole against the bottom of a body of water **2** : to go boating in a punt

³punt *vi* : to play at a gambling game against the banker [French *ponter,* from *ponte* "point in some games", from Spanish *punto* "point", from Latin *punctum*]

⁴punt *vb* **1** : to make a punt **2** : to kick (a ball) by means of a punt [origin unknown]

⁵punt *n* : a kick of a ball which is dropped from the hands and hit before it touches the ground

punt•er \ˈpənt-ər\ *n* : one that punts

punt formation *n* : an offensive football formation in which a back making a punt stands approximately 10 yards (about 9 meters) behind the line and the other backs are in blocking position close to the line of scrimmage

pu•ny \ˈpyü-nē\ *adj* **pu•ni•er; -est** : slight or inferior in power, size, or importance : WEAK [Middle French *puisné* "younger", from *puis* "afterward" + *né* "born"] — **pu•ni•ness** *n*

△ **origin** *Puny* is a spelling adopted to reflect the pronunciation of *puisne,* from the Middle French *puisné,* "younger". The literal meaning of the French *puisné* is "born afterward", and in their earliest uses in English *puisne* and *puny* referred to someone younger than, or of inferior position to, someone else. In this sense it developed a specific legal meaning: a *puisne* (or *puny)* judge is a junior or subordinate judge in the superior courts. Very soon after being borrowed into English *puny* developed from its literal meaning the sense of "slight or inferior in power, vigor, size, or importance."

pup \'pəp\ *n* **:** a young dog; *also* **:** one of the young of various animals (as seals) **[**short for *puppy***]**

pu•pa \'pyü-pə\ *n, pl* **pu•pae** \-ˌpē, -ˌpī\ *or* **pupas :** the stage of an insect (as a bee, moth, or beetle) having complete metamorphosis that occurs between the larva and the adult, is usually enclosed in a cocoon or case, and undergoes internal changes by which larval structures are replaced by those of the adult **[**Latin, "girl, doll"**]** — **pu•pal** \'pyü-pəl\ *adj*

pu•par•i•um \pyü-'par-ē-əm, -'per-\ *n, pl* **pu•par•ia** \-ē-ə\ **:** an outer shell that covers the pupae of some insects (as a fly) and is formed from the skin of the larva **[**New Latin, from *pupa***]**

pu•pate \'pyü-ˌpāt\ *vi* **:** to become a pupa **:** pass through a pupal stage — **pu•pa•tion** \pyü-'pā-shən\ *n*

[1]**pu•pil** \'pyü-pəl\ *n* **1 :** a child or young person in school or in the charge of a tutor **:** STUDENT **2 :** one who has been taught or influenced by a famous or distinguished person **[**Middle French *pupille* "minor ward", from Latin *pupillus* "male ward" (from *pupus* "boy") and *pupilla* "female ward", from *pupa* "girl, doll"**]**

△ **origin** In Latin a *pupa* was either a girl or a doll. Its diminutive *pupilla* had two senses. A person can see himself or herself reflected in miniature, like a little doll, in the eye of another. For this reason the opening in the iris which seems to hold this image was called a *pupilla.* Our English *pupil* was borrowed from the Middle French descendent of the Latin word. In Latin a little girl who was an orphan and a ward was also called a *pupilla,* her masculine counterpart being a *pupillus.* Middle French *pupille* served for both sexes. English *pupil* was originally used for a ward, but in the 16th century the word developed a new meaning, and a *pupil* became a student in the charge of a tutor or in school.

[2]**pupil** *n* **:** the usually round opening in the iris of the eye that contracts and expands to control the amount of light falling on the retina **[**Middle French *pupille,* from Latin *pupilla,* from *pupa* "girl, doll"; from the tiny image of oneself seen reflected in another's eye**]**

pu•pil•age *or* **pu•pil•lage** \'pyü-pə-lij\ *n* **:** the state or period of being a pupil

pup•pet \'pəp-ət\ *n* **1 a :** a small-scale figure (as of a person) usually with a cloth body and hollow head that fits over and is moved by the hand **b :** MARIONETTE **2 :** DOLL 1 **3 :** one whose acts are controlled by an outside force or influence **[**Middle French *poupette,* derived from Latin *pupa* "doll"**]**

pup•pe•teer \ˌpəp-ə-'tiər\ *n* **:** one who manipulates puppets

pup•pet•ry \'pəp-ə-trē\ *n, pl* **-ries :** the production or creation of puppets or puppet shows

pup•py \'pəp-ē\ *n, pl* **puppies :** a young domestic dog; *esp* **:** one less than a year old **[**Middle French *poupée* "doll, toy", derived from Latin *pupa* "doll"**]** — **pup•py•ish** \-ē-ish\ *adj*

pup tent *n* **:** a small low tent for two persons usually consisting of two halves fastened together

pur•blind \'pər-ˌblīnd\ *adj* **1 :** partly blind **2 :** lacking in vision, insight, or understanding **:** OBTUSE **[**obsolete *purblind* "wholly blind", from Middle English *pur blind,* from *pur* "purely, wholly", from *pur* "pure"**]** — **pur•blind•ly** *adv* — **pur•blind•ness** \-ˌblīnd-nəs, -ˌblīn-nəs\ *n*

[1]**pur•chase** \'pər-chəs\ *vt* **1 a :** to obtain by paying money or its equivalent **:** BUY ⟨*purchase* a house⟩ **b :** to obtain by labor, danger, or sacrifice **:** EARN **2 :** to apply a device for obtaining a mechanical advantage to (as something to be moved); *also* **:** to move by a purchase **[**Old French *purchacier* "to seek to obtain", from *pur-* "forward" (from Latin *pro-*) + *chacier* "to chase"**]** — **pur•chas•able** \-chə-sə-bəl\ *adj* — **pur•chas•er** *n*

[2]**purchase** *n* **1 :** an act or instance of purchasing **2 :** something purchased **3 a :** a mechanical hold or advantage applied to the raising or moving of heavy bodies **b :** an apparatus or device by which advantage is gained **4 :** a secure, hold, grasp, or place to stand ⟨could not get a *purchase* on the ledge⟩

pur•dah \'pərd-ə\ *n* **:** seclusion of women from public observation among Muslims and some Hindus especially in India **[**Hindi *parda,* literally, "screen, veil"**]**

pure \'pyu̇r\ *adj* **1 a :** not mixed with anything else ⟨*pure* gold⟩ **b :** free from dust, dirt, or taint ⟨*pure* food⟩ **2 a :** nothing other than **:** SHEER ⟨*pure* nonsense⟩ **b :** ABSTRACT 3a, THEORETICAL ⟨*pure* science⟩ ⟨*pure* mathematics⟩ **3 a :** free from sin or moral guilt; *esp* **:** marked by chastity **b :** of unmixed ancestry **c :** breeding true for one or more characters **[**Old French *pur,* from Latin *purus***]** **syn** see CHASTE — **pure•ness** *n*

pure•blood \-ˌbləd\ *or* **pure–blood•ed** \-'bləd-əd\ *adj* **:** of unmixed ancestry **:** PUREBRED — **pureblood** *n*

pure•bred \-'bred\ *adj* **:** bred from members of a recognized breed, strain, or kind without admixture of other blood over many generations — **pure•bred** \-ˌbred\ *n*

[1]**pu•ree** \pyu̇-'rā, -'rē\ *n* **1 :** a paste or thick liquid suspension usually produced by rubbing cooked food through a sieve **2 :** a thick soup having pureed vegetables as a base **[**French, from *purer* "to purify, strain", from Latin *purare* "to purify", from *purus* "pure"**]**

[2]**puree** *vt* **pu•reed; pu•ree•ing :** to reduce to a pulp by cooking and then rub through a sieve

pure line *n* **:** an essentially homozygous strain (as of Indian corn) usually formed by repeated selfing — **pure–line** *adj*

pure•ly \'pyu̇r-lē\ *adv* **1 :** without admixture of anything injurious or foreign **2 :** MERELY ⟨read *purely* for relaxation⟩ **3 :** in a chaste manner **4 :** WHOLLY 1

[1]**pur•ga•tive** \'pər-gət-iv\ *adj* **:** purging or tending to purge; *esp* **:** causing a usually marked looseness of the bowels ⟨the *purgative* effect of green apples⟩

[2]**purgative** *n* **:** a strong laxative

pur•ga•to•ri•al \ˌpər-gə-'tōr-ē-əl, -'tȯr-\ *adj* **1 :** cleansing of sin **:** EXPIATORY **2 :** of or relating to purgatory

pur•ga•to•ry \'pər-gə-ˌtōr-ē, -ˌtȯr-\ *n, pl* **-ries 1 :** an intermediate state after death in which according to Roman Catholic doctrine the souls of those who die in God's grace but without having made full satisfaction for their sins are purified by suffering **2 :** a place or state of temporary punishment **[**Medieval Latin *purgatorium,* from Late Latin *purgatorius* "purging", from Latin *purgare* "to purge"**]**

[1]**purge** \'pərj\ *vb* **1 a :** to clear of sin or guilt **b :** to cleanse or purify by separating and carrying off impurities **2 :** to become free of impurities or excess matter through a cleansing process **3 :** to remove by cleansing **4 :** to have or cause vigorous and usually repeated evacuation of the bowels **5 :** to get rid of (as undesirable persons) **[**Old French *purgier,* from Latin *purgare* "to purify, purge", from *purus* "pure"**]** — **pur•ga•tion** \ˌpər-'gā-shən\ *n* — **purg•er** *n*

[2]**purge** *n* **1 a :** an act or instance of purging **b :** a ridding of persons regarded as treacherous or disloyal **2 :** something that purges; *esp* **:** PURGATIVE

pu•ri•fi•ca•tion \ˌpyu̇r-ə-fə-'kā-shən\ *n* **:** an act or instance of purifying or of being purified

pu•ri•fi•ca•tor \'pyu̇r-ə-fə-ˌkāt-ər\ *n* **1 :** one that purifies **2 :** a linen cloth used to wipe the chalice after celebration of the Eucharist

pu•rif•i•ca•to•ry \pyu̇r-'if-i-kə-ˌtōr-ē, 'pyu̇r-ə-fə-kə-, -ˌtȯr-\ *adj* **:** serving, tending, or intended to purify

pu•ri•fy \'pyu̇r-ə-ˌfī\ *vb* **-fied; -fy•ing 1 :** to make pure **:** free from anything alien, extraneous, corrupting, polluting, or damaging **2 :** to grow or become pure or clean — **pu•ri•fi•er** \-ˌfī-ər, -ˌfīr\ *n*

Pu•rim \'pu̇r-ˌim, pu̇r-'\ *n* **:** a Jewish holiday celebrated in February or March in commemoration of the deliverance of the Jews from the massacre plotted by Haman **[**Hebrew *pūrīm***]**

pu•rine \'pyu̇r-ˌēn\ *n* **:** any of several bases (as adenine or guanine) that include fundamental constituents of DNA and RNA **[**German *purin,* from Latin *purus* "pure" + New Latin *uricus* "uric" + German *-in* "ine"**]**

pur•ism \'pyu̇r-ˌiz-əm\ *n* **:** rigid adherence to or insistence of nicety especially in use of words — **pur•ist** \-əst\ *n* — **pu•ris•tic** \pyu̇r-'is-tik\ *adj*

pu•ri•tan \'pyu̇r-ət-n\ *n* **1** *cap* **:** a member of a 16th and 17th century Protestant group in England and New England opposing as unscriptural many traditional customs of the Church of England **2 :** one who practices or preaches or follows a stricter moral code than that which prevails **[**probably from

Late Latin *puritas* "purity"] — **puritan** *adj, often cap* — **pu·ri·tan·i·cal** \ˌpyu̇r-ə-ˈtan-i-kəl\ *adj* — **pu·ri·tan·i·cal·ly** \-kə-lē, -klē\ *adv* — **pu·ri·tan·ism** \ˈpyu̇r-ət-n-ˌiz-əm\ *n, often cap*

pu·ri·ty \ˈpyu̇r-ət-ē\ *n* : the quality or state of being pure [Old French *pureté,* from Late Latin *puritas,* from Latin *purus* "pure"]

¹purl \ˈpərl\ *n* : an intertwining of thread through the loop of a stitch along an edge (as in buttonholing) [obsolete *pirl* "to twist"]

²purl *vb* : to knit in purl stitch

³purl *n* **1** : a purling or swirling stream or rill **2** : a gentle murmur or movement (as of purling water) [perhaps of Scandinavian origin]

⁴purl *vi* **1** : EDDY, SWIRL **2** : to make a soft murmuring sound like that of a purling stream

pur·lieu \ˈpərl-ˌyü\ *n* **1 a** : a place of resort : HAUNT **b** *pl* : ²BOUND 3 **2 a** : an outlying or adjacent district **b** *pl* : ENVIRONMENT 1 [Middle English *purlewe* "land severed from a royal forest by perambulation", from Anglo-French *puralé* "perambulation", from Old French *puraler* "to go through", from *pur-* "for, through" + *aler* "to go"]

pur·lin \ˈpər-lən\ *n* : a horizontal member in a roof supporting the rafters [origin unknown]

pur·loin \pər-ˈlȯin, ˌpər-ˈ, ˈpər-ˌ\ *vt* : STEAL 2a, FILCH [Anglo-French *purloigner* "to put away", from Old French *porloigner* "to put off, delay", from *por-* "forward" + *loing* "at a distance", from Latin *longe,* from *longus* "long"] — **pur·loin·er** *n*

purl stitch *n* : a knitting stitch usually made with the yarn at the front of the work by inserting the right needle into the front of a loop on the left needle from the right, catching the yarn with the right needle, and bringing it through to form a new loop — compare KNIT STITCH

¹pur·ple \ˈpər-pəl\ *adj* **1** : of the color purple **2** : highly rhetorical : ORNATE ⟨*purple* prose⟩ [Middle English *purpel,* alteration of *purper,* from Old English *purpuran* "of purple", from *purpure* "purple color", from Latin *purpura,* from Greek *porphyra*]

²purple *n* **1 a** : TYRIAN PURPLE **b** : a color about midway between red and blue **2 a** : cloth dyed purple **b** : a garment of purple cloth; *esp* : a robe worn as an emblem of rank or authority **3** : a mollusk yielding a purple dye and especially the Tyrian purple of ancient times **4** : a pigment or dye that colors purple **5** : imperial or regal rank or power : exalted station

³purple *vb* **pur·pled**; **pur·pling** \ˈpər-pə-ling, -pling\ : to turn purple

pur·plish \ˈpər-pə-lish, -plish\ *adj* : somewhat purple

¹pur·port \ˈpər-ˌpōrt, -ˌpȯrt\ *n* : meaning conveyed, professed, or implied : IMPORT; *also* : SUBSTANCE 1b, GIST [Anglo-French, "content, tenor", from *purporter* "to contain", from Old French *porporter* "to convey", from *por-* "forward" + *porter* "to carry"]

²pur·port \pər-ˈpōrt, ˌpər-ˈ, -ˈpȯrt\ *vt* : to profess outwardly but often deceptively : CLAIM

pur·port·ed *adj* : REPUTED 2, RUMORED — **pur·port·ed·ly** *adv*

¹pur·pose \ˈpər-pəs\ *n* **1 a** : something set up as an end to be attained : INTENTION **b** : RESOLUTION 5b, DETERMINATION **2** : an object or result aimed at or achieved **3** : a subject under discussion [Old French *purpos,* from *purposer* "to purpose", from Latin *proponere* "to propose"] **syn** see INTENTION — **pur·pose·ful** \-fəl\ *adj* — **pur·pose·ful·ly** \-fə-lē\ *adv* — **pur·pose·ful·ness** \-fəl-nəs\ *n* — **pur·pose·less** \-ləs\ *adj* — **on purpose** : by intent : INTENTIONALLY

²purpose *vt* : to have in mind as a purpose : INTEND, PROPOSE

pur·pose·ly \ˈpər-pəs-lē\ *adv* : with a deliberate or express purpose

pur·pos·ive \ˈpər-pə-siv\ *adj* **1** : serving or effecting a useful end though not clearly as a result of design **2** : having or tending to fulfill a conscious purpose or design : PURPOSEFUL — **pur·pos·ive·ly** *adv* — **pur·pos·ive·ness** *n*

purr \ˈpər\ *n* : the characteristic low vibrating murmur of an apparently contented or pleased cat [imitative] — **purr** *vb*

¹purse \ˈpərs\ *n* **1 a** : a small bag or pouch usually closed with a drawstring or snap and used to carry money **b** : a container (as a handbag) used to carry money and often small objects **2 a** : FUND 2b, RESOURCES **b** : a sum of money offered as a prize or present [Old English *purs,* from Medieval Latin *bursa,* from Late Latin, "hide of an ox", from Greek *byrsa*]

²purse *vt* **1** : to put into a purse **2** : PUCKER, KNIT ⟨*purse* one's lips⟩

purse–proud \-ˌprau̇d\ *adj* : proud of one's wealth

purs·er \ˈpər-sər\ *n* : an official on a ship who keeps accounts and supervises the care of passengers

purs·lane \ˈpər-slən, -ˌslān\ *n* : a fleshy-leaved trailing plant with tiny bright yellow flowers that is a common troublesome weed but is sometimes used as a potherb or in salads [Middle French *porcelaine,* from Late Latin *porcillago,* from Latin *porcillaca,* alteration of *portulaca*]

pur·su·ance \pər-ˈsü-əns\ *n* : the act of pursuing or carrying out ⟨in *pursuance* of their plans⟩

pur·su·ant to \-ənt-\ *prep* : in carrying out : in conformance to : according to

pur·sue \pər-ˈsü\ *vt* **1** : to follow in order to overtake and capture or destroy **2** : to try to obtain or accomplish : SEEK ⟨*pursue* pleasure⟩ **3** : to proceed along : FOLLOW ⟨*pursue* a northerly course⟩ **4** : to engage in : PRACTICE ⟨*pursue* a hobby⟩ **5** : HARASS, HAUNT ⟨*pursued* by fears of bankruptcy⟩ **6** : COURT 2a, WOO [Anglo-French *pursuer,* from Old French *poursuir,* from Latin *prosequi,* from *pro-* "forward" + *sequi* "to follow"] **syn** see CHASE — **pur·su·er** *n*

pur·suit \pər-ˈsüt\ *n* **1** : the act of pursuing **2** : an activity that one engages in especially as a vocation [Old French *poursuite,* from *poursuir* "to pursue"]

pur·sui·vant \ˈpər-swi-vənt, -si-\ *n* : a person ranking below a herald but having similar duties [Middle French *poursuivant* "attendant of a herald", literally, "follower", from *poursuir, poursuivre* "to pursue"]

pur·sy \ˈpəs-ē, ˈpər-sē\ *or* **pus·sy** \ˈpəs-ē\ *adj* **pur·si·er** *or* **pus·si·er**; **-est 1** : short-winded especially because of corpulence **2** : too fat especially from self-indulgent or luxurious living [Anglo-French *pursif,* from Middle French *polsif,* from *poulser, polser* "to beat, push, pant"] — **pur·si·ness** *n*

pu·ru·lent \ˈpyu̇r-yə-lənt, ˈpyu̇r-ə-\ *adj* : containing, consisting of, or accompanied by the formation of pus ⟨a *purulent* fever⟩ [Latin *purulentus,* from *pur-, pus* "pus"] — **pu·ru·lence** \-ləns\ *n*

pur·vey \pər-ˈvā, ˌpər-ˈ, ˈpər-ˌ\ *vt* : to supply (as provisions) usually as a business **2** : CIRCULATE 2b [Middle French *porveeir,* from Latin *providēre* "to provide"] — **pur·vey·ance** \-əns\ *n*

pur·vey·or \-ər\ *n* : one that purveys something (as provisions or news); *esp* : CATERER

pur·view \ˈpər-ˌvyü\ *n* **1** : the range or limit of authority, competence, responsibility, concern, or intention **2** : range of vision, understanding, or awareness [Middle English *purveu* "provision of a statute", from Anglo-French *purveu est* "it is provided" (opening phrase of a statute)]

pus \ˈpəs\ *n* : thick cloudy usually yellowish white fluid matter formed at a place of inflammation and infection (as an abscess) and containing white blood cells, tissue debris, and microorganisms [Latin]

¹push \ˈpu̇sh\ *vb* **1 a** : to press against with force in order to drive or impel **b** : to exert or use pressure ⟨*push* on the door⟩ **2** : to thrust forward, downward, or outward ⟨plants *pushing* roots into the soil⟩ **3 a** : to press or urge forward **b** : to carry on with vigor or effectiveness ⟨*push* a campaign⟩ **4** : to bear hard upon so as to involve in difficulty ⟨was *pushed* for money⟩ **5** : to exert oneself continuously, vigorously, or obtrusively to gain an end (as social advancement) **6** : to engage in the sale of (illicit drugs) [Old French *poulser* "to beat, push", from Latin *pulsare,* from *pulsus,* past participle of *pellere* "to drive, strike"] — **push·er** *n*

• **syn** PUSH, SHOVE, THRUST, PROPEL mean to cause to move ahead or aside by force. PUSH implies application of force by a body already in contact with the body to be moved; SHOVE implies a fast or rough pushing of something usually along a surface; THRUST suggests less steadiness and greater violence than PUSH ⟨*thrust* a knife into the crack⟩ PROPEL suggests rapidly driving forward or onward by force applied in any manner.

²push *n* **1** : a vigorous advance against obstacles **2** : a condition or occasion of stress : EMERGENCY **3** : an act of pushing: as **a** : a sudden thrust : SHOVE **b** : a steady application of physical force in a direction away from the body exerting it **c** : a stimulating effect or action ⟨the holiday business gave retail trade a *push*⟩

push–but·ton \ˌpu̇sh-ˌbət-n\ *adj* : using or dependent on complex and more or less automatic mechanisms ⟨*push-button* warfare⟩

push button *n* **:** a small button or knob that when pushed operates something especially by closing an electric circuit

push•cart \'pu̇sh-ˌkärt\ *n* **:** a cart or barrow pushed by hand

push•ing *adj* **1 :** ENTERPRISING **2 :** tactlessly forward **:** PUSHY

push off *vi* **:** to set out **:** LEAVE

push•over \'pu̇sh-ˌō-vər\ *n* **1 :** an opponent easy to defeat or a victim incapable of effective resistance **2 :** someone unwilling or unable to resist the power of a particular attraction or appeal **3 :** something accomplished without difficulty **:** SNAP ⟨the test was a *pushover*⟩

Push•tu \'pəsh-tü\ *variant of* PASHTO

push–up \'pu̇sh-ˌəp\ *n* **:** a conditioning exercise performed in a prone position by bending and straightening the arms while keeping the body straight supported on the hands and toes

pushy \'pu̇sh-ē\ *adj* **push•i•er**; **-est :** aggressive often to an objectionable degree **:** FORWARD — **push•i•ly** \'pu̇sh-ə-lē\ *adv* — **push•i•ness** \'pu̇sh-ē-nəs\ *n*

pu•sil•la•nim•i•ty \ˌpyü-sə-lə-'nim-ət-ē\ *n* **:** the quality or state of being pusillanimous

pu•sil•lan•i•mous \ˌpyü-sə-'lan-ə-məs\ *adj* **:** lacking courage and resolution **:** COWARDLY **[**Late Latin *pusillanimis,* from Latin *pusillus* "very small" (from *pusus* "small child") + *animus* "spirit"**]** — **pu•sil•lan•i•mous•ly** *adv*

[1]puss \'pu̇s\ *n* **1 :** CAT 1a **2 :** GIRL 1 **[**origin unknown**]**

[2]puss *n, slang* **:** FACE 1 **[**Irish Gaelic *pus* "mouth"**]**

puss•ley \'pəs-lē\ *n* **:** PURSLANE **[**by alteration**]**

[1]pussy \'pu̇s-ē\ *n, pl* **puss•ies 1 :** PUSS 1 **2 :** a catkin of the pussy willow

[2]pus•sy \'pəs-ē\ *adj* **pus•si•er**; **-est :** full of or resembling pus

[3]pus•sy *variant of* PURSY

pussy•foot \'pu̇s-ē-ˌfu̇t\ *vi* **1 :** to tread or move warily or stealthily **2 :** to avoid committing oneself **:** HEDGE

pussy willow \ˌpu̇s-ē-\ *n* **:** a willow having large cylindrical silky catkins

pus•tu•lar \'pəs-chə-lər\ *adj* **1 :** of, relating to, marked by, or resembling pustules ⟨a *pustular* eruption⟩ **2 :** covered with pustules ⟨a *pustular* leaf⟩

pus•tule \'pəs-chül\ *n* **1 :** a small elevation of the skin having an inflamed base and containing pus **2 :** a small elevation resembling a pimple or blister **[**Latin *pustula***]**

[1]put \'pu̇t\ *vb* **put**; **put•ting 1 a :** to place in a particular position or relationship ⟨*put* the book down⟩ **b :** to cause to move or go ⟨*put* a fist through the window⟩ ⟨*put* the ball into right field⟩ **c :** to throw with an overhand pushing motion ⟨*put* the shot⟩ **d :** to bring into a specified state or condition ⟨*put* it to use⟩ ⟨*put* the matter right⟩ **2 a :** to cause to suffer something ⟨*put* them to death⟩ **b :** IMPOSE, INFLICT ⟨*put* a special tax on luxuries⟩ **c :** to apply to some end ⟨*put* their skills to use⟩ **3 :** to set before one for judgment or decision (as by a formal vote) **4 :** to give expression to especially in intelligible language **:** TRANSLATE ⟨*put* your feelings into words⟩ ⟨*put* the poem into English⟩ **5 a :** to devote or urge to an activity or end ⟨*put* your mind to the problem⟩ ⟨*put* them to work⟩ **b :** INVEST ⟨*put* money in land⟩ **6 a :** to give as an estimate ⟨*put* the time at about eleven⟩ **b :** ATTACH, ATTRIBUTE ⟨*puts* a high value on friendship⟩ **c :** IMPUTE ⟨*put* the blame on your partner⟩ **7 a :** to commence a voyage ⟨the ship *put* to sea shorthanded⟩ **b :** to take a course ⟨*put* into a sheltered bay⟩ **[**Middle English *putten***]** — **put forth 1 :** to bring into action **:** EXERT **2 :** to produce or send out by growth ⟨*put forth* leaves⟩ **3 :** to start out — **put forward :** PROPOSE ⟨*put forward* a theory⟩ — **put in mind :** REMIND — **put to it :** to give difficulty to ⟨had been *put to it* to keep up⟩ — **put up with :** TOLERATE 1, ENDURE

[2]put *n* **:** a throw made usually with an overhand pushing motion

put about *vb* **:** to change or cause to change course or direction ⟨*put* the ship *about*⟩

put across *vt* **:** to achieve or convey successfully ⟨*put across* a plan⟩ ⟨*put* an idea *across*⟩

pu•ta•tive \'pyüt-ət-iv\ *adj* **:** commonly accepted or supposed to exist ⟨*putative* racial superiority⟩ ⟨a *putative* conspiracy⟩ **[**Late Latin *putativus,* from Latin *putare* "to think"**]** — **pu•ta•tive•ly** *adv*

put away *vt* **1 :** DISCARD 2, RENOUNCE **2 :** to consume by eating or drinking **3 :** to confine especially in a mental institution

put by *vt* **:** to lay aside **:** SAVE ⟨had some money *put by*⟩

put down *vt* **1 :** to bring to an end by force ⟨*put down* a riot⟩ **2 a :** DEPOSE 1, DEGRADE **b :** DISPARAGE, BELITTLE ⟨mentioned my poetry only to *put* it *down*⟩ **c :** DISAPPROVE, CRITICIZE ⟨were *put down* for the way they dressed⟩ **d :** HUMILIATE, SQUELCH ⟨was *put down* with a sharp retort⟩ **3 :** to make ineffective **:** CHECK **4 a :** to write down (as in a list) **b :** to assign to a particular category or cause **5 :** to preserve for future use ⟨*put down* a cask of pickles⟩

put in *vb* **1 :** to make or make as a request, offer, or declaration ⟨*put in* a plea of not guilty⟩ ⟨*put in* for a job at the store⟩ **2 :** to spend (time) at some activity or place ⟨*put in* six hours at the office⟩ **3 :** PLANT ⟨*put in* a crop⟩ **4 :** to call at or enter a place; *esp* **:** to enter a harbor or port

put off *vt* **1 :** DISCONCERT, REPEL ⟨*put off* by their indifference⟩ **2 a :** to hold back to a later time **:** DEFER ⟨*put off* a visit to the dentist⟩ **b :** to induce to wait ⟨*put* the bill collector *off*⟩ **3 :** to rid oneself of

put on *vt* **1 a :** to dress oneself in **b :** to assume as if a garment **:** ADOPT ⟨*put on* airs⟩; *also* **:** FEIGN ⟨*put on* a show of anger⟩ **2 :** EXAGGERATE 1 ⟨they are *putting* it *on* when they make such claims⟩ **3 :** PERFORM, PRODUCE ⟨*put on* an entertaining act⟩ **4 :** to mislead deliberately especially for amusement ⟨you're *putting* me *on*⟩ — **put–on** *adj*

put•out \'pu̇t-ˌau̇t\ *n* **:** the act or an instance of causing a base runner or batter to be out in baseball

put out \pu̇t-'au̇t, 'pu̇t-\ *vb* **1 :** EXERT, USE ⟨*put out* all their strength to move the piano⟩ **2 :** to cause to cease to burn or glow **3 :** PRODUCE ⟨*puts out* a lot of work in eight hours⟩ **4 a :** IRRITATE, PROVOKE ⟨*put out* by our tardiness⟩ **b :** INCONVENIENCE ⟨don't *put* yourself *out* for us⟩ **5 :** to cause to be out (as in baseball) **6 :** to set out from shore

put over *vt* **:** to put across ⟨*put over* a scheme⟩ ⟨they're always trying to *put* something *over* on me⟩

pu•tre•fac•tion \ˌpyü-trə-'fak-shən\ *n* **1 :** the rotting of organic matter; *esp* **:** bacterial or fungal decay of proteins with the formation of foul-smelling incompletely oxidized products **2 :** the state of being putrefied **:** CORRUPTION **[**Late Latin *putrefactio,* from Latin *putrefacere* "to putrefy"**]** — **pu•tre•fac•tive** \-'fak-tiv\ *adj*

pu•tre•fy \'pyü-trə-ˌfī\ *vb* **-fied**; **-fy•ing :** to make or become putrid **:** DECOMPOSE, ROT **[**Latin *putrefacere,* from *putrēre* "to be rotten" + *facere* "to make"**]**

pu•tres•cent \pyü-'tres-nt\ *adj* **:** becoming putrid **:** ROTTING — **pu•tres•cence** \-ns\ *n*

pu•trid \'pyü-trəd\ *adj* **1 a :** being in a state of putrefaction **:** ROTTEN ⟨*putrid* meat⟩ **b :** characteristic of putrefaction **:** FOUL ⟨a *putrid* odor⟩ **2 a :** morally corrupt **b :** totally disagreeable or objectionable **:** VILE **[**Latin *putridus,* from *putrēre* "to be rotten", from *puter, putris* "rotten"**]** — **pu•trid•i•ty** \pyü-'trid-ət-ē\ *n* — **pu•trid•ly** \'pyü-trəd-lē\ *adv* — **pu•trid•ness** *n*

putsch \'pu̇ch\ *n* **:** a secretly plotted and suddenly executed attempt to overthrow a government **[**German**]**

putt \'pət\ *n* **:** a golf stroke made on a putting green to cause the ball to roll toward the hole **[**alteration of [2]*put***]** — **putt** *vb*

put•tee \ˌpə-'tē, pu̇-; 'pət-ē\ *n* **1 :** a cloth strip wrapped around the leg from ankle to knee **2 :** a leather legging secured by a strap or catch or by laces **[**Hindi *paṭṭī* "strip of cloth", from Sanskrit *paṭṭikā***]**

[1]put•ter \'pu̇t-ər\ *n* **:** one that puts

[2]putt•er \'pət-ər\ *n* **:** a golf club used in putting

[3]put•ter \'pət-ər\ *vi* **1 :** to move or act aimlessly or idly **:** DAWDLE **2 :** to work at random **:** TINKER **[**alteration of *potter***]** — **put•ter•er** \-ər-ər\ *n*

put through *vt* **:** to carry to a successful conclusion **:** EFFECT ⟨*put* a reform *through*⟩

putt•ing green \'pət-ing-\ *n* **:** a smooth usually grassy area around the hole into which the ball must be played in golf

put to *vi* **:** to put in to shore (as for shelter)

[1]put•ty \'pət-ē\ *n, pl* **putties :** a cement usually made of whiting and boiled linseed oil beaten or kneaded to the consistency of dough and used in fastening glass in sashes and stopping crevices in woodwork; *also* **:** any of various substances resembling such cement in appearance, consistency, or use **[**French *potée,* literally, "potful", from *pot* "pot"**]**

[2]putty *vt* **put•tied**; **put•ty•ing :** to cement or seal with putty

\ə\ **abut**	\au̇\ **out**	\i\ **tip**	\ȯ\ **saw**	\u̇\ **foot**
\ər\ **further**	\ch\ **chin**	\ī\ **life**	\ȯi\ **coin**	\y\ **yet**
\a\ **mat**	\e\ **pet**	\j\ **job**	\th\ **thin**	\yü\ **few**
\ā\ **take**	\ē\ **easy**	\ng\ **sing**	\t͟h\ **this**	\yu̇\ **cure**
\ä\ **cot, cart**	\g\ **go**	\ō\ **bone**	\ü\ **food**	\zh\ **vision**

put–up \ˌpu̇t-ˌəp\ *adj* : arranged secretly beforehand ⟨a *put-up* job⟩

put up \pu̇t-ˈəp, ˈpu̇t-\ *vb* **1 a :** to prepare for later use ⟨*put up* a lunch⟩; *esp* **:** CAN ⟨*put up* peaches⟩ **b :** to put away out of use ⟨*put up* your sword⟩ **2 :** to nominate for election **3 :** to offer for public sale ⟨*put* the furniture *up* for auction⟩ **4 :** to give or obtain food and shelter **:** LODGE ⟨*put* us *up* overnight⟩ **5 :** BUILD 1, ERECT **6 :** CARRY ON 3 ⟨*put up* a struggle against odds⟩ **7 :** to offer as a prize or stake — **put up to :** INCITE, INSTIGATE — **put up with :** TOLERATE 1, ENDURE

[1]puz•zle \ˈpəz-əl\ *vb* **puz•zled; puz•zling** \ˈpəz-ling, -ə-ling\ **1 :** to confuse the understanding of **:** PERPLEX, BEWILDER **2 :** to solve with difficulty or ingenuity ⟨*puzzled* out the mystery⟩ **3 :** to be uncertain as to action or choice **4 :** to seek for or grope after something in a confused or uncertain manner ⟨*puzzle* over a problem⟩ [origin unknown] — **puz•zler** \ˈpəz-lər, -ə-lər\ *n*

• syn PUZZLE, PERPLEX, MYSTIFY mean to baffle and disturb mentally. PUZZLE suggests some complication or contradiction difficult to understand or explain as a cause of mental confusion; PERPLEX usually adds an implication of causing worry and uncertainty in making a decision; MYSTIFY implies puzzling or perplexing thoroughly often by deliberate intent.

[2]puzzle *n* **1 :** PUZZLEMENT 1 **2 a :** something that puzzles **b :** a question, problem, or contrivance designed for testing ingenuity

puz•zle•ment \ˈpəz-əl-mənt\ *n* **1 :** the state of being puzzled **:** PERPLEXITY **2 :** PUZZLE 2a

py- *or* **pyo-** *combining form* **:** pus ⟨pyemia⟩ ⟨pyorrhea⟩ [Greek *pyon*]

pyc•nom•e•ter \pik-ˈnäm-ət-ər\ *n* **:** a standard vessel for measuring and comparing the densities of liquids or solids [Greek *pyknos* "dense"]

py•emia \pī-ˈē-mē-ə\ *n* **:** infection of the blood with pus-forming bacteria accompanied by multiple abscesses — **py•emic** \-mik\ *adj*

py•gid•i•um \pī-ˈjid-ē-əm\ *n, pl* **-ia** \-ē-ə\ **:** a tail or terminal body region of an invertebrate [New Latin, from Greek *pygidion* "small rump", from *pygē* "rump"] — **py•gid•i•al** \-ē-əl\ *adj*

pyg•my *also* **pig•my** \ˈpig-mē\ *n, pl* **pygmies 1** *often cap* **:** one of a race of dwarfs described by ancient Greek authors **2** *cap* **:** one of a small people of equatorial Africa ranging under five feet in height **3 :** a person or thing very small for its kind **:** DWARF [Latin *pygmaeus* "of a pygmy, dwarfish", from Greek *pygmaios*, from *pygmē*, a measure of length, literally "fist"] — **pygmy** *adj*

py•ja•mas \pə-ˈjä-məz\ *chiefly British variant of* PAJAMAS

py•lon \ˈpī-ˌlän, -lən\ *n* **1 :** a usually massive gateway; *esp* **:** an ancient Egyptian one composed of two flat-topped pyramids and a crosspiece **2 :** a tower for supporting either end of a wire over a long span **3 :** a projection (as a post or tower) marking a prescribed course of flight for an airplane [Greek *pylōn*, from *pylē* "gate"]

py•lo•ric \pī-ˈlōr-ik, pə-, -ˈlȯr-\ *adj* **:** of or relating to the pylorus; *also* **:** of, relating to, or situated in or near the posterior part of the stomach

py•lo•rus \-ˈlōr-əs, -ˈlȯr-\ *n, pl* **-lo•ri** \-ˈlōr-ˌī, -ˈlȯr-, -ˌē\ **:** the opening from the stomach to the intestine of a vertebrate [Late Latin, from Greek *pylōros*, literally, "one who guards a gate", from *pylē* "gate"]

pyo•gen•ic \ˌpī-ə-ˈjen-ik\ *adj* **:** producing pus **:** marked by pus production

py•or•rhea \ˌpī-ə-ˈrē-ə\ *n* **:** a pussy inflammation of the sockets of the teeth leading usually to loosening of the teeth — **py•or•rhe•al** \-ˈrē-əl\ *adj*

pyr- *or* **pyro-** *combining form* **:** fire **:** heat ⟨pyromania⟩ [Greek *pyr* "fire"]

[1]pyr•a•mid \ˈpir-ə-ˌmid\ *n* **1 :** a massive structure built especially in ancient Egypt that usually has a square base and four triangular faces meeting at a point and contains tombs **2 a :** something felt to resemble a pyramid (as in shape or in broad-based organization) ⟨the social *pyramid*⟩ **b :** one of the conical masses that project from the medulla into the cavity of the kidney pelvis **3 :** a polyhedron having for its base a plane figure with three or more angles and for its sides three or more triangles that meet to form the vertex [Latin *pyramid-, pyramis*, from Greek] — **py•ram•i•dal** \pə-ˈram-əd-l, ˌpir-ə-ˈmid-l\ *adj* — **py•ram•i•dal•ly** \-ē\ *adv* — **pyr•a•mid•i•cal** \ˌpir-ə-ˈmid-i-kəl\ *adj*

[2]pyramid *vb* **1 :** to increase rapidly and progressively step by step on a broad base **2 :** to arrange or build up as if on the base of a pyramid

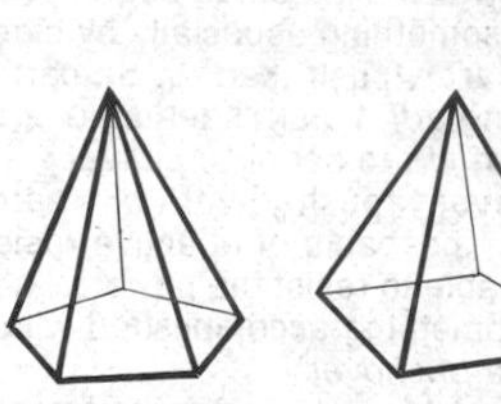

[1]pyramid 3

pyre \ˈpīr\ *n* **:** a combustible heap for burning a dead body as a funeral rite; *also* **:** a pile of material to be burned [Latin *pyra*, from Greek, from *pyr* "fire"]

py•re•noid \pī-ˈrē-ˌnȯid, ˈpī-rə-\ *n* **:** one of the protein bodies in the chromatophores of various lower organisms (as some algae) that act as centers for starch deposition [Greek *pyrēn* "stone of a fruit"]

py•re•thrin \pī-ˈrē-thrən, -ˈreth-rən\ *n* **:** either of two oily liquid esters having insecticidal properties and occurring especially in pyrethrum flowers

py•re•thrum \-ˈrē-thrəm, -ˈreth-rəm\ *n* **1 :** any of several chrysanthemums with finely divided often aromatic leaves including ornamentals as well as important sources of insecticides **2 :** an insecticide made from the dried heads of some Old World pyrethrums [Latin, a plant resembling yarrow, from Greek *pyrethron*, from *pyr* "fire"]

Py•rex \ˈpī-ˌreks\ *trademark* — used for glass and glassware resistant to heat, chemicals, or electricity

pyr•i•dine \ˈpir-ə-ˌdēn\ *n* **:** a toxic water-soluble flammable liquid organic base C_5H_5N of pungent odor used as a solvent and in the manufacture of pharmaceuticals [derived from Greek *pyr* "fire"]

pyr•i•dox•ine *also* **pyr•i•dox•in** \ˌpir-ə-ˈdäk-ˌsēn, -sən\ *n* **:** a crystalline alcohol of the vitamin B_6 group found especially in cereals and convertible in the organism into phosphate compounds that are essential coenzymes [*pyridine* + *ox-* + *-ine*]

pyr•i•form \ˈpir-ə-ˌfȯrm\ *adj* **:** having the form of a pear [Medieval Latin *pyrum* "pear", from Latin *pirum*]

py•rim•i•dine \pī-ˈrim-ə-ˌdēn, pə-\ *n* **:** any of several bases (as cytosine or thymine) that include fundamental constituents of DNA and RNA [alteration of *pyridine*]

py•rite \ˈpī-ˌrīt\ *n* **:** a common mineral FeS_2 that consists of iron disulfide, has a pale brass-yellow color and metallic luster, and is burned in making sulfur dioxide and sulfuric acid [Latin *pyrites* "flint"]

py•rites \pə-ˈrīt-ēz, pī-; ˈpī-ˌrīts\ *n, pl* **pyrites :** any of various metallic-looking sulfides of which pyrite is the commonest [Latin, "flint", from Greek *pyritēs* "of fire", from *pyr* "fire"]

py•ro•lu•site \ˌpī-rō-ˈlü-ˌsīt\ *n* **:** a mineral MnO_2 consisting of manganese dioxide that is of an iron-black or dark steel-gray color and metallic luster, is usually soft, and is the most important ore of manganese [German *pyrolusit*, from Greek *pyr* "fire" + *lousis* "washing", from *louein* "to wash"]

py•rol•y•sis \pī-ˈräl-ə-səs\ *n* **:** chemical change brought about by the action of heat

py•ro•ma•nia \ˌpī-rō-ˈmā-nē-ə, -nyə\ *n* **:** a compulsive urge to start fires — **py•ro•ma•ni•ac** \-nē-ˌak\ *n*

py•rom•e•ter \pī-ˈräm-ət-ər\ *n* **:** an instrument for measuring temperatures especially when above the range of mercurial thermometers — **py•ro•met•ric** \ˌpī-rə-ˈme-trik\ *adj* — **py•ro•met•ri•cal•ly** \-tri-kə-lē, -klē\ *adv* — **py•rom•e•try** \pī-ˈräm-ə-trē\ *n*

py•rope \ˈpī-ˌrōp\ *n* **:** a magnesium-aluminum garnet that is deep red in color and is frequently used as a gem [Middle French *pirope*, a red gem, from Latin *pyropus*, a red bronze, from Greek *pyrōpos*, literally, "fiery-eyed", from *pyr* "fire" + *ōps* "eye"]

py•ro•phor•ic \ˌpī-rə-ˈfȯr-ik, -ˈfär-\ *adj* **1 :** igniting spontaneously **2 :** emitting sparks when scratched or struck especially with steel [Greek *pyrophoros* "fire-bearing", from *pyr* "fire" + *-phoros* "carrying", from *pherein* "to carry"]

py•ro•tech•nic \ˌpī-rə-ˈtek-nik\ *n* **1** *pl* **:** the art of making or the manufacture and use of fireworks **2** *pl* **a :** materials (as fireworks) for flares or signals **b :** a display of fireworks **3 :** a spectacular display (as of oratory) — usually used in pl. [derived from Greek *pyr* "fire" + *technē* "art"] — **pyrotechnic** *also*

py•ro•tech•ni•cal \-ni-kəl\ *adj* — **py•ro•tech•ni•cal•ly** \-ni-kə-le, -klē\ *adv* — **py•ro•tech•nist** \-'tek-nəst\ *n*

py•rox•ene \pī-'räk-ˌsēn\ *n* : any of various silicate minerals that usually contain magnesium or iron [French *pyroxène,* from Greek *pyr* "fire" + *xenos* "stranger"] — **py•rox•e•nic** \ˌpī-ˌräk-'sē-nik\ *adj*

py•rox•y•lin \pī-'räk-sə-lən\ *n* : a flammable substance resembling cotton that is produced chemically from cellulose and used in the manufacture of various products (as celluloid, lacquer, and some explosives) [*pyr-* + Greek *xylon* "wood"]

Pyr•rhic victory \ˌpir-ik-\ *n* : a victory won at excessive cost [*Pyrrhus,* died 272 B.C., king of Epirus who sustained heavy losses in defeating the Romans]

py•ru•vate \pī-'rü-ˌvāt\ *n* : a salt or ester of pyruvic acid

py•ru•vic acid \pī-ˌrü-vik-\ *n* : a 3-carbon liquid organic acid $C_3H_4O_3$ that is an important intermediate in carbohydrate metabolism and can be formed from either glucose or glycogen [*pyr-* + Latin *uva* "grape"; from its importance in fermentation]

Py•thag•o•re•an \pə-ˌthag-ə-'rē-ən, pī-\ *adj* : of, relating to, or associated with the Greek philosopher Pythagoras — **Pythagorean** *n*

Pythagorean numbers *n* : any set of three positive integers (as 3, 4, 5) that satisfy the equation $x^2 + y^2 = z^2$

Pythagorean theorem *n* : a theorem in geometry: the square of the length of the hypotenuse of a right triangle equals the sum of the squares of the lengths of the other two sides

Pyth•i•an \'pith-ē-ən\ *adj* : of or relating to the ancient Greek god Apollo especially as patron deity of Delphi [Latin *pythius* "of Delphi", from Greek *pythios,* from *Pythō* "Pytho", former name of Delphi]

Pythian Games *n pl* : an ancient Panhellenic festival similar to the Olympic Games celebrated at Delphi every four years in honor of Apollo

py•thon \'pī-ˌthän, -thən\ *n* : a large nonpoisonous constricting snake (as a boa); *esp* : any of an Old World genus of large snakes [Latin *Python,* a monstrous serpent killed by Apollo, from Greek *Pythōn*] — **py•tho•nine** \'pī-thə-ˌnīn\ *adj*

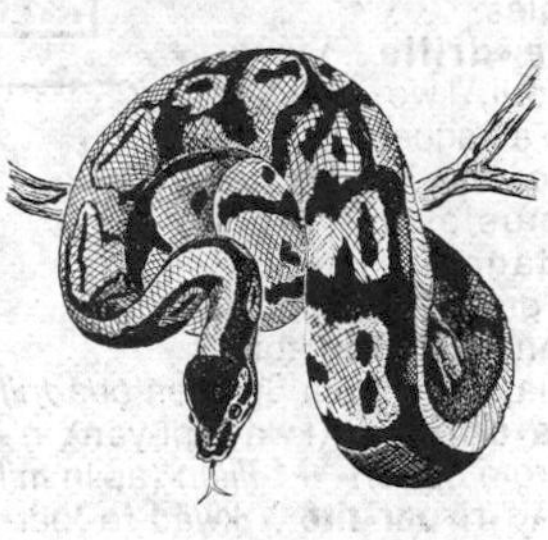
python

py•tho•ness \'pī-thə-nəs, 'pith-ə-\ *n* : a woman supposed to have a spirit of divination; *esp* : a priestess of Apollo held to have prophetic powers [Middle French *pithonisse,* from Late Latin *pythonissa,* from Greek *Pythōn,* spirit of divination, from *Pythō,* seat of the Delphic oracle] — **py•thon•ic** \pī-'thän-ik\ *adj*

pyx \'piks\ *n* : a small round case used to carry the Eucharist to the sick [Medieval Latin *pyxis,* from Latin, "box", from Greek]

Q q—quotient

q \'kyü\ *n, pl* **q's** *or* **qs** \'kyüz\ *often cap* : the seventeenth letter of the English alphabet

Q fever \'kyü-\ *n* : a disease marked by high fever, chills, and muscular pains, caused by a rickettsia, and transmitted by raw milk, by contact, or by ticks [*query*]

qt \'kyü-'tē\ *n, often cap Q & T* : QUIET — usually used in the phrase *on the qt* [abbreviation]

¹quack \'kwak\ *vi* : to utter the characteristic cry of a duck [imitative]

²quack *n* : a cry made by or as if by quacking

³quack *n* **1** : a person who pretends to have medical skill **2** : CHARLATAN [short for earlier *quacksalver,* from obsolete Dutch] — **quack•ery** \'kwak-rē, -ə-rē\ *n*

⁴quack *adj* : of, relating to, or characteristic of a quack; *esp* : pretending to cure diseases

quack grass *n* : a European grass that is naturalized throughout North America as a weed and spreads by creeping rhizomes — called also *couch grass, witchgrass* [derived from Old English *cwice*]

¹quad \'kwäd\ *n* : QUADRANGLE

²quad *n* : a type-metal space that is 1 en or more in width [derived from *quadrate*]

³quad *n* : QUADRUPLET

quad•ran•gle \'kwäd-ˌrang-gəl\ *n* **1** : a 4-sided enclosure especially when surrounded by buildings **2** : the buildings enclosing a quadrangle — **qua•dran•gu•lar** \kwä-'drang-gyə-lər\ *adj*

quad•rant \'kwäd-rənt\ *n* **1** : an instrument for measuring altitudes (as in astronomy or surveying) **2 a** : an arc of 90° : one quarter of a circle **b** : the area bounded by a quadrant and two radii **3** : any of the four quarters into which something is divided by two real or imaginary lines that intersect each other at right angles; *esp* : any of the four parts into which a plane is divided by rectangular coordinate axes lying in that plane [Latin *quadrans* "fourth part"] — **qua•dran•tal** \kwä-'drant-l\ *adj*

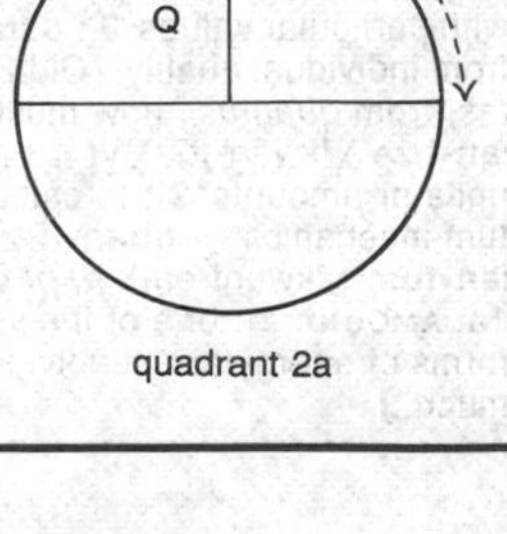

quadrant 2a

qua•draph•o•ny \kwä-'draf-ə-nē\ *n* : the transmission, recording, or reproduction of sound by techniques that utilize four transmission channels [derived from *quadri-* + *-phone*] — **quad•ra•phon•ic** \ˌkwäd-rə-'fän-ik\ *adj*

quad•rat \'kwäd-rət, -ˌrat\ *n* : a usually rectangular plot used for ecological or population studies [alteration of *quadrate*]

quad•rate \'kwäd-ˌrāt, -rət\ *n* : a bony or cartilaginous element on each side of the skull to which the lower jaw is attached in most lower vertebrates [earlier *quadrate* "square or cubical area or object", from Latin *quadratus,* past participle of *quadrare* "to make square"] — **quadrate** *adj*

qua•drat•ic \kwä-'drat-ik\ *adj* : involving terms of second degree at most ⟨a *quadratic* polynomial⟩ — **quadratic** *n*

quadratic equation *n* : an equation containing one term in which the unknown is squared and no term in which it is raised to a higher power

quad•ra•ture \'kwäd-rə-ˌchůr, -chər\ *n* **1** : the process of finding a square equal in area to a given area ⟨*quadrature* of the circle is impossible with ruler and compass⟩ **2** : a configuration in which two celestial bodies have a separation of 90 degrees ⟨Mars in *quadrature* with the sun⟩

qua•dren•ni•al \kwä-'dren-ē-əl\ *adj* **1** : consisting of or lasting for four years **2** : occurring or being done every four years [Latin *quadriennium* "period of four years", from *quadri-* + *annus* "year"] — **qua•dren•ni•al•ly** \-ē-ə-lē\ *adv*

quadri- *or* **quadr-** *or* **quadru-** *combining form* **1** : four **2** : fourth [Latin]

quad•ri•ceps \'kwäd-rə-ˌseps\ *n* : the great extensor muscle of the front of the thigh [*quadri-* + *-ceps* (as in *biceps*)]

quadriceps fem•o•ris \-'fem-ə-rəs\ *n* : QUADRICEPS [New Latin]

¹quad•ri•lat•er•al \ˌkwäd-rə-'lat-ə-rəl, -'la-trəl\ *adj* : having

\ə\ **abut**	\au̇\ **out**	\i\ **tip**	\ȯ\ **saw**	\u̇\ **foot**
\ər\ **further**	\ch\ **chin**	\ī\ **life**	\ȯi\ **coin**	\y\ **yet**
\a\ **mat**	\e\ **pet**	\j\ **job**	\th\ **thin**	\yü\ **few**
\ā\ **take**	\ē\ **easy**	\ng\ **sing**	\th̲\ **this**	\yu̇\ **cure**
\ä\ **cot, cart**	\g\ **go**	\ō\ **bone**	\ü\ **food**	\zh\ **vision**

four sides [Latin *quadrilaterus,* from *quadri-* + *later-, latus* "side"]

2**quadrilateral** *n* : a plane figure of four sides and four angles

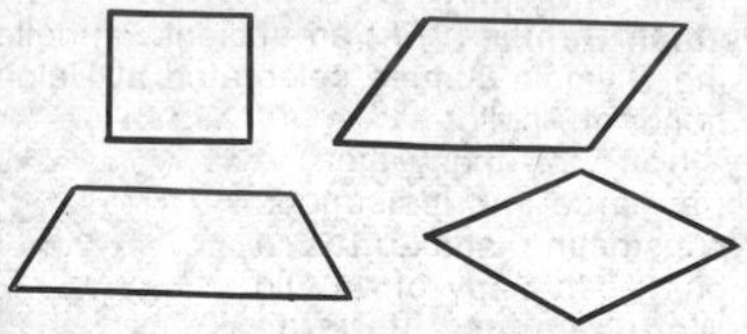

2quadrilateral

qua•drille \kwä-ˈdril, kwə-, kə-\ *n* : a square dance for four couples or music for this dance [French, "group of knights in an exhibition tournament", from Spanish *cuadrilla* "troop"]

qua•dril•lion \kwä-ˈdril-yən\ *n* — see NUMBER table [French, from *quadri-* + *-illion* (as in *million*)]

quad•ri•par•tite \ˌkwäd-rə-ˈpär-ˌtīt\ *adj* **1** : consisting of four parts ⟨a *quadripartite* vault⟩ **2** : shared by four parties or persons ⟨a *quadripartite* agreement⟩

qua•droon \kwä-ˈdrün\ *n* : a person of one-quarter Negro ancestry [Spanish *cuarterón,* from *cuarto* "fourth", from Latin *quartus*]

quad•ru•ped \ˈkwäd-rə-ˌped\ *n* : an animal having four feet — **quadruped** *or* **qua•dru•pe•dal** \kwä-ˈdrü-pəd-l, ˌkwäd-rə-ˈped-\ *adj*

1**qua•dru•ple** \kwä-ˈdrüp-əl, -ˈdrəp-; ˈkwäd-rəp-\ *vb* **qua•dru•pled; qua•dru•pling** \-ling, -ə-ling\ : to make or become four times as great or as many

2**quadruple** *adj* **1** : having four units or members **2** : being four times as great or as many **3** : marked by four beats per measure ⟨*quadruple* meter⟩ [Latin *quadruplus,* from *quadri-* + *-plus* "multiplied by"] — **quadruple** *n*

qua•drup•let \kwä-ˈdrəp-lət, -ˈdrüp-; ˈkwäd-rəp-\ *n* **1** : one of four offspring born at one birth **2** : a combination of four of a kind

1**qua•dru•pli•cate** \kwä-ˈdrü-pli-kət\ *adj* : having or being four corresponding or identical parts or examples [Latin *quadruplicatus,* past participle of *quadruplicare* "to quadruple", from *quadruplic-, quadruplex* "fourfold"]

2**qua•dru•pli•cate** \-plə-ˌkāt\ *vt* **1** : QUADRUPLE **2** : to provide in quadruplicate — **qua•dru•pli•ca•tion** \kwä-ˌdrü-plə-ˈkā-shən\ *n*

3**qua•dru•pli•cate** \kwä-ˈdrü-pli-kət\ *n* **1** : one of four like things **2** : four copies all alike ⟨typed in *quadruplicate*⟩

quaes•tor \ˈkwes-tər\ *n* : one of numerous ancient Roman officials concerned chiefly with financial administration [Latin, from *quaestus,* past participle of *quaerere* "to seek, ask"]

quaff \ˈkwäf, ˈkwaf\ *vb* : to drink deeply or repeatedly [origin unknown] — **quaff** *n*

quag \ˈkwag, ˈkwäg\ *n* : MARSH, BOG [origin unknown]

quag•ga \ˈkwag-ə, ˈkwäg-\ *n* : an extinct wild ass of southern Africa related to the zebras [obsolete Afrikaans]

quag•mire \ˈkwag-ˌmīr, ˈkwäg-\ *n* **1** : soft miry land that gives under the feet **2** : a complex or uncertain position : PREDICAMENT

qua•hog \ˈkwō-ˌhȯg, ˈkwō-, ˈkō-, -ˌhäg\ *n* : a round thick-shelled American clam [of American Indian origin]

quai \ˈkā\ *n* : QUAY [French]

1**quail** \ˈkwāl\ *n, pl* **quail** *or* **quails** : any of various game birds related to the common fowl: as **a** : a stocky short-winged Old World migratory bird occurring in many varieties **b** : any of various small American birds; *esp* : BOBWHITE [Middle French *quaille,* from Medieval Latin *quaccula*]

2**quail** *vi* : to shrink in dread or terror : COWER [Middle French *quailler* "to curdle", from Latin *coagulare*]

quaint \ˈkwānt\ *adj* **1** : unusual or different in character or appearance : ODD **2** : pleasingly old-fashioned or unfamiliar [Old French *cointe* "skilled", from Latin *cognitus,* past participle of *cognoscere* "to know"] — **quaint•ly** *adv* — **quaint•ness** *n*

1**quake** \ˈkwāk\ *vi* **1** : to shake or vibrate usually from shock or instability **2** : to tremble or shudder usually from cold or fear [Old English *cwacian*]

2**quake** *n* : a shaking or trembling; *esp* : EARTHQUAKE

quak•er \ˈkwā-kər\ *n* **1** : one that quakes **2** *cap* : FRIEND 4

Quaker meeting *n* : a meeting of Friends for worship marked often by long periods of silence

qual•i•fi•ca•tion \ˌkwäl-ə-fə-ˈkā-shən\ *n* **1** : something that limits or restricts ⟨agreed without *qualification*⟩ **2 a** : a quality or skill that fits a person (as for an office) ⟨the applicant with the best *qualifications*⟩ **b** : a condition that must be met ⟨a *qualification* for membership⟩

qual•i•fied \ˈkwäl-ə-ˌfīd\ *adj* **1** : having the necessary skill, knowledge, or ability to do something ⟨a *qualified* accountant⟩ **2** : limited or modified in some way ⟨*qualified* agreement⟩ — **qual•i•fied•ly** \-ˌfī-əd-lē, -ˌfīd-lē\ *adv*

qual•i•fi•er \-ˌfī-ər, -ˌfīr\ *n* : one that qualifies: as **a** : one that satisfies specified requirements **b** : a word or word group that limits the meaning of another word or word group : MODIFIER

qual•i•fy \ˈkwäl-ə-ˌfī\ *vb* **-fied; -fy•ing 1 a** : to make less general and more restricted : LIMIT **b** : to make less harsh or strict : MODERATE **c** : to alter the strength or flavor of ⟨*qualify* a liquor⟩ **d** : to limit the meaning of (as a noun) **2** : to characterize by naming a quality : DESCRIBE **3 a** : to fit by training, skill, or ability for a special purpose **b** : CERTIFY, LICENSE ⟨*qualified* to practice law⟩ **4** : to exhibit needed fitness, skill, or ability for some end [Middle French *qualifier,* from Medieval Latin *qualificare,* from Latin *qualis* "of what kind"]

qual•i•ta•tive \ˈkwäl-ə-ˌtāt-iv\ *adj* : of, relating to, or involving quality or kind — **qual•i•ta•tive•ly** *adj*

qualitative analysis *n* : chemical analysis designed to identify the components of a substance or mixture

qual•i•ty \ˈkwäl-ət-ē\ *n, pl* **-ties 1 a** : peculiar and essential character : NATURE **b** : an inherent feature : PROPERTY ⟨hardness is a *quality* of steel⟩ **2** : degree of excellence : GRADE **3** : usually high social status : RANK **4** : a distinguishing attribute : CHARACTERISTIC **5 a** : vividness of hue **b** : TIMBRE [Old French *qualité,* from Latin *qualitas,* from *qualis* "of what kind"]

• **syn** PROPERTY, ATTRIBUTE: QUALITY is a very general term applying to any trait, mark, or character of an individual or of a type; PROPERTY applies to a quality belonging to a thing's essential nature and helping to distinguish and identify its type or species; ATTRIBUTE is a quality ascribed to a thing or being often through lack of definite knowledge of it.

qualm \ˈkwäm, ˈkwälm *also* ˈkwȯm\ *n* **1** : a sudden attack of illness, faintness, or nausea **2** : a sudden fear or misgiving **3** : a feeling of doubt or hesitation in matters of conscience ⟨had no *qualms* about lying⟩ [origin unknown] — **qualmy** \-ē\ *adj*

• **syn** QUALM, SCRUPLE, COMPUNCTION mean a misgiving about what one is doing or going do do. QUALM implies an uneasy fear that one is not following one's conscience or better judgment; SCRUPLE implies doubt of the rightness of an act on grounds of principle; COMPUNCTION implies a spontaneous feeling that one is inflicting a wrong or injustice on someone.

qualm•ish \-ish\ *adj* **1 a** : feeling qualms : SQUEAMISH **b** : overly scrupulous **2** : of, relating to, or producing qualms — **qualm•ish•ly** *adv* — **qualm•ish•ness** *n*

quan•da•ry \ˈkwän-də-rē, -drē\ *n, pl* **-ries** : a state of puzzlement or doubt : DILEMMA [origin unknown] **syn** see PREDICAMENT

quan•ti•fi•er \ˈkwänt-ə-ˌfī-ər, -ˌfīr\ *n* : a term (as *two, all, most,* or *no*) expressive of quantity; *esp* : one that binds the variables in a logical formula

quan•ti•ta•tive \ˈkwänt-ə-ˌtāt-iv, ˈkwän-\ *adj* : of, relating to, expressible as, or involving the measurement of quantity — **quan•ti•ta•tive•ly** *adv* — **quan•ti•ta•tive•ness** *n*

quantitative analysis *n* : chemical analysis designed to determine the amounts or proportions of the components of a substance or mixture

quantitative inheritance *n* : inheritance of a character (as height or skin color in humans) controlled by a group of gene pairs at different chromosomal locations with each pair having a specific quantitative effect

quan•ti•ty \ˈkwänt-ət-ē, ˈkwän-\ *n, pl* **-ties 1 a** : an indefinite amount or number **b** : a large amount or number — often used in pl. **2 a** : the aspect in which a thing is measurable in terms of degree or magnitude **b** : a mathematical expression concerned with particular values **3** : duration of a speech sound as distinct from individual quality [Old French *quantité,* from Latin *quantitas,* from *quantus* "how much, how large"]

quan•tize \ˈkwän-ˌtīz\ *vt* **1** : to subdivide (as energy) into small units or amounts **2** : to calculate or express in terms of quantum mechanics — **quan•ti•za•tion** \ˌkwänt-ə-ˈzā-shən\ *n*

quan•tum \ˈkwänt-əm\ *n, pl* **quan•ta** \ˈkwänt-ə\ **1** : QUANTITY 1a, AMOUNT **2** : one of the very small parcels into which many forms of energy are subdivided [Latin, neuter of *quantus* "how much"]

quantum mechanics *n* : a general mathematical theory dealing with the interactions of matter and radiation in terms of observable quantities only — **quantum mechanical** *adj*

quantum theory *n* : a branch of physical theory based on the concept of the subdivision of radiant energy into finite quanta and applied to numerous processes involving transference or transformation of energy on an atomic or molecular scale

¹quar•an•tine \ˈkwȯr-ən-ˌtēn, ˈkwär-\ *n* **1** : a term during which a ship arriving in port and suspected of carrying contagious disease is forbidden contact with the shore **2** : a restraint upon the activities or movements of persons or the transport of goods designed to prevent the spread of disease or pests **3** : the period during which a person with a contagious disease is under quarantine **4** : a place (as a hospital) where individuals under quarantine are kept **[**Italian *quarantina* "period of 40 days", from Middle French *quarantaine,* from *quarante* "forty", from Latin *quadraginta***]**

²quarantine *vt* : to detain in or exclude by or as if by quarantine : ISOLATE — **quar•an•tin•able** \-ˌtē-nə-bəl\ *adj*

¹quar•rel \ˈkwȯr-əl, ˈkwär-əl, ˈkwȯrl, ˈkwärl\ *n* **1** : a cause of dispute or complaint **2** : a usually angry verbal dispute **[**Middle French *querele* "complaint", from Latin *querela,* from *queri* "to complain"**]**

²quarrel *vi* **-reled** *or* **-relled**; **-rel•ing** *or* **-rel•ling 1** : to find fault ⟨*quarrel* with an idea⟩ **2** : to contend or dispute actively : SQUABBLE — **quar•rel•er** *or* **quar•rel•ler** *n*

quar•rel•some \ˈkwȯr-əl-səm, ˈkwär-əl-, ˈkwȯrl-, ˈkwärl-\ *adj* : apt or inclined to quarrel : CONTENTIOUS — **quar•rel•some•ly** *adv* — **quar•rel•some•ness** *n*

¹quar•ry \ˈkwȯr-ē, ˈkwär-\ *n, pl* **quarries 1** : the object of a chase : GAME; *esp* : game hunted with hawks **2** : PREY 1 **[**Middle English *querre* "entrails of game given to the hounds", from Middle French *cuiree***]**

△ **origin** The *quarry* the hunter stalks is not related to the stonecutter's quarry. The first can be traced to a minor ceremony that was once part of every successful hunt. The hounds were rewarded after the kill with a part of the slain animal's entrails. The French word for this hounds' portion was *cuiree. Cuiree* was borrowed into Middle English as *querre.* The word for the entrails of an animal was later transferred to the animal itself, when considered in the character of game pursued. Now anything pursued is its pursuer's *quarry.*

²quarry *n, pl* **quarries** : an open excavation usually for obtaining building stone, slate, or limestone **[**Middle French *quarriere,* derived from Latin *quadrum* "square"**]**

△ **origin** The stone *quarry* is not so-called because it is sought after, as is game by a hunter, but rather takes its name from the building stones it provides. *Quarriere* was the Middle French word for a quarry, a source of squared stones. Its ultimate source was Latin *quadrum,* which means "square".

³quarry *vt* **quar•ried**; **quar•ry•ing 1** : to dig or take from or as if from a quarry **2** : to make a quarry in — **quar•ri•er** *n*

quart \ˈkwȯrt\ *n* **1** : a unit of measure equal to ¼ gallon — see MEASURE table **2** : a vessel or measure having a capacity of one quart **[**Middle French *quarte* "fourth of a gallon", from *quart* "fourth", from Latin *quartus***]**

¹quar•tan \ˈkwȯrt-n\ *adj* : characterized by an interval of approximately three days between occurrences : occurring on the fourth day **[**Old French *(fievre) quartaine* "quartan fever", from Latin *(febris) quartana,* from *quartanus* "of the fourth", from *quartus* "fourth"**]**

²quartan *n* : an intermittent fever characterized by intervals of approximately 72 hours between attacks; *esp* : a quartan malaria

¹quar•ter \ˈkwȯrt-ər, ˈkwȯt-\ *n* **1** : one of four equal parts **2** : a unit (as of weight or length) that equals one fourth of some larger unit **3 a** : any of four 3-month divisions of a year **b** : a school term of about 12 weeks **c** : QUARTER HOUR **d** : a coin worth a fourth of a dollar; *also* : the sum of 25 cents **e** : one limb of a 4-limbed animal or carcass with the parts near it ⟨a *quarter* of beef⟩ **f** : a fourth part of the moon's period ⟨a moon in its first *quarter*⟩ **g** : one of the four parts into which the horizon may be divided; *also* : a region or direction under such a part **h** : one of the four cardinal points corresponding to the four parts of the horizon; *also* : a compass point **4** : someone or something (as a place, direction, or group) not specified ⟨expecting trouble from another *quarter*⟩ **5 a** : a particular division or district of a city ⟨the foreign *quarter*⟩ **b** : an assigned place or duty station especially of a member of a naval crew ⟨a call to *quarters*⟩ **c** *pl* : living accommodations : LODGING **6** : MERCY; *esp* : a refraining from destroying a defeated enemy **7** : the stern area of a ship's side **[**Old French *quartier,* from Latin *quartarius,* from *quartus* "fourth"**]** — **at close quarters** : at close range or in immediate contact

²quarter *vb* **1 a** : to divide into four equal parts **b** : to separate into parts ⟨peel and *quarter* an orange⟩ **c** : DISMEMBER 1 **2** : to provide with or occupy a lodging **3** : to crisscross an area in many directions ⟨*quartered* the hills looking for the child⟩

³quarter *adj* : consisting of or equal to a quarter

¹quar•ter•back \-ˌbak\ *n* : an offensive football back who calls the signals and directs the offensive play of the team

²quarterback *vt* : to act as quarterback of (a football team)

quarter day *n, chiefly British* : the day which begins a quarter of the year and on which a quarterly payment falls due

quar•ter•deck \-ˌdek\ *n* **1** : the stern area of a ship's upper deck **2** : a part of a deck on a naval vessel set aside for ceremonial and official use

quarterdeck 1

quarter horse *n* : an alert stocky muscular horse capable of high speed for short distances and of great endurance under the saddle **[**from its high speed for distances up to a quarter of a mile**]**

quarter hour *n* **1** : 15 minutes **2** : any of the quarter points of an hour

quar•ter•ing *adj* : coming from a point well abaft the beam of a ship but not directly astern ⟨a *quartering* wind⟩

¹quar•ter•ly \ˈkwȯrt-ər-lē, ˈkwȯt-\ *adv* : at 3-month intervals ⟨interest compounded *quarterly*⟩

²quarterly *adj* : coming during or at the end of each 3-month interval ⟨*quarterly* premium⟩ ⟨*quarterly* meeting⟩

³quarterly *n, pl* **-lies** : a periodical published four times a year

quar•ter•mas•ter \ˈkwȯrt-ər-ˌmas-tər, ˈkwȯt-\ *n* **1** : a petty officer who attends to a ship's steering and signals **2** : an army officer responsible for the clothing and subsistence of a body of troops

quar•tern \ˈkwȯrt-ərn, ˈkwȯt-\ *n* : a fourth part : QUARTER **[**Old French *quarteron* "quarter of a pound, quarter of a hundred", from *quartier* "quarter"**]**

quarter note *n* : a musical note equal in value to one fourth of a whole note

quar•ter•saw \ˈkwȯrt-ər-ˌsȯ, ˈkwȯt-\ *vt* **-sawed**; **-sawed** *or* **-sawn** \-ˌsȯn\; **-saw•ing** : to saw (a log) into quarters and then into planks in which the annual rings are nearly at right angles to the wide face

quarter section *n* : a tract of land that is half a mile square and contains 160 acres (about .647 square kilometer) in the United States government system of land surveying

quar•ter•staff \ˈkwȯrt-ər-ˌstaf\ *n, pl* **-staves** \-ˌstavz, -ˌstāvz\ : a long stout staff formerly used as a weapon

quar•tet *also* **quar•tette** \kwȯr-ˈtet\ *n* **1** : a musical composition for four instruments or voices **2** : a group or set of four **[**Italian *quartetto,* from *quarto* "fourth", from Latin *quartus***]**

quarter note

quar•tile \ˈkwȯr-ˌtīl, ˈkwȯrt-l\ *n* : one of three values that divide a frequency distribution into four equal intervals **[**derived from Latin *quartus* "fourth"**]**

quar•to \ˈkwȯrt-ō\ *n, pl* **quartos** : a book made of sheets of paper each folded twice to make four leaves or eight pages **[**Latin, ablative of *quartus* "fourth"**]**

\ə\ **abut**	\au̇\ **out**	\i\ **tip**	\ȯ\ **saw**	\u̇\ **foot**
\ər\ **further**	\ch\ **chin**	\ī\ **life**	\ȯi\ **coin**	\y\ **yet**
\a\ **mat**	\e\ **pet**	\j\ **job**	\th\ **thin**	\yü\ **few**
\ā\ **take**	\ē\ **easy**	\ng\ **sing**	\t͟h\ **this**	\yu̇\ **cure**
\ä\ **cot, cart**	\g\ **go**	\ō\ **bone**	\ü\ **food**	\zh\ **vision**

quartz \'kwȯrts\ *n* : a common mineral SiO_2 consisting of silica often found in the form of colorless transparent crystals but sometimes (as in amethysts, agates, and jaspers) brightly colored [German *quarz*] — **quartz•ose** \'kwȯrt-ˌsōs\ *adj*

quartz glass *n* : vitreous silica prepared from pure quartz and noted for its transparency to ultraviolet radiation

quartz•ite \'kwȯrt-ˌsīt\ *n* : a compact granular rock composed of quartz and derived from sandstone

qua•sar \'kwā-ˌzär *also* -ˌsär\ *n* : any of various distant celestial objects that resemble stars but emit unusually bright blue and ultraviolet light and radio waves [*quas*i-stell*ar* radio source]

quash \'kwäsh, 'kwȯsh\ *vt* **1** : to make void by judicial action ⟨*quash* an indictment⟩ **2** : to suppress completely : QUELL ⟨*quash* a rebellion⟩ [Middle French *casser, quasser,* from Late Latin *cassare,* from Latin *cassus* "void"]

qua•si \'kwā-ˌzī, -ˌsī; 'kwäz-ē; 'kwäs-; 'kwā-zē\ *adj* : having or legally held to have a likeness to something else ⟨a *quasi* contract⟩

qua•si- \'kwā-ˌzī; -ˌsī; 'kwäz-ē; 'kwäs-; 'kwā-zē\ *combining form* : in some sense or degree : seemingly [Latin *quasi* "as if, as it were, approximately", from *quam* "as" + *si* "if"]

See *quasi-* and 2d element

quasi-academic
quasi-apology
quasi-autobiographical
quasi-automatic
quasi-autonomous
quasi-biography
quasi-blockade
quasi-confidential
quasi-criminal
quasi-diplomacy
quasi-documentary
quasi-dramatic
quasi-experimental
quasi-feudal
quasi-fictional
quasi-governmental
quasi-historical
quasi-history
quasi-independent
quasi-intellectual
quasi-judicial
quasi-legal
quasi-legislative
quasi-legitimate
quasi-liberal
quasi-literary
quasi-living
quasi-medical
quasi-military
quasi-miraculous
quasi-mockery
quasi-monopolistic
quasi-monopoly
quasi-mystic
quasi-mystical
quasi-national
quasi-official
quasi-peace
quasi-permanence
quasi-permanent
quasi-philosophical
quasi-philosophy
quasi-poetic
quasi-poetical
quasi-poetry
quasi-political
quasi-professional
quasi-public
quasi-realism
quasi-religious
quasi-scholarly
quasi-scientific
quasi-technical
quasi-tragic
quasi-vigilante
quasi-voluntarily
quasi-voluntary
quasi-war

qua•si–stel•lar radio source \-'stel-ər-\ *n* : QUASAR

quas•sia \'kwäsh-ə\ *n* : a bitter tonic drug from the heartwood of several tropical trees sometimes used as a mild agent against parasitic worms or as an insecticide [*Quassi,* 18th century Surinam Negro slave who discovered the medicinal value of quassia]

Qua•ter•na•ry \'kwät-ər-ˌner-ē, kwə-'tər-nə-rē\ *n* : the period of the Cenozoic era from the end of the Tertiary to the present time; *also* : the corresponding system of rocks — see GEOLOGIC TIME table [Latin *quaternarius* "consisting of four each", from *quaterni* "four each"] — **Quaternary** *adj*

qua•train \'kwä-ˌtrān\ *n* : a unit or group of four lines of verse [French, from *quatre* "four", from Latin *quattuor*]

qua•tre•foil \'kat-ər-ˌfoil, 'ka-trə-\ *n* **1** : a conventionalized representation of a flower with four petals or of a leaf with four leaflets **2** : a 4-lobed foliation in architecture [Middle English *quaterfoil* "set of four leaves", from Middle French *quatre* "four" + Middle English *-foil* (as in *trefoil*)]

¹qua•ver \'kwā-vər\ *vb* **qua•vered**; **qua•ver•ing** \'kwāv-ring, -ə-ring\ **1** : TREMBLE, SHAKE ⟨*quavering* inwardly⟩ **2** : TRILL 2 **3** : to utter sound in tremulous uncertain tones ⟨a voice that *quavered*⟩ **4** : to utter quaveringly [Middle English *quaveren,* from *quaven* "to tremble"] — **qua•ver•ing•ly** \'kwāv-ring-lē, -ə-ring-\ *adv* — **qua•very** \'kwāv-rē, -ə-rē\ *adj*

²quaver *n* **1** : TRILL 1 **2** : a tremulous sound

quay \'kē, 'kā, 'kwā\ *n* : a paved bank or a solid artificial landing place beside water for convenience in loading and unloading ships [alteration of earlier *key,* from Middle French *cai,* of Celtic origin]

quean \'kwēn\ *n* : a disreputable woman [Old English *cwene*]

quea•sy *also* **quea•zy** \'kwē-zē\ *adj* **quea•si•er**; **-est** **1** : full of doubt : HAZARDOUS **2 a** : causing nausea ⟨*queasy* motion⟩ **b** : suffering from nausea **3 a** : causing uneasiness **b** (1) : DELICATE, SQUEAMISH ⟨a *queasy* conscience⟩ (2) : ill at ease ⟨*queasy* about our debts⟩ [Middle English *coysy, qwesye*] — **quea•si•ly** \-zə-lē\ *adv* — **quea•si•ness** \-zē-nəs\ *n*

que•bra•cho \kā-'bräch-ō, ki-\ *n, pl* **-chos** : a South American tree of the sumac family with dense wood rich in tannins; *also* : its wood or a tannin-rich extract of this used in tanning [American Spanish, alteration of *quiebracha,* from Spanish *quiebra* "it breaks" + *hacha* "ax"]

Que•chua \'kech-wə, -ə-wə\ *n* **1 a** : a member of an Amerindian people of central Peru **b** : a group of peoples constituting the dominant element of the Inca Empire **2** : the language of the Quechua people widely spoken by other Amerindian peoples of southern and western South America [Spanish, from Quechua *kkechúwa* "plunderer, robber"] — **Que•chu•an** \-wən\ *adj or n*

¹queen \'kwēn\ *n* **1** : the wife or widow of a king **2** : a woman who is a monarch **3 a** : a woman eminent in rank, power, or attractions ⟨a society *queen*⟩ **b** : a goddess or a thing personified as female and having supremacy in a specified realm ⟨*queen* of the ocean liners⟩ **c** : an attractive girl or woman; *esp* : a beauty contest winner **4** : the most privileged piece in chess having the power to move in any direction any number of unobstructed squares **5** : a playing card bearing the stylized figure of a queen **6 a** : the fertile fully developed female of social bees, ants, and termites whose function is to lay eggs **b** : a mature female cat [Old English *cwēn* "woman, wife, queen"] — **queen•like** \-ˌlīk\ *adj* — **queen•li•ness** \-lē-nəs\ *n* — **queen•ly** \-lē\ *adv or adj*

²queen *vb* **1** : to act like a queen; *esp* : to put on airs — usually used with *it* **2** : to become or promote to a queen in chess

Queen Anne \kwē-'nan\ *adj* **1** : of or relating to an early 18th century style of furniture characterized by extensive use of upholstery, marquetry, and Oriental fabrics **2** : of or relating to an early 18th century English style of building characterized by unpretentious design, modified classic ornament, and red brickwork in which relief ornament is carved [*Queen Anne* of England]

Queen Anne's lace *n* : WILD CARROT

queen consort *n, pl* **queens consort** : the wife of a reigning king

queen mother *n* : a dowager queen who is mother of the reigning sovereign

queen post *n* : one of two vertical tie posts in a truss (as of a roof)

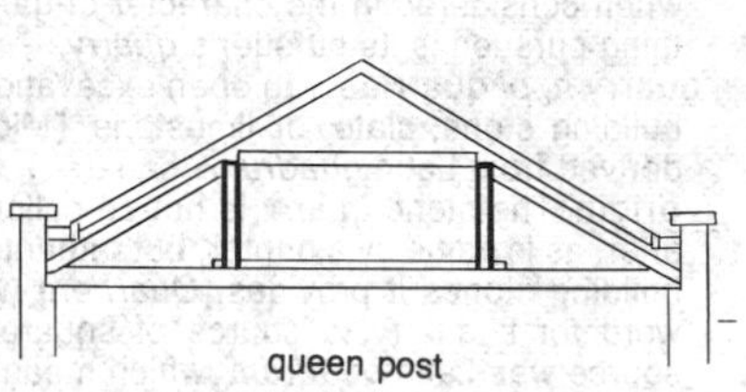

queen post

¹queer \'kwiər\ *adj* **1 a** : differing from what is usual or normal : ODD **b** (1) : ECCENTRIC 2, UNCONVENTIONAL (2) : mildly insane **2 a** *slang* : WORTHLESS 1a, COUNTERFEIT ⟨*queer* money⟩ **b** : QUESTIONABLE 2, SUSPICIOUS **3** : not quite well : QUEASY [origin unknown] **syn** see STRANGE — **queer•ish** \-ish\ *adj* — **queer•ly** *adv* — **queer•ness** *n*

²queer *adv* : QUEERLY

³queer *vt* **1** : to spoil the effect or success of : DISRUPT ⟨*queer* one's plans⟩ **2** : to put or get into an embarrassing or unfavorable situation

quell \'kwel\ *vt* **1** : to put down : SUPPRESS ⟨*quell* a riot⟩ **2** : QUIET 1, PACIFY ⟨*quell* fears⟩ [Old English *cwellan* "to kill"] — **quell•er** *n*

quench \'kwench\ *vt* **1** : to put out ⟨*quench* a fire⟩ ⟨*quench* a lamp⟩ **2** : to bring to an end: as **a** : OVERCOME 1 ⟨*quench* anger⟩ **b** : REPRESS 3 ⟨*quench* rebellion⟩ **c** : SLAKE 2, SATISFY ⟨*quench* thirst⟩ **3** : to cool (as heated steel) suddenly by immersion (as in water or oil) [Old English *-cwencan*] — **quench•able** \'kwen-chə-bəl\ *adj* — **quench•er** *n* — **quench•less** \'kwench-ləs\ *adj*

quern \'kwərn\ *n* : a primitive hand mill for grinding grain [Old English *cweorn*]

quer•u•lous \'kwer-ə-ləs, -yə-ləs\ *adj* **1** : habitually complaining **2** : FRETFUL, PETULANT ⟨a *querulous* voice⟩ [Latin *querulus,* from *queri* "to complain"] — **quer•u•lous•ly** *adv* — **quer•u•lous•ness** *n*

¹que•ry \'kwiər-ē, 'kweər-\ *n, pl* **queries** **1** : QUESTION 1a(1), INQUIRY **2** : a question in the mind : DOUBT **3** : QUESTION MARK [Latin *quaere,* imperative of *quaerere* "to ask"]

[2]**query** *vt* **que•ried**; **que•ry•ing** **1** : to put as a question ⟨"When can I leave?" I *queried*⟩ **2** : to ask questions about especially in order to resolve a doubt ⟨*queried* a statement⟩ **3** : to ask questions of especially with a desire for authoritative information ⟨*queried* the professor about the lesson⟩ **4** : to mark with a query

[1]**quest** \ˈkwest\ *n* **1** : an act or instance of seeking: **a** : PURSUIT, SEARCH ⟨in *quest* of game⟩ **b** : a chivalrous enterprise in medieval romance ⟨the *quest* of the Holy Grail⟩ **2** *obs* : ones who search or make inquiry [Middle French *queste* "search, pursuit", from Latin *quaestus*, past participle of *quaerere* "to seek, ask"]

[2]**quest** *vb* **1** : to go on a quest **2** : to search for : SEEK, PURSUE **3** : to ask for : DEMAND

[1]**ques•tion** \ˈkwes-chən, ˈkwesh-\ *n* **1 a** (1) : an interrogative expression often used to test knowledge (2) : an interrogative sentence or clause **b** : a subject or aspect in dispute or open for discussion : ISSUE; *also* : MATTER 1b **c** (1) : a subject or point of debate or a proposition to be voted on in a meeting ⟨put the *question* to the members⟩ (2) : the bringing of this to a vote **d** : the specific point at issue **2 a** : an act or instance of asking : INQUIRY **b** (1) : OBJECTION, DISPUTE ⟨obey without *question*⟩ (2) : room for doubt or objection ⟨there's no *question* about their honesty⟩ (3) : CHANCE, POSSIBILITY ⟨no *question* of escape⟩ [Middle French, from Latin *quaestio*, from *quaestus*, past participle of *quaerere* "to seek, ask"]

[2]**question** *vb* **1 a** : to ask questions of or about **b** : INQUIRE 2 ⟨a *questioning* mind⟩ **2** : CROSS-EXAMINE ⟨*question* a witness⟩ **3 a** : DOUBT, DISPUTE ⟨*question* a decision⟩ **b** : to subject to analysis : EXAMINE — **ques•tion•er** *n* — **ques•tion•ing•ly** \-che-ning-lē\ *adv*

ques•tion•able \ˈkwes-chə-nə-bəl, ˈkwesh-, *rapid* ˈkwesh-nə-\ *adj* **1** : affording reason for being doubted, questioned, or challenged : not certain or exact : PROBLEMATIC ⟨milk of *questionable* purity⟩ ⟨a *questionable* decision⟩ **2** : attended by well-grounded suspicions of being immoral, crude, false, or unsound : DUBIOUS ⟨*questionable* motives⟩ — **ques•tion•ably** \-blē\ *adv*

question mark *n* : a punctuation mark ? used chiefly at the end of a sentence to indicate a direct question

ques•tion•naire \ˌkwes-chə-ˈnaər, -ˈneər\ *n* : a set of questions to be asked of a number of persons usually in order to gather statistics (as on opinions) [French, from *questionner* "to question"]

quet•zal \ket-ˈsäl, -ˈsal\ *n, pl* **quet•zals** *or* **quet•za•les** \-ˈsäl-ās\ **1** : a Central American bird with narrow crest and brilliant plumage and in the male tail feathers often more than one half meter in length **2** *pl usually quetzales* : the basic monetary unit of Guatemala; *also* : a coin or note representing this unit [American Spanish, from Nahuatl *quetzaltototl*, from *quetzalli* "brilliant tail feather" + *tototl* "bird"]

[1]**queue** \ˈkyü\ *n* **1** : a braid of hair usually worn hanging at the back of the head **2** : a line especially of persons or vehicles [French, literally, "tail", from Latin *cauda*]

[2]**queue** *vb* **queued**; **queu•ing** *or* **queue•ing** **1** : to arrange or form in a queue **2** : to line up or wait in a queue ⟨the crowd *queued* up for tickets⟩ — **queu•er** *n*

[1]**quib•ble** \ˈkwib-əl\ *n* **1** : an evasion of or shift from the point : EQUIVOCATION **2** : a trivial objection or criticism [probably from obsolete *quib* "quibble"]

[2]**quibble** *vi* **quib•bled**; **quib•bling** \ˈkwib-ling, -ə-ling\ **1** : to evade the issue : EQUIVOCATE **2 a** : CAVIL, CARP **b** : BICKER — **quib•bler** \ˈkwib-lər, -ə-lər\ *n*

[1]**quick** \ˈkwik\ *adj* **1** *archaic* : not dead : LIVING, ALIVE **2** : RAPID, SPEEDY: as **a** : fast in understanding, thinking, or learning : mentally agile **b** : reacting with speed and sensitivity **c** : aroused immediately and intensely ⟨*quick* temper⟩ **d** : fast in development or occurrence ⟨a *quick* succession of events⟩ ⟨gave them a *quick* look⟩ **e** : marked by speed, readiness, or promptness of physical movement ⟨walked with *quick* steps⟩ **f** : capable of being speedily prepared ⟨a *quick* dinner⟩ **3** : having a sharp angle ⟨a *quick* turn in the road⟩ [Old English *cwic*] — **quick•ly** *adv* — **quick•ness** *n*

• **syn** SPEEDY: QUICK stresses promptness and the shortness of time in which response, movement, or action takes place ⟨saved by *quick* thinking⟩ ⟨a *quick* answer⟩ SPEEDY implies quickness of successful accomplishment ⟨found a *speedy* solution of the problems⟩ or unusual velocity ⟨a *speedy* runner⟩

[2]**quick** *adv* : in a quick manner

[3]**quick** *n* **1** : a very sensitive area of flesh (as under a fingernail) **2** : the innermost sensibilities ⟨hurt to the *quick* by the remark⟩ **3** : the very center of something : HEART ⟨the *quick* of the matter⟩ [probably of Scandinavian origin]

quick bread *n* : a bread made with a leavening agent that permits immediate baking of the dough or batter mixture

quick•en \ˈkwik-ən\ *vb* **quick•ened**; **quick•en•ing** \ˈkwik-ning, -ə-ning\ **1 a** : to make or become alive : REVIVE **b** : to cause to be enlivened : STIMULATE ⟨curiosity *quickened* my interest⟩ **2** : to make or become more rapid : HASTEN, ACCELERATE ⟨*quickened* their steps⟩ ⟨my pulse *quickened* at the sight⟩ **3** : to show vitality or animation: as **a** : to commence active growth and development ⟨seeds *quickening* in the soil⟩ **b** : to reach the stage of fetal growth at which motion is felt by the mother **4** : to shine more brightly ⟨watched the dawn *quickening* in the east⟩ — **quick•en•er** \ˈkwik-nər, -ə-nər\ *n*

quick–freeze \ˈkwik-ˈfrēz\ *vt* **-froze** \-ˈfrōz\; **-fro•zen** \-ˈfrōz-n\; **-freez•ing** : to freeze (food) for preservation so rapidly that ice crystals formed are too small to rupture the cells and the natural juices and flavor are preserved

quick•ie \ˈkwik-ē\ *n* : something done or made in a hurry

quick•lime \ˈkwik-ˌlīm\ *n* : the first solid product that is obtained by calcining limestone and that develops great heat and becomes crumbly when treated with water

quick•sand \-ˌsand\ *n* : a deep mass of mixed loose sand and water into which heavy objects sink

quick•sil•ver \-ˌsil-vər\ *n* : MERCURY 1a [Old English *cwicseolfor*, from *cwic* "alive" + *seolfor* "silver"]

△ **origin** The metal mercury resembles silver in color, but, unlike silver, mercury is liquid at normal temperatures. It moves, then, like a living thing. The Old English word for mercury was *cwicseolfor*, a compound of *cwic* "alive" and *seolfor* "silver". The descriptive nature of the word *quicksilver*, however, is not native to English. The compound is a translation of the Latin *argentum vivum* found in Pliny and literally meaning "living silver".

quick•step \ˈkwik-ˌstep\ *n* : a spirited march tune usually accompanying a march in quick time

quick–tem•pered \ˈkwik-ˈtem-pərd\ *adj* : easily angered

quick time *n* : a rate of marching in which 120 steps each 30 inches in length are taken in one minute

quick–wit•ted \-ˈwit-əd\ *adj* : quick in perception and understanding : mentally alert — **quick–wit•ted•ness** *n*

[1]**quid** \ˈkwid\ *n, pl* **quid** *also* **quids** *British* : a pound sterling : SOVEREIGN [origin unknown]

[2]**quid** *n* : a wad of something chewable ⟨a *quid* of tobacco⟩ [Old English *cwidu* "cud"]

quid pro quo \ˌkwid-ˌprō-ˈkwō\ *n* : something given or received for something else [New Latin, "something for something"]

qui•es•cent \kwī-ˈes-nt, kwē-\ *adj* **1** : being at rest : INACTIVE **2** : causing no trouble or symptoms [Latin *quiescens*, present participle of *quiescere* "to become quiet, rest", from *quies* "quiet"] **syn** see LATENT — **qui•es•cence** \-ns\ *n* — **qui•es•cent•ly** *adv*

[1]**qui•et** \ˈkwī-ət\ *n* : the quality or state of being quiet : TRANQUILLITY [Latin *quiet-*, *quies* "rest, quiet"] — **on the quiet** : in a secretive manner

[2]**quiet** *adj* **1 a** : marked by little or no motion or activity : CALM **b** : GENTLE, EASYGOING ⟨a *quiet* temperament⟩ **c** : not disturbed ⟨*quiet* reading⟩ **d** : enjoyed in peace and relaxation ⟨a *quiet* cup of tea⟩ **2 a** : free from noise or uproar : STILL **b** : UNOBTRUSIVE, CONSERVATIVE ⟨*quiet* clothes⟩ **3** : SECLUDED 1 ⟨a *quiet* nook⟩ [Middle French, from Latin *quietus*, from past participle of *quiescere* "to become quiet, rest", from *quies* "rest, quiet"] — **qui•et•ly** *adv* — **qui•et•ness** *n*

[3]**quiet** *adv* : in a quiet manner ⟨*quiet*-running engine⟩

[4]**quiet** *vb* **1** : to cause to be quiet : CALM **2** : to become quiet ⟨the audience *quieted* as the curtain rose⟩ — **qui•et•er** *n*

qui•etude \ˈkwī-ə-ˌtüd, -ˌtyüd\ *n* : a quiet state : REPOSE

qui•etus \kwī-ˈēt-əs\ *n* **1** : a final freeing from something (as a debt, a duty, or life itself) **2** : something that quiets or represses **3** : a state of inactivity [Medieval Latin *quietus est* "he is quit", formula of discharge from obligation]

\ə\ **abut**	\aú\ **out**	\i\ **tip**	\ó\ **saw**	\ú\ **foot**
\ər\ **further**	\ch\ **chin**	\ī\ **life**	\ói\ **coin**	\y\ **yet**
\a\ **mat**	\e\ **pet**	\j\ **job**	\th\ **thin**	\yü\ **few**
\ā\ **take**	\ē\ **easy**	\ng\ **sing**	\t͟h\ **this**	\yú\ **cure**
\ä\ **cot, cart**	\g\ **go**	\ō\ **bone**	\ü\ **food**	\zh\ **vision**

1quill \ˈkwil\ *n* **1 a :** a bobbin, spool, or spindle on which filling yarn is wound **b :** a roll of dried bark (as of cinnamon) **c :** a hollow shaft often surrounding another shaft and used in various mechanical devices **2 a :** the hollow horny barrel of a feather; *also* **:** one of the large stiff feathers of a bird's wing or tail **b :** one of the hollow sharp spines of a porcupine or hedgehog **3 :** an article made from or resembling the quill of a feather: as **a :** a pen for writing **b :** a float for a fishing line [Middle English *quil* "hollow reed, bobbin"]

2quill *vt* **:** to pierce or wound with quills ⟨a dog badly *quilled* by a porcupine⟩

1quilt \ˈkwilt\ *n* **1 :** a bed coverlet having two layers of cloth filled with wool, cotton, or down held in place by patterned stitching **2 :** something that is quilted or resembles a quilt [Old French *cuilte* "mattress, quilt", from Latin *culcita* "mattress"]

2quilt *vb* **1 a :** to fill, pad, or line like a quilt **b :** to stitch, sew, or cover with lines or patterns like those used in quilts **c :** to fasten between two pieces of material **2 :** to stitch or sew in layers with padding in between **3 a :** to make quilts **b :** to do quilted work — **quilt•er** *n*

quilt•ing *n* **1 :** the act of one who quilts something **2 :** material that is quilted or used for making quilts

quince \ˈkwins\ *n* **:** the fruit of an Asian tree of the rose family that resembles a hard-fleshed yellow apple and is used especially for marmalade, jelly, and preserves; *also* **:** this tree [Middle English *quynce* "quinces", pl. of *quyn* "quince", from Middle French *coin,* from Latin *cydonium,* from Greek *kydōnion*]

quince

qui•nine \ˈkwī-ˌnīn *also* ˈkwin-ˌīn\ *n* **:** a bitter crystalline alkaloid from cinchona bark used in medicine especially against malaria; *also* **:** a salt of this [Spanish *quina* "cinchona", short for *quinaquina,* from Quechua]

quinine water *n* **:** a carbonated beverage flavored with a small amount of quinine, lemon, and lime

Quin•qua•ge•si•ma \ˌkwing-kwə-ˈjes-ə-mə, -ˈjā-zə-\ *n* **:** the Sunday before Lent [Medieval Latin, from Latin *quinquagesimus* "fiftieth", from *quinquaginta* "fifty"]

quin•quen•ni•al \kwin-ˈkwen-ē-əl\ *adj* **1 :** consisting of or lasting for five years **2 :** occurring or being done every five years [Middle French, from Latin *quinquennium* "period of five years", from *quinque* "five" + *annus* "year"] — **quinquennial** *n* — **quin•quen•ni•al•ly** \-ē-ə-lē\ *adv*

quin•sy \ˈkwin-zē\ *n* **:** a severe inflammation of the throat or adjacent parts with swelling and fever [Middle French *quinancie,* from Late Latin *cynanche,* from Greek *kynanchē,* from *kyn-,kyōn* "dog" + *anchein* "to strangle"]

quint \ˈkwint\ *n* **:** QUINTUPLET

quin•tain \ˈkwint-n\ *n* **:** an object to be tilted at; *esp* **:** a post with a revolving crosspiece that has a target at one end and a sandbag at the other [Middle French *quintaine,* from Latin *quintana* "street in a Roman camp separating the 5th maniple from the 6th where military exercises were performed", from *quintanus* "5th in rank", from *quintus* "fifth"]

quin•tal \ˈkwint-l\ *n* **1 :** HUNDREDWEIGHT **2** — see METRIC SYSTEM table [Middle French, from Medieval Latin *quintale,* from Arabic *qinṭār,* from Late Greek *kentēnarion,* from Late Latin *centenarium,* derived from Latin *centum* "hundred"]

quin•tes•sence \kwin-ˈtes-ns\ *n* **1 :** the purest form of something ⟨melody is the *quintessence* of music⟩ **2 :** the most typical example ⟨manners that were the *quintessence* of courtesy⟩ [derived from Medieval Latin *quinta essentia* "fifth essence, supposed fifth element more subtle than earth, air, fire, or water"] — **quint•es•sen•tial** \ˌkwint-ə-ˈsen-chəl\ *adj*

quin•tet *also* **quin•tette** \kwin-ˈtet\ *n* **1 :** a musical composition or movement for five instruments or voices **2 :** a group or set of five [Italian *quintetto,* from *quinto* "fifth", from Latin *quintus*]

quin•til•lion \kwin-ˈtil-yən\ *n* — see NUMBER table [Latin *quintus* "fifth" + English *-illion* (as in *million*)] — **quin•til•lionth** \-yənth, -yəntth\ *adj or n*

1quin•tu•ple \kwin-ˈtüp-əl, -ˈtyüp-, -ˈtəp-; ˈkwint-əp-\ *adj* **1 :** having five units or members **2 :** being five times as great or as many [Middle French, from Late Latin *quintuplex,* from Latin *quintus* "fifth" + *-plex* "-fold"] — **quintuple** *n*

2quintuple *vb* **quin•tu•pled**; **quin•tu•pling** \-ling, -ə-ling\ **:** to make or become five times as great or as many

quin•tup•let \kwin-ˈtəp-lət, -ˈtüp, -ˈtyüp-; ˈkwint-əp-\ *n* **1 :** a combination of five of a kind **2 :** one of five offspring born at one birth

1quin•tu•pli•cate \kwin-ˈtü-pli-kət, -ˈtyü-\ *adj* **:** having or being five corresponding or identical parts or examples [Latin *quintuplicatus,* past participle of *quintuplicare* "to quintuple", from *quintuplic-, quintuplex* "quintuple"]

2quin•tu•pli•cate \-pli-kət\ *n* **1 :** one of five like things **2 :** five copies all alike ⟨typed in *quintuplicate*⟩

3quin•tu•pli•cate \-plə-ˌkāt\ *vt* **1 :** QUINTUPLE **2 :** to provide in quintuplicate

1quip \ˈkwip\ *n* **1 a :** a clever usually taunting remark **:** GIBE **b :** a witty or funny observation or response **2 :** something strange or eccentric **:** ODDITY [earlier *quippy,* perhaps from Latin *quippe* "indeed", from *quid* "what"] **syn** see JEST — **quip•ster** \-stər\ *n*

2quip *vb* **quipped**; **quip•ping :** to make quips or make quips at

quire \ˈkwīr\ *n* **:** a collection of 24 or sometimes 25 sheets of paper of the same size and quality **:** 1/20 ream [Middle French *quaer* "four sheets of paper folded once, collection of sheets", derived from Latin *quaterni* "four each"]

quirk \ˈkwərk\ *n* **1 :** an abrupt turn, twist, or curve ⟨some *quirk* of fate threw us together⟩ **2 :** a peculiar trait **:** MANNERISM, IDIOSYNCRASY ⟨human beings with their *quirks* and foibles⟩ [origin unknown] — **quirk•i•ly** \ˈkwər-kə-lē\ *adv* — **quirk•i•ness** *n* \-kē-nəs\ *n* — **quirky** \-kē\ *adj*

quirt \ˈkwərt\ *n* **:** a riding whip with a short handle and a rawhide lash [Mexican Spanish *cuarta*]

quis•ling \ˈkwiz-ling\ *n* **:** a traitor who collaborates with the invaders of his or her country especially by serving in a puppet government [Vidkun *Quisling,* died 1945, Norwegian politician]

1quit \ˈkwit\ *adj* **:** released from obligation, charge, or penalty; *esp* **:** FREE ⟨*quit* of unnecessary fears⟩ [Old French *quite,* literally, "at rest", from Latin *quietus* "quiet, at rest"]

2quit *vb* **quit** *also* **quit•ted**; **quit•ting 1 :** to make full payment of ⟨*quit* a debt⟩ **2 :** ACQUIT ⟨the youths *quit* themselves like adults⟩ **3 a :** to depart from or out of **b :** to bring (as a way of thought, acting, or living) to an end **:** STOP ⟨*quit* horsing around⟩ **c :** to give up (an action, activity, or employment) for good ⟨*quit* smoking⟩ ⟨*quit* a job⟩ **4 :** to admit defeat **:** SURRENDER **syn** see STOP

quit•claim \ˈkwit-ˌklām\ *vt* **:** to release or relinquish a legal claim to especially by a quitclaim deed — **quitclaim** *n*

quitclaim deed *n* **:** a legal instrument used to release a right, title, or interest in property to another without warranting the title

quite \ˈkwīt\ *adv* **1 :** WHOLLY 1, COMPLETELY ⟨not *quite* all⟩ **2 :** to an extreme **:** POSITIVELY ⟨not *quite* sure⟩ **3 :** to a considerable extent **:** RATHER ⟨*quite* near⟩ [Middle English, from *quite* "free, quit"]

quit•rent \ˈkwit-ˌrent\ *n* **:** a fixed rent; *esp* **:** one payable to a feudal superior in the place of services

quits \ˈkwits\ *adj* **:** even or equal with another (as by repaying a debt or returning a favor)

quit•tance \ˈkwit-ns\ *n* **1 a :** discharge from a debt or an obligation **b :** a document evidencing quittance **2 :** RECOMPENSE, REQUITAL

quit•ter \ˈkwit-ər\ *n* **:** one that quits; *esp* **:** one that gives up too easily

1quiv•er \ˈkwiv-ər\ *n* **:** a case for holding arrows [Old French *quivre,* of Germanic origin]

2quiver *vi* **quiv•ered**; **quiv•er•ing** \ˈkwiv-ring, -ə-ring\ **:** to move with a slight trembling motion ⟨tall grass *quivering* in the breeze⟩ [Middle English *quiveren*]

3quiver *n* **:** the act or action of quivering

qui vive \kē-ˈvēv, ˈkē-\ *n* **1 :** CHALLENGE 2 **2 :** ALERT, LOOKOUT ⟨on the *qui vive* for prowlers⟩ [French *qui vive?* "long live who?", challenge of a French sentry]

quix•ot•ic \kwik-ˈsät-ik\ *adj* **:** idealistic to an impractical degree; *esp* **:** marked by rash lofty romantic ideas or extravagantly chivalrous action [Don *Quixote,* hero of the novel *Don Quixote de la Mancha* by Cervantes] — **quix•ot•i•cal•ly**

\-'sät-i-kə-lē, -klē\ *adv* — **quix·o·tism** \'kwik-sə-,tiz-əm\ *n*

1quiz \'kwiz\ *n, pl* **quiz·zes** **1** : an eccentric or mocking person **2** : PRACTICAL JOKE **3** : the act or action of quizzing; *esp* : a short oral or written test [origin unknown]

2quiz *vt* **quizzed**; **quiz·zing** **1** : to make fun of : MOCK **2** : to look at inquisitively **3** : to question closely : EXAMINE — **quiz·zer** *n*

quiz·zi·cal \'kwiz-i-kəl\ *adj* **1** : slightly eccentric : ODD **2** : marked by bantering or teasing **3** : INQUISITIVE ⟨a *quizzical* look⟩ — **quiz·zi·cal·ly** \-kə-lē, -klē\ *adv*

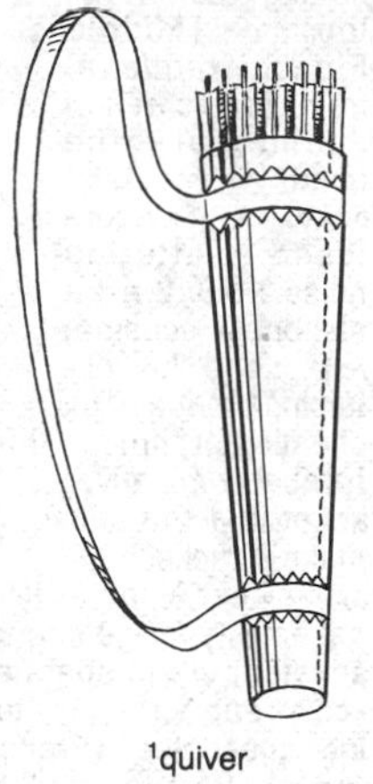

1quiver

quoin \'kȯin, 'kwȯin\ *n* : a solid exterior angle (as of a building); *also* : one of the blocks forming it [alteration of earlier *coin* "corner, coin"]

quoit \'kwȯit, 'kwāt, 'kȯit\ *n* **1** : a flattened ring of iron or circle of rope used in quoits **2** *pl* : a game in which quoits are tossed in an attempt to encircle a peg or come closer than one's opponent [Middle English *coite*]

quon·dam \'kwän-dəm, -,dam\ *adj* : FORMER 1, SOMETIME ⟨a *quondam* friend⟩ [Latin, "at one time, formerly"]

Quon·set \'kwän-sət\ *trademark* — used for a prefabricated shelter set on a foundation of steel trusses and built of a semicircular arching roof of corrugated metal

quo·rum \'kwōr-əm, 'kwȯr-\ *n* : the number of officers or members of a body that when duly assembled is legally competent to transact business [Latin, "of whom"]

quo·ta \'kwōt-ə\ *n* **1** : a proportional part or share; *esp* : the share or proportion assigned to each member of a body **2** : the number or amount constituting a proportional share [Medieval Latin, from Latin *quota pars* "how great a part"]

quot·able \'kwōt-ə-bəl\ *adj* : fit for or worth quoting

quo·ta·tion \kwō-'tā-shən\ *n* **1** : something that is quoted; *esp* : a passage referred to or repeated **2 a** : the act or process of quoting **b** : the naming or publishing of current bids and offers or prices of securities or commodities; *also* : the bids, offers, or prices so named or published

quotation mark *n* : one of a pair of punctuation marks " " or " " or ' ' or ' ' used chiefly to indicate the beginning and the end of a quotation in which the exact phraseology of another or of a text is directly cited

1quote \'kwōt\ *vb* **1 a** : to speak or write (a passage) from another usually with credit acknowledgment **b** : to repeat a passage from especially as authority or illustration ⟨*quote* Shakespeare⟩ **2** : to cite in illustration ⟨*quote* cases⟩ **3 a** : to name (the current price) of a commodity, stock, or bond **b** : to give exact information on **4** : to set off by quotation marks **5** : to give a quotation ⟨the defendant said, and I *quote*, . . .⟩ ⟨*quoted* from the Bible⟩ [Medieval Latin *quotare* "to mark the number of, number references", derived from Latin *quot* "how many"]

2quote *n* **1** : QUOTATION 1 **2** : QUOTATION MARK

quoth \kwōth, 'kwōth\ *vb past, archaic* : SAID — used chiefly in the first and third persons and placed before the subject [Old English *cwæth*, past of *cwethan* "to say"]

quo·tid·i·an \kwō-'tid-ē-ən\ *adj* **1** : belonging to each day ⟨*quotidian* routine⟩ **2** : COMMONPLACE, ORDINARY ⟨*quotidian* drabness⟩ [Middle French *cotidian*, from Latin *quotidianus*, *cotidianus*, from *quotidie* "every day", from *quot* "how many, (as) many as" + *dies* "day"]

quo·tient \'kwō-shənt\ *n* : the number resulting from the division of one number by another [Latin *quotiens* "how many times", from *quot* "how many"]

R r—ryegrass

r \'är\ *n, pl* **r's** *or* **rs** \'ärz\ *often cap*: the 18th letter of the English alphabet

rab·at \'rab-ē, 'rab-ət\ *n* : a black shirtfront often worn with a clerical collar [Middle French]

1rab·bet \'rab-ət\ *n* : a groove or recess cut in the edge or face of a surface especially to receive the edge of another surface (as a panel) [Middle French *rabat* "act of beating down," from *rabattre* "to beat down"]

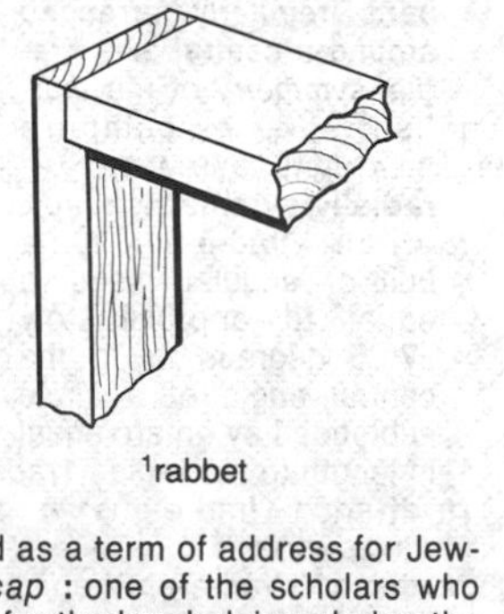

1rabbet

2rabbet *vt* **1** : to cut a rabbet in **2** : to join the edges of (as boards) by a rabbet

rab·bi \'rab-,ī\ *n* **1** *often cap* : MASTER, TEACHER — used as a term of address for Jewish religious leaders **2** *often cap* : one of the scholars who developed the Talmudic basis of orthodox Judaism during the first centuries of the Christian era **3** : a Jew trained professionally and ordained as the official leader of a Jewish congregation [Late Latin, from Greek *rhabbi*, from Hebrew *rabbī* "my master", from *rabh* "master" + *-ī* "my"]

rab·bin·ate \'rab-ə-nət, -,nāt\ *n* **1** : the office or tenure of a rabbi **2** : the whole body of rabbis

rab·bin·ic \rə-'bin-ik, ra-\ *adj* **1** *often cap* : of or relating to rabbis or their writings **2** : of or preparing for the rabbinate — **rab·bin·i·cal** \-'bin-i-kəl\ *adj* — **rab·bin·i·cal·ly** \-i-kə-lē, -klē\ *adv*

rab·bin·ism \'rab-ə-,niz-əm\ *n* : rabbinic teachings and traditions

1rab·bit \'rab-ət\ *n, pl* **rabbits** *also* **rabbit** : a small long-eared burrowing mammal differing from the related hares especially in producing naked young; *also* : its pelt [Middle English *rabet*]

2rab·bit *vi* : to hunt rabbits

rabbit fever *n* : TULAREMIA

rabbit punch *n* : a short chopping blow delivered to the back of the neck or the base of the skull [from the way a rabbit is stunned before being killed and butchered]

rab·ble \'rab-əl\ *n* **1** : a noisy and unruly crowd : MOB **2** : a body of people looked down upon as ignorant and disorderly [Middle English *rabel* "pack of animals"]

rab·ble-rous·er \-,raů-zər\ *n* : one that stirs up the masses of the people especially to hatred or violence

Ra·be·lai·sian \,rab-ə-'lā-zhən, -zē-ən\ *adj* **1** : of, relating to, or characteristic of Rabelais or his works **2** : marked by gross robust humor or extravagant caricature

rab·id \'rab-əd\ *adj* **1** : extremely violent : FURIOUS **2** : going to extreme lengths in expressing or pursuing a feeling, interest, or opinion ⟨a *rabid* sports fan⟩ **3** : affected with rabies ⟨a *rabid* dog⟩ [Latin *rabidus* "mad", from *rabere* "to rage, rave"] — **rab·id·ly** *adv* — **rab·id·ness** *n*

ra·bies \'rā-bēz\ *n* : an acute virus disease of the central nervous system of warm-blooded animals transmitted by the bite of an infected animal and always fatal when untreated — called also *hydrophobia* [Latin "madness", from *rabere* "to rage, rave"] — **ra·bic** \'rā-bik\ *adj*

\ə\ **abut**	\aů\ **out**	\i\ **tip**	\ȯ\ **saw**	\ů\ **foot**
\ər\ **further**	\ch\ **chin**	\ī\ **life**	\ȯi\ **coin**	\y\ **yet**
\a\ **mat**	\e\ **pet**	\j\ **job**	\th\ **thin**	\yü\ **few**
\ā\ **take**	\ē\ **easy**	\ng\ **sing**	\t͟h\ **this**	\yů\ **cure**
\ä\ **cot, cart**	\g\ **go**	\ō\ **bone**	\ü\ **food**	\zh\ **vision**

rac•coon *also* **ra•coon** \ra-ˈkün\ *n, pl* **raccoon** *or* **raccoons** : a small flesh-eating mammal of North America that is chiefly gray, has a bushy ringed tail, and lives chiefly in trees; *also* : its pelt [of American Indian origin]

raccoon

[1]race \ˈrās\ *n* **1** : a strong or rapid current of water or its channel or passage; *esp* : a current of water used for industrial purposes (as turning a mill wheel) **2 a** : a set course or duration of time **b** : the course of life **3 a** : a running in competition **b** *pl* : a meeting for contests in the running especially of horses ⟨off to the *races*⟩ **c** : a contest involving progress toward a goal ⟨the *race* for the governorship⟩ **4** : a track or channel in which something rolls or slides; *esp* : a groove for the balls in a bearing [Old Norse *rās*]

[2]race *vb* **1** : to run in a race **2** : to go, move, or drive at top speed or out of control ⟨the flood *raced* through the valley⟩ **3 a** : to engage in a race with ⟨*race* the champion⟩ **b** : to enter in a race ⟨had a new horse to *race*⟩ **4** : to run (as an engine) at high speed without a load or with the transmission disengaged

[3]race *n* **1 a** : a group of people of common ancestry or stock ⟨scion of a noble *race*⟩; *also* : one unified by community of interests, habits, or characteristics as if by ancestry ⟨the English *race*⟩ **b** : one of the three, four, or five primary divisions commonly recognized in mankind and based on readily observed traits (as skin color) that are transmitted by heredity ⟨the Caucasian *race*⟩ **c** : HUMANITY 4 ⟨the human *race*⟩ **2** : a group of genetically related individuals within a species; *also* : a taxonomic category (as a subspecies or breed) that represents such a group **3** *obsolete* : inherited temperament or disposition [Middle French, "generation", from Italian *razza*]

race•course \ˈrā-ˌskōrs, -ˌskȯrs\ *n* : a course for racing

race•horse \ˈrās-ˌhȯrs\ *n* : a horse bred or kept for racing

ra•ceme \rā-ˈsēm\ *n* : a simple inflorescence with a long axis bearing flowers on short stems in succession toward the apex [Latin *racemus* "bunch of grapes"] — **ra•ce•mose** \ˈras-ə-ˌmōs, rā-ˈsē-\ *adj*

rac•er \ˈrā-sər\ *n* **1** : one that races **2** : any of various slender active American snakes; *esp* : common blacksnake

race•track \ˈrā-ˌstrak\ *n* : a usually oval course for races

ra•chis \ˈrā-kəs, ˈrak-əs\ *n, pl* **ra•chis•es** *also* **ra•chi•des** \ˈrak-ə-ˌdēz, ˈrā-kə-\ **1** : the axis of an inflorescence **2** : an extension of the petiole of a compound leaf that bears the leaflets **3** : the distal part of the shaft of a feather [Greek *rhachis* "spine, backbone"]

ra•cial \ˈrā-shəl\ *adj* **1** : of, relating to, or based on race **2** : existing or occurring between human races ⟨*racial* harmony⟩ — **ra•cial•ly** \-shə-lē\ *adv*

ra•cial•ism \ˈrā-shə-ˌliz-əm\ *n* : RACISM — **ra•cial•ist** \ˈrāsh-ləst, -ə-ləst\ *n* — **ra•cial•is•tic** \ˌrā-shə-ˈlis-tik\ *adj*

rac•i•ly \ˈrā-sə-lē\ *adv* : in a racy manner

rac•i•ness \-sē-nəs\ *n* : the quality or state of being racy

rac•ism \ˈrā-ˌsiz-əm\ *n* **1** : belief that certain races of people are by birth and nature superior to others **2** : discrimination against the members of one or more races based upon racism — **rac•ist** \ˈrā-səst\ *n*

[1]rack \ˈrak\ *n* **1** : a framework for holding fodder for livestock **2** : an instrument of torture on which a body is stretched **3** : a framework, stand, or grating on or in which articles are placed ⟨clothes *rack*⟩ ⟨bicycle *rack*⟩ **4** : a bar with teeth on one face for gearing with a pinion or worm gear [Middle English] — **on the rack** : under great mental or emotional stress

[2]rack *vt* **1** : to torture on the rack **2** : to cause to suffer torture, pain, or anguish ⟨*racked* by a cough⟩ **3** : to stretch or strain violently **syn** see AFFLICT

[3]rack *vi* : to go at a rack [probably alteration of [1]*rock*]

[4]rack *n* : either of two gaits of a horse: **a** : PACE 2b **b** : a fast showy usually artifical 4-beat gait — called also *single-foot*

[5]rack *n* : DESTRUCTION ⟨went to *rack* and ruin⟩ [alteration of *wrack*]

[1]rack•et *also* **rac•quet** \ˈrak-ət\ *n* : a usually long-handled implement used for hitting a ball or shuttlecock (as in tennis or badminton) that consists of an oval open frame strung with a netting (as of nylon) [Middle French *raquette*, from Arabic *rāhah* "palm of the hand"]

[1]racket: *top* tennis, *bottom* badminton

[2]racket *n* **1** : confused clattering noise : DIN **2 a** : a dishonest scheme; *esp* : one for obtaining money by cheating or through threats of violence **b** *slang* : OCCUPATION [probably imitative]

[3]racket *vi* **1** : to engage in active social life **2** : to move with or make a racket

[1]rack•e•teer \ˌrak-ə-ˈtiər\ *n* : a person who engages in an illegal activity for getting money especially by extortion

[2]racketeer *vi* : to operate an illegal racket

ra•con•teur \ˌrak-ˌän-ˈtər, ˌrak-ən-\ *n* : one who excels in telling anecdotes [French, from *raconter* "to tell", from Old French, from *re-* "re-" + *aconter, acompter* "to tell, count"]

ra•coon *variant of* RACCOON

rac•quets \ˈrak-əts\ *n* : a game for two or four played with ball and racket on a 4-walled court

[1]racy \ˈrā-sē\ *adj* **rac•i•er**; **-est** **1** : having the distinctive quality of something in its original or most characteristic form **2 a** : full of zest or vigor : LIVELY **b** : slightly indecent or improper : RISQUÉ, SUGGESTIVE ⟨*racy* stories⟩ [[3]*race*]

[2]racy *adj* **rac•i•er**; **-est** : being long-bodied and lean ⟨a *racy* whippet⟩

ra•dar \ˈrā-ˌdär\ *n* : a device that sends out a powerful beam of radio waves that when reflected back to it from a distant object indicate the position and direction of motion of the object [*ra*dio *d*etecting *a*nd *r*anging]

ra•dar•scope \-ˌskōp\ *n* : the part of a radar apparatus on which the spots of light appear that indicate the position and direction of motion of a distant object [*radar* + oscillo*scope*]

[1]ra•di•al \ˈrād-ē-əl\ *adj* **1** : arranged or having parts arranged like rays coming from a common center **2** : relating to, placed like, or moving along a radius [Medieval Latin *radialis*, from Latin *radius* "spoke, radius, ray"] — **ra•di•al•ly** \-ē-ə-lē\ *adv*

[2]radial *n* **1** : a radial part **2** : a pneumatic tire in which the ply cords are laid at approximately 90° to the center line of the tread — called also *radial-ply tire, radial tire*

radial engine *n* : a usually internal-combustion engine with cylinders arranged radially like the spokes of a wheel

radial symmetry *n* : the condition of having similar parts regularly arranged around a central axis ⟨*radial symmetry* of the starfish⟩ — compare BILATERAL SYMMETRY — **radially symmetrical** *adj*

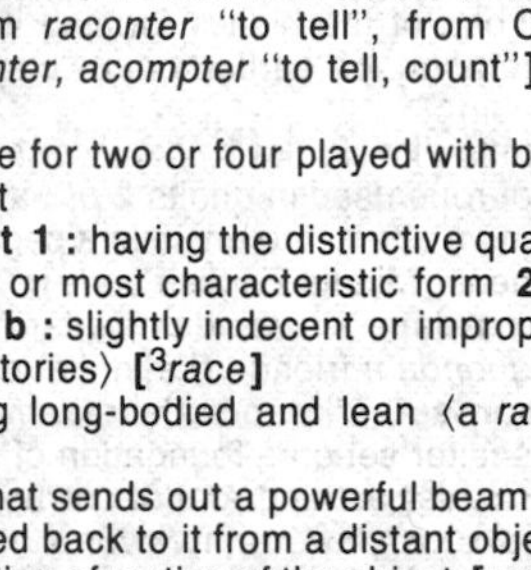

radial symmetry

ra•di•an \ˈrād-ē-ən\ *n* : a unit of angular measure equal to approximately 57.25 degrees or to the central angle of a circle subtended by an arc equal in length to the radius [*radi*us + *-an*]

ra•di•ance \ˈrād-ē-əns\ *n* : the quality or state of being radiant : SPLENDOR

ra•di•ant \ˈrād-ē-ənt\ *adj* **1 a** : giving out or reflecting rays of light ⟨the *radiant* sun⟩ ⟨a *radiant* jewel⟩ **b** : vividly bright and shining ⟨*radiant* eyes⟩ **2** : marked by or expressive of love, confidence, or happiness **3 a** : emitted or transmitted by radiation ⟨*radiant* heat from the sun⟩ **b** : emitting or relating to radiant heat ⟨a *radiant* lamp⟩ — **ra•di•ant•ly** *adv*

radiant energy *n* : energy transmitted in the form of electromagnetic waves (as heat waves, light waves, radio waves, or X rays)

radiant heating *n* : PANEL HEATING

[1]ra•di•ate \ˈrād-ē-ˌāt\ *vb* **1** : to send out rays of or as if of light **2 a** : to come or be sent out from a center in or as if in rays ⟨heat *radiates*⟩ ⟨a story that *radiated* widely⟩ **b** : to send out in rays or as if in rays ⟨stars *radiate* energy⟩ **3** : IRRADIATE 1a,

ILLUMINATE **4** : to spread abroad or around : DISSEMINATE [Latin *radiare,* from *radius* "ray"]

²ra•di•ate \-ē-ət\ *adj* : having rays or radial parts

ra•di•a•tion \ˌrād-ē-ˈā-shən\ *n* **1** : the action or process of radiating; *esp* : the process of emitting radiant energy in the form of waves or particles **2** : something that is radiated: as **a** : energy radiated in the form of waves or particles **b** : biological evolution in a group of organisms that is characterized by spreading into different environments and by divergence of structure ⟨the Devonian *radiation* of fishes⟩ — **ra•di•a•tion•al** \-shnəl, -shən-l\ *adj* — **ra•di•a•tive** \ˈrād-ē-ˌāt-iv\ *adj*

radiation sickness *n* : sickness that results from exposure to radiation and is commonly marked by fatigue, nausea, vomiting, loss of teeth and hair, and in more severe cases by damage to blood-forming tissue with decrease in red and white blood cells and bleeding

ra•di•a•tor \ˈrād-ē-ˌāt-ər\ *n* : one that radiates: as **a** : a device consisting of a series of pipes through which hot water or steam circulates for heating a room **b** : a device for cooling by radiation water (as of an automobile engine) that circulates through a series of tubes

¹rad•i•cal \ˈrad-i-kəl\ *adj* **1** : of, relating to, or proceeding from a root **2** : of or relating to the origin : FUNDAMENTAL ⟨*radical* differences⟩ **3 a** : marked by a sharp departure from the usual or traditional : EXTREME **b** : of, relating to, or disposed to the making of extreme changes in existing views, habits, conditions, or institutions ⟨*radical* ideas⟩; *esp* : of, relating to, or constituting a political group associated with views, practices, and policies of extreme change [Late Latin *radicalis,* from Latin *radic-, radix* "root"] **syn** see LIBERAL — **rad•i•cal•ness** *n*

²radical *n* **1** : ROOT 5 **2** : one who is radical **3** : a group of atoms that is replaceable by a single atom and is capable of remaining unchanged during a series of reactions **4 a** : the indicated root of a mathematical expression **b** : RADICAL SIGN

radical expression *n* : a mathematical expression involving radical signs

rad•i•cal•ism \ˈrad-i-kə-ˌliz-əm\ *n* **1** : the quality or state of being radical **2** : the doctrines or principles of radicals

rad•i•cal•ize \-kə-ˌlīz\ *vt* : to make radical especially in politics — **rad•i•cal•iza•tion** \ˌrad-i-kə-lə-ˈzā-shən\ *n*

rad•i•cal•ly \ˈrad-i-kə-lē, -klē\ *adv* **1** : in origin or essence : NATURALLY **2** : in a radical or extreme manner

radical sign *n* : the sign √ placed before an expression in mathematics to indicate that the square root is to be extracted or that some other root is to be extracted when a corresponding index is placed over the sign

rad•i•cand \ˌrad-ə-ˈkand\ *n* : the expression under a radical sign [derived from Latin *radicari* "to take root", from *radic-, radix* "root"]

radices *pl of* RADIX

rad•i•cle \ˈrad-i-kəl\ *n* : the lower part of the axis of a plant embryo or seedling : the growing tip of the hypocotyl : HYPOCOTYL [Latin *radicula* "small root", from *radic-, radix* "root"] — **ra•dic•u•lar** \ra-ˈdik-yə-lər\ *adj*

radii *pl of* RADIUS

¹ra•dio \ˈrād-ē-ˌō\ *n, pl* **ra•di•os 1** : the sending or receiving of messages or effects and especially sound by means of electromagnetic waves without a connecting wire **2** : a radio message **3** : a radio receiving set **4 a** : a radio transmitting station **b** : a radio broadcasting organization **c** : the radio broadcasting industry [short for *radiotelegraphy*]

²radio *adj* **1** : of, relating to, using, or operated by radiant energy ⟨*radio* communication⟩ **2** : of or relating to electric currents or phenomena of frequencies between about 15 kilohertz and 100,000 megahertz **3 a** : of, relating to, or used in radio or a radio set **b** : controlled or directed by radio

³radio *vb* **1** : to send or communicate by radio **2** : to send a radio message to

radio- *combining form* **1** : radial : radially ⟨*radio*symmetrical⟩ **2 a** : radiant energy : radiation ⟨*radio*active⟩ **b** : radioactive ⟨*radio*carbon⟩ **c** : radio ⟨*radio*telegraph⟩ [French, from Latin *radius* "spoke, radius, ray"]

ra•dio•ac•tive \ˌrād-ē-ō-ˈak-tiv\ *adj* : of, caused by, or exhibiting radioactivity — **ra•dio•ac•tive•ly** *adv*

ra•dio•ac•tiv•i•ty \-ˌak-ˈtiv-ət-ē\ *n* : the property possessed by some elements (as uranium) of spontaneously emitting alpha, beta, and gamma rays by the disintegration of the nuclei of atoms

radio astronomy *n* : astronomy dealing with electromagnetic radiations of radio frequency received from outside the earth's atmosphere — **radio astronomer** *n*

ra•dio•au•to•graph \ˌrād-ē-ō-ˈȯt-ə-ˌgraf\ *n* : AUTORADIOGRAPH — **ra•dio•au•tog•ra•phy** \-ȯ-ˈtäg-rə-fē\ *n*

radio beacon *n* : a radio transmitting station that transmits radio signals for use (as on a landing field) in determining the direction or position of those receiving them

ra•dio•broad•cast \ˌrād-ē-ō-ˈbrȯd-ˌkast\ *vt* : BROADCAST 3a — **ra•dio•broad•cast•er** *n*

radio car *n* : an automobile (as a police car) equipped with two-way radio communications

ra•dio•car•bon \-ˈkär-bən\ *n* : radioactive carbon; *esp* : CARBON 14

ra•dio•cast \ˈrād-ē-ō-ˌkast\ *vt* : BROADCAST 3a — **ra•dio•cast•er** *n*

ra•dio•el•e•ment \ˌrād-ē-ō-ˈel-ə-mənt\ *n* : a radioactive element

radio frequency *n* : any of the electromagnetic wave frequencies intermediate between audio frequencies and infrared frequencies used especially in radio and television transmission

ra•dio•gen•ic \ˌrād-ē-ō-ˈjen-ik\ *adj* : produced by radioactivity

ra•dio•gram \ˈrād-ē-ō-ˌgram\ *n* **1** : RADIOGRAPH **2** : a message sent by radiotelegraphy

¹ra•dio•graph \-ˌgraf\ *n* : a picture produced on a sensitive surface by a form of radiation other than light; *esp* : X-RAY PHOTOGRAPH — **ra•dio•graph•ic** \ˌrād-ē-ō-ˈgraf-ik\ *adj* — **ra•dio•graph•i•cal•ly** \-ˈgraf-i-kə-lē, -klē\ *adv* — **ra•di•og•ra•phy** \ˌrād-ē-ˈäg-rə-fē\ *n*

²radiograph *vt* : to make a radiograph of

³radiograph *vt* : to send a radiogram to

ra•dio•iso•tope \ˌrād-ē-ō-ˈī-sə-ˌtōp\ *n* : a radioactive isotope

ra•di•o•lar•i•an \ˌrād-ē-ō-ˈlar-ē-ən, -ˈler-\ *n* : any of a large order (Radiolaria) of marine protozoans with radiating threadlike pseudopodia and a siliceous skeleton [derived from Late Latin *radiolus* "small sunbeam", from Latin *radius* "ray"]

ra•di•ol•o•gy \ˌrād-ē-ˈäl-ə-jē\ *n* : the use of radiant energy in medicine — **ra•dio•log•ic** \ˌrād-ē-ə-ˈläj-ik\ *adj* — **ra•dio•log•i•cal** \-ˈläj-i-kəl\ *adj* — **ra•di•ol•o•gist** \ˌrād-ē-ˈäl-ə-jəst\ *n*

ra•di•om•e•ter \ˌrād-ē-ˈäm-ət-ər\ *n* : an instrument for measuring the intensity of radiant energy — **ra•dio•met•ric** \ˌrād-ē-ō-ˈme-trik\ *adj* — **ra•di•om•e•try** \-ˈäm-ə-trē\ *n*

ra•dio•nu•clide \ˌrād-ē-ō-ˈnü-ˌklīd, -ˈnyü-\ *n* : a radioactive nuclide

ra•dio•phone \ˈrād-ē-ə-ˌfōn\ *n* : RADIOTELEPHONE

ra•dio•pho•to \ˌrād-ē-ō-ˈfōt-ō\ *n* **1** : a picture transmitted by radio **2** : the process of transmitting a picture by radio

ra•dio•sonde \ˈrād-ē-ō-ˌsänd\ *n* : a miniature radio transmitter that is carried (as by a balloon) aloft with instruments for broadcasting data on humidity, temperature, and pressure [French *sonde* "sounding line"]

ra•dio•tel•e•graph \ˌrād-ē-ō-ˈtel-ə-ˌgraf\ *n* : telegraphy using radio waves — **ra•dio•te•leg•ra•phy** \-tə-ˈleg-rə-fē\ *n*

ra•dio•tel•e•phone \-ˈtel-ə-ˌfōn\ *n* : a telephone (as in a car) that utilizes radio waves wholly or partly instead of connecting wires — **ra•dio•te•le•pho•ny** \-tə-ˈlef-ə-nē, -ˈtel-ə-ˌfō-nē\ *n*

radio telescope *n* : a radio receiver-antenna combination used for observation in radio astronomy

ra•dio•ther•a•py \ˌrād-ē-ō-ˈther-ə-pē\ *n* : the treatment of disease by means of X rays or radioactive substances — **ra•dio•ther•a•pist** \-pəst\ *n*

ra•dio–ul•na \ˌrād-ē-ō-ˈəl-nə\ *n* : a single bone in the forelimb of an amphibian (as a frog) equivalent to the separate radius and ulna of higher forms

radio wave *n* : an electromagnetic wave with radio frequency used in radio, television, or radar communication

rad•ish \ˈrad-ish, ˈred-\ *n* : a pungent fleshy root usually eaten raw; *also* : a plant of the mustard family whose roots are radishes [Old English *rædic,* from Latin *radix* "root, radish"]

ra•di•um \ˈrād-ē-əm\ *n* : an intensely radioactive shining white metallic chemical element that occurs in combination in minute quantities in minerals (as pitchblende), emits alpha particles and gamma rays to form radon, and is used chiefly in luminous materials and in the treatment of cancer — see ELEMENT table [New Latin, from Latin *radius* "ray"]

ra•di•us \ˈrād-ē-əs\ *n, pl* **-dii** \-ē-ˌī\ *also* **-di•us•es 1 :** the bone on the thumb side of the human forearm; *also* **:** a corresponding part of vertebrates above fishes **2 a :** a line segment extending from the center of a circle or sphere to the circumference or surface; *also* **:** its length **b :** a circular area defined by a radius ⟨deer may wander within a *radius* of several miles⟩ **3 :** a radial part or plane [Latin, "spoke, ray, radius"]

ra•dix \ˈrād-iks\ *n, pl* **ra•di•ces** \ˈrād-ə-ˌsēz, ˈrad-\ *or* **ra•dix•es :** the base of a number system [Latin, "root"]

ra•dome \ˈrā-ˌdōm\ *n* **:** a usually plastic housing sheltering the antenna assembly of a radar set [*radar dome*]

ra•don \ˈrā-ˌdän\ *n* **:** a heavy radioactive gaseous chemical element formed by disintegration of radium — see ELEMENT table [derived from *radium*]

rad•u•la \ˈraj-ə-lə\ *n, pl* **-lae** \-ˌlē, -ˌlī\ *also* **-las :** a toothed horny band in mollusks other than bivalves used to tear up and draw food into the mouth [Latin, "scraper", from *radere* "to scrape"] — **rad•u•lar** \-lər\ *adj*

raf•fia \ˈraf-ē-ə\ *n* **:** fiber from a pinnate-leaved palm of Madagascar used especially for baskets and hats [Malagasy *rafia*]

raff•ish \ˈraf-ish\ *adj* **1 :** vulgarly crude or flashy **2 :** marked by a carefree unconventionality [Middle English *raf* "rubbish"] — **raff•ish•ly** *adv* — **raff•ish•ness** *n*

[1]**raf•fle** \ˈraf-əl\ *n* **:** a lottery in which the prize is won by one of the persons buying chances [Middle French *rafle,* a dice game]

[2]**raffle** *vt* **raf•fled; raf•fling** \ˈraf-ling, -ə-ling\ **:** to offer as a prize in a raffle ⟨*raffle* off a turkey⟩

[1]**raft** \ˈraft\ *n* **1 :** a collection of logs or timber fastened together for transportation by water **2 :** a flat structure for support or transportation on water [Middle English *rafte* "rafter, raft", from Old Norse *raptr* "rafter"]

[2]**raft** *vb* **1 :** to transport or move in or by means of a raft **2 :** to make into a raft

[3]**raft** *n* **:** a large amount [alteration of earlier *raff* "jumble, rubbish", from Middle English *raf*]

raf•ter \ˈraf-tər\ *n* **:** any of the parallel beams that support a roof [Old English *ræfter*]

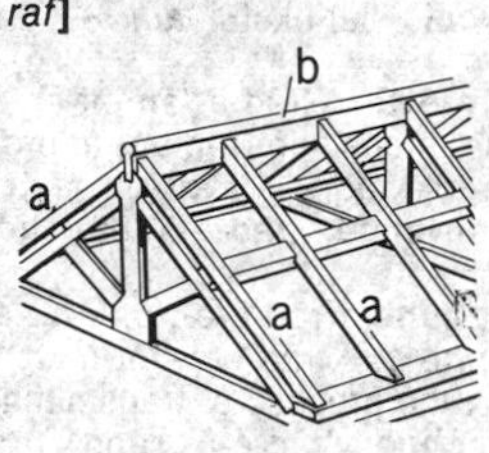

rafter: *a* rafters, *b* ridgepole

[1]**rag** \ˈrag\ *n* **1 a :** a waste or worn piece of cloth **b** *pl* **:** shabby or tattered clothing ⟨dressed in *rags*⟩ **2 :** something felt to resemble a rag of cloth; *esp* **:** SCRAP 2, SHRED ⟨left without a *rag* of self-respect⟩ [Old Norse *rögg* "tuft, shagginess"]

[2]**rag** *vt* **ragged** \ˈragd\; **rag•ging 1 :** to rail at **:** SCOLD **2 :** TEASE 2a, HARASS [origin unknown]

rag•a•muf•fin \ˈrag-ə-ˌməf-ən\ *n* **:** a ragged often disreputable person; *esp* **:** a poorly clothed often dirty child [*Ragamoffyn,* a demon in *Piers Plowman* (1393), attributed to William Langland]

rag•bag \ˈrag-ˌbag\ *n* **1 :** a bag for scraps **2 :** a miscellaneous collection

[1]**rage** \ˈrāj\ *n* **1 a :** violent and uncontrolled anger **:** FURY **b :** a fit of violent anger **2 :** violent action (as of wind or sea) **3 :** CRAZE, VOGUE ⟨was all the *rage*⟩ [Middle French, derived from Latin *rabies* "madness, rage", from *rabere* "to rage, be mad"] **syn** see ANGER

[2]**rage** *vi* **1 :** to be in a rage **2 :** to be in tumult ⟨the storm *raged*⟩ **3 :** to persist or spread uncontrollably ⟨a *raging* epidemic⟩

rag•ged \ˈrag-əd\ *adj* **1 :** roughly unkempt **:** STRAGGLY ⟨a *ragged* lawn⟩ **2 :** having an irregular edge or outline **:** JAGGED ⟨*ragged* cliffs⟩ **3 a :** torn or worn to or as if to tatters ⟨a *ragged* dress⟩ **b :** wearing tattered clothes **4 :** executed in an irregular or uneven manner ⟨played *ragged* defense⟩ — **rag•ged•ly** *adv* — **rag•ged•ness** *n*

rag•gedy \-əd-ē\ *adj* **:** somewhat ragged

rag•gle-tag•gle \ˈrag-əl-ˌtag-əl\ *adj* **:** MOTLEY [derived from *ragtag*]

rag•ing \ˈrā-jing\ *adj* **1 :** causing great pain or distress **2 :** VIOLENT 1, WILD

rag•lan \ˈrag-lən\ *n* **:** a loose overcoat having sleeves that extend to the neckline with slanted seams from the underarm to the neck [F. J. H. Somerset, Baron *Raglan,* died 1855, British field marshal]

rag•man \ˈrag-ˌman\ *n* **:** a collector of or dealer in rags and waste

ra•gout \ra-ˈgü\ *n* **:** a highly seasoned meat stew with vegetables [French *ragoût*]

rag•tag and bob•tail \ˌrag-ˌtag-ən-ˈbäb-ˌtāl\ *n* **:** RABBLE [*ragtag* from [1]*rag* + [1]*tag*]

rag•time \ˈrag-ˌtīm\ *n* **1 :** musical rhythm in which the melody has the accented notes falling on beats that are not usually accented **2 :** music with ragtime rhythm [probably from *ragged* + *time*]

rag•weed \ˈrag-ˌwēd\ *n* **:** any of various chiefly North American weedy herbs related to the daisies that produce pollen highly irritating to the eyes and nasal passages of some persons

rah \ˈrä, ˈrȯ\ *interj* **:** HURRAH — used especially to cheer on a team ⟨*rah, rah,* team⟩

[1]**raid** \ˈrād\ *n* **1 a :** an entering of something hostile or predatory **b :** a surprise attack by a small military force **2 :** a sudden entry of officers of the law [Scottish dialect, from Old English *rād* "ride, raid"]

[2]**raid** *vt* **:** to make a raid on — **raid•er** *n*

[1]**rail** \ˈrāl\ *n* **1 a :** a bar extending from one post or support to another and serving as a guard or barrier **b :** RAILING 1 **2 a :** a bar of rolled steel forming a track for wheeled vehicles **b :** TRACK 1c(2) **c :** RAILROAD [Middle French *reille* "ruler, bar", from Latin *regula* "ruler", from *regere* "to keep straight, rule"]

[2]**rail** *vt* **:** to provide with a railing

[3]**rail** *n, pl* **rails** *or* **rail :** any of a family of small wading birds related to the cranes [Middle French *raale*]

[4]**rail** *vi* **:** to criticize or scold in harsh or abusive language [Middle French *railler* "to mock, rally"] — **rail•er** *n*

rail•ing \ˈrā-ling\ *n* **1 :** a barrier (as a fence or balustrade) consisting of rails and their supports **2 :** material for making rails **:** RAILS

rail•lery \ˈrā-lə-rē\ *n, pl* **-ler•ies :** good-natured ridicule **:** BANTER [French *raillerie,* from *railler* "to mock, rally"]

[1]**rail•road** \ˈrāl-ˌrōd\ *n* **:** a permanent road having a line of rails fixed to ties and laid on a roadbed and providing a track for cars and equipment drawn by locomotives or propelled by self-contained motors; *also* **:** such a road and its assets constituting a single property **:** a railroad company

[2]**railroad** *vb* **1 a :** to transport by railroad **b :** to work for a railroad company **2 a :** to push through hastily or without due consideration ⟨*railroad* a bill into law⟩ **b :** to convict with undue haste and by means of false charges or insufficient evidence — **rail•road•er** *n*

rail•road•ing *n* **:** construction or operation of a railroad

rail•way \ˈrāl-ˌwā\ *n* **1 :** RAILROAD; *esp* **:** a railroad operating with light equipment or within a small area **2 :** a line of track providing a runway for wheels ⟨a cash or parcel *railway* in a department store⟩

rai•ment \ˈrā-mənt\ *n* **:** CLOTHING, GARMENTS [Middle English *rayment,* short for *arrayment,* from *arrayen* "to array"]

[1]**rain** \ˈrān\ *n* **1 a :** water falling in drops condensed from vapor in the atmosphere; *also* **:** the descent of such water **b :** RAINWATER **2 a :** a fall of rain **:** RAINSTORM **b** *pl* **:** the rainy season **3 :** rainy weather **4 :** a heavy fall of particles or bodies; *also* **:** a large outpouring ⟨a *rain* of abuse⟩ [Old English *regn*] — **rain•less** \-ləs\ *adj*

[2]**rain** *vb* **1 :** to fall as water in drops from the clouds **2 :** to send down rain **3 :** to fall like rain ⟨ashes *rained* from the volcano⟩ **4 :** to bestow abundantly ⟨*rain* favors⟩

rain•bow \-ˌbō\ *n* **1 :** an arc or circle that exhibits in concentric bands the colors of the spectrum and that is formed opposite the sun by the refraction and reflection of the sun's rays in raindrops, spray, or mist **2 :** a multicolored array

rainbow runner *n* **:** a large brightly marked blue and yellow food and sport fish of warm seas

rainbow trout *n* **:** a large stout-bodied usually brightly marked trout native to western North America — called also *rainbow;* compare STEELHEAD

rain•coat \ˈrān-ˌkōt\ *n* **:** a coat of waterproof or water-resistant material

rain•drop \-ˌdräp\ *n* **:** a drop of rain

rain•fall \-ˌfȯl\ *n* **1 :** RAIN 2a **2 :** amount of precipitation ⟨an annual *rainfall* of 20 inches⟩

rain forest *n* **:** a usually tropical woodland with a high annual rainfall and lofty trees forming a continuous canopy

rain gauge *n* : an instrument for measuring rainfall

rain•mak•ing \'rān-,mā-king\ *n* : the act or process of producing or attempting to produce rain by artificial means — **rain•mak•er** \-kər\ *n*

rain•proof \'rān-'prüf\ *adj* : impervious to rain

rain•storm \-,stȯrm\ *n* : a storm of or with rain

rain•wa•ter \-,wȯt-ər, -,wät-\ *n* : water fallen as rain

rainy \'rā-nē\ *adj* **rain•i•er; -est** : having much rain : SHOWERY ⟨a *rainy* season⟩

rainy day *n* : a period of want or need ⟨lay something by for a *rainy day*⟩

[1]**raise** \'rāz\ *vb* **1** : to cause or help to rise ⟨*raise* dust⟩ **2 a** : to rouse from sleep : AROUSE **b** : to stir up : INCITE ⟨*raise* a rebellion⟩ **c** : to establish radio communication with **3 a** : to set upright by lifting or building **b** : to lift to a higher position ⟨a fist *raised* in anger⟩ **c** : to place higher in rank or dignity : ELEVATE **d** : HEIGHTEN 1a, INVIGORATE **e** : to end or suspend the operation or validity of ⟨*raise* a siege⟩ **4** : COLLECT ⟨*raise* funds⟩ **5 a** : to foster the growth and development of : GROW ⟨*raise* corn⟩ ⟨*raise* pigs⟩ **b** : to bring up (a child) ⟨was *raised* in the city⟩ **6 a** : to give rise to : PROVOKE **b** : to give voice to ⟨*raise* a cheer⟩ **7** : to bring up for consideration or debate ⟨*raise* an issue⟩ **8 a** : to increase the strength, intensity, or pitch of **b** : to increase the degree or rate of ⟨*raise* the rent⟩ **c** : to multiply (a quantity) by itself a specified number of times **9** : to make light and porous ⟨*raise* dough⟩ **10** : to cause (an elevated injury) to form on the skin ⟨the blow *raised* a welt⟩ [Old Norse *reisa*] **syn** see LIFT — **rais•er** *n*

[2]**raise** *n* **1** : an act or method of raising or lifting **2** : an upward grade : RISE **3 a** : an increase in amount (as of a bet or bid) **b** : an increase in pay

rai•sin \'rāz-n\ *n* : a grape rich in sugar that is dried for food [Middle French, "grape", from Latin *racemus* "cluster of grapes or berries"]

rai•son d'être \,rā-,zō^{n}-'detr\ *n* : reason or justification for existence [French]

ra•ja *or* **ra•jah** \'räj-ə, 'räzh-\ *n* : an Indian or Malay prince or chief [Hindi *rājā*, from Sanskrit *rājan* "king"]

Raj•put *or* **Raj•poot** \'räj-,püt, 'räzh-\ *n* : a member of a former Indo-Aryan dominant military caste of northern India [Hindi *rājpūt*, from Sanskrit *rājaputra* "king's son", from *rājan* "king" + *putra* "son"]

[1]**rake** \'rāk\ *n* : a long-handled garden tool having a bar with teeth or prongs; *also* : a machine for gathering hay [Old English *racu*]

[2]**rake** *vt* **1** : to gather, loosen, or smooth with or as if with a rake **2** : to gain (as money) quickly and in abundance **3 a** : BRUSH 3 **b** : SCRATCH 1 **4 a** : to search through : RANSACK **b** : to search out and gather together ⟨*rake* up old scandals⟩ **5** : to sweep the length of especially with gunfire **6** : to glance over rapidly — **rak•er** *n*

[3]**rake** *vi* : to incline from the perpendicular : SLANT [origin unknown]

[4]**rake** *n* : a slant or slope away from the perpendicular

[5]**rake** *n* : a dissolute person : LIBERTINE [short for earlier *rakehell*]

rake–off \'rā-,kȯf\ *n* : an improper or unlawful commission or profit received by one party in a business deal

[1]**rak•ish** \'rā-kish\ *adj* : of, relating to, or characteristic of a rake — **rak•ish•ly** *adv* — **rak•ish•ness** *n*

[2]**rakish** *adj* **1** : having a smart stylish appearance suggestive of speed ⟨a *rakish* ship⟩ **2** : flashily unconventional or informal : JAUNTY ⟨*rakish* clothes⟩ [probably from [3]*rake;* from the raking masts of pirate ships] — **rak•ish•ly** *adv* — **rak•ish•ness** *n*

rale \'ral, 'räl\ *n* : an abnormal sound accompanying breathing (as in pneumonia) [French *râle*]

ral•len•tan•do \,räl-ən-'tän-dō\ *adv or adj* : with a gradual decrease in tempo — used as a direction in music [Italian, literally, "slowing down"]

[1]**ral•ly** \'ral-ē\ *vb* **ral•lied; ral•ly•ing 1 a** : to bring together for a common purpose **b** : to bring back to order ⟨*rallying* the forces for a second assault⟩ **2** : to rouse for action or from depression or weakness ⟨the medicine *rallied* the patient⟩ **3** : to come together to renew an effort : join in a common cause **4** : RECOVER, REBOUND ⟨the market *rallied* after a slump⟩ **5** : to engage in a rally (as in tennis) [French *rallier*, from Old French *ralier*, from *re-* "re-" + *alier* "to unite, ally"]

[2]**rally** *n, pl* **rallies 1** : the action of rallying **2** : a mass meeting intended to arouse group enthusiasm **3** : a series of strokes interchanged between players (as in tennis) before a point is won

[3]**rally** *vt* **ral•lied; ral•ly•ing** : to tease with good-natured or friendly ridicule [French *railler* "to mock, rally", from Provençal *ralhar* "to babble, joke", derived from Latin *ragere* "to neigh"]

[1]**ram** \'ram\ *n* **1** : a male sheep **2** : BATTERING RAM **3** : a pointed beak on the prow of a ship for piercing an enemy ship **4** : a guided piece for exerting pressure or for driving or forcing something by impact [Old English *ramm*]

[2]**ram** *vb* **rammed; ram•ming 1** : to strike or strike against with violence : CRASH **2** : to rush violently or forcibly ⟨*ram* through traffic⟩ **3** : to force in, down, or together by or as if by driving or pressing **4** : to force passage or acceptance of ⟨*ram* a bill through congress⟩ [Middle English *rammen*, probably from *ram*, n.] — **ram•mer** *n*

Ram•a•dan \'ram-ə-,dän, -,dan\ *n* : the 9th month of the Muhammadan year observed with daily fasting from dawn to sunset [Arabic *Ramaḍān*]

[1]**ram•ble** \'ram-bəl\ *vb* **ram•bled; ram•bling** \-bə-ling, -bling\ **1 a** : to move aimlessly from place to place : WANDER, ROAM **b** : to explore idly **2** : to talk or write in a disjointed or disorganized fashion **3** : to grow or extend irregularly [perhaps from Middle English *romblen*, from *romen* "to roam"]

[2]**ramble** *n* : a leisurely excursion for pleasure; *esp* : a leisurely or aimless walk

ram•bler \'ram-blər\ *n* **1** : one that rambles **2** : a climbing rose with rather small often double flowers in large clusters

rambler 2

ramb•ling \'ram-bling\ *adj* : lacking in logical organization : DISCURSIVE — **ram•bling•ly** \-bling-lē\ *adv*

ram•bouil•let \,ram-bə-'lā\ *n, often cap* : a large sturdy sheep developed in France for mutton and wool [*Rambouillet*, France]

ram•bunc•tious \ram-'bəng-shəs, -'bəngk-\ *adj* : not restrained or orderly : UNRULY [probably derived from *robust*] — **ram•bunc•tious•ly** *adv* — **ram•bunc•tious•ness** *n*

ram•e•kin *or* **ram•e•quin** \'ram-i-kən\ *n* : an individual baking dish [French *ramequin*, a preparation of cheese baked with bread crumbs or eggs, from Low German *ramken*, from *ram* "cream"]

ra•mie \'rā-mē, 'ram-ē\ *n* : an Asian perennial plant of the nettle family; *also* : its strong lustrous bast fiber used as a textile fiber [Malay *rami*]

ram•i•fi•ca•tion \,ram-ə-fə-'kā-shən\ *n* **1** : the act or process of branching **2** : BRANCH 2, OFFSHOOT **3** : OUTGROWTH, CONSEQUENCE ⟨the *ramifications* of a problem⟩

ram•i•fy \'ram-ə-,fī\ *vb* **-fied; -fy•ing** : to spread out or split up into branches or divisions [Middle French *ramifier*, from Medieval Latin *ramificare*, from Latin *ramus* "branch"]

ram•jet engine \,ram-,jet-\ *n* : a jet engine having in its forward end a continuous inlet of air so that there is a compressing effect produced on the air taken in while the engine is in motion

[1]**ramp** \'ramp\ *vi* **1** : to stand or advance menacingly with forelegs or with arms raised **2** : to move or act furiously : STORM [Old French *ramper* "to crawl, rear", of Germanic origin]

[2]**ramp** *n* : a sloping passage or roadway connecting different levels [French *rampe*, from *ramper* "to crawl, rear"]

[1]**ram•page** \'ram-,pāj, ram-', 'ram-'\ *vi* : to rush wildly about : STORM [Scottish]

[2]**ram•page** \'ram-,pāj\ *n* : a course of violent, riotous, or reckless action or behavior — **ram•pa•geous** \ram-'pā-jəs\ *adj* — **ram•pa•geous•ly** *adv* — **ram•pa•geous•ness** *n*

ram•pant \'ram-pənt, -,pant\ *adj* **1** : rearing upon one or both hind legs with forelegs extended **2 a :** marked by a menacing wildness, extravagance, or absence of restraint **b :** unchecked in growth or spread [Middle French, present participle of *ramper* "to crawl, rear"] — **ram•pan•cy** \-pən-sē\ *n* — **ram•pant•ly** *adv*

ram•part \ˈram-ˌpärt, -pərt\ *n* **:** a broad wall or mound of earth raised as a fortification or protective barrier [Middle French]

1ram•rod \ˈram-ˌräd\ *n* **1 :** a rod for ramming home the charge in a muzzle-loading firearm **2 :** a cleaning rod for small arms

2ramrod *adj* **:** marked by rigidity, severity, or stiffness

ram•shack•le \ˈram-ˌshak-əl\ *adj* **:** appearing ready to collapse: as **a :** DILAPIDATED **b :** carelessly or loosely constructed [alteration of earlier *ransackled,* derived from *ransack*]

ra•mus \ˈrā-məs\ *n, pl* **ra•mi** \-ˌmī\ **:** a projecting part or elongated process **:** BRANCH ⟨the *rami* of the lower jaw⟩ [Latin, "branch"]

ran *past of* RUN

1ranch \ˈranch\ *n* **1 :** an establishment for raising horses, cattle, or sheep **2 :** a farm devoted to a specialty ⟨a fruit *ranch*⟩ **3 :** RANCH HOUSE [Mexican Spanish *rancho* "small ranch", from Spanish, "camp, hut", from *ranchearse* "to settle", from Middle French *se ranger* "to arrange oneself"]

2ranch *vi* **:** to live or work or raise livestock on a ranch

ranch•er \ˈran-chər\ *n* **:** one who owns or operates or works on a ranch

ran•che•ro \ran-ˈcheər-ō, rän-\ *n, pl* **-ros :** RANCHER [Mexican Spanish, from *rancho* "small ranch"]

ranch house *n* **:** a one-story house typically with a low-pitched roof

ranch•man \ˈranch-mən\ *n* **:** RANCHER

ran•cho \ˈran-chō, ˈrän-\ *n, pl* **ranchos :** RANCH 1 [Mexican Spanish, "small ranch"]

ran•cid \ˈran-səd\ *adj* **1 :** having the unpleasant smell or taste typical of decomposed oil or fat ⟨*rancid* butter⟩ **2 :** distinctly unpleasant or distasteful; *also* **:** CORRUPT [Latin *rancidus,* from *rancēre* "to be rancid"] — **ran•cid•i•ty** \ran-ˈsid-ət-ē\ *n* — **ran•cid•ness** \ˈran-səd-nəs\ *n*

ran•cor \ˈrang-kər\ *n* **:** intense hatred or spite [Middle French *ranceur,* from Late Latin *rancor* "rancidity, rancor", from Latin *rancēre* "to be rancid"] — **ran•cor•ous** \-kə-rəs, -krəs\ *adj* — **ran•cor•ous•ly** *adv*

1ran•dom \ˈran-dəm\ *n* **:** a haphazard course [Middle French *randon* "impetuosity", from *randir* "to run", of Germanic origin] — **at random :** without definite aim, direction, rule, or method

2random *adj* **1 :** lacking a definite plan, purpose, or pattern **2 :** having a definite and especially an equal probability of occurring ⟨a *random* number⟩; *also* **:** consisting of or relating to such elements selected independently ⟨*random* samples⟩ — **ran•dom•ly** *adv* — **ran•dom•ness** *n*

• **syn** RANDOM, HAPHAZARD, CASUAL mean determined by accident rather than design. RANDOM stresses lack of definite aim or fixed goal or avoidance of regular procedure ⟨*random* collection of furniture⟩ HAPHAZARD applies to what is done without regard for regularity or fitness or ultimate consequences ⟨*haphazard* arrangement of furniture⟩ CASUAL suggests working or acting without deliberation, intention, or purpose ⟨a *casual* tour of the sights⟩

3random *adv* **:** in a random manner

ran•dom•ize \ˈran-də-ˌmīz\ *vt* **:** to make random ⟨carefully *randomized* sampling⟩ — **ran•dom•iza•tion** \ˌran-də-mə-ˈzā-shən\ *n*

rang *past of* RING

1range \ˈrānj\ *n* **1 a :** a series of things in a line **:** ROW ⟨a *range* of mountains⟩ **b :** an aggregate of individuals in one rank **:** CLASS, ORDER **2 :** a cooking stove that has an oven and a flat top with plates or racks to hold utensils over flames or coils **3 a :** a place that may be ranged over **b :** open land over which livestock may roam and feed **c :** the region throughout which a kind of organism or ecological community naturally occurs **4 :** the act of ranging about **5 a (1) :** the horizontal distance to which a projectile can be propelled **(2) :** the maximum distance a vehicle can travel without refueling **b :** a place where shooting is practiced; *also* **:** a special course (as over water) where missiles are tested **6 a :** the space or extent included, covered, or used **:** SCOPE **b :** the extent of pitch covered by a voice or a melody **7 a :** a variation between limits ⟨a wide *range* of patterns⟩ **b :** the difference between the least and greatest of a set of values **8 :** the set of values a function may take on; *esp* **:** the set of values that the dependent variable may take on — compare DOMAIN 4 [Middle English, "row of persons", from Old French *renge,* from *rengier* "to range"]

2range *vb* **1 a :** to set in a row or in the proper order **b :** to place among others in a position or situation **c :** to assign to a category **:** CLASSIFY **2 :** to rove over or through **:** roam at large or freely **3 :** to raise (livestock) on a range **4 :** to determine or give the elevation necessary for (a gun) to propel a projectile to a given distance **5 a :** to correspond in direction or line **:** ALIGN **b :** to extend in a particular direction **6 :** to vary within limits **7 :** to live or occur in or be native to a region [Middle French *ranger,* from Old French *rengier,* from *renc, reng* "line, place, row, rank"]

range finder *n* **:** a device used to determine the distance of an object (as a target)

range•land \ˈrānj-ˌland\ *n* **:** land used or suitable for range

rang•er \ˈrān-jər\ *n* **1 a :** the keeper of a British royal park or forest **b :** an officer charged with patrolling and protecting a forest **2 :** an animal that ranges **3 a :** one of a body of organized armed men who range over a region **b :** a soldier trained in close-range fighting and raiding tactics

rangy \ˈrān-jē\ *adj* **rang•i•er; -est 1 :** having room for ranging **2 :** able to range for considerable distances **3 a :** being long-limbed and long-bodied ⟨*rangy* cattle⟩ **b :** being tall and slender ⟨*rangy* athletes⟩ — **rang•i•ness** *n*

ra•ni *or* **ra•nee** \rä-ˈnē, ˈrän-ē\ *n* **:** the wife of a raja **:** an Indian or Malay queen or princess [Hindi *rānī,* from Sanskrit *rājñī,* feminine of *rājan* "king"]

1rank \ˈrangk\ *adj* **1 :** strong and vigorous and usually coarse in growth ⟨*rank* weeds⟩ **2 :** offensively gross or coarse ⟨*rank* language⟩ **3 :** shockingly conspicuous ⟨*rank* cowardice⟩ **4 :** EXTREME, UTTER ⟨a *rank* amateur⟩ **5 :** unpleasantly strong-smelling **:** RANCID, FOUL [Old English *ranc* "overbearing, strong"] **syn** see FLAGRANT — **rank•ness** *n*

2rank *n* **1 :** ROW, SERIES ⟨*ranks* of houses⟩ **2 :** a line of soldiers in close order side by side **3** *pl* **:** a group of individuals classed together ⟨in the *ranks* of the unemployed⟩ **4 :** relative position or order **:** STANDING **5 :** official grade or status (as in the army or navy) ⟨the *rank* of general⟩ **6 :** position in regard to merit ⟨a musician of the highest *rank*⟩ **7 :** a high social position **8** *pl* **:** the body of enlisted personnel (as in an army) [Middle French *renc, reng,* of Germanic origin]

3rank *vb* **1 :** to arrange in lines or in a regular formation **2 :** to determine the relative position of **:** RATE **3 :** to take precedence of ⟨a captain *ranks* a lieutenant⟩ **4 :** to take or have a position in relation to others **:** be in a class

rank and file *n* **1 :** the enlisted personnel of an armed force **2 :** the ordinary body of an organization or society as distinguished from the leaders

rank•er \ˈrang-kər\ *n* **:** one who serves or has served in the ranks; *esp* **:** a commissioned officer promoted from the ranks

rank•ing *adj* **:** having the highest rank or the foremost position

ran•kle \ˈrang-kəl\ *vb* **ran•kled; ran•kling** \-kə-ling, -kling\ **1 :** to cause anger, irritation, or deep bitterness **2 :** to cause resentment or bitterness in **:** irritate deeply [Middle French *rancler* "to fester", from Old French *draoncler, raoncler,* from *draoncle, raoncle* "festering sore", from Medieval Latin *dracunculus,* from Latin, "small serpent"]

△ **origin** The modern senses of the verb *rankle* are figurative extensions of an earlier meaning, "to fester". The word was borrowed from Middle French *rancler.* The Old French noun *raoncle,* or *draoncle,* from which the verb is derived, means "a festering sore" and comes ultimately from Latin *dracunculus.* This word means literally "small serpent or dragon". In Medieval Latin *dracunculus* was used for a cancerous tumor or ulcer, probably because the form of a tumor was thought to be like that of a small serpent.

ran•sack \ˈran-ˌsak, ran-ˈ, ˈran-ˈ\ *vt* **:** to search thoroughly **:** RUMMAGE; *esp* **:** to search through and steal things of value [Old Norse *rannsaka*] — **ran•sack•er** *n*

1ran•som \ˈran-səm\ *n* **1 :** something (as money) paid or demanded for the freedom of a captured person **2 :** the act of ransoming [Old French *rançon,* from Latin *redemptio* "redemption"]

2ransom *vt* **:** to free from captivity or punishment by paying a price **syn** see RESCUE — **ran•som•er** *n*

1rant \ˈrant\ *vi* **1 :** to talk noisily, excitedly, or wildly ⟨*rant* and rave in anger⟩ **2 :** to scold violently [obsolete Dutch *ranten*] — **rant•er** *n*

2rant *n* **:** ranting speech **:** wild unrestrained language

[1]**rap** \ˈrap\ *n* **1** : a sharp blow or knock **2** *slang* **a** : the blame for an action ⟨took the *rap*⟩ **b** : a criminal charge [Middle English *rappe*]

[2]**rap** *vb* **rapped**; **rap•ping 1** : to give a quick sharp blow : KNOCK ⟨*rap* on the door⟩ **2** : to utter suddenly with force ⟨*rap* out an order⟩

[3]**rap** *n* : the least bit ⟨don't care a *rap*⟩ [perhaps from [1]*rap*]

[4]**rap** *n* : CONVERSATION, TALK [perhaps from *repartee*]

[5]**rap** *vi* **rapped**; **rap•ping** : to talk freely and frankly

ra•pa•cious \rə-ˈpā-shəs\ *adj* **1** : very grasping or greedy **2** : living on prey : PREDATORY [Latin *rapac-, rapax,* from *rapere* "to seize"] — **ra•pa•cious•ly** *adv* — **ra•pa•cious•ness** *n* — **ra•pac•i•ty** \-ˈpas-ət-ē\ *n*

[1]**rape** \ˈrāp\ *n* : a European herb of the mustard family grown as a forage crop and for its seeds which are used as a source of oil and as a bird food [Latin *rapa, rapum* "turnip, rape"]

[2]**rape** *vt* **1** *archaic* : to seize and take away by force **2** : to commit rape on : RAVISH [Latin *rapere*] — **rap•er** *n* — **rap•ist** \ˈrā-pəst\ *n*

[3]**rape** *n* **1** : a seizing by force **2** : sexual intercourse with a woman carried out without her consent and especially by force

ra•phe \ˈrā-fē, -ˌfē\ *n* : a seam or ridge (as at the union of the two lateral halves of an organ or on a seed) [Greek *rhaphē* "seam", from *rhaptein* "to sew"]

[1]**rap•id** \ˈrap-əd\ *adj* : marked by a fast rate of motion, activity, succession, or occurrence : SWIFT [Latin *rapidus* "seizing, sweeping, rapid", from *rapere* "to seize, sweep away"] **syn** see FAST — **rap•id•ly** *adv* — **rap•id•ness** *n*

[2]**rapid** *n* : a part of a river where the current is fast and the surface is usually broken by obstructions — usually used in pl.

rap•id–fire \ˌrap-əd-ˈfīr\ *adj* **1** : firing or adapted for firing shots in rapid succession **2** : marked by rapidity, liveliness, or sharpness ⟨*rapid-fire* questions⟩

ra•pid•i•ty \rə-ˈpid-ət-ē, ra-\ *n* : the quality or state of being rapid

rapid transit *n* : fast public passenger transportation (as by subway) in urban areas

ra•pi•er \ˈrā-pē-ər\ *n* : a straight 2-edged sword with a narrow pointed blade [Middle French *rapiere*]

rapier

rap•ine \ˈrap-ən, -ˌīn\ *n* : the seizing and carrying away of something by force : PILLAGE, PLUNDER [Latin *rapina,* from *rapere* "to seize"]

rap•port \ra-ˈpōr, -ˈpȯr\ *n* : harmonious accord or relation that makes communication possible or easy ⟨the teacher had good *rapport* with the pupils⟩ [French, from *rapporter* "to bring back, refer"]

rap•proche•ment \ˌrap-ˌrōsh-ˈmäⁿ\ *n* : the establishment or a state of cordial relations [French, from *rapprocher* "to bring together", from *re-* "re-" + *approcher* "to approach"]

rap•scal•lion \rap-ˈskal-yən\ *n* : RASCAL 1, SCAMP [alteration of earlier *rascallion,* from *rascal*]

rapt \ˈrapt\ *adj* **1** : carried away with emotion ⟨a *rapt* audience⟩ **2** : wholly absorbed ⟨listened with *rapt* attention⟩ [Latin *raptus,* past participle of *rapere* "to seize, sweep away"] — **rapt•ly** *adv* — **rapt•ness** \ˈrapt-nəs, ˈrap-\ *n*

rap•tor \ˈrap-tər, -ˌtȯr\ *n* : a bird of prey [derived from Latin *raptor* "plunderer", from *rapere* "to seize"]

rap•to•ri•al \rap-ˈtōr-ē-əl, -ˈtȯr-\ *adj* **1** : adapted to seize prey **2** : of, relating to, or being a bird of prey

rap•ture \ˈrap-chər\ *n* : a deeply moving sense of joy, delight, or love — **rap•tur•ous** \ˈrap-chə-rəs, ˈrap-shrəs\ *adj* — **rap•tur•ous•ly** *adv* — **rap•tur•ous•ness** *n*

ra•ra avis \ˌrar-ə-ˈā-vəs, ˌrer-; ˌrär-ə-ˈä-wəs\ *n, pl* **ra•ra avis•es** \-ˈā-və-səz\ *or* **ra•rae aves** \ˌrär-ˌī-ˈä-ˌwās\ : a rare person or thing : RARITY [Latin, "rare bird"]

[1]**rare** \ˈraər, ˈreər\ *adj* : not cooked through — used of meat [Old English *hrēre* "lightly boiled"]

[2]**rare** *adj* **1** : not thick or dense : THIN ⟨the *rare* atmosphere at high altitudes⟩ **2** : unusually fine : EXCELLENT, SPLENDID ⟨a person of *rare* charm⟩ **3** : seldom occurring or found : very uncommon **4** : valuable because of scarcity ⟨a collection of *rare* books⟩ [Latin *rarus*] — **rare•ness** *n*

rare•bit \ˈraər-bət, ˈreər-\ *n* : WELSH RABBIT [by alteration]

rare earth element *n* : any of a series of naturally occurring metallic elements that includes the elements with atomic numbers 58 through 71, usually lanthanum, and sometimes yttrium and scandium

rar•e•fac•tion \ˌrar-ə-ˈfak-shən, ˌrer-\ *n* : the act or process of rarefying : the state of being rarefied [Medieval Latin *rarefactio,* from Latin *rarefacere* "to rarefy"] — **rar•e•fac•tion•al** \-shnəl, -shən-l\ *adj*

rar•e•fy *also* **rar•i•fy** \ˈrar-ə-ˌfī, ˈrer-\ *vb* **-fied**; **-fy•ing 1** : to make or become thin, porous, or less dense **2** : to make or become more spiritual, refined, or abstruse [Middle French *rarefier,* from Latin *rarefacere,* from *rarus* "rare" + *facere* "to make"]

rare•ly \ˈraər-lē, ˈreər-\ *adv* **1** : not often : SELDOM **2** : with rare skill : EXCELLENTLY **3** : UNUSUALLY ⟨a *rarely* beautiful view⟩

rare•ripe \-ˌrīp\ *adj* : early ripe [English dialect *rare* "early" + *ripe*] — **rareripe** *n*

rar•ing \-ing\ *adj* : full of enthusiasm or eagerness [from English dialect *rare* "to rear", alteration of English *rear*]

rar•i•ty \ˈrar-ət-ē, ˈrer-\ *n, pl* **-ties 1** : the quality or state of being rarefied ⟨the *rarity* of the atmosphere⟩ **2** : the fact of being rare: as **a** : EXCELLENCE 1 **b** : SCARCITY **3** : one that is rare ⟨black pearls are *rarities*⟩

ras•cal \ˈras-kəl\ *n* **1** : a mean, unprincipled, or dishonest person : ROGUE **2** : a mischievous person or animal [Middle English *rascaile* "rabble, one of the rabble"]

ras•cal•i•ty \ra-ˈskal-ət-ē\ *n, pl* **-ties** : the act, actions, or character of a rascal

ras•cal•ly \ˈras-kə-lē\ *adj* : of or characteristic of a rascal ⟨a *rascally* trick⟩ — **rascally** *adv*

[1]**rash** \ˈrash\ *adj* **1** : being too hasty in speech or action or in making decisions **2** : showing undue disregard for consequences : RECKLESS ⟨a *rash* act⟩ ⟨regret a *rash* promise⟩ [Middle English, *rasch* "quick"] **syn** see DARING — **rash•ly** *adv* — **rash•ness** *n*

[2]**rash** *n* : a breaking out of the skin with red spots (as in measles) : ERUPTION [obsolete French *rache* "scurf", drived from Latin *rasus,* past participle of *radere* "to scrape, shave"]

rash•er \ˈrash-ər\ *n* : a thin slice of bacon or ham cut for broiling or frying; *also* : a portion consisting of several such slices [perhaps from obsolete *rash* "to cut", from Middle English *rashen*]

[1]**rasp** \ˈrasp\ *vb* **1** : to rub with or as if with a rough file ⟨*rasp* off a rough edge⟩ **2** : to grate harshly upon : IRRITATE ⟨a voice that *rasps* the ear⟩ **3** : to speak or utter in a grating tone ⟨*rasp* out a complaint⟩ **4** : to produce a grating sound [Middle English *raspen*] — **rasp•er** *n*

[2]**rasp** *n* **1** : a coarse file with cutting points instead of lines **2 a** : an act of rasping **b** : a rasping sound, sensation, or effect

rasp•ber•ry \ˈraz-ˌber-ē, -bə-rē, -brē\ *n* **1 a** : any of various black or red edible berries that consist of numerous small drupes on a fleshy receptable and are rounder and smaller than the related blackberries **b** : a bramble that bears raspberries **2** : a sound of contempt made by protruding the tongue between the lips and expelling air so forcibly as to produce a vibration [English dialect *rasp* "raspberry" + English *berry*]

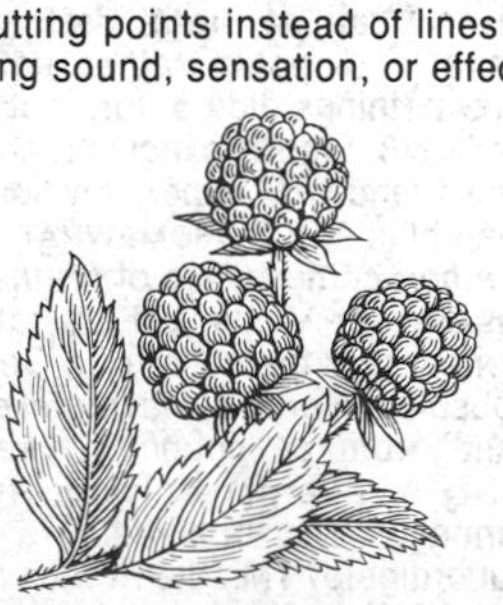

raspberry 1a

raspy \ˈras-pē\ *adj* **rasp•i•er**; **-est 1** : HARSH, GRATING ⟨spoke with a *raspy* twang⟩ **2** : IRRITABLE

[1]**rat** \ˈrat\ *n* **1** : a scaly-tailed gnawing rodent distinguished from

the mouse chiefly by its larger size and by differences in the teeth **2 :** a person who deserts a cause or betrays associates [Old English *ræt*]

[2]**rat** *vi* **rat•ted; rat•ting 1 :** to desert or inform on one's associates **2 :** to catch or hunt rats

rat•able *or* **rate•able** \ˈrāt-ə-bəl\ *adj* **1 :** capable of being rated, estimated, or apportioned **2** *British* **:** TAXABLE — **rat•ably** \-blē\ *adv*

ratch \ˈrach\ *n* **1 :** RATCHET 2 **2 :** a notched bar with which a pawl or detent works to prevent reversal of motion [German *ratsche,* from *ratschen* "to rattle"]

rat cheese *n* **:** CHEDDAR

ratch•et \ˈrach-ət\ *n* **1 :** a mechanism that consists of a bar or wheel having inclined teeth into which a pawl drops so as to allow motion in one direction only **2 :** a pawl or detent for holding or propelling a ratchet wheel [alteration of earlier *rochet,* from French, from Middle French *rocquet* "lance head", of Germanic origin]

ratchet wheel *n* **:** a toothed wheel held in position or turned by an engaging pawl

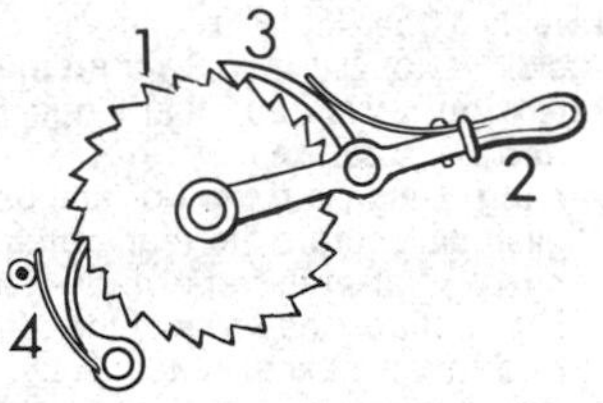

ratchet wheel: *1* wheel, *2* reciprocating lever, *3* pawl for communicating motion, *4* pawl for preventing backward motion

[1]**rate** \ˈrāt\ *vt* **:** to scold violently **:** BERATE [Middle English *raten*]

[2]**rate** *n* **1 :** reckoned value **:** VALUATION **2 a :** a fixed ratio between two things — compare RATE OF EXCHANGE **b** (1) **:** a charge, payment, or price fixed according to a ratio, scale, or standard ⟨the tax *rate*⟩ (2) *British* **:** a local tax — usually used in pl. **3 a :** a quantity, amount, or degree of something measured per unit of something else **b :** an amount of payment or charge based on another amount ⟨interest at the *rate* of six percent⟩ **4 :** relative condition or quality **:** CLASS [Middle French, from Medieval Latin *rata,* from Latin *pro rata parte* "according to a fixed proportion"] — **at any rate :** in any case **:** at least

[3]**rate** *vb* **1 :** CONSIDER, REGARD ⟨was *rated* a good pianist⟩ **2 :** to set an estimate or value on ⟨*rate* houses for tax purposes⟩ **3 :** to determine the rank, class, or position of **:** GRADE ⟨*rate* a seaman⟩ ⟨*rate* a ship⟩ **4 :** to have a rating or rank **:** be classed ⟨*rate* high⟩ **5 :** to set a rate on **6 :** to be qualified for ⟨*rate* a promotion⟩

rate of exchange : the amount of one currency that will buy a given amount of another

rate•pay•er \ˈrāt-ˌpā-ər\ *n, British* **:** TAXPAYER

rat•er \ˈrāt-ər\ *n* **1 :** one that rates; *esp* **:** a person who estimates or determines a rating **2 :** one having a specified rating or class — usually used in combination ⟨first-*rater*⟩

rath•er \ˈrath-ər, ˈrəth-, ˈräth\ *adv* **1 :** more willingly **:** PREFERABLY ⟨I would *rather* not go⟩ **2 :** on the contrary **:** INSTEAD ⟨things did not turn out well; *rather,* they turned out very badly⟩ **3 :** more exactly **:** more properly **:** with better reason ⟨my friend, or, *rather,* my former friend⟩ ⟨to be pitied *rather* than blamed⟩ **4 :** SOMEWHAT ⟨*rather* cold today⟩ [Old English *hrathor,* comparative of *hrathe* "quickly"]

raths•kel•ler \ˈräts-ˌkel-ər, ˈrats-, ˈraths-\ *n* **:** a restaurant patterned after the cellar of a German city hall where beer is sold [obsolete German (now *ratskeller*), "city-hall basement restaurant", from *rat* "council" + *keller* "cellar"]

rat•i•fy \ˈrat-ə-ˌfī\ *vt* **-fied; -fy•ing :** to approve and sanction formally **:** CONFIRM ⟨*ratify* a treaty⟩ ⟨*ratify* the decision of a subordinate⟩ [Middle French *ratifier,* from Medieval Latin *ratificare,* from Latin *ratus* "determined", from past participle of *reri* "to calculate"] — **rat•i•fi•ca•tion** \ˌrat-ə-fə-ˈkā-shən\ *n* — **rat•i•fi•er** \ˈrat-ə-ˌfī-ər, -ˌfīr\ *n*

rat•ing \ˈrāt-ing\ *n* **1 a :** a classification according to grade or rank **b :** a naval specialist classification **2** *chiefly British* **:** a naval enlisted man **3 :** a relative estimate or evaluation **:** STANDING ⟨a good credit *rating*⟩

ra•tio \ˈrā-shō, -shē-ˌō\ *n, pl* **ra•tios 1 :** a fixed or approximate relation in number, quantity, or degree between things or to another thing ⟨the *ratio* of eggs to butter in a cake⟩ ⟨women outnumbered men in the *ratio* of three to one⟩ **2 :** the quotient of one quantity divided by another ⟨the *ratio* of 6 to 3 may be expressed as 6:3, 6/3, and 2⟩ [Latin, "computation, reason"]

ra•ti•o•ci•na•tion \ˌrat-ē-ˌōs-n-ˈā-shən, ˌrash-ē-, -ˌäs-\ *n* **1 :** the process of exact thinking **:** REASONING **2 :** a reasoned train of thought [Latin *ratiocinatio,* from *ratiocinari* "to reckon", from *ratio* "computation, reason"] — **ra•ti•o•ci•na•tive** \-ˈōs-n-ˌāt-iv, -ˈäs-\ *adj*

[1]**ra•tion** \ˈrash-ən, ˈrā-shən\ *n* **1 a :** a food allowance for one day **b :** FOOD, DIET ⟨a salt-free *ration*⟩ — usually used in pl. ⟨had to pack supplies and *rations* on their backs⟩ **2 :** a share especially as determined by supply or allotment by authority ⟨a wartime meat *ration*⟩ [French, from Latin *ratio* "computation, reason"]

[2]**ration** *vt* **ra•tioned; ra•tion•ing** \ˈrash-ning, ˈrāsh-, -ə-ning\ **1 :** to supply with rations ⟨*ration* cattle⟩ **2 a :** to distribute or allot as a ration ⟨the government *rationed* gas⟩ **b :** to use or allot sparingly ⟨the doctor *rations* a diabetic's sugar intake⟩

[1]**ra•tio•nal** \ˈrash-nəl, -ən-l\ *adj* **1 a :** having reason or understanding ⟨*rational* beings⟩ **b :** relating to, based on, or agreeable to reason; *also* **:** SANE ⟨*rational* behavior⟩ **2 :** relating to, consisting of, or being rational numbers ⟨a *rational* fraction⟩ [Latin *rationalis,* from *ratio* "computation, reason"] — **ra•tio•nal•i•ty** \ˌrash-ə-ˈnal-ət-ē\ *n* — **ra•tio•nal•ly** \ˈrash-nə-lē, -ən-l-ē\ *adv*

[2]**rational** *n* **:** something rational; *esp* **:** a rational number or fraction

ra•tio•nale \ˌrash-ə-ˈnal\ *n* **:** a basic reason or explanation [Latin, neuter of *rationalis* "rational"]

ra•tio•nal•ism \ˈrash-nə-ˌliz-əm, -ən-l-ˌiz-\ *n* **:** the theory or practice of guiding one's actions and opinions solely by what seems reasonable — **ra•tio•nal•ist** \-nə-ləst, -ən-l-əst\ *n* — **rationalist** *or* **ra•tio•nal•is•tic** \ˌrash-nə-ˈlis-tik, -ən-l-ˈis-\ *adj* — **ra•tio•nal•is•ti•cal•ly** \-ti-kə-lē, -klē\ *adv*

ra•tio•nal•ize \ˈrash-nə-ˌlīz, -ən-l-ˌīz\ *vb* **1 :** to free (a mathematical equation) from irrational expressions **2 a :** to provide a rational explanation of ⟨*rationalize* a myth⟩ **b :** to justify unreasonable actions or views by seemingly reasonable motives — **ra•tio•nal•iza•tion** \ˌrash-nə-lə-ˈzā-shən, -ən-l-ə-\ *n*

rational number *n* **:** a number expressible as an integer or the quotient of two integers

rational operation *n* **:** one of the arithmetic operations of addition, subtraction, multiplication, and division (except by 0)

rat•like \ˈrat-ˌlīk\ *adj* **:** of, relating to, or resembling a rat

rat•line \ˈrat-lən\ *n* **:** one of the small cross ropes attached to the shrouds of a ship so as to form the steps of a rope ladder [origin unknown]

ratline

rat mite *n* **:** a widely distributed mite that usually feeds on rodents but may cause dermatitis in or transmit typhus to man

rat snake *n* **:** any of various large harmless rat-eating snakes

rat•tan \ra-ˈtan, rə-\ *n* **1 a :** a climbing palm with very long tough stems **b :** a part of one of these stems used especially for walking sticks and wickerwork **2 :** a rattan cane or switch [Malay *rotan*]

rat•ter \ˈrat-ər\ *n* **:** one that catches rats; *esp* **:** a rat-catching dog or cat

[1]**rat•tle** \ˈrat-l\ *vb* **rat•tled; rat•tling** \ˈrat-ling, -l-ing\ **1 :** to make or cause to make a rattle **2 :** to chatter incessantly and aimlessly **3 :** to say or do in a brisk lively fashion ⟨*rattled* off the answers⟩ **4 :** to disturb the composure of **:** UPSET ⟨*rattled* the speaker with questions⟩ [Middle English *ratelen*]

[2]**rattle** *n* **1 :** a series of short sharp sounds **:** CLATTER ⟨the *rattle* of hail on a roof⟩ **2 :** a device (as a toy) for making a rattling sound **3 :** a rattling organ at the end of a rattlesnake's tail made up of horny joints **4 :** a noise in the throat caused by air passing through mucus especially at the approach of death

rat•tler \ˈrat-lər, -l-ər\ *n* **1 :** one that rattles **2 :** RATTLESNAKE

rat•tle•snake \ˈrat-l-ˌsnāk\ *n* **:** any of various venomous American snakes having at the end of the tail horny interlocking joints that rattle when shaken

rat•tle•trap \-ˌtrap\ *n* **:** something rattly or rickety; *esp* **:** an old car — **rattletrap** *adj*

rat•tling \'rat-ling, -l-ing\ *adj* : LIVELY, BRISK ⟨moved at a *rattling* pace⟩ — **rat•tling•ly** \'rat-ling-lē\ *adv*

rat•tly \'rat-lē, -l-ē\ *adj* : likely to rattle : making a rattle ⟨a *rattly* old car⟩

rat•ty \'rat-ē\ *adj* **rat•ti•er; -est 1 :** infested with or suggestive of rats **2 :** SHABBY, UNKEMPT ⟨a *ratty* old overcoat⟩

rau•cous \'rȯ-kəs\ *adj* **1 :** disagreeably harsh or strident ⟨a *raucous* voice⟩ **2 :** boisterously disorderly ⟨a *raucous* party⟩ [Latin *raucus* "hoarse"] — **rau•cous•ly** *adv* — **rau•cous•ness** *n*

rau•wol•fia \rau̇-'wu̇l-fē-ə, rȯ-\ *n* : a medicinal extract from the root of an Indian tree of the dogbane family used in the treatment of hypertension and mental disorders; *also* : this tree [New Latin, a genus of trees, from Leonhard *Rauwolf,* died 1596, German botanist]

1rav•age \'rav-ij\ *n* **1 :** an act or practice of ravaging **2 :** damage resulting from ravaging ⟨the *ravage* of time⟩ [French, from *ravir* "to ravish"]

2ravage *vb* **1 :** to lay waste : PLUNDER **2 :** DESTROY, RUIN ⟨a body *ravaged* by disease⟩ — **rav•ag•er** *n*

• **syn** RAVAGE, DEVASTATE, WASTE mean to lay waste by plundering or destroying. RAVAGE suggests violent often repeated or continuing pillaging and destruction; DEVASTATE implies causing complete ruin and desolation over a wide area; WASTE may suggest destruction as a result of a slow process or may come close to *devastate* or *ravage.*

1rave \'rāv\ *vb* **1 :** to talk irrationally in or as if in delirium **2 :** to declaim wildly **3 :** to talk or utter with extreme enthusiasm [Middle English *raven*] — **rav•er** *n*

2rave *n* **1 :** an act or instance of raving **2 :** an extravagantly favorable criticism

1rav•el \'rav-əl\ *vb* **rav•eled** *or* **rav•elled; rav•el•ing** *or* **rav•el•ling** \'rav-ling, -ə-ling\ **1 :** to separate or undo the texture of : UNRAVEL **2 :** to make plain : SIMPLIFY **3 :** ENTANGLE, CONFUSE [Dutch *rafelen,* from *rafel* "loose thread"] — **rav•el•er** *or* **rav•el•ler** \'rav-lər, -ə-lər\ *n*

2ravel *n* : something that is raveled

rav•el•ing *or* **rav•el•ling** \'rav-ling, -ə-ling, -lən\ *n* : something raveled or frayed; *esp* : a thread raveled out of a fabric

1ra•ven \'rā-vən\ *n* : a glossy black bird about one half meter long of northern regions that is related to the crow and has pointed throat feathers [Old English *hræfn*]

1raven

2raven *adj* : black or glossy like a raven

rav•en•ous \'rav-ə-nəs\ *adj* : very eager for food, satisfaction, or gratification ⟨a *ravenous* appetite⟩ [Middle French *ravineus* "rushing, rapacious", from *raviner* "to rush forward, ravish", from *ravine* "rapine", from Latin *rapina*] — **rav•en•ous•ly** *adv* — **rav•en•ous•ness** *n*

ra•vine \rə-vēn\ *n* : a small narrow steep-sided valley larger than a gully, smaller than a canyon, and usually worn by running water [French, "mountain torrent", from Middle French, "rapine, rush", from Latin *rapina* "rapine"]

rav•i•o•li \,rav-ē-'ō-lē, ,räv-\ *n pl* : little cases of dough containing a filling (as of meat or cheese) that are usually boiled and served with a spicy tomato sauce [Italian, from Italian dialect *raviolo* "little turnip", from *rava* "turnip", from Latin *rapa*]

rav•ish \'rav-ish\ *vt* **1 :** to seize and take away by violence **2 :** to overcome with emotion **3 :** RAPE 2 **4 :** PLUNDER, ROB [Middle French *raviss-,* stem of *ravir* "to ravish", from Latin *rapere* "to seize"] — **rav•ish•er** *n* — **rav•ish•ment** \-mənt\ *n*

rav•ish•ing \'rav-i-shing\ *adj* : unusually attractive, pleasing, or striking — **rav•ish•ing•ly**\-shing-lē\ *adv*

1raw \'rȯ\ *adj* **raw•er**\'rȯ-ər, 'rȯr\; **raw•est**\ 'rȯ-əst\ **1 :** not cooked **2 a (1) :** being in or nearly in the natural state ⟨*raw* furs⟩ : not processed or manufactured ⟨*raw* milk⟩ ⟨*raw* data⟩ **(2)** : lacking a normal or usual finish **b :** not diluted or blended ⟨*raw* spirits⟩ **3 :** having the surface abraded or chafed ⟨a *raw* wound⟩; *also* : irritated as if by chafing ⟨a *raw* sore throat⟩ **4 a** : lacking experience or understanding : GREEN ⟨a *raw* recruit⟩ **b :** lacking comforts or refinements ⟨a *raw* frontier village⟩ **c** : VULGAR, COARSE ⟨a *raw* story⟩ **5 :** disagreeably damp or cold ⟨a *raw* blustery day⟩ [Old English *hrēaw*] — **raw•ly** \'rȯ-lē\ *adv* — **raw•ness** *n*

2raw *n* : a raw place or state — **in the raw 1 :** in a natural or crude state ⟨life *in the raw*⟩ **2 :** NAKED ⟨slept *in the raw*⟩

raw•boned \'rȯ-'bōnd\ *adj* : having little flesh : GAUNT **syn** see LANK

raw deal *n* : an instance of unfair treatment

1raw•hide \'rȯ-,hīd\ *n* **1 :** untanned cattle skin **2 :** a whip of untanned hide

2rawhide *vt* **-hid•ed; -hid•ing** : to whip or drive with or as if with a rawhide

raw material *n* : natural resources in an unprocessed state : material from which useful things can be produced

1ray \'rā\ *n* : any of numerous flat broad fishes (as a skate) that live on the sea bottom and have their eyes on the upper surface of their bodies and the tail long and narrow [Middle French *raie,* from Latin *raia*]

2ray *n* **1 a :** one of the lines of light that appear to radiate from a bright object **b :** a thin beam of radiant energy (as light) **c :** a stream of particles traveling (as in radioactive phenomena) in the same line **2 :** light cast by rays : RADIANCE **3 :** a thin line suggesting a ray: as **a :** any of a group of lines diverging from a common center **b :** HALF LINE **4 :** a plant or animal structure that resembles a ray: as **a :** a band of tissue extending radially in a woody plant stem and usually storing food or conducting raw material **b :** RAY FLOWER **5 :** PARTICLE, TRACE ⟨a *ray* of hope⟩ [Middle French *rai,* from Latin *radius* "rod, spoke, ray"]

3ray *vb* **1 :** to send out rays of or as if of light **2 :** RADIATE 4 **3 :** to subject to radiation

rayed \'rād\ *adj* : having rays or ray flowers

ray flower *n* : one of the flowers with a strap-shaped corolla in the head of a composite plant (as the aster) — called also *ray floret*

ray•less \'rā-ləs\ *adj* : lacking rays or ray flowers

ray•on \'rā-,än\ *n* **1 :** any of a group of smooth textile fibers made from cellulosic material by extrusion through minute holes **2 :** a rayon yarn, thread, or fabric [derived from *2ray*]

raze \'rāz\ *vt* : to destroy utterly by tearing down : DEMOLISH ⟨*raze* a building⟩ [Middle English *rasen* "to erase", from Middle French *raser* "to scrape, erase", from Latin *rasus,* past participle of *radere* "to scrape, shave"]

ra•zor \'rā-zər\ *n* : a sharp cutting instrument used especially to shave off hair [Old French *raseor,* from *raser,* "to scrape, shave, erase"] — **razor** *adj*

ra•zor•back \-,bak\ *or* **razorback hog** *or* **razor–backed hog** \-,bakt-\ *n* : a thin-bodied long-legged half-wild mongrel hog chiefly of the southeastern United States

razor clam *n* : any of numerous marine bivalve mollusks having a long narrow curved thin shell

razz \'raz\ *vt* : to tease mockingly : KID [*raspberry*]

-rd *symbol* — used after the figure 3 to indicate the ordinal number *third* ⟨3*rd*⟩ ⟨53*rd*⟩

1re \'rā\ *n* : the 2d note of the diatonic scale [Medieval Latin]

2re \'rā, 'rē\ *prep* : with regard to [Latin, ablative of *res* "thing"]

re- *prefix* **1 :** again : anew ⟨*re*appear⟩ **2 :** back : backward ⟨*re*call⟩ [Latin *re-, red-* "back, again, against"]

See *re-* and 2d element

reaccelerate	**reacquire**	**readmittance**
reacceleration	**reacquisition**	**readopt**
reaccept	**readapt**	**readoption**
reacclimatization	**readd**	**reaffirm**
reacclimatize	**readdict**	**reaffirmation**
reaccommodate	**readdiction**	**reaffix**
reaccredit	**readdition**	**realign**
reaccreditation	**readdress**	**realignment**
reaccumulate	**readjust**	**reallocate**
reaccumulation	**readjustable**	**reallocation**
reachieve	**readjustment**	**reanalysis**
reachievement	**readmission**	**reanalyze**
reacquaint	**readmit**	**reanesthetize**

\ə\ **abut**	\au̇\ **out**	\i\ **tip**	\ȯ\ **saw**	\u̇\ **foot**
\ər\ **further**	\ch\ **chin**	\ī\ **life**	\ȯi\ **coin**	\y\ **yet**
\a\ **mat**	\e\ **pet**	\j\ **job**	\th\ **thin**	\yü\ **few**
\ā\ **take**	\ē\ **easy**	\ng\ **sing**	\th\ **this**	\yu̇\ **cure**
\ä\ **cot, cart**	\g\ **go**	\ō\ **bone**	\ü\ **food**	\zh\ **vision**

reannex
reannexation
reappear
reappearance
reapplication
reapply
reappoint
reappointment
reapportion
reapportionment
reappraisal
reappraise
reappropriate
reapproval
reapprove
reargue
reargument
rearousal
rearouse
rearranger
rearrest
reascend
reascent
reassail
reassemble
reassembly
reassert
reassertion
reassess
reassessment
reassign
reassignment
reassociate
reassociation
reassort
reassortment
reassume
reassumption
reattach
reattachment
reattack
reattain
reattainment
reattempt
reattribute
reattribution
reaudition
reauthorize
reawake
reawaken
rebait
rebalance
rebaptism
rebaptize
rebid
rebiddable
rebind
reboard
reboil
rebook
reburial
rebury
rebutton
rebuy
recalculate
recalculation
recalibrate
recalibration
recane
recast
recatalog
recentralization
recentralize
recertification
recertify
rechannel
recharge
rechart
recheck
rechristen
recirculate
recirculation
reclassification
reclassify
reclean
recodification
recodify
recolonization
recolonize
recolor
recombination
recombine
recommence
recommencement
recommission
recompilation
recompile
recomplete
recompletion
recomputation
recompute
reconceive
reconception
recondensation
recondense
reconduct
reconfine
reconnect
reconnection
reconquer
reconquest
reconsecrate
reconsecration
reconsolidate
reconsolidation
reconsult
reconsultation
recontact
recontaminate
recontamination
recontour
recontract
reconvene
reconverge
reconvict
reconviction
reconvince
recook
recopy
recross
recultivate
recut
redate
redeal
rededicate
rededication
redefine
redefinition
redeliver
redelivery
redemand
redeposit
redesignate
redetermination
redetermine
redevelop
rediscover
rediscovery
redissolve
redistill
redistribute
redistribution
redivide
redivision
redock
redraft
redraw
redry
reeligibility
reeligible
reembodiment
reembody
reemerge
reemergence
reemergent
reemission
reemit
reemphasis
reemphasize
reenergize
reengage
reengagement
reengrave
reenlist
reenlistment
reenroll
reenter
reentrant
reequip
reerect
reerection
reescalate
reescalation
reestablish
reestablishment
reestimate
reestimation
reevaluate
reevaluation
reexamination
reexamine
reexchange
reexpand
reexpansion
reexperience
reexploration
reexplore
reexport
reexportation
reface
refasten
refeed
refight
refigure
refilm
refilter
refinance
refind
refire
refix
refloat
reflood
reflower
refly
refocus
refold
reformulate
reformulation
refortification
refortify
reframe
refreeze
refry
regather
regild
reglaze
reglue
regrind
regroove
regrow
regrowth
rehear
reheat
rehire
rehospitalization
rehospitalize
rehouse
rehumanize
reidentification
reidentify
reignite
reimmerse
reimmersion
reimplant
reimplantation
reimpose
reimposition
reimprison
reimprisonment
reinclude
reinclusion
reincorporate
reindict
reindictment
reinfest
reinfestation
reinfiltrate
reinfiltration
reinflate
reinflation
reinitiate
reinject
reinjection
reinjure
reinoculate
reinoculation
reinsert
reinsertion
reinspect
reinspection
reinstall
reinstallation
reinstitute
reinstitution
reinstruct
reinsulate
reintegrate
reintegration
reinter
reintroduce
reintroduction
reinvade
reinvasion
reinvent
reinvention
reinvestigate
reinvestigation
reinvigorate
reinvigoration
rejudge
rekeyboard
rekindle
reknit
relabel
relandscape
relaunch
relearn
relend
relet
relicense
relight
reline
reload
relock
relubricate
relubrication
remarry
remeet
remelt
remigrate
remigration
remilitarization
remilitarize
remobilization
remobilize
remoisten
remold
remotivate
remotivation
rename
renationalization
renationalize
renegotiable
renegotiate
renegotiation
reobserve
reoccupation
reoccupy
reoccur
reoccurrence
reoffer
reoperate
reoperation
reorchestrate
reorchestration
reorient
reorientate
reorientation
repack
repaint
repattern
repave
reperk
rephotograph
replan
replaster
replay
repledge
replot
repolarization
repolarize
repolish
repoll
repopularize
repopulate
repopulation
repressurization
repressurize
reprice
reprocess
reprogram
repropose
repurchase
reread
rerecord
reregister
reregistration
reroll
reroof
reroute
resample
resaw
reschedule
reschool
rescore
rescreen
resculpture
reseal
reseat
resee
resegregate
resegregation
resell
reseller
resentence
reset
resettle
resettlement
resew
reshoot
reshoulder
reshow
resilver
resoak
resocialization
resocialize
resod
resolder
resolidification
resolidify
resow
respecification
respecify
respray
respring
restaff
restage
restamp
restart
restimulate
restimulation
restock
restraighten
restrengthen
restring
restructure
restudy
restyle
resubmission
resubmit
resummon
resupply
resurface
resurge
resurrender
resurvey
resuspend
resuspension
resynthesis
resynthesize
resystematize
retabulate
retag
retailor
retarget
retaste
reteach
retelevise
retell
retest
rethink
rethread
retie
retighten
retint
retitle
retrack
retrain
retransfer
retransform
retransformation
retranslate
retransmission
retransmit
retransplant
retransplantation
retrap
retraverse
retry
retune
retype
reupholster
reutilization
reutilize
revaccinate
revaccination
revalidate
revalidation
reverification
reverify
revisit
rewarm
rewash
rewater

rewax	**reweigh**	**rewind**
reweave	**reweld**	**rewire**
rewed	**rewet**	**rewrap**

're \ər, r\ *vb* : ARE ⟨what'*re* you doing⟩ ⟨they'*re* very nice children⟩

re•ab•sorb \ˌrē-əb-'sȯrb, -'zȯrb\ *vt* : to absorb again; *esp* : RESORB — **re•ab•sorp•tion** \-'sȯrp-shən, -'zȯrp-\ *n* — **re•ab•sorp•tive** \-'sȯrp-tiv, -'zȯrp-\ *adj*

1reach \'rēch\ *vb* **1 a** : to stretch out : EXTEND ⟨*reach* out your hand⟩ **b** : to move the arm so as to make a grab ⟨*reached* for a knife⟩ **c** : to touch or grasp by extending a part of the body or an object ⟨couldn't *reach* the apple on the tree⟩ **2 a** : to go as far as ⟨the shadow *reached* the wall⟩ **b** : to extend continuously ⟨the field *reaches* to the highway⟩ **c** : to go or function effectively ⟨as far as the eye can *reach*⟩ **3 a** : to arrive at : come to ⟨*reached* home late⟩; *also* : ACHIEVE ⟨*reached* an understanding⟩ **b** : to get or be delivered to ⟨your message *reached* me⟩ **4** : to communicate with ⟨tried to *reach* you by phone⟩; *also* : to make an impression on : INFLUENCE ⟨couldn't *reach* my own child⟩ **5** : to hand over : PASS ⟨*reach* me the salt⟩ **6** : to sail on a reach [Old English *rǣcan*] — **reach•able** \'rē-chə-bəl\ *adj* — **reach•er** *n*

2reach *n* **1 a** : the action or an act of reaching **b** : the distance or extent of reaching or of ability to reach ⟨you have a long *reach*⟩ **c** : COMPREHENSION, GRASP ⟨the subject was beyond my *reach*⟩ **2** : a continuous unbroken stretch or expanse; *esp* : a straight portion of a stream or river **3** : a course sailed approximately at right angles to the wind

re•act \rē-'akt\ *vb* **1** : to exert a reciprocal or counteracting force or influence — often used with *on* or *upon* **2** : to act or behave in response ⟨*reacted* violently to the suggestion⟩; *also* : to respond to a stimulus **3** : to act in opposition to a force or influence — usually used with *against* ⟨*reacted* against unfair treatment⟩ **4** : to move or tend in a reverse direction ⟨prices *reacted* strongly after a brief drop⟩ **5** : to undergo or make undergo chemical reaction [New Latin *reactus*, past participle of *reagere* "to react", from Latin *re-* + *agere* "to act"]

re•ac•tance \rē-'ak-təns\ *n* : the part of the impedance of an alternating-current circuit due to capacitance and inductance and expressed in ohms

re•ac•tant \-tənt\ *n* : a chemically reacting substance

re•ac•tion \rē-'ak-shən\ *n* **1 a** : the act or process or an instance of reacting **b** : tendency toward a former especially outmoded political or social order or policy **2** : bodily response to or activity aroused by a stimulus: **a** : the response of tissues to a foreign substance (as an allergen or infective agent) **b** : mental or emotional response (as to exhausting effort or one's life situation) **3** : the force that a body subjected to the action of a force from another body exerts in the opposite direction **4 a** : chemical transformation or change : the action between atoms or molecules to form one or more new substances **b** : a process involving change in atomic nuclei — **re•ac•tion•al** \-shnəl, -shən-l\ *adj* — **re•ac•tion•al•ly** \-ē\ *adv*

1re•ac•tion•ary \rē-'ak-shə-ˌner-ē\ *adj* : relating to, marked by, or favoring especially political reaction

2reactionary *n, pl* **-ar•ies** : a reactionary person

reaction time *n* : the time between the beginning of a stimulus and an individual's reaction to it

re•ac•ti•vate \rē-'ak-tə-ˌvāt, 'rē-\ *vb* : to make or become activated again — **re•ac•ti•va•tion** \ˌrē-ˌak-tə-'vā-shən\ *n*

re•ac•tive \rē-'ak-tiv\ *adj* **1** : of or relating to reaction or reactance **2** : reacting or tending to react — **re•ac•tive•ly** *adv* — **re•ac•tive•ness** *n* — **re•ac•tiv•i•ty** \ˌrē-ˌak-'tiv-ət-ē\ *n*

re•ac•tor \rē-'ak-tər\ *n* **1** : one that reacts; *esp* : one that reacts positively to a foreign substance (as in a test for hypersensitivity or a disease) **2 a** : a vat for an industrial chemical reaction **b** : an apparatus in which a chain reaction of fissionable material is initiated and controlled — called also *nuclear reactor*

1read \'rēd\ *vb* **read** \'red\; **read•ing** \'rēd-iŋ\ **1 a** (1) : to go over systematically by sight or touch to take in and understand the meaning of (as letters or symbols) (2) : to study the movements of (a speaker's lips) and so understand what is being said (3) : to utter aloud the printed or written words of (4) : to understand the written form of ⟨*reads* French⟩ **b** : to learn from what one has seen in writing or printing ⟨*read* that they got married⟩ ⟨*read* about your promotion⟩ **c** : to deliver aloud by or as if by reading **d** : to make a study of ⟨*read* law⟩ **e** : PROOFREAD **f** : to hear and understand (a speaker or a transmission) in radio communications ⟨how do you *read* me — over⟩ **2 a** : to interpret the meaning or significance of ⟨*read* palms⟩ **b** : FORETELL, PREDICT **3** : to discover by interpreting outward expression or signs ⟨*read* guilt in their faces⟩ **4 a** : to attribute a meaning to : UNDERSTAND ⟨how do you *read* this passage⟩ **b** : to attribute as an assumption or conjecture ⟨*read* a nonexistent meaning into my words⟩ **5** : to use as a substitute for or in preference to another word or phrase in a particular passage, text, or version ⟨*read* "hurry" for "harry"⟩ **6** : INDICATE ⟨the thermometer *reads* zero⟩ **7 a** : to sense the meaning of (coded information) ⟨data must be *read* before it can be processed⟩ **b** : to sense the coded information on ⟨*read* a punch card⟩ **c** : to cause to be read and transferred to storage ⟨*read* data into memory⟩ **8** : to consist of specific words, phrases, or symbols ⟨the passage *reads* differently in older versions⟩ [Old English *rǣdan* "to advise, interpret, read"] — **read•abil•i•ty** \ˌrēd-ə-'bil-ət-ē\ *n* — **read•able** \'rēd-ə-bəl\ *adj* — **read•able•ness** *n* — **read•ably** \-blē\ *adv* — **read between the lines** : to understand more than is directly stated — **read the riot act 1** : to give an order or warning to cease something **2** : to give a severe reprimand

2read \'red\ *adj* : taught or informed by reading ⟨widely *read* in history⟩

read•er \'rēd-ər\ *n* **1** : one that reads **2** : a device that scans recorded data for input ⟨a card *reader*⟩ **3** : a book for instruction and practice especially in reading

read•er•ship \-ˌship\ *n* **1** : the office or position of a reader **2** : the mass or a particular group of readers

read•i•ly \'red-l-ē\ *adv* : in a ready manner: as **a** : WILLINGLY ⟨*readily* accepted advice⟩ **b** : EASILY ⟨reasons that were *readily* understood⟩

read•ing \'rēd-iŋ\ *n* **1 a** : material read or for reading **b** : extent of material read ⟨a person of vast *reading*⟩ **2** : something that is registered (as on a gauge) ⟨the thermometer *reading* was 70 degrees⟩ **3** : a particular interpretation or performance **4** : the introduction of a proposed bill to a legislative body by reading aloud all or a part of it

reading desk *n* : a desk to support a book in a convenient position for a standing reader

read•out \'rēd-ˌau̇t\ *n* : an electronic device that displays information (as data from a calculator); *also* : the information displayed

1ready \'red-ē\ *adj* **read•i•er**; **-est 1** : prepared for use or action ⟨dinner is *ready*⟩ **2** : APT, LIKELY ⟨*ready* to cry⟩ **3** : WILLING ⟨*ready* to give aid⟩ **4** : notably dexterous, adroit, or skilled ⟨a *ready* wit⟩ **5** : PROMPT ⟨a *ready* answer⟩ **6** : AVAILABLE, HANDY ⟨*ready* money⟩ [Middle English *redy*] — **read•i•ness** \-nəs\ *n*

2ready *vt* **read•ied**; **ready•ing** : to make ready

3ready *n* : the state of being ready; *esp* : preparation of a gun for immediate aiming or firing

ready-made \ˌred-ē-'mād\ *adj* **1** : made beforehand for general sale ⟨*ready-made* clothes⟩ **2** : lacking individuality : COMMONPLACE

ready room *n* : a room in which pilots are briefed and await take-off orders

ready-to-wear \ˌred-ēt-ə-'waər, -'weər\ *adj* : READY-MADE 1

re•agent \rē-'ā-jənt\ *n* : one that reacts or induces a reaction; *esp* : a substance that takes part in or brings about a particular chemical reaction ⟨a fixing *reagent* for tissues⟩ ⟨a *reagent* for etching steel⟩ [New Latin *reagens*, present participle of *reagere* "to react"]

re•agin \rē-'ā-jən, -gən\ *n* : an antibody in the blood of some allergic individuals that can sensitize the skin of normal individuals [*reagent* + *-in*] — **re•agin•ic** \ˌrē-ə-'jin-ik\ *adj* — **re•agin•i•cal•ly** \-'jin-i-kə-lē, -klē\ *adv*

1re•al \'ri-əl, 'ril, 'rē-əl, 'rēl\ *adj* **1** : not artificial, deceptive, seeming, or false : GENUINE ⟨*real* gold⟩ **2 a** : not imaginary : ACTUAL ⟨in *real* life⟩ **b** (1) : belonging to the set of real numbers ⟨the *real* roots of an equation⟩ (2) : taking on only real numbers for values ⟨a *real* variable⟩ **3** : measured by purchasing power ⟨*real* income⟩ [Middle French, from Medieval Latin *realis* "relating to things" and Late Latin *realis* "real, actual";

\ə\ **abut**	\au̇\ **out**	\i\ **tip**	\ȯ\ **saw**	\u̇\ **foot**
\ər\ **further**	\ch\ **chin**	\ī\ **life**	\ȯi\ **coin**	\y\ **yet**
\a\ **mat**	\e\ **pet**	\j\ **job**	\th\ **thin**	\yü\ **few**
\ā\ **take**	\ē\ **easy**	\ŋ\ **sing**	\t͟h\ **this**	\yu̇\ **cure**
\ä\ **cot, cart**	\g\ **go**	\ō\ **bone**	\ü\ **food**	\zh\ **vision**

from Latin *res* "thing, fact"] — **re•al•ness** *n*
• **syn** REAL, ACTUAL, TRUE mean corresponding to known facts. REAL implies an agreement between what a thing seems to be and what it is ⟨this is a *real* diamond⟩ ACTUAL stresses occurrence or existence as action or fact ⟨the *actual* temperature today is higher than predicted⟩ TRUE implies conforming to what is real or actual ⟨a *true* account of the incident⟩ or to a model or standard ⟨prove oneself a *true* friend⟩
²real *n* : a real thing; *esp* : REAL NUMBER
³real *adv* : REALLY, VERY ⟨we had a *real* good time⟩
⁴re•al \rā-ˈäl\ *n, pl* **re•als** *or* **re•ales** \-ˈäl-ās\ : the chief former monetary unit of Spain [Spanish, from *real* "royal", from Latin *regalis*]
real estate *n* : property in houses and land
re•al•gar \rē-ˈal-ˌgär, -gər\ *n* : an orange-red mineral As_4S_4 or AsS consisting of a sulfide of arsenic and having a resinous luster [Medieval Latin, from Catalan, from Arabic *rahj al-ghār* "powder of the mine"]
real image *n* : an image of an object formed by rays of light coming to a focus (as after passing through a lens or after being reflected by a concave mirror)
re•al•ism \ˈri-ə-ˌliz-əm, ˈrē-ə-\ *n* **1** : the belief that objects we perceive through our senses are real and have an existence outside our own minds **2** : the tendency to see situations or difficulties in the light of facts and to deal with them practically **3** : the representation in literature and art of things as they are in life — **re•al•ist** \-ləst\ *n*
re•al•is•tic \ˌri-ə-ˈlis-tik, ˌrē-ə-\ *adj* **1** : true to life or nature ⟨a *realistic* painting⟩ **2** : having or showing an inclination to face facts and to deal with them sensibly ⟨a *realistic* approach⟩ — **re•al•is•it•cal•ly** \-ti-kə-lē, klē\ *adv*
re•al•i•ty \rē-ˈal-ət-ē\ *n, pl* **-ties** **1** : actual existence ⟨doubt the *reality* of sea serpents⟩ **2** : someone or something real or actual ⟨the *realities* of life⟩ **3** : the characteristic of being true to life or to fact
re•al•ize \ˈri-ə-ˌlīz, ˈrē-ə-\ *vt* **1** : to make actual : ACCOMPLISH ⟨*realize* a lifelong ambition⟩ **2** : to convert into money ⟨*realized* their assets⟩ **3** : to bring or get by sale, investment, or effort : GAIN ⟨*realize* a large profit⟩ **4** : to be aware of ⟨*realized* the danger involved⟩ — **re•al•iz•able** \ˈri-ə-ˌlī-zə-bəl, ˈrē-ə-\ *adj* — **re•al•iza•tion** \ˌri-ə-lə-ˈzā-shən, ˌrē-ə-\ *n* — **re•al•iz•er** *n*
re•al•ly \ˈril-ē, ˈrēl-ē, ˈri-ə-lē, ˈrē-ə-lē\ *adv* **1** : in reality : ACTUALLY ⟨didn't *really* mean what I said⟩ **2** : VERY 1, TRULY ⟨a *really* beautiful day⟩
realm \ˈrelm\ *n* **1** : KINGDOM 1, 2 **2** : SPHERE, DOMAIN ⟨the *realm* of fancy⟩ [Old French *realme,* from Latin *regimen* "rule"]
real number *n* : any of the set of numbers (as −2, 3, ⅞, .25, $\sqrt{2}$, π) that includes the rational numbers and the irrational numbers but not the imaginary numbers
real property *n* : property consisting of fixed, permanent, or immovable things (as lands, houses, or fixtures) — compare PERSONAL PROPERTY
Re•al•tor \ˈrē-əl-tər, ˈrēl-, -ˌtȯr\ *collective mark* — used for a real estate agent who is a member of the National Association of Realtors
re•al•ty \ˈrē-əl-tē, ˈrēl-\ *n, pl* **-ties** : REAL ESTATE [*real* + *-ty* (as in *property*)]
¹ream \ˈrēm\ *n* **1** : a quantity of paper being 20 quires or variously 480, 500, or 516 sheets **2** : a great amount — usually used in pl. [Middle French *raime,* from Arabic *rizmah,* literally, "bundle"]
²ream *vt* **1** : to widen the opening of (a hole) : COUNTERSINK **2** : to shape, enlarge, or dress (a hole) with a reamer **3** : to remove by reaming [perhaps from Old English dialect *rēman*]
ream•er \ˈrē-mər\ *n* **1** : a rotating tool with cutting edges for enlarging or shaping a hole **2** : a juice extractor with a ridged and pointed center rising from a shallow dish
re•an•i•mate \rē-ˈan-ə-ˌmāt, ˈrē-\ *vb* : to give life to anew : REVIVE — **re•an•i•ma•tion** \-ˌan-ə-ˈmā-shən\ *n*
reap \ˈrēp\ *vb* **1 a** (1) : to cut with a sickle, scythe, or reaping machine ⟨*reap* rye⟩ (2) : to clear (as a field) of a crop by so cutting **b** : to gather (a crop) by so cutting : HARVEST **2** : to gain as a reward ⟨*reap* the benefit of hard work⟩ [Old English *reopan*]
reap•er \ˈrē-pər\ *n* : one that reaps; *esp* : a machine for reaping grain
¹rear \ˈriər\ *vb* **1** : to erect by building : CONSTRUCT **2 a** : to raise upright **b** : to rise high ⟨skyscrapers *rearing* above the city⟩ **c** : to rise up on the hind legs ⟨the horse *reared* in fright⟩ **3 a** : to undertake the breeding and raising of ⟨*rear* cattle⟩ **b** : to bring up (a person) [Old English *rǣran*]

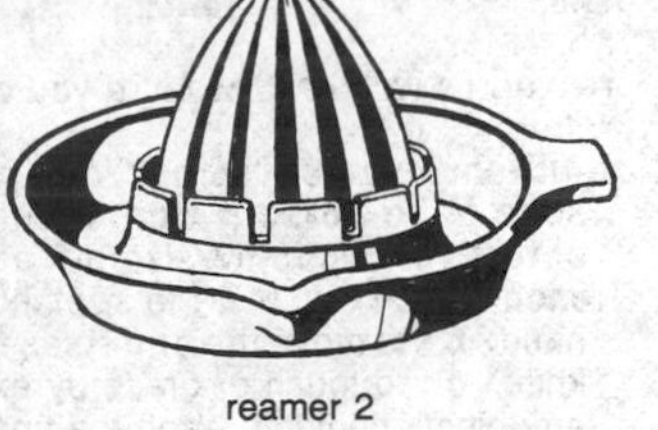
reamer 2

²rear *n* **1** : the back part of something: as **a** : the unit (as of an army) or area farthest from the enemy **b** : BUTTOCK 2 **2** : the space or position at the back ⟨the *rear* of a building⟩ [probably from *rear-* (in such terms as *rear guard*)]
³rear *adj* : being at the back
rear admiral *n* : an officer rank in the Navy and Coast Guard above captain and below vice admiral
rear guard *n* : a military detachment detailed to bring up and protect the rear of a main body or force [Middle French *reregarde,* from *rere* "backward, behind" (from Latin *retro*) + *garde* "guard"]
re•arm \rē-ˈärm, ˈrē-\ *vb* : to arm again especially with new or better weapons — **re•ar•ma•ment** \-ˈär-mə-mənt\ *n*
rear•most \ˈriər-ˌmōst\ *adj* : farthest in the rear
re•ar•range \ˌrē-ə-ˈrānj\ *vt* : to arrange again especially in a different way — **re•ar•range•able** \-ˈrān-jə-bəl\ *adj* — **re•ar•range•ment** \-ˈrānj-mənt\ *n*
¹rear•ward \ˈriər-wərd\ *adj* **1** : located at, near, or toward the rear **2** : directed toward the rear : BACKWARD — **rear•ward•ly** *adv*
²rearward *also* **rear•wards** \-wərdz\ *adv* : at, near, or toward the rear : BACKWARD
¹rea•son \ˈrēz-n\ *n* **1 a** : a statement offered in explanation or justification ⟨gave no *reason* for their absence⟩ **b** : a rational ground or motive ⟨*reasons* for thinking life may exist on Mars⟩ **c** : the thing that makes some fact intelligible : CAUSE **2 a** : the power of comprehending, inferring, or thinking especially in orderly logical ways : INTELLIGENCE **b** : SANITY ⟨almost lost my *reason*⟩ [Old French *raison,* from Latin *ratio* "computation, reason"] **syn** see CAUSE — **in reason** : with reason — **within reason** : within reasonable limits — **with reason** : with good cause : JUSTIFIABLY
²reason *vb* **rea•soned**; **rea•son•ing** \ˈrēz-ning, -n-ing\ **1** : to talk persuasively or to present reasons in order to cause a change of mind ⟨*reason* with someone⟩ **2 a** : to use one's reason or to think in a logical way or manner **b** : to state, formulate, or conclude by use of reason ⟨*reasoned* that both statements couldn't be true⟩ **syn** see THINK
rea•son•able \ˈrēz-nə-bəl, -n-ə-bəl\ *adj* **1 a** : agreeable to reason ⟨a *reasonable* theory⟩ **b** : not extreme or excessive : MODERATE ⟨a *reasonable* request⟩ **c** : INEXPENSIVE ⟨*reasonable* prices⟩ **2 a** : having the faculty of reason : RATIONAL **b** : possessing sound judgment — **rea•son•abil•i•ty** \rēz-nə-ˈbil-ət-ē, -n-ə-\ *n* — **rea•son•able•ness** \ˈrēz-nə-bəl-nəs, -n-ə-\ *n* — **rea•son•ably** \-blē\ *adv*
rea•son•ing *n* **1** : the use of reason; *esp* : the drawing of inferences or conclusions through the use of reason **2** : the reasons used in and the proofs that result from thought
re•as•sur•ance \ˌrē-ə-ˈshu̇r-əns\ *n* : the action of reassuring : the state of being reassured
re•as•sure \ˌrē-ə-ˈshu̇r\ *vt* **1** : to assure anew **2** : to restore to confidence **3** : to insure anew — **re•as•sur•ing•ly** \-ˈshu̇r-ing-lē\ *adv*
re•ata \rē-ˈat-ə, -ˈät-\ *n* : LARIAT [American Spanish]
Re•au•mur \ˌrā-ō-ˈmyu̇r\ *adj* : relating or conforming to a temperature scale on which the boiling point of water is at 80 degrees above the zero of the scale and the freezing point is at zero [René Antoine Ferchault de *Réaumur,* died 1757, French physicist]
reave \ˈrēv\ *vb* **reaved** *or* **reft** \ˈreft\; **reav•ing** *archaic* : PLUNDER, ROB [Old English *rēafian*] — **reav•er** *n*
reb \ˈreb\ *n* : JOHNNY REB [short for *rebel*]
¹re•bate \ˈrē-ˌbāt, ri-ˈ\ *vt* : to make a rebate of : give as a rebate [Middle French *rabattre* "to beat down again", from Old French, from *re-* "re-" + *abattre* "to beat down"] — **re•bat•er** *n*
²re•bate \ˈrē-ˌbāt\ *n* : a return of a portion of a payment

[1]reb•el \'reb-əl\ *adj* **1 a :** opposing or taking arms against the government or ruler **b :** of or relating to rebels **2 :** REBELLIOUS 2, DISOBEDIENT [Old French *rebelle,* from Latin *rebellis,* from *re-* "re-, against" + *bellum* "war"]

[2]rebel *n* **:** one who rebels or participates in a rebellion

[3]re•bel \ri-'bel\ *vi* **re•belled; re•bel•ling 1 a :** to oppose or resist authority or control **b :** to renounce and resist by force the authority of one's government **2 :** to feel or exhibit anger or revulsion

re•bel•lion \ri-'bel-yən\ *n* **1 :** opposition to one in authority or dominance **2 a :** open defiance of or resistance to an established government **b :** an instance of such defiance or resistance **:** REVOLT, UPRISING

• syn UPRISING, REVOLT, REVOLUTION: REBELLION implies open, organized, often armed resistance to authority; UPRISING implies no more than an effort at rebellion; REVOLT suggests an armed uprising that quickly succeeds or fails; REVOLUTION applies to a successful rebellion resulting in a change of government and often of social structure.

re•bel•lious \ri-'bel-yəs\ *adj* **1 :** engaged in rebellion **2 :** inclined to resist or disobey authority **:** INSUBORDINATE — **re•bel•lious•ly** *adv* — **re•bel•lious•ness** *n*

re•birth \rē-'bərth, 'rē-\ *n* **1 :** a new or second birth **2 :** RENAISSANCE 2, REVIVAL

re•born \-'bȯrn\ *adj* **:** experiencing a rebirth

[1]re•bound \ri-'baůnd\ *vi* **1 :** to spring back on striking something **2 :** to recover from setback or frustration [Middle French *rebondir,* from *re-* "re-" + *bondir* "to leap, bound"]

[2]re•bound \'rē-ˌbaůnd, ri-'\ *n* **1 a :** the action of rebounding **:** RECOIL **b :** an upward leap or movement ⟨a sharp *rebound* of the market⟩ **2 :** a basketball or hockey puck that rebounds **3 :** a reaction to setback, frustration, or crisis

re•branch \rē-'branch, 'rē-\ *vi* **:** to form secondary branches

re•broad•cast \rē-'brȯd-ˌkast, 'rē-\ *vt* **-cast** *also* **-cast•ed; -cast•ing 1 :** to broadcast again (a radio or television program being simultaneously received from another source) **2 :** to repeat (a broadcast) at a later time — **rebroadcast** *n*

re•buff \ri-'bəf\ *vt* **:** to refuse or check sharply **:** SNUB [Middle French *rebuffer,* from obsolete Italian *ribuffare*] — **rebuff** *n*

re•build \rē-'bild\ *vb* **-built** \-'bilt\; **-build•ing 1 a :** to make extensive repairs to **b :** to restore to a previous state **2 :** to make extensive changes in **:** REMODEL **3 :** to build again ⟨planned to *rebuild* after the fire⟩

[1]re•buke \ri-'byük\ *vt* **:** to scold or criticize sharply **:** REPRIMAND [Old North French *rebuker*] **syn** see REPROVE — **re•buk•er** *n*

[2]rebuke *n* **:** REPRIMAND, REPROOF

re•bus \'rē-bəs\ *n* **:** a representation of words or syllables by pictures of objects whose names resemble the intended words or syllables in sound; *also* **:** a riddle made up of such pictures or symbols [Latin, "by things", from *res* "thing"]

rebus

re•but \ri-'bət\ *vt* **re•but•ted; re•but•ting 1 :** to contradict or oppose by formal argument, plea, or contrary proof **2 :** to expose the falsity of **:** REFUTE ⟨*rebut* a theory⟩ [Old French *reboter* "to drive back", from *re-* "re-" + *boter* "to butt"] — **re•but•ta•ble** \-'bət-ə-bəl\ *adj*

re•but•tal \ri-'bət-l\ *n* **:** the act of rebutting; *also* **:** argument or proof that rebuts

re•cal•ci•trance \ri-'kal-sə-trəns\ *or* **re•cal•ci•tran•cy** \-trən-sē\ *n* **:** the state of being recalcitrant

re•cal•ci•trant \-trənt\ *adj* **1 :** obstinately defiant of authority or restraint **2 :** not responsive to handling or treatment [Late Latin *recalcitrare* "to be stubbornly disobedient", from Latin, "to kick back", from *re-* + *calcitrare* "to kick", from *calc-, calx* "heel"] **syn** see UNRULY — **recalcitrant** *n*

[1]re•call \ri-'kȯl\ *vt* **1 a :** to ask or order to come back **b :** to bring back to mind usually with some effort **2 :** CANCEL 2a, REVOKE **3 a :** to bring back into existence **b :** to restore to consciousness or awareness **syn** see REMEMBER — **re•call•able** \-'kȯ-lə-bəl\ *adj*

[2]re•call \ri-'kȯl, 'rē-ˌ\ *n* **1 :** a summons to return **2 :** the right or procedure by which an official may be removed by vote of the people on petition **3 :** remembrance of what has been learned or experienced **4 :** the act of revoking; *also* **:** the possibility of being revoked ⟨the matter is beyond *recall*⟩

re•cant \ri-'kant\ *vb* **:** to withdraw or repudiate a statement of opinion or belief formally and publicly [Latin *recantare,* from *re-* + *cantare* "to sing"] — **re•can•ta•tion** \ˌrē-ˌkan-'tā-shən\ *n*

• syn RECANT, RETRACT mean to withdraw publicly something declared or professed. RECANT implies admission of error in something one has openly professed or taught ⟨the candidate *recanted* the challenged position⟩ RETRACT stresses the repudiation of something (as an accusation or an offer) previously put forward ⟨*retracted* their earlier offer⟩

[1]re•cap \rē-'kap, 'rē-\ *vt* **re•capped; re•cap•ping :** to cement, mold, and vulcanize a strip of rubber upon the surface of the tread of (a worn automobile tire)

[2]re•cap \'rē-ˌkap\ *n* **:** a recapped tire

[3]re•cap \ri-'kap, 'rē-\ *vt* **re•capped; re•cap•ping :** RECAPITULATE ⟨now, to *recap* the news⟩

[4]re•cap \'rē-ˌkap, ri-'\ *n* **:** RECAPITULATION

re•ca•pit•u•late \ˌrē-kə-'pich-ə-ˌlāt\ *vb* **:** to repeat briefly **:** SUMMARIZE [Late Latin *recapitulare,* from Latin *re-* + *capitulum* "division of a book", from *caput* "head"]

re•ca•pit•u•la•tion \-ˌpich-ə-'lā-shən\ *n* **1 :** a concise summary **2 :** the supposed repetition in the development of an individual of the evolutionary stages represented in its ancestral types **3 :** the third section of a sonata form — **re•ca•pit•u•la•to•ry** \-'pich-ə-lə-ˌtōr-ē, -ˌtȯr-\ *adj*

re•cap•ture \rē-'kap-chər, 'rē-\ *n* **:** the act of retaking **:** the fact of being retaken **:** RECOVERY — **recapture** *vt*

re•cede \ri-'sēd\ *vi* **1 a :** to move back or away **:** WITHDRAW ⟨the *receding* tide⟩ **b :** to slant backward ⟨a *receding* forehead⟩ **2 :** to grow less **:** CONTRACT [Latin *recedere* "to go back", from *re-* + *cedere* "to go"]

[1]re•ceipt \ri-'sēt\ *n* **1 :** RECIPE **2 :** the act or process of receiving **3 :** something received — usually used in pl. **4 :** a writing acknowledging the receiving of goods or money [Old North French *receite,* from Medieval Latin *recepta,* derived from Latin *recipere* "to receive"]

[2]receipt *vt* **1 :** to give a receipt for or acknowledge the receipt of **2 :** to mark as paid

re•ceiv•able \ri-'sē-və-bəl\ *adj* **1 :** capable of being received **2 :** not yet paid **:** DUE ⟨accounts *receivable*⟩

re•ceiv•ables \-bəlz\ *n pl* **:** amounts of money receivable

re•ceive \ri-'sēv\ *vb* **1 :** to take possession or delivery of **:** come into possession of ⟨*receive* the money⟩ ⟨*receive* a letter⟩ **2 :** to permit to enter one's household or company **:** WELCOME, GREET ⟨*receive* friends⟩ **3 :** to hold a reception ⟨*receive* from four to six o'clock⟩ **4 :** to undergo or be subjected to (an experience or treatment) ⟨*receive* a shock⟩ **5 :** to change incoming radio waves into sounds or pictures [Old North French *receivre,* from Latin *recipere,* from *re-* + *capere* "to take"]

• syn ACCEPT, TAKE: RECEIVE normally implies passiveness but usually suggests physical contact or presence; ACCEPT implies some element of consent or approval but a minimum of physical activity ⟨*accepted* the award and attended a dinner to *receive* it⟩ TAKE may imply seizing or picking up what is offered ⟨*take* a bribe⟩ ⟨*take* a hint⟩ or enduring what is inflicted ⟨*took* many heavy blows⟩

re•ceiv•er \ri-'sē-vər\ *n* **:** one that receives: as **a :** a person appointed to take control of property that is involved in a lawsuit or of a business that is bankrupt or is being reorganized **b (1) :** an apparatus for receiving radio or television broadcasts **(2) :** the portion of a telegraphic or telephonic apparatus that converts electric currents or waves into visible or audible signals **c :** an offensive football player who is eligible to catch a forward pass

re•ceiv•er•ship \-ˌship\ *n* **1 :** the office or function of a receiver **2 :** the state of being in the hands of a receiver

re•cen•cy \'rēs-n-sē\ *n* **:** the quality or state of being recent

re•cent \'rēs-nt\ *adj* **1 a :** of or relating to a time not long past **b :** having lately appeared or come into being **2** *cap* **:** of, relating

\ə\ abut	\aů\ **out**	\i\ **tip**	\ȯ\ **saw**	\ů\ **foot**
\ər\ **further**	\ch\ **chin**	\ī\ **life**	\ȯi\ **coin**	\y\ **yet**
\a\ **mat**	\e\ **pet**	\j\ **job**	\th\ **thin**	\yü\ **few**
\ā\ **take**	\ē\ **easy**	\ng\ **sing**	\t͟h\ **this**	\yů\ **cure**
\ä\ **cot, cart**	\g\ **go**	\ō\ **bone**	\ü\ **food**	\zh\ **vision**

to, or being the present epoch of the Quaternary which is dated from the close of the Pleistocene [Latin *recens*] — **re•cent•ly** *adv* — **re•cent•ness** *n*

• **syn** RECENT, MODERN, LATE mean having taken place, existed, or developed in times close to the present. RECENT is the least precise, suggesting only comparative nearness to the present ⟨*recent* discoveries in nuclear physics⟩ MODERN implies being characteristic of the present age ⟨*modern* methods of teaching⟩ LATE usually implies a series or succession of which the one described is the most recent ⟨the *late* war⟩

re•cep•ta•cle \ri-ˈsep-ti-kəl\ *n* **1 :** something used to receive and contain smaller objects **:** CONTAINER **2 :** the enlarged end of the flower stalk upon which the floral organs are borne **3 :** an electrical fitting (as a socket) into which another fitting may be pushed or screwed for making an electrical connection [Latin *receptaculum,* from *receptare* "to receive", from *receptus,* past participle of *recipere* "to receive"]

re•cep•tion \ri-ˈsep-shən\ *n* **1 :** the act or process of receiving, welcoming, or accepting ⟨our *reception* of the news⟩ ⟨got a cool *reception*⟩ **2 :** the state or fact of being received (as into shelter or membership) **3 :** a social gathering ⟨a wedding *reception*⟩ **4 :** the receiving of a radio or television broadcast [Latin *receptio,* from *receptus,* past participle of *recipere* "to receive"]

re•cep•tion•ist \ri-ˈsep-shə-nəst, -shnəst\ *n* **:** an office employee who greets and assists callers

re•cep•tive \ri-ˈsep-tiv\ *adj* **1 :** open and responsive to ideas **2 :** able to receive and transmit stimuli **:** SENSORY — **re•cep•tive•ly** *adv* — **re•cep•tive•ness** *n* — **re•cep•tiv•i•ty** \ˌrē-ˌsep-ˈtiv-ət-ē, ri-\ *n*

re•cep•tor \ri-ˈsep-tər\ *n* **:** a cell or group of cells that receives stimuli **:** SENSE ORGAN

¹re•cess \ˈrē-ˌses, ri-ˈ\ *n* **1 :** a hidden, secret, or secluded place **2 a :** a space or little hollow set back (as from the main line of a coast) **:** INDENTATION **b :** ALCOVE 1 **3 :** a suspension of business or procedure; *esp* **:** a brief period for relaxation between class or study periods of a school day [Latin *recessus,* from *recedere* "to recede"]

²recess *vb* **1 :** to put into a recess ⟨*recessed* lighting⟩ **2 :** to make a recess in **3 :** to interrupt for or take a recess

re•ces•sion \ri-ˈsesh-ən\ *n* **1 :** the act or fact of receding **2 :** a departing procession (as of clergy and choir at the end of a church service) **3 :** a downturn in business activity; *also* **:** the period of such a downturn

re•ces•sion•al \ri-ˈsesh-nəl, -ən-l\ *n* **:** a hymn or musical piece at the conclusion of a service or program; *also* **:** RECESSION 2

¹re•ces•sive \ri-ˈses-iv\ *adj* **1 :** tending to go back **2 a :** producing an effect on bodily characteristics only when homozygous ⟨*recessive* genes⟩ **b :** exhibited by the body only when the determining gene is homozygous ⟨*recessive* traits⟩ — **re•ces•sive•ly** *adv* — **re•ces•sive•ness** *n*

²recessive *n* **:** a recessive trait or gene; *also* **:** an organism expressing one or more recessive characters

re•cher•ché \rə-ˌsher-ˈshā\ *adj* **1 :** being rare or exotic **2 :** excessively refined **:** PRECIOUS [French, from *rechercher* "to seek out, research"]

rec•i•pe \ˈres-ə-pē, -ˌpē\ *n* **1 :** PRESCRIPTION 3a **2 :** a set of instructions for making something (as a food dish) from various ingredients **3 :** method of procedure ⟨a *recipe* for happiness⟩ [Latin, "take", imperative of *recipere* "to take, receive"]

re•cip•i•ent \ri-ˈsip-ē-ənt\ *n* **:** one that receives ⟨the *recipient* of many honors⟩ [Latin *recipiens,* present participle of *recipere* "to receive"] — **recipient** *adj*

¹re•cip•ro•cal \ri-ˈsip-rə-kəl\ *adj* **1 :** done or felt equally by both sides ⟨*reciprocal* affection⟩ **2 :** related to each other in such a way that one completes the other or is the equivalent of the other **:** mutually corresponding **3 :** of, constituting, or resulting from paired crosses in which the kind that supplies the male parent of the first cross supplies the female parent of the second cross and vice versa [Latin *reciprocus* "returning the same way, alternating", derived from *re-* "back" + *pro-* "forward"] — **re•cip•ro•cal•ly** \-kə-lē, -klē\ *adv*

• **syn** RECIPROCAL, MUTUAL, COMMON mean shared or experienced by each of those involved. RECIPROCAL implies an equal return or counteraction by each of two sides ⟨*reciprocal* lowering of tariffs⟩ MUTUAL applies to feelings or effects shared by two jointly ⟨*mutual* affection⟩ COMMON implies only being shared by others ⟨united in a *common* purpose⟩

²reciprocal *n* **1 :** something in a reciprocal relationship to another **2 :** either of a pair of numbers (as 2/3 and 3/2 or 9 and 1/9) whose product is one

re•cip•ro•cate \ri-ˈsip-rə-ˌkāt\ *vb* **1 :** to give and take mutually **:** EXCHANGE **2 :** to make a return for something **3 :** to move forward and backward alternately ⟨a *reciprocating* mechanical part⟩ — **re•cip•ro•ca•tion** \-ˌsip-rə-ˈkā-shən\ *n* — **re•cip•ro•ca•tor** \-ˈsip-rə-ˌkāt-ər\ *n*

reciprocating engine *n* **:** an engine in which the to-and-fro motion of a piston is transformed into circular motion of the crankshaft

rec•i•proc•i•ty \ˌres-ə-ˈpräs-ət-ē\ *n, pl* **-ties 1 :** mutual dependence, cooperation, or exchange between persons, groups or states **2 :** a mutual exchange of privileges; *esp* **:** a recognition by one of two countries or institutions of the validity of licenses or privileges granted by the other

re•cit•al \ri-ˈsīt-l\ *n* **1 :** a reciting of something; *esp* **:** a story told in detail ⟨the *recital* of their troubles⟩ **2 :** a program of one kind of music ⟨a piano *recital*⟩ **3 :** a public performance by pupils (as music or dancing pupils) — **re•cit•al•ist** \-l-əst\ *n*

rec•i•ta•tion \ˌres-ə-ˈtā-shən\ *n* **1 :** an enumeration or telling in detail **2 :** the act or an instance of reading or repeating aloud especially publicly **3 a :** a student's oral reply to questions **b :** a class period

rec•i•ta•tive \ˌres-tə-ˈtēv, -ə-tə-\ *n* **:** a rhythmically free vocal style that imitates the natural inflections of speech and that is used for dialogue and narrative in operas and oratorios; *also* **:** a passage in this style [Italian *recitativo,* from *recitare* "to recite", from Latin] — **recitative** *adj*

re•cite \ri-ˈsīt\ *vb* **1 :** to repeat from memory or read aloud publicly ⟨*recite* a poem⟩ **2 a :** to give a detailed narration of **b :** STATE 2 **3 :** to answer (as to a teacher) questions about a lesson [Latin *recitare,* from *re-* + *citare* "to summon"] — **re•cit•er** *n*

reck \ˈrek\ *vi* **1 :** CARE 1a, MIND **2** *archaic* **:** to be of interest **:** MATTER [Old English *reccan* "to take heed"]

reck•less \ˈrek-ləs\ *adj* **1 :** marked by lack of caution **:** RASH **2 :** NEGLIGENT 1, IRRESPONSIBLE ⟨*reckless* driving⟩ **syn** see DARING — **reck•less•ly** *adv* — **reck•less•ness** *n*

reck•on \ˈrek-ən\ *vb* **reck•oned; reck•on•ing** \ˈrek-ning, -ə-ning\ **1 a :** COUNT 1a, COMPUTE ⟨*reckon* the days till Christmas⟩ **b :** to estimate by calculation ⟨*reckon* the height of a building⟩ **2 :** CONSIDER 3, REGARD ⟨was *reckoned* among the leaders⟩ **3** *chiefly dialect* **:** THINK, SUPPOSE ⟨*reckoned* they might win⟩ **4 :** to make up or settle an account **5 :** to count on **:** DEPEND ⟨*reckon* on support⟩ [Old English *-recenian* (as in *gerecenian* "to narrate")] — **reck•on•er** \ˈrek-nər, -ə-nər\ *n* — **reckon with :** to take into account — **reckon without :** to fail to take into account

reck•on•ing *n* **1 :** the act or an instance of reckoning: as **a :** ⁴BILL 4, ACCOUNT **b :** COMPUTATION **c :** calculation of a ship's position **2 :** a settling of accounts ⟨a day of *reckoning*⟩ **3 :** a summing up **:** APPRAISAL

re•claim \ri-ˈklām\ *vt* **1 :** to recall from wrong or improper conduct **:** REFORM **2 :** to alter from an undesirable or uncultivated state ⟨*reclaim* swampland for agriculture⟩ **3 :** to obtain from a waste product or by-product **:** RECOVER ⟨*reclaimed* wool⟩ [Old French *reclamer* "to call back", from Latin *reclamare* "to cry out against", from *re-* + *clamare* "to cry out"] — **re•claim•able** \-ˈklā-mə-bəl\ *adj* — **re•claim•er** *n*

rec•la•ma•tion \ˌrek-lə-ˈmā-shən\ *n* **:** the act or process of reclaiming **:** the state of being reclaimed

re•cline \ri-ˈklīn\ *vb* **1 :** to lean or cause to lean backwards **2 :** REPOSE, LIE ⟨*reclining* on the sofa⟩ [Latin *reclinare,* from *re-* + *clinare* "to bend"]

¹re•cluse \ˈrek-ˌlüs, ri-ˈklüs\ *adj* **:** marked by withdrawal from society **:** SOLITARY [Old French *reclus,* literally, "shut up", from Late Latin *reclusus,* past participle of *recludere* "to shut up", from Latin *re-* + *claudere* "to close"] — **re•clu•sive** \ri-ˈklü-siv, -ziv\ *adj*

²recluse *n* **:** a person (as a hermit) who lives away from others

rec•og•ni•tion \ˌrek-ig-ˈnish-ən, ˌrek-əg-\ *n* **1 :** the act of recognizing ⟨their *recognition* of me⟩ **2 :** special attention or notice **3 :** acknowledgment of something done or given (as by making an award) ⟨got a medal in *recognition* of bravery⟩ **4 :** formal acknowledgment of the political existence of a government or nation [Latin *recognitio,* from *recognitus,* past participle of *recognoscere* "to recognize"]

rec•og•niz•able \ˈrek-ig-ˌnī-zə-bəl, ˈrek-əg-\ *adj* **:** capable of being recognized — **rec•og•niz•abil•i•ty** \ˌrek-ig-ˌnī-zə-ˈbil-ət-ē, ˌrek-əg-\ *n* — **rec•og•niz•ably** \ˈrek-ig-ˌnī-zə-blē, -əg-\ *adv*

re•cog•ni•zance \ri-ˈkäg-nə-zəns, -ˈkän-ə-\ *n* **:** a recorded legal promise to do something (as to appear in court)

rec•og•nize \ˈrek-ig-ˌnīz, ˈrek-əg-\ *vt* **1 :** to know and remember upon seeing ⟨*recognize* a person⟩ **2 :** to consent to admit **:** ACKNOWLEDGE ⟨*recognize* one's faults⟩ **3 :** to take approving notice of ⟨*recognize* an act of bravery⟩ **4 :** to acknowledge acquaintance with ⟨*recognize* someone with a nod⟩ **5 :** to acknowledge as entitled to be heard at a meeting ⟨the chair *recognizes* the delegate from Illinois⟩ **6 :** to grant diplomatic recognition to ⟨*recognized* the new government⟩ **[**Middle French *reconoiss-,* stem of *reconoistre* "to recognize", from Latin *recognoscere,* from *re-* + *cognoscere* "to know", from *co-* + *gnoscere* "to come to know"**]**

[1]**re•coil** \ri-ˈkȯil\ *vi* **1 a :** to fall back under pressure ⟨the soldiers *recoiled* before the enemy attack⟩ **b :** to shrink back ⟨*recoil* in horror⟩ **2 :** to spring back to or as if to a starting point ⟨the spring *recoiled* upon release⟩ **[**Old French *reculer,* from *re-* "re-" + *cul* "backside", from Latin *culus***]**

[2]**re•coil** \ri-ˈkȯil, ˈrē-ˌ\ *n* **1 :** REBOUND 1 **2 :** a springing back **3 :** the distance through which something (as a spring) recoils

re•coil•less \ri-ˈkȯil-ləs, ˈrē-ˌ\ *adj* **:** having a minimum of recoil ⟨a *recoilless* gun⟩

rec•ol•lect \ˌrek-ə-ˈlekt\ *vb* **1 :** to bring back to the level of conscious awareness **2 :** to recall to (oneself) something forgotten or overlooked ⟨*recollected* myself and apologized⟩ **[**Medieval Latin *recollectus,* past participle of *recolligere* "to recollect", from Latin, "to gather again"**] syn** see REMEMBER

re–col•lect \ˌrē-kə-ˈlekt\ *vt* **:** to collect again; *esp* **:** RECOVER ⟨*re-collect* one's drooping spirits⟩

rec•ol•lec•tion \ˌrek-ə-ˈlek-shən\ *n* **1 :** the action or power of recalling to mind **:** REMEMBRANCE **2 :** something recalled to the mind **syn** see MEMORY

re•com•bi•nant \rē-ˈkäm-bə-nənt, ˈrē-\ *n* **:** an individual exhibiting genetic recombination

recombinant DNA *n* **:** DNA prepared in the laboratory by breaking up and splicing together DNA from several different species of organisms

re•com•bi•na•tion \ˌrē-ˌkäm-bə-ˈnā-shən\ *n* **:** the production of new combinations of genes especially through genetic crossing-over and the operation of the law of independent assortment

rec•om•mend \ˌrek-ə-ˈmend\ *vt* **1 :** to make a statement in praise of; *esp* **:** to endorse as fit, worthy, or competent ⟨*recommend* a person for a position⟩ **2 :** to put forward or suggest as one's advice, as one's choice, or as having one's support ⟨*recommend* that the matter be dropped⟩ **3 :** to cause to receive favorable attention **[**Medieval Latin *recommendare* "to praise", from Latin *re-* + *commendare* "to commend"**]** — **rec•om•mend•able** \-ˈmen-də-bəl\ *adj* — **rec•om•mend•er** *n*

rec•om•men•da•tion \ˌrek-ə-mən-ˈdā-shən, -ˌmen-\ *n* **1 :** the act of recommending **2 :** something that recommends **3 :** a thing or course of action recommended

re•com•mit \ˌrē-kə-ˈmit\ *vt* **1 :** to refer (as a bill) again to a committee **2 :** to commit again — **re•com•mit•ment** \-mənt\ *n* — **re•com•mit•al** \-ˈmit-l\ *n*

[1]**rec•om•pense** \ˈrek-əm-ˌpens\ *vt* **:** to give compensation to or for **[**Middle French *recompenser,* from Late Latin *recompensare,* from Latin *re-* + *compensare* "to compensate"**]**

[2]**recompense** *n* **:** a return for something done, suffered, or given

rec•on•cil•abil•i•ty \ˌrek-ən-ˌsī-lə-ˈbil-ət-ē\ *n* **:** the quality or state of bring reconcilable

rec•on•cil•able \ˌrek-ən-ˈsī-lə-bəl\ *adj* **:** capable of being reconciled — **rec•on•cil•able•ness** *n*

rec•on•cile \ˈrek-ən-ˌsīl\ *vt* **1 :** to make friendly again ⟨*reconcile* friends who have quarreled⟩ **2 :** SETTLE, ADJUST ⟨*reconcile* differences of opinion⟩ **3 :** to make agree ⟨a story that cannot be *reconciled* with the facts⟩ **4 :** to cause to submit or accept ⟨*reconciled* to hardship⟩ **[**Latin *reconciliare,* from *re-* + *conciliare* "to conciliate"**]** — **rec•on•cile•ment** \-mənt\ *n* — **rec•on•cil•er** *n* — **rec•on•cil•ia•to•ry** \ˌrek-ən-ˈsil-yə-ˌtōr-ē, -ˌtȯr-\ *adj*

rec•on•cil•i•a•tion \ˌrek-ən-ˌsil-ē-ˈā-shən\ *n* **1 :** the action of reconciling **:** the state of being reconciled **2 :** PENANCE 2

rec•on•dite \ˈrek-ən-ˌdīt, ri-ˈkän-\ *adj* **1** *archaic* **:** hidden from sight **:** CONCEALED **2 :** difficult to understand **:** DEEP ⟨a *recondite* subject⟩ **3 :** of, relating to, or dealing with something little known **[**Latin *reconditus,* past participle of *recondere* "to conceal", from *re-* + *condere* "to store up"**]** — **rec•on•dite•ly** *adv* — **rec•on•dite•ness** *n*

re•con•di•tion \ˌrē-kən-ˈdish-ən\ *vt* **:** to restore to good condition (as by repairing or replacing parts) ⟨*recondition* a house⟩

re•con•firm \ˌrē-kən-ˈfərm\ *vt* **:** to confirm again; *also* **:** to establish more strongly — **re•con•fir•ma•tion** \ˌrē-ˌkän-fər-ˈmā-shən\ *n*

re•con•nais•sance \ri-ˈkän-ə-zəns\ *n* **:** a preliminary survey to gain information; *esp* **:** an exploratory military survey of enemy territory **[**French, literally, "recognition", from Middle French *reconoissance,* from *reconoistre* "to recognize"**]**

re•con•noi•ter \ˌrē-kə-ˈnȯit-ər, ˌrek-ə-\ *vb* **:** to make a reconnaissance; *esp* **:** to survey in preparation for military action ⟨*reconnoiter* enemy territory⟩ **[**obsolete French *reconnoître,* literally, "to recognize", from Middle French *reconoistre***]**

re•con•sid•er \ˌrē-kən-ˈsid-ər\ *vb* **:** to consider again especially with a view to change or reversal — **re•con•sid•er•a•tion** \-ˌsid-ə-ˈrā-shən\ *n*

re•con•sti•tute \rē-ˈkän-stə-ˌtüt, ˈrē-, -ˌtyüt\ *vt* **:** to restore to a former condition by adding water

re•con•struct \ˌrē-kən-ˈstrəkt\ *vt* **:** to construct again **:** REBUILD, REMODEL

re•con•struc•tion \ˌrē-kən-ˈstrək-shən\ *n* **1 a :** the action of reconstructing **:** the state of being reconstructed **b** *often cap* **:** the reorganization and reestablishment of the seceded states in the Union after the American Civil War **2 :** something reconstructed

re•con•ver•sion \ˌrē-kən-ˈvər-zhən\ *n* **:** conversion back to a previous state

re•con•vert \ˌrē-kən-ˈvərt\ *vb* **:** to convert back

[1]**re•cord** \ri-ˈkȯrd\ *vb* **1 a** (1) **:** to set down in writing (2) **:** to deposit an authentic official copy of ⟨*record* a deed⟩ **b** (1) **:** to register permanently (2) **:** INDICATE, READ ⟨the thermometer *recorded* 90°⟩ **2 :** to cause (as sound or visual images) to be registered (as on a phonograph disc or magnetic tape) in reproducible form **3 :** REPRODUCE 2 ⟨a voice that *records* well⟩ **4 :** to give evidence of **[**Old French *recorder* "to recall to mind", from Latin *recordari,* from *re-* + *cord-, cor* "heart"**]**

[2]**rec•ord** \ˈrek-ərd, -ˌȯrd\ *n* **1 :** the state or fact of being recorded **2 :** something that records: as **a :** something (as a monument) that recalls or reports past events **b :** an official writing that records the proceedings or acts of a group, organization, or official **c :** an authentic official copy of a document **3 a :** the known or recorded facts regarding something or someone ⟨my school *record*⟩ **b :** the best that has ever been done (as in a particular competition) ⟨broke the long jump *record*⟩ **4 :** something on which sound or visual images have been recorded for later reproduction; *esp* **:** a disc with a spiral groove carrying recorded sound for phonograph reproduction — **off the record :** not for publication — **on record 1 :** in the position of having publicly declared oneself **2 :** in the status of being known, published, or documented

[3]**rec•ord** \ˈrek-ərd\ *adj* **:** setting a record **:** outstanding among other like things ⟨a *record* crop⟩

re•cord•er \ri-ˈkȯrd-ər\ *n* **1 :** one that records **2 :** a municipal judge with criminal and sometimes limited civil jurisdiction **3 :** a fipple flute with eight finger holes

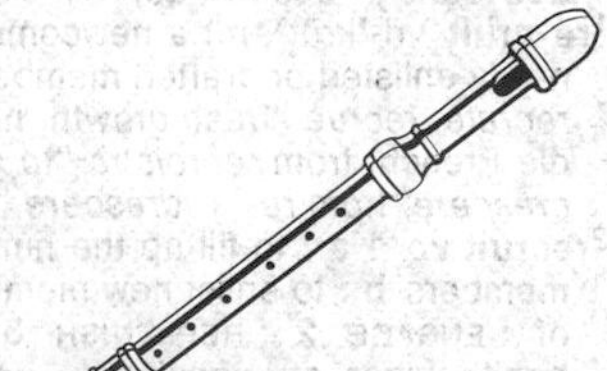

recorder 3

re•cord•ing \ri-ˈkȯrd-ing\ *n* **:** RECORD 4

re•cord•ist \ri-ˈkȯrd-əst\ *n* **:** one who records sound especially on film

rec•ord player \ˈrek-ərd-\ *n* **:** an instrument for playing phonograph records through a loudspeaker

[1]**re•count** \ri-ˈkau̇nt\ *vt* **:** to relate in detail ⟨*recount* an adventure⟩ **[**Middle French *reconter,* from *re-* "re-" + *conter* "to count, relate"**]**

[2]**re•count** \rē-ˈkau̇nt, ˈrē-\ *vb* **:** to count again

\ə\ abut	\au̇\ **out**	\i\ **tip**	\ȯ\ **saw**	\u̇\ **foot**
\ər\ **further**	\ch\ **chin**	\ī\ **life**	\ȯi\ **coin**	\y\ **yet**
\a\ **mat**	\e\ **pet**	\j\ **job**	\th\ **thin**	\yü\ **few**
\ā\ **take**	\ē\ **easy**	\ng\ **sing**	\t͟h\ **this**	\yu̇\ **cure**
\ä\ **cot, cart**	\g\ **go**	\ō\ **bone**	\ü\ **food**	\zh\ **vision**

[3]**re•count** \rē-ˈkau̇nt, ˈrē-ˌ\ *n* **:** a second or fresh count (as of election votes)

re•coup \ri-ˈküp\ *vt* **1 :** to make up for **:** RECOVER ⟨*recoup* a loss⟩ **2 :** REIMBURSE, COMPENSATE ⟨*recoup* a person for losses⟩ [French *recouper* "to cut back", from *re-* "re-" + *couper* "to cut"] — **re•coup•able** \-ˈkü-pə-bəl\ *adj* — **re•coup•ment** \-ˈküp-mənt\ *n*

re•course \ˈrē-ˌkōrs, -ˌkȯrs, ri-ˈ\ **1 :** a turning for assistance or protection ⟨have *recourse* to the law⟩ **2 :** a source of help or strength [Middle French *recours,* from Late Latin *recursus,* from Latin, "act of running back", from *recurrere* "to run back", from *re-* + *currere* "to run"]

re•cov•er \ri-ˈkəv-ər\ *vb* **-cov•ered; -cov•er•ing** \-ˈkəv-ring, -ə-ring\ **1 :** to get back **:** REGAIN ⟨*recover* a lost wallet⟩ **2 :** to bring back to normal position or condition ⟨stumbled, then *recovered* myself⟩ **3 a :** to make up for ⟨*recover* lost time⟩ **b :** to gain by legal process ⟨*recover* damages⟩; *also* **:** to win damages at law **4** *archaic* **:** to come or return to **:** REACH **5 :** RECLAIM ⟨*recover* gold from ore⟩ **6 :** to regain health, consciousness, or self-control [Middle French *recoverer,* from Latin *recuperare*] — **re•cov•er•able** \-ˈkəv-rə-bəl, -ə-rə-\ *adj*

re–cov•er \rē-ˈkəv-ər, ˈrē-\ *vt* **:** to cover again or anew

re•cov•ery \ri-ˈkəv-rē, -ə-rē\ *n, pl* **-er•ies :** the act or process or an instance of recovering; *esp* **:** return to a former normal state (as of health or spirits)

recovery room *n* **:** a hospital room equipped for meeting emergencies following surgery or childbirth

[1]**rec•re•ant** \ˈrek-rē-ənt\ *adj* **1 :** crying for mercy **:** COWARDLY **2 :** unfaithful to duty or allegiance [Middle French, from *recroire* "to renounce one's cause in a trial by battle", from *re-* "re-" + *croire* "to believe", from Latin *credere*]

[2]**recreant** *n* **1 :** COWARD **2 :** one that is unfaithful **:** TRAITOR

[1]**rec•re•ate** \ˈrek-rē-ˌāt\ *vt* **:** to give new life or freshness to [Latin *recreare* "to create anew, restore, refresh", from *re-* + *creare* "to create"] — **rec•re•ative** \-ˌāt-iv\ *adj*

[2]**re•cre•ate** \ˌrē-krē-ˈāt\ *vt* **:** to create anew especially in the imagination — **re•cre•ative** \-ˈāt-iv\ *adj*

rec•re•ation \ˌrek-rē-ˈā-shən\ *n* **:** refreshment of strength and spirits after toil **:** DIVERSION; *also* **:** a means of refreshment or diversion (as a game or exercise) [Middle French, from Latin *recreatio* "restoration to health", from *recreare* "to restore, refresh"] — **rec•re•ation•al** \-shnəl, -shən-l\ *adj*

re•crim•i•nate \ri-ˈkrim-ə-ˌnāt\ *vb* **1 :** to make a return charge against an accuser **2 :** to retort bitterly [Medieval Latin *recriminare,* from Latin *re-* + *criminari* "to accuse", from *crimen* "accusation, crime"] — **re•crim•i•na•tion** \-ˌkrim-ə-ˈnā-shən\ *n* — **re•crim•i•na•to•ry** \-ˈkrim-ə-nə-ˌtōr-ē, -ˌtȯr-\ *adj*

re•cru•des•cense \ˌrē-krü-ˈdes-ns\ *n* **:** a renewal or breaking out again especially of something unhealthful or dangerous ⟨*recrudescence* of an epidemic⟩ [Latin *recrudescere* "to become raw again", from *re-* + *crudescere* "to become raw", from *crudus* "raw"] — **re•cru•desce** \-ˈdes\ *vi* — **re•cru•des•cent** \-ˈdes-nt\ *adj*

[1]**re•cruit** \ri-ˈkrüt\ *n* **:** a newcomer to a field or activity; *esp* **:** a newly enlisted or drafted member of the armed forces [French *recrute, recrue* "fresh growth, new levy of soldiers", from Middle French, from *recroistre* "to grow up again", from Latin *recrescere,* from *re-* + *crescere* "to grow"]

[2]**recruit** *vb* **1 a :** to fill up the number of (as an army) with new members **b :** to enlist new members **c :** to secure the services of **:** ENGAGE **2 :** REPLENISH **3 :** to restore or increase the health, vigor, or intensity of — **re•cruit•er** *n* — **re•cruit•ment** \-ˈkrüt-mənt\ *n*

rect•an•gle \ˈrek-ˌtang-gəl\ *n* **:** a parallelogram all of whose angles are right angles [Medieval Latin *rectangulus* "having a right angle", from Latin *rectus* "right" + *angulus* "angle"]

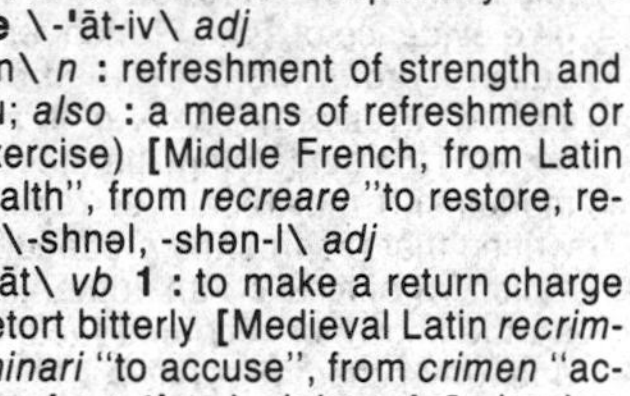
rectangle

rect•an•gu•lar \rek-ˈtang-gyə-lər\ *adj* **1 :** having a flat surface shaped like a rectangle **2 a :** crossing, lying, or meeting at a right angle ⟨*rectangular* axes⟩ **b :** having edges and faces that meet at right angles and faces that are shaped like rectangles ⟨a *rectangular* solid⟩ — **rect•an•gu•lar•i•ty** \rek-ˌtang-gyə-ˈlar-ət-ē\ *n* — **rect•an•gu•lar•ly** \rek-ˈtang-gyə-lər-lē\ *adv*

rectangular coordinate *n* **:** a Cartesian coordinate of a Cartesian coordinate system whose straight-line axes are perpendicular

rec•ti•fi•er \ˈrek-tə-ˌfī-ər, -ˌfīr\ *n* **:** one that rectifies; *esp* **:** a device for converting alternating current into direct current

rec•ti•fy \ˈrek-tə-ˌfī\ *vt* **-fied; -fy•ing 1 :** to set right **:** REMEDY **2 :** to purify (as alcohol) especially by repeated or fractional distillation **3 :** to correct by removing errors **:** ADJUST ⟨*rectify* the calendar⟩ **4 :** to convert (an alternating current) into a direct current [Middle French *rectifier,* from Medieval Latin *rectificare,* from Latin *rectus* "right"] **syn** see CORRECT — **rec•ti•fi•able** \ˈrek-tə-ˌfī-ə-bəl\ *adj* — **rec•ti•fi•ca•tion** \ˌrek-tə-fə-ˈkā-shən\ *n*

rec•ti•lin•e•ar \ˌrek-tə-ˈlin-ē-ər\ *adj* **1 :** moving in, being in, or forming a straight line ⟨*rectilinear* motion⟩ **2 :** characterized by straight lines [Late Latin *rectilineus,* from Latin *rectus* "straight, right" + *linea* "line"] — **rec•ti•lin•e•ar•ly** *adv*

rec•ti•tude \ˈrek-tə-ˌtüd, -ˌtyüd\ *n* **1 :** the quality or state of being straight **2 :** moral integrity [Middle French, from Late Latin *rectitudo,* from Latin *rectus* "straight, right"]

rec•to \ˈrek-tō\ *n, pl* **rectos :** a right-hand page — compare VERSO [New Latin *recto folio* "the page being straight"]

rec•tor \ˈrek-tər\ *n* **1 :** a clergyman in charge of a church or parish **2 :** the priest in charge of certain Roman Catholic religious houses for men **3 :** the head of a university or school [Latin, "guide, director", from *rectus,* past participle of *regere* "to direct"]

rec•to•ry \ˈrek-tə-rē, -trē\ *n, pl* **-ries :** a rector's residence

rec•tum \ˈrek-təm\ *n, pl* **rectums** *or* **rec•ta** \-tə\ **:** the last part of the intestine linking the colon to the anus [New Latin, from *rectum intestinum,* literally, "straight intestine"] — **rec•tal** \-tl\ *adj*

rec•tus \ˈrek-təs\ *n, pl* **rec•ti** \-ˌtī, -ˌtē\ **:** any of several straight muscles (as of the abdomen) [New Latin, from *rectus musculus* "straight muscle"]

re•cum•bent \ri-ˈkəm-bənt\ *adj* **1 :** being in a state of rest **2 :** lying down [Latin *recumbens,* present participle of *recumbere* "to lie down"] — **re•cum•bent•ly** *adv*

re•cu•per•ate \ri-ˈkü-pə-ˌrāt, -ˈkyü-\ *vb* **:** to get back **:** RECOVER; *esp* **:** to regain health or strength [Latin *recuperare*] — **re•cu•per•a•tion** \-ˌkü-pə-ˈrā-shən, -ˌkyü-\ *n*

re•cu•per•a•tive \ri-ˈkü-pə-ˌrāt-iv, -ˈkyü-, -pə-rət-, -prət-\ *adj* **:** of, relating to, or promoting recuperation

re•cur \ri-ˈkər\ *vi* **re•curred; re•cur•ring 1 :** to go or come back in thought or discussion ⟨*recur* to a subject in conversation⟩ **2 :** to come again into the mind ⟨a memory that *recurred* over and over⟩ **3 :** to occur again ⟨the fever *recurred*⟩ [Latin *recurrere* "to run back, return", from *re-* + *currere* "to run"] — **re•cur•rence** \-ˈkər-əns, -ˈkə-rəns\ *n*

re•cur•rent \ri-ˈkər-ənt, -ˈkə-rənt\ *adj* **1 :** returning from time to time ⟨a *recurrent* fever⟩ **2 :** running or turning back in direction ⟨a *recurrent* vein⟩ [Latin *recurrens,* present participle of *recurrere* "to return"] — **re•cur•rent•ly** *adv*

re•curve \rē-ˈkərv, ˈrē-\ *vb* **:** to curve backward or inward

re•cy•cle \rē-ˈsī-kəl, ˈrē-\ *vt* **:** to process (as liquid body waste, glass, or cans) in order to regain for use — **re•cy•cla•ble** \-kə-lə-bəl, -klə-bəl\ *adj*

[1]**red** \ˈred\ *adj* **red•der; red•dest 1 a :** of the color red **b :** having red as a distinguishing color **2 a** (1) **:** flushed usually from emotion (2) **:** RUDDY 1 (3) **:** BLOODSHOT **b :** of a coppery hue **c :** being in the color range between a moderate orange and russet or bay **d :** REDDISH **3 a :** stirring up or approving extreme social or political change especially by force **b** *cap* **:** COMMUNIST **c :** of or relating to a Communist country (as the Soviet Union) [Old English *rēad*] — **red•ly** *adv* — **red•ness** *n*

[2]**red** *n* **1 :** a color whose hue resembles that of fresh blood or the ruby or is that of the long-wave extreme of the visible spectrum **2 :** one that is of a red or reddish color **3 :** a pigment or dye that colors red **4 a :** a person who seeks the overthrow of an existing social or political order **b** *cap* **:** COMMUNIST **5 :** the condition of showing a loss ⟨in the *red*⟩ [sense 5 from the bookkeeping practice of entering debit items in red ink]

re•dact \ri-ˈdakt\ *vt* **1 :** to put in writing **:** FRAME **2 :** to select or adapt for publication [back-formation from *redaction*] — **re•dac•tor** \-ˈdak-tər\ *n*

re•dac•tion \ri-ˈdak-shən\ *n* **1 :** an act or instance of redacting

2 : EDITION 1 [French *rédaction,* derived from Latin *redigere* "to bring back, reduce", from *re-, red-* "re-" + *agere* "to lead"] — **re•dac•tion•al** \-shnəl, -shən-l\ *adj*

red alga *n* : an alga (division Rhodophyta) having predominantly red pigmentation

red•bird \'red-,bərd\ *n* : any of several birds (as a cardinal, several tanagers, or the bullfinch) with predominantly red plumage

red blood cell *n* : one of the hemoglobin-containing cells that carry oxygen to the tissues and are responsible for the red color of vertebrate blood — called also *red blood corpuscle*

red–blood•ed \'red-'bləd-əd\ *adj* : full of spirit and vigor

red•bone \'red-,bōn\ *n* : a speedy medium-sized dark red or red and tan American hound that is used especially for hunting raccoons

red•breast \-,brest\ *n* : a bird (as a robin) with a reddish breast

red•bud \-,bəd\ *n* : an American tree of the pea family with usually pale rosy pink flowers and heart-shaped leaves

red•cap \-,kap\ *n* : a baggage porter

red–car•pet \'red-'kär-pət\ *adj* : marked by ceremonial courtesy ⟨*red-carpet* treatment⟩ [from the traditional laying down of a red carpet for important guests to walk on]

red cedar *n* : an American juniper with fragrant close-grained red wood; *also* : its wood

red cell *n* : RED BLOOD CELL

red cent *n* : a trivial amount

red clover *n* : a Eurasian clover with globe-shaped heads of reddish purple flowers widely grown as a hay, forage, and cover crop

·**red•coat** \'red-,kōt\ *n* : a British soldier especially during the Revolutionary War

red corpuscle *n* : RED BLOOD CELL

red cross *n* : a red-colored cross on a white background used as a badge for hospitals and for members of an international organization that helps the suffering especially in war or disaster areas

[1]redd \'red\ *vb* **redd•ed** *or* **redd**; **redd•ing 1** *chiefly dialect* : to set in order **2** *chiefly dialect* : to make things tidy [Middle English *redden* "to clear"]

[2]redd *n* : the spawning place or nest of a fish [origin unknown]

red deer *n* : the common deer of temperate Europe and Asia related to but smaller than the American elk

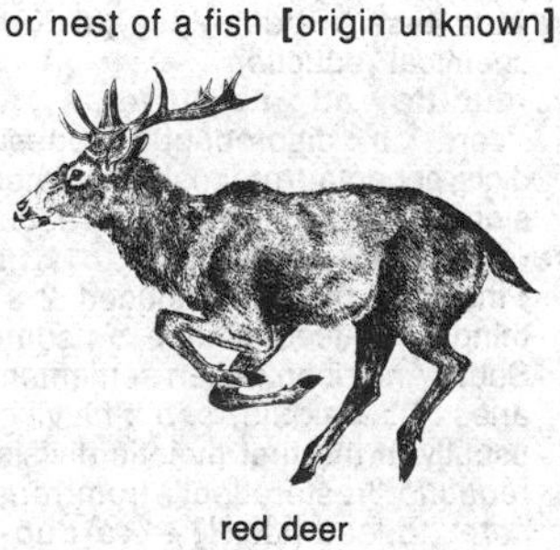
red deer

red•den \'red-n\ *vb* **red•dened**; **red•den•ing** \'red-ning, -n-ing\ : to make or become red or reddish; *esp* : BLUSH 1

red•dish \'red-ish\ *adj* : somewhat red — **red•dish•ness** *n*

rede \'rēd\ *vt* **1** *dialect* : to give counsel to : ADVISE **2** *dialect* : INTERPRET 1, EXPLAIN [Old English *rǣdan* "to advise, interpret, read"]

red•ear \'red-,iər\ *n* : a common American sunfish with orange-red marks on the gill cover

re•dec•o•rate \rē-'dek-ə-,rāt, 'rē-\ *vb* **1** : to freshen or change in appearance : REFURBISH **2** : to freshen or change a decorative scheme — **re•dec•o•ra•tion** \,rē-,dek-ə-'rā-shən\ *n*

re•deem \ri-'dēm\ *vt* **1 a** : to buy back : REPURCHASE **b** : to get or win back **2 a** : to free from captivity usually by paying a ransom **b** : LIBERATE 1 **c** : to free from the bondage of sin **3** : to change for the better : REFORM **4** : REPAIR 1, RESTORE **5 a** : to get back (a pledge) by payment of an amount secured thereby **b** : to remove the obligation of by payment **c** : to change into something of value **6 a** : to atone for : EXPIATE **b** : to offset the bad effect of **7** : to make good : FULFILL ⟨*redeem* a promise⟩ [Middle French *redimer,* from Latin *redimere,* from *re-, red-* "re-" + *emere* "to take, buy"] **syn** see RESCUE — **re•deem•able** \-'dē-mə-bəl\ *adj*

re•deem•er \ri-'dē-mər\ *n* : one that redeems; *esp, cap* : JESUS

red eft *n* : an individual of the reddish terrestrial phase of a common American newt that has also a spotted aquatic phase

re•demp•tion \ri-'dem-shən, -'demp-\ *n* : the act or process or an instance of redeeming [Middle French, from Latin *redemptio,* from *redemptus,* past participle of *redimere* "to redeem"] — **re•demp•tion•al** \-shnəl, -shən-l\ *adj* — **re•demp•tive** \-'dem-tiv, -'demp-\ *adj*

Re•demp•tor•ist \ri-'dem-tə-rəst, -'demp-, -trəst\ *n* : a member of the Roman Catholic Congregation of the Most Holy Redeemer [French *rédemptoriste,* from Late Latin *redemptor* "redeemer", derived from Latin *redimere* "to redeem"]

re•de•sign \,rēd-i-'zīn\ *vt* : to revise in appearance, function, or content — **redesign** *n*

re•de•vel•op•ment \,rēd-i-'vel-əp-mənt\ *n* : the act or process of redeveloping; *esp* : renewal of a blighted area

red•fish \'red-,fish\ *n* : any of various reddish to bright red fishes

red fox *n* : a common fox with orange-red to dusky reddish brown fur

red giant *n* : a very large star with a relatively low surface temperature

red–green blindness *n* : a form of color blindness in which the spectrum is seen in tones of yellow and blue — called also *red-green color blindness*

red gum *n* : SWEET GUM

red–hand•ed \'red-'han-dəd\ *adv or adj* : in the act of committing a crime or misdeed

red•head \'red-,hed\ *n* **1** : a person having red hair **2** : an American duck related to the canvasback but having in the male a brighter reddish head and shorter bill

red heat *n* : the state of being red-hot; *also* : the temperature at which a substance is red-hot

red herring *n* **1** : a herring cured by salting and slow smoking to a dark brown color **2** : something intended to distract attention from the real issue [sense 2 from the practice of drawing a red herring across a trail to confuse hunting dogs]

red–hot \'red-'hät\ *adj* **1** : glowing red with heat **2** : exhibiting or marked by intense emotion, enthusiasm, or energy ⟨a *red-hot* political campaign⟩ **3** : FRESH, NEW ⟨*red-hot* news⟩

re•dia \'rēd-ē-ə\ *n, pl* **re•di•ae** \-ē-,ē\ *also* **re•di•as** : a larva produced within the sporocyst of many trematodes that produces another generation of rediae or develops into a cercaria [Francesco *Redi,* died 1698?, Italian naturalist] — **re•di•al** \-ē-əl\ *adj*

Red Indian *n* : INDIAN 2a

red•in•gote \'red-ing-,gōt\ *n* : a fitted outer garment: as **a** : a woman's lightweight coat open at the front **b** : a dress with a front gore of contrasting material [French, from English *riding coat*]

red•in•te•grate \ri-'dint-ə-,grāt, re-\ *vt, archaic* : to restore to a former or sound state [Latin *redintegrare,* from *re-, red-* "re-" + *integrare* "to integrate"] — **red•in•te•gra•tion** \-,dint-ə-'grā-shən, ,rē-, ,re-\ *n, archaic*

re•di•rect \,rēd-ə-'rekt, ,rē-dī-\ *vt* : to change the course or direction of — **re•di•rec•tion** \-'rek-shən\ *n*

[1]re•dis•count \rē-'dis-,kaůnt, 'rē-; ,rē-dis-'\ *vt* : to discount again — **re•dis•count•able** \-ə-bəl\ *adj*

[2]re•dis•count \rē-'dis-,kaůnt, 'rē-\ *n* : the act or process of rediscounting

re•dis•trict \rē-'dis-trikt, 'rē-\ *vt* : to divide anew into districts; *esp* : to revise the legislative districts of

red jasmine *n* : a widely cultivated frangipani with large terminal clusters of pink, red, or purple fragrant flowers

red lead *n* : a red lead oxide Pb_3O_4 used in storage-battery plates, in glass and ceramics, and as a paint pigment

red–let•ter \'red-'let-ər\ *adj* : memorable especially in a happy or joyful way ⟨a *red-letter* day⟩ [from the practice of marking holy days in red letters in church calendars]

red•line \'red-,līn\ *vb* : to withhold home-loan funds or insurance from neighborhoods held to be poor economic risks : discriminate against in lending or insuring — **red•lin•ing** \-ing\ *n*

Red Man *n* : AMERICAN INDIAN

red maple *n* : a common American maple with reddish twigs and rather soft wood

red marrow *n* : reddish bone marrow that is the seat of blood-cell production

red–neck \ˈred-ˌnek\ *n* : a member of the white Southern rural laboring class

re•do \rē-ˈdü, ˈrē-\ *vt* **-did** \-ˈdid\; **-done** \-ˈdən\; **-do•ing** : to do over or again; *esp* : REDECORATE ⟨*redid* the bedroom in blue⟩

red oak *n* : any of numerous American oaks that have acorns with the inner surface of the shell lined with woolly hairs and leaf veins that usually run beyond the margin of the leaf to form bristles

red ocher *n* : a red earthy hematite used as a pigment

red•o•lence \ˈred-l-əns\ *n* **1** : the quality or state of being redolent **2** : SCENT 1b, AROMA

red•o•lent \-ənt\ *adj* **1** : exuding fragrance : AROMATIC **2 a** : full of a specified fragrance ⟨a room *redolent* of tobacco smoke⟩ **b** : tending to suggest ⟨a city *redolent* of ancient times⟩ [Middle French, from Latin *redolens,* present participle of *redolēre* "to emit a scent", from *re-, red-* "re-" + *olere* "to smell"] — **red•o•lent•ly** *adv*

re•dou•ble \rē-ˈdəb-əl, ˈrē-\ *vb* **1** : to make or become doubled (as in size, amount, or degree) ⟨*redouble* one's efforts⟩ **2** : to double back ⟨the fox *redoubled* on its tracks⟩ **3** : to double again

re•doubt \ri-ˈdau̇t\ *n* : a small often temporary fortification (as for defending a hilltop) [French *redoute,* from Italian *ridotto,* from Medieval Latin *reductus* "secret place", from Latin, "withdrawn", from *reducere* "to lead back"]

re•doubt•able \ri-ˈdau̇t-ə-bəl\ *adj* **1** : arousing fear or dread : FORMIDABLE ⟨a *redoubtable* enemy⟩ **2** : arousing admiring respect : EMINENT ⟨a *redoubtable* scholar⟩ [Middle French *redoutable,* from *redouter* "to dread", from *re-* "re-" + *douter* "to doubt"] — **re•doubt•ably** \-blē\ *adv*

re•doubt•able \ri-ˈdau̇t-ə-bəl\ *adj* **1** : arousing fear or dread : FORMIDABLE ⟨a *redoubtable* enemy⟩ **2** : arousing admiring respect : EMINENT ⟨a *redoubtable* scholar⟩ [Middle French *redoubtable,* from *redouter* "to dread", from *re-* "re-" + *douter* "to doubt"] — **re•doubt•ably** \-blē\ *adv*

re•dound \ri-ˈdau̇nd\ *vi* : to become reflected back especially so as to bring credit or discredit ⟨actions that *redound* to one's credit⟩ [Middle French *redonder* "to overflow", from Latin *redundare,* from *re-, red-* "re-" + *unda* "wave"]

re•dox \ˈrē-ˌdäks\ *n* : OXIDATION-REDUCTION [*red*uction + *ox*idation]

red–pen•cil \ˈred-ˈpen-səl\ *vt* **1** : CENSOR **2** : EDIT 1a, CORRECT

red pepper *n* : CAYENNE PEPPER

red•poll \ˈred-ˌpōl\ *n* : any of several small finches which resemble siskins and in which the males usually have a red or rosy crown

[1]re•dress \ri-ˈdres\ *vt* **1** : to set (as a wrong) right : make amends for : REMEDY, RELIEVE **2** : to correct or amend the faults of [Middle French *redresser,* from Old French *redrecier,* from *re-* "re-" + *drecier* "to make straight", from Latin *directus* "direct"]

[2]re•dress \ri-ˈdres, ˈrē-ˌ\ *n* **1 a** : relief from distress **b** : means or possibility of seeking a remedy **2** : compensation for wrong or loss **3 a** : an act or instance of redressing **b** : CORRECTION 1, RETRIBUTION

red salmon *n* : SOCKEYE

red shift *n* : a displacement of the spectrum of a celestial body toward longer wavelengths

red siskin *n* : a South American finch that is scarlet with black head, wings, and tail and is often kept in captivity

red snapper *n* : any of several reddish sea fishes including some esteemed for food or sport

red snow *n* : snow reddened by various airborne dusts or especially by a growth of reddish algae

red spider *n* : any small web-spinning mite that attacks forage and crop plants

red spruce *n* : a cone-bearing tree of eastern North America that is an important source of lumber and pulpwood

red squirrel *n* : a common North American squirrel that has the upper parts chiefly red — called also *chickaree*

red star *n* : a star having a low surface temperature and a red color

red•start \ˈred-ˌstärt\ *n* **1** : a small red-tailed European thrush **2** : an American fly-catching warbler [*red* + obsolete *start* "tail", from Old English *steort*]

red tape *n* : official routine or procedure especially as marked by delay or inaction [from the red tape formerly used to bind legal documents in England]

red tide *n* : seawater discolored and made toxic by the presence of large numbers of dinoflagellates — compare GYMNODINIUM

redstart 2

red•top \ˈred-ˌtäp\ *n* : any of several grasses with reddish panicles including an important forage and lawn grass of eastern North America

re•duce \ri-ˈdüs, -ˈdyüs\ *vb* **1 a** : to draw together or cause to converge : CONSOLIDATE **b** : to diminish in size, amount, extent, or number ⟨*reduce* the number of accidents⟩; *esp* : to lose weight by dieting **2** : to bring to a specified state or condition ⟨*reduce* anarchy to order⟩ **3** : to force to surrender **4 a** : to bring to a systematic form or character ⟨*reduce* language to writing⟩ ⟨*reduced* their observations to a theorem⟩ **b** : to become converted or equated ⟨their differences *reduced* to a question of semantics⟩ **5** : to correct (as a fracture) by bringing displaced or broken parts back into normal position **6 a** : to lower in grade or rank : DEMOTE **b** : to lower in condition or status ⟨*reduced* to panhandling⟩ **c** : to diminish in strength or intensity **d** : to diminish in value **7 a** : to change the denominations or form of without changing the value **b** : to transpose from one form into another **c** : to change (a mathematical expression) to an equivalent but more fundamental expression ⟨*reduce* a fraction⟩ **8** : to break down (as by crushing or grinding) ⟨*reduce* metal from its ore⟩ **9 a** : to bring to the metallic state by removal of nonmetallic elements **b** : DEOXIDIZE **c** : to combine with or subject to the action of hydrogen **d** (1) : to change (an element or ion) from a higher to a lower oxidation state (2) : to add one or more electrons to (an atom or ion or molecule) [Latin *reducere* "to lead back", from *re-* + *ducere* "to lead"] — **re•duc•er** *n* — **re•duc•ibil•i•ty** \-ˌdü-sə-ˈbil-ət-ē, -ˌdyü-\ *n* — **re•duc•ible** \-ˈdü-sə-bəl, -ˈdyü-\ *adj* — **re•duc•ibly** \-blē\ *adv*

reducing agent *n* : a substance that reduces a chemical compound usually by donating electrons

re•duc•tase \ri-ˈdək-ˌtās, -ˌtāz\ *n* : an enzyme that catalyzes a chemical reduction

re•duc•tio ad ab•sur•dum \ri-ˈdək-tē-ˌō-ˌad-əb-ˈsərd-əm, -ˈzərd-\ *n* : disproof of a proposition by showing that it contradicts accepted propositions when carried to its logical conclusion [Late Latin, literally, "reduction to the absurd"]

re•duc•tion \ri-ˈdək-shən\ *n* **1** : the act or process of reducing : the state of being reduced **2 a** : the amount by which something is reduced in price **b** : something made by reducing **3** : a South American Indian settlement directed by Spanish missionaries **4** : MEIOSIS; *esp* : halving of the chromosome number usually in the first meiotic division [Middle French, from Latin *reductio* "restoration", from *reductus,* past participle of *reducere* "to lead back"] — **re•duc•tion•al** \-shnəl, -shən-l\ *adj* — **re•duc•tive** \-ˈdək-tiv\ *adj*

reduction division *n* : the division of meiosis in which chromosome reduction occurs and which is usually the first of the two meiotic division; *also* : MEIOSIS

re•dun•dan•cy \ri-ˈdən-dən-sē\ *n, pl* **-cies** **1** : the quality or state of being redundant **2** : a lavish or excessive amount **3 a** : unnecessary repetition : PROLIXITY **b** : an act or instance of needless repetition

re•dun•dant \ri-ˈdən-dənt\ *adj* **1 a** : exceeding what is necessary or normal **b** : using more words than necessary : REPETITIOUS **2** : ABUNDANT, PROFUSE [Latin *redundare* "to overflow", from *re-, red-* "re-" + *unda* "wave"] — **re•dun•dant•ly** *adv*

re•du•pli•cate \ri-ˈdü-pli-ˌkāt, ˈrē-, -ˈdyü-\ *vt* **1** : to make or perform again : COPY **2** : to form (a word) by reduplication — **re•du•pli•cate** \-kət\ *adj*

re•du•pli•ca•tion \ri-ˌdü-pli-ˈkā-shən, ˌrē-, -ˌdyü-\ *n* **1** : an act or instance of doubling or reiterating : DUPLICATION **2** : repetition of a radical element or a part of it occurring usually at the beginning of a word and often accompanied by change of the radical vowel — **re•du•pli•ca•tive** \ri-ˈdü-pli-ˌkāt-iv, ˈrē-, -ˈdyü-\ *adj* — **re•du•pli•ca•tive•ly** *adv*

red•wing \ˈred-ˌwing\ *n* **1** : a red-winged European thrush **2** : RED-WINGED BLACKBIRD

red–winged blackbird \ˌred-ˌwingd-, -ˌwing-\ *n* : a North American blackbird of which the adult male is black with a patch of bright scarlet on the wing

red-winged blackbird

red•wood \ˈred-ˌwu̇d\ *n* : a tall cone-bearing timber tree of California that often reaches a height of 300 feet; *also* : its light durable brownish red wood

re•echo \rē-ˈek-ō, ˈrē-\ *vb* : to echo back : REVERBERATE ⟨thunder *reechoed* through the valley⟩

reed \ˈrēd\ *n* **1 a** : any of various tall grasses having slender often prominently jointed stems and growing especially in wet areas **b** : a stem of such a grass **c** : a mass or growth of reeds **2** : ARROW 1 **3** : a musical instrument made of the hollow joint of a plant **4** : an ancient Hebrew unit of length equal to 6 cubits (about 3 meters) **5 a** : a thin elastic tongue (as of cane, wood, metal, or plastic) fastened at one end to the mouthpiece of a musical instrument (as a clarinet) or to a fixture (as a reed block) over an air opening (as in an accordion) and set in vibration by an air current (as the breath) **b** : a reed instrument ⟨the *reeds* of an orchestra⟩ **6** : a device on a loom resembling a comb and used to space warp yarns evenly **[**Old English *hrēod***]**

reed•buck \-ˌbək\ *n, pl* **reedbuck** *also* **reedbucks** : any of several fawn-colored African antelopes with hornless females

reed organ *n* : a keyboard wind instrument in which the wind acts on a set of metal reeds

re•ed•u•cate \rē-ˈej-ə-ˌkāt, ˈrē-\ *vt* : to train again; *esp* : to rehabilitate through education — **re•ed•u•ca•tion** \ˌrē-ˌej-ə-ˈkā-shən\ *n* — **re•ed•u•ca•tive** \rē-ˈej-ə-ˌkāt-iv, ˈrē-\ *adj*

reedy \ˈrēd-ē\ *adj* **reed•i•er**; **-est 1** : abounding in or covered with reeds ⟨a *reedy* marsh⟩ **2** : made of or resembling reeds; *esp* : SLENDER, FRAIL ⟨*reedy* arms⟩ ⟨the *reedy* stem of a goblet⟩ **3** : having the tone quality of a reed instrument ⟨a *reedy* tenor voice⟩ — **reed•i•ly** \ˈrēd-l-ē\ *adv* — **reed•i•ness** \ˈrēd-ē-nəs\ *n*

[1]reef \ˈrēf\ *n* **1** : a part of a sail taken in or let out in regulating size **2** : the reduction in sail area made by reefing **[**Old Norse *rif***]**

[2]reef *vt* : to reduce the area of (a sail) by rolling or folding and tying a portion

[3]reef *n* **1** : a chain of rocks or ridge of sand at or near the surface of water **2** : LODE **[**Dutch *rif***]**

[1]reef•er \ˈrē-fər\ *n* **1** : one that reefs **2** : a close-fitting usually double-breasted jacket of thick cloth

[2]reefer *n* : a marijuana cigarette **[**from *reef* "to roll up like a sail", from *[2]reef***]**

[3]ree•fer \ˈrē-fər\ *n* : REFRIGERATOR; *also* : a refrigerator car, truck, trailer, or ship **[**by alteration**]**

reef knot *n* : a square knot used in reefing a sail

[1]reek \ˈrēk\ *n* **1** : VAPOR 1 **2** : a strong or disagreeable odor **[**Old English *rēc* "smoke"**]** — **reeky** \ˈrē-kē\ *adj*

[2]reek *vi* **1** : to emit smoke or vapor **2** : to have or give off a strong or unpleasant smell ⟨clothes *reeking* of tobacco smoke⟩ **3** : to give a strong impression ⟨a neighborhood that *reeks* of poverty⟩

[1]reel \ˈrēl\ *n* **1** : a revolvable device on which something flexible is wound: as **a** : a small windlass at the butt of a fishing rod for the line **b** : a flanged spool for photographic film **2** : a quantity of something wound on a reel **3** : a frame for drying clothes usually having radial arms on a vertical pole **[**Old English *hrēol***]**

[2]reel *vb* **1** : to wind on or as if on a reel **2** : to bring in (as a hooked fish) by reeling a fishing line : to wind or turn a reel — **reel•able** \ˈrē-lə-bəl\ *adj* — **reel•er** *n*

[3]reel *vi* **1 a** : to whirl around ⟨*reeling* in a dance⟩ **b** : to be in a whirl ⟨heads *reeling* with excitement⟩ **2** : to give way : fall back ⟨soldiers *reeling* in defeat⟩ **3** : STAGGER 1a **[**Middle English *relen*, probably from *[1]reel***]**

[4]reel *n* : a reeling motion

[5]reel *n* : a lively dance originally of the Scottish Highlands; *also* : its music **[**probably from *[4]reel***]**

re•elect \ˌrē-ə-ˈlekt\ *vt* : to elect for another term in office — **re•elec•tion** \-ˈlek-shən\ *n*

reel off *vt* : to recite fluently ⟨*reeled off* the statistics⟩

re•en•act \ˌrē-ə-ˈnakt\ *vt* **1** : to enact again **2** : to perform again — **re•en•act•ment** \-ˈnakt-mənt, -ˈnak-\ *n*

re•en•trance \rē-ˈen-trəns, ˈrē-\ *n* : REENTRY 2, 3

re•en•try \rē-ˈen-trē, ˈrē-\ *n* **1** : a retaking possession especially from a tenant **2** : a second or new entry **3** : the action of reentering the earth's atmosphere after travel in space

[1]reeve \ˈrēv\ *n* : a medieval English manor officer responsible chiefly for enforcing the discharge of feudal obligations **[**Old English *gerēfa***]**

[2]reeve *vt* **rove** \ˈrōv\ *or* **reeved**; **reev•ing 1** : to pass (as a rope) through a hole or opening **2** : to rig for operation by passing a rope through ⟨*reeve* up a set of blocks⟩ **[**origin unknown**]**

[3]reeve *n* : the female of the ruff **[**probably alteration of *ruff***]**

ref \ˈref\ *n* : REFEREE 2

re•fash•ion \rē-ˈfash-ən, ˈrē-\ *vt* : to make over : ALTER

re•fec•tion \ri-ˈfek-shən\ *n* **1** : refreshment of mind, spirit, or body; *esp* : NOURISHMENT **2 a** : the taking of refreshment **b** : food and drink together : REPAST **[**Middle French, from Latin *refectio*, from *reficere* "to restore", from *re-* + *facere* "to make"**]**

re•fec•to•ry \ri-ˈfek-tə-rē, -trē\ *n, pl* **-ries** : a dining hall especially in a monastery or convent **[**Late Latin *refectorium*, from Latin *refectus*, past participle of *reficere* "to restore"**]**

refectory table *n* : a long narrow table with heavy legs

re•fer \ri-ˈfər\ *vb* **re•ferred**; **re•fer•ring 1** : to place in a certain class so far as cause, relationship, or source is concerned ⟨*referred* the defeat to poor training⟩ **2** : to send or direct to a person or place for treatment, help, or information ⟨*refer* a child to a dictionary⟩ **3** : to go for information, advice, or aid ⟨*refer* to the dictionary for the meaning of a word⟩ **4** : to have relation or connection : RELATE ⟨the asterisk *refers* to a footnote⟩ **5** : to submit or hand over to someone else ⟨*refer* a patient to a specialist⟩ **6** : to direct attention : make reference **[**Latin *referre* "to bring back, report, refer", from *re-* + *ferre* "to carry"**]** — **re•fer•able** \ˈref-rə-bəl, -ə-rə-; ri-ˈfər-ə-\ *adj* — **re•fer•rer** \ri-ˈfər-ər\ *n*

• syn REFER, ALLUDE mean to direct attention to something. REFER implies intentional introduction and distinct mention as by direct naming; ALLUDE suggests such indirect mention as is conveyed in a hint, a figure of speech, or other roundabout expression.

[1]ref•er•ee \ˌref-ə-ˈrē\ *n* **1** : a person to whom a legal matter is referred for investigation and report or for settlement **2** : a sports official usually having final authority in administering a game

[2]referee *vb* **-eed**; **-ee•ing** : to act or supervise as a referee

ref•er•ence \ˈref-ərns, ˈref-rəns, -ə-rəns\ *n* **1** : the act of referring or consulting **2** : a bearing on a matter : RELATION ⟨with *reference* to what was said⟩ **3 a** : a remark referring to something : ALLUSION ⟨made *reference* to our agreement⟩ **b** : a sign or indication referring a reader to another passage or book **c** : consultation of information sources ⟨books for ready *reference*⟩ **4 a** : a person to whom inquiries as to the character or ability of another can be made **b** : a statement as to a person's character or ability given by someone familiar with them **c** : a book, passage, or document to which a reader is referred

reference book *n* : a book (as a dictionary, encyclopedia, or almanac) containing useful facts or information

reference mark *n* : a conventional mark (as *, †, or ‡) used in printing or writing to mark a reference

ref•er•en•dum \ˌref-ə-ˈren-dəm\ *n, pl* **-da** \-də\ *or* **-dums** : the principle or practice of submitting to popular vote a measure proposed or passed on by a legislative body or by popular initiative; *also* : a vote on such a measure **[**Latin, neuter of *referendus* "to be referred", from *referre* "to refer"**]**

re•fer•ent \ˈref-rənt, -ə-rənt; ri-ˈfər-ənt\ *n* : something that refers or is referred to; *esp* : the thing a word stands for **[**Latin *referens*, present participle of *referre* "to refer"**]** — **referent** *adj*

re•fer•ral \ri-ˈfər-əl\ *n* **1** : the act or an instance of referring **2** : one that is referred

[1]re·fill \rē-ˈfil, ˈrē-\ *vb* : to fill or become filled again — **re·fill·able** \-ˈfil-ə-bəl\ *adj*

[2]re·fill \ˈrē-ˌfil\ *n* **1** : material used to replace the exhausted supply of a device ⟨a lipstick *refill*⟩ **2** : something provided again; *esp* : a second filling of a medical prescription

re·fine \ri-ˈfīn\ *vb* **1 a** : to come or bring to a pure state ⟨*refine* sugar⟩ **b** : to distill (crude oil) and purify the resulting products **2** : to make or become improved or perfected by pruning or polishing **3** : to free from what is coarse, vulgar, or uncouth **4** : to make improvement by introducing subtleties or distinctions ⟨*refined* upon the older methods⟩ — **re·fin·er** *n*

re·fined \ri-ˈfīnd\ *adj* **1** : freed from impurities : PURE ⟨*refined* gold⟩ ⟨*refined* sugar⟩ **2** : WELL-BRED, CULTURED ⟨very *refined* manners⟩ **3** : carried to a fine point : EXACT ⟨*refined* measurements⟩

re·fine·ment \ri-ˈfīn-mənt\ *n* **1** : the act or process of refining **2** : the quality or state of being refined : CULTIVATION **3 a** : a refined feature or method **b** : SUBTLETY 2 **c** : a feature or device intended to improve or perfect

re·fin·ery \ri-ˈfīn-rē, -ə-rē\ *n, pl* **-er·ies** : a building and equipment for refining or purifying metals, oil, or sugar

re·fin·ish \rē-ˈfin-ish, ˈrē-\ *vt* : to give (as furniture) a new surface — **re·fin·ish·er** *n*

re·fit \rē-ˈfit, ˈrē-\ *vb* **re·fit·ted**; **re·fit·ting** : to get ready for use again : fit out or equip again ⟨*refit* a ship for service⟩ — **re·fit** \ˈrē-ˌfit, rē-ˈ, ˈrē-ˈ\ *n*

re·flect \ri-ˈflekt\ *vb* **1** : to bend or throw back waves of light, sound, or heat ⟨a polished surface *reflects* light⟩ **2** : to give back an image or likeness of as if by a mirror **3** : to bring as a result ⟨your scholarship *reflects* credit on your school⟩ **4** : to cast reproach or blame ⟨our bad conduct *reflects* on our training⟩ **5** : to think seriously and carefully : MEDITATE **[**Latin *reflectere* "to bend back", from *re-* + *flectere* "to bend"**]** **syn** see THINK

re·flec·tance \ri-ˈflek-təns\ *n* : the part of the light falling upon a surface that is reflected

reflecting telescope *n* : REFLECTOR 2

re·flec·tion \ri-ˈflek-shən\ *n* **1** : an instance of reflecting; *esp* : the return of light or sound waves from a surface **2** : the production of an image by or as if by a mirror **3 a** : the action of bending or folding back **b** : a reflected part : FOLD **4** : something produced by reflecting; *esp* : an image given back by a reflecting surface **5** : an often obscure or indirect criticism : REPROACH **6** : a thought, idea, or opinion formed or a remark made as a result of careful thinking **7** : consideration of some subject matter, idea, or purpose **8** : a geometric figure or a graph of an equation that is symmetric to another geometric figure or graph with respect to a line (as an axis of a coordinate system) — **re·flec·tion·al** \-shnəl, -shən-l\ *adj*

re·flec·tive \ri-ˈflek-tiv\ *adj* **1** : capable of reflecting light, images, or sound waves **2** : marked by reflection : THOUGHTFUL **3** : of, relating to, or caused by reflection — **re·flec·tive·ly** *adv* — **re·flec·tive·ness** *n* — **re·flec·tiv·i·ty** \ˌrē-ˌflek-ˈtiv-ət-ē, ri-\ *n*

re·flec·tor \ri-ˈflek-tər\ *n* **1** : one that reflects; *esp* : a polished surface for reflecting light or heat **2** : a telescope in which the principal focusing element is a mirror

[1]re·flex \ˈrē-ˌfleks\ *n* **1 a** : reflected heat, light, or color **b** : a mirrored image **c** : a copy exact in essential or peculiar features **2 a** : an automatic and usually inborn response to a stimulus in which a nerve impulse passes inward from a receptor to a nerve center and thence outward to an effector (as a muscle or gland) without reaching the level of consciousness — compare HABIT **b** *pl* : the power of acting or responding with adequate speed **[**Latin *reflexus*, past participle of *reflectere* "to bend back"**]**

[2]reflex *adj* **1** : produced in reaction, resistance, or return **2** : of, relating to, or produced by a neural reflex ⟨*reflex* action⟩ — **reflex·ly** *adv*

reflex arc *n* : the complete nervous path involved in a reflex

reflex camera *n* : a single- or double-lens camera in which the image formed by the focusing lens is reflected onto a usually ground-glass screen for viewing

re·flexed \ˈrē-ˌflekst, ri-ˈ\ *adj* : bent or curved backward or downward ⟨*reflexed* petals⟩

re·flex·ion \ri-ˈflek-shən\ *chiefly British variant of* REFLECTION

[1]re·flex·ive \ri-ˈflek-siv\ *adj* **1** : REFLEXED **2** : relating to, characterized by, or being a relation that exists between an entity and itself ⟨the relation "is equal to" is *reflexive* but the relation "is the parent of" is not⟩ **3** : of, relating to, or being an action directed back upon the doer or the grammatical subject ⟨*myself* in "I hurt myself" is a *reflexive* pronoun⟩ — **re·flex·ive·ly** *adv* — **re·flex·ive·ness** *n* — **re·flex·iv·i·ty** \ˌrē-ˌflek-ˈsiv-ət-ē, ri-\ *n*

[2]reflexive *n* : a reflexive pronoun or verb

re·flux \ˈrē-ˌfləks\ *n* : a flowing back : EBB

re·for·est \rē-ˈfȯr-əst, ˈrē-, -ˈfär-\ *vt* : to renew forest cover on by seeding or planting — **re·for·es·ta·tion** \ˌrē-ˌfȯr-ə-ˈstā-shən, -ˌfär-\ *n*

[1]re·form \ri-ˈfȯrm\ *vb* **1** : to make better by removal of faults ⟨*reform* the penal system⟩ **2** : to correct or improve one's own character or habits **[**Middle French *reformer*, from Latin *reformare*, from *re-* + *formare* "to form"**]** — **re·form·able** \-ˈfȯr-mə-bəl\ *adj*

[2]reform *n* **1** : improvement of what is bad or corrupt **2** : a removal or correction of an abuse, a wrong, or errors

re-form \rē-ˈfȯrm, ˈrē-\ *vt* : to form or take form again

ref·or·ma·tion \ˌref-ər-ˈmā-shən\ *n* **1** : the act of reforming : the state of being reformed **2** *cap* : a 16th century religious movement marked by rejection or modification of much of the Roman Catholic doctrine and practice and establishment of the Protestant churches — **ref·or·ma·tion·al** \-shnəl, -shən-l\ *adj*

re·for·ma·tive \ri-ˈfȯr-mət-iv\ *adj* : tending or inclined to reform

[1]re·for·ma·to·ry \ri-ˈfȯr-mə-ˌtōr-ē, -ˌtȯr-\ *adj* : tending or intended to reform ⟨*reformatory* measures⟩

[2]reformatory *n, pl* **-ries** : a penal institution to which youthful or first offenders or women are committed for training and rehabilitation

re·formed *adj* **1** : changed for the better **2** *cap* : PROTESTANT; *esp* : of or relating to the Calvinist churches of continental Europe

reformed spelling *n* : any of several methods of spelling English words that use letters with more phonetic consistency than conventional spelling and usually discard some silent letters (as in *thoro* for *thorough*)

re·form·er \ri-ˈfȯr-mər\ *n* **1** : one that works for or urges reform **2** *cap* : a leader of the Reformation

re·form·ism \ri-ˈfȯr-ˌmiz-əm\ *n* : a doctrine, policy, or movement of reform — **re·form·ist** \-məst\ *n*

Reform Judaism *n* : a 19th and 20th century development of Judaism marked by rationalization of belief, simplification of many observances, and affirmation of the religious rather than the national character of Judaism

reform school *n* : a reformatory for youthful offenders

re·fract \ri-ˈfrakt\ *vt* : to subject to refraction **[**Latin *refractus*, past participle of *refringere* "to break open, break up, refract", from *re-* + *frangere* "to break"**]**

refracting telescope *n* : REFRACTOR

re·frac·tion \ri-ˈfrak-shən\ *n* : the bending of a ray when it passes at an angle from one medium (as air) into another (as glass) in which its speed is different — **re·frac·tive** \-ˈfrak-tiv\ *adj* — **re·frac·tiv·i·ty** \ˌrē-ˌfrak-ˈtiv-ət-ē, ri-\ *n*

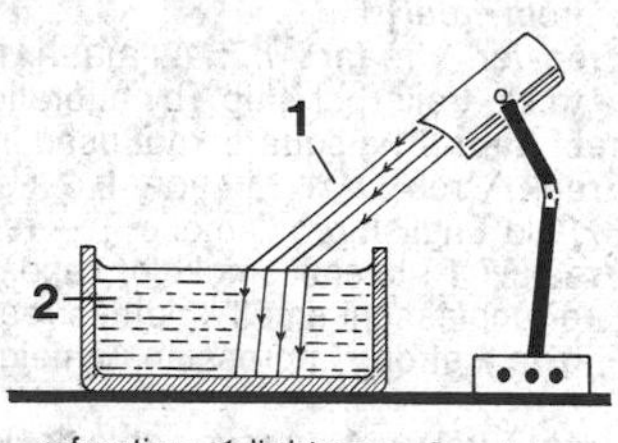

refraction: *1* light rays, *2* water

refractive index *n* : INDEX OF REFRACTION

re·frac·tor \ri-ˈfrak-tər\ *n* : a telescope whose principal focusing element is usually an achromatic lens

[1]re·frac·to·ry \ri-ˈfrak-tə-rē, -trē\ *adj* **1** : resisting control or authority : STUBBORN ⟨a *refractory* child⟩ **2 a** : resistant to treatment **b** : unresponsive to stimulus **3** : difficult to fuse, corrode, or draw out; *esp* : capable of enduring high temperature **[**Latin *refractarius*, from *refragari* "to oppose"**]** **syn** see UNRULY — **re·frac·to·ri·ly** \-tə-rə-lē, -trə-\ *adv* — **re·frac·to·ri·ness** \-tə-rē-nəs, -trē-\ *n*

[2]refractory *n, pl* **-ries** : something refractory; *esp* : a heat-resisting ceramic material

[1]re·frain \ri-ˈfrān\ *vi* : to hold oneself back from some often impulsive course of action ⟨*refrain* from laughing⟩ **[**Middle French *refraindre* "to restrain", from Latin *refringere* "to break up, check, refract"**]** — **re·frain·ment** \-mənt\ *n*

• **syn** REFRAIN, ABSTAIN, FORBEAR mean to keep oneself from doing or indulging in something. REFRAIN suggests the checking of a momentary impulse or inclination ⟨*refrain* from smiling⟩ ABSTAIN implies deliberate renunciation or self-denial on principle ⟨*abstained* from alcohol in any form⟩ FORBEAR suggests self-restraint motivated by compassion, charity, or stoicism.

[2]**refrain** *n* **:** a regularly recurring phrase or verse especially at the end of each stanza of a poem or song **:** CHORUS; *also* **:** the melody of a refrain [Middle French, from *refraindre* "to resound", from Latin *refringere* "to break up, refract"]

re•fran•gi•ble \ri-ˈfran-jə-bəl\ *adj* **:** capable of being refracted [derived from Latin *refringere* "to refract"] — **re•fran•gi•bil•i•ty** \-ˌfran-jə-ˈbil-ət-ē\ *n* — **re•fran•gi•ble•ness** *n*

re•fresh \ri-ˈfresh\ *vb* **1 :** to restore strength and animation to **:** REVIVE ⟨sleep *refreshes* the body⟩ **2 a :** to restore or maintain by renewing supply **:** REPLENISH **b :** STIMULATE ⟨let me *refresh* your memory⟩ **3 :** to restore water to **4 :** to take refreshment **syn** see RENEW

re•fresh•en \-ˈfresh-ən\ *vt* **:** REFRESH 1, 2

re•fresh•er \ri-ˈfresh-ər\ *n* **1 :** something that refreshes **2 :** review or instruction designed especially to keep one up-to-date on professional developments

re•fresh•ing \-ing\ *adj* **:** serving to refresh; *esp* **:** agreeably stimulating because of freshness or newness — **re•fresh•ing•ly** \-ing-lē\ *adv*

re•fresh•ment \ri-ˈfresh-mənt\ *n* **1 :** the act of refreshing **:** the state of being refreshed **2 a :** something that refreshes **b** *pl* **:** a light meal

re•frig•er•ant \ri-ˈfrij-rənt, -ə-rənt\ *n* **:** a substance (as ice, ammonia, or carbon dioxide) used in refrigeration

re•frig•er•ate \ri-ˈfrij-ə-ˌrāt\ *vt* **:** to make or keep cold or cool; *esp* **:** to freeze or chill (food) for preservation [Latin *refrigerare,* from *re-* + *frigerare* "to cool", from *frigor-, frigus* "cold"] — **re•frig•er•a•tion** \ri-ˌfrij-ə-ˈrā-shən\ *n*

re•frig•er•a•tor \ri-ˈfrij-ə-ˌrāt-ər\ *n* **:** a cabinet or room for keeping articles (as food) cool especially by means of a mechanical device

reft *past of* REAVE

re•fu•el \rē-ˈfyü-əl, ˈrē-\ *vb* **:** to provide with or take on additional fuel

ref•uge \ˈref-yüj, -ˌyüj\ *n* **1 :** shelter or protection from danger or distress **2 :** a place that provides shelter or protection ⟨a wildlife *refuge*⟩ [Middle French, from Latin *refugium,* from *refugere* "to escape", from *re-* + *fugere* "to flee"]

ref•u•gee \ˌref-yu̇-ˈjē\ *n* **:** a person who flees for safety especially to a foreign country

re•ful•gence \ri-ˈfu̇l-jəns, -ˈfəl-\ *n* **:** a radiant or resplendent quality or state **:** BRILLIANCE [Latin *refulgentia,* from *refulgēre* "to shine brightly", from *re-* + *fulgēre* "to shine"] — **re•ful•gent** \-jənt\ *adj*

[1]**re•fund** \ri-ˈfənd, ˈrē-ˌfənd\ *vt* **:** to return (money) in restitution or repayment [Latin *refundere,* literally, "to pour back", from *re-* + *fundere* "to pour"] — **re•fund•able** \-ə-bəl\ *adj*

[2]**re•fund** \ˈrē-ˌfənd\ *n* **1 :** the act of refunding **2 :** a sum refunded

[3]**re•fund** \rē-ˈfənd, ˈrē-\ *vt* **:** to fund (a debt) again or anew

re•fur•bish \rē-ˈfər-bish, ˈrē-\ *vt* **:** to brighten or freshen up **:** RENOVATE — **re•fur•bish•ment** \-mənt\ *n*

re•fus•al \ri-ˈfyü-zəl\ *n* **1 :** the act of refusing **2 :** the opportunity or right of refusing or taking before others

[1]**re•fuse** \ri-ˈfyüz\ *vb* **1 :** to decline to accept **:** REJECT ⟨*refused* the money⟩ **2 a :** to show or express positive unwillingness **:** fail deliberately ⟨*refused* to act⟩ **b :** DENY ⟨was *refused* entrance⟩ **3 :** to withhold acceptance, compliance, or permission [Middle French *refuser,* from Latin *refusus,* past participle of *refundere* "to pour back"] — **re•fus•er** *n*

[2]**ref•use** \ˈref-ˌyüs, -ˌyüz\ *n* **1 :** worthless material **2 :** RUBBISH, TRASH [Middle French *refus* "rejection", from *refuser* "to refuse"]

ref•u•ta•tion \ˌref-yu̇-ˈtā-shən\ *n* **:** the act or process of refuting **:** DISPROOF

re•fute \ri-ˈfyüt\ *vt* **:** to prove wrong by argument or evidence **:** show to be false ⟨*refute* a witness's testimony⟩ [Latin *refutare,* literally, "to beat back"] — **re•fut•able** \-ˈfyüt-ə-bəl\ *adj* — **re•fut•ably** \-blē\ *adv* — **re•fut•er** *n*

re•gain \ri-ˈgān\ *vt* **:** to gain or reach again **:** RECOVER ⟨*regained* my health⟩

re•gal \ˈrē-gəl\ *adj* **1 :** of, relating to, or suitable for a sovereign **2 :** notably excellent or magnificent **:** SPLENDID [Latin *regalis,* from *reg-, rex* "king"] — **re•gal•i•ty** \ri-ˈgal-ət-ē\ *n* — **re•gal•ly** \ˈrē-gə-lē\ *adv*

re•gale \ri-ˈgāl\ *vb* **1 :** to treat or entertain lavishly **2 :** to give pleasure and amusement to ⟨*regaled* us with stories⟩ **3 :** to feast oneself **:** FEED [French *régaler,* from Middle French *regale* "party", from *re-* + *galer* "to have a good time"] — **re•gale•ment** \-mənt\ *n*

re•ga•lia \ri-ˈgāl-yə\ *n sing or pl* **1 :** the emblems and symbols (as the crown and scepter) of royalty **2 :** the insignia of an office or order **3 :** special or official dress [Medieval Latin, from Latin *regalis* "regal"]

[1]**re•gard** \ri-ˈgärd\ *n* **1 a :** CONSIDERATION 1, HEED **b :** LOOK 1, GAZE **2 a :** the worth or estimation in which something is held **b** (1) **:** a feeling of respect and affection **:** ESTEEM (2) *pl* **:** friendly greetings implying such feeling ⟨give them my *regards*⟩ **3 :** REFERENCE, RESPECT ⟨this is in *regard* to your unpaid balance⟩ **4 :** an aspect to be considered ⟨nothing to worry about in that *regard*⟩ [Middle French, from *regarder* "to look back at, regard", from *re-* + *garder* "to guard, look at"]

[2]**regard** *vt* **1 :** to pay attention to **2 a :** to show respect or consideration for **b :** to hold in high esteem **3 :** to look at steadily or attentively **4 :** to take into consideration or account **5 :** CONSIDER 3 ⟨*regarded* you as a friend⟩

• **syn** REGARD, RESPECT, ESTEEM, ADMIRE mean to recognize the worth of. REGARD is somewhat formal and requires some qualification ⟨one highly *regarded* in banking circles⟩ RESPECT implies having a good opinion of without suggesting real liking or warmth of feeling; ESTEEM implies high evaluation together with warmth of feeling; ADMIRE implies enthusiastic and often uncritical appreciation.

— **as regards :** with respect to **:** REGARDING

re•gard•ful \ri-ˈgärd-fəl\ *adj* **1 :** OBSERVANT 2, HEEDFUL **2 :** full of or expressing regard **:** RESPECTFUL — **re•gard•ful•ly** \-fə-lē\ *adv* — **re•gard•ful•ness** *n*

re•gard•ing *prep* **:** with respect to **:** CONCERNING

[1]**re•gard•less** \ri-ˈgärd-ləs\ *adj* **:** having or taking no regard **:** HEEDLESS — **re•gard•less•ly** *adv* — **re•gard•less•ness** *n*

[2]**regardless** *adv* **:** despite everything ⟨we are going there *regardless*⟩

re•gat•ta \ri-ˈgät-ə, -ˈgat-\ *n* **:** a boat race or a series of such races [Italian]

[1]**re•gen•cy** \ˈrē-jən-sē\ *n, pl* **-cies 1 :** the office, jurisdiction, or government of a regent or body of regents **2 :** the period of rule of a regent or body of regents

[2]**regency** *adj, often cap* **:** of, relating to, or resembling the furniture or the dress of the regency (1811–20) of George, Prince of Wales

re•gen•er•a•cy \ri-ˈjen-rə-sē, -ə-rə-\ *n* **:** the state of being regenerated

[1]**re•gen•er•ate** \ri-ˈjen-rət, -ə-rət\ *adj* **:** having been regenerated; *esp* **:** spiritually reborn or converted — **re•gen•er•ate•ly** *adv* — **re•gen•er•ate•ness** *n*

[2]**re•gen•er•ate** \ri-ˈjen-ə-ˌrāt\ *vb* **1 :** to cause to be reborn spiritually **2 :** to reform radically for the better ⟨*regenerating* criminals⟩ **3 :** to generate or produce anew; *esp* **:** to renew (a lost or damaged body part) by a new growth of tissue **4 :** to restore to original strength or properties — **re•gen•er•a•tor** \-ˌrāt-ər\ *n*

re•gen•er•a•tion \ri-ˌjen-ə-ˈrā-shən, ˌrē-\ *n* **1 :** an act or the process of regenerating **:** the state of being regenerated **2 :** spiritual renewal or revival

re•gen•er•a•tive \ri-ˈjen-ə-ˌrāt-iv\ *adj* **1 :** of, relating to, or marked by regeneration **2 :** tending to regenerate

re•gent \ˈrē-jənt\ *n* **1 :** one who governs a kingdom during the minority, absence, or disability of the sovereign **2 :** a member of a governing board (as of a state university) [Medieval Latin *regens,* from Latin *regere* "to direct, rule"] — **regent** *adj*

reg•i•cide \ˈrej-ə-ˌsīd\ *n* **1 :** one who murders a king or assists in his death **2 :** the murdering of a king [Latin *reg-, rex* "king"] — **reg•i•cid•al** \ˌrej-ə-ˈsīd-l\ *adj*

re•gime *also* **ré•gime** \rā-ˈzhēm, ri-\ *n* **1 a :** REGIMEN 1 **b :** a regular pattern of occurrence or action **2 a :** mode of rule or management **b :** a form of government ⟨a socialist *regime*⟩ **c**

: *a government in power* **d** : a period of rule ⟨during the last *regime*⟩ [French *régime,* from Latin *regimen* "rule, guidance"]

reg•i•men \'rej-ə-mən, -,men\ *n* **1** : a systematic course of treatment ⟨a strict dietary *regimen*⟩ **2** : REGIME 2b [Latin, "rule", from *regere* "to rule"]

[1]**reg•i•ment** \'rej-mənt, -ə-mənt\ *n* : a military unit consisting of a number of battalions [Middle French, "rule, government", from Late Latin *regimentum,* from Latin *regere* "to rule"] — **reg•i•men•tal** \,rej-ə-'ment-l\ *adj* — **reg•i•men•tal•ly** \-l-ē\ *adv*

[2]**reg•i•ment** \'rej-ə-,ment\ *vt* **1** : to organize rigidly so as to regulate or control **2** : to subject to order or uniformity — **reg•i•men•ta•tion** \,rej-ə-mən-'tā-shən, -,men-\ *n*

reg•i•men•tals \,rej-ə-'ment-lz\ *n pl* **1** : a regimental uniform **2** : military dress

re•gion \'rē-jən\ *n* **1** : an administrative area, division, or district **2 a** : an often indefinite part, portion, or area ⟨cloudy *regions* of the sky⟩; *also* : VICINITY ⟨a pain in the *region* of the heart⟩ **b** : a broad continuous area (as of the earth) ⟨arctic *regions*⟩ **3** : FIELD 2 **4** : a set of points any two points of which can be connected by a line lying wholly within the set together with none, some, or all of the points on its boundary [Middle French, from Latin *regio,* from *regere* "to direct, rule"]

re•gion•al \'rēj-nəl, -ən-l\ *adj* **1** : of, relating to, or characteristic of a region ⟨a *regional* dialect⟩ **2** : affecting a particular region : LOCAL ⟨*regional* pain⟩ — **re•gion•al•ly** \-ē\ *adv*

re•gion•al•ism \'rēj-nəl-,iz-əm, -ən-l-\ *n* **1** : consciousness of and loyalty to a distinct geographical region **2** : emphasis on regional locale and characteristics in art or literature — **re•gion•al•ist** \-əst\ *n or adj* — **re•gion•al•is•tic** \,rēj-nəl-'is-tik, -ən-l-\ *adj*

[1]**reg•is•ter** \'rej-ə-stər\ *n* **1 a** : a written record containing regular entries of items or details **b** : a book for such a record ⟨a *register* of voters⟩ **2 a** : a set of organ pipes of like quality : STOP **b** : the range or a part of the range of a human voice or a musical instrument comprising tones similarly produced or of the same quality **3** : a device (as in a floor or a wall) usually with a grille and shutters that regulate the flow of heated air from a furnace **4** : REGISTRATION, REGISTRY ⟨a port of *register*⟩ **5 a** : an automatic device registering a number or a quantity **b** : a number or quantity so registered **6** : a condition of correct alignment or proper relative position [Middle French *registre,* from Medieval Latin *registrum,* from Late Latin *regesta,* pl., "register", from Latin *regerere* "to bring back, record", from *re-* + *gerere* "to carry"]

[2]**register** *vb* **reg•is•tered; reg•is•ter•ing** \-stə-ring, -string\ **1 a** : to make or secure official entry of in a register : RECORD ⟨*register* a deed⟩ **b** : to enroll formally especially as a voter or student **c** : to record automatically ⟨the thermometer *registered* zero⟩ **2** : to make or adjust so as to correspond exactly **3** : to obtain special protection for (a piece of mail) by prepayment of a fee **4** : to convey an impression of ⟨your face *registered* fear⟩ **5** : to be in correct alignment or register **6** : to make an impression ⟨the name didn't *register*⟩

[3]**register** *n* : REGISTRAR

reg•is•tered *adj* **1** : having the owner's name entered in a register ⟨a *registered* security⟩ **2** : recorded on the basis of pedigree or breed characteristics in the studbook of a breed association

registered nurse *n* : a graduate trained nurse licensed by a state authority

reg•is•tra•ble \'rej-ə-stə-rə-bəl, -strə-bəl\ *adj* : that can be registered

reg•is•trant \'rej-ə-strənt\ *n* : one that registers or is registered

reg•is•trar \'rej-ə-,strär\ *n* : an official recorder or keeper of records [Middle French *registreur,* from *registrer* "to register", from Medieval Latin *registrare,* from *registrum* "register"]

reg•is•tra•tion \,rej-ə-'strā-shən\ *n* **1** : the act of registering **2** : an entry in a register **3** : the number of individuals registered : ENROLLMENT **4** : a document certifying an act of registering ⟨an automobile *registration*⟩

reg•is•try \'rej-ə-strē\ *n, pl* **-tries** **1** : REGISTRATION 3, ENROLLMENT **2** : a ship's nationality as proved by its entry in a register **3** : a place of registration **4** : an official record book or an entry in one

reg•nal \'reg-nᵊl\ *adj* : of or relating to a reign; *esp* : calculated from a monarch's accession to the throne ⟨during the second *regnal* year⟩ [Medieval Latin *regnalis,* from Latin *regnum* "reign"]

reg•nant \'reg-nənt\ *adj* **1** : exercising rule ⟨the queen *regnant*⟩ **2** : having the chief power [Latin *regnare* "to reign", from *regnum* "reign"]

reg•o•lith \'reg-ə-,lith\ *n* : MANTLEROCK [Greek *rhēgos* "blanket" + English *-lith*]

[1]**re•gress** \'rē-,gres\ *n* **1** : an act or the privilege of going or coming back **2** : REENTRY 1 [Latin *regressus,* from *regredi* 'to go back", from *re-* + *gradi* "to go"]

[2]**re•gress** \ri-'gres\ *vb* : to go or cause to go back especially to a former level or condition — **re•gres•sor** \-'gres-ər\ *n*

re•gres•sion \ri-'gresh-ən\ *n* : an act or the fact of regressing: as **a** : progressive decline of something (as a manifestation of disease) **b** : gradual loss of differentiation and function by a body part **c** : reversion of thought or behavior to that characteristic of an earlier level of development

re•gres•sive \ri-'gres-iv\ *adj* **1** : of, relating to, or tending toward regression **2** : decreasing in rate as the base increases ⟨a *regressive* tax⟩ — **re•gres•sive•ly** *adv* — **re•gres•sive•ness** *n*

[1]**re•gret** \ri-'gret\ *vb* **re•gret•ted; re•gret•ting** **1 a** : to mourn the loss or death of **b** : to miss very much **2** : to be very sorry for **3** : to experience regret [Middle French *regreter*] — **re•gret•ta•ble** \-'gret-ə-bəl\ *adj* — **re•gret•ta•bly** \-blē\ *adv* — **re•gret•ter** *n*

[2]**regret** *n* **1** : sorrow caused by circumstances beyond one's ability to remedy **2 a** : an expression of distressing emotion (as sorrow or disappointment) **b** *pl* : a note politely declining an invitation — **re•gret•ful** \-'gret-fəl\ *adj* — **re•gret•ful•ly** \-fə-lē\ *adv* — **re•gret•ful•ness** *n*

re•group \rē-'grüp, 'rē-\ *vb* : to form into a new grouping — **re•group•ment** \-mənt\ *n*

[1]**reg•u•lar** \'reg-yə-lər\ *adj* **1** : belonging to a religious order ⟨*regular* clergy⟩ **2 a** : formed, built, arranged, or ordered according to an established rule, law, principle, or type **b** (1) : being both equilateral and equiangular ⟨a *regular* polygon⟩ (2) : having faces that are congruent regular polygons and all the polyhedral angles congruent ⟨a *regular* polyhedron⟩ **c** : perfectly symmetrical or even; *esp* : having radial symmetry ⟨*regular* flowers⟩ **d** : having or constituting an isometric system ⟨*regular* crystals⟩ **3 a** : ORDERLY, METHODICAL ⟨*regular* habits⟩ **b** : recurring or functioning at fixed or uniform intervals **4 a** : following established or prescribed usages, rules, or discipline **b** : NORMAL 2, CORRECT: as (1) : COMPLETE, ABSOLUTE ⟨a *regular* scoundrel⟩ (2) : thinking or behaving in an acceptable manner **c** : conforming to the normal or usual manner of inflection ⟨*regular* verbs⟩ **5** : of, relating to, or constituting a regular army [Middle French *reguler,* from Late Latin *regularis,* from Latin *regula* "straightedge, rule"] — **reg•u•lar•i•ty** \,reg-yə-'lar-ət-ē\ *n* — **reg•u•lar•ly** \'reg-yə-lər-lē\ *adv*

• **syn** NORMAL, TYPICAL: REGULAR stresses conformity to a rule, standard, or pattern; NORMAL implies lack of deviation from what has been established as the most usual or expected; TYPICAL implies showing all the important traits of a type, class, or group and may suggest lack of strong individuality.

[2]**regular** *n* : one who is regular: as **a** : one of the regular clergy **b** : a soldier in a regular army **c** : a player on an athletic team who usually starts every game

regular army *n* : a permanently organized body that is the standing army of a state

reg•u•lar•ize \'reg-yə-lə-,rīz\ *vt* : to make regular — **reg•u•lar•iz•er** *n*

reg•u•late \'reg-yə-,lāt\ *vt* **1 a** : to govern or direct according to rule **b** : to bring under the control of law or established authority **2** : to reduce to order, method, or uniformity ⟨*regulated* their habits⟩ **3** : to adjust for accurate functioning ⟨*regulate* a clock⟩ [Late Latin *regulare,* from Latin *regula* "rule"] — **reg•u•la•tive** \-,lāt-iv\ *adj* — **reg•u•la•tor** \-,lāt-ər\ *n* — **reg•u•la•to•ry** \-lə-,tōr-ē, -,tȯr-\ *adj*

[1]**reg•u•la•tion** \,reg-yə-'lā-shən\ *n* **1** : the act of regulating : the state of being regulated **2 a** : an authoritative rule dealing with details **b** : a rule or order having the force of law issued by an executive authority **syn** see LAW

[2]**regulation** *adj* : conforming to regulations : OFFICIAL

regulator gene *n* : a gene controlling the production of a genetic repressor

Reg•u•lus \'reg-yə-ləs\ *n* : a bright star in the constellation Leo [Latin, "petty king", from *reg-, rex* "king"]

re·gur·gi·tate \rē-ˈgər-jə-ˌtāt, ˈrē-\ *vb* **:** to throw or be thrown back or out again ⟨*regurgitate* undigested food⟩ [Medieval Latin *regurgitare,* from Latin *re-* + Late Latin *gurgitare* "to engulf", from Latin *gurgit-, gurges* "whirlpool"] — **re·gur·gi·ta·tion** \rē-ˌgər-jə-ˈtā-shən\ *n*

re·ha·bil·i·tate \ˌrē-ə-ˈbil-ə-ˌtāt, ˌrē-hə-ˈbil-\ *vt* **1 a :** to restore to a former status **:** REINSTATE **b :** to restore to good repute **:** reestablish the good name of **2 a :** to restore to a state of efficiency, good management, or repair **b :** to restore to a condition of health or useful and constructive activity [Medieval Latin *rehabilitare,* derived from Latin *re-* + *habilitas* "aptness, ability", from *habilis* "handy, apt", from *habēre* "to have, hold"] — **re·ha·bil·i·ta·tion** \-ˌbil-ə-ˈtā-shən\ *n* — **re·ha·bil·i·ta·tive** \-ˈbil-ə-ˌtāt-iv\ *adj*

re·hash \rē-ˈhash, ˈrē-\ *vt* **:** to present or use (as an argument) again in another form without substantial change or improvement — **re·hash** \ˈrē-ˌhash\ *n*

re·hears·al \ri-ˈhər-səl\ *n* **:** a rehearsing of something: as **a :** a private performance or practice session preparatory to a public appearance **b :** a practice exercise **:** TRIAL

re·hearse \ri-ˈhərs\ *vb* **1 a :** to say again **:** REPEAT **b :** to recount in order **:** ENUMERATE **2 a :** to practice (as a play) for public performance **b :** to train or make proficient (as actors) by rehearsal **3 :** to engage in a rehearsal [Middle French *rehercier,* literally, "to harrow again", from *re-* "re-" + *hercier* "to harrow", from *herce* "harrow", from Latin *hirpex*] — **re·hears·er** *n*

re·hy·drate \rē-ˈhī-ˌdrāt, ˈrē-\ *vt* **:** to restore fluid lost in dehydration to — **re·hy·dra·tion** \ˌrē-ˌhī-ˈdrā-shən\ *n*

reichs·mark \ˈrīk-ˌsmärk\ *n, pl* **reichsmarks** *also* **reichsmark :** the German mark from 1925 to 1948 [German, from *reich* "empire" + *mark* "mark"]

[1]**reign** \ˈrān\ *n* **1 a :** royal authority **:** SOVEREIGNTY **b :** the domination or influence of one resembling a monarch **2 :** the time during which a monarch rules [Old French *regne,* from Latin *regnum,* from *reg-, rex* "king"]

[2]**reign** *vi* **1 a :** to have or exercise sovereign power **:** RULE **b :** to hold office as chief of state with only slight governing powers **2 :** to exercise authority in the manner of a monarch **3 :** to be predominant or prevalent

reign of terror : a period marked by violence that is often committed by those in power and produces widespread terror

re·im·burse \ˌrē-əm-ˈbərs\ *vt* **:** to pay back **:** REPAY [*re-* + obsolete *imburse* "to put in the pocket", from Middle French *embourser,* from Old French *em-* "en-" + *borser* "to get money", from *borse* "purse", from Medieval Latin *bursa*] — **re·im·burs·able** \-ˈbər-sə-bəl\ *adj* — **re·im·burse·ment** \-ˈbərs-mənt\ *n*

[1]**rein** \ˈrān\ *n* **1 :** a line or strap fastened to a bit on each side for controlling an animal — usually used in pl. **2 a :** a restraining influence **:** CHECK ⟨kept the child under a tight *rein*⟩ **b :** controlling or guiding power ⟨seize the *reins* of government⟩ **3 :** complete freedom **:** SCOPE — usually used in the phrase *give rein to* [Middle French *rene,* derived from Latin *retinēre* "to hold back, restrain", from *re-* + *tenēre* "to hold"]

[2]**rein** *vb* **:** to check, control, or stop by or as if by reins

re·in·car·nate \ˌrē-ən-ˈkär-ˌnāt\ *vt* **:** to give a new or different body or form to

re·in·car·na·tion \rē-ˌin-ˌkär-ˈnā-shən\ *n* **1 :** the action of reincarnating **:** the state of being reincarnated **2 :** rebirth in new bodies or forms of life; *esp* **:** a rebirth of a soul in a new human body

rein·deer \ˈrān-ˌdiər\ *n, pl* **reindeer** *also* **reindeers :** any of several large deer of northern regions having antlers in both sexes and including some used as meat and draft animals [Middle English *reindere,* from Old Norse *hreinn* "reindeer" + Middle English *dere* "deer"]

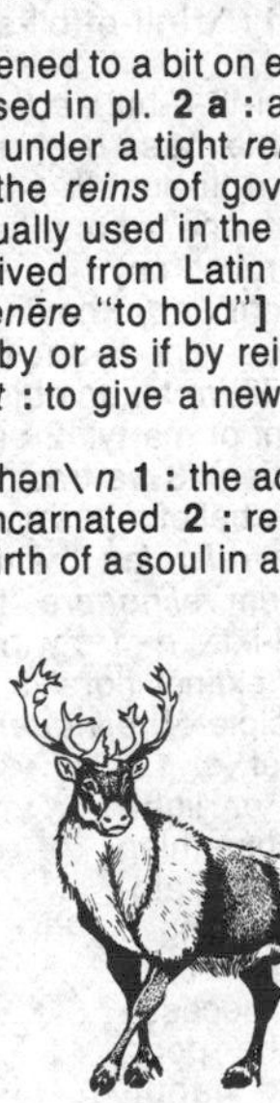

reindeer

reindeer moss *n* **:** a gray, erect, and much-branched lichen of northern and arctic regions important as reindeer food

re·in·fec·tion \ˌrē-ən-ˈfek-shən\ *n* **:** infection following another infection of the same type — **re·in·fect** \-ˈfekt\ *vt*

re·in·force \ˌrē-ən-ˈfōrs, -ˈfȯrs\ *vt* **1 :** to strengthen with new force, assistance, material, or support ⟨*reinforce* a wall⟩ ⟨*reinforce* an argument⟩ **2 :** to strengthen with additional troops or ships **3 :** to stimulate (as a student) so as to increase the frequency of a desired response; *also* **:** to increase the frequency of (a response) by such stimulation [*re-* + *inforce,* alteration of *enforce*]

reinforced concrete *n* **:** concrete in which metal rods, bars, or mesh are embedded for strengthening

re·in·force·ment \ˌrē-ən-ˈfōr-smənt, -ˈfȯr-\ *n* **1 :** the action of reinforcing **:** the state of being reinforced **2 :** something that reinforces

reins \ˈrānz\ *n pl* **1 :** the kidneys or the region thereof **2 :** the seat of the feelings or passions [Middle French, from Latin *renes*]

re·in·state \ˌrē-ən-ˈstāt\ *vt* **:** to restore to possession or to a former position, condition, or capacity ⟨*reinstate* an official⟩ — **re·in·state·ment** \-mənt\ *n*

re·in·ter·pret \ˌrē-ən-ˈtər-prət, *rapid* -pət\ *vt* **:** to interpret again; *esp* **:** to give a new or different interpretation to — **re·in·ter·pre·ta·tion** \-ˌtər-prə-ˈtā-shən, *rapid* -pə-ˈtā-\ *n*

re·in·vest \ˌrē-ən-ˈvest\ *vt* **1 :** to invest again or anew **2 a :** to invest (as income from investments) in additional securities **b :** to invest (as earnings) in a business rather than distribute as dividends or profits — **re·in·vest·ment** \-ˈvest-mənt, -ˈves-\ *n*

re·is·sue \rē-ˈish-ü, ˈrē-\ *vb* **:** to issue again ⟨*reissued* the book in paperback form⟩ — **reissue** *n*

re·it·er·ate \rē-ˈit-ə-ˌrāt\ *vt* **:** to say or do over again or repeatedly **syn** see REPEAT — **re·it·er·a·tion** \rē-ˌit-ə-ˈrā-shən\ *n* — **re·it·er·a·tive** \rē-ˈit-ə-ˌrāt-iv, -rət-\ *adj* — **re·it·er·a·tive·ly** *adv* — **re·it·er·a·tive·ness** *n*

[1]**re·ject** \ri-ˈjekt\ *vt* **1 :** to refuse to accept, submit to, or deal with **2 :** DISCARD 2 **3 :** to refuse to grant or consider **4 :** to subject to immunological rejection ⟨*reject* a heart transplant⟩ [Latin *rejectus,* past participle of *reicere* "to reject", from *re-* + *jacere* "to throw"]

• **syn** REJECT, REPUDIATE, SPURN mean to refuse to accept, receive, or consider something proposed or offered. REJECT stresses a casting back on the source and implies firmness and finality ⟨*rejected* all proposals for a truce⟩ REPUDIATE implies a usually scornful and public thrusting away as unworthy, untrue, or unjustified ⟨now *repudiate* former beliefs⟩ SPURN implies disdain or contempt more strongly than REJECT ⟨*spurned* all marriage proposals⟩

[2]**re·ject** \ˈrē-ˌjekt\ *n* **:** a rejected person or thing

re·jec·tion \ri-ˈjek-shən\ *n* **1 a :** the act of rejecting **:** the state of being rejected **b :** the immunological process of sloughing off foreign tissue or a transplanted organ **2 :** something rejected

re·joice \ri-ˈjȯis\ *vb* **1 :** to give joy to ⟨news that *rejoices* the heart⟩ **2 :** to feel joy ⟨*rejoice* over a friend's good fortune⟩ [Middle French *rejoiss-,* stem of *rejoir* "to rejoice", from *re-* "re-" + *joir* "to rejoice", from Latin *gaudēre*] — **re·joic·er** *n* — **re·joic·ing·ly** \-ˈjȯi-sing-lē\ *adv*

re·joic·ing \-ˈjȯi-sing\ *n* **1 :** the action of one that rejoices **2 :** an instance, occasion, or expression of joy **:** FESTIVITY

re·join *vt* **1** \ˈrē-ˈjȯin, ˈrē-\ **:** to join again **:** return to ⟨*rejoined* my family after a trip⟩ **2** \ri-\ **:** ANSWER 1, REPLY

re·join·der \ri-ˈjȯin-dər\ *n* **:** REPLY; *esp* **:** an answer to a reply [Middle English *rejoiner,* from Middle French *rejoindre* "to rejoin", from *re-* "re-" + *joindre* "to join"]

re·ju·ve·nate \ri-ˈjü-və-ˌnāt\ *vt* **:** to make young or youthful again **:** give new vigor to [*re-* + Latin *juvenis* "young"] — **re·ju·ve·na·tion** \-ˌjü-və-ˈnā-shən\ *n* — **re·ju·ve·na·tor** \-ˈjü-və-ˌnāt-ər\ *n*

[1]**re·lapse** \ri-ˈlaps, ˈrē-ˌ\ *n* **:** the act or fact of relapsing; *esp* **:** a recurrence of illness after a period of improvement [Latin *relapsus,* past participle of *relabi* "to slide back", from *re-* + *labi* "to slide"]

[2]**relapse** *vi* **1 :** to slip or fall back into a former worse state **2 :** SINK, SUBSIDE ⟨*relapsed* into thought⟩ — **re·laps·er** *n*

relapsing fever *n* **:** an epidemic disease marked by recurring

\ə\ **abut**	\au̇\ **out**	\i\ **tip**	\ȯ\ **saw**	\u̇\ **foot**
\ər\ **further**	\ch\ **chin**	\ī\ **life**	\ȯi\ **coin**	\y\ **yet**
\a\ **mat**	\e\ **pet**	\j\ **job**	\th\ **thin**	\yü\ **few**
\ā\ **take**	\ē\ **easy**	\ng\ **sing**	\t͟h\ **this**	\yu̇\ **cure**
\ä\ **cot, cart**	\g\ **go**	\ō\ **bone**	\ü\ **food**	\zh\ **vision**

high fever lasting five to seven days and caused by a spirochete transmitted by the bites of lice or ticks

re•late \ri-ˈlāt\ *vb* **1 :** to give an account of **:** NARRATE ⟨*relate* a story⟩ **2 :** to show or establish a relationship between ⟨*relate* cause and effect⟩ **3 :** to have relationship or connection **:** REFER **4 :** to have meaningful social relationships **[**Latin *relatus,* past participle of *referre* "to carry back, refer"**]** — **re•lat•able** \-ˈlāt-ə-bəl\ *adj* — **re•lat•er** *n*

re•lat•ed *adj* **:** belonging to the same group on the basis of known or determinable qualities ⟨*related* phenomena⟩: as **a** (1) **:** having a common ancestry (2) **:** belonging to the same family by blood or marriage **b :** having close harmonic connection ⟨*related* chords⟩ — **re•lat•ed•ness** *n*

re•la•tion \ri-ˈlā-shən\ *n* **1 :** the act of telling or recounting **:** ACCOUNT **2 :** an aspect or quality (as resemblance) that connects two or more things or parts as being or belonging or working together or as being of the same kind **3 a :** RELATIVE 3 **b :** relationship by blood or marriage **:** KINSHIP **4 :** REFERENCE 2, RESPECT ⟨in *relation* to this⟩ **5 :** the attitude which two or more individuals assume toward one another ⟨race *relations*⟩ **6 a :** the state of being mutually or reciprocally interested (as in social or commercial matters) **b** *pl* (1) **:** AFFAIR 1a, DEALINGS ⟨foreign *relations*⟩ (2) **:** INTERCOURSE 1 — **re•la•tion•al** \-shnəl, -shən-l\ *adj*

re•la•tion•ship \-shən-ˌship\ *n* **1 :** the state or character of being related or interrelated **2 :** KINSHIP; *also* **:** a specific instance or type of this **3 :** a state of affairs existing between those having shared dealings

[1]rel•a•tive \ˈrel-ət-iv\ *n* **1 :** a word referring grammatically to an antecedent **2 :** a thing having a relation to or connection with or necessary dependence upon another thing **3 :** an individual connected with another by blood or marriage

[2]relative *adj* **1 :** introducing a subordinate clause that qualifies an expressed or implied antecedent ⟨*relative* pronouns⟩; *also* **:** introduced by such a connective ⟨a *relative* clause⟩ **2 :** RELEVANT, PERTINENT ⟨questions *relative* to the topic⟩ **3 :** not absolute or independent **:** COMPARATIVE ⟨lived in *relative* isolation⟩ **4 :** having the same key signature — used of major and minor keys and scales **5 :** expressed as the ratio of the specified quantity (as an error in measuring) to the total magnitude (as the value of a measured quantity) or to the mean of all the quantities involved — **rel•a•tive•ly** *adj* — **rel•a•tive•ness** *n*

relative error *n* **:** the ratio of an error in a measured or calculated quantity to the magnitude of that quantity

relative humidity *n* **:** the ratio of the amount of water vapor actually present in the air to the greatest amount possible at the same temperature

rel•a•tiv•i•ty \ˌrel-ə-ˈtiv-ət-ē\ *n* **1 :** the quality or state of being relative; *esp* **:** dependence on something else **2 a :** a theory in physics that equates mass and energy and that describes changes in mass, dimension, and time which are related to velocities approaching the speed of light **b :** an extension of the theory to include a discussion of gravitation and related acceleration phenomena — **rel•a•tiv•ist** \ˈrel-ət-iv-əst\ *n* — **rel•a•tiv•is•tic** \ˌrel-ət-iv-ˈis-tik\ *adj* — **rel•a•tiv•is•ti•cal•ly** \-ti-kə-lē, -klē\ *adv*

re•la•tor \ri-ˈlāt-ər\ *n* **:** one that relates **:** NARRATOR

re•lax \ri-ˈlaks\ *vb* **1 :** to make or become less tense or rigid **:** EASE **2 :** to make or become less severe or rigid ⟨*relax* immigration laws⟩ **3 :** to cast off social restraint, nervous tension, anxiety, or suspicion ⟨couldn't *relax* in crowds⟩ **4 :** to seek rest or recreation **[**Latin *relaxare,* from *re-* + *laxare* "to loosen", from *laxus* "loose"**]** — **re•lax•er** *n*

[1]re•lax•ant \ri-ˈlak-sənt\ *adj* **:** producing relaxation

[2]relaxant *n* **:** a relaxing agent; *esp* **:** a drug causing muscular relaxation

re•lax•a•tion \ˌrē-ˌlak-ˈsā-shən, ri-\ *n* **1 :** the act or fact of relaxing or being relaxed **2 :** a relaxing or diverting state, activity, or pastime **3 :** the lengthening that characterizes inactive muscles

re•laxed \ri-ˈlakst\ *adj* **1 :** lacking in precision or strictness **2 :** set at rest or at ease **3 :** easy of manner **:** INFORMAL — **re•laxed•ly** \-ˈlak-səd-lē, -ˈlaks-tlē\ *adv* — **re•laxed•ness** \-ˈlak-səd-nəs, -ˈlakst-nəs, -ˈlaks-nəs\ *n*

re•lax•in \ri-ˈlak-sən\ *n* **:** a hormone of the corpus luteum that relaxes pelvic ligaments and facilitates childbirth

[1]re•lay \ˈrē-ˌlā\ *n* **1 :** a fresh supply (as of horses or men) arranged to relieve others at various stages especially of a journey or race **2 a :** a race between teams in which each team member successively covers a specified portion of the course or of the total distance **b :** one of the divisions of a relay **3 a :** an electromagnetic device in which the opening or closing of a circuit operates another device **b :** SERVOMOTOR **4 :** the act of passing along by stages; *also* **:** one of such stages **[**Middle French *relais,* from *relaier* "to relay", from *re-* "re-" + *laier* "to leave", derived from Latin *laxare* "to loosen"**]**

[2]re•lay \ˈrē-ˌlā, ri-ˈlā\ *vt* **re•layed; re•lay•ing 1 :** to place in or provide with relays **2 :** to pass along by relays **3 :** to control or operate by a relay

[3]re•lay \rē-ˈlā, ˈrē-\ *vt* **-laid** \-ˈlād\; **-lay•ing :** to lay again ⟨*relay* the patio flagstones⟩

[1]re•lease \ri-ˈlēs\ *vt* **1 :** to set free from restraint, confinement, or servitude **2 :** to relieve from something that holds, burdens, or oppresses **3 :** to give up in favor of another ⟨*release* a claim to property⟩ **4 :** to give permission for publication, performance, exhibition, or sale of at a specified date **[**Old French *relessier,* from Latin *relaxare* "to relax"**] syn** see FREE — **re•leas•abil•i•ty** \-ˌlē-sə-ˈbil-ət-ē\ *n* — **re•leas•able** \-ˈlē-sə-bəl\ *adj*

[2]release *n* **1 :** relief or deliverance from sorrow, suffering, or trouble **2 a :** a discharge from an obligation (as a debt) **b :** a relinquishment of a right or claim; *esp* **:** a conveyance of a right in real property to another **c :** a document embodying a release **3 a :** the act or an instance of liberating or freeing (as from physical restraint) **b :** the act or manner of ending a speech sound **4 :** the state of being freed **5 :** a device adapted to hold or release a mechanism as required **6 a :** the act of permitting performance or publication **b :** the matter released

re•leas•er \ri-ˈlē-sər\ *n* **:** one that releases; *esp* **:** a stimulus that serves as the initiator of complex reflex behavior

rel•e•gate \ˈrel-ə-ˌgāt\ *vt* **1 :** EXILE, BANISH **2 :** to remove or dismiss to a less important or prominent place ⟨*relegate* old books to the attic⟩ **3 :** to submit to someone or something for appropriate action **[**Latin *relegare,* from *re-* + *legare* "to send with a commission", from *leg-, lex* "law"**]** — **rel•e•ga•tion** \ˌrel-ə-ˈgā-shən\ *n*

re•lent \ri-ˈlent\ *vi* **1 :** to become less severe, harsh, or strict **2 :** to let up **:** SLACKEN **[**Middle English *relenten***]**

re•lent•less \-ləs\ *adj* **:** mercilessly hard or harsh — **re•lent•less•ly** *adv* — **re•lent•less•ness** *n*

rel•e•vance \ˈrel-ə-vəns\ *also* **rel•e•van•cy** \-vən-sē\ *n, pl* **-vanc•es** *also* **-van•cies :** relation to the matter at hand **:** PERTINENCE

rel•e•vant \-vənt\ *adj* **:** having relevance ⟨a *relevant* question⟩ **[**Medieval Latin *relevans,* from Latin *relevare* "to raise up, relieve"**]** — **rel•e•vant•ly** *adv*

re•li•abil•i•ty \ri-ˌlī-ə-ˈbil-ət-ē\ *n* **:** the quality or state of being reliable

re•li•able \ri-ˈlī-ə-bəl\ *adj* **:** that can be relied on **:** DEPENDABLE — **re•li•able•ness** *n* — **re•li•ably** \-blē\ *adv*

re•li•ance \ri-ˈlī-əns\ *n* **1 :** the act of relying **2 :** the condition or attitude of one who relies **:** DEPENDENCE **3 :** something or someone relied on

re•li•ant \-ənt\ *adj* **:** having reliance on something or someone **:** TRUSTING — **re•li•ant•ly** *adv*

rel•ic \ˈrel-ik\ *n* **1 :** an object venerated because of association with a saint or martyr **2 :** a surviving ruin or remnant ⟨*relics* of ancient cities⟩ **3 :** a trace of some past or outmoded practice, custom, or belief **:** VESTIGE **[**Old French *relique,* derived from Late Latin *reliquiae* "remains of a martyr", from Latin, "remains", from *relinquere* "to leave behind"**]**

rel•ict \ˈrel-ikt\ *n* **1 :** WIDOW **2 :** a persistent remnant of an otherwise extinct flora or fauna **[**derived from Latin *relictus,* past participle of *relinquere* "to leave behind"**]**

re•lief \ri-ˈlēf\ *n* **1 a :** removal or lightening of something oppressive, painful, or distressing **b :** aid in the form of money or necessities for the poor, aged, or handicapped **c :** military assistance to a post or force in extreme danger **d :** means of breaking monotony or boredom **:** DIVERSION **2 a :** release from sentry or other duty **b :** one that

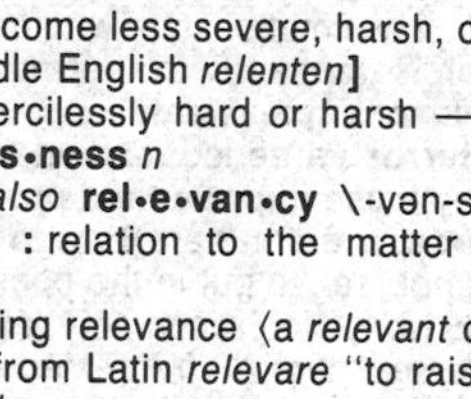

relief 4b

takes the place of another on duty **3 :** legal remedy or redress **4 a :** projection from the background (as of figures in sculpture) **b :** a work of art with such raised figures **c :** vividness or sharpness of outline due to contrast (as of color or shading) **5 :** the elevations or inequalities of a land surface **[**Middle French, from *relever* "to relieve"**]**

relief map *n* **:** a map representing topographic relief

relief pitcher *n* **:** a baseball pitcher who takes over for another during a game

re•lieve \ri-ˈlēv\ *vb* **1 :** to free from pain, discomfort, or distress **:** give aid or help to ⟨*relieve* the poor⟩ ⟨*relieved* by the news⟩ **2 :** to release from a post or duty especially by taking the place of ⟨*relieve* a sentry⟩ **3 :** to remove or lessen the monotony of ⟨a black dress *relieved* by a white collar⟩ **4 :** to put in or stand out in relief **:** give prominence to or set off by contrast (as in sculpture or painting) **[**Middle French *relever* "to raise up, relieve", from Latin *relevare,* from *re-* + *levare* "to raise"**]** — **re•liev•er** *n*

• **syn** RELIEVE, ALLEVIATE, LIGHTEN mean to make something less grievous or more bearable. RELIEVE implies either removing entirely or lifting enough of a burden to make it tolerable; ALLEVIATE suggests temporary or partial lessening of pain or distress; LIGHTEN implies reducing a burdensome or depressing weight ⟨the good news *lightened* their minds⟩

re•li•gion \ri-ˈlij-ən\ *n* **1 a :** the service and worship of God or the supernatural **b :** belief in or devotion to religious faith or observance **c :** the state of a religious **2 :** a set or system of religious attitudes, beliefs, and practices **3 :** a cause, principle, or system of beliefs held to with zeal and faith **[**Latin *religio***]**

re•li•gion•ist \ri-ˈlij-nəst, -ə-nəst\ *n* **:** a person adhering to a religion

¹re•li•gious \ri-ˈlij-əs\ *adj* **1 a :** devoted to God or to the powers or principles believed to govern life ⟨a very *religious* person⟩ **b :** belonging to a religious order ⟨a *religious* house⟩ **2 :** of or relating to religion ⟨*religious* beliefs⟩ **3 :** DEPENDABLE, FAITHFUL **syn** see DEVOUT — **re•li•gious•ly** *adv* — **re•li•gious•ness** *n*

²religious *n, pl* **religious :** a member of a religious order

re•lin•quish \ri-ˈling-kwish\ *vt* **1 :** to withdraw or retreat from **:** ABANDON **2 a :** to desist from **b :** to release a claim to or possession or control of **:** RENOUNCE **3 :** to release or let go (as a grip or hold) **[**Middle French *relinquiss-,* stem of *relinquir* "to relinquish", from Latin *relinquere* "to leave behind", from *re-* + *linquere* "to leave"**]** — **re•lin•quish•ment** \-mənt\ *n*

• **syn** RELINQUISH, YIELD, RESIGN, SURRENDER mean to give up completely. RELINQUISH suggests that some regret, reluctance, or weakness is involved; YIELD implies concession or compliance or submission to force; RESIGN emphasizes voluntary and usually formal relinquishment; SURRENDER implies a giving up after a struggle to retain or resist.

rel•i•quary \ˈrel-ə-ˌkwer-ē\ *n, pl* **-quar•ies :** a small box or shrine in which sacred relics are kept

¹rel•ish \ˈrel-ish\ *n* **1 :** a pleasing appetizing taste **2 :** a small bit added for flavor **:** DASH **3 :** personal liking ⟨*relish* for hard work⟩ **4 :** keen enjoyment of something that satisfies one's tastes, inclination, or desires **5 :** a highly seasoned sauce (as of pickles or mustard) eaten with other food to add flavor **[**Middle English *reles* "taste", from Old French, "something left behind", from *relessier* "to release"**] syn** see TASTE

²relish *vt* **1 :** to add relish to **2 :** to be pleased or gratified by **:** ENJOY **3 :** to eat or drink with pleasure — **rel•ish•able** \-ə-bəl\ *adj*

re•live \rē-ˈliv, ˈrē-\ *vb* **:** to live again or over; *esp* **:** to experience again in imagination

re•lo•cate \rē-ˈlō-ˌkāt, ˈrē-; ˌrē-lō-ˈkāt\ *vb* **1 :** to locate again **2 :** to move to a new location ⟨*relocate* a factory⟩ — **re•lo•cat•able** \-ə-bəl\ *adj* — **re•lo•ca•tion** \ˌrē-lō-ˈkā-shən\ *n*

re•luc•tance \ri-ˈlək-təns\ *n* **:** the quality or state of being reluctant

re•luc•tan•cy \-tən-sē\ *n, pl* **-cies :** RELUCTANCE

re•luc•tant \ri-ˈlək-tənt\ *adj* **:** not willing ⟨*reluctant* to go⟩ **[**Latin *reluctari* "to struggle against", from *re-* + *luctari* "to struggle"**]** — **re•luc•tant•ly** *adv*

re•ly \ri-ˈlī\ *vi* **re•lied; re•ly•ing 1 :** to depend confidently ⟨I know I can *rely* on you⟩ **2 :** to be dependent ⟨*relied* on a spring for water⟩ **[**Middle French *relier* "to connect, rally", from Latin *religare* "to tie back", from *re-* + *ligare* "to tie"**]**

¹re•main \ri-ˈmān\ *vi* **1 a :** to be a part not destroyed, taken, or used up ⟨little *remained* after the fire⟩ **b :** to be something yet to be shown, done, or treated ⟨that *remains* to be proved⟩ **2 :** to stay in the same place or with the same person or group; *esp* **:** to stay behind **3 :** to continue unchanged ⟨the weather *remained* cold⟩ **[**Middle French *remaindre,* from Latin *remanēre,* from *re-* + *manēre* "to stay, remain"**] syn** see STAY

²remain *n* **1 :** a remaining part or trace — usually used in pl. **2** *pl* **:** writings left unpublished at a writer's death **3** *pl* **:** a dead body

¹re•main•der \ri-ˈmān-dər\ *n* **1 a :** a remaining group, part, or trace **b (1) :** the number left after a subtraction **(2) :** the final undivided part after division that is less than the divisor **2 :** a book sold at a reduced price by the publisher after sales have slowed **[**Anglo-French, from Middle French *remaindre* "to remain"**] syn** see BALANCE

²remainder *vt* **re•main•dered; re•main•der•ing** \-də-ring, -dring\ **:** to dispose of (books) as remainders

re•make \rē-ˈmāk, ˈrē-\ *vt* **-made** \-ˈmād\; **-mak•ing :** to make anew or in a different form — **re•make** \ˈrē-ˌmāk\ *n*

¹re•mand \ri-ˈmand\ *vt* **:** to order back: as **a :** to send back (a case) to a lower court for further action **b :** to return to custody pending trial or for further detention **[**Middle French *remander,* from Late Latin *remandare* "to send back word", from Latin *re-* + *mandare* "to order"**]**

²remand *n* **:** the act of remanding **:** the state of being remanded

¹re•mark \ri-ˈmärk\ *vb* **1 :** to take notice of **:** OBSERVE **2 :** to express as an observation or comment **:** SAY **3 :** to make an observation or comment **[**French *remarquer,* from *re-* + *marquer* "to mark"**]**

²remark *n* **1 :** the act of remarking **:** NOTICE **2 :** mention of that which deserves attention or notice **3 :** an expression of opinion or judgment

re•mark•able \ri-ˈmär-kə-bəl\ *adj* **1 :** worthy of being or likely to be noticed **2 :** UNCOMMON, EXTRAORDINARY ⟨a *remarkable* career⟩ — **re•mark•able•ness** *n* — **re•mark•ably** \-blē\ *adv*

re•mar•riage \rē-ˈmar-ij, ˈrē-\ *n* **:** a second or later marriage

re•match \rē-ˈmach, ˈrē-ˌ\ *n* **:** a second match between the same contestants or teams

re•me•di•a•ble \ri-ˈmēd-ē-ə-bəl\ *adj* **:** capable of being remedied — **re•me•di•a•ble•ness** *n* — **re•me•di•a•bly** \-blē\ *adv*

re•me•di•al \ri-ˈmēd-ē-əl\ *adj* **:** intended to remedy or improve ⟨*remedial* measures⟩ ⟨*remedial* reading courses⟩ — **re•me•di•al•ly** \-ē-ə-lē\ *adv*

¹rem•e•dy \ˈrem-əd-ē\ *n, pl* **-dies 1 :** a medicine or treatment that cures or relieves **2 :** something that corrects an evil, rights a wrong, or makes up for a loss **[**Anglo-French *remedie,* from Latin *remedium,* from *re-* + *mederi* "to heal"**]**

²remedy *vt* **-died; -dy•ing :** to provide or serve as a remedy for **:** RELIEVE **syn** see CURE

re•mem•ber \ri-ˈmem-bər\ *vb* **-bered; -ber•ing** \-bə-ring, -bring\ **1 :** to bring to mind or think of again **2 a :** to keep in mind for attention or consideration **b :** to show remembrance of usually by kindness or giving ⟨*remembered* in the will⟩ **3 :** to retain in the memory **4 :** to convey greetings from **[**Middle French *remembrer,* from Late Latin *rememorari,* from *re-* + *memorari* "to be mindful of", from Latin *memor* "mindful"**]** — **re•mem•ber•able** \-bə-rə-bəl, -brə-bəl\ *adj* — **re•mem•ber•er** \-bər-ər\ *n*

• **syn** RECOLLECT, RECALL, REMINISCE: REMEMBER implies a keeping in memory that may be effortless or unwilled; RECOLLECT implies bringing back to mind what is lost or scattered; RECALL suggests an effort to bring back to mind and often to recreate in speech; REMINISCE implies a casual often nostalgic recalling of experiences from long ago.

re•mem•brance \ri-ˈmem-brəns\ *n* **1 :** the state of bearing in mind ⟨let us live in constant *remembrance* of our faults⟩ **2 :** ability to remember **:** MEMORY **3 :** an act of calling to mind ⟨*remembrance* of past wrongs⟩ **4 :** a memory of something ⟨had no *remembrance* of that day⟩ **5 a :** something that serves to keep in or bring to mind **b :** something (as a gift or greeting) expressive of friendly remembrance **syn** see MEMORY

re•mind \ri-ˈmīnd\ *vt* **:** to cause to remember something ⟨*remind* a child that it is bedtime⟩ — **re•mind•er** *n*

rem•i•nisce \ˌrem-ə-ˈnis\ *vi* : to engage in reminiscence **syn** see REMEMBER

rem•i•nis•cence \ˌrem-ə-ˈnis-ns\ *n* **1** : a recalling or telling of past experience ⟨spent an hour in *reminiscence*⟩ **2** : an account of a memorable experience **syn** see MEMORY

rem•i•nis•cent \-nt\ *adj* **1** : of or relating to reminiscence : indulging in reminiscence **2** : tending to remind one (as of something seen or known before) [Latin *reminiscens,* present participle of *reminisci* "to remember"]

re•miss \ri-ˈmis\ *adj* **1** : negligent in the performance of work or duty : CARELESS **2** : showing neglect or disregard : LAX [Latin *remissus,* from *remittere* "to send back, relax"] **syn** see NEGLIGENT — **re•miss•ly** *adv* — **re•miss•ness** *n*

re•mis•si•ble \ri-ˈmis-ə-bəl\ *adj* : capable of being forgiven ⟨*remissible* sins⟩ — **re•mis•si•bly** \-blē\ *adv*

re•mis•sion \ri-ˈmish-ən\ *n* : the act or process of remitting [Old French, from Latin *remissio,* from *remittere* "to send back, remit"]

re•mit \ri-ˈmit\ *vb* **re•mit•ted**; **re•mit•ting** **1 a** : to release from the guilt or penalty of : PARDON ⟨*remit* sins⟩ **b** : to refrain from exacting ⟨*remit* a penalty⟩ **c** : to give relief from (suffering) **2 a** : to lay aside ⟨do not *remit* your care of the garden⟩ **b** : to refrain from **c** : to let slacken : RELAX **3** : to submit or refer for consideration, judgment, decision, or action **4** : to restore or consign to a former status or condition **5** : POSTPONE, DEFER **6** : to send (money) especially in payment **7** : to lessen in intensity or severity often temporarily : MODERATE ⟨the fever *remitted*⟩ [Latin *remittere* "to send back, remit, relax", from *re-* + *mittere* "to send"] — **remit** *n* — **re•mit•ment** \-ˈmit-mənt\ *n* — **re•mit•ta•ble** \-ˈmit-ə-bəl\ *adj* — **re•mit•ter** *n*

re•mit•tal \ri-ˈmit-l\ *n* : REMISSION

re•mit•tance \ri-ˈmit-ns\ *n* **1** : a sum of money remitted **2** : a sending of money (as to a distant place)

re•mit•tent \ri-ˈmit-nt\ *adj* : marked by alternating periods of abatement and increase of symptoms ⟨a *remittent* fever⟩ [Latin *remittens,* present participle of *remittere* "to remit"] — **re•mit•tent•ly** *adv*

rem•nant \ˈrem-nənt\ *n* **1** : a surviving trace ⟨the *remnants* of a great civilization⟩ **2** : something left over ⟨a *remnant* of cloth⟩ [Middle French *remenant,* from *remenoir* "to remain", from Latin *remanēre*]

re•mod•el \rē-ˈmäd-l, ˈrē-\ *vt* : to alter the structure of : partly rebuild

re•mon•strance \ri-ˈmän-strəns\ *n* : an act or instance of remonstrating : PROTEST

re•mon•strant \-strənt\ *adj* : vigorously objecting or opposing — **remonstrant** *n* — **re•mon•strant•ly** *adv*

re•mon•strate \ri-ˈmän-ˌstrāt\ *vb* : to plead in opposition to something : speak in reproof : OBJECT, PROTEST ⟨*remonstrate* with a pupil for being disorderly⟩ [Medieval Latin *remonstrare* "to demonstrate", from Latin *re-* + *monstrare* "to show"]

rem•o•ra \ˈrem-ə-rə\ *n* : a fish having the front upper fin converted into a disk on the head by means of which it clings to other fishes and to ships [Latin, literally, "delay"]

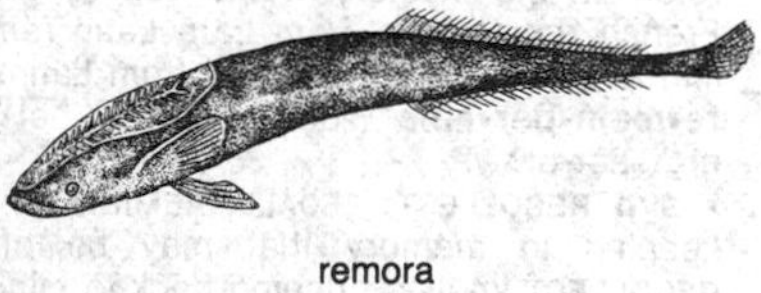

remora

re•morse \ri-ˈmȯrs\ *n* : a deep regret arising from a sense of guilt for past wrongs : SELF-REPROACH [Middle French *remors,* from Medieval Latin *remorsus,* from Latin *remordēre* "to bite again", from *re-* + *mordēre* "to bite"]

re•morse•ful \-fəl\ *adj* : arising from or marked by remorse — **re•morse•ful•ly** \-fə-lē\ *adv* — **re•morse•ful•ness** *n*

re•morse•less \-ləs\ *adj* : being without remorse : MERCILESS — **re•morse•less•ly** *adv* — **re•morse•less•ness** *n*

re•mote \ri-ˈmōt\ *adj* **1** : far off in place or time : not near or recent ⟨the *remote* past⟩ **2** : OUT-OF-THE-WAY, SECLUDED ⟨a *remote* valley⟩ **3** : not closely connected or related **4** : not obvious or striking : SLIGHT ⟨*remote* likeness⟩ **5** : APART, ALOOF ⟨kept themselves *remote* from the dispute⟩ **6** : maintained or operating from a distance ⟨*remote* control⟩ [Latin *remotus,* from *removēre* "to remove"] **syn** see DISTANT — **re•mote•ly** *adv* — **re•mote•ness** *n*

¹re•mount \rē-ˈmau̇nt, ˈrē-\ *vb* : to mount again

²re•mount \ˈrē-ˌmau̇nt, rē-ˈ\ *n* : a fresh horse to take the place of one disabled or exhausted

re•mov•abil•i•ty \ri-ˌmü-və-ˈbil-ət-ē\ *n* : the quality or state of being removable

re•mov•able \ri-ˈmü-və-bəl\ *adj* : that can be removed — **re•mov•able•ness** *n* — **re•mov•ably** \-blē\ *adv*

re•mov•al \ri-ˈmü-vəl\ *n* : the act of removing : the fact of being removed

¹re•move \ri-ˈmüv\ *vb* **1 a** : to change or cause to change to another location, position, station, or residence **b** : to go away **2 a** : to move by lifting, pushing aside, or taking away or off **b** : to yield to being so moved ⟨this cap should *remove* easily⟩ **3** : to dismiss from office **4** : ELIMINATE ⟨*remove* a tumor surgically⟩ [Old French *removoir,* from Latin *removēre,* from *re-* + *movēre* "to move"] — **re•mov•er** *n*

²remove *n* **1** : REMOVAL; *esp* : a change of residence or location **2 a** : a distance or interval separating one thing from another **b** : a degree or stage of separation ⟨at one *remove*⟩

re•moved \ri-ˈmüvd\ *adj* **1** : far away : DISTANT ⟨a home far *removed* from cities⟩ **2** : distant in relationship ⟨the children of your first cousin are your first cousins once *removed*⟩ **syn** see DISTANT

re•mu•da \ri-ˈmüd-ə\ *n* : a herd of horses from which those to be used (as on a ranch) for the day are drawn [American Spanish, "relay of horses", from Spanish, "exchange", from *remudar* "to exchange", from *re-* "re-" + *mudar* "to change", from Latin *mutare*]

re•mu•ner•ate \ri-ˈmyü-nə-ˌrāt\ *vt* : to pay an equivalent to for a service, loss, or expense : COMPENSATE [Latin *remunerare,* from *re-* + *munerare* "to give", from *muner-, munus* "gift"] **syn** see PAY — **re•mu•ner•a•tor** \-ˌrāt-ər\ *n* — **re•mu•ner•a•to•ry** \ri-ˈmyü-nə-rə-ˌtōr-ē, -ˌtȯr-\ *adj*

re•mu•ner•a•tion \ri-ˌmyü-nə-ˈrā-shən\ *n* **1** : an act or fact of remunerating **2** : something that remunerates : COMPENSATION

re•mu•ner•a•tive \ri-ˈmyü-nə-ˌrāt-iv\ *adj* **1** : serving to remunerate **2** : PROFITABLE ⟨made a highly *remunerative* investment⟩ — **re•mu•ner•a•tive•ly** *adv* — **re•mu•ner•a•tive•ness** *n*

Re•nais•sance \ˌren-ə-ˈsäns, -ˈzäns\ *n* **1 a** : the movement or period in Europe between the 14th and 17th centuries marked by a revival of interest in classical arts and literature and by the beginnings of modern science **b** : the neoclassic style of architecture prevailing during the Renaissance **2** *often not cap* : a movement or period marked by a revival of vigorous artistic and intellectual activity [French, from Middle French, "rebirth", from *renaistre* "to be born again", from Latin *renasci,* from *re-* + *nasci* "to be born"]

re•nal \ˈrēn-l\ *adj* : of, relating to, or located in or near the kidneys [Late Latin *renalis,* from Latin *renes* "kidneys"]

renal artery *n* : either of the paired arteries that arise from the dorsal aorta and supply blood to the kidneys

renal vein *n* : either of the paired veins that drain blood from the kidneys into the vena cava

re•na•scence \ri-ˈnas-ns, -ˈnās-\ *n, often cap* : RENAISSANCE 2 — **re•na•scent** \-nt\ *adj*

rend \ˈrend\ *vt* **rent** \ˈrent\ *also* **rend•ed**; **rend•ing** **1** : to remove from place by violence : WREST **2** : to split or tear apart or in pieces by violence **3** : to tear (the hair or clothing) as a sign of anger, grief, or despair **4 a** : to hurt mentally or emotionally **b** : to pierce with sound **c** : to divide (as a nation) into parties [Old English *rendan*]

ren•der \ˈren-dər\ *vt* **ren•dered**; **ren•der•ing** \-də-riŋ, -driŋ\ **1** : DELIVER, GIVE ⟨*render* judgment⟩ **2** : to melt down : extract by heating ⟨*render* lard⟩ **3** : to give up : SURRENDER ⟨*render* one's life for a cause⟩ **4** : to give in return ⟨*render* thanks⟩ **5** : to present a statement of : bring to one's attention ⟨*render* a bill⟩ **6** : to cause to be or become : MAKE ⟨*render* a person helpless⟩ **7** : FURNISH, CONTRIBUTE ⟨*render* aid⟩ **8** : PRESENT, PERFORM ⟨*render* a song⟩ ⟨*render* a salute⟩ **9** : TRANSLATE ⟨*render* Latin into English⟩ [Middle French *rendre* "to give back, yield", derived from Latin *reddere*] — **ren•der•able** \-də-rə-bəl, -drə-bəl\ *adj* — **ren•der•er** \-dər-ər\ *n*

¹ren•dez•vous \ˈrän-di-ˌvü, -dā-\ *n, pl* **ren•dez•vous** \-ˌvüz\ **1 a** : a place appointed for assembling or meeting **b** : a place where people get together : HAUNT **2** : an appointed meeting **3** : the process of bringing two spacecraft together [Middle French, from *rendez vous* "present yourselves"]

[2]rendezvous *vb* **ren•dez•voused** \-ˌvüd\; **ren•dez•vous•ing** \-ˌvü-iŋ\; **ren•dez•vouses** \-ˌvüz\ : to come or bring together at a rendezvous

ren•di•tion \ren-ˈdish-ən\ *n* : the act or result of rendering: as **a** : TRANSLATION **b** : PERFORMANCE 3, INTERPRETATION [obsolete French, from Middle French *reddition,* from Late Latin *redditio,* from Latin *reddere* "to give back, yield"]

[1]ren•e•gade \ˈren-i-ˌgād\ *n* **1** : a deserter from one faith, cause, or allegiance to another **2** : one who rejects lawful or conventional behavior [Spanish *renegado,* from Medieval Latin *renegatus,* from *renegare* "to deny", from Latin *re-* + *negare* "to deny"]

[2]renegade *vi* : to become a renegade

[3]renegade *adj* : TRAITOROUS 1, APOSTATE

ren•e•ga•do \ˌren-i-ˈgäd-ō, -ˈgād-\ *n, pl* **-does** : RENEGADE [Spanish]

re•nege \ri-ˈnig, -ˈneg, -ˈnēg, -ˈnāg\ *vi* **1** : to violate a rule in a card game by failing to follow suit when able **2** : to go back on a promise or commitment [Medieval Latin *renegare* "to deny"] — **re•neg•er** *n*

re•new \ri-ˈnü, -ˈnyü\ *vt* **1** : to make new again : restore to freshness or vigor ⟨strength *renewed* by a night's rest⟩ **2** : to restore to existence : REESTABLISH, RECREATE ⟨*renew* the splendor of a palace⟩ **3** : to do or make again : REPEAT ⟨*renew* a complaint⟩ **4** : to begin again : RESUME ⟨*renewed* efforts to make peace⟩ **5** : to put in a fresh supply of : REPLACE ⟨*renew* the water in a tank⟩ **6** : to grant or obtain an extension of ⟨*renew* a lease⟩

• **syn** RENEW, RESTORE, REFRESH, RENOVATE mean to make like new. RENEW can imply a replacing (as of worn parts or used-up supplies) or a recruiting (as of vigor or health); RESTORE suggests a returning to an original state of soundness or wholeness ⟨*restored* the old mansion⟩ REFRESH implies restoring qualities of liveliness or zest ⟨*refreshed* by a short nap⟩ RENOVATE applies chiefly to material things and suggests making like new but not necessarily like the original ⟨*renovate* the upstairs rooms⟩

re•new•able \ri-ˈnü-ə-bəl, -ˈnyü-\ *adj* : capable of being renewed; *esp* : capable of being replaced by natural ecological cycles or sound management procedures ⟨*renewable* resources like water, wildlife, forests, and grasslands⟩ — **re•new•abil•i•ty** \-ˌnü-ə-ˈbil-ət-ē, -ˌnyü-\ *n*

re•new•al \ri-ˈnü-əl, -ˈnyü-\ *n* **1** : the act of renewing : the state of being renewed **2** : something renewed

re•ni•form \ˈren-ə-ˌfȯrm, ˈrē-nə-\ *adj* : suggesting a kidney in outline ⟨a *reniform* leaf⟩ [Latin *renes* "kidneys"]

ren•net \ˈren-ət\ *n* **1** : the contents of the stomach of an unweaned calf or other animal or the lining membrane of the stomach used for curdling milk **2** : rennin or a substitute used to curdle milk [Middle English, from Old English *gerennan* "to cause to coagulate"]

ren•nin \ˈren-ən\ *n* : a stomach enzyme that coagulates casein and is used commercially to curdle milk in the making of cheese

re•nom•i•nate \rē-ˈnäm-ə-ˌnāt, ˈrē-\ *vt* : to nominate again especially for a succeeding term — **re•nom•i•na•tion** \rē-ˌnäm-ə-ˈnā-shən\ *n*

re•nounce \ri-ˈnau̇ns\ *vt* **1** : to give up, abandon, or resign usually by formal declaration ⟨*renounced* the throne⟩ ⟨*renounce* one's errors⟩ **2** : to refuse further to follow, obey, or recognize : REPUDIATE ⟨*renounce* one's allegiance⟩ [Middle French *renoncer,* from Latin *renuntiare,* from *re-* + *nuntiare* "to report, announce", from *nuntius* "messenger"] — **re•nounce•ment** \-mənt\ *n* — **re•nounc•er** *n*

ren•o•vate \ˈren-ə-ˌvāt\ *vt* : to make like new again : restore to a former state or to good condition [Latin *renovare,* from *re-* + *novare* "to make new", from *novus* "new"] **syn** see RENEW — **ren•o•va•tion** \ˌren-ə-ˈvā-shən\ *n* — **ren•o•va•tor** \ˈren-ə-ˌvāt-ər\ *n*

re•nown \ri-ˈnau̇n\ *n* : a state of being widely acclaimed and highly honored : FAME [Middle French *renon,* from *renomer* "to celebrate", from *re-* + *nomer* "to name", from Latin *nominare,* from *nomen* "name"]

re•nowned \-ˈnau̇nd\ *adj* : having renown : CELEBRATED **syn** see FAMOUS

[1]rent \ˈrent\ *n* **1** : property (as a house) rented or for rent **2** : money paid for the use of property : a periodic payment made by a tenant to the owner for the possession and use of real property **3** : the portion of the national income attributable to land as a factor of production [Old French *rente* "income from a property", derived from Latin *reddere* "to give back, yield"] — **for rent** : available for use or service at a price

[2]rent *vb* **1** : to take and hold property under an agreement to pay rent **2** : to grant the possession and enjoyment of for rent : LET **3** : to be for rent **syn** see HIRE — **rent•able** \-ə-bəl\ *adj*

[3]rent *past of* REND

[4]rent *n* **1** : an opening made by or as if by rending **2** : an act or instance of rending

[1]rent•al \ˈrent-l\ *n* **1** : an amount paid or collected as rent **2** : something rented **3** : an act of renting

[2]rental *adj* **1** : of, relating to, or available for rent **2** : dealing in rental property

rental library *n* : a commercially operated library (as in a store) that lends books at a fixed charge per book per day

rent•er \ˈrent-ər\ *n* : one that rents; *esp* : TENANT

rent•tier \rä^{n}-tyā\ *n* : a person who receives a fixed income from investments [French, from *rente* "income from a property"]

re•num•ber \rē-ˈnəm-bər, ˈrē-\ *vt* : to number again or differently

re•nun•ci•a•tion \ri-ˌnən-sē-ˈā-shən\ *n* : the act or practice of renouncing [Latin *renuntiatio,* from *renuntiare* "to renounce"] — **re•nun•ci•a•tive** \-ˈnən-sē-ˌāt-iv\ *adj* — **re•nun•ci•a•to•ry** \-sē-ə-ˌtōr-ē, -ˌtȯr-\ *adj*

re•open \rē-ˈō-pən, ˈrē-, -ˈōp-m\ *vb* **1** : to open again **2** : to take up again : RESUME

[1]re•or•der \rē-ˈȯrd-ər, ˈrē-\ *vb* **1** : REORGANIZE **2** : to place a reorder or a reorder for

[2]reorder *n* : an order like a previous order from the same supplier

re•or•ga•ni•za•tion \rē-ˌȯrg-nə-ˈzā-shən, ˌrē-, -ə-nə-\ *n* : the act of reorganizing : the state of being reorganized; *esp* : the financial reconstruction of a business concern

re•or•ga•nize \rē-ˈȯr-gə-ˌnīz, ˈrē-\ *vb* : to organize again or anew; *esp* : to bring about a reorganization (as of a business concern) — **re•or•ga•niz•er** *n*

rep *or* **repp** \ˈrep\ *n* : a plain-woven fabric with prominent rounded crosswise ribs [French *reps,* from English *ribs,* pl. of *rib*]

re•pack•age \rē-ˈpak-ij, ˈrē-\ *vt* : to package again and especially differently

[1]re•pair \ri-ˈpaər, -ˈpeər\ *vi* : to make one's way : GO ⟨*repair* to an inner office⟩ [Middle French *repairier* "to go back to one's country", from Late Latin *repatriare,* from Latin *re-* + *patria* "native country"]

[2]repair *vb* **1 a** : to restore by replacing a part or putting together what is damaged : MEND **b** : to restore to a sound or healthy state : RENEW **2** : to make good : REMEDY **3** : to make up for : compensate for [Middle French *reparer,* from Latin *reparare,* from *re-* + *parare* "to prepare"] **syn** see FIX — **re•pair•abil•i•ty** \-ˌpar-ə-ˈbil-ət-ē, -ˌper-\ *n* — **re•pair•able** \-ˈpar-ə-bəl, -ˈper-\ *adj* — **re•pair•er** \-ər\ *n*

[3]repair *n* **1** : the action or process of repairing ⟨make *repairs*⟩ **2** : the result of repairing ⟨a tire with three *repairs*⟩ **3** : good or sound condition ⟨a house in *repair*⟩ **4** : condition with respect to soundness or need of repairing ⟨a house in bad *repair*⟩

re•pair•man \ri-ˈpaər-ˌman, -ˈpeər-, -mən\ *n* : one whose occupation is making repairs ⟨a TV *repairman*⟩

rep•a•ra•ble \ˈrep-rə-bəl, -ə-rə-\ *adj* : capable of being repaired

rep•a•ra•tion \ˌrep-ə-ˈrā-shən\ *n* **1** : the action or process of repairing or restoring : the state of being repaired or restored **2** : a making amends for a wrong or injury done : COMPENSATION **3** : the amends made for a wrong or injury; *esp* : money paid (as by one country to another) in compensation (as for damages in war) [Middle French, from Late Latin *reparatio,* from Latin *reparare* "to repair"]

re•par•a•tive \ri-ˈpar-ət-iv\ *adj* **1** : of, relating to, or effecting repair **2** : serving to make amends

rep•ar•tee \ˌrep-ər-ˈtē, -är-, -ˈtā\ *n* : a clever witty reply; *also* : the making of such replies [French *repartie,* from *repartir* "to retort", from *re-* "re-" + *partir* "to divide, part"]

\ə\ **abut**	\au̇\ **out**	\i\ **tip**	\ȯ\ **saw**	\u̇\ **foot**
\ər\ **further**	\ch\ **chin**	\ī\ **life**	\ȯi\ **coin**	\y\ **yet**
\a\ **mat**	\e\ **pet**	\j\ **job**	\th\ **thin**	\yü\ **few**
\ā\ **take**	\ē\ **easy**	\ng\ **sing**	\t͟h\ **this**	\yu̇\ **cure**
\ä\ **cot, cart**	\g\ **go**	\ō\ **bone**	\ü\ **food**	\zh\ **vision**

re•pass \rē-ˈpas, ˈrē-\ *vb* **1 :** to pass again especially in the opposite direction **:** RETURN **2 :** to cause to pass again **3 :** to adopt again — **re•pas•sage** \-ˈpas-ij\ *n*

re•past \ri-ˈpast\ *n* **:** something taken as food **:** MEAL **[**Middle French, from *repaistre* "to feed", from *re-* "re-" + *paistre* "to feed", from Latin *pascere***]**

re•pa•tri•ate \rē-ˈpā-trē-ˌāt, ˈrē-, -ˈpa-\ *vt* **:** to send or bring back to the country of which one is a citizen ⟨*repatriate* prisoners of war⟩ **[**Late Latin *repatriare* to go back to one's country", from Latin *re-* + *patria* 'native country"**]** — **re•pa•tri•ate** \-trē-ət, -trē-ˌāt\ *n* — **re•pa•tri•a•tion** \ˌrē-ˌpā-trē-ˈā-shən, -ˌpa-\ *n*

re•pay \rē-ˈpā, ˈrē-\ *vb* **-paid; -pay•ing 1 :** to pay back ⟨I've already been *repaid*⟩ ⟨*repay* a loan⟩ **2 :** to make return payment ⟨a lending bank requires proof of ability to *repay*⟩ — **re•pay•able** \-ə-bəl\ *adj* — **re•pay•ment** \-mənt\ *n*

re•peal \ri-ˈpēl\ *vt* **:** REVOKE, ANNUL; *esp* **:** to do away with by legislative enactment **[**Middle French *repeler,* from *re-* + *apeler* "to call, appeal"**]** — **repeal** *n* — **re•peal•able** \-ˈpē-lə-bəl\ *adj* — **re•peal•er** *n*

[1]re•peat \ri-ˈpēt\ *vt* **1 a :** to say or state again **:** REITERATE **b :** to say over from memory **:** RECITE **c :** to say after another **d :** to tell to others ⟨*repeat* gossip⟩ **2 :** to make, do, or perform again ⟨*repeat* a mistake⟩ **3 :** to recur or cause to recur ⟨the cycle *repeats* itself indefinitely⟩ **[**Middle French *repeter,* from Latin *repetere,* from *re-* + *petere* "to go to, seek"**]** — **re•peat•able** \-ə-bəl\ *adj*

• syn REPEAT, REITERATE mean to do or say again. REPEAT is the general term and may apply to one or many actions or utterances; REITERATE stresses exact repetition of something said and may be stronger in implying multiple repetition.

— **repeat oneself :** to say or do the same thing more than once

[2]re•peat \ri-ˈpēt, ˈrē-,\ *n* **1 :** the act of repeating **2 a :** something repeated **b** (1) **:** a musical passage to be repeated in performance (2) **:** a sign consisting of vertical dots placed before and after a passage to be repeated

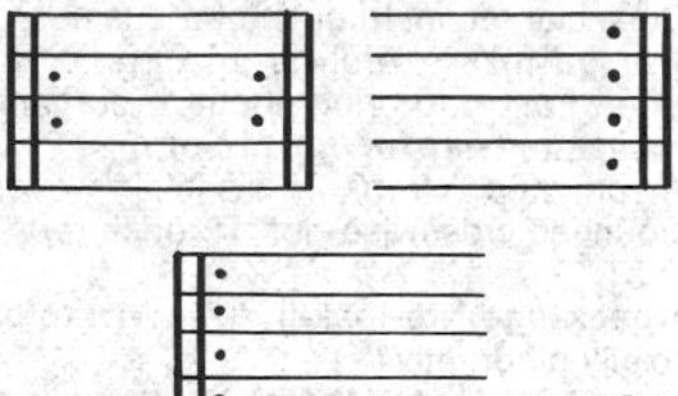

[2]repeat 2b (2)

re•peat•ed \ri-ˈpēt-əd\ *adj* **:** done or happening again and again **:** FREQUENT — **re•peat•ed•ly** *adv*

re•peat•er \ri-ˈpēt-ər\ *n* **:** one that repeats: as **a :** a watch that strikes the time when a spring is pressed **b :** a firearm that fires several times without reloading **c :** an habitual violator of the laws **d :** a student repeating a class or course

repeating decimal *n* **:** a decimal in which after a certain point a particular digit or sequence of digits repeats itself indefinitely — compare TERMINATING DECIMAL

re•pel \ri-ˈpel\ *vb* **re•pelled; re•pel•ling 1 a :** to drive back **:** REPULSE **b :** to fight against **:** RESIST **2 :** to turn away **:** REJECT ⟨*repelled* the insinuation⟩ **3 a :** to drive away **:** DISCOURAGE **b :** to be incapable of adhering to, mixing with, taking up, or holding **c :** to force away or apart or tend to do so by mutual action at a distance **4 :** to cause aversion **:** DISGUST **[**Latin *repellere,* from *re-* + *pellere* "to drive"**]** — **re•pel•ler** *n*

re•pel•lant \ri-ˈpel-ənt\ *adj or n* **:** REPELLENT

[1]re•pel•lent \-ənt\ *adj* **1 :** serving or tending to drive away or ward off **2 :** arousing aversion or disgust **:** REPULSIVE **[**Latin *repellens,* present participle of *repellere* "to repel"**]** **syn** see REPUGNANT — **re•pel•len•cy** \-ən-sē\ *n* — **re•pel•lent•ly** *adv*

[2]repellent *n* **:** something that repels; *esp* **:** a substance employed to prevent insect attacks

re•pent \ri-ˈpent\ *vb* **1 :** to feel sorrow for a wrong action and determine to do what is right **2 :** to feel sorry for or dissatisfied with **:** REGRET ⟨*repent* a rash decision⟩ **[**Old French *repentir,* from *re-* "re-" + *pentir* "to be sorry", from Latin *paenitēre***]** — **re•pent•er** *n*

re•pent•ance \ri-ˈpent-ns\ *n* **:** the action or process of repenting especially for misdeeds or moral shortcomings **syn** see PENITENCE

re•pent•ant \ri-ˈpent-nt\ *adj* **:** feeling or showing repentance — **re•pent•ant•ly** *adv*

re•per•cus•sion \ˌrē-pər-ˈkəsh-ən, ˌrep-ər-\ *n* **1 :** REFLECTION 1, REVERBERATION **2 a :** a reciprocal action or effect **b :** a widespread, indirect, or unforeseen effect of an act, action, or event — **re•per•cus•sive** \-ˈkəs-iv\ *adj*

rep•er•toire \ˈrep-ə-ˌtwär, -ər-\ *n* **1 a :** a list or supply of dramas, operas, pieces, or parts that a company or person is prepared to perform **b :** a supply of skills, devices, or expedients possessed by a person **2 a :** the complete list or supply of dramas, operas, or musical works available for performance **b :** the complete list or supply of skills, devices, or ingredients used in a particular field, occupation, or practice **[**French *répertoire,* from Late Latin *repertorium* "list"**]**

rep•er•to•ry \ˈrep-ər-ˌtōr-ē, -ə-, -ˌtȯr-\ *n, pl* **-ries 1 :** a stock or store of something **:** COLLECTION ⟨a *repertory* of unusual skills⟩ **2 :** REPERTOIRE **[**Late Latin *repertorium* "list", from Latin *reperire* "to find", from *re-* + *parere* "to produce"**]**

rep•e•ti•tion \ˌrep-ə-ˈtish-ən\ *n* **1 :** the act or an instance of repeating **2 :** the fact of being repeated **3 :** something repeated **[**Latin *repetitio,* from *repetere* "to repeat"**]**

rep•e•ti•tious \-ˈtish-əs\ *adj* **:** marked by repetition; *esp* **:** tediously repeating — **rep•e•ti•tious•ly** *adv* — **rep•e•ti•tious•ness** *n*

re•pet•i•tive \ri-ˈpet-ət-iv\ *adj* **:** REPETITIOUS — **re•pet•i•tive•ly** *adv* — **re•pet•i•tive•ness** *n*

re•phrase \rē-ˈfrāz, ˈrē-\ *vt* **:** to state in a different form ⟨let me *rephrase* the question⟩

re•pine \ri-ˈpīn\ *vi* **1 :** to feel or express dejection or discontent **:** COMPLAIN **2 :** to wish discontentedly — **re•pin•er** *n*

re•place \ri-ˈplās\ *vt* **1 :** to put back in a proper or former place ⟨*replace* a card in a file⟩ **2 :** to take the place of **:** SUPPLANT ⟨paper money has *replaced* gold coins⟩ **3 :** to fill the place of **:** supply an equivalent for ⟨*replace* a broken dish⟩ — **re•place•able** \-ˈplā-sə-bəl\ *adj*

• syn REPLACE, SUPPLANT, SUPERSEDE mean to put out of place or into the place of another. REPLACE implies a supplying of a substitute or equivalent for something lost, destroyed, or no longer usable or adequate; SUPPLANT implies taking the place of one forced out by craft or fraud or the replacing of a thing with another newer or better ⟨coal *supplanted* wood for heating⟩ SUPERSEDE implies taking the place of one that has become outmoded, obsolete, or inferior.

re•place•ment \ri-ˈplā-smənt\ *n* **1 :** the act of replacing **:** the state of being replaced **:** SUBSTITUTION **2 :** one that replaces another

replacement set *n* **:** a set of elements any one of which may be used to replace a given variable or placeholder in a mathematical expression (as an equation)

re•plant \rē-ˈplant, ˈrē-\ *vt* **1 :** to set (a plant) to grow again or anew **2 :** to provide with new plants ⟨*replanted* the park⟩

re•plen•ish \ri-ˈplen-ish\ *vt* **:** to fill again **:** bring back to a condition of being full or complete **[**Middle French *repleniss-,* stem of *replenir* "to fill", from *re-* "re-" + *plein* "full", from Latin *plenus***]** — **re•plen•ish•er** *n* — **re•plen•ish•ment** \-ish-mənt\ *n*

re•plete \ri-ˈplēt\ *adj* **1 :** filled to capacity **:** FULL; *esp* **:** full of food **2 :** fully supplied or provided ⟨a book *replete* with illustrations⟩ **3 :** COMPLETE 1a **[**Latin *repletus,* past participle of *replēre* "to fill up", from *re-* + *plēre* "to fill"**]** — **re•plete•ness** *n*

re•ple•tion \ri-ˈplē-shən\ *n* **1 :** the act of eating to excess **:** the state of being fed to excess **:** SURFEIT **2 :** the condition of being filled up or overcrowded **3 :** fulfillment of a need or desire **:** SATISFACTION

rep•li•ca \ˈrep-li-kə\ *n* **1 :** a close reproduction or facsimile especially by the maker of the original **2 :** COPY 1, DUPLICATE **[**Italian, "repetition", from *replicare* "to repeat", from Late Latin, from Latin, "to fold back"**]**

[1]rep•li•cate \ˈrep-lə-ˌkāt\ *vb* **1 :** DUPLICATE 1, REPEAT **2 :** to undergo replication ⟨*replicating* DNA⟩

[2]rep•li•cate \-li-kət\ *n* **:** one of several identical experiments, procedures, or samples

rep•li•ca•tion \ˌrep-lə-ˈkā-shən\ *n* **1 :** ANSWER 1a, REPLY **2 :** precise copying or reproduction; *also* **:** an act or process of this

[1]re•ply \ri-ˈplī\ *vb* **re•plied; re•ply•ing 1 a :** to respond in speech or writing **b :** to give as an answer **2 :** to do something in response; *esp* **:** to return an attack **[**Middle French *replier*

"to fold again", from Latin *replicare* "to fold back", from *re-* + *plicare* "to fold"] — **re•pli•er** \-ˈplī-ər, -ˈplīr\ *n*

[2]**reply** *n, pl* **replies** : something said, written, or done in response

[1]**re•port** \ri-ˈpōrt, -ˈpȯrt\ *n* **1 a** : common talk : an account spread by common talk : RUMOR **b** : FAME, REPUTATION ⟨a person of good *report*⟩ **2** : a usually detailed account or statement ⟨a news *report*⟩ **3** : an explosive noise ⟨the *report* of a gun⟩ [Middle French, from *reporter* "to report", from Latin *reportare,* from *re-* + *portare* "to carry"]

[2]**report** *vb* **1** : to give an account (as of an incident or of one's activities) **2** : to give an account of as a news item ⟨*report* a baseball game⟩ **3** : to make a charge of misconduct against ⟨*report* a schoolmate⟩ **4** : to present oneself ⟨*report* for duty⟩ ⟨*report* at the office⟩ **5** : to make known to the proper authorities ⟨*report* a fire⟩ **6** : to return or present (as a matter officially referred to a committee) with conclusions and recommendations — **re•port•able** \-ə-bəl\ *adj*

re•port•age \ri-ˈpōrt-ij, -ˈpȯrt-, *especially for 2* ˌrep-ər-ˈtäzh\ *n* **1** : the act or process of reporting news **2** : writing intended to report observed or documented events [French, from *reporter* "to report"]

report card *n* : a report on a student's grades that is periodically submitted by a school to the student's parents or guardian

re•port•ed•ly \ri-ˈpōrt-əd-lē, -ˈpȯrt-\ *adv* : according to report

re•port•er \ri-ˈpōrt-ər, -ˈpȯrt-\ *n* : one that reports: as **a** : one that makes authorized statements of law decisions or legislative proceedings **b** : one employed by a newspaper or magazine to gather and write news **c** : one that broadcasts news — **rep•or•to•ri•al** \ˌrep-ər-ˈtōr-ē-əl, ˌrēp-, -ə-ˈtōr-, -ˈtȯr-\ *adj* — **rep•or•to•ri•al•ly** \-ē-ə-lē\ *adv*

[1]**re•pose** \ri-ˈpōz\ *vt* **1** : to place unquestioningly : SET ⟨*repose* trust in a friend⟩ **2** : to place for control, management, or use [derived from Latin *reponere* "to put back, put away, place", from *re-* + *ponere* "to put"]

[2]**repose** *vb* **1** : to lay at rest : put in a restful position ⟨*reposed* my head on a cushion⟩ **2** : to lie at rest : take rest ⟨*reposing* on the couch⟩ [Middle French, *reposer,* from Late Latin *repausare,* from *re-* + *pausare* "to stop", from Latin *pausa* "pause"]

[3]**repose** *n* **1** : a state of resting after exertion or strain; *esp* : rest in sleep **2** : CALM 2, PEACE **3** : cessation or absence of activity, movement, or animation ⟨a face in *repose*⟩

re•pose•ful \ri-ˈpōz-fəl\ *adj* : full of repose : QUIET — **re•pose•ful•ly** \-fə-lē\ *adv* — **re•pose•ful•ness** *n*

re•po•si•tion \ˌrē-pə-ˈzish-ən\ *vt* : to change or restore the position of

re•pos•i•to•ry \ri-ˈpäz-ə-ˌtōr-ē, -ˌtȯr-\ *n, pl* **-ries** **1** : a place or container where something is deposited or stored **2** : a side altar in a Roman Catholic church where the consecrated host is reserved from Holy Thursday until Good Friday **3** : one that contains or stores something nonmaterial ⟨libraries are *repositories* of knowledge⟩ **4** : a person to whom something is confided or entrusted [Latin *repositorium,* from *repositus,* past participle of *reponere* "to put away"]

re•pos•sess \ˌrē-pə-ˈzes\ *vt* **1 a** : to regain possession of **b** : to retake possession of in default of the payment of installments due **2** : put in possession again — **re•pos•ses•sion** \-ˈzesh-ən\ *n*

re•pous•sé \rə-ˌpü-ˈsā\ *adj* **1** : shaped or ornamented with patterns in relief made by hammering or pressing on the reverse side — used of metal **2** : formed in relief [French]

repp *variant of* REP

rep•re•hend \ˌrep-ri-ˈhend\ *vt* : to voice disapproval of : CENSURE [Latin *reprehendere,* literally, "to hold back", from *re-* + *prehendere* "to grasp"]

rep•re•hen•si•ble \ˌrep-ri-ˈhen-sə-bəl\ *adj* : worthy of or deserving censure or blame : CULPABLE — **rep•re•hen•si•ble•ness** *n* — **rep•re•hen•si•bly** \-blē\ *adv*

rep•re•hen•sion \-ˈhen-chən\ *n* : the act of reprehending : REPROOF [Latin *reprehensio,* from *reprehendere* "to reprehend"] — **rep•re•hen•sive** \-ˈhen-siv\ *adj*

rep•re•sent \ˌrep-ri-ˈzent\ *vt* **1** : to present a picture, image, or likeness of : PORTRAY ⟨this picture *represents* a scene at King Arthur's court⟩ **2** : to serve as a sign or symbol of ⟨the flag *represents* our country⟩ **3 a** : to take the place of in some respect **b** : to act for or in the place of (as in a legislative body) **4** : to describe as having a specified character or quality **5** : to serve as a specimen, example, or instance of [Middle French *representer,* from Latin *repraesentare,* from *re-* + *praesentare* "to present"] — **rep•re•sent•able** \-ə-bəl\ *adj* — **rep•re•sent•er** *n*

rep•re•sen•ta•tion \ˌrep-ri-ˌzen-ˈtā-shən\ *n* **1** : one that represents: as **a** : an artistic likeness or image **b** : a sign or symbol of something **2** : a usually formal protest **3** : the act or action of representing or state of being represented (as in a legislative body) — **rep•re•sen•ta•tion•al** \-shnəl, -shən-l\ *adj*

[1]**rep•re•sen•ta•tive** \ˌrep-ri-ˈzent-ət-iv\ *adj* **1** : being a representation ⟨a painting *representative* of a battle⟩ **2** : standing or acting for another especially through delegated authority **3** : of, based upon, or being a government in which the people are represented by persons chosen from among them usually by election **4** : serving as a typical or characteristic example ⟨a *representative* sample⟩ — **rep•re•sen•ta•tive•ly** *adv* — **rep•re•sen•ta•tive•ness** *n*

[2]**representative** *n* **1** : a typical example of a group, class, or quality : SPECIMEN **2 a** : one (as an agent or delegate) that represents another or others **b** : a member of the house of representatives of the United States Congress or a state legislature

re•press \ri-ˈpres\ *vt* **1** : to check by or as if by pressure : CURB **2** : to hold in by self-control ⟨*repress* a laugh⟩ **3** : to put down by force : SUBDUE ⟨*repress* a disturbance⟩ **4** : to prevent the natural or normal expression, activity, or development of ⟨*repress* one's anger⟩ **5** : to exclude from consciousness [Latin *repressus,* past participle of *reprimere* "to check, repress", from *re-* + *premere* "to press"] — **re•pres•sive** \-ˈpres-iv\ *adj* — **re•pres•sive•ly** *adv* — **re•pres•sive•ness** *n* — **re•pres•sor** \-ˈpres-ər\ *n*

re•pressed *adj* **1** : subjected to or marked by usually excessive repression **2** : characterized by restraint

re•pres•sion \ri-ˈpresh-ən\ *n* **1** : the act of repressing : the state of being repressed **2** : a psychological process by which unacceptable wishes or impulses are kept from conscious awareness

re•pres•sor \ri-ˈpres-ər\ *n* : a gene product that interacts with a genetic operator to inhibit its function

[1]**re•prieve** \ri-ˈprēv\ *vt* **1** : to delay the punishment of (as a condemned prisoner) **2** : to give relief or deliverance to for a time [perhaps from Middle French *repris,* past participle of *reprendre* "to take back"]

[2]**reprieve** *n* **1 a** : the act of reprieving : the state of being reprieved **b** : a formal temporary suspension of the execution of a sentence **2** : RESPITE 2

[1]**rep•ri•mand** \ˈrep-rə-ˌmand\ *n* : a severe or formal reproof [French *réprimande,* from Latin *reprimendus* "to be checked", from *reprimere* "to check, repress"]

[2]**reprimand** *vt* : to reprove severely and especially officially **syn** see REPROVE

[1]**re•print** \rē-ˈprint, ˈrē-\ *vt* : to print again — **re•print•er** *n*

[2]**re•print** \ˈrē-ˌprint\ *n* **1** : a new or additional printing without any change in the text of a book already published **2** : a separately printed text or excerpt

re•pri•sal \ri-ˈprī-zəl\ *n* **1** : the use of force short of war by one nation against another in retaliation for damage or loss suffered ⟨economic *reprisals*⟩ **2** : an act of retaliation especially in war [Middle French *reprisaille,* from obsolete Italian *ripresaglia,* from *ripreso,* past participle of *riprendere* "to take back", from *ri-* "re-" + *prendere* "to take", from Latin *prehendere*]

re•prise \ri-ˈprēz\ *n* : a recurrence, renewal, or resumption of an action or a musical passage [Middle French, from *reprendre* "to take back", from *re-* "re-" + *prendre* "to take", from Latin *prehendere*]

re•pro \ˈrē-prō\ *n, pl* **repros** : a clear sharp proof made especially from a letterpress printing surface to serve as photographic copy for a printing plate [short for *reproduction*]

[1]**re•proach** \ri-ˈprōch\ *n* **1 a** : a cause or occasion of blame, discredit, or disgrace **b** : DISCREDIT 1, DISGRACE **2** : the act or action of reproaching : REBUKE [Middle French *reproche,* from *reprochier* "to reproach", derived from Latin *re-* + *prope* "near"] — **re•proach•ful** \-fəl\ *adj* — **re•proach•ful•ly** \-fə-lē\ *adv* — **re•proach•ful•ness** *n*

[2]**reproach** *vt* **1 :** to find fault with : blame for a mistake or failure ⟨*reproached* me for my carelessness⟩ **2 :** to bring into discredit **syn** see REPROVE — **re•proach•able** \-'prō-chə-bəl\ *adj* — **re•proach•er** *n* — **re•proach•ing•ly** \-'prō-ching-lē\ *adv*

[1]**rep•ro•bate** \'rep-rə-,bāt\ *vt* **:** to condemn as unworthy or evil [Late Latin *reprobare,* from Latin *re-* + *probare* "to test, approve"] — **rep•ro•ba•tion** \,rep-rə-'bā-shən\ *n* — **rep•ro•ba•tive** \'rep-rə-,bāt-iv\ *adj* — **rep•ro•ba•to•ry** \-bə-,tōr-ē, -,tòr-\ *adj*

[2]**reprobate** *adj* **1 :** doomed to damnation **2 :** thoroughly disreputable and morally abandoned

[3]**reprobate** *n* **:** a reprobate person

re•pro•duce \,rē-prə-'düs, -'dyüs\ *vb* **1 :** to produce again: as **a :** to give rise to (new individuals of the same kind) **b :** to cause to exist again or anew ⟨*reproduce* water from steam⟩ **c :** to imitate closely ⟨*reproduce* the sound of thunder and footsteps by sound effects⟩ **d :** to present again **e :** to make an image or copy of **f :** to translate (a recording) into sound **2 :** to undergo reproduction ⟨your voice *reproduces* well⟩ **3 :** to produce offspring — **re•pro•duc•er** *n* — **re•pro•duci•bil•i•ty** \-,dü-sə-'bil-ət-ē -,dyü-\ *n* — **re•pro•duc•ible** \-'dü-sə-bəl, -'dyü-\ *adj*

re•pro•duc•tion \,rē-prə-'dək-shən\ *n* **1 :** the act or process of reproducing; *esp* **:** the process by which plants and animals give rise to offspring **2 :** something reproduced : COPY **syn** see DUPLICATE

re•pro•duc•tive \,rē-prə-'dək-tiv\ *adj* **:** of, relating to, capable of, or concerned with reproduction — **re•pro•duc•tive•ly** *adv* — **re•pro•duc•tive•ness** *n* — **re•pro•duc•tiv•i•ty** \-,dək-'tiv-ət-ē\ *n*

re•proof \ri-'prüf\ *n* **:** censure for a fault : REBUKE [Middle French *reprove,* from *reprover* "to reprove"]

re•prove \ri-'prüv\ *vt* **1 :** to scold usually gently or with kindly intent **2 :** to express disapproval of : CENSURE [Middle French *reprover,* from Late Latin *reprobare* "to disapprove, reprobate"] — **re•prov•er** *n*

• **syn** REPROVE, REBUKE, REPRIMAND, REPROACH mean to criticize for faulty behavior. REPROVE may imply a kindly intent and lack of harshness; REBUKE implies a stern or sharp reproving; REPRIMAND implies a severe, formal, often public or official rebuke; REPROACH often suggests displeasure or disappointment expressed in mild scolding.

[1]**rep•tile** \'rep-tl, -,tīl\ *n* **1 :** any of a class (Reptilia) of air-breathing vertebrates comprising the alligators and crocodiles, lizards, snakes, turtles, and extinct related forms and having a bony skeleton and a body usually covered with scales or bony plates **2 :** a groveling or despicable person [Late Latin, from *reptilis* "creeping", from *repere* "to creep"]

[2]**reptile** *adj* **:** characteristic of a reptile : REPTILIAN

[1]**rep•til•i•an** \rep-'til-ē-ən\ *adj* **:** of, relating to, or resembling reptiles

[2]**reptilian** *n* **:** REPTILE 1

re•pub•lic \ri-'pəb-lik\ *n* **1 a :** a government having a chief of state who is not a monarch and who is usually a president **b :** a political unit having such a form of government **2 a :** a government in which supreme power resides in a body of citizens entitled to vote and is exercised by elected officers and representatives responsible to them **b :** a political unit (as a nation) having such a form of government **3 :** a constituent political and territorial unit of the Soviet Union or Yugoslavia [French *république,* from Latin *respublica,* from *res* "thing, wealth" + *publica,* feminine of *publicus* "public"]

[1]**re•pub•li•can** \ri-'pəb-li-kən\ *adj* **1 a :** of, relating to, or having the characteristics of a republic **b :** favoring, supporting, or advocating a republic **2** *cap* **a :** DEMOCRATIC-REPUBLICAN **b :** of, relating to, or constituting a political party in the United States evolving in the mid-19th century and historically associated with business, financial, and some agricultural interests and with favoring a restricted governmental role in social and economic life

[2]**republican** *n* **1 :** one that favors or supports a republican form of government **2** *cap* **a :** a member of a political party advocating republicanism **b :** a member of the Republican party of the United States

re•pub•li•can•ism \-kə-,niz-əm\ *n* **1 :** adherence to or sympathy for a republican form of government **2 :** the principles or theory of republican government **3** *cap* **:** the principles, policy, or practices of the Republican party of the United States

re•pu•di•ate \ri-'pyüd-ē-,āt\ *vt* **1 :** to divorce or separate formally from (a woman) **2 :** to refuse to have anything to do with : DISOWN **3 a :** to refuse to accept **b :** to reject as untrue or unjust ⟨*repudiate* a charge of favoritism⟩ **4 :** to refuse to acknowledge or pay ⟨*repudiate* a debt⟩ [Latin *repudiare,* from *repudium* "divorce"] **syn** see REJECT — **re•pu•di•a•tion** \-,pyüd-ē-'ā-shən\ *n* — **re•pu•di•a•tor** \-'pyüd-ē-,āt-ər\ *n*

re•pug•nance \ri-'pəg-nəns\ *n* **:** deep-rooted dislike : AVERSION, LOATHING

re•pug•nant \-nənt\ *adj* **1 :** CONTRARY, INCOMPATIBLE ⟨punishments *repugnant* to the spirit of the law⟩ **2 :** arousing distaste or aversion ⟨a *repugnant* idea⟩ [Middle French, "opposed, incompatible", from Latin *repugnare* "to fight against", from *re-* + *pugnare* "to fight"] — **re•pug•nant•ly** *adv*

• **syn** REPELLENT, ABHORRENT: REPUGNANT implies arousing one's resistance or loathing by being alien to one's ideas, principles, or tastes; REPELLENT suggests a generally forbidding or unlovely quality that makes one back away; ABHORRENT adds to REPUGNANT an implication of stronger resistance or profound antagonism ⟨police methods *abhorrent* to a free people⟩

[1]**re•pulse** \ri-'pəls\ *vt* **1 :** to drive or beat back : REPEL ⟨*repulse* an attack⟩ **2 :** to repel by discourtesy, coldness, or denial : REBUFF ⟨*repulsed* their advances⟩ **3 :** to cause repulsion in : DISGUST ⟨*repulsed* at the sight⟩ [Latin *repulsus,* past participle of *repellere* "to repel"]

[2]**repulse** *n* **1 :** a cold discourteous rebuff **2 a :** the action of repelling an attacker **b :** the fact of being repelled

re•pul•sion \ri-'pəl-shən\ *n* **1 :** the action of repulsing : the state of being repulsed **2 :** the action of repelling : the force with which bodies, particles, or like forces repel one another **3 :** a feeling of aversion : REPUGNANCE

re•pul•sive \ri-'pəl-siv\ *adj* **1 :** tending or serving to repulse **2 :** arousing aversion or disgust — **re•pul•sive•ly** *adv* — **re•pul•sive•ness** *n*

rep•u•ta•ble \'rep-yət-ə-bəl\ *adj* **:** having a good reputation : RESPECTED — **rep•u•ta•bil•i•ty** \,rep-yət-ə-'bil-ət-ē\ *n* — **rep•u•ta•bly** \'rep-yət-ə-blē\ *adv*

rep•u•ta•tion \,rep-yə-'tā-shən\ *n* **1 :** overall quality or character as seen or judged by people in general ⟨has a bad *reputation*⟩ **2 :** recognition by other people of some characteristic or ability ⟨has the *reputation* of being clever⟩ **3 :** good name : a place in public esteem ⟨lose one's *reputation*⟩ **4 :** FAME ⟨a worldwide *reputation*⟩

[1]**re•pute** \ri-'pyüt\ *vt* **:** BELIEVE 4, CONSIDER ⟨is *reputed* to be a millionaire⟩ [Middle French *reputer,* from Latin *reputare* "to reckon up, think over", from *re-* + *putare* "to reckon"]

[2]**repute** *n* **1 :** REPUTATION ⟨know a person by *repute*⟩ **2 :** FAME, NOTE ⟨a scientist of *repute*⟩

re•put•ed \ri-'pyüt-əd\ *adj* **1 :** having repute ⟨a highly *reputed* lawyer⟩ **2 :** popularly supposed ⟨a *reputed* success⟩ — **re•put•ed•ly** *adv*

[1]**re•quest** \ri-'kwest\ *n* **1 :** an asking for something ⟨a *request* for help⟩ **2 :** something asked for ⟨grant every *request*⟩ **3 :** the condition of being requested ⟨tickets are available upon *request*⟩ **4 :** DEMAND ⟨that book is in great *request*⟩ [Middle French *requeste,* derived from Latin *requirere* "to seek for, require"]

[2]**request** *vt* **1 :** to make a request to or of **2 :** to ask for ⟨*request* a loan⟩ **syn** see ASK — **re•quest•er** *n*

re•qui•em \'rek-wē-əm *also* 'rāk- *or* 'rēk-\ *n* **1 :** a mass for the dead; *also* **:** a musical setting for such a mass **2 :** a musical service or hymn in honor of the dead [Latin, accusative of *requies* "rest"; first word of the introit of the requiem mass]

req•ui•es•cat \,rek-wē-'es-,kät, ,rā-kwē-\ *n* **:** a prayer for the repose of a dead person [Latin, "may he (or she) rest", from *requiescere* "to rest", from *re-* + *quiescere* "to be quiet", from *quies* "quiet"]

re•quire \ri-'kwīr\ *vt* **1 :** ORDER, COMMAND ⟨the law *requires* drivers to observe traffic lights⟩ **2 :** to demand as necessary or essential [Middle French *requerre,* derived from Latin *requirere,* from *re-* + *quaerere* "to seek, ask"] **syn** see DEMAND

re•quire•ment \-mənt\ *n* **:** something required ⟨comply with all *requirements*⟩ ⟨sleep is a *requirement* for health⟩

req•ui•site \'rek-wə-zət\ *adj* **:** needed especially for the fulfillment of a special purpose [Latin *requisitus,* past participle of *requirere* "to require"] **syn** see NECESSARY — **requisite** *n* — **req•ui•site•ness** *n*

[1]**req•ui•si•tion** \,rek-wə-'zish-ən\ *n* **1 :** the act of requiring or demanding **2 :** an authoritative or formal demand or application ⟨a *requisition* for army supplies⟩ **3 :** the condition of being de-

manded or put into use ⟨every car was in *requisition*⟩

[2]**requisition** *vt* **-si·tioned**; **-si·tion·ing** \-ˈzish-ning, -ə-ning\ : to take or get with a requisition ⟨*requisition* fresh supplies⟩

re·quit·al \ri-ˈkwīt-ᵊl\ *n* **1** : the act or action of requiting : the state of being requited **2** : something given in requital

re·quite \ri-ˈkwīt\ *vt* **1 a** : to make return for : REPAY **b** : to retaliate for : AVENGE **2** : to give something to in return for a benefit or service or for an injury [*re-* + obsolete *quite* "to quit, pay"] — **re·quit·er** *n*

[1]**re·run** \rē-ˈrən, ˈrē-\ *vt* : to run again or anew

[2]**re·run** \ˈrē-ˌrən, rē-ˈ, ˈrē-ˈ\ *n* : the act or action or an instance of rerunning; *esp* : presentation of a motion-picture film or television program after its first run

re·sale \ˈrē-ˌsāl, rē-ˈ, ˈrē-ˈ\ *n* : the act or an instance of selling again

re·scind \ri-ˈsind\ *vt* **1** : to make void : CANCEL ⟨*rescind* a contract⟩ **2** : REPEAL ⟨*rescind* a law⟩ [Latin *rescindere* "to cut apart, annul", from *re-* + *scindere* "to cut"] — **re·scind·er** *n*

re·scis·sion \ri-ˈsizh-ən\ *n* : an act of rescinding [Late Latin *rescissio,* from Latin *rescindere* "to annul"]

res·cue \ˈres-kyü\ *vt* : to free from confinement, danger, or evil : SAVE [Middle French *rescourre,* from *re-* + *escourre* "to shake out, wrest away", from Latin *excutere,* from *ex-* + *quatere* "to shake"] — **rescue** *n* — **res·cu·er** *n*

• **syn** DELIVER, REDEEM, RANSOM: RESCUE implies freeing from imminent danger by prompt or viorgous action; DELIVER implies releasing from confinement, temptation, slavery, or suffering; REDEEM implies releasing from bondage or penalties by giving what is demanded or necessary; RANSOM applies specifically to buying out of captivity.

re·search \ri-ˈsərch, ˈrē-ˌ\ *n* **1** : careful or diligent search **2** : studious inquiry or examination; *esp* : investigation or experimentation aimed at the discovery and interpretation of facts, revision of accepted theories or laws in the light of new facts, or practical application of such new or revised theories or laws [Middle French *recerche,* from *recerchier* "to investigate thoroughly", from *re-* + *cerchier* "to search"] — **research** *vb* — **re·search·er** *n*

re·sec·tion \ri-ˈsek-shən\ *n* : the surgical removal of part of an organ or structure [Latin *resectio* "act of cutting off", from *resecare* "to cut off", from *re-* + *secare* "to cut"] — **re·sect** \-ˈsekt\ *vt*

re·seed \rē-ˈsēd, ˈrē-\ *vb* **1** : to sow seed on again or anew **2** : to maintain itself by self-sown seed

re·sem·blance \ri-ˈzem-bləns\ *n* **1 a** : the quality or state of resembling; *esp* : correspondence in appearance or superficial qualities **b** : a point of likeness **2** : REPRESENTATION 1a, IMAGE **syn** see LIKENESS

re·sem·ble \ri-ˈzem-bəl\ *vt* **-bled**; **-bling** \-bə-ling, -bling\ : to be like or similar to [Middle French *resembler,* from *re-* "re-" + *sembler* "to be like, seem", from Latin *similare* "to copy", from *similis* "like"]

re·sent \ri-ˈzent\ *vt* : to feel or show annoyance or ill will over ⟨*resent* criticism⟩ [French *ressentir* "to feel, resent", from *re-* "re-" + *sentir* "to feel", from Latin *sentire*]

re·sent·ful \-fəl\ *adj* **1** : full of resentment : inclined to resent **2** : caused or marked by resentment — **re·sent·ful·ly** \-fə-lē\ *adv* — **re·sent·ful·ness** *n*

re·sent·ment \ri-ˈzent-mənt\ *n* : a feeling of angry displeasure at something regarded as a wrong, insult, or injury

re·ser·pine \ri-ˈsər-ˌpēn, -pən\ *n* : a drug obtained especially from and used similarly to rauwolfia [German *reserpin,* probably derived from New Latin *Rauwolfia serpentina,* a species of rauwolfia]

res·er·va·tion \ˌrez-ər-ˈvā-shən\ *n* **1** : the act of reserving **2** : an arrangement to have something (as a hotel room) held for one's use **3** : something reserved for a special use; *esp* : a tract of public lands so reserved ⟨an Indian *reservation*⟩ **4** : a limiting condition : EXCEPTION ⟨agree without *reservations*⟩

[1]**re·serve** \ri-ˈzərv\ *vt* **1** : to keep in store for future or special use **2** : to retain or hold over to a future time or place : DEFER ⟨*reserve* one's comments on a plan⟩ **3** : to set or have set aside or apart ⟨*reserve* a hotel room⟩ [Middle French *reserver,* from Latin *reservare,* literally, "to keep back", from *servare* "to keep, save"]

[2]**reserve** *n* **1** : something stored or available for future use : STOCK ⟨oil *reserves*⟩ **2** : something reserved for a particular use: as **a** : military forces withheld or available for later use — usually used in pl. **b** : the military forces of a country not part of the regular services **c** : RESERVIST **d** : a tract set apart : RESERVATION **3** : an act of reserving : EXCEPTION **4** : restraint, closeness, or caution in one's words and bearing **5** : money or its equivalent kept on hand or set apart usually to meet obligations **6** : SUBSTITUTE ⟨the *reserves* on the football team⟩

re·served \ri-ˈzərvd\ *adj* **1** : restrained in words and actions ⟨very *reserved* in public⟩ **2** : set aside for future or special use **syn** see SILENT — **re·serv·ed·ly** \-ˈzər-vəd-lē\ *adv* — **re·served·ness** \-ˈzər-vəd-nəs, -ˈzərvd-nəs, -ˈzərv-nəs\ *n*

re·serv·ist \ri-ˈzər-vəst\ *n* : a member of a military reserve

res·er·voir \ˈrez-ərv-ˌwär, -əv-, -ˌwȯr, -ˌȯr\ *n* **1** : a place where something is kept in store; *esp* : an artificial lake where water is collected and kept in quantity for use **2** : an extra supply : RESERVE **3** : an organism in which a parasite that is harmful to some other species lives and multiplies [French *réservoir,* from *réserver* "to reserve"]

reservoir 1

re·shape \rē-ˈshāp, ˈrē-\ *vt* : to give a new form to

re·ship \-ˈship\ *vb* : to ship again; *esp* : to put on board a second time — **re·ship·ment** \-mənt\ *n* — **re·ship·per** *n*

re·shuf·fle \-ˈshəf-əl\ *vt* **1** : to shuffle again **2** : to reorganize usually by redistribution of existing elements ⟨the President *reshuffled* the cabinet⟩ — **reshuffle** *n*

re·side \ri-ˈzīd\ *vi* **1** : to dwell permanently or continuously : have a fixed abode ⟨*reside* in St. Louis⟩ **2** : to be present as an element, quality, or right ⟨the power of veto *resides* in the president⟩ [Latin *residēre* "to sit back, abide", from *re-* + *sedēre* "to sit"] — **re·sid·er** *n*

res·i·dence \ˈrez-əd-əns, -ə-ˌdens\ *n* **1** : the act or fact of residing in a place as a dweller or in discharge of a duty ⟨physicians in *residence* in a hospital⟩ **2 a** : the place where one lives **b** : the status of a legal resident **3 a** : a building used as a home : DWELLING **b** : a unit of housing provided for students **4 a** : the period during which a person resides in a place **b** : a period of active study, research, or teaching at a college or university

res·i·den·cy \ˈrez-əd-ən-sē, -ə-ˌden-\ *n, pl* **-cies** **1** : a usually official place of residence **2** : a territorial unit in which a political resident exercises authority **3** : a period of advanced training in a medical specialty

[1]**res·i·dent** \ˈrez-əd-ənt, -ə-ˌdent\ *adj* **1 a** : living in a place for some length of time **b** : serving in a regular or full-time capacity ⟨a *resident* engineer⟩ **c** : engaged in academic residence or professional residency ⟨a *resident* scholar⟩ ⟨*resident* physicians⟩ **2** : PRESENT 2b ⟨energy *resident* in matter⟩ **3** : not migratory ⟨*resident* birds⟩ [Latin *residens,* present participle of *residēre* "to sit back, abide"]

[2]**resident** *n* **1** : one who resides in a place **2** : a diplomatic agent exercising authority in a protected state **3** : one (as a physician) serving a residency

res·i·den·tial \ˌrez-ə-ˈden-chəl\ *adj* **1** : used as a residence or by residents ⟨a *residential* hotel⟩ **2** : adapted to or occupied by residences ⟨a *residential* neighborhood⟩ **3** : of or relating to residence or residences — **res·i·den·tial·ly** \-ˈdench-lē, -ə-lē\ *adv*

[1]**re·sid·u·al** \ri-ˈzij-ə-wəl, -ˈzij-wəl\ *adj* : being or active as a residue : left over — **re·sid·u·al·ly** \-ē\ *adv*

[2]**residual** *n* **1** : a residual product, substance, or result : REMAINDER **2** : a payment (as to an actor or writer) for a rerun (as of a taped television program) after an initial showing

residual power *n* : power held to remain at the disposal of a government authority if neither forbidden (as by a constitution) or delegated to other authorities

re·sid·u·ary \ri-ˈzij-ə-ˌwer-ē\ *adj* : of, relating to, disposing of, or being a residue ⟨a *residuary* clause in a will⟩

res•i•due \ˈrez-ə-ˌdü, -ˌdyü\ *n* : whatever remains after a part is taken, set apart, or lost : REMNANT, REMAINDER; *esp* : the part of an estate remaining after the payment of all debts and specific devises and bequests [Middle French *residu,* from Latin *residuum,* from *residuus* "left over", from *residēre* "to sit back, remain"]

re•sid•u•um \ri-ˈzij-ə-wəm\ *n, pl* **re•sid•ua** \-ə-wə\ : something residual : RESIDUE, REMAINDER [Latin]

re•sign \ri-ˈzīn\ *vb* **1** : to give up by a formal or official act ⟨*resign* an office⟩ **2** : to give up an office or position **3** : to commit or give over or up : submit or yield deliberately ⟨*resign* oneself to disappointment⟩ [Middle French *resigner,* from Latin *resignare* "to unseal, cancel, resign", from *re-* + *signare* "to sign, seal"] **syn** see RELINQUISH — **re•sign•er** *n*

res•ig•na•tion \ˌrez-ig-ˈnā-shən\ *n* **1 a** : an act of resigning **b** : a written statement that gives notice of this act **2** : the quality or the feeling of a person who is resigned : quiet or patient submission or acceptance

re•signed \ri-ˈzīnd\ *adj* : submitting patiently (as to loss, sorrow, or misfortune) : SUBMISSIVE, UNCOMPLAINING — **re•sign•ed•ly** \-ˈzī-nəd-lē\ *adv* — **re•sign•ed•ness** \-ˈzī-nəd-nəs\ *n*

re•sil•ience \ri-ˈzil-yəns\ *or* **re•sil•ien•cy** \-yən-sē\ *n* **1** : the ability of a body to rebound, recoil, or resume its original size and shape after being compressed, bent, or stretched : ELASTICITY ⟨the *resilience* of rubber⟩ ⟨the *resiliency* of arteries⟩ **2** : the ability to recover from or adjust to misfortune or change

re•sil•ient \-yənt\ *adj* : having resilience: as **a** : capable of withstanding shock without permanent deformation or rupture **b** : SPRINGY ⟨*resilient* turf⟩ **c** : tending to recover readily from fatigue or depression [Latin *resiliens,* present participle of *resilire* "to jump back, recoil", from *re-* + *salire* "to leap"] **syn** see ELASTIC — **re•sil•ient•ly** *adv*

res•in \ˈrez-n\ *n* **1 a** : any of various solid or semisolid fusible natural organic substances that are usually transparent or translucent and yellowish to brown, are formed especially in plant secretions, are soluble in organic solvents but not in water, are electrical nonconductors, and are used chiefly in varnishes, printing inks, plastics, and sizes and in medicine **b** : ROSIN **2** : any of a large class of synthetic products that have some of the physical properties of natural resins but are different chemically and are used chiefly as plastics [Middle French *resine,* from Latin *resina,* from Greek *rhētinē* "pine resin"] — **res•in•ous** \-əs\ *adj*

res•in•oid \-ˌȯid\ *n* : a somewhat resinous substance; *esp* : a thermosetting synthetic resin

¹re•sist \ri-ˈzist\ *vb* **1** : to withstand the force or effect of ⟨*resist* disease⟩ ⟨silver *resists* acids⟩ **2** : to exert oneself to check or defeat **3** : to exert force in opposition [Latin *resistere,* from *re-* + *sistere* "to take a stand"] **syn** see OPPOSE — **re•sist•er** *n*

²resist *n* : something (as a coating) that resists or prevents a particular action

re•sis•tance \ri-ˈzis-təns\ *n* **1 a** : an act or instance of resisting : OPPOSITION **b** : a means of resisting **2** : the ability to resist **3** : an opposing or retarding force **4 a** : the opposition offered by a body or substance to the passage through it of an electric current **b** : a source of electrical resistance **5** *often cap* : an underground organization of a conquered country engaging in sabotage and secret operations against occupation forces and collaborators

re•sis•tant \-tənt\ *adj* : giving or capable of resistance

re•sist•ibil•i•ty \ri-ˌzis-tə-ˈbil-ət-ē\ *n* **1** : the quality or state of being resistible **2** : the ability to resist

re•sist•ible \ri-ˈzis-tə-bəl\ *adj* : capable of being resisted

re•sis•tive \ri-ˈzis-tiv\ *adj* : marked by resistance

re•sis•tiv•i•ty \ri-ˌzis-ˈtiv-ət-ē\ *n, pl* **-ties** **1** : capacity for resisting : RESISTANCE **2** : the longitudinal electrical resistance of a uniform rod of unit length and unit cross-sectional area : the reciprocal of conductivity

re•sist•less \ri-ˈzist-ləs\ *adj* **1** : IRRESISTIBLE **2** : offering no resistance — **re•sist•less•ly** *adv* — **re•sist•less•ness** *n*

re•sis•tor \ri-ˈzis-tər\ *n* : a device offering electrical resistance

res•o•lute \ˈrez-ə-ˌlüt\ *adj* **1** : marked by firm determination **2** : BOLD 1, STEADY [Latin *resolutus,* past participle of *resolvere* "to break up, dissolve"] — **res•o•lute•ly** *adv* — **res•o•lute•ness** *n*

res•o•lu•tion \ˌrez-ə-ˈlü-shən\ *n* **1** : the act or process of reducing to simpler form: as **a** : the act of analyzing a complex idea into simpler ones **b** : the act of answering **c** : the act of determining **2** : the progression of a chord from dissonance to consonance **3** : the process or capability of making distinguishable individual parts, closely adjacent optical images, or sources of light **4** : the subsidence of inflammation especially in a lung **5 a** : something that is resolved **b** : firmness of resolve **6** : a formal expression of the opinion, will, or intent of an official body or assembled group **7** : the point in a literary work (as a play) at which the chief dramatic complication is worked out

¹re•solve \ri-ˈzälv, -ˈzȯlv\ *vb* **1 a** : to break up or separate into component parts; *also* : to change by disintegration **b** : to reduce by analysis **c** : to distinguish between or make independently visible adjacent parts of **2 a** : to clear up : DISPEL ⟨*resolve* doubts⟩ **b** : to find an answer or solution to **3** : to reach a decision about : DETERMINE, DECIDE **4** : to declare or decide by a formal resolution and vote **5** : to work out the resolution of (as a play) **6** : to progress or cause to progress from dissonance to consonance [Latin *resolvere* "to unloose, break up, dissolve", from *re-* + *solvere* "to loosen"] — **re•solv•able** \-ˈzäl-və-bəl, -ˈzȯl-\ *adj* — **re•solv•er** *n*

²resolve *n* **1** : something resolved : DETERMINATION, RESOLUTION **2** : fixity of purpose

re•solved \ri-ˈzälvd, -ˈzȯlvd\ *adj* : RESOLUTE 1, DETERMINED — **re•solv•ed•ly** \-ˈzäl-vəd-lē, -ˈzȯl-\ *adv*

res•o•nance \ˈrez-n-əns\ *n* **1 a** : the quality or state of being resonant **b** (1) : a vibration of large amplitude in a mechanical or electrical system caused by a relatively small periodic stimulus of the same or nearly the same period as the natural vibration period of the system (as when a radio receiving circuit is tuned to a broadcast frequency) (2) : the state of adjustment that produces resonance in a mechanical or electrical system ⟨two circuits in *resonance* with each other⟩ **2 a** : the intensification and enriching of a musical tone by supplementary vibration **b** : a quality imparted to voiced sounds by the configuration of the mouth and pharynx and in some cases also of the nasal cavity **3** : the condition of a molecule, ion, or radical in which two or more representative structures are needed to describe its characteristics

res•o•nant \-n-ənt\ *adj* **1** : continuing to sound : ECHOING **2** : of, relating to, or showing resonance **3** : intensified and enriched by resonance — **res•o•nant•ly** *adv*

res•o•nate \ˈrez-n-ˌāt\ *vi* **1** : to produce or exhibit resonance **2** : REECHO, RESOUND [Latin *resonare* "to resound"]

res•o•na•tor \-ˌāt-ər\ *n* : something (as a device for increasing the resonance of a musical instrument) that resounds or resonates

re•sorb \rē-ˈsȯrb, ˈrē-, -ˈzȯrb\ *vt* : to break down and assimilate (something previously produced) ⟨the tadpole's tail is gradually *resorbed*⟩ [Latin *resorbēre* "to swallow again", from *re-* + *sorbēre* "to suck up"] — **re•sorp•tion** \-ˈsȯrp-shən, -ˈzȯrp-\ *n*

¹re•sort \ri-ˈzȯrt\ *n* **1 a** : one that is looked to for help : REFUGE, RESOURCE **b** : RECOURSE ⟨have *resort* to force⟩ **2 a** : frequent, habitual, or general visiting **b** (1) : a frequently visited place (2) : a place providing recreation and entertainment especially to vacationers [Middle French, "resource, recourse", from *resortir* "to rebound, resort", from *re-* + *sortir* "to escape"] **syn** see RESOURCE

²resort *vi* **1** : to go especially frequently or habitually : REPAIR **2** : to have recourse ⟨*resort* to violence⟩

re•sort•er \ri-ˈzȯrt-ər\ *n* : one that resorts; *esp* : a frequenter of resorts

re•sound \ri-ˈzau̇nd\ *vb* **1** : to become filled with sound : REVERBERATE **2 a** : to sound loudly **b** : to sound or utter in full resonant tones **3** : to become renowned **4** : to extol loudly or widely : CELEBRATE [Middle French *resoner,* from Latin *resonare,* from *re-* + *sonare* "to sound"]

re•sound•ing *adj* **1** : producing or characterized by resonant sound : RESONATING **2 a** : impressively sonorous ⟨a *resounding* name⟩ **b** : DEFINITE, UNEQUIVOCAL ⟨a *resounding* success⟩ — **re•sound•ing•ly** \-ˈzau̇n-diŋ-lē\ *adv*

re•source \ˈrē-ˌsōrs, -ˌzōrs, -ˌsȯrs, -ˌzȯrs, ri-ˈ\ *n* **1** : a new or a reserve source of supply or support **2** *pl* : a usable stock or supply (as of money, products, power, or energy) ⟨America has great natural *resources*⟩ **3** *archaic* : the possibility of relief or recovery **4** : the ability to meet and handle situations : RESOURCEFULNESS **5** : a means of handling a situation or of getting out of difficulty : EXPEDIENT [French *ressource,* from

Old French *ressourse* "relief, resource", from *resourdre* "to relieve", literally, "to rise again", from Latin *resurgere*]

• **syn** RESORT: RESOURCE applies to anything one falls back upon in the absence or failure of usual means ⟨emergency power *resources*⟩ RESORT implies usually one final resource called upon or used only under compulsion or in desperation ⟨used the gun only as a last *resort*⟩

re•source•ful \-fəl\ *adj* : able to meet and deal with difficult situations — **re•source•ful•ly** \-fə-lē\ *adv* — **re•source•ful•ness** *n*

[1]re•spect \ri-'spekt\ *n* **1** : a relation to or concern with something usually specified : REFERENCE ⟨with *respect* to your last letter⟩ **2** : an act of giving particular attention : CONSIDERATION **3 a** : deferential regard : ESTEEM ⟨we've great *respect* for your opinion⟩ **b** : the quality or state of being esteemed : HONOR **c** *pl* : expressions of respect or deference ⟨pay one's *respects*⟩ **4** : PARTICULAR, DETAIL ⟨perfect in all *respects*⟩ [Latin *respectus,* literally, "act of looking back", from *respicere* "to look back, regard", from *re-* + *specere* "to look"] **syn** see DEFERENCE

[2]respect *vt* **1 a** : to consider worthy of high regard : ESTEEM **b** : to avoid interfering with ⟨*respected* their privacy⟩ **2** : to have reference to : CONCERN **syn** see REGARD — **re•spect•er** *n*

re•spect•abil•i•ty \ri-,spek-tə-'bil-ət-ē\ *n* **1** : the quality or state of being respectable **2 a** : respectable persons **b** : a respectable custom : DECENCY

re•spect•able \ri-'spek-tə-bəl\ *adj* **1** : worthy of respect : ESTIMABLE **2** : decent or correct in character or behavior : PROPER ⟨*respectable* people⟩ **3 a** : fair in size or quantity ⟨a *respectable* amount⟩ **b** : moderately good : TOLERABLE **4** : fit to be seen : PRESENTABLE ⟨*respectable* clothes⟩ — **re•spect•able•ness** *n* — **re•spect•ably** \-blē\ *adv*

re•spect•ful \ri-'spekt-fəl\ *adj* : marked by or showing respect — **re•spect•ful•ly** \-fə-lē\ *adv* — **re•spect•ful•ness** *n*

re•spect•ing *prep* : CONCERNING

re•spec•tive \ri-'spek-tiv\ *adj* **1** *obsolete* : PARTIAL 1, DISCRIMINATIVE **2** : OWN, SEPARATE ⟨their *respective* homes⟩ — **re•spec•tive•ness** *n*

re•spec•tive•ly \ri-'spek-tiv-lē\ *adv* : as relating to each : each in the order given

re•spell \rē-'spel, 'rē-\ *vt* : to spell again or in another way; *esp* : to spell out according to a phonetic system ⟨*respelled* pronunciations⟩

re•spi•ra•ble \'res-pə-rə-bəl, -prə-bəl; ri-'spī-rə-\ *adj* : fit for breathing

res•pi•ra•tion \,res-pə-'rā-shən\ *n* **1 a** : the placing (as by breathing) of air or dissolved gases in intimate contact with the circulating medium of a multicellular organism **b** : a single complete act of breathing **2** : the physical and chemical processes by which an organism supplies its cells and tissues with the oxygen needed for metabolism and relieves them of the carbon dioxide formed **3** : CELLULAR RESPIRATION — **res•pi•ra•tion•al** \-shnəl, -shən-l\ *adj*

res•pi•ra•tor \'res-pə-,rāt-ər\ *n* **1** : a device covering the mouth or nose especially to prevent the inhalation of harmful vapors **2** : a device used in artificial respiration

res•pi•ra•to•ry \'res-pə-rə-,tōr-ē, -prə-tōr-; ri-'spī-rə-; -,tór-\ *adj* : of or relating to respiration or the organs of respiration ⟨*respiratory* diseases⟩ ⟨*respiratory* enzymes⟩

respiratory pigment *n* : any of various permanently or intermittently colored complex proteins (as hemoglobin and cytochrome) that function in the transfer of oxygen in cellular respiration

respiratory system *n* : a system of organs that functions in respiration and consists typically in air-breathing vertebrates of the lungs with their nerves and blood vessels, the organs by which the lungs connect with the outside air, and usually the muscles and parts of the skeleton concerned with support and with emptying and filling the lungs

re•spire \ri-'spīr\ *vb* : to engage in respiration; *esp* : BREATHE [Latin *respirare,* from *re-* + *spirare* "to blow, breathe"]

[1]res•pite \'res-pət\ *n* **1** : a temporary delay : POSTPONEMENT; *esp* : REPRIEVE 1b **2** : an interval of rest or relief ⟨a *respite* from toil⟩ [Old French *respit,* from Medieval Latin *respectus,* from Latin, "act of looking back"]

[2]respite *vt* **1** : to grant a respite to **2** : to put off : DELAY

re•splen•dence \ri-'splen-dəns\ *n* : the quality or state of being resplendent : SPLENDOR — **re•splen•den•cy** \-dən-sē\ *n*

re•splen•dent \-dənt\ *adj* : marked by glowing splendor [Latin *resplendens,* present participle of *resplendēre* "to shine back", from *re-* + *splendēre* "to shine"] — **re•splen•dent•ly** *adv*

re•spond \ri-'spänd\ *vb* **1** : to say something in return : REPLY **2** : to react especially favorably in response ⟨*respond* to surgery⟩ [Middle French *respondre,* from Latin *respondēre* "to promise in return, answer", from *re-* + *spondēre* "to promise"]

[1]re•spon•dent \ri-'spän-dənt\ *n* : one who responds: as **a** : one who maintains a thesis in reply **b** : one who answers in various legal proceedings (as in equity or to an appeal) [Latin *respondens,* present participle of *respondēre* "to answer"]

[2]respondent *adj* : RESPONSIVE 1; *esp* : being a respondent at law

re•sponse \ri-'späns\ *n* **1** : the act of replying : ANSWER **2** : words said or sung by the congregation or choir in a religious service **3** : a reaction of an organism to stimulation [Latin *responsum,* from *responsus,* past participle of *respondēre* "to answer"]

re•spon•si•bil•i•ty \ri-,spän-sə-'bil-ət-ē\ *n, pl* **-ties** **1** : the quality or state of being responsible **2** : RELIABILITY, TRUSTWORTHINESS **3** : something for which one is responsible

re•spon•si•ble \ri-'spän-sə-bəl\ *adj* **1** : liable to be called upon to give satisfaction (as for losses or misdeeds) : ANSWERABLE ⟨*responsible* for the damage⟩ **2** : willing and able to fulfill one's obligations : RELIABLE ⟨*responsible* citizens⟩ **3** : requiring a person to take charge of or be trusted with important matters ⟨a *responsible* job⟩ **4** : able to choose for oneself between right and wrong — **re•spon•si•ble•ness** *n* — **re•spon•si•bly** \-blē\ *adv*

re•spon•sive \ri-'spän-siv\ *adj* **1** : giving response : ANSWERING ⟨*responsive* glances⟩ **2** : quick to respond or react sympathetically : SENSITIVE **3** : using responses ⟨*responsive* worship⟩ — **re•spon•sive•ly** *adv* — **re•spon•sive•ness** *n*

[1]rest \'rest\ *n* **1** : REPOSE, SLEEP; *esp* : a bodily state characterized by minimal functional and metabolic activities **2 a** : freedom from activity **b** : a state of motionlessness or inactivity **c** : the repose of death **3** : a place for resting or lodging **4** : peace of mind or spirit **5 a (1)** : a silence in music equivalent in duration to a note of the same value **(2)** : a character representing such a silence **b** : a brief pause in reading **6** : something used for support ⟨leaned against the back *rest*⟩ [Old English]

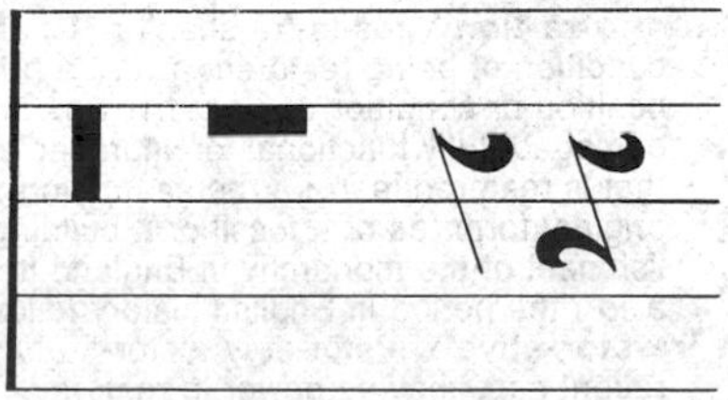

[1]rest 5a (2)

[2]rest *vb* **1 a (1)** : to get rest by lying down; *esp* : SLEEP **(2)** : to give rest to ⟨*rest* yourself on the couch⟩ **b** : to lie dead **2** : to refrain from work or activity **3** : to place or be placed for or as if for support ⟨*rest* one's feet on a hassock⟩ **4 a** : to remain for action or accomplishment ⟨the decision *rests* with you alone⟩ **b** : DEPEND ⟨the success of the flight *rests* on the wind⟩ **c** : to fix or be fixed in trust or confidence ⟨*rested* our hopes on their promise⟩ **5** : to stop voluntarily the introduction of evidence in a law case ⟨the defense *rests*⟩

[3]rest *n* : something that is left over or behind : REMAINDER — used with *the* [Middle French *reste,* from *rester* "to remain", from Latin *restare,* literally, "to stand back", from *re-* + *stare* "to stand"] **syn** see BALANCE

re•state \rē-'stāt, 'rē-\ *vt* : to state again or in another way — **re•state•ment** \-mənt\ *n*

res•tau•rant \'res-tə-rənt, -trənt, -tə-,ränt\ *n* : a public eating place [French, from *restaurer* "to restore", from Latin *restaurare*]

res•tau•ra•teur \,res-tə-rə-'tər\ *also* **res•tau•ran•teur** \-,rän-\ *n* : the operator or proprietor of a restaurant [French *restaurateur,* from Late Latin *restaurator* "restorer", from Latin *restaurare* "to restore"]

\ə\ **abut**	\au̇\ **out**	\i\ **tip**	\ȯ\ **saw**	\u̇\ **foot**
\ər\ **further**	\ch\ **chin**	\ī\ **life**	\ȯi\ **coin**	\y\ **yet**
\a\ **mat**	\e\ **pet**	\j\ **job**	\th\ **thin**	\yü\ **few**
\ā\ **take**	\ē\ **easy**	\ng\ **sing**	\th̲\ **this**	\yu̇\ **cure**
\ä\ **cot, cart**	\g\ **go**	\ō\ **bone**	\ü\ **food**	\zh\ **vision**

rest•ful \'rest-fəl\ *adj* **1** : giving rest ⟨a *restful* chair⟩ **2** : giving a feeling of rest : QUIET ⟨a *restful* scene⟩ — **rest•ful•ly** \-fə-lē\ *adv* — **rest•ful•ness** *n*
rest home *n* : an establishment that provides housing and care for the aged or for convalescents
rest house *n* : a building used for shelter by travelers
rest•ing *adj* **1** : DORMANT ⟨a *resting* spore⟩ **2** : VEGETATIVE 1a ⟨a *resting* nucleus⟩
res•ti•tu•tion \ˌres-tə-'tü-shən, -'tyü-\ *n* : the restoring of something to its rightful owner or the giving of an equivalent (as for loss or damage) ⟨make *restitution* for personal injuries⟩ [Old French, from Latin *restitutio,* from *restituere* "to restore", from *re-* + *statuere* "to set up", from *status* "position, condition, state"]
res•tive \'res-tiv\ *adj* **1** : stubbornly resisting control : BALKY **2** : fidgeting about : UNEASY [Middle French *restif,* from *rester* "to stop behind, remain", from Latin *restare*] — **res•tive•ly** *adv* — **res•tive•ness** *n*
• **syn** RESTIVE, RESTLESS mean showing signs of unrest. RESTIVE implies unwillingness to submit to discipline or follow orders ⟨the colonies were becoming increasingly *restive*⟩ RESTLESS implies constant, aimless activity as from anxiety, boredom, discontent, or discomfort ⟨*restless* children in rainy weather⟩
rest•less \'rest-ləs\ *adj* **1** : lacking rest : giving no rest ⟨a *restless* night⟩ **2** : continuously moving : UNQUIET ⟨the *restless* sea⟩ **3** : marked by or showing unrest especially of mind ⟨*restless* pacing⟩ **syn** see RESTIVE — **rest•less•ly** *adv* — **rest•less•ness** *n*
rest mass *n* : the mass of a body exclusive of additional mass acquired by the body when in motion according to the theory of relativity
re•stor•able \ri-'stōr-ə-bəl, -'stȯr-\ *adj* : fit to be restored or reclaimed
res•to•ra•tion \ˌres-tə-'rā-shən\ *n* **1** : an act of restoring or the condition of being restored: as **a** : a bringing back to a former position or condition **b** : RESTITUTION **c** : a restoring to an undamaged, fully functional, or improved condition **2** : something that is restored; *esp* : a representation or reconstruction of the original form (as of a fossil or a building) **3** *cap* : the reestablishment of the monarchy in England in 1660 under Charles II; *also* : the period in English history following this Restoration
[1]**re•stor•ative** \ri-'stōr-ət-iv, -'stȯr-\ *adj* : of or relating to restoration; *esp* : having power to restore
[2]**restorative** *n* : something that serves to restore to consciousness or health
re•store \ri-'stōr, -'stȯr\ *vt* **1** : to give back : RETURN ⟨*restored* the package to its owner⟩ **2** : to put or bring back into existence or use ⟨*restore* harmony to the club⟩ **3** : to bring back to or put back into a former or original state : RENEW **4** : to put again in possession of something [Old French *restorer,* from Latin *restaurare* "to renew, rebuild", alteration of *instaurare*] **syn** see RENEW — **re•stor•er** *n*
re•strain \ri-'strān\ *vt* **1 a** : to prevent from doing something **b** : CURB, REPRESS ⟨*restrain* one's anger⟩ **2** : to limit, restrict, or keep under control ⟨*restrain* trade⟩ **3** : to deprive of liberty; *esp* : to place under arrest or restraint [Middle French *restraindre,* from Latin *restringere,* from *re-* + *stringere* "to bind tight"] — **re•strain•able** \-'strā-nə-bəl\ *adj* — **re•strain•er** \-'strā-nər\ *n*
re•strained \ri-'strānd\ *adj* : marked by restraint : being without excess or extravagance — **re•strain•ed•ly** \-'strā-nəd-lē\ *adv*
re•straint \ri-'strānt\ *n* **1** : the act of restraining : the state of being restrained ⟨held in *restraint*⟩ **2** : a means of restraining : a restraining force or influence ⟨head *restraints* in a car⟩ ⟨place *restraints* on imports⟩ **3** : control over one's thoughts or feelings : RESERVE ⟨acted with admirable *restraint*⟩ [Middle French *restrainte,* from *restraindre* "to restrain"]
re•strict \ri-'strikt\ *vt* **1** : to confine within bounds : RESTRAIN **2** : to place under restrictions as to use [Latin *restrictus,* past participle of *restringere* "to restrain, restrict"] — **re•strict•ed** *adj* — **re•strict•ed•ly** *adv*
re•stric•tion \ri-'strik-shən\ *n* **1** : something (as a law or rule) that restricts **2** : an act of restricting : the condition of being restricted
re•stric•tive \ri-'strik-tiv\ *adj* **1** : serving or tending to restrict **2** : limiting the reference of a modified word or phrase ⟨*restrictive* clause⟩ — **re•stric•tive•ly** *adv* — **re•stric•tive•ness** *n*
rest room *n* : a room or suite of rooms providing personal facilities (as toilets)
[1]**re•sult** \ri-'zəlt\ *vi* **1** : to come about as an effect of something ⟨disease *results* from infection⟩ **2** : to have something as an effect ⟨a disease that *results* in death⟩ [Medieval Latin *resultare,* from Latin, "to rebound", from *re-* + *saltare* "to leap", from *saltus,* past participle of *salire* "to leap"]
[2]**result** *n* **1** : something that results as a consequence, issue, or conclusion **2** : a beneficial or tangible effect ⟨this method gets *results*⟩ **syn** see EFFECT — **re•sult•ful** \-fəl\ *adj* — **re•sult•less** \-ləs\ *adj*
[1]**re•sult•ant** \ri-'zəlt-nt\ *adj* : derived from or resulting from something else — **re•sult•ant•ly** *adv*
[2]**resultant** *n* **1** : something that results : OUTCOME **2** : a vector equal to the sum of a given set of vectors
re•sume \ri-'züm\ *vb* **1** : to take or occupy again ⟨*resume* your seats⟩ **2** : to begin again or go back to (as after an interruption) ⟨*resume* speaking⟩ [Latin *resumere,* from *re-* + *sumere* "to take"]
ré•su•mé *or* **re•su•me** \'rez-ə-ˌmā\ *n* : SUMMARY; *esp* : a short account of one's career and qualifications prepared typically by someone applying for a job [French *résumé,* from *résumer* "to resume, summarize", from Latin *resumere* "to resume"]
re•sump•tion \ri-'zəm-shən, -'zəmp-\ *n* : the action of resuming ⟨*resumption* of work⟩ [Late Latin *resumptio,* from Latin *resumere* "to resume"]
re•sur•gence \ri-'sər-jəns\ *n* : a rising again into life, activity, or prominence [derived from Latin *resurgens,* present participle of *resurgere* "to rise again"] — **re•sur•gent** \-jənt\ *adj*
res•ur•rect \ˌrez-ə-'rekt\ *vt* **1** : to raise from the dead : bring back to life **2** : to bring to view or into use again ⟨*resurrect* an old song⟩ [back-formation from *resurrection*]
res•ur•rec•tion \ˌrez-ə-'rek-shən\ *n* **1 a** *cap* : the rising of Christ from the dead **b** *often cap* : the rising again to life of all the human dead before the final judgment **2** : RESURGENCE, REVIVAL [Late Latin *resurrectio,* from Latin *resurrectus,* past participle of *resurgere* "to rise again", from *re-* + *surgere* "to rise"] — **res•ur•rec•tion•al** \-shnəl, -shən-l\ *adj*
re•sus•ci•tate \ri-'səs-ə-ˌtāt\ *vb* : to revive from apparent death or from unconsciousness; *also* : REVITALIZE [Latin *resuscitare,* from *re-* + *suscitare* "to stir up", from *sub-, sus-* "up" + *citare* "to put in motion, stir"] — **re•sus•ci•ta•tion** \-ˌsəs-ə-'tā-shən\ *n* — **re•sus•ci•ta•tive** \-'səs-ə-ˌtāt-iv\ *adj*
re•sus•ci•ta•tor \ri-'səs-ə-ˌtāt-ər\ *n* : one that resuscitates; *esp* : an apparatus used to relieve asphyxiation
ret \'ret\ *vb* **ret•ted; ret•ting** : to soak so as to loosen the fiber from the woody tissue ⟨*ret* flax⟩ [Dutch *reten*]
[1]**re•tail** \'rē-ˌtāl, *especially for 2 also* ri-'\ *vb* **1** : to sell in small quantities directly to the ultimate consumer **2** : TELL 2a, RETELL [Middle French *retaillier* "to cut back, divide into pieces", from *re-* "re-" + *taillier* "to cut", from Late Latin *taliare,* from Latin *talea* "twig, cutting"] — **re•tail•er** *n*
[2]**re•tail** \'rē-ˌtāl\ *n* : the sale of commodities or goods in small quantities directly to consumers — **at retail 1** : at a retailer's price **2** : [4]RETAIL
[3]**re•tail** \'rē-ˌtāl\ *adj* : of, relating to, or engaged in the sale of commodities at retail ⟨*retail* trade⟩
[4]**re•tail** \'rē-ˌtāl\ *adv* **1** : in small quantities **2** : from a retailer
re•tain \ri-'tān\ *vt* **1 a** : to keep in possession or use ⟨*retain* knowledge⟩ **b** : to keep in one's employ or service; *esp* : to employ by paying a retainer **2** : to hold secure or intact ⟨lead *retains* heat⟩ [Middle French *retenir,* from Latin *retinēre* "to hold back, keep", from *re-* + *tenēre* "to hold"]
retained object *n* : an object in a passive construction ⟨*me* in *a book was given me* and *book* in *I was given a book* are *retained objects*⟩
[1]**re•tain•er** \ri-'tā-nər\ *n* : a fee paid (as to a lawyer) for advice or services or for a claim upon services in case of need [Middle English *reteiner* "act of withholding", from *reteinen* "to retain" + Anglo-French *-er* (as in *weyver* "waiver")]
[2]**retainer** *n* **1** : one that retains **2** : a servant or follower in a wealthy household
[1]**re•take** \rē-'tāk, 'rē-\ *vt* **-took** \-'tu̇k\; **-tak•en** \-'tā-kən\; **-tak•ing** : to take again; *esp* : to film again
[2]**re•take** \'rē-ˌtāk\ *n* : a second filming or photograph
re•tal•i•ate \ri-'tal-ē-ˌāt\ *vi* : to return like for like; *esp* : to get even [Late Latin *retaliare,* from Latin *re-* + *talio* "legal retaliation"] — **re•tal•i•a•tion** \-ˌtal-ē-'ā-shən\ *n* — **re•tal•i•a•tive**

\-'tal-ē-ˌāt-iv\ *adj* — **re•tal•ia•to•ry** \-'tal-yə-ˌtōr-ē, -ˌtȯr-\ *adj*

re•tard \ri-'tärd\ *vt* **:** to slow up or hold back [Latin *retardare,* from *re-* + *tardus* "slow"] — **re•tard•er** *n*

re•tar•dant \ri-'tärd-nt\ *adj* **:** serving or tending to retard — **retardant** *n*

re•tar•date \ri-'tär-ˌdāt\ *n* **:** one who is retarded mentally

re•tar•da•tion \ˌrē-ˌtär-'dā-shən\ *n* **1 :** an act or instance of retarding **2 :** the extent to which something is retarded **3 :** an abnormal slowness especially of mental or bodily development

re•tard•ed \ri-'tärd-əd\ *adj* **:** slow or limited in intellectual or emotional development or academic progress

retch \'rech, *especially British* 'rēch\ *vb* **:** VOMIT 1; *also* **:** to try to vomit [Old English *hrǣcan* "to spit, clear the throat"]

re•te \'rēt-ē\ *n, pl* **re•tia** \-ē-ə\ **:** an anatomical network (as of nerves or blood vessels) [Latin, "net"]

re•ten•tion \ri-'ten-chən\ *n* **1 :** the act of retaining **:** the state of being retained **2 :** power of or capacity for retaining **3 :** something retained [Latin *retentio,* from *retinēre* "to retain"]

re•ten•tive \ri-'tent-iv\ *adj* **:** having ability to retain; *esp* **:** having a good memory — **re•ten•tive•ly** *adv* — **re•ten•tive•ness** *n*

re•ten•tiv•i•ty \ˌrē-ˌten-'tiv-ət-ē\ *n* **:** the power of retaining; *esp* **:** the capacity for retaining magnetism after the action of the magnetizing force has ceased

ret•i•cence \'ret-ə-səns\ *n* **:** the quality or state of being reticent

ret•i•cent \-sənt\ *adj* **1 :** inclined to be silent or secretive **:** UNCOMMUNICATIVE **2 :** restrained in expression or presentation [Latin *reticens,* present participle of *reticēre* "to keep silent", from *re-* + *tacēre* "to be silent"] **syn** see SILENT — **ret•i•cent•ly** *adv*

re•tic•u•lar \ri-'tik-yə-lər\ *adj* **:** RETICULATE; *also* **:** of, relating to, or being a reticulum

[1]re•tic•u•late \-lət\ *adj* **:** resembling a net [Latin *reticulatus,* from *reticulum* "network", from *rete* "net"] — **re•tic•u•late•ly** *adv*

[2]re•tic•u•late \-ˌlāt\ *vb* **1 :** to divide, mark, or construct so as to form a network **2 :** to distribute by a network **3 :** to become reticulated

re•tic•u•la•tion \ri-ˌtik-yə-'lā-shən\ *n* **:** a reticulate formation **:** NETWORK

ret•i•cule \'ret-i-ˌkyül\ *n* **:** a woman's drawstring bag used especially as a carryall [French *réticule,* from Latin *reticulum* "network, network bag", from *rete* "net"]

re•tic•u•lo•en•do•the•li•al system \ri-'tik-yə-lō-ˌen-də-'thē-lē-əl-\ *n* **:** a system of scattered cells derived from mesenchyme that includes all phagocytic cells in the body except circulating leukocytes [*reticulum* + *endothelium*]

re•tic•u•lum \ri-'tik-yə-ləm\ *n, pl* **-la** \-lə\ **1 :** the second stomach of a ruminant mammal **2 :** a netlike structure [Latin, "network", from *rete* "net"]

ret•i•na \'ret-n-ə, 'ret-nə\ *n, pl* **retinas** *or* **ret•i•nae** \-n-ˌē, -n-ˌī\ **:** the sensory membrane that lines the eye, receives the image formed by the lens, is the immediate instrument of vision, and is connected with the brain by the optic nerve [Medieval Latin] — **ret•i•nal** \'ret-n-əl, 'ret-nəl\ *adj*

ret•i•nal \'ret-n-ˌal, -ˌȯl\ *n* **:** either a yellowish or an orange aldehyde derived from vitamin A that in combination with proteins forms the visual pigments of the retinal rods and cones [derived from *retina*]

ret•i•nene \'ret-n-ˌēn\ *n* **:** RETINAL

ret•i•nue \'ret-n-ˌü, -ˌyü\ *n* **:** the body of retainers who follow a distinguished person **:** SUITE [Middle French *retenue,* from *retenu,* past participle of *retenir* "to retain"]

re•tire \ri-'tīr\ *vb* **1 :** to withdraw or cause to withdraw from action or danger **:** RETREAT **2 :** to withdraw especially for privacy **3 :** to give up or cause to give up one's position or occupation **4 :** to go to bed **5 a :** to withdraw from circulation **:** RECALL **b :** to withdraw (as obsolete equipment) from usual use or service **6 :** to put out (a batter or side) in baseball [Middle French *retirer,* from *re-* "re-" + *tirer* "to draw"]

re•tired \ri-'tīrd\ *adj* **1 :** HIDDEN, SECLUDED ⟨a *retired* spot in the woods⟩ **2 :** withdrawn from active duties or business **3 :** received by or due to a person who has retired ⟨*retired* pay⟩ — **re•tired•ly** \-'tī-rəd-lē, -'tīrd-\ *adv* — **re•tired•ness** \-'tīrd-nəs\ *n*

re•tire•ment \ri-'tīr-mənt\ *n* **:** an act of retiring **:** the state of being retired; *esp* **:** a giving up of one's position or occupation

re•tir•ing \ri-'tīr-ing\ *adj* **:** RESERVED 1, SHY — **re•tir•ing•ly** \-ing-lē\ *adv* — **re•tir•ing•ness** *n*

re•tool \rē-'tül, 'rē-\ *vt* **:** to equip anew with new or different tools ⟨*retool* a factory for making a new product⟩

[1]re•tort \ri-'tȯrt\ *vb* **1 :** to answer back **:** reply angrily or sharply **2 :** to reply (as to an argument) with a counter argument [Latin *retortus,* past participle of *retorquēre* "to twist back, hurl back, retort", from *re-* + *torquēre* "to twist"]

[2]retort *n* **:** a quick, witty, or cutting reply; *esp* **:** one that turns the first speaker's words against him

[3]re•tort \ri-'tȯrt, 'rē-ˌ\ *n* **:** a vessel in which substances are distilled or decomposed by heat [Middle French *retorte,* from Medieval Latin *retorta,* from Latin *retorquēre* "to twist back"; from its shape]

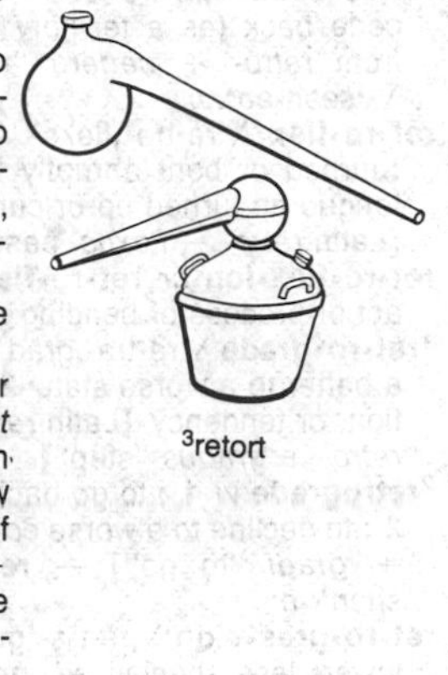

[3]retort

re•touch \rē-'təch, 'rē-\ *vt* **:** to touch up; *esp* **:** to alter (as a photographic negative) in order to produce a more desirable appearance — **re•touch** \'rē-ˌtəch, rē-', 'rē-'\ *n* — **re•touch•er** \rē-'təch-ər, 'rē-\ *n*

re•trace \rē-'trās, 'rē-\ *vt* **:** to trace again or back

re•tract \ri-'trakt\ *vt* **1 :** to draw or pull back or in ⟨a cat can *retract* its claws⟩ **2 :** to take back (as an offer or accusation) **:** WITHDRAW [Latin *retractus,* past participle of *retrahere* "to retract", from *re-* + *trahere* "to draw"] **syn** see RECANT — **re•tract•able** \-'trak-tə-bəl\ *adj*

re•trac•tile \ri-'trak-tl, -ˌtīl\ *adj* **:** capable of being drawn back or in ⟨the *retractile* claws of a cat⟩

re•trac•tion \ri-'trak-shən\ *n* **1 :** a statement retracting something previously said or published **2 :** an act of retracting **:** the state of being retracted

re•trac•tor \ri-'trak-tər\ *n* **:** one that retracts; *esp* **:** a muscle that draws an organ or part in or back — compare PROTRACTOR

[1]re•tread \rē-'tred, 'rē-\ *vt* **re•tread•ed; re•tread•ing :** to cement, mold, and vulcanize a new tread of camelback upon the bare cord fabric of (a worn pneumatic tire)

[2]re•tread \'rē-ˌtred\ *n* **1 :** a new tread on a tire **2 :** a retreaded tire

[1]re•treat \ri-'trēt\ *n* **1 a :** an act or process of withdrawing especially from what is difficult, dangerous, or disagreeable **b :** the usually forced withdrawal of troops from an enemy or from an advanced position **c :** a signal for retreating **d :** a signal given by bugle at the beginning of a military flag-lowering ceremony **e :** a military flag-lowering ceremony **2 :** a place of privacy or safety **:** REFUGE **3 :** a period of group withdrawal for prayer, meditation, and instruction under a director [Middle French *retrait,* from *retraire* "to withdraw", from Latin *retrahere* "to retract, withdraw"]

[2]retreat *vi* **1 :** to make a retreat **2 :** to slope backward

re•trench \ri-'trench\ *vb* **1 :** to cut down (as expenses) **:** REDUCE **2 :** to reduce expenses **:** ECONOMIZE [obsolete French *retrencher,* from Middle French *retrenchier,* from *re-* + *trenchier* "to cut"] — **re•trench•ment** \-mənt\ *n*

re•tri•al \rē-'trī-əl, 'rē-ˌ, -'trīl\ *n* **:** a second trial or experiment

ret•ri•bu•tion \ˌre-trə-'byü-shən\ *n* **:** something given in payment for an offense **:** PUNISHMENT [Middle French, from Late Latin *retributio,* from Latin *retribuere* "to pay back", from *re-* + *tribuere* "to pay"]

re•trib•u•tive \ri-'trib-yət-iv\ *adj* **:** of, relating to, or marked by retribution — **re•trib•u•tive•ly** *adv*

re•trib•u•to•ry \-yə-ˌtōr-ē, -ˌtȯr-\ *adj* **:** RETRIBUTIVE

re•triev•al \ri-'trē-vəl\ *n* **1 :** an act or process of retrieving **2 :** possibility of being retrieved or of recovering

\ə\ **abut**	\au̇\ **out**	\i\ **tip**	\ȯ\ **saw**	\u̇\ **foot**
\ər\ **further**	\ch\ **chin**	\ī\ **life**	\ȯi\ **coin**	\y\ **yet**
\a\ **mat**	\e\ **pet**	\j\ **job**	\th\ **thin**	\yü\ **few**
\ā\ **take**	\ē\ **easy**	\ng\ **sing**	\t͟h\ **this**	\yu̇\ **cure**
\ä\ **cot, cart**	\g\ **go**	\ō\ **bone**	\ü\ **food**	\zh\ **vision**

[1]re·trieve \ri-'trēv\ *vb* **1 :** to find and bring in killed or wounded game ⟨a dog that *retrieves* well⟩ **2 :** to recover, restore, repair, or make good (as a loss or damage) ⟨*retrieve* a damaged reputation⟩ [Middle French *retrouver* "to find again", from *re-* "re-" + *trouver* "to find"] — **re·triev·able** \-'trē-və-bəl\ *adj*

[2]retrieve *n* **1 :** RETRIEVAL **2 :** the successful return of a ball that is difficult to reach or control (as in tennis)

re·triev·er \ri-'trē-vər\ *n* **:** one that retrieves; *esp* **:** a vigorous active medium-sized dog with heavy water-resistant coat developed by crossbreeding and used especially for retrieving game

retro- *prefix* **:** backward **:** back ⟨*retro*rocket⟩ [Latin, from *retro*]

ret·ro·ac·tive \,re-trō-'ak-tiv\ *adj* **:** intended to apply or take effect at a date in the past ⟨a *retroactive* pay raise⟩ — **ret·ro·ac·tive·ly** *adv*

ret·ro·cede \,re-trō-'sēd\ *vb* **1 :** to go back **:** RECEDE **2 :** to cede back (as a territory or jurisdiction) [Latin *retrocedere,* from *retro-* + *cedere* "to go, cede"] — **ret·ro·ces·sion** \-'sesh-ən\ *n*

ret·ro·flex \'re-trə-,fleks\ *or* **ret·ro·flexed** \-,flekst\ *adj* **1 :** turned or bent abruptly backward **2 :** pronounced with the tongue tip turned up or curled back just under the hard palate [Latin *retro-* + *flexus,* past participle of *flectere* "to bend"]

ret·ro·flex·ion *or* **ret·ro·flec·tion** \,re-trə-'flek-shən\ *n* **:** the act or process of bending back **:** the state of being bent back

[1]ret·ro·grade \'re-trə-,grād\ *adj* **1 :** going or inclined to go from a better to a worse state **2 :** having a backward direction, motion, or tendency [Latin *retrogradus* "moving backward", from *retro-* + *gradus* "step"]

[2]retrograde *vi* **1 :** to go back **:** RETREAT ⟨a glacier *retrogrades*⟩ **2 :** to decline to a worse condition [Latin *retrogradi,* from *retro-* + *gradi* "to go"] — **ret·ro·gra·da·tion** \,re-trō-grā-'dā-shən\ *n*

ret·ro·gres·sion \,re-trə-'gresh-ən\ *n* **:** reversion to an earlier, lower, less specialized, or less developed state or condition [derived from Latin *retrogressus,* past participle of *retrogradi* "to move backward", from *retro-* + *gradi* "to step, go"] — **ret·ro·gress** \,re-trə-'gres\ *vi* — **ret·ro·gres·sive** \-'gres-iv\ *adj* — **ret·ro·gres·sive·ly** *adv*

ret·ro·rock·et \'re-trō-,räk-ət\ *n* **:** an auxiliary rocket on an airplane, missile, or spacecraft that produces thrust in a direction opposite to or at an oblique angle to the motion of the object for deceleration

ret·ro·spect \'re-trə-,spekt\ *n* **:** a looking back on things past **:** reflection on past events [*retro-* + *-spect* (as in *prospect*)]

ret·ro·spec·tion \,re-trə-'spek-shən\ *n* **1 :** the act or power of recalling the past **2 :** a review of past events

ret·ro·spec·tive \-'spek-tiv\ *adj* **1 :** of, relating to, characteristic of, or given to retrospection **2 :** affecting things past **:** RETROACTIVE — **ret·ro·spec·tive·ly** *adv*

[1]re·turn \ri-'tərn\ *vb* **1 :** to come or go back **2 :** REPLY, ANSWER **3 :** to make (as a report) officially by submitting a statement ⟨the jury *returned* a verdict⟩ **4 :** to reelect to office ⟨a candidate *returned* by a large majority⟩ **5 :** to bring, carry, send, or put back **:** RESTORE ⟨*return* a book to the library⟩ **6 :** to bring in (as profit) **:** YIELD **7 :** REPAY ⟨*return* borrowed money⟩ **8 :** to send or say in response or reply ⟨*return* thanks⟩ [Middle French *retourner,* from *re-* "re-" + *tourner* "to turn"] — **re·turn·er** *n*

[2]return *n* **1 a :** the act of coming back to or from a place or condition **b :** a regular or frequent returning **:** RECURRENCE ⟨the *return* of spring⟩ **2 a :** a report of the results of balloting — usually used in pl. ⟨election *returns*⟩ **b :** a completed income tax form **3 :** a means for conveying something (as water) back to its starting point **4 a :** the profit from labor, investment, or business **:** YIELD **b :** the rate of profit per unit of cost **5 a :** the act of returning something to a former place, condition, or ownership **b :** something returned **6 :** an answering or retaliatory play: as **a :** the act of hitting a ball back to an opponent (as in tennis) **b :** the running with a football after receiving a kick or intercepting a pass of the other team

[3]return *adj* **:** played, delivered, or given in return ⟨a *return* call⟩ ⟨a *return* game⟩

re·turn·able \ri-'tər-nə-bəl\ *adj* **1 :** that may be returned ⟨*returnable* bottles⟩ **2 :** that must be returned ⟨a library book *returnable* in two weeks⟩

re·turn·ee \ri-,tər-'nē\ *n* **:** one who returns; *esp* **:** one returning to the United States after military service abroad

re·uni·fy \rē-'yü-nə-,fī, 'rē-\ *vt* **:** to restore unity to — **re·uni·fi·ca·tion** \rē-,yü-nə-fə-'kā-shən\ *n*

re·union \rē-'yü-nyən, 'rē-\ *n* **1 :** the act of reuniting **:** the state of being reunited **2 :** a reuniting of persons ⟨a class *reunion*⟩

re·unite \,rē-yü-'nīt\ *vb* **:** to come or bring together again after a separation

re·use \rē-'yüz, 'rē-\ *vt* **:** to use again — **re·us·able** \-'yü-zə-bəl\ *adj* — **re·use** \-'yüs\ *n*

[1]rev \'rev\ *n* **:** a revolution of a motor

[2]rev *vb* **revved; rev·ving :** to operate or cause to operate at an increasing speed of revolution ⟨*rev* up a motor⟩

re·val·u·ate \rē-'val-yə-,wāt, 'rē-\ *vt* **:** REVALUE — **re·val·u·a·tion** \rē-,val-yə-'wā-shən\ *n*

re·val·ue \rē-'val-yü, 'rē-\ *vt* **:** to make a new valuation of

re·vamp \rē-'vamp, 'rē-\ *vt* **1 :** RENOVATE, RECONSTRUCT **2 :** to work over **:** REVISE

re·veal \ri-'vēl\ *vt* **1 :** to make known ⟨*reveal* a secret⟩ **2 :** to show plainly **:** DISPLAY [Middle French *reveler,* from Latin *revelare* "to uncover, reveal", from *re-* + *velare* "to cover", from *velum* "veil"] — **re·veal·able** \-'vē-lə-bəl\ *adj* — **re·veal·er** *n*

re·veal·ment \-'vēl-mənt\ *n* **:** an act of revealing **:** REVELATION

rev·eil·le \'rev-ə-lē\ *n* **:** a signal sounded at about sunrise on a bugle or drum to call soldiers or sailors to duty [French *réveillez,* imperative pl. of *réveiller* "to awaken", from *re-* "re-" + *éveiller* "to awaken", derived from Latin *ex-* + *vigilare* "to keep watch, stay awake"]

[1]rev·el \'rev-əl\ *vi* **rev·eled** *or* **rev·elled; rev·el·ing** *or* **rev·el·ling** \'rev-ling, -ə-ling\ **1 :** to take part in a revel **2 :** to take intense satisfaction ⟨*reveling* in success⟩ [Middle French *reveler,* literally, "to rebel", from Latin *rebellare*] — **rev·el·er** *or* **rev·el·ler** \'rev-lər, -ə-lər\ *n*

[2]revel *n* **:** a noisy or merry celebration or party

rev·e·la·tion \,rev-ə-'lā-shən\ *n* **1 :** an act of revealing or communicating divine truth **2 a :** an act of revealing to view **b :** something that is revealed; *esp* **:** an enlightening or astonishing disclosure [Middle French, from Late Latin *revelatio,* from Latin *revelare* "to reveal"]

Rev·e·la·tion \,rev-ə-'lā-shən\ *n* — see BIBLE table

re·vel·a·to·ry \'rev-ə-lə-,tōr-ē, -,tȯr-, ri-'vel-ə-\ *adj* **:** of, relating to, or characteristic of revelation

rev·el·ry \'rev-əl-rē\ *n, pl* **-ries :** boisterous merrymaking

[1]re·venge \ri-'venj\ *vt* **1 :** to inflict injury in return for ⟨*revenge* an insult⟩ **2 :** to avenge for a wrong done ⟨able to *revenge* themselves on their former persecutors⟩ [Middle French *revengier,* from *re-* + *vengier* "to avenge", from Latin *vindicare*] **syn** see AVENGE — **re·veng·er** *n*

[2]revenge *n* **1 :** an act or instance of revenging **2 :** a desire to repay injury for injury **3 :** an opportunity for getting satisfaction

re·venge·ful \-fəl\ *adj* **:** full of or given to revenge **:** VINDICTIVE — **re·venge·ful·ly** \-fə-lē\ *adv* — **re·venge·ful·ness** *n*

rev·e·nue \'rev-ə-,nü, -,nyü\ *n* **1 :** the income from an investment **2 :** the income that a government collects for public use **3 :** the income produced by a given source [Middle French, from *revenir* "to return", from Latin *revenire,* from *re-* + *venire* "to come"]

rev·e·nu·er \-,nü-ər, -,nyü-\ *n* **:** a revenue officer or boat

revenue stamp *n* **:** a stamp (as on a cigar box) for use as evidence of payment of a tax

re·ver·ber·ant \ri-'vər-brənt, -bə-rənt\ *adj* **:** that reverberates — **re·ver·ber·ant·ly** *adv*

re·ver·ber·ate \ri-'vər-bə-,rāt\ *vi* **:** RESOUND, ECHO ⟨the shot *reverberated* among the hills⟩ [Latin *reverberare* "to cause to rebound", from *re-* + *verberare* "to lash", from *verber* "rod"] — **re·ver·ber·a·tion** \-,vər-bə-'rā-shən\ *n* — **re·ver·ber·a·tive** \-'vər-bə-,rāt-iv\ *adj*

[1]re·ver·ber·a·to·ry \ri-'vər-bə-rə-,tōr-ē, -brə-, -,tȯr-\ *adj* **:** acting by reverberation

[2]reverberatory *n, pl* **-tories :** a furnace or kiln in which heat is radiated from the roof onto the material treated

[1]re·vere \ri-'viər\ *vt* **:** to show devotion and honor to [Latin *revereri,* from *re-* + *vereri* "to fear, respect"]

• **syn** REVERE, REVERENCE, VENERATE, WORSHIP mean to hold in profound respect and honor. REVERE further implies deference and tenderness of feeling ⟨*revered* their grandparents⟩ REVERENCE suggests a self-denying acknowledging of what has a deep and inviolate claim to respect ⟨*reverence* truth⟩ VENERATE implies regarding as holy or sacrosanct especially because of age; WORSHIP implies paying homage to or as if to a divine being ⟨*worship* idols⟩

[2]**revere** *n* : REVERS [by alteration]

[1]**rev•er•ence** \'rev-rəns, 'rev-ə-rəns, 'rev-ərns\ *n* **1 a** : honor or respect felt or shown : DEFERENCE **b** : a feeling of worshipful respect : VENERATION **2** : a gesture of respect (as a bow) **3** : the state of being revered or honored **4** : one held in reverence — used as a title for a member of the clergy **syn** see DEFERENCE

[2]**reverence** *vt* : to regard or treat with reverence **syn** see REVERE

[1]**rev•er•end** \'rev-rənd, 'rev-ə-rənd, 'rev-ərnd\ *adj* **1** : worthy of reverence : REVERED **2** *often cap* : being a member of the clergy — used as a title usually preceded by *the* and followed by a title or a full name ⟨the *Reverend* Mr. Doe⟩ ⟨the *Reverend* John M. Doe⟩ [Middle French, from Latin *reverendus,* from *revereri* "to revere"]

[2]**reverend** *n* : a member of the clergy ⟨the *reverend* spoke at the meeting⟩

rev•er•ent \'rev-rənt, 'rev-ə-rənt, 'rev-ərnt\ *adj* : very respectful : showing reverence [Latin *reverens,* present participle of *revereri* "to revere"] — **rev•er•ent•ly** *adv*

rev•er•en•tial \ˌrev-ə-'ren-chəl\ *adj* **1** : proceeding from or expressing reverence ⟨*reverential* awe⟩ **2** : inspiring reverence — **rev•er•en•tial•ly** \-'rench-lē, -ə-lē\ *adv*

rev•er•ie *or* **rev•ery** \'rev-rē, -ə-rē\ *n, pl* **-er•ies** **1** : DAYDREAM **2** : the condition of being lost in thought [French *rêverie,* from Middle French, "delirium", from *resver, rever* "to wander, be delirious"]

re•vers \ri-'viər, -'veər\ *n, pl* **re•vers** \-'viərz, -'veərz\ : a lapel especially on a woman's garment [French, from Middle French *revers* "turned back, reversed"]

revers

re•vers•al \ri-'vər-səl\ *n* : an act or the process of reversing or being reversed

[1]**re•verse** \ri-'vərs\ *adj* **1** : opposite or contrary to a previous or normal condition ⟨*reverse* order⟩ **2** : acting or operating in a manner contrary to the usual **3** : effecting reverse movement ⟨*reverse* gear⟩ [Middle French *revers,* from Latin *reversus,* past participle of *revertere* "to turn back"] — **re•verse•ly** *adv*

[2]**reverse** *vb* **1** : to turn completely about or upside down or inside out **2** : ANNUL: as **a** : to overthrow or set aside (a legal decision) by a contrary decision **b** : to cause to take an opposite point of view **c** : to change to the contrary ⟨*reverse* a policy⟩ **3 a** : to go or cause to go in the opposite direction **b** : to put (as a car) into reverse — **re•vers•er** *n*

• **syn** REVERSE, TRANSPOSE, INVERT mean to change to the opposite position. REVERSE may imply change in order, direction of motion, or meaning; TRANSPOSE implies a change in order or relative position of units often through exchange of position; INVERT applies chiefly to turning upside down or inside out, less often end for end

[3]**reverse** *n* **1** : something directly contrary to something else : OPPOSITE **2** : an act or instance of reversing; *esp* : a change for the worse ⟨financial *reverses*⟩ **3** : the back part of something **4 a** : a gear that reverses something; *also* : the whole mechanism brought into play when such a gear is used **b** : movement in reverse

re•vers•ibil•i•ty \ri-ˌvər-sə-'bil-ət-ē\ *n* : the quality or state of being reversible

[1]**re•vers•ible** \ri-'vər-sə-bəl\ *adj* : capable of being reversed or of reversing: as **a** : having two finished usable sides ⟨*reversible* fabric⟩ **b** : wearable with either side out ⟨a *reversible* coat⟩ — **re•vers•ibly** \-blē\ *adv*

[2]**reversible** *n* : a reversible fabric or garment

re•ver•sion \ri-'vər-zhən\ *n* **1** : a right of future possession (as of property or a title) **2 a** : an act or the process of returning (as to a former condition) **b** : reappearance of an ancestral character **3** : an act or instance of turning the opposite way : the state of being so turned **4** : a product of reversion (as an organism with atavistic characteristics) [Middle French, from Latin *reversio* "act of turning back", from *revertere* "to turn back"]

re•ver•sion•ary \-zhə-ˌner-ē\ *adj* : of, relating to, constituting, or involving especially a legal reversion

re•vert \ri-'vərt\ *vi* **1** : to come or go back ⟨many *reverted* to savagery⟩ **2** : to undergo reversion [Middle French *revertir,* from *revertere* "to turn back", from *re-* + *vertere* "to turn"] — **re•vert•er** *n* — **re•vert•ible** \-'vərt-ə-bəl\ *adj*

re•vet \ri-'vet\ *vt* **re•vet•ted; re•vet•ting** : to face (as an embankment) with a revetment [French *revêtir,* literally, "to clothe again, dress up", from Latin *revestire,* from *re-* + *vestire* "to clothe"]

re•vet•ment \-mənt\ *n* **1** : a facing (as of stone) to sustain an embankment **2** : EMBANKMENT; *esp* : a protective barricade (as against bomb splinters)

re•vict•ual \rē-'vit-l, 'rē-\ *vb* : to resupply with provisions

[1]**re•view** \ri-'vyü\ *n* **1 a** : a formal military inspection **b** : a military ceremony honoring a person or an event **2** : a general survey ⟨a *review* of the week's news⟩ **3** : an act of inspecting or examining ⟨the auditors' *review* was thorough⟩ **4** : judicial reexamination of the proceedings of a lower court **5 a** : a critical evaluation (as of a book or play) **b** : a magazine devoted chiefly to reviews and essays **6 a** : a retrospective view or survey **b** (1) : renewed study of material previously studied (2) : an exercise facilitating such study **7** : REVUE [Middle French *revue,* from *revoir* "to look over", from *re-* "re-" + *voir* "to see", from Latin *vidēre*]

[2]**review** *vb* **1** : to look at a thing again : study or examine again ⟨*review* a lesson⟩; *esp* : to reexamine judicially **2** : to make a formal inspection of (as troops) **3** : to give a criticism of (as a book or play) **4** : to look back on ⟨*review* accomplishments⟩ — **re•view•er** *n*

re•vile \ri-'vīl\ *vb* **1** : to subject to verbal abuse **2** : to use abusive language : RAIL [Middle French *reviler* "to despise", from *re-* "re-" + *vil* "vile"] — **re•vile•ment** \-mənt\ *n* — **re•vil•er** *n*

re•vis•able \ri-'vī-zə-bəl\ *adj* : capable of being revised

re•vis•al \-zəl\ *n* : an act of revising : REVISION

[1]**re•vise** \ri-'vīz\ *vt* **1** : to look over again in order to correct or improve ⟨*revise* a manuscript⟩ **2** : to make a new, amended, improved, or up-to-date version or arrangement of ⟨*revise* a dictionary⟩ [French *reviser,* from Latin *revisere* "to look at again", from *revisus,* past participle of *revidere* "to see again", from *re-* + *vidēre* "to see"] — **re•vis•er** *or* **re•vi•sor** \-'vī-zər\ *n*

[2]**re•vise** \'rē-ˌvīz, ri-'\ *n* : an act of revising : REVISION

re•vi•sion \ri-'vizh-ən\ *n* **1** : an act of revising (as a manuscript) **2** : a revised version — **re•vi•sion•ary** \-'vizh-ə-ˌner-ē\ *adj*

re•vi•sion•ism \ri-'vizh-ə-ˌniz-əm\ *n* : a movement in revolutionary Marxian socialism favoring an evolutionary spirit — **re•vi•sion•ist** \-'vizh-nəst, -ə-nəst\ *adj or n*

re•vi•so•ry \ri-'vīz-rē, -ə-rē\ *adj* : having the power or purpose to revise ⟨*revisory* body⟩ ⟨a *revisory* function⟩

re•vi•tal•i•za•tion \rē-ˌvīt-l-ə-'zā-shən\ *n* **1** : an act or instance of revitalizing **2** : something revitalized

re•vi•tal•ize \rē-'vīt-l-ˌīz, 'rē-\ *vt* : to give new life or vigor to

re•viv•al \ri-'vī-vəl\ *n* : an act or instance of reviving : the state of being revived: as **a** : a reviving of interest (as in art, literature, or religion) **b** : a new publication or presentation (as of a book or play) **c** : a renewed flourishing ⟨a *revival* of business⟩ **d** : a meeting or series of meetings conducted by a preacher to arouse religious emotions or to make converts

re•viv•al•ism \-'vī-və-ˌliz-əm\ *n* : the often highly emotional spirit or methods characteristic of religious revivals

re•viv•al•ist \ri-'vī-və-ləst\ *n* : one who conducts revivals — **re•viv•al•is•tic** \-ˌvī-və-'lis-tik\ *adj*

re•vive \ri-'vīv\ *vb* **1** : to bring back or come back to life, consciousness, or activity : make or become fresh or strong again **2** : to bring back into use ⟨trying to *revive* an old fashion⟩ [Middle French *revivre,* from Latin *revivere* "to live again", from *re-* + *vivere* "to live"] — **re•viv•er** *n*

re•viv•i•fy \rē-'viv-ə-ˌfī\ *vt* **-fied; -fy•ing** : to give new life to : REVIVE — **re•viv•i•fi•ca•tion** \-ˌviv-ə-fə-'kā-shən\ *n*

rev•o•ca•ble \'rev-ə-kə-bəl\ *adj* : capable of being revoked [Middle French, from Latin *revocabilis,* from *revocare* "to revoke"]

rev•o•ca•tion \ˌrev-ə-'kā-shən\ *n* : an act or instance of revoking

\ə\ **abut**	\au̇\ **out**	\i\ **tip**	\ȯ\ **saw**	\u̇\ **foot**
\ər\ **further**	\ch\ **chin**	\ī\ **life**	\ȯi\ **coin**	\y\ **yet**
\a\ **mat**	\e\ **pet**	\j\ **job**	\th\ **thin**	\yü\ **few**
\ā\ **take**	\ē\ **easy**	\ng\ **sing**	\t͟h\ **this**	\yu̇\ **cure**
\ä\ **cot, cart**	\g\ **go**	\ō\ **bone**	\ü\ **food**	\zh\ **vision**

re•voke \ri-ˈvōk\ *vb* **:** to put an end to (as a law, order, or privilege) by withdrawing, repealing, or canceling **:** ANNUL ⟨*revoke* a driver's license for speeding⟩ **[**Middle French *revoquer,* from Latin *revocare,* literally, "to call back", from *re-* + *vocare* "to call"**]** — **re•vok•er** *n*

1re•volt \ri-ˈvōlt\ *vb* **1 :** to renounce allegiance or subjection (as to a government) **:** REBEL **2 :** to experience or cause to experience disgust or shock ⟨my tender nature *revolts* against such treatment⟩ **[**Middle French *revolter,* from Italian *rivoltare* "to overthrow", derived from Latin *revolvere* "to revolve, roll back"**]** — **re•volt•er** *n*

2revolt *n* **1 :** an act or instance of revolting **2 :** a renunciation of allegiance to a government or other legitimate authority; *esp* **:** INSURRECTION **syn** see REBELLION

re•volt•ing *adj* **:** extremely offensive **:** NAUSEATING — **re•volt•ing•ly** \-ˈvōl-ting-lē\ *adv*

rev•o•lu•tion \ˌrev-ə-ˈlü-shən\ *n* **1 :** the action by a celestial body of going round in an orbit; *also* **:** the time taken to complete one such orbit **2 :** completion of a course (as of years) ⟨a geologic *revolution*⟩ **3 a :** the action or motion of revolving **:** a turning round a center or axis **:** ROTATION **b :** a single complete turn (as of a wheel or a phonograph record) **4 a :** a sudden, radical, or complete change **b :** a fundamental change in political organization; *esp* **:** the overthrow of one government and the substitution of another by the governed **[**Middle French, from Late Latin *revolutio,* from Latin *revolvere* "to revolve, roll back"**] syn** see REBELLION

1rev•o•lu•tion•ary \-shə-ˌner-ē\ *adj* **1 a :** of, relating to, or constituting a revolution ⟨*revolutionary* war⟩ **b (1) :** tending to or promoting revolution **(2) :** RADICAL 3, EXTREMIST **2** *cap* **:** of or relating to the American Revolution

2revolutionary *n, pl* **-ar•ies :** REVOLUTIONIST

rev•o•lu•tion•ist \ˌrev-ə-ˈlü-shə-nəst, -shnəst\ *n* **1 :** one engaged in a revolution **2 :** one who holds or puts forward revolutionary doctrines — **revolutionist** *adj*

rev•o•lu•tion•ize \-shə-ˌnīz\ *vt* **1 :** to overthrow the established government of **2 :** to imbue with revolutionary doctrines **3 :** to change fundamentally or completely (as by a revolution) — **rev•o•lu•tion•iz•er** *n*

re•volve \ri-ˈvälv, -ˈvȯlv\ *vb* **1 :** to turn over at length in the mind ⟨*revolved* the story while I waited⟩ **2 a :** to go round or cause to go round in an orbit **b :** to turn round on or as if on an axis **:** ROTATE **3 :** to come around again **:** RECUR **4 :** to move in response to or dependence on a specified agent ⟨the household *revolves* about the baby⟩ **[**Latin *revolvere* "to roll back, cause to return", from *re-* + *volvere* "to roll"**]** — **re•volv•able** \-ˈväl-və-bəl, -ˈvȯl-\ *adj*

re•volv•er \ri-ˈväl-vər, -ˈvȯl-\ *n* **:** a handgun with a cylinder of several chambers brought successively into line with the barrel and discharged with the same hammer

re•volv•ing *adj* **:** tending to revolve or recur; *esp* **:** recurrently available ⟨*revolving* credit⟩

re•vue \ri-ˈvyü\ *n* **:** a theatrical production consisting typically of brief often satirical sketches and songs — compare MUSICAL **[**French, literally, "review"**]**

re•vul•sion \ri-ˈvəl-shən\ *n* **1 :** a strong pulling or drawing away **:** WITHDRAWAL **2 a :** a sudden or strong reaction or change **b :** a sense of utter repugnance **:** REPULSION **[**Latin *revulsio* "act of tearing away", from *revellere* "to pluck away", from *re-* + *vellere* "to pluck"**]** — **re•vul•sive** \-ˈvəl-siv\ *adj*

re•wake \rē-ˈwāk, ˈrē-\ *or* **re•wak•en** \-ˈwā-kən\ *vb* **:** to waken again or anew

1re•ward \ri-ˈwȯrd\ *vt* **:** to give a reward to or for ⟨*reward* them for their troubles⟩ ⟨*rewarded* our honesty⟩ **[**Old North French *rewarder* "to regard, reward", from *re-* "re-" + *warder* "to watch, guard", of Germanic origin**]** — **re•ward•able** \-ə-bəl\ *adj* — **re•ward•er** *n*

2reward *n* **:** something given or offered in return for a service; *esp* **:** money offered for the return of something lost or stolen or for the capture of a criminal

re•word \rē-ˈwərd, ˈrē-\ *vt* **:** to state in different words ⟨*reword* a question⟩

re•work \rē-ˈwərk, ˈrē-\ *vt* **:** to work again or anew: as **a :** REVISE **b :** to process (used or scrap material) for further use

1re•write \rē-ˈrīt, ˈrē-\ *vt* **-wrote** \-ˈrōt\; **-writ•ten** \-ˈrit-n\ *also* **-writ** \-ˈrit\; **-writ•ing 1 :** to write over again especially in a different form **2 :** to put (material turned in by a reporter) into form for publication in a newspaper — **re•writ•er** *n*

2re•write \ˈrē-ˌrīt\ *n* **:** something (as a newspaper article) rewritten

rex \ˈreks\ *n, pl* **rex•es** *or* **rex :** a mammal of a genetically variant strain characterized by a coat in which the normally longer and coarser guard hairs are shorter than the undercoat or lacking entirely **[**French *castorex,* a variety of rabbit, from Latin *castor* "beaver" + *rex* "king"**]**

rex

rey•nard \ˈrān-ərd, ˈren-\ *n, often cap* **:** FOX 1a **[**Middle French *Renart, Renard,* the fox who is hero of the French beast epic *Roman de Renart***]**

re•zone \rē-ˈzōn, ˈrē-\ *vt* **:** to alter the zoning of

Rh \ˈär-ˈāch\ *adj* **:** of, relating to, or being an Rh factor ⟨an *Rh* antigen⟩

rhad•a•man•thine \ˌrad-ə-ˈman-thən, -ˈmant-\ *adj, often cap* **:** rigorously strict or just **[***Rhadamanthus,* mythical judge in the lower world**]**

Rhae•to–Ro•man•ic \ˌrēt-ō-rō-ˈman-ik\ *n* **:** a Romance language of eastern Switzerland, northeastern Italy, and adjacent parts of Austria **[**Latin *rhaetus* "of Rhaetia (ancient Roman province)" + English *Romanic* "Romance"**]**

rhap•so•dize \ˈrap-sə-ˌdīz\ *vi* **:** to speak or write rhapsodically ⟨*rhapsodize* about a new book⟩ — **rhap•so•dist** \-səd-əst\ *n*

rhap•so•dy \ˈrap-səd-ē\ *n, pl* **-dies 1 :** a written or spoken expression of extravagant praise or ecstasy **2 :** a musical composition of irregular form **[**Latin *rhapsodia* "portion of an epic poem adapted for recitation", from Greek *rhapsōidia* "recitation of selections from epic poetry", from *rhaptein* "to sew, stitch together" + *aidein* "to sing"**]** — **rhap•sod•ic** \rap-ˈsäd-ik\ *or* **rhap•sod•i•cal** \-i-kəl\ *adj* — **rhap•sod•i•cal•ly** \-i-kə-lē, -klē\ *adv*

rhea \ˈrē-ə\ *n* **:** any of several large tall flightless three-toed South American birds that resemble but are smaller than the ostrich **[**New Latin *Rhea,* genus name, probably from Latin, mother of Zeus, from Greek**]**

rhe•ni•um \ˈrē-nē-əm\ *n* **:** a rare heavy hard silvery white metallic chemical element that is used in catalysts and thermocouples — see ELEMENT table **[**New Latin, from Latin *Rhenus* "Rhine river"**]**

rhe•o•stat \ˈrē-ə-ˌstat\ *n* **:** a resistor for regulating an electric current by means of variable resistances **[**Greek *rhein* "to flow" + *-states* "one that stops or steadies", from *histanai* "to cause to stand"**]** — **rhe•o•stat•ic** \ˌrē-ə-ˈstat-ik\ *adj*

rhea

rhe•sus monkey \ˌrē-səs-\ *n* **:** a pale brown Indian monkey often kept in zoos and frequently used in medical research **[**New Latin *Rhesus,* genus of monkeys, from Latin, a mythical king of Thrace**]**

rhet•o•ric \ˈret-ə-rik\ *n* **1 :** the art of speaking or writing effectively; *also* **:** the study or application of the principles and rules of composition **2 a :** skill in the effective use of speech **b :** insincere or pretentious language **[**Middle French *rethorique,* from Latin *rhetorica,* from Greek *rhētorikē,* derived from *rhētōr* "orator, rhetorician", from *eirein* "to say, speak"**]**

rhe•tor•i•cal \ri-ˈtȯr-i-kəl, -ˈtär-\ *adj* **1 a :** of, relating to, or dealing with rhetoric ⟨*rhetorical* studies⟩ **b :** used solely for rhetorical effect ⟨a *rhetorical* question⟩ **2 :** using rhetoric; *esp* **:** pretentious in language — **rhe•tor•i•cal•ly** \-kə-lē, -klē\ *adv* — **rhe•tor•i•cal•ness** \-kəl-nəs\ *n*

rhet•o•ri•cian \ˌret-ə-ˈrish-ən\ *n* **1 a :** a master or teacher of rhetoric **b :** ORATOR **2 :** an eloquent or pretentious writer or speaker

rheum \ˈrüm\ *n* **1 :** a watery discharge from the mucous membranes especially of the eyes or nose **2 :** a condition (as a cold) marked by a rheum [Middle French *reume,* from Latin *rheuma,* from Greek, literally, "flow, flux", from *rhein* "to flow"] — **rheumy** \ˈrü-mē\ *adj*

[1]**rheu•mat•ic** \ru̇-ˈmat-ik\ *adj* **:** of, relating to, characteristic of, or affected with rheumatism — **rheu•mat•i•cal•ly** \-ˈmat-i-kə-lē, -klē\ *adv*

[2]**rheumatic** *n* **:** one affected with rheumatism

rheumatic fever *n* **:** an acute disease especially of young people characterized by fever, by inflammation and pain in and around the joints, and by inflammation of the pericardium and heart valves

rheu•ma•tism \ˈrü-mə-ˌtiz-əm\ *n* **:** any of various conditions characterized by inflammation or pain in muscles, joints, or fibrous tissue ⟨muscular *rheumatism*⟩ — compare RHEUMATOID ARTHRITIS [Latin *rheumatismus* "flux, rheum", from Greek *rheumatismos,* derived from *rheuma* "flux, rheum", from *rhein* "to flow"]

rheu•ma•toid arthritis \ˌrü-mə-ˌtȯid-\ *n* **:** a usually chronic disease of unknown cause characterized especially by pain, stiffness, inflammation, and swelling of joints

Rh factor \är-ˈāch-\ *n* **:** a substance present in the red blood cells inherited according to Mendelian principles and capable of inducing intense antigenic reactions [*rh*esus monkey (in which it was first detected)]

rhine•stone \ˈrīn-ˌstōn\ *n* **:** a brilliant colorless imitation diamond made usually of glass or paste [*Rhine* river]

Rhine wine \ˈrīn-\ *n* **:** a typically light-bodied dry white wine produced in the Rhine valley; *also* **:** a similar wine made elsewhere

rhi•ni•tis \rī-ˈnīt-əs\ *n* **:** inflammation of the mucous membrane of the nose [Greek *rhin-, rhis* "nose"]

rhi•no \ˈrī-nō\ *n, pl* **rhino** *or* **rhinos :** RHINOCEROS

rhi•noc•er•os \rī-ˈnäs-rəs, -ə-rəs\ *n, pl* **-er•os•es** *or* **-er•os :** a large thick-skinned three-toed plant-eating mammal of Africa and Asia that is related to the horse and has one or two heavy upright horns on the snout [Latin *rhinoceros,* from Greek *rhinokerōs,* from *rhin-, rhis* "nose" + *keras* "horn"]

rhinoceros

rhiz- *or* **rhizo-** *combining form* **:** root ⟨*rhizo*sphere⟩ [Greek *rhiza*]

rhi•zo•bi•um \rī-ˈzō-bē-əm\ *n, pl* **-bia** \-bē-ə\ **:** any of a genus of small soil bacteria capable of forming symbiotic nodules on the roots of leguminous plants and of there fixing atmospheric nitrogen [*rhiz-* + Greek *bios* "life"]

rhi•zoid \ˈrī-ˌzȯid\ *n* **:** a structure (as a fungal hypha) that functions like a root in absorption or support — **rhi•zoi•dal** \rī-ˈzȯid-l\ *adj*

rhi•zome \ˈrī-ˌzōm\ *n* **:** a somewhat elongate, often thickened, and usually horizontal underground plant stem that produces shoots above and roots below [Greek *rhizōma* "mass of roots", derived from *rhiza* "root"]

rhi•zo•pod \ˈrī-zə-ˌpäd\ *n* **:** any of a group (Rhizopoda) of usually creeping protozoans having pseudopodia and including the typical amoebas and related forms

rhi•zo•pus \ˈrī-zə-pəs\ *n* **:** any of a genus of mold fungi including economic pests (as the common black mold of bread) causing decay [*rhiz-* + Greek *pous* "foot"]

rhi•zo•sphere \ˈrī-zə-ˌsfiər\ *n* **:** the soil immediately about and influenced by plant roots **:** the rooting zone of a soil

Rh–negative \ˌär-ˌāch-ˈneg-ət-iv\ *adj* **:** lacking Rh factor in the red blood cells

rho \ˈrō\ *n* **:** the 17th letter of the Greek alphabet — Ρ or ρ

Rhode Is•land Red \rō-ˌdī-lənd-, -lən-\ *n* **:** any of an American breed of general-purpose domestic fowls with rich brownish red plumage [*Rhode Island,* United States]

Rho•de•sian man \rō-ˌdē-zhən-, -zhē-ən-\ *n* **:** an extinct African hominid with prominent brow ridges and large face but human palate and dentition [Northern *Rhodesia,* Africa]

rho•di•um \ˈrōd-ē-əm\ *n* **:** a white hard ductile metallic chemical element used in alloys with platinum — see ELEMENT table [New Latin, from Greek *rhodon* "rose"]

rho•do•den•dron \ˌrōd-ə-ˈden-drən\ *n* **:** any of a genus of the heath family of widely grown shrubs and trees with alternate leaves and showy flowers; *esp* **:** one with leathery evergreen leaves as distinguished from a deciduous azalea [Latin, "oleander", from Greek, from *rhodon* "rose" + *dendron* "tree"]

rho•dop•sin \rō-ˈdäp-sən\ *n* **:** a red light-sensitive pigment in the retinal rods of marine fishes and most higher vertebrates that is important in vision in dim light — called also *visual purple;* compare IODOPSIN [Greek *rhodon* "rose" + *opsis* "sight, vision"]

rhomb•en•ceph•a•lon \ˌräm-ˌben-ˈsef-ə-ˌlän\ *n* **:** the parts of the vertebrate brain that develop from the embryonic hindbrain [Greek *rhombos* "rhombus" + English *encephalon*]

rhom•bic \ˈräm-bik\ *adj* **1 :** having the form of a rhombus **2 :** ORTHORHOMBIC

rhom•bo•he•dron \ˌräm-bō-ˈhē-drən\ *n, pl* **-drons** *or* **-dra** \-drə\ **:** a parallelepiped whose faces are rhombuses — **rhom•bo•he•dral** \-drəl\ *adj*

rhom•boid \ˈräm-ˌbȯid\ *n* **:** a parallelogram in which the angles are oblique and adjacent sides are unequal — **rhomboid** *adj* — **rhom•boi•dal** \räm-ˈbȯid-l\ *adj*

rhom•bus \ˈräm-bəs\ *n, pl* **rhom•bus•es** *or* **rhom•bi** \-ˌbī, -ˌbē\ **:** a parallelogram having the sides equal and the angles usually oblique [Latin, from Greek *rhombos*]

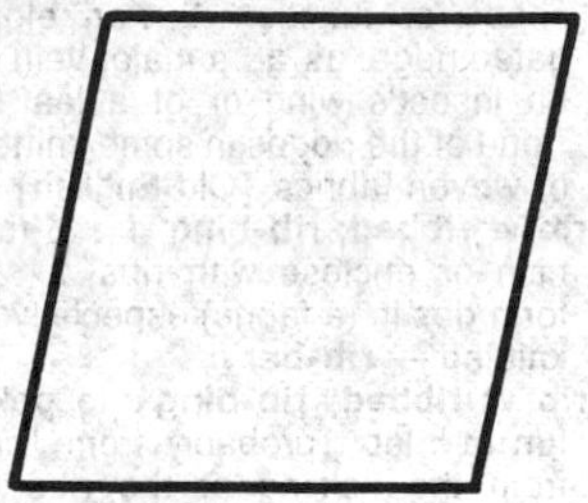
rhombus

Rh–pos•i•tive \ˌär-ˌāch-ˈpäz-ət-iv, -ˈpäz-tiv\ *adj* **:** containing Rh factor in the red blood cells

rhu•barb \ˈrü-ˌbärb\ *n* **1 :** a plant related to buckwheat that has broad green leaves borne on thick juicy pinkish stems often used for food **2 :** a heated dispute or controversy ⟨the pitcher got into a *rhubarb* with the umpire⟩ [Middle French *reubarbe,* from Medieval Latin *reubarbarum,* alteration of *rha barbarum,* literally, "barbarian rhubarb"]

rhumba *variant of* RUMBA

rhumb line \ˈrəm-\ *n* **:** a line on the surface of the earth that makes equal oblique angles with all meridians [Spanish *rumbo*]

[1]**rhyme** *or* **rime** \ˈrīm\ *n* **1 a :** correspondence in terminal sounds of two or more words or lines of verse **b :** one of two or more words thus corresponding in sound **2 a :** rhyming verse **b :** a composition in verse that rhymes [Old French *rime*]

[2]**rhyme** *or* **rime** *vb* **1 :** to make rhymes **:** put into rhyme; *also* **:** to compose rhyming verse **2 :** to end in syllables that form rhymes ⟨words that *rhyme*⟩ **3 :** to be in accord **:** HARMONIZE ⟨colors that *rhyme* well⟩ **4 :** to cause to rhyme **:** use as rhyme ⟨*rhymed* "moon" with "June"⟩ — **rhym•er** *n*

rhyme scheme *n* **:** the arrangement of rhymes in a stanza or a poem

rhyme•ster *or* **rime•ster** \ˈrīm-stər\ *n* **:** an inferior poet **:** a maker of poor verse

rhyn•cho•ce•pha•lian \ˌring-kō-sə-ˈfāl-yən\ *n* **:** the tuatara or a related extinct reptile [derived from Greek *rhynchos* "beak, snout" + *kephalē* "head"]

rhy•o•lite \ˈrī-ə-ˌlīt\ *n* **:** a very acid volcanic rock that is the lava form of granite [German *rhyolith,* from Greek *rhyax* "stream, stream of lava" (from *rhein* "to flow") + German *-lith* "-lite"] — **rhy•o•lit•ic** \ˌrī-ə-ˈlit-ik\ *adj*

rhythm \ˈrit͟h-əm\ *n* **1 a :** a flow of rising and falling sounds in language that is produced in verse by a regular recurrence of stressed and unstressed syllables **:** CADENCE **b :** a particular example or form of rhythm ⟨iambic *rhythm*⟩ **2 a :** a flow of sound in music marked by accented beats coming at regular intervals **b :** a characteristic rhythmic pattern ⟨waltz *rhythm*⟩ **c**

\ə\ **abut**	\au̇\ **out**	\i\ **tip**	\ȯ\ **saw**	\u̇\ **foot**
\ər\ **further**	\ch\ **chin**	\ī\ **life**	\ȯi\ **coin**	\y\ **yet**
\a\ **mat**	\e\ **pet**	\j\ **job**	\th\ **thin**	\yü\ **few**
\ā\ **take**	\ē\ **easy**	\ng\ **sing**	\t͟h\ **this**	\yu̇\ **cure**
\ä\ **cot, cart**	\g\ **go**	\ō\ **bone**	\ü\ **food**	\zh\ **vision**

: the group of instruments in a band providing the rhythm — called also *rhythm section* **3** : a movement or activity in which some action or element recurs regularly ⟨the *rhythm* of breathing⟩ [Latin *rhythmus,* from Greek *rhythmos,* from *rhein* "to flow"] — **rhyth•mic** \ˈrith-mik\ *or* **rhyth•mi•cal** \-mi-kəl\ *adj* — **rhyth•mi•cal•ly** \-mi-kə-lē, -klē\ *adv*

[1]ri•al \rē-ˈȯl, -ˈäl\ *n* **1** *also* **ri•yal** \-ˈȯl, -ˈyȯl, -ˈäl, -ˈyäl\ : the basic monetary unit of Oman **2** : the basic monetary unit of Iran **3** : a coin or note representing one rial [Persian, from Arabic *riyāl* "riyal"]

[2]rial *variant of* RIYAL

ri•al•to \rē-ˈal-tō\ *n, pl* **-tos 1** : a center of business or financial activity **2** : a theater district [*Rialto,* island and district in Venice]

ri•ata \rē-ˈat-ə, -ˈät-\ *n* : LARIAT [American Spanish *reata*]

[1]rib \ˈrib\ *n* **1 a** : one of the paired curved bony or partly cartilaginous rods that are joined to the spinal column, stiffen the walls of the body of most vertebrates, and protect the viscera **b** : a cut of meat including a rib **2** : something (as a structural member of a ship or airplane) resembling a rib in shape or function **3** : an elongated ridge: as **a** : a major vein of an insect's wing or of a leaf **b** : one of the ridges in some knitted or woven fabrics [Old English]

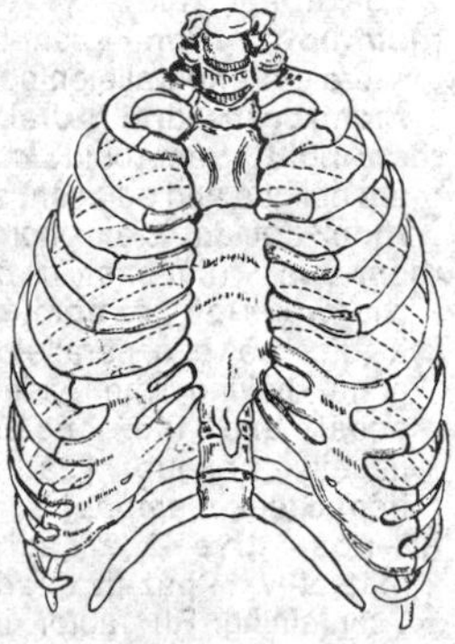

[1]rib 1a

[2]rib *vt* **ribbed**; **rib•bing 1** : to furnish or enclose with ribs **2** : to form ribs in (a fabric) especially in knitting — **rib•ber** *n*

[3]rib *vt* **ribbed**; **rib•bing** : to poke fun at : KID [probably from [1]*rib;* from the tickling of the ribs to cause laughter] — **rib•ber** *n*

rib•ald \ˈrib-əld\ *adj* : marked by or inclined to coarseness and indecency ⟨*ribald* language⟩ ⟨a *ribald* scoffer⟩ [Old French *ribauld* "rascal, wanton", from *riber* "to be wanton", of Germanic origin] **syn** see COARSE — **rib•ald•ry** \-əl-drē\ *n*

rib•and \ˈrib-ənd\ *n* : a ribbon used especially as a decoration [Middle English, alteration of *riban*]

rib•bon \ˈrib-ən\ *n* **1 a** : a narrow closely woven strip of fabric used especially for trimming or for tying or ornamenting packages **b** : a piece of usually multicolored ribbon worn as a military decoration or as a symbol of a medal **c** : a strip of colored ribbon given for winning a place in competition **2** : a long narrow strip resembling a ribbon: as **a** : a board framed into the studs to support the ceiling or floor joists **b** : a strip of inked fabric (as in a typewriter) **3** : SHRED, TATTER — usually used in pl. [Middle English *riban,* from Middle French *riban, ruban*] — **rib•bon•like** \-ˌlīk\ *adj*

rib•bon•fish \-ˌfish\ *n* : any of various very long and greatly compressed sea fishes

ribbon worm *n* : NEMERTEAN

rib•by \ˈrib-ē\ *adj* : having prominent ribs; *also* : GAUNT

rib cage *n* : the bony enclosing wall of the chest consisting chiefly of the ribs and their connectives

ri•bo•fla•vin \ˌrī-bə-ˈflā-vən\ *n* : a yellow crystalline compound that is a growth-promoting member of the vitamin B complex occurring both free (as in milk) and combined (as in liver) [*ribose* + Latin *flavus* "yellow"]

ri•bo•nu•cle•ase \ˌrī-bō-ˈnü-klē-ˌās, -ˈnyü-, -ˌāz\ *n* : an enzyme that catalyzes the hydrolysis of RNA

ri•bo•nu•cle•ic acid \ˌrī-bō-nü-ˌklē-ik-, -nyü-, -ˌklā-\ *n* : RNA [*ribose* + *nucleic acid*]

ri•bo•nu•cle•o•tide \-ˈnü-klē-ə-ˌtīd, -ˈnyü-\ *n* : a ribose-containing nucleotide that occurs especially in RNA

ri•bose \ˈrī-ˌbōs\ *n* : a pentose sugar $C_5H_{10}O_5$ found in the nucleotides of RNA [from *ribonic acid,* an acid obtained by oxidation of ribose, from German *ribonsäure*]

ribosomal RNA *n* : an RNA that is a fundamental structural part of the ribosomes

ri•bo•some \ˈrī-bə-ˌsōm\ *n* : a protoplasmic granule that contains RNA and is a site of protein synthesis [*ribo*nucleic acid + *-some*] — **ri•bo•som•al** \ˌrī-bə-ˈsō-məl\ *adj*

rice \ˈrīs\ *n, pl* **rice** : an annual cereal grass grown in warm wet areas for its seed that is used especially for food; *also* : this seed [Old French *ris,* from Italian *riso,* from Greek *oryza*]

rice•bird \ˈrīs-ˌbərd\ *n* : any of several small birds common in rice fields; *esp* : BOBOLINK

ric•er \ˈrī-sər\ *n* : a kitchen utensil in which soft foods (as boiled potatoes) are pressed through a perforated container as slender strings

rich \ˈrich\ *adj* **1** : having or controlling great wealth **2 a** : having great value ⟨a *rich* harvest⟩ **b** : magnificently impressive : SUMPTUOUS **3** : well supplied with something pleasing or desirable ⟨a land *rich* in resources⟩: as **a** : vivid and deep in color ⟨a *rich* red⟩ **b** : full and mellow in tone and quality ⟨a *rich* voice⟩ **c** : of pleasingly strong odor ⟨*rich* perfumes⟩ **4** : highly productive : FRUITFUL ⟨a *rich* mine⟩ ⟨*rich* soil⟩ **5 a** : highly seasoned, fatty, oily, or sweet ⟨*rich* foods⟩ **b** : high in combustible content ⟨a *rich* fuel mixture⟩ **6** : giving amusement; *also* : LAUGHABLE [Old English *rīce*] — **rich•ness** *n*

rich•en \ˈrich-ən\ *vt* **rich•ened**; **rich•en•ing** \ˈrich-ning, -ə-ning\ : to make rich or richer

rich•es \ˈrich-əz\ *n pl* : things that make one rich : WEALTH [Old French *richesse* "richness", form *riche* "rich", of Germanic origin]

rich•ly \ˈrich-lē\ *adv* **1** : in a rich manner **2** : in full measure : AMPLY ⟨praise *richly* deserved⟩

Rich•ter scale \ˈrik-tər-\ *n* : a logarithmic scale for expressing the intensity of a seismic disturbance (as an earthquake) in terms of the energy dissipated in it [Charles R. *Richter,* born 1900, American seismologist]

[1]rick \ˈrik\ *n* : a stack (as of hay) in the open air [Old English *hrēac*]

[2]rick *vt* : to pile (as hay) in ricks

rick•ets \ˈrik-əts\ *n* : a disease of the young marked especially by soft and deformed bones due to failure to assimilate and use calcium and phosphorus normally and caused by inadequate vitamin D [origin unknown]

rick•ett•sia \rik-ˈet-sē-ə\ *n, pl* **-si•as** *or* **-si•ae** \-sē-ˌē, -sē-ˌī\ : any of various microorganisms sometimes held to be intermediate between bacteria and true viruses that live in cells and include causers of serious diseases (as typhus) [Howard T. *Ricketts,* died 1910, American pathologist] — **rick•ett•si•al** \-sē-əl\ *adj*

rick•ety \ˈrik-ət-ē\ *adj* **1** : affected with rickets **2** : feeble in the joints ⟨a *rickety* old pensioner⟩ **3** : UNSOUND c, SHAKY ⟨a *rickety* wagon⟩

rick•ey \ˈrik-ē\ *n, pl* **rickeys** : a drink containing liquor, lime juice, sugar, and soda water; *also* : a similar drink without liquor [probably from the name *Rickey*]

rick•rack *or* **ric•rac** \ˈrik-ˌrak\ *n* : a flat braid woven to form zigzags and used especially as trimming on clothing [reduplication of [2]*rack*]

rick•sha *or* **rick•shaw** \ˈrik-ˌshȯ\ *n* : a small 2-wheeled covered vehicle pulled by one man and used originally in Japan [alteration of *jinrikisha*]

ricksha

[1]ric•o•chet \ˈrik-ə-ˌshā, *British also* -ˌshet\ *n* : a glancing rebound (as of a bullet off a flat surface); *also* : an object that ricochets [French]

[2]ricochet *vi* **-cheted** \-ˌshād\ *or* **-chet•ted** \-ˌshet-əd\; **-chet•ing** \-ˌshā-ing\ *or* **-chet•ting** \-ˌshet-ing\ : to skip with or as if with glancing rebounds

ri•cot•ta \ri-ˈkȯt-ə\ *n* : a white unripened whey cheese of Italy that resembles cottage cheese [Italian, from *ricuocere* "to cook again", from Latin *recoquere,* from *re-* + *coquere* "to cook"]

ric•tus \ˈrik-təs\ *n* : a gaping grin or grimace [Latin, "open mouth", from *rictus,* past participle of *ringi* "to gape"]

rid \ˈrid\ *vt* **rid** *also* **rid•ded**; **rid•ding** : to make free : RELIEVE — often used in the phrase *be rid of* or *get rid of* [Middle English *ridden* "to clear", from Old Norse *rythja*]

rid•able *or* **ride•able** \ˈrīd-ə-bəl\ *adj* : fit for riding

rid•dance \ˈrid-ns\ *n* : the act of ridding : the state of being rid of

rid•den \'rid-n\ *adj* : extremely concerned with or burdened by — usually used in combination ⟨guilt-*ridden*⟩ ⟨slum-*ridden*⟩

[1]rid•dle \'rid-l\ *n* **1** : a mystifying, misleading, or puzzling question posed as a problem to be solved or guessed : CONUNDRUM **2** : something or someone difficult to understand [Old English *rǣdelse* "opinion, conjecture, riddle"] **syn** see MYSTERY

[2]riddle *vb* **rid•dled**; **rid•dling** \'rid-ling, -l-ing\ **1** : to find the solution of **2** : to set a riddle for : PUZZLE **3** : to speak in riddles or set forth a riddle — **rid•dler** \-lər, -l-ər\ *n*

[3]riddle *n* : a coarse sieve (as for ashes) [Old English *hriddel*]

[4]riddle *vt* **1** : to sift or separate with or as if with a riddle **2 a** : to fill full of holes ⟨a boat *riddled* with shot⟩ **b** : to spread through : PERMEATE ⟨a story *riddled* with lies⟩

[1]ride \'rīd\ *vb* **rode** \'rōd\; **rid•den** \'rid-n\; **rid•ing** \'rīd-ing\ **1 a** : to sit on and control so as to be carried along ⟨*ride* a horse⟩ ⟨*ride* a motorcycle⟩ **b** : to travel in or on as a conveyance ⟨*ride* a bus⟩ ⟨*ride* in an airplane⟩ **2 a** : to be supported by and move with ⟨a ship *riding* the waves⟩ ⟨the bearings *ride* on a cushion of grease⟩ **b** : to float at anchor **c** : to remain afloat through : SURVIVE ⟨*ride* out a storm⟩ **3 a** : to convey in or as if in a vehicle : give a ride to **b** : to travel over a surface ⟨the car *rides* well⟩ **4** : to torment by or as if by constant nagging or teasing **5 a** : to be contingent : DEPEND ⟨all our hopes *ride* on their success⟩ **b** : to be bet ⟨their money is *riding* on the favorite⟩ [Old English *rīdan*]

• **syn** DRIVE: RIDE stresses being borne along on the back of an animal or in a conveyance ⟨*ride* in a train⟩ and implies control only when the rider is mounted astride ⟨*ride* a bicycle⟩ DRIVE implies the action of controlling the movements of an animal or a powered vehicle whether or not the agent is borne along ⟨*drive* a herd of sheep⟩ ⟨*drive* a bus⟩

— **ride for a fall** : to court disaster — **ride roughshod over** : to treat with disdain or abuse

[2]ride *n* **1** : an act of riding; *esp* : a trip on horseback or by vehicle ⟨a *ride* in the country⟩ **2** : a way (as a road or path) for riding **3** : a mechanical device (as at an amusement park) for riding on **4** : a means of transportation ⟨needs a *ride* to work⟩

rid•er \'rīd-ər\ *n* **1** : one that rides **2 a** : an addition to a document often attached on a separate piece of paper **b** : a clause added to a legislative bill to secure a usually distinct object — **rid•er•less** \-ləs\ *adj*

[1]ridge \'rij\ *n* **1** : a raised body part (as along the backbone) **2** : a range of hills or mountains **3** : a raised strip (as of plowed ground) **4** : the line made where two sloping surfaces come together ⟨the *ridge* of a roof⟩ [Old English *hrycg*]

[2]ridge *vb* : to form into or extend in ridges

ridge•ling *or* **ridg•ling** \'rij-ling\ *n* : a male domestic animal that is imperfectly developed sexually or imperfectly castrated [perhaps from [1]*ridge*]

ridge•pole \'rij-,pōl\ *n* **1** : the highest horizontal timber in a sloping roof to which the upper ends of the rafters are fastened **2** : a horizontal support for the top of a tent

ridgy \'rij-ē\ *adj* : having or rising in ridges

[1]rid•i•cule \'rid-ə-,kyül\ *n* : the act of exposing to laughter : DERISION, MOCKERY [Latin *ridiculum* "jest", from *ridiculus* "laughable", from *ridēre* "to laugh"]

[2]ridicule *vt* : to make fun of — **rid•i•cul•er** *n*

• **syn** RIDICULE, DERIDE, MOCK, TAUNT mean to make an object of laughter or scorn. RIDICULE implies an often malicious belittling; DERIDE suggests contemptuous and often bitter ridicule; MOCK implies scorn often expressed ironically as by mimicry or sham deference; TAUNT implies mockery and often jeering insults in an effort to challenge or reproach.

ri•dic•u•lous \rə-'dik-yə-ləs\ *adj* : arousing or deserving ridicule : ABSURD, PREPOSTEROUS **syn** see LAUGHABLE — **ri•dic•u•lous•ly** *adv* — **ri•dic•u•lous•ness** *n*

[1]ri•ding \'rīd-ing\ *n* : one of the three administrative jurisdictions into which Yorkshire, England, was formerly divided [Middle English, derived from Old Norse *thrithjungr* "third part", from *thrithi* "third"]

[2]rid•ing \'rīd-ing\ *n* : the action or state of one that rides

[3]rid•ing *adj* **1** : used for or when riding ⟨a *riding* horse⟩ **2** : operated by a rider ⟨a *riding* plow⟩

rid•ley \'rid-lē\ *n* : a large sea turtle of the western Atlantic [probably from the name *Ridley*]

rife \'rīf\ *adj* **1** : WIDESPREAD 2, PREVALENT ⟨lands where famine is *rife*⟩ **2** : well supplied ⟨the air was *rife* with rumors⟩ [Old English *rȳfe*] — **rife** *adv* — **rife•ly** *adv*

[1]riff \'rif\ *vb* : RIFFLE 3, SKIM ⟨*riff* pages⟩ [short for *riffle*]

[2]riff *n* : a repeated figure in jazz typically supporting a solo improvisation [probably from *refrain*]

[3]riff *vi* : to perform a jazz riff

Riff \'rif\ *n, pl* **Riffs** *or* **Riffi** \'rif-ē\ *or* **Riff** : a Berber of the Rif in northern Morocco

[1]rif•fle \'rif-əl\ *n* **1 a** : a shallow extending across a stream bed and causing broken water **b** : a stretch of water flowing over a riffle **2** : a small wave or succession of small waves : RIPPLE [perhaps alteration of *ruffle*]

[2]riffle *vb* **rif•fled**; **rif•fling** \'rif-ling, -ə-ling\ **1** : to form, flow over, or move in riffles **2** : to ruffle slightly : RIPPLE **3 a** : to flip or leaf through hastily **b** : to manipulate or finger lightly or idly ⟨*riffle* a stack of coins⟩

riff•raff \'rif-,raf\ *n* **1 a** : disreputable persons **b** : RABBLE 2 **2** : RUBBISH, REFUSE [Middle English *ryffe raffe*, from *rif and raf* "every single one", from Middle French *rif et raf* "completely", from *rifler* "to scratch, plunder" + *raffe* "act of sweeping"] — **riffraff** *adj*

[1]ri•fle \'rī-fəl\ *vb* **ri•fled**; **ri•fling** \'rī-fling, -fə-ling\ **1** : to ransack especially with the intent to steal ⟨*rifle* the mail⟩ **2** : to steal and carry away **3** : to engage in ransacking and stealing [Middle French *rifler* "to scratch, file, plunder", of Germanic origin] — **ri•fler** \'rī-flər, -fə-lər\ *n*

△ **origin** The basic meaning of Middle French *rifler* was "to scratch or file". But it was in the extended sense "to plunder or ransack" that the Middle English borrowed the word from the French. Early in the 17th century the French word was borrowed again into English in something closer to its original sense, "to scratch". To *rifle* a gun was to cut spiral grooves into its bore. By functional shift *rifle* became a noun which named such a groove. And by the late 18th century a gun with a rifled bore was itself called a *rifle*.

[2]rifle *vt* **ri•fled**; **ri•fling** : to cut spiral grooves into the bore of ⟨*rifled* arms⟩ ⟨*rifled* pipe⟩ [French *rifler* "to scratch, file"]

[3]rifle *n* **1 a** : a weapon with a rifled bore intended to be fired from the shoulder **b** : a rifled artillery piece **2** *pl* : a body of soldiers armed with rifles

ri•fle•man \'rī-fəl-mən\ *n* **1** : a soldier armed with a rifle **2** : a person skilled in shooting with a rifle

ri•fle•ry \'rī-fəl-rē\ *n* : rifle shooting especially at targets

ri•fling \'rī-fling, -fə-ling\ *n* **1** : the act or process of making spiral grooves **2** : a system of spiral grooves in the bore of a gun causing a projectile when fired to rotate about its longer axis

[1]rift \'rift\ *n* **1 a** : an opening (as a fissure or crevasse) made by splitting or separation **b** : FAULT 4 **2** : BREACH 3a, ESTRANGEMENT [of Scandinavian origin]

[2]rift *vb* : [2]CLEAVE 1a, DIVIDE

[1]rig \'rig\ *vt* **rigged**; **rig•ging** **1** : to fit out (as a ship) with rigging **2** : CLOTHE, DRESS ⟨was *rigged* out in my Sunday clothes⟩ **3** : to furnish with special gear : EQUIP **4** : to set up or fit up often as a makeshift ⟨*rig* a temporary shelter⟩ [Middle English *riggen*]

[2]rig *n* **1** : the distinctive shape, number, and arrangement of sails and masts of a ship ⟨a schooner *rig*⟩ **2** : EQUIPAGE; *esp* : a carriage with its horse **3** : CLOTHING, DRESS **4** : tackle, equipment, or machinery fitted for a specified purpose ⟨oil-drilling *rig*⟩

[3]rig *vt* **rigged**; **rig•ging** : to manipulate or control usually by deceptive or dishonest means ⟨*rig* an election⟩ ⟨*rig* a contest⟩ [from earlier *rig* "swindle", of unknown origin]

rig•a•doon \,rig-ə-'dün\ *or* **ri•gau•don** \rē-gō-dōⁿ\ *n* : a lively dance of the 17th and 18th centuries; *also* : the music for a rigadoon [French *rigaudon*]

rigamarole *variant of* RIGMAROLE

Ri•gel \'rī-jəl, -gəl\ *n* : a bright star in the left foot of the constellation Orion [Arabic *Rijl*, literally, "foot"]

rig•ger \'rig-ər\ *n* **1** : one that rigs **2** : a ship of a specified rig ⟨square-*rigger*⟩

rig•ging \'rig-ing, -ən\ *n* **1 a** : the lines and chains used aboard a ship for supporting masts and spars and controlling sails **b** : a similar network (as in theater scenery) used for support and manipulation **2** : CLOTHING

[1]right \ˈrīt\ *adj* **1 :** RIGHTEOUS 1, UPRIGHT **2 :** being in accordance with what is just, good, or proper ⟨*right* conduct⟩ **3 a :** conforming to a standard **b :** conforming to facts or truth **:** CORRECT ⟨the *right* answer⟩ **4 :** SUITABLE, APPROPRIATE ⟨the *right* person for the job⟩ **5 :** STRAIGHT ⟨a *right* line⟩ **6 :** GENUINE 1, REAL **7 a :** of, relating to, situated on, or being the side of the body which is away from the heart and on which the hand is stronger and more skilled in most people ⟨*right* arm⟩ **b :** located in the same relative position as the right of the body when facing in the same direction as the observer **:** RIGHT-HAND ⟨the *right* side of the road⟩ **8 :** having its axis perpendicular to the base ⟨a *right* cone⟩ **9 :** of, relating to, or being the principal or more prominent side of an object ⟨turn the *right* side out⟩ **10 :** acting or judging in accordance with truth or fact ⟨time proved them *right*⟩ **11 a :** physically or mentally well ⟨did not feel *right*⟩ **b :** being in a correct or proper state ⟨put things *right*⟩ **12 :** most favorable or desired **:** PREFERABLE ⟨live on the *right* side of town⟩ **13** *often cap* **:** of or adhering to the Right in politics [Old English *riht*] — **right•ness** *n*

[2]right *n* **1 :** qualities (as adherence to duty and obedience to lawful authority) that together constitute the ideal of moral propriety **2 :** something to which one has a just claim or which one may properly claim as due ⟨the *right* to respect⟩: as **a :** a power or privilege to which one is justly entitled ⟨one's *right* to vote⟩ **b :** an interest that one has in a property — often used in pl. ⟨mineral *rights*⟩ ⟨film *rights* of a novel⟩ **3 :** the cause of truth or justice **4 :** the location or direction of the right side ⟨the woods on my *right*⟩ **5 a :** the true account or correct interpretation **b :** the quality or state of being factually correct **6** *often cap* **a :** the part of a legislative chamber located to the right of the presiding officer **b :** the members of a continental European legislative body occupying the right and holding more conservative political views than other members **7 a** *cap* **:** individuals sometimes professing opposition to change in the established order and favoring traditional attitudes and practices and sometimes advocating the forced establishment of an authoritarian political order **b** *often cap* **:** a conservative position — **by rights :** with reason or justice **:** PROPERLY — **to rights :** into proper order

[3]right *adv* **1 :** according to right ⟨live *right*⟩ **2 :** EXACTLY, PRECISELY ⟨*right* at my fingertips⟩ **3 :** in a suitable, proper, or desired manner ⟨hold your pen *right*⟩ **4 :** in a direct line or course **:** DIRECTLY ⟨go *right* home⟩ **5 :** according to fact or truth **:** TRULY ⟨guess *right*⟩ **6 a :** all the way ⟨windows *right* to the floor⟩ **b :** COMPLETELY ⟨felt *right* at home⟩ **7 :** IMMEDIATELY ⟨*right* after lunch⟩ **8 :** VERY ⟨a *right* pleasant day⟩ **9 :** on or to the right ⟨looked *right* and left⟩

[4]right *vb* **1 a :** to relieve from wrong **b :** JUSTIFY 1a, VINDICATE **2 a :** to adjust or restore to the proper state or condition **b :** to bring or restore to an upright position ⟨*right* a capsized boat⟩ **3 :** to become upright — **right•er** *n*

right angle *n* **:** the angle that is formed by two lines perpendicular to each other and measures 90 degrees — **right–an•gled** \ˈrīt-ˈang-gəld\ *or* **right–an•gle** \-gəl\ *adj*

right circular cone *n* **:** a cone with a circular base and with the axis joining the vertex to the center of the base perpendicular to the plane of the base

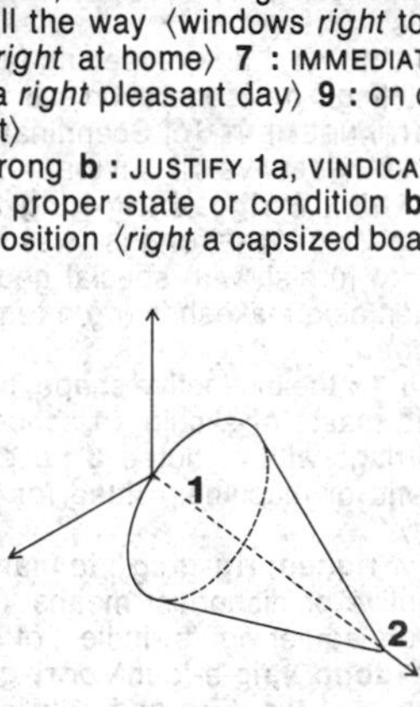

right circular cone: *1* axis, *2* vertex

right circular cylinder *n* **:** a cylinder with the bases circular and with the axis joining the two centers of the bases perpendicular to the planes of the two bases

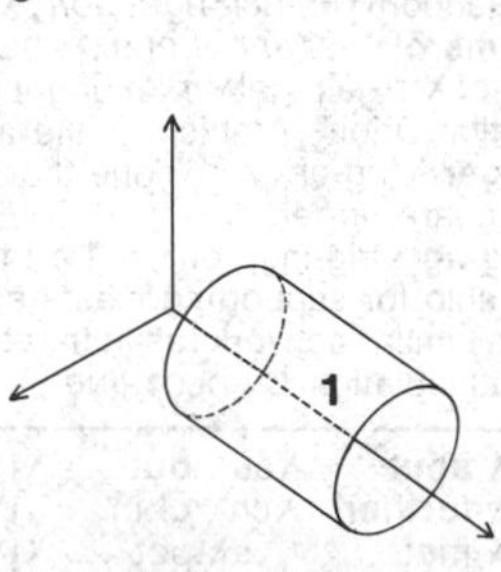

right circular cylinder: *1* axis

righ•teous \ˈrī-chəs\ *adj* **1 :** acting rightly **:** UPRIGHT **2 a :** morally right or justifiable ⟨*righteous* actions⟩ **b :** arising from an outraged sense of justice or morality ⟨*righteous* indignation⟩ [alteration of earlier *rightuous*, from Middle English *rightwise*, *rightwos*, from Old English *rihtwīs*, from *riht* "right" + *wīs* "wise"] — **righ•teous•ly** *adv* — **righ•teous•ness** *n*

right field *n* **1 :** the part of the baseball outfield to the right looking out from the home plate **2 :** the position of the player defending right field — **right fielder** *n*

right•ful \ˈrīt-fəl\ *adj* **1 :** morally right or good **2 a :** having a just or legally enforceable claim **:** LEGITIMATE ⟨the *rightful* owner⟩ **b :** held by right or just claim **:** LEGAL ⟨*rightful* authority⟩ **3 :** PROPER 1, FITTING — **right•ful•ly** \-fə-lē\ *adv* — **right•ful•ness** *n*

right–hand \ˌrīt-ˌhand\ *adj* **1 :** situated on the right **2 :** RIGHT-HANDED 1 **3 :** chiefly relied on **:** almost indispensable

right hand *n* **1 a :** the hand on a person's right side **b :** a reliable or indispensable person **2 a :** the right side **b :** a place of honor

right–hand•ed \ˈrīt-ˈhan-dəd\ *adj* **1 :** using the right hand more skillfully or freely than the left **2 :** done or made with or for the right hand **3 :** having or moving with a clockwise turn or twist — **right–hand•ed•ly** *or* **right–hand•ed** *adv* — **right–hand•ed•ness** *n*

right–hand•er \-ˈhan-dər\ *n* **1 :** a blow struck with the right hand **2 :** a right-handed person

right•ist \ˈrīt-əst\ *n, often cap* **:** an advocate or adherent of the doctrines of the Right — **rightist** *adj, often cap*

right•ly \ˈrīt-lē\ *adv* **1 :** FAIRLY 3, JUSTLY **2 :** PROPERLY 1, FITLY **3 :** according to truth or fact

right–of–way \ˌrīt-əv-ˈwā, -ə-\ *n, pl* **rights–of–way** *also* **right–of–ways 1 :** a legal right of passage over another person's ground **2 a :** the area over which a right-of-way exists **b :** the strip of land over which a public road is built **c :** the land occupied by a railroad especially for its main line **d :** the land used by a public utility (as for a transmission line) **3 :** the right of traffic to take precedence over other traffic

right prism *n* **:** a prism with the lateral edges perpendicular to the two bases and with all the lateral faces rectangles

Right Reverend — used as a title for some high religious officials (as Episcopal bishops)

right–to–work law \ˌrīt-tə-ˈwərk-\ *n* **:** a law banning the union shop and the closed shop

right triangle *n* **:** a triangle having a right angle

right•ward \-wərd\ *adv* **:** toward or on the right — **rightward** *adj*

right whale *n* **:** a large whalebone whale with no fin on the back, a very large head, and small eyes near the angles of the mouth

right wing *n* **1 :** the rightist division of a group **2 :** RIGHT 7 — **right–wing•er** \ˈrīt-ˈwing-ər\ *n*

rig•id \ˈrij-əd\ *adj* **1 :** lacking flexibility **:** STIFF, HARD **2 a :** inflexibly set in opinion **:** UNYIELDING **b :** strictly observed **:** SCRUPULOUS **3 :** HARSH, SEVERE ⟨*rigid* treatment⟩ **4 :** precise and accurate in procedure [Latin *rigidus*, from *rigēre* "to be stiff"] — **ri•gid•i•ty** \rə-ˈjid-ət-ē\ *n* — **rig•id•ly** \ˈrij-əd-lē\ *adv* — **rig•id•ness** *n*

syn RIGID, RIGOROUS, STRICT, STRINGENT mean very severe or stern. RIGID implies uncompromising inflexibility ⟨*rigid* and arbitrary rules⟩ RIGOROUS implies the imposing of hardship and difficulty ⟨*rigorous* training⟩ STRICT emphasizes close conformity to rules, standards, or requirements ⟨*strict* discipline⟩ STRINGENT suggests restrictions or limitations that curb or coerce ⟨*stringent* punishment⟩

rig•ma•role *or* **rig•a•ma•role** \ˈrig-ə-mə-ˌrōl, ˈrig-mə-\ *n* **1 :** confused or meaningless talk **2 :** a complex and often unnecessary procedure [alteration of obsolete *ragman roll* "long list, catalog"]

rig•or \ˈrig-ər, 2 *is also* ˈrī-ˌgȯr\ *n* **1 a :** harsh strictness **:** the quality of being unyielding **:** SEVERITY **b :** an act or instance of rigor **2 :** a tremor caused by a chill **3 :** a condition that makes life difficult or uncomfortable ⟨the *rigors* of frontier life⟩ **4 :** strict precision ⟨logical *rigor*⟩ [Middle French *rigueur*, from Latin *rigor*, literally, "stiffness", from *rigēre* "to be stiff"]

rig•or mor•tis \ˌrig-ər-ˈmȯrt-əs\ *n* **:** transitory rigidity of muscles occurring after death [New Latin, "stiffness of death"]

rig•or•ous \ˈrig-rəs, -ə-rəs\ *adj* **1 :** exercising or favoring rigor **:** very strict **2 :** marked by extremes of temperature or climate **:** HARSH, SEVERE **3 :** extremely accurate **:** PRECISE **syn** see RIGID — **rig•or•ous•ly** *adv* — **rig•or•ous•ness** *n*

rile \ˈrīl\ *vt* **1 :** ROIL 1 **2 :** to make angry [alteration of *roil*]

[1]rill \ˈril\ *n* **:** a very small brook [Dutch *ril* or Low German *rille*]

²rill \'ril\ *or* **rille** \'ril, 'ril-ə\ *n* : any of several long narrow valleys on the moon's surface [German *rille*, literally, "channel made by a small stream", from Low German, "rill"]

¹rim \'rim\ *n* **1 a** : the outer often curved or circular edge or border of something **b** : BRINK 2 **2** : the outer part of a wheel joined to the hub usually by spokes [Old English *rima*] — **rim·less** \-ləs\ *adj*

• **syn** BRIM: RIM applies to the edge of something circular or curving ⟨*rim* of a plate⟩ BRIM applies to the upper inside rim of something hollow ⟨fill the cup to the *brim*⟩

²rim *vb* **rimmed; rim·ming 1** : to furnish with a rim : serve as a rim for : BORDER **2** : to run around the rim of ⟨putts that *rim* the cup⟩ **3** : to form or show a rim

¹rime \'rīm\ *n* **1** : FROST 1c **2** : an accumulation of granular ice tufts on objects that resembles frost in appearance but is formed from supercooled fog or cloud **3** : CRUST 3a, INCRUSTATION [Old English *hrīm*]

²rime *vt* : to cover with or as if with rime

³rime, rimer, rimester *variant of* RHYME, RHYMER, RHYMESTER

rimy \'rī-mē\ *adj* **rim·i·er; -est** : covered with rime : FROSTY

rind \'rīnd\ *n* : the bark of a tree; *also* : a usually hard or tough outer layer (as the skin of a fruit) [Old English] — **rind·ed** \'rīn-dəd\ *adj*

rin·der·pest \'rin-dər-,pest\ *n* : an acute virus disease of cattle and sometimes sheep and goats [German, from *rinder* "cattle" + *pest* "pestilence"]

¹ring \'ring\ *n* **1** : a circular band for holding, connecting, hanging, or pulling ⟨a curtain *ring*⟩ ⟨a key *ring*⟩ or for packing or sealing **2** : a circlet often of precious metal worn on the finger **3 a** : a circular line, figure, or object **b** : an encircling arrangement ⟨a *ring* of suburbs⟩ **c** : a circular or spiral course **4 a** : an often circular space for exhibitions or competitions; *esp* : such a space at a circus **b** : a square enclosure in which boxing matches are held; *also* : the sport of boxing **5** : ANNUAL RING **6** : a combination of persons for a selfish and often corrupt purpose ⟨a drug *ring*⟩ **7** : an arrangement of atoms represented in formulas or models as a ring [Old English *hring*] — **ringed** \'ringd\ *adj* — **ring·like** \'ring-,līk\ *adj*

²ring *vb* **ringed; ring·ing** \'ring-ing\ **1** : to place or form a ring around : ENCIRCLE **2** : to provide with a ring **3** : GIRDLE 3 **4** : to throw a ring over (the mark) in a game where curved objects (as horseshoes) are tossed at a mark **5** : to form or take the shape of a ring

³ring *vb* **rang** \'rang\; **rung** \'rəng\; **ring·ing** \'ring-ing\ **1** : to sound clearly and reasonantly when struck ⟨church bells *ringing*⟩ **2** : to cause to sound especially by striking ⟨*rang* the dinner bell⟩ **3** : to ring a bell as a signal ⟨*ring* for the attendant⟩ **4** : to announce by or as if by ringing ⟨*ring* in the new year⟩ **5 a** : to be filled with reverberating sound : RESOUND ⟨the hall *rang* with cheers⟩ **b** : to have the sensation of being filled with a humming sound ⟨my ears were *ringing*⟩ **6** : to be filled with talk or report ⟨the whole town *rang* with the story⟩ **7** : to repeat often or loudly or earnestly **8** : to have a sound or character expressive of some quality ⟨the story *rings* true⟩ **9 a** : to summon especially by bell **b** *chiefly British* : TELEPHONE 3 — usually used with *up* [Old English *hringan*] — **ring a bell** : to arouse a response ⟨that name *rings a bell*⟩ — **ring down the curtain** : to end a performance or an action — **ring the changes** : to run through a whole range of possibilities

⁴ring *n* **1** : a set of bells **2** : a clear resonant sound made by or as if by vibrating metal **3** : resonant tone : SONORITY **4** : a loud sound continued, repeated, or reverberated **5** : a sound or character expressive of a particular quality ⟨a story with the *ring* of truth⟩ **6 a** : the act or an instance of ringing **b** : a telephone call

ring·bolt \'ring-,bōlt\ *n* : a bolt with a ring through a loop at one end

¹ring·er \'ring-ər\ *n* **1** : one that sounds especially by ringing **2 a** : an often superior or ineligible competitor entered in competition under false representations ⟨charged that a *ringer* had won the feature race⟩ **b** : one that strongly resembles another ⟨you're a dead *ringer* for my cousin⟩

²ringer *n* : one (as a quoit or horseshoe) that encircles or puts a ring around a peg

Ring·er's solution \'ring-ərz-\ *n* : a balanced aqueous ionic solution that is used in physiological experiments to provide a medium essentially isotonic to many animal tissues [Sidney *Ringer*, died 1910, English physician]

ring finger *n* : the third finger of the hand

ring·lead·er \'ring-,lēd-ər\ *n* : a leader of a group engaged especially in improper or unlawful activities

ring·let \'ring-lət\ *n* **1** *archaic* : a small ring or circle **2** : CURL; *esp* : a long curl of hair

ring·mas·ter \'ring-,mas-tər\ *n* : one in charge of performances in a ring (as of a circus)

ring-necked \'ring-'nekt, -'nek, ,ring-,\ *or* **ring-neck** \,ring-,nek\ *adj* : having a ring of color about the neck

ring-necked pheasant *n* : an Old World pheasant with a white neck ring widely introduced in temperate regions as a game bird

ring-necked pheasant

ring·side \'ring-,sīd\ *n* **1** : the area just outside a ring especially in which a contest occurs **2** : a place from which one may have a close view — **ringside** *adj*

ring stand *n* : a metal stand consisting of an upright rod on a rectangular base used with rings and clamps for supporting laboratory apparatus

ring-tailed \'ring-'tāld\ *adj* : having a tail marked with rings of differing colors

ring·toss \-,tȯs, -,täs\ *n* : a game the object of which is to toss a ring so that it will fall over an upright stick

ring·worm \-,wərm\ *n* : a contagious skin disease caused by fungi and characterized by ring-shaped discolored patches

rink \'ringk\ *n* **1 a** : a sheet of ice marked off for curling or ice hockey **b** : a usually artificial sheet of ice for ice-skating **c** : an enclosure for roller-skating **2** : a division of a bowling green large enough for a match **3** : a team in bowls or curling [Middle English *rinc* "area for a contest", from Middle French *renc* "row, rank, place"]

¹rinse \'rins\ *vt* **1** : to cleanse with liquid (as water) **2** : to treat (hair) with a rinse **3** : to remove (as dirt or impurities) by washing lightly or in water only [Middle French *rincer*, derived from Latin *recens* "fresh, recent"] — **rins·er** *n*

²rinse *n* **1** : the act or process of rinsing **2 a** : liquid used for rinsing **b** : a solution that temporarily tints hair

¹ri·ot \'rī-ət\ *n* **1** *archaic* **a** : DEBAUCHERY **b** : unrestrained revelry **2 a** : public violence, tumult, or disorder **b** : a tumultuous disturbance of the public peace by three or more persons assembled together **3** : a random or disorderly abundance especially of color **4** : one that is wildly amusing [Old French, "quarrel, dispute"]

²riot *vb* **1** : REVEL 1 **2** : to create or engage in a riot **3** : to waste or spend recklessly — **ri·ot·er** *n*

riot act *n* : a very strong reproof, reprimand, or warning — used in the phrase *read the riot act* [the *Riot Act*, English law of 1715 providing for the dispersal of riots upon command of legal authority]

riot gun *n* : a small arm used to disperse rioters rather than to inflict serious injury; *esp* : a short-barreled shotgun

ri·ot·ous \'rī-ət-əs\ *adj* **1** : PROFUSE 2, ABUNDANT **2 a** : of the nature of a riot : TURBULENT **b** : taking part in a riot — **ri·ot·ous·ly** *adv* — **ri·ot·ous·ness** *n*

¹rip \'rip\ *vb* **ripped; rip·ping 1** : to tear or split apart or open **2** : to saw or split (wood) with the grain **3** : to slash or slit with or as if with a sharp blade **4** : to rush headlong [probably from Flemish *rippen* "to strip off roughly"] — **rip·per** *n* — **rip into** : to tear into : ATTACK

²rip *n* : a rent made by ripping : TEAR

³rip *n* : a body of water made rough by the meeting of opposing currents or by passing over an irregular bottom [perhaps from ²*rip*]

⁴rip *n* **1** : a worn-out worthless horse **2** : a reckless or dissolute person [perhaps from *reprobate*]

ri·par·i·an \rə-'per-ē-ən, rī-\ *adj* : relating to or living or located on the bank of a natural watercourse (as a stream or river) or sometimes of a lake or a tidewater [Latin *riparius*, from *ripa* "bank, shore"]

rip cord *n* : a cord or wire pulled in making a descent to release the pilot parachute which lifts the main parachute out of its container

rip current *n* : a strong surface current flowing outward from a shore

ripe \ˈrīp\ *adj* **1** : fully grown and developed : MATURE **2** : having mature knowledge, understanding, or judgment **3** : of advanced years ⟨a *ripe* old age⟩ **4 a** : fully arrived : SUITABLE ⟨the time seemed *ripe*⟩ **b** : fully prepared : READY ⟨*ripe* for action⟩ **5** : brought by aging to full flavor or the best state : MELLOW ⟨*ripe* cheese⟩ **6** : ruddy, plump, or full like ripened fruit [Old English *rīpe*] — **ripe•ly** *adv* — **ripe•ness** *n*

rip•en \ˈrī-pən\ *vb* **rip•ened**; **rip•en•ing** \ˈrīp-ning, -ə-ning\ : to grow or make ripe — **rip•en•er** \ˈrīp-nər, -ə-nər\ *n*

rip–off \ˈrip-ˌȯf\ *n* : an act or instance of stealing : THEFT; *also* : a financial exploitation

rip off \rip-ˈȯf, ˈrip-\ *vt* : ROB 1; *also* : STEAL

ri•poste \ri-ˈpōst\ *n* **1** : a fencer's quick return thrust following a parry **2** : a quick retort **3** : a retaliatory maneuver or measure [French, from Italian *risposta*, literally, "answer", from *rispondere* "to answer, respond", from Latin *respondēre*] — **riposte** *vi*

rip•ping \ˈrip-ing\ *adj* : MARVELOUS 3, TERRIFIC [probably from [1]*rip*]

[1]rip•ple \ˈrip-əl\ *vb* **rip•pled**; **rip•pling** \ˈrip-ling, -ə-ling\ **1 a** : to become lightly ruffled or covered with small waves **b** : to flow in small waves **2** : to stir up small waves on ⟨wind *rippling* water⟩ **3** : to flow with a light rise and fall of sound or inflection ⟨laughter *rippling* over the audience⟩ **4** : to impart a wavy motion or appearance to [perhaps from [1]*rip*] — **rip•pler** \ˈrip-lər, -ə-lər\ *n*

[2]ripple *n* **1 a** : the ruffling of the surface of water **b** : a small wave **2** : a sound like that of rippling water

[1]rip•rap \ˈrip-ˌrap\ *n* **1** : a foundation or sustaining wall of stones thrown together without order (as in deep water or on an embankment slope to prevent erosion) **2** : stone used for riprap [obsolete *riprap* "sound of rapping"]

[2]riprap *vt* **rip•rapped**; **rip•rap•ping** **1** : to form a riprap in or on **2** : to strengthen or support with a riprap

rip–roar•ing \ˈrip-ˈrōr-ing, -ˈrȯr-\ *adj* : noisily excited or exciting

rip•saw \ˈrip-ˌsȯ\ *n* : a coarse-toothed saw for cutting wood in the direction of the grain

rip•tide \ˈrip-ˌtīd\ *n* : RIP CURRENT

[1]rise \ˈrīz\ *vi* **rose** \ˈrōz\; **ris•en** \ˈriz-n\; **ris•ing** \ˈrī-zing\ **1 a** : to get up especially from lying, kneeling, or sitting **b** : to get up from sleep or from one's bed **2** : to return from death **3** : to take up arms ⟨*rise* in rebellion⟩ **4** : to respond warmly : APPLAUD — usually used with *to* **5** : to end a session : ADJOURN ⟨the senate *rose* at noon⟩ **6** : to appear above the horizon ⟨the sun *rises* at six⟩ ⟨land *rose* to starboard⟩ **7 a** : to move upward : ASCEND ⟨smoke *rises*⟩ **b** : to extend upward ⟨the hill *rises* to a great height⟩ **8** : to swell in size or volume ⟨the river is *rising*⟩ ⟨dough *rises*⟩ **9 a** : to become heartened or elated ⟨their spirits *rose*⟩ **b** : to increase in intensity ⟨felt my anger *rising*⟩ **10 a** : to go higher in rank : be promoted ⟨*rose* to colonel⟩ **b** : to increase in quantity or number ⟨production *rose* sharply⟩ **c** : to increase in price or be marked by increasing prices ⟨*rising* costs⟩ ⟨a *rising* stock market⟩ **11 a** : to come about : HAPPEN ⟨an ugly rumor had *risen*⟩ **b** : to have a source : ORIGINATE ⟨that river *rises* in the hills⟩ **12** : to exert oneself to meet a challenge ⟨always *rose* to the occasion⟩ [Old English *rīsan*]

[2]rise \ˈrīz\ *n* **1** : an act of rising : a state of having risen **2** : ORIGIN 2a, BEGINNING **3** : the distance or elevation of one point above another **4** : an increase especially in amount, number, volume, or price **5 a** : an upward slope **b** : a spot higher than surrounding ground **6** : an irritated or angry reaction ⟨got a *rise* out of you⟩

ris•er \ˈrī-zər\ *n* **1** : one that rises (as from sleep) **2** : the upright member between two stair treads

ris•i•bil•i•ty \ˌriz-ə-ˈbil-ət-ē\ *n, pl* **-ties** **1** : the ability or inclination to laugh — often used in pl. **2** : LAUGHTER, MERRIMENT

ris•i•ble \ˈriz-ə-bəl\ *adj* **1** : able or inclined to laugh **2** : provoking laughter : FUNNY [Late Latin *risibilis*, from Latin *risus*, past participle of *ridēre* "to laugh"] **syn** see LAUGHABLE

[1]risk \ˈrisk\ *n* **1** : possibility of loss or injury : PERIL **2 a** : the chance of loss or the perils to a person or thing that is insured **b** : a person or thing that is a hazard to an insurer ⟨a poor *risk*⟩ [French *risque*, from Italian *risco*] **syn** see DANGER

riser 2

[2]risk *vt* **1** : to expose to hazard or danger ⟨*risked* my life⟩ **2** : to take the risk or danger of ⟨*risked* breaking my neck⟩ — **risk•er** *n*

risky \ˈris-kē\ *adj* **risk•i•er**; **-est** : involving risk or danger : HAZARDOUS — **risk•i•ness** *n*

ris•qué \ri-ˈskā\ *adj* : bordering on impropriety or indecency : OFF-COLOR [French, from *risquer* "to risk", from *risque* "risk"]

ri•tar•dan•do \ri-ˌtär-ˈdän-dō, ˌrē-\ *adv or adj* : with a gradual slackening in tempo — used as a direction in music [Italian, literally, "retarding"] — **ritardando** *n*

rite \ˈrīt\ *n* **1 a** : a prescribed form for a ceremony **b** : LITURGY 2 **2** : a ceremonial act or action **3** : a division of the Christian church using a distinctive liturgy [Latin *ritus*]

[1]rit•u•al \ˈrich-ə-wəl, ˈrich-əl\ *adj* **1** : of or relating to rites or a ritual ⟨a *ritual* dance⟩ **2** : according to religious law or social custom ⟨*ritual* purity⟩ — **rit•u•al•ly** \-ē\ *adv*

[2]ritual *n* **1** : an established form for a ceremony **2 a** : ritual observance; *esp* : a system of rites **b** : RITE 2 **c** : a formal and customarily repeated act or series of acts

rit•u•al•ism \-ˌiz-əm\ *n* **1** : the use of ritual **2** : excessive devotion to ritual — **rit•u•al•ist** \-əst\ *n* — **rit•u•al•is•tic** \ˌrich-ə-wəl-ˈis-tik, ˌrich-əl-\ *adj* — **rit•u•al•is•ti•cal•ly** \-ti-kə-lē, -klē\ *adv*

ritzy \ˈrit-sē\ *adj* **ritz•i•er**; **-est** : showily elegant : POSH [*Ritz* hotels, noted for their opulence]

[1]ri•val \ˈrī-vəl\ *n* **1 a** : one of two or more trying to reach or obtain something that only one can possess **b** : one who tries to excel **2** : one that equals another in desired qualities : PEER [Latin *rivalis* "one using the same stream as another, rival in love", from *rivalis* "of a stream", from *rivus* "stream"]

△ **origin** *Rival* is derived from Latin *rivalis* which as an adjective means "of a brook or stream", from *rivus*, "brook or stream". As a noun *rivalis* (in its plural forms) refers literally to those who use the same stream as a source of water. Just as neighbors are likely to dispute each other's rights to a common source of water, so too contention is inevitable when two or more persons strive to obtain something that only one can possess. Latin *rivalis* developed a sense relating to rivalry in love, and in this sense it came into English.

[2]rival *adj* : having the same pretensions or claims

[3]rival *vt* **-valed** *or* **-valled**; **-val•ing** *or* **-val•ling** \ˈrīv-ling, -ə-ling\ **1** : to be in competition with **2** : to try to equal or excel **3** : EQUAL 2, MATCH

ri•val•ry \ˈrī-vəl-rē\ *n, pl* **-ries** : the act of rivaling : the state of being a rival : COMPETITION

rive \ˈrīv\ *vb* **rived** \ˈrīvd\; **riv•en** \ˈriv-ən\ *also* **rived**; **riv•ing** \ˈrī-ving\ **1 a** : to tear apart : REND **b** : to split with force or violence **2 a** : to divide into pieces or factions ⟨the church was *riven* with discord⟩ **b** : FRACTURE ⟨a country *riven* by earthquakes⟩ [Old Norse *rīfa*]

riv•er \ˈriv-ər\ *n* **1** : a natural stream of water larger than a brook or creek **2** : a large stream or flow ⟨a *river* of oil⟩ [Old French *rivere*, derived from Latin *riparius* "of a bank or shore", from *ripa* "bank, shore"]

riv•er•bank \ˈriv-ər-ˌbangk\ *n* : the bank of a river

riv•er•bed \-ˌbed\ *n* : the channel occupied or formerly occupied by a river

riv•er•boat \-ˌbōt\ *n* : a boat for use on a river

river horse *n* : HIPPOPOTAMUS

riv•er•ine \ˈriv-ə-ˌrīn, -ˌrēn\ *adj* **1** : relating to, formed by, or resembling a river **2** : living or situated on the banks of a river

riv•er•side \ˈriv-ər-ˌsīd\ *n* : the side or bank of a river

[1]riv•et \ˈriv-ət\ *n* : a single-headed pin or bolt of metal used for uniting two or more pieces by passing the shank through a hole in each piece and then beating or pressing down the plain end so as to make a second head [Middle French, from *river* "to attach, clinch"]

1rivet

2rivet *vt* **1 :** to fasten with or as if with rivets **2 :** to beat or press the end or point of (as a metallic pin, rod, or bolt) so as to form a head **3 :** to attract and hold (as the attention) completely — **riv•et•er** *n*

ri•vi•era \ˌriv-ē-ˈer-ə, ri-ˈvyer-ə\ *n, often cap* **:** a coastal region frequented as a resort area and usually marked by a mild climate [from the *Riviera,* region in France and Italy]

riv•u•let \ˈriv-yə-lət, ˈriv-ə-lət\ *n* **:** a small stream [Italian *rivoletto,* from *rivolo* "brook", from Latin *rivulus* "small stream", from *rivus* "brook, stream"]

1ri•yal \rē-ˈȯl, -ˈyȯl, -ˈäl, -ˈyäl\ *also* **ri•al** \-ˈȯl, -ˈäl\ *n* **1 :** the basic monetary unit of Saudi Arabia **2 :** a coin or note representing one riyal [Arabic *riyāl,* from Spanish *real* "real"]

2riyal *variant of* RIAL

RNA \ˌär-ˌen-ˈā\ *n* **:** any of various nucleic acids that contain ribose and uracil as structural components and are associated with the control of cellular chemical activities — compare DNA, MESSENGER RNA, RIBOSOMAL RNA, TRANSFER RNA [*ribo*nucleic *a*cid]

1roach \ˈrōch\ *n, pl* **roach** *also* **roach•es :** a silver-white greenish-backed European freshwater fish related to the carp; *also* **:** any of several similar or related fishes [Middle French *roche*]

2roach *vt* **:** to brush (the hair) into an arched roll — often used with *up* [origin unknown]

3roach *n* **:** COCKROACH

road \ˈrōd\ *n* **1 :** a place less enclosed than a harbor where ships may ride at anchor — often used in pl. **2 a :** an open way for vehicles, persons, and animals; *esp* **:** one lying outside an urban district **b :** ROADBED 2 **3 :** ROUTE 2, PATH **4 :** RAILWAY [Old English *rād* "ride, journey"] — **on the road 1 :** away from home (as on business) **2 :** in transit through a circuit of performances or games in different locales

road•abil•i•ty \ˌrōd-ə-ˈbil-ət-ē\ *n* **:** the qualities (as steadiness and balance) desirable in an automobile on the road

road•bed \ˈrōd-ˌbed\ *n* **1 :** the foundation of a road or railroad **2 :** the part of the surface of a road traveled by vehicles

road•block \-ˌbläk\ *n* **1 a :** a barricade at a point on a road that can be covered by fire from a defending army **b :** a road barricade set up by law-enforcement officers **2 :** an obstruction in a road **3 :** something that hinders progress

road hog *n* **:** a motorist who obstructs others especially by occupying part of another's traffic lane

road•house \ˈrōd-ˌhau̇s\ *n* **:** a nightclub usually outside city limits

road metal *n* **:** broken stone or cinders used in making and repairing roads or ballasting railroads

road•run•ner \ˈrōd-ˌrən-ər\ *n* **:** a swift-running long-tailed cuckoo of the southwestern United States

1road•side \ˈrōd-ˌsīd\ *n* **:** the strip of land along a road **:** the side of a road

2roadside *adj* **:** situated at the side of a road

road•stead \ˈrōd-ˌsted\ *n* **:** ROAD 1

road•ster \ˈrōd-stər\ *n* **:** an open automobile with one cross seat

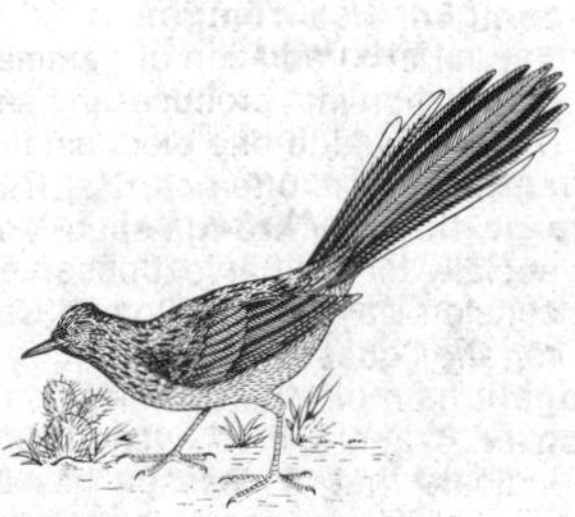

roadrunner

road•way \ˈrōd-ˌwā\ *n* **1 a :** the strip of land over which a road passes **b :** ROAD; *esp* **:** ROADBED 2 **2 :** a railroad right-of-way **3 :** the part of a bridge used by vehicles

road•work \-ˌwərk\ *n* **:** conditioning for an athletic contest (as a boxing match) consisting mainly of long runs

roam \ˈrōm\ *vb* **1 :** to go from place to place aimlessly **:** WANDER ⟨*roam* the hills⟩ **2 :** to travel purposefully and unhindered through a wide area ⟨cattle *roaming* in search of water⟩ [Middle English *romen*] — **roam•er** *n*

1roan \ˈrōn\ *adj* **:** of a base color (as black, red, or brown) dulled and lightened by white hairs [Middle French, from Spanish *roano*]

2roan *n* **1 :** an animal (as a horse) with a roan coat **2 :** the color of a roan horse

1roar \ˈrōr, ˈrȯr\ *vb* **1 :** to utter the characteristic loud prolonged cry of a wild beast (as a lion) or a similar sound **2 a :** to make a loud reverberating sound **b :** to laugh loudly **3 :** to be boisterous or disorderly **4 :** to cause to roar ⟨*roar* a motor⟩ [Old English *rārian*] — **roar•er** \ˈrōr-ər, ˈrȯr-\ *n*

2roar *n* **1 a :** the deep loud cry of a wild beast **b :** a loud deep cry (as of pain or anger) **2 :** a loud continuous confused sound ⟨the *roar* of the crowd⟩

roar•ing *adj* **:** prosperously bustling

1roast \ˈrōst\ *vb* **1 a :** to cook by exposing to dry heat (as in an oven) **b :** to dry and parch by exposure to heat ⟨*roast* coffee⟩ **2 :** to heat (inorganic material) with access of air and without fusing to effect change (as expulsion of volatile matter) ⟨*roast* a sulfide ore⟩ **3 :** to criticize severely **4 :** to undergo roasting [Old French *rostir,* of Germanic origin]

2roast *n* **1 :** a piece of meat roasted or suitable for roasting **2 :** an outing at which food is roasted **3 :** an act of roasting; *esp* **:** severe banter or criticism

3roast *adj* **:** cooked by roasting ⟨*roast* beef⟩

roast•er \ˈrō-stər\ *n* **1 :** one that roasts **2 :** a pan or an appliance for roasting **3 :** something (as a young chicken) suitable for roasting

rob \ˈräb\ *vb* **robbed; rob•bing 1 a :** to take something away from (a person or place) by force, threat, stealth, or trickery ⟨*rob* a store⟩ ⟨*rob* a pedestrian⟩ **b :** to commit robbery **:** STEAL **2 a :** to deprive of something due, expected, or desired **b :** to withhold unjustly or injuriously [Old French *rober,* of Germanic origin] — **rob•ber** *n*

robber fly *n* **:** any of various predaceous flies that usually resemble bumblebees

rob•bery \ˈräb-rē, -ə-rē\ *n, pl* **-ber•ies :** the act or practice of robbing; *esp* **:** larceny from the person or presence of another by violence or threat

1robe \ˈrōb\ *n* **1 :** a long loose or flowing garment: as **a :** one used for ceremonial occasions or as a symbol of office or profession **b :** a garment (as a dressing gown) replacing outer garments for informal wear **2 :** a covering or wrap for the lower body ⟨wrapped the legs in a *robe* at the game⟩ [Old French, "plunder, robe", of Germanic origin]

2robe *vb* **1 :** to clothe, invest, or cover with or as if with a robe **2 :** to put on a robe **3 :** DRESS 2a

rob•in \ˈräb-ən\ *n* **1 :** a small European thrush with yellowish red throat and breast **2 :** a large North American thrush with a gray back, streaked throat, and chiefly dull reddish breast and underparts [short for *Robin redbreast,* from *Robin,* nickname for *Robert*]

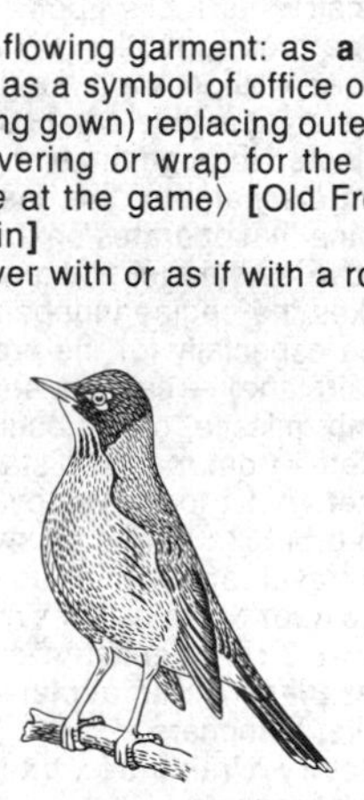

robin 2

ro•bot \ˈrō-ˌbät, -bət\ *n* **1 a :** a machine that looks like a human being and performs various complex acts (as walking or talking) of a human being **b :** an efficient, insensitive, often brutalized person **2 :** an automatic apparatus that performs functions ordinarily ascribed to human beings or operates with what appears to be almost human intelligence **3 :** something guided by automatic controls ⟨a *robot* airplane⟩ ⟨a *robot* factory⟩ [Czech, from *robota* "work"]

△ **origin** In 1923 a play called *R.U.R.* opened in London and New York. The author, Karel Čapek, coined the term *robot* from the Czech *robota,* meaning "work" or "forced labor". In *R.U.R.* (which stands for "Rossum's Universal Robots" in the English

\ə\ **abut**	\au̇\ **out**	\i\ **tip**	\ȯ\ **saw**	\u̇\ **foot**
\ər\ **further**	\ch\ **chin**	\ī\ **life**	\ȯi\ **coin**	\y\ **yet**
\a\ **mat**	\e\ **pet**	\j\ **job**	\th\ **thin**	\yü\ **few**
\ā\ **take**	\ē\ **easy**	\ng\ **sing**	\t͟h\ **this**	\yu̇\ **cure**
\ä\ **cot, cart**	\g\ **go**	\ō\ **bone**	\ü\ **food**	\zh\ **vision**

translation) mechanical men originally designed to perform manual labor become so sophisticated that some advanced models develop the capacity to feel and hate, and eventually they destroy mankind.

ro•bust \rō-ˈbəst, ˈrō-ˌ\ *adj* **1 :** strong and vigorously healthy **:** STURDY **2 :** ROUGH, RUDE ⟨*robust* humor⟩ **3 :** requiring strength or vigor ⟨*robust* work⟩ **4 :** STRONG 7a [Latin *robustus* "oaken, strong", from *robur* "oak, strength"] — **ro•bust•ly** *adv* — **ro•bust•ness** *n*

roc \ˈräk\ *n* **:** a legendary bird of great size and strength believed to inhabit the Indian ocean area [Arabic *rukhkh*]

Ro•chelle salt \rō-ˌshel-\ *n* **:** a hydrated crystalline salt of potassium and sodium that is a mild purgative [La *Rochelle*, France]

roch•et \ˈräch-ət\ *n* **:** a white linen vestment resembling a surplice worn by bishops and privileged prelates [Middle French]

[1]**rock** \ˈräk\ *vb* **1 :** to move back and forth in or as if in a cradle **2 a :** to sway or cause to sway back and forth **b** (1) **:** DAZE 1, STUN (2) **:** DISTURB 2a, b, UPSET [Old English *roccian*] **syn** see SHAKE

[2]**rock** *n* **1 :** a rocking movement **2 :** music usually played on amplified instruments and marked by a heavy beat, repetition of simple phrases, and often country, folk, or blues elements

[3]**rock** *n* **1 :** a large mass of stone forming a cliff, promontory, or peak **2 :** consolidated or unconsolidated solid mineral matter; *also* **:** a particular mass of it **3 :** something (as a support or refuge) like a rock in firmness **4** *slang* **a :** GEM 1 **b :** DIAMOND 1a [Old North French *roque*] — **on the rocks 1 :** in or into a state of destruction or wreckage **2 :** on ice cubes ⟨bourbon *on the rocks*⟩

rock bottom *n* **:** the lowest or most basic part or level — **rock–bottom** *adj*

rock•bound \ˈräk-ˈbau̇nd\ *adj* **:** fringed, surrounded, or covered with rocks **:** ROCKY

rock candy *n* **:** sugar crystallized in large masses

rock crystal *n* **:** transparent quartz

rock•er \ˈräk-ər\ *n* **1 a :** a curving piece of wood or metal on which an object (as a cradle) rocks **b :** a structure or device (as a chair) that rocks upon rockers **2 :** a mechanism that works with a rocking motion **3 :** a rock singer, musician, or song

[1]**rock•et** \ˈräk-ət\ *n* **1 :** a firework consisting of a case containing a combustible composition fastened to a guiding stick and projected through the air by the reaction resulting from the rearward discharge of the gases liberated by combustion **2 :** a jet engine that operates on the same principle as the firework rocket, carries the fuel and oxygen needed for combustion and thus makes the engine independent of the oxygen of the air, and is used especially for the propulsion of a missile or a vehicle (as an airplane) — called also *rocket engine* **3 :** a rocket-propelled bomb, missile, or projectile [Italian *rocchetta*, literally, "small distaff", from *rocca* "distaff", of Germanic origin]

[2]**rocket** *vb* **1 :** to convey by means of a rocket ⟨*rocket* a satellite into orbit⟩ **2 :** to rise up swiftly, spectacularly, and with force **3 :** to travel rapidly in or as if in a rocket

rock•e•teer \ˌräk-ə-ˈtiər\ *n* **1 :** one who fires, pilots, or rides in a rocket **2 :** a scientist who specializes in rocketry

rocket plane *n* **:** an airplane propelled by rockets or armed with rocket launchers

rock•et•ry \ˈräk-ə-trē\ *n* **:** the study of, experimentation with, or use of rockets

rocket ship *n* **:** a rocket-propelled spaceship

rock•fish \ˈräk-ˌfish\ *n* **:** any of various valuable market and sport fishes (as a greenling or striped bass) that live among rocks or on rocky bottoms

rock garden *n* **:** a garden laid out among rocks or decorated with rocks and adapted for the growth of particular kinds of plants (as alpines)

rocking chair *n* **:** a chair mounted on rockers

rocking horse *n* **:** a toy horse mounted on rockers — called also *hobbyhorse*

rock lobster *n* **:** SPINY LOBSTER

rock 'n' roll \ˌräk-ən-ˈrōl\ *n* **:** [2]ROCK 2

rock pigeon *n* **:** a wild bluish gray Old World pigeon

rock–ribbed \ˈräk-ˈribd\ *adj* **1 :** [1]ROCKY 1 **2 :** INFLEXIBLE 2, 3

rock salt *n* **:** common salt in large crystals or masses

rock•weed \ˈräk-ˌwēd\ *n* **:** any of various brown algae commonly growing attached to rocks along shores — called also *fucus*

rock wool *n* **:** mineral wool made by blowing a jet of steam through molten rock or through slag and used chiefly for heat and sound insulation

[1]**rocky** \ˈräk-ē\ *adj* **rock•i•er**; **-est 1 :** abounding in or consisting of rocks **2 :** difficult to impress or affect **:** INSENSITIVE **3 :** firmly held **:** STEADFAST — **rock•i•ness** *n*

[2]**rocky** *adj* **rock•i•er**; **-est 1 :** not stable **:** WOBBLY **2 :** physically upset **:** UNWELL — **rock•i•ness** *n*

Rocky Mountain goat *n* **:** MOUNTAIN GOAT [*Rocky mountains*, North America]

Rocky Mountain sheep *n* **:** BIGHORN

Rocky Mountain spotted fever *n* **:** an acute rickettsial disease marked by chills, fever, prostration, pains in muscles and joints, and a red to purple eruption and transmitted by the bite of a tick

ro•co•co \rə-ˈkō-kō, ˌrō-kə-ˈkō\ *adj* **1 :** of or relating to an 18th century artistic style marked especially by fanciful curved forms **2 :** excessively ornate [French, from *rocaille* "rock-work", from *roc* "rock", from Middle French *roche*] — **rococo** *n*

rod \ˈräd\ *n* **1 :** a straight slender stick or bar ⟨a curtain *rod*⟩: as **a :** a stick used to punish; *also* **:** PUNISHMENT **b :** a pole with a line and usually a reel attached for fishing **c :** a bar for measuring **2 a :** a unit of length — see MEASURE table **b :** a square rod **3 :** any of the rod-shaped sensory bodies in the retina responsive to faint light **4 :** a bacterium shaped like a rod **5** *slang* **:** PISTOL [Old English *rodd*] — **rod•less** \-ləs\ *adj* — **rod•like** \-ˌlīk\ *adj*

rode *past of* RIDE

ro•dent \ˈrōd-nt\ *n* **:** any of an order (Rodentia) of relatively small gnawing mammals (as mice, squirrels, or beavers) having a single pair of upper incisors with a chisel-shaped edge — compare LAGOMORPH [derived from Latin *rodens*, present participle of *rodere* "to gnaw"] — **rodent** *adj*

ro•den•ti•cide \rō-ˈdent-ə-ˌsīd\ *n* **:** an agent that kills or repels rodents — **ro•den•ti•cid•al** \-ˌdent-ə-ˈsīd-l\ *adj*

ro•deo \ˈrōd-ē-ˌō, rə-ˈdā-ō\ *n, pl* **-de•os 1 :** ROUNDUP 1 **2 :** a contest or exhibition of cowboy skills (as riding and roping) [Spanish, from *rodear* "to surround", from *rueda* "wheel", from Latin *rota* "wheel"]

[1]**roe** \ˈrō\ *n, pl* **roe** *or* **roes :** DOE [Old English *rā*]

[2]**roe** *n* **:** the eggs of a fish especially while still bound together in a membrane [Middle English *roof, roughe, row*]

roe•buck \ˈrō-ˌbək\ *n, pl* **roebuck** *or* **roebucks :** ROE DEER; *esp* **:** the male roe deer

roe deer *n* **:** a small active deer of Europe and Asia that has erect antlers forked at the tip and is reddish brown in summer and grayish in winter

roe deer

[1]**roent•gen** *also* **rönt•gen** \ˈrent-gən, ˈrənt-, -jən\ *adj* **:** of or relating to X rays ⟨*roentgen* examinations⟩ [Wilhelm *Röntgen*, died 1923, German physicist]

[2]**roentgen** *also* **röntgen** *n* **:** a unit of x-radiation or gamma radiation equal to the amount of radiation that produces in one cubic centimeter of dry air ionization equal to one electrostatic unit of charge

roentgen ray *n, often cap 1st R* **:** X RAY

Ro•ga•tion Day \rō-ˈgā-shən-\ *n* **:** one of the days of prayer especially for the harvest observed on the three days before Ascension Day and by Roman Catholics also on April 25 [Latin *rogatio* "questioning", from *rogare* "to ask"]

rogations *n pl* **:** the ceremonies of the Rogation Days

rog•er \ˈräj-ər\ *interj* — used especially in radio and signaling to indicate that a message has been received and understood [*Roger*, former communications code word for *r*, initial letter of *received*]

[1]**rogue** \ˈrōg\ *n* **1 a :** TRAMP 1, VAGRANT **b :** a dishonest or worthless person **:** SCOUNDREL **c :** a pleasantly mischievous person **:** SCAMP **2 :** a vicious or lazy animal **3 :** an individual plant or animal with a chance and usually inferior biological variation [origin unknown] — **rogu•ish** \ˈrō-gish\ *adj* — **rogu•ish•ly** *adv* — **rogu•ish•ness** *n*

[2]**rogue** *vi* **rogued**; **rogu•ing** *or* **rogue•ing :** to weed out inferior individuals from a crop

^{3}**rogue** *adj* : being vicious and destructive ⟨*rogue* elephants⟩
rogu•ery \'rō-gə-rē, -grē\ *n, pl* **-er•ies** **1** : the practices or an act characteristic of a rogue **2** : mischievous play
rogues' gallery *n* : a collection of pictures of persons arrested as criminals
roil \'rȯil, *2 is also* 'rīl\ *vt* **1** : to make cloudy or muddy by stirring up sediment ⟨*roil* the water of a brook⟩ **2** : RILE 2 [origin unknown]
roily \'rȯi-lē\ *adj* **roil•i•er**; **-est** **1** : full of sediment or dregs : MUDDY **2** : TURBULENT 2
rois•ter \'rȯi-stər\ *vi* **rois•tered**; **rois•ter•ing** \-stə-riŋ, -striŋ\ : REVEL 1 [from earlier *roister* "roisterer", probably from Middle French *rustre* "boor, lout", derived from Latin *rusticus* "rustic, rural"] — **rois•ter•er** \-stər-ər\ *n*
role *also* **rôle** \'rōl\ *n* **1 a** : a character assigned or assumed **b** : a part played by an actor or singer **2** : FUNCTION 2, 4 ⟨the *role* of enzymes in digestion⟩ [French *rôle*, literally, "roll", from Old French *rolle*]
^{1}**roll** \'rōl\ *n* **1 a** : a written document that may be rolled up : SCROLL **b** : an official list especially of members of a body (as a legislature) **2** : something that is rolled or rounded: as **a** : a quantity (as of fabric or paper) rolled up to form a single package **b** (1) : a food preparation rolled up for cooking or serving (2) : a small piece of baked yeast dough **c** : paper money folded or rolled; *also, slang* : BANKROLL **3** : something that rolls : ROLLER [Old French *rolle*, from Latin *rotula*, "small wheel", from *rota* "wheel"]
^{2}**roll** *vb* **1 a** : to move along a surface by rotation without sliding **b** : to turn over and over **c** : to move about or as if about an axis or point **2 a** : to put a wrapping around **b** : to form into a ball or roll **3** : to make smooth, even, or compact with or as if with a roller **4 a** : to move on rollers or wheels **b** : to begin operating or moving ⟨the new shop got *rolling*⟩ **5 a** : to make or cause to make a full reverberating or continuous beating sound ⟨*roll* a drum⟩ ⟨thunder *rolled*⟩ **b** : to utter with a trill ⟨you *roll* your *r*'s⟩ **6** : to rob (as an unconscious person) usually by going through the pockets **7** : to luxuriate in an abundant supply ⟨*rolling* in money⟩ **8** : ELAPSE, PASS ⟨time *rolls* by⟩ **9** : to flow in a continuous stream ⟨money was *rolling* in⟩ **10** : to have a wavy surface ⟨*rolling* prairies⟩ **11** : to sway from side to side : ROCK ⟨the ship heaved and *rolled*⟩ **12** : to respond to rolling in a specified way ⟨a good paint *rolls* on smoothly⟩ **13** : to move forward : develop and maintain impetus ⟨the team finally got *rolling* in the second half⟩
^{3}**roll** *n* **1 a** : a sound produced by rapid strokes on a drum **b** : a sonorous and often rhythmical flow of speech **c** : a heavy reverberating sound ⟨the *roll* of cannon⟩ **2** : a rolling movement or an action or process involving such movement; *esp* : a swaying or side-to-side movement
roll bar *n* : an overhead metal bar on an automobile that is designed to protect the occupant in case of a turnover
roll call *n* : the act of calling off a list of names (as for checking attendance); *also* : a time for a roll call
^{1}**roll•er** \'rō-lər\ *n* **1 a** : a revolving cylinder over or on which something is moved or which is used to press, shape, or smooth something **b** : a rod on which something (as a map) is rolled up **c** : a small wheel (as of a roller skate) **2** : a long heavy wave on the sea
^{2}**rol•ler** \'rō-lər\ *n* : a canary with a soft trilling song [German, from *rollen* "to roll, reverberate", from Middle French *roller*, derived from Latin *rotula* "small wheel"]
roller bearing *n* : a bearing in which a revolving part turns on rollers held in a circular frame or cage
roll•er coaster \'rō-lər-,kō-stər, 'rō-lē-,kō-\ *n* : an amusement park ride consisting of an elevated railway with sharp curves and steep inclines on which cars roll
roll•er skate *n* : a skate that has wheels instead of a runner — **roller-skate** *vi*
rol•lick \'räl-ik\ *vi* : FROLIC [origin unknown] — **rollick** *n* — **rol•lick•ing** *adj*
rolling mill *n* : an establishment where metal is rolled into plates and bars
rolling pin *n* : a cylinder (as of wood) for rolling out dough
rolling stock *n* : wheeled vehicles owned or used by a railroad or motor carrier
roll•top desk \,rōl-,täp-\ *n* : a writing desk with a cover that rolls back into the frame
roll up *vb* **1** : ACCUMULATE ⟨*rolled up* a majority⟩ **2** : to arrive in a vehicle

ro•ly-po•ly \,rō-lē-'pō-lē\ *n, pl* **-lies** **1** : a pudding made of rolled-out dough spread with a filling, rolled up into a cylinder shape, and baked or steamed **2** : a short stout person or thing [reduplication of *roly*, from ^{2}*roll*] — **roly-poly** *adj*

roller skate

ro•maine \rō-'mān\ *n* : a lettuce with long spoon-shaped leaves and columnar heads [French, from *romain* "Roman", from Latin *Romanus*]
^{1}**Ro•man** \'rō-mən\ *n* **1 a** : a native or resident of Rome **b** : a citizen of the Roman Empire **2** : ROMAN CATHOLIC — often taken to be offensive **3** *not cap* : roman letters or type
^{2}**Roman** *adj* **1** : of or relating to ancient or modern Rome, the people of Rome, or the empire of which Rome was the original capital; *esp* : characteristic of the ancient Romans ⟨*Roman* fortitude⟩ **2** : LATIN 2 **3** *not cap* : of or relating to a type style with upright characters (as in "these words are roman") **4** : of or relating to the see of Rome or the Roman Catholic Church **5** : having a prominent slightly aquiline bridge ⟨a *Roman* nose⟩
ro•man à clef \rō-,mä^{n}-ä-'klā\ *n, pl* **ro•mans à clef** *same or* -,mä^{n}z-ä-\ : a novel in which real persons or actual events figure under disguise [French, literally, "novel with a key"]
Roman candle *n* : a cylindrical firework that discharges at intervals balls or stars of fire
Roman Catholic *adj* : of or relating to the body of Christians having a hierarchy under the pope, a liturgy centered in the Mass, and a body of dogma formulated by the church as the infallible interpreter of revealed truth — **Roman Catholic** *n* — **Roman Catholicism** *n*
^{1}**ro•mance** \rō-'mans, 'rō-,\ *n* **1 a** : a medieval tale based on legend, chivalric love and adventure, and the supernatural **b** : a prose narrative dealing with imaginary characters involved in heroic, adventurous, or mysterious events remote in time or place **c** : a love story **2** : something that lacks basis in fact **3** : the adventurous or glamorous attractiveness of something ⟨the *romance* of the old West⟩ **4** : a love affair **5** *cap* : the Romance languages [Old French *romans* "French, something written in French, romance", from Latin *romanice* "in the Roman manner", derived from *Romanus* "Roman"]
△ **origin** In the last centuries of the Roman Empire the wide variety and distribution of the peoples recognized as Roman citizens led to the gradual change of the Latin language. The developing languages, which in their early stages were local dialects of Latin, were called *romans* (to use the Old French term) to distinguish them from the formal and official language. Most serious literature was still written in Latin, but in France entertaining verse tales were often written in the more popular spoken language, *romans*. The word *romans* came to be used for such a tale and was borrowed, in this sense, into English. Because many of these tales dealt with love, *romance* came to mean simply "a love story", and eventually it developed the sense of "a love affair".
^{2}**romance** *vb* **1** : to exaggerate or invent details or incidents **2 a** : to entertain romantic thoughts or ideas **b** : to carry on a love affair with
Ro•mance \rō-'mans, 'rō-,\ *adj* : of, relating to, or being the languages (as French, Italian, or Spanish) developed from Latin
Roman collar *n* : CLERICAL COLLAR
Ro•man•esque \,rō-mə-'nesk\ *adj* : of or relating to an architectural style developed in Italy and western Europe and characterized in its development after 1000 A.D. by the use of the round arch and vault, decorative use of arcades, and profuse ornament — **Romanesque** *n*
Ro•ma•ni•an *variant of* RUMANIAN
Ro•man•ic \rō-'man-ik\ *adj* : ROMANCE — **Romanic** *n*
Roman numeral *n* : a numeral in a system of notation based on

the ancient Roman system — see NUMBER table

Ro•ma•no \rə-'män-ō, rō-\ *n* : a sharp hard Italian cheese [Italian, "Roman", from Latin *Romanus*]

Ro•mans \'rō-mənz\ *n* — see BIBLE table

Ro•mansh *or* **Ro•mansch** \rō-'mänch\ *n* : the Rhaeto-Romanic dialects spoken in the Grisons, Switzerland, and adjacent parts of Italy [Romansh *romonsch*]

1ro•man•tic \rō-'mant-ik\ *adj* **1 a :** consisting of or resembling a romance ⟨*romantic* writing⟩ **b :** not factual : IMAGINARY ⟨a too *romantic* report of your adventure⟩ **2 a :** UNREALISTIC, IMPRACTICAL **b** *often cap* **:** of, relating to, or exhibiting romanticism **3 :** having a strong emotional or imaginative appeal or association ⟨a *romantic* spot⟩ **4 :** marked by or being passionate love [French *romantique*, from obsolete *romant* "romance", from Old French *romans*] — **ro•man•ti•cal•ly** \-i-kə-lē, -klē\ *adv*

2romantic *n* **1 :** a romantic person, trait, or component **2** *cap* **:** a romantic writer, artist, or composer

ro•man•ti•cism \rō-'mant-ə-,siz-əm\ *n* **1 :** the quality or state of being romantic **2** *often cap* **:** a literary, artistic, and philosophical movement marked by emphasis on the imagination and emotions and especially by an exaltation of primitive and the common people, appreciation of nature, and interest in the remote or melancholy — **ro•man•ti•cist** \-səst\ *n, often cap*

ro•man•ti•cize \rō-'mant-ə-,sīz\ *vb* **1 :** to make romantic : present romantically **2 :** to have romantic ideas — **ro•man•ti•ci•za•tion** \-,mant-ə-sə-'zā-shən\ *n*

Ro•ma•ny \'räm-ə-nē, 'rō-mə-\ *n* **1 :** GYPSY 1 **2 :** the Indic language of the Gypsies [Romany *romani*, adj., "gypsy", from *rom* "gypsy man", from Sanskrit *ḍomba* "man of a low caste of musicians"] — **Romany** *adj*

1romp \'rämp\ *n* **1 :** ROMPER 1 **2 :** boisterous play : FROLIC [derived from 1*ramp*]

2romp *vi* **:** to play in a boisterous way : FROLIC

romp•er \'räm-pər\ *n* **1 :** one that romps **2 :** a child's one-piece garment including pants and a top — usually used in pl.

ron•do \'rän-dō\ *n, pl* **rondos :** a musical composition or movement in which the principal theme recurs several times with contrasting themes in between [Italian *rondò*, from Middle French *rondeau* "song with frequent repetitions of its two themes, rondeau"]

röntgen *variant of* ROENTGEN

rood \'rüd\ *n* **1 :** CROSS 1b, CRUCIFIX **2 :** any of various units of land area; *esp* **:** a British unit equal to ¼ acre (about 1011.7 square meters) [Old English *rōd* "rod, rood"]

1roof \'rüf, 'rụ̇f\ *n, pl* **roofs** \'rüfs, 'rụ̇fs *also* 'rüvz, 'rụ̇vz\ **1 :** the upper covering part of a building; *also* **:** ROOFING **2 :** something (as the vaulted upper boundary of the mouth) resembling a roof in form, position, or function [Old English *hrōf*] — **roofed** \'rüft, 'rụ̇ft\ *adj* — **roof•less** \-ləs\ *adj* — **roof-like** \-,līk\ *adj*

2roof *vt* **:** to cover with or as if with a roof — **roof•er** *n*

roof•ing *n* **:** material for a roof

roof•top \'rüf-,täp, 'rụ̇f-\ *n* **:** ROOF 1; *esp* **:** the outer surface of a usually flat roof ⟨sunning themselves on the *rooftop*⟩

roof•tree \-,trē\ *n* **:** RIDGEPOLE 1

1rook \'rụ̇k\ *n* **:** a common Old World gregarious bird about the size and color of the related American crow [Old English *hrōc*]

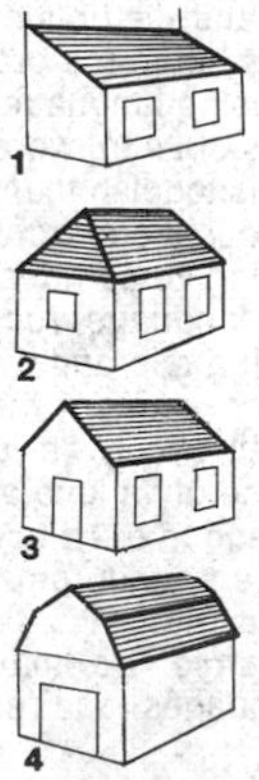

1roof 1. *1* lean-to, *2* hip, *3* saddle, *4* gambrel

2rook *vt* **:** to defraud by cheating or swindling

3rook *n* **:** a chess piece that can move parallel to the edges of the board across any number of unoccupied squares — called also *castle* [Middle French *roc*, from Arabic *rukhkh*, from Persian]

rook•ery \'rụ̇k-ə-rē\ *n, pl* **-er•ies 1 :** the breeding place of a colony of gregarious birds (as rooks) or mammals; *also* **:** the colony itself **2 :** a crowded dilapidated tenement or group of dwellings

rook•ie \'rụ̇k-ē\ *n* **1 :** RECRUIT 1 **2 :** a person who is in the first year of participation in a professional sport [perhaps alteration of *recruit*]

1room \'rüm, 'rụ̇m\ *n* **1 :** unoccupied area : SPACE ⟨*room* to turn the car⟩ **2 a :** a partitioned part of the inside of a building **b :** the people in a room **c** *pl* **:** LODGING 2, APARTMENT **3 :** opportunity or occasion for something : CHANCE ⟨*room* for improvement⟩ [Old English *rūm*] — **roomed** \'rümd, 'rụ̇md\ *adj*

2room *vb* **:** to provide with or occupy lodgings

room•er \'rü-mər, 'rụ̇m-ər\ *n* **:** LODGER

room•ette \rü-'met, rụ̇m-'et\ *n* **:** a small private single room on a railroad sleeping car

room•ful \'rüm-,fụ̇l, 'rụ̇m-\ *n, pl* **roomfuls** \-,fụ̇lz\ *or* **rooms•ful** \'rümz-,fụ̇l, 'rụ̇mz-\ **:** as much or as many as a room will hold; *also* **:** the persons or objects in a room

rooming house *n* **:** a house where rooms are rented to lodgers

room•mate \'rüm-,māt, 'rụ̇m-\ *n* **:** one of two or more persons occupying the same room

roomy \'rü-mē, 'rụ̇m-ē\ *adj* **room•i•er; -est :** having plenty of room : SPACIOUS — **room•i•ness** *n*

1roost \'rüst\ *n* **1 :** PERCH 2a **2 :** a place where birds customarily roost [Old English *hrōst*]

2roost *vb* **:** to settle on or as if on a roost : PERCH

roost•er \'rü-stər\ *n* **:** an adult male domestic fowl; *also* **:** an adult male bird

1root \'rüt, 'rụ̇t\ *n* **1 a :** the usually underground part of a seed plant body that functions as an organ of absorption, aeration, and food storage or as a means of anchorage and support and that differs from a stem especially in lacking nodes, buds, and leaves **b :** a subterranean plant part especially when fleshy and edible **2 a :** the part of a tooth within the socket **b :** the enlarged basal part of a hair within the skin **c :** the basal or central part of a bodily structure or the part by which it is attached ⟨nerve *roots*⟩ ⟨the *root* of the tongue⟩ **3 a :** the cause or origin of something : SOURCE **b :** an underlying support : BASIS **c :** the essential core : HEART **4 a :** a number that when taken as a factor an indicated number of times gives a specified number ⟨2 is a 4th *root* of 16⟩ **b :** a solution of a polynomial equation in one unknown **5 :** a word or part of a word from which other words are derived by adding a prefix or suffix **6 :** the lowest tone of a chord in normal position — compare INVERSION [Old English *rōt*, from Old Norse] **syn** see ORIGIN — **root•ed** \-əd\ *adj* — **root•less** \-ləs\ *adj* — **root•like** \-,līk\ *adj*

2root *vb* **1 a :** to form or enable to form roots **b :** to fix or become fixed by or as if by roots : take root **2 :** to remove altogether often by force ⟨*root* out dissenters⟩

3root *vb* **1 :** to turn up or dig in the earth with the snout **2 :** to poke or dig about [Old English *wrōtan*]

4root \'rüt *also* 'rụ̇t\ *vi* **1 :** to applaud noisily : CHEER ⟨a group of students *rooting* for the football team⟩ **2 :** to encourage or lend support to someone or something ⟨*rooted* for the reform candidate⟩ [perhaps from earlier *rout* "to bellow", from Old Norse *rauta*] — **root•er** *n*

root beer *n* **:** a sweetened carbonated beverage flavored with extracts of roots and herbs

root cap *n* **:** a protective cap of parenchyma cells that covers the terminal meristem in most root tips

root cellar *n* **:** an underground storage area for vegetables (as root crops)

root crop *n* **:** a crop (as turnips or sweet potatoes) grown for its enlarged roots

root hair *n* **:** one of the filamentous outgrowths near the tip of a rootlet that function in absorption of water and minerals

root•let \'rüt-lət, 'rụ̇t-\ *n* **:** a small root

root pressure *n* **:** the chiefly osmotic pressure that contributes to the rise of water into the stems of plants from the roots

root•stock \'rüt-,stäk, 'rụ̇t-\ *n* **1 :** RHIZOME **2 :** a stock for grafting consisting of a root or a piece of root

rooty \'rüt-ē, 'rụ̇t-\ *adj* **root•i•er; -est :** full or consisting of roots ⟨*rooty* soil⟩

1rope \'rōp\ *n* **1 a :** a large stout cord of strands (as of fiber or wire) twisted or braided together **b :** a length of material (as rope or rawhide) suitable for a use; *esp* **:** LARIAT **c :** a hangman's noose **2 :** a row or string consisting of things united by or as if by braiding, twining, or threading ⟨a *rope* of daisies⟩ **3** *pl* **:** special techniques or procedures ⟨show them the *ropes*⟩ [Old English *rāp*]

2rope *vb* **1 a :** to bind, fasten, or tie with a rope or cord **b :** to set off or divide by a rope ⟨*rope* off the street⟩ **c :** LASSO **2 :** to draw as if with a rope : LURE **3 :** to take the form of or twist in the manner of rope — **rop•er** *n*

rope•danc•er \'rōp-,dan-sər\ *n* **:** one that dances, walks, or performs acrobatic feats on a rope high in the air — **rope·danc·ing** \-sing\ *n*

rope·walk \-ˌwȯk\ *n* : a place where rope is made

rope·walk·er \-ˌwȯ-kər\ *n* : an acrobat who walks on a rope high in the air

ropy \ˈrō-pē\ *adj* **rop·i·er; -est** **1** : capable of being drawn into a sticky thread **2** : suggesting rope : STRINGY, SINEWY ⟨*ropy* muscles⟩ — **rop·i·ness** *n*

Roque·fort \ˈrōk-fərt\ *trademark* — used for a cheese made of ewes' milk and ripened in caves

ror·qual \ˈrȯr-kwəl, -ˌkwȯl\ *n* : any of several large whalebone whales having the skin of the throat marked with deep longitudinal furrows [French, from Norwegian *røyrhval,* from Old Norse *reytharhvalr,* from *reythr* "rorqual" + *hvalr* "whale"]

Ror·schach test \ˌrȯr-ˌshäk-, ˌrōr-\ *n* : a personality and intelligence test in which the way a subject interprets blots of ink of varying designs and colors is used to interpret intellectual and emotional factors [Herman *Rorschach,* died 1922, Swiss psychiatrist]

ro·sar·i·an \rō-ˈzar-ē-ən, -ˈzer-\ *n* : a grower or fancier of roses

ro·sa·ry \ˈrōz-rē, -ə-rē\ *n, pl* **-ries** **1** : a string of beads used in counting prayers especially of the Roman Catholic rosary **2** *often cap* : a Roman Catholic devotion consisting of meditation on usually five sacred mysteries during recitation of five decades of Hail Marys of which each is preceded by the Lord's Prayer and followed by the Gloria Patri [Medieval Latin *rosarium,* from Latin, "rose garden", derived from *rosa* "rose"]

△ **origin** *Rosary* comes from Medieval Latin *rosarium,* which in earlier Latin meant literally "a rose garden". It was used metaphorically to refer to a series of prayers, thought of perhaps as a garden of prayers and perhaps influenced by the association in Christian symbolism of the rose with the Virgin Mary and the rose garden with paradise. *Rosarium* was applied by extension to the string of beads as well as to the prayers themselves.

[1]**rose** *past of* RISE

[2]**rose** \ˈrōz\ *n* **1 a** : any of a genus of usually prickly dicotyledonous shrubs with pinnate leaves and showy flowers having five petals in the wild state but being often double in cultivation **b** : the flower of a rose **2** : COMPASS CARD **3** : a moderate purplish red [Old English, from Latin *rosa*] — **rose·like** \-ˌlīk\ *adj*

[3]**rose** *adj* **1** : of, relating to, resembling, or used for the rose **2** : of the color rose

ro·se·ate \ˈrō-zē-ət, -zē-ˌāt\ *adj* **1** : resembling a rose especially in color **2** : overly optimistic — **ro·se·ate·ly** adv

rose·bay \ˈrōz-ˌbā\ *n* : RHODODENDRON; *esp* : one of eastern North America with rosy bell-shaped flowers

rose–breast·ed grosbeak \ˌrōz-ˌbres-təd-\ *n* : a grosbeak of eastern North America that in the male is chiefly black and white with the breast and lining of the wings rose red and in the female is a streaky grayish brown with the lining of the wings orange

rose·bud \ˈrōz-ˌbəd\ *n* : the bud of a rose

rose·bush \-ˌbu̇sh\ *n* : a shrubby rose

rose–col·ored \ˈrōz-ˌkəl-ərd\ *adj* **1** : having a rose color **2** : seeing or seen in a promising light : OPTIMISTIC

rose fever *n* : hay fever occurring in the spring or early summer

rose·fish \ˈrōz-ˌfish\ *n* : a marine food fish of northern Atlantic coasts that is usually rosy red when adult

rose mallow *n* : a usually rosy-flowered hibiscus or hollyhock

rose·mary \ˈrōz-ˌmer-ē\ *n* : a fragrant shrubby mint of southern Europe and Asia Minor used in cookery and in perfumery [Latin *rosmarinus,* from *ros* "dew" + *marinus* "of the sea"]

rose of Shar·on \-ˈshar-ən, -ˈsher-\ : a commonly cultivated Asian small shrubby hibiscus having showy rose, purple, or white flowers [Plain of *Sharon,* Palestine]

ro·se·o·la \ˌrō-zē-ˈō-lə, rō-ˈzē-ə-lə\ *n* : a spotty rose-colored eruption or a condition marked by this; *esp* : GERMAN MEASLES [New Latin, from Latin *roseus* "rosy", from *rosa* "rose"] — **ro·se·o·lar** \-lər\ *adj*

ro·sette \rō-ˈzet\ *n* **1** : an ornament (as of cloth or paper) resembling a rose **2** : a cluster of leaves developed on a plant in crowded whorls either basally (as in a dandelion) or at the apex (as in palms)

rose water *n* : a watery solution of the fragrant constituents of the rose used as a perfume

rose·wood \ˈrōz-ˌwu̇d\ *n* **1** : any of various tropical trees yielding valuable cabinet woods of a dark red or purplish color streaked and variegated with black **2** : the wood of a rosewood

rosette 1

Rosh Ha·sha·nah \ˌrōsh-hə-ˈshō-nə, ˌrōsh-ə-, ˌräsh-, -ˈshän-ə\ *n* : the Jewish New Year observed as a religious holiday in September or October [Hebrew *rōsh hashshānāh,* literally, "beginning of the year"]

[1]**ros·in** \ˈräz-n, ˈrȯz-\ *n* : a translucent amber-colored to almost black brittle resin that is obtained by chemical means from pine trees or from tall oil and is used in making varnish, paper size, soap, and soldering flux and on violin bows [Middle French *resine* "resin"] — **ros·in·ous** \ˈräz-n-əs, ˈräz-nəs, ˈrȯz-\ *adj*

[2]**rosin** *vt* : to rub (as the bow of a violin) with rosin

ros·ter \ˈräs-tər\ *n* : a list usually of personnel; *esp* : one assigning duties [Dutch *rooster,* literally, "gridiron", from *roosten* "to roast"; from the parallel lines]

ros·trum \ˈräs-trəm\ *n, pl* **rostrums** *or* **ros·tra** \-trə\ **1** : a stage or platform for public speaking **2** : a bodily part or process (as a snout or median projection) suggesting a bird's bill [Latin, "beak, ship's beak", from *rodere* "to gnaw"; sense 1 from Latin *Rostra,* speakers' platform in the Roman Forum, from pl. of *rostrum* "beak"] — **ros·tral** \-trəl\ *adj* — **ros·trate** \-ˌtrāt\ *adj*

△ **origin** The Latin word *rostrum,* whose primary meaning is "beak", was derived from the verb *rodere,* "to gnaw". Eventually *rostrum* came to be used to refer to the prow or beak of a ship. In 338 B.C. the beaks of ships captured from the people of Antium (now called Anzio) were used to decorate the orators' platform in the Roman Forum. From this time on, this platform was called *Rostra,* the plural form of *rostrum.* Later *rostra* was used to refer to any platform from which a speaker addressed an assembly. In English the singular form *rostrum* is still so used.

rosy \ˈrō-zē\ *adj* **ros·i·er; -est** **1 a** : of the color rose **b** : having a healthy pink complexion **c** : marked by blushes **2** : characterized by or tending to promote optimism ⟨*rosy* prospects⟩ — **ros·i·ly** \-zə-lē\ *adv* — **ros·i·ness** \-zē-nəs\ *n*

[1]**rot** \ˈrät\ *vb* **rot·ted; rot·ting** **1 a** : to undergo decomposition from the action of bacteria or fungi **b** : to become unsound or weak (as from use or chemical action) **2 a** : to go to ruin : DETERIORATE **b** : to become morally corrupt : DEGENERATE **3** : to cause to decompose or deteriorate with rot [Old English *rotian*] **syn** see DECAY

[2]**rot** *n* **1 a** : the process of rotting : the state of being rotten **b** : something rotten or rotting **2** : a disease of plants or animals marked by the breaking down of tissue; *also* : an area of broken-down tissue **3** : NONSENSE 1 — often used interjectionally

Ro·ta \ˈrōt-ə\ *n* : a tribunal of the papal curia exercising jurisdiction especially in matrimonial cases appealed from diocesan courts [Medieval Latin, from Latin, "wheel"]

Ro·tar·i·an \rō-ˈter-ē-ən\ *n* : a member of one of the major service clubs [*Rotary (club)*]

[1]**ro·ta·ry** \ˈrōt-ə-rē\ *adj* **1 a** : turning on an axis like a wheel ⟨a *rotary* blade⟩ **b** : taking place about an axis ⟨*rotary* motion⟩ **2** : having an important part that turns on an axis ⟨a *rotary* cutter⟩ **3** : characterized by rotation [Medieval Latin *rotarius,* from Latin *rota* "wheel"]

[2]**rotary** *n, pl* **-ries** **1** : a rotary machine **2** : a road junction formed around a central circle about which traffic moves in one direction only

rotary engine *n* **1** : any of various engines (as a turbine) in which power is applied to vanes or similar parts that move in a circular path **2** : a radial engine in which the cylinders revolve about a stationary crankshaft

rotary–wing aircraft *n* : an aircraft supported in flight partially or wholly by rotating airfoils

ro•tate \'rō-ˌtāt\ *vb* **1 :** to turn or cause to turn about an axis or a center : REVOLVE ⟨the earth *rotates*⟩ **2 a :** to do or cause to do something in turn : ALTERNATE ⟨*rotate* on the night shift⟩ **b :** to pass in a series ⟨the seasons *rotate*⟩ **3 :** to grow in rotation ⟨*rotate* alfalfa and corn⟩ [Latin *rotare,* from *rota* "wheel"] — **ro•tat•able** \'rō-ˌtāt-ə-bəl *also* rō-'\ *adj* — **ro•tat•or** \'rō-ˌtāt-ər *also* rō-'\ *n*

ro•ta•tion \rō-'tā-shən\ *n* **1 a :** the act of rotating especially on or as if on an axis **b :** one complete turn **2 a :** return or succession in a recurring series ⟨*rotation* of the seasons⟩ **b :** CROP ROTATION — **ro•ta•tion•al** \-shnəl, -shən-l\ *adj* — **in rotation :** one after another in an orderly sequence

ro•ta•to•ry \'rōt-ə-ˌtōr-ē, -ˌtȯr-\ *adj* **1 :** of, relating to, or producing rotation **2 :** occurring in rotation

rote \'rōt\ *n* **1 :** the use of memory usually with little intelligence ⟨learn by *rote*⟩ **2 :** routine or repetition carried out mechanically or without understanding [Middle English]

ro•te•none \'rōt-n-ˌōn\ *n* **:** a crystalline insecticide obtained from plants (as derris) that is of low toxicity for warm-blooded animals and is used especially in home gardens [Japanese *roten* "derris plant"]

ro•ti•fer \'rōt-ə-fər\ *n* **:** any of a class (Rotifera) of minute aquatic animals having at one end a disk with circles of cilia which in motion look like revolving wheels [derived from Latin *rota* "wheel" + *ferre* "to bear, carry"] — **ro•tif•er•an** \rō-'tif-ə-rən\ *adj or n*

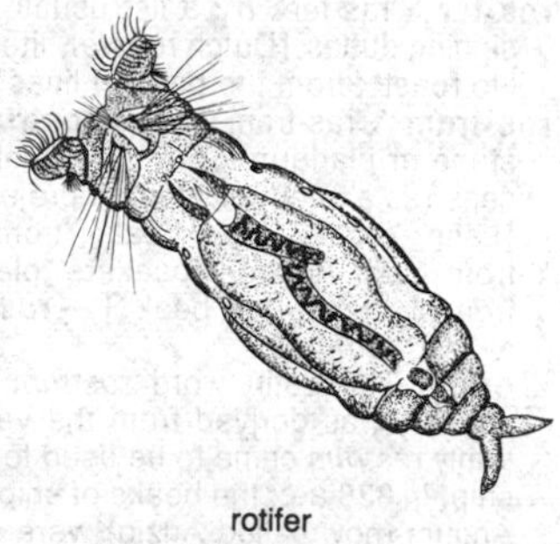
rotifer

ro•tis•ser•ie \rō-'tis-rē, -ə-rē\ *n* **:** an appliance fitted with a spit on which food is rotated before or over a source of heat [French *rôtisserie* "restaurant", from Middle French *rostisserie,* from *rostir* "to roast"]

ro•to \'rōt-ō\ *n, pl* **rotos :** ROTOGRAVURE

ro•to•gra•vure \ˌrōt-ə-grə-'vyu̇r\ *n* **1 a :** a photogravure process in which the impression is produced by a rotary press **b :** a print made by rotogravure **2 :** a section of a newspaper devoted to rotogravure pictures [Latin *rota* "wheel" + English *-o-* + *gravure*]

ro•tor \'rōt-ər\ *n* **1 :** a part that revolves in a stationary part (as in an electrical machine) **2 :** a complete system of horizontal rotating blades that supplies the force supporting an aircraft in flight ⟨the *rotor* of a helicopter⟩ [contraction of *rotator*]

rot•ten \'rät-n\ *adj* **1 :** having rotted : PUTRID ⟨*rotten* fruit⟩ **2 :** morally corrupt **3 :** extremely unpleasant or inferior ⟨*rotten* weather⟩ [Old Norse *rotinn*] — **rot•ten•ly** *adv* — **rot•ten•ness** \-n-nəs\ *n*

rot•ten•stone \'rät-n-ˌstōn\ *n* **:** a decomposed siliceous limestone used for polishing

rot•ter \'rät-ər\ *n* **:** a thoroughly objectionable person

ro•tund \rō-'tənd, 'rō-ˌ\ *adj* **1 :** marked by roundness **2 :** FULL, SONOROUS ⟨*rotund* voices⟩ **3 :** PLUMP, CHUBBY [Latin *rotundus*] — **ro•tun•di•ty** \rō-'tən-dət-ē\ *n* — **ro•tund•ly** \rō-'tənd-lē, 'rō-ˌ\ *adv* — **ro•tund•ness** \rō-'tənd-nəs, -'tən-, 'rō-ˌ\ *n*

ro•tun•da \rō-'tən-də\ *or* **ro•ton•da** \-'tän-\ *n* **1 :** a round building; *esp* **:** one covered by a dome **2 a :** a large round room **b :** a large central area (as in a hotel) [Italian *rotonda,* from Latin *rotundus* "round"]

roué \rü-'ā\ *n* **:** a usually male libertine [French, literally, "broken on the wheel", from *rouer* "to break on the wheel", from Medieval Latin *rotare,* from Latin, "to rotate"; from the feeling that such a person deserves this punishment]

[1]**rouge** \'rüzh, *especially South* 'rüj\ *n* **1 :** any of various cosmetics to color the cheeks or lips red **2 :** a red powder consisting essentially of ferric oxide used in polishing (as gems) and as a pigment [French, from *rouge* "red", from Latin *rubeus* "reddish"]

[2]**rouge** *vb* **1 :** to apply rouge to **2 :** to use rouge

[1]**rough** \'rəf\ *adj* **1 a :** having an uneven surface : not smooth **b :** covered with or made up of coarse and often shaggy hair or bristles ⟨a *rough*-coated terrier⟩ **c :** difficult to travel over or penetrate : WILD ⟨*rough* country⟩ **2 a :** characterized by harshness, violence, or force **b :** DIFFICULT, TRYING ⟨a *rough* day at the office⟩ **3 :** coarse or rugged in character or appearance: as **a :** harsh to the ear **b :** crude in style or expression **c :** marked by a lack of refinement or grace : UNCOUTH **4 :** marked by incompleteness or inexactness ⟨a *rough* draft⟩ ⟨*rough* estimates⟩ [Old English *rūh*] — **rough•ly** *adv* — **rough•ness** *n*

• syn ROUGH, HARSH, RUGGED mean not smooth or even. ROUGH implies having points, bristles, ridges, or projections on the surface ⟨*rough* wood⟩ HARSH implies having a surface or texture that is unpleasant to the touch ⟨*harsh* sand⟩ RUGGED implies irregularity or unevenness of land surface and connotes difficulty of travel ⟨*rugged* mountain roads⟩

[2]**rough** *n* **1 :** uneven ground covered with high grass, brush, and stones; *esp* **:** such ground bordering a golf fairway **2 :** the disagreeable side or aspect ⟨take the *rough* with the smooth⟩ **3 :** something in a crude, unfinished, or preliminary state; *also* **:** such a state ⟨diamonds in the *rough*⟩ **c :** a hasty preliminary drawing or layout **4 :** ROWDY, TOUGH ⟨a gang of *roughs*⟩

[3]**rough** *vt* **1 :** ROUGHEN **2 a :** MANHANDLE, BEAT ⟨*roughed* up by hoodlums⟩ **b :** to subject to unnecessary and intentional violence in a sport **3 :** to shape, make, or dress in a rough or preliminary way ⟨*rough* out a plan⟩ — **rough•er** *n* — **rough it :** to live under primitive conditions

rough•age \'rəf-ij\ *n* **:** coarse bulky food (as bran) that is relatively high in fiber and low in digestible nutrients and assists in movement of materials through the digestive tract

rough–and–ready \ˌrəf-ən-'red-ē\ *adj* **:** crude in nature, method, or manner but effective in action or use

rough–and–tum•ble \-ən-'təm-bəl\ *n* **:** a rough disorderly unrestrained struggle — **rough–and–tumble** *adj*

[1]**rough•cast** \'rəf-ˌkast\ *n* **1 :** a rough model **2 :** a plaster of lime mixed with shells or pebbles used for covering buildings

[2]**roughcast** *vt* **-cast; -cast•ing 1 :** to plaster (as a wall) with roughcast **2 :** to shape or form roughly

rough•dry \-'drī\ *vt* **:** to dry (laundry) without smoothing or ironing — **roughdry** *adj*

rough•en \'rəf-ən\ *vb* **rough•ened; rough•en•ing** \'rəf-ning, -ə-ning\ **:** to make or become rough

rough fish *n* **:** a fish that is neither a sport fish nor an important food for sport fishes

rough•hew \'rəf-'hyü\ *vt* **-hewed; -hewed** *or* **-hewn** \-'hyün\; **-hew•ing 1 :** to hew (as timber) coarsely without smoothing or finishing **2 :** to form crudely

rough–hewn \'rəf-'hyün\ *adj* **:** lacking polish or social graces

rough•house \'rəf-ˌhau̇s\ *n* **:** violence or rough rowdy play — **rough•house** \-ˌhau̇s, -ˌhau̇z\ *vb* — **rough•house** \-ˌhau̇s\ *adj*

rough•ish \'rəf-ish\ *adj* **:** somewhat rough

rough•neck \'rəf-ˌnek\ *n* **:** a rough person; *esp* **:** ROWDY, TOUGH

rough•rid•er \'rəf-'rīd-ər\ *n* **1 :** one who breaks horses to the saddle or rides little-trained horses **2** *cap* **:** a member of the 1st United States Volunteer Cavalry regiment in the Spanish-American War commanded by Theodore Roosevelt

rough•shod \-'shäd\ *adj* **1 :** shod with calked shoes **2 :** marked by force without justice or consideration

rou•lade \rü-'läd\ *n* **:** a slice of meat rolled with or without a stuffing [French, from *rouler* "to roll"]

[1]**rou•lette** \rü-'let\ *n* **1 :** a gambling game in which players bet on which compartment of a revolving wheel a small ball will come to rest in **2 a :** a toothed wheel or disk (as for producing rows of dots on engraved plates or for making short consecutive incisions in paper to facilitate subsequent division) **b :** tiny slits in a sheet of stamps made by a roulette [French, literally, "small wheel", from Old French *roelete,* from *roele* "wheel", from Late Latin *rotella* "small wheel", from Latin *rota* "wheel"]

[2]**roulette** *vt* **:** to make roulettes in

Rou•ma•ni•an \rü-'mā-nē-ən\ *variant of* RUMANIAN

[1]**round** \'rau̇nd\ *adj* **1 a :** shaped like a disk or a ball : having every part of the surface or circumference equidistant from the center **b :** CYLINDRICAL **c :** having a curved outline **2 :** well fleshed : PLUMP **3 a :** COMPLETE, FULL ⟨a *round* dozen⟩ **b :** approximately correct; *esp* **:** exact only to a specific decimal **c :** LARGE ⟨a good *round* sum⟩ **4 a :** BLUNT, OUTSPOKEN **b :** not restrained or toned down ⟨a *round* oath⟩ **5 :** moving in or forming a circle **6 a :** brought to completion or perfection : FINISHED **b :** presented with lifelike fullness or vividness **7 a :** having full or unimpeded resonance or tone **b :** pronounced with rounded lips **8 :** of or relating to handwriting predominantly curved rather than angular [Old French *roont,* from Latin *rotundus*] —

round•ly *adv* — **round•ness** \'raůnd-nəs, 'raůn-\ *n*
^{2}**round** *adv* **:** with a circular motion **:** in a circular course **:** AROUND
^{3}**round** \raůnd, 'raůnd\ *prep* **1 :** in a circle about **:** AROUND **2 :** all during **:** THROUGHOUT ⟨*round* the year⟩
^{4}**round** \'raůnd\ *n* **1 a :** something (as a circle, globe, or ring) that is round **b :** a knot or circle of people or things **2 :** ROUND DANCE 1 **3 :** a song in which three or four voices follow each other around and sing the same melody and words **4 a :** a rung of a ladder or a chair **b :** a rounded molding **5 a :** a circling path or course **b :** motion in a circle or a curving path **6 :** a route or circuit habitually covered **:** a series of customary calls or stops **7 :** a drink apiece served at one time to each person in a group **8 :** a series of recurring routine or repetitive actions or events ⟨a *round* of parties⟩ **9 :** a period of time that recurs in a fixed pattern **10 a :** one shot fired by a weapon or by each man in a military unit **b :** a unit of ammunition consisting of the parts necessary to fire one shot **11 :** a unit of action in a contest or game that occupies a stated period, covers a prescribed distance, includes a specified number of plays, or gives each player one turn **12 :** a demonstrative outpouring or burst ⟨a *round* of applause⟩ **13 :** a cut of beef especially between the rump and the lower leg **14 :** a rounded or curved part — **in the round 1 :** in full sculptured form unattached to a background **:** FREESTANDING **2 :** with a comprehensive view or representation **3 :** with a center stage surrounded by an audience on all sides ⟨theater *in the round*⟩ — **out of round :** not perfectly or adequately round or circular
^{5}**round** \'raůnd\ *vb* **1 a :** to make round **b :** to become round or plump **c :** to pronounce (a sound) with rounding of the lips **2 a :** to go around **b :** to pass part way around **3 :** to form a circle around **4 a :** to bring to completion ⟨*round* out a career⟩ **b :** to become complete **c :** to bring to perfection of style **:** POLISH 3 **5 :** to express as a round number ⟨*round* off to three decimal places⟩ **6 :** to follow a winding course ⟨horses *rounding* into the homestretch⟩ — **round on :** to turn against
^{1}**round•about** \'raůn-də-,baůt\ *n* **1 :** an indirect route **:** DETOUR **2** *British* **a :** MERRY-GO-ROUND **b :** ROTARY 2
^{2}**round•about** \,raůn-də-'baůt\ *adj* **:** not direct
round clam *n* **:** QUAHOG
round dance *n* **1 :** a folk dance in which dancers form a ring and move in a prescribed direction **2 :** a ballroom dance in which couples progress around the room
round•ed \'raůn-dəd\ *n* **1 :** curving or round in shape **2 :** fully developed — **round•ed•ness** *n*
roun•del \'raůn-dl\ *n* **:** a round figure or object; *esp* **:** a circular panel, window, or niche [Old French *rondel,* from *roont* "round"]
roun•de•lay \'raůn-də-,lā\ *n* **1 :** a simple song with a refrain **2 :** a poem with a refrain recurring frequently or at fixed intervals [Middle French *rondelet,* literally, "small circle", from *rondel* "small circle, roundel"]
round•er \'raůn-dər\ *n* **1 :** a person of loose morals or conduct **2** *pl* **:** an English game played with ball and bat somewhat resembling baseball **3 a :** one that rounds by hand or by machine **b :** a tool for making an edge or a surface round
Round•head \'raůnd-,hed\ *n* **:** a Puritan or member of the parliamentary party in England at the time of Charles I and Oliver Cromwell [from the Puritans' cutting their hair short in contrast to the Cavaliers]
round•head•ed \-'hed-əd\ *adj* **:** having a round head; *esp* **:** BRACHYCEPHALIC — **round•head•ed•ness** *n*
round•house \'raůnd-,haůs\ *n* **1 :** a circular building for housing and repairing locomotives **2 :** a cabin or apartment on the after part of a quarterdeck **3 :** a blow in boxing delivered with a wide swing **4 :** a slow wide curve in baseball
round•ish \'raůn-dish\ *adj* **:** somewhat round
round robin *n* **1 a :** a written petition or protest with signatures in a circle so as not to indicate who signed first **b :** a letter sent in turn to the members of a group each of whom signs and forwards it sometimes after adding comment **2 :** a tournament in which every contestant meets every other contestant in turn **3 :** SERIES 1, ROUND [from the name *Robin*]
round–shoul•dered \'raůnd-'shōl-dərd, 'raůn-\ *adj* **:** having the shoulders stooping or rounded
round table *n* **1** *cap R&T* **a :** a large circular table for King Arthur and his knights **b :** the knights of King Arthur **2 :** a meeting of a group of persons for discussion of questions of common interest; *also* **:** the persons meeting for such a purpose
round–the–clock *adj* **:** being in effect, continuing, or lasting 24 hours a day
round trip *n* **:** a trip to a place and back usually over the same route
round•up \'raůn-,dəp\ *n* **1 :** the gathering together of cattle on the range by riding around them and driving them in **2 :** a gathering together of scattered persons or things **3 :** SUMMARY, RÉSUMÉ ⟨the 6 o'clock news *roundup*⟩
round up \raůn-'dəp, 'raůn-\ *vt* **1 :** to collect (cattle) by means of a roundup **2 :** to gather in or bring together
round•worm \'raůn-,dwərm\ *n* **:** a nematode worm (as a hookworm or a trichina); *also* **:** a related round-bodied unsegmented worm as distinguished from a flatworm
^{1}**rouse** \'raůz\ *vb* **1 :** to arouse or become aroused from or as if from sleep **:** AWAKEN **2 :** to become stirred **3 :** to stir up **:** EXCITE [Middle English *rousen*]
^{2}**rouse** *n* **:** an act or instance of rousing; *esp* **:** an excited stir
^{3}**rouse** *n, archaic* **:** CAROUSE
rous•ing \'raů-ziŋ\ *adj* **1 a :** EXCITING ⟨played a *rousing* march⟩ **b :** BRISK, LIVELY ⟨a *rousing* cheer⟩ **2 :** EXCEPTIONAL 2
roust•about \'raů-stə-,baůt\ *n* **:** one who does heavy or unskilled labor (as a deckhand or longshoreman, a laborer in an oil field, or a circus worker who erects and dismantles tents) [from *roust* "to rouse", alteration of *rouse*]
^{1}**rout** \'raůt\ *n* **1 :** a crowd of people; *esp* **:** RABBLE **2 :** DISTURBANCE 3 **3 :** a fashionable gathering **:** RECEPTION [Middle French *route* "troop, defeat", derived from Latin *ruptus,* past participle of *rumpere* "to break"]
^{2}**rout** *vb* **1 :** to search haphazardly **:** RUMMAGE **2 :** to find or bring to light especially with difficulty **:** DISCOVER **3 :** to gouge out or make a furrow in (as wood or metal); *esp* **:** to cut away (as blank parts) from a printing surface (as an engraving or electrotype) **4 a :** to expel by force **:** EJECT ⟨*routed* out of their homes⟩ **b :** to cause to emerge especially from bed **:** ROUSE [alteration of ^{3}*root*]
^{3}**rout** *n* **1 :** a state of wild confusion and disorderly retreat **2 a :** a disastrous defeat **b :** an act or instance of routing [Middle French *route* "troop, defeat"]
^{4}**rout** *vt* **1 :** to disorganize or defeat completely **2 :** to drive out **:** DISPEL
^{1}**route** \'rüt, 'raůt\ *n* **1 a :** a traveled way **:** HIGHWAY **b :** a means of access **:** CHANNEL **2 :** an established, selected, or assigned course of travel ⟨a newspaper *route*⟩ [Old French, derived from Latin *ruptus,* past participle of *rumpere* "to break"]
^{2}**route** *vt* **1 :** to send, forward, or transport by a certain route ⟨*route* traffic around the city⟩ **2 :** to arrange and direct the order and carrying out of (as a series of operations in a factory)
route•man \-mən, -,man\ *n* **:** one who sells or makes deliveries on an assigned route
^{1}**rou•tine** \rü-'tēn\ *n* **1 :** a regular or customary course of procedure **2 :** an often repeated speech **3 :** a fixed piece of entertainment often repeated **:** ACT; *esp* **:** a theatrical number [French, from *route* "route"]
^{2}**routine** *adj* **1 :** being commonplace or uninspired **2 :** done or happening regularly ⟨*routine* inspection⟩ — **rou•tine•ly** *adv*
^{1}**rove** \'rōv\ *vb* **1 :** to move aimlessly **:** ROAM ⟨*rove* about the country⟩ **2 :** to wander through or over ⟨*rove* the seas⟩ [Middle English *roven* "to shoot arrows at marks chosen at random"]
^{2}**rove** *past of* REEVE
rove beetle *n* **:** any of numerous often predatory active beetles with a long body and very short wing cases [perhaps from ^{1}*rove*]
^{1}**ro•ver** \'rō-vər\ *n* **:** PIRATE [Dutch, from *roven* "to rob"]
^{2}**rov•er** \'rō-vər\ *n* **:** one that roves **:** WANDERER, ROAMER
^{1}**row** \'rō\ *vb* **1 :** to propel a boat by means of oars **2 :** to move by or as if by the propulsion of oars **3 :** to be equipped with (a specified number of oars) **4 :** to engage in rowing **5 :** to transport in or as if in a boat propelled by oars [Old English *rōwan*] — **row•er** \'rō-ər, 'rōr\ *n*
^{2}**row** *n* **:** an act or instance of rowing
^{3}**row** *n* **1 :** a group forming a more or less straight line ⟨a *row* of

\ə\ **abut**	\aů\ **out**	\i\ **tip**	\ȯ\ **saw**	\ů\ **foot**
\ər\ **further**	\ch\ **chin**	\ī\ **life**	\ȯi\ **coin**	\y\ **yet**
\a\ **mat**	\e\ **pet**	\j\ **job**	\th\ **thin**	\yü\ **few**
\ā\ **take**	\ē\ **easy**	\ŋ\ **sing**	\t͟h\ **this**	\yů\ **cure**
\ä\ **cot, cart**	\g\ **go**	\ō\ **bone**	\ü\ **food**	\zh\ **vision**

bottles⟩ ⟨corn planted in *rows*⟩ **2 :** an urban street or district — used with a descriptive name ⟨Strivers' *Row*⟩
4row \'rau̇\ *n* **:** a noisy disturbance or quarrel **:** BRAWL [origin unknown]
5row \'rau̇\ *vi* **:** to engage in a row **:** FIGHT, QUARREL
row•an \'rau̇-ən, 'rō-ən\ *n* **1 :** a Eurasian tree of the rose family with flat clusters of white flowers followed by small red pomes; *also* **:** the closely related American mountain ash **2** *or* **row•an•ber•ry** \-ˌber-ē\ **:** the fruit of a rowan [of Scandinavian origin]
row•boat \'rō-ˌbōt\ *n* **:** a boat designed to be rowed
1row•dy \'rau̇d-ē\ *adj* **row•di•er; -est :** coarse or boisterous in behavior **:** ROUGH [perhaps from 4*row*] — **row•di•ness** *n* — **row•dy•ish** \-ē-ish\ *adj* — **row•dy•ism** \-ē-ˌiz-əm\ *n*
2rowdy *n, pl* **rowdies :** a rowdy person **:** TOUGH
1row•el \'rau̇-əl, 'rau̇l\ *n* **:** a revolving disk at the end of a spur with sharp points for goading a horse [Middle French *rouelle* "small wheel", from Late Latin *rotella,* from Latin *rota* "wheel"]

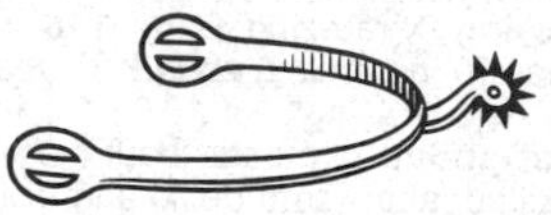
1rowel

2rowel *vt* **-eled** *or* **-elled; -el•ing** *or* **-el•ling :** to goad with or as if with a rowel **:** SPUR
row•en \'rau̇-ən\ *n* **1 :** a stubble field left unplowed for late grazing **2 :** AFTERMATH 1 — often used in pl. [Middle English *rowein*]
row house \'rō-\ *n* **:** one of a series of houses connected by common sidewalls
row•ing \'rō-ing\ *n* **:** the sport of racing long narrow boats propelled by oars
row•lock \'räl-ək, 'rəl-; 'rō-ˌläk\ *n, chiefly British* **:** OARLOCK
1roy•al \'rȯi-əl, 'rȯil\ *adj* **1 a :** of kingly ancestry **b :** of, relating to, or subject to the crown **c :** being in the crown's service ⟨*Royal* Navy⟩ **2 a :** suitable for royalty **:** MAGNIFICENT ⟨a *royal* welcome⟩ **b :** requiring no exertion **:** EASY ⟨no *royal* road to victory⟩ **3 a :** of great size or high quality **b :** established or chartered by the crown ⟨a *royal* colony⟩ [Middle French *roial,* from Latin *regalis,* from *reg-, rex* "king"] — **roy•al•ly** \'rȯi-ə-lē\ *adv*
2royal *n* **:** a small sail on the mast immediately above the topgallant sail
royal blue *n* **:** a vivid purplish blue
roy•al•ist \'rȯi-ə-ləst\ *n* **1 :** a supporter (as during a time of civil war) of a king **2 :** a believer in monarchy as a form of government — **royalist** *adj*
royal jelly *n* **:** a highly nutritious secretion of the pharyngeal glands of the honeybee that is fed to all very young larvae and continuously to queen larvae
royal palm *n* **:** a tall graceful American palm widely planted as an ornamental tree in tropical regions
royal poinciana *n* **:** a showy tropical tree widely planted for its immense racemes of scarlet and orange flowers
roy•al•ty \'rȯi-əl-tē, 'rȯil-tē\ *n, pl* **-ties 1 a :** royal standing or power **b :** a right or privilege of a sovereign (as a percentage of gold or silver taken from mines) **2 :** regal character or bearing **:** NOBILITY **3 a :** persons of royal lineage **b :** a person of royal rank **c :** a privileged class **4 a :** a share of the product or profit reserved by the grantor especially of an oil or mining lease **b :** a payment made to the owner of a patent or copyright for the use of it
-rrhea *also* **-rrhoea** *n combining form* **:** flow **:** discharge ⟨*seborrhea*⟩ [Greek *-rrhoia,* from *rhoia,* from *rhein* "to flow"]
1rub \'rəb\ *vb* **rubbed; rub•bing 1 a :** to move or make move along the surface of a body with pressure **b** (1) **:** to fret or chafe with friction ⟨the new shoes *rubbed*⟩ (2) **:** to cause or cause to feel discontent, irritation, or anger ⟨*rubbed* me the wrong way⟩ **2 a :** to apply or spread by rubbing ⟨*rub* ointment on your chest⟩ **b :** to treat in some way by rubbing ⟨*rub* the surface clean⟩ [Middle English *rubben*]
2rub *n* **1 a :** DIFFICULTY ⟨that's the *rub*⟩ **b :** something (as sharp criticism) that grates the feelings **c :** something that mars or upsets serenity **2 :** the application of friction with pressure ⟨an alcohol *rub*⟩
ru•ba•to \rü-'bät-ō\ *n, pl* **-tos :** fluctuation of speed within a musical phrase typically against a rhythmically steady accompaniment [Italian, literally, "robbed"]
1rub•ber \'rəb-ər\ *n* **1 a :** one that rubs **b :** an instrument or object (as a rubber eraser) used in rubbing, polishing, scraping, or cleaning **c :** something that prevents rubbing or chafing **2 a :** an elastic substance obtained by coagulating the milky juice of various tropical plants **b :** any of various synthetic rubberlike substances **c :** natural or synthetic rubber modified by chemical treatment to increase its useful properties (as toughness and resistance to wear) and used in tires, electrical insulation, and waterproof materials **3 :** something made of or resembling rubber; *esp* **:** a rubber overshoe [sense 2 from its use in erasers] — **rub•ber•like** \-ˌlīk\ *adj* — **rub•bery** \'rəb-rē, -ə-rē\ *adj*
2rubber *n* **:** a contest that consists of an odd number of games and is won by the side that takes a majority (as two out of three) [origin unknown]
rub•ber•ize \'rəb-ə-ˌrīz\ *vt* **:** to coat or impregnate with rubber or a rubber preparation ⟨*rubberized* raincoats⟩
rub•ber•neck \'rəb-ər-ˌnek\ *n* **1 :** an inquisitive person **2 :** TOURIST; *esp* **:** one on a guided tour — **rubberneck** *vi*
rubber plant *n* **:** a tall tropical Asian fig tree that is often dwarfed in pots as a houseplant
rub•ber–stamp \ˌrəb-ər-'stamp\ *vt* **:** to approve, endorse, or dispose of as a matter of routine usually without exercise of judgment or at the command of another
rubber stamp *n* **1 :** a stamp of rubber for making imprints **2 a :** a person who echoes or imitates others **b :** a person or body given to rubber-stamping
rubber tree *n* **:** a South American tree that is a source of rubber and is cultivated in plantations; *also* **:** any tree that yields rubber
rub•bing \'rəb-ing\ *n* **:** an image of a raised, indented, or textured surface obtained by placing paper over it and rubbing the paper with colored material
rubbing alcohol *n* **:** a watery solution of an alcohol used externally especially to soothe or refresh
rub•bish \'rəb-ish\ *n* **:** useless waste or rejected matter **:** TRASH [Middle English *robys*] — **rub•bishy** \'rəb-i-shē\ *adj*
rub•ble \'rəb-əl\ *n* **1 :** rough stone as it comes from the quarry **2 :** waterworn or rough broken stones or bricks used in coarse masonry or in filling courses of walls; *also* **:** RUBBLEWORK **3 :** a mass of rough irregular pieces ⟨a town bombed to *rubble*⟩ [Middle English *robyl*]

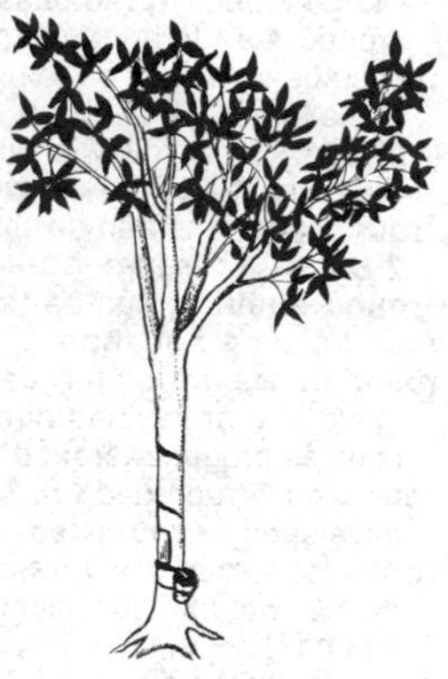
rubber tree

rub•ble•work \'rəb-əl-ˌwərk\ *n* **:** masonry of unsquared or rudely squared stones that are irregular in size and shape
rub•down \'rəb-ˌdau̇n\ *n* **:** a brisk rubbing of the body (as after a bath)
rube \'rüb\ *n* **:** an awkward unsophisticated rustic [*Rube,* nickname for *Reuben*]
1ru•be•fa•cient \ˌrü-bə-'fā-shənt\ *adj* **:** causing redness (as of the skin) [Latin *rubefaciens,* present participle of *rubefacere* "to make red", from *rubeus* "reddish" + *facere* "to make"]
2rubefacient *n* **:** a substance for external application that produces redness of the skin — **ru•be•fac•tion** \-'fak-shən\ *n*
ru•bel•la \rü-'bel-ə\ *n* **:** GERMAN MEASLES [New Latin, from Latin *rubellus* "reddish", from *ruber* "red"]
ru•be•o•la \rü-'bē-ə-lə, ˌrü-bē-'ō-\ *n* **:** MEASLES [New Latin, from Latin *rubeus* "reddish"] — **ru•be•o•lar** \-lər\ *adj*
Ru•bi•con \'rü-bi-ˌkän\ *n* **:** a deliberate irrevocable step or act [Latin *Rubicon-, Rubico,* river of northern Italy forming part of the boundary between Cisalpine Gaul and Italy whose crossing by Julius Caesar in 49 B.C. was regarded by the Senate as an act of war]
ru•bi•cund \'rü-bi-ˌkənd, -kənd\ *adj* **:** somewhat red **:** RUDDY [Latin *rubicundus,* from *rubēre* "to be red"] — **ru•bi•cun•di•ty** \ˌrü-bi-'kən-dət-ē\ *n*
ru•bid•i•um \rü-'bid-ē-əm\ *n* **:** a soft silvery metallic chemical element that decomposes water with violence and bursts into flame spontaneously in air — see ELEMENT table [New Latin,

from Latin *rubidus* "red", from *rubēre* "to be red"]

ru•big•i•nous \rü-'bij-ə-nəs\ *adj* **:** of a rusty red color [Latin *robiginosus, rubiginosus* "rusty", from *robigo* "rust"]

ru•ble \'rü-bəl\ *n* **1 :** the basic monetary unit of the Soviet Union **2 :** a coin representing one ruble [Russian *rubl'*]

rub out *vt* **1 :** to obliterate by rubbing **2 :** KILL 1

ru•bric \'rü-brik\ *n* **1 :** a heading of a part of a book or manuscript done or underlined in a color (as red) different from the rest **2 a** (1) **:** NAME, TITLE; *esp* **:** the title of a law (2) **:** something under which a thing is classed **:** CATEGORY **b :** an authoritative rule; *esp* **:** a rule for conduct of a liturgical service **c :** an explanatory or introductory comment or gloss; *esp* **:** an editorial interpolation **3 :** an established rule or custom [Middle French *rubrique,* literally, "red ocher", from Latin *rubrica,* from *ruber* "red"] — **rubric** *or* **ru•bri•cal** \-bri-kəl\ *adj*

△ **origin** Derived ultimately from Latin *ruber,* "red", *rubric* was originally used in Middle English to name red ocher, a red pigment. Yet in present-day English *rubric* is used to mean "an authoritative rule" or "an explanatory commentary". This semantic transformation is derived from the practice originated centuries ago of putting instructions or explanations in a manuscript or printed book in red ink to contrast with the black ink of the text.

[1]**ru•by** \'rü-bē\ *n, pl* **rubies 1 :** a precious stone that is a deep red corundum **2 a :** the dark red color of the ruby **b :** something resembling a ruby in color [Middle French *rubi,* from Latin *rubeus* "reddish"]

[2]**ruby** *adj* **:** of the color ruby

ruby glass *n* **:** glass of a deep red color containing selenium, an oxide of copper, or chloride of gold

ruck \'rək\ *n* **:** the usual run of persons or things [Middle English *ruke* "pile of combustible material", of Scandinavian origin]

ruck•sack \'rək-,sak, 'rük-, 'rùk-\ *n* **:** KNAPSACK [German]

ruck•us \'rək-əs, 'rük-, 'rùk-\ *n* **:** [4]ROW, DISTURBANCE [probably blend of *ruction* and *rumpus*]

ruc•tion \'rək-shən\ *n* **1 :** a noisy fight **2 :** UPROAR [perhaps from *insurrection*]

rud•der \'rəd-ər\ *n* **:** a flat piece of wood or metal attached to the stern of a boat or the after end of the keel for steering a boat; *also* **:** a similar piece attached to the rear of an aircraft [Old English *rōther* "paddle"]

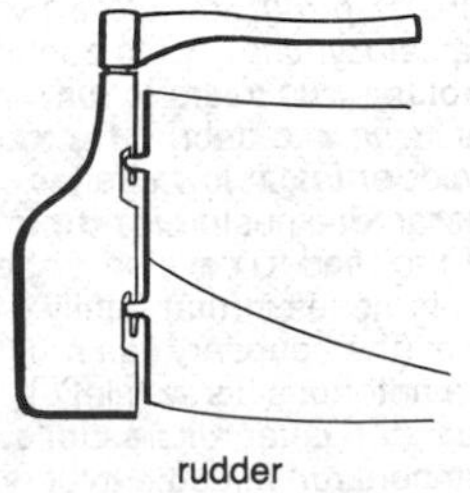
rudder

rud•dle \'rəd-l\ *n* **:** RED OCHER [from earlier *rud* "red ocher", from Old English *rudu* "redness"]

rud•dle•man \-mən\ *n* **:** a dealer in red ocher

rud•dy \'rəd-ē\ *adj* **rud•di•er; -est 1 :** having a healthy reddish color **2 :** REDDISH [Old English *rudig,* from *rudu* "redness"] — **rud•di•ly** \'rəd-l-ē\ *adv* — **rud•di•ness** \'rəd-ē-nəs\ *n*

rude \'rüd\ *adj* **1 :** being in a rough or unfinished state **:** CRUDE **2 :** lacking refinement, delicacy, or culture **3 :** offensive in manner or action **:** DISCOURTEOUS **4 :** FORCEFUL, ABRUPT ⟨a *rude* awakening⟩ [Middle French, from Latin *rudis*] — **rude•ly** *adv* — **rude•ness** *n*

ru•di•ment \'rüd-ə-mənt\ *n* **1 :** an elementary principle or skill — usually used in pl. ⟨the *rudiments* of chess⟩ **2 :** something unformed or undeveloped **:** BEGINNING — usually used in pl. [Latin *rudimentum* "beginning", from *rudis* "raw, rude"] — **ru•di•men•tal** \,rüd-ə-'ment-l\ *adj* — **ru•di•men•ta•ri•ness** \-'ment-ə-rē-nəs, -'men-tre-\ *n* — **ru•di•men•ta•ry** \,rüd-ə-'ment-ə-rē, -'men-trē\ *adj*

[1]**rue** \'rü\ *vt* **rued; ru•ing :** to feel penitence, remorse, or regret for [Old English *hrēowan*]

[2]**rue** *n* **:** REGRET 1, SORROW

[3]**rue** *n* **:** a woody perennial herb with yellow flowers, a strong smell, and bitter-tasting leaves [Middle French, from Latin *ruta,* from Greek *rhytē*]

rue anemone *n* **:** a delicate spring herb of the buttercup family with white flowers

rue•ful \'rü-fəl\ *adj* **1 :** exciting pity or sympathy **:** PITIABLE ⟨a *rueful* tale⟩ **2 :** MOURNFUL, REGRETFUL ⟨took defeat with a *rueful* smile⟩ — **rue•ful•ly** \-fə-lē\ *adv* — **rue•ful•ness** *n*

ru•fes•cent \rü-'fes-nt\ *adj* **:** REDDISH [Latin *rufescens,* present participle of *rufescere* "to become red", from *rufus* "red"]

[1]**ruff** \'rəf\ *n* **1 :** a stiff wheel-shaped collar worn by men and women of the late 16th and early 17th centuries **2 a :** a fringe of long hairs or feathers growing around or on the neck **b :** a common Eurasian sandpiper whose male during the breeding season has a large ruff [probably from *ruffle*] — **ruffed** \'rəft\ *adj*

[2]**ruff** *n* **:** the act of trumping [Middle French *roffle*] — **ruff** *vb*

ruffed grouse *n* **:** a North American grouse with tufts of shiny black feathers on the sides of the neck

ruffed grouse

ruf•fi•an \'rəf-ē-ən\ *n* **:** a coarse brutal person [Middle French *rufian*] — **ruffian** *adj* — **ruf•fi•an•ism** \-ē-ə-,niz-əm\ *n* — **ruf•fi•an•ly** \-ē-ən-lē\ *adj*

[1]**ruf•fle** \'rəf-əl\ *vb* **ruffled; ruf•fling** \'rəf-ling, -ə-ling\ **1 a :** to disturb the smoothness of **:** ROUGHEN ⟨*ruffle* the waters of a pond⟩ **b :** TROUBLE 1a, VEX **2 :** to erect (as feathers) in or like a ruff **3 :** RIFFLE 3, SHUFFLE **4 :** to make into a ruffle [Middle English *ruffelen*]

[2]**ruffle** *n* **1 :** a state or cause of irritation **2 :** an unevenness or disturbance of surface **:** RIPPLE **3 a :** a strip of lace or cloth gathered or pleated on one edge **b :** [1]RUFF 2a — **ruf•fly** \'rəf-lē, -ə-lē\ *adj*

[3]**ruffle** *n* **:** a low vibrating drumbeat that is less loud than a roll [from earlier *ruff* "drumbeat", of imitative origin]

ru•fous \'rü-fəs\ *adj* **:** REDDISH [Latin *rufus* "red"]

rug \'rəg\ *n* **1 :** a piece of thick heavy fabric usually with a nap or pile used as a floor covering **2 :** a floor mat of an animal pelt ⟨bearskin *rug*⟩ **3 :** a lap robe [of Scandinavian origin]

rug•by \'rəg-bē\ *n, often cap* **:** a football game played by teams of 15 players and marked by continuous play featuring kicking, running with the ball, lateral passing, and tackling but without blocking or forward passing [*Rugby* School, Rugby, England]

rug•ged \'rəg-əd\ *adj* **1 :** having a rough uneven surface **:** JAGGED ⟨*rugged* mountains⟩ **2 :** STORMY 2 **3 :** showing signs of strength **:** STURDY ⟨*rugged* pioneers⟩ **4 a :** STERN ⟨*rugged* times⟩ **b :** COARSE 3, RUDE **5 :** presenting a severe test of ability, endurance, or resolution ⟨*rugged* course of training⟩ [Middle English, "shaggy"] **syn** see ROUGH — **rug•ged•ly** *adv* — **rug•ged•ness** *n*

ru•gose \'rü-,gōs\ *adj* **:** full of folds or wrinkles ⟨*rugose* leaves⟩ [Latin *rugosus,* from *ruga* "wrinkle"] — **ru•gose•ly** *adv* — **ru•gos•i•ty** \rü-'gäs-ət-ē\ *n*

[1]**ru•in** \'rü-ən, -,in\ *n* **1 :** physical, moral, economic, or social collapse **2 a :** the state of being ruined **b :** the remains of something destroyed — usually used in pl. ⟨the *ruins* of a city⟩ **3 :** a cause of destruction ⟨greed was my *ruin*⟩ **4 :** the action of destroying, laying waste, or wrecking **5 :** a ruined building, person, or object [Middle French *ruine* "collapse", from Latin *ruina*]

[2]**ruin** *vt* **1 :** to reduce to ruins **:** DEVASTATE ⟨a *ruined* city⟩ **2 a :** to damage irreparably ⟨*ruined* our chances⟩ **b :** BANKRUPT, IMPOVERISH ⟨*ruined* by the depression⟩ — **ru•in•er** *n*

ru•in•ation \,rü-ə-'nā-shən\ *n* **:** RUIN 3

ru•in•ous \'rü-ə-nəs\ *adj* **1 :** DILAPIDATED **2 :** causing or tending to cause ruin **:** DESTRUCTIVE ⟨*ruinous* tax laws⟩ — **ru•in•ous•ly** *adv*

[1]**rule** \'rül\ *n* **1 a :** a prescribed guide for conduct or action **b :** the laws laid down by the founder of a religious order **c :** an accepted procedure, custom, or habit **d :** a legal precept or doctrine **e :** REGULATION, BYLAW ⟨the *rules* of the club⟩ **2 a :** a usually valid generalization **b :** a generally prevailing quality, state, or mode **c :** a regulating principle ⟨the *rules* of harmony⟩ **3 a :** the exercise of authority or control **:** DOMINION **b :** a period of such rule **:** REIGN ⟨during the *rule* of King George III⟩ **4 a :** a strip of material marked off in units used for measuring or ruling

off lengths **b** (1) **:** a metal strip that prints a linear design (2) **:** a linear design produced by or as if by such a strip [Old French *reule,* from Latin *regula* "straightedge, norm, rule", from *regere* "to lead straight, rule"]

²rule *vb* **1 a :** CONTROL 2a, DIRECT **b :** MANAGE 2 **2 a :** to exercise authority or power over **:** GOVERN **b :** to be preeminent in **:** DOMINATE **3 :** to declare authoritatively; *esp* **:** to lay down a legal rule **4 :** to mark with lines drawn along or as if along the straight edge of a ruler **5 a :** to exercise supreme authority **b :** PREDOMINATE 2, PREVAIL **syn** see GOVERN

rule•less \ˈrül-ləs\ *adj* **:** not restrained or regulated by law

rule of thumb 1 : a method based on experience and common sense **2 :** a general principle regarded as roughly correct but not scientifically accurate

rule out *vt* **1 :** to eliminate as a possibility **2 :** to make impossible **:** PREVENT

rul•er \ˈrü-lər\ *n* **1 :** one that rules; *esp* **:** SOVEREIGN **2 :** a smooth-edged strip (as of wood or metal) used as a guide in drawing lines or for measuring

¹rul•ing \ˈrü-liŋ\ *n* **:** an official or authoritative decision or interpretation (as by a judge on a point of law)

²ruling *adj* **1 :** exerting power or authority **2 :** CHIEF ⟨a *ruling* ambition⟩

rum \ˈrəm\ *n* **1 :** an alcoholic liquor distilled from a fermented cane product (as molasses) **2 :** alcoholic liquor [probably from obsolete *rumbullion* "rum"]

Ru•ma•nian *or* **Ro•ma•nian** *also* **Rou•ma•nian** \rü-ˈmā-nē-ən, -nyən\ *n* **1 :** a native or inhabitant of Rumania **2 :** the Romance language of the Rumanians — **Rumanian** *adj*

rum•ba *also* **rhum•ba** \ˈrəm-bə, ˈrüm-\ *n* **1 :** a Cuban dance marked by violent movements **2 :** a ballroom dance imitative of the Cuban rumba [American Spanish]

¹rum•ble \ˈrəm-bəl\ *vb* **rum•bled; rum•bling** \-bə-liŋ, -bliŋ\ **1 :** to make a low heavy rolling sound **2 :** to travel with a low reverberating sound **3 :** to speak or utter in a low rolling tone [Middle English *rumblen*]

²rumble *n* **:** a low heavy continuous reverberating often muffled sound

rumble seat *n* **:** a folding seat in the back of an automobile (as a coupe or roadster) not covered by the top

ru•men \ˈrü-mən\ *n, pl* **ru•mi•na** \-mə-nə\ *or* **rumens :** the large first compartment of the stomach of a ruminant in which cellulose is broken down by the action of symbionts [Latin *rumin-, rumen* "gullet"] — **ru•mi•nal** \-mən-l\ *adj*

¹ru•mi•nant \ˈrü-mə-nənt\ *n* **:** a ruminant mammal

²ruminant *adj* **1 a :** chewing the cud **b :** of or relating to a group (Ruminantia) of even-toed hoofed mammals (as sheep, giraffes, deer, and camels) that chew the cud and have a complex 3- or 4-chambered stomach **2 :** given to or engaged in contemplation **:** MEDITATIVE — **ru•mi•nant•ly** *adv*

ru•mi•nate \ˈrü-mə-ˌnāt\ *vb* **1 :** to engage in contemplation **:** MUSE, MEDITATE **2 :** to chew the cud **:** bring up and chew again what has been chewed slightly and swallowed [Latin *ruminari* "to chew the cud, muse upon", from *rumen* "gullet"] — **ru•mi•na•tion** \ˌrü-mə-ˈnā-shən\ *n* — **ru•mi•na•tive** \ˈrü-mə-ˌnāt-iv\ *adj* — **ru•mi•na•tive•ly** *adv* — **ru•mi•na•tor** \-ˌnāt-ər\ *n*

¹rum•mage \ˈrəm-ij\ *n* **:** a thorough search especially among a confusion of objects or into every section [Middle French *arrimage* "act of packing cargo"]

²rummage *vb* **1 :** to make a thorough search especially by moving about, turning over, or looking through the contents of a place or receptacle ⟨*rummage* through an attic⟩ **2 :** to discover by searching ⟨*rummaged* up what they needed for costumes⟩

rummage sale *n* **:** a sale of miscellaneous and often donated articles

rum•my \ˈrəm-ē\ *n* **:** a card game in which each player tries to be the first to play all cards held in the hand by laying them down in groups of three or more of the same kind or in sequence [perhaps derived from earlier *rum* "queer, odd"]

¹ru•mor \ˈrü-mər\ *n* **1 :** talk or opinion widely current but having no known source **:** HEARSAY **2 :** a statement or report going around without known authority for its truth [Middle French *rumour,* from Latin *rumor*]

²rumor *vt* **ru•mored; ru•mor•ing** \ˈrüm-riŋ, -ə-riŋ\ **:** to tell or spread by rumor

ru•mor•mon•ger \ˈrü-mər-ˌməŋ-gər, -ˌmäŋ-\ *n* **:** one who spreads rumors

rump \ˈrəmp\ *n* **1 :** the back part of an animal's body where the hips and thighs join generally including the buttocks **2 :** a cut of beef between the loin and round **3 :** a small fragment remaining after the separation of the larger part of a group or an area; *esp* **:** a group (as a parliament) carrying on in the name of the original body after the departure or expulsion of a large number of its members [of Scandinavian origin] — **rumped** \ˈrəmt, ˈrəmpt\ *adj*

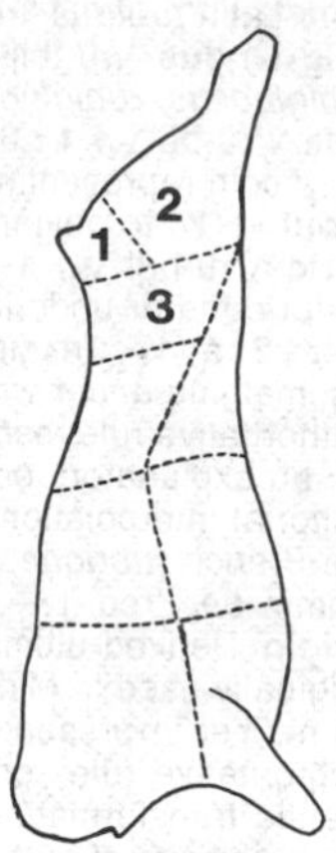

rump 1: *1* rump, *2* round, *3* loin

rum•ple \ˈrəm-pəl\ *vb* **rum•pled; rum•pling** \-pə-liŋ, -pliŋ\ **1 :** WRINKLE, CRUMPLE ⟨*rumple* the bedclothes⟩ **2 :** to make unkempt **:** TOUSLE ⟨*rumpled* my hair⟩ [Dutch *rompelen*]

rum•pus \ˈrəm-pəs\ *n* **:** a noisy commotion [origin unknown]

rumpus room *n* **:** a room (as in the basement of a home) set apart for games, parties, and recreation

¹run \ˈrən\ *vb* **ran** \ˈran\; **run; run•ning 1 a :** to go faster than a walk; *esp* **:** to go steadily by springing steps so that both feet leave the ground for an instant in each step **b :** to move at a fast gallop ⟨*running* horses⟩ **c :** FLEE 1, RETREAT, ESCAPE ⟨dropped the gun and *ran*⟩ **2 a :** to move freely about at will ⟨let the dog *run* loose⟩ **b :** to keep company ⟨*running* with a bad crowd⟩ **c :** to sail in the same direction the wind is blowing **d :** to go about ⟨*running* around without a coat⟩ **3 a :** to go or cause to go rapidly or hurriedly **:** HASTEN **b :** to do or accomplish by or as if by running ⟨*run* errands⟩ **4 a :** to compete in a race **b :** to enter or put forward as a contestant in an election contest **5 a :** to move on or as if on wheels **:** GLIDE ⟨file drawers *running* on ball bearings⟩ **b :** to roll forward rapidly or freely **c :** to ravel lengthwise **6 :** to sing or play a musical passage quickly ⟨*run* up the scale⟩ **7 a :** to go back and forth **:** PLY **b :** to migrate or move in schools; *esp* **:** to ascend a river to spawn ⟨shad are *running* in the river⟩ **8 :** FUNCTION, OPERATE ⟨keep the car *running*⟩ **9 :** to continue in force or operation ⟨the contract has two years to *run*⟩ **10 :** to pass into a specified condition ⟨*run* into debt⟩ **11 a :** to move as a fluid **:** FLOW **b :** MELT ⟨solder *runs* at low heat⟩ **c :** to spread out **:** DISSOLVE ⟨colors guaranteed not to *run*⟩ **d :** to discharge a fluid ⟨a *running* sore⟩ **12 :** to tend to develop a specified quality or feature ⟨they *run* to big noses in that family⟩ **13 a :** to extend through space or time ⟨the boundary line *runs* east⟩ ⟨a family line that *runs* back to a notorious horse thief⟩ **b :** to be in a certain form or expression ⟨the letter *runs* as follows⟩ or order of succession ⟨house numbers *run* in odd numbers from 3 to 57⟩ **14 a :** to occur persistently **:** RECUR ⟨musical talent *runs* in the family⟩ **b :** to exist or occur in a continuous range of variation ⟨the quality *runs* from good to terrible⟩ **c :** to play on stage ⟨the play *ran* for six months⟩ **15 a :** to spread or pass quickly from point to point ⟨chills *ran* up my spine⟩ **b :** to be current **:** CIRCULATE ⟨speculation *ran* rife on who it would be⟩ **16 a :** to bring to a specified condition by or as if by running ⟨*ran* themselves to death⟩ **b :** TRACE ⟨*ran* the rumor to its source⟩ **c :** to keep or maintain (livestock) on or as if on pasturage **17 a :** to pass over or traverse ⟨*ran* the whole range of emotions⟩ **b :** to slip through or past ⟨*run* a blockade⟩ **18 a :** to cause to penetrate or enter **:** THRUST ⟨*ran* a splinter into my toe⟩ **b :** STITCH ⟨*run* a basting⟩ **c :** to cause to pass **:** LEAD ⟨*run* a wire in from the antenna⟩ **d :** to cause to collide ⟨*ran* my head into a post⟩ **e :** SMUGGLE ⟨*run* guns⟩ **19 :** to cause to pass lightly or quickly over, along, or into something ⟨*ran* my eye down the list⟩ **20 a :** to cause or allow to go in a specified manner or direction ⟨*ran* the car off the road⟩ **b :** to carry on **:** MANAGE ⟨*run* a factory⟩ **21 a :** to flow with ⟨streets *ran* blood⟩ **b :** ASSAY ⟨the ore *runs* high in silver⟩ **22 :** to make oneself liable to **:** INCUR ⟨*ran* the risk of discovery⟩ **23 :** to mark out **:** DRAW ⟨*run* a contour line on a map⟩ **24 :** to permit charges to accumulate before settling ⟨*run* an account⟩ ⟨*ran* up a big bill⟩ **25 :** PRINT ⟨*run* the advertisement for three days⟩ [Middle English *rinnen,* v.i. (from Old English *rinnan* and Old Norse *rinna*) and *rennen,* v.t., from Old Norse *renna*] — **run across :** to meet with or discover by chance — **run a fever** *or* **run a temperature :** to have a fever — **run foul of 1 :** to collide with ⟨*ran foul* of a hidden reef⟩ **2 :** to run into conflict with or hostility to ⟨*run foul* of the law⟩ — **run into 1 :** to mount up to ⟨a boat like that one *runs into* money⟩ **2 a :** to collide with **b :** ENCOUNTER, MEET ⟨*ran into* an old friend⟩ — **run riot 1 :** to act wildly or without restraint **2 :** to occur in profusion — **run short :** to become insufficient — **run to seed :** to exhaust vitality in or as if in producing seed

2run *n* **1 a :** an act or the action of running **:** continued rapid movement ⟨broke into a *run*⟩ **b :** a fast gallop **c :** a migrating of fish; *also* **:** fish migrating especially to spawn **d :** a running race ⟨a mile *run*⟩ **e :** a score made in baseball by a base runner reaching home plate **2 a** *chiefly Midland* **:** CREEK 2 **b :** something that flows in the course of an operation or during a particular time ⟨the first *run* of maple sap⟩ **3 a :** the horizontal distance from one point to another **b :** general tendency or direction **4 :** a continuous series or unbroken period especially of things of identical or similar sort: as **a :** a rapid scale passage in vocal or instrumental music **b :** an unbroken course of theatrical performances **c :** an unbroken stretch ⟨a *run* of bad luck⟩ **d :** sudden heavy demands from depositors, creditors, or customers ⟨a *run* on a bank⟩ **5 :** the quantity of work turned out in a continuous operation **6 :** the usual or normal kind ⟨average *run* of college graduates⟩ **7 a :** the distance covered in a period of continuous traveling or sailing ⟨logged the day's *run*⟩ **b :** regular course **:** TRIP ⟨the bus makes four *runs* daily⟩ **c :** freedom of movement in or access to a place or area ⟨has the *run* of the house⟩ **8 a :** a way, track, or path frequented by animals ⟨a deer *run*⟩ **b :** an enclosure for livestock where they may feed or exercise **9 a :** an inclined course (as for skiing) **b :** a track or guide on which something runs **10 :** a ravel in a knitted fabric (as in hosiery) caused by the breaking of stitches — **run•less** \-ləs\ *adj*

run•about \'rən-ə-ˌbau̇t\ *n* **1 :** one who wanders about **:** STRAY **2 :** a light open wagon, roadster, or motorboat

run•a•gate \'rən-ə-ˌgāt\ *n* **1 :** FUGITIVE 1, RUNAWAY 2 **:** VAGABOND [from obsolete *renegate* "renegade", from Medieval Latin *renegatus*]

run•around \'rən-ə-ˌrau̇nd\ *n* **:** deceptive or delaying action especially in response to a request

1run•away \'rən-ə-ˌwā\ *n* **1 :** FUGITIVE 1 **2 :** the act of running away out of control; *also* **:** a horse that is running out of control **3 :** a one-sided victory

2runaway *adj* **1 :** running away **:** FUGITIVE **2 :** accomplished by elopement or during flight ⟨a *runaway* marriage⟩ **3 :** won by or having a long lead **4 :** subject to uncontrolled changes ⟨*runaway* inflation⟩

run away \ˌrən-ə-'wā\ *vi* **1 :** FLEE 1, DESERT ⟨*ran away* from the fight⟩ **2 :** to leave home; *esp* **:** ELOPE ⟨*ran away* to get married⟩ **3 :** to run out of control **:** STAMPEDE, BOLT

run•down \'rən-ˌdau̇n\ *n* **:** an item-by-item report **:** SUMMARY

run–down \'rən-'dau̇n\ *adj* **1 :** being in poor repair **:** DILAPIDATED **2 :** being in poor health **3 :** completely unwound ⟨a *run-down* clock⟩

run down \'rən-'dau̇n, ˌrən-\ *vb* **1 a :** to collide with and knock down **b :** to run against and cause to sink **2 a :** to chase until exhausted or captured **b :** to find by search **:** trace the source of **3 :** DISPARAGE 2 **4 :** to cease to operate because of the exhaustion of motive power **5 :** to deteriorate in physical condition

rune \'rün\ *n* **1 :** one of the characters of an alphabet used by the Germanic peoples from about the 3d to the 13th centuries **2 :** mystic utterance or inscription **3 :** a Finnish or Old Norse poem [Old Norse and Old English *rūn* "mystery, runic character, writing"; sense 3 from Finnish *runo,* of Germanic origin] — **ru•nic** \'rü-nik\ *adj*

rune 1

1rung *past participle of* RING

2rung \'rəŋ\ *n* **1 a :** a rounded part placed as a crosspiece between the legs of a chair **b :** one of the crosspieces of a ladder **2 :** STEP 5a, LEVEL ⟨down a few *rungs* in the social scale⟩ [Old English *hrung* "crossbar, spoke"]

run–in \'rən-ˌin\ *n* **:** ALTERCATION, QUARREL

run•let \'rən-lət\ *n* **:** RUNNEL

run•nel \'rən-ᵊl\ *n* **:** RIVULET, STREAMLET [Old English *rynel*]

run•ner \'rən-ər\ *n* **1 a :** one that runs **:** RACER **b :** BALLCARRIER **c :** BASE RUNNER **2 :** MESSENGER ⟨was a *runner* on Wall Street⟩ **3 :** any of various large active sea fishes **4 a :** either of the longitudinal pieces on which a sled or sleigh slides **b :** the blade of a skate **c :** the support of a drawer or a sliding door **5 a :** a slender creeping branch of a plant; *esp* **:** STOLON 1 **b :** a plant that forms or spreads by runners **6 a :** a long narrow carpet for a hall or staircase **b :** a narrow decorative cloth cover for a table or dresser top

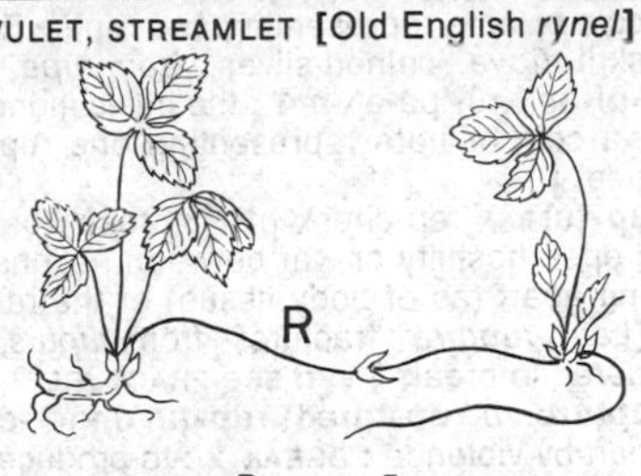

R runner 5a

run•ner–up \'rən-ər-ˌəp\ *n* **:** the competitor in a contest that finishes next to the winner

1run•ning *adj* **1 :** FLUID, RUNNY ⟨a *running* sore⟩ **2 :** INCESSANT, CONTINUOUS ⟨a *running* battle⟩ **3 :** measured in a straight line ⟨buy cloth by the *running* meter⟩ **4 :** CURSIVE ⟨a *running* hand in writing⟩ **5 :** initiated or performed while running or with a running start ⟨a *running* leap⟩ **6 :** fitted or trained for running ⟨*running* track⟩ ⟨*running* horse⟩

2running *adv* **:** in succession **:** CONSECUTIVELY ⟨four days *running*⟩

running board *n* **:** a footboard especially at the side of an automobile

running knot *n* **:** a knot that slips along the line round which it is tied

running light *n* **:** one of the lights carried by a vehicle (as a ship) under way at night that indicate position, size, and direction

running mate *n* **:** a candidate running for a subordinate office (as of vice-president) who is paired with the candidate for the top office on the same ticket

run•ny \'rən-ē\ *adj* **run•ni•er**; **-est :** having a tendency to run ⟨a *runny* nose⟩

run•off \'rən-ˌȯf\ *n* **1 :** water that is removed from soil by natural drainage **2 :** a final contest to decide a previous indecisive contest or series of contests

run off \'rən-'ȯf, ˌrən-\ *vb* **1 :** to produce by or as if by printing ⟨*ran off* a few more copies⟩ **2 :** to cause to be run or played to a finish **3 :** to steal (as cattle) by driving away **4 :** to run away — **run off with :** to carry off **:** STEAL

run–of–the–mill \ˌrən-əv-t͟hə-'mil, ˌrən-ə-t͟hə-\ *adj* **:** not outstanding in quality or rarity **:** AVERAGE

1run–on \'rən-'ȯn, -'än\ *adj* **:** continuing without rhetorical pause from one line of verse into another

2run–on \'rən-ˌȯn, -ˌän\ *n* **:** something (as a dictionary entry) that is run on

run on \'rən-'ȯn, ˌrən-, -'än\ *vb* **1 :** PERSIST 2 **2 :** to talk or narrate at length **3 :** to continue (matter in type) without a break or a new paragraph **4 :** to place or add (as an entry in a dictionary) at the end of a paragraphed item

run–on sentence *n* **:** a sentence containing a comma fault

run out *vi* **1 :** to come to an end **:** EXPIRE **2 :** to become exhausted or used up **:** FAIL — **run out of :** to use up the available supply of

run over *vb* **1 :** OVERFLOW 2, 3 **2 :** to exceed a limit **3 :** to go over, examine, repeat, or rehearse quickly **4 :** to collide with, knock down, and often drive over

runt \'rənt\ *n* **:** an unusually small person or animal [origin unknown] — **runty** \-ē\ *adj*

run through *vt* **1 :** PIERCE 1 **2 :** to spend or consume wastefully and rapidly

run•way \'rən-ˌwā\ *n* **1 :** RUN 8 **2 :** a paved strip of ground on a landing field for the landing and takeoff of airplanes **3 :** a support (as a track, pipe, or trough) on which something runs

ru•pee \rü-'pē, 'rü-ˌpē\ *n* **1 :** the basic monetary unit of India, Mauritius, Nepal, Pakistan, Seychelles, and Sri Lanka **2 :** a coin or note representing one rupee [Hindi *rūpaiyā,* from Sanskrit *rūpya* "coined silver", from *rūpa* "form, beauty"]

ru·pi·ah \rü-ˈpē-ə\ *n* **1 :** the basic monetary unit of Indonesia **2 :** a coin or note representing one rupiah [Hindi *rūpaiyā* "rupee"]

1rup·ture \ˈrəp-chər\ *n* **1 :** breach of peace or concord; *esp* **:** open hostility or war between nations **2 :** a breaking or tearing apart (as of body tissue) or the resulting state **3 :** HERNIA [Latin *ruptura* "fracture", from *ruptus,* past participle of *rumpere* "to break"] **syn** see FRACTURE

2rupture *vb* **rup·tured; rup·tur·ing** \-chə-ring, -shring\ **1 :** to part by violence **:** BREAK **2 :** to produce a rupture in **3 :** to have a rupture

ru·ral \ˈru̇r-əl\ *adj* **:** of or relating to the country, country people or life, or agriculture [Middle French, from Latin *ruralis,* from *rur-, rus* "open land, country"]

rural free delivery *n* **:** the free delivery of mail on routes in country districts — called also *rural delivery*

rural route *n* **:** a mail-delivery route in a rural free delivery area

rur·ban \ˈrər-bən, ˈru̇r-\ *adj* **:** of, relating to, or constituting an area which is chiefly residential but where some farming is carried on [blend of *rural* and *urban*]

ruse \ˈrüs, ˈrüz\ *n* **:** a deceptive stratagem **:** ARTIFICE, SUBTERFUGE **syn** see TRICK [French, from Middle French *ruser* "to dodge, deceive"]

1rush \ˈrəsh\ *n* **:** any of various monocotyledonous often tufted marsh plants with cylindrical often hollow stems used in chair seats and mats [Old English *risc, rysc*] — **rushy** \-ē\ *adj*

2rush *vb* **1 :** to move forward, progress, or act with haste or eagerness or without preparation ⟨*rush* out the door⟩ **2 :** to push or impel on or forward with speed or violence ⟨*rush* them to the hospital⟩ **3 :** to perform in a short time or at a high speed ⟨*rush* a job through⟩ **4 :** CHARGE 4 ⟨*rushed* the hijackers⟩ **5 :** to carry the football in a running play **6 :** to lavish attention on **:** COURT [Middle French *ruser* "to put to flight, dodge, deceive", from Latin *recusare* "to refuse"] — **rush·er** *n*

3rush *n* **1 a :** a violent forward motion ⟨a *rush* of wind⟩ **b :** CHARGE 7, ONSET ⟨led the *rush* on the enemy position⟩ **2 :** a burst of activity, productivity, or speed **3 :** a thronging of people usually to a new place and in search of wealth ⟨gold *rush*⟩ **4 :** a running play in football **5 :** a round of attention usually involving extensive social activity **6 :** the first rapid excitation produced by a narcotic drug

4rush *adj* **:** requiring or marked by special speed or urgency ⟨*rush* orders⟩ ⟨the *rush* season⟩

rusk \ˈrəsk\ *n* **:** a sweet or plain bread baked, sliced, and baked again until dry and crisp [Spanish and Portuguese *rosca* "coil, twisted roll"]

Russ \ˈrəs\ *n, pl* **Russ** *or* **Russ·es :** RUSSIAN 1a [Russian *Rus'*] — **Russ** *adj*

rus·set \ˈrəs-ət\ *n* **1 :** coarse homespun usually reddish brown cloth **2 :** a strong brown **3 :** any of various winter apples with rough russet skins [Old French *rousset,* from *rousset* "reddish brown", from *rous* "reddish brown", from Latin *russus* "red"] — **russet** *adj*

Rus·sian \ˈrəsh-ən\ *n* **1 a :** any of the people of the Soviet Union; *esp* **:** a member of the dominant Slavic-speaking Great Russian ethnic group of Russia **b :** a person of Russian descent **2 :** a Slavic language of the Russian people that is the official language of the Soviet Union — **Russian** *adj*

Russian olive *n* **:** a small Eurasian tree or shrub with usually silvery leaves widely grown in dry windy regions as a hedge and shelter plant

Russian thistle *n* **:** a prickly European herb that is a serious weed in North America

Russian wolfhound *n* **:** BORZOI

Russo- *combining form* **1 :** Russia **:** Russians **2 :** Russian and

1rust \ˈrəst\ *n* **1 a :** the reddish brittle coating chiefly of ferric oxide formed on iron especially when chemically attacked by moist air **b :** a comparable coating produced on other metals by corrosion **2 :** corrosive or injurious influence or effect **3 a :** any of numerous destructive diseases of plants caused by fungi and marked by reddish brown pustular lesions **b :** any of an order (Uredinales) of parasitic fungi that cause plant rusts — compare WHITE RUST **4 :** a strong reddish brown [Old English *rūst*]

2rust *vb* **1 :** to form or cause to form rust **:** become oxidized ⟨iron *rusts*⟩ **2 :** to weaken or degenerate or cause to degenerate especially from inaction, lack of use, or passage of time **:** CORRODE ⟨diplomatic skill that had not *rusted*⟩ **3 :** to turn the color of rust

1rus·tic \ˈrəs-tik\ *adj* **1 :** of, relating to, or suitable for the country **:** RURAL ⟨*rustic* sports⟩ **2 :** made of the rough limbs of trees ⟨*rustic* furniture⟩ **3 :** AWKWARD, BOORISH ⟨*rustic* manners⟩ [Middle French *rustique,* from Latin *rusticus,* from *rus* "open land, country"] — **rus·ti·cal·ly** \-ti-kə-lē, -klē\ *adv* — **rus·tic·i·ty** \ˌrəs-ˈtis-ət-ē\ *n*

2rustic *n* **:** an inhabitant of a rural area; *esp* **:** an unsophisticated one

rus·ti·cate \ˈrəs-ti-ˌkāt\ *vb* **1 :** to go into or reside in the country **2 :** to suspend from school or college — **rus·ti·ca·tion** \ˌrəs-ti-ˈkā-shən\ *n* — **rus·ti·ca·tor** \ˈrəs-ti-ˌkāt-ər\ *n*

1rus·tle \ˈrəs-əl\ *vb* **rus·tled; rus·tling** \ˈrəs-ling, -ə-ling\ **1 :** to make or cause to make a rustle **2 :** to act or move with energy or speed **3 :** to get by or as if by foraging ⟨*rustle* up some food⟩ **4 :** to steal (as cattle) from the range [Middle English *rustelen*]

2rustle *n* **:** a quick succession or confusion of small sounds ⟨the *rustle* of leaves⟩ ⟨the *rustle* among a theater audience⟩

rus·tler \ˈrəs-lər, -ə-lər\ *n* **:** one that rustles cattle

rust·proof \ˈrəst-ˈprüf\ *adj* **:** incapable of rusting

rusty \ˈrəs-tē\ *adj* **rust·i·er; -est 1 :** affected by or as if by rust; *esp* **:** stiff with or as if with rust **2 :** inept and slow through lack of practice or old age **3 a :** of the color rust **b :** dulled in color or appearance by age and use — **rust·i·ly** \ˈrəs-tə-lē\ *adv* — **rust·i·ness** \-tē-nəs\ *n*

1rut \ˈrət\ *n* **:** a state of sexual excitement especially in the male deer; *also* **:** a period in which this occurs [Middle French *rut, ruit* "roar", from Late Latin *rugitus,* from Latin *rugire* "to roar"]

2rut *n* **1 :** a track worn by a wheel or by habitual passage **2 :** a usual or fixed practice **:** a regular course; *esp* **:** a monotonous routine ⟨my life's in a *rut*⟩ [perhaps from Middle French *route* "way, route"] — **rut·ty** \ˈrət-ē\ *adj*

3rut *vt* **rut·ted; rut·ting :** to make a rut in **:** FURROW

ru·ta·ba·ga \ˌrüt-ə-ˈbā-gə, ˌru̇t-, -ˈbeg-ə\ *n* **:** a turnip with a very large yellowish root [Swedish dialect *rotabagge,* from Swedish *rot* "root" + *bagge* "bag"]

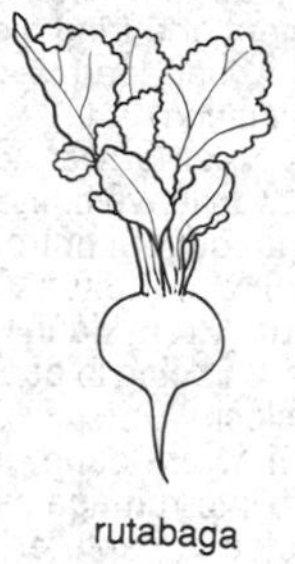

rutabaga

ruth \ˈrüth\ *n* **1 :** compassion for the misery of another **:** PITY **2 :** sorrow for one's own faults **:** REMORSE [Middle English *ruthe,* from *ruen* "to rue"]

Ruth \ˈrüth\ *n* — see BIBLE table

ru·the·ni·um \rü-ˈthē-nē-əm\ *n* **:** a hard brittle grayish rare metallic chemical element used in hardening platinum alloys — see ELEMENT table [New Latin, from Medieval Latin *Ruthenia* "Russia"]

ruth·less \ˈrüth-ləs\ *adj* **:** having no ruth **:** MERCILESS, CRUEL — **ruth·less·ly** *adv* — **ruth·less·ness** *n*

ru·tile \ˈrü-ˌtēl\ *n* **:** a mineral TiO_2 that consists of titanium dioxide usually with a little iron, is mostly of a reddish brown color, and is a major source of titanium [German *rutil,* from Latin *rutilus* "reddish"]

-ry \rē\ *n suffix, pl* **-ries :** -ERY ⟨citizenry⟩ ⟨wizardry⟩ [Old French *-erie, -rie* "-ery"]

rye \ˈrī\ *n* **1 :** a hardy annual cereal grass widely grown for grain and as a cover crop; *also* **:** its seeds **2 :** whiskey distilled from rye or from rye and malt [Old English *ryge*]

rye bread *n* **:** bread made wholly or partly from rye flour

rye·grass \ˈrī-ˌgras\ *n* **:** either of two grasses that are used especially for pasture and as cover crops

S s—systolic

s \'es\ *n, pl* **s's** *or* **ss** \'es-əz\ *often cap* **1 :** the 19th letter of the English alphabet **2 :** a grade rating a student's work as satisfactory **3 :** something shaped like the letter S

[1]-s \s *after a voiceless consonant sound,* z *after a voiced consonant sound or a vowel sound*\ *n pl suffix* **1** — used to form the plural of most nouns that do not end in *s, z, sh, ch,* or *y* following a consonant ⟨heads⟩ ⟨books⟩ ⟨boys⟩ ⟨beliefs⟩, to form the plural of proper nouns that end in *y* following a consonant ⟨Marys⟩, and with or without a preceding apostrophe to form the plural of abbreviations, numbers, letters, and symbols used as nouns ⟨MCs⟩ ⟨4s⟩ ⟨#s⟩ ⟨B's⟩; compare [1]-ES 1 **2** — used to form adverbs denoting usual or repeated action or state ⟨always at home Sundays⟩ ⟨mornings we stop by the newsstand⟩ ⟨goes to school nights⟩ [Old English *-as,* nominative and accusative pl. ending of some masculine nouns; sense 2 from Old English *-es,* genitive sing. ending of nouns (functioning adverbially)]

[2]-s *like* [1]-s\ *vb suffix* — used to form the third person singular present of most verbs that do not end in *s, z, sh, ch,* or in *y* following a consonant ⟨falls⟩ ⟨takes⟩ ⟨plays⟩; compare [2]-ES

[1]'s *like* -'s\ *vb* **1 :** IS ⟨someone's here⟩ **2 :** HAS ⟨who's seen them?⟩ **3 :** DOES ⟨what's it need?⟩

[2]'s \s\ *pron* **:** US — used with *let* ⟨let's⟩

-'s \s *after voiceless consonant sounds other than* s, sh, ch; z *after vowel sounds or voiced consonant sounds other than* z, zh, j; əz *after* s, sh, ch, z, zh, j\ *n suffix or pron suffix* — used to form the possessive of singular nouns ⟨child's⟩, of plural nouns not ending in s ⟨children's⟩, of some pronouns ⟨anyone's⟩, and of word groups functioning as nouns ⟨the book on the shelf's cover⟩ or pronouns ⟨someone else's⟩ [Old English *-es,* genitive singular ending]

sab•a•dil•la \ˌsab-ə-'dil-ə, -'dē-ə, -'dē-yə\ *n* **:** a Mexican plant of the lily family; *also* **:** its seeds used as a source of a poisonous irritant alkaloid and in insecticides [Spanish *cebadilla*]

Sab•ba•tar•i•an \ˌsab-ə-'ter-ē-ən\ *n* **1 :** one who keeps the 7th day of the week as holy **2 :** one who favors strict observance of the Sabbath [Latin *sabbatarius,* from *sabbatum* "Sabbath"] — **Sabbatarian** *adj* — **Sab•ba•tar•i•an•ism** \-ˌiz-əm\ *n*

Sab•bath \'sab-əth\ *n* **1 :** the 7th day of the week observed from Friday evening to Saturday evening as a day of rest and worship by Jews and some Christians **2 :** the day of the week (as among Christians) set aside in a religion for rest and worship [Old French and Old English *sabat,* from Latin *sabbatum,* from Greek *sabbaton,* from Hebrew *shabbāth,* literally, "rest"] **syn** see SUNDAY

sab•bat•i•cal \sə-'bat-i-kəl\ *or* **sab•bat•ic** \-'bat-ik\ *adj* **1 :** of or relating to the Sabbath **2 :** of or relating to a sabbatical year

sabbatical year *n* **:** a leave granted (as to a professor) usually every 7th year for rest, travel, or research — called also *sabbatical leave*

[1]sa•ber *or* **sa•bre** \'sā-bər\ *n* **1 :** a cavalry sword with a curved blade, thick back, and guard **2 a :** a fencing sword with an arched guard that covers the back of the hand and an imaginary full-length cutting edge **b :** the sport of fencing with a saber [French *sabre,* from German dialect *sabel,* of Slavic origin]

[2]saber *or* **sabre** *vt* **sa•bered** *or* **sa•bred**; **sa•ber•ing** *or* **sa•bring** \-bə-ring, -bring\ **:** to strike, cut, or kill with a saber

saber rattling *n* **:** aggressive display of military power

sa•ber–toothed tiger \ˌsā-bər-ˌtüth-'tī-gər, -ˌtütht-\ *n* **:** any of various large prehistoric cats with very long curved upper canine teeth — called also *saber-toothed cat*

Sa•bine \'sā-ˌbīn\ *n* **:** a member of an ancient people of the Apennines northeast of Latium conquered by Rome in 290 B.C. [Latin *Sabinus*] — **Sabine** *adj*

[1]sa•ble \'sā-bəl\ *n, pl* **sable** *or* **sables 1 a :** the color black **b :** black clothing worn in mourning — usually used in pl. **2 a :** a flesh-eating mammal of northern Europe and Asia related to the martens and valued for its soft rich brown fur; *also* **:** a related animal **b :** the fur or pelt of a sable [Middle French, "sable or its fur, the heraldic color black", from Low German *sabel,* of Slavic origin]

[1]sable 2a

[2]sable *adj* **1 :** BLACK 1a **2 :** DARK ⟨the *sable* sky⟩

sa•ble•fish \'sā-bəl-ˌfish\ *n* **:** a large dark spiny-finned fish of the Pacific coast that is a leading market fish with a liver rich in vitamins

sa•bot \sa-'bō, 'sab-ō\ *n* **:** a wooden shoe worn especially in various European countries [French]

[1]sab•o•tage \'sab-ə-ˌtäzh\ *n* **1 :** destruction of an employer's property (as tools or materials) or the hindering of manufacturing by discontented workers **2 :** destructive or obstructive action carried on by enemy agents or sympathizers to hinder a nation's war or defense effort [French, from *saboter* "to clatter with sabots, botch, sabotage", from *sabot* "sabot"]

[2]sabotage *vt* **:** to practice sabotage on

sab•o•teur \ˌsab-ə-'tər, -'tür\ *n* **:** a person who commits sabotage [French, from *saboter* "to sabotage"]

sa•bra \'säb-rə\ *n, often cap* **:** a native Israeli [Modern Hebrew *sābhār,* literally, "prickly pear"]

sac \'sak\ *n* **:** a pouch within an animal or plant often containing a fluid ⟨a synovial *sac*⟩ [French, literally, "bag", from Latin *saccus*] — **sac•cate** \'sak-ˌāt\ *adj* — **sac•like** \'sak-ˌlīk\ *adj*

sac•cha•ride \'sak-ə-ˌrīd\ *n* **:** a simple sugar, combination of sugars, or polymerized sugar

sac•cha•rim•e•ter \ˌsak-ə-'rim-ət-ər\ *n* **:** a device for measuring the amount of sugar in a solution

sac•cha•rin \'sak-rən, -ə-rən\ *n* **:** a very sweet white coal tar derivative that is a calorie-free sweetener

sac•cha•rine \'sak-rən, -ə-rən, -ə-ˌrēn, -ə-ˌrīn\ *adj* **1 a :** of, relating to, or resembling that of sugar ⟨*saccharine* taste⟩ ⟨*saccharine* fermentation⟩ **b :** yielding or containing sugar ⟨*saccharine* fluids⟩ **2 :** overly or ingratiatingly sweet ⟨a *saccharine* smile⟩ [Latin *saccharum* "sugar", from Greek *sakcharon,* derived from Sanskrit *śarkarā* "gravel, sugar"] — **sac•cha•rin•i•ty** \ˌsak-ə-'rin-ət-ē\ *n*

sac•cule \'sak-yül\ *n* **:** a little sac; *esp* **:** the smaller chamber of the membranous labyrinth of the ear — compare UTRICLE [Latin *sacculus* "little bag", from *saccus* "bag"]

sac•cu•lus \'sak-yə-ləs\ *n, pl* **-li** \-ˌlī, -ˌlē\ **:** SACCULE

sac•er•do•tal \ˌsas-ər-'dōt-l, ˌsak-\ *adj* **:** PRIESTLY [Middle French, from Latin *sacerdotalis,* from *sacerdos* "priest", from *sacer* "sacred"] — **sac•er•do•tal•ly** \-l-ē\ *adv*

sac•er•do•tal•ism \-l-ˌiz-əm\ *n* **:** religious belief emphasizing the powers of priests as essential mediators between God and man — **sac•er•do•tal•ist** \-l-əst\ *n*

sac fungus *n* **:** ASCOMYCETE

sa•chem \'sā-chəm\ *n* **:** a North American Indian chief; *esp* **:** an Algonquian chief [of American Indian origin] — **sa•chem•ic** \sā-'chem-ik\ *adj*

sa•chet \sa-'shā\ *n* **:** a small bag that contains a perfumed powder and is used to scent clothes and linens [French, literally, "small bag", from *sac* "bag"]

[1]sack \'sak\ *n* **1 a :** a large bag made of coarse strong material **b :** a small container made of light material (as paper) **2 :** the

\ə\ **abut**	\au̇\ **out**	\i\ **tip**	\ȯ\ **saw**	\u̇\ **foot**
\ər\ **further**	\ch\ **chin**	\ī\ **life**	\ȯi\ **coin**	\y\ **yet**
\a\ **mat**	\e\ **pet**	\j\ **job**	\th\ **thin**	\yü\ **few**
\ā\ **take**	\ē\ **easy**	\ng\ **sing**	\th\ **this**	\yu̇\ **cure**
\ä\ **cot, cart**	\g\ **go**	\ō\ **bone**	\ü\ **food**	\zh\ **vision**

amount contained in a sack **3 a :** a woman's loose-fitting dress **b :** a short usually loose-fitting coat for women and children **4 :** DISMISSAL — usually used with *get* or *give* **5 :** BUNK 2, BED [Old English *sacc* "bag", from Latin *saccus,* from Greek *sakkos,* of Semitic origin]

[2]**sack** *vt* **1 :** to put in a sack **2 :** to dismiss especially in a summary manner

[3]**sack** *n* **:** a usually dry and strong white wine imported to England from the south of Europe especially during the 16th and 17th centuries [Middle French *sec* "dry", from Latin *siccus*]

[4]**sack** *n* **:** the plundering of a captured town [Middle French *sac,* from Italian *sacco* literally, "bag", from Latin *saccus*]

[5]**sack** *vt* **1 :** to plunder after capture **2 :** to strip of valuables **:** LOOT

sack•but \ˈsak-ˌbət, -bət\ *n* **:** a medieval trombone [Middle French *saqueboute,* literally, "hooked lance", from *saquer* "to pull" + *bouter* "to push"]

sack•cloth \ˈsak-ˌklȯth\ *n* **1 :** a coarse cloth suitable for sacks **:** SACKING **2 :** a garment of sackcloth worn as a sign of mourning or penitence

sack coat *n* **:** a man's jacket with a straight unfitted back

sack•ful \ˈsak-ˌfu̇l\ *n, pl* **sackfuls** \-ˌfu̇lz\ *or* **sacks•ful** \ˈsaks-ˌfu̇l\ **:** the quantity that fills a sack

sack•ing \ˈsak-ing\ *n* **:** strong coarse cloth (as burlap) from which sacks are made

sack race *n* **:** a jumping race in which the legs of each competitor are enclosed in a sack

sacque \ˈsak\ *n* **:** a loose lightweight jacket; *esp* **:** an infant's short jacket fastened at the neck [alteration of [1]*sack*]

sa•cral \ˈsak-rəl, ˈsā-krəl\ *adj* **:** of, relating to, or lying near the sacrum

sac•ra•ment \ˈsak-rə-mənt\ *n* **1 :** a formal religious act that is sacred as a sign or symbol of a spiritual reality; *esp* **:** one instituted by Jesus Christ as a means of grace **2** *cap* **:** BLESSED SACRAMENT 2 [Late Latin *sacramentum,* from Latin, "oath of allegiance, obligation", from *sacrare* "to consecrate", from *sacer* "holy, sacred"] — **sac•ra•men•tal** \ˌsak-rə-ˈment-l\ *adj* — **sac•ra•men•tal•ly** \-l-ē\ *adv*

sac•ra•men•tal \ˌsak-rə-ˈment-l\ *n* **:** an action (as a rite) or object (as a rosary) originating in the church but serving as an indirect means of grace by producing devotion

sac•ra•men•tal•ism \-l-ˌiz-əm\ *n* **:** belief in or use of sacramental rites, acts, or objects; *esp* **:** belief that the sacraments are in themselves effective and necessary for salvation — **sac•ra•men•tal•ist** \-l-əst\ *n*

sa•cred \ˈsā-krəd\ *adj* **1 :** set apart in honor of someone ⟨a monument *sacred* to the memory of our heroes⟩ **2 :** HOLY ⟨the *sacred* name of Jesus⟩ **3 :** RELIGIOUS ⟨*sacred* songs⟩ **4 :** requiring or deserving to be held in highest esteem and protected from violation or encroachment ⟨a *sacred* right⟩ ⟨one's *sacred* word⟩ [Middle English, from past participle of *sacren* "to consecrate", from Old French *sacrer,* from Latin *sacrare,* from *sacer* "sacred, holy, cursed"] — **sa•cred•ly** *adv* — **sa•cred•ness** *n*

sacred cow *n* **:** a person or thing immune from criticism [from the veneration of the cow by Hindus]

[1]**sac•ri•fice** \ˈsak-rə-ˌfīs, -fəs\ *n* **1 :** an act of offering to deity something precious; *esp* **:** the killing of a victim on an altar **2 :** something offered in sacrifice **3 :** a giving up of something for the sake of something else; *also* **:** something so given up ⟨the *sacrifices* made by parents⟩ **4 :** loss of something and especially of a profit ⟨sell goods at a *sacrifice*⟩ [Old French, from Latin *sacrificium,* from *sacer* "sacred" + *facere* "to make"]

[2]**sac•ri•fice** \-ˌfīs, -ˌfīz\ *vb* **1 :** to offer as a sacrifice or perform sacrificial rites **2 :** to give up for the sake of something else ⟨*sacrifice* one's free time to help a friend⟩ ⟨*sacrificed* everything to win the election⟩ **3 :** to sell at a loss **4 :** to make a sacrifice hit — **sac•ri•fic•er** *n*

sacrifice fly *n* **:** an outfield fly in baseball that is caught but that is long enough to permit a base runner to score

sacrifice hit *n* **:** a bunt in baseball that allows a base runner to advance one base while the batter is put out

sac•ri•fi•cial \ˌsak-rə-ˈfish-əl\ *adj* **:** of or relating to sacrifice — **sac•ri•fi•cial•ly** \-ˈfish-ə-lē\ *adv*

sac•ri•lege \ˈsak-rə-lij\ *n* **1 :** theft or violation of something consecrated to God **2 :** gross misuse or disrespect of something sacred or precious ⟨it would be a *sacrilege* to cut such splendid trees⟩ [Old French, from Latin *sacrilegium,* derived from *sacer* "sacred" + *legere* "to gather, steal"] — **sac•ri•le•gious** \ˌsak-rə-ˈlij-əs, -ˈlē-jəs\ *adj* — **sac•ri•le•gious•ly** *adv* — **sac•ri•le•gious•ness** *n*

sac•ris•tan \ˈsak-rə-stən\ *n* **:** an officer of a church in charge of the sacristy and ceremonial equipment; *also* **:** SEXTON

sac•ris•ty \ˈsak-rə-stē\ *n, pl* **-ties :** a room in a church where sacred utensils and vestments are kept [Medieval Latin *sacristia,* from *sacrista* "sacristan", from Latin *sacer* "sacred"]

sac•ro•il•i•ac \ˌsak-rō-ˈil-ē-ˌak, ˌsā-krō-\ *n* **:** the region in which the sacrum and ilium join — **sacroiliac** *adj*

sac•ro•sanct \ˈsak-rō-ˌsangt, -ˌsangkt\ *adj* **:** SACRED 4, INVIOLABLE [Latin *sacrosanctus,* probably from *sacro sanctus* "hallowed by a sacred rite"] — **sac•ro•sanc•ti•ty** \ˌsak-rō-ˈsang-tət-ē, -ˈsangk-\ *n*

sa•crum \ˈsak-rəm, ˈsā-krəm\ *n, pl* **sa•cra** \ˈsak-rə, ˈsā-krə\ **:** the part of the vertebral column that is directly connected with or forms a part of the pelvis and in man consists of five united vertebrae [Late Latin *os sacrum* "last bone of the spine", literally, "sacred bone"]

sad \ˈsad\ *adj* **sad•der; sad•dest 1 :** affected with or expressive of grief or unhappiness ⟨*sad* at the loss⟩ ⟨*sad* songs⟩ **2 a :** causing or associated with grief or unhappiness **:** DEPRESSING ⟨*sad* news⟩ **b :** DEPLORABLE, WRETCHED ⟨a *sad* loss of confidence⟩ [Old English *sæd* "sated"] — **sad•ly** *adv*

sad•den \ˈsad-n\ *vb* **sad•dened; sad•den•ing** \ˈsad-ning, -n-ing\ **:** to make or become sad

[1]**sad•dle** \ˈsad-l\ *n* **1 a :** a girthed usually padded and leather-covered seat for a rider on horseback; *also* **:** a comparable part of a driving harness **b :** a seat to be straddled on a vehicle (as a bicycle) **2 :** a ridge connecting two higher land elevations **3 :** a cut of meat consisting of both sides of the back including the loins **4 :** something like a saddle in shape, position, or use; *esp* **:** a support for an object **5 :** a piece of leather across the instep of a shoe [Old English *sadol*] — **in the saddle :** in control or command

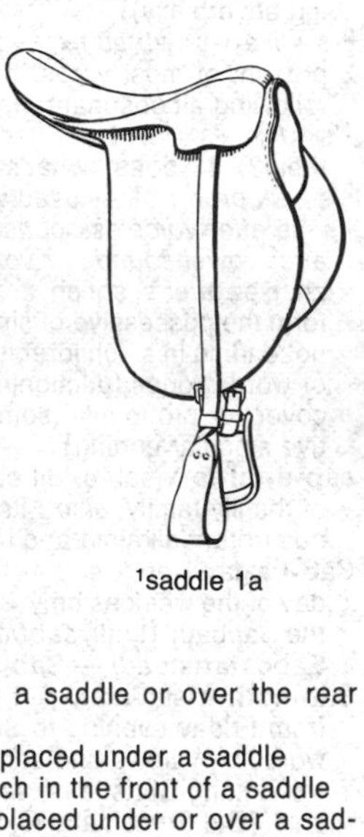

[1]saddle 1a

[2]**saddle** *vb* **sad•dled; sad•dling** \ˈsad-ling, -l-ing\ **1 :** to put a saddle on or on a horse ⟨quickly *saddled* and rode off⟩ **2 :** ENCUMBER 1, BURDEN

sad•dle•bag \ˈsad-l-ˌbag\ *n* **:** a large pouch carried hanging from a saddle or over the rear wheel of a bicycle or motorcycle

saddle blanket *n* **:** a blanket or pad placed under a saddle

sad•dle•bow \ˈsad-l-ˌbō\ *n* **:** the arch in the front of a saddle

sad•dle•cloth \-ˌklȯth\ *n* **:** a cloth placed under or over a saddle

saddle horse *n* **:** a horse suited for or trained for riding

saddle leather *n* **:** vegetable-tanned leather from cattle hide that is used for saddlery; *also* **:** smooth polished leather simulating this

sad•dler \ˈsad-lər\ *n* **:** one that makes, repairs, or sells equipment for horses (as saddles)

saddle roof *n* **:** a roof (as of a tower) having two gables and one ridge

sad•dlery \ˈsad-lə-rē, ˈsad-l-rē\ *n, pl* **-dler•ies :** the work, articles of trade, or shop of a saddler

saddle shoe *n* **:** an oxford-style shoe having a saddle of contrasting color or leather

saddle soap *n* **:** a mild oily soap used for cleansing and conditioning leather

saddle sore *n* **1 :** a sore on the back of a horse from an ill-fitting saddle **2 :** an irritation or sore on parts of a rider's body chafed by the saddle

sad•dle•tree \ˈsad-l-ˌtrē\ *n* **:** the frame of a saddle

Sad•du•cee \ˈsaj-ə-ˌsē, ˈsad-yə-\ *n* **:** a member of a Jewish party of the time of Christ that consisted largely of a priestly aristocracy and that rejected doctrines not in the Law [Old English *sadduce,* from Late Latin *sadducaeus,* from Greek *saddoukaios,* from Hebrew *ṣăddūqī*] — **Sad•du•ce•an** \ˌsaj-ə-ˈsē-ən, ˌsad-yə-\ *adj* — **Sad•du•cee•ism** \ˈsaj-ə-ˌsē-ˌiz-əm, ˈsad-yə-\ *n*

sad•iron \'sad-ˌī-ərn, -ˌīrn\ *n* : a flatiron pointed at both ends and having a removable handle [*sad* "compact, heavy" (from Old English *sæd* "sated") + *iron*]

sa•dism \'sād-ˌiz-əm, 'sad-\ *n* **1** : a perversion in which pleasure is obtained by inflicting physical or mental pain especially upon a loved one **2 a** : pleasure taken in cruelty **b** : excessive cruelty [Marquis de *Sade*, died 1814, French soldier and pervert] — **sa•dist** \-əst\ *n* — **sa•dis•tic** \sə-'dis-tik, sā-\ *adj* — **sa•dis•ti•cal•ly** \-ti-kə-lē, -klē\ *adv*

sad•ness \'sad-nəs\ *n* : the quality, state, or fact of being sad **syn** see MELANCHOLY

sad sack *n* : a very inept person

sa•fa•ri \sə-'fär-ē, -'far-\ *n, pl* **-ris 1** : the caravan and equipment of a hunting expedition especially in eastern Africa **2** : a hunting expedition in eastern Africa **3** : EXPEDITION 1a [Arabic *safarīy* "of a trip"]

¹safe \'sāf\ *adj* **1** : freed from harm or risk : UNHURT **2 a** : secure from threat of danger, harm, or loss **b** : successful in reaching base in baseball **3** : affording safety **4** : not threatening danger : HARMLESS ⟨*safe* medicine⟩ **5 a** : CAUTIOUS ⟨a *safe* policy⟩ **b** : TRUSTWORTHY, RELIABLE ⟨a *safe* guide⟩ [Old French *sauf*, from Latin *salvus* "safe, healthy"] — **safe•ly** *adv* — **safe•ness** *n*

• **syn** SAFE, SECURE mean free from danger. SAFE often implies danger successfully avoided or risk run without harm ⟨arrived *safe* on the other bank of the river⟩ and always suggests present or immediate freedom from threatening harm ⟨stayed *safe* at home⟩ SECURE implies freedom from anxiety or apprehension of loss or danger ⟨locks and alarms designed to make people feel *secure*⟩

²safe *n* : a place or container to keep articles (as valuables) safe

safe–con•duct \'sāf-'kän-ˌdəkt, -dəkt\ *n* **1** : protection given a person passing through a military zone or occupied area **2** : a document authorizing safe-conduct

safe•crack•er \'sāf-ˌkrak-ər\ *n* : one that breaks open safes to steal their contents

safe–de•pos•it box \ˌsāf-di-'päz-ət-\ *n* : a box (as in the vault of a bank) for the safe storage of valuables

¹safe•guard \'sāf-ˌgärd\ *n* : something that protects and gives safety : DEFENSE

²safeguard *vt* : to make safe or secure : PROTECT

safe•keep•ing \'sāf-'kē-ping\ *n* : a keeping or being kept in safety

safe•light \'sā-ˌflīt\ *n* : a darkroom lamp with a filter to screen out rays that are harmful to sensitive film or paper

safe•ty \'sāf-tē\ *n, pl* **safeties 1** : the state of being safe : SECURITY **2** : a protective device (as on a firearm) to prevent accidental operation **3 a** : a football play in which the ball is downed by the offensive team behind its own goal line and which counts two points for the defensive team — compare TOUCHBACK **b** : a defensive football back who plays the deepest position in the secondary

safety belt *n* : a belt fastening a person to an object to prevent falling or injury

safety glass *n* : glass that resists shattering and is formed of two sheets of glass with a sheet of transparent plastic between them

safety island *n* : an area within a roadway from which vehicular traffic is excluded

safety lamp *n* : a miner's lamp constructed to avoid explosion in an atmosphere containing flammable gas usually by enclosing the flame in fine wire gauze

safety match *n* : a match that can be ignited only by striking on a specially prepared surface

safety pin *n* : a pin in the form of a clasp with a guard covering its point

safety razor *n* : a razor with a guard for the blade to prevent deep cuts

safety valve *n* **1** : a valve that opens automatically to prevent accident (as when steam pressure becomes too great) **2** : OUTLET 2

safety zone *n* : a safety island for persons on foot

saf•flow•er \'saf-ˌlau̇-ər, -ˌlau̇r\ *n* : a widely grown Old World herb of the daisy family with large orange or red flower heads yielding a dyestuff and seeds rich in edible oil [Middle French *saffleur*, from Italian *saffiore*, from Arabic *aṣfar*, a yellow plant]

saf•fron \'saf-rən\ *n* **1 a** : a purple-flowered crocus whose deep orange aromatic pungent dried stigmas are used especially to color and flavor foods **b** : these dried usually powdered stigmas **2** : a moderate orange to orange yellow [Old French *safran*, from Medieval Latin *safranum*, from Arabic *za'farān*]

saf•ra•nine *or* **saf•ra•nin** \'saf-rə-ˌnēn, -nən\ *n* : any of various usually red synthetic dyes [from French or German *safran* "saffron"]

¹sag \'sag\ *vi* **sagged**; **sag•ging 1** : to droop, sink, or settle from or as if from pressure or loss of tautness **2** : to lose firmness, resiliency, or vigor ⟨*sagging* spirits⟩ **3** : to decline from a thriving position ⟨a *sagging* economy⟩

²sag *n* : a sagging part or area ⟨the *sag* in a rope⟩; *also* : an instance or amount of sagging

sa•ga \'säg-ə\ *n* **1** : a tale of historic or legendary figures and events of Norway and Iceland **2** : a story of heroic deeds **3** : a long detailed account [Old Norse]

sa•ga•cious \sə-'gā-shəs\ *adj* : keen and farsighted in understanding and judgment : DISCERNING ⟨a *sagacious* judge of character⟩ [Latin *sagac-, sagax*] **syn** see SHREWD — **sa•ga•cious•ly** *adv* — **sa•ga•cious•ness** *n* — **sa•gac•i•ty** \-'gas-ət-ē\ *n*

sag•a•more \'sag-ə-ˌmōr, -ˌmȯr\ *n* **1** : an Algonquian Indian chief subordinate to a sachem **2** : SACHEM [of American Indian origin]

¹sage \'sāj\ *adj* : WISE, PRUDENT ⟨*sage* advice⟩ [Old French, derived from Latin *sapere* "to taste, be wise"] — **sage•ly** *adv* — **sage•ness** *n*

²sage *n* : a very wise person

³sage *n* **1** : a mint with grayish green aromatic leaves used especially in flavoring meats; *also* : SALVIA **2** : SAGEBRUSH [Middle French *sauge*, from Latin *salvia*, from *salvus* "healthy, safe"]

sage•brush \'sāj-ˌbrəsh\ *n* : any of several low shrubby North American plants of the daisy family; *esp* : a common plant with a bitter juice and an odor like a sage that is widespread on alkaline plains of the western United States

sag•it•tal \'saj-ət-l, sə-'jit-\ *adj* : of, relating to, or being the median longitudinal plane of the body [Latin *sagitta* "arrow"] — **sag•it•tal•ly** \-l-ē\ *adv*

Sag•it•tar•i•us \ˌsaj-ə-'ter-ē-əs\ *n* **1** : a zodiacal southern constellation pictured as a centaur shooting an arrow **2** : the 9th sign of the zodiac; *also* : one born under this sign [Latin, literally, "archer", from *sagitta* "arrow"]

sa•go \'sā-gō\ *n, pl* **sagos** : a dry granulated or powdered starch prepared from the pith of a sago palm [Malay *sagu* "sago palm"]

sago palm *n* : a palm or cycad that yields sago; *esp* : any of a genus of tall pinnate-leaved East Indian palms

sa•gua•ro \sə-'wär-ə, -'wär-ō, -'gwär-ō\ *n, pl* **-ros** : a cactus of desert regions of the southwestern United States and Mexico that has a columnar spiny sparsely branched trunk of up to 60 feet and bears white flowers and edible fruit [Mexican Spanish]

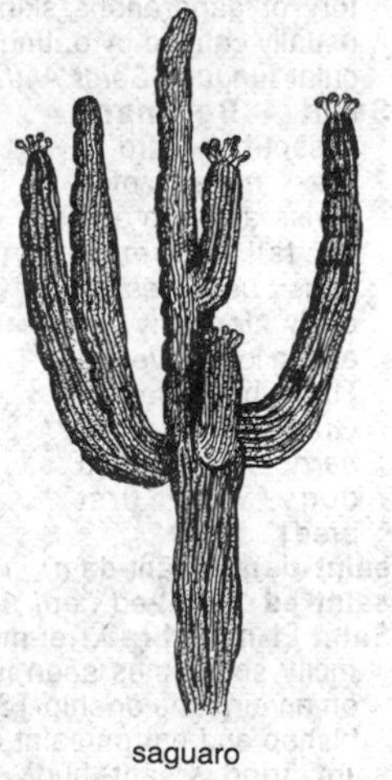
saguaro

sa•hib \'sä-ˌhib, -ˌib, -ˌhēb, -ˌēb, ˌsä-'\ *n* **1** : SIR, MASTER — used especially among Hindus and Muslims in colonial India when addressing or speaking of a European of some social or official status **2** : a European man of some social status living in India — compare MEMSAHIB

said \'sed\ *adj* : AFOREMENTIONED ⟨the *said* parties will abide by the terms of the contract⟩ [from past participle of *say*]

¹sail \'sāl, *as last element in compounds often* səl\ *n* **1 a** : a usually rectangular or triangular piece of fabric by means of which wind is used to propel a wind-powered vessel or craft **b** : the sails of a ship **2** *pl usually* **sail** : a ship equipped with sails **3** : a passage by a sailing boat or ship ⟨go for a *sail*⟩ [Old English *segl*]

[2]**sail** *vb* **1 a :** to travel on water in a sailing vessel; *also* **:** to travel or begin a journey by water ⟨*sailed* for England on the first steamer⟩ **b :** to move or pass over by ship ⟨*sail* the seas⟩ **c :** to function in sailing ⟨a boat that *sails* well⟩; *also* **:** to handle or manage the sailing of ⟨experienced in *sailing* small craft⟩ **2 :** to move effortlessly or gracefully — **sail into :** to attack vigorously or sharply ⟨*sailed into* their dinner⟩ ⟨*sailed into* me for being late⟩

sail•boat \ˈsāl-ˌbōt\ *n* **:** a boat equipped with sails

sail•cloth \-ˌklȯth\ *n* **:** a heavy canvas formerly much used for sails and tents

sail•er \ˈsā-lər\ *n* **:** a ship or boat especially having specified sailing qualities

sail•fish \ˈsāl-ˌfish\ *n* **:** any of a genus of large sea fishes related to the swordfish but having teeth, scales, and a very large fin on the back

sailboat

sail•ing \ˈsā-liŋ\ *n* **1 :** the technical skill of managing a ship **:** NAVIGATION **2 :** the sport of navigating or riding in a sailboat

sail•or \ˈsā-lər\ *n* **1 :** one that sails: as **a :** a member of a ship's crew **b :** a person of the rank of seaman in the Navy **c :** a traveler by water **2 :** a stiff straw hat with a low flat crown and straight circular brim

sail•plane \ˈsāl-ˌplān\ *n* **:** a glider designed to rise in an upward current of air

[1]**saint** \ˈsānt; *when a name follows* ˌsānt *or* sānt *or* sənt\ *n* **1 :** a holy and godly person; *esp* **:** one who is canonized **2 :** a very pious or virtuous person **3** *cap* **:** LATTER-DAY SAINT [Middle French, from Late Latin *sanctus,* from Latin, "sacred", from *sancire* "to make sacred"]

[2]**saint** \ˈsānt\ *vt* **:** CANONIZE

Saint Ag•nes's Eve \-ˌag-nə-səz-ˈēv, -ˌag-nəs-ˈēv\ *n* **:** the night of January 20 when a woman is traditionally held to have a revelation of her future husband [*Saint Agnes*]

Saint An•drew's cross \-ˌan-ˌdrüz-\ *n* **:** a cross having two intersecting oblique bars [*Saint Andrew,* died about 60 A.D., one of the 12 apostles]

Saint An•tho•ny's fire \-ˌan-thə-nēz-, -ˌant-\ *n* **:** an inflammatory or gangrenous skin condition (as erysipelas); *esp* **:** one usually caused by eating rye (as in bread) infected with a particular fungus [*Saint Anthony,* died about 350, Egyptian monk]

Saint Ber•nard \ˌsānt-bər-ˈnärd, -bə-\ *n* **:** any of a Swiss alpine breed of tall powerful dogs used especially formerly in aiding lost travelers [the hospice of Grand *Saint Bernard,* where such dogs were first bred]

Saint Bernard

saint•dom \ˈsānt-dəm\ *n* **:** SAINTHOOD 1

saint•ed \ˈsānt-əd\ *adj* **1 :** SAINTLY, PIOUS **2 :** DECEASED

Saint El•mo's fire \-ˌel-mōz-\ *n* **:** a luminous discharge of electricity sometimes seen in stormy weather at prominent points on an airplane or ship [*Saint Elmo (Erasmus),* died 303, Italian bishop and patron saint of sailors]

saint•hood \ˈsānt-ˌhu̇d\ *n* **1 :** the quality or state of being a saint **2 :** saints as a group

Saint–John's–wort \-ˈjänz-ˌwərt, -ˌwȯrt\ *n* **:** any of a large genus of mostly weedy herbs and shrubs with showy yellow flowers [*Saint John* the Baptist]

saint•ly \ˈsānt-lē\ *adj* **saint•li•er; -est :** relating to, resembling, or befitting a saint **:** HOLY — **saint•li•ness** *n*

Saint Mar•tin's summer \-ˌmärt-nz-ˈsəm-ər, -ˌmärt-n-\ *n* **:** Indian summer when occurring in November [*Saint Martin's Day,* November 11]

Saint Pat•rick's Day \-ˈpa-triks-\ *n* **:** March 17 observed by the Roman Catholic Church in honor of St. Patrick and celebrated as a legal holiday in Ireland in commemoration of his death

saint•ship \ˈsānt-ˌship\ *n* **:** SAINTHOOD 1

Saint Val•en•tine's Day \-ˈval-ən-ˌtīnz-\ *n* **:** February 14 observed as a time for sending valentines [*Saint Valentine,* died about 270, Italian priest]

Saint Vi•tus' dance *or* **Saint Vi•tus's dance** \-ˌvīt-əs-, -əs-əz-\ *n* **:** CHOREA [*Saint Vitus,* 3d century Christian child martyr]

saith \seth, ˈseth, ˈsā-əth\ *archaic present 3d sing of* SAY

[1]**sake** \ˈsāk\ *n* **1 :** END, PURPOSE ⟨for the *sake* of argument⟩ **2 :** GOOD, ADVANTAGE ⟨the *sake* of my country⟩ [Middle English, "dispute, guilt, purpose", from Old English *sacu* "guilt, action at law"]

[2]**sa•ke** *or* **sa•ki** \ˈsäk-ē\ *n* **:** a Japanese alcoholic beverage of fermented rice usually served hot [Japanese *sake*]

sal \ˈsal\ *n* **:** SALT — usually used in combination ⟨*sal* soda⟩ [Latin]

sa•laam \sə-ˈläm\ *n* **1 :** a salutation or ceremonial greeting in the East **2 :** deference shown by bowing very low and placing the right palm on the forehead [Arabic *salām,* literally, "peace"] — **salaam** *vb*

sal•able *or* **sale•able** \ˈsā-lə-bəl\ *adj* **1 :** fit to be sold **2 :** MARKETABLE 2 — **sal•abil•i•ty** \ˌsā-lə-ˈbil-ət-ē\ *n*

sa•la•cious \sə-ˈlā-shəs\ *adj* **1 :** arousing sexual desire or imagination **:** LASCIVIOUS **2 :** LUSTFUL, LECHEROUS [Latin *salac-, salax* "fond of leaping, lustful", from *salire* "to leap"] — **sa•la•cious•ly** *adv* — **sa•la•cious•ness** *n*

sal•ad \ˈsal-əd\ *n* **1 :** a cooked or uncooked food prepared with a savory dressing and usually served cold: as **a :** raw vegetables (as lettuce and tomatoes) served with dressing **b :** a cold dish (as of meat or fish) served singly or in combinations usually on lettuce and with a dressing **2 :** a green vegetable or herb grown for salad [Middle French *salade,* from Provençal *salada,* from *salar* "to salt", from *sal* "salt", from Latin]

salad days *n pl* **:** time of youthful inexperience or indiscretion

salad dressing *n* **:** a sauce for a salad

salad oil *n* **:** a vegetable oil suitable for use in salad dressings

sal•a•man•der \ˈsal-ə-ˌman-dər\ *n* **1 :** a mythical being having the power to endure fire without harm **2 :** any of an order (Caudata) of amphibians superficially resembling lizards but scaleless and covered with a soft moist skin **3 :** something (as a utensil for browning pastry or a portable stove or incinerator) used in connection with fire [Middle French *salamandre,* from Latin *salamandra,* from Greek] — **sal•a•man•drine** \ˌsal-ə-ˈman-drən\ *adj*

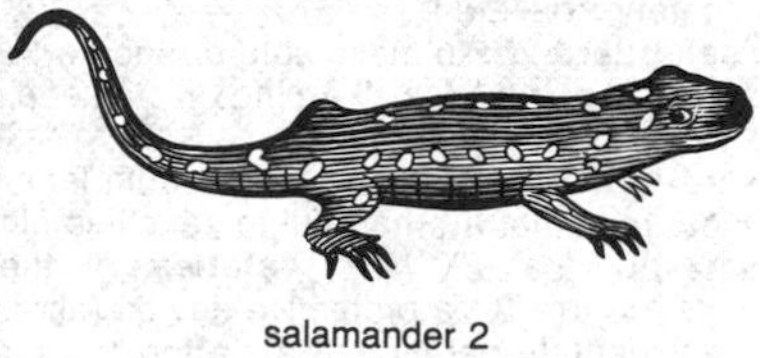
salamander 2

sa•la•mi \sə-ˈläm-ē\ *n* **:** highly seasoned sausage of pork and beef often dried for storage [Italian, pl. of *salame* "salami", from *salare* "to salt", from *sale* "salt", from Latin *sal*]

sal am•mo•ni•ac \ˌsal-ə-ˈmō-nē-ˌak\ *n* **:** AMMONIUM CHLORIDE [Latin *sal ammoniacus,* literally, "salt of Ammon"]

sal•a•ried \ˈsal-rēd, -ə-rēd\ *adj* **:** receiving or yielding a salary

sal•a•ry \ˈsal-rē, -ə-rē\ *n, pl* **-ries :** money paid regularly (as by the year or month) for work or services [Latin *salarium* "salt money, pension, salary", derived from *sal* "salt"] **syn** see WAGE

△ **origin** In the Roman army soldiers were allowed a sum of money to buy salt with, since salt was not always easily come by and was important for more than increasing the savor of food in the days before refrigeration. Later *salarium,* the name for this money, came to be used for the stipend or pension paid to soldiers and still later for payments made to officials of the empire. Latin *salarium,* the source of English *salary,* is derived from *sal,* "salt".

sale \ˈsāl\ *n* **1 :** the act of selling; *esp* **:** the transfer of ownership of property from one person to another for a price **2 :** availability for purchase — usually used in the phrases *for sale* and *on sale* **3 :** public disposal to the highest bidder **:** AUCTION **4 :** a selling of goods at bargain prices **5** *pl* **a :** the business of selling **b :** gross receipts ⟨*sales* are up⟩ [Old English *sala,* from Old Norse]

sales \'sālz\ *adj* : of, relating to, or used in selling
sales check *n* : a piece of paper used by retail stores as a memorandum, record, or receipt of a sale
sales•clerk \-ˌklərk\ *n* : a person employed to sell merchandise in a store
Sa•le•sian \sə-'lē-zhən, sā-\ *n* : a member of the Society of St. Francis de Sales founded by St. John Bosco in Turin, Italy in the 19th century and devoted chiefly to education
sales•man \'sālz-mən\ *n* : one who is employed to sell merchandise either in a territory or in a store — **sales•man•ship** \-ˌship\ *n*
sales•peo•ple \-ˌpē-pəl\ *n pl* : people employed to sell goods or services
sales•per•son \-ˌpər-sən\ *n* : a person employed to sell goods or services
sales register *n* : CASH REGISTER
sales•room \'sālz-ˌrüm, -ˌru̇m\ *n* : a place where goods are displayed for sale
sales tax *n* : a tax on the sale of goods and services that is usually calculated as a percentage of the purchase price and collected by the seller
sales•wom•an \'sālz-ˌwu̇m-ən\ *n* : a woman employed to sell merchandise
Sa•lic \'sā-lik, 'sal-ik\ *adj* : of, relating to, or being a Frankish people that settled on the IJssel river early in the 4th century [Medieval Latin *Salicus,* from Late Latin *Salii* "Salic Franks"]
sal•i•cin \'sal-ə-sən\ *n* : a bitter white crystalline compound found in the bark and leaves of several willows and poplars and used in medicine like salicylic acid [French *salicine,* from Latin *salic-, salix* "willow"]
sa•lic•y•late \sə-'lis-ə-ˌlāt\ *n* : a salt or ester of salicylic acid; *also* : SALICYLIC ACID
sal•i•cyl•ic acid \ˌsal-ə-ˌsil-ik-\ *n* : a crystalline organic acid $C_7H_6O_3$ used especially in the form of salts to relieve pain or fever and in the treatment of rheumatism [derived from Latin *salic-, salix* "willow"]
sa•lience \'sāl-yəns, 'sā-lē-əns\ *n* **1** : the quality or state of being salient **2** : a striking point or feature : HIGHLIGHT
[1]**sa•lient** \'sāl-yənt, 'sā-lē-ənt\ *adj* **1** : jetting upward ⟨a *salient* fountain⟩ **2 a** : projecting beyond a line, surface, or level ⟨a *salient* angle⟩ **b** : standing out conspicuously : PROMINENT ⟨*salient* traits⟩ [Latin *saliens,* present participle of *salire* "to leap"] — **sa•lient•ly** *adv*
[2]**salient** *n* : something that projects outward; *esp* : an outwardly projecting part of a fortification or line of defense
sa•li•en•tian \ˌsā-lē-'en-chən\ *n* : any of an order (Salientia) of amphibians comprising the frogs, toads, and tree toads all of which lack a tail in the adult stage and have long strong hind limbs suited to leaping and swimming [derived from Latin *salire* "to leap"] — **salientian** *adj*
[1]**sa•line** \'sā-ˌlēn, -ˌlīn\ *adj* **1** : consisting of or containing salt ⟨a *saline* solution⟩ **2** : of, relating to, or resembling salt : SALTY ⟨a *saline* taste⟩ ⟨*saline* compounds⟩ [Latin *salinus,* from *sal* "salt"] — **sa•lin•i•ty** \sā-'lin-ət-ē, sə-\ *n*
[2]**saline** *n* **1** : a metallic salt; *esp* : a salt of potassium, sodium, or magnesium with a cathartic action **2** : a saline solution
sal•i•nom•e•ter \ˌsal-ə-'näm-ət-ər\ *n* : an instrument for measuring the amount of salt in a solution
Salis•bury steak \ˌsȯlz-ˌber-ē-, ˌsalz-, -bə-rē, -brē-\ *n* : ground beef mixed with egg, milk, bread crumbs, and seasoning and formed into large patties for cooking [J. H. *Salisbury,* 19th century English physician]
sa•li•va \sə-'lī-və\ *n* : a slightly alkaline secretion of water, mucin, protein, salts, and often a starch-splitting enzyme secreted into the mouth by salivary glands [Latin]
sal•i•vary \'sal-ə-ˌver-ē\ *adj* : of or relating to saliva or the glands that secrete it; *esp* : producing or carrying saliva ⟨*salivary* glands⟩
sal•i•vate \'sal-ə-ˌvāt\ *vi* : to secrete saliva especially in large amounts — **sal•i•va•tion** \ˌsal-ə-'vā-shən\ *n*
Salk vaccine \'sȯk-, 'sȯlk-\ *n* : a polio vaccine that contains virus inactivated with formaldehyde and is administered by injection [Jonas *Salk,* born 1914, American physician]
[1]**sal•low** \'sal-ō\ *n* : any of various Old World broad-leaved willows used especially as sources of charcoal and tanbark [Old English *sealh*]
[2]**sallow** *adj* : of a grayish greenish yellow color [Old English *salu*] — **sal•low•ish** \'sal-ə-wish\ *adj* — **sal•low•ness** \'sal-ō-nəs\ *n*
[3]**sallow** *vt* : to make sallow
[1]**sal•ly** \'sal-ē\ *n, pl* **sallies 1** : an action of rushing or bursting forth; *esp* : a sortie of troops from a defensive position to attack the enemy **2 a** : a brief outbreak : OUTBURST **b** : a witty remark : QUIP **3** : an excursion usually off the beaten track : JAUNT [Middle French *saillie,* from *saillir* "to rush forward", from Latin *salire* "to leap"]
[2]**sally** *vi* **sal•lied**; **sal•ly•ing 1** : to leap out or burst forth suddenly **2** : to set out : DEPART — usually used with *forth*
Sal•ly Lunn \ˌsal-ē-'lən\ *n* : a slightly sweetened yeast-leavened bread [*Sally Lunn,* 18th century English baker]
sal•ma•gun•di \ˌsal-mə-'gən-dē\ *n* **1** : a salad of chopped meats, anchovies, eggs, and vegetables arranged in rows for contrast and served with dressing **2** : a varied mixture : POTPOURRI [French *salmigondis*]
salm•on \'sam-ən\ *n, pl* **salmon** *also* **salmons 1 a** : a large soft-finned game fish of the northern Atlantic related to the trouts and chars and noted as a table fish **b** : any of various related fishes; *esp* : any of a genus of fishes that breed in rivers tributary to the northern Pacific **2** : a strong yellowish pink color resembling that of the flesh of some salmons [Middle French, from Latin *salmo*] — **salm•on•oid** \'sam-ə-ˌnȯid\ *adj or n*

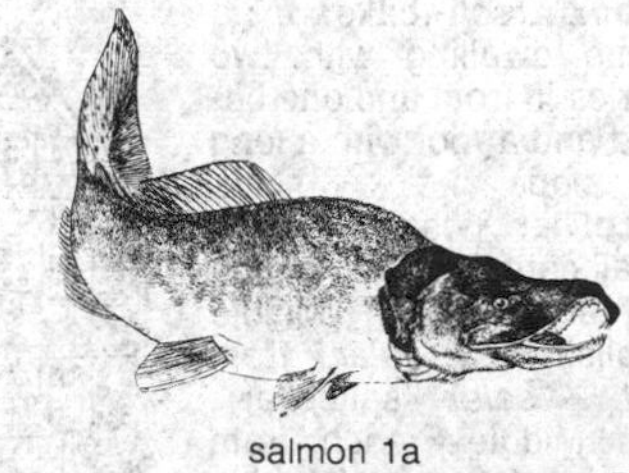
salmon 1a

salm•on•ber•ry \-ˌber-ē\ *n* : a showy red-flowered raspberry of the Pacific coast; *also* : its edible salmon-colored fruit
sal•mo•nel•la \ˌsal-mə-'nel-ə\ *n, pl* **-nellas** *or* **-nella** *also* **-nel•lae** \-'nel-ˌē, -ˌī\ : any of a genus of rod-shaped bacteria that cause food poisoning, gastrointestinal inflammation, or diseases of the genital tract of warm-blooded animals [New Latin, from Daniel E. *Salmon,* died 1914, American veterinarian]
sal•mo•nel•lo•sis \ˌsal-mə-ˌnel-'ō-səs\ *n, pl* **-lo•ses** \-ˌsēz\ : infection with or disease caused by salmonellas
salmon pink *n* : a strong yellowish pink
sa•lon \sə-'län, 'sal-ˌän, sa-'lōⁿ\ *n* **1** : an elegant apartment or living room **2** : a fashionable gathering of notables customarily held at the home of a prominent person **3 a** : a place for the exhibition of art **b** *cap* : an annual art exhibition **4** : a stylish business establishment [French]
sa•loon \sə-'lün\ *n* **1** : an elaborately decorated public apartment or hall (as a large cabin for the social use of a ship's passengers) **2** : a place in which alcoholic beverages are sold and consumed [French *salon,* from Italian *salone,* from *sala* "hall", of Germanic origin]
sal•pi•glos•sis \ˌsal-pə-'gläs-əs\ *n* : any of a genus of Chilean herbs of the potato family that are sometimes grown for their large multicolored funnel-shaped flowers [New Latin, from Greek *salpinx* "trumpet" + *glōssa* "tongue"]
sal•si•fy \'sal-sə-fē, -ˌfī\ *n, pl* **-fies** : a purple-flowered herb of the daisy family that is grown for its long fleshy edible root — called also *oyster plant* [French *salsifis,* from Italian *sassefrica,* from Late Latin *saxifrica,* any of various herbs, from Latin *saxum* "rock" + *fricare* "to rub"]
sal soda \'sal-'sōd-ə\ *n* : a transparent crystalline hydrated sodium carbonate $Na_2CO_3{\cdot}10H_2O$ used in washing and bleaching textiles
[1]**salt** \'sȯlt\ *n* **1 a** : a crystalline compound NaCl that is the chloride of sodium, is abundant in nature, and is used especially for seasoning or preserving food — called also *common salt* **b** *pl* (1) : a mineral or saline mixture (as Epsom salts) used as a laxative or carthartic (2) : SMELLING SALTS **c** : a compound formed by replacement of part or all of the acid hydrogen of an acid by a metal or a radical acting like a metal **2 a** : an ingredient that gives savor, piquancy, or zest : FLAVOR **b** : sharpness of wit : PUNGENCY **c** : COMMON SENSE **d** : DOUBT 3 — of-

ten used in the phrase *with a grain of salt* **e** : the sprinkling of people thought to set a model of excellence for or to give tone to the rest — usually used in the phrase *salt of the earth* **3** : SAILOR ⟨a tale told by an old *salt*⟩ [Old English *sealt*]

2salt *vt* **1 a** : to treat, flavor, or supply with salt ⟨*salt* a dish to taste⟩ **b** : to preserve (food) with salt **2** : to add flavor or zest to (as a story) **3** : to make (as a mine) appear richer by secretly adding valuable mineral

3salt *adj* **1 a** : SALINE, SALTY ⟨*salt* water⟩ **b** : being or inducing the one of the four basic taste sensations produced by table salt **2** : cured or seasoned with salt ⟨*salt* pork⟩ **3** : flooded by the sea ⟨a *salt* pond⟩ **4** : SALTY 3a — **salt•ness** *n*

sal•ta•tion \sal-ˈtā-shən, sȯl-\ *n* : the action of leaping or jumping [Latin *saltatio,* from *saltare* "to leap, dance", from *saltus,* past participle of *salire* "to leap"]

salt away *vt* : to lay away (as money) safely : SAVE

salt•box \ˈsȯlt-ˌbäks\ *n* : a frame dwelling with two stories in front and one behind and a roof with a long rear slope

saltbox

salt•cel•lar \-ˌsel-ər\ *n* : a small container for holding salt at the table [Middle English *salt saler,* from *salt* + *saler* "saltcellar", from Middle French, from Latin *salarius* "of salt", from *sal* "salt"]

salt•er \ˈsȯl-tər\ *n* **1** : one that manufactures or deals in salt **2** : one that salts something (as meat, fish, or hides)

sal•tern \ˈsȯl-tərn\ *n* : a place where salt is made by boiling or evaporation [Old English *sealtern,* from *sealt* "salt" + *ærn* "house"]

salt flat *n* : an area of salt-encrusted land left by evaporation of water (as from a former lake)

salt gland *n* : a gland (as of a seabird) capable of excreting a concentrated salt solution

sal•tine \sȯl-ˈtēn\ *n* : a thin crisp cracker sprinkled with salt

salt lick *n* : LICK 3

salt marsh *n* : flat land subject to overflow by salt water

salt out *vt* : to precipitate, coagulate, or separate (a dissolved substance or sol) from a solution by adding salt

salt•pe•ter \ˈsȯlt-ˈpēt-ər\ *n* **1** : POTASSIUM NITRATE **2** : SODIUM NITRATE [Middle French *salpetre,* from Medieval Latin *sal petrae,* literally, "salt of the rock"]

salt•shak•er \-ˌshā-kər\ *n* : a container with a perforated top for sprinkling salt

salt•wa•ter \ˌsȯlt-ˌwȯt-ər, -ˌwät-\ *adj* : relating to, living in, or consisting of salt water

salt•works \ˈsȯlt-ˌwərks\ *n sing or pl* : a plant where salt is prepared commercially

salty \ˈsȯl-tē\ *adj* **salt•i•er; -est 1** : seasoned with or containing salt often to excess **2** : suggesting the sea or nautical life **3 a** : CAUSTIC ⟨*salty* wit⟩ **b** : SPICY 4, RACY — **salt•i•ness** *n*

sa•lu•bri•ous \sə-ˈlü-brē-əs\ *adj* : favorable to or promoting health [Latin *salubris*] **syn** see HEALTHFUL — **sa•lu•bri•ous•ly** *adv* — **sa•lu•bri•ous•ness** *n* — **sa•lu•bri•ty** \-brət-ē\ *n*

sa•lu•ki \sə-ˈlü-kē\ *n* : any of an old northern African and Asian breed of tall slender swift-footed keen-eyed hunting dogs having long narrow skulls and a smooth silky coat ranging from white or cream to black or black and tan [Arabic *salūqīy* "of Saluq", from *Salūq* "Saluq (ancient city in Arabia)"]

saluki

sal•u•tary \ˈsal-yə-ˌter-ē\ *adj* **1** : promoting health : CURATIVE **2** : producing a beneficial effect ⟨*salutary* advice⟩ [Middle French *salutaire,* from Latin *salutaris,* from *salut-, salus* "health"] **syn** see HEALTHFUL — **sal•u•tar•i•ly** \ˌsal-yə-ˈter-ə-lē\ *adv* — **sal•u•tar•i•ness** \ˈsal-yə-ˌter-ē-nəs\ *n*

sal•u•ta•tion \ˌsal-yə-ˈtā-shən\ *n* **1 a** : an expression of greeting, goodwill, or courtesy **b** *pl* : REGARD 2b(2) **2** : the word or phrase of greeting that conventionally begins a letter — **sal•u•ta•tion•al** \-shnəl, -shən-l\ *adj*

sa•lu•ta•to•ri•an \sə-ˌlüt-ə-ˈtōr-ē-ən, -ˈtȯr-\ *n* : the graduating student usually second highest in rank who gives the salutatory address

1sa•lu•ta•to•ry \sə-ˈlüt-ə-ˌtōr-ē, -ˌtȯr-\ *adj* : expressing salutations or welcome

2salutatory *n, pl* **-ries** : a salutatory address given at a commencement exercise

1sa•lute \sə-ˈlüt\ *vb* **1** : to greet with courteous words or with a sign of respect or goodwill **2 a** : to honor by a conventional military ceremony **b** : to show respect and recognition by assuming a prescribed position or making a prescribed gesture ⟨*salute* an officer⟩ **c** : PRAISE 1 [Latin *salutare,* from *salut-, salus* "health, safety, greeting"] — **sa•lut•er** *n*

2salute *n* **1** : SALUTATION 1, GREETING **2 a** : a sign, token, or ceremony (as a kiss or a bow) expressing goodwill, compliment, or respect **b** : the position or gesture of a person saluting a superior

salv•able \ˈsal-və-bəl\ *adj* : capable of being saved or salvaged [Late Latin *salvare* "to save"]

1sal•vage \ˈsal-vij\ *n* **1** : money paid for saving a wrecked or endangered ship, its cargo, or its passengers **2 a** : the act of saving a ship **b** : the act of saving property in danger **3** : property saved or recovered (as from a wreck or fire) [French, from Middle French *salver* "to save"]

2salvage *vt* : to rescue or save especially from wreckage or ruin — **sal•vage•able** \-ə-bəl\ *adj* — **sal•vag•er** *n*

Sal•var•san \ˈsal-vər-ˌsan\ *trademark* — used for arsphenamine

sal•va•tion \sal-ˈvā-shən\ *n* **1** : deliverance from sin **2** : preservation from destruction or failure **3** : something that saves ⟨the medicine was the patient's *salvation*⟩ [Old French, from Late Latin *salvatio,* from *salvare* "to save"] — **sal•va•tion•al** \-shnəl, -shən-l\ *adj*

1salve \ˈsav, ˈsȧv\ *n* **1** : a healing ointment **2** : an influence or agent that remedies or soothes [Old English *sealf*]

2salve *vt* : to ease or soothe with or as if with a salve

sal•ver \ˈsal-vər\ *n* : a serving tray [French *salve,* from Spanish *salva* "sampling of food to detect poison, tray", from *salvar* "to save, sample food to detect poison", from Late Latin *salvare* "to save"]

sal•via \ˈsal-vē-ə\ *n* : any of a large and widely distributed genus of herbs or shrubs of the mint family; *esp* : a scarlet-flowered sage widely grown for ornament [Latin]

sal•vo \ˈsal-vō\ *n, pl* **salvos** *or* **salvoes 1 a** : a firing at one time of two or more guns in military action or as a salute **b** : the release all at once of a rack of bombs or rockets **c** : a discharge of one gun after another in a battery **d** : the bombs or projectiles released in a salvo **2** : SALUTE 2a, TRIBUTE **3** : a sudden burst (as of cheers) [Italian *salva,* from French *salve,* from Latin, "hail!", imperative of *salvēre* "to be healthy", from *salvus* "healthy, safe"]

sa•ma•ra \ˈsam-ə-rə; sə-ˈmar-ə, -ˈmär-\ *n* : a dry usually one-seeded winged fruit (as of an ash or elm tree) that does not split open when ripe — called also *key* [Latin, "elm seed"]

Sa•mar•i•tan \sə-ˈmar-ət-n, -ˈmer-\ *n* **1** : a native or inhabitant of Samaria **2** *often not cap* : one ready and generous in helping those in distress [Late Latin *samaritanus,* from Greek *samaritēs,* from *Samaria* "Samaria"; sense 2 from the parable of the good Samaritan, Luke 10:30-37] — **samaritan** *adj, often cap*

sa•mar•i•um \sə-ˈmer-ē-əm, -ˈmar-\ *n* : a pale gray lustrous metallic chemical element — see ELEMENT table [New Latin, from French *samarskite,* a mineral, from Colonel von *Samarski,* 19th century Russian mine official]

sam•ba \ˈsam-bə, ˈsäm-\ *n* : a Brazilian dance characterized by a dip and spring upward at each beat of the music [Portuguese] — **samba** *vi*

Sam Browne belt \ˌsam-ˌbraün-\ *n* : a leather belt for a dress uniform supported by a light strap passing over the right shoulder [Sir *Samuel* James *Browne,* died 1901, British army officer]

1same \ˈsām\ *adj* **1 a** : resembling in every relevant respect **b** : conforming in every respect ⟨gave the *same* answer as before⟩ **2 a** : being one without addition, change, or discontinuance : IDENTICAL **b** : being the one under discussion or already referred to ⟨quoted from this *same* book⟩ **3** : corresponding so closely as to be indistinguishable ⟨on the *same* day last year⟩ [Old Norse *samr*]

[2]same *pron* **1 :** something identical with or similar to another **2 :** something previously defined or described
[3]same *adv* **:** in the same manner
same•ness \ˈsām-nəs\ *n* **1 :** the quality or state of being the same **:** IDENTITY **2 :** lack of variety **:** MONOTONY
sam•i•sen \ˈsam-ə-ˌsen\ *n* **:** a 3-stringed Japanese musical instrument resembling a banjo [Japanese]

samisen

sa•mite \ˈsam-ˌīt, ˈsā-ˌmīt\ *n* **:** a rich medieval silk fabric interwoven with gold or silver [Middle French *samit,* from Medieval Latin *examitum,* from Middle Greek *hexamiton,* from Greek *hexanitos* "of 6 threads", from *hex* "six" + *mitos* "warp thread"]
sam•o•var \ˈsam-ə-ˌvär\ *n* **1 :** an urn with a spigot at its base used especially in Russia to boil water for tea **2 :** an urn similar to a Russian samovar with a device for heating the contents [Russian, from *samo-* "self" + *varit'* "to boil"]
samp \ˈsamp\ *n* **:** coarse hominy or a boiled cereal made from it [of American Indian origin]
sam•pan \ˈsam-ˌpan\ *n* **:** a flat-bottomed Chinese skiff usually propelled by two short oars [Chinese (Pekingese dialect) *san[1]pan[3],* from *san[1]* "three" + *pan[3]* "plank"]

sampan

[1]sam•ple \ˈsam-pəl\ *n* **1 :** a representative part or a single item from a larger whole or group **:** SPECIMEN **2 :** a part of a statistical population whose properties are studied to gain information about the whole [Middle French *essample* "example, sample", from Latin *exemplum*]
[2]sample *vt* **sam•pled; sam•pling** \-pə-ling, -pling\ **:** to take a sample of; *esp* **:** to judge the quality of by a sample
[1]sam•pler \ˈsam-plər\ *n* **:** a piece of needlework typically having letters or verses embroidered on it in various stitches as an example of skill
[2]sampler *n* **1 :** one that collects, prepares, or examines samples **2 :** a collection of samples
sample room *n* **:** a room where samples of merchandise are displayed for the inspection of buyers for retail stores
sample space *n* **:** a set in which all the possible outcomes of a statistical experiment (as tossing a pair of dice) are represented as points
sam•pling *n* **1** \ˈsam-pling\ **:** SAMPLE **1 2** \-pə-ling, -pling\ **:** the act, process, or technique of selecting a suitable sample
Sam•u•el \ˈsam-yə-wəl, ˈsam-yəl\ *n* — see BIBLE table
sam•u•rai \ˈsam-ə-ˌrī, -yə-ˌrī\ *n, pl* **samurai 1 :** a feudal military retainer of a Japanese daimyo **2 :** the warrior aristocracy of Japan [Japanese]
san•a•tar•i•um \ˌsan-ə-ˈter-ē-əm\ *n, pl* **-i•ums** *or* **-ia** \-ē-ə\ **:** SANATORIUM
san•a•to•ri•um \ˌsan-ə-ˈtōr-ē-əm, -ˈtȯr-\ *n, pl* **-ri•ums** *or* **-ria** \-ē-ə\ **:** an establishment for the care and treatment especially of convalescents or the chronically ill [New Latin, derived from Latin *sanare* "to heal, cure", from *sanus* "healthy"]
sanc•ti•fy \ˈsang-tə-ˌfī, ˈsangk-\ *vt* **-fied; -fy•ing 1 :** to set apart as sacred **:** CONSECRATE **2 :** to make free from sin **:** PURIFY **3 :** to give moral or social sanction to [Middle French *sanctifier,* from Late Latin *sanctificare,* from Latin *sanctus* "sacred", from *sancire* "to make sacred"] — **sanc•ti•fi•ca•tion** \ˌsang-tə-fə-ˈkā-shən, ˌsangk-\ *n* — **sanc•ti•fi•er** \ˈsang-tə-ˌfī-ər, ˈsangk-,-ˌfīr\ *n*
sanc•ti•mo•ni•ous \ˌsang-tə-ˈmō-nē-əs, ˌsangk-\ *adj* **:** hypocritically devout — **sanc•ti•mo•ni•ous•ly** *adv* — **sanc•ti•mo•ni•ous•ness** *n*
sanc•ti•mo•ny \ˈsang-tə-ˌmō-nē, ˈsangk-\ *n* **:** hypocritical piety [Middle French *sanctimonie* "holiness", from Latin *sanctimonia,* from *sanctus* "holy, sacred"]
[1]sanc•tion \ˈsang-shən, ˈsangk-\ *n* **1 :** a binding or compelling force; *esp* **:** one that determines action in accordance with morality **2 :** explicit or official permission or approval **3 :** an economic or military measure adopted usually by several nations against another nation violating international law [Latin *sanctio,* from *sanctus,* past participle of *sancire* "to make sacred, sanction"]
[2]sanction *vt* **sanc•tioned; sanc•tion•ing** \-shə-ning, -shning\ **1 :** to make valid or binding usually by a formal procedure **2 :** to give effective or authoritative approval or consent to **syn** see APPROVE
sanc•ti•ty \ˈsang-tət-ē, ˈsangk-\ *n, pl* **-ties 1 :** holiness of life and character **2 a :** inviolable quality ⟨the *sanctity* of a promise⟩ **b** *pl* **:** sacred objects, obligations, or rights
sanc•tu•ary \ˈsang-chə-ˌwer-ē, ˈsangk-\ *n, pl* **-ar•ies 1 :** a holy or sacred place **2 :** a building or room for religious worship **3 :** the most sacred part (as near the altar) of a place of worship **4 :** a refuge for wildlife where predators are controlled and hunting is illegal **5 a :** a place of refuge **b :** safety or protection afforded by a sanctuary [Middle French *saintuarie,* from Late Latin *sanctuarium,* from Latin *sanctus* "sacred"]
sanc•tum \ˈsang-təm, ˈsangk-\ *n, pl* **sanctums** *also* **sanc•ta** \-tə\ **1 :** SANCTUARY 1 **2 :** a place where one is free from intrusion [Late Latin, from Latin *sanctus* "sacred"]
Sanc•tus \ˈsang-təs, ˈsangk-, ˈsäng-, ˈsängk-\ *n* **:** an ancient Christian hymn closing the preface of most Christian liturgies and commencing with the words *Sanctus, sanctus, sanctus* or *Holy, holy, holy*
[1]sand \ˈsand\ *n* **1 a :** a loose granular material resulting from the disintegration of rocks **b :** soil containing 85 percent or more of sand and a maximum of 10 percent of clay **2 :** a tract of sand **:** BEACH **3 :** the sand in an hourglass; *also* **:** the moments of a lifetime — usually used in pl. **4 :** firm resolution **:** COURAGE ⟨hasn't the *sand* to object⟩ [Old English]
[2]sand *vt* **1 :** to sprinkle with or as if with sand **2 :** to cover or fill with sand **3 :** to smooth with an abrasive and especially with sandpaper — **sand•er** \ˈsan-dər\ *n*
san•dal \ˈsan-dl\ *n* **1 :** a shoe consisting of a sole strapped to the foot **2 :** a low-cut shoe that fastens by an ankle strap **3 :** a rubber overshoe cut very low [Latin *sandalium,* from Greek *sandalion,* from *sandalon* "sandal"] — **san•daled** *or* **san•dalled** \[1]ˈsan-dld\ *adj*
san•dal•wood \ˈsan-dl-ˌwu̇d\ *n* **:** the close-grained fragrant yellowish heartwood of an Indo-Malayan tree much used in ornamental carving and cabinetwork; *also* **:** the tree that yields this wood [Middle French *sandal,* from Medieval Latin *sandalum,* from Late Greek *santalon,* derived from Sanskrit *candana*]
[1]sand•bag \ˈsand-ˌbag, ˈsan-\ *n* **:** a bag filled with sand (as for use as ballast or as a weapon or in a wall or fortification)
[2]sandbag *vt* **1 :** to bank, stop up, or weight with sandbags **2 a :** to hit or stun with a sandbag **b :** to force by crude means — **sand•bag•ger** *n*
sand•bank \-ˌbangk\ *n* **:** a large deposit of sand
sand•bar \-ˌbär\ *n* **:** a ridge of sand formed in water by tides or currents
[1]sand•blast \-ˌblast\ *n* **:** a stream of sand projected by air or steam (as for engraving, cutting, or cleaning glass or stone)
[2]sandblast *vt* **:** to engrave, cut, or clean with a high-velocity stream of sand — **sand•blast•er** *n*
sand•box \-ˌbäks\ *n* **:** a box for holding sand especially for children to play in
sand•bur \-ˌbər\ *n* **:** any of several weeds of waste places with burry fruit
sand dollar *n* **:** a flat circular sea urchin that lives chiefly in shallow water and on sandy bottoms

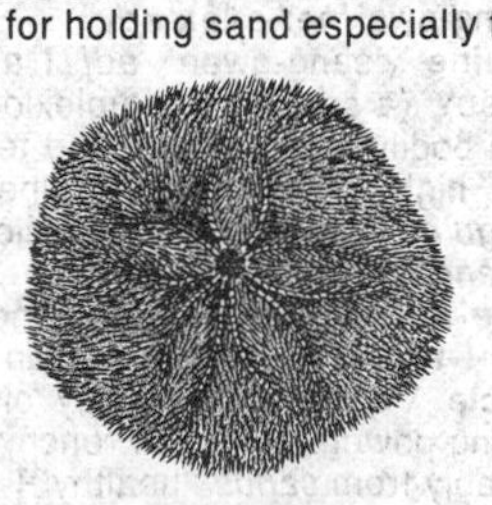

sand dollar

sand•er•ling \ˈsan-dər-ling\ *n* **:** a small largely gray and white sandpiper [perhaps derived from *sand* + *-ling*]

\ə\ abut	\au̇\ out	\i\ tip	\ȯ\ saw	\u̇\ foot
\ər\ further	\ch\ chin	\ī\ life	\ȯi\ coin	\y\ yet
\a\ mat	\e\ pet	\j\ job	\th\ thin	\yü\ few
\ā\ take	\ē\ easy	\ng\ sing	\t͟h\ this	\yu̇\ cure
\ä\ cot, cart	\g\ go	\ō\ bone	\ü\ food	\zh\ vision

sand flea *n* **1 :** a flea found in sandy places **2 :** BEACH FLEA
sand fly *n* **:** any of various small biting two-winged flies
sand·glass \'sand-,glas, 'san-\ *n* **:** an instrument like an hourglass for measuring time by the running of sand
sand·hog \'sand-,hòg, -,häg\ *n* **:** a laborer who works in a caisson in driving underwater tunnels
sand·lot \'san-,dlät, -,lät\ *n* **:** a vacant lot especially when used by youngsters for unorganized sports — **sandlot** *adj* — **sand·lot·ter** *n*
sand·man \'sand-,man, 'san-\ *n* **:** a character in folklore who makes children sleepy supposedly by sprinkling sand in their eyes
1sand·pa·per \-,pā-pər\ *n* **:** paper covered on one side with abrasive material (as sand) glued fast and used for smoothing and polishing
2sandpaper *vt* **:** to rub with sandpaper
sand·pile \-,pīl\ *n* **:** a pile of sand especially for children to play in
sand·pip·er \-,pī-pər\ *n* **:** any of numerous small shorebirds distinguished from the related plovers chiefly by the longer and soft-tipped bill
sand·stone \'sand-,stōn, 'san-\ *n* **:** a sedimentary rock consisting of usually quartz sand and a natural cement
sand·storm \-,stòrm\ *n* **:** a storm of wind (as in a desert) that drives clouds of sand
sand trap *n* **:** an artificial hazard on a golf course consisting of a depression containing sand
1sand·wich \'san-,dwich, -,wich\ *n* **1 :** slices of bread with a filling (as of meat, cheese, or a spread) between them **2 :** something resembling a sandwich [John Montagu, 4th Earl of *Sandwich*, died 1792, English diplomat]
2sandwich *vt* **1 :** to insert between two or more things ⟨plastic *sandwiched* between layers of glass to make safety glass⟩ **2 :** to make a place for **:** CROWD ⟨*sandwich* another activity into a busy schedule⟩
sandwich board *n* **:** two usually hinged boards designed for hanging from the shoulders with one board before and one behind and used especially for advertising
sandwich man *n* **:** a person who advertises or pickets a place of business by wearing a sandwich board
sand·worm \'san-,dwərm, -,wərm\ *n* **:** any of various sand-dwelling polychaete worms; *esp* **:** any of several large burrowing worms often used as bait
sand·wort \'san-,dwərt, -,wərt, -,dwòrt, -,wòrt\ *n* **:** any of various low tufted chickweeds growing in sandy or gritty soil
sandy \'san-dē\ *adj* **sand·i·er; -est 1 :** consisting of, containing, or sprinkled with sand **2 :** of a yellowish gray color
sandy loam *n* **:** a loam low in clay and high in sand
sane \'sān\ *adj* **1 :** mentally sound and healthy **2 :** SENSIBLE 4, RATIONAL [Latin *sanus* "healthy, sane"] — **sane·ly** *adv* — **sane·ness** \'sān-nəs\ *n*
sang *past of* SING
sang·froid \'sä^{n}-'frwä\ *n* **:** self-possession or imperturbability especially under strain [French *sang-froid,* literally, "cold blood"]
san·gui·nary \'sang-gwə-,ner-ē\ *adj* **1 :** BLOODTHIRSTY, MURDEROUS **2 :** BLOODY ⟨a *sanguinary* battle⟩ [Latin *sanguinarius,* from *sanguin-, sanguis* "blood"] — **san·gui·nar·i·ly** \,sang-gwə-'ner-ə-lē\ *adv*
san·guine \'sang-gwən\ *adj* **1 a :** having the color of blood **b :** RUDDY ⟨a *sanguine* complexion⟩ **2 :** SANGUINARY 1 **3 :** having a bodily conformation and temperament marked by sturdiness, high color, and cheerfulness **4 :** CONFIDENT, OPTIMISTIC ⟨*sanguine* about the future⟩ [Middle French *sanguin,* from Latin *sanguineus,* from *sanguin-, sanguis* "blood"] — **san·guine·ly** *adv* — **san·guine·ness** \-gwən-nəs\ *n* — **san·guin·i·ty** \sang-'gwin-ət-ē, san-\ *n*
san·i·cle \'san-i-kəl\ *n* **:** any of several plants held to have healing powers [Middle French, from Medieval Latin *sanicula,* probably from *sanus* "healthy"]
san·i·tar·i·an \,san-ə-'ter-ē-ən\ *n* **:** a specialist in sanitary science and public health ⟨milk *sanitarian*⟩
san·i·tar·i·um \,san-ə-'ter-ē-əm\ *n, pl* **-i·ums** *or* **-ia** \-ē-ə\ **:** SANATORIUM [New Latin, from Latin *sanitas* "health, sanity"]
san·i·tary \'san-ə-,ter-ē\ *adj* **1 :** of or relating to health **:** HYGIENIC ⟨*sanitary* laws⟩ **2 :** free from filth, infection, or dangers to health [French *sanitaire,* from Latin *sanitas* "health"] — **san·i·tar·i·ly** \,san-ə-'ter-ə-lē\ *adv*
sanitary napkin *n* **:** a disposable absorbent pad in a gauze covering used to absorb uterine flow (as during menstruation)
san·i·ta·tion \,san-ə-'tā-shən\ *n* **1 :** the act or process of making sanitary **2 :** the promotion of community hygiene and disease prevention especially by supervision and maintenance of sewage disposal systems, collection and disposal of trash and garbage, and cleaning of streets
san·i·tize \'san-ə-,tīz\ *vt* **:** to make sanitary (as by cleaning or sterilizing) — **san·i·ti·za·tion** \,san-ət-ə-'zā-shən\ *n*
san·i·ty \'san-ət-ē\ *n* **:** the quality or state of being sane [Latin *sanitas* "health, sanity", from *sanus* "healthy, sane"]
San Jo·se scale \,san-ə-,zā-\ *n* **:** a scale insect that is naturalized in the United States probably from Asia and is a most damaging pest to fruit trees [*San Jose,* California]
sank *past of* SINK
sans \sanz, ,sanz\ *prep* **:** WITHOUT [Middle French, from Latin *sine*]
San·skrit \'san-,skrit\ *n* **:** an ancient Indic language that is the classical language of India and of Hinduism [Sanskrit *saṁskṛta,* literally, "perfected"] — **Sanskrit** *adj*
sans ser·if *or* **san·ser·if** \san-'ser-əf\ *n* **:** a letter or typeface with no serifs
san·se·vie·ria \,san-sə-'vir-ē-ə\ *n* **:** any of a genus of tropical Old World herbs with mottled or striped sword-shaped leaves [Raimondo di Sangro, prince of *San Severo,* died 1774, Italian scholar]
San·ta Claus \'sant-ē-,klòz, 'sant-ə-\ *n* **:** the spirit of Christmas personified as a fat, jolly old man in a red suit who distributes toys to children [Dutch *Sinterklaas,* alteration of *Sint Nikolaas* "Saint Nicholas"]
San·ta Ger·tru·dis \,sant-ə-,gər-'trüd-əs\ *n* **:** any of an American breed of cherry-red beef cattle developed from a Brahman-Shorthorn cross and noted for their ability to withstand heat and their resistance to insects [*Santa Gertrudis,* section of the King Ranch, Kingsville, Texas]

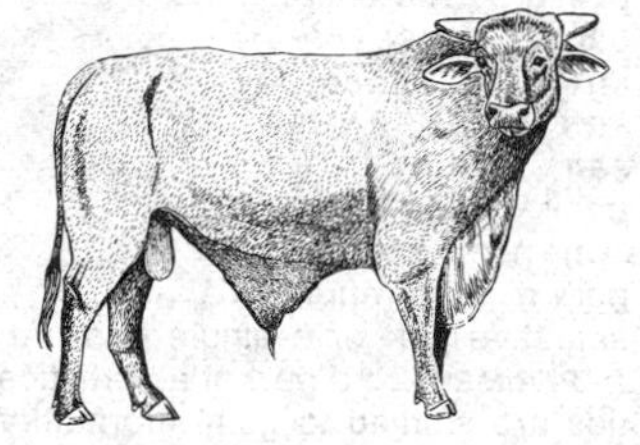
Santa Gertrudis

san·ton·i·ca \san-'tän-i-kə\ *n* **:** the dried unopened flower heads of a wormwood sometimes used as a worm remedy [Latin *herba santonica,* a kind of herb, from *santonicus* "of the Santoni", from *Santoni,* a people of Aquitania]
1sap \'sap\ *n* **1 :** the fluid part of a plant; *esp* **:** a watery solution that circulates through a vascular plant **2 :** VITALITY 2b **3 :** a foolish gullible person [Old English *sæp*]
2sap *vt* **sapped; sap·ping 1 :** UNDERMINE ⟨heavy tides *sapped* the seawall⟩ **2 :** to weaken gradually ⟨the heat *sapped* my strength⟩ [earlier *sap* "extension of a trench to a point beneath an enemy's fortifications", from Middle French *sappe* "hoe", from Italian *zappa*]
sap·head \'sap-,hed\ *n* **:** a weak-minded or foolish person **:** SAP — **sap·head·ed** \-'hed-əd\ *adj*
sa·pi·ence \'sā-pē-əns, 'sap-ē-\ *n* **:** WISDOM 1a
sa·pi·ent \'sā-pē-ənt, 'sap-ē-\ *adj* **:** WISE 1, DISCERNING [Middle French, from Latin *sapiens,* from *sapere* "to taste, be wise"] — **sa·pi·ent·ly** *adv*
sap·less \'sap-ləs\ *adj* **1 :** destitute of sap **:** DRY **2 :** lacking vitality or vigor **:** FEEBLE — **sap·less·ness** *n*
sap·ling \'sap-ling\ *n* **:** a young tree usually not over four inches in diameter at breast height
sap·o·dil·la \,sap-ə-'dil-ə\ *n* **:** a tropical American evergreen tree with hard reddish wood, an edible brownish berry, and a latex that yields chicle [Spanish *zapotillo,* from *zapote* "sapodilla", from Nahuatl *tzapotl*]
sap·o·na·ceous \,sap-ə-'nā-shəs\ *adj* **:** resembling or having the qualities of soap **:** SOAPY [Latin *sapon-, sapo* "soap", of Germanic origin] — **sap·o·na·ceous·ness** *n*
sa·pon·i·fi·ca·tion \sə-,pän-ə-fə-'kā-shən\ *n* **1 :** the hydrolysis of a fat by alkali with formation of a soap together with glycerol **2 :** the hydrolysis by alkali of an ester into the corresponding alcohol and acid — **sa·pon·i·fi·able** \-'pän-ə-,fī-ə-bəl\ *adj* — **sa·pon·i·fi·er** \-,fī-ər, -,fīr\ *n* — **sa·pon·i·fy** \-,fī\ *vb*

sap•per \'sap-ər\ *n* **1 :** a military engineer who constructs field fortifications **2 :** an engineer who lays, detects, and disarms mines

sap•phire \'saf-,īr\ *n* **1 :** a gem variety of corundum occurring in transparent or translucent colorless or colored forms except red; *esp* **:** a transparent rich blue gemstone **2 :** a deep purplish blue [Old French *safir,* from Latin *sapphirus,* from Greek *sappheiros,* from Hebrew *sappīr,* from Sanskrit *śanipriya,* literally, "dear to the planet Saturn", from *Śani* "Saturn" + *priya* "dear"] — **sapphire** *adj*

sap•py \'sap-ē\ *adj* **sap•pi•er; -est 1 :** abounding with sap **2 :** containing much sapwood **3 a :** foolishly sentimental **b :** lacking in good sense **:** SILLY — **sap•pi•ness** *n*

sapr- *or* **sapro-** *combining form* **1 :** rotten **:** putrid **2 :** dead or decaying organic matter ⟨*sapro*phyte⟩ [Greek *sapros*]

sap•ro•phyte \'sap-rə-,fīt\ *n* **:** a plant living on dead or decaying organic matter; *also* **:** any saprophytic organism

sap•ro•phyt•ic \,sap-rə-'fit-ik\ *adj* **:** obtaining food by absorbing dissolved organic material and especially the products of organic breakdown and decay — **sap•ro•phyt•i•cal•ly** \-'fit-i-kə-lē, -klē\ *adv*

sap•suck•er \'sap-,sək-ər\ *n* **:** any of various small American woodpeckers reputed to feed on sap

sapsucker

sap•wood \-,wu̇d\ *n* **:** the younger softer sap-containing and usually lighter-colored wood in the outer portion of a woody stem — compare HEARTWOOD

Sar•a•cen \'sar-ə-sən\ *n* **1 :** a member of a nomadic people of the deserts of Syria and northern Arabia **2 :** ARAB 1 **3 :** one of the Muslim opponents of the Crusaders [Late Latin *Saracenus,* from Late Greek *Sarakēnos*] — **Saracen** *adj* — **Sar•a•cen•ic** \,sar-ə-'sen-ik\ *adj*

sa•ran \sə-'ran\ *n* **:** a tough flexible thermoplastic resin that can be formed into waterproof and chemically resistant products (as filaments, tubing, and coating) [from *Saran Wrap,* a trademark]

sa•ra•pe *variant of* SERAPE

sarc- *or* **sarco-** *combining form* **:** flesh [Greek *sark-, sarx*]

sar•casm \'sär-,kaz-əm\ *n* **1 :** a cutting and often ironic remark **2 :** the use of sarcasms in speech or writing ⟨this is no time to indulge in *sarcasm*⟩ [French *sarcasme,* from Late Latin *sarcasmos,* from Greek *sarkasmos,* from *sarkazein* "to tear flesh, bite the lips, sneer", from *sark-, sarx* "flesh"]

sar•cas•tic \sär-'kas-tik\ *adj* **1 :** given to sarcasm **2 :** containing sarcasm ⟨a *sarcastic* remark⟩ — **sar•cas•ti•cal•ly** \-ti-kə-lē, -klē\ *adv*

sar•co•lem•ma \,sär-kə-'lem-ə\ *n* **:** the thin sheath of a muscle fiber [*sarc-* + Greek *lemma* "husk", from *lepein* "to peel"]

sar•co•ma \sär-'kō-mə\ *n* **:** a malignant tumor arising in tissue of mesodermal origin (as connective tissue or striated muscle) — **sar•co•ma•tous** \sär-'käm-ət-əs, -'kōm-\ *adj*

sar•coph•a•gus \sär-'käf-ə-gəs\ *n, pl* **-gi** \-,gī, -,jī, -,gē\ *or* **-gus•es :** a stone coffin; *esp* **:** one exposed to view in the open air or in a tomb [Latin *sarcophagus (lapis)* "limestone used for coffins", from Greek *(lithos) sarkophagos,* literally, "flesh-eating stone", from *sark-, sarx* "flesh" + *phagein* "to eat"]

sar•dine \sär-'dēn\ *n, pl* **sardines** *also* **sardine 1 :** any of several small or immature fishes of the herring family; *esp* **:** the young of the European pilchard when of a size suitable for preserving for food **2 :** any of various small fishes (as an anchovy) resembling the true sardines or similarly preserved for food [Middle French, from Latin *sardina*]

sar•don•ic \sär-'dän-ik\ *adj* **:** bitterly scornful **:** CYNICAL [French *sardonique,* from Greek *sardonios*] — **sar•don•i•cal•ly** \-'dän-i-kə-lē, -klē\ *adv*

sard•on•yx \sär-'dän-iks, 'särd-n-\ *n* **:** onyx having layers of carnelian [Latin, from Greek]

sar•gas•so \sär-'gas-ō\ *n, pl* **-sos 1 :** GULFWEED, SARGASSUM **2 :** a mass of floating vegetation and especially sargassums [Portuguese *sargaço*]

sar•gas•sum \sär-'gas-əm\ *n* **:** any of a genus of branching brown algae with lateral outgrowths forming leafy segments, air bladders, or spore-bearing structures [New Latin, from *sargasso*]

sa•ri *or* **sa•ree** \'sär-ē\ *n* **:** a garment of Hindu women that consists of a long cloth draped so that one end forms a skirt and the other a head or shoulder covering [Hindi *sāṛī,* from Sanskrit *śāṭī*]

sari

sa•rong \sə-'ro̅ng, -'räng\ *n* **:** a loose skirt made of a long strip of cloth wrapped loosely around the body and worn by men and women of the Malay archipelago and the Pacific islands [Malay *kain sarong* "cloth sheath"]

sar•sa•pa•ril•la \,sas-pə-'ril-ə, ,särs-, -ə-pə-\ *n* **1 a :** any of various tropical American smilaxes **b :** the dried roots of a sarsaparilla plant used especially as a flavoring **2 :** a sweetened carbonated beverage flavored chiefly with birch oil and sassafras [Spanish *zarzaparilla*]

sar•to•ri•al \sär-'tōr-ē-əl, -'tȯr-\ *adj* **:** of or relating to a tailor or tailored clothes ⟨the *sartorial* appearence of a politician⟩ ⟨*satorial* splendor⟩ [Latin *sartor* "tailor", from *sartus,* past participle of *sarcire* "to mend"] — **sar•to•ri•al•ly** \-ē-ə-lē\ *adv*

sar•to•ri•us \-ē-əs\ *n* **:** a muscle that crosses the front of the thigh obliquely and assists in rotating the leg outward to the position assumed in sitting cross-legged [New Latin, from Latin *sartor* "tailor"]

1sash \'sash\ *n* **:** a broad band (as of silk) worn around the waist or over the shoulder [Arabic *shāsh* "muslin"]

2sash *n, pl* **sash** *or* **sash•es :** the framework in which panes of glass are set in a window or door; *also* **:** the movable part of a window ⟨raised the *sash* to let in air⟩ [probably from French *châssis* "chassis"]

sa•shay \sa-'shā\ *vi* **1 :** to strut or move about in an ostentatious manner **2 :** to proceed in a diagonal or sideways manner [French *chassé,* a dance step, from *chasser* "to chase"]

1sass \'sas\ *n* **:** impudent speech [back-formation from *sassy*]

2sass *vt* **:** to talk impudently or disrespectfully to

sassafras

sas•sa•fras \'sas-,fras, -ə-,fras\ *n* **:** a tall eastern North American tree of the laurel family having fragrant yellow flowers and blue-black berries; *also* **:** its dried root bark used especially in medicine or as a flavoring agent [Spanish *sasafrás*]

sassy \'sas-ē\ *adj* **sass•i•er; -est :** given to back talk **:** FRESH [alteration of *saucy*]

sat *past of* SIT

Sa•tan \'sāt-n\ *n* **:** DEVIL 1 [Old English, from Late Latin, from Greek, from Hebrew *śāṭān*] — **sa•tan•ic** \sə-'tan-ik, sā-\ *adj* — **sa•tan•i•cal•ly** \-'tan-i-kə-lē, -klē\ *adv*

satch•el \'sach-əl\ *n* **:** a small bag for carrying clothes or books [Middle French *sachel,* from Latin *sacellus* "small bag", from *saccus* "bag"]

sate \'sāt\ *vt* **1 :** SURFEIT, GLUT **2 :** SATIATE 1 [probably from *satiate*]

sa•teen \sa-'tēn\ *n* **:** a glossy cotton fabric resembling satin [alteration of *satin*]

\ə\ **abut**	\au̇\ **out**	\i\ **tip**	\ȯ\ **saw**	\u̇\ **foot**
\ər\ **further**	\ch\ **chin**	\ī\ **life**	\ȯi\ **coin**	\y\ **yet**
\a\ **mat**	\e\ **pet**	\j\ **job**	\th\ **thin**	\yü\ **few**
\ā\ **take**	\ē\ **easy**	\ng\ **sing**	\t͟h\ **this**	\yu̇\ **cure**
\ä\ **cot, cart**	\g\ **go**	\ō\ **bone**	\ü\ **food**	\zh\ **vision**

sat•el•lite \'sat-l-ˌīt\ *n* **1** : a servile follower **2 a** : a celestial body orbiting another of larger size **b** : a man-made object or vehicle intended to orbit the earth, the moon, or another celestial body **3** : one that is subordinate to or dependent on another; *esp* : a country dominated or controlled by another more powerful country [Middle French, from Latin *satellit-, satelles* "attendant"] — **satellite** *adj*

sa•tia•ble \'sā-shə-bəl\ *adj* : possible to appease or satisfy

¹sa•tiate \'sā-shē-ət, -shət\ *adj* : marked by or feeling satiety

²sa•ti•ate \'sā-shē-ˌāt\ *vt* **1** : to satisfy (as a person or an appetite) fully **2** : SURFEIT [Latin *satiare,* from *satis* "enough"] — **sa•ti•a•tion** \ˌsā-shē-'ā-shən, ˌsā-sē-\ *n*

sa•ti•e•ty \sə-'tī-ət-ē\ *n* **1** : SURFEIT 1, REPLETION **2** : revulsion or disgust that follows overindulgence [Middle French *satieté,* from Latin *satietas,* from *satis* "enough"]

sat•in \'sat-n\ *n* : a fabric (as of silk) with smooth lustrous face and dull back [Middle French] — **satin** *adj*

sat•in•et *or* **sat•in•ette** \ˌsat-n-'et\ *n* : a usually thin silk satin

satin weave *n* : a weave in which warp threads interlace with filling threads to produce a smooth-faced fabric

sat•in•wood \'sat-n-ˌwu̇d\ *n* **1** : a hard yellowish brown wood with a satiny luster **2** : a tree yielding satinwood; *esp* : an East Indian tree of the mahogany family

sat•iny \'sat-n-ē\ *adj* : having the soft lustrous smoothness of satin : resembling satin ⟨*satiny* skin⟩

sat•ire \'sa-ˌtīr\ *n* **1** : a literary work holding up human vices and follies to ridicule or scorn **2** : biting wit, irony, or sarcasm used to expose and discredit vice or folly [Middle French, from Latin *satura, satira,* from *(lanx) satura* "full plate, medley", from *satur* "sated"] — **sa•tir•ic** \sə-'tir-ik\ *or* **sa•tir•i•cal** \-'tir-i-kəl\ *adj* — **sa•tir•i•cal•ly** \-i-kə-lē, -klē\ *adv*

△ **origin** English *satire* is derived from Latin *satira* and its earlier form *satura,* which in classical times meant "a satirical poem". Before the development of this style of satiric poetry, the *satura* was a poem dealing with a number of different subjects. It is this sense of "a poetic medley" that gives us a clue to the early development of the word. This sense of *satura* evolved from the phrase *lanx satura,* literally "a full plate". *Satura* is a form of *satur,* which means "sated" or "full of food". *Lanx satura* once meant a plate filled with various fruits or a dish made from a mixture of many ingredients.

sat•i•rist \'sat-ə-rəst\ *n* : one that satirizes; *esp* : a satirical writer

sat•i•rize \-ˌrīz\ *vb* **1** : to utter or write satires **2** : to criticize or ridicule by means of satire

sat•is•fac•tion \ˌsat-əs-'fak-shən\ *n* **1 a** : fulfillment of a need or want **b** : the quality or state of being satisfied : CONTENTMENT **c** : a cause or means of enjoyment : GRATIFICATION **2** : compensation for a loss or injury : RESTITUTION **3** : convinced assurance or certainty ⟨proved to the *satisfaction* of the court⟩ [Middle French, from Latin *satisfactio* "reparation, amends", from *satisfacere* "to satisfy"]

sat•is•fac•to•ry \ˌsat-əs-'fak-tə-rē, -trē\ *adj* : sufficient or adequate to satisfy : meeting what is asked or demanded — **sat•is•fac•to•ri•ly** \-tə-rə-lē, -trə-\ *adv* — **sat•is•fac•to•ri•ness** \-tə-rē-nəs, -trē-\ *n*

sat•is•fy \'sat-əs-ˌfī\ *vb* **-fied; -fy•ing 1 a** : to carry out the terms of ⟨*satisfy* a contract⟩ **b** : to meet a financial obligation to : PAY **2 a** : to make happy : PLEASE **b** : to gratify to the full : APPEASE ⟨*satisfied* my hunger⟩ **3 a** : CONVINCE ⟨*satisfied* that the defendant is innocent⟩ **b** : to put an end to : DISPEL ⟨*satisfied* all their objections⟩ **4 a** : to conform or be adequate to : MEET ⟨*satisfy* a need⟩ **b** : to make true by fulfilling a condition ⟨values that *satisfy* an equation⟩ ⟨*satisfy* a hypothesis⟩ [Middle French *satisfier,* from Latin *satisfacere,* from *satis* "enough" + *facere* "to do, make"] — **sat•is•fi•able** \ˌsat-əs-'fī-ə-bəl\ *adj* — **sat•is•fy•ing•ly** \'sat-əs-ˌfī-ing-lē\ *adv*

sa•trap \'sā-ˌtrap, 'sa-\ *n* **1** : the governor of a province in ancient Persia **2** : a subordinate ruler; *esp* : a petty tyrant [Latin *satrapes,* from Greek *satrapēs,* from Persian *xshathrapāvan,* literally, "protector of the dominion"]

sa•tra•py \'sā-trə-pē, 'sa-, -ˌtrap-ē\ *n, pl* **-pies** : the territory or jurisdiction of a satrap

sat•u•rant \'sach-ə-rənt\ *n* : something that saturates

sat•u•rate \'sach-ə-ˌrāt\ *vt* **1** : to treat, furnish, or charge with something to the point where no more can be absorbed, dissolved, or retained ⟨air *saturated* with water vapor⟩ **2** : to fill completely with something that permeates or pervades [Latin *saturare,* from *satur* "sated"] — **sat•u•ra•ble** \'sach-rə-bəl, -ə-rə-\ *adv* — **sat•u•ra•tor** \'sach-ə-ˌrāt-ər\ *n*

sat•u•rat•ed \'sach-ə-ˌrāt-əd\ *adj* **1** : steeped in moisture : SOAKED **2 a** : being the most concentrated solution that can remain in the presence of an excess of the dissolved substance **b** : being a compound that does not tend to unite directly with another compound — used especially of organic compounds containing no double or triple bonds **3** : not diluted with white ⟨a *saturated* color⟩

sat•u•ra•tion \ˌsach-ə-'rā-shən\ *n* **1** : the act of saturating : the state of being saturated **2** : chromatic purity : freedom from dilution with white **3** : an overwhelming concentration of military forces or firepower

Sat•ur•day \'sat-ərd-ē\ *n* : the 7th day of the week [Old English *sæterndæg,* literally, "Saturn's day", derived from Latin *Saturnus* "Saturn"]

Sat•urn \'sat-ərn\ *n* : the planet 6th in order from the sun — see PLANET table [*Saturn,* Roman god] — **Sa•tur•ni•an** \sa-'tər-nē-ən\ *adj*

sat•ur•na•lia \ˌsat-ər-'nāl-yə\ *n sing or pl* **1** *cap* : the festival of Saturn in ancient Rome beginning on December 17 **2** : an unrestrained often licentious celebration : ORGY [Latin, derived from *Saturnus* "Saturn"] — **sat•ur•na•lian** \-yən\ *adj*

sat•ur•nine \'sat-ər-ˌnīn\ *adj* : having a sullen or sardonic aspect : GLOOMY, GRAVE [from the supposed character of those born under the planet Saturn] — **sat•ur•nine•ly** *adv*

sa•tyr \'sāt-ər, 'sat-\ *n* **1** : a forest god in Greek mythology often represented as having the ears and tail of a horse or goat and given to boisterous pleasures **2** : a man of lustful or lecherous habits **3** : any of a family of usually brown and gray butterflies often with eyespots on the wings [Latin *satyrus,* from Greek *satyros*] — **sa•tyr•ic** \sā-'tir-ik, sə-, sa-\ *adj*

¹sauce \'sȯs, *4 usually* 'sas\ *n* **1** : a condiment or relish for food; *esp* : one in the form of a liquid or semisolid : DRESSING **2** : something that adds zest or piquancy **3** : cooked fruit eaten with other food or as a dessert ⟨apple *sauce*⟩ **4** : pert or impudent language or actions [Middle French, from Latin *salsus* "salted", from *sallere* "to salt", from *sal* "salt"]

²sauce \'sȯs, *2 usually* 'sas\ *vt* **1** : to add relish or seasoning to **2** : to be rude or impudent to

sauce•pan \'sȯ-ˌspan\ *n* : a small deep cooking pan with a handle

sau•cer \'sȯ-sər\ *n* **1** : a small round shallow dish in which a cup is set at table **2** : something like a saucer especially in shape [Middle French *saussier* "dish for sauce", from *sausse, sauce* "sauce"]

saucy \'sas-ē *also* 'sȯs-ē\ *adj* **sauc•i•er; -est 1** : IMPUDENT, BOLD **2** : IRREPRESSIBLE, PERT **3** : SMART, TRIM ⟨a *saucy* little hat⟩ — **sauc•i•ly** \-ə-lē\ *adv* — **sauc•i•ness** \-ē-nəs\ *n*

sau•er•bra•ten \'sau̇-ər-ˌbrät-n, 'sau̇r-\ *n* : pot-roasted beef marinated in vinegar with seasonings before cooking [German, from *sauer* "sour" + *braten* "roast meat"]

sau•er•kraut \'sau̇-ər-ˌkrau̇t, 'sau̇r-\ *n* : finely cut cabbage fermented in brine [German, from *sauer* "sour" + *kraut* "cabbage"]

sau•ger \'sȯ-gər\ *n* : a pike perch similar to the walleye but smaller; *also* : WALLEYE [origin unknown]

sau•na \'sȯ-nə, 'sau̇-nə\ *n* : a Finnish steam bath; *also* : a bathhouse with steam provided usually by water thrown on hot stones [Finnish]

saun•ter \'sȯnt-ər, 'sänt-\ *vi* : to walk along in an idle or leisurely manner : STROLL [probably from Middle English *santren* "to muse"] — **saunter** *n* — **saun•ter•er** \-ər-ər\ *n*

sau•ri•an \'sȯr-ē-ən\ *n* : any of a group (Sauria) of reptiles including the lizards and in older classifications the crocodiles and various extinct forms (as the dinosaurs) suggesting lizards [derived from Greek *sauros* "lizard"] — **saurian** *adj*

saur•is•chi•an \sȯ-'ris-kē-ən\ *n* : any of an order (Saurischia) of four-footed dinosaurs with a typically reptilian pelvic girdle [derived from Greek *sauros* "lizard" + *ischion* "hip joint"] — **saurischian** *adj*

sau•ro•pod \'sȯr-ə-ˌpäd\ *n* : any of a group (Sauropoda) of large long-necked plant-eating saurischian dinosaurs — **sauropod** *adj*

sau•sage \'sȯ-sij\ *n* : highly seasoned minced meat (as pork) usually stuffed in casings [Old North French *saussiche,* from Late Latin *salsicia,* from Latin *salsus* "salted", from *sallere* "to salt", from *sal* "salt"]

¹sau•té \sō-'tā, sō-\ *n* : a sautéed dish [French, "sautéed", from *sauter* "to jump", from Latin *saltare*] — **sauté** *adj*

[2]**sauté** *vt* **sau•téed** *or* **sau•téd**; **sau•té•ing** : to fry quickly in shallow fat

sau•terne \sō-ˈtərn, sȯ-, -ˈteərn\ *n* : a semisweet golden-colored table wine [French *sauternes,* from *Sauternes,* commune in France]

[1]**sav•age** \ˈsav-ij\ *adj* **1** : not domesticated or under human control ⟨a *savage* bear⟩ **2** : CRUEL 2, FEROCIOUS **3 a** : RUDE 3 **b** : lacking complex or advanced culture : UNCIVILIZED [Middle French *sauvage,* derived from Latin *silvaticus* "of the woods, wild", from *silva* "wood, forest"] **syn** see BARBARIAN — **sav•age•ly** *adv* — **sav•age•ness** *n*

[2]**savage** *n* **1** : a person belonging to a primitive society **2** : a brutal person **3** : a rude or unmannerly person

[3]**savage** *vt* : to attack or treat violently or brutally

sav•age•ry \ˈsav-ij-rē, -ə-rē\ *n, pl* **-ries 1** : the quality of being savage **2** : an act of cruelty or violence **3** : an uncivilized state

sa•van•na *or* **sa•van•nah** \sə-ˈvan-ə\ *n* : a tropical or subtropical grassland containing scattered trees [Spanish *zavana,* of American Indian origin]

sa•vant \sa-ˈvänt, -ˈvän^n; sə-ˈvant, ˈsav-ənt\ *n* : a learned person : SCHOLAR [French, from *savoir* "to know", from Latin *sapere* "to taste, be wise"]

[1]**save** \ˈsāv\ *vb* **1 a** : to deliver from sin **b** : to rescue from danger or harm **c** : to preserve or guard from injury, destruction, or loss **2** : to put aside as a store or reserve; *also* : to put aside money **3 a** : to make unnecessary : AVOID **b** : to prevent an opponent from making, scoring, or winning ⟨a diving catch that *saved* a goal⟩ **4** : MAINTAIN, PRESERVE ⟨*save* appearances⟩ **5** : to avoid unnecessary waste or expense : ECONOMIZE [Old French *salver,* from Late Latin *salvare,* from Latin *salvus* "safe"] — **sav•able** *or* **save•able** \ˈsā-və-bəl\ *adj* — **sav•er** *n*

[2]**save** *n* : a play that prevents an opponent from scoring or winning; *also* : a game that has been saved

[3]**save** \sāv, ˌsāv\ *prep* : EXCEPT ⟨no hope *save* one⟩ [Old French *sauf,* from *sauf,* adj., "safe"]

[4]**save** \sāv, ˌsāv\ *conj* : were it not : ONLY — used with *that*

sav•in \ˈsav-ən\ *n* : any of several mostly low-growing junipers [Middle French *savine,* from Latin *sabina*]

[1]**sav•ing** \ˈsā-viŋ\ *n* **1** : the act of rescuing ⟨the *saving* of lives⟩ **2 a** : something saved ⟨made a *saving* of 50 percent⟩ **b** *pl* : money saved over a period of time

[2]**saving** *adj* **1** : ECONOMICAL 1, THRIFTY **2** : making up for something : COMPENSATORY ⟨a *saving* sense of humor⟩

[3]**saving** *prep* **1** : EXCEPT, SAVE **2** : without disrespect to

[4]**saving** *conj* : EXCEPT

savings account *n* : an interest-bearing account with a bank

savings bank *n* : a bank that receives and invests savings accounts and pays interest to depositors

savings bond *n* : a registered United States bond issued in denominations of $25 to $1000

sav•ior *or* **sav•iour** \ˈsāv-yər\ *n* **1** : one that saves from harm **2** *cap* : a bringer of salvation; *esp* : JESUS [Middle French *saveour,* from Late Latin *salvator,* from *salvare* "to save"]

sa•voir faire \ˌsav-ˌwär-ˈfaər, -ˈfeər\ *n* : ability to do or say the right or graceful thing : TACT [French *savoir-faire,* literally, "knowing how to do"]

[1]**sa•vor** \ˈsā-vər\ *n* **1** : the taste and odor of something ⟨the *savor* of roast meat⟩ **2** : a distinctive quality [Old French, from Latin *sapor*] — **sa•vor•less** \-ləs\ *adj*

[2]**savor** *vb* **sa•vored**; **sa•vor•ing** \ˈsāv-riŋ, -ə-riŋ\ **1** : to have a specified smell or quality **2** : to give flavor to : SEASON **3 a** : to have experience of **b** : to taste or smell with pleasure : RELISH **c** : to delight in : ENJOY — **sa•vor•er** \ˈsā-vər-ər\ *n*

[1]**sa•vory** \ˈsāv-rē, -ə-rē\ *adj* **sa•vor•i•er**; **-est** : pleasing to the taste or smell : APPETIZING — **sa•vor•i•ness** *n*

[2]**sa•vo•ry** \ˈsāv-rē, -ə-rē\ *n, pl* **-ries** : any of a genus of aromatic mints used to season food [Middle English *saverey*]

[1]**sav•vy** \ˈsav-ē\ *vb* **sav•vied**; **sav•vy•ing** : GET 7c, UNDERSTAND ⟨you *savvy* what I mean?⟩ [Spanish *sabe* "he, she, or it knows", from *saber* "to know", from Latin *sapere* "to taste, be wise"]

[2]**savvy** *n* : practical understanding ⟨political *savvy*⟩

[1]**saw** *past of* SEE

[2]**saw** \ˈsȯ\ *n* **1** : a hand or power tool used to cut hard material (as wood, metal, or bone) with a toothed blade or disk **2** : a machine mounting a saw (as a band saw or circular saw) [Old English *sagu*] — **saw•like** \-ˌlīk\ *adj*

[3]**saw** *vb* **sawed** \ˈsȯd\; **sawed** *or* **sawn** \ˈsȯn\; **saw•ing** \ˈsȯ-iŋ, ˈsȯiŋ\ **1** : to cut or form by cutting with a saw **2** : to slice as though with a saw **3** : to make motions as though using a saw ⟨*sawed* at the reins⟩ — **saw•er** \ˈsȯ-ər, ˈsȯr\ *n*

[4]**saw** *n* : a common saying : PROVERB [Old English *sagu* "talk"]

saw•buck \ˈsȯ-ˌbək\ *n* **1** : SAWHORSE **2** *slang* : a 10-dollar bill [sense 2 probably from the resemblance of the Roman numeral X to the ends of a sawhorse]

saw•dust \ˈsȯ-ˌdəst\ *n* : dust or fine particles of wood made by a saw in cutting

saw–edged \ˈsȯ-ˈejd\ *adj* : having a toothed or nicked edge

sawed–off \ˈsȯ-ˌdȯf\ *adj* **1** : having an end sawed off ⟨a *sawed-off* shotgun⟩ **2** : being of less than average height

saw•fish \ˈsȯ-ˌfish\ *n* : any of several mostly tropical rays with a long flattened snout bearing a row of stout toothlike structures along each edge

sawhorse

saw•fly \-ˌflī\ *n* : any of numerous insects that are related to the wasps and bees and usually have in the female a pair of organs for making slits in leaves or stems into which eggs are laid

saw grass *n* : a sedge with sharply toothed leaves

saw•horse \ˈsȯ-ˌhȯrs\ *n* : a frame or rack on which wood is rested while being sawed by hand

saw•log \-ˌlȯg, -ˌläg\ *n* : a log fit for sawing into lumber

saw•mill \-ˌmil\ *n* : a mill or machine for sawing logs

saw•tim•ber \ˈsȯ-ˌtim-bər\ *n* : timber suitable for sawing into lumber

saw•tooth \-ˌtüth\ *adj* : SAW-TOOTHED

saw–toothed \-ˈtütht\ *adj* : having an edge or outline like the teeth of a saw

saw–whet \-ˌhwet, -ˌwet\ *n* : a very small harsh-voiced North American owl largely dark brown above and white beneath [from the resemblance of its cry to the sound of filing a saw]

saw•yer \ˈsȯ-yər, ˈsȯi-ər\ *n* **1** : one that saws timber **2** : any of several large beetles whose larvae bore large holes in timber

sax \ˈsaks\ *n* : SAXOPHONE

sax•horn \ˈsaks-ˌhȯrn\ *n* : one of a family of valved brass instruments having a conical tube, oval shape, and cup-shaped mouthpiece [Antoine J. *Sax,* died 1894, Belgian maker of musical instruments]

sax•i•frage \ˈsak-sə-frij, -ˌfrāj\ *n* : any of a genus of plants with showy 5-parted flowers and usually with leaves growing in tufts close to the ground [Middle French, from Late Latin *saxifraga,* derived from Latin *saxum* "rock" + *frangere* "to break"]

Sax•on \ˈsak-sən\ *n* **1** : a member of a Germanic people invading and conquering England with the Angles and Jutes in the 5th century A.D. and merging with them to form the Anglo-Saxon people **2** : a native or inhabitant of Saxony [Late Latin *Saxones* "Saxons", of Germanic origin] — **Saxon** *adj*

sax•o•phone \ˈsak-sə-ˌfōn\ *n* : a wind instrument with reed mouthpiece, curved conical metal tube, and finger keys [French, from Antoine J. *Sax,* died 1894, Belgian maker of musical instruments] — **sax•o•phon•ic** \ˌsak-sə-ˈfän-ik\ *adj* — **sax•o•phon•ist** \ˈsak-sə-ˌfō-nəst\ *n*

saxophone

sax•tu•ba \ˈsaks-ˈtü-bə, -ˈtyü-\ *n* : a bass saxhorn

[1]**say** \'sā\ *vt* **said** \'sed\; **say•ing** \'sā-iŋ\; **says** \'sez\ **1 a** : to express in words : STATE **b** : to state as opinion or belief : DECLARE **2 a** : UTTER 1b, PRONOUNCE **b** : RECITE, REPEAT ⟨*said* their prayers⟩ **3** : INDICATE, SHOW ⟨the clock *says* five minutes after twelve⟩ [Old English *secgan*] — **say•er** \'sā-ər\ *n*

[2]**say** *n* **1** : an expression of opinion ⟨had my *say*⟩ **2** : the power to decide or help decide

[3]**say** *adv* **1** : ABOUT, APPROXIMATELY ⟨the property is worth, *say*, four million dollars⟩ **2** : for example : AS ⟨if we compress any gas, *say* oxygen⟩

say•ing \'sā-iŋ\ *n* : something frequently said : PROVERB

say–so \'sā-ˌsō\ *n* **1 a** : one's unsupported word or assurance **b** : an authoritative pronouncement ⟨acted on the doctor's *say-so*⟩ **2** : a right of final decision : AUTHORITY

[1]**scab** \'skab\ *n* **1** : scabies of domestic animals **2** : a crust of hardened blood and serum over a wound **3 a** : a contemptible person **b** : a worker who takes the place of a striking worker **4** : any of various plant diseases characterized by crusted spots [of Scandinavian origin]

[2]**scab** *vi* **scabbed**; **scab•bing 1** : to become covered with a scab **2** : to act as a scab

scab•bard \'skab-ərd\ *n* : a sheath for a sword, dagger, or bayonet [Anglo-French *escauberz* "scabbards", of Germanic origin] — **scabbard** *vt*

scab•by \'skab-ē\ *adj* **scab•bi•er**; **-est 1 a** : covered with or full of scabs ⟨*scabby* skin⟩ **b** : diseased with scab ⟨a *scabby* animal⟩ ⟨*scabby* potatoes⟩ **2** : MEAN, CONTEMPTIBLE ⟨a *scabby* trick⟩

sca•bies \'skā-bēz\ *n, pl* **scabies** : an itch or mange caused by mites living as parasites under the skin [Latin]

sca•brous \'skab-rəs *also* 'skāb-\ *adj* **1** : DIFFICULT, KNOTTY ⟨a *scabrous* problem⟩ **2** : rough to the touch ⟨a *scabrous* leaf⟩ **3** : unpleasant, repulsive, or reprehensible in some way [Latin *scaber* "rough, scurfy"] — **sca•brous•ly** *adv* — **sca•brous•ness** *n*

[1]**scad** \'skad\ *n, pl* **scad** *also* **scads** : any of several mostly small sea fishes related to the pompanos [origin unknown]

[2]**scad** *n* **1** : a large number or quantity **2** *pl* : a great abundance ⟨*scads* of money⟩ [probably from English dialect *scald* "a multitude", from [2]*scald*]

scaf•fold \'skaf-əld *also* -ˌōld\ *n* **1 a** : a temporary or movable platform for workmen **b** : a platform on which a criminal is executed (as by hanging) **2** : a supporting framework [Old North French *escafaut*]

scaf•fold•ing \-iŋ\ *n* : a system of scaffolds; *also* : materials for scaffolds

[1]**sca•lar** \'skā-lər, -ˌlär\ *adj* **1** : arranged like a ladder : GRADUATED ⟨a *scalar* chain of authority⟩ **2** : capable of being represented by a point on a scale **3** : of, relating to, or being a scalar or a scalar product [Latin *scalaris*, from *scalae* "stairs, ladders"]

[2]**scalar** *n* **1** : a real number rather than a vector **2** : a quantity (as mass or time) that has a magnitude describable by a real number but no direction

sca•la•re \skə-'laər-ē, -'leər-, -'lär-\ *n* : a black and silver laterally compressed South American fish popular in aquariums [derived from Latin *scalaris* "scalar"; from the barred pattern on its body]

scalar product *n* : a real number that is the product of the lengths of two vectors and the cosine of the angle between them

scal•a•wag *or* **scal•ly•wag** \'skal-i-ˌwag\ *n* **1** : RASCAL 1, SCAMP **2** : a white Southerner acting as a Republican in the time of reconstruction after the Civil War [origin unknown]

[1]**scald** \'skȯld\ *vt* **1** : to burn with or as if with hot liquid or steam **2 a** : to subject to the action of boiling water or steam ⟨*scald* dishes⟩ **b** : to bring to a temperature just below the boiling point ⟨*scald* milk⟩ **3** : SCORCH 1a [Old North French *escalder*, from Late Latin *excaldare* "to wash in warm water", from Latin *ex-* + *calida, calda* "warm water", from *calidus* "warm"]

[2]**scald** *n* **1** : an injury to the body caused by scalding **2** : an act or process of scalding **3** : a plant disease marked especially by discoloration suggesting injury by heat

scald•ing \'skȯl-diŋ\ *adj* **1** : causing the sensation of scalding or burning **2** : BOILING ⟨*scalding* water⟩ **3** : very hot : SCORCHING ⟨the *scalding* sun⟩ **4** : SCATHING, CUTTING ⟨a *scalding* editorial⟩

[1]**scale** \'skāl\ *n* **1 a** : either pan of a balance **b** : BALANCE — usually used in pl. **2** : a device for weighing ⟨a bathroom *scale*⟩ [Old Norse *skāl* "bowl, scale of a balance"]

[2]**scale** *vb* **1** : to weigh in scales **2** : to have a specified weight

[3]**scale** *n* **1** : one of the small rigid flattened plates forming an outer covering on the body especially of a fish or reptile **2** : a small thin part or structure suggesting a fish scale: as **a** : a modified leaf covering a bud of a seed plant **b** : a small dry flake of skin ⟨dandruff *scales*⟩ **3** : SCALE INSECT **4** : a thin layer, coating, or incrustation forming especially on metal (as iron) ⟨boiler *scale*⟩ [Middle French *escale*, of Germanic origin] — **scaled** \'skāld\ *adj* — **scale•less** \'skāl-ləs\ *adj* — **scale•like** \'skāl-ˌlīk\ *adj*

[4]**scale** *vb* **1** : to remove scale or the scales from ⟨*scale* a boiler⟩ ⟨*scale* fish⟩ **2** : to take off in scales or thin layers **3** : to form scale on **4** : to come off in scales or shed scales : FLAKE **5** : to become encrusted with scale **6** : to throw (a flat object) and cause to sail in the air or skip on the water ⟨*scaling* cards into a hat⟩

[5]**scale** *n* **1** : something graduated especially when used as a measure or rule: as **a** : a series of spaces marked by lines and used to measure distances or to register something (as the height of the mercury in a thermometer) **b** : a divided line on a map or chart indicating the length (as an inch) used to represent a larger unit of measure (as a mile) **c** : an instrument consisting of a strip (as of wood, plastic, or metal) with one or more sets of spaces graduated and numbered on its surface for measuring or laying off distances or dimensions **2** : a basis for a system of numbering ⟨the decimal *scale*⟩ **3** : a graduated series ⟨the *scale* of prices⟩ **4** : the size of a picture, plan, or model of a thing in proportion to the size of the thing itself **5** : relative size or degree ⟨do things on a large *scale*⟩ **6** : a standard by which something can be measured or judged **7** : a graduated series of tones going up or down in pitch [Late Latin *scala* "ladder, staircase", from Latin *scalae*, pl., "stairs, ladder"]

[6]**scale** *vb* **1** : to climb by or as if by means of a ladder or rope **2 a** : to arrange in a graduated series ⟨*scale* a test⟩ **b** : to measure by or as if by a scale **c** : to make, regulate, or estimate according to a rate or standard ⟨*scale* down a budget⟩ **syn** see ASCEND

scale insect *n* : any of numerous small insects that are related to the plant lice, include many destructive plant pests, and have winged males, scale-covered females usually structurally degenerate and permanently attached to the host plant, and young that suck the juices of plants

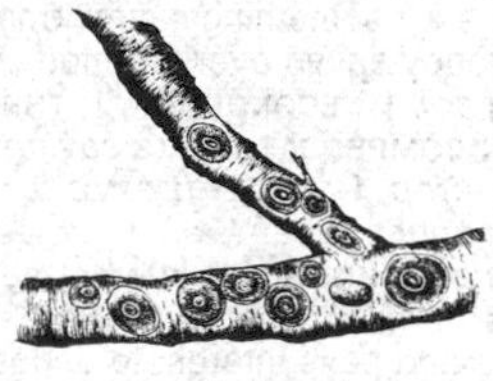
scale insect

scale leaf *n* : a modified usually small and scaly leaf (as of a cypress)

sca•lene \'skā-ˌlēn, skā-'\ *adj* : having the sides unequal ⟨a *scalene* triangle⟩ [Late Latin *scalenus*, from Greek *skalēnos*, literally, "uneven"]

scale•pan \'skāl-ˌpan\ *n* : a pan of a scale for weighing

scal•er \'skā-lər\ *n* : one that scales

scal•lion \'skal-yən\ *n* : a young onion pulled before the bulb has enlarged [Anglo-French *scalun*, derived from Latin *ascalonia caepa* "onion of Ascalon (a seaport in Palestine)"]

[1]**scal•lop** \'skäl-əp, 'skal-\ *n* **1 a** : any of a family of marine bivalve mollusks with the shell radially ribbed **b** : the adductor muscle of a scallop as an article of food **2** : a scallop-shell valve or a similarly shaped dish used for baking **3** : one of a continuous series of circle segments or angular projections forming a border [Middle French *escalope* "shell", of Germanic origin]

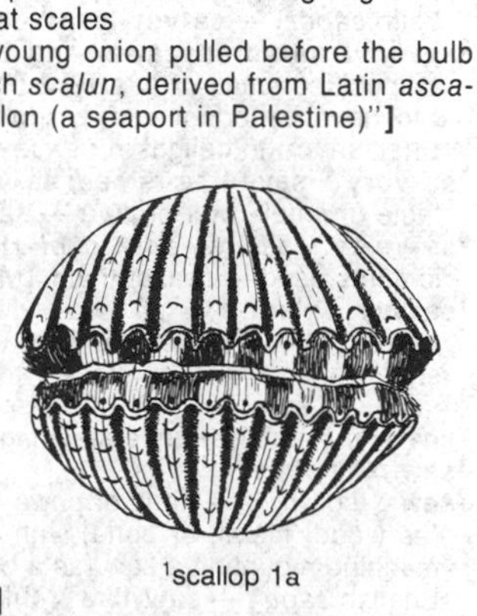
[1]scallop 1a

[2]**scallop** *or* **es•cal•lop** \is-'käl-əp, -'kal-\ *vt* : to bake in a sauce

usually covered with seasoned bread or cracker crumbs ⟨*scalloped* potatoes⟩ **2 :** to shape, cut, or finish in scallops — **scal·lop·er** *n*

scal·ly·wag *variant of* SCALAWAG

[1]**scalp** \ˈskalp\ *n* **1 :** the part of the skin and flesh of the head usually covered with hair **2 :** a part of the human scalp cut or torn from an enemy as a token of victory [of Scandinavian origin]

[2]**scalp** *vt* **1 a :** to deprive of the scalp **b :** to remove an upper or better part from **2 a :** to buy and sell so as to make small quick profits **b :** to buy and resell at greatly increased prices ⟨*scalp* theater tickets⟩ — **scalp·er** *n*

scal·pel \ˈskal-pəl *also* skal-ˈpel\ *n* **:** a small straight thin-bladed knife used especially in surgery [Latin *scalpellum* "small knife", from *scalprum* "chisel, knife", from *scalpere* "to carve"]

scalp lock *n* **:** a long tuft of hair on the crown of the otherwise shaved head of a warrior of some American Indian tribes

scaly \ˈskā-lē\ *adj* **scal·i·er; -est 1 a :** covered with, composed of, or rich in scale or scales **b :** FLAKY 2 **2 :** infested with scale insects ⟨*scaly* fruit⟩ — **scal·i·ness** *n*

[1]**scamp** \ˈskamp\ *n* **1 :** RASCAL 1, ROGUE **2 :** an impish or playful young person [obsolete *scamp* "to roam about idly"]

[2]**scamp** *vt* **:** to perform in a hasty, neglectful, or imperfect manner **:** SKIMP ⟨*scamp* one's work⟩ [perhaps of Scandinavian origin]

scam·per \ˈskam-pər\ *vi* **scam·pered; scam·per·ing** \-pə-ring, -pring\ **:** to run nimbly and playfully [perhaps from obsolete Dutch *schampen* "to flee", from Middle French *escamper*, derived from Latin *ex-* + *campus* "field"] — **scamper** *n*

scan \ˈskan\ *vb* **scanned; scan·ning 1 a :** to read or mark so as to show metrical structure **b :** to conform to a metrical pattern **2 a :** to examine intensively **b :** to make a wide sweeping search of ⟨a fire lookout *scanning* the hills⟩ **c :** to look through or over hastily ⟨*scan* the newspaper⟩ **3 a :** to bring under a moving electron beam for conversion of light and dark image values into corresponding electrical values to be transmitted by television; *also* **:** to move across in successive lines in reproducing a television image ⟨the electron beam *scans* the face of the picture tube⟩ **b :** to direct a succession of radar beams over in searching for a target [Late Latin *scandere*, from Latin, "to climb"] **syn** see SCRUTINIZE — **scan** *n* — **scan·ner** \-ər\ *n*

scan·dal \ˈskan-dl\ *n* **1 :** an offense against faith or morals that causes another to sin **2 :** loss of or damage to reputation caused by actual or apparent violation of morality or propriety **:** DISGRACE ⟨to the *scandal* of the school⟩ **3 a :** something that offends propriety or accepted moral standards or disgraces those associated with it ⟨the slum is a *scandal*⟩ **b :** a person whose conduct offends propriety or morality **4 :** malicious or defamatory gossip ⟨untouched by *scandal*⟩ [Late Latin *scandalum* "stumbling block, offense", from Greek *skandalon*]

scan·dal·ize \ˈskan-də-ˌlīz\ *vt* **1 :** to speak falsely or maliciously of **:** MALIGN **2 :** to offend the moral sense of **:** SHOCK ⟨their actions *scandalized* the neighbors⟩ — **scan·dal·iza·tion** *n* — **scan·dal·iz·er** *n*

scan·dal·mon·ger \ˈskan-dl-ˌməng-gər, -ˌmäng-\ *n* **:** a person who spreads scandal

scan·dal·ous \ˈskan-də-ləs, -dləs\ *adj* **1 :** DEFAMATORY ⟨a *scandalous* story⟩ **2 :** offensive to propriety or morality **:** SHOCKING ⟨*scandalous* behavior⟩ — **scan·dal·ous·ly** *adv* — **scan·dal·ous·ness** *n*

scandal sheet *n* **:** a newspaper or periodical dealing to a large extent in scandal and gossip

Scan·di·na·vian \ˌskan-də-ˈnā-vē-ən, -vyən\ *n* **1 a :** a native or inhabitant of Scandinavia **b :** a person of Scandinavian descent **2 :** the Germanic languages of the Scandinavian peoples including Icelandic, Norwegian, Swedish, and Danish — **Scandinavian** *adj*

scan·di·um \ˈskan-dē-əm\ *n* **:** a silvery white metallic chemical element — see ELEMENT table [New Latin, from Latin *Scandia*, southern part of the Scandinavian peninsula]

scan·sion \ˈskan-chən\ *n* **:** the analysis of verse to show its meter [Late Latin *scansio*, from *scandere* "to scan"]

[1]**scant** \ˈskant\ *adj* **1** *dialect* **:** excessively frugal **:** PARSIMONIOUS **2 a :** barely or scarcely sufficient ⟨paid *scant* attention to me⟩; *esp* **:** not quite coming up to a stated measure ⟨a *scant* cup of milk⟩ **b :** lacking in amplitude or quantity **:** MEAGER, SCANTY ⟨a *scant* amount⟩ **3 :** having a small or insufficient supply ⟨*scant* of breath⟩ [Old Norse *skamt*, neuter of *skammr* "short"] — **scant·ly** *adv* — **scant·ness** *n*

[2]**scant** *adv, dialect* **:** SCARCELY, HARDLY

[3]**scant** *vt* **1 :** to provide with a meager or inadequate portion or share **:** STINT **2 :** to make small, narrow, or meager **:** SKIMP **3 :** to provide an incomplete supply of ⟨*scant* one's efforts⟩ **4 :** to give scant attention to **:** SLIGHT ⟨a subject *scanted* in textbooks⟩

scant·ling \ˈskant-ling, -lən\ *n* **:** a small piece of lumber; *esp* **:** one of the upright pieces in the frame of a house [Middle English *scantilon*, literally, "mason's or carpenter's gauge", from Old North French *escantillon*]

scanty \ˈskant-ē\ *adj* **scant·i·er; -est 1 :** barely enough **2 :** less than normal or needed **:** INSUFFICIENT **syn** see MEAGER — **scant·i·ly** \ˈskant-l-ē\ *adv* — **scant·i·ness** \ˈskant-ē-nəs\ *n*

[1]**scape** \ˈskāp\ *vb* **:** ESCAPE

[2]**scape** *n* **1 :** a leafless flower stalk (as in the tulip) that begins at or beneath the surface of the ground **2 :** the shaft of an animal part (as an antenna or a feather) [Latin *scapus* "shaft, stalk"]

-scape \ˌskāp\ *n combining form* **:** a (specified) type of scene; *also* **:** a pictorial representation of (such a scene) ⟨*moonscape*⟩ [*landscape*]

scape·goat \ˈskāp-ˌgōt\ *n* **1 :** a goat upon whose head are symbolically placed the sins of the people after which he is sent into the wilderness in the biblical ceremony for Yom Kippur **2 :** a person or thing bearing the blame for others [[1]*scape*]

scape·grace \-ˌgrās\ *n* **:** an incorrigible rascal

scap·u·la \ˈskap-yə-lə\ *n, pl* **-lae** \-ˌlē, -ˌlī\ *or* **-las :** SHOULDER BLADE [Latin, "shoulder, shoulder blade"]

[1]**scap·u·lar** \ˈskap-yə-lər\ *n* **1 a :** a long wide band of cloth with an opening for the head worn front and back over the shoulders as part of a monastic habit **b :** a pair of small cloth squares joined by shoulder tapes and worn under the clothing on the breast and back as a sacramental and often also as a badge of a third order or confraternity **2 :** one of the feathers covering the base of a bird's wing [Late Latin *scapulare*, from Latin *scapula* "shoulder"]

[2]**scapular** *adj* **:** of or relating to the shoulder or the shoulder blade

scapular medal *n* **:** a medal worn in place of a sacramental scapular

[1]**scar** \ˈskär\ *n* **1 :** an isolated or protruding rock **2 :** a steep rocky eminence **:** a bare place on the side of a mountain [Old Norse *sker* "skerry"]

[2]**scar** *n* **1 a :** a mark remaining after injured tissue has healed **b :** a mark resembling a scar and usually marking the former point of attachment of some other structure; *esp* **:** one on a stem where a leaf or fruit has separated **2 :** a lasting moral or emotional injury [Middle French *escare* "scab", from Late Latin *eschara*, from Greek, "hearth, scab"] — **scar·less** \-ləs\ *adj*

[3]**scar** *vb* **scarred; scar·ring** *vb* **1 :** to mark with or form a scar **2 :** to do lasting injury to **3 :** to become scarred

scar·ab \ˈskar-əb\ *n* **1 :** a large black or nearly black dung beetle regarded by the ancient Egyptians as symbolic of resurrection and immortality; *also* **:** any of various related beetles **2 :** an ornament or a gem made to represent a scarab [Middle French *scarabee*, from Latin *scarabaeus*]

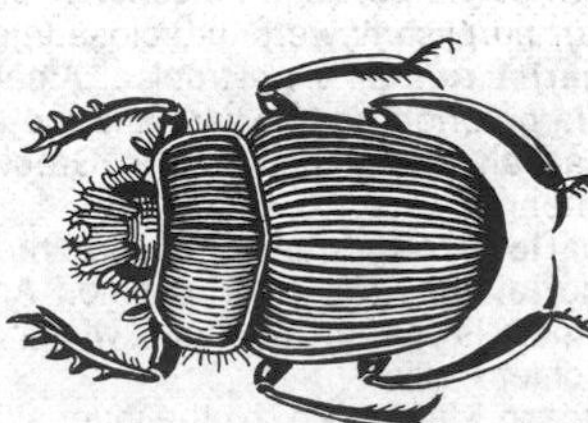

scarab 1

scar·a·mouch *or* **scar·a·mouche** \ˈskar-ə-ˌmüsh, -ˌmüch, -ˌmau̇ch\ *n* **1 :** a cowardly buffoon **2 :** RASCAL, SCAMP [French *Scaramouche*, a stock character in Italian comedy, from Italian *Scaramuccia*]

[1]**scarce** \ˈskeərs, ˈskaərs\ *adj* **:** deficient in quantity or number **:** not plentiful or abundant [Old North French *escars*, derived

from Latin *excerpere* "to pluck out, excerpt"] — **scarce•ness** *n*

²scarce *adv* : SCARCELY, HARDLY

scarce•ly \'sker-slē, 'skar-\ *adv* **1 a** : only just ⟨had *scarcely* got there when they started⟩ **b** : almost not ⟨*scarcely* ever goes out⟩ **2 a** : certainly not ⟨could *scarcely* tell them they were wrong⟩ **b** : probably not ⟨could *scarcely* have found a neater solution⟩

scar•ci•ty \'sker-sət-ē, 'skar-\ *n, pl* **-ties** : the quality or condition of being scarce

¹scare \'skeər, 'skaər\ *vb* **1** : to frighten suddenly : ALARM **2** : to become frightened ⟨they *scare* easily⟩ [Old Norse *skirra*, from *skjarr* "shy, timid"] — **scar•er** *n*

²scare *n* **1** : a sudden fright **2** : a widespread state of alarm : PANIC

scare•crow \'skeər-,krō, 'skaər-\ *n* **1 a** : an object usually suggesting a human figure that is set up to scare birds away from crops **b** : something frightening but harmless **2** : a skinny or ragged person

scare•head \-,hed\ *n* : a big, sensational, or alarming newspaper headline

scare•mon•ger \-,məng-gər, -,mäng-\ *n* : ALARMIST

scare up *vt* : to bring to light or get together with considerable labor or difficulty ⟨managed to *scare up* the necessary money⟩

¹scarf \'skärf\ *n, pl* **scarves** \'skärvz\ *or* **scarfs** \'skärfs\ **1** : a broad band (as of cloth) worn about the shoulders, around the neck, over the head, or about the waist **2** : TIPPET 3 **3** : RUNNER 6 [Old North French *escarpe* "sash, sling"]

²scarf *n* **1** : either of the ends that fit together to form a scarf joint **2** : a joint made by beveling, halving, or notching two pieces to correspond and lapping and bolting them [Middle English *skarf*]

³scarf *or* **scarph** \'skärf\ *vt* : to unite by a scarf joint

scarf•pin \'skärf-,pin\ *n* : TIEPIN

scarf•skin \'skärf-,skin\ *n* : EPIDERMIS 1, CUTICLE; *esp* : that about the base of a nail [¹*scarf*]

scar•i•fy \'skar-ə-,fī, 'sker-\ *vt* **-fied**; **-fy•ing** **1** : to make scratches or small cuts in ⟨*scarify* skin for vaccination⟩ ⟨*scarify* seeds to help them germinate⟩ **2** : to lacerate the feelings of : FLAY [Middle French *scarifier*, from Late Latin *scarificare*, from Latin *scarifare*, from Greek *skariphasthai* "to scratch an outline, sketch"] — **scar•i•fi•ca•tion** \,skar-ə-fə-'kā-shən, ,sker-\ *n* — **scar•i•fi•er** \'skar-ə-,fī-ər, 'sker-, -,fīr\ *n*

scar•la•ti•na \,skär-lə-'tē-nə\ *n* : a usually mild scarlet fever [New Latin, from Medieval Latin *scarlata* "scarlet"] — **scar•la•ti•nal** \-'tēn-l\ *adj*

¹scar•let \'skär-lət\ *n* **1** : scarlet cloth or clothes **2** : a bright red [Medieval Latin *scarlata*, from Persian *sagalāt*, a kind of rich cloth]

²scarlet *adj* : bright red

scarlet fever *n* : an acute contagious disease caused by a blood-attacking streptococcus and marked by fever, inflammation of the nose, throat, and mouth, and a red rash

scarlet pimpernel *n* : a common pimpernel having scarlet, white, or purplish flowers that close in cloudy weather

scarlet runner *n* : a tropical American high-climbing bean with large bright red flowers and red-and-black seeds grown widely as an ornamental and in Great Britain as a preferred table bean

scarlet sage *n* : any of several red-flowered salvias

scarlet tanager *n* : a common American tanager of which the male is scarlet with black wings and the female and young are chiefly olive

¹scarp \'skärp\ *n* **1** : the inner side of a ditch below the parapet of a fortification **2 a** : a line of cliffs produced by faulting or erosion **b** : a low steep slope along a beach caused by wave erosion [Italian *scarpa*]

²scarp *vt* : to cut down vertically or to a steep slope

scar tissue *n* : connective tissue forming a bodily scar

scary *also* **scar•ey** \'skeər-ē, 'skaər-\ *adj* **scar•i•er**; **-est** **1** : causing fright : ALARMING ⟨a *scary* movie⟩ **2** : easily scared : TIMID **3** : marked by fear ⟨a *scary* feeling⟩

¹scat \'skat\ *vi* **scat•ted**; **scat•ting** **1** : to go away quickly — often used interjectionally to drive away an animal (as a cat) **2** : to move fast : SCOOT [*scat*, interj. used to drive away a cat]

²scat *n* : jazz singing with nonsense syllables [perhaps imitative]

³scat *vi* **scat•ted**; **scat•ting** : to improvise nonsense syllables to an instrumental accompaniment : sing scat

¹scathe \'skāth\ *n* : HARM, INJURY [Old Norse *skathi*] — **scathe•less** \-ləs\ *adj*

²scathe *vt* **1** : to do harm to; *esp* : to injure by fire **2** : to assail with withering denunciation

scath•ing \'skā-thing\ *adj* : bitterly severe ⟨a *scathing* rebuke⟩ — **scath•ing•ly** \-thing-lē\ *adv*

sca•tol•o•gy \skə-'täl-ə-jē, ska-\ *n* : interest in or treatment of obscene matters especially in literature [Greek *skat-*, *skōr* "dung"] — **scat•o•log•i•cal** \,skat-l-'äj-i-kəl\ *adj*

scat•ter \'skat-ər\ *vb* **1** : to cause to separate widely **2** : to distribute irregularly **3** : to sow broadcast : STREW **4** : to diffuse, disperse, or reflect (a beam of radiation) in a random manner **5** : to separate from each other and go in various directions ⟨we all *scattered* after graduation⟩ **6** : to occur or fall irregularly or at random [Middle English *scateren*] — **scat•ter•er** \-ər-ər\ *n*

• **syn** SCATTER, DISPERSE, DISPEL, DISSIPATE mean to cause to separate or break up. SCATTER implies forcefully driving parts or units irregularly in many directions; DISPERSE implies a wider separation and complete breaking up of mass or group; DISPEL stresses a driving away or getting rid of as if by scattering; DISSIPATE stresses complete disintegration or dissolution and final disappearance.

scat•ter•brain \-,brān\ *n* : a giddy heedless person incapable of concentration — **scat•ter•brained** \-,brānd\ *adj*

scat•tered \'skat-ərd\ *adj* **1** : not closely associated or organized ⟨*scattered* thoughts⟩ **2** : separated by or occurring at wide irregular intervals ⟨*scattered* showers⟩ **3** : spread over a wide area ⟨a *scattered* settlement⟩ **syn** see INFREQUENT

¹scat•ter•ing \'skat-ə-ring\ *n* **1** : an act or process in which something scatters or is scattered **2** : something scattered; *esp* : a small number or quantity interspersed here and there ⟨a *scattering* of visitors⟩

²scattering *adj* **1** : going in various directions **2** : found or placed far apart and in no order — **scat•ter•ing•ly** *adv*

scatter pin *n* : a small pin used as jewelry and worn usually in groups of two or more on a woman's dress

scatter rug *n* : a rug of such a size that several can be used (as to fill vacant places) in a room

scaup \'skȯp\ *n, pl* **scaup** *or* **scaups** : any of several diving ducks [perhaps from *scalp* "bed of shellfish"; from its fondness for shellfish]

scav•enge \'skav-inj\ *vb* **1** : to remove dirt or refuse from an area **2** : to salvage (usable material) from what has been discarded [back-formation from *scavenger*]

scav•en•ger \'skav-ən-jer\ *n* **1** *chiefly British* : a person employed to remove dirt and refuse from streets **2** : one that scavenges **3** : an organism (as a vulture) that feeds habitually on refuse or carrion [Middle English *skawager* "collector of a toll on goods sold by nonresident merchants", from *skawage* "toll on goods sold by nonresident merchants", from Old North French *escauwage* "inspection"]

△ **origin** In the 14th, 15th, and 16th centuries many English towns and cities levied a tax on goods shown for sale by nonresident merchants in order to put outsiders at a disadvantage in their trade in comparison with local merchants. Middle English *skawage*, the name for this tax, was borrowed from Old North French *escauwage*, "inspection", a word of Germanic origin, related to English *show*. The *skawagers* (or later *scavengers*) of London were officers who collected the *skawage*. The responsibility for keeping the streets clean later fell on their shoulders as well. Now anyone who collects junk is a *scavenger*.

scavenger hunt *n* : a party contest in which players are sent out usually in pairs to obtain without buying unusual objects within a time limit

sce•nar•io \sə-'nar-ē-,ō, -'ner-\ *n, pl* **-i•os** **1 a** : an outline or synopsis of a play **b** : the libretto of an opera **2** : SCREENPLAY **3** : an account or synopsis of a projected course of action or events [Italian, from Latin *scaenarium*, from *scaena*, *scena* "stage, scene"]

sce•nar•ist \-'nar-əst, -'ner-\ *n* : a writer of scenarios

¹scend \'send\ *vi* : to rise or heave upward under the influence of a natural force (as on a wave) [alteration of *send*]

²scend *n* **1** : the upward movement of a pitching ship **2** : the lift of a wave

scene \'sēn\ *n* **1** : one of the subdivisions of a play: as **a** : a division of an act presenting continuous action in one place **b**

: a single situation or unit of dialogue in a play **c** : a motion picture or television episode or sequence **2 a** : a stage setting ⟨change *scenes*⟩ **b** : a view or sight having pictorial quality ⟨a winter *scene*⟩ **3** : the place of an occurrence or action : LOCALE ⟨*scene* of a riot⟩ **4** : an exhibition of anger or indecorous behavior ⟨create a *scene*⟩ [Middle French, "stage", from Latin *scena* "stage, scene", from Greek *skēnē* "temporary shelter, tent, building forming the background for a dramatic performance, stage"] — **behind the scenes 1** : out of public view : in secret **2** : in a position to see or control the hidden workings ⟨the person *behind the scenes*⟩

scen•ery \'sēn-rē, -ə-rē\ *n* **1** : the painted scenes or hangings and accessories used on a theater stage **2** : a picturesque view or landscape ⟨mountain *scenery*⟩

scene•shift•er \'sēn-ˌshif-tər\ *n* : a worker who moves the scenes in a theater

scene–steal•er \-ˌstē-lər\ *n* : an actor who is not the intended center of attraction but who draws attention to himself

sce•nic \'sē-nik\ *adj* **1** : of or relating to the stage, a stage setting, or stage representation ⟨*scenic* effects⟩ **2** : of, relating to, or marked by natural scenery ⟨a *scenic* route⟩ **3** : representing graphically an action, event, or episode ⟨a *scenic* frieze⟩ — **sce•ni•cal** \-ni-kəl\ *adj* — **sce•ni•cal•ly** \-ni-kə-lē, -klē\ *adv*

scenic railway *n* : a miniature railway (as in an amusement park) with artificial scenery along the way

[1]scent \'sent\ *vt* **1 a** : SMELL ⟨the dog *scented* a rabbit⟩ **b** : to get or have an inkling of ⟨*scent* trouble⟩ **2** : to imbue or fill with odor ⟨*scent* a handkerchief⟩ [Middle French *sentir* "to feel, smell", from Latin *sentire* "to perceive, feel"]

[2]scent *n* **1 a** : an odor left by an animal on a surface passed over; *also* : a course of pursuit or discovery ⟨throw one off the *scent*⟩ **b** : a characteristic or particular and usually agreeable odor **2 a** : sense of smell ⟨a keen *scent*⟩ **b** : power of detection ⟨a *scent* for heresy⟩ **3** : INKLING, INTIMATION ⟨a *scent* of trouble⟩ **4** : PERFUME 2 **5** : bits of paper dropped in the game of hare and hounds **6** : an odorous lure for an animal **syn** see SMELL

scent•ed *adj* : having scent; *esp* : PERFUMED

scent•less \'sent-ləs\ *adj* : lacking scent; *esp* : ODORLESS — **scent•less•ness** *n*

scep•ter \'sep-tər\ *n* **1** : a staff or baton borne by a sovereign as an emblem of authority **2** : royal or imperial authority : SOVEREIGNTY [Old French *ceptre*, from Latin *sceptrum*, from Greek *skēptron*] — **scep•tered** \-tərd\ *adj*

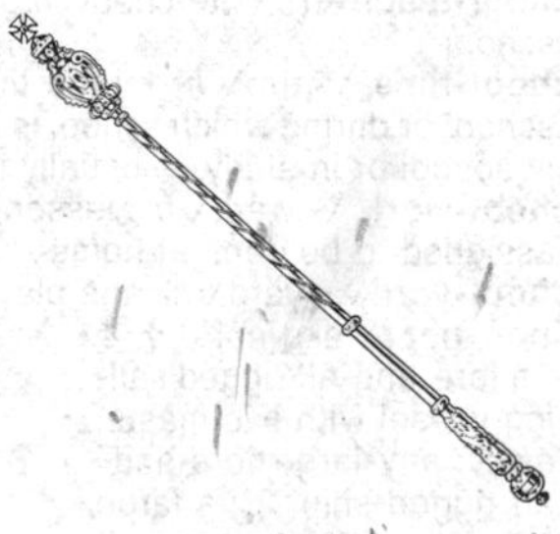

scepter 1

scep•tic \'skep-tik\ *variant of* SKEPTIC

[1]sched•ule \'skej-ül, -əl, *Canadian also* 'shej-, *British usually* 'shed-yül\ *n* **1 a** : a written or printed list, catalog, or inventory **b** : TIMETABLE **2** : PROGRAM 3, AGENDA [Middle French *cedule* "slip of paper, note", from Late Latin *schedula* "slip of paper", from Latin *scheda* "sheet of papyrus"]

[2]schedule *vt* **1** : to place in or as if in a schedule ⟨*schedule* a meeting⟩ **2** : to make a schedule of

schee•lite \'shā-ˌlīt\ *n* : a mineral $CaWO_4$ that is a souce of tungsten and its compounds [German *scheelit*, from Karl W. *Scheele*, died 1786, Swedish chemist]

sche•mat•ic \ski-'mat-ik\ *adj* : of, relating to, or forming a scheme, plan, or diagram : DIAGRAMMATIC — **scematic** *n* — **sche•mat•i•cal•ly** \-'mat-i-kə-lē, -klē\ *adv*

sche•ma•tize \'skē-mə-ˌtīz\ *vt* **1** : to form or form into a scheme or systematic arrangement **2** : to express or depict schematically — **sche•ma•ti•za•tion** \ˌskē-mət-ə-'zā-shən\ *n*

[1]scheme \'skēm\ *n* **1** : a graphic sketch or outline **2** : a concise statement or table **3** : a plan or program of action; *esp* : a crafty or secret one **4** : a systematic or organized design ⟨the color *scheme* of a room⟩ ⟨their whole *scheme* of life⟩ [Latin *schemat-*, *schema* "arrangement, figure", from Greek *schēmat-*, *schēma*, from *echein* "to have, hold, be in (such) a position"] **syn** see PLAN

[2]scheme *vb* **1** : to form a scheme for **2** : to form plans; *also* : to engage in intrigue : PLOT — **schem•er** *n*

schem•ing *adj* : given to forming schemes; *esp* : shrewdly devious and intriguing

scher•zan•do \skert-'sän-dō\ *adv or adj* : in a sportive manner : PLAYFULLY — used as a direction in music indicating style and tempo ⟨allegretto *scherzando*⟩ [Italian, from *scherzare* "to joke", of Germanic origin]

scher•zo \'skert-sō\ *n, pl* **scherzos** *or* **scher•zi** \-sē\ : a sprightly humorous instrumental musical composition or movement commonly in quick triple time [Italian, literally, "joke", from *scherzare* "to joke"]

Schick test \'shik-\ *n* : a serological test to determine whether an individual is susceptible to diphtheria [Béla *Schick*, died 1967, American pediatrician]

schil•ler \'shil-ər\ *n* : a bronzy iridescent luster (as of a mineral) [German]

schil•ling \'shil-ing\ *n* **1** : the basic monetary unit of Austria **2** : a coin representing one schilling [German]

schism \'siz-əm, 'skiz-\ *n* **1** : DIVISION 5, SEPARATION; *also* : lack of harmony : DISCORD **2 a** : formal division in or separation from a church or religious body **b** : the religious offense of promoting schism [Middle French *cisme*, from Late Latin *schismat-*, *schisma*, from Greek, "cleft, division", from *schizein* "to split"]

[1]schis•mat•ic \siz-'mat-ik, skiz-\ *n* : one who creates or takes part in schism

[2]schismatic *adj* : of, relating to, or guilty of schism — **schis•mat•i•cal** \-'mat-i-kəl\ *adj* — **schis•mat•i•cal•ly** \-i-kə-lē, -klē\ *adv*

schis•ma•tist \'siz-mət-əst, 'skiz-\ *n* : SCHISMATIC

schis•ma•tize \-mə-ˌtīz\ *vb* : to take part in or induce into schism

schist \'shist\ *n* : a metamorphic crystalline rock that can be split along approximately parallel planes [French *schiste*, derived from Greek *schizein* "to split"] — **schis•tose** \'shis-ˌtōs\ *adj*

schis•to•some \'shis-tə-ˌsōm\ *n* : any of various elongated trematode worms with the sexes separate that mostly parasitize the blood vessels of birds and mammals and in man cause serious diseases [Greek *schistos* "that may be split" (from *schizein* "to split") + *sōma* "body"] — **schistosome** *adj*

schis•to•so•mi•a•sis \ˌshis-tə-sə-'mī-ə-səs\ *n, pl* **-a•ses** \-ə-ˌsēz\ : infestation with or disease caused by schistosomes

schiz- *or* **schizo-** *combining form* **1** : split : cleft ⟨*schizo*carp⟩ **2** : characterized by or involving cleavage ⟨*schizo*gony⟩ [Greek *schizein* "to split"]

schiz•o•carp \'skiz-ə-ˌkärp, 'skit-sə-\ *n* : a dry compound fruit that splits at maturity into closed one-seeded carpels — **schiz•o•car•pous** \ˌskiz-ə-'kär-pəs, ˌskit-sə-\ *adj*

schiz•oid \'skit-ˌsȯid\ *adj* : characterized by a personality exhibiting shyness, oversensitivity, daydreaming, avoidance of competition or close relationships with people, and often eccentric behavior — **schizoid** *n*

schiz•o•phre•nia \ˌskit-sə-'frē-nē-ə\ *n* : a psychosis characterized by abnormalities of thought, emotion, and behavior including distorted perception of reality, withdrawal from social interaction, emotions inappropriate to the thoughts or behavior associated with them, delusions, and hallucinations [New Latin, from *schiz-* + Greek *phrēn* "mind"] — **schiz•o•phren•ic** \-'fren-ik\ *adj or n*

schle•miel \shlə-'mēl\ *n* : an unlucky bungler : CHUMP [Yiddish *shlumiel*]

schlock \'shläk\ *adj* : of low quality or value ⟨*schlock* merchandise⟩ [Yiddish *shlak*, from *shlak* "curse, cheap merchandise", literally, "blow", from Middle High German *slag*, *slac*] — **schlock** *n*

schm- *or* **shm-** \shm\ *combining form* — used to form a rhyming term of derision by replacing the initial consonant or consonant cluster of a word or by preceding the initial vowel ⟨art, *schm*art, that's just kitsch⟩ ⟨fancy, *schm*ancy, I prefer plain⟩ [Yiddish *shm-*]

schmaltz *or* **schmalz** \'shmȯlts\ *n* : sentimental or florid music or art [Yiddish *shmalts*, literally, "rendered fat", from Middle High German *smalz*] — **schmaltzy** \'shmȯlt-sē\ *adj*

\ə\ **a**but	\aů\ **ou**t	\i\ t**i**p	\ȯ\ s**aw**	\ů\ f**oo**t
\ər\ furth**er**	\ch\ **ch**in	\ī\ l**i**fe	\ȯi\ c**oi**n	\y\ **y**et
\a\ m**a**t	\e\ p**e**t	\j\ **j**ob	\th\ **th**in	\yü\ f**ew**
\ā\ t**a**ke	\ē\ **ea**sy	\ng\ si**ng**	\th\ **th**is	\yů\ c**u**re
\ä\ c**o**t, c**a**rt	\g\ **g**o	\ō\ b**o**ne	\ü\ f**oo**d	\zh\ vi**si**on

schmear \'shmiər\ *n* : a mass or body of similar things — usually used in the phrase *the whole schmear* [Yiddish *shmir* "smear", from *shmiren* "to smear", from Middle High German *smiren*]

schmuck *or* **shmuck** \'shmək\ *n* : a stupid, naive, or foolish person [Yiddish *shmok* "penis, fool", from German *schmuck* "adornment"]

schnapps \'shnaps\ *n, pl* **schnapps** : any of various distilled liquors; *esp* : strong Holland gin [German *schnaps*]

schnau•zer \'shnau̇t-sər; 'shnau̇-zər, 'snau̇-\ *n* : any of an old German breed of terriers with a long head, small ears, and wiry coat [German, from *schnauze* "snout"]

schnauzer

schnit•zel \'shnit-səl, 'snit-\ *n* : a seasoned and garnished veal cutlet [German, "cutlet, shaving, chip"]

schnoz•zle \'shnäz-əl, 'snäz-\ *n, slang* : NOSE [probably from Yiddish *shnoitsl*, from *shnoits* "snout", from German *schnauze*]

scho•la can•to•rum \ˌskō-lə-ˌkan-'tōr-əm, -'tȯr-\ *n, pl* **scholae cantorum** \-ˌlē-, -ˌlā-, -ˌlī-\ : a liturgical choir or choir school [Medieval Latin, "school of singers"]

schol•ar \'skäl-ər\ *n* **1** : one who attends a school or studies under a teacher : PUPIL **2 a** : one who has done advanced study in a special field **b** : a learned person **3** : a holder of a scholarship [Old English *scolere* and Old French *escoler*, from Medieval Latin *scholaris*, derived from Latin *schola* "school"]

schol•ar•ly \-ər-lē\ *adj* : characteristic of or suitable to learned persons : LEARNED, ACADEMIC

schol•ar•ship \-ər-ˌship\ *n* **1** : financial aid given to a student (as by a college or foundation) to assist in the cost of education **2** : the character, qualities, or attainments of a scholar : LEARNING

¹scho•las•tic \skə-'las-tik\ *adj* **1 a** *often cap* : of or relating to Scholasticism ⟨*scholastic* theology⟩ **b** : excessively dogmatic or formal in instruction : PEDANTIC **2** : of or relating to schools or scholars [Latin *scholasticus* "of a school", from Greek *scholastikos*, derived from *scholē* "school"] — **scho•las•ti•cal•ly** \-ti-kə-lē, -klē\ *adv*

²scholastic *n* **1** *cap* : a Scholastic philosopher **2** : a person who prefers or uses scholastic or traditional methods (as in art)

scho•las•ti•cism \skə-'las-tə-ˌsiz-əm\ *n* **1** *cap* : a dominant movement in medieval thought typically using methods of reasoning adapted from Aristotle to interpret systematically the dogmas of Christian faith **2** : close adherence to traditional teachings or methods (as of a school or sect)

scho•li•ast \'skō-lē-ˌast, -lē-əst\ *n* : a maker of scholia : COMMENTATOR, ANNOTATOR [Middle Greek *scholiastēs*, derived from Greek *scholion* "scholium"]

scho•li•um \'skō-lē-əm\ *n, pl* **-lia** \-lē-ə\ *or* **-li•ums 1** : a marginal annotation or comment (as on the text of a classic by an early grammarian) **2** : explanatory or elaborative matter appended to but not essential to a demonstration or a train of reasoning [New Latin, from Greek *scholion* "comment, scholium", from *scholē* "lecture, school"]

¹school \'skül\ *n* **1 a** : a place or establishment for teaching and learning ⟨a *school* of design⟩ ⟨public *schools*⟩ **b** : a faculty or division of an institution of higher learning devoted to teaching, study, and research in a particular field of knowledge ⟨graduate *school*⟩ ⟨the *school* of law⟩ **2** : the physical plant of a school : SCHOOLHOUSE **3 a** : the process of learning or being instructed at a school ⟨found *school* very difficult⟩ **b** : attendance at a school ⟨my last year of *school*⟩ **c** : a session of school ⟨missed *school* yesterday⟩ **d** : the students or the students and faculty of a school ⟨is popular with the whole *school*⟩ **4** : persons holding the same opinions and beliefs or accepting the same intellectual methods or leadership ⟨certain *schools* of thought⟩ [Old English *scōl*, from Latin *schola*, from Greek *scholē* "leisure, discussion, lecture, school"]

△ **origin** The original meaning of the Greek word *scholē*, from which our *school* is derived, was "leisure". To the Greeks it seemed only natural to occupy one's leisure with learning and thinking, and *scholē* came to mean "a place for learning" as well as "leisure". The Romans borrowed the Greek word as *schola* and employed Greek slaves as teachers. Christian missionaries later established schools throughout Europe, and Latin *schola* became Old English *scōl*.

²school *vt* : TEACH, TRAIN; *esp* : to drill in or habituate to something ⟨*school* oneself in patience⟩

³school *n* : a large number of aquatic animals of one kind (as bass) swimming together [Dutch *schole*]

⁴school *vi* : to swim or feed in a school ⟨bluefish are *schooling*⟩

school age *n* : the period of life during which a child is considered mentally and physically fit to attend school and is commonly required to do so by law

school•bag \'skül-ˌbag\ *n* : a bag for carrying schoolbooks and school supplies

school board *n* : a board in charge of local public schools

school•book \'skül-ˌbu̇k\ *n* : a school textbook

school•boy \-ˌbȯi\ *n* : a boy attending elementary or secondary school

school bus *n* : a vehicle used for transporting children to or from school or on activities connected with school

school•child \'skül-ˌchīld\ *n* : a child attending school

school•fel•low \-ˌfel-ō\ *n* : SCHOOLMATE

school•girl \-ˌgərl\ *n* : a girl attending elementary or secondary school

school•house \-ˌhau̇s\ *n* : a building used as a school

school•ing *n* **1** : instruction in school : EDUCATION **2** : the cost of instruction and maintenance at school **3** : the training of an animal and especially a horse to service

School•man \'skül-mən, -ˌman\ *n* : SCHOLASTIC 1

school•marm \-ˌmärm, -ˌmäm\ *or* **school•ma'am** \-ˌmäm, -ˌmam\ *n* **1** : a woman schoolteacher especially in an old-type rural or small-town school **2** : a person who exhibits characteristics (as pedantry and priggishness) popularly attributed to schoolteachers [*school* + *marm*, alteration of *ma'am*]

school•mas•ter \-ˌmas-tər\ *n* : a male schoolteacher

school•mate \-ˌmāt\ *n* : a school companion

school•mis•tress \-ˌmis-trəs\ *n* : a woman schoolteacher

school•room \-ˌrüm, -ˌru̇m\ *n* : CLASSROOM

school•teach•er \-ˌtē-chər\ *n* : a person who teaches in a school

school•time \-ˌtīm\ *n* **1** : the time for beginning a session of school or during which school is held **2** : the period of life spent in school or in study — usually used in pl.

school•work \-ˌwərk\ *n* : lessons done in classes at school or assigned to be done at home

school•yard \-ˌyärd\ *n* : the playground of a school

schoo•ner \'skü-nər\ *n* **1** : a fore-and-aft rigged sailing vessel with two masts; *also* : any large fore-and-aft rigged ship **2** : a large tall glass (as for beer) **3** : PRAIRIE SCHOONER [origin unknown]

schooner 1

schot•tische \'shät-ish, shä-'tēsh\ *n* **1** : a round dance similar to but slower than the polka **2** : music for the schottische [German, from *schottisch* "Scottish"]

schuss \'shu̇s, 'shüs\ *n* **1** : a straight high-speed run on skis **2** : a straightaway downhill skiing course [German, literally, "shot"] — **schuss** *vb*

schwa \'shwä\ *n* **1** : an unstressed vowel that is the usual sound of the first and last vowels of the English word *America* **2** : the symbol ə commonly used for a schwa and sometimes also for a similarly articulated stressed vowel (as in *cut*) [German, from Hebrew *shĕwā*]

sci•at•ic \sī-'at-ik\ *adj* **1** : of, relating to, or situated near the hip **2** : of, relating to, or caused by sciatica [Middle French *sciatique*, from Late Latin *sciaticus*, from Latin *ischiadicus* "of sciatica", from Greek *ischiadikos*, from *ischiad-*, *ischias* "sciatica", from *ischion* "ischium"]

sci•at•i•ca \sī-'at-i-kə\ *n* : pain along the course of a sciatic nerve especially in the back of a thigh; *also* : pain in or near the hips [Medieval Latin, from Late Latin *sciaticus* "sciatic"]

sciatic nerve *n* : either of the pair of largest nerves in the body each of which supplies a leg and the pelvic region and passes out of the pelvis and down the back of the thigh

sci•ence \'sī-əns\ *n* **1 a :** a department of systematized knowledge that is an object of study ⟨the *science* of theology⟩; *esp* **:** one of the natural sciences ⟨chemistry is a *science*⟩ **b :** something (as a sport or technique) that may be studied or learned like systematized knowledge **2 :** knowledge covering general truths or the operation of general laws especially as obtained and tested through the scientific method [Middle French, from Latin *scientia*, from *sciens* "having knowledge", from *scire* "to know"]

science fiction *n* **:** fiction dealing with the impact of actual or imagined scientific developments upon society or individuals; *also* **:** futuristic fiction using an aspect of science as an essential component of the plot

sci•en•tial \sī-'en-chəl\ *adj* **1 :** relating to or producing knowledge or science **2 :** having efficient knowledge **:** CAPABLE

sci•en•tif•ic \,sī-ən-'tif-ik\ *adj* **:** of, relating to, or exhibiting the methods or principles of science — **sci•en•tif•i•cal•ly** \-'tif-i-kə-lē, -klē\ *adv*

scientific method *n* **:** principles and procedures for the systematic pursuit of knowledge involving the recognition and formulation of a problem, the collection of data through observation and experiment, and the formulation and testing of hypotheses

scientific notation *n* **:** the representation of numbers as the product of a decimal between 1 and 10 and a power of 10

sci•en•tism \'sī-ən-,tiz-əm\ *n* **1 :** methods and attitudes typical of or attributed to the natural scientist **2 :** an exaggerated trust in scientific and especially materialistic methods (as for seeking knowledge or solving problems)

sci•en•tist \'sī-ən-təst\ *n* **1 :** one learned in science and especially natural science **:** a scientific investigator **2** *cap* **:** CHRISTIAN SCIENTIST

sci•en•tis•tic \,sī-ən-'tis-tik\ *adj* **1 :** professedly scientific **2 :** relating to or characterized by scientism

scil•la \'sil-ə, 'skil-ə\ *n* **:** any of a genus of Old World bulbous herbs of the lily family often grown for their clusters of pink, blue, or white flowers [Latin, "squill"]

scim•i•tar \'sim-ət-ər, -ə-,tär\ *n* **:** a curved sword used especially by Arabs and Turks [Italian *scimitarra*]

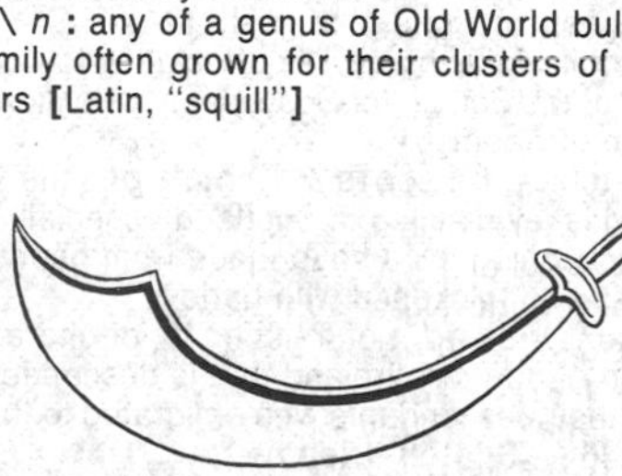

scimitar

scin•til•la \sin-'til-ə\ *n* **:** a very small amount **:** IOTA, TRACE [Latin]

scin•til•late \'sint-l-,āt\ *vi* **1 :** to emit quick flashes of light; *also* **:** SPARKLE 1, TWINKLE **2 :** to perform brilliantly [Latin *scintillare* "to sparkle", from *scintilla* "spark"] **syn** see GLISTEN — **scin•til•lant** \-l-ənt\ *adj* — **scin•til•lant•ly** *adv* — **scin•til•la•tion** \,sint-l-'ā-shən\ *n* — **scin•til•la•tor** \'sint-l-,āt-ər\ *n*

scintillation counter *n* **:** a device for detecting and registering individual scintillations (as in radioactive emission)

sci•o•lism \'sī-ə-,liz-əm\ *n* **:** a superficial show of learning [Late Latin *sciolus* "one whose knowledge is superficial", from Latin *scius* "knowing", from *scire* "to know"] — **sci•o•list** \-ləst\ *n* — **sci•o•lis•tic** \,sī-ə-'lis-tik\ *adj*

sci•on *also* **ci•on** \'sī-ən\ *n* **1 :** a detached living portion of a plant joined to a stock in grafting and usually supplying only aerial parts to a graft **2 :** DESCENDANT, CHILD ⟨a *scion* of a royal stock⟩ [Middle French, *cion*, of Germanic origin]

scis•sion \'sizh-ən\ *n* **:** a dividing of or split in a group or union [French, "division, split", from Late Latin *scissio*, from Latin *scindere* "to split"]

[1]**scis•sor** \'siz-ər\ *n* **:** SCISSORS [Middle French *cisoire*, from Late Latin *cisorium* "cutting instrument", derived from Latin *caedere* "to cut"]

[2]**scissor** *vt* **:** to cut, cut up, or cut off with scissors

scis•sors \'siz-ərz\ *n sing or pl* **1 :** a cutting instrument having two blades so fastened together that the sharp edges slide past each other **2 :** a gymnastic or wrestling feat in which the leg movements suggest the action of scissors

scissors kick *n* **:** a swimming kick used especially in the sidestroke in which the legs come together like scissors

scler- *or* **sclero-** *combining form* **:** hard ⟨*scler*ite⟩ [Greek *sklēros*]

sclera \'skler-ə\ *n* **:** the dense fibrous white or bluish white tissue that covers that portion of the eyeball not covered by the cornea [New Latin, from Greek *sklēros* "hard"]

scler•e•id \'skler-ē-əd\ *n* **:** a supporting cell of a plant that is lignified and often mineralized — called also *stone cell* [derived from *sclerenchyma*]

scle•ren•chy•ma \sklə-'reng-kə-mə\ *n* **:** a protective or supporting tissue in higher plants composed of cells with walls thickened and lignified and often mineralized — compare COLLENCHYMA [*scler-* + *-enchyma* (as in *parenchyma*)] — **scler•en•chy•ma•tous** \,skler-ən-'kim-ət-əs, -'kī-mət-\ *adj*

scler•ite \'skliər-,īt, 'skleər-\ *n* **:** a hard chitinous or calcareous plate or piece (as of the arthropod skeleton)

scle•ro•sis \sklə-'rō-səs\ *n* **:** a usually pathological hardening of tissue especially from increase of connective tissue

scle•rot•ic \sklə-'rät-ik\ *adj* **1 :** being or relating to the sclera **2 :** of, relating to, or affected with or as if with sclerosis

[1]**scoff** \'skäf, 'skȯf\ *n* **:** an expression of scorn, derision, or contempt [Middle English *scof*]

[2]**scoff** *vb* **:** to show or treat with contempt by derisive acts or words **:** MOCK — **scoff•er** *n*

• **syn** SCOFF, SNEER, JEER mean to show contempt in derision or mockery. SCOFF implies insolent or irreverent mockery or derision ⟨*scoffed* at the coach's training rules⟩ SNEER implies an ill-natured contempt often half concealed and conveyed only in the tone of voice or facial expression; JEER suggests loud laughter and coarse or vulgar derision.

scoff•law \-,lȯ\ *n* **:** a contemptuous law violator

[1]**scold** \'skōld\ *n* **1 :** one addicted to abusive language **2 :** one that scolds habitually or persistently [Middle English *scald*, *scold*]

[2]**scold** *vb* **1 :** to find fault noisily **2 :** to rebuke severely or angrily — **scold•er** *n*

sco•lex \'skō-,leks\ *n, pl* **sco•li•ces** *also* **sco•le•ces** \-lə-,sēz\ *or* **sco•lex•es** \-,lek-səz\ **:** the head of a tapeworm [Greek *skōlēx* "worm"]

sco•li•o•sis \,skō-lē-'ō-səs, ,skäl-ē-\ *n, pl* **-o•ses** \-,sēz\ **:** a lateral curvature of the spine — compare KYPHOSIS, LORDOSIS [Greek *skoliōsis* "crookedness of a bodily part", from *skolios* "crooked"] — **sco•li•ot•ic** \-'ät-ik\ *adj*

sconce \'skäns\ *n* **:** a candlestick or group of candlesticks mounted on a plaque and fastened to a wall [Middle French *esconse* "screened lantern", from *escondre* "to hide", from Latin *abscondere*]

sconce

scone \'skōn, 'skän\ *n* **:** a quick bread usually made with oatmeal or barley flour and baked on a griddle [perhaps from Dutch *schoonbrood* "fine white bread", from *schoon* "pure, clean" + *brood* "bread"]

[1]**scoop** \'sküp\ *n* **1 a :** a large shovel (as for shoveling coal) **b :** a tool or utensil shaped like a shovel or a deep spoon for taking up a portion of a loose or soft material ⟨an ice cream *scoop*⟩ **c :** a cutting or gouging tool with a rounded blade **2 :** an act or the action of scooping **:** a motion made with or as if with a scoop **3 a :** the amount held by a scoop ⟨a *scoop* of sugar⟩ **b :** a hole made by scooping **4 :** information of immediate interest; *also* **:** an exclusive news report [Dutch *schope*] — **scoop•ful** \-,fu̇l\ *n*

[2]**scoop** *vt* **1 :** to take out or up or empty with or as if with a scoop **2 :** to make hollow **:** dig out **3 :** BEAT 5a(2) — **scoop•er** *n*

scoot \'sküt\ *vi* **:** to go suddenly and swiftly **:** DART [probably of Scandinavian origin] — **scoot** *n*

\ə\ **abut**	\au̇\ **out**	\i\ **tip**	\ȯ\ **saw**	\u̇\ **foot**
\ər\ **further**	\ch\ **chin**	\ī\ **life**	\ȯi\ **coin**	\y\ **yet**
\a\ **mat**	\e\ **pet**	\j\ **job**	\th\ **thin**	\yü\ **few**
\ā\ **take**	\ē\ **easy**	\ng\ **sing**	\t͟h\ **this**	\yu̇\ **cure**
\ä\ **cot, cart**	\g\ **go**	\ō\ **bone**	\ü\ **food**	\zh\ **vision**

scoot•er \ˈsküt-ər\ *n* **1** : a child's vehicle that consists of a narrow board mounted between two wheels one behind the other with an upright steering handle attached to the front wheel **2** : MOTOR SCOOTER

scop \ˈshōp, ˈskōp, ˈskäp\ *n* : an Old English bard or poet [Old English]

[1]**scope** \ˈskōp\ *n* **1** : space or opportunity for unhampered action or thought ⟨given full *scope* to develop new solutions⟩ **2** : something sought : OBJECT **3** : extent covered, reached, or viewed : RANGE ⟨a subject broad in *scope*⟩ [Italian *scopo* "purpose, goal", from Greek *skopos*]

[2]**scope** *n* : any of various instruments for viewing: as **a** : MICROSCOPE **b** : TELESCOPE **c** : OSCILLOSCOPE **d** : RADARSCOPE [*-scope*]

-scope \ˌskōp\ *n combining form* : means (as an instrument) for viewing or observing ⟨micro*scope*⟩ [Greek *-skopion*]

sco•pol•amine \skō-ˈpäl-ə-ˌmēn, -mən\ *n* : a poisonous alkaloid found in some plants of the potato family and used as a truth serum or especially with morphine as a sedative [German *scopolamin*, from New Latin *Scopolia*, genus of plants + German *amin* "amine"]

-s•co•py \s-kə-pē\ *n combining form, pl* **-pies** : viewing : observation ⟨stereo*scopy*⟩ [Greek *-skopia*, from *skeptesthai* "to watch, look at"]

scor•bu•tic \skȯr-ˈbyüt-ik\ *adj* : of, relating to, or resembling scurvy; *also* : diseased with scurvy [New Latin *scorbutus* "scurvy"] — **scor•bu•ti•cal•ly** \-ˈbyüt-i-kə-lē, -klē\ *adv*

[1]**scorch** \ˈskȯrch\ *vb* **1 a** : to burn superficially usually to the point of changing color, texture, or flavor ⟨*scorch* a roast⟩ ⟨linen *scorches* easily⟩ **b** : to parch and discolor with or as if with intense heat ⟨lawns *scorched* by summer suns⟩ **2** : to distress or embarrass with usually sarcastic censure [Middle English *scorchen*]

[2]**scorch** *n* **1** : a result of scorching **2** : a browning of plant tissues usually from disease or heat

scorched earth *n* : land stripped of anything that could be of use to an invading enemy force

scorch•er \ˈskȯr-chər\ *n* : one that scorches; *esp* : a very hot day

[1]**score** \ˈskōr, ˈskȯr\ *n, pl* **scores 1** *or pl* **score a** : TWENTY **b** : a group of 20 things — often used in combination with a cardinal number ⟨five*score*⟩ **c** *pl* : an indefinite large number ⟨*scores* of cars in the parking lot⟩ **2 a** : a line made with or as if with a sharp instrument **b** : a mark used as a starting point or goal or for keeping account **3 a** : a reckoning kept by making marks on a tally **b** : ACCOUNT 1 **c** : amount due : INDEBTEDNESS **4** : an obligation or grudge kept in mind for requital ⟨looking for an opportunity to settle the *score*⟩ **5 a** : REASON, GROUND ⟨you have nothing to fear on that *score*⟩ **b** : SUBJECT 3c, TOPIC **6** : a musical composition in written or printed notation **7** : a number expressing accomplishment (as in a game or test) or quality (as of a product) ⟨a *score* of 80 out of a possible 100⟩ **8** : the true facts or prospects of a situation ⟨know the *score* on the unemployment situation⟩ [Old Norse *skor* "notch, tally, twenty"]

[2]**score** *vb* **1 a** : to record by or as if by notches on a tally **b** : to keep score in a game or contest **2** : to mark with lines, grooves, scratches, or notches **3** : BERATE, SCOLD **4 a** : to make a score in or as if in a game : TALLY ⟨*score* a run⟩ **b** : to enable (a base runner) to make a score ⟨*scored* the runner from second base with a single⟩ **c** : to have as a value in a game or contest : COUNT ⟨a touchdown *scores* six points⟩ **d** : ACHIEVE 2, WIN **5** : to determine the merit of : GRADE **6** : to write or arrange music for **7 a** : to gain or have the advantage **b** : to be successful — **scor•er** *n*

score•board \ˈskōr-ˌbōrd, ˈskȯr-ˌbȯrd\ *n* : a large board for displaying the score of a game or match

score•card \-ˌkärd\ *n* : a card for recording the score (as of a game)

score•keep•er \-ˌkē-pər\ *n* : an official who records the score during the progress of a game or contest

score•less \-ləs\ *adj* : having no score; *esp* : involving no points or runs

sco•ria \ˈskōr-ē-ə, ˈskȯr-\ *n, pl* **-ri•ae** \-ē-ˌē, -ē-ˌī\ **1** : the refuse from melting of metals or reduction of ores : SLAG **2** : rough vesicular cindery lava [Latin, from Greek *skōria*, from *skōr* "excrement"] — **sco•re•a•ceous** \ˌskōr-ē-ˈā-shəs, ˌskȯr-\ *adj*

[1]**scorn** \ˈskȯrn\ *n* **1** : a feeling of contempt and loathing toward something considered inferior or unworthy **2** : an object of extreme disdain, contempt, or derision [Old French *escarn*, of Germanic origin]

[2]**scorn** *vt* **1** : to hold in or reject with bitter or angry contempt ⟨*scorned* all weaklings⟩ ⟨*scorn* a bribe⟩ **2** : to refuse because of scorn : DISDAIN ⟨*scorned* to reply to the charge⟩ **syn** see DESPISE — **scorn•er** *n*

scorn•ful \ˈskȯrn-fəl\ *adj* : full of scorn : CONTEMPTUOUS — **scorn•ful•ly** \-fə-lē\ *adv* — **scorn•ful•ness** *n*

Scor•pio \ˈskȯr-pē-ˌō\ *n* **1** : a zodiacal southern constellation that is located partly in the Milky Way and adjoins Libra **2** : the 8th sign of the zodiac; *also* : one born under this sign [Latin, from Greek *Skorpios*, literally, "scorpion"]

scor•pi•on \ˈskȯr-pē-ən\ *n* : any of an order (Scorpionida) of arachnids having an elongated body and a narrow segmented tail with a venomous sting at the tip [Old French, from Latin *scorpio*, from Greek *skorpios*]

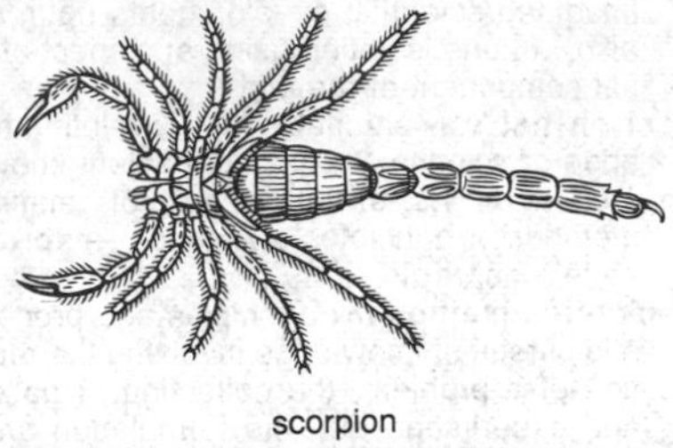
scorpion

scorpion fish *n* : any of a family of large-headed spiny-finned sea fishes including some with poisonous spines

Scor•pi•us \ˈskȯr-pē-əs\ : SCORPIO 1 [Latin, from Greek *Skorpios*, literally, "scorpion"]

Scot \ˈskät\ *n* **1** : any of a Gaelic people of northern Ireland settling in Scotland about A.D. 500 **2 a** : a native or inhabitant of Scotland **b** : a person of Scotch descent [Old English *Scottas* "Irishmen, Scotsmen", from Late Latin *Scotus* "Irishman"]

scotch \ˈskäch\ *vt* **1** : to injure so as to make temporarily harmless **2** : to stamp out : CRUSH ⟨*scotch* a rebellion⟩; *esp* : to end decisively by showing the falsity of ⟨*scotch* a rumor⟩ [Middle English *scocchen* "to gash"]

[1]**Scotch** \ˈskäch\ *adj* **1** : of, relating to, or characteristic of Scotland, the Scotch, or Scots **2** : ECONOMICAL 1, FRUGAL [contraction of *Scottish*]

[2]**Scotch** *n* **1** : SCOTS **2 Scotch** *pl* : the people of Scotland **3** : whiskey distilled in Scotland especially from barley

Scotch broth *n* : a soup made from beef or mutton and vegetables and thickened with barley

Scotch-Irish *adj* : of, relating to, or characteristic of the population of northern Ireland that is descended from Scotch settlers or their descendants who emigrated to the United States before 1846 — **Scotch-Irish** *n*

Scotch•man \ˈskäch-mən\ *n* : a man who is a Scot or is of Scotch descent

Scotch terrier *n* : SCOTTISH TERRIER

Scotch•wom•an \ˈskäch-ˌwu̇m-ən\ *n* : a woman who is a Scot or is of Scotch descent

sco•ter \ˈskōt-ər\ *n, pl* **scoters** *or* **scoter** : any of several sea ducks of northern coasts of Europe and North America [origin unknown]

scot-free \ˈskät-ˈfrē\ *adj* : totally free from obligation, harm, or penalty [from *scot* "money assessed or paid", from Old Norse *skot* "shot, contribution"]

[1]**Scots** \ˈskäts\ *adj* : SCOTCH 1 [Middle English *Scottis*, alteration of *Scottish*]

[2]**Scots** *n* : the English language of Scotland

Scots•man \ˈskät-smən\ *n* : SCOTCHMAN

Scots•wom•an \-ˌswu̇m-ən\ *n* : SCOTCHWOMAN

scot•tie \ˈskät-ē\ *n* : SCOTTISH TERRIER

[1]**Scot•tish** \ˈskät-ish\ *adj* : SCOTCH 1

[2]**Scottish** *n* : SCOTS

Scottish Gaelic *n* : the Gaelic language of Scotland

Scottish terrier *n* : any of an old Scottish breed of terrier with short legs, large head, small erect ears, broad deep chest, and a thick harsh coat

scoun•drel \ˈskau̇n-drəl\ *n* : a mean worthless person : VILLAIN [origin unknown] — **scoundrel** *adj* — **scoun•drel•ly** \-drə-lē\ *adj*

[1]**scour** \ˈskau̇r\ *vb* **1** : to move about or through quickly especially in search **2** : to examine minutely and rapidly [Middle English *scuren*] — **scour•er** *n*

[2]**scour** *vb* **1 a** : to rub hard in order to clean **b** : to remove by rubbing hard and washing ⟨*scour* spots from the stove⟩ **2** : to

free from foreign matter or impurities by or as if by washing ⟨*scour* wool⟩ **3 a :** to clear, dig, or remove by a powerful current of water **b :** to wear away (as by water) **:** ERODE ⟨a stream *scouring* its banks⟩ **4 :** to suffer from diarrhea or dysentery **5 :** to become clean and bright by rubbing [Middle English *scouren*] — **scour•er** *n*

3scour *n* **1 :** an action or result of scouring **2** *pl* **:** DIARRHEA, DYSENTERY

1scourge \ˈskərj\ *n* **1 :** WHIP 1, LASH **2 a :** an instrument of punishment or criticism **b :** a cause of widespread or great affliction [Anglo-French *escorge*, derived from Old French *es-* "ex-" + Latin *corrigia* "whip"]

2scourge *vt* **1 :** to whip severely **:** FLOG **2 :** to subject to affliction **:** DEVASTATE ⟨a region *scourged* by malaria⟩ — **scourg•er** *n*

scouring rush *n* **:** EQUISETUM; *esp* **:** one with harsh abrasive stems formerly used for scouring

1scout \ˈskau̇t\ *vb* **1 :** to go about and observe in search of information ⟨*scout* an area for minerals⟩ ⟨*scouted* around the enemy position⟩ **2 a :** to make a search ⟨*scout* about for firewood⟩ **b :** to find by searching [Middle French *escouter* "to listen", from Latin *auscultare*]

2scout *n* **1 :** the act or an instance of scouting **:** RECONNAISSANCE **2 a :** one sent to obtain information and especially to reconnoiter in war **b :** LOOKOUT 1 **c :** a person who searches for talented newcomers **3 a :** BOY SCOUT **b :** GIRL SCOUT **4 :** FELLOW 4a, GUY

3scout *vb* **1 :** to make fun of **:** MOCK **2 :** to reject scornfully as absurd **:** SCOFF ⟨*scout* a theory⟩ [of Scandinavian origin]

scout car *n* **:** a fast armored military reconnaissance vehicle with four-wheel drive and open top

scout•craft \-ˌkraft\ *n* **:** the craft, skill, or practice of a scout

scout•er \-ər\ *n* **1 :** one that scouts **2 :** a member of the Boy Scouts of America over 18 years of age

scout•ing \ˈskau̇t-iŋ\ *n* **1 :** the action of one that scouts **2 :** the activities of the various boy scout and girl scout movements

scout•mas•ter \ˈskau̇t-ˌmas-tər\ *n* **:** the leader of a band of scouts and especially of a troop of boy scouts

scow \ˈskau̇\ *n* **:** a large flat-bottomed boat with broad square ends used chiefly for transporting sand, gravel, or refuse [Dutch *schouw*]

scow

1scowl \ˈskau̇l\ *vb* **1 :** FROWN 1, GLOWER ⟨*scowled* at my impudence⟩ **2 :** to exhibit or express with a scowl ⟨*scowl* one's displeasure⟩ [Middle English *skoulen*] — **scowl•er** *n*

2scowl *n* **:** a facial expression of displeasure **:** FROWN

1scrab•ble \ˈskrab-əl\ *vb* **scrab•bled; scrab•bling** \ˈskrab-liŋ, -ə-liŋ\ **1 :** SCRAWL, SCRIBBLE **2 :** to scratch or claw about clumsily or frantically **3 a :** to struggle for a foothold **:** SCRAMBLE **b :** to struggle by or as if by scraping or scratching ⟨*scrabble* for a living⟩ [Dutch *schrabbelen* "to scratch"] — **scrab•bler** \ˈskrab-lər, -ə-lər\ *n*

2scrabble *n* **:** an act or instance of scrabbling

scrab•bly \ˈskrab-lē, -ə-lē\ *adj* **scrab•bli•er; -est 1 :** RASPY 1, SCRATCHY **2 :** SPARSE, SCRUBBY ⟨a *scrabbly* garden⟩

1scrag \ˈskrag\ *n* **1 :** a rawboned or scrawny person or animal **2 :** the lean end of a neck of mutton or veal [perhaps from *crag* "neck, throat", from Dutch *crāghe*]

2scrag *vt* **scragged; scrag•ging :** to wring the neck of

scrag•gly \ˈskrag-lē, -ə-lē\ *adj* **scrag•gli•er; -est :** of rough or irregular outline; *also* **:** RAGGED, UNKEMPT

scrag•gy \ˈskrag-ē\ *adj* **scrag•gi•er; -est 1 :** ROUGH 1c, JAGGED **2 :** being lean and long **:** SCRAWNY

scram \ˈskram\ *vi* **scrammed; scram•ming :** to go away at once ⟨*scram*, you're not wanted⟩ [short for *scramble*]

scram•ble \ˈskram-bəl\ *vb* **scram•bled; scram•bling** \-bə-liŋ, -bliŋ\ **1 :** to move or climb hastily on all fours **2 :** to move or act urgently or unceremoniously in trying to win or escape something ⟨*scramble* for front seats⟩ **3 :** SPRAWL 3, STRAGGLE **4 a :** to toss or mix together **:** JUMBLE **b :** to prepare (eggs) by stirring during cooking [perhaps alteration of 1*scrabble*] — **scramble** *n* — **scram•bler** \-bə-lər, -blər\ *n*

1scrap \ˈskrap\ *n* **1** *pl* **:** fragments of discarded or leftover food **2 :** a small bit **:** FRAGMENT ⟨*scraps* of cloth⟩ ⟨not a *scrap* of truth in the story⟩ **3 :** discarded or waste material (as metal) for reprocessing [Old Norse *skrap* "scraps"]

2scrap *vt* **scrapped; scrap•ping 1 :** to break up into scrap ⟨*scrap* a battleship⟩ **2 :** to discard as worthless ⟨*scrap* outworn methods⟩

3scrap *adj* **1 :** made up of odds and ends ⟨a *scrap* meal⟩ **2 :** constituting scrap ⟨*scrap* metal⟩

4scrap *n* **:** 1QUARREL, FIGHT [origin unknown]

5scrap *vi* **scrapped; scrap•ping :** QUARREL 2, FIGHT — **scrap•per** *n*

scrap•book \ˈskrap-ˌbu̇k\ *n* **:** a blank book for mementos (as clippings and pictures)

1scrape \ˈskrāp\ *vb* **1 a :** to remove by repeated strokes of an edged tool ⟨*scrape* off rust⟩ **b :** to clean or smooth by rubbing with an edged tool or abrasive **2 :** to move along or over something with a grating noise **:** GRATE; *also* **:** to damage by such an action ⟨*scrape* a fender⟩ **3 a :** to gather with difficulty and little by little ⟨*scrape* together a few dollars⟩ **b :** to barely make one's way ⟨*scraped* through with low grades⟩ [Old Norse *skrapa*] — **scrap•er** *n*

2scrape *n* **1 a :** the act or process of scraping **b :** a sound, mark, or injury made by scraping **2 :** a bow made by drawing back the foot **3 :** a disagreeable predicament

scrap•ple \ˈskrap-əl\ *n* **:** a seasoned ground mush of cornmeal and bits of meat set in a mold and served sliced and fried [derived from 1*scrap*]

1scrap•py \ˈskrap-ē\ *adj* **scrap•pi•er; -est :** consisting of scraps

2scrappy *adj* **scrap•pi•er; -est 1 :** likely or tending to quarrel **:** QUARRELSOME **2 :** aggressive and determined in spirit — **scrap•pi•ness** *n*

1scratch \ˈskrach\ *vb* **1 :** to scrape or dig with or as if with the claws or nails **2 :** to rub and tear or mark the surface of with something sharp **3 a :** SCRAPE 3 **b :** to work hard and save ⟨have to *scratch* for a living⟩ **4 :** to write or draw on a surface especially hastily or carelessly **:** SCRAWL **5 a :** ERASE, CANCEL **b :** to withdraw (an entry) from competition **6 a :** to use the claws or nails in digging, tearing, or wounding **b :** to scrape or rub oneself (as to relieve itching) **7 :** to make a thin grating sound [blend of English dialect *scrat* "to scratch" and obsolete English *cratch* "to scratch"] — **scratch•er** *n*

2scratch *n* **1 a :** an act or sound of scratching **b :** a mark (as a line) or injury made by scratching **2 a :** the starting line in a race **b :** NOTHING ⟨start from *scratch*⟩ **3 :** satisfactory condition or performance ⟨not up to *scratch*⟩ **4 :** poultry feed scattered especially to induce birds to exercise

3scratch *adj* **1 :** made tentatively or casually ⟨a *scratch* shot⟩ **2 :** put together with little selection ⟨a *scratch* team⟩

scratch hit *n* **:** a batted ball not solidly hit or cleanly played yet credited to the batter as a base hit

scratch line *n* **:** a starting or restraining line in any of several track-and-field events

scratch paper *n* **:** paper suitable for casual writing

scratch test *n* **:** a test for allergic susceptibility made by rubbing an extract of an allergy-producing substance into small breaks or scratches in the skin

scratchy \ˈskrach-ē\ *adj* **scratch•i•er; -est 1 :** likely to scratch or irritate **:** PRICKLY ⟨*scratchy* woolens⟩ **2 :** making a scratching noise **3 :** marked or made with scratches ⟨a *scratchy* surface⟩ **4 :** uneven in quality — **scratch•i•ly** \ˈskrach-ə-lē\ *adv* — **scratch•i•ness** \ˈskrach-ē-nəs\ *n*

scrawl \ˈskrȯl\ *vb* **:** to write or draw awkwardly, hastily, or carelessly **:** SCRIBBLE [origin unknown] — **scrawl** *n* — **scrawl•er** *n* — **scrawl•i•ness** \ˈskrȯ-lē-nəs\ *n* — **scrawly** \ˈskrȯ-lē\ *adj*

scraw•ny \ˈskrȯ-nē\ *adj* **scraw•ni•er; -est :** ill-nourished **:** SKINNY ⟨*scrawny* cattle⟩ [origin unknown] — **scraw•ni•ness** *n*

1scream \ˈskrēm\ *vb* **1 :** to utter a loud shrill prolonged cry or sound; *also* **:** to utter with such a sound ⟨*screamed* my name⟩ **2 :** to produce or give a vivid, startling, or alarming effect ⟨a *screaming* red⟩ ⟨*screaming* headlines⟩ [Middle English *scremen*]

\ə\ **a**but	\au̇\ **ou**t	\i\ t**i**p	\ȯ\ s**aw**	\u̇\ f**oo**t
\ər\ furth**er**	\ch\ **ch**in	\ī\ l**i**fe	\ȯi\ c**oi**n	\y\ **y**et
\a\ m**a**t	\e\ p**e**t	\j\ **j**ob	\th\ **th**in	\yü\ f**ew**
\ā\ t**a**ke	\ē\ **ea**sy	\ŋ\ si**ng**	\th̲\ **th**is	\yu̇\ c**u**re
\ä\ c**o**t, c**a**rt	\g\ **g**o	\ō\ b**o**ne	\ü\ f**oo**d	\zh\ vi**s**ion

[2]**scream** *n* **1 :** a loud shrill prolonged cry or sound **2 :** one that provokes great laughter ⟨you're a *scream* when you get going⟩
• **syn** SHRIEK, SCREECH: SCREAM is the general term for utterance that is sharpened and prolonged by intensity of feeling. SHRIEK may imply an intensified scream or suggest a degree of wildness or lack of control ⟨*shrieks* of dismay⟩ ⟨hysterical *shrieks* of laughter⟩ SCREECH implies a harsh shrillness painful to the hearer and suggesting an unearthly or, often, a comic effect ⟨the *screech* of an angry parrot⟩

scream•er \ˈskrē-mər\ *n* **1 :** one that screams **2 :** any of several large South American birds with spurs on the wings **3 :** a sensationally startling headline

scream•ing•ly \ˈskrē-ming-lē\ *adv* **:** to an extreme degree ⟨*screamingly* funny⟩

[1]**screech** \ˈskrēch\ *vb* **1 :** to utter a high shrill piercing cry usually in terror or pain; *also* **:** to utter with a screech ⟨*screeched* a warning⟩ **2 :** to make a sound like a screech [Middle English *scrichen*] — **screech•er** *n*

[2]**screech** *n* **1 :** a shrill harsh cry usually of terror or pain **2 :** a sound like a screech ⟨*screech* of brakes⟩ **syn** see SCREAM

screech owl *n* **:** any of numerous small New World owls with a pair of tufts of lengthened feathers on the head that resemble ears

screech owl

screed \ˈskrēd\ *n* **:** a lengthy discourse [Old English *scrēade* "fragment, shred"]

[1]**screen** \ˈskrēn\ *n* **1 a :** a device or partition used to hide, restrain, protect, or decorate ⟨a window *screen*⟩; *also* **:** something that serves to shelter, protect, or conceal ⟨a *screen* of fighter planes⟩ ⟨used the store as a *screen* for illegal activities⟩ **b :** a maneuver in various sports whereby a defender is legally cut off from the play **2 :** a sieve or perforated material set in a frame and used for separating finer parts from coarser parts (as of sand) **3 a :** a flat surface upon which a picture or series of pictures is projected; *also* **:** the surface upon which the image appears in a television or radar receiver **b :** the motion-picture industry [Middle French *escren*, from Dutch *scherm*]

[2]**screen** *vb* **1 :** to guard from injury or danger **2 a :** to shelter, protect, or separate with or as if with a screen **b :** to pass (as coal, gravel, or ashes) through a screen to separate the fine part from the coarse; *also* **:** to remove by or as if by a screen **c :** to examine systematically in order to separate into groups; *also* **:** to select or eliminate by this means ⟨*screened* the applicants⟩ **3 :** to provide with a screen especially to keep out insects ⟨*screen* a porch⟩ **4 a :** to project (as a motion-picture film) on a screen **b :** to present in a motion picture **c :** to appear on a motion-picture screen **5 :** to cut off an opponent from a play — **screen•able** \ˈskrē-nə-bəl\ *adj* — **screen•er** *n*

screen•ing \ˈskrē-ning\ *n* **1** *pl* **:** material (as fine coal) separated out by passage through or retention on a screen **2 :** a mesh (as of metal or plastic) used especially for screens

screen pass *n* **:** a forward pass in football in which the receiver is protected by a screen of blockers

screen•play \ˈskrēn-ˌplā\ *n* **:** the written form of a story prepared for motion-picture or television production

screen test *n* **:** a short film sequence testing the ability of a prospective movie actor or actress — **screen–test** *vt*

screen•writ•er \ˈskrēn-ˌrīt-ər\ *n* **:** a writer of screenplays

[1]**screw** \ˈskrü\ *n* **1 a :** a simple machine consisting of a spirally grooved solid cylinder and a correspondingly grooved cylindrical hollow part into which it fits **b :** a nail-shaped or rod-shaped metal piece with a spiral groove and a slotted or recessed head used for fastening pieces of solid material together **2 a :** a screw-shaped form **:** SPIRAL **b :** a turn of a screw; *also* **:** a twist like the turn of a screw **c :** a screw-shaped device (as a corkscrew) **3 :** PROPELLER **4 :** THUMBSCREW 2 [Middle French *escroe* "screw nut", from Medieval Latin *scrofa*, from Latin, "sow"] — **screw•like** \-ˌlīk\ *adj*

[2]**screw** *vb* **1 a** (1) **:** to attach, fasten, or close by means of a screw ⟨*screw* a hinge to a door⟩ (2) **:** to operate, tighten, or adjust by means of a screw ⟨*screw* up a sagging beam with a jack⟩ **b :** to move or cause to move spirally as a screw does; *also* **:** to close or set in position by such an action ⟨*screw* on a lid⟩ ⟨*screw* a jar shut⟩ **2 a :** to twist out of shape **:** CONTORT ⟨a face *screwed* up in pain⟩ **b :** SQUINT 2 **3 :** to increase in amount or capability ⟨*screwed* up my nerve⟩ — **screw•er** *n*

[1]**screw•ball** \ˈskrü-ˌbȯl\ *n* **1 :** a baseball pitch that spins and breaks in the opposite direction to a curve **2 :** NUT 4a

[2]**screwball** *adj* **:** NUTTY 2

screw•driv•er \ˈskrü-ˌdrī-vər\ *n* **:** a tool for turning screws

screw eye *n* **:** a screw having a head in the form of a loop

screw pine *n* **:** any of a genus of tropical plants with slender palmlike stems, often huge prop roots, and terminal crowns of swordlike leaves — called also *pandanus*

screw propeller *n* **:** PROPELLER

screw thread *n* **:** the projecting spiral rib of a screw between the grooves

screw•worm \ˈskrü-ˌwərm\ *n* **:** the grub of a two-winged fly of warm parts of America that develops especially in sores or wounds of mammals

screwy \ˈskrü-ē\ *adj* **screw•i•er; -est 1 :** crazily absurd, eccentric, or unusual **2 :** CRAZY 2a, INSANE

scrib•al \ˈskrī-bəl\ *adj* **:** of, relating to, or due to a scribe ⟨a *scribal* error⟩

scrib•ble \ˈskrib-əl\ *vb* **scrib•bled; scrib•bling** \ˈskrib-ling, -ə-ling\ **:** to write or draw hastily or carelessly [Medieval Latin *scribillare*, from Latin *scribere* "to write"] — **scribble** *n*

scrib•bler \ˈskrib-lər\ *n* **1 :** one that scribbles **2 :** a minor or inferior author

[1]**scribe** \ˈskrīb\ *n* **1 :** a scholar of the Jewish law in New Testament times **2 a :** an official or public secretary or clerk **b :** a copier of manuscripts **3 :** AUTHOR 1; *esp* **:** JOURNALIST [Latin *scriba* "official writer", from *scribere* "to write"]

[2]**scribe** *vt* **:** to mark or make by cutting or scratching with a pointed instrument ⟨*scribe* a line on metal⟩ [probably short for *describe*]

scrib•er \ˈskrī-bər\ *n* **:** a sharp-pointed tool for marking off material (as wood or metal) to be cut

scrim \ˈskrim\ *n* **:** a durable plain-woven usually cotton fabric [origin unknown]

[1]**scrim•mage** \ˈskrim-ij\ *n* **1 :** a confused fight **:** SCUFFLE **2 :** the interplay between two football teams that begins with the snap of the ball and continues until the ball is dead **3 :** practice play between a team's squads or a practice game between two teams [alteration of [1]*skirmish*]

[2]**scrimmage** *vi* **:** to take part in a scrimmage — **scrim•mag•er** *n*

scrimp \ˈskrimp\ *vb* **1 :** STINT 1, SKIMP **2 :** ECONOMIZE 1 [perhaps of Scandinavian origin] — **scrimpy** \ˈskrim-pē\ *adj*

scrim•shaw \ˈskrim-ˌshȯ\ *n* **:** carved or engraved articles made especially by American whalers and from whale ivory [origin unknown] — **scrimshaw** *vb*

scrip \ˈskrip\ *n* **1 :** a document showing that the holder or bearer is entitled to something (as stock or land) **2 :** paper currency or a token issued temporarily (as in an emergency) [short for *script*]

script \ˈskript\ *n* **1 a :** something written **:** TEXT **b :** an original or principal legal document **c** (1) **:** MANUSCRIPT 1 (2) **:** the written text of a stage play, a movie, or a broadcast **2 a :** printed lettering resembling handwritten lettering **b :** written characters **:** HANDWRITING **c :** ALPHABET 1 [Latin *scriptum* "thing written", from *scribere* "to write"]

scrip•to•ri•um \skrip-ˈtōr-ē-əm, -ˈtȯr-\ *n, pl* **-ria** \-ē-ə\ **:** a copying room in a medieval monastery set apart for the scribes [Medieval Latin, from Latin *scribere* "to write"]

scrip•tur•al \ˈskrip-chə-rəl, ˈskrip-shrəl\ *adj* **:** of, relating to, or being in accordance with a sacred writing; *esp* **:** BIBLICAL — **scrip•tur•al•ly** \-ē\ *adv*

scrip•ture \ˈskrip-chər\ *n* **1 a** *cap* **:** the books of the Old and New Testaments or of either of them **:** BIBLE — often used in pl. **b** *often cap* **:** a passage from the Bible **2 :** the sacred writings of any religion **3 :** a body of writings considered authoritative [Latin *scriptura* "writing", from *scribere* "to write"]

script•writ•er \ˈskrip-ˌtrīt-ər\ *n* **:** one that writes scripts for motion pictures or for radio or television programs

scriv•e•ner \ˈskriv-nər, -ə-nər\ *n* **:** a professional copyist or writer **:** SCRIBE [Middle French *escrivein*, derived from Latin *scriba* "scribe"]

scrod \ˈskräd\ *n* : a young fish (as a cod or haddock); *esp* : one split and boned for cooking [perhaps from obsolete Dutch *schrood* "shred"]

scrof•u•la \ˈskrȯf-yə-lə, ˈskräf-\ *n* : tuberculosis of the lymph glands especially in the neck [Medieval Latin, from Late Latin *scrofulae* "swellings of the lymph glands of the neck", from Latin *scrofa* "sow"] — **scrof•u•lous** \-ləs\ *adj*

scroll \ˈskrōl\ *n* **1** : a roll (as of paper or parchment) providing a writing surface; *esp* : one on which something is written or engraved **2** : an ornament suggesting a loosely or partly rolled scroll [Middle English *scrowle,* alteration of *scrowe,* from Middle French *escroue* "scrap, scroll", of Germanic origin]

scroll 1

scroll saw *n* : a saw with a thin blade for cutting curves or irregular designs

scroll•work \ˈskrōl-ˌwərk\ *n* : ornamental work (as in metal or wood) having a scroll or scrolls as its chief feature

scrooge \ˈskrüj\ *n, often cap* : a miserly person [Ebenezer *Scrooge,* character in *A Christmas Carol,* story by Charles Dickens]

scro•tum \ˈskrōt-əm\ *n, pl* **scro•ta** \ˈskrōt-ə\ *or* **scrotums** : the external pouch that in most mammals contains the testes [Latin] — **scro•tal** \ˈskrōt-l\ *adj*

scrounge \ˈskrau̇nj\ *vb* **1** : to hunt or collect by or as if by foraging ⟨*scrounge* around for firewood⟩ **2** : CADGE, WHEEDLE ⟨*scrounge* a dollar from a friend⟩ [from English dialect *scrunge* "to wander about idly"] — **scroung•er** *n*

[1]**scrub** \ˈskrəb\ *n* **1 a** : a stunted tree or shrub **b** : vegetation consisting chiefly of or a tract covered with scrubs **2** : a usually inferior domestic animal of mixed or unknown parentage **3 a** : a person of insignificant size or standing **b** : a player not on the first team [Old English *scrybb* "brushwood"] — **scrub** *adj*

[2]**scrub** *vb* **scrubbed; scrub•bing 1** : to clean with hard rubbing : SCOUR **b** : to remove by or as if by scrubbing **2** : to subject to friction : RUB [of Low German or Scandinavian origin] — **scrub•ber** *n*

[3]**scrub** *n* **1** : an act or instance of scrubbing **2** : one that scrubs

scrub brush *n* : a brush with hard bristles for heavy cleaning

scrub•by \ˈskrəb-ē\ *adj* **scrub•bi•er; -est 1** : inferior in size or quality : STUNTED ⟨*scrubby* cattle⟩ **2** : covered with or consisting of vegetational scrub **3** : lacking distinction : SHABBY [[1]*scrub*]

scrub typhus *n* : an acute rickettsial disease of the western Pacific area that resembles typhus and is transmitted by larval mites — called also *tsutsugamushi disease*

scrub•wom•an \ˈskrəb-ˌwu̇m-ən\ *n* : a woman who hires herself out for cleaning : CHARWOMAN

scruff \ˈskrəf\ *n* : the loose skin of the back of the neck : NAPE [alteration of earlier *scuff,* of unknown origin]

scruffy \-ē\ *adj* **scruff•i•er; -est** : poor and shabby ⟨a *scruffy* hippie⟩ ⟨put on my *scruffiest* jeans⟩ [English dialect *scruff* "something worthless", alteration of *scurf*]

scrump•tious \ˈskrəm-shəs, ˈskrəmp-\ *adj* : DELIGHTFUL, EXCELLENT [probably alteration of *sumptuous*] — **scrump•tious•ly** *adv*

[1]**scrunch** \ˈskrənch\ *vb* **1 a** : to crush together : CRUMPLE **b** : to make or move with a crunching sound **2** : CROUCH 1 [alteration of [1]*crunch*]

[2]**scrunch** *n* : a crunching sound

[1]**scru•ple** \ˈskrü-pəl\ *n* **1** — see MEASURE table **2** : a tiny part or quantity [Latin *scrupulus,* a unit of weight, from *scrupulus* "small sharp stone"]

[2]**scruple** *n* **1** : an ethical consideration or principle that makes one uneasy or inhibits action **2** : SCRUPULOSITY 1 [Middle French *scrupule,* from Latin *scrupulus* "small sharp stone, scruple", from *scrupus* "sharp stone"] **syn** see QUALM

[3]**scruple** *vi* **scru•pled; scru•pling** \-pə-ling, -pling\ : to have scruples

scru•pu•los•i•ty \ˌskrü-pyə-ˈläs-ət-ē\ *n, pl* **-ties 1** : the quality or state of being scrupulous **2** : [2]SCRUPLE 1

scru•pu•lous \ˈskrü-pyə-ləs\ *adj* **1** : having or full of scruples **2** : PUNCTILIOUS **syn** see CAREFUL — **scru•pu•lous•ly** *adv* — **scru•pu•lous•ness** *n*

scru•ta•ble \ˈskrüt-ə-bəl\ *adj* : capable of being deciphered : COMPREHENSIBLE [Late Latin *scrutabilis* "searchable", from Latin *scrutari* "to search, examine"]

scru•ti•nize \ˈskrüt-n-ˌīz\ *vt* : to examine very closely or critically : INSPECT — **scru•ti•niz•er** *n*

• **syn** SCRUTINIZE, SCAN, EXAMINE mean to look at searchingly and critically. SCRUTINIZE stresses close attention to minute detail ⟨*scrutinized* every line of the contract⟩ SCAN suggests a rapid but thorough covering of an entire surface or body of printed matter ⟨*scanned* several newspapers each morning⟩ EXAMINE suggests scrutinizing in order to determine the nature, condition, or quality of a thing ⟨*examined* the gem for flaws⟩

scru•ti•ny \ˈskrüt-n-ē, ˈskrüt-nē\ *n, pl* **-nies 1** : a thorough study, inquiry, or inspection : EXAMINATION **2** : a searching look [Latin *scrutinium,* from *scrutari* "to search, examine", from *scruta* "trash"]

scu•ba \ˈskü-bə, ˈskyü-\ *n* : an apparatus that provides air for breathing while swimming underwater [*s*elf-*c*ontained *u*nderwater *b*reathing *a*pparatus]

scuba diver

scuba diver *n* : a person who dives with scuba gear

[1]**scud** \ˈskəd\ *vi* **scud•ded; scud•ding** : to move or run swiftly especially as if driven forward [probably of Scandinavian origin]

[2]**scud** *n* **1** : the act of scudding **2** : wind-driven clouds or water

[1]**scuff** \ˈskəf\ *vb* **1** : to scrape the feet in walking : SHUFFLE ⟨*scuff* one's feet on the ground⟩ ⟨*scuffed* along the path⟩ **2** : to become rough or scratched through wear ⟨some leathers *scuff* easily⟩ [probably of Scandinavian origin]

[2]**scuff** *n* **1** : a noise or act of scuffing **2** : a flat-soled house slipper

scuf•fle \ˈskəf-əl\ *vb* **scuf•fled; scuf•fling** \ˈskəf-ling, -ə-ling\ **1** : to struggle in a confused way at close quarters **2** : to move with a quick shuffling gait; *also* : SCUFF [probably of Scandinavian origin] — **scuffle** *n* — **scuf•fler** \ˈskəf-lər, -ə-lər\ *n*

[1]**scull** \ˈskəl\ *n* **1 a** : an oar used at the stern of a boat to propel it forward with a side-to-side motion **b** : one of a pair of short oars for use by one person **2** : a long narrow boat usually for racing propelled by one or more persons using sculls [Middle English *sculle*]

[2]**scull** *vb* **1** : to propel by a scull or sculls **2** : to scull a boat — **scull•er** *n*

scul•lery \ˈskəl-rē, -ə-rē\ *n, pl* **-ler•ies** : a room for cleaning and storing dishes and culinary utensils, washing vegetables, and similar domestic work [Middle French *escuelerie* "department of household in charge of dishes", from *escuelle* "bowl", from Latin *scutella* "drinking bowl, tray", from *scutra* "platter"]

scul•lion \ˈskəl-yən\ *n* : a kitchen helper [Middle French *escouillon* "dishcloth", from *escouve* "broom", from Latin *scopa,* literally, "twig"]

scul•pin \ˈskəl-pən\ *n, pl* **sculpins** *also* **sculpin 1** : any of numerous spiny large-headed broad-mouthed usually scaleless fishes **2** : a scorpion fish of the southern California coast sought for food and sport [origin unknown]

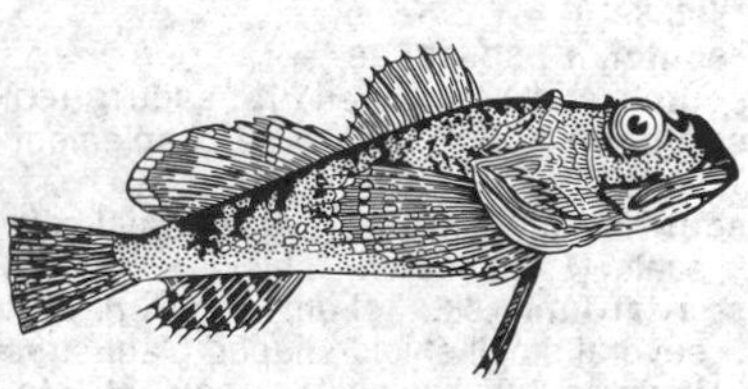
sculpin 1

\ə\ **abut**	\au̇\ **out**	\i\ **tip**	\ȯ\ **saw**	\u̇\ **foot**
\ər\ **further**	\ch\ **chin**	\ī\ **life**	\ȯi\ **coin**	\y\ **yet**
\a\ **mat**	\e\ **pet**	\j\ **job**	\th\ **thin**	\yü\ **few**
\ā\ **take**	\ē\ **easy**	\ng\ **sing**	\t͟h\ **this**	\yu̇\ **cure**
\ä\ **cot, cart**	\g\ **go**	\ō\ **bone**	\ü\ **food**	\zh\ **vision**

sculpt \'skəlpt\ *vb* : SCULPTURE 1, CARVE [French *sculpter,* derived from Latin *sculpere*]

sculp•tor \'skəlp-tər\ *n* : one that sculptures [Latin, from *sculpere* "to carve"]

sculp•tress \-trəs\ *n* : a woman who sculptures

sculp•tur•al \'skəlp-chə-rəl, 'skəlp-shrəl\ *adj* : of, relating to, or resembling sculpture — **sculp•tur•al•ly** \-ē\ *adv*

[1]**sculp•ture** \'skəlp-chər\ *n* **1** : the act, process, or art of carving or cutting hard materials or modeling plastic materials into works of art **2** : work produced by sculpture; *also* : a piece of such work [Latin *sculptura,* from *sculpere* "to carve" alteration of *scalpere*]

[2]**sculpture** *vb* **1 a** : to represent or produce by or subject to sculpture ⟨*sculpture* a model's head⟩ ⟨*sculpture* a statue⟩ ⟨*sculpture* marble⟩ **b** : to adorn with sculpture ⟨*sculpture* a tomb⟩ **2** : to work as a sculptor

[1]**scum** \'skəm\ *n* **1 a** : extraneous matter or impurities risen to or formed on the surface of a liquid **b** : a slimy coating especially on stagnant water **2 a** : foul or worthless things **b** : the lowest class : RABBLE [Dutch *schum*] — **scum•my** \'skəm-ē\ *adj*

[2]**scum** *vi* **scummed**; **scum•ming** : to form or become covered with or as if with scum

scun•ner \'skən-ər\ *n* : an unreasonable or extreme dislike or prejudice [Middle English *skunniren* "to be disgusted"]

scup \'skəp\ *n, pl* **scup** *also* **scups** : either of two porgies of the Atlantic coast of the United States [of American Indian origin]

scup•per \'skəp-ər\ *n* : an opening in the bulwarks of a boat through which water drains overboard [Middle English *skopper*]

scup•per•nong \-ˌnȯng, -ˌnäng\ *n* **1** : MUSCADINE; *esp* : a cultivated muscadine with yellowish green plum-flavored fruits **2** : a wine made from scuppernongs [*Scuppernong,* river and lake in North Carolina]

scurf \'skərf\ *n* **1** : thin dry scales given off by the skin especially in an abnormal skin condition **2** : a substance that sticks to a surface in flakes; *also* : a scaly deposit or covering (as on a plant surface) [of Scandinavian origin] — **scurfy** \'skər-fē\ *adj*

scur•ri•lous \'skər-ə-ləs, 'skə-rə-\ *adj* **1 a** : using or given to coarse language **b** : being vulgar and evil **2** : containing obscenities or crude abuse ⟨*scurrilous* verse⟩ [Latin *scurrilis,* from *scurra* "buffoon"] — **scur•ril•i•ty** \skə-'ril-ət-ē\ *n* — **scur•ri•lous•ly** \'skər-ə-ləs-lē, 'skə-rə-\ *adv* — **scur•ri•lous•ness** *n*

scur•ry \'skər-ē, 'skə-rē\ *vi* **scur•ried**; **scur•ry•ing** : to move briskly : SCAMPER [short for *hurry-scurry,* reduplication of *hurry*] — **scurry** *n*

[1]**scur•vy** \'skər-vē\ *adj* **scur•vi•er**; **-est** : disgustingly mean or contemptible ⟨*scurvy* tricks⟩ [*scurf*] **syn** see CONTEMPTIBLE — **scur•vi•ly** \-və-lē\ *adv* — **scur•vi•ness** \-vē-nəs\ *n*

[2]**scurvy** *n* : a deficiency disease caused by lack of ascorbic acid and marked by spongy gums, loosened teeth, and bleeding into the skin and mucous membranes

scut \'skət\ *n* : a short erect tail (as of a rabbit) [origin unknown]

[1]**scutch** \'skəch\ *vt* : to separate the woody fiber from (flax or hemp) by beating [obsolete French *escoucher,* derived from Latin *excutere* "to beat out", from *ex-* + *quatere* "to shake, strike"]

[2]**scutch** *n* : SCUTCHER

scutch•eon \'skəch-ən\ *n* : ESCUTCHEON

scutch•er \'skəch-ər\ *n* : an implement or machine for scutching

scute \'sküt, 'skyüt\ *n* : an external bony or horny plate or large scale [Latin *scutum* "shield"]

scu•tel•lum \skü-'tel-əm, skyü-\ *n, pl* **-tel•la** \-'tel-ə\ : any of several small shield-shaped plant structures [New Latin, from Latin *scutum* "shield"] — **scu•tel•late** \-'tel-ət\ *adj*

scut•ter \'skət-ər\ *vi* : SCURRY, SCUTTLE [alteration of [4]*scuttle*]

[1]**scut•tle** \'skət-l\ *n* **1** : a shallow open basket (as for grain or garden produce) **2** : a metal pail for carrying coal [Latin *scutella* "drinking bowl, tray", from *scutra* "platter"]

[2]**scuttle** *n* : a small opening (as in the side or deck of a ship or the roof of a house) furnished with a lid; *also* : its lid [Middle English *skottell*]

[3]**scuttle** *vt* **scut•tled**; **scut•tling** \'skət-ling, -l-ing\ **1** : to sink (a boat) intentionally by making holes in the sides or bottom **2** : to injure or end by a deliberate act ⟨*scuttle* a conference⟩

[4]**scuttle** *vi* **scut•tled**; **scut•tling** \'skət-ling, -l-ing\ : SCURRY [probably blend of *scud* and *shuttle*]

[5]**scuttle** *n* **1** : a quick shuffling pace **2** : a short swift run

scut•tle•butt \'skət-l-ˌbət\ *n* : RUMOR 1, GOSSIP [earlier *scuttlebutt* "cask fitted with a spigot to provide drinking water on shipboard, drinking fountain on a ship", from [2]*scuttle*]

scy•pha \'sī-fə\ *n* : any of various small mostly cup-shaped calcareous sponges [New Latin, from Latin *scyphus* "cup"]

scy•phis•to•ma \sī-'fis-tə-mə\ *n, pl* **-mae** \-ˌmē\ *also* **-mas** : a sexually produced scyphozoan larva that repeatedly constricts transversely to form free-swimming medusae [Latin *scyphus* "cup" + Greek *stoma* "mouth"]

scy•pho•zo•an \ˌsī-fə-'zō-ən\ *n* : any of a class (Scyphozoa) of coelenterates comprising mostly large jellyfishes that lack a true polyp stage [Latin *scyphus* "cup" + Greek *zōion* "animal"] — **scyphozoan** *adj*

[1]**scythe** \'sīth, 'sī\ *n* : an implement used for mowing (as grass) and composed of a long curving blade fastened at an angle to a long handle [Old English *sīthe*]

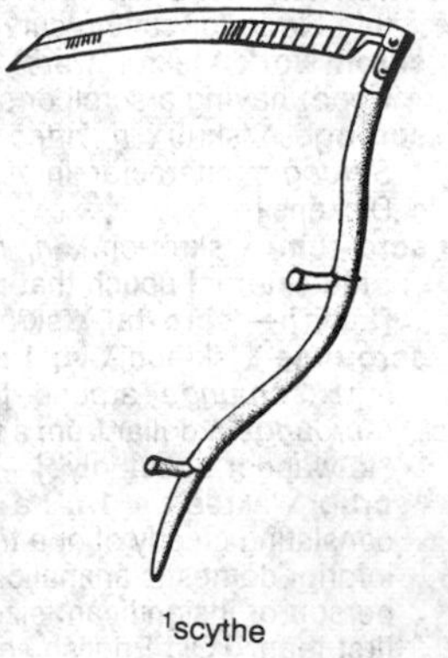

[1]scythe

[2]**scythe** *vt* : to cut with or as if with a scythe : MOW

sea \'sē\ *n* **1 a** : the great body of salty water that covers much of the earth; *also* : the waters of the earth as distinguished from the land and air **b** : a body of salt water less extensive than an ocean ⟨the Mediterranean *sea*⟩ **c** : OCEAN 2 **d** : an inland body of water either salt or fresh ⟨the *Sea* of Galilee⟩ **2 a** : surface motion on a large body of water or its direction ⟨a following *sea*⟩ **b** : rough water : a heavy swell or wave ⟨a high *sea* swept the deck⟩ **3** : something suggesting the sea (as in vastness) ⟨a golden *sea* of wheat⟩ **4** : the seafaring life [Old English *sǣ*] — **sea** *adj* — **at sea 1** : on the sea; *esp* : on a sea voyage **2** : LOST 2c, BEWILDERED — **to sea** : to or on the open waters of the sea

sea anchor *n* : a drag typically of canvas thrown overboard to retard the drifting of a ship or seaplane and to keep its head to the wind

sea anemone *n* : any of numerous usually solitary polyps (order Actiniaria) that have bright and varied colors and a cluster of tentacles and that superficially resemble a flower in form

sea•bag \'sē-ˌbag\ *n* : a cylindrical canvas bag used especially by a sailor for gear (as clothes)

sea bass *n* **1** : any of numerous marine fishes related to but usually smaller and more active than the groupers; *esp* : a food and sport fish of the Atlantic coast of the United States **2** : any of numerous croakers or drums including noted sport and food fishes

sea•beach \'sē-ˌbēch\ *n* : a beach lying along the sea

sea•bed \-ˌbed\ *n* : the floor of a sea or ocean

Sea•bee \'sē-ˌbē\ *n* : a member of a construction battalion of the United States Navy [alteration of *cee* + *bee*; from the initials of *construction battalion*]

sea•bird \'sē-ˌbərd\ *n* : a bird (as a gull or albatross) frequenting the open ocean

sea biscuit *n* : HARDTACK

sea•board \'sē-ˌbōrd, -ˌbȯrd\ *n* : SEACOAST; *also* : the country bordering a seacoast — **seaboard** *adj*

sea•boot \'sē-ˌbüt\ *n* : a very high waterproof boot used especially by sailors and fishermen

sea•borne \-ˌbōrn, -ˌbȯrn\ *adj* **1** : borne over or upon the sea ⟨a *seaborne* invasion⟩ **2** : engaged in or carried on by overseas shipping ⟨*seaborne* trade⟩

sea bread *n* : HARDTACK

sea bream *n* : any of numerous sea fishes related to the perches

sea breeze *n* : a breeze blowing inland from the sea

sea change *n* **1** : a change brought about by the sea **2** : TRANSFORMATION 1

sea chest *n* : a sailor's storage chest for personal property
sea•coast \ˈsē-ˌkōst\ *n* : the shore or border of the land adjacent to the sea
sea cow *n* : MANATEE, DUGONG
sea•craft \ˈsē-ˌkraft\ *n* **1** : seagoing ships **2** : skill in navigation
sea cucumber *n* : any of a class (Holothurioidea) of echinoderms having a long flexible tough muscular body often resembling a cucumber — called also *holothurian*
sea dog *n* : a veteran sailor
sea duty *n* : duty in the United States Navy performed outside the continental United States or specified dependencies thereof
sea eagle *n* : any of various eagles that feed largely on fish
sea fan *n* : a coelenterate with a fan-shaped skeleton that is related to the corals and sea anemones
sea•far•er \ˈsē-ˌfar-ər, -ˌfer-\ *n* : MARINER [*sea* + ¹*fare* + *-er*]
sea•far•ing \-ˌfar-iŋ, -ˌfer-\ *n* **1** : traveling over the sea **2** : the occupation of a sailor — **seafaring** *adj*
sea•food \ˈsē-ˌfüd\ *n* : edible marine fish and shellfish
sea•front \-ˌfrənt\ *n* : the waterfront of a seaside place
sea gate *n* : a gate, beach, or channel that gives access to the sea
sea•girt \-ˌgərt\ *adj* : surrounded by the sea
sea•go•ing \-ˌgō-iŋ\ *adj* : adapted or used for sea travel ⟨*seagoing* ships⟩; *also* : SEAFARING ⟨a *seagoing* nation⟩
sea green *n* **1** : a moderate green or bluish green **2** : a moderate yellow green
sea gull *n* : GULL; *esp* : one frequenting the sea
sea hare *n* : any of various large naked sea mollusks with arched backs and front tentacles that project like ears
sea horse *n* **1** : a fabulous animal half horse and half fish **2** : a small long-snouted fish that is covered with bony plates and has a head that looks like a horse's head
sea is•land cotton \ˌsē-ˌī-lənd-, -ˌī-lən-\ *n, often cap S&I* : a cotton with especially long silky fiber [*Sea Islands,* chain of islands in the Atlantic]
sea king *n* : a Viking chief
¹seal \ˈsēl\ *n, pl* **seals** *also* **seal** **1** : any of numerous marine flesh-eating mammals chiefly of cold regions with limbs modified into webbed flippers adapted primarily to swimming **2 a** : the pelt of a seal **b** : leather made from the skin of a seal [Old English *seolh*]
²seal *vi* : to hunt seals — **seal•er** *n*

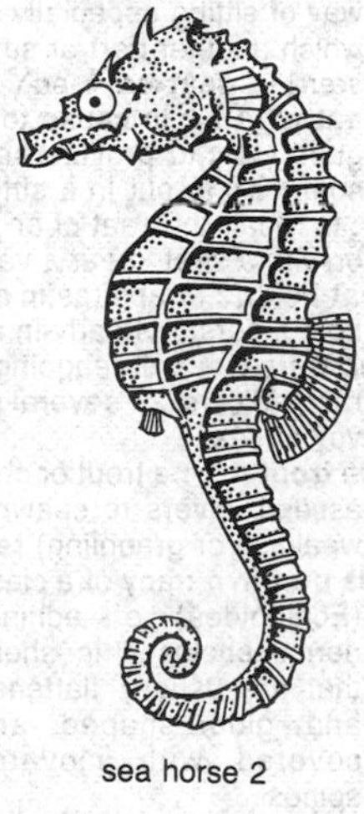
sea horse 2

³seal *n* **1** : a device with an identifying design or words cut into or raised on its surface that can be pressed or stamped (as into paper or wax) to form a mark (as for certifying a signature or authenticating a document); *also* : a piece of wax or a wafer bearing such an impressed mark or the mark itself **2** : a usually ornamental adhesive stamp that may be used to close a letter or package; *esp* : one sold in a fund-raising campaign **3 a** : something (as a pledge) that makes safe or secure ⟨under *seal* of secrecy⟩ **b** : a closure that can be opened only by breaking or tearing ⟨a *seal* on the door of a boxcar⟩ **c** : a tight and perfect closure ⟨test the *seal* of the jars⟩; *also* : a device or an arrangement of material designed to produce such a closure ⟨covered the joint with a thick *seal* of rosin⟩ ⟨the water *seal* of a toilet⟩ [Old French *seel,* from Latin *sigillum,* from *signum* "sign, seal"] — **under seal** : with an authenticating seal affixed
⁴seal *vt* **1** : to mark with or certify or authenticate by or as if by a seal ⟨*seal* a deed⟩ **2** : to close or make fast with or as if with a seal often to prevent or disclose tampering ⟨the sheriff *sealed* the premises⟩ ⟨*seal* a letter with glue⟩ ⟨ice *sealed* the ships into the harbor⟩ **3** : to determine finally and irrevocably ⟨this answer *sealed* our fate⟩ — **seal•er** *n*
sea ladder *n* **1** : a rope ladder or set of steps to be lowered over a ship's side for use in coming aboard (as at sea) **2** : SEA STEPS
sea lamprey *n* : a large lamprey sometimes used as food that is a pest destructive of native fish in the Great Lakes
sea–lane \ˈsē-ˌlān\ *n* : an established sea route
seal•ant \ˈsē-lənt\ *n* : a sealing agent ⟨radiator *sealant*⟩
sea lavender *n* : any of several salt-marsh plants with basal leaves and branching sprays of tiny usually lavender flowers
sea legs *n* : bodily adjustment to the motion of a ship at sea indicated especially by ability to walk steadily and by freedom from seasickness
sea lettuce *n* : ULVA
sea level *n* : the height of the surface of the sea midway between the average high and low tides
sea lily *n* : CRINOID; *esp* : a stalked crinoid
sealing wax *n* : a resinous composition that is plastic when warm and is used for sealing (as letters or dry cells)
sea lion *n* : any of several large Pacific eared seals
seal•skin \ˈsēl-ˌskin\ *n* **1** : the fur or pelt of a fur seal **2** : a garment (as a coat) of sealskin — **sealskin** *adj*
¹seam \ˈsēm\ *n* **1** : the joining or the mark made by the joining of two pieces or edges of material by sewing **2** : the space between adjacent planks of a ship **3 a** : a line left by a cut or wound; *also* : WRINKLE **b** : a layer or stratum (as of mineral) between distinctive layers ⟨coal *seams*⟩ [Old English *sēam*] — **seam•less** \-ləs\ *adj* — **seam•like** \-ˌlīk\ *adj*

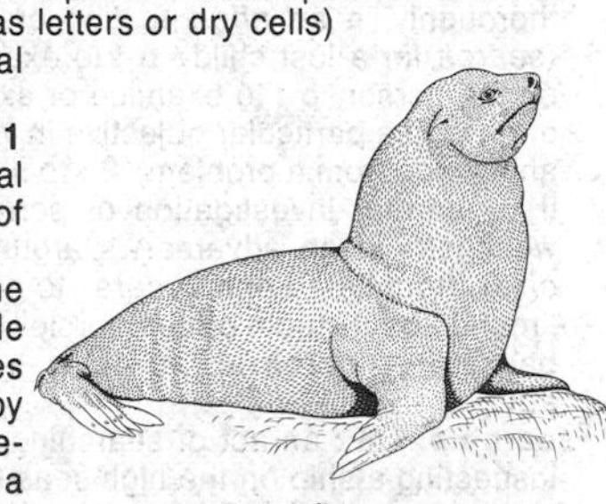
sea lion

²seam *vt* **1** : to join by or as if by sewing **2** : to mark with lines suggesting seams : FURROW ⟨creeks *seam* the valley⟩ — **seam•er** *n*
sea•man \ˈsē-mən\ *n* **1** : SAILOR 1a, MARINER **2** : an enlisted rank in the Navy and Coast Guard above seaman apprentice and below petty officer third class
seaman apprentice *n* : an enlisted rank in the Navy and Coast Guard above seaman recruit and below seaman
seaman recruit *n* : the lowest enlisted rank in the Navy and Coast Guard
sea•man•ship \ˈsē-mən-ˌship\ *n* : the art or skill of handling, working, and navigating a ship
sea•mark \-ˌmärk\ *n* **1** : a line on a coast marking the tidal limit **2** : an elevated object serving as a beacon to mariners
sea mile *n* : NAUTICAL MILE
sea•mount \ˈsē-ˌmau̇nt\ *n* : a submarine mountain
seam•stress \ˈsēm-strəs, ˈsēmp-\ *also* **semp•stress** \ˈsem-strəs, ˈsemp-\ *n* : a woman who sews especially for a living [*seamster, sempster* "tailor" (from Old English *sēamestre,* from *sēam* "seam") + *-ess*]
seamy \ˈsē-mē\ *adj* **seam•i•er**; **-est** **1** : having or showing seams ⟨*seamy* ledges⟩ **2** : UNPLEASANT, SORDID ⟨the *seamy* side of life⟩ — **seam•i•ness** *n*
sé•ance \ˈsā-ˌäns, -ˌäⁿs\ *n* **1** : SESSION 1 **2** : a meeting of persons seeking to communicate with spirits [French, literally, "sitting", from *seoir* "to sit", from Latin *sedēre*]
sea nettle *n* : a stinging jellyfish
sea otter *n* : a large marine otter of northern Pacific coasts that attains a maximum length of nearly six feet and feeds largely on shellfish
sea–ot•ter's–cab•bage \ˌsē-ˌät-ərz-ˈkab-ij\ *n* : a very large Pacific kelp among fronds of which sea otters congregate

sea otter

sea pen *n* : any of numerous coelenterates that are related to the corals and form colonies of a feathery form

sea•plane \'sē-ˌplān\ *n* : an airplane designed to take off from and land on the water

sea•port \-ˌpōrt, -ˌpȯrt\ *n* : a port, harbor, or town accessible to seagoing ships

sea power *n* **1** : a nation having formidable naval strength **2** : naval strength

sea purse *n* : the horny egg case of a skate or of some sharks

[1]**sear** \'siər\ *vb* **1** : to cause withering or drying : PARCH ⟨harsh winds that *sear* and burn⟩ **2** : to burn, scorch, brown, or injure with or as if with sudden application of intense heat [Old English *sēarian* "to become sere", from *sēar* "sere"]

[2]**sear** *n* : a mark or scar left by searing

[1]**search** \'sərch\ *vb* **1 a** : to go through or look carefully and thoroughly in an effort to find or discover ⟨*search* a room⟩ ⟨*search* for a lost child⟩ **b** : to examine for articles concealed on the person **c** : to examine or explore with painstaking care often with a particular objective in view : PROBE ⟨*searching* for an escape from a problem⟩ **2** : to find or come to know by or as if by careful investigation or scrutiny ⟨*searching* out every weakness in an adversary's argument⟩ [Middle French *cerchier,* from Late Latin *circare* "to go about", from Latin *circum* "round about", from *circus* "circle"] — **search•able** \'sər-chə-bəl\ *adj* — **search•er** \-chər\ *n* — **search•ing•ly** \-ching-lē\ *adv*

[2]**search** *n* **1 a** : an act of searching **b** : an act of boarding and inspecting a ship on the high seas (as by a belligerent seeking contraband goods) **2** : a person or party that searches

search•light \'sərch-ˌlīt\ *n* **1** : an apparatus for projecting a beam of light; *also* : a beam of light projected by it **2** : FLASHLIGHT 3

search warrant *n* : a warrant authorizing a search of a specified place for stolen goods or unlawful possessions

sea robin *n* : any of several gurnards

sea–run \ˌsē-ˌrən\ *adj* : ANADROMOUS ⟨a *sea-run* salmon⟩

sea•scape \'sē-ˌskāp\ *n* **1** : a view of the sea **2** : a picture representing a scene at sea

sea scorpion *n* : SCULPIN

sea scout *n* : one enrolled in the Boy Scouts of America program that provides training for older youths in seamanship and water activities

sea serpent *n* : a large marine animal resembling a snake often reported to have been seen but never proved to exist

sea•shell \'sē-ˌshel\ *n* : the shell of a marine animal and especially a mollusk

sea•shore \-ˌshōr, -ˌshȯr\ *n* **1** : land adjacent to the sea : SEACOAST **2** : the ground between the ordinary high-water and low-water marks

sea•sick \-ˌsik\ *adj* : affected with or suggestive of seasickness

sea•sick•ness \-nəs\ *n* : motion sickness experienced on the water

sea•side \'sē-ˌsīd\ *n* : country adjacent to the sea : SEASHORE

sea slug *n* **1** : SEA CUCUMBER **2** : a naked marine gastropod mollusk

sea snake *n* **1** : any of numerous venomous aquatic snakes of warm seas **2** : SEA SERPENT

[1]**sea•son** \'sēz-n\ *n* **1 a** : a suitable or natural time or occasion ⟨a *season* for all things⟩ **b** : a usually brief period of time ⟨willing to wait a *season*⟩ **c** : a particular point in a period or in the course of events ⟨visitors at all *seasons*⟩ **2 a** : a period of the year associated with some recurrent phenomenon or activity ⟨the growing *season*⟩ **b** : a period characterized by a particular kind of weather ⟨a long dry *season*⟩ **c** : one of the four quarters into which the year is commonly divided — compare AUTUMN, SPRING, SUMMER, WINTER **d** : a period of the year associated with a particular event (as a holiday) or phase of human activity (as agriculture, sport, or business) ⟨the Christmas *season*⟩ ⟨the baseball *season*⟩ [Old French *saison,* from Latin *satio* "act of sowing", from *satus,* past participle of *serere* "to sow"] — **in season 1** : at the right or fitting time **2** : at the stage of greatest fitness (as for eating) ⟨peaches are *in season*⟩ **3** : legal to take by hunting or fishing — **out of season** : not in season ⟨fined for hunting *out of season*⟩

[2]**season** *vb* **sea•soned; sea•son•ing** \'sēz-ning, -n-ing\ **1** : to give food better flavor or more zest by adding seasoning ⟨a perfectly *seasoned* stew⟩; *also* : to add seasoning ⟨*season* to taste⟩ **2 a** : to treat so as to be fit for use; *esp* : to prepare (lumber) for use by controlled drying **b** : to make fit by experience ⟨*seasoned* veterans⟩ **3** : to become seasoned [Middle French *assaisoner* "to ripen, season", from *saison* "season"] — **sea•son•er** \'sēz-nər, -n-ər\ *n*

sea•son•able \'sēz-nə-bəl, -n-ə-bəl\ *adj* **1** : occurring in good or proper time : OPPORTUNE ⟨*seasonable* advice⟩ **2** : suitable to the season or circumstances : TIMELY ⟨a *seasonable* frost⟩ — **sea•son•able•ness** *n* — **sea•son•ably** \-blē\ *adv*

sea•son•al \'sēz-nəl, -n-əl\ *adj* : of, relating to, or restricted to a particular season ⟨*seasonal* industries⟩ ⟨*seasonal* activity⟩ — **sea•son•al•ly** \-ē\ *adv*

sea•son•ing \'sēz-ning, -n-ing\ *n* : an ingredient (as a condiment, spice, or herb) added to food primarily for savor

season ticket *n* : a ticket (as to all of a club's home games) valid during a specified time

sea spider *n* : any of a class (Pycnogonida) of small long-legged marine arthropods superficially resembling spiders

sea squirt *n* : any of various simple pouched tunicates

sea star *n* : STARFISH

sea steps *n pl* : projecting metal plates or bars attached to the side of a ship by which it may be boarded

sea stores *n pl* : supplies (as of foodstuffs) laid in before starting on a sea voyage

[1]**seat** \'sēt\ *n* **1 a** : something (as a chair) intended to be sat in or on **b** : the particular part of something on which one rests in sitting ⟨*seat* of the trousers⟩ ⟨a chair *seat*⟩ **c** : the part of the body that bears the weight in sitting : BUTTOCKS **2 a** : a seating accommodation ⟨had three *seats* for the game⟩ **b** : a right of sitting usually as a member ⟨a *seat* in the senate⟩ **c** : MEMBERSHIP ⟨a *seat* on the stock exchange⟩ **3** : a place or area where something is situated or centered ⟨*seats* of higher learning⟩; *esp* : a place (as a capital city) from which authority is exercised ⟨the new *seat* of the government⟩ **4** : posture in or way of sitting especially on horseback **5** : a part or surface on which another part or surface rests ⟨a valve *seat*⟩ [Old Norse *sæti*] — **seat•ed** \-əd\ *adj*

[2]**seat** *vb* **1 a** : to cause to sit or assist in finding a seat ⟨*seat* a guest⟩ **b** : to provide seats for ⟨a theater *seating* 1000 persons⟩ **c** : to put in a sitting position ⟨*seat* oneself at table⟩ **2** : to repair the seat of or provide a new seat for **3** : to fit to, on, or with a seat ⟨*seat* a valve⟩ — **seat•er** *n*

seat belt *n* : straps (as in an automobile or airplane) designed to hold a person steady in a seat

sea train *n* **1** : a seagoing ship equipped for carrying a train of railroad cars **2** : several army or navy transports forming a convoy at sea

sea trout *n* **1** : a trout or char that as an adult inhabits the sea but ascends rivers to spawn **2** : any of various sea fishes (as a weakfish or greenling) resembling trouts

sea urchin *n* : any of a class (Echinoidea) of echinoderms enclosed in shells that are usually flattened and globe-shaped and covered with movable spines

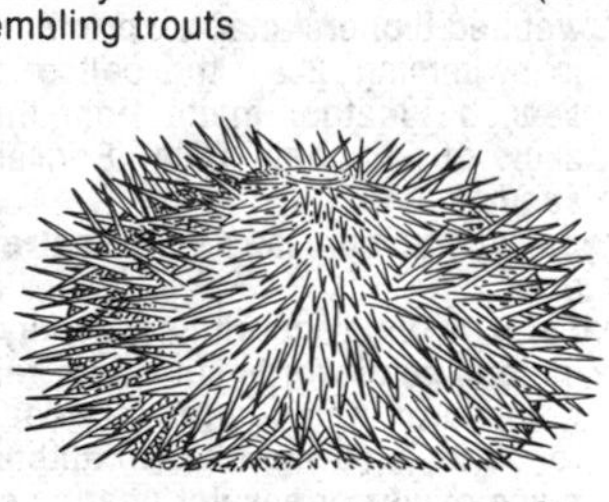

sea urchin

sea•wall \'sē-ˌwȯl\ *n* : a wall or embankment to protect the shore from erosion or to act as a breakwater

sea walnut *n* : CTENOPHORE

[1]**sea•ward** \'sē-wərd\ *also* **sea•wards** \-wərdz\ *adv or adj* : toward the sea

[2]**seaward** *n* : the direction or side away from land and toward the open sea

sea•wa•ter \'sē-ˌwȯt-ər, -ˌwät-\ *n* : water in or from the sea

sea•way \-ˌwā\ *n* **1** : a moderate or rough sea ⟨caught in a *seaway*⟩ **2** : a ship's headway **3** : a route for travel on the sea; *also* : an ocean traffic lane **4** : a deep inland waterway that admits ocean shipping

sea•weed \-ˌwēd\ *n* : a plant growing in the sea; *esp* : a marine alga (as a kelp)

sea•worn \-ˌwōrn, -ˌwȯrn\ *adj* **1** : impaired or eaten away by the sea ⟨*seaworn* shores⟩ **2** : worn out by sea voyaging

sea•wor•thy \-ˌwər-thē\ *adj* : fit or safe for a sea voyage ⟨a *seaworthy* ship⟩ — **sea•wor•thi•ness** *n*

sea wrack *n* : SEAWEED; *esp* : that cast ashore in masses

se•ba•ceous gland \si-ˌbā-shəs-\ *n* : one of the skin glands that secrete an oily lubricating substance into the hair follicles [Latin *sebaceus* "made of tallow", from *sebum* "tallow"]

seb•or•rhea \ˌseb-ə-ˈrē-ə\ *n* **:** excessive secretion and discharge of sebum — **seb•or•rhe•ic** \-ˈrē-ik\ *adj*

se•bum \ˈsē-bəm\ *n* **:** the secretion of the sebaceous glands [Latin, "tallow, grease"]

se•cant \ˈsē-ˌkant, -kənt\ *n* **1 :** a straight line cutting a curve at two or more points **2 :** a trigonometric function that for an acute angle is the ratio of the hypotenuse of a right triangle of which the angle is considered part and the side adjacent to the angle — abbreviation *sec* [Latin *secans,* present participle of *secare* "to cut"]

se•cede \si-ˈsēd\ *vi* **:** to withdraw from an organization (as a nation, church, or political party) [Latin *secedere,* from *se-* "apart" + *cedere* "to go"] — **se•ced•er** *n*

se•ces•sion \si-ˈsesh-ən\ *n* **1 :** the act of seceding **:** a formal withdrawal **2** *often cap* **:** the withdrawal of the 11 southern states from the Union at the start of the Civil War [Latin *secessio,* from *secedere* "to secede"] — **se•ces•sion•ism** \-ˈsesh-ə-ˌniz-əm\ *n* — **se•ces•sion•ist** \-ˈsesh-nəst, -ə-nəst\ *n*

se•clude \si-ˈklüd\ *vt* **:** to keep or shut away from others **:** make inaccessible ⟨*secluded* themselves with a few old friends⟩ ⟨a cottage *secluded* by dense forests⟩ [Latin *secludere,* from *se-* "apart" + *claudere* "to close"]

se•clud•ed *adj* **1 :** screened or hidden from view **2 :** living in seclusion **:** SOLITARY — **se•clud•ed•ly** *adv* — **se•clud•ed•ness** *n*

se•clu•sion \si-ˈklü-zhən\ *n* **1 :** the act of secluding **:** the condition of being secluded **2 :** a secluded or isolated place [Medieval Latin *seclusio,* from Latin *secludere* "to seclude"] — **se•clu•sive** \-ˈklü-siv, -ziv\ *adj* — **se•clu•sive•ly** *adv* — **se•clu•sive•ness** *n*

seco•bar•bi•tal \ˌsek-ō-ˈbär-bə-ˌtȯl\ *n* **:** a barbiturate $C_{12}H_{18}N_2O_3$ that is used chiefly in the form of its bitter powdery sodium salt as a hypnotic and sedative [*Seco*nal, a trademark + *barbital*]

Sec•o•nal \ˈsek-ə-ˌnȯl\ *trademark* — used for secobarbital

[1]**sec•ond** \ˈsek-ənd *also* -ənt\ *adj* **1 :** being number two in a countable series **2 :** being next after the first (as in order, time, or importance) **3 :** ALTERNATE, OTHER ⟨elects a mayor every *second* year⟩ **4 :** resembling or suggesting a prototype **:** ANOTHER ⟨a *second* Solomon⟩ **5 :** having a musical part lower in pitch than or subordinate to another of its kind ⟨*second* violin⟩ ⟨*second* soprano⟩ [Old French, from Latin *secundus* "following, second", from *sequi* "to follow"] — **second** *adv* — **sec•ond•ly** *adv*

[2]**second** *n* **1 a :** number two in a countable series ⟨the *second* of the month⟩ — see NUMBER table **b :** one next after the first (as in the time, order, or importance) **2 :** one who assists or supports another (as in a duel or a boxing match) **3 a :** a musical interval embracing two diatonic degrees **b :** the tone at this interval **4 :** an inferior or flawed article (as of merchandise) **5 :** the act of seconding a motion **6 :** the second gear or speed in an automotive vehicle **7** *pl* **:** a second helping of food

[3]**second** *n* **1 :** the 60th part of a minute of time or of a degree **2 :** an instant of time **:** MOMENT ⟨I'll be back in a *second*⟩ [Medieval Latin *secunda,* from Latin *secundus* "second"; from its being the second sexagesimal division of a unit, as a minute is the first]

[4]**second** *vt* **1 :** to give support or encouragement to **:** ASSIST **2 :** to endorse (a motion or a nomination) so that it may be debated or voted on [Latin *secundare,* from *secundus* "second, favorable"] — **sec•ond•er** *n*

[1]**sec•ond•ary** \ˈsek-ən-ˌder-ē\ *adj* **1 a :** of second rank, importance, or value ⟨*secondary* streams⟩ **b :** of, relating to, or constituting the second strongest of the three or four degrees of stress ⟨the fourth syllable of *basketball team* carries *secondary* stress⟩ **2 a :** derived from something original, primary, or basic **b :** of or relating to the induced current or its circuit in an induction coil or transformer ⟨a *secondary* coil⟩ ⟨*secondary* voltage⟩ **c :** produced by activity of formative tissue and especially cambium other than that at the growing point **3 a :** of, relating to, or being a second order or stage in a sequence or series **b :** of, relating to, or being the second segment of the wing of a bird or the quills of this segment **c :** intermediate between elementary and collegiate ⟨*secondary* school⟩ — **sec•ond•ar•i•ly** \ˌsek-ən-ˈder-ə-lē\ *adv* — **sec•ond•ar•i•ness** \ˈsek-ən-ˌder-ē-nəs\ *n*

[2]**secondary** *n, pl* **-ar•ies :** one that is secondary: as **a :** a defensive football backfield **b :** a secondary feather of a bird

secondary cell *n* **:** STORAGE CELL

secondary emission *n* **:** the emission of electrons from a surface that is bombarded by charged particles

secondary road *n* **1 :** a road not of primary importance **2 :** a road that feeds traffic to a more important road (as a turnpike)

secondary sex characteristic *n* **:** a physical or mental characteristic that appears in members of one sex at puberty or in seasonal breeders at the breeding season and is not directly concerned with reproduction

second base *n* **1 :** the base that must be touched second by a base runner in baseball **2 :** the position of the player defending the area to the right of second base

second base•man \-ˈbā-smən\ *n* **:** a player defending the area to the right of second base

sec•ond–best \ˌsek-ən-ˈbest\ *adj* **:** next to the best

second childhood *n* **:** a state of feebleness or childishness of mind caused by or accompanying old age — called also *dotage*

sec•ond–class \ˌsek-ng-ˈklas, -ən-, -ənd-\ *adj* **1 :** of or relating to a second class **2 a :** INFERIOR 3, MEDIOCRE **b :** socially or economically deprived ⟨*second-class* citizens⟩

second class *n* **1 :** the second and usually next to highest group in a classification **2 :** a class of United States or Canadian mail comprising newspapers and periodicals sent to regular subscribers

Second Coming *n* **:** the coming of Christ on Judgment Day

second–degree burn *n* **:** a burn marked by pain, blistering, and superficial destruction of the skin with fluid infiltration and reddening of the tissues beneath the burn

second growth *n* **:** forest trees that come up naturally after removal of the first growth by cutting or by fire

sec•ond–guess \ˌsek-ng-ˈges, -ən-\ *vt* **1 :** to think out alternative strategies or explanations for after the event **2 a :** OUTWIT **b :** PREDICT — **sec•ond–guess•er** *n*

sec•ond•hand \ˌsek-ən-ˈhand\ *adj* **1 :** taken from someone else ⟨*secondhand* information⟩ **2 :** having had a previous owner ⟨a *secondhand* car⟩ **3 :** selling used goods ⟨a *secondhand* store⟩ — **secondhand** *adv*

second hand \ˈsek-ən-ˌhand\ *n* **:** the hand marking seconds on a timepiece

second lieutenant *n* **:** the lowest officer rank in the Army, Marine Corps, and Air Force

second person *n* **:** a set of words or forms (as verb forms or pronouns) referring to the person or thing addressed in the utterance in which they occur; *also* **:** a word or form belonging to such a set

sec•ond–rate \ˌsek-ən-ˈdrāt, -ˈrāt\ *adj* **:** of second or inferior quality or value **:** MEDIOCRE — **sec•ond–rate•ness** *n* — **sec•ond–rat•er** \-ˈdrāt-ər, -ˈrāt-\ *n*

second sight *n* **:** CLAIRVOYANCE 1

second–story man *n* **:** a burglar who enters a house by an upstairs window

sec•ond–string \ˌsek-ən-ˈstriŋ, -ng-\ *adj* **:** being a substitute player as distinguished from a regular [from the reserve bowstring carried by an archer in case the first breaks]

se•cre•cy \ˈsē-krə-sē\ *n, pl* **-cies 1 :** the habit or practice of keeping secrets **2 :** the quality or state of being hidden or concealed [Middle English *secretee,* from *secre* "secret", from Middle French *secré,* from Latin *secretus*]

[1]**se•cret** \ˈsē-krət\ *adj* **1 a :** hidden or kept from knowledge or view **b :** working with hidden aims or methods **:** UNDERCOVER ⟨a *secret* agent⟩ **2 :** SECLUDED 1 ⟨a *secret* valley⟩ [Middle French, from Latin *secretus,* from *secernere* "to separate, distinguish", from *se-* "apart + *cernere* "to sift"] — **se•cret•ly** *adv*

• **syn** SECRET, COVERT, CLANDESTINE, SURREPTITIOUS mean done without attracting observation. SECRET may imply concealment on any grounds or for any motive ⟨*secret* diplomatic negotiations⟩ COVERT stresses the mere fact of not being open or declared ⟨*covert* envy of a friend⟩ CLANDESTINE implies secrecy usually of a forbidden act ⟨*clandestine* drug trade⟩ SURREPTITIOUS stresses the careful and skillful avoidance of detection as in violating a law or custom or right ⟨*surreptitious* copying from notes⟩

\ə\ **abut**	\au̇\ **out**	\i\ **tip**	\ȯ\ **saw**	\u̇\ **foot**
\ər\ **further**	\ch\ **chin**	\ī\ **life**	\ȯi\ **coin**	\y\ **yet**
\a\ **mat**	\e\ **pet**	\j\ **job**	\th\ **thin**	\yü\ **few**
\ā\ **take**	\ē\ **easy**	\ng\ **sing**	\t͟h\ **this**	\yu̇\ **cure**
\ä\ **cot, cart**	\g\ **go**	\ō\ **bone**	\ü\ **food**	\zh\ **vision**

[2]**secret** *n* **1 a :** something kept hidden or unexplained **:** MYSTERY **b :** something kept from the knowledge of others or shared only confidentially with a few **2 :** a secret condition or place **:** SECRECY ⟨conspired in *secret*⟩ **3 :** something taken to be a key to a desired end ⟨the *secret* of longevity⟩

sec•re•tar•i•at \ˌsek-rə-ˈter-ē-ət\ *n* **1 :** the clerical staff of an organization **2 :** the administrative department of a governmental organization ⟨the United Nations *secretariat*⟩ [French *secrétariat* "office of a secretary, secretariat", from Medieval Latin *secretariatus* "office of a secretary", from *secretarius* "secretary"]

sec•re•tary \ˈsek-rə-ˌter-ē\ *n, pl* **-tar•ies 1 :** a person employed to handle correspondence and routine or detail work for a superior **2 :** an officer of a business corporation or society who has charge of the correspondence and records **3 :** a government official in charge of the affairs of a department ⟨*Secretary* of State⟩ **4 :** a writing desk with a top section for books [Medieval Latin *secretarius* "confidential employee, secretary", derived from Latin *secretus* "secret"] — **sec•re•tari•al** \ˌsek-rə-ˈter-ē-əl\ *adj* — **sec•re•tary•ship** \ˈsek-rə-ˌter-ē-ˌship\ *n*

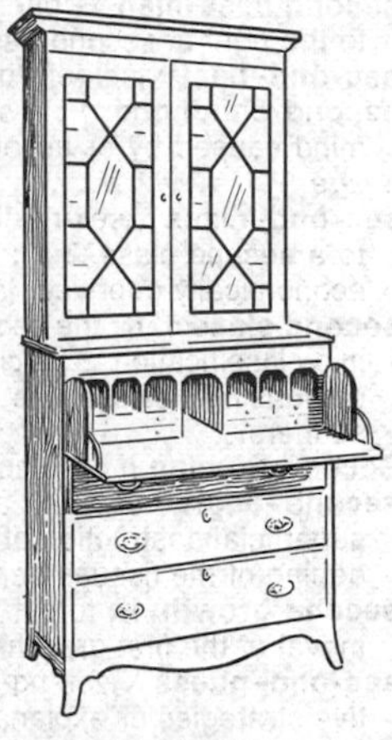
secretary 4

secretary–general *n, pl* **secretaries–general :** a principal administrative officer

secret ballot *n* **:** AUSTRALIAN BALLOT

[1]**se•crete** \si-ˈkrēt\ *vb* **:** to produce and give off a secretion ⟨glands that *secrete* intermittently⟩ [back-formation from *secretion*]

[2]**se•crete** \si-ˈkrēt, ˈsē-krət\ *vt* **:** to deposit or conceal in a hiding place ⟨*secrete* money in one's shoe⟩ [[1]*secret*]

se•cre•tin \si-ˈkrēt-n\ *n* **:** an intestinal hormone capable of stimulating the pancreas and liver to secrete [*secret*ion + *-in*]

se•cre•tion \si-ˈkrē-shən\ *n* **1 :** a concealing or hiding of something **2 a :** the act or process of secreting **b :** a product of glandular activity; *esp* **:** one (as a hormone or enzyme) that performs a specific useful function in the organism [French *sécrétion,* from Latin *secretio* "separation", from *secernere* "to separate", from *se-* "apart" + *cernere* "to sift"] — **se•cre•tion•ary** \-shə-ˌner-ē\ *adj*

se•cre•tive \ˈsē-krət-iv, si-ˈkrēt-\ *adj* **:** disposed to secrecy or concealment **:** not frank or open — **se•cre•tive•ly** *adv* — **se•cre•tive•ness** *n*

se•cre•to•ry \si-ˈkrēt-ə-rē\ *adj* **:** of, relating to, or active in secretion

secret police *n* **:** a police organization operating largely in secrecy and especially to further the political purposes of its government often with terroristic methods

Secret Service *n* **:** a division of the United States Treasury Department charged chiefly with the suppression of counterfeiting and the protection of the president

sect \ˈsekt\ *n* **1 a :** a dissenting or schismatic religious body; *esp* **:** one regarded as extreme or heretical **b :** a religious denomination **2 a :** a group adhering to a distinctive doctrine or to a leader **b :** PARTY 1 **c :** FACTION 1 [Latin *secta* "way of life, class of persons", from *sequi* "to follow"]

[1]**sec•tar•i•an** \sek-ˈter-ē-ən\ *adj* **1 :** of, relating to, or characteristic of a sect or sectarian **2 :** limited in character or scope **:** PAROCHIAL — **sec•tar•i•an•ism** \-ē-ə-ˌniz-əm\ *n*

[2]**sectarian** *n* **1 :** a member of a sect **2 :** a narrow or bigoted person

sec•tar•i•an•ize \sek-ˈter-ē-ə-ˌnīz\ *vb* **1 :** to act as sectarians **2 :** to make sectarian

sec•ta•ry \ˈsek-tə-rē\ *n, pl* **-ries :** a member of a sect

[1]**sec•tion** \ˈsek-shən\ *n* **1 a :** the action or an instance of cutting or separating by cutting **b :** a part set off by or as if by cutting **:** PORTION, SLICE **2 :** a distinct part or portion of a writing: as **a :** a subdivision of a chapter **b :** a distinct component part of a newspaper ⟨sports *section*⟩ **3 :** CROSS SECTION 1b **4 :** a character § used chiefly as a reference mark or to show the beginning of a section **5 :** a piece of land one square mile (about 2.6 square kilometers) in area forming one of the 36 subdivisions of a township **6 :** a distinct part of an area, community, or group of people **7 a :** a division of a railroad sleeping car with an upper and a lower berth **b :** a part of a permanent railroad way under the care of a particular set of men **c :** one of two or more vehicles that run on the same schedule **8 :** one of several component parts (as of a bookcase) that may be assembled or reassembled **9 :** a division of an orchestra composed of one class of instruments ⟨brass *section*⟩ [Latin *sectio,* from *secare* "to cut"]

[2]**section** *vb* **sec•tioned; sec•tion•ing** \-shə-ning, -shning\ **1 :** to cut or separate into or become cut or separated into parts or sections **2 :** to represent in sections (as by a drawing)

sec•tion•al \ˈsek-shnəl, -shən-l\ *adj* **1 a :** of or relating to a section **b :** local or regional rather than general in character ⟨*sectional* interests⟩ **2 :** made up of or divided into sections ⟨a *sectional* sofa⟩ — **sec•tion•al•ly** \-ē\ *adv*

sec•tion•al•ism \ˈsek-shnə-ˌliz-əm, -shən-l-ˌiz-\ *n* **:** an exaggerated devotion to the interests of a region

section gang *n* **:** a gang or crew of track workers employed to maintain a railroad section

section hand *n* **:** a laborer belonging to a section gang

sec•tor \ˈsek-tər, -ˌtȯr\ *n* **1 :** the part of a circle between two radii and their intercepted arc on the circumference **2 :** an area assigned to a military commander to defend **3 :** a distinctive part (as of an economy) ⟨the industrial *sector*⟩ [Latin, "cutter", from *secare* "to cut"] — **sec•to•ri•al** \sek-ˈtōr-ē-əl, -ˈtȯr-\ *adj*

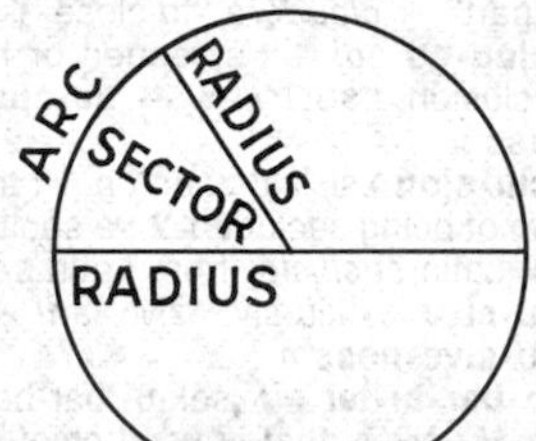

sector 1

[1]**sec•u•lar** \ˈsek-yə-lər\ *adj* **1 a :** of or relating to the worldly or temporal ⟨*secular* concerns⟩ **b :** not openly or specifically religious ⟨*secular* music⟩ **c :** not ecclesiastical or clerical ⟨*secular* courts⟩ **2 :** of or relating to clergy not belonging to a religious order ⟨a *secular* priest⟩ **3 a :** occurring once in an age or a century **b :** existing or continuing through ages or centuries ⟨*secular* enmities⟩ [Old French *seculer,* from Late Latin *saecularis,* from Latin, "coming once in an age", from *saeculum* "breed, generation, age"] — **sec•u•lar•ly** *adv*

[2]**secular** *n* **1 :** a secular ecclesiastic (as a parish priest) **2 :** LAYMAN

sec•u•lar•ism \-lə-ˌriz-əm\ *n* **:** indifference to or rejection or exclusion of religion and religious considerations — **sec•u•lar•ist** \-rəst\ *n* — **secularist** *or* **sec•u•lar•is•tic** \ˌsek-yə-lə-ˈris-tik\ *adj*

sec•u•lar•ize \ˈsek-yə-lə-ˌrīz\ *vt* **1 :** to make secular **2 :** to transfer from ecclesiastical to civil or lay use, possession, or control — **sec•u•lar•iza•tion** \ˌsek-yə-lə-rə-ˈzā-shən\ *n* — **sec•u•lar•iz•er** \ˈsek-yə-lə-ˌrī-zər\ *n*

se•cur•ance \si-ˈkyu̇r-əns\ *n* **:** the act of making secure

[1]**se•cure** \si-ˈkyu̇r\ *adj* **1 a :** easy in mind **:** CONFIDENT **b :** assured in opinion or expectation **:** having no doubt **2 a :** free from danger **b :** free from risk of loss **c :** affording safety **:** INVIOLABLE ⟨a *secure* hideaway⟩ **d :** TRUSTWORTHY, DEPENDABLE ⟨a *secure* foundation⟩ **3 :** SURE 5a, CERTAIN ⟨our victory is *secure*⟩ [Latin *securus* "safe, secure", from *se* "without" + *cura* "care"] **syn** see SAFE — **se•cure•ly** *adv* — **se•cure•ness** *n*

[2]**secure** *vb* **1 a :** to relieve from exposure to danger **:** GUARD, SHIELD ⟨*secure* a supply line from enemy raids⟩ **b :** to put beyond hazard of losing or of not receiving **:** GUARANTEE **c :** to give pledge of payment to (a creditor) or of (an obligation) ⟨*secure* a note with collateral⟩ **2 a :** to take (a person) into custody ⟨*secure* the prisoner⟩ **b :** to make fast **:** SEAL ⟨*secure* a door⟩ **c :** to tie up **:** BERTH ⟨*secure* a boat for the night⟩ **3 a :** to get secure possession of **:** PROCURE ⟨*secure* employment⟩ **b :** to bring about **:** EFFECT **4 :** to release (naval personnel) from work or duty; *also* **:** to stop work — **se•cur•er** *n*

se•cure•ment \si-ˈkyu̇r-mənt\ *n* **:** the act or process of making secure

se•cu•ri•ty \si-ˈkyu̇r-ət-ē\ *n, pl* **-ties 1 :** the quality or state of being secure: as **a :** freedom from danger **:** SAFETY **b :** freedom from fear or anxiety **2 a :** something given, deposited, or pledged to make certain the fulfillment of an obligation ⟨*secur-*

ity for a loan⟩ **b** : SURETY 3 **3** : an evidence of debt or of property ⟨bonds and stock certificates are *securities*⟩ **4 a** : something that secures : PROTECTION **b** : measures taken especially to guard against espionage or sabotage ⟨concern over internal *security*⟩

Security Council *n* : a permanent council of the United Nations having primary responsibility for the maintenance of peace and security

se•dan \si-'dan\ *n* **1** : a portable often covered chair that is designed to carry one person and is borne on poles by two men **2 a** : an enclosed automobile that seats four to seven persons including the driver in a single compartment and has a permanent top **b** : CRUISER 3 [origin unknown]

se•date \si-'dāt\ *adj* : SERIOUS 1, STAID ⟨*sedate* manners⟩ [Latin *sedatus,* from *sedare* "to calm"] — **se•date•ly** *adv* — **se•date•ness** *n*

se•da•tion \si-'dā-shən\ *n* **1** : the inducing of a relaxed easy state especially by the use of sedatives **2** : a state resulting from or like that resulting from sedation

¹sed•a•tive \'sed-ət-iv\ *adj* : tending to calm, moderate, or relieve tension or irritability

²sedative *n* : a sedative agent or drug

sed•en•tary \'sed-n-ˌter-ē\ *adj* **1** : not migratory : SETTLED ⟨*sedentary* birds⟩ **2** : doing or requiring much sitting ⟨a *sedentary* job⟩ **3** : permanently attached ⟨*sedentary* barnacles⟩ [Middle French *sedentaire,* from Latin *sedentarius,* from *sedens,* present participle of *sedēre* "to sit"]

se•der \'sād-ər\ *n, pl* **se•da•rim** \si-'där-əm\ *or* **seders** *often cap* : a Jewish home or community service and ceremonial dinner held on the first and by Orthodox Jews outside Israel on the second evening of the Passover in commemoration of the exodus from Egypt [Hebrew *sēdher* "order"]

sedge \'sej\ *n* : any of a family of usually tufted marsh plants differing from the related grasses in having achenes and solid stems [Old English *secg*] — **sedgy** \'sej-ē\ *adj*

sed•i•ment \'sed-ə-mənt\ *n* **1** : material that settles to the bottom of a liquid **2** : material (as stones and sand) deposited by water, wind, or glaciers [Middle French, from Latin *sedimentum* "settling", from *sedēre* "to sit, sink down"] — **sed•i•ment** \-ˌment\ *vb*

sed•i•men•ta•ry \ˌsed-ə-'ment-ə-rē, -'men-trē\ *adj* **1** : of, relating to, or containing sediment ⟨*sedimentary* deposits⟩ **2** : formed by or from deposits of sediment ⟨limestone and sandstone are *sedimentary* rocks⟩

sed•i•men•ta•tion \ˌsed-ə-mən-'tā-shən, -ˌmen-\ *n* : the action or process of depositing sediment

se•di•tion \si-'dish-ən\ *n* : incitement of resistance to or of insurrection against lawful authority [Middle French, from Latin *seditio,* literally, "separation", from *sed-, se-* "apart" + *itio* "act of going", from *ire* "to go"]

• **syn** SEDITION, TREASON mean a serious breach of allegiance. SEDITION implies acts leading to or exciting commotion or resistance to authority but not including overt acts of violence or betrayal; TREASON implies an overt act aiming at overthrow of government or betrayal to the ememy.

se•di•tious \si-'dish-əs\ *adj* **1** : disposed to arouse, take part in, or be guilty of sedition ⟨a *seditious* agitator⟩ **2** : being or tending to cause sedition ⟨*seditious* statements⟩ — **se•di•tious•ly** *adv* — **se•di•tious•ness** *n*

se•duce \si-'düs, -'dyüs\ *vt* **1** : to persuade to disobedience or disloyalty **2** : to lead astray ⟨*seduced* into crime⟩ **3** : to entice to sexual intercourse **4** : ATTRACT [Latin *seducere* "to lead away", from *se-* "apart" + *ducere* "to lead"] — **se•duce•ment** \-'dü-smənt, -'dyü-\ *n* — **se•duc•er** *n*

se•duc•tion \si-'dək-shən\ *n* **1** : the act of seducing **2** : something that seduces [Latin *seductio* "act of leading aside", from *seducere* "to lead away"]

se•duc•tive \si-'dək-tiv\ *adj* : tending to or having the qualities to seduce — **se•duc•tive•ly** *adv* — **se•duc•tive•ness** *n*

se•duc•tress \-trəs\ *n* : a woman who seduces [obsolete *seductor* "male seducer" + *-ess*]

sed•u•lous \'sej-ə-ləs\ *adj* : diligent in application or pursuit : ASSIDUOUS [Latin *sedulus,* from *sedulo* "sincerely, diligently", from *se* "without" + *dolus* "guile"] — **sed•u•lous•ly** *adv* — **sed•u•lous•ness** *n*

se•dum \'sēd-əm\ *n* : any of a genus of fleshy-leaved herbs including the orpine : STONECROP [Latin, a plant related to sedum]

¹see \'sē\ *vb* **saw** \'sȯ\; **seen** \'sēn\; **see•ing** \'sē-ing\ **1 a** : to perceive by the eye or have the power of sight ⟨*see* a bird⟩ ⟨a person who cannot *see*⟩ **b** : to give or pay attention ⟨*see,* the bus is coming⟩ **c** : to look about **2 a** : to have experience of : UNDERGO ⟨*see* army service⟩ **b** : to come to know : DISCOVER **3 a** : to form a mental picture of : VISUALIZE **b** : to perceive the meaning or importance of : UNDERSTAND **c** : to be aware of : RECOGNIZE **d** : to imagine as a possibility : SUPPOSE ⟨can't *see* how we can lose⟩ **4 a** : to make investigation or inquiry : EXAMINE, WATCH ⟨want to *see* how they handle the problem⟩ **b** : READ ⟨*saw* the story in the paper⟩ **c** : to attend as a spectator ⟨*see* a play⟩ **5 a** : to take care of : provide for ⟨enough to *see* us through⟩ **b** : FINISH ⟨*see* the job through⟩ **c** : HELP, SUPPORT ⟨*saw* me through a bad time⟩ **6** : to make sure ⟨*see* that order is kept⟩ **7 a** : to regard as : JUDGE **b** : to prefer to have ⟨I'll *see* you dead before I accept your terms⟩ **c** : to find acceptable or attractive ⟨still can't *see* the design⟩ **8 a** : to call on : VISIT ⟨*see* a sick friend⟩ **b** (1) : to keep company with especially in courtship or dating ⟨had been *seeing* each other for a year⟩ (2) : to grant an interview to : RECEIVE ⟨the president will *see* you now⟩ **9** : ACCOMPANY, ESCORT ⟨*see* the babysitter home⟩ **10** : to meet (a bet) in poker or to equal the bet of (a player) : CALL [Old English *sēon*]

²see *n* **1** : the city in which a bishop's church is located **2** : the jurisdiction of a bishop : DIOCESE [Old French *se,* from Latin *sedes* "seat"]

see•able \'sē-ə-bəl\ *adj* : capable of being seen

¹seed \'sēd\ *n, pl* **seed** *or* **seeds** **1 a** : the grains or ripened ovules of plants used for sowing **b** : the fertilized ripened ovule of a flowering plant containing an embryo and capable normally of germination to produce a new plant; *also* : a plant structure (as a spore or small dry fruit) capable of producing a new plant **2 a** : MILT, SEMEN **b** : a developmental form of a lower animal suitable for transplanting; *esp* : SPAT **3** : PROGENY ⟨the *seed* of David⟩ **4** : a source of development or growth : GERM ⟨sowed the *seeds* of discord⟩ **5** : something (as a small bubble in glass) that resembles a seed in shape or size [Old English *sǣd*] — **seed** *adj* — **seed•ed** \-əd\ *adj* — **seed•like** \'sēd-ˌlīk\ *adj*

²seed *vb* **1 a** : sow 1a, c, PLANT ⟨*seed* land to grass⟩ **b** : to bear or shed seeds ⟨weeds that *seed* freely⟩ **c** : to remove seeds from ⟨*seed* raisins⟩ **2** : to supply with nuclei (as of crystallization or condensation); *esp* : to treat (a cloud) with solid particles to convert water droplets into ice crystals in an attempt to produce rain **3** : to schedule (tournament players or teams) so that superior ones will not meet in early rounds

seed•bed \'sēd-ˌbed\ *n* : soil or a bed of soil prepared for planting seed

seed•case \-ˌkās\ *n* : a dry hollow fruit (as a pod) enclosing seeds

seed coat *n* : the hardened integuments of a ripened plant ovule forming an outer protective cover on a seed

seed•eat•er \'sēd-ˌēt-ər\ *n* : a bird (as a finch) whose diet consists basically of seeds

seed•er \'sēd-ər\ *n* **1** : a machine for planting or sowing seeds **2** : a device for seeding fruit

seed fern *n* : any of an order (Cycadofilicales) of extinct plants with fronds like ferns and naked seeds

seed leaf *n* : COTYLEDON 2

seed•less \'sēd-ləs\ *adj* : having no seeds ⟨*seedless* grapes⟩

seed•ling \-ling\ *n* **1** : a plant grown from seed **2** : a young plant; *esp* : a tree smaller than a sapling — **seedling** *adj*

seed oyster *n* : a young oyster especially of a size for transplantation

seed pearl *n* : a very small and often irregular pearl

seed plant *n* : a plant that bears seeds : SPERMATOPHYTE

seed•pod \'sēd-ˌpäd\ *n* : POD 1

seeds•man \'sēdz-mən\ *n* **1** : one that sows seed **2** : a dealer in seeds

seed•time \'sēd-ˌtīm\ *n* : the season of sowing

seedy \'sēd-ē\ *adj* **seed•i•er; -est** **1 a** : containing or full of seeds ⟨a *seedy* fruit⟩ **b** : containing many small similar inclusions ⟨glass *seedy* with air bubbles⟩ **2** : inferior in condition or quality: as **a** : SHABBY, RUN-DOWN ⟨*seedy* clothes⟩ **b** : somewhat disreputable : SQUALID ⟨a *seedy* district⟩ ⟨*seedy* entertainment⟩ **c :** slightly unwell ⟨felt *seedy* and went home early⟩ — **seed•i•ly** \'sēd-l-ē\ *adv* — **seed•i•ness** \'sēd-ē-nəs\ *n*

see•ing \'sē-iŋ\ *conj* **:** in view of the fact : inasmuch as — often used with *that* or *as*

Seeing Eye *trademark* — used for a guide dog trained to lead the blind

seek \'sēk\ *vb* **sought** \'sȯt\; **seek•ing 1 :** to resort to : go to ⟨*seek* the shade on a hot day⟩ **2 a :** to go in search of : look for ⟨*seek* a friend⟩ **b :** to make a search or inquiry **c :** to try to discover ⟨*seek* the truth⟩ **3 :** to ask for ⟨*seek* advice⟩ **4 :** to try to acquire or gain ⟨*seek* one's fortune⟩ **5 :** to make an attempt : TRY ⟨*seek* to find a way⟩ [Old English *sēcan*] — **seek•er** *n*

seel \'sēl\ *vt* **:** to close the eyes of (as a hawk) by drawing threads through the eyelids [Middle French *siller,* from Medieval Latin *ciliare,* from Latin *cilium* "eyelid"]

seem \'sēm\ *vi* **1 a** (1) **:** to give the impression of being : APPEAR ⟨*seem* reasonable⟩ (2) **:** to pretend to be **b :** to appear to the observation or understanding ⟨*seemed* to know⟩ **c :** to appear to one's own mind or opinion ⟨*seem* to feel no pain⟩ **2 :** to give evidence of existing or being present ⟨there *seems* no reason for worry [of Scandinavian origin]

[1]**seem•ing** \'sē-miŋ\ *n* **:** external appearance as distinguished from true character : LOOK

[2]**seeming** *adj* **:** apparent on superficial view : OSTENSIBLE ⟨*seeming* enthusiasm⟩ — **seem•ing•ly** \'sē-miŋ-lē\ *adv*

seem•ly \'sēm-lē\ *adj* **seem•li•er; -est 1 :** good-looking : HANDSOME, ATTRACTIVE **2 :** conventionally proper : DECOROUS ⟨*seemly* behavior⟩ **3 :** suited to the occasion, purpose, or person : FIT ⟨a *seemly* reply⟩ [Old Norse *sœ̄miligr,* from *sœ̄mr* "becoming"] — **seem•li•ness** *n* — **seemly** *adv*

seen *past participle of* SEE

seep \'sēp\ *vi* **:** to flow or pass slowly through fine pores or small openings : OOZE ⟨water *seeped* through the wall⟩ [Old English *sipian*]

seep•age \'sē-pij\ *n* **1 :** the process of seeping **2 :** fluid that has seeped through porous material

seer \'siər, *esp for 1 also* 'sē-ər\ *n* **1 :** one that sees **2 a :** one that predicts events or developments : PROPHET **b :** a person credited with extraordinary moral and spiritual insight

seer•ess \'siər-əs\ *n* **:** a woman who is a seer

seer•suck•er \'siər-,sək-ər\ *n* **:** a light fabric of linen, cotton, or rayon usually striped and slightly puckered [Hindi *śīrśaker,* from Persian *shīr-o-shakar,* literally, "milk and sugar"]

[1]**see•saw** \'sē-,sȯ\ *n* **1 :** an alternating up-and-down or backward-and-forward motion or movement; *also* **:** a contest or struggle in which now one side now the other has the lead **2 a :** a pastime in which two children or groups of children ride on opposite ends of a plank balanced in the middle so that one end goes up as the other goes down **b :** the plank or apparatus so used [probably from reduplication of [3]*saw*] — **seesaw** *adj*

[2]**seesaw** *vb* **see•sawed; see•saw•ing 1 a :** to move backward and forward or up and down **b :** to play on a seesaw **2 :** ALTERNATE

seethe \'sēth\ *vb* **1** *archaic* **:** BOIL, STEW **2 :** to soak or saturate in a liquid **3 a :** to be in a state of rapid agitated movement **b :** to churn or foam as if boiling ⟨the river rapids *seethed*⟩ **4 :** to suffer violent internal excitement ⟨*seethed* with rage⟩ [Old English *sēothan*]

[1]**seg•ment** \'seg-mənt\ *n* **1 :** any of the parts into which a thing is divided or naturally separates : SECTION, DIVISION **2 a :** a part cut off from a geometrical figure (as a circle or sphere) by a line or plane; *esp* **:** the part of a circle bounded by a chord and an arc of that circle **b :** a part of a straight line included between two points — called also *line segment* [Latin *segmentum,* from *secare* "to cut"] **syn** see PART — **seg•men•tary** \'seg-mən-,ter-ē\ *adj* — **seg•ment•ed** \'seg-,ment-əd, seg-'ment-\ *adj*

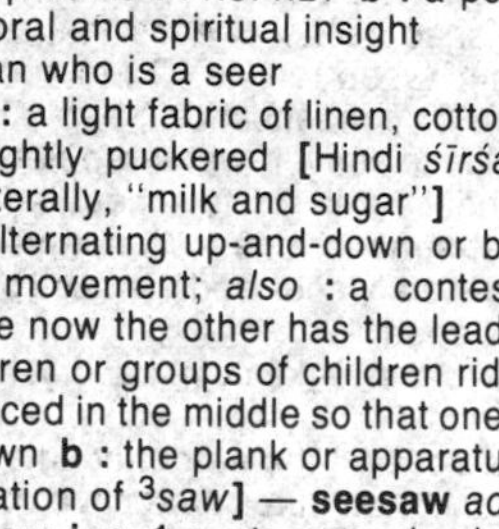

[1]segment 2a

[2]**seg•ment** \'seg-,ment\ *vb* **:** to separate into segments : give off as segments

seg•men•tal \seg-'ment-l\ *adj* **1 :** of, relating to, or having the form of a segment or sector of a circle ⟨*segmental* fanlight⟩ ⟨*segmental* pediment⟩ **2 :** METAMERIC **3 :** of, relating to, or resulting from segmentation : SUBSIDIARY ⟨*segmental* data⟩ — **seg•men•tal•ly** \-l-ē\ *adv*

seg•men•ta•tion \,seg-mən-'tā-shən, -,men-\ *n* **:** the process of dividing into segments; *esp* **:** the formation of many cells from a single cell (as in a developing egg)

se•go lily \,sē-gō-\ *n* **:** a western North American perennial herb of the lily family with bell-shaped flowers white within and largely green without and an edible bulb [Paiute *sego* "bulb of the sego lily"]

[1]**seg•re•gate** \'seg-ri-,gāt\ *vb* **1 :** to separate or set apart from others : ISOLATE; *esp* **:** to separate by races **2 :** to separate from the general mass and collect together (as in crystallization) **3 :** to separate during meiosis [Latin *segregare,* from *se-* "apart" + *greg-, grex* "herd"] — **seg•re•ga•tive** \-,gāt-iv\ *adj*

[2]**seg•re•gate** \-gət, -,gāt\ *n* **:** a segregated individual or class of individuals

seg•re•ga•tion \,seg-ri-'gā-shən\ *n* **1 :** the act or process of segregating : the state of being segregated **2 :** the separation or isolation of a race, class, or ethnic group by discriminatory means (as restriction to an area, barriers to social intercourse, or separate educational facilities)

seg•re•ga•tion•ist \-shə-nəst, -shnəst\ *n* **:** an advocate of segregation especially of races

se•gue \'sāg-wā, 'seg-\ *imperative verb* **:** proceed to what follows without pause — used as a direction in music [Italian, "there follows", from *seguire* "to follow", from Latin *sequi*]

sei•del \'sīd-l\ *n* **:** a large glass for beer [German, from Latin *situla* "bucket"]

sei•gneur \sān-'yər\ *n, often cap* **:** LORD 1a, b, SEIGNIOR [Middle French, from Medieval Latin *senior,* from Latin, adj., "senior"] — **sei•gneur•ial** \-ē-əl\ *adj*

sei•gnior \sān-'yȯr, 'sān-,\ *n* **:** a man of rank or authority; *esp* **:** the feudal lord of a manor [Middle French *seigneur*]

sei•gniory *or* **sei•gnory** \'sān-yə-rē\ *n, pl* **-gnior•ies** *or* **-gnor•ies :** the territory of a lord : DOMAIN

sei•gno•ri•al \sān-'yōr-ē-əl, -'yȯr-\ *adj* **:** of, relating to, or befitting a seignior : MANORIAL

[1]**seine** \'sān \ *n* **:** a large fishing net kept vertical in the water by weights and floats [Old English *segne,* from Latin *sagena,* from Greek *sagēnē*]

[2]**seine** *vb* **:** to fish with or catch with a seine — **sein•er** *n*

seism \'sī-zəm\ *n* **:** EARTHQUAKE [Greek *seismos*]

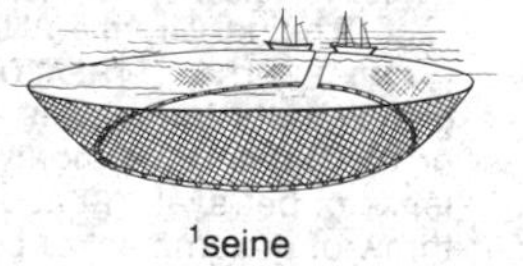
[1]seine

seis•mic \'sīz-mik, 'sīs-\ *adj* **:** of, subject to, or caused by an earthquake or an artificially produced earth vibration — **seis•mi•cal•ly** \-mi-kə-lē, -klē\ *adv*

seis•mo- *combining form* **:** earthquake : vibration ⟨*seismograph*⟩ [Greek *seismos* "shock, earthquake", from *seiein* "to shake"]

seis•mo•gram \'sīz-mə-,gram, 'sīs-\ *n* **:** the record of an earth tremor made by a seismograph

seis•mo•graph \-,graf\ *n* **:** an apparatus for recording the intensity, direction, and duration of earthquakes or similar vibrations of the ground — **seis•mo•graph•ic** \,sīz-mə-'graf-ik, ,sīs-\ *adj* — **seis•mog•ra•phy** \sīz-'mäg-rə-fē, sīs-\ *n*

seis•mol•o•gy \sīz-'mäl-ə-jē, sīs-\ *n* **:** a science that deals with earthquakes and with artificially produced vibrations of the earth — **seis•mo•log•i•cal** \,sīz-mə-'läj-i-kəl, ,sīs-\ *adj* — **seis•mo•log•i•cal•ly** \-kə-lē, -klē\ *adv* — **seis•mol•o•gist** \sīz-'mäl-ə-jəst, sīs-\ *n*

seize \'sēz\ *vb* **1 :** to take possession of : CONFISCATE **2 :** to take possession of by force ⟨*seize* a fortress⟩ **3 :** to take hold of suddenly or with force : CLUTCH **4 :** UNDERSTAND, COMPREHEND ⟨*seize* an idea quickly⟩ **5 :** to take prisoner : ARREST **6 :** to bind together by lashing (as with small cord) ⟨*seize* two ropes⟩ **7 :** to attack or overwhelm suddenly ⟨was *seized* with a fever⟩ **8 a :** to stick fast to or jam with a part in relative motion ⟨the piston *seized*⟩ **b :** to fail to operate due to the seizing of a part ⟨the engine *seized*⟩ [Old French *saisir* "to put in possession of", from Medieval Latin *sacire,* of Germanic origin] **syn** see TAKE — **seiz•er** *n*

seiz•ing \'sē-ziŋ\ *n* **1 :** the operation of fastening together or lashing with small rope or cord **2 a :** the cord used in seizing **b :** the fastening so made

sei•zure \'sē-zhər\ *n* **1 :** the act or process of seizing **:** the state of being seized **2 :** a sudden attack (as of disease) **:** FIT

se•lag•i•nel•la \sə-ˌlaj-ə-'nel-ə\ *n* **:** any of a genus of mossy lower vascular plants [New Latin, from Latin *selagin-, selago,* a kind of plant]

se•lah \'sē-lə, -ˌlä\ *interj* — a term of uncertain meaning found in the Hebrew text of the Psalms and Habakkuk carried over untranslated into some English versions [Hebrew *selāh*]

sel•dom \'sel-dəm\ *adv* **:** in few instances **:** RARELY [Old English *seldan*]

[1]se•lect \sə-'lekt\ *adj* **1 :** chosen from a number or group by fitness or preference **2 a :** of special value or excellence **:** SUPERIOR, CHOICE ⟨a *select* hotel⟩ **b :** carefully or fastidiously chosen often with regard to social, economic, or cultural characteristics ⟨a *select* membership⟩ **3 :** judicious or restrictive in choice **:** DISCRIMINATING [Latin *selectus,* past participle of *seligere* "to select", from *se-* "apart" + *legere* "to gather, pick"] — **se•lect•ness** *n*

[2]select *vb* **:** to take by preference from a number or group **:** pick out **:** CHOOSE

se•lect•ee \sə-ˌlek-'tē\ *n* **:** one inducted into military service under selective service

se•lec•tion \sə-'lek-shən\ *n* **1 :** the act or process of selecting **:** the state of being selected **2 :** one that is selected **:** CHOICE; *also* **:** a collection of selected things **3 :** a natural or artificial process that results or tends to result in the survival and reproduction of some individuals or organisms but not of others with the result that the inherited traits of the survivors are perpetuated

se•lec•tive \sə-'lek-tiv\ *adj* **1 :** of, relating to, or characterized by selection **:** selecting or tending to select **2 :** of, relating to, or constituting the ability of a radio circuit or apparatus to respond to a specific frequency without interference — **se•lec•tive•ly** *adv* — **se•lec•tive•ness** *n* — **se•lec•tiv•i•ty** \si-ˌlek-'tiv-ət-ē, ˌsē-\ *n*

selective service *n* **:** a system under which individuals are called up for military service **:** DRAFT

se•lect•man \sə-'lekt-ˌman, -'lek-, -mən; -ˌlekt-'man, -ˌlek-\ *n* **:** one of a board of elected town officials in all New England states except Rhode Island

se•lec•tor \sə-'lek-tər\ *n* **:** one that selects

sel•e•nite \'sel-ə-ˌnīt\ *n* **:** a variety of gypsum occurring in transparent colorless crystals or crystalline masses [Latin *selenites,* from Greek *selēnitēs lithos,* literally, "stone of the moon", from *selēnē* "moon"; from the belief that it waxed and waned with the moon]

se•le•ni•um \sə-'lē-nē-əm\ *n* **:** a nonmetallic chemical element resembling sulfur in chemical properties that is used chiefly in electronic devices — see ELEMENT table [New Latin, from Greek *selēnē* "moon"]

sel•e•nog•ra•phy \ˌsel-ə-'näg-rə-fē\ *n* **1 :** the science of the physical features of the moon **2 :** the physical features of the moon [Greek *selēnē* "moon"] — **sel•e•nog•ra•pher** \-fər\ *n* — **se•le•no•graph•ic** \ˌsel-ə-nō-'graf-ik, sə-ˌlē-nə-\ *adj*

[1]self \'self, *South also* 'sef\ *pron* **:** MYSELF, HIMSELF, HERSELF ⟨check payable to *self*⟩ [Old English, intensive pron.]

[2]self *adj* **1 :** having a single character or quality throughout; *esp* **:** having one color only ⟨a *self* flower⟩ **2 :** of the same kind (as in color, material, or pattern) as something with which it is used ⟨a *self* belt⟩ ⟨*self* trimming⟩

[3]self \'self\ *n, pl* **selves** \'selvz, *South also* 'sevz\ **1 :** a person regarded as an individual apart from everyone else **2 :** a typical or particular aspect of one's behavior or character ⟨one's true *self*⟩ ⟨your better *self*⟩ **3 :** personal interest or advantage ⟨without thought of *self*⟩

[4]self *vb* **1 :** INBREED **2 :** SELF-POLLINATE

self- *combining form* **1 a :** oneself or itself ⟨*self*-devouring⟩ **b :** of oneself or itself ⟨*self*-abasement⟩ **c :** by oneself or itself ⟨*self*-made⟩ **2 a :** to, with, for, or toward oneself or itself ⟨*self*-addressed⟩ ⟨*self*-satisfaction⟩ **b :** of or in oneself or itself inherently ⟨*self*-evident⟩ **c :** from or by means of oneself or itself ⟨*self*-fertile⟩

self-aban•doned \ˌsel-fə-'ban-dənd\ *adj* **:** abandoned by oneself; *esp* **:** given up to one's impulses

self-abase•ment \ˌsel-fə-'bās-mənt\ *n* **:** humiliation of oneself based on feelings of inferiority, guilt, or shame

self-ab•ne•gat•ing \'sel-'fab-ni-ˌgāt-iŋ\ *adj* **:** SELF-DENYING

self-ab•ne•ga•tion \ˌsel-ˌfab-ni-'gā-shən\ *n* **:** SELF-DENIAL

self-ab•sorbed \ˌsel-fəb-'sȯrbd, -'zȯrbd\ *adj* **:** absorbed in one's own thoughts, activities, or interests

self-ab•sorp•tion \-'sȯrp-shən, -'zȯrp-\ *n* **:** preoccupation with oneself

self-abuse \ˌsel-fə-'byüs\ *n* **1 :** reproach of oneself **2 :** MASTURBATION

self-ac•cu•sa•tion \ˌsel-ˌfak-yə-'zā-shən\ *n* **:** the act or an instance of accusing oneself

self-ac•quired \ˌsel-fə-'kwīrd\ *adj* **:** acquired by oneself

self-act•ing \'sel-'fak-tiŋ\ *adj* **:** acting or capable of acting of or by itself

self-ad•dressed \ˌsel-fə-'drest, 'sel-'fad-ˌrest\ *adj* **:** addressed for return to the sender ⟨*self-addressed* envelopes⟩

self-ad•just•ing \ˌsel-fə-'jəs-tiŋ\ *adj* **:** adjusting by itself ⟨a *self-adjusting* wrench⟩

self-ad•min•is•tered \ˌsel-fəd-'min-ə-stərd\ *adj* **:** administered, managed, or dispensed by oneself

self-ad•mi•ra•tion \ˌsel-ˌfad-mə-'rā-shən\ *n* **:** SELF-CONCEIT

self-ad•vance•ment \ˌsel-fəd-'van-smənt\ *n* **:** the act of advancing oneself

self-af•fect•ed \ˌsel-fə-'fek-təd\ *adj* **:** VAIN 3, CONCEITED

self-ag•gran•dize•ment \ˌsel-fə-'gran-dəz-mənt, -ˌdīz-; ˌsel-ˌfag-rən-'dīz-\ *n* **:** the act or process of making oneself greater (as in power or influence)

self-ag•gran•diz•ing \ˌsel-fə-'gran-ˌdī-ziŋ, 'sel-'fag-rən-\ *adj* **:** acting or seeking to make oneself greater

self-anal•y•sis \ˌsel-fə-'nal-ə-səs\ *n* **:** a systematic attempt by an individual to understand his or her own personality without the aid of another person — **self-an•a•lyt•i•cal** \ˌsel-ˌfan-l-'it-i-kəl\ *adj*

self-ap•plause \ˌsel-fə-'plȯz\ *n* **:** an expression or feeling of approval of oneself

self-ap•point•ed \ˌsel-fə-'pȯint-əd\ *adj* **:** appointed by oneself usually without justification or qualifications ⟨a *self-appointed* censor⟩

self-ap•pro•ba•tion \ˌsel-ˌfap-rə-'bā-shən\ *n* **:** satisfaction with one's actions and achievements

self-as•sert•ing \ˌsel-fə-'sərt-iŋ\ *adj* **1 :** asserting oneself or one's own rights, opinions, or claims **2 :** putting oneself forward in a confident or arrogant manner

self-as•ser•tion \ˌsel-fə-'sər-shən\ *n* **1 :** the act of asserting oneself or one's own rights, opinions, or claims **2 :** the act of asserting one's superiority over others

self-as•ser•tive \-'sərt-iv\ *adj* **:** given to or marked by self-assertion — **self-as•ser•tive•ly** *adv* — **self-as•ser•tive•ness** *n*

self-as•sur•ance \ˌsel-fə-'shu̇r-əns\ *n* **:** SELF-CONFIDENCE

self-as•sured \-'shu̇rd\ *adj* **:** SELF-CONFIDENT — **self-as•sured•ness** \-'shu̇r-əd-nəs, -'shu̇rd-\ *n*

self-aware•ness \ˌsel-fə-'waer-nəs, -'weər-\ *n* **:** an awareness of one's own personality or individuality

self-born \'self-'bȯrn\ *adj* **1 :** arising within the self ⟨*self-born* sorrows⟩ **2 :** springing from a prior self ⟨a phoenix rising *self-born* from the fire⟩

self-cen•tered \'self-'sent-ərd\ *adj* **:** interested chiefly in one's own self **:** SELFISH — **self-cen•tered•ly** *adv* — **self-cen•tered•ness** *n*

self-charg•ing \-'chär-jiŋ\ *adj* **:** that charges itself

self-clos•ing \-'klō-ziŋ\ *adj* **:** closing or shutting automatically after being opened

self-com•mand \ˌself-kə-'mand\ *n* **:** control of one's own behavior and emotions **:** SELF-CONTROL

self-com•pat•i•ble \ˌself-kəm-'pat-ə-bəl\ *adj* **:** capable of effective self-pollination — compare SELF-INCOMPATIBLE

self-com•pla•cent \ˌself-kəm-'plās-nt\ *adj* **:** SELF-SATISFIED, COMPLACENT — **self-com•pla•cen•cy** \-'plās-n-sē\ *n* — **self-com•pla•cent•ly** *adv*

\ə\ **abut**	\au̇\ **out**	\i\ **tip**	\ȯ\ **saw**	\u̇\ **foot**
\ər\ **further**	\ch\ **chin**	\ī\ **life**	\ȯi\ **coin**	\y\ **yet**
\a\ **mat**	\e\ **pet**	\j\ **job**	\th\ **thin**	\yü\ **few**
\ā\ **take**	\ē\ **easy**	\ŋ\ **sing**	\t͟h\ **this**	\yu̇\ **cure**
\ä\ **cot, cart**	\g\ **go**	\ō\ **bone**	\ü\ **food**	\zh\ **vision**

self–com•posed \ˌself-kəm-ˈpōzd\ *adj* : having one's emotions under control — **self–com•pos•ed•ly** \-ˈpō-zəd-lē\ *adv*
self–con•ceit \ˌself-kən-ˈsēt\ *n* : too high an opinion of one's qualities or abilities — **self–con•ceit•ed** \-əd\ *adj*
self–con•cern \ˌself-kən-ˈsərn\ *n* : selfish or morbid concern for oneself — **self–con•cerned** \-ˈsərnd\ *adj*
self–con•dem•na•tion \ˌself-ˌkän-ˌdem-ˈnā-shən, -dəm-\ *n* : condemnation of one's own character or actions
self–con•fessed \ˌself-kən-ˈfest\ *adj* : openly acknowledged
self–con•fi•dence \ˈself-ˈkän-fəd-əns, -fə-ˌdens\ *n* : confidence in oneself and in one's powers and abilities — **self–con•fi•dent** \-fəd-ənt, -fə-ˌdent\ *adj* — **self–con•fi•dent•ly** *adv*
self–con•scious \ˈself-ˈkän-chəs\ *adj* **1** : aware of oneself as an individual **2** : uncomfortably conscious of oneself as an object of the observation of others : ill at ease — **self–con•scious•ly** *adv* — **self–con•scious•ness** *n*
self–con•sis•tent \ˌself-kən-ˈsis-tənt\ *adj* : having each part logically consistent with the rest — **self–con•sis•ten•cy** \-tən-sē\ *n*
self–con•sti•tut•ed \ˈself-ˈkän-stə-ˌtüt-əd, -ˌtyüt-\ *adj* : constituted by oneself
self–con•tained \ˌself-kən-ˈtānd\ *adj* **1** : complete in itself **2 a** : showing self-control **b** : formal and reserved in manner — **self–con•tained•ly** \-ˈtā-nəd-lē, -ˈtān-dlē\ *adv* — **self–con•tained•ness** \-ˈtā-nəd-nəs, -ˈtānd-nəs, -ˈtān-nəs\ *n* — **self–con•tain•ment** \-ˈtān-mənt\ *n*
self–con•tempt \ˌself-kən-ˈtemt, -ˈtempt\ *n* : contempt for oneself
self–con•tent•ed \ˌself-kən-ˈtent-əd\ *adj* : SELF-SATISFIED, COMPLACENT — **self–con•tent** \-ˈtent\ *n* — **self–con•tent•ed•ly** *adv* — **self–con•tent•ed•ness** *n* — **self–con•tent•ment** \-ˈtent-mənt\ *n*
self–con•tra•dic•to•ry \ˌself-ˌkän-trə-ˈdik-tə-rē, -trē\ *adj* : consisting of two contradictory members or parts ⟨a *self-contradictory* statement⟩
self–con•trol \ˌself-kən-ˈtrōl\ *n* : control over one's own impulses, emotions, or acts — **self–con•trolled** \-ˈtrōld\ *adj*
self–cor•rect•ing \ˌself-kə-ˈrek-tiŋ\ *adj* : correcting or compensating for one's own errors or weaknesses
self–cor•rec•tive \-ˈrek-tiv\ *adj* : SELF-CORRECTING
self–cre•at•ed \ˌself-krē-ˈāt-əd\ *adj* : created or appointed by oneself
self–crit•i•cism \ˈself-ˈkrit-ə-ˌsiz-əm\ *n* : the act of or capacity for criticizing one's own faults or shortcomings
self–de•ceiv•ing \ˌself-di-ˈsē-viŋ\ *adj* **1** : given to self-deception ⟨a *self-deceiving* hypocrite⟩ **2** : serving to deceive oneself ⟨*self-deceiving* excuses⟩
self–de•cep•tion \ˌself-di-ˈsep-shən\ *n* : the act of deceiving oneself : the state of being deceived by oneself — **self–de•cep•tive** \-ˈsep-tiv\ *adj*
self–ded•i•ca•tion \ˌself-ˌded-i-ˈkā-shən\ *n* : dedication of oneself to a cause or ideal
self–de•feat•ing \ˌself-di-ˈfēt-iŋ\ *adj* : acting to defeat its own purpose
self–de•fense \ˌself-di-ˈfens\ *n* : the act of defending oneself, one's property, or a close relative
self–de•ni•al \ˌself-di-ˈnī-əl, -ˈnīl\ *n* : the act of refraining from gratifying one's own desires — **self–de•ny•ing** \-ˈnī-iŋ\ *adj*
self–de•pen•dence \ˌself-di-ˈpen-dəns\ *n* : SELF-RELIANCE — **self–de•pen•dent** \-dənt\ *adj*
self–de•pre•ci•a•tion \ˌself-di-ˌprē-shē-ˈā-shən\ *n* : belittlement or undervaluation of oneself
self–de•spair \ˌself-di-ˈspaər, -ˈspeər\ *n* : despair of oneself : HOPELESSNESS
self–de•struct \ˌself-di-ˈstrəkt\ *vi* : to destroy itself
self–de•struc•tion \ˌself-di-ˈstrək-shən\ *n* : destruction of oneself; *esp* : SUICIDE — **self–de•struc•tive** \-ˈstrək-tiv\ *adj*
self–de•ter•mi•na•tion \ˌself-di-ˌtər-mə-ˈnā-shən\ *n* **1** : the act or power of deciding things for oneself **2** : the right of a people to determine the form of government they will have — **self–de•ter•min•ing** \-ˈtər-mə-niŋ\ *adj*
self–de•ter•mined \-ˈtər-mənd\ *adj* : determined by oneself
self–de•vel•op•ment \ˌself-di-ˈvel-əp-mənt\ *n* : development of one's own capabilities or possibilities
self–de•vo•tion \ˌself-di-ˈvō-shən\ *n* : devotion of oneself especially in service or sacrifice
self–de•vour•ing \ˌself-di-ˈvau̇r-iŋ\ *adj* : devouring itself
self–di•rect•ed \ˌself-də-ˈrek-təd, -dī-\ *adj* : directed by oneself; *esp* : not guided or impelled by an outside force or agency ⟨a *self-directed* personality⟩
self–dis•ci•pline \ˈself-ˈdis-ə-plən\ *n* : correction or regulation of oneself for the sake of improvement — **self–dis•ci•plined** \-plənd\ *adj*
self–dis•cov•ery \ˌself-dis-ˈkəv-rē, -ə-rē\ *n* : the act or process of achieving self-knowledge
self–dis•trust \ˌself-dis-ˈtrəst\ *n* : a lack of confidence in oneself : DIFFIDENCE — **self–dis•trust•ful** \-fəl\ *adj*
self–doubt \ˈself-ˈdau̇t\ *n* : a lack of faith in oneself — **self–doubt•ing** \-iŋ\ *adj*
self–ed•u•cat•ed \ˈsel-ˈfej-ə-ˌkāt-əd\ *adj* : educated by one's own efforts without formal instruction — **self–ed•u•ca•tion** \ˌsel-ˌfej-ə-ˈkā-shən\ *n*
self–ef•fac•ing \ˌsel-fə-ˈfā-siŋ\ *adj* : tending to keep oneself in the background : UNASSERTIVE — **self–ef•face•ment** \-ˈfā-smənt\ *n* — **self–ef•fac•ing•ly** \-ˈfā-siŋ-lē\ *adv*
self–em•ployed \ˌsel-fim-ˈplȯid\ *adj* : earning income directly from one's own business, trade, or profession rather than as salary or wages from an employer — **self–em•ploy•ment** \-ˈplȯi-mənt\ *n*
self–es•teem \ˌsel-fə-ˈstēm\ *n* **1** : a proper satisfaction with one's own worth **2** : an inflated opinion of one's own worth
self–ev•i•dent \ˈsel-ˈfev-əd-ənt, -ə-ˌdent\ *adj* : evident without proof or argument — **self–ev•i•dent•ly** *adv*
self–ex•am•i•na•tion \ˌsel-fig-ˌzam-ə-ˈnā-shən\ *n* : an act of examining oneself; *esp* : INTROSPECTION
self–ex•e•cut•ing \ˈsel-ˈfek-sə-ˌkyüt-iŋ\ *adj* : taking effect immediately without implementing legislation ⟨a *self-executing* treaty⟩
self–ex•plain•ing \ˌsel-fik-ˈsplā-niŋ\ *adj* : SELF-EXPLANATORY
self–ex•plan•a•to•ry \-ˈsplan-ə-ˌtōr-ē, -ˌtȯr-\ *adj* : understandable without explanation
self–ex•pres•sion \ˌsel-fik-ˈspresh-ən\ *n* : the expression of one's own personality : assertion of one's individual traits — **self–ex•pres•sive** \-ˈspres-iv\ *adj*
self–feed•er \ˈself-ˈfēd-ər\ *n* : a device for feeding livestock equipped with a feed hopper that automatically supplies a trough
self–fer•tile \ˈself-ˈfərt-ᵊl\ *adj* : fertile by means of its own pollen or sperm — **self–fer•til•i•ty** \ˌself-fər-ˈtil-ət-ē\ *n*
self–fer•til•iza•tion \ˌself-ˌfərt-ᵊl-ə-ˈzā-shən\ *n* : fertilization by pollen or sperm from the same individual — **self–fer•til•ize** \ˈself-ˈfərt-ᵊl-ˌīz\ *vb*
self–flat•tery \ˈself-ˈflat-ə-rē\ *n* : the glossing over of one's own weaknesses or mistakes and the exaggeration of one's own good qualities and achievements
self–for•get•ful \ˌself-fər-ˈget-fəl\ *adj* : having or showing no thought of self or selfish interests — **self–for•get•ful•ly** \-fə-lē\ *adv* — **self–for•get•ful•ness** *n*
self–formed \ˈself-ˈfȯrmd\ *adj* : formed or developed by one's own efforts
self–fruit•ful \ˈself-ˈfrüt-fəl\ *adj* : capable of setting a crop of self-pollinated fruit — **self–fruit•ful•ness** *n*
self–ful•fill•ing \ˌself-fu̇l-ˈfil-iŋ\ *adj* : marked by or achieving self-fulfillment
self–ful•fill•ment \-ˈfil-mənt\ *n* : fulfillment of oneself
self–giv•ing \ˈself-ˈgiv-iŋ\ *adj* : inclined to self-sacrifice : UNSELFISH
self–glo•ri•fi•ca•tion \ˌself-ˌglōr-ə-fə-ˈkā-shən, -ˌglȯr-\ *n* : a feeling or expression of one's own superiority
self–glo•ry \ˈself-ˈglōr-ē, -ˈglȯr-\ *n* : personal vanity : PRIDE
self–gov•ern•ment \ˈself-ˈgəv-ər-mənt; -ˈgəb-m-ənt, -ˈgəv-; -ˈgəv-ərn-mənt\ *n* **1** : SELF-CONTROL **2** : government of a political unit by action of its own people; *esp* : democratic government — **self–gov•erned** \-ˈgəv-ərnd\ *adj* — **self–gov•ern•ing** \-ər-niŋ\ *adj*
self–grat•i•fi•ca•tion \ˌself-ˌgrat-ə-fə-ˈkā-shən\ *n* : the act of pleasing oneself or of satisfying one's desires
self–hard•en•ing \ˈself-ˈhärd-niŋ, -ᵊn-iŋ\ *adj* : hardening by itself or without quenching after heating ⟨*self-hardening* steel⟩
self–heal \ˈself-ˌhēl\ *n* : a low-growing blue-flowered mint supposed to have healing powers
self–help \ˈself-ˈhelp\ *n* : the act or an instance of providing for or helping oneself without depending on others
self–hyp•no•sis \ˌself-hip-ˈnō-səs\ *n* : hypnosis of oneself

self–ig•nite \ˌsel-fig-ˈnīt\ *vi* : to become ignited without flame or spark (as under high compression) — **self–ig•ni•tion** \-ˈnish-ən\ *n*
self–im•age \ˈsel-ˈfim-ij\ *n* : one's conception of oneself or of one's role
self–im•mo•la•tion \ˌsel-ˌfim-ə-ˈlā-shən\ *n* : a deliberate and willing sacrifice of oneself
self–im•por•tance \ˌsel-fim-ˈpȯrt-ⁿs, -ənsˋ\ *n* **1** : an exaggerated estimate of one's own importance : SELF-CONCEIT **2** : arrogant or pompous behavior — **self–im•por•tant** \-ⁿt, -əntˋ\ *adj* — **self–im•por•tant•ly** *adv*
self–im•posed \ˌsel-fim-ˈpōzd\ *adj* : imposed on one by oneself : voluntarily assumed ⟨a *self-imposed* exile⟩
self–im•prove•ment \ˌsel-fim-ˈprüv-mənt\ *n* : improvement of oneself by one's own action
self–in•clu•sive \ˌsel-fin-ˈklü-siv, -ziv\ *adj* : SELF-CONTAINED 1
self–in•com•pat•i•ble \ˌsel-ˌfin-kəm-ˈpat-ə-bəl\ *adj* : incapable of effective self-pollination — compare SELF-COMPATIBLE
self–in•crim•i•na•tion \ˌsel-fin-ˌkrim-ə-ˈnā-shən\ *n* : incrimination of oneself; *esp* : the giving of evidence or answering of questions which could make one subject to criminal prosecution — **self–in•crim•i•nat•ing** \-ˈkrim-ə-ˌnāt-ing\ *adj*
self–in•duced \ˌsel-fin-ˈdüst, -ˈdyüst\ *adj* **1** : induced by oneself **2** : produced by self-induction ⟨a *self-induced* voltage⟩
self–in•duc•tance \-ˈdək-təns\ *n* : inductance that induces an electromotive force in the same circuit as the one in which the current varies
self–in•duc•tion \-ˈdək-shən\ *n* : induction of an electromotive force in a circuit by a varying current in the same circuit
self–in•dul•gence \ˌsel-fin-ˈdəl-jəns\ *n* : overindulgence of one's own appetites, desires, or whims — **self–in•dul•gent** \-jənt\ *adj* — **self–in•dul•gent•ly** *adv*
self–in•flict•ed \ˌsel-fin-ˈflik-təd\ *adj* : inflicted by oneself ⟨a *self-inflicted* wound⟩
self–in•struct•ed \ˌsel-fin-ˈstrək-təd\ *adj* : SELF-TAUGHT
self–in•ter•est \ˈsel-ˈfin-trəst, -ˈfint-ə-rəst\ *n* **1** : one's own interest or advantage **2** : a concern for one's own advantage and well-being — **self–in•ter•est•ed** \-əd\ *adj* — **self–in•ter•est•ed•ness** *n*
self–in•volved \ˌsel-fin-ˈvälvd, -ˈvȯlvd\ *adj* : SELF-ABSORBED
self•ish \ˈsel-fish\ *adj* **1** : concerned excessively or exclusively with oneself : seeking or concentrating on one's own advantage, pleasure, or well-being without regard for others **2** : arising from concern with one's own welfare or advantage in disregard of others ⟨a *selfish* act⟩ — **self•ish•ly** *adv* — **self•ish•ness** *n*
self–jus•ti•fi•ca•tion \ˌself-ˌjəs-tə-fə-ˈkā-shən\ *n* : the act or an instance of making excuses for oneself
self–knowl•edge \ˈself-ˈnäl-ij\ *n* : knowledge of one's own capabilities, character, feelings, or motivations
self•less \ˈsel-fləs\ *adj* : having or showing no concern for self : UNSELFISH — **self•less•ly** *adv* — **self•less•ness** *n*
self–lim•it•ing \ˈsel-ˈflim-ət-ing\ *adj* : limiting oneself or itself
self–lock•ing \ˈsel-ˈfläk-ing\ *adj* : locking by its own action
self–love \ˈsel-ˈfləv\ *n* : love of self: **a** : CONCEIT 1, SELF-CONCEIT **b** : regard for one's own happiness or advantage — **self–lov•ing** \-ing\ *adj*
self–lu•bri•cat•ing \ˈsel-ˈflü-brə-ˌkāt-ing\ *adj* : lubricating itself
self–lu•mi•nous \ˈsel-ˈflü-mə-nəs\ *adj* : having in itself the property of emitting light
self–made \ˈself-ˈmād\ *adj* **1** : made by oneself or itself **2** : raised from poverty or obscurity by one's own efforts
self–mas•tery \ˈself-ˈmas-tə-rē, -trē\ *n* : SELF-COMMAND, SELF-CONTROL
self–ob•ser•va•tion \ˌsel-ˌfäb-sər-ˈvā-shən, -zər-\ *n* **1** : observation of one's own appearance **2** : INTROSPECTION
self–op•er•at•ing \ˈsel-ˈfäp-ə-ˌrāt-ing\ *or* **self–op•er•a•tive** \-ˈfäp-rət-iv, -ə-rət-; -ˈfäp-ə-ˌrāt-\ *adj* : SELF-ACTING
self–opin•ion•at•ed \ˌsel-fə-ˈpin-yə-ˌnāt-əd\ *adj* **1** : CONCEITED **2** : stubbornly holding to one's own opinion
self–orig•i•nat•ed \ˌsel-fə-ˈrij-ə-ˌnāt-əd\ *adj* : originated by oneself or itself
self–per•pet•u•at•ing \ˌself-pər-ˈpech-ə-ˌwāt-ing\ *adj* : capable of continuing or renewing itself indefinitely ⟨*self-perpetuating* board of trustees⟩
self–pity \ˈself-ˈpit-ē\ *n* : pity for oneself — **self–pity•ing** \-ē-ing\ *adj* — **self–pity•ing•ly** \-ing-lē\ *adv*
self–poised \ˈself-ˈpȯizd\ *adj* **1** : balanced without support **2** : having poise through self-command
self–pol•li•nate \ˈself-ˈpäl-ə-ˌnāt\ *vb* : to undergo or cause to undergo self-pollination
self–pol•li•na•tion \ˌself-ˌpäl-ə-ˈnā-shən\ *n* : pollination in which the pollen transferred is from the same flower or sometimes from a genetically identical flower (as of the same plant or clone)
self–por•trait \ˈself-ˈpōr-trət, -ˈpȯr-, -ˌtrāt\ *n* : a portrait of oneself done by oneself
self–pos•sessed \ˌself-pə-ˈzest\ *adj* : composed in mind or manner : CALM — **self–pos•sessed•ly** \-ˈzes-əd-lē, -ˈzest-lē\ *adv*
self–pos•ses•sion \ˌself-pə-ˈzesh-ən\ *n* : control of one's emotions or reactions : COMPOSURE
self–praise \ˈself-ˈprāz\ *n* : praise of oneself
self–pres•er•va•tion \ˌself-ˌprez-ər-ˈvā-shən\ *n* : the keeping of oneself from destruction, injury, or loss
self–pride \ˌself-ˈprīd\ *n* : pride in oneself or in that which relates to oneself
self–pro•claimed \ˌself-prō-ˈklāmd\ *adj* : SELF-STYLED ⟨a *self-proclaimed* genius⟩
self–pro•duced \ˌself-prə-ˈdüst, -ˈdyüst\ *adj* : produced by oneself or itself
self–pro•pelled \ˌself-prə-ˈpeld\ *adj* : containing within itself the means for its own propulsion
self–pro•pel•ling \-ˈpel-ing\ *adj* : SELF-PROPELLED
self–pro•tec•tion \ˌself-prə-ˈtek-shən\ *n* : protection of oneself : SELF-DEFENSE
self–pun•ish•ment \ˈself-ˈpən-ish-mənt\ *n* : punishment of oneself
self–pu•ri•fi•ca•tion \ˌself-ˌpyu̇r-ə-fə-ˈkā-shən\ *n* : purification of oneself ⟨moral *self-purification*⟩
self–ques•tion•ing \ˈself-ˈkwes-chə-ning\ *n* : INTROSPECTION
self–re•al•iza•tion \ˌsel-ˌfrē-ə-lə-ˈzā-shən\ *n* : fulfillment by oneself of the possibilities of one's character or personality
self–re•cord•ing \ˌsel-fri-ˈkȯrd-ing\ *adj* : making a record automatically ⟨*self-recording* instruments⟩
self–re•gard \ˌsel-fri-ˈgärd\ *n* **1** : regard for or consideration of oneself or one's own interests **2** : SELF-RESPECT 1 — **self–re•gard•ing** \-ing\ *adj*
self–reg•is•ter•ing \ˈsel-ˈfrej-ə-stə-ring, -string\ *adj* : registering automatically ⟨a *self-registering* barometer⟩
self–reg•u•lat•ing \ˈsel-ˈfreg-yə-ˌlāt-ing\ *adj* : regulating oneself or itself; *esp* : AUTOMATIC ⟨a *self-regulating* mechanism⟩ — **self–reg•u•la•tion** \ˌsel-ˌfreg-yə-ˈlā-shən\ *n*
self–re•li•ance \ˌsel-fri-ˈlī-ənts\ *n* : reliance on one's own efforts and abilities — **self–re•li•ant** \-ənt\ *adj*
self–re•nun•ci•a•tion \ˌsel-fri-ˌnən-sē-ˈā-shən\ *n* : renunciation of one's own desires or ambitions
self–rep•li•cat•ing \ˈsel-ˈfrep-lə-ˌkāt-ing\ *adj* : duplicating itself ⟨DNA is a *self-replicating* molecule⟩
self–re•proach \ˌsel-fri-ˈprōch\ *n* : the act of blaming or accusing oneself — **self–re•proach•ful** \-fəl\ *adj* — **self–re•proach•ing** \-ˈprō-ching\ *adj*
self–re•pro•duc•ing \ˈsel-ˌfrē-prə-ˈdü-sing, -ˈdyü-\ *adj* : SELF-REPLICATING
self–re•spect \ˌsel-fri-ˈspekt\ *n* **1** : a proper respect for oneself as a human being **2** : regard for one's own standing or position — **self–re•spect•ing** \-ˈspek-ting\ *adj*
self–re•straint \ˌsel-fri-ˈstrānt\ *n* : restraint imposed on oneself : SELF-CONTROL
self–re•veal•ing \ˌsel-fri-ˈvē-ling\ *adj* : marked by self-revelation
self–rev•e•la•tion \ˌsel-ˌfrev-ə-ˈlā-shən\ *n* : revelation of one's own thoughts, feelings, and attitudes especially without deliberate intent
self–re•ward•ing \ˌsel-fri-ˈwȯrd-ing\ *adj* : containing or producing its own reward ⟨a *self-rewarding* virtue⟩
self–righ•teous \ˈsel-ˈfrī-chəs\ *adj* : convinced of one's own righteousness especially in contrast with the actions and beliefs of others — **self–righ•teous•ly** *adv* — **self–righ•teous•ness** *n*

\ə\ **abut**	\au̇\ **out**	\i\ **tip**	\ȯ\ **saw**	\u̇\ **foot**
\ər\ **further**	\ch\ **chin**	\ī\ **life**	\ȯi\ **coin**	\y\ **yet**
\a\ **mat**	\e\ **pet**	\j\ **job**	\th\ **thin**	\yü\ **few**
\ā\ **take**	\ē\ **easy**	\ng\ **sing**	\th̲\ **this**	\yu̇\ **cure**
\ä\ **cot, cart**	\g\ **go**	\ō\ **bone**	\ü\ **food**	\zh\ **vision**

self–right•ing \'sel-'frīt-iŋ\ *adj* : capable of righting itself when capsized ⟨a *self-righting* boat⟩
self–ris•ing \'sel-'frī-ziŋ\ *adj* : rising without the use of leaven ⟨*self-rising* flour⟩
self–sac•ri•fice \'self-'sak-rə-ˌfīs, -fəs\ *n* : sacrifice of oneself or one's interest for others or for a cause or ideal — **self–sac•ri•fic•ing** \-ˌfī-siŋ\ *adj* — **self–sac•ri•fic•ing•ly** \-siŋ-lē\ *adv*
self•same \'self-ˌsām\ *adj* : precisely the same : IDENTICAL — **self•same•ness** *n*
self–sat•is•fac•tion \ˌself-ˌsat-əs-'fak-shən\ *n* : a usually smug satisfaction with oneself, one's position, or one's achievements
self–sat•is•fied \'self-'sat-əs-ˌfīd\ *adj* : feeling or showing self-satisfaction
self–sat•is•fy•ing \-ˌfī-iŋ\ *adj* : giving satisfaction to oneself
self–seal•ing \'self-'sē-liŋ\ *adj* : capable of sealing itself (as after puncture) ⟨a *self-sealing* tire⟩
self–search•ing \'self-'sər-chiŋ\ *adj* : SELF-QUESTIONING
self–seek•er \'self-'sē-kər\ *n* : a person who is interested only in his or her own advantage or pleasure — **self–seek•ing** \-kiŋ\ *n or adj*
self–ser•vice \'self-'sər-vəs\ *n* : the serving of oneself (as in a cafeteria or market) with things to be paid for usually upon leaving — **self–service** *adj*
self–slaugh•ter \'self-'slȯt-ər\ *n* : SUICIDE 1a
self–sow \'self-'sō\ *vi* : to sow itself by dropping seeds or by natural action (as of wind or water)
self–start•er \'self-'stärt-ər\ *n* : a more or less automatic attachment for starting an internal-combustion engine
self–start•ing \-'stärt-iŋ\ *adj* : capable of starting by itself
self–ster•ile \'self-'ster-əl\ *adj* : sterile to its own pollen or sperm — **self–ste•ril•i•ty** \ˌself-stə-'ril-ət-ē\ *n*
self–styled \'self-'stīld\ *adj* : called by oneself ⟨*self-styled* experts⟩
self–suf•fi•cient \ˌself-sə-'fish-ənt\ *adj* **1** : able to take care of oneself without outside help **2** : having great confidence in one's own ability or worth : SECURE — **self–suf•fi•cien•cy** \-ən-sē\ *n*
self–suf•fic•ing \ˌself-sə-'fī-siŋ\ *adj* : SELF-SUFFICIENT 1 — **self–suf•fic•ing•ly** \-'fī-siŋ-lē\ *adv* — **self–suf•fic•ing•ness** *n*
self–sup•port \ˌself-sə-'pōrt, -'pȯrt\ *n* : independent support of oneself or itself — **self–sup•port•ed** \-əd\ *adj* — **self–sup•port•ing** \-iŋ\ *adj*
self–sus•tained \ˌself-sə-'stānd\ *adj* : sustained by oneself
self–sus•tain•ing \-'stā-niŋ\ *adj* **1** : maintaining or able to maintain oneself by independent effort : SELF-SUPPORTING **2** : maintaining or able to maintain itself once started ⟨a *self-sustaining* nuclear reaction⟩
self–taught \'self-'tȯt\ *adj* **1** : having knowledge or skills acquired by one's own efforts without formal instruction **2** : learned by oneself ⟨*self-taught* knowledge⟩
self–treat•ment \'self-'trēt-mənt\ *n* : medication of oneself or treatment of one's ailment without outside medical supervision
self–trust \'self-'trəst\ *n* : SELF-CONFIDENCE
self–un•der•stand•ing \ˌsel-ˌfən-dər-'stan-diŋ\ *n* : SELF-KNOWLEDGE
self–will \'self-'wil\ *n* : stubborn or willful adherence to one's own desires or ideas : OBSTINACY — **self–willed** \-'wild\ *adj*
self–wind•ing \'self-'wīn-diŋ\ *adj* : not needing to be wound by hand : winding by itself ⟨a *self-winding* watch⟩
Sel•juk \'sel-ˌjük, sel-'\ *or* **Sel•ju•ki•an** \sel-'jü-kē-ən\ *adj* **1** : of or relating to any of several Turkish dynasties ruling in western Asia in the 11th, 12th, and 13th centuries **2** : of, relating to, or characteristic of a Turkish people ruled over by a Seljuk dynasty [Turkish *Selçuk,* ancestor of the dynasties] — **Seljuk** *or* **Seljukian** *n*
[1]**sell** \'sel\ *vb* **sold** \'sōld\; **sell•ing** **1** : to deliver up in violation of duty, trust, or loyalty : BETRAY ⟨the traitors *sold* their king to the enemy⟩ **2 a** : to give in exchange especially for money ⟨they *sold* us some fish⟩; *also* : to give in exchange foolishly or dishonorably ⟨sell one's birthright for a mess of pottage⟩ **b** : to work at or deal in the sale of : have or offer for sale ⟨*sells* insurance⟩ ⟨that store *sells* imported foods⟩; *also* : to achieve the sale of ⟨tried *selling* encyclopedias for a while⟩ **3 a** : to find buyers : be bought ⟨that model didn't *sell* very well⟩ **b** : to be for sale ⟨they *sell* for $15 apiece⟩ **4 a** : to make acceptable, believable, or desirable by persuasion ⟨the President couldn't *sell* the program to Congress⟩ **b** : to bring around to a favorable way of thinking ⟨tried to *sell* me on the idea⟩ **c** : to gain acceptance or approval ⟨your idea won't *sell* with them⟩ [Old English *sellan*] — **sell•able** \'sel-ə-bəl\ *adj* — **sell short** **1** : to make a short sale of ⟨*sell* a stock *short*⟩ **2** : to underestimate the ability, strength, or importance of
[2]**sell** *n* **1** : a deliberate deception : HOAX **2** : the act or a type of selling : SALESMANSHIP
sell•er \'sel-ər\ *n* **1** : one that offers for sale or makes a sale **2** : a product selling well or to a specified extent ⟨a good *seller*⟩
seller's market *n* : a market with few goods at relatively high prices — compare BUYER'S MARKET
sell•out \'sel-ˌau̇t\ *n* **1** : the act or an instance of selling out **2** : a performance or exhibition for which all seats are sold
sell out \sel-'au̇t, 'sel-\ *vb* **1 a** : to dispose of one's goods by sale **b** : to sell the goods of usually to meet an obligation **2** : to betray one's cause or associates
selt•zer \'selt-sər\ *n* : an artificially prepared water containing carbon dioxide [German *Selterser wasser* "water of Selters", from *Nieder Selters,* Germany]
sel•va \'sel-və\ *n* : a tropical rain forest [Spanish and Portuguese, "forest", from Latin *silva* "wood, grove"]
sel•vage *or* **sel•vedge** \'sel-vij\ *n* : the edge of cloth so woven that it will not ravel [Middle English *selvage,* probably from Flemish *selvegge, selvage,* from *selv* "self" + *egge* "edge"]
selves *pl of* SELF
se•man•tic \si-'mant-ik\ *adj* **1** : of or relating to meaning in language **2** : of or relating to semantics [Greek *sēmantikos* "significant", from *sēmanein* "to signify, mean", from *sēma* "sign, token"] — **se•man•ti•cal•ly** \-'mant-i-kə-lē, -klē\ *adv*
se•man•ti•cist \si-'mant-ə-səst\ *n* : a specialist in semantics
se•man•tics \si-'mant-iks\ *n* **1** : the study of meanings **2 a** : the meaning or relationship of meaning of a word or set of words ⟨it's just a question of *semantics*⟩ **b** : the careful use of words (as in advertising or political propaganda) to achieve a desired effect on an audience
[1]**sem•a•phore** \'sem-ə-ˌfōr, -ˌfȯr\ *n* **1** : an apparatus for visual signaling (as by the position of one or more movable arms) **2** : a system of visual signaling by two flags held one in each hand [Greek *sēma* "sign, signal"]

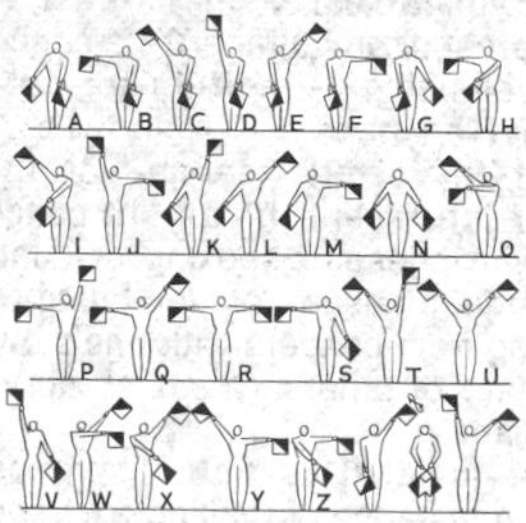

[1]semaphore 2

[2]**semaphore** *vb* : to signal by or as if by semaphore
sem•blance \'sem-bləns\ *n* **1** : outward appearance or show **2 a** : one that resembles another **b** : SIMILARITY 1 [Middle French, from *sembler* "to be like, seem", from Latin *similare* "to copy", from *similis* "like, similar"]
se•men \'sē-mən\ *n, pl* **sem•i•na** \'sem-ə-nə\ *or* **semens** : a viscid whitish fluid of the male reproductive tract consisting of spermatozoa suspended in secretions of accessory glands [Latin, "seed"]
se•mes•ter \sə-'mes-tər\ *n* : one of two usually 18-week terms into which an academic year is often divided [German, from Latin *semestris* "half-yearly", from *sex* "six" + *mensis* "month"] — **se•mes•tral** \-trəl\ *or* **se•mes•tri•al** \-trē-əl\ *adj*
semi- \ˌsem-i, 'sem-, -ē, -ˌī\ *prefix* **1 a** : precisely half of **b** : half in quantity or value : half of or occurring halfway through a specified period of time ⟨*semi*annual⟩ ⟨*semi*centennial⟩ — compare BI- **2** : to some extent : partly : incompletely ⟨*semi*-dry⟩ ⟨*semi*-independent⟩ — compare DEMI-, HEMI- **3 a** : partial : incomplete ⟨*semi*darkness⟩ **b** : having some of the characteristics of ⟨*semi*desert⟩ **c** : in some sense or degree ⟨*semi*governmental⟩ [Latin]
semi•ab•strac•tion \ˌsem-ē-ab-'strak-shən, ˌsem-ˌī-\ *n* : a composition or creation (as in painting or sculpture) in which the subject matter is easily recognizable though the form is stylized — **semi•ab•stract** \-ab-'strakt, -'ab-ˌ\ *adj*
semi•an•nu•al \ˌsem-ē-'an-yə-wəl, ˌsem-ˌī-, -'an-yəl\ *adj* : occurring twice a year — **semi•an•nu•al•ly** \-ē\ *adv*
semi•aquat•ic \-ə-'kwät-ik, -'kwat-\ *adj* : growing in or adjacent to water; *also* : frequenting but not living wholly in water

semi•ar•bo•re•al \-ˌär-ˈbōr-ē-əl, -ˈbȯr-\ *adj* : often inhabiting and frequenting trees
semi•ar•id \-ˈar-əd\ *adj* : characterized by light rainfall; *esp* : having from about 10 to 20 inches (25 to 50 centimeters) of annual precipitation
semi•au•to•mat•ic \-ˌȯt-ə-ˈmat-ik\ *adj* : not fully automatic — **semiautomatic** *n* — **semi•au•to•mat•i•cal•ly** \-ˈmat-i-kə-lē, -klē\ *adv*
semi•au•ton•o•mous \-ȯ-ˈtän-ə-məs\ *adj* : chiefly self-governing within a larger political or organizational entity
semi•cen•ten•a•ry \ˌsem-i-ˌsen-ˈten-ə-rē, ˌsem-ˌī-, -ˈsent-n-ˌer-ē\ *n or adj* : SEMICENTENNIAL
semi•cen•ten•ni•al \-ˌsen-ˈten-ē-əl\ *n* : a 50th anniversary or its celebration — **semicentennial** *adj*
semi•cir•cle \ˈsem-i-ˌsər-kəl\ *n* : a half of a circle bounded by a diameter and half the circumference — **semi•cir•cu•lar** \ˌsem-i-ˈsər-kyə-lər\ *adj*
semicircular canal *n* : any of the loop-shaped tubular parts in the inner ear of vertebrates that together constitute a sensory organ concerned with the maintenance of bodily equilibrium
semi•civ•i•lized \ˌsem-i-ˈsiv-ə-ˌlīzd, ˌsem-ˌī-\ *adj* : partly civilized
semi•clas•si•cal \-ˈklas-i-kəl\ *adj* **1** : having some of the characteristics of the classical: as **a** : of, relating to, or being a musical composition that acts as a bridge between classical and popular music **b** : of, relating to, or being a classical composition that has developed popular appeal **2** : of less importance or of lower quality than the classical ⟨a *semiclassical* theory in physics⟩
semi•co•lon \ˈsem-i-ˌkō-lən\ *n* : a punctuation mark ; used chiefly to separate independent clauses not joined by a conjunction, to separate independent clauses the second of which begins with a conjunctive adverb, or to separate phrases and clauses containing commas
semi•con•duc•tor \ˌsem-i-kən-ˈdək-tər, ˌsem-ˌī-\ *n* : any of a class of solids (as germanium or silicon) whose electrical conductivity is between that of a conductor and that of an insulator — **semi•con•duct•ing** \-tiŋ\ *adj* — **semi•con•duc•tive** \-tiv\ *adj*
semi•con•scious \-ˈkän-chəs\ *adj* : incompletely conscious — **semi•con•scious•ly** *adv* — **semi•con•scious•ness** *n*
semi•crys•tal•line \-ˈkris-tə-lən\ *adj* : partly crystalline
semi•dark•ness \-ˈdärk-nəs\ *n* : partial darkness
semi•des•ert \-ˈdez-ərt\ *n* : an area having some of the characteristics of a desert and often lying between a desert and grassland
semi•de•tached \-di-ˈtacht\ *adj* : forming one of a pair of residences joined into one building by a common sidewall
semi•di•vine \-də-ˈvīn\ *adj* : more than mortal but not fully divine
semi•do•mes•ti•cat•ed \-də-ˈmes-ti-ˌkāt-əd\ *adj* : of, relating to, or living in semidomestication
semi•do•mes•ti•ca•tion \-də-ˌmes-ti-ˈkā-shən\ *n* : a captive state of a wild animal in which its living conditions and often its breeding are controlled by man
semi•dry \ˌsem-i-ˈdrī\ *adj* : fairly dry
semi•dry•ing \ˌsem-i-ˈdrī-iŋ\ *adj* : that dries imperfectly or slowly ⟨cottonseed oil is a *semidrying* oil⟩
semi•ev•er•green \-ˈev-ər-ˌgrēn\ *adj* : HALF-EVERGREEN
[1]**semi•fi•nal** \ˌsem-i-ˈfīn-l\ *adj* **1** : being next to the last in an elimination tournament ⟨*semifinal* pairings⟩ **2** : of or participating in a semifinal
[2]**semi•fi•nal** \ˈsem-i-ˌfīn-l\ *n* : a semifinal match or round — **semi•fi•nal•ist** \ˌsem-i-ˈfīn-l-əst\ *n*
semi•fit•ted \ˌsem-i-ˈfit-əd, ˌsem-ˌī-\ *adj* : partly fitted
semi•flex•i•ble \-ˈflek-sə-bəl\ *adj* : somewhat flexible
semi•flu•id \ˌsem-i-ˈflü-əd, ˌsem-ˌī-\ *adj* : having the qualities of both a fluid and a solid : VISCOUS ⟨fluid and *semifluid* greases⟩ — **semifluid** *n*
semi•for•mal \-ˈfȯr-məl\ *adj* : being or suitable for an occasion of moderate formality ⟨a *semiformal* dinner⟩
semi•gloss \ˈsem-i-ˌgläs, ˈsem-ˌī-, -ˌglȯs\ *adj* : having a low luster ⟨*semigloss* paint⟩
semi•gov•ern•men•tal \ˌsem-i-ˌgəv-ər-ˈment-l, ˌsem-ˌī-, -ˌgəv-ərn-ˈment-l\ *adj* : having some governmental functions and powers
semi•hard \-ˈhärd\ *adj* : moderately hard
semi•hol•i•day \ˌsem-i-ˈhäl-ə-ˌdā, ˌsem-ˌī-\ *n* : a weekday during a religious festival (as Passover) on which ceremonial observances continue but activities forbidden on full festival days are permitted though discouraged
semi–in•de•pend•ent \ˌsem-ē-ˌin-də-ˈpen-dənt, ˌsem-ˌī-\ *adj* : partially independent; *esp* : SEMIAUTONOMOUS
semi•leg•end•ary \ˌsem-i-ˈlej-ən-ˌder-ē, ˌsem-ˌī-\ *adj* : elaborated in legend but having a possible historical existence
semi•liq•uid \ˌsem-i-ˈlik-wəd, ˌsem-ˌī-\ *adj* : having the qualities of both a liquid and a solid : SEMIFLUID ⟨*semiliquid* ice cream⟩ — **semiliquid** *n*
semi•lit•er•ate \-ˈlit-ə-rət, -ˈli-trət\ *adj* **1** : able to read and write on an elementary level **2** : able to read but unable to write
semi•log•a•rith•mic \-ˌlȯg-ə-ˈrith-mik, -ˌläg-\ *also* **semi•log** \ˈsem-i-ˌlȯg, ˈsem-ˌī-, -ˌläg\ *adj* : having one scale logarithmic and the other arithmetic ⟨*semilogarithmic* graph paper⟩
semi•lu•nar \ˌsem-i-ˈlü-nər, ˌsem-ˌī-\ *adj* : shaped like a crescent
semilunar valve *n* : any of the crescent-shaped valvular cusps that occur as a set of three between the heart and the aorta and another of three between the heart and the pulmonary artery
semi•lus•trous \ˌsem-i-ˈləs-trəs, ˌsem-ˌī-\ *adj* : slightly lustrous
semi•mat *or* **semi•matt** *or* **semi•matte** \ˌsem-i-ˈmat, ˌsem-ˌī-\ *adj* : having little luster
semi•moist \-ˈmȯist\ *adj* : slightly moist
semi•mo•nas•tic \-mə-ˈnas-tik\ *adj* : having some features characteristic of a monastic order
[1]**semi•month•ly** \-ˈmənth-lē, -ˈməntth-\ *adj* : done, appearing, or occurring twice a month
[2]**semimonthly** *n* : a semimonthly publication
[3]**semimonthly** *adv* : twice a month
semi•mys•ti•cal \-ˈmis-ti-kəl\ *adj* : having some of the qualities of mysticism
sem•i•nal \ˈsem-ən-l\ *adj* **1** : of, relating to, or consisting of seed or semen **2** : having the character of a creative power, principle, or source : containing or contributing the seeds of later development [Middle French, from Latin *seminalis,* from *semin-, semen* "seed"] — **semi•nal•ly** \-l-ē\ *adv*
seminal vesicle *n* : a pouch on either side of the male reproductive tract that serves for the temporary storage of semen
sem•i•nar \ˈsem-ə-ˌnär\ *n* **1** : a course of study pursued by a group of advanced students doing original research under a professor and exchanging results and discussions **2** : a meeting of a seminar or a room for such meetings [German, from Latin *seminarium* "seedbed"]
sem•i•nar•i•an \ˌsem-ə-ˈner-ē-ən\ *n* : a student in a seminary especially of the Roman Catholic Church
sem•i•nary \ˈsem-ə-ˌner-ē\ *n, pl* **-nar•ies** **1** : an institution of secondary education; *esp* : an academy for girls **2** : an institution for training clergymen [Latin *seminarium* "seedbed", from *semin-, semen* "seed"]
sem•i•nif•er•ous \ˌsem-ə-ˈnif-rəs, -ə-rəs\ *adj* : producing or bearing seed or semen [Latin *semin-, semen* "seed" + English *-iferous*]
seminiferous tubule *n* : any of the coiled threadlike tubules that make up the bulk of the testis and are lined with a germinal epithelium from which the spermatozoa are produced
Sem•i•nole \ˈsem-ə-ˌnōl\ *n* : a member of an Amerindian people of what is now Florida [Creek *simaló-ni, simanó-li,* literally, "wild", from American Spanish *cimarrón*]
semi•no•mad \ˌsem-i-ˈnō-ˌmad, ˌsem-ˌī-\ *n* : a member of a people living usually in portable or temporary dwellings and practicing seasonal migration but having a base camp at which some crops are cultivated — **semi•no•mad•ic** \-nō-ˈmad-ik\ *adj*
semi•of•fi•cial \ˌsem-ē-ə-ˈfish-əl, ˌsem-ˌī-\ *adj* : having some official authority or standing ⟨a *semiofficial* statement⟩ — **semi•of•fi•cial•ly** \-ˈfish-lē, -ə-lē\ *adv*
semi•opaque \-ō-ˈpāk\ *adj* : nearly opaque
semi•pal•mat•ed \ˌsem-i-ˈpal-ˌmāt-əd, ˌsem-ˌī-, -ˈpäm-ˌāt-, -ˈpäl-ˌmāt-\ *adj* : having the anterior toes joined only part way down with a web
semi•per•ma•nent \-ˈpər-mə-nənt\ *adj* **1** : permanent in some

respects **2 :** lasting for an indefinite time
semi•per•me•able \-'pər-mē-ə-bəl\ *adj* **:** partially but not freely or wholly permeable; *esp* **:** permeable to some usually small molecules but not to other usually larger particles ⟨a *semipermeable* membrane⟩ — **semi•per•me•abil•i•ty** \-,pər-mē-ə-'bil-ət-ē\ *n*
semi•po•lit•i•cal \-pə-'lit-i-kəl\ *adj* **:** of, relating to, or involving some political features or activity
semi•post•al \-'pōs-tl\ *n* **:** a postage stamp sold (as for various humanitarian purposes) at a premium over its postal value
semi•pre•cious \-'presh-əs\ *adj* **:** of somewhat less commercial value than precious ⟨*semiprecious* gemstones⟩
semi•pri•vate \-'prī-vət\ *adj* **:** shared with one other or a few others ⟨a *semiprivate* room in a hospital⟩
semi•pro \'sem-i-,prō, 'sem-,ī-\ *adj or n* **:** SEMIPROFESSIONAL
semi•pro•fes•sion•al \,sem-i-prə-'fesh-nəl, -ən-l, ,sem-,ī-\ *adj* **1 :** engaging in an activity for pay or gain but not as a full-time occupation **2 :** engaged in by semiprofessional players ⟨*semiprofessional* baseball⟩ — **semiprofessional** *n* — **semi•pro•fes•sion•al•ly** \-ē\ *adv*
semi•pub•lic \-'pəb-lik\ *adj* **1 :** having some features of a public institution; *esp* **:** maintained as a public service by a private nonprofit organization **2 :** open to some persons outside the regular membership
semi•re•li•gious \-ri-'lij-əs\ *adj* **:** somewhat religious in character
semi•rig•id \-'rij-əd\ *adj* **1 :** rigid to some degree or in some parts **2 :** having a flexible cylindrical gas container with an attached stiffening keel that carries the load ⟨*semirigid* airships⟩
semi•sa•cred \-'sā-krəd\ *adj* **:** SEMIRELIGIOUS
semi•skilled \,sem-i-'skild, ,sem-,ī-\ *adj* **:** having or requiring less training than skilled labor and more than unskilled labor
semi•soft \-'sȯft\ *adj* **:** fairly soft; *esp* **:** firm but easily cut ⟨*semisoft* cheese⟩
semi•sol•id \-'säl-əd\ *adj* **:** having the qualities of both a solid and a liquid ⟨jelly is *semisolid*⟩ — **semisolid** *n*
semi•sweet \-'swēt\ *adj* **:** slightly sweetened ⟨*semisweet* chocolate⟩
Sem•ite \'sem-,īt\ *n* **1 :** a member of any of the peoples descended from Shem **2 :** a member of any of a group of peoples of southwestern Asia chiefly represented by the Jews and Arabs [French *sémite,* from *Sem* "Shem (eldest son of Noah)", from Late Latin, from Greek *Sēm,* from Hebrew *Shēm*]
semi•ter•res•tri•al \,sem-i-tə-'res-trē-əl, ,sem-,ī-, -'res-chəl, -'resh-chəl\ *adj* **1 :** growing on boggy ground **2 :** frequenting but not living wholly on land
¹Se•mit•ic \sə-'mit-ik\ *adj* **1 :** of, relating to, or characteristic of the Semites; *esp* **:** JEWISH **2 :** of, relating to, or constituting a branch of the Afro-Asiatic language family that includes Hebrew, Aramaic, Arabic, and Ethiopic
²Semitic *n* **:** any or all of the Semitic languages
Sem•i•tism \'sem-ə-,tiz-əm\ *n* **1 a :** Semitic character or qualities **b :** a Semitic idiom or expression **2 :** policy favorable to Jews **:** predisposition in favor of Jews
semi•ton•al \,sem-i-'tōn-l, ,sem-,ī-\ *adj* **:** CHROMATIC 2, SEMITONIC — **semi•ton•al•ly** \-l-ē\ *adv*
semi•tone \'sem-i-,tōn, 'sem-,ī-\ *n* **:** the tone at a half step; *also* **:** HALF STEP — **semi•ton•ic** \,sem-i-'tän-ik, ,sem-,ī-\ *adj* — **semi•ton•i•cal•ly** \-'tän-i-kə-lē, -klē\ *adv*
semi•trail•er \'sem-i-,trā-lər, 'sem-,ī-\ *n* **:** a freight trailer that in use is supported at its forward end by the truck tractor; *also* **:** a semitrailer with attached tractor
semi•trans•lu•cent \,sem-i-,trans-'lüs-nt, ,sem-,ī-, -,tranz-\ *adj* **:** partly translucent
semi•trans•par•ent \-'par-ənt, -'per-\ *adj* **:** imperfectly transparent — **semi•trans•par•en•cy** \-ən-sē\ *n*
semi•trop•i•cal \-'träp-i-kəl\ *adj* **:** SUBTROPICAL
semi•trop•ics \-'träp-iks\ *n pl* **:** SUBTROPICS
¹semi•week•ly \-'wē-klē\ *adj* **:** done, appearing, or occurring twice a week — **semiweekly** *adv*
²semiweekly *n* **:** a semiweekly publication
semi•works \'sem-i-,wərks, 'sem-,ī-\ *n pl* **:** a manufacturing plant operating on a limited commercial scale to provide final tests of a new product or process
semi•year•ly \,sem-i-'yiər-lē, ,sem-,ī-\ *adj* **:** done, appearing, or occurring twice a year
sem•o•li•na \,sem-ə-'lē-nə\ *n* **:** the purified middlings of hard wheat (as durum) used for pasta (as macaroni or spaghetti) [Italian *semolino,* from *semola* "bran", from Latin *simila* "finest wheat flour"]
sem•per•vi•vum \,sem-pər-'vī-vəm\ *n* **:** any of a large genus of Old World fleshy herbs of the orpine family often grown as ornamentals [New Latin, from Latin *sempervivus* "ever-living", from *semper* "ever" + *vivus* "living"]
sem•pi•ter•nal \,sem-pi-'tərn-l\ *adj* **:** of never-ending duration **:** ETERNAL [Late Latin *sempiternalis,* from Latin *sempiternus,* from *semper* "ever, always"] — **sem•pi•ter•nal•ly** \-l-ē\ *adv* — **sem•pi•ter•ni•ty** \-'tər-nət-ē\ *n*
sem•pre \'sem-prā\ *adv* **:** ALWAYS — used in music directions [Italian, from Latin *semper*]
semp•stress *variant of* SEAMSTRESS
¹sen \'sen\ *n, pl* **sen 1 :** a Japanese monetary unit equal to ¹⁄₁₀₀ yen **2 :** a coin representing one sen [Japanese]
²sen *n, pl* **sen 1 :** an Indonesian monetary unit equal to ¹⁄₁₀₀ rupiah **2 :** a coin representing one sen [Indonesian *sén,* probably from English *cent*]
sen•ate \'sen-ət\ *n* **1 a :** the supreme council of the ancient Roman republic and empire **b :** the higher chamber in some bicameral legislatures **2 :** the hall or chamber in which a senate meets **3 :** a governing body of some universities charged with maintaining academic standards and regulations [Old French *senat,* from Latin *senatus,* from *senex* "old, old man"]
sen•a•tor \'sen-ət-ər\ *n* **:** a member of a senate — **sen•a•tor•ship** \-,ship\ *n*
sen•a•to•ri•al \,sen-ə-'tōr-ē-əl, -'tȯr-\ *adj* **:** of, relating to, or befitting a senator or a senate ⟨*senatorial* office⟩ ⟨*senatorial* rank⟩
senatorial courtesy *n* **:** a custom of the United States Senate of refusing to confirm a presidential appointment of an official in or from a state when the appointment is opposed by the senators or senior senator of the president's party from that state
send \'send\ *vb* **sent** \'sent\; **send•ing 1 :** to cause to go **:** DISPATCH ⟨*sent* the student home⟩ ⟨*send* a message⟩; *esp* **:** to drive or propel physically ⟨*sent* the ball into right field⟩ **2 :** to cause to happen ⟨whatever fate may *send*⟩ **3 :** to have an agent, order, or request go or be transmitted ⟨*send* out for coffee⟩ ⟨*sent* for their price list⟩; *esp* **:** to transmit an order or request to come or return ⟨the principal *sent* for me⟩ **4 :** to put or bring into a certain condition ⟨the request *sent* them into a tizzy⟩ [Old English *sendan*] — **send•er** *n* — **send packing :** to send off roughly or in disgrace
send-off \'sen-,dȯf\ *n* **:** a demonstration of goodwill and enthusiasm for the beginning of a new venture (as a trip)
Sen•e•ca \'sen-i-kə\ *n, pl* **Seneca** *or* **Senecas :** a member of an Iroquoian people of what is now western New York [Dutch *Sennecaas* "the Seneca, Oneida, Onondaga, and Cayuga people", from Mohican *A'sinnika* "Oneida", translation of Iroquois *Onẽyóde', literally, "standing rock"*]
sen•e•schal \'sen-ə-shəl\ *n* **:** an agent or bailiff who managed a lord's estate in feudal times [Middle French, of Germanic origin]
se•nes•cence \si-'nes-ns\ *n* **1 :** the process of growing old **2 :** the state of being old [Latin *senescens,* present participle of *senescere* "to grow old", from *senex* "old"] — **se•nesce** \si-'nes\ *vi* — **se•nes•cent** \-nt\ *adj*
se•nhor \si-'nyōr, -'nyȯr\ *n, pl* **senhors** *or* **se•nho•res** \-'nyōr-ēs, -'nyȯr-, -ēsh, -ēz, -ēzh\ — used by or to Portuguese-speaking people as a courtesy title equivalent to *Mr.* [Portuguese, from Medieval Latin *senior* "lord, superior", from Latin, adj., "senior"]
se•nho•ra \si-'nyōr-ə, -'nyȯr-\ *n* — used by or to Portuguese-speaking people as a courtesy title equivalent to *Mrs.* [Portuguese, feminine of *senhor*]
se•nho•ri•ta \,sē-nyə-'rēt-ə\ *n* — used by or to Portuguese-speaking people as a courtesy title equivalent to *Miss* [Portuguese, from *senhora*]
se•nile \'sēn-,īl *also* 'sen-\ *adj* **:** of or relating to old age **:** resulting from old age ⟨*senile* weaknesses⟩; *also* **:** having infirmities associated with old age ⟨a *senile* oldster⟩ [Latin *senilis,* from *senex* "old, old man"] — **se•nile•ly** \-,īl-lē\ *adv*
se•nil•i•ty \si-'nil-ət-ē\ *n* **:** the quality or state of being senile; *esp* **:** the physical and mental infirmity of old age
¹se•nior \'sē-nyər\ *n* **1 :** a person older or of higher rank than another **2 :** a student in the last year before graduating from a school of secondary or higher level [Latin, from *senior,* adj.]
²senior *adj* **1 a :** OLDER — used chiefly to distinguish a father

with the same given name as his son and usually placed in its abbreviated form after a surname ⟨John M. Doe, *Sr.*⟩ **b** : having reached the age of retirement ⟨*senior* citizens⟩ **2** : higher in standing or rank ⟨*senior* partner⟩ **3** : of or relating to seniors ⟨the *senior* class⟩ **[**Latin, "older, elder, senior", comparative of *senex* "old"**]**

senior airman *n* : a rank in the Air Force comparable to sergeant that is usually held temporarily by an airman before being appointed sergeant

senior chief petty officer *n* : an enlisted rank in the Navy and Coast Guard above chief petty officer and below master chief petty officer

senior high school *n* : a school usually including grades 10-12

se•nior•i•ty \sēn-'yȯr-ət-ē, -'yär-\ *n* **1** : the quality or state of being senior **2** : a privileged status attained by length of service

senior master sergeant *n* : an enlisted rank in the Air Force above master sergeant and below chief master sergeant

sen•na \'sen-ə\ *n* **1** : CASSIA 2; *esp* : one used medicinally **2** : the dried leaflets of various cassias used as a purgative **[**Arabic *sanā***]**

sen•net \'sen-ət\ *n* : a signal call on a trumpet or cornet for entrance or exit on the stage **[**probably from obsolete *signet* "signal"**]**

sen•night *also* **se'n•night** \'sen-,īt\ *n, archaic* : one week **[**Old English *seofon nihta* "seven nights"**]**

sen•nit \'sen-ət\ *n* **1** : a braided cord or fabric of plaited rope yarns or other small stuff **2** : a straw or grass braid for hats **[**perhaps from French *coussinet* "small cushion, pad", from *coussin* "cushion"**]**

se•nor *or* **se•ñor** \sān-'yȯr\ *n, pl* **senors** *or* **se•ño•res** \-'yōr-ās, -'yȯr-\ — used by or to Spanish-speaking people as a courtesy title equivalent to *Mr.* **[**Spanish *señor*, from Medieval Latin *senior* "superior, lord", from Latin, adj., "senior"**]**

se•no•ra *or* **se•ño•ra** \sān-'yōr-ə, -'yȯr-\ *n* — used by or to Spanish-speaking people as a courtesy title equivalent to *Mrs.* **[**Spanish *señora*, feminine of *señor***]**

se•no•ri•ta *or* **se•ño•ri•ta** \,sān-yə-'rēt-ə\ *n* — used by or to Spanish-speaking people as a courtesy title equivalent to *Miss* **[**Spanish *señorita*, from *señora***]**

sen•sa•tion \sen-'sā-shən, sən-\ *n* **1 a** : awareness (as of noise or heat) or a mental process (as seeing, hearing, or smelling) due to stimulation of a sense organ **b** : an indefinite bodily feeling ⟨a *sensation* of buoyancy⟩ **2** : something that causes or is the object of sensation **3 a** : a state of excited interest or feeling **b** : a cause of such excitement ⟨the play was a *sensation*⟩

sen•sa•tion•al \-shnəl, -shən-l\ *adj* **1** : of or relating to sensation or the senses **2** : arousing or tending to arouse (as by lurid details) an intense and usually superficial interest or emotional reaction ⟨*sensational* news⟩ **3** : exceedingly or unexpectedly excellent or great ⟨a *sensational* diving catch⟩ — **sen•sa•tion•al•ly** \-ē\ *adv*

sen•sa•tion•al•ism \-,iz-əm\ *n* : the use or effect of sensational subject matter or treatment — **sen•sa•tion•al•ist** \-əst\ *n* — **sen•sa•tion•al•is•tic** \-,sā-shnəl-'is-tik, -shən-l-\ *adj*

[1]**sense** \'sens\ *n* **1** : a meaning conveyed or intended; *esp* : one of the meanings a word may bear **2 a** : a specialized animal function or mechanism (as sight, hearing, smell, taste, or touch) basically involving interaction of a stimulus and a sense organ ⟨the pain *sense*⟩ **b** : the sensory mechanisms constituting a unit distinct from other functions (as movement or thought) **3** : conscious awareness or rationality ⟨when they came to their *senses* they saw what they had done⟩ **4 a** : a particular sensation or kind or quality of sensation ⟨a good *sense* of balance⟩ **b** : a definite but often vague awareness ⟨a *sense* of danger⟩ **c** : intellectual appreciation ⟨a *sense* of humor⟩ **5** : INTELLIGENCE 1a, JUDGMENT; *esp* : good judgment **6** : one of two opposite directions describable by the motion of a point, line, or surface **[**Latin *sensus* "sensation, feeling, meaning", from *sentire* "to perceive, feel"**]** **syn** see MEANING

[2]**sense** *vt* **1 a** : to perceive by the senses **b** : to be or become conscious of ⟨*sense* danger⟩ **2** : UNDERSTAND 1 **3** : to detect (as radiation) automatically

sense•ful \'sens-fəl\ *adj* : full of sense : REASONABLE

sense•less \'sen-sləs\ *adj* : destitute of, deficient in, or contrary to sense: as **a** : UNCONSCIOUS ⟨knocked *senseless*⟩ **b** : FOOLISH, STUPID **c** : MEANINGLESS, PURPOSELESS ⟨a *senseless* act⟩ — **sense•less•ly** *adv* — **sense•less•ness** *n*

sense organ *n* : a bodily structure affected by a stimulus (as heat or sound waves) in such a manner as to activate associated sensory nerve fibers which convey impulses to the central nervous system where they are interpreted as corresponding sensations

sen•si•bil•i•ty \,sen-sə-'bil-ət-ē\ *n, pl* **-ties 1** : ability to receive sensations : SENSITIVITY ⟨tactile *sensibility*⟩ **2** : peculiar susceptibility to a pleasurable or painful impression (as praise or a slight) — often used in pl. **3** : awareness of and responsiveness toward something (as emotion in another) **4** : refined sensitiveness in emotion and taste

sen•si•ble \'sen-sə-bəl\ *adj* **1 a** : capable of being perceived by the senses or by reason or understanding **b** : perceptibly large : CONSIDERABLE ⟨a *sensible* error⟩ **2** : capable of receiving sense impressions ⟨*sensible* to pain⟩ **3** : COGNIZANT, AWARE **4** : having or containing good sense or reason : REASONABLE ⟨a *sensible* arrangement⟩ — **sen•si•ble•ness** *n* — **sen•si•bly** \-blē\ *adv*

sen•si•tive \'sen-sət-iv, 'sen-stiv\ *adj* **1** : subject to excitation by or responsive to stimuli **2** : easily or strongly affected or hurt ⟨a *sensitive* child⟩; *esp* : HYPERSENSITIVE ⟨*sensitive* to egg protein⟩ **3 a** : capable of indicating minute differences : DELICATE ⟨*sensitive* scales⟩ **b** : readily affected or changed by various agents or causes (as light or mechanical shock) **c** : high in radio sensitivity **4** : concerned with or involving highly classified government information ⟨appointed to a *sensitive* government post⟩ **[**Middle French *sensitif*, from Medieval Latin *sensitivus*, from Latin *sentire* "to feel"**]** — **sen•si•tive•ly** *adv* — **sen•si•tive•ness** *n*

sensitive fern *n* : a common American fern with fronds very susceptible to frost injury

sensitive plant *n* : any of several mimosas having leaves that fold or droop when touched

sen•si•tiv•i•ty \,sen-sə-'tiv-ət-ē\ *n, pl* **-ties** : the quality or state of being sensitive: as **a** : the capacity of an organism or sense organ to respond to stimulation : IRRITABILITY **b** : HYPERSENSITIVITY **c** : the degree to which a radio receiving set responds to incoming waves

sen•si•tize \'sen-sə-,tīz\ *vb* : to make or become sensitive or 2Hhypersensitive — **sen•si•ti•za•tion** \,sen-sət-ə-'zā-shən\ *n* — **sen•si•tiz•er** \'sen-sə-,tī-zər\ *n*

sen•si•tom•e•ter \,sen-sə-'täm-ət-ər\ *n* : an instrument for measuring sensitivity of photographic material — **sen•si•to•met•ric** \,sen-sət-ə-'me-trik\ *adj* — **sen•si•tom•e•try** \,sen-sə-'täm-ə-trē\ *n*

sen•sor \'sen-,sȯr, 'sen-sər\ *n* : a device that responds to a physical stimulus (as heat or light) and transmits a resulting impulse (as for operating a control)

sen•so•ri•mo•tor \,sens-rē-'mōt-ər, -ə-rē-\ *adj* : of, relating to, or functioning in both sensory and motor aspects of bodily activity

sen•so•ry \'sens-rē, -ə-rē\ *adj* **1** : of or relating to sensation or to the senses **2** : conveying nerve impulses from the sense organs : AFFERENT ⟨*sensory* neurons⟩

sen•su•al \'sench-wəl, -ə-wəl; 'sen-shəl\ *adj* **1** : SENSORY 1 **2** : relating to or consisting in the gratification of the senses or the indulgence of appetite **3 a** : devoted to or preoccupied with the senses or appetites **b** : VOLUPTUOUS 1 **c** : deficient in moral, spiritual, or intellectual interests : WORLDLY; *esp* : IRRELIGIOUS **[**Late Latin *sensualis*, from Latin *sensus* "sense"**]** — **sen•su•al•i•ty** \,sen-chə-'wal-ət-ē\ *n* — **sen•su•al•ly** \'sench-wə-lē, -ə-wə-; 'sen-shə-lē\ *adv*

sen•su•al•ism \'sench-wə-,liz-əm, -ə-wə-, 'sen-shə-,liz-\ *n* : persistent pursuit of sensual pleasures — **sen•su•al•ist** \-ləst\ *n* — **sen•su•al•is•tic** \,sench-wə-'lis-tik, -ə-wə-; ,sen-shə-'lis-\ *adj*

sen•su•al•ize \'sench-wə-,līz, -ə-wə-; 'sen-shə-,līz\ *vt* : to make sensual — **sen•su•al•iza•tion** \,sench-wə-lə-'zā-shən, -ə-wə-; ,sen-shə-lə-\ *n*

sen•su•ous \'sench-wəs, -ə-wəs\ *adj* **1 a** : of or relating to the senses **b** : having strong sensory appeal ⟨*sensuous* pleasure⟩ **2** : characterized by sense impressions or imagery aimed at the senses ⟨*sensuous* description⟩ **3** : highly susceptible to influ-

\ə\ **abut**	\au̇\ **out**	\i\ **tip**	\ȯ\ **saw**	\u̇\ **foot**
\ər\ **further**	\ch\ **chin**	\ī\ **life**	\ȯi\ **coin**	\y\ **yet**
\a\ **mat**	\e\ **pet**	\j\ **job**	\th\ **thin**	\yü\ **few**
\ā\ **take**	\ē\ **easy**	\ng\ **sing**	\th\ **this**	\yu̇\ **cure**
\ä\ **cot, cart**	\g\ **go**	\ō\ **bone**	\ü\ **food**	\zh\ **vision**

ence through the senses — **sen•su•ous•ly** *adv* — **sen•su•ous•ness** *n*

sent *past of* SEND

[1]**sen•tence** \'sent-ns, -nz\ *n* **1 a :** JUDGMENT 2a; *esp* **:** one formally pronounced by a court in a criminal proceeding and specifying the punishment to be inflicted **b :** the punishment so imposed ⟨serve a *sentence* for robbery⟩ **2** *archaic* **:** AXIOM 1 **3 a :** a grammatically self-contained speech unit that expresses an assertion, a question, a command, a wish, or an exclamation, that in writing usually begins with a capital letter and concludes with appropriate end punctuation, and that in speaking is phonetically distinguished by various patterns of stress, pitch, and pauses **b :** a statement in words or symbols (as 3 + 5 = 8) expressing a relationship between mathematical entities **[**Old French, from Latin *sententia,* literally, "feeling, opinion", from *sentire* "to feel"**]** — **sen•ten•tial** \sen-'ten-chəl\ *adj* — **sen•ten•tial•ly** \-chə-lē\ *adv*

[2]**sentence** *vt* **1 :** to pronounce sentence on **2 :** to condemn to a specified punishment

sentence fragment *n* **:** a word, phrase, or clause that lacks the grammatically self-contained structure of a sentence but has in speech the intonation of a sentence and is written and punctuated as if it were a complete sentence

sentence stress *n* **:** the manner in which stresses are distributed on the syllables of words assembled into sentences — called also *sentence accent*

sen•ten•tious \sen-'ten-chəs\ *adj* **1 :** being concise and forceful **:** PITHY **2 :** containing, using, or inclined to use high-sounding empty phrases or pompous sayings **[**Latin *sententiosus,* from *sententia* "sentence, maxim, feeling"**]** — **sen•ten•tious•ly** *adv* — **sen•ten•tious•ness** *n*

sen•tient \'sen-chē-ənt, -chənt\ *adj* **:** capable of feeling **:** conscious of sense impressions ⟨the lowest of *sentient* creatures⟩ **[**Latin *sentiens,* present participle of *sentire* "to feel"**]** — **sentience** \-chē-ənts, -chəns\ *n* — **sen•tient•ly** *adv*

sen•ti•ment \'sent-ə-mənt\ *n* **1 a :** an attitude, thought, or judgment prompted by feeling **b :** a specific view or notion **:** OPINION **2 a :** EMOTION 2 **b :** refined feeling **:** delicate sensibility **c :** emotional idealism **d :** a romantic or nostalgic feeling **[**Medieval Latin *sentimentum,* from Latin *sentire* "to feel"**]** **syn** see FEELING

sen•ti•men•tal \,sent-ə-'ment-l\ *adj* **1 a :** marked or governed by feeling, sensibility, or emotional idealism **b :** resulting from feeling rather than reason or thought **2 :** having an excess or affectation of sentiment or sensibility — **sen•ti•men•tal•ly** \-l-ē\ *adv*

sen•ti•men•tal•ism \-l-,iz-əm\ *n* **1 :** the disposition to favor or indulge in sentiment **2 :** SENTIMENTALITY 2 — **sen•ti•men•tal•ist** \-l-əst\ *n*

sen•ti•men•tal•i•ty \,sent-ə-,men-'tal-ət-ē, -mən-\ *n, pl* **-ties 1 :** the quality or state of being sentimental especially to excess or in affectation **2 :** a sentimental idea or its expression

sen•ti•men•tal•ize \-'ment-l-,īz\ *vb* **1 :** to indulge in sentiment **2 :** to look upon or imbue with sentiment — **sen•ti•men•tal•iza•tion** \-,ment-l-ə-'zā-shən\ *n*

[1]**sen•ti•nel** \'sent-nəl, -n-əl\ *n* **:** one that watches or guards **[**Middle French *sentinelle,* from Italian *sentinella,* from *sentina* "vigilance", from *sentire* "to perceive", from Latin**]**

[2]**sentinel** *vt* **-neled;** *or* **-nelled; -nel•ing** *or* **-nel•ling 1 :** to watch over as a sentinel **2 :** to furnish with a sentinel **3 :** to post as sentinel

sen•try \'sen-trē\ *n, pl* **sentries :** GUARD, WATCH; *esp* **:** a soldier standing guard at a point of passage **[**perhaps from obsolete *sentry* "sanctuary, watch tower"**]**

sentry box *n* **:** a shelter for a sentry on duty

se•pal \'sēp-əl, 'sep-\ *n* **:** one of the modified leaves comprising a flower calyx **[**New Latin *sepalum,* derived from Greek *skepē* "covering"**]**

sep•a•ra•ble \'sep-rə-bəl, -ə-rə-\ *adj* **:** capable of being separated or distinguished — **sep•a•ra•bil•i•ty** \,sep-rə-'bil-ət-ē, -ə-rə-\ *n* — **sep•a•ra•ble•ness** \'sep-rə-bəl-nəs, -ə-rə-\ *n* — **sep•a•ra•bly** \-blē\ *adv*

[1]**sep•a•rate** \'sep-ə-,rāt, 'sep-,rāt\ *vb* **1 a :** to set or keep apart **:** DISCONNECT **b :** to keep distinct in the mind **:** DISTINGUISH ⟨*separate* religion from magic⟩ **c :** SORT ⟨*separate* mail⟩ **d :** to disperse in space or time **:** SCATTER ⟨widely *separated* homesteads⟩ **2 :** to release officially **:** DISCHARGE ⟨was *separated* from the army⟩ **3 :** to block off **:** SEGREGATE **4 :** to isolate or become isolated from a mixture ⟨*separate* cream from milk⟩ **5 :** to become divided or detached **:** come apart **6 a :** to break off an association **:** WITHDRAW **b :** to cease to be or live together especially as husband and wife **7 :** to go in different directions **[**Latin *separare,* from *se-* "apart" +*parare* "to prepare, procure"**]**

• **syn** SEPARATE, DIVIDE, SEVER mean to break or keep apart. SEPARATE may imply any one of several ways or causes such as dispersion, removal of one from others, or presence of an intervening thing; DIVIDE implies separating by cutting or breaking into pieces or sections; SEVER implies violence especially in the removal of a part or member.

[2]**sep•a•rate** \'sep-rət, -ə-rət\ *adj* **1 :** set or kept apart **:** DETACHED **2 :** not shared with another **:** INDIVIDUAL ⟨*separate* rooms⟩ **3 a :** existing by itself **b :** dissimilar in nature or identity ⟨the *separate* pieces of a puzzle⟩ — **sep•a•rate•ly** \-rət-lē, 'sep-ərt-lē\ *adv* — **sep•a•rate•ness** \-rət-nəs\ *n*

[3]**sep•a•rate** \'sep-rət, -ə-rət\ *n* **:** an article of dress designed to be worn interchangeably with others to form various costume combinations

sep•a•ra•tion \,sep-ə-'rā-shən\ *n* **1 :** the act or process of separating **:** the state of being separated **2 a :** a point, line, or means of division **b :** an intervening space **:** GAP **3 a :** a formal separating of husband and wife by agreement but without divorce **b :** termination of a contractual relationship (as employment or military service)

sep•a•rat•ist \'sep-rət-əst, -ə-rət-\ *n, often cap* **:** one that favors separation: as **a** *cap* **:** one of a group of 16th and 17th century English Protestants preferring to separate from rather than to reform the Church of England **b :** an advocate of independence or autonomy for a part of a nation — **sep•a•rat•ism** \-rə-,tiz-əm\ *n* — **separatist** *adj, often cap* — **sep•a•ra•tis•tic** \,sep-rə-'tis-tik, -ə-rə-\ *adj*

sep•a•ra•tive \'sep-ə-,rāt-iv, 'sep-rət-, 'sep-ə-rət-\ *adj* **:** tending toward, causing, or expressing separation

sep•a•ra•tor \'sep-ə-,rāt-ər\ *n* **:** one that separates; *esp* **:** a device for separating liquids (as cream from milk) of different specific gravities or liquids from solids — compare CENTRIFUGE

Se•phar•di \sə-'färd-ē\ *n, pl* **Se•phar•dim** \-'färd-əm\ **:** a member of one of the two great divisions of Jews comprising the occidental branch of European Jews settling in Spain and Portugal — compare ASHKENAZI **[**Hebrew *sĕphāradhī,* from *Sĕphāradh* "Spain", from *sĕphāradh,* a region where Jews were once exiled (Obadiah 1:20)**]** — **Se•phar•dic** \-'färd-ik\ *adj*

[1]**se•pia** \'sē-pē-ə\ *n* **1 :** a brown melanin-containing pigment from the ink of cuttlefishes **2 :** a brownish gray to dark olive brown **[**Latin, "cuttlefish", from Greek *sēpia***]**

[2]**sepia** *adj* **1 :** of the color sepia **2 :** made of or done in sepia ⟨*sepia* print⟩

se•poy \'sē-,pȯi\ *n* **:** a native of India employed as a soldier by a European power **[**Portuguese *sipai,* from Hindi *sipāhī,* from Persian, "cavalryman"**]**

sep•sis \'sep-səs\ *n, pl* **sep•ses** \'sep-,sēz\ **:** a poisoned condition resulting from the spread of bacteria or their poisonous products from a center of infection **[**Greek *sēpsis* "decay", from *sēpein* "to make putrid"**]**

sep•tate \'sep-,tāt\ *adj* **:** divided by or having a septum

Sep•tem•ber \sep-'tem-bər, səp-\ *n* **:** the 9th month of the year **[**Old French *Septembre,* from Latin *September,* from *septem* "seven"; from its having been originally the 7th month of the Roman calendar**]**

sep•ten•ni•al \sep-'ten-ē-əl\ *adj* **1 :** consisting of or lasting for seven years **2 :** occurring or being done every seven years **[**Late Latin *septennium* "period of 7 years", from Latin *septem* "seven" + *-ennium* (as in *biennium* "biennium")**]** — **sep•ten•ni•al•ly** \-ē-ə-lē\ *adv*

sep•tet *also* **sep•tette** \sep-'tet\ *n* **1 :** a musical composition for seven instruments or voices **2 :** a group or set of seven **[**German *septet,* from Latin *septem* "seven"**]**

sep•tic \'sep-tik\ *adj* **1 :** of, relating to, or causing putrefaction **2 :** produced by putrefaction or by disease germs ⟨*septic* poisoning⟩ **[**Latin *septicus,* from Greek *sēptikos,* from *sēpein* "to make putrid"**]**

sep•ti•ce•mia \,sep-tə-'sē-mē-ə\ *n* **:** BLOOD POISONING — **sep•ti•ce•mic** \-'sē-mik\ *adj*

septic sore throat *n* **:** a severe sore throat caused by streptococci and accompanied by fever, prostration, and toxemia

septic tank *n* **:** a tank in which the solid matter of continuously flowing sewage is broken down by bacteria

sep•til•lion \sep-ˈtil-yən\ *n* — see NUMBER table [French, from Latin *septem* "seven" + French *-illion* (as in *million*)]

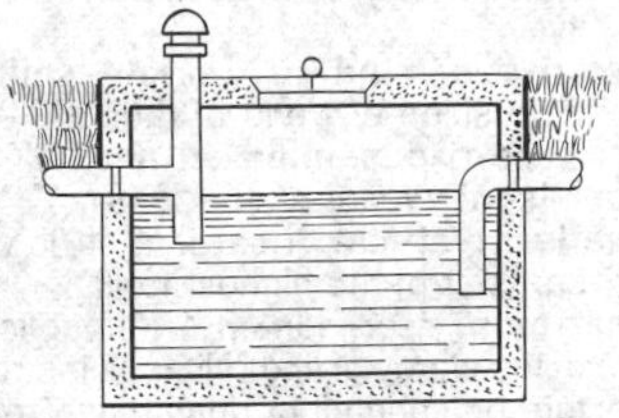
septic tank

sep•tu•a•ge•nar•i•an \ˌsep-ˌtü-ə-jə-ˈner-ē-ən, -ˌtyü-; ˌsep-tə-wə-jə-\ *n* : a person who is 70 or more but less than 80 years old [Late Latin *septuagenarius* "70 years old", derived from Latin *septuaginta* "seventy"] — **septuagenarian** *adj*

Sep•tu•a•ges•i•ma \ˌsep-tə-wə-ˈjes-ə-mə\ *n* : the 3d Sunday before Lent [Late Latin, from Latin *septuagesimus* "70th", from *septuaginta* "seventy"]

Sep•tu•a•gint \sep-ˈtü-ə-jənt, -ˈtyü-; ˈsep-tə-wə-ˌjint\ *n* : a pre-Christian Greek version of the Old Testament used by Greek-speaking Christians [Latin *septuaginta* "seventy"; from the approximate number of its translators]

sep•tum \ˈsep-təm\ *n, pl* **sep•ta** \-tə\ : a dividing wall or membrane especially between bodily spaces or masses of soft tissue [Latin *saeptum* "enclosure, wall", from *saepire* "to fence in", from *saepes* "fence"] — **sep•tal** \ˈsep-tl\ *adj*

[1]**sep•ul•cher** *or* **sep•ul•chre** \ˈsep-əl-kər\ *n* **1** : a place of burial : TOMB **2** : a receptacle for religious relics especially in an altar [Old French *sepulcre*, from Latin *sepulcrum, sepulchrum*, from *sepelire* "to bury"]

[2]**sepulcher** *or* **sepulchre** *vt* **-chered** *or* **-chred**; **-cher•ing** *or* **-chring** \-kə-ring, -kring\ : to place in or as if in a sepulcher : BURY

se•pul•chral \sə-ˈpəl-krəl\ *adj* **1** : of or relating to burial, the grave, or monuments to the dead ⟨a *sepulchral* stone⟩ **2** : DISMAL 1, GLOOMY — **se•pul•chral•ly** \-krə-lē\ *adv*

sep•ul•ture \ˈsep-əl-ˌchu̇r\ *n* **1** : BURIAL **2** : SEPULCHER [Old French, from Latin *sepultura*, from *sepelire* "to bury"]

se•qua•cious \si-ˈkwā-shəs\ *adj* **1** *archaic* : inclined to follow : TRACTABLE **2** : intellectually servile [Latin *sequac-, sequax* "inclined to follow", from *sequi* "to follow"] — **se•qua•cious•ly** *adv* — **se•quac•i•ty** \-ˈkwas-ət-ē\ *n*

se•quel \ˈsē-kwəl\ *n* **1** : an event that follows or comes afterward : RESULT **2** : a literary work that continues a story begun in another [Middle French *sequelle*, from Latin *sequela*, from *sequi* "to follow"]

se•que•la \si-ˈkwel-ə, -ˈkwē-lə\ *n, pl* **-que•lae** \-ˈkwel-ˌē, -ˌī; -ˈkwē-ˌlē\ **1** : an aftereffect of disease or injury **2** : a secondary result : CONSEQUENCE [Latin, "sequel"]

[1]**se•quence** \ˈsē-kwəns, -ˌkwens\ *n* **1** : a continuous or connected series: as **a** : an extended series of poems united by a single theme ⟨a sonnet *sequence*⟩ **b** : three or more playing cards usually of the same suit in consecutive order of rank **c** : a succession of repetitions of a melodic phrase each in a new position **d** : a set of numbers having a definite order fixed by a rule **e** : a succession of scenes developing a single subject or phase of a film story **2** : order of succession **3 a** : CONSEQUENCE 1, RESULT **b** : a subsequent development **4** : continuity of progression [derived from Late Latin *sequentia* "sequel", from Latin *sequi* "to follow"] **syn** see SUCCESSION

[2]**sequence** *vt* : to arrange in a sequence

se•quenc•er \ˈsē-kwən-sər, -ˌkwen-sər\ *n* : a device that determines a sequence

se•quen•cy \-kwən-sē\ *n, pl* **-cies** : SEQUENCE 2, 4

se•quent \ˈsē-kwənt\ *adj* : following in time or as an effect [Latin *sequens*, present participle of *sequi* "to follow"] — **sequent** *n*

se•quen•tial \si-ˈkwen-chəl\ *adj* : SEQUENT — **se•quen•tial•ly** \-chə-lē\ *adv*

se•ques•ter \si-ˈkwes-tər\ *vt* **-tered**; **-ter•ing** \-tə-ring, -tring\ **1** : to set apart : SEGREGATE, WITHDRAW **2** : to take custody of (as personal property) until a demand is satisfied [Middle French *sequestrer*, from Late Latin *sequestrare* "to surrender for safekeeping, set apart", from Latin *sequester* "agent, depositary"]

se•ques•trate \si-ˈkwes-ˌtrāt\ *vt* : SEQUESTER

se•ques•tra•tion \ˌsē-kwəs-ˈtrā-shən, si-ˌkwes-\ *n* : the act of sequestering : the state of being sequestered

se•quin \ˈsē-kwən\ *n* **1** : an old gold coin of Italy and Turkey **2** : a spangle used as an ornament on clothes [French, from Italian *zecchino*, from *zecca* "mint", from Arabic *sikkah* "die, coin"]

se•quined *or* **se•quinned** \-kwənd\ *adj* : ornamented with or as if with sequins

se•quoia \si-ˈkwȯi-ə\ *n* : either of two huge cone-bearing California trees of the pine family that reach a height of over 90 meters: **a** : BIG TREE **b** : REDWOOD [*Sequoya* (George Guess), died 1843, American Indian scholar]

sera *pl of* SERUM

se•rac \sə-ˈrak\ *n* : a pinnacle, sharp ridge, or block of ice among the crevasses of a glacier [French *sérac*, literally, a kind of white cheese, from Medieval Latin *seracium* "whey", from Latin *serum*]

se•ra•glio \sə-ˈral-yō\ *n, pl* **-glios** *also* **-gli** \-yē\ : HAREM 1a [Italian *serraglio* "enclosure, seraglio", partly from Medieval Latin *serraculum* "bar of a door, bolt", from Late Latin *serare* "to bolt"; partly from Turkish *saray* "palace"]

se•ra•pe *or* **sa•ra•pe** \sə-ˈräp-ē, -ˈrap-\ *n* : a colorful woolen shawl worn over the shoulder especially by Mexican men [Mexican Spanish *sarape*]

serape

ser•aph \ˈser-əf\ *n, pl* **ser•a•phim** \-ə-ˌfim\ *or* **seraphs** : an angel of the highest order [Late Latin *seraphim* "seraphs", from Hebrew *śĕrāphīm*]

Serb \ˈsərb\ *n* **1** : a native or inhabitant of the former kingdom of Serbia or of the federal republic of Serbia in Yugoslavia **2** : SERBIAN 2 [Serbian *Srb*] — **Serb** *adj*

Ser•bi•an \ˈsər-bē-ən\ *n* **1** : SERB 1 **2 a** : the Serbo-Croatian language as spoken in Serbia **b** : a literary form of Serbo-Croatian using the Cyrillic alphabet — **Serbian** *adj*

Ser•bo–Cro•atian \ˌsər-bō-krō-ˈā-shən\ *n* **1** : the Slavic language of the Serbs and Croats which is called Serbian when written in the Cyrillic alphabet and Croatian when written in the Roman alphabet **2** : one whose native language is Serbo-Croatian — **Serbo–Croatian** *adj*

sere \ˈsiər\ *adj* : dried up [Old English *sēar* "dry"]

[1]**ser•e•nade** \ˌser-ə-ˈnād\ *n* **1 a** : a complimentary vocal or instrumental performance; *esp* : one given outdoors at night for a woman **b** : a work so performed **2** : a work for chamber orchestra resembling a suite [French *sérénade*, from Italian *serenata*, from *sereno* "clear, calm (of weather)", from Latin *serenus*]

[2]**serenade** *vb* : to entertain with or perform a serenade — **ser•e•nad•er** *n*

ser•en•dip•i•tous \ˌser-ən-ˈdip-ət-əs\ *adj* : obtained or characterized by serendipity ⟨*serendipitous* discoveries⟩

ser•en•dip•i•ty \ˌser-ən-ˈdip-ət-ē\ *n* : the gift of accidentally finding valuable or agreeable things [from its possession by the heroes of the Persian fairy tale *The Three Princes of Serendip*]

[1]**se•rene** \sə-ˈrēn\ *adj* **1 a** : being clear and free of storms ⟨*serene* skies⟩ **b** : shining bright and steady **2** : marked by utter calm : TRANQUIL **3** : AUGUST — used as part of a title ⟨Your *Serene* Highness⟩ [Latin *serenus*] **syn** see CALM — **se•rene•ly** *adv* — **se•rene•ness** \-ˈrēn-nəs\ *n*

[2]**serene** *n* **1** : a serene condition or expanse (as of sky, sea, or light) **2** : SERENITY, TRANQUILLITY

se•ren•i•ty \sə-ˈren-ət-ē\ *n* : the quality or state of being serene

serf \ˈsərf\ *n* : a member of a servile feudal class bound to the soil [French, from Latin *servus* "slave, servant, serf"] — **serf•age** \ˈsər-fij\ *n* — **serf•dom** \ˈsərf-dəm\ *n* — **serf•hood** \-ˌhu̇d\ *n* — **serf•ish** \ˈsər-fish\ *adj* — **serf•ism** \-ˌfiz-əm\ *n*

serge \'sərj\ *n* : a durable twilled fabric having a smooth clear face and a diagonal rib on the front and the back [Middle French *sarge,* derived from Latin *sericus* "of silk", from Greek *sērikos,* from *Sēres,* an eastern Asian people producing silk in ancient times]

ser•gean•cy \'sär-jən-sē\ *n* : the function, office, or rank of a sergeant

ser•geant *also* **ser•jeant** \'sär-jənt\ *n* **1** : a police officer ranking in the United States just below captain or sometimes lieutenant and in England just below inspector **2** : an enlisted rank in the Army and Marine Corps above corporal and below staff sergeant and in the Air Force above airman first class and below staff sergeant [Middle English, literally, "servant", from Old French *sergent,* from Latin *serviens,* present participle of *servire* "to serve"]

sergeant at arms *n* : an officer of an organization (as a court of law) appointed to keep order

sergeant first class *n* : an enlisted rank in the Army above staff sergeant and below master sergeant

sergeant major *n, pl* **sergeants major** *or* **sergeant majors 1** : a noncommissioned officer (as in the Army) serving as chief enlisted assistant in a headquarters **2 a** : an enlisted rank in the Marine Corps above master sergeant **b** : COMMAND SERGEANT MAJOR, STAFF SERGEANT MAJOR

[1]**se•ri•al** \'sir-ē-əl\ *adj* **1** : of, consisting of, or arranged in a series, rank, or row ⟨*serial* order⟩ **2** : appearing in parts or numbers that follow regularly ⟨a *serial* story⟩ — **se•ri•al•ly** \-ē-ə-lē\ *adv*

[2]**serial** *n* **1** : a work appearing (as in a magazine or on television) in parts at intervals **2** : one part of a serial work : INSTALLMENT — **se•ri•al•ist** \-ē-ə-ləst\ *n*

se•ri•al•ize \'sir-ē-ə-,līz\ *vt* : to arrange or present in serial form — **se•ri•al•iza•tion** \,sir-ē-ə-lə-'zā-shən\ *n*

se•ri•a•tim \,sir-ē-'āt-əm, -'at-\ *adv* : in a series : SERIALLY [Medieval Latin, from Latin *series* "series"]

seri•cul•ture \'ser-ə-,kəl-chər\ *n* : the raising of silkworms for silk production [Latin *seri*cum "silk" + English *culture*] — **seri•cul•tur•al** \,ser-ə-'kəlch-rəl, -ə-rəl\ *adj*

se•ries \'siər-ēz, -,ēz\ *n, pl* **series 1 a** : a number of things or events of the same class coming one after another **b** : a group with an order of arrangement exhibiting progression **2** : the indicated sum of a usually infinite sequence of numbers **3** : a succession of volumes or issues published with related subjects or authors, similar format and price, or continuous numbering **4** : a division of rock formations smaller than a system comprising rocks deposited during an epoch **5** : an arrangement of the parts of or elements in an electric circuit whereby all the current passes through each part or element without branching **6** : a group of chemical compounds related in composition and structure [Latin, from *serere* "to join, link together"] **syn** see SUCCESSION — **in series** : in a serial arrangement

series winding *n* : a winding in which the armature coil and the field-magnet coil are in series with the external circuit — **series–wound** \,sir-ēz-'waůnd\ *adj*

ser•if \'ser-əf\ *n* : any of the short lines that cross the ends of the strokes of a printed letter [probably from Dutch *schreef* "stroke, line", from *schriven* "to write", from Latin *scribere*]

seri•graph \'ser-ə-,graf\ *n* : an original color print made by the silk-screen process [Latin *sericum* "silk" + Greek *graphein* "to write, draw"] — **se•rig•ra•pher** \sə-'rig-rə-fər\ *n* — **se•rig•ra•phy** \-fē\ *n*

ser•ine \'seər-,ēn\ *n* : a crystalline amino acid $C_3H_7NO_3$ that occurs as a structural part of many proteins [derived from Latin *sericum* "silk"]

se•rio•com•ic \,sir-ē-ō-'käm-ik\ *adj* : having a mixture of the serious and the comic — **se•rio•com•i•cal•ly** \-'käm-i-kə-lē, -klē\ *adv*

se•ri•ous \'sir-ē-əs\ *adj* **1** : thoughtful or subdued in appearance or manner : SOBER **2 a** : requiring much thought or work ⟨*serious* study⟩ **b** : of or relating to a matter of importance ⟨a *serious* play⟩ **3** : not joking or trifling : EARNEST **4 a** : not easily answered or solved ⟨*serious* objections⟩ **b** : having important or dangerous possible consequences ⟨a *serious* injury⟩ [Late Latin *seriosus,* alteration of Latin *serius*] — **se•ri•ous•ly** *adv* — **se•ri•ous•ness** *n*

• **syn** EARNEST, GRAVE, SOLEMN: SERIOUS implies showing or having a concern for what really matters; EARNEST adds an implication of sincerity or intensity of purpose; GRAVE implies both seriousness and dignity in expression or attitude; SOLEMN suggests an impressive gravity utterly free from levity.

se•ri•ous–mind•ed \,sir-ē-ə-'smīn-dəd\ *adj* : having a serious disposition or trend of thought — **se•ri•ous–mind•ed•ly** *adv* — **se•ri•ous–mind•ed•ness** *n*

ser•jeant *variant of* SERGEANT

serjeant–at–law \,sär-jənt-ət-'lȯ\ *n, pl* **serjeants–at–law** : a barrister of the highest rank

ser•mon \'sər-mən\ *n* **1** : a public speech usually by a member of the clergy giving religious instruction or exhortation **2** : a lecture on conduct or duty [Old French, from Medieval Latin *sermo,* from Latin, "speech, conversation", from *serere* "to join, link together"] — **ser•mon•ic** \,sər-'män-ik\ *adj*

ser•mon•ize \'sər-mə-,nīz\ *vb* **1** : to compose or deliver a sermon : PREACH **2** : to speak or write as if delivering a sermon : LECTURE — **ser•mon•iz•er** *n*

Sermon on the Mount : a talk by Jesus recorded in Matthew 5–7 and Luke 6: 20–49

se•rol•o•gy \sə-'räl-ə-jē\ *n* : a science dealing with serums and especially their reactions and properties — **se•ro•log•ic** \,sir-ə-'läj-ik\ *or* **se•ro•log•i•cal** \-'läj-i-kəl\ *adj* — **se•ro•log•i•cal•ly** \-i-kə-lē, -klē\ *adv* — **se•rol•o•gist** \sə-'räl-ə-jəst\ *n*

se•ro•sa \sə-'rō-zə\ *n* : a usually enclosing serous membrane [New Latin, from *serosus* "serous", from Latin *serum* "serum"] — **se•ro•sal** \-'rō-zəl\ *adj*

se•ro•to•nin \,sir-ə-'tō-nən, ,ser-\ *n* : an amine that causes narrowing of blood vessels and is found especially in the blood serum and gastric mucous membrane of mammals [*serum* + *tonic* + *-in*]

se•rous \'sir-əs\ *adj* : of, relating to, resembling, or producing serum; *esp* : thin and watery ⟨a *serous* fluid⟩

serous membrane *n* : a thin membrane (as the peritoneum) with cells that secrete a serous fluid; *esp* : SEROSA

ser•pent \'sər-pənt\ *n* **1** : SNAKE 1; *esp* : a large snake **2** : DEVIL 1 **3** : a treacherous person [Middle French, from Latin *serpens,* from *serpere* "to creep"]

[1]**ser•pen•tine** \'sər-pən-,tēn, -,tīn\ *adj* **1** : of or resembling a serpent **2** : subtly wily or tempting **3** : winding or turning one way and another ⟨a *serpentine* path⟩ — **ser•pen•tine•ly** *adv*

[2]**serpentine** *n* : something that winds sinuously

[3]**ser•pen•tine** \-,tēn\ *n* : a mineral consisting essentially of a hydrous silicate of magnesium usually having a dull green color and often a mottled appearance

serpent star *n* : BRITTLE STAR

[1]**ser•rate** \sə-'rāt, 'seər-,āt\ *vt* : to mark with serrations : NOTCH [Late Latin *serrare* "to saw", from Latin *serra* "saw"]

[2]**ser•rate** \'seər-,āt, sə-'rāt\ *or* **ser•rat•ed** \'ser-,āt-əd, sə-'rāt-\ *adj* : having a saw-toothed edge ⟨a *serrate* leaf⟩ [Latin *serratus,* from *serra* "saw"]

ser•ra•tion \sə-'rā-shən, se-\ *n* **1** : a serrate condition or formation **2** : one of the teeth in a serrate margin

ser•ried \'ser-ēd\ *adj* : crowded together ⟨*serried* ranks of soldiers⟩ — **ser•ried•ly** *adv* — **ser•ried•ness** *n* [from earlier *serry* "to crowd together", from Middle French *serrer* "to press, crowd", from Late Latin *serare* "to bolt"]

se•rum \'sir-əm\ *n, pl* **serums** *or* **se•ra** \-ə\ : the watery portion of an animal fluid remaining after coagulation: as **a** : BLOOD SERUM **b** : immune blood serum that contains specific immune bodies (as antitoxins or agglutinins) [Latin, "whey, serum"] — **se•ral** \'sir-əl\ *adj*

serum albumin *n* : an albumin or mixture of albumins normally constituting more than half of the blood serum protein and serving to maintain the blood osmotic pressure

serum globulin *n* : a globulin or mixture of globulins occurring in blood serum and containing most of the antibodies of the blood

serum sickness *n* : an allergic reaction to the injection of foreign serum

ser•val \'sər-vəl, ,sər-'val\ *n* : a tawny black-spotted African wildcat with large ears and long legs [French, from Portuguese *lobo serval* "lynx", from Medieval Latin *lupus cervalis,* literally, "cervine wolf"]

ser•vant \'sər-vənt\ *n* : one that serves others; *esp* : one that performs household or personal services [Old French, from *servir* "to serve"]

[1]**serve** \'sərv\ *vb* **1 a** : to be a servant **b** : to give the service and respect due to (a superior); *also* : WORSHIP ⟨*serve* God⟩ **c** : to comply with the commands or demands of : GRATIFY **d**(1)

: to work through or perform a term of service especially in an army or navy (2) : to put in : SPEND ⟨*serve* 30 days in jail⟩ **2 a** : to officiate as a priest or member of the clergy **b** : to assist as server at mass **3 a** : to be of use : answer a purpose ⟨the tree *serves* as shelter⟩ **b** : to be favorable, opportune, or convenient ⟨when the time *serves*⟩ **c** : to be enough or satisfactory for ⟨a pie that will *serve* eight people⟩ **d** : to hold an office : discharge a duty or function ⟨*serve* on a jury⟩ **4 a** : to wait on (as at a table or counter) **b** : to set out or bring portions of (food or drink) **5 a** : to supply with something (as heat or light) needed or desired **b** : to furnish professional services to **6** : to make a serve (as in tennis) **7** : to treat or act toward in a specified way ⟨they *served* me ill⟩ **8 a** : to bring to notice, deliver, or execute as required by law **b** : to make legal service on (a person named in a writ) [Old French *servir,* from Latin *servire* "to be a slave, serve", from *servus* "slave, servant"]

serval

[2]**serve** *n* : the act or privilege of putting the ball or shuttlecock in play (as in tennis or badminton); *also* : a stroke that begins a rally

serv•er \ˈsər-vər\ *n* **1** : one that serves food or drink **2** : the player who puts a ball or shuttlecock in play **3** : the celebrant's assistant at low mass **4** : something (as a tray) used in serving food or drink

[1]**ser•vice** \ˈsər-vəs\ *n* **1** : the occupation or function of serving ⟨in active *service*⟩; *esp* : employment as a servant **2 a** : the work or action performed by one that serves ⟨gives good and quick *service*⟩ **b** : HELP, USE, BENEFIT ⟨be of *service* to them⟩ **c** : contribution to the welfare of others **d** : disposal for use ⟨at your *service*⟩ **3 a** : a form followed in worship or in a religious ceremony ⟨the burial *service*⟩ **b** : a meeting for worship ⟨held an evening *service*⟩ **4** : the act of serving: as **a** : a helpful act : good turn ⟨did us a *service*⟩ **b** : useful labor that does not produce a tangible commodity — usually used in pl. ⟨charge for professional *services*⟩ **c** : the act or privilege of serving (as in tennis) **5** : a set of articles for a particular use ⟨a coffee *service*⟩ **6 a** : an administrative division (as of a government) ⟨the consular *service*⟩ **b** : a nation's military forces or one of these forces ⟨called into the *service*⟩ **7** : a facility supplying some public demand ⟨bus *service*⟩; *esp* : one providing maintenance and repair [Old French, from Latin *servitium* "condition of a slave", from *servus* "slave"]

[1]service 5

[2]**service** *adj* **1 a** : of or relating to the armed services **b** : of, relating to, or constituting a branch of an army that provides service and supplies **2** : used in serving or supplying **3** : intended for everyday use : DURABLE **4** : providing services (as repairs or maintenance)

[3]**service** *vt* : to perform services for : repair or provide maintenance for

[4]**service** *n* : an Old World tree resembling the related mountain ashes but having larger flowers and larger edible fruit; *also* : a related Old World tree with small speckled brown fruits [Old English *syrfe,* from Latin *sorbus*]

ser•vice•able \ˈsər-və-sə-bəl\ *adj* **1** : HELPFUL, USEFUL **2** : wearing well in use — **ser•vice•abil•i•ty** \ˌsər-və-sə-ˈbil-ət-ē\ *n* — **ser•vice•ably** \-blē\ *adv*

ser•vice•ber•ry \ˈsər-vəs-ˌber-ē, *2 is also* ˈsär-\ *n* **1** : the fruit of a service tree **2** : any of various North American trees and shrubs of the rose family that bear showy white flowers and edible purple or red fruits — called also *Juneberry, shadblow, shadbush*

service book *n* : a book setting forth forms of worship used in religious services

service box *n* : the area of the court in which a player stands while serving in various wall and net games

service charge *n* : a fee charged for a particular service often in addition to a standard or basic fee

service club *n* **1** : a club of business or professional people organized for their common benefit and active in community service **2** : a recreation center for enlisted men provided by one of the armed services

service court *n* : a part of the court into which the ball or shuttlecock must be served (as in tennis or badminton)

ser•vice•man \ˈsər-vəs-ˌman, -mən\ *n* **1** : a man who is in the armed forces **2** : a man employed to repair or maintain equipment

service mark *n* : a mark or device used to identify a service (as transportation or insurance) offered to customers

service medal *n* : a medal awarded to a person who does military service in a specified war or campaign

service module *n* : a space vehicle module that contains propellant tanks, fuel cells, and the main rocket engine

service station *n* : a retail station for servicing motor vehicles especially with gasoline and oil

service stripe *n* : a stripe worn on the left sleeve of a military uniform to indicate three years of service in the Army or Air Force or four years in the Navy

ser•vice tree \ˈsər-vəs-\ *n* : [4]SERVICE

ser•vi•ette \ˌsər-vē-ˈet\ *n, chiefly British* : a table napkin [French, from *servir* "to serve"]

ser•vile \ˈsər-vəl, -ˌvīl\ *adj* **1** : of or befitting a slave or an enslaved or menial class ⟨*servile* work⟩ ⟨*servile* flattery⟩ **2** : lacking spirit or independence : SUBMISSIVE ⟨*servile* to authority⟩ [Latin *servilis,* from *servus* "slave"] — **ser•vile•ly** \-vəl-lē, -ˌvīl-lē\ *adv* — **ser•vile•ness** \-vəl-nəs, -ˌvīl-\ *n* — **ser•vil•i•ty** \ˌsər-ˈvil-ət-ē\ *n* [Latin *servilis,* from *servus* "slave"]

serv•ing \ˈsər-ving\ *n* : a portion of food or drink for an individual

Ser•vite \ˈsər-ˌvīt\ *n* : a member of the mendicant Order of Servants of Mary founded at Florence in 1233 [Medieval Latin *Servitae* "Servites", from Latin *servus* "slave, servant"]

ser•vi•tor \ˈsər-vət-ər, -və-ˌtȯr\ *n* : a male servant [Middle French *servitour,* from Late Latin *servitor,* from Latin *servire* "to serve"]

ser•vi•tude \ˈsər-və-ˌtüd, -ˌtyüd\ *n* : a state of subjection to another that constitutes or resembles slavery or serfdom [Middle French, from Latin *servitudo* "slavery", from *servus* "slave"]

ser•vo \ˈsər-vō\ *n, pl* **servos** **1** : SERVOMOTOR **2** : SERVOMECHANISM

ser•vo•mech•a•nism \ˈsər-vō-ˌmek-ə-ˌniz-əm\ *n* : a device for automatically correcting the performance of a mechanism [*servo-* (as in *servomotor*) + *mechanism*]

ser•vo•mo•tor \ˈsər-vō-ˌmōt-ər\ *n* : a motor in a servomechanism that supplements a primary control by correcting position or motion [French *servo-moteur,* from Latin *servus* "slave, servant" + French *moteur* "motor", from Latin *motor* "one that moves"]

ses•a•me \ˈses-ə-mē\ *n* **1** : an East Indian annual erect hairy herb; *also* : its small somewhat flat seeds used as a source of oil and a flavoring agent **2** : OPEN SESAME [Latin *sesama,* from Greek *sēsamē,* of Semitic origin]

sesqui- *combining form* : one and a half times ⟨*sesqui*centennial⟩ [Latin, "one and a half", literally, "and a half", from *semis* "half" + *-que* "and"]

ses•qui•cen•ten•ni•al \ˌses-kwi-sen-ˈten-ē-əl\ *n* : a 150th anniversary or its celebration — **sesquicentennial** *adj*

ses•qui•pe•da•lian \ˌses-kwə-pə-ˈdāl-yən\ *adj* **1** : having many syllables : LONG **2** : given to or characterized by the use of long words [Latin *sesquipedalis,* literally, "a foot and a half long", from *sesqui-* + *ped-, pes* "foot"]

ses•sile \ˈses-ˌīl, -əl\ *adj* **1** : attached directly by the base and not raised upon a stalk or peduncle ⟨a *sessile* leaf⟩ **2** : permanently attached and not free to move about : SEDENTARY ⟨*sessile* polyps⟩ [Latin *sessilis* "of or fit for sitting, low", from *sessus,* past participle of *sedēre* "to sit"]

\ə\ **abut**	\au̇\ **out**	\i\ **tip**	\ȯ\ **saw**	\u̇\ **foot**
\ər\ **further**	\ch\ **chin**	\ī\ **life**	\ȯi\ **coin**	\y\ **yet**
\a\ **mat**	\e\ **pet**	\j\ **job**	\th\ **thin**	\yü\ **few**
\ā\ **take**	\ē\ **easy**	\ng\ **sing**	\t͟h\ **this**	\yu̇\ **cure**
\ä\ **cot, cart**	\g\ **go**	\ō\ **bone**	\ü\ **food**	\zh\ **vision**

ses•sion \'sesh-ən\ *n* **1 :** a meeting or series of meetings of a body (as a court or legislature) to transact business **2 :** the period between the first and last of a series of meetings of a legislative or judicial body **3 :** the ruling body of a Presbyterian congregation **4 :** the period during the year or day in which a school conducts classes **5 :** a meeting or period devoted to an activity ⟨a recording *session*⟩ [Middle French, from Latin *sessio*, literally, "act of sitting", from *sessus*, past participle of *sedēre* "to sit"] — **ses•sion•al** \'sesh-nəl, -ən-l\ *adj*

ses•terce \'ses-ˌtərs\ *n* **:** an ancient Roman coin equal to ¼ denarius [Latin *sestertius*]

ses•tet \se-'stet\ *n* **:** a stanza or poem of six lines; *esp* **:** the last six lines of an Italian sonnet — compare OCTAVE 2 [Italian *sestetto*, from *sesto* "sixth", from Latin *sextus*, from *sex* "six"]

¹set \'set\ *vb* **set**; **set•ting 1 :** to cause to sit **:** place in or on a seat **2 :** to give (a fowl) eggs to hatch or provide (eggs) with suitable conditions for hatching **3 a :** to put or fix in a place, condition, or position ⟨*set* a dish on the table⟩ ⟨*set* a trap⟩ **b :** to put (dough) aside to rise **4 :** to direct with fixed attention ⟨*set* your mind to it⟩ **5 :** to cause to assume a specified condition, relation, or occupation ⟨slaves were *set* free⟩ **6 :** to appoint or assign an office or duty ⟨*set* pickets around the camp⟩ **7 :** APPLY ⟨*set* a match to kindling⟩ **8 :** FIX, PRESCRIBE ⟨*set* a date⟩ **9 a :** to establish as the highest level or best performance ⟨*set* a speed record⟩ **b :** to furnish as a pattern or model ⟨*set* a good example⟩ **c :** to allot as a task ⟨I was *set* the job of dusting⟩ **10 :** to arrange or put into a desired and especially a normal position ⟨*set* a broken bone⟩ ⟨*set* the sails⟩ **11 a :** to put in order for use ⟨*set* the table⟩ **b :** to make scenically ready for a performance ⟨*set* the stage⟩ **c** (1) **:** to arrange (type) for printing (2) **:** to put into type or its equivalent **12 :** to dress (hair) especially by curling or waving **13 a :** to adorn with something attached or separate ⟨a sky *set* with stars⟩ **b :** to fix (as a jewel) in a setting **14 a :** to place in a relative rank or category ⟨*set* duty before pleasure⟩ **b :** VALUE, ESTIMATE ⟨*set* the loss at $2000⟩ **15 a :** to direct to action **b :** to incite to attack or antagonism ⟨war *sets* country against country⟩ **16 :** to put and fix in a direction ⟨*set* our faces toward home⟩ **17 a :** to fix firmly **:** make immobile ⟨*set* my jaw in determination⟩ **b :** to make unyielding or obstinate ⟨*set* your mind against all appeals⟩ **18 :** to become or cause to become firm or solid ⟨the jelly is *setting*⟩ **19 :** to form and bring (fruit or seed) to maturity **20** *chiefly dialect* **:** SIT 1a **21 :** to be becoming **:** be suitable **:** FIT ⟨your behavior doesn't *set* well with your years⟩ **22 :** to cover and warm eggs to hatch them ⟨*setting* hens⟩ **23 :** to become lodged or fixed ⟨the pudding *sets* heavily on the stomach⟩ **24 :** to pass below the horizon **:** go down ⟨the sun *sets*⟩ **25 :** to apply oneself ⟨*set* to work⟩ **26 :** to have a specified direction in motion **:** FLOW ⟨a current that *sets* to the north⟩ **27 :** to dance face-to-face with another in a square dance ⟨*set* to your partner and turn⟩ **28 :** to become permanent ⟨a dye that will not *set*⟩ **29 :** to become whole by knitting ⟨the bone has not *set*⟩ [Old English *settan*] — **set about :** to begin to do ⟨*set about* proving it could be done⟩ — **set aside 1 :** to put to one side **:** DISCARD **2 :** to save for future use **3 :** to reject from consideration **4 :** ANNUL, OVERRULE ⟨the verdict was *set aside* by the court⟩ — **set at :** ATTACK 1, ASSAIL — **set forth 1 :** to make known **:** PUBLISH **2 :** to start out on a journey **:** set out — **set forward 1 :** PROMOTE 2, FURTHER **2 :** to set out on a journey — **set one's heart on :** RESOLVE 3 — **set store :** to consider valuable or worthwhile — used with *by* or *on* — **set to music :** to provide music for (lyrics) — **set upon :** to attack with violence ⟨*set upon* by a band of robbers⟩

²set *adj* **1 :** INTENT, DETERMINED ⟨were *set* on going⟩ **2 :** fixed by authority ⟨a *set* wage⟩ **3 :** INTENTIONAL, PREMEDITATED ⟨did it of *set* purpose⟩ **4 :** reluctant to change **:** OBSTINATE ⟨very *set* in your ways⟩ **5 a :** IMMOVABLE, RIGID ⟨a *set* frown⟩ **b :** BUILT-IN **6 :** remaining unchanged **:** PERSISTENT ⟨*set* defiance⟩ **7 a :** READY 1, PREPARED ⟨all *set* for an early start⟩ **b :** poised to start running or to dive in at the instant a signal is given ⟨ready, get *set*, go⟩

³set *n* **1 :** the act or action of setting **:** the condition of being set **2 :** mental inclination, tendency, or habit **:** BENT **3 :** a number of persons or things of the same kind that belong or are used together **4 :** direction of flow ⟨the *set* of the wind⟩ **5 :** form or carriage of the body or of its parts ⟨the *set* of your shoulders⟩ **6 :** the manner of fitting or of being placed or suspended ⟨the *set* of a coat⟩ **7 :** amount of deflection from a straight line **8 :** permanent change of form (as of metal) due to repeated or excessive stress **9 :** a young plant or a plant part (as a corm or a piece of tuber) suitable for planting or transplanting **10 :** an artificial setting for a scene of a play or movie **11 :** a division of a tennis match won usually by the player or side that first wins six games **12 :** SETTING 6 **13 :** the basic formation in a country-dance or square dance **14 :** a collection of mathematical elements (as numbers or points) **15 :** an electronic apparatus ⟨a radio *set*⟩ ⟨a television *set*⟩

se•ta \'sēt-ə\ *n, pl* **se•tae** \'sē-ˌtē\ **:** a slender usually rigid or bristly and springy organ or part of an animal or plant [Latin *saeta, seta* "bristle"] — **se•tal** \'sēt-l\ *adj*

set•back \'set-ˌbak\ *n* **1 :** a checking of progress **2 :** an unexpected reverse or defeat

set down *vt* **1 :** to cause to sit down **:** SEAT **2 :** to cause or allow to get off a vehicle **:** DELIVER **3 :** to land (an aircraft) on the ground or water **4 :** to put in writing **5 a :** REGARD, CONSIDER ⟨*set* them *down* as crooks⟩ **b :** ATTRIBUTE ⟨*set down* their success to perseverance⟩

¹set-in \ˌset-ˌin\ *adj* **1 :** placed, located, or built as a part of another construction ⟨*set-in* bookcases⟩ **2 :** cut separately and stitched in ⟨*set-in* sleeves⟩

²set-in \'set-ˌin\ *n* **:** something that is set in **:** INSERT

set in *vb* **1 :** INSERT; *esp* **:** to stitch (a small part) within a larger article **2 :** to enter upon a particular state ⟨winter *set in* early⟩ **3 :** to begin to work

set•off \'set-ˌȯf\ *n* **1 :** something that is set off against another thing: **a :** DECORATION 2, ORNAMENT **b :** COUNTERBALANCE 2 **2 :** the discharge of a debt by setting against it a distinct claim in favor of the debtor; *also* **:** the claim itself

set off \set-'ȯf, 'set-\ *vb* **1 a :** to show up by contrast ⟨a pale face *set off* by dark eyes⟩ **b :** ADORN, EMBELLISH ⟨that pin *sets off* the dress⟩ **c :** to set apart **:** make distinct or outstanding ⟨commas *set off* words in a series⟩ **2 a :** OFFSET 1b, COMPENSATE **b :** to make a setoff of **3 a :** to set in motion **:** cause to begin ⟨that story *set* me *off* laughing⟩ **b :** to cause to explode **4 :** to measure off on a surface **:** lay off **5 :** to start out on a course or a journey ⟨*set off* for home⟩

set on *vb* **1 :** ATTACK 1 **2 a :** to urge (as a dog) to attack or pursue **b :** to incite to action **:** INSTIGATE ⟨*set* students *on* to riot⟩ **c :** to set to work **3 :** to go on **:** ADVANCE

set out *vb* **1 :** to state, describe, or recite at length **2 a :** to arrange and present graphically or systematically **b :** to mark out (as a design) **:** lay out the plan of **3 :** to begin with a definite purpose **:** INTEND ⟨*set out* to win⟩ **4 :** to start out on a course, a journey, or a career

set piece *n* **1 :** a realistic piece of stage scenery standing by itself **2 :** a composition (as in literature) executed in a fixed or ideal form often with great artistry and brilliant effect

set point *n* **:** a point that decides a tennis set if won by the side having an advantage in the score

set•screw \'set-ˌskrü\ *n* **1 :** a screw screwed through one part and tightly upon or into another part to prevent relative movement **2 :** a screw for regulating a valve opening or a spring tension

set•tee \se-'tē\ *n* **1 :** a long seat with a back **2 :** a medium-sized sofa with arms and a back [alteration of ¹*settle*]

set•ter \'set-ər\ *n* **1 :** one that sets **2 :** a large long-coated bird dog of a type formerly trained to crouch on finding game but now to point

set theory *n* **:** a branch of mathematics that deals with the nature and relations of sets — **set–theoretic** *adj*

set•ting \'set-ing\ *n* **1 :** the way, position, or direction in which something is set **2 :** the frame or bed in which a gem is set **3 a :** BACKGROUND 3a, b(1), ENVIRONMENT **b :** the time and place of the action of a play or movie **c :** the scenery used in a play or a movie **4 :** the music composed for a text (as a poem) **5 :** the tableware required for arranging a place at a table **6 :** a batch of eggs for incubation

¹set•tle \'set-l\ *n* **:** a wooden bench with arms, a high solid back, and an enclosed base [Old English *setl* "seat, chair"]

²settle *vb* **set•tled**; **set•tling** \'set-ling, -l-ing\ **1 :** to place so as to stay **2 a :** to establish residence in **:** COLONIZE ⟨*settled* the West⟩ **b :** to make one's home ⟨*settle* in the country⟩ **3 a :** to cause to pack down or to become compact by sinking **:** sink gradually or to the bottom **b :** to clarify by causing dregs or impurities to sink **c :** to become clear by depositing sediment **4 a :** to make or become quiet or orderly ⟨reading *settles* my nerves⟩ **b :** to take up an ordered or stable life ⟨marry and *set-*

tle down⟩ **5 a :** to fix or resolve conclusively ⟨*settle* the question⟩ **b :** to establish or secure permanently **6 :** to arrange in a desired position **7 a :** to make or arrange for final disposition of ⟨*settle* an estate⟩ **b :** to bestow or give possession of legally ⟨*settled* property on the child⟩ **c :** to pay in full ⟨*settle* a bill⟩ **8 :** to adjust differences or accounts [Old English *setlan* "to seat, place, settle", from *setl* "seat"]

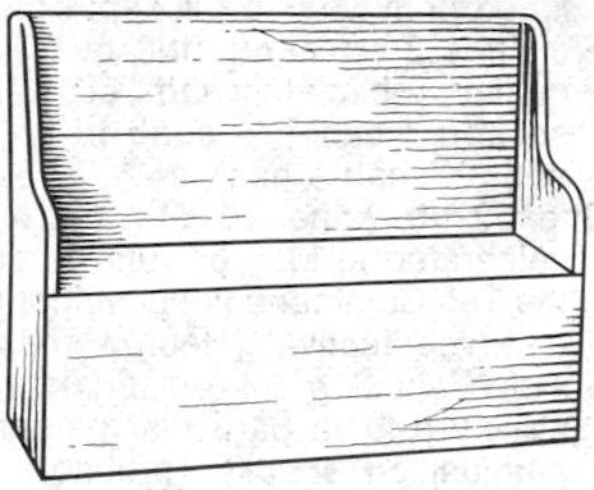

[1]settle

set•tle•ment \ˈset-l-mənt\ *n* **1 :** the act or process of settling **2 :** final payment (as of a bill) **3 a :** a place or region newly settled **b :** a small village **4 :** an institution providing various community services especially to residents of large cities — called also *settlement house* **5 :** an agreement composing differences

set•tler \ˈset-lər, -l-ər\ *n* **:** one that settles (as in a new region)

set•tling \ˈset-ling, -l-ing\ *n* **:** something that settles at the bottom of a liquid **:** SEDIMENT — usually used in pl.

set•tlor \ˈset-ˌlȯr, -l-ˌȯr\ *n* **:** one that makes a settlement or creates a trust of property

set–to \ˈset-ˌtü\ *n, pl* **set–tos** \-ˌtüz\ **:** a usually brief and vigorous fight or argument

set to \set-ˈtü, ˈset-\ *vi* **1 :** to begin actively and earnestly ⟨*set to* and ate with a will⟩ **2 :** to begin fighting

set•up \ˈset-ˌəp\ *n* **1 :** glass, ice, and mixer served to patrons who supply their own liquor **2 :** a task or contest intentionally made easy **3 :** the way in which something is set up **:** ARRANGEMENT

set up \set-ˈəp, ˈset-\ *vb* **1 a :** to assemble the parts of and erect ⟨*set up* a printing press⟩ **b :** to put (a machine) in readiness or adjustment for a tooling operation **2 a :** ELATE, GRATIFY ⟨*set up* by the victory⟩ **b :** to make proud or vain **3 a :** to put forward or extol as a model **b :** to claim (oneself) to be ⟨*set* yourself *up* as an authority⟩ **4 :** FOUND 3, INAUGURATE **5 :** to provide with a means of making a living ⟨*set* them *up* in a new shop⟩ **6 :** to make careful plans for ⟨*set up* a robbery⟩ **7 a :** to treat to (drinks) **b :** to treat (someone) to something **8 :** to make pretensions ⟨*setting up* for a wit⟩ — **set up housekeeping :** to establish one's living quarters — **set up shop :** to establish one's business

sev•en \ˈsev-ən\ *n* **1 :** one more than six; *also* **:** a symbol representing this — see NUMBER table **2 :** the seventh in a set or series **3 :** something having seven units or members [Old English *seofon*] — **seven** *adj or pron*

sev•en•teen \ˌsev-ən-ˈtēn, ˈsev-ən-\ *n* **:** one more than 16; *also* **:** a symbol representing this — see NUMBER table [Old English *seofontēne*] — **seventeen** *adj or pron* — **sev•en•teenth** \-ˈtēnth, -ˈtēntth\ *adj or n*

seventeen–year locust *n* **:** a cicada of the United States with a life of 17 years in the North and 13 years in the South of which the greatest part is spent as a wingless underground nymph that feeds on roots and emerges from the soil to become a short-lived winged adult

sev•enth \ˈsev-ənth, -ənth\ *n, pl* **sev•enths** \ˈsev-əns, -ənths, -ənths\ **1 :** number seven in a countable series — see NUMBER table **2 a :** a musical interval embracing seven degrees **b :** LEADING TONE **c :** the harmonic combination of two tones a seventh apart — **seventh** *adj or adv*

Seventh Day Adventist *n* **:** a member of an evangelical Protestant denomination organized in the United States in 1863 and marked by emphasis on preparation for Christ's Second Coming

seventh heaven *n* **:** a state of extreme joy [from the 7th being the highest of the 7 heavens of Muslim and cabalist doctrine]

sev•en•ty \ˈsev-ən-tē\ *n, pl* **-ties :** ten more than 60; *also* **:** a symbol representing this — see NUMBER table [Old English *seofontig*] — **sev•en•ti•eth** \-tē-əth\ *adj or n* — **seventy** *adj or pron*

sev•en•ty–eight \ˌsev-ən-tē-ˈāt\ *n* **:** a phonograph record for play at 78 revolutions per minute

sev•er \ˈsev-ər\ *vb* **sev•ered; sev•er•ing** \ˈsev-ring, -e-ring\ **1 :** to put or keep apart **:** DIVIDE; *esp* **:** to remove (as a part) by or as if by cutting **2 :** to come or break apart [Middle French *severer,* from Latin *separare*] **syn** see SEPARATE — **sev•er•abil•i•ty** \ˌsev-rə-ˈbil-ət-ē, -ə-rə-\ *n* — **sev•er•able** \ˈsev-rə-bəl, -ə-rə-\ *adj*

[1]**sev•er•al** \ˈsev-rəl, -ə-rəl\ *adj* **1 a :** separate or distinct from one another **:** DIFFERENT ⟨federal union of the *several* states⟩ **b :** PARTICULAR, RESPECTIVE ⟨specialists in their *several* fields⟩ **2 :** more than two but fewer than many ⟨moved *several* inches⟩ [Anglo-French, from Medieval Latin *separalis,* derived from the Latin *separare* "to separate"] — **sev•er•al•ly** \-ē\ *adv*

[2]**several** *pron, pl in construction* **:** an indefinite number more than two and fewer than many ⟨*several* of the guests⟩

sev•er•al•fold \ˌsev-rəl-ˈfōld, -ə-rəl-\ *adj* **1 :** having several parts or aspects **2 :** being several times as large, as great, or as many as some understood size, degree, or amount ⟨a *severalfold* increase⟩ — **severalfold** *adv*

sev•er•al•ty \ˈsev-rəl-tē, -ə-rəl-\ *n* **:** the quality or state of being several **:** DISTINCTNESS, SEPARATENESS

sev•er•ance \ˈsev-rəns, -ə-rəns\ *n* **:** the act or process of severing **:** the state of being severed

severance pay *n* **:** an allowance usually based on length of service that is payable to an employee on termination of employment

se•vere \sə-ˈviər\ *adj* **1 a :** strict in judgment, discipline, or government **b :** strict or stern in bearing or manner **:** AUSTERE **2 :** rigorous in restraint, punishment, or requirement **:** STRINGENT **3 :** strongly critical **4 :** sober or restrained in decoration or manner **:** PLAIN **5 a :** inflicting physical discomfort or hardship **:** HARSH ⟨*severe* winters⟩ **b :** inflicting pain or distress **:** GRIEVOUS ⟨a *severe* wound⟩ **6 :** requiring great effort **:** ARDUOUS ⟨a *severe* test⟩ **7 :** of a great degree **:** MARKED ⟨a *severe* economic depression⟩ [Latin *severus*] — **se•vere•ly** *adv* — **se•vere•ness** *n*

• **syn** SEVERE, STERN, AUSTERE mean showing or requiring strict discipline or firm restraint. SEVERE implies enforcing standards without indulgence or laxity and may suggest harshness; STERN stresses inflexibility and inexorability of temper or character; AUSTERE suggests absence of warmth, color, or feeling and may apply to rigorous simplicity or self-denial.

se•ver•i•ty \sə-ˈver-ət-ē\ *n, pl* **-ties :** the quality or state of being severe

Sè•vres \ˈsev-rə, ˈsev, ˈsevr\ *n* **:** an often elaborately decorated French porcelain [*Sèvres,* France]

sew \ˈsō\ *vb* **sewed; sewn** \ˈsōn\ *or* **sewed; sew•ing 1 :** to join or fasten by stitches made with a flexible thread or filament ⟨*sew* on a button⟩ **2 :** to close or enclose by sewing ⟨*sew* the money in a bag⟩ **3 :** to practice or engage in sewing [Old English *sīwian*]

sew•age \ˈsü-ij\ *n* **:** refuse liquids or waste matter carried off by sewers [[3]*sewer*]

[1]**sew•er** \ˈsō-ər, ˈsōr\ *n* **:** one that sews

[2]**sew•er** \ˈsü-ər, ˈsu̇-ər, ˈsu̇r\ *n* **:** a covered usually underground passage to carry off water and sewage [Middle French *esseweur, seweur,* from *essewer* "to drain", derived from Latin *ex-* + *aqua* "water"]

sew•er•age \ˈsü-ə-rij, ˈsu̇-ər-ij, ˈsu̇r-ij\ *n* **1 :** SEWAGE **2 :** the removal and disposal of sewage and surface water by sewers **3 :** a system of sewers

sew•ing \ˈsō-ing\ *n* **1 :** the act, method, or occupation of one that sews **2 :** material that has been or is to be sewed

sew up *vt* **1 :** to get exclusive use or control of **2 :** to make certain of **:** ASSURE ⟨*sew up* a deal⟩

sex \ˈseks\ *n* **1 :** either of two divisions of organisms distinguished respectively as male and female **2 :** the sum of the structural, functional, and behavioral characteristics of living beings that are ultimately related to reproduction by two interacting parents and that serve to distinguish males and females **3 :** sexual activity or intercourse [Latin *sexus*]

sex- *or* **sexi-** *combining form* **:** six [Latin *sex*]

sex•a•ge•nar•i•an \ˌsek-sə-jə-ˈner-ē-ən, sek-ˌsaj-ə-\ *n* **:** a person who is 60 or more but less than 70 years old [Latin *sexagenarius* "60 years old, of 60", derived from *sexaginta* "sixty"] — **sexagenarian** *adj*

Sex•a•ges•i•ma \ˌsek-sə-ˈjes-ə-mə, -ˈjā-zə-mə\ *n* **:** the second

\ə\ **abut**	\au̇\ **out**	\i\ **tip**	\ȯ\ **saw**	\u̇\ **foot**
\ər\ **further**	\ch\ **chin**	\ī\ **life**	\ȯi\ **coin**	\y\ **yet**
\a\ **mat**	\e\ **pet**	\j\ **job**	\th\ **thin**	\yü\ **few**
\ā\ **take**	\ē\ **easy**	\ng\ **sing**	\t͟h\ **this**	\yu̇\ **cure**
\ä\ **cot, cart**	\g\ **go**	\ō\ **bone**	\ü\ **food**	\zh\ **vision**

Sunday before Lent [Late Latin, from Latin *sexagesimus* "sixtieth"]

sex•a•ges•i•mal \-'jes-ə-məl\ *adj* **:** of, relating to, or based on the number 60 ⟨*sexagesimal* measurement of angles⟩ [Latin *sexagesimus* "sixtieth", from *sexaginta* "sixty"]

sex appeal *n* **:** personal appeal or physical attractiveness for members of the opposite sex

sex cell *n* **:** GAMETE

sex chromosome *n* **:** a chromosome inherited differently in the two sexes that is or is held to be concerned directly with the inheritance of sex

sexed \'sekst\ *adj* **:** having sex or sexual instincts

sex gland *n* **:** GONAD

sex hormone *n* **:** a hormone that affects the growth or function of the reproductive organs or the development of secondary sex characteristics

sex•ism \'sek-ˌsiz-əm\ *n* **:** prejudice or discrimination based on sex — **sex•ist** \'sek-səst\ *adj or n*

sex•less \'sek-sləs\ *adj* **:** lacking sex **:** NEUTER — **sex•less•ness** *n*

sex–linked \'sek-ˌslingt, -ˌslingkt\ *adj* **1 :** located on one sex chromosome but not on the other so that one sex has one allele and the other has two ⟨a *sex-linked* gene⟩ **2 :** characterized by or controlled by sex-linked genes ⟨a *sex-linked* character⟩ — **sex–link•age** \-ˌsling-kij\ *n*

sext \'sekst\ *n, often cap* **:** the fourth of the canonical hours [Latin *sexta* "6th hour of the day", from *sextus* "sixth", from *sex* "six"]

sex•tant \'sek-stənt\ *n* **:** a navigational instrument for measuring the angle between the horizon and the sun or a star in order to determine the latitude (as of a ship) [New Latin *sextans* "6th part of a circle", from Latin, "6th part", from *sextus* "sixth"]

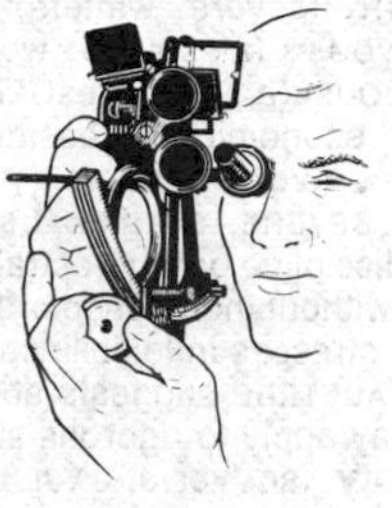
sextant

sex•tet *also* **sex•tette** \sek-'stet\ *n* **1 :** a musical composition for six instruments or voices **2 :** a group or set of six [alteration of *sestet*]

sex•til•lion \sek-'stil-yən\ *n* — see NUMBER table [French, from Latin *sex* "six" + French *-illion* (as in *million*)]

sex•ton \'sek-stən\ *n* **:** a church officer or employee who takes care of the church property and sometimes rings the bell for services and digs graves [Middle French *secrestain*, from Medieval Latin *sacristanus* "sacristan"]

¹sex•tu•ple \sek-'stüp-əl, -'styüp-, -'stəp-; 'sek-stəp-\ *adj* **1 :** having six units or members **2 :** being six times as great or as many [probably from Medieval Latin *sextuplus*, from Latin *sextus* "sixth"] — **sextuple** *n*

²sextuple *vb* **sex•tu•pled**; **sex•tu•pling** \-ling, -ə-ling\ **:** to make or become six times as much or as many

sex•tup•let \sek-'stəp-lət, -'stüp-, -'styüp-; 'sek-stəp-\ *n* **1 :** a combination of six of a kind **2 :** one of six offspring born at one birth

sex•u•al \'seksh-wəl, -ə-wəl; 'sek-shəl\ *adj* **1 :** of, relating to, or associated with sex or the sexes ⟨*sexual* differentiation⟩ ⟨*sexual* conflict⟩ **2 :** having or involving sex ⟨*sexual* reproduction⟩ ⟨*sexual* spores⟩ — **sex•u•al•i•ty** \ˌsek-shə-'wal-ət-ē\ *n* — **sex•u•al•ly** \'seksh-wə-lē, -ə-wə-; 'seksh-lē, -ə-lē\ *adv*

sexual intercourse *n* **:** sexual connection especially between human beings

sexy \'sek-sē\ *adj* **sex•i•er**; **-est :** sexually suggestive or stimulating **:** EROTIC — **sex•i•ness** *n*

sfer•ics \'sfiər-iks, 'sfer-\ *n pl* **:** ATMOSPHERICS [by shortening]

¹sfor•zan•do \sfȯrt-'sän-dō, -'san-\ *adj or adv* **:** played with prominent stress or accent — used of a single note or chord as a direction in music [Italian, literally, "forcing", from *sforzare* "to force"]

²sforzando *n, pl* **-dos** *or* **-di** \-dē\ **:** an accented tone or chord

sh \sh *often prolonged*\ *interj* — used often in prolonged or reduplicated form to urge or command silence or less noise [imitative]

shab•by \'shab-ē\ *adj* **shab•bi•er**; **-est 1 a :** threadbare and faded from wear **b :** ill kept **:** DILAPIDATED **2 :** dressed in worn clothes **3 a :** MEAN, UNFAIR ⟨*shabby* treatment⟩ **b :** inferior in quality [obsolete *shab* "scab, low fellow", from Old English *sceabb* "scab"] — **shab•bi•ly** \'shab-ə-lē\ *adv* — **shab•bi•ness** \'shab-ē-nəs\ *n*

Sha•bu•oth \shə-'vü-ˌōt, -ˌōth, -ˌōs, -əs\ *n* **:** a Jewish holiday celebrated in May or June to commemorate the revelation of the Ten Commandments at Mount Sinai and in biblical times as a harvest festival [Hebrew *shābhu'ōth*, literally, "weeks"]

shack \'shak\ *n* **1 :** HUT, SHANTY **2 :** a room or similar enclosed structure for a particular person or use ⟨a radio *shack*⟩ ⟨an ammunition *shack*⟩ [probably from English dialect *shackly* "rickety"]

¹shack•le \'shak-əl\ *n* **1 :** something (as a manacle or fetter) that confines the legs or arms **2 :** something that checks or prevents free action as if by fetters — usually used in pl. **3 :** a device (as a clevis) for making something fast [Old English *sceacul*]

²shackle *vt* **shack•led**; **shack•ling** \'shak-ling, -ə-ling\ **1 a :** to bind with shackles **b :** to make fast with a shackle **2 :** to deprive of freedom of action **:** HINDER ⟨*shackled* by poverty⟩ **syn** see HAMPER — **shack•ler** \'shak-lər, -ə-lər\ *n*

shad \'shad\ *n, pl* **shad :** any of several deep-bodied food fishes that are closely related to the herrings but ascend rivers in the spring to spawn [Old English *sceadd*]

shad•blow \'shad-ˌblō\ *n* **:** SERVICEBERRY 2

shad•bush \-ˌbu̇sh\ *n* **:** SERVICEBERRY 2

shad•dock \'shad-ək\ *n* **:** a large thick-rinded usually pear-shaped citrus fruit closely related to the grapefruit but often having coarse dry pulp; *also* **:** the tree that bears it [Captain *Shaddock*, 17th century English ship commander]

¹shade \'shād\ *n* **1 a :** partial darkness caused by interception of the rays of light **b :** relative obscurity or retirement **2 :** space sheltered from sunlight **3 :** a vaporous or unreal appearance **4** *pl* **a :** the shadows that gather as darkness comes on **b :** UNDERWORLD 2, HADES **5 :** a disembodied spirit **:** GHOST **6 :** something that intercepts or shelters from light, sun, or heat: as **a :** a device partially covering a lamp so as to reduce glare **b :** a screen usually on a roller for regulating the light or the view through a window **7 a :** the representation of the effect of shade in painting or drawing **b :** a subdued or somber feature **8 a :** a color produced by a pigment or dye mixture having some black in it **b :** a color slightly different from the one under consideration **9 :** a minute difference or variation ⟨*shades* of meaning⟩ **10 :** a facial expression of sadness or displeasure [Old English *sceadu*] **syn** see COLOR — **shade•less** \-ləs\ *adj*

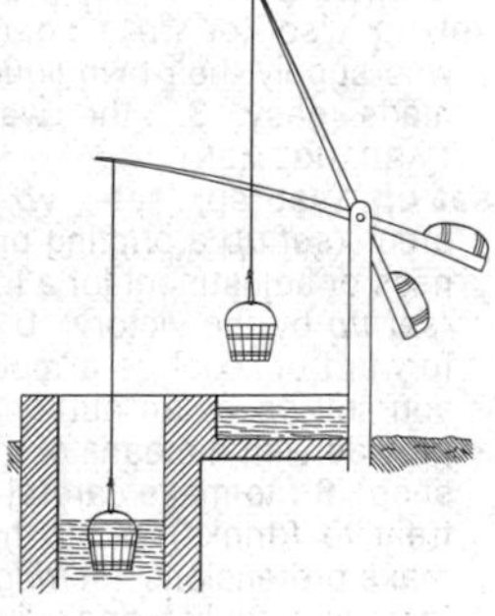
shadoof

²shade *vb* **1 a :** to shelter or screen by intercepting radiated light or heat **b :** to cover with a shade **2 :** to hide partly by or as if by a shadow **3 :** to darken with or as if with a shadow **4 :** to cast into the shade **:** OBSCURE **5 a :** to represent the effect of shade or shadow on **b :** to add shading to **c :** to color so that the shades pass gradually from one to another **6 :** to change by gradual transition or qualification **7 :** to reduce (as a price) slightly — **shad•er** *n*

shad•ing \'shād-ing\ *n* **:** a filling up within outlines to suggest different degrees of light and dark in a picture or drawing

sha•doof \shə-'düf, sha-\ *n* **:** a counterbalanced sweep used since ancient times especially in Egypt for raising water (as for irrigation) [Arabic *shādūf*]

¹shad•ow \'shad-ō\ *n* **1 :** shade within defined bounds **2 :** a reflected image **3 :** shelter from danger or observation **4 a :** an imperfect and faint representation **b :** IMITATION 2, COPY **5 :** the dark figure cast upon a surface by a body blocking rays from a light source **6 :** PHANTOM 1a **7 :** a shaded part of a picture **8 :** a form without substance **:** REMNANT, VESTIGE ⟨are only a *shadow* of your former self⟩ **9 a :** an inseparable companion or follower **b :** one that shadows as a spy or detective **10 :** a small degree or portion **:** TRACE ⟨not a *shadow* of a doubt⟩ **11 :** a gloomy influence [Old English *sceadu* "shade, shadow"] — **shad•ow•less** \-ləs\ *adj* — **shad•ow•like** \-ˌlīk\ *adj*

2shadow *vb* **1 a :** to cast a shadow on **b :** to cast a gloom over **:** CLOUD **2 :** to represent or indicate obscurely or faintly **3 :** to follow especially secretly **:** TRAIL **4 :** to pass gradually or by degrees **5 :** to become overcast with or as if with shadows — **shad•ow•er** \ˈshad-ə-wər\ *n*

3shadow *adj* **1 a :** set up in order to function if the opportunity arises ⟨a *shadow* government⟩ **b :** belonging to a shadow cabinet or shadow government ⟨*shadow* minister of foreign affairs⟩ **2 :** having an indistinct pattern ⟨a *shadow* plaid⟩

shad•ow•box \ˈshad-ō-ˌbäks, -ə-\ *vi* **:** to go through the motions of boxing as if with an imaginary opponent especially during training — **shad•ow•box•ing** *n*

shadow box *n* **:** a shallow enclosing case usually with a glass front in which something is displayed

shadow play *n* **:** a play in which the shadows of the actors are projected on a screen

shad•owy \ˌshad-ə-wē\ *adj* **1 a :** being or resembling a shadow **:** UNREAL **b :** faintly visible **:** INDISTINCT **2 :** being in or obscured by shadow **3 :** SHADY 1

shady \ˈshād-ē\ *adj* **shad•i•er; -est 1 :** producing or affording shade **2 :** sheltered from the sun **3 a :** of questionable merit **b :** DISREPUTABLE — **shad•i•ly** \ˈshād-l-ē\ *adv* — **shad•i•ness** \ˈshād-ē-nəs\ *n*

1shaft \ˈshaft\ *n, pl* **shafts** \ˈshafs, ˈshafts, *in sense 3 also* ˈshavz\ **1 a :** the long handle of a weapon (as a spear) **b :** 1SPEAR 1, LANCE **2 a :** the slender stem of an arrow **b :** ARROW 1 **3 :** POLE; *esp* **:** one of two poles between which a horse is hitched to pull a vehicle **4 :** a narrow beam of light **5 :** something resembling the shaft of an arrow or spear: as **a :** the handle of a tool **b :** a tall monument (as a column) **c :** a vertical opening or passage through the floors of a building ⟨an air *shaft*⟩ **d :** a commonly cylindrical bar used to support rotating pieces or to transmit power or motion by rotation **e :** a vertical or inclined opening of uniform and limited cross section made for finding or mining ore, raising water, or ventilating underground workings **f :** the midrib of a feather **6 a :** a projectile thrown like a spear or shot like an arrow **b :** a scornful or satirical remark **:** BARB **c :** harsh or unfair treatment [Old English *sceaft*]

2shaft *vt* **:** to fit with a shaft

1shag \ˈshag\ *n* **1 a :** a shaggy tangled mass or covering **b :** long coarse or matted fiber or nap **2 :** CORMORANT 1 [Old English *sceacga*]

2shag *vb* **shagged; shag•ging 1 :** to fall or hang in shaggy masses **2 :** to make rough or shaggy

3shag *vt* **shagged; shag•ging 1 :** to chase after; *esp* **:** to run after and return (as a ball) **2 :** to chase away [origin unknown]

shag•bark \ˈshag-ˌbärk\ *n* **:** a hickory with a gray shaggy outer bark that peels off in long strips

shag•gy \ˈshag-ē\ *adj* **shag•gi•er; -est 1 a :** covered with or made up of long, coarse, or matted hair or thick, tangled, or unkempt vegetation **b :** having a rough or hairy surface **2 :** UNKEMPT, SHABBY — **shag•gi•ly** \ˈshag-ə-lē\ *adv* — **shag•gi•ness** \ˈshag-ē-nəs\ *n*

sha•green \sha-ˈgrēn, shə-\ *n* **1 :** an untanned leather covered with small round granulations and usually dyed green **2 :** the rough skin of various sharks and rays [French *chagrin,* from Turkish *çağrı, sağrı*] — **shagreen** *adj*

shah \ˈshä, ˈshȯ\ *n* **:** the sovereign of Iran [Persian *shāh* "king"] — **shah•dom** \ˈshäd-əm, ˈshȯd-\ *n*

1shake \ˈshāk\ *vb* **shook** \ˈshu̇k\; **shak•en** \ˈshā-kən\; **shak•ing 1 :** to move irregularly to and fro **:** QUIVER, TREMBLE ⟨*shaking* with cold⟩ **2 :** to become unsteady **:** TOTTER **3 :** to brandish, wave, or flourish often in a threatening way **4 :** to cause to move in a quick jerky way **5 :** to free oneself from ⟨*shake* off a cold⟩ **6 :** to cause to waver **:** WEAKEN ⟨*shake* one's faith⟩ **7 :** to dislodge or eject by quick jerky movements ⟨*shake* the dust from a cloth⟩ **8 :** to clasp (hands) in greeting or as a sign of goodwill or agreement **9 :** to stir the feelings of **:** UPSET ⟨*shook* me up⟩ [Old English *sceacan*] — **shak•able** *or* **shake•able** \ˈshā-kə-bəl\ *adj*

• syn SHAKE, AGITATE, ROCK mean to move up and down or back and forth with some violence. SHAKE applies to short, rapid movements often for a particular purpose; AGITATE suggests more violent and prolonged tossing or stirring ⟨the washer cleans by *agitating*⟩ ROCK implies a swinging or swaying motion resulting from violent impact or upheaval ⟨a city *rocked* by an earthquake⟩

— **shake a leg 1 :** DANCE 1 **2 :** to hurry up

2shake *n* **1 :** an act of shaking **:** as **a :** an act of shaking hands **b :** an act of shaking oneself **2 a :** a blow or shock that upsets the equilibrium or disturbs the balance of something **b :** EARTHQUAKE **3** *pl* **:** a condition of trembling (as from chill) **4 :** something produced by shaking: as **a :** a fissure in strata **b :** MILK SHAKE **5 :** a wavering, quivering, or alternating motion caused by a blow or shock **6 :** TRILL 1a **7 :** a very brief period of time **:** INSTANT ⟨ready in two *shakes*⟩ **8** *pl* **:** one of importance or ability — usually used in the phrase *no great shakes* **9 :** a shingle split from a piece of log usually three to four feet long ⟨cedar *shakes*⟩ **10 :** 3DEAL 2 ⟨a fair *shake*⟩

shake•down \ˈshāk-ˌdau̇n\ *n* **1 :** an improvised bed (as one made up on the floor) **2 :** a boisterous dance **3 :** an act or instance of shaking someone down; *esp* **:** EXTORTION **4 :** a process or period of adjustment **5 :** a test under operating conditions of something new (as a ship) for defects or to familiarize the operators with it

shake down \shāk-ˈdau̇n, ˈshāk-\ *vb* **1 a :** to take up temporary quarters **b :** to occupy a makeshift bed **2 a :** to become accustomed especially to new surroundings or duties **b :** to settle down **c :** to give a shakedown test to **3 :** to obtain money from in a dishonest or illegal manner and especially by extortion **4 :** to bring about a reduction of

shake•out \ˈshā-ˌkau̇t\ *n* **:** a minor economic recession

shak•er \ˈshā-kər\ *n* **1 :** one that shakes; *esp* **:** any of various utensils or machines used in shaking **2** *cap* **:** a member of a millenarian sect originating in England in 1747 and practicing celibacy and communal living — **Shaker** *adj*

Shake•spear•ean *or* **Shake•spear•ian** \shāk-ˈspir-ē-ən\ *adj* **:** of, relating to, or characteristic of William Shakespeare or his writings

Shakespearean sonnet *n* **:** ENGLISH SONNET

shake–up \ˈshā-ˌkəp\ *n* **:** an act or instance of shaking up; *esp* **:** an extensive and often drastic reorganization ⟨lost my job in an office *shake-up*⟩

shake up \shā-ˈkəp, ˈshā-\ *vt* **1 :** to jar by or as if by a physical shock ⟨the collision *shook* both drivers *up*⟩ **2 :** to make an extensive often drastic reorganization of

sha•ko \ˈshak-ō, ˈshak-ō\ *n, pl* **sha•kos** *or* **sha•koes :** a stiff military cap with a high crown and plume [French, from Hungarian *csákó*]

shako

shaky \ˈshā-kē\ *adj* **shak•i•er; -est 1 a :** lacking stability **b :** lacking in firmness (as of beliefs) **c :** lacking in authority or reliability **:** QUESTIONABLE **2 a :** somewhat unsound in health **b :** characterized by shaking **3 :** likely to give way or break down — **shak•i•ly** \-kə-lē\ *adv* — **shak•i•ness** \-kē-nəs\ *n*

shale \ˈshāl\ *n* **:** a rock that is formed by the consolidation of clay, mud, or silt, has a finely layered structure, and splits easily [Old English *scealu* "shell, scale"] — **shaley** \ˈshā-lē\ *adj*

shall \shəl, shal, ˈshal\ *auxiliary verb, past* **should** \shəd, shu̇d, ˈshu̇d\; *present sing & pl* **shall 1a** — used to express a command or exhortation ⟨you *shall* go⟩ **b** — used in laws, regulations, or directives to express what is mandatory ⟨it *shall* be unlawful to carry firearms⟩ **2a** — used to express what is inevitable or what is likely to happen in the future ⟨we *shall* have to be ready⟩ ⟨we *shall* see⟩ **b** — used to express simple futurity ⟨when *shall* we expect you⟩ **3** — used to express determination ⟨they *shall* not pass⟩ [Old English *sceal* "owe, owes, ought to, must"]

shal•lop \ˈshal-əp\ *n* **:** a small open boat propelled by oars or sails [Middle French *chaloupe*]

\ə\ **abut**	\au̇\ **out**	\i\ **tip**	\ȯ\ **saw**	\u̇\ **foot**
\ər\ **further**	\ch\ **chin**	\ī\ **life**	\ȯi\ **coin**	\y\ **yet**
\a\ **mat**	\e\ **pet**	\j\ **job**	\th\ **thin**	\yü\ **few**
\ā\ **take**	\ē\ **easy**	\ng\ **sing**	\t͟h\ **this**	\yu̇\ **cure**
\ä\ **cot, cart**	\g\ **go**	\ō\ **bone**	\ü\ **food**	\zh\ **vision**

shal•lot \shə-ˈlät\ *n* : a bulbous perennial herb that resembles the related onion and produces small clustered bulbs used in cooking [French *échalote*]

¹**shal•low** \ˈshal-ō\ *adj* **1** : having little depth ⟨*shallow* water⟩ ⟨a *shallow* pan⟩ **2** : lacking in depth of knowledge, thought, or feeling [Middle English *schalowe*] **syn** see SUPERFICIAL — **shal•low•ly** *adv* — **shal•low•ness** *n*

²**shallow** *vb* : to make or become shallow

³**shallow** *n* : a shallow place or area in a body of water — usually used in pl.

sha•lom \shä-ˈlōm, shə-\ *interj* — used as a Jewish greeting and farewell [Hebrew *shālōm* "peace"]

sha•lom alei•chem \ˌshō-lə-mə-ˈlā-kəm, ˌshō-, -kəm\ *interj* — used as a traditional Jewish greeting [Hebrew *shālōm 'alēkhem* "peace unto you"]

shalt \shəlt, shalt, ˈshalt\ *archaic present 2d sing of* SHALL

¹**sham** \ˈsham\ *n* **1** : HOAX 1 **2** : cheap falseness : HYPOCRISY **3** : a decorative piece of cloth simulating an article of personal or household linen and used in place of or over it **4** : an imitation or counterfeit intended to appear genuine **5** : a person who shams [perhaps from English dialect *sham* "shame"]

²**sham** *vb* **shammed**; **sham•ming** : to act intentionally so as to give a false impression : FEIGN

³**sham** *adj* **1** : not genuine : FALSE **2** : having such poor quality as to seem false

sha•man \ˈshäm-ən, ˈshā-mən\ *n, pl* **shamans** : a priest held to cure the sick, to discover the hidden, and to control events by magic [Russian, of Altaic origin]

sha•man•ism \-ˌiz-əm\ *n* : a religion of the Ural-Altaic peoples of northern Asia and Europe marked by belief in gods, demons, and ancestral spirits responsive only to the shamans; *also* : any similar religion — **sha•man•ist** \-əst\ *n or adj* — **sha•man•is•tic** \ˌshäm-ən-ˈis-tik, ˌshā-mən-\ *adj*

sham•ble \ˈsham-bəl\ *vi* **sham•bled**; **sham•bling** \-bə-ling, -bling\ : to walk awkwardly with dragging feet : SHUFFLE [*shamble legs* "malformed legs", from *shamble* "table for exhibition of meat for sale", from Old English *sceamul* "stool, table"] — **shamble** *n*

sham•bles \ˈsham-bəlz\ *n sing or pl* **1** : a place of mass slaughter **2** : a scene or state of great confusion, disorder, or destruction [*shamble* "table for exhibition of meat for sale, meat market"]

sham•bling *adj* : marked by slow awkward movement

¹**shame** \ˈshām\ *n* **1 a** : a painful emotion caused by consciousness of guilt, shortcoming, or impropriety **b** : the susceptibility to such emotion **2** : a condition of humiliating disgrace or disrepute **3 a** : something that brings strong regret, censure, or reproach **b** : a cause of feeling shame [Old English *scamu*]

²**shame** *vt* **1** : to bring shame to : DISGRACE **2** : to put to shame by outdoing **3** : to cause to feel shame **4** : to force by causing to feel guilty ⟨*shamed* into confessing⟩

shame•faced \ˈshām-ˈfāst\ *adj* **1** : showing modesty : BASHFUL **2** : ASHAMED 1 [alteration of earlier *shamefast,* from Old English *scamfæst,* from *scamu* "shame" + *fæst* "fixed, fast"] — **shame•faced•ly** \-ˈfā-səd-lē, -ˈfāst-lē\ *adv* — **shame•faced•ness** \-ˈfā-səd-nəs, -ˈfāst-nəs, -ˈfās-nəs\ *n*

△ **origin** Some English words have been altered so as to give them an apparent relationship to other better-known or better-understood words. Such a process of alteration is called folk etymology. A common word formed by folk etymology is *shamefaced.* Old English *scamfæst* meant "bashful" or "modest" or, more literally, "held fast by shame". The second element of *shamefaced,* then, was originally the same as that of *steadfast.* The similarity of consonant sounds between *-fast* and *-faced* contributed to the alteration of *shamefast* to *shamefaced,* and the belief that modesty or bashfulness is reflected in a person's face probably had some influence too.

shame•ful \ˈshām-fəl\ *adj* **1** : bringing shame : DISGRACEFUL **2** : arousing the feeling of shame : INDECENT — **shame•ful•ly** \-fə-lē\ *adv* — **shame•ful•ness** *n*

shame•less \ˈshām-ləs\ *adj* **1** : having no shame : BRAZEN **2** : showing lack of shame : DISGRACEFUL — **shame•less•ly** *adv* — **shame•less•ness** *n*

sham•mer \ˈsham-ər\ *n* : one that shams

sham•my \ˈsham-ē\ *variant of* CHAMOIS

¹**sham•poo** \sham-ˈpü\ *vt* **1** *archaic* : MASSAGE **2 a** : to wash (as the hair) with soap and water or with a special preparation **b** : to wash the hair of [Hindi *cā̃po,* imperative of *cā̃pnā* "to press, shampoo"] — **sham•poo•er** *n*

²**shampoo** *n, pl* **shampoos** **1** : an act or instance of shampooing **2** : a preparation used in shampooing

sham•rock \ˈsham-ˌräk\ *n* : any of several plants (as a wood sorrel or some clovers) having leaves with three leaflets and used as a floral emblem by the Irish [Irish Gaelic *seamrōg*]

sha•mus \ˈshäm-əs, ˈshā-məs\ *n* **1** *slang* : POLICEMAN **2** *slang* : a private detective [probably from Yiddish *shames* "sexton of a synagogue"]

shang•hai \shang-ˈhī, ˈshang-\ *vt* **shang•haied**; **shang•hai•ing** **1 a** : to put aboard a ship by force often with the help of liquor or drugs **b** : to put by force or threat of force into a place of detention **2** : to put by trickery into an undesirable position [*Shanghai,* China; from the former use of this method to secure sailors for voyages to the Orient] — **shang•hai•er** \-ˈhī-ər, -ˈhīr\ *n*

Shan•gri–la \ˌshang-gri-ˈlä\ *n* **1** : a beautiful imaginary place where life approaches perfection : UTOPIA **2** : a remote usually idyllic hideaway [*Shangri-La,* imaginary community depicted in the novel *Lost Horizon* by James Hilton]

shank \ˈshangk\ *n* **1 a** : the part of the leg between the knee and the ankle in humans or the corresponding part in various other vertebrates **b** : a cut of meat from usually the upper part of a leg **2** : a straight narrow usually essential part of an object: as **a** : a straight shaft (as of an anchor or fishhook) **b** : the stem of a tobacco pipe or the part between the stem and the bowl **c** : the narrow part of the sole of a shoe beneath the instep **3** : a part of a tool that connects the acting part with a part (as a handle) by which it is held or moved ⟨the *shank* of a drill⟩ ⟨the *shank* of a key⟩ **4 a** : the latter part of a period of time **b** : the early or main part of a period of time [Old English *scanca*]

shan't \shant, ˈshant, shȧnt, ˈshȧnt\ : shall not

shan•tung \shan-ˈtəng, ˈshan-\ *n* : a fabric in plain weave having a slightly irregular surface [*Shantung,* China]

shan•ty \ˈshant-ē\ *n, pl* **shanties** : a small roughly built shelter or dwelling : HUT [Canadian French *chantier,* from French, "frame for supporting barrels", from Latin *cantherius* "trellis"]

shan•ty•town \-ˌtau̇n\ *n* : a town or section of a town consisting mostly of shanties

shap•able *or* **shape•able** \ˈshā-pə-bəl\ *adj* **1** : capable of being shaped **2** : SHAPELY

¹**shape** \ˈshāp\ *vb* **1** : FORM 1, CREATE; *esp* : to give a particular form or shape to **2** : to adapt in shape so as to fit neatly and closely **3** : DEVISE 2, PLAN **4** : to embody in definite form ⟨*shaping* a tradition into an epic⟩ **5** : to make fit : ADAPT ⟨learn to *shape* your aims to your abilities⟩ **6** : to determine or direct the course of (as life) **7** : to take on or approach a definite form : DEVELOP — often used with *up* [Old English *scieppan*]

²**shape** *n* **1 a** : the visible characteristic of a particular thing **b** : spatial form **c** : a standard or universally recognized spatial form **2** : bodily contour especially of the trunk : FIGURE **3 a** : PHANTOM 1a, APPARITION **b** : assumed appearance : GUISE **4** : form of embodiment (as in words) : a form (as of thought) that is definite and organized ⟨a plan took *shape*⟩ ⟨got the speech into *shape*⟩ **5** : something having a particular form ⟨the *shape* of society now⟩ **6** : the condition in which one exists at a particular time ⟨in good *shape* for your age⟩ **syn** see FORM — **shaped** *adj*

shape•less \ˈshā-pləs\ *adj* **1** : having no definite shape **2 a** : deprived of usual or normal shape : MISSHAPEN **b** : not shapely — **shape•less•ly** *adv* — **shape•less•ness** *n*

shape•ly \ˈshā-plē\ *adj* **shape•li•er**; **-est** : having a regular or pleasing shape — **shape•li•ness** *n*

shap•en \ˈshā-pən\ *adj* : fashioned in or provided with a definite shape — usually used in combination ⟨an ill-*shapen* body⟩

shard \ˈshärd\ *also* **sherd** \ˈshərd\ *n* **1** : a fragment of something brittle (as pottery) **2** : a small piece : SCRAP [Old English *sceard*]

¹**share** \ˈsheər, ˈshaər\ *n* **1 a** : a portion belonging to, due to, or contributed by an individual **b** : a fair portion **2 a** : the part allotted or belonging to one of a number owning something together **b** : any of the equal portions or interests into which the property of a corporation is divided [Old English *scearu* "cutting, tonsure"]

²**share** *vb* **1** : to divide and distribute in shares : APPORTION — usually used with *out* **2** : to partake of, use, experience, or enjoy with others **3 a** : to give or be given a share in **b** : to have a share — used with *in* — **shar•er** *n*

³**share** *n* : PLOWSHARE [Old English *scear*]

share•crop \'sheər-,kräp, 'shaər-\ *vb* : to farm or produce as a sharecropper
share•crop•per \-,kräp-ər\ *n* : a farmer who works land for a landlord in return for a share of the crop
share•hold•er \-,hōl-dər\ *n* : one that owns a share in a property; *esp* : STOCKHOLDER
[1]**shark** \'shärk\ *n* : any of numerous usually rather large and typically gray marine elasmobranch fishes most of which are active predators and are of economic importance especially for their large livers which are a source of oil and for their hides from which leather is made [origin unknown]
[2]**shark** *n* **1** : a greedy crafty person who takes advantage of the needs of others ⟨a loan *shark*⟩ **2** : a person who excels especially in a particular field ⟨a *shark* at math⟩ [probably from German *schurke* "scoundrel"]
shark•skin \-,skin\ *n* **1** : the hide of a shark or leather made from it **2 a** : a smooth durable woolen or worsted suiting in twill or basket weave with small woven designs **b** : a smooth crisp fabric with a dull finish made usually of rayon in basket weave
shark sucker *n* : REMORA
[1]**sharp** \'shärp\ *adj* **1** : adapted to cutting or piercing: as **a** : having a thin keen edge or fine point **b** : briskly cold : CHILLY **2 a** : keen in intellect : QUICK-WITTED **b** : keen in perception : ACUTE, VIGILANT **c** : keen in attention to one's own interest sometimes to the point of being unethical **3** : keen in spirit or action: as **a** : full of activity : BRISK **b** : capable of acting or reacting strongly; *esp* : CAUSTIC 1 **4** : SEVERE, HARSH: as **a** : inclined to or marked by irritability or anger **b** : causing intense mental or physical distress **c** : cutting in language or import ⟨a *sharp* retort⟩ **5 a** : having a strong odor or flavor ⟨*sharp* cheese⟩ **b** : ACRID 1 **c** : having a strong piercing sound **6 a** : terminating in a point or edge ⟨*sharp* features⟩ **b** : involving an abrupt change in direction ⟨a *sharp* turn⟩ **c** : clear in outline or detail : DISTINCT **d** : set forth with clarity and distinctness ⟨*sharp* contrast⟩ **7 a** : higher by a half step ⟨tone of G *sharp*⟩ **b** : higher than the proper pitch **c** : having a sharp in the signature ⟨key of F *sharp*⟩ **8** : STYLISH, DRESSY [Old English *scearp*] — **sharp•ly** *adv* — **sharp•ness** *n*
• **syn** SHARP, KEEN, ACUTE mean having or showing alert competence and clear understanding. SHARP implies quick perception, clever resourcefulness, or sometimes questionable trickiness ⟨*sharp* traders⟩ KEEN suggests quickness, enthusiasm, and a penetrating mind ⟨a *keen* student of history⟩ ACUTE implies a power to penetrate and may suggest subtlety and sharpness of discrimination ⟨*acute* mathematical reasoning⟩
[2]**sharp** *vb* **1** : to raise in pitch especially by a half step **2** : to sing or play above the proper pitch
[3]**sharp** *adv* **1** : in a sharp manner : SHARPLY **2** : EXACTLY 1, PRECISELY ⟨4 o'clock *sharp*⟩
[4]**sharp** *n* **1** : a musical note or tone one half step higher than a specified note or tone; *also* : a character # on a line or space of the staff indicating such a note or tone **2** : a real or self-styled expert; *also* : SHARPER
sharp•en \'shär-pən\ *vb* **sharp•ened**; **sharp•en•ing** \'shärp-ning, -ə-ning\ : to make or become sharp or sharper — **sharp•en•er** \'shärp-nər, -ə-nər\ *n*
sharp•er \'shär-pər\ *n* : CHEAT 2, SWINDLER
sharp–eyed \'shär-'pīd\ *adj* : having keen sight; *also* : keen in observing or penetrating
sharp•ie *or* **sharpy** \'shär-pē\ *n, pl* **sharp•ies** **1** : a long narrow shallow-draft boat with flat or slightly V-shaped bottom and one or two masts that bear a triangular sail **2 a** : SHARPER **b** : an exceptionally keen or alert person
sharp–nosed \'shärp-'nōzd\ *adj* : keen in smelling
sharp practice *n* : unscrupulous seeking or taking of advantage (as in business)
sharp–set \'shärp-'set\ *adj* **1** : set at a sharp angle or so as to present a sharp edge **2** : eager in appetite or desire — **sharp–set•ness** *n*
sharp•shoot•er \'shärp-,shüt-ər\ *n* : a good marksman especially with a rifle — **sharp•shoot•ing** \-,shüt-ing\ *n*
sharp–sight•ed \-'sīt-əd\ *adj* **1** : having acute sight **2** : mentally keen or alert
sharp–tongued \-'təngd\ *adj* : harsh or bitter in speech
sharp–wit•ted \-'wit-əd\ *adj* : having or showing a keen mind
Shas•ta daisy \'shast-ə-\ *n* : a large-flowered garden daisy that resembles the oxeye daisy [Mount *Shasta,* northern California]
[1]**shat•ter** \'shat-ər\ *vb* **1** : to cause to drop or be dispersed **2** : to break at once into pieces **3** : to damage badly : RUIN ⟨my health had been *shattered*⟩ **4** : to drop or scatter parts (as leaves, petals, or fruit) [Middle English *schateren*]
[2]**shatter** *n* : FRAGMENT 1, SHRED ⟨the vase lay in *shatters*⟩
shat•ter•proof \,shat-ər-'prüf\ *adj* : made so as not to shatter ⟨*shatterproof* glass⟩
[1]**shave** \'shāv\ *vb* **shaved**; **shaved** *or* **shav•en** \'shā-vən\; **shav•ing** **1 a** : to cut off thin slices from (as a board with a plane) **b** : to cut off closely ⟨a lawn *shaven* close⟩ **2** : to make bare or smooth by cutting the hair from ⟨had my head *shaved*⟩ **3** : to cut or pare off by means of an edged instrument (as a razor); *esp* : to remove hair close to the skin with a razor **4** : to come close to or touch lightly in passing [Old English *scafan*]
[2]**shave** *n* **1** : any of various tools for shaving or cutting thin slices **2** : a thin slice : SHAVING **3** : an act or process of shaving **4** : an act of coming very near to
shave•ling \'shāv-ling\ *n* **1** : a tonsured clergyman : PRIEST — usually used disparagingly **2** : STRIPLING
shav•er \'shā-vər\ *n* **1** : one that shaves; *esp* : an electric razor **2** : BOY 1, YOUNGSTER
shave•tail \'shāv-,tāl\ *n* **1** : a pack mule especially when newly broken in **2** : SECOND LIEUTENANT — usually used disparagingly [from the practice of shaving the tails of newly broken mules]
Sha•vi•an \'shā-vē-ən\ *n* : an admirer or devotee of G. B. Shaw, his writings, or his social and political theories [New Latin *Shavius,* latinized form of George Bernard *Shaw*] — **Shavian** *adj*
shav•ing \'shā-ving\ *n* **1** : the act of one that shaves **2** : something shaved off ⟨wood *shavings*⟩
shaw \'shȯ\ *n, dialect* : COPPICE, THICKET [Old English *sceaga*]
[1]**shawl** \'shȯl\ *n* : a square or oblong piece of fabric used especially as a covering for the head or shoulders [Persian *shāl*]
[2]**shawl** *vt* : to wrap in or as if in a shawl
shawm \'shȯm\ *n* : a medieval double-reed woodwind instrument [Middle French *chalemie,* derived from Latin *calamus* "reed", from Greek *kalamos*]
Shaw•nee \shȯ-'nē, shä-\ *n, pl* **Shawnee** *or* **Shawnees** : a member of an Algonquian people originally of the central Ohio valley [Shawnee *Shaawanwaaki*]
shay \'shā\ *n, chiefly dialect* : CHAISE 1 [back-formation from *chaise,* taken as pl.]
[1]**she** \shē, 'shē\ *pron* **1** : that female one who is neither speaker nor hearer ⟨*she* is a doctor⟩ — compare HE, HER, HERS, IT, THEY **2** — used to refer to one regarded as feminine (as by personification) ⟨*she* was a fine ship⟩ [Middle English]
[2]**she** \'shē\ *n* : a female person or animal — often used in combination ⟨*she*-cat⟩ ⟨*she*-cousin⟩
sheaf \'shēf\ *n, pl* **sheaves** \'shēvz\ **1** : a bundle of stalks and ears of grain **2** : something resembling or suggesting a sheaf of grain ⟨a *sheaf* of papers⟩ [Old English *scēaf*] — **sheaf•like** \'shē-,flīk\ *adj*
[1]**shear** \'shiər\ *vb* **sheared**; **sheared** *or* **shorn** \'shōrn, 'shȯrn\; **shear•ing** **1** : to cut the hair or wool from ⟨*shearing* sheep⟩ **2** : to deprive of by or as if by cutting ⟨*shorn* of their power⟩ **3** : to cut or cut through with or as if with shears ⟨*shear* a metal sheet in two⟩ **4** : to become divided or broken under the action of a shear ⟨bolts may *shear* off⟩ [Old English *scieran*] — **shear•er** *n*
[2]**shear** *n* **1 a** : a cutting implement similar or identical to a pair of scissors but typically larger — usually used in pl.; *also* : one blade of a pair of shears **b** : any of various cutting machines operating by the action of opposed cutting edges of metal — usually used in pl. **2** : an action or force that causes or tends to cause two parts of a body to slide on each other in a direction parallel to their plane of contact
sheared \'shiərd\ *adj* : formed or finished by shearing; *esp* : having the pile cut to uniform length ⟨*sheared* beaver⟩
shear•wa•ter \'shiər-,wȯt-ər, -,wät-\ *n* : any of numerous oceanic birds related to the petrels and albatrosses that in flight usually skim close to the waves

sheath \'shēth\ *n, pl* **sheaths** \'shēthz, 'shēths\ **1 :** a case for a blade (as of a knife) **2 :** a covering especially of an anatomical structure suggesting a sheath in form or use **3 :** a woman's close-fitting dress [Old English *scēath*]

sheathe \'shēth\ *vt* **1 :** to put into or as if into a sheath **2 :** to encase or cover with something (as sheets of metal) that protects [Middle English *shethen,* from *shethe* "sheath"] — **sheath•er** *n*

sheath•ing \'shē-thing, -thing\ *n* **:** material used to sheathe something; *esp* **:** the first covering of boards or of waterproof material on the outside wall of a frame house or on a timber roof

sheath knife *n* **:** a knife having a fixed blade and designed to be carried in a sheath

1**sheave** \'shiv, 'shēv\ *n* **:** a grooved wheel **:** PULLEY [Middle English *sheve*]

2**sheave** \'shēv\ *vt* **:** to gather and bind into a sheaf [*sheaf*]

she•bang \shi-'bang\ *n* **:** CONTRIVANCE 2, AFFAIR, CONCERN ⟨the whole *shebang*⟩ [perhaps derived from Irish Gaelic *sībīn* "bad ale"]

1**shed** \'shed\ *vb* **shed; shed•ding 1 a :** to pour forth in drops ⟨*shed* tears⟩ **b :** to cause (blood) to flow by cutting or wounding **c :** to give off or out ⟨the sun *sheds* light⟩ **2 :** to throw off **:** REPEL ⟨the duck's plumage *sheds* water⟩ **3 a :** to rid of **:** DISCARD ⟨*shed* excess weight⟩ ⟨*shed* spores⟩ **b :** to cast aside or let fall (some natural covering) ⟨a snake *sheds* its skin⟩ ⟨the cat is *shedding*⟩ [Old English *scēadan* "to divide, separate"] — **shed•der** *n*

2**shed** *n* **1 :** a slight structure built for shelter or storage ⟨tool *shed*⟩ **2 :** a single-storied building with one or more sides unenclosed ⟨customs *shed*⟩ [probably from Middle English *shade*]

3**shed** *vt* **shed•ded; shed•ding :** to put or house in a shed

she'd \shēd, ˌshēd\ **:** she had **:** she would

sheen \'shēn\ *n* **1 :** a bright or shining condition **2 :** subdued shininess of surface ⟨the *sheen* of satin⟩ [Old English *scīene*] — **sheeny** \'shē-nē\ *adj*

sheep \'shēp\ *n, pl* **sheep 1 :** any of a genus of cud-chewing mammals related to the goats but stockier and lacking a beard in the male; *esp* **:** one long domesticated for its flesh, wool, and other products **2 :** one that is like a sheep (as in being timid, defenseless, or easily led) **3 :** SHEEPSKIN 1 [Old English *scēap*] — **sheep** *adj*

sheep 1: *top* karakul, *bottom* merino

sheep•cote \-ˌkōt, -ˌkät\ *n, chiefly British* **:** SHEEPFOLD

sheep–dip \-ˌdip\ *n* **:** a liquid preparation of toxic chemicals into which sheep are plunged especially to destroy parasitic arthropods

sheep dog *n* **:** a dog used or trained to tend, drive, or guard sheep

sheep•fold \'shēp-ˌfōld\ *n* **:** a pen or shelter for sheep

sheep•herd•er \'shēp-ˌhərd-ər\ *n* **:** a worker in charge of sheep especially on open range — **sheep•herd•ing** \-ˌhərd-ing\ *n*

sheep•ish \'shē-pish\ *adj* **1 :** resembling a sheep in meekness, stupidity, or timidity **2 :** embarassed by consciousness of a fault ⟨a *sheepish* look⟩ — **sheep•ish•ly** *adv* — **sheep•ish•ness** *n*

sheep's eye *n* **:** a shy, longing, and usually amorous glance

sheeps•head \'shēps-ˌhed\ *n* **:** any of several fishes; *esp* **:** a food fish of the Atlantic and Gulf coasts of the United States with broad incisor teeth

sheep•shear•er \'shēp-ˌshir-ər\ *n* **:** one that shears sheep

sheep•shear•ing \-ˌshiər-ing\ *n* **1 :** the act of shearing sheep **2 :** the time or season for shearing sheep

sheep•skin \'shēp-ˌskin\ *n* **1 :** the skin of a sheep or leather prepared from it; *also* **:** PARCHMENT 1 **2 :** DIPLOMA

1**sheer** \'shiər\ *adj* **1 :** very thin or transparent ⟨*sheer* stockings⟩ **2 a :** UTTER ⟨*sheer* nonsense⟩ **b :** taken or acting apart from everything else ⟨by *sheer* force⟩ **3 :** marked by great and unbroken steepness [Middle English *schere* "free from guilt"] *syn* see STEEP — **sheer•ly** *adv* — **sheer•ness** *n*

2**sheer** *adv* **1 :** WHOLLY 1, ALTOGETHER **2 :** straight up or down

3**sheer** *vi* **:** to turn from a course **:** SWERVE [perhaps alteration of 1*shear*]

4**sheer** *n* **:** a turning from or change in the course of a ship

5**sheer** *n* **:** the fore-and-aft curvature from bow to stern of a ship's deck as shown in side elevation [perhaps alteration of 2*shear*]

1**sheet** \'shēt\ *n* **1 :** a broad piece of cloth; *esp* **:** an oblong of cloth used as an article of bedding next to the person **2 a :** a usually rectangular piece of paper **b** *pl* **:** the unbound pages of a book **c :** a newspaper, periodical, or occasional publication **d :** the unseparated postage stamps printed by one impression of a plate on a single piece of paper **3 :** a broad expanse or surface ⟨a *sheet* of ice⟩ **4 :** a portion of something that is thin in comparison to its length and breadth ⟨a *sheet* of plastic⟩ [Old English *scȳte*]

2**sheet** *vt* **1 :** to cover with a sheet **:** SHROUD **2 :** to furnish with sheets

3**sheet** *n* **1 :** a rope or chain that regulates the angle at which a sail is set in relation to the wind **2** *pl* **:** the spaces at either end of an open boat not taken up by seats [Old English *scēata* "lower corner of a sail"]

sheet anchor *n* **1 :** an unusually large anchor especially for use in an emergency **2 :** something that constitutes a main support or dependence in danger

sheet•ing \'shēt-ing\ *n* **:** material in the form of sheets or suitable for forming into sheets

sheet lightning *n* **:** lightning in diffused or sheet form

sheet metal *n* **:** metal in the form of sheets

sheet music *n* **:** music printed on unbound sheets of paper

sheikh *or* **sheik** \'shēk, *for 1 also* 'shāk\ *n* **1 :** an Arab chief **2** *usually sheik* **:** a man held to be irresistibly attractive to romantic young women [Arabic *shaykh*] — **sheik•dom** \-dəm\ *n*

shek•el \'shek-əl\ *n* **1 :** an ancient unit of weight or value; *esp* **:** a Hebrew unit equal to about 252 grains troy (about 16.3 grams) **2 :** a coin weighing one shekel [Hebrew *sheqel*]

shel•drake \'shel-ˌdrāk\ *n* **1 :** any of several Old World ducks; *esp* **:** a common mostly black-and-white European duck slightly larger than the mallard **2 :** MERGANSER [Middle English]

shelf \'shelf\ *n, pl* **shelves** \'shelvz\ **1 a :** a thin flat usually long and narrow piece of firm material fastened horizontally (as on a wall) at a distance from the floor to hold objects **b :** the contents of a shelf **2 :** something resembling a shelf: as **a :** a sandbank or ledge of rocks usually partially submerged **b :** a flat projecting layer of rock [Middle English] — **shelf•like** \'shel-ˌflīk\ *adj* — **on the shelf :** in a state of inactivity or uselessness

shelf fungus *n* **:** a fungus that forms shelflike fruiting bodies

1**shell** \'shel\ *n* **1 a :** a hard rigid outer covering of an animal (as a turtle, oyster, or beetle) **b :** the outer covering of an egg and especially of a bird's egg **c :** the outer covering of a nut, fruit, or seed especially when hard or toughly fibrous **2 :** shell material or shells especially of mollusks; *also* **:** a shell-bearing mollusk **3 :** something that resembles a shell: as **a :** a framework or exterior structure **b :** a casing without substance ⟨the *shell* of my former self⟩ **c :** an edible case for holding a filling ⟨a pastry *shell*⟩ **d :** a reinforced concrete arched or domed roof used primarily over large unpartitioned areas **4 :** an impersonal manner that conceals the presence or absence of feeling **5 :** a narrow light racing boat propelled by two, four, or eight persons pulling oars; *also* **:** SCULL **6 :** any of the spheres defined by the orbits of a group of electrons of approximately equal energy surrounding the nucleus of an atom **7 a :** a hollow projectile for artillery containing an explosive bursting charge **b :** a metal or metal and plastic or paper case which holds the charge of powder and shot or a bullet used with breech-loading small arms **8 :** a plain usually sleeveless blouse or sweater [Old English *sciell*] — **shell** *adj* — **shelled** \'sheld\ *adj* — **shell•work** \'shel-ˌwərk\ *n* — **shelly** \'shel-ē\ *adj*

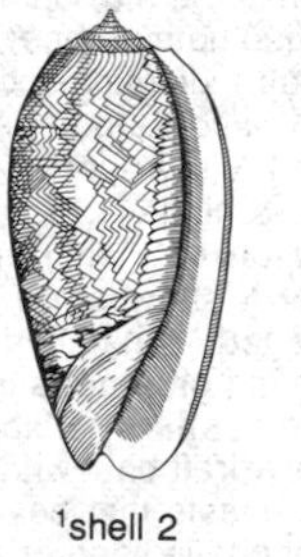
1shell 2

2**shell** *vb* **1 a :** to remove or fall from a natural enclosing cover (as a shell or husk) ⟨*shell* peas⟩ **b :** to remove the grains from (as an ear of Indian corn) **2 :** to shoot shells at, upon, or into **:** BOMBARD

she'll \shēl, shil, ˌshēl\ **:** she shall **:** she will

1**shel•lac** \shə-ˈlak\ *n* **1 :** purified lac **2 :** a preparation of lac dissolved in alcohol that is used in finishing wood [*shell* + *lac*]

2**shellac** *vt* **shel•lacked; shel•lack•ing 1 :** to coat with shellac **2 :** to defeat decisively

shel•lack•ing \shə-ˈlak-ing\ *n* **:** a decisive defeat or sound drubbing ⟨took a *shellacking* in last year's election⟩

shell•back \ˈshel-ˌbak\ *n* **:** an old or veteran sailor

shell bean *n* **:** a bean grown primarily for its edible seeds; *also* **:** these seeds — compare SNAP BEAN

shell•fire \ˈshel-ˌfīr\ *n* **:** a firing or exploding of shells

shell•fish \-ˌfish\ *n* **:** an aquatic invertebrate animal with a shell; *esp* **:** an edible mollusk or crustacean

shell out *vb* **:** PAY 1

shell pink *n* **:** a light yellowish pink

shell•proof \ˈshel-ˈprüf\ *adj* **:** capable of resisting shells or bombs

shell shock *n* **:** a neurotic condition appearing in soldiers exposed to modern warfare — **shell–shock** \ˈshel-ˌshäk\ *vt*

1**shel•ter** \ˈshel-tər\ *n* **1 :** something that covers or affords protection **:** a means or place of protection ⟨fallout *shelter*⟩ **2 :** the state of being covered and protected [origin unknown] — **shel•ter•less** \-ləs\ *adj*

2**shelter** *vb* **shel•tered; shel•ter•ing** \-tə-ring, -tring\ **1 :** to constitute or provide a shelter for **:** PROTECT **2 :** to place under shelter or protection **3 :** to take shelter — **shel•ter•er** \-tər-ər\ *n*

shel•ter•belt \-tər-ˌbelt\ *n* **:** a barrier of trees and shrubs that protects (as soil and crops) from wind and storm and lessens erosion

shelter half *n* **:** one of the halves of a shelter tent

shelter tent *n* **:** a small tent for two persons usually consisting of two interchangeable pieces of waterproof cotton duck that fasten together at an overlap

shel•ty *or* **shel•tie** \ˈshel-tē\ *n, pl* **shelties 1 :** SHETLAND PONY **2 :** SHETLAND SHEEPDOG [probably of Scandinavian origin]

shelve \ˈshelv\ *vb* **1 :** to furnish with shelves ⟨*shelve* a closet⟩ **2 :** to place on a shelf ⟨*shelve* books⟩ **3 a :** to remove from active service **b :** to put off or aside ⟨*shelve* a bill⟩ **4 :** to slope in a formation like a shelf **:** INCLINE — **shelv•er** *n*

shelves *pl of* SHELF

shelv•ing \ˈshel-ving\ *n* **1 :** material for shelves **2 :** a number of shelves

She•ma \shə-ˈmä\ *n* **:** the central creed of Judaism comprising Deuteronomy 6:4–9 and 11:13–21 and Numbers 15:37–41 [Hebrew *shĕmaʿ* "hear", first word of Deuteronomy 6:4]

she•nan•i•gan \shə-ˈnan-i-gən\ *n* **1 :** an underhand trick **2 a :** tricky or questionable conduct **b :** high-spirited or mischievous activity — usually used in pl. [origin unknown]

She•ol \shē-ˈōl, ˈshē-ˌ\ *n* **1 :** the dwelling place of the dead in ancient Hebrew belief **2 :** HELL 1 [Hebrew *Shĕʾōl*]

1**shep•herd** \ˈshep-ərd\ *n* **1 :** a man or boy who tends and guards sheep **:** PASTOR [Old English *scēaphyrde,* from *scēap* "sheep" + *hierde* "herdsman"]

2**shepherd** *vt* **1 :** to tend as a shepherd **2 :** to guide or guard in the manner of a shepherd ⟨*shepherd* tourists through a museum⟩

shepherd dog *n* **:** SHEEP DOG

shep•herd•ess \-ˈshep-ərd-əs\ *n* **:** a woman or girl who tends and guards sheep

shepherd's check *n* **:** a pattern of small even black and white checks; *also* **:** a fabric woven in this pattern — called also *shepherd's plaid*

shepherd's pie *n* **:** a meat pie topped with mashed potatoes

Sher•a•ton \ˈsher-ət-n\ *adj* **:** of or relating to an early 19th century English furniture style characterized by delicate construction, graceful proportions, and the use of straight lines [Thomas *Sheraton,* died 1806, English cabinetmaker]

sher•bet \ˈshər-bət\ *also* **sher•bert** \-bərt\ *n* **1 :** a cold drink of sweetened and diluted fruit juice **2 :** an ice with milk, egg white, or gelatin added [Turkish *şerbet,* from Persian *sharbat,* from Arabic *sharbah* "drink"]

sherd *variant of* SHARD

sher•iff \ˈsher-əf\ *n* **:** a county official charged with keeping the peace and with judicial duties (as executing the processes and orders of courts) [Old English *scīrgerēfa,* from *scīr* "shire" + *gerēfa* "reeve"]

sher•lock \ˈshər-ˌläk\ *n, often cap* **:** DETECTIVE [*Sherlock* Holmes, detective in stories by Sir Arthur Conan Doyle]

Sher•pa \ˈsheər-pə, ˈshər-\ *n* **:** a member of a Tibetan people living on the high southern slopes of the Himalayas and skilled in mountain climbing

sher•ry \ˈsher-ē\ *n, pl* **sherries :** a fortified wine with a distinctive nutty flavor [*Xeres* (now *Jerez),* Spain]

△ **origin** Many wines are named after the places where they are made. The region around the town of *Xeres* (the modern name is *Jerez*) in Spain produced a type of white wine that was introduced to England in the 16th century. At that time the name of the town *Xeres* was often spelled *Sherries* in English — the *sh* represented the best English approximation to the contemporary pronunciation of the Spanish *x*. And the wine from *Xeres* was called *sherris*. But some, judging from the form of the word *sherris* that it was a plural, began to use what they believed was its singular form, *sherry*. This type of derivation by subtraction of a real or supposed affix is called back-formation.

she's \shēz, ˌshēz\ **:** she is **:** she has

Shet•land \ˈshet-lənd\ *n* **1 a :** SHETLAND PONY **b :** SHETLAND SHEEPDOG **2** *often not cap* **a :** a lightweight loosely twisted yarn of Shetland wool used for knitting and weaving **b :** a fabric of Shetland wool

Shetland pony *n* **:** any of a breed of small stocky shaggy hardy ponies originating in the Shetland islands

Shetland sheepdog *n* **:** any of a breed of dogs resembling miniature collies with a profuse long coat developed in the Shetland islands

Shetland pony

Shetland wool *n* **:** fine wool from sheep raised in the Shetland islands; *also* **:** yarn spun from this wool

shew \ˈshō\ *British variant of* SHOW

shib•bo•leth \ˈshib-ə-ləth *also* -ˌleth\ *n* **1 a :** SLOGAN 2 **b :** a use of language that is distinctive of a particular group **2 :** a custom or usage that is a criterion for distinguishing members of one group [Hebrew *shibbōleth* "stream"]

△ **origin** In the 12th chapter of the book of Judges there is an account of a battle between the Gileadites and the Ephraimites. The Ephraimite army was routed, and the retreating Ephraimites tried to cross the Jordan river at a ford held by the Gileadites. Anyone wishing to pass was asked if he were an Ephraimite. If the reply was "no" he was asked to say the word *shibbōleth*. In Hebrew *shibbōleth* means "stream", but on this occasion its meaning was of no importance. Unlike the Gileadites, the Ephraimites could not pronounce an *sh* sound. If a man replied *"sibbōleth"* the Gileadites knew he was an Ephraimite and slew him.

1**shield** \ˈshēld\ *n* **1 :** a broad piece of defensive armor carried on the arm **2 :** one that protects or defends **:** DEFENSE **3 :** ESCUTCHEON **4 a :** a device or part that serves as a protective cover or barrier **b :** a protective structure (as a carapace) of some animals **5 :** something shaped like or resembling a shield: as **a :** a policeman's badge **b :** a decorative or identifying emblem [Old English *scield*]

2**shield** *vt* **1 :** to protect with or as if with a shield **2 :** to cut off from observation **:** HIDE **syn** see DEFEND

1**shift** \ˈshift\ *vb* **1 :** to exchange for or replace by another **:** CHANGE **2 a :** to change the place, position, or direction of **:** MOVE **b :** to make a change in place, position, or direction **c :** to change the gear rotating the transmission shaft of an automobile **3 :** to change phonetically **4 :** to get along **:** MANAGE ⟨left the others to *shift* for themselves⟩ [Old English *sciftan* "to divide, arrange"] — **shift•er** *n*

2**shift** *n* **1 a :** a means or device for effecting an end **b :** a deceitful scheme : DODGE **c** : an expedient tried in difficult circumstances : EXTREMITY **2** : SLIP 5a, CHEMISE **3** : a change in direction ⟨a *shift* in the wind⟩ **4** : a change in place or position **5** : a group who work together in alternation with other groups; *also* : the period during which one such group works **6** : a removal from one person or thing to another : TRANSFER ⟨a *shift* of responsibility⟩ **7** : GEARSHIFT

shift•less \'shift-ləs, 'shif-\ *adj* **1** : lacking in resourcefulness : INEFFICIENT **2** : lacking in ambition or incentive : LAZY — **shift•less•ly** *adv* — **shift•less•ness** *n*

shifty \'shif-tē\ *adj* **shift•i•er; -est** **1 a** : given to deception, evasion, or fraud : TRICKY **b** : capable of evasive movement : ELUSIVE ⟨a *shifty* boxer⟩ **2** : indicative of a tricky nature ⟨*shifty* eyes⟩ — **shift•i•ly** \-tə-lē\ *adv* — **shift•i•ness** \-tē-nəs\ *n*

shil•le•lagh *also* **shil•la•lah** \shə-'lā-lē\ *n* : CUDGEL, CLUB [*Shillelagh,* town in Ireland famed for its oak trees]

shil•ling \'shil-iŋ\ *n* **1 a** : a former British monetary unit equal to 12 pence or 1/20 pound **b** : a coin representing this unit **2** : a monetary unit equal to 1/20 pound and a corresponding coin in any of several countries in or formerly in the British Commonwealth **3** : any of several early American coins **4 a** : the basic monetary unit of Kenya, Somalia, Tanzania, and Uganda **b** : a coin representing this unit [Old English *scilling*]

[1]**shil•ly–shal•ly** \'shil-ē-ˌshal-ē\ *adj* : IRRESOLUTE [reduplication of *shall I*]

[2]**shilly–shally** *n* : INDECISION, IRRESOLUTION

[3]**shilly–shally** *vi* **shil•ly–shal•lied; shil•ly–shal•ly•ing** **1** : to show hesitation or lack of decisiveness : VACILLATE **2** : to waste time : DAWDLE

[1]**shim** \'shim\ *n* : a thin often tapered piece of wood, metal, or stone used to fill in space (as for support or leveling) [origin unknown]

[2]**shim** *vt* **shimmed; shim•ming** : to fill out or level up by the use of a shim

[1]**shim•mer** \'shim-ər\ *vi* **shim•mered; shim•mer•ing** \'shim-riŋ, -ə-riŋ\ **1** : to shine with a wavering light : GLIMMER ⟨leaves *shimmering* in the sunshine⟩ **2** : to appear in a constantly changing wavy form ⟨the *shimmering* heat from the pavement⟩ [Old English *scimerian*]

[2]**shimmer** *n* **1** : a wavering light : subdued sparkle or sheen **2** : a wavering image or effect especially when produced by heat waves — **shim•mery** \'shim-rē, -ə-rē\ *adj*

[1]**shim•my** \'shim-ē\ *n, pl* **shimmies** **1** : a jazz dance characterized by a shaking of the body from the shoulders down **2** : an abnormal vibration especially in the front wheels of an automobile [short for *shimmy-shake,* from *shimmy,* alteration of *chemise*]

[2]**shimmy** *vi* **shim•mied; shim•my•ing** **1** : to shake or quiver in or as if in dancing a shimmy **2** : to vibrate abnormally

[1]**shin** \'shin\ *n* : the front part of the vertebrate leg below the knee [Old English *scinu*]

[2]**shin** *vb* **shinned; shin•ning** **1** : to climb by moving oneself along alternately with the arms or hands and legs ⟨*shin* a tree⟩ **2** : to move forward rapidly on foot

shin•bone \'shin-'bōn, -ˌbōn\ *n* : TIBIA 1a

shin•dig \'shin-ˌdig\ *n* : a festive occasion: as **a** : a social gathering with dancing **b** : a usually large or lavish party [probably alteration of *shindy*]

shin•dy \'shin-dē\ *n, pl* **shindys** *or* **shindies** **1** : SHINDIG a **2** : FRACAS, UPROAR [probably alteration of [1]*shinny*]

[1]**shine** \'shīn\ *vb* **shone** \'shōn\ *or* **shined; shin•ing** **1** : to send out rays of light **2** : to be bright by reflection of light : GLEAM **3** : to show brilliance : be eminent or distinguished ⟨*shine* in conversation⟩ **4** : to have a bright glowing appearance **5** : to be conspicuously evident or clear ⟨human sympathy *shone* through all their actions⟩ **6** : to throw or flash the light of **7** *past & past participle* *shined* : to make bright by polishing ⟨*shine* your shoes⟩ [Old English *scīnan*]

[2]**shine** *n* **1** : brightness caused by the emission or reflection of light **2** : a brilliance of quality or appearance **3** : fair weather : SUNSHINE ⟨will go, rain or *shine*⟩ **4** : a stupid trick or silly caper — usually used in pl. **5** : LIKING, FANCY ⟨took a *shine* to them⟩ **6** : a polish given to shoes

shin•er \'shī-nər\ *n* **1** : one that shines **2** : a silvery fish; *esp* : any of numerous freshwater American fishes related to the carp **3** : BLACK EYE

[1]**shin•gle** \'shiŋ-gəl\ *n* **1** : a small thin piece of building material (as of wood or a composition of asphalt) for laying in overlapping rows as a covering for the roof or sides of a building **2** : a small signboard [Middle English *schingel*]

[2]**shingle** *vt* **shin•gled; shin•gling** \-gə-liŋ, -gliŋ\ **1** : to cover with or as if with shingles **2** : to cut (a woman's hair) with a short tapered line at the back

[3]**shingle** *n* **1** : coarse pebbly gravel on the seashore **2** : a place (as a beach) strewn with shingle [probably of Scandinavian origin]

shin•gler \'shiŋ-gə-lər, -glər\ *n* : one that shingles

shin•gles \'shiŋ-gəlz\ *n* : a virus disease marked by inflammation of one or more ganglia and by pain and skin eruption usually along the course of a single nerve [Medieval Latin *cingulus,* from Latin *cingulum* "girdle", from *cingere* "to gird"]

shin•gly \'shiŋ-gə-lē, -glē\ *adj* : composed of or abounding in shingle ⟨a *shingly* beach⟩

shin•ing *adj* **1** : giving forth or reflecting light **2** : splendidly bright ⟨*shining* newness⟩ **3** : having a distinguished quality ⟨*shining* prose⟩; *esp* : ILLUSTRIOUS ⟨a *shining* example of integrity⟩ — **shin•ing•ly** \'shī-niŋ-lē\ *adv*

[1]**shin•ny** \'shin-ē\ *n* : the game of hockey played with a curved stick and a ball or block of wood by youngsters [perhaps from [1]*shin*]

[2]**shinny** *vi* **shin•nied; shin•ny•ing** : SHIN 1 [[2]*shin*]

shin•plas•ter \'shin-ˌplas-tər\ *n* : a piece of privately issued paper currency; *esp* : one poorly secured and depreciated in value

Shin•to \'shin-ˌtō\ *n* : a religious cult of Japan consisting chiefly in the reverence of the spirits of natural forces, emperors, and heroes [Japanese *shintō*] — **Shin•to•ism** \-ˌiz-əm\ *n* — **Shin•to•ist** \-əst\ *n or adj*

shiny \'shī-nē\ *adj* **shin•i•er; -est** : bright in appearance : SHINING ⟨*shiny* kitchenware⟩ — **shin•i•ness** *n*

[1]**ship** \'ship\ *n* **1 a** : a large seagoing vessel **b** : a square-rigged sailing vessel with three or more masts — compare [5]BARK, BRIG **2** : the crew of a ship **3 a** : AIRSHIP **b** : AIRPLANE **c** : SPACESHIP [Old English *scip*]

[2]**ship** *vb* **shipped; ship•ping** **1 a** : to place or receive on board a ship for transportation by water **b** : to cause to be transported ⟨*ship* grain by rail⟩ **2** : to put in place for use ⟨*ship* the tiller⟩ **3** : to take into a ship or boat ⟨*ship* oars⟩ **4** : to take (as water) over the side **5** : to engage to serve on shipboard

-ship \ˌship\ *n suffix* **1** : state : condition : quality ⟨friend*ship*⟩ **2** : office : dignity : profession ⟨author*ship*⟩ ⟨clerk*ship*⟩ ⟨lord*ship*⟩ **3** : art : skill ⟨seaman*ship*⟩ **4** : something showing, exhibiting, or embodying a quality or state ⟨town*ship*⟩ **5** : one entitled to a (specified) rank, title, or appellation ⟨your Lady*ship*⟩ [Old English *-scipe*]

ship biscuit *n* : HARDTACK

ship•board \'ship-ˌbōrd, -ˌbȯrd\ *n* **1** : the side of a ship **2** : the deck or interior of a ship ⟨met on *shipboard*⟩

ship bread *n* : HARDTACK

ship•build•er \'ship-ˌbil-dər\ *n* : one who designs or builds ships — **ship•build•ing** \-diŋ\ *n*

ship canal *n* : a canal large enough for seagoing ships to use

ship chandler *n* : a dealer in supplies and equipment for ships

ship•lap \'ship-ˌlap\ *n* : wooden sheathing in which the boards are rabbeted so that the edges of each board lap over the edges of adjacent boards to make a flush joint

ship•man \'ship-mən\ *n* **1** : SAILOR 1a **2** : SHIPMASTER

ship•mas•ter \-ˌmas-tər\ *n* : the master or commander of a ship other than a warship

ship•mate \-ˌmāt\ *n* : a fellow sailor

ship•ment \'ship-mənt\ *n* **1** : the act or process of shipping **2** : the goods shipped

ship of the line : a warship large enough to be used for direct engagement of the enemy

ship•own•er \'ship-ˌō-nər\ *n* : the owner of a ship

ship•pa•ble \'ship-ə-bəl\ *adj* : suitable for shipping

ship•per \'ship-ər\ *n* : one that sends goods by any form of conveyance

ship•ping \'ship-iŋ\ *n* **1** : the body of ships in one place or belonging to one port or country **2** : the act or business of one that ships

shipping clerk *n* : one who is employed in a shipping room to assemble, pack, and send out or receive goods

ship•shape \'ship-'shāp\ *adj* : TRIM, TIDY

ship•side \-ˌsīd\ *n* : the area adjacent to shipping that is used for storage and loading of freight and passengers

ship's papers *n pl* : documents required on board a ship including certificates of ownership and registry, logbook, customs clearance, and crew, passenger, and cargo lists

ship·way \ˈship-ˌwā\ *n* **1** : the ways on which a ship is built **2** : SHIP CANAL

ship·worm \ˈship-ˌwərm\ *n* : any of various long-bodied marine clams that resemble worms, burrow in submerged wood, and damage wharf piles and wooden ships

[1]ship·wreck \-ˌrek\ *n* **1** : a wrecked ship or its parts : WRECKAGE **2** : the destruction or loss of a ship **3** : total loss or failure : RUIN [Old English *scipwræc,* from *scip* "ship" + *wræc* "something driven by the sea"]

[2]shipwreck *vt* **1 a** : to cause to experience shipwreck ⟨a *shipwrecked* crew⟩ **b** : RUIN ⟨a *shipwrecked* career⟩ **2** : to destroy (a ship) by grounding or foundering

ship·wright \-ˌrīt\ *n* : a carpenter skilled in ship construction and repair

ship·yard \-ˌyärd\ *n* : a place where ships are built or repaired

shire \ˈshīr, *in place-name compounds* ˌshiər, shər\ *n* : a territorial division of England usually identical with a county [Old English *scīr* "office, shire"]

shirk \ˈshərk\ *vb* **1** : to evade the performance of an obligation ⟨some worked, others *shirked*⟩ **2** : AVOID ⟨*shirked* telling the truth⟩ [origin unknown] — **shirk·er** *n*

shirr \ˈshər\ *vt* **1** : to draw (as cloth) together in a shirring **2** : to bake (eggs removed from the shell) until set [origin unknown]

shirr·ing \ˈshər-iŋ\ *n* : a decorative gathering (as of cloth) made by drawing up the material along two or more parallel lines of stitching

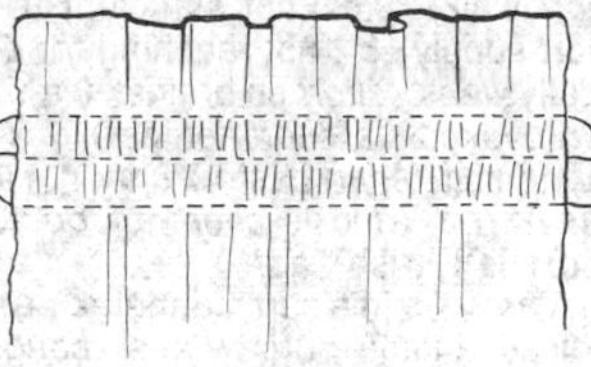

shirring

shirt \ˈshərt\ *n* : a garment for the upper part of the body: as **a** : a loose cloth garment usually having a collar, sleeves, a front opening, and a tail long enough to be tucked inside trousers or a skirt **b** : UNDERSHIRT [Old English *scyrte*]

shirt·front \-ˌfrənt\ *n* : the front of a shirt

shirt·ing \ˈshərt-iŋ\ *n* : fabric suitable for shirts

shirt·mak·er \ˈshərt-ˌmā-kər\ *n* : one that makes shirts

shirt·tail \ˈshərt-ˌtāl\ *n* : the part of a shirt that reaches below the waist especially in the back

shirt·waist \ˈshərt-ˌwāst\ *n* : a woman's tailored garment (as a dress or blouse) with details copied from men's shirts

shish ke·bab \ˈshish-kə-ˌbäb\ *n* : kabob cooked on skewers [Armenian *shish kabab*]

shiv·a·ree \ˌshiv-ə-ˈrē, ˈshiv-ə-ˌrē\ *n* : a noisy mock serenade to a newly married couple [French *charivari*] — **shivaree** *vt*

[1]shiv·er \ˈshiv-ər\ *n* : one of the small pieces into which a brittle thing is broken by sudden violence [Middle English]

[2]shiver *vb* **shiv·ered**; **shiv·er·ing** \ˈshiv-riŋ, -ə-riŋ\ : to break into many small pieces : SHATTER

[3]shiver *vi* **shiv·ered**; **shiv·er·ing** \ˈshiv-riŋ, -ə-riŋ\ : to undergo trembling (as from cold or fear) : QUIVER [Middle English *chiveren*]

[4]shiver *n* : an instance of shivering : QUIVER

shiv·ery \ˈshiv-rē, -ə-rē\ *adj* **1** : characterized by shivers : TREMULOUS ⟨felt *shivery* before the interview⟩ **2** : causing shivers ⟨a *shivery* winter's day⟩ ⟨*shivery* ghost stories⟩

shm- — see SCHM-

shmuck *variant of* SCHMUCK

[1]shoal \ˈshōl\ *adj* : SHALLOW ⟨*shoal* water⟩ [Old English *sceald*]

[2]shoal *n* **1** : a shallow place in a body of water (as the sea or a river) **2** : a sandbank or sandbar that makes the water shallow

[3]shoal *vi* : to become shallow

[4]shoal *n* : a large group (as of fish) : SCHOOL, CROWD [Old English *scolu* "multitude"]

[5]shoal *vi* : [4]SCHOOL, THRONG

shoat \ˈshōt\ *n* : a young hog usually less than one year old [Middle English *shote*]

[1]shock \ˈshäk\ *n* : a pile of sheaves of grain or stalks of Indian corn with the butt ends down [Middle English]

[2]shock *vt* : to collect into shocks

[3]shock *n* **1** : the impact or encounter of individuals or groups in combat **2** : a violent shake or jar : CONCUSSION ⟨an earthquake *shock*⟩ **3 a** : a disturbance in the equilibrium or permanence of something **b** : a sudden or violent disturbance in the mental or emotional faculties **4** : a state of profound bodily depression associated with reduced blood volume and pressure and caused usually by severe especially crushing injuries, hemorrhage, or burns **5** : sudden stimulation of the nerves and convulsive contraction of the muscles caused by the discharge of electricity through the animal body **6 a** : STROKE 5 **b** : CORONARY THROMBOSIS [Middle French *choc,* from *choquer* "to strike against"]

[4]shock *vt* **1 a** : to strike with surprise, terror, horror, or disgust ⟨*shocked* by the city's slums⟩ **b** : to subject to the action of an electrical discharge **2** : to drive by or as if by a shock ⟨*shocked* the public into action⟩

[5]shock *n* : a thick bushy mass (as of hair) [perhaps from [1]*shock*]

shock absorber *n* : a device for absorbing the energy of sudden impulses or shocks in machinery or structures

shock·er \ˈshäk-ər\ *n* : one that shocks; *esp* : a sensational work of fiction or drama

shock·ing *adj* : extremely startling and offensive ⟨a *shocking* crime⟩ — **shock·ing·ly** \-iŋ-lē\ *adv*

shock therapy *n* : the treatment of mental disorder by causing coma or convulsions especially through use of electricity — called also *shock treatment*

shock troops *n pl* : troops chosen for offensive work because of their high morale, training, and discipline

shock wave *n* **1** : BLAST 5c **2** : a compressional wave formed whenever the speed of a body relative to a medium exceeds that at which the medium can transmit sound

shod \ˈshäd\ *adj* **1** : wearing shoes **2** : furnished or equipped with a shoe

[1]shod·dy \ˈshäd-ē\ *n* **1** : a fabric manufactured wholly or partly from reclaimed wool **2** : inferior, imitation, or pretentious articles or matter [origin unknown]

[2]shoddy *adj* **shod·di·er**; **-est** **1** : made of shoddy **2 a** : cheaply imitative : vulgarly pretentious **b** : hastily or poorly done : INFERIOR **c** : SHABBY 1a — **shod·di·ly** \ˈshäd-l-ē\ *adv* — **shod·di·ness** \ˈshäd-ē-nəs\ *n*

[1]shoe \ˈshü\ *n* **1** : an outer covering for the human foot typically made of leather with a thick or stiff sole and an attached heel **2** : something that resembles a shoe in appearance or use: as **a** : HORSESHOE 1 **b** : the runner of a sled **c** : the part of a brake that presses on the wheel of a vehicle **3** : the outside casing of an automobile tire [Old English *scōh*]

[2]shoe *vt* **shod** \ˈshäd\ *also* **shoed** \ˈshüd\; **shoe·ing** **1** : to furnish with a shoe or shoes **2** : to cover for protection, strength, or ornament

shoe·black \ˈshü-ˌblak\ *n* : BOOTBLACK

shoe·horn \-ˌhȯrn\ *n* : a curved piece (as of metal or plastic) to aid in slipping on a shoe

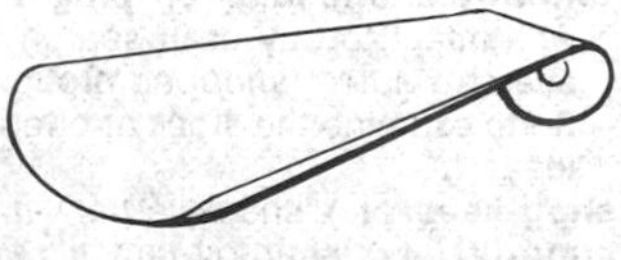

shoehorn

shoe·lace \-ˌlās\ *n* : a lace or string for fastening a shoe

shoe·mak·er \-ˌmā-kər\ *n* : one whose business is making or repairing shoes

shoe·string \-ˌstriŋ\ *n* **1** : SHOELACE **2** : a small or barely adequate amount of money or capital ⟨start a business on a *shoestring*⟩ [sense 2 from shoestrings' being a typical item sold by itinerant vendors]

shoe tree *n* : a foot-shaped device for inserting in a shoe to preserve its shape

sho·far \ˈshō-ˌfär, -fər\ *n, pl* **sho·froth** \shō-ˈfrōt, -ˈfrōth, -ˈfrōs\ : a ram's-horn trumpet used in some synagogue observances [Hebrew *shōphār*]

\ə\ **abut**	\au̇\ **out**	\i\ **tip**	\ȯ\ **saw**	\u̇\ **foot**
\ər\ **further**	\ch\ **chin**	\ī\ **life**	\ȯi\ **coin**	\y\ **yet**
\a\ **mat**	\e\ **pet**	\j\ **job**	\th\ **thin**	\yü\ **few**
\ā\ **take**	\ē\ **easy**	\ŋ\ **sing**	\t͟h\ **this**	\yu̇\ **cure**
\ä\ **cot, cart**	\g\ **go**	\ō\ **bone**	\ü\ **food**	\zh\ **vision**

sho•gun \'shō-gən\ *n* : one of a line of military governors ruling Japan until the revolution of 1867–68 [Japanese *shōgun* "general"] — **sho•gun•ate** \'shō-gə-nət, -ˌnāt\

shone *past of* SHINE

shoo \'shü\ *vt* : to scare, drive, or send away by or as if by crying *shoo* [Middle English *schowe,* interj. used in frightening away an animal]

[1]**shook** *past or chiefly dialect past participle of* SHAKE

[2]**shook** \'shu̇k\ *n* **1** : a set of pieces of lumber for assembling one hogshead, cask, or barrel **2** : a bundle of parts (as of boxes) ready to be put together [origin unknown]

[1]**shoot** \'shüt\ *vb* **shot** \'shät\; **shoot•ing 1 a** : to let fly or cause to be driven forward with force ⟨*shoot* an arrow⟩ **b** : to cause a missile to be driven forth from : DISCHARGE ⟨*shoot* off a gun⟩ **c** : to cause a weapon to discharge a missile ⟨*shoot* at a target⟩ **d** : to carry when discharged ⟨guns that *shoot* many miles⟩ **e** : to send forth with suddenness or intensity ⟨*shot* us a meaningful look⟩ **f** : to propel (as a ball or puck) toward a goal; *also* : to score by so doing ⟨*shoot* a basket⟩ **g** : PLAY ⟨*shoot* a round of golf⟩ ⟨*shoot* craps⟩ **2 a** : to strike with a missile especially from a bow or gun; *esp* : to wound or kill with a missile discharged from a firearm ⟨*shoot* deer⟩ ⟨*shot* a burglar⟩ **b** : to remove or destroy by use of firearms ⟨*shoot* off a lock⟩ **3** : to push or slide into or out of a fastening ⟨*shot* the door bolt⟩ **4** : to set off : DETONATE ⟨*shoot* off fireworks⟩ **5 a** : to push or thrust forward usually abruptly or swiftly ⟨lizards *shooting* out their tongues⟩ **b** : to sprout or grow rapidly ⟨children *shooting* up into adulthood⟩ **6** : to utter or emit rapidly, suddenly, or with force ⟨*shot* out the answer⟩ **7 a** : to go or pass rapidly and precipitately ⟨*shot* out of the office⟩ ⟨the pain *shot* down my arm⟩ **b** : to pass swiftly along ⟨*shoot* the rapids in a canoe⟩ **c** : to stream out suddenly : SPURT **8 a** : to take the altitude of ⟨*shoot* the sun with a sextant⟩ **b** : to take a picture of : PHOTOGRAPH **c** : to film a scene ⟨the director is ready to *shoot*⟩ [Old English *scēotan*] — **shoot•er** *n* — **shoot at** *or* **shoot for** : to aim at : strive for — **shoot the works** : to put forth all one's efforts or available capital

[2]**shoot** *n* **1 a** : the aerial part of a plant : a stem with its leaves and appendages; *also* : a branch or part of a plant developed from a single bud **b** : OFFSHOOT **2 a** : an act or the action of shooting **b** : a hunting trip or party **c** : a shooting match ⟨skeet *shoot*⟩

shooting gallery *n* : a range usually covered and equipped with targets for practice with firearms

shooting iron *n* : FIREARM

shooting star *n* **1** : a meteor appearing as a temporary streak of light in the night sky **2** : a North American perennial herb of the primrose family with entire oblong leaves and showy flowers

[1]**shop** \'shäp\ *n* **1** : a building or room stocked with merchandise for sale : STORE **2** : FACTORY 2, MILL **3 a** : a school laboratory equipped for instruction in manual arts **b** : the art or science of working with tools and machinery **4 a** : a business establishment; *esp* : OFFICE **b** : SHOPTALK [Old English *sceoppa* "booth"]

[2]**shop** *vb* **shopped**; **shop•ping 1** : to examine goods or services with intent to buy or in search of the best buy **2** : to make a search : HUNT ⟨*shopped* around for the best-qualified person⟩ **3** : to examine the stock or offerings of ⟨*shop* the stores for gift ideas⟩

shop•keep•er \'shäp-ˌkē-pər\ *n* : STOREKEEPER

shop•lift•er \'shäp-ˌlif-tər\ *n* : a thief who steals merchandise on display in stores — **shop•lift•ing** \-tiŋ\ *n*

shop•per \'shäp-ər\ *n* **1** : one that shops **2** : one whose occupation is shopping as an agent for customers or for an employer

shopping center *n* : a group of retail and service stores located in a suburban area and provided with extensive parking space

shop steward *n* : a union member elected as the union representative of a shop or department in dealings with the management

shop•talk \'shäp-ˌtȯk\ *n* : the jargon or subject matter peculiar to an occupation or a special area of interest

shop•worn \-ˌwōrn, -ˌwȯrn\ *adj* **1** : faded, soiled, or impaired by remaining too long in a store ⟨*shopworn* merchandise⟩ **2** : stale from excessive use or familiarity ⟨a story on a *shopworn* theme⟩ ⟨full of clichés and *shopworn* anecdotes⟩

sho•ran \'shōr-ˌan, 'shȯr-\ *n* : a system of short-range navigation in which two radar signals transmitted by an airplane are intercepted and rebroadcast to the airplane by two ground stations of known position so as to determine the position of the airplane [*sho*rt-*ra*nge *n*avigation]

[1]**shore** \'shōr, 'shȯr\ *n* : the land bordering a usually large body of water; *esp* : COAST [Middle English]

[2]**shore** *vt* : to give support to : BRACE [Middle English *shoren*]

[3]**shore** *n* : a prop or brace placed beneath or against something to support it

shore•bird \-ˌbərd\ *n* : any of a group (Charadrii) of birds that frequent the seashore

shore leave *n* : a leave of absence to go on shore granted to a sailor or naval officer

shore•line \-ˌlīn\ *n* : the line where a body of water touches the shore; *also* : the strip of land along this line

shore patrol *n* : a branch of a navy that exercises guard and police functions

shor•ing \'shōr-iŋ, 'shȯr-\ *n* : a group of shores ⟨the *shoring* for a wall⟩

shorn *past participle of* SHEAR

[1]**short** \'shȯrt\ *adj* **1 a** : having little length **b** : not tall : LOW **2 a** : not extended in time : BRIEF ⟨a *short* life⟩ **b** : not retentive ⟨a *short* memory⟩ **c** : QUICK, SPEEDY ⟨made *short* work of the job⟩ **d** : seeming to pass quickly ⟨a few *short* years later⟩ **3 a** : being a syllable or speech sound of relatively little duration **b** : being the member of a pair of similarly spelled vowel or vowel-containing sounds that is descended from a vowel short in duration ⟨*short a* in *fat*⟩ ⟨*short i* in *sin*⟩ **4** : limited in distance ⟨a *short* walk⟩ **5 a** : not sufficient in quantity : INADEQUATE ⟨in *short* supply⟩ **b** : not reaching far enough **c** : inherently or basically weak ⟨*short* on brains⟩ **6 a** : ABRUPT 2b, CURT **b** : quickly provoked ⟨a *short* temper⟩ **7** : containing or cooked with shortening ⟨*short* pastry⟩ **8 a** : not lengthy or drawn out **b** : ABBREVIATED ⟨*doc* is *short* for *doctor*⟩ [Old English *scort*] — **short•ish** \-ish\ *adj*

[2]**short** *adv* **1** : in a curt manner **2** : BRIEFLY ⟨*short*-lasting⟩ **3** : at a disadvantage : UNAWARES ⟨caught *short*⟩ **4** : so as to interrupt ⟨took us up *short*⟩ **5** : ABRUPTLY, SUDDENLY ⟨stopped *short*⟩ **6** : at some point before a goal or limit aimed at ⟨the arrow fell *short*⟩

[3]**short** *n* **1** : the sum and substance : UPSHOT ⟨the *short* of it⟩ **2 a** : a short syllable **b** : a short sound or signal **3** *pl* **a** : a by-product of wheat milling that includes the germ, fine bran, and some flour **b** : refuse, clippings, or trimmings discarded in various manufacturing processes **4** : something that is shorter than the usual or regular length **5** *pl* **a** : knee-length or less than knee-length trousers **b** : short underpants **6** : SHORT CIRCUIT — **in short** : by way of summary : BRIEFLY

[4]**short** *vt* : SHORT-CIRCUIT

short•age \'shȯrt-ij\ *n* : a lack in the amount needed : DEFICIT ⟨a *shortage* in the accounts⟩

short•bread \'shȯrt-ˌbred\ *n* : a thick cookie made of flour, sugar, and much shortening

short•cake \-ˌkāk\ *n* **1** : a crisp and often unsweetened biscuit or cookie **2** : a dessert made of usually very short baking-powder-biscuit dough baked and spread with sweetened fruit

short•change \-'chānj\ *vt* **1** : to give less than the correct amount of change to **2** : to deprive of something due : CHEAT — **short•chang•er** *n*

short–cir•cuit \'shȯrt-'sər-kət\ *vb* **1** : to make a short circuit in or have a short circuit **2** : BYPASS

short circuit *n* : a connection of comparatively low resistance accidentally or intentionally made between points in an electric circuit between which the resistance is normally much greater

short•com•ing \'shȯrt-ˌkəm-iŋ, shȯrt-'kəm-, 'shȯrt-'kəm-\ *n* : the state, fact, or an instance of falling below a standard

short•cut \'shȯrt-ˌkət, -'kət\ *n* **1** : a route more direct than that usually taken **2** : a quicker way of doing something

short–day \'shȯrt-ˌdā\ *adj* : flowering or developing to maturity only in response to alternating short light and long dark periods — compare DAY-NEUTRAL, LONG-DAY

short division *n* : mathematical division in which the successive steps are performed without writing out the remainders

short•en \'shȯrt-n\ *vb* **short•ened**; **short•en•ing** \'shȯrt-niŋ, -n-iŋ\ : to make or become short or shorter — **short•en•er** \'shȯrt-nər, -n-ər\ *n*

• **syn** CURTAIL, ABBREVIATE: SHORTEN may imply reduction either in extent or duration; CURTAIL adds an implication of a cutting off that deprives of completeness or adequacy ⟨rain *curtailed* the ceremony⟩ ABBREVIATE applies chiefly to the shortening of the written form of a word or phrase by omission of parts ⟨*Doctor* can be *abbreviated* to *Dr.*⟩

short•en•ing \'shȯrt-niŋg, -n-iŋg\ *n* **1 :** a making or becoming short or shorter **2 :** an edible fat (as butter or lard) used in baking

short•hand \'shȯrt-ˌhand\ *n* **:** a method of writing rapidly by substituting characters, abbreviations, or symbols for letters, words, or phrases **:** STENOGRAPHY — **shorthand** *adj*

short•hand•ed \-'han-dəd\ *adj* **:** short of the regular or necessary number of people

short•horn \'shȯrt-ˌhȯrn\ *n, often cap* **:** any of a breed of red, roan, or white beef cattle originating in the north of England and including good milk-producing strains from which a distinct breed has been evolved — called also *Durham*

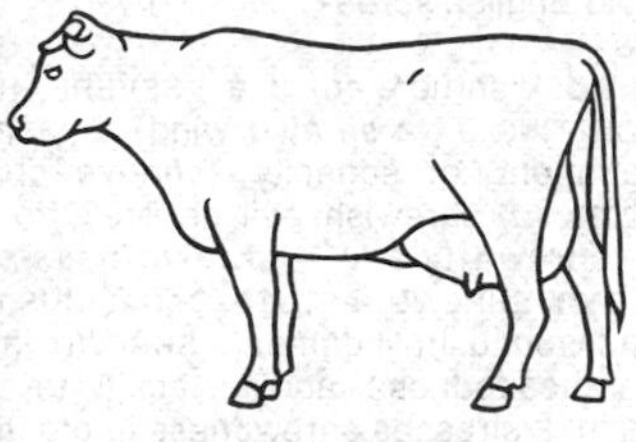

shorthorn

short-horned \-'hȯrnd\ *adj* **:** having short horns or antennae

short-horned grasshopper *n* **:** any of a family of grasshoppers with short antennae

short hundredweight *n* **:** HUNDREDWEIGHT 1

short-lived \'shȯrt-'līvd, -'livd\ *adj* **:** not living or lasting long ⟨*short-lived* happiness⟩ — **short-lived•ness** \'līvd-nəs, -'livd-, -'līv, -'liv-\ *n*

short•ly \'shȯrt-lē\ *adv* **1 a :** in a few words **:** BRIEFLY ⟨put it *shortly*⟩ **b :** in an abrupt manner **:** CURTLY **2 a :** in a short time **:** SOON ⟨will arrive *shortly*⟩ **b :** at a short interval ⟨*shortly* after⟩

short•ness \'shȯrt-nəs\ *n* **:** the quality or state of being short ⟨*shortness* of breath⟩

short order *n* **:** an order for food that can be quickly cooked

short ribs *n pl* **:** a cut of beef consisting of rib ends between the rib roast and the plate

short shrift *n* **1 :** a brief respite from death **2 :** little consideration ⟨gave the matter *short shrift*⟩

short•sight•ed \'shȯrt-'sīt-əd\ *adj* **1 :** NEARSIGHTED, MYOPIC **2 :** characterized by lack of foresight — **short•sight•ed•ly** *adv* — **short•sight•ed•ness** *n*

short•stop \'shȯrt-ˌstäp\ *n* **1 :** the position of the baseball player defending the area on the third-base side of second base **2 :** the player stationed in the shortstop position

short story *n* **:** an invented prose narrative usually dealing with a few characters and aiming at developing a single episode or creating a single mood

short-tem•pered \'shȯrt-'tem-pərd\ *adj* **:** having a quick temper **:** easily angered

short-term \-'tərm\ *adj* **1 :** occurring over or involving a relatively short period of time **2 :** of or relating to a financial transaction based on a term usually of less than a year

short•wave \-'wāv\ *n* **:** a radio wave having a wavelength between 10 and 100 meters

short-wind•ed \-'win-dəd\ *adj* **:** affected with or characterized by shortness of breath

Sho•shone \shə-'shō-nē, -'shōn; 'shō-ˌshōn\ *or* **Sho•sho•ni** \shə-'shō-nē\ *n, pl* **Shoshones** *or* **Shoshoni** *also* **Shoshone** *or* **Shoshonis :** a member of a group of Indian peoples of the Great Basin having an Aztec-related language

[1]**shot** \'shät\ *n* **1 a :** an action of shooting **b :** a directed propelling of a missile (as an arrow, stone, or rocket); *esp* **:** a directed discharge of a gun or cannon **c :** a stroke or throw in a game; *esp* **:** an attempt at scoring **d :** a setting off of an explosive ⟨a nuclear *shot*⟩ **e :** an injection of something (as a medicine or antibody) into the body **2 a** *pl* **shot :** something propelled by shooting; *esp* **:** small lead or steel pellets fired from a shotgun **b :** a metal sphere of iron or brass that is put for distance **3 a :** the distance that a missle is or can be thrown **b :** RANGE, REACH ⟨not within rifle *shot*⟩ **4 :** one that shoots **:** MARKSMAN **5 a :** ATTEMPT, TRY ⟨take another *shot* at the puzzle⟩ **b :** CHANCE ⟨the horse was a 10 to 1 *shot*⟩ **6 :** a remark so directed as to have telling effect **7 a :** PHOTOGRAPH **b :** a single sequence of a motion picture or a television program shot by one camera without interruption **8 a :** a single drink of liquor **b :** a portion (as of medicine) taken at one time **[**Old English *scot***]**

[2]**shot** *adj* **1 a :** having contrasting and changeable color effects **:** IRIDESCENT ⟨blue silk *shot* with silver⟩ **b :** suffused or streaked with a color ⟨hair *shot* with gray⟩ **c :** pervaded by a contrasting element ⟨satire *shot* with sympathy⟩ **2 :** reduced to ruin or collapse ⟨the business was *shot*⟩

shot•gun \'shät-ˌgən\ *n* **:** a gun with a smooth bore used to fire small shot at short range

shot hole *n* **1 :** a drilled hole in which a charge of dynamite is exploded **2 :** a hole made usually by a boring insect

shot put *n* **:** a field event in which the shot is put for distance — **shot-put•ter** \-ˌpu̇t-ər\ *n* — **shot-put•ting** \-ˌpu̇t-iŋg\ *n*

should \shəd, shu̇d, 'shu̇d\ *past of* SHALL — used as an auxiliary verb to express (1) condition or possibility ⟨if you *should* see them, tell them this⟩, (2) obligation or propriety ⟨you *should* brush your teeth regularly⟩, (3) futurity from the point of view in the past ⟨thought I *should* soon be free⟩, (4) what is probable or expected ⟨they *should* be here soon⟩, and (5) politeness in softening a request or assertion ⟨I *should* like some coffee⟩ **[**Old English *sceolde* "owed, was obliged to"**]**

[1]**shoul•der** \'shōl-dər\ *n* **1 a :** the laterally projecting part of the human body formed of the bones and joints by which the arm is connected with the trunk together with the muscles covering these **b :** the corresponding but usually less projecting part of a lower vertebrate **2 :** a cut of meat including the upper joint of the foreleg and adjacent parts **3 :** the part of a garment at the wearer's shoulder **4 :** a part or projection resembling a human shoulder ⟨*shoulder* of a hill⟩ **5 :** either edge of a road; *esp* **:** the part of a road outside of the traveled way **[**Old English *sculdor***]**

[2]**shoulder** *vb* **shoul•dered; shoul•der•ing** \-də-riŋg, -driŋg\ **1 :** to push or thrust with the shoulder **:** JOSTLE ⟨*shouldered* my way through the crowd⟩ **2 a :** to place or bear on the shoulder ⟨*shouldered* the knapsack⟩ **b :** to assume the burden or responsibility of ⟨*shoulder* the blame⟩

shoulder blade *n* **:** a large triangular bone of the back part of the shoulder that is the principal bone of the corresponding half of the shoulder girdle and articulates with the corresponding clavicle or coracoid to form a socket for the humerus of the arm — called also *scapula*

shoulder girdle *n* **:** PECTORAL GIRDLE

shoulder strap *n* **:** a strap that passes over the shoulder and holds up an article or garment

should•est \'shu̇d-əst\ *archaic past 2d sing of* SHALL

shouldn't \'shu̇d-nt\ **:** should not

shouldst \shədst, shu̇dst, 'shu̇dst\ *archaic past 2d sing of* SHALL

[1]**shout** \'shau̇t\ *vb* **1 :** to utter a sudden loud cry ⟨*shouted* with delight⟩ **2 :** to utter in a loud voice ⟨*shouted* insults⟩ **[**Middle English *shouten***]** — **shout•er** *n*

[2]**shout** *n* **:** a loud cry or call

shouting distance *n* **:** easy reach ⟨lived within *shouting distance* of their cousins⟩

[1]**shove** \'shəv\ *vb* **1 :** to push with steady force **2 :** to push carelessly or rudely ⟨*shove* a person out of the way⟩ **[**Old English *scūfan* "to thrust away"**] syn** see PUSH — **shov•er** *n*

[2]**shove** *n* **:** an act or instance of shoving **:** a forcible push

[1]**shov•el** \'shəv-əl\ *n* **1 :** an implement consisting of a broad often curved blade attached to a long handle used for lifting and throwing loose material **2 :** SHOVELFUL **[**Old English *scofl***]**

[2]**shovel** *vb* **shov•eled** *or* **shov•elled; shov•el•ing** *or* **shov•el•ling** \'shəv-liŋg, -ə-liŋg\ **1 :** to take up and throw with a shovel **2 :** to dig or clean out with a shovel **3 :** to throw or convey roughly or in the mass as if with a shovel ⟨*shovel* food into one's mouth⟩

shov•el•er *or* **shov•el•ler** \'shəv-lər, -ə-lər\ *n* **1 :** one that shovels **2 :** any of several river ducks having a large and very broad bill

shov•el•ful \'shəv-əl-ˌfu̇l\ *n, pl* **shovelfuls** \-ˌfu̇lz\ *or* **shov•els•ful** \-əlz-ˌfu̇l\ **:** the amount held by a shovel

shov•el•man \-ˌman, -mən\ *n* **:** one who works with a hand or power shovel

shov•el-nosed \ˌshəv-əl-'nōzd\ *adj* **:** having a broad flat head, nose, or beak

\ə\ **abut**	\au̇\ **out**	\i\ **tip**	\ȯ\ **saw**	\u̇\ **foot**
\ər\ **further**	\ch\ **chin**	\ī\ **life**	\ȯi\ **coin**	\y\ **yet**
\a\ **mat**	\e\ **pet**	\j\ **job**	\th\ **thin**	\yü\ **few**
\ā\ **take**	\ē\ **easy**	\ŋg\ **sing**	\t͟h\ **this**	\yu̇\ **cure**
\ä\ **cot, cart**	\g\ **go**	\ō\ **bone**	\ü\ **food**	\zh\ **vision**

[1]**show** \ˈshō\ *vb* **showed; shown** \ˈshōn\ *or* **showed; show·ing 1 :** to place in sight **:** DISPLAY **2 :** to reveal by one's condition, nature, or behavior **3 :** GRANT, BESTOW ⟨the king *showed* no mercy⟩ **4 :** TEACH ⟨*showed* me how to knit⟩ **5 :** PROVE ⟨the result *showed* that we were right⟩ **6 :** DIRECT, GUIDE ⟨*show* a visitor to the door⟩ **7 :** APPEAR ⟨anger *showed* in their faces⟩ **8 :** to be noticeable ⟨the patch hardly *shows*⟩ **9 :** to finish third or at least third in a horse race [Old English *scēawian* "to look, look at, see"]

• **syn** SHOW, EXHIBIT, DISPLAY mean to present so as to invite notice or attention. SHOW implies enabling another to see or examine ⟨*showed* me a picture of the lake⟩ EXHIBIT implies putting forward openly or publicly ⟨*exhibit* paintings at a gallery⟩ DISPLAY stresses putting in position where others may see to advantage ⟨*display* sale items⟩

[2]**show** *n* **1 :** a demonstrative display ⟨a *show* of strength⟩ **2 a :** a false semblance **:** PRETENSE ⟨made a *show* of friendship⟩ **b :** a more or less true appearance of something **:** SIGN ⟨a *show* of reason⟩ **c :** an impressive display **3 :** something exhibited especially for wonder or ridicule **:** SPECTACLE **4 :** a public presentation: as **a :** a competitive exhibition (as of animals) to demonstrate quality **b :** a theatrical presentation **c :** a radio or television program **d :** ENTERTAINMENT 3 **5 :** ENTERPRISE, AFFAIR ⟨ran the whole *show*⟩ **6 :** third place at the finish of a horse race

show·boat \ˈshō-ˌbōt\ *n* **:** a river steamboat containing a theater and carrying a troupe of actors to give plays at river communities

show·case \-ˌkās\ *n* **:** a glass case or box to display and protect wares in a store or articles in a museum

show·down \-ˌdau̇n\ *n* **:** the final settlement of a contested issue; *also* **:** the test of strength by which a contested issue is resolved

[1]**show·er** \ˈshau̇-ər, ˈshau̇r\ *n* **1 a :** a fall of rain of short duration **b :** a like fall of sleet, hail, or snow **2 :** something resembling a rain shower ⟨a *shower* of sparks⟩ ⟨a *shower* of tears⟩ **3 :** a party given by friends who bring gifts often of a particular kind ⟨a linen *shower* for a bride⟩ **4 :** SHOWER BATH [Old English *scūr*] — **show·ery** \-ē\ *adj*

[2]**shower** *vb* **1 :** to fall in or as if in a shower **2 :** to bathe in a shower bath **3 :** to wet copiously in a spray, fine stream, or drops **4 :** to give in abundance ⟨*showered* them with gifts⟩

[3]**show·er** \ˈshō-ər, ˈshōr\ *n* **:** one that shows **:** EXHIBITOR

shower bath *n* **:** a bath in which water is sprayed on the person; *also* **:** the apparatus that provides such a bath

show·ing \ˈshō-ing\ *n* **1 :** an act of putting something on view **:** EXHIBITION ⟨a *showing* of fall fashions⟩ ⟨a *showing* of a new feature film⟩ **2 :** PERFORMANCE, RECORD ⟨made a good *showing* in the tournament⟩

show·man \ˈshō-mən\ *n* **1 :** the producer of a theatrical show **2 :** a person having a sense or knack for dramatization or visual effectiveness — **show·man·ship** \-ˌship\ *n*

show–off \ˈshō-ˌȯf\ *n* **1 :** conspicuous behavior **2 :** one that shows off

show off \shō-ˈȯf, ˈshō-\ *vb* **1 :** to display proudly **2 :** to seek to attract attention by conspicuous behavior

show·piece \-ˌpēs\ *n* **:** a prime or outstanding example used for exhibition

show·place \-ˌplās\ *n* **:** a place exhibited or regarded as an example of beauty or excellence

show·room \-ˌrüm, -ˌru̇m\ *n* **:** a room used for the display of merchandise or of samples

show up *vb* **1 :** to reveal the true nature of **:** EXPOSE ⟨*showed up* their ignorance⟩ **2 :** ARRIVE ⟨*showed up* late⟩ **3 :** to be visible or evident ⟨*shows up* well in this light⟩

showy \ˈshō-ē\ *adj* **show·i·er; -est 1 :** making an attractive show ⟨*showy* blossoms⟩ **2 :** GAUDY — **show·i·ly** \ˈshō-ə-lē\ *adv* — **show·i·ness** \ˈshō-ē-nəs\ *n*

shrap·nel \ˈshrap-nᵊl\ *n, pl* **shrapnel 1 :** a projectile that consists of a case provided with a powder charge and a large number of usually lead balls and is exploded in flight **2 :** bomb, mine, or shell fragments [Henry *Shrapnel,* died 1842, English artillery officer]

[1]**shred** \ˈshred\ *n* **:** a long narrow strip from a larger body of the same material ⟨*shreds* of cloth⟩; *also* **:** PARTICLE, SCRAP ⟨hadn't a *shred* of evidence⟩ [Old English *scrēade*]

[2]**shred** *vb* **shred·ded; shred·ding 1 :** to cut or tear into shreds **2 :** to break up into shreds — **shred·der** *n*

shrew \ˈshrü\ *n* **1 :** any of numerous small chiefly nocturnal mammals related to the moles, somewhat resembling mice, but having a long pointed snout, very small eyes, and velvety fur **2 :** a woman who scolds or quarrels constantly [Old English *scrēawa*]

shrew 1

shrewd \ˈshrüd\ *adj* **1 a :** SEVERE, HARD ⟨a *shrewd* blow⟩ **b :** CUTTING 2 ⟨a *shrewd* wind⟩ **2 :** marked by cleverness, discernment, or sagacity ⟨*shrewd* observer⟩ [Middle English *shrewed* "shrewish, evil, severe", from *shrewe* "shrew" + *-ed*] — **shrewd·ly** *adv* — **shrewd·ness** *n*

• **syn** SHREWD, ASTUTE, SAGACIOUS mean acute in perception and sound in judgment. SHREWD implies native cleverness, hardheadedness, and an ability to see beneath the surface; ASTUTE stresses shrewdness in practical affairs and especially connotes an ability to act successfully in one's own interests; SAGACIOUS suggests native shrewdness matured by experience into practical wisdom and farsightedness.

shrew·ish \ˈshrü-ish\ *adj* **:** QUARRELSOME, ILL-TEMPERED — **shrew·ish·ly** *adv* — **shrew·ish·ness** *n*

[1]**shriek** \ˈshrēk\ *vb* **1 :** to utter a loud shrill cry or sound **2 :** to utter with a shriek or sharply and shrilly [probably from Middle English *shriken*]

[2]**shriek** *n* **1 :** a shrill usually wild or involuntary cry **2 :** a sound like a shriek ⟨a *shriek* of escaping steam⟩ **syn** see SCREAM

shrie·val \ˈshrē-vəl\ *adj* **:** of or relating to a sheriff [obsolete *shrieve* "sheriff", from Old English *scīrgerēfa*] — **shrie·val·ty** \-tē\ *n*

shrift \ˈshrift\ *n, archaic* **:** the confession of sins to a priest or the hearing of a confession by a priest [Old English *scrift,* from *scrīfan* "to shrive"]

shrike \ˈshrīk\ *n* **:** any of numerous usually largely gray or brownish singing birds that have a strong notched bill hooked at the tip, feed chiefly on insects, and often impale their prey on thorns [perhaps from Old English *scrīc* "thrush"]

[1]**shrill** \ˈshril\ *vb* **:** to utter or emit a sharp piercing sound **:** SCREAM [Middle English *shrillen*]

[2]**shrill** *adj* **1 :** having, emitting, or being a sharp high-pitched tone or sound ⟨a *shrill* whistle⟩ **2 :** accompanied by sharp high-pitched sounds or cries ⟨*shrill* gaiety⟩ **3 :** having an intense or vivid effect on the senses — **shrill** *adv* — **shrill·ness** *n* — **shril·ly** \ˈshril-lē\ *adv*

[3]**shrill** *n* **:** a shrill sound

[1]**shrimp** \ˈshrimp\ *n, pl* **shrimp** *or* **shrimps 1 :** any of numerous small mostly marine crustaceans related to the lobsters and having a long slender body, compressed abdomen, and long legs; *also* **:** any small crustacean resembling a true shrimp **2 :** a very small or puny person or thing [Middle English *shrimpe*]

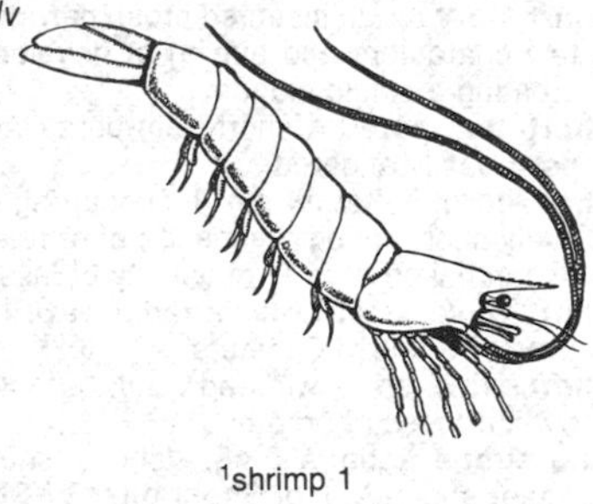
[1]shrimp 1

[2]**shrimp** *vi* **:** to fish for or catch shrimp

[1]**shrine** \ˈshrīn\ *n* **1 :** a case or box for sacred relics (as the bones of a saint) **2 a :** the tomb of a saint **b :** a place in which devotion is paid to a saint or deity **c :** a niche containing a religious image **3 :** a place or object hallowed because of its associations ⟨Westminster Abbey is a *shrine* for tourists⟩ [Old English *scrīn,* from Latin *scrinium* "case, chest"]

[2]**shrine** *vt* **:** ENSHRINE

shrin·er \ˈshrī-nər\ *n* **:** a member of a secret fraternal society called the Ancient Arabic Order of Nobles of the Mystic Shrine

[1]**shrink** \ˈshringk\ *vb* **shrank** \ˈshrangk\ *also* **shrunk** \ˈshrəngk\; **shrunk; shrink·ing 1 :** to contract or curl up the body or part of it **:** HUDDLE, COWER ⟨*shrink* in horror⟩ **2 a :** to become or cause to become smaller or more compacted ⟨the sweater *shrank* when it was washed⟩ **b :** to lose substance or

weight ⟨meat *shrinks* in cooking⟩ **c :** to lessen in amount or value ⟨their fortune *shrank* during the depression⟩ **3 :** to draw back ⟨*shrink* from a quarrel⟩ [Old English *scrincan*] — **shrink•able** \'shring-kə-bəl\ *adj* — **shrink•er** *n*

[2]shrink *n* **1 :** the act of shrinking **2** *slang* **:** PSYCHIATRIST

shrink•age \'shring-kij\ *n* **1 :** the act or process of shrinking **2 :** the amount lost by shrinkage

shrinking violet *n* **:** a bashful or retiring person; *esp* **:** one who shrinks from public recognition

shrive \'shrīv\ *vb* **shrived** *or* **shrove** \'shrōv\; **shriv•en** \'shriv-ən\ *or* **shrived**; **shriv•ing** \'shrī-ving\ **1 :** to hear the confession of and administer the sacrament of penance to **:** PARDON **2 :** to confess one's sins especially to a priest [Old English *scrīfan* "to shrive, prescribe", from Latin *scribere* "to write"]

shriv•el \'shriv-əl\ *vb* **shriv•eled** *or* **shriv•elled**; **shriv•el•ing** *or* **shriv•el•ling** \'shriv-ling, -ə-ling\ **1 :** to draw into wrinkles especially with a loss of moisture **2 :** to reduce or become reduced to weakness, helplessness, or inefficiency [origin unknown] **syn** see WITHER

Shrop•shire \'shräp-,shiər, -shər, *especially in the United States* -,shīr\ *n* **:** any of an English breed of dark-faced hornless mutton-type sheep that yield a heavy fleece [*Shropshire*, England]

[1]shroud \'shraùd\ *n* **1 :** burial garment **:** WINDING-SHEET **2 :** something that covers, screens, or guards ⟨a *shroud* of secrecy⟩ **3 a :** one of the lines leading usually in pairs from the top of a mast to provide lateral support to the mast **b :** one of the cords that suspend the harness of a parachute from the canopy [Old English *scrūd* "garment"]

[2]shroud *vt* **1 a :** to cut off from view **:** SCREEN ⟨trees *shrouded* in heavy mist⟩ **b :** to veil under another appearance ⟨*shrouded* in mystery⟩ **2 :** to dress for burial

Shrove•tide \'shrōv-,tīd\ *n* **:** the period of three days immediately preceding Ash Wednesday [Middle English *schroftide*]

Shrove Tuesday \'shrōv-\ *n* **:** the Tuesday before Ash Wednesday

[1]shrub \'shrəb\ *n* **:** a low usually several-stemmed woody plant — compare HERB, TREE [Old English *scrybb* "brushwood"]

[2]shrub *n* **1 :** a beverage that consists of an alcoholic liquor, fruit juice, fruit rind, and sugar **2 :** a beverage made by adding acidulated fruit juice to iced water [Arabic *sharāb* "beverage"]

shrub•bery \'shrəb-rē, -ə-rē\ *n, pl* **-ber•ies :** a planting or growth of shrubs

shrub•by \'shrəb-ē\ *adj* **shrub•bi•er**; **-est 1 :** consisting of or covered with shrubs **2 :** resembling a shrub

[1]shrug \'shrəg\ *vb* **shrugged**; **shrug•ging :** to raise or draw in the shoulders especially to express lack of interest or dislike [Middle English *schruggen*]

[2]shrug *n* **1 :** an act of shrugging **2 :** a woman's small waist-length or shorter jacket

shrug off *vt* **1 :** to brush aside **:** MINIMIZE **2 :** to shake off **3 :** to remove (a garment) by wriggling out

shrunk•en \'shrəng-kən\ *adj* **1 :** diminished or contracted especially in size or value ⟨the *shrunken* dollar⟩ **2 :** having been subjected to a shrinking process

[1]shuck \'shək\ *n* **1 :** SHELL, HUSK: as **a :** the outer covering of a nut or Indian corn **b :** the shell of an oyster or clam **2 :** something of little value ⟨not worth *shucks*⟩ [origin unknown]

[2]shuck *vt* **1 :** to strip of shucks **2 :** REMOVE ⟨*shucked* their clothes off⟩

[1]shud•der \'shəd-ər\ *vi* **shud•dered**; **shud•der•ing** \'shəd-ring, -ə-ring\ **1 :** to tremble convulsively **:** SHIVER ⟨*shuddered* to think of the accident⟩ **2 :** QUIVER ⟨the train *shuddered* to a halt⟩ [Middle English *shoddren*]

[2]shudder *n* **:** an act of shuddering — **shud•dery** \-ə-rē\ *adj*

[1]shuf•fle \'shəf-əl\ *vb* **shuf•fled**; **shuf•fling** \'shəf-ling, -ə-ling\ **1 :** to mix in a mass confusedly **:** JUMBLE **2 :** to put or thrust aside or under cover **3 a :** to mix (as a pack of cards) so that cards will later appear in random order **b :** to move about, back and forth, or from one place to another **4 a :** to move (as the feet) by sliding along or dragging back and forth without lifting **b :** to perform (as a dance) with a dragging sliding step **5 :** to get into or out of (a situation) especially by trickery **:** WORM ⟨*shuffle* out of a difficulty⟩ **6 :** to act or speak in an evasive manner [perhaps from [1]*shove*] — **shuf•fler** \-lər, -ə-lər\ *n*

[2]shuffle *n* **1 :** evasion of an issue **:** EQUIVOCATION **2 a :** an act of shuffling **b :** a right or turn to shuffle cards **c :** JUMBLE **3 a :** a dragging sliding movement; *esp* **:** a sliding or scraping step in dancing **b :** a dance characterized by such a step

shuf•fle•board \'shəf-əl-,bōrd, -,bȯrd\ *n* **1 :** a game in which players try to push disks into scoring areas of a diagram marked on a smooth surface **2 :** the diagram or court on which shuffleboard is played [alteration of obsolete *shove-board*]

shun \'shən\ *vt* **shunned**; **shun•ning :** to avoid deliberately and especially habitually [Old English *scunian*] — **shun•ner** *n*

shun•pike \'shən-,pīk\ *n* **:** a side road used to avoid tolls on a turnpike

[1]shunt \'shənt\ *vb* **1 :** to turn off to one side **:** SHIFT; *esp* **:** to switch (as a train) from one track to another **2 :** to provide with or divert by means of an electrical shunt **3 :** to travel back and forth [Middle English *shunten* "to flinch"] — **shunt•er** *n*

[2]shunt *n* **:** a means or mechanism for turning or thrusting aside: as **a** *chiefly British* **:** a railroad switch **b :** a conductor joining two points in an electrical circuit so as to form a parallel or alternative path through which a portion of the current may pass

shush \'shəsh, 'shùsh\ *n* **:** a sibilant sound uttered to demand silence [imitative] — **shush** *vt*

shut \'shət\ *vb* **shut**; **shut•ting 1 :** to close or become closed by bringing openings or covering parts together ⟨*shut* one's eyes⟩ **2 :** to prevent entrance to or passage to or from **3 :** to hold within limits by or as if by enclosure **:** IMPRISON ⟨*shut* up in a stalled elevator⟩ **4 :** to cease or cause to cease operation ⟨the epidemic *shut* down the school⟩ [Old English *scyttan*]

shut•down \'shət-,daùn\ *n* **:** a temporary or permanent ending of an activity (as work in a factory)

shut–eye \'shət-,ī\ *n* **:** SLEEP 1

shut–in \,shət-,in\ *adj* **:** confined by illness or incapacity — **shut–in** \'shət-,in\ *n*

shut•off \'shət-,ȯf\ *n* **1 :** something that shuts off **2 :** INTERRUPTION, STOPPAGE

shut•out \'shət-,aùt\ *n* **:** a game or contest in which one side is prevented from scoring

shut out \'shət-'aùt, ,shət-\ *vt* **1 :** to keep out **:** EXCLUDE **2 :** to prevent (an opponent) from scoring in a game or contest

[1]shut•ter \'shət-ər\ *n* **1 :** one that shuts **2 :** a usually movable cover or screen for a window or door **3 :** the part of a camera that opens and closes to expose the film

[2]shutter *vt* **:** to close with or by shutters

shut•ter•bug \-,bəg\ *n* **:** a photography enthusiast

[1]shut•tle \'shət-l\ *n* **1 a :** an instrument used in weaving to carry the thread back and forth from side to side through the threads that run lengthwise **b :** a spindle-shaped device holding the thread in tatting or netting **c :** any of various thread holders for the lower thread of a sewing machine that carry the lower thread through a loop of the upper thread to make a stitch **2 a :** a going back and forth regularly over a specified and often short route by a vehicle **b :** a vehicle used in a shuttle ⟨a *shuttle* bus⟩ [Middle English *shittle, schutylle*]

[2]shuttle *vb* **shut•tled**; **shut•tling** \'shət-ling, -l-ing\ **1 :** to move or travel back and forth frequently **2 :** to move by or as if by a shuttle

[1]shut•tle•cock \'shət-l-,käk\ *n* **:** a lightweight conical object with a rounded often rubber-covered nose used in badminton and usually made of molded plastic or a rounded cork with feathers stuck in one side

[2]shuttlecock *vb* **:** to send, toss, or go to and fro

shut up *vb* **1 :** to cause (a person) to stop talking **2 :** to stop writing or speaking

[1]shy \'shī\ *adj* **shi•er** *or* **shy•er** \'shī-ər, 'shīr\; **shi•est** *or* **shy•est** \'shī-əst\ **1 :** easily frightened **:** TIMID **2 :** disposed to avoid a person or thing **:** DISTRUSTFUL **3 :** hesitant in committing oneself **:** CHARY **4 :** marked by sensitive diffidence **:** BASHFUL **5 :** having less than the proper amount or number **:** SHORT [Old English *scēoh*] — **shy•ly** *adv* — **shy•ness** *n*

• syn BASHFUL, MODEST, COY: SHY implies a timid shrinking from contact or familiarity with others; BASHFUL implies a hesitant shyness characteristic of childhood; MODEST suggests an absence of undue confidence or conceit; COY implies deliberately assumed or affected shyness.

\ə\ **abut**	\aù\ **out**	\i\ **tip**	\ȯ\ **saw**	\ù\ **foot**
\ər\ **further**	\ch\ **chin**	\ī\ **life**	\ȯi\ **coin**	\y\ **yet**
\a\ **mat**	\e\ **pet**	\j\ **job**	\th\ **thin**	\yü\ **few**
\ā\ **take**	\ē\ **easy**	\ng\ **sing**	\t͟h\ **this**	\yù\ **cure**
\ä\ **cot, cart**	\g\ **go**	\ō\ **bone**	\ü\ **food**	\zh\ **vision**

[2]**shy** *vi* **shied; shy•ing 1 :** to draw back in sudden dislike or distaste : RECOIL ⟨*shied* from publicity⟩ ⟨*shied* at the idea of encouraging revolutionaries⟩ **2 :** to start suddenly aside through fright or alarm ⟨the horse *shied* at a blowing paper⟩

[3]**shy** *n, pl* **shies :** a sudden start aside (as of a horse)

[4]**shy** *vt* **shied; shy•ing :** to throw with a jerk : FLING [perhaps from [1]*shy*]

[5]**shy** *n, pl* **shies :** the act of shying : TOSS

shy•ster \'shī-stər\ *n* **:** an unscrupulous lawyer or politician [probably from *Scheuster,* 19th century American attorney frequently rebuked in a New York court for pettifoggery]

si \'sē\ *n* **:** the 7th note of the diatonic scale : TI [Italian]

[1]**Si•a•mese** \ˌsī-ə-'mēz, -'mēs\ *adj* **1 :** of, relating to, or characteristic of Thailand, the Thais, or their language **2 :** exhibiting great resemblance : very like [*Siam* (Thailand); sense 2 from *Siamese twin*]

[2]**Siamese** *n, pl* **Siamese 1 :** THAI 1 **2 :** THAI 2

Siamese cat *n* **:** a slender blue-eyed short-haired domestic cat of a breed of oriental origin with pale body and darker ears, paws, tail, and face

Siamese cat

Siamese twin *n* **:** either of a pair of human or animal twins born joined together [Chang, died 1874, and Eng, died 1874, congenitally united twins born in Siam]

sib \'sib\ *n* **1 :** KINDRED; *also* **:** a group of persons descended from the same real or supposed ancestor **2 :** one closely related to another : a blood relation [Old English *sibb* "related by blood", from *sibb* "kinship"] — **sib** *adj*

Si•be•ri•an husky \sī-ˌbir-ē-ən-\ *n* **:** any of a breed of medium-sized compact dogs developed as sled dogs in northeastern Siberia that resemble the Alaskan malamutes

[1]**sib•i•lant** \'sib-ə-lənt\ *adj* **:** having, containing, or producing the sound of or a sound resembling that of the *s* or the *sh* in *sash* [Latin *sibilare* "to hiss, whistle"]

[2]**sibilant** *n* **:** a sibilant speech sound (as English \s\, \z\, \sh\, \zh\, \ch (=tsh)\, or \j (=dzh)\)

sib•ling \'sib-ling\ *n* **:** a brother or sister without regard to sex

sib•yl \'sib-əl\ *n, often cap* **1 :** any of several ancient prophetesses **2 a :** a female prophet **b :** FORTUNE-TELLER [Latin *sibylla,* from Greek] — **si•byl•ic** *or* **si•byl•lic** \sə-'bil-ik\ *adj* — **sib•yl•line** \'sib-ə-ˌlīn\ *adj*

[1]**sic** *or* **sick** \'sik\ *vt* **sicced** *or* **sicked** \'sikt\; **sic•cing** *or* **sick•ing** \sik-ing\ **:** to attack or cause to attack or chase — usually used as a command to a dog ⟨*sic* 'em⟩ [alteration of *seek*]

[2]**sic** \'sik, 'sēk\ *adv* **:** intentionally so written — used after a printed word or passage to indicate that it reproduces an original ⟨said they seed [*sic*] it all⟩ [Latin, "so, thus"]

sic•ca•tive \'sik-ət-iv\ *n* **:** DRIER 2 [Late Latin *siccativus* "making dry", from Latin *siccare* "to dry", from *siccus* "dry"]

sick \'sik\ *adj* **1 a** (1) **:** affected with disease or ill health (2) **:** of, relating to, or intended for use in sickness ⟨*sick* pay⟩ ⟨a *sick* ward⟩ **b :** NAUSEATED, QUEASY ⟨*sick* to one's stomach⟩ **c :** undergoing menstruation **2 :** spiritually or morally unsound or corrupt **3 a :** sickened by strong emotion ⟨*sick* with shame⟩ **b :** disgusted by some excess ⟨*sick* of flattery⟩ **c :** depressed and longing for something ⟨*sick* at heart⟩ **4 :** mentally or emotionally unsound or disordered ⟨*sick* thoughts⟩ **5 :** lacking or declining in vigor ⟨*sick* crops⟩ ⟨a *sick* market⟩ [Old English *sēoc*]

• **syn** SICK, ILL mean not being in good health. SICK is the common general term in American use but not in British use where ILL is preferred and SICK usually restricted to mean violently nauseated.

sick bay *n* **:** a compartment in a ship used as a dispensary and hospital

sick•bed \'sik-ˌbed\ *n* **:** the bed of a sick person

sick call *n* **1 :** a daily military formation at which individuals who are sick report to the medical officer **2 :** the period during which sick call is held

sick•en \'sik-ən\ *vb* **sick•ened; sick•en•ing** \'sik-ning, -ə-ning\ **:** to make or become sick

sick•en•er \'sik-nər, -ə-nər\ *n* **:** something that sickens, disgusts, or overwhelms

sick•en•ing *adj* **:** causing sickness : NAUSEATING — **sick•en•ing•ly** \'sik-ning-lē, -ə-ning-\ *adv*

sick headache *n* **:** MIGRAINE

sick•ish \'sik-ish\ *adj* **1 :** somewhat nauseated : QUEASY **2 :** somewhat sickening ⟨a *sickish* odor⟩ — **sick•ish•ly** *adv* — **sick•ish•ess** *n*

[1]**sick•le** \'sik-əl\ *n* **1 a :** a cutting tool consisting of a curved metal blade with a short handle **b :** a cutting mechanism (as of a combine) consisting of a bar with a series of cutting elements **2** *cap* **:** a group of six stars in the constellation Leo [Old English *sicol,* from Latin *secula*] — **sickle** *adj*

[1]sickle 1a

[2]**sickle** *vb* **sick•led; sick•ling** \'sik-ling, -ə-ling\ **:** to form into a crescent ⟨the ability of red blood cells to *sickle*⟩

sick leave *n* **1 :** an absence from duty or work permitted because of illness **2 :** the number of days per year allowed an employee for sickness

sickle cell *n* **:** an abnormal red blood cell of crescent shape

sickle-cell anemia *n* **:** a chronic inherited anemia that occurs especially in Negroes and is characterized by sickle cells in the circulating blood

sickle-cell trait *n* **:** an inherited blood condition in which some red blood cells tend to sickle but not usually enough to produce anemia and which occurs especially in Negroes

sick•ly \'sik-lē\ *adj* **sick•li•er; -est 1 :** somewhat unwell; *also* **:** habitually ailing **2 :** produced by or associated with sickness ⟨a *sickly* complexion⟩ ⟨a *sickly* appetite⟩ **3 :** producing or tending to sickness ⟨a *sickly* climate⟩ **4 :** appearing as if sick: **a :** LANGUID, PALE ⟨a *sickly* flame⟩ **b :** WRETCHED, UNEASY ⟨a *sickly* smile⟩ **c :** lacking in vigor : WEAK ⟨a *sickly* plant⟩ **5 :** MAWKISH 2 — **sick•li•ness** \'sik-lē-nəs\ *n* — **sickly** *adv*

sick•ness \'sik-nəs\ *n* **1 :** ill health : ILLNESS **2 :** a specific disease : MALADY **3 :** NAUSEA 1

sick•room \'sik-ˌrüm, -ˌrům\ *n* **:** a room in which a person is confined by sickness

sid•dur \'sid-ər, -ˌůr\ *n, pl* **sid•du•rim** \sə-'důr-əm\ **:** a Jewish prayer book containing Hebrew and Aramaic prayers used in the daily liturgy [Late Hebrew *siddūr,* literally, "order, arrangement"]

[1]**side** \'sīd\ *n* **1 :** the right or left part of the trunk or wall of the body; *also* **:** the entire right or left half of an animal body ⟨a *side* of beef⟩ **2 :** a place, space, or direction with respect to a center line (as of an aisle, river, or street) **3 :** a surface forming a border or face of an object **4 :** an outer portion of a thing considered as facing in a particular direction ⟨the upper *side*⟩ **5 :** a slope or declivity of a hill or ridge **6 a :** a bounding line of a geometrical figure ⟨*side* of a square⟩ **b :** one of the surfaces that delimit a solid; *esp* **:** one of the longer surfaces **c :** either surface of a thin object ⟨one *side* of a record⟩ **7 :** the space beside one **8 :** the attitude or activity of one person or group with respect to another : PART **9 :** a body of partisans or contestants ⟨victory for neither *side*⟩ **10 :** a line of descent traced through either parent **11 :** an aspect or part of something held to be contrasted with some other aspect or part ⟨the better *side* of one's nature⟩ **12 :** MEMBER 3b [Old English *sīde*] — **on the side 1 :** in addition to the main portion **2 :** in addition to a principal occupation ⟨selling insurance *on the side*⟩

[2]**side** *adj* **1 :** of, relating to, or situated on the side ⟨a *side* window⟩ **2 a :** directed toward or from the side ⟨*side* thrust⟩ **b :** in addition to or secondary to something primary ⟨*side* issue⟩ **c :** additional to the main portion ⟨a *side* order of salad⟩

[3]**side** *vb* **1 :** to take sides : join or form sides ⟨*sided* with the rebels⟩ **2 :** to furnish with sides or siding ⟨*side* a house⟩

[4]**side** *n* **:** swaggering or arrogant manner [obsolete *side* "proud, boastful", from Middle English, "wide"]

side arm *n* **:** a weapon (as a sword or pistol) worn at the side or in the belt

side•board \'sīd-ˌbōrd, -ˌbȯrd\ *n* **:** a piece of dining-room furniture with drawers and compartments for dishes, silverware, and table linen

side·burns \ˈsīd-ˌbərnz\ *n pl* **1 :** short side-whiskers worn with a smooth chin **2 :** continuations of the hairline in front of the ears [anagram of *burnsides*]

△ **origin** During the American Civil War, the Union general Ambrose Everett Burnside wore long bushy side-whiskers. His appearance struck the fancy of Washingtonians as he conducted parades and maneuvers with his regiment of Rhode Island volunteers in the early days of the war. This early popularity fostered the fashion for such whiskers, which came to be called *burnsides*. A later anagram of this word gives us *sideburns*.

side·car \ˈsīd-ˌkär\ *n* **:** a one-wheeled car attached to the side of a motorcycle

sid·ed \ˈsīd-əd\ *adj* **:** having sides often of a specified number or kind ⟨one-*sided*⟩ ⟨glass-*sided*⟩

side dish *n* **:** food served in addition to the main course

side effect *n* **:** a secondary and usually unfavorable effect (as of a drug) — called also *side reaction*

side–glance \ˈsīd-ˌglans\ *n* **1 :** a glance directed to the side **2 :** an indirect or slight reference

side issue *n* **:** an issue apart from the main point

side·kick \ˈsīd-ˌkik\ *n* **:** a person closely associated with another as subordinate or partner

side·light \-ˌlīt\ *n* **1 a :** light from the side **b :** incidental or additional information **2 :** the red light on the port side or the green light on the starboard side carried by ships or boats under way at night

[1]side·line \-ˌlīn\ *n* **1 :** a line at right angles to a goal line or end line and marking a side of a court or field of play **2 a :** a line of goods sold in addition to one's principal line **b :** a business or activity pursued in addition to one's regular occupation **3 a :** the space immediately outside the lines along either side of a playing area **b :** the standpoint of persons not immediately participating or concerned — usually used in pl.

[2]sideline *vt* **:** to make unable to play in a game or sport ⟨*sidelined* by an injury⟩

side·lin·er \ˈsīd-ˌlī-nər\ *n* **:** one that remains on the sidelines during an activity **:** one that does not participate

[1]side·ling *or* **si·dling** \ˈsīd-ling\ *adv* **:** in a sidelong direction **:** SIDEWAYS

[2]sideling *or* **sidling** *adj* **1 :** directed toward one side **2 :** SLOPING ⟨*sideling* ground⟩

[1]side·long \ˈsīd-ˌlȯng\ *adv* **1 :** SIDEWAYS ⟨glanced *sidelong* at them⟩ **2 :** on the side [alteration of [1]*sideling*]

[2]sidelong *adj* **1 :** lying or inclining to one side **:** SLANTING **2 a :** directed to one side ⟨*sidelong* looks⟩ **b :** indirect rather than straightforward

side·man \ˈsīd-ˌman\ *n* **:** a member of a band or orchestra and especially a jazz or swing band or orchestra

side·piece \-ˌpēs\ *n* **:** a piece contained in or forming the side of something

si·de·re·al \sī-ˈdir-ē-əl\ *adj* **1 :** of or relating to the stars or constellations **2 :** measured by the apparent motion of fixed stars ⟨*sidereal* time⟩ [Latin *sidereus,* from *sider-, sidus* "star, constellation"]

sid·er·ite \ˈsid-ə-ˌrīt\ *n* **:** a natural carbonate of iron $FeCO_3$ that is a valuable iron ore [German *siderit,* from Greek *sidēros* "iron"]

side·sad·dle \ˈsīd-ˌsad-l\ *n* **:** a saddle in which the rider sits with both legs on the same side of the horse — **sidesaddle** *adv*

side·show \-ˌshō\ *n* **1 :** a minor show offered in addition to a main exhibition (as of a circus) **2 :** an incidental diversion

side·slip \-ˌslip\ *vi* **1 :** to skid sideways — used especially of an automobile **2 :** to slide sideways through the air in a downward direction — **sideslip** *n*

side·spin \-ˌspin\ *n* **:** a rotary motion that causes a ball to spin around a vertical axis

side·split·ting \-ˌsplit-ing\ *adj* **:** extremely funny

side·step \ˈsīd-ˌstep\ *vb* **1 :** to take a side step **2 :** to avoid by a step to the side **3 :** to avoid meeting issues

side step *n* **1 :** a step to the side (as in boxing to avoid a blow) **2 :** a step taken sideways (as in climbing on skis)

side·stroke \-ˌstrōk\ *n* **:** a swimming stroke performed on the side in which the arms are alternately moved forward and both under the water while the legs do a scissors kick

side·swipe \-ˌswīp\ *vt* **:** to strike with a glancing blow along the side ⟨*sideswiped* a parked car⟩

[1]side·track \-ˌtrak\ *n* **1 :** SIDING 1 **2 :** a position or state of secondary importance

[2]sidetrack *vt* **1 :** to transfer from a main railroad line to a siding ⟨*sidetrack* a train⟩ **2 :** to turn aside from a main purpose or use

side·walk \ˈsīd-ˌwȯk\ *n* **:** a usually paved walk for pedestrians at the side of a street

sidewalk superintendent *n* **:** a passerby who stops to watch construction or demolition work

side·wall \ˈsīd-ˌwȯl\ *n* **1 :** a wall forming the side of something **2 :** the side of an automotive tire between the tread shoulder and the bead

side·ward \-wərd\ *or* **side·wards** \-wərdz\ *adv or adj* **:** toward the side

side·way \-ˌwā\ *adv or adj* **:** SIDEWAYS

side·ways \-ˌwāz\ *adv or adj* **1 :** from one side **2 :** with one side forward **3 :** toward one side; *also* **:** ASKANCE

side–wheel·er \ˈsīd-ˌhwē-lər, ˈsīd-ˌwē-\ *n* **:** a steamboat having a paddle wheel on each side

side-wheeler

side–whis·kers \ˈsīd-ˌhwis-kərz, ˈsīd-ˌwis-\ *n pl* **:** whiskers on the side of the face usually worn long with the chin shaven

side·wind·er \ˈsīd-ˌwīn-dər\ *n* **1 :** a heavy swinging blow from the side **2 :** a small rattlesnake of the southwestern United States that moves over sand by thrusting its body diagonally forward in a series of flat S-shaped loops

side·wise \-ˌwīz\ *adv or adj* **:** SIDEWAYS

sid·ing \ˈsīd-ing\ *n* **1 :** a short railroad track connected with the main track by switches at one or more places **2 :** material (as boards or metal pieces) used to cover the outside walls of frame buildings

si·dle \ˈsīd-l\ *vb* **si·dled; si·dling** \ˈsīd-ling, -l-ing\ **1 :** to advance obliquely usually in a furtive or unobtrusive way **2 :** to cause to move or turn sideways [probably back-formation from [2]*sideling*] — **sidle** *n*

siege \ˈsēj\ *n* **1 :** a military blockade of a fortified place **2 :** a continued attempt to gain possession of something **3 :** a persistent attack (as of illness) [Old French *sege* "seat, blockade", derived from Latin *sedēre* "to sit"]

si·en·na \sē-ˈen-ə\ *n* **:** an earthy substance containing oxides of iron and usually of manganese that is brownish yellow when raw and orange red or reddish brown when burnt and is used as a pigment [Italian *terra di Siena,* literally, "Siena earth", from *Siena,* Italy]

si·er·ra \sē-ˈer-ə\ *n* **1 :** a range of mountains especially with jagged peaks **2 :** the country about a sierra [Spanish, literally, "saw", from Latin *serra*]

si·es·ta \sē-ˈes-tə\ *n* **:** an afternoon nap or rest [Spanish, from Latin *sexta hora* "noon", literally, "sixth hour"]

sie·va bean \ˈsē-və-, ˈsiv-ē-\ *n* **:** any of several small-seeded beans closely related to and sometimes classed as lima beans [origin unknown]

[1]sieve \ˈsiv\ *n* **:** a device with meshes or perforations through which finer particles of a mixture (as of ashes, flour, or sand) of various sizes are passed to separate them from coarser ones, through which the liquid is drained from liquid-containing material, or through which soft materials are forced for reduction to fine particles [Old English *sife*]

[2]sieve *vb* **:** to put through a sieve **:** SIFT

sieve plate *n* **1 :** a perforated structure through which water passes into the body of a starfish or other echinoderm **2 :** an area in the end wall of a sieve tube pierced by fine pores

sieve tube *n* **:** a tube that consists of an end-to-end series of thin-walled living cells, is the characteristic element of the phloem, and is held to function chiefly in translocation of organic solutes

\ə\ **abut**	\au̇\ **out**	\i\ **tip**	\ȯ\ **saw**	\u̇\ **foot**
\ər\ **further**	\ch\ **chin**	\ī\ **life**	\ȯi\ **coin**	\y\ **yet**
\a\ **mat**	\e\ **pet**	\j\ **job**	\th\ **thin**	\yü\ **few**
\ā\ **take**	\ē\ **easy**	\ng\ **sing**	\t͟h\ **this**	\yu̇\ **cure**
\ä\ **cot, cart**	\g\ **go**	\ō\ **bone**	\ü\ **food**	\zh\ **vision**

sift \'sift\ *vb* **1 a :** to put through a sieve ⟨*sift* flour⟩ **b :** to separate by putting through a sieve **2 a :** to screen out the valuable or good **:** SELECT **b :** to study or investigate thoroughly **3 :** to scatter by or as if by sifting **4 :** to pass through or as if through a sieve [Old English *siftan*] — **sift•er** *n*

sift•ing *n* **1 :** the act or process of sifting **2** *pl* **:** sifted material ⟨bran mixed with *siftings*⟩

sigh \'sī\ *vb* **1 :** to take or exhale a deep audible breath (as in weariness or grief) **2 :** to make a sound like sighing ⟨wind *sighing* in the branches⟩ **3 :** GRIEVE ⟨*sighing* for the days of my youth⟩ **4 :** to express by sighs [Old English *sīcan*] — **sigh** *n* — **sigh•er** \'sī-ər, 'sīr\ *n*

¹sight \'sīt\ *n* **1 :** something that is seen **:** SPECTACLE **2 a :** a thing that is worth seeing **b :** something ridiculous or disorderly in appearance **3 a :** the process, power, or function of seeing; *esp* **:** the animal sense of which the eye is the receptor organ and by which the position, shape, and color of objects are perceived **b :** mental or spiritual perception **c :** mental view; *esp* **:** JUDGMENT **4 a :** the act of looking at or beholding **b :** INSPECTION ⟨this letter is for your *sight* only⟩ **c :** VIEW, GLIMPSE ⟨I caught *sight* of a friend⟩ **d :** an observation to determine direction or position (as by a navigator) **5 a :** perception of an object by the eye **b :** the range of vision **6 a :** a device (as a small metal bead on a gun barrel) that aids the eye in aiming or in determining the direction of an object **b :** an aim or observation taken by means of such a device [Old English *gesiht* "faculty or act of sight, thing seen"]

²sight *adj* **1 :** based on recognition or comprehension without previous study ⟨*sight* translation⟩ **2 :** payable on presentation ⟨a *sight* draft⟩

³sight *vb* **1 :** to get sight of **2 :** to look at through or as if through a sight **3 :** to aim by means of sights **4 :** to look carefully in a particular direction

sight•ed \'sīt-əd\ *adj* **:** having sight ⟨clear-*sighted*⟩

sight•less \'sīt-ləs\ *adj* **:** lacking sight **:** BLIND — **sight•less•ness** *n*

sight•ly \'sīt-lē\ *adj* **1 :** pleasing to the sight **:** HANDSOME **2 :** affording a good view — **sight•li•ness** *n*

sight–read \'sīt-ˌrēd\ *vb* **sight–read** \-ˌred\; **sight–read•ing** \-ˌrēd-ing\ **:** to read a foreign language or perform music at first sight — **sight reader** \-ˌrēd-ər\ *n*

¹sight–see•ing \'sīt-ˌsē-ing\ *adj* **:** engaged in, devoted to, or used for seeing things and places of interest

²sight–seeing *n* **:** the act or pastime of seeing places of interest — **sight•se•er** \'sīt-ˌsē-ər, -ˌsi-ər, -ˌsir\ *n*

sight unseen *adv* **:** without inspection or appraisal

sig•il \'sij-əl, 'sig-ˌil\ *n* **1 :** SEAL 1, SIGNET **2 :** a sign, word, or device of supposed occult power in astrology or magic [Latin *sigillum,* from *signum* "sign, seal"]

sig•ma \'sig-mə\ *n* **:** the 18th letter of the Greek alphabet — Σ or σ or ς

sig•moid \'sig-ˌmȯid\ *adj* **1 a :** curved like the letter C **b :** curved in two directions like the letter S **2 :** of, relating to, or being the contracted and crooked part of the colon immediately above the rectum [Greek *sigmoeidēs,* from *sigma* "sigma"; from a common form of sigma shaped like the Roman letter C] — **sig•moi•dal•ly** \sig-'mȯid-l-ē\ *adv*

¹sign \'sīn\ *n* **1 a :** a motion or gesture by which a thought is expressed or a command made known **b :** SIGNAL 1a **2 :** a mark having a conventional meaning and used in place of words or to represent a complex notion **3 :** one of the 12 divisions of the zodiac **4 a :** a character (as a flat or sharp) used in musical notation **b :** a character (as ÷ or √) indicating a mathematical operation; *also* **:** one of two characters + and − characterizing a number as positive or negative **5 a :** a lettered board or other display used to identify or advertise a place of business **b :** a posted command, warning, or direction **c :** SIGNBOARD **6 a :** something that serves to indicate the presence or existence of something **:** TOKEN **b :** PRESAGE 1, PORTENT **c :** an objective evidence of plant or animal disease — compare SYMPTOM [Old French *signe,* from Latin *signum* "mark, sign, image, seal"]

²sign *vb* **1 a :** to place a sign upon **b :** to represent or indicate by a sign **2 :** to affix one's signature to **3 :** to communicate by making a sign **4 :** to hire by securing the signature of [Middle French *signer,* from Latin *signare,* from *signum* "sign"] — **sign•er** *n*

¹sig•nal \'sig-nᵊl\ *n* **1 a :** an act, event, or watchword that serves to start some action **b :** something that stirs to action **2 :** a sound or gesture made to give warning or command **3 :** an object placed to give notice or warning **4 a :** the message, sound, or effect transmitted in electronic communication (as radio or television) **b :** a radio wave or electric current that transmits a message or effect (as in radio, television, or telephony) [Middle French, from Medieval Latin *signale,* derived from Latin *signum* "sign"]

²signal *vb* **-naled** *or* **-nalled**; **-nal•ing** *or* **-nal•ling 1 :** to notify by a signal **2 :** to communicate by signals **3 :** to make or send a signal — **sig•nal•er** *n*

³signal *adj* **1 :** distinguished from the ordinary **:** OUTSTANDING ⟨a *signal* achievement⟩ **2 :** used in signaling ⟨a *signal* beacon⟩ — **sig•nal•ly** \'sig-nᵊl-ē\ *adv*

sig•nal•ize \'sig-nᵊl-ˌīz\ *vt* **1 :** to make conspicuous **:** DISTINGUISH **2 :** to point out carefully or distinctly **3 :** to make signals to **:** SIGNAL; *also* **:** INDICATE 1 — **sig•nal•iza•tion** \ˌsig-nᵊl-ə-'zā-shən\ *n*

sig•nal•man \'sig-nᵊl-mən, -ˌman\ *n* **:** one who signals or works with signals

sig•nal•ment \-mənt\ *n* **:** description by peculiar, appropriate, or characteristic marks

sig•na•to•ry \'sig-nə-ˌtōr-ē, -ˌtȯr-\ *n, pl* **-ries :** a signer with another or others; *esp* **:** a government bound with others by a signed convention — **signatory** *adj*

sig•na•ture \'sig-nə-ˌchür, -chər\ *n* **1 :** the name of a person written with his or her own hand **2 :** a letter at the bottom of the first page of a sheet of printed pages (as of a book) to ensure placement in the right order in binding; *also* **:** the sheet itself which when folded becomes one unit of the book **3 a :** KEY SIGNATURE **b :** TIME SIGNATURE **4 :** a tune, musical number, or sound effect or in television a characteristic title or picture used to identify a program, entertainer, or orchestra [Medieval Latin *signatura,* from Latin *signare* "to sign, seal"]

sign•board \'sīn-ˌbōrd, -ˌbȯrd\ *n* **:** a board bearing a notice or sign

¹sig•net \'sig-nət\ *n* **1 :** a seal used in place of a signature on a document **2 :** the impression made by or as if by a signet **3 :** a small intaglio seal (as in a finger ring) [Middle French, from *signe* "sign, seal"]

²signet *vt* **:** to stamp or authenticate with a signet

signet ring *n* **:** a finger ring engraved with a signet

sig•ni•fi•able \'sig-nə-ˌfī-ə-bəl\ *adj* **:** capable of being represented by a sign or symbol

sig•nif•i•cance \sig-'nif-i-kəns\ *n* **1 a :** something that is conveyed as a meaning often obscurely or indirectly **b :** the quality of communicating or implying **2 a :** IMPORTANCE ⟨the industrial *significance* of coal⟩ **b :** the quality of being statistically significant **syn** see MEANING

sig•nif•i•can•cy \-kən-sē\ *n* **:** SIGNIFICANCE

sig•nif•i•cant \-kənt\ *adj* **1 :** having meaning **:** SUGGESTIVE, EXPRESSIVE **2 :** suggesting or containing a disguised or special meaning **3 a :** IMPORTANT 1, WEIGHTY **b :** probably caused by something other than chance ⟨statistically *significant* correlations⟩ **c :** DISTINCTIVE ⟨the difference between the initial sounds of *keel* and *cool* is not *significant* in English⟩ [Latin *significare* "to signify"] — **sig•nif•i•cant•ly** *adv*

significant figures *n pl* **:** the figures of a number beginning with the first figure to the left that is not zero and ending with the last figure to the right that is not zero or is a zero that is considered to be exact — called also *significant digits*

sig•ni•fi•ca•tion \ˌsig-nə-fə-'kā-shən\ *n* **1 :** a signifying by signs **2 :** IMPORT; *esp* **:** the meaning that a term, symbol, or character regularly conveys or is intended to convey **syn** see MEANING

sig•nif•i•ca•tive \sig-'nif-ə-ˌkāt-iv\ *adj* **1 :** INDICATIVE 2 **2 :** SIGNIFICANT 1, SUGGESTIVE — **sig•nif•i•ca•tive•ly** *adv* — **sig•nif•i•ca•tive•ness** *n*

sig•ni•fi•er \'sig-nə-ˌfī-ər, -ˌfīr\ *n* **:** one that signifies **:** SIGN

sig•ni•fy \'sig-nə-ˌfī\ *vb* **-fied**; **-fy•ing 1 :** MEAN 2, DENOTE **2 :** to show by a word, signal, or gesture **3 :** to have significance or importance [Old French *signifier,* from Latin *significare* "to indicate, signify", from *signum* "sign"]

sign language *n* **:** a system of hand gestures used for communication by the deaf or by people speaking different languages

sign off *vi* **:** to announce the end of a message, program, or broadcast and discontinue transmitting

sign of the cross : a gesture of the hand forming a cross especially on forehead, shoulders, and breast to profess Christian faith or ask divine care and blessing

si·gnor \sēn-ˈyȯr, -ˈyȯr\ *n, pl* **signors** *or* **si·gno·ri** \sēn-ˈyōr-ē, -ˈyȯr-\ — used by or to Italian-speaking people as a courtesy title equivalent to *Mr.* [Italian *signore, signor,* from Medieval Latin *senior* "superior, lord", from Latin, adj., "senior"]

si·gno·ra \sēn-ˈyōr-ə, -ˈyȯr-\ *n, pl* **-gnoras** *or* **-gno·re** \-ˈyōr-ā, -ˈyȯr-ā\ — used by or to Italian-speaking people as a courtesy title equivalent to *Mrs.* [Italian, feminine of *signore, signor*]

si·gno·ri·na \ˌsēn-yə-ˈrē-nə\ *n, pl* **-nas** *or* **-ne** \-nā\ — used by or to Italian-speaking people as a courtesy title equivalent to *Miss* [Italian, from *signora*]

sign·post \ˈsīn-ˌpōst\ *n* : a post with a sign on it to direct travelers

Sikh \ˈsēk\ *n* : a believer in a monotheistic religion of India founded about 1500 by a Hindu under Islamic influence and marked by rejection of idolatry and caste [Hindi, literally, "disciple"] — **Sikh** *adj* — **Sikh·ism** \-ˌiz-əm\ *n*

si·lage \ˈsī-lij\ *n* : fodder converted into succulent feed for livestock through processes of anaerobic acid fermentation (as in a silo) [short for *ensilage*]

sild \ˈsil(d)\ *n* : a young herring other than a brisling canned as a sardine in Norway [Norwegian]

[1]**si·lence** \ˈsī-ləns\ *n* **1** : forbearance from speech or noise — often used interjectionally **2** : absence of sound or noise : STILLNESS **3** : absence of mention: **a** : OBLIVION 2, OBSCURITY **b** : SECRECY 2

[2]**silence** *vt* **1** : to stop the noise or speech of : reduce to silence **2** : to restrain from expression **3** : to cause to cease hostile firing by return fire or by destroying

si·lenc·er \ˈsī-lən-sər\ *n* : one that silences; *esp* : a silencing device for small arms

si·lent \ˈsī-lənt\ *adj* **1 a** : not speaking : MUTE, SPEECHLESS **b** : unwilling to speak **2** : free from sound or noise : STILL **3** : UNSPOKEN ⟨*silent* disapproval⟩ **4 a** : making no mention ⟨history is *silent* about this person⟩ **b** : INACTIVE; *esp* : taking no active part in the conduct of a business ⟨a *silent* partner⟩ **5** : not pronounced ⟨*silent b* in *doubt*⟩ [Latin *silens,* from *silēre* "to be silent"] — **si·lent·ly** *adv*

• **syn** TACITURN, RETICENT, RESERVED: SILENT implies a habit of saying no more than is necessary and often less than expected; TACITURN suggests a temperamental disinclination to talk and a sullen avoidance of sociability; RETICENT implies a reluctance to speak out plainly especially about one's personal affairs; RESERVED suggests the restraining influence of caution or formality in checking easy conversation.

silent butler *n* : a container with hinged lid for collecting table crumbs and the contents of ashtrays

si·lex \ˈsī-ˌleks\ *n* : SILICA [Latin, "flint, quartz"]

[1]**sil·hou·ette** \ˌsil-ə-ˈwet\ *n* **1** : a drawing or cutout of the outline of an object filled in with black; *esp* : a profile portrait of this kind **2** : characteristic shape of an object (as an airplane) seen or as if seen against the light [French, from Étienne de *Silhouette,* died 1767, French controller general of finances]

△ **origin** Étienne de Silhouette was French controller general of finances in the mid-18th century. He was extremely close with the state's money as well as his own, so close, in fact, that *à la Silhouette* came to mean "cheaply" for a time. His niggardliness was greeted with ridicule. It was even suggested that one of his economies was the decoration of his house with his outlines, which he made himself, rather than more expensive paintings. Outline drawings, as stingy of detail as Silhouette was of money, were given his name.

[2]**silhouette** *vt* : to represent by a silhouette; *also* : to project upon a background like a silhouette ⟨a flock of geese *silhouetted* against the evening sky⟩

sil·i·ca \ˈsil-i-kə\ *n* : the dioxide of silicon SiO_2 occurring in crystalline, amorphous, and impure forms (as in quartz, opal, and sand) [New Latin, from Latin *silic-, silex* "flint, quartz"]

silica gel *n* : colloidal silica resembling coarse white sand in appearance but possessing many fine pores and therefore extremely adsorbent

sil·i·cate \ˈsil-i-kət, ˈsil-ə-ˌkāt\ *n* : a compound formed from silica and any of various oxides of metals

si·li·ceous *or* **si·li·cious** \sə-ˈlish-əs\ *adj* : of, relating to, or containing silica or a silicate ⟨*siliceous* limestone⟩

si·lic·ic \sə-ˈlis-ik\ *adj* : of, relating to, or derived from silica or silicon

silicic acid *n* : any of various weakly acid substances obtained as gelatinous masses by treating silicates with acids

silicified wood *n* : chalcedony in the form of petrified wood

si·lic·i·fy \sə-ˈlis-ə-ˌfī\ *vt* **-fied; -fy·ing** : to convert into or impregnate with silica — **si·lic·i·fi·ca·tion** \-ˌlis-ə-fə-ˈkā-shən\ *n*

sil·i·con \ˈsil-i-kən, ˈsil-ə-ˌkän\ *n* : a tetravalent nonmetallic chemical element that occurs combined as the most abundant element next to oxygen in the earth's crust and is used especially in alloys — see ELEMENT table [*silica* + *-on* (as in *carbon*)]

silicon carbide *n* : a hard brittle crystalline compound SiC of silicon and carbon used as an abrasive

silicon dioxide *n* : SILICA

sil·i·cone \ˈsil-ə-ˌkōn\ *n* : any of various polymeric organic silicon compounds obtained as oils, greases, or plastics and used especially for water-resistant and heat-resistant lubricants, varnishes, binders, and electric insulators [derived from *silicon*]

sil·i·co·sis \ˌsil-ə-ˈkō-səs\ *n* : a disease of the lungs marked by formation of scar tissue and shortness of breath and caused by prolonged inhaling of silica dusts — **sil·i·cot·ic** \-ˈkät-ik\ *adj or n*

si·lique \sə-ˈlēk\ *n* : a long narrow 2-valved usually many-seeded capsule characteristic of the mustard family [French, from Latin *siliqua* "pod, husk"]

[1]**silk** \ˈsilk\ *n* **1** : a fine continuous protein fiber produced by various insect larvae usually for cocoons; *esp* : a lustrous tough elastic fiber produced by silkworms and used for textiles **2 a** : thread, yarn, or fabric made from silk **b** : a garment of silk **3** : a silky material or filament (as that produced by a spider) ⟨milkweed *silk*⟩; *esp* : the styles of an ear of Indian corn [Old English *seolc*] — **silk** *adj*

[2]**silk** *vi* : to develop the silk ⟨the corn is *silking*⟩

silk cotton *n* : the silky or cottony covering of seeds of a silk-cotton tree; *esp* : KAPOK

silk–cotton tree *n* : any of various tropical trees with palmate leaves and large fruits with the seeds enveloped by silk cotton

silk·en \ˈsil-kən\ *adj* **1** : made or consisting of silk **2** : resembling silk especially in soft lustrous smoothness

silk hat *n* : a hat with a tall cylindrical crown and a silk-plush finish worn by men as a dress hat

silk moth *n* : the silkworm moth

silk screen *n* : a stencil process in which coloring matter is forced onto the material to be printed through the meshes of a silk or organdy screen — called also *silk-screen process*

silk–stocking *adj* **1** : fashionably dressed ⟨a *silk-stocking* audience⟩ **2** : ARISTOCRATIC, WEALTHY ⟨the *silk-stocking* districts of a city⟩

silk·worm \ˈsil-ˌkwərm\ *n* : a moth larva that spins a large amount of strong silk in constructing its cocoon; *esp* : the rough wrinkled hairless yellowish caterpillar of an Asian moth long grown as a source of silk

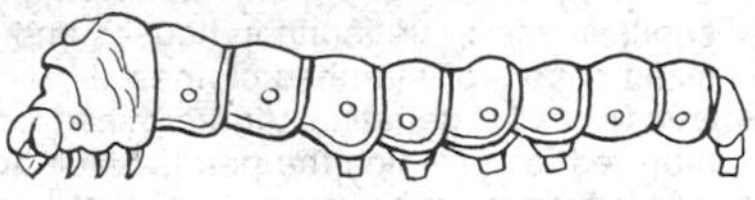

silkworm

silky \ˈsil-kē\ *adj* **silk·i·er; -est 1** : SILKEN 2 **2** : having or covered with fine soft hairs, plumes, or scales — **silk·i·ly** \-kə-lē\ *adv* — **silk·i·ness** \-kē-nəs\ *n*

sill \ˈsil\ *n* **1** : a horizontal piece (as a timber) that forms the lowest member of a framework or supporting structure (as of a house or bridge): as **a** : the horizontal member at the base of a window **b** : the timber or stone at the foot of a door : THRESHOLD **2** : a flat mass of igneous rock injected while molten between other rocks [Old English *syll*]

sillabub *variant of* SYLLABUB

sil·li·man·ite \ˈsil-ə-mə-ˌnīt\ *n* : a brown, grayish, or pale green crystalline mineral that consists of an aluminum silicate [Benjamin *Silliman,* died 1864, American geologist]

\ə\ **abut**	\au̇\ **out**	\i\ **tip**	\ȯ\ **saw**	\u̇\ **foot**
\ər\ **further**	\ch\ **chin**	\ī\ **life**	\ȯi\ **coin**	\y\ **yet**
\a\ **mat**	\e\ **pet**	\j\ **job**	\th\ **thin**	\yü\ **few**
\ā\ **take**	\ē\ **easy**	\ng\ **sing**	\t͟h\ **this**	\yu̇\ **cure**
\ä\ **cot, cart**	\g\ **go**	\ō\ **bone**	\ü\ **food**	\zh\ **vision**

sil•ly \'sil-ē\ *adj* **sil•li•er; -est 1 :** mentally feeble **:** FOOLISH **2 :** contrary to reason **:** ABSURD **3 :** lacking in seriousness **:** TRIFLING [Middle English *sely* "happy, innocent, pitiable, feeble", from Old English *sǣl* "happiness"] — **sil•li•ly** \'sil-ə-lē\ *adv* — **sil•li•ness** \'sil-ē-nəs\ *n* — **silly** *n or adv*

si•lo \'sī-lō\ *n, pl* **silos 1 :** a trench, pit, or especially a tall cylinder (as of wood or concrete) used for making and storing silage **2 :** a deep bin for housing a missile underground [Spanish]

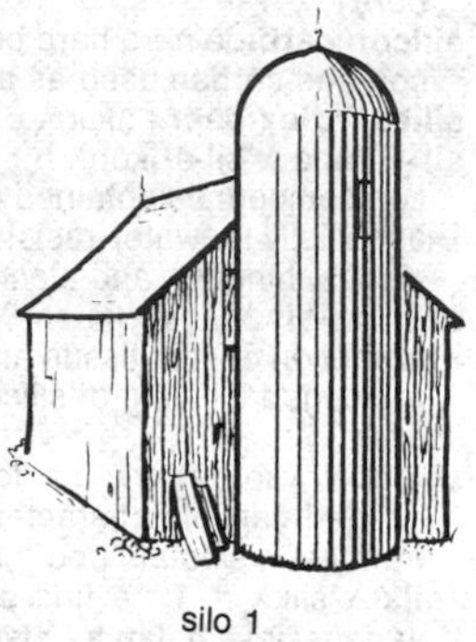
silo 1

¹silt \'silt\ *n* **1 :** loose sedimentary material with rock particles usually 1/20 millimeter or less in diameter; *also* **:** soil containing 80 percent or more of such silt and less than 12 percent of clay **2 :** a deposit of sediment (as by a river) [Middle English *cylte*] — **silty** \'sil-tē\ *adj*

²silt *vb* **:** to become or make choked, obstructed, or covered with silt — **silt•a•tion** \sil-'tā-shən\ *n*

Si•lu•ri•an \sī-'lu̇r-ē-ən, sə-\ *n* **:** the period of the Paleozoic era between the Ordovician and Devonian marked by the beginning of coral-reef building and the appearance of very large crustaceans; *also* **:** the corresponding system of rocks — see GEOLOGIC TIME table [Latin *Silures,* a people of ancient Britain] — **Silurian** *adj*

silvan *variant of* SYLVAN

¹sil•ver \'sil-vər\ *n* **1 :** a white ductile and malleable metallic chemical element that takes a high polish, is usually univalent in compounds, and has high thermal and electric conductivity — see ELEMENT table **2 a :** coin made of silver **b :** articles (as tableware) made of or plated with silver **3 :** a medium gray [Old English *seolfor*]

²silver *adj* **1 :** relating to, made of, or yielding silver ⟨*silver* jewelry⟩ ⟨*silver* ore⟩ **2 :** SILVERY

³silver *vt* **sil•vered; sil•ver•ing** \'silv-ring, -ə-ring\ **1 a :** to cover with silver (as by electroplating) **b :** to coat with a substance (as a metal) resembling silver ⟨*silver* glass with an amalgam⟩ **2 :** to give a silvery appearance to — **sil•ver•er** \'sil-vər-ər\ *n*

silver bromide *n* **:** a compound AgBr extremely sensitive to light and much used for photographic emulsions

silver chloride *n* **:** a compound AgCl sensitive to light and used especially for photographic emulsions

sil•ver•fish \'sil-vər-,fish\ *n* **1 :** any of various silvery fishes (as a tarpon) **2 :** any of various small wingless insects (order Thysanura); *esp* **:** one found in houses and sometimes injurious to sized papers or starched clothes

silver fox *n* **:** a genetically determined color phase of the common red fox in which the pelt is black tipped with white

silver iodide *n* **:** a compound AgI that is sensitive to light and is used in photography, rainmaking, and medicine

silver lining *n* **:** a consoling or hopeful prospect

silver maple *n* **:** a common North American maple with deeply cut leaves that are light green above and silvery white below; *also* **:** its hard close-grained but brittle light brown wood

sil•vern \'sil-vərn\ *adj* **1 :** made of silver **2 :** resembling or characteristic of silver **:** SILVERY

silver nitrate *n* **:** an irritant compound $AgNO_3$ that is used as a chemical reagent, in photography, and in medicine especially as an antiseptic

silver paper *n* **:** a metallic paper with a coating or lamination resembling silver

silver perch *n* **:** any of various somewhat silvery fishes that resemble perch

silver plate *n* **1 :** a plating of silver **2 :** domestic flatware and hollowware of silver or of a base metal plated with silver

silver protein *n* **:** a colloidal light-sensitive preparation of silver and protein used as an antiseptic

silver screen *n* **1 :** a motion-picture screen **2 :** SCREEN 3b

sil•ver•sides \'sil-vər-,sīdz\ *n sing or pl* **:** any of a family of small fishes with a silvery stripe along each side of the body

sil•ver•smith \-,smith\ *n* **:** a person who makes articles of silver

silver spoon *n* **:** WEALTH; *esp* **:** inherited wealth [from the phrase *born with a silver spoon in one's mouth* "born wealthy"]

silver standard *n* **:** a monetary standard under which the currency unit is defined by a stated quantity of silver

sil•ver–tongued \,sil-vər-'təngd\ *adj* **:** ELOQUENT ⟨a *silver-tongued* orator⟩

sil•ver•ware \'sil-vər-,waər, -,weər\ *n* **:** SILVER PLATE 2; *also* **:** FLATWARE

sil•very \'silv-rē, -ə-rē\ *adj* **1 :** having a soft clear ring ⟨a *silvery* voice⟩ **2 :** having the white lustrous sheen of silver — **sil•ver•i•ness** *n*

sil•vi•cul•ture *or* **syl•vi•cul•ture** \'sil-və-,kəl-chər\ *n* **:** FORESTRY; *esp* **:** the science of the culture of forest trees [French, from Latin *silva* "forest" + *cultura* "culture"] — **sil•vi•cul•tur•al** \,sil-və-'kəlch-rəl, -ə-rəl\ *adj* — **sil•vi•cul•tur•al•ly** \-ē\ *adv* — **sil•vi•cul•tur•ist** \-'kəlch-rəst, -ə-rəst\ *n*

Sim•chas To•rah \,sim-käs-'tōr-ə, -'tȯr-\ *n* **:** a Jewish holiday observed in October or November in celebration of the completion of the annual reading of the Torah [Hebrew *śimḥath tōrāh* "rejoicing of the Torah"]

¹sim•i•an \'sim-ē-ən\ *adj* **:** of, relating to, or resembling monkeys [Latin *simia* "ape", from *simus* "snub-nosed", from Greek *simos*]

²simian *n* **:** MONKEY 1

sim•i•lar \'sim-ə-lər\ *adj* **1 :** having characteristics in common **:** COMPARABLE **2 :** not differing in shape but only in size or position ⟨*similar* triangles⟩ [French *similaire,* from Latin *similis* "like, similar"] — **sim•i•lar•ly** *adv*

• **syn** SIMILAR, ANALOGOUS, PARALLEL mean closely resembling each other. SIMILAR implies the possibility of being mistaken for each other; ANALOGOUS applies to things belonging in essentially different categories but nevertheless having many similarities ⟨*analogous* political systems⟩ PARALLEL suggests a marked likeness in the development of two things ⟨the *parallel* careers of two movie stars⟩

sim•i•lar•i•ty \,sim-ə-'lar-ət-ē\ *n, pl* **-ties 1 :** the quality or state of being similar **:** RESEMBLANCE **2 :** a point in which things are similar **:** CORRESPONDENCE **syn** see LIKENESS

sim•i•le \'sim-ə-lē, -,lē\ *n* **:** a figure of speech in which things different in kind or quality are compared by the use of the word *like* or *as* (as in *cheeks like roses*) — compare METAPHOR [Latin, "comparison", from *similis* "like, similar"]

si•mil•i•tude \sə-'mil-ə-,tüd, -,tyüd\ *n* **1 :** a visible likeness **:** IMAGE **2 :** an imaginative comparison **3 :** SIMILARITY

sim•mer \'sim-ər\ *vb* **sim•mered; sim•mer•ing** \'sim-ring, -ə-ring\ **1 :** to stew gently below or just at the boiling point **2 a :** to be in a state of early development ⟨an idea *simmering* in the back of my mind⟩ **b :** to be in inward turmoil **:** SEETHE ⟨*simmered* with fury at the insult⟩ [Middle English *simperen*] — **simmer** *n*

si•mo•ni•ac \sī-'mō-nē-,ak, sə-\ *n* **:** one who practices simony — **simoniac** *or* **si•mo•ni•a•cal** \,sī-mə-'nī-ə-kəl, ,sim-ə-\ *adj* — **si•mo•ni•a•cal•ly** \-'nī-ə-kə-lē, -klē\ *adv*

si•mo•nize \'sī-mə-,nīz\ *vt* **:** to polish with or as if with wax [from *Simoniz,* a trademark]

si•mon–pure \,sī-mən-'pyu̇r\ *adj* **:** of untainted purity or integrity; *also* **:** pretentiously or hypocritically pure [from *the real Simon Pure,* alluding to a character impersonated by another in the play *A Bold Stroke for a Wife* (1718) by Susanna Centlivre]

si•mo•ny \'sī-mə-nē, 'sim-ə-\ *n* **:** the buying or selling of a church office [Late Latin *simonia,* from *Simon* Magus (Acts 8:9–24)]

si•moom \sə-'müm, sī-\ *or* **si•moon** \-'mün\ *n* **:** a hot dry violent wind laden with dust from Asian and African deserts [Arabic *samūm*]

sim•pa•ti•co \sim-'pät-i-,kō, -'pat-\ *adj* **1 :** LIKABLE **2 :** CONGENIAL 2 [Italian, from *simpatia* "sympathy, congeniality", from Latin *sympathia* "sympathy"]

¹sim•per \'sim-pər\ *vi* **sim•pered; sim•per•ing** \-pə-ring, -pring\ **:** to smile in a foolish affected manner [perhaps of Scandinavian origin] — **sim•per•er** \-pər-ər\ *n*

²simper *n* **:** a silly smile **:** SMIRK

sim•ple \'sim-pəl\ *adj* **sim•pler** \-pə-lər, -plər\; **sim•plest** \-pə-ləst, -pləst\ **1 :** free from deceit or vanity **2 a :** of humble origin **b :** lacking in education, experience, or intelligence **3 a** (1) **:** free from complexity or complications ⟨a *simple* melody⟩ (2) **:** expressed in a form in which the indicated operations have been carried out and radicals have been eliminated as far as possible ⟨3x is *simpler* than 6x − 3x⟩ **b :** consisting of only one main clause and no subordinate clauses ⟨*simple* sentence⟩ **c :** not compound ⟨the *simple* noun "boat"⟩ **d** (1) : not subdivided into branches or leaflets (2) : developing from a single ovary ⟨*simple* fruits⟩ **4 a :** UTTER, ABSOLUTE ⟨the *simple* truth⟩ **b :** easily understood or performed ⟨a *simple* explanation⟩ ⟨a *simple* task⟩ [Old French, "plain, uncomplicated, artless", from Latin *simplus, simplex,* literally, "single"] — **sim•ple•ness** \-pəl-nəs\ *n*

• syn SIMPLE, EASY mean not demanding great effort or involving difficulty. SIMPLE stresses lack of complexity or subtlety ⟨a *simple* case of theft⟩ EASY implies offering little resistance to being understood or accomplished or dealt with ⟨an *easy* problem⟩ ⟨an *easy* victory⟩

simple eye *n* **:** an eye having a single lens — compare COMPOUND EYE

simple fraction *n* **:** a fraction having whole numbers for the numerator and denominator — compare COMPLEX FRACTION

simple fracture *n* **:** a breaking of a bone in such a way that the skin is not broken and bone fragments do not protrude

simple interest *n* **:** interest paid or computed on the original principal only of a loan or on the amount of an account

simple machine *n* **:** any of six elementary mechanisms having the elements of which all machines are composed and comprising the lever, the wheel and axle, the pulley, the inclined plane, the wedge, and the screw

sim•ple•mind•ed \ˌsim-pəl-ˈmīn-dəd\ *adj* **:** not subtle **:** UNSOPHISTICATED; *also* **:** FOOLISH — **sim•ple•mind•ed•ly** *adv* — **sim•ple•mind•ed•ness** *n*

simple sugar *n* **:** MONOSACCHARIDE

sim•ple•ton \ˈsim-pəl-tən\ *n* **:** a person lacking in common sense [*simple* + *-ton* (as in surnames such as *Washington*)]

sim•plex \ˈsim-ˌpleks\ *n, pl* **sim•pli•cia** \sim-ˈplish-ə, -ē-ə\ *or* **sim•pli•ces** \ˈsim-plə-ˌsēz\ **:** a word that is not a compound [Latin *simplic-, simplex* "simple, single"] — **sim•pli•cial** \sim-ˈplish-əl\ *adj*

sim•plic•i•ty \sim-ˈplis-ət-ē\ *n, pl* **-ties 1 :** the quality or state of being simple **2 :** freedom from pretense or guile **:** HONESTY **3 a :** directness or clarity of expression **b :** restraint in ornamentation **:** PLAINNESS **4 :** FOLLY 2, SILLINESS [Middle French *simplicité,* from Latin *simplicitas,* from *simplic-, simplex* "simple"]

sim•pli•fy \ˈsim-plə-ˌfī\ *vt* **-fied; -fy•ing :** to make simple or simpler — **sim•pli•fi•ca•tion** \ˌsim-plə-fə-ˈkā-shən\ *n* — **sim•pli•fi•er** \ˈsim-plə-ˌfī-ər, -ˌfīr\ *n*

sim•ply \ˈsim-plē\ *adv* **1 a :** CLEARLY ⟨stated the directions *simply*⟩ **b :** PLAINLY ⟨*simply* dressed⟩ **c :** DIRECTLY, CANDIDLY ⟨told the story as *simply* as a child would⟩ **2 a :** MERELY, SOLELY ⟨eats *simply* to keep alive⟩ **b :** REALLY 1 ⟨*simply* marvelous⟩

sim•u•late \ˈsim-yə-ˌlāt\ *vt* **:** to give the appearance or effect of **:** IMITATE [Latin *simulare* "to copy, represent, feign", from *similis* "like, similar"] — **sim•u•la•tive** \-ˌlāt-iv\ *adj* — **sim•u•la•tor** \-ˌlāt-ər\ *n*

sim•u•la•tion \ˌsim-yə-ˈlā-shən\ *n* **1 :** the act or process of simulating **2 :** a sham object **:** COUNTERFEIT

si•mul•cast \ˈsī-məl-ˌkast\ *vb* **:** to broadcast simultaneously by AM and FM radio or by radio and television [*simul*taneous broad*cast*] — **simulcast** *n*

si•mul•ta•neous \ˌsī-məl-ˈtā-nē-əs, -nyəs\ *adj* **1 :** existing or occurring at the same time **:** COINCIDENT **2 :** satisfied by the same values of the variables ⟨*simultaneous* equations⟩ [derived from Latin *simul* "at the same time"] **syn** see CONTEMPORARY — **si•mul•ta•ne•i•ty** \-tə-ˈnē-ət-ē, -ˈnā-\ *n* — **si•mul•ta•neous•ly** \-ˈtā-nē-ə-slē, -nyə-slē\ *adv* — **si•mul•ta•neous•ness** *n*

¹sin \ˈsin\ *n* **1 :** an offense against God **2 :** MISDEED, FAULT [Old English *synn*]

²sin *vi* **sinned; sin•ning :** to commit a sin

Sin•an•thro•pus \sī-ˈnan-thrə-pəs, -ˈnant-; ˌsī-ˌnan-ˈthrō-\ *n* **:** PEKING MAN [Late Latin *Sinae,* pl., "Chinese" + Greek *anthrōpos* "man"]

¹since \sins, ˈsins\ *adv* **1 :** from a definite past time until now ⟨has stayed there ever *since*⟩ **2 :** before the present time **:** AGO ⟨long *since* dead⟩ **3 :** after a time in the past **:** SUBSEQUENTLY ⟨has *since* become rich⟩ [Middle English *sithens, sins,* from *sithen,* from Old English *siththan,* from *sith tham* "since that"]

²since *prep* **:** from or after a specified time in the past ⟨improvements made *since* 1928⟩ ⟨happy *since* then⟩

³since *conj* **1 :** at a time or times in the past after or later than ⟨have held two jobs *since* I graduated⟩ **2 :** from the time in the past when ⟨ever *since* we were children⟩ **3 :** in view of the fact that **:** BECAUSE ⟨*since* it was raining I wore a hat⟩

sin•cere \sin-ˈsiər\ *adj* **1 a :** free from deceit **:** HONEST ⟨a *sincere* friend⟩ **b :** free from adulteration **:** PURE ⟨a *sincere* doctrine⟩ **2 :** GENUINE 1, REAL ⟨a *sincere* work of art⟩ [Middle French, from Latin *sincerus*] — **sin•cere•ly** *adv* — **sin•cere•ness** *n* — **sin•cer•i•ty** \-ˈser-ət-ē, -ˈsir-\ *n*

sine \ˈsīn\ *n* **:** a trigonometric function that for an acute angle in a right triangle is the ratio between the side opposite the angle and the hypotenuse — abbreviation *sin* [Medieval Latin *sinus,* from Latin, "curve"]

si•ne•cure \ˈsī-ni-kyůr, ˈsin-i-\ *n* **:** an office or position that requires little or no work [Medieval Latin *sine cura* "without cure of souls"]

si•ne die \ˌsī-nē-ˈdī-ˌē, -ˈdī; sin-ē-ˈdē-ˌā\ *adv* **:** for an unspecified period of time **:** INDEFINITELY ⟨the meeting adjourned *sine die*⟩ [Latin, "without day"]

si•ne qua non \ˌsin-i-ˌkwä-ˈnän, -ˈnōn; *also* ˌsī-nē-ˌkwā-ˈnän\ *n* **:** something absolutely essential or indispensable [Late Latin, "without which not"]

sin•ew \ˈsin-yü, ˈsin-ü\ *n* **1 :** TENDON; *esp* **:** one dressed for use as a cord or thread **2 :** solid resilient strength **:** POWER [Old English *seono*]

sine wave *n* **:** a wave form that represents periodic oscillations in which the amplitude of displacement at each point is proportional to the sine of the angle of the displacement

sin•ewy \ˈsin-yə-wē, ˈsin-ə-wē\ *adj* **1 :** full of sinews **:** TOUGH, STRINGY ⟨*sinewy* meat⟩ **2 :** STRONG ⟨*sinewy* arms⟩

sin•fo•nia \ˌsin-fə-ˈnē-ə\ *n, pl* **-nie** \-ˈnē-ˌā\ **1 :** an orchestral musical composition found in 18th century opera **2 :** SYMPHONY 2 [Italian, from Latin *symphonia* "symphony"]

sin•ful \ˈsin-fəl\ *adj* **:** marked by or full of sin **:** WICKED — **sin•ful•ly** \-fə-lē\ *adv* — **sin•ful•ness** *n*

¹sing \ˈsing\ *vb* **sang** \ˈsang\ *or* **sung** \ˈsəng\; **sung; sing•ing** \ˈsing-ing\ **1 a :** to produce musical sounds by means of the voice ⟨*sing* for joy⟩ **b :** to utter with musical sounds ⟨*sing* a song⟩ **c :** CHANT, INTONE ⟨*sing* mass⟩ **2 :** to make pleasing musical sounds ⟨birds *singing* at dawn⟩ **3 :** to make a slight shrill sound ⟨a kettle *singing* on the stove⟩ **4 a :** to tell a story in poetry **:** relate in verse **b :** to express vividly and enthusiastically ⟨*sing* their praises⟩ **5 :** BUZZ, RING ⟨ears *singing* from the sudden descent⟩ **6 :** to act on or affect by singing ⟨*sing* a baby to sleep⟩ **7 a :** to call aloud **:** cry out ⟨*sing* out when you find them⟩ **b :** to divulge information or give evidence [Old English *singan*] — **sing•able** \ˈsing-ə-bəl\ *adj*

²sing *n* **:** a singing especially in company

¹singe \ˈsinj\ *vb* **singed** \ˈsinjd\; **singe•ing** \ˈsin-jing\ **:** to burn superficially or lightly **:** SCORCH; *esp* **:** to remove hair, down, or fuzz from usually by passing briefly over a flame [Old English *sengan*]

²singe *n* **:** a slight burn **:** SCORCH

¹sing•er \ˈsing-ər\ *n* **:** one that sings

²sing•er \ˈsin-jər\ *n* **:** one that singes

singing bird *n* **1 :** SONGBIRD 1 **2 :** a passerine bird

¹sin•gle \ˈsing-gəl\ *adj* **1 :** not married **2 :** unaccompanied by others **3 a** (1) : consisting of or having only one part or feature (2) : of or relating to one of two or more aspects or parts **b :** having but one whorl of petals or ray flowers ⟨a *single* rose⟩ **4 a :** consisting of a separate unique whole **:** INDIVIDUAL ⟨every *single* citizen⟩ **b :** of, relating to, or involving only one person **5 :** FRANK, HONEST ⟨a *single* devotion⟩ **6 :** being a whole ⟨a *single* world⟩ **7 :** engaged in one to one ⟨fight in *single* combat⟩ **8 :** having no equal or like **:** SINGULAR **9 :** designed for the use of one person or family ⟨a *single* house⟩ [Middle French, from Latin *singulus* "one only"] — **sin•gle•ness** *n*

• syn SOLITARY, SOLE, UNIQUE **:** SINGLE implies being unaccompanied or unassisted by any other ⟨operated by a *single* worker⟩ ⟨a *single* line of trees⟩ SOLITARY implies being both single and isolated ⟨a *solitary* oak in a field⟩ SOLE implies being the only one existing or acting ⟨the *sole* reason for refusing⟩ ⟨the *sole* survivor of the wreck⟩ UNIQUE implies being the only one of its kind or character in existence ⟨a *unique* mineral specimen⟩

[2]**single** *n* **1 :** a separate individual person or thing **2 :** a base hit that permits the batter to reach first base **3** *pl* **:** a game (as of tennis or handball) between two players

[3]**single** *vb* **sin•gled; sin•gling** \ˈsiŋ-gə-liŋ, -gliŋ\ **1 :** to select or distinguish (a person or thing) from a number or group — usually used with *out* **2 :** to make a single in baseball

sin•gle–breast•ed \ˌsiŋ-gəl-ˈbres-təd\ *adj* **:** having a center closing with one row of buttons and no lap ⟨a *single-breasted* coat⟩

single entry *n* **:** a method of bookkeeping that shows only one side of a business transaction and usually consists only of a record of accounts with debtors and creditors

single file *n* **:** a line of persons or things arranged one behind another — **single file** *adv*

[1]**sin•gle–foot** \ˈsiŋ-gəl-ˌfu̇t\ *n, pl* **single–foots :** [4]RACK b

[2]**single–foot** *vi* **:** to go at a rack — **sin•gle–foot•er** *n*

sin•gle–hand•ed \ˌsiŋ-gəl-ˈhan-dəd\ *adj* **1 :** managed or done by one person or with one hand **2 :** working alone **:** lacking help — **single–handed** *adv* — **sin•gle–hand•ed•ly** *adv* — **sin•gle–hand•ed•ness** *n*

sin•gle–heart•ed \-ˈhärt-əd\ *adj* **:** characterized by sincerity and unity of purpose — **sin•gle–heart•ed•ly** *adv* — **sin•gle–heart•ed•ness** *n*

sin•gle–mind•ed \-ˈmīn-dəd\ *adj* **1 :** SINCERE, SINGLE-HEARTED **2 :** having one overriding purpose — **sin•gle–mind•ed•ly** *adv* — **sin•gle–mind•ed•ness** *n*

sin•gle–space \-ˈspās\ *vt* **:** to type or print with no blank lines between lines of copy

sin•gle•stick \ˈsiŋ-gəl-ˌstik\ *n* **:** fighting or fencing with a wooden stick or sword held in one hand; *also* **:** the weapon used

sin•glet \ˈsiŋ-glət\ *n, chiefly British* **:** an athletic jersey **:** UNDERSHIRT [from its having only one thickness of cloth]

single tax *n* **:** a tax levied on a single item (as real estate) as the sole source of public revenue

sin•gle•ton \ˈsiŋ-gəl-tən\ *n* **1 :** a playing card that is the only one of its suit originally held in a hand **2 :** an individual distinct from others grouped with it [French, from English *single*]

sin•gle•tree \-ˌtrē\ *n* **:** WHIFFLETREE

sin•gly \ˈsiŋ-gə-lē, -glē\ *adv* **1 :** by or with oneself **:** INDIVIDUALLY **2 :** SINGLE–HANDEDLY

[1]**sing•song** \ˈsiŋ-ˌsȯŋ\ *n* **:** voice delivery marked by a narrow range or a monotonous rise and fall of pitch

[2]**singsong** *adj* **:** having a monotonous cadence or rhythm

[1]**sin•gu•lar** \ˈsiŋ-gyə-lər\ *adj* **1 a :** of or relating to a separate person or thing **:** INDIVIDUAL **b :** of, relating to, or being a word form denoting one person, thing, or instance **c :** of or relating to a single instance or to something considered by itself **2 a :** EXCEPTIONAL 2 **b :** UNIQUE 2 **3 :** being at variance with others **:** PECULIAR ⟨held *singular* views of civic responsibility⟩ [Middle French *singuler,* from Latin *singularis,* from *singulus* "only one"] — **sin•gu•lar•ly** *adv*

[2]**singular** *n* **:** something that is singular; *esp* **:** the singular number, the inflectional form denoting it, or a word in that form

sin•gu•lar•i•ty \ˌsiŋ-gyə-ˈlar-ət-ē\ *n, pl* **-ties 1 :** the quality or state of being singular **2 :** something that is peculiar

sin•gu•lar•ize \ˈsiŋ-gyə-lə-ˌrīz\ *vt* **:** to make singular

Sin•ha•lese *or* **Sin•gha•lese** \ˌsiŋ-gə-ˈlēz, ˌsin-ə-, ˌsin-hə-, -ˌlēs\ *n* **1 :** a member of a people forming a major part of the population of Sri Lanka **2 :** the Indic language of the Sinhalese people [Sanskrit *Siṁhala* "Ceylon"] — **Sinhalese** *adj*

sin•is•ter \ˈsin-ə-stər\ *adj* **1 :** singularly evil or productive of evil **:** BAD **2 :** of, relating to, or situated to the left or on the left side of something **3 :** seriously threatening trouble or disaster **:** OMINOUS [Latin, "on the left side, inauspicious"] — **sin•is•ter•ly** *adv* — **sin•is•ter•ness** *n*

sin•is•tral \ˈsin-ə-strəl\ *adj* **:** of, relating to, or inclined to the left; *esp* **:** LEFT-HANDED — **sin•is•tral•ly** \-strə-lē\ *adv*

[1]**sink** \ˈsiŋk\ *vb* **sank** \ˈsaŋk\ *or* **sunk** \ˈsəŋk\; **sunk; sink•ing 1 :** to move or cause to move downward usually so as to be submerged or buried ⟨feet *sinking* into deep mud⟩ ⟨*sink* a ship⟩ **2 a :** to fall to a lower level ⟨the lake *sank* during the drought⟩ **b :** to make or become lower in pitch or volume ⟨my voice *sank* to a whisper⟩ **c :** to fall to or into an inferior status **:** DECLINE ⟨*sink* into decay⟩ **d :** SET 24 **3 a :** to penetrate or cause to penetrate ⟨*sank* the ax into the tree⟩ **b :** to become absorbed ⟨water *sinking* into dry sand⟩; *also* **:** to be apprehended and retained ⟨the lesson *sank* in⟩ **4 :** to fail in strength, spirits, or health ⟨my heart *sank* as I saw the wreck⟩ ⟨the patient is *sinking* fast⟩ **5 :** to form by digging or boring usually in the earth ⟨*sink* a well⟩ **6 :** RESTRAIN, SUPPRESS ⟨*sinking* my pride, I apologized⟩ **7 :** to invest especially unwisely [Old English *sincan*] — **sink•able** \ˈsiŋ-kə-bəl\ *adj*

[2]**sink** *n* **1 a :** CESSPOOL **b :** SEWER **c :** a stationary basin for washing (as in a kitchen) connected with a drain and usually a water supply **2 :** a place marked by vice, corruption, and filth **3 :** a depression in the land surface; *esp* **:** one having a saline lake with no outlet

sink•age \ˈsiŋ-kij\ *n* **:** the act, process, or extent of sinking

sink•er \ˈsiŋ-kər\ *n* **1 :** one that sinks; *esp* **:** a weight for sinking a line or net **2 :** DOUGHNUT

sink•hole \ˈsiŋk-ˌhōl\ *n* **:** a hollow place in which drainage collects

sinking fund *n* **:** a fund set up and accumulated by usually regular deposits for paying off the principal of a debt

sin•less \ˈsin-ləs\ *adj* **:** free from sin — **sin•less•ly** *adv* — **sin•less•ness** *n*

sin•ner \ˈsin-ər\ *n* **:** one that sins

Sino- *combining form* **1 :** Chinese **2 :** Chinese and [Late Latin *Sinae,* pl., "Chinese", from Greek *Sinai,* from Arabic *Sīn* "China"]

si•no•atri•al node \ˌsī-nō-ˌā-trē-əl-\ *n* **:** a small mass of tissue that is embedded in the musculature of the right atrium of higher vertebrates and that originates the impulses stimulating the heartbeat [*sinus* + *atrium*]

sin•ter \ˈsint-ər\ *vt* **:** to cause to become a coherent mass by heating without melting [German *sinter* "deposit formed by the evaporation of lake water", from Old High German *sintar* "slag"] — **sinter** *n*

sin•u•os•i•ty \ˌsin-yə-ˈwäs-ət-ē\ *n, pl* **-ties 1 :** the quality or state of being sinuous **2 :** something that is sinuous

sin•u•ous \ˈsin-yə-wəs\ *adj* **1 a :** of a serpentine or wavy form **:** WINDING **b :** marked by strong lithe movements **2 :** INTRICATE, COMPLEX [Latin *sinuosus,* from *sinus* "curve"] — **sin•u•ous•ly** *adv* — **sin•u•ous•ness** *n*

si•nus \ˈsī-nəs\ *n* **:** CAVITY, HOLLOW: as **a :** a narrow passage by which pus is discharged **b :** any of several cavities in the skull mostly communicating with the nostrils **c :** a dilatation in a bodily canal or vessel; *also* **:** a space forming a channel (as for the passage of blood) **d :** a cleft or indentation between adjoining lobes (as of a leaf) [Latin, "curve, fold, hollow"]

si•nus•itis \ˌsī-nə-ˈsīt-əs\ *n* **:** inflammation of a sinus especially of the skull

si•nus ve•no•sus \ˌsī-nəs-vi-ˈnō-səs\ *n* **:** an enlarged pouch which adjoins the heart and through which venous blood enters the heart in lower vertebrates and embryos [New Latin, "venous sinus"]

Si•on \ˈsī-ən\ *variant of* ZION

Siou•an \ˈsü-ən\ *n* **1 :** a stock of Indian languages spoken in central and eastern North America **2 :** a member of the Indian peoples speaking Siouan languages

Sioux \ˈsü\ *n, pl* **Sioux** \ˈsü, ˈsüz\ **:** a member of an Amerindian people of the Missouri and northern Mississippi valleys **:** SIOUAN [French, from *Nadowessioux,* from Ojibwa *Nadoweisiw*]

[1]**sip** \ˈsip\ *vb* **sipped; sip•ping 1 :** to drink in small quantities or little by little **2 :** to take sips from **:** TASTE [Middle English *sippen*] — **sip•per** *n*

[2]**sip** *n* **1 :** the act of sipping **2 :** a small amount taken by sipping

[1]**si•phon** *also* **sy•phon** \ˈsī-fən\ *n* **1 a :** a tube bent to form two legs of unequal length by which a liquid can be transferred to a lower level over an intermediate elevation by the pressure of the atmosphere in forcing the liquid up the shorter branch of the tube immersed in it while the excess of weight of the liquid in the longer branch when once filled causes a continuous flow **b** *usually syphon* **:** a bottle for holding carbonated water that is driven out through a bent tube in its

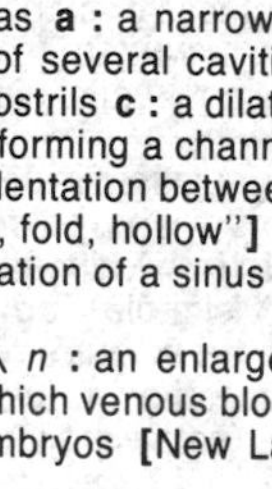

[1]siphon 1a

neck by the pressure of the gas when a valve in the tube is opened **2 :** any of various tubular organs in animals and especially mollusks or arthropods used for drawing in or ejecting fluids [French, from Latin *sipho* "tube, pipe, siphon", from Greek *siphōn*]

2**siphon** *also* **syphon** *vb* **si•phoned**; **si•phon•ing** \'sī-fning, -ə-ning\ **:** to draw off or pass off by or as if by a siphon

si•pho•no•phore \sī-'fän-ə-ˌfōr, 'sī-fə-nə-, -ˌfȯr\ *n* **:** any of an order (Siphonophora) of mostly delicate, transparent, and colored compound hydrozoans

sir \sər, 'sər\ *n* **1** *often cap* **:** a male member of an order of knighthood or a man holding the rank of baronet — used as a title before a full name or a given name ⟨*Sir* Winston Churchill⟩ ⟨*Sir* Winston⟩ **2 a** — used as a usually respectful form of direct address ⟨yes, *sir*⟩ **b** *cap* — used sometimes as a salutation in a letter addressed to high-ranking officials (as a governor) ⟨*Sir:*⟩ [Middle English, from *sire*]

sir•dar \'sər-ˌdär\ *n* **:** a person of high rank or one holding a position of responsibility especially in India [Hindi *sardār*, from Persian]

1**sire** \'sīr\ *n* **1 a :** FATHER 1a **b** *archaic* **:** a male ancestor **:** FOREFATHER **c :** AUTHOR 2, ORIGINATOR **2 a** *archaic* **:** a man of high station or great authority — used formerly as a form of address (as to a king) or as a title **b** — a form of respectful address formerly used for a reigning sovereign **3 :** the male parent of an animal and especially of a domestic animal [Old French, from Latin *senior*, adj., "senior"]

2**sire** *vt* **1 :** BEGET 1, PROCREATE — used especially of domestic animals **2 :** to bring into being **:** ORIGINATE

1**si•ren** \'sī-rən, *for 3 also* sī-'rēn\ *n* **1** *often cap* **:** one of a group of creatures in Greek mythology depicted as birds with the heads and sometimes the breasts and arms of women that lured mariners to destruction by their singing **2 :** a woman held to be insidiously seductive **:** TEMPTRESS **3 a :** an apparatus producing musical tones by the rapid interruption of a current (as of air or steam) by a perforated rotating disk **b :** a device often electrically operated for producing a penetrating warning sound ⟨an ambulance *siren*⟩ ⟨an air-raid *siren*⟩ **4 a :** any of a genus of eel-shaped amphibians with small forelimbs but neither hind legs nor pelvis and with permanent external gills as well as lungs **b :** SIRENIAN [Latin, from Greek *seirēn*]

2**si•ren** \'sī-rən\ *adj* **:** of, relating to, or resembling a siren

si•re•ni•an \sī-'rē-nē-ən\ *n* **:** any of an order (Sirenia) of aquatic plant-eating mammals including the manatee and dugong

siren song *n* **:** an alluring utterance or appeal; *esp* **:** one that is seductive or deceptive

Sir•i•us \'sir-ē-əs\ *n* **:** a star of the constellation Canis Major constituting the brightest star in the heavens — called also *Dog Star* [Latin, from Greek *Seirios*, literally, "glowing"]

sir•loin \'sər-ˌlȯin\ *n* **:** a cut of meat and especially of beef from the part of the hindquarter just in front of the round [Middle French *surlonge*, from *sur* "over" (from Latin *super*) + *loigne, longe* "loin"]

si•roc•co \sə-'räk-ō\ *n, pl* **-cos 1 a :** a hot dust-laden wind from the Libyan desert that blows on the northern Mediterranean coast chiefly in Italy, Malta, and Sicily **b :** a warm moist oppressive southeast wind in the same regions **2 :** a hot or warm wind of cyclonic origin from an arid or heated region [Italian *scirocco, sirocco*, from Arabic *sharq* "east"]

sir•rah *also* **sir•ra** \'sir-ə\ *n, obsolete* — used as a form of address implying inferiority in the person addressed [alteration of *sir*]

sir•ree *also* **sir•ee** \sər-'ē, ˌsər-'ē\ *n* **:** SIR 2a — used as an emphatic form usually after *yes* or *no*

sirup, sirupy *variant of* SYRUP, SYRUPY

si•sal \'sī-səl, -zəl\ *n* **1 :** a strong durable white fiber used for cordage **2 :** a widely grown West Indian agave whose leaves yield sisal [Mexican Spanish, from *Sisal*, Yucatán, Mexico]

sis•kin \'sis-kən\ *n* **:** a small chiefly greenish and yellowish Old World finch related to the goldfinch [German dialect *sisschen*, of Slavic origin]

sis•si•fied \'sis-i-ˌfīd\ *adj* **:** SISSY

sis•sy \'sis-ē\ *n, pl* **sissies :** an effeminate man or boy; *also* **:** a timid or cowardly person [*sis*, short for *sister*] — **sissy** *adj*

sis•ter \'sis-tər\ *n* **1 a** (1) **:** a female human being having the same parents as another person (2) **:** HALF SISTER (3) **:** SISTER-IN-LAW **b :** a female lower animal having a parent in common with another **2** *often cap* **:** a woman who is a member of a religious order — often used as a title ⟨*Sister* Mary Angelica⟩ **3 a :** a woman related to another person by a common tie or interest **b :** one having characteristics similar to another ⟨*sister* ships⟩ **4** *chiefly British* **:** NURSE 2 [Old English *sweoster*]

sis•ter•hood \-ˌhu̇d\ *n* **1 a :** the state of being a sister **b :** sisterly relationship **2 :** a community or society of sisters; *esp* **:** a religious society of women

sis•ter–in–law \'sis-tə-rən-ˌlȯ, -trən-ˌlȯ, -tərn-ˌlȯ\ *n, pl* **sis•ters–in–law** \-tər-zən-\ **1 :** the sister of one's spouse **2 a :** the wife of one's brother **b :** the wife of one's spouse's brother

sis•ter•ly \'sis-tər-lē\ *adj* **:** of, relating to, or typical of a sister — **sisterly** *adv*

sis•trum \'sis-trəm\ *n, pl* **sistrums** *or* **sis•tra** \-trə\ **:** an ancient Egyptian percussion instrument having a thin metal frame with many metal rods that jingle when shaken [Latin, from Greek *seistron*, from *seiein* "to shake"]

1**sit** \'sit\ *vb* **sat** \'sat\; **sit•ting 1 a :** to rest or cause to rest on the buttocks or haunches ⟨*sit* in a chair⟩ ⟨*sat* the baby down to eat⟩ **b :** PERCH 2, ROOST **c :** to keep one's seat upon ⟨*sit* a horse⟩ **d :** SEAT 1b **2 :** to occupy a place as a member of an official body ⟨*sit* in Congress⟩ **3 :** to hold a session **4 :** to cover eggs for hatching **:** BROOD **5 a :** to pose for a portrait or photograph **b :** to serve as a model **6 :** to lie or hang relative to a wearer ⟨the collar *sits* awkwardly⟩ **7 :** to lie or rest in any condition or location ⟨the vase *sits* on the table⟩ ⟨the house *sits* well back from the road⟩ **8 :** to remain inactive ⟨the car *sits* in the garage⟩ **9 :** BABY-SIT [Old English *sittan*] — **sit on 1 :** to hold deliberations about **2 :** REPRESS 4, SQUELCH **3 :** to delay action or decision concerning — **sit on one's hands 1 :** to withhold applause **2 :** to fail to take action — **sit pretty :** to be in a very favorable position — **sit tight :** to maintain one's position without change

2**sit** *n* **1 :** an act or period of sitting **2 :** the way in which a garment fits

si•tar \si-'tär\ *n* **:** an Indian lute with a long neck and a varying number of strings [Hindi *sitār*]

sitar

sit–down \'sit-ˌdau̇n\ *n* **:** a work stoppage in which protesting employees cease working but refuse to leave their place of employment — called also *sit-down strike*

1**site** \'sīt\ *n* **1 :** the actual or planned location (as of a building or town) **2 :** the place or scene of something ⟨famous battle *sites*⟩ ⟨a camp *site*⟩ [Latin *situs* "place, position", from *sinere* "to leave, place, lay"]

2**site** *vt* **:** to place on a site or in position **:** LOCATE

sith \sith, 'sith\ *archaic variant of* SINCE

sit–in \'sit-ˌin\ *n* **1 :** SIT-DOWN **2 :** an act of occupying seats especially in a racially segregated establishment in organized protest

sit out *vt* **:** to refrain from participating in ⟨will *sit* the next dance *out*⟩ ⟨*sat* the war *out*⟩

sit•ter \'sit-ər\ *n* **:** one that sits; *esp* **:** BABY-SITTER

1**sit•ting** \'sit-ing\ *n* **1 :** an act of one that sits; *esp* **:** a single occasion of continuous sitting **2 a :** a brooding over eggs for hatching **b :** SETTING 6 **3 :** SESSION 1

2**sitting** *adj* **1 :** that is setting ⟨a *sitting* hen⟩ **2 :** easily hit ⟨a *sitting* target⟩ **3 a :** used in or for sitting ⟨a *sitting* position⟩ **b :** performed while sitting ⟨a *sitting* shot⟩

sitting duck *n* **:** an easy or defenseless target for attack, criticism, or unscrupulous dealings

sitting room *n* **:** LIVING ROOM

1**sit•u•ate** \'sich-ə-wət, -ˌwāt\ *adj* **:** SITUATED 1 [Medieval Latin *situatus*, past participle of *situare* "to place", from Latin *situs* "place, site"]

\ə\ abut	\au̇\ out	\i\ tip	\ȯ\ saw	\u̇\ foot
\ər\ further	\ch\ chin	\ī\ life	\ȯi\ coin	\y\ yet
\a\ mat	\e\ pet	\j\ job	\th\ thin	\yü\ few
\ā\ take	\ē\ easy	\ng\ sing	\t͟h\ this	\yu̇\ cure
\ä\ cot, cart	\g\ go	\ō\ bone	\ü\ food	\zh\ vision

[2]sit·u·ate \ˈsich-ə-ˌwāt\ *vt* : to place in a site or situation

sit·u·at·ed \-ˌwāt-əd\ *adj* **1** : having a site : LOCATED **2** : CIRCUMSTANCED ⟨not rich but comfortably *situated*⟩

sit·u·a·tion \ˌsich-ə-ˈwā-shən\ *n* **1 a** : the way in which something is placed in relation to its surroundings **b** : SITE 1 **2 a** : position or place of employment : POST, JOB **b** : position in life : STATUS **3** : position with respect to conditions and circumstances ⟨the military *situation*⟩ **4 a** : relative position or combination of circumstances at a certain moment ⟨the *situation* at the beginning of the trial⟩ **b** : a particular or striking complex of affairs at a stage in the action of a narrative or drama — **sit·u·a·tion·al** \-shnəl, -shən-l\ *adj* — **sit·u·a·tion·al·ly** \-ē\ *adv*

sit–up \ˈsit-ˌəp\ *n* : a conditioning exercise performed in a supine position by raising the trunk to a sitting position usually while keeping the legs straight and returning to the original position

sit up \sit-ˈəp\ *vi* **1** : to rise from a lying to a sitting position **2** : to show interest, alertness, or surprise **3** : to stay up beyond the usual bedtime

si·tus \ˈsīt-əs\ *n* : the place where something exists or originates [Latin, "place, site"]

sitz bath \ˈsits-\ *n* : a tub in which one bathes in a sitting position; *also* : a bath so taken especially therapeutically [German *sitzbad,* from *sitz* "act of sitting" + *bad* "bath"]

sitz·mark \ˈsit-ˌsmärk, ˈzit-\ *n* : a depression left in the snow by a skier falling backward [German *sitzmarke,* from *sitz* "act of sitting" + *marke* "mark"]

six \ˈsiks\ *n* **1** : one more than five; *also* : a symbol representing this — see NUMBER table **2** : the sixth in a set or series **3** : something having six units or members; *esp* : a 6-cylinder engine or automobile [Old English *siex*] — **six** *adj or pron* — **at sixes and sevens** : in disorder

six–gun \ˈsiks-ˌgən\ *n* : a 6-chambered revolver

six–o–six *or* **606** \ˌsik-ˌsō-ˈsiks\ *n* : ARSPHENAMINE [from its having been the 606th compound tested and introduced by Paul Ehrlich, died 1915, German bacteriologist]

six–pack \ˈsik-ˌspak\ *n* **1** : a package of six items (as bottles or cans) **2** : the contents of a six-pack

six·pence \ˈsik-spəns, *in the United States also* -ˌspens\ *n* : the sum of six pence; *also* : a British coin no longer issued worth six pence or half a shilling

six·pen·ny \-spə-nē, *in the United States also* -ˌspen-ē\ *adj* : costing or worth sixpence

six–shoot·er \ˈsik-ˈshüt-ər, ˈsiks-\ *n* : SIX-GUN

six·teen \sik-ˈstēn, ˈsik-\ *n* : one more than 15; *also* : a symbol representing this — see NUMBER table [Old English *sixtȳne*] — **sixteen** *adj or pron* — **six·teenth** \-ˈstēnth, -stēntth\ *adj or n*

sixteenth note *n* : a musical note with the time value of 1/16 of a whole note

sixth \ˈsiksth, ˈsikstth, ˈsikst\ *n* : number six in a countable series — see NUMBER table — **sixth** *adj or adv* — **sixth·ly** \-lē\ *adv*

sixth sense *n* : a keen intuitive power

six·ty \ˈsik-stē\ *n, pl* **sixties** : ten more than 50; *also* : a symbol representing this — see NUMBER table [Old English *siextig*] — **six·ti·eth** \-stē-əth\ *adj or n* — **sixty** *adj or pron*

six·ty–fourth note \ˌsik-stē-ˈfōrth-, -ˈfȯrth-\ *n* : a musical note with the time value of 1/64 of a whole note

siz·able *or* **size·able** \ˈsī-zə-bəl\ *adj* : fairly large — **siz·able·ness** *n* — **siz·ably** \-blē\ *adv*

[1]size \ˈsīz\ *n* **1 a** : physical magnitude, extent, or bulk : relative or proportionate dimensions **b** : considerable proportions : BIGNESS **2** : one of a series of graduated measures especially of manufactured articles (as of clothing) conventionally identified by numbers or letters ⟨a *size* 7 hat⟩ **3** : character or status of a person or thing especially with reference to importance, merit, or correspondence to needs **4** : actual state of affairs : true condition ⟨that's about the *size* of it⟩ [Middle French *sise* "assize", short for *assise*]

[2]size *vt* **1** : to make a particular size : bring to proper or suitable size **2** : to arrange, grade, or classify as to size or bulk **3** : to form a judgment of — usually used with *up* ⟨*size* a job up⟩ ⟨*sizing* up the candidates⟩

[3]size *n* : a gluey material (as a preparation of glue, flour, varnish, or resins) used for filling the pores in a surface (as of plaster), as a stiffener (as of fabric), or as an adhesive for applying color or leaf to book edges or covers [Middle English *sise*]

[4]size *vt* : to apply size to

[5]size *adj* : SIZED 1 ⟨bite-*size*⟩

sized \ˈsīzd\ *adj* **1** : having a specified size or bulk ⟨a small-*sized* house⟩ **2** : arranged or adjusted by size

siz·ing \ˈsī-zing\ *n* : [3]SIZE

siz·zle \ˈsiz-əl\ *vb* **siz·zled**; **siz·zling** \ˈsiz-ling, -ə-ling\ **1** : to burn up or sear with or as if with a hissing sound **2** : to make a hissing sound in or as if in burning or frying **3** : SEETHE 4 [perhaps from earlier *siss* "to hiss"] — **sizzle** *n* — **siz·zler** \ˈsiz-lər, -ə-lər\ *n*

skald \ˈskȯld, ˈskäld\ *n* : an ancient Scandinavian poet or writer of history [Old Norse *skāld*] — **skald·ic** \-ik\ *adj*

[1]skate \ˈskāt\ *n* : any of numerous rays with broadly winglike lateral fins [Old Norse *skata*]

[2]skate *n* : a metal runner or a set of two pairs of wheels in tandem on a frame that may be attached to the bottom of a boot for use in gliding over ice or rolling over a hard flat surface; *also* : a boot with an attached runner or wheels [Dutch *schaats* "stilt, skate"]

[3]skate *vi* **1** : to glide on skates propelled by the alternate pushing action of the legs **2** : to slip or glide as if on skates — **skat·er** *n*

[4]skate *n* **1** : a thin awkward-looking or decrepit horse : NAG **2** : FELLOW 4a [probably from English dialect *skite* "offensive person"]

skate·board \ˈskāt-ˌbōrd, -ˌbȯrd\ *n* : a short narrow board with two pairs of wheels mounted on the bottom in such a way that they will turn in the direction that the board is tilted — **skate·board·er** \-ˌbōrd-ər, -ˌbȯrd-\ *n* — **skate·board·ing** \-ing\ *n*

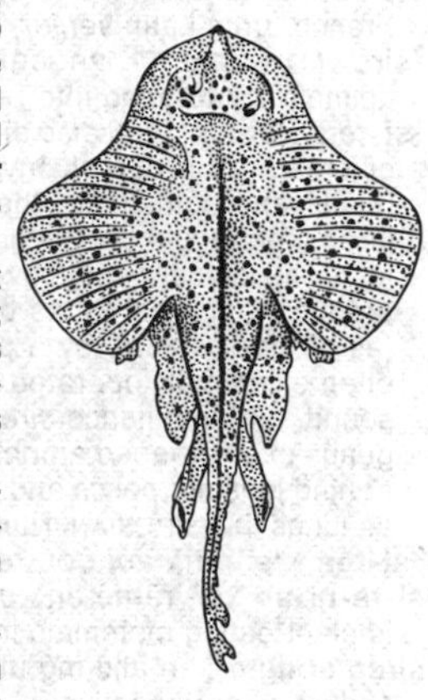

[1]skate

skat·ing \ˈskāt-ing\ *n* : the sport or pastime of gliding on skates; *esp* : competition that involves racing or the performance of fancy maneuvers or dance patterns on skates

ske·dad·dle \ski-ˈdad-l\ *vi* **-dad·dled**; **-dad·dling** \-ˈdad-ling, -l-ing\ : to run away; *esp* : to flee in a panic [origin unknown]

skeet \ˈskēt\ *n* : clay pigeon shooting on a semicircular range with targets thrown from either of two traps so as to provide a variety of shooting angles [Old Norse *skjōta* "to shoot"]

[1]skein \ˈskān\ *n* : a looped length of yarn or thread put up in a loose twist after it is taken from the reel [Middle French *escaigne*]

[2]skein *vt* : to wind into skeins ⟨*skein* yarn⟩

skel·e·tal \ˈskel-ət-l\ *adj* : of, relating or attached to, forming, or resembling a skeleton ⟨*skeletal* muscles⟩ ⟨the *skeletal* system⟩ — **skel·e·tal·ly** \-l-ē\ *adv*

[1]skel·e·ton \ˈskel-ət-n\ *n* **1** : a usually rigid supporting or protecting structure or framework of an organism; *esp* : the framework of bone or sometimes cartilage that supports the soft tissues and protects the internal organs of a vertebrate (as a fish or human) **2** : something reduced to its minimum form or essential parts **3** : an emaciated person or animal **4** : something forming a structural framework **5** : something shameful and kept secret (as in a family) [Greek, neuter of *skeletos* "dried up"]

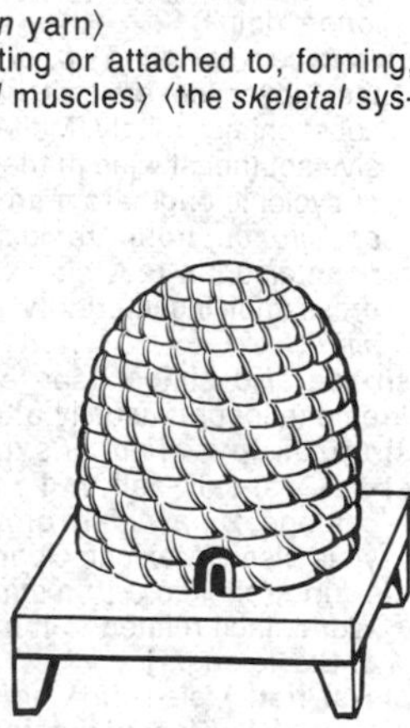

skep

[2]skeleton *adj* : of, consisting of, or resembling a skeleton ⟨a *skeleton* crew⟩

skel·e·ton·ize \ˈskel-ət-n-ˌīz\ *vt* : to produce in or reduce to skeleton form

skel·e·ton·iz·er \-ˌī-zər\ *n* : a

moth or butterfly larva that feeds on leaves reducing them to a skeleton of veins
skeleton key *n* : a key made to open many locks
skel•ter \ˈskel-tər\ *vi* : SCURRY [from *helter-skelter*]
skep \ˈskep\ *n* : a domed beehive made of twisted straw [Old English *sceppe* "basketful", from Old Norse *skeppa* "bushel"]
skep•tic *or* **scep•tic** \ˈskep-tik\ *n* **1** : an adherent or advocate of skepticism **2** : a person slow to believe or ready to question : DOUBTER [Greek *skeptikos,* from *skeptikos* "thoughtful", from *skeptesthai* "to look, consider"]
skep•ti•cal \-ti-kəl\ *adj* : relating to, characteristic of, or marked by skepticism — **skep•ti•cal•ly** \-kə-lē, -klē\ *adv*
skep•ti•cism \ˈskep-tə-ˌsiz-əm\ *n* **1** : the philosophical doctrine that true and absolute knowledge is unattainable **2** : an attitude of doubt, suspicion, or uncertainty especially about religious matters
sker•ry \ˈsker-ē\ *n, pl* **skerries** : a rocky isle : REEF [of Scandinavian origin]
1sketch \ˈskech\ *n* **1 a** : a rough drawing representing the chief features of an object or scene and often made as a preliminary study **b** : a tentative draft (as for a literary work) **2** : a brief description or outline **3 a** : a short literary composition somewhat resembling the short story and the essay but intentionally casual in treatment and familiar in tone **b** : a short instrumental composition **c** : a theatrical piece having a single scene; *esp* : a brief comic skit [Dutch *schets,* from Italian *schizzo* "sketch, splash", from *schizzare* "to splash"]
2sketch *vb* **1** : to make a sketch, rough draft, or outline of **2** : to draw or paint sketches — **sketch•er** *n*
sketch•book \ˈskech-ˌbu̇k\ *n* : a book of or for sketches
sketchy \ˈskech-ē\ *adj* **sketch•i•er**; **-est** **1** : of the nature of a sketch : roughly outlined **2** : lacking in completeness, clearness, or polish — **sketch•i•ly** \ˈskech-ə-lē\ *adv* — **sketch•i•ness** \ˈskech-ē-nəs\ *n*
1skew \ˈskyü\ *vb* **1** : to take an oblique course : move or turn aside : TWIST, SWERVE **2** : to make, set, or cut on the skew **3** : to distort from a true value or symmetrical form [Old North French *escuer* "to shun", of Germanic origin]
2skew *adj* **1** : set, placed, or running obliquely to something else **2** : neither parallel nor intersecting ⟨*skew* lines⟩ — **skew•ness** \ˈskyü-nəs\ *n*
3skew *n* : a deviation from a straight line : SLANT
skew•bald \ˈskyü-ˌbȯld\ *adj* : marked with spots and patches of white and some other color ⟨a *skewbald* horse⟩ [earlier *skewed* "skewbald" + *bald*]
1skew•er \ˈskyü-ər, ˈskyu̇-ər, ˈskyu̇r\ *n* **1** : a pin for keeping meat in form while roasting or for holding small pieces of meat and vegetables for broiling **2** : something shaped or used like a meat skewer [probably from earlier *skiver* "cutter", from *skive* "to cut, pare", of Scandinavian origin]
2skewer *vt* : to fasten or pierce with or as if with a skewer
skew quadrilateral *n* : a quadrilateral in which not all four vertices lie in the same plane
1ski \ˈskē\ *n, pl* **skis** : one of a pair of narrow strips of wood, metal, or plastic curving upward in front that are worn by people for gliding over snow or water [Norwegian, from Old Norse *skīth* "stick, ski"]
2ski *vi* **skied**; **ski•ing** : to glide on skis — **ski•er** *n*
ski boot *n* : a boot or shoe used for skiing; *esp* : a heavy rigid boot that extends above the ankle
1skid \ˈskid\ *n* **1** : a log or plank for supporting something (as above the ground) ⟨put a boat on *skids*⟩ **2** : one of the logs, planks, or rails along or on which something heavy is rolled or slid **3** : a device placed under a carriage wheel to prevent its turning : DRAG **4** : a runner used as part of the landing gear of an airplane or helicopter **5** : the act of skidding : SLIDE [perhaps of Scandinavian origin] — **on the skids** : declining sharply (as in value, status, or prominence)

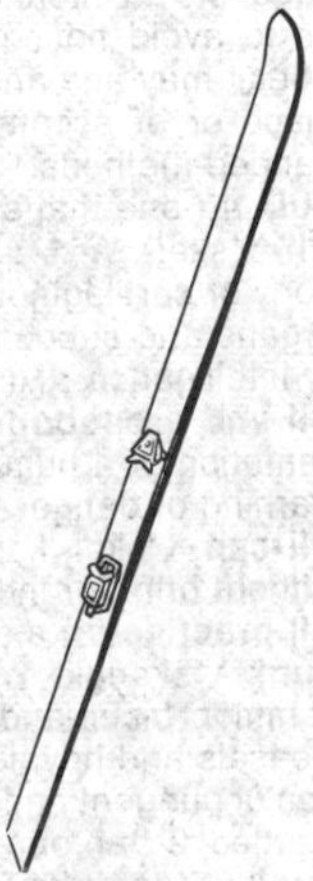
1ski

2skid *vb* **skid•ded**; **skid•ding** **1** : to slow or halt by use of a skid **2** : to haul along, slide, hoist, or store on skids **3 a** : to fail to grip the roadway; *esp* : to slip sideways on the road ⟨the car *skidded* on an icy road⟩ **b** : to slide sideways away from the center of curvature when turning ⟨a *skidding* airplane⟩ **c** : SLIDE, SLIP ⟨*skid* across ice⟩ **4** : to fall rapidly, steeply, or far ⟨the temperature *skidded* to zero⟩
skid•doo *or* **ski•doo** \skid-ˈü\ *vi* : to go away : DEPART [probably alteration of *skedaddle*]
skid row \ˈskid-ˈrō\ *n* : a district of cheap saloons and rooming houses frequented by vagrants and derelicts [from *skid road* "road along which logs are dragged, section of town frequented by loggers"]
skiff \ˈskif\ *n* **1** : a small rowboat or sailboat **2** : a small fast motorboat [Italian *schifo,* of Germanic origin]
ski•ing *n* : the art or sport of sliding and jumping on skis
ski jump *n* : a jump made by a person wearing skis; *also* : a course or track especially prepared for such jumping — **ski jump** *vi*
ski lift *n* : a power-driven conveyor for transporting skiers or sightseers up a long slope or mountainside
skill \ˈskil\ *n* **1** : ability or dexterity that comes from training or practice **2** : a developed or acquired ability : ACCOMPLISHMENT ⟨reading *skills*⟩ [Old Norse *skil* "distinction, knowledge"] **syn** see ART
skilled \ˈskild\ *adj* **1** : having acquired mastery of a skill : EXPERT ⟨a *skilled* mason⟩ **2** : requiring skill and training ⟨a *skilled* trade⟩
• **syn** SKILLFUL: SKILLED applies to one who has mastered the details and technique of a trade, art, or profession ⟨*skilled* craftsmen⟩ SKILLFUL stresses adeptness and dexterity as individual qualities rather than standards ⟨*skillful* performance of a concerto⟩
skil•let \ˈskil-ət\ *n* : a frying pan [Middle English *skelet*]
skill•ful *or* **skil•ful** \ˈskil-fəl\ *adj* **1** : having or displaying skill : EXPERT, DEXTEROUS ⟨a *skillful* debater⟩ **2** : accomplished with skill ⟨*skillful* defense⟩ **syn** see PROFICIENT, SKILLED — **skill•ful•ly** \-fə-lē\ *adv* — **skill•ful•ness** *n*
skill-less *or* **skil•less** \ˈskil-ləs\ *adj* : having no skill — **skill-less•ness** *n*
1skim \ˈskim\ *vb* **skimmed**; **skim•ming** **1 a** : to clear (a liquid) of scum or floating substance : remove (as film or scum) from the surface of a liquid **b** : to remove cream from by skimming **2** : to read, study, or examine superficially and rapidly; *esp* : to glance through (as a book) for the chief ideas or the plot **3** : to throw so as to ricochet along the surface of water **4** : to cover or become covered with or as if with a film or scum **5** : to pass swiftly or lightly over : glide above or near a surface [Middle English *skimmen*]
2skim *n* **1** : a thin layer, coating, or film **2** : the act of skimming **3** : something (as milk) that is skimmed
3skim *adj* **1** : that has been skimmed **2** : made of skim milk ⟨*skim* cheese⟩
skim•mer \ˈskim-ər\ *n* **1** : one that skims; *esp* : a flat perforated scoop or spoon used for skimming **2** : any of several long-winged seabirds related to the terns that fly low over the water **3** : a usually straw flat-crowned hat with a wide straight brim
skim milk *also* **skimmed milk** *n* : milk from which the cream has been taken
skim•ming \ˈskim-ing\ *n* **1** : material skimmed from a liquid **2** : the practice of concealing gambling profits so as to avoid taxes
ski•mo•bile \ˈskē-mō-ˌbēl\ *n* : SNOWMOBILE
skimp \ˈskimp\ *vb* **1** : to give insufficient or barely sufficient attention or effort to or funds for **2** : to save by or as if by skimping [perhaps alteration of *scrimp*]
skimpy \ˈskim-pē\ *adj* **skimp•i•er**; **-est** : deficient (as in supply) especially through skimping : SCANTY — **skimp•i•ly** \-pə-lē\ *adv* — **skimp•i•ness** \-pē-nəs\ *n*
1skin \ˈskin\ *n* **1 a** : the integument of an animal and especially of a small animal or furbearer when separated from the body — compare HIDE **b** : a sheet of parchment or vellum made from a hide **c** : BOTTLE 1b **2 a** : the external limiting layer of an animal

\ə\ **abut**	\au̇\ **out**	\i\ **tip**	\ȯ\ **saw**	\u̇\ **foot**
\ər\ **further**	\ch\ **chin**	\ī\ **life**	\ȯi\ **coin**	\y\ **yet**
\a\ **mat**	\e\ **pet**	\j\ **job**	\th\ **thin**	\yü\ **few**
\ā\ **take**	\ē\ **easy**	\ng\ **sing**	\t͟h\ **this**	\yu̇\ **cure**
\ä\ **cot, cart**	\g\ **go**	\ō\ **bone**	\ü\ **food**	\zh\ **vision**

body especially when forming a tough but flexible cover; *also* : the 2-layered tissue of which this is formed in a vertebrate — compare DERMIS, EPIDERMIS **b** : an outer or surface layer (as a rind) ⟨a sausage *skin*⟩ ⟨apple *skins*⟩ **3** : the life or physical well-being of a person ⟨save one's *skin*⟩ **4** : a sheathing or casing forming the outside surface of a structure (as a ship or airplane) [Old Norse *skinn*] — **skin·less** \-ləs\ *adj* — **skinned** \'skind\ *adj* — **by the skin of one's teeth** : by a very narrow margin — **under one's skin** : beneath one's surface powers of resistance to the point of distressing or irritating

²skin *vb* **skinned**; **skin·ning** **1** : to cover or become covered with or as if with skin **2 a** : to strip, scrape, or rub off the skin of ⟨*skin* a fruit⟩ ⟨*skin* one's knee⟩ **b** : to strip or peel off **3 a** : CHEAT 1, FLEECE **b** : OUTDO **c** : CENSURE, REPRIMAND **4 a** : to climb up or down ⟨*skin* up and down a rope⟩ **b** : to pass or get by with scant room to spare

skin-deep \'skin-'dēp\ *adj* **1** : as deep as the skin **2** : SUPERFICIAL; *esp* : not thorough or lasting in impression

skin-dive \'skin-,dīv\ *vi* : to engage in skin diving — **skin diver** *n*

skin diving *n* : the sport of swimming underwater with a mask, swim fins, and usually a snorkel especially without scuba equipment

skin·flint \'skin-,flint\ *n* : a person who is very hard and grasping in money matters

skin·ful \-,fu̇l\ *n* **1** : the contents of a skin bottle **2** : a large or satisfying quantity especially of liquor

skin game *n* : a swindling game or trick

skin graft *n* : a piece of skin transferred from a donor area to grow new skin at a place denuded (as by burning)

skink \'skingk\ *n* : any of a family of mostly small lizards with small scales [Latin *scincus*, from Greek *skinkos*]

skin·ner \'skin-ər\ *n* **1** : one that removes and processes or deals in skins, pelts, or hides **2** : a driver of draft animals and especially mules

skin·ny \'skin-ē\ *adj* **skin·ni·er**; **-est** **1** : resembling skin : MEMBRANOUS ⟨a *skinny* layer⟩ **2** : very thin : LEAN, EMACIATED — **skin·ni·ness** *n*

skin·ny-dip·ping \'skin-ē-,dip-ing\ *n* : swimming in the nude — **skin·ny-dip·per** \-,dip-ər\ *n*

skin test *n* : a test (as a scratch test) performed on the skin and used in detecting allergic hypersensitivity

skin·tight \'skin-'tīt\ *adj* : closely fitted to the figure

¹skip \'skip\ *vb* **skipped**; **skip·ping** **1 a** : to move or proceed with leaps and bounds **b** : to bound or cause to bound off one point after another **c** : to leap over lightly and nimbly **2** : to depart hurriedly or secretly ⟨*skip* town⟩ **3 a** : to pass over or omit (as an interval, item, or step) **b** : to omit or cause to omit a grade in school in advancing to the next **c** : to pass over without notice or mention **d** : to fail to attend ⟨*skipped* the meeting⟩ **e** : MISFIRE 1 [Middle English *skippen*]

²skip *n* **1 a** : a light bounding step **b** : a gait composed of alternating hops and steps **2** : an act of omission or the thing omitted

³skip *n* : the captain of a side in some games (as curling or lawn bowling) [short for ²*skipper*]

⁴skip *vt* **skipped**; **skip·ping** : to act as skipper of

skip·jack \'skip-,jak\ *n, pl* **skipjacks** *or* **skipjack** : any of various fishes (as a bonito or bluefish) that jump above or play at the surface of the water

ski pole *n* : a pointed pole or stick used as an aid in skiing that is fitted with a strap for the hand at the top and an encircling disk set a little above the point

¹skip·per \'skip-ər\ *n* **1** : one that skips **2 a** : any of numerous small stout-bodied insects of swift erratic flight that differ from the typical butterflies in wing venation and the form of the antennae **b** : any of several small leaping insects ⟨cheese *skippers*⟩

²skipper *n* : the master of a ship; *esp* : the master of a fishing, small trading, or pleasure boat [Dutch *schipper*, from *schip* "ship"]

¹skirl \'skərl, 'skirl\ *vb* : to sound the high shrill tone of the bagpipe [of Scandinavian origin]

²skirl *n* : the high shrill sound of a bagpipe

¹skir·mish \'skər-mish\ *n* **1** : a minor fight in war **2** : a brisk preliminary conflict [Middle French *escarmouche*, from Italian *scaramuccia*, of Germanic origin]

²skirmish *vi* **1** : to engage in a skirmish **2** : to search about (as for supplies) — **skir·mish·er** *n*

¹skirr \'skər\ *vb* **1** : to leave hurriedly : FLEE; *also* : to move rapidly **2** : to pass rapidly over especially in search of something [perhaps from ¹*scour*]

²skirr *n* : WHIR, ROAR [probably imitative]

¹skirt \'skərt\ *n* **1 a** : a free hanging part of a garment extending from the waist down **b** : a separate free hanging garment for women and girls covering the body from the waist down **c** : either of two flaps on a saddle covering the bars on which the stirrups are hung **2** *pl* : the outlying parts of a town or city : OUTSKIRTS **3** : a part or attachment serving as a rim, border, or edging **4** *slang* : GIRL 1b, WOMAN [Old Norse *skyrta* "shirt, kirtle"]

²skirt *vb* **1** : to form or run along the edge of : BORDER **2** : to provide a skirt or border for **3 a** : to go or pass around or about; *esp* : to go around or keep away from in order to avoid danger or discovery **b** : to evade or miss by a narrow margin **4** : to be, lie, or move along an edge, border, or margin — **skirt·er** *n*

skirt·ing \'skərt-ing\ *n* **1** : something that skirts: as **a** : BORDER 1, MARGIN **b** *British* : BASEBOARD **2** : fabric suitable for skirts

ski run *n* : a slope or trail suitable for skiing

ski suit *n* : a warm outfit for winter sports made in one-piece or two-piece style with a jacket top and pants

skit \'skit\ *n* **1** : a satirical or humorous story or sketch; *esp* : a sketch included in a dramatic performance (as a revue) **2** : a short serious dramatic piece; *esp* : one done by amateurs [origin unknown]

ski tow *n* **1** : a power-driven conveyor for pulling skiers to the top of a slope that consists usually of an endless motor-driven moving rope which the skier grasps **2** : SKI LIFT

skit·ter \'skit-ər\ *vb* : to glide or skip lightly or quickly : skim along a surface [probably from English dialect *skite* "to move quickly"]

skit·tish \'skit-ish\ *adj* **1** : lively or frivolous in nature or action **2** : easily frightened : RESTIVE ⟨a *skittish* horse⟩ **3** : hard to deal with or manage : TRICKY **4 a** : tensely nervous or cautious : WARY **b** : inclined to be shy : COY [Middle English] — **skit·tish·ly** *adv* — **skit·tish·ness** *n*

skit·tle \'skit-l\ *n* **1** *pl* : an English version of ninepins played either with wooden disks or a ball **2** : one of the pins used in skittles [perhaps of Scandinavian origin]

skoal \'skōl\ *n* : TOAST 3, HEALTH — often used interjectionally [Danish *skaal*, literally, "cup"]

skua \'skyü-ə\ *n* : JAEGER; *esp* : a large North Atlantic jaeger [New Latin, of Scandinavian origin]

skul·dug·gery *or* **skull·dug·gery** \,skəl-'dəg-rē, -ə-rē\ *n, pl* **-ger·ies** : underhanded or unscrupulous behavior [origin unknown]

¹skulk \'skəlk\ *vi* **1** : to move in a stealthy or furtive manner : SNEAK **2** : to hide or conceal oneself from cowardice or fear or with treacherous intent [of Scandinavian origin] — **skulk·er** *n*

• **syn** SKULK, SLINK, SNEAK mean to go or act so as to escape attention. SKULK may imply shyness or cowardice but often suggests an intent to spy or waylay; SLINK stresses a moving so as to avoid notice rather than keeping actually out of sight; SNEAK may add an implication of furtively entering or leaving a place or of accomplishing a purpose by indirect and underhanded methods.

²skulk *n* : one that skulks

skull \'skəl\ *n* **1** : the vertebrate head skeleton that forms a bony or cartilaginous case enclosing the brain and chief sense organs and supporting the jaws **2** : the seat of understanding or intelligence : MIND [of Scandinavian origin]

skull and crossbones *n, pl* **skulls and crossbones** : a representation of a human skull over crossbones usually used as a warning of danger to life

skull·cap \'skəl-,kap\ *n* : a close-fitting cap; *esp* : a light cap without brim for indoor wear

skull practice *n* : a strategy class for an athletic team

¹skunk \'skəngk\ *n, pl* **skunks** *also* **skunk** **1** : any of various common black-and-white New World mammals related to the weasels and having glands near the anus from which a secretion of pungent and offensive odor is ejected when the animal is startled **2** : an obnoxious person [of American Indian origin]

²skunk *vt* : to defeat decisively; *esp* : to shut out in a game

skunk cabbage *n* : an American perennial marsh herb of the arum family that sends up in early spring a cowl-shaped ill-smelling brownish purple spathe

sky \'skī\ *n, pl* **skies** **1** : the expanse of space that appears to constitute a vault over the earth **2** : HEAVEN 2 **3** : WEATHER, CLIMATE ⟨the weatherman predicts sunny *skies*⟩ [Old Norse *ský* "cloud"]

sky blue *n* : a pale to light blue

sky•borne \'skī-,bōrn, -,bȯrn\ *adj* : AIRBORNE ⟨*skyborne* troops⟩

1skylark

sky•cap \-,kap\ *n* : a person employed to carry hand luggage at an airport [*sky* + *-cap* (as in *redcap*)]

sky•div•ing \-,dī-ving\ *n* : the sport of jumping from an airplane with a parachute at a moderate altitude (as 2000 meters) and performing various maneuvers before opening the parachute or attempting to land on a small target on the ground — **sky diver** *n*

sky•ey \'skī-ē\ *adj* : of or resembling the sky : ETHEREAL

sky–high \'skī-'hī\ *adv or adj* **1 a** : high into the air **b** : to a very high level : SOARING ⟨our spirits rose *sky-high*⟩ ⟨profits were *sky-high*⟩ **2** : in an enthusiastic manner **3** : to bits : APART ⟨blown *sky-high*⟩

sky•jack•er \-,jak-ər\ *n* : one who commandeers a flying airplane (as by coercing the pilot at gunpoint) [*sky* + *-jacker* (as in *hijacker*)] — **sky•jack•ing** \-,jak-ing\ *n*

1sky•lark \'skī-,lärk\ *n* : a common Old World lark that sings as it rises in almost perpendicular flight

2skylark *vi* : to play wild boisterous pranks : FROLIC — **sky•lark•er** *n*

1skunk 1

sky•light \'skī-,līt\ *n* : a window or group of windows in a roof or ceiling

sky•line \-,līn\ *n* **1** : the line where earth and sky seem to meet : HORIZON **2** : an outline against the sky ⟨a *skyline* of tall buildings⟩

sky pilot *n* : CLERGYMAN; *esp* : CHAPLAIN

1sky•rock•et \'skī-,räk-ət\ *n* : ROCKET 1

2skyrocket *vb* : to rise or cause to rise abruptly and rapidly ⟨prices are *skyrocketing*⟩

sky•scrap•er \'skī-,skrā-pər\ *n* : a very tall building

sky•ward \'skī-wərd\ *adv or adj* **1** : toward the sky ⟨gaze *skyward*⟩ **2** : to a higher level

sky•way \'skī-,wā\ *n* **1** : a route used by airplanes : AIR LANE **2** : an elevated highway

sky•writ•ing \'skī-,rīt-ing\ *n* : writing formed in the sky by means of a visible substance (as smoke) emitted from an airplane — **sky•writ•er** \-,rīt-ər\ *n*

slab \'slab\ *n* **1** : a thick slice or plate (as of stone, wood, or bread) **2** : the outside piece cut from a log in squaring it [Middle English *slabbe*]

slab•ber \'slab-ər\ *vb* **slab•bered**; **slab•ber•ing** \'slab-ring, -ə-ring\ : SLOBBER 1, DROOL [probably from Dutch *slabberen*, from *slabben* "to slaver"] — **slabber** *n*

slab–sid•ed \'slab-'sīd-əd\ *adj* : having flat sides; *also* : being tall or long and lank

1slack \'slak\ *adj* **1** : not properly diligent, careful, or prompt : NEGLIGENT **2** : marked by slowness or lack of energy ⟨a *slack* pace⟩ **3 a** : not tight or tightly drawn ⟨a *slack* rope⟩ **b** : lacking in firmness : WEAK ⟨*slack* control⟩ **4** : wanting in activity : DULL ⟨the *slack* season⟩ [Old English *sleac*] — **slack•ly** *adv* — **slack•ness** *n*

2slack *vb* **1 a** : to be or become slack or negligent in performing or doing ⟨*slack* one's vigilance⟩ **b** : MODERATE 1 ⟨the wind *slacked* off⟩ **2** : to shirk or evade work or duty **3** : LOOSEN 2 **4 a** : to cause to abate **b** : SLAKE 4

3slack *n* **1** : cessation in movement or flow **2** : a part of something that hangs loose without strain ⟨the *slack* of a rope⟩ **3** *pl* : pants especially for casual wear **4** : a dull season or period : LULL

4slack *n* : fine screenings of coal containing wastes that make it unusable as fuel unless cleaned [Middle English *sleck*]

slack•en \'slak-ən\ *vb* **slack•ened**; **slack•en•ing** \'slak-ning, -ə-ning\ **1** : to make or become less active : slow up ⟨*slacken* speed⟩ **2** : to make less taut : LOOSEN ⟨*slacken* sail⟩ **3** : SLACK 1a

slack•er \'slak-ər\ *n* : one who shirks work or evades an obligation especially for military service in time of war

slack water *n* : the period at the turn of the tide when there is little or no horizontal motion of tidal water

slag \'slag\ *n* **1** : waste left after the smelting of ore **2** : volcanic lava resembling cinders [Low German *slagge*] — **slag•gy** \'slag-ē\ *adj*

slain *past participle of* SLAY

slake \'slāk, *3 & 4 are also* 'slak\ *vb* **1** *archaic* : to make or become less violent, intense, or severe : ABATE, MODERATE **2** : to relieve or satisfy with water or liquid : QUENCH ⟨*slake* one's thirst⟩ **3** : to become slaked ⟨lime may *slake* spontaneously in moist air⟩ **4 a** : to cause (lime) to heat and crumble by treatment with water : HYDRATE **b** : to alter (lime) by exposure to air with conversion at least in part to a carbonate [Old English *slacian*, from *sleac* "slack"]

sla•lom \'släl-əm\ *n* **1** : skiing in a zigzag or wavy course between upright obstacles (as flags) **2** : a race against time over a zigzag course [Norwegian, literally, "sloping track"]

1slam \'slam\ *n* : the winning of all or all but one of the tricks of a deal in bridge [origin unknown]

2slam *n* **1** : a heavy impact **2 a** : a noisy violent closing **b** : a banging noise especially from the slamming of a door **3** : a cutting or violent criticism [probably of Scandinavian origin]

3slam *vb* **slammed**; **slam•ming** **1** : to strike or beat hard **2** : to shut forcibly and noisily : BANG ⟨*slam* the door⟩ **3 a** : to set or slap down violently or noisily ⟨*slammed* my fist on the table⟩ **b** : to put or set hard : JAM 2 ⟨*slammed* on the brakes⟩ **4** : to make a banging noise **5** : to criticize harshly

slam–bang \'slam-'bang\ *adv or adj* **1** : with noisy violence **2** : HEADLONG, RECKLESSLY

1slan•der \'slan-dər\ *n* **1** : the utterance of false charges or misrepresentations which defame and damage another's reputation **2** : a false and defamatory oral statement about a person — compare LIBEL [Old French *esclandre*, from Late Latin *scandalum* "stumbling block, offense", from Greek *skandalon*] — **slan•der•ous** \-də-rəs, -drəs\ *adj* — **slan•der•ous•ly** *adv* — **slan•der•ous•ness** *n*

2slander *vt* **slan•dered**; **slan•der•ing** \-də-ring, -dring\ : to utter slander against — **slan•der•er** \-dər-ər\ *n*

• **syn** SLANDER, DEFAME, MALIGN mean to injure by speaking ill of. SLANDER stresses the suffering of the victim regardless of the intent of the slanderer ⟨*slandered* by thoughtless tongues⟩ DEFAME stresses the actual loss of or injury to one's good name and repute ⟨turning traitor forever *defamed* the family name⟩ MALIGN usually suggests the operation of hatred, prejudice, or bigotry often by subtle misrepresentation rather than direct accusation ⟨*maligned* and persecuted by evil forces⟩

1slang \'slang\ *n* **1** : language peculiar to a particular group, trade, or pursuit ⟨baseball *slang*⟩ **2** : an informal nonstandard vocabulary composed typically of often short-lived coinages, arbitrarily changed words, and extravagant, forced, or facetious figures of speech [origin unknown] **syn** see DIALECT — **slang** *adj*

2slang *vb* **1** *chiefly British* : to abuse with harsh or coarse language **2** : to use slang or vulgar abuse

slangy \'slang-ē\ *adj* **slang•i•er**; **-est** **1** : of, relating to, or being slang : containing slang **2** : addicted to the use of slang — **slang•i•ly** \'slang-ə-lē\ *adv* — **slang•i•ness** \'slang-ē-nəs\ *n*

1slant \'slant\ *vb* **1** : to turn or incline from a straight line or a level : SLOPE **2** : to interpret or present in accordance with a special viewpoint ⟨stories *slanted* toward young adults⟩ [of Scandinavian origin]

2slant *n* **1** : a slanting direction, line, or plane : SLOPE **2 a** : something that slants **b** : DIAGONAL 3 **3** : a way of looking at something ⟨considered the problem from a new *slant*⟩ **4** : GLANCE 3, LOOK — **slant** *adj*

slant height *n* **1** : the length of a line segment lying in the lateral surface of a right circular cone **2** : the altitude of a lateral face of a regular pyramid

slant•ways \'slant-,wāz\ *adv* : SLANTWISE

slant•wise \-,wīz\ *adv or adj* : so as to slant : at a slant : in a slanting direction or position

¹slap \'slap\ *n* **1** : a quick sharp blow especially with the open hand; *also* : a noise suggesting that of a slap **2** : INSULT 1, SNUB [Low German *slapp*]

²slap *vb* **slapped; slap•ping 1 a** : to strike with or as if with the open hand **b** : to make a sound like that of a slap **2** : to put, place, or throw with careless haste or force ⟨*slapped* down the paper⟩ **3** : to assail verbally : INSULT

³slap *adv* : DIRECTLY 1, SMACK

slap•dash \'slap-,dash, -'dash\ *adv or adj* : in a slipshod manner : HAPHAZARD; *also* : HASTILY

slap down *vt* **1** : to prohibit or restrain usually abruptly and with censure from acting in a specified way : SQUELCH **2** : to put an abrupt stop to : SUPPRESS

slap•jack \'slap-,jak\ *n* **1** : PANCAKE **2** : a card game for children in which each player tries to be first to slap a hand on any jack that is turned face up [²*slap* + *-jack* (as in *flapjack*)]

slap shot *n* : a shot in ice hockey made with a full swing that usually causes the puck to fly through the air

slap•stick \'slap-,stik\ *n* **1** : a device made of two flat sticks so fastened as to make a loud noise when used (as by a clown) to strike a person **2** : comedy stressing farce and horseplay — **slapstick** *adj*

¹slash \'slash\ *vb* **1** : to cut with rough sweeping blows : GASH **2** : to whip or strike with or as if with a cane **3** : to criticize without mercy **4** : to cut slits in (as a skirt) to reveal a color beneath **5** : to reduce sharply : CUT ⟨*slash* prices⟩ [Middle English *slaschen*] — **slash•er** *n*

²slash *n* **1** : an act or result of slashing: as **a** : a long cut or stroke made by slashing **b** : an ornamental slit in a garment **c** : a sharp reduction ⟨budget *slash*⟩ **2** : an open debris-strewn tract in a forest; *also* : the debris in such a tract **3** : DIAGONAL 3

³slash *n* : a low swampy area often overgrown with brush [probably from Old English *plæsc* "marshy pool"]

slash pine *n* : a southern pine important as a source of turpentine and lumber

slash pocket *n* : a pocket suspended on the wrong side of a garment from a finished slit on the right side that serves as its opening

slat \'slat\ *n* : a thin narrow flat strip of wood, plastic, or metal ⟨the *slats* of a blind⟩ [Middle French *esclat* "splinter", from *esclater* "to burst, splinter"] — **slat•ted** \'slat-əd\ *adj*

¹slate \'slāt\ *n* **1** : a fine-grained and usually bluish gray rock that is formed by compression of shales or other rocks and that splits readily into thin layers or plates; *also* : a piece of this (as a shingle) dressed for use **2** : a tablet of material (as slate) used for writing on **3** : something (as a list of candidates) recorded or made public as if written on a slate **4 a** : a dark purplish gray **b** : a gray similar in color to common roofing slate [Middle French *esclat* "splinter"] — **slate** *adj* — **slate•like** \-,līk\ *adj*

²slate *vt* **1** : to cover with slate or a slatelike substance ⟨*slate* a roof⟩ **2** : to register or schedule on or as if on a slate ⟨*slate* a meeting⟩ — **slat•er** \'slāt-ər\ *n*

slath•er \'sla<u>th</u>-ər\ *vt* **slath•ered; slath•er•ing** \'sla<u>th</u>-ring, -ə-ring\ **1** : to spread thickly or lavishly ⟨*slather* jam on bread⟩ **2** : to cover thickly or lavishly ⟨*slather* bread with jam⟩ [from earlier *slather* "great quantity", of unknown origin]

slat•tern \'slat-ərn\ *n* : an untidy slovenly woman [probably from German *schlottern* "to hang loosely, slouch"] — **slat-tern•li•ness** \-lē-nəs\ *n* — **slat•tern•ly** \-lē\ *adj or adv*

slaty \'slāt-ē\ *adj* : of, containing, or characteristic of slate; *also* : gray like slate

¹slaugh•ter \'slȯt-ər\ *n* **1** : the act of killing; *esp* : the butchering of livestock for market **2** : destruction of human lives especially in battle : CARNAGE [of Scandinavian origin]

²slaughter *vt* **1** : to kill (an animal) for food : BUTCHER **2** : to kill ruthlessly or in large numbers : MASSACRE — **slaugh•ter•er** \'slȯt-ər-ər\ *n*

slaugh•ter•house \'slȯt-ər-,hau̇s\ *n* : an establishment where animals are butchered

slaugh•ter•ous \'slȯt-ə-rəs\ *adj* : of or relating to slaughter : MURDEROUS — **slaugh•ter•ous•ly** *adv*

Slav \'släv, 'slav\ *n* : a native speaker of a Slavic language [Medieval Latin *Sclavus*, from Late Greek *Sklabos*, from *Sklabēnoi* "Slavs", of Slavic origin]

¹slave \'slāv\ *n* **1** : a person held in servitude as the property of another **2** : a person who has lost self-control and is dominated by something or someone ⟨a *slave* to drink⟩ **3** : DRUDGE, TOILER [Medieval Latin *sclavus*, from *Sclavus* "Slav"] — **slave** *adj*

△ **origin** In the Middle Ages the warring Germanic peoples subjugated a great part of the Slavic population of east-central Europe. Conquered Slavs were bought and sold as slaves throughout the West. The Slavs' own name for themselves became *Sclavus* in the Latin that served medieval Europe as a universal language. By the 9th or 10th century *sclavus* was used for any human chattel of no matter what origin. This *sclavus* is the ancestor of our English *slave*.

²slave *vi* : to work like a slave : DRUDGE

slave driver *n* **1** : a supervisor of slaves at work **2** : a harsh taskmaster

slave•hold•er \'slāv-,hōl-dər\ *n* : an owner of slaves — **slave-hold•ing** \-diŋ\ *adj or n*

¹sla•ver \'slav-ər, 'slāv-\ *vi* **sla•vered; sla•ver•ing** \'slav-riŋ, 'slāv-, -ə-riŋ\ : DROOL 1b, SLOBBER [of Scandinavian origin]

²slaver *n* : saliva dribbling from the mouth

³slav•er \'slā-vər\ *n* : a person or ship engaged in the slave trade

slav•ery \'slāv-rē, -ə-rē\ *n* **1** : DRUDGERY, TOIL **2 a** : the state of being a slave : SERVITUDE **b** : the practice of owning slaves

slave state *n* : a state of the United States in which slavery was legal until the Civil War

slave trade *n* : traffic in slaves; *esp* : the buying and selling of Negroes for profit prior to the American Civil War

slav•ey \'slā-vē\ *n, pl* **slaveys** : DRUDGE; *esp* : a servant who does general housework

¹Slav•ic \'slav-ik, 'släv-\ *adj* : of, relating to, or characteristic of the Slavs or their languages

²Slavic *n* : a branch of the Indo-European language family including Bulgarian, Czech, Polish, Serbo-Croatian, Slovene, Russian, and Ukrainian

slav•ish \'slā-vish\ *adj* **1** : of or characteristic of a slave : SERVILE **2** : lacking in independence or originality especially of thought ⟨*slavish* dependence on customary ways⟩ ⟨*slavish* imitators⟩ — **slav•ish•ly** *adv* — **slav•ish•ness** *n*

¹Sla•von•ic \slə-'vän-ik\ *adj* : SLAVIC [Medieval Latin *Sclavonia, Slavonia* "land of the Slavs"]

²Slavonic *n* **1** : SLAVIC **2** : OLD CHURCH SLAVONIC

slaw \'slȯ\ *n* : COLESLAW

slay \'slā\ *vb* **slew** \'slü\; **slain** \'slān\; **slay•ing** : to put to death violently : KILL [Old English *slēan* "to strike, slay"] **syn** see KILL — **slay•er** *n*

sleave \'slēv\ *n* : SKEIN [derived from Old English *-slǣfan* "to cut"]

slea•zy \'slē-zē, 'slā-\ *adj* **slea•zi•er; -est 1** : not firmly or closely woven : FLIMSY **2** : made carelessly of inferior material : SHODDY **3** : cheap in character or quality [origin unknown] — **slea•zi•ly** \-zə-lē\ *adv* — **slea•zi•ness** \-zē-nəs\ *n*

¹sled \'sled\ *n* **1** : a vehicle on runners for conveying loads especially over snow or ice **2** : a sled used for coasting on snow-covered slopes [Dutch *sledde*]

²sled *vb* **sled•ded; sled•ding** : to ride or carry on a sled or sleigh — **sled•der** *n*

sled•ding *n* **1** : the use of a sled; *also* : the conditions under which a sled is used **2** : GOING 2 ⟨tough *sledding*⟩

sled dog *n* : a dog trained to draw a sledge especially in the Arctic regions — called also *sledge dog*

¹sledge \'slej\ *n* : SLEDGEHAMMER [Old English *slecg*]

²sledge *n* : a vehicle with low runners that is used for transporting loads especially over snow or ice [Dutch dialect *sleedse*]

³sledge *vb* : to travel with or transport on a sledge

sledge•ham•mer \'slej-,ham-ər\ *n* : a large heavy hammer usually wielded with both hands [¹*sledge*] — **sledgehammer** *adj or vb*

¹sleek \'slēk\ *vb* **1** : to make or become sleek **2** : to cover up : gloss over [Middle English *sliken*]

²sleek *adj* **1 a** : smooth and glossy as if polished ⟨*sleek* dark hair⟩ **b** : having a smooth healthy well-groomed look ⟨*sleek* cattle⟩ **2** : having a prosperous air — **sleek•ly** *adv* — **sleek-ness** *n*

¹sleep \'slēp\ *n* **1** : the natural periodic suspension of consciousness during which the powers of the body are restored **2** : a state resembling sleep: as **a** : a state of torpid inactivity **b** : DEATH 4; *also* : TRANCE, COMA [Old English *slǣp*] — **sleep-like** \-ˌlīk\ *adj*

2**sleep** *vb* **slept** \'slept\; **sleep•ing** **1** : to rest or be in a state of sleep **2** : to have sexual relations **3** : to get rid of or spend in or by sleep ⟨*slept* away my cares⟩ **4** : to provide sleeping space for ⟨the boat *sleeps* six⟩

sleep•er \'slē-pər\ *n* **1** : one that sleeps **2** : a piece of timber, stone, or steel on or near the ground to support a superstructure, keep railroad rails in place, or receive floor joists **3** : SLEEPING CAR **4** : something unpromising or unnoticed that suddenly attains prominence or value

sleeping bag *n* : a bag that is warmly lined or padded for use in sleeping outdoors

sleeping car *n* : a railroad passenger car having berths for sleeping

sleeping pill *n* : a drug and especially a barbiturate that is taken as a tablet or capsule to induce sleep

sleeping sickness *n* **1** : a serious disease found in much of tropical Africa that is marked by fever, protracted lethargy, tremors, and loss of weight is caused by either of two trypanosomes, and is transmitted by tsetse flies **2** : any of various virus diseases of which lethargy or drowsiness is a prominent feature

sleep•less \'slē-pləs\ *adj* **1** : not able to sleep : INSOMNIAC **2** : affording no sleep **3** : unceasingly alert or active — **sleep-less•ly** *adv* — **sleep•less•ness** *n*

sleep out *vi* **1** : to sleep outdoors **2** : to sleep away from home

sleep•walk•er \'slēp-ˌwȯ-kər\ *n* : one that walks in one's sleep : SOMNAMBULIST — **sleep•walk•ing** \-king\ *n*

sleepy \'slē-pē\ *adj* **sleep•i•er**; **-est** **1** : ready to fall asleep : DROWSY **2** : quietly inactive ⟨a *sleepy* village⟩ — **sleep•i•ly** \-pə-lē\ *adv* — **sleep•i•ness** \-pē-nəs\ *n*

sleepy•head \'slē-pē-ˌhed\ *n* : a sleepy person

1**sleet** \'slēt\ *n* **1** : partly frozen rain : a mixture of rain and snow **2** : GLAZE 1 [Middle English *slete*] — **sleety** \'slēt-ē\ *adj*

2**sleet** *vi* : to shower sleet

sleeve \'slēv\ *n* **1** : the part of a garment covering the arm **2** : something like a sleeve in shape or use; *esp* : a tubular part fitting over another part [Old English *slīefe*] — **sleeved** \'slēvd\ *adj* — **sleeve•less** \'slēv-ləs\ *adj*

sleeve•let \'slēv-lət\ *n* : a covering for the forearm to protect clothing from wear or dirt

sleeve target *n* : a tubular cloth target towed by an airplane for use in air and ground antiaircraft gunnery practice

1**sleigh** \'slā\ *n* : a vehicle on runners used for transporting persons or goods on snow or ice [Dutch *slede, slee*]

2**sleigh** *vi* : to drive or travel in a sleigh

sleigh bell *n* : any of various bells commonly attached to a sleigh or to the harness of a horse drawing a sleigh

sleight \'slīt\ *n* : deceitful craftiness : CUNNING; *also* : STRATAGEM [Old Norse *slœgth*, from *slœgr* "sly"]

sleight of hand **1** : skill and dexterity especially in magic tricks **2** : a magic trick requiring sleight of hand

slen•der \'slen-dər\ *adj* **1 a** : spare in frame or flesh; *esp* : gracefully slight **b** : small in circumference in proportion to length or height **2** : limited or inadequate in amount : MEAGER [Middle English *sclendre, slendre*] **syn** see THIN — **slen•der-ly** *adv* — **slen•der•ness** *n*

slen•der•ize \-də-ˌrīz\ *vt* : to make slender

1**sleuth** \'slüth\ *n* : DETECTIVE [short for *sleuthhound*]

△ **origin** A modern English *sleuth* is a detective, but in Middle English the word *sleuth* meant "the track of an animal or person". The word was a borrowing from Old Norse *slōth*. After the 15th century, *sleuth* was seldom used except in compounds like *sleuth-dog* and *sleuthhound*. These were terms for a dog trained to follow a track. The sleuthhound became a symbol of the eager and thorough pursuit of an object. In the 19th century United States the metaphoric *sleuthhound* acquired a more specific meaning and became an epithet for a detective. This new term was soon shortened to *sleuth*.

2**sleuth** *vi* : to act as a detective

sleuth•hound \-ˌhau̇nd\ *n* : a dog that tracks by scent; *esp* : BLOODHOUND [Middle English, from *sleuth* "track of an animal or person", from Old Norse *slōth*]

1**slew** \'slü\ *past of* SLAY

2**slew** *variant of* SLOUGH

3**slew** *variant of* SLUE

4**slew** *also* **slue** *n* : a large number : LOT [Irish Gaelic *sluagh*]

1**slice** \'slīs\ *n* **1** : a thin flat piece cut from something ⟨a *slice* of bread⟩ **2** : a spatula or knife with wedge-shaped blade ⟨fish *slice*⟩ **3** : a path of a ball that deviates from a straight course to the same side as the dominant hand of the player propelling it [Middle French *esclice* "splinter", from *esclicier* "to splinter", of Germanic origin]

2**slice** *vb* **1 a** : to cut with or as if with a knife **b** : to cut into slices **2** : to hit (a ball) so that a slice results — **slic•er** *n*

1**slick** \'slik\ *vt* : to make sleek or smooth [Middle English *sliken*]

2**slick** *adj* **1 a** : having a smooth surface : SLIPPERY **b** : GLIB, TRITE **2 a** : characterized by subtlety or nimble wit; *esp* : WILY **b** : DEFT, SKILLFUL — **slick•ly** *adv* — **slick•ness** *n*

3**slick** *n* **1** : something that is smooth or slippery; *esp* : a smooth patch of water covered with a film of oil **2** : a popular magazine printed on coated stock

slick•er \'slik-ər\ *n* **1** : a long loose raincoat often of oilskin or plastic **2 a** : a clever crook **b** : a usually sophisticated or stylish person : DUDE

1**slide** \'slīd\ *vb* **slid** \'slid\; **slid•ing** \'slīd-ing\ **1 a** : to move or cause to move smoothly over a surface : GLIDE, SLIP ⟨*slide* a dish across the table⟩ ⟨the pen *slides* smoothly over the paper⟩ **b** : to coast on snow or ice **2** : to slip and fall by a loss of footing, balance, or support ⟨the package *slid* from the heap⟩ **3 a** : to move or pass smoothly and easily ⟨the dog *slid* through the brush⟩ **b** : to move, pass, or put unobtrusively, stealthily, or imperceptibly ⟨*slid* quietly into the seat⟩ ⟨time *slid* by⟩ ⟨*slide* the note into my hand⟩ [Old English *slīdan*]

2**slide** *n* **1** : the act or motion of sliding **2** : the descent of a mass (as of earth, rock, or snow) down a slope **3 a** : a surface down which a person or thing slides **b** : something (as a cover for an opening) that operates or adjusts by sliding **4 a** : a glass plate on which is placed an object to be examined under a microscope **b** : a photographic transparency arranged for projection

slide fastener *n* : ZIPPER

slid•er \'slīd-ər\ *n* **1** : one that slides or operates a slide **2** : a pitch in baseball that is thrown like a fastball but breaks slightly in the same direction as a curve

slide rule *n* : an instrument used for rapid calculation that consists in its simple form of a ruler with a lengthwise central sliding piece each of which is graduated with similar logarithmic scales labeled with the corresponding antilogarithms

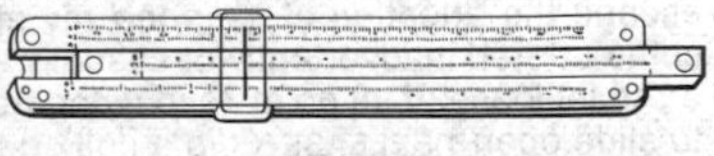
slide rule

slide•way \'slīd-ˌwā\ *n* : a way along which something slides

sliding board *n* : a playground slide

1**slight** \'slīt\ *adj* **1 a** : having a slim or delicate build : not stout or massive in body **b** : lacking in strength or substance : FLIMSY, FRAIL **c** : deficient in weight, solidity, or importance : TRIVIAL **2** : small of its kind or in amount : SCANTY, MEAGER [Middle English, "smooth, slight"] **syn** see THIN — **slight•ly** *adv* — **slight•ness** *n*

2**slight** *vt* : to treat as slight or unimportant: as **a** : to treat with disdain or discourteous indifference **b** : to perform or attend to carelessly and inadequately

3**slight** *n* **1** : an act or an instance of slighting **2** : a humiliating discourtesy

slight•ing *adj* : characterized by disregard or disrespect ⟨a *slighting* remark⟩ — **slight•ing•ly** \-ing-lē\ *adv*

sli•ly *variant of* SLYLY

1**slim** \'slim\ *adj* **slim•mer**; **slim•mest** **1** : of small diameter or thickness in proportion to the height or length : SLENDER **2 a** : inferior in quality or amount : SLIGHT **b** : SCANTY 2, SMALL [Dutch, "bad, inferior"] **syn** see THIN — **slim•ly** *adv* — **slim•ness** *n*

\ə\ **abut**	\au̇\ **out**	\i\ **tip**	\ȯ\ **saw**	\u̇\ **foot**
\ər\ **further**	\ch\ **chin**	\ī\ **life**	\ȯi\ **coin**	\y\ **yet**
\a\ **mat**	\e\ **pet**	\j\ **job**	\th\ **thin**	\yü\ **few**
\ā\ **take**	\ē\ **easy**	\ng\ **sing**	\th\ **this**	\yu̇\ **cure**
\ä\ **cot, cart**	\g\ **go**	\ō\ **bone**	\ü\ **food**	\zh\ **vision**

²slim *vb* **slimmed**; **slim•ming** : to make or become slender
slime \'slīm\ *n* **1** : soft moist earth or clay; *esp* : sticky slippery mud **2** : a soft slippery substance; *esp* : a skin secretion (as of a slug or catfish) [Old English *slīm*]
slime mold *n* : any of a group (Myxomycetes or Mycetozoa) of organisms that are usually held to be lower fungi but sometimes are considered protozoans and that live vegetatively as mobile plasmodia and reproduce by spores
slim–jim \'slim-'jim\ *n* : one that is notably slender [*slim* + *Jim,* nickname for *James*]
slimy \'slī-mē\ *adj* **slim•i•er**; **-est** **1** : of, relating to, or resembling slime : VISCOUS; *also* : covered with or yielding slime **2** : VILE, OFFENSIVE ⟨a *slimy* traitor⟩ — **slim•i•ly** \-mə-lē\ *adv* — **slim•i•ness** \-mē-nəs\ *n*
¹sling \'sling\ *vt* **slung** \'sləng\; **sling•ing** \'sling-ing\ **1** : to toss casually or forcibly : FLING **2** : to throw with a sling [Middle English *slingen*] — **sling•er** \'sling-ər\ *n*
²sling *n* : a slinging or hurling of or as if of a missile
³sling *n* **1 a** : a device for throwing something (as stones) that usually consists of a short strap with strings fastened to its ends and is whirled round to discharge its missile **b** : SLINGSHOT **2 a** : a usually looped line (as of rope) used to hoist, lower, support, or carry something; *esp* : a hanging bandage suspended from the neck to support an arm or hand **b** : a device (as a rope net) for enclosing material to be hoisted by a tackle or crane
⁴sling *vt* **slung** \'sləng\; **sling•ing** \'sling-ing\ **1** : to put in or move or support with a sling ⟨*sling* cargo from a ship's hold⟩ **2** : to cause to become suspended ⟨*sling* a hammock⟩
sling•shot \'sling-,shät\ *n* : a forked stick with an elastic band attached for shooting small stones
slink \'slingk\ *vb* **slunk** \'sləngk\; **slink•ing** : to move or go stealthily (as in fear or shame) [Old English *slincan* "to creep"] **syn** see SKULK
slinky \'sling-kē\ *adj* **slink•i•er**; **-est** **1** : stealthily quiet ⟨*slinky* movements⟩ **2** : sleek and sinuous in outline ⟨a *slinky* evening gown⟩
¹slip \'slip\ *vb* **slipped**; **slip•ping** **1 a** : to move easily and smoothly : SLIDE ⟨the bolt *slipped* back⟩ ⟨*slip* the knife into its sheath⟩ **b** : to move or place quietly or stealthily **c** : to pass without being noted or used ⟨time *slipped* by⟩ ⟨let the opportunity *slip*⟩ **2 a** : to get away from : ELUDE ⟨*slipped* their pursuers⟩ **b** : to get free from ⟨the dog *slipped* its collar⟩ **c** : to escape the attention of ⟨*slipped* my mind⟩ **d** : to utter or become uttered inadvertently or casually ⟨the secret *slipped* out⟩ **e** : to let loose or let go of ⟨*slip* a dog from a leash⟩ **f** : to cause to slide open : RELEASE ⟨*slip* a bolt⟩ **g** : to let (a knitting stitch) pass from one needle to another without working a new stitch **3 a** : to slide out of place, away from a support, or from one's grasp ⟨the dish *slipped* to the floor⟩ **b** : to slide so as to fall or lose balance ⟨*slip* on a grease spot⟩ **c** : to slide or cause to slide especially in putting, passing, or inserting easily or quickly ⟨*slip* into a coat⟩ ⟨*slip* a dress on⟩ **d** : DISLOCATE ⟨*slipped* my shoulder⟩ **e** : to fail to progress or hold normally from or as if from sliding ⟨the loose belt continued to *slip*⟩ **4** : to fall from some level or standard (as of conduct or activity) usually gradually or by degrees ⟨the market *slipped* from an earlier high⟩ [Middle English *slippen,* from Dutch or Low German] — **slip something over** : to foist something on another : get the better of another by trickery
²slip *n* **1 a** : a sloping ramp that extends out into the water and serves for landing or repairing ships **b** : a ship's berth between two piers **2** : the act or an instance of departing secretly or hurriedly **3 a** : a mistake in judgment, policy, or procedure **b** : an unintentional and trivial mistake or fault **4** : the act or an instance of slipping down or out of place ⟨a *slip* on the ice⟩ ⟨a *slip* in stock prices⟩ **5 a** : an undergarment made in dress length with shoulder straps **b** : PILLOWCASE **syn** see ERROR
³slip *n* **1** : a small shoot or twig cut for planting or grafting : CUTTING **2 a** : a long narrow strip of material **b** : a piece of paper used for a memorandum or record ⟨sales *slip*⟩ **3** : a young and slender person [Middle English *slippe*]
⁴slip *vt* **slipped**; **slip•ping** : to take cuttings from (a plant)
⁵slip *n* : thin wet clay used in pottery for casting, for decoration, or as a cement [Old English *slypa* "slime, paste"]
slip•case \'slip-,kās\ *n* : a protective container for books with one open end
slip•cov•er \'slip-,kəv-ər\ *n* : a removable protective covering for an article of furniture
slip•knot \'slip-,nät\ *n* : a knot that slips along a line around which it is made; *esp* : one made by tying an overhand knot around a rope to form an adjustable loop
slip noose *n* : a noose with a slipknot
slip–on \'slip-,ón, -,än\ *n* : an article of clothing (as a glove, shoe, or girdle) that is easily slipped on or off
slip•page \'slip-ij\ *n* **1** : an act, instance, or process of slipping **2 a** : power lost in transmission **b** : the difference between theoretical and actual output (as of power)
slipped disk *n* : a protrusion of one of the cartilage disks between vertebrae with pressure on spinal nerves resulting in low back pain
slip•per \'slip-ər\ *n* : a light low shoe without laces that is easily slipped on or off — **slip•pered** \-ərd\ *adj*
slip•pery \'slip-rē, -ə-rē\ *adj* **slip•per•i•er**; **-est** **1** : having a surface smooth enough to cause one to slide or lose one's hold ⟨a *slippery* floor⟩ **2** : not worthy of trust : TRICKY, UNRELIABLE [Old English *slipor*] — **slip•per•i•ness** *n*
slippery elm *n* : a North American elm with hard wood and fragrant inner bark; *also* : its wood or bark
slip•shod \'slip-'shäd\ *adj* : very careless : SLOVENLY [earlier *slipshod* "wearing loose shoes, shabby", from ¹*slip* + *shod*]
slip•stick \'slip-,stik\ *n* : SLIDE RULE
slip stitch *n* : a concealed stitch for sewing folded edges (as hems) made by alternately running the needle inside the fold and picking up a thread or two from the body of the article
slip•stream \'slip-,strēm\ *n* : the stream of air driven aft by the propeller of an aircraft
slip•up \'slip-,əp\ *n* **1** : MISTAKE **2** : MISCHANCE
slip up \slip-'əp, 'slip-\ *vi* : to make a mistake : BLUNDER
¹slit \'slit\ *vt* **slit**; **slit•ting** **1 a** : to make a slit in : SLASH **b** : to cut off or away : SEVER **2** : to cut into long narrow strips [Middle English *slitten*] — **slit•ter** *n*
²slit *n* : a long narrow cut or opening — **slit** *adj* — **slit•like** \-,līk\ *adj*
slith•er \'slith-ər\ *vb* **slith•ered**; **slith•er•ing** \'slith-ring, -ə-ring\ **1** : to slide or cause to slide on or as if on a loose gravelly surface **2** : to slip or slide like a snake [Old English *slidrian,* from *slīdan* "to slide"]
slith•ery \'slith-rē, -ə-rē\ *adj* : having a slippery surface, texture, or quality
¹sliv•er \'sliv-ər, *2 is usually* 'slīv-\ *n* **1** : a long slender piece cut or torn off : SPLINTER **2** : an untwisted strand of textile fiber as it comes from a carding or combining machine [Middle English *slivere,* from *sliven* "to slice off", from Old English *-slīfan*]
²sliv•er \'sliv-ər\ *vb* **sliv•ered**; **sliv•er•ing** \'sliv-ring, -ə-ring\ : to cut or form into slivers : SPLINTER
slob \'släb\ *n* : a slovenly or boorish person [Irish Gaelic *slab* "mud"]
¹slob•ber \'släb-ər\ *vb* **slob•bered**; **slob•ber•ing** \'släb-ring, -ə-ring\ **1** : to let saliva or liquid dribble from the mouth : DROOL **2** : to show feeling to excess : GUSH [Middle English *sloberen*] — **slob•ber•er** \'släb-ər-ər\ *n*
²slobber *n* **1** : dripping saliva **2** : silly excessive show of feeling — **slob•bery** \'släb-rē, -ə-rē\ *adj*
sloe \'slō\ *n* : the tart bluish black globe-shaped fruit of the blackthorn; *also* : BLACKTHORN 1 [Old English *slāh*]
sloe–eyed \'slō-'īd\ *adj* **1** : having soft dark bluish or purplish black eyes **2** : having slanted eyes
sloe gin *n* : a sweet reddish liqueur flavored chiefly with sloes
slog \'släg\ *vb* **slogged**; **slog•ging** **1** : to hit hard : BEAT **2** : to plod or work doggedly on [origin unknown] — **slog•ger** *n*
slo•gan \'slō-gən\ *n* **1** : a word or phrase that calls to battle **2** : a word or phrase used by a party, a group, or a business to attract attention [Scottish Gaelic *sluagh-ghairm* "army cry"]
slo•gan•eer \,slō-gə-'niər\ *n* : a coiner or user of slogans — **sloganeer** *vi*
sloop \'slüp\ *n* : a fore-and-aft rigged sailing boat with one mast and a single jib [Dutch *sloep*]
¹slop \'släp\ *n* **1** : soft mud : SLUSH **2** : thin tasteless drink or liquid food — usually used in pl. **3** : liquid spilled or splashed **4 a** : food waste (as garbage) or a thin gruel fed to animals **b** : excreted body waste — usually used in pl. [Middle English *sloppe*]
²slop *vb* **slopped**; **slop•ping** **1** : to spill on or over ⟨*slop* milk from a glass⟩ ⟨*slopped* my shirt with gravy⟩ **2** : to feed slop to ⟨*slop* the hogs⟩ **3** : to slouch or lounge about in a sloppy manner ⟨*slop* about the house⟩

1slope \'slōp\ *adj* : being slanted or at an angle [Middle English *slope,* adv., "obliquely"]

2slope *vb* : to take a slanting direction : give a slant to : INCLINE — **slop•er** *n*

3slope *n* **1** : ground that forms a natural or artificial incline **2** : upward or downward slant or inclination or degree of slant **3** : the part of a continent draining to a particular ocean **4 a** : the tangent of the angle made by a straight line with the x-axis **b** : the slope of the line tangent to a plane curve at a point

slop•py \'släp-ē\ *adj* **slop•pi•er; -est 1 a** : wet so as to spatter easily : SLUSHY ⟨a *sloppy* racetrack⟩ **b** : wet with or as if with something slopped over **2** : SLOVENLY, CARELESS ⟨a *sloppy* dresser⟩ **3** : excessively sentimental — **slop•pi•ly** \'släp-ə-lē\ *adv* — **slop•pi•ness** \'släp-ē-nəs\ *n*

1slosh \'släsh\ *n* **1** : SLUSH 1, 2 **2** : the slap or splash of liquid [probably blend of *slop* and *slush*]

2slosh *vb* **1** : to flounder through or splash about in or with water, mud, or slush **2** : to move with a splash

1slot \'slät\ *n* : a long narrow opening, groove, or passage : SLIT, NOTCH [Middle English, "hollow running down the middle of the breast", from Middle French *esclot*]

2slot *vt* **slot•ted; slot•ting** : to cut a slot in

3slot *n, pl* **slot** : the track of an animal (as a deer) [Middle French *esclot* "track"]

sloth \'slóth, 'slōth\ *n* **1** : INDOLENCE, LAZINESS **2** : any of several slow-moving mammals of Central and South America that are related to the armadillos and live in trees where they hang back downward and feed on leaves, shoots, and fruits [Middle English *slouthe,* from *slow*]

sloth 2

sloth•ful \-fəl\ *adj* : LAZY 1, INDOLENT — **sloth•ful•ly** \-fə-lē\ *adv* — **sloth•ful•ness** *n*

slot machine *n* : a machine whose operation is begun when a coin is dropped into a slot

1slouch \'slau̇ch\ *n* **1** : an awkward, lazy, or incompetent person **2** : a gait or posture characterized by ungainly stooping of head and shoulders [origin unknown]

2slouch *vi* : to walk with or assume a slouch — **slouch•er** *n*

slouch hat *n* : a soft usually felt hat with a flexible brim

slouchy \'slau̇-chē\ *adj* **slouch•i•er; -est** : slouching or slovenly in appearance — **slouch•i•ly** \-chə-lē\ *adv* — **slouch•i•ness** \-chē-nəs\ *n*

1slough \'slü, 'slau̇; *in the United States (except New England)* 'slü *is usual for sense 1;* 'slau̇ *is more frequent for sense* 2\ *n* **1** *also* **slew** *or* **slue** \'slü\ : a wet and marshy or muddy place (as a swamp or backwater) **2** : a discouraged, degraded, or dejected state [Old English *slōh*]

2slough \'sləf\ *or* **sluff** *n* **1** : the cast-off skin of a snake **2** : a mass of dead tissue separating from an ulcer **3** : something that may be shed or cast off [Middle English *slughe*]

3slough \'sləf\ *or* **sluff** *vb* : to cast off or become cast off: as **a** : to cast off one's skin or dead tissue from living tissue **b** : to get rid of or discard as irksome, objectionable, or disadvantageous

slough of de•spond \ˌslau̇-əv-di-'spänd, ˌslü-\ : a state of extreme depression [from the *Slough of Despond,* deep bog into which Christian falls in the allegory *Pilgrim's Progress* (1678) by John Bunyan]

slough over \ˌsləf-\ *vt* : to treat as slight or unimportant ⟨trying to *slough over* their own mistakes⟩

Slo•vak \'slō-ˌväk, -ˌvak\ *n* **1** : a member of a Slavic people of eastern Czechoslovakia **2** : the Slavic language of the Slovak people [Slovak *Slovák*] — **Slovak** *adj* — **Slo•vak•i•an** \slō-'väk-ē-ən, -'vak-\ *adj or n*

slov•en \'sləv-ən\ *n* : one habitually negligent of neatness or cleanliness [Middle English *sloveyn* "rascal"]

Slo•vene \'slō-ˌvēn\ *n* **1 a** : a member of a southern Slavic group of people usually classed with the Serbs and Croats and living in Yugoslavia **b** : a native or inhabitant of Slovenia **2** : the language of the Slovenes [German, from Slovene *Sloven*] — **Slovene** *adj* — **Slo•ve•ni•an** \slō-'vē-nē-ən\ *adj or n*

slov•en•ly \'sləv-ən-lē\ *adj* **1 a** : untidy especially in dress or person **b** : lazily slipshod **2** : characteristic of a sloven — **slov•en•li•ness** *n* — **slovenly** *adv*

1slow \'slō\ *adj* **1 a** : mentally dull : STUPID **b** : naturally inert or sluggish **2 a** : lacking in readiness, promptness, or willingness **b** : not hasty **3 a** : moving, flowing, or proceeding without speed or at less than usual speed ⟨*slow* traffic⟩ **b** : not vigorous or active ⟨a *slow* fire⟩ **c** : taking place at a low rate or over a considerable period of time ⟨*slow* growth⟩ **4** : having qualities that hinder or stop rapid progress or action ⟨a *slow* racetrack⟩ **5 a** : registering behind or below what is correct ⟨the clock is *slow*⟩ **b** : that is behind the time at a specified time or place **6** : lacking in activity or liveliness ⟨a *slow* market⟩⟨a *slow* party⟩[Old English *slāw*] — **slow•ly** *adv* — **slow•ness** *n*

2slow *adv* : SLOWLY⟨drive *slow*⟩

3slow *vb* : to make or go slow or slower

slow•down \'slō-ˌdau̇n\ *n* : a slowing down

slow-foot•ed \'slō-'fu̇t-əd\ *adj* : moving at a very slow pace — **slow-foot•ed•ness** *n*

slow•ish \'slō-ish\ *adj* : somewhat slow ⟨a *slowish* reader⟩

slow match *n* : a match or fuse made so as to burn slowly and evenly and used for firing (as of blasting charges)

slow motion *n* : action in a projected motion picture or television program that proceeds at a rate slower than the action photographed or taped

slow•poke \'slō-ˌpōk\ *n* : a very slow person

slow-wit•ted \-'wit-əd\ *adj* : SLOW 1a

sludge \'sləj\ *n* **1** : MUD, MIRE **2** : a muddy or slushy mass, deposit, or sediment; *esp* : precipitated solid matter produced by water and sewage treatment processes [probably alteration of *slush*] — **sludgy** \'sləj-ē\ *adj*

1slue \'slü\ *variant of* SLOUGH

2slue *vb* : to turn, twist, or swing about especially out of a course : VEER [origin unknown]

3slue *n* : an act or instance of sluing

4slue *variant of* SLEW

1slug \'sləg\ *n* **1** : SLUGGARD **2** : any of numerous chiefly terrestrial mollusks that are closely related to the land snails but are long and wormlike and have only a rudimentary shell or none **3** : a smooth soft larva of a sawfly or moth that creeps like a snail [of Scandinavian origin]

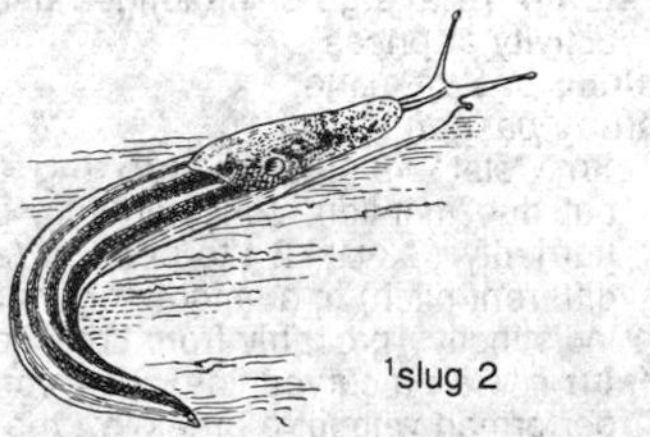

1slug 2

2slug *n* **1** : a small piece of shaped metal: as **a** : a musket ball or bullet **b** : a metal disk for insertion in a slot machine in place of a coin **2** : a line of type cast as one piece **3** : a single drink of liquor : SHOT **4** : the gravitational unit of mass in the fps system to which a pound force can impart an acceleration of one foot per second per second that is equal to about 14.59 kilograms [probably from 1*slug*]

3slug *n* : a heavy blow especially with the fist [perhaps from 2*slug*]

4slug *vb* **slugged; slug•ging** : to strike heavily with or as if with the fist or a bat

slug•abed \'sləg-ə-ˌbed\ *n* : one who stays in bed too long; *also* : SLUGGARD

slug•fest \'sləg-ˌfest\ *n* : a fight or boxing match marked by exchange of heavy blows

slug•gard \'sləg-ərd\ *n* : an habitually lazy person [Middle English *sluggart*] — **sluggard** *adj* — **slug•gard•ly** *adj*

slug•ger \'sləg-ər\ *n* : one (as a batter or boxer) that strikes hard or with heavy blows

slug•gish \'sləg-ish\ *adj* : slow and inactive in movement or reaction by habit or condition — **slug•gish•ly** *adv* — **slug•gish•ness** *n*

¹sluice \'slüs\ *n* **1 :** an artificial passage for water with a gate for controlling its flow or changing its direction **2 :** a body of water held back by a gate or a stream flowing through a gate **3 :** a device (as a water gate) for controlling the flow of water **4 :** a channel that carries off surplus water **5 :** a long inclined trough (as for washing gold-bearing earth or for floating logs to a sawmill) [Middle French *escluse,* from Late Latin *exclusa,* from Latin *excludere* "to shut off, exclude"]

²sluice *vt* **1 :** to draw off by or through a sluice **2 a :** to wash with or in water running through or from a sluice **b :** to drench with a sudden flow

sluice•way \'slü-ˌswā\ *n* **:** an artificial channel into which water is let by a sluice

¹slum \'sləm\ *n* **:** a thickly populated usually urban area marked by crowding, run-down housing, and generally wretched living conditions [origin unknown]

²slum *vi* **slummed; slum•ming :** to visit slums especially out of curiosity or for pleasure — **slum•mer** *n*

slum•ber \'sləm-bər\ *vi* **slum•bered; slum•ber•ing** \-bə-riŋ, -briŋ\ **1 :** to sleep or lie asleep **:** DOZE **2 :** to lie dormant ⟨a *slumbering* volcano⟩ [Middle English *slumberen,* from *slumen* "to doze"] — **slumber** *n* — **slum•ber•er** \-bər-ər\ *n*

slum•ber•ous *or* **slum•brous** \'sləm-bə-rəs, -brəs\ *adj* **1 a :** SLEEPY 1 **b :** QUIET 1a **2 :** inviting slumber ⟨a *slumberous* sound⟩

slumber party *n* **:** an overnight gathering of teenage girls usually at one of their homes at which they dress in nightclothes but pass the night more in talking than sleeping

slum•gul•lion \'sləm-ˌgəl-yən\ *n* **:** a meat stew [perhaps from earlier *slum* "slime" + English dialect *gullion* "mud, cesspool"]

slum•lord \'sləm-ˌlȯrd\ *n* **:** a landlord who receives unusually large profits from substandard properties [*slum* + land*lord*]

¹slump \'sləmp\ *vi* **1 :** to drop or slide down suddenly **:** COLLAPSE **2 :** to assume a drooping posture or carriage **:** SLOUCH **3 :** to fall sharply ⟨sales *slumped*⟩ [probably of Scandinavian origin]

²slump *n* **:** a large or prolonged decline especially in economic activity or prices

slung *past of* SLING

slunk *past of* SLINK

¹slur \'slər\ *vb* **slurred; slur•ring 1 a :** to slide or slip over without due mention, consideration, or emphasis **b :** to perform hurriedly **:** SKIMP **2 :** to perform (successive musical notes of different pitch) in a smooth or connected manner **3 :** to speak indistinctly [probably from Low German *slurrn* "to shuffle"]

²slur *n* **1 a :** a curved line ⌒ or ⌣ connecting notes to be sung or performed without a break **b :** the combination of two or more slurred tones **2 :** a slurring manner of speech

³slur *vb* **slurred; slur•ring 1 :** to cast aspersions upon **:** DISPARAGE **2 :** to make indistinct **:** OBSCURE [Middle English *sloor* "thin mud"]

⁴slur *n* **1 :** an insulting or disparaging remark **2 :** a shaming or degrading effect

slurp \'slərp\ *vb* **:** to eat or drink noisily or with a sucking sound [Dutch *slurpen*] — **slurp** *n*

slur•ry \'slər-ē, 'slə-rē\ *n, pl* **slurries :** a watery mixture of insoluble matter (as mud, lime, or pulverized ore) [Middle English *slory*]

slush \'sləsh\ *n* **1 :** partly melted or watery snow **2 :** soft mud **:** MIRE **3 :** RUBBISH, DRIVEL [perhaps of Scandinavian origin]

slush fund *n* **:** a fund for carrying on corrupt activities (as bribing public officials)

slushy \'sləsh-ē\ *adj* **slush•i•er; -est :** full of or resembling slush ⟨a *slushy* road⟩ ⟨soft *slushy* ice⟩ — **slush•i•ness** *n*

slut \'slət\ *n* **1 :** a slovenly woman **2 :** a lewd woman; *esp* **:** PROSTITUTE [Middle English *slutte*] — **slut•tish** \'slət-ish\ *adj* — **slut•tish•ly** *adv* — **slut•tish•ness** *n*

sly \'slī\ *adj* **sli•er** *also* **sly•er** \'slī-ər, 'slīr\; **sli•est** *also* **sly•est** \'slī-əst\ **1 a :** clever in concealing one's aims or ends ⟨too *sly* to be trusted⟩ **b :** lacking in straightforwardness and candor ⟨a *sly* explanation⟩ **2 :** lightly mischievous **:** ROGUISH [Old Norse *slœgr*] — **sly•ly** *adv* — **sly•ness** *n*

• syn SLY, CRAFTY, ARTFUL, WILY mean apt to attain an end by devious means. SLY stresses furtiveness, lack of candor, and skill in concealing one's aims and methods ⟨a *sly* scheme⟩ CRAFTY suggests skill in deception acquired by experience ⟨a *crafty* trial lawyer⟩ ARTFUL suggests insinuating or ingratiating craftiness ⟨an *artful* matchmaker⟩ WILY stresses cleverness in setting or avoiding traps ⟨the *wily* fox⟩ — **on the sly :** in a stealthy or furtive manner

¹smack \'smak\ *n* **1 :** characteristic or perceptible taste or flavor **2 :** a small quantity [Old English *smæc*]

²smack *vi* **:** to have a flavor, trace, or suggestion ⟨the roast *smacks* of thyme⟩ ⟨such actions *smack* of treachery⟩

³smack *vb* **1 :** to close and open (lips) noisily especially in eating **2 :** to kiss usually loudly or boisterously **3 a :** to make a smack **b :** to hit so as to make a smack [related to Dutch *smacken* "to strike"]

⁴smack *n* **1 :** a quick sharp noise made by rapidly compressing and opening the lips **2 :** a loud kiss **3 :** a sharp slap or blow

⁵smack *adv* **:** in a square and sharp manner **:** DIRECTLY ⟨it hit me *smack* in the face⟩

⁶smack *n* **:** a sailing ship (as a sloop or cutter) used chiefly in coasting and fishing [Dutch *smak* or Low German *smack*]

smack–dab \'smak-'dab\ *adv, dialect* **:** SQUARELY, EXACTLY

smack•er \'smak-ər\ *n* **1 :** one that smacks **2** *slang* **:** DOLLAR 3

¹small \'smȯl\ *adj* **1 :** little in size **2 :** few in numbers or members ⟨a *small* crowd⟩ **3 :** little in amount ⟨a *small* supply⟩ **4 :** not very much or big ⟨*small* success⟩ **5 :** UNIMPORTANT ⟨a *small* matter⟩ **6 :** operating on a limited scale ⟨*small* dealers⟩ **7 :** GENTLE, SOFT ⟨a *small* voice⟩ **8 :** not generous **:** MEAN ⟨a *small* nature⟩ **9 :** made up of small units **10 :** HUMBLE, MODEST ⟨a *small* beginning⟩ **11 :** HUMILIATED, HUMBLED ⟨felt very *small* to be caught cheating⟩ **12 :** LOWERCASE [Old English *smæl*] — **small•ness** *n*

• syn LITTLE: SMALL and LITTLE are often interchangeable but SMALL, contrasting with *large* or *great,* applies more to relative size determined by capacity, value, number ⟨a *small* mouth⟩ ⟨a *small* quantity of salt⟩ LITTLE, contrasting with *big* or *much,* is more absolute in implication and may suggest pettiness, petiteness, insignificance, immaturity ⟨a *little* child⟩ ⟨had *little* hope of success⟩

²small *adv* **1 :** in or into small pieces ⟨cut the meat *small*⟩ **2 :** without force or loudness ⟨speak *small*⟩ **3 :** in a small manner ⟨most businesses begin *small*⟩

³small *n* **1 :** a part smaller and especially narrower than the remainder ⟨the *small* of the back⟩ **2 a** *pl* **:** small-sized products **b** *pl, British* **:** SMALLCLOTHES 2

small arm *n* **:** a firearm fired while held in the hands

small beer *n* **1 :** a weak or inferior beer **2 :** something of small importance **:** TRIVIA

small calorie *n* **:** CALORIE 1a

small change *n* **1 :** money consisting of small coins **2 :** something trifling or petty

small circle *n* **:** a circle on the surface of a sphere whose plane does not pass through the center of the sphere; *esp* **:** such a circle on the surface of the earth — compare GREAT CIRCLE

small•clothes \'smȯl-ˌklōz, -ˌklōthz\ *n pl* **1 :** close-fitting knee breeches worn especially in the 18th century **2 :** small articles of clothing

small–fry \-ˌfrī\ *adj* **1 :** MINOR ⟨a *small-fry* politician⟩ **2 :** of or relating to children

small game *n* **:** birds and small mammals (as rabbits) hunted for sport

small hours *n pl* **:** the early morning hours

small intestine *n* **:** the part of the intestine that lies between the stomach and colon, consists of duodenum, jejunum, and ileum, secretes digestive enzymes, and is the chief seat of the absorption of digested nutrients

small•ish \'smȯ-lish\ *adj* **:** somewhat small

small–mind•ed \'smȯl-'mīn-dəd\ *adj* **:** lacking breadth of mind; *also* **:** typical of a small-minded person — **small–mind•ed•ly** *adv* — **small–mind•ed•ness** *n*

small potatoes *n* **:** someone or something of trivial importance or worth

small•pox \'smȯl-ˌpäks\ *n* **:** an acute contagious virus disease marked by fever and skin eruption with pustules, sloughing, and scar formation

small–scale \-'skāl\ *adj* **1 :** small in scope; *esp* **:** small in output or operation **2 :** having a scale (as one inch to 25 miles) that permits plotting of comparatively little detail ⟨a *small-scale* map⟩

small stores *n pl* **:** articles of clothing sold by a naval supply officer to naval personnel

small talk *n* **:** light or casual conversation

small–time \'smȯl-'tīm\ *adj* **:** of insignificant standing **:** SMALL=

SCALE, MINOR — **small–tim•er** \-'tī-mər\ *n*

smarmy \'smär-mē\ *adj* : exhibiting or marked by smug, ingratiating, or false earnestness : UNCTUOUS [earlier *smarm* "to gush, slobber", of unknown origin]

[1]**smart** \'smärt\ *vi* **1** : to cause or feel a sharp stinging pain **2** : to feel or endure distress, remorse, or embarrassment ⟨*smarts* under criticism⟩ [Old English *smeortan*]

[2]**smart** *adj* **1** : causing smarting **2** : marked by forceful activity or vigorous strength **3** : BRISK 1, SPIRITED **4 a** : mentally alert : BRIGHT **b** : sharp in scheming : SHREWD **5 a** : WITTY, CLEVER **b** : PERT, SAUCY ⟨don't get *smart* with me⟩ **6 a** : stylish or elegant in dress or appearance **b** : SOPHISTICATED 3 **c** : FASHIONABLE 1 **syn** see CLEVER — **smart•ly** *adv* — **smart•ness** *n*

[3]**smart** *adv* : SMARTLY

[4]**smart** *n* **1** : a smarting pain **2** : deep grief or remorse

smart al•eck \'smärt-ˌal-ik, -ˌel-\ *n* : an offensively conceited and bumptious person [*Aleck,* nickname for *Alexander*] — **smart–al•ecky** \-ˌal-ə-kē, -ˌel-\ *or* **smart–aleck** *adj*

smart•en \'smärt-n\ *vb* **smart•ened; smart•en•ing** \'smärt-ning, -n-ing\ **1** : to make smart or smarter : SPRUCE, FRESHEN ⟨*smarten* up an old dress with a new collar⟩ **2** : to make or become more alert or informed ⟨*smarten* up if you don't want to get into trouble⟩

smart set *n* : extremely fashionable society

smart•weed \'smärt-ˌwēd\ *n* : any of various weedy plants with strong acrid juice that are related to the buckwheats

smarty *or* **smart•ie** \'smärt-ē\ *n, pl* **smart•ies** : SMART ALECK

[1]**smash** \'smash\ *vb* **1** : to break in pieces by force : SHATTER ⟨*smash* down a door⟩ ⟨the dish *smashed* on the floor⟩ **2** : to drive, throw, or move with a destructive effect ⟨the ball *smashed* through the window⟩ **3** : WRECK 1b **4** : to go to pieces suddenly : COLLAPSE [perhaps blend of *smack* and *mash*] — **smash•er** *n*

[2]**smash** *n* **1 a** : a smashing blow or attack **b** : a hard overhand stroke (as in tennis) **2** : the condition of being smashed **3 a** : the action or sound of smashing; *esp* : SMASHUP 2 **b** : utter collapse : RUIN; *esp* : BANKRUPTCY **4** : a striking success : HIT ⟨the new play is a *smash*⟩

smash•ing \'smash-ing\ *adj* **1** : that smashes ⟨a *smashing* defeat⟩ **2** : extremely moving, effective, or attractive ⟨a *smashing* performance⟩

smash•up \'smash-ˌəp\ *n* **1** : a complete collapse **2** : a destructive collision of motor vehicles

smat•ter \'smat-ər\ *n* : SMATTERING 2 [Middle English *smatteren* "to chatter, talk ignorantly"]

smat•ter•ing \'smat-ə-ring\ *n* **1** : superficial piecemeal knowledge **2** : a small scattered number

smaze \'smāz\ *n* : a combination of haze and smoke similar to smog in appearance but less damp in consistency [*smoke* + *haze*]

[1]**smear** \'smiər\ *n* **1** : a spot made by or as if by an oily or sticky substance : SMUDGE **2** : material smeared on a surface; *esp* : material prepared for microscopic examination by smearing on a slide **3** : a usually unproven charge or accusation [Old English *smeoru*]

[2]**smear** *vt* **1 a** : to spread or daub with something oily or sticky **b** : to spread over a surface **2** : to stain, smudge, or dirty by or as if by smearing; *also* : to blacken the reputation of **3** : to blot out or blur by or as if by smearing — **smear•er** *n*

smear•case *or* **smier•case** \'smiər-ˌkās\ *n, chiefly Midland* : COTTAGE CHEESE [German *schmierkäse,* from *schmieren* "to smear" + *käse* "cheese"]

smear word *n* : an epithet intended to smear a person or group

smeary \'smiər-ē\ *adj* **smear•i•er; -est 1** : marked by smears **2** : tending to smear

[1]**smell** \'smel\ *vb* **smelled** \'smeld\ *or* **smelt** \'smelt\; **smell•ing 1** : to get the odor of through stimuli affecting the olfactory sense organs of the nose **2** : to detect or become aware of as if by the sense of smell **3** : to exercise the sense of smell **4 a** : to give off an odor **b** : to give off a suggestion of something and especially of something unwholesome or evil ⟨the plan *smells* of trickery⟩ [Middle English *smellen*] — **smell•er** *n* — **smell a rat** : to have a suspicion of something wrong

[2]**smell** *n* **1 a** : the process or power of smelling **b** : the special sense used to perceive odor **2** : the property of a thing that affects the olfactory organs : ODOR **3** : a pervading quality : AURA **4** : an act of smelling

• **syn** ODOR, SCENT, AROMA: SMELL and ODOR may imply either a pleasant or unpleasant sensation though SMELL may cover a wider range of quality, intensity, or source; SCENT implies less strength and suggests a substance, an animal, or a plant giving off a characteristic smell ⟨the *scent* of pine⟩ AROMA suggests a pungent, pervasive, usually pleasant smell ⟨the *aroma* of fresh coffee⟩

smelling salts *n pl* : a usually scented aromatic preparation of an ammonium salt and ammonia water used to relieve faintness

smelly \'smel-ē\ *adj* **smell•i•er; -est** : having a smell and especially a bad smell

[1]**smelt** \'smelt\ *n, pl* **smelts** *or* **smelt** : any of several very small food fishes of coastal or fresh waters that resemble and are related to the trout [Old English]

[2]**smelt** *vt* : to melt or fuse (as ore) usually in order to separate the metal [Dutch or Low German *smelten*]

smelt•er \'smel-tər\ *n* : one that smelts: **a** : a worker in or an owner of a smeltery **b** *or* **smelt•ery** \-tə-rē, -trē\ : an establishment for smelting

smid•gen *or* **smid•geon** *or* **smid•gin** \'smij-ən\ *n* : a small amount : BIT [perhaps from English dialect *smitch* "soiling mark"]

smi•lax \'smī-ˌlaks\ *n* **1** : GREENBRIER **2** : a delicate greenhouse twining plant related to the garden asparagus and having ovate bright green terminal branches in place of leaves [Latin, "bindweed, yew", from Greek]

[1]**smile** \'smīl\ *vb* **1** : to have, produce, or exhibit a smile **2 a** : to look with amusement or ridicule **b** : to be propitious or agreeable ⟨weather *smiled* on our plans⟩ **3** : to express by a smile [Middle English *smilen*] — **smil•er** *n* — **smil•ing•ly** \'smī-ling-lē\ *adv*

[2]**smile** *n* : a change of facial expression in which the eyes brighten and the lips curve slightly upward especially in expression of amusement, pleasure, approval, or scorn — **smile•less** \'smīl-ləs\ *adj* — **smile•less•ly** *adv*

smirch \'smərch\ *vt* **1** : to make dirty, stained, or discolored especially by smearing with something that soils **2** : to bring discredit or disgrace on [Middle English *smorchen*] — **smirch** *n*

smirk \'smərk\ *vi* : to smile in an affected manner : SIMPER [Old English *smearcian* "to smile"] — **smirk** *n*

smirky \'smər-kē\ *adj* : marked by or given to smirking

smite \'smīt\ *vb* **smote** \'smōt\; **smit•ten** \'smit-n\ *or* **smote**; **smit•ing** \'smīt-ing\ **1** : to strike sharply or heavily with the hand or a hand weapon **2 a** : to kill or injure by smiting **b** : to attack or afflict suddenly and injuriously ⟨*smitten* by disease⟩ **3** : to affect like a sudden hard blow ⟨*smitten* with terror⟩ [Old English *smītan*] — **smit•er** \'smīt-ər\ *n*

smith \'smith\ *n* **1** : a worker in metals **2** : MAKER — often used in combination ⟨gun*smith*⟩ ⟨tune*smith*⟩ [Old English]

smith•er•eens \ˌsmith-ə-'rēnz\ *n pl* : small pieces [Irish Gaelic *smidirīn* "small fragment"]

smith•ery \'smith-ə-rē\ *n* **1** : the work, art, or trade of a smith **2** : SMITHY

smith•son•ite \'smith-sə-ˌnīt\ *n* : a usually white or nearly white native zinc carbonate $ZnCO_3$ [James *Smithson,* died 1829, British chemist]

smithy \'smith-ē, 'smith-\ *n, pl* **smith•ies 1** : the workshop of a smith **2** : BLACKSMITH

[1]**smock** \'smäk\ *n* **1** *archaic* : a woman's undergarment; *esp* : CHEMISE **2** : a light loose garment worn usually over regular clothing for protection from dirt [Old English *smoc*]

[2]**smock** *vt* : to embroider or shirr with smocking

smock•ing \'smäk-ing\ *n* : a decorative embroidery or shirring made by gathering cloth in regularly spaced round tucks

smog \'smäg *also* 'smòg\ *n* : fog made heavier and darker by smoke and fumes [blend of *smoke* and *fog*] — **smog•gy** \-ē\ *adj*

smok•able *or* **smoke•able** \'smō-kə-bəl\ *adj* : fit for smoking

[1]**smoke** \'smōk\ *n* **1 a** : the gas of burning organic materials (as coal, wood, or tobacco) made visible by small particles of carbon **b** : a suspension of solid or liquid particles in a gas **2** : a mass or column of smoke **3** : fume or vapor often resulting from the action of heat on moisture **4** : something of little substance,

permanence, or value **5** : something that obscures **6** : something to smoke (as a cigarette); *also* : the smoking of this [Old English *smoca*] — **smoke•like** \'smō-,klīk\ *adj*

²smoke *vb* **1 a** : to emit or exhale smoke **b** : to emit excessive smoke **2** : to inhale and exhale the fumes of burning plant material (as tobacco); *also* : to use in smoking ⟨*smoke* a cigar⟩ **3** : to act on with smoke: as **a** : to drive away by smoke **b** : to blacken or discolor with smoke **c** : to cure by exposure to smoke ⟨*smoked* meat⟩ **d** : to stun (as bees) by smoke

smoke•chas•er \-,chā-sər\ *n* : one that fights forest fires

smoke-filled room \,smōk-,fild-\ *n* : a room (as in a hotel) in which a small group of politicians carry on negotiations

smoke•house \'smōk-,haùs\ *n* : a building where meat or fish is cured by means of dense smoke

smoke jumper *n* : a forest-fire fighter who parachutes to locations otherwise difficult to reach

smoke•less \'smō-kləs\ *adj* : producing or containing little or no smoke ⟨*smokeless* powder⟩ ⟨a *smokeless* sky⟩

smoke out *vt* **1** : to drive out by or as if by smoke **2** : to bring to public knowledge

smok•er \'smō-kər\ *n* **1** : one that smokes **2** : a railroad car or compartment in which smoking is allowed **3** : an informal social gathering for men

smoke screen *n* : a screen of or as if of smoke to hinder observation or detection

smoke•stack \'smōk-,stak\ *n* : a chimney or funnel through which smoke and gases are discharged (as from a ship or factory)

smoke tree *n* : a small shrubby tree of the sumac family often grown for its large panicles of tiny flowers suggesting a cloud of smoke

smoking jacket *n* : a man's easy jacket for home wear

smoking lamp *n* : a lamp on a ship kept lighted during the hours when smoking is allowed

smoking room *n* : a room (as in a hotel or club) set apart for smokers

smoky \'smō-kē\ *adj* **smok•i•er**; **-est 1** : giving off smoke especially in large quantities ⟨*smoky* stoves⟩ **2** : resembling or suggestive of smoke ⟨a *smoky* flavor⟩ **3** : filled with or darkened by smoke ⟨a *smoky* room⟩ ⟨*smoky* ceilings⟩ — **smok•i•ly** \-kə-lē\ *adv* — **smok•i•ness** \-kē-nəs\ *n*

smoky quartz *n* : a yellow or smoky-brown often transparent crystalline quartz

¹smol•der *or* **smoul•der** \'smōl-dər\ *n* : a slow smoky fire [Middle English *smolder*]

²smolder *or* **smoulder** *vi* **smol•dered** *or* **smoul•dered**; **smol•der•ing** *or* **smoul•der•ing** \'smōl-də-ring, -dring\ **1** : to burn sluggishly with smoke and usually without flame ⟨fire was *smoldering* in the grate⟩ **2** : to exist in a state of suppressed activity ⟨a *smoldering* rebellion⟩; *also* : to indicate a suppressed emotion ⟨eyes *smoldering* with anger⟩

smolt \'smōlt\ *n* : a salmon or sea trout when it is about two years old and silvery and first descends to the sea [Middle English]

smooch \'smüch\ *vi* : KISS, PET [alteration of earlier *smouch* "to kiss loudly", of imitative origin] — **smooch** *n*

¹smooth \'smüth\ *adj* **1 a** : having a continuous even curve or surface : not rough ⟨a *smooth* skin⟩ **b** : being without hairs or projections : GLABROUS **c** : causing no resistance to sliding **2** : free from obstacles or difficulties ⟨a *smooth* path⟩ **3** : even and uninterrupted in flow or flight **4** : excessively and often artfully suave : INGRATIATING **5 a** : calm or unruffled in manner or behavior **b** : generally agreeable : COURTEOUS **6** : not sharp or acid : BLAND ⟨a *smooth* sherry⟩ [Old English *smōth*] **syn** see SUAVE — **smooth•ly** *adv* — **smooth•ness** *n*

²smooth *vt* **1** : to make smooth **2 a** : to free from what is harsh or disagreeable : POLISH ⟨*smoothed* out my style⟩ **b** : to make calm : SOOTHE **3** : to minimize (as a fault) in order to allay ill will ⟨*smoothed* things over with apologies⟩ **4** : to free from obstruction or difficulty **5** : to cause to lie evenly and in order ⟨*smooth* out the tablecloth⟩ — **smooth•er** *n*

smooth•bore \'smüth-'bōr, -'bòr\ *adj* : having a smooth-surfaced bore — **smooth•bore** \'smüth-,\ *n*

smooth•en \'smü-thən\ *vb* : to make or become smooth

smooth muscle *n* : muscle made up of spindle-shaped cells with single nuclei and no cross striations that is typical of visceral organs, occurs especially in sheets and rings, and is not under voluntary control — called also *involuntary muscle;* compare STRIATED MUSCLE

smooth-tongued \'smüth-'təngd\ *adj* : ingratiating in speech

smoothy *or* **smooth•ie** \'smü-thē\ *n, pl* **smooth•ies 1 a** : a person with polished manners **b** : a man with an ingratiating manner toward women **2** : a smooth-tongued person

smor•gas•bord \'smòr-gəs-,bòrd, -,bōrd\ *n* : a buffet offering a large variety of foods and dishes [Swedish *smörgåsbord,* from *smörgås* "open sandwich" + *bord* "table"]

smote *past of* SMITE

¹smoth•er \'sməth-ər\ *n* **1** : a dense cloud (as of fog, foam, or dust) **2** : a confused multitude of things [Middle English *smorther* "dense smoke", from *smoren* "to smother", from Old English *smorian* "to suffocate"]

²smother *vb* **smoth•ered**; **smoth•er•ing** \'sməth-ring, -ə-ring\ **1 a** : to overcome by depriving of air or exposing to smoke or fumes : SUFFOCATE **b** : to prevent the development or activity of ⟨*smother* a child with too much care⟩ **2** : to become suffocated **3 a** : to cover up : SUPPRESS ⟨*smother* a yawn⟩ **b** : to overlay thickly : BLANKET ⟨broiled steak *smothered* with mushrooms⟩ **c** : OVERWHELM 1 **d** : CONQUER 3

¹smudge \'sməj\ *vb* **1 a** : to make a smudge on **b** : to soil as if by smudging **2** : to smoke or protect by a smudge fire **3** : to make a smudge or become smudged [Middle English *smogen*]

²smudge *n* **1 a** : a blurry spot or streak : SMEAR **b** : STAIN 2 **2** : a fire made to smoke (as for driving away mosquitoes or protecting fruit from frost) — **smudg•i•ly** \'sməj-ə-lē\ *adv* — **smudg•i•ness** \'sməj-ē-nəs\ *n* — **smudgy** \'sməj-ē\ *adj*

smudge pot *n* : a container in which fuel (as oil) is burned to produce a smudge

smug \'sməg\ *adj* **smug•ger**; **smug•gest** : highly self-satisfied : COMPLACENT [probably from Low German *smuck* "neat"] — **snug•ly** *adv* — **snug•ness** *n*

smug•gle \'sməg-əl\ *vb* **smug•gled**; **smug•gling** \'sməg-ling, -ə-ling\ **1** : to export or import secretly and unlawfully (as to avoid paying duty) ⟨*smuggle* jewels⟩ **2** : to take, bring, or introduce secretly or stealthily [Low German *smuggeln* and Dutch *smokkelen*] — **smug•gler** \'sməg-lər\ *n*

¹smut \'smət\ *vb* **smut•ted**; **smut•ting 1** : to stain, taint, or affect with smut **2** : to become affected by smut [probably from Middle English *smotten* "to stain"]

²smut *n* **1** : matter that soils or blackens; *esp* : a particle of soot **2** : any of various destructive diseases of plants and especially of cereal grasses caused by parasitic fungi that transform plant structures (as seeds) into dark masses of spores; *also* : a fungus causing a smut **3** : obscene or indecent language or matter

smutch \'sməch\ *n* : a dark stain : SMUDGE [probably from ¹*smudge*] — **smutch** *vt* — **smutchy** \-ē\ *adj*

smut•ty \'smət-ē\ *adj* **smut•ti•er**; **-est 1** : soiled with smut ⟨a *smutty* face⟩ **2** : affected with smut fungus **3** : INDECENT ⟨*smutty* jokes⟩ — **smut•ti•ly** \'smət-l-ē\ *adv* — **smut•ti•ness** \'smət-ē-nəs\ *n*

snack \'snak\ *n* : a light meal : LUNCH [Middle English *snake* "bite", from *snaken* "to bite"]

snack bar *n* : a public eating place where snacks are served usually at a counter

snaf•fle \'snaf-əl\ *n* : a simple jointed bit for a bridle [origin unknown] — **snaffle** *vt*

sna•fu \sna-'fü\ *adj* : being in a state of confusion : AWRY [*s*ituation *n*ormal *a*ll *f*ouled *u*p] — **snafu** *n* — **snafu** *vt*

¹snag \'snag\ *n* **1** : a stump or stub of a tree branch especially when embedded under water and not visible from the surface **2** : an uneven or broken projection from a smooth or finished surface **3** : a concealed or unexpected difficulty or hindrance [of Scandinavian origin] — **snag•gy** \'snag-ē\ *adj*

²snag *vt* **snagged**; **snag•ging 1 a** : to catch and usually damage on or as if on a snag ⟨*snagged* my sleeve on a nail⟩ **b** : to halt or impede as if on a snag ⟨the bill was *snagged* in committee⟩ **2** : to catch or obtain by quick action ⟨*snagged* two tickets for the big game⟩

snag•gle•tooth \'snag-əl-'tüth\ *n* : an irregular, broken, or projecting tooth [English dialect *snaggle* "irregular tooth", from ¹*snag*] — **snag•gle•toothed** \,snag-əl-'tütht\ *adj*

snail \'snāl\ *n* **1** : a gastropod mollusk especially when having an external enclosing spiral shell **2** : a slow-moving person or thing [Old English *snægl*]

¹snake \'snāk\ *n* **1** : any of numerous limbless reptiles (suborder Serpentes or Ophidia) with a long tapering body and salivary glands often modified to produce venom which is injected through grooved or tubular fangs **2 :** a despicable or treacherous person [Old English *snaca*] — **snake·like** \'snā-,klīk\ *adj*

snail 1

[2]snake *vb* **1 :** to crawl or move sinuously, silently, or secretly **2 :** to move (as logs) by dragging

snake·bird \'snāk-,bərd\ *n* **:** any of several fish-eating birds related to the cormorants but distinguished by a long slender neck and sharp-pointed bill

snake·bite \-,bīt\ *n* **:** the bite of a snake and especially a venomous snake

snake charmer *n* **:** an entertainer who exhibits a professed power to charm or fascinate venomous snakes

snake dance *n* **:** a group of people moving single file in a wavy path (as in celebration of an athletic victory)

snake doctor *n* **:** DRAGONFLY

snake fence *n* **:** WORM FENCE

snake in the grass 1 : a lurking or unsuspected danger **2 :** a treacherous person pretending to be a friend

snake oil *n* **:** any of various substances or mixtures sold (as by a traveling medicine show) as medicine usually without regard to their medical worth or properties

snake·root \'snā-,krüt, -,kru̇t\ *n* **:** any of various plants mostly with roots reputed to cure snakebites; *also* **:** the root of such a plant

snake·skin \'snāk-,skin\ *n* **:** the skin of a snake or leather made from it

snaky \'snā-kē\ *adj* **snak·i·er; -est 1 :** of or resembling a snake **2 :** abounding in snakes — **snak·i·ly** \-kə-lē\ *adv*

[1]snap \'snap\ *vb* **snapped; snap·ping 1 a :** to close the jaws suddenly **:** seize something sharply with the mouth ⟨fish *snapping* at bait⟩ **b :** to grasp at something eagerly ⟨*snapped* at the chance to travel⟩ **c :** to take possession of promptly and decisively ⟨*snap* up a bargain⟩ **2 :** to speak or utter sharply or irritably ⟨*snap* at a friend⟩ ⟨*snapped* out an answer⟩ **3 a :** to break or break apart suddenly and especially with a sharp sound ⟨the twig *snapped*⟩ **b :** to give way or cause to give way suddenly under stress ⟨my nerves *snapped*⟩ **c :** to bring to a sudden end ⟨*snapped* the opposing team's winning streak⟩ **4 :** to make or cause to make a sharp or crackling sound ⟨*snap* a whip⟩ **5 a :** to close or fit in place with an abrupt movement ⟨the lid *snapped* shut⟩ **b :** to put into or remove from a position by a sudden movement or with a snapping sound ⟨*snap* off a switch⟩ **c :** to close by means of snaps or fasteners ⟨*snapped* up the back of the dress⟩ **6 :** FLASH ⟨eyes *snapping* in anger⟩ **7 a :** to move briskly or sharply ⟨*snapped* to attention⟩ **b :** to put (a football) in play especially by passing or handing backward between the legs **c :** to take a snapshot of [Dutch or Low German *snappen*]

[2]snap *n* **1 :** an abrupt closing (as of the mouth in biting or of scissors in cutting); *esp* **:** a biting or snatching with the teeth or jaws **2 :** CINCH 3a **3 :** a small amount **:** BIT ⟨don't care a *snap*⟩ **4 a :** a sudden snatching at something **b :** a quick short movement **c :** a sudden sharp breaking **5 :** a sound made by snapping something ⟨shut the book with a *snap*⟩ **6 :** a sudden interval of harsh weather ⟨a cold *snap*⟩ **7 :** a catch or fastening that closes or locks with a click ⟨the *snap* of a bracelet⟩ **8 :** a thin brittle cookie **9 :** SNAPSHOT **10 a :** ENERGY 2 **b :** a pleasing vigorous quality **11 :** an act or instance of snapping a football

[3]snap *adj* **1 :** made suddenly or without deliberation ⟨a *snap* judgment⟩ **2 :** shutting or fastening with a click or by means of a device that snaps ⟨a *snap* lock⟩ **3 :** unusually easy ⟨a *snap* course⟩

snap·back \'snap-,bak\ *n* **:** a sudden rebound or recovery

snap back \snap-'bak, 'snap-\ *vi* **:** to make a quick or vigorous recovery ⟨*snap back* after an illness⟩

snap bean *n* **:** a bean grown primarily for its young pods usually used broken in pieces as a cooked vegetable — compare SHELL BEAN

snap·drag·on \'snap-,drag-ən\ *n* **:** any of several garden plants having showy white, crimson, or yellow 2-lipped flowers [from the fancied resemblance of the flowers to the face of a dragon]

snap·per \'snap-ər\ *n, pl* **snappers** *also* **snapper 1 a :** one that snaps **b :** SNAPPING TURTLE **2 a :** any of a large family of active flesh-eating fishes of warm seas important as food and sport fishes **b :** any of several immature fishes (as the young of the bluefish) that resemble a snapper

snapping turtle *n* **:** any of several large edible American aquatic turtles with powerful jaws and a strong musky odor

snap·pish \'snap-ish\ *adj* **1 :** marked by or given to curt irritable speech **:** IRASCIBLE **2 :** inclined to bite ⟨a *snappish* dog⟩ — **snap·pish·ly** *adv* — **snap·pish·ness** *n*

snap·py \'snap-ē\ *adj* **snap·pi·er; -est 1 :** SNAPPISH 1 **2 a :** LIVELY 4 **b :** briskly cold **c :** SMART 6a, STYLISH — **snap·pi·ly** \'snap-ə-lē\ *adv* — **snap·pi·ness** \'snap-ē-nəs\ *n*

snap·shot \'snap-,shät\ *n* **:** a casual photograph made by rapid exposure usually with a small hand-held camera

[1]snare \'snaər, 'sneər\ *n* **1 :** a trap often consisting of a noose for catching small animals or birds **2 :** something by which one is entangled, trapped, or deceived **3 :** one of the catgut strings or metal spirals of a snare drum [Old English *sneare*, from Old Norse *snara*]

[2]snare *vt* **1 :** to capture or entangle by or as if by use of a snare **2 :** to win or attain by skillful or deceptive maneuvers **syn** see CATCH — **snar·er** *n*

snare drum *n* **:** a small double-headed drum with one or more snares stretched across its lower head

[1]snarl \'snärl\ *n* **1 :** a tangle especially of hairs or thread **:** KNOT **2 :** a tangled situation ⟨a traffic *snarl*⟩ [Middle English *snarle*]

[2]snarl *vb* **:** to become or cause to become tangled

[3]snarl *vb* **1 :** to growl with a snapping or gnashing of teeth **2 :** to express anger in a surly harsh way **3 :** to utter with a snarl [obsolete *snar* "to growl"] — **snarl·er** *n*

[4]snarl *n* **:** a surly angry growl

[1]snatch \'snach\ *vb* **1 :** to seize or try to seize something quickly or suddenly ⟨*snatched* at the rope⟩ **2 :** to grasp or take suddenly without permission, ceremony, or right [Middle English *snacchen* "to snap, seize"] **syn** see TAKE — **snatch·er** *n*

[2]snatch *n* **1 a :** a snatching at or of something **b** *slang* **:** an act or instance of kidnapping **2 a :** a short period ⟨slept in *snatches*⟩ **b :** something brief, fragmentary, or hurried ⟨*snatches* of old tunes⟩

snatchy \'snach-ē\ *adj* **:** marked by breaks in continuity

snaz·zy \'snaz-ē\ *adj* **snaz·zi·er; -est :** conspicuously or flashily attractive [origin unknown]

[1]sneak \'snēk\ *vb* **sneaked** \'snēkt\ *also* **snuck** \'snək\; **sneak·ing 1 :** to go stealthily or furtively **:** SLINK **2 :** to put, bring, or take in a furtive or sly manner [related to Old English *snīcan* "to sneak along"] **syn** see SKULK

[2]sneak *n* **1 :** a person who acts in a stealthy, furtive, or sly manner **2 :** the act or an instance of sneaking

[3]sneak *adj* **1 :** carried on secretly **:** CLANDESTINE **2 :** occurring without warning ⟨a *sneak* attack⟩

sneak·er \'snē-kər\ *n* **1 :** one that sneaks **2 :** a usually canvas sports shoe with a pliable rubber sole

sneak·ing \'snē-king\ *adj* **1 :** UNDERHAND 1, FURTIVE **2 a :** not openly expressed or acknowledged ⟨a *sneaking* sympathy⟩ **b :** that is a persistent conjecture ⟨a *sneaking* suspicion⟩ — **sneak·ing·ly** \'snē-king-lē\ *adv*

sneak preview *n* **:** a special advance showing of a movie before its release for public viewing

sneak thief *n* **:** a thief who steals without using violence or forcibly breaking into buildings

sneaky \'snē-kē\ *adj* **sneak·i·er; -est :** UNDERHAND 1 — **sneak·i·ly** \-kə-lē\ *adv* — **sneak·i·ness** \-kē-nəs\ *n*

[1]sneer \'sniər\ *vb* **1 :** to smile with facial contortions expressing scorn or contempt **2 a :** to speak or write in a scornfully jeering manner **b :** to express with a sneer [probably related to Middle High German *snerren* "to chatter, gossip"] **syn** see SCOFF — **sneer·er** *n*

[2]sneer *n* **:** a sneering expression or remark

[1]sneeze \'snēz\ *vi* **:** to expel the breath in a sudden violent audible spasm [Middle English *snesen*, alteration of *fnesen*, from Old English *fnēosan*] — **sneez·er** *n* — **sneeze at :** to treat as

\ə\ **abut**	\au̇\ **out**	\i\ **tip**	\ȯ\ **saw**	\u̇\ **foot**
\ər\ **further**	\ch\ **chin**	\ī\ **life**	\ȯi\ **coin**	\y\ **yet**
\a\ **mat**	\e\ **pet**	\j\ **job**	\th\ **thin**	\yü\ **few**
\ā\ **take**	\ē\ **easy**	\ng\ **sing**	\th\ **this**	\yu̇\ **cure**
\ä\ **cot, cart**	\g\ **go**	\ō\ **bone**	\ü\ **food**	\zh\ **vision**

unimportant ⟨a cool million is nothing to *sneeze at*⟩

2sneeze *n* : an act or fact of sneezing

sneeze•weed \ˈsnēz-ˌwēd\ *n* : a North American yellow-flowered perennial herb whose odor is said to cause sneezing

sneezy \ˈsnē-zē\ *adj* : given to or causing sneezing

snell \ˈsnel\ *n* : a short line by which a fishhook is attached to a longer line [origin unknown]

1snick \ˈsnik\ *vt* : to cut slightly : NICK [probably from obsolete *snick or snee* "to cut and thrust", from Dutch *steken of snijden* "to thrust or cut"]

2snick *n* : a slight often metallic sound : CLICK [imitative]

1snick•er \ˈsnik-ər\ *vi* **snick•ered**; **snick•er•ing** \ˈsnik-ring, -ə-ring\ : to laugh in a covert or partly suppressed way especially at the embarrassment of someone else [imitative]

2snicker *n* : an act or sound of snickering

snide \ˈsnīd\ *adj* **1** : MEAN, LOW ⟨a *snide* trick⟩ **2** : slyly disparaging : INSINUATING ⟨*snide* remarks⟩ [origin unknown]

sniff \ˈsnif\ *vb* **1** : to draw air audibly up the nose **2** : to show or express disdain or scorn ⟨*sniffed* at menial jobs⟩ **3** : to smell or take by inhalation through the nose : INHALE ⟨*sniff* perfume⟩ **4** : to detect by or as if by smelling ⟨*sniff* out trouble⟩ [Middle English *sniffen*] — **sniff** *n* — **sniff•er** *n*

sniff•ish \ˈsnif-ish\ *adj* : SNIFFY, HAUGHTY — **sniff•ish•ly** *adv* — **sniff•ish•ness** *n*

1snif•fle \ˈsnif-əl\ *vi* **snif•fled**; **snif•fling** \ˈsnif-ling, -ə-ling\ **1** : to sniff repeatedly : SNUFFLE **2** : to speak with or as if with sniffling [derived from *sniff*] — **snif•fler** \ˈsnif-lər, -ə-lər\ *n*

2sniffle *n* **1** : an act or sound of sniffling **2** *pl* : a head cold marked by nasal discharge

sniffy \ˈsnif-ē\ *adj* : inclined to sniff haughtily : SUPERCILIOUS — **sniff•i•ly** \ˈsnif-ə-lē\ *adv* — **sniff•i•ness** \ˈsnif-ē-nəs\ *n*

snif•ter \ˈsnif-tər\ *n* : a short-stemmed goblet with a bowl narrowing toward the top [Middle English *snifteren* "to sniff, snort"]

snig•ger \ˈsnig-ər\ *vi* **snig•gered**; **snig•ger•ing** \ˈsnig-ring, -ə-ring\ : SNICKER [by alteration] — **snigger** *n*

1snip \ˈsnip\ *n* **1** : a small piece that is snipped off; *also* : FRAGMENT **2** : an act or sound of snipping **3** : a presumptuous or impertinent person [Dutch or Low German]

2snip *vb* **snipped**; **snip•ping** : to cut or cut off with or as if with shears or scissors; *esp* : to clip suddenly or by bits

1snipe \ˈsnīp\ *n, pl* **snipes** *or* **snipe** : any of several game birds especially of marshy areas that resemble the related woodcocks [of Scandinavian origin]

1snipe

2snipe *vi* **1** : to shoot at a person or persons from a usually concealed vantage point **2** : to aim a snide attack [earlier *snipe* "to shoot snipe"] — **snip•er** \ˈsnī-pər\ *n*

snip•pet \ˈsnip-ət\ *n* : a small part, piece, or thing

snip•py \ˈsnip-ē\ *adj* **snip•pi•er**; **-est** **1** : SHORT-TEMPERED, IRASCIBLE **2** : unduly brief or curt **3** : putting on airs — **snip•pi•ness** *n*

snips \ˈsnips\ *n pl* : hand shears used especially for cutting sheet metal ⟨tin *snips*⟩

snit \ˈsnit\ *n* : a state of irritated agitation [origin unknown]

1snitch \ˈsnich\ *vb* **1** : INFORM, TATTLE ⟨always *snitching* on someone⟩ **2** : to take by stealth; *esp* : PILFER ⟨*snitched* a dime from me⟩ [origin unknown] — **snitch•er** *n*

2snitch *n* : one that snitches; *esp* : INFORMANT

sniv•el \ˈsniv-əl\ *vi* **sniv•eled** *or* **sniv•elled**; **sniv•el•ing** *or* **sniv•el•ling** \ˈsniv-ling, -ə-ling\ **1** : to run at the nose **2** : to snuff mucus up the nose audibly : SNUFFLE **3** : to cry or whine with snuffling **4** : to speak or act in a whining or weakly emotional way [Middle English *snivelen*] — **sniv•el•er** \ˈsniv-lər, -ə-lər\ *n*

snob \ˈsnäb\ *n* **1** : one who obviously imitates, fawningly admires, or vulgarly seeks association with those in a superior position **2 a** : one who looks down on those in an inferior position **b** : one whose attitude is offensively superior (as in matters of taste) [obsolete *snob* "member of the lower classes", from English dialect, "shoemaker"]

snob appeal *n* : qualities in a product (as high price or foreign origin) that appeal to the snobbery in a purchaser

snob•bery \ˈsnäb-rē, -ə-rē\ *n, pl* **-ber•ies** : snobbish conduct or outlook

snob•bish \ˈsnäb-ish\ *adj* : characteristic of or befitting a snob — **snob•bish•ly** *adv* — **snob•bish•ness** *n* — **snob•bism** \ˈsnäb-ˌiz-əm\ *n*

snob•by \ˈsnäb-ē\ *adj* : SNOBBISH

snood \ˈsnüd\ *n* : a net or fabric bag pinned or tied on at the back of a woman's head for holding the hair [Old English *snōd* "hair band"]

snook \ˈsnu̇k, ˈsnük\ *n, pl* **snook** *or* **snooks** : a large vigorous sport and food fish of warm seas related to the perches but resembling a pike [Dutch *snoek*]

snook•er \ˈsnu̇k-ər\ *n* : a variation of pool played with 15 red object balls and 6 object balls of different colors [origin unknown]

1snoop \ˈsnüp\ *vi* : to look or pry especially in a sneaky or meddlesome way [Dutch *snoepen* "to buy or eat on the sly"] — **snoop•er** \ˈsnü-pər\ *n*

2snoop *n* : one that snoops

snoop•er•scope \ˈsnü-pər-ˌskōp\ *n* : a device utilizing infrared radiation for enabling a person to see an object obscured (as by darkness)

snoopy \ˈsnü-pē\ *adj* : given to snooping : NOSY

snoot \ˈsnüt\ *n* **1** : SNOUT 1 **2** : NOSE 1 [Middle English *snute*]

snooty \ˈsnüt-ē\ *adj* **snoot•i•er**; **-est** : haughtily contemptuous : SNOBBISH — **snoot•i•ly** \ˈsnüt-l-ē\ *adv* — **snoot•i•ness** \ˈsnüt-ē-nəs\ *n*

1snooze \ˈsnüz\ *vi* : NAP 1, DOZE [origin unknown] — **snooz•er** *n*

2snooze *n* : a short sleep : NAP

snore \ˈsnōr, ˈsnȯr\ *vi* : to breathe during sleep with a rough hoarse noise [Middle English *snoren*] — **snore** *n* — **snor•er** *n*

1snor•kel \ˈsnȯr-kəl\ *n* **1** : a tube or tubes that can be extended above the surface of the water to supply air to and remove exhaust from a submerged submarine **2** : a tube used by swimmers for breathing with the face under water [German *schnorchel*]

2snorkel *vi* **snor•keled**; **snor•kel•ing** \-kə-ling, -kling\ : to swim on the surface with the face in the water using a snorkel; *also* : to engage in skin diving

1snort \ˈsnȯrt\ *vb* **1** : to force air violently through the nose with a rough harsh sound **2 a** : to express scorn, anger, indignation, or surprise by a snort **b** : to express with a snort ⟨*snort* one's disgust⟩ [Middle English *snorten*] — **snort•er** *n*

2snort *n* **1** : an act or sound of snorting **2** : a drink of usually straight liquor taken in one draft

snout \ˈsnau̇t\ *n* **1 a** : a long projecting nose or muzzle (as of a swine); *also* : the projecting front of the head of various animals (as a weevil) **b** : the human nose especially when large or grotesque **2** : something resembling an animal's snout [Middle English *snute*] — **snout•ed** \-əd\ *adj*

snout beetle *n* : WEEVIL

1snow \ˈsnō\ *n* **1 a** : small white crystals of frozen water formed directly from the water vapor of the air **b** : a fall of snow crystals : a mass of snow crystals fallen to earth **2** : something resembling snow: as **a** : a congealed or crystallized substance resembling snow in appearance ⟨carbon dioxide *snow*⟩ **b** *slang* : COCAINE **c** : small transient light or dark spots on a television or radar screen [Old English *snāw*]

2snow *vb* **1** : to fall or cause to fall in or as snow ⟨*snowed* messages on the senators⟩ **2 a** : to cover, shut in, or imprison with or as if with snow **b** : to charm, persuade, or deceive glibly

1snow•ball \ˈsnō-ˌbȯl\ *n* : a round mass of snow pressed or rolled together

2snowball *vb* **1** : to throw snowballs at **2** : to increase or expand at a rapidly accelerating rate

snow•bank \ˈsnō-ˌbangk\ *n* : a mound or slope of snow

snow•ber•ry \-ˌber-ē\ *n* : a low-growing North American shrub of the honeysuckle family with clusters of pink flowers and white berries

snow•bird \-ˌbərd\ *n* : any of several small birds (as a junco) seen chiefly in winter

snow–blind \-ˌblīnd\ *or* **snow–blind•ed** \-ˈblīn-dəd\ *adj* : affected with snow blindness

snow blindness *n* : inflammation and inability to tolerate light caused by exposure of the eyes to ultraviolet rays reflected from snow or ice

snow•bound \'snō-'bau̇nd\ *adj* : shut in or blockaded by snow
snow•cap \-,kap\ *n* : a covering cap of snow (as on a mountain peak) — **snow•capped** \-,kapt\ *adj*
snow•drift \-,drift\ *n* : a bank of drifted snow
snow•drop \-,dräp\ *n* : an early-blooming plant of the amaryllis family that bears nodding white flowers
snow•fall \-,fȯl\ *n* **1** : a fall of snow **2** : the amount of snow that falls in a single storm or in a given period
snow•field \-,fēld\ *n* : a broad level expanse of snow; *esp* : a mass of perennial snow (as at the head of a glacier)
snow•flake \-,flāk\ *n* : a flake or crystal of snow
snow leopard *n* : a large cat of central Asia with a long heavy pelt blotched with brownish black in summer and almost pure white in winter — called also *ounce*
snow•man \'snō-,man\ *n* : snow shaped to resemble a human figure
snow•mo•bile \'snō-mō-,bēl\ *n* : any of various automotive vehicles for travel on snow [*snow* + auto*mobile*] — **snow•mo•bil•er** \-,bē-lər\ *n* — **snow•mo•bil•ing** \-,bē-liŋ\ *n*
snow–on–the–mountain *n* : a showy white-bracted spurge native to the western United States
snow•plow \'snō-,plau̇\ *n* **1** : any of various devices used for clearing away snow **2** : a method of stopping in skiing in which the tails of the skis are pushed out to either side
[1]**snow•shoe** \-,shü\ *n* : a light oval wooden frame strung with thongs that is attached to the foot to enable a person to walk on soft snow without sinking
[2]**snowshoe** *vi* **snow•shoed**; **snow•shoe•ing** : to travel on snowshoes
snowshoe rabbit *n* : a rather large rabbit of northern North America with heavy fur on the hind feet and a coat that is brown in the summer but usually white in winter — called also *snowshoe hare*

snowshoe rabbit

snow•slide \'snō-,slīd\ *n* : an avalanche of snow
snow•storm \-'stȯrm\ *n* : a storm of falling snow
snow•suit \-,süt\ *n* : a one-piece or two-piece and usually lined garment for winter wear by children
snow tire *n* : an automobile tire with a tread designed to give added traction on snow
snow train *n* : a special train to a place (as a ski resort) suitable for winter sports
snow under *vt* **1** : to overwhelm especially beyond capacity to absorb or deal with something **2** : to defeat by a large margin
snow–white \'snō-'hwīt -'wīt\ *adj* : white as snow
snowy \'snō-ē\ *adj* **snow•i•er**; **-est** **1 a** : marked by snow ⟨a *snowy* day⟩ **b** : covered with snow ⟨*snowy* mountaintops⟩ **2** : whitened by or as if by snow ⟨an orchard *snowy* with apple blossoms⟩ **3** : SNOW-WHITE — **snow•i•ly** \'snō-ə-lē\ *adv* — **snow•i•ness** \'snō-ē-nəs\ *n*
snowy owl *n* : a large chiefly arctic owl that is white or white spotted with brown

snowy owl

[1]**snub** \'snəb\ *vt* **snubbed**; **snub•bing** **1** : to check or stop with a cutting reply : REBUKE **2** : to check (as a line or cable that is running out) suddenly especially by turning around a fixed object (as a post) **3** : to treat with contempt or neglect **4** : to extinguish by stubbing ⟨*snub* out a cigarette⟩ [of Scandinavian origin]
[2]**snub** *n* : an act or an instance of snubbing : REBUFF
[3]**snub** *or* **snubbed** \'snəbd\ *adj* : BLUNT, STUBBY ⟨a *snub* nose⟩ — **snub•ness** *n*
snub•ber \'snəb-ər\ *n* **1** : one that snubs **2** : SHOCK ABSORBER
snub–nosed \'snəb-'nōzd\ *adj* : having a stubby and usually slightly turned-up nose
snuck *past of* SNEAK

[1]**snuff** \'snəf\ *n* : the charred part of the wick of a candle [Middle English *snoffe*]
[2]**snuff** *vt* **1** : to cut or pinch off the snuff of (a candle) so as to brighten the light **2** : EXTINGUISH ⟨*snuff* out a life⟩
[3]**snuff** *vb* **1** : to draw forcibly through or into the nostrils **2** : to sniff inquiringly [related to Dutch *snuffen* "to sniff, snuff"]
[4]**snuff** *n* : the act of snuffing : SNIFF
[5]**snuff** *n* : a preparation of pulverized tobacco to be chewed, placed against the gums, or inhaled through the nostrils [Dutch *snuf,* short for *snuftabak,* from *snuffen* "to sniff, snuff" + *tabak* "tobacco"] — **up to snuff** : meeting an acceptable standard
snuff•box \'snəf-,bäks\ *n* : a small box for holding snuff
[1]**snuff•er** \'snəf-ər\ *n* **1** : a device somewhat like a pair of scissors for cutting and holding the snuff of a candle — usually used in pl. **2** : a device for extinguishing candles

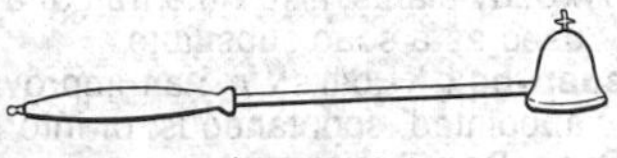
[1]snuffer 2

[2]**snuffer** *n* : one that snuffs or sniffs
[1]**snuf•fle** \'snəf-əl\ *vb* **snuf•fled**; **snuf•fling** \'snəf-liŋ, -ə-liŋ\ **1** : to snuff or sniff usually noisily and repeatedly **2** : to breathe through an obstructed nose with a sniffing sound **3** : to speak in a nasal tone; *also* : WHIMPER, WHINE [related to Dutch *snuffelen* "to snuffle"] — **snuf•fler** \'snəf-lər, -ə-lər\ *n*
[2]**snuffle** *n* : the sound made in snuffling
[1]**snug** \'snəg\ *adj* **snug•ger**; **snug•gest** **1 a** : SEAWORTHY **b** : fitting closely and comfortably ⟨a *snug* coat⟩ **2** : enjoying or affording warm secure shelter and comfort : COZY ⟨a *snug* cottage⟩ **3** : offering safe concealment ⟨a *snug* hideout⟩ [perhaps of Scandinavian origin] — **snug** *adv* — **snug•ly** *adv* — **snug•ness** *n*
[2]**snug** *vb* **snugged**; **snug•ging** **1** : to settle or lie down : NESTLE **2** : to make snug
snug•gery \'snəg-rē, -ə-rē\ *n, pl* **-ger•ies** *chiefly British* : a snug place; *esp* : DEN 4
snug•gle \'snəg-əl\ *vb* **snug•gled**; **snug•gling** \'snəg-liŋ, -ə-liŋ\ **1** : to curl up comfortably or cozily **2** : to draw close especially for comfort or in affection [derived from [2]*snug*]
[1]**so** \sō, 'sō, *especially before an adj or adv followed by "that"* sə\ *adv* **1 a** : in a manner or way that is indicated or suggested ⟨do you really think *so*⟩ ⟨it *so* happened that all were wrong⟩ **b** : in the same manner or way : ALSO ⟨you worked hard and *so* did we⟩ **c** : SUBSEQUENTLY, THEN ⟨and *so* home and to bed⟩ **2 a** : to an indicated or suggested extent or degree ⟨had never been *so* happy⟩ **b** : to a great extent or degree : VERY, EXTREMELY ⟨came home because we loved it *so*⟩ **c** : to a definite but unspecified extent or degree ⟨can only do *so* much in a day⟩ **d** : most certainly : INDEED ⟨you did *so* do it⟩ **3** : THEREFORE, CONSEQUENTLY ⟨the witness is biased and *so* unreliable⟩ [Old English *swā*]
[2]**so** \sō, 'sō\ *conj* **1 a** : with the result that ⟨your diction is good, *so* every word is clear⟩ **b** : in order that ⟨be quiet *so* I can sleep⟩ **2** : provided that — usually preceded by *just* **3 a** : for that reason : THEREFORE ⟨I want to go, *so* I will⟩ **b** — used as an introductory particle ⟨*so* here we are⟩ often to belittle a point being discussed ⟨*so* what?⟩
[3]**so** \'sō\ *adj* **1** : conforming with actual facts : TRUE ⟨said things that were not *so*⟩ **2** : marked by a definite order ⟨your books are always just *so*⟩
[4]**so** \,sō, 'sō\ *pron* **1** : such as has been specified : the same ⟨became insane and remained *so*⟩ **2** : approximately that — ⟨20 years or *so*⟩
[5]**so** \'sō\ *variant of* SOL
[1]**soak** \'sōk\ *vb* **1 a** : to remain steeping in liquid (as water) **b** : to place in a medium to wet or permeate thoroughly **2 a** : to enter or pass through something by or as if by pores : SATURATE **b** : to capture one's full attention ⟨let the remark *soak in*⟩ **3** : to extract by or as if by steeping ⟨*soak* the dirt out⟩

\ə\ **abut**	\au̇\ **out**	\i\ **tip**	\ȯ\ **saw**	\u̇\ **foot**
\ər\ **further**	\ch\ **chin**	\ī\ **life**	\ȯi\ **coin**	\y\ **yet**
\a\ **mat**	\e\ **pet**	\j\ **job**	\th\ **thin**	\yü\ **few**
\ā\ **take**	\ē\ **easy**	\ŋ\ **sing**	\t͟h\ **this**	\yu̇\ **cure**
\ä\ **cot, cart**	\g\ **go**	\ō\ **bone**	\ü\ **food**	\zh\ **vision**

4 : to draw in by or as if by suction or absorption ⟨*soaked* up the sunshine⟩ **5** : to levy an exorbitant charge against ⟨*soaked* the taxpayers⟩ [Old English *socian*] — **soak•er** *n*

2soak *n* **1** : the act or process of soaking : the state of being soaked **2** : DRUNKARD

soak•age \'sō-kij\ *n* **1** : liquid gained by absorption or lost by seepage **2** : the act or process of soaking : the state of being soaked

so–and–so \'sō-ən-ˌsō\ *n, pl* **so–and–sos** *or* **so–and–so's** \-ən-ˌsōz\ : an unnamed or unspecified person or thing

1soap \'sōp\ *n* **1** : a substance that is usually made by the action of alkali on fat, dissolves in water, and is used for washing **2** : a salt of a fatty acid [Old English *sāpe*] — **soap•less** \'sō-pləs\ *adj* — **soap•mak•ing** \'sōp-ˌmā-king\ *n*

2soap *vt* : to rub soap over or into

soap•ber•ry \'sōp-ˌber-ē\ *n* : any of a genus of chiefly tropical woody plants; *also* : the fruit of a soapberry and especially one used as a soap substitute

soap•box \-ˌbäks\ *n* : an improvised platform used by a self-appointed, spontaneous, or informal speaker — **soapbox** *adj*

Soap Box Derby *service mark* — used for a downhill race for youngsters' homemade racing cars without motors or pedals

soap bubble *n* : a hollow iridescent globe formed by blowing a film of soapsuds (as from a pipe)

soap opera *n* : a radio or television serial drama performed usually on a daytime commerical program [from its frequently being sponsored by soap manufacturers]

soap plant *n* : a plant with a part (as leaves or root) that can be used as a soap substitute

soap•stone \'sōp-ˌstōn\ *n* : a soft stone having a soapy feel and composed essentially of talc, chlorite, and often some magnetite

soap•suds \-ˌsədz\ *n pl* : SUDS 1

soap•wort \-ˌwərt, -ˌwȯrt\ *n* : BOUNCING BET

soapy \'sō-pē\ *adj* **soap•i•er**; **-est** **1** : smeared with or full of soap ⟨a *soapy* face⟩ **2** : containing or combined with soap ⟨*soapy* ammonia⟩ **3** : resembling or having the qualities of soap — **soap•i•ly** \-pə-lē\ *adv* — **soap•i•ness** \-pē-nəs\ *n*

1soar \'sōr, 'sȯr\ *vi* **1 a** : to fly aloft or about **b** : to sail or hover in the air often at a great height : GLIDE **2 a** : to move upward in position or status : RISE **b** : to ascend to a higher or more exalted level **3** : to rise majestically [Middle French *essorer* "to air, soar" derived from Latin *ex-* + *aura* "air"] — **soar•er** *n*

2soar *n* : the act of soaring : upward flight

1sob \'säb\ *vb* **sobbed**; **sob•bing** **1** : to cry with convulsive catching of the breath **2** : to make a sound like that of sobbing ⟨the wind *sobbed* through the trees⟩ **3** : to bring to a specified state by sobbing ⟨*sobbed* myself to sleep⟩ **4** : to utter with sobs ⟨*sobbed* out the story⟩ [Middle English *sobben*]

2sob *n* **1** : an act of sobbing **2** : a sound of or like that of sobbing

1so•ber \'sō-bər\ *adj* **so•ber•er** \-bər-ər\; **so•ber•est** \-bə-rəst, -brəst\ **1 a** : sparing or temperate in the use of food and drink **b** : not drunk **2** : SERIOUS 1 **3** : subdued in tone, color, or intensity **4** : having or showing self-control : avoiding extremes of behavior [Middle French *sobre*, from Latin *sobrius*] — **so•ber•ly** \-bər-lē\ *adv* — **so•ber•ness** *n*

2sober *vb* **so•bered**; **so•ber•ing** \-bə-ring, -bring\ : to make or become sober — often used with *up*

so•ber•sid•ed \ˌsō-bər-'sīd-əd\ *adj* : SERIOUS 1

so•ber•sides \'sō-bər-ˌsīdz\ *n sing or pl* : one who is sober-sided

so•bri•e•ty \sə-'brī-ət-ē\ *n* : the quality or state of being sober [Middle French *sobrieté*, from Latin *sobrietas*, from *sobrius* "sober"]

so•bri•quet \'sō-bri-ˌkā, -ˌket, ˌsō-bri-'\ *or* **sou•bri•quet** \'sō-, ˌsō-, 'sü-, ˌsü-\ *n* : a fanciful name or epithet [French]

sob story *n* : a sentimental story designed chiefly to evoke sympathy or sadness

so–called \'sō-'kȯld\ *adj* **1** : commonly or popularly named ⟨the *so-called* pocket veto⟩ **2** : falsely or inaccurately named ⟨your *so-called* friend⟩

soc•cer \'säk-ər\ *n* : a football game with 11 players on a side in which a round ball is advanced by kicking or by propelling it with any part of the body except the hands and arms [by shortening and alteration from *association football*]

so•cia•bil•i•ty \ˌsō-shə-'bil-ət-ē\ *n, pl* **-ties** : the quality or state of being sociable : AFFABILITY; *also* : the act or an instance of being sociable

1so•cia•ble \'sō-shə-bəl\ *adj* **1** : inclined to seek or enjoy companionship : AFFABLE, FRIENDLY ⟨*sociable* people⟩ **2** : leading to friendliness or pleasant social relations [Latin *sociabilis*, from *sociare* "to join, associate", from *socius* "companion"] — **so•cia•ble•ness** *n* — **so•cia•bly** \-blē\ *adv*

2sociable *n* : SOCIAL

1so•cial \'sō-shəl\ *adj* **1 a** : marked by, devoted to, or engaged in for sociability ⟨*social* events⟩ ⟨my *social* life⟩ **b** : SOCIABLE 1 **2 a** : naturally living or growing in groups or communities ⟨bees are *social* insects⟩ **b** : tending to form cooperative and interdependent relationships with one's fellows ⟨humans are *social* beings⟩ **3** : of or relating to human society, the interaction of the group and its members, and the welfare of these members ⟨*social* institutions⟩ ⟨*social* legislation⟩ **4** : of, relating to, or based on status in a particular society ⟨different *social* circles⟩; *also* : of or relating to fashionable society ⟨a *social* leader⟩ [Latin *socialis*, from *socius* "companion, associate"]

2social *n* : an informal social gathering frequently involving a special activity or interest

social climber *n* : one who attempts to gain a higher social position or acceptance in fashionable society

social democracy *n* : a political movement advocating a gradual and peaceful transition from capitalism to socialism by democratic means — **social democrat** *n* — **social democratic** *adj*

social disease *n* **1** : VENEREAL DISEASE **2** : a disease (as tuberculosis) whose frequency is directly related to social and economic factors

so•cial•ism \'sō-shə-ˌliz-əm\ *n* **1** : any of various economic and political theories or social systems based on collective or governmental ownership and administration of the means of production and distribution of goods **2** : a stage of society in Marxist theory transitional between capitalism and communism and distinguished by unequal distribution of goods and pay according to work done — **so•cial•ist** \'sōsh-ləst, -ə-ləst\ *n* — **socialist** *or* **so•cial•is•tic** \ˌsō-shə-'lis-tik\ *adj* — **so•cial•is•ti•cal•ly** \-ti-kə-lē, -klē\ *adv*

so•cial•ite \'sō-shə-ˌlīt\ *n* : a socially prominent person

so•ci•al•i•ty \ˌsō-shē-'al-ət-ē\ *n, pl* **-ties** **1** : SOCIABILITY **2** : the tendency to associate in or to form social groups

so•cial•ize \'sō-shə-ˌlīz\ *vb* **1** : to make social; *esp* : to train so as to develop the qualities essential to group living **2** : to adapt to social needs and uses **3** : to regulate according to the theory or practice of socialism ⟨*socialize* industry⟩ **4** : to take part in the social life around one — **so•cial•iza•tion** \ˌsō-shə-lə-'zā-shən\ *n* — **so•cial•iz•er** \'sō-shə-ˌlī-zər\ *n*

socialized medicine *n* : medical and hospital services for the members of a class or population administered by an organized group (as a state agency) and paid for from funds obtained usually by assessments, philanthropy, or taxation

so•cial•ly \'sōsh-lē,-ə-lē\ *adv* **1** : in a social manner ⟨*socially* popular⟩ **2** : with respect to society ⟨*socially* prominent⟩ **3** : by or through society ⟨*socially* prescribed values⟩

so•cial–mind•ed \ˌsō-shəl-'mīn-dəd\ *adj* : having an interest in society; *esp* : actively interested in social welfare or the well-being of society as a whole

social science *n* **1** : a science (as psychology or sociology) that deals with the institutions and functioning of human society and with the interrelationships of individuals as members of society **2** : a science (as economics) dealing with a particular phase or aspect of human society — **social scientist** *n*

social secretary *n* : a personal secretary employed to handle social correspondence and appointments

social security *n* **1** : the principle or practice of public provision for the economic security and social welfare of the individual and the family **2** *often cap* : a United States government program established in 1935 to include old-age and survivors insurance, contributions to state unemployment insurance, and old-age and disability assistance

social service *n* : an activity designed to promote social welfare

social studies *n pl* : studies (as history, civics, economics, and geography) that deal with human relationships and the functions of society

social welfare *n* : organized public or private social services for the assistance of disadvantaged groups

social work *n* : the art, practice, or profession of extending the benefits of organized society especially through assistance to the economically underprivileged and the socially maladjusted — **social worker** *n*

1so•ci•ety \sə-'sī-ət-ē\ *n, pl* **-et•ies** **1** : companionship with one's associates : COMPANY **2** : the social order or community life considered as a system within which the individual lives ⟨rural *society*⟩ **3** : people in general ⟨the benefit of *society*⟩ **4** : an association of persons for some purpose ⟨a mutual aid *society*⟩ **5** : a part of a community regarded as a unit distinguished by common interests or standards; *esp* : the group or set of fashionable persons **6** : a system of interdependent organisms or biological units; *also* : an assemblage of plants usually of a single species or habit within a larger ecological community [Middle French *societé,* from Latin *societas,* from *socius* "companion"] — **so•ci•etal** \-ət-l\ *adj*

2society *adj* : of, relating to, or characteristic of fashionable society

so•cio•eco•nom•ic \ˌsō-sē-ō-ˌek-ə-'näm-ik, ˌsō-shē-, -ˌē-kə-\ *adj* : of, relating to, or involving a combination of social and economic factors

so•ci•ol•o•gy \ˌsō-sē-'äl-ə-jē, -shē-\ *n* : the science of society, social institutions, and social relationships [French *sociologie,* from Latin *socius* "companion"] — **so•cio•log•i•cal** \ˌsō-sē-ə-'läj-i-kəl, -shē-\ *also* **so•cio•log•ic** \-ə-'läj-ik\ *adj* — **so•cio•log•i•cal•ly** \-i-kə-lē, -klē\ *adv* — **so•ci•ol•o•gist** \-'äl-ə-jəst\ *n*

so•cio•po•lit•i•cal \ˌsō-sē-ō-pə-'lit-i-kəl, ˌsō-shē-\ *adj* : of, relating to, or involving both social and political factors

1sock \'säk\ *n, pl* **socks** *or* **sox** \'säks\ : a knitted or woven covering for the foot usually extending above the ankle and sometimes to the knee [Old English *socc* "low shoe", from Latin *soccus*]

2sock *vb* : to hit, strike, or apply forcefully : deliver a blow [probably of Scandinavian origin]

3sock *n* : a vigorous or violent blow : PUNCH

sock•et \'säk-ət\ *n* **1** : an opening or hollow that receives and holds something ⟨the eye *socket*⟩ **2** : a device to receive and grip the end of something (as a bolt or light bulb) [Anglo-French *soket* "small plowshare", from Old French *soc* "plowshare"]

socket wrench *n* : a wrench usually in the form of a bar and removable socket made to fit a bolt or nut

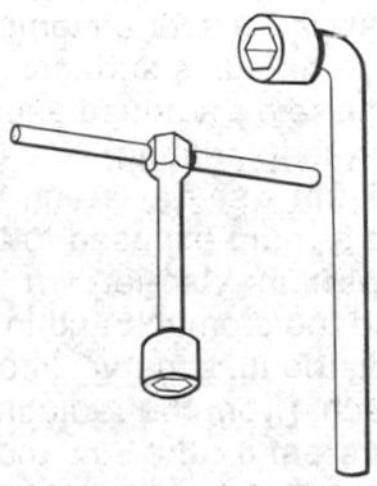
socket wrench

sock•eye \'säk-ˌī\ *n* : a small but commercially important Pacific salmon that spawns in late summer or fall — called also *red salmon* [of American Indian origin]

So•crat•ic \sə-'krat-ik\ *adj* : of or relating to Socrates, his followers, or his philosophical method of systematic doubt and questioning of another

1sod \'säd\ *n* **1 a** : TURF 1 **b** : the grass- and forb-covered surface of the ground **2** : one's native land [Dutch or Low German *sode*]

2sod *vt* **sod•ded; sod•ding** : to cover with sod or turfs

so•da \'sōd-ə\ *n* **1 a** : SODIUM CARBONATE **b** : SODIUM BICARBONATE **c** : SODIUM HYDROXIDE **d** : sodium oxide Na_2O **e** : SODIUM — used in combination ⟨*soda* alum⟩ **2 a** : SODA WATER **b** : SODA POP **c** : a sweet drink consisting of soda water, flavoring, and often ice cream [Italian]

soda ash *n* : commercial sodium carbonate

soda cracker *n* : a cracker leavened with bicarbonate of soda and cream of tartar

soda fountain *n* **1** : an apparatus for drawing soda water **2** : the equipment and counter for the preparation and serving of sodas, sundaes, and ice cream

soda jerk *n* : one who dispenses carbonated drinks and ice cream at a soda fountain

soda lime *n* : a mixture of sodium hydroxide and slaked lime used especially to absorb moisture and gases

so•da•list \'sōd-l-əst, sō-'dal-\ *n* : a sodality member

so•dal•i•ty \sō-'dal-ət-ē\ *n, pl* **-ties** : an organized society or fellowship; *esp* : a devotional or charitable association of Roman Catholic laity [Latin *sodalitas* "comradeship, club", from *sodalis* "comrade"]

soda pop *n* : a bottled soft drink consisting of soda water with added flavoring and a sweet syrup

soda water *n* : a beverage consisting of water highly charged with carbonic acid gas

1sod•den \'säd-n\ *adj* **1 a** : dull or lacking in expression ⟨*sodden* features⟩ **b** : SLUGGISH, UNIMAGINATIVE ⟨*sodden* minds⟩ **2** : heavy with moisture : SATURATED ⟨*sodden* ground⟩ [Middle English *soden,* from past participle of *sethen* "to seethe"] — **sod•den•ly** *adv* — **sod•den•ness** \-n-nəs, -n-əs\ *n*

2sodden *vb* : to make or become sodden

so•di•um \'sōd-ē-əm\ *n* : a soft waxy silver-white metallic element chemically very active and found abundantly in nature always in combined form — see ELEMENT table [New Latin, from English *soda*]

sodium ben•zo•ate \-'ben-zə-ˌwāt\ *n* : a crystalline or granular sodium salt $NaC_7H_5O_2$ used chiefly as a food preservative

sodium bicarbonate *n* : a white crystalline weakly alkaline salt $NaHCO_3$ used especially in baking powders, fire extinguishers, and medicine

sodium carbonate *n* : a sodium salt of carbonic acid: as **a** : a strongly alkaline compound Na_2CO_3 used in making glass, soaps, and chemicals **b** : SAL SODA

sodium chloride *n* : SALT 1a

sodium cyanide *n* : a white poisonous salt NaCN used especially in electroplating, fumigating and treating steel

sodium fluoride *n* : a poisonous crystalline salt NaF that is used in the fluoridation of water and as a pesticide

sodium hydroxide *n* : a white brittle solid NaOH that is a strong caustic base used in making soap, rayon, and paper

sodium hypochlorite *n* : an unstable salt NaOCl used as a bleaching agent and disinfectant

sodium hyposulfite *n* **1** : SODIUM THIOSULFATE **2** : a crystalline water-soluble salt $Na_2S_2O_4$ used especially in dyeing and bleaching

sodium nitrate *n* : a deliquescent crystalline salt $NaNO_3$ found in crude form in Chile and used as a fertilizer and an oxidizing agent and in curing meat

sodium silicate *n* : WATER GLASS 3

sodium thiosulfate *n* : a hygroscopic crystalline salt $Na_2S_2O_3$ used especially as a photographic fixing agent and a reducing or bleaching agent

sodium–vapor lamp *n* : an electric lamp that contains sodium vapor and electrodes between which a luminous discharge takes place

Sod•om \'säd-əm\ *n* : a place notorious for vice or corruption [*Sodom,* city of ancient Palestine destroyed by God for its wickedness (Genesis 18:20, 21; 19:24–28)]

so•fa \'sō-fə\ *n* : a long upholstered seat usually with arms and a back and often convertible into a bed [Arabic *ṣuffah* "long bench"]

so far as *conj* : insofar as

sof•fit \'säf-ət\ *n* : the underside of a part or member of a building and especially of an arch [French *soffite,* from Italian *soffitto,* derived from Latin *suffigere* "to fasten underneath"]

1 soffit

soft \'sȯft\ *adj* **1 a** : having a pleasing, comfortable, or soothing quality or effect : GENTLE, MILD ⟨*soft* breezes⟩ **b** : quiet in pitch or volume ⟨*soft* voices⟩ **c** : not bright or glaring ⟨*soft lighting*⟩ **d** : demanding little effort : EASY ⟨a *soft* job⟩ **e** : smooth or delicate in appearance or texture ⟨*soft* cashmere⟩ **f** : pleasingly mild in taste or odor **2 a** : having a mild gentle nature : DOCILE **b** : lacking in strength or vigor : unfit for prolonged exertion or severe stress : FEEBLE ⟨*soft* from good living⟩ **c** : weak or deficient mentally **d** : advocating or being a moderate or conciliatory policy ⟨took a *soft* stand toward the rebels⟩ **3 a** : yielding to physical pressure ⟨a *soft* mattress⟩ ⟨*soft* metals such as lead⟩ **b** : relatively lacking in hardness ⟨*soft* iron⟩ ⟨*soft* wood⟩ **4**

\ə\ **abut**	\au̇\ **out**	\i\ **tip**	\ȯ\ **saw**	\u̇\ **foot**
\ər\ **further**	\ch\ **chin**	\ī\ **life**	\ȯi\ **coin**	\y\ **yet**
\a\ **mat**	\e\ **pet**	\j\ **job**	\th\ **thin**	\yü\ **few**
\ā\ **take**	\ē\ **easy**	\ng\ **sing**	\t͟h\ **this**	\yu̇\ **cure**
\ä\ **cot, cart**	\g\ **go**	\ō\ **bone**	\ü\ **food**	\zh\ **vision**

: gently or gradually curved or rounded : not harsh or jagged ⟨a range of *soft* hills⟩ **5** : sounding as in *ace* and *gem* respectively — used of *c* and *g* **6 a** : deficient in or free from substances (as calcium and magnesium salts) that prevent lathering of soap ⟨*soft* water⟩ **b** : containing no alcohol ⟨*soft* drinks⟩ **7** : having relatively low penetrating power ⟨*soft* X rays⟩ **8** : occurring at such a speed as to avoid destructive impact ⟨*soft* landing of a spacecraft on the moon⟩ [Old English *sēfte, sōfte*] — **soft•ly** \'sȯft-lē\ *or* **soft** *adv* — **soft•ness** \'sȯft-nəs, 'sȯf-\ *n*

soft•ball \'sȯft-ˌbȯl, 'sȯf-\ *n* : a variation of baseball played on a smaller diamond with a larger ball that is pitched underhanded; *also* : the ball used in this game

soft–boiled \-'bȯild\ *adj* : lightly boiled so that the contents are only partly coagulated ⟨*soft-boiled* eggs⟩

soft coal *n* : BITUMINOUS COAL

soft•en \'sȯ-fən\ *vb* **soft•ened**; **soft•en•ing** \'sȯf-ning, -ə-ning\ **1** : to make or become soft or softer **2** : to lessen the strength or resistance of — **soft•en•er** \'sȯf-nər, -ə-nər\ *n*

soft–finned \'sȯft-'find, 'sȯf-\ *adj* : having fins in which the membrane is supported entirely or mostly by soft or jointed rays — compare SPINY-FINNED

soft•head•ed \'sȯft-'hed-əd\ *adj* : having a weak, unrealistic, or uncritical mind : IMPRACTICAL — **soft•head•ed•ly** *adv* — **soft•head•ed•ness** *n*

soft•heart•ed \-'härt-əd\ *adj* : emotionally responsive : SYMPATHETIC — **soft•heart•ed•ly** *adv* — **soft•heart•ed•ness** *n*

soft–land \-'land\ *vb* : to make or cause to make a soft landing on a celestial body (as the moon) — **soft–land•er** *n*

soft palate *n* : a fold at the back of the hard palate that partially separates the mouth and pharynx

soft–ped•al \'sȯft-'ped-l, 'sȯf-\ *vt* **1** : to use the soft pedal in playing **2** : to play down ⟨*soft-pedal* the issue⟩

soft pedal *n* : a foot pedal on a piano that reduces the volume of sound

soft rot *n* : a mushy, watery, or slimy decay of a plant or plant part usually caused by bacteria or fungi

soft scale *n* : a scale insect more or less active in all stages

soft sell *n* : the use of suggestion or persuasion in selling rather than aggressive pressure

soft–shell \'sȯft-ˌshel, 'sȯf-\ *or* **soft–shelled** \-'sheld\ *adj* : having a soft or fragile shell especially as a result of recent shedding

soft–shoe \'sȯft-'shü, 'sȯf-\ *adj* : of or relating to tap dancing done in soft-soled shoes without metal taps

soft–soap \-'sōp\ *vb* : to soothe or coax with flattery — **soft–soap•er** *n*

soft soap *n* **1** : a semifluid soap **2** : FLATTERY 2

soft–spo•ken \'sȯft-'spō-kən, 'sȯf-\ *adj* : having a mild or gentle voice

soft•ware \'sȯf-ˌtwaər, -ˌtweər\ *n* : the programs and related documentation associated with a computer system; *esp* : computer programs

soft wheat *n* : a wheat with soft starchy kernels high in starch but usually low in gluten

¹soft•wood \'sȯf-ˌtwu̇d\ *n* **1** : the wood of a cone-bearing tree including both soft and hard woods **2** : a tree that yields softwood

²softwood *adj* **1** : having or made of softwood **2** : consisting of immature still pliable tissue ⟨*softwood* cuttings for propagating plants⟩

soft–wood•ed \'sȯf-'twu̇d-əd\ *adj* **1** : having soft wood that is easy to work or finish **2** : SOFTWOOD 1

softy *or* **sof•tie** \'sȯf-tē\ *n, pl* **soft•ies** **1** : a silly or sentimental person **2** : WEAKLING

sog•gy \'säg-ē\ *adj* **sog•gi•er**; **-est** : saturated or heavy with water or moisture [English dialect *sog* "to soak"] — **sog•gi•ly** \'säg-ə-lē\ *adv* — **sog•gi•ness** \'säg-ē-nəs\ *n*

¹soil \'sȯil\ *vb* : to make or become dirty or corrupt [Old French *soiller* "to wallow, soil", from *soil* "pigsty", probably from Latin *suile,* from *sus* "pig"]

²soil *n* **1 a** : SOILAGE, STAIN **b** : moral defilement : CORRUPTION **2** : something that soils or pollutes

³soil *n* **1** : firm land : EARTH **2** : the loose surface material of the earth in which plants grow **3** : COUNTRY 2a, LAND ⟨our native *soil*⟩ **4** : the agricultural life or calling **5** : a medium in which something may take root and grow ⟨slums are fertile *soil* for crime⟩ [Anglo-French, from Latin *solium* "seat"]

soil•age \'sȯi-lij\ *n* : the act of soiling : the condition of being soiled

soil bank *n* : acreage retired from crop cultivation and planted with soil-building crops under a federally sponsored plan that provides subsidies to farmers for the retired land

soil conservation *n* : soil management designed to obtain good yields while improving and protecting the soil

soil•less \'sȯil-ləs\ *adj* : carried on without soil ⟨*soilless* agriculture⟩

soil profile *n* : PROFILE 4

soil science *n* : the science of soils — **soil scientist** *n*

soi•ree *or* **soi•rée** \swä-'rā\ *n* : an evening party or reception [French *soirée* "evening period, evening party", from *soir* "evening", from Latin *sero* "at a late hour", from *serus* "late"]

¹so•journ \'sō-ˌjərn, sō-'\ *n* : a temporary stay [Old French *sojorn,* from *sojorner* "to sojourn", derived from Latin *sub* "under, during" + Late Latin *diurnum* "day"]

²sojourn *vi* : to stay as a temporary resident — **so•journ•er** *n*

¹sol \'sōl\ *also* **so** \'sō\ *n* : the 5th note of the diatonic scale [Medieval Latin]

²sol \'säl, 'sōl\ *n, pl* **so•les** \'sō-ˌlās\ **1** : the basic monetary unit of Peru **2** : a coin or note representing one sol [American Spanish, from Spanish, "sun", from Latin]

³sol \'säl, 'sōl\ *n* : a fluid colloidal system [*solution*]

Sol \'säl\ : SUN 1a [Latin]

¹sol•ace \'säl-əs\ *n* : a relieving of grief or anxiety or a source of this [Old French *solas,* from Latin *solacium,* from *solari* "to console"]

²solace *vt* **1** : to give solace to **2** : to make cheerful **3** : ALLAY, SOOTHE ⟨*solace* grief⟩ **syn** see COMFORT — **sol•ac•er** *n*

so•la•num \sə-'lā-nəm, -'län-, -'lan-\ *n* : any of a large genus of herbs, shrubs, and trees that includes several economically important plants (as the potato and eggplant) [Latin, "nightshade"]

so•lar \'sō-lər, -ˌlär\ *adj* **1** : of, derived from, or relating to the sun **2** : measured by the earth's course in relation to the sun ⟨*solar* time⟩ ⟨*solar* year⟩ **3** : produced or operated by the action of the sun's light or heat ⟨a *solar* furnace⟩; *also* : utilizing the sun's rays [Latin *solaris,* from *sol* "sun"]

solar flare *n* : a sudden temporary outburst of gases from a small area of the sun's surface

solar house *n* : a house equipped to utilize the sun's rays extensively (as in heating)

so•lar•i•um \sō-'lar-ē-əm, sə-, -'ler-\ *n, pl* **-ia** \-ē-ə\ *also* **-i•ums** : a room exposed to the sun [Latin, from *sol* "sun"]

so•lar plexus \'sō-lər-\ *n* **1** : a nerve plexus in the abdomen behind the stomach and in front of the aorta that contains ganglia distributing nerve fibers to the viscera **2** : the pit of the stomach [from the radiating nerve fibers]

solar system *n* : the sun and the planets, asteroids, comets, and meteors that revolve around it

solar wind *n* : plasma continuously ejected from the sun's surface into interplanetary space

sold *past of* SELL

¹sol•der \'säd-ər, 'sȯd-\ *n* : a metal or metallic alloy used when melted to join metallic surfaces; *esp* : an alloy of lead and tin so used [Middle French *soudure,* from *souder* "to solder", from Latin *solidare* "to make solid", from *solidus* "solid"]

²solder *vb* **sol•dered**; **sol•der•ing** \'säd-ring, 'sȯd-, -ə-ring\ **1** : to unite or repair with solder **2** : to become joined or renewed by or as if by the use of solder — **sol•der•er** \-ər-ər\ *n*

soldering iron *n* : a metal device for applying heat in soldering

¹sol•dier \'sōl-jər\ *n* **1 a** : one engaged in military service and especially in the army **b** : an enlisted man or woman **2** : a worker in a cause **3** : a member of a caste of wingless individuals with large heads and jaws among termites and some ants [Old French *soudier,* from *soulde* "pay", from Late Latin *solidus,* a kind of coin, from Latin, "solid"] — **sol•dier•ly** \-lē\ *adj* — **sol•dier•ship** \-ˌship\ *n*

²soldier *vi* **sol•diered**; **sol•dier•ing** \'sōlj-ring, -ə-ring\ **1** : to serve as or act like a soldier **2** : to make a show of activity while really loafing

soldier of fortune : one who follows a military career wherever there is promise of profit, adventure, or pleasure

sol•diery \'sōlj-rē, -ə-rē\ *n, pl* **-dier•ies** : a body of soldiers

¹sole \'sōl\ *n* **1** : the undersurface of a foot **2** : the part of footwear on which the sole of the foot rests **3** : the bottom or lower part of something : the base on which something rests [Middle French, from Latin *solea* "sandal"] — **soled** \'sōld\ *adj*

²sole *vt* : to furnish with a sole ⟨*sole* shoes⟩

³sole *n* : any of a family of small-mouthed flatfishes having reduced fins and small closely set eyes and including valued food fishes; *also* : any of several other market flatfishes [Middle French, from Latin *solea* "sandal, a kind of flatfish"]

⁴sole *adj* **1** : having no companion : ALONE **2 a** : having no sharer ⟨*sole* owner⟩ **b** : being the only one **3** : functioning independently and without assistance or interference ⟨the *sole* judge⟩ **4** : belonging exclusively to the one person, unit, or group named ⟨given *sole* authority⟩ [Middle French *seul,* from Latin *solus*] **syn** see SINGLE — **sole•ness** *n*

so•le•cism \ˈsäl-ə-ˌsiz-əm, ˈsō-lə-\ *n* **1** : an ungrammatical combination of words in a sentence **2** : a breach of etiquette or decorum [Latin *solecismus,* from Greek *soloikismos,* from *soloikos* "speaking incorrectly", literally, "inhabitant of Soloi", from *Soloi,* city in ancient Cilicia where a substandard form of Greek was spoken] — **so•le•cis•tic** \ˌsäl-ə-ˈsis-tik, ˌsō-lə-\ *adj*

sole•ly \ˈsōl-lē, ˈsō-lē\ *adv* **1** : without another : SINGLY, ALONE **2** : EXCLUSIVELY, ENTIRELY ⟨done *solely* for money⟩

sol•emn \ˈsäl-əm\ *adj* **1** : celebrated with religious rites or ceremony : SACRED **2** : FORMAL, STATELY ⟨a *solemn* procession⟩ **3** : done or made seriously and thoughtfully ⟨*solemn* promise⟩ **4** : gravely sober and serious ⟨at this *solemn* moment⟩ **5** : SOMBER ⟨robe of *solemn* black⟩ [Middle French *solempne,* from Latin *sollemnis* "regularly appointed, solemn"] **syn** see SERIOUS — **so•lem•ni•ty** \sə-ˈlem-nət-ē\ *n* — **sol•emn•ly** \ˈsäl-əm-lē\ *adv* — **sol•emn•ness** \-əm-nəs\ *n*

sol•em•nize \ˈsäl-əm-ˌnīz\ *vt* **1** : to observe or honor with solemnity **2** : to perform with pomp or ceremony; *esp* : to celebrate (a marriage) with religious rites **3** : to make solemn : DIGNIFY — **sol•em•ni•za•tion** \ˌsäl-əm-nə-ˈzā-shən\ *n*

so•le•noid \ˈsō-lə-ˌnȯid, ˈsal-ə-\ *n* : a coil of wire commonly in the form of a cylinder that when carrying a current resembles a bar magnet so that a movable core is drawn into the coil when a current flows [French *solénoïde,* derived from Greek *sōlēn* "pipe"] — **so•le•noi•dal** \ˌsō-lə-ˈnȯid-l, ˌsäl-ə-\ *adj*

sole•plate \ˈsōl-ˌplāt\ *n* : the undersurface of a flatiron

sole•print \-ˌprint\ *n* : a print of the sole of the foot; *esp* : one made in the manner of a fingerprint and used for the identification of an infant

¹sol–fa \sōl-ˈfä, ˈsōl-\ *n* **1** : SOL-FA SYLLABLES **2** : SOLMIZATION; *also* : an exercise thus sung

²sol–fa *vb* **1** : to sing the sol-fa syllables **2** : to sing (as a melody) to sol-fa syllables

sol–fa syllables *n pl* : the syllables *do, re, mi, fa, sol, la, ti* used in singing the tones of the scale

soli *pl of* SOLO

so•lic•it \sə-ˈlis-ət\ *vb* **1** : BEG, ENTREAT; *esp* : to approach with a request or plea ⟨*soliciting* employers for jobs⟩ **2** : to appeal for ⟨*solicit* funds⟩ **3** : to accost a person for immoral purposes [Middle French *solliciter* "to disturb, take charge of", from Latin *sollicitare* "to disturb", from *sollicitus* "solicitous"] — **so•lic•i•ta•tion** \-ˌlis-ə-ˈtā-shən\ *n*

so•lic•i•tant \sə-ˈlis-ət-ənt\ *n* : one who solicits

so•lic•i•tor \sə-ˈlis-ət-ər\ *n* **1** : one that solicits; *esp* : an agent that solicits (as contributions to charity) **2** : a British lawyer who advises clients, represents them in the lower courts, and prepares cases for barristers to plead in the higher courts **3** : the chief law officer of a municipality, county, or government department — **so•lic•i•tor•ship** *n*

so•lic•i•tous \sə-ˈlis-ət-əs\ *adj* **1** : full of concern or fears : APPREHENSIVE **2** : anxiously willing : EAGER **3** : extremely careful [Latin *sollicitus,* from *sollus* "whole" + *citus,* past participle of *ciēre* "to move"] **syn** see THOUGHTFUL — **so•lic•i•tous•ly** *adv* — **so•lic•i•tous•ness** *n*

so•lic•i•tude \sə-ˈlis-ə-ˌtüd, -ˌtyüd\ *n* **1** : the state of being solicitous : ANXIETY **2** : excessive care or attention

¹sol•id \ˈsäl-əd\ *adj* **1 a** : having an interior filled with matter : not hollow **b** : written as one word without a hyphen ⟨a *solid* compound⟩ **c** : not interrupted ⟨for three *solid* hours⟩ **2** : having, involving, or dealing with three dimensions or with solids ⟨*solid* geometry⟩ **3 a** : not loose or spongy : COMPACT ⟨a *solid* mass of rock⟩ **b** : neither gaseous nor liquid : HARD, RIGID ⟨*solid* ice⟩ **4** : of good substantial quality or kind ⟨*solid* comfort⟩ ⟨*solid* reasons⟩ **5** : UNANIMOUS, UNITED ⟨we are *solid* for pay increases⟩ **6 a** : thoroughly dependable : RELIABLE ⟨a *solid* citizen⟩ **b** : serious in purpose or character ⟨*solid* reading⟩ **7** : of one substance or character: as **a** : entirely of one metal or containing the minimum of alloy necessary to impart hardness ⟨*solid* gold⟩ **b** : of a single color or tone [Middle French *solide,* from Latin *solidus*] — **solid** *adv* — **sol•id•ly** *adv* — **sol•id•ness** *n*

²solid *n* **1** : a geometrical figure or element (as a cube or sphere) having three dimensions **2** : a solid substance : a substance that does not flow perceptibly under moderate stress

sol•i•dar•i•ty \ˌsäl-ə-ˈdar-ət-ē\ *n, pl* **-ties** : unity based on community of interests, objectives, or standards [French *solidarité,* derived from Latin *solidus* "solid"] **syn** see UNITY

solid geometry *n* : a branch of geometry that deals with figures of three-dimensional space — compare PLANE GEOMETRY

so•lid•i•fy \sə-ˈlid-ə-ˌfī\ *vb* **-fied; -fy•ing** : to make or become solid, compact, or hard — **so•lid•i•fi•ca•tion** \sə-ˌlid-ə-fə-ˈkā-shən\ *n*

so•lid•i•ty \sə-ˈlid-ət-ē\ *n, pl* **-ties 1** : the quality or state of being solid **2** : moral, mental, or financial soundness

solid–state *adj* **1** : relating to the properties, structure, or reactivity of solid material **2** : utilizing the electric, magnetic, or photic properties of solid materials : not utilizing electron tubes

so•lil•o•quist \sə-ˈlil-ə-kwəst\ *n* : one who soliloquizes

so•lil•o•quize \sə-ˈlil-ə-ˌkwīz\ *vi* : to utter a soliloquy : talk to oneself — **so•lil•o•quiz•er** *n*

so•lil•o•quy \sə-ˈlil-ə-kwē\ *n, pl* **-quies 1** : the act of talking to oneself **2** : a dramatic monologue that gives the illusion of being a series of unspoken thoughts [Late Latin *soliloquium,* from Latin *solus* "alone" + *loqui* "to speak"]

sol•i•taire \ˈsäl-ə-ˌtaər, -ˌteər\ *n* **1** : a single gem (as a diamond) set alone **2** : a card game played by one person alone [French, from *solitaire,* adj., "solitary", from Latin *solitarius*]

¹sol•i•tary \ˈsäl-ə-ˌter-ē\ *adj* **1** : being or going alone ⟨a *solitary* traveler⟩ **2** : seldom visited : UNFREQUENTED **3** : being the only one : SOLE ⟨the *solitary* example⟩ **4** : growing or living alone : not forming part of a group or cluster ⟨flowers terminal and *solitary*⟩ ⟨the *solitary* bees⟩ [Latin *solitarius,* from *solitas* "solitude", from *solus* "alone"] — **sol•i•tar•i•ly** \ˌsäl-ə-ˈter-ə-lē\ *adv* — **sol•i•tar•i•ness** \ˈsäl-ə-ˌter-ē-nəs\ *n*

• **syn** SOLITARY, FORLORN, DESOLATE mean isolated from others. SOLITARY implies the absence of any others of the same kind; FORLORN and DESOLATE imply absence or loss of friends and family; applied to places they suggest dreariness and desertion by former inhabitants; DESOLATE may also imply a sense of final and irreparable loss and loneliness. **syn** see in addition SINGLE

²solitary *n, pl* **-tar•ies 1** : RECLUSE, HERMIT **2** : solitary confinement in prison

sol•i•tude \ˈsäl-ə-ˌtüd, -ˌtyüd\ *n* **1** : the quality or state of being alone or remote from society **2** : a lonely place

sol•mi•za•tion \ˌsäl-mə-ˈzā-shən\ *n* : the act, practice, or system of using a set of syllables to denote the tones of a musical scale [French *solmisation,* from *solmiser* "to sing the syllables *do, re, mi, fa, sol, la, ti*", from *sol* "sol" + *mi* "mi" + *-iser* "-ize"]

¹so•lo \ˈsō-lō\ *n, pl* **solos 1** *or pl* **so•li** \ˈsō-lē\ **a** : a musical composition for a single voice or instrument with or without accompaniment **b** : the featured part of a concerto or similar work **2** : an action in which there is only one performer [Italian, from *solo* "alone", from Latin *solus*]

²solo *adv or adj* : without a companion : ALONE

³solo *vi* **so•loed; so•lo•ing** : to perform by oneself; *esp* : to fly an airplane without one's instructor

so•lo•ist \ˈsō-lə-wəst, -ˌlō-əst\ *n* : one who performs a solo

Solomon's seal *n* **1** : an emblem consisting of two triangles forming a 6-pointed star and formerly used as an amulet especially against fever **2** : any of a genus of perennial herbs of the lily family with gnarled rhizomes

Solomon's seal 1

\ə\ **abut**	\au̇\ **out**	\i\ **tip**	\ȯ\ **saw**	\u̇\ **foot**
\ər\ **further**	\ch\ **chin**	\ī\ **life**	\ȯi\ **coin**	\y\ **yet**
\a\ **mat**	\e\ **pet**	\j\ **job**	\th\ **thin**	\yü\ **few**
\ā\ **take**	\ē\ **easy**	\ng\ **sing**	\t͟h\ **this**	\yu̇\ **cure**
\ä\ **cot, cart**	\g\ **go**	\ō\ **bone**	\ü\ **food**	\zh\ **vision**

so•lon \'sō-lən, -ˌlän\ *n* **1** : a wise and skillful lawgiver **2** : a member of a legislative body [*Solon,* died about 559 B.C., Athenian lawgiver]

so long \sō-'lȯŋ\ *interj* — used to express farewell [probably by folk etymology from Irish Gaelic *slán,* literally, "health, security"]

so long as *conj* **1** : during and up to the end of the time that : WHILE **2** : provided that

sol•stice \'säl-stəs, 'sōl-, 'sȯl-\ *n* **1** : the point in the path of the sun at which the sun is farthest from the equator either north or south **2** : the time of the sun's passing a solstice which occurs on June 22d to begin summer in the northern hemisphere and on December 22d to begin winter in the northern hemisphere [Old French, from Latin *solstitium,* from *sol* "sun" + *sistere* "to come to a stop, cause to stand"] — **sol•sti•tial** \säl-'stish-əl, sōl-, sȯl-\ *adj*

sol•u•bil•i•ty \ˌsäl-yə-'bil-ət-ē\ *n, pl* **-ties** **1** : the quality or state of being soluble **2** : the amount of a substance that will dissolve in a given amount of another substance

sol•u•bi•lize \'säl-yə-bə-ˌlīz\ *vt* : to make soluble or increase the solubility of

sol•u•ble \'säl-yə-bəl\ *adj* **1 a** : capable of being dissolved in a fluid ⟨sugar is *soluble* in water⟩ **b** : that can be emulsified ⟨a *soluble* oil⟩ **2** : capable of being solved or explained [Middle French, from Late Latin *solubilis,* from Latin *solvere* "to loosen, solve, dissolve"] — **sol•u•ble•ness** *n* — **sol•u•bly** \-blē\ *adv*

sol•ute \'säl-ˌyüt\ *n* : a dissolved substance [Latin *solutus,* past participle of *solvere* "to dissolve"]

so•lu•tion \sə-'lü-shən\ *n* **1 a** : an action or process of solving **b** (1) : an answer to a problem : EXPLANATION (2) : SOLUTION SET; *also* : a member of a solution set **2 a** : an act or the process by which a solid, liquid, or gaseous substance is uniformly mixed with a liquid or sometimes a gas or solid **b** : a typically liquid uniform mixture formed by the process of solution **c** : the condition of being dissolved **d** : a liquid containing a dissolved substance **3** : a bringing or coming to an end or into a state of discontinuity [Middle French, from Latin *solutio,* from *solvere* "to loosen, solve, dissolve"]

solution set *n* : a set of values that satisfy an equation or inequality; *also* : TRUTH SET

solv•able \'säl-və-bəl, 'sȯl-\ *adj* : capable of being solved — **solv•abil•i•ty** \ˌsäl-və-'bil-ət-ē, ˌsȯl-\ *n*

¹sol•vate \'säl-ˌvāt, 'sȯl-\ *n* : a combination of a solute with a solvent or of a dispersed phase with a dispersion medium [*solvent* + *-ate*]

²solvate *vt* : to convert into a solvate — **sol•va•tion** \säl-'vā-shən, sȯl-\ *n*

solve \'sälv, 'sȯlv\ *vt* : to find a solution for [Latin *solvere* "to loosen, solve, dissolve", from *sed-, se-* "apart" + *luere* "to release"]

sol•ven•cy \'säl-vən-sē, 'sȯl-\ *n, pl* **-cies** : the quality or state of being solvent

¹sol•vent \-vənt\ *adj* **1** : able to pay all legal debts **2** : dissolving or able to dissolve ⟨*solvent* fluids⟩⟨*solvent* action of water⟩ [Latin *solvens,* present participle of *solvere* "to dissolve, pay"] — **sol•vent•ly** *adv*

²solvent *n* **1** : a usually liquid substance capable of dissolving or dispersing one or more other substances **2** : something that provides a solution

So•ma•li \sō-'mäl-ē, sə-\ *n* : a member of a people of Somaliland apparently of mixed Mediterranean and Negroid stock — **Somali** *adj*

so•mat•ic \sō-'mat-ik, sə-\ *adj* **1** : of, relating to, or affecting the body especially as distinguished from the germ plasm or the psyche ⟨*somatic* cells⟩ **2** : of or relating to the wall of the body : PARIETAL [Greek *sōmatikos,* from *sōmat-, sōma* "body"] — **so•mat•i•cal•ly** \-'mat-i-kə-lē, -klē\ *adv*

somatic mutation *n* : a mutation occurring in a somatic cell and inducing a chimera

so•mato•tro•phic hormone \sō-ˌmat-ə-ˌtrō-fik\ *or* **so•mato•tro•pic hormone** \-ˌtrō-pik-\ *n* : GROWTH HORMONE 1

som•ber *or* **som•bre** \'säm-bər\ *adj* **1** : so shaded as to be dark and gloomy **2** : GRAVE, MELANCHOLY ⟨a *somber* mood⟩ **3** : dull or dark colored [French *sombre*] — **som•ber•ly** *or* **som•bre•ly** *adv* — **som•ber•ness** *or* **som•bre•ness** *n*

som•bre•ro \səm-'breər-ō, säm-\ *n, pl* **-ros** : a high-crowned hat of felt or straw with a very wide brim worn especially in the Southwest and Mexico [Spanish, from *sombra* "shade"]

sombrero

¹some \'səm, *sense 2* 'səm *or* səm\ *adj* **1** : being unknown, undetermined, or unspecified ⟨*some* stranger was looking for you⟩ **2 a** : being one, a part, or an unspecified number of something (as a class or group) named or implied ⟨*some* gems are hard⟩ **b** : being of an unspecified amount or number ⟨give me *some* water⟩⟨have *some* apples⟩ **3** : worthy of notice or consideration ⟨that was *some* party⟩ [Old English *sum*]

²some \'səm\ *pron, sing or pl in construction* **1** : one indeterminate quantity, portion, or number as distinguished from the rest ⟨*some* of the milk⟩⟨*some* of the apples⟩ **2** : an indefinite additional amount ⟨ran a mile and then *some*⟩

³some \'səm, ˌsəm\ *adv* **1** : ABOUT ⟨*some* eighty houses⟩ **2** : SOMEWHAT ⟨felt *some* better⟩

¹-some \səm\ *adj suffix* : characterized by a (specified) thing, quality, state, or action ⟨awe*some*⟩⟨burden*some*⟩ [Old English *-sum*]

²-some \səm\ *n suffix* : group of (so many) members and especially persons ⟨four*some*⟩ [Middle English *sum,* pron., "one, some"]

³-some \ˌsōm\ *n combining form* : body ⟨chromo*some*⟩ [Greek *sōma*]

some•body \'səm-ˌbäd-ē, -bəd-\ *pron* **1** : one or some person of unspecified or indefinite identity ⟨*somebody* will come in⟩ **2** : a person of position or importance

some•day \'səm-ˌdā\ *adv* : at some future time

some•how \'səm-ˌhau̇\ *adv* : in one way or another not known or designated : by some means

some•one \-wən, -ˌwən\ *pron* : some person : SOMEBODY

some•place \-ˌplās\ *adv* : SOMEWHERE 1

som•er•sault \'səm-ər-ˌsȯlt\ *n* : a leap or roll in which a person turns forward or backward in a complete revolution with the feet moving up over the head [Middle French *sombresaut* "leap", derived from Latin *super* "over" + *saltus* "leap", from *salire* "to jump"] — **somersault** *vi*

som•er•set \-ˌset\ *n or vi* : SOMERSAULT [by alteration]

¹some•thing \'səm-thiŋ, 'səmp-, *especially in rapid speech or for 2* 'səmp-m\ *pron* **1** : some undetermined or unspecified thing **2** : a person or thing of consequence

²something *adv* **1** : in some degree : SOMEWHAT **2** : EXTREMELY ⟨swears *something* awful⟩

¹some•time \'səm-ˌtīm\ *adv* **1** : at some time in the future ⟨I'll do it *sometime*⟩ **2** : at some not specified or definitely known point of time ⟨*sometime* last night⟩

²sometime *adj* : having been formerly : FORMER ⟨*sometime* mayor of the city⟩

some•times \'səm-ˌtīmz; ˌsəm-', səm-'\ *adv* : at times : now and then : OCCASIONALLY

some•way \'səm-ˌwā\ *also* **some•ways** \-ˌwāz\ *adv* : in some way : SOMEHOW

¹some•what \-ˌhwät, -ˌhwət, -ˌwät, -ˌwət; ˌsəm-', səm-'\ *pron* : SOMETHING 2

²somewhat *adv* : in some degree or measure : SLIGHTLY ⟨*somewhat* relieved⟩

¹some•where \'səm-ˌhweər, -ˌhwaər, -hwər, -ˌwear, -ˌwaər, -wər\ *adv* **1** : in, at, or to a place unknown or unspecified **2** : to or into a stage or period of positive accomplishment ⟨now we're getting *somewhere*⟩ **3** : APPROXIMATELY ⟨*somewhere* about nine o'clock⟩

²somewhere *n* : an undetermined or unnamed place

some•wheres \-ˌhweərz, -ˌhwaərz, -hwərz, -ˌweərz, -ˌwaərz, -wərz\ *adv* : SOMEWHERE 1

so•mite \'sō-ˌmīt\ *n* : one segment of the longitudinal series of segments into which the body of vertebrates and many other animals is divided : METAMERE [Greek *sōma* "body"] — **so•mit•ic** \sō-'mit-ik\ *adj*

som•me•lier \ˌsəm-əl-'yā\ *n, pl* **sommeliers** \-'yā, -'yāz\ : an employee of a restaurant who has charge of wines and their serving [French, from Middle French, "court official charged with transportation of supplies", from Provençal *saumalier* "pack animal driver", from *sauma* "pack animal", from Late

Latin *sagma* "packsaddle", from Greek]

som·nam·bu·lant \säm-ˈnam-byə-lənt\ *adj* **:** walking or addicted to walking while asleep

som·nam·bu·lism \säm-ˈnam-byə-ˌliz-əm\ *n* **:** a sleeping state in which motor acts (as walking) are performed; *also* **:** actions characteristic of this state [derived from Latin *somnus* "sleep" + *ambulare* "to walk"] — **som·nam·bu·list** \-ləst\ *n* — **som·nam·bu·lis·tic** \säm-ˌnam-byə-ˈlis-tik\ *adj*

som·nif·er·ous \säm-ˈnif-rəs, -ə-rəs\ *adj* **:** SOPORIFIC 1a [Latin *somnifer,* from *somnus* "sleep" + *-fer* "-ferous"] — **som·nif·er·ous·ly** *adv*

som·no·lence \ˈsäm-nə-ləns\ *n* **:** the quality or state of being drowsy

som·no·lent \-lənt\ *adj* **:** inclined to or heavy with sleep **:** DROWSY ⟨a *somnolent* village⟩ [Middle French *sompnolent,* from Latin *somnolentus,* from *somnus* "sleep"] — **som·no·lent·ly** *adv*

son \ˈsən\ *n* **1 a :** a male offspring especially of human beings **b :** a male adopted child **c :** a male descendant **2** *cap* **:** the second person of the Trinity **3 :** a person closely associated with or deriving from a formative agent (as a nation, school, or race) ⟨*sons* of modern technology⟩ [Old English *sunu*]

so·nance \ˈsō-nəns\ *n* **:** SOUND

so·nant \ˈsō-nənt\ *adj* **1 :** VOICED 2 **2 :** SYLLABIC 2 [Latin *sonare* "to sound"] — **sonant** *n*

so·nar \ˈsō-ˌnär\ *n* **:** an apparatus that detects the presence and location of submerged objects (as submarines) by reflected sound waves [*so*und *na*vigation *r*anging]

so·na·ta \sə-ˈnät-ə\ *n* **:** an instrumental musical composition typically of three or four movements in contrasting forms and keys [Italian, from *sonare* "to sound", from Latin]

sonata form *n* **:** a musical form consisting basically of an exposition, a development, and a recapitulation used especially for the first movement of a sonata

son·a·ti·na \ˌsän-ə-ˈtē-nə\ *n* **:** a short usually simplified sonata [Italian, from *sonata*]

song \ˈsȯng\ *n* **1 :** the act or art of singing **2 :** poetical composition **:** POETRY **3 a :** a short musical composition of words and music **b :** a collection of such compositions **4 a :** a melody for a lyric poem or ballad **b :** a poem easily set to music **5 :** a small amount ⟨can be bought for a *song*⟩ [Old English *sang*]

song·bird \-ˌbərd\ *n* **1 :** a bird that utters a successon of musical tones **2 :** SINGING BIRD 2

song·fest \-ˌfest\ *n* **:** an informal session of group singing of popular or folk songs

song·ful \-fəl\ *adj* **:** given to singing **:** MELODIOUS — **song·ful·ly** \-fə-lē\ *adv* — **song·ful·ness** *n*

song·less \ˈsȯng-ləs\ *adj* **:** lacking in, incapable of, or not given to song — **song·less·ly** *adv*

Song of Sol·o·mon \-ˈsäl-ə-mən\ — see BIBLE table

song·smith \ˈsȯng-ˌsmith\ *n* **:** a composer of songs

song sparrow *n* **:** a common sparrow of eastern North America noted for its sweet cheerful song

song·ster \ˈsȯng-stər\ *n* **:** one skilled in song **:** SINGER

song·stress \-strəs\ *n* **:** a female singer

song thrush *n* **:** a largely olive-brown Old World thrush noted for its song — called also *mavis, throstle*

song·writ·er \ˈsȯng-ˌrīt-ər\ *n* **:** a person who composes words or music or both especially for popular songs

son·ic \ˈsän-ik\ *adj* **1 :** having a frequency within the audibility range of the human ear — used of waves and vibrations **2 :** utilizing, produced by, or relating to sound waves ⟨*sonic* altimeter⟩ **3 :** of, relating to, or being the speed of sound in air that is about 1192 kilometers per hour at sea level [Latin *sonus* "sound"] — **son·i·cal·ly** \ˈsän-i-kə-lē, -klē\ *adv*

sonic boom *n* **:** a sound resembling an explosion produced when a pressure wave formed at the nose of an aircraft traveling at supersonic speeds reaches the ground

son–in–law \ˈsən-ən-ˌlȯ\ *n, pl* **sons–in–law** \ˈsən-zən-\ **:** the husband of one's daughter

son·net \ˈsän-ət\ *n* **:** a poem of 14 lines usually in iambic pentameter rhyming according to a prescribed scheme — compare ENGLISH SONNET, ITALIAN SONNET [Italian *sonetto,* from Provençal *sonet* "little song", from *son* "sound, song", from Latin *sonus* "sound"]

son·ne·teer \ˌsän-ə-ˈtiər\ *n* **:** a writer of sonnets

sonnet sequence *n* **:** a series of sonnets often having a unifying theme

son·ny \ˈsən-ē\ *n* **:** a young boy — usually used in address

so·nom·e·ter \sə-ˈnäm-ət-ər\ *n* **:** an instrument for demonstrating the mathematical relations of musical tones that consists of a single string stretched on a board and a movable bridge [Latin *sonus* "sound"]

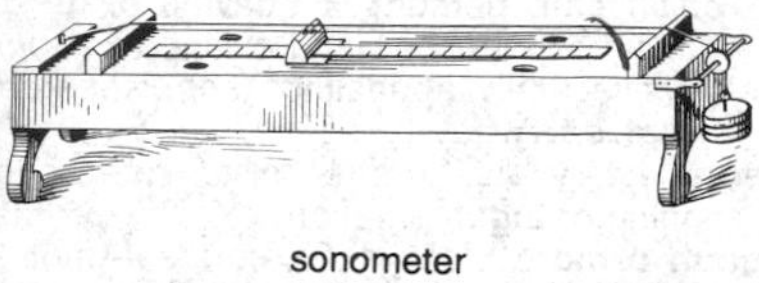

sonometer

so·nor·i·ty \sə-ˈnȯr-ət-ē, -ˈnär-\ *n, pl* **-ties 1 :** the quality or state of being sonorous **:** RESONANCE **2 :** a sonorous tone or speech

so·no·rous \sə-ˈnōr-əs, -ˈnȯr-; ˈsän-ə-rəs\ *adj* **1 :** producing sound (as when struck) **2 :** full or loud in sound **:** RESONANT **3 :** imposing or impressive in effect or style [Latin *sonorus*] — **so·no·rous·ly** *adv* — **so·no·rous·ness** *n*

son·ship \ˈsən-ˌship\ *n* **:** the relationship of son to father

soon \ˈsün, *especially New England* ˈsu̇n\ *adv* **1 :** before long **:** without undue time lapse ⟨*soon* after sunrise⟩ **2 :** PROMPTLY, SPEEDILY ⟨as *soon* as possible⟩ **3 :** before the usual time **4 :** by choice **:** WILLINGLY ⟨I'd *sooner* stay than go⟩ [Old English *sōna* "soon, immediately"]

soot \ˈsu̇t, ˈsət, ˈsüt\ *n* **:** a black substance that is formed by combustion, rises in fine particles, and adheres to the sides of the chimney or pipe conveying the smoke; *esp* **:** the fine powder consisting chiefly of carbon that colors smoke [Old English *sōt*]

¹sooth \ˈsüth\ *adj, archaic* **:** agreeing with or telling the truth [Old English *sōth*]

²sooth *n, archaic* **:** the quality or state of being true

soothe \ˈsüt͟h\ *vb* **1 a :** to please by or as if by attention or concern **:** PLACATE **b :** RELIEVE 1, ALLEVIATE **2 :** to bring comfort, solace, or reassurance [Old English *sōthian* "to prove the truth", from *sōth* "true"]

sooth·ing \ˈsü-t͟hing\ *adj* **:** tending to calm or allay — **sooth·ing·ly** \-t͟hing-lē\ *adv* — **sooth·ing·ness** *n*

sooth·ly \ˈsüth-lē\ *adv, archaic* **:** in truth **:** TRULY

sooth·say·er \ˈsüth-ˌsā-ər\ *n* **:** a person who claims to foretell events — **sooth·say·ing** \-ˌsā-ing\ *n*

sooty \ˈsu̇t-ē, ˈsət-, ˈsüt-\ *adj* **soot·i·er; -est 1 a :** of, relating to, or producing soot **b :** soiled with soot **2 :** of the color of soot — **soot·i·ly** \-l-ē\ *adv* — **soot·i·ness** \-ē-nəs\ *n*

sooty mold *n* **:** a dark layer of fungus mycelium growing in insect honeydew on the leaves of plants; *also* **:** a fungus producing this

¹sop \ˈsäp\ *n* **1** *chiefly dialect* **:** a piece of food dipped or steeped in a liquid (as bread dipped in milk or gravy) **2 :** a bribe, gift, or gesture meant to pacify or win favor [Old English *sopp*]

²sop *vt* **sopped; sop·ping 1 a :** to steep or dip in or as if in liquid **b :** to wet thoroughly **:** SOAK **2 :** to mop up (as water) **3 :** to give a bribe or conciliatory gift to

soph·ism \ˈsäf-ˌiz-əm\ *n* **:** an unsound misleading argument that on the surface seems reasonable

soph·ist \ˈsäf-əst\ *n* **1** *cap* **:** one of a class of ancient Greek teachers of rhetoric, philosophy, and the art of successful living noted for their subtle often specious reasoning **2 :** one who argues by the use of sophisms [Latin *sophista,* from Greek *sophistēs,* literally, "expert, wise man", from *sophizesthai* "to become wise, deceive", from *sophos* "wise"]

so·phis·tic \sə-ˈfis-tik\ *or* **so·phis·ti·cal** \-ti-kəl\ *adj* **:** being clever and subtle but misleading — **so·phis·ti·cal·ly** \-ti-kə-lē, -klē\ *adv*

¹so·phis·ti·cate \sə-ˈfis-tə-ˌkāt\ *vt* **1 :** to alter deceptively; *esp* **:** ADULTERATE **2 :** to deprive of genuineness, naturalness, or simplicity; *esp* **:** to deprive of naiveté and make worldly-wise — **so·phis·ti·ca·tion** \-ˌfis-tə-ˈkā-shən\ *n*

²so·phis·ti·cate \-ˈfis-ti-kət, -tə-ˌkāt\ *n* **:** a sophisticated person

so·phis·ti·cat·ed \-tə-ˌkāt-əd\ *adj* **1 :** not in a natural, pure, or

\ə\ **abut**	\au̇\ **out**	\i\ **tip**	\ȯ\ **saw**	\u̇\ **foot**
\ər\ **further**	\ch\ **chin**	\ī\ **life**	\ȯi\ **coin**	\y\ **yet**
\a\ **mat**	\e\ **pet**	\j\ **job**	\th\ **thin**	\yü\ **few**
\ā\ **take**	\ē\ **easy**	\ng\ **sing**	\t͟h\ **this**	\yu̇\ **cure**
\ä\ **cot, cart**	\g\ **go**	\ō\ **bone**	\ü\ **food**	\zh\ **vision**

original state ⟨a *sophisticated* oil⟩ **2** : deprived of native or original simplicity: as **a** : highly complicated : COMPLEX ⟨*sophisticated* instruments⟩ **b** : WORLDLY-WISE, KNOWING ⟨a *sophisticated* person⟩ **3** : devoid of grossness : SUBTLE: as **a** : finely experienced and aware ⟨a *sophisticated* columnist⟩ **b** : intellectually appealing ⟨*sophisticated* novels⟩ — **so•phis•ti•cat•ed•ly** *adv*

soph•ist•ry \'säf-ə-strē\ *n, pl* **-ries** : subtle but deceptive reasoning or argumentation

soph•o•more \'säf-m-,ōr, -,ȯr; 'säf-,mōr, -,mȯr\ *n* : a student in the second year at college or secondary school [probably from Greek *sophos* "wise" + *mōros* "foolish"]

soph•o•mor•ic \,säf-ə-'mōr-ik, -'mȯr-, -'mär-\ *adj* **1** : of, relating to, or characteristic of a sophomore **2** : conceited and overconfident of knowledge but poorly informed and immature

So•pho•ni•as \,säf-ə-'nī-əs, ,sō-fə-\ *n* — see BIBLE table

¹so•po•rif•ic \,säp-ə-'rif-ik, ,sō-pə-\ *adj* **1 a** : causing or tending to cause sleep **b** : tending to dull awareness or alertness **2** : of, relating to, or characterized by sleepiness or lethargy [derived from Latin *sopor* "deep sleep"]

²soporific *n* : a soporific agent or drug

sop•ping \'säp-ing\ *adj* : very wet : drenched through

sop•py \'säp-ē\ *adj* **sop•pi•er**; **-est** **1** : SOPPING **2** : very wet or slushy

¹so•prano \sə-'pran-ō, -'prän-\ *n, pl* **-pran•os** **1** : the highest voice part in a 4-part chorus — compare ALTO, BASS, TENOR **2 a** : the highest singing voice of women or boys **b** : a singer having such a voice [Italian, from *sopra* "above", from Latin *supra*]

²soprano *adj* **1** : relating to the soprano voice or part **2** : having a high range ⟨*soprano* sax⟩

so•ra \'sōr-ə, 'sȯr-\ *n* : a small short-billed North American rail common in marshes [origin unknown]

sorb \'sȯrb\ *vt* : to take up and hold by either adsorption or absorption [back-formation from *absorb* and *adsorb*]

sor•cer•er \'sȯrs-rər, -ə-rər\ *n* : a person who practices sorcery : WIZARD

sor•cer•ess \'sȯrs-rəs, -ə-rəs\ *n* : a female sorcerer

sor•cer•ous \'sȯrs-rəs, -ə-rəs\ *adj* : of or relating to sorcery

sor•cery \'sȯrs-rē, -ə-rē\ *n* : the use of power gained from the assistance or control of evil spirits especially for divining : WITCHCRAFT [Old French *sorcerie,* from *sorcier* "sorcerer", derived from Latin *sors* "chance, lot"]

sor•did \'sȯrd-əd\ *adj* **1** : DIRTY, FILTHY ⟨*sordid* surroundings⟩ **2** : marked by baseness or grossness : VILE ⟨*sordid* motives⟩ **3** : meanly greedy : COVETOUS **4** : of a dull or muddy color [Latin *sordidus,* from *sordes* "dirt"] — **sor•did•ly** *adv* — **sor•did•ness** *n*

sor•di•no \sȯr-'dē-nō\ *n, pl* **-di•ni** \-nē\ : MUTE 2 [Italian, from *sordo* "silent", from Latin *surdus*]

¹sore \'sōr, 'sȯr\ *adj* **1 a** : causing or tending to cause mental distress ⟨a *sore* subject⟩ **b** : painfully sensitive : TENDER ⟨*sore* muscles⟩ **c** : hurt or inflamed so as to be or seem painful ⟨*sore* runny eyes⟩ **2** : attended by difficulties, hardship, or exertion ⟨in *sore* straits⟩ **3** : made angry ⟨*sore* over a remark⟩ [Old English *sār*] — **sore•ness** *n*

²sore *n* **1** : a localized sore spot on the body; *esp* : one (as an ulcer) with the tissues broken and usually infected **2** : a source of pain or vexation : AFFLICTION

³sore *adv* : SORELY

sore•head \-,hed\ *n* : a person easily angered or disgruntled — **sorehead** *or* **sore•head•ed** \-'hed-əd\ *adj*

sore•ly \-lē\ *adv* : in a sore manner : VERY, EXTREMELY

sore throat *n* : painful throat due to inflammation of the fauces and pharynx

sor•ghum \'sȯr-gəm\ *n* **1** : any of an economically important genus of Old World tropical grasses similar to Indian corn in habit but with the spikelets in pairs on a hairy axis; *esp* : one cultivated for grain, forage, or syrup — compare SORGO **2** : syrup from sorgo [New Latin, from Italian *sorgo*]

sor•go \'sȯr-gō\ *n, pl* **sorgos** : a sorghum grown primarily for its sweet juice from which syrup is made but also used for fodder and silage [Italian]

so•ro•ral \sə-'rōr-əl, -'rȯr-\ *adj* : of, relating to, or characteristic of a sister : SISTERLY [Latin *soror* "sister"]

so•ror•i•ty \sə-'rȯr-ət-ē, -'rär-\ *n, pl* **-ties** : a club of girls or women especially at a college [Medieval Latin *sororitas* "sisterhood", from Latin *soror* "sister"]

sorp•tion \'sȯrp-shən\ *n* : the process of sorbing : the state of being sorbed [back-formation from *absorption* and *adsorption*]

¹sor•rel \'sȯr-əl, 'sär-\ *n* **1** : an animal (as a horse) of a sorrel color **2** : a brownish orange to light brown [Middle French *sorel,* from *sor* "reddish brown"]

²sorrel *n* : any of various plants with sour juice: as **a** : ¹DOCK **b** : WOOD SORREL [Middle French *surele,* from *sur* "sour", of Germanic origin]

¹sor•row \'sär-ō, 'sȯr-\ *n* **1 a** : sadness or anguish due to loss (as of something loved) **b** : a cause of grief or sadness **2** : CONTRITION, REPENTANCE [Old English *sorg*]

• **syn** SORROW, GRIEF, ANGUISH mean distress of mind. SORROW implies a sense of loss often with feelings of guilt and remorse; GRIEF implies a sharp feeling of distress for a definite and immediate cause; ANGUISH implies a torturing grief or dread.

²sorrow *vi* : to feel or express sorrow : GRIEVE

sor•row•ful \-fəl\ *adj* **1** : full of or marked by sorrow **2** : expressive of or inducing sorrow — **sor•row•ful•ly** \-fə-lē\ *adv* — **sor•row•ful•ness** *n*

sor•ry \'sär-ē, 'sȯr-\ *adj* **sor•ri•er**; **-est** **1** : feeling sorrow, regret, or penitence **2** : MOURNFUL 2, SAD **3** : inspiring sorrow, pity, scorn, or ridicule : WRETCHED [Old English *sārig,* from *sār* "sore"] — **sor•ri•ly** \'sär-ə-lē, 'sȯr-\ *adv* — **sor•ri•ness** \'sär-ē-nəs, 'sȯr-\ *n*

¹sort \'sȯrt\ *n* **1** : a group set up on the basis of any characteristic in common : CLASS, KIND **2** : method or manner of acting : WAY **3** : general character or disposition; *also* : PERSON, INDIVIDUAL ⟨you're not a bad *sort* at heart⟩ [Middle French *sorte,* probably from Latin *sors* "chance, lot"] **syn** see KIND — **after a sort** : in a rough or haphazard way — **of sorts** *or* **of a sort** : of an inconsequential or mediocre quality ⟨a poet *of sorts*⟩ — **out of sorts** **1** : out of temper : IRRITABLE **2** : not well

²sort *vb* **1** : to put in a certain place or rank according to kind, class, or nature : CLASSIFY ⟨*sort* mail⟩ ⟨*sort* out colors⟩ **2** *archaic* : AGREE 6, SUIT — **sort•able** \'sȯrt-ə-bəl\ *adj* — **sort•er** *n*

sor•tie \'sȯrt-ē, sȯr-'tē\ *n* **1** : a sudden issuing of troops from a defensive position against the enemy : SALLY **2** : one mission or attack by a single plane [French, from *sortir* "to go out"] — **sortie** *vi*

sort of \,sȯrt-əv, -ə, -ər\ *adv* : to a moderate degree : RATHER

so•rus \'sōr-əs, 'sȯr-\ *n, pl* **so•ri** \'sōr-,ī, 'sȯr-, -ē\ : a cluster of plant reproductive bodies; *esp* : one of the dots on the underside of a fertile fern frond consisting of a cluster of spores [New Latin, from Greek *sōros* "heap"]

SOS \,es-ō-'es, ,es-ə-'wes\ *n* **1** : an internationally recognized signal of distress in radio code ··· ––– ··· used especially by ships calling for help **2** : a call or request for help or rescue

¹so–so \'sō-'sō\ *adv* : neither very badly nor very well

²so–so *adj* : neither very good nor very bad

so•ste•nu•to \,sō-stə-'nüt-ō, ,sȯ-\ *adv or adj* : sustained to or beyond the note's full value — used as a direction in music [Italian, from *sostenere* "to sustain", from Latin *sustinēre*]

sot \'sät\ *n* : an habitual drunkard [Old English *sott* "fool"]

sot•ted \'sät-əd\ *adj* : become stupid or drunken : SOTTISH

sot•tish \'sät-ish\ *adj* : resembling a sot (as in folly or intemperance) — **sot•tish•ly** *adv* — **sot•tish•ness** *n*

sot•to vo•ce \,sät-ō-'vō-chē\ *adv or adj* **1** : under the breath : in an undertone; *also* : PRIVATELY **2** : very softly [Italian *sottovoce,* from *sotto* "under" + *voce* "voice"]

sou \'sü\ *n* : a French bronze coin of the period before 1914 worth 5 centimes or one twentieth of a franc [French, from Old French *sol,* from Late Latin *solidus,* a kind of coin, from Latin, "solid"]

sou•brette \sü-'bret\ *n* **1 a** : a coquettish maid or frivolous young woman in comedies **b** : an actress who plays such a part **2** : a soprano who sings supporting roles in comic opera [French]

sou•bri•quet *variant of* SOBRIQUET

¹souf•flé \sü-'flā, 'sü-,\ *n* : a delicate spongy hot dish lightened in baking by stiffly beaten egg whites [French, from *souffler* "to puff up", from Latin *sufflare,* from *sub-* + *flare* "to blow"]

²soufflé *or* **souf•fléed** \-'flād, -,flād\ *adj* : puffed by or in cooking ⟨*soufflé* omelets⟩

sough \'saů, 'səf\ *vi* : to make a moaning or sighing sound [Old English *swōgan*] — **sough** *n*

sought *past of* SEEK

¹soul \'sōl\ *n* **1** : the spiritual part of a person believed to give life to the body and in many religions regarded as immortal **2 a** : a person's moral and emotional nature ⟨my *soul* rebels against cruelty⟩ **b** : spiritual force : FERVOR **3** : the essential part of something **4** : the moving spirit : LEADER ⟨the *soul* of an enterprise⟩ **5** : EMBODIMENT ⟨a friend who is the *soul* of honor⟩ **6** : a human being : PERSON ⟨a kind *soul*⟩ **7** : a disembodied spirit **8** : a strong positive feeling (as of intense sensitivity and emotional fervor) conveyed especially by black American performers **[**Old English *sāwol***]**

• **syn** SOUL, SPIRIT mean an immaterial entity distinguishable from and superior to the body. SOUL is preferred when the entity is considered as having functions, responsibilities, or a certain destiny ⟨to save one's *soul*⟩ ⟨sell one's *soul* to the devil⟩ SPIRIT is preferred when the quality, movement, or activity is stressed ⟨their *spirits* were refreshed⟩ or opposition to the material part is intended ⟨the *spirit* is willing but the flesh is weak⟩

[2]**soul** *adj* **1** : of, relating to, or characteristic of black Americans or their culture **2** : designed for or controlled by blacks

soul•ful \-fəl\ *adj* : full of or expressing feeling or emotion — **soul•ful•ly** \-fə-lē\ *adv* — **soul•ful•ness** *n*

soul•less \'sōl-ləs\ *adj* : having no soul or no greatness or nobleness of mind or feeling — **soul•less•ly** *adv*

soul–search•ing \'sōl-ˌsər-ching\ *n* : examination of one's conscience especially with regard to motives and values

[1]**sound** \'saund\ *adj* **1** : free from flaw, defect, or decay **2** : free from injury or disease : HEALTHY ⟨a *sound* mind in a *sound* body⟩ **3** : SOLID, FIRM ⟨a building of *sound* construction⟩ **4** : free from error or fallacy : VALID ⟨a *sound* argument⟩ **5** : showing good sense : WISE ⟨*sound* advice⟩ **6** : HONORABLE, HONEST ⟨*sound* principles⟩ **7** : THOROUGH ⟨a *sound* beating⟩ **8** : not disturbed : DEEP ⟨a *sound* sleep⟩ **[**Old English *gesund***]** **syn** see HEALTHY, VALID — **sound•ly** *adv* — **sound•ness** \'saund-nəs, 'saun-\ *n*

[2]**sound** *adv* : SOUNDLY ⟨*sound* asleep⟩

[3]**sound** *n* **1 a** : the sensation experienced through the sense of hearing **b** : a particular auditory impression : NOISE, TONE **c** : mechanical energy that is transmitted by longitudinal pressure waves in a material medium (as air) and is the objective cause of hearing **2 a** : one of the noises that together make up human speech ⟨the *sound* of *th* in *this*⟩ **b** : a sequence of spoken noises ⟨*-cher* of *teacher* and *-ture* of *creature* have the same *sound*⟩ **3 a** : meaningless noise **b** : impression conveyed ⟨the excuse has a suspicious *sound*⟩ **4** : hearing distance : EARSHOT **[**Old French *son,* from Latin *sonus***]**

[4]**sound** *vb* **1 a** : to make or cause to make a sound **b** : RESOUND 1, 2 **c** : to give a summons by sound **2 a** : PRONOUNCE 3 **b** : to put into words : VOICE **3 a** : to make known : PROCLAIM **b** : to order, signal, or indicate by a sound **4** : to make or convey the impression of being : SEEM ⟨*sounds* incredible⟩ **5** : to examine by causing to emit sounds ⟨*sound* the lungs⟩ — **sound•able** \'saun-də-bəl\ *adj*

[5]**sound** *n* **1** : a long passage of water that is wider than a strait and often connects two larger bodies of water or forms a channel between the mainland and an island **2** : the air bladder of a fish **[**Old English *sund* "sea" and Old Norse *sund* "strait"**]**

[6]**sound** *vb* **1 a** : to measure the depth of (as with a sounding line) : FATHOM **b** : to look into or investigate the possibility **2** : to try to find out the views or intentions of : PROBE **3** : to dive down suddenly ⟨a *sounding* whale⟩ **[**Middle French *sonder,* from *sonde* "sounding line"**]**

sound barrier *n* : the sudden large increase in resistance that the air offers to an airplane nearing the speed of sound

sound•board \'saund-ˌbōrd, 'saun-, -ˌbȯrd\ *n* **1** : a thin resonant board so placed in a musical instrument as to reinforce its tones by sympathetic vibration **2** : SOUNDING BOARD 1a

sound box *n* : a hollow chamber in a musical instrument for increasing its sonority

sound effects *n pl* : variously produced effects that are imitative of sounds called for in a script (as of a play or movie)

sound•er \'saun-dər\ *n* : one that sounds; *esp* : an electromagnetic device in a telegraph receiver that makes clicking sounds from which the message can be interpreted

[1]**sound•ing** \'saun-ding\ *n* **1 a** : measurement by sounding **b** : the depth so ascertained **2** : measurement of atmospheric conditions at various heights **3** : a probe, test, or sampling of opinion or intention

[2]**sounding** *adj* **1** : SONOROUS 2, RESONANT **2** : POMPOUS 1, HIGH-SOUNDING — **sound•ing•ly** \-ding-lē\ *adv*

sounding board *n* **1 a** : a structure behind or over a pulpit, rostrum, or platform to give distinctness and sonority to sound **b** : a device or agency that helps spread opinions or utterances **2** : SOUNDBOARD 1

sounding line *n* : a line, wire, or cord weighted at one end and often marked at intervals for sounding

[1]**sound•less** \'saun-dləs\ *adj* : incapable of being sounded : UNFATHOMABLE

[2]**soundless** *adj* : making no sound — **sound•less•ly** *adv*

sound off *vi* **1** : to count cadence while marching **2 a** : to speak up in a loud voice **b** : to voice one's opinions freely and vigorously

sound pollution *n* : NOISE POLLUTION

[1]**sound•proof** \'saund-'prüf, 'saun-\ *adj* : impervious to sound

[2]**soundproof** *vt* : to insulate so as to obstruct the passage of sound

sound track *n* **1** : the area on a motion-picture film that carries the sound record **2** : a recording of the musical score of a motion picture

sound truck *n* : a truck equipped with a loudspeaker

sound waves *n pl* : longitudinal pressure waves in a material medium regardless of whether they constitute audible sound

soup \'süp\ *n* **1** : a liquid food with a meat, fish, or vegetable stock as a base and often containing pieces of solid food **2** : something (as a heavy fog) having or suggesting the consistency of soup **3** : an unfortunate predicament ⟨in the *soup*⟩ **[**French *soupe* "sop, soup", of Germanic origin**]**

soup•çon \süp-'sō^{n}, 'süp-ˌsän\ *n* : a little bit : TRACE **[**French, literally, "suspicion"**]**

souped–up \'süpt-'əp\ *adj* : increased in power or efficiency ⟨a *souped-up* hot rod⟩ **[**English slang *soup* "dope injected into a racehorse to improve its performance", from *soup***]** — **soup up** \süp-'əp, 'süp-\ *vt*

soup kitchen *n* : an establishment dispensing free food (as soup and bread) to the needy

soupy \'sü-pē\ *adj* **soup•i•er; -est** **1** : having the consistency of soup **2** : densely foggy or cloudy

[1]**sour** \'saur\ *adj* **1** : being or inducing the one of the four basic taste sensations characterized by an acid or tart taste ⟨*sour* as vinegar⟩ **2 a** : having undergone a usually acid fermentation ⟨*sour* milk⟩ **b** : indicative of decay : PUTRID ⟨a *sour* odor⟩ **3** : UNPLEASANT, DISAGREEABLE ⟨a *sour* look⟩ ⟨hit a *sour* note⟩ **4** : acid in reaction ⟨*sour* soil⟩ **[**Old English *sūr***]** — **sour•ish** \-ish\ *adj* — **sour•ly** *adv* — **sour•ness** *n*

• **syn** ACID, TART: SOUR usually implies having lost sweetness or freshness through fermentation or spoiling ⟨*sour* cream⟩ ACID applies to things having naturally or normally a biting or stinging taste ⟨*acid* fruits like lemons⟩ TART suggests a sharp but agreeable acidity ⟨*tart* applesauce⟩

[2]**sour** *n* **1** : something sour **2** : the primary taste sensation produced by sour stimuli

[3]**sour** *vb* : to become or make sour

sour ball *n* : a spherical piece of hard candy having a tart flavor

source \'sōrs, 'sȯrs\ *n* **1** : the point of origin of a stream of water : FOUNTAINHEAD **2 a** : a generative force : CAUSE **b** (1) : a point of origin (2) : one that initiates : AUTHOR; *also* : PROTOTYPE 2, MODEL (3) : one that supplies information **3** : a firsthand document or primary reference work **[**Middle French *sourse,* from *sourdre* "to rise, spring forth", from Latin *surgere***]** **syn** see ORIGIN

source book *n* : a fundamental document or record on which subsequent writings, beliefs, or practices are based

sour cherry *n* : a small Old World cherry tree widely grown for its soft tart bright red to nearly black fruits; *also* : its fruit

sour•dough \'saur-ˌdō\ *n* **1** : a leaven of dough in which fermentation is active **2** : an old-time prospector in Alaska or northwestern Canada **[**sense 2 from the use of sourdough for making bread in prospectors' camps**]**

sour grapes *n pl* : the belittling of something that has proven unattainable **[**from the fable ascribed to Aesop of the fox who being unable to reach some grapes he had desired disparaged them as sour**]**

sour gum *n* : a timber tree of the eastern United States with blue=

black fruits and close-grained grayish wood

sour•sop \'saůr-,säp\ *n* : a small tropical American tree related to the custard apple; *also* : its large edible fruit with fleshy spines and a slightly acid fibrous pulp

sou•sa•phone \'sü-zə-,fōn\ *n* : a large circular tuba with a flaring adjustable bell [John P. *Sousa*]

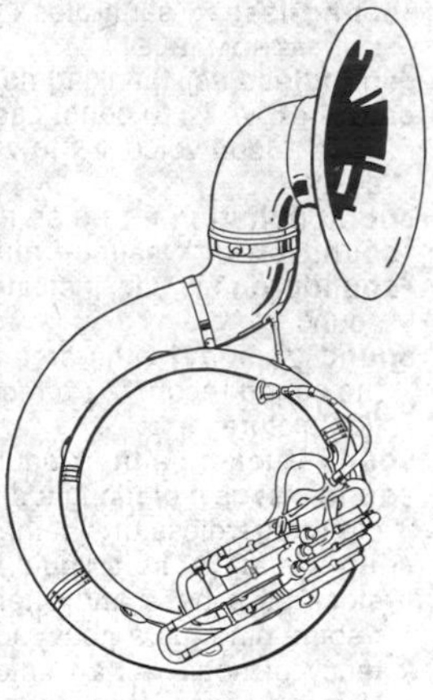

sousaphone

1souse \'saůs\ *vb* **1** : PICKLE **2 a** : to plunge in liquid : IMMERSE **b** : DRENCH 2, SATURATE **3** : to make or become drunk : INEBRIATE [Middle French *souce* "pickling solution", of Germanic origin]

2souse *n* **1** : something pickled; *esp* : seasoned and chopped pork trimmings, fish, or shellfish **2** : an act or instance of drenching **3** : an habitual drunkard

sou•tane \sü-'tän, -'tan\ *n* : CASSOCK [French, from Italian *sottana*, literally, "undergarment", derived from Latin *subtus* "underneath"]

1south \'saůth; *in compounds, as "southwest", also* saů *or* 'saů *especially by seamen*\ *adv* : to, toward, or in the south [Old English *sūth*]

2south *adj* **1** : situated toward or at the south **2** : coming from the south

3south *n* **1 a** : the direction to the right of one facing east **b** : the compass point directly opposite to north **2** *cap* : regions or countries south of a specified or implied point

South African *n* : a native or inhabitant of the Republic of South Africa; *esp* : AFRIKANER — **South African** *adj*

south•bound \'saůth-,baůnd\ *adj* : headed south

1south•east \saů-'thēst, *nautical* saů-'ēst\ *adv* : to, toward, or in the southeast

2southeast *n* **1 a** : the general direction between south and east **b** : the compass point midway between south and east : S 45° E **2** *cap* : regions or countries southeast of a specified or implied point

3southeast *adj* **1** : coming from the southeast **2** : situated toward or at the southeast

south•east•er \saů-'thē-stər, saů-'ē-stər\ *n* **1** : a strong southeast wind **2** : a storm with southeast winds

south•east•er•ly \saů-'thē-stər-lē\ *adv or adj* **1** : from the southeast **2** : toward the southeast

south•east•ern \saů-'thē-stərn\ *adj* **1** *often cap* : of, relating to, or characteristic of a region conventionally designated Southeast **2** : lying toward or coming from the southeast — **south•east•ern•most** \-stərn-,mōst\ *adj*

South•east•ern•er \-stər-nər, -stə-nər\ *n* : a native or inhabitant of a southeastern region (as of the United States)

1south•east•ward \saů-'thēs-twərd\ *adv or adj* : toward the southeast — **south•east•wards** \-twərdz\ *adv*

2southeastward *n* : SOUTHEAST

south•er \'saů-thər\ *n* : a southerly wind

south•er•ly \'səth-ər-lē\ *adv or adj* **1** : from the south **2** : toward the south

south•ern \'səth-ərn\ *adj* **1** *often cap* : of, relating to, or characteristic of a region conventionally designated South **2** : lying toward or coming from the south [Old English *sūtherne*] — **south•ern•most** \-,mōst\ *adj*

Southern Cross *n* : four bright stars in the southern hemisphere situated as if at the extremities of a Latin cross; *also* : the constellation of which these four stars are the brightest

South•ern•er \'səth-ər-nər, 'səth-ə-nər\ *n* : a native or inhabitant of the South (as of the United States)

southern hemisphere *n* : the half of the earth that lies south of the equator

southern lights *n pl* : AURORA AUSTRALIS

south•ern•ly \'səth-ərn-lē\ *adj* **1** : coming from the south **2** : headed south

south•ing \'saů-thing, -thing\ *n* **1** : difference in latitude to the south from the last preceding point of reckoning **2** : southerly progress

south•land \'saůth-,land, -lənd\ *n, often cap* : land in the south : the south of a country or region

south•paw \'saůth-,pȯ\ *n* : LEFT-HANDER; *esp* : a left-handed baseball pitcher — **southpaw** *adj*

south pole *n* **1** *often cap S&P* : the southernmost point of the earth : the southern end of the earth's axis **2** : the pole of a magnet that points toward the south

South•ron \'səth-rən\ *n* : SOUTHERNER: as **a** *chiefly Scottish* : ENGLISHMAN **b** *chiefly South* : a native or inhabitant of the southern states of the United States [Middle English *southren* "southern", from Old English *sūtherne*]

south–southeast *n* : two points east of south : S 22° 30′ E

south–southwest *n* : two points west of south : S 22° 30′ W

1south•ward \'saůth-wərd\ *adv or adj* : toward the south — **south•wards** \-wərdz\ *adv*

2southward *n* : southward direction or part

1south•west \saůth-'west, *nautical* saů-'west\ *adv* : to, toward, or in the southwest

2southwest *n* **1 a** : the general direction between south and west **b** : the compass point midway between south and west : S 45° W **2** *cap* : regions or countries southwest of a specified or implied point

3southwest *adj* **1** : coming from the southwest **2** : situated toward or at the southwest

south•west•er \saůth-'wes-tər, saů-'wes-\ *n* **1** : a strong southwest wind **2** : a storm with southwest winds

south•west•er•ly \-'wes-tər-lē\ *adv or adj* **1** : from the southwest **2** : toward the southwest

south•west•ern \saůth-'wes-tərn\ *adj* **1** *often cap* : of, relating to, or characteristic of a region conventionally designated Southwest **2** : lying toward or coming from the southwest — **south•west•ern•most** \-stərn-,mōst\ *adj*

South•west•ern•er \-tər-nər, -tə-nər\ *n* : a native or inhabitant of a southwestern region (as of the United States)

1south•west•ward \saůth-'wes-twərd\ *adv or adj* : toward the southwest — **south•west•wards** \-twərdz\ *adv*

2southwestward *n* : SOUTHWEST

sou•ve•nir \'sü-və-,niər, ,sü-və-'\ *n* : something that serves as a reminder : MEMENTO [French, literally, "act of remembering", from (*se*) *souvenir* "to remember", from Latin *subvenire* "to come up, come to mind", from *sub-* "up" + *venire* "to come"]

sou'•west•er \saů-'wes-tər\ *n* **1** : SOUTHWESTER **2 a** : a long oilskin coat worn especially at sea during stormy weather **b** : a waterproof hat with wide slanting brim longer in back than in front

sou'wester 2b

1sov•er•eign *also* **sov•ran** \'säv-rən, -ərn, -ə-rən, 'səv-\ *n* **1 a** : one possessing or held to possess sovereignty; *esp* : a monarch exercising supreme authority **b** : one that exercises supreme authority within a limited sphere : CHIEF **c** : an acknowledged leader : ARBITER **2** : a British gold coin no longer used worth one pound sterling

2sovereign *also* **sovran** *adj* **1 a** : supreme in power or authority ⟨a *sovereign* ruler⟩ **b** : politically independent : AUTONOMOUS ⟨a *sovereign* state⟩ **2 a** : SUPREME 2, SUPERLATIVE **b** : EFFECTUAL, POTENT ⟨a *sovereign* remedy for colds⟩ [Middle French *soverain*, derived from Latin *super* "over, above"] **syn** see FREE — **sov•er•eign•ly** *adv*

sov•er•eign•ty \-tē\ *n, pl* **-ties 1 a** : supreme power especially over a political unit **b** : freedom from external control **2** : one that is sovereign; *esp* : an autonomous state

so•vi•et \'sōv-ē-,et, 'säv-, -ē-ət\ *n* **1** : an elected governmental council in a Communist country **2** *pl, cap* **a** : BOLSHEVIK 1 **b** : the people and especially the political and military leaders of the Soviet Union [Russian *sovet*] — **soviet** *adj, often cap* — **so•vi•et•ism** \-,iz-əm\ *n, often cap*

so•vi•et•ize \-,īz\ *vt, often cap* **1** : to bring under Soviet control **2** : to force into conformity with Soviet cultural patterns or governmental policies — **so•vi•et•iza•tion** \,sōv-ē-,et-ə-'zā-shən, ,säv-ē-, -ē-ət-\ *n, often cap*

sov•khoz \säf-'kȯz\ *n, pl* **sov•kho•zy** \-'kȯ-zē\ *or* **sov•khoz•es** : a state-owned farm of the Soviet Union paying wages to the workers — compare KOLKHOZ [Russian, from *sovetskoe khozyaĭstvo* "soviet farm"]

[1]sow \'saù\ *n* : an adult female swine [Old English *sugu*]

[2]sow \'sō\ *vb* **sowed**; **sown** \'sōn\ *or* **sowed**; **sow•ing 1 a** : to plant seed for growth especially by scattering **b** : PLANT 1a **c** : to strew with or as if with seed **d** : to introduce into a selected environment : IMPLANT **2** : to set in motion : FOMENT ⟨*sow* suspicion⟩ **3** : to spread abroad : DISSEMINATE [Old English *sāwan*] — **sow•er** \'sō-ər, 'sōr\ *n*

sow•bel•ly \'saù-,bel-ē\ *n* : fat salt pork or bacon

sow bug \'saù-\ *n* : WOOD LOUSE

sow thistle \'saù-\ *n* : any of a genus of spiny weedy European herbs of the sunflower family widely naturalized (as in North America)

sox *pl of* SOCK

soy \'sòi\ *n* **1** : an oriental brown sauce made from soybeans fermented in brine **2** : SOYBEAN [Japanese *shōyu,* from Chinese (Cantonese dialect) *shī-yaū,* literally, "soybean oil"]

soya \'sòi-ə, 'sòi-yə\ *n* : SOYBEAN [Dutch *soja,* from Japanese *shōyu* "soy"]

soy•bean \'sòi-'bēn, -,bēn\ *n* : a hairy annual Asian plant of the pea family widely grown for its oil-rich and protein-rich edible seeds and for forage and soil improvement; *also* : its seed

soybean

spa \'spä, 'spò\ *n* **1 a** : a mineral spring **b** : a resort with mineral springs **2** : a fashionable resort or hotel [*Spa,* waterihg place in Belgium]

[1]space \'spās\ *n* **1** : a period of time; *also* : its duration **2 a** : a limited extent in one, two, or three dimensions **b** : an extent set apart or available ⟨parking *space*⟩ ⟨floor *space*⟩ **3** : one of the degrees between or above or below the lines of a musical staff **4** : a boundless three-dimensional extent in which objects and events occur and have relative position and direction **5** : the region beyond the earth's atmosphere **6 a** : a blank area separating words or lines **b** : something (as a piece of type) used to produce such a blank area **7** : a set of mathematical points each defined by one or more coordinates **8** : an interval in operation during which a telegraph key is not in contact **9 a** : LINAGE 1 **b** : broadcast time available especially to advertisers [Old French *espace,* from Latin *spatium* "area, room, interval of space or time"]

[2]space *vt* : to place at intervals or arrange with space between — **spac•er** *n*

space charge *n* : an electric charge (as the electrons in the region near the filament of a vacuum tube) distributed throughout a three-dimensional region

space•craft \'spā-,skraft\ *n* : a vehicle designed to operate outside the earth's atmosphere

spaced–out \'spā-'staùt\ *adj* : dazed or stupefied by or as if by a drug

space•flight \'spās-,flīt\ *n* : flight beyond the earth's atmosphere

space heater *n* : a device for heating an enclosed space; *esp* : an often portable device that heats the space in which it is located and has no external heating ducts

space•less \'spā-sləs\ *adj* **1** : having no limits : BOUNDLESS **2** : occupying no space

space•man \'spā-,sman, -smən\ *n* **1** : one who travels outside the earth's atmosphere **2** : a person engaged in any of various fields bearing on flight through outer space

space medicine *n* : a branch of medicine that deals with the effect on the human body of spaceflight

space•port \'spā-,spōrt, -,spòrt\ *n* : an installation for testing and launching rockets, missiles, and satellites

space•ship \'spās-,ship, 'spāsh-\ *n* : SPACECRAFT

space shuttle *n* : a usually two-stage vehicle that is designed to serve as transportation between the earth and an orbiting space station

space station *n* : a manned artificial satellite designed for a fixed orbit about the earth and to serve as a base (as for scientific observation)

space suit *n* : a suit with air supply and provisions to make life in free space possible for its wearer

space writer *n* : a writer paid according to the space his or her matter fills in print

spa•cial *variant of* SPATIAL

spac•ing \'spā-sing\ *n* **1** : an arrangement in space **2** : the distance between any two objects in a usually regular series

spa•cious \'spā-shəs\ *adj* **1** : vast or ample in extent : ROOMY ⟨a *spacious* hall⟩ **2** : large or magnificent in scale : EXPANSIVE — **spa•cious•ly** *adv* — **spa•cious•ness** *n*

[1]spade \'spād\ *n* **1** : a digging implement adapted for being pushed into the ground with the foot **2** : a spade-shaped instrument [Old English *spadu*] — **spade•ful** *n* — **call a spade a spade 1** : to call a thing by its right name however coarse **2** : to speak frankly

[2]spade *vb* : to dig with or use a spade — **spad•er** *n*

[3]spade *n* : a black figure resembling an inverted heart with a short stem at the bottom used to distinguish a suit of playing cards; *also* : a card of the suit bearing spades [Italian *spada* or Spanish *espada* "broad sword"; both from Latin *spatha,* from Greek *spathē* "blade"]

spade•foot \'spād-,fùt\ *n, pl* **spadefoots** : any of several burrowing toads with the feet modified for digging — called also *spadefoot toad*

spade•work \'spād-,wərk\ *n* **1** : work done with a spade **2** : the preliminary hard work in an undertaking

spa•dix \'spād-iks\ *n, pl* **spa•di•ces** \'spād-ə-,sēz\ : a floral spike (as in the arums) with a fleshy or succulent axis usually enclosed in a spathe [Latin, "frond torn from a palm tree", from Greek, from *span* "to draw, pull"]

spadix

spa•ghet•ti \spə-'get-ē\ *n* : pasta made in thin solid strings [Italian, from pl. of *spaghetto* "little string", from *spago* "string"]

spake \'spāk\ *archaic past of* SPEAK

[1]span \'span\ *archaic past of* SPIN

[2]span *n* **1** : the distance from the end of the thumb to the end of the little finger of a spread hand; *also* : an English unit of length equal to 9 inches (about 22.9 centimeters) **2** : an extent, stretch, reach, or spread between two limits: as **a** : a limited space of time ⟨*span* of life⟩ **b** : the spread of an arch, beam, truss, or girder from one support to another; *also* : the portion thus extended [Old English *spann*]

[3]span *vt* **spanned**; **span•ning 1 a** : to measure by or as if by the hand with fingers and thumb extended **b** : MEASURE 3 **2 a** : to reach or extend across ⟨a bridge *spans* the river⟩ **b** : to place or construct a span over : BRIDGE

[4]span *n* : a pair of animals (as mules) driven together [Dutch, from *spannen* "to hitch up"]

span•drel *or* **span•dril** \'span-drəl\ *n* : the sometimes ornamented space between the right or left exterior curve of an arch and an enclosing right angle [derived from Old French *espandre* "to spread out, expand", from Latin *expandere*]

1 spandrel

[1]span•gle \'spang-gəl\ *n* **1** : a small piece of shining metal or plastic used for ornamentation especially on clothes **2** : a small glittering object [Middle English *spangel*]

[2]spangle *vb* **span•gled**; **span•gling** \'spang-gə-ling, -gling\ **1** : to set or sprinkle with or as if with spangles **2** : to glitter as if covered with spangles : SPARKLE

\ə\ **abut**	\aù\ **out**	\i\ **tip**	\ò\ **saw**	\ù\ **foot**
\ər\ **further**	\ch\ **chin**	\ī\ **life**	\òi\ **coin**	\y\ **yet**
\a\ **mat**	\e\ **pet**	\j\ **job**	\th\ **thin**	\yü\ **few**
\ā\ **take**	\ē\ **easy**	\ng\ **sing**	\th\ **this**	\yù\ **cure**
\ä\ **cot, cart**	\g\ **go**	\ō\ **bone**	\ü\ **food**	\zh\ **vision**

Span•iard \ˈspan-yərd\ *n* : a native or inhabitant of Spain [Middle French *Espaignart,* from *Espaigne* "Spain", from Latin *Hispania*]

span•iel \ˈspan-yəl\ *n* **1** : any of numerous small or medium-sized mostly short-legged dogs usually having long wavy hair, feathered legs and tail, and large drooping ears **2** : TOADY [Middle French *espaignol,* literally, "Spaniard", derived from Latin *Hispania* "Spain"]

Span•ish \ˈspan-ish\ *n* **1** : the Romance language of the largest part of Spain and of the countries colonized by Spaniards **2** *pl in construction* : the people of Spain [Middle English *Spainish,* from *Spain*] — **Spanish** *adj*

Spanish American *n* **1** : a native or inhabitant of one of the countries of America in which Spanish is the national language **2** : a resident of the United States whose native language is Spanish and whose culture is of Spanish origin — **Spanish–American** *adj*

Spanish fly *n* : a green blister beetle of southern Europe; *also* : a dried preparation of these formerly used as an aphrodisiac

Spanish mackerel *n* : any of various usually large fishes chiefly of warm seas that resemble or are related to the common mackerel

Spanish moss *n* : an epiphytic plant related to the pineapple that forms pendent tufts of grayish green filaments on trees in the southern United States, Mexico, and the West Indies

Spanish moss

Spanish omelet *n* : an omelet served with a sauce of chopped green pepper, onion, and tomato

Spanish rice *n* : rice cooked with onions, green pepper, and tomatoes

spank \ˈspangk\ *vt* : to strike especially on the buttocks with the open hand [imitative] — **spank** *n*

spank•er \ˈspang-kər\ *n* : the fore-and-aft sail on the mast nearest the stern of a square-rigged ship [origin unknown]

spank•ing \ˈspang-king\ *adj* **1** : remarkable of its kind **2 a** : moving or able to move briskly **b** : being fresh and strong ⟨a *spanking* wind⟩ [origin unknown]

span•ner \ˈspan-ər\ *n* **1** *chiefly British* : WRENCH 2 **2** : a wrench having a jaw or socket to fit a nut or head of a bolt, a pipe, or hose coupling; *esp* : one having a tooth or pin in its jaw to fit a hole or slot in an object [German, "instrument for winding springs", from *spannen* "to stretch"]

span–new \ˈspan-ˈnü, -ˈnyü\ *adj* : BRAND-NEW [Old Norse *spānnȳr,* from *spānn* "chip of wood" + *nȳr* "new"]

span•worm \ˈspan-ˌwərm\ *n* : LOOPER 1

[1]**spar** \ˈspär\ *n* **1** : a stout rounded wood or metal piece (as a mast, boom, or yard) used to support sail rigging **2** : one of the main longitudinal members of the wing of an airplane that carry the ribs [Middle English *sparre*]

[2]**spar** *vi* **sparred; spar•ring 1 a** : BOX; *esp* : to gesture without landing a blow to draw one's opponent or create an opening **b** : to engage in a practice or exhibition bout of boxing **2** : SKIRMISH 1, WRANGLE [probably alteration of [2]*spur*]

[3]**spar** *n* : a sparring match or session

[4]**spar** *n* : any of various nonmetallic somewhat lustrous minerals usually able to be split readily in certain directions [Low German]

[1]**spare** \ˈspaər, ˈspeər\ *vb* **1** : to refrain from destroying, punishing, or harming : be lenient ⟨*spare* a prisoner⟩ **2** : to refrain from attacking or reprimanding ⟨the sermon *spared* no one⟩ **3** : to free from a liability or requirement : EXEMPT ⟨*spare* yourself the trouble⟩ **4** : to refrain from : AVOID ⟨*spare* no cost⟩ **5** : to be frugal or use frugally : STINT ⟨don't *spare* the syrup⟩ **6 a** : to give up as not strictly needed ⟨can you *spare* a dollar⟩ **b** : to have left over or as margin ⟨time to *spare*⟩ [Old English *sparian*]

[2]**spare** *adj* **1** : not being used; *esp* : held for emergency use ⟨a *spare* tire⟩ **2** : being over and above what is needed : SUPERFLUOUS ⟨*spare* time⟩ **3** : not liberal or profuse : MEAGER ⟨a *spare* diet⟩ **4** : healthily lean ⟨a *spare* build⟩ **5** : not abundant or plentiful : SCANTY [Old English *spær*] — **spare•ly** *adv* — **spare•ness** *n*

[3]**spare** *n* **1** : a spare or duplicate piece or part (as an automobile tire) **2 a** : the knocking down of all 10 pins with 2 bowls in a frame in bowling **b** : the score made by this action

spare•able \ˈspar-ə-bəl, ˈsper-\ *adj* : that can be spared

spare•ribs \ˈspaər-ˌribz, ˈspeər-, -ˌibz\ *n pl* : a cut of pork ribs separated from the bacon strip [by folk etymology from Low German *ribbesper* "pickled pork ribs roasted on a spit", from *ribbe* "rib" + *sper* "spear, spit"]

spar•ing \ˈspaər-ing, ˈspeər-\ *adj* **1** : tending to save; *esp* : FRUGAL **2** : SCANTY 2 — **spar•ing•ly** \-ing-lē\ *adv*

[1]**spark** \ˈspärk\ *n* **1 a** : a small particle of a burning substance **b** : a hot glowing particle struck from a larger mass; *esp* : one heated by friction ⟨produce a *spark* by striking steel on flint⟩ **2 a** : a luminous electrical discharge of very short duration between two conductors **b** : the electrical discharge in a spark plug **3** : SPARKLE 1, FLASH **4** : something that sets off a sudden force ⟨the *spark* that set off the rebellion⟩ **5** : SEED 4, GERM [Old English *spearca*]

[2]**spark** *vb* **1 a** : to throw out or produce sparks **b** : to flash or fall like sparks **2** : to respond with enthusiasm **3** : to set off in a burst of activity : ACTIVATE **4** : to stir to activity : INCITE ⟨the captain *sparked* the team to victory⟩ — **spark•er** *n*

[3]**spark** *n* **1** : a foppish young man : GALLANT **2** : SUITOR 3, SWAIN [perhaps of Scandinavian origin]

[4]**spark** *vb* : woo 1a, COURT — **spark•er** *n*

spark arrester *n* : a device for preventing the escape of sparks (as from a smokestack)

spark coil *n* : an induction coil for producing a spark for an internal-combustion engine

sparking plug *n, British* : SPARK PLUG 1

[1]**spar•kle** \ˈspär-kəl\ *vi* **spar•kled; spar•kling** \-kə-ling, -kling\ **1 a** : SPARK 1a **b** : to give off or reflect bright moving points of light **2** : to perform brilliantly **3** : EFFERVESCE ⟨wine that *sparkles*⟩ **4** : to become lively or animated [derived from *spark*] **syn** see FLASH

[2]**sparkle** *n* **1** : a little spark : SCINTILLATION ⟨the *sparkle* of a diamond⟩ **2** : the quality of sparkling **3 a** : ANIMATION, LIVELINESS ⟨the *sparkle* of your wit⟩ **b** : EFFERVESCENCE

spar•kler \ˈspär-klər\ *n* : one that sparkles: as **a** : DIAMOND 1a **b** : a firework that throws off brilliant sparks on burning

sparkling wine *n* : an effervescent red or white wine

spark plug *n* **1** : a part that fits into the cylinder head of an internal-combustion engine and produces the spark for combustion **2** : one that activates or gives impetus to an undertaking — **spark•plug** \ˈspärk-ˌpləg\ *vt*

spark plug 1

sparring partner *n* : one with whom a boxer spars for practice during training

spar•row \ˈspar-ō\ *n* **1** : any of several small dull singing birds related to the finches; *esp* : ENGLISH SPARROW **2** : any of various finches resembling the true sparrows [Old English *spearwa*]

sparrow hawk *n* : any of various small hawks or falcons

sparse \ˈspärs\ *adj* : of few and scattered elements; *esp* : not thickly grown or settled [Latin *sparsus* "spread out", from *spargere* "to scatter"] **syn** see MEAGER — **sparse•ly** *adv* — **sparse•ness** *n* — **spar•si•ty** \ˈspär-sət-ē\ *n*

[1]**Spar•tan** \ˈspärt-n\ *n* **1** : a native or inhabitant of ancient Sparta **2** : a person of great courage and fortitude

[2]**Spartan** *adj* **1** : of or relating to ancient Sparta **2 a** : marked by strict self-discipline and self-denial ⟨a *Spartan* athlete⟩ **b** : marked by simplicity and frugality ⟨*Spartan* living conditions⟩ **c** : undaunted by pain or danger ⟨*Spartan* courage⟩

spar varnish *n* : an exterior waterproof varnish [[1]*spar*]

spasm \ˈspaz-əm\ *n* **1** : an involuntary and abnormal muscular contraction **2** : a sudden violent and temporary effort or emotion [Middle French *spasme,* from Latin *spasmus,* from Greek *spasmos,* from *span* "to draw, pull"]

spas•mod•ic \spaz-ˈmäd-ik\ *adj* **1 :** relating to or affected or characterized by spasm ⟨*spasmodic* movements⟩ **2 :** acting or proceeding fitfully **:** INTERMITTENT ⟨*spasmodic* interest⟩ **3 :** subject to outbursts of emotional excitement **:** EXCITABLE [Greek *spasmōdēs,* from *spasmos* "spasm"] — **spas•mod•i•cal•ly** \-ˈmäd-i-kə-lē, -klē\ *adv*

spas•tic \ˈspas-tik\ *adj* **1 :** of, relating to, or characterized by spasm ⟨*spastic* colon⟩ **2 :** suffering from spastic paralysis ⟨a *spastic* child⟩ [Latin *spasticus,* from Greek *spastikos* "drawing in", from *span* "to draw, pull"] — **spastic** *n* — **spas•ti•cal•ly** \-ti-kə-lē, -klē\ *adv* — **spas•tic•i•ty** \spa-ˈstis-ət-ē\ *n*

spastic paralysis *n* **:** paralysis from rigidly contracted muscles and increased tendon reflexes — compare CEREBRAL PALSY

[1]**spat** \ˈspat\ *past of* SPIT

[2]**spat** *n, pl* **spat** *or* **spats :** a young bivalve mollusk (as an oyster) — usually used collectively [origin unknown]

[3]**spat** *n* **:** a cloth or leather gaiter covering the instep and ankle [short for *spatterdash,* a kind of legging worn as protection from water and mud]

[4]**spat** *n* **1 :** a brief petty quarrel **:** TIFF **2** *chiefly dialect* **:** SLAP 1 **3 :** a sound like that of rain falling in large drops ⟨the *spat* of bullets⟩ [probably imitative]

[5]**spat** *vb* **spat•ted**; **spat•ting 1** *chiefly dialect* **:** SLAP 1a **2 :** to quarrel pettily or briefly **:** TIFF **3 :** to strike with a sound like that of rain falling in large drops

spate \ˈspāt\ *n* **1 :** FLOOD 1a, FRESHET **2 a :** a large number or amount **b :** a sudden or strong outburst **:** RUSH [Middle English]

spathe \ˈspāth\ *n* **:** a sheathing bract or pair of bracts enclosing an inflorescence and especially a spadix [Latin *spatha* "broad sword", from Greek *spathē* "blade"] — **spathed** \ˈspāthd\ *adj*

spa•tial *or* **spa•cial** \ˈspā-shəl\ *adj* **:** relating to, occupying, or having the character of space [Latin *spatium* "space"] — **spa•ti•al•i•ty** \ˌspā-shē-ˈal-ət-ē\ *n* — **spa•tial•ly** \ˈspāsh-lē, -ə-lē\ *adv*

[1]**spat•ter** \ˈspat-ər\ *vb* **1 :** to splash with or as if with a liquid; *also* **:** to soil or spot in this way **2 :** to scatter by splashing ⟨*spatter* mud⟩ **3 :** to injure by aspersion **:** DEFAME ⟨*spatter* a good reputation⟩ **4 a :** to spurt out in scattered drops **b :** to drop with a sound like rain [related to Flemish *spetteren* "to spatter"]

[2]**spatter** *n* **1 :** the act or sound of spattering **:** the state of being spattered **2 a :** a drop or splash spattered on something **b :** a small amount or number **:** SPRINKLE ⟨a *spatter* of applause⟩

spat•ter•dock \ˈspat-ər-ˌdäk\ *n* **:** a common yellow North American water lily

spat•u•la \ˈspach-ə-lə\ *n* **:** a flat thin usually metal implement used especially for spreading or mixing soft substances, scooping, or lifting [Late Latin, "spoon, spatula", from Latin *spatha* "sword, spoon", from Greek *spathē* "blade"]

spat•u•late \ˈspach-ə-lət\ *adj* **:** shaped like a spatula

spav•in \ˈspav-ən\ *n* **:** a bony enlargement of the hock of a horse associated with strain [Middle French *espavain*] — **spav•ined** \-ənd\ *adj*

[1]**spawn** \ˈspȯn, ˈspän\ *vb* **1 a :** to produce or deposit eggs or spawn — used of an aquatic animal **b :** to induce (fish) to spawn **2 :** to bring forth **:** GENERATE ⟨*spawn* ideas⟩ **3 :** to produce young especially in large numbers [Anglo-French *espaundre,* from Old French *espandre* "to spread out, expand", from Latin *expandere*] — **spawn•er** *n*

[2]**spawn** *n* **1 :** the eggs of aquatic animals (as fishes or oysters) that lay many small eggs **2 a :** PRODUCT 2 **b :** offspring produced in large quantities **3 :** the seed, germ, or source of something **4 :** mycelium especially prepared (as in bricks) for propagating mushrooms

spay \ˈspā\ *vt* **:** to remove the ovaries of (a female animal) [Middle French *espeer* "to cut with a sword", from *espee* "sword", from Latin *spatha,* from Greek *spathē* "blade"]

speak \ˈspēk\ *vb* **spoke** \ˈspōk\; **spo•ken** \ˈspō-kən\; **speak•ing 1 :** to utter words with the voice **:** TALK **2 :** to utter by means of words ⟨*speak* the truth⟩ **3 :** to address a gathering **4 :** to mention in speech or writing **5 :** to carry a meaning as if by speech ⟨wore clothes that *spoke* of poverty⟩ **6 :** to make a natural or characteristic sound ⟨the big gun *spoke*⟩ **7 :** to use in talking ⟨*speak* French⟩ [Old English *sprecan, specan*] — **speak•able** \ˈspē-kə-bəl\ *adj*

• **syn** TALK: SPEAK may apply to any articulated sounds ranging from the least to the most coherent; TALK is less technical and less formal and implies a listener and connected discourse or exchange of thoughts.

— **speak for 1 :** to speak in behalf of **:** represent the opinions of **2 :** to apply for **:** CLAIM — **speak out 1 :** to speak loudly and distinctly **2 :** to speak freely — **speak to :** REPROVE 2, REBUKE — **speak up :** to speak out — **speak well for :** to be evidence in favor of — **speak with :** to talk to

speak•easy \ˈspē-ˌkē-zē\ *n* **:** a place where alcoholic drinks are illegally sold

speak•er \ˈspē-kər\ *n* **1 a :** one that speaks **b :** a person who makes a public speech or acts as a spokesman **2 :** the presiding officer of a deliberative assembly ⟨*Speaker* of the House of Representatives⟩ **3 :** LOUDSPEAKER

speak•er•ship \-ˌship\ *n* **:** the position of speaker especially of a legislative body

speak•ing \ˈspē-king\ *adj* **1 :** highly significant or expressive **:** ELOQUENT ⟨*speaking* eyes⟩ **2 :** closely resembling an original ⟨a *speaking* portrait⟩

speaking tube *n* **:** a pipe through which conversation may be conducted (as between different parts of a building)

[1]**spear** \ˈspiər\ *n* **1 :** a thrusting or throwing a weapon with a long shaft and sharp head or blade **2 :** a sharp-pointed instrument with barbs used in spearing fish **3 :** SPEARMAN [Old English *spere*]

[2]**spear** *adj* **:** PATERNAL 1, MALE ⟨the *spear* side of the family⟩ [[1]*spear* — see DISTAFF *origin*]

[3]**spear** *vb* **1 :** to pierce or strike with or as if with a spear **2 :** to thrust with or as if with a spear — **spear•er** *n*

[4]**spear** *n* **:** a usually young blade, shoot, or sprout (as of grass) [alteration of [1]*spire*]

spear•fish \ˈspiər-ˌfish\ *n* **:** any of several large sea fishes related to the marlins and sailfishes

[1]**spear•head** \ˈspiər-ˌhed\ *n* **1 :** the sharp-pointed head of a spear **2 :** a leading element, force, or influence ⟨the *spearhead* of the attack⟩

[2]**spearhead** *vt* **:** to serve as leader or leading element of ⟨*spearhead* an attack⟩

spear•man \ˈspiər-mən\ *n* **:** one (as a soldier) armed with a spear

spear•mint \-ˌmint, -mənt\ *n* **:** a common mint grown for flavoring and especially for its aromatic oil

spearmint

spe•cial \ˈspesh-əl\ *adj* **1 a :** distinguished by some unusual quality ⟨a *special* occasion⟩ **b :** regarded with particular favor ⟨a *special* friend⟩ **2 a :** distinctive in character **:** PECULIAR ⟨a *special* case⟩ **b :** of, relating to, or constituting a species **:** SPECIFIC ⟨a *special* concept⟩ **3 :** additional to what is usual ⟨a *special* edition⟩ **4 :** designed for a particular purpose or occasion ⟨a *special* diet⟩ [Latin *specialis* "individual, particular", from *species* "species"] — **special** *n* — **spe•cial•ly** \ˈspesh-lē, -ə-lē\ *adv*

special delivery *n* **:** a messenger delivery of a piece of mail ahead of the regular carrier delivery for an extra fee

spe•cial•ist \ˈspesh-ləst, -ə-ləst\ *n* **1 :** one who devotes himself or herself to a special occupation or branch of learning ⟨eye *specialist*⟩ **2 :** any of four enlisted ranks in the Army comparable to corporal through sergeant first class — **specialist** *or* **spe•cial•is•tic** \ˌspesh-ə-ˈlis-tik\ *adj*

spe•ci•al•i•ty \ˌspesh-ē-ˈal-ət-ē\ *n, pl* **-ties 1 :** a special mark or quality **2 :** a special object or class of objects **3 a :** a special aptitude or skill **b :** a particular occupation or branch of learning

spe•cial•iza•tion \ˌspesh-lə-ˈzā-shən, -ə-lə-\ *n* **1 :** a making or becoming specialized **2 a :** structural adaptation of a body part to a particular function or of an organism for life in a particular environment **b** : a body part or an organism adapted by specialization

spe•cial•ize \'spesh-ə-ˌlīz\ *vb* **1** : to make particular mention of : PARTICULARIZE **2** : to apply or direct to a specific end or use ⟨*specialized* study⟩ **3** : to concentrate one's efforts in a special activity or field ⟨*specialize* in French⟩ **4** : to undergo specialization; *esp* : to change adaptively

spe•cial•ty \'spesh-əl-tē\ *n, pl* **-ties 1** : a distinctive mark or quality **2 a** : a special object or class of objects; *esp* : a product of a special kind or of special excellence ⟨pancakes were the cook's *specialty*⟩ **b** : the state of being special, distinctive, or peculiar **3** : something in which one specializes or has special knowledge

spe•ci•a•tion \ˌspē-shē-'ā-shən, ˌspē-sē-\ *n* : differentiation into new biological species — **spe•ci•ate** \'spē-shē-ˌāt, -sē-\ *vi*

spe•cie \'spē-shē, -sē\ *n* : money in coin especially of gold or silver [from *in specie* "in kind, in coin", from Latin, "in kind"] — **in specie** : in the same or like form

[1]**spe•cies** \'spē-ˌshēz, -shēz, -ˌsēz, -sēz\ *n, pl* **species 1 a** : a class of individuals with common qualities and a common name : KIND, SORT **b** (1) : a category of biological classification ranking below the genus, comprising related organisms or populations potentially capable of interbreeding, and being designated by a binomial that consists of the name of its genus followed by a Latin or latinized uncapitalized noun or adjective agreeing grammatically with the genus name (2) : an individual or kind belonging to such a species **2** : the consecrated eucharistic elements [Latin, "appearance, kind, species"]

[2]**species** *adj* : belonging to a biological species as distinguished from a horticultural variety ⟨a *species* rose⟩

spec•i•fi•able \'spes-ə-ˌfī-ə-bəl\ *adj* : capable of being specified

[1]**spe•cif•ic** \spi-'sif-ik\ *adj* **1** : of, relating to, or constituting a species **2** : precisely and accurately formulated ⟨a *specific* statement of faith⟩ **3** : having a unique relation to something ⟨*specific* antibodies⟩; *esp* : exerting a distinctive and usually a causative or curative influence ⟨quinine is *specific* for malaria⟩ [Late Latin *specificus*, from Latin *species* "species"] **syn** see EXPLICIT — **spe•cif•i•cal•ly** \-'sif-i-kə-lē, -klē\ *adv* — **spec•i•fic•i•ty** \ˌspes-ə-'fis-ət-ē\ *n*

[2]**specific** *n* **1 a** : something peculiarly adapted to a purpose or use **b** : a drug or remedy specific for a particular disease **2 a** : a characteristic quality or trait **b** : precise details or distinctions : PARTICULARS **c** *pl* : SPECIFICATION 2a

spec•i•fi•ca•tion \ˌspes-fə-'kā-shən, -ə-fə-\ *n* **1** : the act or process of specifying **2 a** (1) : a detailed precise presentation of something or of a plan or proposal for something — often used in pl. ⟨the architect's *specifications* for a new building⟩ (2) : a written description of an invention for which a patent is sought **b** : a single item in such a detailed presentation

specific gravity *n* : the ratio of the weight of a volume of a substance to the weight of an equal volume of some other substance taken as the standard which is water for solids and liquids and air or hydrogen for gases

specific heat *n* **1** : the ratio of the quantity of heat required to raise the temperature of a body one degree to that required to raise the temperature of an equal mass of water one degree **2** : the heat joules required to raise the temperature of one kilogram of a substance one kelvin

spec•i•fy \'spes-ə-ˌfī\ *vt* **-fied**; **-fy•ing 1** : to name or state explicitly or in detail ⟨*specify* the reason for absence⟩ **2** : to include as an item in a specification ⟨*specify* oak flooring⟩ [Old French *specifier*, from Late Latin *specificare*, from *specificus* "specific"] — **spec•i•fi•er** \-ˌfī-ər, -ˌfīr\ *n*

spec•i•men \'spes-ə-mən\ *n* **1** : an item or part typical of a group or whole : SAMPLE **2** : PERSON, SORT ⟨a tough *specimen*⟩ [Latin, from *specere* "to look at"]

spe•ci•os•i•ty \ˌspē-shē-'äs-ət-ē\ *n* : the quality or state of being specious

spe•cious \'spē-shəs\ *adj* : having a false look of truth, fairness, or genuineness ⟨a *specious* argument⟩ [Latin *speciosus* "beautiful, plausible", from *species* "appearance, species"] **syn** see PLAUSIBLE — **spe•cious•ly** *adv* — **spe•cious•ness** *n*

[1]**speck** \'spek\ *n* **1** : a small discoloration or spot especially from dirt or decay **2** : PARTICLE 2a, BIT **3** : something marked or marred with specks [Old English *specca*]

[2]**speck** *vt* : to produce specks on or in

[1]**speck•le** \'spek-əl\ *n* : a little speck [Middle English]

[2]**speckle** *vt* **speck•led**; **speck•ling** \'spek-ling, -ə-ling\ **1** : to mark with speckles **2** : to be distributed in or on like speckles ⟨small lakes *speckled* the land⟩

specs \'speks\ *n pl* : GLASS 2c [contraction of *spectacles*]

spec•ta•cle \'spek-ti-kəl\ *n* **1 a** : something exhibited to view as unusual, notable, or entertaining; *esp* : an eye-catching or dramatic public display **b** : an object of curiosity or contempt ⟨made a *spectacle* of herself at the party⟩ **2** *pl* : GLASS 2c [Middle French, from Latin *spectaculum*, from *spectare* "to watch", from *specere* "to look at"]

spec•ta•cled \-kəld\ *adj* : having or wearing spectacles

[1]**spec•tac•u•lar** \spek-'tak-yə-lər, spək-\ *adj* : of, relating to, or constituting a spectacle — **spec•tac•u•lar•ly** *adv*

[2]**spectacular** *n* : something (as an elaborate television show) that is spectacular

spec•ta•tor \'spek-ˌtāt-ər, spek-'\ *n* : one who watches without being involved or taking part [Latin, from *spectare* "to watch"] — **spectator** *adj*

spec•ter *or* **spec•tre** \'spek-tər\ *n* **1** : GHOST 2 **2** : something that haunts or perturbs the mind [French *spectre*, from Latin *spectrum* "appearance, specter", from *specere* "to look, look at"]

spec•tral \'spek-trəl\ *adj* **1** : of, relating to, or suggesting a specter : GHOSTLY **2** : of, relating to, or made by a spectrum ⟨*spectral* color⟩ — **spec•tral•ly** \-trə-lē\ *adv* — **spec•tral•ness** *n*

spec•tro•gram \'spek-trə-ˌgram\ *n* : a photograph or diagram of a spectrum

spec•tro•graph \'spek-trə-ˌgraf\ *n* : an apparatus for dispersing radiation into a spectrum and photographing or mapping the spectrum — **spec•tro•graph•ic** \ˌspek-trə-'graf-ik\ *adj* — **spec•tro•graph•i•cal•ly** \-'graf-i-kə-lē, -klē\ *adv*

spec•trom•e•ter \spek-'träm-ət-ər\ *n* **1** : an instrument used in determining the index of refraction **2** : a spectroscope fitted for measurements of the spectra observed with it — **spec•tro•met•ric** \ˌspek-trə-'me-trik\ *adj* — **spec•trom•e•try** \spek-'träm-ə-trē\ *n*

spec•tro•scope \'spek-trə-ˌskōp\ *n* : any of various instruments for forming and examining spectra — **spec•tro•scop•ic** \ˌspek-trə-'skäp-ik\ *adj* — **spec•tro•scop•i•cal•ly** \-'skäp-i-kə-lē, -klē\ *adv* — **spec•tros•co•pist** \spek-'träs-kə-pəst\ *n* — **spec•tros•co•py** \-pē\ *n*

spec•trum \'spek-trəm\ *n, pl* **spec•tra** \-trə\ *or* **spec•trums 1 a** : a series of colors formed when a beam of white light is dispersed (as by passing through a prism) so that the component waves are arranged in the order of their wavelengths from red continuing through orange, yellow, green, blue, indigo, and violet **b** : a series of radiations arranged in regular order according to some varying characteristic especially wavelength — compare ELECTROMAGNETIC SPECTRUM **2** : a continuous sequence or range ⟨a wide *spectrum* of political opinions⟩ [Latin, "appearance, specter"]

spec•u•lar \'spek-yə-lər\ *adj* : of, relating to, or having the qualities of a mirror [Latin *specularis*, from *speculum* "mirror"] — **spec•u•lar•ly** *adv*

spec•u•late \'spek-yə-ˌlāt\ *vi* **1 a** : to meditate on or ponder a subject : REFLECT **b** : to think or theorize about something in which evidence is too slight for certainty to be reached **2** : to assume a business risk in hope of gain; *esp* : to buy or sell in expectation of profiting from market fluctuations [Latin *speculari* "to spy out, examine", from *specula* "watchtower", from *specere* "to look"] **syn** see THINK — **spec•u•la•tion** \ˌspek-yə-'lā-shən\ *n* — **spec•u•la•tive** \'spek-yə-lət-iv, -ˌlāt-\ *adj* — **spec•u•la•tive•ly** *adv* — **spec•u•la•tor** \-ˌlāt-ər\ *n*

spec•u•lum \'spek-yə-ləm\ *n, pl* **-la** \-lə\ *also* **-lums 1** : a tubular instrument inserted into a body passage for inspection or medication **2** : a reflector in an optical instrument [Latin, "mirror", from *specere* "to look"]

speech \'spēch\ *n* **1 a** : the communication or expression of thoughts in spoken words **b** : CONVERSATION **2 a** : something that is spoken **b** : a public discourse **3 a** : LANGUAGE 1a, DIALECT **b** : an individual manner or style of speaking **4** : the power of expressing or communicating thoughts by speaking [Old English *sprǣc, spǣc*]

speech area *n* : a brain center associated with the motor control of speech

speech community *n* : a group of people sharing characteristic patterns of vocabulary, grammar, and pronunciation

speech•ify \'spē-chə-ˌfī\ *vi* **-ified**; **-ify•ing** : to make a speech : HARANGUE

speech•less \'spēch-ləs\ *adj* **1** : lacking or deprived of the power of speaking **2** : not speaking for a time : SILENT ⟨*speechless* with surprise⟩ **syn** see DUMB — **speech•less•ly** *adv* — **speech•less•ness** *n*

[1]**speed** \'spēd\ *n* **1** *archaic* : prosperity in an undertaking : SUCCESS **2 a** : the act or state of moving swiftly : SWIFTNESS **b** : rate of motion : VELOCITY **3** : swiftness or rate of performance or action : QUICKNESS **4 a** : the sensitivity of a photographic film, plate, or paper **b** : the light-gathering power of a lens expressed as relative aperture **5** : a transmission gear in automotive vehicles ⟨shift to low *speed*⟩ **6** : METHAMPHETAMINE; *also* : a related drug [Old English *spēd*] **syn** see HASTE

[2]**speed** *vb* **sped** \'sped\ *or* **speed•ed**; **speed•ing** **1 a** : to prosper in an undertaking **b** : to help to succeed : AID **2 a** : to make haste **b** : to go or drive at excessive or illegal speed **3** : to move, work, or take place faster : ACCELERATE **4 a** : to cause to move quickly : HASTEN **b** : to wish Godspeed to **c** : to increase the speed of : ACCELERATE ⟨*speeded* up the engine⟩ — **speed•er** *n*

[3]**speed** *adj* : of, relating to, or regulating speed

speed•ball \'spēd-ˌbȯl\ *n* : a game between 2 teams of 11 players on a football field which is similar to soccer but in which the ball may be kicked or played with the hands

speed•boat \'spēd-ˌbōt\ *n* : a fast launch or motorboat

speed limit *n* : the highest speed a vehicle may legally travel at

speed•om•e•ter \spi-'däm-ət-ər\ *n* **1** : an instrument that measures speed **2** : an instrument that both measures speed and records distance traveled

speed•ster \'spēd-stər\ *n* : one that speeds or is capable of great speed

speed trap *n* : a stretch of road policed by concealed officers or devices (as radar) to catch speeders

speed•up \'spēd-ˌəp\ *n* **1** : ACCELERATION 2 **2** : an employer's demand for accelerated output without increased pay

speed•way \'spēd-ˌwā\ *n* **1** : a road on which more than ordinary speed is allowed **2** : a racecourse for motor vehicles

speed•well \'spēd-ˌwel\ *n* : any of a genus of herbs of the snapdragon family; *esp* : a creeping perennial European herb with small bluish flowers

speedy \'spēd-ē\ *adj* **speed•i•er**; **-est** : rapid in motion or action **syn** see QUICK — **speed•i•ly** \'spēd-l-ē\ *adv* — **speed•i•ness** *n*

spe•le•ol•o•gy \ˌspē-lē-'äl-ə-jē, ˌspel-ē-\ *n* : the scientific study or exploration of caves [Latin *speleum* "cave" (from Greek *spēlaion*) + English *-logy*] — **spe•le•o•log•i•cal** \ˌspē-lē-ə-'läj-i-kəl, ˌspel-ē-\ *adj* — **spe•le•ol•o•gist** \-'äl-ə-jəst\ *n*

[1]**spell** \'spel\ *n* **1 a** : a spoken word or form of words believed to have magic power : INCANTATION **b** : a state of enchantment **2** : a strong compelling influence or attraction [Old English, "talk, tale"]

[2]**spell** *vt* : to put under a spell : BEWITCH

[3]**spell** *vb* **spelled** \'speld, 'spelt\; **spell•ing** **1** : to read or discern slowly and with difficulty — often used with *out* **2 a** : to name, write, or print the letters of in order ⟨*spell* a word⟩ **b** : to constitute the letters of ⟨*c-a-t* spells "cat"⟩ **3** : MEAN, SIGNIFY ⟨another drought may *spell* famine⟩ **4** : to form words with letters [Old French *espeller*, of Germanic origin]

[4]**spell** *vb* **spelled** \'speld\; **spell•ing** **1** : to take the place of for a time : RELIEVE ⟨if we *spell* each other we won't get tired⟩ **2** : to allow an interval of rest to : REST [Old English *spelian*]

[5]**spell** *n* **1** : one's turn at work **2** : a period spent in a job or occupation **3 a** : a short period of time **b** : a stretch of a specified type of weather **4** : a period of bodily or mental distress or disorder : ATTACK, FIT ⟨a *spell* of coughing⟩ ⟨a fainting *spell*⟩

spell•bind \'spel-ˌbīnd\ *vt* **-bound** \-ˌbau̇nd\; **-bind•ing** : to hold by or as if by a spell : FASCINATE [back-formation from *spellbound*]

spell•bind•er \-ˌbīn-dər\ *n* : a speaker of compelling eloquence

spell•bound \-'bau̇nd\ *adj* : held by or as if by a spell

spell•down \'spel-ˌdau̇n\ *n* : SPELLING BEE

spell•er \'spel-ər\ *n* **1** : one that spells words **2** : a book with exercises for teaching spelling

spell•ing \'spel-iŋ\ *n* : the forming of words from letters according to accepted usage; *also* : the letters of a word

spelling bee *n* : a spelling contest in which each contestant is eliminated as soon as he or she misspells a word

spell out *vt* : to make very explicit or emphatic

[1]**spelt** \'spelt\ *n* : a wheat with loose spikes and spikelets that each contain two light-red kernels [Old English, from Late Latin *spelta*, of Germanic origin]

[2]**spelt** *chiefly British past of* SPELL

spel•ter \'spel-tər\ *n* : ZINC; *esp* : zinc cast in slabs for commercial use [probably from Dutch *speauter*]

spe•lunk•ing \spi-'ləŋ-kiŋ, 'spē-ˌ\ *n* : the hobby or practice of exploring caves [Latin *spelunca* "cave", from Greek *spēlynx*] — **spe•lunk•er** \-kər\ *n*

spend \'spend\ *vt* **spent** \'spent\; **spend•ing** **1** : to use up or pay out : EXPEND **2 a** : to wear out : EXHAUST **b** : to consume wastefully : SQUANDER **3** : to cause or permit to elapse : PASS ⟨*spent* the evening reading⟩ [partly from Old English *spendan*, from Latin *expendere* "to expend"; partly from Old French *despendre*, from Latin *dispendere* "to weigh out", from *dis-* + *pendere* "to weigh"] — **spend•er** *n*

spend•able \'spen-də-bəl\ *adj* : available for spending

spending money *n* : money for small personal expenses

spend•thrift \'spend-ˌthrift, 'spen-\ *n* : one who spends lavishly or wastefully — **spendthrift** *adj*

Spen•se•ri•an \spen-'sir-ē-ən\ *adj* : of, relating to, or characteristic of Edmund Spenser or his writings

Spenserian stanza *n* : a stanza consisting of eight lines of iambic pentameter and an alexandrine with a rhyme scheme *ababbcbcc*

spent \'spent\ *adj* **1** : used up **2** : drained of energy or effectiveness [past participle of *spend*]

sperm \'spərm\ *n, pl* **sperm** *or* **sperms** **1 a** : SEMEN **b** : a male gamete **2** : a product (as oil) of the sperm whale [Middle French *esperme*, from Late Latin *sperma*, from Greek, literally, "seed"]

sperm- *or* **spermo-** *or* **sperma-** *or* **spermi-** *combining form* : seed : germ : sperm ⟨*sperma*theca⟩ [Greek *sperma*]

sper•ma•ce•ti \ˌspər-mə-'sēt-ē, -'set-\ *n* : a waxy solid obtained from the oil of cetaceans and especially the sperm whale and used in ointments, cosmetics, and candles [Medieval Latin *sperma ceti* "whale sperm"]

sper•ma•ry \'spərm-rē, -ə-rē\ *n, pl* **-ries** : an organ in which male gametes are developed

spermat- *or* **spermato-** *combining form* : seed : spermatozoon ⟨*spermato*cyte⟩ [Greek *spermat-*, *sperma* "seed, sperm"]

sper•ma•the•ca \ˌspər-mə-'thē-kə\ *n* : a sac for sperm storage in the female reproductive tract of many lower animals — **sper•ma•the•cal** \-kəl\ *adj*

sper•mat•ic \ˌspər-'mat-ik\ *adj* : of or relating to sperm or the male gonad

sper•ma•tid \'spər-mət-əd\ *n* : one of the cells produced in meiosis that differentiate into spermatozoa [derived from Greek *sperma* "seed, sperm"]

sper•ma•ti•um \ˌspər-'mā-shē-əm\ *n, pl* **-tia** \-shē-ə\ : a nonmotile cell functioning or held to function as a male gamete in some lower plants [New Latin, derived from Greek *sperma* "seed, sperm"] — **sper•ma•tial** \-shē-əl, -shəl\ *adj*

sper•mato•cyte \ˌspər-'mat-ə-ˌsīt, 'spər-mət-\ *n* : a cell giving rise to sperm cells

sper•mato•gen•e•sis \ˌspər-mət-ə-'jen-ə-səs, spər-ˌmat-\ *n, pl* **-e•ses** \-ə-ˌsēz\ : the process of male gamete formation including meiosis and transformation of the four resulting spermatids into spermatozoa — **sper•mato•ge•net•ic** \spər-ˌmat-ə-jə-'net-ik, ˌspər-mət-ō-\ *adj*

sper•mato•go•ni•um \ˌspər-mət-ə-'gō-nē-əm, spər-ˌmat-\ *n, pl* **-nia** \-nē-ə\ : a primitive male germ cell [*spermat-* + *gonium* "primitive germ cell", from Greek *gonos* "offspring, seed"] — **sper•mato•go•ni•al** \-nē-əl\ *adj*

sper•mato•phyte \ˌspər-'mat-ə-ˌfīt\ *n* : any of a group (Spermatophyta) of higher plants comprising those that produce seeds and including the gymnosperms and angiosperms — **sper•mato•phyt•ic** \spər-ˌmat-ə-'fit-ik, ˌspər-mət-\ *adj*

sper•mato•zo•on \spər-ˌmat-ə-'zō-ˌän, ˌspər-mət-, -'zō-ən\ *n, pl* **-zoa** \-'zō-ə\ : SPERM CELL [*spermat-* + Greek *zōion* "an-

\ə\ **abut**	\au̇\ **out**	\i\ **tip**	\ȯ\ **saw**	\u̇\ **foot**
\ər\ **further**	\ch\ **chin**	\ī\ **life**	\ȯi\ **coin**	\y\ **yet**
\a\ **mat**	\e\ **pet**	\j\ **job**	\th\ **thin**	\yü\ **few**
\ā\ **take**	\ē\ **easy**	\ŋ\ **sing**	\t͟h\ **this**	\yu̇\ **cure**
\ä\ **cot, cart**	\g\ **go**	\ō\ **bone**	\ü\ **food**	\zh\ **vision**

imal"] — **sper•mato•zo•al** \-'zō-əl\ *adj*

sperm cell *n* : a motile male gamete of an animal usually with rounded or elongate head and a long posterior flagellum — called also *spermatozoon*

sperm nucleus *n* : either of two nuclei derived from the generative nucleus of a pollen grain that function in the double fertilization of a seed plant

sperm oil *n* : a pale yellow oil from the sperm whale used especially as a lubricant

sperm whale \'spərm-\ *n* : a large toothed whale with a closed cavity in the head containing a fluid mixture of spermaceti and oil [short for *spermaceti whale*]

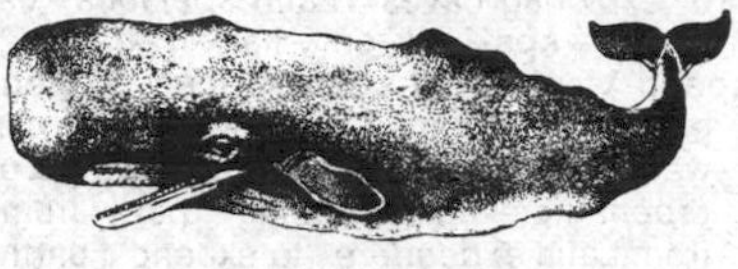

sperm whale

[1]spew \'spyü\ *vb* : to pour forth : VOMIT [Old English *spīwan*] — **spew•er** *n*

[2]spew *n* : matter that is spewed

sphag•num \'sfag-nəm\ *n* **1** : any of a large genus of atypical mosses that grow only in wet acid areas where their remains become compacted with other plant debris to form peat **2** : a mass of sphagnum plants [New Latin, from Latin *sphagnos,* a kind of moss, from Greek] — **sphag•nous** \-nəs\ *adj*

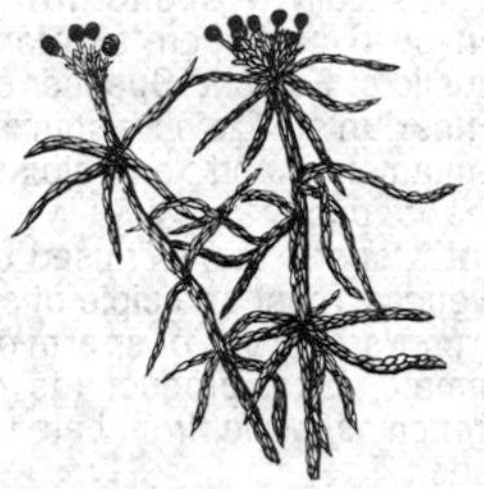

sphagnum 1

sphal•er•ite \'sfal-ə-,rīt\ *n* : a widely distributed ore of zinc composed essentially of zinc sulfide [German *sphalerit,* from Greek *sphaleros* "deceitful"; from its often being mistaken for galena]

sphe•no•don \'sfē-nə-,dän, 'sfen-ə-\ *n* : TUATARA [derived from Greek *sphēn* "wedge" + *odōn* "tooth"]

[1]sphe•noid \'sfē-,nȯid\ *or* **sphe•noi•dal** \sfi-'nȯid-l\ *adj* : of, relating to, or being a winged bone of the base of the cranium [Greek *sphēnoeidēs* "wedge-shaped", from *sphēn* "wedge"]

[2]sphenoid *n* : a sphenoid bone

sphe•nop•sid \sfi-'näp-səd\ *n* : any of a major group (Sphenopsida) of primitive, jointed, and mostly extinct vascular plants including the equisetums [derived from Greek *sphēn* "wedge" + *opsis* "appearance, vision"]

sphere \'sfiər\ *n* **1 a** (1) : the apparent surface of the heavens of which half forms the dome of the visible sky (2) : one of the concentric and eccentric revolving spherical transparent shells in which according to ancient astronomy stars, sun, planets, and moon are set **b** : a globe representing the earth **2 a** : a globular body : BALL **b** : a surface all points of which are equally distant from a center; *also* : the space enclosed by such a surface **3** : natural, normal, or proper place; *esp* : social order or rank **4** : a field or range of influence or significance : PROVINCE [Middle French *espere* "globe, celestial sphere", from Latin *sphaera,* from Greek *sphaira,* literally, "ball"] — **spher•ic** \'sfiər-ik, 'sfer-\ *adj* — **sphe•ric•i•ty** \sfir-'is-ət-ē\ *n*

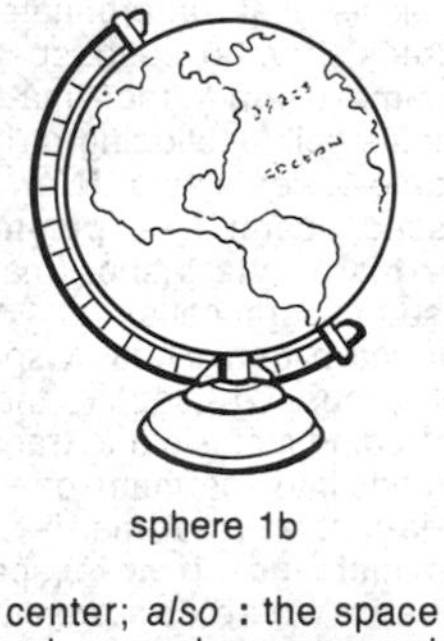

sphere 1b

sphere of influence : an area within which the interests of one nation are paramount

spher•i•cal \'sfir-i-kəl, 'sfer-\ *adj* **1** : having the form of a sphere or of one of its segments **2** : relating to or dealing with a sphere or its properties — **spher•i•cal•ly** \-kə-lē, -klē\ *adv*

spherical aberration *n* : aberration that is caused by the spherical form of a lens or mirror that gives different foci for central and marginal rays

spherical angle *n* : the angle between two intersecting arcs of great circles of a sphere

spherical triangle *n* : a figure analogous to a plane triangle formed by three intersecting arcs of great circles of a sphere

sphe•roid \'sfiər-,ȯid, 'sfeər-\ *n* : a figure resembling a flattened sphere — **sphe•roi•dal** \sfir-'ȯid-l\ *adj* — **sphe•roi•dal•ly** \-'ȯid-l-ē\ *adv*

spher•ule \'sfiər-ül, 'sfeər-, -yül\ *n* : a little sphere or spherical body

spher•u•lite \'sfir-ə-,līt, 'sfer-, -yə-\ *n* : a usually spherical crystalline body of radiating crystal fibers found in vitreous volcanic rocks — **spher•u•lit•ic** \,sfir-ə-'lit-ik, ,sfer-, -yə-\ *adj*

sphery \'sfiər-ē\ *adj* : suggestive of the heavenly spheres ⟨*sphery* eyes⟩ ⟨*sphery* music⟩

sphinc•ter \'sfing-tər, 'sfingk-\ *n* : a muscular ring surrounding and able to contract or close a bodily opening [Late Latin, from Greek *sphinktēr,* literally, "band", from *sphingein* "to bind tight"]

sphinx \'sfings, 'sfingks\ *n* **1 a** : a monster in Greek mythology having typically a lion's body, wings, and the head and bust of a woman **b** : a person whose character, motives, or feelings are enigmatic **2** : an ancient Egyptian image in the form of a recumbent lion having a man's head, a ram's head, or a hawk's head **3** : HAWKMOTH — called also *sphinx moth* [Latin, from Greek]

sphinx 2

sphyg•mo•ma•nom•e•ter \,sfig-mō-mə-'näm-ət-ər\ *n* : an instrument for measuring blood pressure and especially arterial blood pressure [Greek *sphygmos* "pulse" + English *manometer*] — **sphyg•mo•ma•nom•e•try** \-mə-'näm-ə-trē\ *n*

Spi•ca \'spī-kə\ *n* : a bright star in the constellation Virgo [Latin, literally, "spike of grain"]

spi•cate \'spī-,kāt\ *adj* : arranged in the form of a spike ⟨a *spicate* inflorescence⟩ [Latin *spicatus,* past participle of *spicare* "to arrange in a spike", from *spica* "spike of grain"]

[1]spice \'spīs\ *n* **1** : any of various aromatic plant products (as pepper or nutmeg) used to season or flavor foods **2** : something that gives zest or relish **3** : a pungent or fragrant odor : PERFUME [Old French *espice,* from Late Latin *species* "spices", from Latin, "species"]

[2]spice *vt* : to season with or as if with spices

spice box *n* : a box holding or designed to hold spices; *esp* : a box fitted with smaller boxes for holding spices

spice•bush \-,bu̇sh\ *n* : an aromatic shrub of the laurel family with small early yellow flowers

spick–and–span \,spik-ən-'span\ *adj* **1** : BRAND-NEW, FRESH **2** : spotlessly clean and neat [derived from obsolete *spick* "spike" + *span-new*]

spic•ule \'spik-yül\ *n* : a minute slender pointed usually hard body; *esp* : one of the minute calcium or silica-containing bodies that support the tissues of various invertebrates [Latin *spiculum* "point", from *spica* "spike of grain"]

spicy \'spī-sē\ *adj* **spic•i•er; -est 1** : having the quality, flavor, or fragrance of spice **2** : producing or abounding in spices **3** : LIVELY, SPIRITED ⟨a *spicy* temper⟩ **4** : somewhat scandalous or lewd ⟨*spicy* gossip⟩ — **spic•i•ly** \-sə-lē\ *adv* — **spic•i•ness** \-sē-nəs\ *n*

spi•der \'spīd-ər\ *n* **1** : any of an order (Araneida) of arachnids having a body with two main divisions, four pairs of walking legs, and two or more pairs of abdominal organs for spinning threads of silk used in making cocoons for their eggs, nests for themselves, or webs for entangling their prey **2** : a cast-iron frying pan originally made with short feet to stand among coals on the hearth [Middle English *spithre*]

spider crab *n* : any of numerous crabs with extremely long legs and nearly triangular bodies

spider mite *n* : RED SPIDER

spider monkey *n* : any of a genus of New World monkeys with long slender limbs, the thumb absent or rudimentary, and a very long prehensile tail

spi•der•web \'spīd-ər-,web\ *n* **1** : the silken web spun by most spiders and used as a resting place and a trap for small prey **2**

: something like a spiderweb in appearance or function

spi•der•wort \-ˌwərt, -ˌwȯrt\ *n* : any of a genus of monocotyledonous plants with short-lived usually blue or violet flowers

spi•dery \'spīd-ə-rē\ *adj* **1** : resembling a spider; *also* : long and thin like the legs of a spider **2** : resembling a spiderweb **3** : full of spiders

spie•gel•ei•sen \'spē-gə-ˌlī-zᵊn\ *also* **spie•gel** \'spē-gəl\ *n* : a pig iron containing 15 to 30 percent manganese and 4.5 to 6.5 percent carbon [German *spiegeleisen,* from *spiegel* "mirror" + *eisen* "iron"]

[1]spiel \'spēl\ *vb* : to talk volubly or extravagantly [German *spielen* "to play"] — **spiel•er** *n*

[2]spiel *n* : voluble mechanical often extravagant talk; *esp* : a sales pitch

spiffy \'spif-ē\ *adj* **spiff•i•er; -est 1** : fine looking : SMART **2** : EXCELLENT, DELIGHTFUL ⟨a *spiffy* party⟩ [English dialect *spiff* "dandified"]

spig•ot \'spig-ət, 'spik-ət\ *n* **1** : a pin or peg used to stop the vent in a cast **2** : FAUCET [Middle English]

[1]spike \'spīk\ *n* **1** : a very large nail **2 a** : one of a row of pointed irons placed (as on the top of a wall) to prevent passage **b** : one of several metal projections set in the sole and heel of a shoe to improve traction in sports **3** : an unbranched antler of a young deer **4** : a pointed element (as in a graph) [Middle English]

[2]spike *vt* **1** : to fasten or furnish with spikes **2 a** : to disable (a muzzle-loading cannon) temporarily by driving a spike into the vent **b** : to suppress or block completely : QUASH **3** : to pierce or impale with or on a spike **4** : to add alcohol or liquor to (a drink) **5** : to drive (a volleyball) down into the opponent's court with a hard blow

[3]spike *n* **1** : an ear of grain **2** : a long usually rather narrow flower cluster in which the blossoms grow close to the central stem [Latin *spica*]

spiked \'spīkt\ *adj* **1 a** : bearing ears **b** : having a spiky inflorescence ⟨*spiked* flowers⟩ **2** : SPIKY

spike heel *n* : a very high tapering heel used on women's shoes

spike lavender *n* : a European mint related to and used like the true lavender

spike•let \'spī-klət\ *n* : a small or secondary spike; *esp* : one of the small few-flowered bracted spikes that make up the compound inflorescence of a grass or sedge

spike•like \'spī-ˌklīk\ *adj* : resembling a spike

spike•nard \'spīk-ˌnärd\ *n* **1 a** : a fragrant ointment of the ancients **b** : an East Indian aromatic plant of the valerian family from which the ointment may have been derived **2** : an American herb of the ginseng family with an aromatic root and round flower clusters branching off the main stem [Medieval Latin *spica nardi,* literally, "spike of nard"]

spiky \'spī-kē\ *adj* **spik•i•er; -est 1** : having a sharp projecting point **2** : having spikes

spile \'spīl\ *n* **1** : [1]PILE **2** : a small plug used to stop the vent of a cask : BUNG **3** : a spout inserted in a tree to draw off sap [probably from Dutch *spijl* "stake"] — **spile** *vt*

spil•ing \'spī-ling\ *n* : a set of piles : PILING

[1]spill \'spil\ *vb* **spilled** \'spild, 'spilt\ *also* **spilt** \'spilt\; **spill•ing 1** : to cause (blood) to flow **2 a** : to cause or allow unintentionally to fall, flow, or run out **b** : to fall or run out so as to be lost or wasted **3** : to relieve or lessen the pressure of (the wind) on sails by movement of the boat or adjustment of the sail **4** : to fall or cause to fall from one's place ⟨the horse *spilled* its rider⟩ **5** : to let out : DIVULGE **6** : to spread beyond bounds ⟨crowds *spilled* into the street⟩ [Old English *spillan* "to kill, spill"] — **spill•able** \'spil-ə-bəl\ *adj*

[2]spill *n* **1** : an act or instance of spilling; *esp* : a fall from a horse or vehicle **2** : something spilled **3** : SPILLWAY

[3]spill *n* : a slender piece: as **a** : a metallic rod or pin **b** : a small roll or twist of paper or slip of wood for lighting a fire **c** : a roll or cone of paper serving as a container **d** : a peg for plugging a hole : SPILE [Middle English *spille* "wooden splinter"]

spill•age \'spil-ij\ *n* **1** : the act or process of spilling **2** : the quantity that spills

spil•li•kin \'spil-i-kən\ *n* : JACKSTRAW [probably from Dutch *spelleken* "small peg"]

spill•way \'spil-ˌwā\ *n* : a passage for surplus water to run over or around a dam or similar obstruction

spilth \'spilth\ *n* **1** : an act or instance of spilling **2 a** : something spilled **b** : TRASH 1a, RUBBISH

[1]spin \'spin\ *vb* **spun** \'spən\; **spin•ning 1** : to draw out and twist into yarn or thread ⟨*spin* flax⟩ **2 a** : to produce by drawing out and twisting fibers ⟨*spin* thread⟩ **b** : to form threads or a web or cocoon by extruding a viscous rapidly hardening fluid **3 a** : to revolve rapidly : GYRATE **b** : to be dizzy : feel as if turning rapidly **4** : to cause to whirl : TWIRL ⟨*spin* a top⟩ **5 a** : to extend to great length : PROLONG **b** : to make up with the imagination ⟨*spun* a story⟩ **6** : to move swiftly on wheels or in a vehicle **7** : to shape into threadlike form in manufacture; *also* : to manufacture by a whirling process [Old English *spinnan*]

[2]spin *n* **1 a** : the act of spinning or twirling something **b** : whirling motion imparted by spinning : rapid rotation **c** : an excursion in a vehicle especially on wheels **2 a** : an aerial maneuver or flight condition in which an airplane moves downward in a somewhat corkscrew path **b** : a plunging descent or downward spiral **c** : a state of mental confusion

spin•ach \'spin-ich\ *n* : a potherb of the goosefoot family widely grown for its edible leaves [Middle French *espinache,* from Spanish *espinaca,* from Arabic *isfānākh,* from Persian]

[1]spi•nal \'spīn-ᵊl\ *adj* **1** : of, relating to, or situated near the backbone **2** : of, relating to, or affecting the spinal cord ⟨*spinal* nerve cells⟩ — **spi•nal•ly** \-ᵊl-ē\ *adv*

[2]spinal *n* : an anesthetic administered by way of the spinal cord

spinal column *n* : the axial skeleton of the trunk and tail of a vertebrate that consists of a jointed series of vertebrae enclosing and protecting the spinal cord — called also *backbone*

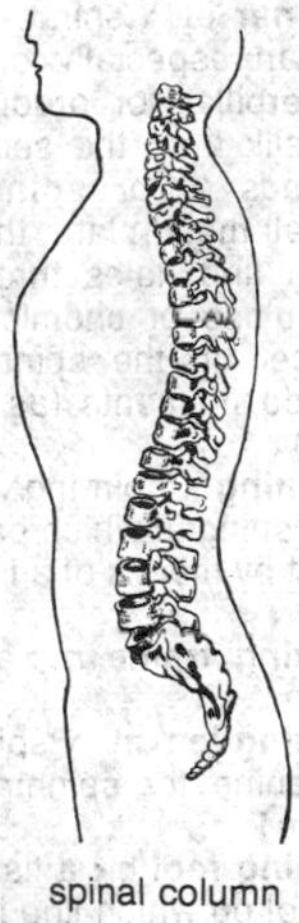
spinal column

spinal cord *n* : the cord of nervous tissue that extends from the brain along the back in the cavity of the spinal column, gives off the spinal nerves, and not only carries impulses to and from the brain but also serves as a center for initiating and coordinating many reflex acts

spinal nerve *n* : any of the paired nerves which arise from the spinal cord and pass to various parts of the trunk and limbs and of which there are normally 31 pairs in man

[1]spin•dle \'spin-dᵊl\ *n* **1 a** : a round stick with tapered ends used to form and twist the yarn in hand spinning **b** : a rod holding a bobbin in a textile machine **2** : something shaped like a spindle (as a figure along which the chromosomes are distributed during mitosis) **3 a** : the bar that actuates the bolt of a lock **b** (1) : a turned often decorative piece of furniture or woodwork ⟨*spindles* of a chair⟩ (2) : NEWEL 2 **c** : a revolving piece usually smaller than a shaft **d** : the part of an axle on which a vehicle wheel turns [Old English *spinel*]

[2]spindle *vi* **spin•dled; spin•dling** \'spin-dling, -ling, -dᵊl-ing\ : to form a long slender stalk usually without flower or fruit

spin•dle–legged \ˌspin-dᵊl-'leg-əd, -'legd\ *adj* : having long thin legs

spin•dle–shanked \ˌspin-dᵊl-'shangt, -'shangkt\ *adj* : SPINDLE-LEGGED

spin•dling \'spin-dling, -ling, -dᵊl-ing\ *adj* : SPINDLY ⟨*spindling* stems⟩

spin•dly \'spin-dlē, -lē, -dᵊl-ē\ *adj* **spin•dli•er; -est** : excessively or abnormally long or tall and thin ⟨*spindly* legs⟩

spin•drift \'spin-ˌdrift\ *n* : spray blown from waves [Scottish *speendrift,* from *speen* "to drive before a wind" + English *drift*]

spine \'spīn\ *n* **1 a** : SPINAL COLUMN **b** : something resembling a spinal column or constituting a central axis or chief support **c** : the back of a book usually lettered with the title and the author's and publisher's names **2** : a stiff pointed process; *esp* : one on a plant that is a modified leaf or leaf part [Latin *spina*

\ə\ **abut**	\au̇\ **out**	\i\ **tip**	\ȯ\ **saw**	\u̇\ **foot**
\ər\ **further**	\ch\ **chin**	\ī\ **life**	\ȯi\ **coin**	\y\ **yet**
\a\ **mat**	\e\ **pet**	\j\ **job**	\th\ **thin**	\yü\ **few**
\ā\ **take**	\ē\ **easy**	\ng\ **sing**	\t͟h\ **this**	\yu̇\ **cure**
\ä\ **cot, cart**	\g\ **go**	\ō\ **bone**	\ü\ **food**	\zh\ **vision**

"thorn, spinal column"] — **spined** \'spīnd\ *adj*

spi•nel \spə-'nel\ *n* **1 :** a hard crystalline mineral $MgAl_2O_4$ consisting of an oxide of magnesium and aluminum that varies from colorless to ruby-red to black and is used as a gem **2 :** any of a group of minerals that are essentially oxides of magnesium, ferrous iron, zinc, or manganese [Italian *spinella,* from *spina* "thorn", from Latin]

spine•less \'spīn-ləs\ *adj* **1 :** free from spines, thorns, or prickles **2 :** having no spinal column **:** INVERTEBRATE **3 :** lacking courage or strength of character — **spine•less•ly** *adv* — **spine•less•ness** *n*

spin•et \'spin-ət\ *n* **1 :** a small early harpsichord usually without legs **2 a :** a small upright piano **b :** a small electronic organ [Italian *spinetta*]

spin•na•ker \'spin-i-kər\ *n* **:** a large triangular sail set on a long light pole in front of the mast and used when reaching or when running before the wind [origin unknown]

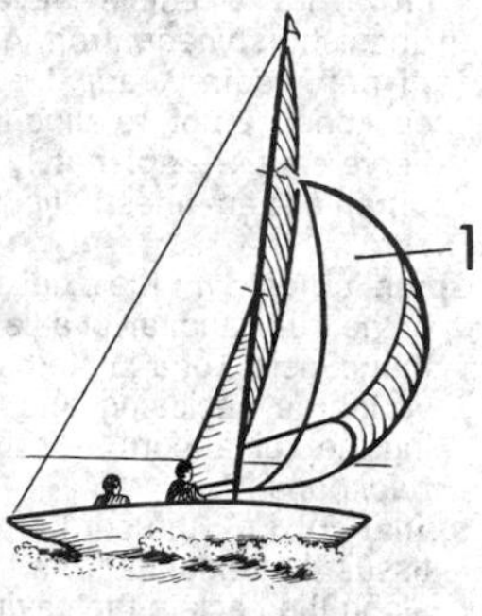

1 spinnaker

spin•ner \'spin-ər\ *n* **1 :** one that spins **2 :** a fishing lure that revolves when drawn through the water

spin•ner•et \ˌspin-ə-'ret\ *n* **1 :** an organ especially of a spider or caterpillar for producing threads of silk from the secretion of silk glands **2** *or* **spin•ner•ette :** a small metal plate, thimble, or cap with fine holes through which a cellulose or chemical solution is forced in the spinning of man-made filaments (as rayon or nylon)

spin•ning \'spin-iŋ\ *n* **:** a method of fishing in which bait or a lure is cast by means of a light flexible rod, a spinning reel, and a light line

spinning frame *n* **:** a machine that draws, twists, and winds yarn

spinning jen•ny \'spin-iŋ-ˌjen-ē\ *n* **:** an early multiple-spindle machine for spinning wool or cotton [*Jenny,* nickname for *Jane*]

spinning reel *n* **:** a fishing reel with an open-faced nonrevolving spool on which line is wound by a moving arm which is locked out of the way during casting to permit the line to spiral off the reel freely

spinning wheel *n* **:** a small domestic hand-driven or foot-driven machine for spinning yarn or thread in which a wheel drives a single spindle

spin–off \'spin-ˌȯf\ *n* **:** a secondary or derived product or effect **:** BY-PRODUCT ⟨household products that are *spin-offs* of missile research⟩

spi•nous \'spī-nəs\ *adj* **:** SPINY 1, 3

spin•ster \'spin-stər\ *n* **1 :** a woman whose occupation is to spin **2 :** an unmarried woman; *esp* **:** one who seems unlikely to marry — **spin•ster•hood** \-ˌhu̇d\ *n* — **spin•ster•ish** \-stə-rish, -strish\ *adj*

spin•thari•scope \spin-'thar-ə-ˌskōp\ *n* **:** an instrument consisting of a fluorescent screen and a magnifying lens system for visual detection of alpha rays [Greek *spintharis* "spark"]

spin the bottle *n* **:** a kissing game in which a bottle is spun to point to the one to be kissed

spi•nule \'spī-nyül\ *n* **:** a tiny spine — **spi•nu•lose** \-nyə-ˌlōs\ *adj*

spiny \'spī-nē\ *adj* **spin•i•er; -est 1 :** having spines, prickles, or thorns **2 :** full of difficulties, obstacles, or annoyances **:** THORNY **3 :** resembling a spine especially in slender pointed form — **spin•i•ness** *n*

spiny anteater *n* **:** ECHIDNA

spiny–finned \ˌspī-nē-'find\ *adj* **:** having fins with one or more stiff unbranched rays without transverse segmentation — compare SOFT-FINNED

spiny–head•ed worm \ˌspī-nē-ˌhed-əd-\ *n* **:** any of a small phylum (Acanthocephala) of unsegmented parasitic worms with a hooked proboscis used for attachment to the intestinal wall of the host

spiny lobster *n* **:** an edible crustacean distinguished from the related true lobster by the simple unenlarged first pair of legs and by the spiny carapace

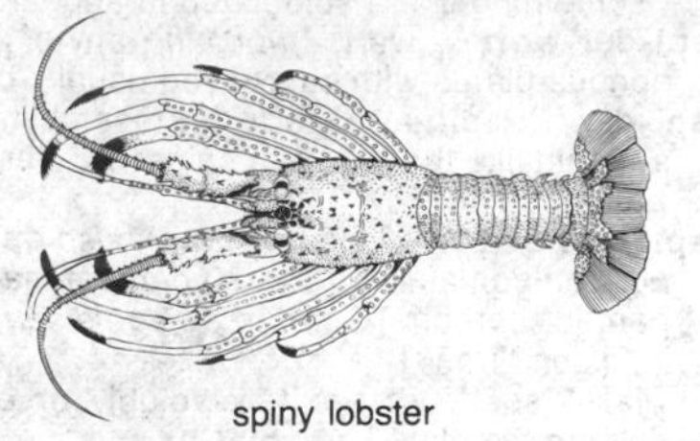
spiny lobster

spir•a•cle \'spir-i-kəl, 'spī-ri-\ *n* **:** a breathing orifice (as a blowhole of a whale or a tracheal opening of an insect) [Latin *spiraculum,* from *spirare* "to breathe"] — **spi•rac•u•lar** \spə-'rak-yə-lər, spī-\ *adj*

[1]**spi•ral** \'spī-rəl\ *adj* **1 :** winding around a center or pole and gradually receding from or approaching it **2 :** HELICAL ⟨the *spiral* form of the thread of a screw⟩ **3 :** of, relating to, or resembling a spiral ⟨a *spiral* staircase⟩ [Medieval Latin *spiralis,* from Latin *spira* "coil"] — **spi•ral•ly** \-rə-lē\ *adv*

[2]**spiral** *n* **1 a :** the path of a point in a plane moving around a central point while continuously moving away from or approaching it **b :** a three-dimensional curve (as a helix) turning about an axis **2 :** a single turn or coil in a spiral object **3 :** something having a spiral form **4 :** a continuously spreading and accelerating increase or decrease ⟨a wage *spiral*⟩

[3]**spiral** *vb* **-raled** *or* **-ralled; -ral•ing** *or* **-ral•ling 1 :** to move in a spiral course **2 :** to form into a spiral

spiral galaxy *n* **:** a galaxy with a central nucleus from which extend concentrations of matter forming curved arms

spi•rant \'spī-rənt\ *n* **:** a consonant (as \f\, \s\, \sh\) uttered with friction of the breath against some part of the oral passage [Latin *spirans,* present participle of *spirare* "to breathe"] — **spirant** *adj*

[1]**spire** \'spīr\ *n* **1 :** a slender tapering blade or stalk (as of grass) **2 :** a sharp pointed tip (as of a tree or antler) **3 a :** a pointed roof especially of a tower **b :** STEEPLE [Old English *spīr*]

[1]spire 3a

[2]**spire** *vi* **:** to shoot up like a spire

[3]**spire** *n* **:** the upper part of a spiral mollusk shell [Latin *spira* "coil", from Greek *speira*]

[4]**spire** *vi* **:** to rise in or as if in a spiral

spi•rea *or* **spi•raea** \spī-'rē-ə\ *n* **:** any of a genus of shrubs of the rose family with small perfect white or pink flowers in dense clusters [Latin, a kind of plant, from Greek *speiraia*]

spired \'spīrd\ *adj* **:** having a spire ⟨a *spired* church⟩

spi•ril•lum \spī-'ril-əm\ *n, pl* **-ril•la** \-'ril-ə\ **:** any of a genus of long curved flagellate bacteria; *also* **:** any spiral filamentous bacterium (as a spirochete) [New Latin, from Latin *spira* "coil"]

[1]**spir•it** \'spir-ət\ *n* **1 :** a life-giving force; *esp* **:** a force within a person held to endow the body with life, energy, and power **:** SOUL **2 a** *cap* **:** HOLY SPIRIT **b :** a supernatural being **:** GHOST, DEVIL **c :** a supernatural being that enters into and controls a person **d :** a bodiless being inhabiting a place or thing **3 :** MOOD, DISPOSITION ⟨in good *spirits*⟩ **4 :** mental vigor or animation **:** VIVACITY **5 :** real meaning or intention ⟨the *spirit* of the law⟩ **6 :** an emotion, frame of mind, or inclination governing one's actions ⟨said in a *spirit* of fun⟩⟨school *spirit*⟩ **7 :** PERSON ⟨a bold *spirit*⟩ **8 a :** a distilled alcoholic liquor — usually used in pl. **b :** an alcoholic solution of a volatile substance ⟨*spirit* of camphor⟩ — often used in pl. [Latin *spiritus,* literally, "breath"] **syn** see SOUL

[2]**spirit** *vt* **1 :** ANIMATE 2, ENCOURAGE **2 :** to carry off or convey secretly or mysteriously

spir•it•ed \'spir-ət-əd\ *adj* **:** full of spirit, courage, or energy — **spir•it•ed•ly** *adv* — **spir•it•ed•ness** *n*

spirit gum *n* **:** a solution (as of gum arabic in ether) used especially for attaching false hair to the skin

spir•it•ism \'spir-ət-ˌiz-əm\ *n* **:** SPIRITUALISM 2a — **spir•it•ist** \-ət-əst\ *n* — **spir•it•is•tic** \ˌspir-ət-'is-tik\ *adj*

spir·it·less \'spir-ət-ləs\ *adj* : lacking animation, cheer, or courage — **spir·it·less·ly** *adv* — **spir·it·less·ness** *n*

spirit level *n* : a level using the position of a bubble in a small tube of liquid (as alcohol) as an indicator

spirits of turpentine *or* **spirit of turpentine** : TURPENTINE 2a

[1]**spir·i·tu·al** \'spir-ich-wel, -ə-wəl, -ich-əl\ *adj* **1** : of, relating to, or consisting of spirit : not bodily or material **2 a** : RELIGIOUS, SACRED ⟨*spiritual* songs⟩ **b** : ecclesiastical rather than lay or temporal **3** : related or joined in spirit : having a spiritual rather than physical relationship **4 a** : of or relating to supernatural beings **b** : of, relating to, or involving spiritualism : SPIRITUALISTIC — **spir·i·tu·al·ly** \-ē\ *adv* — **spir·i·tu·al·ness** *n*

[2]**spiritual** *n* : a religious song originated by blacks especially of the southern United States

spir·i·tu·al·ism \'spir-ich-wə-,liz-əm, -ə-wə-, -ich-ə-,liz-\ *n* **1** : the belief that spirit is the principal aspect of reality **2 a** : a belief that the spirits of the dead communicate with the living **b** *cap* : a movement comprising religious organizations emphasizing spiritualism — **spir·i·tu·al·ist** \-ləst\ *n, often cap* — **spir·i·tu·al·is·tic** \,spir-ich-wə-'lis-tik, -ə-wə-, -ich-ə-'lis-\ *adj*

spir·i·tu·al·i·ty \,spir-ich-ə-'wal-ət-ē\ *n* **1** : concern with religious rather than material values **2** : the quality or state of being spiritual

spir·i·tu·al·ize \'spir-ich-wə-,līz, -ə-wə-, -ich-ə-,līz\ *vt* **1** : to make spiritual especially by freeing from worldly influences **2** : to give a spiritual meaning to or understand in a spiritual sense — **spir·i·tu·al·iza·tion** \,spir-ich-wə-lə-'zā-shən, -ə-wə-, -ich-ə-lə-\ *n*

spir·i·tu·ous \'spir-ich-wəs, -ə-wəs, -ich-əs, 'spir-ət-əs\ *adj* : containing or being distilled alcohol ⟨*spirituous* liquors⟩ — **spir·i·tu·os·i·ty** \,spir-ich-ə-'wäs-ət-ē\ *n*

spi·ro·chete *or* **spi·ro·chaete** \'spī-rə-,kēt\ *n* : any of an order (Spirochaetales) of slender spirally undulating bacteria including those causing syphilis and relapsing fever [Latin *spira* "coil" (from Greek *speira*) + Greek *chaitē* "long hair"] — **spi·ro·che·tal** \,spī-rə-'kēt-l\ *adj*

spi·ro·gy·ra \,spī-rə-'jī-rə\ *n* : any of a genus of freshwater green algae with spiral chlorophyll bands [Greek *speira* "coil" + *gyros* "ring, circle"]

spi·rom·e·ter \spī-'räm-ət-ər\ *n* : an instrument for measuring the air entering and leaving the lungs [Latin *spirare* "to breathe"] — **spi·ro·met·ric** \,spī-rə-'me-trik\ *adj* — **spi·rom·e·try** \spī-'räm-ə-trē\ *n*

spiry \'spīr-ē\ *adj* : resembling a spire especially in slender tapering form; *also* : having spires

[1]**spit** \'spit\ *n* **1** : a slender pointed rod for holding meat over a fire **2** : a small point of land especially of sand or gravel running into a body or water [Old English *spitu*]

[2]**spit** *vt* **spit·ted**; **spit·ting** : to put on or as if on a spit

[3]**spit** *vb* **spit** *or* **spat** \'spat\; **spit·ting 1 a** : to eject saliva from the mouth : EXPECTORATE **b** : to express by or as if by spitting or make a spitting sound ⟨the cat *spat* angrily⟩ ⟨*spitting* a contemptuous reply⟩ **2 a** : to give off usually briskly or vigorously : EMIT ⟨the fire *spat* sparks⟩ **b** : to rain or snow in flurries [Old English *spittan*] — **spit·ter** *n*

[4]**spit** *n* **1 a** : SALIVA **b** : the act of spitting **2** : a frothy secretion produced by spittlebugs **3** : perfect likeness

spit and polish *n* : extreme attention to smartness of appearance especially at the expense of operational efficiency [from the practice of polishing objects such as shoes by spitting on them and then rubbing them with a cloth]

spit·ball \'spit-,bȯl\ *n* **1** : paper chewed and rolled into a ball to be used as a missile **2** : a baseball pitch delivered after the ball has been moistened (as with saliva or sweat) so that it moves erratically

spit curl *n* : a small spiral curl that is usually pressed flat against the forehead, temple, or cheek

[1]**spite** \'spīt\ *n* : petty ill will or malice with a desire to irritate, annoy, or thwart [Middle English, short for *despite*] — **in spite of** : in defiance or contempt of : NOTWITHSTANDING

[2]**spite** *vt* **1** : to treat maliciously (as by shaming or thwarting) **2** : ANNOY, OFFEND ⟨did it to *spite* me⟩

spite·ful \'spīt-fəl\ *adj* : filled with or showing spite : MALICIOUS — **spite·ful·ly** \-fə-lē\ *adv* — **spite·ful·ness** *n*

spit·fire \'spit-,fīr\ *n* : a quick-tempered person

spit·ting image \,spit-n-, ,spit-ing-\ *n* : perfect likeness

spit·tle \'spit-l\ *n* **1** : SALIVA **2** : [4]SPIT 2 [Old English *spǣtl*]

spit·tle·bug \-,bəg\ *n* : any of numerous leaping insects that are related to the cicadas and aphids and have larvae which secrete froth

spittle insect *n* : SPITTLEBUG

spit·toon \spi-'tün\ *n* : a receptacle for spit — called also *cuspidor* [[4]*spit* + *-oon* (as in *balloon*)]

spitz \'spits\ *n* : any of several stocky heavy-coated dogs of northern origin with erect ears and a heavily furred tail tightly curled over the back [German, from *spitz* "pointed"]

splanch·nic \'splangk-nik\ *adj* : of or relating to the viscera : VISCERAL [Greek *splanchnikos*, from *splanchna* "viscera"]

[1]**splash** \'splash\ *vb* **1 a** : to strike or move through a liquid or semifluid substance and cause it to spatter ⟨*splash* water⟩⟨*splash* through mud⟩ **b** : to wet or soil by dashing a liquid on : SPATTER ⟨*splashed* by a passing car⟩; *also* : to cause to soil something by splashing ⟨*splashed* ink on the paper⟩ **2** : to make a splashing sound (as in falling or moving) ⟨a brook *splashing* over rocks⟩ **3 a** : to spread or scatter like a splashed liquid ⟨a painting *splashed* with color⟩ ⟨sunbeams *splashed* through the curtain⟩ **b** : to display prominently ⟨a scandal *splashed* all over the newspaper⟩ [alteration of *plash*] — **splash·er** *n*

[2]**splash** *n* **1** : splashed material; *also* : a spot or daub from or as if from splashed liquid **2** : the sound or action of splashing **3** : a vivid impression created especially by showy activity or appearance; *also:* a showy display — **splash·i·ly** \'splash-ə-lē\ *adv* — **splash·i·ness** \'splash-ē-nəs\ *n* — **splashy** \'splash-ē\ *adj*

splash·down \'splash-,daůn\ *n* : the controlled landing of a spacecraft in the ocean — **splash down** \splash-'daůn, 'splash-\ *vi*

splash guard *n* : a flap suspended behind a rear wheel to prevent tire splash from muddying windshields of following vehicles

[1]**splat** \'splat\ *n* : a single flat thin usually vertical member of a back of a chair [obsolete *splat* "to spread flat", from Middle English *splatten*]

[2]**splat** *n* : a spattering or splashing sound [imitative]

splat·ter \'splat-ər\ *vb* : SPATTER 1, 2, 4 [probably blend of *splash* and *spatter*] — **splatter** *n*

[1]**splay** \'splā\ *vb* **1** : to spread out **2** : to make or become slanting [Middle English *splayen*, short for *displayen* "to display"]

[2]**splay** *n* **1** : a slope or bevel especially of the sides of a door or window **2** : degree of outward slope

[3]**splay** *adj* **1** : turned outward **2** : AWKWARD 2a, UNGAINLY

splay·foot \'splā-,fůt, -'fůt\ *n* : a foot abnormally flattened and spread out : FLATFOOT — **splayfoot** *or* **splay·foot·ed** \-'fůt-əd\ *adj*

spleen \'splēn\ *n* **1** : a very vascular ductless organ near the stomach or intestine of most vertebrates concerned with final destruction of blood cells, storage of blood, and production of lymphocytes **2** : ANGER, MALICE [Latin *splen*, from Greek *splēn*]

spleen·ful \-fəl\ *adj* : SPLENETIC

spleen·wort \-,wərt, -,wȯrt\ *n* : any of a genus of ferns having linear or oblong clusters of spores borne obliquely on the upper side of the frond [from the belief in its power to cure disorders of the spleen]

spleeny \'splē-nē\ *adj* : full of or displaying spleen

splen·dent \'splen-dənt\ *adj* **1** : SHINING 1, LUSTROUS **2** : ILLUSTRIOUS, BRILLIANT [Late Latin *splendens*, from Latin *splendēre* "to shine"]

splen·did \'splen-dəd\ *adj* **1** : possessing or displaying splendor: as **a** : brilliantly shining : RADIANT **b** : SHOWY 1, MAGNIFICENT **2** : ILLUSTRIOUS, GRAND **3** : PRAISEWORTHY, EXCELLENT [Latin *splendidus*, from *splendēre* "to shine"] — **splen·did·ly** *adv* — **splen·did·ness** *n*

• **syn** SPLENDID, GLORIOUS, GORGEOUS mean extraordinarily impressive. SPLENDID implies outshining the usual in brilliance or excellence; GLORIOUS suggests beauty and distinction heightened by radiance; GORGEOUS implies a rich splendor especially in display of color.

splen•dif•er•ous \splen-'dif-rəs, -ə-rəs\ *adj* **1 :** SPLENDID 1, MAGNIFICENT **2 :** deceptively splendid [*splendor* + *-i-* + *-ferous*] — **splen•dif•er•ous•ly** *adv* — **splen•dif•er•ous•ness** *n*

splen•dor \'splen-dər\ *n* **1 a :** great brightness or luster **:** BRILLIANCY ⟨the *splendor* of the sun⟩ **b :** sumptuous display **:** MAGNIFICENCE, POMP ⟨an affair of great *splendor*⟩ **2 :** something splendid or contributing to splendor ⟨surrounded by *splendors* and luxuries⟩ [Anglo-French *splendur,* from Latin *splendor,* from *splendēre* "to shine"] — **splen•dor•ous** *also* **splen•drous** \-də-rəs, -drəs\ *adj*

sple•net•ic \spli-'net-ik\ *adj* **:** marked by bad temper, hatred, or spite [Late Latin *spleneticus,* from Latin *splen* "spleen"] — **sple•net•i•cal•ly** \spli-'net-i-kə-lē, -klē\ *adv*

splen•ic \'splen-ik\ *adj* **:** of, relating to, or located in the spleen

[1]**splice** \'splīs\ *vt* **1 :** to unite (as two ropes) by weaving the strands together **2 :** to unite (as rails or timbers) by lapping the ends together and making them fast [obsolete Dutch *splissen*] — **splic•er** *n*

[2]**splice** *n* **:** a joining or joint made by splicing

spline \'splīn\ *n* **1 :** a thin wood or metal strip used in building construction **2 :** a key that is fixed to one of two connected mechanical parts and fits into a keyway in the other; *also* **:** a keyway for such a key [origin unknown]

[2]splice

[1]**splint** \'splint\ *n* **1 a :** a thin strip of wood interwoven with others in caning **b :** SPLINTER 1 **c :** material or a device used to protect and immobilize a body part (as a broken arm) **2 :** a bony enlargement on the cannon bone of a horse [Low German *splinte, splente*]

[2]**splint** *vt* **:** to support and immobilize with or as if with a splint or splints

splint bone *n* **:** one of the slender rudimentary bones on each side of the cannon bone in the limb of a horse

[1]**splin•ter** \'splint-ər\ *n* **1 a :** a thin piece split or torn off lengthwise **:** SLIVER **b :** a small jagged particle **2 :** a group or faction broken away from a parent body [Dutch] — **splinter** *adj* — **splin•tery** \'splint-ə-rē\ *adj*

[2]**splinter** *vb* **:** to divide or break into splinters

[1]**split** \'split\ *vb* **split; split•ting 1 a :** to divide lengthwise usually along a grain or seam or by layers **:** CLEAVE ⟨wood that *splits* easily⟩ ⟨*split* slate into shingles⟩ **b :** to separate the parts of by interposing something ⟨*split* an infinitive⟩ ⟨the river *split* the town⟩ **2 a :** to tear or break apart **:** BURST ⟨the pants *split* at the seams⟩ **b :** to subject (an atom or atomic nucleus) to artificial disintegration especially by fission **c :** to affect as if by breaking up or tearing apart **:** SHATTER **3 :** to divide into parts or portions: as **a :** to divide between individuals **:** SHARE ⟨the winning team *split* the prize⟩ **b :** to divide into factions, parties, or groups **c :** to mark (a ballot) or cast (a vote) for candidates of different parties **d :** to break down (a chemical compound) into constituents ⟨*split* a fat into glycerol and fatty acids⟩; *also* **:** to remove by such separation ⟨*split* off carbon dioxide⟩ **e :** to divide (stock) by issuing a larger number of shares to existing shareholders usually without increase in total face value [Dutch *splitten*] — **split•ter** *n* — **split hairs :** to make trivial distinctions

[2]**split** *n* **1 :** a product or result of splitting: as **a :** a narrow break made by or as if by splitting **:** CRACK **b :** a part split off or made thin by splitting **c :** a group or faction formed by splitting **d :** a situation in bowling in which two or more pins are left standing after a delivery with one or more pins missing between them **2 :** the act or process of splitting **:** DIVISION ⟨a stock *split*⟩; *esp* **:** a dividing into divergent or antagonistic elements **3 :** the feat of lowering oneself to the floor or leaping into the air with the legs extended in a straight line and in opposite directions

[3]**split** *adj* **:** divided by or as if by splitting ⟨a *split* lip⟩ ⟨*split* families⟩; *also* **:** prepared for use by splitting ⟨*split* hides⟩

split decision *n* **:** a decision in a boxing match reflecting a division of opinion among the referee and judges

split end *n* **:** an offensive end in football who lines up several yards wide of the formation

split infinitive *n* **:** an infinitive having a modifier between the *to* and the verbal (as in "to really start")

split–lev•el \'split-'lev-əl\ *adj* **:** divided vertically so that the floor level of rooms in one part is about midway between the levels of two successive stories in an adjoining part ⟨*split-level* houses⟩ — **split–lev•el** \-ˌlev-əl\ *n*

split personality *n* **:** a personality structure composed of two or more groups of behavior tendencies and attitudes each expressed independently

split rail *n* **:** a fence rail split from a log

split second *n* **:** a very brief period **:** FLASH, INSTANT ⟨happened in a *split second*⟩

split shift *n* **:** a shift of working hours divided into two or more working periods (as morning and evening)

split ticket *n* **:** a ballot cast by a voter who votes for candidates of more than one party

split•ting \'split-ing\ *adj* **:** very severe ⟨a *splitting* headache⟩

splotch \'splăch\ *n* **:** BLOTCH 2, SPOT [perhaps blend of *spot* and *blotch*] — **splotch** *vt* — **splotchy** \'splăch-ē\ *adj*

[1]**splurge** \'splərj\ *n* **1 :** a showy display **2 :** liberal indulgence [perhaps blend of *splash* and *surge*]

splurge *vb* **1 :** to make a showy display **2 :** to indulge oneself or spend lavishly

[1]**splut•ter** \'splət-ər\ *n* **1 :** a confused noise (as of hasty speaking) **2 :** a splashing or sputtering sound [probably alteration of *sputter*] — **splut•tery** \'splət-ə-rē\ *adj*

[2]**splutter** *vb* **1 :** to make a noise as if spitting **2 :** to speak or utter hastily and confusedly — **splut•ter•er** \'splət-ər-ər\ *n*

[1]**spoil** \'spȯil\ *n* **1 a :** plunder taken from an enemy in war or a victim in robbery **:** LOOT **b :** something won usually by effort or skill **:** PREY — usually used in pl. ⟨the *spoils* of the chase⟩ **2 :** earth and rock excavated or dredged **3 :** an object damaged or flawed in the making [Middle French *espoille,* from Latin *spolia,* pl. of *spolium*]

[2]**spoil** *vb* **spoiled** \'spȯild, 'spȯilt\ *or* **spoilt** \'spȯilt\; **spoil•ing 1 :** PLUNDER, ROB **2 a :** to damage seriously **:** RUIN ⟨a crop *spoiled* by floods⟩ **b :** to impair the quality or effect of ⟨a quarrel *spoiled* the celebration⟩ **c :** to decay or lose freshness, value, or usefulness usually through being kept too long **3 :** to damage the character or disposition of by pampering **4 :** to have an eager desire ⟨*spoiling* for a fight⟩ **syn** see DECAY — **spoil•able** \'spȯi-lə-bəl\ *adj* — **spoil•er** *n*

spoil•age \'spȯi-lij\ *n* **1 :** the act or process of spoiling **2 :** something spoiled or wasted **3 :** loss by spoilage

spoils•man \'spȯilz-mən\ *n* **:** one who serves a political party in expectation of receiving a public office

spoil•sport \'spȯil-ˌspōrt, -ˌspȯrt\ *n* **:** one who spoils the sport or pleasure of others

spoils system *n* **:** the practice of distributing public offices and their privileges as plunder to members of the victorious political party

[1]**spoke** \'spōk\ *past & archaic past participle of* SPEAK

[2]**spoke** *n* **1 :** one of the bars radiating from the hub of a wheel to support the rim **2 :** a rung of a ladder [Old English *spāca*]

[3]**spoke** *vt* **:** to furnish with or as if with spokes

spo•ken \'spō-kən\ *adj* **1 a :** expressed in speech rather than writing **:** ORAL ⟨a *spoken* message⟩ **b :** used in speaking ⟨*spoken* English⟩ **2 :** speaking in (such) a manner — used in combination ⟨soft-*spoken*⟩ ⟨plain*spoken*⟩ [past participle of *speak*]

spoke•shave \'spōk-ˌshāv\ *n* **:** a two-handled tool that is used for planing curved pieces of wood [[2]*spoke*]

spokes•man \'spōk-smən\ *n* **:** a man who is a spokesperson [probably from [1]*spoke*]

spokes•per•son \'spōk-ˌspərs-n\ *n, pl* **spokespersons** *or* **spokes•peo•ple** \-ˌspē-pəl\ **:** a person who speaks as a representative of another person or of a group

spokes•wom•an \'spōk-ˌswu̇m-ən\ *n* **:** a woman who is a spokesperson

spo•li•a•tion \ˌspō-lē-'ā-shən\ *n* **:** the act of plundering **:** the state of being plundered especially in war [Latin *spoliatio,* from *spoliare* "to plunder", from *spolium* "spoil"]

spon•dee \'spăn-ˌdē\ *n* **:** a metrical foot consisting of two accented syllables (as in *tom-tom*) [Middle French, from Latin *spondeum* "foot of 2 long syllables", from Greek *spondeios,* from *spondē* "libation"; from its use in music accompanying libations] — **spon•da•ic** \spăn-'dā-ik\ *adj*

[1]**sponge** \'spənj\ *n* **1 a :** an elastic porous mass of fibers that forms the internal skeleton of various marine animals (phylum Porifera) and is able when wetted to absorb water; *also* **:** a piece of this material or of a porous rubber or cellulose product of similar properties used especially for cleaning **b :** any of a phylum (Porifera) of lowly aquatic animals that are essentially double-walled cell colonies and permanently attached as adults **2 :** a pad (as of folded gauze) used in surgery and medicine (as to remove discharges or apply medication) **3 :** one who lives upon others **4 a :** raised dough **b :** a whipped dessert usually containing whites of eggs or gelatin **c :** a metal (as platinum) obtained in porous form usually by reduction without fusion [Old English, from Latin *spongia,* from Greek]

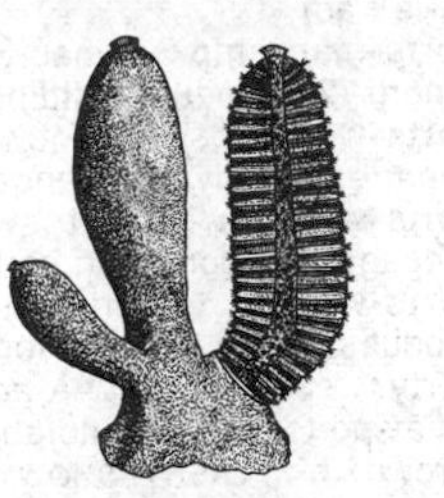

[1]sponge 1b

[2]**sponge** *vb* **1 a :** to cleanse, wipe, or moisten with or as if with a sponge **b :** to erase or destroy with or as if with a sponge **2 :** to absorb with or as if with or like a sponge **3 :** to get something from or live on another by imposing on hospitality or good nature **4 :** to dive or dredge for sponges — **spong•er** *n*

sponge cake *n* **:** a cake made without shortening

sponge rubber *n* **:** cellular rubber resembling a natural sponge in structure used especially for cushions and in weather-stripping

spon•gin \'spən-jən\ *n* **:** a fibrous protein that is the chief constituent of the flexible fibers in sponge skeletons [German, from Latin *spongia* "sponge"]

spongy \'spən-jē\ *adj* **spong•i•er; -est 1 :** resembling a sponge in appearance or absorbency **2 :** soft and full of holes or moisture **:** not firm or solid — **spong•i•ness** *n*

spongy parenchyma *n* **:** a spongy layer of irregular chlorophyll-bearing cells interspersed with air spaces that fills the part of a leaf between the palisade layer and the lower epidermis — called also *spongy layer, spongy tissue*

spon•son \'spän-sən\ *n* **1 :** a projection (as a gun platform) from the side of a ship or a tank **2 :** an air chamber along a canoe or seaplane to increase stability and buoyancy on water [probably from *expansion*]

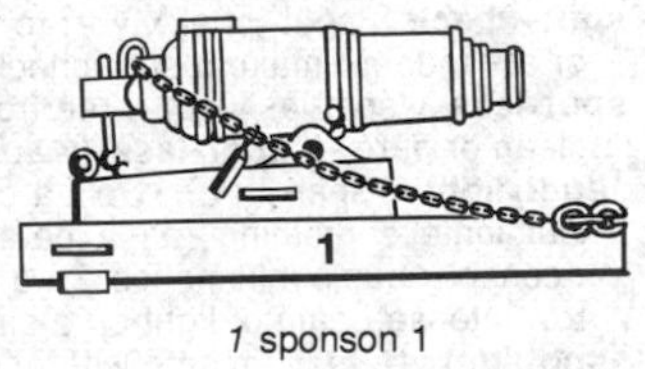

1 sponson 1

[1]**spon•sor** \'spän-sər\ *n* **1 :** a person who takes the responsibility for some other person or thing ⟨agreed to be their *sponsor* at the club⟩ **2 :** GODPARENT **3 :** a person or an organization that pays for or plans and carries out a project or activity; *esp* **:** one that pays the cost of a radio or television program usually in return for limited advertising time [Latin, "guarantor, surety", from *spondēre* "to promise"] — **spon•sor•ship** \'spän-sər-,ship\ *n*

[2]**sponsor** *vt* **spon•sored; spon•sor•ing** \'späns-ring, -ə-ring\ **:** to be or act as sponsor for

spon•ta•ne•ity \,spänt-ən-'ē-ət-ē, ,spänt-n-, -'ā-ət-\ *n* **1 :** the quality or state of being spontaneous **2 :** spontaneous action or movement

spon•ta•ne•ous \spän-'tā-nē-əs\ *adj* **1 :** done, said, or produced freely and naturally ⟨*spontaneous* laughter⟩ **2 :** acting or taking place without apparent external cause or influence ⟨*spontaneous* rebellion⟩ ⟨*spontaneous* recovery from illness⟩ [Late Latin *spontaneus,* from Latin *sponte* "of one's free will"] — **spon•ta•ne•ous•ly** *adv* — **spon•ta•ne•ous•ness** *n*

• syn SPONTANEOUS, IMPULSIVE, INSTINCTIVE, AUTOMATIC mean acting or activated without deliberation. SPONTANEOUS implies lack of prompting and connotes genuineness ⟨*spontaneous* applause⟩ IMPULSIVE implies acting under immediate stress of emotion or spirit of the moment ⟨an *impulsive* act of generosity⟩ INSTINCTIVE stresses spontaneous action involving neither judgment nor conscious intention ⟨*instinctive* shrinking from snakes⟩ AUTOMATIC implies action engaging neither the mind nor the emotions and connotes a predictable response ⟨a soldier's *automatic* obedience to commands⟩

spontaneous combustion *n* **:** a bursting into flame of combustible material through heat produced within itself by chemical action (as oxidation)

spontaneous generation *n* **:** spontaneous origin of organisms directly from lifeless matter — called also *abiogenesis*

[1]**spoof** \'spüf\ *vt* **1 :** to deceive by a hoax **2 :** to make good-natured fun of ⟨a skit *spoofing* big business⟩ [*Spoof,* a hoaxing game invented by Arthur Roberts, died 1933, English comedian]

[2]**spoof** *n* **1 :** HOAX, DECEPTION **2 :** a light good-natured parody

[1]**spook** \'spük\ *n* **:** GHOST 2 [Dutch] — **spook•ish** \'spü-kish\ *adj*

[2]**spook** *vb* **:** to make or become frightened or frantic

spooky \'spü-kē\ *adj* **spook•i•er; -est 1 :** relating to, resembling, or suggesting spooks ⟨a *spooky* movie⟩ **2 :** NERVOUS, SKITTISH ⟨a *spooky* horse⟩ — **spook•i•ness** *n*

spool \'spül\ *n* **1 :** a cylinder which has a rim at each end and usually a hollow center and on which material (as thread or tape) is wound **2 :** material wound on a spool [Middle French *espole,* from Dutch *spoele*] — **spool** *vb*

[1]**spoon** \'spün\ *n* **1 :** an implement that consists of a small shallow bowl with a handle and is used especially in eating and cooking **2 :** something that resembles a spoon in shape [Old English *spōn* "splinter, chip"]

[2]**spoon** *vb* **1 :** to take up and usually transfer in or as if in a spoon **2 :** to make love with kissing and caressing [sense 2 probably from the Welsh custom of an engaged man's presenting his fiancée with an elaborately carved wooden spoon]

spoon•bill \'spün-,bil\ *n* **1 :** any of several wading birds related to the ibises that have the bill broad and flat at the tip **2 :** any of several broad-billed ducks

spoon bread *n, chiefly South & Midland* **:** soft bread made of cornmeal mixed with milk, eggs, shortening, and leavening and served with a spoon

spoonbill 1

spoo•ner•ism \'spü-nə-,riz-əm\ *n* **:** a transposition of usually initial sounds of two or more words (as in *tons of soil* for *sons of toil*) [William A. *Spooner,* died 1930, English clergyman and educator]

spoon-feed \'spün-,fēd\ *vt* **-fed** \-,fed\; **-feed•ing 1 :** to feed by means of a spoon **2 :** to present information to in so complete a manner as to prevent independent thought

spoon•ful \'spün-,fu̇l\ *n, pl* **spoonfuls** \-,fu̇lz\ *also* **spoons•ful** \'spünz-,fu̇l\ **:** as much as a spoon can hold; *esp* **:** TEASPOONFUL

[1]**spoor** \'spu̇r, 'spōr, 'spȯr\ *n* **:** a track or trail especially of a wild animal [Afrikaans]

[2]**spoor** *vb* **:** to track something by a spoor

spor- *or* **sporo-** *combining form* **:** seed **:** spore ⟨*sporo*cyst⟩ [New Latin *spora*]

spo•rad•ic \spə-'rad-ik\ *adj* **:** occurring occasionally, singly, or in scattered instances ⟨*sporadic* outbreaks of disease⟩ [Medieval Latin *sporadicus,* from Greek *sporadikos,* from *sporadēn* "here and there", from *sporas* "scattered"] **syn** see INFREQUENT — **spo•rad•i•cal•ly** \-'rad-i-kə-lē, -klē\ *adv*

spo•ran•gi•o•phore \spə-'ran-jē-ə-,fōr, -,fȯr\ *n* **:** a stalk (as a fungal hypha) that bears sporangia

spo•ran•gi•um \spə-'ran-jē-əm\ *n, pl* **-gia** \-jē-ə\ **:** a sac or case within which usually asexual spores are produced [New Latin, from *spor-* + Greek *angeion* "vessel"] — **spo•ran•gial** \-jē-əl, -jəl\ *adj*

[1]**spore** \'spōr, 'spȯr\ *n* **:** a primitive usually one-celled body produced by plants and some lower animals and capable of devel-

\ə\ **abut**	\au̇\ **out**	\i\ **tip**	\ȯ\ **saw**	\u̇\ **foot**
\ər\ **further**	\ch\ **chin**	\ī\ **life**	\ȯi\ **coin**	\y\ **yet**
\a\ **mat**	\e\ **pet**	\j\ **job**	\th\ **thin**	\yü\ **few**
\ā\ **take**	\ē\ **easy**	\ng\ **sing**	\t͟h\ **this**	\yu̇\ **cure**
\ä\ **cot, cart**	\g\ **go**	\ō\ **bone**	\ü\ **food**	\zh\ **vision**

oping either directly or after fusion with another spore into a new individual in some cases unlike the parent [New Latin *spora* "seed, spore", from Greek, "act of sowing, seed", from *speirein* "to sow"] — **spored** \'spōrd, 'spȯrd\ *adj*

[2]**spore** *vi* : to produce spores or reproduce by spores

spore case *n* : SPORANGIUM

spore mother cell *n* : a cell whose final divisions produce spores usually in groups of four

spo•ro•cyst \'spōr-ə-ˌsist, 'spȯr-\ *n* **1** : a resting cell (as in a slime mold) that may give rise to asexual spores **2** : a sac that is the first asexual reproductive form of some trematode worms and buds off cells from its inner surface — **spo•ro•cys•tic** \ˌspōr-ə-'sis-tik, ˌspȯr-\ *adj*

spo•ro•cyte \'spōr-ə-ˌsīt, 'spȯr-\ *n* : SPORE MOTHER CELL

spo•rog•e•nous \spə-'räj-ə-nəs\ *adj* **1** : producing or adapted to the production of spores ⟨*sporogenous* hyphae⟩ **2** : reproducing by spores

spo•ro•phore \'spōr-ə-ˌfōr, 'spȯr-ə-ˌfȯr\ *n* : the part or organ of a sporophyte that actually produces spores

spo•ro•phyll \'spōr-ə-ˌfil, 'spȯr-\ *n* : a spore-bearing and usually greatly modified leaf (as a stamen or carpel)

spo•ro•phyte \-ˌfīt\ *n* : the individual or generation of a plant having alternating sexual and asexual generations that bears asexual spores — compare GAMETOPHYTE — **spo•ro•phyt•ic** \ˌspōr-ə-'fit-ik, ˌspȯr-\ *adj*

spo•ro•zo•an \ˌspōr-ə-'zō-ən, ˌspȯr-\ *n* : any of a large class (Sporozoa) of strictly parasitic protozoans that have a complicated life cycle usually involving both asexual and sexual generations often in different hosts and that include important pathogens (as the malaria parasites) [derived from *spor-* + Greek *zōion* "animal"] — **sporozoan** *adj*

spo•ro•zo•ite \-'zō-ˌīt\ *n* : a usually motile infective form of some sporozoans that is formed by division of a zygote and initiates an asexual cycle in the new host

spor•ran \'spȯr-ən, 'spär-\ *n* : a pouch of skin with the hair or fur on that is worn in front of the kilt by Highlanders in full dress [Scottish Gaelic *sporan*]

1 sporran

[1]**sport** \'spōrt, 'spȯrt\ *vb* **1 a** : to amuse oneself : FROLIC **b** : to engage in a sport **2** : to speak or act in jest or mockingly : TRIFLE **3** : to display or wear proudly : show off ⟨*sport* a new hat⟩ **4** : to deviate or vary abruptly from type : MUTATE [Middle English *sporten,* short for *disporten* "to disport"]

[2]**sport** *n* **1 a** : a source of diversion : RECREATION **b** : physical activity engaged in for pleasure; *esp* : a particular activity (as hunting or an athletic game) so engaged in **2 a** : PLEASANTRY 2, JEST **b** : MOCKERY 1, DERISION **3 a** : something tossed or driven about in or as if in play ⟨the battered boat became the *sport* of wind and waves⟩ **b** : LAUGHINGSTOCK, BUTT **4 a** : a person who engages in sport **b** : one who lives up to the ideals of sportsmanship **5** : a usually conspicuous mutant individual

[3]**sport** or **sports** \'spōrts, 'spȯrts\ *adj* : relating to, suitable for, or sought for sport ⟨*sport* fish⟩

sport•ing \'spōrt-ing, 'spȯrt-\ *adj* **1 a** : used or suitable for sport; *esp* : bred or trained for use in hunting ⟨a *sporting* dog⟩ **b** : marked by or calling for sportsmanship **c** : involving such risk as a sports contender may expect to take or encounter ⟨a *sporting* chance⟩ **2** : of or relating to dissipation (as gambling)

sport•ive \'spōrt-iv, 'spȯrt-\ *adj* : engaging in sport : FROLICSOME — **sport•ive•ly** *adv* — **sport•ive•ness** *n*

sports car *also* **sport car** *n* : a low usually two-seat open automobile that is especially fast and maneuverable

sports•cast \'spōrt-ˌskast, 'spȯrt-\ *n* : a broadcast dealing with sports events [*sport* + broad*cast*] — **sports•cast•er** *n*

sport shirt *n* : a shirt for casual wear with open neck

sports•man \'spōrt-smən, 'spȯrt-\ *n* **1** : a person who engages in or is interested in sports and especially outdoor sports **2** : a person who is fair and generous and a good loser and a graceful winner — **sports•man•like** \-ˌlīk\ *adj* — **sports•man•ly** \-lē\ *adj*

sports•man•ship \-smən-ˌship\ *n* **1** : skill in or devotion to sports **2** : conduct befitting a good sportsman

sports•wear \-ˌswaər, -ˌsweər\ *n* : clothes suitable for casual wear especially while engaging in or watching sports

sports•wom•an \'spōrt-ˌswu̇m-ən, 'spȯrt-\ *n* : a woman who engages in sports and especially in outdoor sports

sports•writ•er \'spōrts-ˌrīt-ər, 'spȯrts-\ *n* : one who writes about sports especially for a newspaper

sporty \'spōrt-ē, 'spȯrt-\ *adj* **sport•i•er**; **-est** **1** : characteristic of a sportsman **2 a** : notably gay or dissipated : FAST ⟨a *sporty* crowd⟩ **b** : FLASHY, SHOWY ⟨*sporty* new clothes⟩ **3** : SPORT ⟨a *sporty* boat⟩ — **sport•i•ly** \'spōrt-l-ē, 'spȯrt-\ *adv* — **sport•i•ness** \'spōrt-ē-nəs, 'spȯrt-\ *n*

spor•u•la•tion \ˌspōr-yə-'lā-shən, ˌspȯr-\ *n* : formation of or division into spores [New Latin *sporula* "small spore", from *spora* "spore"] — **spor•u•late** \'spōr-yə-ˌlāt, 'spȯr-\ *vi* — **spor•u•la•tive** \-ˌlāt-iv\ *adj*

[1]**spot** \'spät\ *n* **1** : a blemish or stain on character or reputation : FAULT **2 a** : a small area visibly different (as in color, finish, or material) from the surrounding area **b** : an area marred or marked (as by dirt); *also* : a circumscribed surface lesion of disease (as measles) **3 a** : a small quantity or amount **b** : a small or particular place or extent of space ⟨a good *spot* for a picnic⟩ **4 a** : a particular position (as in an organization or on a program) ⟨have a *spot* open in sales⟩ **b** : a position usually of difficulty or embarrassment : FIX [Middle English] — **on the spot** **1** : at once : IMMEDIATELY **2** : at the place of action ⟨make an investigation *on the spot*⟩ **3** : in difficulty or danger

[2]**spot** *vb* **spot•ted**; **spot•ting** **1** : to mark or become marked with or as if with spots : STAIN, BLEMISH ⟨a *spotted* reputation⟩ ⟨white *spots* so easily⟩ **2** : to single out : IDENTIFY, DETECT ⟨*spot* a friend⟩ ⟨*spot* an opportunity⟩; *also* : to locate precisely ⟨*spot* an enemy's position⟩ **3 a** : to lie or occur at intervals in or on ⟨slopes *spotted* with plowed fields⟩ **b** : to place at intervals or in a desired spot ⟨*spot* a picture on the wall⟩ **4** : to remove spots from **5** : to allow a handicap or advantage ⟨was *spotted* 5 points⟩ — **spot•ta•ble** \'spät-ə-bəl\ *adj*

[3]**spot** *adj* **1** : being, originating, or done on the spot or in or for a particular spot ⟨*spot* coverage of the news⟩ **2 a** : paid out upon delivery ⟨*spot* cash⟩ **b** : broadcast between scheduled programs ⟨*spot* announcements⟩ **3** : made at random or restricted to a few places or instances ⟨a *spot* check⟩

spot–check \'spät-ˌchek\ *vb* : to sample or investigate quickly or at random : make a spot check

spot•less \'spät-ləs\ *adj* : free from spot or blemish : perfectly clean or pure — **spot•less•ly** *adv* — **spot•less•ness** *n*

[1]**spot•light** \'spät-ˌlīt\ *n* **1 a** : a projected spot of light used to illuminate something (as a person on a stage) brilliantly **b** : conspicuous public notice **2** : a light designed to direct a narrow intense beam of light on a small area

[2]**spotlight** *vt* : to illuminate with or as if with a spotlight

spot•ted \'spät-əd\ *adj* **1 a** : marked with spots **b** : being sullied : TARNISHED **2** : accompanied by an eruption ⟨a *spotted* fever⟩ **3** : SPOTTY 2

spot•ter \'spät-ər\ *n* **1** : one that makes, applies, or removes spots **2** : one that keeps watch : OBSERVER; *esp* : a civilian who watches for approaching enemy airplanes

spot•ty \'spät-ē\ *adj* **spot•ti•er**; **-est** **1** : SPOTTED 1a **2** : lacking uniformity ⟨did a *spotty* job of cleaning up⟩ — **spot•ti•ly** \'spät-l-ē\ *adv* — **spot•ti•ness** \'spät-ē-nəs\ *n*

spou•sal \'spau̇-zəl, -səl\ *n* : MARRIAGE 2, WEDDING — usually used in pl. — **spousal** *adj*

spouse \'spau̇s *also* 'spau̇z\ *n* : a married person [Old French *espous,* from Latin *sponsus* "betrothed, newly married", from *spondēre* "to promise, betroth"]

[1]**spout** \'spau̇t\ *vb* **1** : to eject (as liquid) in a stream or jet ⟨wells *spouting* oil⟩ **2** : to speak or utter readily, volubly, and at length **3** : to issue with force or in a jet : SPURT ⟨blood *spouted* from the wound⟩ [Middle English *spouten*] — **spout•er** *n*

[2]**spout** *n* **1** : a tube, pipe, or hole through which something (as rainwater) spouts **2** : a jet of liquid; *esp* : WATERSPOUT

[1]**sprain** \'sprān\ *n* **1** : a sudden or violent twist or wrench of a joint with stretching or tearing of ligaments **2** : a sprained condition [origin unknown] **syn** see STRAIN

[2]**sprain** *vt* : to subject to sprain

sprat \'sprat\ *n* : a small European herring closely related to the common herring; *also* : a small or young herring or similar fish (as an anchovy) [Old English *sprott*]

sprawl \'sprȯl\ *vb* **1** : to creep or clamber awkwardly **2** : to lie or sit with arms and legs spread out **3** : to spread or cause to spread out irregularly or awkwardly ⟨a factory *sprawling* over a vast area⟩ [Old English *sprēawlian* "to thrash about"] — **sprawl** *n*

[1]**spray** \'sprā\ *n* **1** : a usually flowering branch or shoot **2** : a decorative flat arrangement of flowers and foliage **3** : something (as an ornament) resembling a spray [Middle English]

[2]**spray** *n* **1** : water flying in small drops or particles (as when blown from waves or thrown up by a waterfall) **2 a** : a jet of vapor or finely divided liquid (as from an atomizer) **b** : a device (as an atomizer or sprayer) by which a spray is dispersed or applied [obsolete *spray* "to sprinkle", from Dutch *sprayen*]

[3]**spray** *vb* **1** : to disperse or apply in a spray **2** : to project spray on or into — **spray•er** *n*

spray gun *n* : a device for spraying paints or insecticides

[1]**spread** \'spred\ *vb* **spread**; **spread•ing 1 a** : to open or expand over a larger area ⟨*spread* out a map⟩ **b** : to stretch out or apart : EXTEND ⟨*spread* your arms wide⟩ **2 a** : SCATTER, STREW ⟨*spread* fertilizer⟩ **b** : to distribute over a period or among a group ⟨*spread* the work to be done⟩ **c** : to apply on a surface ⟨*spread* butter on bread⟩ **d** : COVER, OVERLAY ⟨*spread* a floor with carpet⟩ **e** (1) : to prepare or furnish for dining : SET ⟨*spread* a table⟩ (2) : SERVE ⟨*spread* a banquet⟩ **3 a** : to become or cause to become widely known ⟨the news *spread* rapidly⟩ **b** : to extend the range or incidence of ⟨*spread* a disease⟩ [Old English *sprǣdan*] — **spread•er** *n*

[2]**spread** *n* **1 a** : the act or process of spreading **b** : extent of spreading ⟨the *spread* of a bird's wings⟩ **2** : something spread out: as **a** : EXPANSE **b** *West* : RANCH 1 **c** : a prominent display in a periodical **3** : something spread on or over a surface: as **a** : a food to be spread (as on bread or crackers) **b** : FEAST 1a **c** : a cover for a table or bed **4** : distance between two points

spread–ea•gle \'spred-,ē-gəl\ *vb* **spread–ea•gled**; **spread–ea•gling** \-gə-ling, -gling\ **1** : to stand or move with arms and legs stretched out **2** : to spread over : stretch across

spread eagle *n* **1** : a representation of an eagle with wings raised and legs extended **2** : something resembling or suggesting a spread eagle

spreading adder *n* : HOGNOSE SNAKE

spree \'sprē\ *n* : an unrestrained indulgence in or outburst of an activity ⟨a buying *spree*⟩; *esp* : BINGE [perhaps from Scottish *spreath* "cattle raid, foray", from Scottish Gaelic *sprēidh* "cattle", from Latin *praeda* "booty, prey"]

[1]**sprig** \'sprig\ *n* **1** : a small shoot : TWIG **2** : an ornament resembling a sprig, stemmed flower, or leaf **3** : a small headless nail : BRAD [Middle English *sprigge*]

[2]**sprig** *vt* **sprigged**; **sprig•ging** : to drive sprigs into

spright•ful \'sprīt-fəl\ *adj* : SPRIGHTLY — **spright•ful•ly** \-fə-lē\ *adv* — **spright•ful•ness** *n*

spright•ly \'sprīt-lē\ *adj* **spright•li•er**; **-est** : marked by a gay lightness and liveliness [obsolete *spright* "sprite", alteration of *sprite*] — **spright•li•ness** *n*

[1]**spring** \'spring\ *vb* **sprang** \'sprang\ *or* **sprung** \'sprəng\; **sprung**; **spring•ing** \'spring-ing\ **1a** (1) : DART 2, SHOOT (2) : to be resilient or elastic; *also* : to move by elastic force ⟨the lid *sprang* shut⟩ **b** : to become warped **2** : to issue with speed and force or as a stream **3 a** : to grow as a plant **b** : to issue by birth or descent **c** : to come into being : ARISE **4 a** : to make a leap or series of leaps **b** : to jump up suddenly **5** : to stretch out in height : RISE **6 a** : SPLIT, CRACK ⟨wind *sprang* the mast⟩ **b** : to have (a leak) develop **7** : to cause to operate suddenly ⟨*spring* a trap⟩ **8** : to produce or disclose suddenly or unexpectedly ⟨*sprung* a surprise on us⟩ **9** : to release or cause to be released from custody or confinement [Old English *springan*] — **spring•er** \'spring-ər\ *n*

[2]**spring** *n* **1 a** : a source of supply; *esp* : a source of water issuing from the ground **b** : an ultimate source especially of action or motion **2 a** : the season between winter and summer comprising in the northern hemisphere usually the months of March, April, and May or as reckoned astronomically extending from the March equinox to the June solstice **b** : a time or season of growth or development **3** : an elastic body or device that recovers its original shape when released after being distorted **4 a** : the act or an instance of leaping up or forward : BOUND **b** : capacity for springing : RESILIENCE, BOUNCE

spring beauty *n* : a spring herb that sends up a 2-leaved stem bearing delicate pink flowers

spring•board \'spring-,bōrd, -,bȯrd\ *n* **1** : a flexible board usually secured at one end and used to gain height for gymnastic stunts or diving **2** : a point of departure

spring•bok \'spring-,bäk\ *n, pl* **springbok** *or* **springboks** : a swift and graceful southern African gazelle [Afrikaans, from *spring* "to jump" + *bok* "male goat"]

spring–clean•ing \-'klē-ning\ *n* : the act or process of cleaning a place thoroughly

spring•er spaniel \,spring-ər-\ *n* : a medium-sized largely white sporting dog of English or Welsh origin used chiefly for finding and flushing small game

spring fever *n* : a lazy or restless feeling often associated with the onset of spring

spring•house \'spring-,haůs\ *n* : a small building over a spring used for cool storage (as of dairy products or meat)

spring•let \'spring-lət\ *n* : a little spring : STREAMLET

spring peeper *n* : a small brown tree toad of the eastern United States and Canada with a shrill piping call

spring•tail \'spring-,tāl\ *n* : any of an order (Collembola) of small primitive wingless arthropods that are related to or classed among the insects

spring•tide \'spring-,tīd\ *n* : SPRINGTIME

spring tide *n* : a greater than usual tide occurring at each new moon and full moon

spring•time \'spring-,tīm\ *n* : the season of spring

spring wagon *n* : a light wagon equipped with springs

spring•wood \'spring-,wůd\ *n* : the softer more porous portion of an annual ring of wood that develops early in the growing season — compare SUMMERWOOD

springy \'spring-ē\ *adj* **spring•i•er**; **-est** : having an elastic quality : RESILIENT — **spring•i•ly** \'spring-ə-lē\ *adv* — **spring•i•ness** \'spring-ē-nəs\ *n*

[1]**sprin•kle** \'spring-kəl\ *vb* **sprin•kled**; **sprin•kling** \-kə-ling, -kling\ **1** : to scatter in drops or particles **2 a** : to scatter over **b** : to scatter at intervals in or among : DOT **c** : to wet lightly **3** : to rain lightly in scattered drops [Middle English *sprinclen*] — **sprin•kler** \-kə-lər, -klər\ *n*

[2]**sprinkle** *n* **1** : the act or an instance of sprinkling; *esp* : a light rain **2** : SPRINKLING

sprinkler system *n* : a system for protection against fire in which pipes are distributed for conveying an extinguishing fluid (as water) to outlets

sprin•kling \'spring-kling\ *n* : a limited quantity or amount; *esp* : SCATTERING

[1]**sprint** \'sprint\ *vi* : to run at top speed especially for a short distance [of Scandinavian origin] — **sprint•er** *n*

[2]**sprint** *n* **1** : the act or an instance of sprinting **2** : a race run at or near top speed the whole way : DASH

sprit \'sprit\ *n* : a spar attached to the mast that runs diagonally across a rectangular fore-and-aft sail to support it [Old English *sprēot* "pole, spear"]

sprite \'sprīt\ *n* **1** : GHOST 2 **2 a** : an often mischievous supernatural being **b** : an elfish person [Old French *esprit* "spirit", from Latin *spiritus*]

sprit•sail \'sprit-,sāl, -səl\ *n* : a sail extended by a sprit

sprock•et \'spräk-ət\ *n* **1** : a projection on the rim of a wheel shaped so as to interlock with the links of a chain **2** : a wheel having sprockets [origin unknown]

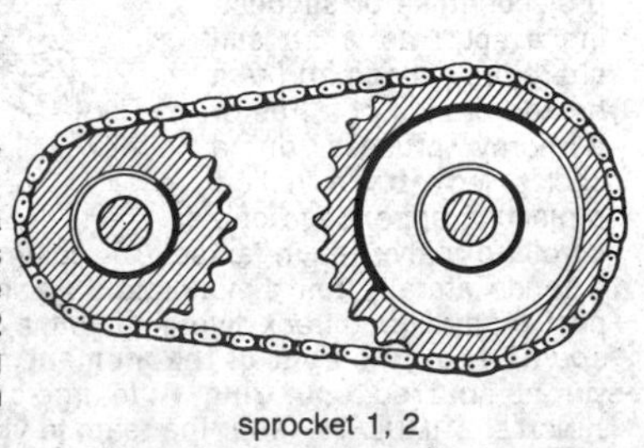
sprocket 1, 2

[1]**sprout** \'spraůt\ *vb* **1** : to send out new growth **2** : to grow rapidly **3** : to cause to sprout ⟨*sprout* oats⟩ [Old English *-sprūtan*]

[2]**sprout** *n* **1** : SHOOT 1a; *esp* : a young shoot (as from a seed or root) **2** *pl* : edible shoots especially of a plant of the mustard family; *also* : a plant (as brussels sprouts) producing them

[1]**spruce** \'sprüs\ *n* : any of a genus of evergreen trees of the

pine family with a conical head of dense foliage and with soft light wood; *also* : its wood [Middle English *Spruce* "Prussia", alteration of *Pruce,* from Old French]

△ **origin** Prussia was formerly called *Pruce* or *Spruce* in English. A number of goods imported from Prussia — *spruce* canvas, *spruce* iron, *spruce* leather — were all very well-thought-of. Perhaps the most important of these Prussian or *Spruce* products was the spruce tree, a tall, straight conifer that was especially desirable for use as the mast of a ship. About the middle of the 17th century, *Spruce* as the name for the country was largely supplanted by *Prussia.* But by this time *spruce* had become well established as the name of the tree.

[2]**spruce** *adj* : neat or smart in appearance : TRIM [perhaps from obsolete *spruce leather* "leather imported from Prussia"] — **spruce•ly** *adv* — **spruce•ness** *n*

[3]**spruce** *vb* : to make or make oneself spruce ⟨*spruce* up a room⟩ ⟨*spruce* up before dinner⟩

sprue \ˈsprü\ *n* : a chronic disease marked especially by fatty diarrhea and dietary deficiency symptoms [Dutch *spruw*]

sprung *past of* SPRING

spry \ˈsprī\ *adj* **spri•er** *or* **spry•er** \ˈsprī-ər, ˈsprīr\; **spri•est** *or* **spry•est** \ˈsprī-əst\ : vigorously active : BRISK [perhaps of Scandinavian origin] — **spry•ly** *adv* — **spry•ness** *n*

[1]**spud** \ˈspəd\ *n* **1** : a tool or device (as for digging, lifting, or cutting) combining the characteristics of spade and chisel **2** : POTATO 2b [Middle English *spudde* "dagger"]

[2]**spud** *vb* **spud•ded**; **spud•ding** : to dig with a spud

[1]**spume** \ˈspyüm\ *n* : frothy matter on liquids : FOAM [Middle French, from Latin *spuma*] — **spu•mous** \ˈspyü-məs\ *adj* — **spumy** \ˈspyü-mē\ *adj*

[2]**spume** *vi* : FROTH 3, FOAM

spu•mo•ni *or* **spu•mo•ne** \spu̇-ˈmō-nē\ *n* : ice cream in layers of different colors, flavors, and textures often with candied fruits and nuts [Italian *spumone,* from *spuma* "foam", from Latin]

spun *past of* SPIN

spun glass *n* : FIBERGLASS

spunk \ˈspəngk\ *n* : SAND 4, PLUCK [earlier *spunk* "tinder", from Scottish Gaelic *spong* "sponge, tinder", from Latin *spongia* "sponge"]

spunky \ˈspəng-kē\ *adj* **spunk•i•er**; **-est** : full of spunk : SPIRITED — **spunk•i•ly** \-kə-lē\ *adv* — **spunk•i•ness** \-kē-nəs\ *n*

spun sugar *n* : a confection or garnish made from boiled sugar syrup drawn out into fine threads and variously shaped or heaped up

[1]**spur** \ˈspər\ *n* **1 a** : a pointed device secured to a rider's heel and used to urge on the horse **b** *pl* : recognition for achievement **2** : a goad to action : STIMULUS **3** : something projecting like or suggesting a spur: as **a** : a stiff sharp projecting part (as a broken branch of a tree or a horny process on a cock's leg) **b** : a hollow projecting appendage of a corolla or calyx (as in larkspur or columbine) **4** : a ridge that extends laterally from a mountain **5** : a short wooden brace of a post **6** : a railroad track diverging from a main line [Old English *spura*] — **on the spur of the moment** : on impulse

[1]spur 1a

[2]**spur** *vb* **spurred**; **spur•ring** **1** : to urge a horse on with spurs **2** : INCITE, STIMULATE ⟨*spur* the team to victory⟩

spurge \ˈspərj\ *n* : any of a family of mostly shrubby plants with a bitter milky juice and often showy bracts surrounding insignificant flowers — compare POINSETTIA [Middle French, "purge, spurge", from *espurgier* "to purge", from Latin *expurgare*]

spur gear *n* : a gear wheel with radial teeth parallel to its axis

spu•ri•ous \ˈspyu̇r-ē-əs\ *adj* : not genuine or authentic : FALSE, COUNTERFEIT [Late Latin *spurius,* from Latin, "bastard"] — **spu•ri•ous•ly** *adv* — **spu•ri•ous•ness** *n*

[1]**spurn** \ˈspərn\ *vt* **1** : to kick aside **2** : to reject with disdain [Old English *spurnan*] **syn** see REJECT — **spurn•er** *n*

[2]**spurn** *n* **1** : KICK 1a (1) **2** : disdainful rejection

spur–of–the–moment *adj* : occurring or developing without prior planning ⟨a *spur-of-the-moment* decision⟩

spurred \ˈspərd\ *adj* **1** : wearing spurs **2** : having one or more spurs ⟨a *spurred* violet⟩

spur•ri•er \ˈspər-ē-ər\ *n* : one that makes spurs

[1]**spurt** \ˈspərt\ *n* : a sudden brief burst of increased effort or activity [origin unknown]

[2]**spurt** *vi* : to make a spurt

[3]**spurt** *vb* **1** : SPOUT 3 **2** : SQUIRT [perhaps related to *sprout*]

[4]**spurt** *n* : a sudden gush : JET

spur track *n* : a track that diverges from a main line

sput•nik \ˈspu̇t-nik, ˈspət-\ *n* : SATELLITE 2b [Russian, literally, "traveling companion", from *s* "with" + *put'* "path"]

[1]**sput•ter** \ˈspət-ər\ *vb* **1** : to spit or squirt particles of food or saliva noisily from the mouth **2** : to speak or utter hastily or explosively in confusion or excitement ⟨*sputtered* out their protests⟩ **3** : to make explosive popping sounds ⟨the motor *sputtered* and died⟩ [related to Dutch *sputteren* "to sputter"] — **sput•ter•er** \-ər-ər\ *n*

[2]**sputter** *n* : the act or sound of sputtering

spu•tum \ˈspyüt-əm, ˈspüt-\ *n, pl* **spu•ta** \-ə\ : material spit or coughed up and made up of saliva and mucous discharges from the respiratory passages [Latin, from *spuere* "to spit"]

[1]**spy** \ˈspī\ *vb* **spied**; **spy•ing** **1** : to watch, inspect, or examine secretly : act as a spy **2** : to catch sight of : SEE ⟨*spied* a friend in the crowd⟩ **3** : to search or search out usually by close study or examination [Old French *espier,* of Germanic origin]

[2]**spy** *n, pl* **spies** **1** : one that secretly watches another so as to obtain information **2** : a person who tries secretly to obtain information for one country in the territory of another usually hostile country

spy•glass \ˈspī-ˌglas\ *n* : a small telescope

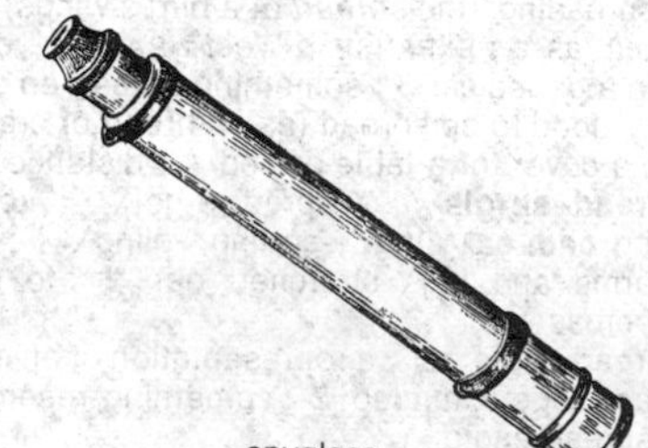

spyglass

squab \ˈskwäb\ *n, pl* **squabs** *or* **squab** : a fledgling bird; *esp* : a fledgling pigeon about four weeks old [probably of Scandinavian origin]

[1]**squab•ble** \ˈskwäb-əl\ *n* : a noisy quarrel usually over trifles [probably of Scandinavian origin]

[2]**squabble** *vi* **squab•bled**; **squab•bling** \ˈskwäb-ling, -ə-ling\ : to quarrel noisily and to no purpose : WRANGLE — **squab•bler** \-lər, -ə-lər\ *n*

squad \ˈskwäd\ *n* **1** : a small organized group of military personnel; *esp* : a tactical unit that can be easily directed in the field **2** : a small group engaged in a common effort or occupation ⟨a football *squad*⟩ [Middle French *esquade,* from Spanish *escuadra* and Italian *squadra,* both derived from Latin *quadrare* "to square"]

squad car *n* : a police automobile connected by a two-way radio with headquarters — called also *cruiser, prowl car*

squad•ron \ˈskwäd-rən\ *n* : any of several units of military organization [Italian *squadrone,* from *squadra* "squad"]

squad room *n* **1** : a room in a barracks used to billet soldiers **2** : a room in a police station where members of the force assemble

squal•id \ˈskwäl-əd\ *adj* **1** : marked by filthiness and degradation from neglect or poverty **2** : morally debased : SORDID [Latin *squalidus*] — **squal•id•ly** *adv* — **squal•id•ness** *n*

[1]**squall** \ˈskwȯl\ *vb* : to utter a raucous cry [of Scandinavian origin] — **squall•er** *n*

[2]**squall** *n* : a raucous cry

[3]**squall** *n* **1** : a sudden violent wind often with rain or snow **2** : a short-lived commotion [probably of Scandinavian origin]

[4]**squall** *vi* : to blow a squall

squally \ˈskwȯ-lē\ *adj* **squall•i•er**; **-est** : marked by squalls : GUSTY, STORMY

squal•or \ˈskwäl-ər\ *n* : the quality or state of being squalid [Latin]

squa•mo•sal \skwə-ˈmō-səl, -zəl\ *adj* : of, relating to, or being a bone of the skull of many vertebrates corresponding to the squamous portion of the temporal bone of humans

squa•mous \ˈskwā-məs, ˈskwä-\ *adj* **1** : covered with or consisting of scales : SCALY **2** : of, relating to, or being the anterior upper portion of the temporal bone of human beings and some other mammals [Latin *squamosus,* from *squama* "scale"]

squan•der \'skwän-dər\ *vb* **squan•dered**; **squan•der•ing** \-də-riŋ, -driŋ\ : to spend extravagantly or wastefully [origin unknown] — **squan•der•er** \-dər-ər\ *n*

[1]**square** \'skwaər, 'skweər\ *n* **1** : an instrument having at least one right angle and two straight edges used to mark or test right angles **2** : a rectangle with all four sides equal **3** : any of the quadrilateral spaces marked out on a board for playing games **4** : the product of a number multiplied by itself **5 a** : an open place or area formed at the meeting of two or more streets **b** : BLOCK 5b, 5c **6** : a person who is overly conventional or conservative [Middle French *esquarre*, derived from Latin *ex-* + *quadrare* "to square"] — **on the square 1** : at right angles **2** : in a fair open manner : HONESTLY — **out of square** : not at an exact right angle

[1]square 2

[2]**square** *adj* **1 a** : having four equal sides and four right angles **b** : forming a right angle ⟨a *square* corner⟩ **2** : raised to the second power **3 a** : of a shape suggesting strength and solidity ⟨a *square* jaw⟩ ⟨*square* shoulders⟩ **b** : rectangular and equilateral in section ⟨a *square* tower⟩ **c** : having a rectangular rather than curving outline **4 a** : converted from a linear unit into a square unit of area having the same length of side ⟨a *square* meter is the area of a square each side of which is a meter⟩ **b** : being of a specified length in each of two equal dimensions ⟨10 meters *square*⟩ **5 a** : exactly adjusted or aligned **b** : FAIR 5a, JUST **c** : leaving no balance : SETTLED **d** : TIED ⟨the golfers were all *square* at the end of the 6th hole⟩ **e** : SUBSTANTIAL 2 ⟨a *square* meal⟩ **6** : being unsophisticated, conservative, or conventional — **square•ly** *adv* — **square•ness** *n*

[3]**square** *vb* **1** : to make square or rectangular ⟨*square* a building stone⟩ **2** : to bring approximately to a right angle ⟨*squared* my shoulders⟩ **3 a** : to multiply (a number) by itself **b** : to find a square equal in area to ⟨*square* a circle⟩ **4** : to agree or make agree : HARMONIZE ⟨your story does not *square* with the facts⟩ **5** : BALANCE, SETTLE ⟨*square* an account⟩ **6** : to mark off into squares **7** : to influence or settle by or as if by a bribe

square away *vb* : to put in order or readiness

square bracket *n* : BRACKET 3a

square dance *n* : a dance for four couples who form a hollow square — **square dancer** *n* — **square dancing** *n*

square deal *n* : an honest and fair transaction or trade

square knot *n* : a knot made of two reverse half-knots and typically used to join the ends of two cords

square measure *n* : a unit or system of units for measuring area — see MEASURE table, METRIC SYSTEM table

square–rigged \'skwaər-'rigd, 'skweər-\ *adj* : having the principal sails extended on yards fastened to the masts horizontally and at their center

square–rig•ger \-'rig-ər\ *n* : a square-rigged vessel

square root *n* : a factor of a number that when squared gives the number ⟨the *square root* of 9 is ±3⟩

square sail \-,sāl, -səl\ *n* : a 4-sided sail used on a square-rigged vessel

square shooter *n* : a just or honest person

square–shoul•dered \-'shōl-dərd\ *adj* : having the shoulders high and well braced back

squar•ish \'skwaər-ish, 'skweər-\ *adj* : somewhat square in form or appearance — **squar•ish•ly** *adv*

[1]**squash** \'skwäsh, 'skwósh\ *vb* **1** : to press or beat into a pulp or flat mass **2** : to put down : SUPPRESS **3** : SQUEEZE, PRESS ⟨*squashed* into the seat⟩ [Middle French *esquasser*, from Latin *ex-* + *quassare* "to shake"] — **squash•er** *n*

[2]**squash** *n* **1** : the sudden fall of a heavy soft body or the sound of such a fall **2** : a squelching sound made by walking on oozy ground or in water-soaked boots **3** : a crushed mass **4** : SQUASH RACQUETS

[3]**squash** *n, pl* **squash•es** *or* **squash** : a fruit of any of various widely grown plants of the gourd family that is used especially as a vegetable and for livestock feed; *also* : a plant that bears squashes [of American Indian origin]

squash bug *n* : a large black American bug injurious to squash vines

squash racquets *n* : a singles or doubles game in a 4-wall court with rackets and a rubber ball

squash tennis *n* : a game resembling squash racquets played with an inflated ball the size of a tennis ball

squashy \'skwäsh-ē, 'skwósh-\ *adj* **squash•i•er**; **-est** : easily squashed : SOFT ⟨a *squashy* pillow⟩ — **squash•i•ly** \'skwäsh-ə-lē, 'skwósh-\ *adv* — **squash•i•ness** \'skwäsh-ē-nəs, 'skwósh-\ *n*

[1]**squat** \'skwät\ *vb* **squat•ted**; **squat•ting 1** : to sit or cause (oneself) to sit on one's haunches or heels **2** : to occupy land as a squatter **3** : CROUCH, COWER ⟨a *squatting* hare⟩ [Middle French *esquatir*, from *es-* "ex-" + *quatir* "to press", derived from Latin *cogere* "to drive together"]

[2]**squat** *n* **1** : the act of squatting **2** : a squatting posture

[3]**squat** *adj* **squat•ter**; **squat•test 1** : sitting with the haunches close above the heels **2 a** : low to the ground **b** : being short and thick — **squat•ly** *adv* — **squat•ness** *n*

squat•ter \'skwät-ər\ *n* **1** : one that squats **2 a** : one that settles on land without right or title or payment of rent **b** : one that settles on public land under government regulation with the purpose of acquiring title

squat•ty \'skwät-ē\ *adj* **squat•ti•er**; **-est** : SQUAT 2

squaw \'skwó\ *n* : an American Indian woman [of American Indian origin]

squaw•fish \-,fish\ *n* : any of several mostly freshwater fishes of western North America

[1]**squawk** \'skwók\ *vi* **1** : to utter a harsh abrupt scream **2** : to complain or protest loudly or vehemently [probably blend of *squall* and *squeak*] — **squawk•er** *n*

[2]**squawk** *n* **1** : a harsh abrupt scream **2** : a noisy complaint

squawk box *n* : an intercom speaker

squaw•root \'skwó-,rüt, -,ru̇t\ *n* : a North American herb that is parasitic on oak and hemlock roots and has a thick stem with yellow fleshy scales

[1]**squeak** \'skwēk\ *vb* **1** : to utter a sharp shrill cry or noise **2** : to pass, succeed, or win by a narrow margin ⟨barely *squeaked* by⟩ **3** : to utter in a shrill piping tone [Middle English *squeken*]

[2]**squeak** *n* **1** : a sharp shrill cry or sound **2** : ESCAPE 1 ⟨a close *squeak*⟩ — **squeaky** \'skwē-kē\ *adj*

[1]**squeal** \'skwēl\ *vb* **1** : to utter a shrill cry or sound **2 a** : to turn informer **b** : COMPLAIN 1, PROTEST **3** : to utter with or as if with a squeal [Middle English *squelen*] — **squeal•er** *n*

[2]**squeal** *n* : a shrill cry or sound

squea•mish \'skwē-mish\ *adj* **1 a** : easily nauseated : QUEASY **b** : affected with nausea **2** : easily shocked or disgusted [Anglo-French *escoymous*] — **squea•mish•ly** *adv* — **squea•mish•ness** *n*

squee•gee \'skwē-,jē\ *n* : a blade of leather or rubber set on a handle and used for spreading or wiping liquid material on, across, or off a surface (as a window) [probably imitative] — **squeegee** *vt*

[1]**squeeze** \'skwēz\ *vb* **1 a** : to exert pressure especially on opposite sides of : COMPRESS **b** : to extract or emit under pressure ⟨*squeeze* juice from a lemon⟩ **c** : to force or thrust by compression : CROWD ⟨two more *squeezed* into the car⟩ **2 a** : to extort money, goods, or services from ⟨*squeezed* their tenants mercilessly⟩ **b** : to cause hardship to : OPPRESS **c** : to reduce the amount of ⟨rising costs *squeezed* profits⟩ **3** : to gain or win by a narrow margin [Old English *cwȳsan*] — **squeez•er** *n*

[2]**squeeze** *n* **1 a** : an act or instance of squeezing : COMPRESSION **b** : HANDSHAKE; *also* : EMBRACE **2** : financial pressure caused by narrowing margins (as between costs and selling price) or by shortages

squeeze bottle *n* : a bottle of flexible plastic that dispenses its contents by being pressed

squeeze play *n* : a baseball play in which a batter attempts to score a runner from third base by bunting

[1]**squelch** \'skwelch\ *n* **1** : a sound of or as if of semiliquid matter under suction ⟨the *squelch* of mud⟩ **2** : a retort that silences an opponent [imitative]

[2]**squelch** *vb* **1 a** : to fall or stamp on so as to crush **b** : to com-

\ə\ **abut**	\au̇\ **out**	\i\ **tip**	\ó\ **saw**	\u̇\ **foot**
\ər\ **further**	\ch\ **chin**	\ī\ **life**	\ói\ **coin**	\y\ **yet**
\a\ **mat**	\e\ **pet**	\j\ **job**	\th\ **thin**	\yü\ **few**
\ā\ **take**	\ē\ **easy**	\ŋ\ **sing**	\t͟h\ **this**	\yu̇\ **cure**
\ä\ **cot, cart**	\g\ **go**	\ō\ **bone**	\ü\ **food**	\zh\ **vision**

pletely suppress : QUELL, SILENCE **2** : to emit or cause to emit a sucking sound **3** : to splash through water, slush, or mire — **squelch•er** *n*

sque•teague \skwi-'tēg\ *n, pl* **squeteague** : any of various weakfishes [of American Indian origin]

squib \'skwib\ *n* **1 a** : a small firecracker **b** : a broken firecracker that burns out with a fizz **2** : a short humorous or satiric writing or speech [origin unknown]

squid \'skwid\ *n, pl* **squid** *or* **squids** : any of numerous 10-armed cephalopod mollusks with a long tapered body, a fin on each side, and usually a slender internal chitinous support [origin unknown]

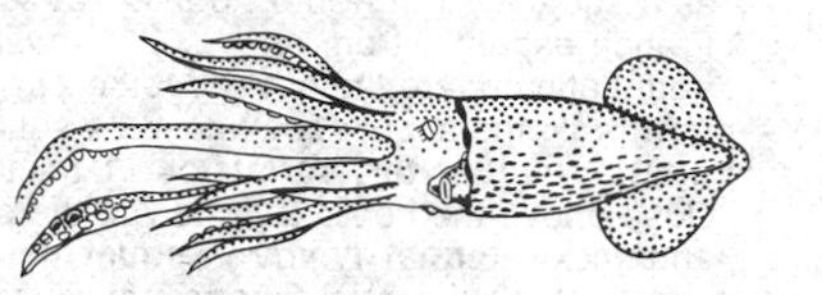
squid

squig•gle \'skwig-əl\ *n* : a short wavy twist or line : CURLICUE [from earlier *squiggle* "to wriggle", blend of *squirm* and *wriggle*]

squill \'skwil\ *n* **1** : a Mediterranean bulbous herb of the lily family with narrow leaves and white flowers; *also* : its bulb used in medicine and in rat poisons **2** : SCILLA [Latin *squilla, scilla,* from Greek *skilla*]

^{1}**squint** \'skwint\ *adj* : affected with cross-eye [Middle English *asquint*]

^{2}**squint** *vi* **1 a** : to look in a squint-eyed manner **b** : to be cross-eyed **2** : to look or peer with eyes closed — **squint•er** *n*

^{3}**squint** *n* : STRABISMUS; *also* : an action or instance of squinting — **squinty** \'skwint-ē\ *adj*

squint–eyed \'skwint-'īd\ *adj* : having eyes that squint

^{1}**squire** \'skwīr\ *n* **1** : one who bears the shield or armor of a knight **2 a** : a male attendant on a great personage **b** : GALLANT 2a, ESCORT **3 a** : a member of the British gentry ranking below a knight and above a gentleman **b** : an owner of a country estate **c** : JUSTICE OF THE PEACE [Old French *esquier,* from Late Latin *scutarius* "guard armed with a shield", from Latin *scutum* "shield"]

^{2}**squire** *vt* : to attend as a squire or escort

squire•archy *or* **squir•archy** \'skwīr-,är-kē\ *n* **1** : the gentry or landed-proprietor class **2** : government by a landed gentry

squirm \'skwərm\ *vi* **1** : to twist about like an eel or a worm **2** : to feel acutely embarrassed ⟨undeserved praise made us *squirm*⟩ [perhaps imitative] — **squirmy** \'skwər-mē\ *adj*

squir•rel \'skwər-əl, 'skwə-rəl, 'skwərl\ *n, pl* **squirrels** *also* **squirrel 1** : any of various small or medium-sized rodents (family Sciuridae); *esp* : one with a long bushy tail and strong hind legs adapted to leaping from branch to branch **2** : the fur of a squirrel [Middle French *esquireul,* derived from Latin *sciurus,* from Greek *skiouros,* from *skia* "shadow" + *oura* "tail"]

squirrel monkey *n* : a small soft-haired South American monkey having a long tail not used for grasping and being colored chiefly yellowish gray with a white face and black nose

^{1}**squirt** \'skwərt\ *vb* : to come forth, drive, or eject in a sudden rapid stream : SPURT [Middle English *squirten*]

^{2}**squirt** *n* **1 a** : an instrument (as a syringe) for squirting a liquid **b** : a small quick stream : JET **c** : the action of squirting **2** : an impudent youngster

squirt gun *n* : WATER PISTOL

squirting cucumber *n* : a Mediterranean plant of the gourd family having a fruit that bursts when ripe forcibly ejecting the seeds

squishy \'skwish-ē\ *adj* : being soft, yielding, and damp [from earlier *squish* "to squash"]

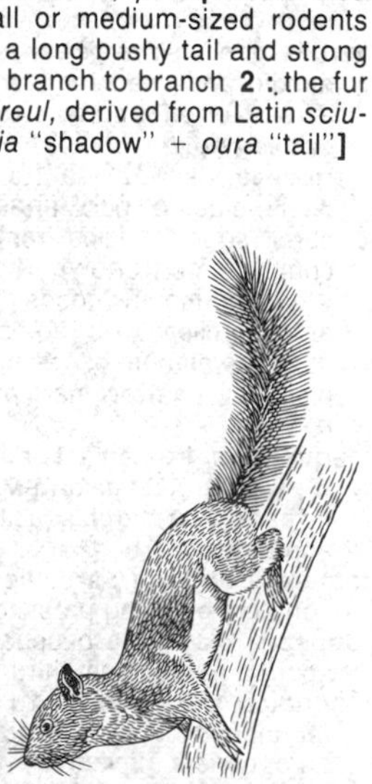
squirrel 1

SS \es-'es, 'es-\ *n* : a unit of Nazis created to serve as bodyguard to Hitler and later expanded to take charge of central security and extermination of undesirables [German, abbreviation for *Schutzstaffel* "elite guard"]

^{1}**-st** — see -EST

^{2}**-st** *symbol* — used after the figure 1 to indicate the ordinal number *first* ⟨1*st*⟩ ⟨71*st*⟩

^{1}**stab** \'stab\ *n* **1** : a wound produced by a pointed weapon **2** : a thrust of a pointed weapon **3** : EFFORT 2, TRY [Middle English *stabbe*]

^{2}**stab** *vt* **stabbed**; **stab•bing 1** : to wound or pierce by the thrust of a pointed weapon **2** : STICK 2 ⟨*stab* a needle into thick cloth⟩ — **stab•ber** *n*

sta•bil•i•ty \stə-'bil-ət-ē\ *n, pl* **-ties** : the quality, state, or degree of being stable: as **a** : the property of a body that causes it to return to its original condition when disturbed (as in balance) **b** : resistance to chemical change or to physical disintegration

sta•bi•lize \'stā-bə-,līz\ *vb* : to make or become stable, steadfast, or firm; *also* : to hold steady (as by means of a stabilizer) — **sta•bi•li•za•tion** \,stā-bə-lə-'zā-shən\ *n*

sta•bi•liz•er \'stā-bə-,lī-zər\ *n* : one (as a chemical or a device) that stabilizes something; *esp* : a fixed surface for stabilizing the motion of an airplane

^{1}**sta•ble** \'stā-bəl\ *n* **1** : a building in which domestic animals are sheltered and fed; *esp* : such a building having stalls or compartments ⟨horse *stable*⟩ **2 a** : the racehorses of one owner **b** : a group of athletes (as boxers) under one management [Old French *estable,* from Latin *stabulum,* from *stare* "to stand"] — **sta•ble•man** \-mən, -,man\ *n*

^{2}**stable** *vb* **sta•bled**; **sta•bling** \-bə-ling, -bling\ : to put, keep, or live in or as if in a stable

^{3}**stable** *adj* **sta•bler** \-bə-lər, -blər\; **sta•blest** \-bə-ləst, -bləst\ **1 a** : firmly established : FIXED ⟨a *stable* community⟩ **b** : not changing or fluctuating ⟨a *stable* income⟩ **c** : LASTING, PERMANENT ⟨*stable* institutions⟩ **2** : steady in purpose : CONSTANT ⟨*stable* personalities⟩ **3 a** : designed so as to develop forces that restore the original condition when disturbed from a condition of equilibrium or steady motion ⟨a *stable* airplane⟩ **b** : able to resist alteration in chemical, physical, or biological properties ⟨a *stable* compound⟩⟨*stable* emulsions⟩ [Old French *estable,* from Latin *stabilis,* from *stare* "to stand"] — **sta•bly** \-bə-lē, -blē\ *adv*

sta•ble•ness \'stā-bəl-nəs\ *n* : STABILITY

sta•bler \-bə-lər, -blər\ *n* : one that keeps a stable

sta•bling *n* : accommodation for animals in a building ⟨*stabling* for six horses⟩

stac•ca•to \stə-'kät-ō\ *adj* **1 a** : cut short or apart in performing : DISCONNECTED ⟨*staccato* notes⟩ **b** : marked by short clear-cut playing or singing of tones or chords ⟨a *staccato* style⟩ **2** : ABRUPT, DISJOINTED ⟨the *staccato* noises of a skipping motor⟩ [Italian, from *staccare* "to detach", derived from Old French *destachier*] — **staccato** *adv* — **staccato** *n*

^{1}**stack** \'stak\ *n* **1** : a large usually conical pile (as of hay, straw, or grain) **2** : an orderly pile of objects usually one on top of the other ⟨a *stack* of dishes⟩ **3** : a vertical pipe (as for carrying off smoke or vapor) **4 a** : a rack with shelves for storing books **b** *pl* : the part of a library in which books are stored in racks **5** : three or more rifles arranged together to stand in the form of a pyramid [Old Norse *stakkr*]

^{2}**stack** *vb* : to arrange in or form a stack : PILE ⟨*stacked* the dishes on the table⟩ — **stack•er** *n*

stack up *vi* : to measure : COMPARE

sta•dia \'stād-ē-ə\ *n* : a surveying method for determination of distances and differences of elevation that uses a telescopic instrument having two horizontal lines through which the marks on a graduated rod are observed; *also* : the instrument or the rod used in this method [Italian, probably from Latin, pl. of *stadium*]

sta•di•um \'stād-ē-əm\ *n, pl* **-dia** \-ē-ə\ *or* **-di•ums 1** : an ancient Greek or Roman unit of length ranging from about 185 to 225 meters **2 a** : a course for footraces in ancient Greece with tiers of seats for spectators **b** *pl usu stadiums* : a large usually unroofed building with tiers of seats for spectators at modern sports events [Latin, from Greek *stadion*]

^{1}**staff** \'staf\ *n, pl* **staffs** \'stafs, 'stavz\ *or* **staves** \'stavz, 'stāvz\ **1 a** : a pole, stick, rod, or bar used as a support or as a sign of authority ⟨a flag hanging limp on its *staff*⟩ **b** : the long handle of a weapon (as a lance or pike) **c** : CLUB 1a, CUDGEL **2** : something that props or sustains ⟨bread is the *staff* of life⟩ **3** : the five horizontal lines with their spaces on which music is written **4** *pl staffs* **a** : a group of persons serving as assistants to or employees under a chief ⟨a hospital *staff*⟩ **b** : a group of officers or aides appointed to assist a civil executive or commanding officer **c :** military officers not eligible for operational command but having administrative duties [Old English *stæf*] — **staff** *adj*

1staff 3 with clef

2staff *vt* **:** to supply with a staff (as of workers)
staff•er \'staf-ər\ *n* **:** a member of a staff
staff sergeant *n* **:** an enlisted rank in the Army above sergeant and below sergeant first class, in the Marine Corps above sergeant and below gunnery sergeant, and in the Air Force above sergeant and below technical sergeant
staff sergeant major *n* **:** an enlisted rank in the Army above master sergeant
1stag \'stag\ *n, pl* **stag** *or* **stags 1 :** an adult male red deer; *also* **:** the male of various other large deer **2 :** a male animal castrated after maturity **3 a :** a social gathering of men only **b :** a man who attends a dance or party unaccompanied by a woman [Old English *stagga*]
2stag *adj* **1 :** intended or suitable for men only ⟨a *stag* party⟩ **2 :** unaccompanied by someone of the opposite sex — **stag** *adv*
stag beetle *n* **:** any of numerous mostly large beetles whose males have long and often branched mandibles
1stage \'stāj\ *n* **1 :** one of the horizontal levels into which a structure is divisible: as **a :** a floor of a building **b :** a shelf or layer especially as one of a series **c :** any of the levels attained by a river above an arbitrary zero point ⟨flood *stage*⟩ **2 :** a raised platform (as a scaffold or landing stage): as **a :** a part of a theater including the acting area **b :** the small platform on which an object is placed for microscopic examination **3 a :** a center of attention **:** scene of action **b :** the theatrical profession or art **4 :** a division or a dividing point: as **a :** a stopping place especially for a stagecoach providing fresh horses and refreshments **b :** the distance between stopping places in a journey **c :** a degree of advance attained (as in a process or undertaking) ⟨an early *stage* of a disease⟩ **d :** one of the distinguishable periods of the growth and development of a plant or animal ⟨the larval *stage* of a beetle⟩; *also* **:** an individual in such a stage **e :** one complete process or step in a sequential or recurrent activity **5 :** STAGECOACH **6 :** a propulsion unit in a rocket with its own fuel and containers [Old French *estage,* derived from Latin *stare* "to stand"] — **on the stage :** in or into the acting profession
2stage *vt* **:** to produce or show publicly on or as if on the stage
stage•coach \'stāj-,kōch\ *n* **:** a horse-drawn passenger and mail coach running on a regular schedule
stage•craft \-,kraft\ *n* **:** the effective management of theatrical devices or techniques
stage direction *n* **:** a description or direction written or printed in a play
stage fright *n* **:** nervousness felt at appearing before an audience
stage•hand \'stāj-,hand\ *n* **:** a stage worker who handles scenery, properties, or lights
stage manager *n* **:** a person who is in charge of the stage and physical aspects of a theatrical production
stag•er \'stā-jər\ *n* **:** an experienced person ⟨an old *stager*⟩
stage•struck \'stāj-,strək\ *adj* **:** fascinated by the stage; *esp* **:** having a strong desire to become an actor
stage whisper *n* **:** a loud whisper by an actor audible to the spectators but supposed not be to heard by persons on the stage
1stag•ger \'stag-ər\ *vb* **stag•gered; stag•ger•ing** \'stag-ring, -ə-ring\ **1 a :** to move unsteadily from side to side as if about to fall **:** REEL **b :** to cause to reel or totter **2 a :** to begin to doubt and waver **:** become less confident **b :** to cause to doubt, waver, or hesitate **3 :** to place or arrange in a zigzag or alternate but regular way [Old Norse *stakra,* from *staka* "to push"] — **stag•ger•er** \'stag-ər-ər\ *n*
2stagger *n* **1** *pl* **:** an abnormal condition of domestic mammals and birds associated with damage to the central nervous system and marked by incoordination and a reeling unsteady gait **2 :** a reeling or unsteady gait or stance
stag•ger•ing *adj* **:** serving to stagger **:** ASTONISHING, OVERWHELMING — **stag•ger•ing•ly** \'stag-ring-lē, -ə-ring-\ *adv*
stag•ing \'stā-jing\ *n* **1 :** SCAFFOLDING **2 :** the putting of a play on the stage **3 :** the assembling of troops or supplies in a particular place
stag•nant \'stag-nənt\ *adj* **1 a :** not flowing in a current or stream **b :** STALE ⟨*stagnant* air⟩ **2 :** DULL, INACTIVE ⟨*stagnant* business⟩ — **stag•nan•cy** \-nən-sē\ *n* — **stag•nant•ly** *adv*
stag•nate \'stag-,nāt\ *vi* **:** to be or become stagnant [Latin *stagnare,* from *stagnum* "body of standing water"] — **stag•na•tion** \stag-'nā-shən\ *n*
stagy \'stā-jē\ *adj* **stag•i•er; -est :** of or resembling the stage; *esp* **:** theatrical or artificial in manner — **stag•i•ly** \-jə-lē\ *adv* — **stag•i•ness** \-jē-nəs\ *n*
1staid \'stād\ *adj* **:** marked by sedateness and often prim self-restraint **:** SOBER, GRAVE [from past participle of *3stay*] — **staid•ly** *adv* — **staid•ness** *n*
2staid *past of* STAY
1stain \'stān\ *vb* **1 :** to soil or discolor especially in spots **2 :** to give color to (as by dyeing) **3 :** to taint with guilt, vice, or corruption [partly from Middle French *desteindre* "to discolor", from *des-* "dis-" + *teindre* "to dye", from Latin *tingere;* partly of Scandinavian origin] — **stain•abil•i•ty** \,stā-nə-'bil-ət-ē\ *n* — **stain•able** \'stā-nə-bəl\ *adj* — **stain•er** *n*
2stain *n* **1 :** a soiled or discolored spot **2 :** a taint of guilt **:** STIGMA **3 :** a preparation (as of dye or pigment) used in staining; *esp* **:** one capable of penetrating the pores of wood — **stain•less** \'stān-ləs\ *adj* — **stain•less•ly** *adv*
stained glass *n* **:** glass colored or stained (as for windows)
stainless steel *n* **:** steel alloyed with chromium and highly resistant to stain, rust, and corrosion
stair \'staər, 'steər\ *n* **1 :** a series of steps or flights of steps for passing from one level to another — often used in pl. ⟨ran down the *stairs*⟩ **2 :** one step of a stairway [Old English *stǣger*]
stair•case \-,kās\ *n* **:** a flight of stairs with the supporting framework, casing, and balusters
stair•way \-,wā\ *n* **:** one or more flights of stairs usually with landings to pass from one level to another
stair•well \-,wel\ *n* **:** a vertical shaft in which stairs are located
1stake \'stāk\ *n* **1 :** a pointed piece (as of wood) driven or to be driven into the ground especially as a marker or support; *also* **:** a similar upright support (as for the load of a vehicle) **2 a :** a post to which a person is bound for execution by burning **b :** execution by burning at a stake **3 a :** something that is staked for gain or loss **b :** the prize in a contest **c :** an interest or share in a commercial venture **4 :** a Mormon territorial unit comprising a number of wards **5 :** GRUBSTAKE [Old English *staca*] — **at stake :** at issue **:** in jeopardy
2stake *vt* **1 a :** to mark the limits of by stakes ⟨*stake* out a mining claim⟩ **b :** to tether to a stake **c :** to fasten up or support (as plants) with stakes **2 a :** BET 1, HAZARD **b :** to back financially; *esp* **:** GRUBSTAKE
sta•lac•tite \stə-'lak-,tīt\ *n* **:** a deposit of calcium carbonate resembling an icicle hanging from the roof or sides of a cavern [Greek *stalaktos* "dripping" from *stalassein* "to let drip"] — **stal•ac•tit•ic** \,stal-,ak-'tit-ik\ *adj*
sta•lag•mite \stə-'lag-,mīt\ *n* **:** a deposit like an inverted stalactite found on the floor of a cave [Greek *stalagma* "drop" or *stalagmos* "dripping"] — **stal•ag•mit•ic** \,stal-,ag-'mit-ik\ *adj*
1stale \'stāl\ *adj* **1 :** tasteless, unpleasant, or unwholesome from age ⟨*stale* food⟩ **2 :** tedious from familiarity ⟨*stale* news⟩ **3 :** WEAK, INEFFECTIVE ⟨felt *stale* and listless after a long illness⟩ [Middle English, "aged" (of ale)] — **stale•ly** \'stāl-lē\ *adv* — **stale•ness** *n*
2stale *vb* **:** to make or become stale

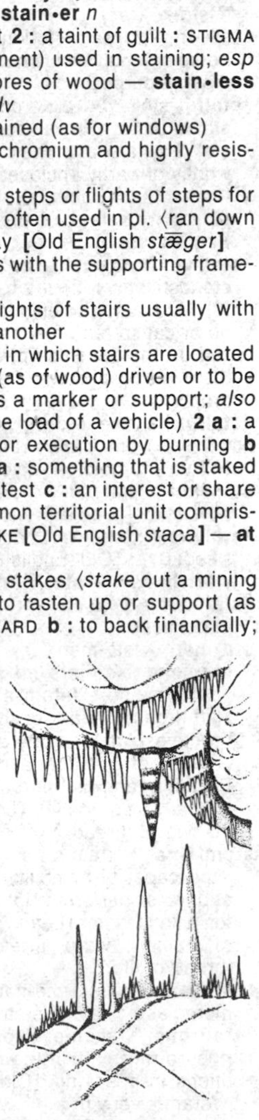
stalactite and stalagmite

\ə\ **abut**	\au̇\ **out**	\i\ **tip**	\ȯ\ **saw**	\u̇\ **foot**
\ər\ **further**	\ch\ **chin**	\ī\ **life**	\ȯi\ **coin**	\y\ **yet**
\a\ **mat**	\e\ **pet**	\j\ **job**	\th\ **thin**	\yü\ **few**
\ā\ **take**	\ē\ **easy**	\ng\ **sing**	\t͟h\ **this**	\yu̇\ **cure**
\ä\ **cot, cart**	\g\ **go**	\ō\ **bone**	\ü\ **food**	\zh\ **vision**

[1]stale·mate \'stäl-,māt\ *n* **1 :** a drawing position in chess in which only the king can move and although not in check can move only into check **2 :** a drawn contest : DEADLOCK [obsolete *stale* "stalemate" (derived from Old French *estal* "position, stall") + *mate*]

[2]stalemate *vt* **:** to bring into a stalemate

Sta·lin·ism \'stäl-ə-,niz-əm, 'stal-\ *n* **:** the theory and practice of communism developed by Stalin from Marxism-Leninism and characterized especially by rigid authoritarianism, widespread use of terror, and often by Russian nationalism — **Sta·lin·ist** \-nəst\ *n or adj*

[1]stalk \'stȯk\ *vb* **1 :** to hunt stealthily ⟨a *stalking* cat⟩ ⟨*stalk* a deer⟩; *also* **:** to go through (an area) in stalking prey **2 :** to walk with haughty or pompous bearing **3 :** to move through or follow usually in a persistent or furtive way ⟨famine *stalked* the land⟩⟨*stalk* a criminal⟩[Old English *bestealcian*] — **stalk·er** *n*

[2]stalk *n* **1 :** the act of stalking **2 :** a stalking gait

[3]stalk *n* **1 :** a plant stem; *esp* **:** the main stem of an herbaceous plant **2 :** a slender supporting or connecting structure **:** PEDUNCLE ⟨the *stalk* of a crinoid⟩[Middle English *stalke*] — **stalked** \'stȯkt\ *adj* — **stalk·less** \'stȯk-ləs\ *adj* — **stalky** \'stȯ-kē\ *adj*

stalk·ing–horse \'stȯ-king-,hȯrs\ *n* **1 :** a horse or a figure like a horse behind which a hunter stalks game **2 :** something used to mask a purpose

[1]stall \'stȯl\ *n* **1 a :** a compartment for a domestic animal in a stable or barn **b :** a space set off (as for parking a motor vehicle) **2 a :** a seat in the chancel of a church with back and sides wholly or partly enclosed **b** *British* **:** a front orchestra seat in a theater **3 :** a booth, stand, or counter at which articles are displayed for sale **4 :** a protective sheath for a finger or toe [Old English *steall*]

[2]stall *vb* **1 :** to put into or keep in a stall **2 :** to bring or come to a standstill: as **a :** MIRE **b** (1) **:** to stop running ⟨the car *stalled*⟩ (2) **:** to cause (an engine) to stop usually unintentionally **c :** to go or cause (as an airplane) to go into a stall

[3]stall *n* **:** the condition of an airfoil or airplane operating so that there is a breakdown of airflow and loss of lift with a tendency to drop

[4]stall *n* **:** a ruse to deceive or delay [English dialect *stale* "lure, decoy", from Anglo-French *estale*]

[5]stall *vb* **:** to hold off, divert, or delay by evasion or deception

stal·lion \'stal-yən\ *n* **:** a male horse; *esp* **:** one kept primarily as a stud [Middle French *estalon*, of Germanic origin]

[1]stal·wart \'stȯl-wərt\ *adj* **1 :** STURDY 1a, STOUT **2 :** VALIANT 1, RESOLUTE [Old English *stǣlwierthe* "serviceable"] — **stal·wart·ly** *adv* — **stal·wart·ness** *n*

[2]stalwart *n* **1 :** a stalwart person **2 :** an unwavering partisan (as in politics)

sta·men \'stā-mən\ *n, pl* **stamens** *also* **sta·mi·na** \'stā-mə-nə, 'stam-ə-\ **:** an organ of a flower that produces male gametes, consists of an anther and a filament, and is morphologically a sporophyll [Latin, "warp, thread"]

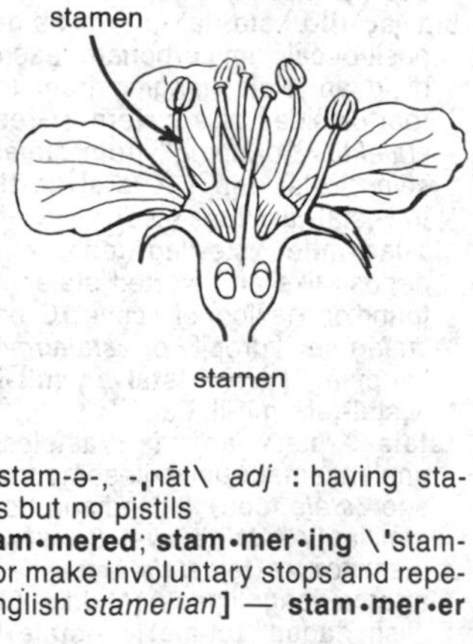

stamen

stam·i·na \'stam-ə-nə\ *n* **:** the capacity or ability to endure or perform a lot or for a long time [Latin, pl. of *stamen* "warp, thread, thread of life"]

sta·mi·nate \'stā-mə-nət, 'stam-ə-, -,nāt\ *adj* **:** having stamens; *esp* **:** having stamens but no pistils

[1]stam·mer \'stam-ər\ *vb* **stam·mered; stam·mer·ing** \'stam-ring, -ə-ring\ **:** to utter with or make involuntary stops and repetitions in speaking [Old English *stamerian*] — **stam·mer·er** \'stam-ər-ər\ *n*

• **syn** STAMMER, STUTTER mean to speak haltingly or stumblingly. STAMMER often suggests a temporary inhibition through fear, embarrassment, or shock ⟨breathlessly *stammered* out thanks⟩ STUTTER suggests an habitual defect of speech although it may imply merely the effect of haste or excitement.

[2]stammer *n* **:** an act or instance of stammering

[1]stamp \'stamp; *1b & 2 are also* 'stämp *or* 'stȯmp\ *vb* **1 a :** to pound or crush with a heavy instrument **b :** to strike or beat forcibly with the bottom of the foot **c :** to bring down forcibly or noisily ⟨*stamp* one's feet⟩ **d :** to extinguish or destroy by or as if by stamping with the foot ⟨*stamp* out racism⟩ **2 :** to walk heavily or noisily **3 a :** IMPRESS, IMPRINT ⟨*stamp* the bill "paid"⟩ **b :** to attach a stamp to ⟨*stamp* a letter⟩ **4 :** to form with a stamp or die **5 :** CHARACTERIZE 1 [Middle English *stampen*] — **stamp·er** *n*

[2]stamp \'stamp\ *n* **1 :** a device or instrument for stamping **2 :** the impression or mark made by stamping **3 :** a distinctive character, indication, or mark **4 :** the act of stamping **5 :** a stamped or printed paper affixed in evidence that a tax has been paid; *also* **:** POSTAGE STAMP

[1]stam·pede \stam-'pēd\ *n* **1 :** a wild headlong rush or flight of frightened animals **2 :** a mass movement of people at a common impulse [American Spanish *estampida*, from Spanish, "crash", from *estampar* "to stamp", of Germanic origin]

[2]stampede *vb* **1 :** to run away or cause (as cattle) to run away in panic **2 :** to act together or cause to act together suddenly and without thought (as in panic)

stamp·ing ground \'stamp-, 'stämp-, 'stȯmp-\ *n* **:** a favorite or habitual resort

stance \'stans\ *n* **1 :** way of standing or being placed **:** POSTURE **2 :** intellectual or emotional attitude ⟨an antiwar *stance*⟩ [Middle French *estance* "position, posture, stay", derived from Latin *stare* "to stand"]

[1]stanch *also* **staunch** \'stȯnch, 'stänch\ *vt* **:** to stop the flowing of; *also* **:** to stop the flow of blood from (a wound) [Middle French *estancher*, derived from Latin *stare* "to stand"] — **stanch·er** *n*

[2]stanch *variant of* STAUNCH

[1]stan·chion \'stan-chən\ *n* **1 :** an upright bar, post, or support **2 :** a device that fits loosely around an animal's neck and limits forward and backward motion (as in a stall) [Middle French *estanchon*, from *estance* "stance, stay, prop"]

[2]stanchion *vt* **:** to provide with stanchions **:** support or secure with or as if with a stanchion

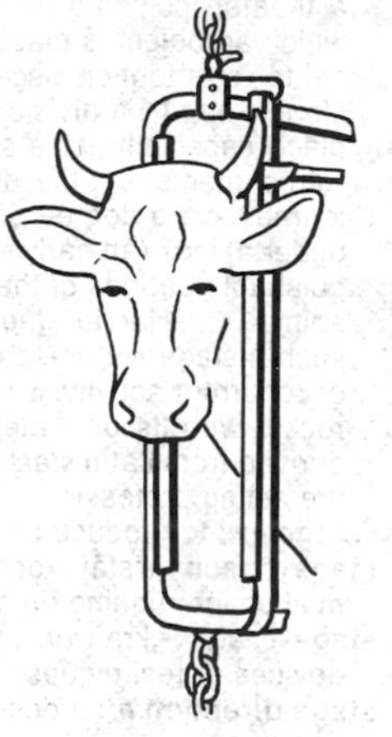
[1]stanchion 2

[1]stand \'stand\ *vb* **stood** \'stu̇d\; **stand·ing 1 a :** to support oneself on the feet in an erect position **b :** to be a specified height when fully erect ⟨*stands* two meters tall⟩ **c** to rise to one's feet **2 a :** to take up or maintain a specified position or posture ⟨*stand* aside⟩ ⟨*stands* first in the class⟩ ⟨where do we *stand* on this question⟩ **b :** to maintain one's position ⟨*stand* fast⟩ **3 :** to be in a particular state or situation ⟨*stands* accused⟩ **4 :** to hold a course at sea ⟨*standing* away from the shore⟩ **5** *chiefly British* **:** to be a candidate **:** RUN **6 a :** to rest, remain, or set upright on a base or lower end ⟨the clock *stood* on the mantle⟩ **b :** to occupy a place or location ⟨a house *standing* on a knoll⟩ **7 a :** to remain stationary or inactive ⟨the car *stood* in the garage⟩ ⟨rainwater *standing* in pools⟩ **b :** to remain in effect ⟨the order *stands*⟩ **8 :** to exist in a definite form ⟨you must take or leave the offer as it *stands*⟩ **9 a :** to endure or undergo successfully **:** BEAR, WITHSTAND ⟨*stand* pain⟩ ⟨able to *stand* an operation⟩ **b :** to submit to ⟨*stand* trial⟩ **10 :** to perform the duty of ⟨*stand* guard⟩ **11 :** to pay for ⟨*stand* drinks⟩ [Old English *standan*] — **stand·er** *n* — **stand by :** to be or remain loyal to ⟨*stood by* us in our hour of need⟩ — **stand for 1 :** to be a symbol for **:** REPRESENT **2 :** to put up with **:** PERMIT — **stand on 1 :** to depend upon **2 :** to insist on — **stand one's ground :** to maintain one's position — **stand pat :** to oppose or resist change

[2]stand *n* **1 :** an act or instance of stopping or staying in one place: as **a :** a halt for defense or resistance ⟨a goal-line *stand*⟩ **b :** a stop made to give a theatrical performance **2 a :** a place or post where one stands **b :** a position with respect to an issue **3 a :** the place occupied by a witness testifying in court **b :** a tier of seats for spectators of an outdoor sport or spectacle **c :** a raised platform (as for a speaker) **4 :** a small often open-air structure for a small retail business **5 :** a support (as a rack or table) on or in which something may be placed ⟨umbrella

STANDARD TIME IN 50 PLACES THROUGHOUT THE WORLD WHEN IT IS
12:00 NOON IN NEW YORK

CITY	TIME	CITY	TIME
[1]Amsterdam, Netherlands	6:00 P.M.	Montreal, Quebec	12:00 NOON
Anchorage, Alaska	7:00 A.M.	[1]Moscow, U.S.S.R.	8:00 P.M.
Bangkok, Thailand	12:00 MIDNIGHT	Ottawa, Ontario	12:00 NOON
Berlin, Germany	6:00 P.M.	[1]Paris, France	6:00 P.M.
Bombay, India	10:30 P.M.	Peking, China	1:00 A.M. next day
[1]Brussels, Belgium	6:00 P.M.	Perth, Australia	1:00 A.M. next day
[2]Buenos Aires, Argentina	2:00 P.M.	Rio de Janeiro, Brazil	2:00 P.M.
Calcutta, India	10:30 P.M.	Rome, Italy	6:00 P.M.
Cape Town, South Africa	7:00 P.M.	Saint John's, Newfoundland	1:30 P.M.
Chicago, Illinois	11:00 A.M.	Salt Lake City, Utah	10:00 A.M.
Delhi, India	10:30 P.M.	San Francisco, California	9:00 A.M.
Denver, Colorado	10:00 A.M.	San Juan, Puerto Rico	1:00 P.M.
Djakarta, Indonesia	12:00 MIDNIGHT	Santiago, Chile	1:00 P.M.
Halifax, Nova Scotia	1:00 P.M.	Shanghai, China	1:00 A.M. next day
Hong Kong	1:00 A.M. next day	Singapore	12:30 A.M. next day
Honolulu, Hawaii	7:00 A.M.	Stockholm, Sweden	6:00 P.M.
Istanbul, Turkey	7:00 P.M.	Sydney, Australia	3:00 A.M. next day
Juneau, Alaska	9:00 A.M.	Tehran, Iran	8:30 P.M.
Karachi, Pakistan	10:00 P.M.	Tokyo, Japan	2:00 A.M. next day
London, England	5:00 P.M.	Toronto, Ontario	12:00 NOON
Los Angeles, California	9:00 A.M.	Vancouver, British Columbia	9:00 A.M.
[1]Madrid, Spain	6:00 P.M.	[1]Vladivostok, U.S.S.R	3:00 A.M. next day
Manila, Philippines	1:00 A.M. next day	Washington, D.C.	12:00 NOON
Mexico City, Mexico	11:00 A.M.	Wellington, New Zealand	5:00 A.M. next day
[2]Montevideo, Uruguay	2:00 P.M.	Winnipeg, Manitoba	11:00 A.M.

[1]Time in France, Spain, Netherlands, Belgium, and the U.S.S.R. is one hour in advance of the standard meridians.
[2]Time in Argentina and Uruguay is one hour in advance of the standard meridian.

stands⟩ **6 :** a group of plants growing in a continuous area ⟨a good *stand* of wheat⟩

[1]**stan•dard** \'stan-dərd\ *n* **1 a :** a figure adopted as an emblem by an organized body of people ⟨the eagle was the Roman legion's *standard*⟩ **b :** the personal flag of the ruler of a state **2 a :** something set up by authority or by general consent as a rule for measuring or as a model ⟨a *standard* of weight⟩ ⟨*standards* of good manners⟩ **b :** the basis of value in a monetary system **3 :** a structure that serves as a support ⟨a lamp *standard*⟩ **4 :** an enlarged upper petal of a flower; *esp* **:** one of the three inner usually erect and incurved petals of an iris **[**Middle French *estandard* "rallying point, standard", of Germanic origin**]**

• syn STANDARD, GAUGE, CRITERION denote a means of determining what a thing should be. STANDARD applies to any definite rule, principle, or measure established by authority or custom ⟨*standards* of education⟩ GAUGE applies to a means of testing a particular dimension (as thickness, depth, or diameter) or a particular quality or aspect ⟨viewed awards as a *gauge* of quality in books⟩ CRITERION may apply to anything used as a test of quality whether or not it is formulated as a rule or principle ⟨the sole *criterion* for passing⟩

[2]**standard** *adj* **1 a :** constituting or conforming to a standard established by law or custom ⟨*standard* weight⟩ **b :** being sound and usable but not of special or the highest quality ⟨*standard* beef⟩ **2 :** regularly and widely used ⟨*standard* practice in the trade⟩ **3 :** having recognized and permanent value ⟨a *standard* reference work⟩ **4 :** substantially uniform and well established by usage in the speech and writing of the educated and widely recognized as acceptable

stan•dard–bear•er \-,bar-ər, -,ber-\ *n* **1 :** one that bears a standard or banner **2 :** the leader of an organization or movement

stan•dard•bred \-,bred\ *n* **:** any of an American breed of light trotting and pacing horses bred for speed and noted for endurance

standard conditions *n pl* **:** a temperature of 0°C and a pressure of 760 millimeters of mercury employed especially in comparison of gas volumes

Standard English *n* **:** the English that with respect to spelling, grammar, pronunciation, and vocabulary is substantially uniform though not devoid of regional differences, that is well established by usage in the formal and informal speech and writing of the educated, and that is widely recognized as acceptable wherever English is spoken and understood

stan•dard•ize \'stan-dər-,dīz\ *vt* **:** to compare with or bring into conformity with a standard — **stan•dard•iza•tion** \,stan-dərd-ə-'zā-shən\ *n*

standard of living : the necessities, comforts, and luxuries that a person or group is accustomed to

standard time *n* **:** the time established by law or by general usage over a region or country — compare ALASKA TIME, ATLANTIC TIME, BERING TIME, CENTRAL TIME, EASTERN TIME, HAWAII TIME, MOUNTAIN TIME, PACIFIC TIME, YUKON TIME

stand•by \'stand-,bī, 'stan-\ *n, pl* **stand•bys :** one available or to be relied upon especially in emergencies

stand by \stand-'bī, 'stand-, stan-, 'stan-\ *vi* **1 :** to be present; *also* **:** to remain aloof **2 :** to be waiting in a state of readiness ⟨please *stand by*⟩

stand down *vi* **:** to leave the witness stand

stand•ee \stan-'dē\ *n* **:** one who occupies standing room

stand–in \'stan-,din\ *n* **1 :** someone employed to occupy a performer's place while lights and camera are readied **2 :** SUBSTITUTE

stand in \stan-'din, 'stan-\ *vi* **:** to act as a stand-in — **stand in with :** to be in a specially favored position with

[1]**stand•ing** \'stan-ding\ *adj* **1 :** upright on the feet or base **:** ERECT ⟨*standing* timber⟩ **2 a :** not flowing **:** STAGNANT **b :** remaining the same for an indeterminate period ⟨a *standing* offer⟩ **c :** continuing in existence or use indefinitely **:** PERMANENT ⟨a *standing* army⟩ ⟨*standing* committees⟩ **3 :** done from a standing position ⟨*standing* jump⟩

[2]**standing** *n* **1 :** the action or position of one that stands **2 :** DURATION ⟨a quarrel of long *standing*⟩; *esp* **:** length of service or experience especially as determining status ⟨postgraduate *standing*⟩ **3 :** position or comparative rank (as in society, a profession, or a competitive activity) ⟨had the highest *standing* on the test⟩; *also* **:** good reputation ⟨people of *standing* in the community⟩

standing room *n* **:** space for standing; *esp* **:** accommodation available for spectators or passengers after all seats are filled

standing wave *n* **:** a vibration of a body or physical system in which the amplitude varies from place to place, is constantly zero at fixed points, and has maxima at other points

stand•off \'stan-,dȯf\ *n* **1 :** a standing off; *esp* **:** ALOOFNESS **2 a :** a counterbalancing effect **b :** TIE 4b, DRAW

\ə\ **abut**	\au̇\ **out**	\i\ **tip**	\ȯ\ **saw**	\u̇\ **foot**
\ər\ **further**	\ch\ **chin**	\ī\ **life**	\ȯi\ **coin**	\y\ **yet**
\a\ **mat**	\e\ **pet**	\j\ **job**	\th\ **thin**	\yü\ **few**
\ā\ **take**	\ē\ **easy**	\ng\ **sing**	\t͟h\ **this**	\yu̇\ **cure**
\ä\ **cot, cart**	\g\ **go**	\ō\ **bone**	\ü\ **food**	\zh\ **vision**

stand off \stan-'dȯf, 'stan-\ *vb* **:** to keep or hold at a distance (as in social intercourse)
stand•off•ish \stan-'dȯ-fish\ *adj* **:** lacking cordiality
stand•out \'stan-ˌdau̇t\ *n* **:** one that is prominent or conspicuous especially because of excellence
stand out \stan-'dau̇t, 'stan-\ *vi* **1 a :** to appear as if in relief **:** PROJECT **b :** to be prominent or conspicuous **2 :** to be stubborn in resolution or resistance
stand•pat \'stand-ˌpat, 'stan-\ *adj* **:** stubbornly conservative — **stand•pat•ter** \-ˌpat-ər\ *n*
stand•pipe \'stand-ˌpīp, 'stan-\ *n* **:** a high vertical pipe or reservoir used to deliver water at uniform pressure
stand•point \-ˌpȯint\ *n* **:** a position from which objects or principles are viewed and according to which they are compared and judged
stand•still \-ˌstil\ *n* **:** a complete stop
stand up *vb* **1 :** to remain sound and intact **2 :** to fail to keep an appointment with — **stand up for :** DEFEND ⟨*stand up for* one's beliefs⟩ — **stand up to 1 :** to meet fairly and fully **2 :** to face boldly
stank *past of* STINK
stan•nic \'stan-ik\ *adj* **:** of, relating to, or containing tin especially with a valence of four [derived from Late Latin *stannum* "tin"]
stan•nous \'stan-əs\ *adj* **:** of, relating to, or containing tin especially when bivalent
stan•za \'stan-zə\ *n* **:** a division of a poem consisting of a series of lines arranged together in a usually recurring pattern of meter and rhyme [Italian, "stay, abode, room, stanza", derived from Latin *stare* "to stand"] — **stan•za•ic** \stan-'zā-ik\ *adj*
sta•pes \'stā-ˌpēz\ *n, pl* **stapes** *or* **sta•pe•des** \'stā-pə-ˌdēz\ **:** the innermost ossicle of the ear of a mammal — compare INCUS, MALLEUS [Medieval Latin, "stirrup"] — **sta•pe•di•al** \stā-'pēd-ē-əl, stə-\ *adj*
staph \'staf\ *n* **:** STAPHYLOCOCCUS
staph•y•lo•coc•cus \ˌstaf-ə-lō-'käk-əs\ *n, pl* **-coc•ci** \-'käk-ˌsī, -ˌī, -ˌsē, -ˌē\ **:** any of various nonmotile spherical bacteria that occur especially in irregular clusters and include parasites of skin and mucous membranes [derived from Greek *staphylē* "bunch of grapes" + *kokkos* "grain, seed"] — **staph•y•lo•coc•cal** \-'käk-əl\ *adj* — **staph•y•lo•coc•cic** \-'käk-sik, -ik\ *adj*
[1]**sta•ple** \'stā-pəl\ *n* **1 :** a U-shaped piece of metal usually with sharp points to be driven into a surface to hold something (as fence wire) in place **2 :** a U-shaped piece of thin wire to be driven through layers of thin material (as paper) and bent over at the ends to fasten them together [Old English *stapol* "post"]
[2]**staple** *vt* **sta•pled; sta•pling** \-pə-ling, -pling\ **:** to fasten with staples
[3]**staple** *n* **1 :** a town established formerly as a center for the sale or exportation of commodities in bulk **2 :** a place of supply **:** SOURCE **3 :** a chief commodity or product of a place **4 a :** something in widespread and constant use or demand **b :** the sustaining or principal element **:** SUBSTANCE **5 :** RAW MATERIAL **6 :** textile fiber (as wool or rayon) of relatively short length that when spun and twisted forms a yarn rather than a filament [Dutch *stapel* "emporium"]
[4]**staple** *adj* **1 :** used, needed, or enjoyed constantly usually by many individuals **2 :** produced regularly or in large quantities **3 :** PRINCIPAL, CHIEF ⟨our *staple* crop⟩
sta•pler \'stā-plər\ *n* **:** a device that staples
[1]**star** \'stär\ *n* **1 :** a natural luminous body visible in the sky especially at night **2 :** a self-luminous gaseous celestial body (as the sun) of great mass whose shape is usually spheroidal and whose size may be as small as the earth's or larger than the earth's orbit **3 a :** a planet or a configuration of the planets that is held in astrology to influence one's destiny or fortune — usually used in pl. **b :** FORTUNE 2, FAME **c** *obsolete* **:** DESTINY 2 **4 a :** a conventional figure with five or more points that represents or resembles a star; *esp* **:** ASTERISK **b :** an often star-shaped ornament or medal worn as a badge of honor, authority, or rank or as the insignia of an order **5 a :** the principal member of a theatrical or operatic company **b :** an outstandingly talented performer **c :** one who stands out among one's peers ⟨one of the brightest *stars* in the legal profession⟩ [Old English *steorra*] — **star•less** \-ləs\ *adj* — **star•like** \-ˌlīk\ *adj*
[2]**star** *vb* **starred; star•ring 1 :** to sprinkle or adorn with stars **2 a :** to mark with a star as being superior **b :** to mark with an asterisk **3 :** to present in the role of a star **4 :** to play the most prominent or important role ⟨will *star* in a new play⟩ **5 :** to perform outstandingly ⟨*starred* at shortstop⟩
[3]**star** *adj* **1 :** of, relating to, or being a star **2 :** being of outstanding excellence ⟨a *star* athlete⟩
[1]**star•board** \'stär-bərd\ *n* **:** the right side of a ship or airplane looking forward — compare [3]PORT [Old English *stēorbord,* from *stēor-* "steering oar" + *bord* "ship's side"]
[2]**starboard** *vt* **:** to turn or put (a helm or rudder) to the right
[3]**starboard** *adj* **:** of, relating to, or situated to starboard
[1]**starch** \'stärch\ *vt* **:** to stiffen with or as if with starch [Middle English *sterchen*]
[2]**starch** *n* **1 :** a white odorless tasteless granular or powdery complex carbohydrate $(C_6H_{10}O_5)_x$ that is the chief storage form of carbohydrate in plants, is an important foodstuff, and is used also in adhesives and sizes, in laundering, and in pharmacy and medicine **2 :** a stiff formal manner **:** FORMALITY **3 :** resolute vigor **:** ENERGY
Star Chamber *n* **:** a court existing in England from the 15th century until 1641 with wide civil and criminal jurisdiction and marked by secret often arbitrary and oppressive procedures
starchy \'stär-chē\ *adj* **starch•i•er; -est 1 :** containing, consisting of, or resembling starch **2 :** consisting of or marked by formality or stiffness — **starch•i•ness** *n*
star-crossed \'stär-ˌkrȯst\ *adj* **:** not favored by the stars **:** ILL-FATED
star•dom \'stärd-əm\ *n* **:** the status or position of a star ⟨rose to *stardom* in Hollywood⟩
star•dust \'stär-ˌdəst\ *n* **:** a feeling or impression of romance, magic, or ethereality
[1]**stare** \'staər, 'steər\ *vb* **1 :** to look fixedly often with wide-open eyes ⟨*stare* at a stranger⟩ **2 :** to show up conspicuously **3 :** to have an effect upon by looking fixedly [Old English *starian*] — **star•er** *n*
[2]**stare** *n* **:** the act or an instance of staring
stare down *vt* **:** to cause to waver or submit by or as if by staring ⟨*stare down* a dog⟩
star•fish \'stär-ˌfish\ *n* **:** any of a class (Asteroidea) of echinoderms having a body of usually five arms radially arranged about a central disk and feeding largely on mollusks (as oysters)

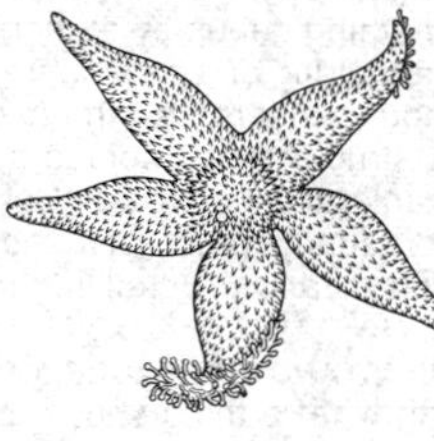
starfish

star•flow•er \-ˌflau̇-ər, -ˌflau̇r\ *n* **:** any of several plants (as a star-of-Bethlehem) having star-shaped 5-petaled flowers
star•gaze \-ˌgāz\ *vi* **1 :** to gaze at stars **2 :** to stare absentmindedly **:** DAYDREAM [back-formation from *stargazer*]
star•gaz•er \-ˌgā-zər\ *n* **:** one that gazes at the stars: as **a :** ASTROLOGER **b :** ASTRONOMER
[1]**stark** \'stärk\ *adj* **1 :** STRONG 1, ROBUST **2 a :** rigid in or as if in death **b :** INFLEXIBLE 3, STRICT ⟨*stark* discipline⟩ **3 :** SHEER, UTTER ⟨*stark* nonsense⟩ **4 a :** BARREN, DESOLATE ⟨a *stark* landscape⟩ **b (1) :** having few or no ornaments **:** BARE **(2) :** HARSH, UNADORNED ⟨*stark* realism⟩ **5 :** sharply delineated [Old English *stearc* "stiff, strong"] — **stark•ly** *adv* — **stark•ness** *n*
[2]**stark** *adv* **1 :** in a stark manner **2 :** WHOLLY 1 ⟨*stark* mad⟩
star•let \'stär-lət\ *n* **:** a young movie actress being coached and publicized for starring roles
star•light \-ˌlīt\ *n* **:** the light given by the stars
star•ling \'stär-ling\ *n* **:** any of a family of usually dark passerine birds that tend to flock together; *esp* **:** a dark brown or in summer glossy greenish black European bird naturalized and often a pest in the United States [Old English *stærlinc,* from *stær* "starling" + *-ling, -linc* "-ling"]
star•lit \'stär-ˌlit\ *adj* **:** lighted by the stars
star–of–Bethlehem *n* **:** any of a genus of plants of the lily family with 5-petaled usually greenish white flowers
star of Beth•le•hem \-'beth-li-ˌhem, -lē-həm, -lē-əm\ **:** a star held to have guided the three wise men to the infant Jesus in Bethlehem
Star of Da•vid \-'dā-vəd\ **:** a hexagram used as a symbol of Judaism
star•ry \'stär-ē\ *adj* **star•ri•er; -est 1 :** adorned with stars

⟨*starry* heavens⟩ **2 :** of, relating to, or consisting of the stars **:** STELLAR ⟨*starry* light⟩ **3 :** shining like stars **:** SPARKLING ⟨*starry* eyes⟩

star•ry–eyed \ˌstär-ē-ˈīd\ *adj* **:** regarding an object or a prospect in an overly favorable light

Stars and Bars *n sing or pl* **:** the first flag of the Confederate States of America having three bars of red, white, and red respectively and a blue union with white stars in a circle representing the seceded states

Stars and Stripes *n sing or pl* **:** the flag of the United States having 13 alternately red and white horizontal stripes and a blue union with one white star for each state

star–span•gled \ˈstär-ˌspang-gəld\ *adj* **:** studded with stars

Star–Spangled Banner *n* **:** STARS AND STRIPES

¹start \ˈstärt\ *vb* **1 :** to move suddenly and sharply **:** react with a quick involuntary movement **2 a :** to issue with sudden force ⟨blood *starting* from the wound⟩ **b :** to come into being, activity, or operation **:** BEGIN **3 :** BULGE ⟨eyes *starting* from their sockets⟩ **4 :** to become or cause to become loosened or forced out of place **5 a :** to begin a course or journey **b :** to range from a specified initial point ⟨the rates *start* at ten dollars⟩ **6 :** to be or cause to be a participant in a game or contest; *esp* **:** to be or cause to be in the lineup at the beginning of a game **7 :** to cause to leave a place of concealment **:** FLUSH **8** *archaic* **:** STARTLE 2, ALARM **9 :** to bring up for consideration or discussion **10 :** to bring into being ⟨*start* a rumor⟩ **11 :** to begin the use or employment of ⟨*start* a fresh loaf of bread⟩ **12 a :** to cause to move, act, or operate ⟨*start* the motor⟩ **b :** to care for during early stages ⟨*start* seedlings indoors⟩ **13 :** to perform the first stages or action of ⟨*started* studying music⟩ [Middle English *sterten*]

²start *n* **1 a :** a quick involuntary bodily reaction **b :** a brief and sudden action or movement **c :** a sudden impulse or outburst **2 :** a beginning of movement, activity, or development **3 :** a lead or advantage at the beginning of a race or competition **:** HEAD START **4 :** a place of beginning **5 :** the act or an instance of being a competitor in a race or a member of a lineup at the beginning of a game

start•er \ˈstärt-ər\ *n* **1 :** one that initiates or sets going: as **a :** an official who gives the signal to begin a race **b :** one who dispatches vehicles **2 a :** one that enters a competition or that regularly appears in a lineup at the beginning of games **b :** one that begins to engage in an activity or process **3 :** one that causes something to begin operating: as **a :** SELF-STARTER **b :** material containing microorganisms used to induce a desired fermentation **4 :** something that is the beginning of a process, activity, or series

¹star•tle \ˈstärt-l\ *vb* **star•tled; star•tling** \ˈstärt-ling, -l-ing\ **1 :** to move or jump suddenly as in surprise or alarm **2 :** to frighten suddenly and usually not seriously **3 :** to cause to start [Middle English *sterilen*, from *sterten* "to start"]

²startle *n* **:** a sudden mild shock (as of surprise or alarm)

star•tling *adj* **:** causing a momentary fright, surprise, or astonishment — **star•tling•ly** \ˈstärt-ling-lē, -l-ing-\ *adv*

star•va•tion \stär-ˈvā-shən\ *n* **:** the act or an instance of starving **:** the state of being starved

starve \ˈstärv\ *vb* **1 :** to die or suffer greatly from lack of food **2** *archaic* **a :** to die of or suffer greatly from cold **b :** to kill with cold **3 :** to suffer or perish or cause to suffer or perish from deprivation ⟨a child *starving* for affection⟩ **4 a :** to kill or subdue with hunger **b :** to deprive of nourishment **c :** to cause to submit as if by depriving of nourishment [Old English *steorfan* "to die"]

starve•ling \-ling\ *n* **:** one thin and weakened by or as if by lack of food

¹stash \ˈstash\ *vt* **:** to store in a usually secret place for future use [origin unknown]

²stash *n* **1 :** hiding place **:** CACHE **2 :** something stored or hidden away

sta•sis \ˈstā-səs, ˈstas-əs\ *n, pl* **sta•ses** \ˈstā-ˌsēz, ˈstas-ˌēz\ **1 :** a slowing or stoppage of a normal bodily flow (as of blood) or rhythmic movement (as of the intestine) **2 :** a state of static balance among opposing tendencies or forces **:** STAGNATION [Greek, "act or condition of standing, stopping", from *histasthai* "to stand"]

stat•able *or* **state•able** \ˈstāt-ə-bəl\ *adj* **:** capable of being stated

¹state \ˈstāt\ *n* **1 a :** mode or condition of being ⟨water in the gaseous *state*⟩ ⟨a *state* of readiness⟩ **b** (1) **:** condition of mind or temperament ⟨in a highly nervous *state*⟩ (2) **:** a condition of abnormal tension or excitement **2 a :** social positon; *esp* **:** high rank **b** (1) **:** elaborate or luxurious style of living (2) **:** formal dignity ⟨travel in *state*⟩ **3 a :** ESTATE 3 **b** *obsolete* **:** a person of high rank **:** NOBLE **4 a :** a politically organized body of people usually occupying a definite territory; *esp* **:** one that is sovereign **b :** the political organization of such a body of people **5 :** the operations or concerns of the government of a country **6 :** one of the units which make up a nation having a federal government ⟨the United *States* of America⟩ **7 :** the territory of a state [Latin *status*, from *stare* "to stand"] — **state•less** \-ləs\ *adj* — **state•less•ness** *n*

²state *adj* **1 :** suitable or used for ceremonial or formal occasions ⟨*state* robes⟩ **2 :** of or relating to a national state or to one of the units which make up a federal government ⟨a *state* church⟩ ⟨a *state* legislature⟩ **3 :** GOVERNMENTAL ⟨*state* secrets⟩

³state *vt* **1 :** to set by regulation or authority **2 :** to express the particulars of especially in words; *also* **:** to express in words ⟨*state* an opinion⟩

state bank *n* **:** a bank chartered by and operating under the laws of a state especially of the United States

state capitalism *n* **:** an economic system in which capital is largely under government ownership and control while other economic relations are little changed from capitalism

state college *n* **:** a college that is financially supported by a state government and often specializes in a branch of technical or professional education

state•craft \ˈstāt-ˌkraft\ *n* **:** the art of conducting state affairs **:** STATESMANSHIP

stat•ed \ˈstāt-əd\ *adj* **1 :** FIXED, REGULAR ⟨at *stated* times⟩ **2 :** set down definitely — **stat•ed•ly** *adv*

stated clerk *n* **:** an executive officer of a Presbyterian governing body (as a synod) ranking below the moderator

State flower *n* **:** a flowering plant selected as the floral emblem of a state of the United States

state•hood \ˈstāt-ˌhu̇d\ *n* **:** the condition of being a state; *esp* **:** the condition or status of one of the states of the United States

state•house \-ˌhau̇s\ *n* **:** the building in which a state legislature sits

state•ly \ˈstāt-lē\ *adj* **state•li•er; -est 1 a :** HAUGHTY, UNAPPROACHABLE **b :** marked by lofty or imposing dignity **2 :** impressive in size or proportions — **state•li•ness** *n* — **stately** *adv*

state•ment \ˈstāt-mənt\ *n* **1 :** the act or process of stating or presenting orally or on paper **2 :** something stated: as **a :** a report of facts or opinions **b :** a single declaration or remark **:** ASSERTION **3 :** PROPOSITION 2 **4 :** a brief summarized record of a financial account ⟨a monthly bank *statement*⟩

state•room \ˈstāt-ˌrüm, -ˌru̇m\ *n* **:** a private room on a boat or ship or on a railroad car

state's evidence *n, often cap S* **1 :** one who gives evidence for the prosecution in United States state or federal criminal proceedings **2 :** evidence for the prosecution in a criminal proceeding

States General *n pl* **:** the assembly of the three orders of clergy, nobility, and third estate in France before the Revolution

¹state•side \ˈstāt-ˌsīd\ *adj* **:** of or relating to the United States as regarded from outside its conterminous limits [(*United*) *States* + *side*]

²stateside *adv* **:** in or to the conterminous states of the United States

states•man \ˈstāt-smən\ *n* **:** a person engaged in fixing the policies and conducting the affairs of a government; *esp* **:** one having unusual wisdom in such matters — **states•man•like** \-ˌlīk\ *adj* — **states•man•ly** \-lē\ *adj* — **states•man•ship** \-ˌship\ *n*

state socialism *n* **:** an economic system with limited socialist characteristics introduced by usually gradual political action

states' rights *n pl* **:** all rights not vested by the Constitution of the United States in the federal government nor forbidden by it to the separate states

state•wide \ˈstāt-ˈwīd\ *adj* **:** including all parts of a state

1stat·ic \'stat-ik\ *adj* **1 :** exerting force by reason of weight alone without motion ⟨*static* load⟩ **2 :** of or relating to bodies at rest or forces in equilibrium **3 :** showing little change **4 a :** marked by a lack of movement, animation, or progress **b :** producing an effect of rest or interruption **5 :** standing or fixed in one place : STATIONARY **6 :** of, relating to, producing, or being stationary charges of electricity (as those produced by friction or induction) **7 :** of, relating to, or caused by radio static [Greek *statikos* "causing to stand", from *histanai* "to cause to stand, weigh"] — **stat·i·cal·ly** \'stat-i-kə-lē, -klē\ *adv*

2static *n* **:** disturbing effects produced in a radio or television receiver by atmospheric or electrical disturbances; *also* **:** the electrical disturbances producing these effects [*static electricity*]

stat·ics \'stat-iks\ *n* **:** a branch of mechanics dealing with the relations of forces that produce equilibrium among material bodies

1sta·tion \'stā-shən\ *n* **1 :** the place or position in which something or someone stands or is assigned to stand or remain **2 :** the act or manner of standing : POSTURE **3 :** a stopping place: as **a :** a regular stopping place in a transportation route **b :** a building at such a stopping place : DEPOT **4 a :** a post or sphere of duty or occupation **b :** a stock farm of Australia or New Zealand **5 :** social standing : RANK **6 :** a place for specialized observation and study of scientific phenomena ⟨a weather *station*⟩ **7 a :** a place established to provide a public service ⟨police *station*⟩ ⟨power *station*⟩ **b :** a branch post office **8 a :** a complete assemblage of radio or television equipment for transmitting or receiving **b :** the place in which such a station is located [Middle French, from Latin *statio,* from *stare* "to stand"]

2station *vt* **sta·tioned; sta·tion·ing** \'stā-shə-niŋ, -shniŋ\ **:** to assign or set in a station or position : POST

sta·tion·ary \'stā-shə-ˌner-ē\ *adj* **1 :** fixed in a station, course, or mode : IMMOBILE ⟨a *stationary* laundry tub⟩ **2 :** unchanging in condition : STABLE

station break *n* **:** a pause in a radio or television broadcast for announcement of the identify of the network or station

sta·tio·ner \'stā-shə-nər, -shnər\ *n* **1** *archaic* **a :** BOOKSELLER **b :** PUBLISHER **2 :** one that sells stationery [Medieval Latin *stationarius,* from *statio* "shop", from Latin, "station"]

sta·tio·nery \'stā-shə-ˌner-ē\ *n* **1 :** materials (as paper, pens, and ink) for writing or typing **2 :** letter paper usually with matching envelopes [*stationer*]

station house *n* **:** a police station

sta·tion·mas·ter \'stā-shən-ˌmas-tər\ *n* **:** an official in charge of the operation of a railroad station

stations of the cross *often cap S&C* **1 :** a series of usually 14 images or pictures especially in a church that represent the stages of Christ's passion **2 :** a devotion involving commemorative meditation before the stations of the cross

station wagon *n* **:** an automobile that has an interior longer than a sedan's, has one or more rear seats readily lifted out or folded to facilitate light trucking, has no separate luggage compartment, and often has a door at the rear end

stat·ism \'stāt-ˌiz-əm\ *n* **:** a concentration of economic controls and planning in the hands of a highly centralized government

sta·tis·tic \stə-'tis-tik\ *n* **:** a single term or datum in a collection of statistics [back-formation from *statistics*]

stat·is·ti·cian \ˌstat-ə-'stish-ən\ *n* **:** one versed in or engaged in compiling statistics

sta·tis·tics \stə-'tis-tiks\ *n sing or pl* **:** a branch of mathematics dealing with the collection, analysis, interpretation, and presentation of masses of numerical data; *also* **:** a collection of such numerical data [German *statistik* "study of political data", derived from Latin *status* "state"] — **sta·tis·ti·cal** \-'tis-ti-kəl\ *adj* — **sta·tis·ti·cal·ly** \-ti-kə-lē, -klē\ *adv*

stato- *combining form* **1 :** resting **2 :** equilibrium ⟨*stato*cyst⟩ [Greek *statos* "stationary", from *histasthai* "to stand"]

stat·o·cyst \'stat-ə-ˌsist\ *n* **:** an organ of equilibrium occurring especially in invertebrate animals and consisting usually of a fluid-filled vesicle in which are suspended calcium-containing particles

stat·o·lith \'stat-l-ˌith\ *n* **:** a calcium-containing body in a statocyst

sta·tor \'stāt-ər\ *n* **:** a stationary part in a machine in or about which a rotor revolves [Latin, "one that stands", from *stare* "to stand"]

stat·u·ary \'stach-ə-ˌwer-ē\ *n, pl* **-ar·ies 1 a :** the art of making statues **b :** a collection of statues **2 :** SCULPTOR — **statuary** *adj*

stat·ue \'stach-ü\ *n* **:** a likeness (as of a person or animal) sculptured, modeled, or cast in a solid substance [Middle French, from Latin *statua,* from *statuere* "to set up", from *status* "position, state"]

stat·u·esque \ˌstach-ə-'wesk\ *adj* **:** resembling a statue especially in well-proportioned or massive dignity — **stat·u·esque·ly** *adv* — **stat·u·esque·ness** *n*

stat·u·ette \ˌstach-ə-'wet\ *n* **:** a small statue

stat·ure \'stach-ər\ *n* **1 :** natural height (as of a person) in an upright position **2 :** quality or status gained by growth, development, or achievement ⟨reached adult *stature*⟩ [Old French, from Latin *statura,* from *stare* "to stand"]

sta·tus \'stāt-əs, 'stat-\ *n* **1 :** position or rank in relation to others : STANDING **2 :** CONDITION, SITUATION ⟨the economic *status* of a country⟩ [Latin, "position, state, status"]

sta·tus quo \ˌstāt-əs-'kwō, ˌstat-\ *n* **:** the existing state of affairs [Latin, "state in which"]

stat·ute \'stach-üt, -ət\ *n* **:** a law enacted by the legislative branch of a government [Old French *statut,* from Late Latin *statutum* "law, regulation", from Latin *statuere* "to set up", from *status* "position, state"] **syn** see LAW

statute mile *n* **:** MILE 1

statute of limitations : a statute assigning a certain time after which rights cannot be enforced by legal action

stat·u·to·ry \'stach-ə-ˌtōr-ē, -ˌtȯr-\ *adj* **1 :** of, relating to, or of the nature of a statute **2 :** enacted, created or regulated by statute

1staunch *variant of* STANCH

2staunch *or* **stanch** \'stȯnch, 'stänch\ *adj* **1 a :** WATERTIGHT, SOUND ⟨a *staunch* ship⟩ **b :** strongly built : SUBSTANTIAL ⟨*staunch* foundations⟩ **2 :** steadfast in loyalty or principle ⟨a *staunch* friend⟩ [Middle French *estanc,* from *estancher* "to stanch"] — **staunch·ly** *adv* — **staunch·ness** *n*

1stave \'stāv\ *n* **1 :** a wooden stick **2 :** one of the narrow strips of wood or narrow iron plates placed edge to edge to form the sides, covering, or lining of a vessel (as a barrel) or structure **3 :** STANZA **4 :** STAFF 3 [back-formation from *staves*]

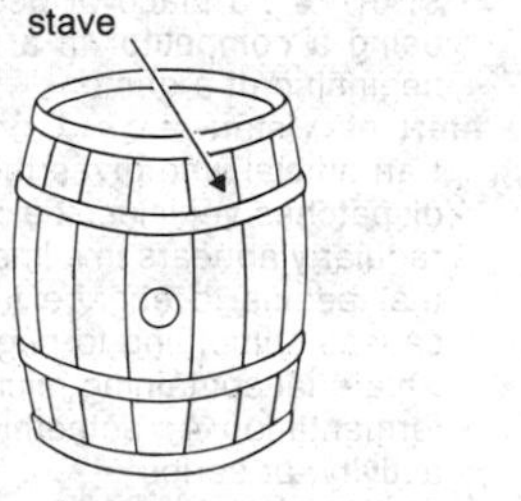

1stave 2

2stave *vb* **staved** *or* **stove** \'stōv\; **stav·ing 1 :** to break in the stave of (a cask) **2 :** to smash a hole in ⟨*stave* in a boat⟩; *also* **:** to crush or break inward ⟨*staved* in several ribs⟩ **3 :** to drive or thrust away **4 :** to become stove in — used of a boat or ship

stave off *vt* **:** to ward or fend off ⟨*stave off* trouble⟩

staves *pl of* STAFF

1stay \'stā\ *n* **:** a strong rope or wire used to steady or brace something (as a mast) [Old English *stæg*]

2stay *vb* **1 :** to fasten (as a smokestack) with stays **2 :** to go about : TACK

3stay *vb* **stayed** \'stād\ *or* **staid** \'stād\; **stay·ing 1 :** to stop going forward : PAUSE **2 :** to continue in a place or condition : REMAIN **3 :** to stand firm **4 :** to take up residence : LODGE **5 :** WAIT **1 6 :** to last out (as a race) **7 :** CHECK, HALT ⟨*stay* an execution⟩ **8 :** ALLAY ⟨*stayed* the unrest⟩ [Middle French *ester* "to stand, stay", from Latin *stare*]

• **syn** STAY, REMAIN, ABIDE, LINGER mean to continue in a place. STAY often implies the status of a guest or visitor; REMAIN suggests a continuing after others have gone; ABIDE may imply either continuing indefinitely in a residence or waiting patiently for an outcome; LINGER implies failing to depart when it is time to do so.

4stay *n* **1 :** the action of halting : the state of being stopped **2 :** a residence or visit in a place

5stay *n* **1 a :** something that serves as a prop : SUPPORT **b :** a thin firm strip (as of whalebone, steel, or plastic) used for stiffening a garment (as a corset) or part (as a shirt collar) **2 :** a corset stiffened with stays — usually used in pl. [Middle French *estaie,* of Germanic origin]

6stay *vt* **1 :** to provide physical or moral support for : SUSTAIN **2 :** to fix on something as a foundation : REST

stay–at–home \ˈstā-ət-ˌhōm\ *n* : one that seldom travels or wanders from home : HOMEBODY
staying power *n* : capacity for endurance
stay•sail \ˈstā-ˌsāl, -səl\ *n* : a fore-and-aft sail hoisted on a stay
stead \ˈsted\ *n* **1** : ADVANTAGE, SERVICE ⟨my knowledge of French stood me in good *stead*⟩ **2** : the office, place, or function ordinarily occupied or carried out by someone or something else ⟨acted in the mayor's *stead*⟩ [Old English *stede* "place, position"]
stead•fast \ˈsted-ˌfast\ *adj* **1 a** : firmly fixed in place **b** : not subject to change ⟨a *steadfast* purpose⟩ **2** : firm in belief, determination, or adherence : LOYAL ⟨*steadfast* friends⟩ [Old English *stedefæst*, from *stede* "place" + *fæst* "fixed, fast"] **syn** see FAITHFUL — **stead•fast•ly** *adv* — **stead•fast•ness** \-ˌfast-nəs, -ˌfas-\ *n*
stead•ing \ˈsted-ing\ *n* : a small farm or homestead [Middle English *steding*, from *stede* "place, farm"]
[1]**steady** \ˈsted-ē\ *adj* **stead•i•er**; **-est** **1 a** : firm in position : FIXED **b** : direct or sure in movement : UNFALTERING **2 a** : REGULAR, UNIFORM ⟨a *steady* pace⟩ **b** : not changing constantly or varying widely **3 a** : not easily moved or upset **b** : constant in feeling, principle, purpose, or attachment : DEPENDABLE **c** : not given to dissipation or disorderly behavior [obsolete *stead* "place, position", from Old English *stede*] — **stead•i•ly** \ˈsted-l-ē\ *adv* — **stead•iness** \ˈsted-ē-nəs\ *n*
• **syn** STEADY, EVEN, UNIFORM mean not varying throughout a course or extent. STEADY implies lack of fluctuation or interruption of movement; EVEN suggests an absence of variation in quality or character; UNIFORM stresses the sameness or alikeness of all the elements of an aggregate, a series, or a set.
[2]**steady** *vb* **stead•ied**; **steady•ing** : to make, keep, or become steady
[3]**steady** *adv* **1** : in a steady manner : STEADILY **2** : on the course set — used as a direction to the helmsman of a ship
[4]**steady** *n, pl* **stead•ies** : one that is steady; *esp* : a boyfriend or girl friend with whom one goes steady
steady state *n* : a dynamically balanced conditon of a system or process that when once established tends to persist
steady state theory *n* : a theory in astronomy: the universe has always existed and has always been expanding with hydrogen being created continuously — compare BIG BANG THEORY
steak \ˈstāk\ *n* **1 a** : a slice of meat cut from a fleshy part of a beef carcass **b** : a similar slice of a specified meat other than beef **2** : a cross-sectional slice of a large fish (as salmon) [Old Norse *steik*]
steak knife n : a table knife having a blade with a sharp often serrated edge
[1]**steal** \ˈstēl\ *vb* **stole** \ˈstōl\; **sto•len** \ˈstō-lən\; **steal•ing** **1** : to come or go secretly, quietly, gradually, or unexpectedly ⟨*stole* out of the room⟩ **2 a** : to take and carry away without right and with intent to keep the property of another **b** : to take entirely to oneself or beyond one's proper share ⟨*steal* the show⟩ **3 a** : to move, transfer, or introduce secretly : SMUGGLE **b** : to accomplish or get in a concealed or unobserved manner ⟨*steal* a nap⟩ **4 a** : to seize, gain, or win by trickery, skill, or daring **b** : to reach a base in baseball by running without the aid of a hit or an error [Old English *stelan*] — **steal•er** *n*
[2]**steal** *n* **1** : the act or an instance of stealing **2** : something offered or purchased at a low price : BARGAIN
stealth \ˈstelth\ *n* : sly or secret action [Middle English *stelthe*]
stealthy \ˈstel-thē\ *adj* **stealth•i•er**; **-est** **1** : slow and secret in action or character **2** : intended to escape observation ⟨*stealthy* glances⟩ — **stealth•i•ly** \-thə-lē\ *adv* — **stealth•i•ness** \-thē-nəs\ *n*
[1]**steam** \ˈstēm\ *n* **1 a** : the invisible vapor into which water is converted when heated to the boiling point **b** : the mist formed by the condensation on cooling of water vapor **2 a** : water vapor kept under pressure so as to supply energy for heating, cooking, or mechanical work; *also* : the power so generated **b** : driving force : POWER ⟨arrived under their own *steam*⟩ **c** : emotional tension ⟨needed to let off a little *steam* after exams⟩ **3 a** : STEAMER 2a **b** : travel by or a trip in a steamer [Old English *stēam*]
[2]**steam** *vb* **1** : to rise or pass off as vapor **2** : to give off steam or vapor **3** : to move or travel by or as if by the agency of steam **4** : to be angry : BOIL **5** : to expose to the action of steam (as for softening or cooking)
steam•boat \-ˌbōt\ *n* : a boat propelled by steam power
steam engine *n* : an engine driven by steam; *esp* : a reciprocating engine having a piston driven in a closed cylinder by steam
steam•er \ˈstē-mər\ *n* **1** : a vessel in which something is steamed **2 a** : a ship propelled by steam **b** : an engine, machine, or vehicle operated by steam
steamer rug *n* : a warm covering for the lap and feet especially of a person sitting on a ship's deck
steamer trunk *n* : a trunk suitable for use in a stateroom of a steamer
steam fitter *n* : one that installs or repairs equipment (as steam pipes) for heating, ventilating, or refrigerating systems — **steam fitting** *n*
steam heating *n* : a system of heating in which steam generated in a boiler is piped to radiators
steam iron *n* : a pressing iron with a compartment holding water that is converted to steam by the iron's heat and emitted through the bottom onto the fabric being pressed
[1]**steam•roll•er** \ˈstēm-ˈrō-lər\ *n* **1** : a machine formerly driven by steam that is equipped with heavy wide rollers for compacting roads and pavements **2** : a power or force that crushes opposition

[1]steamroller 1

[2]**steamroller** *also* **steam•roll** \-ˈrōl\ *vb* **1** : to crush with a steamroller **2 a** : to overcome by greatly superior force **b** : to exert crushing force or pressure with respect to **3** : to move or proceed with irresistible force
steam•ship \ˈstēm-ˌship\ *n* : STEAMER 2a
steam shovel *n* : a power shovel formerly operated by steam
steam table *n* : a table having openings to hold containers of cooked food over steam or hot water circulating beneath them
steam turbine *n* : a turbine that is driven by the pressure of steam discharged at high velocity against the turbine vanes
steamy \ˈstē-mē\ *adj* **steam•i•er**; **-est** : consisting of, characterized by, or full of steam — **steam•i•ly** \-mə-lē\ *adv* — **steam•i•ness** \-mē-nəs\ *n*
ste•ap•sin \stē-ˈap-sən\ *n* : a fat-digesting enzyme in pancreatic juice [Greek *stear* "fat" + English *-psin* (as in *pepsin*)]
stea•rate \ˈstē-ə-ˌrāt, ˈsti-ər-ˌāt, ˈstir-ˌāt\ *n* : a salt or ester of stearic acid
stea•ric acid \stē-ˌar-ik-, ˌstiər-ik-\ *n* : a white crystalline fatty acid obtained by saponifying tallow or other hard fats containing stearin [derived from Greek *stear* "fat, suet"]
stea•rin \ˈstē-ə-rən, ˈsti-ər-ən, ˈstir-ən\ *n* **1** : an ester of glycerol and stearic acid **2** *also* **stea•rine** *same or* -ˌrēn, -ˌēn\ : the solid portion of a fat
ste•atite \ˈstē-ə-ˌtīt\ *n* : a massive talc having a grayish green or brown color : SOAPSTONE [Latin *steatitis*, a precious stone, from Greek, from *steat-*, *stear* "fat"]
steed \ˈstēd\ *n* : HORSE; *esp* : a spirited horse [Old English *stēda* "stallion"]
[1]**steel** \ˈstēl\ *n* **1** : commercial iron that contains carbon in any amount up to about 1.7 percent as an essential alloying constituent and is distinguished from cast iron by its malleability and lower carbon content **2** : an instrument or implement of or characteristically of steel: as **a** : a thrusting or cutting weapon **b** : an instrument (as a fluted round rod with a handle) for sharpening knives **c** : a piece of steel for striking sparks from flint **3** : a hard cold quality suggestive of steel [Old English *stȳle*, *stēle*]
[2]**steel** *vt* **1** : to overlay, point, or edge with steel **2** : to make hard or unbending ⟨*steel* one's heart⟩
[3]**steel** *adj* **1** : made of or resembling steel **2** : of or relating to the production of steel
steel guitar *n* : HAWAIIAN GUITAR

\ə\ **a**but	\au̇\ **ou**t	\i\ t**i**p	\ȯ\ s**aw**	\u̇\ f**oo**t
\ər\ f**ur**ther	\ch\ **ch**in	\ī\ l**i**fe	\ȯi\ c**oi**n	\y\ **y**et
\a\ m**a**t	\e\ p**e**t	\j\ **j**ob	\th\ **th**in	\yü\ f**ew**
\ā\ t**a**ke	\ē\ **ea**sy	\ng\ si**ng**	\t͟h\ **th**is	\yu̇\ c**u**re
\ä\ c**o**t, c**a**rt	\g\ **g**o	\ō\ b**o**ne	\ü\ f**oo**d	\zh\ vi**si**on

steel•head \'stēl-ˌhed\ *n* : a large silvery western North American seagoing trout that ascends rivers to breed and is usually held to be a race of the rainbow trout

steel•ie *also* **steely** \'stē-lē\ *n, pl* **steelies** : a small steel ball used in playing marbles

steel wool *n* : an abrasive material composed of long fine steel shavings and used especially for scouring and burnishing

steel•work \'stēl-ˌwərk\ *n* **1** : work in steel **2** *pl* : an establishment where steel is made — **steel•work•er** \-ˌwər-kər\ *n*

steely \'stē-lē\ *adj* **steel•i•er**; **-est** **1** : made of steel **2** : resembling steel ⟨*steely* determination⟩ — **steel•i•ness** *n*

steel•yard \'stēl-ˌyärd\ *n* : a balance on which something to be weighed is hung from the shorter arm of a lever and is balanced by a weight that slides along the longer arm which is marked with a scale

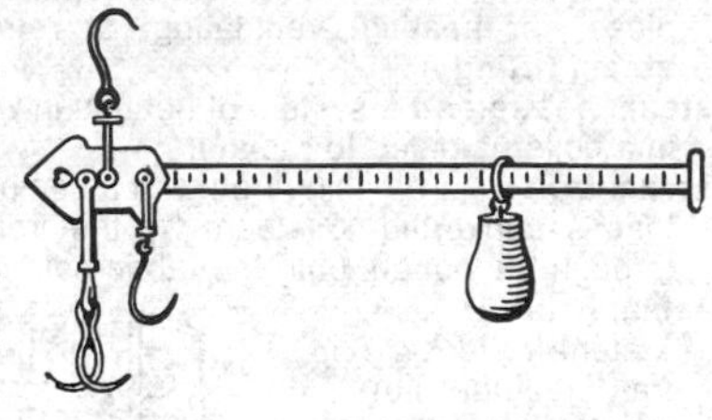

steelyard

[1]steep \'stēp\ *adj* **1** : making a large angle with the plane of the horizon : almost straight up and down **2** : being or characterized by a very rapid decline or increase ⟨a *steep* rise in costs⟩ **3** : difficult to accept, meet, or perform : STIFF ⟨*steep* prices⟩ [Old English *stēap* "high, deep"] — **steep•ly** *adv* — **steep•ness** *n*

• **syn** PRECIPITOUS, SHEER: STEEP implies such sharpness of pitch that ascent or descent is very difficult ⟨*steep* hills⟩ ⟨a *steep* roof⟩ PRECIPITOUS suggests an incline closely approaching the vertical ⟨*precipitous* canyon walls⟩ SHEER implies an unbroken perpendicular expanse ⟨a *sheer* cliff⟩

[2]steep *n* : a place with steep sides or slope

[3]steep *vb* **1 a** : to soak in a liquid (as for softening, bleaching, or extracting a flavor) at a temperature under the boiling point ⟨*steep* tea⟩ **b** : to undergo the process of soaking in a liquid **2** : BATHE, WET **3** : to saturate with or subject thoroughly to (some strong or pervading influence) ⟨*steeped* in learning⟩ [Middle English *stepen*] — **steep•er** *n*

steep•en \'stē-pən\ *vb* **steep•ened**; **steep•en•ing** \'stēp-ning, -ə-ning\ : to make or become steeper ⟨the trail *steepened*⟩

stee•ple \'stē-pəl\ *n* : a tall structure that tops a church tower and usually bears a small spire at the top; *also* : a church tower [Old English *stēpel* "tower"] — **stee•pled** \-pəld\ *adj*

stee•ple•chase \'stē-pəl-ˌchās\ *n* **1 a** : a cross-country race on horseback **b** : a race on a closed course over obstacles (as hedges, walls, and a water jump) **2** : a footrace of usually 3000 meters run over hurdles and a water jump [from the use of church steeples as landmarks to guide the riders] — **stee•ple•chas•er** \-ˌchā-sər\ *n*

stee•ple•jack \-ˌjak\ *n* : one whose work is building smokestacks, towers, or steeples or climbing up the outside of such structures to paint and make repairs

[1]steer \'stiər\ *n* : a domestic bull castrated before sexual maturity; *esp* : an ox being raised for beef [Old English *stēor* "young ox"]

[2]steer *vb* **1 a** : to direct the course or the course of ⟨*steer* by the stars⟩ ⟨*steer* a conversation⟩ **b** : to take or maintain a course ⟨*steer* for home⟩ **c** : to set and hold to (a course) ⟨*steer* a course for home⟩ **2** : to pursue a course of action **3** : to respond to steering ⟨a car that *steers* well⟩ [Old English *stīeran*] — **steer•able** \'stir-ə-bəl\ *adj* — **steer•er** \'stir-ər\ *n* — **steer clear** : to keep entirely away ⟨*steer* clear of arguments⟩

[3]steer *n* : a hint as to procedure : TIP ⟨gave us a bum *steer*⟩

steer•age \'stiər-ij\ *n* **1** : the act or practice of steering; *also* : DIRECTION 1 **2** : a section in a passenger ship for passengers paying the lowest fares [sense 2 from its originally being located near the rudder]

steer•age•way \-ˌwā\ *n* : sufficient forward motion of a boat or ship for it to be able to respond to steering

steering column *n* : the column that encloses the connections to the steering gear of a vehicle (as an automobile)

steering committee *n* : a managing or directing committee

steering gear *n* : a mechanism by which something is steered

steering wheel *n* : a hand-operated wheel by means of which one steers something

steers•man \'stiərz-mən\ *n* : one who steers : HELMSMAN

stego•saur \'steg-ə-ˌsȯr\ *n* : any of a suborder of dinosaurs with strongly developed dorsal bony armor [derived from New Latin *stegosaurus*]

stego•sau•rus \ˌsteg-ə-'sȯr-əs\ *n* : any of a genus of large armored dinosaurs of the Upper Jurassic rocks of Colorado and Wyoming [New Latin, from Greek *stegos* "roof" + *sauros* "lizard"]

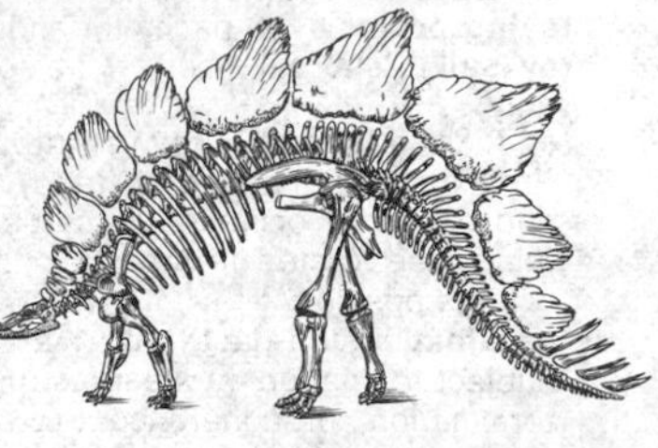

stegosaur

stein \'stīn\ *n* : an earthenware mug especially for beer often having a hinged top; *also* : the quantity of beer that a stein holds [probably from German *steingut* "stoneware", from *stein* "stone" + *gut* "goods"]

stele \'stēl, 'stē-lē\ *n* : the usually cylindrical central vascular portion of the axis of a vascular plant [Greek *stēlē* "pillar"] — **ste•lar** \'stē-lər\ *adj*

stel•lar \'stel-ər\ *adj* **1 a** : of or relating to the stars : ASTRAL ⟨*stellar* light⟩ **b** : composed of stars **2** : of or relating to a theatrical or film star **3** : OUTSTANDING 3 ⟨a *stellar* production⟩ ⟨a *stellar* performance⟩ [Late Latin *stellaris,* from Latin *stella* "star"]

[1]stem \'stem\ *n* **1 a** : the main axis of a plant that develops buds and shoots instead of roots **b** : a plant part (as a petiole or stipe) that supports another **2** : the bow of a ship **3** : a line of ancestry : STOCK; *esp* : a fundamental line from which others have arisen **4** : the part of an inflected word that remains unchanged throughout an inflection **5** : something felt to resemble a plant stem: as **a** : a main or heavy stroke of a letter **b** : the short perpendicular line extending from the head of a musical note **c** : the part of a tobacco pipe from the bowl outward **d** : the slender support of a piece of stemware (as a goblet) **e** : a shaft of a watch [Old English *stefn, stemn*] — **stem•less** \-ləs\ *adj* — **stemmed** \'stemd\ *adj* — **from stem to stern** : THROUGHOUT, THOROUGHLY

[2]stem *vt* **stemmed**; **stem•ming** **1** : to make headway against (as an adverse tide, current, or wind) **2** : to go counter to (something adverse) ⟨*stem* an angry crowd⟩

[3]stem *vb* **stemmed**; **stem•ming** **1** : to have or trace an origin or development : DERIVE ⟨illness that *stems* from an accident⟩ **2** : to remove the stem from — **stem•mer** *n*

[4]stem *vb* **stemmed**; **stem•ming** **1** : to stop, check, or restrain by or as if by damming; *also* : to become checked **2 a** : to push (a ski) out to the side in preparation for turning or to slow down **b** : to retard oneself by forcing the heels of both skis outward from the line of progress [Old Norse *stemma* "to dam up"]

[5]stem *n* : an act or instance of stemming on skis

stem•my \'stem-ē\ *adj* **stem•mi•er**; **-est** : abounding in stems ⟨*stemmy* hay⟩

stem•ware \'stem-ˌwaər, -ˌweər\ *n* : stemmed glass hollowware

stem–wind•ing \-'wīn-ding\ *adj* : wound by an inside mechanism turned by the knurled knob at the outside end of the stem ⟨a *stem-winding* watch⟩ — **stem–wind•er** \-dər\ *n*

stench \'stench\ *n* : an extremely disagreeable smell : STINK [Old English *stenc*]

[1]sten•cil \'sten-səl\ *n* **1** : impervious material (as paper or metal) perforated with lettering or a design through which a substance (as ink) is forced onto a surface to be printed **2** : a pattern, design, or print produced by means of a stencil **3** : a printing process that uses a stencil [Middle French *estanceler* "to ornament with sparkling colors", from *estancele* "spark", derived from Latin *scintilla*]

[2]stencil *vt* **-ciled** *or* **-cilled**; **-cil•ing** *or* **-cil•ling** \-sə-ling, -sling\ **1** : to produce by stencil **2** : to mark or paint with a stencil

stencil paper *n* : strong tissue paper impregnated or coated (as with paraffin) for stencils

steno \'sten-ō\ *n, pl* **sten•os** : STENOGRAPHER

ste•nog•ra•pher \stə-'näg-rə-fər\ *n* **1** : a writer of shorthand **2** : one employed chiefly to take and transcribe dictation

ste•nog•ra•phy \-fē\ *n* **1** : the art or process of writing in shorthand **2** : shorthand especially written from dictation or oral discourse **3** : the making of shorthand notes and subsequent transcription of them [Greek *stenos* "narrow"] — **sten•o•graph•ic** \ˌsten-ə-ˈgraf-ik\ *adj* — **sten•o•graph•i•cal•ly** \-ˈgraf-i-kə-lē, -klē\ *adv*

ste•no•sis \stə-ˈnō-səs\ *n, pl* **-no•ses** \-ˈnō-ˌsēz\ **:** a narrowing or constriction of a bodily passage or orifice [Greek *stenōsis* "act of narrowing", from *stenoun* "to narrow", from *stenos* "narrow"] — **ste•nosed** \-ˈnōzd, -ˈnōst\ *adj* — **ste•not•ic** \-ˈnät-ik\ *adj*

sten•tor \ˈsten-ˌtȯr, ˈstent-ər\ *n* **1 :** a person having a loud voice **2 :** any of a genus of trumpet-shaped ciliate protozoans [Latin, from Greek *Stentōr,* a Greek herald in the Trojan War noted for his loud voice]

sten•to•ri•an \sten-ˈtōr-ē-ən, -ˈtȯr-\ *adj* **:** extremely loud ⟨a *stentorian* voice⟩

[1]**step** \ˈstep\ *n* **1 :** a rest for the foot in ascending or descending: as **a :** STAIR 2 **b :** a ladder rung **2 a** (1) **:** an advance or movement made by raising the foot and bringing it down elsewhere (2) **:** a combination of foot or foot and body movements constituting a unit or a repeated pattern (as in a dance) (3) **:** manner of walking **:** STRIDE ⟨know you by your *step*⟩ **b :** FOOTPRINT **c :** the sound of a footstep **3 a :** the space passed over in one step **b :** a short distance ⟨only a *step* away⟩ **c :** the height of one stair **4** *pl* **:** COURSE, WAY ⟨directed their *steps* for home⟩ **5 a :** a degree, grade, or rank in a scale ⟨one *step* nearer graduation⟩ **b :** a stage in a process **6 :** a block supporting the heel of a mast **7 :** an action, proceeding, or measure often occurring as one in a series **8 :** a steplike offset or part usually occurring in a series **9 :** a musical scale degree [Old English *stæpe*] — **step•like** \-ˌlīk\ *adj* — **stepped** \ˈstept\ *adj*

[2]**step** *vb* **stepped; step•ping 1 a :** to move or take by raising the foot and bringing it down elsewhere or by moving each foot in succession ⟨*stepped* off the curb⟩ ⟨*step* a pace forward⟩ **b :** DANCE 1 **2 a :** to go on foot **:** WALK ⟨*step* outside⟩ **b :** to move briskly ⟨kept us *stepping*⟩ **3 :** to press down with the foot ⟨*step* on a nail⟩ **4 :** to come as if at a single step ⟨*step* into a good job⟩ **5 :** to erect (a mast) by fixing the lower end in a step **6 :** to measure by steps ⟨*step* off 50 meters⟩ **7 :** to make steps in **8 :** to construct or arrange in or as if in steps — **step on it :** to hurry up

step- *combining form* **:** related by virtue of a remarriage (as of a parent) and not by blood ⟨*step*parent⟩ ⟨*step*sister⟩ [Old English *stēop-*]

step•broth•er \ˈstep-ˌbrəth-ər\ *n* **:** a son of one's stepparent by a former marriage

step–by–step \ˌstep-bə-ˈstep\ *adj* **:** marked by successive degrees usually of limited extent **:** GRADUAL

step•child \ˈstep-ˌchīld\ *n* **:** a child of one's spouse by a former marriage

step•daugh•ter \-ˌdȯt-ər\ *n* **:** a daughter of one's spouse by a former marriage

step down \step-ˈdau̇n, ˈstep-\ *vb* **1 :** to give up a position **2 :** to lower the voltage of (a current) by means of a transformer — **step–down** \ˈstep-ˌdau̇n\ *adj*

step•fa•ther \ˈstep-ˌfäth-ər\ *n* **:** the husband of one's mother by a subsequent marriage

step–in \ˈstep-ˌin\ *n* **1 :** an article of clothing that is put on by being stepped into **2** *pl* **:** a woman's brief panties

step•lad•der \ˈstep-ˌlad-ər\ *n* **:** a portable set of steps with a hinged frame for steadying

step•moth•er \-ˌməth-ər\ *n* **:** the wife of one's father by a subsequent marriage

step out *vi* **1 :** to go away from a place usually for a short distance and for a short time **2 :** to go or march at a vigorous or increased pace **3 :** to engage in social activity away from home

step•par•ent \ˈstep-ˌpar-ənt, -ˌper-\ *n* **:** the spouse of one's parent by a subsequent marriage

steppe \ˈstep\ *n* **:** dry usually level largely grass-covered land in regions of wide temperature range (as in southeastern Europe and parts of Asia) [Russian *step'*]

stepped–up \ˈstep-ˈtəp\ *adj* **:** made more vigorous and intensive ⟨a *stepped-up* advertising program⟩

step•per \ˈstep-ər\ *n* **:** one that steps lively (as a fast horse or a dancer)

step•ping–off place \ˌstep-ing-ˈȯf-\ *n* **1 :** the outbound end of a transportation line **2 :** a place from which one leaves

step•ping–stone \ˈstep-ing-ˌstōn\ *n* **1 :** a stone to step on (as in crossing a stream) **2 :** a means of progress or advancement ⟨a *stepping-stone* to success⟩

step rocket *n* **:** a multistage rocket whose sections are fired successively

step•sis•ter \ˈstep-ˌsis-tər\ *n* **:** a daughter of one's stepparent by a former marriage

step•son \-ˌsən\ *n* **:** a son of one's spouse by a former marriage

step stool *n* **:** a stool with one or two steps beneath the seat

step up \step-ˈəp, ˈstep-\ *vb* **1 :** to increase the voltage of (a current) by means of a transformer **2 :** to increase, augment, or advance ⟨*step up* production⟩ **3 :** to come forward — **step–up** \ˈstep-ˌəp\ *adj*

step•wise \ˈstep-ˌwīz\ *adj* **:** marked by steps **:** GRADUAL

-ster \stər\ *n combining form* **1 :** one that does or handles or operates ⟨spin*ster*⟩ ⟨tap*ster*⟩⟨team*ster*⟩ **2 :** one that makes or uses ⟨pun*ster*⟨song*ster*⟩ **3 :** one that is associated with or participates in ⟨game*ster*⟩ ⟨gang*ster*⟩ **4 :** one that is ⟨old*ster*⟩ ⟨young*ster*⟩ [Old English *-estre* "female agent"]

stere \ˈstiər, ˈsteər\ *n* **:** a metric unit of volume equal to one cubic meter [French *stère,* from Greek *stereos* "solid"]

stere- *or* **stereo-** *combining form* **1 :** solid ⟨*stereo*scope⟩ **2 :** stereoscopic ⟨*stereo*microscope⟩ [Greek *stereos*]

ste•reo \ˈster-ē-ˌō, ˈstir-\ *n* **1 :** STEREOTYPE 1 **2 a :** a stereoscopic method, system, or effect **b :** a stereoscopic photograph **3 a :** stereophonic reproduction **b :** a stereophonic sound system — **stereo** *adj*

ste•re•og•ra•phy \ˌster-ē-ˈäg-rə-fē, ˌstir-\ *n* **:** stereoscopic photography — **ste•reo•graph•ic** \-ē-ə-ˈgraf-ik\ *adj*

ste•reo•isom•er•ism \ˌster-ē-ō-ī-ˈsäm-ə-ˌriz-əm, ˌstir-\ *n* **:** isomerism in which atoms are linked in the same order but differ in their spatial arrangement — **ste•reo•iso•mer** \-ˈī-sə-mər\ *n* — **ste•reo•iso•mer•ic** \-ˌī-sə-ˈmer-ik\ *adj*

ste•reo•mi•cro•scope \-ˈmī-krə-ˌskōp\ *n* **:** a microscope having a set of lenses for each eye to make an object appear in three dimensions

ste•reo•phon•ic \ˌster-ē-ə-ˈfän-ik, ˌstir-\ *adj* **:** giving, relating to, or constituting a three-dimensional effect of reproduced sound — compare MONOPHONIC

ste•re•op•ti•con \ˌster-ē-ˈäp-ti-kən, ˌstir-\ *n* **:** a projector for transparent slides [*stere-* + Greek *optikon,* neuter of *optikos* "optic"]

ste•reo•scope \ˈster-ē-ə-ˌskōp, ˈstir-\ *n* **:** an optical instrument with two eyeglasses for helping the observer to combine the images of two pictures taken from points of view a little way apart and thus to get the effect of solidity or depth

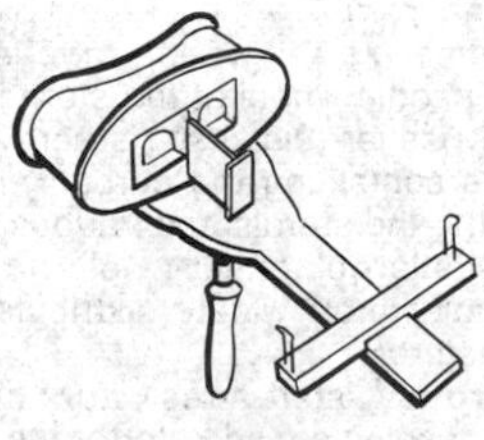
stereoscope

ste•reo•scop•ic \ˌster-ē-ə-ˈskäp-ik, ˌstir-\ *adj* **1 :** of or relating to the stereoscope **2 :** characterized by stereoscopy ⟨*stereoscopic* vision⟩ — **ste•reo•scop•i•cal•ly** \-i-kə-lē, -klē\ *adv*

ste•re•os•co•py \ˌster-ē-ˈäs-kə-pē, ˌstir-\ *n* **:** the seeing of objects in three dimensions

ste•reo•tax•ic \ˌster-ē-ə-ˈtak-sik, ˌstir-\ *adj* **:** of, relating to, or being a technique or apparatus used in neurological research or surgery for directing the tip of a delicate instrument (as a needle or an electrode) in three planes in an attempt to reach a predetermined place in the nervous system and especially the brain [derived from *stere-* + *taxis*] — **ste•reo•tax•i•cal•ly** \-si-kə-lē, -klē\ *adv*

[1]**ste•reo•type** \ˈster-ē-ə-ˌtīp, ˈstir-\ *n* **1 :** a plate made by molding a matrix of a printing surface and making from this a cast in type metal **2 :** something conforming to a general pattern and lacking individual distinguishing marks or qualities; *esp* **:** a standardized mental picture that is held in common by members of a group and that represents an oversimplified opinion, emotional attitude, or uncritical judgment

[2]**stereotype** *vt* **1 :** to make a stereotype from **2 a :** to repeat with-

\ə\ **abut**	\au̇\ **out**	\i\ **tip**	\ȯ\ **saw**	\u̇\ **foot**
\ər\ **further**	\ch\ **chin**	\ī\ **life**	\ȯi\ **coin**	\y\ **yet**
\a\ **mat**	\e\ **pet**	\j\ **job**	\th\ **thin**	\yü\ **few**
\ā\ **take**	\ē\ **easy**	\ng\ **sing**	\th\ **this**	\yu̇\ **cure**
\ä\ **cot, cart**	\g\ **go**	\ō\ **bone**	\ü\ **food**	\zh\ **vision**

out variation **b :** to develop a mental stereotype about — **ste·reo·typ·er** *n*

ste·reo·typed \-ˌtīpt\ *adj* **:** lacking originality or individuality **syn** see TRITE

ste·reo·ty·py \-ˌtī-pē\ *n* **:** the art or process of making or of printing from stereotype plates

ste·rig·ma \stə-ˈrig-mə\ *n, pl* **-ma·ta** \-met-ə\ **:** a filament that supports a spore or chain of spores [Greek *stērigma* "support", from *stērizein* "to prop"]

ster·ile \ˈster-əl\ *adj* **1 :** not able to bear fruit, crops, or offspring **:** not fertile **:** BARREN ⟨*sterile* soil⟩ **2 :** free from living organisms and especially microorganisms ⟨*sterile* dressing for a wound⟩ **3 :** lacking in ideas or originality [Latin *sterilis*] — **ste·ril·i·ty** \stə-ˈril-ət-ē\ *n*

ster·il·ize \ˈster-ə-ˌlīz\ *vt* **:** to make sterile: as **a :** to deprive of the power of reproducing or germinating **b :** to make powerless or useless **c :** to free from living organisms (as bacteria) — **ster·il·iza·tion** \ˌster-ə-lə-ˈzā-shən\ *n* — **ster·il·iz·er** \ˈster-ə-ˌlī-zər\ *n*

¹ster·ling \ˈstər-liŋ\ *n* **1 :** British money **2 :** sterling silver or articles of it [Middle English, "silver penny"]

²sterling *adj* **1 :** of, relating to, or calculated in terms of British sterling **2 a :** a fixed standard of purity usually defined legally as represented by an alloy of 925 parts of silver with 75 parts of copper ⟨*sterling* silver⟩ **b :** made of sterling silver **3 :** conforming to the highest standard ⟨a person of *sterling* quality⟩ — **ster·ling·ly** \-liŋ-lē\ *adv* — **ster·ling·ness** *n*

¹stern \ˈstərn\ *adj* **1 :** hard and severe in nature or manner ⟨a *stern* judge⟩ **2 :** not inviting or attractive **:** FORBIDDING **3 :** showing severity **:** HARSH **4 :** FIRM, RESOLUTE ⟨a *stern* resolve to win⟩ [Old English *styrne*] **syn** see SEVERE — **stern·ly** *adv* — **stern·ness** \ˈstərn-nəs\ *n*

²stern *n* **1 :** the rear end of a boat or ship **2 :** a rear part [Middle English "rudder"]

stern·most \ˈstərn-ˌmōst\ *adj* **:** farthest astern

stern·post \-ˌpōst\ *n* **:** the principal member at the stern of a ship extending from keel to deck

ster·num \ˈstər-nəm\ *n, pl* **sternums** *or* **ster·na** \-nə\ **:** a compound ventral bone or cartilage connecting the ribs or the pectoral girdle or both — called also *breastbone* [New Latin, from Greek *sternon* "chest, breastbone"] — **ster·nal** \ˈstərn-l\ *adj*

stern–wheel·er \-ˈhwē-lər, -ˈwē-lər\ *n* **:** a steamboat having a single paddle wheel at the stern instead of on the sides

ste·roid \ˈstiər-ˌȯid *also* ˈsteər-\ *n* **:** any of numerous compounds containing the carbon ring system of the sterols and including the sterols and various hormones and glycosides

ste·rol \ˈstiər-ˌȯl, ˈsteər-, -ˌōl\ *n* **:** any of various solid alcohols (as cholesterol) widely distributed in animal and plant lipids [*cholesterol*]

ster·to·rous \ˈstərt-ə-rəs\ *adj* **:** characterized by a harsh snoring or gasping sound ⟨*stertorous* breathing⟩ [derived from Latin *stertere* "to snore"] — **ster·to·rous·ly** *adv* — **ster·to·rous·ness** *n*

stet \ˈstet\ *vt* **stet·ted; stet·ting :** to annotate (a word or passage) with or as if with the word *stet* in order to nullify a previous order to delete or omit from a manuscript or printer's proof [Latin, "let it stand", from *stare* "to stand"]

stetho·scope \ˈsteth-ə-ˌskōp *also* ˈsteth-\ *n* **:** an instrument used for listening to sounds produced in the body and especially in the chest [French *stéthoscope*, from Greek *stēthos* "chest"] — **stetho·scop·ic** \ˌsteth-ə-ˈskäp-ik *also* ˌsteth-\ *adj*

ste·ve·dore \ˈstē-və-ˌdōr, -ˌdȯr\ *n* **:** a person whose work is to load and unload ships or boats in port [Spanish *estibador*, from *estibar* "to pack", from Latin *stipare* "to press together"] — **stevedore** *vb*

¹stew \ˈstü, ˈstyü\ *vb* **1 :** to cook in liquid over a low heat **2 :** to become agitated or worried **:** FRET [Middle French *estuver*]

²stew *n* **1 :** food (as meat with vegatables) prepared by slow boiling **2 :** a state of excitement, worry, or confusion

stew·ard \ˈstü-ərd, ˈstu̇-, ˈstyü-, ˈstyu̇-, ˈstu̇rd, ˈstyu̇rd\ *n* **1 :** a manager of a large household, estate, or organization **2 a :** a person employed to supervise the provision and distribution of food (as on a ship) **b :** a worker who serves and attends the needs of passengers (as on a train or ship) [Old English *stīweard*, from *stī, stig* "hall, sty" + *weard* "ward"]

stew·ard·ess \-əs\ *n* **:** a woman who performs the duties of a steward; *esp* **:** one who attends passengers on an airplane

stew·ard·ship \-ˌship\ *n* **:** the office, duties, and obligations of a steward; *also* **:** the individual's responsibility to manage his life and property with proper regard to the rights of others

stib·nite \ˈstib-ˌnīt\ *n* **:** a mineral Sb_2S_3 consisting of a sulfide of antimony occurring in lead-gray crystals of metallic luster [French *stibine*, from Latin *stibium* "antimony", from Greek *stibi*, from Egyptian *stm*]

¹stick \ˈstik\ *n* **1 :** a cut or broken branch or twig especially when dry and dead **2 :** a long slender piece of wood: as **a :** a club or staff used as a weapon **b :** WALKING STICK 1 **c :** an implement used for striking or propelling an object in a game **3 :** something like a stick in shape, origin, or use ⟨a *stick* of dynamite⟩; *esp* **:** an airplane lever operating the elevators and ailerons **4 :** a person who is dull, stiff, and lifeless **5** *pl* **:** remote or rural districts ⟨way out in the *sticks*⟩ [Old English *sticca*]

²stick *vb* **stuck** \ˈstək\; **stick·ing 1 a :** PIERCE 1, STAB **b :** to kill by piercing **2 :** to cause (as a pointed instrument) to penetrate — used with *in, into,* or *through* ⟨*stuck* a needle in my finger⟩ **3 a :** to fasten by thrusting in **b :** IMPALE **c :** to push out, up, or under ⟨*stuck* out my hand⟩ **4 :** to put or set in a specified place or position **5 :** to attach by or as if by causing to adhere to a surface **6 :** to halt the movement or action of ⟨cars got *stuck* in the mud⟩ **7 :** BAFFLE 1, STUMP **8 a :** CHEAT 1, DEFRAUD **b :** to saddle with something disadvantageous or disagreeable ⟨*stuck* with the job of cleaning up⟩ **9 :** to hold to something firmly by or as if by adhesion ⟨the glue *stuck* to my fingers⟩ **10 a :** to remain in a place, situation, or environment **b :** to hold fast or adhere resolutely **:** CLING **11 a :** to become blocked, wedged, or jammed **b :** to be unable to proceed through fear or scruple **12 :** PROJECT 3, PROTRUDE [Old English *stician*]

• **syn** STICK, ADHERE, COHERE, CLING mean to become or remain closely attached. STICK implies being embedded, glued, or cemented in or on something; ADHERE implies a growing together or a process like it; COHERE suggests a sticking together of parts so as to form a unified mass or whole; CLING implies attachment by hanging on with arms or tendrils.

— **stick one's neck out :** to make oneself vulnerable unnecessarily — **stuck on :** infatuated with

³stick *n* **1 :** a thrust with a pointed instrument **:** STAB **2 :** adhesive quality or substance

stick around *vi* **:** to stay or wait about **:** LINGER

stick·ball \ˈstik-ˌbȯl\ *n* **:** baseball adapted for play in small areas using a broomstick and a lightweight ball

stick·er \ˈstik-ər\ *n* **1 :** one (as a brier or knife) that pierces with a point **2 a :** something that adheres (as a bur) or causes adhesion (as glue) **b :** a slip of paper with gummed back that when moistened adheres to a surface

stick·han·dler \ˈstik-ˌhan-dlər, -lər, -dl-ər\ *n* **:** a hockey or lacrosse player adept at maneuvering the ball or puck

stick insect *n* **:** any of various usually wingless insects that are distantly related to the mantises and have a long round body resembling a stick

stick–in–the–mud \ˈstik-ən-thə-ˌməd\ *n* **:** one who is slow, old-fashioned, or unprogressive; *esp* **:** an old fogy

stick·le \ˈstik-əl\ *vi* **stick·led; stick·ling** \ˈstik-liŋ, -ə-liŋ\ **1 :** to contend especially stubbornly and usually on insufficient grounds **2 :** to feel often excessive scruples [Middle English *stightlen*, from *stighten* "to arrange", from Old English *stihtan*]

stick·le·back \ˈstik-əl-ˌbak\ *n* **:** any of numerous small scaleless fishes having two or more free spines in front of the dorsal fin [Old English *sticel* "goad"]

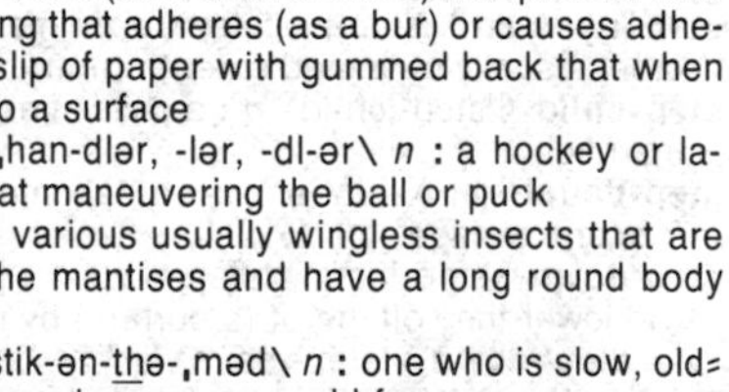

stickleback

stick·ler \ˈstik-lər, -ə-lər\ *n* **1 :** one that insists on exactitude or rigid propriety (as of conduct or dress) **2 :** POSER, PUZZLE

stick·man \ˈstik-ˌman, -mən\ *n* **:** one who handles a stick: as **a :** one who supervises the play at a dice table, calls the decisions, and retrieves the dice **b :** a player in any of various games (as lacrosse) played with a stick

stick out *vb* **1 a :** to jut out **:** PROJECT **b :** to be conspicuous **2 :** to be persistent ⟨*stuck out* for higher wages⟩ **3 :** to put up with : ENDURE

stick•pin \'stick-ˌpin\ *n* : an ornamental pin worn in a necktie

stick shift *n* : a manually operated gearshift mounted on the steering column or floor of an automobile vehicle

stick•tight \'stik-ˌtīt\ *n* : BUR MARIGOLD

stick–to–it•ive•ness \stik-tü-ət-iv-nəs\ *n* : dogged perseverance : TENACITY

stick up \stik-'əp, 'stik-\ *vt* : to rob at the point of a gun — **stick•up** \'stik-ˌəp\ *n*

stick•work \'stik-ˌwərk\ *n* **1** : the use (as in lacrosse) of one's stick in offensive and defensive techniques **2** : batting ability in baseball

sticky \'stik-ē\ *adj* **stick•i•er**; **-est** **1 a** : ADHESIVE, GLUEY ⟨*sticky* syrup⟩ **b** : coated with a sticky substance **2** : HUMID, MUGGY ⟨a hot, *sticky* day⟩ **3** : tending to stick ⟨a *sticky* valve⟩ **4 a** : DISAGREEABLE 1, PAINFUL **b** : DIFFICULT, TROUBLESOME ⟨a *sticky* situation⟩ — **stick•i•ly** \'stik-ə-lē\ *adv* — **stick•i•ness** \'stik-ē-nəs\ *n*

1**stiff** \'stif\ *adj* **1 a** : not easily bent : RIGID **b** : lacking in normal or usual suppleness or mobility ⟨*stiff* muscles⟩ **2 a** : marked by moral courage **b** : STUBBORN 2, UNYIELDING **c** : formally reserved in manner; *also* : lacking in ease or grace **3** : hard fought ⟨drives a *stiff* bargain⟩ **4 a** : exerting great force : STRONG ⟨a *stiff* wind⟩ **b** : POTENT ⟨a *stiff* dose⟩ **5 a** : HARSH, SEVERE ⟨a *stiff* penalty⟩ **b** : difficult to do or cope with ⟨a *stiff* task⟩; *also* : RUGGED ⟨*stiff* terrain⟩ **6** : EXPENSIVE 2, STEEP [Old English *stīf*] — **stiff•ly** *adv* — **stiff•ness** *n*

2**stiff** *adv* **1** : in a stiff manner ⟨frozen *stiff*⟩ **2** : to an extreme degree ⟨bored *stiff*⟩

3**stiff** *n* **1** : CORPSE **2** : PERSON, FELLOW ⟨you lucky *stiff*⟩

stiff–arm \'stif-ˌärm\ *vb* : STRAIGHT-ARM — **stiff–arm** *n*

stiff•en \'stif-ən\ *vb* **stiff•ened**; **stiff•en•ing** \'stif-ning, -ə-ning\ : to make or become stiff or stiffer — **stiff•en•er** \-nər, -ə-nər\ *n*

stiff–necked \'stif-'nekt\ *adj* : arrogantly stubborn

1**sti•fle** \'stī-fəl\ *n* : the joint next above the hock in the hind leg of a four-footed animal (as a horse) corresponding to the knee in humans [Middle English]

2**stifle** *vb* **sti•fled**; **sti•fling** \-fə-ling, -fling\ **1 a** : to kill by depriving of or die from lack of oxygen or air **b** : to smother by or as if by depriving of air ⟨*stifle* a fire⟩ **2** : to check or keep in check by deliberate effort : REPRESS ⟨*stifled* my anger⟩ [Middle English *stuflen*] — **sti•fling•ly** \-fə-ling-lē, -fling-\ *adv*

stig•ma \'stig-mə\ *n, pl* **stig•ma•ta** \stig-'mät-ə, 'stig-mət-ə\ *or* **stigmas** **1 a** : a mark of shame or discredit : STAIN **b** : an identifying mark or characteristic; *esp* : a specific diagnostic sign of a disease **2** *pl* : bodily marks or pains resembling the wounds of the crucified Christ **3 a** : a small spot, scar, or opening on a plant or animal **b** : the part of the pistil of a flower which receives the pollen grains and on which they germinate [Latin *stigmat-, stigma* "mark, brand", from Greek, from *stizein* "to tattoo"] — **stig•mal** \'stig-məl\ *adj* — **stig•mat•ic** \stig-'mat-ik\ *adj* — **stig•mat•i•cal•ly** \-'mat-i-klē, -kə-lē\ *adv*

stig•ma•tize \'stig-mə-ˌtīz\ *vt* : to mark with a stigma; *esp* : to characterize or identify as disgraceful or shameful — **stig•ma•ti•za•tion** \ˌstig-mət-ə-'zā-shən\ *n*

1**stile** \'stīl\ *n* : a step or set of steps for passing over a fence or wall; *also* : TURNSTILE [Old English *stigel*]

2**stile** *n* : one of the vertical members in a frame or panel (as of a window or door) into which the secondary members are fitted [probably from Dutch *stijl* "post"]

sti•let•to \stə-'let-ō\ *n, pl* **-tos** *or* **-toes** **1** : a slender dagger with a blade thick in proportion to its width **2** : a pointed instrument for piercing holes for eyelets or embroidery [Italian, from *stilo* "stylus, dagger", from Latin *stilus* "stylus"]

1**still** \'stil\ *adj* **1 a** : not moving ⟨lying quiet and *still*⟩ **b** : not carbonated ⟨*still* wine⟩ **c** : of, relating to, or being an ordinary photograph as distinguished from a motion picture **2** : uttering no sound : QUIET ⟨be *still* and listen⟩ **3 a** : CALM, TRANQUIL ⟨a *still* lake⟩ **b** : free from noise or turbulence : PEACEFUL [Old English *stille*] — **still•ness** *n*

2**still** *vb* **1 a** : ALLAY 2, CALM ⟨*still* their fears⟩ **b** : to put an end to **2** : to make or become motionless or silent

3**still** *adv* **1** : without motion ⟨sit *still*⟩ **2** *archaic* : ALWAYS, CONTINUALLY **3** — used as a function word to indicate the continuance of an action or condition ⟨*still* lived there⟩ ⟨it's *still* hot⟩ **4** : in spite of that : NEVERTHELESS ⟨those who take the greatest care *still* make mistakes⟩ **5 a** : EVEN ⟨a *still* more difficult problem⟩ **b** : in addition : YET ⟨won *still* another game⟩

4**still** *n* **1** : QUIET, SILENCE **2** : a still photograph; *esp* : one of actors or scenes of a motion picture for publicity or documentary purposes

5**still** *n* **1** : DISTILLERY **2** : apparatus used in distillation [Middle English *stillen* "to distill", short for *distillen*]

still alarm *n* : a fire alarm transmitted (as by telephone call) without sounding the signal apparatus

still•birth \'stil-ˌbərth\ *n* : the birth of a dead fetus

still•born \-'bȯrn\ *adj* **1** : dead at birth **2** : failing from the start : ABORTIVE — **still•born** \-ˌbȯrn\ *n*

still hunt *n* : a quiet pursuing or ambushing (as of game) — **still–hunt** \'stil-ˌhənt\ *vb*

still life *n, pl* **still lifes** \-ˌlīfs, -ˌlīvz\ : a picture consisting predominantly of inanimate objects

still•man \'stil-mən\ *n* **1** : one who runs or operates a still **2** : one who tends distillation equipment (as in an oil refinery)

1**stilt** \'stilt\ *n* **1 a** : one of two poles each with a rest or strap for the foot used to elevate the wearer above the ground in walking **b** : a pile or post serving as one of the supports of a structure above ground or water level **2** *pl also* **stilt** : any of various long-legged three-toed birds related to the avocets that frequent inland ponds and marshes and nest in small colonies [Middle English *stilte*]

2**stilt** *vt* : to raise on or as if on stilts

stilt•ed \'stil-təd\ *adj* **1** : raised on or as if on stilts ⟨a *stilted* arch⟩ **2** : stiffly formal : not easy and natural ⟨*stilted* speech⟩ — **stilt•ed•ly** *adv* — **stilt•ed•ness** *n*

stim•u•lant \'stim-yə-lənt\ *n* **1** : an agent (as a drug) that temporarily increases the functional activity or efficiency of a tissue or organ **2** : STIMULUS ⟨a *stimulant* to trade⟩ **3** : an alcoholic beverage — **stimulant** *adj*

stim•u•late \-ˌlāt\ *vt* **1** : to make active or more active : ANIMATE, AROUSE ⟨*stimulate* industry⟩ **2** : to act on as a physiological stimulus or stimulant [Latin *stimulare*, from *stimulus* "goad, stimulus"] **syn** see PROVOKE — **stim•u•la•tion** \ˌstim-yə-'lā-shən\ *n* — **stim•u•la•tive** \'stim-yə-ˌlāt-iv\ *adj* — **stim•u•la•tor** \-ˌlāt-ər\ *n* — **stim•u•la•to•ry** \-lə-ˌtōr-ē, -ˌtȯr-\ *adj*

stim•u•lus \'stim-yə-ləs\ *n, pl* **-li** \-ˌlī, -ˌlē\ **1** : something that rouses or incites to activity : INCENTIVE ⟨new *stimuli* to business⟩ **2** : an agent (as an environmental change) that directly influences the activity of living protoplasm (as by exciting a sensory organ) [Latin]

1**sting** \'sting\ *vb* **stung** \'stəng\; **sting•ing** \'sting-ing\ **1 a** : to prick painfully especially with a sharp or poisonous process **b** : to affect with or feel sharp, quick, and usually burning pain or smart ⟨hail *stung* their faces⟩ ⟨faces *stinging* from the cold⟩ **2** : to cause to suffer severely ⟨*stung* with remorse⟩ **3** : OVERCHARGE, CHEAT ⟨some people always get *stung*⟩ **4** : to use a stinger [Old English *stingan*]

2**sting** *n* **1 a** : the act of stinging **b** : a wound or pain caused by or as if by stinging **2** : STINGER 2 **3** : a stinging element, force, or quality — **sting•less** \'sting-ləs\ *adj*

sting•a•ree \'sting-ə-rē\ *n* : STINGRAY [by alteration]

sting•er \'sting-ər\ *n* **1** : one that stings; *esp* : a sharp blow or remark **2** : a sharp organ of offense and defense (as of a bee or scorpion) usually adapted to wound by piercing and injecting a poisonous secretion

stinging cell *n* : NEMATOCYST

sting•ray \'sting-ˌrā\ *n* : any of numerous rays with one or more large sharp barbed spines near the base of the whiplike tail capable of inflicting severe wounds

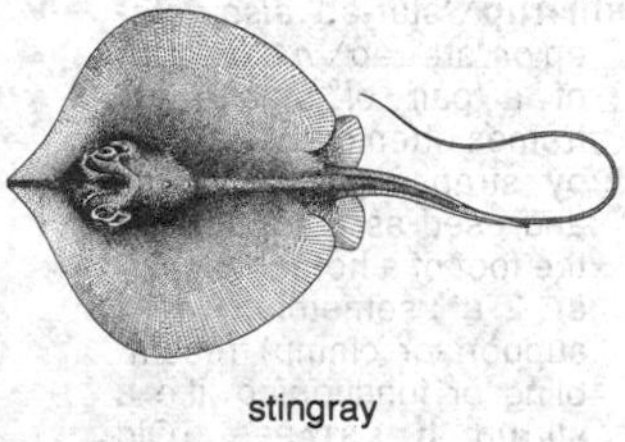
stingray

stin•gy \'stin-jē\ *adj* **stin•gi•er**; **-est** **1** : not generous or liberal : sparing or scant in giving or spending **2** : SCANTY, MEAGER ⟨*stingy* portions⟩ [probably related to *sting*] — **stin•gi•ly** \-jə-lē\ *adv* — **stin•gi•ness** \-jē-nəs\ *n*

\ə\ **abut**	\au̇\ **out**	\i\ **tip**	\ȯ\ **saw**	\u̇\ **foot**
\ər\ **further**	\ch\ **chin**	\ī\ **life**	\ȯi\ **coin**	\y\ **yet**
\a\ **mat**	\e\ **pet**	\j\ **job**	\th\ **thin**	\yü\ **few**
\ā\ **take**	\ē\ **easy**	\ng\ **sing**	\t͟h\ **this**	\yu̇\ **cure**
\ä\ **cot, cart**	\g\ **go**	\ō\ **bone**	\ü\ **food**	\zh\ **vision**

• **syn** CLOSE, PENURIOUS, MISERLY : STINGY implies an unwillingness to spend, give, or share freely and a marked lack of generosity; CLOSE suggests keeping a tight grip on one's money and possessions; PENURIOUS implies a frugality that gives an appearance of actual poverty; MISERLY suggests a sordid avariciousness and a morbid pleasure in hoarding.

[1]**stink** \'stiŋk\ *vb* **stank** \'staŋk\ *or* **stunk** \'stəŋk\; **stunk**; **stink•ing 1 :** to give forth or cause to have a strong and offensive smell ⟨*stink* up a room⟩ **2 :** to be offensive or have something to an offensive degree **3 :** to be of extremely poor quality [Old English *stincan*]

[2]**stink** *n* **1 :** a strong offensive odor : STENCH **2 :** a public outcry against something offensive ⟨raised a *stink* about gambling⟩ — **stinky** \'stiŋ-kē\ *adj*

stink•bug \'stiŋk-,bəg\ *n* **:** any of various true bugs that emit a disagreeable odor

stink•er \'stiŋ-kər\ *n* **1 :** one that stinks **2 :** an offensive or contemptible person

[1]**stint** \'stint\ *vb* **1 :** to limit in share or portion **:** cut short in amount ⟨*stint* the children's milk⟩ **2 :** to be sparing or frugal [Old English *styntan* "to blunt, dull"] — **stint•er** *n*

[2]**stint** *n* **1 :** RESTRICTION 1, LIMITATION **2 :** a definite quantity of work assigned

stipe \'stīp\ *n* **:** a short plant stalk; *esp* **:** one supporting a fern frond or the cap of a mushroom [Latin *stipes* "tree trunk"] — **stiped** \'stīpt\ *adj*

sti•pend \'stī-,pend, -pənd\ *n* **:** a fixed sum of money paid periodically for services or to defray expenses [Latin *stipendium*, from *stips* "gift" + *pendere* "to weigh, pay"] **syn** see WAGE

stip•ple \'stip-əl\ *vt* **stip•pled**; **stip•pling** \'stip-liŋ, -ə-liŋ\ **1 :** to engrave by means of dots and flicks **2 a :** to make (as in paint or ink) by small short touches that together produce an even or softly graded shadow **b :** to apply (as paint) by repeated small touches **3 :** SPECKLE 1, FLECK [Dutch *stippelen* "to spot, dot"] — **stipple** *n* — **stip•pler** \-lər, -ə-lər\ *n*

stip•u•late \'stip-yə-,lāt\ *vb* **:** to make an agreement or arrange as part of an agreement; *esp* **:** to demand or insist on as a condition in an agreement [Latin *stipulari*] — **stip•u•la•tor** \-,lāt-ər\ *n* — **stip•u•la•to•ry** \-lə-,tōr-ē, -,tȯr-\ *adj*

stip•u•la•tion \,stip-yə-'lā-shən\ *n* **1 :** an act of stipulating **2 :** something stipulated; *esp* **:** a condition required as part of an agreement

stip•ule \'stip-yül\ *n* **:** either of a pair of small appendages at the base of the leaf in many plants [Latin *stipula* "stalk"] — **stip•u•lar** \-yə-lər\ *adj* — **stip•u•late** \-yə-lət\ *adj*

[1]**stir** \'stər\ *vb* **stirred**; **stir•ring 1 a :** to make or cause to make a usually slight movement or change of position **b :** to disturb the quiet of **:** AGITATE **2 a :** to alter the relative position of the particles or parts of especially by a continued circular movement **b :** to mix by or as if by stirring **3 :** BESTIR **4 :** to bring into notice or debate **:** RAISE ⟨the answer *stirred* our hopes⟩ **5 a :** to rouse to activity **:** INCITE, QUICKEN ⟨their emotions *stirred*⟩ **b :** to call forth (as a memory) **:** EVOKE ⟨*stirred* thoughts of home⟩ **6 :** to be active or busy [Old English *styrian*] — **stir•rer** *n*

[2]**stir** *n* **1 a :** a state of disturbance or activity **b :** widespread notice and discussion **:** IMPRESSION **2 :** a slight movement **3 :** a stirring movement

stir•ring \'stər-iŋ\ *adj* **1 :** ACTIVE 4 **2 :** giving rise to excitement

stir•rup \'stər-əp *also* 'stir-əp *or* 'stə-rəp\ *n* **1 :** either of a pair of small light frames often of metal hung by straps from a saddle and used as a support for the foot of a horseback rider **2 a :** something (as a support or clamp) resembling or functioning like a stirrup **b :** STAPES [Old English *stigrāp*, literally, "mounting rope"]

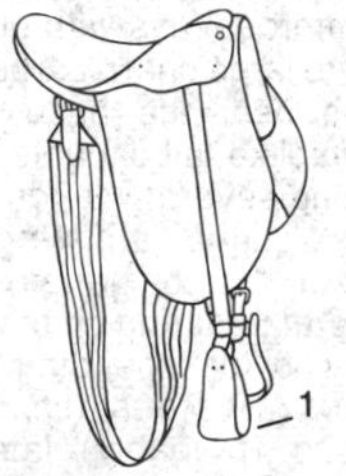

1 stirrup 1

stirrup cup *n* **1 :** a cup of drink (as wine) taken by a rider about to depart **2 :** a farewell cup

[1]**stitch** \'stich\ *n* **1 :** a local sharp and sudden pain especially in the side **2 a :** one in-and-out movement of a threaded needle in sewing, embroidering, or suturing **b :** a portion of thread left in the material after one stitch **3 :** a single piece of clothing ⟨didn't have a *stitch* on⟩ **4 :** a single loop of thread or yarn around an implement (as a knitting needle or crochet hook) **5 :** a stitch or series of stitches formed in a particular way ⟨basting *stitch*⟩ [Old English *stice*] — **in stitches :** in a state of uncontrollable laughter

[2]**stitch** *vb* **1 a :** to join with or as if with stitches **b :** to make, mend, or decorate with or as if with stitches **2 :** to unite by means of staples **3 :** to do needlework **:** SEW — **stitch•er** *n*

stithy \'stit͟h-ē, 'stith-\ *n, pl* **stith•ies 1 :** ANVIL 1 **2 :** SMITHY 1 [Old Norse *stethi*]

sti•ver \'stī-vər\ *n* **1 a :** a former monetary unit of the Netherlands equal to 1/20 gulden **b :** a coin representing one stiver **2 :** something of little value [Dutch *stuiver*]

stoat \'stōt\ *n* **:** the European ermine especially in its brown summer coat [Middle English *stote*]

stob \'stäb\ *n, chiefly dialect* **:** STAKE 1, POST [Middle English, "stump"]

[1]**stock** \'stäk\ *n* **1 a :** STUMP 1b **b** *archaic* **:** a log or block of wood **c** (1) **:** something without life or consciousness (2) **:** a dull, stupid, or lifeless person **2 :** a supporting framework or part: as **a** *pl* **:** a timber frame with holes to contain the feet or feet and hands of an offender undergoing public punishment **b :** the wooden part by which a rifle or shotgun is held during firing **c :** the butt of an implement **3 a :** the main stem of a plant **:** TRUNK **b :** a plant or plant part united with a scion in grafting and supplying mostly underground parts to a graft **4 :** the crosspiece of an anchor **5 a :** the original (as a person, race, or language) from which others derive **:** SOURCE **b :** the descendants of one individual **:** FAMILY, LINEAGE **6 a** (1) **:** the equipment of an establishment (2) **:** farm animals **:** LIVESTOCK **b :** a store or supply accumulated; *esp* **:** the inventory of goods of a merchant or manufacturer **7 a :** the capital that a firm employs in the conduct of business **b :** the proprietorship element in a corporation divided into shares giving to the owners an interest in its assets and earnings and usually voting power **8 :** any of a genus of herbaceous or shrubby plants of the mustard family with clusters of usually sweet-scented flowers **9 :** a wide band or scarf worn about the neck especially by some members of the clergy **10 a :** liquid in which meat, fish, or vegetables have been simmered that is used as a basis for soup, gravy, or sauce **b :** RAW MATERIAL **11 a :** the estimation in which one is held **b :** confidence placed in one **12 :** the production and presentation of plays by a stock company **13 :** a small batholith [Old English *stocc*]

[2]**stock** *vb* **1 :** to fit to or with a stock **2 :** to provide with or acquire stock or a stock ⟨*stock* a family with linens⟩ ⟨*stock* up on sundries⟩ **3 :** to procure or keep a stock of ⟨a store that *stocks* only the finest goods⟩ **4 :** to graze (livestock) on land

[3]**stock** *adj* **1 a :** kept regularly in stock ⟨comes in *stock* sizes⟩ ⟨a *stock* model⟩ **b :** commonly used or brought forward **:** STANDARD ⟨the *stock* answer⟩ **2 a :** kept for breeding purposes ⟨a *stock* mare⟩ **b :** devoted to or used or intended for livestock ⟨*stock* train⟩ ⟨*stock* farm⟩ **3 :** employed in taking care of the stock of merchandise on hand ⟨a *stock* clerk⟩

[1]**stock•ade** \stä-'kād\ *n* **1 :** a line of stout posts set firmly to form a defense **2 a :** an enclosure or pen made with posts and stakes **b :** an enclosure in which prisoners are kept [Spanish *estacada*, from *estaca* "stake", of Germanic origin]

[2]**stockade** *vt* **:** to fortify or surround with a stockade

stock•bro•ker \'stäk-,brō-kər\ *n* **:** one that carries out orders to buy and sell securities — **stock•brok•ing** \-,brō-kiŋ\ *or* **stock•bro•ker•age** \-kə-rij, -krij\ *n*

stock•car \'stäk-,kär\ *n* **:** a railroad boxcar with the sides slatted for ventilation that is used for carrying livestock

stock car *n* **1 :** an automotive vehicle of a model and type kept in stock for regular sales **2 :** a racing car having the basic chassis and body lines of a commercially produced assembly-line model

stock company *n* **1 :** a corporation or joint-stock company whose capital is represented by stock **2 :** a theatrical company attached to a repertory theater; *esp* **:** one without outstanding stars

stock exchange *n* **1 :** a place where organized trading in securities is conducted **2 :** an association of people organized to provide a market among themselves for the purchase and sale of securities

stock•fish \'stäk-,fish\ *n* **:** fish (as cod, haddock, or hake) dried hard in the open air without salt [Dutch *stocvisch*, from *stoc* "stick" + *visch* "fish"]

stock•hold•er \-ˌhōl-dər\ *n* : an owner of stocks : SHAREHOLDER

stock•i•nette *or* **stock•i•net** \ˌstäk-ə-ˈnet\ *n* : a soft elastic usually cotton fabric used especially for bandages and infants' wear [alteration of earlier *stocking net*]

stock•ing \ˈstäk-iŋ\ *n* **1 a** : a usually knit close-fitting covering for the foot and leg **b** : SOCK **2** : something resembling a stocking; *esp* : a ring of distinctive color on the lower part of the leg of an animal [obsolete *stock* "to cover with a stocking", from English dialect *stock* "stocking"] — **stock•inged** \-iŋd\ *adj*

stocking cap *n* : a long knitted cone-shaped cap usually with a tassel or pom-pom worn especially for winter sports or play

stock–in–trade \ˌstäk-ən-ˈtrād, ˈstäk-ən-ˌ\ *n* **1** : the equipment necessary to or used in a trade or business **2** : something held to resemble the standard equipment of a business or person with a trade

stock•man \ˈstäk-mən, -ˌman\ *n* : one occupied as an owner or worker in the raising of livestock

stock market *n* **1** : STOCK EXCHANGE 1 **2** : a market for stocks or for a particular stock

stock•pile \ˈstäk-ˌpīl\ *n* : a reserve supply especially of something essential accumulated within a country for use during a shortage — **stockpile** *vt*

stock•pot \-ˌpät\ *n* : a pot in which soup stock is prepared

stock•room \-ˌrüm, -ˌru̇m\ *n* : a storage place for supplies or goods used in a business

stock–still \-ˈstil\ *adj* : very still : MOTIONLESS

stocky \ˈstäk-ē\ *adj* **stock•i•er; -est** : compact, sturdy, and relatively thick in build : THICKSET — **stock•i•ly** \ˈstäk-ə-lē\ *adv* — **stock•i•ness** \ˈstäk-ē-nəs\ *n*

stock•yard \ˈstäk-ˌyärd\ *n* : a yard for stock; *esp* : one in which livestock are kept temporarily for slaughter, market, or shipping

stodgy \ˈstäj-ē\ *adj* **stodg•i•er; -est 1** : having a thick gluey consistency : HEAVY ⟨*stodgy* bread⟩ **2** : moving in a slow plodding way especially as a result of physical bulkiness **3** : having no excitement : DULL **4** : extremely old-fashioned in attitude or outlook **5 a** : DRAB 2 **b** : DOWDY [earlier *stodge* "to stuff with food"] — **stodg•i•ly** \ˈstäj-ə-lē\ *adv* — **stodg•i•ness** \ˈstäj-ē-nəs\ *n*

sto•gie *or* **sto•gy** \ˈstō-gē\ *n, pl* **stogies** : a slender cylindrical cigar; *also* : CIGAR [*Conestoga*, Pennsylvania]

[1]**sto•ic** \ˈstō-ik\ *n* **1** *cap* : a member of an ancient Greek school of philosophy holding that the wise person should be free from passion, unmoved by joy or grief, and submissive to natural law **2** : one who appears or claims to be indifferent to pleasure or pain [Latin *stoicus*, from Greek *stōïkos*, from *Stoa Poikilē* "the Painted Portico (portico at Athens where Zeno taught)"]

[2]**stoic** *adj* **1** *cap* : of or relating to the Stoics or their doctrines **2** : indifferent to pleasure or pain — **sto•i•cal** \ˈstō-i-kəl\ *adj* — **sto•i•cal•ly** \-i-kə-lē,-klē\ *adv*

sto•icism \ˈstō-ə-ˌsiz-əm\ *n* **1** *cap* : the philosophy of the Stoics **2** : indifference to pleasure or pain : IMPASSIVENESS

stoke \ˈstōk\ *vb* **1** : to stir up or tend (as a fire) : supply (as a furnace) with fuel **2** : to stir up a fire : tend the fires of furnaces **3** : to feed (as oneself) abundantly [Dutch *stoken*]

stoke•hold \-ˌhōld\ *n* **1** : the space in front of the boilers of a ship from which the furnaces are fed **2** : a room containing a ship's boilers

stoke•hole \-ˌhōl\ *n* **1** : the mouth to the grate of a furnace **2** : STOKEHOLD

stok•er \ˈstō-kər\ *n* **1** : one that tends a furnace; *esp* : one that tends a ship's steam boiler **2** : a machine for feeding a fire

[1]**stole** *past of* STEAL

[2]**stole** \ˈstōl\ *n* **1** : a long loose garment : ROBE **2** : a long narrow band worn around the neck by bishops and priests and over the left shoulder by deacons in ceremonies **3** : a long wide scarf or similar covering worn usually across the shoulders [Old English, from Latin *stola*, from Greek *stolē*]

stolen *past participle of* STEAL

stol•id \ˈstäl-əd\ *adj* : having or expressing little or no sensibility : not easily aroused or excited : UNEMOTIONAL ⟨*stolid* peasants⟩ ⟨waited in *stolid* silence⟩ [Latin *stolidus* "dull, stupid"] **syn** see IMPASSIVE — **sto•lid•i•ty** \stä-ˈlid-ət-ē, stə-\ *n* — **stol•id•ly** \ˈstäl-əd-lē\ *adv*

sto•lon \ˈstō-lən, -ˌlän\ *n* **1** : a horizontal branch from the base of a plant that produces new plants from buds at its tip or nodes (as in the strawberry) — called also *runner* **2** : a branch of fungus mycelium spreading over the surface of the medium on which it is growing [Latin *stolon-*, *stolo* "branch, sucker"] — **sto•lon•if•er•ous** \ˌstō-lə-ˈnif-rəs, -ə-rəs\ *adj*

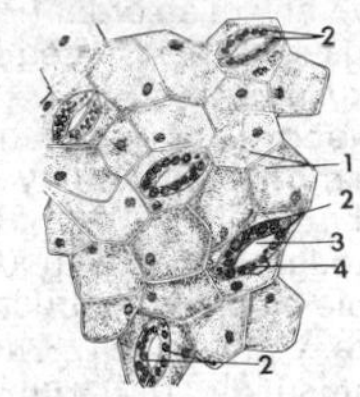

stoma: *1* epithelial cells, *2* guard cells, *3* stoma, *4* chloroplasts

sto•ma \ˈstō-mə\ *n, pl* **sto•ma•ta** \-mət-ə\ *also* **sto•mas** : a small opening like a mouth in form or function; *esp* : one of those giving passage to moisture and gases through the epidermis of a leaf [Greek *stomat-*, *stoma* "mouth"] — **sto•ma•tal** \ˈstō-mət-l\ *adj*

[1]**stom•ach** \ˈstəm-ək, -ik\ *n* **1 a** : a pouch of the vertebrate alimentary canal into which food goes for further mixing and digestion after passing from the mouth down the throat **b** : a cavity with a similar function in an invertebrate animal **c** : the part of the body that contains the stomach : BELLY, ABDOMEN **2 a** : desire for food caused by hunger : APPETITE **b** : INCLINATION, DESIRE ⟨had no *stomach* for bloodshed⟩ **3** *obsolete* **a** : VALOR, SPIRIT **b** : PRIDE 1a **c** : RESENTMENT [Middle French *estomac*, *from* Latin *stomachus* "gullet, esophagus, stomach", from Greek *stomachos*, from *stoma* "mouth"] — **stomach** *adj*

[2]**stomach** *vt* **1** *archaic* : to take offense at **2** : to bear without open reaction or resentment : BROOK

stom•ach•ache \-ˌāk\ *n* : pain in or in the region of the stomach

stom•ach•er \ˈstəm-i-kər, -i-chər\ *n* : the center front section of a bodice appearing through the laces of an outer garment (as in 16th century costume); *also* : a jeweled ornament for the front of a bodice

sto•mach•ic \stə-ˈmak-ik\ *adj* **1** : of or relating to the stomach ⟨*stomachic* vessels⟩ **2** : strengthening or stimulating to the stomach ⟨a *stomachic* medicine⟩ — **stomachic** *n* — **sto•mach•i•cal•ly** \-ˈmak-i-kə-lē, -klē\ *adv*

stomach pump *n* : a suction pump with a flexible tube for removing liquids from the stomach

sto•mate \ˈstō-ˌmāt\ *n* : a leaf stoma usually together with its guard cells [derived from *stoma*]

[1]**stomp** \ˈstämp, ˈstȯmp\ *vb* : STAMP 2 — **stomp•er** *n*

[2]**stomp** *n* **1** : STAMP 4 **2** : a jazz dance characterized by heavy stamping

[1]**stone** \ˈstōn\ *n* **1** : earth or mineral matter hardened in a mass **2** : a piece of rock not as fine as gravel ⟨throw *stones*⟩ **3** : rock used as a material especially for building **4** : a piece of rock used for some special purpose (as for a monument at a grave) **5** : JEWEL, GEM ⟨precious *stones*⟩ **6** : CALCULUS 1 **7** : a hard stony seed or one (as of a plum) enclosed in a stony cover **8** *pl usually* **stone** : any of various units of weight; *esp* : an official British unit equal to 14 pounds (about 6.35 kilograms) [Old English *stān*]

[2]**stone** *vt* **1** : to hurl stones at; *esp* : to kill by hitting with stones **2** : to remove the stones of (a fruit) **3 a** : to rub, scour, or polish (as leather or machined metal) with a stone **b** : to sharpen with a whetstone — **ston•er** *n*

[3]**stone** *adj* : of, relating to, or made of stone

Stone Age *n* : the first known period of prehistoric human culture characterized by the use of stone tools

stone–blind \ˈstōn-ˈblīnd\ *adj* : totally blind — **stone–blindness** \-ˈblīnd-nəs, -ˈblīn-\ *n*

stone–broke \-ˈbrōk\ *adj* : completely broke : lacking funds

stone cell *n* : SCLEREID

stone•crop \ˈstōn-ˌkräp\ *n* : SEDUM; *esp* : a mossy evergreen creeping sedum with pungent leaves

stone•cut•ter \-ˌkət-ər\ *n* **1** : one that cuts, carves, or dresses stone **2** : a machine for dressing stone — **stone•cut•ting** \-ˌkət-iŋ\ *n*

stoned \ˈstōnd\ *adj* **1** : DRUNK 1 **2** : being under the influence of a drug

stone–deaf \ˈstōn-ˈdef\ *adj* : totally deaf — **stone–deaf•ness** *n*

\ə\ **abut**	\au̇\ **out**	\i\ **tip**	\ȯ\ **saw**	\u̇\ **foot**
\ər\ **further**	\ch\ **chin**	\ī\ **life**	\ȯi\ **coin**	\y\ **yet**
\a\ **mat**	\e\ **pet**	\j\ **job**	\th\ **thin**	\yü\ **few**
\ā\ **take**	\ē\ **easy**	\ng\ **sing**	\t͟h\ **this**	\yu̇\ **cure**
\ä\ **cot, cart**	\g\ **go**	\ō\ **bone**	\ü\ **food**	\zh\ **vision**

stone fly *n* : any of an order (Plecoptera) of 4-winged insects with aquatic gilled nymphs used by anglers for bait

stone fruit *n* : DRUPE

stone•ma•son \ˈstōn-ˌmās-ⁿn\ *n* : a mason who builds with stone — **stone•ma•son•ry** \-rē\ *n*

stone wall *n* **1** *chiefly North* : a fence made of stones; *esp* : one built of rough stones without mortar to enclose a field **2** : an immovable block or obstruction (as in public affairs)

stone•ware \ˈstōn-ˌwaər, -ˌweər\ *n* : a strong opaque ceramic ware that is high-fired, well vitrified, and nonporous

stone•work \-ˌwərk\ *n* **1** : a structure or part built of stone : MASONRY **2** : the shaping, preparation, or setting of stone — **stone•work•er** \-ˌwər-kər\ *n*

stone•wort \-ˌwərt, -ˌwȯrt\ *n* : any of a family of freshwater green algae that resemble the equisetums and are often encrusted with calcium-containing deposits

stony *also* **ston•ey** \ˈstō-nē\ *adj* **ston•i•er**; **-est** **1** : abounding in or having the nature of stone : ROCKY **2 a** : insensitive as stone : PITILESS, HARDHEARTED **b** : showing no movement or reaction : EXPRESSIONLESS **3** : STONE-BROKE — **ston•i•ly** \ˈstōn-ˡl-ē\ *adv* — **ston•i•ness** \ˈstō-nē-nəs\ *n*

stood *past of* STAND

stooge \ˈstüj\ *n* **1** : STRAIGHT MAN **2** : one who slavishly follows or serves another [origin unknown] — **stooge** *vi*

stool \ˈstül\ *n* **1 a** : a seat usually without back or arms supported by three or four legs or by a central pedestal **b** : FOOTSTOOL **2 a** : a seat used while defecating or urinating **b** : a discharge of fecal matter [Old English *stōl*]

stool pigeon *n* **1** : a pigeon used as a decoy to draw others within a net **2** : a person acting as a spy or informer especially for the police [probably from the early practice of fastening the decoy bird to a stool]

¹stoop \ˈstüp\ *vb* **1** : to bend forward and downward **2** : to carry the head and shoulders or the upper part of the body bent forward **3** : to descend to doing something that is beneath one : degrade or debase oneself ⟨*stoop* to lying⟩ **4** : to descend swiftly on prey : SWOOP ⟨a hawk *stooping* after a mouse⟩ [Old English *stūpian*]

• **syn** STOOP, CONDESCEND, DEIGN mean to descend from one's real or pretended level of dignity. STOOP may imply a descent from a relatively high plane to a much lower one morally or socially; CONDESCEND implies an unbending by one of high position to meet a social inferior on the same level; DEIGN suggests a haughty or reluctant condescension; CONDESCEND and DEIGN are used chiefly in irony or mild derision.

²stoop *n* **1 a** : an act of bending the body forward **b** : a temporary or habitual forward bend of the back and shoulders **2** : the descent of a bird especially on its prey **3** : a lowering of oneself either in condescension or in submission

³stoop *n* : a porch, platform, or entrance stairway at a house door [Dutch *stoep*]

¹stop \ˈstäp\ *vb* **stopped**; **stop•ping** **1** : to close an opening by filling or blocking it : PLUG ⟨nose *stopped* up by a cold⟩ ⟨*stopped* their ears with cotton⟩ **2** : CHECK, RESTRAIN ⟨*stop* a person from going⟩ **3** : to halt the movement or progress of ⟨*stop* the car⟩ **4** : to instruct one's bank not to honor or pay ⟨*stop* payment on a check⟩ **5** : to change the pitch of (as a violin string) by pressing with the finger **6 a** : to cease activity or operation **b** : to come to an end **7** : to break one's journey ⟨*stopping* with friends for a week⟩ [Old English *-stoppian*, from Latin *stuppa* "oakum, tow"]

• **syn** CEASE, DESIST, QUIT: STOP applies to action or progress or to what is operating or progressing and may imply suddenness or definiteness ⟨*stopped* at the red signal⟩ CEASE applies to states, conditions, or existence and may add a suggestion of gradualness and a degree of finality ⟨*ceased* raining during the night⟩ DESIST implies forbearance or restraint as a motive for stopping or ceasing ⟨*desisted* from further efforts to persuade them⟩ QUIT may stress either finality or abruptness in stopping or ceasing ⟨the engine faltered, sputtered, then *quit* altogether⟩

²stop *n* **1 a** : CESSATION, END **b** : a pause or breaking off in speech **2** : a graduated set of organ pipes of like kind and tone quality **3 a** : something that impedes, obstructs, or brings to a halt : IMPEDIMENT, OBSTACLE **b** : the aperture of a camera lens **c** : a drain plug : STOPPER **4** : a device for arresting or limiting motion **5** : the act of stopping : the state of being stopped : CHECK **6 a** : a halt in a journey : STAY **b** : a stopping place **7a** *chiefly British* : any of several punctuation marks **b** — used in telegrams and cables to indicate a period **8** : a consonant in the articulation of which there is a stage (as in the *p* of *apt* or the *g* of *tiger*) when the breath passage is completely closed

³stop *adj* : serving to stop : designed to stop ⟨*stop* line⟩ ⟨*stop* signal⟩ ⟨*stop* valve⟩

stop•cock \ˈstäp-ˌkäk\ *n* : a cock for stopping or regulating flow (as through a pipe)

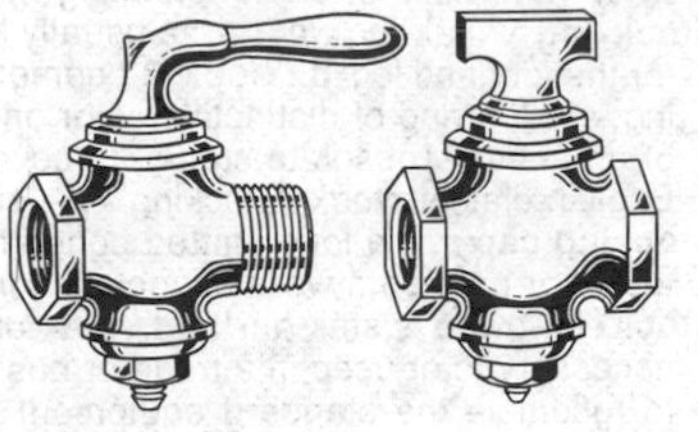

stopcock

stop down *vt* : to reduce the aperture of (a lens) by means of a diaphragm

¹stope \ˈstōp\ *n* : a usually steplike excavation underground for the removal of ore [probably from Low German *stope*, literally, "step"]

²stope *vb* : to mine by means of a stope

stop•gap \ˈstäp-ˌgap\ *n* : something that serves as a temporary substitute : MAKESHIFT

stop knob *n* : one of the handles by which an organist draws or shuts off a particular stop

stop•light \ˈstäp-ˌlīt\ *n* **1** : a light on the rear of a motor vehicle that is illuminated when the driver presses the brake pedal **2** : TRAFFIC SIGNAL

stop•over \ˈstäp-ˌō-vər\ *n* **1** : a stop at an intermediate point in one's journey **2** : a stopping place on a journey

stop•page \ˈstäp-ij\ *n* : the act of stopping : the state of being stopped : HALT, OBSTRUCTION

¹stop•per \ˈstäp-ər\ *n* **1** : one that brings to a halt : CHECK **2** : one that closes, shuts, or fills up; *esp* : something (as a bung or cork) used to plug an opening

²stopper *vt* : to close or secure with or as if with a stopper

stop•ple \ˈstäp-əl\ *n* : something that closes an aperture : STOPPER, PLUG [Middle English *stoppell*, from *stoppen* "to stop"] — **stopple** *vt*

stop street *n* : a street on which a vehicle must stop just before entering a through street

stop•watch \ˈstäp-ˌwäch\ *n* : a watch having a hand that can be started and stopped at will for exact timing (as of a race)

stor•able \ˈstōr-ə-bəl, ˈstȯr-\ *adj* : that may be stored ⟨*storable* commodities⟩ — **storable** *n*

stor•age \ˈstōr-ij, ˈstȯr-\ *n* **1 a** : space or a place for storing **b** : an amount stored **c** : MEMORY 4 **2 a** : the act of storing : the state of being stored **b** : the price charged for storing something

storage battery *n* : a cell or connected group of cells that converts chemical energy into electrical energy by reversible chemical reactions and that may be recharged by passing a current through it in the direction opposite to that of its discharge — called also *storage cell*

sto•rax \ˈstōr-ˌaks, ˈstȯr-\ *n* **1** : a resin related to benzoin and formerly used in incense **2** : a fragrant balsam from trees of the witchhazel family [Late Latin, from Latin *styrax*, from Greek]

¹store \ˈstōr, ˈstȯr\ *vt* **1** : FURNISH, SUPPLY ⟨*store* a ship with provisions⟩ **2** : to lay away : ACCUMULATE ⟨*store* vegetables for winter use⟩ **3 a** : to deposit in a place (as a warehouse) for safekeeping or disposal ⟨*stored* my furniture until I found a new apartment⟩ **b** : to place (as data) in a computer for later use **4** : to provide storage room for : HOLD [Old French *estorer* "to construct, restore, store", from Latin *instaurare* "to renew, restore"]

²store *n* **1** *pl* : accumulated supplies (as of food) ⟨a ship's *stores*⟩ **2** : something stored : STOCK ⟨a *store* of good jokes⟩ **3** : a place where goods are sold : SHOP — **in store** : in a state of imminence : WAITING ⟨there's trouble *in store* for you⟩

³store *adj* : purchased from a store : READY-MADE ⟨*store* clothes⟩ ⟨*store* bread⟩

store cheese *n* : CHEDDAR

store•front \ˈstōr-ˌfrənt, ˈstȯr-\ *n* **1** : the front side of a store or store building facing a street **2** : a building, room, or group of rooms having a storefront — **storefront** *adj*

storefront church *n* : a city church that uses storefront facilities as a meeting place

store•house \ˈstōr-ˌhau̇s, ˈstȯr-\ *n* **1** : a building for storing goods : WAREHOUSE **2** : an abundant supply or source ⟨a *storehouse* of knowledge⟩

store•keep•er \-ˌkē-pər\ *n* **1 :** one that is in charge of supplies **2 :** the operator of a retail store

store•room \-ˌrüm, -ˌrům\ *n* **:** a room in which goods are stored

store•wide \-ˈwīd\ *adj* **:** including all or most merchandise in a store ⟨a *storewide* sale⟩

[1]**sto•ried** \ˈstōr-ēd, ˈstȯr-\ *adj* **1 :** decorated with designs representing scenes from story or history ⟨a *storied* tapestry⟩ **2 :** having an interesting history **:** celebrated in story or history ⟨a *storied* castle⟩

[2]**storied** *or* **sto•reyed** *adj* **:** having stories ⟨a two-*storied* house⟩

stork \ˈstȯrk\ *n* **:** any of various large mostly Old World wading birds having a long stout bill and being related to the herons [Old English *storc*]

storks•bill \ˈstȯrks-ˌbil\ *n* **:** any of several plants of the geranium family with long beaked fruits

[1]**storm** \ˈstȯrm\ *n* **1 a :** a disturbance of the atmosphere accompanied by wind and usually by rain, snow, hail, sleet, or thunder and lightning **b :** a heavy fall of rain, snow, or hail **c :** wind having a speed of 64 to 72 miles per hour **2 :** a disturbed or agitated state **:** a sudden or violent commotion **3 :** a sudden heavy influx or onset **4 :** a heavy discharge of objects (as missiles) **5 :** a tumultuous outburst ⟨a *storm* of protests⟩ **6 :** a violent assault on a defended position [Old English]

[2]**storm** *vb* **1 a :** to blow with violence **b :** to rain, hail, snow, or sleet heavily **2 :** to attack by storm ⟨*stormed* ashore at zero hour⟩ ⟨*storm* the fort⟩ **3 :** to show violent emotion **:** RAGE ⟨*storming* at the delay⟩ **4 :** to rush about violently ⟨the mob *stormed* through the streets⟩ **syn** see ATTACK

storm•bound \-ˌbau̇nd\ *adj* **:** cut off from outside communication by a storm or its effects **:** stopped or delayed by storms

storm door *n* **:** an additional door placed outside an ordinary outside door for protection against severe weather

storm petrel *n* **:** any of various small petrels; *esp* **:** a small sooty black white-marked petrel frequenting the north Atlantic and Mediterranean — called also *Mother Carey's chicken, stormy petrel*

storm petrel

storm trooper *n* **:** a member of a private Nazi army noted for aggressiveness, violence, and brutality

storm window *n* **:** a framed glass window placed outside an ordinary window as a protection against severe weather — called also *storm sash*

stormy \ˈstȯr-mē\ *adj* **storm•i•er; -est 1 :** relating to, characterized by, or indicative of a storm ⟨a *stormy* day⟩ ⟨*stormy* skies⟩ **2 :** marked by turmoil or fury **:** PASSIONATE, TURBULENT ⟨a *stormy* life⟩ — **storm•i•ly** \-mə-lē\ *adv* — **storm•i•ness** \-mē-nəs\ *n*

[1]**sto•ry** \ˈstōr-ē, ˈstȯr-\ *n, pl* **stories 1 a :** an account of incidents or events **b :** ANECDOTE **2 a :** a fictional narrative shorter than a novel; *esp* **:** SHORT STORY **b :** the plot of a narrative or dramatic work **3 :** a widely circulated rumor **4 :** FALSEHOOD 1 **5 :** LEGEND 1a, ROMANCE **6 :** a news article or broadcast [Old French *estorie* "story, history", from Latin *historia*]

[2]**story** *vt* **sto•ried; sto•ry•ing 1** *archaic* **:** to narrate or describe in story **2 :** to adorn with a story or a scene from history

[3]**story** *or* **sto•rey** *n, pl* **stories** *or* **storeys 1 :** a set of rooms on one floor level of a building **2 :** a horizontal division of a building's exterior not necessarily corresponding exactly with the stories within [Medieval Latin *historia* "picture, story of a building", from Latin, "history"; probably from pictures adorning the windows of medieval buildings]

sto•ry•book \ˈstōr-ē-ˌbu̇k, ˈstȯr-\ *n* **:** a book of stories (as for children)

sto•ry•tell•er \-ˌtel-ər\ *n* **:** a teller of stories: as **a :** a relator of anecdotes **b :** a reciter of tales (as in a children's library) **c :** one that tells lies **:** FIBBER **d :** a writer of stories — **sto•ry•tell•ing** \-ˌtel-iŋ\ *adj or n*

stoup \ˈstüp\ *n* **1 :** a container (as a large glass or a tankard) for beverages **2 :** a basin for holy water at the entrance of a church [Middle English *stowp*]

[1]**stout** \ˈstau̇t\ *adj* **1 :** strong of character: as **a :** BOLD 1a, BRAVE **b :** firmly resolute **:** STAUNCH **2 a :** physically strong **:** POWERFUL **b :** STURDY 2a, VIGOROUS **c :** sturdily constructed **:** SOLID ⟨*stout* boots⟩ **3 :** full of energy **:** FORCEFUL **4 :** bulky in body **:** FAT [Old French *estout*, of Germanic origin] — **stout•ish** \ˈstau̇t-ish\ *adj* — **stout•ly** *adv* — **stout•ness** *n*

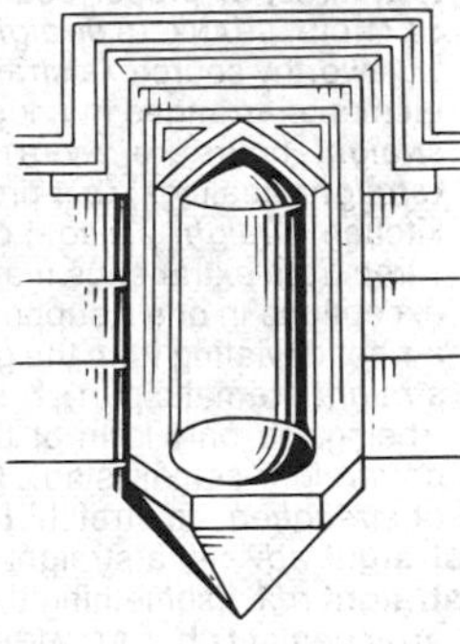
stoup 2

[2]**stout** *n* **1 :** a heavy-bodied dark brew made with roasted malt and a relatively high percentage of hops **2 a :** a fat person **b :** a clothing size for the large figure

stout•en \ˈstau̇t-ⁿn\ *vb* **stout•ened; stout•en•ing** \ˈstau̇t-niŋ, -ⁿn-iŋ\ **:** to make or become stout

stout•heart•ed \ˈstau̇t-ˈhärt-əd\ *adj* **:** BOLD 1a, BRAVE — **stout•heart•ed•ly** *adv* — **stout•heart•ed•ness** *n*

[1]**stove** \ˈstōv\ *n* **1 :** an apparatus that burns fuel or uses electricity to provide heat (as for cooking or heating) **2 :** KILN [Dutch or Low German, "heated room"]

[2]**stove** *past of* STAVE

stove•pipe \ˈstōv-ˌpīp\ *n* **1 :** a metal pipe for carrying off smoke from a stove **2 :** a tall silk hat

sto•ver \ˈstō-vər\ *n* **:** dried stalks of grain with the ears removed that are used as feed for livestock [Anglo-French *estovers* "necessary supplies", from Old French *estoveir* "to be necessary", from Latin *est opus* "there is need"]

stow \ˈstō\ *vt* **1 :** HOUSE 1a, LODGE **2 :** to put away **:** STORE **3 a :** to dispose in an orderly fashion **:** ARRANGE, PACK **b :** to fill with cargo **:** LOAD **4** *slang* **:** to put aside **:** STOP — usually used in the phrase *stow it* **5 :** to cram in (food) — usually used with *away* [Middle English *stowen* "to place", from *stowe* "place", from Old English *stōw*]

stow•age \ˈstō-ij\ *n* **1 a :** an act or process of stowing **b :** goods stowed or to be stowed **2 a :** storage capacity **b :** a place for storage **3 :** STORAGE 2a

stow•away \ˈstō-ə-ˌwā\ *n* **:** one that stows away

stow away \ˌstō-ə-ˈwā, ˈstō-ə-ˌ\ *vi* **:** to conceal oneself aboard a vehicle as a way to obtain transportation

STP \ˌes-ˌtē-ˈpē\ *n* **:** a powerful hallucinogenic drug that is chemically related to amphetamine [from *STP*, a trademark for a motor fuel additive]

stra•bis•mus \strə-ˈbiz-məs\ *n* **:** an eye disorder in which the two eyes cannot be directed to the same point because of a fault of the muscles of the eyeball [Greek *strabismos* "condition of squinting", from *strabizein* "to squint", from *strabos* "squint-eyed"] — **stra•bis•mic** \-mik\ *adj*

[1]**strad•dle** \ˈstrad-ˡl\ *vb* **strad•dled; strad•dling** \ˈstrad-liŋ, -ˡl-iŋ\ **1 :** to part the legs wide **:** stand, sit, or walk with the legs wide apart **2 :** to stand, sit, or be astride of ⟨*straddle* a horse⟩ **3 :** SPRAWL 3 **4 :** to be noncommittal **:** favor or seem to favor two apparently opposite sides ⟨*straddle* an issue⟩ [derived from *stride*] — **strad•dler** \ˈstrad-lər, -ˡl-ər\ *n*

[2]**straddle** *n* **1 :** the act or position of one that straddles **2 :** a noncommittal or uncertain position

strafe \ˈstrāf\ *vt* **:** to fire on (as troops) at close range and especially with machine guns from low-flying airplanes [German *Gott strafe England* "God punish England", slogan of the Germans in World War I] — **straf•er** *n*

strag•gle \ˈstrag-əl\ *vi* **strag•gled; strag•gling** \ˈstrag-liŋ, -ə-liŋ\ **1 :** to wander from a direct course or way **:** ROVE, STRAY **2 :** to trail off from others of its kind **:** spread out irregularly [Middle English *straglen*] — **strag•gler** \-lər, -ə-lər\ *n*

strag•gly \ˈstrag-lē, -ə-lē\ *adj* **strag•gli•er; -est :** spread out or scattered irregularly ⟨a *straggly* beard⟩

[1]**straight** \ˈstrāt\ *adj* **1 a :** free from curves, bends, angles, or

\ə\ **abut**	\au̇\ **out**	\i\ **tip**	\ȯ\ **saw**	\u̇\ **foot**
\ər\ **further**	\ch\ **chin**	\ī\ **life**	\ȯi\ **coin**	\y\ **yet**
\a\ **mat**	\e\ **pet**	\j\ **job**	\th\ **thin**	\yü\ **few**
\ā\ **take**	\ē\ **easy**	\ŋ\ **sing**	\t͟h\ **this**	\yu̇\ **cure**
\ä\ **cot, cart**	\g\ **go**	\ō\ **bone**	\ü\ **food**	\zh\ **vision**

irregularities ⟨*straight* hair⟩ ⟨*straight* timber⟩ **b** : generated by a point moving continuously in the same direction ⟨a *straight* line⟩ **2** : DIRECT, UNINTERRUPTED: as **a** : lying along or holding to a direct or proper course or method ⟨a *straight* thinker⟩ **b** : CANDID, FRANK ⟨a *straight* answer⟩ **c** : coming directly from a trustworthy source ⟨a *straight* tip on the horses⟩ **d** : made up of elements arranged in a logical order; *also* : CONSECUTIVE ⟨five *straight* hours⟩ **e** : VERTICAL 2, UPRIGHT **3 a** : JUST, FAIR ⟨*straight* dealings⟩ **b** : properly ordered or arranged ⟨set the kitchen *straight*⟩; *also* : CORRECT ⟨get the facts *straight*⟩ **4** : free from extraneous matter ⟨*straight* whiskey⟩ **5** : making no exceptions in one's support of a party ⟨vote a *straight* ticket⟩ **6 a** : not deviating from the general norm or prescribed pattern ⟨a *straight* dramatic part⟩ **b** : CONVENTIONAL 1; *esp* : SQUARE 6 **7** : being the only form of financial compensation ⟨salespeople on *straight* commission⟩ [Middle English, from past participle of *strecchen* "to stretch"] — **straight•ness** *n*

²straight *adv* : in a straight manner, course, or line

³straight *n* **1** : something that is straight: as **a** : a straight line or arrangement **b** : STRAIGHTAWAY; *esp* : HOMESTRETCH **c** : a true or honest report or course **2 a** : a sequence (as of shots, strokes, or moves) resulting in a perfect score in a game or contest **b** : first place at the finish of a horse race : WIN **3** : a combination of five cards in sequence in a poker hand **4** : a conventional person

straight A \ˌstrāt-ˌā\ *adj* : having or being a first-class record of achievement

straight angle *n* : an angle whose sides lie in the same straight line and that equals two right angles

straight–arm \ˈstrāt-ˌärm\ *vb* : to ward off an opponent with the arm held straight — **straight–arm** *n*

¹straight•away \ˈstrāt-ə-ˌwā\ *adj* **1** : proceeding in a straight line : continuous in direction : STRAIGHTFORWARD **2** : IMMEDIATE ⟨made a *straightaway* reply⟩

²straightaway *n* : a straight course: as **a** : the straight part of a closed racecourse : STRETCH **b** : a straight and unimpeded stretch of road or way

³straight•away \ˌstrāt-ə-ˈwā\ *adv* : without hesitation or delay : IMMEDIATELY

straight•edge \ˈstrāt-ˌej\ *n* : a bar of wood, metal, or plastic with a straight edge for testing straight lines and surfaces or drawing straight lines

straight•en \ˈstrāt-n\ *vb* **straight•ened**; **straight•en•ing** \ˈstrāt-ning, -n-ing\ **1** : to make or become straight **2** : to put in order ⟨*straighten* up a room⟩ ⟨*straightened* out my accounts⟩ — **straight•en•er** \ˈstrāt-nər, -n-ər\ *n*

straight face *n* : a face showing no emotion and especially no merriment — **straight–faced** \ˈstrāt-ˈfāst\ *adj*

straight flush *n* : a combination of five cards of the same suit in sequence in a poker hand

¹straight•for•ward \strāt-ˈfȯr-wərd, ˈstrāt-\ *also* **straight•for•wards** \-wərdz\ *adv* : in a straightforward way

²straightforward *adj* **1** : proceeding in a straight course or manner : DIRECT, UNDEVIATING **2 a** : OUTSPOKEN, CANDID ⟨a *straightforward* reply⟩ **b** : CLEAR 3c, UNMISTAKABLE — **straight•for•ward•ly** *adv* — **straight•for•ward•ness** *n*

straight man *n* : an entertainer who feeds lines to a comedian

straight off *adv* : at once : IMMEDIATELY

straight razor *n* : a razor with a rigid cutting blade hinged to a case that forms a handle when the razor is open for use

straight•way \ˈstrāt-ˌwā, -ˈwā\ *adv* **1** : in a direct course : DIRECTLY **2** : right away : IMMEDIATELY

¹strain \ˈstrān\ *n* **1 a** : LINEAGE, ANCESTRY **b** : a group of presumed common ancestry that is physiologically but usually not morphologically distinct ⟨a high-yielding *strain* of winter wheat⟩ **c** : SORT 1, KIND **2 a** : inherited or inherent character, quality, or disposition ⟨a *strain* of madness in the family⟩ **b** : TRACE, STREAK ⟨a *strain* of sadness in the story⟩ **3 a** : TUNE 1b, AIR **b** : a passage of verbal or musical expression **4 a** : the general tone of an utterance or of a course of action or conduct **b** : TEMPER 4c, MOOD [Middle English *streen* "progeny, lineage", from Old English *strēon* "gain, acquisition"]

²strain *vb* **1 a** : to draw tight : cause to clasp firmly **b** : to stretch to maximum extension and tautness **2 a** : to exert oneself to the utmost : STRIVE **b** : to injure or undergo injury by overuse, misuse, or excessive pressure ⟨*strain* the heart by overwork⟩ **c** : to cause a change of form or size in (a body) by application of external force **3** : to squeeze or clasp tightly: as **a** : HUG 1 **b** : to compress painfully : CONSTRICT **4 a** : to pass or cause to pass through or as if through a strainer : FILTER **b** : to remove by straining ⟨*strain* lumps out of the gravy⟩ **5** : to stretch beyond a proper limit ⟨*strain* the truth⟩ **6** : to make great difficulty or resistance : BALK ⟨a horse *straining* at the lead⟩ [Middle French *estraindre*, from Latin *stringere*]

³strain *n* : an act of straining or the condition of being strained: as **a** : excessive physical or mental tension **b** : bodily injury from excessive tension, effort, or use ⟨heart *strain*⟩; *esp* : one resulting from a wrench or twist and involving undue stretching of muscles or ligaments ⟨back *strain*⟩ **c** : deformation of a material body under the action of applied forces

• **syn** STRAIN, SPRAIN mean damage to muscles or tendons through overstretching or overexertion. STRAIN may apply to any part of the body; SPRAIN applies chiefly to the tearing of ligaments at a joint by sharp wrenching or twisting.

strained \ˈstrānd\ *adj* **1** : FORCED ⟨a *strained* smile⟩ **2** : pushed by antagonism near to open conflict ⟨*strained* relations between countries⟩

strain•er \ˈstrā-nər\ *n* : one that strains; *esp* : a device (as a screen, sieve, or filter) to retain solid pieces while a liquid passes through

¹strait \ˈstrāt\ *adj* **1** *archaic* **a** : NARROW 1 **b** : limited in space or time **c** : closely fitting : TIGHT **2** *archaic* : STRICT 2b, EXACTING **3 a** : causing distress : DIFFICULT **b** : limited as to means or resources [Old French *estreit*, from Latin *strictus* "strait, strict"] — **strait•ly** *adv* — **strait•ness** *n*

²strait *n* **1 a** *archaic* : a narrow space or passage **b** : a comparatively narrow passageway connecting two large bodies of water — often used in pl. **c** : ISTHMUS **2** : a situation of perplexity or distress — often used in pl. ⟨dire *straits*⟩

strait•en \ˈstrāt-n\ *vt* **strait•ened**; **strait•en•ing** \ˈstrāt-ning, -n-ing\ **1 a** : to make strait or narrow **b** : to hem in : CONFINE **2** *archaic* : to restrict in freedom or scope : HAMPER **3** : to subject to distress, privation, or deficiency ⟨in *straitened* circumstances⟩

strait•jack•et *or* **straight•jack•et** \ˈstrāt-ˌjak-ət\ *n* : a cover or overgarment of strong material (as canvas) used to bind the body and especially the arms closely in restraining a violent prisoner or patient

strait•laced *or* **straight•laced** \ˈstrāt-ˈlāst\ *adj* : excessively strict in manners, morals, or opinion — **strait•laced•ly** \-ˈlā-səd-lē, -lās-tlē\ *adv* — **strait•laced•ness** \-ˈlāst-nəs, -ˈlās-; -ˈlā-səd-nəs\ *n*

strake \ˈstrāk\ *n* : a continuous band of hull planking or plates on a ship; *also* : the width of such a band [Middle English]

stra•mo•ni•um \strə-ˈmō-nē-əm\ *n* : the dried leaves of the jimsonweed used in medicine similarly to belladonna especially in asthma [New Latin, "jimsonweed"]

¹strand \ˈstrand\ *n* : the land bordering a body of water : SHORE, BEACH [Old English]

²strand *vb* **1** : to run, drive, or cause to drift onto a strand : run aground : BEACH **2** : to leave in a strange or an unfavorable place especially without funds or means to depart ⟨*stranded* in a strange city⟩

³strand *n* **1** : one of the threads, strings, or wires twisted to make a cord, rope, or cable; *also* : the rope, cord, or cable into which these strands are twisted **2** : an elongated or twisted and plaited body resembling a rope ⟨a *strand* of pearls⟩ **3** : one of the elements of a complex whole ⟨the *strands* of a legal argument⟩ [Middle English *strond*]

⁴strand *vt* **1** : to form (as a rope) from strands **2** : to play out, twist, or arrange in a strand

strange \ˈstrānj\ *adj* **1** *archaic* : FOREIGN 2 **2** : not native to or naturally belonging in a place : of external origin, kind, or character **3** : not known, heard, or seen before ⟨*strange* surroundings⟩ **4** : causing surprise or wonder : UNUSUAL, BIZARRE ⟨*strange* clothes⟩ **5** : ill at ease ⟨feel *strange* on your first day in school⟩ [Old French *estrange*, from Latin *extraneus*, literally, "external", from *extra* "outside"] — **strange•ly** *adv* — **strange•ness** *n*

• **syn** QUEER, PECULIAR, OUTLANDISH: STRANGE emphasizes unfamiliarity and may apply to what is foreign or unnatural or unaccountable ⟨*strange* behavior⟩ QUEER suggests a dubious, unexpected, often sinister strangeness ⟨a *queer* taste⟩ PECULIAR implies a marked difference from the usual ⟨a *peculiar* hobbling gait⟩ OUTLANDISH implies an uncouth or barbaric strangeness ⟨*outlandish* clothes⟩ ⟨*outlandish* customs⟩

strang•er \ˈstrān-jər\ *n* **1** : one who is strange: as **a** : FOREIGNER **b** : one in the house of another as a guest, visitor, or intruder **c :** a person or thing that is unknown or with whom one is unacquainted **d :** one who does not belong to or is kept from the activities of a group **2 :** one ignorant of or unacquainted with someone or something ⟨a *stranger* to good manners⟩

stran•gle \'strang-gəl\ *vb* **stran•gled**; **stran•gling** \-gə-ling, -gling\ **1 :** to choke to death by squeezing the throat **2 :** to suppress or hinder the rise, expression, or growth of **3 :** to become strangled [Middle French *estrangler,* from Latin *strangulare,* from Greek *strangalan,* from *strangalē* "halter"] — **stran•gler** \-gə-lər, -glər\ *n*

stran•gle•hold \'strang-gəl-ˌhōld\ *n* **1 :** a wrestling hold by which one's opponent is choked **2 :** a force or influence that chokes or suppresses freedom of movement or expression

stran•gu•late \'strang-gyə-ˌlāt\ *vb* **1 :** STRANGLE 1, CONSTRICT **2 :** to become constricted so as to stop circulation ⟨a hernia may *strangulate*⟩ [Latin *strangulare*]

stran•gu•la•tion \ˌstrang-gyə-'lā-shən\ *n* **1 :** an act or process of strangling or strangulating **2 :** the state of being strangled or strangulated

[1]strap \'strap\ *n* **1 :** a band, plate, or loop of metal for binding objects together or for clamping an object in position **2 a :** a narrow usually flat strip or thong of a flexible material and especially leather used variously (as for securing, holding together, or wrapping) **b :** something made of a strap forming a loop ⟨a boot *strap*⟩ **c :** a strip of leather used for flogging **d :** STROP [alteration of *strop*]

[2]strap *vt* **strapped**; **strap•ping** **1 a :** to secure with or attach by means of a strap **b :** BIND, CONSTRICT; *also* **:** to support (as a sprained joint) with strips of adhesive plaster **2 :** to beat or punish with a strap **3 :** STROP **4 :** to cause to suffer from an extreme scarcity ⟨I'm *strapped* for cash⟩

strap•hang•er \'strap-ˌhang-ər\ *n* **:** a standing passenger in a subway, streetcar, bus, or train who clings for support to one of the devices (as short straps) placed along the aisle

strap•less \-ləs\ *adj* **:** having no strap; *esp* **:** made or worn without shoulder straps ⟨a *strapless* gown⟩

strap•per \'strap-ər\ *n* **:** one that is unusually large or robust

strap•ping \'strap-ing\ *adj* **:** having a vigorously sturdy constitution **:** ROBUST

strat•a•gem \'strat-ə-jəm\ *n* **1 a :** a trick in war for deceiving and outwitting the enemy **b :** a cleverly contrived trick or scheme for gaining an end **2 :** skill in ruses or trickery [Italian *stratagemma,* from Latin *strategema,* from Greek *stratēgēma,* from *stratēgein* "to be a general, maneuver", from *stratēgos* "general"] **syn** see TRICK

stra•te•gic \strə-'tē-jik\ *adj* **1 :** of, relating to, or marked by strategy ⟨a *strategic* retreat⟩ **2 a :** important in strategy **:** required for the conduct of war ⟨*strategic* materials⟩ **b :** of great importance within an integrated whole or to a planned effect ⟨emphasized the *strategic* points of the argument⟩ **3 :** designed or trained to strike at the sources of an enemy's power ⟨*strategic* bombers⟩ — **stra•te•gi•cal** \-ji-kəl\ *adj* — **stra•te•gi•cal•ly** \-ji-kə-lē, -klē\ *adv*

strat•e•gist \'strat-ə-jəst\ *n* **:** one skilled in strategy

strat•e•gy \'strat-ə-jē\ *n, pl* **-gies** **1 a** (1) **:** the science and art of using the political, economic, psychological, and military forces of a country so as to support adopted policies in peace or war (2) **:** the science and art of military command exercised to meet the enemy in combat under advantageous conditions **b :** a variety of or instance of the use of strategy **2 a :** a careful plan or method **:** STRATAGEM **b :** the art of devising or employing plans or stratagems to achieve a goal [Greek *stratēgia* "generalship", from *stratēgos* "general", from *stratos* "army" + *agein* "to lead"]

• **syn** TACTICS: STRATEGY applies to the devising of a general plan of attack, defense, or action so as to achieve an end with the forces or means available ⟨attempting to trade blows at close range with a stronger hitter is a mistake in *strategy*⟩ TACTICS applies to the technique of utilizing forces properly or skillfully in action or combat ⟨failing to protect the jaw is poor boxing *tactics*⟩

strath \'strath\ *n* **:** a flat wide river valley or the low-lying grassland along it [Scottish Gaelic *srath*]

stra•tic•u•late \strə-'tik-yə-lət, stra-\ *adj* **:** characterized by thin parallel strata [derived from *stratum*]

strat•i•fy \'strat-ə-ˌfī\ *vb* **-fied**; **-fy•ing** **1 :** to form, deposit, or arrange in strata ⟨*stratified* epithelium⟩⟨a society *stratified* by custom⟩ **2 :** to become arranged in strata — **strat•i•fi•ca•tion** \ˌstrat-ə-fə-'kā-shən\ *n*

stra•tig•ra•phy \strə-'tig-rə-fē\ *n* **1 :** the arrangement of strata **2 :** geology that deals with the origin, composition, distribution, and succession of strata — **strat•i•graph•ic** \ˌstrat-ə-'graf-ik\ *adj*

stra•to•cu•mu•lus \ˌstrāt-ō-'kyü-myə-ləs, ˌstrat-\ *n* **:** stratified cumulus consisting of large balls or rolls of dark cloud which often cover the whole sky especially in winter

strato•sphere \'strat-ə-ˌsfiər\ *n* **:** an upper portion of the atmosphere above approximately 11 kilometers depending on latitude, season, and weather in which temperature changes but little with altitude and clouds of water are rare [French *stratosphère,* from New Latin *stratum* "stratum" + French *sphère* "sphere"] — **strato•spher•ic** \ˌstrat-ə-'sfiər-ik, -'sfer-\ *adj*

stra•tum \'strāt-əm, 'strat-\ *n, pl* **stra•ta** \-ə\ **1 :** a layer of a substance; *esp* **:** one having parallel layers of other kinds lying above or below or both above and below it ⟨a rock *stratum*⟩ ⟨a cold *stratum* in a lake⟩ ⟨deep *stratum* of the skin⟩ **2 a :** a stage of historical or cultural development **b :** a level of society made up of persons with the same or similar social, economic, or cultural status [Latin, "spread, bed", from *sternere* "to spread out"]

stra•tus \'strāt-əs, 'strat-\ *n, pl* **stra•ti** \'strāt-ˌī, 'strat-\ **:** a cloud form extending horizontally over a relatively large area at an altitude of from 600 to 2100 meters [Latin, past participle of *sternere* "to spread out"]

[1]straw \'strò\ *n* **1 a :** stalks of grain after threshing; *also* **:** any dry stalky plant residue ⟨pea *straw*⟩ ⟨pine *straw*⟩ **b :** a natural or artificial heavy fiber used for weaving, plaiting, or braiding **2 :** a dry coarse stem especially of a cereal grass **3 a** (1) **:** something of little value or significance ⟨not worth a *straw*⟩ (2) **:** something too insubstantial to give support or help in a desperate situation ⟨clutch at *straws*⟩ **b :** CHAFF 2 **4 :** a tube for sucking up a beverage [Old English *strēaw*] — **strawy** \'strò-i, 'stròi\ *adj*

[2]straw *adj* **1 a :** made of straw ⟨a *straw* rug⟩ **b :** of, relating to, or used for straw ⟨a *straw* barn⟩ **2 :** of the color of straw **3 :** of little or no value **:** WORTHLESS

straw•ber•ry \'strò-ˌber-ē, -bə-rē, -brē\ *n* **:** an edible juicy red pulpy fruit of a low herb of the rose family with white flowers and long slender runners; *also* **:** this plant [from the appearance of the achenes on the surface] — **strawberry** *adj*

strawberry

strawberry mark *n* **:** a usually red and elevated birthmark that is a small tumor of a blood vessel

strawberry roan *n* **:** a roan horse with a decidedly red ground color

straw boss *n* **:** a foreman of a small gang of workers

straw•flow•er \'strò-ˌflaù-ər, -ˌflaùr\ *n* **:** any of several everlasting flowers

straw•hat theater \ˌstrò-ˌhat-\ *n* **:** a summer theater [from the former fashion of men's wearing straw hats in summer]

straw man *n* **1 :** a weak or imaginary argument or adversary set up only to be easily confuted **2 :** a person set up to serve as a cover for a questionable transaction

straw vote *n* **:** an unofficial vote (as one taken at a chance gathering) to test the relative strength of opposing candidates or issues

[1]stray \'strā\ *vi* **1 :** to wander from company, restraint, or proper limits **:** ROAM **2 a :** to wander from a direct course or at random **b :** ERR 2 [Middle French *estraier,* derived from Latin *extra-* "outside" + *vagari* "to wander"] — **stray•er** *n*

[2]stray *n* **1 a :** a domestic animal wandering at large or lost **b :** a person or thing that strays **:** a detached individual **:** STRAGGLER, WAIF **2 :** a disruptive electrical effect in radio reception not produced by a transmitting station

[3]**stray** *adj* **1** : having strayed ⟨a *stray* cow⟩ **2** : occurring at random or as detached individuals ⟨a few *stray* hairs⟩ ⟨*stray* remarks⟩

[1]**streak** \ˈstrēk\ *n* **1** : a line or mark that is not the same color or texture as its background : STRIPE **2 a** : the color of the fine powder of a mineral obtained by scratching or rubbing against a hard white surface **b** : microorganisms implanted in a line on a solid culture medium **3 a** : a narrow band of light **b** : a lightning bolt **4 a** : TRACE, STRAIN ⟨a *streak* of stubbornness⟩ **b** : a brief run (as of luck) **c** : a consecutive series ⟨a winning *streak*⟩ **5** : a narrow layer ⟨a *streak* of lean in bacon⟩ ⟨a *streak* of ore⟩ [Old English *strica*]

[2]**streak** *vb* **1** : to make streaks on or in **2** : to move swiftly : RUSH

streaked \ˈstrēkt, ˈstrē-kəd\ *adj* : marked with stripes or linear discolorations

streaky \ˈstrē-kē\ *adj* **streak•i•er**; **-est 1** : marked with streaks **2** : VARIABLE 1a, CHANGEABLE ⟨a *streaky* hitter in baseball⟩ — **streak•i•ness** *n*

[1]**stream** \ˈstrēm\ *n* **1** : a body of running water (as a river or brook) flowing on the earth; *also* : a body of flowing fluid (as water or gas) **2 a** : a steady succession **b** : a constantly renewed supply **c** : a continuous moving procession **3** : an unbroken flow (as of gas or particles of matter) **4** : a ray or beam of light **5** : a dominant attitude, group, or line of development [Old English *strēam*] — **on stream** : into production

[2]**stream** *vb* **1 a** : to flow or cause to flow in or as if in a stream **b** : to leave a bright trail **2 a** : to exude a bodily fluid profusely **b** : to become soaked **3** : to trail out at full length **4** : to pour in large numbers **5** : to display fully extended

stream•er \ˈstrē-mər\ *n* **1 a** : a flag that streams in the wind; *esp* : PENNANT **b** : a long narrow wavy strip like or suggesting a banner floating in the wind **c** : BANNER 2 **2** *pl* : AURORA BOREALIS

stream•let \ˈstrēm-lət\ *n* : a small stream

stream•line \-ˌlīn, -ˌlīn\ *vt* **1** : to design or construct with a contour for decreasing resistance to motion through water or air or as if for this purpose **2** : to bring up to date : MODERNIZE **3** : to make simpler or more efficient

stream•lined \-ˈlīnd, -ˌlīnd\ *also* **stream•line** *adj* **1 a** : contoured to reduce resistance to motion through water or air or as if for this purpose **b** : stripped of nonessentials **2** : brought up to date

street \ˈstrēt\ *n* **1 a** : a thoroughfare especially in a city, town, or village usually including sidewalks and being wider than an alley or lane **b** : the part of a street reserved for vehicles **c** : a thoroughfare and the property along it ⟨lived on Maple *Street*⟩ **2** : the people occupying property on a street ⟨the whole *street* was excited⟩ [Old English *strǣt*, from Late Latin *strata* "paved road", from Latin *stratus*, past participle of *sternere* "to spread out"]

street ar•ab \-ˈar-əb, -ˈā-ˌrab\ *n, often cap A* : a homeless vagabond and especially an outcast boy or girl in the streets of a city

street•car \ˈstrēt-ˌkär\ *n* : a vehicle on rails used primarily for transporting passengers and typically operating on city streets

street•light \-ˌlīt\ *n* : a light usually mounted on a pole that forms one in a series spaced at intervals along a public road

street railway *n* : a company operating streetcars or buses

strength \ˈstrength, ˈstrengkth\ *n* **1** : the quality or state of being strong : inherent power **2** : power to resist force : SOLIDITY, TOUGHNESS **3** : power of resisting attack : INVULNERABILITY **4** : legal, logical, or moral force **5 a** : degree of potency of effect or of concentration **b** : intensity of light, color, sound, or odor **6** : force as measured in numbers ⟨an army at full *strength*⟩ **7** : SUPPORT ⟨has enough *strength* in the senate to pass the bill⟩ [Old English *strengthu*] **syn** see POWER — **strength•less** \-ləs\ *adj* — **strength•less•ness** *n*

strength•en \ˈstreng-thən, ˈstrengk-\ *vb* **strength•ened**; **strength•en•ing** \ˈstrength-ning, ˈstrengkth-, -ə-ning\ : to make or become stronger — **strength•en•er** \ˈstrength-nər, ˈstrengkth-, -ə-nər\ *n*

stren•u•os•i•ty \ˌstren-yə-ˈwäs-ət-ē\ *n* : the quality or state of being strenuous

stren•u•ous \ˈstren-yə-wəs\ *adj* **1 a** : vigorously active : ENERGETIC ⟨leads a *strenuous* life⟩ **b** : FERVENT, ZEALOUS ⟨*strenuous* protest⟩ **2** : marked by or calling for energy or stamina : ARDUOUS ⟨*strenuous* work⟩ [Latin *strenuus*] **syn** see VIGOROUS — **stren•u•ous•ly** *adv* — **stren•u•ous•ness** *n*

strep \ˈstrep\ *n* : STREPTOCOCCUS

strep throat *n* : SEPTIC SORE THROAT

strep•to•ba•cil•lus \ˌstrep-tō-ba-ˈsil-əs\ *n* : any of various bacilli in which the individual cells are joined in a chain [Greek *streptos* "twisted, pliant" (from *strephein* "to twist, turn") + New Latin *bacillus*]

strep•to•coc•cus \ˌstrep-tə-ˈkäk-əs\ *n, pl* **strep•to•coc•ci** \-ˈkäk-ˌsī, -ˌī, -ˌsē, -ˌē\ : any of various nonmotile mostly parasitic spherical bacteria that occur in pairs or chains and include important pathogens of man and domestic animals [derived from Greek *streptos* "twisted" + *kokkos* "grain, seed"] — **strep•to•coc•cal** \-ˈkäk-əl\ *adj*

strep•to•my•ces \ˌstrep-tə-ˈmī-ˌsēz\ *n, pl* **streptomyces** *or* **strep•to•my•cetes** \-ˈmī-ˌsēts, -mī-ˈ; -mī-ˈsēt-ēz\ : any of a genus of mostly soil actinomycetes including some that form antibiotics as by-products of their metabolism [derived from Greek *streptos* "twisted" + *mykēs* "fungus"]

strep•to•my•cin \ˌstrep-tə-ˈmīs-n\ *n* : an antibiotic base produced by a soil streptomyces and used especially in the treatment of tuberculosis

[1]**stress** \ˈstres\ *n* **1** : constraining force or influence: as **a** : mutual force or action between surfaces in contact caused by external force (as tension or shear) **b** : a force that tends to distort a body **c** : a factor that induces bodily or mental tension and may be a factor in the causing of disease; *also* : a state of tension resulting from a stress **2** : EMPHASIS, WEIGHT ⟨lay *stress* on a point⟩ **3** : intensity of utterance given to a speech sound, syllable, or word **4** : relative force or prominence of sound in verse; *also* : a syllable having this stress **5** : ACCENT 6a [Middle English *stresse* "stress, distress", from *destresse*, from Old French] — **stress•less** \-ləs\ *adj* — **stress•less•ness** *n*

[2]**stress** *vt* **1** : ACCENT ⟨*stress* the first syllable⟩ **2** : to subject to physical or psychological stress **3** : to lay stress on : EMPHASIZE

stress•ful \-fəl\ *adj* : full of or tending to induce stress — **stress•ful•ly** \-fə-lē\ *adv*

stress mark *n* : a mark used with (as before, after, or over) a written syllable in the respelling of a word to show that this syllable is to be stressed when spoken : ACCENT MARK

[1]**stretch** \ˈstrech\ *vb* **1** : to extend (as one's limbs or body) in a reclining position ⟨*stretch* oneself out on the bed⟩ **2** : to reach out ⟨*stretch* forth an arm⟩ **3 a** : to extend in length or breadth or both : SPREAD **b** : to extend over a continuous period **4** : to cause the limbs of (a person) to be pulled especially in torture **5** : to draw up (one's body) from a cramped, stooping, or relaxed position ⟨awoke and *stretched* myself⟩ **6** : to pull taut **7 a** : to enlarge or distend especially by force **b** : STRAIN 2b **8** : to cause to reach or continue ⟨*stretch* a wire between two posts⟩ **9** : to extend often unduly the scope or meaning of ⟨*stretch* the truth⟩ **10** : to become extended without breaking [Middle English *strecchen*, from Old English *streccan*] — **stretch•abil•i•ty** \ˌstrech-ə-ˈbil-ət-ē\ *n* — **stretch•able** \ˈstrech-ə-bəl\ *adj* — **stretch one's legs** : to take a walk for exercise

[2]**stretch** *n* **1 a** : an exercise of something (as the imagination or understanding) beyond ordinary or normal limits **b** : an extension of the scope or application of something **2** : the extent to which something may be stretched **3** : the act of stretching : the state of being stretched **4 a** : an extent in length or area **b** : a continuous period of time ⟨silent for a *stretch*⟩ **5** : a walk to relieve fatigue **6** : a term of imprisonment **7 a** : either of the straight sides of a racecourse; *esp* : HOMESTRETCH **b** : a final stage **8** : the capacity for being stretched : ELASTICITY

[3]**stretch** *adj* : easily stretched : ELASTIC ⟨*stretch* hosiery⟩

stretch•er \ˈstrech-ər\ *n* **1** : one that stretches; *esp* : a device or machine for stretching or expanding something (as curtains) **2** : a litter (as of canvas) for carrying a disabled or dead person **3** : a rod or bar extending between two legs of a chair or table

stretch•er–bear•er \-ˌbar-ər, -ˌber-\ *n* : one who carries one end of a stretcher

strew \ˈstrü\ *vt* **strewed**; **strewed** *or* **strewn** \ˈstrün\; **strew•ing 1** : to spread (as seeds or flowers) by scattering **2** : to cover by or as if by scattering something over or on **3** : to become dispersed over **4** : to spread abroad : DISSEMINATE [Old English *strewian*]

stria \ˈstrī-ə\ *n, pl* **stri•ae** \ˈstrī-ˌē\ **1** : a tiny groove or channel **2** : a narrow line, band, or groove especially when one of a series [Latin, "furrow, channel"]

stri•at•ed \'strī-ˌāt-əd\ *adj* : marked with lines, bands, or grooves — **stri•a•tion** \strī-'ā-shən\ *n*

striated muscle *n* : muscle that is made up of usually elongated cells with many nuclei and with alternate light and dark cross striations, is typical of the muscles which move the vertebrate skeleton, and is mostly under voluntary control — compare CARDIAC MUSCLE, SMOOTH MUSCLE

strick•en \'strik-ən\ *adj* **1** : hit or wounded by or as if by a missile **2** : afflicted with disease, misfortune, or sorrow [from past participle of *strike*]

strict \'strikt\ *adj* **1** : stringent in requirement or control ⟨under *strict* orders⟩ **2 a** : inflexibly maintained or adhered to : COMPLETE, ABSOLUTE ⟨*strict* secrecy⟩ **b** (1) : rigorously conforming to principle or to a norm ⟨a *strict* Catholic⟩ (2) : severe in discipline **3** : EXACT, PRECISE ⟨in the *strict* meaning of the word⟩ [Latin *strictus,* from *stringere* "to bind tight"] **syn** see RIGID — **strict•ly** *adv* — **strict•ness** \'strikt-nəs, 'strik-\ *n*

stric•ture \'strik-chər\ *n* **1** : an abnormal narrowing of a bodily passage; *also* : the narrowed part **2** : something that closely restrains or limits : RESTRICTION **3** : an adverse criticism : CENSURE [Late Latin *strictura,* from Latin *stringere* "to bind tight"]

¹stride \'strīd\ *vb* **strode** \'strōd\; **strid•den** \'strid-n\; **strid•ing** \'strīd-ing\ **1** : to move over, through, or along with or as if with long measured steps **2** : BESTRIDE, STRADDLE **3** : to take a very long step **4** : to step over [Old English *strīdan*] — **strid•er** \'strīd-ər\ *n*

²stride *n* **1 a** : a step or the distance covered by a step **b** : a cycle of locomotor movements of a four-footed animal completed when the feet regain their initial relative positions; *also* : the distance covered by this **2** : an act or manner of progressing on foot : way of striding ⟨a purposeful *stride*⟩ **3** : a stage of progress : ADVANCE ⟨the *strides* made in the control of tuberculosis⟩

stri•dent \'strīd-nt\ *adj* **1** : sounding harsh, grating, or shrill **2** : unpleasantly discordant ⟨*strident* colors⟩ [Latin *stridens,* past participle of *stridere, stridēre* "to make a harsh noise"] — **stri•den•cy** \-n-sē\ *n* — **stri•dent•ly** *adv*

stri•dor \'strīd-ər, 'strī-ˌdȯr\ *n* : a strident noise [Latin, from *stridere, stridēre* "to make a harsh noise"]

strid•u•late \'strij-ə-ˌlāt\ *vi* : to make a shrill creaking noise by rubbing together special bodily structures — used especially of male insects (as crickets or grasshoppers) [derived from Latin *stridulus* "shrill", from *stridere, stridēre* "to make a harsh noise"] — **strid•u•la•tion** \ˌstrij-ə-'lā-shən\ *n*

strid•u•lous \'strij-ə-ləs\ *adj* : making a shrill creaking sound [Latin *stridulus*] — **strid•u•lous•ly** *adv*

strife \'strīf\ *n* **1** : bitter sometimes violent conflict or dissension ⟨political *strife*⟩ **2** : an act of contention : FIGHT, STRUGGLE [Old French *estrif*]

strife•less \-ləs\ *adj* : free from strife

¹strike \'strīk\ *vb* **struck** \'strək\; **struck** *also* **strick•en** \'strik-ən\; **strik•ing** \'strī-king\ **1** : to take a course : GO ⟨*strike* across the field⟩ **2 a** : to deliver a stroke, blow, or thrust : HIT **b** : to drive or remove by or as if by a blow ⟨*struck* the knife from my hand⟩ **c** : to attack or seize especially with fangs or claws ⟨*struck* by a snake⟩ **3** : to come into contact or collision with **4** : to remove or cancel with or as if with a stroke of the pen ⟨*struck* out a word in the text⟩ **5** : to lower, take down, or take apart ⟨*strike* a flag⟩ ⟨*strike* the tents⟩ **6 a** : to indicate or become indicated by a bell or chime (as of a clock) **b** : to indicate by sounding **7** : to pierce or penetrate or to cause to pierce or penetrate **8** : to make a military attack : FIGHT ⟨*strike* for freedom⟩ **9** : to seize the bait ⟨a fish *struck*⟩ **10** : to begin or cause to grow : take root or cause to take root ⟨some plant cuttings *strike* quickly⟩ **11** : to stop work in order to force an employer to comply with demands **12** : to make a beginning : LAUNCH ⟨the orchestra *struck* into another waltz⟩ **13** : to afflict suddenly : lay low ⟨*struck* down at the height of one's career⟩ **14 a** : to bring into forceful contact ⟨*struck* my knee against the dash⟩ **b** : to thrust oneself forward **c** : to fall on ⟨sunlight *struck* the glass⟩ **d** : to become audible to ⟨a loud sound *strikes* the ear⟩ **15 a** : to affect with a mental or emotional state or a strong emotion ⟨*struck* with horror⟩ **b** : to bring about : INDUCE, CAUSE ⟨the words *struck* fear in them⟩ **c** : to cause to become by or as if by a sudden blow ⟨*struck* them dead⟩ **d** : to produce by stamping with a die or punch ⟨*strike* a medal⟩ **e** : to produce (as fire) by or as if by striking or rubbing **f** : to cause to ignite by friction ⟨*strike* a match⟩ **16** : to agree on the terms of ⟨*strike* a bargain⟩ **17 a** : to play by strokes on the keys or strings **b** : to produce by or as if by playing a musical instrument ⟨*strike* a chord on the piano⟩ **18 a** : to occur to **b** : to appear to **c** : to make a strong impression on : IMPRESS ⟨I was *struck* by its beauty⟩ **19** : to arrive at by computation ⟨*strike* an average⟩ **20 a** : to come to ⟨*strike* the main road⟩ **b** : to run across ⟨the best story I ever *struck*⟩ **21** : to take on : ASSUME ⟨*strike* a pose⟩ [Old English *strīcan* "to stroke, go"]

²strike *n* **1** : an act or instance of striking **2 a** : a work stoppage by a body of workers to force an employer to comply with demands **b** : a temporary stoppage of activities in protest against an act or condition **3** : the direction of the line of intersection of a horizontal plane with an uptilted geological stratum **4** : a pull on a line by a fish in striking **5** : a stroke of good luck; *esp* : a discovery of a valuable mineral deposit **6 a** : a pitched baseball that passes through the strike zone or that is swung at and is charged against the batter **b** : DISADVANTAGE 2, HANDICAP **7** : an act or instance of knocking down all the bowling pins with the first bowl **8 a** : a military attack; *esp* : an air attack on a single objective **b** : a group of airplanes taking part in such an attack

strike•bound \'strīk-ˌbau̇nd\ *adj* : subjected to or shut down by a strike ⟨a *strikebound* factory⟩

strike•break•er \'strīk-ˌbrā-kər\ *n* : a person hired to help break up a strike by workers

strike•break•ing \-king\ *n* : action designed to break up a strike

strike•less \'strī-kləs\ *adj* : marked by the absence of strikes

strike off *vt* **1** : to produce with ease ⟨*strike off* a poem for the occasion⟩ **2** : to depict clearly and exactly

strike•out \'strī-ˌkau̇t\ *n* : an out in baseball resulting from a batter's being charged with three strikes

strike out \strī-'kau̇t, 'strī-\ *vb* **1** : to retire or be retired by a strikeout **2** : to enter upon a course of action ⟨*strike out* on one's own⟩ **3** : to set out vigorously ⟨*struck out* for home immediately⟩

strike•over \'strī-ˌkō-vər\ *n* : an act or instance of striking a typewriter character on a spot already occupied by another character

strik•er \'strī-kər\ *n* : one that strikes: as **a** : a player in any of several games who strikes **b** : the hammer of the striking mechanism of a clock or watch **c** : a worker on strike

strike up *vb* **1** : to begin to play or be played ⟨the band *struck up*⟩ ⟨a waltz *struck up*⟩ **2** : to cause to begin ⟨*strike up* a conversation⟩

strike zone *n* : the area (as between the knees and armpits of a batter) over home plate through which a pitched baseball must pass to be called a strike

strik•ing \'strī-king\ *adj* : REMARKABLE, IMPRESSIVE ⟨a *striking* costume⟩ ⟨a *striking* resemblance⟩ — **strik•ing•ly** \-king-lē\ *adv*

¹string \'string\ *n* **1** : a small cord used to bind, fasten, or tie **2** : a thin tough plant structure; *esp* : the fiber connecting the halves of a bean pod **3 a** : the gut, wire, or plastic cord of a musical instrument **b** *pl* (1) : the stringed instruments of an orchestra (2) : the players of such instruments **4 a** : a group of objects threaded on a string **b** : a series arranged in or as if in a line ⟨a *string* of victories⟩ **c** : the animals and especially horses belonging to or used by one individual **5** : LINE 14 **6** *pl* **a** : contingent conditions or obligations ⟨an agreement with no *strings* attached⟩ **b** : CONTROL 1, DOMINATION [Old English *streng*] — **string•less** \'string-ləs\ *adj* — **on the string** : subject to one's pleasure or influence

²string *vb* **strung** \'strəng\; **string•ing** \'string-ing\ **1** : to equip with strings **2** : to make tense **3 a** : to thread on or as if on a string ⟨*string* beads⟩ **b** : to thread with objects **c** : to tie, hang, or fasten with string **4** : to hang by the neck ⟨*strung* up from a high tree⟩ **5** : to remove the strings of ⟨*string* beans⟩ **6 a** : to extend or stretch like a string ⟨*string* wires from tree to tree⟩ **b** : to set out in a line or series **c** : to move, progress, or lie in a string **d** : to form into strings **7** : FOOL 3, HOAX

string along *vb* **1** : to go along : AGREE ⟨*string along* with the

\ə\ **abut**	\au̇\ **out**	\i\ **tip**	\ȯ\ **saw**	\u̇\ **foot**
\ər\ **further**	\ch\ **chin**	\ī\ **life**	\ȯi\ **coin**	\y\ **yet**
\a\ **mat**	\e\ **pet**	\j\ **job**	\th\ **thin**	\yü\ **few**
\ā\ **take**	\ē\ **easy**	\ng\ **sing**	\t͟h\ **this**	\yu̇\ **cure**
\ä\ **cot, cart**	\g\ **go**	\ō\ **bone**	\ü\ **food**	\zh\ **vision**

majority⟩ **2 :** to keep dangling or waiting ⟨*stringing* customers *along* with false promises⟩

string bass *n* **:** DOUBLE BASS

string bean *n* **:** a bean of one of the older varieties of kidney bean that have stringy fibers on the lines of separation of the pods; *also* **:** SNAP BEAN

string•course \ˈstring-ˌkōrs, -ˌkȯrs\ *n* **:** a horizontal band (as of bricks) in a building forming a part of the design

stringed instrument \ˈstringd-\ *n* **:** a musical instrument (as a violin, harp, or piano) sounded by plucking or striking or by drawing a bow across tense strings

strin•gent \ˈstrin-jənt\ *adj* **1 :** binding, drawing, or pressing tight **2 :** marked by rigor, strictness, or severity especially with regard to rule or standard **[**Latin *stringens,* present participle of *stringere* "to bind tight"**]** **syn** see RIGID — **strin•gen•cy** \-jən-sē\ *n* — **strin•gent•ly** *adv*

string•er \ˈstring-ər\ *n* **1 :** one that strings **2 a :** a long horizontal member in a framed structure or a bridge **b :** one of the inclined sides of a stair supporting the treads and risers **c :** a longitudinal member (as in an airplane fuselage or wing) to reinforce the skin **3 :** one estimated to be of specified excellence or quality or efficiency — usually used in combination ⟨first-*stringer*⟩ ⟨second-*stringer*⟩

string•halt \ˈstring-ˌhȯlt\ *n* **:** lameness of the hind legs of a horse due to muscular spasm — **string•halt•ed** \-ˌhȯl-təd\ *adj*

string•ing \ˈstring-ing\ *n* **:** the gut, silk, or nylon with which a racket is strung

string quartet *n* **1 :** a quartet of performers on stringed instruments usually including a first and second violin, a viola, and a cello **2 :** a composition for string quartet

string tie *n* **:** a narrow necktie

stringy \ˈstring-ē\ *adj* **string•i•er; -est 1 a :** containing, consisting of, or resembling fibrous matter or a string ⟨*stringy* root⟩ ⟨*stringy* hair⟩ **b :** lean and sinewy in build **:** WIRY **2 :** capable of being drawn out to form a string **:** ROPY ⟨a *stringy* precipitate⟩ — **string•i•ness** *n*

[1]**strip** \ˈstrip\ *vb* **stripped** *also* **stript** \ˈstript\; **strip•ping 1 a :** to remove clothing, covering, or surface matter from ⟨*stripped* the baby for a bath⟩ **b :** to remove (as clothing) from a person ⟨*stripped* the gloves from my hands⟩ **c :** UNDRESS ⟨*stripped* and showered⟩ **d :** SKIN, PEEL ⟨*strip* bark from a tree⟩ **2 :** to divest of honors, privileges, or functions **3 a :** to remove unnecessary or superficial matter from ⟨a prose style *stripped* to the bones⟩ **b :** to remove furniture, equipment, or accessories from **4 :** PLUNDER, SPOIL ⟨troops *stripped* the captured town⟩ **5 :** to make bare or clear (as by cutting or grazing) **6 :** DISMANTLE 2, DISASSEMBLE ⟨*strip* a rifle⟩ **7 :** to tear or damage the screw thread of (as a bolt or nut) **[**Old English *-strīpan***]** — **strip•per** *n*

[2]**strip** *n* **1 :** a long narrow piece or area ⟨*strips* of bacon⟩ ⟨a *strip* of land⟩ **2 :** AIRSTRIP **[**perhaps from Low German *strippe* "strap"**]**

strip–crop•ping \ˈstrip-ˌkräp-ing\ *n* **:** the growing of a cultivated crop (as corn) in strips alternating with strips of a sod-forming crop (as hay) arranged to follow land contours and minimize erosion — **strip–crop** \-ˌkräp\ *vb*

[1]**stripe** \ˈstrīp\ *n* **:** a stroke or blow with a rod or lash **[**Middle English**]**

[2]**stripe** *n* **1 :** a line or long narrow section differing in color or texture from parts adjoining **2 a :** a piece of braid (as on the sleeve) to indicate military rank or length of service **b :** CHEVRON 2 **3 :** a distinct variety or sort **:** TYPE ⟨persons of the same political *stripe*⟩ **[**probably from Dutch**]** — **stripe•less** \ˈstrī-pləs\ *adj*

[3]**stripe** *vt* **:** to make stripes on

striped \ˈstrīpt, ˈstrī-pəd\ *adj* **:** having stripes or streaks

striped bass *n* **:** a large sea bass of the Atlantic coast of the United States that has been introduced along the Pacific coast

strip•ling \ˈstrip-ling\ *n* **:** a youth just passing from boyhood to manhood **[**Middle English**]**

strip mine *n* **:** a mine that is worked from the earth's surface by the stripping away of overlying material — **strip–mine** *vt* — **strip miner** *n*

strive \ˈstrīv\ *vi* **strove** \ˈstrōv\ *also* **strived** \ˈstrīvd\; **striv•en** \ˈstriv-ən\ *or* **strived**; **striv•ing** \ˈstrī-ving\ **1 :** to struggle in opposition **:** CONTEND **2 :** to devote serious effort or energy **:** ENDEAVOR ⟨*strive* to win⟩ **[**Old French *estriver,* of Germanic origin**]** **syn** see TRY — **striv•er** \ˈstrī-vər\ *n*

strobe \ˈstrōb\ *n* **1 :** STROBOSCOPE **2 :** a device that uses a flashtube for high-speed illumination (as in photography) — called also *strobe light*

stro•bi•lus \strō-ˈbī-ləs, ˈstrō-bə-\ *n, pl* **-li** \-ˌlī\ **1 :** an aggregation of sporophylls resembling a cone (as in a club moss or equisetum) **2 :** the cone of a gymnosperm **[**Late Latin, "pinecone", from Greek *strobilos* "top, pinecone", from *strobos* "whirl"**]**

stro•bo•scope \ˈstrō-bə-ˌskōp\ *n* **:** an instrument for determining speeds of rotation or frequencies of vibration especially by means of a rapidly flashing light that illuminates an object intermittently **[**Greek *strobos* "whirl"**]** — **stro•bo•scop•ic** \ˌstrō-bə-ˈskäp-ik\ *adj* — **stro•bo•scop•i•cal•ly** \-ˈskäp-i-kə-lē, -klē\ *adv*

strode *past of* STRIDE

[1]**stroke** \ˈstrōk\ *vt* **1 :** to pass the hand over gently in one direction **2 :** to caress by stroking **[**Old English *strācian***]** — **strok•er** *n*

[2]**stroke** *n* **1 :** the act of striking; *esp* **:** a blow with a weapon or implement **2 :** a single unbroken movement; *esp* **:** one of a series of repeated or to-and-fro movements **3 :** a striking of the ball in a game; *esp* **:** a striking or attempt to strike the ball that constitutes the scoring unit in golf **4 :** a sudden action or process producing an impact ⟨a *stroke* of lightning⟩ or unexpected result ⟨a *stroke* of luck⟩ **5 :** sudden weakening or loss of consciousness, sensation, and voluntary motion caused by rupture or obstruction of an artery of the brain (as by a clot) — called also *apoplexy* **6 :** one of a series of propelling movements against a resisting medium ⟨*strokes* of an oar⟩ **7 a :** a vigorous or energetic effort **b :** a delicate or clever touch in a narrative, description, or construction **8 :** the movement or the distance of the movement in either direction of a mechanical part (as a piston rod) having a reciprocating motion **9 a :** the sound of a bell being struck **b :** HEARTBEAT **10 a :** a mark made by a single movement of a tool **b :** one of the lines of a letter of the alphabet **[**Middle English**]**

[3]**stroke** *vt* **1 :** to mark or cancel with a line ⟨*stroked* out my name⟩ **2 :** HIT 1a

stroll \ˈstrōl\ *vb* **:** to walk in a leisurely or idle manner **:** RAMBLE **[**probably from German dialect *strollen***]** — **stroll** *n*

stroll•er \ˈstrō-lər\ *n* **1 :** one that strolls **2 :** a wheeled seat in which a baby may be pushed

stro•ma \ˈstrō-mə\ *n, pl* **stro•ma•ta** \-mət-ə\ **:** a supporting framework in or of an organism: as **a :** the network of connective tissue that supports an animal organ **b :** an irregular mass of fungal hyphae supporting and enclosing spore-bearing structures **[**Latin, "bed covering", from Greek *strōma,* from *stornynai* "to spread out"**]**

strong \ˈstrȯng\ *adj* **strong•er** \ˈstrȯng-gər\; **strong•est** \ˈstrȯng-gəst\ **1 :** having or marked by great physical power **:** ROBUST **2 :** having moral or intellectual power **3 :** having great resources (as of wealth) **4 :** of a specified number ⟨an army ten thousand *strong*⟩ **5 :** being great or striking **:** CLOSE ⟨bears a *strong* resemblance to me⟩ **6 :** FORCEFUL, COGENT ⟨*strong* arguments⟩ **7 :** not mild or weak **:** INTENSE: as **a :** rich in some active agent (as a flavor or extract) ⟨*strong* coffee⟩ **b :** high in saturation and medium in lightness ⟨a *strong* red⟩ **c :** ionizing freely in solution ⟨*strong* acids and bases⟩ **d :** magnifying by refracting greatly ⟨a *strong* lens⟩ **8 :** moving with rapidity or force ⟨*strong* wind⟩ **9 :** ARDENT, ZEALOUS ⟨*strong* advocates of peace⟩ **10 a :** able to withstand stress **:** not easily injured **:** SOLID **b :** not easily subdued or taken ⟨a *strong* fort⟩ **11 :** well established **:** FIRM ⟨*strong* beliefs⟩ **12 :** having or being an offensive or intense odor or flavor **:** RANK **13 :** of, relating to, or constituting a verb or verb conjugation that forms the past tense by a change in the root vowel and the past participle usually by the addition of *-en* with or without change of the root vowel (as *strive, strove, striven* or *drink, drank, drunk*) **[**Old English *strang***]** — **strong** *adv* — **strong•ly** \ˈstrȯng-lē\ *adv*

[1]**strong–arm** \ˈstrȯng-ˈärm\ *adj* **:** having, using, or involving undue force **:** VIOLENT ⟨*strong-arm* methods⟩

[2]**strong–arm** *vt* **1 :** to use force on **:** ASSAULT **2 :** to rob by force

strong•box \ˈstrȯng-ˌbäks\ *n* **:** a strongly made container for money or valuables

strong•hold \-ˌhōld\ *n* **:** a fortified place **:** FORTRESS

strong–mind•ed \-ˈmīn-dəd\ *adj* **:** markedly independent in thought and judgment — **strong–mind•ed•ly** *adv* — **strong–mind•ed•ness** *n*

strong suit *n* **1 :** a long suit containing high cards **2 :** something in which one excels **:** FORTE

stron•tium \'strän-chē-əm, -chəm; 'stränt-ē-əm\ *n* **:** a soft malleable ductile metallic element occurring only in combined form — see ELEMENT table [New Latin, from *strontia* "strontium monoxide", from *Strontian,* village in Scotland]

strontium 90 *n* **:** a heavy radioactive isotope of strontium having the mass number 90 that is present in the fallout from nuclear explosions

¹strop \'sträp\ *n* **:** STRAP; *esp* **:** a usually leather band for sharpening a razor [Old English, "thong for securing an oar", from Latin *struppus* "band, strap", from Greek *strophos*]

²strop *vt* **stropped; strop•ping :** to sharpen (a razor) on a strop

stro•phe \'strō-fē\ *n* **:** a division of a poem **:** STANZA [Greek *strophē,* literally, "turn", from *strephein* "to turn, twist"] — **stro•phic** \'strō-fik, 'sträf-ik\ *adj*

strove *past & chiefly dialect past participle of* STRIVE

struck \'strək\ *adj* **:** closed or affected by a labor strike [past participle of *strike*]

struc•tur•al \'strək-chə-rəl, 'strək-shrəl\ *adj* **1 :** of, relating to, or affecting structure ⟨*structural* defects⟩ ⟨*structural* principles⟩ **2 :** used or formed for use in construction ⟨*structural* steel⟩ — **struc•tur•al•ly** \-ē\ *adv*

structural formula *n* **:** an expanded molecular formula showing the arrangement within the molecule of atoms and of bonds

¹struc•ture \'strək-chər\ *n* **1 :** the action of building **:** CONSTRUCTION **2 a :** something constructed **b :** something made up of interdependent parts in a definite pattern of organization **3 :** manner of construction **:** MAKEUP **4 :** the arrangement or relationship of elements (as particles, parts, or organs) in a substance, body, or system ⟨soil *structure*⟩ ⟨the *structure* of a language⟩ [Latin *structura,* from *struere* "to heap up, build"] — **struc•ture•less** \-ləs\ *adj*

²structure *vt* **struc•tured; struc•tur•ing** \'strək-chə-ring, 'strək-shring\ **:** to form into a structure **:** ORGANIZE

stru•del \'strüd-l, 'shtrüd-l\ *n* **:** a pastry made from a sheet of thin dough rolled up with filling and baked [German, literally, "whirlpool"]

¹strug•gle \'strəg-əl\ *vi* **strug•gled; strug•gling** \'strəg-ling, -ə-ling\ **1 :** to make violent strenuous efforts against opposition **:** STRIVE **2 :** to proceed with difficulty or with great effort ⟨*struggle* through deep snow⟩ [Middle English *struglen*] — **strug•gler** \-lər, -ə-lər\ *n*

²struggle *n* **1 :** a violent effort or exertion **2 :** CONTEST 1, STRIFE

struggle for existence : the competition (as for food, space, or light) between members of a natural population that tends to eliminate less efficient individuals and thereby to increase the chance that the more efficient will pass on their traits

strum \'strəm\ *vb* **strummed; strum•ming :** to play on a stringed instrument by brushing the strings with the fingers [imitative] — **strum•mer** *n*

strum•pet \'strəm-pət\ *n* **:** PROSTITUTE, HARLOT [Middle English]

strung *past of* STRING

¹strut \'strət\ *vb* **strut•ted; strut•ting 1 :** to walk with a stiff proud gait **2 :** to parade (as clothes) with a show of pride [Old English *strūtian* "to exert oneself"] — **strut•ter** *n*

• **syn** STRUT, SWAGGER mean to assume an air of importance. STRUT emphasizes pompous dignity and vanity as expressed by one's gait or bearing; SWAGGER suggests ostentatiousness and insolence or boastfulness especially in one's manners and movements.

²strut *n* **1 :** a bar or brace that resists pressure in the direction of its length **2 :** a pompous step or walk

strych•nine \'strik-ˌnīn, -nən, -ˌnēn\ *n* **:** a bitter poisonous alkaloid that is obtained from nux vomica and related plants, acts as a stimulant to the central nervous system, and is used especially as a rat poison [French, from Latin *strychnos* "nightshade", from Greek]

¹stub \'stəb\ *n* **1 :** STUMP 1b **2 :** something having or worn to a short or blunt shape: as **a :** a pen with a short blunt nib **b :** a short part left after a larger part has been broken off or used up ⟨pencil *stub*⟩ **3 a :** a small part of a check kept as a record of the contents of the check **b :** the part of a ticket returned to the user [Old English *stybb*]

²stub *vt* **stubbed; stub•bing 1 :** to extinguish (as a cigarette) by crushing **2 :** to strike (as one's toe) against an object

stub•ble \'stəb-əl\ *n* **1 :** the stem ends of herbaceous plants and especially cereal grasses remaining attached to the soil after harvest **2 :** a rough surface or growth resembling stubble; *esp* **:** a short growth of beard [Old French *estuble,* from Latin *stipula, stupula,* "stalk, straw"] — **stub•bly** \'stəb-lē, -ə-lē\ *adj*

stub•born \'stəb-ərn\ *adj* **1 a :** having a firm idea or purpose **:** DETERMINED **b :** hard to convince, persuade, or move to action **:** OBSTINATE ⟨*stubborn* as a mule⟩ **2 :** done or continued in an obstinate or persistent manner ⟨*stubborn* refusal⟩ **3 :** difficult to handle, manage, or treat ⟨*stubborn* hair⟩ [Middle English *stuborn*] **syn** see OBSTINATE — **stub•born•ly** *adv* — **stub•born•ness** \-ərn-nəs\ *n*

stub•by \'stəb-ē\ *adj* **stub•bi•er; -est 1 :** resembling a stub especially in shortness and broadness ⟨*stubby* fingers⟩ **2 :** abounding with stubs **:** BRISTLY — **stub•bi•ness** *n*

stuc•co \'stək-ō\ *n, pl* **stuccos** *or* **stuccoes :** a plaster (as of portland cement, sand, and lime) used to cover exterior walls or ornament interior walls [Italian, of Germanic origin] — **stucco** *vt*

stuc•co•work \'stək-ō-ˌwərk\ *n* **:** work done in stucco

stuck *past of* STICK

stuck–up \'stək-'əp\ *adj* **:** CONCEITED, SELF-IMPORTANT

¹stud \'stəd\ *n* **1 :** a group of animals and especially horses kept primarily for breeding; *also* **:** the place where they are kept **2 :** a male animal (as a stallion) kept for breeding [Old English *stōd*] — **at stud :** for breeding as a stud

²stud *n* **1 :** one of the smaller uprights in the framing of the walls of a building to which sheathing, paneling, or laths are fastened **:** SCANTLING **2 a :** a boss, rivet, or nail with a large head used for ornament or protection **b :** a solid button with a shank or eye on the back inserted through an eyelet in a garment as a fastener or ornament **3 :** a piece (as a rod or pin) projecting from a machine and serving chiefly as a support or axis [Old English *studu* "post"]

³stud *vt* **stud•ded; stud•ding 1 :** to furnish (as a building or wall) with studs **2 :** to adorn, cover, or protect with studs **3 :** to mark, decorate, or dot at random ⟨a sky *studded* with stars⟩

stud•book \'stəd-ˌbu̇k\ *n* **:** an official record of the pedigree of purebred animals (as horses or dogs)

stud•ding \'stəd-ing\ *n* **1 :** material for studs **2 :** the studs of a building or wall

stud•ding sail \'stəd-ing-ˌsāl, 'stən-səl\ *n* **:** a light sail set at the side of a principal square sail of a ship [origin unknown]

stu•dent \'stüd-nt, 'styüd-, *especially South* -ənt\ *n* **1 :** LEARNER, SCHOLAR; *esp* **:** one who attends a school or college **2 :** one who studies **:** an attentive and systematic observer ⟨a *student* of life⟩ [Latin *studens,* from *studēre* "to study"]

student government *n* **:** the organization and management of student life, activities, or discipline by various student organizations in a school or college

student teacher *n* **:** a student engaged in practice teaching

stud•horse \'stəd-ˌhȯrs\ *n* **:** a stallion kept especially for breeding

stud•ied \'stəd-ēd\ *adj* **1 :** KNOWLEDGEABLE, LEARNED ⟨well *studied* in math⟩ **2 :** carefully considered or prepared **:** THOUGHTFUL **3 :** produced or marked by conscious design ⟨*studied* indifference⟩ — **stud•ied•ly** *adv* — **stud•ied•ness** *n*

stu•dio \'stüd-ē-ˌō, 'styüd-\ *n, pl* **-di•os 1 a :** the working place of an artist **b :** a place for the study of an art ⟨a dance *studio*⟩ **2 :** a place where motion pictures are made **3 :** a place maintained and equipped for the transmission of radio or television programs [Italian, literally, "study", from Latin *studium*]

studio couch *n* **:** an upholstered usually backless couch that can be made to serve as a double bed by sliding from underneath it the frame of a single cot

stu•di•ous \'stüd-ē-əs, 'styüd-\ *adj* **1 :** given to, concerned with, or tending to promote study ⟨*studious* habits⟩ **2 :** marked by purposeful effort **:** EARNEST — **stu•di•ous•ly** *adv* — **stu•di•ous•ness** *n*

¹study \'stəd-ē\ *n, pl* **stud•ies 1 :** a state of contemplation **:** REVERIE **2 a :** application of the mind to the acquisition of knowledge often about a particular field or topic **b :** a careful examination or analysis of something; *also* : a report or publication on such a study **3** : a building or room devoted to study or literary pursuits **4 a** : a branch or department of learning : SUBJECT **b** : the activity or work of a student **5** : a usually preliminary or elementary artistic production concerned especially with problems of technique ⟨a series of *studies* of classic heads⟩ [Old French *estudie,* from Latin *studium*]

[2]**study** *vb* **stud•ied**; **study•ing 1** : to engage in study or the study of **2** : ENDEAVOR, TRY ⟨*studied* to please the boss⟩ **3** : to consider attentively or in detail especially with the intent of fixing in the mind or of appraising ⟨*studied* the question carefully⟩

study hall *n* **1** : a room in a school set aside for study **2** : a period in a student's day set aside for study and homework

[1]**stuff** \'stəf\ *n* **1** : materials, supplies, or equipment used in some activity: as **a** : a person's or a family's movable possessions (as household goods or baggage) **b** : material to be manufactured, wrought, or used in construction **c** : a finished textile suitable for clothing; *esp* : wool or worsted material **2 a** : writing, discourse, or ideas often of little or temporary worth **b** : actions or talk of a particular and often objectionable kind ⟨how do they get away with such *stuff*⟩ **3 a** : an aggregate of matter ⟨volcanic rock is curious *stuff*⟩ **b** : matter of a particular kind often unspecified ⟨sold tons of the *stuff*⟩ **4 a** : fundamental material : SUBSTANCE ⟨*stuff* of greatness⟩ **b** : subject matter **5** : special knowledge or capability ⟨has the *stuff* to do well here⟩ [Middle French *estoffe,* from *estoffer* "to equip, stock"]

[2]**stuff** *vb* **1 a** : to fill by or as if by packing things in : CRAM **b** : to eat gluttonously **c** : to fill with a stuffing **d** : to stop up : PLUG **2** : to put or push into something especially carelessly or casually ⟨*stuffed* the clothes into the drawer⟩ — **stuff•er** *n*

stuffed shirt *n* : a smug, conceited, and usually pompous person

stuff•ing \'stəf-iŋ\ *n* : material used to stuff something; *esp* : a seasoned mixture used to stuff meat, vegetables, eggs, or poultry

stuff shot *n* : DUNK SHOT

stuffy \'stəf-ē\ *adj* **stuff•i•er**; **-est 1** : SULLEN 1, ILL-HUMORED **2 a** : oppressive to the breathing : CLOSE ⟨a *stuffy* room⟩ **b** : stuffed or choked up ⟨a *stuffy* feeling in my head⟩ **3** : lacking in vitality or interest : DULL **4** : narrowly inflexible in standards of conduct : SELF-RIGHTEOUS — **stuff•i•ly** \'stəf-ə-lē\ *adv* — **stuff•i•ness** \'stəf-ē-nəs\ *n*

stul•ti•fy \'stəl-tə-,fī\ *vt* **-fied**; **-fy•ing 1** : to cause to appear or be stupid, foolish, or absurdly illogical **2** : to make futile or useless especially through weakening or repressive influences ⟨*stultify* initiative⟩ [Late Latin *stultificare* "to make foolish", from Latin *stultus* "foolish"] — **stul•ti•fi•ca•tion** \,stəl-tə-fə-'kā-shən\ *n*

stum•ble \'stəm-bəl\ *vi* **stum•bled**; **stum•bling** \-bə-liŋ, -bliŋ\ **1** : to trip in walking or running; *also* : to walk unsteadily **2 a** : to blunder morally **b** : to speak or act in a blundering or clumsy manner **3** : to come or happen unexpectedly or by chance ⟨*stumbled* on a discovery⟩ [Middle English *stumblen*] — **stumble** *n* — **stum•bler** \-bə-lər, -blər\ *n* — **stum•bling•ly** \-bə-liŋ-lē, -bliŋ-\ *adv*

stum•bling block \'stəm-bliŋ-\ *n* **1** : an impediment to belief or understanding **2** : an obstacle to progress

[1]**stump** \'stəmp\ *n* **1 a** : the base of a bodily part (as an arm or leg) remaining after the rest is removed **b** : the part of a plant and especially a tree remaining attached to the root after the top is cut off **2** : a part (as of a tooth or pencil) remaining after the rest is worn away or lost : STUB **3** : a place or occasion for political public speaking [Middle English *stumpe*]

[2]**stump** *vb* **1 a** : STUB 2 **b** : to walk or walk over heavily or clumsily **2 a** : CHALLENGE 4, DARE **b** : BEWILDER 2, CONFOUND **3** : to clear (land) of stumps **4** : to go about making political speeches or supporting a cause ⟨*stump* the state for the reform candidate⟩ — **stump•er** *n*

stump•age \'stəm-pij\ *n* : the value of standing timber; *also* : uncut timber or the right to cut it

stumpy \'stəm-pē\ *adj* **stump•i•er**; **-est 1** : full of stumps **2** : being short and thick : SQUAT

stun \'stən\ *vt* **stunned**; **stun•ning 1** : to make senseless or dizzy by or as if by a blow **2** : to overcome with astonishment or disbelief : SHOCK ⟨*stunned* by the news⟩ [Old French *estoner* "to astonish", from Latin *ex-* + *tonare* "to thunder"]

stung *past of* STING

stunk *past of* STINK

stun•ner \'stən-ər\ *n* : one that stuns; *esp* : an unusually attractive person

stun•ning \'stən-iŋ\ *adj* **1** : tending or able to stupefy or bewilder ⟨a *stunning* blow⟩ **2** : strikingly lovely or pleasing ⟨a *stunning* dress⟩ — **stun•ning•ly** \-iŋ-lē\ *adv*

[1]**stunt** \'stənt\ *vt* : to hinder the normal growth of : DWARF [English dialect *stunt* "stunted, abrupt"]

[2]**stunt** *n* : a plant disease in which dwarfing occurs

[3]**stunt** *n* : an unusual or difficult feat performed or undertaken usually to gain attention or publicity [probably alteration of *stump* "challenge"]

[4]**stunt** *vi* : to perform stunts

stupe \'stüp, 'styüp\ *n* : a hot wet often medicated cloth applied externally (as to stimulate circulation) [Latin *stuppa* "coarse part of flax, tow", from Greek *styppē*]

stu•pe•fy \'stü-pə-,fī, 'styü-\ *vt* **-fied**; **-fy•ing 1** : to make stupid, dull, or numb by or as if by drugs **2** : ASTONISH, BEWILDER [Middle French *stupefier,* from Latin *stupefacere,* from *stupēre* "to be astonished" + *facere* "to make, do"] — **stu•pe•fac•tion** \,stü-pə-'fak-shən, ,styü-\ *n* — **stu•pe•fi•er** \'stü-pə-,fī-ər, 'styü-, -,fīr\ *n*

stu•pen•dous \stu̇-'pen-dəs, styu̇-\ *adj* : stupefying or amazing especially because of size, complexity, or greatness [Latin *stupendus* "to be wondered at", from *stupēre* "to be astonished"] **syn** see MONSTROUS — **stu•pen•dous•ly** *adv* — **stu•pen•dous•ness** *n*

stu•pid \'stü-pəd, 'styü-\ *adj* **1 a** : slow of mind : OBTUSE **b** : given to unwise decisions or actions **2 a** : dulled in feeling or sensation **b** : incapable of feeling or sensation **3** : marked by or resulting from dullness : SENSELESS ⟨a *stupid* mistake⟩ **4** : DREARY, BORING ⟨a *stupid* plot⟩ [Middle French *stupide,* from Latin *stupidus,* from *stupēre* "to be benumbed, be astonished"] — **stu•pid•ly** *adv* — **stu•pid•ness** *n*

• **syn** STUPID, DULL, DENSE mean lacking in power to take in ideas or impressions. STUPID implies a slow-witted or dazed state of mind that may be either congenital or temporary; DULL suggests a slow or sluggish mind such as results from disease, depression, or shock; DENSE implies a relative imperviousness to new or complex ideas.

stu•pid•i•ty \stu̇-'pid-ət-ē, styu̇-\ *n, pl* **-ties 1** : the quality or state of being stupid **2** : something (as an idea or act) that is stupid

stu•por \'stü-pər, 'styü-\ *n* **1** : a condition characterized by great dulling or suspension of sense or feeling ⟨a drunken *stupor*⟩ **2** : a state of extreme apathy or torpor resulting often from stress or shock [Latin, from *stupēre* "to be benumbed, be astonished"] **syn** see LETHARGY — **stu•por•ous** \-pə-rəs, -prəs\ *adj*

stur•dy \'stərd-ē\ *adj* **stur•di•er**; **-est 1 a** : firmly built or made **b** : HARDY 3 **2 a** : marked by or reflecting physical strength or vigor : ROBUST **b** : FIRM 3, RESOLUTE [Middle English, "brave, stubborn", from Old French *estourdi* "stunned, rash", from *estourdir* "to stun", derived from Latin *ex-* + *turdus* "thrush"] — **stur•di•ly** \'stərd-l-ē\ *adj* — **stur•di•ness** \'stərd-ē-nəs\ *n*

△ **origin** In early medieval Europe the thrush had a reputation for drunkenness and dullwittedness. This bird was believed to gorge itself on grapes until it became quite dizzy. Indeed, the French still have a proverbial phrase *soûl comme une grive,* "drunk as a thrush". A person who is stunned acts dizzy or drunk, and the Old French verb *estourdir,* "to stun", was derived from the Latin name, *turdus,* of the drunk and dizzy thrush. Middle English *sturdy,* borrowed from Old French *estourdi,* "stunned, rash", originally meant "rashly or recklessly brave". *Sturdy* later developed the senses "stubborn, hardy, robust, firm".

stur•geon \'stər-jən\ *n* : any of various usually large long-bodied fishes that have a thick skin with rows of bony plates and are valued for their flesh and especially for their roe which is made into caviar [Old French *estourjon,* of Germanic origin]

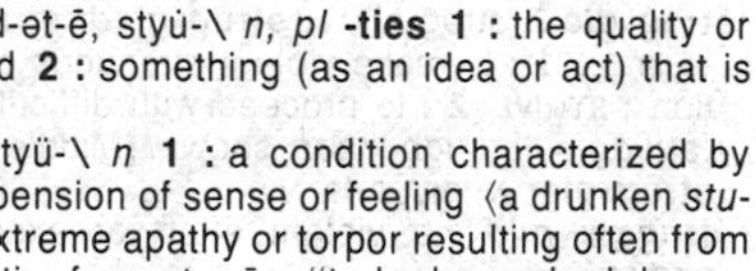

sturgeon

[1]**stut•ter** \'stət-ər\ *vb* : to speak or utter with involuntary repeti-

tion, disruption, or blocking of vocal sounds [Middle English *stutten*] **syn** see STAMMER — **stut•ter•er** \'stət-ər-ər\ *n*

[2]**stutter** *n* **1** : an act or instance of stuttering **2** : a speech disorder involving stuttering accompanied by emotional turmoil

[1]**sty** \'stī\ *n, pl* **sties** *also* **styes** \'stīz\ **1** : a pen or enclosed housing for swine **2** : a filthy, low, or vicious place [Old English *stig*]

[2]**sty** *or* **stye** \'stī\ *n, pl* **sties** *or* **styes** \'stīz\ : an inflamed swelling of a skin gland on the edge of an eyelid [from obsolete *styan*, from Old English *stīgend*, from *stīgan* "ro rise"]

sty•gian \'stij-ən, 'stij-ē-ən\ *adj, often cap* : INFERNAL, GLOOMY ⟨*stygian* darkness⟩ [Latin *stygius*, from Greek *stygios*, from *Styg-, Styx* "Styx"]

[1]**style** \'stīl\ *n* **1 a** : an instrument used by the ancients in writing on waxed tablets **b** : the shadow-producing indicator of a sundial **c** : GRAVER 2 **d** : NEEDLE 3d **e** : a slender prolongation of a plant ovary bearing a stigma at its apex **f** : a slender bodily process of an animal **2** : mode of expressing thought in language; *esp* : one characteristic of an individual, period, school, or nation ⟨ornate *style*⟩ **3** : the custom or plan followed in spelling, capitalization, punctuation, and typographic arrangement and display **4** : mode of address : TITLE **5 a** (1) : manner or method of acting or performing especially in accordance with some standard (2) : a distinctive or characteristic manner **b** : a fashionable manner or mode ⟨dining in *style*⟩ ⟨that dress is out of *style*⟩ **c** : overall excellence, skill, or grace in performance, manner, or appearance [Latin *stilus* "stake, stylus, style of writing"] **syn** see DICTION, FASHION — **style•less** \'stīl-ləs\ *adj*

[2]**style** *vt* **1** : NAME, CALL ⟨*style* themselves scientists⟩ **2 a** : to cause to conform to a customary style **b** : to design and make in accord with the current fashion — **styl•er** *n*

style•book \'stīl-,bu̇k\ *n* : a book explaining, describing, or illustrating the prevailing, accepted, or authorized style ⟨a *stylebook* for printers⟩

sty•let \'stī-lət\ *n* **1** : a slender surgical probe **2** : a style on an animal [French, from Middle French *stilet* "stiletto", from Italian *stiletto*]

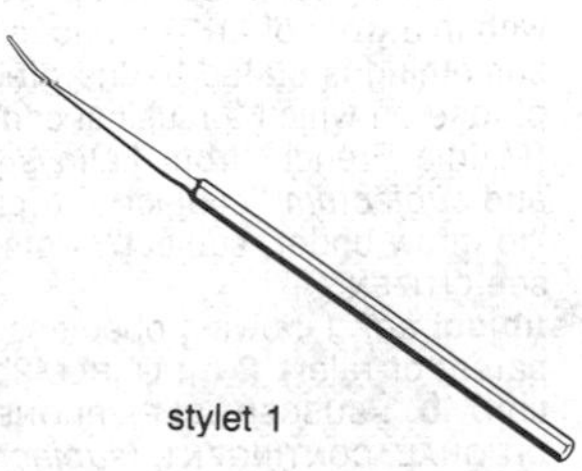

stylet 1

styl•ish \'stī-lish\ *adj* : having style; *esp* : conforming to current fashion — **styl•ish•ly** *adv* — **styl•ish•ness** *n*

styl•ist \'stī-ləst\ *n* **1** : a master or model of style; *esp* : a writer or speaker eminent in matters of style **2** : one who develops, designs, or advises on styles — **sty•lis•tic** \stī-'lis-tik\ *also* **sty•lis•ti•cal** \-ti-kəl\ *adj* — **sty•lis•ti•cal•ly** \-ti-kə-lē, -klē\ *adv*

styl•ize \'stīl-,īz\ *vt* : to conform to a style; *esp* : to represent or design according to a style or stylistic pattern rather than according to nature — **styl•iza•tion** \,stī-lə-'zā-shən\ *n* — **styl•iz•er** \'stīl-,ī-zər\ *n*

sty•lo•bate \'stī-lə-,bāt\ *n* : a continuous flat coping or pavement on which a row of architectural columns is supported [Latin *stylobates*, from Greek *stylobatēs*, from *stylos* "pillar" + *bainein* "to walk, go"]

sty•loid \'stīl-,ȯid\ *adj* : resembling a style ⟨the slender pointed *styloid* process of the ulna⟩

sty•lus \'stī-ləs\ *n, pl* **sty•li** \'stīl-,ī\ *also* **sty•lus•es** \'stī-lə-səz\ **1** : an instrument for writing or marking **2** : NEEDLE 3d [Latin *stilus* "stake, stylus"]

stylus 1 with Roman wax tablet

[1]**sty•mie** \'stī-mē\ *n* : a very distressing and thwarting situation [perhaps from Scottish *stymie* "person with poor eyesight"]

[2]**stymie** *vt* **sty•mied**; **sty•mie•ing** : to present an obstacle to : stand in the way of

styp•tic \'stip-tik\ *adj* : tending to contract or bind : ASTRINGENT; *esp* : tending to check bleeding ⟨*styptic* effect of cold⟩ [Latin *stypticus*, from Greek *styptikos*, from *styphein* "to contract"] — **styptic** *n*

styptic pencil *n* : a cylindrical stick of medicated styptic substance used especially in shaving to stop the bleeding from small cuts

sty•rene \'stī-,rēn\ *n* : a fragrant liquid hydrocarbon used chiefly in making synthetic rubber, resins, and plastics [derived from Latin *styrax* "storax"]

Sty•ro•foam \'stī-rə-,fōm\ *trademark* — used for an expanded rigid polystyrene plastic

sua•sion \'swā-zhən\ *n* : the act of influencing or persuading [Latin *suasio*, from *suadēre* "to urge, persuade"] — **sua•sive** \'swā-siv, -ziv\ *adj* — **sua•sive•ly** *adv* — **sua•sive•ness** *n*

suave \'swäv\ *adj* : smoothly but often superficially polite and agreeable [Middle French, "pleasant, sweet", from Latin *suavis*] — **suave•ly** *adv* — **suave•ness** *n* — **sua•vi•ty** \'swäv-ət-ē\ *n*

• **syn** SUAVE, URBANE, BLAND, SMOOTH mean pleasingly tactful and well-mannered. SUAVE implies a specific ability to deal with others easily and without friction ⟨a *suave* headwaiter⟩ URBANE suggests courtesy and poise developed by wide social experience ⟨an *urbane* outlook on life⟩ BLAND emphasizes mildness of manner and absence of irritating qualities ⟨a *bland*, kindly old soul⟩ SMOOTH usually suggests a deliberately assumed suavity ⟨a *smooth* liar⟩

[1]**sub** \'səb\ *n* : SUBSTITUTE

[2]**sub** *vi* **subbed**; **sub•bing** : to act as a substitute

[3]**sub** *n* : SUBMARINE

sub- *prefix* **1** : under : beneath : below ⟨*sub*aqueous⟩ ⟨*sub*soil⟩ **2 a** : subordinate : secondary ⟨*sub*station⟩ **b** : subdivision of ⟨*sub*committee⟩ ⟨*sub*species⟩ **c** : with repetition (as of a process) so as to form, stress, or deal with subordinate parts or relations ⟨*sub*let⟩ **3** : less than completely, perfectly, or normally : somewhat ⟨*sub*dominant⟩ **4** : falling nearly in the category of and often adjoining : bordering upon ⟨*sub*arctic⟩ [Latin, "under, below, secretly, from below, up, near", from *sub* "under, close to"]

See *sub-* and 2d element

subadolescent
subaffluent
subage
subagency
subagent
suballocation
subaverage
subbase
subbasement
subbranch
subcabinet
subcaste
subcategorization
subcategorize
subcategory
subclassification
subclassify
subclause
subcluster
subcollege
subcollegiate
subcolony
subcommission
subcommunity
subcomponent
subconcept
subcult
subdepartment
subdevelopment
subdialect
subdirector
subdiscipline
subdistrict
subfield
subfile
subframe
subgenre
subglacial
subgoal
subgroup
subhorizontal
subhumid
subice
subindustry
sublethal
sublevel
sublot
submarket
subminimal
subnetwork
subniche
suboceanic
suboptimal
suborganization
subpar
subparagraph
subpart
subpattern
subproblem
subprocess
subproduct
subprogram
subproject
subregion
subroutine
subsea
subsite
subsociety
subspecialty
subsystem
subtask
subtest
subtheme
subtotal
subtreasury
subtribe
subtype
subunit
subvisible
subzone

sub•aer•i•al \,səb-'ar-ē-əl, 'səb-, -'er-; ,səb-ā-'ir-ē-əl\ *adj* : situated or occurring on or close to the surface of the earth ⟨*subaerial* habitat⟩ ⟨*subaerial* roots⟩ — **sub•aer•i•al•ly** \-ē-ə-lē\ *adv*

sub•al•pine \,səb-'al-,pīn, 'səb-\ *adj* **1** : of or relating to the

\ə\ **abut**	\au̇\ **out**	\i\ **tip**	\ȯ\ **saw**	\u̇\ **foot**
\ər\ **further**	\ch\ **chin**	\ī\ **life**	\ȯi\ **coin**	\y\ **yet**
\a\ **mat**	\e\ **pet**	\j\ **job**	\th\ **thin**	\yü\ **few**
\ā\ **take**	\ē\ **easy**	\ng\ **sing**	\t͟h\ **this**	\yu̇\ **cure**
\ä\ **cot, cart**	\g\ **go**	\ō\ **bone**	\ü\ **food**	\zh\ **vision**

region about the foot and lower slopes of the Alps **2** *cap* **:** of, relating to, or growing on upland slopes near timberline

¹sub•al•tern \sə-ˈbȯl-tərn, *especially British* ˈsəb-əl-tərn\ *adj* **:** of low or lower rank **:** SUBORDINATE **[**Late Latin *subalternus,* from Latin *sub-* + *alternus* "alternate"**]**

²subaltern *n* **:** SUBORDINATE; *esp* **:** a commissioned officer in the British army below the rank of captain

sub•aque•ous \ˌsəb-ˈā-kwē-əs, ˈsəb-, -ˈak-wē-\ *adj* **:** formed, occurring, or existing in or under water

sub•arc•tic \-ˈärk-tik, -ˈärt-ik\ *adj* **:** of, relating to, or being regions immediately outside of the arctic circle or regions similar to these in climate or conditions of life

sub•as•sem•bly \ˌsəb-ə-ˈsem-blē\ *n* **:** an assembled unit designed to be incorporated with other units in a finished product

sub•atom•ic \ˌsəb-ə-ˈtäm-ik\ *adj* **:** of or relating to the inside of the atom or particles smaller than atoms

sub•cel•lu•lar \ˌsəb-ˈsel-yə-lər, ˈsəb-\ *adj* **:** of less than cellular scope or level of organization

sub•class \ˈsəb-ˌklas\ *n* **:** a primary division of a class (as in taxonomy)

¹sub•cla•vi•an \ˌsəb-ˈklā-vē-ən\ *adj* **1 :** located under the clavicle **2 :** of, relating to, or being a subclavian part

²subclavian *n* **:** a subclavian part (as an artery or vein)

sub•clin•i•cal \ˌsəb-ˈklin-i-kəl, ˈsəb-\ *adj* **:** not severe enough to be detectable by the usual clinical tests ⟨a *subclinical* infection⟩ — **sub•clin•i•cal•ly** \-kə-lē, -klē\ *adv*

sub•com•mit•tee \ˈsəb-kə-ˌmit-ē, ˌsəb-kə-ˈ\ *n* **:** a subdivision of a committee usually organized for a specific purpose

sub•com•pact \ˈsəb-ˈkäm-ˌpakt\ *n* **:** an automobile smaller than a compact

¹sub•con•scious \ˌsəb-ˈkän-chəs, ˈsəb-\ *adj* **1 :** existing in the mind but not immediately available to consciousness **2 :** imperfectly conscious ⟨a *subconscious* state⟩ — **sub•con•scious•ly** *adv* — **sub•con•scious•ness** *n*

²subconscious *n* **:** the mental activities just below the threshold of consciousness

sub•con•ti•nent \ˈsəb-ˈkänt-n-ənt, -ˈkänt-nənt\ *n* **:** a large landmass (as Greenland) smaller than any of the usually recognized continents; *also* **:** a major subdivision of a continent — **sub•con•ti•nen•tal** \ˌsəb-ˌkänt-n-ˈent-l\ *adj*

¹sub•con•tract \ˌsəb-ˈkän-ˌtrakt, ˈsəb-; ˌsəb-kən-ˈ\ *vb* **1 :** to engage a third party to perform (work included in an original contract) under a subcontract **2 :** to let out or undertake work under a subcontract — **sub•con•trac•tor** \-ˌtrak-tər\ *n*

²sub•con•tract \ˈsəb-ˈkän-ˌtrakt, -ˌkän-\ *n* **:** a contract between a party to an original contract and a third party who usually agrees to supply work or materials required in the original

sub•crit•i•cal \ˌsəb-ˈkrit-i-kəl, ˈsəb-\ *adj* **1 :** less or lower than critical **2 :** of insufficient size to sustain a chain reaction ⟨*subcritical* mass of fissionable material⟩

sub•cul•ture \ˈsəb-ˌkəl-chər\ *n* **1 :** a culture (as of bacteria) derived from another culture; *also* **:** an act or instance of producing a subculture **2 :** a distinguishable subdivision of a culture ⟨a criminal *subculture*⟩

sub•cu•ta•ne•ous \ˌsəb-kyu̇-ˈtā-nē-əs\ *adj* **:** being, living, used, or made under the skin ⟨*subcutaneous* fat⟩ ⟨a *subcutaneous* needle⟩ — **sub•cu•ta•ne•ous•ly** *adv*

sub•dea•con \ˌsəb-ˈdē-kən, ˈsəb-\ *n* **:** a cleric ranking below a deacon; *esp* **:** a cleric in the lowest of the former major orders of the Roman Catholic church

sub•deb \ˈsəb-ˌdeb\ *n* **:** SUBDEBUTANTE

sub•deb•u•tante \ˌsəb-ˈdeb-yu-ˌtänt, ˈsəb-\ *n* **:** a young girl who is about to become a debutante; *also* **:** a girl in her middle teens

sub•di•ac•o•nate \ˌsəb-dī-ˈak-ə-nət\ *n* **:** the office or rank of a subdeacon

sub•di•vide \ˌsəb-də-ˈvīd\ *vb* **1 :** to divide the parts of into more parts **2 :** to divide into several parts; *esp* **:** to divide (a tract of land) into building lots — **sub•di•vid•able** \-də-ˈvīd-ə-bəl\ *adj* — **sub•di•vi•sion** \ˌsəb-də-ˈvizh-ən, ˈsəb-də-ˌ\ *n*

sub•dom•i•nant \ˌsəb-ˈdäm-ə-nənt, ˈsəb-\ *n* **1 :** the 4th tone of the major or minor scale (as F in the scale of C) **2 :** an ecologically important life form subordinate in influence to the dominants of a community — **subdominant** *adj*

sub•due \səb-ˈdü, -ˈdyü\ *vt* **1 :** to conquer and bring into subjection **:** VANQUISH **2 :** to bring under control especially by willpower ⟨*subdued* fear⟩ **3 :** to reduce the intensity or degree of ⟨*subdued* light⟩ **[**Middle French *soduire* "to seduce" from Latin *subducere* "to withdraw", from *sub-* + *ducere* "to lead, draw"**]** **syn** see CONQUER — **sub•du•er** *n*

sub•en•try \ˈsəb-ˌen-trē\ *n* **:** an entry made under a more general entry

su•ber•in \ˈsü-bə-rən\ *n* **:** a complex fatty substance that is the basis of cork **[**French *subérine,* from Latin *suber* "cork"**]**

sub•fam•i•ly \ˈsəb-ˌfam-lē, -ə-lē\ *n* **:** a taxonomic category next below a family

sub•freez•ing \ˈsəb-ˈfrē-zing\ *adj* **:** lower than is required to produce freezing

sub•ge•nus \ˈsəb-ˌjē-nəs\ *n* **:** a category in biological taxonomy below a genus and above a species

sub•grade \ˈsəb-ˌgrād\ *n* **:** a surface of earth or rock leveled off to receive a foundation (as of a road)

sub•head \ˈsəb-ˌhed\ *or* **sub•head•ing** \-ˌing\ *n* **1 :** a heading of a subdivision (as in an outline) **2 :** a subordinate caption, title, or headline

sub•hu•man \ˌsəb-ˈhyü-mən, ˈsəb-, -ˈyü-\ *adj* **:** less than human: as **a :** failing to reach the level (as of intelligence) associated with normal human beings **b :** unsuitable to or unfit for human beings

sub•ja•cent \ˌsəb-ˈjās-nt\ *adj* **:** lying under or below; *also* **:** lower than but not directly below ⟨hills and *subjacent* valleys⟩ **[**Latin *subjacens,* present participle of *subjacēre* "to lie under", from *sub-* + *jacēre* "to lie"**]** — **sub•ja•cen•cy** \-n-sē\ *n* — **sub•ja•cent•ly** *adv*

¹sub•ject \ˈsəb-jikt\ *n* **1 :** one that is placed under authority or control: as **a :** one subject to a monarch and governed by the monarch's law **b :** one who lives in the territory of, enjoys the protection of, and owes allegiance to a sovereign power or state **2 :** the thing or person of which a quality, attribute, or relation is affirmed **3 a :** a department of knowledge or learning **b :** an individual (as a person or plant) that is studied or experimented on; *esp* **:** a dead body for anatomical dissection **c** (1) **:** something about which something is said or done (2) **:** something (as a scene or figure) that is represented or dealt with in a work of art **4 :** a noun or noun equivalent about which something is stated by the predicate **5 :** the principal melodic phrase on which a musical composition or movement is based **[**Middle French, from Latin *subjectus* "one under authority" and *subjectum* "subject of a proposition", both from *subicere* "to throw under, subject", from *sub-* + *jacere* "to throw"**]** **syn** see CITIZEN

²subject *adj* **1 :** owing obedience or allegiance to another (as a parent or ruler) **2 a :** LIABLE 2b, INCLINED ⟨*subject* to temptation⟩ **b :** SUSCEPTIBLE, PRONE ⟨*subject* to colds⟩ **3 :** CONDITIONAL, CONTINGENT ⟨*subject* to approval⟩

³sub•ject \səb-ˈjekt\ *vt* **1 a :** to bring under control or dominion **:** SUBJUGATE **b :** to make amenable to the discipline and control of a superior **2 a :** to make liable **:** PREDISPOSE **b :** to make accountable **:** SUBMIT **3 :** to cause to undergo **:** EXPOSE ⟨*subject* one to ridicule⟩ — **sub•jec•tion** \səb-ˈjek-shən\ *n*

sub•jec•tive \səb-ˈjek-tiv\ *adj* **1 :** of, relating to, or being a subject **2 :** of, relating to, or arising within one's self or mind in contrast to what is outside **:** PERSONAL ⟨*subjective* experience⟩ ⟨*subjective* symptoms of disease⟩ — **sub•jec•tive•ly** *adv* — **sub•jec•tiv•i•ty** \səb-ˌjek-ˈtiv-ət-ē, ˌsəb-\ *n*

subjective complement *n* **:** a grammatical complement relating to the subject of an intransitive verb ⟨in "I had fallen sick" *sick* is a *subjective complement*⟩

subject matter *n* **:** matter presented for consideration in discussion, thought, or study

sub•join \səb-ˈjȯin, ˌsəb-\ *vt* **:** APPEND, ANNEX

sub•ju•gate \ˈsəb-jə-ˌgāt\ *vt* **1 :** to force to submit to control **:** MASTER **2 :** to bring into servitude **:** ENSLAVE **[**Latin *subjugare,* literally, "to bring under the yoke", from *sub-* + *jugum* "yoke"**]** **syn** see CONQUER — **sub•ju•ga•tion** \ˌsəb-jə-ˈgā-shən\ *n* — **sub•ju•ga•tor** \ˈsəb-jə-ˌgāt-ər\ *n*

¹sub•junc•tive \səb-ˈjəng-tiv, -ˈjəngk-\ *adj* **:** of, relating to, or being the grammatical mood that represents a denoted act or state not as fact but as conditional or possible or viewed emotionally (as with doubt or desire) ⟨in "if I were you, I wouldn't go" *were* is in the *subjunctive* mood⟩ **[**Late Latin *subjunctivus,* from Latin *subjungere* "to subordinate", from *sub-* + *jungere* "to join"**]**

²subjunctive *n* **:** the subjunctive mood of a language; *also* **:** a verb in this mood

sub•king•dom \ˈsəb-ˌking-dəm\ *n* **:** a primary division of a taxonomic kingdom

sub•lease \ˈsəb-ˈlēs, -ˌlēs\ *n* : a lease by a tenant of part or all of leased premises to another person — **sublease** *vb*

sub•let \ˈsəb-ˈlet\ *vb* **sub•let**; **sub•let•ting** **1** : to lease or rent all or part of a leased or rented property **2** : SUBCONTRACT 1

¹sub•li•mate \ˈsəb-lə-ˌmāt\ *vt* **1** : to cause to sublime ⟨*sublimate* sulfur⟩ **2** : to direct the expression of (instinctive desires and impulses) from a primitive form to a more socially or culturally acceptable form — **sub•li•ma•tion** \ˌsəb-lə-ˈmā-shən\ *n*

²sub•li•mate \ˈsəb-lə-ˌmāt, -mət\ *n* : a chemical product obtained by sublimation

¹sub•lime \sə-ˈblīm\ *vb* **1** : to pass or cause to pass from a solid to a gaseous state on heating and back to solid form on cooling without apparently passing through a liquid state; *also* : to release or purify by such action ⟨*sublime* sulfur from a mixture⟩ **2** : to make finer or more worthy : convert (something inferior) into something of higher worth [Middle French *sublimer,* from Medieval Latin *sublimare* "to refine, sublime", from Latin, "to elevate", from *sublimis* "sublime, raised on high"] — **sub•lim•er** *n*

²sublime *adj* **1 a** : lofty, grand, or exalted in thought, expression, or manner ⟨a *sublime* prose style⟩ **b** : of outstanding spiritual, intellectual, or moral worth ⟨*sublime* devotion to duty⟩ **2** : inspiring awe : SOLEMN ⟨*sublime* beauty⟩ [Latin *sublimis,* literally, "raised on high", from *sub* "under, up to" + *limen* "threshold, lintel"] — **sub•lime•ly** *adv* — **sub•lime•ness** *n*

sub•lim•i•nal \ˌsəb-ˈlim-ən-l, ˈsəb-\ *adj* **1** : inadequate to produce a sensation or a perception ⟨*subliminal* stimuli⟩ **2** : existing or functioning outside the area of conscious awareness ⟨the *subliminal* mind⟩ ⟨*subliminal* techniques in advertising⟩ [*sub-* + Latin *limin-, limen* "threshold"] — **sub•lim•i•nal•ly** \-l-ē\ *adv*

sub•lim•i•ty \sə-ˈblim-ət-ē\ *n, pl* **-ties** **1** : something sublime **2** : the quality or state of being sublime

sub•lin•gual \ˌsəb-ˈling-gyə-wəl, ˈsəb-, -ˈling-wəl\ *adj* : situated or occurring under the tongue ⟨*sublingual* salivary glands⟩

sub•lux•a•tion \ˌsəb-ˌlək-ˈsā-shən\ *n* : a partial dislocation of a bone or joint [*sub-* + Late Latin *luxatio* "dislocation", from Latin *luxare* "to dislocate", from *luxus* "dislocated"]

sub•ma•chine gun \ˌsəb-mə-ˈshēn-ˌgən\ *n* : a lightweight automatic or semiautomatic portable firearm fired from the shoulder or hip

sub•mar•gin•al \ˌsəb-ˈmärj-nəl, ˈsəb-, -ən-l\ *adj* : less than marginal; *esp* : inadequate for some end or use ⟨farming *submarginal* land⟩ — **sub•mar•gin•al•ly** \-ē\ *adv*

¹sub•ma•rine \ˈsəb-mə-ˌrēn, ˌsəb-mə-ˈ\ *adj* : being, acting, or growing underwater especially in the sea ⟨*submarine* plants⟩ ⟨*submarine* cameras⟩

²submarine *n* **1** : something that functions or operates underwater: as **a** : an underwater explosive mine **b** : a naval combat vessel designed for on-the-surface or underwater operations **2** : a large sandwich made from a long roll filled usually with cold cuts, cheese, onion, lettuce, and tomato

³submarine *vt* : to make an attack on or to sink by means of a submarine

sub•ma•rin•er \ˈsəb-mə-ˌrē-nər, ˌsəb-mə-ˈ; ˌsəb-ˈmar-ə-\ *n* : a member of a submarine crew

¹sub•max•il•lary \ˌsəb-ˈmak-sə-ˌler-ē, ˈsəb-\ *adj* : of, relating to, or situated below the lower jaw

²submaxillary *n, pl* **-lar•ies** : a submaxillary part (as an artery or gland)

sub•me•di•ant \ˌsəb-ˈmēd-ē-ənt, ˈsəb-\ *n* : the 6th tone above the tonic in a diatonic scale

sub•merge \səb-ˈmərj\ *vb* **1** : to put or go under water ⟨the whale *submerged*⟩ **2** : to cover or become covered with or as if with water ⟨floodwaters *submerged* the town⟩ ⟨memories *submerged* by time⟩ [Latin *submergere,* from *sub-* + *mergere* "to plunge"] — **sub•mer•gence** \-ˈmər-jəns\ *n* — **sub•merg•ible** \-ˈmər-jə-bəl\ *adj*

sub•merse \səb-ˈmərs\ *vt* : SUBMERGE [Latin *submersus,* past participle of *submergere* "to submerge"] — **sub•mers•ible** \-ˈmər-sə-bəl\ *adj* — **sub•mer•sion** \-ˈmər-zhən\ *n*

sub•mersed *adj* : growing or adapted to grow underwater

submersible *n* : a boat that is capable of submerging : SUBMARINE

sub•mi•cro•scop•ic \ˌsəb-ˌmī-krə-ˈskäp-ik\ *adj* : too small to be seen in an ordinary light microscope

sub•min•i•a•ture \ˌsəb-ˈmin-ē-ə-ˌchu̇r, ˈsəb-, -ˈmin-i-ˌchu̇r, -chər\ *adj* : very small ⟨*subminiature* electronic equipment⟩

sub•mis•sion \səb-ˈmish-ən\ *n* **1** : an act of submitting something (as for consideration, inspection, or comment) **2** : the condition of being submissive, humble, or compliant **3** : an act of submitting to the authority or control of another [Middle French, from Latin *submissio* "act of lowering", from *submittere* "to lower, submit"]

sub•mis•sive \-ˈmis-iv\ *adj* : inclined or willing to submit to others : YIELDING, MEEK — **sub•mis•sive•ly** *adv* — **sub•mis•sive•ness** *n*

sub•mit \səb-ˈmit\ *vb* **sub•mit•ted**; **sub•mit•ting** **1 a** : to give over or leave to the judgment or approval of someone else : REFER ⟨*submit* an issue for arbitration⟩ **b** : to make available : OFFER ⟨*submit* a report⟩ **2** : to subject to a process or practice **3** : to put forward as an opinion : AFFIRM **4** : to yield to the power or will of another [Latin *submittere* "to lower, submit", from *sub-* + *mittere* "to send"] **syn** see YIELD

sub•mu•co•sa \ˌsəb-myü-ˈkō-zə\ *n* : a supporting layer of loose connective tissue just under a mucous membrane — **sub•mu•co•sal** \-zəl\ *adj* — **sub•mu•cous** \ˌsəb-ˈmyü-kəs, ˈsəb-\ *adj*

¹sub•nor•mal \ˌsəb-ˈnȯr-məl, ˈsəb-\ *adj* : being below what is normal — **sub•nor•mal•i•ty** \ˌsəb-nȯr-ˈmal-ət-ē\ *n* — **sub•nor•mal•ly** \ˌsəb-ˈnȯr-mə-lē, ˈsəb-\ *adv*

²subnormal *n* : one that is below normal; *esp* : a person of subnormal intelligence

sub•or•bit•al \ˌsəb-ˈȯr-bət-l, ˈsəb-\ **1** : situated beneath the eye or its orbit **2** : being or involving less than one orbit ⟨a spacecraft's *suborbital* flight⟩

sub•or•der \ˈsəb-ˌȯrd-ər\ *n* : a subdivision of an order ⟨a soil *suborder*⟩

¹sub•or•di•nate \sə-ˈbȯrd-n-ət, -ˈbȯrd-nət\ *adj* **1** : placed in or occupying a lower class or rank : INFERIOR **2** : submissive to or controlled by authority **3 a** : of, relating to, or being a clause that functions as a noun, adjective, or adverb **b** : grammatically subordinating [Medieval Latin *subordinatus,* past participle of *subordinare* "to subordinate", from Latin *sub-* + *ordinare* "to order"] — **sub•or•di•nate•ly** *adv* — **sub•or•di•nate•ness** *n*

²subordinate *n* : one that is subordinate

³sub•or•di•nate \sə-ˈbȯrd-n-ˌāt\ *vt* : to make subordinate — **sub•or•di•na•tion** \-ˌbȯrd-n-ˈā-shən\ *n* — **sub•or•di•na•tive** \-ˈbȯrd-n-ˌāt-iv\ *adj*

sub•orn \sə-ˈbȯrn\ *vt* : to induce secretly to do an unlawful thing and especially to commit perjury ⟨*suborn* a witness⟩ [Middle French *suborner,* from Latin *subornare,* from *sub-* "secretly" + *ornare* "to furnish, equip"] — **sub•or•na•tion** \ˌsəb-ˌȯr-ˈnā-shən\ *n* — **sub•orn•er** \sə-ˈbȯr-nər\ *n*

sub•phy•lum \ˈsəb-ˌfī-ləm\ *n* : a primary division of a phylum

sub•plot \-ˌplät\ *n* : a subordinate plot in fiction or drama

¹sub•poe•na \sə-ˈpē-nə\ *n* : a writ commanding a person designated in it to appear in court under a penalty for failure to appear [Latin *sub poena* "under penalty"]

²subpoena *vt* **-naed**; **-na•ing** : to serve or summon with a writ of subpoena

sub•po•lar \ˌsəb-ˈpō-lər, ˈsəb-\ *adj* : SUBANTARCTIC, SUBARCTIC

sub•pop•u•la•tion \ˈsəb-ˌpäp-yə-ˈlā-shən\ *n* : an identifiable part of a population

sub ro•sa \ˌsəb-ˈrō-zə\ *adv* : in confidence : SECRETLY [New Latin, literally, "under the rose"; from the old custom of hanging a rose over the council table to indicate that all present were sworn to secrecy]

sub•scribe \səb-ˈskrīb\ *vb* **1 a** : to write (one's name) underneath : SIGN **b** : to give consent or approval by or as if by signing one's name ⟨unwilling to *subscribe* to the agreement⟩ **2 a** : to pledge (a gift or contribution) by writing one's name with the amount ⟨*subscribed* $100 to the fund⟩ **b** : to agree to contribute something; *also* : to make an agreed contribution **3 a** : to enter one's name for a publication or service; *also* : to receive a periodical or service regularly on order ⟨*subscribe* to a newspaper⟩ **b** : to agree to buy and pay for securities especially of a new offering ⟨*subscribed* for 1000 shares⟩ [Latin *subscribere,* literally, "to write beneath", from *sub-* + *scribere* "to write"] — **sub•scrib•er** *n*

sub•script \'səb-,skript\ *n* : a distinguishing symbol or letter written immediately below or below and to the right or left of another character [Latin *subscriptus,* past participle of *subscribere* "to write beneath"] — **subscript** *adj*

sub•scrip•tion \səb-'skrip-shən\ *n* **1** : an act or instance of subscribing **2** : an amount or thing that is subscribed **3** : a purchase of future issues of a periodical [Latin *subscriptio* "signature", from *subscribere* "to write beneath, subscribe"]

sub•se•quent \'səb-si-kwənt, -sə-,kwent\ *adj* : following in time, order, or place : SUCCEEDING [Latin *subsequens,* present participle of *subsequi* "to follow close", from *sub-* "near" + *sequi* "to follow"] — **sub•se•quence** \-sə-,kwens, -si-kwəns\ *n* — **subsequent** *n* — **sub•se•quent•ly** \-,kwent-lē, -kwənt-\ *adv* — **sub•se•quent•ness** \-,kwent-, -kwənt-\ *n*

sub•serve \səb-'sərv\ *vt* **1** : to serve as a means in carrying on or out or in aiding **2** : to promote the welfare or purposes of [Latin *subservire,* from *sub-* + *servire* "to serve"]

sub•ser•vi•ence \səb-'sər-vē-əns\ *also* **sub•ser•vi•en•cy** \-ən-sē\ *n, pl* **-enc•es** *also* **-en•cies** **1** : a subservient or subordinate place or function **2** : slavish obedience

sub•ser•vi•ent \-ənt\ *adj* **1** : useful in an inferior capacity : SUBORDINATE **2** : slavishly obedient : OBSEQUIOUS [Latin *subserviens,* present participle of *subservire* "to subserve"] — **sub•ser•vi•ent•ly** *adv*

sub•set \'səb-,set\ *n* : a mathematical set each of whose elements is included in another set

sub•side \səb-'sīd\ *vi* **1** : to sink or fall to the bottom : SETTLE **2** : to tend downward : DESCEND ⟨the flood *subsided* slowly⟩ **3** : to let oneself settle down ⟨*subside* into a chair⟩ **4** : to become quiet or less : ABATE ⟨as the fever *subsides*⟩ ⟨my anger *subsided*⟩ [Latin *subsidere,* from *sub-* + *sidere* "to sit down, sink"] — **sub•sid•ence** \səb-'sīd-ns, 'səb-səd-əns\ *n*

[1]**sub•sid•i•ary** \səb-'sid-ē-,er-ē, -'sid-ə-rē\ *adj* **1 a** : furnishing aid or support : AUXILIARY ⟨*subsidiary* details⟩ **b** : of secondary importance : TRIBUTARY ⟨*subsidiary* streams⟩ **2** : of, relating to, affected by, or being a subsidy ⟨*subsidiary* payments⟩ [Latin *subsidiarius,* from *subsidium* "reserve troops"] — **sub•sid•i•ar•i•ly** \-,sid-ē-'er-ə-lē\ *adv*

[2]**subsidiary** *n, pl* **-ar•ies** : one that is subsidiary; *esp* : a company wholly controlled by another

sub•si•dize \'səb-sə-,dīz, -zə-\ *vt* : to aid or furnish with a subsidy — **sub•si•di•za•tion** \,səb-səd-ə-'zā-shən, ,səb-zəd-\ *n*

sub•si•dy \'səb-səd-ē, -zəd-\ *n, pl* **-dies** : a grant or gift of money; *esp* : a grant by a government to a private individual, a company, or another government to aid an enterprise beneficial to the public [Latin *subsidium* "reserve troops, support, assistance", from *sub-* "near" + *sedēre* "to sit"]

sub•sist \səb-'sist\ *vi* **1** : to have or continue to have existence **2** : to receive maintenance (as food and clothing) : LIVE [Late Latin *subsistere,* from Latin, "to halt, remain", from *sub-* + *sistere* "to come to a stand"]

sub•sist•ence \səb-'sis-təns\ *n* **1 a** : real being : EXISTENCE **b** : the condition of remaining in existence **2 a** : means of subsisting **b** : the minimum (as of food and shelter) necessary to support life [Late Latin *subsistentia,* from *subsistere* "to subsist"] — **sub•sist•ent** \-tənt\ *adj*

[1]**sub•soil** \'səb-,sȯil\ *n* : a layer of weathered material that lies just under the surface soil

[2]**subsoil** *vt* : to turn, break, or stir the subsoil of

sub•son•ic \,səb-'sän-ik, 'səb-\ *adj* **1** : of, relating to, or being a speed less than that of sound in air **2** : moving, capable of moving, or utilizing air currents moving at a subsonic speed **3** : INFRASONIC 1

sub•spe•cies \'səb-,spē-shēz, -sēz\ *n* : a subdivision of a species: as **a** : a taxonomic category that ranks immediately below a species and designates a physically distinguishable and geographically isolated group whose members interbreed with those of other subspecies of the same species where their ranges overlap **b** : a named subdivision (as a race or variety) of a taxonomic species — **sub•spe•cif•ic** \,səb-spi-'sif-ik\ *adj*

sub•stage \'səb-,stāj\ *n* : an attachment to a microscope by means of which accessories (as a mirror or lamp) are held in place beneath the stage of the instrument

sub•stance \'səb-stəns\ *n* **1 a** : essential nature : ESSENCE ⟨divine *substance*⟩ **b** : a fundamental or characteristic part or quality ⟨the *substance* of the speech⟩ **2 a** : physical material from which something is made or which has discrete existence **b** : matter of particular or definite chemical constitution **3** : material possessions : PROPERTY ⟨a person of *substance*⟩ [Old French, from Latin *substantia,* from *substare* "to stand under", from *sub-* + *stare* "to stand"]

sub•stan•dard \,səb-'stan-dərd, 'səb-\ *adj* **1** : deviating from or falling short of a standard or norm **2** : conforming to a pattern of linguistic usage existing within a speech community but not that of the prestige group in that community

sub•stan•tial \səb-'stan-chəl\ *adj* **1 a** : existing as or in substance : MATERIAL **b** : not imaginary or illusory : REAL ⟨the *substantial* world⟩ **c** : IMPORTANT 1, ESSENTIAL ⟨a *substantial* difference in the stories⟩ **2** : ample to satisfy and nourish ⟨a *substantial* diet⟩ **3 a** : having means : WELL-TO-DO ⟨a *substantial* farmer⟩ **b** : considerable in quantity : significantly large ⟨a *substantial* increase⟩ ⟨a *substantial* wage⟩ **4** : well and sturdily built ⟨*substantial* buildings⟩ **5** : being largely but not wholly what is specified ⟨a *substantial* lie⟩ — **sub•stan•ti•al•i•ty** \-,stan-chē-'al-ət-ē\ *n* — **sub•stan•tial•ly** \-'stanch-lē-, -ə-lē\ *adv*

sub•stan•ti•ate \səb-'stan-chē-,āt\ *vt* **1** : to provide evidence for : PROVE ⟨*substantiate* claims in court⟩ **2** : to give substance or body to : EMBODY — **sub•stan•ti•a•tion** \-,stan-chē-'ā-shən\ *n*

[1]**sub•stan•tive** \'səb-stən-tiv\ *n* : a word or word group functioning syntactically as a noun [Middle French *substantif,* derived from Late Latin *substantivus* "having or expressing substance"] — **sub•stan•ti•val** \,səb-stən-'tī-vəl\ *adj* — **sub•stan•ti•val•ly** \-və-lē\ *adv*

[2]**substantive** *adj* **1** : of, relating to, or being something totally independent **2 a** : real rather than apparent **b** : belonging to the substance of a thing : ESSENTIAL ⟨*substantive* rights⟩ **c** : expressing existence ⟨the *substantive* verb is the verb *to be*⟩ **3** : functioning as a grammatical substantive ⟨a *substantive* clause⟩ **4** : considerable in amount or numbers : SUBSTANTIAL **5** : creating and defining rights and duties ⟨*substantive* law⟩ [Late Latin *substantivus* "having substance", from Latin *substantia* "substance"] — **sub•stan•tive•ly** *adv* — **sub•stan•tive•ness** *n*

sub•sta•tion \'səb-,stā-shən\ *n* : a station subordinate to another station

[1]**sub•sti•tute** \'səb-stə-,tüt, -,tyüt\ *n* : a person or thing that takes the place of another [Latin *substitutus,* past participle of *substituere* "to put in place of", from *sub-* + *statuere* "to set up, place"] — **substitute** *adj*

[2]**substitute** *vb* **1** : to put in the place of another : EXCHANGE **2** : to serve as a substitute : REPLACE — **sub•sti•tu•tion** \,səb-stə-'tü-shən, -'tyü-\ *n* — **sub•sti•tu•tion•al** \-shnəl, shən-l\ *adj* — **sub•sti•tu•tion•al•ly** \-ē\ *adv* — **sub•sti•tu•tion•ary** \-shə-,ner-ē\ *adj*

sub•strate \'səb-,strāt\ *n* **1** : SUBSTRATUM a **2** : the base on which an organism lives or over which it moves ⟨the soil is the *substrate* of most seed plants⟩ **3** : a substance acted upon (as by an enzyme)

sub•stra•tum \'səb-,strāt-əm, -,strat-\ *n* : an underlying support : FOUNDATION: as **a** : the material of which something is made and from which it derives its special qualities **b** : a layer beneath the surface soil : SUBSOIL [Medieval Latin, from Latin *substernere* "to spread under", from *sub-* + *sternere* "to spread"]

sub•struc•ture \'səb-,strək-chər\ *n* : FOUNDATION 2, GROUNDWORK

sub•sume \səb-'süm\ *vt* : to classify within a larger category or under a general principle [Latin *sub-* + *sumere* "to take up"] — **sub•sump•tion** \səb-'səm-shən, -'səmp-\ *n*

sub•sur•face \'səb-,sər-fəs\ *adj* : of, relating to, or involving an area or material beneath a surface (as of the earth) ⟨*subsurface* water⟩

sub•teen \'səb-'tēn\ *n* : a child approaching adolescence; *esp* : a girl under 13 years of age for whom clothing in sizes 8–14 is designed

sub•ten•ant \,səb-'ten-ənt, 'səb-\ *n* : one who rents from a tenant — **sub•ten•an•cy** \-'ten-ən-sē\ *n*

sub•tend \səb-'tend\ *vt* **1 a** : to be opposite to and extend from one side to the other of ⟨a hypotenuse *subtends* a right angle⟩ **b** : to fix the angular extent of with respect to a fixed point or object taken as the vertex ⟨a central angle *subtended* by an arc⟩ **c** : to determine the measure of by marking off the endpoints of ⟨a chord *subtends* an arc⟩ **2** : to underlie so as to include [Latin *subtendere* "to stretch beneath", from *sub-* + *tendere* "to stretch"]

sub·ter·fuge \'səb-tər-,fyüj\ *n* : a device (as a scheme or trick) used to avoid an unpleasant circumstance (as blame) : a deceptive evasion [Late Latin *subterfugium,* from Latin *subterfugere* "to evade", from *subter-* "beneath, secretly" + *fugere* "to flee"]

sub·ter·ra·nean \,səb-tə-'rā-nē-ən, -nyən\ *or* **sub·ter·ra·neous** \-nē-əs, -nyəs\ *adj* **1** : being, living, or operating under the surface of the earth **2** : existing or working in secret : HIDDEN [Latin *subterraneus,* from *sub* "under" + *terra* "earth"] — **sub·ter·ra·ne·an·ly** *adv*

sub·tile \'sət-l, 'səb-tl\ *adj* **sub·til·er** \'sət-lər, -l-ər, 'səb-tə-lər\; **sub·til·est** \'sət-ləst, -l-əst, 'səb-tə-ləst\ **1** : SUBTLE 1a, ELUSIVE **2** : ARTFUL 3b, CRAFTY [Latin *subtilis*] — **sub·tile·ly** \'sət-lē, -l-lē, -l-ē; 'səb-tə-lē\ *adv* — **sub·tile·ness** \'sət-l-nəs, 'səb-tl-\ *n*

sub·til·ty \'sət-l-tē, 'səb-tl-\ *n, pl* **-ties** : SUBTLETY

sub·ti·tle \'səb-,tīt-l\ *n* **1** : a secondary or explanatory title **2** : a printed statement or fragment of dialogue appearing on the screen between the scenes of a silent motion picture or appearing as a translation at the bottom of the screen during the scenes especially of a foreign-language movie — **subtitle** *vt*

sub·tle \'sət-l\ *adj* **sub·tler** \'sət-lər, -l-ər\; **sub·tlest** \'sət-ləst, -l-əst\ **1 a** : DELICATE 1a, ELUSIVE ⟨a *subtle* aroma⟩ **b** : difficult to understand or distinguish : OBSCURE ⟨*subtle* differences in vowel sounds⟩ **2 a** : marked by insight and sensitivity : PERCEPTIVE ⟨a *subtle* mind⟩ **b** : SKILLFUL, EXPERT ⟨*subtle* workmanship⟩; *also* : cleverly made or contrived ⟨a *subtle* mechanism⟩ **3 a** : ARTFUL 3b, WILY **b** : INSIDIOUS ⟨a *subtle* poison⟩ [Old French *soutil,* from Latin *subtilis,* literally, "finely woven", from *sub-* + *tela* "web"] — **sub·tle·ness** \'sət-l-nəs\ *n* — **sub·tly** \'sət-lē, -l-lē, -l-ē\ *adv*

sub·tle·ty \'sət-l-tē\ *n, pl* **-ties** **1** : the quality or state of being subtle **2** : something subtle; *esp* : a fine distinction

sub·ton·ic \,səb-'tän-ik, 'səb-\ *n* : LEADING TONE [from its being a half tone below the upper tonic]

sub·top·ic \'səb-,täp-ik\ *n* : a secondary topic : one of the subdivisions into which a topic may be divided

sub·tract \səb-'trakt\ *vb* : to take away by deducting : perform a subtraction ⟨*subtract* 5 from 9⟩ [Latin *subtractus,* past participle of *subtrahere* "to draw from beneath, withdraw", from *sub-* + *trahere* "to draw"] — **sub·tract·er** *n*

sub·trac·tion \səb-'trak-shən\ *n* **1** : an act or instance of subtracting **2** : the operation of deducting one number from another

sub·trac·tive \-'trak-tiv\ *adj* **1** : tending to subtract **2** : constituting or involving subtraction ⟨a *subtractive* correction⟩

sub·tra·hend \'səb-trə-,hend\ *n* : a number that is to be subtracted from a minuend [Latin *subtrahendus* "to be withdrawn", from *subtrahere* "to withdraw"]

sub·trop·i·cal \,səb-'träp-i-kəl, 'səb-\ *also* **sub·trop·ic** \-'träp-ik\ *adj* : of, relating to, or being the regions bordering on the tropical zone

sub·trop·ics \-'träp-iks\ *n pl* : subtropical regions

sub·urb \'səb-,ərb\ *n* **1 a** : an outlying part of a city or town **b** : a smaller community adjacent to a city **2** *pl* : the residential area adjacent to a city or large town; *also* : ENVIRONS 1 [Latin *suburbium,* from *sub-* "near" + *urbs* "city"] — **sub·ur·ban** \sə-'bər-bən\ *adj or n*

sub·ur·ban·ite \sə-'bər-bə-,nīt\ *n* : one who lives in the suburbs

sub·ur·bia \sə-'bər-bē-ə\ *n* **1** : the suburbs of a city **2** : suburbanites as a distinctive social group **3** : the manners, styles, and customs typical of suburban life

sub·ven·tion \səb-'ven-chən\ *n* : financial support especially in the form of an endowment or a subsidy [Late Latin *subventio* "assistance", from Latin *subvenire* "to come up, come to the rescue", from *sub-* "up" + *venire* "to come"]

sub·ver·sion \səb-'vər-zhən\ *n* : the act of subverting : the state of being subverted; *esp* : a systematic attempt to overthrow or undermine a government or political system by persons working secretly within the country involved [Middle French, from Late Latin *subversio,* from Latin *subvertere* "to subvert"] — **sub·ver·sive** \-'vər-siv, -ziv\ *adj or n* — **sub·ver·sive·ly** *adv*

sub·vert \səb-'vərt\ *vt* **1** : to overturn or overthrow from the foundation : RUIN **2** : to corrupt by undermining the morals, allegiance, or faith of [Middle French *subvertir,* from Latin *subvertere,* literally, "to turn from beneath", from *sub-* + *vertere* "to turn"] — **sub·vert·er** *n*

sub·way \'səb-,wā\ *n* : an underground way; *esp* : a usually electric underground railway

suc·ceed \sək-'sēd\ *vb* **1 a** : to come next after another in possession of an office or estate; *esp* : to inherit sovereignty **b** : to follow after another in order **2** : to turn out well : be successful [Latin *succedere,* from *sub-* "near" + *cedere* "to go"] **syn** see FOLLOW — **suc·ceed·er** *n*

suc·cess \sək-'ses\ *n* **1 a** : degree or measure of succeeding **b** : a favorable completion of something **c** : the gaining of wealth, favor, or prestige **2** : one that succeeds [Latin *successus,* from *succedere* "to succeed"]

suc·cess·ful \-fəl\ *adj* **1** : resulting or terminating in success **2** : gaining or having gained success — **suc·cess·ful·ly** \-fə-lē\ *adv* — **suc·cess·ful·ness** *n*

suc·ces·sion \sək-'sesh-ən\ *n* **1** : the order, action, or right of succeeding to a throne, title, or property **2 a** : a repeated following of one person or thing after another **b** : a process of one-way ecological change in which organisms of one kind are replaced by those of another kind **3** : a number of persons or things that follow one after another [Latin *successio,* from *succedere* "to succeed"] — **suc·ces·sion·al** \-'sesh-nəl, -ən-l\ *adj* — **suc·ces·sion·al·ly** \-ē\ *adv*

• **syn** SEQUENCE, SERIES: SUCCESSION may apply to things of any sort that follow in order of time or place and usually without interruption; SEQUENCE suggests a uniform, logical, or regular succession; SERIES implies that the objects are of a similar nature or stand in similar relation to each other ⟨a *series* of monthly payments⟩

suc·ces·sive \sək-'ses-iv\ *adj* : following in succession or serial order : following each other without interruption ⟨failed in three *successive* tries⟩ **syn** see CONSECUTIVE — **suc·ces·sive·ly** *adv* — **suc·ces·sive·ness** *n*

suc·ces·sor \sək-'ses-ər\ *n* : one that follows: as **a** : one who succeeds to a throne, title, estate, or office **b** : a positive integer obtained from another positive integer by adding 1

suc·cinct \sək-'singt, ,sek-, ,sə-, -'singkt\ *adj* **1** *archaic* **a** : being girded **b** : close-fitting **2** : marked by briefness and compactness of expression : CONCISE [Latin *succinctus,* from *succingere* "to gird from below, tuck up", from *sub-* + *cingere* "to gird"] — **suc·cinct·ly** *adv* — **suc·cinct·ness** *n*

¹suc·cor \'sək-ər\ *n* : RELIEF 1a; *also* : AID, HELP [Old French *sucors,* from Medieval Latin *succursus,* from Latin *succurrere* "to run up, run to help", from *sub-* "up" + *currere* "to run"]

²succor *vt* : to go to the aid of (one in need or distress) : RELIEVE — **suc·cor·er** *n*

suc·co·ry \'sək-rē, -ə-rē\ *n, pl* **-ries** : CHICORY [Middle English *cicoree*]

suc·co·tash \'sək-ə-,tash\ *n* : lima or shell beans and corn cooked together [of American Indian origin]

suc·cu·bus \'sək-yə-bəs\ *n, pl* **suc·cu·bi** \-,bī, -,bē\ : a female demon that lies on people in their sleep [Medieval Latin, from Late Latin *succuba* "prostitute", from Latin *succubare* "to lie under", from *sub-* + *cubare* "to lie, recline"]

¹suc·cu·lent \'sək-yə-lənt\ *adj* **1 a** : full of juice : JUICY **b** : having fleshy tissues designed to conserve moisture ⟨*succulent* plants⟩ **2** : full of vitality, freshness, or richness [Latin *suculentus,* from *sucus* "juice"] — **suc·cu·lence** \-ləns\ *n* — **suc·cu·lent·ly** *adv*

²succulent *n* : a succulent plant (as a cactus)

suc·cumb \sə-'kəm\ *vi* **1** : to yield to superior strength or force or overpowering appeal or desire **2** : to cease to exist : DIE [Latin *succumbere,* from *sub-* + *-cumbere* "to lie down"] **syn** see YIELD

¹such \səch, 'səch, sich, ,sich\ *adj* **1 a** : of a kind or character to be stated or suggested ⟨a bag *such* as a doctor carries⟩ **b** : having a quality to a degree to be indicated ⟨our excitement was *such* that we shouted⟩ **2** : having a quality already specified ⟨deeply moved by *such* acts of kindness⟩ **3** : of so extreme a degree or quality ⟨you're *such* a snob⟩ **4** : of the same class, type, or sort ⟨other *such* clinics throughout the state⟩ [Old English *swilc*]

²such *pron* **1** : such a person or thing ⟨had a plan if it may be called *such*⟩ **2** : someone or something stated, implied, or exemplified ⟨*such* were the Romans⟩ ⟨*such* was the result⟩ **3** : someone or something similar ⟨ships and planes and *such*⟩ — **as such** : in itself ⟨*as such* the gift was worth little⟩

[3]such *adv* **1** : to such a degree : so ⟨*such* tall buildings⟩⟨*such* a fine person⟩ **2** : VERY, ESPECIALLY ⟨hasn't been in *such* good spirits lately⟩ **3** : in such a way

[1]such and such *pron* : something not specified ⟨it's easy to say we want the system to produce *such and such*⟩

[2]such and such *adj* : not named or specified ⟨what we mean when we say that *such and such* a people is civilized⟩

[1]such•like \'səch-ˌlīk\ *adj* : of like kind : SIMILAR

[2]suchlike *pron* : someone or something of the same sort : a similar person or thing

[1]suck \'sək\ *vb* **1 a** : to draw in (liquid) or draw liquid from through suction created by movements of the mouth ⟨*suck* venom from a snakebite⟩ **b** : to draw milk from a breast or udder with the mouth ⟨young pigs *sucking* well⟩ **c** (1) : to consume by applying the lips or tongue to ⟨*suck* a lollipop⟩ (2) : to apply the mouth to and create a sucking action on ⟨suck a bruised finger⟩ **2** : to take something in or up or remove something from by or as if by suction ⟨plants *sucking* moisture from the soil⟩⟨a well *sucked* dry by constant pumping⟩ **3** : to make or cause to make a sound or motion like that of sucking ⟨*suck* in your stomach⟩ **4** : to act in an obsequious way ⟨*sucking* up to the boss⟩ [Old English *sūcan*]

[2]suck *n* **1** : the act of sucking **2** : a sucking movement or force

[1]suck•er \'sək-ər\ *n* **1** : one that sucks **2** : a part of an animal's body used for sucking or for clinging by suction **3** : a secondary shoot from the roots or lower part of a plant **4** : any of numerous freshwater fishes related to the carps but having usually thick soft lips for sucking in food **5** : LOLLIPOP **6 a** : a person easily cheated or deceived **b** : a person irresistibly attracted to something ⟨a *sucker* for new cars⟩

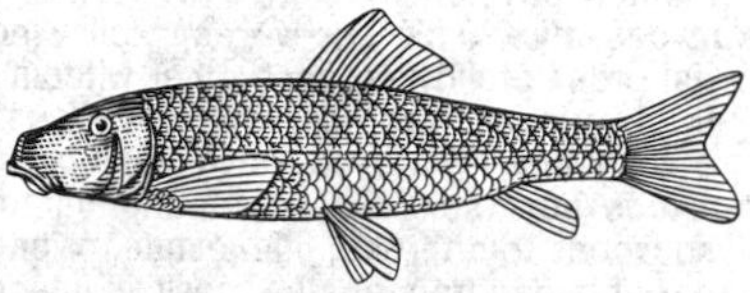
[1]sucker 4

[2]sucker *vb* **suck•ered**; **suck•er•ing** \'sək-ring, -ə-ring\ **1** : to remove suckers from **2** : to have or send out suckers

sucking louse *n* : any of an order (Anoplura) of wingless insects comprising the true lice with mouthparts adapted to sucking body fluids

suck•le \'sək-əl\ *vt* **suck•led**; **suck•ling** \'sək-ling, -ə-ling\ **1 a** : to give milk to from the breast or udder ⟨a mother *suckling* her child⟩ **b** : to bring up : NOURISH **2** : to draw milk from the breast or udder of ⟨lambs *suckling* the ewes⟩ [probably back-formation from *suckling*]

suck•ling \'sək-ling\ *n* : a young unweaned mammal

su•crase \'sü-ˌkrās\ *n* : INVERTASE [French *sucre* "sugar"]

su•cre \'sü-krā\ *n* **1** : the basic monetary unit of Ecuador **2** : a coin representing one sucre [Spanish, from Antonio José de *Sucre,* died 1830, South American liberator]

su•crose \'sü-ˌkrōs\ *n* : a sweet crystalline disaccharide sugar $C_{12}H_{22}O_{11}$ that occurs naturally in most land plants and is the sugar obtained from sugarcane or sugar beets [French *sucre* "sugar"]

suc•tion \'sək-shən\ *n* **1** : the act or process of sucking **2 a** : the action of exerting a force upon something by means of reduced air pressure over part of its surface so that the normal air pressure on another part of its surface pushes or tends to push it toward the region of reduced pressure **b** : force so exerted [Late Latin *suctio,* from Latin *sugere* "to suck"] — **suc•tion•al** \-shən-l, -shnəl\ *adj*

suction cup *n* : a cup-shaped device in which a partial vacuum can be produced when applied to a surface

Su•dan grass \sü-'dan-, -'dän-\ *n* : a vigorous tall-growing annual sorghum widely grown for hay and fodder

Su•dan•ic \sü-'dan-ik\ *n* : the languages neither Bantu nor Hamitic spoken in a belt extending from Senegal to southern Sudan — **Sudanic** *adj*

[1]sud•den \'səd-n\ *adj* **1 a** : happening quickly and unexpectedly ⟨a *sudden* shower⟩ **b** : come upon unexpectedly ⟨a *sudden* turn in the road⟩ **c** : rising or dropping sharply : STEEP ⟨a *sudden* descent to the sea⟩ **2** : marked by or showing hastiness : RASH ⟨a *sudden* decision⟩ **3** : made or brought about in a short time : PROMPT ⟨a *sudden* cure⟩ [Middle French *sodain,* from Latin *subitaneus,* from *subitus* "sudden", from *subire* "to come up", from *sub-* "up" + *ire* "to go"] — **sud•den•ly** *adv* — **sud•den•ness** \'səd-n-nəs, 'səd-n-əs\ *n*

[2]sudden *n, obsolete* : an unexpected occurrence : EMERGENCY — **all of a sudden** *or* **on a sudden** : sooner than was expected : SUDDENLY

sudden death *n* : a period of play to break a tie that terminates a game the moment one side scores or gains a lead

su•do•rif•ic \-'rif-ik\ *adj* : causing or inducing sweat ⟨*sudorific* herbs⟩ [Latin *sudor* "sweat"] — **sudorific** *n*

[1]suds \'sədz\ *n pl* **1** : water mixed with soap or detergent especially when frothy; *also* : the froth on such water **2** *slang* : BEER 1 [probably from Dutch *sudse* "marsh"]

[2]suds *vb* **1** : to wash in suds **2** : to form suds

sudsy \'səd-zē\ *adj* **suds•i•er**; **-est** : full of suds : FROTHY

sue \'sü\ *vb* **1** : to pay court to : WOO **2** : to seek justice from a person by bringing a legal action **3** : to make a request or application : PLEAD — usually used with *for* or *to* ⟨the nation *sued* for peace⟩ [Old French *suivre,* derived from Latin *sequi* "to follow"] — **su•er** *n*

suede *or* **suède** \'swād\ *n* **1** : leather with a napped surface **2** : a cloth fabric finished with a short nap to resemble suede [French *gants de Suède* "Swedish gloves"]

su•et \'sü-ət\ *n* : the hard fat about the kidneys and loins in beef and mutton that yields tallow [Anglo-French *sue,* from Latin *sebum* "tallow, suet"]

suf•fer \'səf-ər\ *vb* **suf•fered**; **suf•fer•ing** \'səf-ring, -ə-ring\ **1** : to feel or endure pain **2** : EXPERIENCE, UNDERGO ⟨*suffer* a defeat⟩ **3** : to bear loss or damage ⟨the business *suffered* during your illness⟩ **4** : to allow especially because of indifference [Old French *souffrir,* from Latin *suffere,* from *sub-* "up" + *ferre* "to bear"] — **suf•fer•able** \'səf-rə-bəl, -ə-rə-\ *adj* — **suf•fer•able•ness** *n* — **suf•fer•ably** \-blē\ *adv* — **suf•fer•er** \'səf-ər-ər\ *n*

suf•fer•ance \'səf-rəns, -ə-rəns\ *n* **1** : consent or approval implied by a lack of interference or failure to enforce a prohibition **2** : power or ability to withstand ⟨pain beyond *sufferance*⟩

suf•fer•ing *n* **1** : the state or experience of one that suffers **2** : mental or physical pain **syn** see DISTRESS

suf•fice \sə-'fīs\ *vb* **1** : to meet or satisfy a need : be sufficient **2** : to be competent or capable **3** : to be enough for [Middle French *suffis-,* stem of *suffire* "to suffice", from Latin *sufficere,* literally, "to put under", from *sub-* + *facere* "to make, do"]

suf•fi•cien•cy \sə-'fish-ən-sē\ *n, pl* **-cies** **1** : sufficient means to meet one's needs : COMPETENCY **2** : the quality or state of being sufficient : ADEQUACY

suf•fi•cient \sə-'fish-ənt\ *adj* **1** : enough to meet the needs of a situation or a proposed end **2** : being a proposition whose truth is adequate to insure the truth of another proposition ⟨*p* is necessary and *sufficient* for *q*⟩ [Latin *sufficiens,* from *sufficere* "to suffice"] — **suf•fi•cient•ly** *adv*

• **syn** ENOUGH, ADEQUATE: SUFFICIENT suggests a fairly exact meeting of a need; ENOUGH is less exact or less formal than SUFFICIENT; ADEQUATE may imply barely meeting a requirement or a moderate standard.

[1]suf•fix \'səf-ˌiks\ *n* : an affix occurring at the end of a word [Latin *suffixus,* past participle of *suffigere* "to fasten underneath", from *sub-* + *figere* "to fasten"] — **suf•fix•al** \-ˌik-səl\ *adj* — **suf•fix•less** \-ˌiks-ləs\ *adj*

[2]suf•fix \'səf-ˌiks, sə-'fiks\ *vt* : to attach as a suffix — **suf•fix•a•tion** \ˌsəf-ˌik-'sā-shən\ *n*

suf•fo•cate \'səf-ə-ˌkāt\ *vb* **1 a** : to stop the breath of (as by strangling or asphyxiation) **b** : to deprive of oxygen; *also* : distress by want of cool fresh air **2** : to hinder or stop the development of **3** : to be or become suffocated; *esp* : to die or suffer from lack of breathable air [Latin *suffocare,* from *sub-* + *fauces* "throat"] — **suf•fo•cat•ing•ly** \-ˌkāt-ing-lē\ *adv* — **suf•fo•ca•tion** \ˌsəf-ə-'kā-shən\ *n* — **suf•fo•ca•tive** \'səf-ə-ˌkāt-iv\ *adj*

[1]suf•fra•gan \'səf-ri-gən\ *n* **1** : a diocesan bishop (as in the Roman Catholic Church and the Church of England) of lower rank than a metropolitan **2** : an Anglican bishop assisting a diocesan bishop and not having the right of succession [Middle French, from Medieval Latin *suffraganeus,* from Latin *suffragium* "support"]

[2]suffragan *adj* **1** : of or being a suffragan **2** : of lower rank than a metropolitan or archiepiscopal see

suf•frage \'səf-rij\ *n* **1** : an intercessory prayer **2** : a vote given in deciding a disputed question or in electing a person to office **3** : the right of voting : FRANCHISE; *also* : the exercise of such right [Latin *suffragium* "vote, support"]

suf•frag•ette \,səf-ri-'jet\ *n* : a woman who supports suffrage for her sex

suf•frag•ist \'səf-ri-jəst\ *n* : one who supports extension of suffrage especially to women

suf•fuse \sə-'fyüz\ *vt* : to spread over or through in the manner of fluid or light : FLUSH, FILL [Latin *suffusus,* past participle of *suffundere* "to pour beneath, suffuse", from *sub-* + *fundere* "to pour"] — **suf•fu•sion** \-'fyü-zhən\ *n* — **suf•fu•sive** \-'fyü-siv, -ziv\ *adj*

Su•fi \'sü-fē\ *n* : a Muslim mystic [Arabic *ṣūfīy*] — **Sufi** *adj* — **Su•fic** \-fik\ *adj* — **Su•fism** \-,fiz-əm\ *n*

1sug•ar \'shu̇g-ər\ *n* **1** : a sweet crystallizable material that consists wholly or essentially of sucrose, is colorless or white when pure, is obtained commercially from sugarcane or sugar beet and less extensively from sorghum, maples, and palms, and is nutritionally important as a source of dietary carbohydrate and as a sweetener and preservative of other foods **2** : any of various water-soluble compounds that vary widely in sweetness and comprise the simpler carbohydrates [Middle French *sucre,* from Medieval Latin *zuccarum,* from Italian *zucchero,* from Arabic *sukkar,* from Persian *shakar,* from Sanskrit *śarkarā*]

2sugar *vb* **sug•ared**; **sug•ar•ing** \'shu̇g-ring, -ə-ring\ **1** : to mix, cover, or sprinkle with sugar **2** : to make something less hard to take or bear **3** : to change to crystals of sugar

sugar beet *n* : a white-rooted beet grown for the sugar in its roots

sugar bush *n* : woods in which sugar maples predominate

sug•ar•cane \'shu̇g-ər-,kān\ *n* : a stout tall perennial grass that has broad leaves and is widely grown in warm regions as a source of sugar

sug•ar•coat \,shu̇g-ər-'kōt\ *vt* **1** : to coat with sugar **2** : to make attractive or agreeable on the surface

sug•ar•house \'shu̇g-ər-,hau̇s\ *n* : a building where sugar is made or refined; *esp* : one where maple sap is boiled in the making of maple syrup and maple sugar

sug•ar•loaf \-,lōf\ *n* **1** : refined sugar molded into a cone **2** : a hill or mountain shaped like a sugarloaf — **sugarloaf** *adj*

sugar maple *n* : a maple of eastern North America with 3-lobed to 5-lobed leaves, hard close-grained wood much used for cabinetwork, and sap that is the chief source of maple syrup and maple sugar

sugar of lead : LEAD ACETATE

sugar pine *n* : a lofty pine of California and Oregon that has large cones often 18 inches long and a soft reddish brown wood used for interior finish and shingles

sugarcane

sug•ar•plum \'shu̇g-ər-,pləm\ *n* : a round piece of candy

sug•ary \'shu̇g-rē, -ə-rē\ *adj* **1** : containing, resembling, or tasting of sugar **2** : affectedly or over sweet

sug•gest \səg-'jest, sə-'jest\ *vt* **1 a** : to put (as a thought, plan, or desire) into a person's mind **b** : to propose as an idea or possibility ⟨*suggest* going for a walk⟩ **2** : to call to mind through close connection or association ⟨that smoke *suggests* a forest fire⟩ [Latin *suggestus,* past participle of *suggerere* "to put under, furnish, suggest", from *sub-* + *gerere* "to carry"] — **sug•gest•er** *n*

• **syn** SUGGEST, HINT, INTIMATE mean to convey an idea indirectly. SUGGEST stresses putting into the mind by association of ideas; HINT implies the use of slight or remote suggestion with a minimum of overt statement; INTIMATE stresses delicacy of suggestion without connoting any lack of candor.

sug•gest•ible \səg-'jes-tə-bəl, sə-'jes-\ *adj* : easily influenced by suggestion — **sug•gest•ibil•i•ty** \-,jes-tə-'bil-ət-ē\ *n*

sug•ges•tion \səg-'jes-chən, sə-'jes-, -'jesh-\ *n* **1 a** : the act or process of suggesting **b** : something suggested **2 a** : the process by which one thought leads to another especially through association of ideas **b** : a means or process of influencing attitudes and behavior hypnotically **3** : a slight indication : TRACE

sug•ges•tive \səg-'jes-tiv, sə-'jes-\ *adj* **1 a** : giving a suggestion : INDICATIVE **b** : full of suggestions : PROVOCATIVE **c** : stirring mental associations **2** : suggesting or tending to suggest something indelicate : RISQUÉ — **sug•ges•tive•ly** *adv* — **sug•ges•tive•ness** *n*

sui•cid•al \,sü-ə-'sīd-l\ *adj* **1** : relating to or of the nature of suicide **2** : marked by an impulse to kill oneself **3 a** : very dangerous to life ⟨*suicidal* risks⟩ **b** : destructive of one's own interests — **sui•cid•al•ly** \-l-ē\ *adv*

sui•cide \'sü-ə-,sīd\ *n* **1 a** : the act of taking one's own life voluntarily **b** : ruin of one's own interests **2** : one that commits or attempts suicide [Latin *sui* "of oneself" + English *-cide*]

sui ge•ner•is \,sü-,ī-'jen-ə-rəs, ,sü-ē-'jen-, -'gen-\ *adj* : forming a class alone : PECULIAR [Latin, "of its own kind"]

1suit \'süt\ *n* **1** : an action or process in a court for enforcing a right or claim **2** : an act or instance of suing or seeking by entreaty; *esp* : COURTSHIP **3** : a number of things used together : SET **4** : a set of garments: as **a** : an outer costume of two or more pieces **b** : a costume to be worn for a special purpose or under particular conditions ⟨gym *suit*⟩ **5 a** : all the playing cards of one kind (as spades or hearts) in a pack; *also* : all the cards of the same suit held by a player ⟨a 5-card *suit*⟩ **b** : all the dominoes bearing the same number on one half of the face [Old French *siute* "act of following, suite", derived from Latin *sequi* "to follow"]

2suit *vb* **1** : to be in harmony : AGREE **2** : to be appropriate or acceptable **3** : to outfit with clothes : DRESS **4** : ADAPT ⟨*suit* the action to the word⟩ **5 a** : to be proper for : BEFIT **b** : to be becoming to **6** : to meet the needs or desires of

suit•able \'süt-ə-bəl\ *adj* **1** : adapted to a use or purpose **2** : satisfying propriety : PROPER ⟨clothes *suitable* to the occasion⟩ **3** : QUALIFIED 1 ⟨*suitable* candidates⟩ **syn** see FIT — **suit•abil•i•ty** \,süt-ə-'bil-ət-ē\ *n* — **suit•able•ness** \'süt-ə-bəl-nəs\ *n* — **suit•ably** \-blē\ *adv*

suit•case \'süt-,kās\ *n* : TRAVELING BAG; *esp* : a rigid flat rectangular one

suite \'swēt, *2c is also* 'süt\ *n* **1** : RETINUE; *esp* : the personal staff accompanying a ruler, diplomat, or dignitary on official business **2** : a group of things forming a unit or making up a collection : SET: as **a** : a group of rooms occupied as a unit : APARTMENT **b** (1) : a 17th and 18th century instrumental musical form consisting of a series of dances in the same or related keys (2) : a modern instrumental composition in a number of usually descriptive movements (3) : an orchestral concert arrangement in suite form of material drawn from a longer work (as a ballet) **c** : a set of matched furniture for a room [French, from Old French *siute*]

suit•ing \'süt-ing\ *n* : fabric for suits of clothes

suit•or \'süt-ər\ *n* **1** : one that petitions or pleads **2** : a party to a suit at law **3** : a man who courts a woman or seeks to marry her

su•ki•ya•ki \skē-'äk-ē, ,su̇k-ē-'äk-ē -'yäk-\ *n* : a dish prepared from meat, soybean curd, and vegetables (as onions, celery, bamboo sprouts, and mushrooms) cooked in soy sauce, sake, and sugar [Japanese, from *suki* "spade" + *yaki* "roast"]

Suk•koth \'su̇k-,ōt, -,ōth, -,ōs\ *n* : a Jewish holiday celebrated in September or October as a harvest festival of thanksgiving and to commemorate the temporary shelters used by the Jews during their wanderings in the wilderness [Hebrew *ḥag has–sukkōth* "feast of the tabernacles"]

sul•cus \'səl-kəs\ *n, pl* **sul•ci** \-,kī, -,kē\ : an anatomical furrow or groove; *esp* : a shallow furrow on the surface of the brain separating adjacent convolutions [Latin] — **sul•cate** \-,kāt\ *adj*

sulf- *combining form* : sulfur : containing sulfur ⟨*sulf*ide⟩

sul•fa \'səl-fə\ *adj* **1** : related chemically to sulfanilamide **2** : of, relating to, or employing sulfa drugs [short for *sulfanilamide*]

sul•fa•di•a•zine \,səl-fə-'dī-ə-,zēn\ *n* : a sulfa drug used especially in the treatment of meningitis, pneumonia, and intestinal infections [*sulfa* + *di-* + *az-* "containing nitrogen" (from French *azote* "nitrogen") + *-ine*]

\ə\ **abut**	\au̇\ **out**	\i\ **tip**	\ȯ\ **saw**	\u̇\ **foot**
\ər\ **further**	\ch\ **chin**	\ī\ **life**	\ȯi\ **coin**	\y\ **yet**
\a\ **mat**	\e\ **pet**	\j\ **job**	\th\ **thin**	\yü\ **few**
\ā\ **take**	\ē\ **easy**	\ng\ **sing**	\t͟h\ **this**	\yu̇\ **cure**
\ä\ **cot, cart**	\g\ **go**	\ō\ **bone**	\ü\ **food**	\zh\ **vision**

sulfa drug *n* : any of various synthetic organic bacteria-inhibiting drugs that are sulfonamides closely related chemically to sulfanilamide

sul•fa•mer•a•zine \ˌsəl-fə-ˈmer-ə-ˌzēn\ *n* : a sulfa drug with uses similar to those of sulfadiazine [*sulfa* + *-mer* (from Greek *meros* "part") + *-azine* (as in *sulfadiazine)*]

sul•fa•nil•a•mide \ˌsəl-fə-ˈnil-ə-ˌmīd, -məd\ *n* : a crystalline compound that is the amide of sulfanilic acid and the parent compound of most of the sulfa drugs [*sulfanilic* + *amide*]

sul•fa•nil•ic acid \ˌsəl-fə-ˌnil-ik-\ *n* : a crystalline acid obtained from aniline and used especially in making dyes [*sulf-* + *aniline* + *-ic*]

sul•fate \ˈsəl-ˌfāt\ *n* : a salt or ester of sulfuric acid

sul•fide \ˈsəl-ˌfīd\ *n* : a compound of sulfur with one or more other elements : a salt or ester of hydrogen sulfide

sul•fite \ˈsəl-ˌfīt\ *n* : a salt or ester of sulfurous acid — **sul•fit•ic** \ˌsəl-ˈfit-ik\ *adj*

sul•fon•amide \ˌsəl-ˈfän-ə-ˌmīd, -ˈfō-nə-, -məd\ *n* : the amide (as sulfanilamide) of a sulfonic acid; *also* : SULFA DRUG

sul•fon•ic acid \ˌsəl-ˌfän-ik-, -ˈfōn-\ *n* : any of numerous acids that may be derived from sulfuric acid by replacement of a hydroxyl group by either an inorganic anion or a univalent organic radical [derived from *sulf-*]

sul•fur *or* **sul•phur** \ˈsəl-fər\ *n* : a nonmetallic element that occurs either free or in combined form, is a constituent of proteins, exists in several forms including yellow crystals, and is used especially in the chemical and paper industries, in rubber vulcanization, and in medicine for treating skin diseases — see ELEMENT table [Latin]

sulfur dioxide *n* : a heavy strong-smelling gas SO_2 that is used especially in making sulfuric acid, in bleaching, as a preservative, and as a refrigerant and is a major air pollutant especially in industrial areas

sul•fu•ric *or* **sul•phu•ric** \ˌsəl-ˈfyu̇r-ik\ *adj* : of, relating to, or containing sulfur especially in a higher valence

sulfuric acid *n* : a heavy corrosive oily strong acid H_2SO_4 that is colorless when pure and is a vigorous oxidizing and dehydrating agent

sul•fu•rous *or* **sul•phu•rous** \ˈsəl-fyə-rəs, -fə-, *also esp for 1* ˌsəl-ˈfyu̇r-əs\ *adj* **1** : of, relating to, or containing sulfur especially in a lower valence **2 a** : of, relating to, or dealing with the fire of hell : INFERNAL **b** : FIERY, INFLAMED ⟨*sulfurous* sermons⟩ **c** : PROFANE, BLASPHEMOUS ⟨*sulfurous* language⟩ — **sul•fu•rous•ly** *adv* — **sul•fu•rous•ness** *n*

sulfurous acid *n* : a weak unstable acid H_2SO_3 known in solution and through its salts and used as a reducing and bleaching agent

sulfur trioxide *n* : a compound SO_3 that is a heavy corrosive liquid when first produced but that changes into a solid form and is a powerful oxidizing agent

1sulk \ˈsəlk\ *vi* : to be moodily silent or ill-humored : nurse a grievance [back-formation from *sulky*]

2sulk *n* **1** : the state of one sulking — often used in pl. ⟨had a case of the *sulks*⟩ **2** : a sulky mood or spell ⟨was in a *sulk*⟩

1sulky \ˈsəl-kē\ *adj* **sulk•i•er**; **-est 1** : inclined to sulk : given to fits of sulking **2** : MALCONTENT, GLOOMY [probably from obsolete *sulke* "sluggish"] **syn** see SULLEN — **sulk•i•ly** \-kə-lē\ *adv* — **sulk•i•ness** \-kē-nəs\ *n*

2sulky *n, pl* **sulk•ies** : a light 2-wheeled vehicle having a seat for the driver only and usually no body [probably from 1*sulky*]

2sulky

sul•len \ˈsəl-ən\ *adj* **1 a** : gloomily or resentfully silent or repressed **b** : suggesting a sullen state ⟨a *sullen* refusal⟩ **2** : dull or somber in sound or color **3** : DISMAL 1, GLOOMY [Middle English *solain* "sullen, solitary"] — **sul•len•ly** *adv* — **sul•len•ness** \ˈsəl-ən-nəs, -ən-əs\ *n*

• **syn** SULLEN, SURLY, SULKY mean showing a forbidding or disagreeable mood. SULLEN implies a gloomy silent bad humor and a refusal to be sociable; SURLY implies rudeness and gruffness especially in response to requests or questions; SULKY suggests childish resentment expressed in fits of peevish sullenness.

sul•ly \ˈsəl-ē\ *vb* **sul•lied**; **sul•ly•ing** : to make or become soiled or tarnished [probably from Middle French *soiller* "to soil"]

sul•phur butterfly \ˌsəl-fər-\ *n* : any of numerous rather small butterflies having usually yellow or orange wings with a black border

sulphur yellow *n* : a brilliant greenish yellow

sul•tan \ˈsəlt-n\ *n* : a sovereign especially of a Muslim state [Middle French, from Arabic *sulṭān*]

sul•tana \ˌsəl-ˈtan-ə\ *n* **1** : a female member of a sultan's family; *esp* : a sultan's wife **2 a** : a pale yellow seedless grape grown for raisins and wine **b** : the raisin of this grape [Italian, from *sultano* "sultan", from Arabic *sulṭān*]

sul•tan•ate \ˈsəlt-n-ˌāt\ *n* **1** : the office, dignity, or power of a sultan **2** : a state or country governed by a sultan

sul•try \ˈsəl-trē\ *adj* **sul•tri•er**; **-est 1** : very hot and humid **2** : burning hot ⟨the *sultry* sun⟩ **3** : SENSUAL, VOLUPTUOUS ⟨*sultry* glances⟩ [derived from *swelter*] — **sul•tri•ly** \-trə-lē\ *adv* — **sul•tri•ness** \-trē-nəs\ *n*

1sum \ˈsəm\ *n* **1** : an indefinite or specified amount of money **2** : the whole amount **3 a** : SUMMARY **b** : GIST **4 a** : the result obtained by the mathematical operation of addition ⟨the *sum* of 5 and 7 is 12⟩ **b** : the limit of the sum of the first *n* terms of an infinite series as *n* increases indefinitely **c** : a problem in arithmetic [Old French *summe*, from Latin *summa*, from *summus* "highest"]

• **syn** AMOUNT, AGGREGATE, TOTAL: SUM indicates the result of simple addition of numbers or particulars; AMOUNT implies the result of accumulating or successive additions; AGGREGATE stresses the notion of the grouping or massing together of distinct individuals; TOTAL stresses the completeness or inclusiveness of the addition.

2sum *vb* **summed**; **sum•ming 1** : to calculate the sum of : COUNT **2** : to reach a sum : AMOUNT — usually used with *to* **3** : SUMMARIZE — usually used with *up* ⟨*sum* up the evidence⟩

su•mac *or* **su•mach** \ˈsü-ˌmak, ˈshü-\ *n* **1** : any of a genus of trees, shrubs, and woody vines with feathery compound leaves turning to brilliant red in autumn and spikes or loose clusters of red or whitish berries — compare POISON IVY, POISON OAK **2** : a material used in tanning and dyeing made of the leaves and other parts of sumac [Middle French *sumac*, from Arabic *summāq*]

Su•mer•i•an \su̇-ˈmer-ē-ən, -ˈmir-\ *n* **1** : a native of Sumer **2** : the language of the Sumerians surviving as a literary language after the rise of Akkadian — **Sumerian** *adj*

sum•ma cum lau•de \ˌsu̇m-ə-ˌku̇m-ˈlau̇d-ə, -ˈlau̇d-ē; ˌsəm-ə-ˌkəm-ˈlȯd-ē\ *adv or adj* : with highest academic distinction ⟨graduated *summa cum laude*⟩ [Latin, "with highest praise"]

sum•mand \ˈsəm-ˌand, ˌsə-ˈmand\ *n* : a term in a summation : ADDEND [Medieval Latin *summandus*, from *summare* "to sum", from Latin *summa* "sum"]

sum•ma•rize \ˈsəm-ə-ˌrīz\ *vb* **1** : to tell in or reduce to a summary **2** : to make a summary — **sum•ma•ri•za•tion** \ˌsəm-rə-ˈzā-shən, -ə-rə-\ *n* — **sum•ma•riz•er** \ˈsəm-ə-ˌrī-zər\ *n*

1sum•ma•ry \ˈsəm-ə-rē\ *adj* **1** : expressing or covering the main points briefly **2** : done without delay or formality : quickly carried out [Medieval Latin *summarius*, from Latin *summa* "sum"] — **sum•mar•i•ly** \ˌsə-ˈmer-ə-lē, ˈsəm-ə-rə-lē\ *adv*

2summary *n, pl* **-ries** : a concise statement of the main ideas (as of a book)

sum•ma•tion \ˌsə-ˈmā-shən\ *n* **1** : the act or process of forming a sum : ADDITION **2** : SUM 2, 3a, 4a **3** : a final part of an argument reviewing points made and expressing conclusions — **sum•ma•tion•al** \-shnəl, -shən-l\ *adj*

1sum•mer \ˈsəm-ər\ *n* **1 a** : the season between spring and autumn comprising usually the months of June, July, and August or as determined astronomically extending from the June solstice to the September equinox **b** : the warmer half of the year **2** : YEAR ⟨a youth of 16 *summers*⟩ **3** : a time or season of fulfillment [Old English *sumor*]

2summer *vb* **sum•mered**; **sum•mer•ing** \ˈsəm-ring, -ə-ring\ **1** : to pass the summer **2** : to keep or carry through the summer; *esp* : to provide with pasture during the summer

3summer *n* : a large horizontal beam or stone used especially in building (as for the lintel of a door or window) [Middle French *somier* "packhorse, beam", derived from Late Latin *sagma* "packsaddle", from Greek]

sum•mer•house \ˈsəm-ər-ˌhau̇s\ *n* : a rustic covered structure in a garden or park to provide a cool shady retreat in summer

summer kitchen *n* : a small building or shed built adjacent to a house and used as a kitchen in warm weather
sum•mer•sault *archaic variant of* SOMERSAULT
summer school *n* : a school or school session conducted in summer enabling students to accelerate progress toward a degree, to make up credits lost through absence or failure, or to round out professional education
summer squash *n* : any of various garden squashes closely related to the typical pumpkins and used as a vegetable while immature and before hardening of the seeds and rind
sum•mer•time \'səm-ər-,tīm\ *n* : the summer season or a period like summer
summer time *n, chiefly British* : DAYLIGHT SAVING TIME
sum•mer•wood \'səm-ər-,wu̇d\ *n* : the harder less porous portion of an annual ring of wood that develops late in the growing season — compare SPRINGWOOD
sum•mery \'səm-rē, -ə-rē\ *adj* : of, resembling, or fit for summer
sum•mit \'səm-ət\ *n* **1** : TOP, APEX; *esp* : the highest point (as of a mountain) **2** : the highest level attainable : PINNACLE **3** : the highest level (as of officials) [Middle French *somete,* from *sum* "top", from Latin *summus* "highest"]
• syn SUMMIT, PEAK, PINNACLE, APEX mean the highest point attained or attainable. SUMMIT implies the topmost level attainable ⟨a view from the *summit*⟩ PEAK suggests the highest among other high points ⟨*peak* of excitement⟩ PINNACLE suggests a dizzying often insecure height ⟨reach a *pinnacle* of success on the stage⟩ APEX implies the point at which all ascending lines converge and contrasts with *base* ⟨*apex* of cultural achievement⟩
sum•mon \'səm-ən\ *vt* **1** : to issue a call to convene **2** : to command by service of a summons to appear in court **3** : to send for : CALL ⟨*summon* a physician⟩ **4** : to call forth or arouse ⟨*summon* up enough courage to act⟩ [Old French *somondre,* from Latin *summonēre* "to remind secretly", from *sub-* "secretly" + *monēre* "to warn"] — **sum•mon•er** *n*
[1]**sum•mons** \'səm-ənz\ *n, pl* **sum•mons•es** **1** : the act of summoning; *esp* : a call by authority to appear at a place named or to attend to some duty **2** : a warning or notice to appear in court **3** : a call, signal, or knock that summons
[2]**summons** *vt* : SUMMON 2
sum•mum bo•num \,su̇m-əm-'bō-nəm, ,səm-\ *n* : the supreme or greatest good [Latin]
su•mo \'sü-mō\ *n* : a Japanese form of wrestling in which each competitor seeks to force the opponent out of the ring or make the opponent touch the ground with any part of the body other than the soles of the feet [Japanese *sumō*]
sump \'səmp\ *n* : a pit or reservoir serving as a receptacle or as a drain for fluids [Middle English *sompe* "swamp"]
sump•ter \'səm-tər, 'səmp-\ *n* : a pack animal [Middle French *sometier* "driver of a packhorse", derived from Late Latin *sagma* "packsaddle", from Greek]
sump•tu•ary \'səm-chə-,wer-ē, 'səmp-\ *adj* **1** : designed to regulate personal expenses and especially to prevent luxury **2** : designed to regulate habits on moral or religious grounds [Latin *sumptuarius,* from *sumptus* "expense"]
sump•tu•ous \'səm-chə-wəs, 'səmp-, -chəs\ *adj* : involving large expense : LUXURIOUS ⟨a *sumptuous* feast⟩ [Middle French *sumptueux,* from Latin *sumptuosus,* from *sumptus* "expense", from *sumere* "to take, spend"] — **sump•tu•ous•ly** *adv* — **sump•tu•ous•ness** *n*
sum total *n* **1** : a total arrived at through the counting of sums **2** : total result : TOTALITY ⟨the *sum total* of weeks of discussion was a deadlock⟩
[1]**sun** \'sən\ *n* **1 a** : the luminous celestial body around which the planets revolve, from which they receive heat and light, and which has a mean distance from the earth of 93,000,000 miles (150,000,000 kilometers) and a diameter of 864,000 miles (1,390,000 kilometers) **b** : a celestial body like the sun **2** : the heat or light radiated from the sun : SUNSHINE **3** : one resembling the sun usually in brilliance **4** : the rising or setting of the sun ⟨from *sun* to *sun*⟩ [Old English *sunne*]
[2]**sun** *vb* **sunned**; **sun•ning** **1** : to expose to or as if to the rays of the sun **2** : to sun oneself
sun•baked \'sən-,bākt\ *adj* **1** : baked by exposure to sunlight ⟨*sunbaked* bricks⟩ **2** : heated, parched, or compacted especially by excessive sunlight
sun•bath \'sən-,bath, -,bȧth\ *n* : exposure to sunlight or a sunlamp
sun•bathe \-,bāth\ *vi* : to take a sunbath — **sun•bath•er** \-,bāthər\ *n*
sun•beam \-,bēm\ *n* : a ray of sunlight
sun•bird \-,bərd\ *n* : any of a family of brightly colored Old World birds suggesting hummingbirds
sun•bon•net \-,bän-ət\ *n* : a woman's bonnet with a wide brim framing the face and usually a ruffle at the back to protect the neck from the sun
[1]**sun•burn** \-,bərn\ *vb* **1** : to burn or discolor by the sun **2** : to cause or undergo sunburn
[2]**sunburn** *n* : a skin inflammation caused by excessive exposure to sunlight
sun•burst \'sən-,bərst\ *n* **1** : a burst of sunlight especially through a break in the clouds **2** : a stylized representation of a sun surrounded by rays
sun•dae \'sən-dē\ *n* : a portion of ice cream served with topping (as crushed fruit or nuts) [probably alteration of *Sunday*]
[1]**Sun•day** \'sən-dē\ *n* : the 1st day of the week : the Christian Sabbath [Old English *sunnandæg,* literally, "day of the sun"]
• syn SABBATH: SUNDAY is the name of the first day of the week; SABBATH is the institution of observing one day of the week as a period of rest and worship, the day being Sunday for most Christians, Saturday for Jews and some Christians.
[2]**Sunday** *adj* **1** : of, relating to, or associated with Sunday **2** : AMATEUR, DILETTANTE ⟨*Sunday* painters⟩
[3]**Sunday** *vi* : to spend Sunday ⟨was *Sundaying* in the country⟩
Sunday best *n* : one's best clothes
Sunday punch *n* : a blow in boxing capable of knocking out an opponent; *also* : a devastating blow
Sunday School *n* : a school held on Sunday for religious education
sun deck *n* : a deck of a ship or a roof or terrace used for sunbathing
sun•der \'sən-dər\ *vb* **sun•dered**; **sun•der•ing** \-də-ring, -dring\ : to break, force, or come apart or in two : sever especially with violence [Old English *gesundrian, syndrian*]
sun•dew \'sən-,dü, -,dyü\ *n* : any of a genus of bog herbs that trap and digest insects with their hairy glandular leaves

sundew

sun•di•al \-,dī-əl, -,dīl\ *n* : a device to show the time of day by the position of the shadow cast on a plate or disk typically by an upright indicator
sun dog *n* : PARHELION
sun•down \'sən-,dau̇n\ *n* : SUNSET 2
sun•dries \'sən-drēz\ *n pl* : miscellaneous small articles or items
sun•drops \'sən-,dräps\ *n sing or pl* : a day-flowering herb similar to the related evening primrose
[1]**sun•dry** \'sən-drē\ *adj* : VARIOUS 3 ⟨for *sundry* reasons⟩ [Old English *syndrig* "separate, distinct"]
[2]**sundry** *pron, pl in construction* : various ones — usually used in the phrase *all and sundry*
sun•fast \'sən-,fast\ *adj* : resistant to fading by sunlight ⟨*sunfast* dyes⟩
sun•fish \-,fish\ *n* **1** : a large sea fish with a very deep, short, and flat body, high fins, and a small mouth **2** : any of a family of American freshwater fishes that are related to the perches and usually have a deep compressed body and a metallic luster

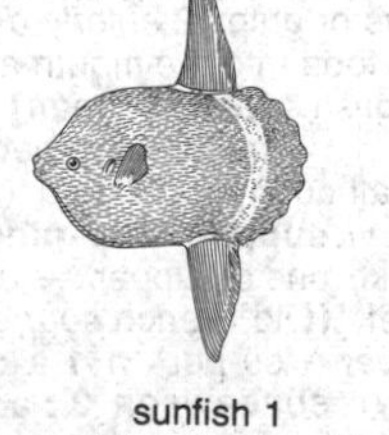
sunfish 1

sun•flow•er \-,flau̇-ər, -,flau̇r\ *n* : any of a genus of tall herbs related to the daisies that are often grown for their showy yellow-rayed flower heads and for their oil-rich seeds

sung *past of* SING

Sung \'su̇ŋ\ *n* : a Chinese dynasty dated A.D. 960–1279 and marked by cultural refinement and achievements in philosophy, literature, and art [Chinese (Pekingese dialect) *Sung*[4]]

sun•glass•es \'sən-ˌglas-əz\ *n pl* : tinted glasses that protect the eyes from sunlight

sun–god \'sən-ˌgäd\ *n* : a god that represents or personifies the sun in various religions

sunk *past of* SINK

sunk•en \'səŋ-kən\ *adj* **1** : submerged especially in the depths of a body of water ⟨*sunken* ships⟩ **2** : fallen in : HOLLOW ⟨*sunken* cheeks⟩ **3 a** : lying in a depression ⟨a *sunken* garden⟩ **b** : constructed below the general floor level ⟨a *sunken* living room⟩

sun•lamp \'sən-ˌlamp\ *n* : an electric lamp designed to emit radiation of wavelengths from ultraviolet to infrared

sun•less \'sən-ləs\ *adj* : lacking sunlight : GLOOMY

sun•light \-ˌlīt\ *n* : the light of the sun : SUNSHINE

sun•lit \-ˌlit\ *adj* : lighted by or as if by the sun

sun•ny \'sən-ē\ *adj* **sun•ni•er**; **-est 1** : bright with or warmed by sunshine ⟨a *sunny* day⟩ ⟨*sunny* rooms⟩ **2** : MERRY 1, CHEERFUL ⟨*sunny* dispositions⟩ — **sun•ni•ly** \'sən-l-ē\ *adv* — **sun•ni•ness** \'sən-ē-nəs\ *n*

sun parlor *n* : a glass-enclosed porch or living room with a sunny exposure — called also *sun porch, sun-room*

sun•rise \'sən-ˌrīz\ *n* **1** : the apparent rising of the sun above the horizon; *also* : the accompanying atmospheric effects **2** : the time at which the sun rises

sun•set \-ˌset\ *n* **1** : the apparent descent of the sun below the horizon; *also* : the accompanying atmospheric effects **2** : the time at which the sun sets **3** : a period of decline; *esp* : old age

sun•shade \-ˌshād\ *n* : something used as a protection from the sun's rays: as **a** : PARASOL **b** : AWNING

sun•shine \-ˌshīn\ *n* **1 a** : the sun's light or direct rays **b** : the warmth and light given by the sun's rays **c** : a spot or surface on which the sun's light shines **2** : something that radiates warmth, cheer, or happiness — **sun•shiny** \-ˌshī-nē\ *adj*

sun•spot \-ˌspät\ *n* : one of the dark spots that appear from time to time on the sun's surface and are usually visible only with the telescope

sun•stroke \-ˌstrōk\ *n* : heatstroke caused by direct exposure to the sun

sun•struck \-ˌstrək\ *adj* : affected or touched by the sun

sun•suit \-ˌsüt\ *n* : an outfit (as of halter and shorts) worn usually for sunbathing and play

sun•tan \-ˌtan\ *n* **1** : a browning of the skin from exposure to the rays of the sun **2** *pl* : a tan-colored summer uniform — **sun•tanned** \-ˌtand\ *adj*

sun•up \'sən-ˌəp\ *n* : SUNRISE

[1]**sun•ward** \-wərd\ *or* **sun•wards** \-wərdz\ *adv* : toward the sun

[2]**sunward** *adj* : facing the sun

sun•wise \'sən-ˌwīz\ *adv* : CLOCKWISE

[1]**sup** \'səp\ *vb* **supped**; **sup•ping 1** : to take or drink in swallows or gulps **2** *chiefly dialect* : to take food and especially liquid food into the mouth a little at a time (as from a spoon) [Old English *sūpan, suppan*]

[2]**sup** *n* : a mouthful especially of liquor or broth : SIP; *also* : a small quantity of liquid ⟨a *sup* of tea⟩

[3]**sup** *vi* **supped**; **sup•ping 1** : to eat the evening meal **2** : to make one's supper — used with *on* or *off* ⟨*supped* on roast beef⟩ [Old French *souper,* from *soupe* "sop, soup"]

[1]**su•per** \'sü-pər\ *n* **1 a** : SUPERNUMERARY 2 **b** : SUPERINTENDENT, SUPERVISOR **2** : a removable upper story of a beehive **3** : a superfine grade or extra large size

[2]**super** *adj* **1** : very good or valuable **2** : very large, powerful, or great ⟨a *super* bomb⟩ ⟨*super* secrecy⟩ [short for *superfine*] — **super** *adv*

super- *prefix* **1 a** : over and above : higher in quantity, quality, or degree than : more than ⟨*super*human⟩ **b** : in addition : extra ⟨*super*tax⟩ **c** : exceeding or so as to exceed a norm ⟨*super*heat⟩ **2 a** : situated or placed above, on, or at the top of ⟨*super*structure⟩ **b** : next above or higher ⟨*super*tonic⟩ **3** : constituting a more inclusive category than that specified ⟨*super*family⟩ **4** : superior in status, title, or position ⟨*super*power⟩ [Latin, "over, above, in addition to", from *super* "over, above, on top of"]

See *super-* and 2d element

superadministrator
superambitious
superathlete
superbomb
superbomber
superbright
superbureaucrat
supercautious
supercautiously
superchic
superclean
supercold
supercolossal
supercomfortable
supercompetitive
superconfidence
superconfident
superconservative
superconvenient
supercop
supercorporation
superdangerous
superdedicated
superdense
superdiplomat
supereffective
superefficiency
superefficient
superenergetic
superenthusiasm
superenthusiastic
superexcited
superfast
supergood
supergovernment
supergroup
superhard
superhero
superheroine
superhit
superintellectual
superintelligence
superintelligent
superintense
superintensity
superlong
superloud
superluxury
supermasculine
supermassive
supermodern
supernation
supernational
supernurse
superpark
superpatriot
superpatriotic
superpatriotism
superpersonal
superplane
superplayer
superpolite
superport
superpowerful
superproductive
superproficient
superrefined
superrich
superromantic
supersafe
supersalesman
supersalesmanship
superscout
supersecrecy
supersecret
supersecurity
superserious
supership
supersize
supersized
supersleuth
superslick
supersmooth
supersoft
supersophisticated
superspecial
superspecialist
superspecialization
superspecialized
superspectacle
superspectacular
superspeedy
superspy
superstate
superstatesman
superstore
superstrength
superstrong
supersubtle
supersubtlety
supersuccess
supersuccessful
supersurgeon
supersweet
supersystem
supertanker
superthick
superthin
superthriller
supertight
supertough
supertrained
supervirtuoso
superwave
superweak
superweapon
superwide
superzealous

su•per•a•ble \'sü-pə-rə-bəl, -prə-bəl\ *adj* : capable of being overcome or conquered ⟨*superable* odds⟩ [Latin *superabilis,* from *superare* "to surmount", from *super* "over"] — **su•per•a•ble•ness** *n* — **su•per•a•bly** \-blē\ *adv*

su•per•abound \ˌsü-pə-rə-'bau̇nd\ *vi* : to abound or prevail greatly or to excess

su•per•abun•dant \-'bən-dənt\ *adj* : more than ample : EXCESSIVE — **su•per•abun•dance** \-dəns\ *n* — **su•per•abun•dant•ly** *adv*

su•per•add \ˌsü-pə-'rad\ *vt* : to add over and above something or in extra or superfluous amount — **su•per•ad•di•tion** \'pə-rə-'dish-ən\ *n*

su•per•an•nu•ate \ˌsü-pə-'ran-yə-ˌwāt\ *vb* **1 a** : to make or declare obsolete or out-of-date **b** : to retire and pension because of age or infirmity **2** : to become retired or antiquated [back-formation from *superannuated*] — **su•per•an•nu•a•tion** \-ˌran-yə-'wā-shən\ *n*

su•per•an•nu•at•ed *adj* **1** : too old or outmoded for work or use **2** : retired on a pension [Medieval Latin *superannuatus,* past participle of *superannuari* "to be too old", from Latin *super-* + *annus* "year"]

su•perb \sü-'pərb\ *adj* : extremely fine, brilliant, or splendid ⟨a *superb* craftsman⟩ ⟨*superb* palaces⟩ [Latin *superbus* "excellent, proud", from *super* "above"] — **su•perb•ly** *adv* — **su•perb•ness** *n*

su•per•car•go \ˌsü-pər-'kär-gō\ *n* : an officer on a merchant ship in charge of the commercial concerns of the voyage [Spanish *sobrecargo,* from *sobre-* "over" (from Latin *super-*) + *cargo* "load, charge"]

su•per•charge \'sü-pər-ˌchärj\ *vt* **1** : to supply a charge to the intake of (as an engine) at a pressure higher than that of the surrounding atmosphere **2** : PRESSURIZE 1

su•per•char•ger \-ˌchär-jər\ *n* : a device (as a blower or compressor) for increasing the volume air charge of an internal-combustion engine or for pressurizing the cabin of an airplane

su•per•cil•i•ous \ˌsü-pər-'sil-ē-əs\ *adj* : haughtily scornful [Latin *superciliosus,* from *supercilium* "eyebrow, haughtiness"] — **su•per•cil•i•ous•ly** *adv* — **su•per•cil•i•ous•ness** *n*

su•per•con•duc•tiv•i•ty \ˌsü-pər-ˌkän-ˌdək-ˈtiv-ət-ē\ *n* **:** a complete disappearance of electrical resistance in various metals at temperatures near absolute zero — **su•per•con•duc•tive** \-kən-ˈdək-tiv\ *adj* — **su•per•con•duc•tor** \-kən-ˈdək-tər\ *n*

su•per•cool \ˌsü-pər-ˈkül\ *vt* **:** to cool below the freezing point without solidification or crystallization

su•per•ego \ˌsü-pə-ˈrē-gō\ *n* **:** the one of the three divisions of the psyche in psychoanalytic theory that is only partly conscious, represents the incorporation of parental conscience and the rules of society, and functions to reward and punish through a system of moral attitudes, conscience, and a sense of guilt — compare EGO 3, ID

su•per•em•i•nent \-ˈrem-ə-nənt\ *adj* **:** extremely high, distinguished, or conspicuous — **su•per•em•i•nence** \-nəns\ *n* — **su•per•em•i•nent•ly** *adv*

su•per•er•o•ga•tion \ˌsü-pə-ˌrer-ə-ˈgā-shən\ *n* **:** the act of performing more than is required by duty, obligation, or need [Medieval Latin *supererogatio,* from *supererogare* "to perform beyond the call of duty", derived from Latin *super-* + *e-* + *rogare* "to ask"]

su•per•erog•a•to•ry \ˌsü-pə-ri-ˈräg-ə-ˌtōr-ē, -ˌtȯr-\ *adj* **1 :** observed or performed to an extent not demanded or needed **2 :** SUPERFLUOUS, NONESSENTIAL

su•per•fam•i•ly \ˈsü-pər-ˌfam-lē, -ə-lē\ *n* **:** a category of taxonomic classification ranking next above a family

su•per•fi•cial \ˌsü-pər-ˈfish-əl\ *adj* **1 a :** of or relating to a surface **b :** situated on or near or affecting only the surface **2 :** concerned only with the obvious or apparent **:** not profound or thorough **:** SHALLOW [Late Latin *superficialis,* from Latin *superficies* "surface", from *super-* + *facies* "face"] — **su•per•fi•ci•al•i•ty** \-ˌfish-ē-ˈal-ət-ē\ *n* — **su•per•fi•cial•ly** \-ˌfish-lē, -ə-lē\ *adv* — **su•per•fi•cial•ness** \-ˈfish-əl-nəs\ *n*

• **syn** SUPERFICIAL, CURSORY, SHALLOW mean lacking in depth, solidity, or completeness. SUPERFICIAL implies a concern only with what appears at the surface or at first glance; CURSORY suggests a neglect of details through haste or indifference; SHALLOW is usually derogatory and implies lack of depth in knowledge, reasoning, emotions, or character.

su•per•fi•cies \-ˈfish-ēz, -ē-ˌēz\ *n, pl* **superficies 1 :** the surface of a body or the boundary of a region of space **2 :** the external aspects or appearance of a thing [Latin, "surface"]

su•per•fine \ˌsü-pər-ˈfīn\ *adj* **1 :** very refined **:** FINICKY **2 :** very finely divided **3 :** of high quality or grade

su•per•flu•i•ty \ˌsü-pər-ˈflü-ət-ē\ *n, pl* **-ties 1 :** EXCESS 1a, OVERSUPPLY **2 :** something unnecessary or more than enough

su•per•flu•ous \su̇-ˈpər-flə-wəs\ *adj* **:** exceeding what is sufficient or necessary **:** EXTRA [Latin *superfluus,* from *superfluere* "to overflow", from *super-* + *fluere* "to flow"] — **su•per•flu•ous•ly** *adv* — **su•per•flu•ous•ness** *n*

su•per•gi•ant \ˈsü-pər-ˌjī-ənt\ *n* **:** a star of very great luminosity and enormous size

su•per•heat \ˌsü-pər-ˈhēt\ *vt* **1 a :** to heat (a liquid) above the boiling point without converting into vapor **b :** to heat (steam) to a higher temperature than the normal boiling point of water **2 :** to heat very much or excessively — **su•per•heat•er** *n*

su•per•het•er•o•dyne \ˌsü-pər-ˈhet-ə-rə-ˌdīn\ *adj* **:** of or relating to a form of radio reception in which beats are produced of a frequency above audibility but below that of the received signals and the current of the beat frequency is then rectified, amplified, and finally rectified again so as to reproduce the sound [*super*sonic + *heterodyne*] — **superheterodyne** *n*

su•per•high frequency \ˈsü-pər-ˌhī-\ *n* **:** a radio frequency in the range between 3000 and 30,000 megacycles — abbreviation *SHF*

su•per•high•way \ˌsü-pər-ˈhī-ˌwā\ *n* **:** a broad highway designed for high-speed traffic

su•per•hu•man \-ˈhyü-mən, -ˈyü-\ *adj* **1 :** being above the human **:** DIVINE **2 :** exceeding normal human power, size, or capability **:** HERCULEAN ⟨*superhuman* effort⟩ — **su•per•hu•man•ly** *adv*

su•per•im•pose \ˌsü-pə-rim-ˈpōz\ *vt* **:** to place or lay over or above something — **su•per•im•pos•able** \-ˈpō-zə-bəl\ *adj* — **su•per•im•po•si•tion** \-ˌrim-pə-ˈzish-ən\ *n*

su•per•in•cum•bent \-rin-ˈkəm-bənt\ *adj* **:** lying or resting and usually exerting pressure on something else [Latin *superincumbens,* present participle of *superincumbere* "to lie on top of", from *super-* + *incumbere* "to lie down on"] — **su•per•in•cum•bent•ly** *adv*

su•per•in•duce \-rin-ˈdüs, -ˈdyüs\ *vt* **:** to introduce as an addition over or above something already existing [Latin *superinducere,* from *super-* + *inducere* "to lead in"] — **su•per•in•duc•tion** \-ˈdək-shən\ *n*

su•per•in•tend \ˌsü-pə-rin-ˈtend, ˌsü-prin-, ˌsü-pərn-\ *vt* **:** to have or exercise the charge and oversight of **:** DIRECT [Late Latin *superintendere,* from Latin *super-* + *intendere* "to attend, direct attention to"]

su•per•in•tend•ence \-ˈten-dəns\ *or* **su•per•in•tend•en•cy** \-dən-sē\ *n, pl* **-enc•es** *or* **-en•cies :** the act, duty, or office of superintending or overseeing

su•per•in•tend•ent \-ˈten-dənt\ *n* **:** a person who oversees, manages, or maintains something ⟨a building *superintendent*⟩ ⟨*superintendent* of schools⟩ [Medieval Latin *superintendens,* from Late Latin *superintendere* "to superintend"]

[1]**su•pe•ri•or** \su̇-ˈpir-ē-ər\ *adj* **1 :** situated higher up **:** UPPER: as **a :** situated above or anterior or dorsal to another and especially a corresponding part ⟨a *superior* artery⟩ **b :** attached to and arising from a plant ovary ⟨a *superior* calyx⟩ **c :** free from the calyx or other floral envelope ⟨a *superior* plant ovary⟩ **2 a :** of higher rank, quality, or importance **b :** greater in quantity or numbers **3 :** courageously or serenely indifferent (as to something painful or disheartening) **4 a :** excellent of its kind **b :** affecting or assuming an air of superiority **:** SUPERCILIOUS **5 :** more comprehensive ⟨a genus is *superior* to a species⟩ [Middle French *superieur,* from Latin *superior,* comparative of *superus* "upper", from *super* "over, above"] — **su•pe•ri•or•i•ty** \-ˌpir-ē-ˈȯr-ət-ē, -ˈär-\ *n* — **su•pe•ri•or•ly** \-ˈpir-ē-ər-lē\ *adv*

[2]**superior** *n* **1 :** one who is above another in rank, station, or office; *esp* **:** the head of a religious house or order **2 :** one that surpasses another in quality or merit

superior court *n* **1 :** a court intermediate between inferior courts and higher appellate courts **2 :** a court with juries having original jurisdiction

superiority complex *n* **:** an exaggerated opinion of oneself

superior vena cava *n* **:** a large vein that returns blood from the head and forelimbs to the heart

su•per•ja•cent \ˌsü-pər-ˈjās-nt\ *adj* **:** lying above or upon ⟨*superjacent* rocks⟩ [Latin *superjacens,* present participle of *superjacēre* "to lie over", from *super-* + *jacēre* "to lie"]

su•per•jet \ˈsü-pər-ˌjet\ *n* **:** a supersonic jet airplane

[1]**su•per•la•tive** \su̇-ˈpər-lət-iv\ *adj* **1 :** of, relating to, or constituting the degree of grammatical comparison that denotes an extreme or unsurpassed level or extent **2 :** surpassing all others **:** SUPREME **3 :** EXCESSIVE, EXAGGERATED [Middle French *superlatif,* from Late Latin *superlativus,* from Latin *superlatus,* past participle of *superferre* "to carry over, raise high", from *super-* + *ferre* "to carry"] — **su•per•la•tive•ly** *adv* — **su•per•la•tive•ness** *n*

[2]**superlative** *n* **1 :** the superlative degree or a superlative form in a language **2 :** the superlative or utmost degree of something **:** ACME; *also* **:** something that is superlative

su•per•man \ˈsü-pər-ˌman\ *n* **:** a man with exceptional powers [translation of German *übermensch*]

su•per•mar•ket \-ˌmär-kət\ *n* **:** a self-service retail market selling foods and household merchandise

su•per•nal \su̇-ˈpərn-l\ *adj* **1 a :** being or coming from on high **b :** being or seeming more than earthly ⟨*supernal* beauty⟩ ⟨*supernal* joy⟩ **2 :** located or originating in the sky [Middle French, from Latin *supernus,* from *super* "over, above"] — **su•per•nal•ly** \-l-ē\ *adv*

su•per•na•tant \ˌsü-pər-ˈnāt-nt\ *adj* **:** floating on the surface [Latin *supernatare* "to float", from *super-* + *natare* "to swim"] — **supernatant** *n*

su•per•nat•u•ral \ˌsü-pər-ˈnach-rəl, -ə-rəl\ *adj* **1 :** of or relating to an order of existence beyond the visible observable universe; *esp* **:** of or relating to God or a god, demigod, spirit, or demon **2 a :** departing from what is usual or normal especially so as to appear to transcend the laws of nature **b :** attributed to

\ə\ abut	\au̇\ out	\i\ tip	\ȯ\ saw	\u̇\ foot
\ər\ further	\ch\ chin	\ī\ life	\ȯi\ coin	\y\ yet
\a\ mat	\e\ pet	\j\ job	\th\ thin	\yü\ few
\ā\ take	\ē\ easy	\ng\ sing	\th̲\ this	\yu̇\ cure
\ä\ cot, cart	\g\ go	\ō\ bone	\ü\ food	\zh\ vision

an invisible agent (as a ghost or spirit) — **supernatural** *n* — **su•per•nat•u•ral•ly** \-'nach-rə-lē, -ə-rə-; -'nach-ər-lē\ *adv* — **su•per•nat•u•ral•ness** \-'nach-rəl-nəs, -ə-rəl-\ *n*

su•per•nat•u•ral•ism \-'nach-rə-,liz-əm, -ə-rə-\ *n* **1 :** the quality or state of being supernatural **2 :** belief in a supernatural power and order of existence — **su•per•nat•u•ral•ist** \-ləst\ *n or adj* — **su•per•nat•u•ral•is•tic** \-,nach-rə-'lis-tik, -ə-rə-\ *adj*

su•per•nor•mal \-'nȯr-məl\ *adj* **1 :** exceeding the normal or average **2 :** being beyond natural human powers — **su•per•nor•mal•ly** \-mə-lē\ *adv*

su•per•no•va \-'nō-və\ *n* **:** a star that is a nova in which the maximum luminosity may reach 100 million times that of the sun

¹su•per•nu•mer•ary \,sü-pər-'nü-mə-,rer-ē, -'nyü-\ *adj* **1 :** exceeding the stated or prescribed number **2 :** SUPERFLUOUS [Late Latin *supernumerarius,* from Latin *super-* + *numerus* "number"]

²supernumerary *n, pl* **-ar•ies 1 :** a supernumerary person or thing **2 :** an actor employed to play a small usually nonspeaking part (as in a mob scene or spectacle)

su•per•phos•phate \,sü-pər-'fäs-,fāt\ *n* **:** a soluble mixture of phosphates used as fertilizer

su•per•po•si•tion \,sü-pər-pə-'zish-ən\ *n* **:** the act or process of laying one thing over or above another especially so that they coincide ⟨*superposition* of congruent triangles⟩ [French, from Late Latin *superpositio,* from Latin *superponere* "to superpose", from *super-* + *ponere* "to place"] — **su•per•pose** \,sü-pər-'pōz\ *vt*

su•per•pow•er \'sü-pər-,paů-ər, -,paůr\ *n* **:** an extremely powerful nation

su•per•sat•u•rate \,sü-pər-'sach-ə-,rāt\ *vt* **:** to add something to beyond saturation — **su•per•sat•u•ra•tion** \-,sach-ə-'rā-shən\ *n*

su•per•scribe \'sü-pər-,skrīb\ *vt* **:** to write or engrave on the top or outside; *esp* **:** to write (as a name or address) on the outside or cover of [Latin *superscribere,* from *super-* + *scribere* "to write"]

su•per•script \'sü-pər-,skript\ *n* **:** a distinguishing symbol or letter written immediately above or above and to the right or left of another character [Latin *superscriptus,* past participle of *superscribere* "to superscribe"] — **superscript** *adj*

su•per•scrip•tion \,sü-pər-'skrip-shən\ *n* **1 :** the act of superscribing **2 :** something superscribed on something else **:** INSCRIPTION; *esp* **:** ADDRESS

su•per•sede \,sü-pər-'sēd\ *vt* **1 :** to force out of use as inferior **2 :** to take the place, room, or position of **3 :** to displace in favor of another **:** SUPPLANT [Middle French *superseder* "to refrain from", from Latin *supersedēre* "to be superior to, refrain from", from *super-* + *sedēre* "to sit"] **syn** see REPLACE — **su•per•sed•er** *n* — **su•per•se•dure** \-'sē-jər\ *n*

su•per•sen•si•tive \-'sen-sət-iv, -'sen-stiv\ *adj* **:** HYPERSENSITIVE — **su•per•sen•si•tive•ly** *adv* — **su•per•sen•si•tive•ness** *n* — **su•per•sen•si•tiv•i•ty** \-,sen-sə-'tiv-ət-ē\ *n*

su•per•ses•sion \,sü-pər-'sesh-ən\ *n* **:** the act of superseding **:** the state of being superseded [Medieval Latin *supersessio,* from Latin *supersedēre* "to refrain from"] — **su•per•ses•sive** \-'ses-iv\ *adj*

su•per•son•ic \-'sän-ik\ *adj* **1 :** making or being a sound higher than the human ear's audibility limit of about 20,000 cycles per second ⟨*supersonic* vibrations⟩ **2 :** utilizing, produced by, or relating to supersonic waves or vibrations ⟨*supersonic* disintegration of a substance⟩ **3 :** of, being, or relating to speeds from one to five times the speed of sound in air **4 :** moving, capable of moving, or utilizing air currents moving at supersonic speed ⟨a *supersonic* airplane⟩ — **su•per•son•i•cal•ly** \-'sän-i-kə-lē, -klē\ *adv*

su•per•son•ics \-'sän-iks\ *n* **:** the science of supersonic phenomena

su•per•star \'sü-pər-,stär\ *n* **:** a star (as in sports or the movies) who is considered extremely talented, has great public appeal, and who can usually command a high salary — **su•per•star•dom** \-dəm\ *n*

su•per•sti•tion \,sü-pər-'stish-ən\ *n* **1 :** beliefs or practices resulting from ignorance, fear of the unknown, or belief in fate, omens, magic, or chance as governing principles **2 :** an attitude of resignation toward or fear of nature, the unknown, or God resulting from superstition [Middle French *supersticion,* from Latin *superstitio,* from *superstes* "standing over (as witness or survivor)", from *super-* + *stare* "to stand"] — **su•per•sti•tious** \-'stish-əs\ *adj* — **su•per•sti•tious•ly** *adv* — **su•per•sti•tious•ness** *n*

su•per•struc•ture \'sü-pər-,strək-chər\ *n* **:** something (as the part of a building above the basement or of a ship above the main deck) built upon an underlying or more fundamental base ⟨the social *superstructure*⟩ — **su•per•struc•tur•al** \-,strək-chə-rəl, -,strək-shrəl\ *adj*

su•per•tax \'sü-pər-,taks\ *n* **:** SURTAX

su•per•ton•ic \,sü-pər-'tän-ik\ *n* **:** the second tone of the musical scale

su•per•vene \,sü-pər-'vēn\ *vi* **:** to take place as an additional or unexpected development [Latin *supervenire,* from *super-* + *venire* "to come"]

su•per•vise \'sü-pər-,vīz\ *vt* **:** to be in charge of **:** SUPERINTEND [Medieval Latin *supervisus,* past participle of *supervidēre* "to supervise", from Latin *super-* + *vidēre* "to see"] — **su•per•vi•sion** \,sü-pər-'vizh-ən\ *n*

su•per•vi•sor \'sü-pər-,vī-zər\ *n* **:** one that supervises; *esp* **:** an administrative officer in charge of a business, government, or school unit or operation — **su•per•vi•so•ry** \,sü-pər-'vīz-rē, -ə-rē\ *adj*

su•per•wom•an \'sü-pər-,wům-ən\ *n* **:** a woman with exceptional powers

su•pi•na•tion \,sü-pə-'nā-shən\ *n* **:** rotation of the hand or forearm so as to bring the palm facing upward or forward [Latin *supinare* "to lay on the back", from *supinus* "supine"] — **su•pi•nate** \'sü-pə-,nāt\ *vb*

su•pi•na•tor \'sü-pə-,nāt-ər\ *n* **:** a muscle that produces the motion of supination

¹su•pine \sů-'pīn\ *adj* **1 :** lying on the back or with the face upward **2 :** showing mental or moral slackness **:** APATHETIC [Latin *supinus*] **syn** see PRONE — **su•pine•ly** *adv* — **su•pine•ness** \-'pīn-nəs\ *n*

²su•pine \'sü-,pīn\ *n* **:** a Latin verbal noun having an accusative of purpose in *-um* and an ablative of specification in *-u*

sup•per \'səp-ər\ *n* **1 :** the evening meal when dinner is taken at midday **2 :** refreshments or a meal served late in the evening [Old French *souper,* from *souper* "to sup"]

sup•plant \sə-'plant\ *vt* **1 :** to take the place of (another) especially by force or treachery **2 a :** to remove and supply a substitute for ⟨efforts to *supplant* the vernacular⟩ **b :** to gain the place of especially by reason of superiority [Middle French *supplanter,* from Latin *supplantare* "to overthrow by tripping up", from *sub-* + *planta* "sole of the foot"] **syn** see REPLACE — **sup•plan•ta•tion** \sə-,plan-'tā-shən\ *n* — **sup•plant•er** \sə-'plant-ər\ *n*

¹sup•ple \'səp-əl\ *adj* **sup•pler** \'səp-lər, -ə-lər\; **sup•plest** \'səp-ləst, -ə-ləst\ **1 a :** yielding easily and often submissively to the wishes of others **b :** readily adaptable to new situations **2 a :** capable of being bent or folded without creases or breaks **:** PLIANT ⟨*supple* leather⟩ **b :** able to bend or twist with ease and grace **:** LIMBER ⟨*supple* legs of a dancer⟩ [Old French *souple,* from Latin *supplex* "submissive, suppliant", literally, "bending under"] — **sup•ple•ness** \-əl-nəs\ *n*

²supple *vt* **sup•pled; sup•pling** \'səp-ling, -ə-ling\ **:** to make supple

¹sup•ple•ment \'səp-lə-mənt\ *n* **1 :** something that completes or makes an addition ⟨diet *supplements*⟩ ⟨the *supplement* at the back of the book⟩ **2 :** an angle or arc that when added to a given angle or arc equals 180 degrees [Latin *supplementum,* from *supplēre* "to fill up, complete, supply"] — **sup•ple•men•tal** \,səp-lə-'ment-l\ *adj* — **sup•ple•men•ta•tion** \,səp-lə-,men-'tā-shən\ *n*

²sup•ple•ment \'səp-lə-,mənt\ *vt* **:** to add to **:** fill a deficiency of

sup•ple•men•ta•ry \,səp-lə-'ment-ə-rē, -'men-trē\ *adj* **1 :** added as a supplement **:** ADDITIONAL **2 :** being or related to a supplement or a supplementary angle

supplementary angle *n* **:** either of two angles or arcs whose sum is 180 degrees — usually used in pl.

¹sup•pli•ant \'səp-lē-ənt\ *n* **:** one who supplicates [Middle French, from *supplier* "to supplicate", from Latin *supplicare*]

²suppliant *adj* **:** earnestly and humbly imploring — **sup•pli•ant•ly** *adv*

sup•pli•cant \'səp-li-kənt\ *n* **:** one who supplicates — **supplicant** *adj* — **sup•pli•cant•ly** *adv*

sup•pli•cate \'səp-lə-,kāt\ *vb* **1 :** to make a humble appeal; *esp* **:** to pray to God **2 :** to ask for or of earnestly and humbly

: BESEECH [Latin *supplicare,* from *supplex* "submissive, suppliant"] — **sup·pli·ca·tion** \ˌsəp-lə-ˈkā-shən\ *n* — **sup·pli·ca·to·ry** \ˈsəp-li-kə-ˌtōr-ē -ˌtȯr-\ *adj*

[1]**sup·ply** \sə-ˈplī\ *vt* **sup·plied**; **sup·ply·ing** **1** : to add as a supplement **2** : to provide for : SATISFY ⟨to *supply* their wants⟩ **3** : to provide or furnish with ⟨*supply* provisions⟩ **4** : to satisfy the needs or wishes of ⟨*supply* them with fuel⟩ [Middle French *soupleier,* from Latin *supplēre* "to fill up, supply", from *sub-* "up" + *plēre* "to fill"] — **sup·pli·er** \-ˈplī-ər, -ˈplīr\ *n*

[2]**supply** *n, pl* **supplies** **1 a** : the quantity or amount (as of a commodity) needed or available **b** : PROVISION 2, STORE — usually used in pl. **2** : the act or process of filling a want or need : PROVISION **3** : the quantities of goods or services offered for sale at a particular time or at one price

[1]**sup·port** \sə-ˈpōrt, -ˈpȯrt\ *vt* **1** : to endure bravely or quietly : BEAR **2a** (1) : to promote the interests or cause of (2) : to uphold or defend as valid or right : ADVOCATE (3) : to argue or vote for **b** : ASSIST, HELP **c** : to act in a lesser role with (a star actor) **d** : SUBSTANTIATE 1, VERIFY **3** : to pay the costs of : MAINTAIN **4 a** : to hold up or in position or serve as a foundation or prop for **b** : to maintain (the price of a commodity) at a high level by purchases or loans **5** : to keep (something) going : SUSTAIN [Middle French *supporter,* from Latin *supportare* "to carry", from *sub-* + *portare* "to carry"] — **sup·port·able** \-ə-bəl\ *adj* — **sup·port·able·ness** *n* — **sup·port·ably** \-blē\ *adv*

[2]**support** *n* **1** : the act or process of supporting : the condition of being supported **2** : one that supports

sup·port·er \sə-ˈpōrt-ər, -ˈpȯrt-\ *n* : one that supports; *esp* : ADVOCATE 2

sup·port·ive \sə-ˈpōrt-iv, -ˈpȯrt-\ *adj* : furnishing or intended to furnish support

sup·pose \sə-ˈpōz\ *vb* **1** : to take as true or as a fact for the sake of argument : lay down as a hypothesis ⟨*suppose* a fire should break out⟩ **2** : to hold as an opinion : BELIEVE ⟨they *supposed* they were on the right bus⟩ **3** : THINK, GUESS ⟨who do you *suppose* will win⟩ ⟨I *suppose* so⟩ [Middle French *supposer,* derived from Latin *supponere* "to put under, substitute", from *sub-* + *ponere* "to put, place"]

sup·posed \sə-ˈpōzd, *in the phrase "supposed to" often* -ˈpōz, -ˈpōs, -ˈpōst\ *adj* **1** : usually mistakenly believed **2 a** : required by authority ⟨she was *supposed* to practice two hours daily⟩ **b** : given permission ⟨you're not *supposed* to do that⟩ — **sup·pos·ed·ly** \-ˈpō-zəd-lē\ *adv*

sup·po·si·tion \ˌsəp-ə-ˈzish-ən\ *n* **1** : something that is supposed : HYPOTHESIS **2** : the act of supposing [Late Latin *suppositio,* derived from Latin *supponere* "to put under"] — **sup·po·si·tion·al** \-ˈzish-nəl, -ən-l\ *adj* — **sup·po·si·tion·al·ly** \-ē\ *adv*

sup·po·si·tious \-ˈzish-əs\ *adj* : SUPPOSITITIOUS

sup·pos·i·ti·tious \sə-ˌpäz-ə-ˈtish-əs\ *adj* **1** : fraudulently substituted : SPURIOUS **2** : of the nature of a supposition : HYPOTHETICAL [Latin *suppositicius,* from *supponere* "to put under, substitute"] — **sup·pos·i·ti·tious·ly** *adv* — **sup·pos·i·ti·tious·ness** *n*

sup·pos·i·to·ry \sə-ˈpäz-ə-ˌtōr-ē, -ˌtȯr-\ *n, pl* **-ries** : a solid but readily meltable cone or cylinder of usually medicated material for insertion into a bodily passage or cavity (as the rectum) [Medieval Latin *suppositorium,* derived from Latin *supponere* "to put under"]

sup·press \sə-ˈpres\ *vt* **1** : to put down by authority or force : SUBDUE **2 a** : to keep from being made known **b** : to stop the publication or circulation of **3 a** : to exclude from consciousness **b** : to hold back : RESTRAIN ⟨*suppress* a cough⟩ **4** : to inhibit the growth or development of : STUNT [Latin *suppressus,* past participle of *supprimere* "to suppress", from *sub-* + *premere* "to press"] — **sup·press·ible** \-ə-bəl\ *adj* — **sup·pres·sion** \-ˈpresh-ən\ *n* — **sup·pres·sive** \-ˈpres-iv\ *adj* — **sup·pres·sor** \-ˈpres-ər\ *n*

sup·pu·rate \ˈsəp-yə-ˌrāt\ *vi* : to form or give off pus [Latin *suppurare,* from *sub-* + *pur-, pus* "pus"] — **sup·pu·ra·tion** \ˌsəp-yə-ˈrā-shən\ *n* — **sup·pu·ra·tive** \ˈsəp-yə-ˌrāt-iv\ *adj*

supra- *prefix* **1** : SUPER- 2a ⟨*supra*orbital⟩ **2** : transcending ⟨*supra*national⟩ [Latin, from *supra* "above, beyond"]

su·pra·na·tion·al \ˌsü-prə-ˈnash-nəl, -ˈnash-ən-l\ *adj* : transcending national boundaries or authority

su·pra·or·bit·al \-ˈȯr-bət-l\ *adj* : situated or occurring above the orbit of the eye

[1]**su·pra·re·nal** \-ˈrēn-l\ *adj* : situated above or in front of the kidneys; *esp* : ADRENAL

[2]**suprarenal** *n* : a suprarenal part; *esp* : ADRENAL GLAND

su·prem·a·cist \sü-ˈprem-ə-səst\ *n* : an advocate of supremacy of a particular group (as a race)

su·prem·a·cy \sü-ˈprem-ə-sē\ *n, pl* **-cies** : the quality or state of being supreme; *also* : supreme authority or power [*supreme* + *-acy* (as in *primacy*)]

• **syn** SUPREMACY, ASCENDANCY mean a being first in rank, power, or influence. SUPREMACY implies definite superiority over all others ⟨*supremacy* in steel production⟩ ASCENDANCY implies domination of one by another which may or may not involve supremacy ⟨seeking to keep one's *ascendancy* over an old rival⟩

su·preme \sü-ˈprēm\ *adj* **1** : highest in rank or authority **2** : highest in degree or quality **3** : ULTIMATE, FINAL ⟨the *supreme* sacrifice⟩ [Latin *supremus,* superlative of *superus* "upper", from *super* "over, above"] — **su·preme·ly** *adv* — **su·preme·ness** *n*

Supreme Being *n* : GOD 1

supreme court *n* : the highest court of the United States consisting of a chief justice and eight associate justices; *also* : a similar body in many states

sur- *prefix* : over : above ⟨*sur*tax⟩ [Old French, from Latin *super-*]

sur·cease \ˈsər-ˌsēs, ˌsər-ˈ\ *n* : CESSATION; *esp* : a temporary respite or end [Middle French *sursis,* past participle of *surseoir* "to desist, take a respite", from Latin *supersedēre* "to be superior to, refrain from", from *super-* + *sedēre* "to sit"]

[1]**sur·charge** \ˈsər-ˌchärj\ *vt* **1 a** : OVERCHARGE 1 **b** : to charge an extra fee usually for a special service **2** : to burden with an excess physical or emotional load **3** : to mark (as a stamp) with a surcharge

[2]**surcharge** *n* **1** : an additional tax or charge **2** : an excessive load **3 a** : an overprint on a stamp; *esp* : one that alters the denomination **b** : a stamp bearing such an overprint

sur·cin·gle \ˈsər-ˌsing-gəl\ *n* : a band or girth passing around the body of a horse to bind a saddle or pack fast to the horse's back [Middle French *surcengle,* from *sur-* + *cengle* "girdle", from Latin *cingulum*]

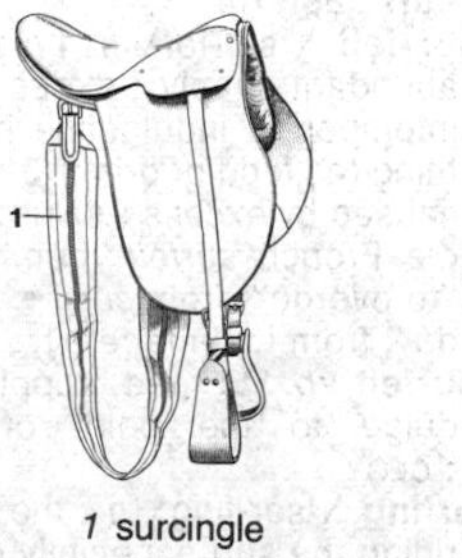

1 surcingle

sur·coat \ˈsər-ˌkōt\ *n* : an outer coat or cloak; *esp* : a tunic worn over armor

[1]**surd** \ˈsərd\ *adj* : VOICELESS — used of speech sounds [Latin *surdus* "deaf, silent, stupid"]

[2]**surd** *n* **1** : an irrational root (as $\sqrt{3}$) **2** : a surd speech sound

[1]**sure** \ˈshu̇r, *especially South* ˈshōr\ *adj* **1** : firmly established : STEADFAST ⟨a *sure* foundation⟩ **2** : RELIABLE, TRUSTWORTHY **3** : marked by or given to feelings of intuitive certainty **4** : admitting of no doubt : CERTAIN **5 a** : bound to happen : INEVITABLE ⟨*sure* disaster⟩ **b** : destined as if by fate ⟨*sure* to win⟩ [Middle French *sur,* from Latin *securus* "secure"] — **sure·ness** *n*

• **syn** SURE, CERTAIN, POSITIVE mean having no doubt of one's opinion or conclusion. SURE usually stresses the subjective or intuitive feeling of assurance ⟨I am *sure* I have seen that face before⟩ CERTAIN implies basing a conclusion on definite grounds or indubitable evidence; POSITIVE intensifies sureness and may imply opinionated conviction or forceful expression of it.

— **for sure** : without doubt : with certainty — **to be sure** **1** : SURELY 1b, CERTAINLY **2** : it must be acknowledged

[2]**sure** *adv* : SURELY

sure·fire \-ˈfīr\ *adj* : certain to get results : DEPENDABLE

sure·foot·ed \-ˈfu̇t-əd\ *adj* : not liable to stumble or fall — **sure·foot·ed·ness** *n*

sure·ly \ˈshu̇r-lē\ *adv* **1 a** : with assurance : CONFIDENTLY **b**

: without doubt : CERTAINLY ⟨will *surely* be there⟩ **2 :** INDEED I, REALLY — often used as an intensive ⟨I *surely* am tired this afternoon⟩

sure•ty \'shu̇r-ət-ē, 'shu̇rt-ē\ *n, pl* **sureties 1 :** sure knowledge : CERTAINTY **2 :** a pledge for the fulfillment of an undertaking : GUARANTEE **3 :** one who assumes legal liability for another's debt, default, or failure to do a duty — **sure•ty•ship** \-ē-ˌship\ *n*

[1]surf \'sərf\ *n* **1 :** the swell of the sea that breaks upon the shore **2 :** the foam, splash, and sound of breaking waves **[**origin unknown**]**

[2]surf *vi* : to ride the surf : engage in surfing — **surf•er** *n*

[1]sur•face \'sər-fəs\ *n* **1 :** the outside of an object or body **2 :** a plane or curved two-dimensional locus of points ⟨the *surface* of a sphere⟩ **3 :** the external or superficial aspect of something ⟨on the *surface,* the statement appears to be true⟩ **4 :** a complete airfoil **[**French, from *sur-* + *face***]** — **surface** *adj* — **surfaced** \-fəst\ *adj*

[2]surface *vb* **1 :** to give a surface to: as **a :** to plane (as lumber) smooth **b :** to apply a surface layer to **2 :** to come to the surface ⟨the submarine *surfaced*⟩ — **sur•fac•er** *n*

surface tension *n* : the property of a liquid that causes its surface to act like an elastic sheet and that is due to the cohesive force exerted on surface molecules by interior molecules

sur•fac•ing \'sər-fə-sing\ *n* : material forming or used to form a surface (as on a road)

surf•board \'sərf-ˌbōrd, -ˌbȯrd\ *n* : a buoyant board used in the sport of surfing — **surfboard** *vi* — **surf•board•er** *n*

surfboard

surf•boat \-ˌbōt\ *n* : a boat for use in heavy surf

surf casting *n* : the technique or act of casting artificial or natural bait into the open ocean or in a bay where waves break on a beach — **surf caster** *n*

[1]sur•feit \'sər-fət\ *n* **1 :** an overabundant supply : EXCESS **2 :** an intemperate indulgence in something (as food or drink) **3 :** disgust caused by excess : SATIETY **[**Middle French *surfait,* from *surfaire* "to overdo", from *sur-* + *faire* "to do", from Latin *facere***]**

[2]surfeit *vb* : to feed, supply, or indulge to the point of surfeit : CLOY

surfing \'sər-fing\ *n* : the sport of riding the surf especially on a surfboard

[1]surge \'sərj\ *vi* **1 :** to rise and fall actively **2 :** to rise and move or roll forward in or as if in waves or billows ⟨the sea *surged*⟩ ⟨a crowd of people *surged* toward the door⟩ **3 :** to rise suddenly to an abnormal value — used especially of current or voltage **[**Middle French *sourge-,* stem of *sourdre* "to rise, surge", from Latin *surgere* "to go straight up, rise", from *sub-* "up" + *regere* "to lead straight"**]**

[2]surge *n* **1 :** a swelling, rolling, or sweeping forward like that of a wave **2 :** a large wave or billow : SWELL **3 :** a transient sudden rise of current or voltage in an electrical circuit

sur•geon \'sər-jən\ *n* : a physician who specializes in surgery **[**Anglo-French *surgien,* from Old French *cirurgien,* from *cirurgie* "surgery"**]**

sur•gery \'sərj-rē, -ə-rē\ *n, pl* **-ger•ies 1 :** a branch of medicine concerned with the correction of physical defects, the repair and healing of injuries, and the treatment of diseased conditions especially by operations **2 :** work done by a surgeon : OPERATION **3 a** *British* : a physician's or dentist's office **b :** a room or area where surgery is performed **[**Old French *cirurgie, surgerie,* from Latin *chirurgia,* from Greek *cheirourgia,* derived from *cheir* "hand" + *ergon* "work"**]**

sur•gi•cal \'sər-ji-kəl\ *adj* : of, relating to, or associated with surgeons or surgery ⟨*surgical* skills⟩ ⟨*surgical* implements⟩ ⟨*surgical* fevers⟩ — **sur•gi•cal•ly** \-kə-lē, -klē\ *adv*

sur•ly \'sər-lē\ *adj* **sur•li•er**; **-est :** irritably sullen and churlish in mood or manner **[**Middle English *sirly* "lordly, imperious", from *sir***]** **syn** see SULLEN — **sur•li•ness** *n*

[1]sur•mise \sər-'mīz\ *vb* : to imagine or infer on slight grounds : GUESS **[**Middle French *surmis,* past participle of *surmetre* "to accuse", from Latin *supermittere* "to throw on", from *super-* + *mittere* "to send"**]** **syn** see CONJECTURE

[2]sur•mise \sər-'mīz, 'sər-ˌ\ *n* : a thought or idea based on scanty evidence : CONJECTURE

sur•mount \sər-'mau̇nt\ *vt* **1 :** to rise above or prevail over : OVERCOME ⟨*surmount* an obstacle⟩ **2 :** to get to the top of : CLIMB **3 :** to stand or lie at the top of : CROWN ⟨a cross *surmounts* the church steeple⟩ — **sur•mount•able** \-ə-bəl\ *adj*

[1]sur•name \'sər-ˌnām\ *n* : the name borne in common by members of a family **[**earlier *surname* "added name, nickname"**]**

[2]surname *vt* : to give a surname to

sur•pass \sər-'pas\ *vt* **1 :** to be greater, better, or stronger than : EXCEED **2 :** to go beyond the reach, powers, or capacity of **syn** see EXCEED — **sur•pass•able** \-ə-bəl\ *adj*

sur•plice \'sər-pləs\ *n* : a loose white tunic worn at service by a member of the clergy or choir **[**Old French *surpliz,* from Medieval Latin *superpellicium,* from *super-* + *pellicium* "coat of skins", derived from Latin *pellis* "skin"**]**

surplice

sur•plus \'sər-ˌpləs, -pləs\ *n* : the amount that remains when use or need is satisfied : EXCESS **[**Middle French, from Medieval Latin *superplus,* from Latin *super-* + *plus* "more"**]** — **surplus** *adj*

sur•plus•age \-ij\ *n* **1 :** SURPLUS **2 :** excessive or nonessential matter

surplus value *n* : the difference in Marxist theory between the value of work done by labor and the wages paid by the employer

[1]sur•prise \sər-'prīz, sə-'prīz\ *n* **1 a :** an attack made without warning **b :** a taking unawares ⟨we were taken by *surprise*⟩ **2 :** something that surprises **3 :** the state of being surprised : ASTONISHMENT **[**Middle French, from *surprendre* "to take over, surprise", from *sur-* + *prendre* "to take"**]**

[2]surprise *vt* **1 :** to attack unexpectedly; *also* : to capture by an unexpected attack **2 :** to take unawares : come upon unexpectedly **3 :** to strike with wonder or amazement because unexpected

• **syn** SURPRISE, ASTONISH, ASTOUND mean to impress strongly through unexpectedness. SURPRISE stresses causing an effect through being unexpected at a particular time or place rather than by being essentially unusual or novel; ASTONISH implies surprising so greatly as to seem incredible; ASTOUND stresses the shock of astonishment.

sur•pris•ing *adj* : of a kind to cause surprise — **sur•pris•ing•ly** \-'prī-zing-lē\ *adv*

sur•re•al•ism \sə-'rē-ə-ˌliz-əm\ *n* : a modern movement in art and literature with the aim of expressing subconscious mental activities through fantastic or incongruous imagery or unnatural juxtapositions and combinations — **sur•re•al•ist** \-ləst\ *n or adj* — **sur•re•al•is•tic** \-ˌrē-ə-'lis-tik\ *adj* — **sur•re•al•is•ti•cal•ly** \-ti-kə-lē, -klē\ *adv*

[1]sur•ren•der \sə-'ren-dər\ *vb* **sur•ren•dered**; **sur•ren•der•ing** \-də-ring, -dring\ **1 :** to give over to the power, control, or possession of another especially under compulsion ⟨*surrendered* the fort⟩ **2 :** to give oneself up into the power of another especially as a prisoner **3 :** to give oneself over to something (as an influence or course of action) **[**Middle French *surrendre,* from *sur-* + *rendre* "to yield"**]** **syn** see RELINQUISH

[2]surrender *n* : the giving of oneself or something into the power of another person or thing

sur•rep•ti•tious \ˌsər-əp-'tish-əs, ˌsə-rəp-\ *adj* : done, made, or acquired by stealth : CLANDESTINE, STEALTHY **[**Latin *surrepticius,* from *surripere* "to snatch secretly", from *sub-* + *rapere* "to seize"**]** **syn** see SECRET — **sur•rep•ti•tious•ly** *adv* — **sur•rep•ti•tious•ness** *n*

sur•rey \'sər-ē, 'sə-rē\ *n, pl* **surreys :** a four-wheel two-seated horse-drawn pleasure carriage **[***Surrey,* England**]**

sur•ro•gate \'sər-ə-ˌgāt, 'sə-rə-, -gət\ *n* **1 :** DEPUTY 1, SUBSTITUTE **2 :** a local judicial officer in some states having jurisdiction over the settling of estates **[**Latin *surrogatus,* past participle of *surrogare* "to substitute", from *sub-* + *rogare* "to ask"] — **surrogate** *adj*

[1]sur•round \sə-ˈraund\ *vt* : to enclose on all sides : ENCIRCLE, ENCOMPASS [Middle French *suronder* "to overflow", from Late Latin *superundare,* from Latin *super-* + *unda* "wave"]

surrey

[2]surround *n* : something (as a border or edging) that surrounds

sur•round•ings \-ˈraun-dingz\ *n pl* : ENVIRONMENT 1

sur•sum cor•da \ˌsur-səm-ˈkord-ə\ *n* **1** *often cap S&C* : a versicle exhorting thanksgiving to God **2** : something inspiriting [Late Latin, "(lift) up (your) hearts"]

sur•tax \ˈsər-ˌtaks\ *n* : an additional tax over and above a general tax

sur•tout \sər-ˈtü, ˌsər-\ *n* : a long close-fitting overcoat [French, from *sur* "over" + *tout* "all"]

sur•veil•lance \sər-ˈvā-ləns *also* -ˈvāl-yəns *or* -ˈvā-əns\ *n* : close watch [French, from *surveiller* "to watch over", from *sur-* + *veiller* "to watch", from Latin *vigilare,* from *vigil* "watchful"]

sur•veil•lant \-ˈvā-lənt *also* -ˈvāl-yənt *or* -ˈvā-ənt\ *n* : one that keeps another under surveillance

[1]sur•vey \sər-ˈvā, ˈsər-ˌ\ *vt* **sur•veyed; sur•vey•ing 1** : to look over and examine closely **2** : to determine the form, boundaries, and position of (as a piece of land) **3** : to view or study as a whole : make a survey of [Middle French *surveeir,* from *sur-* + *veeir* "to see", from Latin *vidēre*] — **sur•vey•or** \sər-ˈvā-ər\ *n*

[2]sur•vey \ˈsər-ˌvā, sər-ˈ\ *n, pl* **surveys 1** : the action or an instance of surveying **2** : something that is surveyed **3** : a careful examination to learn certain facts ⟨a *survey* of the school system⟩ **4** : a history or description that covers a large subject briefly ⟨a *survey* of world history⟩ **5 a** : the process of determining and making a record of the outline, measurements, and position of any part of the earth's surface especially by use of geometry and trigonometry **b** : an organization engaged in surveying **6** : a measured plan and description (as of a portion of land or of a road)

sur•vey•ing \sər-ˈvā-ing\ *n* **1** : the occupation of making land surveys **2** : a branch of applied mathematics concerned with the accurate measurement and representation of the earth's surface

sur•viv•al \sər-ˈvī-vəl\ *n* **1** : a living or continuing longer than another or beyond something ⟨*survival* of the soul after death⟩ **2** : the continuation of life despite difficult conditions ⟨techniques for *survival* in the desert⟩ **3** : one that survives

survival of the fittest : NATURAL SELECTION

sur•vive \sər-ˈvīv\ *vb* **1** : to remain alive or in existence : live on **2** : to remain alive after the death of ⟨the parents *survived* their child⟩ **3** : to continue to exist or live after ⟨*survived* the flood⟩ [Middle French *survivre* "to outlive", from Latin *supervivere,* from *super-* + *vivere* "to live"] — **sur•vi•vor** \-ˈvī-vər\ *n*

sus•cep•ti•bil•i•ty \sə-ˌsep-tə-ˈbil-ət-ē\ *n, pl* **-ties 1** : the quality or state of being susceptible; *esp* : lack of ability to resist some outside agent (as a pathogen or drug) : SENSITIVITY **2 a** : a susceptible temperament or constitution **b** *pl* : FEELING 2b, SENSIBILITIES

sus•cep•ti•ble \sə-ˈsep-tə-bəl\ *adj* **1** : capable of submitting to an action, process, or operation ⟨a theory *susceptible* to proof⟩ **2** : open, subject, or unresistant to some stimulus, influence, or agency ⟨persons *susceptible* to colds⟩ **3** : easily influenced or affected [Late Latin *susceptibilis,* from Latin *suscipere* "to take up", from *sub-, sus-* "up" + *capere* "to take"] — **sus•cep•ti•ble•ness** *n* — **sus•cep•ti•bly** \-blē\ *adv*

[1]sus•pect \ˈsəs-ˌpekt, sə-ˈspekt\ *adj* : regarded with or deserving suspicion [Middle French, from Latin *suspectus,* from *suspicere* "to suspect"]

[2]sus•pect \ˈsəs-ˌpekt\ *n* : one who is suspected

[3]sus•pect \sə-ˈspekt\ *vb* **1** : to have doubts of : DISTRUST **2** : to believe to be guilty on slight evidence or without proof ⟨*suspected* me of theft⟩ **3** : to imagine to be or be true, likely, or probable : SURMISE **4** : to be suspicious [Latin *suspectare,* from *suspicere* "to look up at, regard with awe, suspect", from *sub-* "up" + *specere* "to look at"]

sus•pend \sə-ˈspend\ *vb* **1** : to bar temporarily from any privilege or office ⟨*suspend* a student from school⟩ **2 a** : to stop or do away with (as an activity) for a time ⟨*suspend* publication⟩ **b** : to defer on specified conditions ⟨*suspend* sentence on an offender⟩ ⟨*suspend* judgment⟩ **3** : to cease for a time from operation or activity **4 a** : HANG; *esp* : to hang so as to be free on all sides except at the point of support ⟨*suspend* a ball by a thread⟩ **b** : to keep from falling or sinking by some invisible support (as buoyancy) ⟨dust *suspended* in the air⟩ [Old French *suspendre,* from Latin *suspendere,* from *sub-, sus-* "up" + *pendere* "to cause to hang, weigh"]

suspended animation *n* : temporary suspension of the vital functions (as in persons nearly drowned)

sus•pend•er \sə-ˈspen-dər\ *n* **1** : one that suspends **2** : a device by which something may be suspended; *esp* : either of two supporting bands worn across the shoulders to support pants, skirt, or belt — usually used in pl. ⟨a pair of *suspenders*⟩

sus•pense \sə-ˈspens\ *n* **1** : temporary cessation : SUSPENSION **2** : mental uncertainty: **a** : ANXIETY 1a **b** : pleasant excitement as to a decision or outcome ⟨a novel of *suspense*⟩ **3** : the state of being undecided : lack of certainty ⟨our next move was still in *suspense*⟩ [Middle French, from *suspendre* "to suspend"] — **sus•pense•ful** \-fəl\ *adj*

sus•pen•sion \sə-ˈspen-chən\ *n* **1** : the act of suspending or the state or period of being suspended: as **a** : temporary removal from office or privileges **b** : temporary withholding (as of belief or decision) **c** : temporary setting aside of a law or rule **2** : the act of hanging : the state of being hung **3 a** : the state of a substance when its particles are mixed with but undissolved in a fluid or solid; *also* : a substance in this state **b** : a system consisting of a solid dispersed in a solid, liquid, or gas usually in particles of larger than colloidal size **4** : something suspended **5 a** : a device by which something is suspended **b** : the system of devices (as springs) supporting the upper part of a vehicle on the axles [Late Latin *suspensio,* from Latin *suspendere* "to suspend"]

suspension bridge *n* : a bridge that has its roadway suspended from two or more cables usually passing over towers and securely anchored at the ends

suspension points *n pl* : usually three spaced periods used to show the omission of a word or word group

sus•pen•sive \sə-ˈspen-siv\ *adj* **1** : stopping temporarily **2** : characterized by suspense, suspended judgment, or indecisiveness — **sus•pen•sive•ly** *adv*

sus•pen•sor \sə-ˈspen-sər\ *n* : a suspending part or structure; *esp* : a group of cells supporting a plant embryo or zygospore

sus•pen•so•ry \sə-ˈspens-rē, -ə-rē\ *adj* : fitted or serving to suspend something **2** : temporarily leaving something undetermined

suspensory ligament *n* : a fibrous membrane holding the iris of the eye in place

[1]sus•pi•cion \sə-ˈspish-ən\ *n* **1** : the act or an instance of suspecting or being suspected **2** : a state of mental uneasiness and uncertainty : DOUBT **3** : a slight touch or trace : SUGGESTION ⟨just a *suspicion* of garlic⟩ [Latin *suspicio,* from *suspicere* "to suspect"] **syn** see DOUBT

[2]suspicion *vt* **sus•pi•cioned; sus•pi•cion•ing** \-ˈspish-ning, -ə-ning\ *chiefly substandard* : SUSPECT

sus•pi•cious \sə-ˈspish-əs\ *adj* **1** : arousing or tending to arouse suspicion **2** : disposed to suspect : DISTRUSTFUL **3** : indicative of suspicion ⟨a *suspicious* glance⟩ — **sus•pi•cious•ly** *adv* — **sus•pi•cious•ness** *n*

sus•pire \sə-ˈspīr\ *vi* : to draw a long deep breath : SIGH [Latin *suspirare,* from *sub-* + *spirare* "to breathe"] — **sus•pi•ra•tion** \ˌsəs-pə-ˈrā-shən\ *n*

sus•tain \sə-ˈstān\ *vt* **1** : to give support or relief to **2** : to supply with sustenance : NOURISH **3** : to keep up : PROLONG ⟨*sustain* the growth in the economy⟩ **4** : to support the weight of : CARRY **5** : to keep up the spirits or courage of **6 a** : to bear up under : ENDURE **b** : UNDERGO 1 ⟨*sustained* a serious wound⟩ **7** : to support as true, legal, valid, or just ⟨the court *sustained* the

\ə\ abut	\au\ **out**	\i\ **tip**	\o\ **saw**	\u\ **foot**
\ər\ further	\ch\ **chin**	\ī\ life	\oi\ coin	\y\ **yet**
\a\ mat	\e\ **pet**	\j\ **job**	\th\ **thin**	\yü\ **few**
\ā\ take	\ē\ **easy**	\ng\ **sing**	\th\ this	\yu\ cure
\ä\ cot, cart	\g\ **go**	\ō\ bone	\ü\ **food**	\zh\ vision

earlier verdict〉 **8** : PROVE 2a, CONFIRM [Old French *sustenir,* from Latin *sustinēre* "to hold up, sustain", from *sub-, sus-* "up" + *tenēre* "to hold"] — **sus•tain•able** \-'stā-nə-bəl\ *adj* — **sus•tain•er** *n*

sustaining program *n* : a radio or television program that is paid for by a station or network and has no commercial sponsor

sus•te•nance \'səs-tə-nəns\ *n* **1 a** : means of support, maintenance, or subsistence **b** : FOOD; *also* : NOURISHMENT **2** : the act of sustaining : the state of being sustained; *esp* : a supplying with the necessaries of life [Old French, from *sustenir* "to sustain"]

su•sur•ra•tion \,sü-sə-'rā-shən\ *n* : a rustling or whispering sound [Late Latin *susurratio,* from Latin *susurrare* "to whisper"]

sut•ler \'sət-lər\ *n* : one formerly let to follow an army or establish a store on a post and sell food and provisions [Dutch *soeteler,* from Low German *suteler* "sloppy worker, camp cook"]

sut•tee \sə-'tē, ,sə-'tē\ *n* : the act or custom of a Hindu widow allowing herself to be cremated on the funeral pile of her husband; *also* : a woman so cremated [Sanskrit *satī* "wife who performs suttee", literally, "good woman", from *sat* "true, good"]

1su•ture \'sü-chər\ *n* **1 a** : a strand or fiber used to sew parts of the living body; *also* : a stitch made with this **b** : the act or process of sewing with sutures **2 a** : the line of union in an immovable joint (as between the bones of the skull); *also* : such a joint **b** : a furrow at the junction of adjacent bodily parts; *esp* : a line along which a fruit dehisces [Latin *sutura* "seam, suture", from *suere* "to sew"] — **su•tur•al** \'süch-rəl, -ə-rəl\ *adj* — **su•tur•al•ly** \-ē\ *adv*

2suture *vt* **su•tured**; **su•tur•ing** \'süch-ring, -ə-ring\ : to unite, close, or secure with sutures 〈*suture* a wound〉

su•zer•ain \'süz-rən, -ə-rən, 'süz-ə-,rān\ *n* **1** : a feudal lord : OVERLORD **2** : a state controlling the foreign relations of another but allowing it internal sovereignty [French, from Middle French *sus* "up" + *-erain* (as in *soverain* "sovereign")] — **su•zer•ain•ty** \-tē\ *n*

svelte \'sfelt\ *adj* **1** : slender and graceful in form **2** : URBANE, SUAVE [French, from Italian *svelto,* from *svellere* "to pluck out", from Latin *evellere,* from *e-* + *vellere* "to pluck"]

Sven•ga•li \sfen-'gäl-ē\ *n* : one who attempts to exert a dominant and sometimes evil influence over another [*Svengali,* evil hypnotist in the novel *Trilby* by George du Maurier, died 1896, British artist and novelist]

1swab *or* **swob** \'swäb\ *n* **1 a** : MOP; *esp* : a yarn mop **b** : a wad of absorbent material usually wound around one end of a small stick and used for applying medication or for removing material (as from a wound or lesion); *also* : a specimen taken with a swab **c** : a sponge attached to a long handle for cleaning the bore of a firearm **2** : SAILOR 1a [probably from Dutch *swabbe*]

2swab *or* **swob** *vt* **swabbed** *or* **swobbed**; **swab•bing** *or* **swob•bing** : to use a swab on

swad•dle \'swäd-l\ *vt* **swad•dled**; **swad•dling** \'swäd-ling, -l-ing\ **1** : to wrap (an infant) with swaddling clothes **2** : to wrap closely : SWATHE [Middle English *swadelen*]

swaddling clothes *n pl* **1** : narrow strips of cloth wrapped around an infant to restrict movement **2** : limitations or restrictions imposed upon the immature or inexperienced

swag \'swag\ *n* **1 a** : something hanging in a curve between two points : FESTOON **b** : a suspended cluster **2** : goods acquired by unlawful means : LOOT [earlier *swag* "to sway", probably of Scandinavian origin]

1swage \'swāj, 'swej\ *n* : a tool used by metalworkers to shape material to a desired form [Middle French *souage* "ornamental border"]

2swage *vt* : to shape by means of a swage

1swag•ger \'swag-ər\ *vi* **swag•gered**; **swag•ger•ing** \'swag-ring, -ə-ring\ **1** : to conduct oneself in an arrogant or overbearing manner; *esp* : to walk with an air of superiority **2** : BOAST 1, 2, BRAG [probably from *swag* "to sway"] **syn** see STRUT — **swag•ger•er** \'swag-ər-ər\ *n* — **swag•ger•ing•ly** \-ring-lē, -ə-ring-\ *adv*

2swagger *n* : an act or instance of swaggering

swagger stick *n* : a short light stick usually covered with leather or tipped with metal

Swa•hi•li \swä-'hē-lē\ *n* **1** : a member of a Bantu-speaking people of Zanzibar and the adjacent coast of Africa **2** : a Bantu language that is a trade and governmental language over much of East Africa and in the Congo region [Arabic *sawāḥil,* pl. of *sāḥil* "coast"]

swain \'swān\ *n* **1** : RUSTIC, PEASANT; *esp* : SHEPHERD **2** : a male admirer or suitor : BEAU [Old Norse *sveinn* "boy, servant"]

swale \'swāl\ *n* : a small, low-lying and usually wet stretch of land [Middle English, "shade"]

1swal•low \'swäl-ō\ *n* **1** : any of a family of small long-winged migratory passerine birds that are noted for their graceful flight and have usually a deeply forked tail **2** : any of several swifts that superficially resemble swallows [Old English *swealwe*]

2swallow *vb* **1 a** : to take into the stomach through the mouth and throat **b** : to perform the actions used in swallowing something **2** : to envelop or take in as if by swallowing 〈was *swallowed* up by the crowd〉 **3** : to accept without question, protest, or resentment 〈a hard story to *swallow*〉 **4** : to take back : RETRACT 〈had to *swallow* those words〉 **5** : to keep from expressing or showing : REPRESS 〈*swallow* one's anger〉 **6** : to utter (as words) indistinctly [Old English *swelgan*] — **swal•low•er** \'swäl-ə-wər\ *n*

3swallow *n* **1** : an act of swallowing **2** : an amount that can be swallowed at one time

swal•low•tail \'swäl-ō-,tāl\ *n* **1** : a deeply forked and tapering tail (as of a swallow) **2** : any of various large butterflies with the border of the hind wing drawn out into a process resembling a tail — **swal•low•tailed** \,swäl-ō-'tāld\ *adj*

swam *past of* SWIM

swa•mi \'swäm-ē\ *n* : a Hindu mystic or religious teacher — used as a title [Hindi *svāmī,* from Sanskrit *svāmin* "owner, lord", from *sva* "one's own"]

1swamp \'swämp, 'swȯmp\ *n* : wet spongy land or a tract of this often partially or intermittently covered with water and usually overgrown with shrubs and trees — compare MARSH [Middle English *sompe,* from Dutch *somp* "morass"] — **swamp•i•ness** \-pē-nəs\ *n* — **swampy** \'swäm-pē, 'swȯm-\ *adj*

2swamp *vb* **1 a** : to cause to capsize in water or fill with water and sink **b** : to fill with or as if with water : SUBMERGE **2** : to overwhelm by an excess of something (as enemies or work)

swamp buggy *n* : a vehicle used to negotiate swampy terrain: as **a** : an amphibious tractor **b** : a flat-bottomed boat driven by an airplane propeller

swamp•land \'swäm-,pland, 'swȯm-\ *n* : SWAMP

swamp loosestrife *n* : a woody marsh herb of eastern North America that has clusters of magenta flowers and colonizes the edge of open water in swamps and bogs

swan

swan \'swän\ *n, pl* **swans** *also* **swan** : any of various heavy-bodied long-necked mostly pure white aquatic birds related to but larger than the geese [Old English]

swan dive *n* : a headfirst forward dive made with the back arched, the head back, the arms out to either side, and the legs together

1swank \'swangk\ *vi* : to show off : SWAGGER [perhaps from Middle High German *swanken* "to sway"]

2swank *n* : a sometimes flashy show of elegance or pretense

3swank *or* **swanky** \'swang-kē\ *adj* **swank•er** *or* **swank•i•er**; **-est 1** : characterized by showy display : OSTENTATIOUS **2** : fashionably elegant : SMART — **swank•i•ly** \'swang-kə-lē\ *adv* — **swank•i•ness** \-kē-nəs\ *n*

swans•down \'swänz-,daun\ *n* **1** : the very soft white down of the swan **2** : a heavy cotton flannel with a thick nap on the face

swan song *n* **1** : a song of unusual beauty formerly thought to be sung by a dying swan **2** : a farewell appearance or final act or pronouncement

1swap *also* **swop** \'swäp\ *vb* **swapped**; **swap•ping** : to give in exchange : make an exchange : BARTER [Middle English *swappen* "to strike"; from the practice of striking hands in closing a business deal]

2swap *n* : EXCHANGE 1, TRADE

sward \'swȯrd\ *n* : the grassy surface of land : TURF [Old English *sweard* "skin, rind"]

1**swarm** \ˈswȯrm\ *n* **1 :** a great number of honeybees emigrating together from a hive in company with a queen to start a new colony elsewhere; *also* **:** a colony of honeybees settled in a hive **2 :** an extremely large number massed together and usually in motion [Old English *swearm*]

2**swarm** *vb* **1 :** to form and depart from a hive in a swarm **2 :** to migrate, move, or gather in a crowd **:** THRONG **3 :** to contain or fill with a swarm **:** TEEM — **swarm•er** *n*

3**swarm** *vb* **:** to climb with the hands and feet; *esp* **:** SHIN ⟨*swarm* up a pole⟩ [origin unknown]

swarm spore *n* **:** a tiny motile spore

swart \ˈswȯrt\ *adj* **:** SWARTHY [Old English *sweart*] — **swart•ness** *n*

swar•thy \ˈswȯr-t͟hē, -thē\ *adj* **swar•thi•er; -est :** of a dark color, complexion, or cast **:** DUSKY [derived from *swart*] — **swar•thi•ness** *n*

1**swash** \ˈswäsh\ *n* **1 a :** a body of splashing water **b :** a narrow channel of water lying within a sandbank or between a sandbank and the shore **2 :** a dashing of water against or upon something **3 :** SWAGGER [probably imitative]

2**swash** *vb* **1 :** BLUSTER 2, SWAGGER **2 :** to make violent noisy movements **3 :** to move or cause to move with a splashing sound

swash•buck•ler \-ˌbək-lər\ *n* **:** a boasting soldier or blustering ruffian **:** BRAVO [2*swash* + *buckler*] — **swash•buck•le** \-ˌbək-əl\ *vi* — **swash•buck•ling** \-ˌbək-ling\ *adj or n*

swas•ti•ka \ˈswäs-ti-kə *also* swä-ˈstē-kə\ *n* **:** a symbol or ornament in the form of a Greek cross with the ends of the arms extended at right angles all in the same rotary direction [Sanskrit *svastika,* from *svasti* "welfare", from *su-* "well" + *asti* "he is"; from its being regarded as a good luck symbol]

swat \ˈswät\ *vb* **swat•ted; swat•ting :** to hit with a quick hard blow [English dialect *swat* "to squat", alteration of *squat*] — **swat** *n* — **swat•ter** *n*

swatch \ˈswäch\ *n* **1 a :** a sample piece (as of fabric) or a collection of samples **b :** a typical sample **2 :** PATCH ⟨a *swatch* of color⟩ [origin unknown]

swath \ˈswäth, ˈswȯth\ *or* **swathe** \ˈswät͟h, ˈswȯt͟h, ˈswāt͟h\ *n* **1 a :** the sweep of a scythe or machine in mowing or the path cut in one course **b :** a row of cut grain or grass **2 :** a long broad strip or belt ⟨a long *swath* of land⟩ **3 :** a space devastated as if by a scythe [Old English *swæth* "footstep, trace"]

1**swathe** \ˈswät͟h, ˈswȯt͟h, ˈswāt͟h\ *vt* **1 :** to bind, wrap, or swaddle with or as if with a bandage **2 :** ENVELOP [Old English *swathian*]

2**swathe** \ˈswät͟h, ˈswȯt͟h, ˈswāt͟h\ *or* **swath** \ˈswät͟h, ˈswäth, ˈswȯt͟h, ˈswȯth\ *n* **1 :** a band used in swathing **2 :** an enveloping medium

1**sway** \ˈswā\ *vb* **1 a :** to swing or cause to swing slowly back and forth from a base or pivot **b :** to move gently from an upright to a leaning position **2 :** to hold sway **:** act as ruler or governor **3 :** to fluctuate or veer between one point, position, or opinion and another **4 :** to cause to turn aside (as from a thought or course of action) **5 :** to exert a guiding or controlling influence upon [Middle English *sweyen* "to fall, swoon"] **syn** see INFLUENCE — **sway•er** *n*

• **syn** SWAY, OSCILLATE, VIBRATE, WAVER mean to move back and forth. SWAY implies a slow swinging or teetering movement as of something large and heavy; OSCILLATE suggests a relatively rapid and rhythmic alternation of direction; VIBRATE applies especially to the very rapid oscillation of an elastic body under stress or impact; WAVER stresses irregular movement suggestive of reeling or tottering. **syn** see in addition INFLUENCE

2**sway** *n* **1 :** the action or an instance of swaying or of being swayed **:** an oscillating, fluctuating, or sweeping motion **2 :** an inclination or deflection caused by or as if by swaying **3 a :** a controlling force or influence **b :** sovereign power **:** DOMINION

sway•back \ˈswā-ˈbak\ *n* **:** a sagging or abnormally hollow back (as of a horse) — **sway•backed** \-ˈbakt\ *adj*

swear \ˈswaər, ˈsweər\ *vb* **swore** \ˈswōər, ˈswȯər\; **sworn** \ˈswōrn, ˈswȯrn\; **swear•ing 1 :** to utter or take solemnly (an oath) **2 a :** to assert as true or promise under oath **b :** to assert or promise emphatically or earnestly **3 a :** to administer an oath to ⟨*swear* the witness⟩ **b :** to bind by an oath ⟨*swore* them to secrecy⟩ **4 :** to bring into a specified state by swearing ⟨*swear* your life away⟩ **5 :** to take an oath **6 :** to use profane or obscene language **:** CURSE [Old English *swerian*] — **swear•er** *n* — **swear by :** to place great confidence in — **swear off :** to vow to abstain from ⟨*swear off* smoking⟩

swear in *vt* **:** to induct into office by administration of an oath

swear out *vt* **:** to procure (a warrant for arrest) by making a sworn accusation

swear•word \ˈswaər-ˌwərd, ˈsweər-\ *n* **:** a profane or dirty word

1**sweat** \ˈswet\ *vb* **sweat** *or* **sweat•ed; sweat•ing 1 :** to give off perceptible salty moisture through the openings of the sweat glands **:** PERSPIRE **2 :** to give off or cause to give off moisture **3 :** to collect drops of moisture ⟨stones *sweat* at night⟩ **4 a :** to work so hard that one perspires **:** TOIL ⟨*sweat* over a lesson⟩ **b :** to undergo anxiety or mental distress **5 :** to soak with sweat ⟨*sweat* a collar⟩ **6 :** to get rid of or lose by perspiring ⟨*sweat* off weight⟩ ⟨*sweat* out a fever⟩ **7 :** to drive hard **:** OVERWORK; *esp* **:** to force to work hard at low wages and under bad conditions ⟨a factory that *sweats* its employees⟩ **8 :** to heat (as solder) so as to melt and cause to run especially between surfaces to unite them; *also* **:** to unite by such means ⟨*sweat* a pipe joint⟩ [Old English *swǣtan,* from *swāt* "sweat"] — **sweat blood :** to work or worry intensely

2**sweat** *n* **1 :** hard work **:** DRUDGERY **2 :** fluid excreted from the sweat glands of the skin **:** PERSPIRATION **3 :** moisture issuing from or gathering in drops on a surface **4 :** the condition of one sweating or sweated **5 :** a state of anxiety or impatience

sweat•band \ˈswet-ˌband\ *n* **1 :** a band lining the inner edge of a hat or cap to prevent sweat damage **2 :** a band of material worn around the head or wrist to absorb sweat

sweat•er \ˈswet-ər\ *n* **1 :** one that sweats or causes sweating **2 :** a knitted or crocheted jacket or pullover

sweat gland *n* **:** a gland of the skin that secretes perspiration and opens by a minute pore in the skin

sweat out *vt* **1 :** to endure or wait through the course of **2 :** to work one's way painfully through or to

sweat pants *n pl* **:** pants having a drawstring waist and elastic cuffs at the ankle that are worn especially by athletes in warming up

sweat shirt *n* **:** a loose collarless usually long-sleeved pullover of heavy cotton jersey

sweat•shop \ˈswet-ˌshäp\ *n* **:** a shop or factory in which workers are employed for long hours at low wages and under unhealthy conditions

sweaty \ˈswet-ē\ *adj* **sweat•i•er; -est 1 :** wet or stained with or smelling of sweat **2 :** causing sweat ⟨*sweaty* work⟩ — **sweat•i•ly** \ˈswet-l-ē\ *adv* — **sweat•i•ness** \ˈswet-ē-nəs\ *n*

swede \ˈswēd\ *n* **1** *cap* **a :** a native or inhabitant of Sweden **b :** a person of Swedish descent **2 :** RUTABAGA

Swed•ish \ˈswēd-ish\ *n* **1 :** the Germanic language spoken in Sweden **2** *pl in construction* **:** the people of Sweden — **Swedish** *adj*

1**sweep** \ˈswēp\ *vb* **swept** \ˈswept\; **sweep•ing 1 a :** to remove from a surface with or as if with a broom or brush **b :** to remove or take with a single continuous forceful action **c :** to drive or carry along with irresistible force **2 a :** to clean with or as if with a broom or brush **b :** to move across or along swiftly, violently, or overwhelmingly **c :** to win an overwhelming victory in or on ⟨*sweep* the elections⟩ **3 :** to touch in passing with a swift continuous movement **4 :** to go with stately or sweeping movements **5 :** to trace the outline of (as a curve or angle) **6 :** to cover the entire range of **7 :** to move or extend in a wide curve or range [Middle English *swepen*] — **sweep•er** *n*

2sweep 1a

2**sweep** *n* **1 :** something that sweeps or works with a sweeping motion: as **a :** a long pole pivoted on a post and used to raise and lower a bucket (as in a well) **b :** a long oar **c :** a windmill sail **2 a :** an act or instance of sweeping; *esp* **:** a clearing out or away with or as if with a broom **b :** an overwhelming victory (as

\ə\ **abut**	\au̇\ **out**	\i\ **tip**	\ȯ\ **saw**	\u̇\ **foot**
\ər\ **further**	\ch\ **chin**	\ī\ **life**	\ȯi\ **coin**	\y\ **yet**
\a\ **mat**	\e\ **pet**	\j\ **job**	\th\ **thin**	\yü\ **few**
\ā\ **take**	\ē\ **easy**	\ng\ **sing**	\t͟h\ **this**	\yu̇\ **cure**
\ä\ **cot, cart**	\g\ **go**	\ō\ **bone**	\ü\ **food**	\zh\ **vision**

the winning of all the contests or prizes in a competition) **3 a :** a movement of great range and force **b :** a curving or circular course or line **c :** the compass of a sweeping movement : SCOPE **d :** a broad extent **4 :** CHIMNEY SWEEP

sweep•back \ˈswēp-ˌbak\ *n* **:** the backward slant of an airplane wing in which the outer portion of the wing is downstream from the inner portion

sweep hand *n* **:** SWEEP-SECOND

¹sweep•ing *n* **1 :** the act or action of one that sweeps ⟨gave the room a good *sweeping*⟩ **2** *pl* **:** things collected by sweeping : REFUSE

²sweeping *adj* **1 a :** moving or extending in a wide curve or over a wide area **b :** having a curving line or form **2 a :** EXTENSIVE ⟨*sweeping* reforms⟩ **b :** broadly and indiscriminately inclusive ⟨*sweeping* generalizations⟩ — **sweep•ing•ly** \ˈswē-ping-lē\

sweep net *n* **:** a bag-shaped net with a handle used by entomologists for catching insects by sweeping it over vegetation

sweep–sec•ond \ˈswēp-ˌsek-ənd, -ənt\ *n* **:** a hand marking seconds on a timepiece mounted concentrically with the other hands and read on the minute dial

sweep•stakes \-ˌstāks\ *n sing or pl, also* **sweep•stake** \-ˌstāk\ **1 a :** a race or contest in which the entire prize may be awarded to the winner **b :** a horse race in which the stake awarded to the winner or distributed among the top finishers is made up at least in part of the entry fees or money contributed by the owners of the horses **2 :** CONTEST 1, COMPETITION **3 :** any of various lotteries [Middle English *swepestake* "one who wins all the stakes in a game", from *swepen* "to sweep" + *stake*]

¹sweet \ˈswēt\ *adj* **1 a :** pleasing to the taste **b :** being or inducing the one of the four basic taste sensations that is typically induced by table sugar **c :** having a relatively large sugar content **2 a :** pleasing to the mind or feelings : AGREEABLE **b :** marked by gentle good humor or kindliness **c :** FRAGRANT **d :** delicately pleasing to the ear or eye **e :** SACCHARINE 2, CLOYING **3 :** much loved : DEAR **4 a :** not sour or rancid : not decaying or stale : WHOLESOME **b :** not salt or salted : FRESH ⟨*sweet* water⟩ **c :** free from excessive acidity ⟨*sweet* soil⟩ **d :** free from noxious gases and odors [Old English *swēte*] — **sweet•ly** *adv* — **sweet•ness** *n* — **sweet on :** in love with

²sweet *adv* **:** in a sweet way

³sweet *n* **1 :** something that is sweet to the taste: as **a :** a food (as a candy or preserve) having a high sugar content **b** *British* : DESSERT **c** *British* : CANDY 2 **2 :** a sweet taste sensation **3 :** a pleasant or gratifying experience, possession, or state **4 :** DARLING

sweet alyssum *n* **:** a perennial European herb of the mustard family often grown for its clusters of small fragrant usually white flowers

sweet basil *n* **:** a common basil that has white flowers tinged with purple and is used especially in seasoning

sweet•bread \ˈswēt-ˌbred\ *n* **:** the thymus or pancreas especially of a young animal used as food

sweet•bri•er \-ˌbrī-ər, -ˌbrīr\ *n* **:** an Old World rose with stout recurved prickles and white to deep rosy pink single flowers — called also *eglantine*

sweet cherry *n* **:** a white-flowered Eurasian cherry widely grown for its large sweet-flavored fruits; *also* **:** its fruit

sweet cic•e•ly \-ˈsis-lē, -ə-lē\ *n, pl* **-lies :** any of several herbs of the carrot family with white flowers and an aromatic root [*cicely* from Latin *seselis,* from Greek]

sweet clover *n* **:** any of a genus of tall erect plants of the pea family widely grown for soil improvement or hay

sweet corn *n* **:** an Indian corn with kernels containing much sugar and adapted for table use when immature

sweet gum

sweet•en \ˈswēt-n\ *vb* **sweet•ened; sweet•en•ing** \ˈswēt-ning, -n-ing\ **:** to make or become sweet — **sweeten•er** \ˈswēt-nər, -n-ər\ *n*

sweet•en•ing *n* **1 :** the act or process of making sweet **2 :** something that sweetens

sweet fern *n* **:** a small North American shrub of the wax-myrtle family with sweet-scented or aromatic leaves

sweet flag *n* **:** a perennial marsh herb of the arum family with long leaves and a pungent rhizome

sweet gum *n* **:** an American timber tree with palmately lobed leaves, hard reddish wood, and a long-stemmed woody fruit resembling a bur; *also* **:** its wood

sweet•heart \ˈswēt-ˌhärt\ *n* **1 :** DARLING **2 :** the person one is in love with : LOVER

sweet•ing \ˈswēt-ing\ *n* **1** *archaic* : SWEETHEART **2 :** a sweet apple

sweet•ish \ˈswēt-ish\ *adj* **:** somewhat and often unpleasantly sweet — **sweet•ish•ly** *adv*

sweet marjoram *n* **:** an aromatic European herb with dense spikelike flower clusters

sweet•meat \ˈswēt-ˌmēt\ *n* **:** a food rich in sugar: as **a :** a candied or crystallized fruit **b :** CANDY 2

sweet pea *n* **:** a garden plant with slender climbing stems and large fragrant flowers; *also* **:** its flower

sweet pea

sweet pepper *n* **:** a large mild-flavored thick-walled capsicum fruit; *also* **:** a plant bearing this

sweet potato *n* **1 :** a tropical vine related to the morning glory with variously shaped leaves and purplish flowers; *also* **:** its large sweet starchy tuberous root that is cooked and eaten as a vegetable **2 :** OCARINA

sweet•shop \ˈswēt-ˌshäp\ *n, chiefly British* **:** a candy store

sweet sorghum *n* **:** SORGO

sweet tooth *n* **:** a craving or fondness for sweet food

sweet wil•liam \swēt-ˈwil-yəm\ *n, often cap W* **:** a widely grown Eurasian pink with small white to deep red or purple flowers often showily spotted, banded, or mottled and borne in flat clusters on erect stalks [from the name *William*]

¹swell \ˈswel\ *vb* **swelled; swelled** *or* **swol•len** \ˈswō-lən\; **swell•ing 1 a :** to expand or distend abnormally esp. by internal pressure or growth ⟨a *swollen* tree trunk⟩ ⟨the sprained ankle *swelled* badly⟩ **b :** to increase in size, number, or intensity **c :** to form a bulge or rounded elevation **2 :** to fill or become filled with pride and arrogance **3 :** to fill or become filled with emotion [Old English *swellan*]

²swell *n* **1 a :** the condition of being protuberant **b :** a rounded elevation **2 :** a long often massive crestless wave or succession of waves **3 a :** a gradual increase and decrease of the loudness of a musical sound; *also* **:** a sign < > indicating a swell **b :** a device used in an organ for governing loudness **4 a :** a person dressed in the height of fashion **b :** a person of high social position or outstanding competence

³swell *adj* **1 :** STYLISH, FASHIONABLE **2 :** EXCELLENT, FIRST-RATE

swelled head *n* **:** an exaggerated opinion of oneself : SELF-CONCEIT — **swelled–head•ed** \ˈsweld-ˈhed-əd\ *adj* — **swelled–head•ed•ness** *n*

swell•ing \ˈswel-ing\ *n* **1 :** something that is swollen; *esp* **:** an abnormal bodily protuberance or localized enlargement **2 :** the condition of being swollen

¹swel•ter \ˈswel-tər\ *vb* **swel•tered; swel•ter•ing** \ˈswel-tring, -tə-ring\ **1 :** to suffer, sweat, or be faint from heat **2 :** to oppress with heat [Middle English *sweltren,* from *swelten* "to die, be overcome by heat", from Old English *sweltan* "to die"]

²swelter *n* **1 :** a state of oppressive heat **2 :** an excited or overwrought state of mind ⟨in a *swelter*⟩

swel•ter•ing *adj* **:** oppressively hot — **swel•ter•ing•ly** \-tə-ring-lē, -tring-\ *adv*

swept *past of* SWEEP

swept–back \ˈswept-ˈbak, ˈswep-\ *adj* **:** possessing sweepback

¹swerve \ˈswərv\ *vb* **:** to turn aside suddenly from a straight line or course ⟨*swerved* to avoid an oncoming car⟩ [Old English *sweorfan* "to wipe, grind away"]

• **syn** SWERVE, VEER mean to turn aside from a straight course. SWERVE may suggest a physical, mental, or moral turning that may be small in degree but is usually sudden or sharp; VEER implies a sharp change in course or direction.

²swerve *n* : an act or instance of swerving

¹swift \'swift\ *adj* **1** : moving or capable of moving with great speed **2** : occurring suddenly or within a very short time ⟨*swift* changes⟩ **3** : quick to act or respond ⟨*swift* in thought and deed⟩ [Old English] **syn** see FAST — **swift·ly** *adv* — **swift·ness** \'swift-nəs, 'swif-\ *n*

²swift *adv* : SWIFTLY ⟨*swift*-flowing⟩

³swift *n* **1** : any of several lizards that run swiftly **2** : any of numerous small and usually sooty black birds that are related to the hummingbirds but superficially resemble swallows

¹swig \'swig\ *n* : a quantity drunk at one time : DRAFT [origin unknown]

²swig *vb* **swigged**; **swig·ging** : to drink in gulps ⟨*swig* cider⟩ — **swig·ger** *n*

¹swill \'swil\ *vb* **1** : WASH 2, DRENCH **2** : to drink great drafts of : consume freely, greedily, or to excess **3** : to feed (as a pig) with swill [Old English *swillan*] — **swill·er** *n*

²swill *n* **1** : food for animals (as swine) composed of edible refuse mixed with liquid **2** : GARBAGE, REFUSE **3** : a draft of liquor

¹swim \'swim\ *vb* **swam** \'swam\; **swum** \'swəm\; **swim·ming** **1 a** : to move through water by natural means (as the action of limbs, fins, or tail) **b** : to move quietly and smoothly : GLIDE **2 a** : to float on or in or be covered with or as if with a liquid ⟨toy boats *swimming* in the tub⟩ ⟨meat that *swam* in fat⟩ **b** : to experience or suffer from or as if from vertigo ⟨my head *swam* in the stuffy room⟩ **3** : to surmount difficulties **4** : to cross by propelling oneself through water ⟨*swim* a stream⟩ [Old English *swimman*] — **swim·ma·ble** \'swim-ə-bəl\ *adj* — **swim·mer** *n*

²swim *n* **1** : an act or period of swimming **2** : a temporary dizziness or unconsciousness **3** : the main current of activity ⟨be in the *swim*⟩

swim bladder *n* : the air bladder of a fish

swim fin *n* : a rubber shoe with the front expanded into a paddle for use in skin diving or scuba diving

swim·mer·et \ˌswim-ə-'ret\ *n* : one of a series of small appendages under the abdomen of many crustaceans that are used especially for swimming or for carrying eggs

swimmer's itch *n* : an itchy skin inflammation caused by superficial invasion of the skin by larval trematode worms that are not normally parasites of human beings

swim·ming *adj* : marked by, adapted to, or used in or for swimming

swim·ming·ly \-ing-lē\ *adv* : very well : SPLENDIDLY

swimming pool *n* : a tank (as of concrete or plastic) made for swimming

swim·my \'swim-ē\ *adj* : verging on, causing, or affected by dizziness — **swim·mi·ly** \'swim-ə-lē\ *adv* — **swim·mi·ness** \'swim-ē-nəs\ *n*

swim·suit \'swim-ˌsüt\ *n* : a suit for wear for swimming

¹swin·dle \'swin-dl\ *vb* **swin·dled**; **swin·dling** \-dling, -dl-ing\ : to deprive of something by deception or fraud [back-formation from *swindler*, from German *schwindler* "giddy person", from *schwindeln* "to be dizzy"] **syn** see CHEAT — **swin·dler** \-dlər, -dl-ər\ *n*

²swindle *n* : an act or instance of swindling : FRAUD

swine \'swīn\ *n, pl* **swine** **1** : any of a family of stout-bodied short-legged hoofed mammals with a thick bristly skin and a long mobile snout; *esp* : a domesticated animal derived from the European wild boar and widely raised for meat **2** : a contemptible person [Old English *swīn*]

swine·herd \-ˌhərd\ *n* : one who tends swine

¹swing \'swing\ *vb* **swung** \'swəng\; **swing·ing** \'swing-ing\ **1 a** : to wield with a sweep or flourish ⟨*swing* an axe⟩ **b** : to cause to sway to and fro or turn on an axis; *also* : to face or move in another direction **2 a** : to hang or be hung so as to permit swaying or turning ⟨*swing* a hammock⟩ **b** : to die by hanging **c** : to move freely to and fro from or rotate about a point of suspension ⟨the door *swung* open⟩ **d** : to hang freely from a support **e** : to shift or fluctuate between extremes ⟨the market *swung* sharply downward⟩ **3** : to handle successfully : MANAGE ⟨learning to *swing* a new job⟩ **4** : to play or sing (as a melody) in the style of swing music : perform swing music **5 a** : to move along rhythmically **b** : to start up in a smooth vigorous manner ⟨*swing* into action⟩ **c** : to hit at something with a sweeping movement [Old English *swingan* "to beat, fling oneself, rush"] — **swing·able** \'swing-ə-bəl\ *adj* — **swing·ably** \-blē\ *adv* — **swing·er** \'swing-ər\ *n*

²swing *n* **1** : an act of swinging **2** : a swinging movement, blow, or rhythm: as **a** : a regular to-and-fro movement of or as if of a suspended body **b** : a steady pulsing rhythm (as in poetry or music); *also* : dancing to swing music **c** : a repeated shifting from one condition, form, or position to another **3** : the distance through which something swings ⟨a pendulum with a 25-centimeter *swing*⟩ **4** : a swinging seat usually hung by overhead ropes **5** : a curving course or outline or one beginning and ending at the same point ⟨took a *swing* through the hills⟩ **6** : a style of jazz in which the melody is freely interpreted and improvised on by the individual players within a steadily maintained rhythm — **swing** *adj*

swin·gle·tree \'swing-gəl-ˌtrē\ *n* : WHIFFLETREE [Middle English *swingel* "instrument for beating flax, cudgel"]

swing shift *n* : the work shift between the day and night shifts (as from 4 p.m. to midnight)

swin·ish \'swī-nish\ *adj* : of, suggesting, or befitting swine : BEASTLY — **swin·ish·ly** *adv* — **swin·ish·ness** *n*

¹swipe \'swīp\ *n* : a strong sweeping blow [probably alteration of *sweep*]

²swipe *vb* **1** : to strike or wipe with a sweeping motion **2** : STEAL 2a, PILFER

¹swirl \'swərl\ *n* **1** : a whirling mass or motion : EDDY **2** : whirling confusion **3** : a twisting shape or mark [Middle English]

²swirl *vb* **1** : to move with or pass in a swirl **2** : to be marked with or arranged in swirls **3** : to cause to swirl — **swirl·ing·ly** \'swər-ling-lē\ *adv*

¹swish \'swish\ *vb* : to make, move, or strike with a rustling or hissing sound [imitative] — **swish·ing·ly** \-ing-lē\ *adv*

²swish *n* **1** : a prolonged hissing sound (as of a whip cutting the air) or a light rustling sound (as of silk in friction) **2** : a swishing movement — **swishy** \-ē\ *adj*

Swiss \'swis\ *n* **1** *pl* **Swiss** **a** : a native or inhabitant of Switzerland **b** : a person of Swiss decent **2** *often not cap* : a fine sheer cotton fabric often with raised dots originally made in Switzerland **3** : a mild elastic hard cheese with large holes [Middle French *Suisse*, from Middle High German *Swīzer*, from *Swīz* "Switzerland"] — **Swiss** *adj*

Swiss chard *n* : CHARD

¹switch \'swich\ *n* **1** : a slender flexible whip, rod, or twig **2** : an act of switching: as **a** : a blow with a switch **b** : a shift from one to another ⟨a *switch* of political parties⟩ **3** : a tuft of long hairs at the end of the tail of an animal (as a cow) **4 a** : a device made usually of two movable rails and necessary connections and designed to turn a locomotive or train from one track to another **b** : a railroad siding **5** : a device for making, breaking, or changing the connections in an electrical circuit **6** : a strand of added or artificial hair used in some coiffures [perhaps from Dutch *swijch* "twig"]

²switch *vb* **1** : to strike or whip with or as if with a switch **2** : to lash from side to side : WHISK ⟨a cat *switching* its tail⟩ **3** : to turn, shift, or change by operating a switch ⟨*switch* a train onto a siding⟩ ⟨*switch* off the light⟩ **4** : to change one for another : EXCHANGE ⟨*switched* methods to improve production⟩ ⟨*switched* to a different brand⟩ — **switch·er** *n*

switch·back \'swich-ˌbak\ *n* : a zigzag road or arrangement of tracks for overcoming a steep grade

switch·blade knife \ˌswich-ˌblād-\ *n* : a pocketknife having the blade spring-operated so that pressure on a release catch causes it to fly open

switch·board \'swich-ˌbōrd, -ˌbȯrd\ *n* : an apparatus (as in a telephone exchange) consisting of a panel on which are mounted electric switches so arranged that a number of circuits may be connected, combined, and controlled

switch–hit·ter \'swich-'hit-ər\ *n* : a baseball player who can bat either left-handed or right-handed

switch·man \'swich-mən\ *n* : one who attends a railroad switch

switch·yard \-ˌyärd\ *n* : a place where railroad cars are switched from one track to another and trains are made up

Swit·zer \'swit-sər\ *n* : SWISS 1 [Middle High German *Swīzer*]

¹swiv·el \'swiv-əl\ *n* : a device joining two parts so that one or both can pivot freely (as on a bolt or pin) [Middle English]

[2]swivel *vb* **swiv•eled** *or* **swiv•elled; swiv•el•ing** *or* **swiv•el•ling** \'swivling, -ə-ling\ **:** to turn on or as if on a swivel
swivel chair *n* **:** a chair that swivels on its base
swiv•et \'swiv-ət\ *n* **:** a state of extreme agitation ⟨in a *swivet*⟩ [origin unknown]
swiz•zle stick \'swiz-əl-\ *n* **:** a stick used to stir mixed drinks [*swizzle,* a kind of cocktail]
swob *variant of* SWAB
swollen *past participle of* SWELL
[1]swoon \'swün\ *vi* **1 :** FAINT 2 **2 :** to drift or fade imperceptibly [Middle English *swounen*] — **swoon•er** *n* — **swoon•ing•ly** \'swü-ning-lē\ *adv*
[2]swoon *n* **1 :** a partial or total loss of consciousness; *also* **:** a dazed enraptured state **2 :** a dreamy flow (as of music)
[1]swoop \'swüp\ *vb* **1 :** to descend or pounce suddenly ⟨the eagle *swooped* down on its prey⟩ **2 :** to carry off abruptly [Old English *swāpan* "to sweep"]
[2]swoop *n* **:** an act or instance of swooping
swoosh \'swüsh, 'swůsh,\ *vb* **:** to make, move, or discharge with a rushing sound [imitative] — **swoosh** *n*
swop *variant of* SWAP
sword \'sōrd, 'sȯrd\ *n* **1 :** a weapon having a long usually sharp-pointed and sharp-edged blade **2 :** something that kills or punishes as effectively as a sword **3 :** military power or the use of it **:** WAR [Old English *sweord*] — **sword•like** \-ˌlīk\ *adj* — **at swords' points :** mutually antagonistic
sword cane *n* **:** a cane that conceals a sword or dagger blade
sword dance *n* **:** any of several folk dances in which performers hold, swing, or dance around swords — **sword dancer** *n*
sword•fish \'sōrd-ˌfish, 'sȯrd-\ *n* **:** a very large oceanic food fish having a long swordlike beak formed by the bones of the upper jaw

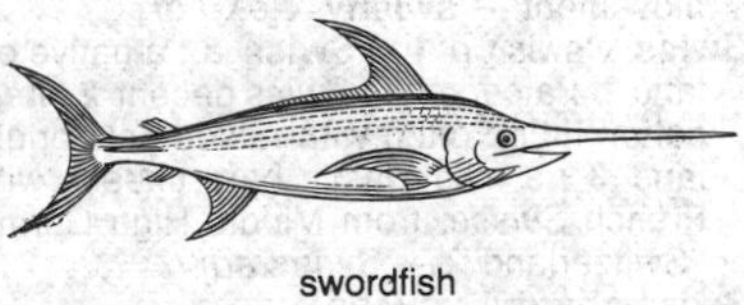
swordfish

sword grass *n* **:** a grass or sedge having leaves with a sharp or toothed edge
sword knot *n* **:** an ornamental cord or tassel tied to the hilt of a sword
sword•play \-ˌplā\ *n* **:** the art or skill of using a sword especially in fencing
swords•man \'sōrdz-mən, 'sȯrdz-\ *n* **1 :** one who fights with a sword **2 :** one skilled in the use of the sword **:** FENCER
swords•man•ship \-ˌship\ *n* **:** SWORDPLAY
sword•tail \'sōrd-ˌtāl, 'sȯrd-\ *n* **:** a small brightly marked Central American topminnow with many color varieties that is often kept in tropical aquariums
swore *past of* SWEAR
sworn *past participle of* SWEAR
swum *past participle of* SWIM
swung *past of* SWING
syc•a•more \'sik-ə-ˌmōr, -ˌmȯr\ *n* **1 :** a common fig tree of Egypt and Asia Minor **2 :** a Eurasian maple with yellow flowers in long clusters **3 :** a large spreading American plane tree with light-brown flaky bark and round fruits like buttons [Middle French *sicamor,* from Latin *sycomorus,* from Greek *sykomoros*]

sycamore 3

syc•o•phant \'sik-ə-fənt\ *n* **:** a servile self-seeking flatterer **:** PARASITE [Latin *sycophanta* "informer, swindler, sycophant", from Greek *sykophantēs* "informer"] — **syc•o•phan•cy** \-fən-sē\ *n* — **syc•o•phan•tic** \ˌsik-ə-'fant-ik\ *adj* — **syc•o•phan•ti•cal•ly** \-'fant-i-kə-lē, -klē\ *adv*
sy•enite \'sī-ə-ˌnīt\ *n* **:** an igneous rock composed chiefly of feldspar [Latin *Syenites lapis* "stone of Syene", from *Syene,* ancient city in Egypt] — **sy•enit•ic** \ˌsī-ə-'nit-ik\ *adj*
syl•la•bary \'sil-ə-ˌber-ē\ *n, pl* **-bar•ies :** a series or set of written characters each one of which is used to represent a syllable
syl•lab•ic \sə-'lab-ik\ *adj* **1 :** of, relating to, or denoting syllables ⟨*syllabic* accent⟩ **2** *of a consonant* **:** not accompanied in the same syllable by a vowel ⟨\n\ is *syllabic* in \'bät-n-ē\ botany but is nonsyllabic in \'bät-nē\⟩ **3 :** characterized by distinct enunciation or separation of syllables — **syl•lab•i•cal•ly** \-'lab-i-kə-lē, -klē\ *adv*
syl•lab•i•ca•tion \sə-ˌlab-ə-'kā-shən\ *n* **:** the forming of syllables **:** the division of words into syllables — **syl•lab•i•cate** \-'lab-ə-ˌkāt\ *vb*
syl•lab•i•fi•ca•tion \sə-ˌlab-ə-fə-'kā-shən\ *n* **:** SYLLABICATION
syl•lab•i•fy \sə-'lab-ə-ˌfī\ *vt* **-fied; -fy•ing :** to form or divide into syllables
[1]syl•la•ble \'sil-ə-bəl\ *n* **1 :** a unit of spoken language that consists of one or more vowel sounds alone or of a syllabic consonant alone or of either with one or more consonant sounds preceding or following **2 :** one or more letters (as *syl, la,* and *ble*) in a word (as *syl•la•ble*) usually set off from the rest of the word by a centered dot or a hyphen and treated as guides to dividing a word at the end of a line **3 :** the smallest conceivable expression or unit of something ⟨not the least *syllable* of wit⟩ [Middle French *sillabe,* from Latin *syllaba,* from Greek *syllabē,* from *syllambanein* "to combine", from *syn-* + *lambanein* "to take"]
[2]syllable *vt* **syl•la•bled; syl•la•bling** \-bə-ling, -bling\ **:** to express or utter in syllables
syl•la•bub *or* **sil•la•bub** \'sil-ə-ˌbəb\ *n* **1 :** a drink or dessert made by curding milk or cream usually with wine **2 :** a dessert of sweetened milk or cream beaten to a froth and flavored with wine or liquor [origin unknown]
syl•la•bus \-bəs\ *n, pl* **-bi** \-ˌbī, -ˌbē\ *or* **-bus•es :** a summary outline (as of a course of study) [Latin *sillybus* "label for a book", from Greek *sillybos*]
syl•lo•gism \'sil-ə-ˌjiz-əm\ *n* **1 :** a brief form for stating an argument from the general to the particular that consists of two statements and a conclusion that must be true if these two statements are true ⟨"all lawbreakers deserve punishment; this person is a lawbreaker; therefore this person deserves punishment" is a *syllogism*⟩ **2 :** deductive reasoning [Middle French *silogisme,* from Latin *syllogismus,* from Greek *syllogismos,* from *syllogizesthai* "to reason deductively", derived from *syn-* + *logos* "reckoning, word"] — **syl•lo•gis•tic** \ˌsil-ə-'jis-tik\ *adj* — **syl•lo•gis•ti•cal•ly** \-ti-kə-lē, -klē\ *adv*
sylph \'silf\ *n* **1 :** an imaginary aerial spirit **2 :** a slender graceful woman [New Latin *sylphus*] — **sylph•like** \'sil-ˌflīk\ *adj*
syl•van *also* **sil•van** \'sil-vən\ *adj* **1 a :** living or located in the woods or forest **b :** of, relating to, or characteristic of the woods or forest **2 :** abounding in woods or trees **:** WOODED [Medieval Latin *silvanus, sylvanus,* from Latin *silva, sylva* "woods"]
syl•vat•ic \sil-'vat-ik\ *adj* **:** occurring in or affecting wild animals ⟨*sylvatic* plague⟩ [Latin *silvaticus* "of the woods, wild", from *silva* "woods"]
sylviculture *variant of* SILVICULTURE
sym- — see SYN-
sym•bi•ont \'sim-ˌbī-änt, -bē-\ *n* **:** an organism living in symbiosis; *esp* **:** the smaller member of a symbiotic pair [derived from Greek *symbioun* "to live together"] — **sym•bi•on•tic** \ˌsim-ˌbī-'änt-ik, -bē-\ *adj*
sym•bi•o•sis \ˌsim-ˌbī-'ō-səs, -bē-\ *n, pl* **-o•ses** \-'ō-ˌsēz\ **:** the living together in intimate association or close union of two unlike organisms especially when mutually beneficial [German *symbiose,* from Greek *symbiōsis* "state of living together", from *symbioun* "to live together", derived from *syn-* + *bios* "life"] — **sym•bi•ot•ic** \-'ät-ik\ *adj* — **sym•bi•ot•i•cal•ly** \-i-kə-lē, -klē\ *adv*
sym•bol \'sim-bəl\ *n* **1 :** something that stands for something else; *esp* **:** something concrete that represents or suggests another thing that cannot in itself be represented or visualized **:** EMBLEM ⟨the cross is the *symbol* of Christianity⟩ **2 :** a letter, character, or sign used (as to represent a quantity, position, relationship, direction, or something to be done) instead of a word or group of words ⟨the sign + is the *symbol* for addition⟩ [derived from Greek *symbolon* "token of identity to be verified by matching it with its other half, symbol", from *symballein* "to throw together, compare", from *syn-* + *ballein* "to throw"]
sym•bol•ic \sim-'bäl-ik\ *or* **sym•bol•i•cal** \-'bäl-i-kəl\ *adj* **1**

: of, relating to, or using symbols or symbolism ⟨a *symbolic meaning*⟩ **2** : having the function or significance of a symbol — **sym•bol•i•cal•ly** \-i-kə-lē, -klē\ *adv*

sym•bol•ism \'sim-bə-,liz-əm\ *n* **1** : the art or practice of using symbols or indicating symbolically (as in art or literature) **2** : a system of symbols or representations ⟨the language and *symbolism* of set theory⟩

sym•bol•ist \-ləst\ *n* **1** : a user of symbols or symbolism (as in artistic expression) **2** : an expert in the interpretation or explanation of symbols — **symbolist** *or* **sym•bol•is•tic** \,sim-bə-'lis-tik\ *adj*

sym•bol•ize \'sim-bə-,līz\ *vb* **1** : to serve as a symbol of ⟨a lion *symbolizes* courage⟩ **2** : to use symbols : represent by a symbol or set of symbols — **sym•bol•iza•tion** \,sim-bə-lə-'zā-shən\ *n* — **sym•bol•iz•er** \'sim-bə-,lī-zər\ *n*

sym•met•ri•cal \sə-'me-tri-kəl\ *or* **sym•met•ric** \-trik\ *adj* **1** : having, involving, or exhibiting symmetry: as **a** : having corresponding points whose connecting lines are bisected by a given point or perpendicularly bisected by a given line or plane ⟨*symmetrical* curves⟩ **b** : capable of division by a longitudinal plane into similar halves ⟨a *symmetrical* leaf⟩ **c** : having the same number of members in each whorl of floral leaves ⟨*symmetrical* flowers⟩ **2** *symmetric* : being a relation or expression for which the terms may be interchanged without altering the value, character, or truth ⟨*R* is a *symmetric* relation if *aRb* implies *bRa*⟩ — **sym•met•ri•cal•ly** \-tri-kə-lē, -klē\ *adv* — **sym•met•ri•cal•ness** \-kəl-nəs\ *n*

sym•me•try \'sim-ə-trē\ *n, pl* **-tries** **1** : balanced proportions; *also* : beauty of form arising from balanced proportions **2** : correspondence in size, shape, and relative position of parts on opposite sides of a dividing line or median plane or about a center of axis — compare BILATERAL SYMMETRY, RADIAL SYMMETRY [Latin *symmetria,* from Greek, derived from *syn-* + *metron* "measure"]

sym•pa•thet•ic \,sim-pə-'thet-ik\ *adj* **1 a** : appropriate to one's mood or disposition : CONGENIAL ⟨a *sympathetic* environment⟩ **b** : favorably impressed or inclined ⟨*sympathetic* with their aims⟩ **c** : marked by kindly or pleased appreciation **2** : given to or arising from sympathy, compassion, friendliness, and sensitivity to others ⟨a *sympathetic* person⟩ ⟨*sympathetic* strikes⟩ ⟨a *sympathetic* remark⟩ **3 a** : of or relating to the sympathetic nervous system **b** : mediated by or acting on the sympathetic nerves — **sym•pa•thet•i•cal•ly** \-'thet-i-kə-lē, -klē\ *adv*

sympathetic nervous system *n* : the part of the autonomic nervous system that contains chiefly nerve fibers secreting adrenaline at nerve synapses and that tends to depress secretion, decrease the tone and contractility of smooth muscle, and cause the contraction of blood vessels — compare PARASYMPATHETIC NERVOUS SYSTEM

sympathetic vibration *n* : a vibration produced in one body by vibrations of exactly the same period in a neighboring body

sym•pa•thize \'sim-pə-,thīz\ *vi* **1** : to react or respond in sympathy **2** : to be in accord or harmony **3 a** : to share in some distress, suffering, or grief **b** : to express sympathy **4** : to be in sympathy intellectually ⟨*sympathize* with a proposal⟩ — **sym•pa•thiz•er** *n*

sym•pa•tho•mi•met•ic \,sim-pə-thō-mə-'met-ik, -mī-\ *adj* : resembling the action of the sympathetic nervous system in physiological effect ⟨*sympathomimetic* drugs⟩

sym•pa•thy \'sim-pə-thē\ *n, pl* **-thies** **1** : a relationship between persons or things wherein whatever affects one similarly affects the other **2 a** : inclination to think or feel alike : emotional or intellectual accord forming a bond of goodwill **b** : tendency to favor or support **3** : the act of or capacity for entering into or sharing the feelings or interests of another [Latin *sympathia,* from Greek *sympatheia,* derived from *syn-* + *pathos* "feelings, experience"]

sym•pat•ric \sim-'pa-trik\ *adj* : occurring in the same area or region ⟨*sympatric* species of birds⟩ [*syn-* + Greek *patra* "fatherland", from *patēr* "father"]

sym•phon•ic \sim-'fän-ik\ *adj* **1** : HARMONIOUS 1 **2** : of, relating to, or suggesting a symphony or symphony orchestra — **sym•phon•i•cal•ly** \-'fän-i-kə-lē, -klē\ *adv*

sym•pho•ny \'sim-fə-nē, 'simp-\ *n, pl* **-nies** **1** : harmonious arrangement (as of sound or color) **2 a** : a usually long and complex sonata for symphony orchestra **b** : something resembling a symphony in complexity or variety **3 a** : SYMPHONY ORCHESTRA **b** : a symphony orchestra concert [Old French *symphonie* "harmony of sounds", from Latin *symphonia,* from Greek *symphōnia,* derived from *syn-* + *phōnē* "voice, sound"]

symphony orchestra *n* : a large orchestra of wind, string, and percussion instruments that plays symphonic works

sym•phy•sis \'sim-fə-səs, 'simp-\ *n, pl* **-phy•ses** \-fə-,sēz\ : a largely or completely immovable joint between bones especially with the surfaces connected by pads of cartilage without a joint membrane [Greek, "state of growing together", from *symphyesthai* "to grow together", from *syn-* + *phyein* "to make grow, bring forth"] — **sym•phy•se•al** \,sim-fə-'sē-əl, ,simp-\ *adj*

sym•po•si•um \sim-'pō-zē-əm *also* -zhē-əm, -zhəm\ *n, pl* **-sia** \-zē-ə, -zhē-ə, -zhə\ *or* **-si•ums** **1** : a formal meeting at which several speakers deliver short addresses on a topic or on related topics **2 a** : a collection of opinions on a subject **b** : DISCUSSION 2 [Latin, "drinking party after a banquet", from Greek *symposion,* from *sympinein* "to drink together", from *syn-* + *pinein* "to drink"]

symp•tom \'sim-təm, 'simp-\ *n* **1** : a change in an organism indicative of disease or physical abnormality; *esp* : one (as headache) that is directly perceptible only to the individual affected — compare SIGN 6c **2** : INDICATION 2; *also* : [1]TRACE 5a [Late Latin *symptomat-, symptoma,* from Greek *symptōma* "occurrence, attribute, symptom", from *sympiptein* "to occur", from *syn-* + *piptein* "to fall"] — **symp•tom•less** \-ləs\ *adj*

symp•tom•at•ic \,sim-tə-'mat-ik, ,simp-\ *adj* **1 a** : being a symptom (as of disease) ⟨*symptomatic* of smallpox⟩ **b** : concerned with or affecting symptoms ⟨*symptomatic* medicine⟩ **2** : CHARACTERISTIC, INDICATIVE ⟨reaction to a scandal as *symptomatic* of the public's concern⟩ — **symp•tom•at•i•cal•ly** \-'mat-i-kə-lē, -klē\ *adv*

syn- *or* **sym-** *prefix* : with : along with : together ⟨*sym*patric⟩ ⟨*syn*gamy⟩ [Greek, from *syn* "with, together with"]

syn•a•gogue *or* **syn•a•gog** \'sin-ə-,gäg\ *n* **1** : a Jewish congregation **2** : the house of worship and communal center of a Jewish congregation [Old French *synagoge,* from Late Latin *synagoga,* from Greek *synagōgē* "assembly, synagogue", from *synagein* "to bring together", from *syn-* + *agein* "to lead"] — **syn•a•gog•al** \,sin-ə-'gäg-əl\ *adj*

[1]**syn•apse** \'sin-,aps, sə-'naps\ *n* : the point at which a nervous impulse passes from one neuron to another [Greek *synapsis* "juncture", from *synaptein* "to fasten together", from *syn-* + *haptein* "to fasten"]

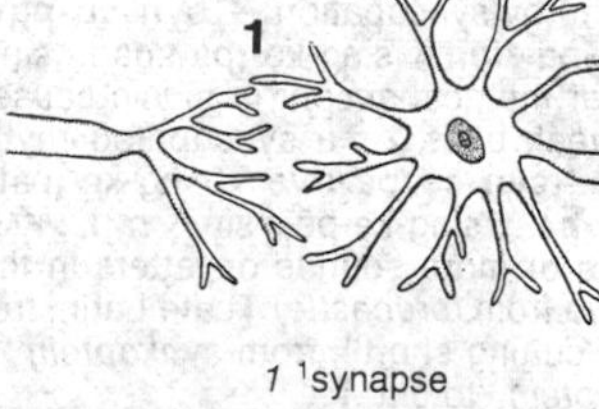

1 [1]synapse

[2]**synapse** *vi* : to form a synapse or come together in synapsis

syn•ap•sis \sə-'nap-səs\ *n, pl* **-ap•ses** \-,sēz\ *n* : the association of homologous chromosomes that occurs in the first meiotic prophase and is the mechanism for crossing over [Greek, "juncture"] — **syn•ap•tic** \-'nap-tik\ *adj*

[1]**sync** \'singk\ *n* : SYNCHRONIZATION, SYNCHRONISM — **sync** *adj*

[2]**sync** *vb* **synced** \'singt, 'singkt\; **sync•ing** \'sing-king\ : SYNCHRONIZE

synchro- *combining form* : synchronized : synchronous ⟨*synchro*flash⟩ ⟨*synchro*mesh⟩

syn•chro–cy•clo•tron \,sing-krō-'sī-klə-,trän, ,sin-\ *n* : a modified cyclotron that achieves greater energies for the charged particles

syn•chro•flash \'sing-krō-,flash, 'sin-\ *adj* : employing or produced with a mechanism that fires a flash bulb the instant the camera shutter opens

syn•chro•mesh \-,mesh\ *adj* : designed for effecting synchronized shifting of gears — **synchromesh** *n*

syn•chro•nism \'sing-krə-,niz-əm, 'sin-\ *n* **1** : the quality or state of being synchronous **2** : chronological arrangement of historical events and personages so as to indicate coincidence or coexistence — **syn•chro•nis•tic** \ˌsing-krə-ˈnis-tik, ˌsin-\ *adj*

syn•chro•nize \ˈsing-krə-ˌnīz, ˈsin-\ *vb* **1 :** to happen at the same time **:** agree in time **2 a :** to cause to agree in time ⟨*synchronize* your watches⟩ **b :** to represent, arrange, or tabulate according to dates or time ⟨*synchronize* the events of European history⟩ **3 :** to make (as two gears) synchronous in operation — **syn•chro•ni•za•tion** \ˌsing-krə-nə-ˈzā-shən, ˌsin-\ *n* — **syn•chro•niz•er** \ˈsing-krə-ˌnī-zər, ˈsin-\ *n*

synchronized swimming *n* **:** exhibition or competitive swimming in which usually two or more swimmers move in such a way as to form constantly changing patterns in the water with their movements synchronized with each other and with a musical accompaniment

syn•chro•nous \ˈsing-krə-nəs, ˈsin-\ *adj* **1 :** happening or existing at the same time **:** SIMULTANEOUS ⟨*synchronous* meetings⟩ **2 :** working, moving, or occurring together at the same rate and at the proper time with respect to each other ⟨*synchronous* beat of a bird's wings⟩; *esp* **:** having the same period and phase ⟨*synchronous* vibration⟩ [Late Latin *synchronos,* from Greek, from *syn-* + *chronos* "time"] — **syn•chro•nous•ly** *adv* — **syn•chro•nous•ness** *n*

synchronous motor *n* **:** an electric motor having a speed strictly proportional to the frequency of the operating current

syn•chro•tron \ˈsing-krə-ˌträn, ˈsin-\ *n* **:** an apparatus for imparting very high speeds to charged particles

syn•cline \ˈsin-ˌklīn\ *n* **:** a trough of stratified rock in which the beds dip toward each other from either side — compare ANTICLINE [back-formation from *synclinal,* from Greek *syn-* + *klinein* "to lean"] — **syn•cli•nal** \sin-ˈklīn-l\ *adj*

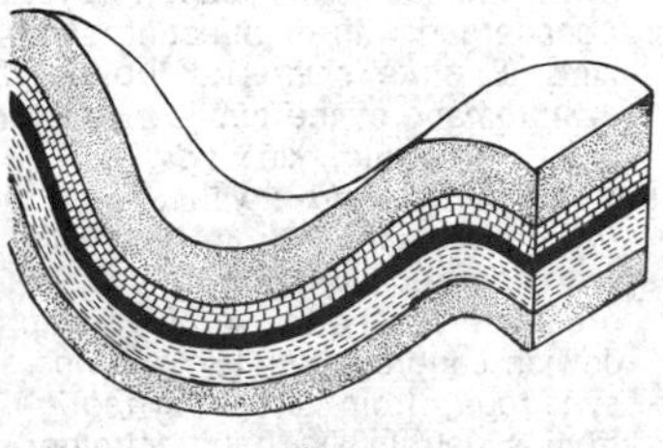
syncline

syn•co•pate \ˈsing-kə-ˌpāt, ˈsin-\ *vt* **1 a :** to shorten or produce by syncope **b :** to cut short **2 :** to modify or affect (musical rhythm) by syncopation — **syn•co•pa•tor** \-ˌpāt-ər\ *n*

syn•co•pa•tion \ˌsing-kə-ˈpā-shən, ˌsin-\ *n* **1 :** a shifting of the regular metrical accent in music caused typically by stressing the weak beat **2 :** a syncopated rhythm, passage, or dance step — **syn•co•pa•tive** \ˈsing-kə-ˌpāt-iv, ˈsin-\ *adj*

syn•co•pe \ˈsing-kə-pē, ˈsin-\ *n* **1 :** FAINT, SWOON **2 :** the loss of one or more sounds or letters in the interior of a word (as *fo'c'sle* from *forecastle)* [Late Latin, from Greek *synkopē,* literally, "cutting short", from *synkoptein* "to cut short", from *syn-* + *koptein* "to cut"]

syn•cy•tium \sin-ˈsish-əm, -ˈsish-ē-əm\ *n, pl* **-tia** \-ə\ **:** a multinucleate mass of protoplasm usually resulting from fusion of cells [New Latin, from *syn-* + *cyt-*] — **syn•cy•tial** \-ˈsish-əl\ *adj*

syn•di•cal•ism \ˈsin-di-kə-ˌliz-əm\ *n* **1 :** a revolutionary doctrine advocating seizure of control of the economy and the government by workers through use of direct means (as the general strike) **2 :** a system of economic organization in which industries are owned and managed by the workers [French *syndicalisme,* from *chambre syndicale* "trade union"] — **syn•di•cal** \ˈsin-di-kəl\ *adj* — **syn•di•cal•ist** \-ləst\ *adj or n*

[1]**syn•di•cate** \ˈsin-di-kət\ *n* **1 :** an association of persons officially authorized to undertake some duty or negotiate some business **2 a :** a group of persons or concerns who combine to carry out a particular transaction **b :** a loose association of racketeers in control of organized crime **c :** a European labor union **3 :** a business concern that sells materials for publication in a number of newspapers or periodicals simultaneously **4 :** a group of newspapers under one management [French *syndicat,* from *syndic* "municipal magistrate", from Latin *syndicus* "representative", from Greek *syndikos* "advocate, representative", from *syn-* + *dikē* "judgment, case at law"] **syn** see MONOPOLY

[2]**syn•di•cate** \ˈsin-də-ˌkāt\ *vb* **1 :** to subject to or manage as a syndicate **2 :** to sell (as a cartoon) to a publication syndicate **3 :** to unite to form a syndicate — **syn•di•ca•tion** \ˌsin-də-ˈkā-shən\ *n* — **syn•di•ca•tor** \ˈsin-də-ˌkāt-ər\ *n*

syn•drome \ˈsin-ˌdrōm\ *n* **:** a group of signs and symptoms that occur together and characterize a particular abnormality [Greek *syndromē,* from *syn-* + *dramein* "to run"]

syn•er•gid \sə-ˈnər-jəd, ˈsin-ər-\ *n* **:** either of two small cells of the embryo sac of a seed plant lying near the micropyle of the ovule [derived from Greek *synergos* "working together"]

syn•er•gism \ˈsin-ər-ˌjiz-əm\ *n* **:** cooperative action of discrete agencies such that the total effect is greater than the sum of the effects taken independently [derived from Greek *synergos* "working together", from *syn-* + *ergon* "work"] — **syn•er•gist** \-jəst\ *n*

syn•er•gis•tic \ˌsin-ər-ˈjis-tik\ *adj* **:** of, relating to, or able to function in synergism ⟨a *synergistic* reaction⟩ ⟨*synergistic* drugs⟩ — **syn•er•gis•ti•cal•ly** \-ti-kə-lē, -klē\ *adv*

syn•ga•my \ˈsing-gə-mē\ *n* **:** FERTILIZATION b

syn•od \ˈsin-əd\ *n* **1 :** an ecclesiastical assembly or council: as **a :** the governing assembly of an Episcopal province **b :** a Presbyterian governing body ranking above the presbytery **c :** a regional or national organization of Lutheran congregations **2 :** a group assembled (as for consultation) **:** MEETING, CONVENTION ⟨a *synod* of cooks⟩ [Late Latin *synodus,* from Greek *synodos* "meeting, assembly", from *syn-* + *hodos* "way, journey"] — **syn•od•al** \-əd-l\ *adj*

syn•od•i•cal \sə-ˈnäd-i-kəl\ *or* **syn•od•ic** \-ˈnäd-ik\ *adj* **1 :** of or relating to a synod **:** SYNODAL **2 :** relating to conjunction; *esp* **:** relating to the period between two successive conjunctions of the same celestial bodies

syn•o•nym \ˈsin-ə-ˌnim\ *n* **1 :** one of two or more words of the same language that have the same or nearly the same meaning in some or all senses **2 :** a symbolic or figurative name **3 :** a taxonomic name rejected as being incorrectly applied or incorrect in form [Latin *synonymum,* from Greek *synōnymon,* derived from *syn-* + *onyma* "name"] — **syn•o•nym•i•ty** \ˌsin-ə-ˈnim-ət-ē\ *n*

syn•on•y•mize \sə-ˈnän-ə-ˌmīz\ *vt* **:** to give or analyze the synonyms of (a word)

syn•on•y•mous \sə-ˈnän-ə-məs\ *adj* **:** having the character of a synonym; *also* **:** alike in meaning or significance — **syn•on•y•mous•ly** *adv*

syn•on•y•my \sə-ˈnän-ə-mē\ *n, pl* **-mies 1 a :** the study or discrimination of synonyms **b :** a list or collection of synonyms often defined and discriminated from each other **2 :** the quality or state of being synonymous

syn•op•sis \sə-ˈnäp-səs\ *n, pl* **-op•ses** \-ˈäp-ˌsēz\ **:** a condensed statement or outline (as of a narrative or treatise) **:** SUMMARY, ABSTRACT [Late Latin, from Greek, literally, "comprehensive view", from *synopsesthai* "to be going to see together", from *syn-* + *opsesthai* "to be going to see"]

syn•op•tic \sə-ˈnäp-tik\ *adj* **1 :** affording a general view of a whole ⟨a daily *synoptic* weather chart of Canada⟩ **2 :** showing or characterized by comprehensiveness or breadth of view ⟨a *synoptic* genius⟩ **3 a :** presenting or sharing the same or a common view **b** *often cap* **:** of or relating to the first three Gospels of the New Testament [Greek *synoptikos,* from *synopsesthai* "to be going to see together"] — **syn•op•ti•cal** \-ti-kəl\ *adj* — **syn•op•ti•cal•ly** \-ti-kə-lē, -klē\ *adv*

syn•o•vi•al \sə-ˈnō-vē-əl\ *adj* **:** of or relating to the connective tissue membrane that lines joint capsules and secretes a transparent viscid lubricating fluid [New Latin *synovia* "fluid secreted by synovial membranes"]

syn•tac•tic \sin-ˈtak-tik\ *adj* **:** of, relating to, or according to the rules of syntax [Greek *syntaktikos* "arranging together", from *syntassein* "to arrange together"] — **syn•tac•ti•cal** \-ti-kəl\ *adj* — **syn•tac•ti•cal•ly** \-ti-kə-lē, -klē\ *adv*

syn•tax \ˈsin-ˌtaks\ *n* **1 :** connected or orderly system or arrangement **2 a :** the way in which words are put together to form phrases, clauses, or sentences **b :** the part of grammar dealing with this [Late Latin *syntaxis,* from Greek, from *syntassein* "to arrange together", from *syn-* + *tassein* "to arrange"]

syn•the•sis \ˈsin-thə-səs, ˈsint-\ *n, pl* **-the•ses** \-thə-ˌsēz\ **1 :** the composition or combination of parts or elements so as to form a whole; *esp* **:** the production of a substance by union of chemically simpler substances **2 a :** the combining of often diverse conceptions into a coherent whole; *also* **:** the complex so formed **b :** deductive reasoning from general principles or causes to particular effects **c :** the final stage of a dialectic process combining thesis and antithesis into a new whole [Greek, from *syntithenai* "to put together", from *syn-* + *tithenai* "to put, place"] — **syn•the•sist** \-səst\ *n*

syn•the•size \-ˌsīz\ *vt* **:** to combine or produce by synthesis

syn•the•siz•er \-ˌsī-zər\ *n* **1 :** one that synthesizes **2 :** a computer-controlled device that creates and modifies sound (as for producing music)

1syn•thet•ic \sin-'thet-ik\ *adj* **1 :** of or relating to synthesis **2 :** produced artificially : MAN-MADE ⟨*synthetic* rubber⟩ ⟨*synthetic* fibers such as rayon⟩ [Greek *synthetikos* "of composition", from *syntithenai* "to put together"] **syn** see ARTIFICIAL — **syn•thet•i•cal•ly** \-'thet-i-kə-lē, -klē\ *adv*

2synthetic *n* **:** a product of chemical synthesis

synthetic division *n* **:** a simplified method for dividing a polynomial by another polynomial of the first degree by writing down only the coefficients of the several powers of the variable and changing the sign of the constant term in the divisor in order to replace the usual subtractions by additions — called also *synthetic substitution*

syph•i•lis \'sif-ləs, -ə-ləs\ *n* **:** a chronic contagious usually venereal disease caused by a spirochete and marked by three stages extending over many years [New Latin, from *Syphilus,* hero of the poem *Syphilis sive Morbus Gallicus* (*Syphilis or the French disease*) (1530) by Girolamo Fracastoro] — **syph•i•lit•ic** \ˌsif-ə-'lit-ik\ *adj or n*

sy•phon *variant of* SIPHON

Syr•a•cuse watch glass \'sir-ə-ˌkyüs-, -ˌkyüz-\ *n* **:** a small circular flat-bottomed dish of thick glass that has a shallow depression and is used in biology (as for culturing or staining) — called also *Syracuse dish* [*Syracuse,* New York]

Syr•i•ac \'sir-ē-ˌak\ *n* **1 :** a literary language based on an eastern Aramaic dialect and used as the literary and liturgical language by several Eastern Christian churches **2 :** Aramaic spoken by Christian communities [Latin *syriacus* "Syrian", from Greek *syriakos,* from *Syria,* ancient country in Asia] — **Syriac** *adj*

sy•rin•ga \sə-'ring-gə\ *n* **:** PHILADELPHUS [New Latin, "lilac", from Greek *syring-, syrinx* "panpipe"]

1sy•ringe \sə-'rinj *also* 'sir-inj\ *n* **:** a device used to inject fluids into or withdraw them from the body or its cavities [Medieval Latin *syringa,* from Greek *syring-, syrinx* "panpipe, tube"]

2syringe *vt* **:** to irrigate or cleanse with or as if with a syringe

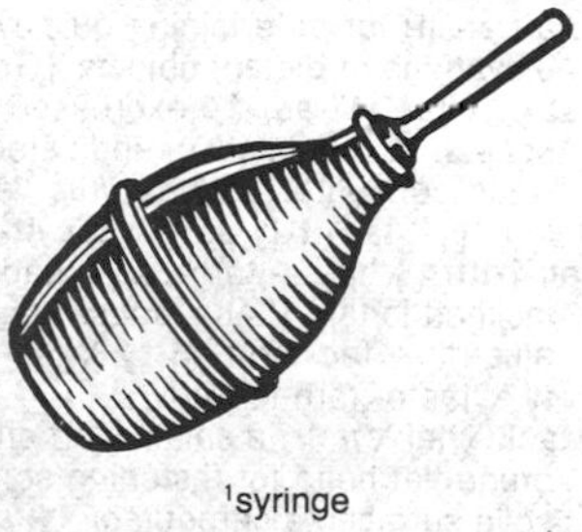
1syringe

syr•inx \'sir-ings, -ingks\ *n, pl* **sy•rin•ges** \sə-'ring-ˌgēz, -'rin-ˌjēz\ *or* **syr•inx•es** \'sir-ing-səz, -ingk-\ **1 :** PANPIPE **2 :** the vocal organ of birds that is a special modification of the lower part of the trachea or of the bronchi or of both [Greek] — **sy•rin•ge•al** \sə-'ring-gē-əl, -'rin-jē-\ *adj*

syr•up *or* **sir•up** \'sər-əp, 'sir-əp, 'sə-rəp\ *n* **1 :** a thick sticky solution of sugar and water often flavored or medicated **2 :** the concentrated juice of a fruit or plant [Middle French *sirop,* from Medieval Latin *syrupus,* from Arabic *sharāb*] — **syr•upy** *or* **sir•upy** \-ē\ *adj*

sys•tem \'sis-təm\ *n* **1 a** (1) **:** a group of objects or units so combined as to form a whole and work, function, or move interdependently and harmoniously ⟨a railroad *system*⟩ ⟨steam heating *systems*⟩ ⟨a park *system*⟩ (2) **:** a set of simultaneous equations or inequalities **b** (1) **:** a body that functions as a whole ⟨a *system* weakened by disease⟩ (2) **:** a group of bodily organs that together carry on one or more vital functions ⟨the nervous *system*⟩ **c :** a particular form of societal organization ⟨the capitalist *system*⟩ **d :** a major division of rocks usually greater than a series **2 a :** an organized set of doctrines or principles usually designed to explain the ordering or functioning of some whole **b :** a method of classifying, symbolizing, or schematizing ⟨a decimal *system* of numbers⟩ ⟨taxonomic *systems*⟩ **3 :** harmonious arrangement or pattern : ORDER [Late Latin *systemat-, systema,* from Greek *systēmat-, systēma,* from *synistanai* "to combine", from *syn* + *histanai* "to cause to stand"] — **sys•tem•less** \-ləs\ *adj*

sys•tem•at•ic \ˌsis-tə-'mat-ik\ *adj* **1 :** relating to or forming a system ⟨*systematic* thought⟩ **2 :** presented or formulated as a system **3 a :** methodical in procedure or plan ⟨*systematic* investigation⟩ **b :** carried on or acting with thoroughness or persistency ⟨*systematic* attacks on the defendant's credibility⟩ **4 :** of, relating to, or concerned with classification : TAXONOMIC — **sys•tem•at•i•cal** \-'mat-i-kəl\ *adj* — **sys•tem•at•i•cal•ly** \-i-kə-lē, -klē\ *adv* — **sys•tem•at•ic•ness** *n*

systematic error *n* **:** an error (as one caused by an incorrect ruler) in data that is due to the method of measurement or observation and not due to chance

sys•tem•at•ics \-'mat-iks\ *n sing or pl* **1 a :** the science or technique of classification **b :** the classification and study of organisms with regard to their natural relationships : TAXONOMY **2 :** a system of classification

sys•tem•a•tist \'sis-tə-mət-əst, sis-'tem-ət-\ *n* **1 :** a maker or follower of a system **2 :** TAXONOMIST

sys•tem•a•tize \'sis-tə-mə-ˌtīz\ *vt* **:** to make into or arrange according to a system — **sys•tem•a•ti•za•tion** \ˌsis-tə-mət-ə-'zā-shən\ *n* — **sys•tem•a•tiz•er** \'sis-tə-mə-ˌtī-zər\ *n*

sys•tem•ic \sis-'tem-ik\ *adj* **:** of, relating to, or common to a system: as **a :** affecting the body generally ⟨a *systemic* disease⟩ **b :** relating to or being part of the systemic circulation ⟨*systemic* arteries⟩ **c :** acting by being taken into bodily systems and making the organism toxic to a pest (as a mite or insect) — **sys•tem•i•cal•ly** \-'tem-i-kə-lē, -klē\ *adv*

systemic circulation *n* **:** the part of the blood circulation concerned with distribution of blood to the tissues as distinguished from the part concerned with gaseous exchange in the lungs

sys•tem•ize \'sis-tə-ˌmīz\ *vt* **:** SYSTEMATIZE — **sys•tem•iza•tion** \ˌsis-tə-mə-'zā-shən\ *n*

sys•to•le \'sis-tə-lē\ *n* **:** the contraction of the heart by which the blood is forced onward and the circulation kept up [Greek *systolē* "contraction", from *systellein* "to contract", from *syn-* + *stellein* "to send"] — **sys•tol•ic** \sis-'täl-ik\ *adj*

T t—type metal

t \'tē\ *n, pl* **t's** *or* **ts** \'tēz\ *often cap* **:** the 20th letter of the English alphabet — **to a T :** to perfection [short for *to a tittle*]

't \t\ *pron* **:** IT ⟨'*twill do*⟩

1tab \'tab\ *n* **1 a :** a short projection used as an aid for filing, pulling, or hanging **b :** a small insert, addition, or remnant ⟨license plate *tab*⟩ **c :** an appendage or extension of something; *esp* **:** one of a series of small pendants forming a decorative border or edge of a garment **d :** a small auxiliary airfoil hinged to a control surface (as a trailing edge) to help stabilize an airplane in flight **2 a :** SURVEILLANCE, WATCH ⟨keep *tab* on the situation⟩ **b :** a creditor's statement : BILL, CHECK **3 :** TABULATOR 6 [origin unknown]

2tab *vt* **tabbed; tab•bing 1 :** to furnish or ornament with tabs **2 :** to single out ⟨*tabbed* as a bright prospect⟩

tab•ard \'tab-ərd\ *n* **1 :** a tunic worn by a knight over his armor and emblazoned with his arms **2 :** a herald's official cape or coat displaying his lord's arms [Old French *tabart*]

1tab•by \'tab-ē\ *n, pl* **tabbies :** a domestic cat with a gray or tawny coat striped and mottled with black; *also* **:** a female cat [French *tabis* "silk taffeta with moiré finish", from Medieval Latin *attabi,* from Arabic *'attābī*]

2tabby *adj* **:** striped and mottled with darker color ⟨*tabby* fur⟩

\ə\ **abut**	\au̇\ **out**	\i\ **tip**	\ȯ\ **saw**	\u̇\ **foot**
\ər\ **further**	\ch\ **chin**	\ī\ **life**	\ȯi\ **coin**	\y\ **yet**
\a\ **mat**	\e\ **pet**	\j\ **job**	\th\ **thin**	\yü\ **few**
\ā\ **take**	\ē\ **easy**	\ng\ **sing**	\th\ **this**	\yu̇\ **cure**
\ä\ **cot, cart**	\g\ **go**	\ō\ **bone**	\ü\ **food**	\zh\ **vision**

tab·er·na·cle \'tab-ər-,nak-əl\ *n* **1 a** *often cap* **:** a tent sanctuary used by the Israelites during the Exodus **b :** a dwelling place **2 :** an ornamental locked box fixed to the middle of the altar and used for reserving bread consecrated at Mass **3 :** a house of worship; *esp* **:** a building or shelter used for evangelistic services [Old French, from Latin *tabernaculum* "tent", from *taberna* "hut, tavern"]

[1]**ta·ble** \'tā-bəl\ *n* **1 :** TABLET 1a **2 a :** a piece of furniture consisting of a smooth flat slab fixed on legs **b :** FOOD, FARE ⟨sets a good *table*⟩ **c :** an act of assembling to eat **:** MEAL **d :** a group of people assembled at or as if at a table **3 a :** a systematic arrangement of data in rows or columns for ready reference ⟨a *table* of weights⟩ **b :** LIST, SYNOPSIS ⟨the *table* of contents⟩ **4 a :** TABLELAND **b :** a horizontal stratum [Old English *tabule* and Old French *table*, both from Latin *tabula* "board, tablet, list"]

[2]**table** *vt* **ta·bled; ta·bling** \-bə-ling, -bling\ **1 :** TABULATE **2 :** to remove (a parliamentary motion) from consideration indefinitely **3 :** to put on a table

tab·leau \'tab-,lō, ta-'blō\ *n, pl* **tableaus** *or* **tab·leaux** \-,lōz, -'blōz\ **:** a lifelike representation of a scene or event by an appropriate grouping of persons who remain silent and motionless [French, derived from Old French *table* "table"]

ta·ble·cloth \'tā-bəl-,klȯth\ *n* **:** a covering spread over a dining table before the places are set

ta·ble d'hôte \,täb-əl-'dōt, ,tab-\ *n* **1 :** a meal served to all guests of a hotel at a stated hour and fixed price **2 :** a complete meal of several courses offered in a restaurant or hotel at a fixed price — compare A LA CARTE [French, literally, "host's table"]

ta·ble·land \'tā-bəl-,land, -,and\ *n* **:** a broad level elevated area **:** PLATEAU

table linen *n* **:** linen (as tablecloths and napkins) for the table

table salt *n* **:** salt for use at the table and in cooking

ta·ble·spoon \'tā-bəl-,spün\ *n* **1 :** a large spoon used for serving rather than eating **2 :** TABLESPOONFUL

ta·ble·spoon·ful \,tā-bəl-'spün-,fu̇l, 'tā-bəl-,\ *n, pl* **-spoonfuls** \-,fu̇lz\ *or* **-spoons·ful** \-'spünz-,fu̇l, -,spünz-\ **1 :** as much as a tablespoon can hold **2 :** a unit of measure used especially in cookery equal to one half fluidounce (about 14.8 milliliters) or three teaspoonfuls

table sugar *n* **:** SUCROSE

tab·let \'tab-lət\ *n* **1 a :** a flat slab or plaque suited for or bearing an inscription **b :** a collection of sheets of writing paper glued together at one edge **2 a :** a compressed or molded block of a solid material **:** CAKE **b :** a small mass of medicated material usually in the shape of a disk [Middle French *tablete*, from *table* "tablet, table"]

table talk *n* **:** informal conversation at or as if at a dining table

table tennis *n* **:** a game resembling tennis that is played on a 9-by-5-foot table with wooden paddles and a small hollow plastic ball

ta·ble·top \'tā-bəl-,täp\ *n* **:** the top of a table — **tabletop** *adj*

ta·ble·ware \'tā-bəl-,waər, -,weər\ *n* **:** utensils (as of china, glass, or silver) for table use

table wine *n* **:** a still wine of not more than 14 percent alcohol by volume usually served with food

[1]**tab·loid** \'tab-,lȯid\ *adj* **:** compressed or condensed into small scope ⟨*tabloid* information⟩ [from *Tabloid*, a trademark applied to a concentrated form of drugs and chemicals]

[2]**tabloid** *n* **:** a newspaper about half the page size of an ordinary newspaper that contains news in condensed form and much photographic matter

[1]**ta·boo** *also* **ta·bu** \tə-'bü, ta-\ *adj* **:** prohibited by a taboo [Tongan (a Polynesian language of the Tonga islands) *tabu*]

[2]**taboo** *also* **tabu** *n, pl* **taboos** *also* **tabus** **1 :** a prohibition against touching, saying, or doing something for fear of immediate harm from a mysterious superhuman force **2 :** a prohibition imposed by social custom

[3]**taboo** *also* **tabu** *vt* **:** to place under a taboo

ta·bor \'tā-bər\ *n* **:** a small drum with one head used to accompany a pipe played by the same person [Old French] — **ta·bor·er** \-bər-ər\ *n*

tab·o·ret *or* **tab·ou·ret** \,tab-ə-'ret, -'rā\ *n* **1 :** a low stool without arms or back **2 :** a small ornamental stand (as for a plant) [French *tabouret*, literally, "small drum", from Middle French *tabor, tabour* "drum"]

tab·u·lar \'tab-yə-lər\ *adj* **1 :** having a flat surface **2 a :** arranged or entered in a table **b :** computed by means of a table [Latin *tabularis* "of boards", from *tabula* "board, tablet"] — **tab·u·lar·ly** *adv*

tabor

ta·bu·la ra·sa \,tab-yə-lə-'räz-ə, -'räs-\ *n, pl* **ta·bu·lae ra·sae** \-,lī-'räz-,ī, -'räs-\ **:** the mind in its hypothetical primary blank or empty state before receiving outside impressions [Latin, "smoothed (wax) tablet"]

tab·u·late \'tab-yə-,lāt\ *vt* **:** to put into tabular form — **tab·u·la·tion** \,tab-yə-'lā-shən\ *n*

tab·u·la·tor \'tab-yə-,lāt-ər\ *n* **:** one that tabulates: as **a :** a business machine that sorts and selects information from marked or perforated cards **b :** a device on a typewriter or billing machine for arranging data in columns

tac·a·ma·hac \'tak-ə-mə-,hak\ *n* **1 :** any of several aromatic oleoresins used in ointments and plasters and for incense **2 :** BALSAM POPLAR [Spanish *tacamahaca*, from Nahuatl *tecamaca*]

tach \'tak\ *n* **:** TACHOMETER

ta·chis·to·scope \tə-'kis-tə-,skōp\ *n* **:** an apparatus for the brief exposure of visual stimuli [Greek *tachistos*, superlative of *tachys* "swift"]

ta·chom·e·ter \ta-'käm-ət-ər, tə-\ *n* **:** a device for indicating speed of rotation (as of the crankshaft of an automobile engine) [Greek *tachos* "speed"]

tachy·car·dia \,tak-i-'kärd-ē-ə\ *n* **:** rapid heart action [Greek *tachys* "swift" + *kardia* "heart"]

ta·chym·e·ter \ta-'kim-ət-ər, tə-\ *n* **:** a surveying instrument (as a transit) for determining quickly the distances, bearings, and elevations of distant objects [Greek *tachys* "swift"]

tac·it \'tas-ət\ *adj* **1 :** expressed or carried on without words or speech **2 :** implied or indicated but not actually expressed ⟨*tacit* consent⟩ [Latin *tacitus* "silent", from *tacēre* "to be silent"] — **tac·it·ly** *adv* — **tac·it·ness** *n*

tac·i·turn \'tas-ə-,tərn\ *adj* **:** habitually or temperamentally disinclined to talk [Latin *taciturnus*, from *tacitus* "silent"] **syn** see SILENT — **tac·i·tur·ni·ty** \,tas-ə-'tər-nət-ē\ *n* — **tac·i·turn·ly** \'tas-ə-,tərn-lē\ *adv*

[1]**tack** \'tak\ *n* **1 :** a small short sharp-pointed nail usually with a broad flat head for fastening some light object or material to a solid surface ⟨a carpet *tack*⟩ **2 a :** a rope used to hold in place the forward lower corner of the lowest sail on any square-rigged mast of a ship **b :** the lower forward corner of a fore-and-aft sail **3 a :** the direction a vessel is sailing as shown by the way the sails are trimmed; *also* **:** the movement of a vessel with respect to the direction of the wind ⟨on the port *tack*⟩ **b :** a change of course from one tack to another **4 :** a zigzag movement on land **5 :** a course or method of action ⟨on the wrong *tack*⟩ **6 :** a slight or temporary sewing or fastening [Middle English *tak* "fastener"]

[2]**tack** *vb* **1 :** ATTACH; *esp* **:** to fasten or affix with tacks **2 :** to join in a slight or hasty manner **3 :** to add as a supplement **4 :** to change the direction of a sailing vessel when sailing close-hauled by putting the helm alee and shifting the sails **5 a :** to sail in a different direction by a tack **b :** to follow a zigzag course **c :** to modify one's policy or an attitude abruptly — **tack·er** *n*

[3]**tack** *n* **:** STUFF 3b; *esp* **:** FOODSTUFF [origin unknown]

[4]**tack** *n* **:** equipment for riding horses **:** stable gear [perhaps short for *tackle*]

tack·i·ness \'tak-ē-nəs\ *n* **:** the quality or state of being tacky

[1]**tack·le** \'tak-əl, *nautical often* 'tāk-\ *n* **1 :** a set of the equipment used in a particular activity **:** GEAR ⟨fishing *tackle*⟩ **2 a :** a ship's rigging **b :** an assemblage of ropes and pulleys arranged to gain mechanical advantage for hoisting and pulling **3 a :** the act or an instance of tackling **b :** either of two football linemen who line up inside the ends [Middle English *takel*]

[2]**tackle** *vt* **tack·led; tack·ling** \'tak-ling, -ə-ling\ **1 :** HARNESS ⟨*tackle* up the horses⟩ **2 a :** to seize, take hold of, or grapple with especially in order to stop or subdue **b** (1) **:** to seize and stop or throw down (a player) in football (2) **:** to obstruct (an opponent playing the ball) so as to cause loss of possession of

the ball (as in soccer) **3 :** to set about dealing with ⟨*tackle* the job of cleaning up⟩ — **tack•ler** \-lər, -ə-lər\ *n*

[1]tacky \ˈtak-ē\ *adj* **tack•i•er; -est :** barely sticky to the touch : ADHESIVE ⟨*tacky* varnish⟩

[2]tacky *adj* **tack•i•er; -est 1 a :** characterized by lack of good breeding **b :** SHABBY 1b, SEEDY **2 a :** marked by lack of style or good taste : DOWDY **b :** marked by cheap showiness : GAUDY [from earlier *tacky* "low-class person"]

ta•co \ˈtäk-ō\ *n, pl* **tacos** \-ōz, -ōs\ **:** a sandwich made of a tortilla rolled up with or folded over a filling [Mexican Spanish]

tac•o•nite \ˈtak-ə-ˌnīt\ *n* **:** a flinty rock high enough in iron content to constitute a low-grade iron ore [*Taconic* moutain range, United States]

tact \ˈtakt\ *n* **:** a keen understanding of how to act in getting along with others; *esp* **:** the ability to deal with others without offending them [French, "sense of touch", from Latin *tactus*, from *tangere* "to touch"]

tact•ful \ˈtakt-fəl\ *adj* **:** having or showing tact — **tact•ful•ly** \-fə-lē\ *adv* — **tact•ful•ness** *n*

[1]tac•tic \ˈtak-tik\ *adj* **:** of, relating to, or showing biological taxis [Greek *taktikos* "of order", from *tassein* "to arrange"]

[2]tactic *n* **1 :** a method of employing forces in combat **2 :** a planned action or maneuver for accomplishing an end

tac•ti•cal \ˈtak-ti-kəl\ *adj* **1 a :** of or relating to combat tactics **b :** of, relating to, or designed for air attack in close support of friendly ground forces ⟨*tactical* air force⟩ **2 a :** of or relating to small-scale actions serving a larger purpose **b :** skillful in planning or maneuvering — **tac•ti•cal•ly** \-kə-lē, -klē\ *adv*

tac•ti•cian \tak-ˈtish-ən\ *n* **:** one skilled in tactics

tac•tics \ˈtak-tiks\ *n sing or pl* **1 a :** the science and art of disposing and maneuvering forces in combat **b :** the art or skill of employing available means to accomplish an end **2 :** a system or mode of procedure [Greek *taktika*, from *taktikos* "of order, of tactics", from *tassein* "to arrange, place in battle formation"] **syn** see STRATEGY

tac•tile \ˈtak-tl, -ˌtīl\ *adj* **1 :** perceptible by touch **2 :** of, relating to, or used in the sense of touch [Latin *tactilis*, from *tangere* "to touch"] — **tac•til•i•ty** \tak-ˈtil-ət-ē\ *n*

tact•less \ˈtak-tləs\ *adj* **:** having or showing no tact — **tact•less•ly** *adv* — **tact•less•ness** *n*

tac•tu•al \ˈtak-chə-wəl, -chəl\ *adj* **:** TACTILE [Latin *tactus* "sense of touch", from *tangere* "to touch"] — **tac•tu•al•ly** \-ē\ *adv*

tad \ˈtad\ *n* **:** BOY 1 [probably from Old English *tāde* "toad"]

tad•pole \ˈtad-ˌpōl\ *n* **:** an aquatic frog or toad larva typically having a long tail, rounded body, and gills [Middle English *taddepol*, from *tode* "toad" + *polle* "head, poll"]

tadpole

tael \ˈtāl\ *n* **1 :** any of various units of weight of eastern Asia **2 :** any of various Chinese units of value based on the value of a tael weight of silver [Portuguese, from Malay *tahil*]

tae•nia \ˈtē-nē-ə\ *n, pl* **-ni•ae** \-nē-ˌē\ *or* **-ni•as 1 :** an ancient Greek fillet **2 :** a band on a Doric order separating the frieze from the architrave **3 :** TAPEWORM [Latin, from Greek *tainia*]

taf•fe•ta \ˈtaf-ət-ə\ *n* **:** a crisp plain-woven lustrous fabric of various fibers used especially for women's clothing [Middle French *taffetas*, from Italian *taffetà*, from Turkish *tafta*, from Persian *tāftah* "woven"]

taff•rail \ˈtaf-ˌrāl, -rəl\ *n* **:** the rail around the stern of a ship [Dutch *tafereel*]

taf•fy \ˈtaf-ē\ *n, pl* **taffies :** a candy usually of molasses or brown sugar boiled and pulled until porous and light-colored [origin unknown]

[1]tag \ˈtag\ *n* **1 :** a loose hanging piece of cloth : TATTER **2 :** a metal or plastic binding on an end of a shoelace **3 :** a piece of hanging or attached material **4 a :** a brief quotation used for emphasis or effect **b :** TAG LINE **5 :** a marker used for identification or classification ⟨price *tag*⟩ [Middle English *tagge*]

[2]tag *vb* **tagged; tag•ging 1 :** to provide or mark with or as if with a tag **2 :** to attach as an addition : APPEND **3 :** to follow closely and persistently **4 :** LABEL 2

[3]tag *n* **1 :** a children's game in which one player is it and chases the others and tries to tag one of them to make that player it **2 :** an act or instance of touching a base runner with the ball in baseball [origin unknown]

[4]tag *vt* **tagged; tag•ging 1 a :** to touch in or as if in a game of tag **b :** to put out (a runner in baseball) by touching with the ball **2 :** to hit solidly : catch with a blow

Ta•ga•log \tə-ˈgäl-əg, -ˌȯg\ *n* **1 :** a member of a people of central Luzon **2 :** an Austronesian language of the Tagalog people [Tagalog]

tag•along \ˈtag-ə-ˌlȯng\ *n* **:** one that persistently and often annoyingly follows the lead of another

tag end *n* **1 :** the last part **2 :** a miscellaneous or random fragment

tag line *n* **1 :** a final line (as in a play or joke); *esp* **:** one that serves to clarify a point or create a dramatic effect **2 :** a phrase identified with an individual, group, or product : SLOGAN

tag up *vi* **:** to touch a base in baseball before running after a fly ball is caught

Ta•hi•tian \tə-ˈhē-shən\ *n* **1 :** a native or inhabitant of Tahiti **2 :** the Polynesian language of the Tahitians — **Tahitian** *adj*

Tai \ˈtī\ *n, pl* **Tai :** a member of a group of peoples of southeast Asia

tai•ga \ˈtī-gə\ *n* **:** swampy northern forest of cone-bearing trees (as pines, spruces, and firs) beginning where the tundra ends [Russian *taĭga*]

[1]tail \ˈtāl\ *n* **1 :** the rear end or a lengthened growth from the rear end of the body of an animal **2 :** something resembling an animal's tail ⟨*tail* of a kite⟩ **3** *pl* **:** full evening dress for men **4 :** the back, last, lower, or inferior part of something **5 :** the reverse of a coin — usually used in pl. ⟨*tails*, I win⟩ **6 :** a spy (as a detective) who follows someone **7 :** the rear part of an airplane consisting of horizontal and vertical stabilizing surfaces with attached control surfaces **8 :** the trail of a fugitive in flight [Old English *tægel*] — **tailed** \ˈtāld\ *adj* — **tail•less** \ˈtāl-ləs\ *adj* — **tail•like** \ˈtāl-ˌlīk\ *adj*

[2]tail *adj* **1 :** being at the rear ⟨*tail* gunner⟩ **2 :** coming from the rear ⟨*tail* wind⟩

[3]tail *vb* **1 a :** to make or furnish with a tail **b :** to follow or be drawn behind like a tail **2 :** to place the end of (as a rafter) in a wall or other support **3 :** to follow closely for purposes of observation : SHADOW **4 :** to grow progressively smaller, fainter, or more scattered — usually used with *off*

tail•back \ˈtāl-ˌbak\ *n* **:** the offensive football back who lines up farthest from the line of scrimmage

tail•board \-ˌbōrd, -ˌbȯrd\ *n* **:** TAILGATE

tail•bone \-ˈbōn, -ˌbōn\ *n* **:** a hind or lower vertebra; *also* **:** COCCYX

tail end *n* **1 :** the hindmost end ⟨the *tail end* of the line⟩ **2 :** the concluding period ⟨the *tail end* of the season⟩

tail fin *n* **:** CAUDAL FIN

[1]tail•gate \ˈtāl-ˌgāt\ *n* **:** a gate at the back end of a vehicle (as a station wagon) that can be let down for loading and unloading

[2]tailgate *vb* **:** to drive dangerously close behind

tail•ing \ˈtā-ling\ *n* **1** *pl* **:** refuse material separated as residue in the preparation of various products (as grain or ores) **2 :** the part of a projecting stone or brick inserted in a wall

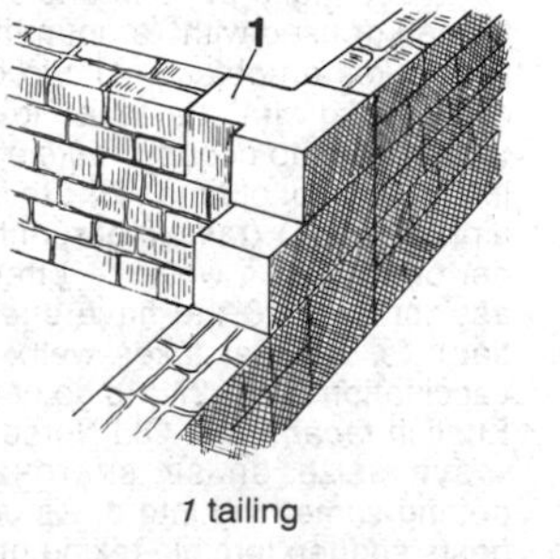

1 tailing

tail lamp *n* **:** TAILLIGHT

tail•light \ˈtāl-ˌlīt\ *n* **:** a red warning light mounted at the rear of a vehicle

[1]tai•lor \ˈtā-lər\ *n* **:** one whose occupation is making or altering outer garments [Old French *tailleur*, from *taillier* "to cut", from Late Latin *taliare*, from Latin *talea* "twig, cutting"]

[2]tailor *vt* **1 a :** to make or fashion as the work of a tailor **b :** to

make or adapt to suit a special need or purpose **2** : to fit with clothes **3** : to style with trim straight lines and details completed by hand
tai•lored \-lərd\ *adj* **1** : made by a tailor **2** : fashioned or fitted to resemble a tailor's work **3** : CUSTOM-MADE
tai•lor•ing *n* **1 a** : the business or occupation of a tailor **b** : the work or workmanship of a tailor **2** : the making or adapting of something to suit a particular purpose
tai•lor–made \ˌtā-lər-ˈmād\ *adj* **1** : made by or as if by a tailor; *esp* : characterized by precise fit and simplicity of style **2** : made or seeming to have been made to suit a particular need
tail•piece \ˈtāl-ˌpēs\ *n* **1** : a piece added at the end **2** : a device from which the strings of a stringed instrument are stretched to the pegs **3** : an ornament placed below the text matter of a page (as at the end of a chapter) **4** : a beam tailed in a wall and supported by a header
tail pipe *n* **1** : the pipe discharging the exhaust gases from the muffler of an automotive engine **2** : the part of a jet engine that carries the exhaust gases rearward
tail plane *n* : the horizontal tail surfaces of an airplane
tail•race \ˈtāl-ˌrās\ *n* : the part of a millrace below the waterwheel or turbine
tail•spin \-ˌspin\ *n* **1** : SPIN 2a **2** : a collapse into depression or confusion
tail wind *n* : a wind moving in the same general direction as an aircraft or ship
¹taint \ˈtānt\ *vt* **1** : to touch or affect slightly with something bad **2** : SPOIL 2c, DECAY **3** : to contaminate morally : CORRUPT [Middle English *taynten* "to affect by attainder", from Middle French *ataint*, past participle of *ataindre* "to affect by attainder, attain"]
²taint *n* **1** : a trace of decay : STAIN, BLEMISH **2** : a contaminating influence — **taint•less** \-ləs\ *adj*
¹take \ˈtāk\ *vb* **took** \ˈtu̇k\; **tak•en** \ˈtā-kən\; **tak•ing 1** : to get into one's hands : GRASP ⟨*take* my hand⟩ **2** : CAPTURE ⟨*take* a fort⟩ **3** : WIN ⟨*take* first prize⟩ **4** : to get possession of (as by buying or capturing) ⟨decided to *take* the house⟩ ⟨*took* several trout with hook and line⟩ **5** : to seize and affect suddenly ⟨*taken* with a fever⟩ **6** : CHARM, DELIGHT ⟨were much *taken* with our new acquaintance⟩ **7** : EXTRACT ⟨*take* material from an encyclopedia⟩ **8** : REMOVE, SUBTRACT ⟨*take* 78 from 112⟩; *also* : to put an end to (as life) **9** : to find out by testing or examining ⟨*take* a patient's temperature⟩ **10** : SELECT ⟨*take* your choice⟩ **11** : ASSUME ⟨*take* office⟩ **12** : ABSORB ⟨this cloth *takes* dye well⟩ **13 a** : to be affected by : CONTRACT ⟨*took* a fit⟩ ⟨*took* cold⟩ **b** : BECOME ⟨*took* sick⟩ **14** : ACCEPT, FOLLOW ⟨*take* my advice⟩ **15** : to introduce into the body ⟨*take* medicine⟩ **16 a** : to submit to ⟨*took* the punishment without complaint⟩ **b** : WITHSTAND ⟨*takes* a punch well⟩ **17** : to subscribe to ⟨*takes* two newspapers⟩ **18** : UNDERSTAND ⟨*take* a nod to mean *yes*⟩ **19** : FEEL ⟨*take* pride in one's work⟩ ⟨*take* offense⟩ **20** : to be formed or used with ⟨a noun that *takes* an *s* in the plural⟩ ⟨this verb *takes* an object⟩ **21** : to convey, lead, carry, or cause to come along with one **22 a** : to avail oneself of ⟨*take* shelter⟩ **b** : to proceed to occupy ⟨*take* a chair⟩ **23** : NEED, REQUIRE ⟨this job *takes* a lot of time⟩ **24** : to obtain an image or copy of ⟨*take* a photograph⟩ ⟨*take* fingerprints⟩ **25** : to set out to make, do, or perform ⟨*take* a walk⟩ — often used with *on* ⟨*took* on a new assignment⟩ **26** : to have effect (as by adherence or absorption) ⟨a dye that *takes* well⟩; *also* : to establish a take ⟨the vaccination *took*⟩ **27** : to go or get away ⟨*take* to the hills⟩ [Old English *tacan*, from Old Norse *taka*]
• **syn** SEIZE, GRASP, SNATCH: TAKE applies to any manner of getting something into one's possession or control; SEIZE suggests sudden forcible taking of something tangible ⟨*seized* the thief in the act of *taking* the money⟩ GRASP stresses a laying hold so as to have firmly in possession ⟨*grasped* the handrail⟩ SNATCH suggests more suddenness but less force than SEIZE ⟨*snatched* a doughnut and ran out⟩ **syn** see in addition BRING, RECEIVE
— **take advantage of 1** : to use to advantage : profit by **2** : to impose upon : EXPLOIT — **take after 1** : to take as an example : FOLLOW **2** : to look like : RESEMBLE — **take care** : to be careful : exercise caution or prudence — **take care of** : to attend to or provide for the needs, operation, or treatment of — **take effect 1** : to become operative **2** : to produce a result as expected or intended : be effective — **take for** : to suppose to be; *esp* : to suppose mistakenly to be — **take for granted 1** : to assume as true, real, or expected **2** : to value too lightly — **take hold** : to become attached or established : take effect — **take into account** : to make allowance for — **take in vain** : to use (a name) profanely or without proper respect — **take issue** : to take up the opposite side — **take part** : PARTICIPATE — **take place** : to come about or occur : HAPPEN — **take stock** : INVENTORY, ASSESS — **take the cake** : to be remarkable or unbelievable — **take the count 1** : to be knocked out in a boxing match **2** : to go down in defeat — **take the floor** : to rise (as in a meeting) to make an address — **take to 1** : to take in hand : take care of **2** : to apply or devote oneself to (as a practice, habit, or occupation) ⟨*take* to begging⟩ **3** : to adapt oneself to : respond to **4** : to conceive a liking for — **take to task** : to call to account for a shortcoming : REPROVE
²take *n* **1** : an act or the action of taking (as by seizing, accepting, or coming into possession) **2** : something that is taken: **a** : money taken in **b** : SHARE, CUT ⟨wanted a bigger *take*⟩ **c** : the quantity (as of game) taken at one time : CATCH **d** (1) : a scene recorded (as on film or videotape) at one time without stopping the camera (2) : a sound recording made during a single recording period (3) : a trial recording **3 a** : a bodily reaction that indicates a successful immunization especially against smallpox **b** : a successful union of a graft **4** : mental response or reaction ⟨delayed *take*⟩
take back *vt* : RETRACT, WITHDRAW ⟨*take back* what you said⟩
¹take•down \ˈtāk-ˌdau̇n\ *adj* : constructed so as to be readily taken apart ⟨a *takedown* rifle⟩
²takedown *n* : the action or an act of taking down: as **a** : the action of humiliating **b** : the action of taking apart **c** : the act of bringing one's wrestling opponent to the mat from a standing position
take down \tāk-ˈdau̇n, ˈtāk-\ *vb* **1 a** : to pull to pieces **b** : DISASSEMBLE **2** : to lower the spirit or vanity of : HUMBLE **3 a** : to write down **b** : to record by mechanical means **4** : to become seized or attacked especially by illness ⟨*took down* with the mumps⟩
take–home pay \ˈtāk-ˌhōm-\ *n* : the money left in one's pay after all deductions (as taxes) have been made : the money one actually gets on payday
take in *vt* **1** : to draw into a smaller compass ⟨*take in* a slack line⟩: **a** : FURL ⟨*take in* the sail⟩ **b** : to make (a garment) smaller by enlarging seams or tucks **2 a** : to receive as a guest or inmate **b** : to give shelter to **3 a** : to receive in payment or as a return **b** : to receive (work) into one's house to be done for pay ⟨*take in* washing⟩ **4** : to encompass within fixed limits : COMPRISE, INCLUDE **5** : ATTEND ⟨*take in* a movie⟩ **6** : to receive into the mind : PERCEIVE, COMPREHEND ⟨paused to *take* the situation *in*⟩ **7** : to impose upon : CHEAT, DECEIVE ⟨*taken in* by a hard luck story⟩
taken *past participle of* TAKE
take•off \ˈtā-ˌkȯf\ *n* **1** : an imitation especially in the form of caricature **2 a** : a rise or leap from a surface in making a jump or flight or an ascent in an airplane **b** : an action of starting out or setting out **3** : a spot at which one takes off **4** : a mechanism for transmission of the power of an engine or vehicle to operate some other mechanism
take off \tā-ˈkȯf, ˈtā-\ *vb* **1** : REMOVE ⟨*take* your hat *off*⟩ **2** : RELEASE ⟨*take* the brake *off*⟩ **3** : to spend (time) away from work or duty ⟨*took* two weeks *off* in August⟩ **4 a** : to copy from an original : REPRODUCE **b** : MIMIC 1, 2 **5** : to take away : DETRACT **6 a** : to start off or away : set out ⟨*took off* without delay⟩ **b** : to branch off (as from a main stream or stem) **c** : to begin a leap or spring **d** : to leave the surface : begin flight
take on *vb* **1** : to contend with or face as an opponent **2** : ENGAGE, HIRE ⟨*took* me *on* for the summer⟩ **3** : to assume or acquire (as an appearance or quality) as or as if one's own **4** : to show one's feelings especially of grief or anger in a demonstrative way
take•out \ˈtā-ˌkau̇t\ *n* : the action or an act of taking out
take out \tā-ˈkau̇t, ˈtā-\ *vb* **1** : to remove by cleansing **2** : to find release for : EXPEND ⟨*took* their frustration *out* on us⟩ **3** : to escort and usually pay the way especially on a social occasion **4** : to take as an equivalent in another form ⟨*took* the debt *out* in goods⟩ **5** : to obtain from the proper authority ⟨*take out* a charter⟩ **6** : to start on a course : set out — **take it out on** : to expend anger, vexation, or frustration in harassment of
take–over \ˈtā-ˌkō-vər\ *n* : the action or an act of taking over
take over \tā-ˈkō-vər, ˈtā-\ *vb* : to assume control or possession of or responsibility for something ⟨*took over* the government⟩

take–up \'tā-ˌkəp\ *n* **1 :** the action of taking something up (as by gathering, contraction, absorption, or adjustment) **2 :** a device for tightening or drawing in

take up \tā-'kəp, 'tā-\ *vb* **1 :** to remove by lifting or pulling up **2 :** to accept or adopt for the purpose of assisting **3 :** to take or accept (as a belief, idea, or practice) as one's own **4 :** to respond favorably to (as a bet, challenge, or proposal) **5 :** to make a beginning where another has left off — **take up for :** to take the part or side of — **take up with :** to begin to associate with

¹tak•ing \'tā-king\ *n* **1 :** a state of violent agitation and distress **2** *pl* **:** receipts especially of money : PROFIT

²taking *adj* **1 :** very attractive **2 :** CONTAGIOUS

talc \'talk\ *n* **:** a soft mineral consisting of a basic silicate of magnesium that is usually whitish, greenish, or grayish with a soapy feel and occurs in flaky, granular, or fibrous masses [Middle French, "mica", from Medieval Latin *talk*, from Arabic *ṭalq*]

tal•cum powder \'tal-kəm-\ *n* **:** a cosmetic powder composed of perfumed talc or talc and a mild antiseptic [Medieval Latin *talcum* "mica", from earlier *talk*]

tale \'tāl\ *n* **1 :** an oral relation or recital ⟨a *tale* of woe⟩ **2 :** a story about an imaginary event ⟨a fairy *tale*⟩ **3 :** a false story : LIE **4 :** a piece of harmful gossip ⟨all sorts of *tales* were going around about them⟩ **5 a :** COUNT 1, TALLY **b :** a number of things taken together : TOTAL [Old English *talu*]

tale•bear•er \-ˌbar-ər, -ˌber-\ *n* **:** one that spreads gossip, scandal, or idle rumors : GOSSIP — **tale•bear•ing** \-ing\ *adj or n*

tal•ent \'tal-ənt\ *n* **1 :** any of several ancient units of weight and money value (as a unit of Palestine and Syria equal to 3000 shekels (about 49 kilograms) or a Greek unit equal to 6000 drachmas (about 26 kilograms) **2 :** the abilities, power, and gifts a person is born with **3 a :** a special often creative or artistic aptitude **b :** general intelligence or mental power : ABILITY **4 :** persons of talent in a field or activity [Old English *talente*, from Latin *talentum*, from Greek *talanton*; senses 2–4 from the parable of the talents in Matthew 25:14–30] — **tal•ent•ed** \-ən-təd\ *adj*

• **syn** GENIUS: TALENT suggests a marked special ability without implying a mind of extraordinary power ⟨a *talent* for singing⟩ GENIUS may also imply marked talent but more often suggests an inborn creative intelligence far above ordinary ⟨true *genius* usually appears very early in life⟩

talent scout *n* **:** a person engaged in discovering and recruiting people of talent (as in music or a sport)

talent show *n* **:** a show consisting of a series of individual performances (as singing) by amateurs who may be selected for special recognition as performing talent

ta•ler *also* **tha•ler** \'täl-ər\ *n* **:** any of numerous silver coins issued by various German states from the 15th to the 19th centuries [German *thaler*, *taler*, short for *joachimsthaler*, from Sankt *Joachimsthal*, Bohemia, where the first talers were made]

tales•man \'tālz-mən, 'tā-lēz-\ *n* **:** a person added to a jury usually from among bystanders to make up a deficiency in the available number of jurors [Middle English *tales* "talesmen", from Medieval Latin *tales de circumstantibus* "such (persons) of the bystanders"; from the wording of the writ summoning them]

tale–tell•er \'tāl-ˌtel-ər\ *n* **1 :** one who tells tales or stories **2 :** TALEBEARER — **tale–tell•ing** \-ing\ *adj or n*

tal•is•man \'tal-ə-smən, -əz-mən\ *n, pl* **talismans :** a ring or stone carved with symbols and believed to have magical powers : CHARM [French, from Italian *talismano*, from Arabic *ṭilsam*, from Middle Greek *telesma*, literally, "consecration"] — **tal•is•man•ic** \ˌtal-ə-'sman-ik, -əz'man-\ *adj* — **tal•is•man•i•cal•ly** \-i-kə-lē, -klē\ *adv*

¹talk \'tȯk\ *vb* **1 :** to deliver or express in speech : UTTER ⟨*talk* sense⟩ **2 :** to make the subject of conversation or discourse : DISCUSS ⟨*talk* business⟩ **3 :** to persuade, affect, or cause by talking ⟨*talked* them into agreeing⟩ **4 :** to use (a language) for conversing or communicating : SPEAK ⟨can *talk* Italian⟩ **5 a :** to express or exchange ideas by means of spoken words : CONVERSE **b :** to convey information or communicate in any way (as with signs or sounds) **c :** to use speech : SPEAK ⟨babies can't *talk*⟩ **6 a :** to speak idly : PRATE **b :** GOSSIP **c :** to reveal secret or confidential information **7 :** to give a talk : LECTURE [Middle English *talken*] **syn** see SPEAK — **talk•er** *n* — **talk back :** to answer impertinently — **talk turkey :** to speak frankly or bluntly

²talk *n* **1 :** the act or an instance of talking : SPEECH **2 :** a way of speaking : LANGUAGE **3 :** pointless or fruitless discussion : VERBIAGE **4 :** a formal discussion, negotiation, or exchange of views : CONFERENCE **5 :** RUMOR, GOSSIP **6 :** the topic of interested comment, conversation, or gossip ⟨it's the *talk* of the village⟩ **7 :** an analysis or discussion presented in an informal manner

talk•ative \'tȯ-kət-iv\ *adj* **:** fond of talking — **talk•ative•ness** *n*

• **syn** TALKATIVE, GARRULOUS, VOLUBLE mean fond of talking. TALKATIVE implies a readiness to talk and engage in conversation; GARRULOUS suggests wordy, rambling, or tedious talkativeness ⟨a *garrulous* old politician⟩ VOLUBLE suggests keeping up an uninterrupted seemingly endless flow of talk ⟨a *voluble* salesclerk who wouldn't quit⟩

talk down *vb* **1 :** to overcome or silence by argument or by loud talking **2 :** to speak in a condescending or superior way

talk•ie \'tȯ-kē\ *n* **:** a motion picture with a synchronized sound track [*talk* + *movie*]

talking book *n* **:** a phonograph or tape recording of a reading of a book or magazine designed chiefly for the use of the blind

talking machine *n* **:** PHONOGRAPH

talk•ing–to \'tȯ-king-ˌtü\ *n* **:** REPRIMAND, LECTURE ⟨father gave them a severe *talking-to*⟩

talk out *vt* **:** to clarify or settle by oral discussion ⟨*talk out* their differences⟩

talk over *vt* **:** to have a talk about : DISCUSS

talk up *vt* **1 :** to discuss favorably : ADVOCATE **2 :** to speak clearly or directly

talky \'tȯ-kē\ *adj* **talk•i•er; -est 1 :** fond of talking : TALKATIVE **2 :** containing too much talk

tall \'tȯl\ *adj* **1 a :** great in stature or height **b :** of a specified height ⟨five feet *tall*⟩ **2 a :** large or formidable in amount, extent, or degree ⟨a *tall* order to fill⟩ **b :** FLOWERY 2, GRANDILOQUENT ⟨*tall* talk⟩ **c :** INCREDIBLE, IMPROBABLE ⟨a *tall* story⟩ [Middle English "brave, handsome"] — **tall** *adv* — **tall•ish** \'tȯ-lish\ *adj* — **tall•ness** *n*

tall•boy \'tȯl-ˌbȯi\ *n* **1 :** HIGHBOY **2 :** a double chest of drawers

tal•lith \'täl-əs, -ət, -əth\ *n, pl* **tal•li•thim** \ˌtäl-ə-'sēm, -'tēm, -'thēm\ **:** a shawl with fringed corners traditionally worn over the head or shoulders by Jewish men during morning prayers [Hebrew *ṭallīth* "cover, cloak"]

tall oil \'täl-, 'tȯl-\ *n* **:** a resinous by-product from the manufacture of chemical wood pulp used especially in making soaps, coatings, and oils [German *tallöl*, from Swedish *tallolja*, from *tall* "pine" + *olja* "oil"]

tal•low \'tal-ō\ *n* **:** the white nearly tasteless solid rendered fat of cattle and sheep used chiefly in soap, margarine, candles, and lubricants [Middle English *talgh*, *talow*] — **tal•lowy** \'tal-ə-wē\ *adj*

¹tal•ly \'tal-ē\ *n, pl* **tallies 1 :** a device for recording business transactions; *esp* **:** a rod notched with marks representing numbers and serving as a record of a transaction and of the amount due or paid **2 a :** a reckoning or recorded account; *also* **:** a total recorded **b :** a score or point made (as in a game) **3 a :** a part that corresponds to an opposite or companion member : COMPLEMENT **b :** CORRESPONDENCE 1a [Medieval Latin *talea*, from Latin, "twig, cutting"]

²tally *vb* **tal•lied; tal•ly•ing 1 :** to keep a reckoning of : COUNT **2 :** to make a tally : SCORE **3 :** MATCH 4, AGREE

tal•ly•ho \ˌtal-ē-'hō\ *n, pl* **tallyhos :** a call of a huntsman at the sight of the fox [probably from French *taïaut*, a cry used to excite hounds in deer hunting]

tal•ly•man \'tal-ē-mən\ *n* **1** *British* **:** one who sells goods on the installment plan **2 :** one who tallies, checks, or keeps an account or record (as of a receipt of goods)

Tal•mud \'täl-ˌmu̇d, 'tal-məd\ *n* **:** the authoritative body of Jewish tradition [Hebrew *talmūdh*, literally, "instruction"] — **tal•mu•dic** \tal-'mü̇d-ik, -'myüd-, -'məd-, täl-'mu̇d-\ *also* **tal•mu•di•cal** \-i-kəl\ *adj, often cap* — **tal•mud•ism** \'täl-ˌmu̇d-ˌiz-əm, 'tal-məd-\ *n, often cap* — **tal•mud•ist** \-əst\ *n, often cap*

\ə\ **abut**	\au̇\ **out**	\i\ **tip**	\ȯ\ **saw**	\u̇\ **foot**
\ər\ **further**	\ch\ **chin**	\ī\ **life**	\ȯi\ **coin**	\y\ **yet**
\a\ **mat**	\e\ **pet**	\j\ **job**	\th\ **thin**	\yü\ **few**
\ā\ **take**	\ē\ **easy**	\ng\ **sing**	\t͟h\ **this**	\yu̇\ **cure**
\ä\ **cot, cart**	\g\ **go**	\ō\ **bone**	\ü\ **food**	\zh\ **vision**

tal•on \ˈtal-ən\ *n* **1** : the claw of an animal and especially of a bird of prey **2** : a part or object shaped like or suggestive of a claw [Middle French, "heel, spur", derived from Latin *talus* "ankle, anklebone"] — **tal•oned** \-ənd\ *adj*

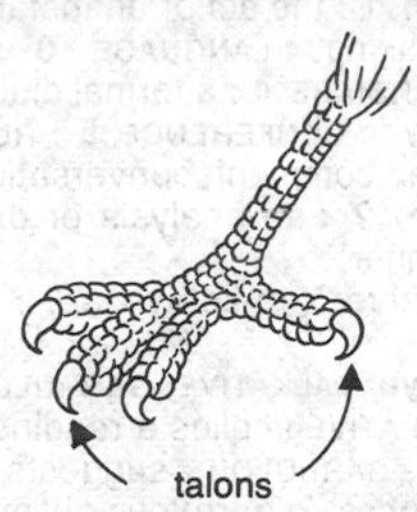

talon 1

¹ta•lus \ˈtā-ləs\ *n* : rock debris at the base of a cliff [French, "sloping ground", from Latin *talutium* "slope indicating presence of gold under the soil"]

²talus *n, pl* **ta•li** \ˈtā-ˌlī\ **1** : the bone that in man bears the weight of the body and with the tibia and fibula forms the ankle joint — called also *anklebone* **2** : the entire ankle [Latin]

tam \ˈtam\ *n* : TAM-O'-SHANTER

tam•able *or* **tame•able** \ˈtā-mə-bəl\ *adj* : capable of being tamed

ta•ma•le \tə-ˈmäl-ē\ *n* : ground meat seasoned with chili, rolled in cornmeal dough, wrapped in corn husks, and steamed [Mexican Spanish *tamales*, pl. of *tamal* "tamale", from Nahuatl *tamalli*]

tam•a•rack \ˈtam-ə-ˌrak\ *n* : any of several American larches; *also* : their wood [origin unknown]

tam•a•rind \ˈtam-ə-rənd, -ˌrind\ *n* : a tropical tree of the pea family with hard yellowish wood, feathery leaves, and red-striped yellow flowers; *also* : its pod which has an acid pulp used for preserves or in drinks [Spanish *tamarindo*, from Arabic *tamr hindī*, literally, "Indian date"]

tam•a•risk \ˈtam-ə-ˌrisk\ *n* : any of a genus of chiefly desert shrubs having tiny narrow leaves and masses of minute flowers [Late Latin *tamariscus*, from Latin *tamarix*]

¹tam•bour \ˈtam-ˌbu̇r, tam-ˈ\ *n* **1** : ¹DRUM 1 **2 a** : an embroidery frame; *esp* : a set of two interlocking hoops between which cloth is stretched before stitching **b** : embroidery made on a tambour frame **3** : a rolling top or front (as of a desk) of narrow strips of wood glued on canvas [French, from Arabic *ṭanbūr*, from Persian *tabīr*]

²tambour *vb* **1** : to embroider (cloth) with tambour **2** : to work at a tambour frame — **tam•bour•er** *n*

tam•bou•rine \ˌtam-bə-ˈrēn\ *n* : a small drum; *esp* : a shallow one-headed drum with loose metallic disks at the sides that is played by shaking, striking with the hand, or rubbing with the thumb

tambourine

¹tame \ˈtām\ *adj* **1** : reduced from a state of native wildness especially so as to be tractable and useful to humans : DOMESTICATED **2** : made docile and submissive : SUBDUED **3** : lacking spirit, zest, or interest : INSIPID [Old English *tam*] — **tame•ly** *adv* — **tame•ness** *n*

²tame *vb* **1 a** : to make or become tame **b** : to subject to cultivation **2** : to deprive of spirit : HUMBLE, SUBDUE **3** : to tone down : SOFTEN — **tam•er** *n*

tame•less \ˈtām-ləs\ *adj* : not tamed or tamable

Ta•mil \ˈtam-əl, ˈtäm-\ *n* **1** : a Dravidian language of Madras state and of northern and eastern Sri Lanka **2** : a Tamil-speaking person

tam–o'–shan•ter \ˈtam-ə-ˌshant-ər\ *n* : a cap of Scottish origin with a tight headband, wide flat circular crown, and often a pompon in the center [*Tam o' Shanter*, hero of the poem *Tam o' Shanter* by Robert Burns]

tamp \ˈtamp\ *vt* **1** : to fill up (a drill hole) above a blasting charge with material (as sand) **2** : to drive in or down by a succession of light or medium blows : COMPACT ⟨*tamp* wet concrete⟩ [probably from Middle English *tampion* "plug", from Middle French *tapon, tampon*, of Germanic origin] — **tamp•er** *n*

tam•per \ˈtam-pər\ *vi* **tam•pered**; **tam•per•ing** \-pə-ring, -pring\ **1** : to use underhand or improper methods (as bribery) **2 a** : to interfere so as to cause a weakening or change for the worse **b** : to try foolish or dangerous experiments : MEDDLE [probably from Middle French *temprer* "to temper, mix, meddle"] — **tam•per•er** \-pər-ər\ *n*

tam-o'-shanter

tam•pi•on \ˈtam-pē-ən, ˈtäm-\ *n* : a wooden plug or a metal or canvas cover for the muzzle of a gun [Middle English, "plug"]

¹tam•pon \ˈtam-ˌpän\ *n* : a plug (as of cotton) introduced into a cavity usually to check bleeding or absorb secretions [French, literally, "plug"]

²tampon *vt* : to plug with a tampon

tam–tam \ˈtam-ˌtam, ˈtäm-ˌtäm\ *n* **1** : TOM-TOM **2** : GONG 1 [Hindi *ṭamṭam*]

¹tan \ˈtan\ *vb* **tanned**; **tan•ning 1** : to convert (hide) into leather by treatment with a solution (as of tannin-rich bark) **2** : to make or become tan or brown by exposure to the sun **3** : THRASH 2, WHIP [Middle French *tanner*, from Medieval Latin *tannare*, from *tannum* "tanbark"]

²tan *n* **1** : TANBARK 1 **2** : a tanning material or its active agent (as tannin) **3** : a brown color imparted to the skin by exposure to the sun or weather **4** : a light yellowish brown [French, from Medieval Latin *tannum*]

³tan *adj* **tan•ner**; **tan•nest** : of the color tan

tan•a•ger \ˈtan-i-jər\ *n* : any of a family of American birds related to the finches that have brightly colored males and inferior songs [Portuguese *tangará*, from Tupi]

tan•bark \ˈtan-ˌbärk\ *n* **1** : bark rich in tannin that is used in tanning **2** : a surface (as a circus ring) covered with spent tanbark

¹tan•dem \ˈtan-dəm\ *n* **1 a** : a 2-seated carriage drawn by horses harnessed one before the other; *also* : a team so harnessed **b** : TANDEM BICYCLE **2** : a group of two or more arranged one behind the other or used or acting in conjunction [Latin, "at last, at length" (taken to mean "lengthwise")]

△ **origin** When a pair of horses pulls a carriage, the two are usually harnessed side by side. But there is a type of carriage that is drawn by two horses harnessed one before the other. This carriage owes its name, *tandem*, to a rather contorted Latin-English pun. The Latin word *tandem* means "at length, at last, finally". We do not know who the punster was who first suggested that a carriage pulled by horses arranged lengthwise, "at length", should be called a *tandem*, but he or she need not have been a scholar. The Latin word is not a rare one and would be known to any student, however shallow, of the language. In English *tandem* came eventually to be used for any arrangement of things or of people one behind another.

²tandem *adv or adj* : one after or behind another

tandem bicycle *n* : a bicycle for two or more persons sitting tandem

tandem bicycle

¹tang \ˈtang\ *n* **1** : a projecting part (as on a knife, file, or sword) to connect with the handle **2 a** : a sharp distinctive often lingering flavor **b** : a pungent odor **3 a** : a faint suggestion : TRACE **b** : a distinguishing characteristic that sets apart or gives a special individuality [of Scandinavian origin] — **tanged** \ˈtangd\ *adj*

²tang *n* : any of various large coarse seaweeds (as a rockweed) [of Scandinavian origin]

³tang *vb* : CLANG, RING [imitative]

⁴tang *n* : a sharp twanging sound

Tang \ˈtäng\ *n* : a Chinese dynasty dated A.D. 618–907 and marked by wide contacts with other cultures and by the development of printing and the flourishing of poetry and art [Chinese (Pekingese dialect) *t'ang²*]

tan•ge•lo \ˈtan-jə-ˌlō\ *n, pl* **-los** : a hybrid between a tangerine and a grapefruit; *also* : its fruit [blend of *tangerine* and *pomelo* "grapefruit" (from Dutch *pompelmoes*)]

tan·gen·cy \ˈtan-jən-sē\ *n, pl* **-cies :** the quality or state of being tangent

1tan·gent \-jənt\ *adj* **1 a :** touching a curve or surface at only one point in the given location ⟨straight line *tangent* to a curve⟩ **b** (1) **:** having a common tangent line at a point ⟨*tangent* curves⟩ (2) **:** having a common tangent plane at a point ⟨*tangent* surfaces⟩ **2 :** diverging from an original purpose or course **:** IRRELEVANT ⟨*tangent* remarks⟩ [Latin *tangens*, present participle of *tangere* "to touch"]

2tangent *n* **1 :** the trigonometric function that for an acute angle is the ratio between the side opposite to the angle when it is considered part of a right triangle and the side adjacent — abbreviation *tan* **2 a :** a line tangent to a curve **b :** the part of a tangent to a plane curve between the point of tangency and the horizontal axis **3 :** an abrupt change of course **:** DIGRESSION ⟨went off on a *tangent* and never got to the point⟩

tan·gen·tial \tan-ˈjen-chəl\ *adj* **1 :** TANGENT **2 :** acting along or lying in a tangent ⟨*tangential* forces⟩ **3 :** DIVERGENT, DIGRESSIVE ⟨*tangential* comment⟩ — **tan·gen·tial·ly** \-ˈjench-lē, -ə-lē\ *adv*

tan·ger·ine \ˈtan-jə-ˌrēn, ˌtan-jə-ˈ\ *n* **1 :** MANDARIN 3; *esp* **:** one grown for its deep orange loose-skinned fruit especially in the United States and southern Africa **2 :** the fruit of the tangerine [French *Tanger* "Tangier, Morocco"]

1tan·gi·ble \ˈtan-jə-bəl\ *adj* **1 a :** capable of being perceived especially by the sense of touch **:** PALPABLE **b :** having substance or reality ⟨a *tangible* advantage⟩ **:** MATERIAL **2 :** capable of being appraised at an actual or approximate value ⟨*tangible* assets⟩ [Late Latin *tangibilis*, from Latin *tangere* "to touch"] — **tan·gi·bil·i·ty** \ˌtan-jə-ˈbil-ət-ē\ *n* — **tan·gi·ble·ness** \ˈtan-jə-bəl-nəs\ *n* — **tan·gi·bly** \-blē\ *adv*

2tangible *n* **:** something tangible; *esp* **:** a tangible asset

1tan·gle \ˈtang-gəl\ *vb* **tan·gled; tan·gling** \-gə-ling, -gling\ **1 :** to make or become involved so as to hamper or embarrass **:** be or become entangled ⟨hopelessly *tangled* in argument⟩ **2 :** to twist or become twisted together into a mass hard to straighten out again [Middle English *tangilen*]

2tangle *n* **1 :** a tangled twisted mass (as of vines) confusedly interwoven **2 :** a complicated or confused state or condition **3 :** DISPUTE, ARGUMENT ⟨had a *tangle* with their neighbor⟩

tan·gle·ment \ˈtang-gəl-mənt\ *n* **:** ENTANGLEMENT

tan·gly \ˈtang-gə-lē, -glē\ *adj* **tan·gli·er; -est :** full of tangles

1tan·go \ˈtang-gō\ *n, pl* **tangos :** a ballroom dance of Spanish-American origin with a variety of steps and postures; *also* **:** music for this dance [American Spanish]

2tango *vi* **:** to dance the tango

tan·gram \ˈtang-grəm, ˈtan-\ *n* **:** a Chinese puzzle made by cutting a square of thin material into a number of pieces which can be recombined into many different figures [perhaps from Chinese (Pekingese dialect) *t'ang*^{2} "Chinese" + English *-gram*]

tangy \ˈtang-ē\ *adj, sometimes* **tang·i·er; -est :** having or suggestive of a tang ⟨a *tangy* smell⟩ — **tang·i·ness** *n*

1tank \ˈtangk\ *n* **1 :** a usually large receptacle for holding, transporting, or storing liquids **2 :** an enclosed heavily armed and armored combat vehicle that moves on endless-belt treads [Portuguese *tanque*, alteration of *estanque*, from *estancar* "to stanch"]

2tank *vt* **:** to place, store, or treat in a tank

tank·age \ˈtang-kij\ *n* **1 :** the capacity or contents of a tank **2 :** dried animal residues usually freed from the fat and gelatin and used as fertilizer and in feeds **3 :** fees charged for storage in tanks

tan·kard \ˈtang-kərd\ *n* **:** a tall one-handled drinking vessel; *esp* **:** a silver or pewter mug with a lid [Middle English]

tankard

tank·er \ˈtang-kər\ *n* **1 a :** a ship fitted with tanks for carrying liquid in bulk **b :** a vehicle (as a truck or trailer) on which a tank is mounted to carry liquids **2 :** a cargo airplane for transporting fuel

tank farm *n* **:** an area with tanks for storage of oil

tank town *n* **:** a small town [from the fact that formerly trains stopped at such towns only to take on water]

tan·nage \ˈtan-ij\ *n* **:** the act, process, or result of tanning

tan·ner \ˈtan-ər\ *n* **:** one that tans hides

tan·nery \ˈtan-rē, -ə-rē\ *n, pl* **tan·ner·ies :** a place where tanning is carried on

tan·nic acid \ˌtan-ik-\ *n* **:** TANNIN

tan·nin \ˈtan-ən\ *n* **:** any of various substances of plant origin used in tanning and dyeing, in inks, and as an astringent [French, from *tanner* "to tan"]

tan·ning *n* **1 :** the art or process by which a skin is tanned **2 :** a browning of the skin by sunlight **3 :** WHIPPING

tan·nish \ˈtan-ish\ *adj* **:** somewhat tan

tan·sy \ˈtan-zē\ *n, pl* **tansies :** any of a genus of mostly weedy herbs related to the daisies; *esp* **:** one with finely cut leaves, aromatic odor, and very bitter taste [Old French *tanesie*, from Medieval Latin *athanasia*, from Greek, "immortality"]

tan·ta·lize \ˈtant-l-ˌīz\ *vt* **:** to tease or torment by or as if by presenting something desirable to the view but continually keeping it out of reach [*Tantalus*] — **tan·ta·liz·er** *n*

tan·ta·liz·ing *adj* **:** possessing a quality that arouses or stimulates desire or interest; *also* **:** mockingly out of reach — **tan·ta·liz·ing·ly** \-ˌī-zing-lē\ *adv*

tan·ta·lum \ˈtant-l-əm\ *n* **:** a hard ductile gray-white acid-resisting metallic chemical element found combined in rare minerals — see ELEMENT table [New Latin, from Latin *Tantalus* "Tantalus"; from its inability to absorb acid]

tan·ta·mount \ˈtant-ə-ˌmau̇nt\ *adj* **:** equal in value, meaning, or effect [obsolete *tantamount*, n., "equivalent", from Anglo-French *tant amunter* "to amount to as much"]

tan·tara \tan-ˈtar-ə, -ˈtär-\ *n* **:** the blare of a trumpet or horn [Latin *taratantara*]

1tan·tivy \tan-ˈtiv-ē\ *adv or adj* **:** at a gallop **:** HEADLONG [origin unknown]

2tantivy *n* **:** a rapid gallop or ride **:** a headlong rush

tan·trum \ˈtan-trəm\ *n* **:** a fit of bad temper [origin unknown]

tan·yard \ˈtan-ˌyärd\ *n* **:** the section or part of a tannery housing tanning vats

Tao \ˈdau̇, ˈtau̇\ *n* **:** the ultimate principle of the universe in Taoism [Chinese (Pekingese dialect) *tao*^{4}, literally, "way"]

Tao·ism \-ˌiz-əm\ *n* **1 :** a Chinese mystical philosophy traditionally founded by Lao-tzu in the 6th century B.C. that teaches conformity to the Tao by unassertive action and simplicity **2 :** a religion developed from Taoist philosophy and Buddhist and folk religion and concerned with obtaining long life and good fortune often by magical means — **Tao·ist** \-əst\ *adj or n* — **Tao·is·tic** \dau̇-ˈis-tik, tau̇-\ *adj*

1tap \ˈtap\ *n* **1 a :** FAUCET, SPIGOT **b :** liquor drawn through a tap **2 :** the procedure of removing fluid from a container or cavity by tapping **3 :** a tool for forming an internal screw thread **4 :** an intermediate point in an electric circuit where a connection may be made [Old English *tæppa* "tap of a cask"] — **on tap 1 :** ready to be drawn ⟨ale *on tap*⟩ **2 :** on hand **:** AVAILABLE

2tap *vt* **tapped; tap·ping 1 :** to release or cause to flow by piercing or by drawing a plug from the containing vessel or cavity ⟨*tap* wine from a cask⟩ **2 a :** to pierce so as to let out or draw off a fluid ⟨*tap* maple trees⟩ **b :** to draw from or upon ⟨*tap* the nation's resources⟩ **c :** to connect into (a telephone or telegraph wire) to get information; *also* **:** to connect into (an electrical circuit) **3 :** to form a female screw in by means of a tap — **tap·per** *n*

3tap *vb* **tapped; tap·ping 1 :** to strike or rap lightly especially with a slight sound ⟨*tap* the desk with a pencil⟩ ⟨*tap* on the window⟩ **2 :** to make or produce by repeated light blows ⟨a woodpecker *tapped* a hole in the tree⟩ **3 :** to repair (a shoe) by putting a half sole on **4 :** SELECT; *esp* **:** to elect to membership (as in a fraternity or sorority) [Middle French *taper* "to strike with the flat of the hand", of Germanic origin] — **tap·per** *n*

4tap *n* **1 :** a light usually audible blow; *also* **:** its sound **2 :** HALF SOLE **3 :** a small metal plate for the sole or heel of a shoe (as for tap dancing)

ta·pa \ˈtäp-ə, ˈtap-\ *n* **:** the bark of a tree pounded to make a coarse cloth usually decorated with geometric patterns; *also* **:** this cloth [Tahitian]

tap dance *n* **:** a dance tapped out audibly with the feet —

\ə\ **abut**	\au̇\ **out**	\i\ **tip**	\ȯ\ **saw**	\u̇\ **foot**
\ər\ **further**	\ch\ **chin**	\ī\ **life**	\ȯi\ **coin**	\y\ **yet**
\a\ **mat**	\e\ **pet**	\j\ **job**	\th\ **thin**	\yü\ **few**
\ā\ **take**	\ē\ **easy**	\ng\ **sing**	\t͟h\ **this**	\yu̇\ **cure**
\ä\ **cot, cart**	\g\ **go**	\ō\ **bone**	\ü\ **food**	\zh\ **vision**

tap–dance \'tap-,dans\ *vi* — **tap dancer** *n* — **tap dancing** *n*

[1]**tape** \'tāp\ *n* **1 :** a narrow band of woven fabric **2 :** a string stretched breast-high above the finishing line of a footrace **3 :** a narrow flexible strip or band **4 :** MAGNETIC TAPE [Old English *tæppe*]

[2]**tape** *vt* **1 :** to fasten, tie, bind, cover, or support with tape **2 :** to measure with a tape measure **3 :** to record on magnetic tape

tape deck *n* **1 a :** a mechanism that moves a tape past a head (as for magnetic recording) **b :** a device that contains such a mechanism, that provides usually for the recording as well as the playback of magnetic tapes, and that usually has to be connected to a separate audio system **2 :** a self-contained device for the playback of recorded magnetic tapes

tape•line \'tā-,plīn\ *n* **:** TAPE MEASURE

tape measure *n* **:** a tape marked off in units (as inches or centimeters) and used for measuring

[1]**ta•per** \'tā-pər\ *n* **1 a :** a long waxed wick used especially for lighting lamps, pipes, or fires; *also* **:** a slender candle **b :** a feeble light **2 a :** a tapering form or figure **b :** gradual lessening of thickness, diameter, or width in an elongated object **c :** a gradual decrease [Old English]

[2]**taper** *vb* **ta•pered**; **ta•per•ing** \-pə-ring, -pring\ **1 :** to make or become gradually smaller toward one end **2 :** to diminish gradually

tape–re•cord \,tā-pri-'kȯrd\ *vt* **:** to make a recording of on magnetic tape — **tape recorder** *n* — **tape recording** *n*

taper off *vb* **:** to stop or decrease gradually

tap•es•try \'tap-ə-strē\ *n, pl* **-tries :** a heavy textile used especially as a wall hanging or furniture covering [Middle French *tapisserie*, from *tapisser* "to carpet", from *tapis* "carpet", from Greek *tapēs*] — **tap•es•tried** \-strēd\ *adj*

tapestry carpet *n* **:** a carpet in which the designs are printed in colors on the threads before the fabric is woven

tape•worm \'tāp-,wərm\ *n* **:** a flatworm with a segmented body that is parasitic when adult in the intestine of vertebrates **:** CESTODE

tap•hole \'tap-,hōl\ *n* **:** a hole for a tap; *esp* **:** a hole at or near the bottom of a furnace or ladle through which molten metal or slag can be tapped

tap•i•o•ca \,tap-ē-'ō-kə\ *n* **:** a usually granular preparation of cassava starch used especially in puddings and as a thickening in liquid foods [Spanish and Portuguese, from Tupi *typyóca*]

ta•pir \'tā-pər\ *n, pl* **tapir** *or* **tapirs :** any of several large inoffensive chiefly nocturnal hoofed mammals of tropical America, Malaya, and Sumatra that have long flexible snouts and are related to the horses and rhinoceroses [Tupi *tapiíra*]

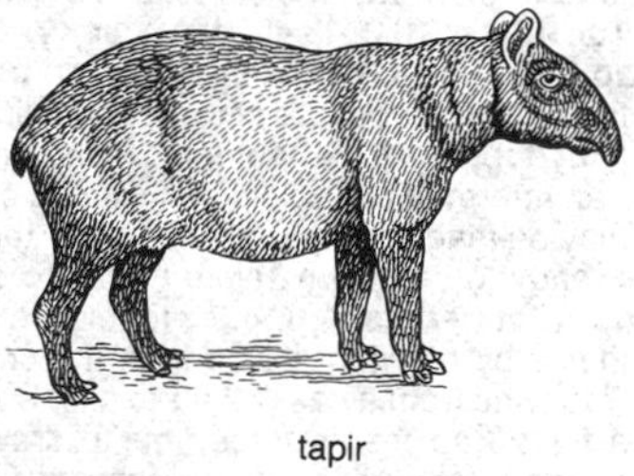

tapir

tap•pet \'tap-ət\ *n* **:** a lever or projection moved by some other piece (as a cam) or intended to tap or touch something else to cause a particular motion [[3]*tap*]

tap•room \'tap-,rüm, -,ru̇m\ *n* **:** BARROOM

tap•root \-,rüt, -,ru̇t\ *n* **:** a large strong root that grows vertically downward and gives off smaller lateral roots — compare FIBROUS ROOT [[1]*tap*]

taps \'taps\ *n sing or pl* **:** the last bugle call at night blown as a signal that lights are to be put out; *also* **:** a similar call blown at military funerals and memorial services [probably from earlier *taptoo* "tattoo"]

tap•ster \'tap-stər\ *n* **:** BARTENDER

[1]**tar** \'tär\ *n* **1 :** a dark usually odorous viscous liquid obtained by destructive distillation of organic material (as wood, coal, or peat) **2 :** a residue present in tobacco smoke that contains combustion by-products (as resins, acids, and phenols) [Old English *teoru*]

[2]**tar** *vt* **tarred**; **tar•ring :** to treat or smear with or as if with tar

tar•an•tel•la \,tar-ən-'tel-ə\ *n* **:** a vivacious folk dance of southern Italy in 6/8 time [Italian, from *Taranto*, Italy]

ta•ran•tu•la \tə-'ranch-lə, -ə-lə; -'rant-l-ə\ *n* **1 :** a large European spider whose bite was once thought to cause an uncontrollable desire to dance **2 :** any of a family of large hairy American spiders that are mostly rather sluggish and essentially harmless to humans [Medieval Latin, from Italian *tarantola*, from *Taranto*, Italy]

tar•boosh *also* **tar•bush** \tär-'büsh, 'tär-,\ *n* **:** a usually red hat similar to the fez worn alone or as part of a turban especially by Muslim men [Arabic *ṭarbūsh*]

tar•dy \'tärd-ē\ *adj* **tar•di•er**; **-est 1 :** moving or progressing slowly **2 :** being late or delayed [Middle French *tardif*, derived from Latin *tardus*] — **tar•di•ly** \'tärd-l-ē\ *adv* — **tar•di•ness** \'tärd-ē-nəs\ *n*

[1]**tare** \'taər, 'teər\ *n* **1 a :** VETCH; *also* **:** its seed **b :** a weed of grainfields mentioned in the Bible **2** *pl* **:** an undesirable element [Middle English]

[2]**tare** *n* **:** a deduction of weight made to allow for the weight of a container or vehicle [Middle French, from Italian *tara*, from Arabic *ṭarḥa*] — **tare** *vt*

targe \'tärj\ *n, archaic* **:** a light shield [Old French]

tar•get \'tär-gət\ *n* **1 a :** a mark to shoot at **b :** an object of ridicule or criticism **c :** a goal to be achieved **:** OBJECTIVE **2 :** the surface usually of platinum or tungsten upon which the cathode rays within an X-ray tube are focused and from which the X rays are emitted [Middle French *targette* "small shield", from *targe* "light shield", of Germanic origin]

target date *n* **:** the date set for an event or for the completion of a project, goal, or quota

tar•iff \'tar-əf\ *n* **1 a :** a schedule of duties imposed by a government on imported or in some countries exported goods **b :** a duty or rate of duty imposed in such a schedule **2 :** a schedule of rates or charges of a business or public utility [Italian *tariffa*, from Arabic *ta'rīf* "notification"]

tar•la•tan \'tär-lət-n\ *n* **:** a thin stiff transparent muslin [French *tarlatane*]

tar•mac \'tär-,mak\ *n* **:** a tarmacadam road, apron, or runway [from *Tarmac*, a trademark]

Tar•mac \'tär-,mak\ *trademark* — used for a bituminous binder for surfacing roads

tar•mac•ad•am \,tär-mə-'kad-əm\ *n* **1 :** a pavement made by putting tar over courses of crushed stone and then rolling **2 :** a material of tar and aggregates mixed in a plant and shaped on the roadway [*tar* + *macadam*]

tarn \'tärn\ *n* **:** a small mountain lake or pool usually of glacial origin [of Scandinavian origin]

[1]**tar•nish** \'tär-nish\ *vb* **1 :** to make or become dull, dim, or discolored ⟨silver *tarnishes*⟩ **2 :** to lessen the prestige or quality of ⟨a *tarnished* reputation⟩ [Middle French *terniss-*, stem of *ternir* "to tarnish"] — **tar•nish•able** \-ə-bəl\ *adj*

[2]**tarnish** *n* **1 :** tarnished condition **2 :** a surface film (as of oxide or sulfide) formed on metal

ta•ro \'tär-ō, 'tar-, 'ter-\ *n, pl* **taros :** a plant of the arum family grown throughout the tropics for its edible starchy tuberous rootstocks; *also* **:** this rootstock [Tahitian and Maori]

tarp \'tärp\ *n* **:** TARPAULIN

tar paper *n* **:** a felt (as of asbestos) coated or impregnated with tar for use in building

tar•pau•lin \tär-'pȯ-lən, 'tär-pə-\ *n* **:** waterproofed material and especially canvas used in sheets for protecting exposed objects [probably derived from *tar* + *pall*]

tar•pon \'tär-pən\ *n, pl* **tarpon** *or* **tarpons :** a large silvery sport fish common off the Florida coast [origin unknown]

tar•ra•gon \'tar-ə-,gän, -gən\ *n* **:** a small European wormwood grown for its pungent aromatic foliage used especially in vinegar and cookery [Middle French *targon*, from Medieval Latin *tarchon*, from Arabic *ṭarkhūn*]

[1]**tar•ry** \'tar-ē\ *vi* **tar•ried**; **tar•ry•ing 1 :** to be tardy **:** DELAY, LINGER **2 :** to abide in or at a place **:** SOJOURN [Middle English *tarien*]

[2]**tar•ry** \'tär-ē\ *adj* **:** of, resembling, or covered with tar

[1]**tar•sal** \'tär-səl\ *adj* **:** of or relating to the tarsus

[2]**tarsal** *n* **:** a tarsal part (as a bone or cartilage)

tar•si•er \'tär-sē-,ā, -sē-ər\ *n* **:** any of several small nocturnal arboreal East Indian mammals related to the lemurs [French, from *tarse* "tarsus"] — **tar•si•oid** \-sē-,ȯid\ *adj or n*

tar•so•meta•tar•sus \'tär-sō-'met-ə-,tär-səs\ *n* **:** the large compound bone of the tarsus of a bird; *also* **:** the segment of the limb it supports

tar•sus \'tär-səs\ *n, pl* **tar•si** \-,sī, -,sē\ **1 :** the part of the vertebrate foot between the metatarsus and the leg; *also* **:** the small bones that support this part of the foot **2 :** the shank of a bird's leg **3 :** the distal part of the limb of an arthropod [New

Latin, from Greek *tarsos* "wickerwork mat, flat of the foot, ankle"]

[1]**tart** \'tärt\ *adj* **1** : agreeably sharp to the taste : pleasantly acid **2** : SARCASTIC 1, CAUSTIC [Old English *teart* "sharp, severe"] **syn** see SOUR — **tart•ly** *adv* — **tart•ness** *n*

[2]**tart** *n* **1** : a small pie or pastry shell containing jelly, custard, or fruit **2** : PROSTITUTE [Middle French *tarte*]

tar•tan \'tärt-n\ *n* **1** : a plaid textile design of Scottish origin usually distinctively patterned to designate a clan **2** : a fabric or garment with tartan design [probably from Middle French *tiretaine* "linsey-woolsey"]

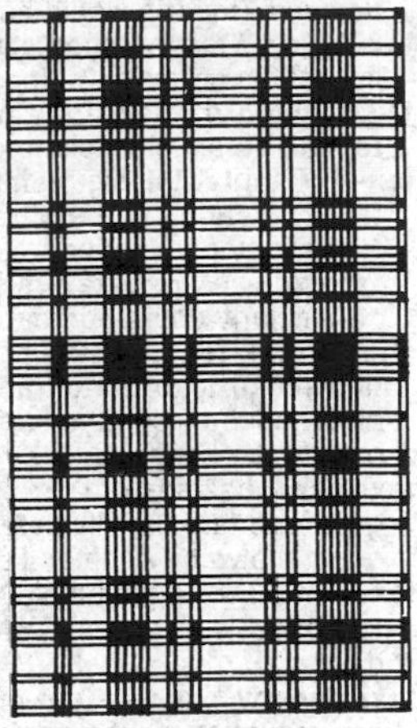
tartan 1

[1]**tar•tar** \'tärt-ər\ *n* **1** : a substance consisting essentially of cream of tartar found in the juice of grapes and deposited in wine casks as a reddish crust or sediment **2** : a hard crust of saliva, food residue, and various calcium salts that forms on the teeth [Medieval Latin *tartarum*]

[2]**tartar** *n* **1** *cap* : a native or inhabitant of Tatary **2** : a bad-tempered or unexpectedly formidable person [Middle French *Tartare*, probably from Medieval Latin *Tartarus*, from Persian *Tātār*] — **Tartar** *adj* — **Tar•tar•i•an** \tär-'tar-ē-ən, -'ter-\ *adj*

tartar emetic *n* : a poisonous salt of sweetish metallic taste that is used in dyeing and in medicine especially in the treatment of amebic dysentery

tar•tar•ic acid \tär-ˌtar-ik-\ *n* : a strong organic acid $C_4H_6O_6$ that occurs in four forms, is usually obtained from grape tartar, and is used especially in food and medicines and in photography

tar•tar sauce *or* **tar•tare sauce** \ˌtärt-ər-\ *n* : mayonnaise with chopped pickles, olives, capers, and parsley [French *sauce tartare*]

tart•ish \'tärt-ish\ *adj* : somewhat tart — **tart•ish•ly** *adv*

tart•let \'tärt-lət\ *n* : a small tart

tar•trate \'tär-ˌtrāt\ *n* : a salt or ester of tartaric acid

Tar•zan \'tärz-n, 'tär-ˌzan\ *n* : a strong agile person of heroic proportions and bearing [*Tarzan*, hero of adventure stories by Edgar Rice Burroughs]

task \'task\ *n* : a piece of work especially as assigned by another : DUTY, FUNCTION [Old North French *tasque*, from Medieval Latin *tasca* "tax or service imposed by a feudal superior", from *taxare* "to tax"]

• **syn** TASK, DUTY, ASSIGNMENT, JOB mean a piece of work to be done. TASK implies work imposed by one in authority or by circumstance ⟨every child had a daily *task* to perform⟩ DUTY implies an obligation to perform or responsibility for performance ⟨the limits of their *duties* as guardians⟩ ASSIGNMENT implies a definite limited task assigned by one in authority; JOB applies to a piece of work one is asked to do or agrees to do voluntarily ⟨a helper to do *jobs* around the house⟩ and often stresses quality or difficulty of performance ⟨did a good *job* on the research project⟩

task force *n* : a temporary grouping especially of military units to accomplish a particular objective

task•mas•ter \'task-ˌmas-tər\ *n* : one who imposes a task or burdens another with labor

task•mis•tress \-ˌmis-trəs\ *n* : a girl or woman who is a taskmaster

task•work \-ˌwərk\ *n* **1** : PIECEWORK **2** : hard work

Tas•ma•ni•an devil \taz-ˌmā-nē-ən-\ *n* : a powerful stocky burrowing flesh-eating marsupial of Tasmania

Tasmanian wolf *n* : a flesh-eating marsupial formerly common in Australia that somewhat resembles a dog

[1]**tas•sel** \'tas-əl, *oftenest of corn* 'täs-, 'tòs-\ *n* **1** : a hanging ornament made of a bunch of cords of even length fastened at one end **2** : something resembling a tassel; *esp* : the terminal male inflorescence of Indian corn [Old French, "clasp, tassel", from Latin *taxillus* "small die"]

[2]**tassel** *vb* **-seled** *or* **-selled**; **-sel•ing** *or* **-sel•ling** \-ə-ling, -ling\ : to adorn with or put forth tassels

[1]**taste** \'tāst\ *vb* **1** : EXPERIENCE ⟨*taste* the joy of flying⟩ **2** : to try or determine the flavor of by taking a little into the mouth **3** : to eat or drink especially in small quantities **4** : to distinguish or recognize as if by the sense of taste **5** : to have a specific flavor [Old French *taster* "to touch, taste", derived from Latin *taxare* "to touch"]

Tasmanian wolf

[2]**taste** *n* **1 a** : a small amount tasted **b** : a small sample of experience ⟨first *taste* of battle⟩ **2** : the one of the special senses that perceives and distinguishes the sweet, sour, bitter, or salty quality of a dissolved substance and is mediated by receptors in the taste buds of the tongue **3 a** : the objective quality of a dissolved substance perceptible to the sense of taste **b** : a complex sensation resulting from usually combined stimulation of the senses of taste, smell, and touch : FLAVOR **4** : the distinctive quality of an experience **5** : individual preference : INCLINATION **6 a** : critical judgment, discernment, or appreciation **b** : manner or aesthetic quality indicative of discernment or appreciation

• **syn** TASTE, RELISH, GUSTO, ZEST mean a liking for something that gives pleasure. TASTE may imply a natural or acquired specific liking or interest; RELISH suggests a capability for keen gratification of appetite or other senses; GUSTO implies a heartiness in relishing that goes with vitality or high spirits; ZEST implies an eagerness for and keen perception of a thing's peculiar pleasure.

taste bud *n* : any of the sensory organs by which taste is perceived and which lie chiefly in the tongue

taste•ful \'tāst-fəl\ *adj* : having, showing, or conforming to good taste — **taste•ful•ly** \-fə-lē\ *adv* — **taste•ful•ness** *n*

taste•less \'tāst-ləs\ *adj* **1** : lacking flavor : FLAT, INSIPID **2** : not having or showing good taste ⟨*tasteless* decorations⟩ — **taste•less•ly** *adv* — **taste•less•ness** *n*

tast•er \'tā-stər\ *n* : one that tastes: as **a** : a person who samples food or drink prepared for another usually to test for poison **b** : a person able to taste the chemical phenylthiocarbamide

tasty \'tā-stē\ *adj* **tast•i•er**; **-est** **1** : pleasing to the taste : SAVORY **2** : TASTEFUL — **tast•i•ly** \-stə-lē\ *adv* — **tast•i•ness** \-stē-nəs\ *n*

tat \'tat\ *vb* **tat•ted**; **tat•ting** : to work at or make by tatting [back-formation from *tatting*]

Ta•tar \'tät-ər\ *n* : a member of any of numerous chiefly Turkic peoples of the Soviet Union found mainly in the Tatar Republic, the north Caucasus, the Crimea, and parts of Siberia [Persian *Tātār*, of Turkic origin]

tat•ter \'tat-ər\ *n* **1** : a part torn and left hanging : SHRED **2** *pl* : tattered clothing [of Scandinavian origin] — **tatter** *vb*

tat•ter•de•ma•lion \ˌtat-ərd-i-'māl-yən, -'mal-, -ē-ən\ *n* : a person dressed in ragged clothing : RAGAMUFFIN [origin unknown]

tat•tered \'tat-ərd\ *adj* **1** : wearing ragged clothes ⟨a *tattered* barefoot child⟩ **2** : torn in shreds : RAGGED ⟨a *tattered* flag⟩

tat•ter•sall \'tat-ər-ˌsòl\ *n* **1** : a pattern of colored lines enclosing squares of solid background **2** : a fabric woven or printed in a tattersall pattern [*Tattersall's* horse market, London, England]

tat•ting \'tat-ing\ *n* **1** : a handmade lace formed usually by looping and knotting with a single thread and a small shuttle **2** : the act or process of making tatting [origin unknown]

[1]**tat•tle** \'tat-l\ *vb* **tat•tled**; **tat•tling** \'tat-ling, -l-ing\ **1** : CHATTER 2, PRATTLE **2** : to tell secrets [Dutch *tatelen*]

[2]**tattle** *n* **1** : idle talk : CHATTER **2** : GOSSIP 2, TALEBEARING

tat•tler \'tat-lər, -l-ər\ *n* **1** : TATTLETALE **2** : any of various slender long-legged shorebirds (as the willet and yellowlegs) with a loud and frequent call

tat•tle•tale \'tat-l-ˌtāl\ *n* : one that tattles : INFORMER

[1]**tat•too** \ta-'tü\ *n, pl* **tattoos** **1 a** : a call sounded shortly before

taps as notice to go to quarters **b** : an outdoor military exercise given by troops as evening entertainment **2** : a rapid rhythmic rapping ⟨hoofs beating a *tattoo* on the road⟩ [Dutch *taptoe*, from the phrase *tap toe!* "taps shut!"]

^{2}**tattoo** *n* : an indelible mark or figure fixed on the body by insertion of pigment under the skin or by production of scars [Tahitian *tatau*]

^{3}**tattoo** *vt* **1** : to mark or color (the skin) with a tattoo **2** : to mark the skin with (a tattoo) — **tat•too•er** *n*

tau \ˈtau̇, ˈtȯ\ *n* : the 19th letter of the Greek alphabet — Τ or τ

taught *past of* TEACH

taunt \ˈtȯnt, ˈtänt\ *vt* : to reproach or challenge in a mocking or insulting way : jeer at [perhaps from Middle French *tenter* "to try, tempt"] **syn** see RIDICULE — **taunt** *n* — **taunt•er** *n* — **taunt•ing•ly** \-iŋ-lē\ *adv*

taupe \ˈtōp\ *n* : a brownish gray [French, literally, "mole", from Latin *talpa*]

tau•rine \ˈtȯr-ˌīn\ *adj* **1** : of or relating to a bull **2** : of or relating to the common domestic cattle as distinguished from Indian humped cattle [Latin *taurinus*, from *taurus* "bull"]

Tau•rus \ˈtȯr-əs\ *n* **1** : a zodiacal constellation that contains the Pleiades and Hyades **2** : the 2d sign of the zodiac; *also* : one born under this sign [Latin, literally, "bull"]

taut \ˈtȯt\ *adj* **1 a** : tightly drawn : not slack ⟨a *taut* rope⟩ **b** : HIGH-STRUNG, TENSE ⟨*taut* nerves⟩ **2 a** : kept in proper order or condition ⟨a *taut* ship⟩ **b** : not loose or flabby : FIRM [Middle English *tought*] **syn** see TIGHT — **taut•ly** *adv* — **taut•ness** *n*

taut•en \ˈtȯt-n\ *vb* **taut•ened**; **taut•en•ing** \ˈtȯt-niŋ, -n-iŋ\ : to make or become taut

tau•tog \ˈtȯ-ˌtȯg\ *n* : an edible fish related to the wrasses and found along the Atlantic coast of the United States — called also *blackfish* [of American Indian origin]

tau•tol•o•gy \tȯ-ˈtäl-ə-jē\ *n, pl* **-gies** : needless repetition of an idea, statement, or word; *also* : an instance of such repetition ⟨"a beginner who has just started" is a *tautology*⟩ [Late Latin *tautologia*, from Greek, from *tautologos* "tautologous", from *tauto* "the same" (contraction of *to auto*) + *legein* "to say"] — **tau•to•log•i•cal** \ˌtȯt-l-ˈäj-i-kəl\ *adj* — **tau•to•log•i•cal•ly** \-kə-lē, -klē\ *adv* — **tau•tol•o•gous** \tȯ-ˈtäl-ə-gəs\ *adj* — **tau•tol•o•gous•ly** *adv*

tav•ern \ˈtav-ərn\ *n* **1** : an establishment where alcoholic beverages are sold to be drunk on the premises **2** : INN 1 [Old French *taverne*, from Latin *taberna*, literally, "shed, hut, shop", from *trabs* "beam"]

tav•ern•er \ˈtav-ər-nər, ˈtav-ə-nər\ *n* : one that keeps a tavern

taw \ˈtȯ\ *n* **1** : a playing marble used as a shooter **2** : the line from which players shoot at marbles [origin unknown]

taw•dry \ˈtȯd-rē, ˈtäd-\ *adj* **taw•dri•er**; **-est** : cheap and gaudy in appearance and quality [*tawdry lace* "tie of lace for the neck", from *Saint Audrey* (Etheldreda), died 679, queen of Northumbria] **syn** see GAUDY — **taw•dri•ly** \-rə-lē\ *adv* — **taw•dri•ness** \-rē-nəs\ *n*

△ **origin** When Etheldreda, queen of Northumbria, renounced her husband and her royal position for the veil of a nun, she was soon appointed abbess of a monastery in the Isle of Ely. She was renowned for her saintliness and is said to have died of a swelling in her throat, which she took as a judgment upon her fondness for wearing necklaces in her youth. An annual fair was held in Saint Etheldreda's honor on 17 October, and her name became simplified to *Saint Audrey*. At these fairs cheap knickknacks were sold, among them a type of necklace called "Saint Audrey's lace", which was eventually altered to "tawdry lace". *Tawdry* came to be used for other cheap finery and is now an adjective meaning "cheap and gaudy".

^{1}**taw•ny** \ˈtȯ-nē, ˈtän-ē\ *adj* **taw•ni•er**; **-est** : of the color tawny [Middle French *tanné*, past participle of *tanner* "to tan"] — **taw•ni•ness** *n*

^{2}**tawny** *n, pl* **tawnies** : a brownish orange to light brown color

^{1}**tax** \ˈtaks\ *vt* **1** : to levy a tax on **2** : to call to account : CENSURE ⟨*taxed* them with neglect of their duties⟩ **3** : to make heavy and rigorous demands on : subject to excessive stress ⟨the job *taxed* my strength⟩ [Middle French *taxer*, from Medieval Latin *taxare*, from Latin, "to feel, estimate, censure", from *tangere* "to touch"] — **tax•abil•i•ty** \ˌtak-sə-ˈbil-ət-ē\ *n* — **tax•able** \ˈtak-sə-bəl\ *adj* — **tax•er** *n*

^{2}**tax** *n* **1 a** : a charge usually of money imposed by authority upon persons or property for public purposes **b** : a sum levied on members of an organization to defray expenses **2** : a heavy demand ⟨the trip would be too great a *tax* on your health⟩

tax•a•tion \tak-ˈsā-shən\ *n* **1** : the action of taxing; *esp* : the imposition of taxes **2** : income obtained from taxes

tax evasion *n* : deliberate failure to pay taxes usually by false reports of taxable income or property

tax-ex•empt \ˌtak-sig-ˈzemt, -ˈzempt\ *adj* **1** : exempted from a tax **2** : bearing interest free from federal or state income tax ⟨*tax-exempt* securities⟩

^{1}**taxi** \ˈtak-sē\ *n, pl* **tax•is** \-sēz\ *also* **tax•ies** : TAXICAB; *also* : a similarly operated boat or airplane

^{2}**taxi** *vb* **tax•ied**; **taxi•ing** *or* **taxy•ing**; **tax•is** *or* **tax•ies** **1 a** : to ride in a taxicab **b** : to transport by taxi **2** : to operate or move at low speed along the surface of the ground ⟨*taxied* the plane over to the hangar⟩

taxi•cab \ˈtak-sē-ˌkab\ *n* : an automobile that carries passengers for a fare usually determined by the distance traveled and often shown by a meter [earlier *taxi*meter *cab*]

taxi dancer *n* : a girl employed by a dance hall, café, or cabaret to dance with patrons who pay a certain amount for each dance

taxi•der•my \ˈtak-sə-ˌdər-mē\ *n* : the art of preparing, stuffing, and mounting skins of animals [derived from Greek *taxis* "arrangement" + *derma* "skin"] — **taxi•der•mic** \ˌtak-sə-ˈdər-mik\ *adj* — **taxi•der•mist** \ˈtak-sə-ˌdər-məst\ *n*

taxi•me•ter \ˈtak-sē-ˌmēt-ər\ *n* : an instrument for use in a hired vehicle (as a taxicab) for automatically showing the fare due [French *taximètre*, from German *taxameter*, from Medieval Latin *taxa* "tax, charge" (from *taxare* "to tax") + German *-meter* "-meter"]

tax•is \ˈtak-səs\ *n, pl* **tax•es** \ˈtak-ˌsēz\ : reflex movement by a freely motile organism in relation to a source of stimulation (as a light or a temperature or chemical gradient); *also* : a reflex reaction involving such movement — compare TROPISM [Greek, "arrangement", from *tassein* "to arrange"]

taxi stand *n* : a place where taxis may park awaiting hire

tax•on \ˈtak-ˌsän\ *n, pl* **taxa** \-sə\ *also* **tax•ons** : a taxonomic group or entity; *also* : its name in a formal system of nomenclature [back-formation from *taxonomy*]

tax•on•o•my \tak-ˈsän-ə-mē\ *n* **1** : the study of scientific classification : SYSTEMATICS **2 a** : CLASSIFICATION 2a(1) **b** : orderly classification of plants and animals according to their presumed natural relationships [French *taxonomie*, from Greek *taxis* "arrangement" + *nemein* "to control, distribute"] — **tax•o•nom•ic** \ˌtak-sə-ˈnäm-ik\ *adj* — **tax•o•nom•i•cal•ly** \-ˈnäm-i-kə-lē, -klē\ *adv* — **tax•on•o•mist** \tak-ˈsän-ə-məst\ *n*

tax•pay•er \ˈtak-ˌspā-ər\ *n* : one that pays or is subject to a tax

tax•us \ˈtak-səs\ *n, pl* **tax•us** \-səs\ : YEW 1a [Latin]

TB \tē-ˈbē, ˈtē-\ *n* : TUBERCULOSIS [*TB* (abbreviation for *tubercle bacillus*)]

T-bone \ˈtē-ˌbōn\ *n* : a small beefsteak from behind the ribs containing a T-shaped bone and a small piece of tenderloin

tea \ˈtē\ *n* **1 a** : a shrub related to the camellia that has lance-shaped leaves and fragrant white flowers and is grown mainly in China, Japan, India, and Ceylon **b** : the leaves and leaf buds of this plant prepared for use in beverages usually by immediate curing by heat or by such curing following a period of fermentation **2** : an aromatic beverage prepared from tea leaves by steeping them in boiling water **3** : any of various plants used like tea; *also* : an infusion from their leaves used medicinally or as a beverage **4 a** : a late afternoon serving of tea and a light meal **b** : a party or reception at which tea is served **5** *slang* : MARIJUANA 2 [Chinese (Amoy dialect) *t'e*]

tea 1a

tea bag *n* : a cloth or filter-paper bag holding enough tea for an individual serving

tea ball *n* : a perforated metal ball that holds tea leaves and is used in brewing tea in a pot or cup

tea•ber•ry \ˈtē-ˌber-ē\ *n* : CHECKERBERRY [from the use of its leaves as a substitute for tea]

tea biscuit *n, British* : CRACKER 2, COOKIE

teach \'tēch\ *vb* **taught** \'tȯt\; **teach•ing** **1 a :** to cause to know or understand ⟨*taught* us German⟩ **b :** to assist in learning how to do something : show how ⟨*teach* a child to read⟩ **2 :** to guide the studies of : INSTRUCT ⟨*teach* a class⟩ **3 :** to give lessons in : instruct pupils in ⟨*teach* music⟩ **4 :** to be or work as a teacher ⟨was *teaching* in Chicago⟩ **5 :** to cause to learn : cause to know the consequences of an action ⟨*taught* by experience⟩ [Old English *tǣcan*]
• **syn** INSTRUCT, EDUCATE, TRAIN: TEACH applies to any manner of imparting information or skill so that others may learn; INSTRUCT suggests methodical or formal teaching ⟨*instructed* them in swimming⟩ EDUCATE suggests providing formal schooling for fostering mental, moral, and physical growth and maturity and usually stresses book learning; TRAIN stresses the end in view and usually implies practice and drill as the means to that end ⟨*train* an apprentice in a trade⟩ ⟨toilet-*train* a young child⟩
syn see in addition LEARN

teach•able \'tē-chə-bəl\ *adj* **1 :** capable of being taught; *esp* **:** apt and willing to learn **2 :** well adapted for use in teaching ⟨a *teachable* textbook⟩ — **teach•abil•i•ty** \ˌtē-chə-'bil-ət-ē\ *n*

teach•er \'tē-chər\ *n* **:** one that teaches; *esp* **:** one whose occupation is to instruct

teachers college *n* **:** a college for the training of teachers usually offering a full 4-year course and granting a bachelor's degree

teach–in \'tē-ˌchin\ *n* **:** a get-together especially of college students and faculty for discussion especially of a controversial public issue

teach•ing *n* **1 :** the act, practice, or profession of a teacher **2 :** something taught; *esp* **:** DOCTRINE — **teaching** *adj*

teaching aid *n* **:** a device (as a record player, map, or picture) used by a teacher to supplement classroom instruction

teaching machine *n* **:** any of various mechanical devices that present programmed instruction and are operated by the student

tea•cup \'tē-ˌkəp\ *n* **:** a cup usually holding less than 250 milliliters that is used with a saucer for hot beverages — **tea•cup•ful** \'tē-ˌkəp-ˌfu̇l\ *n*

tea dance *n* **:** a dance held in the late afternoon

tea•house \'tē-ˌhau̇s\ *n* **:** a public house or restaurant where tea and light refreshments are sold

teak \'tēk\ *n* **:** a tall East Indian timber tree of the vervain family; *also* **:** its hard durable yellowish brown wood [Portuguese *teca,* of Dravidian origin]

tea•ket•tle \'tē-ˌket-l\ *n* **:** a covered kettle with a handle and spout for boiling water

teak•wood \'tē-ˌkwu̇d\ *n* **:** TEAK

teal \'tēl\ *n, pl* **teal** *or* **teals :** any of several small short-necked ducks of Europe and America [Middle English *tele*]

[1]**team** \'tēm\ *n* **1 :** a group of animals: as **a :** two or more draft animals harnessed to the same vehicle or implement; *also* **:** one or more animals with harness and attached vehicle **b :** a brood especially of young pigs or ducks **c :** a matched group of animals for exhibition **2 :** a number of persons associated together in work or activity: as **a :** a group on one side (as in football or a debate) **b :** CREW 2, GANG [Old English *tēam* "group of draft animals"]

[2]**team** *vb* **1 :** to yoke or join in a team **2 :** to haul with or drive a team **3 :** to form a team ⟨*team* up together⟩

team handball *n* **:** a game developed from soccer which is played between two teams of seven players and in which the ball is thrown, caught, and dribbled with the hands

team•mate \'tēm-ˌmāt\ *n* **:** a fellow member of a team

team•ster \'tēm-stər, 'tēmp-\ *n* **:** one who drives a team or truck especially as an occupation

team•work \'tēm-ˌwərk\ *n* **:** the work or activity of a number of persons acting in close association as members of a unit ⟨*teamwork* won the game⟩

tea•pot \'tē-ˌpät\ *n* **:** a vessel with a spout for brewing and serving tea

[1]**tear** \'tiər\ *n* **1 :** a drop of the salty liquid that keeps the eye and the inner eyelids moist **2** *pl* **:** an act of crying or grieving ⟨burst into *tears*⟩ **3 :** a transparent drop of fluid or hardened fluid matter (as resin) [Old English *tæhher, tēar*] — **teary** \'tiər-ē\ *adj*

[2]**tear** *vi* **:** to shed tears

[3]**tear** \'taər, 'teər\ *vb* **tore** \'tōər, 'tȯər\; **torn** \'tōrn, 'tȯrn\; **tear•ing** **1 a :** to separate or pull apart by force : REND **b :** LACERATE ⟨*tear* the skin⟩ **2 :** to divide or disrupt by the pull of contrary forces ⟨a mind *torn* by doubts⟩ **3 :** to remove by force ⟨children *torn* from their families⟩ **4 :** to cause or make by force or violent means ⟨*tore* a hole in the wall⟩ **5 :** to move or act with violence, haste, or force ⟨*tore* down the street⟩ [Old English *teran*] — **tear•er** *n*

[4]**tear** \'taər, 'teər\ *n* **1 a :** the act of tearing **b :** damage from being torn; *esp* **:** a torn place **2 a :** a hurried pace : HURRY **b :** SPREE ⟨go on a *tear*⟩

tear down *vt* **1 a :** to cause to decompose or disintegrate : DESTROY **b :** VILIFY 2, DENIGRATE **2 :** to take apart : DISASSEMBLE

tear•drop \'tiər-ˌdräp\ *n* **1 :** [1]TEAR 1 **2 :** something (as a pendent gem) shaped like a dropping tear

tear•ful \'tiər-fəl\ *adj* **:** flowing with, accompanied by, or causing tears — **tear•ful•ly** \-fə-lē\ *adv* — **tear•ful•ness** *n*

tear gas *n* **:** a solid, liquid, or gaseous substance that on dispersion in the atmosphere blinds the eyes with tears — **tear•gas** \'tiər-ˌgas\ *vt*

tear•jerk•er \'tiər-ˌjər-kər\ *n* **:** an extravagantly pathetic story, play, film, or broadcast — **tear•jerk•ing** \-king\ *adj*

tea•room \'tē-ˌrüm, -ˌru̇m\ *n* **:** a small restaurant serving light meals

tea rose *n* **:** any of numerous hybrid garden bush roses descended chiefly from a Chinese rose and valued especially for their abundant large usually tea-scented blossoms

tear•stain \'tiər-ˌstān\ *n* **:** a spot or streak left by tears — **tear-stained** \-ˌstānd\ *adj*

[1]**tease** \'tēz\ *vt* **1 a :** to disentangle and lay parallel by combing or carding ⟨*tease* wool⟩ **b :** TEASEL **2 a :** to annoy persistently : PESTER **b :** TANTALIZE [Old English *tǣsan*] — **teas•er** *n*

[2]**tease** *n* **1 :** the act of teasing : the state of being teased **2 :** one that teases

[1]**tea•sel** *or* **tea•zel** *or* **tea•zle** \'tē-zəl\ *n* **1 a :** an Old World prickly herb with flower heads that are covered with stiff hooked bracts — called also *fuller's teasel* **b :** a plant related to the teasel **2 a :** a dried flower head of the fuller's teasel used to raise a nap on woolen cloth **b :** a wire substitute for the fuller's teasel [Old English *tǣsel*]

[1]teasel 1a

[2]**teasel** *vt* **tea•seled** *or* **tea•selled**; **tea•sel•ing** *or* **tea•sel•ling** \'tēz-ling, -ə-ling\ **:** to raise a nap on (cloth) with teasels

tea•spoon \'tē-ˌspün, -'spün\ *n* **1 :** a small spoon used especially for eating soft foods and stirring beverages **2 :** TEASPOONFUL

tea•spoon•ful \-ˌfu̇l\ *n, pl* **-spoon•fuls** \-ˌfu̇lz\ *or* **-spoons•ful** \-ˌspünz-ˌfu̇l, -'spünz-\ **1 :** as much as a teaspoon can hold **2 :** a unit of measure used especially in cookery equal to 1⅓ fluidrams (about 4.9 milliliters) or one third of a tablespoonful

teat \'tit, 'tēt\ *n* **1 :** the protuberance through which milk is drawn from an udder or breast : NIPPLE **2 :** a small projection (as on a mechanical part) [Old French *tete,* of Germanic origin] — **teat•ed** \-əd\ *adj*

tea time \'tē-ˌtīm\ *n* **:** the customary time for tea : late afternoon or early evening

tea wagon *n* **:** a small table on wheels used in serving tea and light refreshments

tech•ne•tium \tek-'nē-shē-əm, -shəm\ *n* **:** a metallic chemical element obtained by bombarding molybdenum and in the fission of uranium — **syn** see ELEMENT table [New Latin, from Greek *technētos,* derived from *technē* "art"]

tech•nic \'tek-nik, *for 1 also* tek-'nēk\ *n* **1 :** TECHNIQUE 1 **2** *pl* **:** TECHNOLOGY 1a

tech•ni•cal \'tek-ni-kəl\ *adj* **1 a :** having special usually practical knowledge especially of a mechanical or scientific subject ⟨*technical* experts⟩ **b :** marked by or characteristic of special-

\ə\ **abut**	\au̇\ **out**	\i\ **tip**	\ȯ\ **saw**	\u̇\ **foot**
\ər\ **further**	\ch\ **chin**	\ī\ **life**	\ȯi\ **coin**	\y\ **yet**
\a\ **mat**	\e\ **pet**	\j\ **job**	\th\ **thin**	\yü\ **few**
\ā\ **take**	\ē\ **easy**	\ng\ **sing**	\t͟h\ **this**	\yu̇\ **cure**
\ä\ **cot, cart**	\g\ **go**	\ō\ **bone**	\ü\ **food**	\zh\ **vision**

ization ⟨a *technical* language⟩ **2 :** of or relating to a particular subject; *esp* **:** of or relating to a practical subject organized on scientific principles ⟨*technical* training⟩ **3 :** existing by application of laws or rules **4 :** of or relating to technique ⟨a dancer with great *technical* virtuosity⟩ **5 :** of, relating to, or produced by commercial processes ⟨*technical* sulfuric acid⟩ **[**Greek *technikos* "of art, skillful", from *technē* "art, skill"**]** — **tech•ni•cal•ly** \-kə-lē, -klē\ *adv*

technical foul *n* **:** a foul that is less serious than a personal foul (as in lacrosse) or that involves unsportsmanlike conduct (as in basketball)

tech•ni•cal•i•ty \ˌtek-nə-ˈkal-ət-ē\ *n, pl* **-ties 1 :** the quality or state of being technical **2 :** something technical; *esp* **:** a detail meaningful only to a specialist

technical knockout *n* **:** the termination of a boxing match when one boxer is unable or is declared by the referee to be unable to continue

technical sergeant *n* **:** an enlisted rank in the Air Force above staff sergeant and below master sergeant

tech•ni•cian \tek-ˈnish-ən\ *n* **:** a specialist in the technical details or in the technique of a subject, art, or occupation

tech•nique \tek-ˈnēk\ *n* **1 :** the way in which technical details are treated (as by a writer) or basic physical movements are used (as by a dancer); *also* **:** ability in such treatment or use ⟨faultless piano *technique*⟩ **2 a :** technical methods (as in scientific research) ⟨laboratory *technique*⟩ **b :** a method of accomplishing a desired aim ⟨a *technique* for handling complaints⟩ **[**French, from *technique* "technical", from Greek *technikos***]**

tech•noc•ra•cy \tek-ˈnäk-rə-sē\ *n* **:** management of society by technical experts — **tech•no•crat** \ˈtek-nə-ˌkrat\ *n*

tech•no•log•i•cal \ˌtek-nə-ˈläj-i-kəl\ *or* **tech•no•log•ic** \-ˈläj-ik\ *adj* **:** of, relating to, or characterized or caused by technology ⟨*technological* advance⟩ — **tech•no•log•i•cal•ly** \-ˈläj-i-kə-lē, -klē\ *adv*

tech•nol•o•gy \tek-ˈnäl-ə-jē\ *n, pl* **-gies 1 a :** applied science **b :** a technical method of achieving a practical purpose **2 :** the means employed to provide objects for human sustenance and comfort **[**Greek *technologia* "systematic treatment of an art", from *technē* "art" + *-logia* "-logy"**]** — **tech•nol•o•gist** \-jəst\ *n*

ted•dy bear \ˈted-ē-\ *n* **:** a stuffed toy bear **[***Teddy*, nickname of President Theodore Roosevelt; from a cartoon showing him sparing the life of a bear cub while hunting**]**

Te Deum \tā-ˈdā-əm, tē-ˈdē-\ *n, pl* **Te Deums :** a hymn of praise to God **[**Late Latin *Te Deum laudamus* "Thee, God, we praise"**]**

te•dious \ˈtēd-ē-əs, ˈtē-jəs\ *adj* **:** tiresome because of length or dullness **:** BORING — **te•dious•ly** *adv* — **te•dious•ness** *n*

te•di•um \ˈtēd-ē-əm\ *n* **:** the quality or state of being tedious **:** TEDIOUSNESS, BOREDOM **[**Latin *taedium* "disgust, irksomeness", from *taedēre* "to disgust, weary"**]**

tee \ˈtē\ *n* **:** the area from which a golf ball is struck in starting play on a hole; *also* **:** a tiny mound or a small peg with concave top on which the ball is set to be struck **[**origin unknown**]**

teem \ˈtēm\ *vi* **1 :** to become filled to overflowing **:** ABOUND ⟨lakes *teeming* with fish⟩ **2 :** to be present in large quantity **[**Old English *tīeman*, *tǣman* "to bring forth, give birth to"**]**

teen \ˈtēn\ *adj* **:** TEENAGE

teen•age \ˈtē-ˌnāj\ *or* **teen•aged** \ˈtē-ˌnājd\ *adj* **:** of, being, or relating to people in their teens

teen•ag•er \-ˌnā-jər\ *n* **:** a teenage person

teens \ˈtēnz\ *n pl* **1 :** the numbers 13 through 19; *esp* **:** the years 13 through 19 in a lifetime or century **2 :** teenage people **[***-teen* (as in *thirteen*)**]**

tee•ny \ˈtē-nē\ *adj* **tee•ni•er; -est :** TINY **[**by alteration**]**

tee off *vi* **1 :** to drive a golf ball from a tee at the beginning of play on a hole **2 :** BEGIN 1, START

tee•pee *variant of* TEPEE

tee shirt *variant of* T-SHIRT

tee•ter \ˈtēt-ər\ *vi* **1 a :** to move unsteadily **:** WOBBLE **b :** WAVER 1, VACILLATE **2 :** SEESAW 1b **[**Middle English *titeren***]** — **teeter** *n*

tee•ter•board \-ˌbōrd, -ˌbȯrd\ *n* **1 :** SEESAW 2b **2 :** a board placed on a raised support in such a way that a person standing on one end of the board is thrown into the air if another person jumps on the opposite end

tee•ter–tot•ter \ˈtēt-ər-ˌtät-ər\ *n* **:** SEESAW 2b

teeth *pl of* TOOTH

teethe \ˈtēth\ *vi* **teethed; teeth•ing :** to cut one's teeth **:** grow teeth

teeth•ridge \ˈtē-ˌthrij\ *n* **:** the inner surface of the gums of the upper front teeth

tee•to•tal•er *or* **tee•to•tal•ler** \ˈtē-ˈtōt-l-ər\ *n* **:** a person who practices or advocates teetotalism **[***total* + *total* (abstinence)**]**

tee•to•tal•ism \-l-ˌiz-əm\ *n* **:** the principle or practice of complete abstinence from drinking alcoholic beverages

Tef•lon \ˈtef-ˌlän\ *trademark* — used for synthetic fluorine-containing resins used especially for molded articles and for nonstick coatings (as for frying pans)

tek•tite \ˈtek-ˌtīt\ *n* **:** a glassy body of probably meteoric origin and of rounded but indefinite shape **[**Greek *tēktos* "molten", from *tēkein* "to melt"**]**

tele- *or* **tel-** *combining form* **1 :** at a distance ⟨*tele*communication⟩ ⟨*tele*pathy⟩ **2 a :** telegraph ⟨*tele*typewriter⟩ **b :** television ⟨*tele*course⟩ **[**Greek *tēle* "far off"**]**

tele•cam•era \ˈtel-i-ˌkam-rə, -ə-rə\ *n* **:** a television camera

tele•cast \ˈtel-i-ˌkast\ *vb* **telecast** *also* **tele•cast•ed; tele•cast•ing [***tele-* + broad*cast***]** **:** to broadcast by television — **telecast** *n* — **tele•cast•er** *n*

tele•com•mu•ni•ca•tion \ˌtel-i-kə-ˌmyü-nə-ˈkā-shən\ *n* **1 :** communication at a distance (as by cable, radio, telegraph, telephone, or television) **2 :** a science that deals with telecommunication

tele•course \ˈtel-i-ˌkōrs, -ˌkȯrs\ *n* **:** a course of study conducted over television

tele•ge•nic \ˌtel-ə-ˈjen-ik, -ˈjēn-\ *adj* **:** suitable for television broadcast — **tele•ge•ni•cal•ly** \-i-kə-lē, -klē\ *adv*

tele•gram \ˈtel-ə-ˌgram, *South also* -grəm\ *n* **:** a message sent by telegraph

[1]tele•graph \-ˌgraf\ *n* **:** an apparatus for communication at a distance by coded signals; *esp* **:** an apparatus, system, or process for communication at a distance by electric transmission of such signals over wire — **tele•graph•ic** \ˌtel-ə-ˈgraf-ik\ *adj* — **tele•graph•i•cal•ly** \-ˈgraf-i-kə-lē, -klē\ *adv*

[2]telegraph *vt* **1 a :** to send by or as if by telegraph **b :** to send a telegram to **c :** to send (as flowers or money) by means of a telegraphic order **2 :** to make known by signs especially unknowingly and in advance ⟨*telegraph* a punch⟩ — **te•leg•ra•pher** \tə-ˈleg-rə-fər\ *n* — **te•leg•ra•phist** \-fəst\ *n*

te•leg•ra•phy \tə-ˈleg-rə-fē\ *n* **:** the use or operation of a telegraph apparatus or system

tele•ki•ne•sis \ˌtel-i-kə-ˈnē-səs, -kī-\ *n* **:** the apparent production of motion in objects (as by a spiritualistic medium) without physical contact or other explainable means **[***tele-* + Greek *kinēsis* "motion", from *kinein* "to move"**]**

tele•me•ter \ˈtel-ə-ˌmēt-ər\ *n* **:** an electrical apparatus for measuring something (as pressure, speed, or temperature), transmitting the result especially by radio to a distant station, and there indicating the measurement — **telemeter** *vb* — **tele•met•ric** \ˌtel-ə-ˈme-trik\ *adj* — **tele•met•ri•cal•ly** \-tri-kə-lē, -klē\ *adv* — **te•lem•e•try** \tə-ˈlem-ə-trē\ *n*

te•le•ol•o•gist \ˌtel-ē-ˈäl-ə-jəst, ˌtē-lē-\ *n* **:** a specialist or believer in teleology

te•le•ol•o•gy \ˌtel-ē-ˈäl-ə-jē, ˌtē-lē-\ *n* **:** a doctrine that attributes a purpose to nature or that explains natural phenomena as directed toward a goal **[**Greek *telos* "end, purpose"**]** — **te•le•o•log•i•cal** \ˌtel-ē-ə-ˈläj-i-kəl, ˌtē-lē-\ *adj*

te•le•ost \ˈtel-ē-ˌäst, ˈtē-lē-\ *n* **:** any of a group (Teleostei or Teleostomi) of fishes comprising those with a bony rather than a cartilaginous skeleton **[**derived from Greek *teleios* "complete, perfect" (from *telos* "end") + *osteon* "bone"**]** — **teleost** *adj* — **te•le•os•te•an** \ˌtel-ē-ˈäs-tē-ən, ˌtē-lē-\ *adj or n*

te•lep•a•thy \tə-ˈlep-ə-thē\ *n* **:** apparent communication from one mind to another by means other than the known physical senses — **tele•path** \ˈtel-ə-ˌpath\ *n* — **tele•path•ic** \ˌtel-ə-ˈpath-ik\ *adj* — **tele•path•i•cal•ly** \-ˈpath-i-kə-lē, -klē\ *adv*

[1]tele•phone \ˈtel-ə-ˌfōn\ *n* **:** an instrument for reproducing sounds at a distance; *esp* **:** one in which sound is converted into electrical impulses for transmission by wire or radio

[2]telephone *vb* **1 :** to communicate by telephone **2 :** to send by telephone **3 :** to speak to by telephone — **tele•phon•er** *n*

tele•phon•ic \ˌtel-ə-ˈfän-ik\ *adj* **1 :** conveying sound to a distance **2 :** of, relating to, or conveyed by telephone

te•leph•o•ny \tə-ˈlef-ə-nē *also* ˈtel-ə-ˌfō-\ *n* **:** the use or operation of an apparatus for transmission of sounds between widely removed points with or without connecting wires

1tele·pho·to \ˌtel-ə-ˈfōt-ō\ *adj* : TELEPHOTOGRAPHIC; *esp* : being a camera lens designed to give a large image of a distant object
2telephoto *n* : a telephoto lens
Telephoto *trademark* — used for an apparatus for transmitting photographs electrically or for a photograph so transmitted
tele·pho·tog·ra·phy \ˌtel-ə-fə-ˈtäg-rə-fē\ *n* **1** : FACSIMILE 2 **2** : the photography of distant objects (as by a camera provided with a telephoto lens) — **tele·pho·to·graph·ic** \-ˌfōt-ə-ˈgraf-ik\ *adj*
tele·play \ˈtel-ə-ˌplā\ *n* : a play written for television
tele·print·er \ˈtel-ə-ˌprint-ər\ *n* : TELETYPEWRITER
Tele·Promp·Ter \ˈtel-ə-ˌpräm-tər, -ˌprämp-\ *trademark* — used for a device for presenting a script in front of an actor or speaker on television
1tele·scope \ˈtel-ə-ˌskōp\ *n* **1** : a usually tubular optical instrument for viewing distant objects by means of the refraction of light rays through a lens or the reflection of light rays by a concave mirror — compare REFLECTOR, REFRACTOR **2** : any of various tubular magnifying optical instruments **3** : RADIO TELESCOPE

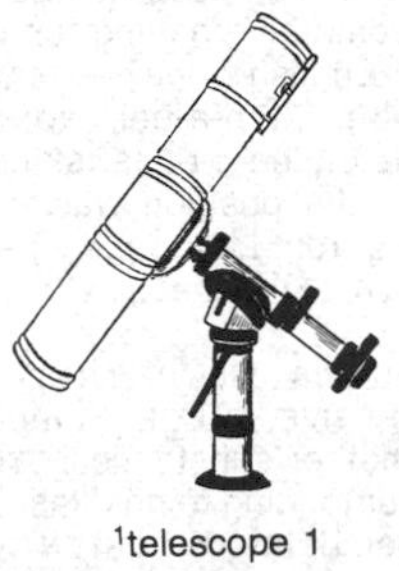
1telescope 1

2telescope *vb* **1** : to slide or pass or cause to slide or pass one within another like the cylindrical sections of a hand telescope **2** : CONDENSE 1, COMPRESS
tele·scop·ic \ˌtel-ə-ˈskäp-ik\ *adj* **1 a** : of, with, or relating to a telescope **b** : suitable for seeing or magnifying distant objects **2** : seen or discoverable only by a telescope ⟨*telescopic* stars⟩ **3** : able to discern objects at a distance **4** : having parts that telescope — **tele·scop·i·cal·ly** \-ˈskäp-i-kə-lē, -klē\ *adv*
tele·thon \ˈtel-ə-ˌthän\ *n* : a long television program usually to solicit funds (as for a charity) [*tele-* + *-thon* (as in *marathon*)]
Tele·type \ˈtel-ə-ˌtīp\ *trademark* — used for a teletypewriter
tele·type·writ·er \ˌtel-ə-ˈtīp-ˌrīt-ər\ *n* : a printing device resembling a typewriter that is used to send and receive telephonic signals
tele·typ·ist \ˈtel-ə-ˌtī-pəst\ *n* : one that operates a teletypewriter
tele·view \ˈtel-ə-ˌvyü\ *vi* : to observe or watch by means of a television receiver — **tele·view·er** *n*
tele·vise \ˈtel-ə-ˌvīz\ *vt* : to pick up and usually broadcast (as a sports event) by television [back-formation from *television*]
tele·vi·sion \ˈtel-ə-ˌvizh-ən\ *n* **1** : an electronic system of transmitting images of fixed or moving objects together with sound over a wire or through space by apparatus that converts light and sound into electrical waves and reconverts them into visible light rays and audible sound **2** : a television receiving set **3 a** : the television broadcasting industry **b** : television as a medium of communication
television tube *n* : PICTURE TUBE
te·lio·spore \ˈtē-lē-ə-ˌspōr, -ˌspȯr\ *n* : a thick-walled spore forming the final stage in the life cycle of a rust fungus and giving rise to a basidium [Greek *teleios* "complete" (from *telos* "end") + English *spore*]
tell \ˈtel\ *vb* **told** \ˈtōld\; **tell·ing** **1** : COUNT, ENUMERATE ⟨all *told*, there were 30 students⟩ **2 a** : to relate in detail : NARRATE ⟨*tell* a story⟩ **b** : to make a narration ⟨*told* about our trip⟩ **c** : SAY, UTTER ⟨*tell* a lie⟩ **3 a** : to make known : REVEAL ⟨*tell* a secret⟩ **b** : to express in words ⟨can't *tell* you how pleased we are⟩ **4** : to report to : INFORM **5** : ORDER, DIRECT ⟨*told* me to wait⟩ **6** : to ascertain by observing : find out ⟨can *tell* you're honest⟩ **7** : to act as a talebearer ⟨*tell* on a cheater⟩ **8** : to have a marked effect ⟨the pressure *told* on them⟩ **9** : to serve as evidence ⟨smiles *telling* of success⟩ [Old English *tellan*]
tell·er \ˈtel-ər\ *n* **1** : one that relates or communicates ⟨a *teller* of tales⟩ **2** : a person appointed to count votes **3** : a bank employee who receives and pays out money
tell·ing \ˈtel-iŋ\ *adj* : producing a marked effect ⟨a *telling* argument⟩ ⟨a *telling* blow⟩ — **tell·ing·ly** \-iŋ-lē\ *adv*
tell off *vt* **1 a** : to number and set apart **b** : to assign to a special duty **2** : SCOLD 2, TONGUE-LASH
tell·tale \ˈtel-ˌtāl\ *n* **1 a** : GOSSIP 1, TALEBEARER **b** : an outward sign : INDICATION **2 a** : a device for indicating or recording something **b** : a railroad warning device (as a row of long strips hanging over tracks near the approach to a low overhead bridge) — **telltale** *adj*
tel·lu·ride \ˈtel-yə-ˌrīd\ *n* : a binary compound of tellurium with another element or a radical
tel·lu·ri·um \tə-ˈlu̇r-ē-əm, te-\ *n* : a chemical element that resembles selenium and sulfur in properties and that occurs in crystalline form, in a dark amorphous form, or combined with metals — see ELEMENT table [New Latin, from Latin *tellur-, tellus* "earth"]
tel·ly \ˈtel-ē\ *n, pl* **tellys** *also* **tellies** *chiefly British* : TELEVISION
telo·phase \ˈtē-lə-ˌfāz, ˈtel-ə-\ *n* : the final stage of mitosis in which the spindle disappears and two new nuclei appear each with a set of chromosomes; *also* : a corresponding stage in meiosis [Greek *telos* "end"]
tel·son \ˈtel-sən\ *n* : the terminal segment of the body of an arthropod or segmented worm; *esp* : that of a crustacean forming the middle lobe of the tail [Greek, "end of a plowed field"]
tem·blor \ˈtem-blər, -ˌblȯr, -ˌblōr\ *n* : EARTHQUAKE [Spanish, literally, "trembling", from *temblar* "to tremble", from Medieval Latin *tremulare*]
tem·er·ar·i·ous \ˌtem-ə-ˈrer-ē-əs, -ˈrar-\ *adj* : marked by temerity : rashly or presumptuously daring [Latin *temerarius*, from *temere* "at random, rashly"] — **tem·er·ar·i·ous·ly** *adv*
te·mer·i·ty \tə-ˈmer-ət-ē\ *n, pl* **-ties** : unreasonable or foolhardy contempt of danger or opposition : RECKLESSNESS [Latin *temeritas*, from *temere* "at random, rashly"]
• **syn** AUDACITY: TEMERITY suggests boldness arising from reckless or heedless contempt of danger ⟨had the *temerity* to challenge the dictatorial order⟩ AUDACITY implies a disregard of restraints imposed by prudence or convention ⟨had the *audacity* to come to the party uninvited⟩
1tem·per \ˈtem-pər\ *vb* **tem·pered**; **tem·per·ing** \ˈtem-pə-riŋ, -priŋ\ **1** : MODERATE, SOFTEN ⟨*temper* justice with mercy⟩ **2** : to control by reducing : SUBDUE ⟨*temper* one's anger⟩ **3** : to bring to the desired consistency or texture ⟨*temper* modeling clay⟩ **4** : to bring (as steel) to the desired hardness by heating and cooling **5** : to be or become tempered [Old English *temprian* and Old French *temprer*, both from Latin *temperare* "to moderate, mix, temper"] — **tem·per·able** \-pə-rə-bəl, -prə-bəl\ *adj*
2temper *n* **1** : characteristic tone : TREND, TENDENCY ⟨the *temper* of the times⟩ **2** : high quality of mind or spirit : COURAGE, METTLE **3** : the state of a substance with respect to certain desired qualities (as hardness, elasticity, or workability) ⟨the *temper* of a knife blade⟩ **4 a** : a characteristic cast of mind or state of feeling : DISPOSITION **b** : calmness of mind : COMPOSURE ⟨lost my *temper*⟩ **c** : state of feeling or frame of mind at a particular time usually dominated by a single strong emotion **d** : a state of anger **e** : a tendency to anger ⟨has a hot *temper*⟩ **syn** see MOOD
tem·pera \ˈtem-pə-rə\ *n* : a process of painting in which an albuminous or colloidal medium (as egg yolk) is employed as a vehicle instead of oil [Italian *tempera*, literally, "temper"]
tem·per·a·ment \ˈtem-pə-rə-mənt, -prə-mənt\ *n* **1** : characteristic mode of emotional response ⟨is of a nervous *temperament*⟩ **2** : excessive sensitiveness or irritability [Latin *temperamentum* "mixture, makeup, constitution", from *temperare* "to mix, temper"]
tem·per·a·ment·tal \ˌtem-pə-rə-ˈment-l, -prə-ˈment-\ *adj* **1** : of, relating to, or arising from temperament ⟨*temperamental* peculiarities⟩ **2 a** : marked by extreme sensitivity and impulsive changes of mood ⟨a *temperamental* singer⟩ **b** : unpredictable in behavior or performance ⟨a *temperamental* car⟩ — **tem·per·a·men·tal·ly** \-l-ē\ *adv*
tem·per·ance \ˈtem-pə-rəns, -prəns, -pərns\ *n* **1** : moderation in action, thought, or feeling : RESTRAINT **2** : habitual moderation in the indulgence of the appetites or passions; *esp* : moderation in or abstinence from the use of intoxicating drink

\ə\ **abut**	\au̇\ **out**	\i\ **tip**	\ȯ\ **saw**	\u̇\ **foot**
\ər\ **further**	\ch\ **chin**	\ī\ **life**	\ȯi\ **coin**	\y\ **yet**
\a\ **mat**	\e\ **pet**	\j\ **job**	\th\ **thin**	\yü\ **few**
\ā\ **take**	\ē\ **easy**	\ŋ\ **sing**	\t͟h\ **this**	\yu̇\ **cure**
\ä\ **cot, cart**	\g\ **go**	\ō\ **bone**	\ü\ **food**	\zh\ **vision**

tem•per•ate \'tem-pə-rət, -prət\ *adj* **1** : marked by moderation: as **a** : not excessive or extreme **b** : moderate in satisfying one's needs or desires **c** : moderate in the use of liquor **d** : marked by self-control : RESTRAINED ⟨*temperate* speech⟩ **2** : having, found in, or associated with a moderate climate ⟨*temperate* heat⟩ **3** : existing as a prophage in infected cells and rarely causing lysis ⟨*temperate* bacteriophages⟩ **syn** see MODERATE — **tem•per•ate•ly** *adv* — **tem•per•ate•ness** *n*

temperate zone *n, often cap T & Z* : the area or region between the tropic of Cancer and the arctic circle or between the tropic of Capricorn and the antarctic circle

tem•per•a•ture \'tem-pər-ˌchu̇r, -pə-ˌchu̇r, -pə-rə-ˌchu̇r, -prə-ˌchu̇r, -chər\ *n* **1** : the degree of hotness or coldness of something (as air, water, or the body) as shown by a thermometer **2** : FEVER 1 ⟨has a *temperature*⟩

tem•pered \'tem-pərd\ *adj* **1** : made moderate ⟨stylishness *tempered* with good taste⟩ **2** : brought to the desired state (as of hardness, toughness, or flexibility) ⟨*tempered* steel⟩ ⟨*tempered* glass⟩ **3** : having a particular kind of temper — used in combination ⟨short-*tempered*⟩

tem•pest \'tem-pəst\ *n* **1** : an extensive violent wind; *esp* : one accompanied by rain, hail, or snow **2** : TUMULT 1, UPROAR [Old French *tempeste,* from Latin *tempestas* "season, weather, storm", from *tempus* "time"]

tem•pes•tu•ous \tem-'pes-chə-wəs, -'pesh-\ *adj* : STORMY 2, VIOLENT — **tem•pes•tu•ous•ly** *adv* — **tem•pes•tu•ous•ness** *n*

Tem•plar \'tem-plər\ *n* **1** : a knight of a religious military order established early in the 12th century in Jerusalem to protect pilgrims and Christ's burial place **2** : KNIGHT TEMPLAR 2 [Old French *templier,* from Medieval Latin *templarius,* from Latin *templum* "temple"]

tem•plate *or* **tem•plet** \'tem-plət\ *n* **1** : a gauge, pattern, or mold (as a thin plate or board) used as a guide to the form of a piece being made **2** : a molecule (as of RNA) in a biological system that carries the genetic code for another molecule [probably derived from French *temple,* a part of a loom]

[1]tem•ple \'tem-pəl\ *n* **1** : a building for worship: as **a** *often cap* : one of three successive national sanctuaries in ancient Jerusalem **b** : a building for Mormon sacred ordinances **c** : a synagogue of Reform or Conservative Judaism **2** : a local lodge of a fraternal order [Old English *tempel* and Old French *temple,* both from Latin *templum*] — **tem•pled** \-pəld\ *adj*

[2]temple *n* : the flattened space on each side of the forehead of man and some other mammals [Middle French, derived from Latin *tempora,* pl., "temples"]

tem•po \'tem-pō\ *n, pl* **tem•pi** \-pē\ *or* **tempos** **1** : the rate of speed of a musical piece or passage indicated by one of a series of directions (as largo, presto, or allegro) and often by an exact metronome marking **2** : rate of motion or activity : PACE [Italian, literally, "time", from Latin *tempus*]

[1]tem•po•ral \'tem-pə-rəl, -prəl\ *adj* **1** : of or relating to time as opposed to eternity : TEMPORARY **2 a** : of or relating to earthly life **b** : of or relating to nonreligious matters [Latin *temporalis,* from *tempor-, tempus* "time"] — **tem•po•ral•ly** \-ē\ *adv*

[2]temporal *adj* : of or relating to the temples or to the sides of the skull behind the orbits [Middle French, derived from Latin *tempora* "temples"] — **tem•po•ral•ly** \-ē\ *adv*

temporal bone *n* : a compound bone of the side of the human skull

tem•po•ral•i•ty \ˌtem-pə-'ral-ət-ē\ *n, pl* **-ties** **1 a** : civil or political as distinguished from spiritual or church power or authority **b** : church property or income — often used in pl. **2** : the quality or state of being temporal

tem•po•rary \'tem-pə-ˌrer-ē\ *adj* : lasting for a limited time [Latin *temporarius,* from *tempor-, tempus* "time"] — **tem•po•rar•i•ly** \ˌtem-pə-'rer-ə-lē\ *adv* — **tem•po•rar•i•ness** \'tem-pə-ˌrer-ē-nəs\ *n*

temporary duty *n* : temporary military service away from one's regular unit

tem•po•rize \'tem-pə-ˌrīz\ *vi* **1** : to act to suit the time or occasion : yield to current or dominant opinion : COMPROMISE **2** : to draw out negotiations so as to gain time : DELAY [Middle French *temporiser,* from Medieval Latin *temporizare* "to pass the time", from Latin *tempor-, tempus* "time"] — **tem•po•ri•za•tion** \ˌtem-pə-rə-'zā-shən\ *n* — **tem•po•riz•er** \'tem-pə-ˌrī-zər\ *n*

tempt \'temt, 'tempt\ *vt* **1** : to entice to do wrong by promising pleasure or gain **2 a** *obsolete* : to make trial of : TEST **b** : to try presumptuously : PROVOKE ⟨*tempted* fate by speeding⟩ **c** : to risk the dangers of **3 a** : to induce to do something : INCITE ⟨*tempt* one to folly⟩ **b** : to cause to be strongly inclined : almost move or persuade ⟨was *tempted* to call it quits⟩ [Old French *tempter, tenter,* from Latin *temptare, tentare* "to feel, try, tempt"] — **tempt•able** \'tem-tə-bəl, 'temp-\ *adj*

temp•ta•tion \tem-'tā-shən, temp-\ *n* **1** : the act of tempting : the state of being tempted especially to evil : ENTICEMENT **2** : something tempting

tempt•er \'tem-tər, 'temp-\ *n* : one that tempts

tempt•ing *adj* : that attracts strongly ⟨a *tempting* offer⟩ — **tempt•ing•ly** \'tem-ting-lē, 'temp-\ *adv*

tempt•ress \'tem-trəs, 'temp-\ *n* : a woman who tempts

ten \'ten\ *n* **1** : one more than nine; *also* : a symbol representing this — see NUMBER table **2** : the tenth in a set or series **3** : something having ten units or members **4** : a 10-dollar bill [Old English *tīene*] — **ten** *adj or pron*

ten•a•ble \'ten-ə-bəl\ *adj* : capable of being held, maintained, or defended : DEFENSIBLE ⟨a *tenable* argument⟩ ⟨retreated since the position was not *tenable*⟩ [French, from *tenir* "to hold", from Latin *tenēre*] — **ten•a•bil•i•ty** \ˌten-ə-'bil-ət-ē\ *n* — **ten•a•ble•ness** \'ten-ə-bəl-nəs\ *n* — **ten•a•bly** \-blē\ *adv*

te•na•cious \tə-'nā-shəs\ *adj* **1 a** : not easily pulled apart : COHESIVE, TOUGH ⟨a *tenacious* metal⟩ **b** : tending to adhere to another substance : STICKY ⟨*tenacious* burs⟩ **2 a** : holding fast or tending to hold fast : PERSISTENT, STUBBORN ⟨*tenacious* of their rights⟩ **b** : RETENTIVE ⟨a *tenacious* memory⟩ [Latin *tenac-, tenax* "tending to hold fast", from *tenēre* "to hold"] — **te•na•cious•ly** *adv* — **te•na•cious•ness** *n*

te•nac•i•ty \tə-'nas-ət-ē\ *n* : the quality or state of being tenacious

ten•an•cy \'ten-ən-sē\ *n, pl* **-cies** **1** : the temporary possession or occupancy of another's property; *also* : the period of such occupancy or possession **2** : the ownership of property

[1]ten•ant \'ten-ənt\ *n* **1 a** : the owner or possessor of real estate or sometimes personal property **b** : one who occupies or temporarily possesses property of another; *esp* : one who rents or leases (as a house) from a landlord **2** : OCCUPANT, DWELLER [Middle French, from *tenir* "to hold"]

[2]tenant *vt* : to hold or occupy as a tenant : INHABIT — **ten•ant•able** \-ən-tə-bəl\ *adj*

tenant farmer *n* : a farmer who works land owned by another and pays rent either in cash or in shares of produce

ten•ant•less \'ten-ənt-ləs\ *adj* : having no tenants

ten•ant•ry \'ten-ən-trē\ *n, pl* **-ries** **1** : the condition of being a tenant **2** : a group of tenants

ten–cent store \'ten-'sent-\ *n* : FIVE-AND-TEN

tench \'tench\ *n, pl* **tench** *or* **tench•es** : a Eurasian freshwater fish related to the dace and noted for its ability to survive outside water [Middle French *tenche,* from Late Latin *tinca*]

Ten Commandments *n pl* : the commandments of God given to Moses on Mount Sinai

[1]tend \'tend\ *vb* **1** : to pay attention ⟨*tend* strictly to business⟩ **2** : to take care of : CULTIVATE ⟨*tend* a garden⟩ **3** : to have charge of as caretaker or overseer **4** : to manage the operation of ⟨*tend* a machine⟩ [Middle English *tenden,* short for *attenden* "to attend"]

[2]tend *vi* **1** : to move or turn in a certain direction : LEAD ⟨the road *tends* to the right⟩ **2** : to have a tendency : to be likely ⟨people who *tend* to slouch⟩ [Middle French *tendre* "to stretch, tend", from Latin *tendere*]

ten•dance \'ten-dəns\ *n* : watchful care : ATTENDANCE

ten•den•cy \'ten-dən-sē\ *n, pl* **-cies** **1 a** : direction or approach toward a place, object, effect, or limit **b** : a proneness to a particular kind of thought or action : PROPENSITY **2** : the purposeful trend of something written or said : AIM [Medieval Latin *tendentia,* from Latin *tendere* "to stretch, tend"]

• **syn** TENDENCY, TREND, DRIFT, TENOR mean movement in a particular direction. TENDENCY implies an ever-present inclination or force sending one in a particular direction ⟨had a *tendency* to exaggerate⟩ ⟨counteracts the *tendency* of engines to knock⟩ TREND implies a general direction maintained in spite of irregularities and more often subject to change than TENDENCY ⟨*trends* in current fiction⟩ DRIFT suggests a tendency determined by external influences ⟨the present *drift* toward centralization⟩ or it may apply to an underlying trend of a discourse ⟨lost the *drift* of the conversation⟩ TENOR stresses a clearly perceptible direction and a continuous, undeviating course.

ten•den•tious *also* **ten•den•cious** \ten-'den-chəs\ *adj* : marked by a tendency in favor of a particular point of view : BIASED — **ten•den•tious•ly** *adv* — **ten•den•tious•ness** *n*

¹ten•der \'ten-dər\ *adj* **1 a** : having a soft or yielding texture : easily broken, cut, or damaged : FRAGILE **b** : easily chewed : SUCCULENT **2 a** : physically weak : DELICATE **b** : IMMATURE, YOUNG ⟨children of *tender* years⟩ **c** : incapable of resisting cold ⟨*tender* shrubs⟩ **3** : FOND, LOVING ⟨a *tender* look⟩ **4 a** : showing care : CONSIDERATE ⟨*tender* regard⟩ **b** : highly susceptible to impressions or emotions : IMPRESSIONABLE ⟨a *tender* conscience⟩ **5 a** : appropriate or conducive to a delicate or sensitive constitution or character : GENTLE, MILD ⟨*tender* breeding⟩ ⟨*tender* irony⟩ **b** : delicate or soft in quality or tone **6 a** : sensitive to touch : easily hurt ⟨a *tender* scar⟩ **b** : sensitive to injury or insult : TOUCHY ⟨*tender* pride⟩ **c** : demanding careful and sensitive handling : TICKLISH ⟨a *tender* situation⟩ [Old French *tendre,* Latin *tener*] — **ten•der•ly** *adv* — **ten•der•ness** *n*

²tend•er \'ten-dər\ *n* : one that tends or takes care: as **a** : a ship employed to serve other ships (as by supplying provisions) **b** : a boat that carries passengers or freight between shore and a larger ship **c** : a vehicle attached to a locomotive for carrying a supply of fuel and water

³ten•der *n* **1** : an offer of money in payment of a debt **2** : an offer or proposal made for acceptance; *esp* : an offer of a bid for a contract **3** : something that may by law be offered in payment; *esp* : MONEY [Middle French *tendre* "to stretch, stretch out, offer, tend"]

⁴ten•der *vt* **ten•dered**; **ten•der•ing** \-də-ring, -dring\ **1** : to make a tender of ⟨*tender* the amount of rent⟩ **2** : to present for acceptance : PROFFER ⟨*tendered* my resignation⟩

ten•der•foot \'ten-dər-,fu̇t\ *n, pl* **-feet** \-,fēt\ *also* **-foots** **1** : a person who is not hardened to a rough outdoor life; *esp* : a newcomer in a recent settlement (as on a frontier) **2** : an inexperienced beginner : NOVICE

ten•der•heart•ed \,ten-dər-'härt-əd\ *adj* : easily moved to love, pity, or sorrow : COMPASSIONATE — **ten•der•heart•ed•ly** *adv* — **ten•der•heart•ed•ness** *n*

ten•der•ize \'ten-də-,rīz\ *vt* : to make (meat) tender — **ten•der•iza•tion** \,ten-də-rə-'zā-shən\ *n* — **ten•der•iz•er** \'ten-də-,rī-zər\ *n*

ten•der•loin \'ten-dər-,lȯin\ *n* **1** : a strip of tender meat on each side of the backbone : a fillet of beef or pork **2** : a district of a city largely devoted to vice [sense 2 from such a district's making possible a luxurious diet for a corrupt police officer]

ten•di•nous \'ten-də-nəs\ *adj* **1** : of, relating to, or resembling a tendon **2** : consisting of tendons : SINEWY [New Latin *tendinosus,* from *tendin-, tendo* "tendon", from Medieval Latin *tendon-, tendo*]

ten•don \'ten-dən\ *n* : a tough cord or band of fibrous tissue connecting a muscle to some other part (as a bone) and transmitting the force exerted by the muscle [Medieval Latin *tendon-, tendo,* from Latin *tendere* "to stretch"]

tendon of Achilles \-ə-'kil-ēz\ : the strong tendon by which the large muscles of the lower leg are connected to the bone of the heel [from the story that Achilles was vulnerable only on the heel]

ten•dril \'ten-drəl\ *n* **1** : a leaf, stipule, or stem modified into a slender spirally coiling sensitive organ serving to attach a plant to its support **2** : something (as a ringlet of hair) that curls like a tendril [perhaps from Middle French *tendron,* alteration of *tendon,* literally, "tendon"] — **ten•driled** *or* **ten•drilled** \-drəld\ *adj* — **ten•dril•ous** \-drə-ləs\ *adj*

Ten•e•brae \'ten-ə-,brā, -,brī, -,brē\ *n sing or pl* : the office of matins and lauds for the three days before Easter commemorating the sufferings and death of Christ with a progressive extinguishing of candles [Medieval Latin, from Latin, "darkness"]

1080 *also* **ten–eighty** \te-'nāt-ē\ *n* : a poisonous substance used to kill rodents [from its laboratory serial number]

ten•e•ment \'ten-ə-mənt\ *n* **1 a** : a house used as a dwelling : RESIDENCE **b** : APARTMENT 1, FLAT **c** : TENEMENT HOUSE **2** : a dwelling place ⟨the soul's *tenement,* the body⟩ [Middle French, from Medieval Latin *tenementum,* from Latin *tenēre* "to hold"]

tenement house *n* : APARTMENT BUILDING; *esp* : one barely meeting minimum standards of sanitation, safety, and comfort and housing poorer families

ten•et \'ten-ət\ *n* : a principle, belief, or doctrine generally held to be true; *esp* : one held in common by members of an organization, group, or profession [Latin, "he holds", from *tenēre* "to hold"] **syn** see DOCTRINE

ten•fold \'ten-,fōld, -'fōld\ *adj* **1** : having 10 units or members **2** : of or equal to 1000 percent — **tenfold** *adv*

ten•nis \'ten-əs\ *n* : a game that is played with rackets and a light elastic ball by two players or pairs of players on a level court divided by a low net [Middle English *tenetz, tenys*]

tennis shoe *n* : a lightweight canvas or leather shoe with a pliable sole for wear when playing tennis

¹ten•on \'ten-ən\ *n* : a projecting part in a piece of material (as wood) for insertion into a mortise to make a joint [Old French, from *tenir* "to hold", from Latin *tenēre*]

²tenon *vt* **1** : to unite by a tenon **2** : to cut or fit for insertion in a mortise

¹ten•or \'ten-ər\ *n* **1** : the general drift of something spoken or written **2 a** : the voice part next to the lowest in a 4-part chorus — compare ALTO, BASS, SOPRANO **b** : the highest natural adult male voice **c** : a singer having such a voice **d** : an instrument playing a part between that of an alto and a bass **3** : a continuance in a course, movement or activity : TREND [Old French, from Latin *tenor* "uninterrupted course", from *tenēre* "to hold"] **syn** see TENDENCY

²tenor *adj* : of, relating to, or being the tenor in music

ten•pen•ny \,ten-,pen-ē\ *adj* : equal to, worth, or costing ten pennies

tenpenny nail *n* : a nail 3 inches (7.62 centimeters) long [from its original price per hundred]

ten•pin \'ten-,pin\ *n* **1** : a bottle-shaped bowling pin 15 inches (38.1 centimeters) high **2** *pl* : a bowling game using 10 tenpins and a large ball with each player allowed to bowl 2 balls in each of 10 frames

ten•pound•er \'ten-'pau̇n-dər\ *n* : LADYFISH

tens digit *n* : the numeral (as 5 in 456) occupying the tens place in a number expressed in the Arabic system of writing numbers

¹tense \'tens\ *n* **1** : a distinction of form in a verb to express distinction of time **2** : a particular inflectional form or set of inflectional forms of a verb expressing a specific time distinction [Middle French *tens* "time, tense", from Latin *tempus*]

²tense *adj* **1** : stretched tight : made taut : RIGID **2 a** : feeling or showing nervous tension : HIGH-STRUNG **b** : marked by strain or suspense **3** : produced with the speech muscles in a relatively tense state ⟨the *tense* vowels \ē\ and \ü\⟩ — compare LAX [Latin *tensus,* from *tendere* "to stretch"] **syn** see TIGHT — **tense•ly** *adv* — **tense•ness** *n*

³tense *vb* : to make or become tense ⟨*tensed* up and played a poor game⟩

ten•sile \'ten-səl *also* 'ten-,sīl\ *adj* **1** : capable of stretching or being stretched : DUCTILE **2** : of or relating to tension

tensile strength *n* : the greatest longitudinal stress a substance can bear without tearing apart

¹ten•sion \'ten-chən\ *n* **1 a** : the act or action of stretching or the condition or degree of being stretched to stiffness : TAUTNESS ⟨*tension* of a muscle⟩ **b** : STRESS 1c **2 a** : either of two balancing forces causing or tending to cause extension of a body **b** : the condition in an elastic body resulting from elongation **c** : PRESSURE ⟨oxygen *tension* in lake water⟩ **3 a** : a state of mental unrest often with signs of physiological stress **b** : a state of latent hostility or opposition between individuals or groups **4** : VOLTAGE ⟨a high-*tension* wire⟩ **5** : a device to produce a desired tension (as in a loom) [Latin *tensio,* from *tendere* "to stretch"] — **ten•sion•al** \'tench-nəl, -ən-l\ *adj* — **ten•sion•less** \'ten-chən-ləs\ *adj*

²tension *vt* : to subject to tension

ten•si•ty \'ten-sət-ē\ *n, pl* **-ties** : the quality or state of being tense

ten•sor \'ten-sər, 'ten-,sȯr\ *n* : a muscle that stretches a part

tens place *n* : the place two to the left of the decimal point in a number expressed in the Arabic system of writing numbers

ten–strike \'ten-,strīk\ *n* : a strike in bowling

¹tent \'tent\ *n* **1** : a collapsible shelter (as of canvas or nylon) stretched and held in place by poles and used especially as temporary housing (as by campers) **2 :** something that resembles a tent or that serves as a shelter; *esp* **:** a canopy or enclosure placed over the head and shoulders to retain vapors or oxygen administered medically **3 :** the web of a tent caterpillar [Old French *tente,* derived from Latin *tendere* "to stretch"]

²tent *vb* **1 :** to live or lodge in a tent **2 :** to cover with or as if with a tent

ten•ta•cle \'tent-i-kəl\ *n* **1 :** one of the long flexible processes usually about the head or mouth of an animal (as a worm or fish) used especially for feeling, grasping, or handling **2 :** something suggesting a tentacle; *esp* **:** a sensitive hair on a plant [New Latin *tentaculum,* from Latin *tentare* "to feel, touch"] — **ten•ta•cled** \-kəld\ *adj* — **ten•tac•u•lar** \ten-'tak-yə-lər\ *adj*

ten•ta•tive \'tent-ət-iv\ *adj* **1 :** not fully worked out or developed **:** not final ⟨*tentative* plans⟩ **2 :** HESITANT, UNCERTAIN ⟨a *tentative* smile⟩ [Medieval Latin *tentativus,* from Latin *tentare* "to feel, try"] — **ten•ta•tive•ly** *adv* — **ten•ta•tive•ness** *n*

tent caterpillar *n* **:** any of several destructive gregarious caterpillars that construct large silken webs on trees

ten•ter \'tent-ər\ *n* **:** a frame or endless track with hooks or clips along two sides that is used for drying and stretching cloth [Middle English *teyntur*]

ten•ter•hook \'tent-ər-,huk\ *n* **:** a sharp hooked nail used especially for fastening cloth on a tenter — **on tenterhooks :** in a state of uneasiness, strain, or suspense

tenth \'tenth, 'tentth\ *n* **1 :** number 10 in a countable series — see NUMBER table **2 :** one of 10 equal parts — **tenth** *adj or adv*

tent stitch *n* **:** a short stitch slanting to the right that is used (as in embroidery) to form even lines of solid background

ten•u•ous \'ten-yə-wəs\ *adj* **1 :** not dense **:** RARE ⟨a *tenuous* fluid⟩ **2 :** not thick **:** SLENDER ⟨a *tenuous* rope⟩ **3 :** having little substance or strength **:** FLIMSY, WEAK ⟨a *tenuous* hold on reality⟩ [Latin *tenuis* "thin, tenuous"] — **te•nu•i•ty** \te-'nü-ət-ē, tə-, -'nyü-\ *n* — **ten•u•ous•ly** \'ten-yə-wəs-lē\ *adv* — **ten•u•ous•ness** *n*

ten•ure \'ten-yər\ *n* **1 :** the act, right, manner, or term of holding something (as real property, a position, or an office) **2 :** GRASP 3, HOLD [Old French, derived from Latin *tenēre* "to hold"] — **ten•ur•i•al** \te-'nyur-ē-əl\ *adj* — **ten•ur•i•al•ly** \-ē-ə-lē\ *adv*

ten•ured \'ten-yərd\ *adj* **:** having tenure ⟨*tenured* teachers⟩

te•o•sin•te \,tā-ō-'sint-ē\ *n* **:** a large annual fodder grass of Mexico and Central America closely related to and possibly ancestral to maize [Mexican Spanish, from Nahuatl *teocentli,* from *teotl* "god" + *centli* "ear of corn"]

te•pee *or* **ti•pi** *also* **tee•pee** \'tē-,pē\ *n* **:** a conical tent usually of skins used by some American Indians [of American Indian origin]

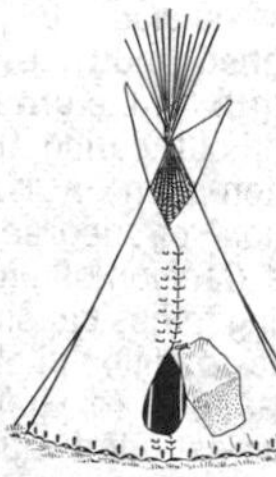
tepee

tep•id \'tep-əd\ *adj* **1 :** moderately warm **:** LUKEWARM ⟨a *tepid* bath⟩ **2 :** lacking enthusiasm or conviction **:** HALFHEARTED ⟨a *tepid* interest⟩ [Latin *tepidus,* from *tepēre* "to be moderately warm"] — **te•pid•i•ty** \tə-'pid-ət-ē, te-\ *n* — **tep•id•ly** \'tep-əd-lē\ *adv* — **tep•id•ness** *n*

te•qui•la \tə-'kē-lə\ *n* **:** a Mexican liquor made by redistilling mescal [Spanish, from *Tequila,* district of Mexico]

tera- \'ter-ə\ *combining form* **:** trillion [Greek *teras* "monster"]

ter•bi•um \'tər-bē-əm\ *n* **:** a usually trivalent metallic highly reactive chemical element — see ELEMENT table [New Latin, from *Ytterby,* Sweden]

terce \'tərs\ *or* **tierce** \'tiərs\ *n, often cap* **:** the third of the canonical hours [Middle French *terce, tierce,* from *terz* "third", from Latin *tertius*]

ter•cen•ten•a•ry \,tər-,sen-'ten-ə-rē; tər-'sent-n-,er-ē, 'tər-\ *n, pl* **-ries :** a 300th anniversary or its celebration [Latin *ter* "three times"] — **tercentenary** *adj*

ter•cen•ten•ni•al \,tər-,sen-'ten-ē-əl\ *adj or n* **:** TERCENTENARY

ter•cet \'tər-sət\ *n* **:** a unit or group of three lines of verse [Italian *terzetto,* from *terzo* "third", from Latin *tertius*]

ter•e•binth \'ter-ə-,binth, -,bintth\ *n* **:** a small European tree related to the sumac that yields an oleoresin [Middle French *terebinthe,* from Latin *terebinthus,* from Greek *terebinthos*]

te•re•do \tə-'rēd-ō, -'rād-\ *n, pl* **-re•dos** *or* **-red•i•nes** \-'red-n-,ēz\ **:** SHIPWORM [Latin, from Greek *terēdōn*]

ter•gi•ver•sate \'tər-ji-vər-,sāt\ *vi* **:** to desert one's party or position; *esp* **:** EQUIVOCATE 1 [Latin *tergiversari* "to turn the back, shuffle", from *tergum* "back" + *versare* "to turn," from *versus,* past participle of *vertere* "to turn"] — **ter•gi•ver•sa•tion** \,tər-ji-vər-'sā-shən\ *n* — **ter•gi•ver•sa•tor** \'tər-ji-vər-,sāt-ər\ *n*

ter•gum \'tər-gəm\ *n, pl* **ter•ga** \-gə\ **:** the back of an animal; *also* **:** a plate on the back of an arthropod [Latin, "back"]

¹term \'tərm\ *n* **1 :** END, TERMINATION; *also* **:** a point in time assigned to something (as payment of rent or interest) **2 :** a fixed extent of time especially as set by law, custom, or some recurrent phenomenon ⟨the governor served two *terms*⟩ ⟨ready for the new school *term*⟩ **3** *pl* **:** provisions determining the nature and scope of something and especially of an agreement **4 a :** a word or expression that has a precise meaning in some uses or is peculiar to a particular field ⟨legal *terms*⟩ **b** *pl* **:** diction of a specified kind ⟨spoke in glowing *terms* of their prospects⟩ **5 a :** a mathematical expression connected with another by a plus or minus sign **b :** an element of a fraction or proportion or of a series or sequence **6** *pl* **a :** mutual relationship **:** FOOTING ⟨on good *terms*⟩ **b :** AGREEMENT, CONCORD ⟨came to *terms* with their employer⟩ [Old French *terme* "boundary, end", from Latin *terminus*] — **in terms of :** with respect to ⟨considered *in terms of* today's wages⟩

²term *vt* **:** to apply a term to **:** CALL, NAME

¹ter•ma•gant \'tər-mə-gənt\ *n* **:** an overbearing quarrelsome woman **:** SHREW [Middle English *Termagant,* an imaginary Muslim deity represented in medieval plays as a boisterous character]

²termagant *adj* **:** noisily quarrelsome

¹ter•mi•nal \'tər-mən-l\ *adj* **1 a :** of or relating to an end, extremity, boundary, or terminus ⟨*terminal* pillar⟩ **b :** growing at the end of a branch or stem ⟨*terminal* bud⟩ **2 a :** of, relating to, or occurring in a term or each term **b :** occurring at or contributing to the end of life ⟨*terminal* illness⟩ **3 :** occurring at or constituting the end of a period or series — **ter•mi•nal•ly** \-l-ē\ *adv*

²terminal *n* **1 :** a part that forms the end **2 :** a device attached to the end (as of a wire) for convenience in making electrical connections **3 a :** either end of a carrier line (as a railroad or shipping line) with its handling and storage facilities, offices, and stations; *also* **:** a usually major freight or passenger station **b :** a town at the end of a carrier line **:** TERMINUS **4 :** a device (as a teletypewriter) through which a user can communicate with a computer

terminal side *n* **:** a straight line that rotates about a point on another line in generating an angle

ter•mi•nate \'tər-mə-,nāt\ *vb* **1 a :** to bring to or come to an end **:** CLOSE **b :** to form the conclusion of **:** form an ending **2 :** to serve as a limit to **:** BOUND **3 :** to extend only to a limit (as a point or line); *esp* **:** to reach a terminus [Latin *terminare,* from *terminus* "end"] **syn** see CLOSE — **ter•mi•na•ble** \-mə-nə-bəl\ *adj* — **ter•mi•na•tive** \-,nāt-iv\ *adj*

terminating decimal *n* **:** a decimal that can be expressed in a finite number of figures — compare REPEATING DECIMAL

ter•mi•na•tion \,tər-mə-'nā-shən\ *n* **1 :** end in time or existence **:** CONCLUSION ⟨*termination* of life⟩ **2 :** a limit in space or extent **:** BOUND **3 :** the last part of a word **:** SUFFIX; *esp* **:** an inflectional ending **4 :** the act of terminating **syn** see END — **ter•mi•na•tion•al** \-shnəl, -shən-l\ *adj*

ter•mi•na•tor \'tər-mə-,nāt-ər\ *n* **1 :** one that terminates **2 :** the dividing line between the illuminated and the unilluminated part of the moon's or a planet's disk

ter•mi•nol•o•gy \,tər-mə-'näl-ə-jē\ *n, pl* **-gies :** the technical or special terms used in a business, art, science, or special subject ⟨the *terminology* of law⟩ [Medieval Latin *terminus* "term, expression", from Latin, "boundary, end"] — **ter•mi•no•log•i•cal** \,tərm-nə-'läj-i-kəl, ,tərm-ən-l-'äj-\ *adj*

term insurance *n* **:** insurance for a specified period that pays only for losses suffered during this period

ter•mi•nus \'tər-mə-nəs\ *n, pl* **-ni** \-,nī, -,nē\ *or* **-nus•es 1 :** final goal **:** finishing point **2 :** a post or stone marking a boundary **3 a :** either end of a transportation line or travel route **b :** the station or the town or city at such a place **4 :** EXTREMITY, TIP ⟨the *terminus* of a glacier⟩ [Latin, "boundary, end"]

ter•mite \'tər-ˌmīt\ *n* : any of an order (Isoptera) of pale-colored soft-bodied social insects that have winged sexual forms, wingless sterile workers, and often soldiers, feed on wood, and include some very destructive to wooden structures and trees — called also *white ant* **[**Late Latin *termit-, termes,* a worm that eats wood**]**

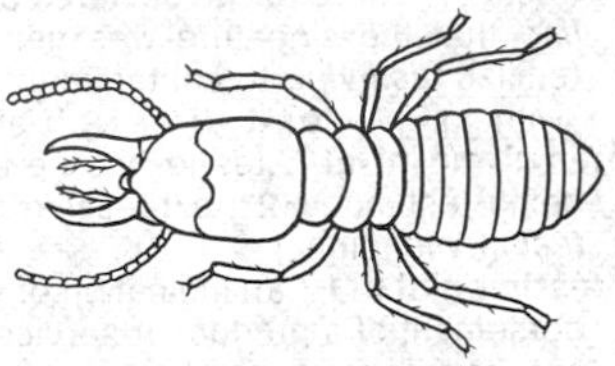

termite

term paper *n* : a major written assignment in a school or college course representative of a student's individual research and study in a subject area — called also *term report*

tern \'tərn\ *n* : any of numerous sea gulls that are smaller and slenderer in body and bill than typical gulls and have narrower wings, often forked tails, black cap, and white body **[**of Scandinavian origin**]**

ter•na•ry \'tər-nə-rē\ *adj* **1 :** of, relating to, or proceeding by threes **2 :** having three elements or parts **[**Latin *ternarius,* from *terni* "three each"**]**

ter•pene \'tər-ˌpēn\ *n* : any of various hydrocarbons $(C_5H_8)_n$ found especially in essential oils, resins, and balsams and used mostly as solvents and in organic synthesis **[**German *terpentin* "turpentine"**]**

terp•si•cho•re•an \ˌtərp-sik-ə-'rē-ən\ *adj* **:** of or relating to dancing **[***Terpsichore,* Greek muse of dancing**]**

[1]**ter•race** \'ter-əs\ *n* **1 a :** a flat roof or open platform **:** BALCONY, DECK **b :** a relatively level paved or planted area adjoining a building **2 :** a raised embankment with the top leveled; *also* **:** one of a series of banks or ridges formed in a slope to conserve moisture and soil for agriculture **3 a** (1) **:** a row of houses on raised ground or a sloping site (2) **:** a group of such houses **b :** a strip of park in the middle of a street **c :** STREET **[**Middle French, "pile of earth, terrace", from Provençal *terrassa,* from *terra* "earth", from Latin**]**

[2]**terrace** *vt* **:** to make into a terrace or supply with terraces ⟨the front yard had been *terraced* down to the road⟩

ter•ra–cot•ta \ˌter-ə-'kät-ə\ *n, pl* **terra–cottas 1 :** glazed or unglazed fired earthenware **2 :** a brownish orange **[**Italian *terra cotta,* literally, "baked earth"**]**

ter•ra fir•ma \-'fər-mə\ *n* **:** dry land **:** solid ground **[**New Latin, literally, "solid land"**]**

ter•rain \tə-'rān, te-\ *n* **:** the surface features of a tract of land ⟨a rough *terrain*⟩ **[**French, "land, ground", from Latin *terrenum,* derived from *terra* "earth, land"**]**

ter•ra•pin \'ter-ə-pən, 'tar-\ *n* **:** any of various edible North American turtles living in fresh or brackish water **[**of American Indian origin**]**

ter•rar•i•um \tə-'rar-ē-əm, -'rer-\ *n, pl* **-ia** \-ē-ə\ *or* **-i•ums :** a vivarium without standing water **[**Latin *terra* "earth land" + *-arium* (as in *aquarium*)**]**

ter•raz•zo \tə-'raz-ō, -'rät-sō\ *n* **:** a mosaic flooring made by embedding small pieces of marble or granite in mortar **[**Italian, literally, "terrace"**]**

ter•res•tri•al \tə-'res-trē-əl, -'res-chəl, -'resh-chəl\ *adj* **1 a :** of or relating to the earth or its inhabitants ⟨*terrestrial* magnetism⟩ **b :** PROSAIC 2, COMMONPLACE **2 :** of or relating to land as distinct from air or water ⟨*terrestrial* transportation⟩ **3 a :** living on or in or growing from land ⟨*terrestrial* plants⟩ ⟨*terrestrial* birds⟩ **b :** of or relating to terrestrial organisms ⟨*terrestrial* habits⟩ **[**Latin *terrestris,* from *terra* "earth"**]** — **terrestrial** *n* — **ter•res•tri•al•ly** \-ē\ *adv*

ter•ri•ble \'ter-ə-bəl\ *adj* **1 :** causing terror or awe **:** FEARFUL, DREADFUL ⟨a *terrible* disaster⟩ **2 a :** hard to bear usually because of excess of some quality ⟨*terrible* cold⟩ **b :** very bad or extremely unpleasant ⟨had a *terrible* time⟩ **c :** of notably inferior quality ⟨did a *terrible* job of painting⟩ **[**Middle French, from Latin *terribilis,* from *terrēre* "to frighten"**]** — **ter•ri•bly** \-blē\ *adv*

ter•ri•er \'ter-ē-ər\ *n* **:** any of various usually small dogs originally used by hunters to dig for small game and attack the quarry underground or drive it out **[**French *chien terrier,* literally, "earth dog"**]**

ter•rif•ic \tə-'rif-ik\ *adj* **1 :** TERRIBLE 1, FRIGHTFUL ⟨*terrific* destruction⟩ **2 :** EXTRAORDINARY, ASTOUNDING ⟨*terrific* speed⟩; *esp* **:** TREMENDOUS ⟨a *terrific* explosion⟩ **3 :** unusually fine **:** MAGNIFICENT ⟨the party was *terrific*⟩ — **ter•rif•i•cal•ly** \-'rif-i-kə-lē, -klē\ *adv*

ter•ri•fy \'ter-ə-ˌfī\ *vt* **-fied; -fy•ing :** to fill with or move to some action by terror

ter•ri•fy•ing \-ˌfī-ing\ *adj* **:** causing terror or great apprehension — **ter•ri•fy•ing•ly** *adv*

[1]**ter•ri•to•ri•al** \ˌter-ə-'tōr-ē-əl, -'tȯr-\ *adj* **1 a :** of or relating to territory or a territory ⟨a *territorial* government⟩ **b :** of or relating to or organized chiefly for home defense ⟨a *territorial* army⟩ **2 :** of, relating to, or exhibiting territoriality ⟨*territorial* birds⟩ — **ter•ri•to•ri•al•ly** \-ē-ə-lē\ *adv*

[2]**territorial** *n* **:** a member of a territorial military unit

ter•ri•to•ri•al•ism \ˌter-ə-'tōr-ē-ə-ˌliz-əm, -'tȯr-\ *n* **:** TERRITORIALITY

ter•ri•to•ri•al•i•ty \ˌter-ə-ˌtōr-ē-'al-ət-ē, -ˌtȯr-\ *n* **:** the pattern of behavior associated with the defense of a male animal's territory

ter•ri•to•ri•al•ize \-'tōr-ē-ə-ˌlīz, -'tȯr-\ *vt* **:** to organize on a territorial basis — **ter•ri•to•ri•al•iza•tion** \-ˌtōr-ē-ə-lə-'zā-shən, -ˌtȯr-\ *n*

territorial waters *n pl* **:** the waters under the sovereign jurisdiction of a nation or state including both marginal sea and inland waters

ter•ri•to•ry \'ter-ə-ˌtōr-ē, -ˌtȯr-\ *n, pl* **-ries 1 :** a geographical area belonging to or under the jurisdiction of a government **b :** an administrative subdivision of a country (as the Soviet Union) **c :** a part of the United States not included within any state but organized with a separate legislature **d :** a geographical area dependent upon an external government but having some degree of autonomy **2 a :** an indeterminate geographical area **b :** a field of knowledge or interest **3 a :** an assigned area ⟨a salesman's *territory*⟩ **b :** an area that is occupied and defended by a male bird or mammal **[**Latin *territorium,* from *terra* "land"**]**

ter•ror \'ter-ər\ *n* **1 :** a state of intense fear **2 a :** a cause of fear or anxiety **b :** a dreadful person or thing; *esp* **:** an obnoxious child **3 a :** REIGN OF TERROR **b :** the deliberate use of violence and brutality especially as a political weapon **[**Middle French *terreur,* from Latin *terror,* from *terrēre* "to frighten"**]**

ter•ror•ism \'ter-ər-ˌiz-əm\ *n* **:** systematic use of terror especially as a means of gaining some political end — **ter•ror•ist** \-ər-əst\ *adj or n* — **ter•ror•is•tic** \ˌter-ər-'is-tik\ *adj*

ter•ror•ize \'ter-ər-ˌīz\ *vt* **1 :** to fill with terror or anxiety **2 :** to coerce by threat or violence — **ter•ror•iza•tion** \ˌter-ər-ə-'zā-shən\ *n*

ter•ry \'ter-ē\ *n, pl* **terries :** an absorbent fabric with a loose pile of uncut loops — called also *terry cloth* **[**perhaps from French *tiré,* past participle of *tirer* "to draw"**]**

terse \'tərs\ *adj* **:** using as few words as possible without loss of force or clearness **:** being brief and effective **:** SUCCINCT **[**Latin *tersus* "clean, neat", from *tergēre* "to wipe off"**]** — **terse•ly** *adv* — **terse•ness** *n*

[1]**ter•tian** \'tər-shən\ *adj* **:** recurring at approximately 48-hour intervals ⟨a *tertian* fever⟩ **[**Latin *tertianus,* from *tertius* "third"**]**

[2]**tertian** *n* **:** an intermittent fever that recurs at approximately 48-hour intervals; *esp* **:** a tertian malaria

[1]**ter•ti•ary** \'tər-shē-ˌer-ē\ *n, pl* **-ar•ies 1 :** a member of a monastic third order especially of lay people **2** *cap* **:** the Tertiary period or system of rocks

[2]**tertiary** *adj* **1 a :** of 3d rank, importance, or value **b :** of, relating to, or constituting the 3d strongest of three or four degrees of stress ⟨the 3d syllable of *basketball team* carries *tertiary* stress⟩ **2** *cap* **:** of, relating to, or being the first period of the Cenozoic era or the corresponding system of rocks marked by the formation of high mountains (as the Alps and Himalayas) and the dominance of mammals on land — see GEOLOGIC TIME table **3 :** formed by the substitution of three atoms or groups ⟨a *tertiary* salt⟩ **4 :** occurring in or being a 3d stage **[**Latin *tertiarius,* from *tertius* "third"**]**

ter•za ri•ma \ˌtert-sə-'rē-mə\ *n* **:** a verse form consisting of tercets usually in iambic pentameter with an interlaced rhyme scheme (as *aba, bcb, cdc*) **[**Italian, literally, "third rhyme"**]**

\ə\ **abut**	\au̇\ **out**	\i\ **tip**	\ȯ\ **saw**	\u̇\ **foot**
\ər\ **further**	\ch\ **chin**	\ī\ **life**	\ȯi\ **coin**	\y\ **yet**
\a\ **mat**	\e\ **pet**	\j\ **job**	\th\ **thin**	\yü\ **few**
\ā\ **take**	\ē\ **easy**	\ng\ **sing**	\th̲\ **this**	\yu̇\ **cure**
\ä\ **cot, cart**	\g\ **go**	\ō\ **bone**	\ü\ **food**	\zh\ **vision**

tes•la \'tes-lə\ *n* : a unit of magnetic flux density in the mks system [Nikola *Tesla,* died 1943, American electrician and inventor]

tes•sel•late \'tes-ə-,lāt\ *vt* : to form into or adorn with mosaic [Late Latin *tessellare* "to pave with tesserae", from Latin *tessella* "small tessera", from *tessera*] — **tes•sel•la•tion** \,tes-ə-'lā-shən\ *n*

tes•sel•lat•ed \'tes-ə-,lāt-əd\ *adj* : made of or resembling mosaic; *esp* : having a checkered appearance

tes•sera \'tes-ə-rə\ *n, pl* **-ser•ae** \-,rē, -,rī\ **1** : a small tablet (as of wood, bone, or ivory) used by the ancient Romans as a ticket, tally, voucher, or means of identification **2** : a small piece (as of marble, glass, or tile) used in mosaic work [Latin]

¹test \'test\ *n* **1 a** : a critical examination, observation, or evaluation : TRIAL ⟨put their courage to the *test*⟩ **b** : something that tries quality or resistance ⟨ideas that can only be judged by the *test* of time⟩ **2** : a means of testing: as **a** : a procedure, reaction, or reagent used to identify or differentiate something ⟨a *test* for starch⟩ ⟨a series of allergy *tests*⟩ **b** : an examination (as in school) intended to measure the skill, knowledge, intelligence, capacities, or aptitudes **3** : a result of or rating based on a test ⟨a boiler of 300 kilograms *test*⟩ [Middle French, "vessel in which metals were assayed, cupel", from Latin *testum* "earthen vessel"]

△ **origin** Latin *testum* was a general word for an earthen vessel. In the Middle Ages its French descendant, *test,* was the word for a specific type of vessel used in the assaying of precious metals, a cupel. A cupel is a shallow porous cup. When impure silver or gold is heated in it, the impurities are absorbed in the porous material, leaving a relatively pure button of silver or gold. As the name for a cupel, *test* was borrowed into English in the 14th century. It was later used figuratively. To "put something to the test" was to make trial of it, to determine its quality or genuineness, as a precious metal might be tried in a cupel.

²test *vb* **1** : to put to test or proof : TRY **2 a** : to undergo a test **b** : to achieve a rating on the basis of tests **3** : to use tests as a means of analysis or diagnosis ⟨*test* for copper⟩ ⟨*test* for allergens⟩ — **test•able** \'tes-tə-bəl\ *adj*

³test *n* : a firm or rigid outer covering (as a shell) of many invertebrates [Latin *testa* "shell"]

tes•ta \'tes-tə\ *n, pl* **tes•tae** \-,tē, -tī\ : the hard outer coat of a seed [Latin, "shell"]

tes•ta•ceous \tes-'tā-shəs\ *adj* : consisting of or resembling shell ⟨stone of *testaceous* composition⟩ **2** : of reddish to yellowish brown

tes•ta•cy \'tes-tə-sē\ *n, pl* **-cies** : the state of being testate

tes•ta•ment \'tes-tə-mənt\ *n* **1 a** *archaic* : a covenant between God and man **b** *cap* : either of two chief divisions of the Bible **2 a** : a tangible proof or tribute **b** : an expression of conviction : CREDO **3** : a legal instrument by which a person determines the disposition of his or her property after death [Late Latin *testamentum* "covenant, holy scripture", from Latin, "last will", from *testari* "to call to witness, make a will", from *testis* "witness"] — **tes•ta•men•ta•ry** \,tes-tə-'ment-ə-rē, -'men-trē\ *adj*

tes•tate \'tes-,tāt, -tət\ *adj* : having a valid will ⟨a person dying *testate*⟩ [Latin *testatus,* past participle of *testari* "to make a will"]

tes•ta•tor \'tes-,tāt-ər, tes-'\ *n* : a person who leaves a will in force at death

tes•ta•trix \tes-'tā-triks\ *n* : a female testator

test ban *n* : a self-imposed ban on the atmospheric testing of nuclear weapons by countries having such weapons

test case *n* **1** : a representative case whose outcome is likely to serve as a precedent **2** : a proceeding brought by agreement or on an understanding of the parties to obtain a decision as to the constitutionality of a statute

test•cross \'test-,krȯs, 'tes-\ *n* : a cross between an individual expressing a recessive trait and one expressing a dominant trait to determine whether or not the latter is heterozygous

test•ed \'tes-təd\ *adj* : subjected to or qualified through testing ⟨time-*tested* principles⟩ ⟨tuberculin-*tested* cattle⟩

¹tes•ter \'tēs-tər, 'tes-\ *n* : a canopy over a bed, pulpit, or altar [Middle French *testiere* "head covering", from *teste* "head", from Late Latin *testa* "skull", from Latin, "shell"]

²test•er \'tes-tər\ *n* : one that tests

tes•ti•cle \'tes-ti-kəl\ *n* : TESTIS [Latin *testiculus,* from *testis*] — **tes•tic•u•lar** \tes-'tik-yə-lər\ *adj*

tes•ti•fy \'tes-tə-,fī\ *vb* \-**fied**; **-fy•ing 1 a** : to make a statement based on personal knowledge or belief : give evidence ⟨*testify* in court⟩ **b** : to declare solemnly (as under oath) ⟨*testified* that the signature was genuine⟩ **2** : to serve as a sign ⟨smiles *testifying* to contentment⟩ [Latin *testificari,* from *testis* "witness"] — **tes•ti•fi•er** \-,fī-ər, -,fīr\ *n*

¹tes•ti•mo•ni•al \,tes-tə-'mō-nē-əl\ *adj* **1** : of, relating to, or being testimony **2** : expressive of appreciation or esteem ⟨a *testimonial* dinner⟩

²testimonial *n* **1** : an indication of worth or quality: as **a** : an endorsement of a product or service ⟨writing *testimonials* for patent medicines⟩ **b** : a character reference : letter of recommendation **2** : an expression of appreciation : TRIBUTE

tes•ti•mo•ny \'tes-tə-,mō-nē\ *n, pl* **-nies 1 a** : the tablets inscribed with the Mosaic law or the ark containing them **b** : a divine decree attested in the Scriptures **2 a** : evidence based on observation or knowledge : authoritative evidence **b** : a solemn declaration usually made orally by a witness under oath in response to interrogation by a lawyer or authorized public official **3** : an open acknowledgement or profession (as of religious experience) [Latin *testimonium* "evidence, witness", from *testis* "witness"]

tes•tis \'tes-təs\ *n, pl* **tes•tes** \'tes-,tēz\ : a male reproductive gland [Latin, "witness, testis"]

tes•tos•ter•one \te-'stäs-tə-,rōn\ *n* : a potent male sex hormone that is produced by special cells of the testis or made synthetically [derived from *testis* + *sterol*]

test paper *n* : paper saturated with a reagent that changes color in testing for various substances

test pilot *n* : a pilot employed to put new airplanes through severe tests

test tube *n* : a usually plain tube of thin glass closed at one end and used especially in chemistry and biology

tes•tu•do \tes-'tüd-ō, -'tyüd-\ *n, pl* **-dos** : a cover of overlapping shields or a shed wheeled up to a wall used by the ancient Romans to protect an attacking force [Latin, literally, "tortoise, tortoise shell"]

tes•ty \'tes-tē\ *adj* **tes•ti•er**; **-est 1** : easily annoyed : IRRITABLE **2** : marked by impatience or ill humor ⟨*testy* remarks⟩ [Anglo-French *testif* "headstrong", from Old French *teste* "head"] **syn** see IRASCIBLE — **tes•ti•ly** \-tə-lē\ *adv* — **tes•ti•ness** \-tē-nəs\ *n*

te•tan•ic \te-'tan-ik\ *adj* : of, relating to, or being tetanus or tetany — **te•tan•i•cal•ly** \-'tan-i-kə-lē, -klē\ *adv*

tet•a•nus \'tet-n-əs, 'tet-nəs\ *n* **1** : an acute infectious disease characterized by tonic spasm of voluntary muscles especially of the jaw and caused by the toxin of a clostridium bacillus which usually enters a wound and multiplies in damaged tissue **2** : prolonged contraction of a muscle resulting from rapidly repeated motor impulses [Latin, from Greek *tetanos,* from *tetanos* "stretched, rigid"]

tet•a•ny \'tet-n-ē, 'tet-nē\ *n* : a condition marked by tonic spasm of muscles and associated usually with deficient parathyroid secretion and faulty mineral balance

tetchy \'tech-ē\ *adj* **tetchi•er**; **-est** : irritably or peevishly sensitive : TOUCHY [perhaps from obsolete *tetch* "habit"]

¹tête-à-tête \,tāt-ə-'tāt\ *adv* : in private [French, literally, "head to head"]

²tête-à-tête \'tāt-ə-,tāt, *2 is also* 'tēt-ə-,tēt\ *n* **1** : a private conversation between two persons **2** : a seat for two persons facing each other

³tête-à-tête \,tāt-ə-,tāt\ *adj* : being face to face : PRIVATE

¹teth•er \'teth-ər\ *n* **1** : a line (as of rope or chain) by which an animal is fastened so as to restrict its range **2** : the limit of one's strength or resources : SCOPE ⟨at the end of my *tether*⟩ [Middle English *tethir*]

²tether *vt* **teth•ered**; **teth•er•ing** \'teth-ring, -ə-ring\ : to fasten or restrain by or as if by a tether

tet•ra \'te-trə\ *n* : any of various small brightly colored South American fishes often bred in tropical aquariums [New Latin *Tetragonopterus,* former genus name, from Late Latin *tetragonum* "quadrangle" + Greek *pteron* "wing"]

tetra- *or* **tetr-** *combining form* : four : having four : having four parts ⟨*tetra*valent⟩ [Greek]

tet•ra•chlo•ride \,te-trə-'klōr-,īd, -'klȯr-\ *n* : a chloride containing four atoms of chlorine

tet•ra•chord \'te-trə-,kȯrd\ *n* : a diatonic series of four tones : half an octave

tet•ra•cy•cline \,te-trə-'sī-,klēn\ *n* : a yellow crystalline broad-spectrum antibiotic produced by a soil actinomycete or synthetically

tet•rad \'te-ˌtrad\ *n* : a group or arrangement of four: as **a** : a group of four cells produced by the successive divisions of a mother cell **b** : an arrangement of chromosomes by fours in the first meiotic prophase due to early splitting of paired chromosomes [Greek *tetrad-*, *tetras*, from *tetra-*] — **te•trad•ic** \te-'trad-ik\ *adj*

tet•ra•eth•yl•lead \ˌte-trə-ˌeth-əl-'led\ *n* : a heavy oily poisonous liquid PbC_4H_{20} used as an antiknock agent

tet•ra•he•dron \ˌte-trə-'hē-drən\ *n, pl* **-drons** *or* **-dra** \-drə\ : a polyhedron of four faces — **tet•ra•he•dral** \-drəl\ *adj*

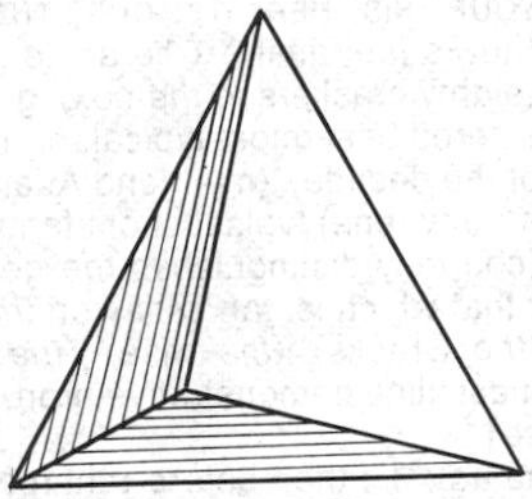

tetrahedron

te•tra•hy•dro•can•nab•i•nol \-ˌhi-drə-kə-'nab-ə-ˌnȯl, -ˌnōl\ *n* : THC [*tetra-* + *hydr-* "hydrogen" + *cannabis* + *-in* + *-ol*]

te•tral•o•gy \te-'träl-ə-jē, -'tral-\ *n, pl* **-gies** : a series of four connected works (as operas or novels)

te•tram•e•ter \te-'tram-ət-ər\ *n* : a line of verse consisting of four metrical feet [Greek *tetrametron*, derived from *tetra-* + *metron* "measure"]

tet•ra•ploid \'te-trə-ˌplȯid\ *adj* : having or being a chromosome number four times the monoploid number ⟨a *tetraploid* cell⟩ — **tetraploid** *n* — **tet•ra•ploi•dy** \-ˌplȯid-ē\ *n*

tet•ra•pod \'te-trə-ˌpäd\ *n* : a vertebrate (as a frog, bird, or cat) with two pairs of limbs

tet•rarch \'te-ˌträrk, 'tē-\ *n* : a governor of the 4th part of a province (as of ancient Rome) [Latin *tetrarcha*, from Greek *tetrarchēs*, from *tetra-* + *archein* "to rule"] — **te•trar•chic** \te-'trär-kik, tē-\ *adj*

te•trar•chy \'te-ˌträr-kē, 'tē-\ *n, pl* **-chies** : government by four persons ruling jointly

tet•ra•va•lent \ˌte-trə-'vā-lənt\ *adj* : having a valence of four

tet•rode \'te-ˌtrōd\ *n* : a vacuum tube with four electrodes

te•trox•ide \te-'träk-ˌsīd\ *n* : a compound of an element or radical with four atoms of oxygen

Teu•ton \'tüt-n, 'tyüt-n\ *n* **1** : a member of an ancient probably Germanic or Celtic people **2** : a member of a people speaking a language of the Germanic branch of the Indo-European language family; *esp* : GERMAN [Latin *Teutoni* "Teutons"]

¹Teu•ton•ic \tü-'tän-ik, tyü-\ *adj* : of, relating to, or characteristic of the Teutons — **Teu•ton•i•cal•ly** \-'tän-i-kə-lē, -klē\ *adv*

²Teutonic *n* : GERMANIC

tex•as \'tek-səs, -siz\ *n* : a structure on an upper deck of a steamer containing the officers' cabins and having the pilothouse in front or on top [*Texas*, state of the United States; from the fact that cabins on Mississippi steamboats were once named after states and the officers' cabins were the largest]

Texas fever *n* : an infectious disease of cattle transmitted by a tick and caused by a protozoan that multiplies in the blood and destroys the red blood cells

texas leagu•er \-'lē-gər\ *n* : a fly that falls between the infielders and the outfielders [*Texas League*, a baseball minor league]

Texas Ranger *n* : a member of a mounted police force in Texas

text \'tekst\ *n* **1 a** : the original written or printed words and form of a literary work **b** : an edited or emended copy of an original work ⟨several *texts* of the play are in print⟩ **2 a** : the main body of printed or written matter on a page **b** : the principal part of a book exclusive of front and back matter **3 a** : a passage of Scripture chosen for the subject of a sermon; *also* : a passage providing a basis (as for a speech) **b** : a source of information or authority **4** : TEXTBOOK ⟨a history *text*⟩ **5** : a subject on which one writes or speaks : THEME, TOPIC [Middle French *texte*, from Latin *textus* "texture, context", from *texere* "to weave"]

text•book \'tekst-ˌbu̇k, 'teks-\ *n* : a book used in the study of a subject; *esp* : one that presents the principles of a subject

tex•tile \'tek-ˌstīl 'teks-tl\ *n* **1** : CLOTH 1; *esp* : a woven or knit cloth **2** : a fiber, filament, or yarn used in making cloth [Latin, from *textilis* "woven", from *texere* "to weave"] — **textile** *adj*

tex•tu•al \'teks-chə-wəl, -chəl\ *adj* : of, relating to, or based on a text — **tex•tu•al•y** \-ē\ *adv*

textual criticism *n* **1** : the study of a literary work that aims to establish the original text **2** : a critical study of literature emphasizing a close reading and analysis of the text — **textual critic** *n*

¹tex•ture \'teks-chər\ *n* **1** : something (as cloth) formed by or as if by weaving **2 a** : the structure, feel, and appearance of a textile that result from the kind and arrangement of its threads ⟨the harsh *texture* of burlap⟩ **b** : similar qualities dependent on the nature and arrangement of the constituent particles of a substance ⟨a gritty *texture*⟩ ⟨rock with a very fine *texture*⟩ **3** : an essential or identifying part or quality ⟨the truly American *texture* of the experience⟩ [Latin *textura*, from *texere* "to weave"] — **tex•tur•al** \-chə-rəl\ *adj* — **tex•tured** \-chərd\ *adj*

²texture *vt* : to give a particular and especially a rough texture to ⟨*texture* a ceiling⟩

T formation *n* : an offensive football formation in which the fullback lines up behind the quarterback and one halfback lines up on either side of the fullback

¹-th — see -ETH

²-th *or* **-eth** *adj suffix* — used in forming ordinal numbers ⟨hundred*th*⟩ ⟨forti*eth*⟩ [Old English *-tha*]

³-th *n suffix* **1** : act or process ⟨spil*th*⟩ **2** : state or condition ⟨dear*th*⟩ [Old English]

Thai \'tī\ *n* **1** : a native or inhabitant of Thailand **2** : the official language of Thailand — **Thai** *adj*

thal•a•mus \'thal-ə-məs\ *n, pl* **-mi** \-ˌmī, -ˌmē\ : the largest subdivision of the diencephalon forming a coordinating center through which incoming nerve impulses are directed to appropriate parts of the brain cortex [New Latin, from Greek *thalamos* "chamber"] — **tha•lam•ic** \thə-'lam-ik\ *adj*

tha•las•sic \thə-'las-ik\ *adj* **1** : of or relating to the sea or ocean **2** : of or relating to seas or gulfs as distinguished from oceans [French *thalassique*, from Greek *thalassa* "sea"]

tha•ler *variant of* TALER

tha•lid•o•mide \thə-'lid-ə-ˌmīd, -məd\ *n* : a sedative and hypnotic drug $C_{13}H_{10}N_2O_4$ found to cause malformation of infants born to mothers using it during pregnancy [derived from *naphthalene* + *amide*]

thal•lic \'thal-ik\ *adj* : of, relating to, or containing thallium especially with a valence of three

thal•li•um \'thal-ē-əm\ *n* : a poisonous metallic chemical element resembling lead in physical properties — see ELEMENT table [New Latin, from Greek *thallos* "young shoot"; from the green line in its spectrum]

thal•lo•phyte \'thal-ə-ˌfīt\ *n* : any of a primary division (Thallophyta) of the plant kingdom comprising plants with single-celled sex organs or with sex organs of which all cells give rise to gametes and including the algae, fungi, and lichens [derived from Greek *thallos* "young shoot" + *phytos* "plant"] — **thal•lo•phyt•ic** \ˌthal-ə-'fit-ik\ *adj*

thal•lous \'thal-əs\ *adj* : of, relating to, or containing thallium with a valence of one

thal•lus \'thal-əs\ *n, pl* **thal•li** \'thal-ˌī, -ˌē\ *or* **thal•lus•es** : the thallophytic plant body characterized by lack of differentiation into distinct members (as stem, leaves, or roots) and by growth that is not confined to an apical point [New Latin, from Greek *thallos* "young shoot", from *thallein* "to sprout"] — **thal•loid** \'thal-ˌȯid\ *adj*

than \t͟hən, t͟han, 't͟han\ *conj* **1** — used as a function word after a comparative adjective or adverb to introduce the second part of a comparison expressing inequality ⟨older *than* I am⟩ ⟨easier said *than* done⟩ **2** — used as a function word to indicate difference of kind, manner, or identity; used especially with some adjectives and adverbs that express diversity ⟨anywhere else *than* at home⟩ [Old English *thonne*, *thænne* "then, than"]

thane \'thān\ *n* **1** : a free retainer of an Anglo-Saxon lord; *esp* : one holding lands of the king and performing military service **2** : a Scottish feudal lord [Old English *thegn*]

thank \'thangk\ *vt* **1** : to express gratitude to ⟨*thanked* them for the present⟩ **2** : to hold responsible ⟨had only themselves to

thank for their loss⟩ [Old English *thancian*]
thank•ful \'thangk-fəl\ *adj* **1 :** conscious of benefit received **2 :** expressive of thanks **3 :** well pleased **:** GLAD **syn** see GRATEFUL — **thank•ful•ly** \-fə-lē\ *adv* — **thank•ful•ness** *n*
thank•less \'thang-kləs\ *adj* **1 :** not expressing or feeling gratitude **:** UNGRATEFUL **2 :** not likely to obtain thanks ⟨a *thankless* task⟩ — **thank•less•ly** *adv* — **thank•less•ness** *n*
thanks \'thangks\ *n pl* **1 :** kindly or grateful thoughts **:** GRATITUDE ⟨express my *thanks* for their kindness⟩ **2 :** an expression of gratitude ⟨return *thanks* before the meal⟩ — often used in an utterance containing no verb and serving as a courteous and somewhat informal expression of gratitude ⟨many *thanks*⟩ [Old English *thanc* "thought, gratitude"]
thanks•giv•ing \thangs-'giv-ing, thangks-\ *n* **1 :** the act of giving thanks **2 :** a prayer expressing gratitude **3** *cap* **:** THANKSGIVING DAY
Thanksgiving Day *n* **:** the 4th Thursday in November observed as a legal holiday in the United States for public thanksgiving to God
thank•wor•thy \'thang-,kwər-t͟hē\ *adj* **:** worthy of thanks or gratitude **:** MERITORIOUS
thank–you–ma'am \'thangk-yu̇-,mam, -yē, -ē-\ *n* **:** a bump or depression in a road [probably from its causing a nodding of the head]
¹that \t͟hat, 't͟hat\ *pron, pl* **those** \t͟hōz, 't͟hōz\ **1 a :** the person, thing, or idea indicated, mentioned, or understood from the situation ⟨*that* is my father⟩ **b :** the time, action, or event specified ⟨after *that* we went to bed⟩ **c :** the kind or thing specified as follows ⟨the purest water is *that* produced by distillation⟩ **2 a :** the one farther away or less immediately under observation or discussion ⟨*those* are elms and these are maples⟩ **b :** the former one **3 a :** the one **:** the thing **:** the kind **:** SOMETHING, ANYTHING ⟨what's *that* you say⟩ **b** *pl* **:** some persons ⟨*those* who think the time has come⟩ [Old English *thæt,* neuter demonstrative pron. and definite article]
²that *adj, pl* **those 1 :** being the person, thing, or idea specified, mentioned, or understood ⟨*that* child did it⟩ **2 :** the farther away or less immediately under observation or discussion ⟨this chair or *that* one⟩
³that \t͟hət, t͟hat, ,t͟hat\ *conj* **1 a** (1) — used to introduce a noun clause that is usually the subject or object of a verb or a predicate nominative ⟨said *that* they were afraid⟩ (2) — used to introduce a subordinate clause that is joined as complement to a noun or adjective ⟨certain *that* this is true⟩ ⟨the certainty *that* this is true⟩ ⟨the fact *that* you are here⟩ **b** — used to introduce an exclamatory clause expressing surprise, sorrow, or indignation ⟨*that* it should come to this⟩ **2a** — used to introduce a subordinate clause expressing purpose or desired result ⟨saved money so *that* they could buy bicycles⟩ **b** — used to introduce an exclamatory clause expressing a wish ⟨oh, *that* they were here⟩ **3** — used to introduce a subordinate clause expressing a reason or cause ⟨delighted *that* you could come⟩ **4** — used to introduce a subordinate clause expressing result, consequence, or effect ⟨worked so hard *that* they became exhausted⟩
⁴that \t͟hət, t͟hat, ,t͟hat\ *pron* **1** — used as a function word to introduce a relative clause and to serve as a substitute within that clause for the substantive modified by that clause ⟨the house *that* Jack built⟩ **2 a :** at which **:** in which **:** on which **:** by which **:** with which **:** to which ⟨each year *that* the lectures are given⟩ **b :** according to what **:** to the extent of what — used after a negative ⟨has never been there *that* I know of⟩ **syn** see WHO
⁵that \'t͟hat\ *adv* **1 :** to such an extent ⟨a nail about *that* long⟩ **2 :** VERY, EXTREMELY ⟨it's not *that* important⟩
¹thatch \'thach\ *vt* **:** to cover with or as if with thatch [Old English *theccan* "to cover"] — **thatch•er** *n*
²thatch *n* **1 :** a plant material (as straw) for use as roofing **2 :** a cover (as a roof) of thatch or as if of thatch ⟨a *thatch* of unruly hair⟩
¹thaw \'tho̊\ *vb* **1 :** to melt or cause to melt **:** reverse the effect of freezing ⟨ice on the pond is *thawing*⟩ **2 a :** to become so warm or mild as to melt ice or show **b :** to recover from chilling ⟨the skiers *thawed* out in front of the fire⟩ **3 :** to grow less cold or reserved in manner **:** become more friendly [Old English *thawian*]
²thaw *n* **1 :** the action, fact, or process of thawing **2 :** a warmth of weather sufficient to thaw ice
THC \,tē-,āch-'sē\ *n* **:** a physiologically active liquid from hemp plant resin that is the chief intoxicant in marijuana — called also *tetrahydrocannabinol* [tetrahydrocannabinol]
¹the *before consonant and especially South sometimes vowel sounds* t͟hə; *before vowel sounds* t͟hē; *1g is often* 't͟hē\ *definite article* **1 a :** that (one) or those (ones) previously mentioned or clearly understood from the context or situation ⟨put *the* cat out⟩ **b :** that unique (one) **:** that (one) existing as only one at a time ⟨*the* Lord⟩ ⟨*the* Pope⟩ **c :** that (one) or those (ones) near in space, time, or thought ⟨news of *the* day⟩ **d :** that (one) or those (ones) best known to the speaker or writer or to the hearer or reader ⟨*the* President⟩ ⟨*the* courts will decide⟩ **e :** MY, YOUR, HIS, HER, ITS, OUR, THEIR ⟨grabbed me by *the* collar⟩ ⟨how's *the* family⟩ ⟨*the* ankle is better today⟩ **f :** EACH, EVERY ⟨eighty crackers to *the* box⟩ **g :** that (one) or those (ones) considered best, most typical, or most worth singling out ⟨*the* poet of the decade⟩ ⟨my friend Adams is not one of *the* Adamses⟩ **2 a :** any (one) typical of or standing for an entire class so named ⟨courtesy distinguishes *the* gentleman⟩ ⟨good for *the* soul⟩ **b :** that which is ⟨an essay on *the* sublime⟩ **3 :** all those that are ⟨*the* Greeks⟩ ⟨*the* wise⟩ ⟨*the* aristocracy⟩ [Old English *thē,* masculine demonstrative pron. and definite article, alteration of *sē*]
²the *adv* **1 :** than before **:** than otherwise — used before a comparative ⟨none *the* wiser for attending⟩ **2 a :** to what extent ⟨*the* sooner the better⟩ **b :** to that extent ⟨the sooner *the* better⟩ **3 :** beyond all others ⟨likes this *the* best⟩ [Old English *thȳ* "by that", from *thæt* "that"]
the- *or* **theo-** *combining form* **:** god **:** God ⟨*the*ism⟩ [Greek *theos*]
the•ater *or* **the•atre** \'thē-ət-ər, *sometimes* 'thē-,āt-ər\ *n* **1 :** a building or area for dramatic performances or for showing movies **2 :** a place resembling a theater in form or use; *esp* **:** a room often with rising tiers of seats for assemblies (as for a lecture) **3 :** a place of enactment of significant events or action ⟨a *theater* of war⟩ **4 :** dramatic literature or performance [Middle French *theatre,* from Latin *theatrum,* from Greek *theatron,* from *theasthai* "to view", from *thea* "act of seeing"]
the•a•ter•go•er \-,gō-ər, -,gōr\ *n* **:** a person who frequently goes to the theater — **the•a•ter•go•ing** \-,gō-ing\ *n*
theater–in–the–round *n* **:** ARENA THEATER
the•at•ri•cal \thē-'a-tri-kəl\ *adj* **1 :** of or relating to the theater or the presentation of plays ⟨a *theatrical* costume⟩ **2 :** marked by pretense or artificiality of emotion **:** not natural and simple **:** SHOWY ⟨a *theatrical* acceptance speech⟩ **syn** see DRAMATIC — **the•at•ri•cal•ism** \-kə-,liz-əm\ *n* — **the•at•ri•cal•i•ty** \-,a-trə-'kal-ət-ē\ *n* — **the•at•ri•cal•ly** \-'a-tri-kə-lē, -klē\ *adv*
the•at•ri•cals \thē-'a-tri-kəlz\ *n pl* **1 :** the performance of plays ⟨amateur *theatricals*⟩ **2 :** the arts of acting and stagecraft
the•at•rics \-triks\ *n pl* **1 :** THEATRICALS 1 **2 :** staged or contrived effects
the•ca \'thē-kə\ *n, pl* **the•cae** \'thē-,sē, -,kē\ **:** an envelope or sheath enclosing an organism or one of its parts **:** CAPSULE, TEST [New Latin, from Greek *thēkē* "case"] — **the•cal** \'thē-kəl\ *adj* — **the•cate** \-,kāt\ *adj*
the•co•dont \'thē-kə-,dänt\ *n* **:** any of an order (Thecodontia) of Triassic reptiles held to be ancestral to the dinosaurs, crocodiles, and birds [derived from Greek *thēkē* "case" + *odont-, odous* "tooth"] — **thecodont** *adj*
thee \t͟hē, 't͟hē\ *pron, objective case of* THOU
theft \'theft\ *n* **:** the act of stealing: as **a :** LARCENY **b :** unlawful taking (as by embezzlement or burglary) of property [Old English *thīefth*]
thegn \'thān\ *n* **:** THANE 1 [Old English]
their \t͟hər, t͟heər, t͟haər, ,t͟heər, ,t͟haər\ *adj* **1 :** of or relating to them or themselves especially as possessors, agents, or objects of an action ⟨*their* clothes⟩ ⟨*their* deeds⟩ ⟨*their* being seen⟩ **2 :** his or her **:** HIS, HER, ITS — used with an indefinite 3d person singular antecedent ⟨anyone in *their* right mind⟩ [Old Norse *theirra,* pron.]
theirs \'t͟heərz, 't͟haərz\ *pron, sing or pl in construction* **1 :** that which belongs to them **:** those which belong to them — used without a following noun as an equivalent in meaning to the adjective *their* **2 :** his or hers **:** HIS, HERS — used with an indefinite 3d person singular antecedent ⟨I will do my part if everybody else will do *theirs*⟩
the•ism \'thē-,iz-əm\ *n* **:** belief in the existence of a god or gods; *esp* **:** belief in the existence of God as creator and ruler of the universe — **the•ist** \'thē-əst\ *n* — **the•is•tic** \thē-'is-tik\

adj — **the•is•ti•cal** \-'is-ti-kəl\ *adj* — **the•is•ti•cal•ly** \-ti-kə-lē, -klē\ *adv*

-theism *n combining form* **:** belief in (such) a god or (such or so many) gods ⟨mono*theism*⟩

-theist *n combining form* **:** believer in (such) a god or (such or so many) gods ⟨mono*theist*⟩

them \thəm, əm, them, 'them, *after* p, b, v, f *also* ᵊm\ *pron, objective case of* THEY

theme \'thēm\ *n* **1 :** a subject of discourse, artistic representation, or musical composition **2 :** a written exercise **:** COMPOSITION [Latin *themat-, thema,* from Greek, literally, "something laid down", from *tithenai* "to put"] — **the•mat•ic** \thi-'mat-ik\ *adj* — **the•mat•i•cal•ly** \-'mat-i-kə-lē, -klē\ *adv*

theme song *n* **1 :** a melody recurring so often in a musical play that it characterizes the production or one of its characters **2 :** SIGNATURE 4

them•selves \thəm-'selvz, them-\ *pron pl* **1 a :** those identical ones that are they — used reflexively or for emphasis ⟨nations that govern *themselves*⟩ ⟨they *themselves* were present⟩; compare THEY **b :** himself or herself **:** HIMSELF, HERSELF — used with an indefinite 3d person singular antecedent ⟨nobody can call *themselves* worthy⟩ **2 :** their normal, healthy, or sane condition or selves ⟨were *themselves* again after a night's rest⟩

[1]then \then, 'then\ *adv* **1 :** at that time **2 a :** soon after that ⟨walked to the door, *then* turned⟩ **b :** following next after in order **c :** in addition **:** BESIDES **3 a :** in that case **b :** according to that ⟨your mind is made up, *then*⟩ **c :** as it appears ⟨the cause, *then,* is established⟩ **d :** as a necessary consequence ⟨if you were there, *then* you saw them⟩ [Old English *thonne, thænne*]

[2]then \'then\ *n* **:** that time ⟨wait until *then*⟩

[3]then \'then\ *adj* **:** existing or acting at or belonging to the time mentioned ⟨the *then* king⟩

thence \'thens, 'thens\ *adv* **1 :** from that place **2** *archaic* **:** from that time **:** THENCEFORTH **3 :** from that fact or circumstance **:** THEREFROM [Middle English *thanne, thannes,* from Old English *thanon*]

thence•forth \-,fōrth, -,fȯrth\ *adv* **:** from that time forward **:** THEREAFTER

thence•for•ward \thens-'fȯr-wərd, thens-\ *also* **thence•for•wards** \-wərdz\ *adv* **:** onward from that place or time **:** THENCEFORTH

theo- — see THE-

the•oc•ra•cy \thē-'äk-rə-sē\ *n, pl* **-cies 1 :** government of a country by officials regarded as divinely guided **2 :** a country governed by a theocracy — **theo•crat** \'thē-ə-,krat\ *n* — **theo•crat•ic** \,thē-ə-'krat-ik\ *adj* — **theo•crat•i•cal•ly** \-'krat-i-kə-lē, -klē\ *adv*

the•od•o•lite \thē-'äd-l-,īt\ *n* **:** a surveyor's instrument for measuring horizontal and usually also vertical angles [New Latin *theodelitus*] — **the•od•o•lit•ic** \-,äd-l-'it-ik\ *adj*

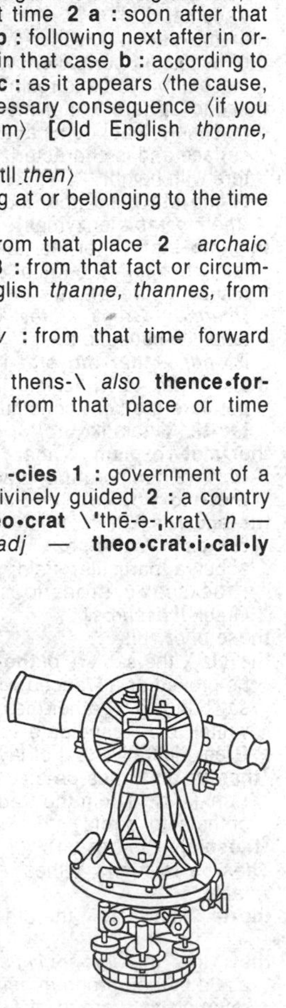

theodolite

theo•lo•gian \,thē-ə-'lō-jən\ *n* **:** a specialist in theology

theo•log•i•cal \,thē-ə-'läj-i-kəl\ *adj* **:** of or relating to theology — **theo•log•i•cal•ly** \-kə-lē, -klē\ *adv*

theological virtue *n* **:** a spiritual grace (as faith, hope, or charity) held to perfect the natural virtues

the•ol•o•gy \thē-'äl-ə-jē\ *n, pl* **-gies 1 :** the study and interpretation of religious faith, practice, and experience; *esp* **:** thought about God and his relation to the world **2 :** a course of professional religious training

the•o•rem \'thē-ə-rəm, 'thi-ər-əm, 'thir-əm\ *n* **1 :** a formula, proposition, or statement (as in logic) that has been or is to be proved from other formulas or propositions **2 :** an idea accepted or proposed as a demonstrable truth **:** PROPOSITION [Late Latin *theorema,* from Greek *theōrēma,* from *theōrein* "to look at", derived from *thea* "act of seeing"]

the•o•ret•i•cal \,thē-ə-'ret-i-kəl\ *also* **the•o•ret•ic** \-'ret-ik\ *adj* **1 a :** relating to or having the character of theory **:** ABSTRACT **b :** confined to theory or speculation **:** SPECULATIVE ⟨*theoretical* mechanics⟩ **2 :** given to or skilled in theorizing **3 :** existing only in theory **:** HYPOTHETICAL [Late Latin *theoreticus,* from Greek *theōrētikos,* from *theōrein* "to look at"] — **the•o•ret•i•cal•ly** \-i-kə-lē, -klē\ *adv*

the•o•re•ti•cian \,thē-ə-rə-'tish-ən\ *n* **:** THEORIST

the•o•rist \'thē-ə-rəst, 'thi-ər-əst, 'thir-əst\ *n* **:** a person who theorizes

the•o•rize \'thē-ə-,rīz\ *vb* **-rized; -riz•ing :** to form a theory **:** SPECULATE — **the•o•ri•za•tion** \,thē-ə-rə-'zā-shən\ *n* — **the•o•riz•er** \'thē-ə-,rī-zər\ *n*

the•o•ry \'thē-ə-rē, 'thi-ər-ē, 'thir-ē\ *n, pl* **-ries 1 :** the general or abstract principles of a body of fact, a science, or an art ⟨music *theory*⟩ — compare PRACTICE **2 :** a plausible or scientifically acceptable general principle or body of principles offered to explain phenomena ⟨the wave *theory* of light⟩ **3 a :** a hypothesis assumed for the sake of argument or investigation **b :** SUPPOSITION 1, CONJECTURE **4 :** abstract thought **:** SPECULATION [Late Latin *theoria,* from Greek *theōria,* from *theōrein* "to look at"] **syn** see HYPOTHESIS

the•os•o•phy \thē-'äs-ə-fē\ *n* **1 :** belief about God and the world held to be based on mystical insight **2** *often cap* **:** the beliefs of a modern movement originating in the United States in 1875, following chiefly Buddhist and Hindu philosophies, and seeking to promote universal brotherhood and spiritual growth [Medieval Latin *theosophia,* from Late Greek, from Greek *theos* "god" + *sophia* "wisdom"] — **the•o•soph•i•cal** \,thē-ə-'säf-i-kəl\ *adj* — **the•o•soph•i•cal•ly** \-'säf-i-kə-lē, -klē\ *adv* — **the•os•o•phist** \thē-'äs-ə-fəst\ *n*

ther•a•peu•tic \,ther-ə-'pyüt-ik\ *adj* **:** of, relating to, or dealing with healing and especially with remedies for diseases **:** MEDICINAL ⟨a *therapeutic* dose of arsenic⟩ ⟨*therapeutic* studies⟩ [Greek *therapeutikos,* from *therapeuein* "to attend, treat", from *theraps* "attendant"] — **ther•a•peu•ti•cal•ly** \-'pyüt-i-kə-lē, -klē\ *adv*

ther•a•peu•tics \-'pyüt-iks\ *n* **:** a branch of medical science dealing with the use of remedies

ther•a•pist \'ther-ə-pəst\ *n* **:** one specializing in therapy; *esp* **:** a person trained in methods of treatment and rehabilitation other than the use of drugs or surgery ⟨a speech *therapist*⟩

the•rap•sid \thə-'rap-səd\ *n* **:** any of an order (Therapsida) of Permian and Triassic reptiles held to be ancestral to the mammals [perhaps from Greek *theraps* "attendant"]

ther•a•py \'ther-ə-pē\ *n, pl* **-pies :** therapeutic treatment of bodily, mental, or social disorders or maladjustment [Greek *therapeia,* from *therapeuein* "to treat"]

[1]there \'thaər, 'theər\ *adv* **1 :** in or at that place ⟨stand over *there*⟩ **2 :** to or into that place **3 :** at that point or stage ⟨*there* the plot thickens⟩ **4 :** in that matter, respect, or relation ⟨*there* you have a choice⟩ **5** — used interjectionally to express satisfaction, approval, soothing, or defiance ⟨*there,* I'm through⟩ [Old English *thær*]

[2]there \thaər, theər, ,thaər, ,theər, *1 is also* thər\ *pron* **1** — used as the grammatical subject in a sentence in which the logical subject appears in the predicate (1) usually after a form of *be* as an auxiliary verb ⟨*there* are some people waiting to see you⟩ or as a full verb ⟨*there* might be something wrong⟩ or (2) rarely after a full verb other than *be* ⟨*there* arose a great howl⟩ **2** — used as an indefinite substitute for a name ⟨hi *there*⟩

[3]there *like*[1]\ *n* **1 :** that place or position **2 :** that point ⟨you take it from *there*⟩

[4]there *like*[1]\ *adj* — used for emphasis especially after a demonstrative pronoun or a noun modified by a demonstrative adjective ⟨those people *there* can tell you⟩

there•abouts *or* **there•about** \,thar-ə-'bau̇ts, ,ther-, -ə-'bau̇t\ *adv* **1 :** near that place or time **2 :** about that amount or number ⟨fifty people or *thereabouts*⟩

there•af•ter \tha-'raf-tər, the-\ *adv* **:** after that

there•at \-'rat\ *adv* **1 :** at that place **2 :** at that occurrence **:** on that account

there•by \thaər-'bī, theər-\ *adv* **1 :** by that **:** by that means ⟨made a friend *thereby*⟩ **2 :** connected with or with reference to that ⟨*thereby* hangs a tale⟩

\ə\ **abut**	\au̇\ **out**	\i\ **tip**	\ȯ\ **saw**	\u̇\ **foot**
\ər\ **further**	\ch\ **chin**	\ī\ **life**	\ȯi\ **coin**	\y\ **yet**
\a\ **mat**	\e\ **pet**	\j\ **job**	\th\ **thin**	\yü\ **few**
\ā\ **take**	\ē\ **easy**	\ng\ **sing**	\th\ **this**	\yu̇\ **cure**
\ä\ **cot, cart**	\g\ **go**	\ō\ **bone**	\ü\ **food**	\zh\ **vision**

there·for \-ˈfȯr\ *adv* : for or in return for that ⟨issued bonds *therefor*⟩

there·fore \ˈthaər-ˌfōr, ˈthear-, -ˌfȯr\ *adv* **1 a** : for that reason : CONSEQUENTLY **b** : because of that **c** : on that ground **2** : to that end

there·from \thaər-ˈfrəm, theər-, -ˈfräm\ *adv* : from that or it ⟨learned much *therefrom*⟩

there·in \tha-ˈrin, the-\ *adv* **1** : in or into that place, time, or thing ⟨the world and all *therein*⟩ **2** : in that particular or respect ⟨*therein* they disagreed⟩

there·in·af·ter \ˌthar-in-ˈaf-tər, ˌther-\ *adv* : in the following part of that matter (as writing, document, or speech)

there·of \tha-ˈrəv, the-, -ˈräv\ *adv* **1** : of that or it **2** : from that cause or particular : THEREFROM

there·on \-ˈrȯn, -ˈrän\ *adv* : on that ⟨a table with a vase set *thereon*⟩

there·to \thaər-ˈtü, theər-\ *adv* : to that ⟨signed my name *thereto*⟩

there·to·fore \ˈthart-ə-ˌfōr, ˈthert-, -ˌfȯr\ *adv* : up to that time

there·up·on \ˈthar-ə-ˌpȯn, ˈther-, -ˌpän\ *adv* **1** : on that matter : THEREON ⟨they disagreed *thereupon*⟩ **2** : THEREFORE **3** : immediately after that : at once

there·with \thaər-ˈwith, theər-, -ˈwith\ *adv* : with that ⟨led a simple life and was happy *therewith*⟩

there·with·al \ˈthaər-with-ˌȯl, ˈtheər-, -with-\ *adv* **1** *archaic* : BESIDES **2** : THEREWITH

therm- *or* **thermo-** *combining form* : heat ⟨*therm*ion⟩ ⟨*thermo*stat⟩ [Greek *thermē*]

[1]**ther·mal** \ˈthər-məl\ *adj* : of, relating to, or caused by heat : WARM, HOT — **ther·mal·ly** \-mə-lē\ *adv*

[2]**thermal** *n* : a rising body of warm air

thermal pollution *n* : the discharge of heated liquid (as water) into natural waters at a temperature harmful to the surrounding ecosystem

thermal spring *n* : a spring whose water is warmer than the locality in which it is situated

therm·ion \ˈthər-ˌmī-ən, -ˌmī-ˌän\ *n* : an electrically charged particle emitted by an incandescent substance — **therm·ion·ic** \ˌthər-mī-ˈän-ik\ *adj*

therm·is·tor \ˈthər-ˌmis-tər\ *n* : an electrical resistor made of a material whose resistance varies sharply in a known manner with the temperature [*therm*al re*sistor*]

ther·mo·cline \ˈthər-mə-ˌklīn\ *n* : a layer of water in a body of water (as a lake) separating an upper warmer lighter oxygen-rich zone from a lower colder heavier oxygen-poor zone

ther·mo·cou·ple \ˈthər-mə-ˌkəp-əl\ *n* : a thermoelectric couple used to measure temperature differences

ther·mo·dy·nam·ics \ˌthər-mō-dī-ˈnam-iks, -də-\ *n* : physics that deals with the mechanical action or relations of heat — **ther·mo·dy·nam·ic** \-ik\ *adj* — **ther·mo·dy·nam·i·cal·ly** \-ˈnam-i-kə-lē, -klē\ *adv*

ther·mo·elec·tric \ˌthər-mō-i-ˈlek-trik\ *adj* : of or relating to phenomena involving relations between the temperature and the electrical condition in a metal or in contacting metals

thermoelectric couple *n* : a union of two conductors (as bars or wires of dissimilar metals joined at their extremities) for producing a thermoelectric current

ther·mo·elec·tric·i·ty \ˌthər-mō-i-ˌlek-ˈtris-ət-ē, -ˈtris-tē\ *n* : electricity produced by the direct action of heat (as by the unequal heating of a circuit composed of two dissimilar metals)

ther·mo·graph \ˈthər-mə-ˌgraf\ *n* : a self-recording thermometer

ther·mo·la·bile \ˌthər-mō-ˈlā-ˌbīl, -bəl\ *adj* : unstable when heated ⟨many enzymes and vitamins are *thermolabile*⟩ — compare THERMOSTABLE — **ther·mo·la·bil·i·ty** \-lā-ˈbil-ət-ē\ *n*

ther·mom·e·ter \thər-ˈmäm-ət-ər, thə-ˈmäm-\ *n* : an instrument for measuring temperature commonly by means of the expansion or contraction of mercury or alcohol as indicated by its rise or fall in a thin glass tube alongside a scale — **ther·mo·met·ric** \ˌthər-mə-ˈme-trik\ *adj* — **ther·mo·met·ri·cal·ly** \-tri-kə-lē, -klē\ *adv*

ther·mom·e·try \thər-ˈmäm-ə-trē, thə-ˈmäm-\ *n* : the measurement of temperature

ther·mo·nu·cle·ar \ˌthər-mō-ˈnü-klē-ər, -ˈnyü-\ *adj* **1** : of or relating to the transformations in the nucleus of atoms of low atomic weight (as hydrogen) that require a very high temperature (as in the hydrogen bomb or in the sun) ⟨a *thermonuclear* reaction⟩ ⟨a *thermonuclear* weapon⟩ **2** : of, utilizing, or relating to a thermonuclear bomb ⟨*thermonuclear* war⟩

ther·mo·phile \ˈthər-mə-ˌfīl\ *n* : an organism growing at a high temperature — **ther·mo·phil·ic** \ˌthər-mə-ˈfil-ik\ *adj*

ther·mo·pile \ˈthər-mə-ˌpīl\ *n* : an apparatus consisting of a number of thermoelectric couples combined so as to multiply the effect and used for generating electric currents or for determining intensities of radiation

ther·mo·plas·tic \ˌthər-mə-ˈplas-tik\ *adj* : having the property of softening or fusing when heated and of hardening again when cooled ⟨*thermoplastic* synthetic resins⟩ — **thermoplastic** *n*

ther·mo·reg·u·la·tor \ˌthər-mō-ˈreg-yə-ˌlāt-ər\ *n* : a device (as a thermostat) for the regulation of temperature

ther·mos \ˈthər-məs\ *n* : VACUUM BOTTLE [from *Thermos*, a former trademark]

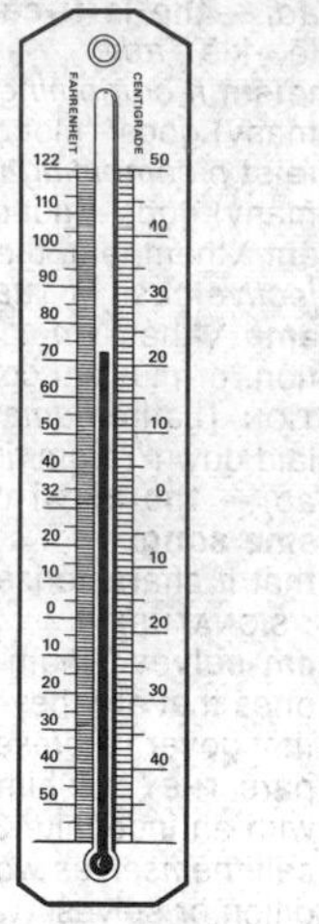

thermometer

ther·mo·set·ting \ˈthər-mō-ˌset-ing\ *adj* : having the property of becoming permanently rigid when heated or cured ⟨a *thermosetting* synthetic resin⟩

ther·mo·sphere \ˈthər-mə-ˌsfiər\ *n* : the part of the earth's atmosphere that begins at about 80 kilometers above the earth's surface and is characterized by a steady increase in temperature with height

ther·mo·sta·ble \ˌthər-mō-ˈstā-bəl\ *adj* : stable when heated ⟨*thermostable* enzymes⟩ — compare THERMOLABILE

ther·mo·stat \ˈthər-mə-ˌstat\ *n* : an automatic device for regulating temperature (as of a heating system); *also* : a device for actuating fire alarms or for controlling automatic sprinklers [*therm-* + Greek *-statēs* "one that stops or steadies", from *histanai* "to cause to stand"] — **ther·mo·stat·ic** \ˌthər-mə-ˈstat-ik\ *adj* — **ther·mo·stat·i·cal·ly** \-ˈstat-i-kə-lē, -klē\ *adv*

ther·mo·tax·is \ˌthər-mə-ˈtak-səs\ *n* : a taxis in which a temperature gradient constitutes the directive factor — **ther·mo·tac·tic** \-ˈtak-tik\ *adj*

ther·mot·ro·pism \ˌthər-ˈmä-trə-ˌpiz-əm\ *n* : a tropism in which a temperature gradient determines the orientation — **ther·mo·trop·ic** \ˌthər-mə-ˈträp-ik\ *adj*

the·sau·rus \thi-ˈsȯr-əs\ *n, pl* **-sau·ri** \-ˈsȯr-ˌī, -ˌē\ *or* **-sau·rus·es** \-ˈsȯr-ə-səz\ **1** : a book of words or of information about a particular field; *esp* : a dictionary of synonyms **2** : TREASURY 3, STOREHOUSE [Latin, "treasure, collection", from Greek *thēsauros*]

these *pl of* THIS

the·sis \ˈthē-səs\ *n, pl* **the·ses** \ˈthē-ˌsēz\ **1** : a proposition to be proved or advanced without proof : HYPOTHESIS **2** : an essay bringing together the results of original research; *esp* : one written by a candidate for an academic degree [Latin, from Greek, literally, "act of laying down", from *tithenai* "to put"]

[1]**thes·pi·an** \ˈthes-pē-ən\ *adj, often cap* : relating to the drama : DRAMATIC [from the tradition that Thespis was the originator of the actor's role]

[2]**thespian** *n* : ACTOR 1b

Thes·sa·lo·nians \ˌthes-ə-ˈlō-nyənz, -nē-ənz\ *n* — see BIBLE table

the·ta \ˈthāt-ə\ *n* : the 8th letter of the Greek alphabet — Θ or θ

they \thā, ˈthā\ *pron, pl in construction* **1 a** : those ones — used as 3d person pronoun serving as the plural of *he, she,* or *it* or referring to a group of two or more individuals not all of the same sex ⟨*they* dance well⟩ **b** : [1]HE 2 — often used with an indefinite 3d person singular antecedent ⟨anyone can leave if *they* like⟩ **2** : PEOPLE 1 — used in a generic sense ⟨as lazy as *they* come⟩ ⟨*they* say it will rain⟩ [Old Norse *their*]

they'd \thād, ˌthād\ : they had : they would

they'll \thāl, ˌthāl, thel\ : they shall : they will

they're \thər, theər, ˌtheər, ˌthā-ər\ : they are

they've \thāv, ˌthāv\ : they have

thi- *or* **thio-** *combining form* : containing sulfur ⟨*thio*urea⟩ [Greek *theion* "sulfur"]

thi·a·mine \ˈthī-ə-mən, -ˌmēn\ *also* **thi·a·min** \-mən\ *n* : a vitamin of the vitamin B complex essential to normal metabolism and nerve function and widely distributed in plants and animals — called also *vitamin B, vitamin B_1* [*thiamine* alteration of *thiamin,* from *thi-* + *-amin* (as in *vitamin*)]

¹thick \'thik\ *adj* **1 a :** having or being of relatively great depth or extent from one surface to its opposite ⟨a *thick* plank⟩ **b :** heavily built : THICKSET **2 a :** close-packed : DENSE ⟨*thick* forest⟩ **b :** occurring in large numbers : NUMEROUS **c :** viscous in consistency ⟨*thick* syrup⟩ **d :** SULTRY, STUFFY ⟨air *thick* with smoke⟩ **e :** marked by haze, fog, or mist ⟨*thick* weather⟩ **f :** impenetrable to the eye ⟨*thick* fog⟩ **g :** extremely intense ⟨*thick* silence⟩ **3 :** measuring in thickness ⟨12 inches *thick*⟩ **4 a :** imperfectly articulated : INDISTINCT ⟨*thick* speech⟩ **b :** PRONOUNCED ⟨a *thick* French accent⟩ **c :** producing inarticulate speech ⟨a *thick* tongue⟩ **5 :** OBTUSE 1, STUPID **6 :** associated on close terms : INTIMATE [Old English *thicce*] — **thick•ish** \-ish\ *adj* — **thick•ly** *adv*

²thick *n* **1 :** the most crowded or active part ⟨in the *thick* of battle⟩ **2 :** the part of greatest thickness

³thick *adv* **:** THICKLY

thick and thin *n* **:** every difficulty and obstacle ⟨stood by their friend through *thick and thin*⟩

thick•en \'thik-ən\ *vb* **thick•ened; thick•en•ing** \'thik-ning, -ə-ning\ **1 :** to make or become thick, dense, or viscous **2 :** to add to the depth or diameter of **3 a :** to make inarticulate : BLUR ⟨alcohol *thickened* their speech⟩ **b :** to grow blurred or obscure **4 :** to grow broader or bulkier **5 :** to grow complicated or keen ⟨the plot *thickens*⟩ — **thick•en•er** \'thik-nər, -ə-nər\ *n*

thick•en•ing *n* **1 :** the act of making or becoming thick **2 :** something used to thicken (as flour in a gravy) **3 :** a thickened part or place

thick•et \'thik-ət\ *n* **1 :** a thick usually circumscribed growth of shrubbery, small trees, or underbrush **2 :** something resembling a thicket in density or impenetrability : TANGLE [Old English *thiccet,* from *thicce* "thick"] — **thick•et•ed** \-ət-əd\ *adj*

thick•head•ed \'thik-'hed-əd\ *adj* **1 :** having a thick head **2 :** mentally dull

thick•ness \'thik-nəs\ *n* **1 :** the quality or state of being thick **2 :** the smallest of the three dimensions of something ⟨length, width, and *thickness* of a board⟩ **3 :** viscous consistency ⟨the *thickness* of honey⟩ **4 :** the thick part of something **5 :** CONCENTRATION 3, DENSITY **6 :** dullness of mind **7 :** LAYER, PLY, SHEET ⟨a single *thickness* of canvas⟩

thick•set \'thik-'set\ *adj* **:** of short stout build : STOCKY

thick–skinned \-'skind\ *adj* **1 :** having a thick skin **2 :** CALLOUS 2, INSENSITIVE

thick–wit•ted \-'wit-əd\ *adj* **:** dull or slow of mind : STUPID

thief \'thēf\ *n, pl* **thieves** \'thēvz\ **:** one that steals [Old English *thēof*] — **thiev•ish** \'thē-vish\ *adj* — **thiev•ish•ly** *adv* — **thiev•ish•ness** *n*

thieve \'thēv\ *vb* **1 :** to commit a theft **2** *chiefly British* **:** to take by stealth : STEAL

thiev•ery \'thēv-rē, -ə-rē\ *n, pl* **-er•ies :** the action of stealing : THEFT

thigh \'thī\ *n* **1 a :** the segment of the vertebrate hind limb extending from the hip to the knee and supported by a single large bone; *also* **:** the next outer segment in a bird or in a four-footed animal in which the true thigh is obscured **b :** the femur of an insect **2 :** something resembling or covering a thigh [Old English *thēoh*]

thigh•bone \-'bōn, -,bōn\ *n* **:** FEMUR 1

thig•mo•tax•is \,thig-mə-'tak-səs\ *n* **:** a taxis in which contact (as with a rigid surface) is the directive factor [Greek *thigma* "contact", from *thinganein* "to touch"]

thig•mot•ro•pism \thig-'mä-trə-,piz-əm\ *n* **:** a tropism in which contact (as with a rigid surface) is the orienting factor

thim•ble \'thim-bəl\ *n* **1 :** a cap or cover used in sewing to protect the finger that pushes the needle **2 :** a grooved ring of thin metal used to fit in a loop in a wire or rope **3 :** a fixed or movable ring, tube, or lining in a hole [Middle English *thymbyl,* probably from Old English *thȳmel* "covering for the thumb", from *thūma* "thumb"]

thim•ble•ber•ry \-,ber-ē\ *n* **:** any of several American raspberries or blackberries with thimble-shaped fruit

thim•ble•ful \-,fu̇l\ *n* **1 :** as much as a thimble will hold **2 :** a very small quantity

¹thim•ble•rig \'thim-bəl-,rig\ *n* **:** a swindling trick in which a small ball or pea is quickly shifted from under one to another of three small cups to fool a spectator guessing its location

²thimblerig *vt* **1 :** to swindle by thimblerig **2 :** to cheat by trickery — **thim•ble•rig•ger** *n*

¹thin \'thin\ *adj* **thin•ner; thin•nest 1 a :** having little extent from one surface to its opposite ⟨*thin* paper⟩ **b :** measuring little in cross section or diameter ⟨*thin* rope⟩ **2 :** not dense in arrangement or distribution ⟨*thin* hair⟩ **3 :** not plump or fat : LEAN **4 a :** more fluid or rarefied than normal ⟨*thin* air⟩ **b :** not well filled or supplied : SCANTY ⟨a *thin* market⟩ **5 :** lacking substance or strength ⟨*thin* broth⟩ ⟨a *thin* excuse⟩ **6 :** somewhat feeble, shrill, and lacking in resonance ⟨a *thin* voice⟩ [Old English *thynne*] — **thin•ly** *adv* — **thin•ness** \'thin-nəs\ *n* — **thin•nish** \'thin-ish\ *adj*

• syn THIN, SLENDER, SLIM, SLIGHT mean not thick, broad, abundant, or dense. THIN implies comparatively little extension between surfaces or in diameter ⟨a *thin* layer of ice⟩ ⟨*thin* wire⟩ or it may imply lack of substance, richness, or abundance ⟨*thin* soup⟩ ⟨a *thin* hedge⟩ SLENDER implies leanness often with graceful proportions ⟨*slender* columns⟩ SLIM suggests scantiness or fragile slenderness ⟨a *slim* paycheck⟩ SLIGHT implies thinness and smallness ⟨a person of *slight* build⟩

²thin *adv* **thin•ner; thin•nest :** THINLY ⟨*thin*-clad⟩

³thin *vb* **thinned; thin•ning :** to make or become thin or thinner: **a :** to reduce in thickness or depth **b :** to make less dense or viscous **c :** DILUTE 2, WEAKEN **d :** to cause to lose flesh **e :** to reduce in number or bulk

¹thine \t͟hīn, 't͟hīn\ *adj, archaic* **:** THY — used especially before a word beginning with a vowel [Old English *thīn*]

²thine \'t͟hīn\ *pron, sing or pl in construction* **:** that which belongs to thee : those which belong to thee — used without a following noun as an equivalent in meaning to the adjective *thy*; used especially in ecclesiastical or literary language

thing \'thing\ *n* **1 a :** a matter of concern : AFFAIR ⟨many *things* to do⟩ **b** *pl* **:** state of affairs in general or within a specified or implied sphere ⟨*things* are improving⟩ **c :** a particular state of affairs : SITUATION ⟨look at this *thing* another way⟩ **d :** EVENT, CIRCUMSTANCE ⟨that shooting was a terrible *thing*⟩ **2 a :** DEED, ACT, ACCOMPLISHMENT ⟨do great *things*⟩ **b :** a product of work or activity ⟨likes to build *things*⟩ **c :** the aim of effort or activity ⟨the *thing* is to get well⟩ **3 a :** a separate and distinct item or object : ENTITY; *esp* **:** a physical object **b :** an inanimate object as distinguished from a living being **4 a** *pl* **:** PERSONAL PROPERTY ⟨pack your *things*⟩ **b :** an article of clothing ⟨not a *thing* to wear⟩ **c** *pl* **:** equipment or utensils especially for a particular purpose ⟨bring the tea *things*⟩ **5 :** an object or entity not precisely designated or capable of being designated ⟨how do you use this *thing*⟩ **6 a :** DETAIL, POINT ⟨checks every little *thing*⟩ **b :** a material or substance of a specified kind ⟨avoid starchy *things*⟩ **7 a :** a spoken or written observation or point **b :** IDEA, NOTION ⟨say the first *thing* you think of⟩ **c :** a piece of news or information ⟨couldn't get a *thing* out of the prisoner⟩ **8 :** INDIVIDUAL; *esp* **:** PERSON ⟨you poor *thing*⟩ **9 :** the proper or fashionable way of behaving, talking, or dressing ⟨it is the *thing* to do⟩ **10 a :** an irrational fear or obsession ⟨have a *thing* about snakes⟩ **b :** something with strong personal appeal ⟨students allowed to do their own *thing*⟩ [Old English, "thing, assembly"]

thing•am•a•bob \'thing-ə-mə-,bäb\ *n* **:** THINGAMAJIG

thing•am•a•jig *or* **thing•um•a•jig** \'thing-ə-mə-,jig\ *n* **:** something that is hard to classify or whose name is unknown or forgotten [derived from *thing*]

thing•um•my \'thing-ə-mē\ *n, pl* **-mies :** THINGAMAJIG [derived from *thing*]

¹think \'thingk\ *vb* **thought** \'thȯt\; **think•ing 1 :** to form or have in the mind **2 :** INTEND, PLAN ⟨*thought* to return early⟩ **3 a :** to have as an opinion : BELIEVE ⟨*think* it's so⟩ **b :** to regard as : CONSIDER ⟨*think* the rule unfair⟩ **4 :** to reflect on : PONDER ⟨*think* the matter over⟩ **5 :** to call to mind : REMEMBER ⟨couldn't *think* of the name⟩ **6 :** to create or devise by thinking ⟨*think* up a caption for the picture⟩ **7 :** to subject to the processes of logical thought ⟨*think* things out⟩ **8 :** to exercise the powers of judgment, conception, or inference : REASON **9 a :** to have the mind engaged in reflection : MEDITATE ⟨*thinking* sadly of the past⟩ **b** : to consider the suitability ⟨*thought* of you for captain⟩ **10** : to have a view or opinion ⟨*think* of myself as a skier⟩ **11** : to have concern ⟨*think* of just yourself⟩ **12** : EXPECT 4a ⟨*thought* to find them at home⟩ [Old English *thencan*] — **think•able** \'thing-kə-bəl\ *adj* — **think•er** *n*

• **syn** THINK, REFLECT, REASON, SPECULATE mean to use one's powers of conception, judgment, or inference. THINK may apply to any mental activity but often suggests attainment of clear ideas or conclusions; REFLECT suggests unhurried consideration of something recalled to mind; REASON stresses orderly logical thinking especially in reaching a conclusion; SPECULATE implies reasoning but stresses the uncertain, theoretical, or problematic character of the conclusions ⟨*speculated* on the probable consequences of a nuclear war⟩

— **think better of** : to reconsider and make a wiser decision — **think much of** : to view with satisfaction — usually used in negative constructions ⟨didn't *think much of* the idea⟩

²think *n* : an act of thinking ⟨has another *think* coming⟩

¹think•ing *n* **1** : the action of using one's mind to produce thoughts **2 a** : OPINION, JUDGMENT ⟨it is, to my *thinking*, utter nonsense⟩ **b** : THOUGHT 3b

²thinking *adj* : marked by use of the intellect : RATIONAL — **think•ing•ly** \'thing-king-lē\ *adv* — **think•ing•ness** *n*

thinking cap *n* : a state or mood in which one thinks ⟨put on your *thinking cap*⟩

think piece *n* : a news article consisting chiefly of background material and personal opinion and analysis

thin•ner \'thin-ər\ *n* : one that thins; *esp* : a volatile liquid (as turpentine) used to thin paint

thin–skinned \'thin-'skind\ *adj* **1** : having a thin skin **2** : unduly sensitive to criticism or insult : TOUCHY

thio- — see THI-

thio•urea \ˌthī-ō-yu̇-'rē-ə\ *n* : a colorless crystalline bitter compound $CS(NH_2)_2$ analogous to and resembling urea that is used especially as a photographic and organic chemical reagent

thi•ram \'thī-ˌram\ *n* : a sulfur-containing fungicide and seed disinfectant [derived from Greek *theion* "sulfur"]

¹third \'thərd\ *adj* **1** : being number three in a countable series **2** : being next after the second (as in order, time, or importance) **3** : being one of three equal parts [Old English *thridda, thirdda*] — **third** *adv* — **third•ly** *adv*

²third *n* **1** : number three in a countable series — see NUMBER table **2** : one of three equal parts **3 a** : a musical interval of three degrees or a tone at this interval **b** : the harmonic combination of two tones a third apart **4** : the third gear or speed of an automotive vehicle **5** : one next after a second (as in time, order, or importance)

third base *n* **1** : the base that must be touched third by a base runner in baseball **2** : the position of the player defending the area around third base

third base•man \-'bā-smən\ *n* : the player defending the area around third base

third class *n* : the class next below second class in a classification ⟨travel by *third class* to Europe⟩; *esp* : a class of United States mail including various printed matter and merchandise that weighs less than 16 ounces and is open to inspection — **third–class** *adj or adv*

third degree *n* : severe or brutal treatment of a prisoner (as by police) in order to get information or a confession

third–degree burn *n* : a burn in which there is destruction of the whole thickness of the skin and sometimes of deeper tissues with loss of fluid and often shock

third dimension *n* : thickness, depth, or apparent thickness or depth that confers solidity on an object — **third–di•men•sion•al** *adj*

third estate *n* : the third of the traditional political orders : COMMON 3a; *also* : MIDDLE CLASS

third force *n* : a grouping (as of political parties or international powers) intermediate between two opposing political forces

third order *n, often cap T&O* **1** : an organization composed of lay people living in secular society under a religious rule and directed by a religious order **2** : a congregation especially of teaching or nursing sisters affiliated with a religious order

third party *n* **1** : a person other than the principals ⟨a *third party* to a divorce proceeding⟩ **2** : a political party operating usually for a limited time in addition to the two major parties in a 2-party system

third person *n* : a set of words or forms (as verb forms or pronouns) referring to someone or something that is neither the speaker or writer of the utterance in which they occur nor the one to whom that utterance is addressed; *also* : a word or form belonging to such a set

third rail *n* : a metal rail which is parallel to the tracks and through which electric current is led to the motors of an electric locomotive

third–rate \'thər-'drāt\ *adj* : of third quality or value; *esp* : worse than second-rate — **third–rat•er** \-'drāt-ər\ *n*

third world *n, often cap T&W* : a group of nations mostly of Africa and Asia claiming to be aligned with neither the Communist nor non-Communist blocs

¹thirst \'thərst\ *n* **1** : a feeling of dryness in the mouth and throat associated with a desire for liquids; *also* : the bodily condition (as of dehydration) that induces this **2** : an ardent desire : LONGING ⟨a *thirst* for knowledge⟩ [Old English *thurst*]

²thirst *vi* **1** : to feel thirsty : suffer thirst **2** : to have a strong desire : LONG

thirsty \'thər-stē\ *adj* **thirst•i•er**; **-est** **1 a** : feeling thirst **b** : lacking moisture : ARID ⟨*thirsty* land⟩ **c** : highly absorbent ⟨*thirsty* towels⟩ **2** : having a strong desire : AVID ⟨*thirsty* for knowledge⟩ — **thirst•i•ly** \-stə-lē\ *adv* — **thirst•i•ness** \-stē-nəs\ *n*

thir•teen \ˌthər-'tēn, ˌthərt-, 'thər-, 'thərt-\ *n* : one more than 12; *also* : a symbol representing this — see NUMBER table [Old English *thrēotīne*] — **thirteen** *adj or pron* — **thir•teenth** \-'tēnth, -'tēntth\ *adj or n*

thir•ty \'thərt-ē\ *n, pl* **thirties** **1** : ten more than 20; *also* : a symbol representing this — see NUMBER table **2** *pl* : the numbers 30 to 39; *esp* : the years 30 to 39 in a lifetime or century **3** : a mark or sign of completion **4** : the 2d point scored by a side in a game of tennis **5** : a 30 caliber machine gun — usually written .30 [Old English *thrītig*] — **thir•ti•eth** \-ē-əth\ *n or adj* — **thirty** *adj or pron*

thir•ty–eight \ˌthərt-ē-'āt\ *n* : a 38 caliber pistol — usually written .38

thirty–second note *n* : a musical note having the time value of one thirty-second of a whole note

thir•ty–thir•ty \ˌthərt-ē-'thərt-ē\ *n* : a rifle that fires a 30 caliber cartridge having a 30 grain powder charge — usually written .30-30

thir•ty–three \-'thrē\ *n* : a phonograph record for play at 33⅓ revolutions per minute — usually written 33

thir•ty–two \-'tü\ *n* : a 32 caliber pistol — usually written .32

¹this \t͟his, 't͟his, t͟həs\ *pron, pl* **these** \t͟hēz 't͟hēz\ **1a** (1) : the person, thing, or idea that is present or near in place, time, or thought or that has just been mentioned ⟨*these* are my hands⟩ (2) : what is stated in the following phrase, clause, or discourse ⟨I can only say *this:* they aren't here⟩ **b** : this time or place ⟨hoped to return before *this*⟩ **2 a** : the one nearer or more immediately under observation ⟨*this* is iron and that is tin⟩ **b** : the latter one [Old English *thes* (masculine), *this* (neuter)]

²this *adj, pl* **these** **1 a** : being the one that is present or near in place, time, or thought or that has just been mentioned ⟨*this* book is mine⟩ ⟨early *this* morning⟩ ⟨all *these* years⟩ **b** : being one not previously mentioned — used especially in narrative to give a sense of immediacy or vividness ⟨I had on *this* bright red shirt⟩ **2** : being the nearer at hand or more immediately under observation or discussion ⟨*this* car or that one⟩

³this \'t͟his\ *adv* : to the degree or extent indicated by something immediately present ⟨didn't expect to wait *this* long⟩

this•tle \'this-əl\ *n* : any of various prickly plants of the daisy family with often showy heads of mostly tubular flowers [Old English *thistel*] — **this•tly** \'this-lē, -ə-lē\ *adj*

this•tle•down \-əl-ˌdau̇n\ *n* : the down from the ripe flower head of a thistle

thistle tube *n* : a funnel tube usually of glass with a bulging top and flaring mouth

¹thith•er \'thit͟h-ər *also* 'thit͟h-\ *adv* : to that place : THERE [Old English *thider*]

²thither *adj* : being on the other and farther side : more remote

thith•er•to \-ˌtü\ *adv* : until that time

tho \'t͟hō, t͟hō, ˌt͟hō\ *adv or conj* : THOUGH

thole \'thōl\ *also* **thole•pin** \-ˌpin\ *n* : a pin set in the gunwale of a boat as a pivot for an oar [Old English *thol*]

Tho•mism \'tō-ˌmiz-əm\ *n* : the scholastic philosophical and theological system of Saint Thomas Aquinas — **Tho•mist** \-məst\ *n or adj* — **Tho•mis•tic** \tō-'mis-tik\ *adj*

Thomp•son submachine gun \'täm-sən-, 'tämp-\ *n* : a submachine gun with a pistol grip and stock for firing from the shoulder — called also *tommy gun* [John T. *Thompson,* died 1940, American army officer]

thong \'thȯng\ *n* : a strip of leather used especially for fastening something [Old English *thwong*]

thoracic duct *n* : the chief lymphatic vessel carrying lymph back to the bloodstream especially from the abdomen and lower limbs, lying along the front of the spinal column, and opening into the left subclavian vein

tho•rax \'thōr-,aks, 'thȯr-\ *n, pl* **tho•rax•es** *or* **tho•ra•ces** \'thōr-ə-,sēz, 'thȯr-\ **1** : the part of the body of a mammal between the neck and the abdomen; *also* : its cavity in which the heart and lungs lie **2** : the middle of the three chief divisions of the body of an insect [Latin *thorac-, thorax* "breastplate, thorax", from Greek *thōrak-, thōrax*] — **tho•rac•ic** \thə-'ras-ik\ *adj*

Tho•ra•zine \'thōr-ə-,zēn, 'thȯr-\ *trademark* — used for chlorpromazine

tho•ria \'thōr-ē-ə, 'thȯr-\ *n* : a powdery white oxide of thorium used especially in crucibles and optical glass [New Latin, from *thorium*]

tho•ri•um \'thōr-ē-əm, 'thȯr-\ *n* : a radioactive metallic chemical element that occurs combined in minerals — see ELEMENT table [New Latin, from Old Norse *Thōrr* "Thor"]

thorn \'thȯrn\ *n* **1** : a woody plant bearing sharp processes (as briers, prickles, or spines); *esp* : HAWTHORN **2 a** : a sharp rigid process on a plant; *esp* : one that is a short, rigid, sharp-pointed, and leafless branch **b** : a sharp rigid process on an animal **3** : something that causes distress or irritation [Old English] — **thorned** \'thȯrnd\ *adj* — **thorn•less** \'thȯrn-ləs\ *adj* — **thorn•like** \-,līk\ *adj*

thorn apple *n* **1** : the fruit of a hawthorn; *also* : HAWTHORN **2** : JIMSONWEED

thorn•bush \'thȯrn-,bu̇sh\ *n* **1** : any of various spiny or thorny shrubs or small trees **2** : a low growth of thorny shrubs especially of dry tropical regions

thorny \'thȯr-nē\ *adj* **thorn•i•er**; **-est** **1** : full of or covered with thorns : SPINY **2** : DIFFICULT, TRYING ⟨a *thorny* problem⟩ — **thorn•i•ness** *n*

thoro \'thər-ō, 'thə-rō\ *nonstandard variant of* THOROUGH

tho•ron \'thōr-,än, 'thȯr-\ *n* : a gaseous radioactive isotope of radon [New Latin, from *thorium*]

thor•ough \'thər-ō, 'thə-rō\ *adj* **1** : being such to the fullest degree : EXHAUSTIVE, COMPLETE ⟨a *thorough* search⟩ ⟨*thorough* success⟩ **2** : careful about detail : PAINSTAKING ⟨a very *thorough* worker⟩ [Middle English *thorow,* from *thorow* "through", from Old English *thurh*] — **thor•ough•ly** *adv* — **thor•ough•ness** *n*

[1]**thor•ough•bred** \'thər-ə-,bred, 'thə-rə-\ *adj* **1 a** *cap* : of, relating to, or being a member of the Thoroughbred breed of horses **b** : PUREBRED ⟨*thoroughbred* dogs⟩ **2** : marked by grace and elegance

[2]**thoroughbred** *n* **1** *cap* : any of an English breed of light speedy horses kept chiefly for racing and originating from crosses between English mares of uncertain ancestry and Arab stallions **2** : a purebred or pedigreed animal **3** : a person of sterling qualities

thor•ough•fare \-,faər, -,feər\ *n* **1** : a public way connecting two streets : a street or road open at both ends **2** : a main road : a busy street

thor•ough•go•ing \,thər-ə-'gō-ing, ,thə-rə-\ *adj* : marked by thoroughness or zeal ⟨*thoroughgoing* cooperation⟩

thorp \'thȯrp\ *n, archaic* : VILLAGE 1, HAMLET [Old English]

those *pl of* THAT

[1]**thou** \t͟hau̇, 't͟hau̇\ *pron* : the one spoken to — used especially in ecclesiastical or literary language; compare THEE, THINE, THY, YE, YOU [Old English *thū*]

[2]**thou** \'thau̇\ *n, pl* **thou** *or* **thous** : a thousand of something (as dollars)

[1]**though** \'t͟hō\ *adv* : HOWEVER 2, NEVERTHELESS ⟨not for long, *though*⟩ [of Scandinavian origin]

[2]**though** \t͟hō, ,t͟hō\ *conj* **1** : in spite of the fact that ⟨*though* it was raining, we went for a walk⟩ **2** : even if : even supposing ⟨determined to fight for truth *though* they should die for it⟩

[1]**thought** *past of* THINK

[2]**thought** \'thȯt\ *n* **1 a** : the act or process of thinking **b** : serious consideration : careful attention ⟨give *thought* to the future⟩ **2 a** : power of thinking and especially of reasoning and judging **b** : power of imagining or comprehending ⟨beauty beyond *thought*⟩ **3 a** : a product of thinking (as an idea, fancy, or invention) ⟨idle *thoughts*⟩ ⟨a pleasing *thought*⟩ **b** : the intellectual product or the organized views and principles of a period, place, group, or individual ⟨modern scientific *thought*⟩ **4** : a slight amount : BIT ⟨add just a *thought* more salt to the stew⟩ [Old English *thōht*]

thought•ful \'thȯt-fəl\ *adj* **1 a** : absorbed in thought : MEDITATIVE **b** : characterized by careful reasoned thinking **2 a** : having thought : HEEDFUL **b** : given to heedful anticipation of the needs of others — **thought•ful•ly** \-fə-lē\ *adv* — **thought•ful•ness** *n*

• **syn** THOUGHTFUL, CONSIDERATE, SOLICITOUS mean mindful of others. THOUGHTFUL implies unselfish concern and ability to anticipate another's needs; CONSIDERATE implies kind concern for the feelings of others; SOLICITOUS implies deep concern and suggests anxiety for the welfare of another ⟨*solicitous* about our family⟩

thought•less \'thȯt-ləs\ *adj* **1 a** : insufficiently alert : CARELESS **b** : RECKLESS 1, RASH **2** : devoid of thought : INSENSATE **3** : lacking concern for others : INCONSIDERATE — **thought•less•ly** *adv* — **thought•less•ness** *n*

thought–out \-'au̇t\ *adj* : produced or arrived at through careful and thorough consideration

thou•sand \'thau̇z-nd, 'thau̇z-n\ *n, pl* **thousands** *or* **thousand** **1** : ten times 100; *also* : a symbol representing this — see NUMBER table **2** : a very large or indefinitely great number [Old English *thūsend*] — **thousand** *adj*

thou•sand–leg•ger \,thau̇-n-'leg-ər, -'dleg-ər\ *n* : MILLIPEDE

thousands digit *n* : the numeral (as 1 in 1456) occupying the thousands place in a number expressed in the Arabic system of writing numbers

thousands place *n* : the place four to the left of the decimal point in a number expressed in the Arabic system of writing numbers

thou•sandth \'thau̇z-nth, -ntth\ *n* **1** : one of 1000 equal parts **2** : number 1000 in a countable series — see NUMBER table — **thousandth** *adj*

thrall \'thrȯl\ *n* **1** : SLAVE 1; *also* : SERF **2** : the condition of a thrall : SLAVERY [Old English *thræl,* from Old Norse *thræll*] — **thrall•dom** *or* **thral•dom** \-dəm\ *n*

[1]**thrash** \'thrash\ *vb* **1** : THRESH 1 **2** : to beat soundly or strike about with or as if with a stick or whip : FLOG; *also* : DEFEAT **3** : to swing, beat, or stir about in the manner of a rapidly moving flail ⟨*thrash* one's arms⟩ **4** : to go over again and again ⟨*thrash* the matter over in your mind⟩ [alteration of *thresh*]

[2]**thrash** *n* : an act of thrashing

[1]**thrash•er** \'thrash-ər\ *n* : one that thrashes or threshes

[2]**thrasher** *n* : any of numerous long-tailed American singing birds that resemble thrushes and include notable singers and mimics [probably alteration of *thrush*]

[1]**thread** \'thred\ *n* **1** : a thin continuous filament ⟨the spider's sticky *thread*⟩; *esp* : a textile cord made by twisting together strands of spun fiber (as cotton, flax, or silk) **2 a** : something (as a streak or slender stream) suggesting a filament ⟨a *thread* of light⟩ **b** : SCREW THREAD **3** : a line of reasoning or train of thought that connects the parts in a sequence of ideas or events ⟨lost the *thread* of the story⟩ [Old English *thrǣd*] — **thread•like** \-,līk\ *adj*

[2]**thread** *vb* **1** : to put a thread in working position in (as a needle) **2 a** : to pass something through in the manner of a thread ⟨*thread* a pipe with wire⟩ **b** : to make one's way through or between : wind a way ⟨*threading* narrow alleys⟩ **3** : to put together on or as if on a thread : STRING ⟨*thread* beads⟩ **4** : to interweave with or as if with threads : INTERSPERSE ⟨dark hair *threaded* with silver⟩ **5** : to form a screw thread on or in **6** : to draw out into a thread when dripped from a spoon — **thread•er** *n*

thread•bare \'thred-,baər, -,beər\ *adj* **1** : having the nap worn off so that the thread shows : SHABBY **2** : having lost freshness and interest from overuse **syn** see TRITE — **thread•bare•ness** *n*

thread•worm \-,wərm\ *n* : a slender nematode worm (as a pinworm)

thready \'thred-ē\ *adj* **thread·i·er**; **-est** **1** : consisting of or bearing fibers or filaments ⟨a *thready* bark⟩ **2** : having the form or appearance of a thread **3** : lacking in fullness, body, or vigor : THIN ⟨a *thready* voice⟩ ⟨a *thready* pulse⟩ — **thread·i·ness** *n*

threat \'thret\ *n* **1** : an expression of an intent to do harm or something wrong or foolish **2** : something that threatens [Old English *thrēat* "coercion"]

threat·en \'thret-n\ *vb* **threat·ened**; **threat·en·ing** \'thret-ning, -n-ing\ **1** : to utter threats : make threats against ⟨*threaten* trespassers⟩ **2** : to give signs or warning of : PORTEND ⟨clouds *threatening* rain⟩ **3** : to be an imminent danger to : MENACE — **threat·en·er** \'thret-nər, -n-ər\ *n* — **threat·en·ing·ly** \'thret-ning-lē, -n-ing-lē\ *adv*

• **syn** THREATEN, MENACE mean to announce or forecast impending danger or evil. THREATEN applies to a probable occurrence of evil or affliction; it may imply an impersonal warning of trouble, punishment, or retribution ⟨the drought *threatened* starvation⟩ MENACE implies alarming by a hostile or fearful aspect or character ⟨nuclear arms that *menace* humanity⟩

three \'thrē\ *n* **1** : one more than two; *also* : a symbol representing this — see NUMBER table **2** : the third in a set or series **3** : something having three units or members [Old English *thrīe* (masculine), *thrēo* (feminine and neuter)] — **three** *adj or pron*

three–base hit *n* : TRIPLE 2

3–D \'thrē-'dē\ *n* : the three-dimensional form or a picture produced in it

three–deck·er \'thrē-'dek-ər\ *n* **1** : a ship having three decks; *also* : a warship carrying guns on three decks **2** : something having three floors, tiers, or layers; *esp* : a sandwich with three slices of bread and two layers of filling

three–dimensional *adj* **1** : of, relating to, or having three dimensions **2** : giving the illusion of depth or varying distances — used of a pictorial representation or a sound system

three·fold \'thrē-,fōld, -'fōld\ *adj* **1** : having three units or members **2** : of or amounting to 300 percent — **threefold** *adv*

three–gait·ed \-'gāt-əd\ *adj* : trained to use the walk, trot, and canter ⟨*three-gaited* saddle horses⟩

three–hand·ed \-'han-dəd\ *adj* : played or to be played by three players ⟨*three-handed* bridge⟩

Three Hours *n* : a service of devotion between noon and three o'clock on Good Friday

three–legged \'thrē-'leg-əd, -'legd\ *adj* : having three legs ⟨a *three-legged* stool⟩

three–legged race *n* : a race between pairs of competitors with each pair having their adjacent legs bound together

three–mile limit *n* : an area of the sea extending three miles out from shore included in the territorial jurisdiction of a state

three·pence \'threp-əns, 'thrip-, 'thrəp-, *United States also* 'thrē-,pens\ *n, pl* **threepence** *or* **three·penc·es** : the sum of three pence; *also* : a British coin no longer issued worth threepence

three·pen·ny \'threp-nē, 'thrip-, 'thrəp-, -ə-nē, *United States also* 'thrē-,pen-ē\ *adj* **1** : costing or worth threepence **2** : of little value : POOR

three–point landing *n* : an airplane landing in which the two main wheels of the landing gear and the tail wheel or skid or the nose wheel touch the ground simultaneously

three–ring circus *n* **1** : a circus with simultaneous performances in three rings **2** : something confusing, engrossing, or entertaining

three R's *n pl* : the fundamentals taught in elementary school; *esp* : reading, writing, and arithmetic [from the phrase *reading, 'riting, and 'rithmetic*]

three·score \'thrē-'skōr, -'skȯr\ *adj* : SIXTY

three·some \'thrē-səm\ *n* : a group of three persons or things

three–spined stickleback \,thrē-,spīnd-, -,spīn-\ *n* : a stickleback of fresh and brackish waters that typically has three dorsal spines

thren·o·dy \'thren-əd-ē\ *n, pl* **-dies** : a song of lamentation or sorrow : DIRGE [Greek *thrēnōidia*, from *thrēnos* "dirge" + *aeidein* "to sing"]

thre·o·nine \'thrē-ə-,nēn\ *n* : an amino acid that is essential to normal nutrition [probably derived from *threose*, a sugar, probably derived from Greek *erythros* "red"]

thresh \'thrash, 'thresh\ *vb* **1 a** : to separate seed from (a harvested plant) mechanically **b** : to separate (grain) from straw **2** : THRASH ⟨*thresh* over a problem⟩ ⟨*threshed* about in bed⟩ [Old English *threscan*]

thresh·er \-ər\ *n* **1** : one that threshes; *esp* : THRESHING MACHINE **2** : a large common shark having a long curved upper lobe on its tail with which it is said to thresh the water to round up the fish on which it feeds — called also *thresher shark*

thresher 2

threshing machine *n* : a machine for separating grain or seeds from straw

thresh·old \'thresh-,hōld, -,ōld\ *n* **1** : the sill of a door **2 a** : GATE 1, DOOR, ENTRANCE **b** : a place of beginning : OUTSET ⟨at the *threshold* of an adventure⟩ **3** : the point or level at which a physiological or psychological effect begins to be produced ⟨*threshold* of pain⟩ [Old English *threscwald*] — **threshold** *adj*

threw *past of* THROW

thrice \'thrīs\ *adv* **1** : three times **2** : to a high degree : GREATLY [Middle English *thrie, thries*, from Old English *thriga*]

thrift \'thrift\ *n* **1** : careful management especially of money **2** : a tufted stemless herb having heads of pink or white flowers growing on mountains and seacoasts [Old Norse, "prosperity", from *thrīfask* "to thrive"]

thrift·less \'thrift-ləs\ *adj* : wasteful of money or resources — **thrift·less·ness** *n*

thrifty \'thrif-tē\ *adj* **thrift·i·er**; **-est** **1** : inclined to save : SAVING **2** : thriving through industry and frugality : PROSPEROUS **3** : thriving in health and growth ⟨*thrifty* cattle⟩ — **thrift·i·ly** \-tə-lē\ *adv* — **thrift·i·ness** \-tē-nəs\ *n*

thrill \'thril\ *vb* **1 a** : to experience or cause to experience a sudden intense feeling of excitement **b** : to have or cause to have a shivering or tingling sensation **2** : VIBRATE 3, TREMBLE ⟨a voice *thrilling* with emotion⟩ [Old English *thyrlian* "to pierce", from *thyrel* "hole", from *thurh* "through"] — **thrill** *n*

thrill·er \-ər\ *n* : one that produces thrills; *esp* : a work of fiction or drama designed to hold the interest by the use of a high degree of action, intrigue, adventure, or suspense

thrips \'thrips\ *n, pl* **thrips** : any of an order (Thysanoptera) of small to tiny sucking insects most of which feed often destructively on plant juices [Latin, "worm that bores in wood", from Greek]

thrive \'thrīv\ *vi* **thrived** *or* **throve** \'thrōv\; **thriv·en** \'thriv-ən\ *or* **thrived**; **thriv·ing** \'thrī-ving\ **1** : to grow vigorously : do well **2** : to gain in wealth or possessions : PROSPER, FLOURISH [Old Norse *thrīfask*] — **thriv·er** \'thrī-vər\ *n* — **thriv·ing·ly** \-ving-lē\ *adv*

throat \'thrōt\ *n* **1** : the part of the neck in front of the spinal column; *also* : the passage through it to the stomach and lungs **2** : something resembling the throat especially in being an entrance, a passageway, a constriction, or a narrowed part [Old English *throte*] — **throat·ed** \-əd\ *adj*

throat·latch \-,lach\ *n* : a strap of a bridle or halter passing under a horse's throat

throaty \'thrōt-ē\ *adj* **throat·i·er**; **-est** : uttered or produced from or as if from low in the throat ⟨a *throaty* voice⟩ — **throat·i·ly** \'thrōt-l-ē\ *adv* — **throat·i·ness** \'thrōt-ē-nəs\ *n*

[1]**throb** \'thräb\ *vi* **throbbed**; **throb·bing** **1** : to pulsate or pound with abnormal force or rapidity : PALPITATE **2** : to beat or vibrate rhythmically [Middle English *throbben*]

[2]**throb** *n* : a single beat of a pulsating movement or sensation : PULSATION

throe \'thrō\ *n* : a condition of struggle and anguish : PANG, SPASM — usually used in pl. ⟨death *throes*⟩ ⟨*throes* of childbirth⟩ [Old English *thrawu, thrēa* "threat, pain"]

thromb- *or* **thrombo-** *combining form* : blood clot : clotting of blood ⟨*thromb*in⟩ ⟨*thrombo*plastic⟩ [Greek *thrombos* "clot"]

throm·bin \'thräm-bən\ *n* : a proteolytic enzyme that is formed from prothrombin and assists the clotting of blood by promoting conversion of fibrinogen to fibrin

throm·bo·cyte \-bə-,sīt\ *n* : BLOOD PLATELET; *also* : an invertebrate cell with similar function — **throm·bo·cyt·ic** \,thräm-bə-'sit-ik\ *adj*

throm·bo·em·bo·lism \,thräm-bō-'em-bə-,liz-əm\ *n* : a blocking of a blood vessel by an embolus that has broken away from a thrombus and become lodged elsewhere

throm•bo•plas•tin \-'plas-tən\ *n* : a complex protein substance found especially in blood platelets that functions in the clotting of blood — **throm•bo•plas•tic** \-'plas-tik\ *adj*

throm•bo•sis \thräm-'bō-səs\ *n, pl* **-bo•ses** \-'bō-,sēz\ : the formation or presence of a blood clot within a blood vessel during life — **throm•bot•ic** \-'bät-ik\ *adj*

throm•bus \'thräm-bəs\ *n, pl* **throm•bi** \-,bī, -,bē\ : a clot of blood formed within a blood vessel and remaining attached to its place of origin — compare EMBOLUS [New Latin, from Greek *thrombos* "clot"]

¹throne \'thrōn\ *n* **1 a** : the chair occupied by a high dignitary (as a king, queen, or bishop) during formal or ceremonial occasions **b** : the seat of a deity or devil **2** : royal power and dignity : SOVEREIGNTY [Old French *trone*, from Latin *thronus*, from Greek *thronos*]

²throne *vt* : to seat on a throne : ENTHRONE

throne room *n* : a formal audience room containing the throne of a sovereign

¹throng \'thrȯng\ *n* **1 a** : a multitude of assembled persons **b** : a large number : CROWD **2** : a crowding together of many individuals [Old English *thrang*] **syn** see MULTITUDE

²throng *vb* **thronged**; **throng•ing** \'thrȯng-ing\ **1** : to crowd upon or into ⟨shoppers *thronged* the store⟩ **2** : to crowd together in great numbers

thros•tle \'thräs-əl\ *n* : ¹THRUSH; *esp* : SONG THRUSH [Old English]

¹throt•tle \'thrät-l\ *vb* **throt•tled**; **throt•tling** \'thrät-ling, -l-ing\ **1 a** : to impede or check the breathing of : CHOKE, STRANGLE **b** : to prevent or check expression or activity of : SUPPRESS **2 a** : to obstruct the flow of (as fuel to an engine) by closing a valve **b** : to reduce the speed of (an engine) by such means [Middle English *throtlen*, from *throte* "throat"] — **throt•tler** \'thrät-lər, -l-ər\ *n*

²throttle *n* : a valve controlling the volume of steam or of fuel (as gasoline) delivered to the cylinders of an engine; *also* : a lever controlling this valve [perhaps from English dialect *thropple* "throat"]

throt•tle•hold \'thrät-l-,hōld\ *n* : a vicious, strangling, or repressive control

¹through *also* **thru** \thrü, 'thrü\ *prep* **1 a** : in at one side and out at the opposite side of ⟨drove *through* the town⟩ **b** : by way of ⟨left *through* the window⟩ **c** : in the midst of : AMONG ⟨highway *through* the trees⟩ **2 a** : by means of ⟨succeeded *through* perseverance⟩ **b** : because of ⟨failed *through* ignorance⟩ **3** : over the whole surface or extent of ⟨all *through* the country⟩ **4 a** : from the beginning to the end of : DURING ⟨*through* the summer⟩ **b** : to and including ⟨Monday *through* Friday⟩ [Old English *thurh, thuruh*] **syn** see BY

²through *also* **thru** \'thrü\ *adv* **1 a** : from one end or side to the other ⟨the shield was pierced *through*⟩ **b** : over the whole distance ⟨shipped *through* to Boston⟩ **2 a** : from beginning to end ⟨read the book *through* at one sitting⟩ **b** : to completion, conclusion, or accomplishment ⟨see it *through*⟩ **3** : to the core : COMPLETELY ⟨was wet *through*⟩ **4** : into the open : OUT ⟨break *through*⟩

³through *also* **thru** \'thrü\ *adj* **1 a** : extending from one surface to another ⟨a *through* mortise⟩ **b** (1) : admitting free or continuous passage : DIRECT ⟨a *through* street⟩ (2) : affording right of way **2 a** (1) : going from point of origin to destination without change or reshipment ⟨a *through* train⟩ (2) : of or relating to such movement ⟨a *through* ticket⟩ **b** : initiated at and destined for points outside a local zone ⟨*through* traffic⟩ **3 a** : arrived at completion or accomplishment ⟨*through* with the job⟩ **b** : having no further strength or resources; *also* : no longer needed or wanted ⟨you're *through* — that was your last chance⟩

¹through•out \thrü-'au̇t\ *adv* **1** : in or to every part : EVERYWHERE ⟨of one color *throughout*⟩ **2** : during the whole time or action : from beginning to end ⟨remained loyal *throughout*⟩

²throughout *prep* **1** : in or to every part of ⟨*throughout* the house⟩ **2** : during the whole time of ⟨*throughout* the evening⟩

through•way *variant of* THRUWAY

throve *past of* THRIVE

¹throw \'thrō\ *vb* **threw** \'thrü\; **thrown** \'thrōn\; **throw•ing** **1** : to propel through the air by a forward motion of the hand and arm **2** : to propel through the air in any way **3** : to cause to fall ⟨the wrestler *threw* the opponent⟩ ⟨a horse shied and *threw* the rider⟩ **4 a** : to put suddenly in a certain condition or position ⟨*thrown* out of work by automation⟩ **b** : to form or shape on a potter's wheel **5** : to put on or take off hastily ⟨*throw* on a coat⟩ **6** : to twist two or more fibers of (as silk) to form one thread **7** : to make a cast of or at dice **8** : SHED ⟨a snake *throws* its skin⟩ **9** : to move quickly ⟨*throw* in reinforcements⟩ **10** : to lose (a game or contest) intentionally ⟨was paid to *throw* the fight⟩ **11** : to move (as a switch or a lever) to an open or closed position **12** : to act as host for : put on ⟨*throw* a party⟩ [Old English *thrāwan* "to cause to twist or turn"] — **throw•er** \'thrō-ər, 'thrōr\ *n*

• **syn** FLING, HURL, TOSS : THROW is interchangeable with the other terms but basically implies a movement of the arm propelling an object through the air; FLING stresses less control and more force in throwing and may suggest an emotional basis for the action ⟨madly rushed to the window and *flung* it open⟩ HURL implies power as in throwing a massive weight ⟨ocean waves *hurling* their weight upon the shore⟩ TOSS suggests a light or aimless upward throwing ⟨leaves *tossed* by the wind⟩

²throw *n* **1 a** : an act of throwing, hurling, or flinging **b** (1) : one's turn to throw something (as dice) (2) : the number thrown with a cast of dice **c** : a method of throwing an opponent in wrestling or judo **2** : the distance a missile is or may be thrown **3 a** : a light coverlet **b** : a woman's scarf or light wrap

throw•away \'thrō-ə-,wā\ *n* : a handbill or circular distributed free

throw away \,thrō-ə-'wā\ *vt* **1** : to get rid of : DISCARD **2** : SQUANDER, WASTE

throw•back \'thrō-,bak\ *n* : reversion to an earlier type or phase; *also* : an instance or product of such reversion

throw back \thrō-'bak, 'thrō-\ *vt* **1** : to cause to rely : make dependent **2** : REFLECT 1

throw in *vt* : to add as a supplement or bonus

throw off *vt* **1 a** : to free oneself from **b** : to cast off often in a hurried or vigorous manner **c** : DIVERT 1 ⟨was *thrown off* the scent⟩ **2** : to give off : EMIT **3** : to produce in an offhand manner **4** : to cause to make a mistake : MISLEAD ⟨was *thrown off* in my calculations⟩

throw out *vt* **1 a** : to remove from a place, office, or employment usually in a sudden or unexpected manner **b** : to reject or get rid of as worthless or unnecessary **2** : to give expression to : UTTER ⟨*threw out* some thoughts for consideration⟩ **3** : to give forth from within : EMIT ⟨the flowers *threw out* a nice fragrance⟩ **4** : to cause to project : EXTEND **5** : to make a throw that enables a teammate in baseball to put out (a base runner) **6** : DISENGAGE ⟨*throw out* the clutch⟩

throw over *vt* : to forsake despite bonds of attachment or duty

throw rug *n* : SCATTER RUG

throw up *vb* **1** : to raise quickly ⟨*throw up* the window⟩ **2** : to give up : QUIT ⟨just want to *throw* the whole thing *up*⟩ **3** : to build hurriedly **4** : VOMIT 1 **5** : to mention repeatedly by way of reproach ⟨*throw up* a past mistake⟩

thru *variant of* THROUGH

¹thrum \'thrəm\ *vb* **thrummed**; **thrum•ming** **1** : to play or pluck a stringed instrument idly : STRUM **2** : to sound with a monotonous hum : recite tiresomely or monotonously [imitative]

²thrum *n* : the monotonous sound of thrumming

¹thrush \'thrəsh\ *n* : any of a large family of small or medium-sized birds that are mostly of a plain color often with spotted underparts and include many excellent singers [Old English *thrysce*]

²thrush *n* : a fungal disease especially of infants marked by white patches in the mouth [probably of Scandinavian origin]

¹thrust \'thrəst\ *vb* **thrust**; **thrust•ing** **1** : to push or drive with force : SHOVE **2** : to cause to enter or pierce something by or as if by pushing **3** : to push forth : EXTEND ⟨*thrust* out roots⟩ **4** : INTERJECT, INTERPOLATE **5** : to press or force the acceptance of upon someone **6** : to make a thrust, stab, or lunge with or as if with a pointed weapon [Old Norse *thrȳsta*] **syn** see PUSH

²thrust *n* **1 a** : a push or lunge with a pointed weapon **b** : a verbal attack **c** : a military assault **2 a** : a strong continued pressure **b** : the sideways pressure of one part of a structure against another part (as of an arch against an abutment) **c** (1) : the force exerted endwise through a propeller shaft to give forward motion (2) : the forwardly directed reaction force produced by a high-speed jet of fluid discharged rearward from a nozzle (as in a jet engine) **3 a** : a forward or upward push **b** : a movement (as by a group of people) in a specified direction

thru•way *or* **through•way** \ˈthrü-ˌwā\ *n* : EXPRESSWAY

[1]**thud** \ˈthəd\ *vi* **thud•ded; thud•ding** : to move or strike so as to make a thud [probably from Old English *thyddan* "to thrust"]

[2]**thud** *n* **1** : [5]BLOW 1 **2** : a dull sound : THUMP

thug \ˈthəg\ *n* : a brutal ruffian or assassin : GANGSTER, KILLER [Hindi *ṭhag*, literally, "thief", from Sanskrit *sthaga* "rogue"] — **thug•gery** \ˈthəg-ə-rē\ *n*

△ **origin** *Thug* was used in English in the early 19th century as a transliteration of Hindi *ṭhag*, which literally means "thief", but which was applied specifically to the members of a group of professional robbers and murderers active in India from the 16th to the 19th century who strangled their victims. The word caught on in English, especially in the United States, and is now used generically to label a brutal ruffian, gangster, or killer.

Thu•le \ˈthü-lē, ˈthyü-\ *n* : the northernmost part of the habitable ancient world [Latin, from Greek *Thoulē*]

thu•li•um \ˈthü-lē-əm, ˈthyü-\ *n* : a rare metallic chemical element — see ELEMENT table [New Latin, from Latin *Thule* "Thule"]

[1]**thumb** \ˈthəm\ *n* **1** : the short thick first digit of the human hand opposable to the other fingers; *also* : the corresponding digit in lower animals **2** : the part of a glove or mitten that covers the thumb [Old English *thūma*]

[2]**thumb** *vt* **1 a** : to leaf through with the thumb : TURN ⟨*thumb* the pages of a book⟩ **b** : to soil or wear by or as if by repeated thumbing ⟨a well-*thumbed* book⟩ **2** : to request or obtain (a ride) in a passing automobile by signaling with the thumb

[1]**thumb•nail** \ˈthəm-ˌnāl, -ˈnāl\ *n* : the nail of the thumb

[2]**thumb•nail** \ˌthəm-ˌnāl\ *adj* : CONCISE, BRIEF ⟨a *thumbnail* sketch⟩

thumb•print \ˈthəm-ˌprint\ *n* : a print or impression made by the thumb

thumb•screw \ˈthəm-ˌskrü\ *n* **1** : a screw having a flat-sided or knurled head so that it may be turned by the thumb and forefinger **2** : an instrument of torture for squeezing the thumb by a screw

thumb•tack \-ˌtak\ *n* : a tack with a broad flat head for pressing into a board or wall with the thumb

[1]**thump** \ˈthəmp\ *vb* **1** : to strike or beat with or as if with something thick or heavy so as to cause a dull sound **2** : to beat heavily : POUND ⟨my heart *thumped* at the sight⟩ **3** : to inflict or emit a thump [imitative]

[2]**thump** *n* : a blow or knock with or as if with something blunt or heavy; *also* : the sound made by such a blow

thump•ing *adj* : impressively large, great, or excellent ⟨a *thumping* majority⟩

[1]**thun•der** \ˈthən-dər\ *n* **1 a** : the loud sound that follows a flash of lightning and is caused by sudden expansion of the air in the path of the electrical discharge **b** *archaic* : a discharge of lightning **2** : a loud utterance or threat **3** : BANG, RUMBLE ⟨the *thunder* of guns⟩ [Old English *thunor*]

[2]**thunder** *vb* **thun•dered; thun•der•ing** \-də-riŋ, -driŋ\ **1** : to produce thunder ⟨it *thundered*⟩ **2** : to produce a sound like thunder ⟨horses *thundered* down the road⟩ **3** : ROAR, SHOUT ⟨the crowd *thundered* its approval⟩ — **thun•der•er** \-dər-ər\ *n*

thun•der•bolt \ˈthən-dər-ˌbōlt\ *n* **1** : a single discharge of lightning with the accompanying thunder **2 a** : a person or thing likened to lightning in suddenness, effectiveness, or destructive power **b** : a verbal lambasting

thun•der•clap \-ˌklap\ *n* **1** : a crash of thunder **2** : something sharp, loud, or sudden like a clap of thunder

thun•der•cloud \-ˌklau̇d\ *n* : a dark storm cloud that produces lightning and thunder

thun•der•head \-ˌhed\ *n* : a rounded mass of cumulus cloud often appearing before a thunderstorm

thun•der•ing *adj* : awesomely great, intense, or unusual ⟨a *thundering* success⟩ — **thun•der•ing•ly** \-də-riŋ-lē, -driŋ-\ *adv*

thunder lizard *n* : BRONTOSAURUS

thun•der•ous \ˈthən-də-rəs, -drəs\ *adj* **1** : full of or marked by thunder ⟨*thunderous* clouds⟩ **2** : as loud as thunder : very loud ⟨*thunderous* applause⟩ — **thun•der•ous•ly** *adv*

thun•der•show•er \ˈthən-dər-ˌshau̇-ər, -ˌshau̇r\ *n* : a shower accompanied by lightning and thunder

thun•der•storm \-ˌstȯrm\ *n* : a storm accompanied by lightning and thunder

thun•der•struck \-ˌstrək\ *adj* : stunned or astonished as if struck by a thunderbolt ⟨*thunderstruck* when they heard the news⟩

thu•ri•ble \ˈthu̇r-ə-bəl, ˈthyu̇r-, ˈthər-\ *n* : CENSER [Middle French, from Latin *thuribulum*, from *thur-, thus* "incense", from Greek *thyos*, from *thyein* "to sacrifice"]

thu•ri•fer \-ə-fər\ *n* : one who carries a censer [Latin, "incense-bearing", from *thur-, thus* "incense" + *ferre* "to carry"]

Thurs•day \ˈthərz-dē\ *n* : the 5th day of the week [Old English *thursdæg*, from Old Norse *thōrsdagr*, literally, "day of Thor"]

thus \ˈt͟həs\ *adv* **1** : in this or that manner or way **2** : to this degree or extent : so ⟨a mild winter *thus* far⟩ **3** : because of this or that : HENCE **4** : as an example [Old English]

thwack \ˈthwak\ *vt* : to strike with or as if with something flat or heavy : WHACK [imitative] — **thwack** *n*

[1]**thwart** \ˈthwȯrt, *nautical often* ˈthȯrt\ *adv* : ATHWART [Old Norse *thvert*, from *thverr* "transverse, oblique"]

[2]**thwart** *adj* : situated or placed across something else : TRANSVERSE, OBLIQUE

[3]**thwart** *vt* **1** : OPPOSE 2, BAFFLE **2** : to defeat the hopes or aspirations of **syn** see FRUSTRATE — **thwart•er** *n*

[4]**thwart** *n* : a rower's seat extending across a boat

thwart•wise \-ˌwīz\ *adv or adj* : CROSSWISE 2

thy \t͟hī, ˌt͟hī\ *adj, archaic* : of or relating to thee or thyself especially as possessor, agent, or object of an action — used especially in ecclesiastical or literary language [Old English *thīn*]

thyme \ˈtīm *also* ˈthīm\ *n* : any of a genus of mints with small pungent aromatic leaves; *esp* : one grown for use in seasoning and formerly in medicine [Middle French *thym*, from Latin *thymum*, from Greek *thymon*, from *thyein* 'to make a burnt offering, sacrifice"]

thy•mine \ˈthī-ˌmēn\ *n* : a pyrimidine base $C_5H_6N_2O_2$ that is one of the four bases coding genetic information in the polynucleotide chain of DNA — compare ADENINE, CYTOSINE, GUANINE [German *thymin*, from New Latin *thymus* "thymus"]

thy•mol \ˈthī-ˌmȯl, -ˌmōl\ *n* : a crystalline compound $C_{10}H_{14}O$ of aromatic odor and antiseptic properties used as a fungicide and preservative [*thyme*]

thy•mus \ˈthī-məs\ *n, pl* **thy•mus•es** *or* **thy•mi** \-ˌmī\ : a largely lymphoid glandular structure of uncertain function that is present in most young vertebrates typically at the base of the neck and that tends to disappear or to become rudimentary in the adult [New Latin, from Greek *thymos*] — **thy•mic** \-mik\ *adj*

thymy *or* **thym•ey** \ˈtī-mē *also* ˈthī-\ *adj* : abounding in or fragrant with thyme

thy•ro•cal•ci•to•nin \ˌthī-rō-ˌkal-sə-ˈtō-nən\ *n* : a protein hormone from the thyroid gland that tends to lower the level of calcium in the blood plasma — called also *calcitonin*

[1]**thy•roid** \ˈthī-ˌrȯid\ *adj* **1** : of, relating to, or being a large endocrine gland of most vertebrates that lies at the base of the neck and produces an iodine-containing hormone which affects especially growth, development, and metabolic rate **2** : of, relating to, or being the chief cartilage of the larynx [Greek *thyreoeidēs* "shield-shaped, thyroid", from *thyreos* "oblong shield", from *thyra* "door"]

[2]**thyroid** *n* **1** : a thyroid gland or cartilage; *also* : a part (as an artery or nerve) associated with either of these **2** : a preparation of mammalian thyroid gland used medicinally

thyroid–stimulating hormone *n* : a hormone secreted by the pituitary gland that regulates the formation and secretion of thyroid hormone

thy•ro•tro•pic hormone \ˌthī-rə-ˌtrō-pik-, -ˌträp-ik-\ *n* : THYROID-STIMULATING HORMONE

thy•rox•ine *or* **thy•rox•in** \thī-ˈräk-ˌsēn, -sən\ *n* : the hormone of the thyroid gland or a preparation or derivative of this used to treat thyroid disorders

thy•self \t͟hī-ˈself\ *pron, archaic* : YOURSELF — used especially in ecclesiastical or literary language

ti \ˈtē\ *n* : the 7th note of the diatonic scale [alteration of *si*]

ti•ara \tē-ˈar-ə, -ˈer-, -ˈär-\ *n* **1** : a 3-tiered crown worn by the pope **2** : a decorative band or semicircular ornament for the head for formal wear by women [Latin, "royal Persian headdress", from Greek]

tiara 2

Ti•bet•an \tə-'bet-n\ *n* **1** : a member of the Mongoloid native race of Tibet modified in the west and south by intermixture with Indian peoples and in the east with Chinese **2** : the language of the Tibetan people — **Tibetan** *adj*

tib•ia \'tib-ē-ə\ *n, pl* **-i•ae** \-ē-,ē, -ē-,ī\ *also* **-i•as** **1 a** : the inner and usually larger of the two bones of the vertebrate hind limb between the knee and ankle — called also *shinbone* **b** : the fourth joint of the leg of an insect between the femur and tarsus **2** : an ancient flute originally fashioned from an animal's leg bone [Latin] — **tib•i•al** \-ē-əl\ *adj*

tib•io•fib•u•la \,tib-ē-ō-'fib-yə-lə\ *n* : a single bone that replaces the tibia and fibula in a frog or toad

tic \'tik\ *n* : local and habitual twitching of particular muscles especially of the face [French]

[1]tick \'tik\ *n* : any of numerous bloodsucking arachnids that are larger than the related mites, attach themselves to warm-blooded vertebrates to feed, and include important vectors of infectious diseases [Middle English *tyke*]

[2]tick *n* **1** : a light rhythmic audible tap or beat (as of a clock); *also* : a series of such ticks **2** : a small spot or mark; *esp* : one used to direct attention to something, to check an item on a list, or to represent a point on a scale [Middle English *tek*]

[3]tick *vb* **1 a** : to make the sound of a tick or a series of ticks **b** : to mark, count, or announce by or as if by ticking beats ⟨a meter *ticking* off the cab fare⟩ **2** : to operate as or in the manner of a functioning mechanism : RUN ⟨tried to understand what made them *tick*⟩ **3** : to mark with a written tick : CHECK ⟨*ticking* off names on a list⟩

[4]tick *n* **1** : the fabric case of a mattress, pillow, or bolster; *also* : a mattress consisting of a tick and its filling **2** : TICKING [Middle English *tike*, probably derived from Latin *theca* "cover", from Greek *thēkē* "case"]

[5]tick *n* : CREDIT, TRUST; *also* : a credit account ⟨bought on *tick*⟩ [short for *ticket*]

ticked \'tikt\ *adj* **1** : marked with small spots **2** : banded with two or more colors ⟨*ticked* hairs in the coat of a rabbit⟩

tick•er \'tik-ər\ *n* : something that ticks or produces a ticking sound: as **a** : WATCH 6 **b** : a telegraphic receiving instrument that automatically prints off stock quotations or news on a paper ribbon **c** *slang* : HEART 1a

ticker tape *n* : the paper ribbon on which a telegraphic ticker prints off its information

[1]tick•et \'tik-ət\ *n* **1 a** : a document that serves as a certificate, license, or permit; *esp* : a mariner's or airman's certificate **b** : TAG, LABEL ⟨price *ticket*⟩ **2** : a summons or warning issued to a traffic offender **3** : a document or token showing that a fare or admission fee has been paid **4** : a list of candidates for nomination or election **5** : a slip or card recording a transaction or undertaking or giving instructions ⟨sales *ticket*⟩ ⟨a driver's trip *ticket*⟩ ⟨repair *ticket*⟩ [obsolete French *etiquet* (now *étiquette*) "label", from Middle French *estiquet*, from *estiquier* "to attach", from Dutch *steken* "to stick"]

[2]ticket *vt* **1** : to attach a ticket to : LABEL; *also* : DESIGNATE **2** : to serve with a traffic ticket

ticket agent *n* **1** : one who acts as an agent of a transportation company to sell tickets for travel **2** : one who sells theater and entertainment tickets — **ticket agency** *n*

ticket-of-leave *n, pl* **tickets-of-leave** : a license or permit formerly given in the United Kingdom and the British Commonwealth to a convict to go free subject to certain conditions

tick•ing \'tik-ing\ *n* : a strong fabric used in upholstering and as a covering for mattresses and pillows

[1]tick•le \'tik-əl\ *vb* **tick•led**; **tick•ling** \'tik-ling, -ə-ling\ **1** : to have a tingling or prickling sensation ⟨my back *tickles*⟩ **2 a** : to excite or stir up agreeably : PLEASE ⟨food that *tickles* the palate⟩ **b** : to provoke to laughter or merriment : AMUSE **3** : to touch a body part lightly so as to excite the surface nerves and cause uneasiness, laughter, or spasmodic movements [Middle English *tikelen*]

[2]tickle *n* **1** : something that tickles **2** : a tickling sensation **3** : the act of tickling

tick•ler \'tik-lər, -ə-lər\ *n* **1** : one that tickles **2** : a file arranged to bring matters to timely attention

tick•lish \'tik-lish, -ə-lish\ *adj* **1** : sensitive to tickling **2 a** : TOUCHY, OVERSENSITIVE ⟨*ticklish* about being bald⟩ **b** : easily overturned : UNSTABLE ⟨a canoe is *ticklish* to handle⟩ **3** : requiring delicate handling : CRITICAL ⟨a *ticklish* subject⟩ ⟨a *ticklish* situation⟩ — **tick•lish•ly** *adv* — **tick•lish•ness** *n*

tick•tack•toe *also* **tic-tac-toe** \,tik-,tak-'tō\ *or* **tit-tat-toe** \,ti-,tat-'tō, ,ti-,tə-'tō\ *n* : a game in which two players alternately put Xs and Os in compartments of a figure formed by two vertical lines crossing two horizontal lines with each player trying to get a row of three Xs or three Os before the opponent does [*tic-tac-toe*, a former game in which players with eyes shut brought down a pencil on a slate marked with numbers and scored the number hit]

tick•tock \'tik-'täk, -,täk\ *n* : the ticking sound of a large clock [imitative]

tick trefoil *n* : any of various plants of the pea family having leaves with three leaflets and rough sticky fruits [[1]*tick*]

tid•al \'tīd-l\ *adj* **1** : of or relating to tides : periodically rising and falling or flowing and ebbing ⟨*tidal* waters⟩ **2** : dependent (as to the time of arrival or departure) on the state of the tide ⟨a *tidal* steamer⟩ — **tid•al•ly** \-l-ē\ *adv*

tidal wave *n* **1 a** : an unusually high sea wave that sometimes follows an earthquake **b** : an unusual rise of water alongshore due to strong winds **2** : something overwhelming (as a sweeping majority vote or an irresistible impulse)

tid•bit \'tid-,bit\ *or* **tit•bit** \'tit-,bit\ *n* **1** : a choice morsel of food **2** : a choice or pleasing bit (as of news) [perhaps from *tit-* (as in *titmouse*) + *bit*]

tid•dle•dy•winks *or* **tid•dly•winks** \'tid-l-ē-,wings, 'tid-l-dē-, 'tid-lē-, -,wingks\ *n* : a game in which players try to snap small disks from a flat surface into a small container [probably from English dialect *tiddly* "little"]

[1]tide \'tīd\ *n* **1 a** *obsolete* : a space of time : PERIOD **b** : a fit or opportune time : OPPORTUNITY **c** : an ecclesiastical anniversary or festival; *also* : its season **2 a** (1) : the alternate rising and falling of the surface of the ocean that occurs twice a day and is caused by the gravitational attraction of the sun and moon occurring unequally on different parts of the earth (2) : a less marked rising and falling of an inland body of water **b** : FLOOD TIDE 1 **3** : something that fluctuates like the tides of the sea : VICISSITUDE ⟨the *tides* of fortune⟩ **4** : a flowing stream : CURRENT [Old English *tīd* "time"]

[2]tide *vb* **1** : to drift or cause to drift with the tide **2** : to enable to surmount or endure a difficulty ⟨the money *tided* us over⟩

tide•land \-,land, -lənd\ *n* **1** : land overflowed during flood tide **2** : land underlying the ocean beyond the low-water limit of the tide but within a nation's territorial waters — often used in pl.

tide•mark \'tīd-,märk\ *n* **1 a** : a high-water or sometimes low-water mark left by tidal water or a flood **b** : a mark placed to indicate this point **2** : the point to which something has risen or below which it has fallen

tide pool *n* : a pool left (as in a rock basin) by an ebbing tide

tide•wa•ter \'tīd-,wȯt-ər, -,wät-\ *n* **1** : water overflowing land at flood tide **2** : low-lying coastal land

tid•ing \'tīd-ing\ *n* : a piece of news — usually used in pl. ⟨good *tidings*⟩ [Old English *tīdung*, from *tīdan* "to happen"]

[1]ti•dy \'tīd-ē\ *adj* **ti•di•er**; **-est** **1** : properly filled out : PLUMP **2** : ADEQUATE, SATISFACTORY ⟨a *tidy* arrangement⟩ **3 a** : neat and orderly in appearance or habits : well ordered and cared for **b** : METHODICAL, PRECISE ⟨a *tidy* mind⟩ **4** : LARGE, SUBSTANTIAL ⟨a *tidy* sum⟩ [Middle English, "timely, in good condition", from *tide* "time"] — **ti•di•ly** \'tīd-l-ē\ *adv* — **ti•di•ness** \'tīd-ē-nəs\ *n*

[2]tidy *vb* **ti•died**; **ti•dy•ing** **1** : to put in order ⟨*tidy* a room⟩ **2** : to make things tidy ⟨*tidying* up after supper⟩

[3]tidy *n, pl* **tidies** : a piece of fancywork used to protect the back, arms, or headrest of a chair or sofa from wear or soiling

[1]tie \'tī\ *n* **1 a** : a line, ribbon, or cord used for fastening, uniting, or drawing something closed; *esp* : SHOELACE **b** (1) : a structural element (as a beam) holding two pieces together : a tension member in a construction (2) : one of the transverse supports to which railroad rails are fastened **2** : something that serves as a connecting link: as **a** : a moral or legal obligation to someone or something **b** : a bond of kinship or affection **3** : a curved line that joins two musical notes indicating the same pitch used to denote a single tone sustained through the time value of the two **4 a** : an equality in number (as of votes or scores) **b** : equality in a contest; *also* : a contest that ends in a draw **5** : a method or style of tying or knotting **6** : something that is knotted or is to be knotted when worn: as **a** : NECKTIE **b** : a low laced shoe : OXFORD [Old English *tēag*]

2tie *vb* **tied; ty•ing** \ˈtī-iŋ\ *or* **tie•ing 1 a** : to fasten, attach, or close by means of a tie **b** : to form a knot or bow in ⟨*tie* your scarf⟩ **c** : to make by tying separate parts together ⟨*tied* a wreath⟩ ⟨*tie* a fishing fly⟩ **2 a** : to unite in marriage **b** : to unite (musical notes) by a tie **3** : to restrain or constrain the acts of **4 a** (1) : to make or have an equal score with in a contest (2) : to cause to be a tie ⟨*tied* the score⟩ **b** : to come up with something equal to : EQUAL **5** : to make a tie: as **a** : to make a bond or connection **b** : to make the same score **c** : to be connected : fit in

tie–in \ˈtī-ˌin\ *n* : something that ties in, relates, or connects

tie in \tī-ˈin, ˈtī-\ *vb* : to connect mechanically or logically in a system ⟨the pipeline *ties in* here⟩

tie•pin \-ˌpin\ *n* : an ornamental pin used to hold the ends of a necktie in place

1tier \ˈtiər\ *n* : a row, rank, or layer of articles; *esp* : one of two or more rows arranged one above another [Middle French *tire* "rank", of Germanic origin]

2tier *vb* **1** : to place or arrange in tiers **2** : to rise in tiers

3ti•er \ˈtī-ər, ˈtīr\ *n* : one that ties

tierce \ˈtiərs\ *often cap, variant of* TERCE

tier•cel \ˈtiər-səl\ *n* : a male hawk — compare FALCON [Middle French *tercel*, derived from Latin *tertius* "third"]

tiered \ˈtiərd\ *adj* : having or arranged in tiers, rows, or layers

tie–up \ˈtī-ˌəp\ *n* **1** : a suspension of traffic or business (as by a strike or lockout or a mechanical breakdown) **2** : CONNECTION 4b, ASSOCIATION ⟨looking for a helpful financial *tie-up*⟩

tie up \tī-ˈəp, ˈtī-\ *vt* **1** : to attach, fasten, or bind securely; *also* : to wrap up and fasten **2 a** : to use in such a manner as to make unavailable for other purposes **b** : to restrain from operation or progress ⟨traffic was *tied up* for miles⟩ **3** : DOCK ⟨the ferry *ties up* at the south slip⟩ **4** : to place in or assume a relationship with something else ⟨this *ties up* with what was said before⟩

1tiff \ˈtif\ *n* : a petty quarrel [origin unknown]

2tiff *vi* : to have a minor quarrel

tif•fin \ˈtif-ən\ *n* : a midday meal : LUNCHEON [probably derived from obsolete English *tiff* "to eat between meals"]

ti•ger \ˈtī-gər\ *n, pl* **tigers** *also* **tiger 1 a** : a large Asian flesh-eating mammal of the cat family having a tawny coat transversely striped with black **b** : any of several large wildcats (as the jaguar or cougar) **c** : TIGER CAT 2 **2** : a fierce and bloodthirsty person or quality [Old English *tiger* and Old French *tigre*, both from Latin *tigris*, from Greek, of Iranian origin] — **ti•ger•like** \-gər-ˌlīk\ *adj*

tiger 1a

tiger beetle *n* : any of numerous active flesh-eating beetles having larvae that tunnel in the soil

tiger cat *n* **1** : any of various wildcats (as the serval, ocelot, or margay) of moderate size and variegated coloration **2** : a striped or sometimes blotched tabby cat

ti•ger•ish \ˈtī-gə-rish, -grish\ *adj* : suggesting a tiger (as in grace, fierceness, or vigor) — **ti•ger•ish•ly** *adv* — **ti•ger•ish•ness** *n*

tiger lily *n* : a common Asian lily widely grown for its nodding orange-colored flowers densely spotted with black

tiger moth *n* : any of a family of stout-bodied moths usually with broad striped or spotted wings

tiger salamander *n* : a common black or brown yellow-blotched North American salamander

tiger shark *n* : a large brown or gray shark of warm seas that is often a man-eater

1tight \ˈtīt\ *adj* **1** : so close in structure as not to permit passage of a fluid or light ⟨a *tight* roof⟩ **2 a** : fixed very firmly in place ⟨loosen a *tight* jar cover⟩ **b** : not slack or loose : TAUT ⟨a *tight* knot⟩ **c** : fitting too closely for comfort or free movement **3** : neat and orderly in arrangement or design : SNUG **4** : difficult to get through or out of : TRYING ⟨in a *tight* situation⟩ **5 a** : firm in control ⟨kept a *tight* hand on the business⟩ **b** : STINGY 1, MISERLY **6** : packed or compressed to the limit : entirely full **7** : DRUNK 1 **8** : low in supply : SCARCE ⟨*tight* loan money⟩ **9** : sound and free from cracks or breaks ⟨*tight* lumber⟩ [of Scandinavian origin] — **tight•ly** *adv* — **tight•ness** *n*

• **syn** TIGHT, TAUT, TENSE mean drawn or stretched to the limit. TIGHT may imply a binding, constricting, or jamming encirclement, or the removal of the smallest opening or looseness; TAUT suggests the pulling of a rope or fabric until there is no give or slack; TENSE often adds to TAUT the suggestion of strain impairing normal functioning ⟨*tense* muscles⟩

2tight *adv* **1** : in a tight manner ⟨the door was shut *tight*⟩ **2** : SOUND ⟨sleep *tight*⟩

tight•en \ˈtīt-n\ *vb* **tight•ened; tight•en•ing** \ˈtīt-niŋ, -n-iŋ\ : to make or become tight or tighter — **tight•en•er** \ˈtīt-nər, -n-ər\ *n*

tight end *n* : an offensive football end who lines up within two yards of the tackle

tight•fist•ed \ˈtīt-ˈfis-təd\ *adj* : MISERLY, STINGY

tight–lipped \-ˈlipt\ *adj* **1** : having the lips closed tight (as in determination) **2** : reluctant to speak

tight•rope \ˈtīt-ˌrōp\ *n* : a rope or wire stretched taut for acrobats to perform on

tights \ˈtīts\ *n pl* : a skintight garment covering the body from the neck down or from the waist down

tight•wad \ˈtīt-ˌwäd\ *n* : a stingy person

tight•wire \-ˌwīr\ *n* : a tightrope made of wire

ti•gress \ˈtī-grəs\ *n* : a female tiger

tike *variant of* TYKE

til•de \ˈtil-də\ *n* : a mark ~ placed especially over the letter *n* (as in Spanish *señor* "sir") to denote the sound \nʸ\ or over vowels (as in Portuguese *profissão* "profession") to indicate nasality [Spanish, from Medieval Latin *titulus* "tittle"]

1tile \ˈtīl\ *n* **1** *pl* **tiles** *or* **tile a** : a flat or curved piece of fired clay, stone, or concrete used especially for roofs, floors, or walls **b** : a hollow or concave piece of fired clay or concrete used for a drain **2** : TILING 2b **3** : a thin piece of resilient material (as linoleum or rubber) for covering floors or walls [Old English *tigele*, from Latin *tegula*]

2tile *vt* **1** : to cover with tiles **2** : to install drainage tile in — **til•er** *n*

til•ing \ˈtī-liŋ\ *n* **1** : the act of one who tiles **2 a** : TILES **b** : a surface of tiles

1till \tl, təl, til, ˌtil\ *prep or conj* : UNTIL [Old English *til*]

2till \ˈtil\ *vt* : to work (land) by plowing, sowing, and raising crops [Old English *tilian*] — **till•able** \-ə-bəl\ *adj*

3till \ˈtil\ *n* : a receptacle (as a drawer) for money [Anglo-French *tylle*]

4till \ˈtil\ *n* : unstratified glacial drift consisting of clay, sand, gravel, and boulders intermingled [origin unknown]

till•age \ˈtil-ij\ *n* **1** : the operation of tilling land **2** : cultivated land

1till•er \ˈtil-ər\ *n* : one that tills : CULTIVATOR

2til•ler \ˈtil-ər\ *n* **1** : a lever used to turn the rudder of a boat from side to side **2** : a steering wheel for the rear wheels or trailer section of a vehicle (as a fire truck) — called also *tiller wheel* [Middle French *telier* "stock of a crossbow", literally, "beam of a loom", from Medieval Latin *telarium*, from Latin *tela* "web"]

3til•ler *n* : SPROUT 1, STALK; *esp* : one from the base of a cereal grass [Old English *telgor, telgra* "twig, shoot"]

4til•ler *vi* : to put forth tillers ⟨the oats are *tillering*⟩

til•ler•man \ˈtil-ər-mən\ *n* : STEERSMAN

1tilt \ˈtilt\ *vb* **1** : to cause to slope : INCLINE **2** : to move or shift so as to lean or incline : SLANT **3** : to engage in a combat with lances : JOUST [Middle English *tilten*] — **tilt•er** *n*

2tilt *n* **1** : a contest on horseback in which two combatants charging with lances try to unhorse each other : JOUST **2 a** : a verbal encounter involving sharp exchanges : ALTERCATION **b** : SPEED 2a — used in the phrase *at full tilt* **3 a** : the act of tilting : the state or position of being tilted **b** : a sloping surface

tilth \'tilth\ *n* **1** : cultivation of the soil **2** : cultivated land : TILLAGE **3** : the state of being tilled [Old English, from *tilian* "to till"]

tim•bal \'tim-bəl\ *n* : KETTLEDRUM [French *timbale*, from Spanish *atabal*, from Arabic *aṭ-ṭabl* "the drum"]

[1]**tim•ber** \'tim-bər\ *n* **1** : wood for use in making something **2** : a squared or dressed and usually large piece of wood **3** : wooded land or growing trees constituting a source of timber **4** : a curving frame branching outward from the keel of a ship that is usually composed of several pieces united : RIB [Old English, "building, wood"] — **timber** *adj*

[2]**timber** *vt* **tim•bered; tim•ber•ing** \-bə-ring, -bring\ : to frame, cover, or support with timbers

tim•bered \'tim-bərd\ *adj* **1** : furnished with, made of, or covered with timber **2** : having walls framed by exposed timbers

timber hitch *n* : a knot used to secure a line to a log or spar

tim•ber•ing \'tim-bə-ring, -bring\ *n* : a set of timbers : timber construction

tim•ber•land \'tim-bər-ˌland\ *n* : wooded land especially with marketable timber

tim•ber•line \-ˌlīn\ *n* : the upper limit of tree growth in mountains or high latitudes

timber wolf *n* : a large usually gray North American wolf extinct over much of the eastern and southern parts of its range

timber wolf

tim•ber•work \'tim-bər-ˌwərk\ *n* : a timber construction

tim•bre \'tam-bər, 'tim-\ *n* : the quality given to a sound by its overtones: as **a** : the resonance by which the ear recognizes and identifies a voiced speech sound **b** : the tone distinctive of a singing voice or a musical instrument [French, from Middle French, "bell struck by a hammer", from Old French, "drum", derived from Greek *tympanon*]

tim•brel \'tim-brəl\ *n* : a small hand drum or tambourine [Middle English *timbre* "tambourine", from Old French, "drum"] — **tim•brelled** \-brəld\ *adj*

[1]**time** \'tīm\ *n* **1 a** : the measured or measurable period during which an action, process, or condition exists or continues : DURATION **b** : LEISURE ⟨*time* for reading⟩ **2** : the point or period when something occurs : OCCASION **3** : an appointed, fixed, or customary moment or hour for something to happen, begin, or end ⟨arrived ahead of *time*⟩ **4 a** : an historical period : AGE **b** : a division of geologic chronology **c** : conditions at present or at some specified period — usually used in pl. ⟨*times* are hard⟩ ⟨move with the *times*⟩ **d** : the present time ⟨issues of the *time*⟩ **5 a** : LIFETIME **b** : a period or term especially of military service **c** : a prison sentence **6** : SEASON 2 **7 a** : rate of speed : TEMPO **b** : the grouping of the beats of music : RHYTHM **8 a** : a moment, hour, day, or year as indicated by a clock or calendar ⟨what *time* is it⟩ **b** : any of various systems (as sidereal or solar) of reckoning time **9 a** : one of a series of recurring instances or repeated actions ⟨told you many *times*⟩ **b** *pl* (1) : multiplied instances ⟨five *times* greater⟩ (2) : equal fractional parts of which an indicated number equals a comparatively greater quantity ⟨seven *times* smaller⟩ **c** : TURN ⟨three *times* at bat⟩ **10** : finite as contrasted with infinite duration **11** : a person's experience during a specified period or on a particular occasion ⟨a good *time*⟩ **12 a** : the period of one's work ⟨make up *time*⟩ **b** : an hourly pay rate **13 a** : the playing time of a game **b** : TIME-OUT ⟨called *time* to make a substitution⟩ [Old English *tīma*] — **at the same time** : HOWEVER 2, NEVERTHELESS — **at times** : now and then — **from time to time** : once in a while : OCCASIONALLY — **in no time** : in the shortest possible time — **in time 1** : early enough **2** : in the course of time : EVENTUALLY **3** : in correct rhythm or tempo — **on time 1** : at the time set : PUNCTUALLY **2** : on an installment payment plan : on credit

[2]**time** *vt* **1 a** : to arrange or set the time of : SCHEDULE **b** : to regulate (a watch) to keep correct time **2** : to set the tempo, speed, or duration of **3** : to cause to keep time with something **4** : to determine or record the time, duration, or rate of **5** : to adjust (as a mechanical part) so that an action occurs at a desired instant

[3]**time** *adj* **1 a** : of or relating to time **b** : recording time **2** : timed to ignite or explode at a specific moment ⟨a *time* bomb⟩

time and a half *n* : payment of a worker (as for overtime) at one and a half times the regular wage rate

time capsule *n* : a container holding historical records or objects representative of current culture that is deposited (as in a cornerstone) for preservation until discovery by some future age

time card *n* : a card used with a time clock to record an employee's starting and quitting times each day or on each job

time clock *n* : a clock that stamps an employee's starting and quitting times on a time card

timed \'tīmd\ *adj* **1** : made to occur at or in a set time ⟨a *timed* explosion⟩ **2** : done or taking place at a time of a specified sort ⟨an ill-*timed* arrival⟩

time deposit *n* : a bank deposit payable a specified number of days after deposit or upon advance notice to the bank

time exposure *n* : exposure of a photographic film for a definite time usually of more than one half second; *also* : a photograph taken by such exposure

time–hon•ored \'tī-ˌmän-ərd\ *adj* : honored or respected because of age or long-established usage

time•keep•er \'tīm-ˌkē-pər\ *n* **1** : TIMEPIECE **2** : a clerk who keeps records of the time worked by employees **3** : an official who keeps track of the time in an athletic game or contest — **time•keep•ing** \-ping\ *n*

time•less \'tīm-ləs\ *adj* **1 a** : having no beginning or end : UNENDING **b** : not restricted to a particular time or date **2** : not affected by time — **time•less•ly** *adv* — **time•less•ness** *n*

time lock *n* : a lock controlled by clockwork to prevent its being opened before a set time

time•ly \'tīm-lē\ *adj* **time•li•er; -est 1** : coming early or at the right time : OPPORTUNE **2** : appropriate or adapted to the times or the occasion ⟨a *timely* book⟩ — **time•li•ness** *n*

time–out \'tī-'mau̇t\ *n* : a suspension of play in an athletic game

time•piece \'tīm-ˌpēs\ *n* : a device (as a clock or watch) to measure the passage of time

tim•er \'tī-mər\ *n* : one that times: as **a** : TIMEPIECE **b** : a device in the ignition system of an internal-combustion engine that causes the spark to be produced in the cylinder at the correct time **c** : a device (as a clock) that indicates by an audible signal the end of an interval of time or that automatically starts or stops a device

times \ˌtīmz\ *prep* : multiplied by ⟨two *times* two is four⟩

time–sav•er \'tīm-ˌsā-vər\ *n* : something that saves time

time•sav•ing \'tīm-ˌsā-ving\ *adj* : intended or serving to lessen the amount of time needed to do something ⟨a *timesaving* device⟩

time•serv•er \-ˌsər-vər\ *n* : a person who only does what everyone else does or what pleases a supervisor — **time•serv•ing** \-ving\ *adj or n*

time–sharing \'tīm-ˌsheər-ing, -ˌshaər-\ *n* : use of a computer system by many users at the same time in such a way that each user has the impression of being the only user of the system

time signature *n* : a fractional sign placed just after the key signature whose denominator indicates the kind of note (as a quarter note) taken as the time unit for the beat and whose numerator indicates the number of these to the measure

time•ta•ble \'tīm-ˌtā-bəl\ *n* **1** : a table of departure and arrival times (as of trains, buses, or airplanes) **2** : a schedule showing a planned order or sequence

time•worn \-ˌwōrn, -ˌwȯrn\ *adj* **1** : worn or impaired by time **2 a** : AGE-OLD, ANCIENT ⟨*time-worn* procedures⟩ **b** : HACKNEYED, STALE ⟨a *timeworn* joke⟩

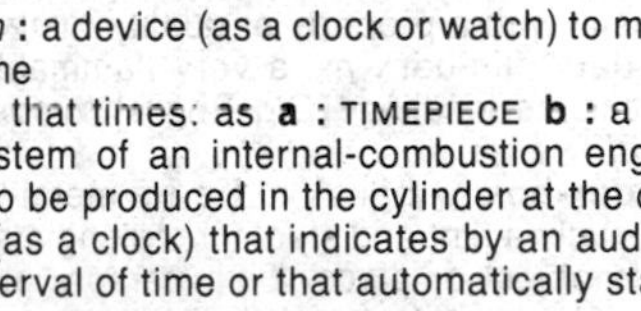
time signature: *1* 3/4 time, *2* common time

time zone *n* : a geographical region within which the same standard time is used

\ə\ **abut**	\au̇\ **out**	\i\ **tip**	\ȯ\ **saw**	\u̇\ **foot**
\ər\ **further**	\ch\ **chin**	\ī\ **life**	\ȯi\ **coin**	\y\ **yet**
\a\ **mat**	\e\ **pet**	\j\ **job**	\th\ **thin**	\yü\ **few**
\ā\ **take**	\ē\ **easy**	\ng\ **sing**	\th\ **this**	\yu̇\ **cure**
\ä\ **cot, cart**	\g\ **go**	\ō\ **bone**	\ü\ **food**	\zh\ **vision**

tim•id \'tim-əd\ *adj* **:** lacking in courage or self-confidence **:** FEARFUL, SHY [Latin *timidus*, from *timēre* "to fear"] — **ti•mid•i•ty** \tə-'mid-ət-ē\ *n* — **tim•id•ly** \'tim-əd-lē\ *adv*

tim•ing *n* **1 :** selection for maximum effect of the precise moment for beginning or doing something **2 :** observation and recording (as by a stopwatch) of the elapsed time of an act, action, or process

tim•o•rous \'tim-rəs, -ə-rəs\ *adj* **1 :** of a timid disposition **:** AFRAID **2 :** expressing or suggesting timidity [Middle French *timoureus*, from Medieval Latin *timorosus*, from Latin *timor* "fear", from *timēre* "to fear"] — **tim•o•rous•ly** *adv* — **tim•o•rous•ness** *n*

tim•o•thy \'tim-ə-thē\ *n* **:** a European grass with long cylindrical spikes widely grown for hay [probably after *Timothy* Hanson, 18th century American farmer said to have introduced it from New England to the southern states]

Tim•o•thy \'tim-ə-thē\ *n* — *see* BIBLE table

tim•pa•ni *or* **tym•pa•ni** \'tim-pə-nē\ *n pl* **:** a set of two or three kettledrums played by one performer [Italian *timpani*, pl. of *timpano* "kettledrum", from Latin *tympanum* "drum"] — **tim•pa•nist** \-nəst\ *n*

¹tin \'tin\ *n* **1 :** a soft bluish white lustrous crystalline metallic chemical element that is malleable and ductile at ordinary temperatures and that is used as a protective coating in tinfoil and in soft solders and alloys — see ELEMENT table **2 a :** a box, can, pan, vessel, or a sheet made of tinplate **b :** a sealed can holding food [Old English] — **tin** *adj*

²tin *vt* **tinned; tin•ning 1 :** to cover or plate with tin or an alloy of tin **2** *chiefly British* **:** to put up or pack in tins **:** CAN

tinct \'tingt, 'tingkt\ *n* **:** TINCTURE 1 — **tinct** adj

¹tinc•ture \'ting-chər, 'tingk-\ *n* **1 :** a substance that colors, dyes, or stains **2 :** a slight admixture **:** TRACE **3 :** an alcoholic solution of a medicinal substance [Latin *tinctura* "act of dyeing", from *tingere* "to tinge"]

²tincture *vt* **1 :** to tint or stain with a color **:** TINGE **2 :** to infuse or instill with a property or quality **:** IMPREGNATE

tin•der \'tin-dər\ *n* **:** a very flammable substance that can be used as kindling [Old English *tynder*] — **tin•dery** \-də-rē\ *adj*

tin•der•box \-ˌbäks\ *n* **1 a :** a metal box for holding tinder and usually a flint and steel for striking a spark **b :** a highly flammable object or place **2 :** a person, place, or situation likely to erupt into strife or conflict

tine \'tīn\ *n* **:** a slender pointed projecting part **:** PRONG ⟨the *tines* of a fork⟩ [Old English *tind*]

tin•ea \'tin-ē-ə\ *n* **:** any of several fungous diseases of the skin; *esp* **:** RINGWORM [Latin, "worm, moth"] — **tin•e•al** \-ē-əl\ *adj*

tin fish *n, slang* **:** TORPEDO 2b

tin•foil \'tin-ˌfȯil\ *n* **1 :** a thin metal sheeting usually of aluminum or tin-lead alloy **2 :** SILVER PAPER

ting \'ting\ *n* **:** a high-pitched sound (as from a light stroke on a glass) [Middle English *tingen* "to ting"] — **ting** *vb*

tinge \'tinj\ *vt* **tinged; tinge•ing** *or* **ting•ing** \'tin-jing\ **1 a :** to color slightly **:** TINT **b :** to affect or modify with a slight odor or taste **2 :** to modify in character ⟨respect *tinged* with envy⟩ [Latin *tingere* "to dip, tinge"] — **tinge** *n*

tin•gle \'ting-gəl\ *vi* **tin•gled; tin•gling** \-gə-ling, -gling\ **:** to feel a ringing, stinging, prickling, or thrilling sensation; *also* **:** to cause such a sensation ⟨the story *tingles* with suspense⟩ [Middle English *tinglen*, alteration of *tinklen* "to tinkle, tingle"] — **tingle** *n* — **tin•gly** \-gə-lē, -glē\ *adj*

tin hat *n* **:** a metal helmet

tin•horn \'tin-ˌhȯrn\ *n* **:** a pretentious or boastful person (as a gambler) with little money, power, or ability

¹tin•ker \'ting-kər\ *n* **1 :** a mender of household utensils (as pots and pans) who usually travels from place to place **2 :** an unskilled mender **:** BUNGLER [Middle English *tinkere*]

²tinker *vi* **tin•kered; tin•ker•ing** \-kə-ring, -kring\ **:** to work in the manner of a tinker; *esp* **:** to repair or adjust something in an unskilled or experimental manner — **tin•ker•er** \-kər-ər\ *n*

tinker's damn *or* **tinker's dam** *n* **:** something absolutely worthless [probably from the tinkers' reputation for blasphemy]

¹tin•kle \'ting-kəl\ *vb* **tin•kled; tin•kling** \-kə-ling, -kling\ **1 :** to make or emit a tinkle **2 a :** to cause to make a tinkle **b :** to produce by tinkling ⟨*tinkle* a tune on the piano⟩ [Middle English *tinklen*, from *tinken* "to tinkle"]

²tinkle *n* **:** a series of short high ringing or clinking sounds — **tin•kly** \-kə-lē, -klē\ *adj*

tin•man \'tin-rˌ ən\ *n* **:** TINSMITH

tin•ni•tus \'ti..-ə-təs\ *n* **:** a usually subjective sensation of noise (as a ringing or roaring) [Latin, "ringing, tinnitus", from *tinnire* "to ring"]

tin•ny \'tin-ē\ *adj* **tin•ni•er; -est 1 :** of, abounding in, or yielding tin **2 :** resembling or suggestive of tin: as **a :** LIGHT, CHEAP ⟨a *tinny* watch⟩ **b :** thin in tone ⟨a *tinny* voice⟩ — **tin•ni•ly** \'tin-l-ē\ *adv* — **tin•ni•ness** \'tin-ē-nəs\ *n*

Tin Pan Alley *n* **:** a district occupied chiefly by composers or publishers of popular music; *also* **:** the body of such composers or publishers

tin•plate \'tin-'plāt\ *n* **:** thin sheet iron or steel coated with tin — **tin–plate** *vt*

¹tin•sel \'tin-səl\ *n* **1 :** a thread, strip, or sheet of metal, paper, or plastic used to produce a glittering and sparkling appearance (as in fabrics, yarns, or decorations) **2 :** something superficially attractive or glamorous but of little real worth [Middle French *estincelle*, *etincelle* "spark, spangle", from Latin *scintilla* "spark"]

²tinsel *adj* **1 :** made of or covered with tinsel **2 :** cheaply gaudy **:** TAWDRY

³tinsel *vt* **-seled** *or* **-selled; -sel•ing** *or* **-sel•ling** \-sə-ling, -sling\ **1 :** to adorn with or as if with tinsel **2 :** to give a superficial brightness to

tin•sel•ly \'tin-sə-lē, -slē\ *adj* **:** TINSEL

tin•smith \'tin-ˌsmith\ *n* **:** a worker who makes or repairs things of metal (as tin)

¹tint \'tint\ *n* **1 :** a slight or pale coloring **:** TINGE ⟨white without a *tint* of yellow⟩ **2 :** a color produced by a pigment or dye mixture having some white in it **3 :** a usually slight modifying quality or characteristic **4 :** dye for the hair [Latin *tinctus* "act of dyeing", from *tingere* "to tinge"] **syn** see COLOR — **tint•er** *n*

²tint *vt* **:** to impart or apply a tint to **:** COLOR

tin•tin•nab•u•la•tion \ˌtin-tə-ˌnab-yə-'lā-shən\ *n* **1 :** the ringing or sounding of bells **2 :** a jingling or tinkling sound as if of bells [Latin *tintinnabulum* "bell", from *tintinnare* "to ring, jingle"]

tin•type \'tin-ˌtīp\ *n* **:** an early photograph consisting of a positive image taken directly on a thin iron plate having a darkened surface

tin•ware \-ˌwaər, -ˌweər\ *n* **:** articles made of tinplate

tin•work \-ˌwərk\ *n* **1 :** work in tin **2** *pl* **:** an establishment where tin is smelted, rolled, or otherwise worked

ti•ny \'tī-nē\ *adj* **ti•ni•er; -est :** very small or diminutive **:** MINUTE [Middle English *tine*] — **ti•ni•ness** *n*

¹tip \'tip\ *n* **1 :** the pointed or rounded end of something **:** END **2 :** a small piece or part serving as an end, cap, or point [Middle English] — **tipped** \'tipt\ *adj*

²tip *vt* **tipped; tip•ping 1 a :** to furnish with a tip **b :** to cover or decorate the tip of **2 :** to affix (an insert) in a book — often used with *in* **3 :** to remove the ends of (as plant shoots)

³tip *vb* **tipped; tip•ping 1 :** OVERTURN, UPSET ⟨*tipped* over a glass⟩ **2 :** TILT 2 ⟨the bench *tipped* on the uneven floor⟩ **3 :** to raise and tilt forward in salute ⟨*tipped* my hat⟩ [Middle English *tipen*] — **tip the scales 1 :** to register weight **2 :** to shift the balance of power or influence

⁴tip *n* **:** the act or an instance of tipping **:** TILT

⁵tip *n* **:** a light touch or blow **:** TAP [Middle English *tippe*]

⁶tip *vt* **tipped; tip•ping :** to strike lightly **:** TAP

⁷tip *vb* **tipped; tip•ping 1 :** to give a gratuity to ⟨*tip* a waitress⟩ **2 :** to give gratuities ⟨was miserly about *tipping*⟩ [perhaps from ⁶*tip*]

⁸tip *n* **:** a gift or small sum of money tendered for a service **:** GRATUITY

⁹tip *n* **:** an item of authoritative or confidential information ⟨a *tip* on a sure winner in a horse race⟩ [perhaps from ⁷*tip*]

¹⁰tip *vt* **tipped; tip•ping :** to give information or advice often in a secret or confidential manner ⟨was *tipped* off as to what would happen⟩

tip•cart \'tip-ˌkärt\ *n* **:** a cart whose body can be tipped on the frame to empty its contents

tip•cat \-ˌkat\ *n* **:** a game in which one player using a bat lightly strikes a tapered wooden peg and as it flies up strikes it again to drive it as far as possible while fielders try to recover it; *also* **:** the peg used in this game

ti•pi *variant of* TEPEE

tip–off \'tip-ˌȯf\ *n* **:** ⁹TIP, WARNING

tip•per \'tip-ər\ *n* **:** one that tips

tip•pet \'tip-ət\ *n* **1 :** a long hanging part of a garment (as on a sleeve or cape) **2** : a shoulder cape usually with hanging ends **3** : a long black scarf worn over the robe by members of the Anglican clergy [Middle English *tipet*]

[1]tip•ple \'tip-əl\ *vi* **tip•pled; tip•pling** \'tip-ling, -ə-ling\ : to drink liquor especially continuously in small amounts [back-formation from obsolete *tippler* "barkeeper", from Middle English *tipeler*] — **tip•pler** \'tip-lər, -ə-lər\ *n*

[2]tipple *n* : an intoxicating beverage : DRINK

[3]tipple *n* **1** : an apparatus by which loaded cars are emptied by tipping **2** : the place where tipping is done; *esp* : a coal-screening plant [derived from *tip*]

tip•staff \'tip-,staf\ *n, pl* **tip•staves** \-,stavz, -,stāvz\ : an officer (as a constable or bailiff) who bears a staff [obsolete *tipstaff* "staff tipped with metal"]

tip•ster \'tip-stər\ *n* : one who gives or sells tips especially for gambling or speculation

tip•sy \'tip-sē\ *adj* **tip•si•er; -est 1** : unsteady, staggering, or foolish from the effects of alcohol : somewhat drunk **2** : ASKEW ⟨a *tipsy* angle⟩ [[3]*tip* + *-sy* (as in *tricksy*)] — **tip•si•ly** \-sə-lē\ *adv* — **tip•si•ness** \-sē-nəs\ *n*

[1]tip•toe \'tip-,tō, -'tō\ *n* : the tip of a toe; *also* : the ends of the toes — **on tiptoe 1** : on the tips of one's toes **2** : ALERT 1, EXPECTANT

[2]tiptoe *adv* : on or as if on tiptoe ⟨walk *tiptoe*⟩

[3]tiptoe *adj* **1** : marked by standing or walking on tiptoe **2** : CAUTIOUS ⟨a *tiptoe* approach⟩

[4]tiptoe *vi* : to stand, raise oneself, or walk on or as if on tiptoe

[1]tip–top \'tip-'täp, -,täp\ *n* : the highest point : SUMMIT

[2]tip–top *adj* : EXCELLENT, FIRST-RATE — **tip–top** *adv*

ti•rade \tī-'rād, 'tī-,\ *n* : a long furious usually abusive speech [French, "shot, tirade", from Italian *tirata*, from *tirare* "to draw, shoot"]

[1]tire \'tīr\ *vb* **1** : to become weary **2** : to exhaust or greatly decrease the physical strength of : FATIGUE **3** : to wear out the patience or attention of : bore completely [Old English *tēorian, tȳrian*]

[2]tire *n* **1** : a metal hoop forming the tread of a wheel **2 a** : a rubber cushion that encircles a wheel and usually consists of a rubber-and-fabric covering containing a cavity or a separate inner tube that is filled with compressed air **b** : the external rubber-and-fabric covering of a pneumatic tire that uses an inner tube [probably from earlier *tire* "headband", from Middle English *attire* "attire"]

tired \'tīrd\ *adj* **1** : WEARY 1 **2 a** : FED UP ⟨I'm *tired* of all this nonsense⟩ **b** : HACKNEYED ⟨*tired* old jokes⟩ — **tired•ly** *adv* — **tired•ness** *n*

tire•less \'tīr-ləs\ *adj* : not easily tired ⟨a *tireless* worker⟩ — **tire•less•ly** *adv* — **tire•less•ness** *n*

tire•some \'tīr-səm\ *adj* : WEARISOME, TEDIOUS — **tire•some•ly** *adv* — **tire•some•ness** *n*

tire•wom•an \'tīr-,wu̇m-ən\ *n* : a lady's maid [derived from *attire*]

tir•ing–room \'tī-ring-,rüm, -,ru̇m\ *n* : a dressing room especially in a theater [derived from *attire*]

'tis \tiz, 'tiz\ : it is

tis•sue \'tish-ü\ *n* **1 a** : a fine lightweight often sheer fabric **b** : MESH, NETWORK, WEB ⟨a *tissue* of lies⟩ **2** : a piece of soft absorbent paper used especially as a handkerchief or for removing cosmetics **3** : a mass or layer of cells usually of one kind that together with their intercellular substance form one of the structural materials of a plant or an animal — compare ORGAN; CONNECTIVE TISSUE, EPITHELIUM, PARENCHYMA [Old French *tissu*, a rich fabric, from *tistre* "to weave", from Latin *texere*]

tissue paper *n* : a thin gauzy paper often used to wrap delicate articles

[1]tit \'tit\ *n* : TEAT [Old English]

[2]tit *n* : TITMOUSE; *also* : any of various small plump often long-tailed birds

ti•tan \'tīt-n\ *n* **1** *cap* : one of a family of giants ruling the universe until overthrown by the Olympian gods **2** : one of gigantic size, power, or achievement [Greek]

ti•ta•nate \'tīt-n-,āt\ *n* **1** : any of various oxides of titanium and another metal **2** : a titanium ester

ti•tan•ess \'tīt-n-əs\ *n, often cap* : a female titan

ti•tan•ic \tī-'tan-ik\ *adj* **1** *cap* : of, relating to, or resembling the Titans **2** : vast in size, force, or power : COLOSSAL

ti•ta•ni•um \tī-'tā-nē-əm, tə-\ *n* : a silvery gray light strong metallic chemical element found combined in various minerals and used in alloys (as steel) — see ELEMENT table [New Latin, from Greek *Titan* "Titan"]

titanium dioxide *n* : an oxide TiO_2 of titanium used especially as a white pigment

titanium white *n* : titanium dioxide used as a pigment

ti•tan•o•there \tī-'tan-ə-,thiər\ *n* : any of various large often horned extinct mammals distantly related to the horses [derived from Greek *Titan* "Titan" + *thērion* "wild animal"]

tit•bit *variant of* TIDBIT

tit for tat \,tit-fər-'tat\ : an equivalent given in return (as for an injury) : RETALIATION [alteration of earlier *tip for tap*]

[1]tithe \'tīth\ *vb* **1** : to pay or give a tithe **2** : to levy a tithe on [Old English *teogothian*, from *teogotha* "tenth"] — **tith•er** *n*

[2]tithe *n* **1** : a tenth part paid in kind or money as a voluntary contribution or as a tax especially for the support of a religious establishment **2 a** : TENTH 2 **b** : a small part

ti•tian \'tish-ən\ *adj, often cap* : of a brownish orange color [*Titian*, Italian painter]

tit•il•late \'tit-l-,āt\ *vt* **1** : TICKLE 2 **2** : to excite pleasurably [Latin *titillare*] — **tit•il•la•tion** \,tit-l-'ā-shən\ *n* — **tit•il•la•tive** \'tit-l-,āt-iv\ *adj*

tit•i•vate *or* **tit•ti•vate** \'tit-ə-,vāt\ *vb* : to dress up : spruce up : SMARTEN [perhaps from *tidy* + *-vate* (as in *renovate*)] — **tit•i•va•tion** \,tit-ə-'vā-shən\ *n*

[1]ti•tle \'tīt-l\ *n* **1 a** : RIGHT, PRIVILEGE; *esp* : the elements constituting legal ownership **b** : a legal document (as a deed) that is evidence of a right **2** : something that justifies or substantiates a claim **3 a** : a descriptive or general heading (as of a chapter in a book) **b** : the heading of an act or statute or of a legal action or proceeding **4** : the distinguishing name of a written, printed, or filmed production or of a musical composition or a work of art **5** : a division of a legal document or a book or bill; *esp* : one larger than a section or article **6** : an appellation of dignity or honor attached to a person or family (as by hereditary right) ⟨a *title* of nobility⟩ **7** : CHAMPIONSHIP 2a ⟨won the batting *title*⟩ [Old French, from Latin *titulus* "inscription, title"]

[2]title *vt* **ti•tled; ti•tling** \'tīt-ling, -l-ing\ : to call by a title : TERM

ti•tled \'tīt-ld\ *adj* : having a title especially of nobility

title deed *n* : the deed constituting the evidence of a person's legal ownership

ti•tle•hold•er \'tīt-l-,hōl-dər\ *n* : one that holds a title; *esp* : CHAMPION

title page *n* : a page of a book bearing the title and usually the names of the author and publisher and the place of publication

title role *n* : a part or character that gives a play or movie its name

ti•tlist \'tīt-l-əst, 'tīt-ləst\ *n* : TITLEHOLDER

tit•mouse \'tit-,mau̇s\ *n, pl* **tit•mice** \-,mīs\ : any of numerous small tree-dwelling and insect-eating birds related to the nuthatches but longer tailed [Middle English *titmose*]

Ti•to•ism \'tēt-ō-,iz-əm\ *n* : nationalistic policies and practices followed by a communist state independently of the Soviet Union especially as practiced in Yugoslavia by Marshal Tito

ti•trate \'tī-,trāt\ *vt* : to subject to titration [French *titre* "title, proportion of gold or silver in a coin", from Old French *title* "label, title"]

ti•tra•tion \tī-'trā-shən\ *n* : the process of determining the strength of a solution or the concentration of a substance in solution by finding the smallest amount of a reagent required to cause a given effect (as color change) in reaction with a known volume of the test solution

ti•tri•met•ric \,tī-trə-'me-trik\ *adj* : determined by titration — **ti•tri•met•ri•cal•ly** \-tri-kə-lē, -klē\ *adv*

tit–tat–toe *variant of* TICKTACKTOE

tit•ter \'tit-ər\ *vi* : to laugh in a nervous or partly suppressed manner [imitative] — **titter** *n*

tit•tle \'tit-l\ *n* **1** : a point or small sign used as a diacritical mark in writing or printing **2** : a very small part or amount [Medieval Latin *titulus*, from Latin, "inscription, title"]

tit•tle–tat•tle \'tit-l-,tat-l\ *n* : GOSSIP 2 [reduplication of *tattle*] — **tittle–tattle** *vi*

tit•u•lar \'tich-lər, -ə-lər\ *adj* **1 a** : existing in title only **b** : having the title belonging to an office or dignity without its duties or responsibilities **2 :** bearing a title **3 :** of, relating to, or being a title [Latin *titulus* "title"] — **tit•u•lar•ly** *adv*

titular bishop *n* **:** a Roman Catholic bishop with the title of but without jurisdiction in a defunct see (as in Christian lands under Muslim control)

tiz•zy \'tiz-ē\ *n, pl* **tizzies :** a highly excited and distracted state of mind [origin unknown]

tme•sis \'mē-səs, tə-'mē-səs\ *n* **:** separation of parts of a compound word by the intervention of one or more words (as *what place soever* for *whatsoever place*) [Late Latin, from Greek *tmēsis* "act of cutting", from *temnein* "to cut"]

TNT \,tē-,en-'tē\ *n* **:** TRINITROTOLUENE [*tri*nitro*t*oluene]

[1]**to** \tə, tu̇, tü, 'tü; *before vowels usually* tə; *after* -t (*as in "want"*) *often* ə\ *prep* **1 a :** in the direction of and reaching ⟨walked *to* school⟩ **b :** in the direction of **:** so as to approach ⟨on the way *to* town⟩ **c :** close against **:** ON ⟨applied polish *to* the table⟩ **d :** as far as ⟨stripped *to* the waist⟩ **2 a :** for the purpose of **:** FOR ⟨came *to* our aid⟩ **b :** in honor of ⟨a toast *to* the winner⟩ **c :** so as to become or bring about ⟨broken *to* pieces⟩ **3 a :** BEFORE ⟨ten minutes *to* five⟩ **b :** UNTIL ⟨from eight *to* five⟩ **4 a :** being a part or accessory of ⟨a key *to* the door⟩ **b :** with the accompaniment of ⟨sang *to* the music⟩ **5 a :** in an indicated relation with ⟨similar *to* that one⟩ **b** (1) **:** in accordance with ⟨add salt *to* taste⟩ (2) **:** within the range of ⟨*to* my knowledge⟩ **c :** contained, occurring, or included in ⟨400 *to* the box⟩ **6 a :** as regards ⟨agreeable *to* everyone⟩ **b :** affecting as the receiver or beneficiary of an action ⟨gave it *to* me⟩ **c :** for no one except ⟨had a room *to* myself⟩ **7** — used to indicate that the following verb is an infinitive ⟨wants *to* go⟩ and often used by itself at the end of a clause to stand for an infinitive ⟨don't want *to*⟩ [Old English *tō*]

[2]**to** \'tü\ *adv* **1** — used as a function word to indicate direction toward ⟨run *to* and fro⟩ **2 :** into contact, position, or attachment especially with a frame (as of a door) ⟨wind blew the door *to*⟩ **3 :** to the matter or business at hand ⟨the boxers set *to* with a flurry of blows⟩ **4 :** to a state of consciousness or awareness ⟨brought me *to* with smelling salts⟩ **5 :** at hand **:** BY ⟨saw the moose close *to*⟩

toad \'tōd\ *n* **:** any of numerous tailless leaping amphibians that as compared with the related frogs are generally more terrestrial in habit and squatter and shorter in build and have weaker hind limbs and rough, dry, and warty rather than smooth and moist skin [Old English *tāde*]

toad•eat•er \-,ēt-ər\ *n* **:** TOADY

toad•fish \-,fish\ *n* **:** any of various marine fishes with a large thick head, a wide mouth, and scaleless slimy skin

toad•flax \-,flaks\ *n* **:** BUTTER-AND-EGGS

toad•stone \'tōd-,stōn\ *n* **:** a stone or similar object held to have formed in the head or body of a toad and formerly often worn as a charm or an antidote to poison

toad•stool \'tōd-,stül\ *n* **:** a fungus having an umbrella-shaped cap **:** MUSHROOM; *esp* **:** one that is poisonous or inedible

[1]**toady** \'tōd-ē\ *n, pl* **toad•ies :** a person who flatters or fawns upon another in the hope of receiving favors

[2]**toady** *vi* **toad•ied; toady•ing :** to behave as a toady — **toady•ism** \-ē-,iz-əm\ *n*

to–and–fro \,tü-ən-'frō\ *adj* **:** forward and backward ⟨*to-and-fro* motion⟩ ⟨*to-and-fro* visiting⟩

[1]**toast** \'tōst\ *vb* **1 :** to make (as bread) crisp, hot, and brown by heat **2 :** to warm thoroughly; *also* **:** to become toasted [Middle French *toster,* from Late Latin *tostare* "to roast", from Latin *torrēre* "to dry, parch"]

[2]**toast** *n* **1 :** sliced toasted bread browned on both sides by heat **2 a :** a person whose health is drunk or something in honor of which persons drink **b :** a highly admired person **3 :** an act of proposing or of drinking in honor of a toast [sense 2 from the use of pieces of spiced toast to flavor drinks]

[3]**toast** *vt* **:** to propose or drink to as a toast

toast•er \'tō-stər\ *n* **:** one that toasts; *esp* **:** an electrical appliance for toasting

toast•mas•ter \'tōst-,mas-tər, 'tōs-\ *n* **:** a person who presides at a banquet and introduces the after-dinner speakers

toast•mis•tress \-,mis-trəs\ *n* **:** a girl or woman who presides as toastmaster

to•bac•co \tə-'bak-ō\ *n, pl* **-cos 1 :** any of a genus of chiefly American plants of the potato family with sticky foliage and tubular flowers; *esp* **:** a tall erect annual South American herb grown for its leaves **2 :** the leaves of cultivated tobacco prepared for use in smoking or chewing or as snuff **3 :** manufactured products of tobacco (as cigars or cigarettes); *also* **:** smoking as a practice [Spanish *tabaco,* of American Indian origin]

tobacco mosaic *n* **:** any of a complex of virus diseases of tobacco and related plants

to•bac•co•nist \tə-'bak-ə-nəst\ *n* **:** a dealer in tobacco especially at retail

to–be \tə-'bē\ *adj* **:** that is to be **:** FUTURE — usually used in combination ⟨a bride-*to-be*⟩

To•bi•as \tə-'bī-əs\ *n* — see BIBLE table

To•bit \'tō-bət\ *n* — see BIBLE table

[1]**to•bog•gan** \tə-'bäg-ən\ *n* **1 :** a long flat-bottomed light sled made without runners and curved up at the front **2 :** a downward course or a sharp decline [Canadian French *tobogan,* of American Indian origin]

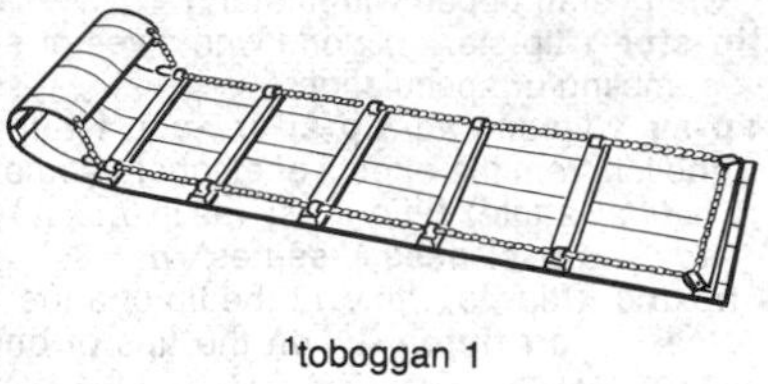

[1]toboggan 1

[2]**toboggan** *vi* **1 :** to coast on a toboggan **2 :** to decline suddenly and sharply (as in value) — **to•bog•gan•er** *n* — **to•bog•gan•ist** \tə-'bäg-ə-nəst\ *n*

to•by \'tō-bē\ *n, pl* **tobies** *often cap* **:** a small jug, pitcher, or mug modeled in the form of a stout man with a cocked hat for the brim [*Toby,* nickname from the name *Tobias*]

toc•ca•ta \tə-'kät-ə\ *n* **:** a musical composition usually for organ or harpsichord in a free style [Italian, from *toccare* "to touch"]

to•coph•er•ol \tō-'käf-ə-,rȯl, -,rōl\ *n* **:** any of various fat-soluble phenolic compounds with varying degrees of antioxidant and vitamin E activity [derived from Greek *tokos* "childbirth, offspring" + *pherein* "to carry, bear"]

toc•sin \'täk-sən\ *n* **1 :** an alarm bell or the ringing of it **2 :** a warning signal [Middle French *toquassen,* from Provençal *tocasenh,* from *tocar* "to touch, ring" + *senh* "sign, bell", from Latin *signum* "sign"]

[1]**to•day** \tə-'dā\ *adv* **1 :** on or for this day **2 :** at the present time **:** NOWADAYS

[2]**today** *n* **:** the present day, time, or age

tod•dle \'täd-l\ *vi* **tod•dled; tod•dling** \'täd-ling, -l-ing\ **:** to walk with short tottering steps in the manner of a young child [origin unknown] — **toddle** *n* — **tod•dler** \'täd-lər, -l-ər\ *n*

tod•dy \'täd-ē\ *n, pl* **toddies 1 :** the sap of various mostly East Indian palms often fermented to form an alcoholic liquor **2 :** a hot drink consisting of an alcoholic liquor, water, sugar, and spices [Hindi *tāṛī,* from *tāṛ,* a kind of palm, from Sanskrit *tāla*]

to–do \tə-'dü\ *n, pl* **to–dos** \-'düz\ **:** BUSTLE, STIR

[1]**toe** \'tō\ *n* **1 a :** one of the jointed members that make up the front end of a vertebrate foot **b :** the front end or part of a foot or hoof **c :** the forepart of something (as a shoe) worn on the foot **2 :** something that resembles the toe of a foot especially in form or position ⟨the *toe* of a golf club⟩ [Old English *tā*] — **toe•less** \-ləs\ *adj*

[2]**toe** *vb* **toed; toe•ing 1 :** to furnish with a toe ⟨*toe* off a sock in knitting⟩ **2 :** to touch, reach, or drive with the toe ⟨*toe* a football⟩ **3 :** to drive (as a nail) slantwise; *also* **:** to fasten by nails so driven **4 :** to stand or walk so that the toes assume an indicated position or direction ⟨*toe* in⟩ — **toe the line :** to conform rigorously to a rule or standard

toed \'tōd\ *adj* **1 :** having a toe or such or so many toes — used especially in combination ⟨5-*toed*⟩ **2 :** driven obliquely ⟨a *toed* nail⟩; *also* **:** secured by toed nails

toe dance *n* **:** a dance executed on the tips of the toes — **toe–dance** \'tō-,dans\ *vi* — **toe dancer** *n*

toe•hold \'tō-,hōld\ *n* **1 :** a small foothold **:** a means of progressing **2 :** a hold in which the offensive wrestler bends or twists the opponent's foot

[1]**toe•nail** \'tō-,nāl, -'nāl\ *n* **:** a nail of a toe

[2]**toenail** *vt* **:** to fasten by toed nails **:** TOE

tof•fee *or* **tof•fy** \'tȯ-fē, 'täf-ē\ *n, pl* **toffees** *or* **toffies :** brittle but tender candy made by boiling sugar and butter together [alteration of *taffy*]

tog \'täg, 'tȯg\ *vt* **togged; tog•ging :** to put togs on **:** DRESS

⟨*togged* out in the latest fashion⟩

to•ga \'tō-gə\ *n* : the loose outer garment worn in public by citizens of ancient Rome; *also* : a similar loose wrap or a professional, official, or academic gown [Latin] — **to•gaed** \-gəd\ *adj*

toga

to•geth•er \tə-'ge*th*-ər\ *adv* **1** : in or into one group, body, or place ⟨gathered *together*⟩ **2** : in or into association, union, or contact with each other ⟨in business *together*⟩ ⟨the doors banged *together*⟩ **3 a** : at one time ⟨they all cheered *together*⟩ **b** : in succession : without intermission ⟨work for hours *together*⟩ **4 a** : in or by combined effort : JOINTLY ⟨worked *together* to clear the road⟩ **b** : in or into agreement ⟨get *together* on a plan⟩ **c** : so as to form an integrated or coherent whole ⟨put words *together* in sentences⟩ **5** : considered as a whole : in the aggregate ⟨gave more than all the others *together*⟩ [Old English *togædere,* from *tō* "to" + *gædere* "together"] — **to•geth•er•ness** *n*

tog•gery \'täg-rē, 'tȯg-, -ə-rē\ *n, pl* **-ger•ies** : CLOTHING

[1]tog•gle \'täg-əl\ *n* **1** : a crosspiece attached to the end of or to a loop in a rope, chain, or belt to prevent slipping or to serve as a fastening or as a grip for tightening **2** : TOGGLE JOINT; *also* : a device with a toggle joint [origin unknown]

[2]toggle *vt* **tog•gled; tog•gling** \'täg-ling, -ə-ling\ **1** : to fasten with or as if with a toggle **2** : to furnish with a toggle

toggle joint *n* : a device consisting of two bars jointed together end to end but not in line so that when a force is applied to the joint tending to straighten it pressure will be exerted on the parts fixed at the ends of the bars

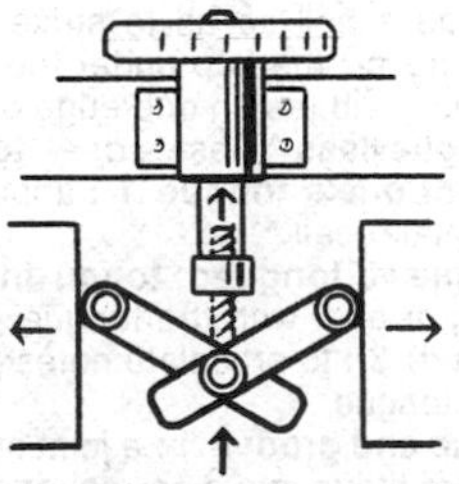
toggle joint

toggle switch *n* : an electric switch depending on a toggle joint with a spring to open or close the circuit when a projecting lever is pushed through a small arc

togs \'tägz, 'tȯgz\ *n pl* : CLOTHING; *esp* : a set of clothes and accessories for a specified use ⟨riding *togs*⟩ [English slang *tog* "coat", probably derived from Latin *toga* "toga"]

[1]toil \'tȯil\ *n* : long hard tiring labor : DRUDGERY [Anglo-French *toyl* "struggle, battle", from Old French *toeil* "battle, confusion", from *toeillier* "to disturb, dispute", from Latin *tudiculare* "to crush, grind", derived from *tudes* "hammer"] — **toil•ful** \-fəl\ *adj* — **toil•ful•ly** \-fə-lē\ *adv*

[2]toil *vi* **1** : to work hard and long : LABOR **2** : PLOD 1, TRUDGE ⟨*toiling* up a steep hill⟩ — **toil•er** *n*

[3]toil *n* : something that involves or holds one fast : SNARE, TRAP — usually used in pl. [Middle French *toile* "cloth, net", from Latin *tela* "web", from *texere* "to weave"]

[1]toi•let \'tȯi-lət\ *n* **1** : the act or process of dressing and grooming oneself **2 a** : BATHROOM **b** : a fixture for defecation and urination; *esp* : WATER CLOSET [Middle French *toilette* "cloth put over the shoulders while dressing the hair or shaving", from *toile* "cloth", from Latin *tela* "web"]

[2]toilet *vb* **1** : to dress and groom oneself **2** : to help (a child) use the toilet

toilet paper *n* : a thin sanitary absorbent paper for bathroom use chiefly after defecation or urination

toi•let•ry \'tȯi-lə-trē\ *n, pl* **-ries** : an article or preparation used in grooming oneself — usually used in pl.

toilet soap *n* : a mild often perfumed and colored soap that is used for washing oneself

toi•lette \twä-'let\ *n* **1** : TOILET 1 **2 a** : formal or fashionable attire or style of dressing **b** : a particular costume or outfit [French]

toilet water *n* : a perfumed liquid containing a high percentage of alcohol for use in or after a bath or as a skin freshener

toil•some \'tȯil-səm\ *adj* : marked by or full of toil or fatigue : LABORIOUS — **toil•some•ly** *adv* — **toil•some•ness** *n*

toil•worn \-ˌwōrn, -ˌwȯrn\ *adj* : showing the effects of or worn out by long hard work

To•kay \tō-'kā\ *n* : a sweet usually dark gold dessert wine made near Tokaj, Hungary; *also* : a similar wine made elsewhere

toke \'tōk\ *n, slang* : a puff on a marijuana cigarette [origin unknown]

[1]to•ken \'tō-kən\ *n* **1** : an outward sign or expression ⟨*tokens* of grief⟩ **2** : SYMBOL, EMBLEM ⟨the white flag is a *token* of surrender⟩ **3 a** : SOUVENIR, KEEPSAKE **b** : a small part representing the whole : INDICATION ⟨a mere *token* of future benefits⟩ **4 a** : something given or shown as a guarantee (as of identity, right, or authority) **b** : a piece resembling a coin issued for use (as for fare on a bus) [Old English *tācen*] — **by the same token** : for the same reason

[2]token *adj* **1** : done or given in partial fulfillment of an obligation or undertaking ⟨a *token* payment⟩ **2** : MINIMAL, PERFUNCTORY ⟨*token* resistance⟩

to•ken•ism \'tō-kə-ˌniz-əm\ *n* : the policy or practice of making only a token effort (as in integrating races)

token money *n* **1** : money of regular government issue having a greater face value than intrinsic value **2** : privately issued tokens for use as money

tol•booth \'tōl-ˌbüth, 'tō-, 'täl-, 'tȯl-\ *n* **1** *Scottish* : a town or market hall **2** *Scottish* : JAIL, PRISON [Middle English *tolbothe* "tollbooth, town hall, jail"]

tol•bu•ta•mide \täl-'byüt-ə-ˌmīd\ *n* : a sulfonamide that lowers blood sugar level and is used in the treatment of diabetes [*tolu*ene + *butyric* + *amide*]

told *past of* TELL

tole \'tōl\ *n* : usually japanned or painted sheet metal (as tinplate) used mostly for decorative objects (as trays or boxes) and finished in various colors often with stenciled designs [French *tôle* "sheet metal", from French dialect, "table, slab", from Latin *tabula* "board, tablet"]

To•le•do \tə-'lēd-ō\ *n, pl* **-dos** : a finely tempered sword of a kind made in Toledo, Spain

tol•er•a•ble \'täl-rə-bəl, -ə-rə-; 'täl-ər-bəl\ *adj* **1** : capable of being borne or endured **2** : moderately good or agreeable : PASSABLE — **tol•er•a•bil•i•ty** \ˌtäl-rə-'bil-ət-ē, -ə-rə-\ *n* — **tol•er•a•bly** \'täl-rə-blē, -ə-rə-; 'täl-ər-blē\ *adv*

tol•er•ance \'täl-rəns, -ə-rəns\ *n* **1** : relative capacity to endure or adapt physiologically to an unfavorable environmental factor **2 a** : sympathy or indulgence for beliefs or practices differing from one's own **b** : the act of allowing something : TOLERATION **3** : allowable deviation from a standard — **tol•er•ant** \-rənt\ *adj* — **tol•er•ant•ly** *adv*

tol•er•ate \'täl-ə-ˌrāt\ *vt* **1** : to allow to be done or to exist : put up with : ENDURE **2** : to show tolerance toward ⟨plants that *tolerate* drought⟩ ⟨*tolerate* a drug⟩ [Latin *tolerare*] — **tol•er•a•tion** \ˌtäl-ə-'rā-shən\ *n* — **tol•er•a•tor** \'täl-ə-ˌrāt-ər\ *n*

[1]toll \'tōl\ *n* **1** : a tax paid for a privilege (as the use of a highway or bridge) **2** : a charge paid for a service (as placing a long-distance telephone call) **3** : a ruinous price; *esp* : cost in life or misery [Old English]

[2]toll *vt* : to take as toll; *also* : to take a toll from

[3]toll *vb* **1** : to sound (a bell) by pulling the rope **2** : to signal or announce by the sounding of a bell ⟨the clock *tolled* the hour⟩ ⟨bells *tolling* the alarm⟩ **3** : to sound with slow measured strokes [Middle English *tollen*]

[4]toll *n* : the sound of a tolling bell

toll•booth \'tōl-ˌbüth\ *n* : a booth where tolls are paid

toll call *n* : a long-distance telephone call at charges above a local rate

toll•gate \'tōl-ˌgāt\ *n* : a point where vehicles stop to pay a toll

toll•house \-ˌhau̇s\ *n* : a house or booth where tolls are collected

Tol•tec \'tōl-ˌtek, 'täl-\ *n* : a member of a Nahuatlan people of central and southern Mexico [Spanish *tolteca,* of American Indian origin] — **Tol•tec•an** \-ən\ *adj*

\ə\ **abut**	\au̇\ **out**	\i\ **tip**	\ȯ\ **saw**	\u̇\ **foot**
\ər\ **further**	\ch\ **chin**	\ī\ **life**	\ȯi\ **coin**	\y\ **yet**
\a\ **mat**	\e\ **pet**	\j\ **job**	\th\ **thin**	\yü\ **few**
\ā\ **take**	\ē\ **easy**	\ng\ **sing**	*th*\ **this**	\yu̇\ **cure**
\ä\ **cot, cart**	\g\ **go**	\ō\ **bone**	\ü\ **food**	\zh\ **vision**

tol•u•ene \'täl-yə-,wēn\ *n* : a hydrocarbon similar to benzene but less volatile, less flammable, and less toxic that is used especially as a solvent and in organic synthesis [Spanish *tolú,* a balsam from which toluene was distilled, from Santiago de *Tolú,* Colombia]

tom \'täm\ *n* : the male of various animals ⟨a *tom* swan⟩: as **a** : TOMCAT **b** : GOBBLER [*Tom,* nickname for *Thomas*]

[1]**tom•a•hawk** \'täm-i-,hök\ *n* : a light ax used as a weapon by North American Indians [of American Indian origin]

[2]**tomahawk** *vt* : to cut, strike, or kill with a tomahawk

to•ma•to \tə-'māt-ō, -'mät-\ *n, pl* **-toes** **1** : any of a genus of South American herbs of the potato family; *esp* : one widely grown for its edible fruits **2** : the usually large, rounded, and red or yellow pulpy fruit of a tomato [Spanish *tomate,* from Nahuatl *tomatl*]

tomb \'tüm\ *n* **1 a** : GRAVE **b** : a place of burial **2** : a house, chamber, or vault for the dead **3** : a building or structure resembling a tomb [Anglo-French *tumbe,* from Late Latin *tumba* "sepulchral mound", from Greek *tymbos*]

tom•boy \'täm-,bȯi\ *n* : a girl of boyish behavior — **tom•boy•ish** \-ish\ *adj* — **tom•boy•ish•ness** *n*

tomb•stone \'tüm-,stōn\ *n* : GRAVESTONE

tom•cat \'täm-,kat\ *n* : a male cat

tom•cod \-,käd\ *n* : any of several small fishes resembling the related common codfish

Tom, Dick, and Harry \,täm-,dik-ən-'har-ē\ *n* : the ordinary person : ANYONE — often used with *every* ⟨helps every *Tom, Dick, and Harry* in need⟩

tome \'tōm\ *n* : BOOK 1a; *esp* : a large or scholarly book [Latin *tomus,* from Greek *tomos* "section, tome", from *temnein* "to cut"]

to•men•tose \tō-'men-,tōs, 'tō-mən-\ *adj* : covered with densely matted hairs ⟨a *tomentose* leaf⟩ [Latin *tomentum* "cushion stuffing"]

tom•fool \'täm-'fül\ *n* : a great fool : BLOCKHEAD — **tomfool** *adj* — **tom•fool•ery** \täm-'fül-rē, -ə-rē\ *n*

Tom•my \'täm-ē\ *n, pl* **Tommies** : a British soldier [*Thomas* Atkins, name used as model in official army forms]

tom•my gun \'täm-ē-,gən\ *n* : SUBMACHINE GUN [*Thompson* submachine gun]

tom•my•rot \'täm-ē-,rät\ *n* : NONSENSE 1 [English dialect *tommy* "fool" + *rot*]

[1]**to•mor•row** \tə-'mär-ō, -'mȯr-\ *adv* : on or for the day after today [Old English *tō morgen,* from *tō* "to" + *morgen* "morrow, morning"]

[2]**tomorrow** *n* **1** : the day after today **2** : FUTURE 1a ⟨the world of *tomorrow*⟩

Tom Thumb \'täm-'thəm\ *n* : a very small individual [*Tom Thumb,* legendary English dwarf]

tom–tom \'täm-,täm, 'təm-,təm\ *n* : a usually long narrow small-headed drum commonly beaten with the hands [Hindi *ṭamṭam*]

-t•o•my \t-ə-mē\ *n combining form, pl* **-tomies** : cutting : incision ⟨tracheo*tomy*⟩ [Greek *-tomos* "that cuts", from *temnein* "to cut"]

ton \'tən\ *n, pl* **tons** *also* **ton** **1** : any of various units of weight: **a** — see MEASURE table **b** : METRIC TON **2 a** : a unit of internal capacity for ships equal to 100 cubic feet (about 2.83 cubic meters) **b** : a unit approximately equal to the volume of a long ton weight of seawater used in reckoning the displacement of ships and equal to 35 cubic feet (about .99 cubic meters) **c** : a unit of volume for cargo freight usually reckoned at 40 cubic feet (about 1.13 cubic meters) **3** : a great quantity : LOT — often used in pl. ⟨*tons* of money⟩ [Middle English *tunne,* a unit of weight or capacity, from Old English *tunne* "tun"]

ton•al \'tōn-l\ *adj* **1** : of, relating to, or having tonality **2** : of or relating to tone or tonicity — **ton•al•ly** \-l-ē\ *adv*

to•nal•i•ty \tō-'nal-ət-ē\ *n, pl* **-ties** : tonal quality: as **a** : the character of a musical composition dependent on its key or on the relation of its tones and chords to a keynote **b** : the arrangement or interrelation of color tones of a picture

[1]**tone** \'tōn\ *n* **1 a** : quality of vocal or musical sound **b** : a sound of definite pitch or vibration **c** : pitch, inflection, or modulation of voice especially as an individual characteristic, a mode of emotional expression, or a linguistic device ⟨a shrill *tone*⟩ ⟨in angry *tones*⟩ **2** : a style or way of speaking or writing ⟨a scholarly *tone*⟩ **3** : general character, quality, or trend ⟨the depressing *tone* of your thoughts⟩ **4 a** : color quality or value : a tint or shade of color ⟨decorated in soft *tones*⟩ **b** : a color that modifies another ⟨gray with a blue *tone*⟩ **5 a** : a healthy state of the body or any of its parts; *also* : a state of normal tension and responsiveness to stimulation **b** : healthy elasticity : RESILIENCY [Latin *tonus* "tension, tone", from Greek *tonos,* literally "act of stretching"] — **toned** \'tōnd\ *adj*

[2]**tone** *vb* **1** : to give a particular intonation or inflection to **2** : to impart tone to : STRENGTHEN ⟨medicine to *tone* up the system⟩ **3** : to soften, blend, or harmonize in color, appearance, or sound — **ton•er** *n*

tone arm *n* : the movable part of a phonograph that carries the pickup and permits the needle to follow the record groove

tone–deaf \'tōn-,def\ *adj* : relatively insensitive to differences in musical pitch

tone language *n* : a language (as Chinese) in which variations in tone distinguish words of different meaning that otherwise would sound alike

tong \'täng, 'tȯng\ *vb* **1** : to take, hold, or handle with tongs **2** : to use tongs especially in taking or handling something — **tong•er** \'täng-ər, 'tȯng-\ *n*

tongs \'tängz, 'tȯngz\ *n pl* : any of numerous grasping devices commonly having two pieces joined at one end by a pivot or hinged like scissors [Old English *tang*]

[1]**tongue** \'təng\ *n* **1 a** : a fleshy movable process of the floor of the mouth in most vertebrates that bears sensory organs and small glands and functions especially in taking and swallowing food and in human beings as a speech organ **b** : an analogous part of various invertebrate animals **2** : the flesh of a tongue (as of the ox or sheep) used as food **3** : the power of communication through speech **4 a** : LANGUAGE; *esp* : a spoken language **b** : manner or quality of utterance with respect to tone or sound, meaning, or the intention of the speaker ⟨a clever *tongue*⟩ **c** : ecstatic usually unintelligible utterance accompanying religious excitation **5** : something resembling an animal's tongue in being elongated and fastened at one end only: as **a** : a movable pin in a buckle **b** : a metal piece suspended inside a bell so as to strike against the sides as the bell is swung **c** : the flap under the lacing of a shoe **6** : a projecting ridge or rib (as on one edge of a board) [Old English *tunge*] — **tongue•less** \-ləs\ *adj* — **tongue•like** \-,līk\ *adj* — **on the tip of one's tongue** **1** : about to be spoken **2** : just escaping mental recall

[2]**tongue** *vb* **tongued**; **tongu•ing** \'təng-ing\ **1** : to touch or lick with or as if with the tongue **2** : to cut a tongue on ⟨*tongue* a board⟩ **3** : to articulate notes on a wind instrument by means of the tongue

tongue and groove *n* : a joint made by a tongue on one edge of a board fitting into a corresponding groove on the edge of another board

tongue in cheek *adv* : with insincerity, irony, or whimsical exaggeration — **tongue-in-cheek** *adj*

tongue–lash \'təng-,lash\ *vb* : SCOLD 2, BERATE — **tongue–lash•ing** n

tongue–tied \-,tīd\ *adj* : unable to speak clearly or freely usually from abnormal shortness of the membrane under the tongue or from shyness

tongue twister *n* : a word, phrase, or sentence difficult to articulate because of a succession of similar consonant sounds

[1]**ton•ic** \'tän-ik\ *adj* **1 a** : of, relating to, or marked by tension and especially muscular tension : exhibiting tonus **b** : producing or tending to produce healthy muscular condition and reaction **c** : being or marked by excessive and prolonged muscular contraction ⟨*tonic* convulsions⟩ **2 a** : improving physical or mental tone : INVIGORATING **b** : yielding a tonic substance **3** : relating to or based on the first tone of a scale ⟨*tonic* harmony⟩ **4** : bearing a principal stress or accent ⟨a *tonic* syllable⟩ [Greek *tonikos,* from *tonos* "tension, tone"] — **ton•i•cal•ly** \'tän-i-kə-lē, -klē\ *adv*

[2]**tonic** *n* **1** : a tonic agent (as a drug) **2** : the first degree of a major or minor musical scale **3** : a voiced sound

to•nic•i•ty \tō-'nis-ət-ē\ *n* : the quality of having tone and especially healthy vigor of body or mind

[1]**to•night** \tə-'nīt\ *adv* : on this present night or the night following this present day

[2]**tonight** *n* : the night that ends the present day

ton•nage \'tən-ij\ *n* **1 a** : a duty on ships based on cargo capacity **b** : a duty on goods per ton transported **2** : ships in terms of the total number of tons registered or carried or of their carrying capacity **3 a** : the cubical content of a merchant ship in units of 100 cubic feet (about 2.83 cubic meters) **b** : the displacement of a warship **4 :** total weight in tons shipped, carried, or mined [Middle English, "duty levied on every tun of imported wine", from Old French *tonne* "tun", from Medieval Latin *tunna,* of Celtic origin]

ton•neau \tə-ˈnō\ *n* **:** the rear seating compartment of an automobile; *also* **:** the entire seating compartment [French, literally, "tun", derived from Old French *tonne*]

ton•sil \ˈtän-səl\ *n* **:** either of a pair of masses of lymphoid tissue that lie one on each side of the throat at the back of the mouth [Latin *tonsillae* "tonsils"] — **ton•sil•lar** \-sə-lər\ *adj*

ton•sil•lec•to•my \ˌtän-sə-ˈlek-tə-mē\ *n, pl* **-mies :** the surgical removal of the tonsils

ton•sil•li•tis \-ˈlīt-əs\ *n* **:** inflammation of the tonsils

ton•so•ri•al \tän-ˈsōr-ē-əl, -ˈsȯr-\ *adj* **:** of or relating to a barber or a barber's work [Latin *tonsorius,* from *tondēre* "to shear"]

ton•sure \ˈtän-chər\ *n* **1 :** the Roman Catholic or Eastern rite of admission to the clergy by the clipping or shaving of the head **2 :** the shaven crown or patch worn by monks and many clerics [Latin *tonsura* "act of shearing", from *tondēre* "to shear"] — **ton•sured** \-chərd\ *adj*

to•nus \ˈtō-nəs\ *n* **:** TONE 5a; *esp* **:** the state of partial contraction characteristic of normal muscle [Latin, "tension, tone"]

too \tü, ˈtü\ *adv* **1 :** ALSO, BESIDES ⟨sell the house and furniture *too*⟩ **2 a :** OVER 3, EXCESSIVELY ⟨it's *too* late⟩ **b :** to such a degree as to be regrettable ⟨this has gone *too* far⟩ **c :** VERY ⟨only *too* glad to help⟩ **3 :** SO 2d, INDEED ⟨I didn't! You did *too!*⟩ [Old English *tō* "to, too"]

took *past of* TAKE

[1]**tool** \ˈtül\ *n* **1 :** an instrument (as a hammer, saw, or wrench) used or worked by hand or by a machine; *also* **:** a machine that operates tools for shaping work **2 a :** an instrument or apparatus used in performing an operation or necessary in the practice of a vocation or profession ⟨a scholar's books are *tools*⟩ **b :** a means to an end **3 :** a person used or manipulated by another **:** DUPE [Old English *tōl*] **syn** see IMPLEMENT

[2]**tool** *vb* **1 :** DRIVE ⟨*tooled* along the road⟩ **2 :** to shape, form, or finish with a tool; *esp* **:** to letter or ornament (as a book cover) by means of hand tools **3 :** to equip a plant or industry with machines and tools for production — often used with *up*

tool•box \ˈtül-ˌbäks\ *n* **:** a chest for tools

tool•head \ˈtül-ˌhed\ *n* **:** a part of a machine in which a tool or toolholder is clamped and which is provided with adjustments to bring the tool into the desired position

tool•hold•er \-ˌhōl-dər\ *n* **:** a short steel bar having a shank at one end to fit into the toolhead of a machine and a clamp at the other end to hold small interchangeable cutting bits

tool•house \-ˌhau̇s\ *n* **:** a building (as in a garden) for storing tools

tool•mak•er \ˈtül-ˌmā-kər\ *n* **:** a machinist who specializes in the construction, repair, maintenance, and calibration of the tools, jigs, fixtures, and instruments of a machine shop

tool•mak•ing \-ˌmā-king\ *n* **:** the act, process, or art of making tools

tool•room \-ˌrüm, -ˌru̇m\ *n* **:** a room where tools are kept; *esp* **:** a room in a machine shop in which tools are made, stored, or loaned out to the workers

tool•shed \-ˌshed\ *n* **:** TOOLHOUSE

[1]**toot** \ˈtüt\ *vb* **1 :** to sound a short blast ⟨a horn *tooted*⟩ **2 :** to blow or sound (an instrument) especially so as to produce short blasts ⟨*toot* a whistle⟩ [probably imitative] — **toot•er** *n*

[2]**toot** *n* **:** a short blast (as on a horn); *also* **:** a sound resembling such a blast

[3]**toot** *n* **:** a drinking bout **:** SPREE ⟨went on a *toot*⟩ [Scottish *toot* "to drink heavily"]

tooth \ˈtüth\ *n, pl* **teeth** \ˈtēth\ **1 a :** one of the hard bony structures borne especially on the jaws of vertebrates and used for seizing and chewing food and as weapons **b :** any of various usually hard and sharp processes especially about the mouth of an invertebrate **2 :** TASTE, LIKING ⟨a *tooth* for sweets⟩ **3 :** a projection resembling or suggesting the tooth of an animal in shape, arrangement, or action ⟨the *tooth* of a saw⟩ **4 :** one of the projections on the rim of a cogwheel **:** COG **5 a :** something that injures, tortures, devours, or destroys ⟨sailed into the *teeth* of the hurricane⟩ **b** *pl* **:** effective means of enforcement **6 :** a roughness of surface produced by mechanical or artificial means [Old English *tōth*] — **toothed** \ˈtütht\ *adj* — **tooth•less** \ˈtüth-ləs\ *adj* — **tooth•like** \-ˌlīk\ *adj* — **to the teeth :** FULLY, COMPLETELY ⟨armed *to the teeth*⟩

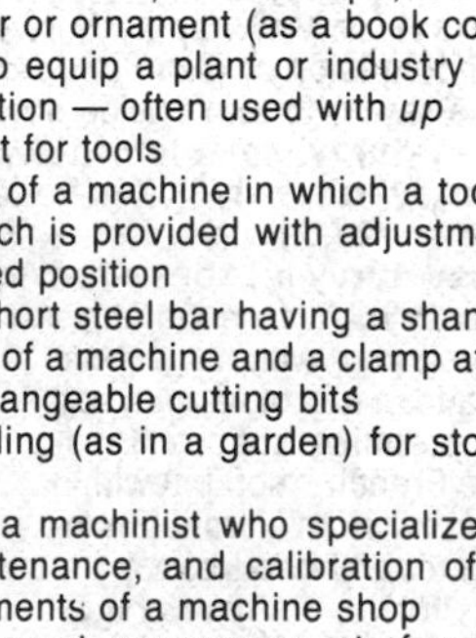

tooth 1a: *1* enamel, *2* dentine, *3* pulp

tooth•ache \ˈtü-ˌthāk\ *n* **:** pain in or about a tooth

tooth and nail *adv* **:** with every available means **:** all out ⟨fight *tooth and nail*⟩

tooth•brush \ˈtüth-ˌbrəsh\ *n* **:** a brush for cleaning the teeth

toothed whale *n* **:** any of a group (Odontoceti) of whales with numerous simple conical teeth

tooth•paste \ˈtüth-ˌpāst\ *n* **:** a paste dentifrice

tooth•pick \-ˌpik\ *n* **:** a pointed instrument (as a small tapering piece of wood) used for removing food particles lodged between the teeth

tooth powder *n* **:** a dentifrice in powder form

tooth shell *n* **:** any of a class (Scaphopoda) of marine mollusks with a tapering tubular shell; *also* **:** this shell

tooth•some \ˈtüth-səm\ *adj* **1 :** pleasing to the taste **:** DELICIOUS ⟨a *toothsome* dessert⟩ **2 :** physically attractive **:** LOVELY — **tooth•some•ly** *adv* — **tooth•some•ness** *n*

toothy \ˈtü-thē\ *adj* **tooth•i•er; -est :** having or showing prominent teeth ⟨a *toothy* grin⟩ — **tooth•i•ly** \-thə-lē\ *adv*

[1]**top** \ˈtäp\ *n* **1 a :** the highest point, level, or part ⟨the *top* of the hill⟩ **b :** the upper end, edge, or surface ⟨the *top* of the page⟩ ⟨filled the glass to the *top*⟩ **2 :** the stalk and leaves of a plant and especially of one with edible roots ⟨beet *tops*⟩ **3 :** an integral part serving as an upper piece, lid, or covering ⟨a pajama *top*⟩ ⟨put the *top* on the jar⟩ **4 :** the highest position or rank **:** ACME ⟨reached the *top* of the profession⟩; *also* **:** one in such a position ⟨secrets known only to the *top*⟩ [Old English] — **topped** \ˈtäpt\ *adj* — **off the top of one's head :** in an impromptu way — **on top of 1 :** in control of ⟨was *on top of* the job⟩ **2 :** in sudden unexpected nearness to ⟨the motorboat was *on top of* us⟩ **3 :** in addition to — **on top of the world :** in a position of great success, happiness, or fame

[2]**top** *vt* **topped; top•ping 1 :** to remove or cut the top of ⟨*top* a tree⟩ **2 a :** to cover with a top **:** provide, form, or serve as a top for **b :** to supply with a decorative or protective finish or a final touch ⟨*topped* the sundae with nuts⟩ ⟨a meal *topped* off with coffee⟩ **3 a :** to be or become higher than ⟨the flood *topped* the dike⟩ **b :** to be superior to ⟨*topped* the record⟩ **c :** to gain ascendancy over **:** DOMINATE **4 a :** to rise to, reach, or be at the top of **b :** to go over the top of **5 :** to strike (a ball) above the center creating topspin or sometimes making a weak stroke

[3]**top** *adj* **1 :** of, relating to, or being at the top **2 :** LEADING 1, CHIEF **3 :** of the highest quality, amount, or degree ⟨*top* value⟩

[4]**top** *n* **:** a commonly cylindrical or cone-shaped toy that has a point on which it is made to spin [Old English]

to•paz \ˈtō-ˌpaz\ *n* **1 :** a hard mineral consisting of a silicate of aluminum and occurring in crystals of various colors with the yellow variety being the one usually cut and prized as a gem **2 :** a gem (as a yellow sapphire) resembling the true topaz [Old French *topace,* from Latin *topazus,* from Greek *topazos*]

top billing *n* **1 :** the position at the top of a theatrical bill usually featuring the star's name **2 :** prominent emphasis, featuring, or advertising

top boot *n* **:** a high boot often with light-colored leather bands around the upper part

top•coat \ˈtäp-ˌkōt\ *n* **:** a lightweight overcoat

top•cross \-ˌkrȯs\ *n* **:** a cross between a superior or purebred male and inferior female stock to improve the average quality of the progeny; *also* **:** an offspring from such a cross

top dog *n* **:** one that is in a position of authority especially by winning in a hard-fought competition

top drawer *n* **:** the highest level of society, authority, or excellence

tope \ˈtōp\ *n* **:** a widely distributed small shark with a liver rich in vitamin A [origin unknown]

\ə\ **abut**	\au̇\ **out**	\i\ **tip**	\ȯ\ **saw**	\u̇\ **foot**
\ər\ **further**	\ch\ **chin**	\ī\ **life**	\ȯi\ **coin**	\y\ **yet**
\a\ **mat**	\e\ **pet**	\j\ **job**	\th\ **thin**	\yü\ **few**
\ā\ **take**	\ē\ **easy**	\ng\ **sing**	\t͟h\ **this**	\yu̇\ **cure**
\ä\ **cot, cart**	\g\ **go**	\ō\ **bone**	\ü\ **food**	\zh\ **vision**

to·pee *or* **to·pi** \tō-ˈpē, ˈtō-pē\ *n* : a lightweight helmet-shaped hat made of pith or cork [Hindi *ṭopī*]

top·er \ˈtō-pər\ *n* : a heavy drinker; *esp* : DRUNKARD [obsolete *tope,* interjection used to wish good health before drinking]

top flight *n* : TOP DRAWER — **top–flight** \ˈtäp-ˈflīt\ *adj*

Top 40 *n pl* : the 40 best-selling phonograph records for a given period

top·gal·lant \täp-ˈgal-ənt, ˈtäp-, tə-ˈgal-\ *n* : the sail just above a topsail and below the royal on a square-rigged ship

top hat *n* : a tall-crowned hat usually of beaver or silk

top–heavy \ˈtäp-ˌhev-ē\ *adj* : having the top part too heavy for the lower part

To·phet \ˈtō-fət\ *n* : HELL 2 [Hebrew *tōpheth,* shrine south of ancient Jerusalem where human sacrifices were performed to Moloch (Jeremiah 7:31)]

[1]**to·pi·ary** \ˈtō-pē-ˌer-ē\ *adj* : of, relating to, or being the training and trimming of woody plants into odd or ornamental shapes; *also* : characterized by such work [Latin *topiarius,* from *topia* "ornamental gardening", from Greek *topos* "place"]

[2]**topiary** *n, pl* **-ar·ies** : topiary art or gardening; *also* : a topiary garden

top·ic \ˈtäp-ik\ *n* **1** : a heading in an outlined argument or exposition **2** : the subject of a discourse or a section of it : THEME [Latin *Topica,* a work by Aristotle on forms of argument, from Greek *Topika,* derived from *topos* "place, commonplace"]

top·i·cal \ˈtäp-i-kəl\ *adj* **1 a** : of or relating to a place **b** : local or designed for local application ⟨a *topical* remedy⟩ ⟨a *topical* anesthetic⟩ **2 a** : of, relating to, or arranged by topics ⟨a *topical* outline⟩ **b** : referring to the topics of the day or place : of local or temporary interest [Greek *topikos,* from *topos* "place"] — **top·i·cal·i·ty** \ˌtäp-ə-ˈkal-ət-ē\ *n* — **top·i·cal·ly** \ˈtäp-i-kə-lē, -klē\ *adv*

topic sentence *n* : a sentence that states the main thought of a paragraph or of a larger unit of discourse

top·knot \ˈtäp-ˌnät\ *n* **1** : an ornament (as a bow) forming a headdress or worn as part of a hairstyle **2** : a crest of feathers or hair on the top of the head

1 topknot 2

top·less \ˈtäp-ləs\ *adj* **1** : being without a top **2 a** : wearing no clothing on the upper body **b** : featuring topless waitresses or entertainers

top·lofty \ˈtäp-ˌlȯf-tē\ *also* **top·loft·i·cal** \täp-ˈlȯf-ti-kəl\ *adj* : very superior in air or attitude : HAUGHTY — **top·loft·i·ness** \ˈtäp-ˌlȯf-tē-nəs\ *n*

top·mast \-ˌmast, -məst\ *n* : the mast that is next above the lower mast and topmost in a fore-and-aft rig

top milk *n* : the cream-rich upper layer of unhomogenized milk that has stood in a container

top·min·now \ˈtäp-ˌmin-ō\ *n* : any of a large family of small viviparous surface-feeding fishes

top·most \-ˌmōst\ *adj* : highest of all : UPPERMOST

top–notch \-ˈnäch\ *adj* : of the highest quality : FIRST-RATE — **top·notch·er** \-ˈnäch-ər\ *n*

to·pog·ra·pher \tə-ˈpäg-rə-fər\ *n* : one skilled in topography

to·po·graph·ic \ˌtäp-ə-ˈgraf-ik, ˌtō-pə-\ *adj* : TOPOGRAPHICAL 1

to·po·graph·i·cal \-ˈgraf-i-kəl\ *adj* **1** : of, relating to, or concerned with topography ⟨a *topographical* engineer⟩ **2** : of, relating to, or concerned with the artistic representation of a particular locality ⟨*topographical* paintings⟩ — **to·po·graph·i·cal·ly** \-kə-lē, -klē\ *adv*

to·pog·ra·phy \tə-ˈpäg-rə-fē\ *n* **1** : the art or practice of detailing on maps or charts natural and man-made features of a place or region especially so as to show elevations **2** : the configuration of a surface including its relief and the position of its natural and man-made features ⟨a map showing *topography*⟩ [Late Latin *topographia,* from Greek, from *topographein* "to describe a place", from *topos* "place" + *graphein* "to write"]

to·pol·o·gy \tə-ˈpäl-ə-jē, tō-\ *n* **1** : topographical study of a particular place; *esp* : the history of a region as indicated by its topography **2** : the anatomy of a particular region of the body **3** : a branch of mathematics concerned with those properties of geometric figures that do not change when the shape of the figure is subjected to continuous change — **to·po·log·i·cal** \ˌtäp-ə-ˈläj-i-kəl, ˌtō-pə-\ *adj* — **to·pol·o·gist** \tə-ˈpäl-ə-jəst, tō-\ *n*

top·per \ˈtäp-ər\ *n* **1** : one that is at or on the top **2 a** : SILK HAT **b** : OPERA HAT **3** : something (as a joke) that caps everything preceding **4** : a woman's usually short and loose-fitting lightweight outer coat

[1]**top·ping** \ˈtäp-ing\ *n* **1** : something that forms a top; *esp* : GARNISH 2 **2** : the action of one that tops

[2]**topping** *adj* **1** : highest in rank or eminence **2** *chiefly British* : SUPERIOR 4a, EXCELLENT

top·ple \ˈtäp-əl\ *vb* **top·pled; top·pling** \ˈtäp-ling, -ə-ling\ **1** : to fall or cause to fall from or as if from being top-heavy **2** : to be or seem unsteady : TOTTER **3** : OVERTHROW ⟨*topple* a government⟩ [derived from [2]*top*]

tops \ˈtäps\ *adj* : topmost in quality, ability, popularity, or eminence ⟨*tops* in your profession⟩

top·sail \ˈtäp-ˌsāl, -səl\ *also* **top·s'l** \-səl\ *n* **1** : the sail next above the lowermost sail on a mast in a square-rigged ship **2** : the sail set above and sometimes on the gaff in a fore-and-aft rigged ship

top secret *adj* : demanding inviolate secrecy among top officials or a select few

top sergeant *n* : FIRST SERGEANT 1

top·side \ˈtäp-ˈsīd\ *adv or adj* **1** : on deck **2** : to or on the top or surface

top·sides \-ˌsīdz\ *n pl* : the top portion of the outer surface of a ship on each side above the waterline

top·soil \-ˌsȯil\ *n* : surface soil; *esp* : the organic layer in which plants have most of their roots and which the farmer turns over in plowing

top·spin \ˈtäp-ˌspin\ *n* : rotary motion imparted to a ball causing it to rotate forward in the direction of movement [[1]*top*]

top·sy–tur·vi·ness \ˌtäp-sē-ˈtər-vē-nəs\ *n* : the quality or state of being topsy-turvy

[1]**top·sy–tur·vy** \ˌtäp-sē-ˈtər-vē\ *adv* **1** : upside down **2** : in utter confusion or disorder [probably derived from [1]*top* + obsolete *terve* "to turn upside down"]

[2]**topsy–turvy** *adj* : turned topsy-turvy : totally disordered — **top·sy–tur·vi·ly** \-ˈtər-və-lē\ *adv* — **top·sy–tur·vy·dom** \-ˈtər-vēd-əm\ *n*

[3]**topsy–turvy** *n* : TOPSY-TURVINESS

toque \ˈtōk\ *n* : a woman's small hat without a brim made in any of various soft close-fitting shapes [Middle French, "soft hat with a narrow brim", from Spanish *toca* "headdress"]

toque

tor \ˈtȯr\ *n* : a high craggy hill [Old English *torr*]

To·rah \ˈtōr-ə, ˈtȯr-; ˈtȯi-rə\ *n* **1** : LAW 3b **2** : the body of wisdom and law found in the Jewish Scripture and oral tradition **3** : a leather or parchment scroll of the Pentateuch used in a synagogue for liturgical purposes [Hebrew *tōrāh*]

[1]**torch** \ˈtȯrch\ *n* **1** : a flaming light made of something (as resinous wood) that burns brightly and usually carried in the hand **2** : something (as wisdom or knowledge) likened to a torch as giving light or guidance **3** : any of various portable devices for producing a hot flame — compare BLOWTORCH **4** *chiefly British* : FLASHLIGHT 3 [Old French *torche* "bundle of twisted straw or tow"]

[2]**torch** *vt* : to set on fire with or as if with a torch

torch·bear·er \ˈtȯrch-ˌbar-ər, -ˌber-\ *n* **1** : one that carries a torch **2** : one that is in the forefront of a movement, campaign, or crusade

torch·light \ˈtȯrch-ˌlīt\ *n* : light given by torches

torch singer *n* : a singer of torch songs

torch song *n* : a popular sentimental song of unrequited love

tore *past of* TEAR

to·re·ador \ˈtȯr-ē-ə-ˌdȯr, ˈtōr-, ˈtär-\ *n* : BULLFIGHTER [Spanish, from *torear* "to fight bulls", from *toro* "bull", from Latin *taurus*]

to·re·ro \tə-ˈreər-ō\ *n, pl* **-ros** : BULLFIGHTER [Spanish, from Late Latin *taurarius,* from Latin *taurus* 'bull']

tori *pl of* TORUS

to•rii \'tōr-ē-,ē, 'tȯr-\ *n, pl* **torii** : a Japanese gateway of light construction built at the approach to a Shinto temple [Japanese]

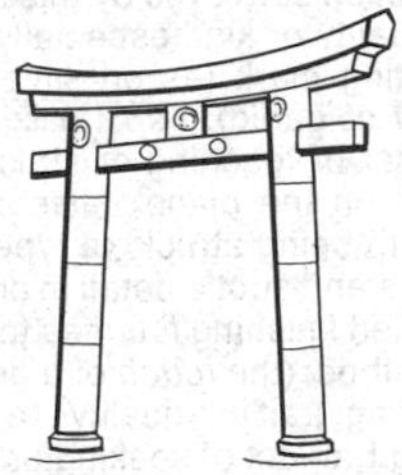

torii

[1]tor•ment \'tȯr-,ment\ *n* **1** : the infliction of torture (as by rack or wheel) **2** : extreme physical or mental pain or anguish : AGONY **3** : a source of irritation or pain [Old French, from Latin *tormentum* "torture", from *torquēre* "to twist"]

[2]tor•ment \tȯr-'ment, 'tȯr-,\ *vt* **1 a** : to cause severe suffering of body or mind to **b** : to cause worry or vexation to : TROUBLE ⟨a mystery that has *tormented* us for years⟩ **2** : DISTORT 1, TWIST **syn** see AFFLICT — **tor•men•tor** \-ər\ *n*

torn *past participle of* TEAR

tor•na•dic \tȯr-'nād-ik, -'nad-\ *adj* : relating to, characteristic of, or being a tornado

tor•na•do \tȯr-'nād-ō\ *n, pl* **-does** *or* **-dos** : a violent destructive whirling wind accompanied by a funnel-shaped cloud that progresses in a narrow path over the land [Spanish *tronada* "thunderstorm", from *tronar* "to thunder", from Latin *tonare*]

[1]tor•pe•do \tȯr-'pēd-ō\ *n, pl* **-does 1** : ELECTRIC RAY **2 a** : a submarine mine **b** : a self-propelled cigar-shaped submarine missile filled with an explosive charge **3 a** : a charge of explosive enclosed in a container or case **b** : a small firework that explodes when thrown against a hard object [Latin, literally, "numbness", from *torpēre* "to be numb"]

[2]torpedo *vt* **1** : to hit or sink (a ship) with a naval torpedo **2** : to destroy or nullify altogether : WRECK ⟨*torpedo* a plan⟩

torpedo boat *n* : a small fast boat for firing torpedoes

torpedo–boat destroyer *n* : a large, fast, and powerful armed torpedo boat originally intended principally for the destruction of torpedo boats but later used also as a formidable torpedo boat

tor•pid \'tȯr-pəd\ *adj* **1 a** : having lost motion or the power of exertion or feeling : DORMANT ⟨a bear *torpid* in its winter sleep⟩ **b** : sluggish in functioning or acting ⟨a *torpid* mind⟩ **2** : lacking in energy or vigor : APATHETIC, DULL [Latin *torpidus,* from *torpēre* "to be numb"] — **tor•pid•i•ty** \tȯr-'pid-ət-ē\ *n* — **torpid•ly** \'tȯr-pəd-lē\ *adv*

tor•por \'tȯr-pər\ *n* **1** : temporary loss or suspension of motion or feeling : extreme sluggishness ⟨the *torpor* of bears in winter⟩ **2** : APATHY 2, DULLNESS [Latin, from *torpēre* "to be numb"] **syn** see LETHARGY

torque \'tȯrk\ *n* : a force which produces or tends to produce rotation or twisting [Latin *torquēre* "to twist"]

tor•rent \'tȯr-ənt, 'tär-\ *n* **1** : a violent or rushing stream of a liquid (as water or lava) **2** : a large, rapid, or violent flow (as of orders, activity, or abuse) : SURGE [French, from Latin *torrens,* from *torrens* "burning, seething, rushing", from *torrēre* "to parch, burn"]

tor•ren•tial \tȯ-'ren-chəl, tə-\ *adj* **1 a** : relating to or having the character of a torrent ⟨*torrential* rains⟩ **b** : caused by or resulting from action of rapid streams ⟨*torrential* gravel⟩ **2** : resembling a torrent in violence or rapidity of flow — **tor•ren•tial•ly** \-'rench-lē, -ə-lē\ *adv*

tor•rid \'tȯr-əd, 'tär-\ *adj* **1 a** : parched with heat especially of the sun ⟨*torrid* sands⟩ **b** : giving off intense heat **2** : ARDENT, PASSIONATE ⟨*torrid* love letters⟩ [Latin *torridus,* from *torrēre* "to parch"] — **tor•rid•i•ty** \tō-'rid-ət-ē\ *n* — **tor•rid•ly** \'tȯr-əd-lē, 'tär-\ *adv* — **tor•rid•ness** *n*

torrid zone *n* : the belt of the earth between the tropics over which the sun is vertical at some period of the year

tor•sion \'tȯr-shən\ *n* **1** : the act or process of turning or twisting **2** : the state of being twisted [Late Latin *torsus,* past participle of Latin *torquēre* "to twist"] — **tor•sion•al** \-shnəl, -shən-l\ *adj*

tor•so \'tȯr-sō\ *n, pl* **torsos** *or* **tor•si** \-,sē\ **1** : the trunk of a sculptured representation of a human body; *esp* : the trunk of a statue whose head and limbs are mutilated **2** : something (as a piece of writing) that is mutilated or left unfinished **3** : the human trunk [Italian, literally, "stalk", from Latin *thyrsus,* from Greek *thyrsos*]

tort \'tȯrt\ *n* : a wrongful act which does not involve a breach of contract and for which the injured party can recover damages in a civil action [Middle French, from Medieval Latin *tortum,* from Latin *tortus* "twisted", from *torquēre* "to twist"]

torte \'tȯrt-ə, 'tȯrt\ *n, pl* **tor•ten** \'tȯrt-n\ *or* **tortes** : a cake made of many eggs and often grated nuts or dry bread crumbs and usually covered with a rich frosting [German]

tor•ti•lla \tȯr-'tē-ə, -'tē-yə\ *n* : a round thin cake made from cornmeal or flour [American Spanish, from Spanish *torta* "cake", from Late Latin, "round loaf of bread"]

tor•toise \'tȯrt-əs\ *n* : any of an order (Testudinata) of reptiles : TURTLE; *esp* : a land turtle [Middle French *tortue*]

[1]tor•toise•shell \'tȯrt-əs-,shel, -əsh-,shel\ *n* : a mottled horny substance that covers the bony shell of some sea turtles and is used in inlaying and in making various ornamental articles

[2]tortoiseshell *adj* : made of or resembling tortoiseshell especially in spotted brown and yellow coloring

tor•to•ni \tȯr-'tō-nē\ *n* : ice cream made of heavy cream often with minced almonds and chopped maraschino cherries and often flavored with rum [probably from *Tortoni,* 19th century Italian restaurateur in Paris]

tor•tu•ous \'tȯrch-wəs, -ə-wəs\ *adj* **1** : marked by repeated twists, bends, or turns : WINDING ⟨a *tortuous* stream⟩ **2 a** : marked by devious or indirect tactics : CROOKED, TRICKY **b** : confusingly roundabout ⟨the *tortuous* workings of the law⟩ [Middle French *tortueux,* from Latin *tortuosus,* from *tortus* "twist", from *torquēre* "to twist"] — **tor•tu•ous•ly** *adv* — **tor•tu•ous•ness** *n*

[1]tor•ture \'tȯr-chər\ *n* **1** : the infliction of intense pain especially to punish or obtain a confession **2 a** : physical or mental anguish : AGONY **b** : something that causes agony [French, from Late Latin *tortura,* from Latin *torquēre* "to twist"]

[2]torture *vt* **tor•tured**; **tor•tur•ing** \'tȯrch-ring, -ə-ring\ **1** : to punish or coerce by inflicting excruciating pain **2** : to cause intense suffering to : TORMENT **3** : to twist or wrench out of shape : DISTORT **syn** see AFFLICT — **tor•tur•er** \'tȯr-chər-ər\ *n*

tor•tur•ous \'tȯrch-rəs, -ə-rəs\ *adj* : causing torture : cruelly painful — **tor•tur•ous•ly** *adv*

to•rus \'tōr-əs, 'tȯr-\ *n, pl* **to•ri** \'tōr-,ī, 'tȯr-, -,ē\ **1** : a large molding of convex profile commonly occurring as the lowest molding in the base of a column **2** : a doughnut-shaped surface generated by a circle rotated about an axis in its plane that does not intersect the circle [Latin, "protuberance, bulge, torus molding"]

To•ry \'tōr-ē, 'tȯr-\ *n, pl* **Tories 1 a** : a member of a British political group of the 18th and early 19th centuries favoring royal authority and the established church and seeking to preserve the traditional political structure — compare WHIG **b** : CONSERVATIVE 1b **2** : an American supporting the cause of the British Crown during the American Revolution : LOYALIST **3** *often not cap* : an extreme conservative especially in politics and economics [Irish Gaelic *tōraidhe* "pursued man, robber"; from Irish royalists outlawed in the 17th century] — **Tory** *adj*

[1]toss \'tȯs, 'täs\ *vb* **1** : to keep throwing here and there or backward and forward : cause to pitch or roll ⟨waves *tossed* the ship about⟩ **2** : to throw with a quick light motion ⟨*toss* a ball into the air⟩ **3** : to lift with a sudden motion ⟨*toss* the head⟩ **4** : to pitch or bob about rapidly ⟨a canoe *tossing* on the waves⟩ **5** : to accomplish, provide, or dispose of easily ⟨*tossed* off a few verses⟩ **6** : to be restless : fling oneself about ⟨*toss* in one's sleep⟩ **7** : to stir or mix lightly ⟨*toss* a salad⟩ **8** : to decide an issue by flipping a coin [probably of Scandinavian origin] **syn** see THROW

[2]toss *n* **1** : the state or fact of being tossed **2 a** : an act or instance of tossing **b** : a deciding by chance and especially by flipping a coin

toss–up \-,əp\ *n* **1** : TOSS 2b **2** : an even chance

[1]tot \'tät\ *n* **1** : a small child : TODDLER **2** : SHOT 8a [origin unknown]

[2]tot *vb* **tot•ted**; **tot•ting** : to add together : TOTAL — usually used with *up* [*tot.,* abbreviation of *total*]

[1]to•tal \'tōt-l\ *adj* **1** : making up or being the whole : ENTIRE ⟨the *total* amount⟩ **2** : ABSOLUTE 4, UTTER ⟨*total* ruin⟩ **3** : mak-

\ə\ **abut**	\au̇\ **out**	\i\ **tip**	\ȯ\ **saw**	\u̇\ **foot**
\ər\ **further**	\ch\ **chin**	\ī\ **life**	\ȯi\ **coin**	\y\ **yet**
\a\ **mat**	\e\ **pet**	\j\ **job**	\th\ **thin**	\yü\ **few**
\ā\ **take**	\ē\ **easy**	\ng\ **sing**	\th\ **this**	\yu̇\ **cure**
\ä\ **cot, cart**	\g\ **go**	\ō\ **bone**	\ü\ **food**	\zh\ **vision**

ing use of every available means to accomplish a single objective ⟨*total* war⟩ [Middle French, from Medieval Latin *totalis,* from Latin *totus* "whole, entire"]

^{2}**total** *n* **1 :** a product of addition **:** SUM **2 :** an entire quantity **:** AMOUNT **syn** see SUM

^{3}**total** *vt* **to•taled** *or* **to•talled**; **to•tal•ing** *or* **to•tal•ling 1 :** to add up **:** COMPUTE **2 :** to amount to **:** NUMBER

total eclipse *n* **:** an eclipse in which one celestial body is completely obscured by the shadow or body of another

to•tal•i•tar•i•an \tō-ˌtal-ə-ˈter-ē-ən\ *adj* **1 :** of, relating to, or being a political regime based on subordination of the individual to the state and strict control of all aspects of life especially by use of force **2 :** advocating or characteristic of such a regime [*total* + *-itarian* (as in *authoritarian*)] **— totalitarian** *n* **— to•tal•i•tar•i•an•ism** \-ē-ə-ˌniz-əm\ *n*

to•tal•i•ty \tō-ˈtal-ət-ē\ *n, pl* **-ties 1 :** an aggregate amount **:** SUM, WHOLE **2 :** the quality or state of being total **:** ENTIRETY

to•tal•ize \ˈtōt-l-ˌīz\ *vt* **1 :** to add up **:** TOTAL **2 :** to express as a whole

to•tal•ly \ˈtōt-l-ē\ *adv* **1 :** in a total manner **:** WHOLLY **2 :** as a whole **:** in toto

^{1}**tote** \ˈtōt\ *vt* **1 :** to carry by hand **:** LUG **2 :** HAUL 2c, CONVEY [origin unknown] **— tot•er** *n*

^{2}**tote** *n* **:** a large handbag — called also *tote bag*

to•tem \ˈtōt-əm\ *n* **:** an object (as an animal or plant) or a representation of an object serving as the emblem of a family or clan and often as a reminder of its ancestry [Ojibwa *ototeman* "his totem"] **— to•tem•ic** \tō-ˈtem-ik\ *adj*

totem pole *n* **:** a pole carved and painted with totemic symbols that is erected before the houses of some northwest coast Indians

totem pole

^{1}**tot•ter** \ˈtät-ər\ *vi* **1 a :** to tremble or rock as if about to fall **:** SWAY **b :** to become unstable **:** threaten to collapse **2 :** to move unsteadily **:** STAGGER, WOBBLE [Middle English *toteren*] **— tot•ter•ing•ly** \ˈtät-ə-ring-lē\ *adv* **— tot•tery** \ˈtät-ə-rē\ *adj*

^{2}**totter** *n* **:** an unsteady gait **:** WOBBLE

tou•can \ˈtü-ˌkan, tü-ˈ\ *n* **:** any of a family of fruit-eating birds of tropical America with brilliant coloring and a very large but light and thin-walled bill [French, from Portuguese *tucano,* from Tupi]

toucan

^{1}**touch** \ˈtəch\ *vb* **1 :** to feel or handle (as with fingers or hands) ⟨loved to *touch* soft velvet⟩ **2 :** to come close **:** VERGE ⟨actions *touching* on treason⟩ **3 a :** to take into the hands or mouth ⟨never *touches* meat⟩ **b :** to put hands on in any way or degree ⟨don't *touch* the exhibits⟩ ⟨wouldn't *touch* your money⟩; *esp* **:** HARM ⟨swore they hadn't *touched* the child⟩ **4 :** to persuade to give or lend ⟨*touched* me for $10⟩ **5 :** to cause to be briefly in contact with something ⟨*touched* spurs to the horse⟩ ⟨*touch* a match to kindling⟩ **6 a :** to meet without overlapping or penetrating **:** ADJOIN **b :** to rival in quality or value ⟨this car doesn't *touch* my old one⟩ **7 :** to speak or tell of especially in passing ⟨barely *touched* on domestic politics⟩ **8 :** to affect the interest of **:** CONCERN ⟨a problem *touching* everyone⟩ **9 a :** to affect physically; *esp* **:** to harm slightly by or as if by contact ⟨fruit *touched* by frost⟩ **b :** to give a delicate tint, line, or expression to ⟨lips *touched* with a smile⟩ **10 :** to move emotionally ⟨*touched* by your loyalty⟩ **11 :** to make a brief incidental stop in part ⟨*touched* at several ports⟩ [Old French *tuchier*] **— touch•able** \-ə-bəl\ *adj* **— touch•er** *n*

^{2}**touch** *n* **1 :** a light stroke, tap, or blow **2 :** the act or fact of touching or being touched **3 a :** the special sense by which light pressure is perceived ⟨fabric soft to the *touch*⟩ **b :** a particular sensation conveyed by this sense **:** FEEL ⟨the soft *touch* of silk⟩ **4 :** quality or kind especially as attested by authority; *also* **:** an attesting mark (as on silver) **5 :** a small amount **:** TRACE ⟨a *touch* of garlic⟩; *esp* **:** a light attack ⟨a *touch* of fever⟩ **6 :** a manner of touching or striking the keys of a keyboard ⟨a firm *touch* on the piano⟩; *also* **:** the character of response of the keys to being struck ⟨a typewriter with a stiff *touch*⟩ **7 :** an effective and subtle detail in creating or improving an artistic work ⟨applied finishing *touches* to the portrait⟩ **8 :** distinctive manner or method ⟨the *touch* of a genius⟩ **9 :** a characteristic or distinguishing trait or quality ⟨a classic *touch* to your writing⟩ **10 slang :** an act of seeking or getting a gift or loan **11 :** a state of contact or communication ⟨let's keep in *touch*⟩

touch and go *n* **:** a highly uncertain or precarious situation **— touch-and-go** *adj*

touch•back \ˈtəch-ˌbak\ *n* **:** a situation in football in which the defending team downs the ball behind its own goal line after receiving a kick or intercepting a pass

touch•down \-ˌdau̇n\ *n* **1 a :** the act of touching a football to the ground behind an opponent's goal **b :** a score of six points in American football made by carrying the ball over the opponent's goal line **2 :** the act or moment of touching down (as with an airplane or spacecraft)

touch down \təch-ˈdau̇n, ˈtəch-\ *vi* **:** to reach the ground **:** LAND

tou•ché \tü-ˈshā\ *interj* — used to acknowledge a hit in fencing or the success of an argument [French, from *toucher* "to touch", from Old French *tuchier*]

touched \ˈtəcht\ *adj* **:** slightly unbalanced mentally

touch football *n* **:** football chiefly characterized by the substitution of touching for tackling

touch•hole \ˈtəch-ˌhōl\ *n* **:** the vent in old-time cannons or firearms through which the charge was ignited

^{1}**touch•ing** *prep* **:** in reference to **:** CONCERNING

^{2}**touching** *adj* **:** arousing tenderness or compassion **— touch•ing•ly** \-ing-lē\ *adv*

touch-me-not \ˈtəch-mē-ˌnät\ *n* **:** IMPATIENS [from the bursting of the ripe pods when touched]

touch off *vt* **1 :** to describe or characterize with precision **2 a :** to cause to explode by or as if by touching with fire **b :** to release or start with sudden violence ⟨*touched off* a riot⟩

touch•stone \ˈtəch-ˌstōn\ *n* **1 :** a black stone formerly used to test the purity of gold and silver by the streak left on the stone when rubbed by the metal **2 :** a test or standard for judging something

touch system *n* **:** a method of typewriting that assigns a particular finger to each key and makes it possible to type without looking at the keyboard

touch-type \ˈtəch-ˌtīp\ *vi* **:** to type by the touch system

touch up *vt* **1 :** to improve or perfect by small additional strokes or alterations **2 :** to stimulate by or as if by a flick of a whip

touch•wood \ˈtəch-ˌwu̇d\ *n* **:** ^{3}PUNK

touchy \ˈtəch-ē\ *adj* **touch•i•er; -est 1 :** marked by readiness to take offense on slight provocation **2 :** acutely sensitive or irritable ⟨a *touchy* swelling⟩ **3 :** calling for tact, care, or caution in treatment ⟨a *touchy* subject⟩ **syn** see IRASCIBLE **— touch•i•ly** \ˈtəch-ə-lē\ *adv* **— touch•i•ness** \ˈtəch-ē-nəs\ *n*

^{1}**tough** \ˈtəf\ *adj* **1 :** able to undergo great strain **:** flexible and not brittle ⟨*tough* fibers⟩ **2 :** not easily chewed ⟨*tough* meat⟩ **3 :** able to stand hard work and hardship **:** ROBUST ⟨a *tough* body⟩ **4 a :** hard to influence **:** STUBBORN ⟨a *tough* bargainer⟩ **b :** very difficult ⟨a *tough* problem⟩ **5 :** ROWDY, LAWLESS ⟨a *tough* neighborhood⟩ **6 :** free from softness or sentimentality ⟨a *tough* approach to delinquency⟩; *esp* **:** marked by firm uncompromising determination ⟨a *tough* foreign policy⟩ [Old English *tōh*] **— tough•ly** *adv* **— tough•ness** *n*

^{2}**tough** *n* **:** a vicious and unruly person; *also* **:** ROWDY

tough•en \ˈtəf-ən\ *vb* **tough•ened; tough•en•ing** \ˈtəf-ning, -ə-ning\ **:** to make or become tough

tough-mind•ed \ˈtəf-ˈmīn-dəd\ *adj* **:** realistic or unsentimental in temper or habitual point of view

tou•pee \tü-ˈpā\ *n* **:** a usually small wig or hairpiece for a man [French *toupet* "forelock", of Germanic origin]

^{1}**tour** \ˈtu̇r, *1 is also* ˈtau̇r\ *n* **1 :** a period of work or duty ⟨a long *tour* abroad⟩ **2 :** a trip or excursion usually ending at the point of beginning ⟨a *tour* of the city⟩ [Middle French, from Old French *tourn, tour* "lathe, circuit, turn", from Latin *tornus* "lathe"]

[2]**tour** *vb* : to make a tour of : travel as a tourist
tour de force \ˌtu̇rd-ə-ˈfōrs, -ˈfȯrs\ *n, pl* **tours de force** *same*\ : a feat of strength, skill, or ingenuity [French]
touring car *n* : an old-fashioned open automobile with two cross seats, usually four doors, and a folding top
tour•ist \ˈtu̇r-əst\ *n* : one who travels for pleasure — **tourist** *adj*
tourist class *n* : economy accommodation on a ship, airplane, or train
tourist court *n* : MOTEL
tourist home *n* : a house in which rooms are available for rent to transients
tour•ma•line \ˈtu̇r-mə-lən, -ˌlēn\ *n* : a mineral of variable color that is a complex silicate and when transparent is cut for use as a gemstone [Sinhalese *toramalli* "carnelian"]
tour•na•ment \ˈtu̇r-nə-mənt *also* ˈtər- *or* ˈtȯr-\ *n* **1 a** : a contest of skill and courage between armored knights fighting with blunted lances or swords **b** : a series of knightly contests occurring at one time and place **2** : a series of athletic contests, sports events, or games for a championship ⟨a tennis *tournament*⟩ [Old French *torneiement* "to engage in a tournament", from *torn, tourn* "lathe, circuit, turn"]
tour•ney \ˈtu̇r-nē *also* ˈtər- *or* ˈtȯr-\ *n, pl* **tourneys** : TOURNAMENT [Middle French *tornei,* from *torneier* "to engage in a tournament"]
tour•ni•quet \ˈtu̇r-ni-kət, ˈtər-\ *n* : a device (as a bandage twisted tight with a stick) to check bleeding [French, from *tourner* "to turn"]
[1]**tou•sle** \ˈtau̇-zəl, -səl\ *vt* **tou•sled**; **tou•sling** \ˈtau̇z-ling, ˈtau̇s-, -ə-ling\ : DISHEVEL, RUMPLE ⟨*tousled* hair⟩ [Middle English *touselen*]
[2]**tousle** *n* : a tangled mass or condition
[1]**tout** \ˈtau̇t\ *vb* **1** : to solicit or canvass for patronage, trade, votes, or support **2 a** *chiefly British* : to spy about at racing stables and tracks to get information to be used in betting **b** : to provide tips on racehorses [Middle English *tuten* "to peer"]
[2]**tout** *n* : one who touts: as **a** : one who solicits patronage **b** : one who gives tips or solicits bets on a horse race
[3]**tout** *vt* : to praise or publicize insistently or excessively [alteration of [1]*toot*]
tout•er \ˈtau̇t-ər\ *n* : TOUT
[1]**tow** \ˈtō\ *vt* : to draw or pull along behind : HAUL [Old English *togian*]
[2]**tow** *n* **1** : an act or instance of towing or the fact or condition of being towed **2** : a line or rope for towing **3** : something (as a tugboat or barge) that tows or is towed — **in tow 1** : in the state or course of being towed **2** : under guidance or protection : in the position of a follower
[3]**tow** *n* **1** : short broken fiber from flax, hemp, or jute used for yarn, twine, or stuffing **2** : yarn or cloth made of tow [Old English *tow-* "spinning"]
tow•age \ˈtō-ij\ *n* **1** : the act of towing **2** : the price paid for towing
[1]**to•ward** \ˈtō-ərd, ˈtȯ-ərd, ˈtōrd, ˈtȯrd\ *adj* **1** *also* **to•wards** \ˈtō-ərdz, ˈtȯ-ərdz, ˈtōrdz, ˈtȯrdz\ **a** : coming soon : IMMINENT ⟨could move fast enough if a meal was *toward*⟩ **b** : happening at the moment : AFOOT **2 a** *obsolete* : quick to learn : APT **b** : PROPITIOUS 3 ⟨a *toward* breeze⟩ [Old English *tōweard* "facing, imminent", from *tō* "to" + *-weard* "-ward"]
[2]**to•ward** \tō-ərd, ˈtō-, twō-, ˈtwō-; tōrd, ˈtōrd, twōrd, ˈtwōrd; tə-ˈwȯrd\ *or* **to•wards** *same followed by* z\ *prep* **1** : in the direction of ⟨driving *toward* town⟩ **2 a** : along a course leading to ⟨efforts *toward* reconciliation⟩ **b** : in relation to ⟨attitude *toward* life⟩ **3** : so as to face ⟨the back was *toward* me⟩ **4** : not long before ⟨*toward* noon⟩ **5** : in order to provide part of the payment for ⟨save *toward* a college education⟩
tow•boat \ˈtō-ˌbōt\ *n* **1** : TUGBOAT **2** : a compact shallow-draft boat for pushing barges on inland waterways
[1]**tow•el** \ˈtau̇-əl, ˈtau̇l\ *n* : a cloth or piece of absorbent paper for wiping or drying [Old French *toaille,* of Germanic origin]
[2]**towel** *vb* **-eled** *or* **-elled**; **-el•ing** *or* **-el•ling 1** : to rub or dry with a towel **2** : to use a towel
tow•el•ing *or* **tow•el•ling** \ˈtau̇-ling, -ə-ling\ *n* : material for towels
[1]**tow•er** \ˈtau̇-ər, ˈtau̇r\ *n* **1** : a building or structure typically higher than it is wide and high relative to its surroundings that may stand apart (as a campanile) or be attached (as a church belfry) to a larger structure and that may be of skeleton framework (as an observation or transmission tower) **2** : a towering citadel : FORTRESS [Old English *torr* and Old French *tur,* both from Latin *turris,* from Greek *tyrsis*] — **tow•ered** \ˈtau̇-ərd, ˈtau̇rd\ *adj*

[1]tower 1

[2]**tower** *vi* : to reach or rise to a great height
tow•er•ing *adj* **1** : impressively high or great : IMPOSING **2** : reaching a high point of intensity ⟨a *towering* rage⟩ **3** : going beyond proper bounds : EXCESSIVE ⟨*towering* ambition⟩
tower wagon *n* : a wagon or motortruck with a high adjustable platform on which workers can stand
tow•head \ˈtō-ˌhed\ *n* : a person having flaxen hair — **tow•head•ed** \-ˈhed-əd\ *adj*
to•whee \ˈtō-ˌhē, ˈtō-ē, tō-ˈhē\ *n* **1** : a finch of eastern North America having the male black, white, and rufous — called also *chewink* **2** : any of numerous American finches related to the towhee [imitative]
to wit \tə-ˈwit\ *adv* : that is to say : NAMELY [Middle English *to witen,* literally, "to know"]
tow•line \ˈtō-ˌlīn\ *n* : a line used in towing
town \ˈtau̇n\ *n* **1 a** : a heavily populated area as distinguished from surrounding rural territory; *esp* : one larger than a village but smaller than a city **b** : CITY 1a **c** : an English village having a periodic fair or market **2 a** : the city or urban life as contrasted with the country **b** : TOWNSPEOPLE 1 **3** : a New England territorial and political unit usually containing both rural and urban areas under a single town government — called also *township* [Old English *tūn* "enclosure, village, town"] — **town** *adj*
town clerk *n* : an official who keeps the town records
town crier *n* : an old-time town officer making public proclamations
town hall *n* : a public building used for town-government offices and meetings
town house *n* **1** : the city residence of one having a countryseat or a chief residence elsewhere **2** : a house connected to another by a common sidewall
town meeting *n* : a meeting of inhabitants or taxpayers of a town to transact public business
towns•folk \ˈtau̇nz-ˌfōk\ *n pl* : TOWNSPEOPLE
town•ship \ˈtau̇n-ˌship\ *n* **1 a** : TOWN 3 **b** : a unit of local government in some northeastern and north central states **c** : a subdivision of the county especially in the southern United States **2** : a division of territory in surveys of United States public land containing 36 sections or 36 square miles (about 93.2 square kilometers)
towns•man \ˈtau̇nz-mən\ *n* **1** : a native or resident of a town or city **2** : a fellow citizen of a town
towns•peo•ple \-ˌpē-pəl\ *n pl* **1** : the inhabitants of a town or city **2** : town-dwelling or town-bred persons
towns•wom•an \-ˌwu̇m-ən\ *n* **1** : a woman native or resident of a town or city **2** : a woman who is a fellow citizen of a town
tow•path \ˈtō-ˌpath, -ˌpȧth\ *or* **towing path** *n* : a path (as along a canal) traveled by men or animals towing boats
tow•rope \ˈtō-ˌrōp\ *n* : a line used in towing
tow truck *n* : WRECKER 4
tox- *or* **toxi-** *or* **toxo-** *combining form* : poisonous : poison ⟨*toxemia*⟩ [Latin *toxicum* "poison"]
tox•a•phene \ˈtäk-sə-ˌfēn\ *n* : a chlorine-containing insecticide [from *Toxaphene,* a former trademark]
tox•emia \täk-ˈsē-mē-ə\ *n* : an abnormal condition associated with the presence of toxic substances in the blood — **tox•emic** \-mik\ *adj*
tox•ic \ˈtäk-sik\ *adj* **1** : of, relating to, or caused by a poison or toxin **2** : POISONOUS [Late Latin *toxicus,* from Latin *toxicum* "poison", from Greek *toxikon* "arrow poison", derived from *toxon* "bow, arrow"] — **tox•ic•i•ty** \täk-ˈsis-ət-ē\ *n*

\ə\ **abut**	\au̇\ **out**	\i\ **tip**	\ȯ\ **saw**	\u̇\ **foot**
\ər\ **further**	\ch\ **chin**	\ī\ **life**	\ȯi\ **coin**	\y\ **yet**
\a\ **mat**	\e\ **pet**	\j\ **job**	\th\ **thin**	\yü\ **few**
\ā\ **take**	\ē\ **easy**	\ng\ **sing**	\t͟h\ **this**	\yu̇\ **cure**
\ä\ **cot, cart**	\g\ **go**	\ō\ **bone**	\ü\ **food**	\zh\ **vision**

tox•i•col•o•gy \ˌtäk-si-ˈkäl-ə-jē\ *n* : a science that deals with poisonous materials and their effect and with the problems involved in their use and control — **tox•i•co•log•i•cal** \-kə-ˈläj-i-kəl\ *adj* — **tox•i•co•log•i•cal•ly** \-i-kə-lē, -klē\ *adv* — **tox•i•col•o•gist** \-ˈkäl-ə-jəst\ *n*
tox•in \ˈtäk-sən\ *n* : a complex usually unstable substance that is a metabolic product of a living organism (as a bacterium), that is very poisonous when introduced directly into the tissues but is usually destroyed by the digestive process when taken by mouth, and that typically induces antibody formation ⟨tetanus *toxin*⟩ — compare ANTITOXIN, TOXOID
tox•in–an•ti•tox•in \ˈtäk-sə-ˈnant-i-ˌtäk-sən\ *n* : a mixture of a toxin and its antitoxin used especially formerly in immunizing against a disease (as diphtheria)
tox•oid \ˈtäk-ˌsȯid\ *n* : a toxin (as of tetanus) treated so as to destroy its poisonous effects while leaving it still capable of causing the formation of antibodies when injected into the body
[1]**toy** \ˈtȯi\ *n* **1** : something (as a trinket) of small or no real value or importance : TRIFLE **2** : something for a child to play with **3** : something tiny; *esp* : an animal of a breed or variety characterized by exceptionally small size [Middle English *toye* "dalliance"] — **toy** *adj* — **toy•like** \-ˌlīk\ *adj*
[2]**toy** *vi* : to amuse oneself as if with a toy : PLAY, TRIFLE ⟨*toy* with an idea⟩ — **toy•er** *n*
toy•on \ˈtȯi-ˌän\ *n* : an ornamental evergreen shrub of the rose family that is native to the North American Pacific coast and has white flowers succeeded by persistent bright red berries [American Spanish *tollon*]
tra•bec•u•la \trə-ˈbek-yə-lə\ *n, pl* **-lae** \-ˌlē, -ˌlī\ *also* **-las** : a small anatomical bar, rod, or septum often bridging a gap or forming part of a framework ⟨spleen *trabeculae*⟩ [Latin, "little beam", from *trabs, trabes* "beam"] — **tra•bec•u•lar** \-lər\ *adj*
[1]**trace** \ˈtrās\ *n* **1** : a mark or line left by something that has passed : TRAIL, TRACK; *also* : FOOTPRINT **2** : a sign or evidence of some past thing : VESTIGE ⟨*traces* of an earlier civilization⟩ **3** : something traced or drawn (as a line); *esp* : the marking made by a recording instrument (as a seismograph or kymograph) **4** : the intersection of a line or plane with a plane **5 a** : a minute amount or indication ⟨a *trace* of red⟩ **b** : an amount of a chemical constituent not quantitatively determined because of minuteness [Middle French, from *tracier* "to trace"]
• **syn** TRACE, VESTIGE, TRACK mean a sign left by something that has passed. TRACE may suggest any line or mark or discernible effect ⟨*traces* of a deer in the snow⟩ ⟨*traces* of their native dialect in their speech⟩ VESTIGE applies to tangible remains, as a fragment, remnant, or relic ⟨*vestiges* of a primitive society⟩ TRACK suggests a continuous line that can be followed ⟨hounds on the *track* of a fox⟩
[2]**trace** *vb* **1 a** : DELINEATE 1, SKETCH **b** : to form (as letters or figures) carefully or painstakingly **c** : to copy (as a drawing) by following lines or letters seen through a transparent superimposed sheet **d** : to make a graphic instrumental record of ⟨*trace* the heart action⟩ **e** : to adorn with linear ornamentation (as tracery) **2 a** : to follow the footprints, track, or trail of **b** : to study out or follow the development and progress of in detail or step by step **3** : to be traceable historically ⟨a family that *traces* to the Norman conquest⟩ [Middle French *tracier,* derived from Latin *trahere* "to pull, draw"]
[3]**trace** *n* **1** : either of two straps, chains, or lines of a harness for attaching a horse to something (as a vehicle) to be drawn **2** : one or more vascular bundles supplying a leaf or twig [Middle French *trais,* pl. of *trait* "pull, draft, tract", from Latin *tractus* "act of drawing", from *trahere* "to pull, draw"]
trace•able \ˈtrā-sə-bəl\ *adj* **1** : capable of being traced **2** : that can be attributed ⟨a failure *traceable* to laziness⟩ — **trace•ably** \-blē\ *adv*
trace element *n* : a chemical element used by organisms in minute quantities and held essential to their physiology
trace•less \ˈtrās-ləs\ *adj* : having or leaving no trace — **trace•less•ly** *adv*
trac•er \ˈtrā-sər\ *n* **1 a** : a person who traces missing persons or property **b** : an inquiry sent out in tracing something lost in transit **2** : a draftsman who traces designs, patterns, or markings **3** : a device (as a stylus) used in tracing **4 a** : ammunition containing a chemical composition to mark the flight of projectiles by a trail of smoke or fire **b** : a substance and especially a labeled element or atom used to trace the course of a chemical or biological process
trac•ery \ˈtrās-rē, -ə-rē\ *n, pl* **-er•ies** **1** : architectural ornamental work with branching lines; *esp* : decorative openwork in the upper part of a Gothic window **2** : a decorative interlacing of lines suggestive of Gothic tracery — **trac•er•ied** \-rēd\ *adj*

tracery 1

tra•chea \ˈtrā-kē-ə\ *n, pl* **-che•ae** \-kē-ˌē, -kē-ˌī\ *also* **-che•as** **1** : the main trunk of the system of tubes by which air passes to and from the lungs in vertebrates **2** : one of the air-conveying tubules forming the respiratory system of most insects and many other arthropods [Medieval Latin, from Late Latin *trachia,* from Greek *tracheia artēria* "rough artery", from *trachys* "rough"] — **tra•che•al** \-kē-əl\ *adj* — **tra•che•ate** \-kē-ˌāt, -ət\ *adj*
tracheal gill *n* : one of the external gills that connect with the tracheae of some aquatic insect larvae or nymphs
tra•cheid \ˈtrā-kē-əd, -ˌkēd\ *n* : a long tubular xylem cell that functions in conduction and support and has tapering closed ends and thickened lignified walls [derived from *trachea*]
tra•cheo•phyte \ˈtrā-kē-ə-ˌfīt\ *n* : any of a division (Tracheophyta) comprising green plants with a vascular system that contains tracheids or tracheal elements and including ferns and related plants and the seed plants
tra•che•ot•o•my \ˌtrā-kē-ˈät-ə-mē\ *n, pl* **-mies** : the surgical operation of cutting into the trachea especially through the skin
tra•cho•ma \trə-ˈkō-mə\ *n* : a chronic contagious eye disease marked by inflammation of the conjunctiva, caused by a rickettsia, and sometimes causing blindness [Greek *trachōma,* from *trachys* "rough"] — **tra•chom•a•tous** \-ˈkäm-ət-əs, -ˈkōm-\ *adj*
trac•ing \ˈtrā-sing\ *n* **1** : the act of one that traces **2** : something that is traced
[1]**track** \ˈtrak\ *n* **1 a** : detectable evidence (as the wake of a ship, a line of footprints, or a wheel rut) that something has passed **b** : a path made by repeated footfalls : TRAIL **c** (1) : a course laid out especially for racing (2) : the parallel rails of a railroad **d** : any of a series of parallel paths on a magnetic tape **2** : the course along which something moves **3 a** : a sequence of events or a train of ideas : SUCCESSION **b** : awareness of a fact or progression ⟨lose *track* of the time⟩ **4 a** : the width of a wheeled vehicle from wheel to wheel **b** : either of two endless metal belts on which a tracklaying vehicle (as a tank) travels **5** : track-and-field sports; *esp* : those performed on a racing track [Middle French *trac*] **syn** see TRACE — **in one's tracks** : where one is at the moment : on the spot : INSTANTLY ⟨dropped the deer *in its tracks*⟩
[2]**track** *vb* **1** : to follow the tracks or traces of : TRAIL **2** : to observe or plot the moving path of (as a spacecraft or missile) with instruments **3** : to pass over : TRAVERSE **4** : to make tracks upon or with ⟨*track* up the floor with muddy feet⟩ ⟨*track* mud all over the floor⟩ — **track•er** *n*
track•age \ˈtrak-ij\ *n* **1** : lines of railway track **2 a** : a right to use the tracks of another railroad **b** : the charge for such right
track–and–field \ˌtrak-ən-ˈfēld\ *adj* : of, relating to, or being any of various competitive athletic events (as running, jumping, and weight throwing) performed on a running track or on the adjacent field
track•lay•ing \ˈtrak-ˌlā-ing\ *adj* : of, relating to, or being a vehicle that travels on two endless metal belts
track•less \ˈtrak-ləs\ *adj* : having no track : PATHLESS — **track•less•ly** *adv* — **track•less•ness** *n*
[1]**tract** \ˈtrakt\ *n, often cap* : verses of Scripture (as from the Psalms) used between the gradual and the Gospel at some masses [Medieval Latin *tractus,* from Latin, "action of drawing, extension"; from its being sung without a break by one voice]
[2]**tract** *n* : a pamphlet or leaflet intended to draw attention or gain support for something (as a political or religious movement) [Latin *tractatus* "treatise", from *tractare* "to draw out, handle, treat"]
[3]**tract** *n* **1 a** : an indefinite stretch especially of land ⟨broad *tracts*

of prairie⟩ **b** : a defined area especially of land ⟨a garden *tract*⟩ **2** : a system of body parts or organs that collectively serve some special purpose ⟨the digestive *tract*⟩ **[**Latin *tractus* "action of drawing, extension", from *trahere* "to pull, draw"**]**

trac•ta•ble \'trak-tə-bəl\ *adj* **1** : easily led, taught, or controlled : DOCILE ⟨a *tractable* horse⟩ **2** : easily handled, managed, or wrought : MALLEABLE **[**Latin *tractabilis,* from *tractare* "to handle, treat"**]** — **trac•ta•bil•i•ty** \,trak-tə-'bil-ət-ē\ *n* — **trac•ta•ble•ness** \'trak-tə-bəl-nəs\ *n* — **trac•ta•bly** \-blē\ *adv*

trac•tion \'trak-shən\ *n* **1** : the act of drawing : the state of being drawn; *also* : the force exerted in drawing **2** : the drawing of a vehicle by motive power; *also* : the motive power employed **3** : the adhesive friction of a body on a surface on which it moves ⟨the *traction* of a wheel on a rail⟩ **4** : a pulling force exerted on a skeletal structure (as in a fracture) by means of a special device; *also* : a state of tension caused by such a pulling force ⟨a leg in *traction*⟩ **[**Medieval Latin *tractio,* from Latin *trahere* "to draw"**]** — **trac•tion•al** \-shnəl, -shən-l\ *adj*

trac•tive \'trak-tiv\ *adj* : serving to pull : used in pulling

trac•tor \'trak-tər\ *n* **1** : a 4-wheeled or tracklaying rider-controlled automotive vehicle used especially for drawing implements (as agricultural) or for bearing and propelling such implements **2** : a smaller 2-wheeled apparatus controlled usually through handlebars by a walking operator **3** : a truck with short chassis used in combination with a trailer for the highway hauling of freight **[**Latin *tractus,* past participle of *trahere* "to pull, draw"**]**

tractor 1

[1]trade \'trād\ *n* **1** : a customary course of action : PRACTICE **2 a** : the business or work in which one engages regularly : OCCUPATION **b** : an occupation requiring manual or mechanical skill : CRAFT **c** : the persons engaged in an occupation business, or industry **3 a** : the business of buying and selling or bartering commodities : COMMERCE **b** : BUSINESS 1b ⟨was in the novelty *trade*⟩ **4 a** : an act or instance of trading : TRANSACTION; *esp* : an exchange of property without use of money **b** : a firm's customers : CLIENTELE **c** : the concerns engaged in a business or industry **[**Middle English, "path, track, course of action", from Low German, "path"**]** **syn** see BUSINESS

[2]trade *vb* **1 a** : to give in exchange for another commodity : BARTER; *also* : to make an exchange of **b** : to buy and sell (as stock) regularly **2 a** : to engage in the exchange, purchase, or sale of goods **b** : to make one's purchases : SHOP

[3]trade *adj* **1** : of, relating to, or used in trade **2** : intended for persons in a business or industry ⟨a *trade* journal⟩ **3** : of, composed of, or representing the trades or trade unions **4** : of or associated with a trade wind ⟨the *trade* belts⟩

trade acceptance *n* : a time draft for the amount of a purchase drawn by the seller on the buyer and bearing the buyer's acceptance

trade dollar *n* : a United States silver dollar issued from 1873 to 1885 for use in oriental trade

trade-in \'trād-,in\ *n* : something given in trade usually as part payment of the price of another

trade in \trād-'in, 'trād-\ *vt* : to turn in as usually part payment for a purchase ⟨*trade* an old car *in* on a new one⟩

[1]trade•mark \-,märk\ *n* : a device (as a word) pointing distinctly to the origin or ownership of merchandise to which it is applied and legally reserved to the exclusive use of the owner as maker or seller

[2]trademark *vt* : to secure trademark rights for : register the trademark of

trade name *n* **1** : the name by which an article is called in its own trade **2** : a name that is given by a manufacturer or merchant to a product to distinguish it as made or sold by him and that may be used and protected as a trademark **3** : the name under which a firm does business

trad•er \'trād-ər\ *n* **1** : a person who trades **2** : a ship engaged in trade

trade school *n* : a secondary school teaching the skilled trades

trades•man \'trādz-mən\ *n* **1** : one who runs a retail store : SHOPKEEPER **2** : a worker in a skilled trade : CRAFTSMAN

trades•peo•ple \-,pē-pəl\ *n pl* : people (as shopkeepers) engaged in trade

trade union *n* : LABOR UNION; *esp* : CRAFT UNION — compare INDUSTRIAL UNION — **trade unionism** *n* — **trade unionist** *n*

trade wind *n* : a wind blowing almost continually in the same course, from northeast to southwest in a belt north of the equator and from southeast to northwest in one south of the equator **[**[1]*trade* ("habitual course")**]**

trading post *n* : a station or store of a trader or trading company established in a sparsely settled region

trading stamp *n* : a printed stamp given as a premium to a retail customer to be accumulated and redeemed in merchandise

tra•di•tion \trə-'dish-ən\ *n* : the handing down of information, beliefs, or customs from one generation to another; *also* : something thus handed down **[**Latin *traditio* "action of handing over, tradition", from *tradere* "to hand over, hand down", from *trans-* + *dare* "to give"**]** — **tra•di•tion•al** \-'dish-nəl, -ən-l\ *adj* — **tra•di•tion•al•ly** \-ē\ *adv*

tra•di•tion•al•ism \-'dish-nə-,liz-əm, -ən-l-,iz-\ *n* : the doctrines or practices of those who follow or accept tradition — **tra•di•tion•al•ist** \-nə-ləst, -ən-l-əst\ *n or adj* — **tra•di•tion•al•is•tic** \-,dish-nə-'lis-tik, -ən-l-'is-\ *adj*

tra•duce \trə-'düs, -'dyüs\ *vt* : to injure the reputation of by falsehood or misrepresentation : DEFAME **[**Latin *traducere* "to lead across, transfer, degrade", from *trans-* + *ducere* "to lead"**]** — **tra•duce•ment** \-mənt\ *n* — **tra•duc•er** *n*

[1]traf•fic \'traf-ik\ *n* **1 a** : import and export trade **b** : the business of buying and selling **2** : communication or dealings between individuals or groups **3 a** : the movement (as of vehicles or pedestrians) through an area or along a route **b** : the vehicles or pedestrians moving along a route **4** : the passengers or cargo carried by a transportation system **[**Middle French *trafique,* from Italian *traffico,* from *trafficare* "to traffic"**]**

[2]traffic *vb* **traf•ficked; traf•fick•ing** : to carry on traffic : TRADE, DEAL — **traf•fick•er** *n*

traffic circle *n* : ROTARY 2

traffic island *n* : a paved or planted island in a roadway designed to guide the flow of traffic

traffic signal *n* : an electrically operated signal (as a system of colored lights) for controlling traffic — called also *traffic light*

trag•a•canth \'traj-ə-,kanth, 'trag-, -,kantth\ *n* : a gum from various Old World plants related to the American locoweeds that swells in water and is used in the arts and in pharmacy — called also *gum tragacanth* **[**Middle French *tragacanthe,* from Latin *tragacantha,* from Greek *tragakantha,* from *tragos* "goat" + *akantha* "thorn"**]**

tra•ge•di•an \trə-'jēd-ē-ən\ *n* **1** : a writer of tragedies **2** : an actor of tragic roles

tra•ge•di•enne \trə-,jēd-ē-'en\ *n* : an actress who plays tragic roles **[**French *tragédienne,* from *tragédie* "tragedy"**]**

trag•e•dy \'traj-əd-ē\ *n, pl* **-dies** **1** : a serious drama having a sorrowful or disastrous conclusion **2 a** : a disastrous event : CALAMITY **b** : MISFORTUNE 2 **3** : tragic quality or element **[**Middle French *tragedie,* from Latin *tragoedia,* from Greek *tragōidia,* from *tragos* "goat" + *aeidein* "to sing"**]**

△ **origin** Our word *tragedy* is derived from Greek *tragōidia,* a compound of *tragos,* "goat", and *aeidein,* "to sing". The Greeks' reasons for calling this dramatic form "goat song" are obscure. Tragedy developed in the 6th and 5th centuries B.C. out of the performance of originally lyric recitations. Prizes were sometimes given for dramatic performances, and it may be that competition for the prize of a goat accounts for the word *tragōidia.* Another possibility is that a goat was sacrificed in earlier religious rituals out of which tragedy may have developed. A third theory is that tragedy developed out of the performance of lyric hymns to the god Dionysus in which the chorus was dressed as satyrs, mythical beings with some of the attributes of goats.

trag•ic \'traj-ik\ *adj* **1** : of, marked by, or expressive of tragedy **2 a** : dealing with or treated in tragedy ⟨the *tragic* hero⟩ **b** : appropriate to or typical of tragedy **3 a** : regrettably serious or unpleasant **b** : marked by a sense of tragedy — **trag•i•cal** \-i-kəl\ *adj* — **trag•i•cal•ly** \-i-kə-lē, -klē\ *adv* — **trag•i•cal•ness** \-i-kəl-nəs\ *n*

tragi•com•e•dy \ˌtraj-i-ˈkäm-əd-ē\ *n* **:** a drama or a situation blending tragic and comic elements — **tragi•com•ic** \-ˈkäm-ik\ *or* **tragi•com•i•cal** \-ˈkäm-i-kəl\ *adj*

1trail \ˈtrāl\ *vb* **1 a :** to drag or draw along behind ⟨the horse *trailed* its reins⟩ **b :** to hang down or rest on or creep over the ground ⟨*trailing* vines⟩ **2 :** to lag behind **:** do poorly in relation to others **3 :** to carry or bring along as a burden or bother **4 :** to follow in the tracks of **:** PURSUE ⟨dogs *trailing* a fox⟩ **5 :** to hang or let hang so as to touch the ground ⟨a *trailing* skirt⟩ **6 :** to form a trail **:** STRAGGLE ⟨smoke *trailed* from the chimney⟩ **7 :** DWINDLE ⟨the sound *trailed* off⟩ [Middle French *trailler* "to tow", derived from Latin *tragula* "sledge, dragnet"] **syn** see CHASE

2trail *n* **1 :** something that trails or is trailed: as **a :** the train of a gown **b :** the part of a gun carriage that rests on the ground when the piece is ready for action **2 a :** something that follows or moves along as if being drawn along **:** TRAIN **b** (1) **:** the streak produced by a meteor (2) **:** a line produced photographically by the moving image of a celestial body ⟨star *trails*⟩ **3 a :** a trace or mark left by something that has passed or been drawn along ⟨a *trail* of blood⟩ **b :** a track made by passage through a wilderness **:** a beaten path **c :** a marked path through a forest or mountainous region

trail•blaz•er \-ˌblā-zər\ *n* **1 :** one that marks or points out a trail to guide others **:** PATHFINDER **2 :** PIONEER 1 — **trail•blaz•ing** \-zing\ *adj*

trail•er \ˈtrā-lər\ *n* **1 :** a trailing plant **2 a :** a vehicle designed to be hauled (as by a tractor) **b :** a vehicle designed to serve wherever parked as a dwelling or as a place of business

trailer park *n* **:** an area equipped to provide space for house trailers — called also *trailer camp, trailer court*

trailing arbutus *n* **:** ARBUTUS 2

trailing edge *n* **:** the rearmost edge of an airfoil

1train \ˈtrān\ *n* **1 :** a part of a gown that trails behind the wearer **2 :** RETINUE **3 :** a moving file of persons, vehicles, or animals **4 a :** order designed to lead to some result **b :** an orderly succession or sequence ⟨a *train* of thought⟩ **c :** accompanying circumstances **d :** SEQUEL 1, AFTERMATH **5 :** a line of combustible material (as gunpowder) laid to lead fire to a charge **6 :** a series of moving machine parts (as gears) for transmitting and modifying motion **7 a :** a connected line of railroad cars with or without a locomotive **b :** an automotive tractor with one or more trailer units [Middle French, from *trainer* "to draw, drag"]

2train *vb* **1 :** to direct the growth of (a plant) usually by bending, pruning, and tying **2 a :** to teach something (as a skill, profession, or trade) to ⟨was *trained* in the law⟩ **b :** to teach (an animal) to obey **3 :** to make ready (as by exercise) for a test of skill **4 :** to aim (as a gun) at a target **5 :** to undergo instruction, discipline, or drill [Middle French *trainer* "to draw, drag"] **syn** see TEACH — **train•able** \ˈtrā-nə-bəl\ *adj* — **train•ee** \trā-ˈnē\ *n*

train•er \ˈtrā-nər\ *n* **1 :** one that trains **2 :** a member of the staff for an athletic team responsible for treating ailments and minor injuries

train•ing \ˈtrā-ning\ *n* **1 :** the course followed by one who trains or is being trained ⟨take nursing *training*⟩ **2 :** the condition of one who has trained for a test or contest **syn** see EDUCATION

train•load \ˈtrān-ˈlōd\ *n* **:** the full freight or passenger capacity of a railroad train

train•man \ˈtrān-mən, -ˌman\ *n* **:** a member of a railroad train crew supervised by a conductor

traipse \ˈtrāps\ *vi* **:** to walk or tramp about [origin unknown] — **traipse** *n*

trait \ˈtrāt\ *n* **:** a distinguishing quality (as of personality or physical makeup) **:** PECULIARITY, CHARACTERISTIC [Middle French, literally, "act of drawing", from Latin *tractus,* from *trahere* "to draw, drag"]

trai•tor \ˈtrāt-ər\ *n* **1 :** one who betrays another's trust or is false to an obligation or duty **2 :** one who commits treason [Old French *traitre,* from Latin *traditor,* from *tradere* "to hand over, betray", from *trans-* + *dare* "to give"]

trai•tor•ous \ˈtrāt-ə-rəs, ˈtrā-trəs\ *adj* **1 :** guilty or capable of treason **2 :** constituting treason — **trai•tor•ous•ly** *adv*

trai•tress \ˈtrā-trəs\ *or* **trai•tor•ess** \ˈtrāt-ə-rəs, ˈtrā-trəs\ *n* **:** a girl or woman who is a traitor

tra•jec•to•ry \trə-ˈjek-tə-rē, -trē\ *n, pl* **-ries :** the curve that a moving body (as a planet in its orbit, a projectile, or a rocket) describes in space [Latin *trajectus,* past participle of *traicere* "to cause to cross, cross", from *trans-* + *jacere* "to throw"]

tram \ˈtram\ *n* **1 :** a cart or wagon running on rails (as in a mine) **2** *chiefly British* **:** STREETCAR **3 :** the carriage of an overhead conveyor [English dialect, "shaft of a wheelbarrow"]

tram•car \-ˌkär\ *n* **1** *chiefly British* **:** STREETCAR **2 :** TRAM 1

tram•line \-ˌlīn\ *n, British* **:** a streetcar line

1tram•mel \ˈtram-əl\ *n* **1 :** a net for catching birds or fish **2 :** something hindering activity, progress, or freedom **:** RESTRAINT — usually used in pl. **3 :** an adjustable pothook for a fireplace crane **4 :** a compass for drawing large circles that consists of a beam with two sliding parts — usually used in pl. [Middle French *tremail,* from Late Latin *tremaculum,* from Latin *tres* "three" + *macula* "mesh, spot"]

2trammel *vt* **tram•meled** *or* **tram•melled**; **tram•mel•ing** *or* **tram•mel•ling** \ˈtram-ling, -ə-ling\ **1 :** to catch or hold in or as if in a net **:** ENMESH **2 :** to prevent or hinder the free play of **:** CONFINE

1tramp \ˈtramp, *1 & 2 are also* ˈträmp, ˈtrȯmp\ *vb* **1 :** to walk heavily **2 :** to tread on forcibly and repeatedly **:** TRAMPLE **3 a :** to wander through or travel on foot **b :** to travel as a tramp [Middle English *trampen*] — **tramp•er** *n*

2tramp \ˈtramp, *3 is also* ˈträmp, ˈtrȯmp\ *n* **1 :** a begging or thieving vagrant **2 :** a walking trip **:** HIKE **3 :** the succession of sounds made by the beating of marching feet **4 :** a ship not making regular trips but taking cargo to any port whenever it is offered — called also *tramp steamer*

tram•ple \ˈtram-pəl\ *vb* **tram•pled**; **tram•pling** \-pə-ling, -pling\ **1 :** to tramp or tread heavily so as to bruise, crush, or injure ⟨the cattle *trampled* on the young wheat⟩ **2 :** to tread underfoot **:** stamp on **3 :** to inflict pain, injury, or loss by ruthless or heartless treatment ⟨*trample* on the rights of a friend⟩ [Middle English *tramplen,* from *trampen* "to tramp"] — **tram•ple** *n* — **tram•pler** \-pə-lər, -plər\ *n*

tram•po•line \ˌtram-pə-ˈlēn, ˈtram-pə-ˌ\ *n* **:** a resilient canvas sheet or web supported by springs in a metal frame used as a springboard and landing area for performing jumps and flips [Spanish *trampolín,* from Italian *trampolino,* of Germanic origin] — **tram•po•lin•er** \-ˈlē-nər, -ˌlē-\ *n* — **tram•po•lin•ist** \-nəst\ *n*

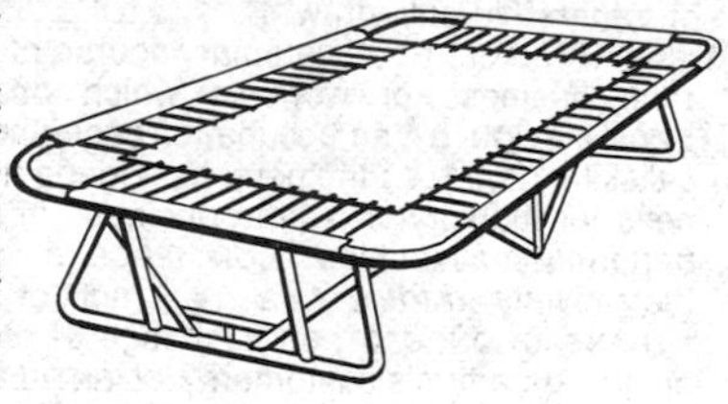

trampoline

tram•po•lin•ing \-ˈlē-ning, -ˌlē-\ *n* **:** the sport of jumping and performing acrobatic feats on a trampoline

tram•way \ˈtram-ˌwā\ *n* **1 :** a road or way for trams **2** *British* **:** a streetcar line

trance \ˈtrans\ *n* **1 :** a state of partly suspended animation or inability to function **:** STUPOR **2 :** a sleeplike state (as of deep hypnosis) **3 :** a state of profound abstraction or absorption **:** ECSTASY [Middle French *transe,* from *transir* "to pass away, swoon", from Latin *transire* "to cross over, pass away", from *trans-* + *ire* "to go"]

tran•quil \ˈtrang-kwəl, ˈtran-\ *adj* **1 :** free from agitation, disturbance, or turmoil **:** SERENE **2 :** STABLE 1b [Latin *tranquillus*] **syn** see CALM — **tran•quil•ly** \-kwə-lē\ *adv* — **tran•quil•ness** *n*

tran•quil•ize *or* **tran•quil•lize** \-kwə-ˌlīz\ *vb* **:** to make or become tranquil or relaxed; *esp* **:** to relieve of mental tension and anxiety usually by means of drugs

tran•quil•iz•er \-ˌlī-zər\ *n* **:** one that tranquilizes; *esp* **:** a drug used to reduce mental disturbance (as anxiety and tension)

tran•quil•li•ty *or* **tran•quil•i•ty** \tran-ˈkwil-ət-ē, trang-\ *n* **:** the quality or state of being tranquil

trans- *prefix* **1 :** on or to the other side of **:** across **:** beyond ⟨*trans*atlantic⟩ **2 :** through **3 :** so or such as to change or transfer ⟨*trans*location⟩ ⟨*trans*ship⟩ [Latin *trans-, tra-,* from *trans* "across, beyond"]

See *trans-* and 2d element

transbay	**transculturally**	**transinsular**
transborder	**transdesert**	**transisthmian**
transchannel	**transequatorial**	**transpeninsular**
transcultural	**transgenerational**	**transworld**

trans•act \trans-'akt, tranz-\ *vt* **1** : to carry through : bring about : NEGOTIATE ⟨*transact* a sale⟩ **2** : to carry on : CONDUCT ⟨*transact* business⟩ [Latin *transactus,* past participle of *transigere* "to drive through, transact", from *trans-* + *agere* "to drive"] — **trans•ac•tor** \-'ak-tər\ *n*

trans•ac•tion \-'ak-shən\ *n* **1** : an act, process, or instance of transacting **2 a** : something transacted; *esp* : a business deal **b** *pl* : the record of the meeting of a society — **trans•ac•tion•al** \-shnəl, -shən-l\ *adj*

trans•at•lan•tic \ˌtrans-ət-'lant-ik, ˌtranz-\ *adj* : extending across or situated beyond the Atlantic ocean

trans•ceiv•er \trans-'ē-vər, tranz-\ *n* : a radio transmitter-receiver that uses many of the same components for transmission and reception [*trans*mitter + *receiver*]

tran•scend \tran-'send\ *vt* **1** : to rise above or go beyond the limits of : EXCEED **2** : SURPASS ⟨a poem *transcending* all others⟩ [Latin *transcendere* "to climb across, transcend", from *trans-* + *scandere* "to climb"] **syn** see EXCEED

tran•scend•ence \-'sen-dəns\ *also* **tran•scend•en•cy** \-dən-sē\ *n* : the quality or state of being transcendent

tran•scend•ent \-dənt\ *adj* **1** : exceeding usual limits **2** : extending or lying beyond the limits of ordinary experience [Latin *transcendens,* present participle of *transcendere* "to transcend"] — **tran•scend•ent•ly** *adv*

tran•scen•den•tal \ˌtran-ˌsen-'dent-l, ˌtran-sən-\ *adj* **1** : TRANSCENDENT 1 **2** : incapable of being the root of an algebraic equation with rational coefficients ⟨π is a *transcendental* number⟩ **3** : of or relating to transcendentalism — **tran•scen•den•tal•ly** \-l-ē\ *adv*

tran•scen•den•tal•ism \-l-ˌiz-əm\ *n* : a philosophy holding that ultimate reality is unknowable and asserting the primacy of the spiritual over the material and empirical — **tran•scen•den•tal•ist** \-l-əst\ *adj or n*

trans•con•ti•nen•tal \ˌtrans-ˌkänt-n-'ent-l\ *adj* : extending or going across a continent ⟨*transcontinental* flight⟩

tran•scribe \tran-'skrīb\ *vt* **1 a** : to make a written copy of **b** : to make a copy of (dictated or recorded matter) in longhand or on a typewriter **2 a** : to represent (speech sounds) by means of phonetic symbols **b** : to transfer (data) from one recording form to another **c** : to record (as on magnetic tape) for later broadcast **3** : to make a musical transcription of **4** : to broadcast by electrical transcription **5** : to cause (as DNA) to undergo genetic transcription [Latin *transcribere,* from *trans-* + *scribere* "to write"] — **tran•scrib•er** *n*

tran•script \'tran-ˌskript\ *n* **1** : a written, printed, or typed copy **2** : an official copy (as of a student's educational record) [Medieval Latin *transcriptum,* from Latin *transcribere* "to transcribe"]

tran•scrip•tion \tran-'skrip-shən\ *n* **1** : an act, process, or instance of transcribing **2** : COPY 1, TRANSCRIPT: as **a** : an arrangement of a musical composition for some instrument or voice other than the original **b** : ELECTRICAL TRANSCRIPTION **3** : the process of constructing a messenger RNA molecule using a DNA molecule as a template with resulting transfer of genetic information to the messenger RNA — compare TRANSLATION 4 — **tran•scrip•tion•al** \-shnəl, -shən-l\ *adj* — **tran•scrip•tion•al•ly** \-ē\ *adv*

trans•duc•er \trans-'dü-sər, tranz-, -'dyü-\ *n* : a device that is actuated by power from one system and supplies power in any other form to a second system [Latin *transducere* "to lead across", from *trans-* + *ducere* "to lead"]

[1]**tran•sect** \tran-'sekt\ *vt* : to cut transversely [*trans-* + Latin *sectus,* past participle of *secare* "to cut"] — **tran•sec•tion** \-'sek-shən\ *n*

[2]**tran•sect** \'tran-ˌsekt\ *n* : a sample area (as of vegetation) usually in the form of a long continuous strip

tran•sept \'tran-ˌsept\ *n* : the part forming the arms of a cross-shaped church [Latin *trans-* + *saeptum* "enclosure, wall", from *saepire* "to fence in", from *saepes* "fence"]

[1]**trans•fer** \trans-'fər, 'trans-ˌ\ *vb* **trans•ferred**; **trans•fer•ring** **1 a** : to convey from one person, place, or situation to another : TRANSPORT **b** : to cause to pass from one to another : TRANSMIT **2** : to make over the possession or ownership of : CONVEY **3** : to print or otherwise copy from one surface to another by contact **4** : to move to a different place, region, or situation; *esp* : to withdraw from one educational institution to enroll at another **5** : to change from one vehicle or transportation line to another [Latin *transferre,* from *trans-* + *ferre* "to carry"] — **trans•fer•abil•i•ty** \ˌtrans-ˌfər-ə-'bil-ət-ē\ *n* — **trans•fer•able** \trans-'fər-ə-bəl\ *adj* — **trans•fer•al** \-'fər-əl\ *n* — **trans•fer•rer** \-'fər-ər\ *n*

[2]**trans•fer** \'trans-ˌfər\ *n* **1** : conveyance of right, title, or interest in real or personal property from one person to another **2** : an act, process, or instance of transferring : TRANSFERENCE **3** : one that transfers or is transferred; *esp* : a graphic image transferred by contact from one surface to another **4** : a place where a transfer is made (as of trains to ferries) **5** : a ticket entitling a passenger on a public conveyance to continue the journey on another route

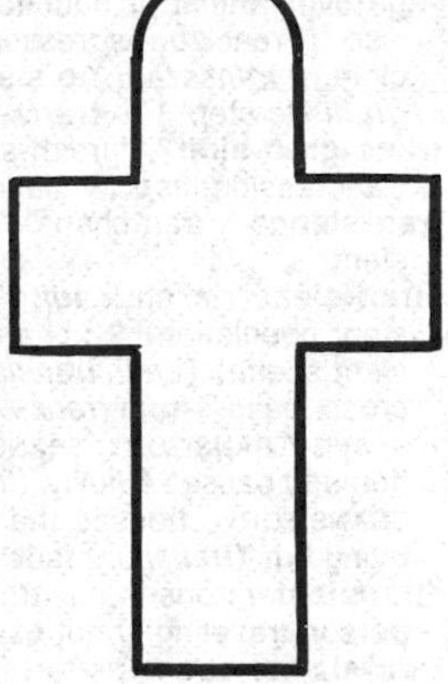
transept

trans•fer•ee \ˌtrans-fər-'ē\ *n* **1** : a person to whom a conveyance is made **2** : one transferred

trans•fer•ence \trans-'fər-əns\ *n* : an act, process, or instance of transferring : TRANSFER

trans•fer•or \ˌtrans-fər-'ȯr\ *n* : one that transfers a title, right, or property

trans•fer RNA \'trans-ˌfər-\ *n* : a relatively small RNA that transfers a particular amino acid to a growing protein at the site of protein synthesis during genetic translation

trans•fig•u•ra•tion \ˌtrans-ˌfig-yə-'rā-shən, -ˌfig-ə-'rā-\ *n* **1** : a change of form or appearance; *esp* : a glorifying or exalting change **2** *cap* **a** : the supernatural change in the appearance of Jesus on the mountain **b** : a church festival on August 6 commemorating this

trans•fig•ure \trans-'fig-yər, *especially British* -'fig-ər\ *vt* : to give a new and typically exalted or spiritual appearance to **syn** see TRANSFORM

trans•fix \trans-'fiks\ *vt* **1** : to pierce through with or as if with a pointed weapon : IMPALE **2** : to hold motionless by or as if by piercing — **trans•fix•ion** \-'fik-shən\ *n*

trans•form \trans-'fȯrm\ *vb* **1 a** : to change in composition, structure, or character : CONVERT **b** : to change in outward appearance **2** : to change in mathematical form without altering value or meaning **3** : to change (a current) in potential (as from high voltage to low) or in type (as from alternating to direct) — **trans•form•able** \-'fȯr-mə-bəl\ *adj* — **trans•for•ma•tive** \-'fȯr-mət-iv\ *adj*

• **syn** TRANSFORM, METAMORPHOSE, TRANSMUTE, TRANSFIGURE mean to change something into a different thing. TRANSFORM implies a change in form, nature, or function ⟨*transform* a desert into a fertile plain⟩ METAMORPHOSE suggests an abrupt or striking alteration induced as if supernaturally or by natural (as chemical) agencies ⟨the ugly duckling *metamorphosed* into a swan⟩ TRANSMUTE implies a change from a lower to a higher element or thing ⟨the artist *transmutes* ordinary scenes into extraordinary ones⟩ TRANSFIGURE implies a change that exalts and glorifies.

trans•for•ma•tion \ˌtrans-fər-'mā-shən\ *n* **1** : an act, process, or instance of transforming or being transformed **2** : the operation of changing (as by rotation or mapping) one mathematical configuration or expression into another in accordance with a mathematical rule **3** : genetic modification of a cell and especially of a bacterium by introduction of DNA from a genetically different source

trans•form•er \trans-'fȯr-mər\ *n* : one that transforms; *esp* : a device without moving parts for changing an electric current into one of different voltage by electromagnetic induction

trans•fuse \trans-'fyüz\ *vt* **1 a** : to cause to pass from one to another : TRANSMIT **b** : to spread into or through : PERMEATE **2 a** : to transfer (as blood or saline) into a vein of a human or animal **b** : to subject (a patient) to transfusion [Latin *transfusus,* past participle of *transfundere* "to transfuse", from *trans-* + *fundere* "to pour"] — **trans•fus•able** \-'fyü-zə-bəl\ *adj* — **trans•fu•sion** \-'fyü-zhən\ *n*

\ə\ **abut**	\au̇\ **out**	\i\ **tip**	\ȯ\ **saw**	\u̇\ **foot**
\ər\ **further**	\ch\ **chin**	\ī\ **life**	\ȯi\ **coin**	\y\ **yet**
\a\ **mat**	\e\ **pet**	\j\ **job**	\th\ **thin**	\yü\ **few**
\ā\ **take**	\ē\ **easy**	\ng\ **sing**	\t͟h\ **this**	\yu̇\ **cure**
\ä\ **cot, cart**	\g\ **go**	\ō\ **bone**	\ü\ **food**	\zh\ **vision**

trans·gress \trans-ˈgres, tranz-\ *vb* **1 :** to go beyond limits set by : VIOLATE ⟨*transgress* the divine law⟩ **2 :** to pass beyond or go over a limit or boundary **3 :** to violate a command or law : SIN [French *transgresser,* from Latin *transgressus,* past participle of *transgredi* "to step beyond or across", from *trans-* + *gradi* "to step"] — **trans·gres·sor** \-ˈgres-ər\ *n*

trans·gres·sion \-ˈgresh-ən\ *n* **:** an act, process, or instance of trangressing; *esp* **:** violation of a law, command, or duty

tran·sience \ˈtran-chəns\ *n* **:** the quality or state of being transient

[1]**tran·sient** \-chənt\ *adj* **1 :** not lasting or staying long ⟨a *transient* population⟩ **2 :** changing in form or appearance ⟨a *transient* scene⟩ [Latin *transiens,* present participle of *transire* "to cross, pass", from *trans-* + *ire* "to go"] — **tran·sient·ly** *adv*
• syn TRANSIENT, TRANSITORY: TRANSIENT applies to what is short in duration and passes quickly ⟨*transient* guests⟩ ⟨*transient* as music⟩ TRANSITORY stresses the inevitability of changing, ending, or dying out ⟨*transitory* fads and fashions⟩

[2]**transient** *n* **:** one that is transient: as **a :** a transient guest **b :** a person traveling about usually in search of work

tran·sis·tor \tran-ˈzis-tər, -ˈsis-\ *n* **:** an electronic device similar to the electron tube in use (as amplification and rectification) consisting of a small block of a semiconductor (as germanium) that has at least three electrodes [[1]*trans*fer + *resistor;* from its transferring an electrical signal across a resistor]

tran·sis·tor·ize \-tə-ˌrīz\ *vt* **:** to equip (a device) with transistors

[1]**tran·sit** \ˈtrans-ət, ˈtranz-\ *n* **1 a :** an act, process, or instance of passing through or over : PASSAGE **b :** transporting of persons or things from one place to another ⟨goods lost in *transit*⟩ **c :** local transportation of people by public conveyance or a system of such transportation **2 a :** passage of a celestial body over the meridian of a place or through the field of a telescope **b :** passage of a smaller body (as Venus) across the disk of a larger (as the sun) **3 :** a theodolite with the telescope mounted so that it can be transited [Latin *transitus,* from *transire* "to cross, pass", from *trans-* + *ire* "to go"]

[2]**transit** *vb* **1 :** to make a transit **2 a :** to pass or cause to pass over or through **b :** to pass across **3 :** to turn (a telescope) about the horizontal transverse axis in surveying

transit instrument *n* **1 :** a telescope mounted at right angles to a horizontal east-west axis and used with a clock and chronograph for observing the time of transit of a celestial body over the meridian of a place **2 :** TRANSIT 3

tran·si·tion \trans-ˈish-ən, tranz-\ *n* **1 :** a passing from one state, stage, place, or subject to another : CHANGE ⟨*transition* from war to peacetime⟩ **2 :** a musical passage leading from one section of a piece to another — **tran·si·tion·al** \-ˈish-nəl, -ən-l\ *adj* — **tran·si·tion·al·ly** \-ē\ *adv*

tran·si·tive \ˈtrans-ət-iv, ˈtranz-\ *adj* **1 :** characterized by having or containing a direct object ⟨a *transitive* verb⟩ **2 :** relating to or being a relation such that if *A* is so related to *B* and *B* is so related to *C,* then *A* is so related to *C* ⟨equality is a *transitive* relation⟩ **3 :** of, relating to, or involving transition — **tran·si·tive·ly** *adv* — **tran·si·tive·ness** *n* — **tran·si·tiv·i·ty** \ˌtrans-ə-ˈtiv-ət-ē, ˌtranz-\ *n*

tran·si·to·ry \ˈtrans-ə-ˌtōr-ē, ˈtranz-, -ˌtȯr-\ *adj* **:** lasting only a short time : SHORT-LIVED, TEMPORARY ⟨the *transitory* pleasures of the world⟩ **syn** see TRANSIENT — **tran·si·to·ri·ly** \ˌtrans-ə-ˈtōr-ə-lē, ˌtranz-, -ˈtȯr-\ *adv* — **tran·si·to·ri·ness** \ˈtrans-ə-ˌtōr-ē-nəs, ˈtranz-, -ˌtȯr-\ *n*

trans·late \trans-ˈlāt, tranz-\ *vb* **1 :** to bear or change from one place, state, form, or appearance to another : TRANSFER, TRANSFORM ⟨*translate* plans into action⟩ **2 a :** to turn from one language into another **b :** to transfer or turn from one set of symbols into another : TRANSCRIBE **c :** to express in different words : PARAPHRASE **3 :** to subject (as genetic information) to translation in protein synthesis [Latin *translatus,* past participle of *transferre* "to transfer, translate"] — **trans·lat·abil·i·ty** \-ˌlāt-ə-ˈbil-ət-ē\ *n* — **trans·lat·able** \-ˈlāt-ə-bəl\ *adj* — **trans·la·tor** \-ˈlāt-ər\ *n*

trans·la·tion \trans-ˈlā-shən, tranz-\ *n* **1 :** an act, process, or instance of translating **2 :** the product of translating ⟨a German *translation* of the novel⟩ **3 :** a rigid motion of a mathematical figure equivalent to a transformation of coordinates in which the new axes are parallel to the old ones **4 :** the process of forming a protein molecule at the site of protein synthesis from information contained in messenger RNA — compare TRANSCRIPTION 3 — **trans·la·tion·al** \-shnəl, -shən-l\ *adj*

trans·lit·er·ate \trans-ˈlit-ə-ˌrāt, tranz-\ *vt* **:** to represent or spell in the characters of another alphabet [*trans-* + Latin *littera* "letter"] — **trans·lit·er·a·tion** \-ˌlit-ə-ˈrā-shən\ *n*

trans·lo·cate \ˈtrans-lō-ˌkāt, ˈtranz-, trans-ˈ, tranz-ˈ\ *vt* **:** to transfer by translocation

trans·lo·ca·tion \ˌtrans-lō-ˈkā-shən, ˌtranz-\ *n* **:** a changing of location : DISPLACEMENT: as **a :** the conducting of soluble material from one part of a plant to another **b :** exchange of parts between nonhomologous chromosomes

trans·lu·cence \trans-ˈlüs-ns, tranz-\ *or* **trans·lu·cen·cy** \-n-sē\ *n* **:** the quality or state of being translucent

trans·lu·cent \-nt\ *adj* **1 :** shining or glowing through : LUMINOUS **2 :** admitting and diffusing light so that objects beyond cannot be clearly distinguished ⟨frosted glass is *translucent*⟩ [Latin *translucens,* present participle of *translucēre* "to shine through", from *trans-* + *lucēre* "to shine"] **syn** see CLEAR — **trans·lu·cent·ly** *adv*

trans·ma·rine \ˌtrans-mə-ˈrēn, ˌtranz-\ *adj* **:** being or coming from beyond or across the sea

trans·mi·gra·tion \ˌtrans-ˌmī-ˈgrā-shən, ˌtranz-\ *n* **1 :** the changing of one's home from one country to another : MIGRATION **2 :** the passing of a soul into another body after death — **trans·mi·grate** \trans-ˈmī-ˌgrāt, tranz-\ *vi* — **trans·mi·gra·to·ry** \-ˈmī-grə-ˌtōr-ē, -ˌtȯr-\ *adj*

trans·mis·si·ble \trans-ˈmis-ə-bəl, tranz-\ *adj* **:** capable of being transmitted ⟨*transmissible* diseases⟩ — **trans·mis·si·bil·i·ty** \-ˌmis-ə-ˈbil-ət-ē\ *n*

trans·mis·sion \-ˈmish-ən\ *n* **1 :** an act, process, or instance of transmitting something **2 :** the passage of radio waves in the space between transmitting and receiving stations; *also* **:** the act or process of transmitting by radio or television **3 :** an assembly of parts including the speed-changing gears and the propeller shaft by which power is transmitted from an automobile engine to the live axle **4 :** something transmitted [Latin *transmissio,* from *transmittere* "to transmit"] — **trans·mis·sive** \-ˈmis-iv\ *adj* — **trans·mis·siv·i·ty** \ˌtrans-mis-ˈiv-ət-ē, ˌtranz-\ *n*

trans·mit \trans-ˈmit, tranz-\ *vb* **trans·mit·ted; trans·mit·ting** **1 a :** to send or transfer from one person or place to another : FORWARD **b :** to transfer by or as if by inheritance **c :** to convey (infection) abroad or to another **2 a** (1) **:** to cause (as light or force) to pass or be passed through space or a medium (2) **:** to admit the passage of ⟨glass *transmits* light⟩ **b :** to send out a signal either by radio waves or over a wire [Latin *transmittere,* from *trans-* + *mittere* "to send"] — **trans·mit·ta·ble** \-ˈmit-ə-bəl\ *adj* — **trans·mit·tal** \-ˈmit-l\ *n*

trans·mit·ter \-ˈmit-ər\ *n* **1 :** one that transmits ⟨a *transmitter* of disease⟩ **2 :** the part of a telephone that includes the mouthpiece and a mechanism that picks up sound waves and sends them over the wire **3 :** the device in a telegraph system that sends out messages **4 :** the apparatus that sends out radio or television signals

trans·mog·ri·fy \trans-ˈmäg-rə-ˌfī, tranz-\ *vt* **-fied; -fy·ing :** to change or alter often with grotesque or humorous effect [origin unknown] — **trans·mog·ri·fi·ca·tion** \-ˌmäg-rə-fə-ˈkā-shən\ *n*

trans·mu·ta·tion \ˌtrans-myü-ˈtā-shən, ˌtranz-\ *n* **:** an act or instance of transmuting or being transmuted: as **a :** the hypothetical changing of base metals into gold or silver **b :** the changing of one element or nuclide into another either naturally or artificially — **trans·mut·a·tive** \trans-ˈmyüt-ət-iv, tranz-\ *adj*

trans·mute \trans-ˈmyüt, tranz-\ *vb* **1 :** to change in form, appearance, or nature especially to a higher form **2 :** to subject (as an element or base metal) to transmutation **3 :** to undergo transmutation [Latin *transmutare,* from *trans-* + *mutare* "to change"] **syn** see TRANSFORM — **trans·mut·able** \-ˈmyüt-ə-bəl\ *adj*

trans·na·tion·al \trans-ˈnash-nəl, ˈtrans-, tranz-, ˈtranz-, -ən-l\ *adj* **:** extending beyond national boundaries

trans·oce·an·ic \ˌtrans-ˌō-shē-ˈan-ik, ˌtranz-\ *adj* **1 :** being or living beyond the ocean **2 :** crossing or extending across the ocean ⟨*transoceanic* cables⟩

tran·som \ˈtran-səm\ *n* **1 :** a transverse piece in a structure : CROSSPIECE: as **a :** LINTEL **b :** a horizontal crossbar in a window, over a door, or between a door and a window or fanlight above it **2 :** a window above a door or above another window built on and commonly hinged to a transom [probably from Latin *transtrum,* from *trans* "across"]

tran·son·ic *also* **trans–son·ic** \trans-ˈsän-ik, tran-ˈsän-\ *adj* **1**

: being or relating to a speed approximating the speed of sound in air — often used of aeronautical speeds between 600 and 900 miles per hour (about 950 to 1450 kilometers per hour) **2** : moving, capable of moving, or utilizing air currents moving at a transonic speed ⟨*transonic* bomber⟩ [*trans-* + *-sonic* (as in *supersonic*)]

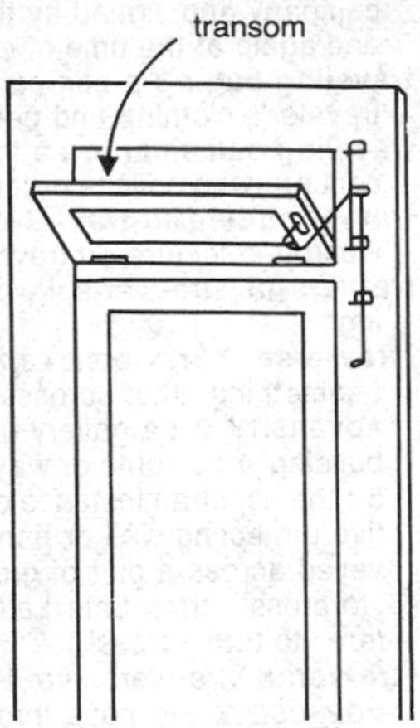

transom 2

trans•pa•cif•ic \ˌtrans-pə-'sif-ik\ *adj* : crossing, extending across, or situated beyond the Pacific ocean

trans•par•ence \trans-'par-əns, -'per-\ *n* : TRANSPARENCY 1

trans•par•en•cy \-ən-sē\ *n, pl* **-cies 1** : the quality or state of being transparent **2** : a picture or design on glass, thin cloth, paper, or film viewed by light shining through it or by projection

trans•par•ent \-ənt\ *adj* **1 a** (1) : having the property of transmitting light so that bodies lying beyond are entirely visible (2) : allowing the passage of a specified form of radiation (as X rays or ultraviolet light) **b** : fine or sheer enough to be seen through ⟨*transparent* gauze⟩ **2 a** : FRANK 1, GUILELESS **b** : easily detected or seen through : OBVIOUS ⟨*transparent* falsehood⟩ [Medieval Latin *transparens,* present participle of *transparēre* "to show through", from Latin *trans-* + *parere* "to show oneself, appear"] **syn** see CLEAR — **trans•par•ent•ly** *adv* — **trans•par•ent•ness** *n*

tran•spi•ra•tion \ˌtrans-pə-'rā-shən\ *n* : the act or process or an instance of transpiring; *esp* : the passage of watery vapor from a living body through a membrane or pores — compare PERSPIRATION

tran•spire \trans-'pīr\ *vb* **1 a** : to pass off or give passage to (a fluid) through small openings; *esp* : to excrete (watery vapor) through a membrane or pores ⟨a large tree may *transpire* tons of water in a season⟩ **b** : to escape in the form of a vapor especially from a living body **2** : to give off vaporous material (as watery vapor from the surfaces of leaves) **3** : to pass in the form of a vapor from a living body **4** : to become known or apparent **5** : to come to pass [Middle French *transpirer,* from Latin *trans-* + *spirare* "to breathe"] **syn** see HAPPEN

[1]**trans•plant** \trans-'plant\ *vb* **1** : to lift and reset (a plant) in another soil or situation **2** : to remove from one place and settle or introduce elsewhere : TRANSPORT **3** : to transfer (an organ or tissue) from one part or individual to another **4** : to tolerate or adapt to being transplanted — **trans•plant•able** \-ə-bəl\ *adj* — **trans•plan•ta•tion** \ˌtrans-ˌplan-'tā-shən\ *n* — **trans•plant•er** \trans-'plant-ər\ *n*

[2]**trans•plant** \'trans-ˌplant\ *n* **1** : the act or process of transplanting **2** : something or someone transplanted

trans•po•lar \trans-'pō-lər, 'trans-\ *adj* : going or extending across either of the polar regions

[1]**trans•port** \trans-'pōrt, -'pȯrt\ *vt* **1** : to convey from one place to another : CARRY **2** : ENRAPTURE ⟨*transported* with delight⟩ **3** : to send to a penal colony overseas [Latin *transportare,* from *trans-* + *portare* "to carry"] — **trans•port•abil•i•ty** \-ˌpōrt-ə-'bil-ət-ē -ˌpȯrt-\ *n* — **trans•port•able** \-'pōrt-ə-bəl, -'pȯrt-\ *adj* — **trans•port•er** *n*

[2]**trans•port** \'trans-ˌpōrt, -ˌpȯrt\ *n* **1** : the act of transporting : TRANSPORTATION **2** : strong or intensely pleasurable emotion : ECSTASY, RAPTURE ⟨*transports* of joy⟩ **3 a** : a ship for carrying soldiers or military equipment **b** : a vehicle used to transport persons or goods **c** : a system of public transportation

trans•por•ta•tion \ˌtrans-pər-'tā-shən\ *n* **1** : an act, process, or instance of transporting or being transported **2** : banishment to a penal colony **3 a** : means of conveyance or travel from one place to another **b** : public conveyance of passengers or goods especially as a commercial enterprise

trans•pose \trans-'pōz\ *vt* **1** : TRANSFORM 1a **2** : TRANSLATE 2 **3** : to transfer from one place or period to another : SHIFT **4** : to change the relative place or normal order of **5** : to write or perform (a musical composition) in a different key **6** : to bring (a term) from one side of an algebraic equation to the other with change of sign [Middle French *transposer,* from Latin *transponere* "to change the position of", from *trans-* + *ponere* "to put, place"] **syn** see REVERSE — **trans•pos•able** \-'pō-zə-bəl\ *adj* — **trans•po•si•tion** \ˌtrans-pə-'zish-ən\ *n*

trans•sex•u•al \trans-'seksh-wəl, 'trans-, -ə-wəl, -'sek-shəl\ *n* : a person genetically of one sex who has a strong urge to belong to the opposite sex which may be carried to the point of undergoing surgery to modify the sex organs to mimic those of the opposite sex — **transsexual** *adj* — **trans•sex•u•al•ism** \-wə-ˌliz-əm, -shə-ˌliz-\ *n*

trans•ship \tran-'ship, trans-\ *vb* : to transfer for further transportation from one means of transport to another — **trans•ship•ment** \-mənt\ *n*

tran•sub•stan•ti•ate \ˌtran-səb-'stan-chē-ˌāt\ *vb* : to change into another substance [Medieval Latin *transubstantiare,* from Latin *trans-* + *substantia* "substance"]

tran•sub•stan•ti•a•tion \-ˌstan-chē-'ā-shən\ *n* **1** : an act or instance of transubstantiating or being transubstantiated **2** : the change in the consecrated bread and wine at Mass in substance but not in appearance to the body and blood of Christ

trans•ura•ni•um \ˌtran-shə-'rā-nē-əm, ˌtran-zhə-\ *or* **trans•ura•nic** \-'ran-ik, -'rā-nik\ *adj* : having an atomic number greater than that of uranium

trans•ver•sal \trans-'vər-səl, tranz-\ *n* : a line that intersects a system of lines

[1]**trans•verse** \trans-'vərs, tranz-', 'trans-ˌ, 'tranz-\ *adj* : lying or being across : set crosswise [Latin *transversus,* from *transvertere* "to turn across", from *trans-* + *vertere* "to turn"] — **trans•verse•ly** *adv*

[2]**trans•verse** \'trans-ˌvərs, 'tranz-\ *n* : something transverse

trans•ves•tism \trans-'ves-ˌtiz-əm, tranz-\ *n* : adoption of the dress and often the behavior of the opposite sex [German *transvestismus,* from Latin *trans-* + *vestire* "to clothe"] — **trans•ves•tite** \-'ves-ˌtīt\ *adj or n*

[1]**trap** \'trap\ *n* **1** : a device (as a snare or pitfall) for catching animals; *esp* : one that holds by springing shut suddenly **2** : something by which one is caught or stopped unawares **3 a** : a device for hurling clay pigeons into the air **b** : SAND TRAP **4** : a light usually one-horse carriage with springs **5** : any of various devices for preventing passage of something often while allowing other matter to proceed **6** : a device for drains or sewers consisting of a bend or partitioned chamber in which the liquid forms a seal to prevent the passage of sewer gas **7** *pl* : a group of percussion instruments (as in a dance or jazz band) [Old English *treppe* and Old French *trape*]

[2]**trap** *vb* **trapped; trap•ping 1 a** : to catch in or as if in a trap **b** : to place in a restricted position : CONFINE **2** : to provide with a trap **3** : to separate out (as water from steam) **4** : to engage in trapping animals **syn** see CATCH — **trap•per** *n*

[3]**trap** *vt* **trapped; trap•ping** : to decorate with or as if with trappings [Middle English *trappen,* from *trappe* "cloth", from Middle French *drap*]

[4]**trap** *or* **trap•rock** \'trap-'räk\ *n* : any of various fine-grained igneous rocks used especially in road making [Swedish *trapp,* from *trappa* "stair", from Low German *trappe*]

trap•door \'trap-'dōr, -'dȯr\ *n* : a lifting or sliding door covering an opening in a roof, ceiling, or floor

trap–door spider *n* : any of various spiders that build silk-lined underground nests topped with a hinged lid

tra•peze \tra-'pēz\ *n* : an acrobatic apparatus consisting of a short horizontal bar suspended at a height by two parallel ropes [French *trapèze,* from New Latin *trapezium* "trapezium"]

tra•pez•ist \-'pē-zəst\ *n* : a performer on the trapeze

tra•pe•zi•um \trə-'pē-zē-əm\ *n, pl* **-zi•ums** *or* **-zia** \-zē-ə\ **1** : a quadrilateral having no two sides parallel **2** *British* : TRAPEZOID 2

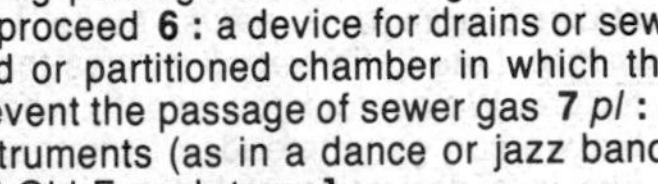
trapezium 1

\ə\ **a**but	\au̇\ **ou**t	\i\ t**i**p	\ȯ\ s**aw**	\u̇\ f**oo**t
\ər\ f**ur**ther	\ch\ **ch**in	\ī\ l**i**fe	\ȯi\ c**oi**n	\y\ **y**et
\a\ m**a**t	\e\ p**e**t	\j\ **j**ob	\th\ **th**in	\yü\ f**ew**
\ā\ t**a**ke	\ē\ **ea**sy	\ng\ si**ng**	\th\ **th**is	\yu̇\ c**u**re
\ä\ c**o**t, c**a**rt	\g\ **g**o	\ō\ b**o**ne	\ü\ f**oo**d	\zh\ vi**si**on

[New Latin, from Greek *trapezion,* literally, "small table", from *trapeza* "table", from *tra-* "four" + *peza* "foot "]

tra•pe•zi•us \-zē-əs\ *n* : a large flat triangular superficial muscle of each side of the back [New Latin, from *trapezium;* from the figure formed by the two muscles]

trap•e•zoid \'trap-ə-,zȯid\ *n* **1** *British* : TRAPEZIUM 1 **2** : a quadrilateral having only two sides parallel — **trap•e•zoi•dal** \,trap-ə-'zȯid-l\ *adj*

trap•ping \'trap-ing\ *n* **1** : CAPARISON 1 — usually used in pl. **2** *pl* : outward decoration or signs ⟨the *trappings* of success⟩

Trap•pist \'trap-əst\ *n* : a monk of an austere branch of the Cistercian Order [French *trappiste,* from La *Trappe,* France, where the branch was established] — **Trappist** *adj*

traps \'traps\ *n pl* : personal belongings : LUGGAGE [Middle English *trappe* "cloth"]

trap•shoot•ing \'trap-,shüt-ing\ *n* : shooting at clay pigeons thrown from a trap into the air away from the shooters — **trap-shoot•er** \-,shüt-ər\ *n*

trash \'trash\ *n* **1** : something worth little or nothing: as **a** : [1]JUNK 2a, RUBBISH **b** : empty talk : NONSENSE **c** : low-grade or worthless artistic matter **2** : something in a crumbled or broken condition or mass; *esp* : debris from pruning or processing plant material **3** : a worthless or shameful person; *also* : RIFFRAFF [of Scandinavian origin]

trashy \'trash-ē\ *adj* **trash•i•er; -est** : resembling trash : WORTHLESS — **trash•i•ness** *n*

trat•to•ria \,trät-ə-'rē-ə\ *n* : an eating house : RESTAURANT [Italian]

trau•ma \'trau̇-mə, 'trȯ-\ *n, pl* **trau•ma•ta** \-mət-ə\ *or* **traumas** **1 a** : a bodily injury caused by a physical force applied from without ⟨surgical *trauma*⟩ **b** : a disordered psychic or behavioral state resulting from stress or injury **2** : a cause of trauma [Greek *traumat-, trauma* "wound"] — **trau•mat•ic** \trə-'mat-ik, trȯ-, trau̇-\ *adj* — **trau•mat•i•cal•ly** \-'mat-i-kə-lē, -klē\ *adv*

[1]**tra•vail** \trə-'vāl, 'trav-,āl\ *n* **1 a** : work especially of a painful or laborious nature : TOIL **b** : a piece of work : TASK **c** : AGONY 1a, TORMENT **2** : LABOR 1c, CHILDBIRTH [Old French from *travaillier* "to torture, travail", derived from Late Latin *tripalis* "having 3 stakes", from *tri-* + *palus* "stake"]

△ **origin** Late Latin *trepalium* was the name of an instrument of torture. We do not know exactly what the *trepalium* looked like, but we can get some idea from the word's etymology. *Trepalium* is a derivative of Latin *tripalis,* which means "having 3 stakes". Although only *trepalium* is found in documents that still exist, we can assume that there was also another form, *tripalium. Travaillier,* "to torture", an Old French descendant of this *tripalium,* early developed the extended and milder senses "to trouble", "to labor or toil", and "to weary". The noun *travail,* "labor, toil", derived from the verb *travaillier,* was borrowed form Old French into English.

[2]**travail** *vi* : to work hard : TOIL

[1]**trav•el** \'trav-əl\ *vb* **trav•eled** *or* **trav•elled; trav•el•ing** *or* **trav•el•ling** \'trav-ling, -ə-ling\ **1** : to journey from place to place or to a distant place **2** : to journey from place to place selling or taking orders **3 a** : to move or advance from one place to another **b** : to undergo transportation **c** : to walk or run with a basketball in violation of the rules **4** : to journey through or over : TRAVERSE ⟨this trail can be *traveled* only on horseback⟩ [Old French *travaillier* "to travail"]

△ **origin** In the Middle Ages the most striking thing about *travel* was its difficulty. A journey cost a great deal of wearisome effort, so that a pilgrimage to a distant religious shrine, for example, was an act of real devotion. The verb *travail* developed in English the specific sense "to go on a journey". *Travel,* originally a variant spelling of *travail,* has attached itself to this particular sense and so become a separate word.

[2]**travel** *n* **1 a** : the act of traveling : PASSAGE **b** : JOURNEY, TRIP — often used in pl. **2** *pl* : an account of one's travels **3** : the number traveling : TRAFFIC **4 a** : MOVEMENT ⟨the *travel* of satellites around the earth⟩ **b** : the motion of a piece of machinery; *esp* : reciprocating motion

travel agency *n* : an agency engaged in selling arranging, or furnishing information about personal transportation or travel — called also *travel bureau* — **travel agent** *n*

trav•eled *or* **trav•elled** \'trav-əld\ *adj* **1** : experienced in travel **2** : used by travelers ⟨a *traveled* road⟩

trav•el•er *or* **trav•el•ler** \'trav-lər, -ə-lər\ *n* : one that travels

traveler's check *n* : a draft purchased from a bank or express company and signed by the purchaser at the time of purchase and again at the time of cashing

traveling bag *n* : a bag carried by hand and designed to hold a traveler's clothing and personal articles

traveling salesman *n* : a traveling representative of a business concern who solicits orders

trav•el•ogue *also* **trav•el•og** \'trav-ə-,lȯg, -,läg\ *n* : a usually illustrated lecture on travel [*travel* + *-logue*]

tra•vers•al \trə-'vər-səl\ *n* : the act or an instance of traversing

[1]**trav•erse** \'trav-ərs, *especially for 5 also* trə-'vərs\ *n* **1** : something that crosses or lies across **2** : OBSTACLE, ADVERSITY **3** : a gallery extending from side to side in a large building **4** : a route or way across or over (as a zigzag course) **5** : the act or an instance of traversing : CROSSING **6** : a protective projecting wall or bank of earth in a trench **7** : a line surveyed across a plot of ground [Middle French, from *traverser* "to cross", from Late Latin *transversare,* from Latin *transvertere* "to turn across"]

[2]**tra•verse** \trə-'vərs\ *vb* **1** : to go against or act in oppostion to : OPPOSE **2** : to pass through, across, or over **3** : to make a study of : EXAMINE **4** : to ascend, descend, or cross (a slope or gap) at an angle **5** : to move back and forth or from side to side **6** : to move or turn laterally : SWIVEL **7** : to climb or ski at an angle or in a zigzag course — **tra•vers•able** \-'vər-sə-bəl\ *adj* — **tra•vers•er** *n*

[3]**trav•erse** \'trav-ərs, -,ərs; trə-'vərs\ *adj* : lying across : TRANSVERSE

trav•erse jury \'trav-ərs-\ *n* : PETIT JURY

trav•er•tine \'trav-ər-,tēn, -tən\ *n* : a massive usually layered calcium carbonate formed by deposition from spring waters or especially from hot springs [French *travertin,* from Italian *tivertino, travertino,* from Latin *tiburtinus* "of Tivoli", from *Tibur* "Tivoli"]

[1]**trav•es•ty** \'trav-ə-stē\ *n, pl* **-ties** **1** : a burlesque and usually grotesque translation or imitation **2** : an inferior imitation or likeness ⟨a *travesty* of justice⟩ [obsolete *travesty* "disguised, parodied", from French *travestir* "to disguise", from Italian *travestire,* from *tra-* "trans-" + *vestire* "to dress", from Latin, from *vestis* "garment"] **syn** see CARICATURE

[2]**travesty** *vt* **-tied; -ty•ing** : to make a travesty of : PARODY

tra•vois \trə-'vȯi, 'trav-,ȯi\ *n, pl* **tra•vois** \-'vȯiz, -,ȯiz\ *also* **tra•vois•es** \-'vȯi-zəz, -,ȯi-zəz\ : a vehicle used by the Amerindians of the Great Plains consisting of two trailing poles serving as shafts and bearing a platform or net for the load [Canadian French *travois*]

[1]**trawl** \'trȯl\ *vb* : to fish or catch with a trawl [probably from Dutch *tragelen*]

[2]**trawl** *n* : a large conical net dragged along the sea bottom in fishing

trawl•er \'trȯ-lər\ *n* : a person or vessel that fishes by trawling

tray \'trā\ *n* : an open receptacle with flat bottom and low rim for holding, carrying, or exhibiting articles ⟨a serving *tray*⟩ ⟨the *trays* of a trunk⟩ [Old English *trīg, trēg*]

treach•er•ous \'trech-rəs, -ə-rəs\ *adj* **1** : guilty of or inclined to treachery **2 a** : not reliable ⟨a *treacherous* memory⟩ **b** : giving a false appearance of safety ⟨*treacherous* quicksand⟩ — **treach•er•ous•ly** *adv* — **treach•er•ous•ness** *n*

treach•ery \'trech-rē, -ə-rē\ *n, pl* **-er•ies** **1** : violation of allegiance or of faith and confidence : TREASON **2** : an act of treason [Old French *trecherie,* from *trechier* "to deceive"]

trea•cle \'trē-kəl\ *n* **1** *chiefly British* : MOLASSES **2** : something (as a tone of voice) heavily sweet and cloying [Middle French *triacle,* an antidote against poison, from Latin *theriaca,* from Greek *thēriakē* "antidote against a poisonous bite", derived from *thēr* "wild animal"] — **trea•cly** \-kə-lē, -klē\ *adj*

[1]**tread** \'tred\ *vb* **trod** \'träd\; **trod•den** \'träd-n\ *or* **trod; tread•ing** **1 a** : to step or walk on or over **b** : to walk along : FOLLOW **2 a** : to beat or press with the feet : TRAMPLE **b** : to bring under control or put down by force **3 a** : to form by treading ⟨*tread* a path⟩ **b** : to execute by stepping or dancing ⟨*tread* a measure⟩ **4 a** : to set foot **b** : to put one's foot : STEP [Old English *tredan*] — **tread•er** *n* — **tread water** : to keep the body nearly upright in the water and the head above water by a treading motion of the feet usually aided by the hands

[2]**tread** *n* **1** : a mark made by or as if by treading **2** : the action, manner, or sound of treading **3 a** : the part of a sole that touches the ground **b** : the part of a wheel that bears on a road or rail; *esp* : the thickened face of an automobile tire **4** : the

distance between the points of contact with the ground of the two front wheels or the two rear wheels of a vehicle **5 :** the horizontal part of a step

[1]**trea•dle** \'tred-l\ *n* **:** a lever or other device pressed by the foot to drive a machine [Old English *tredel* "step of a stair", from *tredan* "to tread"]

[2]**treadle** *vb* **trea•dled; trea•dling** \'tred-ling, -l-ing\ **:** to operate a treadle or operate the treadle of

tread•mill \'tred-ˌmil\ *n* **1 :** a device moved by persons treading on steps set around the rim of a wide wheel or by animals walking on an endless belt **2 :** a wearisome or monotonous routine

trea•son \'trēz-n\ *n* **1 :** the betrayal of a trust **:** TREACHERY **2 :** the offense of attempting by overt acts to overthrow the government of the state to which one owes allegiance or to bring about its defeat in war [Old French *traison,* from Medieval Latin *traditio,* from Latin, "act of handing over, teaching, tradition"] **syn** see SEDITION

△ **origin** *Treason* and *tradition* are derived from the same Latin source. Latin *traditio* means "teaching" or "tradition", but these senses are developed from its literal sense, "the act of handing over something". Tradition is maintained by passing information from one generation to another, whereas treason is committed when someone who has been entrusted with information passes it on to someone else. The difference in form between the two words can be accounted for by the fact that *treason* came to us through Old French, where *traditio* underwent sound change, while *tradition* was later borrowed directly from Latin.

trea•son•able \'trēz-nə-bəl, -n-ə-bəl\ *adj* **:** relating to, consisting of, or involving treason — **trea•son•ably** \-blē\ *adv*

trea•son•ous \'trēz-nəs, -n-əs\ *adj* **:** TREASONABLE

[1]**trea•sure** \'trezh-ər, 'trāzh-\ *n* **1 a** (1) **:** wealth (as money, jewels, or precious metals) stored up or hoarded ⟨buried *treasure*⟩ (2) **:** RICHES **b :** a store of money in reserve **2 :** something of great worth or value; *also* **:** a person esteemed as rare or precious [Old French *tresor,* from Latin *thesaurus,* from Greek *thēsauros*]

[2]**treasure** *vt* **trea•sured; trea•sur•ing** \'trezh-ring, 'trāzh-, -ə-ring\ **1 :** to collect and store up (something of value) for future use **2 :** to hold or keep as precious **:** CHERISH — **trea•sur•able** \'trezh-rə-bəl, 'trāzh-, -ə-rə-\ *adj*

treasure hunt *n* **:** any of various games in which each player or team tries to be first to find whatever has been hidden (as by finding and following a series of hidden clues)

trea•sur•er \'trezh-rər, 'trezh-ər-ər, 'trāzh-\ *n* **:** a person trusted with charge of a treasure or a treasury; *esp* **:** an officer of a club, business, or government who has charge of money taken in and paid out — **trea•sur•er•ship** \-ˌship\ *n*

treasure trove \'trezh-ər-ˌtrōv, 'trāzh-\ *n* **1 :** treasure found buried in the ground or hidden away and of unknown ownership **2 :** a discovery or something discovered that is full of things to be treasured [Anglo-French *tresor trové,* literally, "found treasure"]

trea•sury \'trezh-rē, 'trāzh-, -ə-rē\ *n, pl* **trea•sur•ies 1 a :** a place in which stores of wealth are kept **b :** the place of deposit and disbursement of collected funds; *esp* **:** one where public revenues are deposited, kept, and disbursed **c :** funds kept in a place of deposit **2** *cap* **:** a governmental department in charge of finances **3 :** a repository for treasures ⟨a *treasury* of poems⟩

treasury note *n* **:** a currency note issued by the United States Treasury in payment for silver bullion purchased under the Sherman Silver Purchase Act of 1890

[1]**treat** \'trēt\ *vb* **1 :** to discuss terms of accommodation or settlement **:** NEGOTIATE **2 a :** to deal with a matter especially in writing **:** DISCOURSE ⟨books *treating* of crime⟩ **b :** to present or represent artistically **c :** to deal with **:** HANDLE **3 a :** to pay for another's entertainment **b :** to provide with free food, entertainment, or enjoyment **4 a :** to behave or act toward **:** USE ⟨*treat* a horse cruelly⟩ **b :** to regard and deal with in a specified manner ⟨*treat* as confidential⟩ **5 :** to care for or deal with medically or surgically **6 :** to subject to some action ⟨*treat* soil with lime⟩ [Old French *traitier,* from Latin *tractare* "to handle, deal with, treat", from *trahere* "to draw"] — **treat•er** *n*

[2]**treat** *n* **1 :** an entertainment given without expense to those invited **2 :** an especially unexpected source of pleasure or amusement ⟨the *treat* of seeing you again⟩

treat•able \'trēt-ə-bəl\ *adj* **:** that can be treated; *esp* **:** responsive to medical or surgical treatment — **treat•abil•i•ty** \ˌtrēt-ə-'bil-ət-ē\ *n*

trea•tise \'trēt-əs\ *n* **:** a book or an article treating a subject systematically ⟨a *treatise* on war⟩ [Anglo-French *tretiz,* from Old French *traitier* "to treat"]

treat•ment \'trēt-mənt\ *n* **1 :** the act or manner or an instance of treating someone or something **2 :** a substance or technique used in treating

trea•ty \'trēt-ē\ *n, pl* **treaties :** an agreement or arrangement made by negotiation; *esp* **:** a contract between two or more states or sovereigns [Middle French *traité,* from Medieval Latin *tractatus,* from Latin, "treatment", from *tractare* "to treat"]

treaty port *n* **:** a port or inland city of China, Japan, and Korea formerly open by treaty to foreign commerce

[1]**tre•ble** \'treb-əl\ *n* **1 a :** the highest of the four voice parts in vocal music **:** SOPRANO **b :** a singer or instrument taking this part **c :** a high-pitched voice, tone, or sound **d :** the upper half of the musical pitch range **2 :** something triple in construction, uses, amount, number, or value [Middle English]

[2]**treble** *adj* **1 a :** having three parts **b :** triple in number or amount **2 a :** relating to or having the range of a musical treble ⟨*treble* voices⟩ **b :** high-pitched **:** SHRILL [Middle French, from Latin *triplus* "triple"] — **tre•bly** \'treb-lē, -ə-lē\ *adv*

[3]**treble** *vb* **tre•bled; tre•bling** \'treb-ling, -ə-ling\ **1 :** to make or become three times the size, amount, or number ⟨*treble* its weight⟩ **2 :** to sing treble

treble clef *n* **1 :** a clef that places G above middle C on the second line of the staff **2 :** TREBLE STAFF [from its use for the notation of treble parts]

treble staff *n* **:** the musical staff carrying the treble clef

[1]**tree** \'trē\ *n* **1 a :** a woody perennial plant having a single usually tall main stem with few or no branches on its lower part **b :** a shrub or herb that looks like a tree ⟨rose *trees*⟩ ⟨a banana *tree*⟩ **2 :** a piece of wood (as a post or pole) usually adapted to a particular use or forming part of a structure or implement **3 :** something in the form of or felt to resemble a tree: as **a :** a diagram that depicts a branching from an original stem ⟨genealogical *tree*⟩ **b :** a much-branched system of channels especially in an animal body ⟨the vascular *tree*⟩ [Old English *trēow*] — **tree•less** \-ləs\ *adj* — **tree•like** \-ˌlīk\ *adj*

[2]**tree** *vt* **treed; tree•ing 1 a :** to drive to or up a tree ⟨*treed* by a bull⟩ **b :** to bring to bay **2 :** to furnish or fit with a tree

tree farm *n* **:** an area of forest land managed to ensure continuous commercial production — **tree farmer** *n*

tree fern *n* **:** a tropical fern with a woody stalk and a crown of large often feathery fronds

tree frog *n* **:** any of numerous tailless amphibians that frequent trees — called also *tree toad*; compare SPRING PEEPER

tree house *n* **:** a structure (as a playhouse) built among the branches of a tree

tree line *n* **:** TIMBERLINE

tree of heaven : AILANTHUS

tree ring *n* **:** ANNUAL RING

tree shrew *n* **:** any of a family of tree-dwelling insect-eating mammals sometimes classified as true insectivores and sometimes as primitive primates

tree toad *n* **:** TREE FROG

tree•top \'trē-ˌtäp\ *n* **:** the topmost part of a tree

trefoil 2

tre•foil \'trē-ˌfȯil, 'tref-ˌȯil\ *n* **1 a :** CLOVER **b :** any of several herbs of the pea family having leaves with three leaflets **2 :** an ornament or symbol in the form of a 3-parted leaf [Middle French *trefeuil,* from Latin *trifolium,* from *tri-* + *folium* "leaf"]

trek \'trek\ *vi* **trekked; trek•king 1** *chiefly southern Africa* **:** to migrate by ox wagon or in a train of such wagons **2 :** to make one's way arduously [Afrikaans, from Dutch *trecken* "to pull, haul, migrate"] — **trek** *n* — **trek•ker** *n*

[1]**trel•lis** \'trel-əs\ *n* **:** a frame of latticework used especially as a screen or a support for climbing plants [Middle French *treliz*

\ə\ **abut**	\au̇\ **out**	\i\ **tip**	\ȯ\ **saw**	\u̇\ **foot**
\ər\ **further**	\ch\ **chin**	\ī\ **life**	\ȯi\ **coin**	\y\ **yet**
\a\ **mat**	\e\ **pet**	\j\ **job**	\th\ **thin**	\yü\ **few**
\ā\ **take**	\ē\ **easy**	\ng\ **sing**	\t͟h\ **this**	\yu̇\ **cure**
\ä\ **cot, cart**	\g\ **go**	\ō\ **bone**	\ü\ **food**	\zh\ **vision**

"fabric of coarse weave, trellis", derived from Latin *tri-* + *liceum* "thread"]

²**trellis** *vt* **1 :** to provide with or train on a trellis ⟨*trellis* a vine⟩ **2 :** to cross or interlace on or through **:** INTERWEAVE

trel•lis•work \ˈtrel-ə-ˌswərk\ *n* **:** LATTICEWORK

trem•a•tode \ˈtrem-ə-ˌtōd\ *n* **:** any of a class (Trematoda) of parasitic flatworms including the flukes [derived from Greek *trēmatōdēs* "pierced with holes", from *trēma* "hole", from *tetrainein* "to bore"] — **trematode** *adj*

¹**trem•ble** \ˈtrem-bəl\ *vi* **trem•bled**; **trem•bling** \-bə-ling, -bling\ **1 :** to shake involuntarily (as with fear or cold) **:** SHIVER **2 :** to move, sound, or occur as if shaken or tremulous **3 :** to be affected with fear or doubt ⟨*tremble* for the safety of a friend⟩ [Middle French *trembler,* from Medieval Latin *tremulare,* from Latin *tremulus* "tremulous"] — **trem•bler** \-bə-lər, -blər\ *n*

²**tremble** *n* **1 :** a fit or spell of involuntary shaking or quivering **2 :** a tremor or series of tremors

trem•bly \ˈtrem-bə-lē, -blē\ *adj* **:** marked by trembling

tre•men•dous \tri-ˈmen-dəs\ *adj* **1 :** such as may excite trembling or arouse dread, awe, or terror **:** DREADFUL **2 :** astonishing by reason of extreme size, power, greatness, or excellence [Latin *tremendus,* from *tremere* "to tremble"] **syn** see MONSTROUS — **tre•men•dous•ly** *adv* — **tre•men•dous•ness** *n*

trem•o•lo \ˈtrem-ə-ˌlō\ *n, pl* **-los 1 a :** the rapid reiteration of a musical tone or of alternating tones to produce a tremulous effect **b :** a perceptible rapid variation of pitch in singing similar to the vibrato of a stringed instrument **2 :** a mechanical device in an organ for causing a tremulous effect [Italian, from *tremolo* "tremulous", from Latin *tremulus*]

trem•or \ˈtrem-ər\ *n* **1 :** a trembling or shaking usually from weakness or disease **2 :** a quivering or vibratory motion (as of the earth or a leaf) **3 :** a feeling of uncertainty or insecurity [Middle French *tremour,* from Latin *tremor,* from *tremere* "to tremble"]

trem•u•lous \ˈtrem-yə-ləs\ *adj* **1 :** characterized by or affected with trembling or tremors ⟨*tremulous* hands⟩ **2 :** affected with timidity **:** TIMOROUS ⟨a shy *tremulous* child⟩ **3 :** such as is caused by a tremulous state ⟨a *tremulous* smile⟩ **4 :** exceedingly sensitive [Latin *tremulus,* from *tremere* "to tremble"] — **trem•u•lous•ly** *adv* — **trem•u•lous•ness** *n*

¹**trench** \ˈtrench\ *n* **1 a :** a long narrow cut in land **:** DITCH **b :** a long ditch protected by a bank of earth thrown before it that is used to shelter soldiers **2 :** a long narrow steep-sided depression in the ocean floor [Middle French *trenche* "act of cutting", from *trenchier* "to cut"]

²**trench** *vb* **1 :** to protect with or as if with a trench **2 :** to cut a trench in **:** DITCH **3 :** to come close **:** VERGE ⟨the answer *trenched* on impudence⟩

tren•chan•cy \ˈtren-chən-sē\ *n* **:** the quality of being trenchant

tren•chant \ˈtren-chənt\ *adj* **1 :** having a sharp edge or point **:** CUTTING ⟨a *trenchant* blade⟩ ⟨*trenchant* sarcasm⟩ **2 :** sharply clear **:** PENETRATING ⟨a *trenchant* analysis of a situation⟩ **3 :** mentally energetic [Middle French, present participle of *trenchier* "to cut"] **syn** see INCISIVE — **tren•chant•ly** *adv*

trench coat *n* **1 :** a waterproof overcoat with a removable lining designed for wear in trenches **2 :** a loose double-breasted raincoat with deep pockets, a belt, and straps on the shoulders

¹**tren•cher** \ˈtren-chər\ *n* **:** a wooden platter for serving food [Middle French *trencheoir* "platter for carving", from *trenchier* "to cut"]

²**trench•er** \ˈtren-chər\ *n* **:** one that digs trenches

tren•cher•man \-mən\ *n* **1 :** a hearty eater **2** *archaic* **:** HANGER-ON, SPONGER

trench fever *n* **:** a rickettsial disease marked by fever and pain (as in joints) and transmitted by the body louse

trench foot *n* **:** a painful foot disorder resembling frostbite and resulting from exposure to cold and wet

trench knife *n* **:** a knife with a strong double-edged 8-inch blade suited for hand-to-hand fighting

trench mouth *n* **1 :** VINCENT'S ANGINA **2 :** VINCENT'S INFECTION

¹**trend** \ˈtrend\ *vi* **1 a :** to extend in a general direction **b :** to veer in a new direction **:** BEND **2 a :** to show a tendency **:** INCLINE **b :** SHIFT ⟨opinions *trending* toward conservatism⟩ [Old English *trendan* "to turn, revolve"]

²**trend** *n* **1 :** general direction taken ⟨easterly *trend* of the shoreline⟩ **2 a :** a prevailing tendency or inclination ⟨economic *trends*⟩ **b :** a general movement **:** SWING **c :** a current style or preference **d :** a line of development **syn** see TENDENCY

tre•pan \tri-ˈpan\ *vt* **tre•panned**; **tre•pan•ning :** to remove a disk from (the skull) [Medieval Latin *trepanum* "trephine", from Greek *trypanon* "auger", from *trypan* "to bore", from *trypa* "hole"] — **trep•a•na•tion** \ˌtrep-ə-ˈnā-shən\ *n*

tre•pang \tri-ˈpang\ *n* **:** any of several large Pacific sea cucumbers that are used dried especially by the Chinese for making soup — called also *bêche-de-mer* [Malay *tĕripang*]

tre•phine \ˈtrē-ˌfīn\ *n* **:** a surgical instrument for cutting out circular sections (as of bone or corneal tissue) [French *tréphine,* from obsolete English *trafine,* from Latin *tres fines* "three ends"]

trep•i•da•tion \ˌtrep-ə-ˈdā-shən\ *n* **1** *archaic* **:** a tremulous motion **2 :** a state of alarm **:** FEAR [Latin *trepidatio,* from *trepidare* "to tremble", from *trepidus* "agitated"]

trepo•ne•ma \ˌtrep-ə-ˈnē-mə\ *n, pl* **-ma•ta** \-mət-ə\ *or* **-mas :** any of a genus of spirochetes that parasitize warm-blooded animals and include organisms causing syphilis and yaws [New Latin, derived from Greek *trepein* "to turn" + *nēma* "thread"] — **trepo•ne•mal** \-məl\ *adj*

¹**tres•pass** \ˈtres-pəs, -ˌpas\ *n* **1 a :** a violation of morals **:** TRANSGRESSION; *esp* **:** SIN **b :** an unwarranted infringement **2 a** (1) **:** an unlawful act committed on the person, property, or rights of another (2) **:** a court action for injuries done by such an act **b :** the tort of wrongful entry on real property [Old French *trespas,* from *trespasser* "to go across, trespass", from *tres* "across" (from Latin *trans*) + *passer* "to pass"]

²**trespass** *vi* **1 :** ERR 1, SIN **2 :** to commit a trespass; *esp* **:** to enter unlawfully upon the land of another — **tres•pass•er** *n*

tress \ˈtres\ *n* **1** *archaic* **:** a plait of hair **:** BRAID **2 a :** a long lock of hair **b** *pl* **:** long unbound hair [Old French *trece*]

tres•tle \ˈtres-əl\ *n* **1 :** a braced frame that consists usually of a horizontal piece with spreading legs at each end and that supports something (as a tabletop or drawing board) **2 :** a braced framework of timbers or steel for carrying a road or railroad over a depression [Middle French *trestel,* derived from Latin *transtillum* "small beam", from *transtrum* "traverse beam, transom"]

tres•tle•work \-ˌwərk\ *n* **:** a system of connected trestles supporting a structure (as a bridge)

trews \ˈtrüz\ *n pl* **:** tight-fitting trousers usually of tartan; *esp* **:** close-cut tartan shorts worn under the kilt in Highland dress [Scottish Gaelic *triubhas*]

trey \ˈtrā\ *n, pl* **treys :** a card or die with three spots [Middle French *treis, treie,* from Latin *tres* "three"]

tri- *combining form* **1 :** three **:** having three elements or parts ⟨*tri*axial⟩ ⟨*tri*graph⟩ **2 :** into three ⟨*tri*sect⟩ **3 a :** thrice ⟨*tri*weekly⟩ **b :** every third ⟨*tri*monthly⟩ [Latin (from *tri-, tres*) and Greek, from *tri-, treis*]

tri•able \ˈtrī-ə-bəl\ *adj* **:** liable or subject to judicial or quasi-judicial examination or trial ⟨a case *triable* without a jury⟩ — **tri•able•ness** *n*

tri•ad \ˈtrī-ˌad *also* -əd\ *n* **1 :** a union or group of three usually closely related persons or things **2 :** a chord of three tones consisting of a root with its third and fifth and constituting the harmonic basis of tonal music [Latin *triad-, trias,* from Greek, from *treis* "three"] — **tri•ad•ic** \trī-ˈad-ik\ *adj* — **tri•ad•i•cal•ly** \-ˈad-i-kə-lē, -klē\ *adv*

¹**tri•al** \ˈtrī-əl, ˈtrīl\ *n* **1 :** the action or process of testing something (as by use or examination) **2 :** formal examination before a court of justice of the matter in issue in a civil or criminal case **3 :** a test of faith, patience, or stamina **4 :** a tryout or experiment to test quality, value, or usefulness **5 :** ATTEMPT, EFFORT [Anglo-French, from *trier* "to try"]

²**trial** *adj* **1 :** of, relating to, or used in a trial **2 :** made or done as a test or experiment **3 :** used or tried out in a test or experiment

trial and error *n* **:** the trying of this and that until something succeeds

trial balance *n* **:** a list of the debit and credit balances of accounts in a ledger at a given date made primarily to verify their equality

trial balloon *n* **1 :** a balloon sent up to test air currents and wind velocity **2 :** a project or scheme tentatively announced in order to test public opinion

trial run *n* **:** a testing exercise

tri•an•gle \ˈtrī-ˌang-gəl\ *n* **1 :** a polygon having three sides **2 a :** a musical percussion instrument made of a rod of steel bent into the form of a triangle open at one angle **b :** a drafting instrument consisting of a thin flat right-angled triangle with acute angles of 45 degrees or of 30 degrees and 60 degrees

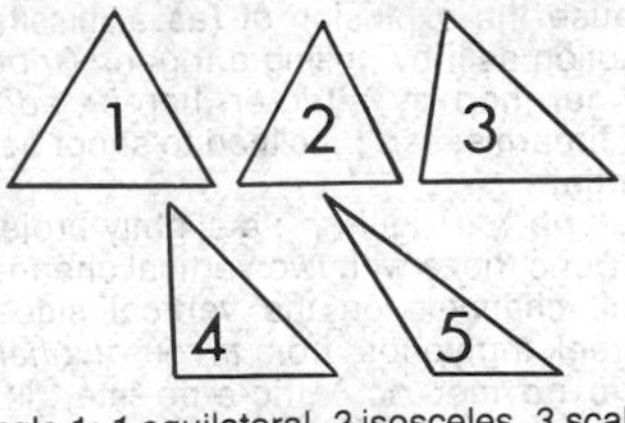

triangle 1: *1* equilateral, *2* isosceles, *3* scalene, *4* right, *5* obtuse

tri·an·gu·lar \trī-ˈang-gyə-lər\ *adj* **1 a :** of, relating to, or having the form of a triangle **b :** having a triangular base or principal surface ⟨a *triangular* pyramid⟩ **2 :** of, relating to, or involving three parts or persons ⟨a *triangular* love affair⟩ — **tri·an·gu·lar·i·ty** \trī-ang-gyə-ˈlar-ət-ē\ *n* — **tri·an·gu·lar·ly** \trī-ˈang-gyə-lər-lē\ *adv*

1tri·an·gu·late \trī-ˈang-gyə-lət\ *adj* **:** consisting of or marked with triangles

2tri·an·gu·late \-ˌlāt\ *vt* **1 :** to divide into triangles **2 :** to survey, map, or determine by triangulation

tri·an·gu·la·tion \trī-ˌang-gyə-ˈlā-shən\ *n* **:** the measurement of the elements necessary to determine the network of triangles into which any part of the earth's surface is divided in surveying

Tri·as·sic \trī-ˈas-ik\ *n* **:** the earliest period of the Mesozoic era; *also* **:** the corresponding system of rocks — see GEOLOGIC TIME table [Latin *trias* "triad"; from the 3 subdivisions of the European Triassic] — **Triassic** *adj*

tri·atom·ic \ˌtrī-ə-ˈtäm-ik\ *adj* **:** having three atoms in the molecule

tri·ax·i·al \trī-ˈak-sē-əl, ˈtrī-\ *adj* **:** having or involving three axes

trib·al \ˈtrī-bəl\ *adj* **:** of, relating to, or characteristic of a tribe ⟨*tribal* customs⟩ — **trib·al·ly** \-bə-lē\ *adv*

trib·al·ism \-bə-ˌliz-əm\ *n* **1 :** tribal consciousness and loyalty; *esp* **:** exaltation of the tribe above other groups **2 :** strong loyalty within a social group

tribe \ˈtrīb\ *n* **1 :** a usually primitive social group comprising numerous families, clans, or generations **2 :** a group of persons having a common character, occupation, or interest **3 a :** a taxonomic category of variable rank; *also* **:** a natural group irrespective of taxonomic rank ⟨the cat *tribe*⟩ **b :** a group of closely related animals or strains within a breed [Latin *tribus* "a division of the Roman people, tribe"]

tribes·man \ˈtrībz-mən\ *n* **:** a member of a tribe

trib·u·la·tion \ˌtrib-yə-ˈlā-shən\ *n* **:** distress or suffering resulting from oppression, persecution, or affliction; *also* **:** a trying experience [Old French *tribulacion,* from Latin *tribulatio,* from *tribulare* "to press, oppress", from *tribulum* "nail-studded board used in threshing", from *terere* "to rub"]

tri·bu·nal \trī-ˈbyün-l, trib-ˈyün-\ *n* **1 :** the seat of a judge **:** TRIBUNE **2 :** a court of justice **3 :** something that decides or determines ⟨the *tribunal* of public opinion⟩ [Latin, "platform for magistrates", from *tribunus* "tribune"]

trib·u·nate \ˈtrib-yə-ˌnāt, trib-ˈyü-nət\ *n* **:** the office, function, or term of office of a tribune

1trib·une \ˈtrib-ˌyün, trib-ˈyün\ *n* **1 a :** one of six officers of a Roman legion who functioned in turn as its commander **b :** a Roman official under the monarchy and the republic with the function of protecting the plebeian citizen from arbitrary action by patrician magistrates **2 :** a defender of the people especially against arbitrary abuse of authority [Latin *tribunus,* from *tribus* "tribe"] — **trib·une·ship** \-ˌship\ *n*

2tribune *n* **:** a platform from which an assembly is addressed [French, from Italian *tribuna,* from Latin *tribunal*]

1trib·u·tary \ˈtrib-yə-ˌter-ē\ *adj* **1 :** paying tribute to another **:** SUBJECT **2 :** paid or owed as tribute **3 :** CONTRIBUTORY **4 :** flowing into a larger stream or lake

2tributary *n, pl* **-tar·ies 1 :** a ruler or state that pays tribute **2 :** a stream feeding a larger stream or a lake

trib·ute \ˈtrib-ˌyüt, -yət\ *n* **1 a :** a payment made by one ruler or nation to another to show submission or to secure peace or protection **b :** a tax to raise money for this payment **c :** the obligation to pay tribute ⟨nations under *tribute*⟩ **2 :** something given or contributed voluntarily as due or deserved **:** a gift or service showing respect, gratitude, or affection ⟨a floral *tribute*⟩; *esp* **:** PRAISE, CREDIT [Latin *tributum,* from *tribuere* "to allot, pay", from *tribus* "tribe"]

trice \ˈtrīs\ *n* **:** a brief space of time **:** INSTANT — used chiefly in the phrase *in a trice* [Middle English *trise,* literally, "pull", from *trisen* "to pull", from Dutch, "to hoist"]

tri·ceps \ˈtrī-ˌseps\ *n, pl* **tri·ceps·es** *also* **triceps :** a muscle that arises from three heads; *esp* **:** the great extensor muscle along the back of the upper arm [Latin, "3-headed", from *tri-* + *caput* "head"]

tri·cer·a·tops \trī-ˈser-ə-ˌtäps\ *n* **:** a large plant-eating Cretaceous dinosaur with three horns, a bony hood or crest on the neck, and hoofed toes [Greek *tri-* + *kerat-, keras* "horn" + *ōps* "face"]

triceratops

-trices *pl of* -TRIX

tri·chi·na \trə-ˈkī-nə\ *n, pl* **-nae 1 :** a small slender nematode worm that in the larval state is parasitic in the voluntary muscles of flesh-eating mammals (as human and hog) **2 :** TRICHINOSIS [New Latin, from Greek *trichinos* "made of hair", from *trich-, thrix* "hair"] — **tri·chi·nal** \trə-ˈkīn-l\ *adj* — **tri·chi·nous** \ˈtrik-ə-nəs, trə-ˈkī-nəs\ *adj*

trich·i·no·sis \ˌtrik-ə-ˈnō-səs\ *n, pl* **-no·ses** \-ˈnō-ˌsēz\ **:** a disease caused by trichinae and marked especially by muscular pain, difficulty in breathing, fever, and edema

tricho·cyst \ˈtrik-ə-ˌsist\ *n* **:** any of the minute lassoing or stinging organs of a protozoan [Greek *trich-, thrix* "hair"]

tri·chome \ˈtrik-ˌōm, ˈtrī-ˌkōm\ *n* **:** a threadlike outgrowth; *esp* **:** an epidermal filament on a plant [German *trichom,* from Greek *trichōma* "growth of hair", from *trich-, thrix* "hair"]

tricho·mo·nad \ˌtrik-ə-ˈmō-ˌnad, -ˈmō-nəd\ *n* **:** any of a genus of flagellated protozoans parasitic in various animals including humans [Greek *trich-, thrix* "hair" + Late Latin *monad-, monas* "monad"]

tricho·mo·ni·a·sis \ˌtrik-ə-mə-ˈnī-ə-səs\ *n, pl* **-a·ses** \-ə-ˌsēz\ **:** infection with or disease caused by trichomonads; *esp* **:** a human vaginal inflammation with a persistent discharge

tri·chot·o·mous \trī-ˈkät-ə-məs\ *adj* **:** divided or dividing into three parts or into threes **:** THREEFOLD ⟨*trichotomous* branching⟩ [Late Greek *trichotomein* "to trisect", from Greek *tricha* "in three" (from *treis* "three") + *temnein* "to cut"] — **tri·chot·o·mous·ly** *adv* — **tri·chot·o·my** \-mē\ *n*

1trick \ˈtrik\ *n* **1 a :** a crafty procedure or practice meant to deceive or defraud **b :** a mischievous act **:** PRANK **c :** an indiscreet or childish action **d :** a dexterous or ingenious feat designed to puzzle or amuse ⟨a juggler's *tricks*⟩ **2 a :** an habitual peculiarity of behavior or manner **b :** a characteristic and identifying feature ⟨a *trick* of speech⟩ **c :** an optical illusion ⟨a mere *trick* of the light⟩ **3 a :** a quick or artful way of getting a result **:** KNACK **b :** a technical device (as of an art or craft) ⟨the *tricks* of stage technique⟩ **4 :** the cards played in one round of a card game often used as a scoring unit **5 :** a working shift [Old North French *trique,* from *trikier* "to deceive, cheat"]

• syn TRICK, RUSE, STRATAGEM, WILE mean an indirect means to gain an end. TRICK may imply deception, roguishness, or illusion and either an evil or harmless end; RUSE stresses an attempt to mislead by a false impression; STRATAGEM implies a ruse to entrap or outwit and suggests a more or less carefully laid-out plan; WILE suggests an attempt to entrap or deceive with false allurements.

2trick *adj* **1 :** of, relating to, or involving tricks or trickery ⟨*trick* dice⟩ **2 :** somewhat defective and unreliable ⟨a *trick* knee⟩

3trick *vt* **1 :** to deceive by cunning or artifice **:** CHEAT **2 :** to dress or adorn especially fancifully or ornately ⟨*tricked* out in a gaudy uniform⟩

trick·ery \ˈtrik-rē, -ə-rē\ *n, pl* **-er·ies :** the use of tricks to deceive or defraud **syn** see DECEPTION

1trick·le \ˈtrik-əl\ *vi* **trick·led; trick·ling** \ˈtrik-ling, -ə-ling\ **1 :** to flow or fall in drops **2 :** to flow in a thin gentle stream [Middle English *triklen*]

\ə\ **abut**	\au̇\ **out**	\i\ **tip**	\ȯ\ **saw**	\u̇\ **foot**
\ər\ **further**	\ch\ **chin**	\ī\ **life**	\ȯi\ **coin**	\y\ **yet**
\a\ **mat**	\e\ **pet**	\j\ **job**	\th\ **thin**	\yü\ **few**
\ā\ **take**	\ē\ **easy**	\ng\ **sing**	\t͟h\ **this**	\yu̇\ **cure**
\ä\ **cot, cart**	\g\ **go**	\ō\ **bone**	\ü\ **food**	\zh\ **vision**

²trickle *n* : a trickling stream
trick or treat *n* : a children's Halloween practice of asking for treats from door to door under threat of playing tricks on householders who refuse
trick•ster \ˈtrik-stər\ *n* : one who tricks or cheats
tricky \ˈtrik-ē\ *adj* **trick•i•er**; **-est** **1** : of or characteristic of a trickster : SLY **2** : requiring skill, aptitude, or caution : DELICATE **3** : TRICK 2 — **trick•i•ly** \ˈtrik-ə-lē\ *adv* — **trick•i•ness** \ˈtrik-ē-nəs\ *n*
tri•clin•ic \trī-ˈklin-ik, ˈtrī-\ *adj* : having three unequal axes intersecting at oblique angles — used especially of a crystal
¹tri•col•or \ˈtrī-ˌkəl-ər\ *n* : a flag of stripes of three colors ⟨the French *tricolor*⟩
²tricolor *or* **tri•col•ored** \ˈtrī-ˌkəl-ərd\ *adj* : having or using three colors
tri•corn \ˈtrī-ˌkòrn\ *adj* : having three horns or corners [Latin *tricornis,* from *tri-* + *cornu* "horn"]
tri•corne *or* **tri•corn** \ˈtrī-ˌkòrn\ *n* : COCKED HAT
tri•cor•nered \ˈtrī-ˈkòr-nərd\ *adj* : having three corners
tri•cot \ˈtrē-kō, ˈtrī-kət\ *n* **1** : a plain run-resistant knitted fabric (as for underwear) **2** : a twilled clothing fabric of wool or wool and cotton [French, from *tricoter* "to knit"]
¹tri•cus•pid \trī-ˈkəs-pəd, ˈtrī-\ *adj* : having three cusps
²tricuspid *n* : a tooth having three cusps
tri•cus•pid valve \trī-ˌkəs-pəd-\ *n* : a valve of three flaps that prevents return of blood from the right ventricle to the right atrium [Latin *tricuspid-, tricuspis* "having 3 points", from *tri-* + *cuspis* "point"]
tri•cy•cle \ˈtrī-ˌsik-əl\ *n* : a 3-wheeled vehicle propelled by pedals, hand levers, or a motor [French from Greek *tri-* + *kykles* "wheel"]
tri•dent \ˈtrīd-nt\ *n* : a 3-pronged spear [Latin *trident-, tridens,* from *tri-* + *dent-, dens* "tooth"]
tri•di•men•sion•al \ˌtrīd-ə-ˈmench-nəl, -ən-l\ *adj* : of or relating to three dimensions
trid•u•um \ˈtrij-ə-wəm, ˈtrid-yə-\ *n* : a period of three days of prayer usually preceding a Roman Catholic feast [Latin, "period of 3 days"]
tried \ˈtrīd\ *adj* : found good, faithful, or trustworthy through experience or testing [from past participle of *try*]
tri•en•ni•al \trī-ˈen-ē-əl, ˈtrī-\ *adj* **1** : consisting of or lasting for three years **2** : occurring or being done every three years — **triennial** *n* — **tri•en•ni•al•ly** \-ē-ə-lē\ *adv*
tri•en•ni•um \trī-ˈen-ē-əm\ *n, pl* **-ni•ums** *or* **-nia** \-ē-ə\ : a period of three years [Latin, from *tri-* + *annus* "year"]
tri•er \ˈtrī-ər, ˈtrīr\ *n* : one that tries
¹tri•fle \ˈtrī-fəl\ *n* **1** : something of little value or importance; *esp* : an insignificant amount **2** *chiefly British* : a dessert of sponge cake spread with jam or jelly covered with custard and whipped cream [Old French *trufe, trufle* "mockery"]
²trifle *vb* **tri•fled**; **tri•fling** \-fə-ling, -fling\ **1 a** : to talk in a jesting or mocking manner with intent to mislead **b** : to act in a heedless or frivolous way : PLAY **2** : to waste time **3** : to spend or waste in trifling or on trifles ⟨*trifle* away money⟩ **4** : to handle something idly : TOY — **tri•fler** \-fə-lər, -flər\ *n*
tri•fling \ˈtrī-fling\ *adj* : lacking in significance or solid worth: as **a** : FRIVOLOUS ⟨*trifling* talk⟩ **b** : TRIVIAL ⟨a *trifling* gift⟩
tri•fo•li•ate \trī-ˈfō-lē-ət, ˈtrī-\ *adj* : having three leaves ⟨a *trifoliate* plant⟩ **2** : TRIFOLIOLATE
tri•fo•li•o•late \trī-ˈfō-lē-ə-ˌlāt, ˈtrī-\ *adj* : having three leaflets ⟨a *trifoliolate* leaf⟩
tri•fur•cate \trī-ˈfər-kət, ˈtrī-, -ˌkāt; ˈtrī-fər-ˌkāt\ *adj* : TRICHOTOMOUS [Latin *trifurcus,* from *tri-* + *furca* "fork"] — **tri•fur•cate** \ˈtrī-fər-ˌkāt, trī-ˈfər-\ *vi* — **tri•fur•ca•tion** \ˌtrī-fər-ˈkā-shən\ *n*
¹trig \ˈtrig\ *adj* : stylishly trim : SMART, NEAT [Middle English, "trusty, nimble", of Scandinavian origin]
²trig *n* : TRIGONOMETRY
tri•gem•i•nal nerve \trī-ˌjem-ən-l-\ *n* : either of the 5th pair of cranial nerves that supply motor and sensory fibers mostly to the face — called also *trigeminal* [Latin *trigeminus* "threefold", from *tri-* + *geminus* "twin"]
¹trig•ger \ˈtrig-ər\ *n* : a movable lever attached to a catch that when released by pressure allows a mechanism to go into action; *esp* : the part of the lock of a firearm that releases the hammer and so fires the gun [Dutch *trekker,* from *trekken* "to pull, draw"] — **trigger** *adj* — **trig•gered** \-ərd\ *adj*
²trigger *vb* **trig•gered**; **trig•ger•ing** \ˈtrig-ring, -ə-ring\ **1** : to fire by pulling a mechanical trigger ⟨*trigger* a rifle⟩; *also* : to cause the explosion of (as a missile) **2** : to initiate or set in motion as if by pulling a trigger ⟨*triggered* a fight⟩
trig•ger–hap•py \ˈtrig-ər-ˌhap-ē\ *adj* : irresponsible in the use of firearms; *esp* : inclined to shoot before clearly identifying the target
tri•glyph \ˈtrī-ˌglif\ *n* : a slightly projecting rectangular tablet in a Doric frieze with two vertical channels and two corresponding half channels on the vertical sides [Latin *triglyphus,* from Greek *triglyphos,* from *tri-* + *glyphein* "to carve"]
trig•o•no•met•ric \ˌtrig-ə-nə-ˈme-trik\ *also* **trig•o•no•met•ri•cal** \-tri-kəl\ *adj* : of, relating to, or in accordance with trigonometry — **trig•o•no•met•ri•cal•ly** \-tri-kə-lē, -klē\ *adv*
trigonometric function *n* : a function (as the sine, cosine, tangent, cotangent, secant, or cosecant) of an arc or angle most simply expressed in terms of the ratios of pairs of sides of a right-angled triangle — called also *circular function*
trig•o•nom•e•try \ˌtrig-ə-ˈnäm-ə-trē\ *n* : the study of the properties of triangles and trigonometric functions and of their applications [Greek *trigōnon* "triangle", derived from *tri-* + *gōnia* "angle"]
tri•graph \ˈtrī-ˌgraf\ *n* : three letters spelling a single consonant, vowel, or diphthong ⟨"eau" in "beau" is a *trigraph*⟩ — **tri•graph•ic** \trī-ˈgraf-ik\ *adj*
tri•he•dral \trī-ˈhē-drəl, ˈtrī-\ *adj* **1** : having three faces ⟨*trihedral* angle⟩ **2** : of or relating to a trihedral angle — **trihedral** *n*
tri•lat•er•al \trī-ˈlat-ə-rəl, ˈtrī-, -ˈla-trəl\ *adj* : having three sides — **tri•lat•er•al•i•ty** \ˌtrī-ˌlat-ə-ˈral-ət-ē\ *n* — **tri•lat•er•al•ly** \trī-ˈlat-ə-rə-lē, ˈtrī-, -ˈla-trə-\ *adv*
tri•lin•gual \trī-ˈling-gwəl, -gyə-wəl\ *adj* **1** : of, containing, or expressed in three languages **2** : using or able to use three languages especially with the fluency characteristic of a native speaker — **tri•lin•gual•ly** \-gwə-lē\ *adv*
¹trill \ˈtril\ *n* **1 a** : the alternation of two musical tones a scale degree apart — called also *shake* **b** : VIBRATO 1 **2** : a sound resembling a musical trill : WARBLE **3** : the rapid vibration of one speech organ against another (as of the tip of the tongue against the teethridge); *also* : a speech sound so made [Italian *trillo,* from *trillare* "to thrill"]
²trill *vb* **1** : to utter as or with a trill **2** : to play or sing with a trill : QUAVER — **trill•er** n
tril•lion \ˈtril-yən\ *n* **1** — see NUMBER table **2** : a very large number [French, from *tri-* "tri-" + *-illion* (as in *million*)] — **trillion** *adj* — **tril•lionth** \-yənth, -yəntth\ *adj or n*
tril•li•um \ˈtril-ē-əm\ *n* : any of a genus of herbs of the lily family with short rhizomes and an erect stem bearing a whorl of three leaves and a large solitary 3-petaled flower [New Latin, from Swedish *trilling* "triplet"; from its 3 leaves]
tri•lo•bite \ˈtrī-lə-ˌbīt\ *n* : any of a group (Trilobita) of extinct Paleozoic marine arthropods having a segmented body divided by longitudinal furrows on the back into three lobes [derived from Greek *trilobos* "three-lobed", from *tri-* + *lobos* "lobe"]
tril•o•gy \ˈtril-ə-jē\ *n, pl* **-gies** : a series of three literary or musical compositions that are closely related and develop a single theme
¹trim \ˈtrim\ *vb* **trimmed**; **trim•ming** **1 a** : to decorate with something (as ribbons or ornaments) : ADORN **b** : to arrange a display of goods in (a shop window) **2 a** : to administer a beating or defeat to **b** : CHEAT 1, SWINDLE **3 a** : to make trim and neat especially by cutting or clipping **b** : to free of excess or unnecessary matter by or as if by cutting ⟨*trim* a budget⟩ **4 a** : to cause (a ship or boat) to assume a desirable position in the water by arrangement of ballast, cargo, or passengers; *also* : to adjust (as an airplane, blimp, or submarine) for horizontal movement or for motion upward or downward **b** : to adjust (as a sail) to a desired position **5** : to maintain neutrality between opposing parties [Old English *trymian* "to strengthen, arrange", from *trum* "strong, firm"]
²trim *adj* **trim•mer**; **trim•mest** : neat, orderly, and compact in line or structure — **trim•ly** *adv* — **trim•ness** *n*
³trim *adv* : TRIMLY
⁴trim *n* **1 a** : the readiness of a ship for sailing **b** : the readiness of a person or thing for action or use : FITNESS **2 a** : material used for ornament or trimming **b** : the woodwork in the finish of a building especially around openings **c** : the interior furnishings of an automobile **3 a** : the position of a ship or boat especially with reference to the horizontal **b** : the relation between the plane of a sail and the direction of the ship **4** : something that is trimmed off

tri•ma•ran \'trī-mə-ˌran, ˌtrī-mə-'\ *n* **:** a sailboat consisting of three hulls side by side [*tri-* + *-maran* (as in *catamaran*)]

tri•mes•ter \trī-'mes-tər, 'trī-ˌ\ *n* **1 :** a period of three or about three months **2 :** one of three terms into which an academic year is sometimes divided [French *trimestre,* from Latin *trimestris* "of 3 months", from *tri-* + *mensis* "month"] — **tri•mes•tral** \trī-'mes-trəl\ *adj* — **tri•mes•tri•al** \trī-'mes-trē-əl\ *adj*

trim•e•ter \'trim-ət-ər\ *n* **:** a line consisting of three metrical feet [Latin *trimetrus,* from Greek *trimetros* "having 3 measures", from *tri-* + *metron* "measure"]

trim•mer \'trim-ər\ *n* **1 a :** one that trims articles **b :** an instrument or machine with which trimming is done **2 :** a beam that holds the end of a header in floor framing **3 :** WEATHERCOCK 2

trim•ming \'trim-ing\ *n* **1 :** the action of one that trims **2 :** a severe defeat **3 :** something that trims, ornaments, or completes ⟨the *trimming* on a hat⟩ ⟨roast turkey and all the *trimmings*⟩ **4** *pl* **:** parts removed by trimming

tri•month•ly \trī-'mənth-lē, 'trī-, -'mənth-\ *adj* **:** occurring every three months

tri•mo•tor \'trī-ˌmōt-ər\ *n* **:** an airplane powered with three engines

trine \'trīn\ *adj* **:** THREEFOLD, TRIPLE [Middle French *trin,* from Latin *trinus,* from *trini* "three each"]

trin•i•tar•i•an \ˌtrin-ə-'ter-ē-ən\ *adj* **1** *cap* **:** of or relating to the Trinity, the doctrine of the Trinity, or adherents to that doctrine **2 :** having three parts or aspects

Trinitarian *n* **:** one who subscribes to the doctrine of the Trinity — **Trin•i•tar•i•an•ism** \-ē-ə-ˌniz-əm\ *n*

tri•ni•tro•tol•u•ene \ˌtrī-ˌnī-trō-'täl-yə-ˌwēn\ *n* **:** a flammable toxic compound $C_7H_5N_3O_6$ obtained by nitrating toluene and used as a high explosive and in chemical synthesis — called also *TNT*

Trin•i•ty \'trin-ət-ē\ *n, pl* **-ties 1 :** the unity of Father, Son, and Holy Spirit as three persons in one Godhead **2** *not cap* **:** TRIAD 1 **3 :** TRINITY SUNDAY [Old French *trinité,* from Late Latin *trinitas* "state of being threefold", from Latin *trinus* "threefold"]

Trinity Sunday *n* **:** the 8th Sunday after Easter

Trin•i•ty•tide \'trin-ət-ē-ˌtīd\ *n* **:** the season of the church year between Trinity Sunday and Advent

trin•ket \'tring-kət\ *n* **1 :** a small ornament (as a jewel or ring) **2 :** a thing of little value **:** TRIFLE [perhaps from Middle English *trenket* "small knife", from Old North French *trenquet*]

trin•ket•ry \'tring-kə-trē\ *n* **:** small items of personal ornament

[1]**tri•no•mi•al** \trī-'nō-mē-əl\ *n* **1 :** a polynomial of three terms **2 :** a biological taxonomic name consisting of three terms of which the first denotes the genus, the second the species, and the third the particular variety or subspecies named in full by the combination [*tri-* + *-nomial* (as in *binomial*)]

[2]**trinomial** *adj* **1 :** consisting of three terms **2 :** of or relating to trinomials

trio \'trē-ō\ *n, pl* **tri•os 1 a :** a musical composition for three voice parts or three instruments **b :** a dance by three people **c :** the performers of a musical or dance trio **2 :** a group or set of three [French, from Italian, from Latin *tri-, tres* "three"]

tri•ode \'trī-ˌōd\ *n* **:** a vacuum tube with three electrodes

tri•o•let \'trī-ə-lət, 'trē-\ *n* **:** a poem or stanza of eight lines in which the first line is repeated as the fourth and seventh and the second line as the eighth and which has a rhyme scheme of *ABaAabAB* [French]

tri•ose \'trī-ˌōs\ *n* **:** either of two monosaccharides containing three carbon atoms

tri•ox•ide \trī-'äk-ˌsīd, 'trī-\ *n* **:** an oxide containing three atoms of oxygen

[1]**trip** \'trip\ *vb* **tripped; trip•ping 1 a :** to move (as in dancing or walking) with light quick steps **b :** to perform (as a dance) lightly or nimbly **2 :** to catch one's foot while walking or running **:** cause to stumble **3 a :** to make or cause to make a mistake **:** SLIP, BLUNDER **b :** to catch in a misstep, fault, or blunder; *also* **:** EXPOSE **4 :** to put (as a mechanism) into operation usually by release of a catch or detent; *also* **:** to become operative [Middle French *triper,* of Germanic origin]

[2]**trip** *n* **1 :** an act of causing another to lose footing **2 a :** VOYAGE, JOURNEY ⟨a *trip* to Europe⟩ **b :** a single visit or round having a specific aim or recurring regularly ⟨a *trip* to the dentist's⟩ ⟨the milkman's daily *trip*⟩ **3 :** ERROR 4, MISSTEP **4 :** a quick light step **5 :** a faltering step **:** STUMBLE **6 a :** the action of tripping mechanically **b :** a device (as a catch) for tripping a mechanism **7 :** an intense sensory and especially visionary experience undergone by a person who has taken a psychedelic drug

tri•par•tite \trī-'pär-ˌtīt, 'trī-\ *adj* **1 :** having three parts **2 :** having three corresponding parts or copies **3 :** made between or involving three parties — **tri•par•tite•ly** *adv*

tripe \'trīp\ *n* **1 :** stomach tissue of a ruminant and especially of the ox for use as food **2 :** TRASH 1 [Old French]

trip–ham•mer \'trip-ˌham-ər\ *n* **:** a massive hammer raised by machinery and then tripped to fall on the work below

triph•thong \'trif-ˌthȯng, 'trip-\ *n* **1 :** a 3-element speech sound **2 :** TRIGRAPH [*tri-* + *-phthong* (as in *diphthong*)]

[1]**tri•ple** \'trip-əl\ *vb* **tri•pled; tri•pling** \'trip-ling, -ə-ling\ **1 :** to make or become three times as great or as many **:** multiply by three **2 :** to make a triple in baseball

[2]**triple** *n* **1 a :** a triple sum, quantity, or number **b :** a combination, group, or series of three **2 :** a base hit that enables the batter to reach third base

[3]**triple** *adj* **1 :** having three units or members **2 :** being three times as great or as many **3 :** three times repeated [Latin *triplus,* from *tri-* + *-plus* "-fold"]

triple jump *n* **:** a track-and-field event in which competitors jump for distance from a running start combining in succession a hop, a stride, and a jump

triple play *n* **:** a play in baseball by which three players are put out

triple point *n* **:** the condition of temperature and pressure under which the gaseous, liquid, and solid phases of a substance can exist in equilibrium

tri•ple–space \ˌtrip-əl-'spās\ *vb* **1 :** to type (copy) leaving two blank lines between lines of copy **2 :** to type on every third line

tri•plet \'trip-lət\ *n* **1 :** a unit of three lines of verse **2 :** a combination, set, or group of three **3 :** one of three offspring born at one birth **4 :** a group of three notes played in the time of two of the same value **5 :** CODON

[1]**tri•plex** \'trip-ˌleks, 'trī-ˌpleks\ *adj* **:** TRIPLE 1 [Latin, from *tri-* + *plex* "-fold"]

[2]**triplex** *n* **:** something that is triplex

[1]**trip•li•cate** \'trip-li-kət\ *adj* **:** having or being three corresponding or identical parts or examples [Latin *triplicatus,* past participle of *triplicare* "to triple", from *triplic-, triplex* "triplex"]

[2]**triplicate** *n* **1 :** one of three like things **2 :** three copies all alike

[3]**trip•li•cate** \-lə-ˌkāt\ *vt* **1 :** to make triple **2 :** to provide in triplicate — **trip•li•ca•tion** \ˌtrip-lə-'kā-shən\ *n*

trip•lo•blas•tic \ˌtrip-lō-'blas-tik\ *adj* **:** having three primary germ layers

trip•loid \'trip-ˌlȯid\ *adj* **:** having or being a chromosome number three times the monoploid number — **triploid** *n* — **trip•loi•dy** \-ˌlȯid-ē\ *n*

tri•ply \'trip-lē, -ə-lē\ *adv* **:** in a triple degree, amount, or manner

tri•pod \'trī-ˌpäd\ *n* **1 :** something (as a container or stool) resting on three legs **2 :** a three-legged stand (as for a camera) [Latin *tripod-, tripus,* from Greek *tripod-, tripous,* derived from *tri-* + *pod-, pous* "foot"] — **tripod** *or* **trip•o•dal** \'trip-əd-l, 'trī-ˌpäd-\ *adj*

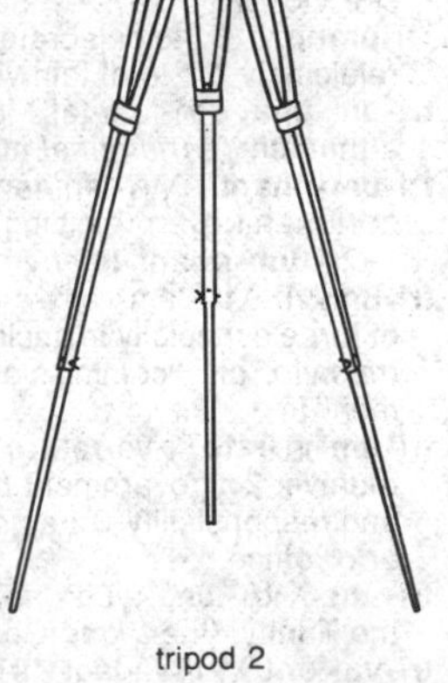

tripod 2

trip•per \'trip-ər\ *n* **1** *chiefly British* **:** EXCURSIONIST **2 :** a tripping device or mechanism

trip•ping•ly \'trip-ing-lē\ *adv* **1 :** in a nimble manner **2 :** in a fluent manner

trip•tych \'trip-tik, -ˌtik\ *n* **1 :** an ancient Roman writing tablet with three waxed leaves hinged together **2 :** a picture or carving in three panels side by side [Greek *triptychos* "having 3 folds", from *tri-* + *ptychē* "fold"]

tri•reme \'trī-ˌrēm\ *n* **:** an ancient galley having three banks of oars [Latin *triremis,* from *tri-* + *remus* "oar"]

\ə\ **abut**	\au̇\ **out**	\i\ **tip**	\ȯ\ **saw**	\u̇\ **foot**
\ər\ **further**	\ch\ **chin**	\ī\ **life**	\ȯi\ **coin**	\y\ **yet**
\a\ **mat**	\e\ **pet**	\j\ **job**	\th\ **thin**	\yü\ **few**
\ā\ **take**	\ē\ **easy**	\ng\ **sing**	\th\ **this**	\yu̇\ **cure**
\ä\ **cot, cart**	\g\ **go**	\ō\ **bone**	\ü\ **food**	\zh\ **vision**

tri•sac•cha•ride \trī-ˌsak-ə-ˌrīd, ˈtrī-\ *n* : any sugar that yields on complete hydrolysis three monosaccharide molecules

tri•sect \ˈtrī-ˌsekt, trī-ˈ\ *vt* : to divide into three usually equal parts [*tri-* + Latin *sectus,* past participle of *secare* "to cut"] — **tri•sec•tion** \ˈtrī-ˌsek-shən, trī-ˈ\ *n* — **tri•sec•tor** \ˈtrī-ˌsek-tər, trī-ˈ\ *n*

tri•so•di•um \ˌtrī-ˌsōd-ē-əm\ *adj* : containing three atoms of sodium in the molecule

tri•so•mic \trī-ˈsō-mik, ˈtrī-\ *adj* : having one or a few chromosomes triploid in an otherwise diploid set — **trisomic** *n* — **tri•so•my** \ˈtrī-ˌsō-mē\ *n*

triste \ˈtrēst\ *adj* : SAD, MOURNFUL; *also* : WISTFUL [French, from Latin *tristis*]

tri•syl•lab•ic \ˌtrī-sə-ˈlab-ik\ *adj* : having three syllables — **tri•syl•lab•i•cal•ly** \-ˈlab-i-kə-lē, -klē\ *adv* — **tri•syl•la•ble** \ˈtrī-ˌsil-ə-bəl, trī-ˈ, ˈtrī-ˈ\ *n*

trite \ˈtrīt\ *adj* : so common that the novelty has worn off : STALE, HACKNEYED ⟨a *trite* remark⟩ [Latin *tritus,* from *terere* "to rub, wear away"] — **trite•ly** *adv* — **trite•ness** *n*

• **syn** TRITE, HACKNEYED, STEREOTYPED, THREADBARE mean lacking freshness and power to interest or compel attention. TRITE applies to a once effective phrase or idea spoiled by long familiarity; HACKNEYED stresses being worn out by overuse so as to become dull and meaningless; STEREOTYPED implies falling invariably into the same pattern or form; THREADBARE applies to something that has been used so often it no longer can be interesting.

tri•ti•um \ˈtrit-ē-əm, ˈtrish-ē-\ *n* : a radioactive isotope of hydrogen with atoms of about three times the mass of ordinary light hydrogen atoms [New Latin, from Greek *tritos* "third"]

trit•o•ma \ˈtrit-ə-mə\ *n* : any of a genus of African herbs of the lily family often grown for their spikes of showy red or yellow flowers [New Latin, from Greek *tritomos* "cut thrice", from *tri-* + *temnein* "to cut"]

tri•ton \ˈtrīt-n\ *n* : any of various large sea snails with a heavy conical shell; *also* : this shell [*Triton,* son of Poseidon]

trit•u•rate \ˈtrich-ə-ˌrāt\ *vt* **1** : CRUSH 3, GRIND **2** : to reduce to a fine powder by rubbing or grinding [Late Latin *triturare* "to thresh", from Latin *tritura* "act of rubbing, threshing", from *tritus,* past participle of *terere* "to rub"] — **trit•u•ra•ble** \-rə-bəl\ *adj* — **trit•u•rate** \-rət\ *n* — **trit•u•ra•tion** \ˌtrich-ə-ˈrā-shən\ *n* — **trit•u•ra•tor** \ˈtrich-ə-ˌrāt-ər\ *n*

[1]**tri•umph** \ˈtrī-əmf, -əmpf\ *n* **1** : an ancient Roman ceremonial honoring a victorious general **2** : joy or exultation over victory or success **3 a** : a military victory or conquest **b** : a notable success [Middle French *triumphe,* from Latin *triumphus*] **syn** see VICTORY

[2]**triumph** *vi* **1** : to celebrate victory or success often boastfully or rejoicingly **2** : to obtain victory : PREVAIL, WIN

tri•um•phal \trī-ˈəm-fəl, -ˈəmp-\ *adj* : of, relating to, or used in a triumph ⟨a *triumphal* march⟩

tri•um•phant \trī-ˈəm-fənt, -ˈəmp-\ *adj* **1** : VICTORIOUS, CONQUERING **2** : rejoicing for or celebrating victory : EXULTANT — **tri•um•phant•ly** *adv*

tri•um•vir \trī-ˈəm-vər\ *n* : one of a commission or ruling body of three especially in ancient Rome [Latin, back-formation from *triumviri,* pl., "commission of 3 men", from *trium virum* "of 3 men"]

tri•um•vi•rate \-və-rət\ *n* **1** : the office or term of office of a triumvir **2** : government by three persons who share authority and responsibility **3** : a group of three persons who share power or office

tri•une \ˈtrī-ˌün, -ˌyün\ *adj* : three in one; *esp* : of or relating to the Trinity ⟨the *triune* God⟩ [Latin *tri-* + *unus* "one"]

tri•va•lent \trī-ˈvā-lənt, ˈtrī-\ *adj* : having a valence of three — **tri•va•lence** \-ləns\ *or* **tri•va•len•cy** \-lən-sē\ *n*

triv•et \ˈtriv-ət\ *n* **1** : a three-legged stand or support; *esp* : one for holding a kettle near the fire **2** : an ornamental metal plate on very short legs used under a hot dish to protect the table [Old English *trefet*]

triv•ia \ˈtriv-ē-ə\ *n sing or pl* : unimportant matters or facts [Latin, "crossroads", pl. of *trivium*]

triv•i•al \ˈtriv-ē-əl\ *adj* **1** : ORDINARY 2a, COMMONPLACE **2** : of little worth or importance : INSIGNIFICANT [Latin *trivialis* "found everywhere, commonplace, trivial", from *trivium* "crossroads", from *tri-* + *via* "way"] — **triv•i•al•ly** \-ē-ə-lē\ *adv*

triv•i•al•i•ty \ˌtriv-ē-ˈal-ət-ē\ *n, pl* **-ties** **1** : the quality or state of being trivial **2** : something trivial : TRIFLE

trivial name *n* **1** : the second term of a taxonomic binomial **2** : a common or vernacular name of an organism or chemical

[1]**tri•week•ly** \trī-ˈwē-klē, ˈtrī-\ *adj* **1** : occurring, appearing, or done three times a week **2** : occurring, appearing, or done every three weeks — **triweekly** *adv*

[2]**triweekly** *n* : a triweekly publication

-trix \triks, ˌtriks\ *n suffix, pl* **-tri•ces** \trə-ˌsēz, ˈtrī-sēz\ *or* **-trix•es** \trik-səz, ˌtrik-\ **1** : female that does or is associated with a (specified) thing ⟨avia*trix*⟩ **2** : geometric line, point, or surface ⟨genera*trix*⟩ [Latin, feminine of *-tor,* suffix denoting an agent]

tRNA \ˌtē-ˌär-ˌen-ˈā, ˈtē-ˌär-ˌen-ˌā\ *n* : TRANSFER RNA

tro•chan•ter \trō-ˈkant-ər\ *n* : a small segment immediately external to the coxa of the leg of an insect [Greek *trochantēr* "rough process at the upper part of the femur"]

tro•che \ˈtrō-kē, *British also* ˈtrōsh\ *n* : a usually circular medicinal tablet or lozenge used especially as a demulcent [earlier *trochisk,* from Late Latin *trochiscus,* from Greek *trochiskos,* from *trochos* "wheel", from *trechein* "to run"]

tro•chee \ˈtrō-ˌkē\ *n* : a metrical foot consisting of one accented syllable followed by one unaccented syllable (as in *hungry*) [French *trochée,* from Latin *trochaeus,* from Greek *trochaios,* derived from *trochē* "run, course", from *trechein* "to run"] — **tro•cha•ic** \trō-ˈkā-ik\ *adj*

troch•le•ar nerve \ˌträk-lē-ər-\ *n* : either of the 4th pair of cranial nerves which control movements of some of the eye muscles — called also *trochlear* [*trochlea* "anatomical structure resembling a pulley", from Latin, "block of pulleys", from Greek *trochileia*]

trocho•phore \ˈträk-ə-ˌfōr, -ˌfȯr\ *n* : a free-swimming ciliated larva typical of marine annelid worms but occurring also in several other invertebrate groups [derived from Greek *trochos* "wheel" + *pherein* "to carry"]

trod *past of* TREAD

trodden *past participle of* TREAD

trog•lo•dyte \ˈträg-lə-ˌdīt\ *n* : CAVEMAN 1; *also* : a person felt to resemble a troglodyte especially in unsocial habits [Latin *troglodytae,* pl., from Greek *trōglodytai,* from *trōglē* "hole, cave" + *dyein* "to enter"] — **trog•lo•dyt•ic** \ˌträg-lə-ˈdit-ik\ *adj*

troi•ka \ˈtrȯi-kə\ *n* **1** : a Russian vehicle drawn by three horses abreast; *also* : a team for such a vehicle **2** : a group of three [Russian *troĭka,* from *troe* "three"]

Tro•jan \ˈtrō-jən\ *n* **1** : a native or inhabitant of ancient Troy **2** : one who shows pluck, endurance, or determined energy [Latin *trojanus* "of Troy", from *Troia, Troja* "Troy", from Greek *Trōïa*] — **Trojan** *adj*

Trojan horse *n* : one intended to undermine or subvert from within [from the large hollow wooden horse filled with Greek soldiers and introduced within the walls of Troy by a stratagem during the Trojan War]

[1]**troll** \ˈtrōl\ *vb* **1 a** : to sing the parts of (as a round or catch) in succession **b** : to sing loudly or in a jovial way **2** : to speak or recite in a rolling voice **3** : to fish or fish for with a hook and line drawn through the water (as behind a slowly moving boat) [Middle English *trollen* "to roll"] — **troll•er** *n*

[2]**troll** *n* **1** : a lure or a line with its lure and hook used in trolling **2** : a song sung in parts successively : ROUND

[3]**troll** *n* : a dwarf or giant of Teutonic folklore inhabiting caves or hills [Norwegian *troll* and Danish *trold,* from Old Norse *troll* "giant, demon"]

trol•ley *or* **trol•ly** \ˈträl-ē\ *n, pl* **trolleys** *or* **trollies** **1 a** : a device for carrying current from a wire to an electrically driven vehicle **b** : TROLLEY CAR **2** : a wheeled carriage running on an overhead rail or track [probably from earlier *troll* "to roll", from Middle English *trollen*]

trolley bus *n* : a bus powered by electric power from two overhead wires

trolley car *n* : a streetcar that runs on tracks and gets its electric power through a trolley

trol•lop \ˈträl-əp\ *n* **1** : a slovenly woman : SLATTERN **2** : a loose woman : WANTON [probably from German dialect *trolle*]

trom•bone \träm-ˈbōn, trəm-, ˌtram-\ *n* : a brass wind instrument that has a cupped mouthpiece, that consists of a long cylindrical metal tube bent twice upon itself and ending in a bell, and that has a movable slide with which to vary the pitch [Italian, from *tromba* "trumpet", of Germanic origin] — **trom•bon•ist** \-ˈbō-nəst\ *n*

-tron \ˌträn\ *n suffix* **1** : vacuum tube **2** : device for the manipulation of subatomic particles ⟨cyclo*tron*⟩ [Greek, suffix denoting an instrument]

[1]troop \'trüp\ *n* **1 a** : a group of soldiers **b** : a cavalry unit corresponding to an infantry company **c** *pl* : armed forces **2** : a collection of beings or things : COMPANY **3** : a unit of boy or girl scouts under a leader [Middle French *troupe* "company, herd", of Germanic origin]

[1]trombone

[2]troop *vi* **1** : to move or gather in crowds **2** : ASSOCIATE 1 ⟨a dove *trooping* with crows⟩

troop•er \'trü-pər\ *n* **1** : an enlisted member of a cavalry unit **2 a** : a mounted police officer **b** : a state police officer

troop•ship \'trüp-,ship\ *n* : a ship for carrying troops : TRANSPORT

trop- *or* **tropo-** *combining form* : turn : turning : change ⟨*tro*pism⟩ ⟨*tropo*sphere⟩ [Greek *tropos*, from *trepein* "to turn"]

trope \'trōp\ *n* : the use of a word or expression in a figurative sense : FIGURE OF SPEECH [Latin *tropus*, from Greek *tropos* "turn, way, trope"]

tro•phic \'trō-fik\ *adj* **1** : of or relating to nutrition : NUTRITIONAL ⟨*trophic* disorders⟩ **2** : [3]TROPIC [French *trophique*, from Greek *trophikos*, from *trophē* "nourishment", from *trephein* "to nourish"] — **tro•phi•cal•ly** \-fi-kə-lē, -klē\ *adv*

tro•phy \'trō-fē\ *n, pl* **trophies** **1 a** : a memorial of an ancient Greek or Roman victory raised on the field of battle **b** : a representation of such a memorial (as on a medal) **2** : something won or given in victory or conquest especially when preserved or mounted as a memorial **3** : MEMENTO [Middle French *trophee*, from Latin *tropaeum, trophaeum*, from Greek *trepaion*, derived from *tropē* "turn, rout", from *trepein* "to turn"] — **trophied** \-fēd\ *adj*

-tro•phy \trə-fē\ *n combining form, pl* **-trophies** : nutrition : nurture : growth ⟨hyper*trophy*⟩ [Greek *-trophia*, from *trephein* "to nourish"]

[1]trop•ic \'träp-ik\ *n* **1** : either of the two parallels of the earth's latitude that are approximately 23½ degrees north of the equator and approximately 23½ degrees south of the equator **2** *pl, often cap* : the region lying between the two tropics [Latin *tropicus* "of the solstice", from Greek *tropikos*, from *tropē* "turn"; from the fact that their projections on the celestial sphere mark the sun's declination at the solstices]

[2]tropic *adj* : of, relating to, or occurring in the tropics : TROPICAL

[3]tro•pic \'trō-pik\ **1** : of, relating to, or characteristic of tropism or of a tropism **2** *of a hormone* : influencing the activity of a specified gland

trop•i•cal *for 1* 'träp-i-kəl, *for 2* 'trōp- *also* 'träp-\ *adj* **1** : of, located in, or used in the tropics **2** : FIGURATIVE 2 — **trop•i•cal•ly** \-kə-lē, -klē\ *adv*

tropical aquarium *n* : an aquarium kept at a uniform warmth and used especially for tropical fish

tropical cyclone *n* : a cyclone in the tropics usually characterized by winds rotating at the rate of 75 miles (about 120 kilometers) an hour or more

tropical fish *n* : any of various small usually showy fishes of exotic origin often kept in the tropical aquarium

tropical storm *n* : a tropical cyclone with strong winds of less than hurricane intensity

tropic bird *n* : any of several web-footed oceanic birds related to the gannets that are mostly white with a little black and a very long central pair of tail feathers

tropic of Cancer : the parallel of latitude that is approximately 23½ degrees north of the equator and is the northernmost latitude reached by the overhead sun [from the sign of the zodiac which its celestial projection intersects]

tropic of Capricorn : the parallel of latitude that is approximately 23½ degrees south of the equator and is the southernmost latitude reached by the overhead sun [from the sign of the zodiac which its celestial projection intersects]

tro•pism \'trō-,piz-əm\ *n* : involuntary orientation by an organism or one of its parts that involves turning or curving and is a positive or negative response to a source of stimulation; *also* : a reflex reaction involving such movement [Greek *tropos* "turn", from *trepein* "to turn"] — **tro•pis•tic** \trō-'pis-tic\ *adj*

tro•po•pause \'trōp-ə-,pȯz, 'träp-\ *n* : the region at the top of the troposphere

tro•po•sphere \'trōp-ə-,sfiər, 'träp-\ *n* : the portion of the atmosphere which is below the stratosphere, which extends outward about 11 to 16 kilometers from the earth's surface, and in which generally temperature decreases rapidly with altitude and clouds form [Greek *tropos* "turn"] — **tro•po•spher•ic** \,trōp-ə-'sfiər-ik, ,träp-, -'sfer-\ *adj*

[1]trot \'trät\ *n* **1 a** (1) : a moderately fast gait of a four-footed animal (as a horse) in which the legs move in diagonal pairs (2) : a jogging gait of humans that falls between a walk and a run **b** : a ride on horseback **2** : PONY 3 [Middle French, from *troter* "to trot", of Germanic origin]

[2]trot *vb* **trot•ted**; **trot•ting** **1 a** : to ride, drive, or go at a trot **b** : to cause to go at a trot **2** : to proceed briskly : HURRY

[1]troth \'träth, 'trȯth, 'trōth *or with* th\ *n* **1** : loyal or pledged faithfulness : FIDELITY **2** : one's pledged word; *also* : BETROTHAL [Old English *trēowth*]

[2]troth *vt* : BETROTH, PLEDGE

trot out *vt* : to bring forward for display

Trots•ky•ism \'trät-skē-,iz-əm, 'trȯt-\ *n* : the Communist principles developed by or associated with Leon Trotsky and usually including adherence to the concept of worldwide revolution — **Trots•ky•ist** \-skē-əst\ *n or adj* — **Trots•ky•ite** \-skē-,īt\ *n or adj*

trot•ter \'trät-ər\ *n* : one that trots; *esp* : a standardbred horse trained for harness racing

trou•ba•dour \'trü-bə-,dōr, -,dȯr, -,důr\ *n* : a poet-musician of medieval France and Italy [French, from Provençal *trobador*, from *trobar* "to compose"]

[1]trou•ble \'trəb-əl\ *vb* **trou•bled**; **trou•bling** \'trəb-ling, -ə-ling\ **1 a** : to agitate or become agitated mentally or spiritually : WORRY, DISTURB **b** : to produce physical disorder in : AFFLICT ⟨*troubled* with deafness⟩ **c** : to put to exertion or inconvenience ⟨may I *trouble* you for the salt⟩ **2** : to put into confused motion ⟨wind *troubled* the sea⟩ **3** : to make an effort : take pains ⟨do not *trouble* to come⟩ [Old French *tourbler, troubler*, derived from Latin *turbidare*, from *turbidus* "turbid, troubled"]

[2]trouble *n* **1 a** : the quality or state of being troubled : MISFORTUNE ⟨help people in *trouble*⟩ **b** : an instance of distress or annoyance **2 a** : civil disorder or agitation ⟨labor *trouble*⟩ **b** : an effort made : PAIN 4 ⟨took the *trouble* to call⟩ **c** (1) : a condition of physical distress (2) : DISEASE, AILMENT (3) : MALFUNCTION ⟨engine *trouble*⟩ ⟨*trouble* with the plumbing⟩ **d** : a personal characteristic that is a handicap or a source of distress ⟨laziness is your *trouble*⟩ **e** : a troubling thing ⟨the *trouble* is that you're wrong⟩ **syn** see EFFORT

trou•ble•mak•er \'trəb-əl-,mā-kər\ *n* : a person who causes dissension

trou•ble•shoot•er \-,shüt-ər\ *n* **1** : a skilled worker employed to locate trouble and make repairs in machinery and technical equipment **2** : one that is expert in resolving disputes or problems — **trou•ble•shoot** \-,shüt\ *vb*

trou•ble•some \'trəb-əl-səm\ *adj* **1** : giving trouble or anxiety : VEXATIOUS ⟨a *troublesome* infection⟩ **2** : DIFFICULT 2a, BURDENSOME — **trou•ble•some•ly** *adv* — **trou•ble•some•ness** *n*

trou•blous \'trəb-ləs, -ə-ləs\ *adj* **1 a** : full of trouble ⟨*troublous* times⟩ **b** : STORMY ⟨*troublous* seas⟩ **2** : that disturbs or troubles ⟨*troublous* dreams⟩ — **trou•blous•ly** *adv* — **trou•blous•ness** *n*

trough \'trȯf, 'trȯth\ *n, pl* **troughs** \'trȯfs, 'trȯvz, 'trȯths, 'trȯthz, 'trȯz\ **1 a** : a long shallow often V-shaped receptacle for the drinking water or feed of domestic animals **b** : any of various domestic or industrial containers **2 a** : a conduit, drain, or channel for water; *esp* : a gutter along the eaves **b** : a long and narrow or shallow depression (as between waves or hills) **3** : the low point in a cycle; *esp* : an elongated area of low barometric pressure [Old English *trog*]

trounce \'trau̇ns\ *vt* : to thrash or punish severely: as **a** : FLOG, CUDGEL **b** : to defeat decisively [origin unknown]

[1]troupe \'trüp\ *n* : COMPANY, TROOP; *esp* : a group of stage performers [Middle French, of Germanic origin]

²troupe *vi* : to travel in a troupe; *also* : to perform as a member of a stage troupe — **troup•er** *n*

trou•sers \'trau̇-zərz\ *n pl* : PANTS 1 [earlier *trouse*, from Scottish Gaelic *triubhas*]

trous•seau \'trü-,sō\ *n, pl* **trous•seaux** \-,sōz\ *or* **trous•seaus** : the personal possessions of a bride [French, from *trousse* "bundle", from *trousser* "to truss"]

trout \'trau̇t\ *n, pl* **trout** *also* **trouts 1** : any of various food and sport fishes mostly smaller than the related salmons and restricted to cool clear fresh waters **2** : any of various fishes felt to resemble the true trouts — compare SEA TROUT [Old English *trūht*, from Late Latin *trocta, tructa*, a kind of fish with sharp teeth, from Greek *trōktēs*, literally, "gnawer", from *trōgein* "to gnaw"]

trout lily *n* : DOGTOOTH VIOLET [probably from its speckled leaves]

trove \'trōv\ *n* **1** : DISCOVERY 2, FIND **2** : a valuable collection : TREASURE; *also* : HAUL 2a [short for *treasure trove*]

trow \'trō\ *vb* **1** *obsolete* : BELIEVE 2, 3, TRUST **2** *archaic* : THINK 3, SUPPOSE [Old English *trēowan*]

¹trow•el \'trau̇-əl, 'trau̇l\ *n* **1** : a small hand tool consisting of a flat blade with a handle used for spreading and smoothing mortar or plaster **2** : a small hand tool with a curved blade used by gardeners [Middle French *truelle*, from Late Latin *truella*, derived from Latin *trua* "ladle"]

²trowel *vt* **-eled** *or* **-elled**; **-el•ing** *or* **-el•ling** : to smooth, mix, or apply with a trowel

troy \'trȯi\ *adj* : expressed in troy weight [*Troyes*, France]

troy weight *n* : a series of units of weight based on a pound of 12 ounces and the ounce of 20 pennyweights or 480 grains — see MEASURE table

tru•ant \'trü-ənt\ *n* : one who shirks duty; *esp* : one who stays out of school without permission [Old French, "vagrant", of Celtic origin] — **tru•an•cy** \-ən-sē\ *n* — **truant** *adj*

truant officer *n* : one employed by a public-school system to investigate cases of truancy

truce \'trüs\ *n* **1** : a temporary interruption of fighting by mutual agreement of the combatants : ARMISTICE **2** : a temporary rest especially from a disagreeable state or activity [Middle English *trewes*, pl. of *trewe* "agreement", from Old English *trēow* "fidelity"]

¹truck \'trək\ *vb* : to exchange goods : BARTER [Old French *troquer*]

²truck *n* **1** : BARTER **2** : goods for barter or for small trade **3** : close association : TRAFFIC **4** : payment of wages in goods instead of cash **5** : vegetables grown for market **6** : small articles of little value; *also* : RUBBISH

³truck *n* **1** : a small wooden cap at the top of a flagpole or mast **2** : a vehicle (as a small flat-topped car on wheels, a two-wheeled barrow with long handles, or a strong heavy wagon or automobile) for carrying heavy articles **3 a** : a swiveling carriage with springs and one or more pairs of wheels used to carry an end of a railroad car or a locomotive **b** : a short heavy-duty automotive vehicle equipped with a swiveling device for hauling a trailer; *also* : a truck with attached trailer [probably from Latin *trochus* "iron hoop", from Greek *trochos* "wheel"]

⁴truck *vb* **1** : to transport on or by truck **2** : to be employed as a truck driver

truck•age \'trək-ij\ *n* **1** : money paid for hauling on a truck **2** : carriage by truck

truck•er \'trək-ər\ *n* **1** : one whose business is transporting goods by truck **2** : a truck driver

truck farm *n* : a farm growing vegetables for market — **truck farmer** *n*

truck•ing \'trək-ing\ *n* : the process or business of transporting goods on trucks

truck•le \'trək-əl\ *vi* **truck•led**; **truck•ling** \'trək-ling, -ə-ling\ : to act in a servile way : yield to the will of another : SUBMIT ⟨*truckle* to a conqueror⟩ [from the lower position of the truckle bed] — **truck•ler** \-lər, -ə-lər\ *n*

truckle bed *n* : TRUNDLE BED [Middle English *trocle* "small wheel, pulley", from Latin *trochlea* "block of pulleys"]

truck•line \'trək-,līn\ *n* : a carrier using trucks and related freight vehicles

truck•man \'trək-mən\ *n* **1** : TRUCKER **2** : a member of a fire department unit that operates a ladder truck

truck system *n* : the system of paying wages in goods instead of cash

truc•u•lent \'trək-yə-lənt *also* 'trük-\ *adj* **1** : feeling or displaying ferocity : CRUEL, SAVAGE **2** : DESTRUCTIVE, DEADLY **3** : very bitter and harsh **4** : AGGRESSIVE, BELLIGERENT [Latin *truculentus*, from *truc-, trux* "fierce"] — **truc•u•lence** \-ləns\ *also* **truc•u•len•cy** \-lən-sē\ *n* — **truc•u•lent•ly** *adv*

¹trudge \'trəj\ *vb* **1** : to walk or march steadily and usually laboriously **2** : to walk or march along or over [origin unknown] — **trudg•er** *n*

²trudge *n* : a long tiring walk : TRAMP

trud•gen stroke \'trəj-ən-\ *n* : a swimming stroke in which a double overarm motion is combined with a scissors kick [John *Trudgen*, 19th century English swimmer]

¹true \'trü\ *adj* **1** : STEADFAST 2, LOYAL **2** *archaic* : TRUTHFUL **3** : that can be relied on : CERTAIN **4 a** : corresponding to fact or actuality : ACCURATE, CORRECT **b** : logically necessary **5** : SINCERE ⟨*true* friendship⟩ **6** : properly so called : GENUINE ⟨lichens have no *true* stems⟩ ⟨whales are *true* but not typical mammals⟩; *also* : TYPICAL ⟨the *true* cats⟩ **7** : that is fitted or formed or that functions accurately **8** : RIGHTFUL, LEGITIMATE ⟨the *true* owner⟩ ⟨our *true* ruler⟩ **9** : determined with reference to the earth's axis rather than the magnetic poles ⟨*true* north⟩ [Old English *trēowe*] **syn** see REAL — **true•ness** *n*

²true *n* **1** : TRUTH 2a(1), REALITY — usually used with *the* **2** : the quality or state of being accurate (as in alignment or adjustment) — used in the phrases *in true* and *out of true*

³true *vt* **trued**; **true•ing** *also* **tru•ing** : to make level, square, balanced, or concentric : bring to desired mechanical accuracy or form

⁴true *adv* **1** : in a truthful manner **2 a** : TRULY 3 ⟨the bullet flew straight and *true*⟩ **b** : without variation from type ⟨breed *true*⟩

true bill *n* : a bill of indictment endorsed by a grand jury as justifying prosecution of the accused

true–blue \'trü-'blü\ *adj* : marked by unswerving loyalty (as to a party)

true•born \-,bȯrn\ *adj* : genuinely such by birth ⟨a *trueborn* American⟩

true bug *n* : BUG 1b

true discount *n* : the interest discounted in advance on a note and computed on the principal of the note — compare BANK DISCOUNT

true–false test *n* : a test consisting of a series of statements to be marked as true or false

true•heart•ed \'trü-'härt-əd\ *adj* : STEADFAST 2, LOYAL

true–life \,trü-,līf\ *adj* : true to life ⟨a *true-life* story⟩

true•love \'trü-,ləv\ *n* : one truly beloved or loving : SWEETHEART

true lover's knot *n* : a complicated ornamental knot not easily untied and symbolic of mutual love — called also *truelove knot*

true rib *n* : one of the ribs connected directly with the sternum by cartilages and in human beings constituting the first seven pairs

truf•fle \'trəf-əl, 'trüf-\ *n* : the usually dark wrinkled edible subterranean fruiting body of a European fungus; also : this fungus [Middle French *truffe*, from Provençal *trufa*, derived from Latin *tuber* "tuber, truffle"]

tru•ism \'trü-,iz-əm\ *n* : an obvious truth — **tru•is•tic** \trü-'is-tik\ *adj*

trull \'trəl\ *n* : TROLLOP 2, STRUMPET [obsolete German *trulle*]

tru•ly \'trü-lē\ *adv* **1** : SINCERELY — often used in a letter as a complimentary close after *yours* **2** : ⁴TRUE 1 **3** : with exactness of construction or operation : ACCURATELY 4a : INDEED — often used as an intensive ⟨*truly*, you are nice⟩ or interjectionally to express astonishment or doubt **b** : without pretense : GENUINELY **5** : as it ought to be

¹trump \'trəmp\ *n* **1** : TRUMPET 1 **2** : a sound of trumpeting [Old French *trompe*]

²trump *n* **1 a** : a card of a suit whose cards will win over any card of any other suit **b** : the suit whose cards are trumps for a particular hand — often used in pl. **2** : a dependable and exemplary person [alteration of ¹*triumph*]

³trump *vb* **1** : to take with a trump ⟨*trump* a trick⟩ **2** : to play a trump **3** : to get the better of : OUTDO

trumped–up \'trəm-'təp, 'trəmp-\ *adj* : MADE-UP 2, SPURIOUS ⟨*trumped-up* charges⟩

trum•pery \'trəm-pə-rē, -prē\ *n, pl* **-per•ies 1 a** : trivial or useless articles : JUNK **b** : worthless nonsense **2** *archaic* : tawdry finery [Middle French *tromperie* "deceit", from *tromper* "to deceive"] — **trumpery** *adj*

¹trum•pet \'trəm-pət\ *n* **1** : a wind instrument consisting of a long cylindrical metal tube commonly once or twice curved and ending in a bell **2** : a trumpet player **3** : something that resembles a trumpet or its tonal quality: as **a** : a funnel-shaped instrument (as a megaphone) for collecting, directing, or intensifying sound ⟨an ear *trumpet*⟩ **b** (1) : a very loud voice (2) : a penetrating cry (as of an elephant) [Middle French *trompette,* from Old French *trompe*] — **trum•pet•like** \-ˌlīk\ *adj*

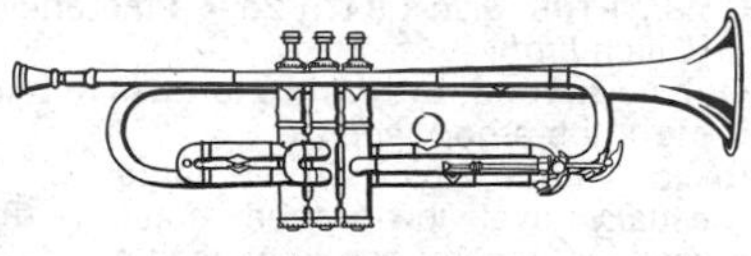

[1]trumpet 1

[2]trumpet *vb* **1** : to blow a trumpet **2** : to sound or proclaim on or as if on a trumpet ⟨*trumpeted* the news⟩ **3** : to make a sound similar to that of a trumpet

trumpet creeper *n* : a North American woody vine with pinnate leaves and large red trumpet-shaped flowers — called also *trumpet vine*

trum•pet•er \'trəm-pət-ər\ *n* **1** : a trumpet player; *esp* : one that gives signals with a trumpet **2 a** : a rare pure white North American wild swan noted for its sonorous voice **b** : any of an Asian breed of pigeons with a rounded crest and heavily feathered feet

trump up *vt* **1** : to concoct especially with intent to deceive : FABRICATE, INVENT ⟨*trump up* false charges⟩ **2** *archaic* : to cite as support for an action or claim : ALLEGE

trun•cate \'trəng-ˌkāt, 'trən-\ *vt* : to shorten by or as if by cutting off [Latin *truncare,* from *truncus* "trunk"] — **trun•ca•tion** \ˌtrəng-'kā-shən, ˌtrən-\ *n*

trun•cat•ed \-ˌkāt-əd\ *adj* **1** : having the apex replaced by a plane section and especially by one parallel to the base ⟨a *truncated* cone⟩ **2 a** : cut short **b** : lacking an expected or normal element (as a syllable) at beginning or end

[1]trun•cheon \'trən-chən\ *n* **1** : a shattered spear or lance **2 a** *obsolete* : CLUB 1a, BLUDGEON **b** : BATON 1 **c** : a police officer's club : BILLY [Middle French *tronchon,* derived from Latin *truncus* "trunk"]

[2]truncheon *vt, archaic* : to beat with a truncheon

[1]trun•dle \'trən-dl\ *n* **1** : a small wheel or roller **2** : a low-wheeled cart or truck [Old English *trendel* "circle, ring, wheel"]

[2]trundle *vb* **trun•dled**; **trun•dling** \'trən-dling, -dl-ing\ **1 a** : to propel by causing to rotate : ROLL ⟨*trundled* a wheelbarrow⟩ **b** : to progress by revolving **2** : to transport in a wheeled vehicle — **trun•dler** \-dlər, -dl-ər\ *n*

trundle bed *n* : a low bed usually on casters that can be slid under a higher bed — called also *truckle bed*

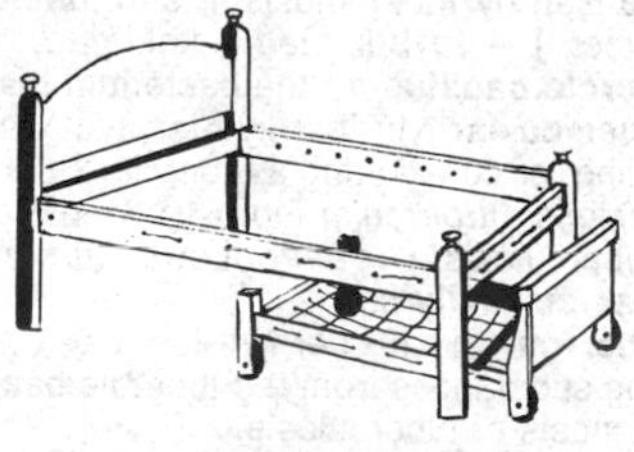

trundle bed

trunk \'trəngk\ *n* **1 a** : the main stem of a tree apart from branches or roots **b** : the body of a person or lower animal apart from the head and limbs **c** : the main or basal part of something ⟨the *trunk* of an artery⟩ **2 a** : a box or chest for holding clothes or other goods especially for traveling **b** : the enclosed space usually in the rear of an automobile for carrying articles (as luggage) **3** : the long flexible muscular nose of an elephant; *also* : PROBOSCIS **4** : TRUNK LINE [Middle French *tronc,* from Latin *truncus* "tree trunk, torso"]

trunk hose *n pl* : short full breeches reaching about halfway down the thigh worn chiefly in the late 16th and early 17th centuries

trunk line *n* **1** : a system handling long-distance through traffic **2 a** : a main supply channel **b** : a direct link

trun•nion \'trən-yən\ *n* : PIVOT 1, PIN; *esp* : either of two opposite projections on which a cannon is supported and elevated [French *trognon* "core, stump"]

[1]truss \'trəs\ *vt* **1 a** : to secure tightly : BIND ⟨they *trussed* up their victim⟩ **b** : to arrange for cooking by binding close the wings or legs of ⟨*truss* a turkey⟩ **2** : to support, strengthen, or stiffen by a truss [Old French *trousser*] — **truss•er** *n*

[2]truss *n* **1** : a rigid framework of beams, bars, or rods ⟨a *truss* for a roof⟩ **2** : a device worn to hold a hernia in place

truss bridge *n* : a bridge supported mainly by trusses

[1]trust \'trəst\ *n* **1 a** : assured reliance on the character, ability, strength, or truth of someone or something **b** : one in which confidence is placed **2 a** : dependence on something future or contingent : HOPE **b** : reliance on future payment for goods delivered : CREDIT **3 a** : a legal right or interest in property that one does not actually own ⟨income received under a *trust* established by their parents⟩ **b** : property held or managed by one person or concern (as a bank or trust company) for the benefit of another **c** : a combination of firms or corporations formed by a legal agreement; *esp* : one that reduces or threatens to reduce competition **4 a** : something (as a public office) committed to one to be used or cared for in the interest of another **b** : responsible charge or office **c** : CUSTODY, CARE [Middle English] **syn** see MONOPOLY — **in trust** : in the care or possession of a trustee

[2]trust *vb* **1 a** : to place confidence : DEPEND ⟨*trust* in God⟩ ⟨*trust* to luck⟩ **b** : to be confident : HOPE **2** : to commit or place in one's care or keeping : ENTRUST **3 a** : to rely on the truthfulness or accuracy of : BELIEVE **b** : to place confidence in : rely on **c** : to hope or expect confidently ⟨*trusted* to find oil on the land⟩ **4 a** : to sell or deliver on credit **b** : to extend credit to — **trust•er** *n*

trust•bust•er \'trəst-ˌbəs-tər\ *n* : one that seeks to break up business trusts; *esp* : a federal official who prosecutes trusts under the antitrust laws — **trust–bust•ing** \-ting\ *n*

trust company *n* : a corporation and especially a bank organized to perform fiduciary functions

trust•ee \ˌtrəs-'tē\ *n* **1** : a person to whom property is legally committed in trust **2** : a country charged with the supervision of a trust territory

trust•ee•ship \-ˌship\ *n* **1** : the office or function of a trustee **2** : supervisory control by one or more countries over a trust territory

trust•ful \'trəst-fəl\ *adj* : full of trust : CONFIDING — **trust•ful•ly** \-fə-lē\ *adv* — **trust•ful•ness** *n*

trust fund *n* : property (as money or securities) settled or held in trust

trust•ing \'trəs-ting\ *adj* : having trust, faith, or confidence : TRUSTFUL — **trust•ing•ly** \-ting-lē\ *adv*

trust territory *n* : a non-self-governing territory placed under an administrative authority by the Trusteeship Council of the United Nations

trust•wor•thy \'trəst-ˌwər-t͟hē\ *adj* : worthy of confidence : DEPENDABLE — **trust•wor•thi•ly** \-t͟hə-lē\ *adv* — **trust•wor•thi•ness** \-t͟hē-nəs\ *n*

[1]trusty \'trəs-tē\ *adj* **trust•i•er**; **-est** : TRUSTWORTHY

[2]trusty \'trəs-tē, ˌtrəs-'tē\ *n, pl* **trust•ies** : a trusty or trusted person; *esp* : a convict considered trustworthy and allowed special privileges

truth \'trüth\ *n, pl* **truths** \'trü͟thz, 'trüths\ **1 a** *archaic* : FIDELITY 1a, CONSTANCY **b** : sincerity in action, character, and utterance **2** : something that is real or true: as **a** (1) : the real state of things : FACT (2) : the body of real things, events, and facts : ACTUALITY **b** (1) : a judgment, proposition, idea, or statement that is true or accepted as true ⟨the *truths* of science⟩ (2) : the body of such truths **3** : the property of being in accord with what is, has been, or must be [Old English *trēowth* "fidelity"] — **in truth** : in fact : ACTUALLY

truth•ful \'trüth-fəl\ *adj* : telling or inclined to tell the truth — **truth•ful•ly** \-fə-lē\ *adv* — **truth•ful•ness** *n*

truth serum *n* : a hypnotic or anesthetic held to induce a subject under questioning to talk freely

truth set *n* : a set of the elements that can be substituted to make a set of open sentences true

[1]try \'trī\ *vb* **tried**; **try•ing** **1 a** : to examine or investigate judicially **b** : to conduct the trial of **2 a** : to put to test or trial **b** : to test to the limit or breaking point : STRAIN ⟨*try one's* patience⟩ **3** : to melt down and obtain in a pure state : RENDER ⟨*try* lard from fat pork⟩ **4** : to make an attempt : ENDEAVOR [Anglo-French *trier,* from Old French, "to pick out, sift"]

\ə\ **abut**	\au̇\ **out**	\i\ **tip**	\ȯ\ **saw**	\u̇\ **foot**
\ər\ **further**	\ch\ **chin**	\ī\ **life**	\ȯi\ **coin**	\y\ **yet**
\a\ **mat**	\e\ **pet**	\j\ **job**	\th\ **thin**	\yü\ **few**
\ā\ **take**	\ē\ **easy**	\ng\ **sing**	\t͟h\ **this**	\yu̇\ **cure**
\ä\ **cot, cart**	\g\ **go**	\ō\ **bone**	\ü\ **food**	\zh\ **vision**

• **syn** ATTEMPT, STRIVE: TRY suggests effort or experiment made in the hope of determining facts or of testing or proving something ⟨*tried* various occupations⟩ ATTEMPT suggests a beginning of or venturing upon something and often implies failure ⟨*attempted* to break through the enemy lines⟩ STRIVE implies great exertion against great difficulty and suggests persistent effort ⟨*strive* to achieve lasting peace⟩ — **try one's hand :** to attempt something for the first time

²try *n, pl* **tries :** an experimental trial **:** ATTEMPT

try for point : an attempt made after scoring a touchdown in football to kick a goal so as to score an additional point or to again carry the ball across the opponents' goal line or complete a forward pass in the opponents' end zone so as to score one or two additional points

try•ing \ˈtrī-iŋ\ *adj* **:** causing distress or annoyance

try on \trī-ˈȯn, ˈtrī-, -ˈän\ *vt* **:** to put on (a garment) in order to test the fit — **try–on** \ˈtrī-ˌȯn, -ˌän\ *n*

try•out \ˈtrī-ˌau̇t\ *n* **:** an experimental performance or demonstration: as **a :** a testing of one's ability to perform especially as an athlete or actor **b :** a test performance of a play before its formal opening

try out \trī-ˈau̇t, ˈtrī-\ *vi* **:** to compete for a position especially on an athletic team or for a part in a play

try•pano•so•ma \trip-ˌan-ə-ˈsō-mə\ *n* **:** TRYPANOSOME

try•pano•some \trip-ˈan-ə-ˌsōm\ *n* **:** any of a genus of parasitic flagellate protozoans that invade the blood of various vertebrates including man, are usually transmitted by the bite of an insect, and include causers of serious disease (as sleeping sickness) [New Latin *Trypanosoma,* genus name, from Greek *trypanon* "auger" + *sōma* "body"]

try•pano•so•mi•a•sis \trip-ˌan-ə-sə-ˈmī-ə-səs\ *n, pl* **-a•ses** \-ə-ˌsēz\ **:** infection with or disease caused by trypanosomes

tryp•sin \ˈtrip-sən\ *n* **:** an enzyme from pancreatic juice that breaks down protein in an alkaline medium [Greek *tryein* "to wear down" + English *-psin* (as in *pepsin*)] — **tryp•tic** \ˈtrip-tik\ *adj*

tryp•sin•o•gen \trip-ˈsin-ə-jən\ *n* **:** the inactive form of trypsin present in the pancreas

tryp•to•phan \ˈtrip-tə-ˌfan\ *or* **tryp•to•phane** \-ˌfān\ *n* **:** a crystalline amino acid that is widely distributed in protein and that is essential to animal life [derived from *trypsin* + Greek *phanēs* "appearing", from *phainein* "to show"]

try square *n* **:** an instrument used for laying off right angles and testing whether work is square

tryst \ˈtrist, *especially British* ˈtrīst\ *n* **1 :** an agreement (as between lovers) to meet **2 :** an appointed meeting or meeting place [Old French *triste* "watch post"]

tsar \ˈzär, ˈtsär, ˈsär\ *variant of* CZAR

tset•se \ˈset-sē, ˈtset-, ˈsēt-, ˈtsēt-, ˈtēt-\ *n, pl* **tsetse** *or* **tseses :** any of a genus of two-winged flies mostly of Africa south of the Sahara desert that include vectors of human and animal trypanosomes — called also *tsetse fly* [Afrikaans, of Bantu origin]

T–shirt \ˈtē-ˌshərt\ *n* **:** a collarless short-sleeved cotton undershirt for men; *also* **:** a jersey outer shirt of similar design [from its being shaped like a T]

T square *n* **:** a ruler with a crosspiece or head at one end used in making parallel lines

tsu•na•mi \su̇-ˈnäm-ē, tsu̇-\ *n* **:** TIDAL WAVE 1a [Japanese] — **tsu•na•mic** \-ˈnäm-ik\ *adj*

tsu•tsu•ga•mu•shi disease \ˌsüt-sə-gə-ˈmü-shē-, ˌtsüt-, ˌtüt-, -ˈgäm-ü-shē-\ *n* **:** SCRUB TYPHUS [Japanese *tsutsugamushi* "scrub typhus mite", from *tsutsuga* "sickness" + *mushi* "insect"]

Tua•reg \ˈtwä-ˌreg\ *n* **:** a member of the dominant nomadic people of the central and western Sahara and the Middle Niger [Arabic *Tawāriq*]

tu•a•ta•ra \ˌtü-ə-ˈtär-ə\ *n* **:** a large spiny four-footed reptile of islands off the coast of New Zealand that has a vestigial third eye and is the only survivor of a once widely distributed order [Maori *tuatàra*]

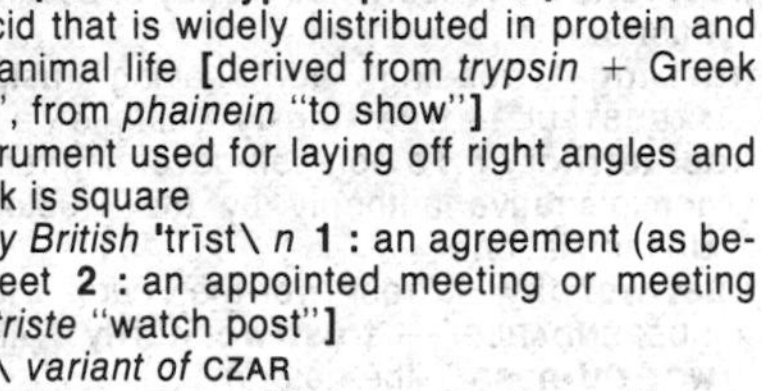

tuatara

¹tub \ˈtəb\ *n* **1 :** a wide low vessel originally formed with wooden staves, round bottom, and hoops **2 :** an old or slow boat **3 :** BATHTUB; *also* **:** BATH 2a **4 :** the amount that a tub will hold [Dutch *tubbe*]

²tub *vb* **tubbed**; **tub•bing :** to wash or bathe in a tub — **tub•ba•ble** \ˈtəb-ə-bəl\ *adj*

tu•ba \ˈtü-bə, ˈtyü-\ *n* **:** a large usually oval low-pitched brass wind instrument; *esp* **:** one with a conical tube and a cup-shaped mouthpiece [Italian, from Latin, "trumpet"]

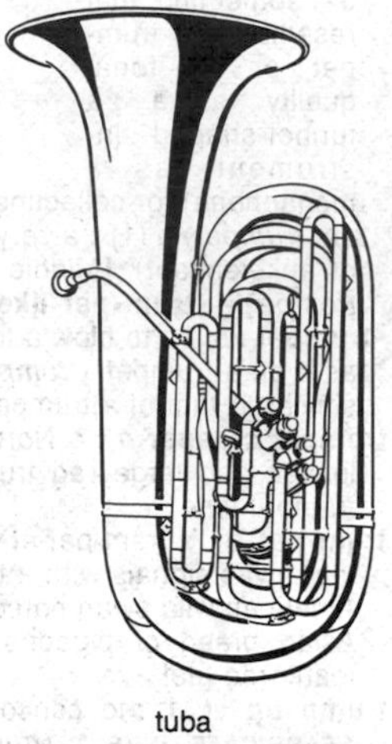

tuba

tub•al \ˈtü-bəl, ˈtyü-\ *adj* **:** of, relating to, or involving a tube

tub•by \ˈtəb-ē\ *adj* **tub•bi•er**; **-est :** PUDGY, CHUBBY

tube \ˈtüb, ˈtyüb\ *n* **1 a :** a hollow elongated cylinder; *esp* **:** one to convey fluids **b :** a slender channel within a plant or animal body **:** DUCT **2 :** any of various usually cylindrical structures or devices: as **a :** a round container from which a paste is dispensed by squeezing **b** (1) **:** TUNNEL (2) *British* **:** SUBWAY **c :** the basically cylindrical part connecting the mouthpiece and bell of a wind instrument **d :** INNER TUBE **e :** ELECTRON TUBE **f :** VACUUM TUBE **g :** TELEVISION ⟨watching the *tube*⟩ [French, from Latin *tubus*] — **tubed** \ˈtübd, ˈtyübd\ *adj* — **tube•like** \ˈtü-ˌblīk, ˈtyü-\ *adj*

tube foot *n* **:** one of the small flexible tubular processes of most echinoderms that are extensions of the water-vascular system used especially in locomotion and grasping

tube•less \ˈtü-bləs, ˈtyü-\ *adj* **:** lacking a tube; *esp* **:** being a pneumatic tire that does not depend on an inner tube for airtightness

tube nucleus *n* **:** a nucleus of a pollen grain that is held to control growth of the pollen tube — compare GENERATIVE NUCLEUS

tu•ber \ˈtü-bər, ˈtyü-\ *n* **:** a plant underground resting stage consisting of a short fleshy stem bearing minute scale leaves each with a bud in its axil potentially able to produce a new plant — compare BULB, CORM **2 :** a fleshy root or rhizome resembling a tuber [Latin, "lump, tuber, truffle"]

tu•ber•cle \ˈtü-bər-kəl, ˈtyü-\ *n* **1 :** a small knobby prominence or outgrowth especially on a plant or animal **2 :** a small abnormal lump in the substance of an organ or in the skin; *esp* **:** one caused by tuberculosis [Latin *tuberculum,* from *tuber* "lump, tuber"] — **tu•ber•cled** \-kəld\ *adj*

tubercle bacillus *n* **:** the bacterium that causes tuberculosis

tu•ber•cu•lar \tu̇-ˈbər-kyə-lər, tyu̇-\ *adj* **1 :** relating to, resembling, or constituting a tubercle **2 :** characterized by tubercular lesions ⟨*tubercular* leprosy⟩ **3 :** of, relating to, or affected with tuberculosis **:** TUBERCULOUS ⟨*tubercular* meningitis⟩ — **tu•ber•cu•lar•ly** *adv*

tu•ber•cu•lin \tu̇-ˈbər-kyə-lən, tyu̇-\ *n* **:** a sterile liquid containing substances from the tubercle bacillus that is used in the diagnosis of tuberculosis

tuberculin test *n* **:** a test for hypersensitivity to tuberculin as an indication of past or present tubercular infection

tu•ber•cu•lo•sis \tu̇-ˌbər-kyə-ˈlō-səs, tyu̇-\ *n* **:** a communicable disease of some vertebrates caused by the tubercle bacillus and typically marked by wasting, fever, and formation of cheesy tubercles that in human beings occur mostly in the lungs

tu•ber•cu•lous \tu̇-ˈbər-kyə-ləs, tyu̇-\ *adj* **2 :** TUBERCULAR 1 **2 :** being or affected or associated with tuberculosis ⟨a *tuberculous* process⟩ ⟨*tuberculous* peritonitis⟩ — **tu•ber•cu•lous•ly** *adv*

tube•rose \ˈtü-ˌbrōz, ˈtyü- (*by folk etymology*); *also* ˈtü-bə-ˌrōz, ˈtyü-, -bə-ˌrōs\ *n* **:** a Mexican bulbous herb of the amaryllis family grown for its spike of fragrant white flowers [Latin *tuberosus* "tuberous", from *tuber* "tuber"]

tu•ber•os•i•ty \ˌtü-bə-ˈräs-ət-ē, ˌtyü-\ *n, pl* **-ties :** a rounded prominence; *esp* **:** one on a bone usually serving for the attachment of muscles or ligaments

tu•ber•ous \ˈtü-bə-rəs, ˈtyü-, -brəs\ *adj* **1 a :** consisting of or resembling a tuber **b :** bearing tubers **2 :** of, relating to, or being a plant tuber or tuberous root — **tu•ber•ous•ly** *adv*

tu•bi•fex \ˈtü-bə-ˌfeks, ˈtyü-\ *n, pl* **-fex** *or* **-fex•es** : any of a genus of slender reddish oligochaete worms that live in tubes in fresh or brackish water and are widely used as food for aquarium fish [New Latin *Tubifex*, genus name, from Latin *tubus* "tube" + *facere* "to make"]

tub•ing \ˈtü-biŋ, ˈtyü-\ *n* **1** : material in the form of a tube; *also* : a length or piece of tube **2** : a series or system of tubes

tu•bu•lar \ˈtü-byə-lər, ˈtyü-\ *adj* **1** : having the form of or consisting of a tube **2** : made or provided with tubes — **tu•bu•lar•i•ty** \ˌtü-byə-ˈlar-ət-ē, ˌtyü-\ *n*

tu•bule \ˈtü-byül, ˈtyü-\ *n* : a small tube; *esp* : a long slender anatomical channel

1tuck \ˈtək\ *vb* **1 a** : to pull up or draw together into folds **b** : to make a tuck in **2** : to put or fit into a snug position or place ⟨a cottage *tucked* away in the hill⟩ **3 a** : to push in the loose end of so as to hold tightly ⟨*tuck* in your shirt⟩ **b** : to cover by tucking in bedclothes ⟨a child *tucked* in for the night⟩ [Old English *tūcian* "to ill-treat"]

2tuck *n* **1** : a fold stitched into cloth to shorten, decorate, or control fullness **2** : an act or instance of tucking

3tuck *n* : VIGOR 1, ENERGY [probably from *2tuck*]

1tuck•er \ˈtək-ər\ *n* **1** : one that tucks **2** : a piece of lace or cloth in the neckline of a dress

2tucker *vt* **tuck•ered**; **tuck•er•ing** \ˈtək-riŋ, -ə-riŋ\ : EXHAUST — often used with *out* [derived from Old English *tūcian* "to ill-treat"]

-tude \ˌtüd, ˌtyüd\ *n suffix* : -NESS ⟨exacti*tude*⟩ [Latin *-tudin-, -tudo*]

Tu•dor \ˈtüd-ər, ˈtyüd-\ *adj* **1** : of or relating to the English royal family ruling from 1485 to 1603 **2** : of, relating to, or characteristic of the Tudor period [Henry *Tudor* (Henry VII of England)] — **Tudor** *n*

Tues•day \ˈtüz-dē, ˈtyüz-\ *n* : the 3d day of the week [Old English *tīwesdæg*, literally, "day of Tiu (god of war)"]

tu•fa \ˈtü-fə, ˈtyü-\ *n* **1** : TUFF **2** : a porous rock formed as a deposit from springs or streams [Italian *tufo*, from Latin *tophus*] — **tu•fa•ceous** \tü-ˈfā-shəs, tyü-\ *adj*

tuff \ˈtəf\ *n* : a rock composed of the finer kinds of volcanic detritus [Middle French *tuf*, from Italian *tufo*] — **tuff•a•ceous** \ˌtə-ˈfā-shəs\ *adj*

tuf•fet \ˈtəf-ət\ *n* **1** : TUFT 1a **2** : a low seat [alteration of *tuft*]

1tuft \ˈtəft\ *n* **1 a** : a small cluster of long flexible outgrowths (as hairs or feathers) **b** : a bunch of soft fluffy threads cut off short and used as ornament **2** : CLUMP 1, CLUSTER [Middle French *tufe*] — **tuft•ed** \ˈtəf-təd\ *adj* — **tufty** \ˈtəf-tē\ *adj*

2tuft *vt* **1** : to provide or adorn with a tuft **2** : to make (as a mattress) firm by stitching at intervals and sewing on tufts

1tug \ˈtəg\ *vb* **tugged**; **tug•ging** **1 a** : to pull hard **b** : to move by pulling hard : DRAG, HAUL **2** : to struggle in opposition : CONTEND **3** : to tow with a tugboat [Middle English *tuggen*] — **tug•ger** *n*

2tug *n* **1 a** : a harness trace **b** : a rope or chain used for pulling **2 a** : an act or instance of tugging : PULL **b** : a strong pulling force **3 a** : a straining effort **b** : a struggle between opposing individuals or opposite forces **4** : TUGBOAT

tug•boat \ˈtəg-ˌbōt\ *n* : a strongly built powerful boat used for towing and pushing (as ships in harbors)

tug–of–war \ˌtəg-əv-ˈwȯr, ˌtəg-ə-\ *n, pl* **tugs–of–war** **1** : a struggle for supremacy **2** : an athletic contest in which two teams pull against each other at opposite ends of a rope

tu•i•tion \tu-ˈish-ən, tyü-\ *n* **1** : the act or profession of teaching : INSTRUCTION **2** : the price of or payment for instruction [Old French *tuicion* "guardianship", from Latin *tuitio*, from *tueri* "to look at, look after"] — **tu•i•tion•al** \-ˈish-nəl, -ən-l\ *adj*

tu•la•re•mia \ˌtü-lə-ˈrē-mē-ə, ˌtyü-\ *n* : an infectious bacterial disease of rodents, man, and some domestic animals transmitted especially by the bites of insects and in man marked by symptoms (as fever) of toxemia [New Latin, from *Tulare* county, California] — **tu•la•re•mic** \-mik\ *adj*

tu•le \ˈtü-lē\ *n* : either of two large coarse sedges growing on wet land of the southwestern United States [Spanish, from Nahuatl *tullin*]

tu•lip \ˈtü-ləp, ˈtyü-\ *n* : any of a genus of Eurasian bulbous herbs of the lily family that have linear or broadly lance-shaped leaves and are widely grown for their showy flowers; *also* : the flower or bulb of a tulip [New Latin *tulipa*, from Turkish *tülbend* "turban"]

tulip tree *n* : a tall North American timber tree of the magnolia family with large greenish yellow tulip-shaped flowers and soft white wood used especially for cabinetwork and woodenware

tulle \ˈtül\ *n* : a sheer often stiffened silk, rayon, or nylon net used chiefly for veils, evening dresses, or ballet costumes [French, from *Tulle*, France]

tulip

tul•li•bee \ˈtəl-ə-ˌbē\ *n* : any of several American whitefishes; *esp* : a common cisco that is a commercially important food fish [Canadian French *toulibi*]

1tum•ble \ˈtəm-bəl\ *vb* **tum•bled**; **tum•bling** \-bə-liŋ, -bliŋ\ **1 a** : to perform gymnastic feats of rolling and turning **b** : to turn end over end in falling or flight **2 a** : to fall suddenly and helplessly **b** : to suffer a sudden decline, downfall, or defeat : COLLAPSE **3** : to move or go hurriedly and confusedly **4** : to come to understand **5** : to cause to tumble (as by pushing) **6 a** : to toss together into a confused mass **b** : RUMPLE [Middle English *tumblen*, from *tumben* "to dance", from Old English *tumbian*]

2tumble *n* **1** : something tumbled **2** : an act or instance of tumbling

tum•ble•bug \ˈtəm-bəl-ˌbəg\ *n* : a large stout-bodied beetle that rolls dung into small balls, buries them in the ground, and lays eggs in them

tum•ble•down \ˌtəm-bəl-ˌdau̇n\ *adj* : DILAPIDATED, RAMSHACKLE

tum•bler \ˈtəm-blər\ *n* **1** : one that tumbles: as **a** : GYMNAST, ACROBAT **b** : a pigeon that habitually somersaults backward in flight **2** : a drinking glass without foot or stem and originally with pointed or convex base **3** : a movable part in a lock that must be adjusted (as by a key) before the bolt can be thrown **4** : a device or mechanism for tumbling (as a revolving cage in which clothes are dried)

tum•ble•weed \ˈtəm-bəl-ˌwēd\ *n* : a plant that breaks away from its roots in autumn and is blown about by the wind

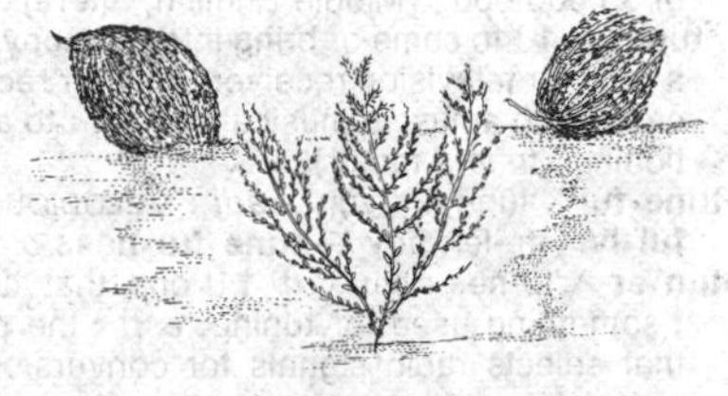
tumbleweed

tum•bling \ˈtəm-bə-liŋ, -bliŋ\ *n* : the skill, practice, or sport of executing acrobatic feats (as somersaults, rolls, and handsprings) on a mat usually without apparatus

tum•brel *or* **tum•bril** \ˈtəm-brəl\ *n* : a farmer's cart used during the French Revolution to carry condemned persons to the guillotine [Old French *tumberel* "tipcart", from *tomber* "to tumble", of Germanic origin]

tu•mes•cence \tü-ˈmes-ns, tyü-\ *n* : a swelling or becoming swollen or the resulting state [Latin *tumescens*, present participle of *tumescere* "to swell up", from *tumēre* "to swell"] — **tu•mes•cent** \-nt\ *adj*

tu•mid \ˈtü-məd, ˈtyü-\ *adj* **1** : marked by swelling ⟨*tumid* flesh⟩ **2** : TURGID 2, BOMBASTIC [Latin *tumidus*, from *tumēre* "to swell"] — **tu•mid•i•ty** \tü-ˈmid-ət-ē, tyü-\ *n*

tum•my \ˈtəm-ē\ *n, pl* **tummies** : STOMACH 1c [baby-talk for *stomach*]

tu•mor \ˈtü-mər, ˈtyü-\ *n* : a swollen or distended part; *esp* : an abnormal mass of tissue that is not inflammatory, arises without obvious cause from cells of preexistent tissue, and possesses no physiologic function [Latin, from *tumēre* "to swell"] — **tu•mor•like** \-ˌlīk\ *adj* — **tu•mor•ous** \ˈtüm-rəs, ˈtyüm-, -ə-rəs\ *adj*

\ə\ **abut**	\au̇\ **out**	\i\ **tip**	\ȯ\ **saw**	\u̇\ **foot**
\ər\ **further**	\ch\ **chin**	\ī\ **life**	\ȯi\ **coin**	\y\ **yet**
\a\ **mat**	\e\ **pet**	\j\ **job**	\th\ **thin**	\yü\ **few**
\ā\ **take**	\ē\ **easy**	\ŋ\ **sing**	\t͟h\ **this**	\yu̇\ **cure**
\ä\ **cot, cart**	\g\ **go**	\ō\ **bone**	\ü\ **food**	\zh\ **vision**

tump•line \ˈtəm-ˌplīn\ *n* **:** a sling formed by a strap slung over the forehead or chest used for carrying a pack on the back or in hauling loads [*tump* of American Indian origin]

tu•mult \ˈtü-ˌməlt, ˈtyü-\ *n* **1 :** violent and disorderly commotion or disturbance (as of a crowd) with uproar and confusion **2 :** violent agitation of mind or feelings [Middle French *tumulte*, from Latin *tumultus*]

tu•mul•tu•ous \tü-ˈməl-chə-wəs, tyü-, -chəs\ *adj* **:** marked by tumult and especially by violent turbulence or upheaval — **tu•mul•tu•ous•ly** *adv* — **tu•mul•tu•ous•ness** *n*

tu•mu•lus \ˈtü-myə-ləs, ˈtyü-\ *n, pl* **-li** \-ˌlī, -ˌlē\ **:** an artificial hillock or mound usually over an ancient grave [Latin]

tun \ˈtən\ *n* **1 :** a large cask for liquids and especially wine **2 :** the capacity of a tun as a varying liquid measure; *esp* **:** a measure of 252 gallons (about 954 liters) [Old English *tunne*]

1tu•na \ˈtü-nə\ *n* **:** any of several flat-jointed prickly pears; *also* **:** the edible fruit of a tuna [Spanish, of American Indian origin]

2tu•na \ˈtü-nə, ˈtyü-\ *n, pl* **tuna** *or* **tunas :** any of several mostly large active sea fishes (as an albacore or bonito) related to the mackerels and valued for food and sport [American Spanish, from Spanish *atún*, from Arabic *tūn*, from Latin *thunnus*, from Greek *thynnos*]

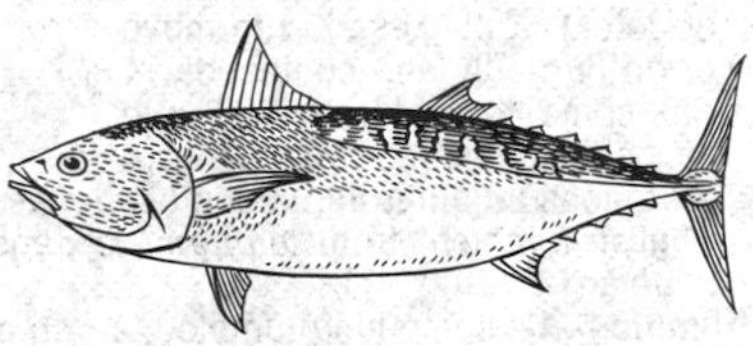

2tuna

tun•able \ˈtü-nə-bəl, ˈtyü-\ *adj* **:** capable of being tuned — **tun•able•ness** *n* — **tun•ably** \-blē\ *adv*

tun•dra \ˈtən-drə *also* ˈtu̇n-\ *n* **:** a treeless plain of arctic and subarctic regions [Russian, of Finno-Ugric origin]

1tune \ˈtün, ˈtyün\ *n* **1 a :** a musical composition or air **b :** a dominant theme **2 :** correct musical pitch or consonance ⟨the piano was not in *tune*⟩ **3 a :** AGREEMENT, HARMONY ⟨in *tune* with the times⟩ **b :** general attitude ⟨you'll change your *tune* after you read this⟩ **4 :** AMOUNT, EXTENT ⟨a subsidy to the *tune* of $5,000,000⟩ [Middle English, alteration of *tone*]

2tune *vb* **1 :** to come or bring into harmony **:** ATTUNE **2 :** to adjust a radio or television receiver to either receive or reject a broadcast **3 :** to adjust in musical pitch **4 :** to adjust for precise functioning ⟨*tune* a motor⟩

tune•ful \ˈtün-fəl, ˈtyün-\ *adj* **:** MELODIOUS 1, MUSICAL — **tune•ful•ly** \-fə-lē\ *adv* — **tune•ful•ness** *n*

tun•er \ˈtü-nər, ˈtyü-\ *n* **1 :** one that tunes ⟨piano *tuner*⟩ **2 :** something used for tuning; *esp* **:** the part of a receiving set that selects radio signals for conversion into audio or visual signals

tune–up \ˈtü-ˌnəp, ˈtyü-\ *n* **1 :** a general adjustment to ensure efficient functioning ⟨a motor *tune-up*⟩ **2 :** a preliminary trial **:** WARM-UP

tung \ˈtəŋ\ *n* **:** TUNG TREE

tung•sten \ˈtəŋ-stən, ˈtəŋk-\ *n* **:** a gray-white heavy ductile hard metallic chemical element that is used especially for electrical purposes and in hardening alloys (as steel) — called also *wolfram*; see ELEMENT table [Swedish, from *tung* "heavy" + *sten* "stone"]

tung tree *n* **:** any of several trees whose seeds yield a drying oil; *esp* **:** a Chinese tree widely grown in warm regions [Chinese (Pekingese dialect) *t'ung*2]

Tun•gu•sic \tu̇ŋ-ˈgü-zik, tən-\ *n* **:** a subfamily of Altaic languages spoken in Manchuria and northward [*Tungus*, a Mongoloid people of eastern Siberia, from Russian] — **Tungusic** *adj*

tu•nic \ˈtü-nik, ˈtyü-\ *n* **1 :** a simple belted knee-length or longer slip-on garment worn by ancient Greeks and Romans **2 :** a long usually plain and close-fitting jacket with high collar worn especially as part of a uniform **3 :** a blouse or jacket reaching to or just below the hips [Latin *tunica*, of Semitic origin]

tu•ni•ca \ˈtü-ni-kə, ˈtyü-\ *n, pl* **-cae** \-nə-ˌkē, -ˌkī\ **:** an enveloping integument, membrane, or layer of animal or plant tissue [Latin, "tunic, membrane"]

tu•ni•cate \ˈtü-ni-kət, ˈtyü-, -nə-ˌkāt\ *n* **:** any of a major group (Tunicata) of lowly marine chordates with a reduced nervous system and an outer cuticular covering **:** SEA SQUIRT — **tunicate** *adj*

tuning fork *n* **:** a 2-pronged metal instrument that gives a fixed tone when struck and is useful for tuning musical instruments and ascertaining standard pitch

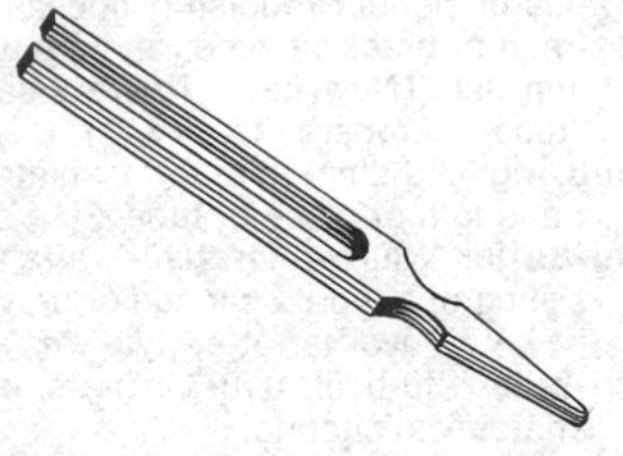

tuning fork

1tun•nel \ˈtən-l\ *n* **:** an enclosed passage (as a tube or conduit); *esp* **:** one underground (as under an obstruction or in a mine [Middle French *tonel* "tun", from Old French *tonne*, from Medieval Latin *tunna*, of Celtic origin] — **tun•nel-like** \-l-ˌlīk, -l-ˌīk\ *adj*

2tunnel *vb* **-neled** *or* **-nelled**; **-nel•ing** *or* **-nel•ling** \ˈtən-ling, -l-iŋ\ **:** to make or use a tunnel or form a tunnel in — **tun•nel•er** \ˈtən-lər, -l-ər\ *n*

tun•ny \ˈtən-ē\ *n, pl* **tunnies** *also* **tunny :** 2TUNA [derived from Latin *thunnus*]

tu•pe•lo \ˈtü-pə-ˌlō, ˈtyü-\ *n, pl* **-los 1 :** any of a genus of mostly North American trees of the dogwood family; *esp* **:** BLACK GUM **2 :** the pale soft easily worked wood of a tupelo [Creek *ito opilwa* "swamp tree"]

Tu•pi \tü-ˈpē, ˈtü-ˌ\ *n* **1 :** a member of a group of peoples of the Amazon valley **2 :** the language of the Tupi people

tup•pence *variant of* TWOPENCE

tuque \ˈtük, ˈtyük\ *n* **:** a warm knitted usually pointed stocking cap [Canadian French, from French *toque*]

tur•ban \ˈtər-bən\ *n* **1 :** a headdress worn chiefly in countries of the eastern Mediterranean and southern Asia especially by Muslims and made of a cap around which is wound a long cloth **2 :** a close-fitting hat without a brim [Middle French *turbant*, from Italian *turbante*, from Turkish *tülbend*, from Persian *dulband*] — **tur•baned** *or* **tur•banned** \-bənd\ *adj*

tur•bel•lar•i•an \ˌtər-bə-ˈler-ē-ən, -ˈlar-\ *n* **:** any of a class (Turbellaria) of mostly aquatic and free-living flatworms; *esp* **:** PLANARIAN [derived from Latin *turbellae* "bustle, stir", from *turba* "confusion, crowd"] — **turbellarian** *adj*

tur•bid \ˈtər-bəd\ *adj* **1 a :** thick or opaque with matter in suspension ⟨a *turbid* stream⟩ **b :** heavy with smoke or mist **:** DENSE **2 :** confused in thought or feeling [Latin *turbidus* "confused, turbid", from *turba* "confusion, crowd"] — **tur•bid•i•ty** \ˌtər-ˈbid-ət-ē\ *n* — **tur•bid•ly** \ˈtər-bəd-lē\ *adv* — **tur•bid•ness** *n*

1tur•bi•nate \ˈtər-bə-nət\ *adj* **:** of, relating to, or being the thin bony or cartilaginous plates on the walls of the nasal passages [Latin *turbinatus* "shaped like a top", from *turbo* "top"]

2turbinate *n* **:** a turbinate bone or cartilage

tur•bine \ˈtər-bən, -ˌbīn\ *n* **:** an engine whose central driving shaft is fitted with vanes whirled around by the pressure of water or hot gases (as steam or exhaust gases) [French, from Latin *turbo* "top, whirlwind"]

tur•bo \ˈtər-bō\ *n, pl* **turbos 1 :** TURBINE **2 :** TURBOSUPERCHARGER

tur•bo- *combining form* **1 :** coupled directly to a driving turbine **2 :** consisting of or incorporating a turbine ⟨*turbo*jet engine⟩

tur•bo•jet \ˈtər-bō-ˌjet\ *n* **:** an airplane powered by turbojet engines

turbojet engine *n* **:** an airplane propulsion system in which the power developed by a turbine is used to drive a compressor that supplies air to a burner and hot gases from the burner pass through the turbine and thence to a rearward-directed thrust-producing exhaust nozzle

tur•bo•prop \ˈtər-bō-ˌpräp\ *n* **1 :** TURBO-PROPELLER ENGINE **2 :** an airplane powered by turbo-propeller engines

tur•bo-pro•pel•ler engine \ˌtər-bō-prə-ˈpel-ər-\ *n* **:** a jet engine having a turbine-driven propeller and designed to produce thrust principally by means of a propeller although additional thrust is usually obtained from the hot exhaust gases which issue in a jet

tur•bo•su•per•charg•er \-ˈsü-pər-ˌchär-jər\ *n* **:** a turbine compressor driven by hot exhaust gases of an airplane engine for feeding rarefied air at high altitudes into the carburetor of the engine at sea-level pressure so as to increase engine power

tur•bot \ˈtər-bət\ *n, pl* **turbot** *also* **turbots :** a large brownish European flatfish that is a popular food fish; *also* **:** any of various flatfishes resembling this [Old French *tourbot*]

tur•bu•lence \ˈtər-byə-ləns\ *n* **:** the quality or state of being turbulent: as **a :** wild commotion **b :** irregular atmospheric motion especially when characterized by up and down currents **c :** departure in a fluid from a smooth flow

tur•bu•len•cy \-lən-sē\ *n, pl* **-cies** *archaic* **:** TURBULENCE

tur•bu•lent \-lənt\ *adj* **1 :** causing unrest, violence, or disturbance **2 :** characterized by agitation or tumult **:** TEMPESTUOUS **[**Latin *turbulentus*, from *turba* "confusion, crowd"**]** — **tur•bu•lent•ly** *adv*

turbulent flow *n* **:** a fluid flow in which the velocity at a given point varies erratically in magnitude and direction

Tur•co- *or* **Tur•ko-** *combining form* **:** Turkish **:** Turkish and

tu•reen \tə-ˈrēn, tyü-\ *n* **:** a deep bowl from which food (as soup) is served **[**French *terrine*, from *terrin* "earthen", derived from Latin *terra* "earth"**]**

turf \ˈtərf\ *n, pl* **turfs** \ˈtərfs\ *or* **turves** \ˈtərvz\ **1 :** the upper layer of soil bound by grass and plant roots into a thick mat; *also* **:** a piece of this — called also *sod* **2 a :** PEAT 2 **b :** a piece of peat dried for fuel **3 a :** a track or course for horse racing **b :** the sport or business of horse racing **[**Old English**]** — **turfy** \ˈtər-fē\ *adj*

turf•man \ˈtərf-mən\ *n* **:** a devotee of horse racing; *esp* **:** one who owns and races horses

tur•ges•cent \ˌtər-ˈjes-nt\ *adj* **:** becoming turgid, distended, or inflated **[**Latin *turgescens*, present participle of *turgescere* "to swell", from *turgēre* "to be swollen"**]** — **tur•ges•cence** \-ns\ *n*

tur•gid \ˈtər-jəd\ *adj* **1 a :** affected with swelling ⟨*turgid* limbs⟩ **b :** exhibiting turgor **2 :** excessively embellished in style or language **:** BOMBASTIC, POMPOUS **[**Latin *turgidus*, from *turgēre* "to be swollen"**]** — **tur•gid•i•ty** \ˌtər-ˈjid-ət-ē\ *n* — **tur•gid•ly** \ˈtər-jəd-lē\ *adv* — **tur•gid•ness** *n*

tur•gor \ˈtər-gər, -ˌgȯr\ *n* **:** the normal state of firmness and tension typical of living cells **[**Late Latin, "turgidity", from Latin *turgēre* "to be swollen"**]**

Turk \ˈtərk\ *n* **1 :** a member of any of numerous Asian peoples speaking Turkic languages who live in the region ranging from the Adriatic to the Sea of Okhotsk **2 :** a native or inhabitant of Turkey **[**Middle French *Turc*, from Medieval Latin *Turcus*, from Turkish *Türk***]**

tur•key \ˈtər-kē\ *n, pl* **turkeys 1 :** a large American bird which is related to the common fowl, is of wide range in North America, and is domesticated in most parts of the world **2 :** FLOP 2, FAILURE **3** *slang* **a :** SUCKER 6a **b :** FOOL 1, DOPE **[***Turkey*; from confusion with the guinea fowl, supposed to be imported from Turkish territory**]**

turkey buzzard *n* **:** an American vulture common in South and Central America and in the southern United States — called also *turkey vulture*

turkey 1

tur•key–cock \ˈtər-kē-ˌkäk\ *n* **1 :** GOBBLER **2 :** a strutting pompous person

turkey shoot *n* **:** a contest of marksmanship with a gun at a moving target with a turkey offered as a prize

Tur•ki \ˈtər-ˌkē, ˈtu̇r-\ *n* **:** any central Asian Turkic language **[**Persian *turkī*, from *Turk* "Turk", from Turkish *Türk***]**

Turk•ic \ˈtər-kik\ *n* **:** a subfamily of Altaic languages including Turkish — **Turkic** *adj*

[1]**Turk•ish** \ˈtər-kish\ *adj* **1 :** of, relating to, or characteristic of Turkey, the Turks, or Turkish **2 :** TURKIC

[2]**Turkish** *n* **:** the Turkic language of Turkey

Turkish bath *n* **:** a bath in which the bather passes through a series of steam rooms of increasing temperature and then receives a rubdown, massage, and cold shower

Turkish coffee *n* **:** a drink made by boiling powdered coffee in a thin sugar syrup

Turkish delight *n* **:** a jellylike or gummy confection usually cut in cubes and dusted with sugar — called also *Turkish paste*

Turkish towel *n* **:** a towel made of cotton terry cloth

Tur•ko•man *or* **Tur•co•man** \ˈtər-kə-mən\ *n, pl* **Turkomans** *or* **Turcomans :** a member of a group of peoples living chiefly in the Turkmen, Uzbek, and Kazakh republics of the Soviet Union **[**Medieval Latin *Turcomannus*, from Persian *Turkmān*, from *turkmān* "resembling a Turk", from *Turk* "Turk", from Turkish *Türk***]**

tur•mer•ic \ˈtər-mə-rik *also* ˈtü-mə-, ˈtyü-\ *n* **1 :** an East Indian herb of the ginger family; *also* **:** its aromatic rootstock powdered for use as a condiment, yellow dye, or stimulant **2 :** any of several plants resembling turmeric **[**Middle French *terre merite* "saffron", from Medieval Latin *terra merita*, literally, "deserving or deserved earth"**]**

tur•moil \ˈtər-ˌmȯil\ *n* **:** an utterly confused or extremely agitated state or condition **[**origin unknown**]**

[1]**turn** \ˈtərn\ *vb* **1 a :** to move or cause to move around an axis or center **:** ROTATE, REVOLVE ⟨wheels *turning* slowly⟩ ⟨*turn* a crank⟩; *also* **:** to operate or cause to operate by so turning ⟨*turn* a key in a lock⟩ **b :** to whirl giddily **:** become dizzy ⟨your head will *turn* at the height⟩ **c :** to have as a center (as of interest) or a decisive factor ⟨their decision must *turn* on circumstances⟩ ⟨the story *turns* about the fate of a family⟩ **d :** to think over **:** PONDER **e :** to execute by revolving ⟨*turn* handsprings⟩ **2 a :** to alter or reverse in position usually by moving through an arc ⟨*turn* toward your partner⟩: as (1) **:** to dig or plow so as to invert ⟨*turn* the soil⟩ (2) **:** to make over by reversing the material and resewing ⟨*turn* a collar⟩ **b :** to disturb or upset the order or state or balance of ⟨everything was *turned* topsy-turvy⟩ **c :** to injure by a sudden twist **:** WRENCH ⟨*turned* my ankle⟩ **3 :** to change or cause to change ⟨water *turned* to ice⟩: as **a** (1) **:** TRANSFORM ⟨*turn* wild land into fruitful farms⟩ (2) **:** BECOME ⟨*turn* traitor⟩ **b :** TRANSLATE 2a, PARAPHRASE **c :** to exchange for something else ⟨*turn* property into cash⟩ **d :** to cause to spoil **:** SOUR ⟨*turned* milk⟩ **e :** to change in color ⟨leaves *turning* in the fall⟩ **f :** to cause to be **:** MAKE ⟨hair *turned* white by sorrow⟩ **g :** to be inconstant **:** VARY **4 a :** to take or cause to take or move in another, an opposite, or a particular direction ⟨*turned* the overflow into an old stream bed⟩ ⟨the road *turns* to the left⟩ ⟨*turned* the car around⟩ ⟨when the tide *turns*⟩; *also* **:** to go around ⟨*turn* a corner⟩ **b :** to alter from a previous or anticipated course ⟨these few votes *turned* the election⟩ **c** (1) **:** to change one's behavior or attitude to opposition or hostility ⟨felt the world had *turned* against them⟩; *also* **:** DEFECT (2) **:** to attack suddenly and usually unexpectedly and violently ⟨the dog *turned* on a neighbor⟩ **d :** to bring to bear **:** TRAIN ⟨*turn* a weapon on an enemy⟩; *also* **:** to direct or point usually toward or away from something ⟨*turned* their thoughts homeward⟩ **e :** to influence toward a change (as in one's way of life) **f :** DEVOTE 1, APPLY ⟨*turned* their skills to the service of the poor⟩ **g :** to cause to recoil ⟨*turns* their own argument against them⟩ **h :** to drive or send from or to a specified place or condition ⟨*turn* cattle into a field⟩ ⟨*turn* mutineers adrift⟩ **i :** to seek out as a source ⟨*turn* to a friend for help⟩ **5 a :** to give a rounded form to by means of a lathe and cutting tool **b :** to give a well-rounded or graceful shape or form to ⟨*turn* the heel of a sock⟩ ⟨*turned* a phrase⟩ **c :** to become or cause to become bent or curved ⟨the edge of the knife had *turned*⟩ **6 :** to gain in the course of business ⟨*turning* a quick profit⟩ **[**Old English *tyrnan, turnian* and Old French *torner, tourner*, both from Latin *tornare* "to turn on a lathe", from *tornus* "lathe", from Greek *tornos***]** — **turn a deaf ear :** to refuse to listen — **turn a hair :** to be or become upset or frightened — **turn one's back on 1 :** REJECT 1 **2 :** ABANDON 3 — **turn one's hand** *or* **turn a hand :** to set to work **:** apply oneself usefully — **turn one's head :** to cause to have great notions of pride or conceit — **turn tail :** to run away **:** FLEE — **turn the scale :** to prove decisive — **turn the trick :** to bring about the desired result or effect — **turn turtle :** CAPSIZE, OVERTURN

[2]**turn** *n* **1 :** the action or an act of turning about a center or axis ⟨each *turn* of the wheel⟩ **2 a :** a change or changing of direction, course, or position **b :** a place where something turns **:** BEND, CURVE ⟨at the *turn* of the road⟩ **c** (1) **:** a change or changing of condition or trend ⟨took a *turn* for the better⟩ ⟨a *turn* in the weather⟩ (2) **:** a usually sudden and brief attack or spell of nerves or faintness ⟨gave me a *turn*⟩ **d :** a musical ornament consisting of a group of notes including the one next above and next below the principal note **3 :** an act affecting

\ə\ **abut**	\au̇\ **out**	\i\ **tip**	\ȯ\ **saw**	\u̇\ **foot**
\ər\ **further**	\ch\ **chin**	\ī\ **life**	\ȯi\ **coin**	\y\ **yet**
\a\ **mat**	\e\ **pet**	\j\ **job**	\th\ **thin**	\yü\ **few**
\ā\ **take**	\ē\ **easy**	\ng\ **sing**	\th\ **this**	\yu̇\ **cure**
\ä\ **cot, cart**	\g\ **go**	\ō\ **bone**	\ü\ **food**	\zh\ **vision**

another ⟨did me a very bad *turn*⟩ **4 a :** a period of action or activity : SPELL ⟨each took a *turn* at the job⟩ **b :** place or appointed time in a succession or scheduled order ⟨wait one's *turn* at the dentist's⟩ **5 :** special purpose or need ⟨it served my *turn*⟩ **6 :** a short walk or ride ⟨took a *turn* through the park⟩ **7 a :** distinctive quality or character ⟨a neat *turn* of phrase⟩ **b :** the form in accord with which something is fashioned : CAST ⟨a peculiar *turn* of mind⟩ **c :** the state or manner of being coiled or twisted; *also* : a single round (as of a rope) ⟨took a *turn* around a post to hold the horse⟩ **d :** a special twist or interpretation ⟨gave the old tale a new *turn*⟩ **8 :** particular or special aptitude or skill : BENT ⟨a *turn* for languages⟩ — **at every turn** : CONSTANTLY, CONTINUOUSLY — **to a turn** : to perfection

turn•about \ˈtər-nə-ˌbau̇t\ *n* : a change or reversal of direction, trend, policy, or role

turn•around \-ˌrau̇nd\ *n* : a space permitting the turning around of a vehicle

turn away *vb* **1 :** DEFLECT, AVERT **2 a :** to send away : REJECT, DISMISS **b :** to refuse admittance or acceptance to **3 :** to start to go away : DEPART

turn back *vb* **1 :** to refer to an earlier time or place **2 :** to drive back or away **3 :** to stop the advance of : CHECK

turn•buck•le \ˈtərn-ˌbək-əl\ *n* : a link with a screw thread at one or both ends used for tightening a rod or stay by pulling together the ends that it connects

turn•coat \ˈtərn-ˌkōt\ *n* : one who forsakes his or her party or principles; *esp* : TRAITOR

turn down \ˌtərn-ˈdau̇n, ˈtərn-\ *vt* **1 :** to turn upside down : INVERT **2 :** to reduce in intensity by turning a control ⟨*turn down* the volume⟩ **3 :** REJECT ⟨*turned down* the offer⟩ — **turn•down** \ˌtərn-ˌdau̇n\ *adj or n*

turn•er \ˈtər-nər\ *n* : one that turns or is used for turning ⟨cake *turner*⟩; *esp* : one that forms articles with a lathe

Tur•ner's syndrome \ˈtər-nərz-\ *n* : a genetically determined condition associated with the presence of one X chromosome and no Y chromosome and characterized by an outwardly female bodily type with incomplete and infertile sex organs [Henry Hubert *Turner*, died 1970, American physician]

turn•ery \ˈtər-nə-rē\ *n, pl* **-er•ies** : the work, products, or shop of a turner

turn in *vb* **1 :** to give up or hand over ⟨*turn in* extra supplies⟩ **2 :** to inform on : BETRAY **3 :** PRODUCE, DO ⟨*turn in* good work⟩ **4 :** to turn from a road or path so as to enter ⟨*turn in* at the gate⟩ **5 :** to go to bed

turning point *n* : a point at which a significant change occurs

tur•nip \ˈtər-nəp\ *n* : either of two biennial herbs of the mustard family with thick roots eaten as a vegetable or fed to stock: **a :** one with hairy leaves and usually white and flattened roots **b :** RUTABAGA [probably from [1]*turn* + English dialect *neep* "turnip", from the rounded root]

turn•key \ˈtərn-ˌkē\ *n, pl* **turnkeys** : one who has charge of a prison's keys : JAILER

turn•off \ˈtər-ˌnȯf\ *n* **1 :** a turning off **2 :** a place where one turns off

turn off \ˌtər-ˈnȯf, ˈtər-\ *vt* **1 :** DISMISS, DISCHARGE ⟨*turn off* employees⟩ **2 :** to turn aside or aside from something ⟨*turn off* a puzzling question⟩ ⟨*turned off* into a side road⟩ **3 :** to stop the functioning or flow of by or as if by turning a control ⟨*turn* the light *off*⟩ **4 :** to cause to lose interest or responsiveness

turn on *vt* **1 :** to cause to function or flow by or as if by turning a control ⟨*turn* the water *on* full⟩ ⟨*turn on* the lights⟩ ⟨*turned on* all my charm⟩ **2 a :** to undergo or cause to undergo an intense often visionary experience by taking a drug; *also* : to cause to get high **b :** to excite or become excited pleasurably ⟨rock music *turns* me *on*⟩

turn•out \ˈtər-ˌnau̇t\ *n* **1 :** an act of turning out **2 :** a gathering of people for a special purpose **3 :** a widened space (as in a highway) for vehicles to pass or park **4 :** a clearing out and cleaning **5 a :** a carriage with its team and equipment **b :** an outfit of clothes : COSTUME **6 :** YIELD, OUTPUT

turn out \ˌtər-ˈnau̇t, ˈtər-\ *vb* **1 :** to put out of some shelter : EVICT **2 :** to empty of contents; *also* : CLEAN **3 :** to make with rapidity or regularity **4 :** to equip, dress, or finish in a careful or elaborate way **5 :** to turn off (as a light) **6 :** to call (as a guard) from rest or shelter **7 a :** to come out in answer to a summons ⟨*turn out* for practice⟩ **b :** to get out of bed **8 a :** to prove in the end ⟨*turned out* to be a spy⟩ **b :** END 2 ⟨how did the game *turn out*⟩

[1]**turn•over** \ˈtər-ˌnō-vər\ *n* **1 :** an act or result of turning over : UPSET **2 :** a shifting usually in position or opinion **3 :** a reorganization especially of personnel **4 :** a filled pastry with one half of the crust turned over the other **5 :** the amount of business done or work accomplished; *also* : the rate at which material is processed **6 :** the buying, selling, and replacing of goods considered as one complete process ⟨the annual *turnover* in shoes⟩ **7 :** the number of employees hired in a given time to replace those leaving or discharged

[2]**turn•over** \ˌtər-ˌnō-vər\ *adj* : capable of being turned over

turn over \ˌtər-ˈnō-vər, ˈtər-\ *vb* **1 a :** to turn from an upright position : OVERTURN **b :** OPERATE, RUN ⟨engines *turning over* slowly⟩ **2 :** to examine or search by shifting item by item ⟨*turning over* old letters⟩ **3 :** to think over : meditate on ⟨*turn over* a problem in search of a solution⟩ **4 :** to hand over : TRANSFER **5 a :** to receive and dispose of (as a stock of merchandise) usually in the course of business **b :** to do business to the amount of ⟨expected to *turn over* $1000 a week⟩ **6 :** to heave with nausea ⟨your stomach will *turn over* with shock⟩

turn•pike \ˈtərn-ˌpīk\ *n* **1 :** a toll bar : TOLLGATE **2 a :** a toll road; *esp* : a toll expressway **b :** a main road [Middle English *turnepike* "revolving frame bearing spikes and serving as a barrier", from *turnen* "to turn" + *pike*]

turn•spit \-ˌspit\ *n* **1 :** one that turns a spit **2 :** a rotatable spit

turn•stile \-ˌstīl\ *n* : a post with arms pivoted on the top set in a passageway so that persons can pass through only on foot one by one

turn•stone \-ˌstōn\ *n* : any of various widely distributed migratory shorebirds resembling the related plovers and sandpipers

turnstone

turn•ta•ble \-ˌtā-bəl\ *n* : a revolvable platform: as **a :** a platform with a track for turning wheeled vehicles **b :** LAZY SUSAN **c :** a rotating platform that carries a phonograph record

turn to \ˈtərn-ˈtü\ *vi* : to apply oneself to work : act vigorously

turn•up \ˌtər-ˌnəp\ *adj* **1 :** turned up ⟨a *turnup* nose⟩ **2 :** made or fitted to be turned up ⟨a *turnup* collar⟩

turn up \ˌtər-ˈnəp, ˈtər-\ *vb* **1 :** to bring or come to light unexpectedly or after being lost ⟨the papers will *turn up*⟩ **2 :** to raise or increase by or as if by adjusting a control ⟨*turn up* the heat⟩ **3 a :** to turn out to be ⟨*turned up* missing⟩ **b :** to become evident : APPEAR ⟨that name is always *turning up*⟩ **c :** to put in an appearance ⟨*turned up* half an hour late⟩ **4 :** to happen unexpectedly — **turn up one's nose :** to show scorn or disdain

tur•pen•tine \ˈtər-pən-ˌtīn\ *n* **1 :** an oleoresin obtained from various conifers (as some pines and firs) **2 a :** an essential oil obtained from turpentines by distillation and used especially as a solvent and thinner — called also *gum turpentine* **b :** a similar oil obtained by distillation or carbonization of pinewood — called also *wood turpentine* [Medieval Latin *terbentina* "oleoresin obtained from the terebinth", derived from Latin *terebinthus* "terebinth"]

tur•pi•tude \ˈtər-pə-ˌtüd, -ˌtyüd\ *n* : inherent baseness : DEPRAVITY ⟨moral *turpitude*⟩ [Middle French, from Latin *turpitudo*, from *turpis* "vile, base"]

turps \ˈtərps\ *n* : TURPENTINE

tur•quoise \ˈtər-ˌkwȯiz, -ˌkȯiz\ *n* **1 :** a mineral that is a blue, bluish green, or greenish gray hydrous basic copper aluminum phosphate, takes a high polish, and sometimes is valued as a gem **2 :** a light greenish blue [Middle French *turquoyse*, from *turquoys* "Turkish", from *Turc* "Turk"]

tur•ret \ˈtər-ət, ˈtə-rət, ˈtu̇r-ət\ *n* **1 :** a little tower often at a corner of a building **2 a :** a pivoted and revolvable holder in a machine tool **b :** a device (as on a microscope or television camera) for holding several lenses **3 : a** gunner's fixed or movable enclosure in an airplane **b :** a revolving structure on a warship or on a tank in which guns are mounted [Middle French *torete*, from *tor, tur* "tower"] — **tur•ret•ed** \-əd\ *adj*

[1]**tur•tle** \ˈtərt-l\ *n, archaic* : TURTLEDOVE [Old English *turtla*, from Latin *turtur*]

[2]**turtle** *n, pl* **turtles** *also* **turtle** : any of an order (Testudinata) of

land, freshwater, and marine reptiles with a toothless horny beak and a bony shell which encloses the trunk and into which the head, limbs, and tail usually may be withdrawn — compare TERRAPIN, TORTOISE [probably from French *tortue*]

tur•tle•back \ˈtərt-l-ˌbak\ *n* : a raised convex surface — **turtle-back** *or* **tur•tle-backed** \ˌtərt-l-ˈbakt\ *adj*

tur•tle•dove \ˈtərt-l-ˌdəv\ *n* : any of several small wild pigeons especially of an Old World genus noted for cooing [[1]*turtle*]

tur•tle•neck \-ˌnek\ *n* : a high close-fitting turnover collar used especially for sweaters; *also* : a sweater with a turtleneck

tur•tling \ˈtərt-ling, -l-ing\ *n* : the action or process of catching turtles

turves *pl of* TURF

[1]**Tus•can** \ˈtəs-kən\ *n* **1** : a native or inhabitant of Tuscany **2 a** : the Italian language spoken in Tuscany **b** : the standard literary dialect of Italian [Latin *tuscanus*, adj., "Etruscan", from *Tusci* "Etruscans"]

[2]**Tuscan** *adj* : of, relating to, or characteristic of Tuscany, the Tuscans, or Tuscan

Tus•ca•ro•ra \ˌtəs-kə-ˈrōr-ə, -ˈrȯr-\ *n* : a member of an Iroquoian people originally of what is now North Carolina and later of New York and Ontario [Tuscarora *Ska-ru-rĕ*^{n}, literally, "Indian hemp gatherers"]

[1]**tush** \ˈtəsh\ *n* : a long pointed tooth [Old English *tūsc*] — **tushed** \ˈtəsht\ *adj*

[2]**tush** *interj* — used to express disdain or reproach [Middle English *tussch*]

[1]**tusk** \ˈtəsk\ *n* **1** : a long greatly enlarged tooth (as of an elephant, walrus, or boar) that projects when the mouth is closed and serves for gathering food or as a weapon **2** : a tooth-shaped part [Old English *tūx*] — **tusked** \ˈtəskt\ *adj*

[2]**tusk** *vt* : to dig up or gash with a tusk

tusk•er \ˈtəs-kər\ *n* : an animal with tusks; *esp* : a male elephant with two normally developed tusks

[1]**tus•sle** \ˈtəs-əl\ *vi* **tus•sled**; **tus•sling** \ˈtəs-ling, -ə-ling\ : to struggle roughly : SCUFFLE [Middle English *tussillen*]

[2]**tussle** *n* **1** : a physical contest or struggle : SCUFFLE **2** : a rough argument, controversy, or struggle against difficult odds

tus•sock \ˈtəs-ək\ *n* : a compact tuft especially of grass or sedge; *also* : a hummock in marsh bound together by plant roots [origin unknown] — **tus•socky** \ˈtəs-ə-kē\ *adj*

tussock moth *n* : any of numerous dull-colored moths that usually have wingless females and larvae with long tufts of hair

tut \a *t-sound made by suction rather than explosion; often read as* ˈtət\ *or* **tut-tut** *interj* — used to express disapproval or disbelief [origin unknown]

tu•tee \tü-ˈtē, tyü-\ *n* : one who is being tutored

tu•te•lage \ˈtüt-l-ij, ˈtyüt-\ *n* **1** : an act of guarding or protecting : GUARDIANSHIP **2** : the state of being under a guardian or tutor; *also* : the right, power, or influence of a tutor over a pupil **3** : INSTRUCTION [Latin *tutela* "protection, guardian", from *tueri* "to look at, guard"]

tu•te•lar \ˈtüt-l-ər, ˈtyüt-\ *adj* : TUTELARY

tu•te•lary \ˈtüt-l-ˌer-ē, ˈtyüt-\ *adj* **1** : having the guardianship of a person or a thing ⟨*tutelary* deities⟩ **2** : of or relating to a guardian ⟨*tutelary* authority⟩

[1]**tu•tor** \ˈtüt-ər, ˈtyüt-\ *n* : a person charged with the instruction and guidance of another: as **a** : a private teacher **b** : a college teacher especially in a British university who guides the individual studies of undergraduates in a particular field **c** : a college or university teacher ranking below an instructor **d** : a college or university officer having administrative or counseling functions [Latin, "guardian, tutor", from *tueri* "to look at, guard"] — **tu•tor•ship** \-ˌship\ *n*

[2]**tutor** *vb* : to teach usually individually

[1]**tu•to•ri•al** \tü-ˈtōr-ē-əl, tyü-, -ˈtȯr-\ *adj* : of, relating to, or involving a tutor

[2]**tutorial** *n* : a class conducted by a tutor for one student or a small number of students

tut•ti-frut•ti \ˌtüt-ē-ˈfrüt-ē\ *n* : a confection or ice cream containing chopped usually candied fruits [Italian *tutti frutti*, literally, "all fruits"]

tu•tu \ˈtü-tü\ *n* : a very short projecting skirt worn by a ballerina [French, from baby talk *cucu*, *tutu* "backside", alteration of *cul*]

tu-whit tu-whoo \tə-ˌhwit-tə-ˈhwü, -ˌwit-tə-ˈwü\ *n* : the cry of an owl [imitative]

tux \ˈtəks\ *n* : TUXEDO

tux•e•do \ˌtək-ˈsēd-ō\ *n, pl* **-dos** *or* **-does** : a semiformal dress suit for men [*Tuxedo* Park, New York]

tutu

△ **origin** *Tuxedo* can be traced back to a Delaware Indian word meaning "wolf". The Delawares of eastern North America belonged to three groups whose totems were the turkey, the turtle, and the wolf. *P'tuksit*, the Delaware word for "wolf", was used as a name for the third group. In the 18th century European Americans gave the name of the P'tuksit, anglicized as *Tuxedo*, to a village in southeastern New York. In the 1880's a large tract of land called Tuxedo Park, near the village and on the shore of Tuxedo Lake, became a fashionable resort community. It was here, near the turn of the century, that some young men began to wear dress jackets without tails. The new style which they made popular was soon called *tuxedo*.

tu•yere \twē-ˈeər\ *n* : a nozzle through which an air blast is delivered to a forge or blast furnace [French *tuyère*, from *tuyau* "pipe"]

tv \ˈtē-ˈvē\ *n, often cap T & V* : TELEVISION [*television*]

twa \ˈtwȧ\ *or* **twae** \ˈtwȧ, ˈtwē\ *Scottish variant of* TWO

twad•dle \ˈtwäd-l\ *n* : silly idle talk : DRIVEL [probably alteration of English dialect *twattle*]

twain \ˈtwān\ *n* **1** : TWO **2** : COUPLE, PAIR [Old English *twēgen*, adj. and pron., "two"]

[1]**twang** \ˈtwang\ *n* **1** : a harsh quick ringing sound like that of a plucked bowstring **2 a** : nasal speech or resonance **b** : the characteristic speech of a region, locality, or group of people [imitative]

[2]**twang** *vb* **twanged**; **twang•ing** \ˈtwang-ing\ **1** : to sound or cause to sound with a twang **2** : to speak with a nasal intonation

[1]**tweak** \ˈtwēk\ *vt* : to pinch and pull with a sudden jerk and twist [Old English *twiccian* "to pluck"]

[2]**tweak** *n* : an act of tweaking : PINCH

tweed \ˈtwēd\ *n* **1** : a rough woolen fabric made usually in twill weaves **2** *pl* : tweed clothing; *esp* : a tweed suit [Scottish *tweel* "twill", from Middle English *twyll*]

tweedy \ˈtwēd-ē\ *adj* **tweed•i•er**; **-est** **1** : of or resembling tweed **2 a** : given to wearing tweeds **b** : informal or suggestive of the outdoors in taste or habits

tweet \ˈtwēt\ *n* : CHIRP [imitative] — **tweet** *vb*

tweet•er \ˈtwēt-ər\ *n* : a small loudspeaker responsive only to the higher acoustic frequencies and reproducing sounds of high pitch

tweeze \ˈtwēz\ *vt* : to pluck or remove with tweezers [back-formation from *tweezers*]

tweez•ers \ˈtwē-zərz\ *n pl* : a small metal instrument that is used for plucking, holding, or manipulating, and consists of two legs joined at one end [obsolete *tweeze* "case for small implements", from French *étui*]

Twelfth Day *n* : EPIPHANY 1

Twelfth Night *n* **1** : the eve preceding Epiphany **2** : the evening of Epiphany

twelve \ˈtwelv\ *n* **1** : one more than 11; *also* : a symbol representing this — see NUMBER table **2** *cap* : the twelve original disciples of Jesus **3** : the 12th in a set or series **4** : something having 12 units or members [Old English *twelf*] — **twelve** *adj or pron* — **twelfth** \ˈtwelfth, ˈtwelftth\ *n* — **twelfth** *adj or adv*

twelve•month \-ˌmənth, -ˌməntth\ *n* : YEAR

twen•ty \ˈtwent-ē\ *n, pl* **twenties** : one more than 19; *also* : a symbol representing this — see NUMBER table [Old English *twēntig*] — **twenty** *adj or pron* — **twen•ti•eth** \-ē-əth\ *adj or n*

\ə\ **abut**	\au̇\ **out**	\i\ **tip**	\ȯ\ **saw**	\u̇\ **foot**
\ər\ **further**	\ch\ **chin**	\ī\ **life**	\ȯi\ **coin**	\y\ **yet**
\a\ **mat**	\e\ **pet**	\j\ **job**	\th\ **thin**	\yü\ **few**
\ā\ **take**	\ē\ **easy**	\ng\ **sing**	\th\ **this**	\yu̇\ **cure**
\ä\ **cot, cart**	\g\ **go**	\ō\ **bone**	\ü\ **food**	\zh\ **vision**

twen•ty–one \ˌtwent-ē-ˈwən\ *n* : BLACKJACK 3

twen•ty–twen•ty *or* **20/20** \ˌtwent-ē-ˈtwent-ē\ *adj* : of normal acuity ⟨*twenty-twenty* vision⟩ [from the custom of testing vision chiefly at a distance of 20 feet]

twen•ty–two \ˌtwent-ē-ˈtü\ *n* : a 22-caliber rifle or pistol — usually written .22

twerp *also* **twirp** \ˈtwərp\ *n* : a silly, insignificant, or contemptible person [origin unknown]

twice \ˈtwīs\ *adv* : two times ⟨*twice* absent⟩ ⟨*twice* two is four⟩ [Middle English *twiges, twies,* from Old English *twiga*]

twice–born \-ˈbȯrn\ *adj* : having undergone a spiritual rebirth or regeneration through religious conversion or renewal or by an initiation ceremony

twice–laid \-ˈlād\ *adj* : made from the ends of rope and strands of used rope ⟨*twice-laid* rope⟩

twice–told \ˌtwīs-ˌtōld\ *adj* **1** : narrated twice **2** : HACKNEYED, TRITE — used chiefly in the phrase *a twice-told tale*

[1]**twid•dle** \ˈtwid-l\ *vb* **twid•dled**; **twid•dling** \ˈtwid-ling, -l-ing\ **1** : to be busy with trifles : FIDDLE **2** : to rotate lightly or idly ⟨*twiddle* one's thumbs⟩ [origin unknown]

[2]**twiddle** *n* : an act of twiddling : TURN, TWIST

[1]**twig** \ˈtwig\ *n* : a small shoot or branch [Old English *twigge*] — **twigged** \ˈtwigd\ *adj* — **twig•gy** \ˈtwig-ē\ *adj*

[2]**twig** *vb* **twigged**; **twig•ging** : to catch on : NOTICE, UNDERSTAND [perhaps from Scottish Gaelic *tuig* "I understand"]

twi•light \ˈtwī-ˌlīt\ *n* **1 a** : the light from the sky between full night and sunrise or between sunset and full night **b** : the time of twilight **2 a** : a state of indistinctness **b** : a period of decline [Middle English, from *twi-* "two" + *light*] — **twilight** *adj*

twilight sleep *n* : a state produced by injection of morphine and scopolamine in which awareness and memory of pain is dulled or effaced

[1]**twill** \ˈtwil\ *n* **1** : a fabric with a twill weave **2** : a textile weave that produces a pattern of diagonal lines or ribs [Middle English *twyll,* from Old English *twilic* "having a double thread", from Latin *bilic-, bilix,* from *bi-* + *licium* "thread"]

[2]**twill** *vt* : to make (cloth) with a twill weave

[1]**twin** \ˈtwin\ *adj* **1** : born with one other or as a pair at one birth ⟨my *twin* brother⟩ ⟨*twin* girls⟩ **2 a** : made up of two similar, related, or connected members or parts **b** : paired in a close or necessary relationship **c** : having or consisting of two identical units **d** : being one of a pair ⟨*twin* city⟩ [Old English *twinn* "twofold"]

[2]**twin** *n* **1** : either of two offspring born together **2** : one of two persons or things closely related to or resembling each other

[3]**twin** *vb* **twinned**; **twin•ning** **1** : to bring together in close association : COUPLE **2** : MATCH 4 **3** : to bring forth twins

twin bill *n* : DOUBLEHEADER

[1]**twine** \ˈtwīn\ *n* **1** : a strong string of two or more strands twisted together **2 a** : an act of interlacing **b** : TANGLE [Old English *twīn*]

[2]**twine** *vb* **1 a** : to twist together **b** : to form by twining **2 a** : to coil or cause to coil about a support **b** : WRAP ⟨*twined* their arms about each other⟩ **3** : MEANDER 1, WIND

[1]**twinge** \ˈtwinj\ *vb* **twinged**; **twing•ing** *or* **twinge•ing** : to affect with or feel a sudden sharp local pain [Old English *twengan* "to pinch"]

[2]**twinge** *n* **1** : a sudden sharp stab of pain **2** : a moral or emotional pang

[1]**twin•kle** \ˈtwing-kəl\ *vb* **twin•kled**; **twin•kling** \ˈtwing-kə-ling, -kling\ **1** : to shine or cause to shine with a flickering or sparkling light : SCINTILLATE **2** : to appear bright with merriment **3** : to move or flutter rapidly : FLIT [Old English *twinclian*] — **twin•kler** \-kə-lər, -klər\ *n*

[2]**twinkle** *n* **1** : a wink of the eyelids **2** : a very brief period : TWINKLING **3** : SPARKLE, FLICKER ⟨that *twinkle* in your eye⟩ — **twin•kly** \-kə-lē, -klē\ *adj*

twin•kling \ˈtwing-kə-ling, -kling, *for 1b* -kling\ *n* **1 a** : a winking of the eye **b** : INSTANT ⟨in a *twinkling*⟩ **2** : SCINTILLATION

twin–screw \ˈtwin-ˈskrü\ *adj* : having a right-handed and a left-handed propeller parallel to each other on each side of the plane of the keel

[1]**twirl** \ˈtwərl\ *vb* **1** : to revolve or cause to revolve rapidly : SPIN, WHIRL ⟨*twirl* a baton⟩ **2** : to pitch in a baseball game **3** : CURL, TWIST ⟨*twirl* one's hair⟩ [perhaps of Scandinavian origin] — **twirl•er** *n*

[2]**twirl** *n* **1** : an act of twirling **2** : COIL, WHORL

twirp *variant of* TWERP

[1]**twist** \ˈtwist\ *vb* **1** : to unite by winding one thread, strand, or wire around another **2** : TWINE 2a, COIL **3 a** : to turn so as to sprain or hurt ⟨*twisted* my ankle⟩ **b** : to alter the meaning of : PERVERT ⟨*twisted* the facts⟩ **c** : CONTORT ⟨*twist* one's face into a grin⟩ **d** : to pull off, rotate, or break by a turning force **e** : WARP 1a **4** : to follow a winding course **5 a** : to turn or change shape under a turning force **b** : SQUIRM, WRITHE ⟨*twisting* in their seats⟩ **6** : to turn around [Middle English *twisten,* from Old English *-twist* "rope"]

[2]**twist** *n* **1** : something formed by twisting or winding: as **a** : a thread, yarn, or cord formed by twisting two or more strands together **b** : a baked piece of twisted dough **c** : tobacco leaves twisted into a thick roll **2 a** : an act of twisting : the state of being twisted **b** : a spiral turn or curve **3 a** : a turning aside : DEFLECTION **b** : ECCENTRICITY ⟨a *twist* of speech⟩ **c** : a distortion of meaning ⟨gave the facts a *twist*⟩ **4 a** : an unexpected turn or development **b** : GIMMICK ⟨a new *twist* in advertising⟩

twist•er \ˈtwis-tər\ *n* **1** : one that twists **2** : a tornado, waterspout, or dust devil in which the rotatory ascending movement of a column of air is visible

twit \ˈtwit\ *vt* **twit•ted**; **twit•ting** : to poke fun at gently [Old English *ætwītan* "to reproach", from *æt* "at" + *wītan* "to blame"]

[1]**twitch** \ˈtwich\ *vb* **1** : to move or pull with a sudden motion **2** : PLUCK ⟨*twitched* at my sleeve⟩ **3** : to move jerkily [Middle English *twicchen*]

[2]**twitch** *n* **1** : an act of twitching **2 a** : a short sharp contraction of muscle fibers **b** : a slight jerk of a body part

[1]**twit•ter** \ˈtwit-ər\ *vb* **1** : to utter successive chirping sounds **2 a** : to talk in a chattering fashion **b** : GIGGLE, TITTER **3** : to shake with agitation : FLUTTER [Middle English *twiteren*]

[2]**twitter** *n* **1** : a trembling agitation **2** : a succession of chirping sounds **3** : a light chattering — **twit•tery** \-ə-rē\ *adj*

twixt \twikst, ˈtwikst\ *prep* : BETWEEN [Middle English *twix,* short for *betwix, betwixt*]

two \ˈtü\ *n* **1** : one more than one; *also* : a symbol representing this — see NUMBER table **2** : the second in a set or series **3** : something having two units or members [Old English *twā,* adj. and pron. (feminine and neuter)] — **two** *adj or pron*

two–base hit *n* : DOUBLE 1b

two–bit \ˌtü-ˌbit\ *adj* **1** : of the value of two bits **2** : being cheap, petty, or small-time

two bits *n sing or pl* **1** : QUARTER 3d **2** : something of small worth or importance

[1]**two–by–four** \ˌtü-bə-ˈfōr, -ˈfȯr\ *adj* **1** : measuring two units (as inches) by four **2** : very small or petty

[2]**two–by–four** *n* : a piece of lumber approximately 2 by 4 inches (5.1 by 10.2 centimeters) as sawed and usually 1⅝ by 3⅝ inches (4.1 by 9.2 centimeters) if dressed

two–dimensional *adj* **1** : having two dimensions **2** : lacking depth of characterization ⟨*two-dimensional* fiction⟩

two–faced \ˈtü-ˈfāst\ *adj* **1** : having two faces **2** : deceptively false in speech or manner — **two–faced•ly** \-ˈfā-səd-lē, -ˈfāst-lē\ *adv*

two–fist•ed \ˈtü-ˈfis-təd\ *adj* : VIRILE, VIGOROUS

two•fold \ˈtü-ˌfōld, -ˈfōld\ *adj* **1** : having two units or members **2** : of or equaling 200 percent — **twofold** *adv*

2, 4–D \ˌtü-ˌfōr-ˈdē, -ˌfȯr-\ *n* : a white crystalline organic compound used as a weed killer

two–hand•ed \ˈtü-ˈhan-dəd\ *adj* **1** : used with both hands ⟨a *two-handed* sword⟩ **2** : requiring two persons ⟨a *two-handed* saw⟩ **3** : having or efficient with two hands

two•pence \ˈtəp-əns, *United States also* ˈtü-ˌpens\ *also* **tuppence** \ˈtəp-əns\ *n* : the sum of two pence

two•pen•ny \ˈtəp-nē, -ə-nē, *United States also* ˈtü-ˌpen-ē\ *adj* : of the value of or costing twopence

two–ply \ˈtü-ˈplī\ *adj* : consisting of two strands or thicknesses

two•some \ˈtü-səm\ *n* : a group of two persons or things

two–step \ˈtü-ˌstep\ *n* **1** : a ballroom dance executed in march or polka time **2** : a piece of music for the two-step — **two–step** *vi*

two–time \ˈtü-ˌtīm\ *vt* : to be unfaithful or treacherous to; *esp* : to be sexually unfaithful to (a spouse or lover)

two–way *adj* : involving two elements or allowing movement or use in two directions or manners

two–winged fly \ˌtü-ˌwingd-\ *n* : any of a large order (Diptera) of winged or rarely wingless insects (as a housefly, mosquito, or gnat) that have the anterior wings functional and the posterior wings reduced to balancers and that have segmented often headless, eyeless, and legless larvae

-ty *n suffix* : -ITY [Old French *-té*, from Latin *-tat-*, *-tas*]

ty•coon \tī-'kün\ *n* **1** : SHOGUN **2** : a business executive of exceptional wealth and power [Japanese *taikun*, from Chinese (Pekingese dialect) *ta*[4] "great" + *chün*[1] "ruler"]

△ **origin** The shoguns were commanders-in-chief of the Japanese army, and so great was their influence that for centuries they were the real rulers of Japan, though they acted in the name of the emperor. When Commodore Matthew Perry went to Japan in 1853, he seems to have thought he was negotiating with the emperor when in fact his antagonist was the shogun. The honorific *taikun* was used to describe the shogun to visiting Westerners. This title, borrowed from Chinese *ta*[4] *chün*[1], "great ruler", was more impressive than *shogun*, "general". Japanese *taikun*, usually spelled *tycoon* in English, caught on in the United States after Perry's expedition fired the public imagination. It was occasionally extended to describe any powerful person. Later specialization of meaning set in and *tycoon* became a term for an industrial magnate.

tying *present participle of* TIE

tyke *also* **tike** \'tīk\ *n* **1** : DOG 1a, CUR **2** : a small child [Old Norse *tīk* "bitch"]

tympani *variant of* TIMPANI

tym•pan•ic \tim-'pan-ik\ *adj* **1** : of, relating to, or being a tympanum **2** : resembling a drum

tympanic membrane *n* : EARDRUM

tym•pa•num \'tim-pə-nəm\ *n, pl* **-na** \-nə\ *also* **-nums 1 a** (1) : EARDRUM (2) : MIDDLE EAR **b** : a thin tense membrane covering an organ of hearing or of sound-production of an insect **2 a** : the recessed usually triangular face of a pediment within the frame made by the upper and lower cornices **b** : the space within an arch and above a lintel or a subordinate arch [Latin, "drum, architectural panel", from Greek *tympanon* "drum"]

[1]type \'tīp\ *n* **1 a** : a person or thing believed to foreshadow or symbolize another **b** (1) : one having qualities of a higher category : MODEL (2) : a specimen or series of specimens on which a taxonomic species or subspecies is actually based **2 a** : a rectangular block typically of metal or wood bearing a relief character from which an inked print is made **b** : a collection of such blocks or the letters printed from them **c** : characters (as numbers, letters, or punctuation marks) for printing ⟨the *type* for this book has been photocomposed⟩ **3 a** : general form or character common to a number of individuals that distinguishes them as an identifiable class ⟨horses of draft *type*⟩ **b** : a particular kind, class, or group : SORT ⟨a seedless *type* of orange⟩ [Latin *typus* "image", from Greek *typos* "blow, impression, model", from *typtein* "to strike, beat"] **syn** see KIND

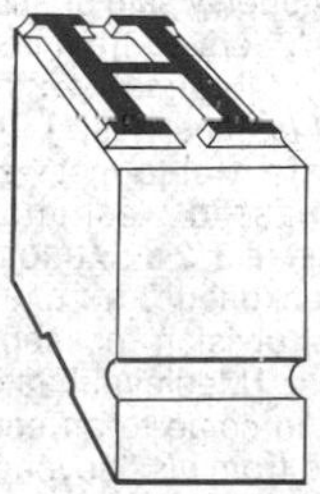

[1]type 2a

[2]type *vb* **1** : TYPIFY **2** : TYPEWRITE **3** : to identify as belonging to a type: as **a** : to determine the natural type of (as a blood sample) **b** : TYPECAST — **typ•able** *or* **type•able** \'tī-pə-bəl\ *adj*

type•cast \'tīp-,kast\ *vt* **1** : to cast (an actor or actress) in a part calling for the same characteristics as those he or she possesses **2** : to cast (an actor or actress) repeatedly in the same type of role

type•face \'tīp-,fās\ *n* : all type of a single design

type•found•er \-,faun-dər\ *n* : one engaged in the design and production of metal printing type for hand composition — **type•found•ing** \-diŋ\ *n* — **type•found•ry** \-drē\ *n*

type metal *n* : an alloy that consists essentially of lead, antimony, and tin and is used in making printing type

type•script \-,skript\ *n* : something that is typewritten [*type* + manu*script*]

type•set \'tīp-,set\ *vt* **-set; -set•ting** : to set in type : COMPOSE

type•set•ter \-,set-ər\ *n* : one that sets type for printing — **type•set•ting** \-,set-iŋ\ *n*

type•write \'tī-,prīt\ *vb* : to write with a typewriter

type•writ•er \'tī-,prīt-ər\ *n* **1** : a machine for writing in characters similar to those produced by printer's type by means of keyboard-operated types striking through an inked ribbon **2** : TYPIST

type•writ•ing \-,prīt-iŋ\ *n* **1** : the act or study of or skill in using a typewriter **2** : the printing done with a typewriter

typh•lo•sole \'tif-lə-,sōl\ *n* : a fold of the wall that projects into the cavity of the intestine of some invertebrates (as the earthworm) [Greek *typhlos* "blind" + *sōlēn* "pipe"]

ty•phoid \'tī-,fȯid, tī-', 'tī-'\ *adj* : of, relating to, or being typhoid fever

typhoid fever *n* : a communicable bacterial disease marked especially by fever, diarrhea, prostration, headache, and intestinal inflammation — called also *typhoid* [derived from New Latin *typhus*]

ty•phoon \tī-'fün\ *n* : a tropical cyclone occurring in the region of the Philippines or the China sea [earlier *touffon*, from Arabic *tūfān* "hurricane", from Greek *typhōn* "whirlwind"]

ty•phus \'tī-fəs\ *n* : a severe rickettsial disease marked by high fever, stupor alternating with delirium, intense headache, and a dark red rash and transmitted especially by body lice [New Latin, from Greek *typhos* "fever"]

typ•i•cal \'tip-i-kəl\ *adj* **1** : being or having the nature of a type ⟨*typical* species⟩ **2** : combining or exhibiting the essential characteristics of a group ⟨a *typical* suburban house⟩ **syn** see REGULAR — **typ•i•cal•i•ty** \,tip-ə-'kal-ət-ē\ *n* — **typ•i•cal•ly** \'tip-i-kə-lē, -klē\ *adv* — **typ•i•cal•ness** \-kəl-nəs\ *n*

typ•i•fy \'tip-ə-,fī\ *vt* **-fied; -fy•ing 1** : PREFIGURE 1, REPRESENT **2** : to have or embody the essential or main characteristics of

typ•ist \'tī-pəst\ *n* : one who typewrites

ty•po \'tī-pō\ *n, pl* **typos** : a typographical error

ty•pog•ra•pher \tī-'päg-rə-fər\ *n* **1** : COMPOSITOR **2** : PRINTER a **3** : a specialist in the choice and arrangement of type matter

ty•pog•ra•phy \-fē\ *n* : the style, arrangement, or appearance of typeset matter — **ty•po•graph•ic** \,tī-pə-'graf-ik\ *adj* — **ty•po•graph•i•cal** \-'graf-i-kəl\ *adj* — **ty•po•graph•i•cal•ly** \-i-kə-lē, -klē\ *adv*

typy *or* **typ•ey** \'tī-pē\ *adj* **typ•i•er; -est** : of superior bodily conformation ⟨a *typy* steer⟩

ty•ran•ni•cal \tə-'ran-i-kəl, tī-\ *also* **ty•ran•nic** \-'ran-ik\ *adj* : *of, relating to, or characteristic of a tyrant or tyranny* : DESPOTIC — **ty•ran•ni•cal•ly** \-'ran-i-kə-lē, -klē\ *adv*

tyr•an•nize \'tir-ə-,nīz\ *vb* **1** : to act like a tyrant **2** : to treat tyrannically — **tyr•an•niz•er** *n*

ty•ran•no•saur \tə-'ran-ə-,sȯr, tī-\ *n* : a very large American flesh-eating dinosaur of the Cretaceous having small forelegs and walking on its hind legs [derived from Greek *tyrannos* "tyrant" + *sauros* "lizard"]

tyrannosaur

ty•ran•no•sau•rus \tə-,ran-ə-'sȯr-əs, tī-\ *n* : TYRANNOSAUR

tyr•an•nous \'tir-ə-nəs\ *adj* : *marked by tyranny*; *esp* : *unjustly severe* — **tyr•an•nous•ly** *adv*

tyr•an•ny \'tir-ə-nē\ *n, pl* **-nies 1 a** : a government in which absolute power is held by a single ruler **b** : the office, authority, and administration of such a ruler **2** : arbitrary and despotic government; *esp* : rigorous, cruel, and oppressive government **3** : SEVERITY, RIGOR ⟨the *tyranny* of the alarm clock⟩ **4** : a tyrannical act [Middle French *tyrannie*, from Medieval Latin *tyrannia*, from Latin *tyrannus* "tyrant"]

ty•rant \'tī-rənt\ *n* **1** : an absolute ruler unrestrained by law or constitution **2 a** : a ruler who exercises absolute power in an oppressive or brutal manner **b** : one resembling such a tyrant in the harsh use of authority or power [Old French *tyran*, *tyrant*, *tyrannus*, from Greek *tyrannos*]

tyrant flycatcher *n* : any of a family of large American flycatchers with a flattened bill usually hooked at the tip

tyre *chiefly British variant of* TIRE

Tyr•i•an purple \ˌtir-ē-ən-\ *n* : a synthetic crimson or purple dye formerly obtained by the ancient Greeks and Romans from gastropod mollusks [*Tyre*, city of ancient Phoenicia]

ty•ro \ˈtī-rō\ *n, pl* **tyros** : a beginner in learning [Latin *tiro* "young soldier, tyro"]

ty•ro•sine \ˈtī-rə-ˌsēn\ *n* : an amino acid obtained by hydrolysis of proteins [derived from Greek *tyros* "cheese"]

tzar \ˈzär, ˈtsär, ˈsär\ *variant of* CZAR

U

u—Uzbek

u \ˈyü\ *n, pl* **u's** *or* **us** \ˈyüz\ *often cap* : the 21st letter of the English alphabet

ubiq•ui•tous \yü-ˈbik-wət-əs\ *adj* : existing or being everywhere at the same time : widely or generally present [from *ubiquity*, from Latin *ubique* "everywhere"] — **ubiq•ui•tous•ly** *adv* — **ubiq•ui•tous•ness** *n* — **ubiq•ui•ty** \-wət-ē\ *n*

U–boat \ˈyü-ˈbōt\ *n* : a German submarine [German *u-boot*, short for *unterseeboot*, literally, "undersea boat"]

ud•der \ˈəd-ər\ *n* **1** : a large bag-shaped organ consisting of two or more mammary glands enclosed in a common envelope and each provided with a nipple **2** : a mammary gland [Old English *ūder*]

UFO \ˌyü-ef-ˈō\ *n, pl* **UFO's** *or* **UFOs** \-ˈōz\ : an unidentified flying object; *esp* : FLYING SAUCER [*u*nidentified *f*lying *o*bject]

ugh *often read as* ˈəg *or* ˈək *or* ˈə\ *interj* — used to indicate the sound of a cough or grunt or to express disgust or horror [probably imitative]

ug•li•fy \ˈəg-li-ˌfī\ *vt* **-fied**; **-fy•ing** : to make ugly

ug•ly \ˈəg-lē\ *adj* **ug•li•er**; **-est** **1** : FRIGHTFUL ⟨an *ugly* wound⟩ **2 a** : offensive to the sight : UNSIGHTLY **b** : offensive or unpleasing to any sense ⟨an *ugly* smell⟩ **3** : morally offensive or objectionable **4 a** : likely to cause inconvenience or discomfort : TROUBLESOME ⟨an *ugly* situation⟩ **b** : SURLY ⟨an *ugly* disposition⟩ — **ug•li•ness** *n* [Old Norse *uggligr*, from *uggr* "fear"]

ugly duckling *n* : an unpromising child or thing actually capable of developing into a person or thing worthy of attention or respect [*The Ugly Duckling*, story by Hans Christian Andersen in which a supposed ugly duckling develops into a swan]

Ugri•an \ˈü-grē-ən, ˈyü-\ *n* : a member of the eastern division of the Finno-Ugric peoples [obsolete Russian *Ugre* "Hungarians"] — **Ugrian** *adj*

uh–huh *two* m*'s separated by the voiceless sound* h, ən-hən, ˈən-ˌhən\ *interj* — used to indicate affirmation, agreement, or gratification [probably imitative]

uh•lan \ˈü-ˌlän, ˈü-lən, ˈyü-lən\ *n* : one of a body of Prussian light cavalry originally modeled on Tatar lancers [German, from Polish *ulan*, from Turkish *oğlan* "boy, servant"]

uin•ta•there \yü-ˈint-ə-ˌthiər\ *n* : any of a genus of extinct plant-eating ungulate mammals that somewhat resembled elephants [*Uinta* county, Wyoming + Greek *thērion* "beast"]

ukase \yü-ˈkās, -ˈkāz, ˈyü-ˌ; ˈü-ˌkäz\ *n* : an edict especially of a Russian emperor or government [French, from Russian *ukaz*]

Ukrai•ni•an \yü-ˈkrā-nē-ən\ *n* **1** : a native or inhabitant of the Ukraine **2** : the Slavic language of the Ukrainian people — **Ukrainian** *adj*

uku•le•le \ˌyü-kə-ˈlā-lē, ˌü-kə-\ *n* : a small guitar popularized in Hawaii that is strung usually with four strings and is played with the fingers or a pick [Hawaiian *ʻukulele*, from *ʻuku* "flea" + *lele* "jumping"]

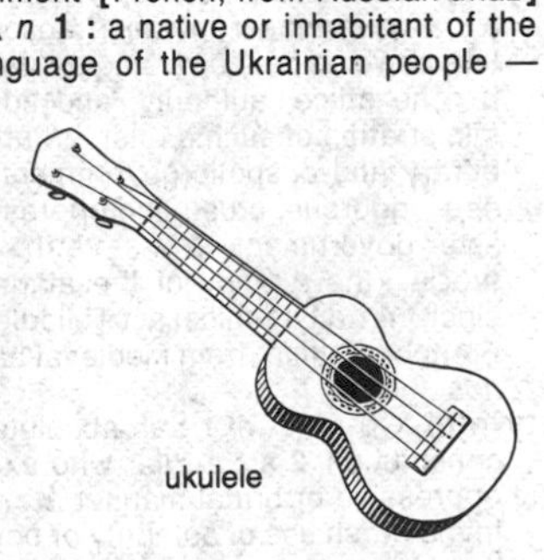

ukulele

-u•lar \yə-lər, ə-lər\ *adj suffix* : of, relating to, or resembling ⟨valv*ular*⟩ [Latin *-ularis*, from *-ulus*, *-ula*, *-ulum* "-ule" + *-aris* "-ar"]

ul•cer \ˈəl-sər\ *n* **1** : a slow-healing open sore that often discharges pus **2** : something that festers and corrupts like an open sore [Latin *ulcer-*, *ulcus*]

ul•cer•ate \ˈəl-sə-ˌrāt\ *vb* : to become affected with or cause an ulcer : cause an ulcer in ⟨an *ulcerated* wound⟩ — **ul•cer•ation** \ˌəl-sə-ˈrā-shən\ *n*

ul•cer•ous \ˈəls-rəs, -ə-rəs\ *adj* **1** : of or marked by ulceration ⟨*ulcerous* lesions⟩ **2** : affected with an ulcer

-ule \ˌül, ˌyül\ *n suffix* : little one ⟨lob*ule*⟩ [Latin *-ulus, -ula, -ulum*]

ul•lage \ˈəl-ij\ *n* : the amount that a container (as a cask) lacks of being full [Middle French *eullage* "act of filling a cask", from *eullier* "to fill a cask", from Old French *ouil* "eye, bunghole", from Latin *oculus* "eye"]

ul•na \ˈəl-nə\ *n, pl* **ulnas** *or* **ul•nae** \-ˌnē, -ˌnī\ : the bone on the little-finger side of the human forearm; *also* : a corresponding part of vertebrates above fishes [Latin, "elbow"] — **ul•nar** \-nər\ *adj*

ul•ster \ˈəl-stər\ *n* : a long loose overcoat of heavy material [*Ulster*, Ireland]

ul•te•ri•or \ˌəl-ˈtir-ē-ər\ *adj* **1** : situated beyond or on the farther side **2** : lying farther away : more remote **3** : going beyond what is openly said or shown ⟨*ulterior* motives⟩ [Latin, "farther, further", derived from *uls* "beyond"] — **ul•te•ri•or•ly** *adv*

ul•ti•ma \ˈəl-tə-mə\ *n* : the last syllable of a word [Latin, feminine of *ultimus* "last"]

¹ul•ti•mate \ˈəl-tə-mət\ *adj* **1 a** : most remote in space or time : FARTHEST **b** : last in a progression : FINAL **c** : EVENTUAL **d** : EXTREME 3 **2 a** : ABSOLUTE, SUPREME ⟨*ultimate* truths⟩ **b** : finally reckoned **3 a** : BASIC ⟨*ultimate* reality⟩ **b** : not capable of further division or separation : ELEMENTAL **4** : being the greatest [Medieval Latin *ultimatus* "last", from Late Latin *ultimare* "to come to an end", from Latin *ultimus* "last, farthest", derived from *uls* "beyond"] **syn** see LAST — **ul•ti•mate•ly** *adv* — **ul•ti•mate•ness** *n*

²ultimate *n* : something ultimate

Ul•ti•ma Thu•le \ˌəl-tə-mə-ˈthü-lē, -ˈthyü-\ *n* : THULE [Latin, "farthest Thule"]

ul•ti•ma•tum \ˌəl-tə-ˈmāt-əm, -ˈmät-\ *n, pl* **-tums** *or* **-ta** \-ə\ : a final proposition, condition, or demand; *esp* : one whose rejection will bring about an end of negotiations and a resort to direct action (as by force) [New Latin, from Medieval Latin *ultimatus* "last"]

ul•ti•mo \ˈəl-tə-ˌmō\ *adj* : of or occurring the month preceding the present [Latin *ultimo mense* "in the last month"]

¹ul•tra \ˈəl-trə\ *adj* : going beyond others or beyond due limit : EXTREME [*ultra-*]

²ultra *n* : EXTREMIST

ultra- *prefix* **1** : beyond in space : on the other side of ⟨*ultra*violet⟩ **2** : beyond the range or limits of : transcending ⟨*ultra*microscopic⟩ ⟨*ultra*sonic⟩ **3** : beyond what is ordinary, proper, or moderate : excessively ⟨*ultra*modern⟩ [Latin, from *ultra* "beyond", derived from *uls* "beyond"]

See *ultra-* and 2d element

ultra-adventurous
ultrabright
ultracalm
ultracareful
ultracasual
ultracautious
ultrachic
ultracivilized
ultraclean
ultracommercial
ultraconservative
ultraconvenient
ultrafashionable
ultrafast
ultrafastidious
ultrafeminine
ultrafinicky
ultrafirm
ultraglamorous
ultrahazardous
ultrahigh
ultraintelligent
ultralarge
ultraleft
ultraleftism
ultraleftist
ultraliberal
ultraliberalism
ultralow
ultramasculine
ultramilitant
ultranationalism
ultranationalist
ultranationalistic
ultraorthodox
ultrapatriotic

ultrapatriotism
ultrapermissive
ultrapessimism
ultrapessimist
ultrapessimistic
ultrapolite
ultraposh
ultrapowerful
ultrapractical
ultraprecision
ultraprivate
ultraprolific
ultrapure
ultrapurification
ultrapurify
ultraradical
ultrarapid
ultrarare
ultrarational
ultrarealism
ultrarealist
ultrarealistic
ultrarefined
ultrarespectable
ultrarevolutionary
ultrarich
ultrarightist
ultraromantic
ultrasafe
ultrasecret
ultrasecretive
ultrasensitive
ultraserious
ultrasharp
ultrasmall
ultrasophisticated
ultrastory
ultrastylish
ultrathin
ultrawide

ul•tra•cen•tri•fuge \,əl-trə-'sen-trə-,fyüj\ *n* : a high-speed centrifuge able to separate small (as colloidal) particles — **ul•tra•cen•trif•u•gal** \-,sen-'trif-yə-gəl, -'trif-i-gəl\ *adj* — **ul•tra•cen•tri•fu•ga•tion** \-,sen-trə-fyü-'gā-shən\ *n*

ul•tra•high frequency \,əl-trə-,hī-\ *n* : any radio frequency in the range between 300 and 3000 megahertz — abbreviation *UHF*

[1]**ul•tra•ma•rine** \,əl-trə-mə-'rēn\ *n* **1** : a deep blue pigment **2** : a vivid blue

[2]**ultramarine** *adj* : situated beyond the sea

ul•tra•mi•cro \,əl-trə-'mī-krō\ *adj* : being or dealing with something smaller than micro

ul•tra•mi•cro•scope \,əl-trə-'mī-krə-,skōp\ *n* : an apparatus that uses scattered light to view particles too small to be seen with an ordinary microscope

ul•tra•mi•cro•scop•ic \-,mī-krə-'skäp-ik\ *adj* **1** : too small to be seen with an ordinary microscope **2** : of or relating to an ultramicroscope — **ul•tra•mi•cro•scop•i•cal•ly** \-'skäp-i-kə-lē, -klē\ *adv*

ul•tra•mod•ern \,əl-trə-'mäd-ərn\ *adj* : extremely or excessively modern in idea, style, or tendency — **ul•tra•mod•ern•ist** \-ər-nəst\ *n*

ul•tra•short \-'shȯrt\ *adj* : very short; *esp* : having a wavelength below 10 meters

[1]**ul•tra•son•ic** \-'sän-ik\ *adj* : SUPERSONIC — **ul•tra•son•i•cal•ly** \-'sän-i-kə-lē, -klē\ *adv*

[2]**ultrasonic** *n* : a supersonic wave or frequency

ul•tra•son•ics \-'sän-iks\ *n* : SUPERSONICS

ul•tra•sound \,əl-trə-'saůnd\ *n* : vibrations of the same physical nature as sound but with frequencies above the range of human hearing

ul•tra•vi•o•let \-'vī-ə-lət\ *adj* **1** : situated beyond the visible spectrum at its violet end and having a wavelength shorter than those of visible light but longer than those of X rays **2** : relating to, producing, or employing ultraviolet radiation — **ultraviolet** *n*

ultraviolet light *n* : ultraviolet radiation

ul•u•late \'əl-yə-,lāt\ *vi* : to utter a howl or wail [Latin *ululare*] — **ul•u•lant** \-lənt\ *adj* — **ul•u•la•tion** \,əl-yə-'lā-shən\ *n*

ul•va \'əl-və\ *n* : any of a genus of green marine algae with a thin flat edible thallus — called also *sea lettuce* [Latin, "sedge"]

um•bel \'əm-bəl\ *n* : an inflorescence typical of the carrot family in which the flower stalks appear to spring from the same point to form a flat or rounded flower cluster [Latin *umbella* "umbrella"] — **um•beled** *or* **um•belled** \-bəld\ *adj* — **um•bel•late** \'əm-bə-,lāt, ,əm-'bel-ət\ *adj*

um•ber \'əm-bər\ *n* **1** : a brown earth valuable as a pigment **2 a** : a moderate to dark yellowish brown **b** : a moderate brown [probably from obsolete *umber* "shade, color", from Middle French *umbre* "shade, shadow", from Latin *umbra*] — **umber** *adj*

um•bil•i•cal \,əm-'bil-i-kəl\ *adj* : of, relating to, or adjacent to the navel

umbilical cord *n* : a cord arising from the navel that connects the fetus with the placenta

um•bil•i•cate \,əm-'bil-i-kət\ *or* **um•bil•i•cat•ed** \-'bil-ə-,kāt-əd\ *adj* : having or suggesting an umbilicus — **um•bil•i•ca•tion** \,əm-,bil-ə-'kā-shən\ *n*

um•bil•i•cus \,əm-'bil-i-kəs\ *n, pl* **-bil•i•ci** \-'bil-ə-,kī, -,kē, -,sī\ *or* **-bil•i•cus•es 1 a** : a depression in the abdominal wall at the point of attachment of the umbilical cord to the fetus **b** : any of several morphological depressions (as the hilum of a seed) **2** : a central point [Latin]

um•bles \'əm-bəlz\ *n pl* : the entrails of an animal and especially of a deer used as food [Middle English *nombles, umbles,* from Middle French *nomble* "fillet of beef, pork loin", from Latin *lumbulus* "little loin", from *lumbus* "loin"]

um•bo \'əm-bō\ *n, pl* **um•bo•nes** \,əm-'bō-nēz\ *or* **umbos 1** : the boss of a shield **2** : a rounded anatomical elevation; *esp* : one of the lateral prominences just above the hinge of a bivalve shell [Latin] — **um•bo•nate** \'əm-bə-,nāt\ *adj*

um•bra \'əm-brə\ *n, pl* **umbras** *or* **um•brae** \-brē, -,brī\ **1** : a shaded area **2** : the conical part of the shadow of a celestial body excluding all light from the primary source **3** : the central dark part of a sunspot [Latin, "shade, shadow"]

um•brage \'əm-brij\ *n* **1 a** : SHADE 1a **b** : a growth (as of tangled branches) that gives shade **2** : RESENTMENT, OFFENSE ⟨take *umbrage* at a remark⟩ [Middle French, derived from Latin *umbra*] — **um•bra•geous** \,əm-'brā-jəs\ *adj*

△ **origin** English *umbrage* originally meant "shade, shadow". This is also the meaning of its ultimate Latin source, *umbra. Umbrage* was often used figuratively, and in the 17th century the word took on the pejorative sense "a shadow of suspicion cast on someone". From this usage it was but a short semantic leap to "resentment, offense", which is the sense used in the common phrases "give umbrage" and "take umbrage".

um•brel•la \,əm-'brel-ə\ *n* **1** : a collapsible shade for protection against weather consisting of fabric stretched over hinged ribs radiating from a center pole; *esp* : a small one for carrying in the hand **2** : the bell-shaped or saucer-shaped largely jellylike body proper of most jellyfishes [Italian *ombrella,* from Latin *umbella,* from *umbra* "shade"]

umbrella 1

umbrella plant *n* : an African sedge that has large terminal whorls of slender leaves and is often grown as a houseplant

umbrella tree *n* **1** : an American magnolia having large leaves clustered at the ends of the branches **2** : any of various trees or shrubs resembling an umbrella especially in the arrangement of leaves or the shape of the crown

Um•bri•an \'əm-brē-ən\ *n* **1 a** : a member of a people of ancient Italy occupying Umbria **b** : a native or inhabitant of the Italian province of Umbria **2** : the Italic language of ancient Umbria — **Umbrian** *adj*

umi•ak *also* **oo•mi•ak** \'ü-mē-,ak\ *n* : an open Eskimo boat made of a wooden frame covered with hide [Eskimo]

umiak

[1]**um•laut** \'ům-,laůt, 'üm-\ *n* **1 a** : the change of a vowel caused by partial assimilation to a succeeding sound **b** : a vowel resulting from such partial assimilation **2** : a diacritical mark ¨ placed especially over a German vowel to indicate umlaut [German, from *um-* "around" + *laut* "sound"]

[2]**umlaut** *vt* **1** : to produce by umlaut **2** : to write or print an umlaut over

[1]**um•pire** \'əm-,pīr\ *n* **1** : one having authority to decide finally a controversy or question between parties **2** : an official in a sport who conducts the game and rules on plays [Middle English *oumpere,* from *noumpere* (the phrase *a noumpere* being understood as *an oumpere*), from Middle French *nomper* "not equal, not paired", from *non-* + *per* "equal", from Latin *par*]

[2]**umpire** *vb* : to supervise or act as umpire ⟨*umpire* a baseball game⟩

\ə\ **abut**	\aů\ **out**	\i\ **tip**	\ȯ\ **saw**	\ů\ **foot**
\ər\ **further**	\ch\ **chin**	\ī\ **life**	\ȯi\ **coin**	\y\ **yet**
\a\ **mat**	\e\ **pet**	\j\ **job**	\th\ **thin**	\yü\ **few**
\ā\ **take**	\ē\ **easy**	\ng\ **sing**	\th\ **this**	\yů\ **cure**
\ä\ **cot, cart**	\g\ **go**	\ō\ **bone**	\ü\ **food**	\zh\ **vision**

ump•teen \ˈəm-ˈtēn, ˈəmp-, ˌəm-, ˌəmp-\ *adj* **:** very many **:** indefinitely numerous [blend of earlier *umpty* "such and such" and *-teen* (as in *thirteen*)] — **ump•teenth** \-ˈtēnth, -ˈtēntth\ *adj*

¹un- \ˌən, ˈən\ *prefix* **1 :** not **:** IN-, NON- — in adjectives formed from adjectives ⟨*un*certain⟩ ⟨*un*skilled⟩ or participles ⟨*un*dressed⟩ and in nouns formed from nouns ⟨*un*concern⟩ **2 :** opposite of **:** contrary to — in adjectives formed from adjectives ⟨*un*constitutional⟩ or participles ⟨*un*believing⟩ and in nouns formed from nouns ⟨*un*reason⟩ [Old English]

²un- *prefix* **1 :** do the opposite of **:** reverse (a specified action) **:** DE- 1a, DIS- 1a — in verbs formed from verbs ⟨*un*bend⟩ ⟨*un*dress⟩ ⟨*un*fold⟩ **2 a :** deprive of **:** remove (a specified thing) from **:** remove — in verbs formed from nouns ⟨*un*frock⟩ ⟨*un*sex⟩ **b :** release from **:** free from — in verbs formed from nouns ⟨*un*hand⟩ **c :** remove from **:** extract from **:** bring out of — in verbs formed from nouns ⟨*un*bosom⟩ **d :** cause to cease to be — in verbs formed from nouns ⟨*un*man⟩ **3 :** completely ⟨*un*loose⟩ [Old English *on-*, *un-*, alteration of *and-* "against"]

See *un-* and 2d element

unabrasive
unabrasiveness
unabsorbable
unabsorbed
unabsorbent
unacademic
unacademically
unaccented
unaccentuated
unacceptability
unacceptable
unacceptably
unaccepted
unacclimated
unacclimatized
unaccommodating
unaccomplished
unaccredited
unachievable
unachieved
unacknowledged
unacquainted
unactable
unacted
unadaptable
unadapted
unaddressed
unadjusted
unadmirable
unadmitted
unadoptable
unadvantageous
unadventurous
unadvertised
unadvisable
unaesthetic
unaffectionate
unaffectionately
unaffiliated
unaffluent
unaffordable
unafraid
unaged
unaggressive
unaggressively
unaggressiveness
unagile
unaging
unaided
unair-conditioned
unalienated
unalike
unalleviated
unallied
unallocated
unallowable
unaltered
unambiguous
unambiguously
unambitious
unambitiously
unamenable
unamendable
unamended
unamiable
unamplified
unamusing
unanalyzable
unanalyzed
unanimated
unannotated
unannounced
unanointed
unanonymous
unanswered
unanticipated
unapologetic
unapologetically
unappalled
unapparent
unappeased
unappetizing
unappetizingly
unappreciated
unappreciative
unapproachability
unapproachable
unapproachableness
unapproachably
unapproached
unappropriated
unapproved
unarguable
unarguably
unaristocratic
unarmored
unarrested
unarrogant
unarticulated
unartistic
unashamed
unashamedly
unaspirated
unaspiring
unassailed
unassigned
unassimilable
unassimilated
unassisted
unassociated
unassuaged
unastronomical
unathletic
unattainable
unattempted
unattended
unattested
unattractive
unattractively
unattractiveness
unattributable
unaudited
unauspicious
unauthentic
unauthenticated
unauthorized
unavailability
unavailable
unavowed
unawakened
unawarded
unawed
unbaked
unbaptized
unbeautified
unbeautiful
unbeautifully
unbefitting
unbelligerent
unbeloved
unbemused
unbigoted
unbitter
unblamable
unblamed
unbleached
unblemished
unblended
unblotted
unboastful
unbookish
unborrowed
unbothered
unbought
unbowdlerized
unbracketed
unbranded
unbreakable
unbridgeable
unbridged
unbrilliant
unbrotherly
unbruised
unbrushed
unbudgeted
unbudging
unburied
unburnable
unburned
unburnished
unburnt
unbusinesslike
unbusy
uncalcified
uncalled
uncanceled
uncanonical
uncapitalized
uncaptured
uncared-for
uncaring
uncarpeted
uncashed
uncastrated
uncataloged
uncatchable
uncaught
uncelebrated
uncensored
uncensured
uncertified
unchallenged
unchallenging
unchanged
unchanging
unchaperoned
uncharacteristic
uncharacteristically
uncharismatic
uncharming
unchary
unchastened
unchecked
unchic
unchivalrous
unchivalrously
unchristened
unchronicled
unciliated
unclad
unclaimed
unclarity
unclassifiable
unclear
uncleared
unclimbable
unclimbed
unclog
uncloistered
unclouded
uncluttered
uncoated
uncoerced
uncollected
uncollectible
uncolored
uncombed
uncombined
uncomely
uncomforted
uncomic
uncommanding
uncommercial
uncompanionable
uncompensated
uncompetitive
uncompetitively
uncompetitiveness
uncomplaining
uncomplainingly
uncompleted
uncomplicated
uncompounded
uncomprehended
uncomprehending
uncomprehensible
uncompromised
unconcealable
unconcealed
unconfessed
unconfident
unconfined
unconfirmed
unconfused
uncongenial
unconnected
unconquered
unconscientious
unconsecrated
unconsolidated
unconstrained
unconsumed
uncontainable
uncontaminated
uncontemporary
uncontested
uncontradicted
uncontrived
uncontrolled
uncontroversial
uncontroversially
unconverted
unconvinced
unconvincing
unconvincingly
uncooked
uncooperative
uncoordinated
uncordial
uncorrected
uncorroborated
uncorrupt
uncorrupted
uncorruptible
uncountable
uncourageous
uncourteous
uncowed
uncreative
uncredited
uncrippled
uncriticized
uncropped
uncrossable
uncrowded
uncultivable
uncultivated
uncultured
uncurbed
uncured
uncurious
uncurtained
uncustomarily
uncustomary
uncynical
uncynically
undamaged
undamped
undaring
undated
undazzled
undecidable
undecipherable
undecked
undeclared
undecorated
undefeatable
undefeated
undefended
undefiled
undefinable
undefined
undeformed
undeliverable
undelivered
undemanding
undemocratic
undemocratically
undenominational
undependable
undescribable
undeserved
undeservedly
undeserving
undesired
undetachable
undetectable
undetected
undeterminable
undetermined
undeterred
undeveloped
undiagnosable
undiagnosed
undialectical
undifferentiated
undigested
undigestible
undignified
undiluted
undiminished
undiminishing
undimmed
undiplomatic
undiplomatically
undischarged
undisciplined
undisclosed
undiscouraged
undiscoverable
undiscovered
undiscriminating
undiscussed
undismayed
undisputable
undisputably
undisputed
undissolved
undistinguishable
undistinguished
undistorted
undistracted
undistributed
undisturbed
undivided
undivulged
undoctored
undoctrinaire
undocumented
undogmatic
undomesticated
undoubtable
undoubting
undrained
undramatic
undrinkable
undutiful
undutifully
undutifulness
undyed
undynamic
uneager
uneatable
uneaten
unedifying
unedited
uneducable
uneducated
unelected
unembarrassed
unembellished
unemotional
unemotionally
unemphatic
unemphatically
unenclosed
unencouraging
unencumbered
unendorsed
unendurable
unendurably

unenduring
unenforceable
unenforced
unengaged
unenjoyable
unenlarged
unenlightened
unenlightening
unenterprising
unenthusiastic
unenthusiastically
unenticing
unenviable
unenvied
unenvious
unequipped
unescapable
unessential
unesthetic
unethical
unevaluated
unexaggerated
unexamined
unexcavated
unexcelled
unexcitable
unexcited
unexciting
unexotic
unexpectable
unexpended
unexpired
unexplainable
unexplained
unexploded
unexploited
unexplored
unexportable
unexposed
unexpressed
unexpressible
unexpurgated
unextinguished
unfaded
unfading
unfaltering
unfalteringly
unfanatical
unfashionable
unfashionably
unfastidious
unfathomable
unfazed
unfeasible
unfed
unfeminine
unfenced
unfermentable
unfermented
unfertile
unfertilized
unfilled
unfiltered
unfired
unflamboyant
unflattering
unflavored
unflustered
unflyable
unfocused
unfond
unforced
unforeseeable
unforeseen
unforgivable
unforgiving
unformulated
unfortified
unfossiliferous
unframed
unfree
unfrozen
unfulfilled
unfunctional
unfunny
unfurnished
unfused
unfussy
ungallant
ungallantly
ungarnished
ungenial
ungenteel
ungentle
ungentlemanly
ungerminated
ungifted
unglamorized
unglamorous
unglazed
ungoverned
ungraded
ungrammatical
ungrammatically
ungraspable
unguessable
unguided
unhackneyed
unhampered
unhardened
unharmed
unharmonious
unharvested
unhatched
unhealable
unhealed
unheated
unheeded
unheeding
unhelpful
unheralded
unheroic
unhesitant
unhesitantly
unhesitating
unhesitatingly
unhindered
unhip
unhired
unhistorical
unhonored
unhoped-for
unhoused
unhumorous
unhurt
unhygienic
unhysterical
unidealized
unidentifiable
unidentified
unideological
unidiomatic
unilluminated
unillustrated
unimaginable
unimaginably
unimaginative
unimpaired
unimpassioned
unimpeded
unimportance
unimportant
unimposing
unimpressed
unimpressible
unimpressionable
unimpressive
uninclined
unincorporated
unincubated
unindexed
unindicted
unindustrialized
uninfected
uninflammable
uninflected
uninfluenced
uninformed
uninhabitable
uninhabited
uninitiated
uninjured
uninoculated
uninspected
uninspired
uninspiring
uninstructed
uninstructive
uninsulated
uninsurable
uninsured
unintegrated
unintellectual
unintelligible
unintelligibly
unintended
unintentional
unintentionally
uninteresting
unintermitted
unintermittent
uninterruptible
unintimidated
uninventive
uninvested
uninvited
uninviting
uninvolved
unirradiated
unirrigated
unissued
unjointed
unjustifiable
unjustifiably
unjustified
unkept
unknowable
unknowing
unknowingly
unknowledgeable
unkosher
unlabeled
unlabored
unladylike
unlamented
unleavened
unliberated
unlicensed
unlighted
unlikable
unlined
unlit
unliterary
unlobed
unlovable
unloved
unloving
unmagnetized
unmalicious
unmalleable
unmanageable
unmanly
unmapped
unmarked
unmarketable
unmarred
unmarried
unmasculine
unmatchable
unmatched
unmatching
unmated
unmeasurable
unmeasured
unmechanized
unmediated
unmelodious
unmemorable
unmentioned
unmerchantable
unmerited
unmet
unmetabolized
unmethodical
unmilitary
unmilled
unmindful
unmixed
unmodern
unmodernized
unmodified
unmodulated
unmolested
unmonitored
unmortgaged
unmotivated
unmounted
unmovable
unmoving
unmusical
unnameable
unnamed
unnaturalized
unnavigable
unnecessary
unneeded
unneighborly
unnewsworthy
unnoted
unnoticeable
unnoticed
unnourishing
unobjectionable
unobliging
unobservable
unobservant
unobserved
unobserving
unobstructed
unobtainable
unobvious
unofficial
unofficially
unopenable
unopened
unopposed
unordered
unorganizable
unoriginal
unorthodox
unorthodoxly
unostentatious
unostentatiously
unowned
unoxygenated
unpaid
unpainted
unpalatable
unparasitized
unpardonable
unpardonably
unpardoned
unpartisan
unpartitioned
unpassable
unpasteurized
unpatentable
unpatient
unpatriotic
unpatterned
unpaved
unpedantic
unpedigreed
unperceived
unperceptive
unperformable
unperformed
unpersuadable
unpersuaded
unpersuasive
unperturbed
unphilosophic
unphilosophical
unphotogenic
unphotographed
unpicturesque
unplanned
unplausible
unplayable
unpleased
unpleasing
unplowed
unpoetic
unpoetical
unpoliced
unpolished
unpolluted
unposed
unpowered
unpractical
unpracticed
unpredictability
unpredictable
unpredictably
unpremeditated
unprepared
unpreparedness
unprepossessing
unprescribed
unpresentable
unpressed
unpressured
unpressurized
unpretty
unpreventable
unprinted
unprivileged
unprocessed
unprocurable
unproductive
unproductively
unprogrammed
unprogressive
unprompted
unpronounceable
unpronounced
unpropertied
unpropitious
unproportionate
unproportioned
unprosperous
unprotected
unprotesting
unprovable
unproved
unproven
unprovided
unprovoked
unpruned
unpublicized
unpublishable
unpublished
unpunctual
unpunctuality
unpunished
unpurchasable
unpure
unquenchable
unquestioned
unradical
unraised
unranked
unratified
unrationed
unravished
unreachable
unrealizable
unrealized
unreasoned
unreceptive
unreceptivity
unreclaimable
unrecognizable
unrecognizably
unrecognized
unreconcilable
unreconciled
unrecorded
unrecoverable
unredeemed
unredressed
unrefined
unreflecting
unreflective
unreformed
unrefuted
unregarded
unregistered
unregulated
unrehearsed
unreimbursed
unreinforced
unrelated
unrelaxed
unrelaxing
unreliability
unreliable
unrelieved
unreligious
unreluctant
unremarkable
unremembered
unreminiscent
unremitted
unremovable
unremunerated
unremunerative
unrepaid
unrepentant
unrepentantly
unreported
unrepresentative
unrepresented
unrepressed
unreproduced
unreproved

unrequited
unresistant
unresisting
unresolvable
unresolved
unresonant
unresourceful
unrespectable
unrestful
unrestricted
unretouched
unreturnable
unrevealed
unrevenged
unreviewed
unrevised
unrevolutionary
unrewarded
unrewarding
unrhymed
unrhythmic
unrhythmical
unridable
unripened
unromantic
unromantically
unromanticized
unroofed
unruled
unrushed
unsafe
unsaid
unsaintly
unsalable
unsalaried
unsalted
unsalvageable
unsanctified
unsanctioned
unsanitary
unsaponifiable
unsaponified
unsated
unsatisfactorily
unsatisfactoriness
unsatisfactory
unsatisfiable
unsatisfied
unsatisfying
unsavable
unscalable
unscaled
unscarred
unscented
unscheduled
unscholarly
unscreened
unscriptural
unseasoned
unseaworthy
unsecretive
unsectarian
unsecured
unseeable
unseeing
unsegmented
unselfconfident
unselfconscious
unselfconsciously
unselfconsciousness
unsensational
unsensitized
unsensual
unsent
unsentimental
unsentimentally
unseparated
unserious
unserved
unserviceable
unshaded
unshadowed
unshakable
unshaken
unshapely
unshared
unsharp
unshaved
unshaven
unshed
unsheltered
unshielded
unshorn
unshrinkable
unshrinking
unsifted
unsigned
unsilent
unsingable
unsinkable
unslaked
unsmiling
unsmilingly
unsmokable
unsoiled
unsold
unsoldierly
unsolicited
unsolicitous
unsolid
unsolvable
unsolved
unsorted
unsown
unspecialized
unspecifiable
unspecific
unspecified
unspectacular
unspent
unspiritual
unsplit
unspoiled
unspoken
unsponsored
unsportsmanlike
unsprayed
unspun
unsquared
unstained
unstandardized
unstatesmanlike
unstereotyped
unsterile
unsterilized
unstinted
unstinting
unstrained
unstratified
unstructured
unstylish
unstylishly
unsubdued
unsubsidized
unsubstantiated
unsubtle
unsuggestible
unsuited
unsullied
unsuperstitious
unsupervised
unsupported
unsuppressible
unsure
unsurely
unsureness
unsurfaced
unsurpassable
unsurpassed
unsurprised
unsurprising
unsurprisingly
unsusceptible
unsuspected
unsuspecting
unsuspenseful
unsuspicious
unsustainable
unsustained
unswayed
unsweetened
unsworn
unsympathetic
unsympathizing
unsynchronized
unsystematic
unsystematically
unsystematized
untactful
untagged
untainted
untalented
untamable
untamed
untapped
untarnishable
untarnished
untaxed
unteachable
untechnical
untempered
untenanted
untended
unterrified
untestable
untested
unthanked
unthawed
untheatrical
unthoughtful
unthreatened
unthreatening
unthreateningly
unthrifty
unthrilling
untillable
untilled
untired
untiring
untouched
untraceable
untractable
untraditional
untrained
untrammeled
untransferable
untranslatable
untranslated
untrapped
untraveled
untreatable
untreated
untrimmed
untrod
untrodden
untroubled
untroublesome
untrustworthiness
untrustworthy
untufted
untunable
untypical
untypically
ununderstandable
unupholstered
unusable
unuseful
unutilized
unuttered
unvaluable
unvaried
unvarying
unventilated
unverifiable
unverified
unversed
unviability
unviable
unvisited
unvulcanized
unwanted
unwarlike
unwarranted
unwatched
unwatered
unwavering
unwaveringly
unwaxed
unweaned
unwearable
unwearying
unweathered
unwed
unwedded
unweeded
unwelcome
unwelded
unwilling
unwillingly
unwillingness
unwinking
unwinnable
unwished
unwitnessed
unwomanly
unwon
unwooded
unworkable
unworked
unworkmanlike
unworried
unwounded
unwoven
unwrinkled
unwrought

un•abashed \ˌən-ə-ˈbasht\ *adj* **:** not abashed — **un•abash•ed•ly** \-ˈbash-əd-lē\ *adv*

un•abat•ed \ˌən-ə-ˈbāt-əd\ *adj* **:** not abated **:** at full strength or force — **un•abat•ed•ly** *adv*

un•able \ˌən-ˈā-bəl, ˈən-\ *adj* **:** not able **:** INCAPABLE

un•abridged \ˌən-ə-ˈbrijd\ *adj* **1 :** not abridged **:** COMPLETE ⟨an *unabridged* reprint of a novel⟩ **2 :** complete of its class **:** not based on one larger ⟨an *unabridged* dictionary⟩

un•ac•com•mo•dat•ed \ˌən-ə-ˈkäm-ə-ˌdāt-əd\ *adj* **:** not accommodated **:** UNPROVIDED

un•ac•com•pa•nied \ˌən-ə-ˈkəmp-nēd, -ə-nēd\ *adj* **:** not accompanied; *esp* **:** being without instrumental accompaniment

un•ac•count•able \ˌən-ə-ˈkau̇nt-ə-bəl\ *adj* **1 :** not to be accounted for **:** INEXPLICABLE **2 :** not to be called to account **:** not responsible — **un•ac•count•abil•i•ty** \-ˌkau̇nt-ə-ˈbil-ət-ē\ *n* — **un•ac•count•ably** \ˌən-ə-ˈkau̇nt-ə-blē\ *adv*

un•ac•count•ed \-ˈkau̇nt-əd\ *adj* **:** not accounted or made clear — often used with *for*

un•ac•cus•tomed \ˌən-ə-ˈkəs-təmd\ *adj* **1 :** UNUSUAL, UNFAMILIAR ⟨*unaccustomed* scenes⟩ **2 :** not used **:** not habituated ⟨*unaccustomed* to travel⟩

una cor•da \ˌü-nə-ˈkȯrd-ə\ *adv or adj* **:** with soft pedal depressed — used as a direction in piano music **[**Italian, literally, "one string"**]**

una corda pedal *n* **:** SOFT PEDAL 1

un•adorned \ˌən-ə-ˈdȯrnd\ *adj* **:** not adorned **:** lacking embellishment or decoration

un•adul•ter•at•ed \ˌən-ə-ˈdəl-tə-ˌrāt-əd\ *adj* **:** free from adulterants **:** PURE — **un•adul•ter•at•ed•ly** *adv*

un•ad•vised \ˌən-əd-ˈvīzd\ *adj* **1 :** done without due consideration **:** RASH **2 :** not prudent — **un•ad•vis•ed•ly** \-ˈvī-zəd-lē\ *adv*

un•af•fect•ed \ˌən-ə-ˈfek-təd\ *adj* **1 :** not influenced or changed mentally, physically, or chemically **2 :** free from affectation **:** GENUINE — **un•af•fect•ed•ly** *adv* — **un•af•fect•ed•ness** *n*

un•alien•able \ˌən-ˈāl-yə-nə-bəl, ˈən-, -ˈā-lē-ə-nə-\ *adj* **:** INALIENABLE

un•aligned \ˌən-l-ˈīnd\ *adj* **:** not associated with any one of competing international blocs ⟨*unaligned* nations⟩

un•al•loyed \ˌən-l-ˈȯid\ *adj* **:** free from all admixture **:** PURE ⟨*unalloyed* metal⟩ ⟨*unalloyed* bliss⟩

un•al•ter•able \ˌən-ˈȯl-trə-bəl, -tə-rə-, ˈən-\ *adj* **:** not capable of being changed ⟨*unalterable* hatred⟩ — **un•al•ter•ably** \-blē\ *adv*

un–Amer•i•can \ˌən-ə-ˈmer-ə-kən\ *adj* **:** not American **:** not characteristic of or consistent with American customs or principles — **un–Amer•i•can•ism** \-kə-ˌniz-əm\ *n*

un•aneled \ˌən-ə-ˈnēld\ *adj, archaic* **:** not having received extreme unction **[**earlier *anele* "to anoint", from Old English *an* "on" + *ele* "oil", from Latin *oleum***]**

una•nim•i•ty \ˌyü-nə-ˈnim-ət-ē\ *n* **:** the quality or state of being unanimous

unan•i•mous \yu̇-ˈnan-ə-məs\ *adj* **1 :** being of one mind **:** agreeing completely **2 :** assented to by all ⟨a *unanimous* vote⟩ **[**Latin *unanimus,* from *unus* "one" + *animus* "mind"**]** — **unan•i•mous•ly** *adv*

un•an•swer•able \ˌən-ˈans-rə-bəl, -ə-rə-, ˈən-\ *adj* **:** not answerable; *esp* **:** IRREFUTABLE ⟨the arguments were *unanswerable*⟩

un•ap•peal•able \ˌən-ə-ˈpē-lə-bəl\ *adj* **:** not appealable **:** not subject to appeal

un•ap•peal•ing \ˌən-ə-ˈpē-liŋ\ *adj* : lacking appeal

un•ap•peas•able \ˌən-ə-ˈpē-zə-bəl\ *adj* : not to be appeased : IMPLACABLE — **un•ap•peas•ably** \-blē\ *adv*

un•apt \ˌən-ˈapt, ˈən-\ *adj* **1** : UNSUITABLE, INAPPROPRIATE **2** : not accustomed and not likely **3** : DULL, BACKWARD ⟨*unapt* students⟩ — **un•apt•ly** \-ˈap-tlē, -lē\ *adv* — **un•apt•ness** \-ˈap-nəs, -ˈapt-\ *n*

un•arm \ˌən-ˈärm, ˈən-\ *vt* : DISARM 1

un•armed \-ˈärmd\ *adj* : not armed or armored

un•asked \ˌən-ˈaskt, -ˈast, -ˈáskt, -ˈást, ˈən-\ *adj* : not asked or asked for

un•as•sail•able \ˌən-ə-ˈsā-lə-bəl\ *adj* : not assailable : not liable to doubt, attack, or question — **un•as•sail•ably** \-blē\ *adv*

un•as•ser•tive \ˌən-ə-ˈsərt-iv\ *adj* : not assertive : MODEST, SHY

un•as•sum•ing \ˌən-ə-ˈsü-miŋ\ *adj* : not bold or forward : MODEST — **un•as•sum•ing•ly** \-miŋ-lē\ *adv* — **un•as•sum•ing•ness** *n*

un•at•tached \ˌən-ə-ˈtacht\ *adj* **1** : not attached **2** : not married or engaged

un•avail•ing \ˌən-ə-ˈvā-liŋ\ *adj* : of no avail : not successful : VAIN — **un•avail•ing•ly** \-liŋ-lē\ *adv*

un•avoid•able \ˌən-ə-ˈvȯid-ə-bəl\ *adj* : not avoidable — **un•avoid•ably** \-blē\ *adv*

[1]**un•aware** \ˌən-ə-ˈwaər, -ˈweər\ *adv* : UNAWARES

[2]**unaware** *adj* : not aware : IGNORANT — **un•aware•ness** *n*

un•awares \-ˈwaərz, -ˈweərz\ *adv* **1** : without warning : by surprise ⟨taken *unawares*⟩ **2** : without knowing

un•backed \ˌən-ˈbakt, ˈən-\ *adj* **1** : not supported or encouraged **2** : having no back

un•bal•ance \ˌən-ˈbal-əns, ˈən-\ *vt* : to put out of balance

un•bal•anced \-ənst\ *adj* **1** : not in equilibrium **2** : mentally deranged **3** : not adjusted so as to make credits equal to debits ⟨an *unbalanced* account⟩

un•bal•last•ed \ˌən-ˈbal-ə-stəd, ˈən-\ *adj* : not furnished with or steadied by ballast : UNSTEADY

un•bar \ˌən-ˈbär, ˈən-\ *vt* : to remove a bar from : UNBOLT, OPEN

un•barred \-ˈbärd\ *adj* **1** : not secured by a bar : UNLOCKED **2** : not marked with bars

un•bear•able \ˌən-ˈbar-ə-bəl, ˈən-, -ˈber-\ *adj* : greater than can be borne ⟨*unbearable* pain⟩ — **un•bear•ably** \-blē\ *adv*

un•beat•able \-ˈbēt-ə-bəl\ *adj* : not capable of being defeated

un•beat•en \-ˈbēt-ⁿn\ *adj* **1** : not pounded or beaten **2** : not traveled **3** : not defeated

un•be•com•ing \ˌən-bi-ˈkəm-iŋ\ *adj* : not becoming : UNSUITABLE **syn** see INDECOROUS — **un•be•com•ing•ly** \-iŋ-lē\ *adv* — **un•be•com•ing•ness** *n*

un•be•known \ˌən-bi-ˈnōn\ *or* **un•be•knownst** \-ˈnōnst\ *adj* : happening without one's knowledge : UNKNOWN — usually used with *to*

un•be•lief \ˌən-bə-ˈlēf\ *n* : the withholding or absence of belief : DOUBT

• **syn** DISBELIEF, INCREDULITY: UNBELIEF suggests withholding of belief especially in religious matters ⟨warned against skepticism and *unbelief*⟩ DISBELIEF stresses rejection of what is asserted or stated ⟨a firm *disbelief* in ghosts⟩ INCREDULITY implies a skeptical attitude ⟨received the news with *incredulity*⟩ and suggests rejection on general grounds rather than immediate evidence.

un•be•liev•able \-ˈlē-və-bəl\ *adj* : too improbable for belief — **un•be•liev•ably** \-blē\ *adv*

un•be•liev•er \-ˈlē-vər\ *n* **1** : one who does not believe : DOUBTER **2** : one who does not believe in a particular religious faith

un•be•liev•ing \-ˈlē-viŋ\ *adj* : marked by unbelief — **un•be•liev•ing•ly** \-viŋ-lē\ *adv*

un•bend \ˌən-ˈbend, ˈən-\ *vb* **-bent** \-ˈbent\; **-bend•ing** **1** : to free from being bent : make or become straight **2** : to make or become less stiff or more affable : RELAX

un•bend•ing \ˌən-ˈben-diŋ, ˈən-\ *adj* : formal and distant in manner

un•be•seem•ing \ˌən-bi-ˈsē-miŋ\ *adj* : not befitting : UNBECOMING

un•bi•ased \ˌən-ˈbī-əst, ˈən-\ *adj* : free from bias ⟨an *unbiased* opinion⟩; *esp* : UNPREJUDICED **syn** see FAIR

un•bid•den \-ˈbid-ⁿn\ *also* **un•bid** \-ˈbid\ *adj* : not bidden : UNASKED

un•bind \-ˈbīnd\ *vt* **-bound** \-ˈbau̇nd\; **-bind•ing** **1** : to remove a band from : free from fastenings **2** : to set free : RELEASE

un•bit•ted \-ˈbit-əd\ *adj* : UNRESTRAINED 1, UNBRIDLED

un•blenched \-ˈblencht\ *adj* : not disconcerted : UNDAUNTED

un•blessed *also* **un•blest** \-ˈblest\ *adj* **1** : not blessed **2** : EVIL 1a

un•blush•ing \-ˈbləsh-iŋ\ *adj* **1** : not blushing **2** : SHAMELESS, UNABASHED — **un•blush•ing•ly** \-iŋ-lē\ *adv*

un•bod•ied \-ˈbäd-ēd\ *adj* **1** : having no body; *also* : freed from the body **2** : FORMLESS

un•bolt \ˌən-ˈbōlt, ˈən-\ *vt* : to open or unfasten by withdrawing a bolt

un•bolt•ed \-ˈbōl-təd\ *adj* : not sifted ⟨*unbolted* flour⟩

un•born \-ˈbȯrn\ *adj* **1** : not born : not brought into life **2** : still to appear : FUTURE ⟨*unborn* generations⟩

un•bos•om \-ˈbu̇z-əm\ *vb* **1** : to give expression to : DISCLOSE, REVEAL **2** : to disclose one's thoughts or feelings

un•bound \-ˈbau̇nd\ *adj* : not bound: as **a** (1) : not fastened or tied up (2) : not confined ⟨an *unbound* spirit⟩ **b** : not having the leaves fastened together ⟨an *unbound* book⟩

un•bound•ed \-ˈbau̇n-dəd\ *adj* : having no limits ⟨*unbounded* space⟩ ⟨*unbounded* enthusiasm⟩

un•bowed \ˌən-ˈbau̇d, ˈən-\ *adj* : not bowed down; *esp* : not subdued

un•brace \-ˈbrās\ *vt* **1** : to free or detach by or as if by untying or removing a brace or bond **2** : to make feeble : WEAKEN

un•braid \-ˈbrād\ *vt* : to separate the strands of

un•branched \ˌən-ˈbrancht, ˈən-\ *adj* : free from or not divided into branches ⟨a straight *unbranched* trunk⟩ ⟨a leaf with *unbranched* veins⟩

un•bred \-ˈbred\ *adj* : not bred : never having been bred ⟨an *unbred* heifer⟩

un•bri•dled \-ˈbrīd-ˀld\ *adj* **1** : not confined by a bridle **2** : UNRESTRAINED ⟨greeted the star's appearance with *unbridled* enthusiasm⟩

un•bro•ken \-ˈbrō-kən\ *adj* **1** : not damaged : WHOLE **2** : not subdued or tamed ⟨an *unbroken* colt⟩ **3** : not interrupted : CONTINUOUS ⟨an *unbroken* row of trees⟩

un•buck•le \ˌən-ˈbək-əl, ˈən-\ *vt* : to unfasten the buckle of

un•build \-ˈbild\ *vt* : to pull down : DEMOLISH, RAZE

un•built \-ˈbilt\ *adj* **1** : not built : not yet constructed **2** : not built on ⟨an *unbuilt* plot⟩

un•bur•den \-ˈbərd-ⁿn\ *vt* **1** : to free from a burden **2** : to relieve oneself of (as cares, fears, or worries) : cast off

un•but•ton \-ˈbət-ⁿn\ *vt* : to unfasten the buttons of (as a garment)

un•but•toned \-nd\ *adj* **1 a** : not buttoned **b** : not provided with buttons **2** : not under constraint

un•cage \ˌən-ˈkāj, ˈən-\ *vt* : to release from or as if from a cage

un•called–for \-ˈkȯld-ˌfȯr\ *adj* : not called for : not needed or wanted : not proper ⟨an *uncalled-for* remark⟩

un•can•ny \-ˈkan-ē\ *adj* **1** : seeming to have a supernatural character or origin : MYSTERIOUS **2** : being beyond what is normal or expected : suggesting superhuman or supernatural powers ⟨an *uncanny* sense of direction⟩ **syn** see WEIRD — **un•can•ni•ly** \-ˈkan-ˀl-ē\ *adv*

un•cap \-ˈkap\ *vt* : to remove a cap or covering from

un•ceas•ing \-ˈsē-siŋ\ *adj* : never ceasing : CONTINUOUS, INCESSANT — **un•ceas•ing•ly** \-ˈsē-siŋ-lē\ *adv*

un•cer•e•mo•ni•ous \ˌən-ˌser-ə-ˈmō-nē-əs\ *adj* : acting without or lacking ordinary courtesy — **un•cer•e•mo•ni•ous•ly** *adv* — **un•cer•e•mo•ni•ous•ness** *n*

un•cer•tain \ˌən-ˈsərt-ⁿn, ˈən-\ *adj* **1** : not determined or fixed ⟨an *uncertain* quantity⟩ **2** : subject to chance or change : not dependable ⟨an *uncertain* temper⟩ **3** : not sure ⟨*uncertain* of the truth⟩ **4** : not definitely known — **un•cer•tain•ly** *adv* — **un•cer•tain•ness** \-ⁿn-nəs, -ⁿn-əs\ *n*

un•cer•tain•ty \-ⁿn-tē\ *n* **1** : lack of certainty **2** : something that is uncertain **syn** see DOUBT

un•chain \ˌən-ˈchān, ˈən-\ *vt* : to free by or as if by removing a chain : set loose

un•chancy \-'chan-sē\ *adj* **1** *chiefly Scottish* : ILL-FATED **2** *chiefly Scottish* : DANGEROUS
un•change•able \-'chān-jə-bəl\ *adj* : not changing or to be changed : IMMUTABLE — **un•change•able•ness** *n* — **un•change•ably** \-blē\ *adv*
un•charged \-'chärjd\ *adj* : having no electric charge
un•char•i•ta•ble \-'char-ət-ə-bəl\ *adj* : lacking in charity; *esp* : severe in judging others — **un•char•i•ta•ble•ness** *n* — **un•char•i•ta•bly** \-blē\ *adv*
un•chart•ed \-'chärt-əd\ *adj* : not recorded or plotted on a map, chart, or plan : UNKNOWN
un•chaste \-'chāst\ *adj* : not chaste : lacking in chastity — **un•chaste•ly** *adv* — **un•chaste•ness** \-'chāst-nəs, -'chās-\ *n* — **un•chas•ti•ty** \-'chas-tət-ē\ *n*
un•chris•tian \-'kris-chən\ *adj* **1** : not of the Christian faith **2 a** : contrary to the Christian spirit or character **b** : BARBAROUS 2 UNCIVILIZED
un•cir•cum•cised \,ən-'sər-kəm-,sīzd, 'ən-\ *adj* **1** : not circumcised **2** : spiritually impure : HEATHEN — **un•cir•cum•ci•sion** \,ən-,sər-kəm-'sizh-ən\ *n*
un•civ•il \,ən-'siv-əl, 'ən-\ *adj* **1** : not civilized : BARBAROUS **2** : lacking in courtesy : ILL-MANNERED
un•civ•i•lized \-'siv-ə-,līzd\ *adj* **1** : not civilized : BARBAROUS **2** : remote from civilization : WILD
un•clasp \-'klasp\ *vb* **1** : to open the clasp of **2** : to loosen a hold or grip or the hold or grip of
un•clas•si•fied \-'klas-ə-,fīd\ *adj* : not classified; *esp* : not subject to a security classification
un•cle \'əng-kəl\ *n* **1** : the brother of one's father or mother **2** : the husband of one's aunt **3** — used as a cry of surrender ⟨was forced to cry *uncle*⟩ [Old French, from Latin *avunculus* "mother's brother"]
un•clean \,ən-'klēn, 'ən-\ *adj* **1** : morally or spiritually impure **2** : prohibited by ritual law for use or contact **3** : DIRTY 1, FILTHY — **un•clean•ness** \-'klēn-nəs\ *n*
[1]**un•clean•ly** \-'klen-lē\ *adj* : morally or physically unclean — **un•clean•li•ness** *n*
[2]**un•clean•ly** \-'klēn-lē\ *adv* : in an unclean manner
un•clench \-'klench\ *vb* : to open from a clenched position : RELAX
Un•cle Sam \,əng-kəl-'sam\ *n* **1** : the United States government personified **2** : the American nation or people [expansion of *U.S.*, abbreviation of *United States*]
Uncle Tom \-'täm\ *n* : a black eager to win the approval of whites and willing to cooperate with them [*Uncle Tom*, pious and faithful slave in the novel *Uncle Tom's Cabin* by Harriet Beecher Stowe]
un•cloak \,ən-'klōk, 'ən-\ *vb* **1** : to remove a cloak or cover from **2** : REVEAL 1, UNMASK **3** : to take off a cloak
un•close \-'klōz\ *vb* : OPEN
un•closed \-'klōzd\ *adj* : not closed or settled : not concluded
un•clothe \-'klōth\ *vt* : to strip of clothes or a covering
un•clothed \-'klōthd\ *adj* : not clothed
un•coil \,ən-'kȯil, 'ən-\ *vb* : to release or become released from a coiled state : UNWIND
un•coined \-'kȯind\ *adj* **1** : not minted ⟨*uncoined* metal⟩ **2** : not fabricated : NATURAL
un•com•fort•able \-'kəm-fərt-ə-bəl, -'kəmp-; -'kəmf-tə-bəl, -'kəmp-, -'kəmpf-, -'kəm-, -tər-\ *adj* **1** : causing discomfort ⟨an *uncomfortable* chair⟩ **2** : feeling discomfort : UNEASY — **un•com•fort•ably** \-blē\ *adv*
un•com•mit•ted \,ən-kə-'mit-əd\ *adj* : not committed; *esp* : not pledged to a particular belief, allegiance, or program
un•com•mon \,ən-'käm-ən, 'ən-\ *adj* **1** : not ordinarily encountered : UNUSUAL ⟨when airplanes were *uncommon*⟩ **2** : EXTRAORDINARY 1, EXCEPTIONAL ⟨a run of *uncommon* luck⟩ — **un•com•mon•ly** *adv* — **un•com•mon•ness** \-ən-nəs\ *n*
un•com•mu•ni•ca•tive \,ən-kə-'myü-nə-,kāt-iv, -ni-kət-\ *adj* : not inclined to talk or give out information : RESERVED
un•com•pli•men•ta•ry \,ən-,käm-plə-'ment-ə-rē, -'men-trē\ *adj* : not complimentary : DEROGATORY
un•com•pro•mis•ing \,ən-'käm-prə-,mī-zing, 'ən-\ *adj* : not making or accepting a compromise : making no concessions — **un•com•pro•mis•ing•ly** \-zing-lē\ *adv*
un•con•cern \,ən-kən-'sərn\ *n* **1** : lack of care or interest : INDIFFERENCE **2** : freedom from excessive concern or anxiety **syn** see INDIFFERENCE
un•con•cerned \-'sərnd\ *adj* **1** : not involved : having no part or interest **2** : not anxious or upset : free of worry — **un•con•cern•ed•ly** \-'sər-nəd-lē\ *adv* — **un•con•cern•ed•ness** \-nəd-nəs\ *n*
un•con•di•tion•al \,ən-kən-'dish-nəl, -'dish-ən-l\ *adj* : not limited : ABSOLUTE, UNQUALIFIED ⟨*unconditional* surrender⟩ — **un•con•di•tion•al•ly** \-ē\ *adv*
un•con•di•tioned \-'dish-ənd\ *adj* **1** : not subject to conditions **2** : not dependent on conditioning or learning : INHERENT
un•con•form•able \,ən-kən-'fȯr-mə-bəl\ *adj* **1** : not conforming **2** : exhibiting geological unconformity — **un•con•form•ably** \-blē\ *adv*
un•con•for•mi•ty \,ən-kən-'fȯr-mət-ē\ *n* **1** : lack of continuity in deposition between rock strata in contact due especially to weathering **2** : the surface of contact between strata exhibiting unconformity
un•con•quer•able \,ən-'käng-krə-bəl, -kə-rə-, 'ən-\ *adj* : incapable of being conquered or overcome — **un•con•quer•ably** \-blē\ *adv*
un•con•scio•na•ble \-'känch-nə-bəl, -ə-nə-\ *adj* **1** : not guided or controlled by conscience **2** : EXCESSIVE, UNREASONABLE ⟨paid an *unconscionable* price⟩ **3** : shockingly unfair or unjust ⟨*unconscionable* sales practices⟩ [earlier *conscionable* "conscientious", derived from *conscience*] — **un•con•scio•na•bly** \-blē\ *adv*
[1]**un•con•scious** \-'kän-chəs\ *adj* **1** : not aware ⟨*unconscious* of the risk⟩ **2 a** : of or relating to the unconscious **b** : having lost consciousness ⟨knocked *unconscious* by a fall⟩ **3** : not realized by oneself : not consciously done ⟨an *unconscious* mistake⟩ — **un•con•scious•ly** *adv* — **un•con•scious•ness** *n*
[2]**unconscious** *n* : the part of one's mental life that is not ordinarily available to consciousness and is manifested in spontaneous overt behavior (as slips of the tongue) or in dreams
un•con•sid•ered \,ən-kən-'sid-ərd\ *adj* **1** : not considered or worth consideration **2** : not resulting from consideration or study
un•con•sti•tu•tion•al \,ən-,kän-stə-'tüsh-nəl, -'tyüsh-, -ən-l\ *adj* : not according to or consistent with the constitution of a state or society — **un•con•sti•tu•tion•al•i•ty** \-,tü-shə-'nal-ət-ē, -,tyü-\ *n* — **un•con•sti•tu•tion•al•ly** \-'tüsh-nə-lē, -'tyüsh-, -ən-l-ē\ *adv*
un•con•trol•la•ble \,ən-kən-'trō-lə-bəl\ *adj* : incapable of being controlled : UNGOVERNABLE — **un•con•trol•la•bly** \-blē\ *adv*
un•con•ven•tion•al \,ən-kən-'vench-nəl, -ən-l\ *adj* : not conventional: as **a** : not bound by or in accordance with convention **b** : being out of the ordinary — **un•con•ven•tion•al•i•ty** \-,ven-chə-'nal-ət-ē\ *n* — **un•con•ven•tion•al•ly** \-'vench-nə-lē, -ən-l-ē\ *adv*
un•cork \,ən-'kȯrk, 'ən-\ *vt* **1** : to draw a cork from **2 a** : to release from a sealed or pent-up state ⟨*uncork* a surprise⟩ **b** : to let go : RELEASE ⟨*uncork* a wild pitch⟩
un•count•ed \-'kaůnt-əd\ *adj* **1** : not counted **2** : INNUMERABLE
un•cou•ple \-'kəp-əl\ *vt* **-cou•pled**; **-cou•pling** \-'kəp-ling, -ə-ling\ **1** : to loose (hunting dogs) to seek game **2** : DISCONNECT ⟨*uncouple* railroad cars⟩
un•couth \-'küth\ *adj* **1** : strange, awkward, and clumsy in shape or appearance **2** : vulgar in conduct or speech : CRUDE [Old English *uncūth* "strange, unfamiliar", from [1]*un-* + *cūth* "known"]
un•cov•er \-'kəv-ər\ *vb* **1** : to make known : bring to light : DISCLOSE, REVEAL **2** : to expose to view by removing some covering **3 a** : to take the cover from **b** : to remove the hat from; *also* : to take off the hat as a token of respect
un•cov•ered \-'kəv-ərd\ *adj* : not covered or supplied with a covering
un•cre•at•ed \,ən-krē-'āt-əd\ *adj* **1** : not existing by creation : ETERNAL **2** : not yet created
un•crit•i•cal \,ən-'krit-i-kəl, 'ən-\ *adj* **1** : not critical : lacking in discrimination **2** : showing lack or improper use of critical standards or procedures — **un•crit•i•cal•ly** \-kə-lē, -klē\ *adv*
un•cross \-'krȯs\ *vb* : to change from a crossed position
un•crown \-'kraůn\ *vt* : to take the crown from : DEPOSE
un•crys•tal•lized \-'kris-tə-,līzd\ *adj* : not crystallized; *esp* : not in final form ⟨an *uncrystallized* plan⟩
unc•tion \'əng-shən, 'əngk-\ *n* **1** : the act of anointing as a rite of consecration or healing **2** : exaggerated, assumed, or superficial earnestness of language or manner [Latin *unctio*, from *unguere* "to anoint"]
unc•tu•ous \'əng-chə-wəs, -chəs, 'əngk-; 'əngsh-wəs,

ˈəngksh-\ *adj* **1 :** being like an ointment especially in smooth greasy texture or appearance **2 :** full of unction in speech and manner; *esp* **:** insincerely smooth **[**Medieval Latin *unctuosus,* from Latin *unctum* "ointment", from *unguere* "to anoint"**]** — **unc·tu·ous·ly** *adv* — **unc·tu·ous·ness** *n*

un·curl \ˌən-ˈkərl, ˈən-\ *vb* **:** to make or become straightened out from a curled or coiled position

un·cut \ˌən-ˈkət, ˈən-\ *adj* **1 :** not cut down or cut into **2 :** not shaped by cutting ⟨an *uncut* diamond⟩ **3** *of a book* **:** not having the folds of the leaves slit **4 :** not abridged or curtailed

un·daunt·ed \ˌən-ˈdȯnt-əd, -ˈdänt-\ *adj* **:** not daunted **:** not discouraged or dismayed **:** FEARLESS — **un·daunt·ed·ly** *adv*

un·de·ceive \ˌən-di-ˈsēv\ *vt* **:** to free from deception, illusion, or error

un·de·cid·ed \ˌən-di-ˈsīd-əd\ *adj* **1 :** not yet decided **:** not settled ⟨the question is still *undecided*⟩ **2 :** not having decided **:** uncertain what to do ⟨still *undecided* about it⟩ — **un·de·cid·ed·ly** *adv*

un·de·mon·stra·tive \ˌən-di-ˈmän-strət-iv\ *adj* **:** restrained or reserved in expression of feeling — **un·de·mon·stra·tive·ly** *adv* — **un·de·mon·stra·tive·ness** *n*

un·de·ni·able \ˌən-di-ˈnī-ə-bəl\ *adj* **1 :** plainly true **:** INCONTESTABLE **2 :** unquestionably excellent or genuine ⟨an applicant with *undeniable* references⟩ — **un·de·ni·able·ness** *n* — **un·de·ni·ably** \-blē\ *adv*

1un·der \ˈən-dər\ *adv* **1 :** in or into a position below or beneath something ⟨the duck surfaced, then went *under* again⟩ **2 :** below some quantity, level, or norm ⟨10 dollars or *under*⟩ — often used in combination ⟨*under*played the part⟩ **3 :** in or into a condition of subjection, subordination, or unconsciousness ⟨the ether put me *under*⟩ **4 :** so as to be covered or hidden ⟨turned *under* by the plow⟩ **[**Old English**]**

2un·der \ˌən-dər, ˈən-\ *prep* **1 a :** lower than and overhung, surmounted, or sheltered by ⟨*under* sunny skies⟩ ⟨*under* a tree⟩ **b :** below the surface of ⟨swimming *under* water⟩ **c :** in or into such a position as to be covered or concealed by ⟨wore a sweater *under* the coat⟩ ⟨the moon went *under* a cloud⟩ **2 a :** subject to the authority or guidance of ⟨served *under* the general⟩ **b :** subject to the action, operation, or effect of ⟨*under* pressure⟩ ⟨*under* an anesthetic⟩ **3 :** within the group or designation of ⟨*under* this heading⟩ **4 a :** less or lower than (as in size, amount, or rank) ⟨all weights *under* 12 ounces⟩ ⟨nobody *under* a colonel⟩ **b :** below the standard or required degree of ⟨*under* legal age⟩ **syn** see BELOW

3under \ˈən-dər\ *adj* **1 a :** lying or placed below, beneath, or on the ventral side **b :** facing or protruding downward — often used in combination ⟨*under*surface of a leaf⟩ **2 :** lower in rank or authority **:** SUBORDINATE **3 :** lower than usual, proper, or desired in amount, quality, or degree

un·der·achiev·er \ˌən-də-rə-ˈchē-vər\ *n* **:** a student who fails to reach his or her scholastic potential

un·der·act \ˌən-də-ˈrakt\ *vb* **:** to perform feebly or with restraint: as **a :** to perform (a dramatic part) with less than the necessary skill or vigor **b :** to perform with restraint for greater dramatic impact or personal force

un·der·ac·tive \ˌən-də-ˈrak-tiv\ *adj* **:** having an abnormally low degree of activity ⟨an *underactive* thyroid gland⟩ — **un·der·ac·tiv·i·ty** \-rak-ˈtiv-ət-ē\ *n*

un·der·age \ˌən-də-ˈrāj\ *adj* **:** of less than mature or legal age

1un·der·arm \ˌən-də-ˌrärm\ *adj* **1 :** placed under or on the underside of the arm ⟨*underarm* seams⟩ **2 :** UNDERHAND 2 ⟨an *underarm* toss⟩

2un·der·arm \ˌən-də-ˈrärm\ *adv* **:** with an underarm motion

3un·der·arm \ˈən-də-ˌrärm\ *n* **1 :** ARMPIT **2 :** the part of a garment that covers the underside of the arm

un·der·bel·ly \ˈən-dər-ˌbel-ē\ *n* **:** the under surface of a body or mass; *also* **:** a vulnerable area

un·der·bid \ˌən-dər-ˈbid\ *vb* **-bid; -bid·ding 1 :** to bid less than (a competing bidder) **2 :** to bid too low (as in cards) — **un·der·bid·der** *n*

un·der·body \ˈən-dər-ˌbäd-ē\ *n* **:** the lower or ventral part of an animal's body

un·der·bred \ˌən-dər-ˈbred\ *adj* **1 :** marked by lack of good breeding **:** ILL-BRED **2 :** of inferior or mixed breed ⟨an *underbred* dog⟩

un·der·brush \ˈən-dər-ˌbrəsh\ *n* **:** shrubs and small trees growing among large trees **:** UNDERGROWTH

un·der·car·riage \-ˌkar-ij\ *n* **1 :** a supporting framework (as of an automobile) **2 :** the landing gear of an airplane

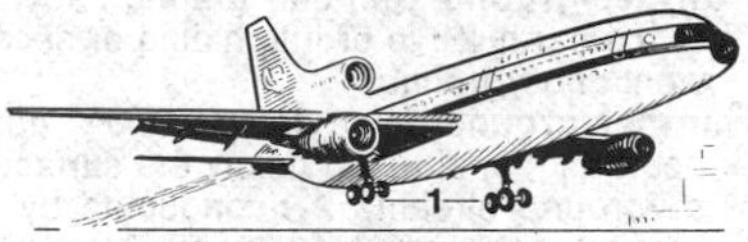

1 undercarriage 2

un·der·charge \ˌən-dər-ˈchärj\ *vt* **:** to charge (as a person) too little — **un·der·charge** \ˈən-dər-ˌ\ *n*

un·der·class·man \ˌən-dər-ˈklas-mən\ *n* **:** a member of the freshman or sophomore class

un·der·clothes \ˈən-dər-ˌklōz, -ˌklōthz\ *n pl* **:** UNDERWEAR

un·der·cloth·ing \-ˌklō-thing\ *n* **:** UNDERWEAR

un·der·coat \-ˌkōt\ *n* **1 :** a coat or jacket worn under another **2 :** a growth of short hair or fur partly concealed by a longer growth ⟨a dog's *undercoat*⟩ **3 :** a coat (as of paint) applied as a base for another coat **4 :** UNDERCOATING — **undercoat** *vt*

un·der·coat·ing \-ˌkōt-ing\ *n* **:** a special waterproof coating applied to the undersurfaces of a vehicle

un·der·cool \ˌən-dər-ˈkül\ *vt* **:** SUPERCOOL

un·der·cov·er \-ˈkəv-ər\ *adj* **:** acting or done in secret; *esp* **:** employed or engaged in spying or secret investigation

un·der·croft \ˈən-dər-ˌkrȯft\ *n* **:** a subterranean room; *esp* **:** a vaulted chamber under a church **[**Middle English, from *under* + *crofte* "crypt", from Dutch, from Latin *crypta***]**

un·der·cur·rent \ˈən-dər-ˌkər-ənt, -ˌkə-rənt\ *n* **1 :** a current below the upper currents or surface **2 :** a hidden tendency of opinion or feeling often contrary to the one publicly shown

1un·der·cut \ˌən-dər-ˈkət\ *vb* **-cut; -cut·ting 1 a :** to cut away the under part of ⟨*undercut* a vein of ore⟩ **b :** to cut away a base or material below a surface **2 :** to cut away material from the underside of (an object) so as to leave an overhanging portion in relief **3 :** to offer to sell at lower prices than or to work for lower wages than (a competitor) **4 :** to strike (the ball) in golf or tennis obliquely downward so as to give a backspin or height to the shot

2un·der·cut \ˈən-dər-ˌkət\ *n* **:** the action or result of cutting away from the underside of something

un·der·de·vel·oped \ˌən-dər-di-ˈvel-əpt\ *adj* **1 :** not normally or adequately developed ⟨*underdeveloped* muscles⟩ **2 :** failing to reach a potential level of economic development (as from lack of capital) ⟨the *underdeveloped* nations⟩

un·der·do \ˌən-dər-ˈdü\ *vt* **-did** \-ˈdid\; **-done** \-ˈdən\; **-do·ing** \-ˈdü-ing\ **:** to do less thoroughly than one can; *esp* **:** to cook (as meat) rare

un·der·dog \ˈən-dər-ˌdȯg\ *n* **1 :** the loser or predicted loser in a struggle **2 :** a victim of injustice or persecution

un·der·done \ˌən-dər-ˈdən\ *adj* **:** not thoroughly cooked **:** RARE ⟨*underdone* steak⟩

un·der·draw·ers \ˈən-dər-ˌdrȯ-ərz, -ˌdrȯrz\ *n pl* **:** UNDERPANTS

un·der·es·ti·mate \ˌən-də-ˈres-tə-ˌmāt\ *vt* **1 :** to estimate as being less than the actual size, quantity, or number **2 :** to place too low a value on **:** UNDERRATE — **un·der·es·ti·mate** \-mət\ *n* — **un·der·es·ti·ma·tion** \-ˌres-tə-ˈmā-shən\ *n*

un·der·ex·pose \ˌən-də-rik-ˈspōz\ *vt* **:** to expose (a photographic plate or film) for less time than is needed — **un·der·ex·po·sure** \-ˈspō-zhər\ *n*

un·der·feed \ˌən-dər-ˈfēd\ *vt* **-fed** \-ˈfed\; **-feed·ing 1 :** to feed too little **2 :** to feed with fuel from the underside

un·der·foot \ˌən-dər-ˈfu̇t\ *adv* **1 :** under the feet **2 :** in the way ⟨a puppy always *underfoot*⟩

un·der·fur \ˈən-dər-ˌfər\ *n* **:** the thick soft fur lying beneath the longer and coarser hair of a mammal

un·der·gar·ment \-ˌgär-mənt\ *n* **:** a garment to be worn under another

un·der·gird \ˌən-dər-ˈgərd\ *vt* **1 :** to make secure underneath **2 :** to brace up **:** STRENGTHEN

un·der·go \ˌən-dər-ˈgō\ *vt* **-went** \-ˈwent\; **-gone** \-ˈgȯn, -ˈgän\; **-go·ing** \-ˈgō-ing\ **1 :** to submit or be subjected to **:** ENDURE ⟨*undergo* an operation⟩ **2 :** to pass through **:** EXPERIENCE ⟨*undergo* a change⟩

\ə\ **abut**	\au̇\ **out**	\i\ **tip**	\ȯ\ **saw**	\u̇\ **foot**
\ər\ **further**	\ch\ **chin**	\ī\ **life**	\ȯi\ **coin**	\y\ **yet**
\a\ **mat**	\e\ **pet**	\j\ **job**	\th\ **thin**	\yü\ **few**
\ā\ **take**	\ē\ **easy**	\ng\ **sing**	\th\ **this**	\yu̇\ **cure**
\ä\ **cot, cart**	\g\ **go**	\ō\ **bone**	\ü\ **food**	\zh\ **vision**

un•der•grad•u•ate \-ˈgraj-wət, -ə-wət, -ə-ˌwāt\ *n* : a student at a college or university who has not received a first degree

¹un•der•ground \ˌən-dər-ˈgrau̇nd\ *adv* **1** : beneath the surface of the earth **2** : in or into hiding or secret operation ⟨the party went *underground*⟩

²un•der•ground \ˈən-dər-ˌgrau̇nd\ *adj* **1** : being, growing, operating, or situated below the surface of the ground ⟨an *underground* stream⟩ **2** : conducted by secret means ⟨*underground* resistance movement⟩ **3** : produced or published outside the establishment ⟨*underground* newspapers⟩; *also* : of or relating to the avant-garde underground ⟨an *underground* theater⟩

³un•der•ground \ˈən-dər-ˌgrau̇nd\ *n* **1** : a space under the surface of the ground; *esp* : an underground railway **2** : a secret political movement or group; *esp* : an organized body working in secret to overthrow a government or an occupying power **3** : a group or movement that functions outside the establishment

Underground Railroad *n* : a system of cooperation among active antislavery people in the United States before 1863 by which fugitive slaves were secretly helped to reach the North or Canada

un•der•growth \ˈən-dər-ˌgrōth\ *n* : low growth on the floor of a forest including seedlings and saplings, shrubs, and herbs

¹un•der•hand \ˈən-dər-ˌhand\ *adv* **1** : in an underhand or secret way **2** : with an underhand motion ⟨bowl *underhand*⟩ ⟨pitch *underhand*⟩

²underhand *adj* **1** : marked by secrecy, chicanery, and deception : SLY **2** : performed with the hand brought forward and up from below the level of the shoulder ⟨an *underhand* pitch⟩

un•der•hand•ed \ˌən-dər-ˈhan-dəd\ *adj or adv* : UNDERHAND — **un•der•hand•ed•ly** *adv* — **un•der•hand•ed•ness** *n*

¹un•der•lay \ˌən-dər-ˈlā\ *vt* **-laid** \-ˈlād\; **-lay•ing** **1** : to provide a layer of something beneath often as a support or backing ⟨*underlay* shingles with tar paper⟩ **2** : to raise or support by something laid under

²un•der•lay \ˈən-dər-ˌlā\ *n* : something that is laid under

un•der•lie \ˌən-dər-ˈlī\ *vt* **-lay** \-ˈlā\; **-lain** \-ˈlān\; **-ly•ing** \-ˈlī-ing\ **1** : to be situated under **2** : to form the foundation of : SUPPORT ⟨ideas *underlying* the revolution⟩

un•der•line \ˈən-dər-ˌlīn, ˌən-dər-ˈ\ *vt* **1** : to draw a line under **2** : STRESS 3 — **un•der•line** \ˈən-dər-ˌlīn\ *n*

un•der•ling \ˈən-dər-ling\ *n* : one who is under the orders of another : SUBORDINATE, INFERIOR

un•der•lip \ˌən-dər-ˈlip\ *n* : the lower lip

un•der•ly•ing \ˌən-dər-ˌlī-ing\ *adj* **1** : lying under or below ⟨the *underlying* rock is shale⟩ **2** : FUNDAMENTAL, BASIC ⟨*underlying* principles⟩

un•der•mine \ˌən-dər-ˈmīn\ *vt* **1** : to dig out or wear away the supporting earth beneath ⟨*undermine* a wall⟩ **2** : to weaken or wear away secretly or gradually ⟨*undermine* a government⟩

un•der•most \ˈən-dər-ˌmōst\ *adj* : lowest in relative position — **undermost** *adv*

¹un•der•neath \ˌən-dər-ˈnēth\ *prep* **1** : directly under **2** : under subjection to [Old English *underneothan,* from *under* + *neothan* "below"]

²underneath *adv* **1** : under or below an object or a surface : BENEATH **2** : on the lower side

un•der•nour•ished \ˌən-dər-ˈnər-isht, -ˈnə-risht\ *adj* : supplied with insufficient nourishment and especially foods for sound health and growth — **un•der•nour•ish•ment** \-ˈnər-ish-mənt, -ˈnə-rish-\ *n*

un•der•pants \ˈən-dər-ˌpans\ *n pl* : short or long pants worn under an outer garment

un•der•part \-ˌpärt\ *n* **1** : a part lying on the lower side especially of a bird or mammal **2** : a subordinate or auxiliary part or role

un•der•pass \-ˌpas\ *n* : a passage underneath something (as for a road passing under a railroad or another road)

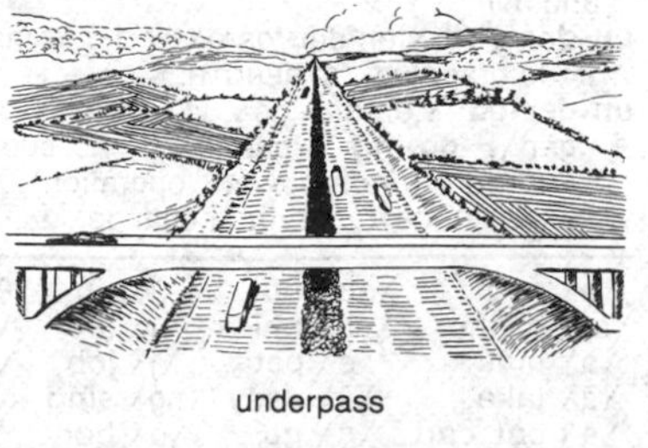
underpass

un•der•pay \ˌən-dər-ˈpā\ *vt* **-paid** \-ˈpād\; **-pay•ing** : to pay too little

un•der•pin \-ˈpin\ *vt* **1** : to form part of, strengthen, or replace the foundation of ⟨*underpin* a structure⟩ **2** : SUPPORT, SUBSTANTIATE ⟨*underpin* an argument with evidence⟩

un•der•pin•ning \ˈən-dər-ˌpin-ing\ *n* **1** : the material and construction (as a foundation) used for support of a structure **2** : PROP, SUPPORT **3** : a person's legs — usually used in pl.

un•der•play \ˌən-dər-ˈplā\ *vb* : to handle without exaggeration; *esp* : to play down ⟨*underplay* a dramatic role⟩

un•der•plot \ˈən-dər-ˌplät\ *n* : a dramatic plot that is subordinate to the main action

un•der•priv•i•leged \ˌən-dər-ˈpriv-lijd, -ə-lijd\ *adj* **1** : deprived of some of the basic economic and social rights that others enjoy **2** : of or relating to underprivileged people

un•der•pro•duc•tion \ˌən-dər-prə-ˈdək-shən\ *n* : production of less than enough to satisfy demand or of less than the usual amount

un•der•rate \ˌən-dər-ˈrāt, -də-ˈrāt\ *vt* : to rate too low : UNDERVALUE

un•der•run \-ˈrən\ *n* : the amount by which something produced falls below an estimate

un•der•score \ˈən-dər-ˌskōr, -ˌskȯr\ *vt* **1** : to draw a line under : UNDERLINE **2** : STRESS 3 — **underscore** *n*

¹un•der•sea \ˌən-dər-ˌsē\ *adj* **1** : being or carried on under the sea or under the surface of the sea ⟨*undersea* oil deposits⟩ **2** : designed for use under the surface of the sea ⟨an *undersea* fleet⟩

²un•der•sea \ˌən-dər-ˈsē\ *or* **un•der•seas** \-ˈsēz\ *adv* : under the sea : beneath the surface of the sea

under secretary *n* : a secretary immediately subordinate to a principal secretary ⟨*under secretary* of state⟩

un•der•sell \ˌən-dər-ˈsel\ *vt* **-sold** \-ˈsōld\; **-sell•ing** : to sell articles cheaper than ⟨*undersell* a competitor⟩

un•der•sexed \-ˈsekst\ *adj* : having little sexual desire

un•der•shirt \ˈən-dər-ˌshərt\ *n* : a collarless undergarment with or without sleeves

un•der•shoot \ˌən-dər-ˈshüt\ *vt* **-shot** \-ˈshät\; **-shoot•ing** **1** : to shoot short of or below (a target) **2** : to fall short of (a runway) in landing an airplane

un•der•shot \ˌən-dər-ˌshät\ *adj* **1** : having the lower incisor teeth or lower jaw projecting beyond the upper when the mouth is closed **2** : moved by water passing beneath ⟨*undershot* wheel⟩

un•der•side \ˈən-dər-ˌsīd, ˌən-dər-ˈ\ *n* : the side or surface lying underneath

un•der•signed \ˈən-dər-ˌsīnd\ *n, pl* **undersigned** : one who signs his or her name at the end of a document

un•der•sized \ˌən-dər-ˈsīzd\ *adj* : smaller than is usual or standard ⟨*undersized* trout⟩

un•der•skirt \ˈən-dər-ˌskərt\ *n* : a skirt worn under an outer skirt; *esp* : PETTICOAT

un•der•slung \ˌən-dər-ˈsləng\ *adj* **1** : suspended so as to extend below the axles ⟨an *underslung* automobile frame⟩ **2** : having a low center of gravity

un•der•spin \ˈən-dər-ˌspin\ *n* : BACKSPIN

un•der•stand \ˌən-dər-ˈstand\ *vb* **-stood** \-ˈstu̇d\; **-stand•ing** **1** : to grasp the meaning of : COMPREHEND **2** : to have thorough knowledge of ⟨*understand* the arts⟩ **3** : GATHER, INFER ⟨we *understand* that you're leaving today⟩ **4** : INTERPRET, EXPLAIN ⟨I *understand* the letter to be a refusal⟩ **5** : to have a sympathetic attitude ⟨you just don't *understand* about these things⟩ **6** : to accept as settled ⟨it is *understood* that I will pay⟩ **7** : to supply in thought as if expressed ⟨"to be married" is commonly *understood* after the word *engaged*⟩ [Old English *understandan,* from *under* + *standan* "to stand"] — **un•der•stand•abil•i•ty** \-ˌstan-də-ˈbil-ət-ē\ *n* — **un•der•stand•able** \-ˈstan-də-bəl\ *adj* — **un•der•stand•ably** \-blē\ *adv*

¹un•der•stand•ing \ˌən-dər-ˈstan-ding\ *n* **1** : mental grasp : COMPREHENSION **2** : the ability to understand and judge ⟨a person of *understanding*⟩ **3 a** : agreement of opinion and feeling **b** : a mutual agreement informally or tacitly entered into ⟨an economic *understanding* between two nations⟩

²understanding *adj* **1** : endowed with understanding **2** : PATIENT 2, TOLERANT, SYMPATHETIC — **un•der•stand•ing•ly** \-ˈstan-ding-lē\ *adv*

un•der•state \ˌən-dər-ˈstāt\ *vt* **1** : to represent as less than is the case **2** : to state with restraint especially for greater effect — **un•der•state•ment** \-mənt\ *n*

un•der•stood \ˌən-dər-ˈstu̇d\ *adj* **1** : fully apprehended **2 a** : agreed on **b** : IMPLICIT 1

un•der•sto•ry \'ən-dər-ˌstōr-ē, -ˌstȯr-\ *n* : the plants of a forest undergrowth; *also* : an underlying layer of low vegetation

[1]**un•der•study** \'ən-dər-ˌstəd-ē, ˌən-dər-'\ *vb* **1** : to study an actor's part in order to substitute in an emergency **2** : to prepare as understudy to (as an actor)

[2]**un•der•study** \'ən-dər-ˌstəd-ē\ *n* : one who is prepared to act another's part or take over another's duties

un•der•sur•face \-ˌsər-fəs\ *n* : UNDERSIDE

un•der•take \ˌən-dər-'tāk\ *vt* **-took** \-'tu̇k\; **-tak•en** \-'tā-kən\; **-tak•ing** **1** : to take in hand : set about ⟨*undertake* a task⟩ **2** : to put oneself under obligation to perform : AGREE ⟨*undertake* to deliver a package⟩ **3** : GUARANTEE 2, PROMISE

un•der•tak•er \'ən-dər-ˌtā-kər\ *n* : one whose business is to prepare the dead for burial and to take charge of funerals

un•der•tak•ing \'ən-dər-ˌtā-king, ˌən-dər-'; *2 is* 'ən-dər-ˌ *only*\ *n* **1** : the act of one that undertakes something (as a project) **2** : the business of an undertaker **3** : something undertaken : ENTERPRISE **4** : PROMISE 1, GUARANTEE

un•der•ten•ant \'ən-dər-ˌten-ənt\ *n* : SUBTENANT

un•der–the–count•er *adj* : covert and usually unlawful ⟨*under-the-counter* liquor sales⟩ [from the hiding of illicit wares under the counters of stores where they are sold]

un•der•tone \'ən-dər-ˌtōn\ *n* **1** : a low or subdued tone ⟨spoke in an *undertone*⟩ **2** : a subdued color

un•der•tow \-ˌtō\ *n* : a current beneath the surface of the water that moves away from or along the shore while the surface water above it moves toward the shore

un•der•val•ue \ˌən-dər-'val-yü\ *vt* **1** : to value below the real worth **2** : to set little value on — **un•der•val•u•a•tion** \-ˌval-yə-'wā-shən\ *n*

un•der•wa•ter \ˌən-dər-ˌwȯt-ər, -ˌwät-\ *adj* : lying, growing, worn, or operating below the surface of the water — **un•der•wa•ter** \-'wȯt-, -'wät-\ *adv*

un•der•way \ˌən-dər-ˌwā\ *adj* : occurring, performed, or used while traveling or in motion ⟨*underway* refueling⟩

under way \-'wā\ *adv* **1** : in motion; *esp* : not at anchor or aground **2** : into motion from a standstill **3** : in progress : AFOOT ⟨preparations were *under way*⟩ [probably from Dutch *onderweg*, from earlier *onderwegen*, literally, "under or among the ways"]

un•der•wear \'ən-dər-ˌwaər, -ˌweər\ *n* : clothing worn next to the skin and under other clothing

[1]**un•der•weight** \ˌən-dər-'wāt\ *n* : weight below what is normal, average, or necessary

[2]**underweight** *adj* : weighing less than the normal or requisite amount

[1]**un•der•wing** \'ən-dər-ˌwing\ *n* : either of the posterior pair of wings of an insect

[2]**underwing** *adj* : located or growing beneath or on the under surface of a wing ⟨*underwing* coverts⟩

un•der•wood \'ən-dər-ˌwu̇d\ *n* : UNDERBRUSH, UNDERGROWTH

un•der•wool \-ˌwu̇l\ *n* : short woolly underfur

un•der•world \-ˌwərld\ *n* **1** *archaic* : WORLD 2 **2** : the place of departed souls : HADES **3** : a social level regarded as below the level of ordinary life; *esp* : the world of organized crime

un•der•write \'ən-dər-ˌrīt, -də-; ˌən-dər-', -də-\ *vt* **-wrote** \-ˌrōt, -'rōt\; **-writ•ten** \-ˌrit-n, -'rit-n\; **writ•ing** \-ˌrīt-ing, -'rīt-\ **1** : to write under or at the end of something else **2 a** : to put one's name to (an insurance policy) and thereby become answerable for a designated loss or damage **b** : to insure life or property **3** : to subscribe to : agree to ⟨refused to *underwrite* the government's foreign policy⟩ **4 a** : to agree to purchase (a security issue) usually on a fixed date at a fixed price with a view to public resale **b** : to guarantee financial support of ⟨*underwrite* an expedition⟩ — **un•der•writ•er** \'ən-dər-ˌrīt-ər, 'ən-də-\ *n*

[1]**un•de•sir•able** \-'zī-rə-bəl\ *adj* : not desirable : OBJECTIONABLE — **un•de•sir•abil•i•ty** \ˌzī-rə-'bil-ət-ē\ *n* — **un•de•sir•able•ness** \-'zī-rə-bəl-nəs\ *n* — **un•de•sir•ably** \-blē\ *adv*

[2]**undesirable** *n* : one that is undesirable

un•de•vi•at•ing \ˌən-'dē-vē-ˌāt-ing, 'ən-\ *adj* : keeping a true course : UNSWERVING — **un•de•vi•at•ing•ly** \-ing-lē\ *adv*

un•dies \'ən-dēz\ *n pl* : UNDERWEAR; *esp* : women's underwear

un•dine \ˌən-'dēn, 'ən-ˌ\ *n* : WATER NYMPH [New Latin *undina*, from Latin *unda* "wave"]

un•di•rect•ed \ˌən-də-'rek-təd, -dī-\ *adj* : not directed, planned, or guided ⟨*undirected* efforts⟩

un•dis•guised \ˌən-dis-'gīzd\ *adj* : OPEN 2c

un•do \ˌən-'dü, 'ən-\ *vb* **-did** \-'did\; **-done** \-'dən\; **-do•ing** \-'dü-ing\ **1** : to make or become unfastened or loosened **2** : to make of no effect or as if not done : NULLIFY **3 a** : to ruin the worldly means, reputation, or hopes of ⟨*undone* by greed⟩ **b** : UPSET 3a — **un•do•er** *n*

un•do•able \-'dü-ə-bəl\ *adj* : that cannot be done

un•do•ing \ˌən-'dü-ing\ *n* **1** : the act of loosening or unfastening **2** : RUIN; *also* : a cause of ruin **3** : ANNULMENT, REVERSAL

un•done \ˌən-'dən, 'ən-\ *adj* : not done or finished

un•doubt•ed \-'dau̇t-əd\ *adj* : not doubted or doubtful : CERTAIN ⟨*undoubted* proof of guilt⟩ — **un•doubt•ed•ly** *adv*

un•drape \-'drāp\ *vt* : to strip of drapery : UNVEIL

un•draw \-'drȯ\ *vt* **-drew** \-'drü\; **-drawn** \-'drȯn\; **-draw•ing** : to draw (as a curtain) aside : OPEN

un•dreamed \ˌən-'dremt, -'drempt, -'drēmd, 'ən-\ *also* **un•dreamt** \-'dremt, -'drempt\ *adj* : not dreamed or thought of — usually used with *of*

[1]**un•dress** \ˌən-'dres, 'ən-\ *vb* **1** : to remove the clothes of **2** : to take off one's clothes

[2]**undress** *n* **1** : informal dress: as **a** : a loose robe or dressing gown **b** : ordinary dress **2** : a state of nudity

un•dressed \-'drest\ *adj* : not dressed: as **a** : partially, improperly, or informally clothed **b** : not fully processed or finished ⟨*undressed* hides⟩ **c** : not cared for or tended ⟨an *undressed* wound⟩ ⟨*undressed* fields⟩

un•due \-'dü, -'dyü\ *adj* **1** : not due : not yet payable **2** : going beyond what is proper or fit

un•du•lant \'ən-jə-lənt, 'ən-dyə-, -də-\ *adj* : rising and falling in waves

undulant fever *n* : a persistent human bacterial disease marked by fluctuating fever, pain and swelling in the joints, and great weakness

un•du•late \'ən-jə-ˌlāt, 'ən-dyə-, -də-\ *vb* **1** : to form or move in waves : FLUCTUATE **2** : to rise and fall in volume, pitch, or cadence **3** : to present a wavy appearance [Late Latin *undula* "small wave", from Latin *unda* "wave"]

un•du•la•tion \ˌən-jə-'lā-shən, ˌən-dyə-, -də-\ *n* **1 a** : the action of undulating **b** : a wavelike motion to and fro in a fluid or elastic medium : VIBRATION **2** : a wavy appearance or form

un•du•la•to•ry \'ən-jə-lə-ˌtōr-ē, 'ən-dyə-, -də-, -ˌtȯr-\ *adj* : of or relating to undulation; *also* : UNDULANT

un•du•ly \ˌən-'dü-lē, -'dyü-, 'ən-\ *adv* : in an undue manner : EXCESSIVELY

un•dy•ing \-'dī-ing\ *adj* : not dying : IMMORTAL

un•earned \-'ərnd\ *adj* : not gained by labor, service, or skill ⟨*unearned* income⟩

un•earth \ˌən-'ərth, 'ən-\ *vt* **1 a** : to dig up out of the earth **b** : to drive out of the ground ⟨*unearth* a badger⟩ **2** : UNCOVER 1, DISCOVER ⟨*unearth* a secret⟩

un•earth•ly \-lē\ *adj* **1** : not earthly: as **a** : SUPERNATURAL 2 ⟨*unearthly* beings⟩ **b** : STRANGE 4, EERIE ⟨an *unearthly* light⟩ **2** : not usual or reasonable ⟨an *unearthly* hour to get up⟩ — **un•earth•li•ness** *n*

un•easy \ˌən-'ē-zē, 'ən-\ *adj* **1** : not easy in manner : AWKWARD **2** : disturbed by pain or worry : RESTLESS **3** : UNSTABLE ⟨an *uneasy* truce⟩ — **un•eas•i•ly** \-'ē-zə-lē\ *adv* — **un•eas•i•ness** \-'ē-zē-nəs\ *n*

un•em•ploy•able \ˌən-im-'plȯi-ə-bəl\ *adj* : not acceptable for employment — **unemployable** *n*

un•em•ployed \-'plȯid\ *adj* : not employed: **a** : not being used **b** : not engaged in a gainful occupation — **unemployed** *n*

un•em•ploy•ment \ˌən-im-'plȯi-mənt\ *n* : the state of being out of work : involuntary idleness of workers

unemployment benefit *n* : money paid at regular intervals to an unemployed worker (as by an employer or a government agency)

un•end•ing \ˌən-'en-ding, 'ən-\ *adj* : being without ending : ENDLESS — **un•end•ing•ly** \-ding-lē\ *adv*

[1]**un•equal** \-'ē-kwəl\ *adj* **1 a** : not of the same measurement, quantity, or number as another **b** : not like or not the same as another in degree, worth, or status **2** : not uniform : VARIABLE,

UNEVEN **3** : badly balanced or matched ⟨an *unequal* fight⟩ **4** : INADEQUATE, INSUFFICIENT ⟨timber *unequal* to the strain⟩ — **un•equal•ly** \-kwə-lē\ *adv*

²unequal *n* : one that is not equal to another

un•equaled \-'ē-kwəld\ *adj* : not equaled : MATCHLESS

un•equiv•o•cal \,ən-i-'kwiv-ə-kəl\ *adj* : leaving no doubt : CLEAR — **un•equiv•o•cal•ly** \-kə-lē, -klē\ *adv*

un•err•ing \,ən-'eər-ing, -'ər-ing, 'ən-\ *adj* : making no errors : UNFAILING — **un•err•ing•ly** \-ing-lē\ *adv*

un•even \,ən-'ē-vən, 'ən-\ *adj* **1** : ODD 2a **2 a** : not even : not level or smooth : RUGGED ⟨large *uneven* teeth⟩ ⟨*uneven* handwriting⟩ **b** : varying from the straight or parallel **c** : not uniform : IRREGULAR ⟨*uneven* combustion⟩ **d** : varying in quality ⟨an *uneven* performance⟩ **3** : UNEQUAL 3 — **un•even•ly** *adv* — **un•even•ness** \-vən-nəs\ *n*

un•event•ful \,ən-i-'vent-fəl\ *adj* : not eventful : lacking interesting or noteworthy happenings ⟨an *uneventful* trip⟩ — **un•event•ful•ly** \-fə-lē\ *adv*

un•ex•am•pled \,ən-ig-'zam-pəld\ *adj* : having no example or parallel : UNPRECEDENTED

un•ex•cep•tion•able \,ən-ik-'sep-shnə-bəl, -shə-nə-\ *adj* : not open to objection or criticism : beyond reproach : UNIMPEACHABLE [¹*un-* + obsolete *exception* "to take exception, object" + *-able*] — **un•ex•cep•tion•able•ness** *n* — **un•ex•cep•tion•ably** \-blē\ *adv*

un•ex•cep•tion•al \-'sep-shnəl, -shən-l\ *adj* : ORDINARY 1

un•ex•pect•ed \,ən-ik-'spek-təd\ *adj* : not expected or foreseen — **un•ex•pect•ed•ly** *adv* — **un•ex•pect•ed•ness** *n*

un•ex•pres•sive \,ən-ik-'spres-iv\ *adj* : INEXPRESSIVE

un•fail•ing \-'fā-ling\ *adj* **1** : CONSTANT 1 **2** : EVERLASTING, INEXHAUSTIBLE ⟨an *unfailing* topic of interest⟩ **3** : INFALLIBLE 2, SURE — **un•fail•ing•ly** *adv* — **un•fail•ing•ness** *n*

un•fair \-'faər, -'feər\ *adj* **1** : marked by injustice, partiality, or deception : UNJUST, DISHONEST **2** : not equitable in business dealings — **un•fair•ly** *adv* — **un•fair•ness** *n*

un•faith \,ən-'fāth, 'ən-', 'ən-,\ *n* : absence of faith : DISBELIEF

un•faith•ful \,ən-'fāth-fəl, 'ən-\ *adj* : not faithful: **a** : not adhering to vows, allegiance, or duty : DISLOYAL **b** : not faithful to marriage vows **c** : INACCURATE ⟨an *unfaithful* translation⟩ — **un•faith•ful•ly** \-fə-lē\ *adv* — **un•faith•ful•ness** *n*

un•fa•mil•iar \,ən-fə-'mil-yər\ *adj* **1** : not well known : STRANGE ⟨an *unfamiliar* place⟩ **2** : not well acquainted ⟨*unfamiliar* with the subject⟩ — **un•fa•mil•iar•i•ty** \-,mil-'yar-ət-ē, -,mil-ē-'ar-\ *n* — **un•fa•mil•iar•ly** \-'mil-yər-lē\ *adv*

un•fas•ten \,ən-'fas-n, 'ən-\ *vb* : to make or become loose : UNDO

un•fa•vor•able \-'fāv-rə-bəl, -ə-rə-; -'fā-vər-bəl\ *adj* **1 a** : not disposed to favor **b** : expressing disapproval : NEGATIVE **2** : not propitious : DISADVANTAGEOUS — **un•fa•vor•able•ness** *n* — **un•fa•vor•ably** \-blē\ *adv*

un•feel•ing \-'fē-ling\ *adj* **1** : lacking feeling : INSENSATE **2** : lacking kindness or sympathy : HARDHEARTED — **un•feel•ing•ly** \-ling-lē\ *adv* — **un•feel•ing•ness** *n*

un•feigned \,ən-'fānd, 'ən-\ *adj* : not feigned or hypocritical : GENUINE — **un•feigned•ly** \-'fā-nəd-lē, -'fān-dlē\ *adv*

un•fet•ter \,ən-'fet-ər, 'ən-\ *vt* : LIBERATE 1, EMANCIPATE

un•fil•ial \-'fil-ē-əl, -'fil-yəl\ *adj* : not observing the obligations of a child to a parent : UNDUTIFUL

un•fin•ished \-'fin-isht\ *adj* : not finished; *esp* : not brought to the final desired state

¹un•fit \-'fit\ *adj* : not fit: **a** : not adapted to a purpose : UNSUITABLE **b** : not qualified : INCOMPETENT **c** : physically or mentally unsound — **un•fit•ly** *adv* — **un•fit•ness** *n*

²unfit *vt* : to make unfit : DISABLE, DISQUALIFY

un•fix \,ən-'fiks, 'ən-\ *vt* **1** : to loosen from a fastening : DETACH, DISENGAGE **2** : to make unstable : UNSETTLE

un•flag•ging \-'flag-ing\ *adj* : CONSTANT 1 — **un•flag•ging•ly** *adv*

un•flap•pa•ble \-'flap-ə-bəl\ *adj* : not easily upset or panicked : COOL [¹*un-* + *flap* "state of excitement" (from ¹*flap*) + *-able*]

un•fledged \-'flejd\ *adj* **1** : not feathered or ready for flight **2** : IMMATURE, CALLOW ⟨an *unfledged* writer⟩

un•flinch•ing \-'flin-ching\ *adj* : STEADFAST 1b, 2 — **un•flinch•ing•ly** \-ching-lē\ *adv*

un•fold \-'fōld\ *vb* **1 a** : to spread or cause to spread or straighten out from a folded position or arrangement **b** : UNWRAP **2 a** : BLOOM 1 **b** : DEVELOP ⟨as the story *unfolds*⟩ **3** : to open out or cause to open out gradually to view or understanding

un•for•get•ta•ble \,ən-fər-'get-ə-bəl\ *adj* : incapable of being forgotten : lasting in memory — **un•for•get•ta•bly** \-blē\ *adv*

un•formed \,ən-'fórmd\ *adj* : not arranged in regular shape, order, or relations; *esp* : IMMATURE

¹un•for•tu•nate \-'fórch-nət, -ə-nət\ *adj* **1 a** : not fortunate : UNLUCKY **b** : marked or accompanied by or resulting in misfortune **2 a** : INAPPROPRIATE ⟨an *unfortunate* choice of words⟩ **b** : DEPLORABLE ⟨an *unfortunate* lack of taste⟩ — **un•for•tu•nate•ly** *adv*

²unfortunate *n* : an unfortunate person; *esp* : a social outcast

un•found•ed \,ən-'faun-dəd, 'ən-\ *adj* : lacking a sound basis : GROUNDLESS ⟨an *unfounded* accusation⟩

un•fre•quent•ed \,ən-frē-'kwent-əd; ,ən-'frē-kwənt-, 'ən-\ *adj* : not often visited or traveled over

un•friend•ed \,ən-'fren-dəd, 'ən-\ *adj* : having no friends

un•friend•ly \,ən-'fren-dlē, -lē, 'ən-\ *adj* **1 a** : not friendly or social **b** : not kind : HOSTILE ⟨an *unfriendly* greeting⟩ **2** : not favorable ⟨an *unfriendly* environment⟩ — **un•friend•li•ness** *n*

un•frock \-'fräk\ *vt* : to deprive (as a priest) of the right to exercise the functions of office

un•fruit•ful \-'früt-fəl\ *adj* **1** : not bearing fruit or offspring **2** : not producing a desired result ⟨*unfruitful* efforts⟩ — **un•fruit•ful•ly** \-fə-lē\ *adv* — **un•fruit•ful•ness** *n*

un•fund•ed \,ən-'fən-dəd, 'ən-\ *adj* : not funded : FLOATING ⟨an *unfunded* debt⟩

un•furl \-'fərl\ *vb* : to loose from a furled state : UNFOLD ⟨*unfurl* a flag⟩

un•gain•ly \-'gān-lē\ *adj* **1** : AWKWARD 1, CLUMSY **2** : AWKWARD 2b [earlier *gainly* "graceful", from Old English *gēn* "direct, straight", from Old Norse *gegn*] — **un•gain•li•ness** *n*

un•gen•er•ous \-'jen-rəs, -ə-rəs\ *adj* **1** : PETTY 3, MEAN **2** : STINGY 1 — **un•gen•er•ous•ly** *adv*

un•gird \,ən-'gərd, 'ən-\ *vt* : to free from a restraining band or girdle : UNBIND

un•glue \-'glü\ *vt* : to separate by or as if by dissolving an adhesive

un•glued \-'glüd\ *adj, slang* : emotionally upset : DISTRAUGHT

un•god•ly \-'gäd-lē, *also* -'gód-\ *adj* **1** : not godly: as **a** : IRRELIGIOUS **b** : WICKED 1, EVIL **2** : UNREASONABLE 2, OUTRAGEOUS ⟨got up at an *ungodly* hour⟩ ⟨an *ungodly* hat⟩ — **un•god•li•ness** *n*

un•gov•ern•able \-'gəv-ər-nə-bəl\ *adj* : not capable of being governed, guided, or restrained **syn** see UNRULY — **un•gov•ern•ably** \-blē\ *adv*

un•grace•ful \-'grās-fəl\ *adj* : not graceful : AWKWARD — **un•grace•ful•ly** \-fə-lē\ *adv* — **un•grace•ful•ness** *n*

un•gra•cious \-'grā-shəs\ *adj* **1** : not courteous : RUDE **2** : not pleasing : DISAGREEABLE — **un•gra•cious•ly** *adv* — **un•gra•cious•ness** *n*

un•grate•ful \,ən-'grāt-fəl, 'ən-\ *adj* **1** : not thankful for favors **2** : not pleasing : DISAGREEABLE ⟨an *ungrateful* task⟩ — **un•grate•ful•ly** \-fə-lē\ *adv* — **un•grate•ful•ness** *n*

un•ground•ed \-'graun-dəd\ *adj* **1** : GROUNDLESS, UNFOUNDED **2** : not instructed or informed

un•grudg•ing \-'grəj-ing\ *adj* : free from envy or unwillingness

un•guard•ed \-'gärd-əd\ *adj* **1** : vulnerable to attack **2** : free from guile or wariness — **un•guard•ed•ly** *adv*

un•guent \'əng-gwənt, 'ən-; 'ən-jənt\ *n* : a soothing or healing salve : OINTMENT [Latin *unguentum*, from *unguere* "to anoint"]

¹un•gu•late \'əng-gyə-lət, 'ən-, -,lāt\ *adj* **1** : having hoofs **2** : of or relating to the ungulates [Late Latin *ungulatus*, from Latin *ungula* "hoof", from *unguis* "nail, hoof"]

²ungulate *n* : any of a group (Ungulata) consisting of the hoofed mammals and including the ruminants, swine, horses, tapirs, rhinoceroses, elephants, and hyraxes of which most are plant-eating and many horned

un•hal•lowed \,ən-'hal-ōd, 'ən-\ *adj* **1** : not blessed or holy **2** : IMPIOUS a, PROFANE

un•hand \,ən-'hand, 'ən-\ *vt* : to remove the hand from : let go

un•hand•some \-'han-səm\ *adj* : not handsome: as **a** : not beautiful : HOMELY **b** : lacking in courtesy or taste — **un•hand•some•ly** *adv*

un·handy \-'han-dē\ *adj* **1** : hard to handle : INCONVENIENT ⟨a thick *unhandy* volume⟩ **2** : lacking in skill or dexterity : AWKWARD — **un·handi·ness** *n*
un·hap·py \-'hap-ē\ *adj* **1** : not fortunate : UNLUCKY ⟨an *unhappy* mistake⟩ **2** : not cheerful : SAD, MISERABLE **3** : INAPPROPRIATE — **un·hap·pi·ly** \-'hap-ə-lē\ *adv* — **un·hap·pi·ness** \-'hap-i-nəs\ *n*
un·har·ness \-'här-nəs\ *vt* : to remove a harness from
un·health·ful \-'helth-fəl\ *adj* : UNHEALTHY 1
un·healthy \-'hel-thē\ *adj* **1** : not conducive to health ⟨an *unhealthy* climate⟩ **2** : not in good health : SICKLY **3 a** : DANGEROUS 1, RISKY **b** : causing harm : INJURIOUS **c** : CORRUPT 1, DEPRAVED — **un·health·i·ly** \-thə-lē\ *adv* — **un·health·i·ness** \-thē-nəs\ *n*
un·heard \,ən-'hərd, 'ən-\ *adj* **1** : not perceived by the ear **2** : not given a hearing ⟨*unheard* protests⟩
un·heard-of \-,əv, -,äv\ *adj* : previously unknown : UNPRECEDENTED
un·hinge \,ən-'hinj, 'ən-\ *vt* **1** : to remove (as a door) from the hinges **2** : to make unstable : UNSETTLE, DISRUPT ⟨a mind *unhinged* by grief⟩
un·hitch \-'hich\ *vt* : to free from or as if from being hitched
un·ho·ly \-'hō-lē\ *adj* **1** : not holy : PROFANE, WICKED **2** : SHOCKING, OUTRAGEOUS ⟨an *unholy* noise⟩ — **un·ho·li·ness** *n*
un·ho·mog·e·nized \-hə-'mäj-ə-,nīzd, -hō-\ *adj* : that has not been homogenized
un·hood \-'hu̇d\ *vt* : to remove a hood or covering from
un·hook \-'hu̇k\ *vt* **1** : to remove from a hook **2** : to unfasten by releasing a hook
un·horse \-'hȯrs\ *vt* : to dislodge from or as if from a horse : UNSEAT
un·hou·seled \-'hau̇-zəld\ *adj, archaic* : not having received the Eucharist especially just before death [derived from earlier *housel* "Eucharist", from Old English *hūsel* "sacrifice, Eucharist"]
un·hur·ried \-'hər-ēd, -'hə-rēd\ *adj* : not hurried : LEISURELY — **un·hur·ried·ly** *adv*
uni- *prefix* : one : single ⟨*uni*cellular⟩ [Latin, from *unus* "one"]
Uni·ate \'ü-nē-,at, 'yü-\ *or* **Uni·at** *n* : a Christian of a church adhering to an Eastern rite but accepting papal authority [Russian *uniyat,* from Polish *uniat,* from *unja* "union", from Late Latin *unio*] — **Uniate** *adj*
uni·ax·i·al \,yü-nē-'ak-sē-əl\ *adj* **1** : having only one axis **2** : of or relating to only one axis — **uni·ax·i·al·ly** \-sē-ə-lē\ *adv*
uni·cam·er·al \,yü-ni-'kam-rəl, -ə-rəl\ *adj* : having or consisting of a single legislative chamber [Late Latin *camera* "chamber"] — **uni·cam·er·al·ly** \-rə-lē\ *adv*
uni·cel·lu·lar \-'sel-yə-lər\ *adj* : having or consisting of a single cell — **uni·cel·lu·lar·i·ty** \-,sel-yə-'lar-ət-ē\ *n*
uni·corn \'yü-nə-,kȯrn\ *n* : a fabulous animal generally depicted with the body and head of a horse, the hind legs of a stag, the tail of a lion, and a single horn on its forehead [Old French *unicorne,* from Late Latin *unicornis,* from Latin *uni-* + *cornu* "horn"]
uni·cy·cle \'yü-ni-,sī-kəl\ *n* : a vehicle that has a single wheel and is usually propelled by pedals [*uni-* + *-cycle* (as in *tricycle*)]

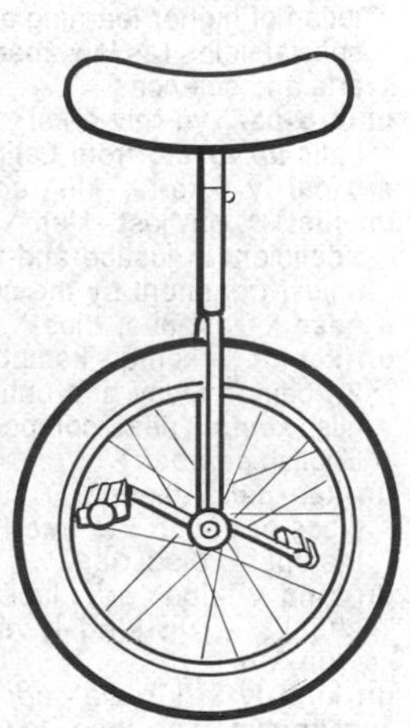
unicycle

uni·di·rec·tion·al \,yü-ni-də-'rek-shnəl, -dī-, -shən-l\ *adj* : having, moving in, or responsive in a single direction ⟨a *unidirectional* antenna⟩
[1]**uni·form** \'yü-nə-,fȯrm\ *adj* **1** : having always the same form, manner, or degree : not varying or variable **2** : of the same form with others : conforming to one rule **syn** see STEADY — **uni·for·mi·ty** \,yü-nə-'fȯr-mət-ē\ *n* — **uni·form·ly** \'yü-nə-,fȯrm-lē, ,yü-nə-'\ *adv* — **uni·form·ness** *n*
[2]**uniform** *vt* : to clothe with a uniform
[3]**uniform** *n* : distinctive dress worn by members of a particular group (as an army or a police force)
uni·for·mi·tar·i·an·ism \,yü-nə-,fȯr-mə-'ter-ē-ə-,niz-əm\ *n* : a geological doctrine that existing processes acting in the same manner as at present are sufficient to account for all geological changes
uni·fy \'yü-nə-,fī\ *vt* **-fied; -fy·ing** : to make into a unit or a coherent whole : UNITE — **uni·fi·able** \-,fī-ə-bəl\ *adj* — **uni·fi·ca·tion** \,yü-nə-fə-'kā-shən\ *n* — **uni·fi·er** \'yü-nə-,fī-ər, -,fīr\ *n*
uni·lat·er·al \,yü-ni-'lat-ə-rəl, -'la-trəl\ *adj* : of, relating to, affecting, or done by one side only ⟨*unilateral* paralysis⟩ ⟨*unilateral* disarmament⟩ — **uni·lat·er·al·ly** \-ē\ *adv*
un·im·peach·able \,ən-im-'pē-chə-bəl\ *adj* : not impeachable : not liable to accusation : IRREPROACHABLE — **un·im·peach·ably** \-blē\ *adv*
un·im·proved \-'prüvd\ *adj* : not improved: as **a** : not tilled, built upon, or otherwise prepared for use ⟨*unimproved* land⟩ **b** : not used or employed advantageously **c** : not selectively bred for better quality or productiveness
un·in·hib·it·ed \,ən-in-'hib-ət-əd\ *adj* : free from inhibition; *esp* : unrestrainedly informal — **un·in·hib·it·ed·ly** *adv*
un·in·tel·li·gent \,ən-in-'tel-ə-jənt\ *adj* : lacking intelligence : UNWISE, IGNORANT — **un·in·tel·li·gent·ly** *adv*
un·in·ter·est·ed \,ən-'int-ə-,res-təd, 'ən-; -'in-trəs-, -,tres-; -'int-ərs-, -'int-ə-rəs-\ *adj* **1** : having no interest and especially no property interest **2** : not having the mind or feelings engaged : not having the curiosity or sympathy aroused
• **syn** DISINTERESTED: UNINTERESTED in discriminating use means having no interest and implies being indifferent through lack of sympathy for or curiosity toward something; DISINTERESTED in comparable use suggests a freedom from concern for personal or financial advantage that enables one to judge, advise, or act without bias.
un·in·ter·rupt·ed \,ən-,int-ə-'rəp-təd\ *adj* : not interrupted : CONTINUOUS — **un·in·ter·rupt·ed·ly** *adv* — **un·in·ter·rupt·ed·ness** *n*
union \'yün-yən\ *n* **1 a** : an act or instance of uniting two or more things into one: as (1) : the formation of a single political unit from two or more separate and independent units (2) : a uniting in marriage (3) : the growing together of severed parts **b** : a unified condition : COMBINATION, JUNCTION **2** : something formed by a combining of parts or members: as **a** : a confederation of independent individuals (as nations or persons) for a common purpose **b** : a political unit constituting an organic whole formed from several units that may have been previously independent **c** : LABOR UNION **d** *cap* : an organization on a college or university campus providing recreational, social, cultural, and sometimes dining facilities; *also* : the building housing it **e** : the set of all elements that belong to one or more of a collection of two or more sets **3 a** : a device symbolizing national unity that is borne on a flag **b** : the upper inner corner of a flag **4 a** : a device for connecting parts (as of a machine) **b** : a coupling for pipes [Middle French, from Late Latin *unio,* from Latin *unus* "one"] **syn** see UNITY

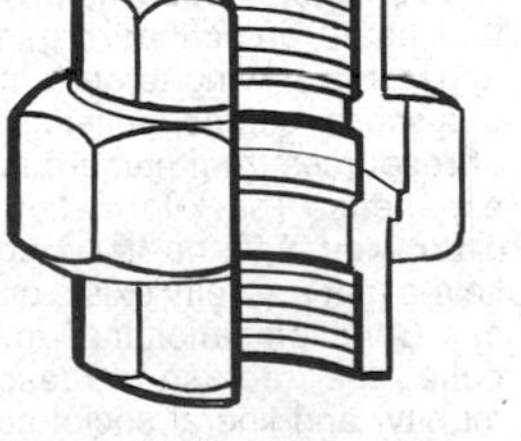
union 4b

Union *adj* : of, relating to, or being the side favoring the federal union in the United States Civil War
union card *n* : a card certifying personal membership in good standing in a labor union
union·ism \'yün-yə-,niz-əm\ *n* **1** : the principle or policy of forming or adhering to a union **2** *cap* : adherence to the policy of a firm federal union prior to or during the United States Civil War **3** : the principles, theory, or system of trade unions — **union·ist** \-yə-nəst\ *n, often cap*
union·ize \'yün-yə-,nīz\ *vt* : to cause to become a member of or subject to the rules of a labor union : form into a labor union — **union·iza·tion** \,yün-yə-nə-'zā-shən\ *n*

\ə\ **abut**	\au̇\ **out**	\i\ **tip**	\ȯ\ **saw**	\u̇\ **foot**
\ər\ **further**	\ch\ **chin**	\ī\ **life**	\ȯi\ **coin**	\y\ **yet**
\a\ **mat**	\e\ **pet**	\j\ **job**	\th\ **thin**	\yü\ **few**
\ā\ **take**	\ē\ **easy**	\ng\ **sing**	\t͟h\ **this**	\yu̇\ **cure**
\ä\ **cot, cart**	\g\ **go**	\ō\ **bone**	\ü\ **food**	\zh\ **vision**

union jack *n, often cap U & J* **1 :** a jack consisting of the part of a national flag that signifies union **2 :** the national flag of the United Kingdom

union shop *n* **:** an establishment in which the employer is free to hire nonunion workers but retains them on the payroll only on condition of their becoming members of the union within a specified time

union suit *n* **:** an undergarment with shirt and pants in one piece

uni•pa•ren•tal \ˌyü-ni-pə-ˈrent-l\ *adj* **:** having or involving a single parent; *also* **:** PARTHENOGENETIC — **uni•pa•ren•tal•ly** \-l-ē\ *adv*

uni•po•lar \ˌyü-ni-ˈpō-lər\ *adj* **:** having, produced by, or acting by a single magnetic or electrical pole — **uni•po•lar•i•ty** \-pō-ˈlar-ət-ē, -pə-\ *n*

unique \yu̇-ˈnēk\ *adj* **1 :** being the only one of its kind **2 :** very unusual **:** NOTABLE **[**French, from Latin *unicus,* from *unus* "one"**]** **syn** see SINGLE — **unique•ly** *adv* — **unique•ness** *n*

uni•sex \ˈyü-nə-ˌseks\ *adj* **:** common to males and females ⟨*unisex* clothing⟩

uni•sex•u•al \ˌyü-ni-ˈsek-shəl, -shwəl, -shə-wəl\ *adj* **:** of, relating to, or restricted to one sex: **a :** male or female but not hermaphroditic **b :** DICLINOUS ⟨a *unisexual* flower⟩ — **uni•sex•u•al•i•ty** \-ˌsek-shə-ˈwal-ət-ē\ *n* — **uni•sex•u•al•ly** \-ˈsek-shə-lē, -shwə-lē, -shə-wə-lē\ *adv*

uni•son \ˈyü-nə-sən, -zən\ *n* **1 a :** identity in musical pitch **b :** the condition of being tuned or sounded at the same pitch or at an octave **2 :** harmonious agreement **:** CONCORD **[**Middle French, from Medieval Latin *unisonus* "having the same sound", from Latin *uni-* + *sonus* "sound"**]** — **in unison :** in perfect agreement **:** so as to harmonize exactly

unit \ˈyü-nət\ *n* **1 a :** the first and least natural number **:** ONE **b :** a single quantity regarded as a whole in calculation **2 :** a definite quantity (as of length, time, or value) adopted as a standard of measurement; *esp* **:** an amount of work used in calculating student credits **3 a :** a single thing, person, or group that is a constituent of a whole **b :** a part of a military establishment that has a prescribed organization **c :** a piece or complex of apparatus serving to perform one particular function **d :** a part of a school course focusing on a central theme and making use of resources from numerous subject areas and the pupils' own experience **[**back-formation from *unity***]**

uni•tar•i•an \ˌyü-nə-ˈter-ē-ən\ *n* **1 a** *often cap* **:** one who believes that the deity exists only in one person **b** *cap* **:** a member of a Christian denomination that stresses individual freedom of belief, the free use of reason in religion, a united world community, and liberal social action **2 :** an advocate of unity or a unitary system — **unitarian** *adj, often cap* — **uni•tar•i•an•ism** \-ē-ə-ˌniz-əm\ *n, often cap*

uni•tary \ˈyü-nə-ˌter-ē\ *adj* **1 a :** of or relating to a unit **b :** based on or characterized by unity or units **2 :** having the character of a unit **:** WHOLE

unit circle *n* **:** a circle with its center at the origin of a coordinate system and its radius one unit of length long

unite \yu̇-ˈnīt\ *vb* **1 a :** to put or come together to form a single unit **b :** to cause to adhere **c :** to link by a legal or moral bond **2 :** to become one or as if one **3 :** to join in a legal action **:** act in concert **[**Late Latin *unitus,* past participle of *unire* "to unite", from Latin *unus* "one"**]** **syn** see JOIN — **unit•er** *n*

unit•ed \yu̇-ˈnīt-əd\ *adj* **1 :** made one or as if one **2 :** relating to or produced by joint action **3 :** being in agreement **:** HARMONIOUS — **unit•ed•ly** *adv*

unit•ize \ˈyü-nət-ˌīz\ *vt* **:** to convert into a unit

units digit \ˈyü-nəts-\ *n* **:** the numeral (as 6 in 456) occupying the units place in a number expressed in the Arabic system of writing numbers

units place *n* **:** the place immediately to the left of the decimal point in a number expressed in the Arabic system of writing numbers

uni•ty \ˈyü-nət-ē\ *n, pl* **-ties 1 :** the quality or state of being one **:** ONENESS **2 :** a condition of harmony **:** CONCORD **3 :** continuity without change (as in purpose or action) **4 :** a definite mathematical quantity or combination of quantities taken as one or for which 1 is made to stand in calculation **5 :** relevance of all the parts in an artistic or literary work to a single main idea **:** oneness of effect or style **6 :** a totality of related parts **[**Old French *unité,* from Latin *unitas,* from *unus* "one"**]**

• syn UNITY, SOLIDARITY, UNION mean the character of a thing that is a whole composed of many parts. UNITY implies oneness gained by the interdependence of its varied parts; SOLIDARITY implies such unity in a group, class, or community that enables it to show undivided strength as through opinion or influence ⟨working-class *solidarity*⟩ UNION implies a thorough integration of parts and their harmonious cooperation ⟨the *union* of the thirteen states into a nation⟩

uni•va•lent \ˌyü-ni-ˈvā-lənt\ *adj* **:** having a chemical valence of one

[1]uni•valve \ˈyü-ni-ˌvalv\ *adj* **:** having or consisting of one valve

[2]univalve *n* **:** a univalve mollusk shell or a mollusk having such a shell

uni•ver•sal \ˌyü-nə-ˈvər-səl\ *adj* **1 :** including or covering all or a whole without limit or exception **2 :** present or occurring everywhere or under all conditions ⟨*universal* cultural patterns⟩ **3 a :** embracing a major part or the greatest portion ⟨*universal* practices⟩ **b :** comprehensively broad and versatile ⟨a *universal* genius⟩ **4 :** adapted or adjustable to meet varied requirements (as of use, shape, or size) ⟨a *universal* wrench⟩ — **uni•ver•sal•i•ty** \-ˌvər-ˈsal-ət-ē\ *n* — **uni•ver•sal•ly** \-ˈvər-sə-lē, -slē\ *adv* — **uni•ver•sal•ness** \-səl-nəs\ *n*

• syn UNIVERSAL, GENERAL mean of all or of the whole. UNIVERSAL implies reference to each individual without exception in the category considered ⟨*universal* franchise⟩ GENERAL implies reference to all or nearly all ⟨the theory has *general* but not *universal* acceptance⟩

universal donor *n* **:** a person with type O blood

uni•ver•sal•ism \ˌyü-nə-ˈvər-sə-ˌliz-əm\ *n, often cap* **1 :** a theological doctrine that all people will eventually be saved **2 :** the principles and practices of a liberal Christian denomination founded in the 18th century to uphold belief in universal salvation and now united with Unitarianism — **uni•ver•sal•ist** \-sə-ləst, -sləst\ *n or adj, often cap*

uni•ver•sal•ize \-ˈvər-sə-ˌlīz\ *vt* **:** to make universal — **uni•ver•sal•iza•tion** \-ˌvər-sə-lə-ˈzā-shən\ *n*

universal joint *n* **:** a shaft coupling capable of transmitting rotation from one shaft to another not in a straight line with it

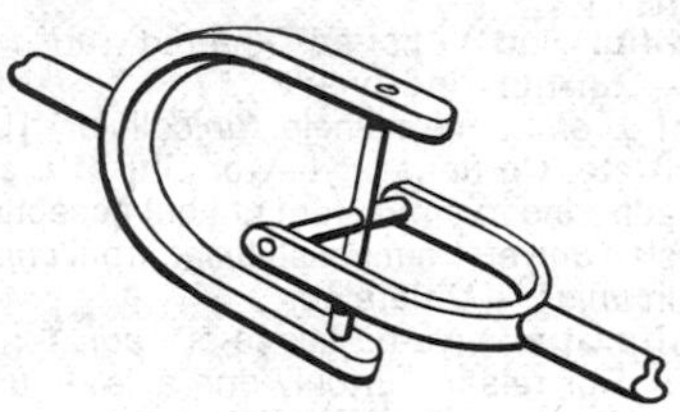

universal joint

uni•verse \ˈyü-nə-ˌvərs\ *n* **1 :** the whole body of things and phenomena observed or postulated **:** COSMOS **2 a :** a systematic whole held to arise by and persist through the direct intervention of divine power **b :** the world of human experience **3 a :** MILKY WAY GALAXY **b :** an aggregate of stars comparable to the Milky Way galaxy **[**Latin *universum,* from *universus* "entire, whole", from *uni-* + *versus* "turned toward", from *vertere* "to turn"**]** **syn** see EARTH

uni•ver•si•ty \ˌyü-nə-ˈvər-sət-ē, -ˈvər-stē\ *n, pl* **-ties :** an institution of higher learning authorized to grant degrees in various special fields (as law, medicine, and theology) as well as in the arts and sciences

univ•o•cal \yü-ˈniv-ə-kəl\ *adj* **:** having one meaning only **[**Late Latin *univocus,* from Latin *uni-* + *voc-, vox* "voice"**]** — **univ•o•cal•ly** \-kə-lē, -klē\ *adv*

un•just \ˌən-ˈjəst, ˈən-\ *adj* **:** characterized by injustice **:** deficient in justice and fairness **:** WRONGFUL ⟨complained of *unjust* treatment by the court⟩ — **un•just•ly** *adv* — **un•just•ness** \-ˈjəst-nəs, -ˈjəs-\ *n*

un•kempt \-ˈkemt, -ˈkempt\ *adj* **1 :** not combed ⟨*unkempt* hair⟩ **2 :** being messy and untidy **:** DISHEVELED **[**un- + Middle English *kempt* "neat, combed", from *kemben* "to comb", from Old English *cemban***]**

un•ken•nel \-ˈken-l\ *vt* **1 a :** to drive (as a fox) from a hiding place or den **b :** to free (dogs) from a kennel **2 :** to bring into the open **:** DISCLOSE

un•kind \-ˈkīnd\ *adj* **:** lacking in kindness or sympathy **:** HARSH, CRUEL — **un•kind•ly** *adv* — **un•kind•ness** \-ˈkīnd-nəs, -ˈkīn-\ *n*

un•kind•ly \-ˈkīn-dlē\ *adj* **:** UNKIND — **un•kind•li•ness** *n*

[1]un•known \ˌən-ˈnōn, ˈən-\ *adj* **:** not known; *also* **:** having an unknown value ⟨find the *unknown* parts of the triangle⟩

[2]unknown *n* **:** something that is unknown; *esp* **:** an unknown quantity usually symbolized in mathematics by one of the last letters of the alphabet

Unknown Soldier *n* : an unidentified soldier whose body is selected to receive national honors as a representative of all of that nation who died in a war

un·lace \ˌən-ˈlās, ˈən-\ *vt* : to loose by undoing a lacing

un·lade \-ˈlād\ *vb* **1** : to take the load or cargo from **2** : to discharge cargo

un·lash \-ˈlash\ *vt* : to untie the lashing of : LOOSE, UNDO

un·latch \-ˈlach\ *vb* **1** : to open or loose by lifting the latch **2** : to become loosed or opened

un·law·ful \-ˈlȯ-fəl\ *adj* **1** : not lawful : contrary to law : ILLEGAL **2** : not morally right or conventional **3** : ILLEGITIMATE 1 — **un·law·ful·ly** \-fə-lē, -flē\ *adv* — **un·law·ful·ness** \-fəl-nəs\ *n*

un·lay \-ˈlā\ *vb* **-laid** \-ˈlād\; **-lay·ing 1** : to untwist the strands of (as a rope) **2** : UNTWIST 2

un·lead·ed \-ˈled-əd\ *adj* **1** : stripped of lead **2** : not mixed with lead or lead compounds ⟨*unleaded* fuel⟩

un·learn \-ˈlərn\ *vt* : to put out of one's knowledge or memory

un·learned \-ˈlər-nəd *for 1,* -ˈlərnd *for 2, 3*\ *adj* **1** : having little formal learning or education **2** : not learned by study : not known ⟨lessons *unlearned* by many⟩ **3** : not learned by previous experience ⟨breathing is *unlearned* behavior⟩

un·leash \-ˈlēsh\ *vt* : to free from or as if from a leash : let loose ⟨*unleash* a dog⟩ ⟨the storm *unleashed* its fury⟩

un·less \ən-ˈles, ˌən-, *in some contexts* ᵊn-, ᵊm-, ᵊng-\ *conj* : except on the condition that ⟨will fail *unless* we work harder⟩ [Middle English *onlesse,* from *on* + *lesse* "less"]

un·let·tered \ˌən-ˈlet-ərd, ˈən-\ *adj* **1** : not educated **2** : ILLITERATE

[1]**un·like** \ˌən-ˈlīk, ˈən-\ *prep* **1** : different from ⟨feeling completely *unlike* a hero⟩ **2** : not characteristic of ⟨it was *unlike* you to be inquisitive⟩ **3** : differently from ⟨behaving *unlike* your associates⟩

[2]**unlike** *adj* : not like: as **a** : marked by dissimilarity : DIFFERENT ⟨the children are quite *unlike*⟩ **b** : UNEQUAL ⟨*unlike* amounts⟩ — **un·like·ness** *n*

un·like·li·hood \ˌən-ˈlī-klē-ˌhu̇d, ˈən-\ *n* **1** : the quality or state of being unlikely **2** : something unlikely

un·like·ly \-ˈlī-klē\ *adj* **1** : not likely : IMPROBABLE **2** : likely to fail : UNPROMISING — **un·like·li·ness** *n*

un·lim·ber \ˌən-ˈlim-bər, ˈən-\ *vb* : to prepare for action [earlier *unlimber* "to ready a gun for use by removing it from the vehicle to which it is attached", from *limber* "2-wheeled vehicle to which a gun may be attached", from Middle English *lymour* "shaft of a cart"]

un·lim·it·ed \-ˈlim-ət-əd\ *adj* **1** : lacking any controls **2** : BOUNDLESS, INFINITE **3** : not restricted by exceptions

un·link \-ˈlingk\ *vt* **1** : to unfasten the links of **2** : to separate by or as if by unlinking a chain

un·list·ed \-ˈlis-təd\ *adj* : not appearing upon a list: as **a** : not listed on an organized securities exchange ⟨*unlisted* stocks⟩ **b** : not in the telephone book ⟨an *unlisted* number⟩

un·liv·able \-ˈliv-ə-bəl\ *adj* : not fit to live in or with

un·live \-ˈliv\ *vt* : to live down : ANNUL, REVERSE

un·load \-ˈlōd\ *vb* **1 a** : to take away or off : REMOVE ⟨*unload* cargo⟩; *also* : to get rid of **b** : to take a load from ⟨*unload* a ship⟩; *also* : UNBURDEN ⟨*unload* your mind of worries⟩ **2** : to get rid of a load or burden ⟨the ship is *unloading* now⟩ **3** : to sell in volume : DUMP ⟨*unload* surplus goods⟩

un·lock \-ˈläk\ *vb* **1** : to open or unfasten through release of a lock ⟨*unlock* the door⟩ ⟨the chest won't *unlock*⟩ **2** : RELEASE ⟨*unlock* a flood of emotions⟩ **3** : DISCLOSE, REVEAL ⟨*unlock* the secrets of nature⟩

un·looked–for \-ˈlu̇kt-ˌfȯr\ *adj* : not foreseen

un·loose \ˌən-ˈlüs, ˈən-\ *vt* **1** : to relax the strain of ⟨*unloose* a grip⟩ **2** : to release from or as if from restraints : set free **3** : to loosen the ties of : UNDO

un·loos·en \-ˈlüs-n\ *vt* : UNLOOSE

un·love·ly \-ˈləv-lē\ *adj* : having no charm or appeal ⟨an *unlovely* disposition⟩ — **un·love·li·ness** *n*

un·lucky \-ˈlək-ē\ *adj* **1** : marked by bad luck or failure **2** : likely to bring misfortune **3** : producing dissatisfaction : REGRETTABLE — **un·luck·i·ly** \-ˈlək-ə-lē\ *adv* — **un·luck·i·ness** \-ˈlək-ē-nəs\ *n*

un·make \-ˈmāk\ *vt* **-made** \-ˈmād\; **-mak·ing 1** : to cause to disappear : DESTROY **2** : to deprive of rank or office : DEPOSE **3** : to change the nature of

un·man \-ˈman\ *vt* : to deprive of courage, strength, or vigor

un·manned \ˌən-ˈmand, ˈən-\ *adj* : having no crew aboard ⟨*unmanned* spacecraft⟩

un·man·nered \-ˈman-ərd\ *adj* **1** : lacking good manners : RUDE **2** : UNAFFECTED 2 — **un·man·nered·ly** *adv*

[1]**un·man·ner·ly** \-ˈman-ər-lē\ *adv* : in an unmannerly fashion

[2]**unmannerly** *adj* : RUDE 3, IMPOLITE — **un·man·ner·li·ness** *n*

un·mask \ˌən-ˈmask, ˈən-\ *vb* **1** : to strip of a mask or disguise : EXPOSE ⟨*unmask* a traitor⟩ **2** : to take off one's own disguise (as at a masquerade)

un·mean·ing \-ˈmē-ning\ *adj* : having no meaning : SENSELESS

un·meant \-ˈment\ *adj* : not meant : UNINTENTIONAL

un·meet \-ˈmēt\ *adj* : not meet : UNSUITABLE, IMPROPER

un·men·tion·able \-ˈmench-nə-bəl, -ə-nə-\ *adj* : not fit or proper to be talked about — **unmentionable** *n*

un·mer·ci·ful \ˌən-ˈmər-si-fəl, ˈən-\ *adj* : not merciful : MERCILESS, CRUEL — **un·mer·ci·ful·ly** \-fə-lē, -flē\ *adv*

un·mis·tak·able \ˌən-mə-ˈstā-kə-bəl\ *adj* : not capable of being mistaken or misunderstood : CLEAR, OBVIOUS — **un·mis·tak·ably** \-blē\ *adv*

un·mit·i·gat·ed \ˌən-ˈmit-ə-ˌgāt-əd, ˈən-\ *adj* **1** : not softened or lessened **2** : THOROUGH, UTTER ⟨an *unmitigated* liar⟩ ⟨*unmitigated* impudence⟩ — **un·mit·i·gat·ed·ly** *adv*

un·moor \-ˈmu̇r\ *vb* **1** : to loose from or as if from moorings **2** : to cast off moorings

un·mor·al \-ˈmȯr-əl, -ˈmär-\ *adj* : having no moral quality or relation : being neither moral nor immoral — **un·mor·al·ly** \-ə-lē\ *adv*

un·moved \-ˈmüvd\ *adj* **1** : not disturbed emotionally ⟨seemed *unmoved* by the news⟩ **2 a** : remaining in the same place **b** : firmly set ⟨*unmoved* in our purpose⟩

un·muf·fle \-ˈməf-əl\ *vt* : to free from something that muffles

un·muz·zle \-ˈməz-əl\ *vt* : to remove a muzzle from

un·my·elin·at·ed \-ˈmī-ə-lə-ˌnāt-əd\ *adj* : lacking a myelin sheath

un·nail \ˌən-ˈnāl, ˈən-\ *vt* : to unfasten by removing nails

un·nat·u·ral \ˌən-ˈnach-rəl, ˈən-, -ə-rəl\ *adj* **1** : not being in accordance with nature or consistent with a normal course of events **2 a** : not according with normal feelings or behavior : PERVERSE, ABNORMAL **b** : ARTIFICIAL ⟨their heartiness was forced and *unnatural*⟩ **c** : STRANGE, IRREGULAR ⟨an *unnatural* alliance⟩ — **un·nat·u·ral·ly** \-ˈnach-rə-lē, -ə-rə-, -ˈnach-ər-lē\ *adv* — **un·nat·u·ral·ness** \-ˈnach-rəl-nəs, -ə-rəl-\ *n*

un·nec·es·sar·i·ly \ˌən-ˌnes-ə-ˈser-ə-lē\ *adv* **1** : not by necessity ⟨spent money *unnecessarily*⟩ **2** : to an unnecessary degree ⟨*unnecessarily* harsh⟩

un·nec·es·sary \ˌən-ˈnes-ə-ˌser-ē, ˈən-\ *adj* : not necessary ⟨a guide is *unnecessary* since the trail is clearly marked⟩

un·nerve \ˌən-ˈnərv, ˈən-\ *vt* : to deprive of nerve, courage, or self-control

un·num·bered \ˌən-ˈnəm-bərd, ˈən-\ *adj* **1** : INNUMERABLE ⟨*unnumbered* stars⟩ **2** : not having an identifying number ⟨*unnumbered* page⟩

un·ob·tru·sive \ˌən-əb-ˈtrü-siv, -ziv\ *adj* : not obtrusive : not blatant or aggressive : INCONSPICUOUS — **un·ob·tru·sive·ly** *adv* — **un·ob·tru·sive·ness** *n*

un·oc·cu·pied \ˌən-ˈäk-yə-ˌpīd, ˈən-\ *adj* **1** : not busy : UNEMPLOYED **2** : not occupied : EMPTY

un·or·ga·nized \ˌən-ˈȯr-gə-ˌnīzd, ˈən-\ *adj* : not subjected to organization: as **a** : not formed or brought into an integrated or ordered whole **b** : not organized into unions ⟨*unorganized* labor⟩

un·pack \ˌən-ˈpak, ˈən-\ *vb* **1** : to separate and remove things packed **2** : to open and remove the contents of ⟨*unpack* a trunk⟩

un·paired \-ˈpaərd, -ˈpeərd\ *adj* **1** : not paired; *esp* : not matched or mated **2** : situated in the median plane of the body ⟨an *unpaired* fin⟩

un·par·al·leled \-ˈpar-ə-ˌleld\ *adj* : having no parallel; *esp* : having no equal or match

un·par·lia·men·ta·ry \ˌən-ˌpär-lə-ˈment-ə-rē, -ˌpärl-yə-, -ˈmen-trē\ *adj* : contrary to parliamentary practice or rules

\ə\ **abut**	\au̇\ **out**	\i\ **tip**	\ȯ\ **saw**	\u̇\ **foot**
\ər\ **further**	\ch\ **chin**	\ī\ **life**	\ȯi\ **coin**	\y\ **yet**
\a\ **mat**	\e\ **pet**	\j\ **job**	\th\ **thin**	\yü\ **few**
\ā\ **take**	\ē\ **easy**	\ng\ **sing**	\th\ **this**	\yu̇\ **cure**
\ä\ **cot, cart**	\g\ **go**	\ō\ **bone**	\ü\ **food**	\zh\ **vision**

un•peg \ˌən-ˈpeg, ˈən-\ *vt* : to open by or as if by removing a peg
un•peo•ple \ˌən-ˈpē-pəl, ˈən-\ *vt* : DEPOPULATE
un•pile \-ˈpīl\ *vb* : to separate or become separated from a pile
un•pin \-ˈpin\ *vt* : to undo by or as if by removing a pin
un•pleas•ant \-ˈplez-ⁿt\ *adj* : not pleasant : not amiable or agreeable — **un•pleas•ant•ly** *adv*
un•pleas•ant•ness \-ˈplez-ⁿt-nəs\ *n* **1** : the quality or state of being unpleasant **2** : an unpleasant situation, experience, or event
un•plumbed \ˌən-ˈpləmd, ˈən-\ *adj* **1** : not tested or measured with a plumb line **2** : not thoroughly explored
un•po•lit•i•cal \ˌən-pə-ˈlit-i-kəl\ *adj* : not interested or engaged in politics
un•pop•u•lar \ˌən-ˈpäp-yə-lər, ˈən-\ *adj* : not popular : viewed or received unfavorably : disliked by many people — **un•pop•u•lar•i•ty** \ˌən-ˌpäp-yə-ˈlar-ət-ē\ *n*
un•prec•e•dent•ed \ˌən-ˈpres-ə-ˌdent-əd, ˈən-\ *adj* : having no precedent : NOVEL — **un•prec•e•dent•ed•ly** *adv*
un•prej•u•diced \ˌən-ˈprej-əd-əst, ˈən-\ *adj* : not prejudiced : IMPARTIAL
un•pre•ten•tious \ˌən-pri-ˈten-chəs\ *adj* : not pretentious : not showy or pompous : SIMPLE, MODEST — **un•pre•ten•tious•ly** *adv* — **un•pre•ten•tious•ness** *n*
un•prin•ci•pled \ˌən-ˈprin-sə-pəld, ˈən-, -sə-bəld, -spəld\ *adj* : lacking moral principles : UNSCRUPULOUS
un•print•able \-ˈprint-ə-bəl\ *adj* : unfit to be printed
un•pro•fes•sion•al \ˌən-prə-ˈfesh-nəl, ˈən-, -ən-ˡl\ *adj* : not professional; *esp* : not conforming to the standards of a profession — **un•pro•fes•sion•al•ly** \-ē\ *adv*
un•prof•it•able \ˌən-ˈpräf-ət-ə-bəl, ˈən-, -ˈpräf-tə-bəl\ *adj* : producing no profit, gain, or result — **un•prof•it•able•ness** *n* — **un•prof•it•ably** \-blē\ *adv*
un•prom•is•ing \-ˈpräm-ə-sing\ *adj* : appearing unlikely to prove worthwhile or result favorably — **un•prom•is•ing•ly** \-sing-lē\ *adv*
un•qual•i•fied \-ˈkwäl-ə-ˌfīd\ *adj* **1** : not fit : lacking necessary qualifications **2** : not modified or restricted by reservations ⟨an *unqualified* denial⟩ — **un•qual•i•fied•ly** \-ˌfī-əd-lē, -ˌfīd-\ *adv*
un•ques•tion•able \-ˈkwes-chə-nə-bəl, -ˈkwesh-, *rapid* -ˈkwesh- nə-\ *adj* **1** : acknowledged as beyond question or doubt ⟨*unquestionable* authority⟩ **2** : not questionable : INDISPUTABLE ⟨*unquestionable* evidence⟩ — **un•ques•tion•ably** \-blē\ *adv*
un•ques•tion•ing \-ˈkwes-chə-ning, -ˈkwesh-\ *adj* : not questioning : accepting without hesitation ⟨*unquestioning* trust in God⟩ — **un•ques•tion•ing•ly** \-ning-lē\ *adv*
un•qui•et \-ˈkwī-ət\ *adj* **1** : not quiet : TURBULENT **2** : physically, emotionally, or mentally restless : UNEASY — **un•qui•et•ly** *adv* — **un•qui•et•ness** *n*
un•quote \ˈən-ˌkwōt\ *n* — used orally to indicate the end of a direct quotation
un•rav•el \ˌən-ˈrav-əl, ˈən-\ *vb* **1** : to separate the threads of : DISENTANGLE ⟨*unravel* a snarl⟩ **2** : SOLVE ⟨*unravel* a mystery⟩ **3** : to become unraveled
un•read \-ˈred\ *adj* **1** : not read ⟨an *unread* book⟩ **2** : not well informed through reading
un•read•able \-ˈrēd-ə-bəl\ *adj* **1** : too dull or unattractive to read ⟨a drab *unreadable* dissertation⟩ **2** : not legible or decipherable : ILLEGIBLE — **un•read•abil•i•ty** \ˌən-ˌrēd-ə-ˈbil-ət-ē\ *n*
• **syn** UNREADABLE, ILLEGIBLE mean difficult or impossible to read. ILLEGIBLE usually implies a physical impossibility of making out letters or signs ⟨*illegible* handwriting⟩ UNREADABLE more often implies a psychological impossibility of continuing to read with interest or pleasure ⟨a novel now thought *unreadable*⟩
un•ready \ˌən-ˈred-ē, ˈən-\ *adj* : not ready or qualified ⟨*unready* to deal with a crisis⟩ — **un•read•i•ness** *n*
un•re•al \-ˈri-əl, -ˈril, -ˈrē-əl, -ˈrēl\ *adj* : lacking in reality, substance, or genuineness
un•re•al•is•tic \ˈən-ˌri-ə-ˈlis-tik, -ˌrē-ə-\ *adj* : not realistic : inappropriate to reality or fact — **un•re•al•is•ti•cal•ly** \-ti-kə-lē, -klē\ *adv*
un•re•al•i•ty \ˌən-rē-ˈal-ət-ē\ *n* **1 a** : the quality or state of being unreal **b** : something unreal, insubstantial, or visionary **2** : ineptitude in dealing with reality
un•rea•son \ˌən-ˈrēz-ⁿn, ˈən-\ *n* : the absence of reason or sanity
un•rea•son•able \-ˈrēz-nə-bəl, -ⁿn-ə-bəl\ *adj* **1 a** : not governed by or acting according to reason ⟨*unreasonable* people⟩ **b** : not conformable to reason : ABSURD ⟨*unreasonable* arguments⟩ **2** : exceeding the bounds of reason or moderation ⟨*unreasonable* suspicion⟩ **syn** see IRRATIONAL — **un•rea•son•able•ness** *n* — **un•rea•son•ably** \-blē\ *adv*
un•rea•son•ing \-ˈrēz-ning, -ⁿn-ing\ *adj* : not reasoning; *esp* : not using or showing the use of reason as a guide or control ⟨*unreasoning* fear⟩ ⟨the *unreasoning* beasts⟩ — **un•rea•son•ing•ly** *adv*
un•re•con•struct•ed \ˌən-ˌrē-kən-ˈstrək-təd\ *adj* : not reconciled to some political, economic, or social change; *esp* : holding stubbornly to principles, beliefs, or views that are held to be outmoded
un•reel \ˌən-ˈrēl, ˈən-\ *vb* : to unwind from or as if from a reel
un•re•gen•er•ate \ˌən-ri-ˈjen-rət, -ə-rət\ *adj* : not reborn spiritually : not at peace with God : SINFUL, WICKED
un•re•lent•ing \ˌən-ri-ˈlent-ing\ *adj* **1** : not softening or yielding in determination : HARD, STERN **2** : not letting up or weakening in vigor or pace — **un•re•lent•ing•ly** \-ing-lē\ *adv*
un•re•mit•ting \ˌən-ri-ˈmit-ing\ *adj* : not stopping : UNCEASING ⟨hard *unremitting* labor⟩ — **un•re•mit•ting•ly** \-ing-lē\ *adv*
un•re•serve \ˌən-ri-ˈzərv\ *n* : absence of reserve : FRANKNESS
un•re•served \ˌən-ri-ˈzərvd\ *adj* **1** : not held in reserve : not kept back **2** : having or showing no reserve in manner or speech — **un•re•serv•ed•ly** \-ˈzər-vəd-lē\ *adv* — **un•re•served•ness** \-ˈzər-vəd-nəs, -ˈzərvd-nəs, -ˈzərv-nəs\ *n*
un•re•spon•sive \ˌən-ri-ˈspän-siv\ *adj* : not responsive — **un•re•spon•sive•ly** *adv* — **un•re•spon•sive•ness** *n*
un•rest \ˌən-ˈrest, ˈən-\ *n* : a disturbed or uneasy state
un•re•strained \ˌən-ri-ˈstrānd\ *adj* **1** : not restrained : IMMODERATE **2** : free of constraint : SPONTANEOUS — **un•re•strain•ed•ly** \-ˈstrā-nəd-lē\ *adv*
un•re•straint \-ˈstrānt\ *n* : lack of restraint
un•rid•dle \ˌən-ˈrid-ˡl, ˈən-\ *vt* : to find the explanation of : SOLVE
un•righ•teous \-ˈrī-chəs\ *adj* **1** : not righteous : SINFUL, WICKED **2** : UNJUST, UNCALLED-FOR ⟨*unrighteous* interference⟩ — **un•righ•teous•ly** *adv* — **un•righ•teous•ness** *n*
un•rip \-ˈrip\ *vt* : to rip or slit up : cut or tear open
un•ripe \-ˈrīp\ *adj* **1** : not ripe : IMMATURE **2** : UNREADY, UNSEASONABLE — **un•ripe•ness** *n*
un•ri•valed *or* **un•ri•valled** \-ˈrī-vəld\ *adj* : having no rival : INCOMPARABLE, UNEQUALED
un•robe \ˌən-ˈrōb, ˈən-\ *vb* : DISROBE, UNDRESS
un•roll \-ˈrōl\ *vb* **1** : to unwind a roll of : open out ⟨*unroll* a carpet⟩ **2** : to spread out like a scroll for reading or inspection **3** : to be or seem to be unrolled ⟨the scene *unrolled* under the speeding plane⟩
un•roof \-ˈrüf, -ˈru̇f\ *vt* : to strip off the roof or covering of
un•root \-ˈrüt, -ˈru̇t\ *vt* : to tear up by the roots : UPROOT
un•round \-ˈrau̇nd\ *vt* : to pronounce (a sound) without, or with decreased, rounding of the lips — **un•round•ed** \-ˈrau̇n-dəd\ *adj*
un•ruf•fled \-ˈrəf-əld\ *adj* **1** : not upset or agitated **2** : not ruffled : SMOOTH ⟨*unruffled* water⟩
un•ruly \ˌən-ˈrü-lē, ˈən-\ *adj* : not yielding readily to rule or restraint : hard to handle or manage ⟨an *unruly* temper⟩ ⟨an *unruly* horse⟩ — **un•rul•i•ness** *n*
• **syn** UNGOVERNABLE, REFRACTORY, RECALCITRANT: UNRULY implies lack of discipline or incapacity for discipline and often connotes waywardness or turbulence of behavior ⟨*unruly* children⟩ UNGOVERNABLE implies either an escape from control or guidance or a state of being unsubdued and incapable of controlling the self or being controlled by others ⟨*ungovernable* rage⟩ ⟨*ungovernable* stampeding cattle⟩ REFRACTORY stresses resistance to attempts to manage or to mold ⟨special schools for *refractory* children⟩ RECALCITRANT suggests determined resistance to or defiance of authority ⟨sabotage by a *recalcitrant* populace⟩
un•sad•dle \ˌən-ˈsad-ˡl, ˈən-\ *vb* **1 a** : to remove the saddle from a horse **b** : to remove a saddle from **2** : UNHORSE
un•sat•u•rate \-ˈsach-rət, -ə-rət\ *n* : an unsaturated chemical compound
un•sat•u•rat•ed \-ˈsach-ə-ˌrāt-əd\ *adj* **1** : capable of absorbing or dissolving more of something ⟨an *unsaturated* salt solution⟩ **2** : able to form a new product by direct chemical combination

with another substance; *esp* : containing double or triple bonds between carbon atoms ⟨an *unsaturated* acid⟩ — **un•sat•u•ra•tion** \ˌən-ˌsach-ə-ˈrā-shən\ *n*

un•saved \ˌən-ˈsāvd, ˈən-\ *adj* : not saved; *esp* : not rescued from eternal punishment

un•sa•vory \-ˈsāv-rē, -ə-rē\ *adj* **1** : having little or no taste **2** : having a bad taste or smell **3** : morally offensive ⟨an *unsavory* character⟩ — **un•sa•vor•i•ly** \-ˈsāv-rə-lē, -ə-rə-\ *adv*

un•say \-ˈsā\ *vt* **-said** \-ˈsed\; **-say•ing** \-ˈsā-iŋ\ : to take back (something said) : RETRACT, WITHDRAW

un•scathed \ˌən-ˈskāthd, ˈən-\ *adj* : wholly unharmed : not injured

un•schooled \-ˈsküld\ *adj* : not schooled : UNTAUGHT

un•sci•en•tif•ic \ˌən-ˌsī-ən-ˈtif-ik\ *adj* **1** : not used in scientific work **2** : not according with the principles and methods of science — **un•sci•en•tif•i•cal•ly** \-ˈtif-i-kə-lē, -klē\ *adv*

un•scram•ble \ˌən-ˈskram-bəl, ˈən-\ *vt* **1** : to separate into original components : RESOLVE, CLARIFY **2** : to restore (as a radio message) to intelligible form

un•screw \-ˈskrü\ *vb* **1** : to remove the screws from **2** : to loosen or withdraw by turning

un•scru•pu•lous \-ˈskrü-pyə-ləs\ *adj* : UNPRINCIPLED — **un•scru•pu•lous•ly** *adv* — **un•scru•pu•lous•ness** *n*

un•seal \-ˈsēl\ *vt* : to break or remove the seal of : OPEN

un•seam \-ˈsēm\ *vt* : to open the seams of

un•search•able \-ˈsər-chə-bəl\ *adj* : impossible to explore or examine ⟨the *unsearchable* ways of God⟩ — **un•search•ably** \-blē\ *adv*

un•sea•son•able \-ˈsēz-nə-bəl, -ˈsēz-n-ə-\ *adj* : not seasonable : happening or coming at the wrong time : UNTIMELY — **un•sea•son•able•ness** *n* — **un•sea•son•ably** \-blē\ *adv*

un•seat \ˌən-ˈsēt, ˈən-\ *vt* **1** : to dislodge from a seat especially on horseback **2** : to dislodge from a place or position; *esp* : to remove from political office

[1]**un•seem•ly** \-ˈsēm-lē\ *adj* : not suitable or proper : UNBECOMING ⟨*unseemly* bickering in public⟩ **syn** see INDECOROUS

[2]**unseemly** *adv* : in an unseemly manner

un•seen \-ˈsēn\ *adj* : not seen or perceived : INVISIBLE

un•seg•re•gat•ed \-ˈseg-ri-ˌgāt-əd\ *adj* : not segregated; *esp* : free from racial segregation

un•self•ish \-ˈsel-fish\ *adj* : not selfish : GENEROUS — **un•self•ish•ly** *adv* — **un•self•ish•ness** *n*

un•set•tle \ˌən-ˈset-l, ˈən-\ *vb* : to move or loosen from a settled state : make or become displaced or disturbed

un•set•tled \-ˈset-ld\ *adj* **1** : not settled : not fixed (as in position or character) ⟨*unsettled* weather⟩ **2** : not calm or tranquil ⟨*unsettled* waters⟩ **3** : not decided in mind ⟨*unsettled* what to do⟩ **4** : not paid ⟨an *unsettled* account⟩; *also* : not disposed of according to law ⟨an *unsettled* estate⟩ **5** : not occupied by settlers ⟨an *unsettled* region⟩

un•sew \ˌən-ˈsō, ˈən-\ *vt* **-sewed**; **-sewn** \-ˈsōn\ *or* **-sewed**; **-sew•ing** : to undo the sewing of

un•sex \-ˈseks\ *vt* : to deprive of sex or of qualities typical of one's sex

un•shack•le \-ˈshak-əl\ *vt* : to loose from shackles

un•shaped \-ˈshāpt\ *adj* : not shaped: as **a** : not dressed or finished to final form ⟨an *unshaped* timber⟩ **b** : imperfect in form or formulation ⟨*unshaped* ideas⟩

un•shap•en \-ˈshā-pən\ *adj* : UNSHAPED **[**Middle English, from [1]*un-* + *shapen,* past participle of *shapen* "to shape"**]**

un•sheathe \-ˈshēth\ *vt* : to draw from or as if from a sheath or scabbard ⟨*unsheathe* a sword⟩

un•ship \ˌən-ˈship, ˈən-\ *vb* **1** : to remove from a ship **2** : to remove or become removed from position ⟨*unship* an oar⟩

un•shod \-ˈshäd\ *adj* : lacking shoes

un•sight•ly \-ˈsīt-lē\ *adj* : unpleasant to the sight : UGLY ⟨an *unsightly* scar⟩ — **un•sight•li•ness** *n*

un•skilled \-ˈskild\ *adj* **1** : not skilled; *esp* : not skilled in a specified branch of work : lacking technical training **2** : not requiring skill ⟨*unskilled* jobs⟩ **3** : marked by lack of skill ⟨*unskilled* writing⟩

un•skill•ful \-ˈskil-fəl\ *adj* : lacking in skill or proficiency — **un•skill•ful•ly** \-fə-lē\ *adv* — **un•skill•ful•ness** *n*

un•sling \-ˈsliŋ\ *vt* **-slung** \-ˈsləŋ\; **-sling•ing** \-ˈsliŋ-iŋ\ : to remove from being slung

un•snap \-ˈsnap\ *vt* : to loosen or free by or as if by undoing a snap

un•snarl \-ˈsnärl\ *vt* : to straighten out a snarl in

un•so•cia•bil•i•ty \ˌən-ˌsō-shə-ˈbil-ət-ē\ *n* : the quality or state of being unsociable

un•so•cia•ble \ˌən-ˈsō-shə-bəl, ˈən-\ *adj* **1** : having or showing a preference for avoiding society or conversation : SOLITARY, RESERVED **2** : not conducive to sociability — **un•so•cia•ble•ness** *n* — **un•so•cia•bly** \-blē\ *adv*

un•so•cial \-ˈsō-shəl\ *adj* **1** : not social : not seeking or given to association **2** : ANTISOCIAL 1 — **un•so•cial•ly** \-ˈsōsh-lē, -ə-lē\ *adv*

un•so•phis•ti•cat•ed \ˌən-sə-ˈfis-tə-ˌkāt-əd\ *adj* : not sophisticated: as **a** : not changed or corrupted : GENUINE **b** (1) : not worldly-wise : lacking sophistication (2) : lacking adornment or complexity of structure : PLAIN, SIMPLE

un•so•phis•ti•ca•tion \-ˌfis-tə-ˈkā-shən\ *n* : lack of sophistication

un•sought \ˌən-ˈsȯt, ˈən-\ *adj* : not sought : not searched for or asked for ⟨*unsought* honors⟩

un•sound \-ˈsau̇nd\ *adj* : not sound: as **a** : not healthy or whole **b** : not mentally normal : not wholly sane **c** : not firmly made, placed, or fixed **d** : not valid or true — **un•sound•ly** *adv* — **un•sound•ness** \-ˈsau̇nd-nəs, -ˈsau̇n-\ *n*

un•spar•ing \-ˈspaər-iŋ, -ˈspeər-\ *adj* **1** : not merciful : HARD, RUTHLESS **2** : not frugal : LIBERAL — **un•spar•ing•ly** \-iŋ-lē\ *adv*

un•speak•able \-ˈspē-kə-bəl\ *adj* **1** : impossible to express in words **2** : extremely bad ⟨*unspeakable* conduct⟩ — **un•speak•ably** \-blē\ *adv*

un•sphere \-ˈsfiər\ *vt* : to remove (as a planet) from a sphere

un•spot•ted \ˌən-ˈspät-əd, ˈən-\ *adj* : not spotted : free from spot or stain; *esp* : free from moral stain

un•sprung \-ˈsprəŋ\ *adj* : not sprung; *esp* : not equipped with springs

un•sta•ble \-ˈstā-bəl\ *adj* : not stable : not firm or fixed : not constant: as **a** : not steady in action or movement **b** : wavering in purpose or intent ⟨*unstable* beliefs⟩; *also* : having defective emotional control ⟨an *unstable* person⟩ **c** : readily changing in chemical composition or physical state or properties ⟨an *unstable* emulsion⟩; *esp* : tending to decompose spontaneously ⟨an *unstable* atomic nucleus⟩ — **un•sta•ble•ness** *n* — **un•sta•bly** \-bə-lē, -blē\ *adv*

un•state \-ˈstāt\ *vt* : to deprive of state, dignity, or rank

un•steady \-ˈsted-ē\ *adj* : lacking in stability or regularity — **un•stead•i•ly** \-ˈsted-l-ē\ *adv* — **un•stead•i•ness** \-ˈsted-ē-nəs\ *n*

un•stick \-ˈstik\ *vt* **-stuck** \-ˈstək\; **-stick•ing** : to release from being stuck or bound

un•stint•ing•ly \-ˈstint-iŋ-lē\ *adv* : without limit : FREELY ⟨gave *unstintingly* of their time⟩

un•stop \-ˈstäp\ *vt* **1** : to free from an obstruction : OPEN **2** : to remove a stopper from

un•strap \-ˈstrap\ *vt* : to remove or loose a strap from

un•stressed \-ˈstrest\ *adj* : not stressed; *esp* : not bearing a stress or accent

un•string \-ˈstriŋ\ *vt* **-strung** \-ˈstrəŋ\; **-string•ing** \-ˈstriŋ-iŋ\ **1** : to loosen or remove the strings of **2** : to remove from a string **3** : to make weak, disordered, or unstable

un•stud•ied \-ˈstəd-ēd\ *adj* **1** : not acquired by study **2** : not planned with a certain effect in mind : NATURAL

un•sub•stan•tial \ˌən-səb-ˈstan-chəl\ *adj* : lacking substance, firmness, or strength — **un•sub•stan•ti•al•i•ty** \-ˌstan-chē-ˈal-ət-ē\ *n* — **un•sub•stan•tial•ly** \-ˈstanch-lē, -ə-lē\ *adv*

un•suc•cess•ful \ˌən-sək-ˈses-fəl\ *adj* : not meeting with or producing success — **un•suc•cess•ful•ly** \-fə-lē\ *adv*

un•suit•able \ˌən-ˈsüt-ə-bəl, ˈən-\ *adj* : not fitting : UNBECOMING, INAPPROPRIATE — **un•suit•abil•i•ty** \-ˌsüt-ə-ˈbil-ət-ē\ *n* — **un•suit•ably** \-ˈsüt-ə-blē\ *adv*

un•sung \-ˈsəŋ\ *adj* **1** : not sung **2** : not praised (as in song or verse) : not publicized ⟨*unsung* heroes⟩

un•swathe \-ˈswäth, -ˈswȯth, -ˈswāth\ *vt* : to free from something that swathes

un•swear \-ˈswaər, -ˈsweər\ *vb* **-swore** \-ˈswōər, -ˈswȯər\; **-sworn** \-ˈswōrn -ˈswȯrn\; **-swear•ing** *archaic* : RECANT, RETRACT

\ə\ abut	\au̇\ **out**	\i\ **tip**	\ȯ\ **saw**	\u̇\ **foot**
\ər\ **further**	\ch\ **chin**	\ī\ **life**	\ȯi\ **coin**	\y\ **yet**
\a\ **mat**	\e\ **pet**	\j\ **job**	\th\ **thin**	\yü\ **few**
\ā\ **take**	\ē\ **easy**	\ŋ\ **sing**	\th\ **this**	\yu̇\ **cure**
\ä\ **cot, cart**	\g\ **go**	\ō\ **bone**	\ü\ **food**	\zh\ **vision**

un•swerv•ing \-ˈswər-viŋ\ *adj* **1** : not swerving or turning aside **2** : STEADY ⟨*unswerving* loyalty⟩

un•sym•met•ri•cal \ˌən-sə-ˈme-tri-kəl\ *also* **un•sym•met•ric** \-trik\ *adj* : not symmetrical : ASYMMETRIC — **un•sym•met•ri•cal•ly** \-tri-kə-lē, -klē\ *adv*

un•tan•gle \ˌən-ˈtaŋ-gəl, ˈən-\ *vt* **1** : to remove a tangle from **2** : to straighten (as something complex or confused) out : RESOLVE **syn** see EXTRICATE

un•taught \-ˈtȯt\ *adj* **1** : not instructed or trained : IGNORANT **2** : NATURAL, SPONTANEOUS ⟨*untaught* kindness⟩

un•teth•er \-ˈteth-ər\ *vt* : to free from a tether

un•think•able \-ˈthiŋ-kə-bəl\ *adj* : not to be thought of or considered as possible ⟨*unthinkable* cruelty⟩

un•think•ing \-ˈthiŋ-kiŋ\ *adj* **1** : not taking thought : HEEDLESS, UNMINDFUL **2** : not indicating thought or reflection **3** : not having the power of thought — **un•think•ing•ly** \-kiŋ-lē\ *adv*

un•thought–of \-ˈthȯt-ˌəv, -ˌäv\ *adj* : not thought of : not considered : not imagined

un•thread \-ˈthred\ *vt* **1** : to draw or take out a thread from **2** : to loosen the threads or connections of **3** : to make one's way through ⟨*unthread* a maze⟩

un•throne \-ˈthrōn\ *vt* : to remove from or as if from a throne

un•ti•dy \-ˈtīd-ē\ *adj* **1** : not neat : CARELESS, SLOVENLY **2 a** : not neatly organized or carried out **b** : tending to cause a lack of neatness — **un•ti•di•ly** \-ˈtīd-l-ē\ *adv* — **un•ti•di•ness** \-ˈtīd-ē-nəs\ *n*

un•tie \-ˈtī\ *vb* **-tied**; **-ty•ing** *or* **-tie•ing** **1** : to free from something that ties, fastens, or restrains : UNBIND **2 a** : to disengage the knotted parts of **b** : DISENTANGLE, RESOLVE **3** : to become loosened or unbound

¹un•til \ən-ˌtil, -tl, -ˌtel, ˌən-, *in some contexts* ᵊn-, ᵊm-, ᵊŋ-\ *prep* : up to the time of ⟨stayed *until* morning⟩ **[**Middle English, from *un-* "to, until" + *til* "till"**]**

²until *conj* **1** : up to the time that ⟨played *until* it got dark⟩ **2** : to the point or degree that ⟨ran *until* I was breathless⟩

¹un•time•ly \ˌən-ˈtīm-lē, ˈən-\ *adv* **1** : at an inopportune time : UNSEASONABLY **2** : too soon

²untimely *adj* **1** : occurring or done before the due, natural, or proper time : too early : PREMATURE ⟨*untimely* death⟩ **2** : UNSEASONABLE ⟨an *untimely* joke⟩ ⟨*untimely* frost⟩ — **un•time•li•ness** *n*

un•ti•tled \-ˈtīt-ld\ *adj* **1** : having no title especially of nobility **2** : not named ⟨an *untitled* painting⟩

un•to \ˈən-tə, -tü\ *prep* : TO **[**Middle English, from *un-* "to, until" + *to***]**

un•told \ˌən-ˈtōld, ˈən-\ *adj* **1** : not told : not revealed ⟨*untold* secrets⟩ ⟨a story yet *untold*⟩ **2** : not counted : VAST, NUMBERLESS ⟨*untold* resources⟩

¹un•touch•able \-ˈtəch-ə-bəl\ *adj* **1 a** : forbidden to the touch **b** : exempt from criticism or control **2** : being out of reach **3** : disagreeable or defiling to the touch — **un•touch•abil•i•ty** \-ˌtəch-ə-ˈbil-ət-ē\ *n*

²untouchable *n* : one that is untouchable; *esp* : a member of a large formerly segregated hereditary group in India having in traditional Hindu belief the quality of defiling by contact a member of a higher caste

un•to•ward \ˌən-ˈtō-ərd, -ˈtȯ-ərd, -ˈtōrd, -ˈtȯrd, ˈən-\ *adj* **1** : difficult to manage : STUBBORN, WILLFUL ⟨an *untoward* child⟩ **2** : INCONVENIENT, TROUBLESOME ⟨an *untoward* encounter⟩ — **un•to•ward•ly** *adv* — **un•to•ward•ness** *n*

un•tread \ˌən-ˈtred, ˈən-\ *vt* **-trod** \-ˈträd\; **-trod•den** \-ˈträd-n\; **-tread•ing** *archaic* : to tread back : RETRACE

un•tried \-ˈtrīd\ *adj* **1** : not tested or proved by experience or trial ⟨*untried* soldiers⟩ **2** : not tried in court ⟨a backlog of *untried* cases⟩

un•true \-ˈtrü\ *adj* **1** : not faithful : DISLOYAL **2** : not according with a standard of correctness : not level or exact **3** : not according with the facts : FALSE — **un•tru•ly** \-ˈtrü-lē\ *adv*

un•truth \-ˈtrüth\ *n* **1** : lack of truthfulness : FALSITY **2** : something that is untrue : FALSEHOOD

un•truth•ful \-ˈtrüth-fəl\ *adj* : not containing or telling the truth : FALSE, INACCURATE ⟨*untruthful* report⟩ — **un•truth•ful•ly** \-fə-lē\ *adv* — **un•truth•ful•ness** *n*

un•tuck \-ˈtək\ *vt* : to release from a tuck or from being tucked up

un•tune \-ˈtün, -ˈtyün\ *vt* **1** : to put out of tune **2** : DISARRANGE, DISCOMPOSE

un•tu•tored \ˌən-ˈtüt-ərd, -ˈtyüt-, ˈən-\ *adj* **1** : lacking schooling **2** : not gained from instruction : NATIVE ⟨*untutored* shrewdness⟩

un•twine \-ˈtwīn\ *vb* **1** : to unwind the twisted or tangled parts of **2** : to remove by unwinding **3** : to become disentangled or unwound

un•twist \-ˈtwist\ *vb* **1** : to separate the twisted parts of : UNTWINE **2** : to become untwined

un•used \-ˈyüzd, *in the phrase "unused to" usually* -ˈyüs, -ˈyüst\ *adj* **1** : not habituated : UNACCUSTOMED 2 **2** : not used: as **a** : never yet used : NEW **b** : not now being used **c** : not used up ⟨*unused* vacation⟩

un•usu•al \-ˈyüzh-wəl, -ə-wəl, -ˈyüzh-əl\ *adj* : not usual : UNCOMMON, RARE — **un•usu•al•ly** \-ˈyüzh-wə-lē, -ə-wə-, -ˈyüzh-lē, -ˈyüzh-ə-lē\ *adv* — **un•usu•al•ness** \-ˈyüzh-wəl-nəs, -ə-wəl-, -ˈyüzh-əl-\ *n*

un•ut•ter•able \-ˈət-ə-rə-bəl\ *adj* : not capable of being put into words : INEXPRESSIBLE — **un•ut•ter•ably** \-blē\ *adv*

un•val•ued \ˌən-ˈval-yüd, ˈən-\ *adj* **1** : not important or prized **2** : not appraised

un•var•nished \-ˈvär-nisht\ *adj* **1** : not embellished or glossed over : PLAIN, STRAIGHTFORWARD ⟨the *unvarnished* truth⟩ **2** : not covered with or as if with varnish

un•veil \-ˈvāl\ *vb* **1** : to remove a veil or covering from ⟨*unveil* a statue⟩ **2** : to remove a concealing cover

un•ver•bal•ized \-ˈvər-bə-ˌlīzd\ *adj* : not put into words or given conscious expression

un•vo•cal \-ˈvō-kəl\ *adj* : not eloquent or outspoken

un•voiced \-ˈvȯist\ *adj* **1** : not verbally expressed **2** : VOICELESS 2

un•war•rant•able \-ˈwȯr-ənt-ə-bəl, -ˈwär-\ *adj* : not justifiable : INEXCUSABLE — **un•war•rant•ably** \-blē\ *adv*

un•wary \-ˈwaər-ē, -ˈweər-\ *adj* : easily fooled or surprised : HEEDLESS, GULLIBLE — **un•war•i•ly** \-ˈwar-ə-lē, -ˈwer-\ *adv* — **un•war•i•ness** \-ˈwar-ē-nəs, -ˈwer-\ *n*

un•wea•ried \-ˈwiər-ēd\ *adj* : not tired : FRESH

un•weave \ˌən-ˈwēv, ˈən-\ *vt* **-wove** \-ˈwōv\; **-wo•ven** \-ˈwō-vən\; **-weav•ing** : DISENTANGLE, RAVEL

un•well \-ˈwel\ *adj* **1** : being in poor health : AILING, SICK **2** : undergoing menstruation

un•wept \-ˈwept\ *adj* : not mourned

un•whole•some \-ˈhōl-səm\ *adj* : detrimental to physical, mental, or moral well-being : UNHEALTHY

un•wieldy \-ˈwēl-dē\ *adj* : not easily handled or managed because of size or weight : AWKWARD, CLUMSY, CUMBERSOME ⟨an *unwieldy* tool⟩ — **un•wield•i•ness** *n*

un•willed \-ˈwild\ *adj* : not willed : INVOLUNTARY

un•wind \-ˈwīnd\ *vb* **-wound** \-ˈwau̇nd\ *also* **-wind•ed**; **-wind•ing** **1 a** : to cause to uncoil : wind off **b** : to become uncoiled or untangled **c** : to free from or as if from a binding or wrapping **2** : to make or become free of tension : RELAX

un•wise \-ˈwīz\ *adj* : not wise : FOOLISH — **un•wise•ly** *adv*

un•wit•ting \-ˈwit-iŋ\ *adj* **1** : not intended : INADVERTENT **2** : not knowing : UNAWARE — **un•wit•ting•ly** \-iŋ-lē\ *adv*

un•wont•ed \-ˈwȯnt-əd, -ˈwōnt-\ *adj* **1** : being out of the ordinary : RARE, UNUSUAL **2** *archaic* : not accustomed by experience — **un•wont•ed•ly** *adv* — **un•wont•ed•ness** *n*

un•world•ly \-ˈwərl-dlē\ *adj* **1** : not of this world; *esp* : SPIRITUAL **2 a** : not wise in the ways of the world : NAIVE **b** : not moved by worldly considerations — **un•world•li•ness** *n*

un•worn \-ˈwōrn, -ˈwȯrn\ *adj* **1** : not damaged by use or wear **2** : not worn : NEW

un•wor•thy \ˌən-ˈwər-thē, ˈən-\ *adj* **1** : BASE, DISHONORABLE ⟨*unworthy* duties⟩ **2** : of insufficient merit or worth ⟨*unworthy* to be trusted⟩ — **un•wor•thi•ly** \-thə-lē\ *adv* — **un•wor•thi•ness** \-thē-nəs\ *n*

un•wrap \-ˈrap\ *vt* : to remove the wrapping from

un•writ•ten \-ˈrit-n\ *adj* **1** : not put in writing : ORAL, TRADITIONAL **2** : containing no writing : BLANK

unwritten law *n* : law based chiefly on custom rather than legislative enactments

un•yield•ing \ˌən-ˈyēl-diŋ, ˈən-\ *adj* **1** : marked by lack of softness or flexibility **2** : marked by firmness or stubbornness

un•yoke \-ˈyōk\ *vt* **1** : to free (as oxen) from a yoke **2** : SEPARATE 1a, DISCONNECT

un•zip \-ˈzip\ *vb* : to open by means of a zipper

¹up \ˈəp\ *adv* **1 a** : in or to a higher position or level : away from the center of the earth **b** : from beneath a surface (as ground or water) **c** : from below the horizon **d** : in or into an upright position **e** : out of bed **2** : with greater strength, force, or energy

⟨speak *up*⟩ **3 a :** in or into a better or more advanced state **b :** in or into a state of greater intensity or activity ⟨stir *up* a fire⟩ **4 a :** into existence, evidence, or knowledge ⟨the missing ring turned *up*⟩ **b :** into consideration ⟨brought the matter *up*⟩ **5 :** into possession or custody **6 a :** WHOLLY 1, COMPLETELY ⟨eat it *up*⟩ **b** — used for emphasis ⟨clean *up* a room⟩ **7 :** ASIDE, BY ⟨lay *up* supplies⟩ ⟨put my car *up* for the winter⟩ **8 :** into a state of closure or confinement ⟨button *up*⟩ ⟨seal *up* a package⟩ **9 a :** so as to arrive or approach ⟨came *up* the drive⟩ **b :** in a direction conventionally opposite to down **c :** so as to be even with, overtake, or arrive at ⟨catch *up*⟩ ⟨keep *up* with the times⟩ **10 :** in or into parts ⟨tear *up* paper⟩ ⟨blow *up* a bridge⟩ **11 :** to a stop ⟨pull *up*⟩ ⟨drew *up* at the curb⟩ **12 a :** AHEAD ⟨went one *up* on their opponent⟩ **b :** for each side ⟨score was 15 *up*⟩ [Old English]

[2]**up** *adj* **1 a :** risen above the horizon **b :** being out of bed **c :** relatively high ⟨the river is *up*⟩ ⟨prices are *up*⟩ **d :** raised so as to be open ⟨windows are *up*⟩ **e :** put together ⟨the house is *up* but not finished⟩ **f :** grown above a surface ⟨the corn is *up*⟩ **g :** moving, inclining, or directed upward or in a direction regarded as up ⟨the *up* escalator⟩ **2 a :** marked by agitation, excitement, or activity ⟨was eager to be *up* and doing⟩ **b :** going on **:** taking place ⟨find out what is *up*⟩ **3 :** come to an end ⟨your time is *up*⟩ **4 :** well informed ⟨always *up* on the news⟩ **5 :** being ahead or in advance of an opponent ⟨was three games *up* in the series⟩ **6 a :** presented for or under consideration ⟨*up* for reelection⟩ **b :** charged before a court ⟨was *up* for robbery⟩ — **up to 1 :** capable of performing or dealing with ⟨was fully *up to* the job⟩ **2 :** engaged in ⟨what are you *up to*⟩ **3 :** being the responsibility of ⟨it's *up to* me⟩

[3]**up** *vb* **upped** *or in 1* **up; upped, up·ping; ups** *or in 1* **up 1 :** to act abruptly or surprisingly — usually followed by *and* and another verb ⟨they *up* and left⟩ **2 :** to rise from a lying or sitting position **3 :** to move or cause to move upward **:** ASCEND, RAISE

[4]**up** \ˌəp, 'əp\ *prep* **1 :** to, toward, or at a higher point of ⟨*up* the hill⟩ **2 a** (1) **:** toward the source of ⟨*up* the river⟩ (2) **:** toward the northern part of ⟨*up* the coast⟩ **b :** to, toward, or in the inner part of **3 :** ALONG ⟨walking *up* the street⟩

[5]**up** \'əp\ *n* **1 :** an upward course or slope **2 :** a period or state of prosperity or success ⟨have my *ups* and downs⟩

up–and–coming \ˌəp-ən-'kəm-iŋ, ˌəp-m-\ *adj* **:** alertly active and likely to advance or succeed

up–and–down \ˌəp-m-'dau̇n, ˌəp-ən-\ *adj* **1 :** marked by alternate upward and downward movement, action, or surface **2 :** very steep **:** PERPENDICULAR

Upa·ni·shad \ü-'pän-ə-ˌshäd, yü-'pan-ə-ˌshad\ *n* **:** one of a class of Vedic philosophical treatises [Sanskrit *upaniṣad*]

[1]**up·beat** \'əp-ˌbēt\ *n* **:** an unaccented beat in a musical measure; *esp* **:** the last beat of the measure

[2]**upbeat** *adj* **:** marked by optimism **:** OPTIMISTIC, CHEERFUL

up·braid \ˌəp-'brād\ *vt* **:** to criticize or scold severely or vehemently [Old English *ūpbregdan*] — **up·braid·er** *n*

up·bring·ing \'əp-ˌbriŋ-iŋ\ *n* **:** early training; *esp* **:** a particular way of bringing up a child

up·chuck \'əp-ˌchək\ *vb* **:** VOMIT 1

up·com·ing \ˌəp-ˌkəm-iŋ\ *adj* **:** being in the near future **:** FORTHCOMING

[1]**up–coun·try** \ˌəp-ˌkən-trē\ *adj* **:** of or relating to the interior of a country or a region — **up–coun·try** \'əp-\ *n*

[2]**up–coun·try** \'əp-'kən-trē\ *adv* **:** to or in the interior of a country or a region

up·date \ˌəp-'dāt\ *vt* **:** to bring up to date — **up·date** \'əp-ˌdāt\ *n*

up·draft \'əp-ˌdraft, -ˌdraft\ *n* **:** an upward movement of gas (as air)

up·end \ˌə-'pend\ *vb* **:** to set, stand, or rise on end

[1]**up·grade** \'əp-ˌgrād\ *n* **1 :** an upward grade or slope **2 a :** INCREASE 1 ⟨crime is on the *upgrade*⟩ **b :** a rise toward a better state — **up·grade** \-'grād\ *adv*

[2]**up·grade** \-ˌgrād\ *vt* **:** to raise to a higher grade or position

up·growth \'əp-ˌgrōth\ *n* **:** the process of increasing (as in height or complexity) **:** DEVELOPMENT; *also* **:** a product or result of this

up·heav·al \ˌəp-'hē-vəl, ə-'pē-\ *n* **1 :** the action or an instance of upheaving especially of part of the earth's crust **2 :** an instance of violent agitation or change

up·heave \ˌəp-'hēv, ə-'pēv\ *vb* **-heaved; -heav·ing :** to heave or lift up from beneath — **up·heav·er** *n*

[1]**up·hill** \'əp-'hil\ *adv* **1 :** upward on a hill or incline **2 :** against difficulties

[2]**up·hill** \'əp-ˌhil\ *adj* **1 a :** situated on elevated ground **b :** going or directed toward higher ground **2 :** requiring much effort

up·hold \ˌəp-'hōld\ *vt* **-held** \-'held\; **-hold·ing 1 a :** to give support to **b :** to support against an opponent **2 a :** to keep elevated **b :** to lift up — **up·hold·er** *n*

up·hol·ster \ˌəp-'hōl-stər, əp-'hōl-; ə-'pōl-\ *vt* **-stered; -ster·ing** \-stə-riŋ, -striŋ\ **:** to furnish with or as if with upholstery [back-formation from *upholstery*] — **up·hol·ster·er** \-stər-ər, -strər\ *n*

up·hol·stery \-stə-rē, -strē\ *n, pl* **-ster·ies :** materials (as fabric, padding, and springs) used to make a soft covering especially for a seat [Middle English *upholdester* "upholsterer", from *upholden* "to uphold, maintain"]

up·keep \'əp-ˌkēp\ *n* **1 :** the act or cost of maintaining in good condition **:** MAINTENANCE **2 :** the state of being maintained

up·land \'əp-lənd, -ˌland\ *n* **:** high land especially at some distance from the sea — **upland** *adj*

upland cotton *n* **:** any of various usually short-staple cottons cultivated especially in the United States

upland plover *n* **:** a large sandpiper of eastern North America that frequents fields and uplands

upland plover

[1]**up·lift** \əp-'lift, ˌəp-\ *vb* **1 :** to lift up **:** ELEVATE **2 :** to improve the condition of especially spiritually, socially, or intellectually — **up·lift·er** *n*

[2]**up·lift** \'əp-ˌlift\ *n* **:** an act, process, or result of uplifting: as **a :** the uplifting of a part of the earth's surface **b :** moral or social improvement; *also* **:** a movement to make such improvement **c :** influences intended to uplift

up·most \'əp-ˌmōst\ *adj* **:** UPPERMOST

up·on \ə-'pȯn, -'pän, -ˌpən, -pən\ *prep* **:** ON

[1]**up·per** \'əp-ər\ *adj* **1 :** higher in physical position, rank, or order **2 :** constituting the smaller and senior branch of a bicameral legislature **3** *cap* **:** of, relating to, or constituting a later geologic period or formation ⟨*Upper* Cretaceous⟩ **4 :** being toward the interior **:** further inland ⟨the *upper* Amazon⟩ **5 :** NORTHERN ⟨*upper* New York state⟩

[2]**upper** *n* **:** one that is upper: as **a :** the parts of a shoe or boot above the sole **b :** an upper tooth or denture **c :** an upper berth

[3]**upper** *n* **:** a stimulant drug; *esp* **:** AMPHETAMINE

up·per·case \ˌəp-ər-'kās\ *adj* **:** CAPITAL 2 [from the printer's practice of keeping capitals in the upper of two typecases] — **uppercase** *n*

upper class *n* **:** a social class occupying a position above the middle class and having the highest status in a society — **up·per–class** *adj*

up·per·class·man \ˌəp-ər-'klas-mən\ *n* **:** a junior or senior in a college or high school

upper crust *n* **:** the highest social class or group

up·per·cut \'əp-ər-ˌkət\ *n* **:** a swinging blow (as in boxing) directed upward with a bent arm — **uppercut** *vb*

upper hand *n* **:** ADVANTAGE 1, BETTER

up·per·most \'əp-ər-ˌmōst\ *adv* **:** in or into the highest or most prominent position — **uppermost** *adj*

up·per·part \-ˌpärt\ *n* **:** a part lying on the upper side (as of a bird)

up·pish \'əp-ish\ *adj* **:** UPPITY — **up·pish·ness** *n*

up·pi·ty \'əp-ət-ē\ *adj* **:** putting on airs of superiority **:** ARROGANT [probably from *up* + *-ity* (as in *persnickity*, variant of *persnickety*)] — **up·pi·ty·ness** *n*

up·raise \ˌə-'prāz, ə-\ *vt* **:** to raise or lift up **:** ELEVATE

[1]**up·right** \'əp-ˌrīt\ *adj* **1 a :** PERPENDICULAR 2, VERTICAL **b :** erect in carriage or posture **c :** having the main axis or a main part perpendicular **2 :** morally correct **:** HONEST, HONORABLE —

\ə\ **abut**	\au̇\ **out**	\i\ **tip**	\ȯ\ **saw**	\u̇\ **foot**
\ər\ **further**	\ch\ **chin**	\ī\ **life**	\ȯi\ **coin**	\y\ **yet**
\a\ **mat**	\e\ **pet**	\j\ **job**	\th\ **thin**	\yü\ **few**
\ā\ **take**	\ē\ **easy**	\ŋ\ **sing**	\t͟h\ **this**	\yu̇\ **cure**
\ä\ **cot, cart**	\g\ **go**	\ō\ **bone**	\ü\ **food**	\zh\ **vision**

up·right·ly *adv* — **up·right·ness** *n*
2upright *n* **1** : the state of being upright : PERPENDICULAR ⟨a pillar out of *upright*⟩ **2** : something upright **3** : UPRIGHT PIANO
upright piano *n* : a piano with vertical frame and strings

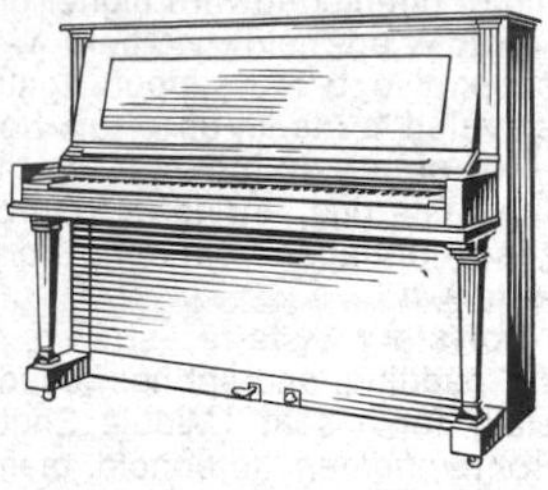
upright piano

1up·rise \ˌə-ˈprīz\ *vi* **up·rose** \-ˈprōz\; **up·ris·en** \-ˈpriz-n\; **up·ris·ing** \-ˈprī-ziŋ\ **1** : to rise to a higher positon **2** : to get up (as from sleep or a sitting position) — **up·ris·er** *n*
2up·rise \ˈəp-ˌrīz\ *n* **1** : an act or instance of uprising **2** : an upward slope
up·ris·ing \ˈəp-ˌrī-ziŋ\ *n* : an act or instance of rising up; *esp* : a usually localized revolt **syn** see REBELLION
up·roar \ˈəp-ˌrōr, -ˌrȯr\ *n* : a state of commotion, excitement, or violent disturbance [by folk etymology from Dutch *oproer,* from *op* "up" + *roer* "motion"]
up·roar·i·ous \ˌəp-ˈrōr-ē-əs, -ˈrȯr-\ *adj* **1** : marked by uproar **2** : extremely funny — **up·roar·i·ous·ly** *adv* — **up·roar·i·ous·ness** *n*
up·root \ˌə'prüt, -ˈprủt\ *vt* **1** : to remove by or as if by pulling up by the roots **2** : to displace from a country or traditional habitat — **up·root·er** *n*
1up·set \ˌəp-ˈset, əp-\ *vb* **-set; -set·ting** **1** : to thicken and shorten (as a heated bar of iron) by hammering on the end : SWAGE **2** : to force or be forced out of the usual upright, level, or proper position : OVERTURN, CAPSIZE **3 a** : to disturb emotionally **b** : to make somewhat ill **4 a** : to throw into disorder : DISARRANGE **b** : INVALIDATE ⟨*upset* a will⟩ **c** : to defeat unexpectedly — **up·set·ter** *n*
2up·set \ˈəp-ˌset\ *n* **1** : an act or result of upsetting : a state of being upset **2 a** : a minor physical disorder ⟨a stomach *upset*⟩ **b** : an emotional disturbance **3 a** : a part of a rod (as the head on a bolt) that is upset **b** : a swage used in upsetting
up·shot \ˈəp-ˌshät\ *n* : final result : OUTCOME
up·side \ˈəp-ˌsīd\ *n* : the upper side or part
up·side down \ˌəp-ˌsīd-ˈdaủn\ *adv* **1** : with the upper and the lower parts reversed in position **2** : in or into great disorder [Middle English *up so doun,* from *up* + *so* + *doun* "down"] — **upside–down** *adv*
up·si·lon \ˈyüp-sə-ˌlän, ˈəp-, -lən\ *n* : the 20th letter of the Greek alphabet — Υ or υ
1up·stage \ˈəp-ˈstāj\ *adv* : toward or at the rear of a stage
2upstage *adj* **1** : of or relating to the rear of a stage **2** : HAUGHTY
3up·stage \ˌəp-ˈstāj\ *vt* : to steal the show from [earlier *upstage* "to force (an actor) to face away from the audience by staying upstage"]
1up·stairs \ˈəp-ˈstaərz, -ˈsteərz\ *adv* **1** : up the stairs : to or on a higher floor **2** : to or at a high altitude or higher position
2up·stairs \-ˌstaərz, -ˌsteərz\ *adj* **1** : situated above the stairs **2** : of or relating to the upper floors
3up·stairs \ˈəp-ˈ, ˈəp-ˌ\ *n* : the part of a building above the ground floor
up·stand·ing \ˌəp-ˈstan-diŋ, ˈəp-ˌ\ *adj* **1** : ERECT 1a **2** : marked by integrity : HONEST — **up·stand·ing·ness** *n*
1up·start \ˌəp-ˈstärt\ *vi* : to jump up suddenly
2up·start \ˈəp-ˌstärt\ *n* : one that has risen suddenly (as from a low position to wealth or power) : PARVENU; *esp* : one that claims more personal importance than is warranted — **up·start** \ˌəp-ˌ\ *adj*
1up·state \ˈəp-ˌstāt\ *adj* : of, relating to, or characteristic of a part of a state away from a large city and especially to the north — **up·state** \ˈəp-ˈstāt\ *adv*
2upstate *n* : an upstate region — **up·stat·er** \-ˈstāt-ər\ *n*
up·stream \ˈəp-ˈstrēm\ *adv* : at or toward the source of a stream — **upstream** *adj*
up·stroke \ˈəp-ˌstrōk\ *n* : an upward stroke (as of a pen)
up·surge \ˈəp-ˌsərj\ *n* : a rapid or sudden rise
up·sweep \ˈəp-ˌswēp\ *vb* **-swept** \-ˌswept\; **-sweep·ing** : to sweep upward : curve or slope upward — **upsweep** *n*
up·swept \ˈəp-ˌswept\ *adj* : swept upward
up·swing \ˈəp-ˌswiŋ\ *n* : an upward swing; *esp* : a marked increase or rise (as in activity)
up·take \ˈəp-ˌtāk\ *n* **1** : UNDERSTANDING, COMPREHENSION ⟨quick on the *uptake*⟩ **2** : a flue leading upward **3** : an act or instance of absorbing and incorporating especially into a living organism [Scottish *uptake* "to understand"]
up·throw \ˈəp-ˌthrō\ *n* : an upward displacement (as of a rock stratum) : UPHEAVAL
up·thrust \ˈəp-ˌthrəst\ *n* : an upward thrust; *esp* : an uplift of part of the earth's crust
up·tight \ˈəp-ˈtīt, ˌəp-ˈ, əp-ˈ; ˌəp-ˌ\ *adj* **1** : TENSE, UNEASY **2** : ANGRY, INDIGNANT **3** : rigidly conventional
up·tilt \ˌəp-ˈtilt\ *vt* : to tilt upward
up to *prep* **1** : as far as a designated part or place ⟨sank *up to* my hips⟩ **2** : to or in fulfillment of ⟨write *up to* the standard⟩ **3 a** : to the limit of ⟨guesses ran *up to* 1000⟩ **b** : as many or as much as ⟨carry *up to* 10 tons⟩ **4** : UNTIL, TILL ⟨from dawn *up to* dusk⟩
up–to–date *adj* **1** : extending up to the present time **2** : abreast of the times (as in style or technique) : MODERN — **up–to–date·ness** *n*
up·town \ˈəp-ˈtaủn\ *adv* : toward, to, or in the upper part of a town — **up·town** \ˌəp-ˌtaủn\ *adj*
up·trend \ˈəp-ˌtrend\ *n* : a tendency upward
1up·turn \ˈəp-ˌtərn, ˌəp-ˈ\ *vb* **1** : to turn up or over **2** : to turn or direct upward
2up·turn \ˈəp-ˌtərn\ *n* : an upward turn (as toward better conditions or higher prices)
1up·ward \ˈəp-wərd\ *or* **up·wards** \-wərdz\ *adv* **1** : in a direction from lower to higher **2** : toward a higher or better condition **3** : toward a greater amount or higher number, degree, or rate
2upward *adj* : directed toward or situated in a higher place or level — **up·ward·ly** *adv* — **up·ward·ness** *n*
upwards of *also* **upward of** *adv* : more than : in excess of
up·well \ˌəp-ˈwel\ *vi* : to well up
up·well·ing \ˌəp-ˈwel-iŋ\ *n* : the movement of deeper, cooler, and often nutrient-rich layers of ocean water to the surface
up·wind \ˈəp-ˈwind\ *adv or adj* : in the direction from which the wind is blowing
ur- *or* **uro-** *combining form* **1** : urine ⟨*ur*ic⟩ **2** : urinary tract ⟨*uro*logy⟩ **3** : urinary and ⟨*uro*genital⟩ **4** : urea ⟨*ur*acil⟩ [Greek *ouron*]
ura·cil \ˈyủr-ə-ˌsil, -səl\ *n* : a pyrimidine base $C_4H_4N_2O_2$ that is one of the four bases coding genetic information in the polynucleotide chain of RNA — compare ADENINE, CYTOSINE, GUANINE [derived from *ur-* + *acetic*]
Ural–Al·ta·ic \ˌyủr-ə-lal-ˈtā-ik\ *n* : a language type showing agglutination and occurring especially in languages of Eurasia [*Ural* mountains + *Altai* mountains] — **Ural–Altaic** *adj*
Ural·ic \yủ-ˈral-ik\ *n* : a language family comprising the Finno-Ugric languages and some languages of northwest Siberia
ura·nic \yủ-ˈran-ik, -ˈrā-nik\ *adj* : of, relating to, or containing uranium
ura·ni·nite \yủ-ˈrā-nə-ˌnīt\ *n* : a mineral that is a black oxide of uranium, contains also various metals (as thorium and lead), and is the chief ore of uranium [German *uranin,* from New Latin *uranium*]
ura·ni·um \yủ-ˈrā-nē-əm\ *n* : a silvery heavy radioactive metallic chemical element that is found especially in pitchblende and uraninite and exists naturally as a mixture of three isotopes of mass number 234, 235, and 238 — see ELEMENT table [New Latin, from *Uranus*]
uranium 238 *n* : an isotope of uranium of mass number 238 that absorbs high-energy neutrons to form a uranium isotope of mass number 239 which then decays through neptunium to form plutonium of mass number 239
uranium 235 *n* : a light isotope of uranium of mass number 235 that when bombarded with low-energy neutrons undergoes rapid fission into smaller atoms with the release of neutrons and atomic energy
ura·nous \yủ-ˈrā-nəs, ˈyủr-ə-\ *adj* : of, relating to, or containing uranium especially with a lower valence than in uranic compounds
Ura·nus \ˈyủr-ə-nəs, yủ-ˈrā-\ *n* : the planet 7th in order from the sun — see PLANET table [*Uranus,* a Greek god]
urate \ˈyủr-ˌāt\ *n* : a salt of uric acid
ur·ban \ˈər-bən\ *adj* : of, relating to, characteristic of, or constituting a city [Latin *urbanus,* from *urbs* "city"]
ur·bane \ˌər-ˈbān\ *adj* : notably polite or finished in manner : SUAVE [Latin *urbanus* "urban, urbane"] **syn** see SUAVE — **ur·bane·ly** *adv*

△ **origin** The advantages of city over country life (and vice versa) have been debated for many years, and this debate is reflected in our vocabulary. Alongside of *urban,* "relating to or characteristic of a city", we have *urbane,* which developed the sense of "smoothly courteous or polite" from the belief (encouraged by city dwellers especially) that the social life of the city is more suave and polished than life in the country. Both *urban* and *urbane* come from the Latin *urbanus,* from *urbs,* "city".

ur•ban•ite \'ər-bə-ˌnīt\ *n* **:** one living in a city

ur•ban•i•ty \ˌər-'ban-ət-ē\ *n, pl* **-ties 1 :** the quality or state of being urbane **2** *pl* **:** urbane acts or conduct

ur•ban•ize \'ər-bə-ˌnīz\ *vt* **1 :** to cause to take on urban characteristics ⟨*urbanized* areas⟩ **2 :** to impart an urban way of life to — **ur•ban•iza•tion** \ˌər-bə-nə-'zā-shən\ *n*

urban renewal *n* **:** a construction program to replace or restore substandard buildings in an urban area

ur•chin \'ər-chən\ *n* **1 :** HEDGEHOG 1 **2 :** a mischievous youngster **3 :** SEA URCHIN [Middle French *herichon,* from Latin *ericius*]

Ur•du \'u̇r-dü, 'ər-\ *n* **:** an Indic language that is an official literary language of Pakistan and is widely used in India [Hindi *urdū-zabān,* literally, "camp language"]

-ure *n suffix* **1 :** act **:** process ⟨expos*ure*⟩ **2 a :** office **:** function **b :** body performing (such) a function ⟨legislat*ure*⟩ [Latin *-ura*]

urea \yu̇-'rē-ə\ *n* **:** a soluble nitrogen-containing compound that is found in mammalian urine and is an end product of protein breakdown [New Latin, from French *urée,* from *urine* "urine"] — **ure•ic** \-'rē-ik\ *adj*

ure•ase \'yu̇r-ē-ˌās, -ˌāz\ *n* **:** an enzyme that promotes the hydrolysis of urea

ure•dio•spore \yu̇-'rēd-ē-ə-ˌspōr, -ˌspȯr\ *or* **ure•do•spore** \-'rēd-ə-\ *n* **:** one of the one-celled spores of a rust fungus that spread the disease by infecting new plants [derived from Latin *uredo* "burning, blight", from *urere* "to burn"]

ure•mia \yu̇-'rē-mē-ə\ *n* **:** accumulation in the blood usually in severe kidney disease of constituents normally eliminated in the urine resulting in a severe toxic condition — **ure•mic** \-mik\ *adj*

ure•ter \'yu̇r-ət-ər\ *n* **:** a duct that carries urine from a kidney to the bladder or cloaca [Greek *ourētēr,* from *ourein* "to urinate"] — **ure•ter•al** \yu̇-'rēt-ə-rəl\ *or* **ure•ter•ic** \ˌyu̇r-ə-'ter-ik\ *adj*

ure•thra \yu̇-'rē-thrə\ *n, pl* **-thras** *or* **-thrae** \-thrē\ **:** the canal that in most mammals carries off the urine from the bladder and in the male serves also as a genital duct [Late Latin, from Greek *ourēthra,* from *ourein* "to urinate"] — **ure•thral** \-thrəl\ *adj*

¹urge \'ərj\ *vt* **1 :** to present, advocate, or demand earnestly ⟨continually *urging* reform⟩ **2 a :** to try to persuade or sway ⟨*urge* a guest to stay longer⟩ **b :** to serve as a motive or reason for **3 :** to press or move to some course or activity (as greater speed) ⟨*urge* on a runner⟩ [Latin *urgēre*] — **urg•er** *n*

²urge *n* **1 :** the act or process of urging **2 :** a force or impulse that urges; *esp* **:** a continuing impulse toward an activity or goal

ur•gent \'ər-jənt\ *adj* **1 a :** calling for immediate attention **:** PRESSING ⟨*urgent* appeals⟩ **b :** conveying a sense of urgency ⟨an *urgent* manner⟩ **2 :** urging insistently [Middle French, from Latin *urgens,* present participle of *urgēre* "to urge"] — **ur•gen•cy** \-jən-sē\ *n* — **ur•gent•ly** *adv*

uric \'yu̇r-ik\ *adj* **:** of, relating to, or found in urine

uric acid *n* **:** a white odorless nearly insoluble nitrogen-containing acid that is present in small quantity in mammalian urine and is the chief nitrogen-containing excretion in birds and lower forms

uri•nal \'yu̇r-ən-l\ *n* **1 :** a receptacle for urine **2 :** a place for urinating

uri•nal•y•sis \ˌyu̇r-ə-'nal-ə-səs\ *n, pl* **uri•nal•y•ses** \-ə-ˌsēz\ **:** the analysis of urine

uri•nary \'yu̇r-ə-ˌner-ē\ *adj* **1 :** relating to, occurring in, or constituting the organs concerned with the formation and discharge of urine ⟨*urinary* bladder⟩ **2 :** of, relating to, or used for urine **3 :** excreted as or in urine

uri•nate \'yu̇r-ə-ˌnāt\ *vi* **:** to discharge urine — **uri•na•tion** \ˌyu̇r-ə-'nā-shən\ *n*

urine \'yu̇r-ən\ *n* **:** waste material that is secreted by the kidney, is rich in end products of protein metabolism together with salts and pigments, and is usually a yellowish liquid in mammals but semisolid in birds and reptiles [Middle French, from Latin *urina*]

urn \'ərn\ *n* **1 :** a vessel that typically has the form of a vase on a pedestal and often is used for preserving the ashes of the dead **2 :** a closed vessel usually with a spigot for serving a hot beverage ⟨coffee *urn*⟩ [Latin *urna*]

urn 2

uro- — see UR-

uro•dele \'yu̇r-ə-ˌdēl\ *n* **:** any of an order (Caudata) of amphibians (as newts) with a tail throughout life [French *urodèle,* derived from Greek *oura* "tail" + *dēlos* "evident, showing"] — **urodele** *adj*

uro•gen•i•tal \ˌyu̇r-ō-'jen-ə-tl\ *adj* **:** of, relating to, or being the organs or functions of excretion and reproduction

urol•o•gy \yu̇-'räl-ə-jē\ *n* **:** a branch of medical science dealing with the urinary or urogenital tract and its disorders — **uro•log•ic** \ˌyu̇r-ə-'läj-ik\ *or* **uro•log•i•cal** \-'läj-i-kəl\ *adj* — **urol•o•gist** \yu̇-'räl-ə-jəst\ *n*

uro•pod \'yu̇r-ə-ˌpäd\ *n* **:** either of the flat lateral appendages of the last abdominal segment of a crustacean [derived from Greek *oura* "tail" + *pod-, pous* "foot"]

uro•style \'yu̇r-ə-ˌstīl\ *n* **:** a bony rod made of fused vertebrae that forms the end of the spinal column of a frog or toad [derived from Greek *oura* "tail" + *stylos* "pillar"]

Ur•sa Ma•jor \ˌər-sə-'mā-jər\ *n* **:** the most conspicuous of the northern constellations that is situated near the north pole of the heavens and contains the stars forming the Big Dipper two of which are in a line indicating the direction of the North Star — called also *Great Bear* [Latin, literally, "greater bear"]

Ursa Mi•nor \-'mī-nər\ *n* **:** the constellation including the north pole of the heavens and the stars that form the Little Dipper with the North Star at the tip of the handle — called also *Little Bear* [Latin, literally, "lesser bear"]

Ur•su•line \'ər-sə-lən, -ˌlīn, -ˌlēn\ *n* **:** a member of a teaching order of nuns founded in Italy in 1535 [Saint *Ursula,* legendary Christian martyr] — **Ursuline** *adj*

ur•ti•car•ia \ˌərt-ə-'kar-ē-ə, -'ker-\ *n* **:** HIVES [New Latin, from Latin *urtica* "nettle"] — **ur•ti•car•i•al** \-ē-əl\ *adj*

urus \'yu̇r-əs\ *n* **:** an extinct large long-horned wild ox of the German forests held to be a wild ancestor of domestic cattle [Latin, of Germanic origin]

us \əs, 'əs\ *pron, objective case of* WE [Old English *ūs*]

us•able \'yü-zə-bəl\ *adj* **:** suitable or fit for use ⟨*usable* waste⟩ — **us•abil•i•ty** \ˌyü-zə-'bil-ət-ē\ *n* — **us•ably** \'yü-zə-blē\ *adv*

us•age \'yü-sij, -zij\ *n* **1 a :** firmly established and generally accepted practice or procedure **b :** the way in which words and phrases are actually used in a language community **2 a :** the action or mode of using **:** USE **b :** manner of treating **:** TREATMENT ⟨ill *usage*⟩ **syn** see HABIT

¹use \'yüs\ *n* **1 a :** the act or practice of using something often so as to get an effect or benefit ⟨put knowledge to *use*⟩ **b :** the fact or state of being used ⟨a dish in daily *use*⟩ **c :** way of using ⟨the proper *use* of tools⟩ **2 a :** the privilege or benefit of using something ⟨had the *use* of a car⟩ **b :** the ability or power to use something (as a limb or faculty) **3 a :** FUNCTION 2 ⟨what's the *use* of this dial⟩ **b :** the quality of being suitable for employment **:** USEFULNESS ⟨old clothes that are still of some *use*⟩ **c :** legitimate employment or application ⟨took only what I had *use* for⟩ **4 :** ESTEEM, LIKING ⟨had no use for modern art⟩ [Old French *us,* from Latin *usus,* from *uti* "to use"]

²use \'yüz\ *vb* **used** \'yüzd, *in the phrase "used to" usually* 'yüs, 'yüst\; **us•ing** \'yü-zing\ **1 :** to put into action or service **:** EMPLOY **2 :** to consume or take (as liquor or drugs) regularly **3 :** to carry out a purpose or action by means of **:** UTILIZE ⟨*use* tact⟩ **4 :** to expend or consume by putting to use ⟨the car *uses* a lot of gas⟩ **5 :** to behave toward **:** TREAT ⟨*used* the prisoners cruelly⟩ **6** — used in the past with *to* to indicate a former practice, fact, or state ⟨claims winters *used* to be harder⟩ ⟨how they

used to quarrel as children⟩ — **us•er** \ˈyü-zər\ *n*
• **syn** EMPLOY, UTILIZE: use implies availing oneself of something as a means or instrument to an end; EMPLOY suggests the use of a person or thing that is available because idle, inactive, or disengaged; UTILIZE suggests the discovery of a new, profitable, or practical use for something ⟨how to *utilize* scrap metal⟩

used \ˈyüzd, *in the phrase "used to" usually* ˈyüs, ˈyüst\ *adj* **1** : employed in accomplishing something **2** : that has endured use; *esp* : SECONDHAND ⟨a *used* car⟩ **3** : made familiar by experience : ACCUSTOMED

use•ful \ˈyüs-fəl\ *adj* : capable of being put to use : USABLE ⟨*useful* scraps of material⟩; *also* : of a kind to be valuable or productive ⟨a *useful* invention⟩ — **use•ful•ly** \-fə-lē\ *adv* — **use•ful•ness** *n*

use•less \ˈyü-sləs\ *adj* : having or being of no use : WORTHLESS — **use•less•ly** *adv* — **use•less•ness** *n*

¹ush•er \ˈəsh-ər\ *n* **1** : an officer who walks before a person of rank **2** : one who escorts persons to seats (as in a theater) [Middle French *ussier,* literally, "doorkeeper", derived from Latin *ostium, ustium* "door"]

²usher *vt* **ush•ered; ush•er•ing** \ˈəsh-ring, -ə-ring\ **1** : to conduct to a place **2** : INAUGURATE, INTRODUCE ⟨*usher* in a new era⟩

usu•al \ˈyüzh-wəl, -ə-wəl, ˈyüzh-əl\ *adj* **1** : accordant with usage, custom, or habit : NORMAL **2** : commonly or ordinarily used ⟨my *usual* route⟩ **3** : found in ordinary practice or in the ordinary course of events : ORDINARY [Late Latin *usualis,* from Latin *usus* "use"] — **usu•al•ly** \ˈyüzh-wə-lē, -ə-wə-, ˈyüzh-lē, ˈyüzh-ə-lē, *rapid* ˈyüz-lē\ *adv* — **usu•al•ness** \ˈyüzh-wəl-nəs, -ə-wəl-, ˈyüzh-əl-\ *n*
• **syn** CUSTOMARY, HABITUAL, ACCUSTOMED: USUAL stresses the absence of strangeness or unexpectedness; CUSTOMARY applies to what accords with the practices, conventions, or usages of an individual or community ⟨their *customary* dress for dinner⟩ HABITUAL suggests a practice settled or established by much repetition ⟨*habitual* frown⟩ ACCUSTOMED is less emphatic than HABITUAL and suggests something that is noticed or expected by others ⟨*accustomed* graciousness⟩

usu•fruct \ˈyü-zə-ˌfrəkt\ *n* : the legal right of using and enjoying the fruits or profits of something belonging to another [Latin *usufructus,* from *usus et fructus* "use and enjoyment"]

usu•rer \ˈyü-zhər-ər, ˈyüzh-rər\ *n* : one that lends money especially at an excessively high rate of interest

usu•ri•ous \yu̇-ˈzhu̇r-ē-əs, -ˈzu̇r-\ *adj* : practicing, involving, or constituting usury ⟨*usurious* interest⟩ — **usu•ri•ous•ly** *adv* — **usu•ri•ous•ness** *n*

usurp \yu̇-ˈsərp *also* -ˈzərp\ *vt* : to seize and hold by force or without right ⟨*usurp* a throne⟩ [Middle French *usurper,* from Latin *usurpare,* from *usu* "by use" + *rapere* "to seize"] — **usur•pa•tion** \ˌyü-sər-ˈpā-shən *also* ˌyü-zər-\ *n* — **usurp•er** \yu̇-ˈsər-pər *also* -ˈzər-\ *n*

usu•ry \ˈyüzh-rē, -ə-rē\ *n, pl* **usuries 1** : the lending of money with an interest charge for its use **2** : an excessive rate or amount of interest charged; *esp* : interest above an established legal rate [Medieval Latin *usuria,* from Latin *usura,* from *usus,* past participle of *uti* "to use"]

Ute \ˈyüt\ *n, pl* **Ute** *or* **Utes** : a member of a group of Indian peoples of what is now Colorado and Utah having an Aztec-related language [Ute *Yuta*]

uten•sil \yu̇-ˈten-səl\ *n* **1** : an instrument or vessel used in a household and especially a kitchen **2** : an article serving a useful purpose [Middle French *utensile* "vessels for domestic use", from Latin *utensilia,* from *utensilis* "useful", from *uti* "to use"] **syn** see IMPLEMENT

uter•us \ˈyüt-ə-rəs\ *n, pl* **uteri** \-ˌrī, -ˌrē\ *also* **uter•us•es 1** : an organ of the female mammal for containing and usually for nourishing the young during development previous to birth — called also *womb* **2** : a structure in some lower animals analogous to the uterus of mammals in which eggs or young develop [Latin] — **uter•ine** \-rən, -ˌrīn\ *adj*

utile \ˈyüt-l, ˈyü-ˌtīl\ *adj* : USEFUL [Middle French, from Latin *utilis*]

¹util•i•tar•i•an \yü-ˌtil-ə-ˈter-ē-ən\ *n* : an advocate or adherent of utilitarianism

²utilitarian *adj* **1** : of or relating to utilitarianism **2 a** : of or relating to utility **b** : aiming at usefulness rather than beauty **c** : serving a useful purpose

util•i•tar•i•an•ism \-ē-ə-ˌniz-əm\ *n* : a doctrine that one's conduct should be determined by the usefulness of its consequences; *esp* : a theory that the aim of action should be the greatest happiness of the greatest number

¹util•i•ty \yü-ˈtil-ət-ē\ *n, pl* **-ties 1** : fitness for some purpose or worth to some end **2** : something useful or designed for use **3 a** : PUBLIC UTILITY **b** (1) : a public service or a commodity provided by a public utility (2) : equipment or a piece of equipment (as plumbing in a house) to provide such or a similar service [Middle French *utilité,* from Latin *utilitas,* from *utilis* "useful", from *uti* "to use"]

²utility *adj* **1** : capable of serving as a substitute in various roles or positions ⟨*utility* infielder⟩ **2** : being of a usable but inferior grade ⟨*utility* beef⟩ **3** : serving primarily for usefulness rather than beauty : UTILITARIAN ⟨*utility* furniture⟩ **4** : designed for general use

uti•lize \ˈyüt-l-ˌīz\ *vt* : to make use of : convert to use **syn** see USE — **uti•liz•able** \-ˌī-zə-bəl\ *adj* — **uti•li•za•tion** \ˌyüt-l-ə-ˈzā-shən\ *n* — **uti•liz•er** *n*

ut•most \ˈət-ˌmōst, *especially South* -məst\ *adj* **1** : situated at the farthest or most distant point : EXTREME **2** : of the greatest or highest degree, quantity, number, or amount [Old English *ūtmest,* superlative adj., from *ūt,* adv., "out"] — **utmost** *n*

uto•pia \yu̇-ˈtō-pē-ə\ *n* **1** *often cap* : a place of ideal perfection especially in laws, government, and social conditions **2** : an impractical scheme for social improvement [*Utopia,* imaginary ideal country in *Utopia* by Sir Thomas More, from Greek *ou* "not, no" + *topos* "place"] — **uto•pi•an** \-pē-ən\ *adj or n, often cap*

△ **origin** In 1516 Sir Thomas More published his book *Utopia,* in which the social and economic conditions of Europe, outlined in Book I, are compared with those of an ideal society described in Book II, a society established on an imaginary island off the shore of the New World. That such an ideal state is unattainable in reality is implied by the name More gave to this island, *Utopia,* which literally means "no place". In modern English *utopia* has become a generic term for any place of ideal perfection. Less optimistically *utopia* has also come to mean an impractical scheme for social improvement.

utri•cle \ˈyü-tri-kəl\ *n* : the larger chamber of the membranous labyrinth of the ear into which the semicircular canals open — compare SACCULE [Latin *utriculus* "small leather bag", from *uter* "leather bag" — **utric•u•lar** \yu̇-ˈtrik-yə-lər\ *adj*

utric•u•lus \yu̇-ˈtrik-yə-ləs\ *n* : UTRICLE [Latin, "small bag"]

¹ut•ter \ˈət-ər\ *adj* : ABSOLUTE, TOTAL ⟨an *utter* impossibility⟩ ⟨*utter* strangers⟩ [Old English *ūtera* "outer", comparative adj., from *ūt,* adv., "out"] — **ut•ter•ly** *adv*

²utter *vt* **1** : to send forth as a sound **2** : to express in usually spoken words **3** : PASS 16a [Middle English *uttren* "to put forth, offer for sale", from *utter,* adv., "outside", from Old English *ūtor,* comparative of *ūt* "out"] — **ut•ter•able** \ˈət-ə-rə-bəl\ *adj* — **ut•ter•er** \ˈət-ər-ər\ *n*

ut•ter•ance \ˈət-ə-rəns\ *n* **1** : something uttered; *esp* : an oral or written statement **2** : the action of uttering with the voice : SPEECH **3** : power, style, or manner of speaking

ut•ter•most \ˈət-ər-ˌmōst\ *adj* : EXTREME 3, UTMOST — **uttermost** *n*

uvu•la \ˈyü-vyə-lə\ *n, pl* **-las** *or* **-lae** \-ˌlē, -ˌlī\ : the pendent fleshy lobe in the middle of the rear border of the soft palate [Medieval Latin, from Latin *uva* "grape, uvula"]

uvu•lar \-lər\ *adj* **1** : of or relating to the uvula ⟨*uvular* glands⟩ **2** : produced with the aid of the uvula ⟨*uvular* r⟩

ux•o•ri•ous \ˌək-ˈsōr-ē-əs, -ˈsȯr-; ˌəg-ˈzōr-, -ˈzȯr-\ *adj* : excessively fond of or submissive to a wife [Latin *uxorius,* from *uxor* "wife"] — **ux•o•ri•ous•ly** *adv* — **ux•o•ri•ous•ness** *n*

Uz•bek \ˈu̇z-ˌbek, ˈəz-\ *n* : a member of a people of Turkestan and especially of the Uzbek Soviet Socialist Republic

V v—vying

v \ˈvē\ *n, pl* **v's** *or* **vs** \ˈvēz\ *often cap* **1** : the 22d letter of the English alphabet **2** : five in Roman numerals

va·can·cy \ˈvā-kən-sē\ *n, pl* **-cies** **1 a** : a vacating of an office, post, or property **b** : the time such office or property is vacant **2** : a vacant office, post, or tenancy ⟨two *vacancies* in a building⟩ **3** : empty space ⟨stare into *vacancy*⟩ **4** : the state of being vacant

va·cant \ˈvā-kənt\ *adj* **1** : having no occupant : not being used ⟨a *vacant* room⟩ ⟨*vacant* chairs⟩ **2** : free from business or care : LEISURE ⟨a few *vacant* hours⟩ **3** : STUPID 3, FOOLISH ⟨a *vacant* laugh⟩ [Old French, from Latin *vacans,* present participle of *vacare* "to be empty, be free"] **syn** see EMPTY — **va·cant·ly** *adv* — **va·cant·ness** *n*

va·cate \ˈvā-ˌkāt, vā-ˈ\ *vt* **1** : to make void : ANNUL ⟨*vacate* an agreement⟩ **2** : to make vacant : leave empty ⟨*vacate* a building⟩ ⟨*vacate* a position⟩ [Latin *vacare* "to be empty, be free"]

1**va·ca·tion** \vā-ˈkā-shən, və-\ *n* **1** : a respite or a time of respite from something : INTERMISSION **2 a** : a period during which activity (as of a school) is suspended **b** : a period of freedom from work granted to an employee for rest and relaxation **3** : a period spent away from home or business in travel or recreation ⟨had a restful *vacation* at the beach⟩ **4** : an act or an instance of vacating

2**vacation** *vi* **-tioned; -tion·ing** \-shə-ning, -shning\ : to take or spend a vacation ⟨*vacation* in July⟩

va·ca·tion·er \-shə-nər, -shnər\ *n* : a person taking a vacation

va·ca·tion·ist \-shə-nəst, -shnəst\ *n* : VACATIONER

va·ca·tion·land \-shən-ˌland\ *n* : an area with recreational attractions and facilities for vacationers

vac·ci·nate \ˈvak-sə-ˌnāt\ *vt* : to inoculate (a person) with cowpox virus in order to produce immunity to smallpox; *also* : to administer a vaccine to usually by injection — **vac·ci·na·tor** \-ˌnāt-ər\ *n*

vac·ci·na·tion \ˌvak-sə-ˈnā-shən\ *n* **1** : the act of vaccinating **2** : the scar left by vaccinating

vac·cine \vak-ˈsēn, ˈvak-ˌ\ *n* : material (as a preparation of killed or modified virus or bacteria) used in vaccinating [Latin *vaccinus* "of cows", from *vacca* "cow"] — **vaccine** *adj*

△ origin Our word *vaccine* was derived from Latin *vacca,* "cow". The Latin adjective *vaccinus,* "of or from cows", was borrowed into English as *vaccine,* which was originally used as an adjective with the same meaning as the Latin. A substance derived from a cow infected with cowpox would be called a *vaccine* substance. In the late 18th century the English physician Edward Jenner discovered that inoculation with a form of cowpox was an effective preventive of smallpox. The substance used in such inoculation came to be called a *vaccine.*

vac·cin·ia \vak-ˈsin-ē-ə\ *n* : COWPOX [New Latin, from Latin *vaccinus* "of cows"] — **vac·cin·i·al** \-ē-əl\ *adj*

vac·il·late \ˈvas-ə-ˌlāt\ *vi* **1** : FLUCTUATE ⟨a *vacillating* stock market⟩ **2** : to incline first to one course or opinion and then to another : WAVER [Latin *vacillare* "to sway, waver"] **syn** see HESITATE — **vac·il·la·tion** \ˌvas-ə-ˈlā-shən\ *n* — **vac·il·la·tor** \ˈvas-ə-ˌlāt-ər\ *n* — **vac·il·la·to·ry** \-lə-ˌtōr-ē, -ˌtȯr-\ *adj*

vac·il·lat·ing·ly \ˈvas-ə-ˌlāt-ing-lē\ *adv* : in a vacillating manner

va·cu·i·ty \va-ˈkyü-ət-ē, və-\ *n, pl* **-ties** **1** : an empty space **2 a** : the state, fact, or quality of being vacuous **b** : vacancy of mind **3** : something (as a remark or idea) that is vacuous or inane

vac·u·ole \ˈvak-yə-ˌwōl\ *n* : a usually fluid-filled cavity in tissues or in the protoplasm of an individual cell [French, literally, "small vacuum", from Latin *vacuum*] — **vac·u·o·lar** \ˌvak-yə-ˈwō-lər, -lär\ *adj*

vac·u·ous \ˈvak-yə-wəs\ *adj* **1** : EMPTY 1 **2** : marked by lack of ideas or intelligence : STUPID ⟨a *vacuous* expression⟩ **3** : having no serious occupation : IDLE [Latin *vacuus*] — **vac·u·ous·ly** *adv* — **vac·u·ous·ness** *n*

1**vac·u·um** \ˈvak-yü-əm, -ˌyüm, -yəm\ *n, pl* **-u·ums** *or* **-ua** \-yə-wə\ **1 a** : a space absolutely devoid of matter **b** : a space partially exhausted (as to the highest degree possible) by artificial means (as an air pump); *also* : the degree of such exhaustion **2 a** : a vacant space **b** : a state of isolation from outside influences **3** : a device creating or utilizing a partial vacuum; *esp* : VACUUM CLEANER [Latin, from *vacuus* "empty"]

2**vacuum** *adj* : of, containing, producing, or making use of a partial vacuum

3**vacuum** *vt* : to use a vacuum device (as a vacuum cleaner) upon

vacuum bottle *n* : a container with a vacuum between an inner and an outer wall used to keep liquids either hot or cold

vacuum cleaner *n* : an electrical appliance for cleaning (as floors or carpets) by suction

vac·u·um·ize \ˈvak-yü-ˌmīz, -yü-ə-ˌmīz\ *vt* **1** : to produce a vacuum in **2** : to clean, dry or pack by a vacuum mechanism or in a vacuum container

vac·u·um–packed \ˌvak-yü-əm-ˈpakt, -yüm-, -yəm-\ *adj* : having much of the air removed before being sealed ⟨a *vacuum-packed* can of coffee⟩

vacuum pump *n* : a pump for exhausting gas from an enclosed space

vacuum tube *n* : an electron tube evacuated to a high degree of vacuum

va·de me·cum \ˌväd-ē-ˈmē-kəm, ˌväd-ē-ˈmā-\ *n, pl* **vade mecums** **1** : a book for ready reference : MANUAL **2** : something regularly carried about by a person [Latin, "go with me"]

1**vag·a·bond** \ˈvag-ə-ˌbänd\ *adj* **1** : moving from place to place without a fixed home ⟨*vagabond* minstrels⟩ **2 a** : of, relating to, or characteristic of a wanderer **b** : leading an unsettled, irresponsible, or disreputable life [Middle French, from Latin *vagabundus,* from *vagari* "to wander"]

2**vagabond** *n* : one who leads a vagabond life; *esp* : TRAMP — **vag·a·bond·age** \-ˌbän-dij\ *n* — **vag·a·bond·ism** \-ˌbän-ˌdiz-əm\ *n*

vag·a·bond·ish \-ˌbän-dish\ *adj* : of, relating to, or characteristic of a vagabond

va·gar·i·ous \vā-ˈger-ē-əs, və-, -ˈgar-\ *adj* : marked by vagaries — **va·gar·i·ous·ly** *adv*

va·ga·ry \ˈvā-gə-rē; və-ˈgeər-ē, -ˈgaər-, vā-\ *n, pl* **-ries** : an eccentric or unpredictable manifestation, action, or notion [probably from Latin *vagari* "to wander"] **syn** see CAPRICE

va·gi·na \və-ˈjī-nə\ *n, pl* **-nae** \-nē\ *or* **-nas** **1** : a canal that leads from the uterus to the external opening of the genital canal **2** : SHEATH 2; *esp* : an ensheathing leaf base [Latin, literally, "sheath"] — **vag·i·nal** \ˈvaj-ən-l\ *adj*

va·gran·cy \ˈvā-grən-sē\ *n, pl* **-cies** **1** : VAGARY **2** : the state, action, or offense of being vagrant or a vagrant

1**va·grant** \ˈvā-grənt\ *n* **1 a** : one who wanders idly from place to place without a home or apparent means of support **b** : a person classed as a vagrant by statute **2** : one that leads a wandering life [probably from Middle French *waucrant, wacrant* "wandering", from *waucrer, wacrer* "to roll, wander", of Germanic origin]

2**vagrant** *adj* **1** : wandering about from place to place usually with no means of support **2 a** : having a fleeting, wayward, or inconstant quality **b** : having no fixed course : RANDOM ⟨*vagrant* thoughts⟩

va·grom \ˈvā-grəm\ *adj* : VAGRANT ⟨a *vagrom* thought⟩

vague \ˈvāg\ *adj* **1 a** : not clearly expressed : stated in indefi-

\ə\ abut	\au̇\ out	\i\ tip	\ȯ\ saw	\u̇\ foot
\ər\ further	\ch\ chin	\ī\ life	\ȯi\ coin	\y\ yet
\a\ mat	\e\ pet	\j\ job	\th\ thin	\yü\ few
\ā\ take	\ē\ easy	\ng\ sing	\th\ this	\yu̇\ cure
\ä\ cot, cart	\g\ go	\ō\ bone	\ü\ food	\zh\ vision

nite terms ⟨*vague* accusations⟩ **b :** not having a precise meaning **2 :** not clearly felt, grasped, or understood **:** INDISTINCT ⟨*vague* ideas⟩ ⟨a *vague* longing⟩ **3 :** not thinking or expressing one's thoughts clearly or precisely ⟨*vague* about dates and places⟩ **4 :** not sharply outlined **:** HAZY, SHADOWY [Middle French, from Latin *vagus,* literally, "wandering"] **syn** see OBSCURE — **vague•ly** *adv* — **vague•ness** *n*

va•gus \ˈvā-gəs\ *n, pl* **va•gi** \ˈvā-ˌgī, -ˌjī\ **:** VAGUS NERVE — **va•gal** \ˈvā-gəl\ *adj*

vagus nerve *n* **:** either of the 10th pair of cranial nerves that arise from the medulla and supply autonomic sensory and motor fibers mostly to the viscera [New Latin *vagus nervus,* literally, "wandering nerve"]

vail \ˈvāl\ *vt* **:** to lower especially as a sign of respect or submission [Middle French *valer,* short for *avaler* "to let fall", from *aval* "downward", from *a* "to" + *val* "valley"]

vain \ˈvān\ *adj* **1 :** WORTHLESS ⟨*vain* promises⟩ **2 :** not succeeding **:** FUTILE ⟨a *vain* attempt⟩ **3 :** proud of one's looks or abilities **:** CONCEITED [Old French, from Latin *vanus* "empty, vain"] — **vain•ly** *adv* — **vain•ness** \ˈvān-nəs\ *n*

• **syn** VAIN, FUTILE mean producing no result. VAIN usually implies simple failure to achieve a purpose or succeed in an attempt ⟨made a *vain* attempt at finishing⟩ FUTILE may suggest completeness of failure or folly of undertaking ⟨a *futile* effort to escape⟩

— in vain 1 : to no purpose **:** without success **2 :** in an irreverent or blasphemous manner

vain•glo•ri•ous \vān-ˈglōr-ē-əs, ˈvān-, -ˈglȯr-\ *adj* **:** marked by vainglory **:** BOASTFUL — **vain•glo•ri•ous•ly** *adv* — **vain•glo•ri•ous•ness** *n*

vain•glo•ry \ˈvān-ˌglōr-ē, -ˌglȯr-\ *n* **1 :** excessive or ostentatious pride in onself and one's achievements **2 :** vain display or show **:** VANITY

vair \ˈvaər, ˈveər\ *n* **:** the bluish gray and white fur of a squirrel prized for ornament during the Middle Ages [Old French, from *vair* "variegated", from Latin *varius* "variegated, various"]

val•ance \ˈval-əns, ˈvāl-\ *n* **1 :** a drapery hung along the edge of a bed, table, altar, canopy, or shelf **2 :** a short drapery or wood or metal frame used as a decorative heading to conceal the top of curtains and fixtures [Middle English *vallance*]

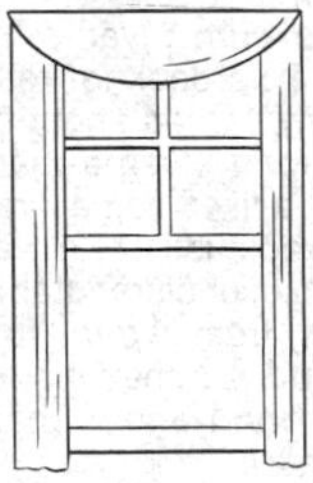

valance 2

vale \ˈvāl\ *n* **:** VALLEY 1, DALE [Old French *val,* from Latin *valles, vallis*]

val•e•dic•tion \ˌval-ə-ˈdik-shən\ *n* **:** an act or utterance of leave-taking **:** FAREWELL [Latin *valedicere* "to say farewell", from *vale* "farewell" + *dicere* "to say"]

vale•dic•to•ri•an \ˌval-ə-ˌdik-ˈtōr-ē-ən, -ˈtȯr-\ *n* **:** the student usually of the highest rank in a graduating class who delivers the valedictory oration at commencement exercises

[1]**vale•dic•to•ry** \-ˈdik-tə-rē, -trē\ *adj* **:** of or relating to leave-taking **:** FAREWELL; *esp* **:** given at a leave-taking ceremony (as school commencement exercises)

[2]**valedictory** *n, pl* **-ries :** a valedictory oration or statement

va•lence \ˈvā-ləns\ *n* **1 a :** the degree of combining power of an element or radical as shown by the number of atomic weights of a univalent element (as hydrogen) with which the atomic weight of the element will combine or for which it can be substituted **b :** a unit of valence ⟨the four *valences* of carbon⟩ **2 :** relative capacity to unite, react, or interact (as with antigens or a biological substrate) [Late Latin *valentia* "power, capacity", from Latin *valēre* "to be strong"]

Va•len•ci•ennes \və-ˌlen-sē-ˈen, ˌval-ən-sē-, -ˈenz\ *n* **:** a fine handmade lace [*Valenciennes,* France]

-va•lent \ˈvā-lənt\ *adj combining form* **:** having a (specified) valence or valences ⟨poly*valent*⟩ ⟨uni*valent*⟩

val•en•tine \ˈval-ən-ˌtīn\ *n* **1 :** a sweetheart chosen or honored (as by a gift) on Saint Valentine's Day **2 :** a gift or greeting sent or given on Saint Valentine's Day

Valentine Day *or* **Valentine's Day** *n* **:** SAINT VALENTINE'S DAY

va•le•ri•an \və-ˈlir-ē-ən\ *n* **1 :** any of a genus of perennial herbs mostly with flat-topped clusters of flowers and with roots and rootstock having medicinal properties **2 :** a drug consisting of the dried roots and rootstocks of the garden heliotrope [Medieval Latin *valeriana*]

va•let \ˈval-ət, ˈval-ˌā, va-ˈlā\ *n* **:** a male servant or hotel employee who takes care of a man's clothes and performs personal services [Middle French *vaslet, varlet, valet* "page, domestic servant", from Medieval Latin *vassus* "servant, vassal"]

val•e•tu•di•nar•i•an \ˌval-ə-ˌtüd-n-ˈer-ē-ən, -ˌtyüd-\ *n* **:** a person of a weak or sickly constitution; *esp* **:** one whose chief concern is his or her invalidism [Latin *valetudinarius* "sickly, infirm", from *valetudo* "state of health, sickness", from *valēre* "to be strong, be well"] — **valetudinarian** *adj* — **val•e•tu•di•nar•i•an•ism** \-ˌiz-əm\ *n*

Val•hal•la \val-ˈhal-ə\ *n* **:** the hall of Odin to which the Valkyries take heroes slain in battle [German *Walhalla,* from Old Norse *Valhöll,* literally, "hall of the slain"]

val•iance \ˈval-yəns\ *n* **:** VALOR

val•ian•cy \-yən-sē\ *n* **:** VALOR

[1]**val•iant** \ˈval-yənt\ *adj* **1 :** boldly brave **:** COURAGEOUS ⟨a *valiant* leader⟩ **2 :** HEROIC ⟨*valiant* fighting⟩ [Middle French *vaillant,* from *valoir* "to be of worth", from Latin *valēre* "to be strong"] — **val•iant•ly** *adv* — **val•iant•ness** *n*

[2]**valiant** *n* **:** a valiant person

val•id \ˈval-əd\ *adj* **1 :** founded on truth or fact **:** WELL-GROUNDED ⟨*valid* reasons⟩ **2 :** binding in law **:** SOUND ⟨a *valid* contract⟩ [Medieval Latin *validus,* from Latin, "strong", from *valēre* "to be strong"] — **va•lid•i•ty** \və-ˈlid-ət-ē, va-\ *n* — **val•id•ly** \ˈval-əd-lē\ *adv* — **val•id•ness** n

• **syn** VALID, SOUND, COGENT mean having such force as to compel consideration and usually acceptance. VALID implies being supported by objective truth or generally accepted authority; SOUND implies being based on solid fact and reasoning; COGENT stresses soundness or lucidness that makes argument or evidence conclusive.

val•i•date \ˈval-ə-ˌdāt\ *vt* **1 :** to make valid **2 :** to support or confirm on a sound or authoritative basis — **val•i•da•tion** \ˌval-ə-ˈdā-shən\ *n*

va•line \ˈval-ˌēn, ˈvā-ˌlēn\ *n* **:** a crystalline essential amino acid $C_5H_{11}NO_2$ that occurs especially in fibrous proteins [derived from *valeric acid,* an acid that occurs in the roots of valerian, from *valerian*]

va•lise \və-ˈlēs\ *n* **:** TRAVELING BAG [French, from Italian *valigia*]

Val•i•um \ˈval-ē-əm\ *trademark* — used for diazepam

Val•kyr•ie \val-ˈkir-ē\ *n* **:** one of the maidens of Odin who in Norse mythology choose the heroes to be slain in battle and conduct them to Valhalla [Old Norse *valkyrja,* literally, "chooser of the slain"]

val•ley \ˈval-ē\ *n, pl* **valleys 1 :** an elongate depression of the earth's surface usually between ranges of hills or mountains **2 a :** DEPRESSION 2, HOLLOW **b :** the place of meeting of two slopes of a roof forming a drainage channel [Old French *valee,* from *val* "valley, vale"]

val•or \ˈval-ər\ *n* **:** personal bravery in combat [Middle French *valour,* from Medieval Latin *valor,* "value, valor", from Latin *valēre* "to be strong"] **syn** see COURAGE

val•or•ous \ˈval-ə-rəs\ *adj* **1 :** possessing or showing valor **:** BRAVE ⟨*valorous* soldiers⟩ **2 :** marked by or performed with valor ⟨*valorous* feats⟩ — **val•or•ous•ly** *adv*

valse \väls\ *n* **:** WALTZ; *esp* **:** a concert waltz [French, from German *walzer*]

[1]**valu•able** \ˈval-yə-bəl, -yə-wə-bəl\ *adj* **1 a :** having monetary value **b :** worth a great deal of money **2 :** having value **:** of great use or service ⟨*valuable* information⟩ **syn** see COSTLY — **valu•able•ness** *n* — **valu•ably** \-blē\ *adv*

[2]**valuable** *n* **:** a personal possession (as a jewel) of relatively great monetary value ⟨stored *valuables* in the safe⟩

val•u•ate \ˈval-yə-ˌwāt\ *vt* **:** to place a value on **:** APPRAISE — **val•u•a•tor** \-ˌwāt-ər\ *n*

val•u•a•tion \ˌval-yə-ˈwā-shən\ *n* **1 :** the act or process of valuing; *esp* **:** appraisal of property **2 :** the estimated or determined value **3 :** judgement or appreciation of worth or character — **val•u•a•tion•al** \-shnəl, -shən-l\ *adj* — **val•u•a•tion•al•ly** \-ē\ *adj*

[1]**val•ue** \ˈval-yü\ *n* **1 :** a fair return in goods, services, or money for something exchanged **2 :** the amount of another commodity for which a given thing can be exchanged; *esp* **:** the amount of money that something will bring **3 :** relative worth, utility or importance **:** degree of excellence **4 a :** a numerical quantity assigned or computed **b :** the magnitude of a physical quantity **c**

: the sound or sounds answering to a letter or orthographic item ⟨the *value* of *a* in *ate*⟩ **5** : the relative duration of a musical note **6 a** : relative lightness or darkness of a color : LUMINOSITY **b** : the relation of one part in a picture to another with respect to lightness and darkness **7** : something having or held to have real worth or merit ⟨the *values* of the old and young are often very different⟩ **8** : DENOMINATION 4 [Middle French, derived from Latin *valēre* "to be worth, be strong"] **syn** see WORTH

²value *vt* **1 a** : to estimate or assign the monetary worth of : APPRAISE ⟨*value* a necklace⟩ **b** : to rate or scale in usefulness, importance, or general worth **2** : to consider or rate highly : PRIZE, ESTEEM ⟨*valued* their friendship⟩ — **valu•er** \-yə-wər\ *n*

val•ued \ˈval-yüd, -yəd\ *adj* : highly regarded : greatly prized

val•ue•less \ˈval-yü-ləs, -yə-\ *adj* : of no value : WORTHLESS

valve \ˈvalv\ *n* **1** : a structure especially in a bodily channel (as a vein) that closes temporarily to obstruct passage of material or permits movement of a fluid in one direction only **2 a** : a mechanical device by which the flow of liquid, gas, or loose material in bulk may be started, stopped, or regulated by a movable part; *also* : the movable part of such a device **b** : a device in a brass wind instrument for quickly varying the tube length in order to change the tone by some definite interval **c** *chiefly British* : ELECTRON TUBE **3** : one of the pair of pieces comprising the hinged shell of some shell-bearing animals and especially of bivalve mollusks **4** : one of the segments or pieces into which a ripe seed capsule or pod separates [Latin *valva* "leaf of a double door"] — **valved** \ˈvalvd\ *adj*

val•vu•lar \ˈval-vyə-lər\ *adj* **1** : resembling or functioning as a valve; *also* : opening by valves **2** : of or relating to a valve especially of the heart

va•moose \və-ˈmüs, va-\ *vi, slang* : to depart quickly : SCRAM [Spanish *vamos* "let us go"]

¹vamp \ˈvamp\ *n* : the part of a shoe upper or boot upper covering especially the forepart of the foot and sometimes also extending forward over the toe or backward to the back seam of the upper [Old French *avantpié* "sock", from *avant-* "fore-" + *pié* "foot", from Latin *pes*]

²vamp *vt* **1 a** : to provide (a shoe) with a new vamp **b** : to piece (something old) with a new part : PATCH ⟨*vamp* up old sermons⟩ **2** : INVENT ⟨*vamp* up an excuse⟩

³vamp *n* : a woman who uses her charm or wiles to seduce and exploit men [short for *vampire*]

⁴vamp *vt* : to practice seductive wiles on

vam•pire \ˈvam-ˌpīr\ *n* **1** : the body of a dead person believed to come from the grave at night and suck the blood of persons asleep **2 a** : one who lives by preying on others **b** : a woman who exploits and ruins her lover **3** : VAMPIRE BAT [French, from German *vampir*, of Slavic origin] — **vam•pir•ism** \-ˌpīr-ˌiz-əm\ *n*

vampire bat *n* : any of three South and Central American bats that feed on blood and are dangerous to man and domestic animals especially as vectors of disease (as rabies)

²van 1

¹van \ˈvan\ *n* : VANGUARD

²van *n* **1** : a usually enclosed wagon or motortruck used for transportation of goods or animals **2** *chiefly British* : an enclosed railroad freight or baggage car [short for *caravan*]

va•na•di•um \və-ˈnād-ē-əm\ *n* : a grayish malleable metallic chemical element found combined in minerals and used especially to form alloys (as of steel) — see ELEMENT table [New Latin, from Old Norse *Vanadīs* "Freya (goddess of love and beauty)"]

Van Al•len radiation belt \va-ˈnal-ən-, və-\ *n* : a belt of intense ionizing radiation that surrounds the earth in the outer atmosphere [James A. *Van Allen* , born 1914, American physicist]

van•dal \ˈvan-dl\ *n* **1** *cap* : one of a Germanic people overrunning Gaul, Spain, and northern Africa in the 4th and 5th centuries A.D., and in 455 sacking Rome **2** : one who willfully destroys, damages, or defaces public or private property [Latin *Vandalii* "Vandals", of Germanic origin] — **vandal** *adj, often cap*

van•dal•ism \ˈvan-dl-ˌiz-əm\ *n* : willful or malicious destruction or defacement of public or private property

van•dal•is•tic \ˌvan-dl-ˈis-tik\ *adj* : of, relating to, or committing vandalism

van•dal•ize \ˈvan-dl-ˌiz\ *vt* : to subject to vandalism

Van de Graaff generator \ˌvan-də-ˌgraf-\ *n* : ELECTROSTATIC GENERATOR [Robert J. *Van de Graaff*, died 1967, American physicist]

Van•dyke \van-ˈdīk\ *n* : a trim pointed beard [Sir Anthony *Vandyke*]

Vandyke

vane \ˈvān\ *n* **1** : a movable device attached to an elevated object (as a spire) for showing the direction of the wind **2** : a flat or curved extended surface attached to an axis and moved by wind or water ⟨the *vanes* of a windmill⟩; *also* : a device revolving in a manner resembling this and moving in water or air ⟨the *vanes* of a propeller⟩ **3 a** : the flat expanded part of a feather — called also *web* **b** : a feather fastened to the shaft near the nock of an arrow [Old English *fana* "banner"] — **vaned** \ˈvānd\ *adj*

van•guard \ˈvan-ˌgärd\ *n* **1** : the troops moving at the head of an army **2** : the forefront of an action or movement or those in the forefront [Middle French *avant-garde*, from *avant-* "fore-" + *garde* "guard"]

va•nil•la \və-ˈnil-ə, -ˈnel-\ *n* **1** : any of a genus of tropical American climbing orchids **2 a** : VANILLA BEAN **b** : the flavoring extract from the vanilla bean [Spanish *vainilla*, from *vaina* "sheath", from Latin *vagina*]

vanilla bean *n* : the long pod of a vanilla that is an important article of commerce for the flavoring extract that it yields

vanilla 1: *1* flowering branch, *2* vanilla bean

va•nil•lin \ˈvan-l-ən\ *n* : a compound that is the chief fragrant component of vanilla

van•ish \ˈvan-ish\ *vi* **1** : to pass quickly from sight : DISAPPEAR **2** : to pass completely from existence [Middle French *evaniss-*, stem of *evanir* "to vanish", from Latin *evanescere*, from *e-* + *vanescere* "to vanish", from *vanus* "empty, vain"] — **van•ish•er** *n*

vanishing cream *n* : a cosmetic preparation that is less oily than cold cream and is used chiefly as a foundation for face powder

vanishing point *n* **1** : a point at which receding parallel lines seem to meet **2** : a point at which something disappears or ceases to exist

vanishing point 1

van•i•ty \ˈvan-ət-ē\ *n, pl* **-ties** **1** : something that is vain **2** : the quality or fact of being vain: as **a** : an empty or worthless state **b** : a state of futility **c** : inflated pride in oneself or one's appearance **3** : a fashionable article or knickknack **4 a** : ³COMPACT 1 **b** : DRESSING TABLE [Old French *vanité*, from Latin *vanitas*, from *vanus* "empty, vain"]

vanity fair *n, often cap V & F* : a scene or place marked by frivolity and pointless show [*Vanity-Fair*, a fair held in the frivolous town of Vanity in John Bunyan's *Pilgrim's Progress*]

van•quish \'vang-kwish, 'van-\ *vt* **1** : to overcome in battle : subdue completely **2** : to gain mastery over (as an emotion or temptation or a competitor) : DEFEAT [Middle French *venquis,* preterit of *veintre* "to conquer", from Latin *vincere*] **syn** see CONQUER — **van•quish•able** \-ə-bəl\ *adj* — **van•quish•er** *n*

van•tage \'vant-ij\ *n* **1** : superiority in a contest **2** : a position giving a strategic advantage, commanding perspective, or comprehensive view **3** : ADVANTAGE 3 [Anglo-French, from Middle French *avantage* "advantage"]

van•ward \'van-wərd\ *adj* : located in the vanguard : ADVANCED — **vanward** *adv*

vap•id \'vap-əd\ *adj* : lacking liveliness, tang, briskness, or force : FLAT, UNINTERESTING ⟨*vapid* remark⟩ ⟨*vapid* smile⟩ [Latin *vapidus* "flat tasting"] **syn** see INSIPID — **va•pid•i•ty** \va-'pid-ət-ē\ *n* — **vap•id•ly** \'vap-əd-lē\ *adv* — **vap•id•ness** *n*

[1]**va•por** \'vā-pər\ *n* **1** : fine particles of matter (as fog or smoke) floating in the air and clouding it **2** : a substance in a gaseous state; *esp* : such a substance that is liquid under ordinary conditions **3** : something insubstantial or fleeting [Middle French *vapeur,* from Latin *vapor* "steam, vapor"]

[2]**vapor** *vi* **va•pored**; **va•por•ing** \-pə-ring, -pring\ **1 a** : to rise or pass off in vapor **b** : to emit vapor **2** : to indulge in bragging, blustering, or idle talk — **va•por•er** \-pər-ər\ *n*

va•por•ing \'vā-pə-ring, -pring\ *n* : the act or speech of one that vapors; *esp* : an idle, extravagant, or high-flown expression or speech

va•por•ish \'vā-pə-rish, -prish\ *adj* **1** : resembling or suggestive of vapor **2** : given to fits of depression or hysteria — **va•por•ish•ness** *n*

va•por•ize \'vā-pə-,rīz\ *vb* : to turn from a liquid or solid into vapor — **va•por•iz•able** \-,rī-zə-bəl\ *adj* — **va•por•iza•tion** \,vā-pə-rə-'zā-shən\ *n*

va•por•iz•er \'vā-pə-,rī-zər\ *n* : a device that vaporizes something (as a fuel oil or a medicated liquid)

vapor lock *n* : a partial or complete interruption of fuel flow in an internal-combustion engine caused by the formation of bubbles of vapor in the fuel-feeding system

va•por•ous \'vā-pə-rəs, -prəs\ *adj* **1** : consisting or characteristic of vapor **2** : containing or obscured by vapors : MISTY **3** : UNSUBSTANTIAL, VAGUE — **va•por•ous•ly** *adv* — **va•por•ous•ness** *n*

vapor pressure *n* : the pressure exerted by a vapor that is in equilibrium with its solid or liquid form — called also *vapor tension*

vapor trail *n* : CONTRAIL

va•pory \'vā-pə-rē, -prē\ *adj* : VAPOROUS

va•que•ro \vä-'keər-ō\ *n pl* **-ros** : a ranch hand : COWBOY [Spanish, from *vaca* "cow", from Latin *vacca*]

var•ia \'ver-ē-ə, 'var-\ *n pl* : MISCELLANY; *esp* : a literary miscellany [Latin, neuter pl. of *varius* "various"]

[1]**vari•able** \'ver-ē-ə-bəl, 'var-\ *adj* **1 a** : able or apt to vary : CHANGEABLE ⟨*variable* winds⟩ **b** : FICKLE, INCONSTANT **2 a** : characterized by variations **b** : not true to type : ABERRANT ⟨a *variable* species of wheat⟩ **3** : having the characteristics of a variable — **vari•abil•i•ty** \,ver-ē-ə-'bil-ət-ē, ,var-\ *n* — **vari•able•ness** \'ver-ē-ə-bəl-nəs, 'var-\ *n* — **vari•ably** \-blē\ *adv*

[2]**variable** *n* **1** : something that is variable **2 a** : a quantity that may assume any one of a set of values **b** : a symbol in a mathematical expression representing a variable

variable star *n* : a star whose brightness changes usually in more or less regular periods

vari•ance \'ver-ē-əns, 'var-\ *n* **1** : the fact, quality, or state of being variable or variant : DIFFERENCE ⟨yearly *variance* in crops⟩ **2** : the fact or state of being in disagreement : DISSENSION, DISPUTE — **at variance** : not in harmony or agreement

[1]**vari•ant** \'ver-ē-ənt, 'var-\ *adj* **1** : differing from others of its kind or class and especially from others regarded as representing a norm, standard, or type **2** : being one of two or more similar but not identical forms with the same meaning ⟨a *variant* spelling⟩

[2]**variant** *n* : one of two or more individuals exhibiting usually slight differences: as **a** : one that exhibits variation from a type or norm **b** : one of two or more different spellings or pronunciations of the same word

vari•a•tion \,ver-ē-'ā-shən, ,var-\ *n* **1 a** : the act or process of varying : the state or fact of being varied **b** : an instance of varying **c** : the extent to which or range in which a thing varies **2** : DECLINATION 5 **3** : the repetition of a musical theme with modifications in rhythm, tune, harmony, or key **4 a** : divergence in biological characters from those typical or usual to an organism or group **b** : an individual or group exhibiting variation — **vari•a•tion•al** \-shnəl, -shən-l\ *adj* — **vari•a•tion•al•ly** \-ē\ *adv*

vari•col•ored \'ver-i-,kəl-ərd, 'var-\ *adj* : having various colors : VARIEGATED ⟨*varicolored* marble⟩

var•i•cose \'var-ə-,kōs\ *adj* : abnormally swollen or dilated ⟨*varicose* veins⟩ [Latin *varicosus* "full of dilated veins", from *varic-, varix* "dilated vein"]

var•i•cos•i•ty \,var-ə-'käs-ət-ē\ *n, pl* **-ties** **1** : the quality or state of being varicose **2** : a varicose part or lesion (as of a vein)

var•ied \'veər-ēd, 'vaər-\ *adj* **1** : having numerous forms or types : DIVERSE **2** : VARIEGATED 2 — **var•ied•ly** *adv*

var•ie•gate \'ver-ē-ə-,gāt, 'ver-i-,gāt, 'var-\ *vt* **1** : to diversify in external appearance especially with different colors **2** : to make interesting by variety [Latin *variegare,* from *varius* "various"] — **var•ie•ga•tion** \,ver-ē-ə-'gā-shən, ,ver-i-'gā-, ,var-\ *n* — **var•ie•ga•tor** \'ver-ē-ə-,gāt-ər, 'ver-i-,gāt-, 'var-\ *n*

var•ie•gat•ed \'ver-ē-ə-,gāt-əd, 'ver-i-,gāt-, 'var-\ *adj* **1** : VARIED 1 **2** : having patches, stripes, or marks of different colors ⟨*variegated* flowers⟩

va•ri•ety \və-'rī-ət-ē\ *n, pl* **-eties** **1** : the quality or state of having different forms or types **2** : a number or collection of different things : ASSORTMENT ⟨the store stocks a large *variety* of goods⟩ **3 a** : something differing from others of the same general kind **b** : any of various groups of plants or animals within a species that are distinguished from other groups by characteristics not constant enough or too trivial to distinguish species **4** : entertainment consisting of successive unrelated performances (as dances, skits, or acrobatic feats) [Latin *varietas,* from *varius* "various"] — **va•ri•etal** \-ət-l\ *adj* — **va•ri•etal•ly** \-l-ē\ *adv*

variety store *n* : a retail store that carries a large variety of usually inexpensive merchandise

va•ri•o•la \,ver-ē-'ō-lə, ,var-; və-'rī-ə-lə\ *n* : any of several virus diseases (as smallpox or cowpox) marked by a pustular eruption [Late Latin, "pustule"]

var•i•o•rum \,ver-ē-'ōr-əm, ,var-, -'ȯr-\ *n* : an edition or text especially of a classical author with notes by different persons and often with variant readings of the text [Latin *cum notis variorum* "with the notes of various persons"]

var•i•ous \'ver-ē-əs, 'var-\ *adj* **1** : marked by variation or variety (as in appearance or properties) : of differing kinds ⟨*various* enterprises use metals⟩ ⟨my *various* responsibilities⟩ **2 a** : differing one from another : UNLIKE ⟨animals as *various* as cat and mouse⟩ **b** : VARIANT ⟨*various* readings are known⟩ **3** : consisting of an indefinite number greater than one ⟨*various* schemes⟩ ⟨stop at *various* towns⟩ [Latin *varius*] — **var•i•ous•ly** *adv* — **var•i•ous•ness** *n*

vari•sized \'ver-i-,sīzd, 'var-\ *adj* : of various sizes

va•ris•tor \va-'ris-tər, ve-\ *n* : an electrical resistor whose resistance depends on the applied voltage [*vari-* "varied" (from Latin *varius*) + *resistor*]

var•let \'vär-lət\ *n* **1** *archaic* : [2]RETAINER 2 **2** : a low fellow [Middle French, "young nobleman, page", from Medieval Latin *vassus* "servant, vassal"]

var•mint \'vär-mənt\ *n* **1** : an animal or bird considered a pest **2** : a contemptible person : RASCAL [alteration of *vermin*]

[1]**var•nish** \'vär-nish\ *n* **1 a** : a liquid preparation that is spread like paint and dries to a hard lustrous typically transparent coating **b** : the covering or glaze given by the application of varnish **2** : deceptive outer appearance [Middle French *vernis*] — **var•nishy** \-ē\ *adj*

[2]**varnish** *vt* : to cover with or as if with varnish — **var•nish•er** *n*

var•si•ty \'vär-sət-ē, -stē\ *n, pl* **-ties** : a principal squad representing a university, college, school, or club [from *university*] — **varsity** *adj*

varve \'värv\ *n* : a pair of layers of alternately finer and coarser silt or clay believed to comprise an annual cycle of deposition in a body of still water [Swedish *varv* "turn, layer"]

vary \'veər-ē, 'vaər-\ *vb* **var•ied**; **vary•ing** : to differ or cause to differ: as **a** : to make a usually minor or partial change in ⟨the rule must not be *varied*⟩ **b** : to give variety to : DIVERSIFY ⟨*vary* a diet⟩ ⟨a program *varied* to avoid monotony⟩ **c :** to exhibit or undergo change ⟨*varying* skies⟩⟨the accuracy of the several chapters *varies* greatly⟩; *also* **:** to be different ⟨laws *vary* from state to state⟩ **d :** to take on increasing or decreasing values from a mathematical set ⟨*y varies* inversely with *x*⟩ **e :** to diverge structurally or physiologically from typical members of a group **[**Latin *variare,* from *varius* "various"**] syn** see CHANGE — **vary•ing•ly** \-ing-lē\ *adv*

varying hare *n* **:** any of several hares having white fur in winter

va•sa ef•fer•en•tia \ˈvā-zə-ˌef-ə-ˈren-chē-ə, -chə\ *n pl* **:** the 12 to 20 tubes that lead from the testis to the vas deferens and except near their beginning are greatly convoluted and form the compact head of the epididymis **[**New Latin, literally, "efferent vessels"**]**

vas•cu•lar \ˈvas-kyə-lər\ *adj* **:** of, relating to, or being an anatomical vessel (as a vein, artery, or vascular bundle) or a system of these; *also* **:** supplied with or made up of such vessels and especially blood vessels ⟨a *vascular* tumor⟩ **[**Latin *vasculum* "small vessel", from *vas* "vessel"**]** — **vas•cu•lar•i•ty** \ˌvas-kyə-ˈlar-ət-ē\ *n*

vascular bundle *n* **:** a unit of the vascular system of a higher plant consisting usually of xylem and phloem together with parenchyma cells and fibers

vascular cambium *n* **:** a ring of meristem between the phloem and xylem of a vascular plant which gives rise to phloem on its outer side and xylem on its inner side

vascular cylinder *n* **:** STELE

vas•cu•lar•iza•tion \ˌvas-kyə-lə-rə-ˈzā-shən\ *n* **:** the development of vessels in tissue

vascular plant *n* **:** a plant having a specialized conducting system that includes xylem and phloem **:** TRACHEOPHYTE

vascular ray *n* **:** a band of xylem and phloem tissue from the pith through the wood of a woody vascular plant that conducts food and water laterally and looks in a cross section of a stem like a spoke of a wheel

vascular tissue *n* **:** a specialized conducting tissue of higher plants that consists essentially of phloem and xylem and forms a continuous system throughout the body

vas•cu•lum \ˈvas-kyə-ləm\ *n, pl* **-la** \-lə\ **:** a usually metal and commonly cylindrical covered box used in collecting botanical specimens **[**Latin, "small vessel"**]**

vas de•fer•ens \ˈvas-ˈdef-ə-rənz, -ˌrenz\ *n, pl* **va•sa de•fer•en•tia** \ˌvas-ə-ˌdef-ə-ˈren-chē-ə, -chə\ **:** a duct conveying sperm especially in a higher vertebrate **[**New Latin, literally, "vessel that brings down"**]**

vase *United States* ˈvās *also* ˈvāz, *Canadian* ˈvāz *also* ˈväz, *British* ˈväz\ *n* **:** a usually round vessel of greater depth than width used chiefly for ornament or for flowers

va•sec•to•my \və-ˈsek-tə-mē, vā-ˈzek-\ *n, pl* **-mies :** surgical removal of part of the vas deferens especially to induce permanent sterility

Vas•e•line \ˈvas-ə-ˌlēn, ˌvas-ə-ˈ\ *trademark* — used for petrolatum

va•so•con•stric•tion \ˌvā-zō-kən-ˈstrik-shən\ *n* **:** narrowing of the diameter of blood vessels **[**Latin *vas* "vessel"**]** — **vaso•con•stric•tive** \-ˈstrik-tiv\ *adj*

va•so•con•stric•tor \-ˈstrik-tər\ *n* **:** an agent (as a sympathetic nerve fiber or a drug) that induces or initiates vasoconstriction

va•so•di•la•ta•tion \ˌvā-zō-ˌdil-ə-ˈtā-shən, -ˌdī-lə-\ *or* **vaso•di•la•tion** \-dī-ˈlā-shən\ *n* **:** widening of the diameter of blood vessels

va•so•di•la•tor \-dī-ˈlāt-ər, -ˈdī-ˌ\ *n* **:** an agent (as a parasympathetic nerve fiber or a drug) that induces or initiates vasodilatation

va•so•mo•tor \ˌvā-zə-ˈmōt-ər\ *adj* **:** of, relating to, or being nerves or centers controlling the size of blood vessels

va•so•pres•sin \ˌvā-zō-ˈpres-n\ *n* **:** a protein hormone secreted by the pituitary gland that increases blood pressure and decreases urine flow **[**from *Vasopressin,* a former trademark**]**

vas•sal \ˈvas-əl\ *n* **1 :** a person under the protection of a feudal lord to whom homage and fealty are vowed **:** a feudal tenant **2 :** one in a subservient or subordinate position **[**Middle French, from Medieval Latin *vassallus,* from *vassus* "servant, vassal", of Celtic origin**]** — **vassal** *adj*

vas•sal•age \ˈvas-ə-lij\ *n* **1 :** the condition of being a vassal **2 :** homage and loyalty due a lord from his vassal **3 :** a position of subordination or submission (as to a political power)

[1]**vast** \ˈvast\ *adj* **:** very great in size, amount, degree, intensity, or especially in extent **[**Latin *vastus*] **syn** see ENORMOUS — **vast•ly** *adv* — **vast•ness** \ˈvast-nəs, ˈvas-\ *n*

[2]**vast** *n* **:** a boundless space **:** IMMENSITY

vasty \ˈvas-tē\ *adj* **vast•i•er; -est :** VAST, IMMENSE

vat \ˈvat\ *n* **:** a large vessel (as a cistern, tub, or barrel) especially for liquids **[**Old English *fæt*]

vat dye *n* **:** a textile dye in a colorless reduced solution in which material to be dyed is steeped and which on exposure to air is oxidized and deposited in the fibers of the material — **vat-dyed** \ˈvat-ˈdīd\ *adj*

vat•ic \ˈvat-ik\ *adj* **:** of or relating to a prophet **[**Latin *vates* "seer, prophet"**]**

Vat•i•can \ˈvat-i-kən\ *n* **:** the headquarters or the government of the Roman Catholic Church **[**Latin *Vaticanus* "Vatican Hill (in Rome)"**]**

vau•de•ville \ˈvȯd-vəl, ˈväd-, ˈvōd-, -ə-vəl, -ˌvil\ *n* **:** light theatrical entertainment featuring usually unrelated variety acts (as songs, dances, and sketches) **[**French, from Middle French *vaudevire, vaudeville* "satirical song", from *vau-de-Vire* "valley of Vire (town in France where such songs were composed)"**]** — **vau•de•vil•lian** \ˌvȯd-ˈvil-yən, ˌväd-, ˌvōd-, -ə-ˈvil\ *adj or n*

[1]**vault** \ˈvȯlt\ *n* **1 a :** an arched structure of masonry usually forming a ceiling or roof **b :** something suggesting a vault especially in arched or domed structure ⟨the blue *vault* of the sky⟩ **2 a :** a space covered by an arched structure, *esp* **:** an underground passage or room **b :** an underground storage compartment **c :** a room or compartment for the safekeeping of valuables **3 a :** a burial chamber **b :** a case usually of metal or concrete in which a casket is enclosed at burial **[**Middle French *voute*]

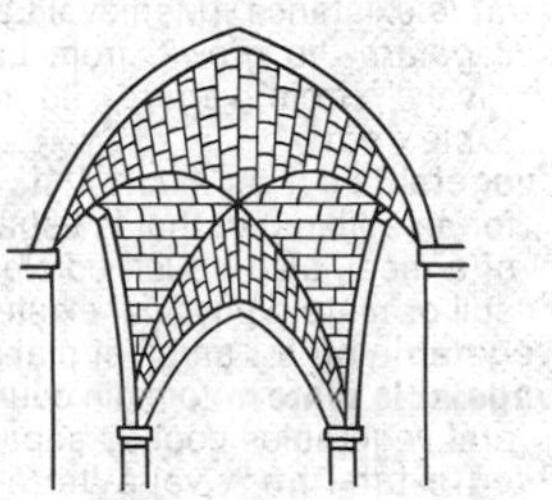

[1]vault 1a

[2]**vault** *vt* **:** to form or cover with or as if with a vault **:** ARCH

[3]**vault** *vb* **:** to execute a leap using the hands or a pole to lift and support the body; *also* **:** to leap over **[**Middle French *volter,* from Italian *voltare,* derived from Latin *volvere* "to roll"**]** — **vault•er** \ˈvȯl-tər\ *n*

[4]**vault** *n* **:** an act of vaulting; *also* **:** LEAP

vault•ed \ˈvȯl-təd\ *adj* **1 :** built in the form of a vault **2 :** covered with a vault

vault•ing \-ting\ *adj* **:** leaping upwards ⟨*vaulting* sparks⟩ ⟨*vaulting* spirits⟩; *esp* **:** straining unreasonably or arrogantly toward the heights ⟨a *vaulting* ambition⟩

vaulting horse *n* **:** a padded rectangular or cylindrical form supported off the floor over which gymnasts vault in competition

[1]**vaunt** \ˈvȯnt, ˈvänt\ *vb* **:** BRAG, BOAST **[**Middle French *vanter,* from Late Latin *vanitare,* from Latin *vanitas* "vanity"**]** — **vaunt•er** *n* — **vaunt•ing•ly** \-ing-lē\ *adv*

[2]**vaunt** *n* **1 :** a vainglorious display (as of worth or accomplishment) **2 :** a bragging assertive speech

vaunt•ful \-fəl\ *adj* **:** BOASTFUL, VAINGLORIOUS

've \v, əv\ *vb* **:** HAVE ⟨we've been there⟩

veal \ˈvēl\ *n* **1 :** CALF 1a; *esp* **:** VEALER **2 :** the flesh of a young calf **[**Middle French *veel,* from Latin *vitellus* "small calf", from *vitulus* "calf"**]**

veal•er \ˈvē-lər\ *n* **:** a calf grown for or suitable for veal

vec•tor \ˈvek-tər\ *n* **1 :** a quantity that has magnitude, direction, and sense **2 :** an organism (as an insect) that transmits a pathogen **[**Latin, "carrier", from *vectus,* past participle of *vehere* "to carry"**]** — **vec•to•ri•al** \vek-ˈtōr-ē-əl, -ˈtȯr-\ *adj* — **vec•to•ri•al•ly** \-ē-ə-lē\ *adv*

Ve•da \ˈvād-ə\ *n* **:** any of a primary class of Hindu sacred writings; *esp* **:** any of four canonical collections of hymns, prayers, and liturgical formulas **[**Sanskrit, literally, "knowledge"**]**

Ve•dan•ta \vā-ˈdänt-ə, və-, -ˈdant-\ *n* **:** an orthodox system of Hindu philosophy **[**Sanskrit *Vedānta,* literally, "end of the Veda"**]** — **Ve•dan•tic** \-ik\ *adj*

\ə\ **abut**	\au̇\ **out**	\i\ **tip**	\ȯ\ **saw**	\u̇\ **foot**
\ər\ **further**	\ch\ **chin**	\ī\ **life**	\ȯi\ **coin**	\y\ **yet**
\a\ **mat**	\e\ **pet**	\j\ **job**	\th\ **thin**	\yü\ **few**
\ā\ **take**	\ē\ **easy**	\ng\ **sing**	\t͟h\ **this**	\yu̇\ **cure**
\ä\ **cot, cart**	\g\ **go**	\ō\ **bone**	\ü\ **food**	\zh\ **vision**

ve•dette *or* **vi•dette** \vi-'det\ *n* : a mounted sentinel stationed in advance of pickets [French, from Italian *veletta, vedetta*]

Ve•dic \'vād-ik\ *adj* : of or relating to the Vedas, the language in which they are written, or Hindu history and culture between 2000 B.C. and 500 B.C.

veep \'vēp\ *n* : VICE-PRESIDENT [from *v.p.,* abbreviation for *vice-president*]

[1]**veer** \'viər\ *vb* : to change direction or course : TURN; *esp* : to shift in a clockwise direction ⟨the wind *veered* from northwest to northeast⟩ [Middle French *virer*] **syn** see SWERVE — **veer•ing•ly** \-ing-lē\ *adv*

[2]**veer** *n* : a change in course or direction

vee•ry \'viər-ē\ *n, pl* **veeries** : a tawny brown thrush common in woodlands of the eastern United States [perhaps imitative]

Ve•ga \'vē-gə, 'vā-\ *n* : a bright star in the constellation Lyra [New Latin, from Arabic (al-Nasr) *al-Wāqi',* literally, "the falling (vulture)"]

[1]**veg•e•ta•ble** \'vej-tə-bəl, 'vej-ət-ə-bəl\ *adj* **1** : of, relating to, or made up of plants ⟨the *vegetable* kingdom⟩⟨*vegetable* growth⟩ **2** : obtained from plants ⟨*vegetable* oils⟩⟨*vegetable* drugs⟩ **3** : suggesting that of a plant (as in monotony) ⟨a *vegetable* existence⟩ [Medieval Latin *vegetabilis* "vegetative", from *vegetare* "to grow", from Latin, "to animate", from *vegetus* "lively", from *vegēre* "to rouse, excite"] — **veg•e•ta•bly** \-blē\ *adv*

[2]**vegetable** *n* **1 a** : PLANT 1 **b** : a usually herbaceous plant grown for an edible part that is usually eaten with the principal course of a meal; *also* : such edible part **2** : a human being having a dull or merely physical existence

vegetable oil *n* : an oil of plant origin

vegetable plate *n* : a main course without meat consisting of several vegetables cooked separately and served on one plate

[1]**veg•e•tar•i•an** \,vej-ə-'ter-ē-ən\ *n* : one who excludes meat from the diet; *esp* : one who believes in or practices living solely on vegetables, fruits, grains, and nuts — **veg•e•tar•i•an•ism** \-ē-ə-,niz-əm\ *n*

[2]**vegetarian** *adj* : of, relating to, or suitable for vegetarians

veg•e•tate \'vej-ə-,tāt\ *vb* **1** : to live or grow in the manner of a plant; *esp* : to lead a passive effortless existence **2** : to establish vegetation in or on ⟨richly *vegetated* slopes⟩ [Medieval Latin *vegetare* "to grow"]

veg•e•ta•tion \,vej-ə-'tā-shən\ *n* **1** : the act or process of vegetating **2** : inert existence **3** : plant life or cover (as of an area) — **veg•e•ta•tion•al** \-shnəl, -shən-l\ *adj*

veg•e•ta•tive \'vej-ə-,tāt-iv\ *adj* **1 a** : of, relating to, or functioning in nutrition and growth as contrasted with reproduction ⟨the stem and leaf are *vegetative* organs⟩ **b** : of, relating to, or involving propagation by other than sexual means **2** : VEGETATIONAL ⟨*vegetative* cover⟩ **3** : affecting, arising from, or relating to involuntary bodily functions : AUTONOMIC ⟨*vegetative* nerves⟩ **4** : VEGETABLE 3 — **veg•e•ta•tive•ly** *adv* — **veg•e•ta•tive•ness** *n*

ve•he•ment \'vē-ə-mənt\ *adj* : marked by forceful energy : POWERFUL ⟨a *vehement* wind⟩: as **a** : intensely emotional : IMPASSIONED, FERVID ⟨*vehement* patriotism⟩⟨*vehement* denunciations⟩ **b** : deeply felt ⟨*vehement* suspicion⟩ [Middle French, from Latin *vehemens*] — **ve•he•mence** \-məns\ *n* — **ve•he•ment•ly** *adv*

ve•hi•cle \'vē-,ik-əl, -,hik-, 'vē-ə-kəl\ *n* **1** : a medium through which something is administered, transmitted, expressed, achieved, or displayed ⟨movies are *vehicles* of ideas⟩⟨turpentine is a common *vehicle* for paint⟩ **2** : something used to transport persons or goods : CONVEYANCE [French *véhicule,* from Latin *vehiculum* "carriage, conveyance", from *vehere* "to carry"]

ve•hic•u•lar \vē-'hik-yə-lər\ *adj* **1** : of, relating to, or designed for vehicles and especially motor vehicles **2** : serving as a vehicle

V–8 \'vē-'āt\ *n* : an internal-combustion engine having two banks of four cylinders each with the banks at an angle to each other; *also* : an automobile having such an engine [from the resemblance of the angle formed by the two banks to the letter V]

[1]**veil** \'vāl\ *n* **1 a** : a length of cloth or net worn especially by women over the head and shoulders or attached to a hat or headdress and sometimes (as in eastern countries) drawn also over the face **b** : a concealing curtain or cover of cloth **c** : something that covers or obscures like a veil ⟨a *veil* of secrecy⟩ **2** : the vows or life of a nun ⟨take the *veil*⟩ [Old North French *veile,* from Latin *vela,* pl. of *velum* "veil"]

[2]**veil** *vt* : to cover, provide, obscure, or conceal with or as if with a veil

veil•ing \'vā-ling\ *n* **1** : VEIL 1a **2** : a light sheer fabric (as net or chiffon) suitable for veils

[1]**vein** \'vān\ *n* **1** : LODE **2 a** : one of the tubular branching vessels that carry blood from the capillaries toward the heart **b** : one of the vascular bundles forming the framework of a leaf **c** : one of the thickened ribs that stiffen the wings of an insect **3** : something like a vein usually in irregular linear form or in forming a channel ⟨underground water *veins*⟩; *esp* : a wavy band or streak (as of a different color or texture) ⟨a marble with greenish *veins*⟩ **4 a** : a distinctive mode of expression : STYLE ⟨writing in a humorous *vein*⟩ **b** : a pervasive element or quality : STRAIN ⟨a *vein* of mysticism in one's character⟩ **c** : [1]MOOD [Old French *veine,* from Latin *vena*] — **vein•al** \'vān-l\ *adj* — **veined** \'vānd\ *adj* — **veiny** \'vā-nē\ *adj*

[2]**vein** *vt* : to form veins in or mark with veins

vein•ing \'vā-ning\ *n* : a pattern of veins : VENATION

vein•let \'vān-lət\ *n* : a small vein especially of a leaf

ve•lar \'vē-lər\ *adj* **1** : of, relating to, or forming a velum and especially the soft palate **2** : formed with the back of the tongue touching or near the soft palate ⟨the *velar* \k\ of \'kül\ *cool*⟩ — **velar** *n*

veld *or* **veldt** \'velt, 'felt\ *n* : open grassland especially of southern Africa usually with scattered shrubs or trees [Afrikaans *veld,* from Dutch, "field"]

vel•le•ity \ve-'lē-ət-ē\ *n, pl* **-ities 1** : the lowest degree of volition **2** : a slight wish or tendency : INCLINATION [Latin *velle* "to wish, will"]

vel•lum \'vel-əm\ *n* **1** : a fine-grained unsplit lambskin, kidskin, or calfskin prepared especially for writing on or for binding books **2** : a strong cream-colored paper resembling vellum [Middle French *veelin,* from *veel* "calf"] — **vellum** *adj*

ve•loc•i•pede \və-'läs-ə-,pēd\ *n* : a lightweight wheeled vehicle propelled by the rider; *esp* : TRICYCLE [French *vélocipède,* from Latin *veloc-, velox* "quick" + *ped-, pes* "foot"]

velocipede

ve•loc•i•ty \və-'läs-ət-ē, -'läs-tē\ *n, pl* **-ties 1** : quickness of motion : SPEED ⟨the *velocity* of sound⟩ **2** : time rate of linear motion in a given direction **3** : rate of occurrence or action : RAPIDITY [Middle French *velocité,* from Latin *velocitas,* from *veloc-, velox* "quick"]

ve•lour *or* **ve•lours** \və-'lůr\ *n, pl* **velours** \-'lůrz\ : a usually heavy fabric with a pile or napped surface resembling velvet [French *velours,* from Old French *velous,* from Latin *villosus* "shaggy", from *villus,* "shaggy hair"]

ve•lum \'vē-ləm\ *n* : a membrane or anatomical partition likened to a veil or curtain; *esp* : SOFT PALATE [Latin, "curtain, veil"]

[1]**vel•vet** \'vel-vət\ *n* **1** : a usually silk or synthetic fabric with a thick soft short pile **2** : something suggesting velvet (as in softness); *esp* : the soft vascular skin covering the developing antlers of a deer **3** : an unanticipated gain or profit [Middle English *veluet, velvet,* from Middle French *velu* "shaggy", derived from Latin *villus* "shaggy hair"]

[2]**velvet** *adj* **1** : made of or covered with velvet **2** : resembling or suggesting velvet : VELVETY

velvet ant *n* : any of various solitary burrowing usually brightly colored wasps with the females wingless

vel•ve•teen \,vel-və-'tēn\ *n* : a cotton fabric made in imitation of velvet

vel•vety \'vel-vət-ē\ *adj* **1** : soft and smooth like velvet ⟨*velvety* fur⟩ **2** : smooth to the taste

ven- *or* **veni-** *combining form* : vein ⟨*ven*ation⟩ ⟨*veni*puncture⟩ [Latin *vena*]

ve•na ca•va \,vē-nə-'kā-və\ *n, pl* **ve•nae ca•vae** \,vē-ni-'kā-vē\ : one of the large veins by which the blood is returned to the right atrium of the heart in an air-breathing vertebrate [New Latin, literally, "hollow vein"]

ve•nal \'vēn-l\ *adj* **1** : willing to take bribes : open to corrupt influences ⟨*venal* officials⟩ **2 :** influenced by bribery **:** CORRUPT ⟨*venal* conduct⟩ [Latin *venalis* "for sale", from *venus* "sale"] — **ve•nal•i•ty** \vi-'nal-ət-ē\ *n* — **ve•nal•ly** \'vēn-l-ē\ *adv*

ve•na•tion \ve-'nā-shən, vē-\ *n* **:** an arrangement or system of veins ⟨the *venation* of the hand⟩ ⟨the *venation* of a leaf⟩ — **ve•na•tion•al** \-shnəl, -shən-l\ *adj*

vend \'vend\ *vb* **:** to sell or offer for sale especially as a hawker or peddler ⟨*vend* fruit⟩ [Latin *vendere* "to sell", from *venum dare* "to give for sale"] — **vend•er** \'ven-dər\ *or* **ven•dor** \'ven-dər, ven-'dȯr\ *n* — **vend•ible** *or* **vend•able** \'ven-də-bəl\ *adj*

vend•ee \ven-'dē\ *n* **:** one to whom a thing is sold **:** BUYER

ven•det•ta \ven-'det-ə\ *n* **:** a feud marked by bitter hostility and motivated by a desire for revenge [Italian, literally, "revenge", from Latin *vindicta*]

vending machine *n* **:** a slot machine for vending merchandise

ven•di•tion \ven-'dish-ən\ *n* **:** the act of selling **:** SALE

ven•due \ven-'dü, vän-, -'dyü\ *n* **:** AUCTION [obsolete French, from *vendre* "to sell", from Latin *vendere*]

[1]**ve•neer** \və-'niər\ *n* **1 :** a thin sheet of a material: as **a :** a layer of a valuable or beautiful wood to be glued to an inferior wood **b :** any of the thin layers bonded together to form plywood **2 :** a protective or ornamental facing (as of brick or stone) **3 :** a superficial or deceptively attractive appearance **:** GLOSS ⟨a *veneer* of courtesy⟩ [German *furnier*, from *furnieren* "to veneer", from French *fournir* "to furnish"]

[2]**veneer** *vt* **:** to overlay with a veneer — **ve•neer•er** *n*

ven•er•a•ble \'ven-ər-bəl, -ər-ə-bəl, 'ven-rə-bəl\ *adj* **1** *often cap* **:** deserving to be venerated — used as a title usually preceded by *the* before the name of an Episcopal archdeacon or a Roman Catholic in the first stage of canonization ⟨the *Venerable* John M. Doe⟩ ⟨the *Venerable* Mother Ann-Marie⟩ **2 :** made sacred by association (as religious or historic) **3 a :** calling forth respect through age, character, and attainments **b :** impressive by reason of age ⟨*venerable* pines⟩ — **ven•er•a•bil•i•ty** \,ven-rə-'bil-ət-ē, -ə-rə-\ *n* — **ven•er•a•ble•ness** \'ven-ər-bəl-nəs, -ər-ə-bəl-, 'ven-rə-bəl-\ *n* — **ven•er•a•bly** \-blē\ *adv*

ven•er•ate \'ven-ə-,rāt\ *vt* **:** to regard with reverential respect or with admiration and deference [Latin *venerari*, from *vener-*, *venus* "love, charm"] **syn** see REVERE — **ven•er•a•tor** \-,rāt-ər\ *n*

ven•er•a•tion \,ven-ə-'rā-shən\ *n* **1 :** a feeling of reverence or deep respect **:** DEVOTION **2 :** the act of venerating **:** the state of being venerated ⟨*veneration* of saints⟩

ve•ne•re•al \və-'nir-ē-əl\ *adj* **:** of or relating to sexual intercourse or to diseases transmitted by it ⟨a *venereal* infection⟩ [Latin *venereus*, from *vener-*, *venus* "love, sexual desire"]

venereal disease *n* **:** a contagious disease (as syphilis) that is usually transmitted by sexual intercourse with an infected person

[1]**ven•ery** \'ven-ə-rē\ *n* **1 :** the art, act, or practice of hunting **2 :** animals that are hunted **:** GAME [Middle French *venerie*, from *vener* "to hunt", from Latin *venari*]

[2]**venery** *n* **:** the pursuit of or indulgence in sexual pleasure; *also* **:** SEXUAL INTERCOURSE [Medieval Latin *veneria*, from Latin *vener-*, *venus* "love, sexual desire"]

vene•sec•tion *or* **veni•sec•tion** \'ven-ə-,sek-shən, 'vēn-\ *n* **:** the operation of opening a vein to draw off blood [New Latin *venae sectio*, literally, "cutting of a vein"]

ve•ne•tian blind \və-,nē-shən-\ *n* **:** a blind having thin horizontal slats that can be set at different angles to vary the amount of light admitted [*Venetian* "of Venice, Italy"]

Venetian red *n* **:** an earthy hematite used as a pigment; *also* **:** a synthetic iron oxide pigment

ven•geance \'ven-jəns\ *n* **:** punishment inflicted in return for an injury or offense **:** RETRIBUTION [Old French, from *vengier* "to avenge", from Latin *vindicare*, from *vindic-*, *vindex* "avenger"] — **with a vengeance 1 :** with great force **2 :** to an extreme degree

venge•ful \'venj-fəl\ *adj* **1 :** filled with a desire for revenge **:** VINDICTIVE **2 :** serving to gain revenge — **venge•ful•ly** \-fə-lē\ *adv* — **venge•ful•ness** *n*

V–en•gine \'vē-'en-jən\ *n* **:** an internal-combustion engine whose cylinders are arranged in two banks forming an acute angle

veni- — see VEN-

ve•nial \'vē-nē-əl, -nyəl\ *adj* **:** of a kind that can be pardoned **:** FORGIVABLE, EXCUSABLE ⟨*venial* faults⟩ [Old French, from Late Latin *venialis*, from Latin *venia* "indulgence, pardon"] — **ve•ni•al•ly** \-ē\ *adv* — **ve•ni•al•ness** *n*

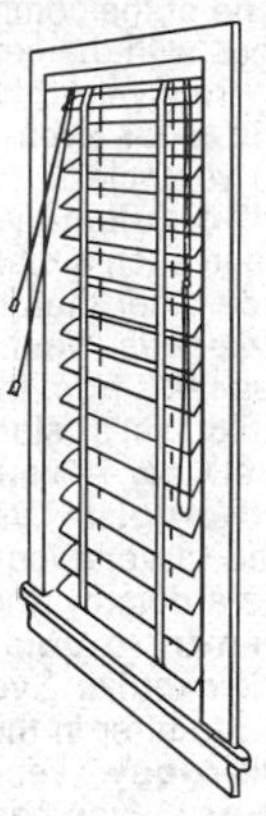
venetian blind

ven•in \'ven-ən\ *n* **:** a toxic component of snake venom [*venom* + *-in*]

ve•ni•punc•ture \'vēn-ə-,pəng-chər, 'ven-, -,pəngk-\ *n* **:** a puncturing of a vein usually to draw off blood or to introduce medication

ve•ni•re \və-'nī-rē\ *n* **:** a panel from which a jury is drawn

ve•ni•re fa•ci•as \və-,nī-rē-'fā-shē-əs\ *n* **:** a writ summoning persons to appear in court to serve as jurors [Medieval Latin, "you should cause to come"]

ven•i•son \'ven-ə-sən *also* -ə-zən\ *n, pl* **venisons** *also* **venison 1 :** the edible flesh of a wild animal taken by hunting **2 :** the flesh of a deer [Old French *veneison* "hunting, game", from Latin *venatio*, from *venari* "to hunt"]

Venn diagram \'ven-\ *n* **:** a diagram using circles or ellipses to represent relations between and operations on sets [John *Venn*, died 1923, English logician]

ven•om \'ven-əm\ *n* **1 :** poisonous matter normally secreted by an animal (as a snake, scorpion, or bee) and communicated chiefly by biting or stinging **2 a :** a spiteful malicious state of mind **b :** a venomous utterance [Old French *venim*, derived from Latin *venenum* "magic charm, drug, poison"]

ven•om•ous \'ven-ə-məs\ *adj* **1 :** filled with venom: as **a :** POISONOUS **b :** SPITEFUL, MALIGNANT ⟨*venomous* words⟩ **2 :** secreting and using venom ⟨*venomous* snakes⟩ — **ven•om•ous•ly** *adv* — **ven•om•ous•ness** *n*

ve•nous \'vē-nəs\ *adj* **1 :** of, relating to, or full of veins ⟨a *venous* rock⟩ ⟨a *venous* system⟩ **2 :** being purplish red oxygen-deficient blood present in most veins — **ve•nous•ly** *adv*

[1]**vent** \'vent\ *vt* **1 a :** to provide with an outlet **b :** to serve as an outlet for ⟨chimneys *vent* smoke⟩ **2 :** to give often forceful or emotional expression to ⟨*vent* one's anger⟩ **3 :** to relieve by venting [Middle English *venten*]

[2]**vent** *n* **1 :** a means of release **:** OUTLET **2 :** an opening for the escape or passage of something: as **a :** ANUS **b :** FUMAROLE

[3]**vent** *n* **:** a slit in a garment and especially in the lower part of a seam [Middle French *fente* "slit, fissure", from *fendre* "to split", from Latin *findere*]

ven•ter \'vent-ər\ *n* **:** a protuberant and often hollow anatomical structure [Latin, "belly, womb"]

ven•ti•fact \'vent-ə-,fakt\ *n* **:** a stone worn, polished, or faceted by windblown sand [Latin *ventus* "wind" + English *-ifact* (as in *artifact*)]

ven•ti•late \'vent-l-,āt\ *vt* **1 :** to discuss freely and openly **:** make public ⟨*ventilate* a complaint⟩ **2 a :** to expose to air and especially to a current of fresh air **b :** to provide with ventilation ⟨*ventilate* a room by fans⟩ [Late Latin *ventilare*, from Latin, "to fan, winnow", derived from *ventus* "wind"] — **ven•ti•la•tive** \-,āt-iv\ *adj*

ven•ti•la•tion \,vent-l-'ā-shən\ *n* **1 :** the act or process of ventilating **2 :** circulation of air ⟨a room with good *ventilation*⟩ **3 :** a system or means of providing fresh air

ven•ti•la•tor \'vent-l-,āt-ər\ *n* **:** one that ventilates; *esp* **:** a contrivance for introducing fresh air or expelling foul or stagnant air

ven•tral \'ven-trəl\ *adj* **1 :** of or relating to the belly **:** ABDOMINAL **2 :** of or relating to or located on or near the surface of the body that in humans is the front but in most other animals is the lower surface ⟨a fish's *ventral* fins⟩ [French, from Latin *ventralis*, from *venter* "belly"] — **ven•tral•ly** \-trə-lē\ *adv*

ven•tri•cle \'ven-tri-kəl\ *n* **:** a cavity of a bodily part or organ: as **a :** a chamber of the heart which receives blood from a corresponding atrium and from which blood is forced into the arteries **b** : one of the communicating cavities in the brain that are continuous with the central canal of the spinal cord [Latin *ventriculus,* from *venter* "belly"]

ven•tric•u•lar \ven-ˈtrik-yə-lər, vən-\ *adj* : of, relating to, or being a ventricle

ven•tril•o•quism \ven-ˈtril-ə-ˌkwiz-əm\ *n* : the production of the voice in such a manner that the sound appears to come from a source other than the vocal organs of the speaker [Late Latin *ventriloquus* "ventriloquist", from Latin *venter* "belly" + *loqui* "to speak"; from the belief that the voice is produced from the ventriloquist's stomach] — **ven•tri•lo•qui•al** \ˌven-trə-ˈlō-kwē-əl\ *adj* — **ven•tri•lo•qui•al•ly** \-kwē-ə-lē\ *adv*

ven•tril•o•quist \ven-ˈtril-ə-kwəst\ *n* : one who uses or is skilled in ventriloquism; *esp* : a professional entertainer who holds a dummy and apparently carries on conversation with it — **ven•tril•o•quis•tic** \ˌven-ˌtril-ə-ˈkwis-tik\ *adj*

ven•tril•o•quize \ven-ˈtril-ə-ˌkwīz\ *vb* : to use ventriloquism; *also* : to utter in the manner of a ventriloquist

ven•tril•o•quy \ven-ˈtril-ə-kwē\ *n* : VENTRILOQUISM

[1]**ven•ture** \ˈven-chər\ *vb* **ven•tured**; **ven•tur•ing** \ˈvench-ring, -ə-ring\ **1** : to expose to hazard : RISK ⟨*ventured* their savings on the stock market⟩ **2** : to face the risks and dangers of : BRAVE ⟨*ventured* the stormy sea⟩ **3** : to offer at the risk of rebuff or censure ⟨*venture* an opinion⟩ ⟨I *venture* to disagree⟩ **4** : to proceed despite danger ⟨*ventured* down the cliff⟩ [Middle English *venteren,* from *aventuren,* from *aventure* "adventure"] — **ven•tur•er** \ˈvench-rər, -ə-rər\ *n*

[2]**venture** *n* **1** : an undertaking involving chance, risk, or danger; *esp* : a speculative business enterprise **2** : a venturesome act

ven•ture•some \ˈven-chər-səm\ *adj* **1** : inclined to court danger or take risks : DARING ⟨a *venturesome* hunter⟩ **2** : involving risk : HAZARDOUS ⟨a *venturesome* journey⟩ **syn** see ADVENTUROUS — **ven•ture•some•ly** *adv* — **ven•ture•some•ness** *n*

ven•tur•ous \ˈvench-rəs, -ə-rəs\ *adj* **1** : VENTURESOME 1 ⟨*venturous* spirit⟩ **2** : HAZARDOUS ⟨*venturous* enterprises⟩ — **ven•tur•ous•ly** *adv* — **ven•tur•ous•ness** *n*

ven•ue \ˈven-ˌyü\ *n* **1** : the place in which events from which a legal action arises are claimed to take place **2** : the place from which the jury is drawn and in which trial is held in a venue action [Middle French, "action of coming", from *venir* "to come", from Latin *venire*]

ven•ule \ˈvēn-yül, ˈven-\ *n* : a small vein; *esp* : one of the minute veins connecting blood capillaries with larger veins

Ve•nus \ˈvē-nəs\ *n* : the planet 2d in order from the sun — see PLANET table [*Venus,* Roman goddess]

Ve•nu•sian \vi-ˈnü-zhən, -ˈnyü-\ *adj* : of or relating to the planet Venus — **Venusian** *n*

Venus's-flower-basket \ˌvē-nəs-əz-ˈflau̇-ər-ˌbas-kət, ˌvē-nəs-ˈflau̇-, -ˈflau̇r-ˌbas-\ *or* **Venus flower basket** *n* : a tubular or cornucopia-shaped sponge with a delicate glassy silica-containing skeleton

Ve•nus's-fly•trap \ˌvē-nəs-əz-ˈflī-ˌtrap, ˌvē-nəs-ˈflī-\ *or* **Venus flytrap** *n* : an insect-eating plant of the sundew family that grows along the Carolina coast and has the leaf apex modified into an insect trap

Venus's-flytrap

ve•ra•cious \və-ˈrā-shəs\ *adj* **1** : TRUTHFUL, HONEST **2** : marked by truth : ACCURATE, TRUE [Latin *verac-, verax,* from *verus* "true"] — **ve•ra•cious•ly** *adv* — **ve•ra•cious•ness** *n*

ve•rac•i•ty \və-ˈras-ət-ē\ *n, pl* **-ties 1** : devotion to the truth : TRUTHFULNESS **2** : conformity with truth or fact **3** : something true

ve•ran•da *or* **ve•ran•dah** \və-ˈran-də\ *n* : a long roofed gallery extending along one or more sides of a building [Hindi *varaṇḍā*]

verb \ˈvərb\ *n* : a word that characteristically is the grammatical center of a predicate and expresses an act, occurrence, or mode of being and that in various languages is inflected (as for agreement with the subject or for tense) — compare [2]AUXILIARY 2, COPULA [Middle French *verbe,* from Latin *verbum* "word, verb"]

[1]**ver•bal** \ˈvər-bəl\ *adj* **1 a** : consisting of or carried on in words ⟨a baby not yet capable of *verbal* communication⟩ **b** : of, relating to, or involving words only rather than meaning or substance or effective action **2** : of, relating to, or formed from a verb ⟨*verbal* adjectives⟩ **3** : spoken rather than written ⟨a *verbal* contract⟩ ⟨*verbal* instructions⟩ **4** : word-for-word : VERBATIM ⟨*verbal* translation⟩ [Late Latin *verbalis,* from Latin *verbum* "word"] **syn** see ORAL — **ver•bal•ly** \-bə-lē\ *adv*

[2]**verbal** *n* : a word that combines characteristics of a verb with those of a noun or adjective

ver•bal•ism \ˈvər-bə-ˌliz-əm\ *n* **1** : a verbal expression : TERM **2** : words used as if they were more important than the realities they represent **3 a** : a wordy expression of little meaning **b** : the quality or state of being wordy

ver•bal•ist \ˈvər-bə-ləst\ *n* **1** : one who stresses words above substance or reality **2** : a person who uses words skillfully — **ver•bal•is•tic** \ˌvər-bə-ˈlis-tik\ *adj*

ver•bal•ize \ˈvər-bə-ˌlīz\ *vb* **1** : to speak or write in wordy or empty fashion **2** : to express or express something in words : describe verbally **3** : to convert into a verb — **ver•bal•iza•tion** \ˌvər-bə-lə-ˈzā-shən\ *n* — **ver•bal•iz•er** \ˈvər-bə-ˌlī-zər\ *n*

verbal noun *n* : a noun derived directly from a verb or verb stem and in some uses having the sense and constructions of a verb

ver•ba•tim \ˌvər-ˈbāt-əm\ *adv or adj* : word for word : in the same words : LITERAL ⟨a *verbatim* translation⟩ ⟨took down the speech *verbatim*⟩ [Medieval Latin, from Latin *verbum* "word"]

ver•be•na \ˌvər-ˈbē-nə\ *n* : VERVAIN; *esp* : any of numerous garden plants of hybrid origin widely grown for their showy spikes of white, pink, red, or blue flowers which are borne in profusion over a long season [New Latin, genus of plants, from Latin *verbenae* "sacred boughs"]

ver•bi•age \ˈvər-bē-ij\ *n* **1** : excess of words in proportion to sense or content **2** : DICTION 1, WORDING ⟨concise *verbiage*⟩

ver•bo•ten \vər-ˈbōt-n, fər-\ *adj* : forbidden usually by authority and often unreasonably [German, "forbidden"]

ver•bose \ˌvər-ˈbōs\ *adj* : excessively wordy : PROLIX — **ver•bose•ly** *adv* — **ver•bose•ness** *n* — **ver•bos•i•ty** \-ˈbäs-ət-ē\ *n*

ver•dant \ˈvərd-nt\ *adj* **1 a** : green in color ⟨*verdant* grass⟩ **b** : green with growing plants ⟨*verdant* fields⟩ **2** : lacking experience or judgment [Middle French *verdoyant,* from *verdoyer* "to be green", from *verd, vert* "green", from Latin *viridis,* from *virēre* "to be green"] — **ver•dan•cy** \-n-sē\ *n* — **ver•dant•ly** *adv*

ver•dict \ˈvər-dikt\ *n* **1** : the decision of a jury on the matter submitted to them in trial **2** : an opinion held or expressed [Anglo-French *verdit,* from Old French *ver dit* "true dictum"]

ver•di•gris \ˈvərd-ə-ˌgrēs, -ˌgris\ *n* **1** : a green or greenish blue poisonous pigment produced by the action of acetic acid on copper **2** : a green or bluish carbonate of copper formed on copper, bronze, or brass surfaces [Old French *vert de Grice,* literally, "green of Greece"]

ver•dure \ˈvər-jər\ *n* : the greenness of growing vegetation; *also* : such vegetation itself [Middle French, from *verd* "green"] — **ver•dured** \-jərd\ *adj* — **ver•dur•ous** \ˈvərj-rəs, -ə-rəs\ *adj* — **ver•dur•ous•ness** *n*

[1]**verge** \ˈvərj\ *n* **1 a** : a staff carried as an emblem of authority or office **b** : an area around a place or within which jurisdiction is exercised **2 a** : something that borders, limits, or bounds : EDGE, BOUNDARY ⟨the *verge* of the sea⟩ **b** : BRINK, THRESHOLD ⟨on the *verge* of bankruptcy⟩ [Middle French, from Latin *virga* "rod, stripe"]

[2]**verge** *vi* **1** : to be contiguous ⟨Canada *verges* on the United States⟩ **2** : to be on the verge ⟨courage that *verged* on recklessness⟩

[3]**verge** *vi* **1** : to move or extend in some direction or toward some condition : INCLINE **2** : to be in transition or change [Latin *vergere* "to bend, incline"]

verg•er \ˈvər-jər\ *n* **1** *chiefly British* : an attendant who carries a verge (as before a bishop or justice) **2** : a church official who keeps order during services or serves as an usher or a sacristan

ver•i•fi•able \ˈver-ə-ˌfī-ə-bəl\ *adj* : capable of being verified —

ver•i•fi•able•ness *n* — **ver•i•fi•ably** \-blē\ *adv*
ver•i•fy \'ver-ə-ˌfī\ *vt* **-fied; -fy•ing 1 :** to prove to be true or correct : CONFIRM **2 :** to check or test the accuracy of [Middle French *verifier,* from Medieval Latin *verificare,* from Latin *verus* "true"] **syn** see CONFIRM — **ver•i•fi•ca•tion** \ˌver-ə-fə-'kā-shən\ *n* — **ver•i•fi•er** \'ver-ə-ˌfī-ər, -ˌfīr\ *n*
ver•i•ly \'ver-ə-lē\ *adv* **:** in fact : CERTAINLY [Middle English *verraily,* from *verray* "very"]
veri•sim•i•lar \ˌver-ə-'sim-lər, -ə-lər\ *adj* **:** having the appearance of truth : PROBABLE [Latin *verisimilis,* from *veri similis* "like the truth"] — **veri•sim•i•lar•ly** *adv*
veri•si•mil•i•tude \-sə-'mil-ə-ˌtüd, -ˌtyüd\ *n* **1 :** the quality or state of being verisimilar **2 :** something verisimilar
ver•i•ta•ble \'ver-ət-ə-bəl\ *adj* **:** ACTUAL, TRUE — **ver•i•ta•ble•ness** *n* — **ver•i•ta•bly** \-blē\ *adv*
ver•i•ty \'ver-ət-ē\ *n, pl* **-ties 1 :** the quality or state of being true or real **2 :** something true **3 :** VERACITY 1 [Middle French *verité,* from Latin *veritas,* from *verus* "true"]
ver•juice \'vər-ˌjüs\ *n* **1 :** the sour juice of crab apples or unripe fruit (as grapes) or an acid liquor made from this **2 :** sourness of disposition or manner [Middle French *vert jus,* literally, "green juice"]
ver•meil *n* **1** \'vər-məl, -ˌmāl\ **:** VERMILION **2** \veər-'mā\ **:** gilded silver, bronze, or copper [Middle French, from *vermeil,* adj., "bright red, vermilion"] — **vermeil** *adj*
vermi- *combining form* **:** worm ⟨*vermi*fuge⟩ [Latin *vermis*]
ver•mi•cel•li \ˌvər-mə-'chel-ē, -'sel-\ *n* **:** a food like spaghetti but of smaller diameter [Italian, from pl. of *vermicello* "little worm", from *verme* "worm", from Latin *vermis*]
ver•mic•u•late \ˌvər-'mik-yə-lət\ *or* **ver•mic•u•lat•ed** \-ˌlāt-əd\ *adj* **:** TORTUOUS 2b, INVOLUTE [Latin *vermiculatus,* from *vermiculus* "little worm", from *vermis* "worm"] — **ver•mic•u•la•tion** \-ˌmik-yə-'lā-shən\ *n*
ver•mic•u•lite \ˌvər-'mik-yə-ˌlīt\ *n* **:** any of numerous minerals that are usually altered micas whose granules expand greatly at high temperatures to give a lightweight absorbent heat-resistant material used especially in seedbeds and as insulation [Latin *vermiculus* "little worm", from *vermis* "worm"]
vermiform appendix *n* **:** APPENDIX 2a
ver•mi•fuge \'vər-mə-ˌfyüj\ *n* **:** an agent that expels or destroys parasitic worms [*vermi* + Latin *fugare* "to put to flight"]
ver•mil•ion *or* **ver•mil•lion** \vər-'mil-yən\ *n* **1 :** a bright red pigment; *esp* **:** one consisting of a sulfide of mercury **2 :** a vivid reddish orange color [Old French *vermeillon,* from *vermeil,* adj., "bright red, vermilion", from Late Latin *vermiculus* "kermes", from Latin, "little worm", from *vermis* "worm"]
ver•min \'vər-mən\ *n, pl* **vermin 1 :** small common harmful or objectionable animals (as fleas or mice) that are difficult to control **2 :** an offensive person [Middle French, from Latin *vermis* "worm"]
ver•min•ous \'vər-mə-nəs\ *adj* **1 :** consisting of or full of vermin ⟨*verminous* houses⟩ **2 :** caused by vermin ⟨*verminous* disease⟩ — **ver•min•ous•ly** *adv*
ver•mouth \vər-'müth\ *n* **:** a fortified wine flavored with aromatic herbs and used as an aperitif or in mixed drinks [French *vermout,* from German *wermut* "wormwood"]
[1]**ver•nac•u•lar** \vər-'nak-yə-lər, və-'nak-\ *adj* **1 :** using a language or dialect native to a region or country rather than a literary, cultured, or foreign language **2 :** of, relating to, or used in the normal spoken form of a language [Latin *vernaculus* "native", from *verna* "slave born in his master's house, native"] — **ver•nac•u•lar•ly** *adv*
[2]**vernacular** *n* **1 :** a vernacular language **2 :** the mode of expression of a group or class **3 :** a common name of a plant or animal as distinguished from the latinized taxonomic name
ver•nal \'vərn-l\ *adj* **1 :** of, relating to, or occurring in the spring ⟨the *vernal* equinox⟩ ⟨*vernal* sunshine⟩ **2 :** fresh or new like the spring; *also* **:** YOUTHFUL [Latin *vernalis,* from *vernus* "vernal", from *ver* "spring"] — **ver•nal•ly** \-l-ē\ *adv*
ver•nal•ize \'vərn-l-ˌīz\ *vt* **:** to hasten the flowering and fruiting of (plants) by treating seeds, bulbs, or seedlings so as to shorten the vegetative period — **ver•nal•iza•tion** \ˌvərn-l-ə-'zā-shən\ *n*
ver•na•tion \vər-'nā-shən\ *n* **:** the arrangement of foliage leaves within the bud [derived from Latin *vernare* "to behave as in spring", from *vernus* "vernal"]
ver•ni•er \'vər-nē-ər\ *n* **1 :** a short scale made to slide along the divisions of a graduated instrument for indicating parts of divisions **2 :** a small auxiliary device used with a main device to obtain fine adjustment [Pierre *Vernier,* died 1637, French mathematician]
vernier caliper *n* **:** a caliper gauge with a graduated beam and a sliding jaw having a vernier
ve•ron•i•ca \və-'rän-i-kə\ *n* **:** SPEEDWELL [New Latin]
ver•ru•cose \və-'rü-ˌkōs\ *adj* **:** covered with warty elevations [Latin *verrucosus,* from *verruca* "wart"]
ver•sa•tile \'vər-sət-l\ *adj* **1 :** changing or fluctuating readily : VARIABLE **2 :** taking in a variety of subjects, fields, or skills; *also* **:** turning with ease from one thing or position to another **3 :** having many uses or applications [Latin versatilis "turning easily", from *versare* "to turn", from *versus,* past participle of *vertere* "to turn"] — **ver•sa•tile•ly** \-sət-l-lē, -sət-l-ē\ *adv* — **ver•sa•tile•ness** \-l-nəs\ *n* — **ver•sa•til•i•ty** \ˌvər-sə-'til-ət-ē\ *n*
[1]**verse** \'vərs\ *n* **1 :** a line of metrical writing **2 a :** light or superficial metrical writing **b :** POETRY ⟨Elizabethan *verse*⟩ **c :** POEM ⟨read the group some *verses*⟩ **3 :** STANZA **4 :** one of the short divisions into which a chapter of the Bible is traditionally divided [Old French *vers,* from Latin *versus,* literally, "turning", from *vertere* "to turn"]
[2]**verse** *vb* **:** VERSIFY
[3]**verse** *vt* **:** to familiarize by study or experience ⟨*verse* oneself in history⟩ [back-formation from *versed,* from Latin *versatus,* past participle of *versari* "to be active, be occupied (in)", passive of *versare* "to turn"]
ver•si•cle \'vər-si-kəl\ *n* **1 :** a short verse or sentence said or sung in public worship by a leader and followed by a response from the people **2 :** a little verse [Latin *versiculus* "small verse", from *versus* "verse"]
ver•si•fi•ca•tion \ˌvər-sə-fə-'kā-shən\ *n* **1 :** the making of verses **2 :** metrical arrangement of poetry
ver•si•fy \'vər-sə-ˌfī\ *vb* **-fied; -fy•ing 1 :** to compose or turn into verse **2 :** to relate or describe in verse — **ver•si•fi•er** \-ˌfī-ər, -ˌfīr\ *n*
ver•sion \'vər-zhən\ *n* **1 :** a translation from another language; *esp* **:** a translation of the Bible or a part of it **2 a :** an account or description from one point of view especially as contrasted with another **b :** an adaptation of a literary or musical work ⟨a stage *version* of the novel⟩ **3 :** a form or variation of an original ⟨an experimental *version* of the plane⟩ **4 :** manual turning of the fetus in the uterus to aid delivery [Middle French, from Medieval Latin *versio* "act of turning", from *vertere* "to turn"] — **ver•sion•al** \'vərzh-nəl, -ən-l\ *adj*
ver•so \'vər-sō\ *n, pl* **versos :** a left-hand page — compare RECTO [New Latin *verso folio* "the page being turned"]
verst \'vərst\ *n* **:** a Russian unit of distance equal to 0.6629 miles (about 1.067 kilometers) [French *verste* and German *werst,* both from Russian *versta*]
ver•sus \'vər-səs, -səz\ *prep* **1 :** AGAINST 2a ⟨United States *versus* Doe⟩ **2 :** in contrast to or as the alternative of ⟨free trade *versus* protection⟩ [Medieval Latin, "towards, against", derived from Latin *vertere* "to turn"]
vert \'vərt\ *n* **:** the heraldic color green [Middle French *vert* "green"]
ver•te•bra \'vərt-ə-brə\ *n, pl* **-brae** \-ˌbrē, -ˌbrā\ *or* **-bras :** one of the bony or cartilaginous segments composing the spinal column that in higher vertebrates have a short nearly cylindrical body with ends articulating with adjacent vertebrae and a bony arch enclosing the spinal cord [Latin, "joint, vertebra", from *vertere* "to turn"]

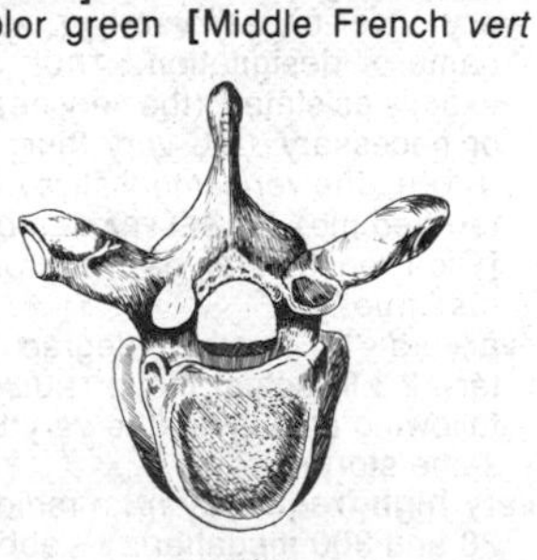
vertebra

ver•te•bral \vər-'tē-brəl\ *adj* **:** of, relating to, or made up of vertebrae : SPINAL — **ver•te•bral•ly** \-ē\ *adv*
vertebral column *n* **:** SPINAL COLUMN
[1]**ver•te•brate** \'vərt-ə-brət, -ˌbrāt\ *adj* **1 a :** having a spinal col-

\ə\ **abut**	\au̇\ **out**	\i\ **tip**	\ȯ\ **saw**	\u̇\ **foot**
\ər\ **further**	\ch\ **chin**	\ī\ **life**	\ȯi\ **coin**	\y\ **yet**
\a\ **mat**	\e\ **pet**	\j\ **job**	\th\ **thin**	\yü\ **few**
\ā\ **take**	\ē\ **easy**	\ng\ **sing**	\t͟h\ **this**	\yu̇\ **cure**
\ä\ **cot, cart**	\g\ **go**	\ō\ **bone**	\ü\ **food**	\zh\ **vision**

umn **b :** of or relating to the vertebrates **2 :** having a strong framework suggesting vertebrae

[2]vertebrate *n* **:** any of a primary division (Vertebrata) of chordates comprising animals (as mammals, birds, reptiles, amphibians, or fishes) with a segmented spinal column together with a few primitive forms in which the backbone is represented by a notochord

ver•tex \'vər-ˌteks\ *n, pl* **ver•ti•ces** \'vərt-ə-ˌsēz\ *also* **ver•tex•es** **1 a :** the point opposite to and farthest from a base of a figure **b :** the common endpoint of the sides of an angle **c :** a point where the axis of an ellipse, parabola, or hyperbola intersects the curve itself **d :** ZENITH 1 **2 :** the top of the head **3 :** the highest point **:** SUMMIT, APEX [Latin *vertic-, vertex* "whirlpool, top of the head, summit", from *vertere* "to turn"]

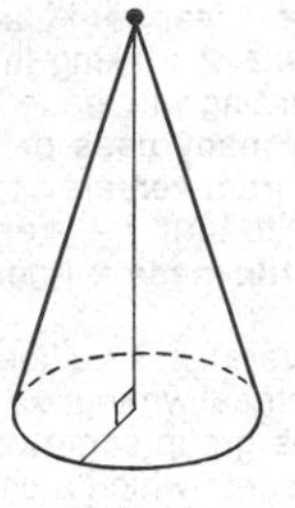
vertex 1a

ver•ti•cal \'vərt-i-kəl\ *adj* **1 :** situated at the highest point **:** directly overhead or in the zenith **2 :** perpendicular to the plane of the horizon or to a primary axis **:** UPRIGHT **3 :** relating to or composed of separate units on different levels ⟨a *vertical* business organization⟩ — **vertical** *n* — **ver•ti•cal•i•ty** \ˌvərt-ə-'kal-ət-ē\ *n* — **ver•ti•cal•ly** \'vərt-i-kə-lē, -klē\ *adv* — **ver•ti•cal•ness** \-kəl-nəs\ *n*

• **syn** VERTICAL, PERPENDICULAR, PLUMB mean being at right angles to a base line. VERTICAL suggests a line or direction rising straight upward toward a zenith; PERPENDICULAR may stress the stiff straightness of a line making a right angle with any other line, not necessarily a horizontal one; PLUMB stresses an exact verticality determined (as with a plumb line) by earth's gravity.

vertical angle *n* **:** one of two angles that have the same vertex and are on opposite sides of two intersecting straight lines

vertical circle *n* **:** a great circle of the celestial sphere whose plane is perpendicular to that of the horizon

vertical file *n* **:** a collection especially of pamphlets and clippings maintained (as in a library) to answer brief questions or to provide information not easily located elsewhere

ver•ti•go \'vərt-i-ˌgō\ *n, pl* **-goes** *or* **-gos** **:** a dizzy or giddy state [Latin, from *vertere* "to turn"]

ver•vain \'vər-ˌvān\ *n* **:** any of a genus of mostly American herbaceous or shrubby plants with often showy heads or spikes of 5-parted regular flowers — called also *verbena* [Middle French *verveine,* from Latin *verbenae* "sacred boughs"]

verve \'vərv\ *n* **1 :** the spirit and enthusiasm that animate artistic composition or performance **:** VIVACITY **2 :** ENERGY 1, VITALITY [French, from Latin *verba,* pl. of *verbum* "word"]

[1]very \'ver-ē\ *adj* **ver•i•er; -est** **1 a :** properly entitled to the name or designation **:** TRUE **b :** ACTUAL 1, REAL **2 a :** being exactly as stated ⟨the *very* heart of the city⟩ **b :** exactly suitable or necessary ⟨the *very* thing for the purpose⟩ **3 :** ABSOLUTE, UTTER ⟨the *veriest* fool alive⟩ **4 :** MERE, BARE ⟨the *very* thought terrified me⟩ **5 :** SELFSAME, IDENTICAL ⟨the *very* person I saw⟩ [Old French *verai,* derived from Latin *verax* "truthful", from *verus* "true"]

[2]very *adv* **1 :** to a high degree ⟨a *very* hot day⟩ ⟨*very* much better⟩ **2 :** in actual fact **:** TRULY — used to give emphasis to a following adjective ⟨the *very* best store in town⟩ ⟨told the *very* same story⟩

very high frequency *n* **:** a radio frequency in the range between 30 and 300 megahertz — abbreviation *VHF*

Very light \ˌver-ē-, ˌviər-ē-\ *n* **:** a pyrotechnic signal in a system of signaling using white or colored balls of fire shot from a special pistol [Edward W. *Very,* died 1910, American naval officer]

very low frequency *n* **:** a radio frequency in the range between 3 and 30 kilohertz — abbreviation *VLF*

Very Reverend — used as a title for various religious officials (as cathedral deans and canons and rectors of Roman Catholic seminaries and colleges)

ves•i•cant \'ves-i-kənt\ *n* **:** an agent (as a drug or a plant substance) that causes blistering [Latin *vesica* "bladder, blister"] — **vesicant** *adj*

ves•i•cle \'ves-i-kəl\ *n* **1 :** a membranous and usually fluid-filled pouch (as a cyst or vacuole) in a plant or animal; *also* **:** a small abnormal elevation of the outer layer of skin enclosing a watery liquid **:** BLISTER **2 :** a small cavity especially in mineral or rock [Middle French *vesicule,* from Latin *vesicula* "small bladder", from *vesica* "bladder"] — **ve•sic•u•lar** \və-'sik-yə-lər\ *adj* — **ve•sic•u•lar•ly** *adv*

[1]ves•per \'ves-pər\ *n* **1** *cap* **:** EVENING STAR **2 :** a vesper bell **3** *archaic* **:** EVENING 1 [Latin, "evening, evening star"]

[2]vesper *adj* **:** of or relating to vespers or the evening

ves•pers \'ves-pərz\ *n, pl, often cap* **1 :** the sixth of the canonical hours **2 :** a late afternoon or evening worship service

ves•per•tine \'ves-pər-ˌtīn\ *adj* **:** of, relating to, or occurring in the evening ⟨*vespertine* shadows⟩ [Latin *vespertinus,* from *vesper* "evening"]

ves•sel \'ves-əl\ *n* **1 a :** a hollow or concave utensil (as a hogshead, bottle, kettle, cup, or bowl) for holding something **b :** a person held to be the recipient of a quality (as grace) **2 :** a structure built for transportation on water **:** BOAT, SHIP; *esp* **:** one larger than a rowboat **3 a :** a tube or canal (as an artery) in which a body fluid is contained and conveyed or circulated **b :** a conducting tube in a vascular plant [Old French *vaissel,* from Late Latin *vascellum,* from Latin *vas* "vase, vessel"]

[1]vest \'vest\ *vb* **1 a :** to place or give (as a right, authority, or title) into the possession or discretion of some person or body ⟨powers *vested* in the presidency⟩ **b :** to become legally vested ⟨the title *vests* in the purchaser⟩ **2 a :** to clothe with or as if with a garment; *esp* **:** to garb in clerical vestments **b :** to put on garments and especially clerical vestments [Middle French *vestir* "to clothe, invest", from Latin *vestire* "to clothe", from *vestis* "clothing, garment"]

[2]vest *n* **1 a :** a sleeveless garment typically worn under a suit coat **b :** a protective usually sleeveless garment (as a life preserver) that extends to the waist **2 :** a plain or decorative piece used to fill in the front neckline of a woman's outer garment (as a coat, or gown) [French *veste* "robe, jacket", from Italian, from Latin *vestis* "garment"]

[2]vest 1a

ves•tal \'ves-tl\ *n* **1 :** a virgin consecrated to the Roman goddess Vesta and to the service of a sacred fire perpetually kept burning on her altar — called also *vestal virgin* **2 :** a chaste woman — **vestal** *adj*

vested interest *n* **1 :** an interest (as in an existing economic or political arrangement) in which the holder has a strong personal commitment **2 :** one having a vested interest in something

vest•ee \ve-'stē\ *n* **1 :** DICKEY; *esp* **:** one made to resemble a vest and worn under a coat **2 :** VEST 2

ves•ti•ary \'ves-tē-ˌer-ē, 'ves-chē-\ *n, pl* **-ar•ies** **1 :** a room where clothing is kept **2 :** CLOTHING; *esp* **:** clerical vestments [Old French *vestiarie* "vestry"]

ves•tib•u•lar \ve-'stib-yə-lər\ *adj* **:** of, relating to, or functioning as a vestibule

ves•ti•bule \'ves-tə-ˌbyül\ *n* **1 a :** a passage or room between the outer door and the interior of a building **:** LOBBY **b :** an enclosed entrance at the end of a railway passenger car **2 :** any of various bodily cavities mostly serving as or resembling an entrance to some other cavity or space; *esp* **:** the central cavity of the labyrinth of the ear [Latin *vestibulum*]

ves•tige \'ves-tij\ *n* **1 a :** a visible sign left by something vanished or lost **b :** a minute remaining amount **2 :** a small and imperfectly developed bodily part or organ that remains from one more fully developed in an earlier stage of the individual, in a past generation, or in closely related forms [French, from Latin *vestigium* "footprint, track, vestige"] **syn** see TRACE — **ves•ti•gial** \ve-'stij-əl, -'stij-ē-əl\ *adj* — **ves•ti•gial•ly** \-ē\ *adv*

vest•ment \'vest-mənt, 'ves-\ *n* **1 a :** an outer garment; *esp* **:** a ceremonial or official robe **b** *pl* **:** CLOTHING, GARB **2 :** a covering resembling a garment **3 :** a ceremonial garment worn by a person officiating at a religious service — **vest•ment•al** \vest-ˈment-l, ves-\ *adj*

vest–pock•et \ˌvest-ˌpäk-ət\ *adj* **1** : adapted to fit into the vest pocket **2** : of very small size or scope

ves•try \ˈves-trē\ *n, pl* **vestries 1 a** : SACRISTY **b** : a room used for church meetings and classes **2 a** : the business meeting of an English parish; *also* : the parishioners assembled for it **b** : an elective body administering the business affairs of an Episcopal parish [probably from Middle French *vestiarie,* from Medieval Latin *vestiarium,* from Latin *vestire* "to clothe"]

ves•try•man \-mən\ *n* : a member of a vestry

ves•try•wom•an \-ˌwu̇m-ən\ *n* : a woman who is a member of a vestry

ves•ture \ˈves-chər\ *n* **1 a** : a covering garment (as a robe or vestment) **b** : CLOTHING, APPAREL **2** : something that covers like a garment

[1]vet \ˈvet\ *n* : VETERINARIAN, VETERINARY

[2]vet *vt* **vet•ted; vet•ting 1** *chiefly British* : to provide veterinary care for (an animal) or medical care for (a person) **2** : to subject to expert appraisal or correction

[3]vet *adj or n* : VETERAN

vetch \ˈvech\ *n* : any of a genus of herbaceous twining plants related to the pea that include valuable fodder and soil-building plants [Old North French *veche,* from Latin *vicia*]

vet•er•an \ˈvet-ə-rən, ˈve-trən\ *n* **1** : a person who has had long experience in an occupation or skill and especially in war **2** : a former member of the armed forces [Latin *veteranus* "soldier of long experience", derived from *veter-, vetus* "old"]

Veterans Day *n* : November 11 observed as a legal holiday in commemoration of the end of hostilities in 1918 and 1945

vet•er•i•nar•i•an \ˌvet-ə-rən-ˈer-ē-ən, ˌve-trən-, ˌvet-n-\ *n* : one qualified and authorized to treat diseases and injuries of animals

[1]vet•er•i•nary \ˈvet-ə-rən-ˌer-ē, ˈve-trən-, ˈvet-n-\ *adj* : of, relating to, or being the medical care of animals and especially domestic animals [derived from Latin *veterinus* "of beasts of burden"]

[2]veterinary *n, pl* **-nar•ies** : VETERINARIAN

[1]veto \ˈvēt-ō\ *n, pl* **vetoes 1** : an authoritative rejection or prohibition **2 a** : a power of one branch of a government to forbid or prohibit the carrying out of projects attempted by another department; *esp* : the power of a chief executive to prevent a measure passed by a legislature from becoming law **b** : the exercise of such authority **c** : a power possessed by members of a body (as the United Nations Security Council) to prohibit action by the body [Latin, "I forbid", from *vetare* "to forbid"]

[2]veto *vt* : to refuse to admit or approve : PROHIBIT; *esp* : to refuse assent to (a legislative bill) so as to prevent enactment or cause reconsideration — **ve•to•er** \ˈvēt-ˌō-ər, -ˌōr\ *n*

vex \ˈveks\ *vt* **vexed** *also* **vext; vex•ing 1 a** : to bring trouble, distress, or agitation to **b** : to irritate or annoy by petty provocations : HARASS **c** : PUZZLE 1, BAFFLE **2** : to debate or discuss at length ⟨a *vexed* question⟩ **3** : to shake or toss about [Middle French *vexer,* from Latin *vexare*]

vex•a•tion \vek-ˈsā-shən\ *n* **1** : the quality or state of being vexed : IRRITATION **2** : the act of vexing : ANNOYANCE **3** : a cause of trouble or worry

vex•a•tious \-shəs\ *adj* **1 a** : causing vexation ⟨a *vexatious* child⟩ **b** : intended to harass ⟨a *vexatious* lawsuit⟩ **2** : full of disorder or stress — **vex•a•tious•ly** *adv* — **vex•a•tious•ness** *n*

via \ˌvī-ə, ˌvē-ə\ *prep* **1** : by way of **2** : through the medium of; *also* : by means of [Latin, ablative of *via* "way"]

vi•a•ble \ˈvī-ə-bəl\ *adj* **1** : capable of living; *esp* : born alive with such form and development of organs as to be normally capable of living **2** : capable of growing or developing ⟨*viable* seeds⟩ ⟨*viable* eggs⟩ **3** : WORKABLE ⟨a *viable* plan⟩ [French, from *vie* "life", from Latin *vita*] — **vi•a•bil•i•ty** \ˌvī-ə-ˈbil-ət-ē\ *n* — **vi•a•bly** \ˈvī-ə-blē\ *adv*

vi•a•duct \ˈvī-ə-ˌdəkt\ *n* : a bridge with high supporting towers or piers for carrying a road or railroad over something (as a gorge or a highway) [Latin *via* "way, road" + English *-duct* (as in *aqueduct*)]

vi•al \ˈvī-əl, ˈvīl\ *n* : a small vessel for liquids (as medicines or chemicals) [Middle French *fiole,* from Provençal *fiola,* from Latin *phiala,* from Greek *phialē*]

vi•and \ˈvī-ənd\ *n* **1** : an item of food **2** *pl* : PROVISION 2, FOOD [Middle French *viande,* from Medieval Latin *vivanda* "food", derived from Latin *vivere* "to live"]

vi•at•i•cum \vī-ˈat-i-kəm, vē-\ *n, pl* **-cums** *or* **-ca** \-kə\ **1** : money or provisions for a journey **2** : Communion given to a person in danger of death [Latin, "traveling money", from *viaticus* "of a journey", from *via* "way"]

viaduct

vi•brant \ˈvī-brənt\ *adj* **1 a** (1) : oscillating or pulsating rapidly (2) : pulsating with life, vigor, or activity ⟨a *vibrant* personality⟩ **b** (1) : readily set in vibration (2) : RESPONSIVE 2, SENSITIVE **2** : sounding as a result of vibration : RESONANT — **vi•bran•cy** \-brən-sē\ *n* — **vi•brant•ly** \-brənt-lē\ *adv*

vi•bra•phone \ˈvī-brə-ˌfōn\ *n* : a percussion musical instrument resembling the xylophone but having metal bars and motor-driven resonators for sustaining the tone and producing a vibrato — **vi•bra•phon•ist** \-ˌfō-nəst\ *n*

vi•brate \ˈvī-ˌbrāt\ *vb* **1** : to swing or move back and forth ⟨a *vibrating* pendulum⟩ **2** : to set in vibration **3** : to oscillate very rapidly so as to produce a quivering effect or sound : SHAKE, QUIVER ⟨guitar strings *vibrate* when plucked⟩ **4** : to respond sympathetically : THRILL **5** : WAVER 1, FLUCTUATE [Latin *vibrare*] **syn** see SWAY

vi•bra•tile \ˈvī-brət-l, -brə-ˌtīl\ *adj* **1** : characterized by vibration **2** : adapted to or used in vibratory motion ⟨the *vibratile* organs of insects⟩

vi•bra•tion \vī-ˈbrā-shən\ *n* **1 a** : the action of vibrating : the state of being vibrated **b** : motion or a movement to and fro : OSCILLATION ⟨the *vibration* of a pendulum⟩ **c** : a periodic motion of the particles of an elastic body or medium rapidly to and fro (as when a stretched cord is pulled or struck and produces a musical tone or when particles of air transmit sounds to the ear) **d** : a quivering or trembling motion ⟨*vibration* of a house caused by a passing truck⟩ **2** : vacillation in opinion or action : WAVERING — **vi•bra•tion•al** \-shnəl, -shən-l\ *adj* — **vi•bra•tion•less** \-shən-ləs\ *adj*

vi•bra•to \vi-ˈbrät-ō, vī-\ *n, pl* **-tos 1** : a slightly trembling effect given to vocal or instrumental tone by slight and rapid variations in pitch **2** : TREMOLO 1b [Italian, from *vibrare* "to vibrate", from Latin]

vi•bra•tor \ˈvī-ˌbrāt-ər\ *n* **1** : one that vibrates or causes vibration **2** : an electromagnetic device that converts low direct current to pulsating direct current or alternating current

vi•bra•to•ry \ˈvī-brə-ˌtōr-ē, -ˌtȯr-\ *adj* **1** : consisting in, capable of, or causing vibration **2** : characterized by vibration : VIBRANT

vib•rio \ˈvib-rē-ˌō\ *n, pl* **-ri•os** : any of a genus of short rigid motile bacteria that are typically shaped like a comma or an S and include serious pathogens (as of Asiatic cholera) [New Latin, from Latin *vibrare* "to vibrate"] — **vib•ri•on•ic** \ˌvib-rē-ˈän-ik\ *adj*

vi•bris•sa \vī-ˈbris-ə, və-\ *n, pl* **vi•bris•sae** \vī-ˈbris-ē; və-ˈbris-ē, -ˌī\ : any of the stiff mostly tactile hairs especially about the face in many mammals [Latin] — **vi•bris•sal** \-ˈbris-əl\ *adj*

vi•bur•num \vī-ˈbər-nəm\ *n* : any of a genus of widely distributed shrubs or trees of the honeysuckle family with simple leaves and white or rarely pink flowers in broad clusters [Latin]

vic•ar \ˈvik-ər\ *n* **1** : AGENT; *esp* : an administrative deputy **2** : an Anglican parish priest who does not hold the right to the tithes **3** : a member of the Episcopal clergy in charge of a mission or a dependent parish [Latin *vicarius,* from *vicarius* "vicarious"] — **vic•ar•ship** \-ˌship\ *n*

vic•ar•age \ˈvik-rij, -ə-rij\ *n* : the benefice or house of a vicar

vicar apostolic *n, pl* **vicars apostolic** : a Roman Catholic titular bishop who administers an ecclesiastical territory not organized as a diocese

vicar–general *n, pl* **vicars–general** : an administrative deputy of

\ə\ **abut**	\au̇\ **out**	\i\ **tip**	\ȯ\ **saw**	\u̇\ **foot**
\ər\ **further**	\ch\ **chin**	\ī\ **life**	\ȯi\ **coin**	\y\ **yet**
\a\ **mat**	\e\ **pet**	\j\ **job**	\th\ **thin**	\yü\ **few**
\ā\ **take**	\ē\ **easy**	\ng\ **sing**	\t͟h\ **this**	\yu̇\ **cure**
\ä\ **cot, cart**	\g\ **go**	\ō\ **bone**	\ü\ **food**	\zh\ **vision**

a Roman Catholic or Anglican bishop or of the head of a religious order

vi•car•i•al \vī-'ker-ē-əl, və-, -'kar-\ *adj* **1 :** VICARIOUS 1 **2 :** of or relating to a vicar

vi•car•i•ate \-ē-ət\ *n* **:** the office, jurisdiction, or tenure of a vicar

vi•car•i•ous \vī-'ker-ē-əs, və-, -'kar-\ *adj* **1 :** serving instead of someone or something else **2 :** performed or suffered by one person as a substitute for another or to the benefit of another ⟨*vicarious* sacrifice⟩ **3 :** experienced or realized through imaginative or sympathetic participation in the experience of another ⟨*vicarious* pleasure⟩ [Latin *vicarius,* from *vicis* "change, alternation, stead"] — **vi•car•i•ous•ly** *adv* — **vi•car•i•ous•ness** *n*

Vicar of Christ : the Roman Catholic pope

[1]**vice** \'vīs\ *n* **1 a :** moral depravity or corruption **:** WICKEDNESS **b :** a moral fault or failing **c :** a minor fault **:** FOIBLE **2 :** BLEMISH, DEFECT **3 :** an undesirable behavior pattern in a domestic animal **4 :** sexual immorality; *esp* **:** PROSTITUTION [Old French, from Latin *vitium* "fault, vice"]

[2]**vice** *n, chiefly British* **:** VISE

[3]**vi•ce** \'vī-sē\ *prep* **:** in the place of [Latin, ablative of *vicis* "change, alternation, stead"]

vice- \vīs, 'vīs, ˌvīs\ *prefix* **:** one that takes the place of ⟨*vice*-president⟩

See *vice-* and 2d element

vice-chairman	**vice-consul**	**vice-premier**
vice-chairwoman	**vice-dean**	**vice-principal**
vice-chamberlain	**vice-director**	**vice-rector**
vice-chancellor	**vice-marshal**	**vice-regent**
vice-chancellorship	**vice-mayor**	**vice-secretary-general**
vice-commander		

vice admiral *n* **:** an officer rank in the Navy and Coast Guard above rear admiral and below admiral

vi•cen•ni•al \vī-'sen-ē-əl\ *adj* **:** occurring once every 20 years [Late Latin *vicennium* "period of 20 years", from Latin *vicies* "20 times" + *annus* "year"]

vice–pres•i•dent \vīs-'prez-əd-ənt, 'vīs-, -'prez-dənt *also* -ə-ˌdent\ *n* **:** an official (as of a government) whose rank is next below that of the president and who takes the place of the president when necessary — **vice–pres•i•den•cy** \-'prez-əd-ən-sē, -'prez-dən-sē *also* -ə-ˌden-sē\ *n* — **vice–pres•i•den•tial** \ˌvīs-ˌprez-ə-'den-chəl\ *adj*

vice•re•gal \-'rē-gəl\ *adj* **:** of or relating to a viceroy or viceroyalty — **vice•re•gal•ly** \-gə-lē\ *adv*

vice•reine \'vīs-ˌrān\ *n* **1 :** the wife of a viceroy **2 :** a woman who is a viceroy [French, from *vice-* "vice-" + *reine* "queen", from Latin *regina,* from *reg-, rex* "king"]

vice•roy \'vīs-ˌrȯi\ *n* **1 :** the governor of a country or province who represents a sovereign **2 :** a black and orange American butterfly resembling but smaller than the monarch [Middle French *vice-roi,* from *vice-* "vice-" + *roi* "king", from Latin *reg-, rex*] — **vice•roy•ship** \-ˌship\ *n*

vice•roy•al•ty \'vīs-ˌrȯi-əl-tē, -ˌrȯil-tē\ *n* **:** the office, jurisdiction, or term of service of a viceroy

vice ver•sa \ˌvī-si-'vər-sə, vīs-'vər-, 'vīs-'vər-\ *adv* **:** with the order changed **:** CONVERSELY [Latin]

vi•chys•soise \ˌvish-ē-'swäz, ˌvē-shē-\ *n* **:** a soup of pureed leeks or onions and potatoes, cream, and chicken stock that is usually served cold [French, from *vichyssois* "of Vichy", from *Vichy,* France]

Vi•chy water \'vish-ē-\ *n* **:** a natural sparkling mineral water from Vichy, France; *also* **:** an imitation of or substitute for this

vic•i•nage \'vis-n-ij, 'vis-nij\ *n* **:** VICINITY 2

vic•i•nal \'vis-n-əl, 'vis-nəl\ *adj* **:** of or relating to a limited district **:** LOCAL

vi•cin•i•ty \və-'sin-ət-ē\ *n, pl* **-ties 1 :** the quality or state of being near **:** PROXIMITY **2 :** a surrounding area or district **3 :** NEIGHBORHOOD 2b [Middle French *vicinité,* from Latin *vicinitas,* from *vicinus* "neighboring", from *vicus* "row of houses, village"]

vi•cious \'vish-əs\ *adj* **1 a :** given to vice **:** WICKED **b :** constituting vice **:** IMMORAL **2 a :** DEFECTIVE 1, FAULTY **b :** INVALID **3 :** IMPURE b, NOXIOUS **4 a :** dangerously aggressive ⟨a *vicious* dog⟩ **b :** extreme in degree, power, or effect **:** FIERCE ⟨a *vicious* storm⟩ **5 :** MALICIOUS, SPITEFUL ⟨*vicious* slander⟩ — **vicious•ly** *adv* — **vi•cious•ness** *n*

vicious circle *n* **1 :** a chain of events in which the apparent solution of one difficulty creates a new problem that makes the original difficulty worse **2 :** an argument or definition that assumes as true something that is to be proved or defined

vi•cis•si•tude \və-'sis-ə-ˌtüd, vī-, -ˌtyüd\ *n* **:** a change or succession from one thing to another; *esp* **:** an often unfavorable event or situation that occurs by chance ⟨the *vicissitudes* of the weather⟩ [Middle French, from Latin *vicissitudo,* from *vicissim* "in turn", from *vicis* "change, alternation"] — **vi•cis•si•tu•di•nous** \-ˌsis-ə-'tüd-n-əs, -'tyüd-\ *adj*

vic•tim \'vik-təm\ *n* **1 :** a living being offered as a sacrifice in a religious rite **2 :** an individual injured or killed (as by disease or accident) **3 :** a person cheated, fooled, or damaged by someone else or by an impersonal force ⟨a mugger's *victim*⟩ ⟨a *victim* of circumstance⟩ [Latin *victima*]

vic•tim•ize \'vik-tə-ˌmīz\ *vt* **:** to make a victim of especially by deception **:** CHEAT — **vic•tim•iza•tion** \ˌvik-tə-mə-'zā-shən\ *n* — **vic•tim•iz•er** \'vik-tə-ˌmī-zər\ *n*

vic•tor \'vik-tər\ *n* **:** one that defeats an enemy or opponent **:** WINNER [Latin, from *victus,* past participle of *vincere* "to conquer, win"] — **victor** *adj*

vic•to•ria \vik-'tōr-ē-ə, -'tȯr-\ *n* **1 :** a low four-wheeled pleasure carriage for two with a folding top and a raised seat in front for the driver **2 :** an old-fashioned automobile with a folding top that usually extends over the rear seat only **3 :** any of a genus of very large South American water lilies with immense rose-white flowers [*Victoria,* queen of England]

victoria 1

[1]**Vic•to•ri•an** \vik-'tōr-ē-ən, -'tȯr-\ *adj* **1 :** of or relating to the reign of Queen Victoria of England or the art, literature, or taste of her time **2 :** typical of the moral standards or conduct of the age of Victoria especially when regarded as stuffy or hypocritical — **Vic•to•ri•an•ism** \-ē-ə-ˌniz-əm\ *n*

[2]**Victorian** *n* **:** a person living during Queen Victoria's reign; *esp* **:** a typical figure of that time

Vic•to•ri•an•ize \-ē-ə-ˌnīz\ *vt* **:** to make Victorian (as in style or taste)

vic•to•ri•ous \vik-'tōr-ē-əs, -'tȯr-\ *adj* **:** having won a victory ⟨a *victorious* army⟩ ⟨*victorious* strategy⟩ — **vic•to•ri•ous•ly** *adv* — **vic•to•ri•ous•ness** *n*

vic•to•ry \'vik-tə-rē, -trē\ *n, pl* **-ries 1 :** the overcoming of an enemy or opponent **2 :** achievement of success in a struggle against odds or difficulties [Middle French *victorie,* from Latin *victoria,* derived from *vincere* "to conquer, win"]

• syn VICTORY, CONQUEST, TRIUMPH mean a successful outcome in a contest or struggle. VICTORY stresses the fact of winning against an opponent or against odds ⟨the *victory* of good over evil⟩ CONQUEST implies the subjugation of a defeated opponent ⟨the *conquest* of Mexico⟩ TRIUMPH suggests acclaim and personal satisfaction to the victor following a brilliant victory or achievement ⟨the *triumphs* of the space flights⟩

[1]**vict•ual** \'vit-l\ *n* **1 :** food usable by humans **2** *pl* **a :** supplies of food **b :** food prepared and served [Middle French *vitaille,* from Late Latin *victualia* "victuals", derived from Latin *victus* "nourishment", from *vivere* "to live"]

[2]**victual** *vb* **-ualed** *or* **-ualled; -ual•ing** *or* **-ual•ling 1 :** to supply with food **2 :** EAT 1, 2 **3 :** to lay in provisions

vict•ual•ler *or* **vict•ual•er** \'vit-l-ər\ *n* **1 :** the keeper of a restaurant or tavern **2 :** one that furnishes provisions (as to an army or a ship)

vi•cu•ña *or* **vi•cu•na** \vi-'kün-yə, vī-; vī-'kü-nə, və-, -'kyü-\ *n* **1 :** a wild ruminant of the Andes that is related to the domesticated llama and alpaca **2 a :** the wool from the vicuña's fine lustrous undercoat **b :** a fabric made of vicuña wool; *also* **:** a sheep's-wool imitation of this [Spanish *vicuña,* from Quechua *wikúña*]

vi•de \'vīd-ē, 'vē-ˌdā\ *imperative verb* **:** SEE — used to direct a reader to another item [Latin, from *vidēre* "to see"]

vi•de•li•cet \və-'del-ə-ˌset, vī-; vi-'dā-li-ˌket\ *adv* **:** that is to say **:** NAMELY — abbreviation *viz.* [Latin, from *vidēre* "to see" + *licet* "it is permitted"]

[1]vid•eo \'vid-ē-,ō\ *adj* : relating to or used in the transmission or reception of the television image ⟨*video* channel⟩ — compare AUDIO [Latin *vidēre* "to see" + English *-o* (as in *audio*)]

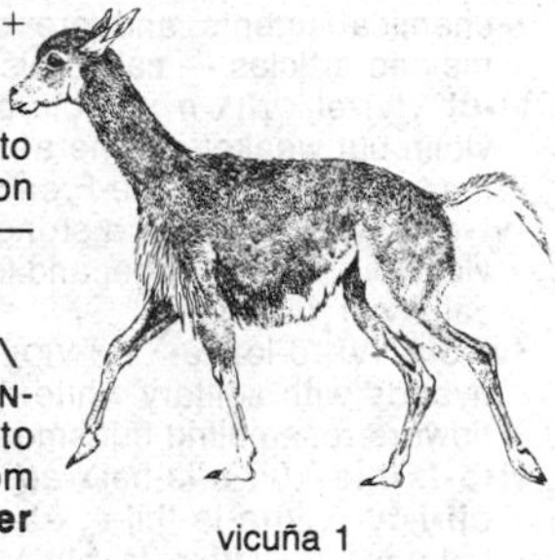

vicuña 1

[2]video *n* : TELEVISION

vid•eo•tape \'vid-ē-ō-,tāp\ *vt* : to make a recording of (a television production) on magnetic tape — **videotape** *n*

vi•dette *variant of* VEDETTE

vie \'vī\ *vi* **vied**; **vy•ing** \'vī-ing\ : to strive for superiority : CONTEND [Middle French *envier* "to invite, challenge, wager", from Latin *invitare* "to invite"] — **vi•er** \'vī-ər, 'vīr\ *n*

Vi•en•na sausage \vē-,en-ə-\ *n* : a short slender frankfurter [*Vienna*, Austria]

Viet•nam•ese \vē-,et-nə-'mēz, ,vyet-, ,vē-ət-, ,vēt-, -na-, -nä-, -'mēs\ *n, pl* **Vietnamese** **1** : a native or inhabitant of Vietnam **2** : the language of the largest group in Vietnam and the official language of the country — **Vietnamese** *adj*

[1]view \'vyü\ *n* **1** : the act of seeing or examining : INSPECTION; *also* : SURVEY **2** : manner of looking at or regarding something : OPINION, JUDGMENT ⟨state one's *views*⟩ **3** : SCENE, PROSPECT ⟨the *view* from my window⟩ **4** : extent or range of vision : SIGHT ⟨the planes passed out of *view*⟩ **5** : something that is looked toward or kept in sight : OBJECT ⟨studied hard with a *view* to getting an A⟩ **6** : the foreseeable future ⟨no hope in *view*⟩ **7** : a pictorial representation [Middle French *veue, vue,* from *veeir, voir* "to see", from Latin *vidēre*] — **in view of** : in regard to : in consideration of — **on view** : open to public inspection : on exhibition

[2]view *vt* **1** : SEE, WATCH ⟨*view* a film⟩ **2** : to look at attentively : SCRUTINIZE **3** : to survey or examine mentally : CONSIDER ⟨*view* all sides of a question⟩

view•er \'vyü-ər\ *n* **1** : one that views; *esp* : a person who watches television **2** : an optical device used in viewing ⟨a *viewer* for photographic transparencies⟩

view•less \'vyü-ləs\ *adj* **1** : INVISIBLE, UNSEEN **2** : affording no view **3** : expressing no views or opinions — **view•less•ly** *adv*

view•point \'vyü-,pȯint\ *n* : POINT OF VIEW, STANDPOINT

vi•ges•i•mal \vī-'jes-ə-məl\ *adj* : based on the number 20 [Latin *vicesimus, vigesimus* "twentieth"]

vig•il \'vij-əl\ *n* **1 a** : a watch formerly kept on the night before a religious feast with devotions **b** : the day before a religious feast **c** : prayers or devotional services held in the evening or at night — usually used in pl. **2** : the act of keeping awake when sleep is customary; *also* : a period of wakefulness **3** : an act or period of watchful observation : WATCH ⟨the soldiers kept *vigil* all night⟩ [Old French *vigile,* from Latin *vigilia* "wakefulness, watch", from *vigil* "awake, watchful"]

vig•i•lant \'vij-ə-lənt\ *adj* : alertly watchful especially to avoid danger **syn** see WATCHFUL — **vig•i•lance** \-ləns\ *n* — **vig•i•lant•ly** \-lənt-lē\ *adv*

vig•i•lan•te \,vij-ə-'lant-ē\ *n* : a member of a local volunteer group organized to suppress and punish crime especially where official law enforcement seems inadequate [Spanish, "watchman, guard", from *vigilante* "vigilant"]

[1]vi•gnette \vin-'yet\ *n* **1** : a small decorative design or picture put on or just before a title page or at the beginning or end of a chapter **2** : a picture that shades off gradually into the surrounding ground **3** : a brief word picture : SKETCH [French, from *vigne* "vine"] — **vi•gnett•ist** \-'yet-əst\ *n*

[2]vignette *vt* **1** : to finish (as a photograph) in the manner of a vignette **2** : to describe briefly — **vi•gnett•er** *n*

vig•or \'vig-ər\ *n* **1** : active physical or mental strength or energy ⟨the full *vigor* of youth⟩ **2** : INTENSITY, FORCE ⟨the *vigor* of their quarrel⟩ [Middle French, from Latin, from *vigēre* "to be vigorous"]

vi•go•ro•so \,vig-ə-'rō-sō\ *adj or adv* : energetic in style — used as a direction in music [Italian, literally, "vigorous"]

vig•or•ous \'vig-rəs, -ə-rəs\ *adj* **1** : having vigor : ROBUST ⟨*vigorous* youth⟩ ⟨a *vigorous* plant⟩ **2** : done with force and energy ⟨a *vigorous* protest⟩ ⟨*vigorous* exercise⟩ — **vig•or•ous•ly** *adv* — **vig•or•ous•ness** *n*

• **syn** VIGOROUS, ENERGETIC, STRENUOUS mean having great vitality and force. VIGOROUS suggests active strength and implies undiminishing freshness or robustness ⟨still *vigorous* in their old age⟩ ENERGETIC suggests a capacity for intense activity ⟨*energetic* young people⟩ STRENUOUS suggests a preference for coping with the arduous and challenging ⟨*strenuous* objections⟩ ⟨*strenuous* exercise⟩

vig•our \'vig-ər\ *chiefly British variant of* VIGOR

Vi•king \'vī-king\ *n* : any of the Norse plunderers of the European coasts in the 8th to 10th centuries [Old Norse *vikingr*]

vile \'vīl\ *adj* **1** : of little worth or account **2 a** : morally base : WICKED ⟨*vile* deeds⟩ **b** : physically repulsive : FOUL ⟨*vile* living quarters⟩ **3** : tending to degrade ⟨*vile* tasks⟩ **4** : CONTEMPTIBLE, DESPICABLE ⟨a *vile* temper⟩ [Old French *vil,* from Latin *vilis*] — **vile•ly** \'vīl-lē\ *adv* — **vile•ness** *n*

vil•i•fy \'vil-ə-,fī\ *vt* **-fied**; **-fy•ing** **1** : to lower in estimation or importance : DEGRADE **2** : to utter slanderous and abusive statements against : DEFAME — **vil•i•fi•ca•tion** \,vil-ə-fə-'kā-shən\ *n* — **vil•i•fi•er** \'vil-ə-,fī-ər, -,fīr\ *n*

vil•la \'vil-ə\ *n* **1** : a country estate **2** : the rural or suburban residence of a wealthy person [Italian, from Latin]

vil•lage \'vil-ij\ *n* **1** : a settlement usually larger than a hamlet and smaller than a town **2** : the residents of a village ⟨the whole *village* knows about it⟩ [Middle French, from *ville* "farm, village", from Latin *villa* "country estate"]

vil•lag•er \'vil-ij-ər\ *n* : an inhabitant of a village

vil•lain \'vil-ən\ *n* **1** : VILLEIN **2** : an uncouth ill-mannered person : BOOR **3** : a thorough-going scoundrel or criminal **4** : a scoundrel in a story or play **5** : a person or thing blamed for an evil or difficulty [Middle English *vilain, vilein*]

△ **origin** In the feudal society of medieval Europe a villein was a member of one of the lower classes, at some times and places a free man and at others fully bound in service to a lord. Because the higher classes often look on the lower as inferior, Middle English *vilein* or *vilain* developed the depreciatory sense of "a person of uncouth mind and manners". This disparaging tendency gained in strength and currency through the common equation of manners and morals, so that the modern *villain* is a scoundrel or criminal or a person or thing blamed for a particular evil or difficulty.

vil•lain•ess \'vil-ə-nəs\ *n* : a girl or woman who is a villain

vil•lain•ous \'vil-ə-nəs\ *adj* **1** : befitting a villain : DEPRAVED **2** : highly objectionable : WRETCHED — **vil•lain•ous•ly** *adv* — **vil•lain•ous•ness** *n*

vil•lainy \'vil-ə-nē\ *n, pl* **-lain•ies** **1 a** : villainous conduct **b** : a villainous act **2** : villainous character : WICKEDNESS

vil•la•nelle \,vil-ə-'nel\ *n* : a verse form running on two rhymes and consisting typically of five tercets and a quatrain in which the first and third lines of the opening tercet recur alternately at the end of the other tercets and together as the last two lines of the quatrain [French, from Italian *villanella*]

vil•lein \'vil-ən, 'vil-,ān, vil-'ān\ *n* **1** : a free peasant of any of various feudal classes **2** : an unfree peasant ranking as a slave of his or her feudal lord but as free in legal relations with others [Middle English *vilain, vilein,* from Middle French, from Medieval Latin *villanus,* from Latin *villa* "country estate"]

vil•len•age \'vil-ə-nij\ *n* **1** : tenure of land given by a feudal lord to a villein **2** : the status of a villein

vil•lous \'vil-əs\ *adj* : having soft long hairs ⟨leaves *villous* underneath⟩ [Latin *villosus* "rough, shaggy", from *villus* "shaggy hair"] — **vil•los•i•ty** \vil-'äs-ət-ē\ *n*

vil•lus \'vil-əs\ *n, pl* **vil•li** \'vil-,ī, -ē\ : a small slender usually vascular process; *esp* : one of the tiny finger-shaped processes of the mucous membrane of the small intestine that function in the absorption of nutriments [Latin, "shaggy hair"]

vim \'vim\ *n* : robust energy and enthusiasm : VITALITY [Latin, accusative of *vis* "strength"]

vin•ai•grette \,vin-i-'gret\ *n* : a small ornamental box or bottle with perforated top used for holding an aromatic preparation (as smelling salts) [French, from *vinaigre* "vinegar"]

vin•ca \'ving-kə\ *n* : [1]PERIWINKLE [New Latin, from Latin *pervinca*]

\ə\ **abut**	\au̇\ **out**	\i\ **tip**	\ȯ\ **saw**	\u̇\ **foot**
\ər\ **further**	\ch\ **chin**	\ī\ **life**	\ȯi\ **coin**	\y\ **yet**
\a\ **mat**	\e\ **pet**	\j\ **job**	\th\ **thin**	\yü\ **few**
\ā\ **take**	\ē\ **easy**	\ng\ **sing**	\t͟h\ **this**	\yu̇\ **cure**
\ä\ **cot, cart**	\g\ **go**	\ō\ **bone**	\ü\ **food**	\zh\ **vision**

Vin•cen•tian \vin-ˈsen-chən\ *n* **:** a member of the Roman Catholic Congregation of the Mission founded in 1625 by St. Vincent de Paul and devoted to missions and seminaries — **Vincentian** *adj*

Vin•cent's angina \ˌvin-sənts-, va^n-ˌsä^{n}z-\ *n* **:** a contagious disease marked by ulceration of the mucous membrane of the mouth and adjacent parts and caused by a bacterium often in association with a spirochete — compare VINCENT'S INFECTION [Jean Hyacinthe *Vincent,* died 1950, French bacteriologist]

Vincent's infection *n* **:** a bacterial infection of the respiratory tract and mouth marked by destructive ulceration especially of the mucous membranes — compare VINCENT'S ANGINA

vin•ci•ble \ˈvin-sə-bəl\ *adj* **:** capable of being overcome or subdued **:** SURMOUNTABLE [Latin *vincibilis,* from *vincere* "to conquer"]

vin•cu•lum \ˈving-kyə-ləm\ *n, pl* **-lums** *or* **-la** \-lə\ **1 :** a unifying bond **:** LINK, TIE **2 :** a straight horizontal mark placed over two or more members of a mathematical expression as a symbol of grouping (as in $a-\overline{b-c}=a-[b-c]$) [Latin, from *vincire* "to bind"]

vin•di•cate \ˈvin-də-ˌkāt\ *vt* **1 a :** EXONERATE, ABSOLVE **b** (1) **:** CONFIRM 2, SUBSTANTIATE (2) **:** to provide defense for **:** JUSTIFY **c :** to protect from attack or encroachment **:** DEFEND **2 :** to maintain a right to **:** ASSERT [Latin *vindicare* "to lay claim to, avenge", from *vindic-, vindex* "claimant, avenger"] **syn** see MAINTAIN — **vin•di•ca•tor** \-ˌkāt-ər\ *n* — **vin•di•ca•to•ry** \-kə-ˌtōr-ē, -ˌtȯr-\ *adj*

vin•di•ca•tion \ˌvin-də-ˈkā-shən\ *n* **:** the act of vindicating **:** the state of being vindicated; *esp* **:** justification against denial or censure

vin•dic•tive \vin-ˈdik-tiv\ *adj* **1 a :** inclined to seek revenge **:** VENGEFUL **b :** intended for or involving revenge **2 :** intended to cause pain or anguish **:** SPITEFUL [Latin *vindicta* "revenge", from *vindicare* "to avenge"] — **vin•dic•tive•ly** *adv* — **vin•dic•tive•ness** *n*

[1]**vine** \ˈvīn\ *n* **1 :** GRAPE 2 **2 :** a plant whose stem requires support and which climbs by tendrils or twining or creeps along the ground; *also* **:** the stem of such a plant [Old French *vigne,* from Latin *vinea* "vine, vineyard", derived from *vinum* "wine"]

[2]**vine** *vi* **:** to form or grow in the manner of a vine

vin•eal \ˈvin-ē-əl, ˈvīn-\ *adj* **:** of or relating to wine [Latin *vineal-is* "of vines", from *vinea* "vine"]

vine•dress•er \ˈvīn-ˌdres-ər\ *n* **:** one that cultivates and prunes grapevines

vin•e•gar \ˈvin-i-gər\ *n* **1 :** a sour liquid obtained by fermentation of cider, wine, or malt and used to flavor or preserve foods **2 :** ill humor **3 :** VIM [Old French *vinaigre,* from *vin* "wine" (from Latin *vinum*) + *aigre* "keen, sour", from Latin *acer* "sharp"]

vinegar eel *n* **:** a tiny roundworm often found in vinegar or acid fermenting vegetable matter

vin•e•gar•ish \ˈvin-i-gə-rish, -grish\ *adj* **:** VINEGARY 2

vin•e•gary \-gə-rē, -grē\ *adj* **1 :** resembling vinegar **:** SOUR **2 :** disagreeable or bitter in character or manner **:** CRABBED

vin•ery \ˈvīn-rē, -ə-rē\ *n, pl* **-er•ies :** an area or building in which vines are grown

vine•yard \ˈvin-yərd\ *n* **:** a planting of grapevines — **vine•yard•ist** \-əst\ *n*

vingt–et–un \ˌvan-ˌtā-ˈən\ *n* **:** BLACKJACK 3 [French, literally, "twenty-one"]

vi•ni•cul•ture \ˈvin-ə-ˌkəl-chər, ˈvī-nə-\ *n* **:** VITICULTURE

vi•nos•i•ty \vī-ˈnäs-ət-ē\ *n* **:** the characteristic body, flavor, and color of a wine

vi•nous \ˈvī-nəs\ *adj* **1 :** of, relating to, or made with wine ⟨*vinous* medications⟩ **2 :** showing the effects of the use of wine [Latin *vinosus,* from *vinum* "wine"]

vin•tage \ˈvint-ij\ *n* **1 a** (1) **:** the grapes or wine produced during one season (2) **:** WINE; *esp* **:** a wine of a particular type, region, and year and usually of superior quality **b :** a collection or category of comparable persons or things **2 :** the act or time of gathering grapes or making wine **3 a :** a period of origin or manufacture ⟨a piano of 1845 *vintage*⟩ **b :** length of existence **:** AGE [Middle French *vendenge,* from Latin *vindemia,* from *vinum* "wine, grapes" + *demere* "to take off"] — **vintage** *adj*

vint•ner \ˈvint-nər\ *n* **:** a wine merchant [Old French *vinetier,* derived from Latin *vinum* "wine"]

viny \ˈvī-nē\ *adj* **vin•i•er; -est 1 :** of, relating to, or resembling vines ⟨*viny* plants⟩ **2 :** covered with or abounding in vines

vi•nyl \ˈvīn-l\ *n* **1 :** a univalent radical $CH_2=CH$ derived from ethylene by removal of one hydrogen atom **2 :** a polymer of a vinyl compound or a product made from one ⟨*vinyl* upholstery⟩ [Latin *vinum* "wine"]

vinyl resin *n* **:** any of a group of elastic resins that are resistant to chemical agents and are used for protective coatings and molded articles — called also *vinyl plastic*

vi•ol \ˈvī-əl, ˈvīl\ *n* **:** an old bowed stringed instrument like the violin but weaker in tone and simpler in construction and playing technique [Middle French *viole,* from Provençal *viola*]

[1]**vi•o•la** \vē-ˈō-lə\ *n* **:** a stringed musical instrument similar to a violin but slightly larger and lower in pitch [Italian, from Provençal, "viol"]

[2]**vi•ola** \vī-ˈō-lə, vē-\ *n* **:** VIOLET 1a; *esp* **:** any of various garden hybrids with solitary white, yellow, or purple often variegated flowers resembling but smaller than typical pansies [Latin]

vi•o•la•ble \ˈvī-ə-lə-bəl\ *adj* **:** that can be violated — **vi•o•la•bil•i•ty** \ˌvī-ə-lə-ˈbil-ət-ē\ *n* — **vi•o•la•ble•ness** \ˈvī-ə-lə-bəl-nəs\ *n* — **vi•o•la•bly** \-blē\ *adv*

vi•o•late \ˈvī-ə-ˌlāt\ *vt* **1 :** to fail to keep or observe ⟨*violate* the law⟩ **2 :** to do harm to the person or the chastity of; *esp* **:** RAPE **3 :** PROFANE, DESECRATE ⟨vandals *violated* the church⟩ **4 :** DISTURB 2a, b [Latin *violare*] — **vi•o•la•tor** \-ˌlāt-ər\ *n*

vi•o•la•tion \ˌvī-ə-ˈlā-shən\ *n* **:** the act of violating **:** the state of being violated: as **a :** TRANSGRESSION **b :** an act of irreverence or desecration **c :** DISTURBANCE 1, 3 **d :** [3]RAPE 2

vi•o•lence \ˈvī-ə-ləns\ *n* **1 :** the use of physical force in a way that harms a person or a person's property **2 :** injury especially to something that deserves respect or reverence ⟨does *violence* to our principles⟩ **3 a :** intense, furious, and often destructive action or force ⟨the *violence* of the storm⟩ **b :** vehement feeling or expression **:** FERVOR **4 :** improper or damaging alteration (as of the wording or the meaning of a text)

vi•o•lent \-lənt\ *adj* **1 :** marked by extreme force or sudden intense activity ⟨a *violent* attack⟩ ⟨*violent* storms⟩ **2 a :** notably furious or vehement ⟨a *violent* denunciation⟩; *also* **:** excited or mentally disordered to the point of loss of self-control ⟨the patient became *violent* and had to be restrained⟩ **b :** EXTREME, INTENSE ⟨*violent* pain⟩ **3 :** caused by force ⟨a *violent* death⟩ [Middle French, from Latin *violentus*] — **vi•o•lent•ly** *adv*

vi•o•let \ˈvī-ə-lət\ *n* **1 a :** any of a genus of herbaceous or shrubby plants having alternate leaves with stipules and both aerial and underground flowers; *esp* **:** one with small usually solid-colored flowers as distinguished from the usually larger-flowered violas and pansies **b :** any of several plants of other genera — compare DOGTOOTH VIOLET **2 :** a reddish blue [Middle French *violete,* from *viole* "violet", from Latin *viola*]

vi•o•lin \ˌvī-ə-ˈlin\ *n* **1 :** a bowed stringed instrument with four strings that has a shallower body and a more curved bridge than the viol **2 :** VIOLINIST [Italian *violino,* from *viola* "viola"]

violin 1

vi•o•lin•ist \-ˈlin-əst\ *n* **:** one who plays the violin

vi•o•list \vē-ˈō-ləst\ *n* **:** one who plays the viola

vi•o•lon•cel•list \ˌvī-ə-lən-ˈchel-əst, ˌvē-\ *n* **:** CELLIST

vi•o•lon•cel•lo \ˌvī-ə-lən-ˈchel-ō, ˌvē-\ *n* **:** CELLO [Italian, from *violone* "double bass", from *viola* "viola, viol"]

VIP \ˌvē-ˌī-ˈpē\ *n, pl* **VIPs** \-ˈpēz\ **:** a person of great influence or prestige [*v*ery *i*mportant *p*erson]

vi•per *n* \ˈvī-pər\ *n* **1 a :** any of a family of sluggish heavy-bodied broad-headed Old World venomous snakes with hollow tubular fangs **b :** PIT VIPER **c :** a venomous or reputedly venomous snake **2 :** a malicious or treacherous person [Middle French *vipere,* from Latin *vipera*] — **vi•per•ine** \-pə-ˌrīn\ *adj*

vi•per•ish \ˈvī-pə-rish, -prish\ *adj* **:** given to spiteful abusive speech **:** VENOMOUS

vi•per•ous \ˈvī-pə-rəs, -prəs\ *adj* **1 :** of or relating to vipers **2 :** having the qualities attributed to vipers **:** SPITEFUL, VENOMOUS ⟨a *viperous* treachery⟩ — **vi•per•ous•ly** *adv*

vi•ra•go \və-ˈräg-ō, -ˈrāg-; ˈvir-ə-ˌgō\ *n, pl* **-goes** *or* **-gos 1 :** a woman of great stature, strength, and courage **2 :** a loud overbearing woman [Latin *viragin-, virago,* from *vir* "man"] — **vi•rag•i•nous** \və-ˈraj-ə-nəs\ *adj*

vi·ral \ˈvī-rəl\ *adj* : of, relating to, or caused by a virus

vir·eo \ˈvir-ē-ˌō\ *n, pl* **-e·os** : any of a family of small insect-eating songbirds that are chiefly olive-green or grayish in color [Latin, a small bird, from *virēre* "to be green"]

vir·ga \ˈvər-gə\ *n* : wisps of precipitation evaporating before reaching the ground [Latin, "branch, streak in the sky suggesting rain"]

1**vir·gin** \ˈvər-jən\ *n* **1** : an unmarried woman devoted to religion **2** : a person who has not had sexual intercourse [Old French *virgine,* from Latin *virgin-, virgo* "young woman, virgin"]

2**virgin** *adj* **1** : being, characteristic of, or befitting a virgin : MODEST **2** : not soiled or marred ⟨*virgin* snow⟩; *esp* : not altered by human activity ⟨*virgin* soil⟩ **3** : being used or worked for the first time or produced by a simple extractive process ⟨*virgin* wool⟩ ⟨*virgin* oil⟩

1**vir·gin·al** \ˈvər-jən-l\ *adj* : of, relating to, characteristic of, or suitable for a virgin or virginity; *esp* : CHASTE — **vir·gin·al·ly** \-l-ē\ *adv*

2**virginal** *n* : a small rectangular spinet having no legs and only one wire to a note

virgin birth *n* **1** : birth from a virgin **2** *often cap V & B* : the theological doctrine that Jesus was miraculously begotten of God and born of a virgin mother

Vir·gin·ia creeper \vər-ˌjin-yə-, -ˌjin-ē-ə-\ *n* : a common North American tendril-climbing vine of the grape family having leaves with five leaflets and bluish black berries — called also *woodbine* [*Virginia,* United States]

Virginia deer *n* : WHITE-TAILED DEER

Virginia reel *n* : a country-dance in which all couples in turn participate in a series of figures

vir·gin·i·ty \vər-ˈjin-ət-ē\ *n, pl* **-ties** : the quality or state of being virgin; *esp* : MAIDENHOOD

virgin's bower *n* : any of several usually small-flowered and climbing clematises

Vir·go \ˈvər-gō, ˈviər-\ *n* **1** : a zodiacal constellation due south of the handle of the Dipper **2** : the 6th sign of the zodiac; *also* : one born under this sign [Latin, literally, "virgin"]

vir·gule \ˈvər-gyül\ *n* : DIAGONAL 3 [French, from Latin *virgula* "little rod", from *virga* "branch, rod"]

vir·i·des·cent \ˌvir-ə-ˈdes-nt\ *adj* : slightly green : GREENISH [Latin *viridis* "green"]

vir·ile \ˈvir-əl, ˈviər-ˌīl\ *adj* **1** : having the nature, powers, or qualities of a man **2 a** : ENERGETIC, VIGOROUS **b** : MASTERFUL 1, FORCEFUL [Latin *virilis,* from *vir* "man, male"]

vi·ril·i·ty \və-ˈril-ət-ē\ *n* : the quality or state of being virile: **a** : MANHOOD **b** : manly vigor : MASCULINITY

vi·rol·o·gy \vī-ˈräl-ə-jē\ *n* : a branch of science that deals with viruses — **vi·ro·log·i·cal** \ˌvī-rə-ˈläj-i-kəl\ *adj* — **vi·rol·o·gist** \vī-ˈräl-ə-jəst\ *n*

vir·tu·al \ˈvərch-wəl, -ə-wəl; ˈvər-chəl\ *adj* : being in essence or effect but not in fact or name ⟨the *virtual* ruler of the country⟩ [Medieval Latin *virtualis* "possessed of powers or virtues", from Latin *virtus* "strength, virtue"] — **vir·tu·al·i·ty** \ˌvər-chə-ˈwal-ət-ē\ *n* — **vir·tu·al·ly** \ˈvərch-wə-lē, -ə-wə-; ˈvərch-lē, -ə-lē\ *adv*

virtual focus *n* : a point from which divergent rays (as of light) seem to originate but do not actually do so (as in the image of a point source seen in a plane mirror)

virtual image *n* : an image formed of virtual foci

vir·tue \ˈvər-chü\ *n* **1** : conformity to a standard of right : MORALITY **2** : a particular moral excellence ⟨justice and charity are *virtues*⟩ **3 a** : an active beneficial power ⟨quinine has *virtue* in the treatment of malaria⟩ **b** : a desirable or commendable quality or trait : MERIT ⟨the *virtues* of country life⟩ **4** : chastity especially in a woman [Old French *virtu, vertu,* from Latin *virtus* "manliness, courage, virtue", from *vir* "man"]

△ **origin** From *vir,* meaning "man", the Romans derived the word *virtus* to denote the sum of the excellent qualities of men, including physical strength, valorous conduct, and moral rectitude. The Christian church stressed the moral virtues, and French *virtu* or *vertu,* developed from Latin *virtus,* was used specifically to mean "morality". The French word was borrowed into English in the 13th century. In the 14th century *virtue* came to be applied to any quality, moral or otherwise, felt to be excellent. By the end of the 16th century the sense "chastity, purity" appeared, especially in reference to women.

— **by virtue of** *or* **in virtue of** : through the force of : by authority of

vir·tu·os·i·ty \ˌvər-chə-ˈwäs-ət-ē\ *n, pl* **-ties** : great technical skill in the practice of the fine arts

vir·tu·o·so \ˌvər-chə-ˈwō-sō, -zō\ *n, pl* **-sos** *or* **-si** \-sē, -zē\ **1** : one skilled in or having a taste for the fine arts **2** : one who excels in the technique of an art; *esp* : a highly skilled musical performer [Italian, from *virtuoso* "virtuous, skilled"] — **virtuoso** *adj*

vir·tu·ous \ˈvər-chə-wəs\ *adj* **1 a** : having or exhibiting virtue **b** : morally excellent **2** : CHASTE 1 — **vir·tu·ous·ly** *adv* — **vir·tu·ous·ness** *n*

vir·u·lent \ˈvir-ə-lənt, -yə-\ *adj* **1 a** : marked by a rapid, severe, and malignant course ⟨a *virulent* infection⟩ **b** : able to overcome bodily defensive mechanisms ⟨a *virulent* pathogen⟩ **2** : extremely poisonous or venomous : NOXIOUS **3** : full of malice [Latin *virulentus,* from *virus* "poison"] — **vir·u·lence** \-ləns\ *or* **vir·u·len·cy** \-lən-sē\ *n* — **vir·u·lent·ly** *adv*

vi·rus \ˈvī-rəs\ *n* **1 a** : any of a large group of submicroscopic infective agents that are held by some to be living organisms and by others to be complex protein molecules containing nucleic acids and comparable to genes, that are capable of growth and multiplication only in living cells, and that cause various important diseases in man, lower animals, or plants; *also* : any of various infective agents (as a true virus or a rickettsia) that remain active after passing through a filter too fine for a bacterium to pass — called also *filterable virus* **b** : a disease caused by a virus **2** : something that poisons the mind or spirit [Latin, "slimy liquid, poison"]

1**vi·sa** \ˈvē-zə *also* -sə\ *n* : an endorsement made on a passport by the proper authorities denoting that it has been examined and that the bearer may proceed [French, from Latin *visus,* past participle of *vidēre* "to see"]

2**visa** *vt* **vi·saed** \-zəd, -səd\; **vi·sa·ing** \-zə-ing, -sə-ing\ : to give a visa to

vis·age \ˈviz-ij\ *n* **1** : the face or countenance of a person or sometimes a lower animal **2** : ASPECT, APPEARANCE ⟨grimy *visage* of a mining town⟩ [Old French, from *vis* "face", from Latin *visus* "sight", from *vidēre* "to see"] — **vis·aged** \-ijd\ *adj*

1**vis-à-vis** \ˌvēz-ə-ˈvē, ˌvēs- *also* -ä-ˈvē\ *n, pl* **vis-à-vis** \-ˈvē, -ˈvēz\ **1** : one that is face to face with another **2 a** : ESCORT 1b, DATE **b** : COUNTERPART **3** : TÊTE-À-TÊTE 1 [French, literally, "face to face"]

2**vis-à-vis** *prep* **1** : face to face with : OPPOSITE **2** : in relation to **3** : as compared with

3**vis-à-vis** *adv* : in company : TOGETHER

viscera *pl of* VISCUS

vis·cer·al \ˈvis-ə-rəl\ *adj* **1 a** : felt in or as if in the viscera ⟨*visceral* sensation⟩ **b** : of, relating to, or being the viscera : SPLANCHNIC **2** : not intellectual : INSTINCTIVE ⟨a *visceral* reaction⟩ — **vis·cer·al·ly** \-rə-lē\ *adv*

vis·cid \ˈvis-əd\ *adj* **1** : VISCOUS, STICKY **2** : covered with a sticky layer [Late Latin *viscidus,* from Latin *viscum* "birdlime"] — **vis·cid·i·ty** \vis-ˈid-ət-ē\ *n* — **vis·cid·ly** \ˈvis-əd-lē\ *adv*

vis·co·elas·tic \ˌvis-kō-i-ˈlas-tik\ *adj* : having both viscous and elastic properties in appreciable degree ⟨*viscoelastic* asphalt⟩

vis·com·e·ter \vis-ˈkäm-ət-ər\ *n* : an instrument with which to measure viscosity — **vis·co·met·ric** \ˌvis-kə-ˈme-trik\ *adj*

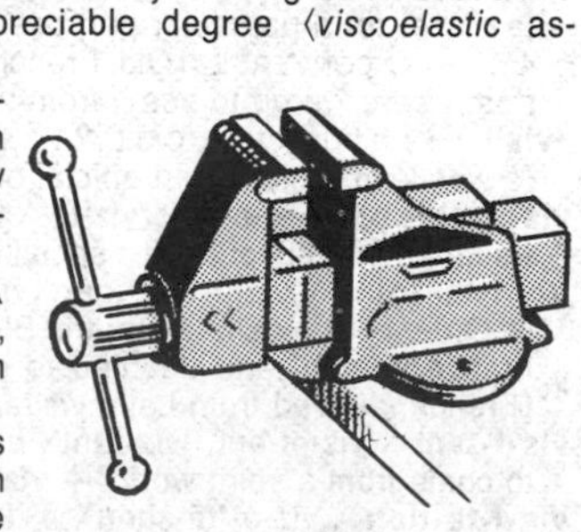

vise

1**vis·cose** \ˈvis-ˌkōs, -ˌkōz\ *adj* **1** : VISCOUS **2** : of, relating to, or made from viscose

2**viscose** *n* **1** : a viscous golden-brown solution made by treating cellulose with caustic alkali solution and carbon disulfide and used in making rayon **2** : viscose rayon

vis·cos·i·ty \vis-ˈkäs-ət-ē\ *n, pl* **-ties** : the quality of being viscous; *esp* : a tendency of a liquid to flow slowly resulting from friction of its molecules ⟨an oil of high *viscosity*⟩

\ə\ **abut**	\au̇\ **out**	\i\ **tip**	\ȯ\ **saw**	\u̇\ **foot**
\ər\ **further**	\ch\ **chin**	\ī\ **life**	\ȯi\ **coin**	\y\ **yet**
\a\ **mat**	\e\ **pet**	\j\ **job**	\th\ **thin**	\yü\ **few**
\ā\ **take**	\ē\ **easy**	\ng\ **sing**	\t͟h\ **this**	\yu̇\ **cure**
\ä\ **cot, cart**	\g\ **go**	\ō\ **bone**	\ü\ **food**	\zh\ **vision**

vis•count \ˈvī-ˌkau̇nt\ *n* : a member of the British peerage ranking below an earl and above a baron [Middle French *viscomte,* from Medieval Latin *vicecomes,* from Late Latin *vice-* "vice-" + *comes* "count"] — **vis•count•cy** \-sē\ *n* — **vis•county** \-ˌkau̇nt-ē\ *n*

vis•count•ess \-ˌkau̇nt-əs\ *n* **1** : the wife or widow of a viscount **2** : a woman who holds the rank of viscount in her own right

vis•cous \ˈvis-kəs\ *adj* **1** : somewhat sticky or glutinous : ADHESIVE **2** : having or characterized by viscosity [Late Latin *viscosus,* from Latin *viscum* "birdlime"] — **vis•cous•ly** *adv* — **vis•cous•ness** *n*

vis•cus \ˈvis-kəs\ *n, pl* **vis•cera** \ˈvis-ə-rə\ : an internal organ of the body; *esp* : one (as the heart, liver, or intestine) located in the great cavity of the trunk proper [Latin]

vise \ˈvīs\ *n* : any of various tools having two jaws for holding work that operate usually by a screw, lever, or cam [Middle French *vis* "something winding", from Latin *vitis* "vine"]

vis•i•bil•i•ty \ˌviz-ə-ˈbil-ət-ē\ *n* **1** : the quality or state of being visible **2** : the degree of clearness of the atmosphere especially as affording clear vision toward the horizon

vis•i•ble \ˈviz-ə-bəl\ *adj* **1** : capable of being seen : apparent to the eye ⟨stars *visible* to the naked eye⟩ **2** : APPARENT, DISCOVERABLE ⟨has no *visible* means of support⟩ [Latin *visibilis,* from *vidēre* "to see"] — **vis•i•ble•ness** *n* — **vis•i•bly** \-blē\ *adv*

Visi•goth \ˈviz-ə-ˌgäth\ *n* : a member of the western division of the Goths — called also *West Goth;* compare OSTROGOTH [Late Latin *Visigothi* "Visigoths"] — **Visi•goth•ic** \ˌviz-ə-ˈgäth-ik\ *adj*

¹vi•sion \ˈvizh-ən\ *n* **1 a** : something seen in a dream, trance, or ecstasy **b** : an object of imagination **c** : GHOST 2, APPARITION **2 a** : the act or power of imagination **b** : unusual discernment or foresight **3 a** : the act or power of seeing : SIGHT **b** : the special sense by which the qualities of an object (as color, luminosity, texture, or shape and size) constituting its appearance are perceived and which is mediated by the eye **4** : something seen; *esp* : a lovely or charming sight [Old French, from Latin *visio,* from *vidēre* "to see"] — **vi•sion•al** \ˈvizh-nəl, -ən-l\ *adj* — **vi•sion•al•ly** \-ē\ *adv* — **vi•sion•less** \ˈvizh-ən-ləs\ *adj*

²vision *vt* **vi•sioned**; **vi•sion•ing** \ˈvizh-ning, -ə-ning\ : IMAGINE, ENVISION ⟨couldn't *vision* it happening⟩

¹vi•sion•ary \ˈvizh-ə-ˌner-ē\ *adj* **1** : given to dreaming or imagining **2** : resembling a vision especially in fanciful or impractical quality ⟨*visionary* schemes⟩ — **vi•sion•ar•i•ness** *n*

²visonary *n, pl* **-ar•ies** **1** : one who sees visions : SEER **2** : one whose ideas or projects are impractical : DREAMER

¹vis•it \ˈviz-ət\ *vb* **vis•it•ed** \ˈviz-ət-əd, ˈviz-təd\; **vis•it•ing** \ˈviz-ət-ing, ˈviz-ting\ **1** : to come to or upon as a reward, affliction, or punishment **2** : to go to see in order to comfort or help **3 a** : to pay a call upon as an act of friendship or courtesy **b** : to go or come to see in an official or professional capacity **c** : to dwell with temporarily as a guest **d** : to go to see or stay at (a place) for a particular purpose (as business or sightseeing) **4** : CHAT, CONVERSE [Old French *visiter,* from Latin *visitare,* from *visere* "to go to see", from *vidēre* "to see"]

²visit *n* **1** : a brief stay : CALL **2** : a stay as a guest or nonresident ⟨a weekend *visit*⟩ **3** : an official or professional call

vis•it•able \ˈviz-ət-ə-bəl, ˈviz-tə-\ *adj* **1** : subject to or allowing visitation or inspection **2** : socially eligible to receive visits

Vis•i•tan•dine \ˌviz-ə-ˈtan-ˌdēn\ *n* : a nun of the Roman Catholic Order of the Visitation of the Blessed Virgin Mary founded in France in 1610 and devoted to contemplation and education [French, derived from Latin *visitare* "to visit"]

vis•i•tant \ˈviz-ət-ənt, ˈviz-tənt\ *n* : VISITOR; *esp* : one thought to come from a spirit world — **visitant** *adj*

vis•i•ta•tion \ˌviz-ə-ˈtā-shən\ *n* **1** : VISIT; *esp* : an official visit (as for inspection) **2 a** : an instance of divine favor or wrath **b** : a severe trial : AFFLICTION **3** *cap* **a** : the visit of the Virgin Mary to Elizabeth before the birth of Elizabeth's son John the Baptist **b** : a church festival on July 2 commemorating this visit — **vis•i•ta•tion•al** \-shnəl, -shən-l\ *adj*

visiting nurse *n* : a nurse employed to visit sick persons or perform public-health services in a community

vis•i•tor \ˈviz-ət-ər, ˈviz-tər\ *n* : one that visits: as **a** : one that makes formal visits of inspection **b** : GUEST 1a **c** : TOURIST, TRAVELER

vi•sor \ˈvī-zər\ **1** : the front piece of a helmet; *esp* : a movable upper piece **2** : a projecting part (as on a cap or an automobile windshield) to protect or shade the eyes [Anglo-French *viser,* from Old French *visiere,* from *vis* "face", from Latin *visus* "sight", from *vidēre* "to see"] — **vi•sored** \-zərd\ *adj* — **vi•sor•less** \-zər-ləs\ *adj*

vis•ta \ˈvis-tə\ *n* **1** : a distant view through or along an avenue or opening : PROSPECT **2** : an extensive mental view (as over a stretch of time or a series of events) [Italian, "sight", from *vedere* "to see", from Latin *vidēre*]

vi•su•al \ˈvizh-wəl, -ə-wəl; ˈvizh-əl\ *adj* **1** : of, relating to, or used in vision ⟨*visual* organs⟩ **2** : attained or maintained by sight ⟨*visual* impressions⟩ **3** : VISIBLE 1 **4** : producing mental images : VIVID **5** : of, relating to, or employing visual aids [Late Latin *visualis,* from Latin *visus* "sight", from *vidēre* "to see"] — **vi•su•al•ly** \-ē\ *adv*

visual acuity *n* : the relative capacity of the visual organ to resolve detail

visual aid *n* : an instructional device (as a chart, map, or model) that appeals chiefly to vision; *esp* : an educational movie or filmstrip

vi•su•al•ize \ˈvizh-wə-ˌlīz, -ə-wə-; ˈvizh-ə-ˌlīz\ *vb* : to make visible; *esp* : to see or form a mental image of : ENVISAGE — **vi•su•al•iz•able** \-ˌlī-zə-bəl\ *adj* — **vi•su•al•iza•tion** \ˌvizh-wə-lə-ˈzā-shən, -ə-wə-; ˌvizh-ə-lə-\ *n* — **vi•su•al•iz•er** \ˈvizh-wə-ˌlī-zər, -ə-wə-, ˈvizh-ə-ˌlī-\ *n*

visual purple *n* : a photosensitive red or purple pigment in the retinal rods of various vertebrates; *esp* : RHODOPSIN

vi•ta \ˈvēt-ə, ˈvīt-ə\ *n, pl* **vi•tae** \ˈvē-ˌtī, ˈvīt-ē\ : a brief autobiographical sketch [Latin, literally, "life"]

vi•tal \ˈvīt-l\ *adj* **1** : of, relating to, or characteristic of life : showing the qualities of living things ⟨*vital* activites⟩ **2** : concerned with or necessary to the maintenance of life ⟨*vital* organs⟩ **3** : full of vitality : ANIMATED **4** : of first importance : BASIC [Middle French, from Latin *vitalis* "of life", from *vita* "life"] **syn** see ESSENTIAL — **vi•tal•ly** \-l-ē\ *adv*

vital capacity *n* : the breathing capacity of the lungs expressed as the number of cubic inches or cubic centimeters of air that can be forcibly exhaled after a full inspiration

vi•tal•ism \ˈvīt-l-ˌiz-əm\ *n* : the doctrine that the life processes are not wholly explainable by the laws of physics and chemistry and that life is in some part self-determining — compare MECHANISM — **vi•tal•ist** \-l-əst\ *n* — **vi•tal•is•tic** \ˌvīt-l-ˈis-tik\ *adj*

vi•tal•i•ty \vī-ˈtal-ət-ē\ *n, pl* **–ties** **1 a** : the peculiarity distinguishing the living from the nonliving **b** : capacity to live and develop; *also* : physical or mental vigor especially when highly developed **2 a** : power of enduring or continuing ⟨the *vitality* of bad habits⟩ **b** : lively and animated character : VIGOR

vi•tal•ize \ˈvīt-l-ˌīz\ *vt* : to give vitality to : ANIMATE — **vi•tal•iza•tion** \ˌvīt-l-ə-ˈzā-shən\ *n*

vi•tals \ˈvīt-lz\ *n pl* **1** : vital organs **2** : essential parts

vital signs *n pl* : the pulse rate, respiratory rate, body temperature, and sometimes blood pressure of a person

vital statistics *n pl* : statistics relating to births, deaths, marriages, health, and disease

vi•ta•min \ˈvīt-ə-mən\ *n* : any of various organic substances that are essential in minute quantities to the nutrition of most animals and some plants, act in the regulation of metabolic processes but do not provide energy or serve as building units, and are present in natural foodstuffs or sometimes produced within the body [Latin *vita* "life" + English *amine*]

vitamin A *n* : a fat-soluble vitamin or vitamin mixture found especially in animal products (as egg yolk, milk, or fish-liver oils) whose lack causes injury to epithelial tissues (as in the eye with resulting visual defects)

vitamin B *n* **1** : VITAMIN B COMPLEX **2** *or* **vitamin B_1** : THIAMINE

vitamin B complex *n* : a group of water-soluble vitamins found widely in foods that include essential coenzymes and growth factors — called also *B complex;* compare BIOTIN, CHOLINE, NICOTINIC ACID, PANTOTHENIC ACID, THIAMINE

vitamin B_6 \-ˈbē-ˈsiks\ *n* : pyridoxine or a closely related compound

vitamin B_{12} \-ˈbē-ˈtwelv\ *n* : a complex cobalt-containing member of the vitamin B complex that occurs especially in liver, is essential to normal blood formation, neural function, and growth, and is used especially in treating pernicious anemia

vitamin B_2 \-ˈbē-ˈtü\ *n* : RIBOFLAVIN

vitamin C *n* : a water-soluble vitamin $C_6H_8O_6$ that is present especially in fruits and leafy vegetables, apparently functions as an enzyme in certain bodily oxidations and syntheses, and is used medicinally in the prevention and treatment of scurvy — called also *ascorbic acid*

vitamin D *n* : any or all of several fat-soluble vitamins that are chemically related to steroids, are essential for normal bone and tooth structure, and are found especially in fish-liver oils, egg yolk, and milk or produced by activation (as by ultraviolet irradiation) of sterols

vitamin E *n* : any of several tocopherols of which the lack in various mammals and birds is associated with infertility, muscular dystrophy, or vascular abnormalities and which occur especially in leaves and in seed-germ oils

vitamin G *n* : RIBOFLAVIN

vitamin H *n* : BIOTIN

vitamin K *n* : any of several fat-soluble vitamins essential for the clotting of blood because of their role in the production of prothrombin [Danish *k*oagulation "coagulation"]

vi•tel•line \vī-'tel-ən, və-\ *adj* : of, relating to, resembling, or producing yolk [derived from Latin *vitellus* "yolk", literally, "small calf"]

vi•ti•ate \'vish-ē-,āt\ *vt* **1** : to injure the quality of : SPOIL, DEBASE **2** : to destroy the validity of ⟨fraud *vitiates* a contract⟩ [Latin *vitiare,* from *vitium* "fault, vice"] — **vi•ti•a•tion** \,vish-ē-'ā-shən\ *n* — **vi•ti•a•tor** \'vish-ē-,āt-ər\ *n*

vi•ti•cul•ture \'vit-ə-,kəl-chər, 'vīt-ə-\ *n* : the growing of grapes [Latin *vitis* "vine"] — **vi•ti•cul•tur•al** \,vit-ə-'kəlch-rəl, -ə-rəl, ,vīt-\ *adj* — **vi•ti•cul•tur•ist** \-'kəlch-rəst, -ə-rəst\ *n*

vit•i•li•go \,vit-l-'ī-gō, -'ē-gō\ *n* : a skin disorder in which smooth white spots appear on the body [Latin, a skin disease]

vit•re•ous \'vi-trē-əs\ *adj* **1** : of, relating to, derived from, or resembling glass : GLASSY ⟨*vitreous* rocks⟩ ⟨a *vitreous* luster⟩ **2** : of, relating to, or being the vitreous humor [Latin *vitreus,* from *vitrum* "glass"] — **vit•re•ous•ness** *n*

vitreous humor *n* : the clear colorless transparent jelly that fills the eyeball posterior to the lens

vit•ri•fy \'vi-trə-,fī\ *vb* **-fied; -fy•ing** : to change into glass or a glassy substance by heat and fusion [French *vitrifier,* from Latin *vitrum* "glass"] — **vit•ri•fi•able** \-,fī-ə-bəl\ *adj* — **vit•ri•fi•ca•tion** \,vi-trə-fə-'kā-shən\ *n*

vit•ri•ol \'vi-trē-əl\ *n* **1 a** : a sulfate of any of various metals (as copper, iron, or zinc) **b** : OIL OF VITRIOL **2** : bitter feelings or harsh speech [Middle French, from Medieval Latin *vitriolum,* derived from Latin *vitreus* "vitreous"] — **vit•ri•ol•ic** \,vi-trē-'äl-ik\ *adj*

vit•tle \'vit-l\ *n* : VICTUAL

vi•tu•per•ate \vī-'tü-pə-,rāt, və-, -'tyü-\ *vb* : to abuse or censure severely : use harsh condemning language [Latin *vituperare,* from *vitium* "fault" + *parare* "to make"] — **vi•tu•per•a•tive** \-'tü-pə-rət-iv, -pə-,rāt-, -prət-iv, -'tyü-\ *adj* — **vi•tu•per•a•tive•ly** *adv* — **vi•tu•per•a•tor** \-pə-,rāt-ər\ *n* — **vi•tu•per•a•to•ry** \-rə-,tōr-ē, -,tòr-\ *adj*

vi•tu•per•a•tion \-,tü-pə-'rā-shən, -,tyü-\ *n* : sustained and bitter railing and condemnation **syn** see ABUSE

vi•va \'vē-və, -,vä\ *interj* — used to express approval or goodwill [Italian, "long live", from *vivere* "to live", from Latin]

vi•va•ce \vē-'väch-ā, vi-, -ē\ *adv or adj* : in a brisk spirited manner — used as a direction in music [Italian, "vivacious"]

vi•va•cious \və-'vā-shəs *also* vī-\ *adj* : lively in temper or conduct : SPRIGHTLY [Latin *vivac-, vivax,* literally, "long-lived", from *vivere* "to live"] **syn** see LIVELY — **vi•va•cious•ly** *adv* — **vi•va•cious•ness** *n*

vi•vac•i•ty \-'vas-ət-ē\ *n* : the quality or state of being vivacious

vi•var•i•um \vī-'var-ē-əm, -'ver-\ *n, pl* **-ia** \-ē-ə\ *or* **-i•ums** : an enclosure for keeping or raising and observing animals or plants indoors; *esp* : such an enclosure for terrestrial animals — called also *terrarium* [Latin, "park, preserve", from *vivus* "alive"]

[1]vi•va vo•ce \,vī-və-'vō-sē, ,vē-və-'vō-chā\ *adv* : by word of mouth : ORALLY [Medieval Latin, "with the living voice"]

[2]viva voce *adj* : expressed or conducted by word of mouth : ORAL

viv•id \'viv-əd\ *adj* **1** : having the appearance of vigorous life or freshness : very lively ⟨a *vivid* personality⟩ **2** : very strong or intense : of very high saturation ⟨a *vivid* red⟩ **3** : producing a strong or clear impression on the senses : SHARP; *esp* : producing distinct mental images ⟨a *vivid* description⟩ **4** : acting clearly and vigorously ⟨a *vivid* imagination⟩ [Latin *vividus,* from *vivere* "to live"] **syn** see GRAPHIC — **viv•id•ly** *adv* — **viv•id•ness** *n*

viv•i•fy \'viv-ə-,fī\ *vt* **-fied; -fy•ing 1** : to provide with the quality or appearance of life : ANIMATE **2** : to make vivid [Middle French *vivifier,* from Late Latin *vivificare,* derived from Latin *vivus* "alive"] — **viv•i•fi•ca•tion** \,viv-ə-fə-'kā-shən\ *n* — **viv•i•fi•er** \'viv-ə-,fī-ər, -,fīr\ *n*

vi•vip•a•rous \vī-'vip-rəs, -ə-rəs\ *adj* : producing living young from within the body rather than from eggs [Latin *viviparus,* from *vivus* "alive" + *parere* "to produce"] — **vi•vi•par•i•ty** \,vī-və-'par-ət-ē\ *n* — **vi•vip•a•rous•ly** \vī-'vip-rəs-lē, -ə-rəs-\ *adv*

vivi•sec•tion \,viv-ə-'sek-shən\ *n* : the cutting of or operation on a living animal usually for scientific investigation; *also* : animal experimentation especially if considered to cause distress to the subject [Latin *vivus* "alive" + English *section*] — **vivi•sect** \'viv-ə-,sekt\ *vb* — **vivi•sec•tion•al** \,viv-ə-'sek-shnəl, -shən-l\ *adj* — **vivi•sec•tion•al•ly** \-ē\ *adv* — **vivi•sec•tion•ist** \-'sek-shə-nəst, -shnəst\ *n* — **vivi•sec•tor** \'viv-ə-,sek-tər\ *n*

vix•en \'vik-sən\ *n* **1** : a female fox **2** : a quick-tempered argumentative woman [Middle English *fixen,* from Old English *fyxe,* feminine of *fox*] — **vix•en•ish** \-sə-nish, -snish\ *adj* — **vix•en•ish•ly** *adv*

viz•ard \'viz-ərd, -,ärd\ *n* : a mask formerly worn especially for disguise [Middle English *viser* "mask, visor"]

vi•zier \və-'ziər\ *n* : a high executive officer of various Muslim countries and especially of the former Turkish Empire [Turkish *vezir,* from Arabic *wazīr*] — **vi•zier•ial** \-'zir-ē-əl\ *adj* — **vi•zier•ship** \-'ziər-,ship\ *n*

vo•ca•ble \'vō-kə-bəl\ *n* : a word composed of various sounds or letters without regard to its meaning [Middle French, "term, name", from Latin *vocabulum,* from *vocare* "to call"]

vo•cab•u•lary \vō-'kab-yə-,ler-ē\ *n, pl* **-lar•ies 1** : a list or collection of words or of words and phrases usually alphabetically arranged and explained or defined **2** : a sum or stock of words employed by a language, group, individual, or work or in a field of knowledge [Middle French *vocabulaire,* probably from Medieval Latin *vocabularium,* derived from Latin *vocabulum* "name, term", from *vocare* "to call"]

vocabulary entry *n* : a word (as the noun *book*), hyphened or open compound (as the adjective *light-headed* or the noun *book review*), word element (as the affix *pro-*), abbreviation (as *agt*), verbalized symbol (as *Na*), or term (as *point of view*) entered alphabetically in a dictionary for the purpose of definition or identification or expressly included as an inflectional form (as the noun *mice* or the verb *saw*) or as a derived form (as the noun *godlessness* or the adverb *globally*) or related phrase (as *one for the book*) run on at its base word and usually set in a type (as boldface) readily distinguishable from that of the lightface text which defines, explains, or identifies the entry

[1]vo•cal \'vō-kəl\ *adj* **1 a** : uttered by the voice : ORAL **b** : VOICED 2 **2** : relating to, composed or arranged for, or sung by the human voice ⟨*vocal* music⟩ **3** : VOCALIC **4** : given to expressing oneself freely or insistently : OUTSPOKEN **5** : of, relating to, or resembling the voice [Latin *vocalis,* from *voc-, vox* "voice"] — **vo•cal•ly** \-kə-lē\ *adv*

[2]vocal *n* **1** : a vocal sound **2** : a solo for a singer especially when accompanied by a dance or jazz band

vocal cords *n pl* : either of two pairs of elastic folds of mucous membrane that project into the cavity of the larynx and that play a major role in the production of vocal sounds — called also *vocal folds*

vo•cal•ic \vō-'kal-ik\ *adj* **1** : marked by or consisting of vowels **2** : of, relating to, or functioning as a vowel [Latin *vocalis* "vowel", from *vocalis* "vocal"] — **vo•cal•i•cal•ly** \-i-kə-lē, -klē\ *adv*

vo•cal•ist \'vō-kə-ləst\ *n* : [1]SINGER

vo•cal•iza•tion \,vō-kə-lə-'zā-shən\ *n* : an act, process, or instance of vocalizing

vo•cal•ize \'vō-kə-,līz\ *vb* **1 a** : to give vocal expression to **b** : SING; *esp* : to sing without words (as in practicing) **2 a** : VOICE 2 **b** : to convert to a vowel — **vo•cal•iz•er** *n*

\ə\ **abut**	\au̇\ **out**	\i\ **tip**	\ȯ\ **saw**	\u̇\ **foot**
\ər\ **further**	\ch\ **chin**	\ī\ **life**	\ȯi\ **coin**	\y\ **yet**
\a\ **mat**	\e\ **pet**	\j\ **job**	\th\ **thin**	\yü\ **few**
\ā\ **take**	\ē\ **easy**	\ng\ **sing**	\th̲\ **this**	\yu̇\ **cure**
\ä\ **cot, cart**	\g\ **go**	\ō\ **bone**	\ü\ **food**	\zh\ **vision**

vo•ca•tion \vō-'kā-shən\ *n* **1 :** a summons or strong inclination to a particular state or course of action; *esp* **:** a divine call to the religious life **2 a :** the work in which a person is regularly employed **:** OCCUPATION **b :** the persons engaged in a particular occupation **3 :** the special function of an individual or group **:** ROLE **[**Latin *vocatio* "summons", from *vocare* "to call"**]**
• syn AVOCATION: VOCATION denotes one's livelihood; AVOCATION denotes a leisure occupation which may or may not bring remuneration.

vo•ca•tion•al \-shnəl, -shən-l\ *adj* **1 :** of, relating to, or concerned with a vocation **2 :** concerned with choice or of training in a skill or trade to be pursued as a career ⟨*vocational* guidance⟩ ⟨a *vocational* school⟩ — **vo•ca•tion•al•ly** \-ē\ *adv*

vo•ca•tion•al•ism \-ˌiz-əm\ *n* **:** emphasis on vocational training in education

voc•a•tive \'väk-ət-iv\ *adj* **:** of, relating to, or constituting a grammatical case marking the one addressed **[**Middle French *vocatif,* from Latin *vocativus,* from *vocare* "to call"**]** — **vocative** *n* — **voc•a•tive•ly** *adv*

vo•cif•er•ant \vō-'sif-ə-rənt\ *adj* **:** VOCIFEROUS — **vo•cif•er•ance** \-rəns\ *n*

vo•cif•er•ate \vō-'sif-ə-ˌrāt\ *vb* **:** to cry out or utter loudly **:** CLAMOR, SHOUT **[**Latin *vociferari,* from *voc-, vox* "voice" + *ferre* "to carry"**]** — **vo•cif•er•a•tion** \-ˌsif-ə-'rā-shən\ *n* — **vo•cif•er•a•tor** \-'sif-ə-ˌrāt-ər\ *n*

vo•cif•er•ous \vō-'sif-rəs, -ə-rəs\ *adj* **:** making a loud outcry **:** NOISY, CLAMOROUS — **vo•cif•er•ous•ly** *adv* — **vo•cif•er•ous•ness** *n*

vod•ka \'väd-kə\ *n* **:** a colorless and unaged alcoholic liquor distilled fom a mash (as of rye or wheat) **[**Russian, from *voda* "water"**]**

vogue \'vōg\ *n* **1 a :** popular approval or favor **:** POPULARITY **b :** a period of popularity **2 :** something or someone in fashion at a particular time **[**Middle French, "action of rowing, course, fashion", from Italian *voga,* from *vogare* "to row"**]** **syn** see FASHION — **vogue** *adj*

vogu•ish \'vō-gish\ *adj* **1 :** following the fashion **:** SMART **2 :** suddenly or temporarily popular

[1]**voice** \'vȯis\ *n* **1 a :** sound produced by vertebrates by means of lungs, larynx, or syrinx; *esp* **:** sound so produced by human beings **b :** musical sound produced by the vocal cords and resonated by the cavities of the head and throat **c :** the quality of the sound produced by the voice ⟨a squeaky *voice*⟩ **2 a :** the ability to produce vocal sound **:** power of speech **b :** the ability to produce musical tones **c :** the quality of the vocal mechanism with respect to the production of musical tones ⟨in good *voice* today⟩ **d :** the use of the voice in speaking, acting, or singing **3 :** something resembling or likened to a vocal utterance ⟨the *voice* of conscience⟩ **4 :** distinction of form or a system of inflections of a verb to indicate the relation of the subject of the verb to the action which the verb expresses **5 a :** wish, choice, or opinion openly or formally expressed ⟨the *voice* of the people⟩ **b :** right of expression **:** SUFFRAGE, SAY **6 :** a medium of expression ⟨the newspaper was the *voice* of conservatism⟩ **7 a :** [1]SINGER **b :** one of the melodic parts of a vocal or instrumental composition **8 :** expiration of air with the vocal cords drawn close so as to vibrate audibly ⟨consonants pronounced with *voice*⟩ **[**Old French *vois,* from Latin *voc-, vox***]** — **with one voice :** UNANIMOUSLY

[2]**voice** *vt* **1 :** UTTER, EXPRESS ⟨*voiced* serious objections to our proposal⟩ **2 :** to pronounce (as a consonant) with voice

voice box *n* **:** LARYNX

voiced \'vȯist\ *adj* **1 a :** furnished with a voice ⟨soft-*voiced*⟩ **b :** expressed in language ⟨a frequently *voiced* opinion⟩ **2 :** uttered with vocal cord vibration ⟨a *voiced* consonant⟩

voice•less \'vȯi-sləs\ *adj* **1 :** having no voice **:** MUTE **2 :** not voiced ⟨a *voiceless* consonant⟩ — **voice•less•ly** *adv* — **voice•less•ness** *n*

voice part *n* **:** VOICE 7b

voice•print \'vȯi-ˌsprint\ *n* **:** an individually distinctive pattern of certain voice characteristics that is spectrographically produced **[***voice* + *-print* (as in *fingerprint*)**]**

[1]**void** \'vȯid\ *adj* **1 :** containing nothing ⟨*void* space⟩ **2 :** not containing or occupied by something usual or normal ⟨hearts *void* of mercy⟩ ⟨a *void* chair⟩ ⟨left the presidency *void*⟩ **3 :** of no legal force or effect ⟨a *void* marriage⟩

[2]**void** *n* **1 a :** empty space **b :** an unfilled opening **2 :** LACK 1, DEFICIENCY **3 :** a feeling of want or hollowness **4 :** absence of cards of a particular suit in a hand as dealt

[3]**void** *vt* **1 :** to make empty or vacant **:** CLEAR **2 :** DISCHARGE, EMIT ⟨*void* excrement⟩ **3 :** NULLIFY, ANNUL ⟨*void* a contract⟩ — **void•er** *n*

void•able \'vȯid-ə-bəl\ *adj* **:** capable of being voided

voile \'vȯil\ *n* **:** a soft sheer fabric of silk, cotton, rayon, or wool used especially for curtains or women's summer clothing **[**French, "veil", from Latin *velum***]**

vo•lan•te \vō-'län-tā\ *adj* **:** moving with light rapidity — used as a direction in music **[**Italian, literally, "flying", from Latin *volare* "to fly"**]**

vo•lar \'vō-lər, -ˌlär\ *adj* **:** relating to the palm of the hand or the sole of the foot **[**Latin *vola* "palm, sole"**]**

[1]**vol•a•tile** \'väl-ət-l\ *adj* **1 :** readily becoming a vapor at a relatively low temperature ⟨a *volatile* solvent⟩ **2 a :** LIGHTHEARTED, LIVELY ⟨a *volatile* mind⟩ **b :** easily aroused ⟨a *volatile* temper⟩ **3 a :** tending or likely to erupt into violent action ⟨a *volatile* situation⟩ **b :** subject to often sudden change ⟨a *volatile* market⟩ **[**French, "flying, volatile", from Latin *volatilis* "flying", from *volare* "to fly"**]** — **vol•a•tile•ness** *n* — **vol•a•til•i•ty** \ˌväl-ə-'til-ət-ē\ *n*

[2]**volatile** *n* **:** a volatile substance

vol•a•til•ize \'väl-ət-l-ˌīz\ *vb* **:** to pass off or cause to pass off in vapor — **vol•a•til•iza•tion** \ˌväl-ət-l-ə-'zā-shən\ *n*

[1]**vol•ca•nic** \väl-'kan-ik, vȯl- *also* -'kān-\ *adj* **1 a :** of or relating to a volcano ⟨a *volcanic* eruption⟩ **b :** having volcanoes ⟨a *volcanic* region⟩ **c :** made of materials from volcanoes ⟨*volcanic* dust⟩ **2 :** explosively violent **:** VOLATILE ⟨*volcanic* passions⟩ — **vol•ca•ni•cal•ly** \-i-kə-lē, -klē\ *adv*

[2]**volcanic** *n* **:** a volcanic rock

volcanic glass *n* **:** natural glass produced by the cooling of molten lava too rapidly to permit crystallization

vol•ca•nism \'väl-kə-ˌniz-əm, 'vȯl-\ *n* **:** volcanic activity

vol•ca•no \väl-'kā-nō, vȯl-\ *n, pl* **-noes** *or* **-nos :** a vent in the earth's crust from which molten or hot rock and steam issue; *also* **:** a hill or mountain composed wholly or in part of ejected volcanic material **[**Italian *vulcano,* from Latin *Volcanus, Vulcanus* "Vulcan"**]**

vol•ca•nol•o•gy \ˌväl-kə-'näl-ə-jē, ˌvȯl-\ *n* **:** a branch of science that deals with volcanic phenomena — **vol•ca•no•log•i•cal** \-kən-l-'äj-i-kəl\ *adj* — **vol•ca•nol•o•gist** \-kə-'näl-ə-jəst\ *n*

vole \'vōl\ *n* **:** any of various small rodents closely related to the lemmings and muskrats but in general resembling stocky mice or rats **[**of Scandinavian origin**]**

vole

vo•li•tion \vō-'lish-ən, və-\ *n* **1 :** the act or power of making one's own choices or decisions ⟨they do not do this of their own *volition*⟩ **2 :** the ending of an act or exercise of willing **[**French, from Medieval Latin *volitio,* from Latin *velle* "to will, wish"**]** — **vo•li•tion•al** \-'lish-nəl, -ən-l\ *adj*

[1]**vol•ley** \'väl-ē\ *n, pl* **volleys 1 a :** a flight of missiles (as arrows or bullets) **b :** simultaneous discharge of a number of missile weapons (as rifles) **2 a :** a return of the ball before it touches the ground (as in tennis or volleyball) **b :** a kick of the ball in soccer before it rebounds **c :** the exchange of the shuttlecock in badminton following the serve **3 :** a bursting forth of many things at once ⟨a *volley* of bubbles⟩ ⟨a *volley* of curses⟩ **[**Middle French *volee* "flight", from *voler* "to fly," from Latin *volare***]**

[2]**volley** *vb* **vol•leyed; vol•ley•ing 1 :** to discharge in a volley **2 :** to propel an object (as a ball) while it is in the air before it touches the ground

vol•ley•ball \'väl-ē-ˌbȯl\ *n* **:** a game played by volleying a large inflated ball over a net

vol•plane \'väl-ˌplān, 'vȯl-\ *vi* **:** to glide in or as if in an airplane **[**French *vol plané* "gliding flight"**]**

volt \'vōlt\ *n* **:** a unit of electrical potential difference and electromotive force equal to the difference of potential between two points in a conducting wire carrying a constant current of one ampere when the power dissipated between these two points is equal to one watt **[**Alessandro *Volta,* died 1827, Italian physicist**]**

volt·age \ˈvōl-tij\ *n* : potential difference expressed in volts

voltage divider *n* : a resistor or series of resistors provided with taps at certain points and used to provide various potential differences from a single power source

vol·ta·ic \väl-ˈtā-ik, vōl-, vȯl-\ *adj* : of, relating to, or producing direct electric current by chemical action (as in a battery) [Alessandro *Volta*]

voltaic cell *n* : an apparatus for generating electricity through chemical action on two unlike metals in an electrolyte

voltaic pile *n* : ^{3}PILE 3a

vol·ta·me·ter \vōl-ˈtam-ət-ər, ˈvōl-tə-ˌmēt-\ *n* : an apparatus for measuring the quantity of electricity passed through a conductor by the amount of electrolysis produced [*voltaic* + *-meter*]

volt–am·pere \ˈvōl-ˈtam-ˌpiər\ *n* : a unit of electric measurement equal to the product of a volt and an ampere that for direct current constitutes a measure of power equivalent to a watt

volte–face \ˌvȯlt-ˈfäs, ˌvȯlt-ə-\ *n* : reversal of attitude especially in policy : ABOUT-FACE [French, from Italian *voltafaccia,* from *voltare* "to turn" + *faccia* "face"]

volt·me·ter \ˈvōlt-ˌmēt-ər\ *n* : an instrument for measuring in volts the differences of potential between different points of an electrical circuit

vol·u·ble \ˈväl-yə-bəl\ *adj* : characterized by ready or rapid speech : GLIB, FLUENT [Latin *volubilis,* from *volvere* "to roll"] **syn** see TALKATIVE — **vol·u·bil·i·ty** \ˌväl-yə-ˈbil-ət-ē\ *n* — **vol·u·bly** \ˈväl-yə-blē\ *adv*

vol·ume \ˈväl-yəm, -yüm\ *n* **1** : BOOK ⟨a dozen *volumes* on the shelf⟩ **2** : any of a series of books forming a complete work or collection ⟨the 5th *volume* of an encyclopedia⟩ **3 a** : space occupied **b** : measure of a bounded space especially in cubic units ⟨find the *volume* of the cylinder⟩ **4 a** : a usually shapeless body or mass ⟨a *volume* of gas⟩ **b** : a considerable quantity ⟨*volumes* of smoke⟩ **5** : intensity or quantity of sound ⟨turn up the *volume* on the radio⟩ [Middle French, from Latin *volumen* "roll, book", from *volvere* "to roll] **syn** see BULK

△ **origin** The earliest books were rolls of papyrus. The Romans took their name for such a roll, *volumen,* from the verb *volvere,* "to roll". Later, books were made of parchment, which, unlike papyrus, could be folded and bound. This eliminated the need for rolls. French *volume,* from Latin *volumen,* originally referred to papyrus rolls but was later used for bound books as well. The French word was borrowed into English in the 14th century. By the 16th century *volume* had acquired the additional sense "the size (of a book)", which led to the development of a generalized sense, "quantity, amount, or mass (of anything)". In the 19th century *volume* acquired the meaning "strength" or "intensity" in reference to sound.

vol·u·meter \ˈväl-yü-ˌmēt-ər\ *n* : an instrument for measuring volumes (as of gases or liquids) directly or (as of solids) by displacement of a liquid

vol·u·met·ric \ˌväl-yə-ˈme-trik\ *adj* : of or relating to the measurement of volume — **vol·u·met·ri·cal·ly** \-tri-kə-lē, -klē\ *adv*

vo·lu·mi·nous \və-ˈlü-mə-nəs\ *adj* **1** : having many folds, coils, or convolutions **2 a** : filling or capable of filling a large volume or several volumes ⟨a *voluminous* correspondence⟩ **b** : writing or speaking much or at great length ⟨a *voluminous* writer⟩ [Late Latin *voluminosus* "full of folds", from Latin *volumen* "roll, book"] — **vo·lu·mi·nous·ly** *adv* — **vo·lu·mi·nous·ness** *n*

vol·un·tar·i·ly \ˌväl-ən-ˈter-ə-lē\ *adv* : of one's own free will

^{1}**vol·un·tary** \ˈväl-ən-ˌter-ē\ *adj* **1** : done, given, or made in accordance with one's own free will or choice ⟨*voluntary* assistance⟩ **2** : not accidental : INTENTIONAL ⟨*voluntary* manslaughter⟩ **3** : of or relating to the will : controlled by the will ⟨*voluntary* behavior⟩ [Latin *voluntarius,* from *voluntas* "will", from *velle* "to will, wish"]

• **syn** VOLUNTARY, INTENTIONAL, DELIBERATE, WILLFULL mean done or brought about of one's own accord. VOLUNTARY implies spontaneousness and freedom from compulsion ⟨*voluntary* contributions⟩ or stresses control of the will ⟨*voluntary* eye movements⟩ INTENTIONAL stresses consciousness of purpose ⟨an *intentional* oversight⟩ DELIBERATE implies full consciousness of the nature of an intended action ⟨a *deliberate* insult⟩ WILLFUL implies an obstinate determination to follow one's own will and a refusal to learn or obey.

^{2}**voluntary** *n, pl* **-tar·ies** : an organ piece often improvised and played before, during, or after a religious service

voluntary muscle *n* : muscle (as most striated muscle) under voluntary control

^{1}**vol·un·teer** \ˌväl-ən-ˈtiər\ *n* **1** : one who enters into a service or offers to serve of his or her own free will; *esp* : one who enters into military service voluntarily **2** : a volunteer plant [French *volontaire,* from *volontaire* "voluntary", from Latin *voluntarius*]

^{2}**volunteer** *adj* **1** : of, relating to, or consisting of volunteers ⟨a *volunteer* army⟩ **2** : growing spontaneously without direct human care especially from seeds lost from a previous crop

^{3}**volunteer** *vb* **1** : to offer or bestow voluntarily ⟨*volunteered* one's services⟩ **2** : to offer oneself as a volunteer

vo·lup·tu·ary \və-ˈləp-chə-ˌwer-ē\ *n, pl* **-ar·ies** : one whose chief interest is luxury and the gratification of sensual appetites — **voluptuary** *adj*

vo·lup·tu·ous \-chə-wəs, -chəs\ *adj* **1** : giving pleasure to the senses : providing sensual or sensuous gratification ⟨*voluptuous* furnishings⟩ ⟨*voluptuous* dancers⟩ **2** : given to or spent in the enjoyment of pleasure and luxury ⟨a *voluptuous* holiday⟩ **3** : having sensual appeal ⟨*voluptuous* dancing⟩ ⟨a *voluptuous* figure⟩ [Latin *voluptuosus,* from *voluptas* "pleasure"]

vo·lute \və-ˈlüt\ *n* **1** : a spiral or scroll-shaped form **2** : a spiral scroll-shaped ornament forming the chief feature of the Ionic capital [Latin *voluta,* from *volvere* "to roll"] — **vo·lute** *or* **vo·lut·ed** \-ˈlüt-əd\ *adj*

vol·va \ˈväl-və, ˈvȯl-\ *n* : a membraneous sac or cup about the base of the stem in many mushrooms [Latin *volva, vulva* "integument"] — **vol·vate** \-ˌvāt\ *adj*

1 volva

vol·vox \-ˌväks\ *n* : any of a genus of green flagellates that form spherical colonies [New Latin, from Latin *volvere* "to roll"]

vo·mer \ˈvō-mər\ *n* : a bone of the lower skull of most vertebrates that in human beings forms part of the nasal septum [Latin, "plowshare"] — **vo·mer·ine** \-mə-ˌrīn\ *adj*

^{1}**vom·it** \ˈväm-ət\ *n* : an act or instance of ejecting the contents of the stomach through the mouth; *also* : the matter ejected [Middle French, from Latin *vomitus,* from *vomere* "to vomit"]

^{2}**vomit** *vb* **1** : to eject the contents of the stomach through the mouth **2** : DISGORGE 2 ⟨lava *vomited* from the volcano⟩ — **vom·it·er** *n*

vom·i·tus \ˈväm-ət-əs\ *n* : material discharged by vomiting [Latin]

^{1}**voo·doo** \ˈvüd-ü\ *n, pl* **voodoos** **1** : a religion derived from African ancestor worship, practiced chiefly by Negroes of Haiti, and consisting largely of magic and sorcery **2 a** : one who deals in spells and necromancy **b (1)** : a sorcerer's spell **(2)** : a hexed object [Louisiana French *voudou,* of African origin] — **voodoo** *adj*

^{2}**voodoo** *vt* : to bewitch by or as if by means of voodoo : HEX

voo·doo·ism \ˈvüd-ü-ˌiz-əm\ *n* **1** : VOODOO 1 **2** : the practice of witchcraft — **voo·doo·ist** \ˈvüd-ˌü-əst\ *n* — **voo·doo·is·tic** \ˌvüd-ü-ˈis-tik\ *adj*

vo·ra·cious \vȯ-ˈrā-shəs, və-\ *adj* **1** : greedy in eating : RAVENOUS ⟨a *voracious* appetite⟩ **2** : excessively eager : INSATIABLE ⟨a *voracious* reader⟩ [Latin *vorac-, vorax,* from *vorare* "to devour"] — **vo·ra·cious·ly** *adv* — **vo·ra·cious·ness** *n* — **vo·rac·i·ty** \-ˈras-ət-ē\ *n*

vor·tex \ˈvȯr-ˌteks\ *n, pl* **vor·ti·ces** \ˈvȯrt-ə-ˌsēz\ *also* **vor·tex·es** \ˈvȯr-ˌtek-səz\ **1** : a mass of fluid and especially of a liquid having a whirling motion that tends to form a cavity in the center and to draw things toward this cavity; *esp* : WHIRLPOOL, EDDY **2** : a whirling mass (as a whirlwind, tornado, or waterspout); *also* : the eye of a cyclone [Latin *vertic-, vertex, vortic-, vortex* "whirlpool", from *vertere* "to turn"]

vor·ti·cal \ˈvȯrt-i-kəl\ *adj* : of, relating to, or resembling a vortex

\ə\ **abut**	\au̇\ **out**	\i\ **tip**	\ȯ\ **saw**	\u̇\ **foot**
\ər\ **further**	\ch\ **chin**	\ī\ **life**	\ȯi\ **coin**	\y\ **yet**
\a\ **mat**	\e\ **pet**	\j\ **job**	\th\ **thin**	\yü\ **few**
\ā\ **take**	\ē\ **easy**	\ng\ **sing**	\t͟h\ **this**	\yu̇\ **cure**
\ä\ **cot, cart**	\g\ **go**	\ō\ **bone**	\ü\ **food**	\zh\ **vision**

vor•ti•cel•la \ˌvȯrt-ə-'sel-ə\ *n, pl* **-cel•lae** \-'sel-ē\ *or* **-cellas** : any of a genus of stalked bell-shaped ciliates [New Latin, from Latin *vortic-, vortex* "whirlpool"]
vor•tic•i•ty \vȯr-'tis-ət-ē\ *n* : the state of a fluid in vortical motion
vo•ta•rist \'vōt-ə-rəst\ *n* : VOTARY
vo•ta•ry \'vōt-ə-rē\ *n, pl* **-ries 1 a** : ENTHUSIAST, DEVOTEE **b** : a devoted adherent or admirer **2** : a devout or zealous worshiper [Latin *votum* "vow"]
[1]**vote** \'vōt\ *n* **1 a** : a formal expression of opinion or will; *esp* : one given as an indication of approval or disapproval of a proposal or a candidate for office **b** : the total number of such expressions of opinion made known at a single time (as at an election) **c** : BALLOT 1 **2** : the collective opinion of a body of persons expressed by voting **3** : the right to cast a vote : SUFFRAGE **4 a** : the act or process of voting ⟨bring the issue to a *vote*⟩ **b** : a method of voting **5 a** : VOTER **b** : a group of voters with common characteristics ⟨the farm *vote*⟩ [Latin *votum* "vow, wish", from *vovēre* "to vow"]
[2]**vote** *vb* **1** : to express one's wish or choice by a vote : cast a vote **2** : to make into law by a vote ⟨*vote* an income tax⟩ **3** : ELECT ⟨*vote* someone into office⟩ **4** : to declare by common consent **5** : PROPOSE 1, SUGGEST
vote•less \'vōt-ləs\ *adj* : having no vote; *esp* : denied the political franchise
vot•er \'vōt-ər\ *n* : one that votes or has the legal right to vote
voting machine *n* : a mechanical device for recording and counting votes cast on it in an election
vo•tive \'vōt-iv\ *adj* **1** : offered or performed in fulfillment of a vow or in gratitude or devotion **2** : consisting of or expressing a vow, wish, or desire ⟨a *votive* prayer⟩ [Latin *votivus*, from *votum* "vow"]
votive mass *n* : a mass celebrated for a special intention (as for a wedding or funeral) in place of the mass of the day
vouch \'vau̇ch\ *vb* **1** *archaic* **a** : ASSERT 1, AFFIRM **b** : ATTEST **2** : to give a guarantee : become surety ⟨I'll *vouch* for your honesty⟩ **3 a** : to supply supporting evidence or testimony **b** : to give personal assurance ⟨*vouch* for the truth of a story⟩ [Middle French *vocher* "to summon into court to give warranty", from Latin *vocare* "to call, summon", from *voc-, vox* "voice"]
vouch•er \'vau̇-chər\ *n* **1** : a person who vouches for another **2** : a document that serves to establish the truth of something; *esp* : a paper (as a receipt) showing payment of a bill or debt
vouch•safe \vau̇ch-'sāf, 'vau̇ch-ˌ\ *vt* : to grant in the manner of one doing a favor : condescend to give or grant
vous•soir \vü-'swär\ *n* : one of the wedge-shaped pieces forming an arch or vault [French, derived from Latin *volvere* "to roll"]
[1]**vow** \'vau̇\ *n* : a solemn promise or assertion; *esp* : one by which one binds oneself to an act, service, or condition [Old French *vou*, from Latin *votum*, from *vovēre* "to vow"]
[2]**vow** *vb* **1** : to make a vow : promise solemnly **2** : to bind or consecrate by a vow
[3]**vow** *vt* : AVOW, DECLARE [short for *avow*]
vow•el \'vau̇-əl, 'vau̇l\ *n* **1** : a speech sound in the articulation of which the oral part of the breath channel is not blocked and is not constricted enough to cause audible friction **2** : a letter representing a vowel; *esp* : any of the letters *a, e, i, o, u,* and sometimes *y* in English [Middle French *vouel*, from Latin *vocalis*, from *vocalis* "vocal"] — **vow•el•like** \'vau̇-əl-ˌlīk, 'vau̇l-\ *adj*
vox po•pu•li \'väk-'späp-yə-ˌlī, -yə-lē\ *n* : popular sentiment [Latin, "voice of the people"]
[1]**voy•age** \'vȯi-ij, 'vȯ-ij, 'voij\ *n* **1** : a journey by water : CRUISE **2** : a journey through air or space [Old French *voiage* "journey", from Latin *viaticum* "traveling money", from *viaticus* "of a journey", from *via* "way"]
[2]**voyage** *vb* **1** : to take a trip : TRAVEL **2** : to pass over or cover in traveling ⟨*voyage* the briny deep⟩ — **voy•ag•er** *n*
voya•geur \ˌvȯi-ə-'zhər, ˌvwä-yä-\ *n* : a person employed by a fur company to transport goods and people to and from remote stations in the Northwest [Canadian French, from French, "traveler"]
Vul•ca•ni•an \ˌvəl-'kā-nē-ən\ *adj* : of or relating to Vulcan or to working in metals (as iron)
vul•can•ism \'vəl-kə-ˌniz-əm\ *n* : VOLCANISM
vul•can•ite \-ˌnīt\ *n* : a hard vulcanized rubber
vul•can•ize \'vəl-kə-ˌnīz\ *vt* : to treat (rubber or similar plastic material) chemically in order to give useful properties (as elasticity, strength, or stability) [Latin *Vulcanus* "Vulcan, fire"] — **vul•can•iza•tion** \ˌvəl-kə-nə-'zā-shən\ *n* — **vul•can•iz•er** \'vəl-kə-ˌnī-zər\ *n*
vul•gar \'vəl-gər\ *adj* **1** : generally used, applied, or accepted **2** : VERNACULAR **3 a** : of or relating to the common people : PLEBEIAN **b** : of the usual, typical, or ordinary kind **4 a** : lacking in cultivation, perception, or taste : COARSE **b** : ostentatious or excessive in expenditure or display : PRETENTIOUS **5** : offensive in language : OBSCENE, PROFANE [Latin *vulgaris* "of the mob, vulgar", from *vulgus* "mob, common people"] **syn** see COARSE — **vul•gar•ly** *adv*
vul•gar•i•an \ˌvəl-'gar-ē-ən, -'ger-\ *n* : a vulgar person
vul•gar•ism \'vəl-gə-ˌriz-əm\ *n* **1 a** : a word or expression originated or used chiefly by illiterate persons **b** : a coarse word or phrase **2** : VULGARITY 1
vul•gar•i•ty \ˌvəl-'gar-ət-ē\ *n, pl* **-ties 1** : the quality or state of being vulgar **2** : something vulgar
vul•gar•ize \'vəl-gə-ˌrīz\ *vt* **1** : to make generally known or liked : POPULARIZE **2** : to make vulgar : COARSEN — **vul•gar•iza•tion** \ˌvəl-gə-rə-'zā-shən\ *n* — **vul•gar•iz•er** \'vəl-gə-ˌrī-zər\ *n*
Vulgar Latin *n* : the nonliterary Latin of ancient Rome including the speech of plebeians and the informal speech of the educated established by comparative evidence as the chief source of the Romance languages
Vul•gate \'vəl-ˌgāt\ *n* : a Latin version of the Bible authorized and used by the Roman Catholic Church [Late Latin *vulgata editio* "edition in general circulation"]
vul•ner•a•ble \'vəln-rə-bəl, -ə-rə-; 'vəl-nər-bəl\ *adj* **1** : capable of being wounded **2** : open to attack or damage ⟨a *vulnerable* fort⟩ **3** : liable to increased penalties but entitled to increased bonuses in a game of contract bridge [Late Latin *vulnerabilis*, from Latin *vulnerare* "to wound", from *vulner-, vulnus* "wound"] — **vul•ner•a•bil•i•ty** \ˌvəln-rə-'bil-ət-ē, -ə-rə-\ *n* — **vul•ner•a•bly** \'vəln-rə-blē, -ə-rə-; 'vəl-nər-blē\ *adv*
vul•pine \'vəl-ˌpīn\ *adj* : of, relating to, or resembling a fox especially in cunning : CRAFTY [Latin *vulpinus*, from *vulpes* "fox"]
vul•ture \'vəl-chər\ *n* **1** : any of various large birds that are related to the hawks and eagles but have weaker claws and the head usually naked and that subsist chiefly or entirely on carrion **2** : a greedy or predatory person [Latin *vultur*]

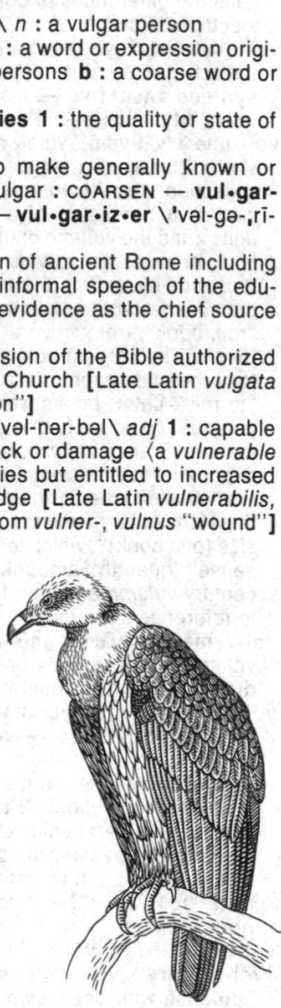
vulture 1

vul•va \'vəl-və\ *n, pl* **vul•vae** \-ˌvē, -ˌvī\ : the external parts of the female genital organs; *also* : the opening between their projecting parts [Latin, "integument, womb"] — **vul•val** \'vəl-vəl\ *or* **vul•var** \-vər, -ˌvär\ *adj*
vying *present participle of* VIE

W w—wyandotte

w \ˈdəb-əl-ˌyü, -yə, *rapid* ˈdəb-ə-yə, ˈdəb-yə\ *n, pl* **w's** *or* **ws** \-ˌyüz, -yəz\ *often cap* **:** the 23d letter of the English alphabet

wab•ble \ˈwäb-əl\ *variant of* WOBBLE

Wac \ˈwak\ *n* **:** a member of the Women's Army Corps [*W*omen's *A*rmy *C*orps]

wacky \ˈwak-ē\ *adj* **wack•i•er; -est :** absurdly or amusingly eccentric or irrational **:** CRAZY [perhaps from English dialect *whacky* "fool"] — **wack•i•ly** \ˈwak-ə-lē\ *adv* — **wack•i•ness** \ˈwak-ē-nəs\ *n*

^{1}**wad** \ˈwäd\ *n* **1 :** a small mass, bundle, or tuft ⟨plugged the hole with *wads* of clay⟩: as **a :** a soft mass of usually light fibrous material **b :** a pliable pad or plug (as of felt) used to retain a powder charge in a gun or cartridge **2 a :** a considerable amount (as of money) **b :** a roll of paper money [origin unknown]

^{2}**wad** *vt* **wad•ded; wad•ding 1 :** to form into a wad ⟨*wad* up a handkerchief⟩ **2 :** to push a wad into ⟨*wad* a gun⟩ **3 :** to hold in by a wad ⟨*wad* a bullet in a gun⟩ **4 :** to stuff or line with soft material

wad•ding \ˈwäd-ing\ *n* **1 :** wads or material for making wads **2 :** a soft mass or sheet of short loose fibers used for stuffing or padding

^{1}**wad•dle** \ˈwäd-l\ *vi* **wad•dled; wad•dling** \ˈwäd-ling, -l-ing\ **:** to walk with short steps swaying from side to side like a duck [derived from *wade*] — **wad•dler** \ˈwäd-lər, -l-ər\ *n*

^{2}**waddle** *n* **:** an awkward clumsy swaying gait

^{1}**wade** \ˈwād\ *vb* **1 :** to step in or through a medium (as water) offering more resistance than air **2 :** to move or proceed with difficulty or labor ⟨*wade* through a dull book⟩ ⟨*wade* into a task⟩ **3 :** to pass or cross by wading ⟨*wade* a stream⟩ [Old English *wadan*]

^{2}**wade** *n* **:** an act of wading ⟨a *wade* in the brook⟩

wad•er \ˈwād-ər\ *n* **1 :** one that wades **2 :** WADING BIRD **3** *pl* **:** high waterproof boots or trousers for wading

wa•di \ˈwäd-ē\ *n* **:** a stream bed or valley especially of southwestern Asia and northern Africa that is usually dry except during the rainy season [Arabic *wādiy*]

wading bird *n* **:** any of many long-legged birds including the shorebirds and various inland water birds (as cranes and herons) that wade in water in search of food

wading pool *n* **:** a shallow pool of portable or permanent construction used by children for wading

Waf \ˈwaf\ *n* **:** a member of the women's component of the United States Air Force [*W*omen in the *A*ir *F*orce]

wa•fer \ˈwā-fər\ *n* **1 a :** a thin crisp cake or cracker **b :** a round thin piece of unleavened bread used in the sacrament of Communion **2 :** something (as a piece of candy or an adhesive seal) resembling a wafer especially in thin round form [Old North French *waufre,* of Germanic origin]

waf•fle \ˈwäf-əl\ *n* **:** a crisp cake of batter baked in a waffle iron [Dutch *wafel*]

waffle iron *n* **:** a cooking utensil with two hinged metal parts that shut upon each other and impress surface projections on waffles being cooked

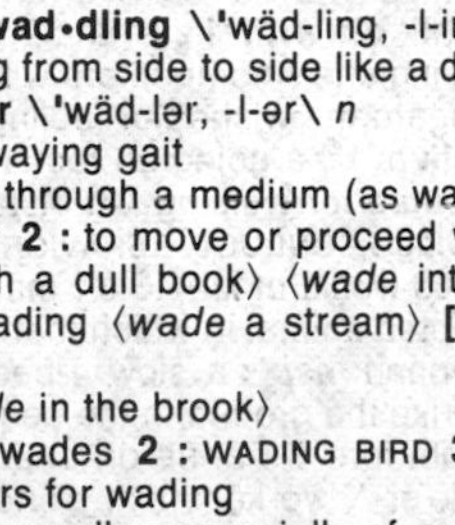

waffle iron

^{1}**waft** \ˈwäft, ˈwaft\ *vb* **:** to move or cause to move or go lightly by or as if by the impulse of wind or waves [Dutch or Low German *wachten* "to watch, guard"] — **waft•er** *n*

^{2}**waft** *n* **1 :** WHIFF 1a **2 :** a slight movement (as of air) **:** PUFF

^{1}**wag** \ˈwag\ *vb* **wagged; wag•ging 1 :** to swing to and fro or from side to side ⟨the dog *wagged* its tail⟩ **2 :** to move in chatter or gossip ⟨scandal caused tongues to *wag*⟩ [Middle English *waggen*] — **wag•ger** *n*

^{2}**wag** *n* **:** an act of wagging **:** SHAKE

^{3}**wag** *n* **:** WIT 4, JOKER [probably from obsolete *waghalter* "person who deserves hanging"]

^{1}**wage** \ˈwāj\ *vb* **1 :** to engage in or carry on ⟨*wage* war⟩ ⟨*wage* a campaign⟩ **2 :** to be waged ⟨the fight *waged* wildly⟩ [Old North French *wagier* "to pledge, give as security", from *wage* "pledge"]

^{2}**wage** *n* **1 :** a payment for labor or services usually according to contract and on an hourly, daily, or piecework basis — often used in pl. **2** *pl* **:** RECOMPENSE, REWARD [Old North French *wage* "pledge, wage", of Germanic origin]
• syn WAGE, SALARY, STIPEND, FEE mean the price paid for labor or services. WAGE implies a regular amount paid on an hourly or daily basis and typically at weekly intervals especially for chiefly physical labor; SALARY and STIPEND apply to a fixed amount paid usually at longer intervals for services requiring training or special ability; STIPEND may also imply a grant or allowance rather than direct pay for work done; FEE applies to the sum asked for the services of a doctor, lawyer, artist, or other professional.

wage earner *n* **:** one that works for wages or salary

^{1}**wa•ger** \ˈwā-jər\ *n* **1 :** something risked on an uncertain event **:** STAKE **2 :** an act of betting **:** GAMBLE [Anglo-French *wageure* "pledge, bet", from Old North French *wagier* "to pledge"]

^{2}**wager** *vb* **wa•gered; wa•ger•ing** \ˈwāj-ring, -ə-ring\ **:** to risk on an outcome **:** VENTURE; *esp* **:** GAMBLE — **wa•ger•er** \ˈwā-jər-ər\ *n*

wag•gery \ˈwag-ə-rē\ *n, pl* **-ger•ies 1 :** mischievous fun **:** PLEASANTRY **2 :** JEST 1a; *esp* **:** PRACTICAL JOKE

wag•gish \ˈwag-ish\ *adj* **1 :** resembling or characteristic of a wag **:** FROLICSOME **2 :** done or made in or for sport ⟨a *waggish* trick⟩ — **wag•gish•ly** *adv* — **wag•gish•ness** *n*

wag•gle \ˈwag-əl\ *vb* **wag•gled; wag•gling** \ˈwag-ling, -ə-ling\ **:** to move backward and forward or from side to side **:** WAG 1 [derived from ^{1}*wag*] — **waggle** *n* — **wag•gly** \ˈwag-lē, -ə-lē\ *adj*

wag•on \ˈwag-ən\ *n* **1 :** a four-wheeled vehicle; *esp* **:** one drawn by animals and used for carrying goods **2 :** a child's four-wheeled cart **3 :** STATION WAGON **4 :** PATROL WAGON [Dutch *wagen*] — **wag•on•er** \ˈwag-ə-nər\ *n* — **on the wagon :** abstaining from alcoholic liquors

wagon 1

wag•on•ette \ˌwag-ə-ˈnet\ *n* **:** a light wagon with two facing seats along the sides in back of a transverse front seat

wa•gon–lit \vȧ-gōⁿ-lē\ *n, pl* **wagons–lits** *or* **wagon–lits** \-gō^{n}-lē\ **:** a railroad sleeping car [French, from *wagon* "railroad car" + *lit* "bed"]

wagon master *n* **:** a person in charge of one or more wagons especially for transporting freight

wagon train *n* **:** a group of wagons (as of pioneers) traveling overland

wag•tail \ˈwag-ˌtāl\ *n* **:** any of numerous slender mostly Old World birds related to the pipits and having a very long tail that is habitually jerked up and down

\ə\ **abut**	\au̇\ **out**	\i\ **tip**	\ȯ\ **saw**	\u̇\ **foot**
\ər\ **further**	\ch\ **chin**	\ī\ **life**	\ȯi\ **coin**	\y\ **yet**
\a\ **mat**	\e\ **pet**	\j\ **job**	\th\ **thin**	\yü\ **few**
\ā\ **take**	\ē\ **easy**	\ng\ **sing**	\t͟h\ **this**	\yu̇\ **cure**
\ä\ **cot, cart**	\g\ **go**	\ō\ **bone**	\ü\ **food**	\zh\ **vision**

1**wa•hoo** \'wä-,hü, 'wȯ-\ *n, pl* **wahoos :** a shrubby North American tree having bright autumn foliage and fruit with scarlet capsules which open to expose scarlet seeds [Creek *ûhawhu*]

2**wahoo** *n, pl* **wahoos :** a large vigorous mackerel that is a common food and sport fish in warm seas [origin unknown]

waif \'wāf\ *n* **1 :** something found without an owner and especially by chance **2 :** STRAY 1b; *esp* **:** a homeless child [Old North French, "lost, unclaimed"]

1**wail** \'wāl\ *vb* **1 :** to express sorrow audibly **:** LAMENT **2 :** to make a sound suggestive of a mournful cry **3 :** to express dissatisfaction plaintively **:** COMPLAIN [of Scandinavian origin] — **wail•er** *n*

2**wail** *n* **1 a :** a usually prolonged cry or sound expressing grief or pain **b :** a sound suggestive of this ⟨the *wail* of an air-raid siren⟩ **2 :** an irritable expressing of grievance **:** COMPLAINT

wail•ful \'wāl-fəl\ *adj* **:** SORROWFUL, MOURNFUL ⟨the *wailful* sound of distant bagpipes⟩ — **wail•ful•ly** \-fə-lē\ *adv*

wain \'wān\ *n* **:** a usually large and heavy vehicle for farm use [Old English *wægn*]

1**wain•scot** \'wān-skət, -,skōt, -,skät\ *n* **1 :** a usually paneled and wooden lining of an interior wall **2 :** the lower three or four feet of an interior wall when finished differently from the remainder of the wall [Dutch *wagenschot*]

2**wainscot** *vt* **-scot•ed** *or* **-scot•ted; -scot•ing** *or* **-scot•ting :** to line with or as if with boards or paneling

wain•scot•ing \-,skōt-ing, -,skät-, -skət-\ *or* **wain•scot•ting** \-,skät-, -skət-\ *n* **:** material for wainscot; *also* **:** WAINSCOT

wain•wright \'wān-,rīt\ *n* **:** a maker and repairer of wagons [Old English *wægnwyrhta,* from *wægn* "wagon" + *wyrhta* "worker, maker"]

waist \'wāst\ *n* **1 a :** the usually narrowed part of the body between the chest and hips **b :** the greatly constricted front part of the abdomen of some insects (as a wasp) **2 :** a part resembling the human waist especially in narrowness or central position ⟨the *waist* of a ship⟩ ⟨the *waist* of a violin⟩ **3 :** a garment or the part of a garment that covers the body from the neck to the waist [Middle English *wast*]

waist•band \'wāst-,band, 'wās-\ *n* **:** a band (as of trousers or a skirt) fitting around the waist

waist•coat \'wāst-,kōt, 'wās-; 'wes-kət\ *n, chiefly British* **:** VEST 1a — **waist•coat•ed** \-əd\ *adj*

waist•line \'wāst-,līn\ *n* **1 a :** WAIST 1a **b :** the circumference of the waist at its narrowest point **2 :** the part of a garment surrounding the waist

1**wait** \'wāt\ *vb* **1 :** to remain inactive in readiness (as for action) or expectation (as of a coming event) **:** AWAIT ⟨*wait* for sunrise⟩ ⟨*wait* your turn⟩ ⟨*wait* for orders⟩ **2 :** POSTPONE, DELAY ⟨*wait* dinner for a guest⟩ **3 :** to attend as a waiter or waitress **:** SERVE ⟨*wait* tables⟩ ⟨*wait* at a luncheon⟩ [Old North French *waitier* "to watch", of Germanic origin] — **wait on** *or* **wait upon 1 a :** to attend as a servant **b :** to supply the wants of **:** SERVE ⟨*wait on* a customer⟩ **2 :** to make a formal call on — **wait up :** to delay going to bed

2**wait** *n* **1 a :** a hidden or concealed position — used chiefly in the expression *lie in wait* **b :** a state or attitude of watchfulness and expectancy **2 :** an act or period of waiting

wait•er \'wāt-ər\ *n* **1 :** one that waits upon another; *esp* **:** a man who waits on table (as in a restaurant) **2 :** a tray on which something is carried

waiting game *n* **:** a strategy in which one or more participants withhold action temporarily in the hope of having a favorable opportunity for more effective action later

waiting list *n* **:** a list or roster of those waiting (as for election to a club or appointment to a position)

waiting room *n* **:** a room (as in a doctor's office) for the use of persons waiting

wait•ress \'wā-trəs\ *n* **:** a girl or woman who waits on table

waive \'wāv\ *vt* **1 :** to give up claim to ⟨*waive* the right to answer⟩ **2 :** to put off the consideration of **:** POSTPONE [Old North French *weyver,* from *waif* "lost, unclaimed"]

waiv•er \'wā-vər\ *n* **1 :** the act of waiving a right, claim, or privilege **2 :** a document containing the declaration of a waiver [Anglo-French *weyver,* from Old North French *weyver* "to waive"]

1**wake** \'wāk\ *vb* **waked** \'wākt\ *or* **woke** \'wōk\; **waked** *or* **wo•ken** \'wō-kən\; **wak•ing 1 :** to be or remain awake **2 :** AROUSE 1 — often used with *up* [Old English *wacan* "to awake" and *wacian* "to be awake"] — **wak•er** *n*

2**wake** *n* **:** a watch held over the body of a dead person prior to burial and sometimes accompanied by festivity

3**wake** *n* **:** the track left by a moving body (as a ship) in the water; *also* **:** a track or path left [of Scandinavian origin] — **in the wake of 1 :** close behind and on the same course **2 :** as a result of

wake•ful \'wāk-fəl\ *adj* **:** not sleeping or able to sleep — **wake•ful•ly** \-fə-lē\ *adv* — **wake•ful•ness** *n*

wak•en \'wā-kən\ *vb* **wak•ened; wak•en•ing** \'wāk-ning, -ə-ning\ **:** AROUSE 1 — often used with *up* — **wak•en•er** \'wāk-nər, -ə-nər\ *n*

wake–rob•in \'wā-,kräb-ən\ *n* **:** TRILLIUM

Wal•den•ses \wȯl-'den-,sēz\ *n pl* **:** a Christian sect arising in southern France in the 12th century, adopting Calvinist doctrines in the 16th century, and later living chiefly in Piedmont [Medieval Latin, from Peter *Waldo,* 12th century French heretic] — **Wal•den•sian** \-'den-chən\ *adj or n*

Wal•dorf salad \,wȯl-,dȯrf-\ *n* **:** a salad made typically of diced apples, celery, and nuts and dressed with mayonnaise [*Waldorf*–Astoria Hotel, New York City]

wale \'wāl\ *n* **1 a :** a streak or ridge made on the skin usually by a rod or whip **b :** a narrow raised surface or ridge (as on corduroy) **2 :** one of the extra-strong strakes on the sides of a wooden ship just above the waterline [Old English *walu*]

1**walk** \'wȯk\ *vb* **1 a :** to move or cause to move along on foot usually at a natural unhurried gait ⟨*walk* to town⟩ ⟨*walk* a horse up a hill⟩ **b :** to pass over, through, or along by walking ⟨*walk* the streets⟩ **c :** to perform or affect by walking ⟨*walk* guard⟩ **2 :** to follow a course of action or way of life **:** BEHAVE **3 :** to take or cause to take first base with a base on balls **4 :** to move or cause to move in a manner suggestive of walking ⟨*walked* my fingers across the table⟩ [Old English *wealcan* "to roll, toss"] — **walk away from 1 :** to outrun or get the better of without difficulty **2 :** to survive (an accident) with little or no injury — **walk off with 1 :** STEAL 2 **2 :** to win or gain especially by outdoing one's competitors without difficulty — **walk over :** to disregard the wishes or feelings of

2**walk** *n* **1 :** a going on foot ⟨go for a *walk*⟩ **2 :** a place, path, or course for walking **3 :** distance to be walked **4 a :** manner of living **:** CONDUCT, BEHAVIOR **b :** social or economic status ⟨various *walks* of life⟩ **5 a :** manner of walking **b :** a gait of a four-footed animal in which there are always at least two feet on the ground; *esp* **:** a slow 4-beat gait of a horse in which the feet strike the ground in the sequence left hind, left fore, right hind, right fore **6 :** BASE ON BALLS

walk•er \'wȯ-kər\ *n* **1 :** one that walks **2 :** something used in walking; *esp* **:** a framework designed to support one who walks with difficulty

walk•ie–talk•ie \,wȯ-kē-'tȯ-kē\ *n* **:** a small portable radio set for receiving and sending messages

walk–in \'wȯ-,kin\ *adj* **:** large enough to be walked into ⟨a *walk-in* refrigerator⟩

walking fern *n* **:** any of a genus of ferns that form new plants at the tips of the long fronds

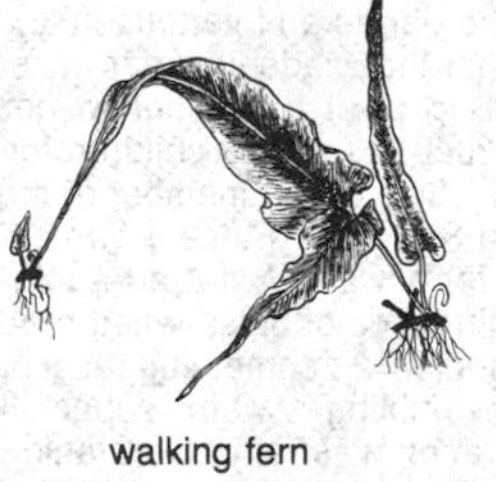
walking fern

walking papers *n pl* **:** DISMISSAL, DISCHARGE

walking stick *n* **1 :** a stick used in walking **2** *usually* **walk•ing•stick :** STICK INSECT

walk–on \'wȯ-,kȯn, -,kän\ *n* **:** a small usually nonspeaking part in a dramatic production

walk•out \'wȯ-,kau̇t\ *n* **1 :** STRIKE 2a **2 :** the leaving of a meeting or organization as an expression of disapproval

walk out \wȯ-'kau̇t, 'wȯ-\ *vi* **1 :** to go on strike **2 :** to leave suddenly often as an expression of disapproval — **walk out on :** ABANDON 3, DESERT

walk•over \'wȯ-,kō-vər\ *n* **:** a one-sided contest or an easy or uncontested victory

walk–up \'wȯ-,kəp\ *n* **:** a building or apartment house without an elevator — **walk–up** \,wȯ-,kəp\ *adj*

walk•way \'wȯ-,kwā\ *n* **:** a passage for walking **:** WALK

1**wall** \'wȯl\ *n* **1 :** a structure (as of brick or stone) raised to some height and meant to enclose or shut off a space; *esp* **:** a side of a room or building **2 :** a material layer enclosing space ⟨the heart *wall*⟩ ⟨the *walls* of a boiler⟩ **3 :** something like a wall;

esp : something that acts as a barrier or defense ⟨a *wall* of reserve⟩ [Old English *weall,* from Latin *vallum* "rampart"] — **walled** \ˈwȯld\ *adj* — **wall–like** \ˈwȯl-ˌlīk\ *adj*

[2]wall *vt* **1** : to provide, separate, or surround with or as if with a wall ⟨*wall* in the garden⟩ **2** : to close (an opening) with or as if with a wall ⟨*wall* up a door⟩

wal•la•by \ˈwäl-ə-bē\ *n, pl* **-bies** *also* **-by** : any of various small or medium–sized usually brightly colored kangaroos [*wolabā,* native name in New South Wales, Australia]

wall•board \ˈwȯl-ˌbōrd, -ˌbȯrd\ *n* : a structural material (as of wood pulp, gypsum, or plastic) made in large rigid sheets and used especially for sheathing interior walls and ceilings

wal•let \ˈwäl-ət\ *n* **1** : a bag or sack for carrying things on a journey **2 a** : BILLFOLD **b** : a pocketbook with compartments (as for change and cards) [Middle English *walet*]

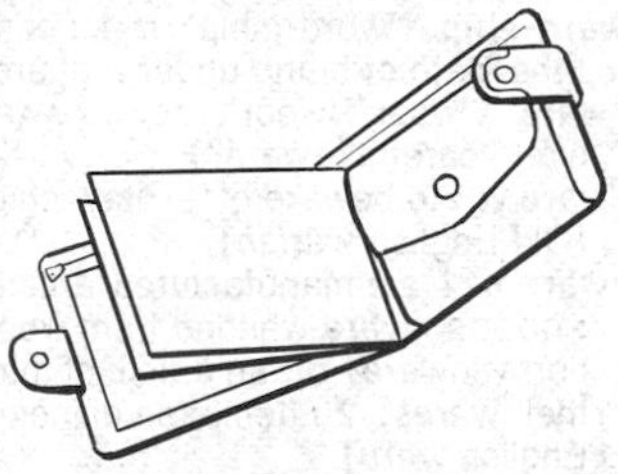
wallet 2b

wall•eye \ˈwȯ-ˌlī\ *n* **1 a** : an eye with a whitish iris or an opaque white cornea **b** : an eye that turns outward showing more than a normal amount of white; *also* : the condition of having such eyes **2** : a large vigorous American freshwater food and sport fish that has prominent eyes and is related to the perches but resembles the true pike — called also *walleyed pike* [back-formation from *walleyed,* from Old Norse *vagl-eygr,* from *vagl* "beam, roost" + *eygr* "eyed"] — **wall•eyed** \-ˈlīd\ *adj*

wall•flow•er \ˈwȯl-ˌflau̇-ər, -ˌflau̇r\ *n* **1** : any of several Old World perennial plants of the mustard family; *esp* : one widely grown for its showy fragrant flowers **2** : a person who from shyness or unpopularity remains on the sidelines of a social activity (as a dance)

Wal•loon \wä-ˈlün\ *n* : a member of a chiefly Celtic people of southern and southeastern Belgium and adjacent parts of France [Middle French *Wallon,* of Germanic origin] — **Walloon** *adj*

[1]wal•lop \ˈwäl-əp\ *n*) : **1** : a powerful blow or impact **2** : the ability (as of a boxer) to hit hard [Old North French *walop* "gallop", from *waloper* "to gallop"]

[2]wallop *vt* **1** : to beat soundly : TROUNCE **2** : to hit with force : SOCK — **wal•lop•er** *n*

wal•lop•ing \ˈwäl-ə-piŋ\ *adj* **1** : very large **2** : exceptionally fine or impressive

[1]wal•low \ˈwäl-ō\ *vi* **1** : to roll about in or as if in deep mud ⟨elephants *wallowing* in the river⟩ **2 a** : to enjoy or indulge oneself in something without restraint **b** : to become abundantly supplied ⟨*wallow* in luxury⟩ **3** : to become or remain helpless ⟨allowed to *wallow* in ignorance⟩ [Old English *wealwian* "to roll"]

[2]wallow *n* **1** : an act or instance of wallowing **2** : a muddy or dust–filled area used by animals for wallowing

wall•pa•per \ˈwȯl-ˌpā-pər\ *n* : decorative paper for the walls of a room — **wallpaper** *vb*

wall plug *n* : an electric receptacle in a wall

Wall Street \ˈwȯl-\ *n* : the influential financial interests of the United States economy [*Wall Street,* New York City, on which the New York Stock Exchange is located]

wal•nut \ˈwȯl-ˌnət, -nət\ *n* **1 a** : an edible nut with a furrowed usually rough shell; *also* : any of a genus of trees related to the hickories that produce such nuts **b** : the usually reddish to dark brown wood of a walnut widely used for cabinetwork and veneers **c** : a hickory nut or tree **2** : a moderate reddish brown [Old English *wealhhnutu,* literally, "foreign nut", from *wealh* "Welshman, foreigner" + *hnutu* "nut"]

△ <u>**origin**</u> Walnut trees have been cultivated in so many countries for so many centuries that the early distribution and origin of the walnut cannot now be clearly discerned. It would appear, however, that the walnut was known to southern Europe for some time before it was introduced into England. The walnut's Old English name, *wealhhnutu,* means literally "foreign nut". It was apparently so called to distinguish the walnut of southern Europe from the nut native to more northern countries, the hazelnut.

Wal•pur•gis Night \väl-ˈpu̇r-gəs-\ *n* : the eve of May Day on which witches are held to ride to a satanic rendezvous [German *Walpurgis* "Saint Walburga (died A. D. 779, English saint whose feast day falls on May Day)"]

wal•rus \ˈwȯl-rəs, ˈwäl-\ *n, pl* **walrus** *or* **wal•rus•es** : either of two large mammals of northern seas related to the seals and hunted especially for the hide, the ivory tusks of the males, and oil [Dutch, of Scandinavian origin]

walrus

[1]waltz \ˈwȯls, ˈwȯlts\ *n* **1** : a round dance in 3/4 time with strong accent on the first beat **2** : music for or suitable for waltzing [German *walzer,* from *walzen* "to roll, dance"]

[2]waltz *vb* **1 a** : to dance a waltz **b** : to dance a waltz with **2** : to advance easily or conspicuously — **waltz•er** *n*

wam•pum \ˈwäm-pəm\ *n* **1** : beads of shells strung in strands, belts, or sashes and used by North American Indians as money and ornaments **2** *slang* : MONEY 1 [of American Indian origin]

wan \ˈwän\ *adj* **1 a** : SICKLY, PALLID ⟨a *wan* complexion⟩ **b** : lacking vitality : FEEBLE **2** : DIM 1, FAINT **3** : LANGUID ⟨a *wan* smile⟩ [Old English, "dark, livid"] — **wan•ly** *adv* — **wan•ness** \ˈwän-nəs\ *n*

wand \ˈwänd\ *n* **1** : a slender rod used by conjurers or magicians **2** : the rigid tube between nozzle and hose of a vacuum cleaner [Old Norse *vöndr* "slender stick"]

wan•der \ˈwän-dər\ *vb* **wan•dered**; **wan•der•ing** \-də-riŋ, -driŋ\ **1** : to move about aimlessly or without a fixed course or goal : RAMBLE **2 a** : to deviate (as from a course) : STRAY **b** : to go astray morally : ERR **c** : to lose normal mental contact (as in delirium or madness) [Old English *wandrian*] — **wander** *n* — **wan•der•er** \-dər-ər\ *n*

wandering Jew *n* : any of several mostly creeping plants of the spiderwort family [the *Wandering Jew,* legendary person condemned to wander the earth until Christ's 2d coming for having mocked Him on the day of the crucifixion]

wan•der•lust \ˈwän-dər-ˌləst\ *n* : strong longing to travel [German, from *wandern* "to wander" + *lust* "desire, pleasure"]

[1]wane \ˈwān\ *vi* **1** : to grow smaller or less: as **a** : to diminish in phase or intensity — used chiefly of the moon **b** : to become less brilliant or powerful : DIM **2** : to fall gradually from power, prosperity, or influence : DECLINE [Old English *wanian*]

[2]wane *n* **1** : the act or process of waning **2** : a period or time of waning; *esp* : the period from full phase of the moon to the new moon

wan•gle \ˈwaŋ-gəl\ *vb* **wan•gled**; **wan•gling** \-gə-liŋ, -gliŋ\ **1 a** : to obtain by sly, roundabout, or underhand means **b** : to use trickery or devious means to achieve an end **2 a** : to adjust or manipulate for personal ends **b** : to make or get (one's way) by devious means : FINAGLE [perhaps alteration of *waggle*] — **wan•gler** \-gə-lər, -glər\ *n*

Wan•kel engine \ˌväŋ-kəl-, ˌwaŋ-\ *n* : an internal-combustion rotary engine that has a rounded triangular rotor functioning as a piston and rotating in a space in the engine and that has only two major moving parts [Felix *Wankel,* born 1902, German engineer]

[1]want \ˈwȯnt *also* ˈwänt, ˈwənt\ *vb* **1** : to be without : LACK ⟨this coat is *wanting* a button⟩ **2** : to fall short by ⟨you *want* one year of being 13⟩ **3 a** : to feel or suffer the need of ⟨cannot get the rest I *want*⟩ **b** : to suffer from a need ⟨never *wanted* for anything⟩ **4** : NEED, REQUIRE ⟨our house *wants* painting⟩ **5** : to desire earnestly : WISH ⟨*wants* to go to college⟩ [Old Norse *vanta*] **syn** see DESIRE

[2]want *n* **1 a** : a lack of a required or usual amount **b** : great need : DESTITUTION **2** : something wanted : NEED, DESIRE

want ad *n* : an advertisement stating that something (as an employee or a specified item) is wanted

[1]want•ing *adj* **1** : not present or in evidence : ABSENT **2 a** : falling below standards or expectations **b :** lacking in ability or capacity **:** DEFICIENT

2wanting *prep* **1 :** WITHOUT ⟨a book *wanting* a cover⟩ **2 :** LESS, MINUS ⟨a month *wanting* two days⟩

1wan•ton \ˈwȯnt-ᵊn, ˈwänt-\ *adj* **1 :** FROLICSOME ⟨*wanton* play⟩ ⟨a *wanton* breeze⟩ **2 :** LEWD 1, BAWDY; *also* **:** SENSUAL **3 a :** MERCILESS, INHUMANE ⟨*wanton* cruelty⟩ **b :** having no just cause **:** MALICIOUS ⟨a *wanton* attack⟩ **4 :** UNRESTRAINED 1, EXTRAVAGANT ⟨*wanton* luxury⟩ [Middle English, "unruly"] — **wan•ton•ly** *adv* — **wan•ton•ness** \-ᵊn-nəs\ *n*

2wanton *n* **:** a wanton individual; *esp* **:** a lascivious person

3wanton *vb* **1 :** to be wanton or act wantonly **2 :** to pass or waste wantonly

wa•pi•ti \ˈwäp-ət-ē\ *n, pl* **-ti** *or* **-tis :** ELK 1b [of American Indian origin]

1war \ˈwȯr\ *n* **1 a :** a state or period of armed hostile conflict between states or nations **b :** the science of warfare **2 a :** a state of hostility, conflict, or antagonism **b :** a struggle between opposing forces or for a particular end ⟨a *war* against disease⟩ [Old North French *werre,* of Germanic origin]

2war *vi* **warred; war•ring 1 :** to engage in warfare **2 :** to be in conflict

1war•ble \ˈwȯr-bəl\ *n* **1 :** a melodious succession of low pleasing sounds **2 :** a musical trill **3 :** the action of warbling [Old North French *werble* "tune", of Germanic origin]

2warble *vb* **war•bled; war•bling** \-bə-liŋ, -bliŋ\ **1 :** to sing in a trilling manner or with many turns and variations **2 :** to express by or as if by warbling

3warble *n* **:** a swelling under the hide (as of the back of cattle) caused by the maggot of a warble fly; *also* **:** such a maggot [perhaps of Scandinavian origin] — **war•bled** \-bəld\ *adj*

warble fly *n* **:** any of various two-winged flies whose larvae are warbles

war•bler \ˈwȯr-blər\ *n* **1 :** one that warbles **:** SINGER **2 a :** any of numerous small Old World singing birds many of which are noted songsters and are closely related to the thrushes **b :** any of numerous small brightly colored American songbirds with a usually weak and unmusical song — called also *wood warbler*

war•bon•net \ˈwȯr-ˌbän-ət\ *n* **:** an American Indian ceremonial headdress with a feathered extension down the back

war chest *n* **:** a fund accumulated for a specific purpose, action, or campaign

war crime *n* **:** a crime (as genocide or maltreatment of prisoners) committed during or in connection with war — usually used in pl. — **war criminal** *n*

war cry *n* **1 :** a cry used by a body of fighters in war **2 :** a slogan used especially to rally people to a cause

1ward \ˈwȯrd\ *n* **1 :** a guarding or being under guard; *esp* **:** CUSTODY **2 a :** a division (as a cell or block) of a prison **b :** a division in a hospital **3 a :** an electoral or administrative division of a city **b :** a local Mormon congregation **4 :** a projecting ridge of metal in a lock casing or keyhole permitting only the insertion of a key with a corresponding notch; *also* **:** a corresponding notch in a key **5 a :** a person (as a child) who is under the care of a court or a guardian **b :** a person, group, or territory under the protection or tutelage of a government [Old English *weard*] — **ward•ed** \-əd\ *adj*

2ward *vt* **1 :** to keep watch over **:** GUARD **2 :** to turn aside **:** DEFLECT — usually used with *off* ⟨*ward* off a cold⟩ [Old English *weardian*]

1-ward \wərd\ *also* **-wards** \wərdz\ *adj suffix* **1 :** that moves, tends, faces, or is directed toward ⟨wind*ward*⟩ **2 :** that occurs or is situated in the direction of ⟨left*ward*⟩ [Old English *-weard*]

2-ward *or* **-wards** *adv suffix* **1 :** in a (specified) spatial or temporal direction ⟨after*ward*⟩ ⟨up*wards*⟩ **2 :** toward a (specified) point, position, or area ⟨coast*ward*⟩ ⟨heaven*wards*⟩

war dance *n* **:** a dance performed by primitive peoples as preparation for battle or in celebration of victory

war•den \ˈwȯrd-ᵊn\ *n* **1 :** one having care or charge of something **:** GUARDIAN **2 :** the governor of a town, district, or fortress **3 a :** an official charged with special duties or with the enforcement of specified laws ⟨game *wardens*⟩ ⟨air raid *wardens*⟩ **b :** an official in charge of a prison **4 a :** a lay officer of an Episcopal parish **b :** any of various British college officials [Old North French *wardein,* from *warder* "to guard", of Germanic origin] — **war•den•ship** \-ˌship\ *n*

ward•er \ˈwȯrd-ər\ *n* **:** a person who keeps guard [Anglo-French *wardere,* from *warde* "act of guarding", of Germanic origin]

ward heeler *n* **:** a local worker for a political boss [from his following at the heels of a political boss]

ward•ress \ˈwȯr-drəs\ *n* **:** a woman supervising female prisoners (as in a jail)

ward•robe \ˈwȯr-ˌdrōb\ *n* **1 :** a room, closet, or chest where clothes are kept **2 :** a collection of wearing apparel (as of one person or for one activity) [Old North French *warderobe,* from *warder* "to guard" + *robe* "robe"]

ward•room \ˈwȯr-ˌdrüm, -ˌdrům\ *n* **:** the space in a warship allotted for living quarters to the officers excepting the captain; *esp* **:** the mess assigned to them

ward•ship \ˈwȯrd-ˌship\ *n* **1 :** care and protection of a ward **2 :** the state of being under a guardian

1ware \ˈwaər, ˈweər\ *adj* **:** AWARE, CONSCIOUS [Old English *wær* "careful, aware"]

2ware *vt* **:** to beware of — used chiefly as a command to hunters [Old English *warian*]

3ware *n* **1 a :** manufactured articles or products of art or craft **:** GOODS ⟨*ware* whittled from wood⟩ — often used in combination ⟨tin*ware*⟩ **b :** an article of merchandise ⟨peddlers hawking their *wares*⟩ **2 :** items (as dishes) of fired clay **:** POTTERY [Old English *waru*]

1ware•house \ˈwaər-ˌhaůs, ˈweər-\ *n* **:** a place for storing merchandise or commodities — **ware•house•man** \-mən\ *n*

2ware•house \-ˌhaůz, -ˌhaůs\ *vt* **:** to deposit, store, or stock in or as if in a warehouse

ware•room \-ˌrüm, -ˌrům\ *n* **:** a room in which goods are exhibited for sale

war•fare \ˈwȯr-ˌfaər, -ˌfeər\ *n* **1 a :** military operations between enemies **:** WAR **b :** an activity undertaken by one country to weaken or destroy another ⟨economic *warfare*⟩ **2 :** a struggle between competitors ⟨industrial *warfare*⟩

war•fa•rin \ˈwȯr-fə-rən\ *n* **:** a crystalline compound that deters blood clotting and is used as a rodent poison and in medicine [*W*isconsin *A*lumni *R*esearch *F*oundation (its patentee) + cou*marin,* a chemical]

war footing *n* **:** the condition of being prepared to undertake or maintain war

war•head \ˈwȯr-ˌhed\ *n* **:** the section of a missile containing the explosive, chemical, or incendiary charge

war–horse \-ˌhȯrs\ *n* **1 :** a horse used in war **:** CHARGER **2 :** a veteran soldier or public person (as a politician)

war•less \ˈwȯr-ləs\ *adj* **:** free from war

war•like \-ˌlīk\ *adj* **1 :** fit for, disposed to, or fond of war ⟨a *warlike* people⟩ **2 :** of, relating to, or useful in war ⟨*warlike* supplies⟩ **3 :** befitting or characteristic of war or of soldiers **syn** see MARTIAL

war•lock \-ˌläk\ *n* **:** a man practicing the black arts **:** SORCERER — compare WITCH [Old English *wǣrloga* "one that breaks faith, the Devil", from *wǣr* "faith" + *lēogan* "to lie"]

war•lord \-ˌlȯrd\ *n* **1 :** a very high military leader **2 :** a military commander exercising local civil power by force

1warm \ˈwȯrm\ *adj* **1 a :** having or giving out heat to a moderate or adequate degree ⟨*warm* food⟩ ⟨a *warm* stove⟩ **b :** serving to retain heat (as of the body) ⟨*warm* clothes⟩ **c :** feeling or inducing sensations of heat ⟨*warm* from exertion⟩ ⟨a *warm* walk⟩ **2 a :** showing or marked by strong feeling **:** ARDENT ⟨a *warm* supporter⟩ ⟨a *warm* temperament⟩ **b :** marked by tense excitement or hot anger ⟨a *warm* debate⟩ **3 :** marked by or tending toward injury, distress, or pain ⟨gave the enemy a *warm* reception⟩ **4 :** newly made **:** FRESH ⟨a *warm* scent⟩ **5 a :** giving a pleasant impression of warmth or friendliness ⟨a *warm* greeting⟩ **b :** of a color or tone that suggests warmth ⟨a *warm* red⟩ **6 :** near to a goal or answer [Old English *wearm*] — **warm•ly** *adv* — **warm•ness** *n*

2warm *vb* **1 :** to make or become warm **2 a :** to give a feeling of warmth or vitality to **b :** to experience feelings of affection or pleasure ⟨*warmed* to the young guests⟩ **3 :** to reheat (cooked food) for eating **4 a :** to make or become ready by some preliminary action ⟨*warm* up the car⟩ **b :** to become ardent or interested ⟨a speaker *warming* to the topic⟩

3warm *adv* **:** WARMLY — usually used in combination ⟨*warm*-clad⟩

warm–blood•ed \ˈwȯrm-ˈbləd-əd\ *adj* **1 :** able to maintain a relatively high and constant body temperature that is essentially independent of the environment **2 :** warm in feeling **:** ARDENT — **warm–blood•ed•ness** *n*

warmed–over \'wȯrm-'dō-vər\ *adj* **1 :** heated again ⟨*warmed-over* beans⟩ **2 :** not fresh or new **:** STALE ⟨*warmed-over* ideas⟩

warm•er \'wȯr-mər\ *n* **:** one that warms; *esp* **:** a device for keeping something warm ⟨a hand *warmer*⟩

warm front *n* **:** an advancing edge of a warm air mass

warm•heart•ed \'wȯrm-'härt-əd\ *adj* **:** marked by warmth of feeling — **warm•heart•ed•ness** *n*

warming pan *n* **:** a long-handled covered pan filled with live coals and formerly used to warm a bed

warm•ish \'wȯr-mish\ *adj* **:** somewhat warm

war•mon•ger \'wȯr-ˌməng-gər, -ˌmäng-\ *n* **:** one who urges or attempts to stir up war **:** JINGO — **war•mon•ger•ing** \-gə-ring, -gring\ *n*

warmth \'wȯrmth, 'wȯrmpth\ *n* **:** the quality or state of being warm: as **a :** emotional intensity (as of enthusiasm, anger, or love) **b :** a glowing effect produced by or as if by the use of warm colors

warm–up \'wȯr-ˌməp\ *n* **:** the act or an instance of warming up; *also* **:** a procedure (as a set of exercises) used in warming up

warm up \wȯr-'məp, 'wȯr-\ *vi* **1 :** to engage in exercise or practice especially before entering a game or contest **2 :** to approach a state of violence, conflict, or danger

warn \'wȯrn\ *vt* **1 a :** to give notice to beforehand especially of danger or evil **b :** ADMONISH 1 **c :** to call to one's attention **:** INFORM **2 :** to order to go or stay away **[**Old English *warnian***]** — **warn•er** *n*

• syn CAUTION: WARN may range from simple notification of something to be watched for to threats of violence or reprisal; CAUTION stresses giving advice that suggests the need of taking care or watching out.

1warn•ing \'wȯr-ning\ *n* **1 :** the act of warning **:** the state of being warned ⟨had *warning* of the risk⟩ **2 :** something that warns or serves to warn

2warning *adj* **:** serving as an alarm, signal, summons, or admonition ⟨a *warning* bell⟩ ⟨*warning* shots⟩ — **warn•ing•ly** \-ning-lē\ *adv*

war of nerves : a conflict characterized by psychological tactics (as bluff, threats, and intimidation) designed primarily to create confusion, indecision, or breakdown of morale

1warp \'wȯrp\ *n* **1 a :** a series of yarns extended lengthwise in a loom and crossed by the woof **b :** FOUNDATION 2, BASE **2 a :** a twist or curve that has developed in something originally flat or straight ⟨a *warp* in a door panel⟩ **b :** a mental twist or aberration **[**Old English *wearp***]**

1warp 1a: *light* warp, *dark* woof

2warp *vb* **1 a :** to turn or twist out of shape; *also* **:** to become so turned or twisted **b :** to cause to judge, choose, or act wrongly **:** PERVERT **c :** DISTORT 1, FALSIFY **2 :** to arrange (yarns) so as to form a warp **3 :** to move (as a ship) by hauling on a line attached to a fixed object **[**Old English *weorpan* "to throw"**]** — **warp•er** *n*

war paint *n* **1 :** paint put on parts of the body (as the face) by American Indians on going to war **2 :** ceremonial dress; *also* **:** FINERY **3 :** MAKEUP 2

war•path \'wȯr-ˌpath, -ˌpȧth\ *n* **1 :** the route taken by a party of American Indians going on a warlike expedition **2 :** a hostile course of action or frame of mind

war•plane \-ˌplān\ *n* **:** a military airplane; *esp* **:** one armed for combat

1war•rant \'wȯr-ənt, 'wär-\ *n* **1 a :** SANCTION 2, AUTHORIZATION **b :** GROUND 2, JUSTIFICATION **2 :** evidence of authority or authorization: as **a :** a legal writ authorizing an officer to make an arrest, seizure, or search **b :** a certificate of appointment issued to a warrant officer **[**Old North French *warant* "protector, warrant", of Germanic origin**]**

2warrant *vt* **1 a :** to declare or maintain positively **:** be sure that **b :** to assure (a person) that what is said is true **2 :** to guarantee (something) to be as it appears or as it is represented **3 :** to guarantee security or immunity to **:** SECURE **4 :** to give sanction to ⟨the law *warrants* this procedure⟩ **5 a :** to give proof of **:** ATTEST **b :** GUARANTEE 1 **6 :** to serve as adequate reason for **:** JUSTIFY — **war•rant•able** \'wȯr-ənt-ə-bəl, 'wär-\ *adj* — **war•rant•able•ness** *n* — **war•rant•ably** \-blē\ *adv* — **war•ran•tor** \ˌwȯr-ən-'tȯr, ˌwär-; 'wȯr-ənt-ər, 'wär-\ *also* **war•rant•er** \'wȯr-ənt-ər, 'wär-\ *n*

war•ran•tee \ˌwȯr-ən-'tē, ˌwär-\ *n* **:** the person to whom a warranty is made

warrant officer *n* **:** an officer in the armed forces holding rank by virtue of a warrant and ranking below a commissioned officer and above a noncommissioned officer

war•ran•ty \'wȯr-ənt-ē, 'wär-\ *n, pl* **-ties :** an explicit or implied statement that a situation or thing is as it appears or is represented to be; *esp* **:** a usually written guarantee of a product's integrity and of the maker's responsiblity for the repair or replacement of defective parts **[**Old North French *warantie,* from *warantir* "to guarantee, warrant", from *warant* "warrant"**]**

war•ren \'wȯr-ən, 'wär-\ *n* **1 :** a place for keeping small game (as hare or pheasant) **2 :** an area where rabbits breed **3 :** a crowded tenement or district **[**Old North French *warenne***]**

war•rior \'wȯr-yər; 'wȯr-ē-ər, 'wär-ē-\ *n* **:** a person engaged or experienced in warfare **[**Old North French *werreieur,* from *werreier* "to make war", from *werre* "war"**]**

war•ship \'wȯr-ˌship\ *n* **:** a government ship used for war purposes; *esp* **:** one armed for combat

wart \'wȯrt\ *n* **1 :** an irregular growth on the skin often caused by a virus **2 :** a protuberance (as on a plant) resembling a wart **[**Old English *wearte***]** — **wart•ed** \'wȯrt-əd\ *adj* — **warty** \-ē\ *adj*

wart•hog \'wȯrt-ˌhȯg, -ˌhäg\ *n* **:** any of a genus of African wild hogs with two pairs of rough warty protuberances on the face and large protruding tusks

warthog

war•time \'wȯr-ˌtīm\ *n* **:** a period of war

war whoop *n* **:** a war cry especially of American Indians

wary \'waər-ē, 'weər-\ *adj* **war•i•er; -est :** very cautious; *esp* **:** watchfully prudent in detecting and escaping danger **[**Old English *wær* "careful, aware, wary"**]** — **war•i•ly** \'war-ə-lē, 'wer-\ *adv* — **war•i•ness** \'war-ē-nəs, 'wer-\ *n*

was *past 1st & 3d sing of* BE **[**Old English, 1st and 3d singular past indicative of *wesan* "to be"**]**

1wash \'wȯsh, 'wäsh\ *vb* **1 :** to cleanse with or as if with water **2 :** to wet thoroughly with liquid **3 :** to flow along the border of ⟨waves *wash* the shore⟩ **4 :** to pour or flow in a stream or current ⟨the river *washes* against its banks⟩ **5 :** to move or carry by the action of water ⟨a passenger *washed* overboard⟩ **6 :** to cover or daub lightly with a liquid (as whitewash or varnish) **7 :** to run water over in order to separate valuable matter from refuse ⟨*wash* sand for gold⟩ **8 :** to undergo laundering ⟨a shirt that *washes* well⟩ **9 :** to stand a test for truthfulness ⟨that story won't *wash*⟩ **10 :** to wear or be worn by water ⟨heavy rain *washed* away the road⟩ **[**Old English *wascan***]** — **wash one's hands of :** to deny interest in, responsibility for, or further connection with

2wash *n* **1 a :** the act or process or an instance of washing or being washed **b :** articles to be or being washed **2 :** the surging action of waves or its sound **3 a :** a piece of ground washed by the sea or river **b :** BOG, MARSH **c :** a shallow body of water or creek **d** *West* **:** the dry bed of a stream — called also *dry wash* **4 :** worthless especially liquid waste **:** REFUSE **5 a :** a sweep or splash especially of color made by or as if by a long stroke of a brush **b :** a thin coat of paint (as watercolor) **c :** a thin liquid used for coating a surface (as a wall) **6 :** LOTION **7 :** loose or eroded surface material of the earth (as rock debris) transported and deposited by running water **8 a :** BACKWASH 1 **b :** a disturbance in the air produced by the passage of an airfoil or propeller

3wash *adj* **:** WASHABLE

wash•able \'wȯsh-ə-bəl, 'wäsh-\ *adj* **:** capable of being washed

\ə\ **abut**	\au̇\ **out**	\i\ **tip**	\ȯ\ **saw**	\u̇\ **foot**
\ər\ **further**	\ch\ **chin**	\ī\ **life**	\ȯi\ **coin**	\y\ **yet**
\a\ **mat**	\e\ **pet**	\j\ **job**	\th\ **thin**	\yü\ **few**
\ā\ **take**	\ē\ **easy**	\ng\ **sing**	\t͟h\ **this**	\yu̇\ **cure**
\ä\ **cot, cart**	\g\ **go**	\ō\ **bone**	\ü\ **food**	\zh\ **vision**

without damage ⟨a *washable* silk⟩ — **wash·abil·i·ty** \ˌwȯsh-ə-ˈbil-ət-ē, ˌwäsh-\ *n*
wash and wear *adj* : of, relating to, or being a fabric or garment that needs little or no ironing after washing
wash·ba·sin \ˈwȯsh-ˌbās-ⁿn, ˈwäsh-\ *n* : WASHBOWL
wash·board \-ˌbōrd, -ˌbȯrd\ *n* : a corrugated rectangular surface to scrub clothes on
wash·bowl \-ˌbōl\ *n* : a large bowl or sink for water especially to wash one's hands and face
wash·cloth \-ˌklȯth\ *n* : a cloth for washing one's face and body — called also *washrag*
wash drawing *n* : watercolor painting in or chiefly in washes
washed–out \ˈwȯsh-ˈtau̇t, ˈwäsh-\ *adj* **1** : faded in color **2** : depleted of vigor or animation
washed–up \-ˈtəp\ *adj* **1** : left with no effective power, capacity, or opportunity for recovery **2** *usually* **washed up** : ready to quit especially from disgust : THROUGH
wash·er \ˈwȯsh-ər, ˈwäsh-\ *n* **1** : one that washes; *esp* : WASHING MACHINE **2** : a ring (as of metal or rubber) used to make something fit tightly or to prevent rubbing

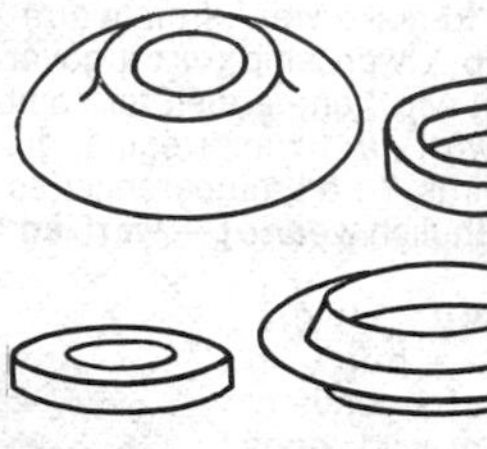

washer 2

wash·er·man \-mən\ *n* : LAUNDRYMAN; *also* : a man operating any of various industrial washing machines
wash·er·wom·an \-ˌwu̇m-ən\ *n* : LAUNDRESS; *esp* : one who takes in washing
wash·house \ˈwȯsh-ˌhau̇s, ˈwäsh-\ *n* : a building used or equipped for washing; *esp* : one for washing clothes
wash·ing \ˈwȯsh-iŋ, ˈwäsh-\ *n* **1** : material obtained by washing **2** : a thin covering or coat ⟨a *washing* of silver⟩ **3** : articles washed or to be washed
washing machine *n* : a machine for washing; *esp* : one for washing clothes and household linen
washing soda *n* : SAL SODA
Wash·ing·ton pie \ˌwȯsh-iŋ-tən-, ˌwäsh-\ *n* : cake layers put together with a jam or jelly filling [George *Washington*]
Washington's Birthday *n* **1** : February 22 formerly observed as a legal holiday in most of the United States **2** : the third Monday in February observed as a legal holiday in most of the United States — called also *Presidents' Day* [George *Washington*]
wash·out \ˈwȯsh-ˌau̇t, ˈwäsh-\ *n* **1** : the washing out or away of earth especially in a roadbed by a freshet; *also* : a place where earth is washed away **2** : one that fails to measure up : FAILURE; *esp* : one who fails in a course of training or study
wash out \wȯsh-ˈau̇t, ˈwȯsh-, wäsh-, ˈwäsh-\ *vb* **1 a** : to cause to fade by laundering **b** : to deplete the strength or vitality of **c** : to eliminate as useless or unsatisfactory : REJECT **2** : to become depleted of color or vitality : FADE **3** : to fail to measure up (as to a standard)
wash·rag \ˈwȯsh-ˌrag, ˈwäsh-\ *n* : WASHCLOTH
wash·room \-ˌrüm, -ˌru̇m\ *n* : a room equipped with washing and toilet facilities : LAVATORY
wash·stand \-ˌstand\ *n* **1** : a stand holding articles needed for washing one's face and hands **2** : a washbowl permanently set in place and attached to water pipes and drainpipes
wash·tub \-ˌtəb\ *n* : a tub for washing (as clothes)
wash up *vt* : FINISH 1 ⟨the scandal *washed* them *up*⟩
wash·wom·an \ˈwȯsh-ˌwu̇m-ən, ˈwäsh-\ *n* : WASHERWOMAN
washy \ˈwȯsh-ē, ˈwäsh-\ *adj* **wash·i·er**; **-est 1** : WEAK, WATERY ⟨*washy* tea⟩ **2** : lacking in color : PALLID **3** : lacking in vigor, individuality, or definiteness
wasn't \ˈwəz-ⁿt, ˈwäz-\ : was not
wasp \ˈwäsp, ˈwȯsp\ *n* : a winged insect related to the bees and ants that has a slender body with the abdomen attached by a narrow stalk and in females and workers a powerful sting [Old English *wæps, wæsp*]
WASP or Wasp \ˈwäsp, ˈwȯsp\ *n* : an American of North European and especially English Protestant ancestry and background [white Anglo-Saxon Protestant]
wasp·ish \ˈwäs-pish, ˈwȯs-\ *adj* **1** : SNAPPISH, IRRITABLE ⟨a *waspish* retort⟩ **2** : resembling a wasp in form; *esp* : slightly built — **wasp·ish·ly** *adv* — **wasp·ish·ness** *n*
wasp waist *n* : a very slender waist

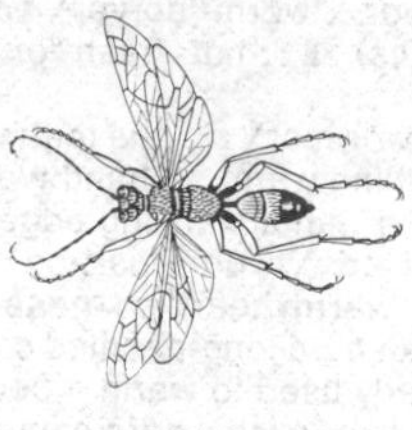

wasp

[1]was·sail \ˈwäs-əl *also* wä-ˈsāl\ *n* **1** : an early English toast to someone's health **2** : a liquor that is made of ale or wine, spices, and often baked apples and that is served in a large bowl usually at Christmas **3** : riotous drinking [Old Norse *ves heill* "be well"]
[2]wassail *vb* **1** : to indulge in wassail : CAROUSE **2** : to drink to the health of
was·sail·er \ˈwäs-ə-lər *also* wä-ˈsā-lər\ *n* **1** : one that carouses : REVELER **2** *archaic* : one who goes about singing carols
Was·ser·mann test \ˈwäs-ər-mən-, ˈväs-\ *n* : a test of the blood for the detection of syphilis [August von *Wassermann*, died 1925, German bacteriologist]
wast \wəst, wäst, ˈwäst\ *archaic past 2d sing of* BE
wast·age \ˈwā-stij\ *n* : loss by use, decay, erosion, or leakage or through wastefulness
[1]waste \ˈwāst\ *n* **1 a** : a sparsely settled or barren region : DESERT **b** : uncultivated land **c** : a broad and empty expanse (as of water) **2** : the act or an instance of wasting : the state of being wasted **3** : gradual loss or decrease by use, wear, or decay **4 a** : damaged, defective, or superfluous material produced by a manufacturing process: as (1) : material rejected during a textile manufacturing process (2) : fluid (as steam) allowed to escape without being utilized **b** (1) : refuse (as garbage, sewage, or rubbish) that accumulates about habitations ⟨collection of city *wastes*⟩ (2) : material (as excrement) that is produced by a living body and is of no value to the organism that produces it [Old North French *wast*, from *wast*, adj., "desolate, waste", from Latin *vastus*]
[2]waste *vb* **1** : to lay waste usually by violence : DEVASTATE ⟨lands *wasted* by war⟩ **2** : to wear away or impair gradually : CONSUME ⟨fields *wasted* by erosion⟩ **3** : to spend or use carelessly : SQUANDER **4** : to lose or cause to lose weight, strength, or vitality — often used with *away* **5 a** : to become diminished in bulk or substance **b** : to become consumed **syn** see RAVAGE
[3]waste *adj* **1** : being wild and uninhabited : DESOLATE **2** : being ruined or devastated **3** : discarded as worthless, defective, or useless
waste·bas·ket \ˈwāst-ˌbas-kət, ˈwās-\ *n* : an open receptacle for trash
waste·ful \ˈwāst-fəl\ *adj* : given to or marked by waste — **waste·ful·ly** \-fə-lē\ *adv* — **waste·ful·ness** *n*
waste·land \ˈwāst-ˌland\ *n* : barren or uncultivated land
waste·pa·per \ˈwāst-ˈpā-pər, ˈwās-\ *n* : paper discarded as used, superfluous, or not fit for use
waste pipe *n* : a pipe for carrying off waste fluid
waste product *n* : material resulting from a process (as of metabolism or manufacture) that is of no further use to the system producing it
wast·er \ˈwā-stər\ *n* : one that wastes or squanders
wast·rel \ˈwā-strəl\ *n* : WASTER, SPENDTHRIFT [derived from [2]*waste*]
[1]watch \ˈwäch, ˈwȯch\ *vb* **1** : to stay awake intentionally (as at the bedside of a sick person) **2 a** : to be on the alert or on the lookout **b** : to keep guard ⟨*watch* outside the door⟩ **3** : to keep one's eyes on : keep in view ⟨*watch* a game⟩ **4** : to observe so as to prevent harm or danger ⟨*watch* a brush fire carefully⟩ **5** : to keep oneself informed about ⟨*watch* a competitor's career⟩ **6** : to be on the alert for the chance to make use of ⟨*watched* my opportunity⟩ [Old English *wæccan*] — **watch·er** *n* — **watch it** : to look out : be careful — **watch one's step** : to proceed with great care — **watch over** : to have charge of
[2]watch *n* **1 a** : the act of keeping awake to guard, protect, or attend **b** : a state of alert and continuous attention **c** : close observation : SURVEILLANCE **2** : one of the indeterminate wakeful intervals marking the passage of night — usually used in pl. **3** : one that watches : LOOKOUT **4 a** : a body of sentinels making up a guard **b** : a watchman or body of watchmen formerly assigned to patrol the streets **5 a** : a portion of time during which a part of a ship's company is on duty **b** : the part of a

ship's company on duty during a particular watch **c** : a period of duty : SHIFT **6** : a portable timepiece designed to be worn (as on the wrist) or carried in the pocket

watch·band \-ˌband\ *n* : the bracelet or strap of a wristwatch

watch·case \-ˌkās\ *n* : the outside covering of a watch

watch·dog \-ˌdȯg\ *n* **1** : a dog kept to guard property **2** : a watchful guardian

watch·ful \-fəl\ *adj* : steadily attentive and alert especially to danger — **watch·ful·ly** \-fə-lē\ *adv* — **watch·ful·ness** *n*

• **syn** WATCHFUL, VIGILANT, ALERT mean being on the lookout especially for opportunity or danger. WATCHFUL is the general and least explicit term for this; VIGILANT suggests maintaining a keen, unremitting watchfulness; ALERT stresses readiness or promptness in meeting danger or seizing opportunity.

watch glass *n* **1** : a glass that is usually convex outwardly and used for covering a watch dial **2** : a small circular glass dish used especially in laboratory work

watch·mak·er \ˈwäch-ˌmā-kər\ *n* : one that makes or repairs watches or clocks — **watch·mak·ing** \-kiŋ\ *n*

watch·man \-mən\ *n* : a person who keeps watch : GUARD

watch night *n* : a devotional service lasting until after midnight especially on New Year's Eve

watch out *vi* : to be vigilant — often used with *for*

watch·tow·er \ˈwäch-ˌtau̇-ər, -ˌtau̇r\ *n* : a tower for a lookout

watch·word \-ˌwərd\ *n* **1** : a secret word used as a signal or sign of recognition **2** : a motto used as a slogan or rallying cry

[1]**wa·ter** \ˈwȯt-ər, ˈwät-\ *n* **1 a** : the liquid that descends from the clouds as rain, forms streams, lakes, and seas, and is a major constituent of all living matter and that is an odorless, tasteless, very slightly compressible oxide of hydrogen H_2O **b** : a natural mineral water — usually used in pl. **2** *pl* : a band of seawater bordering on and under the control of a country ⟨sailing Canadian *waters*⟩ **3** : travel or transportation on water ⟨came by *water*⟩ **4** : the level of water at a particular state of the tide : TIDE **5** : liquid containing or resembling water: as **a** : a pharmaceutical or cosmetic preparation made with water **b** : a watery fluid (as tears, urine, or sap) formed or circulating in a living body **6 a** : the transparency and luster of a precious stone and especially a diamond **b** : a wavy lustrous pattern (as of a textile) **[**Old English *wæter***]** — **above water** : out of difficulty — **in deep water** : in serious difficulties

[2]**water** *vb* **1** : to moisten or soak with water **2 a** : to supply with water ⟨*water* horses⟩ **b** : to get or take water **3** : to treat with or as if with water; *esp* : to impart a lustrous appearance and wavy pattern to (cloth) by calendering **4 a** : to dilute by or as if by adding water **b** : to increase the total stated value of (stock) without a corresponding addition to capital **5** : to form or secrete water or watery matter (as tears or saliva)

water ballet *n* : a synchronized sequence of movements performed by a group of swimmers

water bed *n* : a bed whose mattress is a plastic bag filled with water

water beetle *n* : any of numerous oval flattened aquatic beetles that swim by means of their fringed hind legs which act together as oars

water bird *n* : a swimming or wading bird — compare WATERFOWL

water blister *n* : a blister with a clear watery content

water bloom *n* : an accumulation of algae and especially of blue-green algae at or near the surface of a body of water; *also* : an alga causing this

water boatman *n* : any of various aquatic bugs with one pair of legs modified into paddles

wa·ter·borne \ˈwȯt-ər-ˌbōrn, ˈwät-, -ˌbȯrn\ *adj* : supported or carried by water

water boy *n* : one who keeps a group (as of laborers) supplied with drinking water

wa·ter·buck \ˈwȯt-ər-ˌbək, ˈwät-\ *n, pl* **waterbuck** *or* **waterbucks** : any of various Old World antelopes that commonly frequent streams or wetlands

water buffalo *n* : an often domesticated Asian buffalo somewhat resembling a large ox

water chestnut *n* : any of several aquatic herbs with edible fruits or tubers; *also* : the edible part

water clock *n* : an instrument designed to measure time by the fall or flow of water

water closet *n* **1** : a compartment or room for defecation and urination into a toilet bowl : BATHROOM **2** : a toilet bowl along with its accessories

wa·ter·col·or \ˈwȯt-ər-ˌkəl-ər, ˈwät-\ *n* **1** : a paint whose liquid part is water **2** : the art of painting with water color **3** : a picture or design painted with watercolor — **wa·ter·col·or·ist** \-ˌkəl-ə-rəst\ *n*

water buffalo

wa·ter–cool \ˌwȯt-ər-ˈkül, ˌwät-\ *vt* : to cool by means of water and especially circulating water (as in a water jacket)

wa·ter·course \ˈwȯt-ər-ˌkōrs, ˈwät-, -ˌkȯrs\ *n* **1** : a bed over which or channel through which water flows **2** : a stream of water (as a river, brook, or underground stream)

wa·ter·craft \-ˌkraft\ *n* **1** : skill in water activities (as managing boats) **2** : craft for water transport

wa·ter·cress \-ˌkres\ *n* : any of several water-loving cresses; *esp* : a perennial cress found chiefly in springs or running water and used in salads or as a potherb

water cycle *n* : HYDROLOGIC CYCLE

water dog *n* : a large salamander; *esp* : MUD PUPPY

wa·ter·er \ˈwȯt-ər-ər, ˈwät-\ *n* : one that waters

wa·ter·fall \ˈwȯt-ər-ˌfȯl, ˈwät-\ *n* : a perpendicular or very steep descent of the water of a stream

water flea *n* : any of various small active dark or brightly colored freshwater crustaceans (as a cyclops)

wa·ter·fowl \ˈwȯt-ər-ˌfau̇l, ˈwät-\ *n* **1** : a bird that frequents water; *esp* : a swimming bird **2 waterfowl** *pl* : swimming game birds as distinguished from upland game birds and shorebirds

wa·ter·front \-ˌfrənt\ *n* : land or a section of an urban area bordering on a body of water

water gap *n* : a pass in a mountain ridge through which a stream runs

water gas *n* : a poisonous flammable gaseous mixture that consists chiefly of carbon monoxide and hydrogen, is usually made by blowing air and then steam over red-hot coke or coal, and is used as a fuel

water gate *n* **1** : a gate (as of a building) giving access to a body of water **2** : FLOODGATE 1

water glass *n* **1** : a glass vessel (as a drinking glass) for holding water **2** : an instrument consisting of an open box or tube with a glass bottom used for examining objects in or under water **3** : a water-soluble substance that consists usually of sodium silicate in the form of a glassy mass, a stony powder, or dissolved in water as a syrupy liquid and is used as a protective coating and in preserving eggs

water hemlock *n* : any of a genus of poisonous plants of the carrot family; *esp* : a tall Eurasian perennial herb

water hole *n* **1** : a natural hole or hollow containing water **2** : a hole in a surface of ice

water hyacinth *n* : a showy South American floating aquatic plant that often clogs waterways in the southern United States

water ice *n* : a frozen dessert of water, sugar, and flavoring

watering can *n* : a vessel usually with a perforated spout used to sprinkle water especially on plants

watering place *n* **1** : a place where water may be obtained; *esp* : one where animals and especially livestock come to drink **2** : a health or recreational resort featuring mineral springs or water activities

wa·ter·ish \ˈwȯt-ə-rish, ˈwät-\ *adj* : somewhat watery — **wa·ter·ish·ness** *n*

water jacket *n* : an outer casing which holds water or through which water circulates for cooling something

water jump *n* : an obstacle (as in a steeplechase) consisting of a pool, stream, or ditch of water

wa·ter·less \ˈwȯt-ər-ləs, ˈwät-\ *adj* **1** : lacking water : DRY **2** : not requiring water (as for cooling or cooking) — **wa·ter·less·ly** *adj* — **wa·ter·less·ness** *n*

water lily *n* : any of a family of aquatic plants with rounded floating leaves and usually showy flowers

wa•ter•line \'wȯt-ər-,līn, 'wät-\ *n* : any of several lines that are marked upon the outside of a ship and correspond with the surface of the water when it is afloat on an even keel

wa•ter•logged \-,lȯgd, -,lägd\ *adj* : so filled or soaked with water as to be heavy or hard to manage ⟨a *waterlogged* boat⟩ [*water* + *log* "to accumulate in the hold"]

wa•ter•loo \,wȯt-ər-'lü, ,wät-\ *n* : a decisive defeat [*Waterloo,* Belgium, scene of Napoleon's defeat in 1815]

water lily

water main *n* : a pipe or conduit for conveying water (as from a reservoir)

[1]**wa•ter•mark** \-,märk\ *n* **1** : a mark that indicates a line to which water has risen **2** : a mark (as the maker's name or trademark) made in paper during manufacture and visible when the paper is held up to the light

[2]**watermark** *vt* : to mark (paper) with a watermark

wa•ter•mel•on \'wȯt-ər-,mel-ən, 'wät-\ *n* **1** : a large oblong or rounded fruit with a hard green or white rind often striped or variegated, a sweet watery pink, yellowish, or red pulp, and many seeds **2** : a widely grown African vine of the gourd family whose fruits are watermelons

water meter *n* : an instrument for recording the quantity of water passing through a particular outlet

water moccasin *n* : a venomous semiaquatic pit viper of the southern United States closely related to the copperhead

water mold *n* : an aquatic fungus

water nymph *n* : a minor female divinity (as a naiad) associated with a body of water

water oak *n* : any of several American oaks that thrive in wet soil

water of crystallization : water of hydration present in many crystallized substances

water of hydration : water chemically combined with a substance to form a hydrate that can be expelled (as by heating) without essentially altering the composition of the substance

water ouzel *n* : any of several birds related to the thrushes that dive into swift mountain streams and walk on the bottom in search of food — called also *dipper*

water pipe *n* **1** : a pipe for conveying water **2** : a tobacco-smoking device so arranged that the smoke is drawn through water

water pistol *n* : a toy pistol designed to throw a jet of liquid — called also *squirt gun, water gun*

water plantain *n* : any of a genus of marsh or aquatic herbs with acrid sap and 3-petaled flowers

water polo *n* : a goal game played in water by teams of swimmers using a ball resembling a soccer ball

wa•ter•pow•er \'wȯt-ər-,pau̇-ər, 'wät-, -,pau̇r\ *n* : the power of moving water used to run machinery (as for generating electricity)

[1]**wa•ter•proof** \,wȯt-ər-'prüf, ,wät-\ *adj* : not letting water through; *esp* : covered or treated with a material (as a solution of rubber) to prevent penetration by water — **wa•ter•proof•ness** *n*

[2]**wa•ter•proof** \'wȯt-ər-,, 'wät-\ *n* **1** : a waterproof fabric **2** *chiefly British* : RAINCOAT

[3]**wa•ter•proof** \,wȯt-ər-', ,wät-\ *vt* : to make waterproof — **wa•ter•proof•er** *n*

wa•ter•proof•ing \-'prü-fing\ *n* **1 a** : the act or process of making something waterproof **b** : the condition of being made waterproof **2** : something (as a coating) capable of imparting waterproofness

water rat *n* **1** : a rodent that frequents water **2** : a waterfront loafer or petty thief

wa•ter–re•pel•lent \,wȯt-ər-ri-'pel-ənt, ,wȯt-ə-ri-, ,wät-\ *adj* : treated with a finish that is resistant to penetration by water but not waterproof

wa•ter–re•sis•tant \-ri-'zis-tənt\ *adj* : WATER-REPELLENT

water scorpion *n* : any of various large aquatic bugs with the end of the abdomen prolonged by a long breathing tube

wa•ter•shed \'wȯt-ər-,shed, 'wät-\ *n* **1** : a dividing ridge (as a mountain range) separating one drainage area from others **2** : the whole area that drains into a particular river or lake **3** : a crucial or dividing point, line, or factor

wa•ter•side \-,sīd\ *n* : the land bordering a body of water

water–ski *vi* : to ski on water while towed by a speedboat

water ski *n* : a ski used on water

water•ski•ing \'wȯt-ər-,skē-ing, 'wät-\ *n* : the sport of planing on water skis when towed by a motorboat

water snake *n* : any of numerous snakes frequenting or inhabiting fresh waters and feeding largely on aquatic animals

wa•ter–soak \'wȯt-ər-,sōk, 'wät-\ *vt* : to soak in water

water spaniel *n* : a rather large spaniel with a heavy curly coat used especially for retrieving waterfowl

wa•ter•spout \'wȯt-ər-,spau̇t, 'wät-\ *n* **1** : a pipe for carrying off water from a roof **2** : a tornado occurring over a body of water

water sprite *n* : a sprite inhabiting or haunting water

water strider *n* : any of various long-legged bugs that move about on the surface of the water

water table *n* : the upper limit of the ground wholly saturated with water

wa•ter•tight \,wȯt-ər-'tīt, ,wät-\ *adj* **1** : of such tight construction or fit as to be waterproof **2** : leaving no possibility of misunderstanding or evasion — **wa•ter•tight•ness** *n*

water tower *n* **1** : a tower or standpipe serving as a reservoir to deliver water **2** : a fire apparatus having a vertical pipe that can be extended to various heights and supplied with water under high pressure

water vapor *n* : the vapor of water especially when below the boiling temperature and in diffused form (as in the atmosphere)

water–vascular system *n* : a system of vessels in echinoderms containing a circulating watery fluid that is used for the movement of tentacles and tube feet and may also function in excretion and respiration

water wave *n* : a method or style of setting hair by dampening with water and forming into waves — **wa•ter–waved** \'wȯt-ər-,wāvd, 'wät-\ *adj*

wa•ter•way \'wȯt-ər-,wā, 'wät-\ *n* : a channel or a body of water by which ships can travel

wa•ter•weed \-,wēd\ *n* : a weedy aquatic plant usually with inconspicuous flowers — compare WATER LILY

wa•ter•wheel \-,hwēl, -,wēl\ *n* : a wheel made to turn by a flow of water against it

water wings *n pl* : an air-filled device to give support to a person learning to swim

wa•ter•works \'wȯt-ər-,wərks, 'wät-\ *n pl* : the system of reservoirs, channels, mains, and pumping and purifying equipment by which a water supply is obtained and distributed (as to a city)

wa•ter•worn \-,wōrn, -,wȯrn\ *adj* : worn, smoothed, or polished by the action of water

wa•tery \'wȯt-ə-rē, 'wät-\ *adj* **1** : of or having to do with water ⟨a *watery* grave⟩ **2** : containing, full of, or giving out water ⟨*watery* clouds⟩ **3** : similar to water : THIN, WEAK ⟨*watery* tea⟩ **4** : being soft and soggy ⟨*watery* turnips⟩ — **wa•ter•i•ness** *n*

Wat•son–Crick model \,wät-sən-'krik-\ *n* : a model of DNA structure in which the molecule is a double-stranded helix cross-linked by pairs of purine and pyrimidine bases joined by hydrogen bonds with adenine paired with thymine and cytosine paired with guanine [J. D. *Watson,* born 1928, American biologist and F. H. C. *Crick,* born 1916, English biologist]

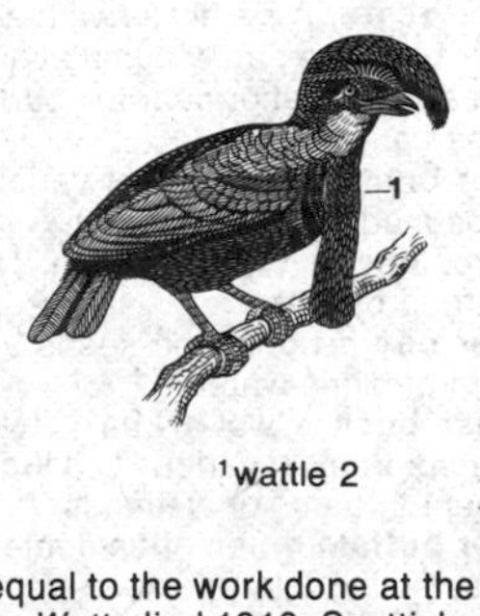

[1]wattle 2

watt \'wät\ *n* : a unit of power equal to the work done at the rate of one joule per second [James *Watt,* died 1819, Scottish engineer]

watt•age \-ij\ *n* : amount of power expressed in watts

watt–hour \'wät-'au̇r\ *n* : a unit of work or energy equivalent to the power of one watt operating for one hour

[1]**wat•tle** \'wät-l\ *n* **1 a** : a structure of poles interwoven with

slender branches, withes, or reeds and used especially formerly in building **b** : material for such construction **c** *pl* : poles laid on a roof to support thatch **2** : a fleshy process hanging usually about the head or neck (as of a bird) **3** : ACACIA 1 [Old English *watel*] — **wat•tled** \-ld\ *adj*

[2]**wattle** *vt* **wat•tled**; **wat•tling** \'wät-ling, -l-ing\ **1** : to form or build of or with wattle **2 a** : to form into wattle : interlace to form wattle **b** : to unite or make solid by interweaving light flexible material

watt•me•ter \'wät-ˌmēt-ər\ *n* : an instrument for measuring electric power in watts

[1]**wave** \'wāv\ *vb* **1** : to float, play, or shake in an air current : move or cause to move loosely to and fro : FLUTTER **2** : to motion with the hands or with something held in them in signal or salute **3 a** : to become moved or brandished to and fro ⟨a sword *waving* under my nose⟩ **b** : BRANDISH, FLOURISH ⟨*waved* a pistol menacingly⟩ **4** : to move before the wind with a wavelike motion ⟨fields of *waving* grain⟩ **5** : to follow or cause to follow a curving line or take a wavy form [Old English *wafian* "to wave with the hands"]

[2]**wave** *n* **1** : a moving swell or crest on the surface of water **2** : a wavelike formation or shape ⟨a *wave* in the hair⟩ **3** : a waving motion (as of the hand or a flag) **4** : FLOW, GUSH ⟨a *wave* of color swept the child's face⟩ **5** : a surge or rapid increase ⟨a *wave* of buying⟩ ⟨a heat *wave*⟩ **6** : a disturbance that transfers energy progressively from point to point and that may take the form of an elastic deformation or of a variation of pressure, electric or magnetic intensity, electric potential, or temperature ⟨a light *wave*⟩ — **wave•like** \-ˌlīk\ *adj*

Wave \'wāv\ *n* : a woman serving in the United States Navy [*W*omen *A*ccepted for *V*olunteer *E*mergency Service]

waved \'wāvd\ *adj* : having a wavelike form or outline: as **a** : marked by undulations ⟨the *waved* cutting edge of a bread knife⟩ **b** : having wavy lines of color ⟨*waved* cloth⟩

wave form *n* : a usually graphic representation of the shape of a wave

wave•length \'wāv-ˌlength, -ˌlengkth\ *n* : the distance (as from crest to crest) in the line of advance of a wave from any one point to the next corresponding point

wave•less \-ləs\ *adj* : having no waves : CALM — **wave•less•ly** *adv*

wave•let \-lət\ *n* : a little wave : RIPPLE

wave mechanics *n* : a branch of physics dealing with the wave nature of elementary particles

[1]**wa•ver** \'wā-vər\ *vi* **wa•vered**; **wa•ver•ing** \'wāv-ring, -ə-ring\ **1** : to swing back and forth uncertainly between choices : fluctuate in opinion, allegiance, or direction **2 a** : to weave or sway unsteadily to and fro : REEL, TOTTER **b** : QUIVER, FLICKER ⟨*wavering* flames⟩ **c** : FALTER 3 **3** : to give an unsteady sound : QUAVER [Middle English *waveren*] **syn** see HESITATE, SWAY — **wa•ver•er** \'wā-vər-ər\ *n* — **wa•ver•ing•ly** \'wāv-ring-lē, -ə-ring-\ *adv*

[2]**waver** *n* : an act of wavering, quivering, or fluttering

wavy \'wā-vē\ *adj* **wav•i•er**; **wav•i•est** : having waves : moving in waves ⟨*wavy* hair⟩ ⟨a *wavy* surface⟩ — **wav•i•ly** \-və-lē\ *adv* — **wav•i•ness** \-vē-nəs\ *n*

[1]**wax** \'waks\ *n* **1** : a yellowish plastic substance secreted by bees and used by them for constructing the honeycomb — called also *beeswax* **2** : any of various substances resembling beeswax in physical or chemical properties: as **a** : a plant or animal product that is harder and less greasy than a typical fat **b** : a solid mixture of higher hydrocarbons **c** : EARWAX **3** : something likened to wax as soft, impressionable, or readily molded [Old English *weax*] — **wax•like** \-ˌlīk\ *adj*

[2]**wax** *vt* : to treat or rub with wax

[3]**wax** *vi* **1** : to grow larger or greater: as **a** : to grow in volume or duration ⟨a stream *waxing* with melting snows⟩ **b** : to increase in apparent size and brightness ⟨the moon *waxes* toward the full⟩ **2** : to pass from one state to another : BECOME ⟨the party *waxed* merry⟩ [Old English *weaxan*]

[4]**wax** *n* **1** : INCREASE 1, GROWTH **2** : the period from the new moon to the full phase of the moon

wax bean *n* : a kidney bean with pods that are yellow when fit for use as snap beans

waxed paper *n* : paper treated with wax to make it impervious to water and grease

wax•en \'wak-sən\ *adj* **1** : made of wax **2** : resembling wax (as in pliability, pallor, or lustrous smoothness)

wax myrtle *n* : a shrub of eastern North America having small hairless hard berries with a thick coating of white wax used for candles; *also* : a related shrub of the west coast of the United States

wax•wing \'wak-ˌswing\ *n* : any of several American and Eurasian birds that are mostly brown with a showy crest and velvety plumage

waxwing

wax•work \'wak-ˌswərk\ *n* **1** : an effigy in wax usually of a person **2** *pl* : an exhibition of wax effigies

waxy \'wak-sē\ *adj* **wax•i•er**; **-est** **1** : covered with wax ⟨a *waxy* surface⟩ ⟨*waxy* berries⟩ **2** : resembling wax : WAXEN ⟨a *waxy* pallor⟩ — **wax•i•ness** *n*

[1]**way** \'wā\ *n* **1 a** : a track for travel or passage : PATH, ROAD, STREET **b** : an opening for passage (as through a crowd or a gate) ⟨no *way* out⟩ **2** : the course traveled from one place to another : ROUTE ⟨knew the *way* home⟩ **3 a** : a course of action ⟨chose the easy *way*⟩ **b** : opportunity, capability, or fact of doing as one pleases ⟨determined to have our *way*⟩ **c** : POSSIBILITY ⟨no two *ways* about it⟩ **4 a** : method in which something is done or happens ⟨a new *way* of painting⟩ ⟨the *way* the mind works⟩ **b** : FEATURE, RESPECT ⟨a good worker in many *ways*⟩ **c** : the usual or characteristic state of affairs ⟨as is the *way* with dreams⟩ **d** : STATE, CONDITION ⟨that's the *way* things are⟩ ⟨was in a bad *way* with rheumatism⟩ **5 a** : a particular or characteristic mode or trick of behavior ⟨it's just my *way*⟩ **b** : a regular continued course (as of life or action) ⟨championing the American *way*⟩ ⟨people met in the *way* of business⟩; *also* : a body of ethical or religious practice (as the Christian religion) **6 a** : the length of a course : DISTANCE ⟨still a *way* from success⟩ **b** : progress along a course ⟨earning my *way* through school⟩ **7** : something (as a locality) having direction as an attribute ⟨come this *way*⟩ ⟨out our *way*⟩ ⟨stroking the fur the wrong *way*⟩ **8 a** : room or chance to progress or advance ⟨make *way* for the queen⟩ **b** : place for something else ⟨slums torn down to make *way* for parks⟩ **9 a** : a guiding track that eases passage or movement **b** *pl* : an inclined support on which a ship is built and from which it is launched **10** : CATEGORY, KIND ⟨get what you need in the *way* of supplies⟩ **11** : motion or speed of a boat through the water ⟨making slow *way* down the harbor⟩ [Old English *weg*] — **by way of 1** : for the purpose of ⟨*by way of* illustration⟩ **2** : by the route through : VIA — **out of the way 1** : WRONG, IMPROPER **2** : SECLUDED 1, REMOTE — **under way 1** : in motion through the water **2** : in progress

[2]**way** *adj* : of, connected with, or constituting an intermediate point on a route ⟨*way* station⟩

[3]**way** *adv* : [1]AWAY 7, FAR ⟨*way* back in the woods⟩

way•bill \'wā-ˌbil\ *n* : a document prepared by the carrier of a shipment of goods and containing details of the shipment, route, and charges

way•far•er \-ˌfar-ər, -ˌfer-\ *n* : a traveler especially on foot — **way•far•ing** \-ˌfar-ing, -ˌfer-\ *adj*

way•lay \'wā-ˌlā\ *vt* **-laid** \-ˌlād\; **-lay•ing** : to wait for and attack or intercept

Way of the Cross : STATIONS OF THE CROSS

-ways \ˌwāz\ *adv suffix* : in (such) a way, course, direction, or manner ⟨side*ways*⟩ [Middle English, from *ways*, genitive of *way*]

ways and means *n pl* : methods and resources for accomplishing something and especially for raising money needed by a state; *also* : a legislative committee concerned with this function

way•side \'wā-ˌsīd\ *n* : the side of or land adjacent to a road or path — **wayside** *adj*

way•ward \'wā-wərd\ *adj* **1** : taking an irregular or improper

\ə\ **abut**	\au̇\ **out**	\i\ **tip**	\ȯ\ **saw**	\u̇\ **foot**
\ər\ **further**	\ch\ **chin**	\ī\ **life**	\ȯi\ **coin**	\y\ **yet**
\a\ **mat**	\e\ **pet**	\j\ **job**	\th\ **thin**	\yü\ **few**
\ā\ **take**	\ē\ **easy**	\ng\ **sing**	\th\ **this**	\yu̇\ **cure**
\ä\ **cot, cart**	\g\ **go**	\ō\ **bone**	\ü\ **food**	\zh\ **vision**

way : DISOBEDIENT ⟨*wayward* children⟩ **2** : CONTRARY, PERVERSE ⟨their *wayward* behavior⟩ **3** : following no clear principle : UNPREDICTABLE [Middle English, from *awayward* "turned away"] — **way•ward•ly** *adv* — **way•ward•ness** *n*

way•worn \-ˌwōrn, -ˌwȯrn\ *adj* : wearied by traveling

we \wē, ˈwē\ *pron, pl in construction* **1** : I and one or more others — used as pronoun of the 1st person plural; compare I, OUR, OURS, US **2** : I — used by sovereigns; used by writers to keep an impersonal character [Old English *wē*]

weak \ˈwēk\ *adj* **1** : lacking strength: as **a** : deficient in physical vigor : FEEBLE ⟨*weak* as a kitten⟩ **b** : not able to sustain or resist much weight, pressure, or strain ⟨a *weak* rope⟩ **c** : deficient in vigor of mind or character; *also* : resulting from or indicative of such deficiency ⟨a *weak* policy⟩ **d** : DILUTE ⟨*weak* tea⟩ **2** : not factually grounded or logically presented ⟨a *weak* argument⟩ **3 a** : not able to function properly ⟨*weak* eyes⟩ **b** : lacking skill or proficiency; *also* : indicative of such a lack ⟨math's my *weakest* subject⟩ **c** : wanting in vigor of expression or effect **4 a** : not having or exerting authority ⟨a *weak* government⟩ **b** : INEFFECTIVE, IMPOTENT ⟨*weak* measures to control crime⟩ **5** : of, relating to, or constituting an English verb or verb conjugation that forms the past tense and past participle by adding the suffix *-ed* or *-d* or *-t* **6** : bearing the minimal degree of stress occurring in the language ⟨a *weak* syllable⟩ [Old Norse *veikr*] — **weak•ly** *adv*

weak•en \ˈwē-kən\ *vb* **weak•ened**; **weak•en•ing** \ˈwēk-ning, -ə-ning\ : to make or become weak or weaker

weak•fish \ˈwēk-ˌfish\ *n* : any of several marine food fishes related to the perches; *esp* : a common sport and market fish of the eastern coast of the United States [Dutch *weekvis*, from *week* "soft" + *vis* "fish"; from its tender flesh]

weak•heart•ed \-ˈhärt-əd\ *adj* : lacking courage : FAINTHEARTED

weak–kneed \ˈwēk-ˈnēd\ *adj* : lacking willpower or determination : IRRESOLUTE

weak•ling \ˈwē-kling\ *n* : one that is weak in body or character — **weakling** *adj*

weak•ly \ˈwē-klē\ *adj* **weak•li•er**; **-est** : FEEBLE 1, WEAK — **weak•li•ness** *n*

weak–mind•ed \ˈwēk-ˈmīn-dəd\ *adj* **1** : lacking in judgment or good sense : FOOLISH **2** : FEEBLE-MINDED — **weak–mind•ed•ness** *n*

weak•ness \ˈwēk-nəs\ *n* **1** : the quality or state of being weak; *also* : an instance or period of being weak **2** : DEFECT, FAULT **3** : an object of special desire or fondness

[1]**weal** \ˈwēl\ *n* : WELL-BEING, PROSPERITY [Middle English *wele*, from Old English *wela*]

[2]**weal** *n* : WELT 2a [alteration of *wale*]

weald \ˈwēld\ *n* **1** : a heavily wooded area : FOREST **2** : a wild or uncultivated usually upland region [the *Weald*, wooded district in southeastern England]

wealth \ˈwelth\ *n* **1** : abundance of possessions or resources : AFFLUENCE **2** : abundant supply : PROFUSION ⟨a *wealth* of detail⟩ **3 a** : all property that has a money or an exchange value **b** : all material objects that have economic utility; *esp* : those in existence at any one time [Middle English *welthe*, from *wele* "weal"]

wealthy \ˈwel-thē\ *adj* **wealth•i•er**; **-est 1** : having wealth : AFFLUENT **2** : characterized by abundance — **wealth•i•ly** \-thə-lē\ *adv* — **wealth•i•ness** \-thē-nəs\ *n*

wean \ˈwēn\ *vt* **1** : to accustom (as a child) to take food otherwise than by nursing **2** : to turn (one) away from something long desired or followed ⟨*wean* a child from a bad habit⟩ [Old English *wenian* "to accustom, wean"] — **wean•er** *n*

wean•ling \-ling\ *n* : one newly weaned — **weanling** *adj*

weap•on \ˈwep-ən\ *n* **1** : something (as a gun, knife, or club) that may be used to fight with **2** : a means by which one contends against another ⟨propaganda is a *weapon* of war⟩ [Old English *wǣpen*]

weap•on•less \-ləs\ *adj* : lacking weapons : UNARMED

weap•on•ry \-rē\ *n* **1** : the science of designing and making weapons **2** : aggregate of weapons

[1]**wear** \ˈwaər, ˈweər\ *vb* **wore** \ˈwōr, ˈwȯr\; **worn** \ˈwōrn, ˈwȯrn\; **wear•ing 1 a** : to bear on the person or use habitually for clothing or adornment ⟨*wore* a jacket⟩ **b** : to carry on the person ⟨*wear* a watch⟩ **2** : to have or show an appearance of ⟨*wore* a happy smile⟩ **3 a** : to impair, diminish, or decay by use or attrition ⟨the dress finally *wore* to bits⟩ ⟨letters on the stone *worn* away by weathering⟩ **b** : to produce gradually by attrition ⟨*wear* a hole in the rug⟩ **c** : to exhaust or lessen the strength of : WEARY, FATIGUE ⟨*worn* by care and toil⟩ **4** : to stand up under use or the passage of time ⟨a coat that has *worn* well⟩ **5** : to lessen or fail with the passage of time ⟨nagging *wore* my patience away⟩ ⟨the day *wore* on⟩ **6** : to go or cause to go about by turning the stern to the wind [Old English *werian*] — **wear•able** \ˈwar-ə-bəl, ˈwer-\ *adj* — **wear•er** \-ər\ *n* — **wear on** : IRRITATE 1, FRAY

[2]**wear** *n* **1** : the act of wearing : the state of being worn : USE ⟨clothes for everyday *wear*⟩ **2** : clothing or an article of clothing usually of a particular kind or for a special occasion or use ⟨casual *wear*⟩ **3** : wearing quality : durability under use **4** : the result of wearing or use : diminution or impairment due to use ⟨*wear*-resistant surface⟩

wear and tear *n* : the loss or injury to which something is subjected by or in the course of use; *esp* : normal depreciation

wear down *vt* : to weary and overcome by persistent effort or pressure

wea•ri•less \ˈwir-ē-ləs\ *adj* : not subject to fatigue — **wea•ri•less•ly** *adv*

wear•ing \ˈwaər-ing, ˈweər-\ *adj* : subjecting to or inflicting wear; *esp* : that fatigues ⟨a *wearing* journey⟩ — **wear•ing•ly** \-ing-lē\ *adv*

wea•ri•some \ˈwir-ē-səm\ *adj* : causing weariness : TIRESOME — **wea•ri•some•ly** *adv* — **wea•ri•some•ness** *n*

wear off *vt* : to diminish gradually (as in effect)

wear out *vb* **1** : to make or become useless by wear **2** : to weary especially to exhaustion

[1]**wea•ry** \ˈwiər-ē\ *adj* **wea•ri•er**; **-est 1** : worn out in strength, endurance, vigor, or freshness **2** : expressing or characteristic of weariness **3** : having one's patience, tolerance, or pleasure exhausted — used with *of* [Old English *wērig*] — **wea•ri•ly** \ˈwir-ə-lē\ *adv* — **wea•ri•ness** \ˈwir-ē-nəs\ *n*

[2]**weary** *vb* **wea•ried**; **wea•ry•ing** : to become or make weary

wea•sand \ˈwēz-nd\ *n* : THROAT 1, GULLET; *also* : WINDPIPE [Middle English *wesand*]

[1]**wea•sel** \ˈwē-zəl\ *n, pl* **weasel** *or* **weasels** : any of various small slender active flesh-eating mammals related to the minks [Old English *weosule*]

[2]**weasel** *vi* **wea•seled**; **wea•sel•ing** \ˈwēz-ling, -ə-ling\ **1** : to speak evasively : EQUIVOCATE **2** : to escape from or evade a situation or obligation — often used with *out* [*weasel word*]

weasel word *n* : a word or statement that is deliberately vague, ambiguous, or misleading [from the weasel's reputed habit of sucking the contents from an egg while leaving the shell superficially intact]

[1]**weath•er** \ˈwet͟h-ər\ *n* **1** : state of the atmosphere with respect to heat or cold, wetness or dryness, calm or storm, clearness or cloudiness **2** : a particular and especially a disagreeable atmospheric state [Old English *weder*] — **under the weather** : somewhat ill or drunk

[2]**weather** *adj* : WINDWARD — compare LEE

[3]**weather** *vb* **weath•ered**; **weath•er•ing** \ˈwet͟h-ring, -ə-ring\ **1 a** : to expose to or endure the action of the elements **b** : to alter (as in color or texture) by exposure to the weather **2** : to sail or pass to the windward of **3** : to bear up against and come safely through ⟨*weather* a storm⟩

weath•er•abil•i•ty \ˌwet͟h-rə-ˈbil-ət-ē, -ə-rə-\ *n* : capability of withstanding weather ⟨*weatherability* of a plastic⟩

weath•er–beat•en \ˈwet͟h-ər-ˌbēt-n\ *adj* **1** : worn or damaged by the weather **2** : toughened or colored by the weather

weath•er•board \-ˌbōrd, -ˌbȯrd\ *n* : CLAPBOARD, SIDING

weath•er•board•ing \-ˌbōrd-ing, -ˌbȯrd-\ *n* : SIDING 2

weath•er–bound \-ˌbau̇nd\ *adj* : restrained or forced to be inactive by bad weather

weather bureau *n* : a government organization that collects weather reports, formulates weather predictions and storm warnings, and compiles weather statistics

weath•er•cock \-ˌkäk\ *n* **1** : a vane often in the figure of a rooster mounted so as to turn freely with the wind and show the wind's direction **2** : one that changes readily or often especially according to public opinion

weath•er•glass \-ˌglas\ *n* : a simple instrument for showing changes in atmospheric pressure by the changing level of liquid in a spout connected with a closed reservoir

weath•er•ing *n* : alteration of exposed objects by action of the elements; *esp* : physical disintegration and chemical decomposition of earth materials at or near the earth's surface

weath•er•man \ˈwet͟h-ər-ˌman\ *n* : one who reports and forecasts the weather : METEOROLOGIST

weather map *n* : a chart showing the principal meteorological features at a given hour over an extended region

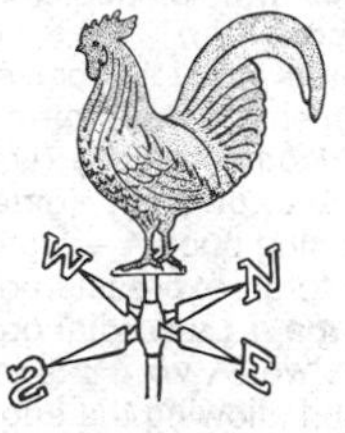
weathercock 1

weath•er•proof \ˌweth-ər-ˈprüf\ *adj* : able to withstand exposure to weather without damage or loss of function — **weatherproof** *vt* — **weath•er•proof•ness** *n*

weather station *n* : a station for taking, recording, and reporting meteorological observations

weather strip *n* : a strip of material used to make a seal where a door or window joins the sill or casing — **weather-strip** *vt*

weather vane *n* : VANE 1

weath•er•worn \-ˌwōrn, -ˌwȯrn\ *adj* : worn by exposure to the weather

[1]**weave** \ˈwēv\ *vb* **wove** \ˈwōv\; **wo•ven** \ˈwō-vən\; **weav•ing 1 a** : to form by interlacing strands of material; *esp* : to make (cloth) on a loom by interlacing warp and filling threads **b** : to interlace (as threads) into a fabric and especially cloth **2** : SPIN 2b **3 a** : to produce by elaborately combining elements ⟨*weave* a plot⟩ **b** : to unite in a coherent whole **c** : to introduce as an appropriate element : work in ⟨*wove* the episodes into a story⟩ ⟨*weave* a moral into a tale⟩ **4** : to direct or move in a winding or zigzag course especially to avoid obstacles ⟨*weaving* through traffic⟩ [Old English *wefan*] — **weav•er** *n*

[2]**weave** *n* : a pattern or method of weaving ⟨a coarse loose *weave*⟩

[3]**weave** *vi* : to move in a wavering manner from side to side : SWAY [Middle English *weven* "to move to and fro, wave"]

weav•er•bird \ˈwē-vər-ˌbərd\ *n* : any of a family of Old World birds that resemble finches and mostly construct elaborate nests of interlaced vegetation

weaverbird

weaver finch *n* : WEAVERBIRD

[1]**web** \ˈweb\ *n* **1** : a fabric on a loom or in process of being removed from a loom **2 a** : COBWEB 1 **b** : SNARE, ENTANGLEMENT ⟨caught in a *web* of fear⟩ **3** : a membrane of an animal or plant; *esp* : one uniting toes (as of many birds) **4** : the plate connecting the upper and lower flanges of a girder or rail **5** : NETWORK ⟨a *web* of highways⟩ **6** : VANE 3a **7** : a continuous sheet of paper manufactured or undergoing manufacture or a reel of this for use in a rotary printing press [Old English] — **web•by** \ˈweb-ē\ *adj* — **web•like** \ˈweb-ˌlīk\ *adj*

[2]**web** *vb* **webbed**; **web•bing 1** : to cover or provide with webs or a network **2** : to form a web

webbed \ˈwebd\ *adj* : having or joined by a web ⟨*webbed* feet⟩

web•bing \ˈweb-ing\ *n* : a strong closely woven tape used especially for straps, harness, or upholstery

web•foot \ˈweb-ˈfu̇t\ *n* : a foot having webbed toes — **web–foot•ed** \-əd\ *adj*

web•worm \ˈweb-ˌwərm\ *n* : any of various mostly gregarious caterpillars that spin large webs

wed \ˈwed\ *vb* **wed•ded** *also* **wed**; **wed•ding 1** : to marry or get married **2** : to unite firmly [Old English *weddian*]

we'd \wēd, ˌwēd\ : we had : we should : we would

wed•ding \ˈwed-ing\ *n* **1** : a marriage ceremony usually with accompanying festivities **2** : a joining in close association

[1]**wedge** \ˈwej\ *n* **1** : a piece of wood or metal tapered to a thin edge and used especially to split wood or rocks and in lifting heavy weights — compare SIMPLE MACHINE **2** : something (as a piece of pie or land or a formation of wild geese) shaped like a wedge **3** : a thing that serves to make a gradual opening or cause a change in something ⟨use every concession as an entering *wedge*⟩ [Old English *wecg*]

[2]**wedge** *vt* **1** : to fasten or tighten by or as if by driving in a wedge **2** : to press or force (something) into a narrow space ⟨*wedged* paper around the loose window⟩ **3** : to separate or split with or as if with a wedge

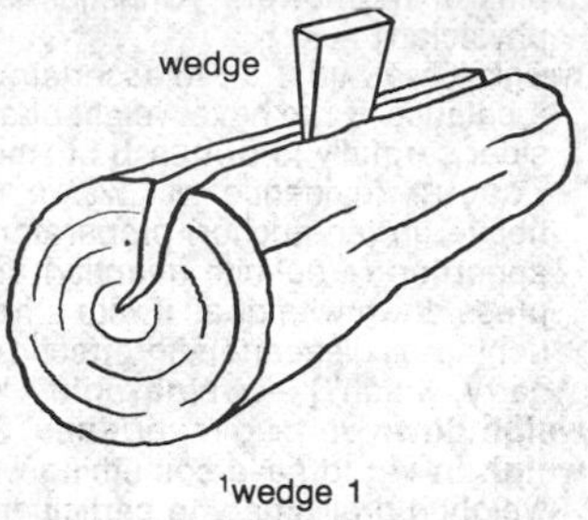

[1]wedge 1

Wedg•wood \ˈwej-ˌwu̇d\ *trademark* — used for ceramic wares

wed•lock \ˈwed-ˌläk\ *n* : the state of being married : MARRIAGE [Old English *wedlāc* "marriage bond", from *wedd* "pledge" + *-lāc*, suffix denoting activity] — **out of wedlock** : with the natural parents not legally married to each other

Wednes•day \ˈwenz-dē\ *n* : the 4th day of the week [Old English *wōdnesdæg*, literally, "day of Odin"]

wee \ˈwē\ *adj* **1** : very small : TINY **2** : very early ⟨*wee* hours of the morning⟩ [Middle English *we*, from *we* "little bit", from Old English *wǣge* "weight"]

[1]**weed** \ˈwēd\ *n* **1** : a plant of no value and usually of rank growth; *esp* : one that tends to overgrow or choke out more desirable plants **2** : something (as an obnoxious thing or person) like a weed [Old English *wēod*] — **weed•less** \-ləs\ *adj*

[2]**weed** *vb* **1** : to free from or remove weeds or something harmful, inferior, or superfluous **2** : to get rid of (weeds or unwanted items) ⟨*weed* out the loafers from the crew⟩ — **weed•er** *n*

[3]**weed** *n* **1** : GARMENT — often used in pl. **2** : dress worn (as by a widow) as a sign of mourning — usually used in pl. [Old English *wǣd*]

weedy \ˈwēd-ē\ *adj* **weed•i•er**; **-est 1** : abounding with or consisting of weeds ⟨a *weedy* field⟩ **2** : resembling a weed especially in rapid growth **3** : noticeably lean and scrawny : LANKY ⟨*weedy* cattle⟩

week \ˈwēk\ *n* **1 a** : seven successive days ⟨was sick for a *week*⟩ **b** : a calendar period of seven days beginning with Sunday and ending with Saturday ⟨the last *week* of the month⟩ **2** : the working or school days of the calendar week ⟨had a hard *week*⟩ [Old English *wicu*]

week•day \-ˌdā\ *n* : a day of the week except Sunday or sometimes except Saturday and Sunday

week•days \-ˌdāz\ *adv* : on weekdays repeatedly : on any weekday ⟨takes a bus *weekdays*⟩

[1]**week•end** \ˈwē-ˌkend\ *n* : the end of the week; *esp* : the period between the close of one working or school week and the beginning of the next

[2]**weekend** *vi* : to spend the weekend

week•ends \-ˌendz, -ˌenz\ *adv* : on weekends repeatedly : on any weekend ⟨travels *weekends*⟩

[1]**week•ly** \ˈwē-klē\ *adj* **1** : occurring, done, produced, or issued every week **2** : computed in terms of one week — **weekly** *adv*

[2]**weekly** *n, pl* **weeklies** : a weekly publication

wee•ny \ˈwē-nē\ *adj* : exceptionally small [*wee* + *tiny*]

weep \ˈwēp\ *vb* **wept** \ˈwept\; **weep•ing 1 a** : to express emotion and especially sorrow by shedding tears : CRY **b** : to pour forth (tears) from the eyes **2** : to give off (liquid) slowly or in drops : OOZE [Old English *wēpan*] — **weep•er** \ˈwē-pər\ *n*

weep•ing \ˈwē-ping\ *adj* **1** : TEARFUL **2** : RAINY **3** : having slender pendent branches ⟨a *weeping* willow⟩

weepy \ˈwē-pē\ *adj* **weep•i•er**; **-est** : inclined to weep : TEARFUL

wee•vil \ˈwē-vəl\ *n* : any of a large group (Rhynchophora) of mostly small beetles having the head long and usually curved downward to form a snout bearing the jaws at the tip and including many very injurious to plants or plant products [Old English *wifel*] — **wee•vily** *or* **wee•vil•ly** \ˈwēv-lē, -ə-lē\ *adj*

weft \ˈweft\ *n* **1 a** : WOOF 1 **b** : yard used for the woof **2** : material made by spinning or weaving [Old English]

wei•ge•la \wī-ˈjē-lə\ *n* : any of a genus of showy shrubs of the honeysuckle family; *esp* : a Chinese shrub widely grown for its

pink or red flowers [Christian E. *Weigel*, died 1831, German physician]
weigh \'wā\ *vb* **1 a** : to ascertain the heaviness of by or as if by a balance **b** : to have weight or a specified weight **2 a** : to consider carefully : PONDER **b** : to merit consideration as important : COUNT ⟨evidence will *weigh* heavily against them⟩ **3** : to heave up (an anchor) preparatory to sailing **4** : to measure or apportion (a definite quantity) on or as if on a scale **5 a** : to press down with or as if with a heavy weight **b** : to have a saddening or disheartening effect [Old English *wegan* "to move, carry, weigh"] — **weigh·able** \'wā-ə-bəl\ *adj* — **weigh·er** *n*
weigh down *vt* **1** : OVERBURDEN **2** : OPPRESS 1, DEPRESS
weigh in *vi* : to have something weighed; *esp* : to have oneself weighed preliminary to participation in a sports event
[1]**weight** \'wāt\ *n* **1 a** : quantity as determined by weighing ⟨sold by *weight*⟩ **b** : the property of a body that is measurable by weighing and that depends on the interaction of its mass with a gravitational field **c** : the standard or established amount that something should weigh ⟨coin of full *weight*⟩ **d** : something with weight : material substance ⟨adding *weight* to the load⟩ **2 a** : a quantity or portion weighing a usually specified amount ⟨take equal *weights* of flour and butter⟩ **b** : the amount that something weighs ⟨worth its *weight* in gold⟩ **c** : relative heaviness (as of a textile) — usually used in combination **3 a** : a unit (as a pound or kilogram) of weight or mass — see MEASURE table, METRIC SYSTEM table **b** : an integrated system of such units **4 a** : an object (as a piece of metal) of known weight for balancing a scale in weighing other objects **b** : a heavy object used to hold, press down, or counterbalance something else ⟨clock *weights*⟩ **c** : a heavy object (as a metal ball or barbell) heaved or lifted in athletic contests or exercises **5 a** : something heavy : LOAD ⟨skill in handling *weights*⟩ **b** : a mental or emotional burden ⟨had a *weight* on my conscience⟩ **6 a** : relative importance or claim to consideration : NOTE ⟨opinions that carry *weight*⟩ **b** : the greater or more impressive part ⟨the *weight* of the evidence favors this view⟩ [Old English *wiht*]
[2]**weight** *vt* **1** : to load or make heavy with or as if with a weight **2** : to oppress with a burden ⟨*weighted* down with cares⟩ **3** : to assign a relative importance to (as in a statistical study)
weight·less \'wāt-ləs\ *adj* : having little weight : lacking apparent gravitational pull — **weight·less·ly** *adv* — **weight·less·ness** *n*
weight lifter *n* : one that lifts barbells in competition or as an exercise — **weight lifting** *n*
weighty \'wāt-ē\ *adj* **weight·i·er**; **-est 1** : having much weight : HEAVY **2 a** : of much importance or consequence : SERIOUS ⟨*weighty* problems⟩ **b** : expressing seriousness : SOLEMN ⟨a *weighty* manner⟩ **3** : exerting authority or influence ⟨*weighty* arguments⟩ — **weight·i·ly** \'wāt-l-ē\ *adv* — **weight·i·ness** \'wāt-ē-nəs\ *n*
wei·ma·ra·ner \ˌvī-mə-'rän-ər, 'wī-mə-ˌ\ *n* : any of a German breed of large gray short-haired sporting dogs [German, from *Weimar*, Germany]
weir \'waər, 'weər, 'wiər\ *n* **1** : a fence set in a stream to catch fish **2** : a dam in a stream to raise the water level or divert its flow [Old English *wer*]
weird \'wiərd\ *adj* **1** : of, relating to, or caused by witchcraft or the supernatural : MAGICAL **2** : of strange or extraordinary character : ODD, FANTASTIC [Middle English *werd* "fate", from Old English *wyrd*] — **weird·ly** *adv* — **weird·ness** *n*
△ **origin** *Weird* is derived from an Old English noun *wyrd*, meaning "fate". The Middle English form *werd* is found primarily as a noun in Scottish and northern contexts. Not until the 15th century is this word recorded in an attributive or adjectival position, and then only in the combination *weird sister*. The Weird Sisters were the three Fates. Finally in the 18th century *weird* began to appear in other contexts as an adjective meaning "magical", "odd", or "fantastic".
• **syn** WEIRD, EERIE, UNCANNY mean mysteriously strange or fantastic. WEIRD may imply unearthliness or simply extreme queerness or oddness; EERIE suggests an uneasy or fearful consciousness of the presence of mysterious and malign spirits; UNCANNY applies especially to abilities or perceptions so remarkable as to seem magical.
Weird Sisters *n pl* : the three Fates
Welch \'welch\ *variant of* WELSH
[1]**wel·come** \'wel-kəm\ *interj* — used to express a greeting to a guest or newcomer upon arrival [Old English *wilcume*, from *wilcuma* "desirable guest"]
[2]**welcome** *vt* **1** : to greet hospitably and with courtesy **2** : to meet or face with pleasure ⟨*welcomed* criticism of the report⟩ — **wel·com·er** *n*
[3]**welcome** *adj* **1** : received gladly into one's presence or companionship ⟨a *welcome* visitor⟩ **2** : giving pleasure : PLEASING ⟨a *welcome* rainfall⟩ ⟨*welcome* news⟩ **3** : willingly permitted to do, have, or enjoy something ⟨anyone is *welcome* to use the swimming pool⟩ **4** — used in the phrase "You're welcome" as a reply to an expression of thanks
[4]**welcome** *n* : a cordial greeting or reception
[1]**weld** \'weld\ *vb* **1** : to join (pieces of metal or plastic) by heating and allowing the edges to flow together or by hammering or pressing together **2** : to join as if by welding ⟨*welded* together in friendship⟩ **3** : to become or be capable of being welded ⟨not all metals *weld* well⟩ [Middle English *wellen* "to boil, well, weld"] — **weld·er** *n*
[2]**weld** *n* **1** : a welded joint **2** : union by welding
weld·ment \'weld-mənt\ *n* : a unit formed by welding together an assembly of pieces
wel·fare \'wel-ˌfaər, -ˌfeər\ *n* **1** : the state of doing well especially in respect to happiness, well-being, or prosperity **2** : WELFARE WORK **3** : RELIEF 1b [Middle English, from *wel faren* "to fare well"] — **welfare** *adj*
welfare state *n* : a nation or state that assumes primary responsibility for the individual and social welfare of its citizens
welfare work *n* : organized efforts for the social betterment of a group in society — **welfare worker** *n*
wel·kin \'wel-kən\ *n* **1** : SKY 1 **2** : AIR 1a [Old English *wolcen* "cloud, sky"]
[1]**well** \'wel\ *n* **1 a** : an issue of water from the earth : a pool fed by a spring **b** : a source of supply : WELLSPRING ⟨was a *well* of information⟩ **2** : a hole sunk into the earth to reach a natural deposit (as of water, oil, or gas) **3** : an enclosure in the middle of a ship's hold around the pumps **4** : an open space extending vertically through floors of a structure (as for a staircase) **5** : something suggesting a well (as in being damp, cool, deep, or dark) [Old English *welle*]
[2]**well** *vi* : to rise to the surface and flow forth ⟨tears *welled* from their eyes⟩ [Middle English *wellen*]
[3]**well** *adv* **bet·ter** \'bet-ər\; **best** \'best\ **1 a** : in a pleasing or desirable manner ⟨the party turned out *well*⟩ **b** : in a good or proper manner ⟨did the work *well*⟩ **2** : in a full or generous manner ⟨eat *well*⟩ ⟨the orchard bore *well*⟩ **3** : with reason or courtesy : PROPERLY ⟨we could not very *well* refuse⟩ **4** : in all respects ⟨a *well*-deserved ovation⟩ **5** : in an intimate way ⟨know a person *well*⟩ **6** : MUCH 1a, FAR ⟨*well* ahead⟩ ⟨*well* over the quota⟩ **7** : without trouble or difficulty ⟨I could *well* have gone⟩ **8** : EXACTLY 1a ⟨remember it *well*⟩ [Old English *wel*] — **as well 1** : in addition : ALSO ⟨other features *as well*⟩ **2** : without real loss or gain : EQUALLY ⟨might *as well* stop here⟩
[4]**well** *interj* **1** — used to express surprise or expostulation **2** — used to begin a discourse or to resume one that was interrupted
[5]**well** *adj* **1** : SATISFACTORY, PLEASING ⟨all's *well* that ends well⟩ **2 a** : PROSPEROUS 2, WELL-OFF **b** : being in satisfactory condition or circumstances **3** : ADVISABLE, DESIRABLE ⟨not *well* to anger them⟩ **4 a** : free or recovered from infirmity or disease : HEALTHY **b** : made sound or whole ⟨the wound is nearly *well*⟩ **5** : being a cause for thankfulness : FORTUNATE ⟨it is *well* that this has happened⟩ **syn** see HEALTHY
we'll \wēl, ˌwēl\ : we shall : we will
well–ad·vised \ˌwel-əd-'vīzd\ *adj* : acting wisely or properly : based on wise counsel ⟨was *well-advised* to follow the doctor's orders⟩ ⟨*well-advised* restraint⟩
wel·la·way \ˌwel-ə-'wā\ *interj* — used to express sorrow or lamentation [Old English *weilāwei*, from *wā lā wā* "woe! lo! woe!"]
well–be·ing \'wel-'bē-ing\ *n* : the state of being happy, healthy, or prosperous : WELFARE
well–be·loved \ˌwel-bi-'ləvd\ *adj* **1** : sincerely and deeply loved **2** : sincerely respected — used in various ceremonial forms of address
well·born \'wel-'bȯrn\ *adj* : born of good stock either socially or genetically
well–bred \-'bred\ *adj* : having or displaying good breeding : REFINED
well–con·di·tioned \ˌwel-kən-'dish-ənd\ *adj* **1** : characterized by proper disposition, morals, or behavior **2** : having a good physical condition : SOUND ⟨a *well-conditioned* animal⟩

well–de•fined \ˌwel-di-ˈfīnd\ *adj* : having clearly distinguishable limits or boundaries ⟨a *well-defined* scar⟩ ⟨a *well-defined* collection is a mathematical set⟩
well–dis•posed \-dis-ˈpōzd\ *adj* : disposed to be friendly, favorable, or sympathetic ⟨*well-disposed* to our plan⟩
well–done \ˈwel-ˈdən\ *adj* **1** : rightly or properly performed **2** : cooked thoroughly
well–fa•vored \ˈwel-ˈfā-vərd\ *adj* : good-looking : HANDSOME — **well–fa•vored•ness** *n*
well–fixed \-ˈfikst\ *adj* : well-off financially
well–found \-ˈfau̇nd\ *adj* : fully furnished : properly equipped ⟨a *well-found* ship⟩
well–found•ed \-ˈfau̇n-dəd\ *adj* : based on sound reasoning, information, judgment, or grounds ⟨your suspicion was *well-founded:* the suspect is wanted for armed robbery⟩
well–groomed \-ˈgrümd, -ˈgru̇md\ *adj* **1** : well dressed and extremely neat **2** : made neat, tidy, and attractive down to the smallest details ⟨a *well-groomed* lawn⟩
well–ground•ed \-ˈgrau̇n-dəd\ *adj* : having a firm foundation : WELL-FOUNDED
well•head \ˈwel-ˌhed\ *n* **1 a** : the source of a spring or a stream **b** : principal source **2** : the top of or a structure built over a well
well–heeled \ˈwel-ˈhēld\ *adj* : WELL-FIXED
well–known \-ˈnōn\ *adj* : fully or widely known
well–mean•ing \-ˈmē-ning\ *adj* : having or based on good intentions
well–nigh \-ˈnī\ *adv* : ALMOST, NEARLY
well–off \ˈwel-ˈȯf\ *adj* : being in good condition or circumstances; *esp* : well supplied with material possessions
well–or•dered \-ˈȯrd-ərd\ *adj* : having an orderly procedure or arrangement ⟨a *well-ordered* household⟩
well–read \-ˈred\ *adj* : well informed or deeply versed through reading ⟨*well-read* in history⟩
well–spoken \-ˈspō-kən\ *adj* **1** : having a good command of language : speaking well and especially courteously **2** : spoken with propriety ⟨*well-spoken* words⟩
well•spring \ˈwel-ˌspring\ *n* **1** : FOUNTAINHEAD 1 **2** : a source of continual supply
well–timed \ˈwel-ˈtīmd\ *adj* : occurring opportunely : TIMELY
well–to–do \ˌwel-tə-ˈdü\ *adj* : having more than adequate material resources : PROSPEROUS
well–turned \ˈwel-ˈtərnd\ *adj* **1** : pleasingly shaped : SHAPELY **2** : pleasingly and appropriately expressed ⟨a *well-turned* phrase⟩
well–wish•er \ˈwel-ˌwish-ər\ *n* : one that wishes well to another — **well–wish•ing** \-ˌwish-ing\ *adj or n*
well–worn \-ˈwōrn, -ˈwȯrn\ *adj* **1 a** : worn by much use ⟨*well-worn* shoes⟩ **b** : made stale by overuse : TRITE ⟨a *well-worn* quotation⟩ **2** : worn well or properly ⟨*well-worn* honors⟩
welsh *or* **welch** \ˈwelsh, ˈwelch\ *vi* : to cheat by avoiding payment of bets [probably from *Welsh,* adj.] — **welsh•er** *n*
Welsh *also* **Welch** \ˈwelsh *also* ˈwelch\ *n* **1 Welsh** *pl* : the natives or inhabitants of Wales **2** : the Celtic language of the Welsh people [Old English *wǣlisc* "Celtic, Welsh, foreign", from *Wealh* "Celt, Welshman, foreigner", of Celtic origin] — **Welsh** *adj* — **Welsh•man** \-mən\ — **Welsh•wom•an** \-ˌwu̇m-ən\ *n*
Welsh cor•gi \-ˈkȯr-gē\ *n* : a short-legged long-backed dog with foxy head occurring in two varieties of Welsh origin: **a** : CARDIGAN **b** : PEMBROKE WELSH CORGI [Welsh *corgi,* from *cor* "dwarf" + *ci* "dog"]
Welsh rabbit *n* : melted often seasoned cheese poured over toast or crackers
Welsh rare•bit \-ˈraər-bət, -ˈreər-\ *n* : WELSH RABBIT [by alteration]
[1]**welt** \ˈwelt\ *n* **1** : the narrow strip of leather between a shoe upper and sole to which other parts are stitched **2 a** : a ridge or lump raised on the skin usually by a blow **b** : a heavy blow [Middle English *welte*]
[2]**welt** *vt* **1** : to furnish with a welt **2 a** : to raise a welt on ⟨mosquitoes *welted* my arms⟩ **b** : to hit hard
[1]**wel•ter** \ˈwel-tər\ *vi* **1 a** : to twist or roll one's body about : WALLOW **b** : to rise and fall or toss about in or with waves **2** : to become deeply sunk, soaked, or involved ⟨*weltered* in misery⟩ **3** : to be in turmoil [Middle English *welteren*]
[2]**welter** *n* **1** : a state of wild disorder : TURMOIL **2** : a chaotic mass or jumble ⟨a *welter* of conflicting regulations⟩
[3]**welter** *n* : WELTERWEIGHT [probably from [1]*welt*]
wel•ter•weight \-ˌwāt\ *n* : a boxer weighing more than 135 but not over 147 pounds [[3]*welter*]
wen \ˈwen\ *n* : a cyst formed by obstruction of a skin gland and filled with fatty material [Old English *wenn*]
wench \ˈwench\ *n* **1** : a young woman : GIRL **2** : a female servant [Middle English *wenchel, wenche* "child", from Old English *wencel*]
wend \ˈwend\ *vb* : to direct one's course : proceed on (one's way) [Old English *wendan*]
went *past of* GO [Middle English, past of *wenden* "to wend"]
wen•tle•trap \ˈwent-l-ˌtrap\ *n* : any of a family of marine snails with usually tall-spired sculptured white shells; *also* : one of the shells [Dutch *wenteltrap* "winding stair"]
wept *past of* WEEP
were *past 2d sing, past pl, or past subjunctive of* BE [Old English *wǣron,* past pl., *wǣre,* past subjunctive sing., *wǣren,* past subjunctive pl. of *wesan* "to be"]
we're \wiər, ˌwiər, wər, ˌwər\ : we are
weren't \wərnt, ˈwərnt, ˈwər-ənt\ : were not
were•wolf \ˈwiər-ˌwu̇lf, ˈwər-, ˈweər-\ *n, pl* **were•wolves** \-ˌwu̇lvz\ : a person held to be transformed or able to transform into a wolf [Old English *werwulf,* from *wer* "man" + *wulf* "wolf"]
wert \wərt, ˈwərt\ *archaic past 2d sing of* BE
wes•kit \ˈwes-kət\ *n* : VEST 1a [alteration of *waistcoat*]
Wes•ley•an \ˈwes-lē-ən, ˈwez-\ *adj* **1** : of or relating to John or Charles Wesley **2** : of or relating to the Methodism taught by John Wesley — **Wesleyan** *n* — **Wes•ley•an•ism** \-lē-ə-ˌniz-əm\ *n*
[1]**west** \ˈwest\ *adv* : to, toward, or in the west [Old English]
[2]**west** *adj* **1** : situated toward or at the west **2** : coming from the west
[3]**west** *n* **1 a** : the general direction of sunset **b** : the compass point directly opposite to east **2** *cap* : regions or countries west of a specified or implied point **3** : the end of a church opposite the chancel
west•bound \ˈwest-ˌbau̇nd, ˈwes-\ *adj* : headed west
west•er \ˈwes-tər\ *vi* **wes•tered; wes•ter•ing** \-tə-ring, -tring\ : to turn or move westward
[1]**west•er•ly** \ˈwes-tər-lē\ *adv or adj* **1** : from the west **2** : toward the west
[2]**westerly** *n, pl* **-lies** : a wind from the west
[1]**west•ern** \ˈwes-tərn\ *adj* **1** *often cap* : of, relating to, or characteristic of a region conventionally designated West **2** : lying toward or coming from the west **3** *cap* : of or relating to the Roman Catholic or Protestant segment of Christianity ⟨*Western* liturgies⟩ [Old English *westerne*] — **west•ern•most** \-ˌmōst\ *adj*
[2]**western** *n* **1** : one that is produced in or characteristic of a western region and especially the western United States **2** *often cap* : a novel, story, motion picture, or broadcast dealing with life in the western United States during the latter half of the 19th century
West•ern•er \ˈwes-tər-nər, -tə-nər\ *n* : a native or inhabitant of the West (as of the United States)
western hemisphere *n* : the half of the earth comprising North and South America and surrounding waters
western hemlock *n* : a commercially important hemlock ranging from Alaska to California and having leaves without pale lines on the underside
west•ern•ize \ˈwes-tər-ˌnīz\ *vt* : to give western characteristics to — **west•ern•iza•tion** \ˌwes-tər-nəˈzā-shən\ *n*
western larch *n* : an important timber tree of western North America with pale green sharply pointed leaves and oblong cones; *also* : its wood
western pine beetle *n* : a bark beetle destructive to various pines of the western United States
West Germanic *n* : a subdivision of the Germanic languages including English, Frisian, Dutch, and German
West Goth *n* : VISIGOTH
West Highland white terrier *n* : a small white long-coated dog of a breed developed in Scotland
west•ing \ˈwes-ting\ *n* **1** : difference in longitude to the west

from the last preceding point of reckoning **2** : westerly progress
west–northwest *n* : two points north of west : W 22°30′N
west–southwest *n* : two points south of west : W 22°30′S
[1]**west·ward** \ˈwes-twərd\ *adv or adj* : toward the west — **westwards** \-twərdz\ *adv*
[2]**westward** *n* : westward direction or part
[1]**wet** \ˈwet\ *adj* **wet·ter**; **wet·test** **1 a** : consisting of, containing, covered with, or soaked with liquid (as water) **b** : RAINY **2** : still moist enough to smudge or smear ⟨*wet* paint⟩ **3** : permitting or openly supporting the manufacture and sale of alcoholic liquor **4** : involving the use or presence of liquid ⟨*wet* processes⟩ **5** : perversely wrong ⟨you're all *wet*⟩ [Old English *wǣt*] — **wet·ly** *adv* — **wet·ness** *n* — **wet behind the ears** : lacking experience : IMMATURE
[2]**wet** *n* **1** : WATER; *also* : MOISTURE **2** : rainy weather : RAIN **3** : a supporter of a wet liquor policy
[3]**wet** *vb* **wet** *or* **wet·ted**; **wet·ting** **1** : to make or become wet **2** : to urinate or urinate in or on — **wet one's whistle** : to take a drink especially of liquor
wet·back \ˈwet-ˌbak\ *n* : a Mexican who enters the United States illegally (as by wading the Rio Grande)
wet blanket *n* : one that quenches or dampens enthusiasm or pleasure — **wet–blanket** *vt*
wet down *vt* : to dampen by sprinkling with water
weth·er \ˈweth-ər\ *n* : a male sheep castrated before sexual maturity [Old English]
wet·land \ˈwet-ˌland\ *n* : land containing much soil moisture : swampy or boggy land
wet–nurse \ˈwet-ˈnərs\ *vt* **1** : to tend as a wet nurse **2** : to give constant and often excessive care to
wet nurse *n* : one that cares for and suckles young not her own
wet suit *n* : a close-fitting rubber suit (as for a skin diver) that traps a thin layer of water against the body to hold body heat
wet·ta·ble \ˈwet-ə-bəl\ *adj* : capable of being wetted — **wet·ta·bil·i·ty** \ˌwet-ə-ˈbil-ət-ē\ *n*
wetting agent *n* : a substance that when adsorbed on a surface reduces its tendency to repel a liquid
wet·tish \ˈwet-ish\ *adj* : somewhat wet : MOIST
wet wash *n* : laundry returned damp and not ironed
we've \wēv, ˌwēv\ : we have
[1]**whack** \ˈhwak, ˈwak\ *vb* **1** : to strike with a smart or resounding blow **2** : to cut with or as if with a whack : CHOP [probably imitative] — **whack·er** *n*
[2]**whack** *n* **1** : a smart or resounding blow; *also* : the sound of or as if of such a blow **2** : PORTION, SHARE ⟨we must each pay our *whack*⟩ **3** : CONDITION; *esp* : proper working order ⟨the machine is out of *whack*⟩ **4 a** : an opportunity or attempt to do something : CHANCE **b** : a single action or occasion : TIME ⟨marked a hundred papers at a *whack*⟩
whack·ing \ˈhwak-ing, ˈwak-\ *adj* : very large : WHOPPING
whack up *vt* : to divide into shares
[1]**whale** \ˈhwāl, ˈwāl\ *n, pl* **whale** *or* **whales** **1** : an aquatic mammal (order Cetacea) that superficially resembles a large fish and is valued commercially for its oil, flesh, and sometimes whalebone; *esp* : one of the larger members of this group **2** : a person or thing impressive in size or qualities ⟨a *whale* of a story⟩ [Old English *hwæl*]
[2]**whale** *vt* **1** : THRASH **2** : to strike or hit hard [origin unknown]
whale·boat \-ˌbōt\ *n* **1** : a long narrow rowboat made with both ends sharp and raking, often steered with an oar, and used by whalers for hunting whales **2** : a long narrow rowboat or motorboat resembling the original whaleboats that is often carried by warships and merchant ships
whale·bone \-ˌbōn\ *n* : a horny substance found in two rows of long plates attached along the upper jaw of whalebone whales
whalebone whale *n* : any of various usually large whales having whalebone instead of teeth
whal·er \ˈhwā-lər, ˈwā-\ *n* **1** : a person or ship engaged in whale fishing **2** : WHALEBOAT 2
whale shark *n* : a very large harmless shark of tropical seas
whal·ing \ˈhwā-ling, ˈwā-\ *n* : the occupation of catching whales and extracting commercial products from them
[1]**wham** \ˈhwam, ˈwam\ *n* **1** : the loud sound of a hard impact **2** : a solid blow [imitative]
[2]**wham** *vb* **whammed**; **wham·ming** : to propel, strike, or beat so as to produce a loud impact
wham·my \ˈhwam-ē, ˈwam-\ *n, pl* **whammies** **1** : a supernatural power held to bring bad luck **2** : a magic curse or spell [probably from [1]*wham*]

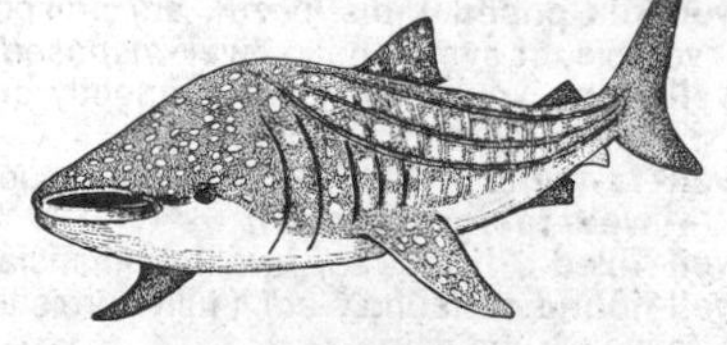
whale shark

[1]**whang** \ˈhwang, ˈwang\ *vb* **1** : to propel or strike with force **2** : to beat or work with force or violence [Middle English *thong, thwang* "thong"]
[2]**whang** *n* : a loud sharp vibrant or resonant sound [imitative]
wharf \ˈhwȯrf, ˈwȯrf\ *n, pl* **wharves** \ˈhwȯrvz, ˈwȯrvz\ *also* **wharfs** : a structure built along or out from the shore of navigable waters so that ships may lie alongside to receive and discharge cargo and passengers [Old English *hwearf*]
wharf·age \ˈhwȯr-fij, ˈwȯr-\ *n* **1** : the provision or the use of a wharf **2** : the charge for the use of a wharf
wharf·in·ger \-fən-jər\ *n* : the operator or manager of a commercial wharf [derived from *wharfage*]
wharf·mas·ter \ˈhwȯrf-ˌmas-tər, ˈwȯrf-\ *n* : WHARFINGER
[1]**what** \hwät, ˈhwät, hwət, ˈhwət, wät, ˈwät, wət, ˈwət\ *pron* **1 a** — used as an interrogative in asking about the identity, nature, or value of a thing ⟨*what* is this⟩ ⟨*what* do they earn⟩ ⟨*what* is wealth without friends⟩ or about the character, occupation, or position of a person ⟨*what* do you think I am, a fool⟩ **b** — used as an exclamation expressing surprise or excitement and frequently introducing a question ⟨*what,* no breakfast⟩ **c** — used in expressions directing attention to a statement that the speaker is about to make ⟨you know *what*⟩ **2** : that which : the one or ones that ⟨no income but *what* I get from my writings⟩ **3** : WHATEVER 1a ⟨say *what* you will⟩ [Old English *hwæt,* neuter of *hwā* "who"]
[2]**what** *adv* **1 a** : in what respect : HOW **b** : how much ⟨*what* do you care⟩ **2** — used with *with* to introduce a prepositional phrase that expresses cause ⟨kept busy *what* with studies and extracurricular activities⟩
[3]**what** *adj* **1 a** — used as an interrogative expressing inquiry about the identity or nature of a person, object, or matter ⟨*what* minerals do we export⟩ **b** : how remarkable or surprising ⟨*what* a suggestion⟩ ⟨*what* a charming view⟩ **2** : WHATEVER 1a
[1]**what·ev·er** \hwät-ˈev-ər, wät-, hwət-, ˌhwət-, wət-, ˌwət-\ *pron* **1 a** : anything or everything that ⟨take *whatever* is needed⟩ **b** : no matter what ⟨obey orders, *whatever* happens⟩ **2** : [1]WHAT 1a — used to express astonishment or perplexity ⟨*whatever* do you mean by that⟩
[2]**whatever** *adj* **1 a** : any . . . that : all . . . that ⟨take *whatever* action is needed⟩ **b** : no matter what **2** : of any kind at all ⟨no food *whatever*⟩
what·not \ˈhwät-ˌnät, ˈhwət-, ˈwät-, ˈwət-\ *n* : a light open set of shelves for bric-a-brac
what·so·ev·er \ˌhwät-sə-ˈwev-ər, ˌhwət-, ˌwät-, ˌwət-\ *pron or adj* : WHATEVER
wheal \ˈhwēl, ˈwēl\ *n* : a suddenly formed elevation of the skin surface: as **a** : WELT 2a **b** : a flat burning or itching eminence on the skin [alteration of *wale*]
wheat \ˈhwēt, ˈwēt\ *n* **1** : a cereal grain that yields a fine white flour, is the chief breadstuff of temperate climates, and is important in animal feeds — compare BRAN, MIDDLINGS **2** : any of a genus of grasses grown in most temperate areas for the wheat they yield; *esp* : an annual cereal grass with long dense flower spikes and white to dark red grains that is the chief source of wheat and is known only in cultivation [Old English *hwǣte*] — **wheat·en** \-n\ *adj*
wheat cake *n* : a pancake made of wheat flour
wheat·ear \ˈhwēt-ˌiər, ˈwēt-\ *n* : a small white-rumped northern bird related to the whinchat [earlier *wheatears,* probably derived from *white* + Old English *ears* "backside"]
wheat germ *n* : the embryo of the wheat kernel separated in milling and used especially as a source of vitamins
wheat rust *n* : a destructive disease of wheat caused by rust fungi; *also* : a fungus causing a wheat rust
whee \ˈhwē, ˈwē\ *interj* — used to express delight or high spirits [probably imitative]
whee·dle \ˈhwēd-l, ˈwēd-\ *vt* **whee·dled**; **whee·dling** \ˈhwēd-ling, ˈwēd-, -l-ing\ **1** : to coax or entice by soft words or flattery **2** : to gain or get by wheedling [origin unknown]

[1]wheel \'hwēl, 'wēl\ *n* **1 :** a disk or circular frame capable of turning on a central axis **2 :** something that is like a wheel (as in being round or in turning on an axis) **3 :** a device the main part of which is a wheel **4 :** BICYCLE **5 :** a circular frame which when turned controls some apparatus **6 a :** a curving or circular movement **b :** a turning movement of troops or ships in line in which the units preserve alignment and relative positions as they change direction **7 a :** a moving power **:** MECHANISM ⟨the *wheels* of government⟩ **b :** a person of importance especially in an organization [Old English *hwēol*] — **wheeled** \'hwēld, 'wēld\ *adj* — **wheel•less** \'hwēl-ləs, 'wēl-\ *adj*

[2]wheel *vb* **1 :** to carry or move on wheels or in a vehicle with wheels ⟨*wheel* a load into the barn⟩ **2 :** to turn or cause to turn on an axis or in a circle **:** REVOLVE ⟨the earth *wheels* about the sun⟩ **3 :** to change direction as if revolving on an axis ⟨*wheeled* about⟩ — **wheel and deal :** to pursue one's interests especially in a shrewd or unscrupulous manner

wheel and axle *n* **:** a simple machine consisting of a grooved wheel turned by a cord or chain with a rigidly attached axle (as for winding up a weight) together with the supporting standards

wheel animalcule *n* **:** ROTIFER — called also *wheel animal*

wheel•bar•row \'hwēl-ˌbar-ō, 'wēl-\ *n* **:** a small vehicle with handles and one or more wheels for carrying small loads

wheel•base \-ˌbās\ *n* **:** the distance in inches between the front and rear axles of an automotive vehicle

wheel•chair \-ˌcheər, -ˌchaər\ *n* **:** a chair on wheels used especially by invalids

wheel•er \'hwē-lər, 'wē-\ *n* **1 :** one that wheels **2 :** WHEELHORSE 1 **3 :** something (as a vehicle or ship) that has wheels — used especially in combinations ⟨side-*wheeler*⟩

wheel•er–deal•er \ˌhwē-lər-'dē-lər, ˌwē-\ *n* **:** a shrewd operator especially in business or politics [from the phrase *wheel and deal*]

wheel•horse \'hwēl-ˌhȯrs, 'wēl-\ *n* **1 :** a horse in a position nearest the wheels in a tandem or similar arrangement **2 :** a steady and effective worker especially in a political body

wheel•house \-ˌhau̇s\ *n* **:** PILOTHOUSE

wheels•man \'hwēlz-mən, 'wēlz-\ *n* **:** one who steers with a wheel; *esp* **:** HELMSMAN

wheel•wright \'hwēl-ˌrīt, 'wēl-\ *n* **:** a man whose occupation is to make or repair wheels and wheeled vehicles

[1]wheeze \'hwēz, 'wēz\ *vi* **1 :** to breathe with difficulty usually with a whistling sound **2 :** to make a sound resembling that of wheezing [Middle English *whesen*] — **wheez•i•ly** \'hwē-zə-lē, 'wē-\ *adv* — **wheez•i•ness** \-zē-nəs\ *n* — **wheezy** \-zē\ *adj*

[2]wheeze *n* **1 :** a sound of wheezing **2 a :** an old joke **b :** a trite saying

whelk \'hwelk, 'welk, 'wilk\ *n* **:** any of numerous large marine snails; *esp* **:** one much used as food in Europe [Old English *weoloc*]

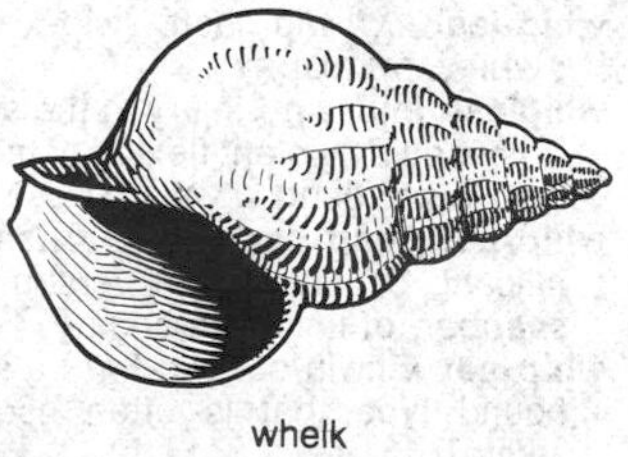

whelk

whelm \'hwelm, 'welm\ *vt* **:** to overcome or engulf completely [Middle English *whelmen*]

[1]whelp \'hwelp, 'welp\ *n* **1 :** one of the young of various flesh-eating mammals and especially of the dog **2 :** CUR 2 [Old English *hwelp*]

[2]whelp *vb* **1 :** to give birth to (whelps) **2 :** to bring forth whelps

[1]when \hwen, 'hwen, wen, 'wen, hwən, wən\ *adv* **1 :** at what time ⟨asked us *when* it happened⟩ **2 :** at or during which time ⟨an era *when* the arts decayed⟩ [Old English *hwanne, hwenne*]

[2]when *conj* **1 a :** at or during the time that **:** WHILE ⟨we go *when* we can⟩ **b :** just after the time that ⟨left *when* the bell rang⟩ **c :** every time that ⟨smile *when* you say that⟩ **2 :** in the event that **:** IF ⟨*when* you cheat you hurt youself⟩ **3 :** in spite of the fact that **:** THOUGH ⟨gave up politics *when* I might have made a great career in it⟩

[3]when \ˌhwen, ˌwen\ *pron* **:** what or which time ⟨since *when* have you known that⟩

whence \hwens, 'hwens, wens, 'wens\ *adv* **1 :** from what place, source, or cause ⟨*whence* come all these doubts⟩ **2 :** from or out of which ⟨the stock *whence* I sprang⟩ [Middle English *whenne, whennes,* from Old English *hwanon*]

[1]when•ev•er \hwe-'nev-ər, we-, hwə-, wə-\ *conj* **:** at any or every time that ⟨stop *whenever* you wish⟩

[2]whenever *adv* **:** at whatever time ⟨available *whenever* needed⟩

when•so•ev•er \'hwen-sə-ˌwev-ər, 'wen-\ *conj* **:** WHENEVER

[1]where \'hweər, 'hwaər, 'weər, 'waər, ˌhwər, ˌwər; *or without stress*\ *adv* **1 :** at, in, or to which place, circumstances, or respect ⟨*where* are we going⟩ ⟨*where* am I wrong⟩ **2 :** in, at, or to which ⟨the house *where* I was born⟩ **3 :** from what place or source ⟨*where* did you get that idea⟩ [Old English *hwǣr*]

[2]where *conj* **1 a :** at or in the place at or in which ⟨stay *where* you are⟩ **b :** to the place at, in, or to which ⟨went *where* we had promised to go⟩ **2 :** WHEREVER ⟨sit *where* you please⟩ **3 :** in a case, situation, or respect in which ⟨outstanding *where* endurance is called for⟩

[3]where \'hweər, 'hwaər, 'weər, 'waər\ *n* **1 :** PLACE, LOCATION ⟨the *where* and the how of the accident⟩ **2 :** what place, source, or cause ⟨*where* are you from⟩

[1]where•abouts \-ə-ˌbau̇ts\ *also* **where•about** \-ˌbau̇t\ *adv* **:** about where **:** near what place ⟨*whereabouts* is the house⟩

[2]whereabouts *n sing or pl* **:** the place or general locality where a person or thing is

where•as \hwer-'az, hwar-, wer-, war-, hwər-, wər-\ *conj* **1 :** in view of the fact that **:** SINCE — used especially to introduce a preamble **2 :** while on the contrary ⟨water puts out fire, *whereas* alcohol burns⟩

where•at \-'at\ *conj* **1 :** at or toward which **2 :** as a result of which **:** WHEREUPON

where•by \hweər-'bī, hwaər-, weər-, waər-, hwər-, wər-\ *conj* **:** by, through, or in accordance with which

[1]where•fore \'hweər-ˌfōr, 'hwaər-, 'weər-, 'waər-, -ˌfȯr\ *adv* **1 :** for what reason or purpose **:** WHY **2 :** THEREFORE 1 [Middle English *wherfor, wherfore,* from *wher* "where" + *for, fore* "for"]

[2]wherefore *n* **:** a statement giving an explanation **:** REASON

where•from \-ˌfrəm, -ˌfräm\ *conj* **:** from which

[1]where•in \hwer-'in, hwar-, wer-, war-, hwər-, wər-\ *adv* **:** in what **:** in what particular or respect ⟨*wherein* was I wrong⟩

[2]wherein *conj* **1 :** in which **:** WHERE ⟨the city *wherein* they live⟩ **2 :** during which ⟨the epoch *wherein* feudalism arose⟩

where•of \-'əv, -'äv\ *conj* **1 :** of what ⟨I know *whereof* I speak⟩ **2 :** of which or whom ⟨books *whereof* the best are lost⟩

where•on \-'ȯn, -'än\ *adv* **:** on which ⟨the base *whereon* it rests⟩

where•so•ev•er \'hwer-sə-ˌwev-ər, 'hwar-, 'wer-, 'war-\ *conj, archaic* **:** WHEREVER 1

[1]where•to \-ˌtü\ *adv* **:** to what place or purpose

[2]whereto *conj* **:** to which

where•un•to \hwer-'ən-tü, hwar-, wer-, war-, hwər-, wər-\ *adv or conj* **:** WHERETO

where•up•on \'hwer-ə-ˌpȯn, 'hwar-, 'wer-, 'war-, -ˌpän\ *conj* **1 :** on which **2 :** closely following and as a result of which

[1]wher•ev•er \hwer-'ev-ər, hwar-, wer-, war-, hwər-, wər-\ *adv* **:** where in the world ⟨*wherever* did you get that hat⟩

[2]wherever *conj* **1 :** at, in, or to whatever place ⟨thrive *wherever* they go⟩ **2 :** in any circumstance in which ⟨*wherever* it is possible, I try to help⟩

[1]where•with \'hweər-ˌwith, 'hwaər-, 'weər-, 'waər-, -ˌwith\ *conj* **:** with or by means of which ⟨we lack tools *wherewith* to repair the damage⟩

[2]wherewith *adv, obsolete* **:** with what

where•with•al \'hweər-wi*th*-ˌȯl, 'hwaər-, 'weər-, 'waər-, -with-\ *n* **:** MEANS, RESOURCES; *esp* **:** MONEY

wher•ry \'hwer-ē, 'wer-\ *n, pl* **wherries :** any of various light boats; *esp* **:** a long light rowboat pointed at both ends [Middle English *whery*]

[1]whet \'hwet, 'wet\ *vt* **whet•ted; whet•ting 1 :** to sharpen by rubbing on or with something (as a stone) ⟨*whet* a knife⟩ **2 :** to make keen ⟨*whet* the appetite⟩ [Old English *hwettan*]

[2]whet *n* **1 :** GOAD 2 **2 :** APPETIZER; *also* **:** a drink of liquor

wheth•er \'hwe*th*-ər, 'we*th*-, ˌhwe*th*-ər, ˌwə*th*-, hwə*th*-, wə*th*-\

conj **1 a** (1) **:** if it is or was true that ⟨ask *whether* they are going⟩ (2) **:** if it is or was better ⟨uncertain *whether* to go or stay⟩ **b :** whichever is or was the case, namely, that ⟨*whether* we succeed or fail, we must try⟩ **2 :** EITHER ⟨seated us together *whether* by accident or design⟩ [Old English *hwæther, hwether,* from *hwæther, hwether,* pron., "which of two"]

whet•stone \ˈhwet-ˌstōn, ˈwet-\ *n* **:** a stone for whetting sharp-edged tools

whew *often read as* ˈhwü, ˈwü, ˈhyü; *the interjection is a whistle ending with a voiceless* ü\ *n* **1 :** a whistling sound **2 :** a sound like a half-formed whistle uttered as an exclamation — used interjectionally chiefly to express amazement, discomfort, or relief [imitative]

whey \ˈhwā, ˈwā\ *n* **:** the watery part of milk that separates after the milk sours and thickens [Old English *hwæg*] — **whey•ey** \ˈhwā-ē\ *adj*

[1]**which** \hwich, wich, ˈhwich, ˈwich\ *adj* **1 :** being what one or ones out of a group — used as an interrogative ⟨*which* coat should I wear⟩ ⟨knew *which* one would win⟩ **2 :** WHICHEVER ⟨it will not fit, turn it *which* way you like⟩ [Old English *hwilc* "of what kind, which"]

[2]**which** *pron* **1 :** what one or ones out of a group — used as an interrogative ⟨*which* of those houses do you live in⟩ ⟨*which* of you want tea and *which* want lemonade⟩ ⟨they are swimming or canoeing, I don't know *which*⟩ **2 :** WHICHEVER ⟨take *which* you like⟩ **3** — used to introduce a relative clause and to serve as a substitute within that clause for the substantive modified by that clause; used in any grammatical relation except that of a possessive; used especially in reference to animals, inanimate objects, groups, or ideas ⟨the records *which* I bought⟩ **syn** see WHO

[1]**which•ev•er** \hwich-ˈev-ər, wich-\ *pron* **:** whatever one or ones out of a group ⟨take two of the four elective subjects, *whichever* you prefer⟩

[2]**whichever** *adj* **:** being whatever one or ones out of a group **:** no matter which ⟨*whichever* way you go⟩

which•so•ev•er \ˌhwich-sə-ˈwev-ər, ˌwich-\ *pron or adj* **:** WHICHEVER

whicker \ˈhwik-ər, ˈwik-\ *vi* **:** WHINNY [imitative] — **whicker** *n*

[1]**whiff** \ˈhwif, ˈwif\ *n* **1 a :** a quick puff or slight gust especially of air, odor, gas, smoke, or spray **b :** an inhalation of odor, gas, or smoke **2 :** a slight trace **:** HINT [imitative]

[2]**whiff** *vb* **1 a :** to expel, puff out, or blow away in or as if in whiffs **b :** SMOKE 2 **2 :** to inhale an odor

whif•fle•tree \ˈhwif-əl-ˌtrē, ˈwif-\ *or* **whip•ple•tree** \ˈhwip-əl-, ˈwip-\ *n* **:** the pivoted swinging bar to which the traces of a harness are fastened and by which a vehicle or implement is drawn [perhaps derived from *whip* + *tree*]

Whig \ˈhwig, ˈwig\ *n* **1 :** a member or supporter of a British political group of the 18th and early 19th centuries seeking to limit royal authority and increase parliamentary power — compare TORY **2 :** an American favoring independence from Great Britain during the American Revolution **3 :** a member or supporter of a 19th century American political party formed in opposition to the Jacksonian Democrats [*Whiggamore* "member of a Scottish group that marched to Edinburgh in 1648 to oppose the court party"] — **Whig** *adj* — **Whig•gish** \-ish\ *adj*

[1]**while** \ˈhwīl, ˈwīl\ *n* **1 :** a period of time ⟨stay here for a *while*⟩ **2 :** the time and effort used (as in the performance of an action) **:** TROUBLE ⟨worth your *while*⟩ [Old English *hwīl*]

[2]**while** *conj* **1 a :** during the time that ⟨take a nap *while* I'm out⟩ **b :** as long as ⟨*while* there's life there's hope⟩ **2 :** in spite of the fact that **:** THOUGH

[3]**while** *vt* **:** to cause to pass especially without boredom or in a pleasant manner — usually used with *away* ⟨*while* away the time⟩

[1]**whi•lom** \ˈhwī-ləm, ˈwī-\ *adv, archaic* **:** FORMERLY [Middle English, literally, "at times", from Old English *hwīlum,* from *hwīl* "time, while"]

[2]**whilom** *adj* **:** FORMER ⟨our *whilom* friends⟩

whilst \ˈhwīlst, ˈwīlst\ *conj, chiefly British* **:** WHILE

whim \ˈhwim, ˈwim\ *n* **:** a sudden wish, desire, or change of mind **:** a sudden notion or fancy [earlier *whim-wham,* of unknown origin] **syn** see CAPRICE

whim•brel \ˈhwim-brəl, ˈwim-\ *n* **:** a small European curlew [perhaps imitative]

[1]**whim•per** \ˈhwim-pər, ˈwim-\ *vi* **whim•pered; whim•per•ing** \-pə-ring, -pring\ **1 :** to make a low whining or broken sound **2 :** to complain with or as if with a whimper [imitative]

[2]**whimper** *n* **:** a low whining or broken sound

whim•si•cal \ˈhwim-zi-kəl, ˈwim-\ *adj* **1 :** full of whims **:** CAPRICIOUS ⟨a *whimsical* person⟩ **2 :** resulting from or characterized by whim or caprice **:** ERRATIC ⟨*whimsical* behavior⟩ — **whim•si•cal•i•ty** \ˌhwim-zə-ˈkal-ət-ē, ˌwim-\ *n* — **whim•si•cal•ly** \ˈhwim-zi-kə-lē, ˈwim-, -klē\ *adv* — **whim•si•cal•ness** \-kəl-nəs\ *n*

whim•sy *or* **whim•sey** \ˈhwim-zē, ˈwim-\ *n, pl* **whimsies** *or* **whimseys 1 :** WHIM **2 :** a fanciful or fantastic device, object, or creation especially in writing or art [derived from *whim-wham* "whim"]

whin \ˈhwin, ˈwin\ *n* **:** FURZE [of Scandinavian origin]

whin•chat \ˈhwin-ˌchat, ˈwin-\ *n* **:** a small brown and buff European singing bird of grassy meadows

[1]**whine** \ˈhwīn, ˈwīn\ *vi* **1 :** to utter a whine or similar sound **2 :** to complain with or as if with a whine [Old English *hwīnan* "to whiz"] — **whin•er** *n* — **whin•ing•ly** \ˈhwī-ning-lē, ˈwī-\ *adv*

[2]**whine** *n* **1 :** a prolonged usually high-pitched plaintive or distressed cry or a similar sound **2 :** a complaint uttered with or as if with a whine — **whiny** *or* **whin•ey** \ˈhwī-nē, ˈwī-\ *adj*

[1]**whin•ny** \ˈhwin-ē, ˈwin-\ *vi* **whin•nied; whin•ny•ing :** to neigh especially in a low or gentle way [probably imitative]

[2]**whinny** *n, pl* **whinnies 1 :** NEIGH **2 :** a sound resembling a neigh

[1]**whip** \ˈhwip, ˈwip\ *vb* **whipped; whip•ping 1 :** to move, snatch, or jerk very quickly and forcefully ⟨*whip* out a gun⟩ **2 a :** to strike (as with a lash or rod) especially as a punishment; *also* **:** SPANK **b :** to drive or urge on by or as if by using a whip **3 a :** to bind or wrap (as a rope) with cord in order to protect, strengthen, or prevent unraveling **b :** to wind or wrap around something **4 :** to defeat utterly **:** TROUNCE **5 :** to stir up **:** AROUSE ⟨*whip* up enthusiasm⟩ **6 :** to produce in a hurry ⟨*whip* up a short article⟩ **7 :** to beat (as eggs or cream) into a froth **8 :** to gather or hold together for united action ⟨*whipped* the doubtful members into line⟩ **9 a :** to move nimbly or briskly **b :** to thrash about flexibly like a whiplash ⟨a flag *whipping* in the wind⟩ [Middle English *whippen*] — **whip•per** *n*

[2]**whip** *n* **1 :** an instrument consisting usually of a handle and lash forming a flexible rod that is used for whipping **2 :** a stroke or cut with or as if with a whip **3 a :** a dessert containing one or more whipped ingredients **b :** a kitchen utensil used in whipping **4 :** one that handles a whip; *esp* **:** a driver of horses **5 :** a member of a legislative body appointed by a party to enforce discipline and to secure the attendance of party members at important sessions **6 :** a whipping or thrashing motion **7 :** a flexible radio antenna — called also *whip antenna* — **whip•like** \ˈhwip-ˌlīk, ˈwip-\ *adj*

whip•cord \ˈhwip-ˌkȯrd, ˈwip-\ *n* **1 :** a thin tough cord made of braided or twisted hemp or catgut **2 :** a cloth of hard-twisted yarns that has fine diagonal cords or ribs

whip hand *n* **:** positive control **:** ADVANTAGE

whip•lash \ˈhwip-ˌlash, ˈwip-\ *n* **1 :** the lash of a whip **2 :** WHIPLASH INJURY

whiplash injury *n* **:** injury to the spine often with concussion that is caused by violent flexing of the head and neck (as in an automobile accident)

whip•per•snap•per \ˈhwip-ər-ˌsnap-ər, ˈwip-\ *n* **:** a small, insignificant, or impertinent person [alteration of earlier *snippersnapper,* of unknown origin]

whip•pet \ˈhwip-ət, ˈwip-\ *n* **:** a small swift slender dog of greyhound type that is often used for racing [probably from [1]*whip*]

whipping boy *n* **:** SCAPEGOAT 2 [from the former practice of maintaining a boy to share the education of a prince and be punished in the prince's stead]

whipping post *n* **:** a post to which offenders are tied to be legally whipped

whip•ple•tree *variant of* WHIFFLETREE

whip•poor•will \ˌhwip-ər-ˈwil, ˌwip-; ˈhwip-ər-ˌ, ˈwip-\ *n* **:** an insect-eating bird of the eastern United States and Canada that is active at night and is often heard at nightfall and just before dawn

[1]**whip•saw** \ˈhwip-ˌsȯ, ˈwip-\ *n* **1 :** a narrow saw tapering from butt to point and having hook teeth **2 :** a crosscut saw operated by two people [[2]*whip*]

[2]**whipsaw** *vt* **whip•sawed; whip•saw•ing 1 :** to saw with a whipsaw **2 :** to victimize in two opposite ways at once, by a two-phase operation, or by the combined action of two opponents

whip scorpion *n* **:** any of an order (Pedipalpida) of arachnids somewhat resembling true scorpions but having a long slender tail process and no sting

whippoorwill

whip•worm \ˈhwip-ˌwərm, ˈwip-\ *n* : any of a family of parasitic roundworms with a body thickened behind and very long and slender in front; *esp* : one of the human intestine

1whir *also* **whirr** \ˈhwər, ˈwər\ *vb* **whirred; whir•ring** : to fly, revolve, or move rapidly with a whir [Middle English *quirren*]

2whir *also* **whirr** *n* : a continuous fluttering or vibrating sound made by something in rapid motion

1whirl \ˈhwərl, ˈwərl\ *vb* **1** : to move or drive in a circle or curve especially with force or speed **2 a** : to turn or cause to turn on or around an axis : SPIN **b** : to turn about abruptly : WHEEL **3** : to pass, move, or go quickly **4** : to become giddy or dizzy : REEL [Middle English *whirlen*] — **whirl•er** \ˈhwər-lər, ˈwər-\ *n*

2whirl *n* **1 a** : a rapid whirling movement **b** : something whirling ⟨a *whirl* of dust⟩ **2 a** : COMMOTION 2 **b** : a confused or giddy mental state ⟨my head's in a *whirl*⟩ **3** : an experimental attempt : TRY ⟨why don't you give it a *whirl*⟩

whirl•i•gig \ˈhwər-li-ˌgig, ˈwər-\ *n* **1** : a toy that has a whirling motion **2** : one that continuously whirls or changes; *also* : a whirling course (as of events) [Middle English *whirlegigg*, from *whirlen* "to whirl" + *gigg* "top"]

whirligig beetle *n* : any of a family of swift-moving beetles that live mostly on the surface of water

whirl•pool \ˈhwərl-ˌpül, ˈwərl-\ *n* : water moving rapidly in a circle so as to produce a depression in the center into which floating objects may be drawn : EDDY, VORTEX

whirl•wind \-ˌwind\ *n* **1** : a small rotating windstorm marked by an inward and upward spiral motion of the lower air **2** : a confused rush : WHIRL

whirly•bird \ˈhwər-lē-ˌbərd, ˈwər-\ *n* : HELICOPTER

1whish \ˈhwish, ˈwish\ *vb* **1** : to urge on or cause to move with a whish **2** : to make a whizzing or swishing sound **3** : to move with a whish especially at high speed : WHIZ [imitative]

2whish *n* : a rushing sound : SWISH

1whisk \ˈhwisk, ˈwisk\ *n* **1** : a quick light brushing or sweeping motion ⟨a *whisk* of the hand⟩ **2 a** : a usually wire kitchen implement for beating food **b** : WHISK BROOM [Middle English *wisk*]

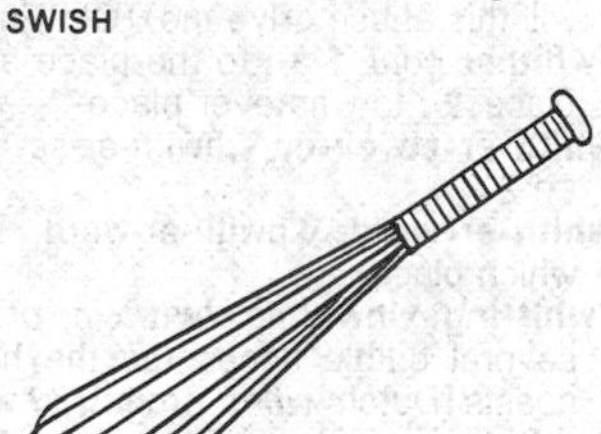
1whisk 2a

2whisk *vb* **1** : to move nimbly and quickly ⟨squirrels *whisked* up the trees⟩ **2** : to move or convey briskly ⟨*whisked* the children off to bed⟩ **3** : to mix or fluff up by or as if by beating with a whisk ⟨*whisk* eggs⟩ **4** : to brush or wipe off lightly ⟨*whisk* crumbs from a table⟩

whisk broom *n* : a small broom with a short handle

whis•ker \ˈhwis-kər, ˈwis-\ *n* **1 a** : a hair of the beard **b** *pl* : the part of the beard growing on the sides of the face or on the chin **c** : HAIRBREADTH ⟨lost the race by a *whisker*⟩ **2** : one of the long projecting hairs or bristles growing near the mouth of an animal (as a cat or bird) [derived from 2*whisk*] — **whis•kered** \-kərd\ *adj*

whis•key *or* **whis•ky** \ˈhwis-kē, ˈwis-\ *n, pl* **whiskeys** *or* **whiskies** : a distilled alcoholic liquor made from fermented mash of grain (as rye, corn, barley, or wheat) [Irish Gaelic *uisce beathadh* and Scottish Gaelic *uisge beatha*, literally, "water of life"]

1whis•per \ˈhwis-pər, ˈwis-\ *vb* **whis•pered; whis•per•ing** \-pə-ring, -pring\ **1** : to speak very low or under the breath **2** : to tell or utter by whispering ⟨*whisper* a secret⟩ **3** : to make a low rustling sound ⟨*whispering* leaves⟩ [Old English *hwisperian*] — **whis•per•er** \-pər-ər\ *n*

2whisper *n* **1 a** : an act or instance of whispering; *esp* : speech without vibration of the vocal cords **b** : a sibilant sound that resembles whispered speech **2 a** : RUMOR ⟨*whispers* of a scandal⟩ **b** : HINT 2a, TRACE

whispering campaign *n* : the systematic spreading of derogatory rumors or charges especially against a candidate for public office

whist \ˈhwist, ˈwist\ *n* : a card game for four players from which bridge developed [earlier *whisk*, probably from 3*whisk*; from whisking up the tricks]

1whis•tle \ˈhwis-əl, ˈwis-\ *n* **1** : a device by which a shrill sound is produced ⟨a tin *whistle*⟩ ⟨a steam *whistle*⟩ **2 a** : a shrill clear sound produced by forcing breath out or air in through puckered lips **b** : the sound or signal produced by a whistle or as if by whistling; *esp* : the shrill clear note of a bird or other animal [Old English *hwistle*]

2whistle *vb* **whis•tled; whis•tling** \ˈhwis-ling, ˈwis-, -ə-ling\ **1 a** : to make a whistle through the puckered lips **b** : to utter a shrill note or call resembling a whistle **c** : to make a shrill clear sound especially by rapid movement ⟨bullets *whistled* by⟩ **d** : to blow or sound a whistle **2** : to signal, order, or summon someone or something by or as if by whistling ⟨*whistle* to a dog⟩ **3** : to send, bring, signal, or call by or as if by whistling ⟨*whistle* the dog back⟩ **4** : to produce, utter, or express by whistling ⟨*whistle* a tune⟩ — **whis•tler** \ˈhwis-lər, ˈwis-, -ə-lər\ *n*

1whis•tle–stop \ˈhwis-əl-ˌstäp, ˈwis-\ *n* **1 a** : a small station at which trains stop only on signal **b** : a small community **2** : a brief personal appearance by a political candidate usually on the rear platform of a touring train

2whistle–stop *vi* : to tour especially in a political campaign with many brief personal appearances in small communities

whit \ˈhwit, ˈwit\ *n* : the smallest part imaginable : BIT ⟨cared not a *whit*⟩ [Old English *wiht* "creature, thing, bit"]

1white \ˈhwīt, ˈwīt\ *adj* **1 a** : free from color **b** : of the color of new snow or milk; *esp* : of the color white **c** : light or pale in color ⟨*white* wine⟩ ⟨lips *white* with fear⟩ **d** : lustrous pale gray : SILVERY; *also* : made of silver **2 a** : of, relating to, or being a member of a group or race characterized by relatively light pigmentation **b** *slang* : FAIR 5a, HONEST **3** : free from spot or blemish: as **a** : free from moral impurity : INNOCENT **b** : unmarked by writing or printing **c** : not intended to cause harm ⟨a *white* lie⟩ ⟨*white* magic⟩ **d** : FAVORABLE, FORTUNATE ⟨a *white* day in my life⟩ **4 a** : wearing or clothed in white **b** : marked by the presence of snow : SNOWY ⟨a *white* Christmas⟩ **5** : very ardent : PASSIONATE ⟨in a *white* fury⟩ **6** : ultraconservative or reactionary in political outlook and action [Old English *hwīt*] — **white•ly** *adv* — **white•ness** *n*

2white *n* **1** : the color of fresh snow **2** : a white or light-colored thing or part: as **a** : a mass of albuminous material surrounding the yolk of an egg **b** : the white part of the ball of the eye **c** : the light-colored pieces in a two-handed board game (as chess) or the player by whom these are played **3** : one that is or approaches the color white **4** : a person belonging to a light-skinned race **5** : a member of a conservative or reactionary political group

white ant *n* : TERMITE

white bass *n* : a North American freshwater food fish

white•beard \ˈhwīt-ˌbiərd, ˈwīt-\ *n* : an old man : GRAYBEARD

white blood cell *n* : a blood cell that does not contain hemoglobin : LEUKOCYTE

white•cap \ˈhwīt-ˌkap, ˈwīt-\ *n* : a wave crest breaking into white foam

white cedar *n* : any of various North American timber trees: as **a** : a strong-scented evergreen swamp tree that somewhat resembles an arborvitae but has smaller leaves **b** : a common arborvitae

white cell *n* : LEUKOCYTE

white clover *n* : a Eurasian clover with round heads of white flowers that is widely used in lawns and pastures and is an important honey plant — called also *Dutch clover, white Dutch clover*

white–col•lar \ˈhwīt-ˈkäl-ər, ˈwīt-\ *adj* : of, relating to, or being the group of salaried employees whose duties do not call for the wearing of work clothes or protective clothing

white corpuscle *n* : LEUKOCYTE
white crappie *n* : a silvery North American sunfish highly esteemed as a panfish and often used for stocking small ponds
white dwarf *n* : a small very dense whitish star of high surface temperature and low luminosity
white elephant *n* **1** : something requiring much care and expense and yielding little profit **2** : an object no longer wanted by its owner though not without value to others **[**from the fact that in parts of India pale-colored elephants are considered sacred and are maintained without being required to work**]**
white-faced \ˈhwīt-ˈfāst, ˈwīt-\ *adj* **1** : having a wan pale face **2** : having the face white in whole or in part ⟨a *white-faced* steer⟩
white feather *n* : a mark or symbol of cowardice ⟨show the *white feather*⟩ **[**from the superstition that a white feather in the plumage of a gamecock is a mark of a poor fighter**]**
white•fish \ˈhwīt-ˌfish, ˈwīt-\ *n* : any of various freshwater food fishes related to the salmons and trouts and mostly greenish above and silvery white below
white flag *n* : a flag of plain white used as a sign of truce or of surrender
white•fly \ˈhwīt-ˌflī, ˈwīt-\ *n* : any of various small white winged insects related to the scale insects and especially destructive to greenhouse plants
white friar *n, often cap W & F* : CARMELITE **[**from the white habit**]**
white gold *n* : a pale alloy of gold especially with nickel or palladium that resembles platinum in appearance
white goods *n pl* **1** : cotton or linen fabrics or articles (as sheets or towels) **2** : major household appliances (as stoves)
white grub *n* : a grub that is the larva of a june beetle and a destructive pest of grass roots
White•hall \ˈhwīt-ˌhȯl, ˈwīt-\ *n* : the British government **[***Whitehall,* street of London in which are located the chief offices of the British government**]**
white•head \ˈhwīt-ˌhed, ˈwīt-\ *n* : a small whitish elevation of the skin caused by accumulation of oil gland secretion when the duct of the gland is blocked by a thin layer of skin cells
white heat *n* **1** : a temperature at which a body (as of metallic or ceramic material) becomes brightly incandescent so as to appear white **2** : a state of intense mental or physical strain, emotion, or activity
White Horde *n* : a Mongolian people powerful in Russia in the 14th century
white-hot \ˈhwīt-ˈhät, ˈwīt-\ *adj* : being at or radiating white heat
White House *n* : the executive department of the United States government **[**the *White House,* mansion in Washington, D.C. assigned to the use of the president of the United States**]**
white lead *n* : a heavy white poisonous carbonate of lead chiefly used as a pigment
white-liv•ered \ˈhwīt-ˈliv-ərd, ˈwīt-\ *adj* : COWARDLY 1, LILY-LIVERED
white matter *n* : whitish nerve tissue that consists largely of nerve fibers sheathed in a fatty material and underlies the gray matter of the brain and spinal cord or forms nerves
whit•en \ˈhwīt-n, ˈwīt-\ *vb* **whit•ened; whit•en•ing** \ˈhwīt-ning, ˈwīt-, -n-ing\ : to make or become white or whiter
• **syn** WHITEN, BLANCH, BLEACH mean to make or grow white or whiter. WHITEN implies making white often by the application or addition of a white substance ⟨*whiten* stained linen with a bleach⟩ BLANCH implies the removal or withdrawal of color especially from living tissue ⟨*blanch* plants by growing them in darkness⟩ BLEACH implies the action of sunlight or chemicals in removing color.
whit•en•er \ˈhwīt-nər, ˈwīt-, -n-ər\ *n* : one that whitens; *esp* : an agent (as a bleach) used to impart whiteness to something
white oak *n* : any of various oaks with acorns that mature in one year and leaf veins that never extend beyond the margin of the leaf; *also* : the hard, strong, durable, and moisture-resistant wood of a white oak
white paper *n* : a government report on a subject
white pepper *n* : a pungent seasoning that consists of the fruit of the East Indian pepper ground after the outer husk has been removed
white perch *n* : a small silvery sea bass of the coast and coastal streams of the eastern United States
white pine *n* : a tall-growing pine of eastern North America with needles in clusters of five; *also* : its wood which is much used in building construction
white-pine blister rust *n* : a destructive disease of white pine caused by a rust fungus that passes part of its life on currant or gooseberry bushes; *also* : this fungus
white potato *n* : POTATO 2b
white rust *n* : any of various plant diseases caused by lower fungi and marked by production of masses of white spores that escape through ruptures in the host tissue; *also* : a fungus causing a white rust
white sale *n* : a sale of white goods
white sauce *n* : a sauce consisting essentially of milk, cream, or stock with flour and seasoning
white sea bass *n* : a large Pacific croaker closely related to the Atlantic weakfishes
white shark *n* : GREAT WHITE SHARK
white•tail \ˈhwīt-ˌtāl, ˈwīt-\ *n* : WHITE-TAILED DEER
white-tailed deer *n* : a North American deer with forward-arching antlers and with a rather long tail white on the underside — called also *Virginia deer*

white-tailed deer

white tie *n* : formal evening dress for men
white•wall \ˈhwīt-ˌwȯl, ˈwīt-\ *n* : an automobile tire having a white band on the sidewall
white walnut *n* : BUTTERNUT 2
[1]**white•wash** \ˈhwīt-ˌwȯsh, ˈwīt-, -ˌwäsh\ *vt* **1** : to whiten with whitewash **2** : to clear of a charge of wrongdoing by offering excuses, hiding facts, or conducting a superficial investigation — **white•wash•er** *n*
[2]**whitewash** *n* **1** : a composition (as of lime and water) for whitening structural surfaces **2** : a covering up or glossing over of something (as wrongdoing)
white•wood \ˈhwīt-ˌwu̇d, ˈwīt-\ *n* **1** : any of various trees with pale or white wood: as **a** : COTTONWOOD **b** : TULIP TREE **2** : the wood of a whitewood and especially of the tulip tree
[1]**whith•er** \ˈhwith-ər, ˈwith-\ *adv* **1** : to what place ⟨*whither* will they go⟩ **2** : to what situation, position, degree, or end ⟨*whither* will this abuse drive me⟩ **[**Old English *hwider***]**
[2]**whither** *conj* **1 a** : to the place at, in, or to which **b** : to which place **2** : to whatever place
whith•er•so•ev•er \ˌhwith-ər-sə-ˈwev-ər, ˌwith-\ *conj* : [2]WHITHER 2
whith•er•ward \ˈhwith-ər-wərd, ˈwith-\ *adv* : toward what or which place
[1]**whit•ing** \ˈhwīt-ing, ˈwīt-\ *n, pl* **whiting** *or* **whitings** : any of several edible fishes (as the hake) found mostly near seacoasts **[**Dutch *witinc,* from *wit* "white"**]**
[2]**whiting** *n* : calcium carbonate prepared as fine powder and used especially as a pigment and extender, in putty, and in rubber compounding
whit•ish \ˈhwīt-ish, ˈwīt-\ *adj* : somewhat white
Whit•sun \ˈhwit-sən, ˈwit-\ *adj* : of, relating to, or observed on Whitsunday or at Whitsuntide
Whit•sun•day \-sən-dē, -sən-ˌdā\ : PENTECOST 2 **[**Old English *hwīta sunnandæg,* literally, "white Sunday"**]**
Whit•sun•tide \-sən-ˌtīd\ *n* : the week beginning with Whitsunday; *esp* : the first three days of this week
whit•tle *vb* **whit•tled; whit•tling** \ˈhwit-ling, ˈwit-,-l-ing\ **1 a** : to pare or cut off chips from the surface of (wood) with a knife **b** : to shape or form by paring or cutting **c** : to cut or shape something by or as if by whittling it **2** : PARE 2 **[**Middle English *thwitel, whittel* "large knife", from *thwiten* "to whittle", from Old English *thwītan***]** — **whit•tler** \ˈhwit-lər, ˈwit-,-l-ər\ *n*
[1]**whiz** *or* **whizz** \ˈhwiz, ˈwiz\ *vb* **whizzed; whiz•zing** **1** : to buzz, whir, or hiss like a speeding object (as an arrow) passing through air **2** : to fly or move swiftly with a whiz **3** : to rotate very rapidly **[**imitative**]** — **whiz•zer** *n*
[2]**whiz** *or* **whizz** *n, pl* **whiz•zes** **1** : a hissing, buzzing, or whirring sound **2** : a movement or passage of something accompanied by a whizzing sound
[3]**whiz** *n, pl* **whiz•zes** : WIZARD 2 **[**probably from *wizard***]**
whiz•bang *or* **whizz•bang** \ˈhwiz-ˌbang, ˈwiz-\ *n* : one that is consipicuous for noise, speed, or startling effect

whiz–bang *adj* : EXCELLENT, FIRST-CLASS
who \hü, ˈhü, ü\ *pron* **1** : what or which person or persons — used as an interrogative ⟨*who* was elected president⟩⟨find out *who* they are⟩; used by reputable writers, though disapproved by some grammarians, as the object of a verb or a following preposition ⟨*who* did you meet⟩⟨*who* is it for⟩ **2** : the person or persons that : WHOEVER **3** — used as a function word to introduce a relative clause; used especially in reference to persons but also in reference to groups, to animals, or to inanimate objects ⟨my friend, *who* was a lawyer⟩ ⟨a generation *who* has grown up⟩ ⟨dogs *who* bark too much⟩⟨earlier sources *who* disagree⟩; used by speakers on all educational levels and by many reputable writers though disapproved by some grammarians, as the object of a verb or a following preposition ⟨a person *who* you all know well⟩ [Old English *hwā*]
• **syn** WHO, WHICH, THAT are relative pronouns. WHO is used usually of persons ⟨my friend, *who* is older than I⟩⟨those *who* believe in miracles⟩ WHICH refers to animals, to inanimate objects, or to ideas or situations expressed but not named (replacing *and that*)⟨you are in trouble, *which* is why I am here⟩ THAT may be used of persons, animals, or things in restrictive clauses ⟨the first one *that* spoke to me⟩ ⟨the car *that* just went by⟩ but not in descriptive (nonrestrictive) clauses referring to persons; WHICH is less usual than THAT in restrictive clauses referring to things except when it follows a preposition ⟨the table on *which* it sat⟩
whoa \ˈwō, ˈhō, ˈhwō\ *imperative verb* — a command (as to a draft animal) to stand still [Middle English *whoo*]
who•dun•it \hü-ˈdən-ət\ *n* : a detective story or mystery story presented as a novel, play, or motion picture [*who done it?*]
who•ev•er \hü-ˈev-ər\ *pron* : whatever person : no matter who — used in any grammatical relation except that of a possessive
[1]**whole** \ˈhōl\ *adj* **1** : being in healthy or sound condition : free from defect or damage : WELL ⟨careful nursing made me *whole* again⟩ **2** : having all its proper parts or elements ⟨*whole* milk⟩ **3 a** : constituting the total sum of : ENTIRE ⟨gave their *whole* time to study⟩ **b** : each or all of the ⟨the *whole* 10 days⟩ **4 a** : constituting an undivided unit ⟨a *whole* roast suckling pig⟩ **b** : directed to one end ⟨give it your *whole* attention⟩ **5 a** : seemingly complete or total ⟨the *whole* sky was red⟩ **b** : very great ⟨feels a *whole* lot better⟩ [Old English *hāl*] — **whole•ness** *n*
• **syn** WHOLE, ENTIRE, PERFECT mean not lacking or faulty in any particular. WHOLE suggests a completeness or perfection that is normal and can be sought, gained, or regained ⟨education makes a person *whole*⟩ ENTIRE implies wholeness deriving from integrity, soundness, or completeness with nothing omitted or taken away; PERFECT implies the soundness and excellence of every part or element often as an unattainable or theoretical state ⟨one's idea of the *perfect* novel⟩
[2]**whole** *n* **1** : a complete amount or sum : a number, aggregate, or totality lacking no part, member, or element **2** : something constituting a complex unity : an orderly system or organization of parts fitting or working together as one — **whole•ness** *n* — **on the whole 1** : in view of all the circumstances or conditions : all things considered **2** : in general : in most instances : TYPICALLY
whole•heart•ed \ˈhōl-ˈhärt-əd\ *adj* : undivided in purpose, enthusiasm, or will : HEARTY ⟨*wholehearted* support⟩ — **whole•heart•ed•ly** *adv* — **whole•heart•ed•ness** *n*
whole hog *n* : the whole way or farthest limit : ALL ⟨go the *whole hog*⟩ — **whole–hog** \ˈhōl-ˈhȯg, -ˈhäg\ *adj or adv* — **whole–hog•ger** \-ˈhȯg-ər, -ˈhäg-\ *n*
whole note *n* : a musical note equal in value to four quarter notes or two half notes to one measure
whole number *n* : INTEGER
[1]**whole•sale** \ˈhōl-ˌsāl\ *n* : the sale of goods in large quantities usually for resale by a retail merchant
[2]**wholesale** *adj* **1** : of, relating to, or engaged in wholesaling ⟨a *wholesale* grocer⟩⟨*wholesale* prices⟩ **2** : done on a large scale ⟨*wholesale* slaughter⟩ — **wholesale** *adv*
[3]**wholesale** *vb* : to sell at wholesale — **whole•sal•er** *n*
whole•some \ˈhōl-səm\ *adj* **1** : promoting mental, spiritual, or bodily health or well-being ⟨*wholesome* advice⟩ ⟨a *wholesome* environment⟩ **2** : sound in body, mind, or morals **3** : based on well-grounded fear : PRUDENT ⟨*wholesome* respect for the law⟩ **syn** see HEALTHFUL — **whole•some•ly** *adv* — **whole•some•ness** *n*
whole–souled \-ˈsōld\ *adj* : WHOLEHEARTED
whole step *n* : a musical interval comprising two half steps — called also *whole tone*
whole wheat *adj* : made of ground entire wheat kernels
whol•ly \ˈhōl-lē, ˈhō-lē\ *adv* **1** : to the full or entire extent : COMPLETELY ⟨*wholly* incompetent⟩ **2** : to the exclusion of other things : SOLELY
whom \hüm, ˈhüm, üm\ *pron, objective case of* WHO — used as an interrogative or relative; used as object of a verb or a preceding preposition ⟨to *whom* was it given⟩ or less frequently as the object of a following preposition ⟨the person *whom* you spoke to⟩ though now often considered stilted especially as an interrogative and especially in oral use [Old English *hwām*, dative of *hwā* "who"]
whom•ev•er \hü-ˈmev-ər\ *pron, objective case of* WHOEVER
whom•so \ˈhüm-sō\ *pron, objective case of* WHOSO
whom•so•ev•er \ˌhüm-sə-ˈwev-ər\ *pron, objective case of* WHOSOEVER
[1]**whoop** \ˈhüp, ˈhwüp, ˈhu̇p, ˈhwu̇p, ˈwüp\ *vb* **1** : to shout or call loudly and vigorously especially in eagerness, enthusiasm, or enjoyment ⟨the kids *whooped* with joy⟩ **2** : to make the sound that follows an attack of coughing in whooping cough **3** : to go or pass with a loud noise **4 a** : to utter or express with a whoop **b** : to urge, drive, or cheer on with a whoop [Middle French *houpper*] — **whoop it up 1** : to celebrate riotously : CAROUSE **2** : to stir up enthusiasm
[2]**whoop** *n* **1** : a whooping sound or utterance: as **a** : a shout of hunters or of persons in battle or pursuit **b** : a loud booming cry of a bird (as an owl or crane) **c** : a crowing sound accompanying the intake of breath after a coughing attack in whooping cough **2** : WHIT, BIT ⟨not worth a *whoop*⟩
[1]**whoop•ee** \ˈhwu̇p-ˌē, ˈwu̇p-; ˈhwü-ˌpē, ˈhü-, ˈwü-\ *interj* — used to express delight or high spirits [derived from [2]*whoop*]
[2]**whoopee** *n* : boisterous convivial fun
whooping cough *n* : an infectious bacterial disease especially of children marked by a convulsive spasmodic cough sometimes followed by a crowing intake of breath — called also *pertussis*
whooping crane *n* : a large white nearly extinct North American crane
whoop•la \ˈhüp-ˌlä, ˈhwüp-, ˈhu̇p-, ˈhwu̇p-\ *n* **1** : a noisy commotion **2** : boisterous merrymaking [alteration of *hoopla*]
whoops \ˈwu̇ps, ˈu̇ps\ *interj* : OOPS
[1]**whoosh** \ˈhwüsh, ˈwüsh, ˈhwu̇sh, ˈwu̇sh\ *vb* : to move with an explosive or hissing rush [imitative]
[2]**whoosh** *n* : a swift or explosive rush
whop \ˈhwäp, ˈwäp\ *vt* **whopped**; **whop•ping 1** : BEAT, HIT ⟨*whopped* me with a bat⟩ **2** : WHIP 4 [Middle English *wappen, whappen* "to throw, strike"]
whop•per \ˈhwäp-ər, ˈwäp-\ *n* **1** : an unusually large thing **2** : a big lie
whop•ping \ˈhwäp-ing, ˈwäp-\ *adj* : very large or great
[1]**whore** \ˈhōr, ˈhȯr, ˈhu̇r\ *n* : PROSTITUTE [Old English *hōre*]
[2]**whore** *vi* : to have unlawful sexual intercourse as or with a whore
whorl \ˈhwȯrl, ˈwȯrl, ˈhwərl, ˈwərl\ *n* **1** : a row of parts (as leaves or petals) encircling an axis and especially a stem **2** : something that whirls, coils, or spirals or whose form suggests such movement **3** : one of the turns of a univalve shell [Middle English *wharle, whorle*] — **whorled** \ˈhwȯrld, ˈhwərld\ *adj*
whor•tle•ber•ry \ˈhwərt-l-ˌber-ē, ˈwərt-\ *n* : a European blueberry with a blackish berry : BILBERRY; *also* : its berry [Middle English *hurtilberye*, from Old English *horte* "whortleberry"]
[1]**whose** \hüz, ˈhüz, üz\ *adj* : of or relating to whom or which especially as possessor or possessors, agent or agents, or object or objects of an action ⟨asked *whose* cars they were⟩ ⟨*whose* plays are greater than Shakespeare's?⟩ ⟨the book *whose* publication was announced⟩ [Middle English *whos*, genitive of *who, what*]
[2]**whose** \hüz, ˈhüz\ *pron* : that which belongs to whom — used without a following noun as a pronoun equivalent in meaning to the adjective *whose*
whose•so•ev•er \ˌhüz-sə-ˈwev-ər\ *adj* : of or relating to whomsoever

whoso \ˈhü-ˌsō\ *pron* : WHOEVER
who•so•ev•er \ˌhü-sə-ˈwev-ər\ *pron* : WHOEVER
1**why** \hwī, ˈhwī, wī, ˈwī\ *adv* : for what cause, reason, or purpose ⟨*why* did you do it⟩ [Old English *hwȳ*, from *hwæt* "what"]
2**why** *conj* **1** : the cause, reason, or purpose for which ⟨know *why* you did it⟩ ⟨that is *why* you did it⟩ **2** : for which : on account of which ⟨know the reason *why* you did it⟩
3**why** \ˈhwī, ˈwī\ *n, pl* **whys** : REASON, CAUSE ⟨the *why* of sexist prejudice⟩
4**why** \wī, ˌwī, hwī, ˌhwī\ *interj* — used to express mild surprise, hesitation, approval, disapproval, or impatience ⟨*why*, here's what I was looking for⟩
whyd•ah \ˈhwid-ə, ˈwid-\ *n* : any of various mostly black and white African weaverbirds often kept as cage birds [from earlier *widow (bird)*; from its long black tail feathers resembling a widow's veil]
wick \ˈwik\ *n* : a cord, strip, or ring of loosely woven material through which a liquid (as melted tallow, wax, or oil) is drawn by capillary action to the top in a candle, lamp, or oil stove for burning [Old English *wēoce*]
wick•ed \ˈwik-əd\ *adj* **1** : morally bad : EVIL **2 a** : FIERCE, VICIOUS ⟨a *wicked* dog⟩ **b** : inclined to mischief : ROGUISH ⟨a *wicked* glance⟩ **3 a** : REPUGNANT, VILE ⟨a *wicked* odor⟩ **b** : causing or likely to cause harm or trouble ⟨a *wicked* storm⟩ [Middle English *wicke*] — **wick•ed•ly** *adv* — **wick•ed•ness** *n*
wick•er \ˈwik-ər\ *n* **1** : a flexible twig or osier : WITHE **2** : WICKERWORK [of Scandinavian origin] — **wicker** *adj*
wick•er•work \-ˌwərk\ *n* : work of osiers, twigs or rods : BASKETRY
wick•et \ˈwik-ət\ *n* **1** : a small gate or door; *esp* : one in or near a larger one **2** : a small window with a grille or grate (as at a ticket office) **3** : either of the 2 sets of 3 rods topped by 2 crosspieces at which the ball is bowled in cricket **4** : an arch or hoop in croquet [Old North French *wiket*, of Germanic origin]
wick•et•keep•er \-ˌkē-pər\ *n* : the player who plays immediately behind the wicket in cricket
wick•ing \ˈwik-ing\ *n* : material for wicks
wick•i•up \ˈwik-ē-ˌəp\ *n* : a cone-shaped American Indian hut consisting of a rough frame covered with reed mats, grass, or brushwood [of American Indian origin]

wickiup

1**wide** \ˈwīd\ *adj* **1** : covering a vast area ⟨the *wide* world⟩ **2** : having a specified extent from side to side ⟨cloth 54 inches *wide*⟩ **3** : having a generous measure across : BROAD ⟨the road isn't very *wide*⟩ **4** : opened as far as possible ⟨eyes *wide* with wonder⟩ **5** : not limited : EXTENSIVE ⟨*wide* experience⟩ **6** : far from the goal, mark, or truth ⟨a *wide* guess⟩ [Old English *wīd*] **syn** see BROAD — **wide•ly** *adv* — **wide•ness** *n*
2**wide** *adv* **1 a** : over a great distance of extent ⟨searched far and *wide*⟩ **b** : over a specified distance, area, or extent ⟨expanded the business country-*wide*⟩ **2 a** : so as to leave much space or distance between ⟨*wide* apart⟩ **b** : so as to pass at or clear by a considerable distance ⟨ran *wide* around left end⟩ **3** : FULLY 1 ⟨opened my eyes *wide*⟩
wide–awake \ˌwīd-ə-ˈwāk\ *adj* : fully awake; *also* : knowingly watchful : ALERT — **wide–awake•ness** *n*
wide–eyed \ˈwīd-ˈīd\ *adj* **1** : having the eyes wide open especially with wonder or astonishment **2** : marked by unsophisticated or uncritical acceptance or admiration : NAIVE ⟨*wide-eyed* innocence⟩
wide•mouthed \-ˈmau̇thd, -ˈmau̇tht\ *adj* **1** : having a wide mouth ⟨*widemouthed* jars⟩ **2** : having one's mouth opened wide (as in awe)
wid•en \ˈwīd-n\ *vb* **wid•ened**; **wid•en•ing** \ˈwīd-ning, -n-ing\ : to make or become wide or wider : BROADEN — **wid•en•er** *n*
wide receiver *n* : an offensive football player principally used to catch passes who lines up several yards wide of the formation
wide•spread \ˈwīd-ˈspred\ *adj* **1** : widely extended ⟨*widespread* wings⟩ **2** : widely distributed or prevalent ⟨*widespread* hostility⟩
wid•geon *also* **wi•geon** \ˈwij-ən\ *n, pl* **widgeon** *or* **widgeons** : any of several freshwater ducks between the teal and the mallard in size [origin unknown]
wid•ish \ˈwīd-ish\ *adj* : somewhat wide
1**wid•ow** \ˈwid-ō\ *n* **1** : a woman who has lost her husband by death; *esp* : one who has not remarried **2** : GRASS WIDOW [Old English *widuwe*] — **wid•ow•hood** \-ˌhu̇d\ *n*
2**widow** *vt* : to cause to become a widow ⟨*widowed* by war⟩
wid•ow•er \ˈwid-ə-wər\ *n* : a man who has lost his wife by death and has not married again — **wid•ow•er•hood** \-ˌhu̇d\ *n*
widow's peak *n* : a point formed by the hair on the forehead
widow's walk *n* : a railed observation platform atop a usually coastal house
width \ˈwidth, ˈwitth\ *n* **1** : a distance from side to side : the measurement taken at right angles to the length : BREADTH **2** : largeness of extent or scope **3** : a measured and cut piece of material ⟨a *width* of calico⟩ ⟨a *width* of lumber⟩ [1*wide*]
width•ways \-ˌwāz\ *adv* : WIDTHWISE
width•wise \-ˌwīz\ *adv* : in the direction of width
wield \ˈwēld\ *vt* **1** : to handle effectively ⟨*wield* a broom⟩ **2** : to exert one's authority by means of ⟨*wield* influence⟩ [Old English *wieldan*] — **wield•er** *n*
wieldy \ˈwēl-dē\ *adj* : capable of wielding or being wielded

widow's peak

wie•ner \ˈwē-nər, -nē, ˈwin-ē\ *n* : FRANKFURTER [German *wienerwurst* "Vienna sausage"]
Wie•ner schnit•zel \ˈvē-nər-ˌshnit-səl, ˌsnit-; ˈwē-nər-ˌsnit-\ *n* : a thin breaded veal cutlet served with a garnish [German, literally, "Vienna cutlet"]
wife \ˈwīf\ *n, pl* **wives** \ˈwīvz\ **1 a** *dialect* : WOMAN 1, 4 **b** : a woman acting in a specified capacity — used in combination ⟨house*wife*⟩ **2** : a married woman [Old English *wīf*] — **wife•hood** \ˈwīf-ˌhu̇d, ˈwī-ˌfu̇d\ *n* — **wife•less** \ˈwī-fləs\ *adj*
wife•ly \ˈwī-flē\ *adj* **wife•li•er**; **-est** : of, relating to, or befitting a wife — **wife•li•ness** *n*
wig \ˈwig\ *n* : a manufactured covering of natural or artificial hair for the head; *also* : TOUPEE [short for *periwig*]
wig•gle \ˈwig-əl\ *vb* **wig•gled**; **wig•gling** \ˈwig-ling, -ə-ling\ **1** : to move to and fro with quick jerky or shaking motions : JIGGLE ⟨*wiggled* my toes⟩ **2** : to proceed with twisting and turning movements : WRIGGLE [Middle English *wiglen*] — **wiggle** *n*
wig•gler \ˈwig-lər, -ə-lər\ *n* **1** : one that wiggles **2** : a larval or pupal mosquito — called also *wriggler*
wig•gly \ˈwig-lē, -ə-lē\ *adj* **wig•gli•er**; **-est** **1** : tending to wiggle ⟨a *wiggly* worm⟩ **2** : WAVY ⟨*wiggly* lines⟩
wight \ˈwīt\ *n* : a living being : CREATURE [Old English *wiht* "creature, thing"]
1**wig•wag** \ˈwig-ˌwag\ *vb* **wig•wagged**; **-wag•ging** **1** : to signal by or as if by a flag or light waved according to a code **2** : to make or cause to make a signal (as with the hand or arm) [English dialect *wig* "to move" + English *wag*]
2**wigwag** *n* **1** : the art or practice of wigwagging **2** : the act of wigwagging
wig•wam \ˈwig-ˌwäm\ *n* : an American Indian hut having typically an arched framework of poles overlaid with bark, rush mats, or hides [of American Indian origin]
wil•co \ˈwil-kō\ *interj* — used especially in radio and signaling to indicate that a message received will be complied with [*will comply*]

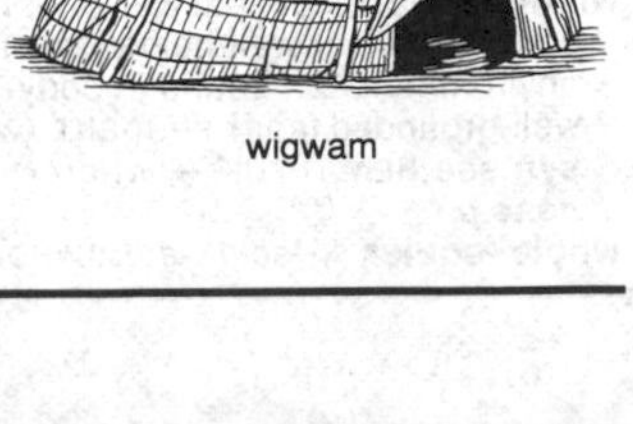
wigwam

1**wild** \ˈwīld\ *adj* **1 a** : living

in a state of nature and not ordinarily tame or domesticated ⟨*wild* duck⟩ **b :** growing or produced without the aid and care of humans ⟨*wild* honey⟩; *also* **:** related to or resembling a corresponding cultivated or domesticated organism ⟨*wild* plum⟩ **c :** of or relating to wild organisms ⟨the *wild* state⟩ **2 :** not inhabited or cultivated ⟨*wild* land⟩ **3 a :** UNRULY ⟨a *wild* rage⟩ ⟨*wild* mobs⟩ **b :** TURBULENT, STORMY ⟨a *wild* night⟩ **c :** EXTRAVAGANT, FANTASTIC ⟨*wild* colors⟩ ⟨*wild* ideas⟩ **d :** indicative of strong passion, desire, or emotion ⟨a *wild* stare⟩ **4 :** UNCIVILIZED 1, SAVAGE **5 a :** deviating from the natural or expected course ⟨a *wild* price increase⟩ **b :** having no basis in fact ⟨a *wild* guess⟩ **6 :** capable of having any value designated by the holder ⟨poker with deuces *wild*⟩ **[**Old English *wilde***]** — **wild•ly** *adv* — **wild•ness** \ˈwīld-nəs, ˈwīl-\ *n*

[2]wild *n* **1 :** WILDERNESS **2 :** a natural uncultivated or undomesticated state or existence

[3]wild *adv* **1 :** in a wild manner **2 :** without regulation or control ⟨running *wild*⟩

wild and woolly *adj* **:** marked by a boisterous and untamed lack of polish and refinement ⟨a *wild and wooly* town⟩

wild boar *n* **:** an Old World wild hog that has contributed to the ancestry of most domestic swine

wild boar

wild carrot *n* **:** a widely naturalized white-flowered Eurasian weed that is probably the original of the cultivated carrot — called also *Queen Anne's lace*

[1]wild•cat \ˈwīld-ˌkat, ˈwīl-\ *n, pl* **wildcats** *or* **wildcat 1 :** any of various small or medium-sized cats (as the lynx or ocelot) **2 :** a savage quick-tempered person

[2]wildcat *adj* **1 a :** financially irresponsible or unreliable ⟨*wildcat* banks⟩ **b :** issued by a wildcat bank ⟨*wildcat* currency⟩ **2 :** operating, produced, or carried on outside the bounds of standard or legitimate business practices **3 :** of, relating to, or being an oil or gas well drilled in territory not known to be productive **4 :** begun by a group of workers without union approval or in violation of a contract ⟨a *wildcat* strike⟩

[3]wildcat *vi* **-cat•ted; -cat•ting :** to prospect and drill an experimental oil or gas well or mine shaft in territory not known to be productive — **wild•cat•ter** *n*

wil•de•beest \ˈwil-də-ˌbēst\ *n, pl* **wildebeests** *also* **wildebeest :** GNU **[**Afrikaans *wildebees,* from *wilde* "wild" + *bees* "beast, ox"**]**

wil•der•ness \ˈwil-dər-nəs\ *n* **:** an uncultivated and uninhabited region **:** wild or waste land **[**Middle English, from *wildern* "wild", from Old English *wilddēoren* "of wild beasts"**]**

wilderness area *n* **:** an area (as of national forest land) set aside for preservation of natural conditions for scientific or recreational purposes

wild–eyed \ˈwīl-ˈdīd\ *adj* **1 :** having a wild expression in the eyes **2 :** consisting of or favoring extreme measures ⟨*wild-eyed* schemes⟩

wild•fire \ˈwīld-ˌfīr, ˈwīl-\ *n* **1 :** a sweeping and destructive fire **2 :** GREEK FIRE

wild flower *n* **:** the flower of a wild or uncultivated plant; *also* **:** a plant bearing wild flowers

wild•fowl \ˈwīld-ˌfau̇l, ˈwīl-\ *n* **:** a game bird; *esp* **:** a game waterfowl (as a wild duck or goose) — **wild•fowl•er** \-ˌfau̇-lər\ *n* — **wild•fowl•ing** \-liŋ\ *n*

wild geranium *n* **:** a geranium of the eastern United States with rosy purple or white flowers

wild ginger *n* **:** a North American perennial woodland herb with pungent creeping rhizomes and bluntly heart-shaped leaves

wild–goose chase *n* **:** a fruitless pursuit or search

wild•ing \ˈwīl-diŋ\ *n* **:** a plant or animal growing or living in the wild — **wilding** *adj*

wild land *n* **:** WILDERNESS, WASTELAND

wild•life \ˈwīl-ˌdlīf, -ˌlīf\ *n* **:** creatures that are neither human nor domesticated; *esp* **:** mammals, birds, and fishes hunted by man — **wildlife** *adj*

wild•ling \ˈwīl-dliŋ, -liŋ\ *n* **:** a wild plant or animal

wild marjoram *n* **:** OREGANO

wild oat *n* **1 :** any of several wild grasses closely related to the cultivated oat **2** *pl* **:** offenses and indiscretions blamed on youthful high spirits — usually used in the phrase *sow one's wild oats*

wild pansy *n* **:** a common and long-cultivated European viola which has small short-spurred flowers usually blue or purple mixed with white and yellow and from which most of the garden pansies are derived — called also *heartsease, Johnny-jump-up*

wild parsley *n* **:** any of various wild plants of the carrot family with finely divided leaves

wild pitch *n* **:** a pitched ball that cannot be stopped by the catcher and that allows a base runner to advance

wild rice *n* **:** a tall aquatic North American perennial grass yielding an edible grain

wild type *n* **:** the typical form of an organism as ordinarily encountered in nature as contrasted with mutant individuals

wild West *n* **:** the western United States in its frontier period

wild•wood \ˈwīl-ˌdwu̇d, -ˌwu̇d\ *n* **:** a wood unaltered or unfrequented by humans

[1]wile \ˈwīl\ *n* **1 :** a trick or stratagem intended to tempt or deceive **2 :** TRICKERY, GUILE **[**Middle English *wil***]** **syn** see TRICK

[2]wile *vt* **:** LURE, ENTICE ⟨the balmy weather *wiled* them from their work⟩

[1]will \wəl, l, ^{ə}l, əl, wil, ˈwil\ *vb, past* **would** \wəd, d, əd, wu̇d, ˈwu̇d\; *present sing & pl* **will 1 :** DESIRE, WISH ⟨call it what you *will*⟩ **2 —** used as an auxiliary verb (1) to express desire, willingness, or in negative constructions refusal ⟨*will* you have another helping⟩ ⟨no one *would* do it⟩ ⟨they *won't* stop pestering me⟩, (2) to express frequent, customary, or habitual action or natural tendency ⟨*will* get angry over nothing⟩, (3) to express simple futurity ⟨tomorrow we *will* go⟩ (4) to express capability or sufficiency ⟨the back seat *will* hold three⟩, (5) to express probability or recognition and often to serve as the equivalent to the simple verb ⟨that *will* be the mail carrier ringing the doorbell⟩, (6) to express determination or willfulness ⟨I *will* go despite them⟩, and (7) to express a command ⟨you *will* do as I say⟩ **[**Old English *wille***]**

[2]will \ˈwil\ *n* **1 :** wish or desire often combined with determination ⟨the *will* to win⟩ **2 :** something desired; *esp* **:** a choice or determination of one having authority or power **3 :** the act, process, or experience of willing **:** VOLITION **4 :** the process or power of wishing, choosing, desiring, or intending **5 :** SELF-CONTROL ⟨a person of iron *will*⟩ **6 :** a legal declaration in which a person states how his or her property is to be disposed of after death **[**Old English *willa* "will, desire"**]** — **at will :** as or whenever one wishes

[3]will \ˈwil\ *vb* **1 :** to dispose of by or as if by a will **:** BEQUEATH **2 a :** to determine by an act of choice ⟨*willed* myself to sleep⟩ **b :** DECREE, ORDAIN ⟨Providence *wills* it⟩ **c :** INTEND, PURPOSE ⟨I *willed* it so⟩ **3 :** to exercise the will

willed \ˈwild\ *adj* **:** having a will especially of a specified kind ⟨strong-*willed*⟩

wil•lem•ite \ˈwil-ə-ˌmīt\ *n* **:** a mineral Zn_2SiO_4 of variable color that consists of zinc silicate occurring in prisms and in massive or granular forms **[**German *willemit,* from *Willem* (William) I, died 1843, king of the Netherlands**]**

wil•let \ˈwil-ət\ *n, pl* **willet :** a large shorebird of the eastern and Gulf coasts and the central parts of North America **[**imitative**]**

will•ful *or* **wil•ful** \ˈwil-fəl\ *adj* **1 :** stubbornly wanting one's own way **:** OBSTINATE **2 :** done deliberately **:** INTENTIONAL ⟨*willful* murder⟩ **syn** see VOLUNTARY — **will•ful•ly** \-fə-lē\ *adv* — **will•ful•ness** *n*

wil•lies \ˈwil-ēz\ *n pl* **:** a fit of nervousness **:** JITTERS **[**origin unknown**]**

will•ing \ˈwil-iŋ\ *adj* **1 :** being agreeable and ready ⟨*willing* to go⟩ **2 :** prompt to act or respond ⟨*willing* workers⟩ **3 :** done, borne, or accepted by choice of without reluctance **:** VOLUNTARY ⟨*willing* obedience⟩ — **will•ing•ly** \-iŋ-lē\ *adv* — **will•ing•ness** *n*

wil•li•waw \ˈwil-i-ˌwȯ\ *n* **1 :** a sudden violent gust of cold land air common along mountainous coasts of high latitudes **2 :** a violent commotion or agitation **[**origin unknown**]**

will–less \ˈwil-ləs\ *adj* **1 :** involving no exercise of the will ⟨*will-less* obedience⟩ **2 :** not exercising the will

will–o'–the–wisp \ˌwil-ə-thə-ˈwisp\ *n* **1 :** IGNIS FATUUS 1 **2 :** a delusive goal or hope [*Will* (nickname for *William*) + *of* + *the* + *wisp*]

wil•low \ˈwil-ō\ *n* **1 :** any of a large genus of trees and shrubs bearing catkins of flowers without petals and including forms of value for wood, osiers, or tanbark and a few ornamentals **2 :** an object made of willow wood; *esp* **:** a cricket bat [Old English *welig*] — **willow** *adj* — **wil•low•like** \-ˌlīk\ *adj*

willow herb *n* **:** any of a genus of herbs of the evening-primrose family; *esp* **:** FIREWEED 1

willow oak *n* **:** an oak with lance-shaped leaves

wil•low•ware \ˈwil-ə-ˌwaər, ˈwil-ō-, -ˌweər\ *n* **:** china that is usually blue and white and that is decorated with a design featuring a large willow tree by a little bridge

wil•lowy \ˈwil-ə-wē\ *adj* **1 :** full of willows **2 :** gracefully tall and slender

will•pow•er \ˈwil-ˌpau̇-ər, -ˌpau̇r\ *n* **:** the ability to stick with something and not be stopped, changed, or talked out of it **:** DETERMINATION

wil•ly–nil•ly \ˌwil-ē-ˈnil-ē\ *adv or adj* **:** by compulsion **:** without choice ⟨rushed us along *willy-nilly*⟩ [alteration of *will I nill* (archaic negative of *will*) *I* or *will ye nill ye* or *will he nill he*]

[1]**wilt** \wəlt, wilt, ˈwilt\ *archaic present 2d sing of* WILL

[2]**wilt** \ˈwilt\ *vb* **1 :** to lose or cause to lose freshness and become limp **:** DROOP ⟨*wilting* roses⟩ **2 :** to grow weak or faint **:** LANGUISH [Middle English *welken*]

[3]**wilt** \ˈwilt\ *n* **1 :** an act or instance of wilting **:** the state of being wilted **2 :** a plant disorder (as various fungus diseases) in which the soft tissues lose their turgor and droop and often shrivel

wily \ˈwī-lē\ *adj* **wil•i•er; -est :** full of guile **:** TRICKY **syn** see SLY — **wil•i•ness** *n*

wim•ble \ˈwim-bəl\ *n* **:** any of various instruments for boring holes [Anglo-French, from Dutch *wimmel* "auger"]

[1]**wim•ple** \ˈwim-pəl\ *n* **:** a cloth covering worn outdoors over the head and around the neck and chin by women especially in the late medieval period and by some nuns [Old English *wimpel*]

[2]**wimple** *vb* **wim•pled; wim•pling** \-pə-ling, -pling\ **1 :** to cover with or as if with a wimple **2 :** to cause to ripple **:** RIPPLE **3 :** to fall or lie in folds

[1]**win** \ˈwin\ *vb* **won** \ˈwən\; **win•ning 1 :** to be first or best in or as if in a contest **:** SUCCEED **2 :** to get possession of by effort **3 a :** to gain in or as if in battle or contest ⟨*win* land from the sea⟩ **b :** to be the victor in ⟨*won* the war⟩ **4 :** to obtain by work **:** EARN **5 :** to seek and gain the favor or support of; *also* **:** to gain the affections of or a promise of marriage from [Old English *winnan* "to struggle"]

[2]**win** *n* **:** VICTORY; *esp* **:** first place at the finish of a horse race

wince \ˈwins\ *vi* **:** to shrink back involuntarily (as from pain) **:** FLINCH [Middle English *wenchen* "to be impatient, dart about"] — **wince** *n*

winch \ˈwinch\ *n* **:** a machine that has a roller on which rope is coiled for hauling or hoisting [Old English *wince*]

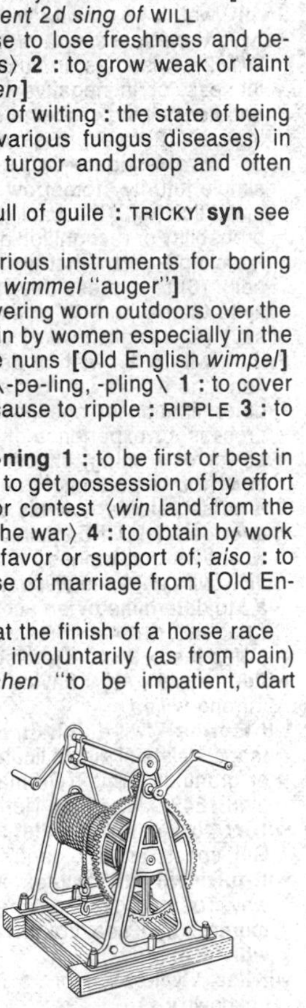

winch

[1]**wind** \ˈwind\ *n* **1 :** a movement of the air of any velocity **2 :** a force or agency that carries along or influences ⟨the *winds* of change⟩ **3 a :** BREATH **b :** the pit of the stomach **:** SOLAR PLEXUS **4 :** gas generated in the stomach or the intestines **5 :** something insubstantial; *esp* **:** idle words **6 a :** air carrying a scent (as of a hunter or game) **b :** slight information especially about something secret ⟨got *wind* of our plans⟩ **7 a :** wind instruments especially as distinguished from strings and percussion **b** *pl* **:** players of wind instruments **8 a :** a point of the compass; *esp* **:** one of the cardinal points **b :** the direction from which the wind is blowing [Old English] — **get the wind up :** to become excited or alarmed — **have the wind of 1 :** to be to windward of **2 :** to be on the scent of **3 :** to have a superior position to — **in the wind :** about to happen **:** ASTIR, AFOOT — **near the wind 1 :** CLOSE-HAULED **2 :** close to a point of danger **:** near the permissible limit — **off the wind :** away from the direction from which the wind is blowing — **under the wind 1 :** to leeward **2 :** in a place protected from the wind **:** under the lee

[2]**wind** *vt* **1 :** to get a scent of ⟨the dogs *winded* game⟩ **2 :** to cause to be out of breath **3 :** to allow (as a horse) to rest so as to catch the breath

[3]**wind** \ˈwīnd, ˈwind\ *vt* **wind•ed** \ˈwīn-dəd, ˈwin-\ *or* **wound** \ˈwau̇nd\; **wind•ing :** to sound by blowing ⟨*wind* a horn⟩ [[1]*wind*]

[4]**wind** \ˈwīnd\ *vb* **wound** \ˈwau̇nd\ *also* **wind•ed; wind•ing 1 :** WARP 1a, BEND **2 :** to have a curving course or shape ⟨a river *winding* through the valley⟩ **3 :** to move or lie so as to encircle ⟨vines *winding* around a tree⟩ **4 :** to turn when lying at anchor **5 a :** ENTANGLE 2 **b :** to introduce sinuously or stealthily **:** INSINUATE **6 a :** to encircle or cover with something pliable **b :** to turn completely or repeatedly about an object **:** COIL, TWINE ⟨*wind* thread on a spool⟩ **c :** to hoist or haul by means of a rope or chain and a windlass ⟨*wind* up a pail⟩ **d** (1) **:** to tighten the spring of ⟨*wind* a clock⟩ ⟨*wind* up a toy train⟩ (2) **:** CRANK ⟨*wound* down the car window⟩ **e :** to raise to a high level (as of excitement or tension) **7 a :** to cause to move in a curving line or path **b :** to traverse on a curving course ⟨the river *winds* the valley⟩ [Old English *windan* "to twist, brandish"]

[5]**wind** \ˈwīnd\ *n* **:** TURN 7c ⟨took a *wind* around the post⟩

wind•age \ˈwin-dij\ *n* **1 :** the influence of the wind in turning the course of a projectile **2 :** the amount of deflection caused by the wind

wind•bag \ˈwind-ˌbag, ˈwin-\ *n* **:** a person who talks a lot without saying anything important

wind•blown \-ˌblōn\ *adj* **:** blown or looking as if blown by the wind

wind•bound \-ˌbau̇nd\ *adj* **:** prevented from sailing by a contrary or a high wind

wind•break \-ˌbrāk\ *n* **:** something (as a growth of trees or shrubs) serving to break the force of wind

Wind•break•er \-ˌbrā-kər\ *trademark* — used for a wind-resistant outer jacket with fitted cuffs and waistband

wind–bro•ken \-ˌbrō-kən\ *adj* **:** having an impaired ability to breathe because of disease ⟨*wind-broken* horses⟩

wind•burn \-ˌbərn\ *n* **:** skin irritation caused by wind — **wind-burned** \-ˌbərnd\ *adj*

wind•chill \ˈwind-ˌchil, ˈwin-\ *or* **windchill index** *n* **:** a still-air temperature that would have the same cooling effect on exposed human flesh as a given combination of temperature and wind speed — called also *windchill factor*

wind cone *n* **:** WIND SOCK

wind•fall \ˈwind-ˌfȯl, ˈwin-\ *n* **1 :** something (as a tree or fruit) blown down by the wind **2 :** an unexpected or sudden gift, gain, or advantage

wind•flow•er \-ˌflau̇-ər, -ˌflau̇r\ *n* **:** ANEMONE

wind gap *n* **:** a notch in the crest of a mountain ridge

wind•ing \ˈwīn-ding\ *n* **:** material (as wire) wound or coiled about an object (as an armature); *also* **:** a single turn of the wound material

wind•ing–sheet \-ˌshēt\ *n* **:** a sheet used to wrap a corpse for burial **:** SHROUD

wind instrument *n* **:** a musical instrument (as a flute or horn) played by blowing

wind•jam•mer \ˈwind-ˌjam-ər, ˈwin-\ *n* **:** a sailing ship or one of its crew

wind•lass \ˈwin-dləs\ *n* **:** a winch used especially on ships for hauling and hoisting [Middle English *wyndas, wyndlas,* from Old Norse *vindāss,* from *vinda* "to wind" + *āss* "pole"]

[1]**wind•mill** \ˈwind-ˌmil, ˈwin-\ *n* **:** a mill or a machine (as for pumping water) worked by the wind turning sails or vanes at the top of a tower

[2]**windmill** *vb* **:** to move or cause to move like the vanes of a windmill

win•dow \ˈwin-dō\ *n* **1 :** an opening especially in the wall of a building for admission of light and air usually closed by casements or sashes containing glass **2 :** WINDOWPANE **3 :** something suggestive of or functioning like a window (as a shutter, opening, or valve) [Old Norse *vindauga,* from *vindr* "wind" + *auga* "eye"]

window box *n* **:** a box designed to hold growing plants on a windowsill

window dressing *n* **1 :** display of merchandise in a store window **2 :** a showing made to create a good but sometimes false impression

window envelope *n* **:** an envelope having a transparent panel through which the address on the enclosure is visible

win·dow·pane \-ˌpān\ *n* : a pane in a window

window seat *n* : a seat built into a window recess

window shade *n* : a shade or curtain for a window

win·dow–shop \-ˌshäp\ *vi* : to look at the displays in store windows without going inside the stores to make purchases — **win·dow–shop·per** *n*

win·dow·sill \-ˌsil\ *n* : the horizontal member at the bottom of a window opening

wind·pipe \ˈwind-ˌpīp, ˈwin-\ *n* : a firm tubular passage connecting the pharynx and lungs : TRACHEA

wind–pollinated *adj* : pollinated by pollen borne by the wind

wind·proof \ˈwind-ˈprüf, ˈwin-\ *adj* : resistant to the passage of wind ⟨a *windproof* jacket⟩

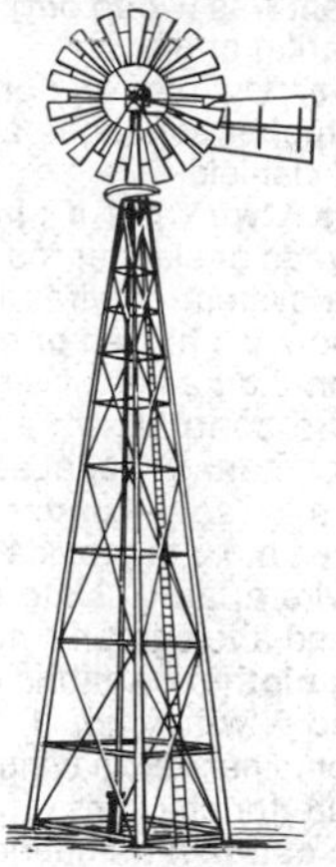

[1]windmill

[1]wind·row \ˈwin-ˌdrō, -ˌrō\ *n* **1** : hay raked up into a row to dry **2** : a row of something (as sand or dry leaves) heaped up by or as if by the wind

[2]windrow *vt* : to put into windrows

wind·screen \ˈwind-ˌskrēn, ˈwin-\ *n, British* : an automobile windshield

wind·shield \-ˌshēld\ *n* : a transparent screen (as of glass) in front of the occupants of a vehicle to protect them from the wind

wind sock *n* : a truncated cloth cone open at both ends and mounted in an elevated position to indicate the direction of the wind — called also *wind sleeve*

Wind·sor chair \ˈwin-zər-\ *n* : a wooden chair with spindle back and raking legs [*Windsor,* England]

Windsor knot *n* : a symmetrical knot used for tying neckties

wind sprint *n* : a sprint performed as a training exercise to develop the breathing capacity especially during exertion

wind·storm \ˈwind-ˌstȯrm, ˈwin-\ *n* : a storm marked by high wind with little or no precipitation

wind·swept \-ˌswept\ *adj* : swept by or as if by wind ⟨*windswept* plains⟩

wind tunnel *n* : an enclosed passage through which air is blown against structures (as airplanes) to test the effect of wind pressure on them

[1]wind·up \ˈwīn-ˌdəp\ *n* **1 a** : the act of bringing to an end **b** : a concluding act or part : FINISH **2** : a preliminary swing of the arms before pitching a baseball

[2]windup *adj* : operated by a spring wound by hand ⟨*windup* toy⟩

wind up \wīn-ˈdəp, ˈwīn-\ *vb* **1** : to bring or come to a conclusion : END **2** : to put in order : SETTLE **3** : to arrive in a place, situation, or condition at the end or as a result of a course of action ⟨and that's how we happened to *wind up* in Baltimore⟩ ⟨*wound up* as millionaires⟩ **4** : to give a preliminary swing to the arm (as before pitching a baseball)

[1]wind·ward \ˈwin-dwərd, -wərd\ *adj* : moving or situated toward the direction from which the wind is blowing — compare LEEWARD

[2]windward *n* : the side or direction from which the wind is blowing

wind–wing \ˈwin-ˌdwing, -ˌwing\ *n* : a small panel in an automobile window that can be turned outward for ventilation

windy \ˈwin-dē\ *adj* **wind·i·er**; **-est** **1** : having or exposed to wind ⟨a *windy* day⟩ ⟨a *windy* prairie⟩ **2** : given to or marked by useless talk ⟨a *windy* speaker⟩ — **wind·i·ly** \-də-lē\ *adv* — **wind·i·ness** \-dē-nəs\ *n*

[1]wine \ˈwīn\ *n* **1 a** : a beverage made from fermented grape juice containing varying percentages of alcohol **b** : a beverage made from the usually fermented juice of other fruits (as peaches or berries) **2** : something that invigorates or intoxicates **3** : a dark red [Old English *wīn,* from Latin *vinum*]

[2]wine *vt* : to treat to wine ⟨*wined* and dined their friends⟩

wine cellar *n* : a room for storing wines; *also* : a stock of wines

wine·grower \ˈwīn-ˌgrō-ər, -ˌgrōr\ *n* : one that cultivates a vineyard and makes wine

wine·press \-ˌpres\ *n* : a vat in which juice is squeezed from grapes

win·ery \ˈwīn-rē, -ə-rē\ *n, pl* **-er·ies** : a wine-making establishment

wine·shop \ˈwīn-ˌshäp\ *n* : a tavern that specializes in serving wine

wine·skin \-ˌskin\ *n* : a bag made from the skin of an animal and used for holding wine

win·ey *variant of* WINY

[1]wing \ˈwing\ *n* **1** : one of the movable feathered or membranous paired appendages by means of which a bird, bat, or insect is able to fly **2** : an appendage or part likened to a wing in shape, appearance, or position: as **a** : a flat or broadly expanded plant or animal part : ALA ⟨the *wings* of the nose⟩ ⟨a stem with woody *wings*⟩; *esp* : either lateral petal of a pealike flower **b** : a sidepiece at the top of an armchair **c** : one of the airfoils that develop a major part of the lift which supports a heavier-than-air aircraft **3** : a means of flight or rapid progress **4** : the act or manner of flying : FLIGHT **5** : a side or outlying region or district **6** : a part or feature projecting from and subordinate to the main or central part ⟨the rear *wing* of the house⟩ **7** *pl* : the area at the side of the stage out of sight **8 a** : a section of an army or fleet **b** : one of the offensive positions or players on each side of a center position in various team sports **9 a** : either of two opposing groups in an organization : FACTION **b** : a section of a legislative chamber representing a distinct group or faction [of Scandinavian origin] — **wing·like** \-ˌlīk\ *adj* — **on the wing** : in flight : FLYING — **under one's wing** : under one's protection : in one's charge or care

[1]wing 1: *1* coverts, *2* primary feathers, *3* secondary feathers

[2]wing *vb* **1** : to go with or as if with wings : FLY **2** : to wound in the wing ⟨*wing* a bird⟩; *also* : to wound without killing ⟨*wing* a deer⟩

wing case *n* : ELYTRON

wing chair *n* : an upholstered armchair with high solid back and sides that provide a rest for the head and protection from drafts

wing·ding \ˈwing-ˌding\ *n* : a wild or lively or lavish party [origin unknown]

winged \ˈwingd *also except for 1b* ˈwing-əd\ *adj* **1 a** : having wings **b** : having wings of a specified character — used in combination **2 a** : ELEVATED 2a **b** : SWIFT 1, RAPID

wing·less \ˈwing-ləs\ *adj* : having no wings or very rudimentary wings — **wing·less·ness** *n*

wing·man \-mən\ *n* : a pilot who flies somewhat behind and to the side of the leader of a flying formation

wing nut *n* : a nut with wings affording a grip for the thumb and finger

wings \ˈwingz\ *n pl* : insignia consisting of a stylized pair of outspread bird's wings

wing·span \ˈwing-ˌspan\ *n* : WINGSPREAD; *esp* : the distance between the tips of an airplane's wings

wing·spread \-ˌspred\ *n* : the spread of the wings; *esp* : the distance between the tips of the fully extended wings of a winged animal

[1]wink \ˈwingk\ *vb* **1** : to close and open the eyes quickly : BLINK **2** : to avoid seeing : pretend not to look : pay no attention ⟨*wink* at a violation of the law⟩ **3** : TWINKLE 1, FLICKER **4** : to close and open one eye quickly as a signal or hint [Old English *wincian*] — **wink·er** \ˈwing-kər\ *n*

• **syn** WINK, BLINK mean to close and open one's eyelids. WINK implies light, rapid, usually involuntary motion or the partial closing of an eye in a mischievous or teasing way. BLINK often implies involuntary motion suggesting a dazzled or dazed state or a struggle against drowsiness; in figurative use WINK implies connivance or indulgence, BLINK suggests shirking or evasion.

\ə\ **abut**	\au̇\ **out**	\i\ **tip**	\ȯ\ **saw**	\u̇\ **foot**
\ər\ **further**	\ch\ **chin**	\ī\ **life**	\ȯi\ **coin**	\y\ **yet**
\a\ **mat**	\e\ **pet**	\j\ **job**	\th\ **thin**	\yü\ **few**
\ā\ **take**	\ē\ **easy**	\ng\ **sing**	\t͟h\ **this**	\yu̇\ **cure**
\ä\ **cot, cart**	\g\ **go**	\ō\ **bone**	\ü\ **food**	\zh\ **vision**

²wink *n* **1** : a brief period of sleep : NAP **2 a** : a hint or sign given by winking the eye **b** : an act of winking **3** : the time of a wink : INSTANT

win•kle \ˈwiŋ-kəl\ *n* : ²PERIWINKLE

win•na•ble \ˈwin-ə-bəl\ *adj* : able to be won

Win•ne•ba•go \ˌwin-ə-ˈbā-gō\ *n, pl* **-go** *or* **-gos** *or* **-goes** : a member of a Siouan people of the western shores of Lake Michigan

win•ner \ˈwin-ər\ *n* : one that wins

winner's circle *n* : an enclosure near the finish line of a racetrack where the winning horse and jockey are brought for photographs and awards

¹win•ning \ˈwin-iŋ\ *n* **1** : the act of one that wins : VICTORY **2** : something won; *esp* : money won at gambling — often used in pl.

²winning *adj* : ATTRACTIVE, CHARMING ⟨a *winning* smile⟩ — **win•ning•ly** \-iŋ-lē\ *adv*

win•now \ˈwin-ō\ *vt* **1 a** : to remove (as chaff from grain) by a current of air **b** : to subject (as grain) to a current of air to remove waste **2** : to get rid of (something unwanted) or to sort or separate (something) as if by winnowing [Old English *windwian*]

win•now•er \ˈwin-ə-wər\ *n* : one that winnows; *esp* : a winnowing machine

wino \ˈwī-nō\ *n, pl* **win•os** : one who is habitually drunk especially on wine

win•some \ˈwin-səm\ *adj* **1** : causing joy or pleasure : WINNING, CHARMING **2** : CHEERFUL 1a, HAPPY [Old English *wynsum*, from *wynn* "joy"] — **win•some•ly** *adv* — **win•some•ness** *n*

¹win•ter \ˈwint-ər\ *n* **1 a** : the season between autumn and spring comprising in the northern hemisphere usually the months of December, January, and February or as determined astronomically extending from the December solstice to the March equinox **b** : the colder half of the year **2** : YEAR ⟨many *winters* ago⟩ **3** : a time or season of inactivity or decay [Old English]

²winter *vb* **win•tered**; **win•ter•ing** \ˈwint-ə-riŋ, ˈwin-triŋ\ **1** : to pass or live through the winter ⟨the cattle *wintered* on the range⟩ **2** : to keep, feed, or manage during the winter ⟨*winter* livestock⟩

³winter *adj* : occurring in or surviving the winter; *esp* : sown in autumn for harvesting in the following spring or summer ⟨*winter* wheat⟩ ⟨*winter* rye⟩

win•ter•ber•ry \ˈwint-ər-ˌber-ē\ *n* : any of various American hollies with bright red berries persistent through the winter

win•ter•green \ˈwint-ər-ˌgrēn\ *n* **1** : any of several low-growing evergreen plants related to the heaths; *esp* : one with white bell-shaped flowers followed by spicy red berries **2** : an essential oil from the common wintergreen or its flavor; *also* : something flavored with it

win•ter•ize \ˈwint-ə-ˌrīz\ *vt* : to make ready for winter — **win•ter•iza•tion** \ˌwint-ə-rə-ˈzā-shən\ *n*

win•ter–kill \ˈwint-ər-ˌkil\ *vb* : to kill (as a plant) by exposure to winter conditions; *also* : to die as a result of such exposure — **winterkill** *n*

winter melon *n* : a muskmelon with smooth rind and sweet white or greenish flesh that keeps well

winter quarters *n pl* : a winter residence or station (as of a military unit)

winter squash *n* : any of various squashes or pumpkins that keep well in storage

win•ter•tide \ˈwint-ər-ˌtīd\ *n* : WINTERTIME

win•ter•time \-ˌtīm\ *n* : the winter season

win through *vi* : to survive difficulties and reach a desired or satisfactory end

win•try \ˈwin-trē\ *adj* **win•tri•er**; **-est 1** : of or characteristic of winter : coming in winter : having to do with winter ⟨*wintry* weather⟩ **2** : CHILLY 3, COLD, CHEERLESS ⟨a *wintry* welcome⟩ — **win•tri•ly** \-trə-lē\ *adv* — **win•tri•ness** \-trē-nəs\ *n*

winy *or* **win•ey** \ˈwī-nē\ *adj* **1** : having the taste or qualities of wine **2** : crisply fresh ⟨*winy* autumn breezes⟩

¹wipe \ˈwīp\ *vt* **1** : to clean or dry by rubbing ⟨*wipe* dishes⟩ **2** : to remove by or as if by rubbing ⟨*wipe* away tears⟩ ⟨*wipe* up spilled milk⟩ **3** : to pass or draw over a surface ⟨*wiped* a hand across my face⟩ [Old English *wīpian*]

²wipe *n* **1** : an act or instance of wiping **2** : something used for wiping

wipe•out \ˈwī-ˌpau̇t\ *n* : a fall from a surfboard

wipe out \wī-ˈpau̇t, ˈwī-\ *vt* **1** : to destroy completely ⟨the regiment was *wiped out*⟩ **2** : to ruin financially ⟨was *wiped out* by a market crash⟩

wip•er \ˈwī-pər\ *n* : one that wipes; *esp* : a device in the form of a rubber squeegee attached to an oscillating arm for wiping a windshield

¹wire \ˈwīr\ *n* **1 a** : metal in the form of a usually very flexible thread or slender rod **b** : a thread or rod of metal **2** *usually pl* **a** : a system of wires used to operate the puppets in a puppet show **b** : hidden or secret influences on a person or organization **3 a** : a line of wire for conducting electrical current — compare CORD 3b **b** : a telephone or telegraph wire or system **c** : TELEGRAM, CABLEGRAM [Old English *wīr*] — **wire•like** \-ˌlīk\ *adj* — **under the wire** : at the last moment

²wire *vb* **1** : to provide with wire; *also* : to provide with electricity ⟨*wire* a farm⟩ **2** : to send or send word to by telegraph **3** : to send a telegraphic message — **wir•able** \ˈwī-rə-bəl\ *adj*

wire cloth *n* : a fabric of woven metallic wire (as for strainers)

wired \ˈwīrd\ *adj* **1** : reinforced or bound with wire ⟨a *wired* container⟩ **2** : having a netting or fence of wire ⟨a *wired* enclosure for chickens⟩

wire gauge *n* : a gauge especially for measuring the diameter of wire or thickness of sheet metal

wire•haired \ˈwīr-ˈhaərd, -ˈheərd\ *adj* : having a stiff wiry outer coat of hair

¹wire•less \ˈwīər-ləs\ *adj* **1** : having no wire **2** *chiefly British* : of or relating to radiotelegraphy, radiotelephony, or radio

²wireless *n* **1** : WIRELESS TELEGRAPHY **2** : RADIOTELEPHONY **3** *chiefly British* : RADIO — **wireless** *vb*

wireless telegraphy *n* : telegraphy carried on by radio waves and without connecting wires

wire•man \ˈwīr-mən\ *n* : a maker of or worker with wire; *esp* : LINEMAN 1

Wire•pho•to \ˈwīr-ˈfōt-ō\ *trademark* — used for a photograph transmitted by electrical signals over telephone wires

wire–pull•er \-ˌpu̇l-ər\ *n* : one who uses secret or underhand means to influence the acts of a person or organization — **wire–pull•ing** \-ˌpu̇l-iŋ\ *n*

wire recorder *n* : a magnetic recorder using magnetic wire

wire recording *n* : magnetic recording on magnetic wire; *also* : the recording made by this process

wire rope *n* : a rope formed wholly or chiefly of wires

wire service *n* : a news agency that sends out syndicated news copy by wire to subscribers

wire•tap \ˈwīr-ˌtap\ *vi* : to tap a telephone or telegraph wire to get information — **wiretap** *n* — **wire•tap•per** *n*

wire•worm \-ˌwərm\ *n* : the slender hard-coated larva of various click beetles that is often destructive to roots

wir•ing \ˈwīr-iŋ\ *n* **1** : the act of providing or using wire **2** : a system of wires; *esp* : an arrangement of wires used for electric distribution

wiry \ˈwīr-ē\ *adj* **wir•i•er**; **wir•i•est 1** : of, relating to, or resembling wire **2** : being slender yet strong and sinewy — **wir•i•ness** \ˈwī-rē-nəs\ *n*

wis•dom \ˈwiz-dəm\ *n* **1 a** : accumulated learning : KNOWLEDGE **b** : ability to discern inner qualities and relationships : INSIGHT **c** : good sense : JUDGMENT **2** : a wise attitude or course of action **3** : the teachings of the ancient sages **4** *cap* — see BIBLE table [Old English *wīsdōm*, from *wīs* "wise"]

Wisdom of Sol•o•mon \-ˈsäl-ə-mən\ — see BIBLE table

wisdom tooth *n* : the last tooth of the full set on each half of each jaw in man [from its being cut usually in the late teens when children were formerly believed to be approaching wisdom]

¹wise \ˈwīz\ *n* : WAY 4a, FASHION — used in such phrases as *in any wise, in no wise, in this wise* [Old English *wīse*]

²wise *adj* **1** : having or showing wisdom, good sense, or good judgment : SENSIBLE **2** : aware of what is going on : INFORMED ⟨was *wise* to our plans⟩ **3** : INSOLENT 1, FRESH [Old English *wīs*] — **wise•ly** *adv*

³wise *vb* : to make or become informed or knowledgeable — usually used with *up*

-wise \ˌwīz\ *adv combining form* **1 a** : in the manner of **b** : in the position or direction of ⟨clock*wise*⟩ ⟨length*wise*⟩ **2** : with regard to : in respect of [Old English *-wīsan*, from *wīse* "manner"]

wise•acre \ˈwī-ˌzā-kər\ *n* : one who pretends to knowledge or cleverness : SMART ALECK [Dutch *wijssegger* "soothsayer", from Old High German *wīzzago*]

¹wise•crack \ˈwīz-ˌkrak\ *n* : a clever, flippant, or sarcastic remark **syn** see JEST

[2]wisecrack *vb* : to make a wisecrack : QUIP — **wise•crack•er** *n*

wise guy \'wīz-,gī\ *n* : SMART ALECK

wi•sen•hei•mer \'wīz-n-,hī-mər\ *n* : one who has the air of knowing all about something or everything : WISEACRE [[2]*wise* + German *-enheimer* (as in German family names such as *Guggenheimer, Oppenheimer*)]

wi•sent \'vē-,zent\ *n* : a nearly extinct European bison [German]

wisent

[1]wish \'wish\ *vb* **1** : to have a desire : long for : WANT ⟨*wish* you were here⟩ ⟨*wish* for a puppy⟩ **2** : to form or express a desire concerning ⟨*wish* you a merry Christmas⟩ **3** : to request by expressing a desire ⟨I *wish* you to go now⟩ [Old English *wȳscan*] **syn** see DESIRE — **wish•er** *n*

[2]wish *n* **1 a** : an act or instance of wishing : WANT, DESIRE **b** : an object of desire : GOAL **2 a** : an expressed will or desire **b** : a request or order expressed as a wish **3** : an invocation of usually good fortune on someone

wish•bone \'wish-,bōn\ *n* : a forked bone in front of the breastbone of a bird consisting chiefly of the fused clavicles [from the superstition that when two people pull it apart the one getting the longer fragment will be granted a wish]

wisteria

wish•ful \'wish-fəl\ *adj* **1** : having a wish : DESIROUS **2** : based on wishes rather than fact ⟨*wishful* thinking⟩ — **wish•ful•ly** \-fə-lē\ *adv* — **wish•ful•ness** *n*

wishy–washy \'wish-ē-,wósh-ē, -,wäsh-\ *adj* **1** : INSIPID **2** : weak in character or determination [reduplication of *washy*]

wisp \'wisp\ *n* **1** : a small bunch of hay or straw **2 a** : a thin strip or fragment **b** : a thready streak ⟨a *wisp* of smoke⟩ **c** : something frail, slight, or fleeting ⟨a *wisp* of a smile⟩ [Middle English] — **wispy** \'wis-pē\ *adj*

wist \'wist\ *vt, archaic* : KNOW [earlier *wis,* from *iwis* "certainly", from Old English *gewis* "certain"]

wis•tar•ia \wis-'tir-ē-ə *also* -'ter-\ *n* : WISTERIA

wis•te•ria \wis-'tir-ē-ə\ *n* : any of a genus of chiefly Asian mostly woody vines of the pea family having compound leaves and showy blue, white, purple, or rose pealike flowers in long hanging clusters [Caspar Wistar, died 1818, American physician]

wist•ful \'wist-fəl\ *adj* : full of unfulfilled longing or desire : YEARNING [blend of *wishful* and obsolete *wistly* "intently"] — **wist•ful•ly** \-fə-lē\ *adv* — **wist•ful•ness** *n*

[1]wit \'wit\ *vb* **wist** \'wist\; **wit•ting**; *present 1st & 3d sing* **wot** \'wät\ *archaic* : KNOW, LEARN [Old English *witan*]

[2]wit *n* **1** : reasoning power : INTELLIGENCE **2** : mental soundness : SANITY — usually used in pl. ⟨scared out of my *wits*⟩ **3 a** : mental capability and resourcefulness — often used in pl. ⟨live by one's *wits*⟩ **b** : the ability to relate seemingly unlike things so as to illuminate or amuse **4** : one noted for making witty remarks [Old English]

• **syn** WIT, HUMOR mean a mode of expression intended to arouse amusement. WIT is more purely intellectual than HUMOR and depends for its effect chiefly on verbal ingenuity or swift perception, especially of the incongruous; HUMOR implies an ability to perceive the ludicrous, the comical, and the absurd in human life and to express these sympathetically and without bitterness.

— **at one's wit's end** *or* **at one's wits' end** : at a loss for a means of solving a problem

wi•tan \'wi-,tän\ *n pl* : members of the witenagemot [Old English, pl. of *wita* "sage, adviser"]

[1]witch \'wich\ *n* **1** : a person believed to have magic powers **2** : an ugly old woman : HAG [Old English *wicca* (masculine) and *wicce* (feminine)]

[2]witch *vb* **1** : BEWITCH **2** : DOWSE

witch•craft \'wich-,kraft\ *n* : the power or practices of a witch : SORCERY

witch doctor *n* : a professional worker of magic in a primitive society resembling a shaman or medicine man

witch•ery \'wich-rē, -ə-rē\ *n, pl* **-er•ies 1 a** : the practice of witchcraft : SORCERY **b** : an act of witchcraft **2** : an irresistible fascination : CHARM

witch•es'–broom \'wich-əz-,brüm, -,brům\ *n* : an abnormal tufted growth of small branches on a tree or shrub caused especially by fungi or viruses

[1]witch•grass \'wich-,gras\ *n* : QUACK GRASS [probably alteration of *quitch* (*grass*), from Old English *cwice*]

[2]witchgrass *n* : a North American grass with slender brushy panicles that is often a weed on cultivated land [[1]*witch*]

witch ha•zel \'wich-,hā-zəl\ *n* **1** : any of a genus of shrubs with slender-petaled yellow flowers borne in late fall or early spring; *esp* : one of eastern North America that blooms in the fall **2** : an alcoholic solution of material from the bark of the common witch hazel used as a soothing and mildly astringent lotion [Old English *wice,* a tree with pliant branches]

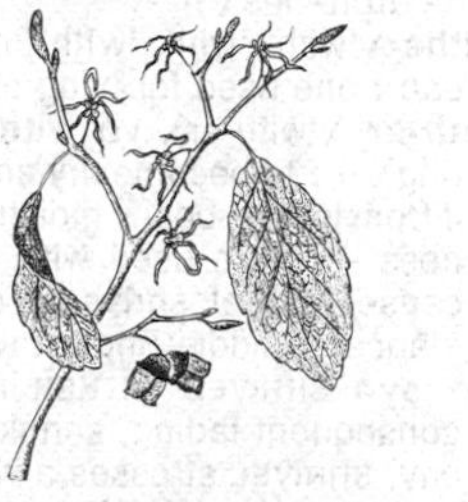
witch hazel 1

witch–hunt \-,hənt\ *n* **1** : a searching out and persecution of persons accused of witchcraft **2** : the searching out and deliberate harassment of those (as political opponents) with unpopular views — **witch–hunt•er** *n*

witch•ing \'wich-ing\ *adj* **1** : of, relating to, or suitable for sorcery or supernatural occurrences ⟨the *witching* hour⟩ **2** : very attractive

wi•te•na•ge•mot *or* **wi•te•na•ge•mote** \'wit-n-ə-gə-,mōt\ *n* : an Anglo-Saxon council of nobles, prelates, and officials convened to advise the king on administrative and judicial matters [Old English *witena gemōt,* from *wita* "sage, adviser" + *gemōt* "assembly"]

with \wit͟h, 'wit͟h, with, 'with\ *prep* **1 a** : in opposition to : AGAINST ⟨fought *with* a neighbor⟩ **b** : so as to be separated from ⟨parting *with* friends⟩ **2** : in mutual relation to ⟨talking *with* a friend⟩ ⟨trade *with* other countries⟩ **3** : as regards : TOWARD ⟨angry *with* me⟩ **4 a** : compared to : equal to ⟨on equal terms *with* the others⟩ **b** : on the side of ⟨voted *with* the majority⟩ **c** : as well as ⟨can sing *with* the best of them⟩ **5 a** : in the judgment or estimation of ⟨in good standing *with* our classmates⟩ **b** : in the experience or practice of ⟨*with* them a promise is a real obligation⟩ **6 a** : by means of ⟨write *with* a pen⟩ **b** : because of ⟨danced *with* joy⟩ **7** : having or showing as manner of action or attendant circumstance ⟨spoke *with* ease⟩ ⟨stood there *with* hat in hand⟩ **8 a** : in possession of ⟨animals *with* horns⟩ ⟨arrived *with* the news⟩ **b** : characterized or distinguished by ⟨a person *with* a hot temper⟩ **9 a** : in the company of ⟨went to the movies *with* me⟩ : in addition to ⟨your money, *with* ours, will be enough⟩ **b** : inclusive of ⟨costs five dollars *with* the tax⟩ **c** : that contains ⟨tea *with* sugar⟩ **10 a** : at the time of ⟨*with* the outbreak of war they went home⟩ : at the same time as ⟨rose *with* the sun⟩ **b** : in proportion to ⟨the pressure varies *with* the depth⟩ **11** : in the possession or care of ⟨left the money *with* your cousin⟩ **12** : in spite of ⟨*with* all your cleverness, you failed⟩ **13** : in the direction of ⟨drift *with* the current⟩ ⟨easier to run *with* the wind than against it⟩ [Old English, "against, from, with"] **syn** see BY

[1]with•al \wit͟h-'ól, with-\ *adv* **1** : together with this : BESIDES **2** : on the other hand : NEVERTHELESS [Middle English, from *with* + *all, al* "all"]

[2]withal *prep, archaic* : WITH — used with a preceding relative or interrogative pronoun as its object

with•draw \wit͟h-'dró, with-\ *vb* **-drew** \-'drü\; **-drawn** \-'drón\; **-draw•ing 1** : to take back or away usually from a

\ə\ **abut**	\aů\ **out**	\i\ **tip**	\ó\ **saw**	\ů\ **foot**
\ər\ **further**	\ch\ **chin**	\ī\ **life**	\ói\ **coin**	\y\ **yet**
\a\ **mat**	\e\ **pet**	\j\ **job**	\th\ **thin**	\yü\ **few**
\ā\ **take**	\ē\ **easy**	\ng\ **sing**	\t͟h\ **this**	\yů\ **cure**
\ä\ **cot, cart**	\g\ **go**	\ō\ **bone**	\ü\ **food**	\zh\ **vision**

holder, a place, or a condition : REMOVE ⟨*withdraw* money from the bank⟩ ⟨the troops were *withdrawn* from combat⟩ **2** : to call back (as from consideration or circulation) : RECALL, RESCIND ⟨*withdrew* the nomination⟩ ⟨*withdraw* the product⟩; *also* : RETRACT, RECANT ⟨*withdrew* the remarks and apologized⟩ **3 a** : to go away : RETREAT, LEAVE ⟨*withdrew* to the country⟩ **b** : to end one's participation or involvement in something ⟨ready to *withdraw* from the firm⟩ [Middle English *withdrawen,* from *with* "from" + *drawen* "to draw"] — **with•draw•able** \-ˈdrȯ-ə-bəl\ *adj*

with•draw•al \-ˈdrȯ-əl, -ˈdrȯl\ *n* : an act or instance of withdrawing (as a removal, a retreat, or a retraction)

with•drawn \-ˈdrȯn\ *adj* **1** : OUT-OF-THE-WAY 1, SECLUDED ⟨*withdrawn* mountain communities⟩ **2** : socially detached and unresponsive ⟨a *withdrawn* manner⟩ — **with•drawn•ness** \-ˈdrȯn–nəs\ *n*

withe \ˈwith, ˈwith, ˈwīth\ *n* : a slender flexible branch or twig; *esp* : one used for tying or binding [Old English *withthe*]

with•er \ˈwith-ər\ *vb* **with•ered**; **with•er•ing** \ˈwith-ring, -ə-ring\ **1** : to become dry and sapless; *esp* : to shrivel from or as if from loss of bodily moisture **2** : to lose vitality, force, or freshness — often used with *away* **3** : to cause to wither **4** : to cause to feel shriveled or blighted ⟨*withered* them with a glance⟩ [Middle English *widren*]

• **syn** SHRIVEL: WITHER implies the loss of vital moisture with consequent fading, shrinking, and approaching death and decay; SHRIVEL stresses a wrinkling and shrinking as by drought or intense heat or blight.

with•er•ing *adj* : acting or serving to destroy ⟨a *withering* fire from the enemy⟩ ⟨*withering* criticism⟩

with•er•ite \ˈwith-ə-ˌrīt\ *n* : a mineral $BaCO_3$ consisting of a carbonate of barium occurring as crystals and in masses [German *witherit,* from William *Withering,* died 1799, English physician]

with•ers \ˈwith-ərz\ *n pl* : the ridge between the shoulder bones of a horse; *also* : the corresponding part in other four-footed animals [probably derived from Old English *wither* "against"]

with•hold \with-ˈhōld, with-\ *vt* **-held** \-ˈheld\; **-hold•ing 1** : to hold back : RESTRAIN ⟨*withhold* an angry answer⟩; *also* : RETAIN **2** : to refrain from granting, giving, or allowing ⟨*withhold* permission⟩ **3** : to deduct (withholding tax) from income [Middle English *withholden,* from *with* "from" + *holden* "to hold"] — **with•hold•er** *n*

withholding tax *n* : a tax withheld from income at the source

¹with•in \with-ˈin, with-\ *adv* **1** : in or into the interior : INSIDE **2** : inside oneself : INWARDLY ⟨calm without but furious *within*⟩ [Old English *withinnan,* from *with* + *innan* "inwardly, within", from *in*]

²within *prep* **1** — used to indicate enclosure or containment ⟨*within* the house⟩ ⟨*within* each mind⟩ **2** : falling inside expressed or implied limits: as **a** : before the end of ⟨left *within* a week⟩ **b** : inside the limitations of ⟨live *within* one's means⟩ **c** : in or into the scope, sphere, or range of ⟨*within* reach⟩ ⟨*within* sight⟩

³within *n* : an inner place or area ⟨revolt from *within*⟩

¹with•out \with-ˈaùt, with-\ *prep* **1** : OUTSIDE 1, 2 **2 a** : not having : LACKING ⟨*without* food⟩ **b** : with absence or omission of ⟨listened *without* answering⟩ [Old English *withūtan,* from *with* + *ūtan* "outside", from *ūt* "out"]

²without *adv* **1** : on the outside **2** : with something lacking or absent ⟨has learned to do *without*⟩

³without *n* : an outer place or area ⟨came from *without*⟩

with•stand \with-ˈstand, with-\ *vt* **-stood** \-ˈstùd\; **-stand•ing** : to stand against : RESIST; *esp* : to oppose (as an attack or bad influence) successfully [Old English *withstandan,* from *with* "against" + *standan* "to stand"] **syn** see OPPOSE

withy \ˈwith-ē\ *n, pl* **with•ies** : OSIER 1 [Old English *wīthig*]

wit•less \ˈwit-ləs\ *adj* : lacking wit or understanding : FOOLISH — **wit•less•ly** *adv* — **wit•less•ness** *n*

wit•loof \ˈwit-ˌlōf\ *n* : CHICORY; *also* : ENDIVE 2 [Dutch dialect *witloof* "chicory", from Dutch *wit* "white" + *loof* "foliage"]

¹wit•ness \ˈwit-nəs\ *n* **1 a** : an attesting of a fact or event : TESTIMONY **b** : public testimony to a religious faith **2** : one that gives evidence; *esp* : one who testifies in a cause or before a court **3 a** : one present at a transaction so as to be able to testify to its having taken place **b** : one who has personal knowledge or experience of something **4** : something serving as evidence or proof : SIGN **5** *cap* : JEHOVAH'S WITNESS [Old English *witnes* "knowledge, testimony, witness", from ²*wit*]

²witness *vb* **1** : to bear witness : ATTEST, TESTIFY **2** : to furnish legal witness of ⟨*witness* the making of a will⟩ **3** : to furnish proof of : INDICATE **4** : to be a witness of ⟨thousands *witnessed* the parade⟩

witness stand *n* : an area from which a witness gives evidence in a court

wit•ted \ˈwit-əd\ *adj* : having wit or understanding — usually used in combination ⟨dull-*witted*⟩

wit•ti•cism \ˈwit-ə-ˌsiz-əm\ *n* : a witty saying [*witty* + *-cism* (as in *criticism*)]

wit•ting•ly \ˈwit-ing-lē\ *adv* : with knowledge or awareness of what one is doing : CONSCIOUSLY

wit•ty \ˈwit-ē\ *adj* **wit•ti•er**; **-est** : marked by or full of wit ⟨a *witty* writer⟩ ⟨a *witty* remark⟩ — **wit•ti•ly** \ˈwit-l-ē\ *adv* — **wit•ti•ness** \ˈwit-ē-nəs\ *n*

wive \ˈwīv\ *vb* **1** : to marry a woman **2** : to take for a wife [Old English *wīfian,* from *wīf* "woman, wife"]

wives *pl of* WIFE

wiz•ard \ˈwiz-ərd\ *n* **1** : MAGICIAN 1, SORCERER **2** : a very clever or skillful person ⟨a *wizard* at chess⟩ [Middle English *wysard,* from *wis, wys* "wise"]

wiz•ard•ry \ˈwiz-ər-drē\ *n, pl* **-ries 1** : the art of practices of a wizard : SORCERY **2** : extraordinary skill or ability

wiz•ened \ˈwiz-nd\ *also* **wiz•en** \ˈwiz-n\ *adj* : dried, shriveled, and wrinkled especially with age [Old English *wisnian* "to dry up, wither"]

woad \ˈwōd\ *n* : a European herb of the mustard family formerly grown for the blue dyestuff yielded by its leaves; *also* : this dyestuff [Old English *wād*]

¹wob•ble *also* **wab•ble** \ˈwäb-əl\ *vb* **wob•bled**; **wob•bling** \ˈwäb-ling, -ə-ling\ **1 a** : to move or cause to move with an irregular rocking or side-to-side motion **b** : TREMBLE, QUAVER ⟨a voice that *wobbles*⟩ **2** : WAVER 1 [probably from Low German *wabbeln*] — **wob•bler** \ˈwäb-lər, -ə-lər\ *n* — **wob•bly** \ˈwäb-lē, -ə-lē\ *adj*

²wobble *also* **wabble** *n* : a wobbling action or movement ⟨the wheel had a bad *wobble*⟩

¹woe \ˈwō\ *interj* — used to express grief, regret, or distress [Old English *wā*]

²woe *n* **1** : a condition of deep suffering from misfortune, affliction, or grief **2** : CALAMITY, MISFORTUNE ⟨economic *woes*⟩

woe•be•gone \ˈwō-bi-ˌgȯn, -ˌgän\ *adj* : exhibiting great woe, sorrow, or misery ⟨*woebegone* faces⟩ [Middle English *wo begon,* from *wo* "woe" + *begon,* past participle of *begon* "to go about, beset", from Old English *begān,* from *be-* + *gān* "to go"]

woe•ful *also* **wo•ful** \ˈwō-fəl\ *adj* **1** : full of woe : WRETCHED **2** : involving or bringing woe ⟨a *woeful* sight⟩ **3** : PALTRY, DEPLORABLE ⟨a *woeful* lack of knowledge⟩ — **woe•ful•ly** \-fə-lē, -flē\ *adv* — **woe•ful•ness** \-fəl-nəs\ *n*

woke *past of* WAKE

woken *past participle of* WAKE

wold \ˈwōld\ *n* : an upland plain or stretch of rolling country without woods [Old English *weald, wald* "forest"]

¹wolf \ˈwùlf\ *n, pl* **wolves** \ˈwùlvz\ *also* **wolf 1** : any of several large erect-eared bushy-tailed predatory mammals that resemble the related dogs and tend to hunt in packs — compare COYOTE, JACKAL **2 a** (1) : a person resembling a wolf (as in ferocity or guile) (2) : a man forward and zealous in attentions to women **b** : dire poverty ⟨trying to keep the *wolf* from the door⟩ [Old English *wulf*] — **wolf•ish** \ˈwùl-fish\ *adj* — **wolf•like** \ˈwùl-ˌflīk\ *adj* — **wolf in sheep's clothing** : one who hides a hostile intention behind a friendly manner

²wolf *vt* : to eat greedily : DEVOUR

wolf•hound \ˈwùlf-ˌhaùnd\ *n* : any of several large dogs used especially formerly in hunting large animals (as wolves)

wol•fram \ˈwùl-frəm\ *n* : TUNGSTEN [German]

wol•fram•ite \ˈwùl-frə-ˌmīt\ *n* : a brownish or grayish mineral that consists of an iron manganese tungstate, occurs in crystals and masses, and is a source of tungsten

wolf spider *n* : any of various active wandering ground spiders

wol•ver•ine \ˌwùl-və-ˈrēn\ *n* : a blackish shaggy-furred flesh-eating mammal of northern North America that is related to the martens and sables and is noted especially for its strength [probably derived from *wolv-* (as in *wolves*)]

wom•an \ˈwùm-ən\ *n, pl* **wom•en** \ˈwim-ən\ **1** : an adult female person **2** : WOMANKIND **3** : a feminine nature : womanly character **4** : a female servant or attendant [Old English *wīfman,* from *wīf* "woman, wife" + *man* "person, man"] —

woman *adj*

wom•an•hood \'wu̇m-ən-ˌhu̇d\ *n* **1** : the state of being a woman **2** : womanly qualities **3** : WOMANKIND

wom•an•ish \'wu̇m-ə-nish\ *adj* **1** : characteristic of a woman **2** : suitable to a woman rather than to a man — **wom•an•ish•ly** *adv* — **wom•an•ish•ness** *n*

wolverine

wom•an•kind \'wu̇m-ən-ˌkīnd\ *n* : female human beings

wom•an•like \-ˌlīk\ *adj* : resembling or characteristic of a woman : WOMANLY

wom•an•ly \-lē\ *adj* **1** : having qualities held to be appropriate to a woman **2** : befitting an adult woman ⟨*womanly* qualities⟩ — **wom•an•li•ness** *n*

woman suffrage *n* : the possession and exercise of the suffrage by women

womb \'wüm\ *n* **1** : UTERUS 1 **2** : a place where something is generated or developed [Old English] — **wombed** \'wümd\ *adj*

wom•bat \'wäm-ˌbat\ *n* : any of several stocky burrowing Australian marsupials resembling small bears [native name in New South Wales, Australia]

wom•en•folk \'wim-ən-ˌfōk\ *or* **wom•en•folks** \-ˌfōks\ *n pl* : WOMANKIND

1**won** \'wən\ *past of* WIN

2**won** \'wo̊n\ *n* **1** : the basic monetary unit of North Korea and South Korea **2** : a coin representing this unit [Korean *wån*]

1**won•der** \'wən-dər\ *n* **1 a** : a cause of astonishment or surprise : MARVEL **b** : MIRACLE **2 a** : a feeling (as of awed astonishment or of uncertainty) aroused by something extraordinary or affecting **b** : the quality of exciting wonder ⟨the charm and *wonder* of the scene⟩ [Old English *wundor*]

2**wonder** *vb* **won•dered**; **won•der•ing** \-də-riŋ, -driŋ\ **1** : to feel surprise or amazement **2** : to feel curiosity or doubt ⟨*wondered* about the cost⟩ — **won•der•er** \-dər-ər\ *n*

wonder drug *n* : a medicinal substance of outstanding effectiveness

won•der•ful \'wən-dər-fəl\ *adj* **1** : exciting wonder : MARVELOUS **2** : unusually good : ADMIRABLE — **won•der•ful•ly** \-fə-lē, -flē\ *adv* — **won•der•ful•ness** \-fəl-nəs\ *n*

won•der•land \'wən-dər-ˌland, -lənd\ *n* **1** : a fairylike imaginary realm **2** : a place that excites admiration or wonder ⟨a scenic *wonderland*⟩

won•der•ment \-mənt\ *n* **1** : a state or feeling of wonder : ASTONISHMENT, SURPRISE **2** : curiosity about something

won•der–work•er \-ˌwər-kər\ *n* : one that performs wonders

won•drous \'wən-drəs\ *adj* : WONDERFUL 1, MARVELOUS — **wondrous** *adv, archaic* — **won•drous•ly** *adv* — **won•drous•ness** *n*

1**wont** \'wo̊nt, 'wōnt\ *adj* : ACCUSTOMED 2, USED ⟨as they are *wont* to do⟩ [Middle English, from past participle of *wonen* "to dwell, be used to", from Old English *wunian*]

2**wont** *n* : CUSTOM, USAGE ⟨according to our *wont*⟩

won't \wōnt, 'wōnt, 'wənt\ : will not

wont•ed \'wo̊nt-əd, 'wōnt-\ *adj* : ACCUSTOMED 2, USUAL ⟨took my *wonted* rest⟩ — **wont•ed•ly** *adv* — **wont•ed•ness** *n*

woo \'wü\ *vb* **1 a** : to try to gain the love of : make love : COURT **b** : to try to win over ⟨a young author trying to *woo* the reader⟩ **2** : to seek usually urgently to gain or bring about ⟨a clever auctioneer *wooing* dollars from the audience⟩ [Old English *wōgian*]

1**wood** \'wu̇d\ *n* **1 a** : a dense growth of trees usually greater in extent than a grove and smaller than a forest — often used in pl. ⟨a thick *woods* runs along the ridge⟩ **b** : WOODLAND **2** : a hard fibrous substance that is basically xylem and makes up the greater part of the stems and branches of trees or shrubs beneath the bark; *also* : this material suitable or prepared for some use (as burning or building) **3** : something made of wood; *esp* : a golf club having a wooden head [Old English *wudu*] — **out of the woods** : escaped from peril or difficulty

2**wood** *adj* **1** : WOODEN 1 **2** : suitable for cutting or working wood ⟨*wood* chisels⟩ **3** *or* **woods** \'wu̇dz\ : living or growing in woods

wood alcohol *n* : METHANOL

wood anemone *n* : any of several anemones that grow in open woodlands

wood•bin \'wu̇d-ˌbin\ *n* : a bin for holding firewood

wood•bine \'wu̇d-ˌbīn\ *n* : any of several climbing vines of Europe and America (as a honeysuckle or the Virginia creeper) [Old English *wudubinde*, from *wudu* "wood" + *bindan* "to tie, bind"; from its winding around trees]

wood block *n* : WOODCUT

wood–carv•er \'wu̇d-ˌkär-vər\ *n* : a person who carves usually ornamental objects of wood — **wood carv•ing** \-viŋ\ *n*

woodchuck

wood•chop•per \-ˌchäp-ər\ *n* : one engaged especially in chopping down trees

wood•chuck \-ˌchək\ *n* : a grizzled thickset marmot of the northeastern United States and Canada; *also* : a related rodent of mountainous western North America [by folk etymology from Ojibwa *otchig* "fisher, marten" or Cree *otcheck* "fisher"]

wood•cock \-ˌkäk\ *n, pl* **woodcocks** *or* **woodcock** : either of two long-billed mottled and usually brown birds related to the snipe; *esp* : an American upland bird prized as a game bird

woodcock

wood•craft \-ˌkraft\ *n* **1** : knowledge about the woods and how to take care of oneself in them **2** : skill in working with or making things of wood

wood•cut \-ˌkət\ *n* **1** : a printing surface consisting of a wooden block with a usually pictorial design cut with the grain **2** : a print from a woodcut

wood•cut•ter \-ˌkət-ər\ *n* : one that cuts wood especially as an occupation

wood duck *n* : a showy American duck that nests in trees and in the male has a large crest and plumage varied with green, purple, black, white, and chestnut

wood•ed \'wu̇d-əd\ *adj* : covered with trees

wood•en \'wu̇d-n\ *adj* **1** : made of wood **2 a** : lacking flexibility : STIFF ⟨a *wooden* expression⟩ **b** : lacking ease, interest, or zest ⟨written in a *wooden* style⟩ — **wood•en•ly** *adv* — **wood•en•ness** \-n-nəs\ *n*

wood engraving *n* **1** : the art or process of cutting a design upon wood and especially upon the end grain of wood for use as a printing surface; *also* : such a printing surface **2** : a design printed from a wood engraving

wood•en•ware \'wu̇d-n-ˌwaər, -ˌweər\ *n* : articles made of wood for domestic use

wood ibis *n* : a large wading bird closely related to the Old World storks that frequents wooded swamps of South and Central America and the southern United States

1**wood•land** \'wu̇d-lənd, -ˌland\ *n* : land covered with woody vegetation : FOREST — **wood•land•er** \-ər\ *n*

2**woodland** *adj* **1** : of, relating to, or being woodland **2** : growing or living in woodland

wood•lot \'wu̇d-ˌlät\ *n* : an area of trees kept usually to meet fuel and timber needs

wood louse *n* : a small flat grayish crustacean that lives especially under stones and bark — called also *pill bug, sow bug*

wood•man \'wu̇d-mən\ *n* : WOODSMAN

wood•note \-ˌnōt\ *n* : a sound or call (as of a bird) natural in a wood

wood nymph *n* : a nymph living in the woods or a particular tree — called also *dryad*

wood•peck•er \ˈwu̇d-ˌpek-ər\ *n* **:** any of numerous usually brightly marked birds with specialized feet and stiff spiny tail feathers used in climbing or resting on tree trunks and a very hard bill used to drill into trees for insect food or to excavate nesting cavities

woodpecker

wood•pile \-ˌpīl\ *n* **:** a pile of wood and especially firewood
wood pulp *n* **:** pulp from wood used in making cellulose derivatives (as paper or rayon)
wood pussy *n* **:** SKUNK 1
wood rat *n* **:** any of numerous native voles of the southern and western United States with soft pale fur, well-furred tails, and large ears
wood ray *n* **:** XYLEM RAY
woods *variant of* WOOD
wood•shed \ˈwu̇d-ˌshed\ *n* **:** a shed for storing wood and especially firewood
woods•man \ˈwu̇dz-mən\ *n* **:** one who frequents or works in the woods; *esp* **:** one skilled in woodcraft
wood sorrel *n* **:** any of a genus of herbs with acid sap, compound leaves, and regular 5-petaled flowers; *esp* **:** a stemless herb having leaves with three leaflets that is held to be the original shamrock
woodsy \ˈwu̇d-zē\ *adj* **:** relating to or suggestive of woods
wood thrush *n* **:** a large thrush of eastern North America noted for its loud clear song
wood turning *n* **:** the art or process of fashioning useful articles from wooden pieces or blocks by means of a lathe — **wood-turn•er** *n*
wood turpentine : TURPENTINE 2b
wood warbler *n* **:** WARBLER 2b
wood•wax•en \ˈwu̇d-ˌwak-sən\ *n* **:** a low bushy yellow-flowered Eurasian shrub of the pea family grown for ornament or formerly as the source of a yellow dye [Old English *wuduweaxe*]
wood•wind \ˈwu̇d-ˌwind\ *n* **1 :** one of a group of wind instruments including flutes, clarinets, oboes, bassoons, and sometimes saxophones **2** *pl* **:** the woodwind section of a band or orchestra — **woodwind** *adj*
wood•work \-ˌwərk\ *n* **:** work made of wood; *esp* **:** interior fittings (as moldings or stairways) of wood
wood•work•ing \-ˌwər-king\ *n* **:** the act, process, or occupation of working with wood — **wood•work•er** \-kər\ *n* — **woodworking** *adj*
woody \ˈwu̇d-ē\ *adj* **wood•i•er**; **-est 1 :** abounding or overgrown with trees **2 :** of or containing wood or wood fibers **:** LIGNEOUS **3 :** characteristic of or resembling wood ⟨a *woody* texture⟩ — **wood•i•ness** *n*
woo•er \ˈwü-ər\ *n* **:** one that woos **:** SUITOR
woof \ˈwu̇f, ˈwüf\ *n* **1 :** the threads that cross the warp in a woven fabric **2 :** a woven fabric or its texture [Old English *ōwef,* from *on* + *wefan* "to weave"]

woof 1: *dark* woof, *light* warp

woof•er \ˈwu̇f-ər\ *n* **:** a loudspeaker that is usually larger than a tweeter, is responsive only to the lower acoustic frequencies, and is used for reproducing sounds of low pitch [from *woof* "to make a low gruff sound", of imitative origin]
wool \ˈwu̇l\ *n* **1 :** the heavy soft wavy or curly undercoat of various mammals and especially the sheep **2 :** a product of wool; *esp* **:** a woven fabric or garment of such fabric **3 a :** dense hair especially on a plant **b :** material (as of glass or metal) drawn or formed into a thready mass **c :** short thick often crisp curly hair on a human head [Old English *wull*] — **wooled** \ˈwu̇ld\ *adj*
[1]**wool•en** *or* **wool•len** \ˈwu̇l-ən\ *adj* **1 :** made of wool — compare WORSTED **2 :** of or relating to the manufacture or sale of woolen products ⟨a *woolen* mill⟩
[2]**woolen** *or* **woollen** *n* **1 :** a fabric made of wool **2 :** garments of woolen fabric — usually used in pl.
wool•gath•er•ing \ˈwu̇l-ˌgath-ring, -ə-ring\ *n* **:** idle daydreaming
[1]**wool•ly** *also* **wooly** \ˈwu̇l-ē\ *adj* **wool•li•er**; **-est 1 a :** of, relating to, or bearing wool **b :** resembling wool **2 :** lacking in clearness **:** BLURRY ⟨*woolly* thinking⟩ **3 :** marked by a lack of order or restraint — **wool•li•ness** *n*
[2]**wool•ly** *also* **wool•ie** *or* **wooly** \ˈwu̇l-ē\ *n, pl* **wool•lies :** a garment made from wool; *esp* **:** underclothing of knitted wool — usually used in pl.
woolly aphid *n* **:** any of several plant lice that secrete a dense coating of woolly wax filaments
woolly bear *n* **:** any of various rather large very hairy moth caterpillars
woolly mammoth *n* **:** a heavy-coated mammoth of the colder parts of the Northern Hemisphere known from fossil remains, from palaeolithic drawings, and from entire frozen bodies unearthed in Siberia

woolly mammoth

wool•sack \ˈwu̇l-ˌsak\ *n* **1 :** a sack for wool **2 :** the official seat of the lord chancellor or his deputy in the House of Lords
woo•zy \ˈwü-zē\ *adj* **woo•zi•er**; **-est 1 :** having the senses dulled **2 :** affected with dizziness, mild nausea, or weakness **:** SICK [probably alteration of *oozy*] — **woo•zi•ly** \-zə-lē\ *adv* — **woo•zi•ness** \-zē-nəs\ *n*
Worces•ter•shire sauce \ˌwu̇s-tər-ˌshiər-, ˌwu̇s-tə-, -shər\ *n* **:** a pungent sauce originally made in Worcester, England, of ingredients that include soy, vinegar, and garlic
[1]**word** \ˈwərd\ *n* **1 a :** something that is said **b** *pl* **:** TALK, DISCOURSE **c :** a brief remark or conversation **2 a :** a speech sound or series of speech sounds that symbolizes and communicates a meaning without being divisible into smaller units capable of independent use **b :** a written or printed character or combination of characters representing a spoken word **c :** a combination of electrical or magnetic impulses conveying a unit of information in communication and computer work **3 :** ORDER, COMMAND ⟨don't advance until you get the *word*⟩ **4** *often cap* **a :** LOGOS **b :** GOSPEL 1a **c :** the expressed or manifested mind and will of God **5 :** NEWS 1, INFORMATION ⟨got *word* of the accident⟩ **6 :** PROMISE, DECLARATION **7 :** a quarrelsome utterance or conversation — usually used in pl. ⟨they had *words* and parted in anger⟩ **8 :** a verbal signal **:** PASSWORD [Old English] — **in a word :** in short — **in so many words :** in precisely these words — **word for word :** in the exact words **:** VERBATIM
[2]**word** *vt* **:** to express in words **:** PHRASE
word•age \ˈwərd-ij\ *n* **:** a quantity or number of words
word•book \ˈwərd-ˌbu̇k\ *n* **:** VOCABULARY 1, DICTIONARY
word class *n* **:** a linguistic form class whose members are words; *esp* **:** PART OF SPEECH
word–hoard \ˈwərd-ˌhōrd, -ˌhȯrd\ *n* **:** a supply of words **:** VOCABULARY
word•ing \ˈwərd-ing\ *n* **1 :** expression in words **2 :** the manner or style of expressing in words **:** PHRASING
word•less \ˈwərd-ləs\ *adj* **1 :** not expressed in or accompanied by words **2 :** SILENT 1a, SPEECHLESS — **word•less•ly** *adv* — **word•less•ness** *n*
word of mouth : oral communication
word order *n* **:** the order of arrangement of words in a phrase, clause, or sentence
word•play \ˈwərd-ˌplā\ *n* **:** verbal wit
word stress *n* **:** the manner in which stresses are distributed on the syllables of a word — called also *word accent*
wordy \ˈwərd-ē\ *adj* **word•i•er**; **-est :** using or containing many or too many words **:** VERBOSE — **word•i•ly** \ˈwərd-l-ē\ *adv* — **word•i•ness** \ˈwərd-ē-nəs\ *n*
wore *past of* WEAR
[1]**work** \ˈwərk\ *n* **1 a :** the use of strength or ability to get something done **b :** the activity engaged in as a means of livelihood **:** OCCUPATION; *also* **:** the place of one's employment ⟨didn't go to *work* today⟩ **c :** something that needs to be done **:** TASK

⟨we've *work* to do⟩ **2 :** the energy expended by a force acting over a given distance **3 a :** a particular method or manner of working ⟨careful police *work*⟩ **b :** the manner or quality of working : WORKMANSHIP ⟨careless *work*⟩ **4** *pl* **:** a place where industrial labor is carried on : PLANT, FACTORY ⟨a locomotive *works*⟩ **5** *pl* **:** the working or moving parts of a mechanical device ⟨the *works* of a watch⟩ **6 :** a product of effort, exertion, or skill ⟨their *work* with retarded children⟩; *esp* **:** an artistic production **7** *pl* **:** performance of moral or religious acts ⟨salvation achieved through good *works*⟩ **8 :** effective operation : EFFECT **9 :** the material that is operated on at some stage in a process ⟨place the *work* to the right of the machine⟩ **10** *pl* **:** everything possessed, available, or appropriate ⟨ordered a hot dog with the *works*⟩ [Old English *werc, weorc*] — **at work 1 :** engaged in working : BUSY; *esp* **:** engaged in one's regular occupation **2 :** having effect — **in the works :** in process of preparation, development, or completion — **out of work :** without regular employment : JOBLESS

2**work** *adj* **1 :** suitable or styled for wear while working ⟨*work* clothes⟩ **2 :** used for work ⟨a *work* elephant⟩

3**work** *vb* **worked** \ˈwərkt\ *or* **wrought** \ˈrȯt\; **work•ing 1 :** to bring to pass : EFFECT **2 :** to fashion or create by expending labor or exertion upon **3 a :** to prepare for use by stirring or kneading **b :** to bring into a desired form by a gradual process of cutting, hammering, scraping, pressing, or stretching ⟨*work* cold steel⟩ **4 :** to set or keep in motion or operation ⟨a pump *worked* by hand⟩ **5 :** to solve (a problem) by reasoning or calculation **6 a :** to cause to toil or labor : get work out of ⟨*work* horses on the road⟩ **b :** to make use of : EXPLOIT **c :** to control or guide the operation of **7 :** to carry on an operation through or in or along ⟨an angler *working* a stream⟩ **8 a :** to get (as oneself or an object) into or out of a condition or position by stages ⟨*work* the nut loose⟩ **b :** CONTRIVE, ARRANGE ⟨if we can *work* it⟩ **9 a :** to practice trickery or deception on for some end ⟨*worked* the management for a free ticket⟩ **b :** EXCITE, PROVOKE ⟨*work* oneself into a rage⟩ **10 a :** to exert oneself physically or mentally especially in sustained effort for a purpose or under compulsion or necessity **b :** to perform a task requiring sustained effort or repeated operations **c :** to perform work regularly for wages **11 :** to function or operate according to plan or design **12 :** to produce the desired effect : SUCCEED ⟨the oil *worked* well⟩ **13 :** to make way slowly and with difficulty **14 :** to react in a specified way to being worked ⟨this wood *works* easily⟩ **15 a :** to be in agitation or restless motion **b :** FERMENT **c :** to move slightly in relation to another part **d :** to get into a specific condition by slow or imperceptible movements ⟨the knot *worked* loose⟩ [Old English *wyrcan*] — **work at :** to be engaged or occupied in — **work on 1 :** AFFECT ⟨*worked on* our sympathies⟩ **2 :** to strive to influence or persuade — **work one's way :** to advance slowly especially against resistance or obstructions

work•able \ˈwər-kə-bəl\ *adj* **1 :** capable of being worked **2 :** FEASIBLE 1, PRACTICABLE — **work•abil•i•ty** \ˌwər-kə-ˈbil-ət-ē\ *n* — **work•able•ness** \ˈwər-kə-bəl-nəs\ *n*

work•a•day \ˈwər-kə-ˌdā\ *adj* **1 :** relating to or suited for working days **2 :** PROSAIC 2, ORDINARY [obsolete *workyday* "workday"]

work•bag \ˈwərk-ˌbag\ *n* **:** a bag for implements or materials for work; *esp* **:** a bag for needlework

work•bas•ket \-ˌbas-kət\ *n* **:** a basket for needlework

work•bench \-ˌbench\ *n* **:** a bench on which work especially of mechanics, machinists, and carpenters is performed

work•book \-ˌbu̇k\ *n* **1 :** a booklet outlining a course of study **2 :** a workman's manual **3 :** a record book of work done **4 :** a student's individual book of problems to be solved directly on the pages

work•box \-ˌbäks\ *n* **:** a box for work instruments and materials

work•day \-ˌdā\ *n* **1 :** a day on which work is performed as distinguished from Sunday or a holiday **2 :** the period of time in a day during which work is performed — **workday** *adj*

worked \ˈwərkt\ *adj* **:** that has been subjected to some process of development, treatment, or manufacture

worked up *adj* **:** emotionally aroused : EXCITED ⟨all *worked up* over the coming wedding⟩

work•er \ˈwər-kər\ *n* **1 a :** one that works **b :** a member of the working class **2 :** one of the members of a colony of social ants, bees, wasps, or termites that are incompletely developed sexually and usually sterile and that perform most of the labor and protective duties of the colony

work farm *n* **:** a farm on which persons convicted of minor law violations are confined and put to work

work force *n* **1 :** the workers engaged in a specific activity ⟨the factory's *work force*⟩ **2 :** the number of workers potentially assignable for any purpose ⟨the nation's *work force*⟩

work•horse \ˈwərk-ˌhȯrs\ *n* **1 :** a horse used chiefly for labor **2 a :** a person who undertakes arduous labor **b :** a markedly useful or durable vehicle, craft, or machine

work•house \-ˌhau̇s\ *n* **1** *British* **:** POORHOUSE **2 :** an institution where persons who have committed minor law violations are confined

1**work•ing** \ˈwər-king\ *adj* **1 a :** doing work especially for a living ⟨*working* people⟩ **b :** that functions ⟨a *working* model⟩ **2 :** good enough to allow work to be done ⟨a *working* majority⟩ ⟨had a *working* knowledge of French⟩ **3 a :** of, relating to, or occupied with work ⟨*working* hours⟩ **b :** used or fit for use in work ⟨*working* clothes⟩

2**working** *n* **:** an excavation or group of excavations made in mining, quarrying, or tunneling — usually used in pl.

working class *n* **:** the class of people who are employed for wages usually in manual labor — **working–class** *adj*

work•ing•man \ˈwər-king-ˌman\ *n* **:** one who works for wages usually at manual labor or in industry

working papers *n pl* **:** official documents legalizing the employment of a minor

work•ing•wom•an \ˈwər-king-ˌwu̇m-ən\ *n* **:** a woman who works for wages

work•less \ˈwər-kləs\ *adj* **:** being without work : UNEMPLOYED — **work•less•ness** *n*

work•man \ˈwərk-mən\ *n* **1 :** WORKINGMAN **2 :** ARTISAN, CRAFTSMAN

work•man•like \-ˌlīk\ *or* **work•man•ly** \-lē\ *adj* **:** exhibiting good workmanship : SKILLFUL

work•man•ship \ˈwərk-mən-ˌship\ *n* **1 :** the art or skill of an artisan : CRAFTSMANSHIP **2 :** the quality or character of a piece of work ⟨the excellent *workmanship* of the desk⟩

workmen's compensation insurance *n* **:** insurance that reimburses an employer for damages that are required to be paid to an employee for injury occurring in the scope and course of employment

work of art : a product of one of the fine arts; *esp* **:** a painting or sculpture of high artistic quality

work off *vt* **:** to get rid of by work or activity ⟨*work off* anger⟩ ⟨*work off* a debt⟩

work•out \ˈwər-ˌkau̇t\ *n* **:** a practice or period of exercise to test or improve one's fitness especially for athletic competition, ability, or performance

work out \wər-ˈkau̇t, ˈwər-\ *vb* **1 :** to bring about by labor and exertion **2 a :** SOLVE **b :** to bring about especially by resolving difficulties ⟨*work out* a compromise⟩ **c :** DEVELOP, ELABORATE ⟨*work out* a plan⟩ **3 :** to discharge (as a debt) by labor **4 :** to exhaust (as a mine) by working **5 a :** to prove effective, practicable, or suitable **b :** to amount to a total or calculated figure — usually used with *to* **6 :** to go through a training session especially in an athletic specialty

work over *vt* **1 :** to do over : REWORK **2 :** to beat up ⟨was *worked over* in a dark alley⟩

work•room \ˈwər-ˌkrüm, -ˌkru̇m\ *n* **:** a room used especially for manual work

work•shop \ˈwərk-ˌshäp\ *n* **1 :** a small establishment where manufacturing or handicrafts are carried on **2 :** a seminar emphasizing free discussion, exchange of ideas, and practical methods and given mainly for adults already employed in the field

work•ta•ble \-ˌtā-bəl\ *n* **:** a table for holding working materials and implements (as for needlework)

work up *vt* **1 :** to stir up : ROUSE **2 :** to produce by mental or physical work

work•week \ˈwər-ˌkwēk\ *n* **:** the hours or days of work in a calendar week ⟨40-hour *workweek*⟩ ⟨a 5-day *workweek*⟩

work•wom•an \-ˌkwu̇m-ən\ *n* **:** a woman who works especially at manual labor or in industry

world \ˈwərld\ *n* **1 :** the earth with its inhabitants and all things upon it **2 :** people in general : HUMANITY **3 :** worldly affairs ⟨withdraw from the *world*⟩ **4 :** the system of created things : UNIVERSE **5 :** a part or section of the earth or its inhabitants by itself **6 :** a state of existence : scene of life and action ⟨the *world* of the future⟩ **7 :** a great number or quantity ⟨a *world* of troubles⟩ **8 :** a distinctive class of persons or their sphere of interest ⟨the musical *world*⟩ **9 :** a heavenly body especially if inhabited **[**Old English *woruld* "human existence, this world, age", literally, "age of man"**]** **syn** see EARTH — **in the world :** among innumerable possibilities : EVER — used as an intensive ⟨what *in the world* is it⟩ — **out of this world :** of extraordinary excellence : SUPERB

world–beat•er \ˈwərld-ˌbēt-ər\ *n* **:** one that excels all others of its kind : CHAMPION

world•ling \ˈwərl-dling, -ling\ *n* **:** a person engrossed in the concerns of this present world

world•ly \ˈwərl-dlē, -lē\ *adj* **world•li•er; -est 1 :** of, relating to, or devoted to this world and its pursuits rather than to spiritual affairs **2 :** WORLDLY-WISE **syn** see EARTHLY — **world•li•ness** *n*

world•ly–mind•ed \ˌwərl-dlē-ˈmīn-dəd, -lē-\ *adj* **:** devoted to or engrossed in worldly interests — **world•ly–mind•ed•ness** *n*

world•ly–wise \ˈwərl-dlē-ˌwīz, -lē-\ *adj* **:** having a practical and often shrewd understanding of human affairs

world power *n* **:** a political unit (as a nation) powerful enough to affect the entire world by its influence or actions

world series *n, often cap W & S* **:** a series of baseball games played each fall between the pennant winners of the major leagues to decide the professional championship

world war *n* **:** a war involving all or most of the chief nations of the world; *esp, cap both Ws* **:** either of two such wars of the 20th century

world–wea•ri•ness \ˈwərld-ˌwir-ē-nəs\ *n* **:** fatigue from or boredom with the life of the world and especially with material pleasures — **world–wea•ry** \-ˌwiər-ē\ *adj*

world•wide \ˈwərl-ˈdwīd\ *adj* **:** extended throughout the world

[1]**worm** \ˈwərm\ *n* **1 a :** EARTHWORM; *also* **:** any annelid worm **b :** any of various small long usually naked and soft-bodied creeping animals (as a maggot or planarian) **2 a :** a human being who is an object of contempt, loathing, or pity : WRETCH **b :** something that inwardly torments or devours **3** *pl* **:** infestation with or disease caused by parasitic worms **4 :** something (as a mechanical device) spiral in form or appearance: as **a :** the thread of a screw **b :** a short revolving screw whose threads gear with the teeth of a worm wheel or rack **[**Old English *wyrm* "serpent, worm"**]** — **worm** *adj* — **worm•like** \-ˌlīk\ *adj*

[2]**worm** *vb* **1 :** to move or cause to move or proceed sinuously or insidiously ⟨spies *worm* into important positions⟩ ⟨*wormed* out of the crowd⟩ **2 :** to insinuate or introduce (oneself) by devious or subtle means **3 :** to free (as a dog) from worms **4 :** to obtain or extract by artful or insidious questioning or by pleading, asking, or persuading ⟨*wormed* the truth out of me⟩ — **worm•er** *n*

worm–eat•en \ˈwər-ˌmēt-n\ *adj* **1 a :** eaten or burrowed by worms ⟨*worm-eaten* timber⟩ **b :** marked with pits **2 :** WORN-OUT, ANTIQUATED

worm fence *n* **:** a zigzag fence consisting of interlocking rails supported by crossed poles — called also *snake fence*

worm gear *n* **1 :** WORM WHEEL **2 :** a gear of a worm and a worm wheel working together

worm•hole \ˈwərm-ˌhōl\ *n* **:** a hole or passage burrowed by a worm

worm•seed \-ˌsēd\ *n* **:** any of various plants (as a goosefoot) whose seeds possess vermifuge properties

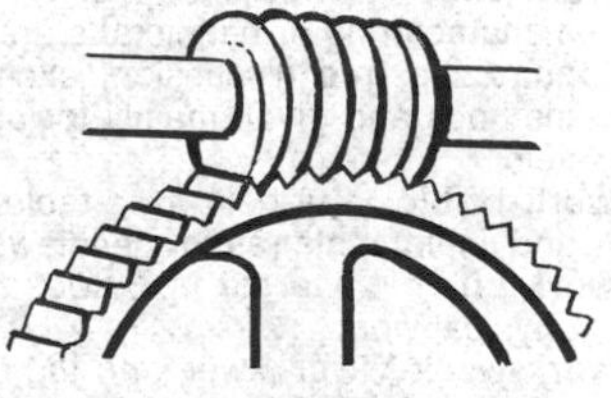

worm gear 2

worm wheel *n* **:** a toothed wheel that meshes with the thread of a worm

worm•wood \ˈwərm-ˌwu̇d\ *n* **1 :** any of a genus of woody herbs related to the daisies; *esp* **:** a European plant yielding a bitter slightly aromatic dark green oil used in absinthe **2 :** something bitter or grievous **[**Middle English *wormwode,* from Old English *wermōd***]**

wormy \ˈwər-mē\ *adj* **worm•i•er; -est 1 :** containing, infested with, or damaged by worms ⟨*wormy* flour⟩ ⟨*wormy* timbers⟩ **2 :** resembling or suggestive of a worm

worn *past participle of* WEAR

worn–out \ˈwōr-ˈnau̇t, ˈwȯr-\ *adj* **:** exhausted or used up by or as if by wear

wor•ri•ment \ˈwər-ē-mənt, ˈwə-rē-\ *n* **:** an act or instance of worrying; *also* **:** TROUBLE, WORRY

wor•ri•some \-səm\ *adj* **1 :** causing distress or worry **2 :** inclined to worry or fret — **wor•ri•some•ly** *adv*

[1]**wor•ry** \ˈwər-ē, ˈwə-rē\ *vb* **wor•ried; wor•ry•ing 1 a :** to shake and tear or mangle with the teeth ⟨a puppy *worrying* an old shoe⟩ **b :** to torment with persistent attacks **2 :** to cause to be anxious : FRET ⟨the late hour *worried* my parents⟩ **3 :** to feel or express great anxiety **[**Old English *wyrgan* "to strangle"**]** **syn** see ANNOY — **wor•ri•er** *n*

[2]**worry** *n, pl* **worries 1 :** ANXIETY 1 **2 :** a cause of anxiety : TROUBLE

wor•ry•wart \-ˌwȯrt\ *n* **:** a person who worries without reasonable cause

[1]**worse** \ˈwərs\ *adj* **1 :** of more inferior quality, value, or condition **2 a :** more unfavorable, unpleasant, or painful; *esp* **:** more unwell ⟨I was *worse* the next day⟩ **b :** more faulty, unsuitable, or incorrect **c :** less skillful or efficient **3 :** bad, evil, or corrupt in a greater degree : more reprehensible ⟨is failing *worse* than cheating?⟩ **[**Old English *wyrsa***]**

[2]**worse** *n* **:** one that is worse

[3]**worse** *adv* **:** in a worse manner : to a worse extent or degree

wors•en \ˈwərs-n\ *vb* **wors•ened; wors•en•ing** \ˈwərs-ning, -n-ing\ **:** to make or become worse

[1]**wor•ship** \ˈwər-shəp\ *n* **1 :** reverence offered a divine being or supernatural power; *also* **:** the expression of such reverence **2 :** extravagant respect or admiration for or devotion to an object of esteem ⟨*worship* of the dollar⟩ **[**Old English *weorthscipe* "worthiness, respect, reverence", from *weorth* "worthy, worth" + *-scipe* "-ship"**]**

[2]**worship** *vb* **-shiped** *or* **-shipped; -ship•ing** *or* **-ship•ping 1 :** to honor or reverence as a divine being or supernatural power **2 :** to regard with extravagant respect, honor, or devotion : IDOLIZE **3 :** to perform or take part in worship or an act of worship **syn** see REVERE — **wor•ship•er** *or* **wor•ship•per** *n*

wor•ship•ful \-fəl\ *adj* **1** *archaic* **:** EMINENT, NOTABLE **2 :** giving worship or veneration — **wor•ship•ful•ly** \-fə-lē\ *adv* — **wor•ship•ful•ness** *n*

[1]**worst** \ˈwərst\ *adj* **1 :** most bad, evil, ill, or corrupt **2 a :** most unfavorable, unpleasant, or painful **b :** most unsuitable, faulty, unattractive, or ill-conceived **c :** least skillful or efficient **3 :** most wanting in quality, value, or condition **[**Old English *wyrsta***]** — **the worst way :** very much ⟨wanted a car in *the worst way*⟩

[2]**worst** *n* **:** one that is worst

[3]**worst** *adv* **1 :** to the extreme degree of badness or inferiority **2 :** to the greatest degree

[4]**worst** *vt* **:** to get the better of : DEFEAT

wor•sted \ˈwu̇s-təd, ˈwərs-\ *n* **1 :** a smooth compact yarn from long wool fibers used especially for firm napless fabrics, carpeting, or knitting **2 :** a fabric made from worsted yarns **[***Worstead,* England**]** — **worsted** *adj*

[1]**wort** \ˈwərt, ˈwȯrt\ *n* **:** PLANT 1; *esp* **:** an herbaceous plant — usually used in combination **[**Old English *wyrt* "root, herb, plant"**]**

[2]**wort** *n* **:** a dilute solution of sugars obtained by infusion from malt and fermented to form beer **[**Old English *wyrt***]**

[1]**worth** \ˈwərth\ *prep* **1 a :** equal in value to **b :** having possessions or income equal to **2 :** deserving of ⟨well *worth* the effort⟩ **[**Old English *weorth* "having value, worthy"**]**

[2]**worth** *n* **1 a :** monetary value **b :** the equivalent of a specified amount or figure ⟨a dollar's *worth* of cheese⟩ **2 :** the value of something measured by its qualities or by the esteem in which it is held **3 a :** moral or personal value **b :** EXCELLENCE 1, MERIT **4 :** the value of one's property

• syn VALUE, PRICE: WORTH applies to what is intrinsically excellent, admirable, useful, or desirable; VALUE may imply the immediate estimation of the worth of something to an individual or at a particular time or place; PRICE applies to what is actually exchanged for something else and may or may not imply an equivalent intrinsic worth.

worth•ful \ˈwərth-fəl\ *adj* **1 :** full of merit : HONORABLE **2 :** having value : VALUABLE — **worth•ful•ness** *n*

worth·less \ˈwərth-ləs\ *adj* **1 a :** lacking worth **:** VALUELESS **b :** USELESS **2 :** DESPICABLE, LOW — **worth·less·ly** *adv* — **worth·less·ness** *n*

worth·while \ˈwərth-ˈhwīl, -ˈwīl\ *adj* **:** being worth the time or effort spent — **worth·while·ness** *n*

[1]**wor·thy** \ˈwər-th̲ē\ *adj* **wor·thi·er; -est 1 a :** having worth or value **:** ESTIMABLE **b :** MERITORIOUS, HONORABLE **2 :** having sufficient worth ⟨you are *worthy* of the honor⟩ — **wor·thi·ly** \-th̲ə-lē\ *adv* — **wor·thi·ness** \-th̲ē-nəs\ *n*

[2]**worthy** *n, pl* **worthies :** a worthy person

wot *present 1st & 3d sing of* WIT

would \wəd, əd, d, ˈwu̇d\ *past of* WILL **1 a** *archaic* **:** WISHED, DESIRED **b** *archaic* **:** wish for **:** WANT **c :** strongly desire **:** WISH ⟨I *would* I were young again⟩ **2** — used as an auxiliary verb (1) with *rather* or *sooner* to express preference between alternatives ⟨*would* sooner die than face them⟩, (2) to express wish, desire, or intent ⟨those who *would* forbid gambling⟩, (3) to express willingness or preference, (4) to express plan or intention ⟨said they *would* come⟩, (5) to express custom or habitual action ⟨we *would* meet often for lunch⟩, (6) to express consent or choice ⟨*would* put it off if they could⟩, (7) to express contingency or possibility ⟨if they were coming, they *would* be here now⟩, (8) to express completion of a statement of desire, request, or advice ⟨we wish that you *would* go⟩, and (9) to express probability or presumption in past or present time ⟨*would* have won if I had not started late⟩ **3 :** COULD ⟨the barrel *would* hold 20 gallons⟩ **4** — used as an auxiliary verb (1) to express a request with which voluntary compliance is expected ⟨*would* you please help us⟩ and (2) to express doubt or uncertainty ⟨the explanation *would* seem satisfactory⟩ **5 :** SHOULD ⟨knew I *would* enjoy the trip⟩ ⟨*would* be glad to know the answer⟩ [Old English *wolde*]

would-be \ˌwu̇d-ˌbē\ *adj* **:** desiring or professing to be ⟨a *would-be* poet⟩

wouldn't \ˈwu̇d-nt\ **:** would not

wouldst \wədst, wu̇dst, ˈwu̇dst, wətst\ *or* **would·est** \ˈwu̇d-əst\ *archaic past 2d sing of* WILL

[1]**wound** \ˈwünd\ *n* **1 :** an injury involving cutting or breaking of bodily tissue (as by violence, accident, or surgery) **2 :** a mental or emotional hurt or blow [Old English *wund*]

[2]**wound** *vb* **1 :** to cause a wound to or in **2 :** to inflict a wound ⟨a *wounding* remark⟩

[3]**wound** \ˈwau̇nd\ *past of* WIND

wove *past of* WEAVE

woven *past participle of* WEAVE

[1]**wow** \ˈwau̇\ *interj* — used to express strong feeling (as pleasure or surprise) [probably imitative]

[2]**wow** *n* **:** a distortion in reproduced sound consisting of a slow rise and fall in pitch caused by speed variation in the reproducing system [imitative]

[1]**wrack** \ˈrak\ *n* **1 :** RUIN 1, DESTRUCTION **2 :** a remnant of something destroyed [Old English *wræc* "misery, punishment, something driven by the sea"]

[2]**wrack** *n* **1 :** a wrecked ship **2 :** a piece of wreckage [Dutch or Low German *wrak*]

[3]**wrack** *vt* **:** to utterly ruin **:** WRECK

[4]**wrack** *vt* **:** [2]RACK 2, 3

[5]**wrack** *n* **:** [1]RACK 2

wraith \ˈrāth\ *n, pl* **wraiths** \ˈrāths *also* ˈrath̲z\ **1 a :** an apparition of a living person seen usually as an exact likeness and just before death **b :** GHOST 2 **2 :** an insubstantial appearance of something **:** SHADOW [origin unknown]

[1]**wran·gle** \ˈrang-gəl\ *vb* **wran·gled; wran·gling** \-gə-ling, -gling\ **1 :** to dispute angrily or peevishly **:** BICKER **2 :** ARGUE 2 **3 :** to obtain by persistent arguing **4 :** to herd and care for (livestock and especially horses) on the range [Middle English *wranglen*]

[2]**wrangle** *n* **1 :** an angry, noisy, or prolonged dispute or quarrel **2 :** the action or process of wrangling

wran·gler \-gə-lər, -glər\ *n* **1 :** one that wrangles or bickers **2 :** a ranch hand who takes care of the saddle horses

[1]**wrap** \ˈrap\ *vb* **wrapped; wrap·ping 1 a :** to cover especially by winding or folding ⟨*wrap* a baby in a blanket⟩ **b :** to envelop and secure (as for transportation or storage) ⟨*wrap* a gift⟩ **c :** to enclose by grasping or embracing **d :** to coil, fold, draw, or twine about something **2 a :** to envelop closely or completely **b :** to involve completely **:** ENGROSS ⟨*wrapped* up in a hobby⟩ **3 :** to conceal or obscure as if by enveloping ⟨a city *wrapped* in darkness⟩ **4 :** to put on clothing **:** DRESS ⟨*wrapped* up warm⟩ **5 :** to be subject to covering, enclosing, or packaging ⟨*wraps* up into a small package⟩ [Middle English *wrappen*]

[2]**wrap** *n* **1 a :** a covering that encloses something **b :** an article of clothing that may be wrapped round a person; *esp* **:** an outer garment (as a coat or shawl) **2 :** a single turn or convolution of something wound round an object **3** *pl* **a :** RESTRAINT 2 **b :** SECRECY ⟨a plan kept under *wraps*⟩

[1]**wrap·around** \ˌrap-ə-ˌrau̇nd\ *adj* **1 :** made to be wrapped around the body ⟨a *wraparound* skirt⟩ **2 :** shaped to follow a contour ⟨*wraparound* sunglasses⟩

[2]**wraparound** \ˈrap-ə-ˌrau̇nd\ *n* **:** a wraparound garment

wrap·per \ˈrap-ər\ *n* **1 :** that in which something is wrapped: as **a** (1) **:** JACKET 2c (2) **:** the paper cover of a book not bound in boards **b :** a paper wrapped around a newspaper or magazine in the mail **2 :** one that wraps **3 :** a wraparound article of clothing

wrap·ping \ˈrap-ing\ *n* **:** something used to wrap an object **:** WRAPPER

wrap-up \ˈrap-ˌəp\ *n* **:** a summarizing report

wrap up \rap-ˈəp, ˈrap-\ *vt* **1 :** to bring to a usually successful conclusion **:** END **2 :** to make a single comprehensive report of

wrasse \ˈras\ *n* **:** any of various usually brilliantly colored spiny-finned fishes with a long deep narrow body that include important food fishes especially of warm seas [Cornish *gwragh,* "old woman, hag, wrasse"]

wrasse

wrath \ˈrath\ *n* **1 :** violent vengeful anger **2 :** retributory punishment for sin or crime [Old English *wrǣththo,* from *wrāth* "wroth"] **syn** see ANGER — **wrathy** \-ē\ *adj*

wrath·ful \ˈrath-fəl\ *adj* **1 :** filled with wrath **:** IRATE **2 :** arising from, marked by, or indicative of wrath ⟨a *wrathful* expression⟩ — **wrath·ful·ly** \-fə-lē\ *adv* — **wrath·ful·ness** *n*

wreak \ˈrēk\ *vt* **1 :** to exact as a punishment **:** INFLICT ⟨*wreak* vengeance⟩ **2 :** to give free scope or rein to ⟨*wreaked* their wrath⟩ [Old English *wrecan* "to drive, punish, avenge"]

wreath \ˈrēth\ *n, pl* **wreaths** \ˈrēth̲z, ˈrēths\ **:** something (as a garland or chaplet) intertwined into a circular shape ⟨a *wreath* of smoke⟩⟨a *wreath* of flowers⟩ [Old English *writha*]

wreathe \ˈrēth̲\ *vb* **1 :** to twist or contort so as to show folds or creases ⟨a face *wreathed* in smiles⟩ **2 a :** to shape into a wreath **b :** to take on the shape of a wreath **:** move or extend in circles or spirals ⟨smoke *wreathed* upward⟩ **c :** to cause to coil about something **3 :** to encircle or adorn with or as if with a wreath ⟨ivy *wreathed* the pole⟩

[1]**wreck** \ˈrek\ *n* **1 :** goods cast upon the land by the sea after a shipwreck **2 :** the action of breaking up or destroying something usually by accident ⟨injured in the *wreck* of a train⟩ **3 :** the broken remains of something wrecked or otherwise ruined **4 :** something disabled or in a state of ruin or dilapidation; *also* **:** an individual broken in health or strength [Anglo-French *wrek,* of Scandinavian origin]

[2]**wreck** *vt* **1 a :** SHIPWRECK 2 **b :** to damage or ruin by breaking up ⟨*wreck* a building⟩ ⟨*wreck* a friendship⟩ **c :** to involve in disaster or ruin **2 :** WREAK 1

wreck·age \ˈrek-ij\ *n* **1 :** the act of wrecking **:** the state of being wrecked **2 :** the remains of a wreck

wreck·er \ˈrek-ər\ *n* **1 :** one that wrecks **2 :** a person who searches for or works on wrecks of ships **3 :** a ship used in salvaging wrecks **4 :** a truck equipped to remove wrecked or disabled automotive vehicles — called also *tow truck*

wrecking bar *n* **:** a small crowbar with a claw for pulling nails at one end and a slight bend for prying at the other end

wren \ˈren\ *n* **1 :** any of a large family of small mostly brown singing birds with short rounded wings and short erect tail **2**

\ə\ **abut**	\au̇\ **out**	\i\ **tip**	\ȯ\ **saw**	\u̇\ **foot**
\ər\ **further**	\ch\ **chin**	\ī\ **life**	\ȯi\ **coin**	\y\ **yet**
\a\ **mat**	\e\ **pet**	\j\ **job**	\th\ **thin**	\yü\ **few**
\ā\ **take**	\ē\ **easy**	\ng\ **sing**	\th̲\ **this**	\yu̇\ **cure**
\ä\ **cot, cart**	\g\ **go**	\ō\ **bone**	\ü\ **food**	\zh\ **vision**

: any of various small singing birds resembling the true wrens in size and habits [Old English *wrenna*]

[1]**wrench** \'rench\ *vb* **1** : to move with a violent twist **2** : to pull, strain, or tighten with violent twisting **3** : to injure or disable by a violent twisting or straining **4** : to change (as the meaning of a word) violently **5** : to snatch forcibly : WREST **6** : to cause to suffer anguish : RACK [Old English *wrencan*]

[2]**wrench** *n* **1 a** : a violent twisting or a pull with or as if with twisting **b** : a sharp twist or sudden jerk straining muscles or ligaments; *also* : the resultant injury (as of a joint) **c** : a distorting or perverting alteration **d** : acute emotional distress : sudden violent mental change **2** : a hand or power tool for holding, twisting, or turning an object (as a bolt or nut)

[1]**wrest** \'rest\ *vt* **1** : to pull, force, or move by violent wringing or twisting movements **2** : to gain with difficulty by or as if by force or violence ⟨*wrest* a living⟩ ⟨*wrest* the power from the king⟩ **3 a** : to divert to an unnatural or improper use **b** : DISTORT ⟨they *wrest* my every word⟩ [Old English *wrǣstan*] — **wrest•er** *n*

[2]**wrest** *n* : a forcible twist : WRENCH

[1]**wres•tle** \'res-əl\ *vb* **wres•tled**; **wres•tling** \'res-ling, -ə-ling\ **1** : to grapple with an opponent in an attempt to trip or throw the opponent down **2** : to contend against in wrestling **3** : to struggle for mastery (as with something difficult) ⟨*wrestle* with a problem⟩ [Old English *wrǣstlian,* from *wrǣstan* "to wrest"] — **wres•tler** \'res-lər\ *n*

[2]**wrestle** *n* : the action or an instance of wrestling : STRUGGLE

wres•tling \'res-ling\ *n* : the sport of hand-to-hand combat between two unarmed contestants who seek to throw each other

wretch \'rech\ *n* **1** : a miserable unhappy person **2** : a base, despicable, or vile person [Old English *wrecca* "outcast"]

wretch•ed \'rech-əd\ *adj* **1** : deeply afflicted, dejected, or distre sed : MISERABLE **2** : very or annoyingly bad ⟨a *wretched* accident⟩ **3 a** : being or appearing mean or contemptible ⟨a *wretched* trick⟩ **b** : very poor in quality or ability : INFERIOR ⟨*wretched* workmanship⟩ — **wretch•ed•ly** *adv* — **wretch•ed•ness** *n*

wrig•gle \'rig-əl\ *vb* **wrig•gled**; **wrig•gling** \'rig-ling, -ə-ling\ **1** : to move to and fro with short writhing motions like a worm : SQUIRM ⟨*wriggled* in the chair⟩ ⟨*wriggled* my toes⟩ **2** : to move or progress by wriggling **3** : to extricate or insinuate oneself or reach a goal by maneuvering, ingratiating, or deceiving ⟨*wriggle* out of a difficulty⟩ [Middle English *wrigglen*] — **wriggle** n — **wrig•gly** \'rig-lē, -ə-lē\ *adj*

wrig•gler \'rig-lər, -ə-lər\ *n* : one that wriggles; *esp* : WIGGLER 2

wright \'rīt\ *n* : a workman in wood : CARPENTER — usually used in combination ⟨ship*wright*⟩⟨wheel*wright*⟩ [Old English *wyrhta, wryhta* "worker, maker"]

wring \'ring\ *vt* **wrung** \'rəng\; **wring•ing** \'ring-ing\ **1** : to squeeze or twist especially so as to make dry or to extract moisture or liquid ⟨*wring* wet clothes⟩ **2** : to get by or as if by twisting or pressing ⟨*wring* the truth out of you⟩ **3 a** : to twist so as to strain or sprain **b** : to twist together (clasped hands) as a sign of anguish **4** : to place or insert by a twisting movement **5** : to affect painfully as if by wringing : TORMENT ⟨a tragedy that *wrung* our hearts⟩ **6** : to shake (a hand) vigorously in greeting [Old English *wringan*] — **wring** *n*

wring•er \'ring-ər\ *n* : one that wrings; *esp* : a machine or device for pressing out liquid or moisture ⟨clothes *wringer*⟩

[1]**wrin•kle** \'ring-kəl\ *n* **1** : a crease or small fold on a surface (as in the skin or in cloth) **2 a** : METHOD 1, TECHNIQUE; *also* : information about a method : HINT **b** : an innovation in method, technique, or equipment : NOVELTY ⟨the latest *wrinkle*⟩ [Middle English] — **wrin•kly** \-kə-lē, -klē\ *adj*

[2]**wrinkle** *vb* **wrin•kled**; **wrin•kling** \-kə-ling, -kling\ *vb* : to develop or cause to develop wrinkles

wrist \'rist\ *n* : the joint or the region of the joint between the human hand and the arm or a corresponding part on a lower animal [Old English]

wrist•band \'rist-,band, 'ris-\ *n* **1** : the part of a sleeve covering the wrist **2** : a band encircling the wrist

wrist•let \'rist-lət, 'ris-\ *n* : a band encircling the wrist; *esp* : a close-fitting knitted band worn for warmth

wrist pin *n* : a stud or pin that forms a journal for a connecting rod

wrist•watch \'ris-,twäch\ *n* : a small watch attached to a bracelet or strap to fasten about the wrist

writ \'rit\ *n* **1** : something written : WRITING ⟨Holy *Writ*⟩ **2 a** : a legal order in writing signed by a court or judicial officer **b** : a written order constituting a symbol of the power and authority of the issuer ⟨where the king's *writ* has no force⟩ [Old English]

writ•able \'rīt-ə-bəl\ *adj* : capable of being put in writing

write \'rīt\ *vb* **wrote** \'rōt\; **writ•ten** \'rit-n\ *also* **writ** \'rit\; **writ•ing** \'rīt-ing\ **1** : to form letters or words with pen or pencil ⟨learn to read and *write*⟩ **2** : to form the letters or the words of (as on paper) : INSCRIBE ⟨*write* one's name⟩ ⟨*write* a check⟩ **3** : to put down on paper : give expression to in writing ⟨*write* an account of the circus⟩ **4** : to make up and set down for others to read : COMPOSE ⟨*write* a book⟩ ⟨*wrote* music⟩ **5** : to pen, dictate, or typewrite a letter to ⟨*write* the president⟩ **6** : to communicate by letter : CORRESPOND **7** : to be fitted for writing ⟨this pen *writes* easily⟩ **8** : to transfer (as data) from the memory of a computer to an output device ⟨*write* data onto magnetic tape⟩ [Old English *wrītan* "to scratch, draw, inscribe"]

write down *vb* **1** : to record in written form **2 a** : to reduce in status, rank, or value **b** : to play down in writing **3** : to write so as to appeal to a less sophisticated audience ⟨*write down* to meet the needs of children⟩

write in *vt* : to insert (a name not listed on a ballot or voting machine) in an appropriate space — **write–in** \'rīt-,in\ *n*

write off *vt* **1** : to reduce the estimated value of : DEPRECIATE **2** : to take off the books : CANCEL ⟨*write off* a bad debt⟩ — **write–off** \'rīt-,ȯf\ *n*

write out *vt* : to put in writing; *esp* : to put into a full and complete written form

writ•er \'rīt-ər\ *n* **1** : AUTHOR 1 **2** : one that can write

writer's cramp *n* : a painful spasmodic cramp of muscles of the hand or fingers which usually has a psychological cause

write–up \'rīt-,əp\ *n* : a written account (as in a newspaper); *esp* : a flattering article

write up \rīt-'əp, 'rīt-\ *vt* **1 a** : to write an account of : DESCRIBE **b** : to put into finished written form **2** : to bring up to date the writing of **3** : to increase the book value of

writhe \'rīth\ *vb* **1** : to twist and turn this way and that ⟨*writhe* in pain⟩ **2** : to suffer with shame or confusion : SQUIRM [Old English *wrīthan*]

writ•ing \'rīt-ing\ *n* **1 a** : the act or process of one that writes : the formation of letters to express words and ideas **b** : HANDWRITING **2 a** : something (as a letter, book, or document) that is written or printed **b** : INSCRIPTION 1 **3** : a style or form of composition **4** : the occupation of a writer

writing desk *n* : a desk often with a sloping top for writing on

writing paper *n* : paper intended for writing on with ink

writ of assistance : a writ issued (as by British authorities in the American colonies) to an officer (as a sheriff) to aid in the search for smuggled or illegal goods

[1]**wrong** \'rȯng\ *n* **1 a** : an injurious, unfair, or unjust act **b** : a violation of the legal rights of another; *esp* : TORT **2** : principles, practices, or conduct contrary to justice, goodness, equity, or law ⟨know right from *wrong*⟩ **3 a** : the state, position, or fact of being or doing wrong **b** : the state of being guilty [Old English *wrang,* of Scandinavian origin]

[2]**wrong** *adj* **wrong•er** \'rȯng-ər\; **wrong•est** \'rȯng-əst\ **1** : not according to the moral standard : SINFUL, IMMORAL **2** : not right or proper according to a code, standard, or convention : IMPROPER **3** : not according to truth or facts : INCORRECT **4** : not satisfactory (as in condition, results, health, or temper) **5** : not in accordance with one's needs or intent ⟨took the *wrong* bus⟩ **6** : being the side of something opposite to the principal one, naturally turned down, inward, or away, or least finished or polished ⟨the *wrong* side of a fabric⟩ — **wrong** *adv* — **wrong•ly** \'rȯng-lē\ *adv* — **wrong•ness** *n*

[3]**wrong** *vt* **wronged**; **wrong•ing** \'rȯng-ing\ **1** : to do wrong to : INJURE, HARM **2** : to make unjust remarks about : DISHONOR, MALIGN — **wrong•er** \'rȯng-ər\ *n*

wrong•do•er \'rȯng-'dü-ər\ *n* : a person who does wrong and especially moral wrong — **wrong•do•ing** \-'dü-ing\ *n*

wrong•ful \'rȯng-fəl\ *adj* **1** : WRONG, UNJUST ⟨a *wrongful* act⟩ **2** : UNLAWFUL 1 — **wrong•ful•ly** \-fə-lē\ *adv* — **wrong•ful•ness** *n*

wrong•head•ed \'rȯng-'hed-əd\ *adj* : stubborn in adherence to wrong opinion or principles : PERVERSE — **wrong•head•ed•ly** *adv* — **wrong•head•ed•ness** *n*

wrote *past of* WRITE

wroth \'rȯth *also* 'rōth\ *adj* : filled with wrath : ANGRY [Old English *wrāth*]

[1]**wrought** *past of* WORK

[2]**wrought** \'rȯt\ *adj* **1** : worked into shape by artistry or effort **2**

: elaborately decorated **3** : processed for use **4** : beaten into shape by tools ⟨*wrought* metals⟩ **5** : deeply stirred ⟨gets easily *wrought* up⟩

wrought iron *n* : a commercial form of iron that is tough, malleable, and relatively soft

wrung *past of* WRING

wry \'rī\ *adj* **wri•er** \'rī-ər, 'rīr\; **wri•est** \'rī-əst\ **1 a** : turned abnormally to one side **b** : twisted in expression of disgust or displeasure ⟨*wry* lips⟩ **2** : cleverly and often ironically or grimly humorous [earlier *wry* "to twist", from Old English *wrigian* "to turn"] — **wry•ly** *adv* — **wry•ness** *n*

wry•neck \'rī-ˌnek\ *n* : a disorder marked by a twisting of the neck and an unnatural position of the head

wurst \'wərst, 'wu̇rst, 'wu̇st, 'wu̇sht\ *n* : SAUSAGE [German]

wy•an•dotte \'wī-ən-ˌdät\ *n* : any of an American breed of medium-sized domestic fowls [probably from *Wyandot,* member of a group of American Indians]

X x—xylophonist

¹x \'eks\ *n, pl* **x's** *or* **xs** \'ek-səz\ *often cap* **1** : the 24th letter of the English alphabet **2** : 10 in Roman numerals **3** : an unknown quantity

△ **origin** The standard use of the letter *x* to designate an unknown quantity goes back to the practice of René Descartes, 17th century French mathematician and philosopher. Descartes, in his book *La géométrie* ("Geometry"), used the first letters of the alphabet for known quantities and the final letters, *x, y, z* (and most commonly *x*), for unknowns. Later mathematicians have simply followed Descartes's example.

²x *vt* **x-ed** *also* **x'd** *or* **xed** \'ekst\; **x-ing** *or* **x'ing** \'ek-sing\ **1** : to mark with an *x* **2** : to cancel or cover over with a series of *x's* — usually used with *out*

xan•tho•phyll \'zan-thə-ˌfil\ *n* : any of several neutral yellow carotenoid pigments that are usually oxygen derivatives of carotenes [French *xanthophylle,* from Greek *xanthos* "yellow" + *phyllon* "leaf"] — **xan•tho•phyl•lic** \ˌzan-thə-'fil-ik\ *adj*

x-ax•is \'ek-ˌsak-səs\ : the axis in a plane Cartesian coordinate system parallel to which abscissas are measured

X chromosome *n* : a sex chromosome that carries factors for femaleness and usually occurs paired in each female zygote and cell and single in each male zygote and cell in species in which the male typically has two unlike sex chromosomes — compare Y CHROMOSOME

x-co•or•di•nate \ˌek-skō-'ȯrd-nət, -n-ət, -n-ˌāt\ *n* : ABSCISSA

xe•bec \'zē-ˌbek, zi-'\ *n* : a usually 3-masted Mediterranean sailing ship typically having lateen sails [probably from French *chebec,* from Arabic *shabbāk*]

xe•non \'zē-ˌnän, 'zen-ˌän\ *n* : a heavy gaseous chemical element occurring in air in minute quantities — see ELEMENT table [Greek, neuter of *xenos* "strange"]

xebec

xe•no•pho•bia \ˌzen-ə-'fō-bē-ə, ˌzēn-\ *n* : fear and hatred of strangers or foreigners or of anything that is strange or foreign [Greek *xenos* "strange, stranger"] — **xe•no•phobe** \'zen-ə-ˌfōb, 'zēn-\ *n* — **xe•no•pho•bic** \ˌzen-ə-'fō-bik, ˌzēn-\ *adj*

xer- *or* **xero-** *combining form* : dry ⟨*xer*ic⟩ ⟨*xero*phyte⟩ [Greek *xēros*]

xe•ric \'zir-ik, 'zer-\ *adj* **1** : low or deficient in available moisture for the support of life **2** : XEROPHYTIC — **xe•ri•cal•ly** \'zir-i-kə-lē, -klē\ *adv*

xe•rog•ra•phy \zə-'räg-rə-fē, zir-'äg-\ *n* : the formation of pictures or copies of graphic matter by the action of light on an electrically charged surface in which the latent image is developed with powders — **xe•ro•graph•ic** \ˌzir-ə-'graf-ik\ *adj*

xe•roph•thal•mia \ˌzir-ˌäf-'thal-mē-ə, -ˌäp-'thal-\ *n* : a dry thickened lusterless condition of the eyeball resulting from a severe systemic deficiency of vitamin A — **xe•roph•thal•mic** \-mik\ *adj*

xe•ro•phyte \'zir-ə-ˌfīt\ *n* : a plant adapted for growth with a limited water supply especially by means of mechanisms that limit transpiration or that provide for the storage of water — **xe•ro•phyt•ic** \ˌzir-ə-'fit-ik\ *adj*

xe•rox \'zier-ˌäks, 'zē-ˌräks\ *vt* : to copy on a Xerox machine

Xerox *trademark* — used for a xerographic copier

xi \'zī, 'ksī\ *n* : the 14th letter of the Greek alphabet — Ξ or ξ

x-in•ter•cept \'ek-'sint-ər-ˌsept\ *n* : the x-coordinate of a point where a line, curve, or surface intersects the x-axis

Xmas \'kris-məs *also* 'ek-sməs\ *n* : CHRISTMAS [X, symbol for Christ, from the Greek letter chi (X), initial of *Christos* "Christ"]

△ **origin** Since the 16th century *Xmas* has been used in English as a short form of *Christmas. X* as a symbol for Christ is derived from the Greek, where *chi* (X) is the initial letter of *Christos,* the Greek form of *Christ.* The word *Xmas* is usually pronounced like *Christmas,* although a pronunciation of the letter *x* plus *-mas* as in *Christmas* is also heard.

x-ra•di•a•tion \ˌeks-ˌrād-ē-'ā-shən\ *n, often cap X* **1** : exposure to X rays **2** : radiation consisting of X rays

x-ray \'eks-ˌrā\ *vt, often cap X* : to examine, treat, or photograph with X rays

X ray \'eks-ˌrā\ *n* **1** : any of the electromagnetic radiations of the same nature as light rays but of very short wavelength that are generated by a stream of electrons striking against a metal surface in vacuum and that are able to penetrate various thicknesses of solids and act on photographic film like light and to cause a fluorescent screen to emit light **2** : a photograph especially of conditions inside the surface of a body taken by the use of X rays [translation of German *x-strahl*] — **X-ray** *adj*

△ **origin** In 1895 Wilhelm Conrad Röntgen was conducting experiments on the properties of cathode rays. He noticed that a fluorescent surface in the neighborhood of a cathode-ray tube would become luminous even if shielded. A thick metal object placed before the tube would cast a dark shadow on the fluorescent surface, but an object made of a less dense substance like wood would cast only a weak shadow. Röntgen's explanation was that the tube produced some kind of invisible radiation that could pass through substances not transparent to ordinary light. Because he did not know the nature of this radiation he had discovered, he named it *x-strahl,* which was translated into English as *X ray.*

X-ray photograph *n* : a shadow picture made with X rays

X-ray therapy *n* : medical treatment (as of a cancer) by controlled application of X rays

X-ray tube *n* : a vacuum tube in which a concentrated stream of electrons strikes a metal target and produces X rays

xyl- *or* **xylo-** *combining form* : wood ⟨*xylo*phone⟩ [Greek *xylon*]

xy•lem \'zī-ləm, -ˌlem\ *n* : a complex tissue of higher plants that transports water and dissolved materials upward, functions also in support and storage, lies internal to the phloem, and typically constitutes the woody part (as of a plant stem) [German, from Greek *xylon* "wood"] — **xy•la•ry** \'zī-lə-rē\ *adj*

xylem ray *n* : a vascular ray or portion of a vascular ray located in xylem — compare PHLOEM RAY

xy•lene \'zī-ˌlēn\ *n* : a colorless flammable liquid obtained from wood tar, coal tar, coke-oven gas, or petroleum and used chiefly as a solvent

\ə\ **abut**	\au̇\ **out**	\i\ **tip**	\ȯ\ **saw**	\u̇\ **foot**
\ər\ **further**	\ch\ **chin**	\ī\ **life**	\ȯi\ **coin**	\y\ **yet**
\a\ **mat**	\e\ **pet**	\j\ **job**	\th\ **thin**	\yü\ **few**
\ā\ **take**	\ē\ **easy**	\ng\ **sing**	\t͟h\ **this**	\yu̇\ **cure**
\ä\ **cot, cart**	\g\ **go**	\ō\ **bone**	\ü\ **food**	\zh\ **vision**

xy·lol \ˈzī-ˌlȯl, -ˌlōl\ *n* : XYLENE
xy·lo·phone \ˈzī-lə-ˌfōn\ *n* : a musical instrument consisting of a series of wooden bars graduated in length to sound the musical scale and played by striking with two wooden hammers — **xy·lo·phon·ist** \-ˌfō-nəst\ *n*

Y y—yurt

y \ˈwī\ *n, pl* **y's** *or* **ys** \ˈwīz\ *often cap* : the 25th letter of the English alphabet
^{1}**-y** *also* **-ey** \ē\ *adj suffix* **-ier**; **-iest** **1 a** : characterized by : full of ⟨clayey⟩ ⟨dirty⟩ ⟨muddy⟩ **b** : having the character of : composed of ⟨icy⟩ ⟨waxy⟩ **c** : like : like that of ⟨homey⟩ ⟨stagy⟩ ⟨wintry⟩ **d** : devoted to : addicted to : enthusiastic over ⟨horsey⟩ **2 a** : tending or inclined to ⟨chatty⟩ ⟨sleepy⟩ **b** : giving occasion for (specified) action ⟨chewy⟩ **c** : performing (specified) action ⟨curly⟩ **3 a** : somewhat : rather : -ISH ⟨chilly⟩ **b** : having (such) characteristics to a marked degree or in an affected or superficial way [Old English *-ig*]
^{2}**-y** \ē\ *n suffix, pl* **-ies** **1** : state : condition : quality ⟨beggary⟩ **2** : activity, place of business, or goods dealt with ⟨laundry⟩ **3** : whole body or group ⟨soldiery⟩ [Old French *-ie*, from Latin *-ia*, from Greek *-ia, -eia*]
^{3}**-y** *n suffix, pl* **-ies** : instance of a (specified) action ⟨entreaty⟩ ⟨inquiry⟩ [Anglo-French *-ie*, from Latin *-ium*]
^{4}**-y** — see -IE
^{1}**yacht** \ˈyät\ *n* : any of various sailing or motor-driven vessels that are used especially for pleasure cruising or racing [obsolete Dutch *jaght*, from Low German *jacht*, short for *jachtschiff*, literally, "hunting ship"]

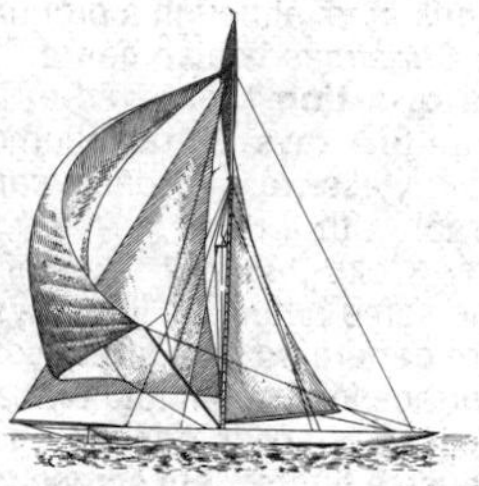
^{1}yacht

△ **origin** In the 16th century the Dutch began building light, fast ships designed to chase the ships of pirates and smugglers from the Dutch coast. The Dutch appropriately called this type of vessel *jaght*, which is a derivative of a Low German word for a fast, light sailing vessel, *jachtschiff*, meaning literally "hunting ship". The ship was introduced into England in 1660 when the Dutch East India Company presented one to King Charles II, who used it as a pleasure boat. The ship's design was copied by British shipbuilders for those wealthy gentlemen who desired and could afford such pleasure craft.
^{2}**yacht** *vi* : to race or cruise in a yacht
yacht·ing *n* : the action, fact, or sport of racing or cruising in a yacht
yachts·man \ˈyät-smən\ *n* : a person who owns or sails a yacht
ya·hoo \ˈyā-hü, ˈyä-\ *n, pl* **yahoos** : a crude or rowdy person [*Yahoo*, member of a race of brutes in Swift's *Gulliver's Travels* who have the form and the vices of people]
Yah·weh \ˈyä-ˌwā, -ˌvā\ *also* **Yah·veh** \-ˌvā\ *n* : the God of the Hebrews [Hebrew *Yahweh*]
^{1}**yak** \ˈyak\ *n, pl* **yaks** *also* **yak** : a large long-haired wild or domesticated ox of Tibet and adjacent elevated parts of central Asia [Tibetan *gyak*]
^{2}**yak** *n* : persistant or voluble talk [probably imitative] — **yak** *vi*

^{1}yak

y'all \ˈyȯl\ *pron, chiefly South* : YOU-ALL
yam \ˈyam\ *n* **1** : an edible starchy tuberous root that is a staple food in tropical areas; *also* : a plant distantly related to the lilies that produces these **2** : a moist-fleshed and usually orange-fleshed sweet potato [Portuguese *inhame* and Spanish *ñame*, of African origin]
yam·mer \ˈyam-ər\ *vi* **yam·mered**; **yam·mer·ing** \ˈyam-ring, -ə-ring\ **1** : to complain persistently **2** : CHATTER 2 [Old English *geōmrian* "to lament"] — **yammer** *n*
yang \ˈyäng\ *n* : the masculine active principle (as of light, heat, or dryness) in nature that in Chinese cosmic philosophy combines with yin to produce all that comes to be [Chinese (Pekingese dialect) *yang*^{2}]
yank \ˈyangk\ *n* : a strong sudden pull : JERK [origin unknown] — **yank** *vb*
Yank \ˈyangk\ *n* : YANKEE
Yan·kee \ˈyang-kē\ *n* **1 a** : a native or inhabitant of New England **b** : a native or inhabitant of the northern United States **2** : a native or inhabitant of the United States [origin unknown] — **Yankee** *adj*
yan·qui \ˈyäng-kē\ *n, often cap* : a citizen of the United States as distinguished from a Latin American [Spanish, from English *Yankee*]
^{1}**yap** \ˈyap\ *vi* **yapped**; **yap·ping** **1** : YELP **2** : to talk with shrill insistence : SCOLD [imitative]
^{2}**yap** *n* **1** : YELP : **2** : shrill insistent talk : CHATTER **3** *slang* : MOUTH 1b
^{1}**yard** \ˈyärd\ *n* **1** : any of various units of measure; *esp* : a unit of length equal in the United States to 0.9144 meter — see MEASURE table **2** : a long spar that supports and spreads the head of a square sail, lateen, or lugsail [Old English *gierd* "twig, measure, yard"]

1 ^{1}yard 2

^{2}**yard** *n* **1 a** : a small usually enclosed area open to the sky and adjacent to a building **b** : the grounds of a building or group of buildings **2 a** : an enclosure for livestock **b** : an area with its buildings and facilities set aside for a particular business or activity **c** : a system of railroad tracks for storage and maintenance of cars and making up trains **3** : a locality where deer herd in winter [Old English *geard* "enclosure, yard"]
^{3}**yard** *vb* : to drive into, gather, or confine in or as if in a yard
yard·age \ˈyärd-ij\ *n* : a total number of yards; *also* : the length, extent, or volume of something as measured in yards
yard·arm \ˈyärd-ˌärm\ *n* : either end of the yard of a square-rigged ship
yard goods *n pl* : fabrics sold by the yard
yard·man \ˈyärd-mən, -ˌman\ *n* **1** : one who is employed to do outdoor work (as mowing lawns) **2** : one who works in or about a yard (as a lumberyard or a railroad yard)
yard·mas·ter \-ˌmas-tər\ *n* : a person in charge of operations in a railroad yard
yard·stick \-ˌstik\ *n* **1** : a measuring stick a yard long **2** : a rule or standard by which something is measured or judged : CRITERION
^{1}**yarn** \ˈyärn\ *n* **1 a** : textile fiber (as spun wool, cotton, flax, or silk) for use in weaving, knitting, or the manufacture of thread **b** : a strand of material (as metal, glass, or asbestos) for uses comparable to those of a textile yarn **2** : an interesting or exciting often made-up story [Old English *gearn*]
^{2}**yarn** *vi* : to tell a yarn
yarn-dye \-ˈdī\ *vt* : to dye before weaving or knitting
yar·row \ˈyar-ō\ *n* : a strong-scented herb related to the daisies that has finely divided leaves and white or rarely pink flowers in

flat clusters [Old English *gearwe*]
yat•a•ghan \'yat-ə-ˌgan\ *n* : a long knife or short saber common among Muslims that is made without a cross guard and usually with a double curve to the edge [Turkish *yatağan*]

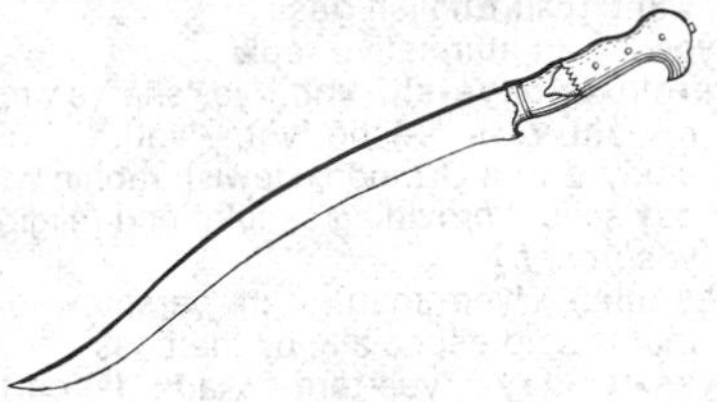
yataghan

yau•pon \'yü-ˌpän *also* 'yō-, 'yȯ-\ *n* : a holly of the southern United States with smooth leaves used as a substitute for tea [of American Indian origin]
yaw \'yȯ\ *vi* : to turn abruptly from a straight course : SWERVE, VEER ⟨a heavy sea made the ship *yaw*⟩ [origin unknown] — **yaw** *n*
yawl \'yȯl\ *n* : a 2-masted fore-and-aft rigged sailing vessel with a mizzenmast abaft the rudder — compare KETCH [Low German *jolle*]

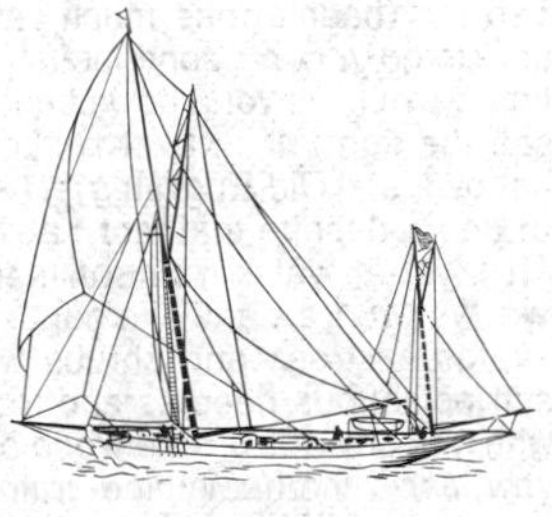
yawl

¹yawn \'yȯn, 'yän\ *vb* **1** : to open wide : GAPE **2** : to open the mouth wide usually as an involuntary reaction to fatigue or boredom **3** : to utter with a yawn [Old English *ginian, geonian*] — **yawn•er** *n*
²yawn *n* : a deep usually involuntary intake of breath through the wide-open mouth
yawn•ing *adj* **1** : wide open : CAVERNOUS ⟨a *yawning* hole⟩ **2** : showing fatigue or boredom by yawns ⟨a *yawning* audience⟩
¹yawp *or* **yaup** \'yȯp\ *vi* **1** : to make a raucous noise : SQUAWK **2** : CLAMOR 2, COMPLAIN [Middle English *yolpen*] — **yawp•er** *n*
²yawp *also* **yaup** *n* : a raucous noise : SQUAWK
yaws \'yȯz\ *n sing or pl* : a tropical disease caused by a spirochete and marked by ulcerating surface lesions with later bone involvement [of American Indian origin]
y–ax•is \'wī-ˌak-səs\ *n* : the axis in a plane Cartesian coordinate system parallel to which ordinates are measured
Y chromosome *n* : a sex chromosome occurring in male zygotes and cells in species in which the male typically has two unlike sex chromosomes — compare X CHROMOSOME
yclept \i-'klept\ *or* **ycleped** \-'klēpt, -'klept\ *adj, archaic* : known as : CALLED [Middle English, from Old English *geclipod,* past participle of *clipian* to cry out, name]
y–co•or•di•nate \ˌwī-kō-'ȯrd-nət, -n-ət, -n-ˌāt\ *n* : ORDINATE
¹ye \yē, 'yē\ *pron* : YOU 1 — used originally only as a plural pronoun of the 2d person in the subjective case and now used especially in ecclesiastical or literary language and in various English dialects [Old English *gē*]
²ye \yē, yə, *or like* THE\ *definite article, archaic* : THE [Old English *thē* "the"; from the use of early printers of *y* to represent þ (th) of manuscripts]
△ **origin** The use of *ye* instead of *the* to suggest an earlier time is the result of changes in handwriting styles which took place before the introduction of printing in England. The alphabet used by the Anglo-Saxons included several letters not found in the Latin alphabet but borrowed from the runic alphabet used by several early Germanic peoples. One of these letters was þ, called *thorn,* which represented the sounds now most often indicated by *th* in English. This letter was used in the Middle English period as well, but by the end of the 14th century the written form of the thorn was often indistinguishable from that of *y.* After 1400, the thorn fell into disuse, and early printers, having no form of thorn in their type fonts, often simply used a *y* in its place.
¹yea \'yā\ *adv* **1** : YES — used in oral voting **2** — used as a function word to introduce a more explicit or emphatic phrase [Old English *gēa*]
²yea *n* **1** : ASSENT, AFFIRMATION **2 a** : an affirmative vote **b** : a person casting a yea vote
yeah \'ye-ə, 'yeü, 'ya-ə\ *adv* : YES
year \'yiər\ *n* **1** : the period of one apparent revolution of the sun around the ecliptic or of the earth's revolution around the sun amounting to approximately 365¼ days **2 a** : a period of 365 days or in leap year 366 days beginning January 1 **b** : a period of time equal to this but beginning at a different time ⟨a fiscal *year*⟩ **3** : a continuous period of time that constitutes the period of some event (as revolution of a planet about its sun) or activity whether greater or less than the calendar year ⟨a school *year* of less than six months⟩ [Old English *gēar*]
year•book \-ˌbu̇k\ *n* **1** : a book published yearly especially as a factual report **2** : a school publication recording the history and activities of a graduating class
year•ling \-liŋ\ *n* : one that is a year old: as **a** : an animal in the second year of its age **b** : a racehorse between January 1st of the year after the year in which it was foaled and the next January 1st — **yearling** *adj*
year•long \-'lȯŋ\ *adj* : lasting through a year
year•ly \-lē\ *adj* **1** : computed in terms of one year **2** : occurring, done, produced, or acted upon every year : ANNUAL — **yearly** *adv*
yearn \'yərn\ *vb* **1** : to feel a longing or craving **2** : to feel tenderness or compassion [Old English *giernan*] **syn** see LONG — **yearn•er** *n*
yearn•ing *n* : a tender or urgent longing
year of grace : a year of the Christian era ⟨the *year of grace* 1979⟩
year–round \'yiər-'rau̇nd, 'yiə-'rau̇nd\ *adj* : effective, employed, or operating for the full year : not seasonal ⟨a *year-round* resort⟩
yeast \'yēst, 'ēst\ *n* **1 a** : a substance that occurs especially in sweet liquids in which it promotes alcoholic fermentation, consists largely of cells of a tiny fungus, and is used especially in the making of alcoholic liquors and as a leaven in baking **b** : a commercial product containing yeast plants in a moist or dry medium **c** : any of various tiny fungi that are usually one-celled and reproduce by budding; *esp* : one present and functionally active in a yeast froth or sediment **2** : foam or froth especially of waves **3** : something that causes ferment or activity [Old English *gist*] — **yeasty** \'yē-stē, 'ē-stē\ *adj*
yegg \'yeg, 'yāg\ *n* : SAFECRACKER; *also* : ROBBER [origin unknown]
¹yell \'yel\ *vb* **1** : to utter a loud cry, scream, or shout **2** : to give a cheer usually in unison **3** : to utter or declare with or as if with a yell : SHOUT [Old English *giellan*] — **yell•er** *n*
²yell *n* **1** : SCREAM 1, SHOUT **2** : a usually rhythmic cheer used especially in schools to encourage athletic teams
¹yel•low \'yel-ō\ *adj* **1 a** : of the color yellow **b** : yellowish from age, disease, or discoloration **c** : having a yellow complexion or skin **2 a** : featuring sensational or scandalous items or ordinary news sensationally distorted ⟨*yellow* journalism⟩ **b** : COWARDLY 1 [Old English *geolu*] — **yel•low•ish** \'yel-ə-wish\ *adj*
²yellow *vb* : to make or turn yellow
³yellow *n* **1 a** : a color whose hue resembles that of ripe lemons or sunflowers or is that of the portion of the spectrum lying between green and orange **b** : a pigment or dye that colors yellow **2** : something yellow or marked by a yellow color **3** *pl* **a** : JAUNDICE **b** : any of several plant virus diseases marked by yellowing of the foliage and stunting
yellow–dog contract *n* : a now illegal employment contract under which a worker agreed not to join a labor union during the period of his or her employment
yellow fever *n* : a destructive infectious disease of warm regions marked by sudden onset, prostration, fever, jaundice, and often hemorrhage and caused by a virus transmitted by a mosquito — called also *yellow jack*
yellow–fever mosquito *n* : a small dark-colored mosquito that is the usual vector of yellow fever
yellow–green alga *n* : any of a division (Chrysophyta) of algae with the chlorophyll masked by brown or yellow pigment
yel•low•ham•mer \'yel-ō-ˌham-ər, 'yel-ə-\ *n* **1** : a common European finch having the male largely bright yellow **2** : YELLOW-

\ə\ **abut**	\au̇\ **out**	\i\ **tip**	\ȯ\ **saw**	\u̇\ **foot**
\ər\ **further**	\ch\ **chin**	\ī\ **life**	\ȯi\ **coin**	\y\ **yet**
\a\ **mat**	\e\ **pet**	\j\ **job**	\th\ **thin**	\yü\ **few**
\ā\ **take**	\ē\ **easy**	\ŋ\ **sing**	\t͟h\ **this**	\yu̇\ **cure**
\ä\ **cot, cart**	\g\ **go**	\ō\ **bone**	\ü\ **food**	\zh\ **vision**

SHAFTED FLICKER [Old English *amore* "yellowhammer"]

yellow jack *n* **1 :** YELLOW FEVER **2 :** a flag raised on ships in quarantine

yellow jacket *n* **:** any of various small yellow-marked social wasps that commonly nest in the ground

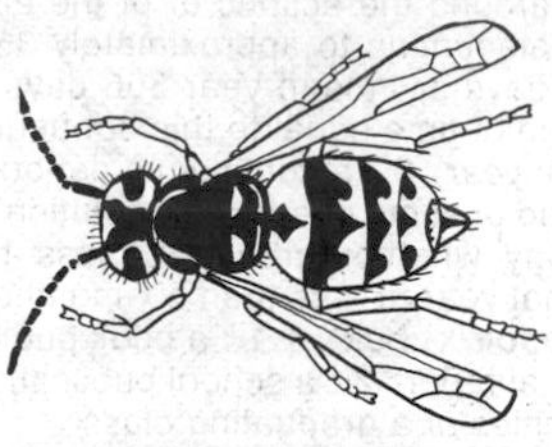
yellow jacket

yellow jessamine *n* **:** a twining evergreen shrub related to the nux vomica and grown in warm regions for its fragrant yellow flowers — called also *yellow jasmine*

yel•low•legs \ˈyel-ō-ˌlegz, ˈyel-ə-, -ˌlāgz\ *n sing or pl* **:** either of two American shorebirds with long yellow legs

yellow ocher *n* **1 :** a yellow mixture of limonite usually with clay and silica used as a pigment **2 :** a moderate orange yellow

yellow perch *n* **:** a common American perch that is yellowish with broad green bars and is an excellent sport and table fish

yellow pine *n* **:** the yellowish resinous wood of any of several American pines; *also* **:** a pine (as the longleaf pine or ponderosa pine) that yields such wood

yel•low–shaft•ed flicker \ˌyel-ō-ˌshaf-təd-, ˌyel-ə-\ *n* **:** a common large woodpecker of eastern North America with a black crescent on the breast, red nape, white rump, and yellow shafts to the tail and wing feathers — called also *yellowhammer*

yellow spot *n* **:** MACULA LUTEA

yel•low•tail \ˈyel-ō-ˌtāl, ˈyel-ə-\ *n, pl* **-tail** *or* **-tails :** any of various fishes having a yellow or yellowish tail and including several food and sport fishes

yel•low•throat \-ˌthrōt\ *n* **:** a largely olive American warbler with yellow breast and throat

yel•low•wood \-ˌwu̇d\ *n* **:** any of various trees having yellowish wood or yielding a yellow extract; *also* **:** this wood

[1]yelp \ˈyelp\ *vi* **:** to utter a yelp or a similar sound [Old English *gielpan* "to boast, exult"]

[2]yelp *n* **:** a sharp quick shrill bark or cry

[1]yen \ˈyen\ *n, pl* **yen 1 :** the basic monetary unit of Japan **2 :** a coin or note representing one yen [Japanese *en*]

[2]yen *n* **:** an intense desire **:** URGE, LONGING ⟨have a *yen* to travel⟩ [Chinese (Cantonese dialect) *in-yăn* "craving for opium", from *in* "opium" + *yăn* "craving"]

△ **origin** During the 18th and 19th centuries China suffered under the encouragement, which amounted to virtual enforcement, of widespread opium addiction by foreign nations whose traders found the drug profitable. In the mid-19th century many Chinese immigrated to the United States, and the word *in-yăn*, "craving for opium", came with them. In English the Chinese syllables became assimilated to *yen-yen*. Eventually the word was shortened to *yen* and generalized from a craving for opium to any strong desire.

yeo•man \ˈyō-mən\ *n* **1 a :** an attendant or officer in a royal or noble household **b :** a naval petty officer who performs clerical duties **2 :** a small farmer who cultivates his own land; *esp* **:** one of a class of English freeholders below the gentry [Middle English *yoman*]

yeo•man•ly \-lē\ *adj* **:** becoming to a yeoman **:** STURDY, SELF-RELIANT, LOYAL

yeoman of the guard : a member of a military corps of the British royal household serving as ceremonial attendants of the sovereign

yeo•man•ry \ˈyō-mən-rē\ *n* **1 :** the body of yeomen and especially of small landed proprietors **2 :** a British volunteer cavalry force created from yeomen in 1761 and incorporated in 1907 into the territorial force

yeoman's service *or* **yeoman service** *n* **:** great and loyal service, assistance, or support

-yer — see -ER

yer•ba ma•té \ˌyer-bə-ˈmä-ˌtā, ˌyər-\ *n* **:** MATÉ [American Spanish *yerba mate*, from *yerba* "herb" + *mate* "maté"]

[1]yes \ˈyes, ˈyeu̇, ˈe-ə, ˈe-yə *are four of many variants*\ *adv* **1** — used to express assent, agreement, or affirmation ⟨are you ready? *Yes*, I am⟩ **2** — used to introduce correction or contradiction of a negative assertion, direction, or request ⟨don't say that! *Yes*, I will⟩ **3** — used to introduce a more emphatic or explicit phrase ⟨we are glad, *yes*, very glad to see you⟩ **4** — used to indicate interest or attentiveness ⟨*yes*, what is it you want⟩ [Old English *gēse*]

[2]yes *n* **:** an affirmative reply

ye•shi•va *or* **ye•shi•vah** \yə-ˈshē-və\ *n, pl* **-shivas** *or* **-shivahs** *or* **-shi•voth** \-ˌshē-ˈvōt, -ˈvōth\ **1 :** a school for Talmudic study **2 :** an Orthodox Jewish rabbinical seminary **3 :** a Jewish day school providing secular and religious instruction [Hebrew *yĕshībhāh*]

yes–man \ˈyes-ˌman\ *n* **:** a person who agrees with everything that is said especially by the boss

[1]yes•ter•day \ˈyes-tərd-ē\ *adv* **1 :** on the day before today **2 :** only a short time ago [Old English *geistran dæg*, from *geistran* "yesterday" + *dæg* "day"]

[2]yesterday *n* **1 :** the day before today **2 :** time not long past ⟨*yesterday's* fashions⟩ **3 :** past time — usually used in pl.

yes•ter•year \ˈyes-tər-ˌyiər\ *n* **1 :** last year **2 :** the recent past [*yester*day + *year*]

[1]yet \yet, ˈyet\ *adv* **1 a :** in addition **:** BESIDES ⟨gives *yet* another reason⟩ **b :** EVEN 2b ⟨a *yet* higher speed⟩ **2 a** (1) **:** up to now **:** so far ⟨hasn't done much *yet*⟩ (2) **:** at this or that time ⟨not time to go *yet*⟩ **b :** continuously up to the present or a specified time **:** STILL ⟨is *yet* a new country⟩ **c :** at a future time ⟨may *yet* see the light⟩ **3 :** NEVERTHELESS, HOWEVER ⟨led a quiet, *yet* happy life⟩ [Old English *gīet*]

[2]yet *conj* **:** despite that fact **:** BUT

ye•ti \ˈyet-ē, ˈyāt-\ *n* **:** ABOMINABLE SNOWMAN [Tibetan]

yew \ˈyü\ *n* **1 a :** any of a genus of evergreen trees and shrubs with stiff poisonous needles and fruits with a fleshy aril **b :** the wood of a yew; *esp* **:** the heavy fine-grained wood of an Old World yew that is used for bows and small articles **2** *archaic* **:** an achery bow made of yew [Old English *īw*]

yew 1a

Yid•dish \ˈyid-ish\ *n* **:** a High German language spoken by Jews chiefly in eastern Europe and areas to which Jews from eastern Europe have migrated and commonly written in Hebrew characters [Yiddish *yidish*, short for *yidish daytsh*, literally, "Jewish German"] — **Yiddish** *adj*

[1]yield \ˈyēld\ *vb* **1 :** to give up possession of on claim or demand **:** hand over possession of **2 :** to give (oneself) up to an inclination, temptation, or habit **3 a :** to bear or bring forth as a natural product especially as a result of cultivation **b :** to furnish as return or result of expended effort **c :** to produce as return from an expenditure or investment **:** furnish as profit or interest **d :** to produce as revenue **:** bring in **4 :** to be fruitful or productive **5 :** to give up and cease resistance or contention **6 :** to give way to pressure or influence **:** submit to urging, persuasion, or entreaty **7 :** to give way under physical force so as to bend, stretch, or break **8 a :** to give place or precedence **:** acknowledge the superiority of someone else **b :** to give way to or become succeeded by someone or something else [Old English *gieldan*] — **yield•er** *n*

• **syn** SUBMIT, SUCCUMB: YIELD may apply to any sort or degree of giving way before force, argument, persuasion, or entreaty; SUBMIT suggests full surrendering after resistance or conflict to the will or control of another; SUCCUMB suggests weakness and helplessness on the part of the one giving way or the overwhelming power of the opposing force. **syn** see in addition RELINQUISH

[2]yield *n* **:** something yielded **:** PRODUCT; *esp* **:** the amount or quantity produced or returned ⟨*yield* of wheat per acre⟩

yield•ing *adj* **1 :** lacking rigidity or stiffness **:** FLEXIBLE ⟨a *yielding* mass⟩ **2 :** disposed to submit or comply ⟨a cheerful *yielding* nature⟩

yin \ˈyin\ *n* **:** the feminine passive principle (as of darkness, cold, or wetness) in nature that in Chinese cosmic philosophy combines with yang to produce all that comes to be [Chinese (Pekingese dialect) *yin*[1]]

y–in•ter•cept \ˌwī-ˈint-ər-ˌsept\ *n* **:** the coordinate of a point where a line, curve, or surface intersects the y-axis

yip \ˈyip\ *vi* **:** YELP [imitative] — **yip** *n*

yip·pee \ˈyip-ē\ *interj* — used to express exuberant delight or triumph

-yl \əl, ᵊl, il, ˌil\ *n combining form* : chemical and usually univalent radical ⟨eth*yl*⟩⟨hydrox*yl*⟩ [Greek *hylē* "matter, material", literally, "wood"]

[1]**yo·del** \ˈyōd-ᵊl\ *vb* **-deled** *or* **-delled**; **-del·ing** *or* **-del·ling** \ˈyōd-ling, -ᵊl-ing\ : to sing by suddenly changing from the natural voice to falsetto and the reverse; *also* : to shout or call in this manner [German *jodeln*] — **yo·del·er** \ˈyōd-lər, -ᵊl-ər\ *n*

[2]**yodel** *n* : a song or refrain sung by yodeling; *also* : a yodeled shout

yo·ga \ˈyō-gə\ *n* **1** *cap* : a Hindu theistic philosophy **2** : a system of exercises for attaining bodily or mental control and well-being [Sanskrit, literally, "yoking"] — **yo·gic** \-gik\ *adj*

yo·gi \ˈyō-gē\ *or* **yo·gin** \-gən, -ˌgin\ *n* **1** : a person who practices yoga **2** *cap* : an adherent of Yoga philosophy [Sanskrit *yogin,* from *yoga*]

yo·gurt *or* **yo·ghurt** \ˈyō-gərt\ *n* : a slightly acid semifluid milk food made of skimmed cow's milk and milk solids fermented by cultures of bacteria, often flavored (as with fruit), and sometimes frozen [Turkish *yoğurt*]

[1]**yoke** \ˈyōk\ *n, pl* **yokes** **1 a** : a wooden bar or frame by which two draft animals (as oxen) are coupled at the heads or necks for working together **b** : a frame fitted to a person's shoulders to carry a load in two equal portions **c** : a clamp or similar piece that embraces two parts to hold or unite them in position **2** *pl usually* **yoke** : two animals yoked together **3 a** : an oppressive agency ⟨freed from the tyrant's *yoke*⟩ **b** : SERVITUDE, BONDAGE **c** : TIE, LINK ⟨the *yoke* of matrimony⟩ **4** : a fitted or shaped piece at the top of a skirt or at the shoulder of various garments [Old English *geoc*]

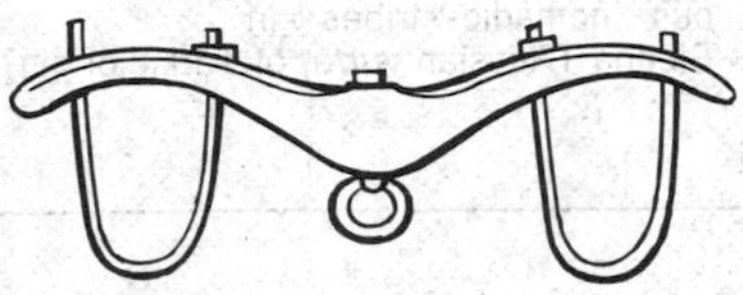

[1]yoke 1a

[2]**yoke** *vb* **1 a** : to put a yoke on or couple with a yoke **b** : to attach (a draft animal) to something **2** : to join as if by a yoke **3** : to put to work

yoke·fellow \ˈyōk-ˌfel-ō\ *n* : a close companion : MATE

yo·kel \ˈyō-kəl\ *n* : RUSTIC, BUMPKIN [perhaps from English dialect *yokel,* a kind of woodpecker]

yolk \ˈyōk, ˈyelk *also* ˈyōlk\ *n* **1 a** : the yellow inner mass of the egg of a bird or reptile **b** : the material stored in an ovum that supplies food material to the developing embryo **2** : oily material in raw sheep wool [Old English *geoloca,* from *geolu* "yellow"] — **yolk** *adj* — **yolked** *adj* — **yolky** *adj*

yolk sac *n* : a membranous sac that is attached to many embryos, encloses food yolk, and is continuous with the intestinal cavity

yolk stalk *n* : a narrow tubular stalk connecting the yolk sac with the embryo

Yom Kip·pur \ˌyōm-ki-ˈpu̇r, ˌyȯm-, ˌyäm-, -ˈkip-ər\ *n* : a Jewish holiday observed in September or October with fasting and prayer as a day of atonement [Hebrew *yōm kippūr,* from *yōm* "day" + *kippūr* "atonement"]

[1]**yon** \ˈyän\ *adj* : YONDER [Old English *geon*]

[2]**yon** *adv* **1** : YONDER **2** : THITHER ⟨ran hither and *yon*⟩

[1]**yond** \ˈyänd\ *adv, archaic* : YONDER [Old English *geond*]

[2]**yond** *adj, dialect* : YONDER

[1]**yon·der** \ˈyän-dər\ *adv* : at or to that place : over there [Middle English, from *yond* + *-er* (as in *hither*)]

[2]**yonder** *adj* **1** : farther removed : more distant ⟨the *yonder* side of the river⟩ **2** : being at a distance within view ⟨*yonder* hills⟩

yore \ˈyōr, ˈyȯr\ *n* : time long past — usually used in the phrase *of yore* [Old English *geāra* "long ago", from *gēar* "year"]

York·ist \ˈyȯr-kəst\ *adj* : of or relating to the English royal house that ruled from 1461 to 1485 — compare LANCASTRIAN [Edward, Duke of *York* (Edward IV of England)] — **Yorkist** *n*

York·shire \ˈyȯrk-ˌshiər, -shər\ *n* : a white swine of any of several breeds or strains originated in Yorkshire, England

York·shire pudding \ˌyȯrk-ˌshiər, -shər-\ *n* : a batter of eggs, flour, and milk baked in meat drippings [*Yorkshire,* England]

you \yü, ˈyü, yə, yē\ *pron* **1** : the one or ones spoken to — used as the pronoun of the 2d person singular or plural in any grammatical relation except that of a possessive ⟨*you* are my friends⟩ ⟨can I pour *you* a cup of tea⟩; used formerly only as a plural pronoun of the 2d person in the dative or accusative case as direct or indirect object of a verb or as object of a preposition; compare THEE, THOU, YE, YOUR, YOURS **2** : [2]ONE 1b [Old English *ēow,* dative and accusative of *gē* "you"]

you–all \yü-ˈȯl, ˈyü-ˌȯl, ˈyȯl\ *pron* : YOU — usually used in addressing two or more persons or sometimes one person as representing also another or others

you'd \yüd, ˌyüd, yu̇d, ˌyu̇d, yəd\ : you had : you would

you'll \yül, ˌyül, yu̇l, ˌyu̇l, yəl\ : you shall : you will

[1]**young** \ˈyəŋ\ *adj* **youn·ger** \ˈyəŋ-gər\; **youn·gest** \ˈyəŋ-gəst\ **1 a** : being in the first or an early stage of life, growth, or development **b** : JUNIOR 1a **2** : having little experience **3 a** : recently come into being : NEW ⟨the *young* democracies⟩ **b** : YOUTHFUL 4 ⟨*young* mountains⟩ **4** : of, relating to, or having the characteristics of youth or a young person [Old English *geong*] — **young·ness** \ˈyəŋ-nəs\ *n*

[2]**young** *n, pl* **young** **1** *pl* **a** : young persons : YOUTH **b** : immature offspring especially of lower animals **2** : a single recently born or hatched animal — **with young** : PREGNANT — used of animals

young·ber·ry \ˈyəŋ-ˌber-ē\ *n* : the large sweet reddish black fruit of a hybrid between a trailing blackberry and a southern dewberry grown in the western and southern United States; *also* : the bramble that bears this fruit [B. M. *Young,* 20th century American fruit grower]

youn·ger \ˈyəŋ-gər\ *n* : an inferior in age : JUNIOR — usually used with a possessive pronoun ⟨is several years my *younger*⟩

youn·gest \ˈyəŋ-gəst\ *n* : one that is the least old

young·ish \ˈyəŋ-ish\ *adj* : somewhat young

young·ling \ˈyəŋ-liŋ\ *n* : one that is young : a young person or animal — **youngling** *adj*

young·ster \ˈyəŋ-stər\ *n* **1** : a young person : YOUTH **2** : CHILD 2a

Young Turk *n* : an insurgent or a member of an insurgent group in a political party [*Young Turks,* a 20th century revolutionary party in Turkey]

youn·ker \ˈyəŋ-kər\ *n* **1** : a young man **2** : CHILD 2a, YOUNGSTER [Dutch *jonker* "young nobleman"]

your \yər, yu̇r, ˈyu̇r, yōr, ˈyōr, yȯr, ˈyȯr\ *adj* **1** : of or relating to you or yourself or yourselves especially as possessor or possessors, agent or agents, or object or objects of an action ⟨*your* house⟩⟨*your* contributions⟩ ⟨*your* discharge⟩ **2** : of or relating to one or oneself ⟨when you face the north, east is at *your* right⟩ [Old English *ēower*]

you're \yər, yu̇r, ˌyu̇r, yōr, ˌyōr, yȯr, ˌyȯr\ : you are

yours \yu̇rz, ˈyōrz, ˈyȯrz\ *pron, sing or pl in construction* : that which belongs to you : those which belong to you — used without a following noun as an equivalent in meaning to the adjective *your;* often used especially with an adverbial modifier in the complimentary close of a letter ⟨*yours* truly⟩

your·self \yər-ˈself\ *pron* **1 a** : that identical one that is you — used reflexively or for emphasis ⟨don't hurt *yourself*⟩ ⟨do it *yourself*⟩ **b** : your normal, healthy, or sane condition or self **2** : ONESELF

your·selves \-ˈselvz\ *pron pl* **1** : those identical ones that are you — used reflexively or for emphasis ⟨get *yourselves* a treat⟩ ⟨carry them *yourselves*⟩ **2** : your normal, healthy, or sane conditions or selves

youth \ˈyüth\ *n, pl* **youths** \ˈyüt͟hz, ˈyüths\ **1** : the time of life marked by growth and development; *esp* : the period between childhood and maturity **2 a** : a young man **b** : young persons — usually pl. in construction ⟨the *youth* of the nation are a fine lot⟩ **3** : YOUTHFULNESS [Old English *geoguth*]

youth·ful \ˈyüth-fəl\ *adj* **1** : of, relating to, or appropriate to youth **2** : being young and not yet mature **3** : FRESH 2b (1), VIGOROUS ⟨*youthful* grandparents⟩ **4** : having accomplished or undergone little erosion ⟨a *youthful* valley⟩⟨*youthful* streams⟩ — **youth·ful·ly** \-fə-lē\ *adv* — **youth·ful·ness** *n*

youth hostel *n* : HOSTEL 2

you've \yüv, ˌyüv, yəv\ : you have

\ə\ **abut**	\au̇\ **out**	\i\ **tip**	\ȯ\ **saw**	\u̇\ **foot**
\ər\ **further**	\ch\ **chin**	\ī\ **life**	\ȯi\ **coin**	\y\ **yet**
\a\ **mat**	\e\ **pet**	\j\ **job**	\th\ **thin**	\yü\ **few**
\ā\ **take**	\ē\ **easy**	\ŋ\ **sing**	\t͟h\ **this**	\yu̇\ **cure**
\ä\ **cot, cart**	\g\ **go**	\ō\ **bone**	\ü\ **food**	\zh\ **vision**

yowl \ˈyau̇l\ *vi* : HOWL 1 [Middle English *yowlen*] — **yowl** *n*

yo-yo \ˈyō-ˌyō\ *n, pl* **yo-yos** *also* **yo-yoes** : a thick divided disk that is made to fall and rise to the hand by unwinding and rewinding on a string [native name in the Philippines]

yt·ter·bi·um \i-ˈtər-bē-əm, ə-\ *n* : a metallic chemical element that occurs in several minerals — see ELEMENT table [New Latin, from *Ytterby,* Sweden]

yt·tri·um \ˈi-trē-əm\ *n* : a metallic chemical element usually included among the rare earth elements with which it occurs in minerals — see ELEMENT table [New Latin, from *yttria* "yttrium oxide", from *Ytterby,* Sweden]

yu·an \ˈyü-ən, yu̇-ˈän\ *n, pl* **yuan** **1** : the basic monetary unit of China **2** : a coin or note representing one yuan [Chinese (Pekingese dialect) *yüan*[2]]

yucca

yuc·ca \ˈyək-ə\ *n* : any of a genus of plants of the lily family growing in dry regions and having stiff sharp-pointed fibrous leaves mostly in a rosette at the base and whitish flowers usually in erect clusters [Spanish *yuca*]

Yu·kon time \ˈyü-ˌkän-\ *n* : the time of the 9th time zone west of Greenwich that includes Yukon Territory and part of southern Alaska

yule \ˈyül\ *n, often cap* : the feast of the nativity of Jesus Christ : CHRISTMAS [Old English *geōl*]

yule log *n, often cap Y* : a large log formerly put on the hearth on Christmas Eve as the foundation of the fire

yule·tide \ˈyül-ˌtīd\ *n, often cap* : the Christmas season : CHRISTMASTIDE

yum·my \ˈyəm-ē\ *adj* : highly attractive or pleasing : DELECTABLE [*yum-yum,* interj. expressing pleasure in the taste of food]

yurt \ˈyu̇rt\ *n* : a light round tent of skins or felt stretched over a lattice framework used by various nomadic tribes in Siberia [Russian *yurta,* of Turkic origin]

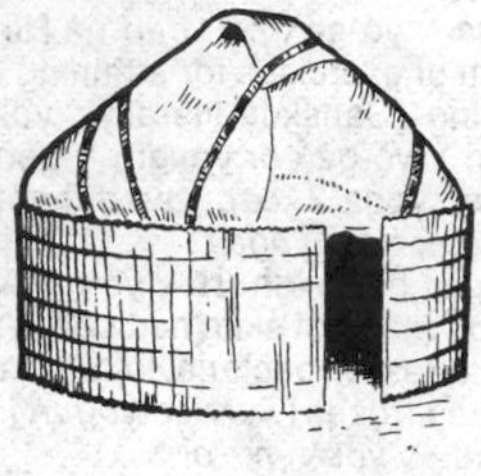
yurt

Z z—zymogenic

z \ˈzē, *British & Canadian* ˈzed\ *n, pl* **z's** *or* **zs** *often cap* : the 26th and last letter of the English alphabet

Zach·a·ri·as \ˌzak-ə-ˈrī-əs\ *n* — see BIBLE table

[1]**za·ny** \ˈzā-nē\ *n, pl* **zanies** **1** : CLOWN 2a, MERRY-ANDREW **2** : BUFFOON 1 [Italian *zanni,* from *Zanni,* nickname for *Giovanni* "John"]

△ **origin** In the 16th century the Italian theater developed a form of comedy improvised from standard situations and stock characters. One of these characters is a subordinate fool, clown, acrobat, or mountebank who mimics ludicrously the tricks of his principal. In Italian the stock name for such a character is *Zanni,* a nickname (in the dialect of Lombardy) for the name *Giovanni,* the Italian form of *John.* Italian *zanni* was soon borrowed into English, and by the early 17th century English *zany* was used for anyone who makes a laughingstock of himself, a buffoon.

[2]**zany** *adj* **za·ni·er**; **-est** **1** : being or having the characteristics of a zany **2** : fantastically or irrationally ludicrous : CRAZY — **za·ni·ly** \ˈzān-l-ē\ *adv* — **za·ni·ness** \ˈzā-nē-nəs\ *n*

zap \ˈzap\ *interj* — used to indicate a sudden or instantaneous occurrence [imitative]

zeal \ˈzēl\ *n* : eagerness and ardent interest in pursuit of something : FERVOR [Late Latin *zelus,* from Greek *zēlos*]
• **syn** ENTHUSIASM: ZEAL implies energetic and unflagging pursuit of an aim or devotion to a cause; ENTHUSIASM suggests lively or eager interest in or admiration for a proposal or cause or activity.

zeal·ot \ˈzel-ət\ *n* **1** *cap* : one of a fanatical sect of ancient Judea bitterly opposing the Roman domination of Palestine **2** : a zealous person; *esp* : a fanatical partisan [Late Latin *zelotes,* from Greek *zēlōtēs,* from *zēlos* "zeal"] — **zeal·ot·ry** \ˈzel-ə-trē\ *n*

zeal·ous \ˈzel-əs\ *adj* : filled with, characterized by, or due to zeal ⟨*zealous* missionaries⟩ — **zeal·ous·ly** *adv* — **zeal·ous·ness** *n*

ze·bra \ˈzē-brə\ *n, pl* **zebras** *also* **zebra** : any of several fleet African mammals related to the horse but distinctively and conspicuously patterned in stripes of black or dark brown and white or buff [Italian, from Spanish *cebra*]

ze·bu \ˈzē-bü, -byü\ *n* : an Asian ox domesticated and differentiated into many breeds and distinguished from European cattle with which it crosses freely by a large fleshy hump over the shoulders and a loose skin prolonged into dewlap and folds [French *zébu*]

Zech·a·ri·ah \ˌzek-ə-ˈrī-ə\ *n* — see BIBLE table

zed \ˈzed\ *n, chiefly British* : the letter *z* [Middle French *zede,* from Late Latin *zeta* "zeta", from Greek *zēta*]

zebu

ze·in \ˈzē-ən\ *n* : a protein from Indian corn used especially in making textile fibers, plastics, and adhesives [New Latin *Zea,* genus including Indian corn, from Greek *zea* "wheat"]

zeit·geist \ˈtsīt-ˌgīst, ˈzīt-\ *n* : the general intellectual, moral, and cultural state of an era [German, from *zeit* "time" + *geist* "spirit"]

zemst·vo \ˈzemst-vō, ˈzempst-, -və\ *n, pl* **zemstvos** : one of the district and provincial assemblies established in Russia in 1864 [Russian]

Zen \ˈzen\ *n* : a Japanese Buddhist sect that stresses the attainment of enlightenment by direct intuition through meditation rather than through intellectual concepts [Japanese, "religious meditation", from Chinese (Pekingese dialect) *ch'an*[2], derived from Sanskrit *dhyāna,* from *dhyāti* "he thinks"]

ze·nith \ˈzē-nəth\ *n* **1** : the point in the heavens directly overhead **2** : the highest point : PEAK, SUMMIT ⟨the *zenith* of our civilization⟩ [Middle French *cenith,* from Medieval Latin, from Spanish *zenit, cenit,* from Arabic *samt* (ar-ra's) "way (of the head)"]

ze·nith·al \-əl\ *adj* : of, relating to, or located at or near the zenith

ze·o·lite \ˈzē-ə-ˌlīt\ *n* : any of various silicates chemically related to the feldspars that are used especially in water softening [Swedish *zeolit,* from Greek *zein* "to boil"] — **ze·o·lit·ic** \ˌzē-ə-ˈlit-ik\ *adj*

Zeph·a·ni·ah \ˌzef-ə-ˈnī-ə\ *n* — see BIBLE table

zeph·yr \ˈzef-ər\ *n* **1 a** : a breeze from the west **b** : a gentle breeze **2 a** : a fine soft wool yarn **b** : any of various lightweight fabrics and articles of clothing [Latin *Zephyrus,* god of the west wind, west wind, from Greek *Zephyros*]

zep·pe·lin \ˈzep-lən, -ə-lən\ *n* : a rigid airship consisting of a cylindrical covered frame supported by internal gas cells

[Count Ferdinand von *Zeppelin,* died 1917, German airship manufacturer]

ze•ro \ˈzē-rō, ˈziər-ō\ *n, pl* **zeros** *also* **zeroes** **1 :** a number denoting absence of all quantity; *also* **:** a symbol representing this number — see NUMBER table **2 a :** the point of departure in reckoning; *also* **:** the point from which the graduation of a scale (as of a speedometer) commences **b :** a value or reading of zero; *esp* **:** the temperature represented by the zero mark on a thermometer **3 :** a person or thing having no importance or significance **:** NONENTITY **4 a :** a state of total absence or neutrality **:** NOTHING **b :** the lowest point **:** NADIR [Italian, from Medieval Latin *zephirum,* from Arabic *ṣifr*]

²zero *adj* **1 a :** of, relating to, or being a zero **b** (1) **:** amounting to zero ⟨a *zero* growth rate⟩ (2) **:** having no modified inflectional form ⟨*zero* plurals⟩ **2 a :** limiting vision to 50 feet or less ⟨*zero* cloud ceiling⟩ **b :** limited to 165 feet or less ⟨*zero* visibility⟩

³zero *vb* **1 :** to determine or adjust the zero of ⟨*zero* a meter⟩ **2 :** to concentrate firepower (as of artillery) on the exact range of — usually used with *in* **3 :** to adjust fire on a specific target — usually used with *in*

zero hour *n* **1 :** the hour at which a planned military movement is scheduled to start **2 :** the moment at which something significant, vital, or crucial is to begin or take place [from its being marked by the count of zero in a countdown]

zero–zero *adj* **:** characterized by or being atmospheric conditions that reduce ceiling and visibility to zero ⟨*zero-zero* weather⟩

zest \ˈzest\ *n* **1 :** a quality of enhancing enjoyment **:** PIQUANCY **2 :** keen enjoyment **:** RELISH, GUSTO [French, "orange or lemon peel used as flavoring"] **syn** see TASTE — **zest•ful** \-fəl\ *adj* — **zest•ful•ly** \-fə-lē\ *adv* — **zest•ful•ness** *n* — **zesty** \ˈzes-tē\ *adj*

△ **origin** *Zest* was borrowed into English in the 17th century from the French *zest* (now spelled *zeste*), meaning "orange or lemon peel". Where the French got the word we do not know. The peels of citrus fruits are still used to add flavoring to food and drinks, and the earliest citations for *zest* in English refer to the peel of such fruit used in this way. By the early 18th century, however, the sense was extended beyond the culinary domain, and *zest* was used to refer to a quality that adds enjoyment or piquancy to something.

ze•ta \ˈzāt-ə\ *n* **:** the 6th letter of the Greek alphabet — Z or ζ

¹zig \ˈzig\ *n* **:** one of the sharp turns or changes or a straight section of a zigzag course [*zig*zag]

²zig *vi* **zigged; zig•ging :** to execute a turn or follow a section of a zigzag course

zig•gu•rat \ˈzig-ə-ˌrat\ *n* **:** an ancient Mesopotamian temple tower consisting of a lofty pyramidal structure built in successive stages with outside staircases and a shrine at the top [Akkadian *ziggurratu* "pinnacle"]

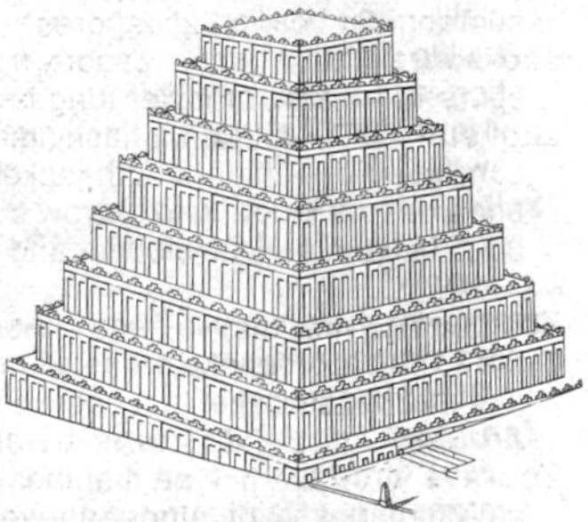

ziggurat

¹zig•zag \ˈzig-ˌzag\ *n* **1 :** a line or course made up of sharp opposite angles or turns at short and rather regular intervals; *also* **:** something (as a road or path) that takes such a course **2 :** one of the units making up a zigzag **:** a sharp angle or turn with the lines enclosing it ⟨the road followed a *zigzag* around the obstruction⟩ [French]

²zigzag *adv* **:** in or by a zigzag path or course

³zigzag *adj* **:** having short sharp turns or angles

⁴zigzag *vi* **zig•zagged; zig•zag•ging :** to lie in, proceed along, or consist of a zigzag course

zilch \ˈzilch\ *adj or n* **:** ZERO [by alteration]

zil•lion \ˈzil-yən\ *n* **:** a large indeterminate number [*z* + *-illion* (as in *million*)] — **zillion** *adj*

zinc \ˈzingk\ *n* **:** a bluish white metallic chemical element that tarnishes only slightly in moist air at ordinary temperatures and is used especially as a protective coating for iron — see ELEMENT table [German *zink*]

zinc blende *n* **:** SPHALERITE [German *blende* "sphalerite", from *blenden* "to blind"]

zinc chloride *n* **:** a poisonous caustic deliquescent salt $ZnCl_2$ used especially as a wood preservative and catalyst

zinc•ic \ˈzing-kik\ *adj* **:** relating to, containing, or resembling zinc

zinc•ite \ˈzing-ˌkīt\ *n* **:** a brittle deep-red to orange-yellow mineral consisting of zinc oxide that occurs in massive or granular form

zinc ointment *n* **:** an ointment containing about 20 percent of zinc oxide used in treating skin diseases

zinc oxide *n* **:** a white solid ZnO used especially as a pigment, in compounding rubber, and in pharmaceutical and cosmetic preparations

zinc sulfide *n* **:** a fluorescent compound ZnS used as a white pigment and as the light-producing substance in fluorescent lamps and television tubes

zinc white *n* **:** a white pigment used especially in house paints and glazes that consists of zinc oxide

¹zing \ˈzing\ *n* **1 :** a shrill humming noise **2 :** VITALITY 2b, VIM [imitative]

²zing *vi* **:** to move with or make a high-pitched hum ⟨tires *zinging* on wet pavement⟩

zinj•an•thro•pus \zin-ˈjan-thrə-pəs, -ˈjant-; ˌzin-ˌjan-ˈthrō-\ *n, pl* **-pi** \-ˌpī, -ˌpē\ *or* **-pus•es :** any of a genus of fossil hominids based on a skull found in eastern Africa, characterized by very low brow and large molars, and tentatively assigned to the Lower Pleistocene [New Latin, from Arabic *Zīnj* "eastern Africa" + Greek *anthrōpos* "human being"]

zin•nia \ˈzin-ē-ə, ˈzin-yə, ˈzēn-\ *n* **:** any of a small genus of tropical American herbs related to the daisies and having showy flower heads with long-lasting ray flowers [Johann G. *Zinn,* died 1759, German physician]

Zi•on \ˈzī-ən\ *n* **1 a :** the Jewish people **:** ISRAEL **b :** the Jewish homeland as a symbol of Judaism or of Jewish national aspiration **c :** the ideal nation or society envisaged by Judaism **2** *also* **Si•on** \ˈsī-ən\ **:** HEAVEN 2a **3 :** UTOPIA 1 [*Zion,* citadel in Palestine which was the nucleus of Jerusalem, derived from Hebrew *Ṣīyōn*]

Zi•on•ism \ˈzī-ə-ˌniz-əm\ *n* **:** a theory, plan, or movement for setting up a Jewish national or religious community in Palestine; *esp* **:** one strongly supporting the nation of Israel — **Zi•on•ist** \-nəst\ *adj or n* — **Zi•on•is•tic** \ˌzī-ə-ˈnis-tik\ *adj*

¹zip \ˈzip\ *vb* **zipped; zip•ping 1 :** to move or act with speed and vigor **2 :** to travel with a sharp hissing or humming sound **3 :** to add zest, interest, or life to — often used with *up* [imitative of the sound of a speeding object]

²zip *n* **1 :** a sudden sharp hissing or sibilant sound **2 :** ENERGY 2, VIM

³zip *vb* **zipped; zip•ping :** to close or open or attach by means of a zipper [back-formation from *zipper*]

zip gun *n* **:** a gun that is made from a toy pistol or a length of pipe, has a firing pin that is usually powered by a rubber band, and fires a .22 caliber bullet

zip•per \ˈzip-ər\ *n* **:** a fastener consisting of two rows of metal or plastic teeth on strips of tape and a sliding piece that closes an opening by drawing the teeth together [from *Zipper,* a former trademark]

zip•pered \-ərd\ *adj* **:** equipped with a zipper

zip•py \ˈzip-ē\ *adj* **zip•pi•er; -est :** full of zip **:** BRISK, SNAPPY

zi•ram \ˈzī-ˌram\ *n* **:** an organic zinc salt used especially as a fungicide [*zinc* + *-ram* (as in *thiram*)]

zir•con \ˈzər-ˌkän, -kən\ *n* **1 :** a crystalline mineral $ZrSiO_4$ which is a silicate of zirconium and of which several transparent varieties are used as gemstones **2 :** a gem cut from zircon [German *zirkon,* from French *jargon,* from Italian *giargone*]

zir•co•nia \ˌzər-ˈkō-nē-ə\ *n* **:** ZIRCONIUM OXIDE

zir•con•ic \ˌzər-ˈkän-ik\ *adj* **:** of, relating to, or containing zirconium

zir•co•ni•um \ˌzər-ˈkō-nē-əm\ *n* **:** a steel-gray strong ductile metallic chemical element with a high melting point that is highly resistant to corrosion and is used especially in alloys — see ELEMENT table [New Latin, from English *zircon*]

zirconium oxide *n* **:** a white crystalline compound ZrO_2 used especially in refractories, in thermal and electric insulation, in abrasives, and in enamels and glazes

\ə\ **abut**	\au̇\ **out**	\i\ **tip**	\ȯ\ **saw**	\u̇\ **foot**
\ər\ **further**	\ch\ **chin**	\ī\ **life**	\ȯi\ **coin**	\y\ **yet**
\a\ **mat**	\e\ **pet**	\j\ **job**	\th\ **thin**	\yü\ **few**
\ā\ **take**	\ē\ **easy**	\ng\ **sing**	\t͟h\ **this**	\yu̇\ **cure**
\ä\ **cot, cart**	\g\ **go**	\ō\ **bone**	\ü\ **food**	\zh\ **vision**

zith•er \ˈzith-ər, ˈzith-\ *n* : a stringed musical instrument having usually 30 to 40 strings over a flat soundboard played with the tips of the fingers and a plectrum [German, from Latin *cithara* "lyre", from Greek *kithara*] — **zith•er•ist** \-ə-rəst\ *n*

zither

zlo•ty \ˈzlot-ē, zə-ˈlȯt-\ *n, pl* **zlo•tys** \-ēz\ *also* **zlo•ty** **1** : the basic monetary unit of Poland **2** : a coin representing one zloty [Polish *złoty*]

zo- *or* **zoo-** *combining form* : animal : animal kingdom or kind ⟨zooid⟩ ⟨zoology⟩ [Greek *zōion* "animal"]

zo•di•ac \ˈzōd-ē-ˌak\ *n* **1** : a zone in the heavens that encompasses the apparent paths of all the principal planets except Pluto, that has as its central line the apparent path of the sun, and that is divided into 12 constellations or signs each taken for astrological purposes to extend 30 degrees of longitude **2** : a figure representing the signs of the zodiac and their symbols [Middle French *zodiaque*, from Latin *zodiacus*, from Greek *zōidiakos*, derived from *zōidion* "carved figure, sign of the zodiac", from *zōion* "animal, figure"] — **zo•di•a•cal** \zō-ˈdī-ə-kəl, zə-\ *adj*

THE SIGNS OF THE ZODIAC

NUMBER	NAME	SYMBOL	SUN ENTERS
1	Aries the Ram	♈	March 21
2	Taurus the Bull	♉	April 20
3	Gemini the Twins	♊	May 21
4	Cancer the Crab	♋	June 22
5	Leo the Lion	♌	July 23
6	Virgo the Virgin	♍	August 23
7	Libra the Balance	♎	September 23
8	Scorpio the Scorpion	♏	October 24
9	Sagittarius the Archer	♐	November 22
10	Capricorn the Goat	♑	December 22
11	Aquarius the Water Bearer	♒	January 20
12	Pisces the Fishes	♓	February 19

-zoic \ˈzō-ik\ *adj combining form* : of, relating to, or being a (specified) geological era ⟨Archeozoic⟩ [Greek *zōē* "life"]

zom•bie *also* **zom•bi** \ˈzäm-bē\ *n* : a human in the West Indies without will or the power of speech and capable only of automatic movement who is held to have died and been reanimated but often believed to have been drugged [of African origin]

△ **origin** Our *zombie* was originally a deity in Africa. In West African voodoo cults, the *zombie* was the python-god. He was later transplanted with African slaves to the West Indies and the southern United States. *Zombie* was also used for a certain power associated with the snake deity, which could enter a corpse and reanimate it. A dead body brought back to life by this power was likewise called a *zombie*.

zon•al \ˈzōn-l\ *adj* **1** : of, relating to, or having the form of a zone **2** : of, relating to, or being a soil or major soil group marked by well-developed characteristics that are determined primarily by the action of climate and organisms especially vegetation — compare AZONAL, INTRAZONAL

zo•na•tion \zō-ˈnā-shən\ *n* : distribution or arrangement in zones; *esp* : distribution of organisms in biogeographic zones

[1]**zone** \ˈzōn\ *n* **1** : any of five great divisions of the earth's surface with respect to latitude and temperature — compare FRIGID ZONE, TEMPERATE ZONE, TORRID ZONE **2** *archaic* : GIRDLE, BELT **3 a** : an encircling anatomical structure **b** : an area that supports a similar flora and fauna throughout its extent **c** : a distinctive belt, layer, or series of layers of earth materials (as rock) **4** : a region or area set off as distinct from surrounding or adjoining parts or created for a particular purpose: as **a** : a zoned section (as of a city) **b** : any of the eight concentric bands of territory centered on a given United States parcel-post shipment point to which mail is charged at a single rate [Latin *zona* "belt, zone", from Greek *zōnē*]

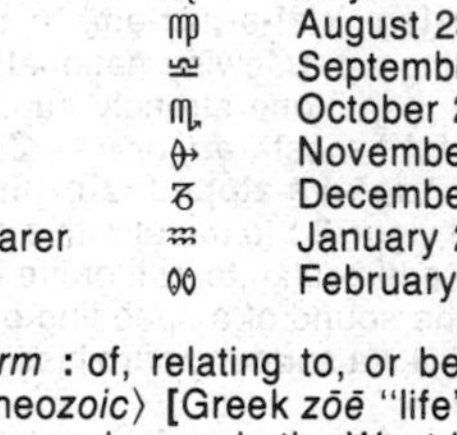

[1]zone 1

[2]**zone** *vt* **1** : to surround with a zone : ENCIRCLE **2** : to arrange in or mark off into zones; *esp* : to divide (as a city) into sections reserved for different purposes

zoo \ˈzü\ *n, pl* **zoos** : a garden or park where living animals are kept for exhibition [short for *zoological garden*]

zoo- — see ZO-

zoo•ge•og•ra•phy \ˌzō-ə-jē-ˈäg-rə-fē\ *n* : a branch of biogeography concerned with the geographical distribution of animals — **zoo•geo•graph•ic** \-ˌjē-ə-ˈgraf-ik\ *or* **zoo•geo•graph•i•cal** \-ˈgraf-i-kəl\ *adj* — **zoo•geo•graph•i•cal•ly** \-i-kə-lē, -klē\ *adv*

zo•oid \ˈzō-ˌȯid\ *n* : an entity (as a phagocyte) that resembles (as in independent motility) but is not wholly the same as a separate individual organism; *esp* : a more or less independent animal (as a polyp of a colonial coral) produced by other than direct sexual methods

zo•o•log•i•cal \ˌzō-ə-ˈläj-i-kəl\ *adj* **1** : of, relating to, or occupied with zoology **2** : of, relating to, or affecting lower animals often as distinguished from man ⟨*zoological* infections⟩ — **zo•o•log•i•cal•ly** \-i-kə-lē, -klē\ *adv*

zoological garden *n* : ZOO

zo•ol•o•gy \zō-ˈäl-ə-jē, zə-ˈwäl-\ *n* **1** : a science that deals with animals and is the branch of biology concerned with the animal kingdom and animal life **2 a** : animal life : FAUNA **b** : the properties of vital phenomena exhibited by an animal, animal type, or group — **zo•ol•o•gist** \-jəst\ *n*

[1]**zoom** \ˈzüm\ *vb* **1** : to move with a loud low hum or buzz **2** : to climb for a short time at an angle greater than that which can be maintained in steady flight ⟨the airplane *zoomed* and vanished in the distance⟩ **3** : to focus a camera or microscope using a special lens that permits the apparent distance of the object to be varied **4** : to cause to zoom [imitative]

[2]**zoom** *n* **1** : an act or process of zooming **2** : a zooming sound

zoom lens *n* : a camera lens in which the image size can be varied continuously so that the image remains in focus at all times

zoo•par•a•site \ˌzō-ə-ˈpar-ə-ˌsīt\ *n* : a parasitic animal

zoo•plank•ton \ˌzō-ə-ˈplang-tən, -ˈplangk-, -ˌtän\ *n* : animal life of the plankton — **zoo•plank•ton•ic** \-ˌplang-ˈtän-ik, -ˌplangk-\ *adj*

zoo•spo•ran•gi•um \ˌzō-ə-spə-ˈran-jē-əm\ *n* : a spore case or sporangium bearing zoospores

zoo•spore \ˈzō-ə-ˌspōr, -ˌspȯr\ *n* : a flagellated motile asexual spore of an alga or lower fungus

zoot suit \ˈzüt-ˌsüt\ *n* : a flashy man's suit of the 1940s typically consisting of a thigh-length jacket with wide padded shoulders and trousers tapering to narrow cuffs [coined by Harold C. Fox, born 1910, American clothier and bandmaster] — **zoot–suit•er** \-ər\ *n*

Zo•ro•as•tri•an \ˌzōr-ə-ˈwas-trē-ən, ˌzȯr-\ *adj* : of or relating to the Persian prophet Zoroaster or the religion founded by him and marked by belief in a cosmic war between good and evil — **Zoroastrian** *n* — **Zo•ro•as•tri•an•ism** \-trē-ə-ˌniz-əm\ *n*

Zou•ave \zü-ˈäv\ *n* **1** : a member of a French infantry unit originally composed of Algerians wearing a colorful uniform and conducting a quick spirited drill **2** : a member of a military unit modeled on the Algerian Zouaves [French, from Berber *Zwāwa*, an Algerian tribe]

zounds \ˈzaünz, ˈzwaünz, ˈzünz, ˈzwünz\ *interj* — used as a mild oath [euphemism for *God's wounds*]

zoy•sia \ˈzȯi-shə, zhə, -sē-ə, -zē-ə\ *n* : any of a genus of creeping perennial grasses having fine wiry leaves and includng some used as lawn grasses [Karl von *Zois*, died 1800, German botanist]

zuc•chet•to \zü-ˈket-ō, tsü-\ *n, pl* **-tos** : a small round skullcap worn by Roman Catholic ecclesiastics in colors that vary according to the rank of the wearer [Italian, from *zucca* "gourd, head", from Late Latin *cucutia* "gourd"]

zuc•chi•ni \zü-ˈkē-nē\ *n, pl* **-ni** *or* **-nis** : a summer squash of bushy growth with smooth slender cylindrical dark green fruits [Italian, pl. of *zucchino* "small gourd, squash", from *zucca* "gourd" from Late Latin *cucutia*]

Zu•lu \ˈzü-lü\ *n* **1** : a member of a Bantu-speaking people of Natal **2** : a Bantu language of the Zulus — **Zulu** *adj*

Zu•ni \ˈzü-ne\ *or* **Zu•ñi** \ˈzün-yē\ *n, pl* **Zuni** *or* **Zunis** *or* **Zuñi**

or **Zuñis** : a member of an Indian people of the Southwest [American Spanish]

zwie•back \ˈswē-ˌbak, ˈswī-, ˈzwē-, ˈzwī-, -ˌbäk\ *n* : a bread enriched with eggs that is baked and then sliced and toasted until dry and crisp [German, literally, "twice baked"]

Zwing•li•an \ˈzwing-lē-ən, ˈswing-, -glē-; ˈtsfing-lē-ən\ *adj* : of or relating to Ulrich Zwingli or his doctrine that in the Lord's Supper there is an influence of Christ upon the soul but that the true body of Christ is present by the contemplation of faith and not in essence or reality — **Zwinglian** *n*

zyg- *or* **zygo-** *combining form* **1** : yoke ⟨*zygo*morphic⟩ **2** : concerned with or produced in sexual reproduction ⟨*zygo*spore⟩ [Greek *zygon*]

zy•go•mat•ic \ˌzī-gə-ˈmat-ik\ *adj* : of, relating to, being, or situated in the region of the arched bony support of the part of the cheek below and to the side of the orbit [Greek *zygōmat-, zygōma* "zygomatic arch", from *zygoun* "to yoke", from *zygon* "yoke"]

zy•go•mor•phic \-ˈmȯr-fik\ *adj* : bilaterally symmetrical in respect to but one axis

zy•go•spore \ˈzī-gə-ˌspōr, -ˌspȯr\ *n* : a plant spore that is formed by conjugation of two similar sexual cells, usually serves as a resting spore, and ultimately produces the sporophyte — compare OOSPORE

zy•gote \ˈzī-ˌgōt\ *n* : a cell formed by the union of two gametes; *also* : the developing individual produced from such a cell [Greek *zygōtos* "yoked", from *zygoun* "to yoke", from *zygon* "yoke"] — **zy•got•ic** \zī-ˈgät-ik\ *adj* — **zy•got•i•cal•ly** \-ˈgät-i-kə-lē, -klē\ *adv*

-zy•gous \ˈzī-gəs\ *adj combining form* : having (such) a zygotic constitution ⟨hetero*zygous*⟩

zym- *or* **zymo-** *combining form* **1** : fermentation ⟨*zym*ase⟩ **2** : enzyme ⟨*zymo*gen⟩ [Greek *zymē* "leaven"]

zy•mase \ˈzī-ˌmās, -ˌmāz\ *n* : an enzyme or enzyme complex that promotes fermentation of monosaccharides

-zyme \ˌzīm\ *n combining form* : enzyme ⟨lyso*zyme*⟩

zy•mo•gen \ˈzī-mə-jən\ *n* : an inactive precursor of an enzyme as secreted by glandular cells and requring activation (as by an acid) before it can function — **zy•mo•gen•ic** \ˌzī-mə-ˈjen-ik\ *adj*

ABBREVIATIONS AND SYMBOLS FOR CHEMICAL ELEMENTS

For a list of special abbreviations used in this dictionary see page 15a preceding the vocabulary.

Most of these abbreviations have been normalized to one form. Variation in use of periods, in typeface, and in capitalization is frequent and widespread (as *mph*, *MPH*, *m.p.h.*, *Mph*).

a absent, acre, answer, are, atto-
A ace, ampere, argon
Å angstrom unit
AA Alcoholics Anonymous, associate in arts, author's alterations
A and M agricultural and mechanical
AAR against all risks
AB able-bodied seaman, bachelor of arts [New Latin *artium baccalaureus*]
abbr abbreviation
ABC American Broadcasting Company
abl ablative
abp archbishop
abs absolute, abstract
abstr abstract
ac account
Ac actinium
AC alternating current, before Christ [Latin *ante Christum*], area code
acad academic, academy
acc, accus accusative
accel accelerando
acct account, accountant
ack acknowledge, acknowledgment
act active, actor, actual
ACT American College Test, Australian Capital Territory
actg acting
AD after date, anno Domini
ADC aide-de-camp, Aid to Dependent Children
addn addition
ad int ad interim
adj adjective, adjunct, adjustment, adjutant
ad loc to or at the place [Latin *ad locum*]
ADM admiral
admin administration
adv adverb, advertisement, advertising
ad val ad valorem
advt advertisement
AEF American Expeditionary Force
aet, aetat of age, aged [Latin *aetatis*]
AF air force, audio frequency
AFB air force base
AFDC Aid to Families with Dependent Children
afft affidavit
AFL-CIO American Federation of Labor and Congress of Industrial Organizations
Afr Africa, African
Ag silver [Latin *argentum*]
agcy agency
agric agricultural, agriculture
agt agent
AK Alaska
aka also known as
Al aluminum
AL Alabama, American Legion
Ala Alabama
Alb Albania, Albanian
alc alcohol
ald alderman
alg algebra
alk alkaline
alt alternate, altitude
Alta Alberta
a.m., AM ante meridiem
Am America, American, americium
AM amplitude modulation, master of arts [New Latin *artium magister*]
amb ambassador
amdt amendment
Amer America, American
amp ampere
amt amount
AMU atomic mass unit
anal analogy, analysis, analytic
anat anatomical, anatomy
anc ancient
ann annals, annual
anon anonymous, anonymously
ans answer
ant antonym
Ant Antarctica
anthrop anthropology
antilog antilogarithm
AO account of
ap apostle, apothecaries'
AP additional premium, American plan, arithmetic progression, Associated Press
APO army post office
app apparatus, appendix
appl applied
approx approximate, approximately
Apr April
apt apartment, aptitude
aq aqua, aqueous
ar arrival, arrive
Ar argon
AR accounts receivable, Arkansas
Arab Arabian, Arabic
arch architect, architecture
archeol archeology
arith arithmetic
Ariz Arizona
Ark Arkansas
arr arranged, arrival, arrive
art article, artificial
As arsenic
AS Anglo-Saxon
assn association
assoc associate, association
asst assistant
astrol astrologer, astrology
astron astronomer, astronomy
ASV American Standard Version
At astatine
Atl Atlantic
atm atmosphere, atmospheric
at. no. atomic number
att attached, attention, attorney
attn attention
attrib attributive, attributively
atty attorney
at. wt. atomic weight
Au gold [Latin *aurum*]
Aug August
AUS Army of the United States
Austral Australian
auth authentic, author, authorized
aux, auxil auxiliary
av avenue, average, avoirdupois
AV ad valorem, audiovisual, Authorized Version
avdp avoirdupois
ave avenue
avg average
avn aviation
AZ Arizona

b back, book, born
B bachelor, Bible, bishop, boron
Ba barium
BA bachelor of arts
bal balance
bar barometer, barometric, barrel
Bart baronet
BBC British Broadcasting Corporation
bbl barrel, barrels
BC before Christ, British Columbia
BCS bachelor of commercial science
bd board, bound
BD bachelor of divinity, bank draft, bills discounted, brought down
bd ft board foot
bdl, bdle bundle
Be beryllium
BE bill of exchange
Belg Belgian, Belgium
bet between
BeV billion electron volts
bf boldface
BF board foot, brought forward
bg background, bag
Bi bismuth
bib Bible, biblical
BID twice a day [Latin *bis in die*]
biog biographer, biographical, biography
biol biologic, biological, biologist, biology
bk bank, book, break
Bk berkelium
bkg banking, bookkeeping
bkt basket, bracket
bl bale, barrel
BL bill of lading
bldg building
blvd boulevard
BM basal metabolism, board measure, bowel movement
BMR basal metabolic rate
BO body odor, box office, branch office, buyer's option
BOQ bachelor officers' quarters
bor borough
bot botanical, botanist, botany, bottle, bottom, bought
bp baptized, birthplace, bishop
BP bills payable, blood pressure, blueprint, boiling point
bpl birthplace
BPW Board of Public Works
br branch
Br Britain, British, bromine
BR bills receivable
Braz Brazil, Brazilian
brig brigade, brigadier
Brit Britain, British
bro brother, brothers
bros brothers
BS bachelor of science, balance sheet, bill of sale
BSA Boy Scouts of America
BSc bachelor of science
bskt basket
Bt baronet
btry battery
Btu British thermal unit
bu bureau, bushel
bull bulletin
bur bureau
bus business
BV Blessed Virgin

BWI British West Indies
bx box

c carat, cent, centi-, centimeter, century, chapter, circa, copyright
C capacitance, carbon, Celsius, centigrade
ca centare, circa
Ca calcium
CA California, chartered accountant, chief accountant, chronological age
CAF, C and F cost and freight
cal calendar, caliber, calorie (small)
Cal California, calorie (large)
Calif California
Can, Canad Canada, Canadian
canc canceled
cap capacity, capital, capitalize, capitalized
CAP Civil Air Patrol
caps capitals, capsule
Capt captain
card cardinal
CARE Cooperative for American Remittances to Everywhere
cat catalog
CATV community antenna television
Cb columbium
CB citizens band
CBC Canadian Broadcasting Corporation
CBD cash before delivery
CBS Columbia Broadcasting System
cc cubic centimeter
CC carbon copy, common carrier
cd candela, candle, cord
Cd cadmium
CD carried down, civil defense
CDR commander
CDT Central daylight time
Ce cerium
CE chemical engineer, civil engineer
cen central
cent centigrade, central, century
cert certificate, certification, certified, certify
cf compare [Latin *confer*]
Cf californium
CF carried forward
CFI cost, freight, and insurance
cg, cgm centigram
CG coast guard
cgs centimeter-gram-second
ch chain, chapter, church
CH clearinghouse, courthouse, customhouse
chap chapter
chem chemical, chemist, chemistry
chg change, charge
Chin Chinese
chm chairman, checkmate
chron chronicle, chronology
CI cost and insurance
CIA Central Intelligence Agency
CIF cost, insurance, and freight
C in C commander in chief
cir circle, circuit, circular, circumference
circ circular
cit citation, cited, citizen
civ civil, civilian
ck cask, check
cl centiliter, class
Cl chlorine
CL carload
clk clerk
clo clothing
cm centimeter
Cm curium
CM Congregation of the Mission
cml commercial
CN credit note
CNO chief of naval operations
CNS central nervous system
co company, county
Co cobalt
CO cash order, Colorado, commanding officer, conscientious objector
c/o care of
COD cash on delivery, collect on delivery
C of C Chamber of Commerce
C of S chief of staff
cog cognate
col colonial, colony, color, colored, column, counsel
Col colonel, Colorado
coll college
collat collateral
colloq colloquial
Colo Colorado
colog cologarithm
com commander, commerce, commissioner, committee, common
comb combination, combined, combining
comdg commanding
comdr commander
comdt commandant
coml commercial
comm commission, commonwealth
comp comparative, compensation, compiled, compiler, composition, compound
comr commissioner
con consolidated, consul
conc concentrated
cond conductivity
conf conference, cofidential
Confed Confederate
cong congress, congressional
conj conjunction
Conn Connecticut
cons conservative, consonant
consol consolidated
const constant, constitution, constitutional
constr construction
cont containing, contents, continent, continental, continued, control
contd continued
contg containing
contr contract, contraction
contrib contribution, contributor
corp corporal, corporation
corr corrected, correction, correspondence, corresponding
cos companies, cosine, counties
COS cash on shipment, chief of staff
cosec cosecant
cot cotangent
cp compare, coupon
CP candlepower, chemically pure, communist party
CPA certified public accountant
cpd compound
Cpl corporal
CPO chief petty officer
CPS cycles per second
CQ charge of quarters
cr credit, creditor
Cr chromium
cresc crescendo
crit critical, criticism, criticized
cryst crystalline, crystallized
cs case, cases
Cs cesium
CS civil service
C/S cycles per second
CSA Confederate States of America
csc cosecant
CSF cerebrospinal fluid
CST Central standard time
ct carat, cent, count, court
CT Central time, certified teacher, Connecticut
ctn carton
ctr center, counter
cu cubic
Cu copper [Latin *cuprum*]
cur currency, current
CV cardiovascular
CW continuous waves
CWO cash with order, chief warrant officer
cwt hundredweight
cyc, cycl cyclopedia
cyl cylinder
CZ Canal Zone

d date, daughter, day, dead, deceased, deci-, degree, penny, pence [Latin *denarius, denarii*]
D Democrat, deuterium, diameter
da deka-
DA days after acceptance, deposit account, district attorney
dag dekagram
dal dekaliter
dam dekameter
Dan Danish
DAR Daughters of the American Revolution
dat dative
db debenture, decibel
DBH diameter at breast height
dbl double
DC da capo, direct current, District of Columbia, doctor of chiropractic, double crochet
DD days after date, demand draft, doctor of divinity
DDD direct distance dialing
DDS doctor of dental science, doctor of dental surgery
DE Delaware
deb debenture
dec deceased, decrease, decrescendo
Dec December
def defendant, definite, definition
deg degree
del delegate, delegation
Del Delaware
dely delivery
Dem Democrat, Democratic
Den Denmark
dent dental, dentist, dentistry
dep depart, departure, deposit, deputy
dept department
der, deriv derivation, derivative
det detached, detachment, detail, determine
DEW distant early warning
DF damage free
DFC Distinguished Flying Cross
DFM Distinguished Flying Medal
dg decigram
DG by the grace of God [Late Latin *Dei gratia*], director general
DH designated hitter
dia, diam diameter
diag diagonal, diagram
dial dialect
dict dictionary
dif, diff difference
dig digest
dil dilute
dim dimension, diminished, diminuendo, diminutive
dir director
disc discount
dist distance, district
distn distillation
distr distribute, distribution
div divided, dividend, division, divorced
dk dark, deck, dock
dkg dekagram
dkl dekaliter
dkm dekameter
dks dekastere
dl deciliter
DLitt, DLit doctor of letters, doctor of literature
DLO dead letter office
dm decimeter
DMZ demilitarized zone
dn down
do ditto
DOA dead on arrival
doc document
DOD Department of Defense
dol dollar
dom domestic, dominion
doz dozen
DP data processing, double play
dpt department
dr debtor, dram, drive, drum
Dr doctor
ds decistere
DS days after sight, dal segno

DSC Distinguished Service Cross
DSM Distinguished Service Medal
DSO Distinguished Service Order
DSP died without issue [Latin *decessit sine prole*]
DST daylight saving time
Du Dutch
dup duplex, duplicate
DV Douay Version, Deo volente
DVM doctor of veterinary medicine
dwt pennyweight
DX distance
Dy dysprosium
dz dozen

E east, eastern, energy, English, error, excellent
ea each
E and OE errors and omissions excepted
EB eastbound
eccl ecclesiastic, ecclesiastical
ECG electrocardiogram
ecol ecological, ecology
econ economics, economist, economy
Ecua Ecuador
ed edited, edition, editor, education
ED extra duty
EDT Eastern daylight time
educ education, educational
EEG electroencephalogram, electroencephalograph
e.g. for example [Latin *exempli gratia*]
Eg Egypt, Egyptian
EHF extremely high frequency
EKG electrocardiogram, electrocardiograph [German *elektrokardiogramm*]
el, elev elevation
elec electric, electrical, electricity
elem elementary
embryol embryology
emer emeritus
emf electromotive force
emp emperor, empress
emu electromagnetic unit
enc, encl enclosure
ency, encyc encyclopedia
eng engine, engineer, engineering
Eng England, English
engr engineer, engraved, engraver, engraving
enl enlarged, enlisted
ENS ensign
entom, entomol entomological, entomology
env envelope
EOM end of month
EP European plan, extended play
eq equal, equation
equip equipment
equiv equivalency, equivalent
Er erbium
Es einsteinium
Esk Eskimo
esp especially
Esq, Esqr esquire
est established, estimate, estimated
EST Eastern standard time
esu electrostatic unit
ET eastern time
ETA estimated time of arrival
et al and others [Latin *et alii*]
etc et cetera
ETD estimated time of departure
ethnol ethnologist, ethnology
et seq and the following one [Latin *et sequens*], and the following ones [Latin *et sequentes* or *et sequentia*]
Eu europium
Eur Europe, European
EV electron volt
evap evaporate
ex example, exchange, executive, express, extra
exc excellent, except
exch exchange, exchanged
exec executive
exp expense, experiment, experimental, export, express
expt experiment
exptl experimental
ext extension, exterior, external, externally, extra, extract

f and the following one, farad, female, feminine, femto-, focal length, folio, force, forte, frequency
F Fahrenheit, filial generation, fluorine, French
FAA Federal Aviation Administration
fac facsimile, faculty
FADM fleet admiral
Fah, Fahr Fahrenheit
FAO Food and Agriculture Organization of the United Nations
FAS free alongside ship
fath fathom
FB freight bill
FBI Federal Bureau of Investigation
FCC Federal Communications Commission
fcp foolscap
fcy fancy
FDA Food and Drug Administration
FDIC Federal Deposit Insurance Corporation
Fe iron [Latin *ferrum*]
Feb February
fed federal, federation
fem female, feminine
FEPC Fair Employment Practices Commission
ff and the following ones, folios, fortissimo
FHA Federal Housing Administration
FICA Federal Insurance Contributions Act
FIFO first in, first out
fig figurative, figuratively, figure
fin finance, financial, finish
Finn Finnish
fl flanker, floor, flourished [Latin *floruit*], fluid
FL, Fla Florida
fl dr fluidram
Flem Flemish
fl oz fluidounce
fm fathom
Fm fermium
FM frequency modulation
fn footnote
fo, fol folio
FOB free on board
FOC free of charge
for foreign, forestry
FOR free on rail
FOS free on steamer
FOT free on truck
fp freezing point
fpm feet per minute
FPO fleet post office
fps feet per second, foot-pound-second
fr father, friar, from
Fr francium, French
freq frequency, frequent, frequently
Fri Friday
front frontispiece
FRS Federal Reserve System
frt freight
frwy freeway
FSH follicle-stimulating hormone
ft feet, foot, fort
ft lb foot-pound
fur furlong
fut future
fwd foreword, forward
FYI for your information

g acceleration of gravity, gauge, gram, gravity
G German, giga-, good
ga gauge
Ga gallium, Georgia
GA general agent, general assembly, general average, Georgia
gal gallery, gallon
galv galvanized
gar garage
GAW guaranteed annual wage
gaz gazette, gazetteer
GB Great Britain
GCA ground-controlled approach
GCD greatest common divisor
GCF greatest common factor
Gd gadolinium
gds goods
Ge germanium
gen general, genitive, genus
genl general
geog geographic, geographical, geography
geol geologic, geological, geology
geom geometric, geometrical, geometry
ger gerund
Ger German, Germany
GHQ general headquarters
gi gill
GI gastrointestinal, general issue, government issue
Gib Gibraltar
Gk Greek
gm gram
GM general manager, grand master, guided missile
GMT Greenwich mean time
GNP gross national product
GOP Grand Old Party (Republican)
Goth Gothic
gov government, governor
govt government
gp group
GP general practice, general practitioner, geometric progression
GPO general post office, Government Printing Office
GQ general quarters
gr grade, grain, gram, gravity, gross
Gr Greece, Greek
grad graduate, graduated
gram grammar, grammatical
GRAS generally recognized as safe
gro gross
GSA Girl Scouts of America
gt great
Gt Brit Great Britain
GU genitourinary, Guam

h hard, hardness, hecto-, heroin, hour, husband
H hit, hydrogen
ha hectare
Hb hemoglobin
HBM Her Britannic Majesty, His Britannic Majesty
HC House of Commons
HCF highest common factor
hd head
HD heavy-duty
hdbk handbook
hdkf handkerchief
hdwe hardware
He helium
HE high explosive, His Eminence, His Excellency
Heb Hebrew
HEW Department of Health, Education, and Welfare
hf half
Hf hafnium
HF high frequency
hg hectogram, hemoglobin
Hg mercury [Latin *hydrargyrum*]
hgt height
HH Her Highness, His Highness, His Holiness
HI Hawaii, high intensity
hist historian, historical, history
hl hectoliter
HL House of Lords
hm hectometer
HM Her Majesty, Her Majesty's, His Majesty, His Majesty's
HMS Her Majesty's ship, His Majesty's ship
Ho holmium
hon honor, honorable, honorary
hor horizontal
hort horticultural, horticulture
hosp hospital
HP high pressure, horsepower
HQ headquarters
hr here, hour

HR House of Representatives
HRH Her Royal Highness, His Royal Highness
HS high school
ht height
HT Hawaiian time, high-tension
Hung Hungarian, Hungary
hwy highway
hy henry
hyp hypothesis, hypothetical
Hz hertz

I interstate, intransitive, iodine, island, isle
Ia, IA Iowa
IAA indoleacetic acid
ib, ibid ibidem
ICBM intercontinental ballistic missile
ICC Interstate Commerce Commission
ICJ International Court of Justice
id idem
ID Idaho, identification
i.e. that is [Latin *id est*]
IF intermediate frequency
IL Illinois
ill, illus, illust illustrated, illustration
Ill Illinois
ILS instrument landing system
imit imitative
imp imperative, imperfect, imperial, import, imported
imperf imperfect
in inch, inlet
In indium
IN Indiana
inc incomplete, incorporated, increase
incl including, inclusive
incog incognito
ind independent, index, industrial, industry
Ind Indian, Indiana
indef indefinite
indic indicative
inf infantry, infinitive
infl influenced
INP International News Photo
INRI Jesus of Nazareth, King of the Jews [Latin *Iesus Nazarenus Rex Iudaeorum*]
ins inches, insurance
insol insoluble
inst instant, institute, institution, institutional
instr instructor, instrument, instrumental
int interest, interior, intermediate, internal, international, intransitive
interj interjection
interrog interrogative
intl, intnl international
intrans intransitive
introd introduction
inv inventor, invoice
iq the same as [Latin *idem quod*]
Ir iridium, Irish
IRBM intermediate range ballistic missile
Ire Ireland
irreg irregular
is island, isle
ISBN International Standard Book Number
Isr Israel, Israeli
ISV International Scientific Vocabulary
It Italian, Italy
ital italic, italicized
Ital Italian
IU international unit
IV intravenous, intravenously
IW Isle of Wight
IWW Industrial Workers of the World

J jack, joule
Jam Jamaica
Jan January
Jap Japan, Japanese
JCC Junior Chamber of Commerce
JCS joint chiefs of staff
jct junction
JD justice department, juvenile delinquent
jg junior grade
jour journal, journeyman
JP jet propulsion, justice of the peace
jr, jun junior
JRC Junior Red Cross
jt, jnt joint
junc junction
juv juvenile
JV junior varsity

k karat, kilo-, kilogram, knit
K Kelvin, king, potassium [Latin *kalium*]
Kans Kansas
kc kilocycle
KC Kansas City, King's Counsel
kcal kilocalorie
kc/s kilocycles per second
KD knocked down
kg kilogram
KG knight of the Garter
KIA killed in action
KJV King James Version
KKK Ku Klux Klan
kl kiloliter
km kilometer
KP kitchen police
Kr krypton
KS Kansas
kt karat, knight
kv kilovolt
kw kilowatt
kwhr, kwh kilowatt-hour
Ky, KY Kentucky

l late, left, liter, long
L lake, large, Latin, pound [Latin *libra*]
La lanthanum, Louisiana
LA law agent, Los Angeles, Louisiana
Lab Labrador
lang language
lat latitude
Lat Latin
lb pound [Latin *libra*]
lc lowercase
LC landing craft, Library of Congress
LCD least common denominator, lowest common denominator
LCL less-than-carload lot
LCM least common multiple, lowest common multiple
ld load, lord
LD lethal dose
ldg landing, loading
lect lecture, lecturer
leg legal, legato, legislative, legislature
legis legislation, legislative, legislature
LEM lunar excursion module
lf lightface
LF low frequency
lg large, long
LH left hand, luteinizing hormone
li link
Li lithium
LI Long Island
lib liberal, librarian, library
lieut lieutenant
LIFO last in, first out
lin lineal, linear
liq liquid, liquor
lit liter, literal, literally, literary, literature
lith, litho lithographic, lithography
LittD, LitD doctor of letters, doctor of literature
ll lines
LLD doctor of laws
LM lunar module
loc cit in the place cited [Latin *loco citato*]
log logarithm
Lond London
long longitude
loq he speaks, she speaks [Latin *loquitur*]
LP low pressure
LPN licensed practical nurse
Lr lawrencium
LS left side, letter signed, place of the seal [Latin *locus sigilli*]
lt light
Lt lieutenant
LT long ton
LTC, Lt Col lieutenant colonel
ltd limited
LTH luteotropic hormone
LTL less-than-truckload lot
ltr letter, lighter
Lu lutetium
lub lubricant, lubricating
lv leave

m male, maritime, married, masculine, mass, meridian, meter, mile, milli-, minute, molal, molality, month, moon, noon [Latin *meridies*]
M mach, medium, mega-, molar, molarity, monsieur, thousand [Latin *mille*]
ma milliampere
MA Massachusetts, master of arts, mental age, Middle Ages
mach machine, machining, machinist
mag magazine, magnesium, magnetism, magneto, magnitude
Maj major
man manual
Man Manitoba
manuf manufacture, manufacturing
mar maritime
Mar March
masc masculine
Mass Massachusetts
math mathematical, mathematician
max maximum
mb millibar
mc megacycle
MC member of Congress
Md Maryland, mendelevium
MD doctor of medicine, Maryland, months after date, muscular dystrophy
mdse merchandise
MDT Mountain daylight time
Me Maine
ME Maine, mechanical engineer, medical examiner, Middle English
meas measure
mech mechanical, mechanics
med medical, medicine, medieval, medium
meg megohm
mem member, memoir, memorial
mer meridian
met meteorological, meteorology, metropolitan
meteorol meteorological, meteorology
MeV million electron volts
Mex Mexican, Mexico
MF medium frequency, mezzo forte, microfiche
mfd manufactured
mfg manufacturing
mfr manufacture, manufacturer
mg milligram
Mg magnesium
mgr manager, monseigneur, monsignor
mgt management
mi mile, mileage, mill
MI, Mich Michigan
MIA missing in action
mid middle
mil military
min minim, minimum, mining, minor, minute
Minn Minnesota
misc miscellaneous
Miss Mississippi
mixt mixture
mk mark
mks meter-kilogram-second
ml milliliter
MLD median lethal dose, minimum lethal dose
Mlle mademoiselle
mm millimeter
MM messieurs
Mme madame
Mn manganese
MN Minnesota
mo month
Mo Missouri, molybdenum
MO mail order, medical officer, Missouri, modus operandi, money order
mod moderate, modern, modulo, modulus
modif modification
mol mole, molecular, molecule

mol wt molecular weight
MOM middle of month
Mon Monday
Mont Montana
mos months
MP melting point, member of parliament, metropolitan police, military police, military policeman
mpg miles per gallon
mph miles per hour
mRNA messenger RNA
MS manuscript, master of science, Mississippi, motor ship, multiple sclerosis
MSc master of science
msec millisecond
MSG, MSgt master sergeant
msgr monseigneur, monsignor
MSS manuscripts
MST Mountain standard time
mt mount, mountain
MT metric ton, Montana, Mountain time
mtg meeting, mortgage
mtge mortgage
mtn mountain
mun, munic municipal
mus museum, music, musical, musician
mv millivolt
Mv mendelevium
mym myriameter

n nano-, net, neuter, noon, note, noun, number
N nitrogen, normal, north, northern
Na sodium [Latin *natrium*]
NA no account, North America, not applicable
NAACP National Association for the Advancement of Colored People
NAS naval air station
NASA National Aeronautics and Space Administration
nat national, native, natural
natl national
NATO North Atlantic Treaty Organization
naut nautical
nav naval, navigable, navigation
Nb niobium
NB New Brunswick, northbound, nota bene
NBC National Broadcasting Company
NBS National Bureau of Standards
NC no charge, North Carolina
NCE New Catholic Edition
NCO noncommissioned officer
Nd neodymium
ND no date, North Dakota
N Dak North Dakota
Ne neon
NE Nebraska, New England, northeast
NEB New English Bible
Nebr, Neb Nebraska
NED New English Dictionary
neg negative
Neth Netherlands
neurol neurological, neurology
neut neuter
Nev Nevada
NF no funds
Nfld Newfoundland
NG national guard, no good
NH New Hampshire
Ni nickel
NJ New Jersey
NL night letter
NM, N Mex New Mexico
no north, number
No nobelium
nom nominative
non seq non sequitur
Nor, Norw Norway, Norwegian
NOS not otherwise specified
Nov November
Np neptunium
NP no protest, notary public
NPN nonprotein nitrogen
NS New Style, not specified, Nova Scotia
NSF not sufficient funds
NSW New South Wales
NT New Testament, Northern Territory
NTP normal temperature and pressure
nt wt, n wt net weight
numis numismatic, numismatics
NV Nevada
NW northwest
NWT Northwest Territories
NY New York
NYC New York City
NZ New Zealand

o ocean, ohm
O Ohio, oxygen
o/a on or about
OAS Organization of American States
ob he died, she died [Latin *obiit*], obstetrical, obstetrician
obj object, objective
obl oblique, oblong
obs obsolete
obv obverse
oc ocean
OC officer candidate
occas occasionally
OCS officer candidate school
oct octavo
Oct October
OD officer of the day, olive drab, on demand, overdose, overdraft, overdrawn
OE Old English
OED Oxford English Dictionary
off office, officer, official
OFM Order of Friars Minor
OG original gum
OH Ohio
OK, Okla Oklahoma
Ont Ontario
op work [Latin *opus*]
OP Order of Preachers, out of print
op cit in the work cited [Latin *opere citato*]
opp opposite
opt optical, optician, optics, optional
OR operating room, Oregon, owner's risk
orch orchestra
ord order, ordnance
Oreg, Ore Oregon
org organic, organization, organized
orig original, originally, originator
ornith ornithology
Os osmium
OS Old Style, ordinary seaman, out of stock
OSB Order of Saint Benedict
OT occupational therapy, Old Testament, overtime
OTS officers' training school
oz ounce, ounces

p page, participle, past, pence, penny, per, piano, pico-, pint, proton, purl
P parental generation, pawn, phosphorus, pressure
pa per annum
Pa Pennsylvania, protactinium
PA passenger agent, Pennsylvania, power of attorney, press agent, private account, public address, purchasing agent
Pac Pacific
paleon paleontology
pam pamphlet
Pan Panama
P and L profit and loss
par paragraph, parallel, parish
part participial, participle, particular
pass passenger, passive
pat patent
path, pathol pathological, pathology
payt payment
Pb lead [Latin *plumbum*]
pc percent, piece, postcard
PC Peace Corps
pct percent, percentage
pd paid
Pd palladium
PD per diem, police department, potential difference
PDT Pacific daylight time
PE physical education, printer's error
PEI Prince Edward Island
pen peninsula
Penn, Penna Pennsylvania
per period, person
perf perfect, perforated, performance
perh perhaps
perm permanent
perp perpendicular
pers person, personal, personnel
Pers Persia, Persian
pert pertaining
pf, pfd preferred
PFC private first class
pg page
PG postgraduate
pharm pharmaceutical, pharmacist, pharmacy
PhD doctor of philosophy [Latin *philosophiae doctor*]
philos philosopher, philosophy
phon phonetics
photog photographic, photography
phr phrase
phys physical, physician, physics
physiol physiologist, physiology
pizz pizzicato
pk park, peak, peck
pkg package
pkt packet, pocket
PKU phenylketonuria
pkwy parkway
pl place, plate, plural
pm premium
p.m., PM post meridiem
Pm promethium
PM paymaster, police magistrate, postmaster, postmortem, prime minister, provost marshal
pmk postmark
pmt payment
PN promissory note
Po polonium
PO petty officer, post office
POC port of call
POD pay on delivery
POE port of embarkation, port of entry
Pol Poland, Polish
polit political, politician
poly polytechnic
pop popular, population
POR pay on return
Port Portugal, Portuguese
pos position, positive
poss possessive
POW prisoner of war
pp pages, pianissimo
PP parcel post, past participle, postpaid, prepaid
ppd postpaid, prepaid
PPS an additional postscript [Latin *post postscriptum*]
ppt precipitate
pptn precipitation
PQ Province of Quebec
pr pair, price, printed
Pr praseodymium
PR payroll, public relations, Puerto Rico
prec preceding
pred predicate
pref preface, preference, preferred, prefix
prem premium
prep preparatory, preposition
pres present, president
prev previous, previously
prf proof
prim primary, primitive
prin principal, principle
PRO public relations officer
prob probable, probably, problem
proc proceedings
prod production
prof professional, professor
prom promontory
pron pronoun, pronounced, pronunciation
prop property, proposition, proprietor
pros prosody
Prot Protestant
prov province, provincial, provisional
prox proximo

PS postscript [Latin *postscriptum*], public school
PSAT Preliminary Scholastic Aptitude Test
pseud pseudonym, pseudonymous
psf pounds per square foot
psi pounds per square inch
PST Pacific standard time
psych psychology
psychol psychologist, psychology
pt part, payment, pint, point, port
Pt platinum
PT Pacific time, physical therapy, physical training
PTA Parent-Teacher Association
pte private (British)
ptg printing
PTO Parent-Teacher Organization, please turn over
PTV public television
Pu plutonium
pub public, publication, published, publisher, publishing
publ publication, published, publisher
pvt private
PW prisoner of war
pwt pennyweight
PX please exchange, post exchange

q quart, quarto, query, question, quintal, quire
Q quartile, queen
QC Queen's Counsel
QED which was to be demonstrated [Latin *quod erat demonstrandum*]
QEF which was to be done [Latin *quod erat faciendum*]
QEI which was to be found out [Latin *quod erat inveniendum*]
QID four times a day [Latin *quater in die*]
Qld, Q'land Queensland
QM quartermaster
QMC quartermaster corps
QMG quartermaster general
qq v which see [Latin pl. *quae vide*]
qr quarter, quire
qt quantity, quart
qto quarto
qty quantity
qu, ques question
quad quadrant
Que Quebec
quot quotation
qv which see [Latin *quod vide*]
qy query

r rare, right, river, roentgen
R rabbi, radical — used especially of a univalent hydrocarbon radical, radius, regular, Republican, resistance, rook, run
Ra radium
RA regular army, royal academy
RAAF Royal Australian Air Force
rad radian, radiator, radical, radio, radius
RADM rear admiral
RAF Royal Air Force
Rb rubidium
RBC red blood cells, red blood count
RBI run batted in
RC Red Cross, Roman Catholic
RCAF Royal Canadian Air Force
RCMP Royal Canadian Mounted Police
rd road, rod, round
RD rural delivery
RDA Recommended Daily Allowance
Re rhenium
rec receipt, record, recording, recreation
recd received
recip reciprocal, reciprocity
rec sec recording secretary
rect receipt, rectangle, rectangular, rectified
ref reference, referred, reformed, refunding
refl reflex, reflexive
refrig refrigerating, refrigeration
reg region, register, registered, regular, regulation
regt regiment
rel relating, relative, released, religion, religious
relig religion
rep report, reporter, representative, republic
Rep Republican
repl replace, replacement
rept report
req require, required, requisition
res research, reserve, residence, resolution
resp respective, respectively
ret retain, retired, return
retd retained, retired, returned
rev revenue, reverse, review, reviewed, revised, revision, revolution
Rev reverend
RF radio frequency
RFD rural free delivery
Rh rhodium
RH right hand
RI Rhode Island
RIP may he [she] rest in peace [Latin *requiescat in pace*]
rit ritardando
riv river
rm ream, room
Rn radon
RN registered nurse, Royal Navy
rnd round
RNZAF Royal New Zealand Air Force
ROG receipt of goods
Rom Roman, Romance, Romania, Romanian
ROTC Reserve Officers' Training Corps
rpm revolutions per minute
RPO railway post office
rps revolutions per second
rpt repeat, report
RQ respiratory quotient
RR railroad, rural route
RS recording secretary, revised statutes, right side, Royal Society
RSFSR Russian Soviet Federated Socialist Republic
RSV Revised Standard Version
RSVP please reply [French *répondez s'il vous plaît*]
RSWC right side up with care
rt right
rte route
Ru ruthenium
Rum Rumania, Rumanian
Russ Russia, Russian
RW right worshipful, right worthy
rwy, ry railway

s scruple, second, secondary, section, semi, series, shilling, sine, singular, son, stere
S saint, senate, short, signor, small, south, southern, sulfur
SA Salvation Army, sex appeal, South Africa, South America, South Australia, subject to approval, without date [Latin *sine anno*]
SAC Strategic Air Command
SAM surface-to-air missile
sanit sanitary, sanitation
Sask Saskatchewan
sat saturate, saturated, saturation
Sat Saturday
SAT Scholastic Aptitude Test
S Aust South Australia
sb substantive
Sb antimony [Latin *stibium*]
SB bachelor of science [New Latin *scientiae baccalaureus*], southbound
SBN Standard Book Number
sc scale, scene, science, scilicet, small capitals
Sc scandium, Scots
SC South Carolina, supreme court
Scand Scandinavia, Scandinavian
sch school
sci science, scientific
scil scilicet
Scot Scotland, Scottish
script scripture
SD sea-damaged, sight draft, sine die, South Dakota, special delivery, stage direction
S Dak South Dakota
Se selenium
SE southeast
SEATO Southeast Asia Treaty Organization
sec according to [Latin *secundum*], secant, second, secondary, secretary, section
sect section, sectional
secy secretary
sel select, selected, selection
sem semicolon, seminar, seminary
sen senate, senator, senior
sep separate, separated
sepn separation
Sept, Sep September
seq the following one [Latin *sequens*]
seqq the following ones [Latin pl. *sequentia*]
ser serial, series, service
serg, sergt sergeant
serv service
sf science fiction, sforzando
SF sinking fund
SFC sergeant first class
sfz sforzando
sg specific gravity
SG senior grade, sergeant, solicitor general, surgeon general
Sgt sergeant
sh share
Shak Shakespeare
SHF superhigh frequency
shpt, shipt shipment
sht sheet
shtg shortage
Si silicon
SI International System of Units [French *Système International d'Unités*]
sig signal, signature, signor
sin sine
sing singular
SJ Society of Jesus
Skt Sanskrit
SL salvage loss, sea level
sm small
Sm samarium
SM master of science [New Latin *scientiae magister*], sergeant major
Sn tin [Late Latin *stannum*]
so south, southern
SO seller's option
soc social, society
sociol sociologist, sociology
sol solicitor, soluble, solution
soln solution
SOP standard operating procedure, standing operating procedure
soph sophomore
sp special, species, specific, specimen, spelling, spirit
Sp Spain, Spanish
SP shore patrol, shore patrolman, shore police, without issue [Latin *sine prole*]
Span Spanish
SPCA Society for the Prevention of Cruelty to Animals
SPCC Society for the Prevention of Cruelty to Children
spec special, specifically
specif specific, specifically
sp gr specific gravity
spp species
sq squadron, square
sr senior
Sr senor, sister, strontium
SR seaman recruit
Sra senora
Sres señores
SRO standing room only
Srta senorita
SS saints, steamship, Sunday school
SSG, SSgt staff sergeant
ssp subspecies
SSR Soviet Socialist Republic
SSS Selective Service System

SST supersonic transport
st stanza, state, stitch, stone, street
St saint
ST short ton
sta station, stationary
stat immediately [Latin *statim*], statute
stbd starboard
std standard
STD doctor of sacred theology [Latin *sacrae theologiae doctor*]
Ste saint (female) [French *sainte*]
stg, ster sterling
stk stock
STP standard temperature and pressure
str steamer
stud student
sub subtract, suburb
subj subject, subjunctive
suff sufficient, suffix
Sun Sunday
sup above [Latin *supra*], superior, supplement, supplementary, supply
supp, suppl supplement, supplementary
supt superintendent
surg surgeon, surgery, surgical
surv survey, surveying, surveyor
SV under the word [Latin *sub verbo* or *sub voce*]
Sw, Swed Sweden, Swedish
SW shipper's weight, shortwave, southwest
SWA South-West Africa
Switz Switzerland
syl, syll syllable
sym symbol, symmetrical
syn synonym, synonymous, synonymy
syst system

t teaspoon, temperature, terα-, ton, transitive, troy, true
T tablespoon, tritium
Ta tantalum
tan tangent
Tas, Tasm Tasmania
taxon taxonomic, taxonomy
tb tablespoon, tablespoonful
Tb terbium
TB trial balance
tbs, tbsp tablespoon, tablespoonful
Tc technetium
tchr teacher
TD touchdown
TDN total digestible nutrients
Te tellurium
tech technical, technically, technician, technological, technology
tel telegram, telegraph, telephone
teleg telegraphy
temp in the time of [Latin *tempore*], temperature, temporary
Tenn Tennessee
ter terrace, territory
terr territory
Tex Texas
TGIF thank God it's Friday
Th thorium, Thursday
ThD doctor of theology [New Latin *theologiae doctor*]
theat theater, theatrical
theol theological, theology
therm thermometer
Thurs, Thu Thursday
Ti titanium
TID three times a day [Latin *ter in die*]
tinct tincture
TKO technical knockout
tkt ticket
Tl thallium
TL total loss
TLC tender loving care
Tm thulium
TM trademark
TMV tobacco mosaic virus
tn ton, town, train
TN Tennessee, true north
tnpk turnpike
TO telegraph office, turn over
topog topography
tot total
tp title page, township
tpk, tpke turnpike
tr translated, translation, translator, transpose
trans transaction, transitive, translated, translation, translator, transportation
transl translated, translation
transp transportation
treas treasurer, treasury
trib tributary
TSgt technical sergeant
TSH thyroid-stimulating hormone
tsp teaspoon, teaspoonful
TT teletypewriter, tuberculin tested
Tues, Tu Tuesday
Turk Turkey, Turkish
TVA Tennessee Valley Authority
TX Texas

u unit
U university, uranium
UAR United Arab Republic
UC upper case
ugt urgent
UHF ultrahigh frequency
UK United Kingdom
ult ultimate, ultimo
UN United Nations
UNESCO United Nations Educational, Scientific, and Cultural Organization
UNICEF United Nations Children's Fund
univ universal, university
UNRWA United Nations Relief and Works Agency
UPI United Press International
US United States
USA United States Army, United States of America
USAF United States Air Force
USCG United States Coast Guard
USDA United States Department of Agriculture
USM United States Mail
USMC United States Marine Corps
USN United States Navy
USO United Service Organizations
USP United States Pharmacopeia
USPS United States Postal Service
USS United States ship
USSR Union of Soviet Socialist Republics
usu usual, usually
UT Utah
UV ultraviolet
UW underwriter

v vector, velocity, verb, verse, versus, vice, vide, voice, volume, vowel
V electric potential, vanadium, victory, volt, voltage
Va Virginia
VA Veterans Administration, vice admiral, Virginia, visual aid
VADM vice admiral
val value, valued
var variable, variant, variation, variety, various
vb verb, verbal
VC vice-chancellor, vice-consul, Victoria Cross
VD venereal disease
veg vegetable
vel vellum, velocity
Ven venerable
vert vertebrate, vertical
VFD volunteer fire department
VFW Veterans of Foreign Wars
VG very good
VHF very high frequency
vi see below [Latin *vide infra*], verb intransitive
VI Virgin Islands
vic vicinity
Vic Victoria
vil village
vis visibility, visual
VISTA Volunteers in Service to America
viz videlicet
VLF very low frequency
VNA Visiting Nurse Association
voc vocative
vocab vocabulary
vol volcano, volume, volunteer
VOR very-high-frequency omnirange
vou voucher
VP vice-president
vs see above [Latin *vide supra*], verse, versus
vss verses, versions
vt verb transitive
Vt, VT Vermont
VTOL vertical takeoff and landing
VTR video tape recorder
Vulg Vulgate
vv verses, vice versa

w water, watt, week, weight, wide, width, wife, with
W tungsten [German *wolfram*], west, western, work
WA Washington
WAC Women's Army Corps
WAF Women in the Air Force
war warrant
Wash Washington
W Aust Western Australia
WAVES Women Accepted for Volunteer Emergency Service
WB water ballast, waybill, westbound
WBC white blood cells
WC water closet, without charge
WCTU Women's Christian Temperance Union
wd wood, word, would
Wed Wednesday
wh which, white
WH watt-hour
whf wharf
WHO World Health Organization
whr watt-hour
whs, whse warehouse
whsle wholesale
WI West Indies, Wisconsin
WIA wounded in action
wid widow, widower
Wis, Wisc Wisconsin
wk week, work
WL wavelength
wmk watermark
WO warrant officer
w/o without
wpm words per minute
wrnt warrant
wt weight
WV, W Va West Virginia
WW world war
WY, Wyo Wyoming

XD, x div ex dividend
Xe xenon
XI, x in, x int ex interest
XL extra large, extra long
Xn Christian
Xnty Christianity

y yard, year
Y YMCA, yttrium
Yb ytterbium
yd yard
YMCA Young Men's Christian Association
YMHA Young Men's Hebrew Association
yr year, younger, your
yrbk yearbook
yrs years, yours
YT Yukon Territory
Yug Yugoslavia
YWCA Young Women's Christian Association
YWHA Young Women's Hebrew Association

z zero, zone
Z atomic number
Zn zinc
zool zoological, zoology
ZPG zero population growth
Zr zirconium

SIGNS AND SYMBOLS

BIOLOGY

○ an individual, specifically, a female—used chiefly in inheritance charts

□ an individual, specifically, a male—used chiefly in inheritance charts

♀ female

♂ *or* ♁ male

× crossed with; hybrid

+ wild type

F_1 offspring of the first generation

F_2 offspring of the second generation

F_3, F_4, F_5 offspring of the third, fourth, fifth, etc., generation

BUSINESS

a/c account ⟨in a/c with⟩

@ at; each ⟨4 apples @ 10¢ = 40¢⟩

/ *or* ℘ per

c/o care of

number if it precedes a numeral ⟨track #3⟩; pounds if it follows ⟨a 5 # sack of sugar⟩

℔ pound; pounds

% percent

‰ per thousand

$ dollars

¢ cents

£ pounds

© copyrighted

® registered trademark

CHEMISTRY

(For element symbols see ELEMENT table)

+ signifies "plus", "and", "together with", and is used between the symbols of substances brought together for, or produced by, a reaction; placed to the right of a symbol above the line, it signifies a unit charge of positive electricity: Ca^{++} denotes the ion of calcium, which carries two positive charges

— signifies a single "bond", or unit of attractive force or affinity, and is used between the symbols of elements or groups which unite to form a compound: H—Cl for HCl, H—O—H for H_2O; placed to the right of a symbol above the line, it signifies a unit charge of negative electricity: Cl^- denotes a chlorine ion carrying a negative charge

· is often used: (1) to indicate a single bond (as H·Cl for H–Cl) or (2) to denote the presence of a single unpaired electron (as H·) or (3) to separate parts of a compound regarded as loosely joined (as $CuSO_4 \cdot 5H_2O$)

⌬ *or* ◎ denotes the benzene ring

= indicates a double bond; placed to the right of a symbol above the line, it signifies two unit charges of negative electricity (as $SO_4^{=}$, the negative ion of sulfuric acid, carrying two negative charges)

: indicates a double bond (as $H_2C{:}CH_2$) or an unshared pair of electrons (as $:NH_3$)

( ) mark groups within a compound [as in $C_6H_4(CH_3)_2$, the formula for xylene which contains two methyl groups (CH_3)]

= gives or forms

→ gives, leads to, or is converted to

⇄ forms and is formed from; is in equilibrium with

↓ indicates precipitation of the substance

↑ indicates that the substance passes off as a gas

pH hydrogen-ion concentration

MATHEMATICS

+ plus; positive—used also to indicate omitted figures or an approximation ⟨3.141 +⟩

− minus; negative

± plus or minus (the square root of $4a^2$ is $\pm 2a$); more or less than ⟨a deviation of ± 2⟩

× multiplied by; times ⟨6 × 4 = 24⟩—also indicated by placing a dot between the factors ⟨6·4 = 24⟩ or by writing factors other than numerals without signs

÷ divided by ⟨24 ÷ 6 = 4⟩—also indicated by writing the divisor under the dividend with a line between ⟨$\frac{24}{6} = 4$⟩ or or by writing the divisor after the dividend with a diagonal between ⟨3/8⟩

= equals ⟨6 + 2 = 8⟩

≠ *or* ⧣ is not equal to

> is greater than ⟨6>5⟩

< is less than ⟨3<4⟩

≧ *or* ≥ is greater than or equal to

≦ *or* ≤ is less than or equal to

≯ is not greater than

≮ is not less than

≈ is approximately equal to

≡ is identical to

∼ equivalent; similar

≅ is congruent to

∶ is to; the ratio of

∴ therefore

∞ infinity

0 zero

∠ angle; the angle ⟨∠ABC⟩

∟ right angle ⟨∟ABC⟩

⊥ the perpendicular; is perpendicular to ⟨AB ⊥ CD⟩

∥ parallel; is parallel to ⟨AB ∥ CD⟩

⊙ *or* ○ circle

△ triangle

□ square

▭ rectangle

√ *or* $\sqrt{}$ root—used without a figure to indicate a square root ⟨as in $\sqrt{4} = 2$⟩ or with an index above the sign to indicate another degree ⟨as in $\sqrt[3]{3}$, $\sqrt[5]{7}$⟩; also denoted by a fractional index at the right of a number whose denominator expresses the degree of the root ⟨$3^{1/3} = \sqrt[3]{3}$⟩

( ) parentheses, [ ] brackets, { } braces — indicate that the quantities enclosed by them are to be taken together

π pi; the number 3.14159+; the ratio of the circumference of a circle to its diameter

! —used to indicate the product of all the whole numbers up to and including a given preceding number

e *or* ϵ (1) the number 2.7182818+; the base of the natural system of logarithms (2) the eccentricity of a conic section

° degree ⟨60°⟩

′ minute; foot ⟨30′⟩—used also to distinguish between different values of the same variable or between different variables (as *a′*, *a″*, *a‴*, usually read *a* prime, *a* double prime, *a* triple prime)

″ second, inch ⟨30″⟩

², ³, etc. —used as exponents placed above and at the right of an expression to indicate that it is raised to a power whose degree is indicated by the figure ⟨a^2, the square of *a*⟩

n —used as a constant denoting an unspecified degree, order, class, or power

i imaginary unit; $+\sqrt{-1}$

∪ union of two sets

∩ intersection of two sets

⊂ is included in, is a subset of

⊃ contains as a subset

∈ *or* ϵ is an element of

∉ is not an element of

Λ *or* 0 *or* ϕ *or* { } null set

MISCELLANEOUS

& and

&c etcetera; and so forth

/ diagonal *or* slant *or* solidus *or* virgule—used to mean "or" (as in *and/or*), "and/or" (as in *dead/wounded*), "per" (as in *feet/second*); used to indicate the end of a line of verse; used to separate the figures of a date (4/4/81)

< derived from, > whence derived, + and, * assumed — used in etymologies

† died—used especially in genealogies

☧ monogram from Greek XP signifying Jesus

LXX Septuagint

✡ Star of David

☥ ankh

℣ versicle

℟ response

✳ —used in Roman Catholic and Anglican service books to divide each verse of a psalm, indicating where the response begins

✠ *or* + —used in some service books to indicate where the sign of the cross is to be made; also used by certain Roman Catholic and Anglican prelates as a sign of the cross preceding their signatures

f/ *or* *f:* relative aperture of a photographic lens

☠ poison

℞ take—used on prescriptions

☢ civil defense

(For Roman numerals see NUMBER table)

MUSIC

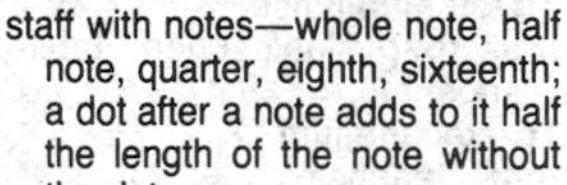

staff with notes—whole note, half note, quarter, eighth, sixteenth; a dot after a note adds to it half the length of the note without the dot

𝄞 G clef; treble clef—used to indicate that the second line represents the first G above middle C

𝄢 F clef; bas clef—used to indicate that the second line represents the first F below middle C

♯ sharp

♭ flat

♮ natural—used to annul the effect of a previous ♯ or ♭; the *sharps* or *flats* placed at the beginning of a composition or section are called collectively the *key signature*

𝄪 double sharp—used to raise a note two half steps

𝄫 double flat—used to lower a note two half steps

𝄆 𝄇 repeat—used to indicate the beginning and end respectively of a passage to be played or sung twice

< crescendo

> decrescendo, diminuendo

<> swell

rests—whole, half, quarter, eighth, & sixteenth

Triplet—three notes grouped together under a curved line or bracket. The three notes have a total duration that two of those notes would ordinarily receive.

2/4 two counts per measure

3/4 three counts per measure

4/4 four counts per measure

6/8 six counts per measure

𝄴 common time: four counts per measure

𝄋 dal segno (D.S.)—repeat from the sign

𝄐 hold, pause

sforzando—strong accent

staccato—shorten value of note and substitute a rest

REFERENCE MARKS

* asterisk *or* star

† dagger

‡ double dagger

§ section *or* numbered clause

‖ parallels

¶ *or* ⁋ paragraph

WEATHER

barometer, changes of:

/ Rising, then falling

/ Rising, then steady; or rising, then rising more slowly

/ Rising steadily, or unsteadily

✓ Falling or steady, then rising; or rising, then rising more quickly

— Steady, same as 3 hours ago

\ Falling, then rising, same or lower than 3 hours ago

\ Falling, then steady; or falling, then falling more slowly

\ Falling steadily, or unsteadily

^ Steady or rising, then falling; or falling, then falling more quickly

◎ calm

○ clear

◐ cloudy (partly)

● cloudy (completely overcast)

drifting or blowing snow

, drizzle

≡ fog

freezing rain

front, cold

warm

occluded

stationary

)(funnel clouds

∞ haze

hurricane

tropical storm

• rain

rain and snow

rime

sandstorm or dust storm

▽ shower(s)

shower of rain

shower of hail

sleet

* snow

thunderstorm

visibility reduced by smoke

BIOGRAPHICAL, BIBLICAL, AND MYTHOLOGICAL NAMES

This section constitutes a pronouncing dictionary of the names of important figures from contemporary life, history, biblical tradition, legend, and myth likely to be of interest to the student. Names containing connectives like *d', de, di, van,* or *von* are alphabetized generally under the part of the name following the connective. When two sets of dates are given, the first set indicates the dates of the person's birth and death, and the second pertains only to the particular office, honor, or achievement which it immediately follows. If a person has a second name, a nickname, or an epithet that students commonly encounter, it is given in italics usually immediately after the birth and death dates.

Aar•on \\'ar-ən, 'er-\\ brother of Moses; 1st high priest of the Hebrews

Abel \\'ā-bəl\\ son of Adam and Eve; killed by his brother Cain

Abra•ham \\'ā-brə-ˌham\\ Old Testament patriarch; founder of the Hebrew people

Achil•les \\ə-'kil-ēz\\ Greek warrior in the Trojan War

Ac•tae•on \\ak-'tē-ən\\ hunter in Greek mythology who is turned into a stag and killed by his own hounds for having seen Artemis bathing

Ad•am \\'ad-əm\\ the first man in biblical tradition

Ad•ams \\'ad-əmz\\ John 1735–1826 2d president of the United States (1797–1801)

Adams John Quin·cy \\'kwin-zē, -sē\\ 1767–1848 6th president of the United States (1825–29); son of John Adams

Adams Samuel 1722–1803 American patriot

Ad•dams \\'ad-əmz\\ Jane 1860–1935 American social worker; Nobel prize winner (1931)

Ad•di•son \\'ad-ə-sən\\ Joseph 1672–1719 English essayist

Ado•nis \\ə-'dän-əs, -'dō-nəs\\ beautiful youth in Greek mythology who is loved by Aphrodite

Ae•a•cus \\'ē-ə-kəs\\ son of Zeus; the original leader of the Myrmidons and later a judge of the underworld

Ae•ne•as \\i-'nē-əs\\ Trojan hero in classical mythology

Ae•o•lus \\'ē-ə-ləs\\ god of the winds in classical mythology

Aes•chy•lus \\'es-kə-ləs, 'ēs-\\ 525–456 B.C. Greek dramatist

Aes•cu•la•pi•us \\'es-kyə-'lā-pē-əs\\ — see ASCLEPIUS

Ae•sop \\'ē-ˌsäp, -səp\\ *about* 620–*about* 560 B.C. Greek writer of fables

Ag•a•mem•non \\ˌag-ə-'mem-ˌnän, -nən\\ legendary king of Mycenae; leader of the Greeks in the Trojan War

Aggeus — see HAGGAI

Agla•ia \\ə-'glī-ə, -'glā-ə\\ one of the three Graces in Greek mythology — compare EUPHROSYNE, THALIA

Ag•nes \\'ag-nəs\\ Saint *died* 304 A.D. Christian martyr

Ag•rip•pi•na \\ˌag-rə-'pī-nə, -'pē-\\ 13 B.C.?–33 A.D. mother of Caligula

Ahab \\'ā-ˌhab\\ king of Israel in the 9th century B.C.; husband of Jezebel

Ahu•ra Maz•da \\ə-ˌhùr-ə-'maz-də, ä-ˌhùr-\\ god of goodness and light in Zoroastrianism

Ajax \\'ā-ˌjaks\\ Greek hero in the Trojan War who kills himself because the armor of Achilles is awarded to Odysseus

Alad•din \\ə-'lad-n\\ youth in the *Arabian Nights' Entertainments* who comes into possession of a magic lamp and ring

Al•a•ric \\'al-ə-rik\\ 370?–410 A.D. king of the Visigoths; conqueror of Rome

Al•ber•tus Mag•nus \\al-'bərt-ə-'smag-nəs\\ Saint 1193? (or 1206?)–1280 *Albert* Count *von Boll·städt* \\-'bòl-ˌshtet\\ German philosopher and theologian

Al•ci•bi•a•des \\ˌal-sə-'bī-ə-ˌdēz\\ *about* 450–404 B.C. Athenian general

Al•cott \\'òl-kət\\ Louisa May 1832–88 American author

Al·ex·an·der \ˌal-ig-ˈzan-dər, ˌel-\ name of 8 popes: especially **VI** *(Rodrigo Lanzol y Borja)* 1431?–1503 (pope 1492–1503)
Alexander name of 3 emperors of Russia: **I** 1777–1825 (reigned 1801–25); **II** 1818–81 (reigned 1855–81); **III** 1845–94 (reigned 1881–94)
Alexander III of Macedon 356–323 B.C. *the Great* king (336–323)
Al·fon·so XIII \al-ˈfän-sō, -zō\ 1886–1941 king of Spain (1886–1931; deposed)
Al·fred \ˈal-frəd, -fərd\ 849–899 *the Great* king of the West Saxons (871–899)
Al·len \ˈal-ən\ Ethan 1738–89 American Revolutionary soldier
Am·brose \ˈam-ˌbrōz\ Saint 340?–397 A.D. bishop of Milan and church father
Amerigo Vespucci — see VESPUCCI
Am·herst \ˈam-ərst, -ˌərst\ Baron Jeffrey *or* Jeffery 1717–97 British general in America
Amon \ˈäm-ən\ ancient Egyptian god often worshiped as a supreme deity identified with the sun-god Ra
Amos \ˈā-məs\ Hebrew prophet of the 8th century B.C.
Amund·sen \ˈäm-ən-sən\ Roald 1872–1928 Norwegian explorer; discovered the South Pole (1911)
An·a·ni·as \ˌan-ə-ˈnī-əs\ early Christian struck dead for lying
An·chi·ses \an-ˈkī-sēz, ang-\ father of Aeneas
An·der·sen \ˈan-dər-sən\ Hans Christian 1805–75 Danish writer of fairy tales
An·der·son \ˈan-dər-sən\ Marian 1902– American contralto
An·drea del Sar·to \än-ˌdrā-ə-ˌdel-ˈsärt-ō\ 1486–1531 Florentine painter
An·dro·cles \ˈan-drə-ˌklēz\ legendary Roman slave spared in the arena by a lion from whose foot he had years before taken a thorn
An·drom·a·che \an-ˈdräm-ə-kē\ wife of Hector
An·drom·e·da \an-ˈdräm-ə-də\ Ethiopian princess rescued from a monster by her future husband Perseus
Angelico Fra — see FIESOLE
Anne \ˈan\ 1665–1714 daughter of James II; queen of Great Britain (1702–14)
An·tho·ny \ˈan-thə-nē, *chiefly British* ˈan-tə-nē\ Saint *about* 250–350 A.D. Egyptian monk
Anthony Mark — see ANTONIUS
Anthony Susan Brownell 1820–1906 American suffragist
Anthony of Padua Saint 1195–1231 Franciscan monk
An·tig·o·ne \an-ˈtig-ə-nē\ daughter of Oedipus and Jocasta
An·to·ni·nus \ˌan-tə-ˈnī-nəs\ Marcus Au·re·lius \ȯ-ˈrēl-yəs, -ˈrē-lē-əs\ 121–180 A.D. Roman emperor (161–180); Stoic philosopher
An·to·ni·us \an-ˈtō-nē-əs\ Marcus 83?–30 B.C. *Mark* or *Marc An·to·ny* or *An·tho·ny* \ˈan-thə-ne, *chiefly British* ˈan-tə-nē\ Roman general
Aph·ro·di·te \ˌaf-rə-ˈdīt-ē\ Greek goddess of love and beauty whose Roman counterpart is Venus
Apol·lo \ə-ˈpäl-ō\ *or* **Phoe·bus** \ˈfē-bəs\ god of sunlight, prophecy, music, and poetry in classical mythology
Apol·lyon \ə-ˈpäl-yən, -ˈpäl-ē-ən\ the angel of hell in the book of Revelation
Aqui·nas \ə-ˈkwī-nəs\ Saint Thomas 1225–74 Italian theologian
Arach·ne \ə-ˈrak-nē\ Lydian girl in Greek mythology who is changed into a spider for challenging Athena to a contest in weaving
Ar·chi·me·des \ˌär-kə-ˈmēd-ēz\ 287?–212 B.C. Greek mathematician
Ares \ˈaər-ēz, ˈeər-; ˈā-ˌrēz\ Greek god of war whose Roman counterpart is Mars
Ar·e·thu·sa \ˌar-ə-ˈthü-zə, -ˈthyü-\ a wood nymph changed by Artemis into a fountain
Ar·gus \ˈär-gəs\ hundred-eyed monster in Greek mythology
Ar·i·ad·ne \ˌar-ē-ˈad-nē\ daughter of Minos who gives Theseus the thread whereby he escapes from the labyrinth built by Daedalus
Ar·is·ti·des *or* **Ar·is·tei·des** \ˌar-ə-ˈstīd-ēz\ 530?–?468 B.C. *the Just* Athenian statesman and general
Ar·is·toph·a·nes \ˌar-ə-ˈstäf-ə-ˌnēz\ 448?–?380 B.C. Greek dramatist
Ar·is·tot·le \ˈar-ə-ˌstät-l\ 384–322 B.C. Greek philosopher
Ari·us \ə-ˈrī-əs; ˈar-ē-əs, ˈer-\ *died* 336 A.D. Greek theologian
Ar·min·i·us \är-ˈmin-ē-əs\ Jacobus 1560–1609 *Jacob Har·men·sen* \ˈhär-mən-sən\ or **Her·mansz** \ˈheər-ˌmäns\ Dutch theologian
Arm·strong \ˈärm-ˌstrȯŋ\ Louis 1900–1971 *Satch·mo* \ˈsach-ˌmō\ American jazz musician
Armstrong Neil Alden 1930– American astronaut; first man on the moon (1969)
Ar·nold \ˈärn-ld\ Benedict 1741–1801 American Revolutionary general and traitor
Arnold Matthew 1822–88 English poet, essayist, and critic
Ar·te·mis \ˈärt-ə-məs\ *or* **Phoe·be** \ˈfē-bē\ Greek goddess of the moon, wild animals, and hunting whose Roman counterpart is Diana
Ar·thur \ˈär-thər\ legendary king of the Britons whose story is based on traditions of a 6th century military leader — **Ar·thu·ri·an** \är-ˈthu̇r-ē-ən, -ˈthyu̇r-\ *adj*
Arthur Chester Alan 1829–86 21st president of the United States (1881–85)
As·cle·pi·us \ə-ˈsklē-pē-əs\ Greek god of medicine whose Roman counterpart is Aesculapius
Ashur \ˈä-ˌshu̇r\ *or* **As·sur** \ˈä-ˌsu̇r\ chief god of Assyria
As·tar·te \ə-ˈstärt-ē\ Phoenician goddess of love and fertility
As·tor \ˈas-tər\ John Jacob 1763–1848 American (German-born) fur trader and capitalist
At·a·lan·ta \ˌat-l-ˈant-ə\ beautiful fleet-footed heroine of Greek legend who challenges her suitors to a race and is defeated when she stops to pick up three golden apples dropped by one of the suitors
Ath·el·stan \ˈath-əl-ˌstan\ 895–940 A.D. king of England (*about* 924–940)
Athe·ne \ə-ˈthē-nē\ *or* **Athe·na** \-nə\ *or* **Pal·las** \ˈpal-əs\ Greek goddess of wisdom whose Roman counterpart is Minerva
At·las \ˈat-ləs\ Titan forced to bear the heavens on his shoulders
Atreus \ˈā-ˌtrüs, -trē-əs\ legendary king of Mycenae; father of Agamemnon and Menelaus
At·ro·pos \ˈa-trə-ˌpäs, -pəs\ the one of the three Fates in classical mythology who cuts off the thread of life — compare CLOTHO, LACHESIS
At·ti·la \ˈat-l-ə, ə-ˈtil-ə\ 406?–453 A.D. *the Scourge of God* king of the Huns
Au·du·bon \ˈȯd-ə-bən, -ˌbän\ John James 1785–1851 American (Haitian-born) artist and naturalist
Au·gus·tine \ˈȯ-gə-ˌstēn; ȯ-ˈgəs-tən, ə-\ Saint 354–430 A.D. church father; bishop of Hippo (396–430)
Augustine Saint *died* 604 A.D. *Apostle of the English* 1st archbishop of Canterbury (601–604)
Au·gus·tus \ȯ-ˈgəs-təs, ə-\ *or* **Augustus Caesar** *or* **Oc·ta·vi·an** \äk-ˈtā-vē-ən\ 63 B.C.–14 A.D. *Gaius Julius Caesar Octavianus* 1st Roman emperor 27 B.C.–14 A.D.
Au·ro·ra \ə-ˈrōr-ə, ȯ-, -ˈrȯr-\ — see EOS
Aus·ten \ˈȯs-tən, ˈäs-\ Jane 1775–1817 English author
Bac·chus \ˈbak-əs\ — see DIONYSUS
Bach \ˈbäk, ˈbäk\ Johann Sebastian 1685–1750 German composer and organist
Ba·con \ˈbā-kən\ Francis 1561–1626 1st Baron *Ver·u·lam* \ˈver-ə-ləm, -yə-\ Viscount *Saint Al·bans* \sānt-ˈȯl-bənz, sənt-\ English philosopher and author
Bacon Roger, Friar 1214?–94 English philosopher
Ba·den–Pow·ell \ˌbād-n-ˈpō-əl\ Robert Stephenson Smyth 1857–1941 English founder of Boy Scout movement
Bal·boa, de \bal-ˈbō-ə\ Vasco Núñez 1475–1519 Spanish explorer; discovered Pacific Ocean (1513)
Baltimore Lord — see George CALVERT
Bal·zac, de \ˈbȯl-ˌzak, ˈbal-, *French* bál-zák\ Honoré 1799–1850 French author
Baptist — see JOHN *the Baptist*
Ba·rab·bas \bə-ˈrab-əs\ prisoner released in preference to Christ at the demand of the multitude
Barbarossa — see FREDERICK 1
Bar·num \ˈbär-nəm\ Phineas Taylor 1810–91 American showman
Bar·rie \ˈbar-ē\ Sir James Matthew 1860–1937 Scottish author
Bar·ry·more \ˈbar-i-ˌmōr, -ˌmȯr\ family of American actors: Maurice 1847–1905; his wife Georgiana Emma 1856–93; their children Lionel 1878–1954, Ethel 1879–1959, and John Blythe 1882–1942
Bar·thol·di \bär-ˈtäl-dē, -ˈtȯl-, -ˈthäl-, -ˈthȯl-\ Frédéric Auguste 1834–1904 French sculptor; works include Statue of Liberty
Bar·tók \ˈbar-ˌtäk, -ˌtȯk\ Bé·la \ˈbā-lə\ 1881–1945 Hungarian composer

Bar•ton \'bärt-n\ Clara 1821–1912 founder of American Red Cross Society
Ba•sil \'baz-əl, 'bās-, 'bas-, 'bāz-\ Saint 330?–?379 A.D. *the Great* church father; bishop of Caesarea
Bau•de•laire \bōd-'laər, -'leər\ Charles Pierre 1821–67 French poet
Beau•re•gard \'bōr-ə-ˌgärd, 'bȯr-\ Pierre Gustave Toutant 1818–93 American Confederate general
Beck•et, à \ə-'bek-ət, ä-\ Saint Thomas 1118?–70 archbishop of Canterbury (1162–70)
Bede \'bēd\ Saint 673–735 A.D. *the Venerable Bede* English historian and theologian
Beel•ze•bub \bē-'el-zi-ˌbəb, 'bēl-zi-, 'bel-\ prince of the demons identified with Satan in the New Testament
Bee•tho•ven, van \'bā-ˌtō-vən\ Ludwig 1770–1827 German composer
Bell \'bel\ Alexander Graham 1847–1922 American (Scottish-born) inventor of the telephone
Bel•ler•o•phon \bə-'ler-ə-fən, -ˌfän\ hero in Greek mythology who slays the monster Chimera with the help of his horse Pegasus
Bel•li•ni \bə-'lē-nē\ Vincenzo 1801–35 Italian composer
Bel•low \'bel-ō\ Saul 1915– American (Canadian-born) author; Nobel prize winner (1976)
Ben•e•dict \'ben-ə-dikt\ name of 15 popes: especially **XIV** *(Prospero Lambertini)* 1675–1758 (pope 1740–58); **XV** *(Giacomo della Chiesa)* 1854–1922 (pope 1914–22)
Benedict of Nur•sia \'nər-shə, -shē-ə\ Saint 480?–?543 A.D. Italian founder of Benedictine order
Be•nét \bə-'nā\ Stephen Vincent 1898–1943 American author
Ben•ja•min \'benj-mən, -ə-mən\ Jacob's youngest son; ancestor of one of the 12 tribes of Israel
Ben•tham \'ben-thəm\ Jeremy 1748–1832 English jurist and philosopher
Ben•ton \'bent-n\ Thomas Hart 1889–1975 American painter
Be•o•wulf \'bā-ə-ˌwu̇lf\ legendary Geatish warrior and hero of the Old English poem *Beowulf*
Be•ring \'biər-ing, 'beər-\ Vitus 1680–1741 Danish navigator; discovered Bering Strait and Bering Sea
Ber•lin \bər-'lin, ˌbər-\ Irving 1888– American (Russian-born) composer
Ber•li•oz \'ber-lē-ˌōz\ (Louis) Hector 1803–69 French composer
Ber•ni•ni \bər-'nē-nē\ Giovanni Lorenzo 1598–1680 Italian sculptor, architect, and painter
Bes•se•mer \'bes-ə-mər\ Sir Henry 1813–98 English engineer
Beyle Marie Henri — see STENDHAL
Bierce \'biərs\ Ambrose (Gwinnett) 1842–?1914 American author
Bis•marck, von \'biz-ˌmärk\ Prince Otto Eduard Leopold 1815–98 1st chancellor of German Empire (1871–90)
Bi•zet \bē-'zā\ Alexandre César Léopold 1838–75 *Georges* French composer
Black Hawk \'blak-ˌhȯk\ 1767–1838 American Indian chief
Black•stone \'blak-ˌstōn, *chiefly British* -stən\ Sir William 1723–80 English jurist
Black•well \'blak-ˌwel, -wəl\ Elizabeth 1821–1910 American (English-born) physician
Blake \'blāk\ William 1757–1827 English poet and artist
Bloom•er \'blü-mər\ Amelia Jenks 1818–94 American social reformer
Boc•cac•cio \bō-'käch-ē-ˌō, -'käch-ō\ Giovanni 1313–75 Italian author
Bohr \'bōr, 'bȯr\ Niels 1885–1962 Danish physicist
Bo•leyn \bu̇-'lin, 'bu̇l-ən\ Anne 1507–36 2d wife of Henry VIII of England; mother of Elizabeth I
Bo•lí•var Si•món \sē-ˌmōn-bə-'lē-ˌvär, ˌsī-mən-'bäl-ə-vər\ 1783–1830 South American liberator
Bo•na•parte \'bō-nə-ˌpärt\ *or Italian* **Buo•na•par•te** \ˌbwȯn-ə-'pärt-ē\ Corsican family: Jérôme 1784–1860 king of Westphalia; Joseph 1768–1844 king of Naples and Spain; Louis 1778–1846 king of Holland; Lucien 1775–1840 prince of Canino *all brothers of Napoleon I*
Bon•i•face \'bän-ə-fəs, -ˌfās\ Saint 680?–755 A.D. *Winfrid* or *Wynfrith* English missionary in Germany
Boniface name of 9 popes: especially **VIII** *(Benedetto Caetani)* 1235?–1303 (pope 1294–1303)
Boone \'bün\ Daniel 1734–1820 American pioneer
Booth \'büth\ John Wilkes 1838–65 assassin of Abraham Lincoln
Booth \'büth, *chiefly British* 'bü<u>th</u>\ William 1829–1912 English founder of Salvation Army
Bo•re•as \'bōr-ē-əs, 'bȯr-\ Greek god of the north wind
Bor•gia \'bȯr-ˌjä, -jə, -zhə\ Cesare 1475 (or 1476)–1507 Italian cardinal and military leader; son of Rodrigo Borgia
Borgia Lucrezia 1480–1519 duchess of Ferrara; daughter of Rodrigo Borgia
Borgia Rodrigo 1431?–1503 — see Pope ALEXANDER VI
Bo•ro•din \ˌbȯr-ə-'dēn, ˌbär-\ Aleksandr Porfirevich 1834–87 Russian composer
Bosch \'bäsh, 'bȯsh, *Dutch* 'bäs, 'bȯs\ Hieronymus *about* 1450–1516 Dutch painter
Bos•co \'bäs-kō, 'bȯs-\ Saint John 1815–88 Italian priest; founder of the Salesians
Bos•well \'bäz-ˌwel, -wəl\ James 1740–95 Scottish biographer of Samuel Johnson
Bot•ti•cel•li \ˌbät-ə-'chel-ē\ Sandro 1444?–1510 Italian painter
Boyle \'bȯil\ Robert 1627–91 British physicist and chemist
Brad•bury \'brad-ˌber-ē, -bə-rē, -brē\ Ray Douglas 1920– American author
Brad•dock \'brad-ək\ Edward 1695–1755 British general in America
Brad•ford \'brad-fərd\ William 1590–1657 Pilgrim father; 2d governor of Plymouth colony
Brad•street \'brad-ˌstrēt\ Anne 1612?–72 American poet
Brah•ma \'bräm-ə\ creator god of the Hindu sacred triad — compare SIVA, VISHNU
Brahms \'brämz\ Johannes 1833–97 German composer
Braille \'brāl, 'brī\ Louis 1809–52 French blind teacher of the blind
Bran•deis \'bran-ˌdīs, -ˌdīz\ Louis Dembitz 1856–1941 American jurist
Brezh•nev \'brezh-ˌnef\ Leonid Ilyich 1906– Russian politician; 1st secretary of Communist party (1964–); president of the U.S.S.R. (1960–64; 1977–)
Bri•an Bo•ru \ˌbrī-ən-bə-'rü\ 926–1014 king of Ireland (1002–14)
Brig•id \'brij-əd, 'brē-əd\ Saint 453–523 A.D. a patron saint of Ireland
Brit•ten \'brit-n\ (Edward) Benjamin 1913–76 English composer
Bron•të \'bränt-ē, 'brän-ˌtā\ family of English writers: Charlotte 1816–55 and her sisters Emily 1818–48 and Anne 1820–49
Brown \'brau̇n\ John *Old Brown of Osa·wat·o·mie* \ˌō-sə-'wät-ə-mē\ 1800–59 American abolitionist
Brow•ning \'brau̇-ning\ Elizabeth Barrett 1806–61 English poet; wife of Robert
Browning Robert 1812–89 English poet
Broz \'brōz, 'brȯz\ *or* **Bro•zo•vitch** \'brō-zə-ˌvich, 'brȯ-\ Josip 1892– *Ti·to* \'tēt-ō\ Yugoslav marshal; prime minister (1945–53); president (1953–)
Bruce \'brüs\ Robert 1274–1329 liberator and king (1306–29) of Scotland
Bruck•ner \'bru̇k-nər\ Anton 1824–96 Austrian composer
Brue•ghel *or* **Breu•ghel** \'brü-gəl, 'brȯi-\ Pieter *the Elder* 1520?–69 Flemish painter
Brun•hild \'brün-ˌhilt\ legendary Germanic queen won by Siegfried for Gunther
Bru•tus \'brüt-əs\ Marcus Junius 85?–42 B.C. Roman politician; one of Julius Caesar's assassins
Bry•an \'brī-ən\ William Jennings 1860–1925 American lawyer and politician
Bry•ant \'brī-ənt\ William Cul•len \'kəl-ən\ 1794–1878 American poet
Bu•chan•an \byü-'kan-ən, bə-\ James 1791–1868 15th president of the United States (1857–61)
Buck \'bək\ Pearl 1892–1973 American author; Nobel prize winner (1938)
Buddha — see GAUTAMA BUDDHA
Buffalo Bill — see William Frederick CODY
Bunche \'bənch\ Ralph Johnson 1904–71 American diplomat
Bun•yan \'bən-yən\ John 1628–88 English preacher and author
Bur•bank \'bər-ˌbangk\ Luther 1849–1926 American horticulturist
Bur•goyne \'bər-ˌgȯin, ˌbər-'\ John 1722–92 British general in America
Burke \'bərk\ Edmund 1729–97 British statesman and writer
Burns \'bərnz\ Robert 1759–96 Scottish poet
Burn•side \'bərn-ˌsīd\ Ambrose Everett 1824–81 American general

Burr \'bər\ Aaron 1756–1836 vice-president of the United States (1801–05)
Bur•roughs \'bər-,ōz, 'bə-,rōz\ Edgar Rice 1875–1950 American author
But•ler \'bət-lər\ Samuel 1835–1902 English author
By•ron \'bī-rən\ 6th Baron 1788–1824 *George Gordon Byron* English poet
Cab•ot \'kab-ət\ John 1450–98 Italian navigator; explored coast of North America for England
Ca•bri•ni \kə-'brē-nē\ Saint Frances Xavier 1850–1917 *Mother Cabrini* 1st American (Italian-born) to be canonized (1946)
Cad•mus \'kad-məs\ founder of Thebes in Greek mythology
Caed•mon \'kad-mən\ *flourished about* 670 A.D. English poet
Cae•sar \'sē-zər\ Gaius Julius 100–44 B.C. Roman general, statesman, and writer
Cain \'kān\ son of Adam and Eve; brother and murderer of Abel
Cal•houn \kal-'hün\ John Caldwell 1782–1850 vice-president of the United States (1825–32)
Ca•lig•u•la \kə-'lig-yə-lə\ 12–41 A.D. *Gaius Caesar* Roman emperor (37–41)
Cal•li•o•pe \kə-'lī-ə-pē\ Greek Muse of heroic poetry
Cal•vert \'kal-vərt\ George 1580?–1632 1st Baron *Baltimore* English proprietary in America
Cal•vin \'kal-vən\ John 1509–64 French theologian and reformer
Ca•lyp•so \kə-'lip-sō\ sea nymph who keeps Odysseus for seven years on an island
Ca•mus \kà-mū̅e\ Albert 1913–60 French author
Ca•nute \kə-'nüt, -'nyüt\ 994?–1035 king of England (1016–35); of Denmark (1018–35); of Norway (1028–35)
Ča•pek \'chäp-,ek\ Karel 1890–1938 Czech author
Capet Hugh — see HUGH CAPET
Car•lyle \kär-'līl, 'kär-,\ Thomas 1795–1881 Scottish essayist and historian
Car•ne•gie \'kär-nə-gē, kär-'neg-ē\ Andrew 1835–1919 American (Scottish-born) industrialist and philanthropist
Carroll Lewis — see DODGSON
Car•son \'kärs-n\ Christopher 1809–68 *Kit* American frontiersman
Car•ter \'kärt-ər\ James Earl, Jr. 1924– *Jimmy* 39th president of the United States (1977–)
Car•tier \kär-'tyā, 'kärt-ē-,ā\ Jacques 1491–1557 French navigator; discovered Saint Lawrence river
Ca•ru•so \kə-'rü-sō, -zō\ En·ri·co \en-'rē-kō\ 1873–1921 Italian tenor
Car•ver \'kär-vər\ George Washington 1864–1943 American botanist
Ca•sals \kə-'sälz, -'zälz\ Pablo 1876–1973 Spanish-born cellist, conductor, and composer
Ca•sa•no•va \,kaz-ə-'nō-və, ,kas-\ Giacomo Girolamo 1725–98 Italian adventurer
Cas•san•dra \kə-'san-drə\ daughter of Priam endowed with the gift of prophecy but fated never to be believed
Cas•satt \kə-'sat\ Mary 1845–1926 American painter
Cas•tor \'kas-tər\ the mortal twin of Pollux in classical mythology
Cas•tro \'kas-trō, 'käs-\ Fi·del \fē-'del\ 1927– Cuban premier (1959–)
Cath•er \'ka*th*-ər\ Willa Sibert 1873–1947 American author
Cath•er•ine \'kath-rən, -ə-rən\ name of 1st, 5th, and 6th wives of Henry VIII of England: Catherine of Aragon 1485–1536; Catherine Howard 1520?–42; Catherine Parr 1512–48
Catherine I 1684?–1727 wife of Peter the Great; empress of Russia (1725–27)
Catherine II 1729–96 *the Great* empress of Russia (1762–96)
Cat•i•line \'kat-l-,īn\ 108?–62 B.C. Roman politician; conspired against Rome
Ca•to \'kāt-ō\ Marcus Porcius 234–149 B.C. *the Elder; the Censor* Roman statesman
Cato Marcus Porcius 95–46 B.C. *the Younger* Roman Stoic philosopher; great-grandson of the preceding
Ca•tul•lus \kə-'təl-əs\ Gaius Valerius 84?–54 B.C. Roman poet
Cax•ton \'kak-stən\ William 1422?–91 first English printer
Ce•ci•lia \sə-'sēl-yə, -'sil-\ Saint 2d or 3d century A.D. Roman martyr; patron saint of music
Cel•li•ni \chə-'lē-nē\ Benvenuto 1500–71 Italian goldsmith and sculptor
Cer•ber•us \'sər-bə-rəs, -brəs\ 3-headed dog in classical mythology who guards the entrance to Hades
Ce•res \'siər-,ēz\ — see DEMETER
Cer•van•tes Saa•ve•dra, de \sər-'van-,tēz-,sä-ə-'vā-drə\ Miguel 1547–1616 Spanish author
Cé•zanne \sā-'zan\ Paul 1839–1906 French painter
Cha•gall \shə-'gäl, -'gal\ Marc 1887– Russian painter in France
Cham•ber•lain \'chām-bər-lən\ (Arthur) Neville 1869–1940 British prime minister (1937–40)
Cham•plain, de \sham-'plān, shäⁿ-plaⁿ\ Samuel 1567?–1635 French explorer in America; founder of Quebec
Char•le•magne \'shär-lə-,mān\ 742–814 A.D. *Charles the Great* or *Charles I* Frankish king (768–814); emperor of the West (800–814)
Charles \'chärlz\ name of 10 kings of France: especially **I** 823–877 A.D. (reigned 840–877) *the Bald;* Holy Roman emperor as *Charles II* (875–877); **IV** 1294–1328 (reigned 1322–28) *the Fair;* **V** 1337–80 (reigned 1364–80) *the Wise;* **VI** 1368–1422 (reigned 1380–1422) *the Mad* or *the Beloved;* **VII** 1403–61 (reigned 1422–61) *the Victorious*; **IX** 1550–74 (reigned 1560–74); **X** 1757–1836 (reigned 1824–30)
Charles name of 2 kings of Great Britain: **I** 1600–49 (reigned 1625–49) *Charles Stuart;* **II** 1630–85 (reigned 1660–85) son of Charles I
Charles 1948– son of Elizabeth II; prince of Wales (invested 1969)
Charles I 1887–1922 *Charles Francis Joseph* emperor of Austria and (as *Charles IV*) king of Hungary (1916–18)
Charles V 1500–58 Holy Roman emperor (1519–56); king of Spain as *Charles I* (1516–56)
Charles XII 1682–1718 king of Sweden (1697–1718)
Charles Edward Stuart 1720–88 *the Young Pretender; (Bonnie) Prince Charlie* British prince
Charles Mar•tel \mär-'tel\ 689?–741 A.D. grandfather of Charlemagne; Frankish ruler (715–741)
Char•on \'kar-ən, 'ker-\ boatman in Greek mythology who ferries the souls of the dead across the river Styx to the entrance of Hades
Cha•teau•bri•and, de \sha-,tō-brē-'äⁿ\ Vi·comte \vē-kōⁿt\ Francois René 1768–1848 French author
Chau•cer \'chò-sər\ Geoffrey 1340?-1400 English poet
Che•khov \'chek-,òf, -òv\ Anton Pavlovich 1860–1904 Russian author
Cheops — see KHUFU
Ches•ter•field \'ches-tər-,fēld\ 4th Earl of 1694–1773 English statesman and author
Ches•ter•ton \'ches-tərt-n\ Gilbert Keith 1874–1936 English author
Chiang Kai-shek \jē-'äng-'kī-'shek, 'chang-\ 1887–1975 Chinese general and statesman; president of China (1948–49; Taiwan, 1950–75)
Chi•ron \'kī-rən, 'kī-,rän\ wise centaur and tutor to many heroes in Greek mythology
Cho•pin \'shō-,pan, -,paⁿ\ Fréderic François 1810–49 Polish pianist and composer
Chou En-lai \'jō-'en-'lī\ 1898–1976 Chinese Communist politician; premier (1949–76)
Christ Jesus — see JESUS
Chris•tie \'kris-tē\ Agatha 1891–1976 English author
Chry•sos•tom \'kris-əs-təm, kris-'äs-təm\ Saint John 345?–407 A.D. church father; patriarch of Constantinople
Chur•chill \'chər-,chil, 'chərch-,hil\ Randolph Henry Spencer 1849–95 *Lord Randolph Churchill* British statesman
Churchill Sir Winston Leonard Spencer 1874-1965 British prime minister (1940–45; 1951–55); son of Lord Randolph Churchill
Cic•ero \'sis-ə-,rō\ Marcus Tullius 106–43 B.C. Roman statesman, orator, and writer
Cid, the \'sid\ 1040?–99 *Rodrigo* (or *Ruy*) *Díaz de Bi·var* \bē-'vär\ Spanish soldier and hero
Cir•ce \'sər-sē\ enchantress in Greek mythology who turns her victims into beasts
Clark \'klärk\ George Rogers 1752–1818 American soldier and frontiersman
Clark William 1770–1838 American explorer (with Meriwether Lewis)
Clay \'klā\ Henry 1777–1852 American statesman and orator
Cle•men•ceau \,klem-ən-'sō, klā-mäⁿ-sō\ Georges 1841–1929 *the Tiger* French statesman
Clem•ens \'klem-ənz\ Samuel Langhorne 1835–1910 pseudonym *Mark Twain* \'twān\ American author

Clem•ent \'klem-ənt\ name of 14 popes
Cle•o•pa•tra \ˌklē-ə-'pa-trə, -'pā-, -'pä-\ 69–30 B.C. queen of Egypt (51–49; 48–30)
Cleve•land \'klēv-lənd\ (Stephen) Grover 1837–1908 22d and 24th president of the United States (1885–89; 1893–97)
Clio \'klī-ō, 'klē-\ Greek Muse of history
Clo•tho \'klō-thō\ the one of the three Fates in classical mythology who spins the thread of life — compare ATROPOS, LACHESIS
Clo•vis I \'klō-vəs\ 466?–511 A.D. Frankish king (481–511)
Cly•tem•nes•tra \ˌklīt-əm-'nes-trə\ wife of Agamemnon
Co•chise \kō-'chēs\ *died* 1874 Apache Indian chief
Co•dy \'kōd-ē\ William Frederick 1846–1917 *Buffalo Bill* American frontiersman and entertainer
Co•han \'kō-ˌhan\ George Michael 1878–1942 American actor and composer
Cole•ridge \'kōl-rij, 'kō-lə-rij\ Samuel Taylor 1772–1834 English poet
Co•lette \kò-'let\ Sidonie Gabrielle Claudine 1873–1954 French author
Co•lum•bus \kə-'ləm-bəs\ Christopher 1451–1506 Italian navigator; discovered America (1492)
Con•fu•cius \kən-'fyü-shəs\ about 551–479 B.C. Chinese philosopher
Con•rad \'kän-ˌrad\ Joseph 1857–1924 British (Ukrainian-born of Polish parents) author
Con•stan•tine \'kän-stən-ˌtēn, -ˌtīn\ 280?–337 A.D. *the Great* Roman emperor (306-337)
Cook \'kük\ Captain James 1728–79 English navigator
Coo•lidge \'kü-lij\ (John) Calvin 1872–1933 30th president of the United States (1923–29)
Coo•per \'kü-pər, 'küp-ər\ James Fen·i·more \'fen-ə-ˌmōr, -ˌmòr\ 1789–1851 American author
Co•per•ni•cus \kō-'pər-ni-kəs\ Nicolaus 1473–1543 Polish astronomer
Cop•land \'kō-plənd\ Aaron 1900– American composer
Corn•wal•lis \kòrn-'wäl-əs\ Charles 1st Marquis 1738–1805 British general and statesman
Co•ro•na•do, de \ˌkòr-ə-'näd-ō, ˌkär-\ Francisco Vásquez 1510–54 Spanish explorer of southwestern United States
Cor•tes *or* **Cor•tez** \kòr-'tez, 'kòr-ˌ\ Hernando 1485–1547 Spanish conqueror of Mexico
Cow•per \'kü-pər, 'küp-ər, 'kaù-pər\ William 1731–1800 English poet
Crane \'krān\ Stephen 1871–1900 American author
Crazy Horse \'krā-zē-ˌhòrs\ 1849?–77 Sioux Indian chief
Cres•si•da \'kres-əd-ə\ Trojan woman who in medieval legend is unfaithful to her lover Troilus
Crock•ett \'kräk-ət\ David 1786–1836 *Davy* American frontiersman
Croe•sus \'krē-səs\ *died* 546 B.C. king of Lydia (560–546)
Crom•well \'kräm-ˌwel, 'krəm-, -wəl\ Oliver 1599–1658 English general and stateman; lord protector of England (1653–58)
Cro•nus \'krō-nəs\ Titan dethroned by his son Zeus
Cu•pid \'kyü-pəd\ — see EROS
Cu•rie \kyù-'rē, 'kyùr-ē\ Marie 1867–1934 French (Polish-born) chemist; Nobel prize winner (1903, 1911)
Curie Pierre 1859–1906 French chemist; husband of Marie; Nobel prize winner (1903)
Cus•ter \'kəs-tər\ George Armstrong 1839–76 American general
Cyb•e•le \'sib-ə-lē\ nature goddess of ancient Asia Minor incorporated into classical mythology
Cy•ra•no de Ber•ge•rac, de \ˌsir-ə-ˌnō-də-'ber-zhə-ˌrak\ Savinieu 1619–55 French poet and soldier
Cyr•il \'sir-əl\ Saint 827–869 A.D. Apostle to the Slavs; brother of Methodius
Cy•rus \'sī-rəs\ 600?–529 B.C. *the Great* or *the Elder* king of Persia (550–529)
Cyrus 424?–401 B.C. *the Younger* Persian prince and satrap
Dae•da•lus \'ded-l-əs, 'dēd-\ builder in Greek mythology of the Cretan labyrinth and inventor of wings by which he and his son Icarus escape from it
Dal•ton \'dòlt-n\ John 1766–1844 English chemist and physicist
Dam•o•cles \'dam-ə-ˌklēz\ courtier of ancient Syracuse held to have been seated at a banquet beneath a sword hung by a single hair
Da•mon \'dā-mən\ a Sicilian held to have pledged his life for his condemned friend Pythias
Da•na \'dā-nə\ Richard Henry 1815–82 American author
Dan•aë \'dan-ə-ˌē\ mother of Perseus; visited by Zeus as a shower of gold during her imprisonment
Dan•iel \'dan-yəl\ Hebrew prophet captive in Babylon who was saved from death in a lions' den by his faith in God
Dan•te \'dän-tā, 'dan-, -tē\ 1265–1321 Italian poet
Daph•ne \'daf-nē\ nymph transformed into a laurel tree to escape the pursuing Apollo
Dare \'daər, 'deər\ Virginia 1587–? first child born in America of English parents
Da•ri•us I \də-'rī-əs\ 558?–486 B.C. *the Great* king of Persia (521-486)
Dar•row \'dar-ō\ Clarence Seward 1857–1938 American lawyer
Dar•win \'där-wən\ Charles Robert 1809–82 English naturalist
Da•vid \'dā-vəd\ the 2d king of Israel who in his youth killed Goliath; successor to Saul and father of Solomon
David Saint 6th century A.D. patron saint of Wales
Da•vid \dä-'vēd\ Jacques Louis 1748–1825 French painter
Da•vis \'dā-vəs\ Jefferson 1808–89 president of the Confederate States of America (1861–65)
Da•vy \'dā-vē\ Sir Humphry 1778–1829 English chemist
Debs \'debz\ Eugene Victor 1855–1926 American socialist
De•bus•sy \ˌdeb-yù-'sē, ˌdāb-; də-'byü-sē\ Claude Achille 1862–1918 French composer
De•ca•tur \di-'kāt-ər\ Stephen 1779–1820 American naval officer
De•foe \di-'fō\ Daniel *about* 1660–1731 English author
De•gas \də-'gä\ (Hilaire Germain) Edgar 1834–1917 French painter
de Gaulle \di-'gōl, -'gòl\ Charles André Joseph Marie 1890–1970 French general; president of Fifth Republic (1959–69)
De•la•croix \ˌdel-ə-'krwä, -'kwä\ (Ferdinand Victor) Eugene 1798–1863 French painter
de la Mare \ˌdel-ə-'maər, -'meər\ Walter John 1873–1956 English author
De•li•lah \di-'lī-lə\ mistress and betrayer of Samson
De•me•ter \di-'mēt-ər\ Greek goddess of agriculture whose Roman counterpart is Ceres
De Mille \də-'mil\ Agnes George 1906?– American choreographer
De Mille Cec·il \'ses-əl\ Blount \'blənt\ 1881–1959 American movie producer
De•mos•the•nes \di-'mäs-thə-ˌnēz\ 385?–322 B.C. Athenian orator and statesman
De•nis *or* **De•nys** \'den-əs, də-nē\ Saint 3d century A.D. 1st bishop of Paris; patron saint of France
De Quin•cey \di-'kwin-sē, -'kwin-zē\ Thomas 1785–1859 English author
Des•cartes \dā-'kärt\ René 1596–1650 French mathematician and philosopher
de So•to \di-'sōt-ō\ Hernando *or* Fernando 1500?–42 Spanish explorer in America; discovered Mississippi River (1541)
Dew•ey \'dü-ē, 'dyü-\ George 1837–1917 American admiral
Dewey John 1859–1952 American philosopher and educator
Di•ana \dī-'an-ə\ — see ARTEMIS
Di•as *or* **Di•az** \'dē-ˌäsh\ Bartholomeu 1450?–1500 Portuguese navigator; 1st to sail around the southern tip of South America
Dick•ens \'dik-ənz\ Charles John Huffam 1812–1870 *Boz* \'bäz, 'bōz\ English author
Dick•in•son \'dik-ən-sən\ Emily Elizabeth 1830–86 American poet
Di•de•rot \dē-'drō, 'dēd-ə-ˌrō\ Denis 1713–84 French philosopher and author
Di•do \'dīd-ō\ legendary queen of Carthage who entertains and falls in love with Aeneas and stabs herself upon his departure
Di•o•cle•tian \ˌdī-ə-'klē-shən\ 245–313 A.D. Roman emperor (284–305)
Di•og•e•nes \dī-'äj-ə-ˌnēz\ 412?–323 B.C. Greek Cynic philosopher
Di•o•me•des \ˌdī-ə-'mēd-ēz\ Greek warrior in the Trojan War
Di•o•ny•sus \ˌdī-ə-'nī-səs, -'nē-\ Greek god of wine and fertility whose Roman counterpart is Bacchus
Dis \'dis\ — see PLUTO
Dis•ney \'diz-nē\ Walter Elias 1901–66 American animated-film producer
Dis•rae•li \diz-'rā-lē\ Benjamin 1804–81 1st Earl of *Beacons·field* \'bē-kənz-ˌfēld\ British prime minister (1868; 1874–80)
Dix \'diks\ Dorothea Lynde 1802–87 American social reformer
Dodg•son \'däj-sən, 'däd-\ Charles Lut·widge \'lət-wij\

1832–98 pseudonym *Lewis Car·roll* \'kar-əl\ English mathematician and author
Dom·i·nic \'däm-ə-nik\ Saint 1170–1221 Spanish-born founder of the Dominican order of friars
Do·mi·tian \də-'mish-ən\ 51–96 A.D. Roman emperor (81–96)
Don·i·zet·ti \ˌdän-əd-'zet-ē, ˌdōn, -ə-'zet-\ Gaetano 1797–1848 Italian composer
Donne \'dən\ John *about* 1572–1631 English poet and clergyman
Dos·to·ev·ski \ˌdäs-tə-'yef-skē, -'yev-\ Fëdor Mikhailovich 1821–81 Russian author
Doug·las \'dəg-ləs\ Stephen Arnold 1813–61 American statesman
Doug·lass \'dəg-ləs\ Frederick 1817?–95 American abolitionist
Doyle \'dȯil\ Sir Arthur Co·nan \'kō-nən, 'kō-\ 1859–1930 British author and physician
Dra·co \'drā-kō\ late 7th century B.C. Athenian lawgiver
Drake \'drāk\ Sir Francis 1540?–96 English navigator and admiral
Drei·ser \'drī-sər, -zər\ Theodore 1871–1945 American author
Drey·fus \'drī-fəs, 'drā-\ Alfred 1859–1935 French army officer
Dry·den \'drīd-n\ John 1631–1700 English author
Du Bois \dü-'bȯis, dyü-\ William Edward Burghardt 1868–1963 American educator
Du·mas \dü-'mä, dyü-; 'dü-ˌmä, 'dyü-\ Alexandre 1802–70 *Dumas père* \'peər\ French author
Dumas Alexandre 1824–95 *Dumas fils* \'fēs\ French author
Dun·bar \'dən-ˌbär\ Paul Laurence 1872–1906 American poet
Dun·can \'dəng-kən\ Isadora 1878–1927 American dancer
Dü·rer \'dür-ər, 'dyür-, 'dᵫr-\ Albrecht 1471–1528 German painter and engraver
Du·se \'dü-zā\ Eleanora 1859–1924 Italian actress
Dvo·řák \də-'vȯr-ˌzhäk, 'vȯr-ˌzhäk\ Anton 1841–1904 Czech composer
Ea·kins \'ā-kənz\ Thomas 1844–1916 American artist
Ear·hart \'eər-ˌhärt, 'iər-\ Amelia 1898–1937 American aviator
Ed·dy \'ed-ē\ Mary Baker 1821–1910 American founder of the Christian Science Church
Ed·i·son \'ed-ə-sən\ Thomas Alva 1847–1931 American inventor
Ed·ward \'ed-wərd\ name of 8 post-Norman kings of England: **I** 1239–1307 (reigned 1272–1307) *Longshanks;* **II** 1284–1327 (reigned 1307–27); **III** 1312–77 (reigned 1327–77); **IV** 1442–83 (reigned 1461–70; 1471–83); **V** 1470–83 (reigned 1483); **VI** 1537–53 (reigned 1547–53) son of Henry VIII and Jane Seymour; **VII** 1841–1910 (reigned 1901–10) *Albert Edward* son of Queen Victoria; **VIII** 1894–1972 (reigned 1936; abdicated) *Duke of Windsor* son of George V
Edward 1330–76 *the Black Prince* son of Edward III; prince of Wales
Edward 1002?–66 *the Confessor* king of the English (1042–66)
Ed·wards \'ed-wərdz\ Jonathan 1703–58 American theologian
Ein·stein \'īn-ˌstīn\ Albert 1879–1955 American (German-born) physicist; Nobel prize winner (1921)
Ei·sen·how·er \'īz-n-ˌhau̇-ər, -ˌhau̇r\ Dwight David 1890–1969 American general; 34th president of the United States (1953–61)
Elec·tra \i-'lek-trə\ sister of Orestes who aids him in avenging their father's murder
El·gar \'el-ˌgär, -gər\ Sir Edward 1857–1934 English composer
Eli \'ē-ˌlī\ early Hebrew judge and priest
Eli·jah \i-'lī-jə\ *or* **Eli·as** \i-'lī-əs\ Hebrew prophet of the 9th century B.C.
El·iot \'el-ē-ət, 'el-yət\ George 1819–80 pseudonym of *Mary Ann Evans* English author
Eliot Thomas Stearns 1888–1965 British (American-born) poet and critic
Elis·a·beth \i-'liz-ə-bəth\ mother of John the Baptist
Eli·sha \i-'lī-shə\ Hebrew prophet; disciple and successor of Elijah
Eliz·a·beth I \i-'liz-ə-bəth\ 1533-1603 daughter of Henry VIII and Anne Boleyn; queen of England (1558–1603)
Elizabeth II 1926– daughter of George VI; queen of Great Britain (1952–)
Em·er·son \'em-ər-sən\ Ralph Waldo 1803–82 American essayist and poet
Em·ped·o·cles \em-'ped-ə-ˌklēz\ 5th century B.C. Greek philosopher and statesman
En·dym·i·on \em-'dim-ē-ən\ beautiful youth loved by the moon goddess Selene in classical mythology
Eos \'ē-ˌäs\ Greek goddess of dawn whose Roman counterpart is Aurora
Ep·i·cu·rus \ˌep-i-'kyu̇r-əs\ 342?–270 B.C. Greek philosopher
Eras·mus \i-'raz-məs\ Desiderius 1466?–1536 Dutch scholar
Er·a·to \'er-ə-ˌtō\ Greek Muse of lyric and especially love poetry
Er·ic \'er-ik\ 10th century *the Red* Norwegian navigator
Ericsson, Leif — see LEIF ERICSSON
Eriny·es \i-'rin-ē-ˌēz\ *or* **Eu·men·i·des** \yü-'men-ə-ˌdēz\ the Furies in Greek mythology
Eris \'ir-əs, 'er-\ Greek goddess of discord
Ernst \'eərnst, 'ərnst\ Max 1891–1976 German painter
Eros \'eər-ˌäs, 'iər-\ Greek god of love whose Roman counterpart is Cupid
Esau \'ē-ˌsȯ\ son of Isaac and Rebekah; elder twin brother of Jacob to whom he sold his birthright
Es·ther \'es-tər\ Hebrew woman who became Xerxes' queen during the Babylonian captivity and delivered her people from destruction
Eu·clid \'yü-kləd\ *flourished about* 300 B.C. Greek mathematician
Eumenides — see ERINYES
Eu·phos·y·ne \yu̇-'fräs-n-ē\ one of the three Graces in Greek mythology — compare AGLAIA, THALIA
Eu·rip·i·des \yu̇-'rip-ə-ˌdēz\ 480?–406 B.C. Greek dramatist
Eu·ro·pa \yu̇-'rō-pə\ Phoenician princess abducted by Zeus disguised as a white bull
Eu·ryd·i·ce \yu̇-'rid-ə-sē\ wife of Orpheus
Eu·ter·pe \yü-'tər-pē\ Greek Muse of music
Eve \'ēv\ the first woman in biblical tradition; wife of Adam
Eze·kiel \i-'zē-kyəl, -kē-əl\ Hebrew prophet of the 6th century B.C.
Ez·ra \'ez-rə\ Hebrew priest, scribe, and reformer of the 5th century B.C.
Fa·bi·us \'fā-bē-əs\ *died* 203 B.C. *Quintus Fabius Maximus Verrucosus Cunc·ta·tor* \'kəngk-ˌtāt-ər\ Roman general against Hannibal
Fahr·en·heit \'far-ən-ˌhīt, 'fär-\ Gabriel Daniel 1686–1736 German physicist
Far·a·day \'far-ə-ˌdā, -əd-ē\ Michael 1791–1867 English chemist and physicist
Far·ra·gut \'far-ə-gət\ David Glasgow 1801–70 American admiral
Faulk·ner \'fȯk-nər\ William 1897–1962 American author; Nobel prize winner (1949)
Faust \'fau̇st\ Doctor Johann (or Georgius) 1480?–1540? German magician and astrologer; basis of legend of Faust
Faust *or* **Fau·stus** \'fau̇-stəs, 'fȯ-\ magician and astrologer in legend and literature who sells his soul to the devil for worldly experience and power
Fawkes \'fȯks\ Guy 1570–1606 English conspirator
Fer·di·nand I \'fərd-n-ˌand\ *died* 1065 *the Great* king of Castile (1033–65); of Navarre and León (1037–65); emperor of Spain (1056–65)
Ferdinand V of Castile or **II** of Aragon 1452–1516 *the Catholic* king of Castile (1474–1504); of Aragon (1479–1516); of Naples (1504–16); founder of the Spanish monarchy
Fer·mi \'feər-mē\ Enrico 1901–54 American (Italian-born) physicist; Nobel prize winner (1938)
Fiel·ding \'fēl-ding\ Henry 1707–54 English author
Fie·so·le, da \fē-'ā-zə-ˌlā, -lē\ Giovanni 1387–1455 *Fra An·ge·li·co* \an-'jel-i-ˌkō\ Italian painter
Fill·more \'fil-ˌmōr, -ˌmȯr\ Millard 1800–74 13th president of the United States (1850–53)
Fitz·ger·ald \fits-'jer-əld\ Francis Scott Key 1896–1940 American author
Fitz·Ger·ald \fits-'jer-əld\ Edward 1809–83 English poet
Flau·bert \flō-'beər\ Gustave 1821–80 French author
Flem·ing \'flem-ing\ Sir Alexander 1881–1955 British bacteriologist; Nobel prize winner (1945)
Flo·ra \'flōr-ə, 'flȯr-\ Roman goddess of flowers
Flying Dutchman legendary Dutch mariner condemned to sail the seas until Judgment Day
Foch \'fȯsh, 'fäsh\ Ferdinand 1851–1929 French general; marshal of France (1918)
Ford \'fōrd, 'fȯrd\ Gerald Rudolph 1913– 38th president of the United States (1974–77)
Ford Henry 1863–1947 American automobile manufacturer

Fos•ter \'fós-tər, 'fäs-\ Stephen Collins 1826–64 American songwriter
Fox \'fäks\ George 1624–91 English founder of Society of Friends (Quakers)
Fran•cis I \'fran-səs\ 1494–1547 king of France (1515–47)
Francis II 1768–1835 last Holy Roman emperor (1792–1806); emperor of Austria (as *Francis I*) (1804–35)
Francis Ferdinand 1863–1914 archduke of Austria; assassinated
Francis Joseph I 1830–1916 emperor of Austria (1848–1916)
Francis of As•si•si \ə-'sē-sē, -zē, -'sis-ē\ Saint 1182–1226 Italian friar; founder of Franciscan order
Franck \'frängk\ César Auguste 1822–90 Belgian-French organist and composer
Fran•co \'fräng-kō, 'frang-\ Francisco 1892–1975 Spanish general and head of state
Frank•lin \'frang-klən\ Benjamin 1706–90 American statesman, philosopher, and inventor
Fred•er•ick I \'fred-rik, -ə-rik\ 1123?–90 *Frederick Bar·baros·sa* \,bär-bə-'räs-ə, -'rós-\ Holy Roman emperor (1152–90)
Frederick II 1194–1250 Holy Roman emperor (1215–50); king of Sicily (1198–1250)
Frederick IX 1899–1972 king of Denmark (1947–72)
Frederick I 1657–1713 king of Prussia (1701–13)
Frederick II 1712–86 *the Great* king of Prussia (1740–86)
Fré•mont \'frē-,mänt\ John Charles 1813–90 American general and explorer
Freud \'fróid\ Sigmund 1856–1939 Austrian neurologist; founder of psychoanalysis
Fron•te•nac, de \'fränt-n-,ak\ Comte *de Pal·lu·au* \pá-lwʸō\ *et* 1620–98 French general and colonial administrator
Frost \'fróst\ Robert Lee 1874–1963 American poet
Ful•ton \'fúlt-n\ Robert 1765–1815 American inventor
Ga•bri•el \'gā-brē-əl\ one of the four archangels named in Hebrew tradition — compare MICHAEL, RAPHAEL, URIEL
Ga•ga•rin \gə-'gär-ən\ Yu·ri \'yür-ē\ Alekseyevich 1934–68 Russian cosmonaut; 1st man in space (1961)
Gage \'gāj\ Thomas 1721–87 British general in America
Gains•bor•ough \'gānz-,bər-ə, -bə-rə, -brə\ Thomas 1727–88 English painter
Gal•a•had \'gal-ə-,had\ knight of the Round Table who finds the Holy Grail
Gal•a•tea \,gal-ə-'tē-ə\ an ivory statue of a maiden carved by Pygmalion in Greek legend and given life by Aphrodite in response to the sculptor's prayer
Ga•len \'gā-lən\ *about* 130–*about* 200 A.D. Greek physician and writer
Ga•li•lei \,gal-ə-'lā-,ē\ Ga·li·leo \,gal-ə-'lē-ō, -'lā-\ 1564–1642 *Galileo* Italian astronomer and physicist
Gall \'gól\ 1840?–94 Sioux Indian leader
Ga•lois \gal-'wä\ Évariste 1811–32 French mathematician
Gals•wor•thy \'golz-,wər-thē\ John 1867–1933 English author; Nobel prize winner (1932)
Ga•ma, da \'gam-ə, 'gäm-\ Vasco 1469?–1524 Portuguese navigator
Gan•y•mede \'gan-i-,mēd\ cupbearer of Zeus
Gar•field \'gär-,fēld\ James Abram 1831–81 20th president of the United States (1881)
Gar•i•bal•di \,gar-ə-'ból-dē\ Giuseppe 1807–82 Italian patriot
Gar•ri•son \'gar-ə-sən\ William Lloyd 1805–79 American abolitionist
Gau•guin \gō-gaⁿ\ (Eugène Henri) Paul 1848–1903 French painter
Gauss \'gaùs\ Karl Friedrich 1777–1855 German mathematician and astronomer
Gau•ta•ma Bud•dha \,gaùt-ə-mə-'büd-ə, -'bùd-\ 563?–?483 B.C. Indian founder of Buddhism
Ga•wain \gə-'wān, 'gä-,wān, 'gaù-ən\ nephew of King Arthur; knight of the Round Table
Gay \'gā\ John 1685–1732 English author
Gen•ghis Khan \,jeng-gə-'skän, ,geng-\ 1162–1227 Mongol conqueror
George \'jórj\ Saint *died about* 303 A.D. Christian martyr; patron saint of England
George name of 6 kings of Great Britain: **I** 1660–1727 (reigned 1714–27); **II** 1683–1760 (reigned 1727–60); **III** 1738–1820 (reigned 1760–1820); **IV** 1762–1830 (reigned 1820–30); **V** 1865–1936 (reigned 1910–36); **VI** 1895–1952 (reigned 1936–52)
George I 1845–1913 king of Greece (1863–1913)
George II 1890–1947 king of Greece (1922–23; 1935–47)
George David Lloyd — see LLOYD GEORGE
Ge•ron•i•mo \jə-'rän-ə-,mō\ 1829–1909 Apache Indian chief
Gersh•win \'gərsh-wən\ George 1898–1937 American composer
Gib•bon \'gib-ən\ Edward 1737–94 English historian
Gide \'zhēd\ André 1869–1951 French author; Nobel prize winner (1947)
Gid•e•on \'gid-ē-ən\ Hebrew hero noted for his defeat of the Midianites
Gil•bert \'gil-bərt\ Sir William Schwenck 1836–1911 English librettist and poet; collaborated with Sir Arthur S. Sullivan
Giot•to \'jót-tō, 'jó-tō, jē-'ät-ō\ 1266?–1337 *Giotto di Bondone* Florentine painter, architect, and sculptor
Glad•stone \'glad-,stōn, *chiefly British* -stən\ William Ewart 1809–98 British prime minister (1868–74; 1880–85; 1886; 1892–94)
Glenn \'glen\ John Herschel 1921– American astronaut; 1st American to orbit the earth (1962)
God•dard \'gäd-ərd\ Robert Hutchings 1882–1945 American physicist
Go•di•va \gə-'dī-və\ Saxon lady noted in legend for riding naked through the streets of Coventry to relieve the town of a burdensome tax levied by her husband
Goeb•bels \'gərb-əlz, 'gœb-əls\ Joseph Paul 1897–1945 German Nazi propagandist
Goe•thals \'gō-thəlz\ George Washington 1858–1928 American general and engineer
Goe•the, von \'gər-tə, 'gœ-tə\ Johann Wolfgang 1749–1832 German author
Gogh, van \van-'gō, -'gäk, -kók\ Vincent 1853–90 Dutch painter
Go•gol \'gó-gəl, 'gō-,gól\ Nikolai Vasilievich 1809–52 Russian author
Gold•smith \'gōld-,smith, 'gōl-\ Oliver 1728–74 British author
Go•li•ath \gə-'lī-əth\ Philistine giant held in the Old Testament to have been killed by David with a sling
Gom•pers \'gäm-pərz\ Samuel 1850–1924 American (British-born) labor leader
Good•year \'gùd-,yiər, 'gùj-,iər\ Charles 1800–60 American inventor
Gor•gas \'gór-gəs\ William Crawford 1854–1920 American army surgeon
Gor•ki \'gór-kē\ Maksim 1868–1936 pseudonym of *Aleksei Maksimovich Pesh·kov* \'pesh-,kóf, -,kóv\ Russian author
Gou•nod \'gü-,nō\ Charles François 1818–93 French composer
Go•ya y Lu•cien•tes, de \'gói-ə-,ē-,lü-sē-,en-,tās\ Francisco José 1746–1828 Spanish painter
Grac•chus \'grak-əs\ Gaius Sempronius 153–121 B.C. and his brother Tiberius Sempronius 163–133 B.C. *the Grac·chi* \'grak-,ī\ Roman statesmen
Gra•ham \'grā-əm, 'gra-əm, 'gram\ Martha 1894?– American dancer
Grant \'grant\ Ulysses Simpson 1822–85 *Ulysses Hiram* (baptized *Hiram Ulysses*) *Grant* American general; 18th president of the United States (1869–77)
Gray \'grā\ Thomas 1716–71 English poet
Gre•co, El \'grek-ō, 'gräk-, 'grēk-\ 1548?–?1614 or ?1625 *Domenico Teotocopulo* Spanish (Cretan-born) painter
Gree•ley \'grē-lē\ Horace 1811–72 American journalist and politician
Greene \'grēn\ Graham 1904– British author
Greene Nathanael 1742–86 American Revolutionary general
Greg•o•ry \'greg-rē, -ə-rē\ name of 16 popes: especially **I** Saint 540?–604 A.D. *the Great* (pope 590–604); **VII** Saint *(Hil·debrand* \'hil-də-,brand\) 1020?–85 (pope 1073–85); **XIII** 1502–85 (pope 1572–85)
Grey \'grā\ Lady Jane 1537–54 English noblewoman beheaded as a possible rival for the throne
Grey (Pearl) Zane 1875–1939 American author
Grieg \'grēg, 'grig\ Edvard Hagerup 1843–1907 Norwegian composer
Grimm \'grim\ Jacob 1785–1863 and his brother Wilhelm 1786–1859 German philologists and fairy tale writers
Guin•e•vere \'gwin-ə-,viər, 'gwen-\ wife of King Arthur and mistress of Lancelot in Arthurian legend
Gun•ther \'gùnt-ər\ Burgundian king and husband of Brunhild in Germanic legend
Gu•ten•berg \'güt-n-,bərg\ Johann 1400?–?68 *Johann Gensfleisch* German inventor of printing from movable type

Ha•dri•an \'hā-drē-ən\ 76–138 A.D. Roman emperor (117–138)
Ha•gar \'hā-,gär, -gər\ concubine of Abraham driven into the desert with her son Ishmael because of Sarah's jealousy
Hag•gai \'hag-ē-,ī, 'hag-,ī\ *or* **Ag•ge•us** \a-'gē-əs\ Hebrew prophet of the 6th century B.C.
Hai•le Se•las•sie \,hī-lē-sə-'las-ē, -'läs-\ 1892–1975 emperor of Ethiopia (1930–36; 1941–74); dethroned
Hale \'hāl\ Edward Everett 1822–1909 American clergyman and author
Hale Nathan 1755–76 American Revolutionary officer; hanged as a spy by the British
Hal•sey \'hȯl-sē, -zē\ William Frederick 1882–1959 American admiral
Ham \'ham\ son of Noah; ancestor of the Hamitic peoples in biblical tradition
Ha•man \'hā-mən\ Old Testament enemy of the Jews hanged for plotting their destruction
Ha•mil•car Bar•ca \hə-'mil-,kär-'bär-kə, 'ham-əl-\ 270?–228 B.C. Carthaginian general; father of Hannibal
Ham•il•ton \'ham-əl-tən, -əlt-n\ Alexander 1755–1804 American statesman
Hamilton Edith 1867–1963 American classicist
Ham•mu•ra•bi \,ham-ə-'räb-ē\ king of Babylon (about 1955–1913 B.C. or earlier) and lawgiver
Ham•sun \'häm-sən\ Knut 1859–1952 pseudonym of *Knut Pedersen* Norweigian author; Nobel prize winner (1920)
Han•cock \'han-,käk\ John 1737–93 American statesman; 1st signer of Declaration of Independence
Han•del \'han-dl\ George Frederick 1685–1759 British (German-born) composer
Han•dy \'han-dē\ William Christopher 1873–1958 *W. C.* American blues musician
Han•ni•bal \'han-ə-bəl\ 247–183 B.C. Carthaginian general against Rome
Har•de•ca•nute \,härd-i-kə-'nüt, -'nyüt\ 1019?–42 king of the English (1040–42); king of Denmark (1035–42)
Har•ding \'härd-ing\ Warren Gamaliel 1865–1923 29th president of the United States (1921–23)
Har•dy \'härd-ē\ Thomas 1840–1928 English author
Har•greaves \'här-,grēvz\ James *died* 1778 English inventor of the spinning jenny
Har•old I \'har-əld\ *died* 1040 *Harold Hare·foot* \'haər-,fůt, 'heər-\ king of the English (1035–40)
Harold II 1022?–66 king of the English (1066)
Har•ris \'har-əs\ Joel Chandler 1848–1908 American author
Har•ri•son \'har-ə-sən\ Benjamin 1833–1901 23d president of the United States (1889–93); grandson of William Henry Harrison
Harrison William Henry 1773–1841 American general; 9th president of the United States (1841)
Harte \'härt\ Francis Brett 1836–1902 *Bret* American author
Har•vey \'här-vē\ William 1578–1657 English physician and anatomist
Haw•thorne \'hȯ-,thȯrn\ Nathaniel 1804–64 American author
Haydn \'hīd-n\ (Franz) Joseph 1732–1809 Austrian composer
Hayes \'hāz\ Rutherford Birchard 1822–93 19th president of the United States (1877–81)
Haz•litt \'haz-lət, 'hāz-\ William 1778–1830 English essayist
Hearst \'hərst\ William Randolph 1863–1951 American newspaper publisher
He•be \'hē-bē\ Greek goddess of youth; cupbearer of the gods
Hec•ate \'hek-ət-ē\ Greek goddess associated especially with the underworld, the moon, and witchcraft
Hec•tor \'hek-tər\ son of Priam and bravest of the Trojans in the Trojan War; slain by Achilles
Hec•u•ba \'hek-yə-bə\ wife of Priam and mother of Hector and Paris
He•gel \'hā-gəl\ Georg Wilhelm Friedrich 1770–1831 German philosopher
Hei•deg•ger \'hī-,deg-ər, 'hīd-i-gər\ Martin 1889–1976 German philosopher
Hei•ne \'hī-nə *also* -nē\ Heinrich 1797–1856 German author
Hel•en of Troy \,hel-ə-nəv-'trȯi\ wife of Menelaus whose abduction by Paris caused the Trojan War
He•li•os \'hē-lē-,ōs, -əs\ Greek sun-god whose Roman counterpart is Sol
Hem•ing•way \'hem-ing-,wā\ Ernest Miller 1899–1961 American author; Nobel prize winner (1954)
Hen•ley \'hen-lē\ William Ernest 1849–1903 English author
Hen•ry \'hen-rē\ name of 8 kings of England: **I** 1068–1135 (reigned 1100–35); **II** 1133–89 (reigned 1154–89); **III** 1207–72 (reigned 1216–72); **IV** 1367–1413 (reigned 1399–1413); **V** 1387–1422 (reigned 1413–22); **VI** 1421–71 (reigned 1422–61; 1470–71); **VII** 1457–1509 (reigned 1485–1509); **VIII** 1491–1547 (reigned 1509–47)
Henry name of 4 kings of France: **I** 1008–60 (reigned 1031–60); **II** 1519–59 (reigned 1547–59); **III** 1551–89 (reigned 1574–89); **IV** 1553–1610 *Henry of Navarre* (reigned 1589–1610)
Henry O. — see William Sydney PORTER
Henry Patrick 1736–99 American statesman and orator
He•phaes•tus \hi-'fes-təs, -'fēs-\ Greek god of fire and of metalworking whose Roman counterpart is Vulcan
He•ra \'hir-ə, 'hē-rə\ Greek goddess of women and marriage whose Roman counterpart is Juno; sister and wife of Zeus
Her•bert \'hər-bərt\ Victor 1859–1924 American (Irish-born) composer and conductor
Her•cu•les \'hər-kyə-,lēz\ *or* **Her•a•cles** *also* **Her•a•kles** \'her-ə-,klēz\ hero in classical mythology noted for his strength and for performing 12 labors imposed on him by Hera
Her•maph•ro•di•tus \hər-,maf-rə-'dīt-əs\ son of Hermes and Aphrodite who is joined with a nymph into one body
Her•mes \'hər-,mēz, -mēz\ Greek god whose Roman counterpart is Mercury; herald and messenger for the other gods and protector of travelers
He•ro \'hē-rō, 'hiər-ō\ priestess of Aphrodite loved by Leander
Her•od \'her-əd\ 73?–4 B.C. *the Great* Roman king of Judea (37–4)
Herod An•ti•pas \'ant-ə-,pas, -pəs\ *died* after 40 A.D. Roman tetrarch of Galilee (4 B.C.–40 A.D.); son of Herod the Great
He•rod•o•tus \hi-'räd-ə-təs\ 5th century B.C. Greek historian
Her•rick \'her-ik\ Robert 1591–1674 English poet
He•si•od \'hē-sē-əd, 'hes-ē-\ 8th century B.C. Greek poet
Hes•se \'hes-ə\ Hermann 1877–1962 German author
Hes•tia \'hes-tē-ə; 'hes-chə, 'hesh-\ Greek goddess of the hearth and domestic activity whose Roman counterpart is Vesta
Hey•er•dahl \'hā-ər-,däl, 'hī-\ Thor 1914– Norwegian explorer and author
Hi•a•wa•tha \,hī-ə-'wȯ-thə, ,hē-ə-, -'wäth-ə\ 16th century Mohawk chieftain and hero of Iroquoian legend
Hick•ok \'hik-,äk\ James Butler 1837–76 *Wild Bill* American scout and United States marshal
Hildebrand — see GREGORY VII
Hil•la•ry \'hil-ə-rē\ Sir Edmund Percival 1919– New Zealand mountaineer who with Tenzing Norgay first reached the summit of Mount Everest (1953)
Hil•ton \'hilt-n\ James 1900–54 English novelist
Hin•den•burg, von \'hin-dən-,bərg, -,bůrg\ Paul 1847–1934 German field marshal; president of Germany (1925–34)
Hip•poc•ra•tes \hip-'äk-rə-,tēz\ 460?–?377 B.C. *father of medicine* Greek physician
Hi•ro•hi•to \,hir-ō-'hē-tō\ 1901– emperor of Japan (1926–)
Hit•ler \'hit-lər\ Adolf 1889–1945 German (Austrian-born) chancellor (1933–45)
Hobbes \'häbz\ Thomas 1588–1679 English philosopher
Ho•garth \'hō-,gärth\ William 1697–1764 English painter and engraver
Hol•bein \'hōl-,bīn, 'hȯl-\ Hans father 1465?–1524 and son 1497?–1543 German painters
Holmes \'hōmz, 'hōlmz\ Oliver Wendell 1809–94 American physician and author
Holmes Oliver Wendell 1841–1935 American jurist; son of the preceding
Ho•mer \'hō-mər\ *flourished* 850 B.C. or earlier; Greek epic poet
Homer Winslow 1836–1910 American painter
Hook•er \'hůk-ər\ Thomas 1586–1647 English puritan clergyman; a founder of Connecticut
Hoo•ver \'hü-vər\ Herbert Clark 1874–1964 31st president of the United States (1929–33)
Hoover John Edgar 1895–1972 American criminologist; director of the Federal Bureau of Investigation (1924–72)
Hop•kins \'häp-kənz\ Gerard Manley 1844–89 English poet and priest
Hor•ace \'hȯr-əs, 'här-\ 65–8 B.C. Roman poet
Ho•rae \'hōr-,ē, 'hȯr-, -,ī\ Greek goddesses of the seasons
Ho•ra•tius \hə-'rā-shē-əs, -shəs\ hero in Roman legend noted for his defense of a bridge over the Tiber against the Etruscans
Ho•sea \hō-'zē-ə, -'zā-\ *or* **Osee** \'ō-zē, ō-'zā-ə\ Hebrew prophet of the 8th century B.C.

Hous•man \ˈhau̇-smən\ Alfred Edward 1859–1936 English classical scholar and poet
Hous•ton \ˈhyü-stən, ˈyü-\ Samuel 1793–1863 *Sam* American general; president of the Republic of Texas (1836–38; 1841–44)
Howe \ˈhau̇\ Elias 1819–67 American inventor of the sewing machine
Howe Julia 1819–1910 née *Ward* American suffragist and reformer
How•ells \ˈhau̇-əlz\ William Dean 1837–1920 American author
Hud•son \ˈhəd-sən\ Henry *died* 1611 English navigator; explored North America
Hudson William Henry 1841–1922 English naturalist and author
Hugh Ca•pet \ˈkā-pət, ˈkap-ət, ka-ˈpā\ 940?–996 A.D. king of France (987–996)
Hughes \ˈhyüz *also* ˈyüz\ Charles Evans 1862–1948 chief justice of the United States Supreme Court (1930–41)
Hughes (James) Langston 1902–67 American author
Hu•go \ˈhyü-gō, yü-\ Victor Marie 1802–85 French author
Hume \ˈhyüm *also* ˈyüm\ David 1711–76 Scottish philosopher and historian
Huss *or* **Hus** \ˈhəs, ˈhu̇s\ John *or* Jan *about* 1374–1415 Bohemian religious reformer
Hus•sein I \hü-ˈsān\ 1935– king of Jordan (1953–)
Hux•ley \ˈhək-slē\ Aldous Leonard 1894–1963 English author
Hy•ge•ia \hī-ˈjē-ə, -yə\ Greek goddess of health
Hy•men \ˈhī-mən\ Greek god of marriage
Hy•pe•ri•on \hī-ˈpir-ē-ən\ Titan; father of Eos, Selene, and Helios
Ib•sen \ˈib-sən, ˈip-\ Henrik 1828–1906 Norwegian author
Ic•a•rus \ˈik-ə-rəs\ son of Daedalus who falls into the sea when the wax of his artificial wings melts as he flies too near the sun
Ig•na•tius \ig-ˈnā-shē-əs, -shəs\ *Saint Ignatius of Loy•o•la* \lȯi-ˈō-lə\ 1491–1556 Spanish soldier and priest; founded the Society of Jesus
In•no•cent \ˈin-ə-sənt\ name of 13 popes: especially **II** *died* 1143 (pope 1130–43); **III** 1161–1216 (pope 1198–1216); **IV** *died* 1254 (pope 1243–54); **XI** 1611–89 (pope 1676–89)
Iph•i•ge•nia \ˌif-ə-jə-ˈnī-ə\ daughter of Agamemnon offered by him as a sacrifice but saved and made a priestess of Artemis
Iris \ˈī-rəs\ goddess of the rainbow and a messenger of the gods in Greek mythology
Ir•ving \ˈər-viŋ\ Washington 1783–1859 American author
Isaac \ˈī-zik, -zək\ Hebrew patriarch; son of Abraham and father of Jacob
Is•a•bel•la I \ˌiz-ə-ˈbel-ə\ 1451–1504 queen of Castile (1474–1504); wife of Ferdinand V of Castile
Isa•iah \ī-ˈzā-ə\ Hebrew prophet of the 8th century B.C.
Iseult — see ISOLDE
Ish•ma•el \ˈish-mē-əl, -mā-\ outcast son of Abraham and Hagar
Ish•tar \ˈish-ˌtär\ chief goddess of the Babylonian and Assyrian pantheons
Isis \ˈī-səs\ Egyptian goddess of motherhood and fertility; wife of Osiris
Isol•de \i-ˈzōl-də\ *or* **Iseult** \is-ˈült, iz-\ Irish princess married to King Mark of Cornwall and loved by Tristram
Ivan III \ē-ˈvän, ˈī-vən\ **Va•si•lie•vich** \və-ˈsil-yə-ˌvich\ 1440–1505 *Ivan the Great* grand duke of Russia (1462–1505)
Ivan IV Vasilievich 1530–84 *Ivan the Terrible* ruler of Russia (1533–84)
Ives \ˈīvz\ Charles Edward 1874–1954 American composer
Jack•son \ˈjak-sən\ Andrew 1767–1845 American general; 7th president of the United States (1829–37)
Jackson Thomas Jonathan 1824–63 *Stonewall* American Confederate general
Ja•cob \ˈjā-kəb\ Hebrew patriarch; son of Isaac and Rebekah and younger twin brother of Esau
James \ˈjāmz\ one of the 12 apostles; son of Zebedee and brother of the apostle John
James *the Less* one of the 12 apostles; son of Alphaeus
James name of 2 kings of Great Britain: **I** 1566–1625 (reigned 1603–25); king of Scotland as *James VI* (reigned 1567–1603); **II** 1633–1701 (reigned 1685–88)
James Henry 1843–1916 British (American-born) author
James William 1842–1910 American psychologist and philosopher; brother of Henry James
Ja•nus \ˈjā-nəs\ Roman god of gates and doors and of beginnings and endings conventionally portrayed as having two opposite faces
Ja•pheth \ˈjā-fəth\ son of Noah; ancestor of the Medes and Greeks in biblical tradition
Ja•son \ˈjās-n\ hero in Greek mythology noted for his successful quest of the Golden Fleece
Jay \ˈjā\ John 1745–1829 American jurist and statesman; 1st chief justice of the United States Supreme Court (1789–95)
Jef•fer•son \ˈjef-ər-sən\ Thomas 1743–1826 3d president of the United States (1801–09)
Jen•ner \ˈjen-ər\ Edward 1749–1823 English physician
Jer•e•mi•ah \ˌjer-ə-ˈmī-ə\ Hebrew prophet of the 6th and 7th centuries B.C.
Je•rome \jə-ˈrōm\ Saint 340?–420 A.D. church father and biblical translator
Je•sus \ˈje-zəs, -zəz\ 4?B.C.–?29 A.D. *Jesus Christ* founder of the Christian religion
Jez•e•bel \ˈjez-ə-ˌbel\ queen of Israel noted for her wickedness; wife of Ahab
Joan of Arc \ˌjō-nə-ˈvärk\ Saint 1412–1431 *the Maid of Orleans* French national heroine
Job \ˈjōb\ Old Testament patriarch who endured afflictions with fortitude and faith
Jo•cas•ta \jō-ˈkas-tə\ queen of Thebes who unknowingly marries her son Oedipus
Jo•el \ˈjō-əl\ Hebrew prophet of the Old Testament
John \ˈjän\ *the Baptist* forerunner and baptizer of Jesus
John one of the 12 apostles held to be the author of the fourth Gospel, three Epistles, and the Book of Revelation
John name of 21 popes: especially **XXIII** *(Angelo Giuseppe Roncalli)* 1881–1963 (pope 1958–63)
John 1167?–1216 *John Lack•land* \ˈlak-ˌland\ king of England (1199–1216)
John of Gaunt \-ˈgȯnt, -ˈgänt\ 1340–99 Duke of Lancaster; son of Edward III of England
John•son \ˈjän-sən\ Andrew 1808–75 17th president of the United States (1865–69)
Johnson Lyndon Baines 1908–73 36tn president of the United States (1963–69)
Johnson Samuel 1709–84 *Dr. Johnson* English lexicographer and author
Jo•liet *or* **Jol•liet** \zhȯl-ˈyā\ Louis 1645–1700 French-Canadian explorer
Jo•nah \ˈjō-nə\ Hebrew prophet who in biblical tradition is cast overboard during a storm, is swallowed by a great fish, and is vomited up after three days in its belly
Jon•a•than \ˈjän-ə-thən\ son of Saul and friend of David
Jones \ˈjōnz\ John Paul 1747–92 American (Scottish-born) naval officer
Jon•son \ˈjän-sən\ Benjamin 1573?–1637 *Ben* English author
Jo•seph \ˈjō-zəf *also* -səf\ Hebrew patriarch who was sold into slavery by his jealous brothers, and became a ruler in Egypt and saved his father Jacob and his brothers in time of famine
Joseph 1840?–1904 Nez Percé Indian chief
Joseph *Saint* husband of Mary, the mother of Jesus
Jo•se•phine \ˈjō-zə-ˌfēn *also* -sə-\ 1763–1814 1st wife of Napoleon I; empress of France (1804–09)
Joseph of Ar•i•ma•thea \-ˌar-ə-mə-ˈthē-ə\ *Saint* wealthy member of the Sanhedrin who placed the body of Jesus in his own tomb
Jo•se•phus \jō-ˈsē-fəs\ *Flavius* 37–?100 A.D. Jewish historian
Josh•ua \ˈjäsh-wə, -ə-wə\ Hebrew leader and successor of Moses during the settlement of the Israelites in Canaan
Jove \ˈjōv\ — see ZEUS
Joyce \ˈjȯis\ James 1882–1941 Irish author
Ju•dah \ˈjüd-ə\ son of Jacob; ancestor of one of the 12 tribes of Israel
Ju•das \ˈjüd-əs\ *or* **Judas Is•car•i•ot** \-is-ˈkar-ē-ət\ one of the 12 apostles; betrayer of Jesus
Ju•das Mac•ca•bae•us \ˈjud-ə-ˌsmak-ə-ˈbē-əs\ *died* 160 B.C. Jewish patriot
Ju•lian \ˈjül-yən\ 331–363 A.D. *the Apostate* Roman emperor (361–363)
Ju•li•ana \ˌjü-lē-ˈan-ə\ 1909– queen of the Netherlands (1948–); daughter of Wilhelmina
Jung \ˈyu̇ŋ\ Carl Gustav 1875–1961 Swiss psychologist
Ju•no \ˈjü-nō\ — see HERA
Ju•pi•ter \ˈjü-pət-ər\ — see ZEUS
Jus•tin•i•an I \ˌjə-ˈstin-ē-ən\ 483–565 A.D. *the Great* Byzantine emperor (527–565)
Ju•ve•nal \ˈjü-vən-l\ 60?–?140 A.D. Roman satirist

Kaf•ka \ˈkäf-kə, ˈkaf-\ Franz 1883–1924 Austrian author
Kalb \ˈkälp, ˈkalb\ Johann 1721–80 Baron *de Kalb* \di-ˈkalb\ German general in American Revolutionary army
Kant \ˈkant, ˈkänt\ Immanuel 1724–1804 German philosopher
Keats \ˈkēts\ John 1795–1821 English poet
Kel•ler \ˈkel-ər\ Helen Adams 1880–1968 American deaf and blind lecturer
Kel•vin \ˈkel-vən\ 1st Baron 1824–1907 *William Thomson* British mathematician and physicist
Kempis Thomas a — see THOMAS A KEMPIS
Ken•ne•dy \ˈken-əd-ē\ John Fitzgerald 1917–63 35th president of the United States (1961–63)
Kennedy Robert Francis 1925–68 American lawyer; attorney general of the United States (1961–64); brother of John F. Kennedy
Ke•o•kuk \ˈkē-ə-ˌkək\ 1788?–?1848 American Indian chief
Kep•ler \ˈkep-lər\ Johannes 1571–1630 German astronomer
Ke•ren•ski \ˈker-ən-skē\ Aleksandr Feodorovich 1881–1970 Russian revolutionist
Key \ˈkē\ Francis Scott 1779–1843 American lawyer; author of "The Star-Spangled Banner"
Keynes \ˈkānz\ 1st Baron 1883–1946 *John Maynard Keynes* English economist — **Keynes•ian** \ˈkān-zē-ən\ *adj or n*
Khayyám Omar — see OMAR KHAYYÁM
Khru•shchev \kru̇sh-ˈchȯf, -ˈȯf, -ˈchȯv, -ˈȯv, -ˈchef, -ˈef, ˈkrüsh-\ Ni·ki·ta \nə-ˈkēt-ə\ Sergeevich 1894–1971 premier of U.S.S.R. (1958–64)
Khu•fu \ˈkü-ˌfü\ *or Greek* **Che•ops** \ˈkē-ˌäps\ king of Egypt (about 2900–2877 B.C.) and pyramid builder
Kidd \ˈkid\ William 1645?–1701 *Captain Kidd* Scottish pirate
Kier•ke•gaard \ˈkir-kə-ˌgärd, -ˌgär, -ˌgȯr\ Sören Aabye 1813–55 Danish philosopher and theologian
King \ˈking\ Ernest Joseph 1878–1956 American admiral
King Martin Luther, Jr. 1929–68 American clergyman and civil rights leader; Nobel prize winner (1964)
Kip•ling \ˈkip-ling\ Rud·yard \ˈrəd-yərd, ˈrəj-ərd\ 1865–1936 English author
Kis•sin•ger \ˈkis-n-jər\ Henry Alfred 1923– American (German-born) scholar and government official; United States secretary of state (1973–77); Nobel prize winner (1973)
Klee \ˈklā\ Paul 1879–1940 Swiss painter
Knox \ˈnäks\ John 1505–72 Scottish religious reformer
Koch \ˈkȯk, ˈkȯk, ˈkōk, ˈkōk, ˈkäk, ˈkäk\ Robert 1843–1910 German bacteriologist; Nobel prize winner (1905)
Kos•ciusz•ko \ˌkäs-ē-ˈəs-ˌkō, kȯsh-ˈchu̇sh-kō\ Thaddeus 1746–1817 Polish patriot; brigadier general in American Revolutionary army
Krish•na \ˈkrish-nə\ deity or deified hero of later Hinduism worshiped as an incarnation of Vishnu
Kriss Kringle — see SANTA CLAUS
Ku•blai Khan \ˌkü-blə-ˈkän, -ˌblī-\ 1216–94 founder of Mongol dynasty in China; grandson of Genghis Khan
Lach•e•sis \ˈlak-ə-səs\ the one of the three Fates in classical mythology who determines the length of the thread of life — compare ATROPOS, CLOTHO
La•fa•yette, de \ˌläf-ē-ˈet, ˌlaf-\ Marquis 1757–1834 French general and statesman; major general in American Revolutionary army
La Fon•taine, de \lə-ˌfän-ˈtān, -ˌfōⁿ-ˈten\ Jean 1621–95 French writer of fables
La•ius \ˈlā-əs, ˈlī-\ king of Thebes slain by his son Oedipus
La•marck, de \lə-ˈmärk\ Chevalier 1744–1829 French naturalist
Lamb \ˈlam\ Charles 1775–1834 English author
Lan•ce•lot \ˈlan-sə-ˌlät\ knight of the Round Table and lover of Queen Guinevere in Arthurian legend
Lang•land \ˈlang-lənd\ William 1332?–?1400 English poet
Lang•ley \ˈlang-lē\ Samuel Pierpont 1834–1906 American astronomer and airplane pioneer
La•oc•o•ön \lā-ˈäk-ə-ˌwan\ Trojan priest killed with his two sons by sea serpents after warning the Trojans against the wooden horse
Lao–tzu *or* **Lao–tse** *or* **Lao–tze** \ˈlau̇d-ˈzə\ 604?–?531 B.C. Chinese philosopher; founder of Taoism
La•place, de \lə-ˈpläs\ Marquis Pierre Simon 1749–1827 French astronomer and mathematician
La Roche•fou•cauld, de \lä-ˌrȯsh-ˌfü-ˈkō, -ˌrōsh-\ Duc Francois 1613–80 French author and moralist
La Salle, de \lə-ˈsal\ Sieur 1643–87 French explorer in North America
La•voi•sier \ləv-ˈwäz-ē-ˌā\ Antoine Laurent 1743–94 French chemist
Law•rence \ˈlȯr-əns, ˈlär-\ David Herbert 1885–1930 English author
Lawrence Sir Thomas 1769–1830 English painter
Lawrence Thomas Edward 1888–1935 *Lawrence of Arabia* British archaeologist, soldier, and author
Laz•a•rus \ˈlaz-rəs, -ə-rəs\ brother of Mary and Martha raised by Jesus from the dead
Lazarus beggar in the biblical parable of the rich man and the beggar
Le•an•der \lē-ˈan-dər\ youth in Greek mythology who swims the Hellespont nightly to visit his lover Hero
Le•da \ˈlēd-ə\ Spartan princess in Greek mythology who is visited by Zeus in the form of a swan
Lee \ˈlē\ Ann 1736–84 English mystic; founder of Shaker society in the United States
Lee Henry 1756–1818 *Light-Horse Harry* American general
Lee Robert Edward 1807–70 American Confederate general; son of Henry Lee
Leeu•wen•hoek *or* **Leu•wen•hoek, van** \ˈlā-vən-ˌhu̇k\ Anton 1632–1723 Dutch naturalist
Leib•niz *or* **Leib•nitz, von** \ˈlīb-nəts, ˈlīp-nits\ Baron Gottfried Wilhelm 1646–1716 German philosopher and mathematician
Leif Er•ic•son \ˈlā-ˈver-ik-sən, ˈlē-ˈfer-\ *flourished* 1000 Norwegian mariner; son of Eric the Red
Le•nin \ˈlen-ən\ V. I. 1870–1924 *Vladimir Ilyich Ul·ya·nov* \ül-ˈyän-əf, -ˌȯf, -ˌȯv\ Russian Communist leader
Leo \ˈlē-ō\ name of 13 popes: especially **I** Saint 390?–461 A.D. (pope 440–461); **III** Saint 750?–816 A.D. (pope 795–816); **XIII** 1810–1903 (pope 1878–1903)
Leonardo da Vinci — see VINCI
Le•on•ca•val•lo \ˌlā-ˌōn-kə-ˈväl-ō\ Ruggiero 1858–1919 Italian composer and librettist
Le•on•i•das \lē-ˈän-əd-əs\ 5th century B.C. Greek hero; king of Sparta (490?–480)
Lep•i•dus \ˈlep-əd-əs\ Marcus Aemilius *died* 13 B.C. Roman triumvir
Les•seps, de \lā-ˈseps, ˈles-əps\ Vicomte Ferdinand Marie 1805–94 French diplomat; promotor of Suez Canal
Le•to \ˈlēt-ō\ mother of Apollo and Artemis by Zeus
Le•vi \ˈlē-ˌvī\ son of Jacob; ancestor of one of the 12 tribes of Israel
Lew•is \ˈlü-əs\ John Llewellyn 1880–1969 American labor leader
Lewis Meriwether 1774–1809 American explorer (with William Clark)
Lewis (Harry) Sinclair 1885–1951 American author; Nobel prize winner (1930)
Lin•coln \ˈling-kən\ Abraham 1809–65 16th president of the United States (1861–65)
Lind•bergh \ˈlind-ˌbərg, ˈlin-\ Charles Augustus 1902–74 American aviator
Lin•nae•us \lə-ˈnē-əs, -ˈnā-\ Carolus 1707–78 *Carl von Lin·né* \lə-ˈnā\ Swedish botanist
Lip•pi \ˈlip-ē\ Fra Fi·lip·po \fə-ˈlip-ō\ *or* Lip·po \ˈlip-ō\ 1406?–69 Florentine painter
Lis•ter \ˈlis-tər\ Joseph 1827–1912 English surgeon
Liszt \ˈlist\ Franz 1811–86 Hungarian pianist and composer
Liv•ing•stone \ˈliv-ing-stən\ David 1813–73 Scottish explorer in Africa
Livy \ˈliv-ē\ 59 B.C.–17 A.D. Roman historian
Lloyd George \ˈlȯid-ˈjȯrj\ David 1863–1945 1st Earl of *Dwy·for* \ˈdü-ē-ˌvȯr\ British prime minister (1916–22)
Locke \ˈläk\ John 1632–1704 English philosopher
Lo•hen•grin \ˈlō-ən-ˌgrin\ son of Parsifal and knight of the Holy Grail in German legend
Long•fel•low \ˈlȯng-ˌfel-ō\ Henry Wads·worth \ˈwädz-wərth, -ˌwərth\ 1807–82 American poet
Lo•re•lei \ˈlōr-ə-ˌlī, ˈlȯr-\ siren in German legend whose beauty and song lured sailors to destruction on a reef in the Rhine
Lot \ˈlät\ nephew of Abraham in biblical tradition whose wife was turned into a pillar of salt for looking back during their flight from Sodom
Lou•is \ˈlü-ē, ˈlü-əs\ name of 18 kings of France: especially **IX** Saint 1214–70 (reigned 1226–70); **XI** 1423–83 (reigned 1461–83); **XII** 1462–1515); (reigned 1498–1515); **XIII** 1601–43 (reigned 1610–43); **XIV** 1638–1715 (reigned 1643–1715); **XV** 1710–74 (reigned 1715–74); **XVI** 1754–93 (reigned 1774–92;

guillotined); **XVII** 1785–95 (nominally reigned 1793–95); **XVIII** 1755–1824 (reigned 1814–15; 1815–24)
Louis Napoleon — see NAPOLEON III
Louis Phi•lippe \fi-'lēp\ 1773–1850 *the Citizen King* king of the French (1830–48)
Low•ell \'lō-əl\ Amy 1874–1925 American poet
Lowell James Russell 1819–91 American author
Loyola — see IGNATIUS
Lu•cre•tius \lü-'krē-shē-əs, -shəs\ 96?–55 B.C. Roman poet and philosopher
Luke \'lük\ physician and companion of the apostle Paul held to be the author of the third Gospel and of the Book of Acts
Lu•na \'lü-nə\ — see SELENE
Lu•ther \'lü-thər\ Martin 1483–1546 German Reformation leader
Ly•on \'lī-ən\ Mary 1797–1849 American educator
Lyt•ton \'lit-n\ 1st Baron 1803–73 *Edward George Earle Lytton Bul·wer-Lytton* \ˌbu̇l-wər-\ English author
Mac•Ar•thur \mə-'kär-thər\ Douglas 1880–1964 American general
Ma•cau•lay \mə-'kȯ-lē\ Thomas Babington 1st Baron 1800–59 English author and statesman
Mc•Car•thy \mə-'kärth-ē\ Joseph Raymond 1908–57 American politician
Mc•Clel•lan \mə-'klel-ən\ George Brinton 1826–85 American general
Mc•Cor•mick \mə-'kȯr-mik\ Cyrus Hall 1809–84 American inventor of a mechanical reaper
Ma•chi•a•vel•li \ˌmak-ē-ə-'vel-ē\ Niccolò 1469–1527 Italian political philosopher
Mc•Kin•ley \mə-'kin-lē\ William 1843–1901 25th president of the United States (1897–1901)
Mad•i•son \'mad-ə-sən\ James 1751–1836 4th president of the United States (1809–17)
Ma•don•na \mə-'dän-ə\ Mary the mother of Jesus
Mae•ter•linck \'māt-ər-ˌlingk *also* 'met-, 'mat-\ Count Maurice 1862–1949 Belgian author
Ma•gel•lan \mə-'jel-ən\ Ferdinand 1480?–1521 Portuguese navigator
Mah•ler \'mäl-ər\ Gustav 1860–1911 Austrian composer
Mahomet *or* **Mahomed** — see MUHAMMAD
Mal•a•chi \'mal-ə-ˌkī\ Hebrew prophet of the 5th century B.C.
Malcolm X \ˌmal-kə-'meks\ 1925–65 American civil rights leader
Mal•o•ry \'mal-rē, -ə-rē\ Sir Thomas *flourished* 1470 English author
Mal•thus \'mal-thəs\ Thomas Robert 1766–1834 English economist
Ma•net \ma-'nā, mä-\ Édouard 1832–83 French painter
Mann \'man\ Horace 1796–1859 American educator
Mann \'män, 'man\ Thomas 1875–1955 American (German-born) author; Nobel prize winner (1929)
Mao Tse–tung \ˌmau̇d-zə-'du̇ng, ˌmau̇-zə-, ˌmau̇t-sə-\ 1893–1976 Chinese Communist leader
Ma•rat \mə-'rä\ Jean Paul 1743–93 French (Swiss-born) revolutionist; assassinated
Mar•co•ni \mär-'kō-nē\ Marchese Guglielmo 1874–1937 Italian electrical engineer and inventor; Nobel prize winner (1909)
Marcus Aurelius — see ANTONINUS
Ma•ria The•re•sa \mə-ˌrē-ə-tə-'rā-sə, -'rā-zə\ 1717–80 wife of Emperor Francis I; queen of Hungary and Bohemia
Ma•rie An•toi•nette \mə-'rē-ˌan-twə-'net, -tə-'net\ 1755–93 daughter of Maria Theresa and wife of Louis XVI of France; guillotined
Mark \'märk\ evangelist held to be the author of the second Gospel
Mar•lowe \'mär-ˌlō\ Christopher 1564–93 English dramatist
Mar•quette \mär-'ket\ Jacques 1637–75 *Père* \ˌpiər, ˌpeər\ *Marquette* Jesuit missionary and explorer in America
Mars \'märz\ — see ARES
Mar•shall \'mär-shəl\ George Catlett 1880–1959 American general and diplomat
Marshall John 1755–1835 American jurist; chief justice of the United States Supreme Court (1801–35)
Martel Charles — see CHARLES MARTEL
Mar•tha \'mär-thə\ sister of Lazarus and Mary and friend of Jesus
Mar•tial \'mär-shəl\ *about* 40–*about* 102 A.D. Roman epigrammatist
Mar•tin \'märt-n, mår-taⁿ\ Saint 315?–?399 A.D. *Martin of Tours* \-'tu̇r\ a patron saint of France
Marx \'märks\ Karl 1818–83 German political philosopher and socialist
Mary \'meər-ē, 'maər-ē, 'mā-rē\ mother of Jesus
Mary sister of Lazarus and Martha
Mary I 1516–58 *Mary Tudor; Bloody Mary* queen of England (1553–58)
Mary II 1662–94 joint British sovereign with William III (1689–94)
Mary Mag•da•lene \-'mag-də-ˌlēn, -ˌmag-də-'lēn-nē\ woman healed of evil spirits by Jesus; identified with the repentant sinner who anointed Jesus' feet
Mary Stuart 1542–87 *Mary, Queen of Scots* queen of Scotland (1542–67; beheaded)
Ma•sca•gni \mä-'skän-yē, ma-\ Pietro 1863–1945 Italian composer
Mase•field \'mās-ˌfēld\ John 1878–1967 English author
Mas•sa•soit \ˌmas-ə-'sȯit\ *died* 1661 Indian chief in eastern Massachusetts
Mas•se•net \ˌmas-n-'ā, ma-'snā\ Jules Émile Frédéric 1842–1912 French composer
Math•er \'mat͟h-ər, 'math-\ Cotton 1663–1728 American clergyman and author
Mather Increase 1639–1723 American clergyman and author; father of Cotton Mather
Ma•tisse \ma-'tēs, mə-\ Henri 1869–1954 French painter
Mat•thew \'math-yü\ one of the 12 apostles; held to be the author of the first gospel
Maugham \'mȯm\ William Somerset 1874–1965 English author
Mau•pas•sant, de \ˌmō-pə-'säⁿ\ (Henri René Albert) Guy 1850–93 French author
Max•i•mil•ian \ˌmak-sə-'mil-yən\ 1832–67 emperor of Mexico (1864–67); brother of Francis Joseph I
Maximilian I 1459–1519 Holy Roman emperor (1493–1519)
Maximilian II 1527–76 Holy Roman emperor (1564–76)
Max•well \'mak-ˌswel, -swəl\ James Clerk \'klärk\ 1831–79 Scottish physicist
Ma•za•rin \ˌmaz-ə-'raⁿ\ Jules 1602–61 French cardinal and statesman
Maz•zi•ni \mät-'sē-nē, mäd-'zē-\ Giuseppe 1805–72 Italian patriot and revolutionist
Mead Margaret 1901–78 American anthropologist
Mea•ny \'mē-nē\ George 1894– American labor leader
Me•dea \mə-'dē-ə\ enchantress in Greek mythology who helps Jason to win the Golden Fleece and kills her children when he deserts her
Me•di•ci, de' \'med-ə-chē\ Catherine 1519–89 *Catherine de Médicis* \ˌmād-ə-'sē, -'sēs\ queen of Henry II of France
Medici, de' Lorenzo 1449–92 *Lorenzo the Magnificent* Florentine ruler, statesman, and patron of the arts
Me•du•sa \mi-'dü-sə, -'dyü-, -zə\ a Gorgon slain by Perseus
Mel•pom•e•ne \mel-'päm-ə-nē\ Greek Muse of tragedy
Mel•ville \'mel-ˌvil\ Herman 1819–91 American author
Men•del \'men-dl\ Gregor Johann 1822–84 Austrian botanist and monk
Men•de•le•ev \ˌmen-də-'lā-əf\ Dmitri Ivanovich 1834–1907 Russian chemist
Men•dels•sohn–Bar•thol•dy \'men-dl-sən-bär-'tȯl-dē, -'thȯl-\ Ludwig Felix 1809–47 German composer, pianist, and conductor
Men•e•la•us \ˌmen-l-'ā-əs\ king of Sparta, brother of Agamemnon, and husband of Helen of Troy
Meph•is•toph•e•les \ˌmef-ə-'stäf-ə-ˌlēz\ a chief devil in the Faust legend
Mer•ca•tor \ˌmər-'kāt-ər\ Gerhardus 1512–94 Flemish geographer
Mer•cu•ry \'mər-kyə-rē, -kə-rē, -krē\ — see HERMES
Mere•e•dith \'mer-əd-əth\ George 1828–1909 English author
Mer•lin \'mər-lən\ prophet and magician in Arthurian legend
Me•tho•di•us \mə-'thōd-ē-əs\ Saint *died* 885 A.D. Apostle to the Slavs; brother of Cyril
Me•thu•se•lah \mə-'thüz-lə, -'thyüz-, ə-lə\ Old Testament patriarch held to have lived 969 years
Met•ter•nich, von \'met-ər-nik, -nik\ Prince Klemens Wenzel Nepomuk Lothar 1773–1859 Austrian statesman
Mey•er•beer \'mī-ər-ˌbiər, -ˌbeər\ Giacomo 1791–1864 German composer
Mi•cah \'mī-kə\ Hebrew prophet of the 8th century B.C.
Mi•chael \'mī-kəl\ one of the four archangels named in Hebrew

tradition; cast Satan and his followers out of heaven — compare GABRIEL, RAPHAEL, URIEL

Mi·chel·an·ge·lo Buo·nar·ro·ti \ˌmī-kə-ˈlan-jə-ˌlō-ˌbwȯn-ə-ˈrȯt-ē, ˌmik-ə-ˈlan-, ˌmē-kə-ˈlän-\ 1475–1564 Italian sculptor, painter, architect, and poet

Mi·das \ˈmīd-əs\ legendary king of Phrygia having the power to turn everything he touched into gold

Mil·lay \mil-ˈā\ Edna St. Vincent 1892–1950 American poet

Mil·ler \ˈmil-ər\ Arthur 1915– American author

Mil·let \mē-ˈyā, mi-lā\ Jean Francois 1814–75 French painter

Mil·li·kan \ˈmil-i-kən\ Robert Andrew 1868–1953 American physicist; Nobel prize winner (1923)

Milne \ˈmiln, ˈmil\ Alan Alexander 1882–1956 English author

Mil·ti·ades \mil-ˈtī-ə-ˌdēz\ 540?–?489 B.C. Athenian general

Mil·ton \ˈmilt-n\ John 1608–74 English poet

Mi·ner·va \mə-ˈnər-və\ — see ATHENE

Mi·nos \ˈmī-nəs\ king and lawgiver of Crete; son of Zeus and Europa; after death a judge in Hades

Min·o·taur \ˈmin-ə-ˌtȯr, ˈmī-nə-\ monster of Greek mythology shaped half like a man and half like a bull

Min·u·it \ˈmin-yə-wət\ Peter 1580–1638 Dutch colonial administrator in America

Mi·ró \mē-ˈrō\ Joan \zhü-ˈän\ 1893– Spanish painter

Mith·ras \ˈmith-rəs\ Persian god of light who was the savior hero of an oriental mystery cult for men flourishing in the late Roman empire — **Mith·ra·ic** \mith-ˈrā-ik\ *adj* — **Mith·ra·ism** \ˈmith-rə-ˌiz-əm\ *n* — **Mith·ra·ist** \mith-ˈrā-əst, ˈmith-rā-ˌist\ *n*

Mne·mos·y·ne \ni-ˈmäs-n-ē\ Greek goddess of memory and mother of the Muses by Zeus

Mo·dred \ˈmō-drəd, ˈmäd-rəd\ knight of the Round Table and rebellious nephew of King Arthur

Mohammed — see MUHAMMAD

Mo·liere \mōl-ˈyeər, ˈmōl-ˌ\ 1622–73 pseudonym of *Jean Baptist Poque·lin* \pō-klaⁿ, -kə-laⁿ\ French actor and dramatist

Mol·och \ˈmäl-ək, ˈmō-ˌläk\ *or* **Mol·ech** \ˈmäl-ək, ˈmō-ˌlek\ a Semitic deity worshiped through the sacrifice of children

Mo·lo·tov \ˈmäl-ə-ˌtȯf, ˈmȯl-, ˈmōl-, -ˌtȯv\ Vyacheslav Mikhailovich 1890– Russian statesman

Mo·net \mō-ˈnā\ Claude 1840–1926 French painter

Mon·roe \mən-ˈrō\ James 1758–1831 5th president of the United States (1817–25)

Mon·taigne, de \män-ˈtān, mōⁿ-tenʸ\ Michel Eyquem 1533–92 French essayist

Mont·calm de Saint-Véran, de \mänt-ˈkäm-də-ˌsaⁿ-vā-ˈräⁿ, -ˈkälm-\ Marquis Louis Joseph 1712–59 French field marshal in Canada

Mon·tes·quieu, de \ˌmänt-əs-ˈkyü, -ˈkyər, -ˈkyœ\ Baron de La Brède et 1689–1755 French political philosopher

Mon·tes·so·ri \ˌmänt-ə-ˈsōr-ē, -ˈsȯr-\ Maria 1870–1952 Italian physician and educator

Mon·te·ver·di \ˌmänt-ə-ˈveərd-ē, -ˈvərd-\ Claudio Giovanni Antonio 1567–1643 Italian composer

Mon·te·zu·ma II \ˌmänt-ə-ˈzü-mə\ 1480?–1520 last Aztec emperor of Mexico (1502–20)

Moore \ˈmōr, ˈmȯr, ˈmu̇r\ Marianne Craig 1887–1972 American poet

Moore Thomas 1779–1852 Irish poet

Mor·de·cai \ˈmȯrd-i-ˌkī\ cousin of Esther who saved the Jews from the destruction planned by Haman

More \ˈmōr, ˈmȯr\ Sir Thomas 1478–1535 *Saint* English statesman and author

Mor·gan \ˈmȯr-gən\ Sir Henry 1635?–88 English buccaneer

Morgan John Pierpont 1837–1913 American financier

Mor·pheus \ˈmȯr-fē-əs, -ˌfyüs, -ˌfüs\ Greek god of dreams

Mor·ris \ˈmȯr-əs, ˈmär-\ William 1834–1896 English poet, artist, and socialist

Morse \ˈmȯrs\ Samuel Finley Breese 1791–1872 American artist and inventor of the electrical telegraph

Mo·ses \ˈmō-zəz *also* -zəs\ Hebrew prophet and lawgiver and liberator of the Israelites from Egypt

Mo·zart \ˈmōt-ˌsärt\ Wolfgang Amadeus 1756–91 Austrian composer

Mu·ham·mad \mō-ˈham-əd, -häm- *also* mü-\ *or* **Mo·ham·med** \mō-ˈhäm-əd\ *also* **Ma·ho·met** \məˈhäm-ət, ˈmā-ə-mət\ *or* **Ma·hom·ed** \mə-ˈhäm-əd\ 570–632 A.D. Arab prophet and founder of Islam

Mus·so·li·ni \ˌmü-sə-ˈlē-nē, ˌmu̇s-ə-\ *Be·ni·to* \bə-ˈnēt-ō\ 1883–1945 *Il Du·ce* \ēl-ˈdü-chā\ Italian premier (1922–45); executed

My·ron \ˈmī-rən\ 5th century B.C. Greek sculptor

Na·bo·kov \nə-ˈbȯ-kəf, -ˌkȯf\ Vladimir Vladimirovich 1899–1977 American (Russian-born) author

Na·hum \ˈnā-əm, -həm\ Hebrew prophet of the 7th century B.C.

Na·o·mi \nā-ˈō-mē\ mother-in-law of the Old Testament heroine Ruth

Na·pier \ˈnā-pē-ər, -ˌpiər; nə-ˈpiər\ John 1550–1617 *Laird of Mer·chis·ton* \ˈmər-kə-stən\ Scottish mathematician

Na·po·leon I \nə-ˈpōl-yən, -ˈpō-lē-ən\ *or* **Napoleon Bo·na·parte** \ˈbō-nə-ˌpärt\ 1769–1821 emperor of the French (1804–15) — **Na·po·le·on·ic** \nə-ˌpō-lē-ˈän-ik\ *adj*

Napoleon III 1808–73 *Louis Napoleon* emperor of the French (1852–70); son of Louis Bonaparte and nephew of Napoleon I

Nar·cis·sus \när-ˈsis-əs\ beautiful youth in Greek legend punished by being made to pine away for love of his own image and transformed into the narcissus

Nas·ser \ˈnäs-ər, ˈnas-\ Ga·mal \gə-ˈmäl\ Ab·del \ˈab-dl\ 1918–70 Egyptian politician; president of Egypt (1956–70)

Na·tion \ˈnā-shən\ Car·ry \ˈkar-ē\ Amelia 1846–1911 American social reformer

Neb·u·chad·nez·zar \ˌneb-yə-kəd-ˈnez-ər, ˌneb-ə-kəd-\ *also* **Neb·u·cha·drez·zar** \-kə-ˈdrez-\ *died* 562 B.C. king of Babylon (605–562) B.C.; conqueror of Jerusalem

Ne·he·mi·ah \ˌnē-ə-ˈmī-ə, ˌnē-hə-\ Hebrew leader of the 5th century B.C.

Neh·ru \ˈneər-ˌü, ˈnā-ˌrü\ Ja·wa·har·lal \jə-ˈwä-hər-ˌläl\ 1889–1964 Indian nationalist; 1st prime minister (1947–64)

Nel·son \ˈnel-sən\ Horatio Viscount 1758–1805 British admiral

Nem·e·sis \ˈnem-ə-səs\ Greek goddess who gives humans the punishment that they deserve

Nep·tune \ˈnep-ˌtün, -ˌtyün\ — see POSEIDON

Ne·ro \ˈnē-ˌrō, ˈniər-ˌō\ 37–68 A.D. Roman emperor (54–68)

Nes·tor \ˈnes-tər\ aged and wise counselor of the Greeks in the Trojan War

New·man \ˈnü-mən, ˈnyü-\ John Henry 1801–90 English cardinal and author

New·ton \ˈnüt-n, ˈnyüt-\ Sir Isaac 1642–1727 English mathematician and physicist

Nich·o·las \ˈnik-ləs, -ə-ləs\ Saint 4th century A.D. bishop of Myra, Asia Minor; patron saint of children — see SANTA CLAUS

Nicholas I 1796–1855 czar of Russia (1825–55)

Nicholas II 1868–1918 czar of Russia (1894–1917); deposed and executed by the Bolsheviks

Nietz·sche \ˈnē-chə, -chē\ Friedrich Wilhelm 1844–1900 German philosopher

Night·in·gale \ˈnīt-n-ˌgāl, -ing-\ Florence 1820–1910 English nurse and philanthropist

Ni·jin·sky \nə-ˈzhin-skē, -ˈjin-\ Was·law \ˈvät-släf\ 1890–1950 Russian dancer

Ni·ke \ˈnī-kē\ Greek goddess of victory usually represented as winged and as carrying a wreath and a palm branch

Nim·itz \ˈnim-əts\ Chester William 1885–1966 American admiral

Nim·rod \ˈnim-ˌräd\ mighty hunter and ruler described in the Old Testament

Ni·o·be \ˈnī-ə-bē, nī-ˈō-bē\ legendary Theban queen whose boasting impels the gods to slay her children and who is turned into a stone from which her tears continue to flow

Nix·on \ˈnik-sən\ Richard Mil·hous \ˈmil-ˌhau̇s\ 1913– 37th president of the United States (1969–74)

No·ah \ˈnō-ə\ Old Testament patriarch and builder of the ark in which he, his family, and living creatures of every kind survived the Flood

No·bel \nō-ˈbel\ Alfred Bernhard 1833–96 Swedish manufacturer, inventor, and philanthropist who established the Nobel prizes

Nos·tra·da·mus \ˌnäs-trə-ˈdā-məs, ˌnōs-trə-ˈdäm-əs\ 1503–66 French physician and astrologer

Noyes \ˈnoiz\ Alfred 1880–1958 English poet

Oba·di·ah \ˌō-bə-ˈdī-ə\ Hebrew prophet of Old Testament times

Ober·on \ˈō-bə-ˌrän, -rən\ king of the fairies in medieval legend and in Shakespeare's *A Midsummer Night's Dream*

O'·Ca·sey \ō-ˈkā-sē\ Sean 1880–1964 Irish dramatist

Oce·anus \ō-ˈsē-ə-nəs\ god of the great outer sea that in Greek mythology encircles the earth

Octavian — see AUGUSTUS

Odin \ˈōd-n\ chief god in Norse mythology identified with Woden

Odys·seus \ō-ˈdish-ˌüs, -ˈdis-ˌyüs, -ˈdis-ē-əs\ *or* **Ulys·ses** \yü-ˈlis-ēz\ king of Ithaca and Greek leader in the Trojan War who after the war wanders 10 years before reaching home

Oe•di•pus \'ed-ə-pəs, 'ēd-\ son of the king and queen of Thebes who according to Greek legend unknowingly kills his father and marries his mother as foretold by an oracle

Of•fen•bach \'ȯf-ən-ˌbäk, -ˌbäk\ Jacques 1819–80 French composer

Ogle•thorpe \'ō-gəl-ˌthȯrp\ James Edward 1696–1785 English general and philanthropist; founder of Georgia

O'•Keeffe \ō-'kēf\ Georgia 1887– American painter

Olaf I \'ō-ləf, -läv\ 969–1000 king of Norway (995–1000)

Olaf II 995?–1030 *Saint Olaf* king of Norway (1016–28)

Olav V 1903– king of Norway (1957–)

Omar Khay•yam \ˌō-ˌmär-ˌkī-'äm, -'yäm, -'am, -'yam\ *died about* 1123 Persian poet and astronomer

O'•Neill \ō-'nēl\ Eugene Gladstone 1888–1953 American dramatist; Nobel prize winner (1936)

Ores•tes \ə-'res-tēz, ȯ-\ son of Agamemnon and Clytemnestra who avenges his father's murder by slaying his mother and her lover

Or•pheus \'ȯr-ˌfyüs, -fē-əs\ poet and musician of Greek mythology who almost rescues his wife Eurydice from Hades by charming Pluto and Persephone with his lyre

Or•well \'ȯr-ˌwel, -wəl\ George 1903–50 pseudonym of *Eric Blair* English author — **Or•well•ian** \ȯr-'wel-ē-ən\ *adj*

Osce•o•la \ˌäs-ē-'ō-lə, ˌō-sē-\ 1800?–38 Seminole Indian chief

Osee \'ō-zē, ō-'zā-ə\ — see HOSEA

Osi•ris \ō-'sī-rəs\ great god of the underworld and judge of the dead in ancient Egyptian mythology

Otis \'ōt-əs\ James 1725–83 American Revolutionary statesman

Ot•to \'ät-ō\ 912–973 A.D. *the Great* Holy Roman emperor (936–973)

Ov•id \'äv-əd\ 43 B.C.–? 17 A.D. Roman poet

Ow•en \'ō-ən\ Robert 1771–1858 Welsh social reformer

Paine \'pān\ Thomas 1737–1809 American (English-born) political philosopher and author

Pa•le•stri•na, da \ˌpal-ə-'strē-nə\ Giovanni Pierluigi 1526?–94 Italian composer

Pal•las \'pal-əs\ *or* **Pallas Athene** — see ATHENE

Pan \'pan\ Greek god of forests, pastures, flocks, and shepherds represented as having the legs and sometimes the ears and horns of a goat

Pan•da•rus \'pan-də-rəs\ procurer of Cressida for Troilus in medieval legend

Pan•do•ra \pan-'dōr-ə, -'dȯr-\ woman to whom Zeus gave a box enclosing all human ills which escaped when she opened it

Par•a•cel•sus \ˌpar-ə-'sel-səs\ Philippus Aureolus 1493–1541 Swiss-born alchemist and physician

Par•is \'par-əs\ son of Priam whose abduction of Helen of Troy led to the Trojan War

Park \'pärk\ Mungo 1771–1806 Scottish explorer of the Niger

Park•man \'pärk-mən\ Francis 1823–93 American historian

Par•nell \pär-'nel\ Charles Stewart 1846–91 Irish nationalist

Par•si•fal \'pär-zi-ˌfäl, -sə-ˌfȯl\ knight of the Holy Grail

Pas•cal \pas-'kal, pás-kál\ Blaise 1623–62 French mathematician and philosopher

Pas•ter•nak \'pas-tər-ˌnak\ Boris Leonidovich 1890–1960 Russian author; Nobel prize winner (1958)

Pas•teur \pas-'tər\ Louis 1822–95 French chemist and microbiologist

Pat•rick \'pa-trik\ Saint 389?–?461 A.D. bishop and patron saint of Ireland

Pa•tro•clus \pə-'trō-kləs, -'träk-ləs\ Greek slain in the Trojan War by Hector and avenged by his friend Achilles

Pat•ton \'pat-n\ George Smith 1885–1945 American general

Paul \'pȯl\ Saint *died about* 67 A.D. *Apostle to the Gentiles* author of several New Testament epistles — **Paul•ine** \'pȯ-ˌlīn\ *adj*

Paul name of 6 popes: especially **III** 1468–1549 (pope 1534–49); **V** 1552–1621 (pope 1605–21); **VI** *(Giovanni Battista Montini)* 1897–1978 (pope 1963–1978)

Paul Bun•yan \'pȯl-'bən-yən\ giant lumberjack in American folklore

Pau•ling \'pȯ-ling\ Linus Carl 1901– American chemist; Nobel prize winner (1954, 1962)

Pav•lov \'päv-ˌlȯf, 'pav-, -ˌlȯv\ Ivan Petrovich 1849–1936 Russian physiologist; Nobel prize winner (1904)

Pa•vlo•va \'pav-lə-və, pav-'lō-və\ Anna 1885–1931 Russian ballerina

Pea•ry \'piər-ē\ Robert Edwin 1856–1920 American arctic explorer

Peg•a•sus \'peg-ə-səs\ winged horse in Greek mythology

Pe•nel•o•pe \pə-'nel-ə-pē\ wife of Odysseus who waits faithfully for him during his 20 years' absence

Penn \'pen\ William 1644–1718 English Quaker; founder of Pennsylvania

Pepys \'pēps\ Samuel 1633–1703 English diarist

Per•ce•val \'pər-sə-vəl\ Arthurian knight who wins a sight of the Holy Grail

Per•i•cles \'per-ə-ˌklēz\ *died* 429 B.C. Athenian statesman

Per•ry \'per-ē\ Matthew Calbraith 1794–1858 American commodore

Perry Oliver Hazard 1785–1819 American naval officer; brother of Matthew Perry

Per•seph•o•ne \pər-'sef-ə-nē\ *or* **Pro•ser•pi•na** \prə-'sər-pə-nə\ *or* **Pros•er•pine** \'präs-ər-ˌpīn\ daughter of Zeus and Demeter; abducted by Pluto and made his wife and queen

Per•seus \'pər-ˌsüs, -sē-əs\ son of Zeus and Danaë; slayer of Medusa

Per•shing \'pər-shing, -zhing\ John Joseph 1860–1948 American general

Pé•tain \pā-ta^{n}\ Henri Philippe 1856–1951 French general; marshal of France; premier of Vichy France (1940–44)

Pe•ter \'pēt-ər\ Saint *died about* 64 A.D. *Si·mon Peter* \'sī-mən-\ fisherman chosen to become one of the 12 apostles; considered by Roman Catholics to be the 1st pope

Peter I 1672–1725 *the Great* czar of Russia (1682–1725)

Peter the Hermit 1050?–?1115 French preacher of the 1st Crusade

Pe•trarch \'pē-ˌträrk, 'pe-\ Francesco *Pe·trar·ca* \pā-'trär-kə\ 1304–74 Italian poet — **Pe•trarch•an** \pē-'trär-kən, pe-\ *adj*

Phae•dra \'fē-drə\ daughter of Minos and wife of Theseus; hanged herself after her stepson Hippolytus resisted her advances

Pha•ë•thon \'fā-ət-n; 'fā-ə-tən, -ˌthän\ son of Helios permitted for a day to drive the chariot of the sun and struck down with a thunderbolt by Zeus to keep the world from being set on fire

Phid•i•as \'fid-ē-əs\ 5th century B.C. Greek sculptor

Phil•ip \'fil-əp\ Saint; one of the 12 apostles

Philip *died* 1676 American Indian chief

Philip name of 6 kings of France: especially **II** *or* **Philip Augustus** 1165–1223 (reigned 1180–1223); **IV** 1268–1314 (reigned 1285–1314) *the Fair*; **VI** 1293–1350 (reigned 1328–50)

Philip name of 5 kings of Spain: especially **II** 1527–98 (reigned 1556–98); **V** 1683–1746 (reigned 1700–46)

Philip II 382–336 B.C. king of Macedon (359–336); father of Alexander the Great

Philip Prince 1921– consort of Elizabeth II of Great Britain; 3d Duke of Edinburgh (from 1947)

Phoebe — see ARTEMIS

Phoebus — see APOLLO

Pi•cas•so \pi-'käs-ō, -'kas-\ Pablo 1881–1973 Spanish painter and sculptor in France

Pick•ett \'pik-ət\ George Edward 1825–75 American Confederate general

Pierce \'piərs\ Franklin 1804–69 14th president of the United States (1853–57)

Pilate — see PONTIUS PILATE

Pin•dar \'pin-dər, -ˌdär\ 522?–443 B.C. Greek poet

Pi•ran•del•lo \ˌpir-ən-'del-ō\ Luigi 1867–1936 Italian author; Nobel prize winner (1934)

Pi•sis•tra•tus *or* **Pei•sis•tra•tus** \pī-'sis-trət-əs, pə-\ *died* 527 B.C. tyrant of Athens

Pitt \'pit\ William 1708–78 Earl of Chatham; English statesman

Pitt William 1759–1806 English prime minister (1783–1801; 1804–06); son of the preceding

Pi•us \'pī-əs\ name of 12 popes: especially **VII** 1742–1823 (pope 1800–23); **IX** 1792–1878 (pope 1846–78); **X** 1835–1914 (pope 1903–14); **XI** 1857–1939 (pope 1922–39); **XII** 1876–1958 (pope 1939–58)

Pi•zar•ro \pə-'zär-ō\ Francisco 1470?–1541 Spanish conqueror of Peru

Planck \'plängk\ Max Karl Ernst Ludwig 1858–1947 German physicist; Nobel prize winner (1918)

Pla•to \'plāt-ō\ 427?–347 B.C. Greek philosopher

Plau•tus \'plȯt-əs\ Titus Maccius 254?–184 B.C. Roman dramatist

Pliny \'plin-ē\ 23–79 A.D. *the Elder* Roman scholar

Pliny 62–113 A.D. *the Younger* Roman author; nephew of the preceding

Plu•tarch \'plü-ˌtärk\ 46?–?120 A.D. Greek biographer

Plu•to \'plüt-ō\ god of the dead and the lower world in Greek mythology whose Roman counterpart is Dis

Po•ca•hon•tas \,pō-kə-'hänt-əs\ 1595?–1617 American Indian princess reputed to have saved the life of Captain John Smith; daughter of Powhatan

Poe \'pō\ Edgar Allan 1809–49 American author

Polk \'pōk\ James Knox 1795–1849 11th president of the United States (1845–49)

Pol•lux \'päl-əks\ immortal twin of Castor in classical mythology

Po•lo \'pō-lō\ Mar·co \'mär-kō\ 1254?–?1324 Italian merchant who traveled to Asia

Pol•y•hym•nia \,päl-i-'him-nē-ə\ Greek Muse of sacred song and later of learning

Poly•phe•mus \,päl-ə-'fē-məs\ Cyclops whom Odysseus blinded in order to escape from his cave

Po•mo•na \pə-'mō-nə\ ancient Italian goddess of fruit trees and gardens

Pom•pa•dour, de \'päm-pə-,dōr, -,dȯr, -,dür\ Marquise 1721–64 mistress of Louis XV of France

Pom•pey \'päm-pē\ 106–48 B.C. *the Great* Roman general and statesman

Ponce de Le•ón \,päns-də-'lē-ən, ,pän-sə-,dā-lē-'ōn\ Juan 1460?–1521 Spanish explorer; discovered Florida (1513)

Pon•ti•ac \'pänt-ē-,ak\ *died* 1769 Ottawa Indian chief

Pon•tius Pi•late \,pän-chəs-'pī-lət, ,pən-\ 1st century A.D. Roman procurator of Judea; tried and condemned Jesus

Pope \'pōp\ Alexander 1688–1744 English poet

Por•ter \'pōrt-ər, 'pȯrt-\ Cole Albert 1891–1964 American composer and songwriter

Porter David Dixon 1813–1891 American admiral

Porter Katherine Anne 1890– American author

Porter William Sydney 1862–1910 pseudonym *O. Hen·ry* \ō-'hen-rē,'ō-\ American author

Po•sei•don \pə-'sīd-n\ Greek god of the sea whose Roman counterpart is Neptune

Pot•ter \'pät-ər\ Beatrix 1866–1943 British author and illustrator

Pound \'pau̇nd\ Ezra Loomis 1885–1972 American poet

Pow•ha•tan \,pau̇-ə-'tan, pau̇-'hat-n\ 1550?–1618 American Indian chief; father of Pocahontas

Prax•it•e•les \prak-'sit-l-,ēz\ 4th century B.C. Athenian sculptor

Pri•am \'prī-əm, -,am\ king of Troy during the Trojan War; father of Hector and Paris

Priest•ley \'prēst-lē\ Joseph 1733–1804 English clergyman and chemist

Pro•crus•tes \prə-'krəs-tēz, pə-, prō-\ robber in Greek mythology who forces travelers to fit one of two unequally long beds by stretching their bodies or cutting off their legs

Pro•kof•iev \prə-'kȯf-yəf, -,yef, -,yev\ Sergei Sergeevich 1891–1953 Russian composer

Pro•me•theus \prə-'me-thyüs, -thüs, -thē-əs\ Titan tortured by Zeus for stealing fire from heaven as a gift to the human race

Proserpina *or* **Proserpine** — see PERSEPHONE

Pro•tag•o•ras \prō-'tag-ə-rəs\ 5th century B.C. Greek philosopher and teacher

Pro•teus \'prō-,tyüs, -,tüs; 'prōt-ē-əs\ Greek sea god capable of assuming different forms

Proust \'prüst\ Marcel 1871–1922 French novelist

Psy•che \'sī-kē\ beautiful princess in classical mythology loved by Cupid

Ptol•e•my \'täl-ə-mē\ name of 14 kings of Egypt: especially **I** 367?–283 B.C. (reigned 323–285); **II** 309–246 B.C. (reigned 285–246)

Ptolemy 2d century A.D. Alexandrian astronomer, geographer, and mathematician

Puc•ci•ni \pü-'chē-nē\ Giacomo 1858–1924 Italian composer

Puck — see ROBIN GOODFELLOW

Pu•las•ki \pə-'las-kē, pyü-\ Casimir 1748?–79 Polish soldier in American Revolution

Pu•lit•zer \'pu̇l-ət-sər, 'pyü-lət-sər\ Joseph 1847–1911 American (Hungarian-born) journalist

Push•kin \'pu̇sh-kən\ Aleksander Sergeevich 1799–1837 Russian author

Pyg•ma•lion \pig-'māl-yən, -'mā-lē-ən\ sculptor and king of Cyprus — see GALATEA

Pyr•a•mus \'pir-ə-məs\ legendary Babylonian youth who dies for the love of Thisbe

Py•thag•o•ras \pə-'thag-ə-rəs, pī-\ *died about* 497 B.C. Greek philosopher and mathematician

Pyth•i•as \'pith-ē-əs\ condemned man for whom Damon stands as hostage and who is granted freedom because of his friend's devotion

Quin•til•ian \kwin-'til-yən\ 1st century A.D. Roman rhetorician

Ra \'rä, 'rȯ\ god of the sun and chief deity of ancient Egypt

Ra•be•lais \'rab-ə-,lā, ,rab-ə-'lā\ François 1494?–1553 French author

Ra•chel \'rā-chəl\ one of the wives of Jacob

Rach•ma•ni•noff \räk-'män-ə-,nȯf, rak-'man-, -,nȯv\ Sergei Wassilievitch 1873–1943 Russian composer, pianist, and conductor

Ra•cine \ra-'sēn, rə-\ Jean Baptiste 1639–99 French dramatist

Ra•leigh *or* **Ra•legh** \'rȯl-ē, 'räl- *also* 'ral-\ Sir Walter 1552?–1618 English navigator and historian

Ra•ma \'räm-ə\ deity or deified hero of later Hinduism worshiped as an incarnation of Vishnu

Ram•say \'ram-zē\ Sir William 1852–1916 British chemist; Nobel prize winner (1904)

Ram•ses \'ram-,sēz\ *or* **Ram•e•ses** \'ram-ə-,sēz\ name of 12 kings of Egypt: especially **II** (reigned 1292–1225 B.C.); **III** (reigned 1198–1167 B.C.)

Ra•pha•el \'raf-ē-əl, 'rā-fē-\ one of the four archangels named in Hebrew tradition — compare GABRIEL, MICHAEL, URIEL

Ra•pha•el \'raf-ē-əl, 'rā-fē-, 'räf-ē-\ 1483–1520 Italian painter

Ras•pu•tin \ra-'spyüt-n, -'spüt-, -'spu̇t-\ Grigori Efimovich 1871?–1916 Russian monk

Ra•vel \rə-'vel, ra-\ Mau·rice \mō-'rēs\ Joseph 1875–1937 French composer

Re•bek•ah *or* **Re•bec•ca** \ri-'bek-ə\ wife of Isaac

Red Cloud \'red-,klau̇d\ 1822–1909 Sioux Indian chief

Reed \'rēd\ Walter 1851–1902 American army surgeon

Re•marque \rə-'märk\ Erich Maria 1898–1970 American (German-born) author

Rem•brandt van Rijn *or* **Ryn** \'rem-,brant-vän-'rīn\ 1606–69 Dutch painter

Re•mus \'rē-məs\ son of Mars slain by his twin brother Romulus

Re•noir \ren-'wär, 'ren-,wär\ Pierre Auguste 1841–1919 French painter

Re•vere \ri-'viər\ Paul 1735–1818 American patriot and silversmith

Reyn•olds \'ren-ldz, -lz\ Sir Joshua 1723–92 English painter

Rhodes \'rōdz\ Cecil John 1853–1902 British administrator and financier in South Africa

Rich•ard \'rich-ərd\ name of 3 kings of England: **I** 1157–99 (reigned 1189–99) *the Lion-Hearted;* **II** 1367–1400 (reigned 1377–99); **III** 1452–85 (reigned 1483–85)

Rich•ard•son \'rich-ərd-sən\ Samuel 1689–1761 English author

Ri•che•lieu, de \'rish-əl-,ü, -,yü; rē-shə-lyœ\ Duc 1585–1642 French cardinal and statesman

Rim•ski–Kor•sa•kov \,rim-skē-'kȯr-sə-,kȯf, ,rimp-, -,kȯv, -,kȯr-sə-'\ Nikolai Andreevich 1844–1908 Russian composer

Ri•ve•ra \ri-'ver-ə\ Diego 1886–1957 Mexican painter

Robes•pierre, de \'rōbz-,piər, -,pyeər; ,rō-,bes-'pyeər\ Maximilien François Marie Isidore 1758–94 French revolutionist; guillotined

Rob•in Good•fel•low \,räb-ən-'gu̇d-,fel-ō\ *or* **Puck** \'pək\ mischievous sprite in English folklore

Rob•in Hood \,räb-ən-'hu̇d\ legendary English outlaw noted for his skill in archery and for his robbing the rich to help the poor

Rob•in•son \'räb-ən-sən\ Edwin Arlington 1869–1935 American poet

Ro•cham•beau, de \,rō-,sham-'bō\ Comte 1725–1807 French general who joined forces with American revolutionists; marshal of France (1791)

Rocke•fel•ler \'räk-i-,fel-ər, 'räk-,fel-\ John Davison father 1839–1937 and son 1874–1960 American oil magnates and philanthropists

Ro•din \'rō-,daⁿ, -,daⁿn\ François Auguste René 1840–1917 French sculptor

Roent•gen *or* **Rönt•gen** \'rent-gən, 'rənt-, -jən\ Wilhelm Conrad 1845–1923 German physicist; Nobel prize winner (1901)

Ro•land \'rō-lənd\ stalwart defender of the Christians against the Saracens in the Charlemagne legends who was killed at Roncesvalles in 778 A.D.

Röl•vaag \'rōl-,väg\ Ole \'ō-lə\ Ed·vart \'ed-,värt\ 1876–1931 Norwegian-born educator and author in America

Ro•ma•nov *or* **Ro•ma•noff** \rō-'män-əf, 'rō-mə-,näf\ Mikhail Feodorovich 1596–1645 1st czar of Russia (1613–45)

Rom•mel \'räm-əl\ Erwin 1891–1944 German field marshal

Rom·u·lus \ˈräm-yə-ləs\ son of Mars and twin brother of Remus; legendary founder and 1st king of Rome (753–716 B.C.)
Roo·se·velt \ˈrō-zə-vəlt (*Roosevelts' usual pronunciation*), -ˌvelt *also* ˈrü-\ (Anna) Eleanor 1884–1962 American lecturer and writer; wife of Franklin Delano Roosevelt
Roosevelt Franklin Del·a·no \ˈdel-ə-ˌnō\ 1882–1945 32d president of the United States (1933–45)
Roosevelt Theodore 1858–1919 26th president of the United States (1901–09); Nobel prize winner (1906)
Root \ˈrüt, ˈru̇t\ Elihu 1845–1937 American lawyer and statesman; Nobel prize winner (1912)
Ross \ˈrȯs\ Betsy 1752–1836 maker of first American flag
Ros·set·ti \rō-ˈzet-ē, -ˈset-\ Christina Georgina 1830–94 English poet; sister of Dante Gabriel Rossetti
Rossetti Dante Gabriel 1828–82 English painter and poet
Ros·si·ni \rȯ-ˈsē-nē, rə-\ Gioacchino Antonio 1792–1868 Italian composer
Ros·tand \rȯ-stäⁿ, ˈräs-ˌtand\ Edmond 1868–1918 French author
Roth·schild \ˈrȯths-ˌchīld, ˈrȯth-, ˈrȯs-; *German* ˈrōt-ˌshilt\ Meyer Amschel 1743–1812 German financier
Rothschild Nathan Meyer 1777–1836 financier in London; son of the preceding
Rous·seau \rü-ˈsō, ˈrü-ˌ\ Jean Jacques 1712–78 French (Swiss-born) philosopher and author
Ru·bens \ˈrü-bənz\ Peter Paul 1577–1640 Flemish painter
Ru·bin·stein \ˈrü-bən-ˌstīn\ An·ton \än-ˈtȯn\ 1829–94 Russian pianist and composer
Rumford, Count — see THOMPSON
Ru·pert \ˈrü-pərt\ Prince 1619–82 nephew of Charles I of England; German-English general and admiral
Rus·kin \ˈrəs-kən\ John 1819–1900 English author
Rus·sell \ˈrəs-əl\ Bertrand Arthur William 3d Earl 1872–1970 English mathematician and philosopher; Nobel prize winner (1950)
Ruth \ˈrüth\ Moabite woman who became the wife of Boaz and ancestress of David
Ruth·er·ford \ˈrəth-ər-fərd, ˈrəth-ə-, ˈrəth-\ Ernest 1st Baron 1871–1937 British physicist; Nobel prize winner (1908)
Sa·dat, el- \ˌel-sə-ˈdat, -ˈdät\ Anwar 1918– president of the United Arab Republic (1970–)
Saint-Gau·dens \sānt-ˈgȯd-nz, sənt-\ Augustus 1848–1907 Irish-born sculptor in America
Saint Nicholas — see NICHOLAS, SANTA CLAUS
Saint-Saëns \saⁿ-säⁿs\ (Charles) Camille 1835–1921 French composer
Sal·a·din \ˈsal-əd-ən\ 1138–93 sultan of Egypt and Syria
Sal·in·ger \ˈsal-ən-jər\ Jerome David 1919– American author
Salk \ˈsȯk, ˈsȯlk\ Jonas Edward 1914– American physician
Sa·lo·me \sə-ˈlō-mē\ niece of Herod Antipas given the head of John the Baptist as a reward for her dancing
Sa·mo·set \ˈsam-ə-ˌset, sə-ˈmäs-ət\ *died about* 1653 Indian leader; friend of the Pilgrims
Sam·son \ˈsam-sən, ˈsamp-\ Hebrew hero of great physical strength who wreaked havoc among the Philistines
Sam·u·el \ˈsam-yəl, -yə-wəl\ Hebrew judge; 1st of the great prophets
Sand \ˈsand, ˈsäⁿd, ˈsäⁿnd, ˈsäⁿ\ George 1804–76 pseudonym of *Amandine Aurore Lucie* French author
Sand·burg \ˈsand-ˌbərg, ˈsan-\ Carl 1878–1967 American author
San·ta Claus \ˈsant-ē-ˌklȯz, ˈsant-ə-\ *or* **Saint Nich·o·las** \sānt-ˈnik-ləs, sənt-, -ˈnik-ə-ləs\ *or* **Kriss Krin·gle** \ˈkris-ˈkring-gəl\ a jolly old man of modern myth who developed from the legends and traditions associated with Saint Nicholas of Myra and who delivers presents to good children at Christmastime
Sap·pho \ˈsaf-ō\ *flourished about* 600 B.C. Greek poet
Sa·rah \ˈser-ə, ˈsar-ə, ˈsā-rə\ wife of Abraham and mother of Isaac
Sar·gent \ˈsär-jənt\ John Singer 1856–1925 American painter
Sar·gon II \ˈsär-ˌgän, -gən\ *died* 705 B.C. king of Assyria (722–705)
Sar·tre \ˈsärtr\ Jean-Paul 1905– French philosopher and author
Sat·urn \ˈsat-ərn\ ancient Roman god of agriculture held to have reigned during a golden age
Saul \ˈsȯl\ 1st king of Israel
Saul *or* **Saul of Tarsus** the apostle Paul
Sa·vo·na·ro·la \ˌsav-ə-nə-ˈrō-lə, sə-ˌvän-ə-ˈrō-\ Gi·ro·la·mo \ji-ˈrȯl-ə-ˌmō\ 1452–98 Italian friar and reformer; executed
Scar·lat·ti \skär-ˈlät-ē\ Alessandro 1659–1725 and his son Domenico 1685–1757 Italian composers
Sche·her·a·zade \shə-ˌher-ə-ˈzäd, -ˈzäd-ə, -ˈzäd-ē\ fictional wife of the sultan of India and narrator of the tales in the *Arabian Nights' Entertainments*
Schil·ler, von \ˈshil-ər\ Johann Christoph Friedrich 1759–1805 German author
Scho·pen·hau·er \ˈshō-pən-ˌhau̇-ər, -ˌhau̇r\ Arthur 1788–1860 German philosopher
Schu·bert \ˈshü-bərt, -ˌbert\ Franz Peter 1797–1828 Austrian composer
Schu·mann \ˈshü-ˌmän, -mən\ Robert 1810–56 German composer
Schweit·zer \ˈshwīt-sər, ˈswīt-, ˈshvīt-\ Albert 1875–1965 French Protestant clergyman, philosopher, physician, and music scholar; Nobel prize winner (1952)
Scip·io \ˈsip-ē-ˌō, ˈskip-\ **Aemilianus Af·ri·ca·nus** \ˌaf-rə-ˈkan-əs\ **Numantinus** Publius Cornelius 185–129 B.C. *Scipio the Younger* Roman general; adopted grandson of Scipio the Elder
Scipio Africanus Publius Cornelius 237–183 B.C. *Scipio the Elder* Roman general
Scott \ˈskät\ Dred \ˈdred\ 1795?–1858 American slave; central figure in United States lawsuit
Scott Sir Walter 1771–1832 Scottish author
Scott Winfield 1786–1866 American general
Se·le·ne \sə-ˈlē-nē, -nə\ goddess of the moon in Greek mythology whose Roman counterpart is Luna
Se·leu·cus I \sə-ˈlü-kəs\ 358?–280 B.C. ruler (306–280) of a Greek dynasty in Syria
Sen·e·ca \ˈsen-i-kə\ 4 B.C.?–A.D. 65 Roman philosopher and dramatist
Sen·nach·er·ib \sə-ˈnak-ə-rəb\ *died* 681 B.C. king of Assyria (705–681); son of Sargon II
Se·quoya \si-ˈkwȯi-ə\ 1770?–1843 Cherokee Indian scholar
Se·ton \ˈsēt-n\ Saint Elizabeth Ann Bayley 1774–1821 *Mother Seton* American religious leader
Sew·ard \ˈsü-ərd, ˈsu̇-ərd, ˈsu̇rd\ William Henry 1801–72 American statesman; secretary of state (1861–69)
Shake·speare \ˈshāk-ˌspiər\ William 1564–1616 English dramatist and poet
Shaw \ˈshȯ\ George Bernard 1856–1950 British author
Shel·ley \ˈshel-ē\ Mary Woll·stone·craft \ˈwu̇l-stən-ˌkraft\ 1797–1851 English novelist; wife of Percy Bysshe Shelley
Shelley Percy Bysshe \ˈbish\ 1792–1822 English poet
Shem \ˈshem\ eldest son of Noah; ancestor of the Semitic peoples in biblical tradition
Shep·ard \ˈshep-ərd\ Alan Bartlett 1923– American astronaut; 1st American in space (1961)
Sher·i·dan \ˈsher-əd-n\ Philip Henry 1831–88 American general
Sheridan Richard Brins·ley \ˈbrinz-lē\ 1751–1816 Irish dramatist
Sher·man \ˈshər-mən\ John 1823–1900 American statesman; brother of William Tecumseh Sherman
Sherman William Tecumseh 1820–91 American general
Shiva — see SIVA
Si·be·lius \sə-ˈbāl-yəs, -ˈbā-lē-əs\ Jean 1865–1957 Finnish composer
Sid·ney \ˈsid-nē\ Sir Philip 1554–86 English poet
Sieg·fried \ˈsig-ˌfrēd, ˈsēg-\ hero in Germanic legend noted especially for winning the hoard of the Nibelungs and for slaying a dragon
Sig·urd \ˈsig-ˌu̇rd, ˈsig-ərd\ hero in Norse mythology who slays a dragon
Si·kor·sky \sə-ˈkȯr-skē\ Igor Ivan 1889–1972 American (Russian-born) aeronautical engineer
Si·mon \ˈsī-mən\ — see PETER
Simon *or* **Simon the Zealot** one of the 12 apostles
Sind·bad the Sailor \ˈsin-ˌbad-\ citizen of Baghdad whose adventures are narrated in the *Arabian Nights' Entertainments*
Sis·y·phus \ˈsis-i-fəs\ legendary king of Corinth condemned to roll a heavy stone up a hill in Hades only to have it roll down again as it nears the top — **Sis·y·phe·an** \ˌsis-i-ˈfē-ən\ *adj*
Sit·ting Bull \ˌsit-ing-ˈbu̇l\ 1834–90 Sioux leader
Si·va \ˈshiv-ə, ˈsiv-; ˈshē-və, ˈsē-\ *or* **Shi·va** \ˈshiv-ə, ˈshē-və\ god of destruction in the Hindu sacred triad — compare BRAHMA, VISHNU — **Si·va·ism** \-ˌiz-əm\ *n*
Smith \ˈsmith\ Adam 1723–90 Scottish economist
Smith John 1580–1631 English colonist in America

Smith Joseph 1805–44 American founder of the Mormon Church
Smol·lett \'smäl-ət\ Tobias George 1721–71 British author
Soc·ra·tes \'säk-rə-,tēz\ 470?–399 B.C. Greek philosopher
Sol \'säl\ — see HELIOS
Sol·o·mon \'säl-ə-mən\ son of David and 10th-century B.C. king of Israel noted for his wisdom
Soph·o·cles \'säf-ə-,klēz\ 496?–406 B.C. Greek dramatist
Sou·sa \'sü-zə, 'sü-sə\ John Philip 1854–1932 American bandmaster and composer
Sou·they \'saù-thē, 'səth-ē\ Robert 1774–1843 English author
Spaatz \'späts\ Carl 1891–1974 American general
Spar·ta·cus \'spärt-ə-kəs\ *died* 71 B.C. Roman slave and gladiator from Thrace; leader of a slave rebellion
Spen·ser \'spen-sər\ Edmund 1552?–99 English poet
Spi·no·za \spin-'ō-zə\ Baruch *or* Benedict 1632–77 Dutch philosopher
Squan·to \'skwän-tō, 'skwòn-\ *died* 1622 Indian friend of the Pilgrims
Sta·lin \'stäl-ən, 'stal-, -,ēn\ Joseph 1879–1953 *Iosif Vissarionovich Dzhu·gash·vi·li* \,jü-gəsh-'vē-lē\ Russian Communist leader
Stan·dish \'stan-dish\ Myles *or* Miles 1584?–1656 English colonist in America
Stan·ley \'stan-lē\ Sir Henry Morton 1841–1904 British explorer in Africa
Stan·ton \'stant-n\ Elizabeth Cady 1815–1902 American suffragist
Steele \'stēl\ Sir Richard 1672–1729 British author
Stein \'stīn\ Gertrude 1874–1946 American author
Stein·beck \'stīn-,bek\ John Ernst 1902–1968 American author; Nobel prize winner (1962)
Stein·metz \'stīn-,mets, 'shtīn-\ Charles Proteus 1865–1923 American (German-born) electrical engineer and inventor
Sten·dhal \sten-'däl, stan-, *French* staⁿ-dàl\ 1783–1842 pseudonym of *Marie Henri Beyle* \'bel\ French author
Ste·phen \'stē-vən\ *Saint* the 1st Christian martyr; stoned to death
Stephen 1097?–1154 *Stephen of Blois* king of England (1135–54)
Sterne \'stərn\ Laurence 1713–68 British author
Steu·ben, von \'stü-bən, 'styü-, 'shtòi-\ Baron Friedrich Wilhelm Ludolf Gerhard Augustin 1730–94 Prussian-born general in America
Ste·ven·son \'stē-vən-sən\ Adlai Ewing 1900–65 American statesman
Stevenson Robert Louis Balfour 1850–94 Scottish author
Stowe \'stō\ Harriet Elizabeth 1811–96 née *Beecher* American author
Stra·di·va·ri \,strad-ə-'vär-ē, -'var-, -'ver-\ Antonio 1644–1737 *Antonius Strad·i·var·i·us* \,strad-ə-'var-ē-əs, -'ver-\ Italian violin maker
Strauss \'straùs, 'shtraùs\ Johann father 1804–49 and his sons Johann 1825–99 and Josef 1827–70 Austrian composers
Strauss Ri·chard \'rik-,ärt, 'rik-\ 1864–1949 German composer
Stra·vin·sky \strə-'vin-skē\ Igor \'ē-,gòr\ Fëdorovich 1882–1971 American (Russian-born) composer
Stu·art \'stü-ərt, 'styü-, 'styù-, 'styùrt\ — see CHARLES I, MARY STUART
Stuart Charles — see CHARLES EDWARD STUART
Stuart Gilbert Charles 1755–1828 American painter
Stuart James Ewell Brown 1833–64 *Jeb* American Confederate general
Stuy·ve·sant \'stī-və-sənt\ Peter 1592–1672 Dutch administrator in America
Sue·to·ni·us \swē-'tō-nē-əs, sü-ə-'tō-\ 2d century A.D. Roman biographer and historian
Su·lei·man I \'sü-lā-,män, -li-\ 1496?–1566 *the Magnificent* Ottoman sultan (1520–66)
Sul·la \'səl-ə\ 138–78 B.C. Roman general and statesman
Sul·li·van \'səl-ə-vən\ Sir Arthur Seymour 1842–1900 English composer; collaborated with Sir William S. Gilbert
Sullivan Louis Henri 1856–1924 American architect
Sum·ner \'səm-nər\ Charles 1811–74 American statesman
Sun Yat-sen \'sùn-'yät-'sen\ 1866–1925 Chinese statesman
Swift \'swift\ Jonathan 1667–1745 English (Irish-born) author
Swin·burne \'swin-,bərn, -bərn\ Algernon Charles 1837–1909 English poet
Tac·i·tus \'tas-ət-əs\ Cornelius 55?–after 117 A.D. Roman historian

Taft \'taft\ William Howard 1857–1930 27th president of the United States (1909–13); chief justice of the United States Supreme Court (1921–30)
Tal·ley·rand–Pé·ri·gord, de \'tal-ē-,rand-,per-ə-'gòr, -,ran-, *French* tàl-e-räⁿ, tàl-räⁿ\ Charles Maurice 1754–1838 French statesman
Tam·er·lane \'tam-ər-,lān\ *or* **Tam·bur·laine** \'tam-bər-,lān\ 1336?–1405 *Timur Lenk* Mongol conqueror
Tan·cred \'tang-krəd\ 1078?–1112 Norman leader in first crusade
Ta·ney \'tò-nē\ Roger Brooke 1777–1864 American jurist; chief justice of the United States Supreme Court (1836–64)
Tann·häu·ser \'tän-,hòi-zər\ knight and minnesinger of Germanic legend noted for his stay with Venus in the Venusberg cavern and his subsequent repentance
Tan·ta·lus \'tant-l-əs\ legendary king of Lydia condemned to stand up to his chin in a pool of water in Hades and beneath fruit-laden boughs only to have the water or fruit recede at each attempt to eat or drink
Tay·lor \'tā-lər\ Zachary 1784–1850 *Old Rough-and-Ready* American general; 12th president of the United States (1849–50)
Tchai·kov·sky \chī-'kòf-skē, chə-, -'kòv-\ Pëtr Ilich 1840–93 Russian composer
Te·cum·seh \tə-'kəm-sə, -'kəmp-, -sē\ 1768–1813 Shawnee Indian chief
Te·lem·a·chus \tə-'lem-ə-kəs\ son of Odysseus and Penelope who aids his father in the slaying of his mother's suitors
Ten·ny·son \'ten-ə-sən\ Alfred 1st Baron 1809–92 English poet
Ter·ence \'ter-əns\ 185?–159 B.C. Roman dramatist
Terp·sich·o·re \,tərp-'sik-ə-rē\ Greek Muse of dancing and choral song
Thack·er·ay \'thak-rē, -ə-rē\ William Makepeace 1811–63 English author
Tha·les \'thā-,lēz\ 640?–546 B.C. Greek philosopher
Tha·lia \thə-'lī-ə\ Greek Muse of comedy and pastoral poetry
Thalia one of the three Graces in Greek mythology — compare AGLAIA, EUPHROSYNE
The·mis·to·cles \thə-'mis-tə-,klēz\ 527?–?460 B.C. Athenian general and statesman
The·oc·ri·tus \thē-'äk-rət-əs\ 3d century B.C. Greek poet
The·od·o·ric \thē-'äd-ə-rik\ 454?–526 A.D. *the Great* king of the Ostrogoths (474–526)
The·o·do·sius I \,thē-ə-'dō-shəs, -shē-əs\ 346?–395 A.D. *the Great* Roman general and emperor (379–395)
The·re·sa *or* **Te·re·sa** \tə-'rē-sə, -'rā-sə, -'rā-zə\ Saint 1515–82 Spanish Carmelite nun, mystic, and author
The·seus \'thē-,süs, -sē-əs\ hero in Greek mythology who slays Procrustes and the Minotaur and conquers the Amazons and marries their queen
Thes·pis \'thes-pəs\ 6th century B.C. Greek poet
The·tis \'thēt-əs\ sea goddess and mother of Achilles
This·be \'thiz-bē\ legendary Babylonian maiden who dies for the love of Pyramus
Thom·as \'täm-əs\ Saint; one of the 12 apostles; demanded proof of Christ's resurrection
Thomas Dyl·an \'dil-ən\ 1914–53 British poet
Thomas à Becket — see BECKET
Thomas a Kem·pis \ə-'kem-pəs, ä-'kem-\ 1380–1471 German priest and author
Thomp·son \'täm-sən, 'tämp-\ Benjamin 1753–1814 Count *Rum·ford* \'rəm-fərd, 'rəmp-\ British (American-born) physicist and statesman
Thor \'thòr\ Norse god of thunder, weather, and crops
Tho·reau \thə-'rō, thò-; 'thòr-ō\ Henry David 1817–62 American author
Thu·cyd·i·des \thü-'sid-ə-,dēz, thyü-\ 471?–?400 B.C. Greek historian
Thur·ber \'thər-bər\ James Grover 1894–1961 American author
Ti·be·ri·us \tī-'bir-ē-əs\ 42 B.C.–37 A.D. Roman emperor (14–37)
Tim·o·thy \'tim-ə-thē\ disciple of the apostle Paul
Tin·to·ret·to, Il \,tin-tə-'ret-ō\ *Jacopo Robusti* 1518–94 Italian painter
Ti·re·si·as \tī-'rē-sē-əs, -zē-əs\ legendary blind soothsayer of Thebes who predicts the doom of Oedipus
Ti·ta·nia \tə-'tān-yə, -'tän-, tī-'tān-\ queen of the fairies and wife of Oberon in Shakespeare's *A Midsummer Night's Dream*
Ti·tian \'tish-ən\ 1477–1576 Italian painter

Tito — see BROZ
Ti•tus \'tīt-əs\ associate of the apostle Paul
Titus 40?–81 A.D. Roman emperor (79–81)
Tocque•ville, de \'tōk-,vil, 'tȯk-, 'täk-, -,vēl, -vəl\ Alexis Charles 1805–59 French statesman and author
Tol•kien \'tōl-,kēn, 'tōl-, 'täl-\ John Ronald Reuel 1892–1973 English author
Tol•stoy *or* **Tol•stoi** \tōl-'stȯi, tōl-', täl-', 'tōl-,, 'tōl-,, 'täl-,\ Count Lev Nikolaevich 1828–1910 Russian author
Tou•louse–Lau•trec, de \tü-,lüz-lō-'trek\ Henri 1864–1901 French painter
Tra•jan \'trā-jən\ 52 or 53–117 A.D. Roman emperor (98–117)
Tris•tram \'tris-trəm\ *or* **Tris•tan** \'tris-tən, -,tän, -,tan\ hero of medieval romance who drinks a love potion and ultimately dies with the Irish princess Isolde
Tri•ton \'trīt-n\ son of Poseidon who is half man and half fish
Troi•lus \'trȯi-ləs, 'trō-ə-ləs\ son of Priam who in medieval legend loves Cressida but loses her to Diomedes
Trots•ky *or* **Trots•ki** \'trät-skē, 'trȯt-\ Leon 1879–1940 *Leib* or *Lev Davydovich Bronstein* Russian Communist leader
Tru•deau \'trü-dō, trü-'\ Pierre Elliott 1919– prime minister of Canada (1968–)
Tru•man \'trü-mən\ Harry S 1884–1972 33d president of the United States (1945–53)
Tub•man \'təb-mən\ Harriet 1820?–1913 American abolitionist
Tur•ner \'tər-nər\ Joseph Mallord William 1775–1851 English painter
Tut•ankh•a•men \,tü-,tang-'käm-ən, -,täng-\ *or* **Tut•enkh•a•mon** \-,teng-'käm-ən\ *flourished about* 1358 B.C. king of Egypt
Twain, Mark — see CLEMENS
Tweed \'twēd\ William Marcy 1823–78 *Boss Tweed* American politician
Ty•ler \'tī-lər\ John 1790–1862 10th president of the United States (1841–45)
Ulysses — see ODYSSEUS
Up•dike \'əp-,dīk\ John 1932– American author
Ura•nia \yu̇-'rā-nē-ə, -nyə\ Greek Muse of astronomy
Ura•nus \'yu̇r-ə-nəs, yu̇-'rā-nəs\ the heavens personified in Greek mythology as the father of the Titans and ruler of the universe until overthrown by his son Cronus
Ur•ban \'ər-bən\ name of 8 popes: especially **II** 1042?–99 (pope 1088–99)
Urey \'yu̇r-ē\ Harold Clayton 1893– American chemist; Nobel prize winner (1934)
Uri•el \'yu̇r-ē-əl\ one of the four archangels named in Hebrew tradition — compare GABRIEL, MICHAEL, RAPHAEL
Uther \'ü-thər, 'yü-, 'ə-\ *or* **Uther Pen•drag•on** \-pen-'drag-ən, -'pen-,\ father of Arthur in Arthurian legend
Va•le•ri•an \və-'lir-ē-ən\ *died* ?269 A.D. Roman emperor (253–260)
Van Bu•ren \van-'byu̇r-ən, vən-\ Martin 1782–1862 8th president of the United States (1837–41)
Van•dyke *or* **Van Dyck** \van-'dīk, vən-\ Sir Anthony 1599–1641 Flemish-born painter in England
Ve•ga, de \'vā-gə\ Lo·pe \'lō-pā\ 1562–1635 Spanish dramatist
Ve•láz•quez *or* **Ve•lás•quez** \və-'las-kəs\ Diego Rodriguez de Silva y 1599–1660 Spanish painter
Ve•nus \'vē-nəs\ — see APHRODITE
Ver•di \'veərd-ē\ Giuseppe 1813–1901 Italian composer
Ver•gil *or* **Vir•gil** \'vər-jəl\ 70–19 B.C. Roman poet — **Ver•gil•i•an** *or* **Vir•gil•i•an** \,vər-'jil-ē-ən\ *adj*
Verne Jules \'jülz-'vərn, 'zhw̅e̅l-'veərn\ 1828–1905 French author
Ve•ro•ne•se \,ver-ə-'nā-sē, -'nā-zē\ Paolo 1528–88 Italian painter
Ves•puc•ci \ve-'spü-chē\ Ame·ri·go \,äm-ə-'rē-gō\ 1451–1512 *Amer·i·cus Ves·pu·cius* \ə-'mer-ə-kəs-,ves-'pyü-shəs, -shē-əs\ Italian navigator for whom America was named
Ves•ta \'ves-tə\ — see HESTIA
Vic•tor Em•man•u•el I \'vik-tər-i-'man-yə-wəl, -'man-yəl\ 1759–1824 king of Sardinia (1802–21)
Victor Emmanuel II 1820–78 king of Sardinia (1849–61); 1st king of Italy (1861–78)
Victor Emmanuel III 1869–1947 king of Italy (1900–46)
Vic•to•ria \vik-tōr-ē-ə, -'tȯr-\ Alexandrina 1819–1901 queen of Great Britain (1837–1901)
Vil•lon \vē-'ōⁿ, -'yōⁿ\ François 1431–after 1462 French poet
Vin•cent de Paul \,vin-sənt-də-'pȯl\ Saint 1581?–1660 French priest; founder of the Vincentians
Vin•ci, da \'vin-chē, 'vēn-\ Le·o·nar·do \,lē-ə-'närd-ō, ,lā-\ 1452–1519 Florentine painter, sculptor, architect, and engineer
Virgin Mary mother of Jesus
Vish•nu \'vish-nü\ god of preservation in the Hindu sacred triad — compare BRAHMA, SIVA
Vi•val•di \vi-'väl-dē, -'vȯl-\ Antonio 1675?–1741 Italian violinist and composer
Vol•taire \vōl-'taər, vȯl-, väl-, -'teər\ 1694–1778 *François Marie Arouet* French author
Von Braun \vän-'brau̇n, fən-, vən-\ Wern·her \'veər-nər\ 1912–1977 American (German-born) engineer
Vul•can \'vəl-kən\ — see HEPHAESTUS
Wag•ner \'väg-nər\ (Wilhelm) Ri·chard \'rik-,ärt, 'rik̲-\ 1813–83 German composer
Wal•pole \'wȯl-,pōl, 'wäl-\ Horace 1717–97 4th Earl of *Or·ford* \'ȯr-fərd\ English author
Wal•ton \'wȯlt-n\ Izaak \'ī-zik, -zək\ 1593–1683 English author
War•ren \'wȯr-ən, 'wär-\ Earl 1891– American lawyer and politician; chief justice of the United States Supreme Court (1953–69)
Wash•ing•ton \'wȯsh-ing-tən, 'wäsh-\ Book·er \'bu̇k-ər\ Tal·ia·ferro \'täl-ə-vər\ 1856–1915 American educator
Washington George 1732–99 American general; 1st president of the United States (1789–97)
Watt \'wät\ James 1736–1819 Scottish inventor
Wayne \'wān\ Anthony 1745–96 *Mad Anthony* American Revolutionary general
We•ber, von \'vā-bər\ Baron Karl Maria Friedrich Ernst 1786–1826 German composer and conductor
Web•ster \'web-stər\ Daniel 1782–1852 American statesman
Webster Noah 1758–1843 American lexicographer
Wel•ling•ton \'wel-ing-tən\ 1st Duke of 1769–1852 *Arthur Wellesley; the Iron Duke* British general and statesman
Wells \'welz\ Herbert George 1866–1946 English author
Wes•ley \'wes-lē, 'wez-\ John 1703–91 English founder of Methodism
West \'west\ Benjamin 1738–1820 American painter in England
Wes•ting•house \'wes-ting-,hau̇s\ George 1846–1914 American inventor
Whar•ton \'hwȯrt-n, 'wȯrt-\ Edith Newbold 1862–1937 American author
Whis•tler \'hwis-lər, 'wis-\ James Abbott McNeill 1834–1903 American artist
Whit•man \'hwit-mən, 'wit-\ Walt 1819–92 American poet
Whit•ney \'hwit-nē, 'wit-\ Eli 1765–1825 American inventor of the cotton gin
Whit•ti•er \'hwit-ē-ər, 'wit-\ John Greenleaf 1807–92 American poet
Wilde \'wīld\ Oscar Fingal O'Flahertie Wills 1854–1900 Irish author
Wil•der \'wīl-dər\ Thornton Niven 1897–1975 American author
Wil•hel•mi•na \,wil-,hel-'mē-nə, ,wil-ə-'mē-\ 1880–1962 queen of the Netherlands (1890–1948)
Wil•liam \'wil-yəm\ name of 4 kings of England: **I** 1027–87 (reigned 1066–87) *the Conqueror;* **II** 1056?–1100 (reigned 1087–1100) *Ru·fus* \'rü-fəs\; **III** 1650–1702 (reigned 1689–1702); **IV** 1765–1837 (reigned 1830–37)
William I 1533–84 *the Silent* prince of Orange and founder of the Dutch Republic
William I 1797–1888 king of Prussia (1861–88) and emperor of Germany (1871–88)
William II 1859–1941 emperor of Germany and king of Prussia (1888–1918; abdicated)
Wil•liam Tell \,wil-yəm-'tel\ legendary Swiss patriot sentenced to shoot an apple from his son's head
Wil•liams \'wil-yəmz\ Roger 1603?–1683 English-born clergyman; founder of Rhode Island
Williams Tennessee 1911– *Thomas Lanier Williams* American dramatist
Williams William Carlos 1883–1963 American author and physician
Wil•son \'wil-sən\ (Thomas) Wood·row \'wu̇d-rō\ 1856–1924 28th president of the United States (1913–21); Nobel prize winner (1919)
Windsor, Duke of — see EDWARD VIII
Win•throp \'win-thrəp, 'wint-\ John 1588–1649 English colonist

in America; 1st governor of Massachusetts Bay Colony
Wo·den \'wōd-n\ chief god in Anglo-Saxon mythology identified with Odin
Wolfe \'wu̇lf\ James 1724–59 British general
Wolfe Thomas Clayton 1900–38 American author
Wol·sey \'wu̇l-zē\ Thomas 1475?–1530 English cardinal and statesman
Woolf \'wu̇lf\ Virginia 1882–1941 née *Stephen* English author
Words·worth \'wərdz- wərth, -,wərth\ William 1770–1850 English poet
Wren \'ren\ Sir Christopher 1632–1723 English architect
Wright \'rīt\ Frank Lloyd 1869–1959 American architect
Wright Or·ville \'ȯr-vəl\ 1871–1948 and his brother Wilbur 1867–1912 American pioneers in aviation
Wyc·liffe \'wik-,lif, -ləf\ John 1320?–84 English reformer and Bible translator
Wy·eth \'wī-əth\ Andrew Newell 1917– American painter
Xa·vi·er \'zā-vē-ər, ig-'zā-\ Saint Francis 1506–52 *Apostle of the Indies* Spanish Jesuit missionary
Xen·o·phon \'zen-ə-fən\ 434?–?355 B.C. Greek historian and soldier
Xer·xes I \'zərk-,sēz\ 519?–465 B.C. *the Great* son of Darius I; king of Persia (486–465); assassinated
Yeats \'yāts\ William Butler 1865–1939 Irish author
Young \'yəng\ Brig·ham \'brig-əm\ 1801–77 American Mormon leader
Zech·a·ri·ah \,zek-ə-'rī-ə\ Hebrew prophet of the 6th century B.C.
Zeng·er \'zeng-ər, 'zeng-gər\ John Peter 1697–1746 American (German-born) journalist and printer
Ze·no \'zē-nō\ 4th–3d century B.C. Greek philosopher; founder of Stoic school
Zeph·a·ni·ah \,zef-ə-'nī-ə\ Hebrew prophet of the 7th century B.C.
Zeph·y·rus \'zef-ə-rəs\ Greek god of the west wind
Zeus \'züs\ chief Greek god, ruler of the elements (as lightning and rain), and husband of Hera; Roman counterpart is Jupiter or Jove
Zo·la \'zō-lə, 'zō-,lä, zō-'lä\ Émile 1840–1902 French author
Zo·ro·as·ter \'zōr-ə-,was-tər, 'zȯr-\ *or* **Za·ra·thus·tra** \,zar-ə-'thüs-trə, -'thəs-\ 6th century B.C. founder of Persian religion
Zwing·li \'zwing-lē, 'swing-, -glē; 'tsfing-lē\ Huldreich *or* Ulrich 1484–1531 Swiss Reformation leader

GEOGRAPHICAL NAMES

This section constitutes a pronouncing dictionary of current and historical place names likely to be of interest to the student. It complements the general vocabulary by entering many derivative adjectives and nouns of geographical names, such as **Florentine** at **Florence** and **Libyan** at **Libya.**

In the entries the letters [N], [E], [S], and [W] singly or in combination indicate direction and are not part of a place name. They may represent either the name of the direction (as *north*) or the adjective derived from it (as *northern*); thus, west-northwest of Santiago appears as [WNW] of Santiago and southern California appears as [S] California. The only other special abbreviations used in this section are U.S. for United States, and U.S.S.R. for Union of Soviet Socialist Republics. All heights and distances are given in metric units.

Aa·chen \'äk-ən\ *or French* **Aix–la–Cha·pelle** \,āk-,slä-shə-'pel, ,ek-\ city West Germany [WSW] of Cologne
Aar·hus \'ȯr-,hüs\ city [E] central Denmark
Aba·dan \,äb-ə-'dän, ,ab-ə-'dan\ city [W] Iran on Abadan Island in Shatt-al-Arab delta
Abe·o·ku·ta \,ab-ē-'ō-kət-ə\ city [SW] Nigeria [S] of Ibadan
Ab·er·deen \,ab-ər-'dēn\ **1** *or* **Ab·er·deen·shire** \-,shiər, -shər\ former county [NE] Scotland **2** city [NE] Scotland — **Ab·er·do·ni·an** \-'dō-nē-ən\ *adj or n*
Ab·i·djan \,ab-i-'jän\ city, capital of Ivory Coast
Abu Dha·bi \,äb-ü-'däb-ē\ city, capital of Abu Dhabi sheikdom & of United Arab Emirates
Abruz·zi \ä-'brüt-sē\ region central Italy on the Adriatic [E] of Latium
Ab·ys·sin·ia \,ab-ə-'sin-ē-ə, -'sin-yə\ — see ETHIOPIA — **Ab·ys·sin·i·an** \-ē-ən, -yən\ *adj or n*
Aca·dia \ə-'kād-ē-ə\ *or French* **Aca·die** \á-ká-dē\ NOVA SCOTIA — an early name
Acadia National Park section of coast of Maine including areas on Mount Desert Island & Isle au Haut
Aca·pul·co \,äk-ə-'pül-kō, ,ak-\ city [S] Mexico on the Pacific
Ac·ar·na·nia \,ak-ər-'nā-nē-ə, -'nā-nyə\ district [W] Greece on Ionian sea
Accad — see AKKAD
Ac·cra \ə-'krä\ city, capital of Ghana
Achaea \ə-'kē-ə\ *or* **Acha·ia** *or Greek* **Akhaïa** \ə-'kī-ə, -'kā-ə, -'kā-yə\ district [S] Greece in [N] Peloponnesus
Ach·er·on \'ak-ə-,rän, -rən\ a river of Hades in Greek mythology
Acon·ca·gua \,ak-ən-'käg-wə, ,äk-, -əng-\ mountain 6960 meters [W] Argentina; highest in the Andes & western hemisphere
Açores — see AZORES
Ac·ti·um \'ak-shē-əm, 'ak-tē-\ promontory & ancient town [W] Greece in [NW] Acarnania
Ada·na \'äd-ə-nə, -,nä; ə-'dän-ə\ city [S] Turkey
Ad·dis Aba·ba \,ad-ə-'sab-ə-bə\ city, capital of Ethiopia
Ad·e·laide \'ad-l-,ād\ city, capital of South Australia
Aden \'äd-n, 'ād-, 'ad-\ **1** former British protectorate [S] Arabia [E] of Yemen **2** former British colony in [SW] Aden Protectorate **3** city, national capital of People's Democratic Republic of Yemen
Aden, Gulf of arm of Indian ocean between the People's Democratic Republic of Yemen (Arabia) & Somalia (Africa)
Adi·ge \'äd-ə-,jā\ river 354 kilometers long [N] Italy flowing [SE] into the Adriatic
Ad·i·ron·dack \,ad-ə-'rän-,dak\ mountains [NE] New York; highest Mount Marcy 1629 meters
Ad·mi·ral·ty \'ad-mrəl-tē, -mə-rəl-\ **1** island [SE] Alaska in [N] Alexander archipelago **2** islands [W] Pacific [N] of New Guinea in Bismarck archipelago; belong to Papua New Guinea
Adri·at·ic \,ā-drē-'at-ik, ,ad-rē-\ sea arm of Mediterranean between Italy & Balkan peninsula
Ae·ge·an \i-'jē-ən\ sea arm of Mediterranean between Asia Minor & Greece
Ae·gi·na \i-'jī-nə\ *or Greek* **Aí·yi·na** \'ā-yē-,nä\ island & ancient state [SE] Greece in Saronic gulf
Ae·o·lis \'ē-ə-ləs\ *or* **Ae·o·lia** \ē-'ō-lē-ə, -'ōl-yə\ ancient country [NW] Asia Minor
Afars and the Issas, French Territory of the — see DJIBOUTI 1
Af·ghan·i·stan \af-'gan-ə-,stan\ country [W] Asia [E] of Iran; capital, Kabul
Af·ri·ca \'af-ri-kə\ continent of eastern hemisphere [S] of Mediterranean
Aga·na \ə-'gän-yə\ town, capital of Guam
Ag·as·siz Lake \'ag-ə-sē\ prehistoric lake 1130 kilometers long in region comprising present [S] Manitoba, [E] Saskatchewan, [NW] Minnesota, & [E] North Dakota

Agra \'äg-rə\ city [N] India in [W] Uttar Pradesh
Agri Dagi *or* **Aghri Dagh** — see ARARAT
Aguas•ca•lien•tes \,äg-wə-,skäl-'yen-,tās\ **1** state central Mexico **2** city, its capital, [NE] of Guadalajara
Agul•has, Cape \ə-'gəl-əs\ headland Republic of South Africa in [S] Cape Province; most southerly point of Africa, at 34° 50′ [S] latitude
Agulhas Current warm current of the Indian Ocean flowing [SW] along [SE] coast of Africa
Ahag•gar \ə-'häg-ər, ,ä-hə-'gär\ *or* **Hog•gar** \'häg-ər, hə-'gär\ mountains [S] Algeria in [W] central Sahara; highest Tahat 3000 meters
Ah•mad•abad *or* **Ah•med•abad** \'äm-əd-ə-,bäd\ city [W] India in Gujarat
Ah•mad•na•gar *or* **Ah•med•na•gar** \,äm-əd-'nəg-ər\ city [W] India in Maharashtra [E] of Bombay
Ah•ven•an•maa \'äk-və-,nän-,mä, 'ä-və-\ *or Swedish* **Åland** \'ō-,länd\ archipelago [SW] Finland in Baltic sea
Aisne \'ān\ river 282 kilometers long [N] France flowing from Argonne Forest into the Oise
Aix-la-Chapelle — see AACHEN
Aj•mer \,əj-'miər, -'meər\ city [NW] India in central Rajasthan [SW] of Delhi
Aka•shi \ä-'käsh-ē\ city Japan in [SW] Honshu [W] of Kobe
Aki•ta \ä-'kēt-ə, 'äk-i-,tä\ city Japan in [N] Honshu on Sea of Japan
Ak•kad *or* **Ac•cad** \'ak-,ad, 'äk-,äd\ **1** [N] division of ancient Babylonia **2** *or* **Aga•de** \ə-'gäd-ə\ ancient city, its capital
Akmolinsk — see TSELINOGRAD
Ak•ron \'ak-rən\ city [NE] Ohio
Al•a•bama \,al-ə-'bam-ə\ state [SE] U.S.; capital, Montgomery — **Al•a•bam•i•an** \-'bam-ē-ən\ *or* **Al•a•bam•an** \-'bam-ən\ *adj or n*
Alas•ka \ə-'las-kə\ **1** peninsula [SW] Alaska [SW] of Cook inlet **2** state of U.S. in [NW] North America; capital, Juneau **3** mountain range [S] Alaska extending from Alaska peninsula to Yukon boundary — **Alas•kan** \-kən\ *adj or n*
Alaska, Gulf of inlet of Pacific off [S] Alaska between Alaska peninsula on [W] & Alexander archipelago on [E]
Al•ba Lon•ga \,al-bə-'lȯng-gə\ ancient city central Italy in Latium [SE] of Rome
Al•ba•nia \al-'bā-nē-ə, -nyə\ country [S] Europe in Balkan peninsula on Adriatic; capital, Tirane
Al•ba•ny \'ȯl-bə-nē\ city, capital of New York
Al•be•marle \'al-bə-,märl\ sound inlet of Atlantic in [NE] North Carolina
Al•bert, Lake \'al-bərt\ lake [E] Africa between Uganda & Zaire in course of Nile
Al•ber•ta \al-'bərt-ə\ province [W] Canada; capital, Edmonton — **Al•ber•tan** \-'bərt-n\ *adj or n*
Albert Nile — see NILE
Al•bi•on \'al-bē-ən\ **1** island of Great Britain **2** ENGLAND
Albis — see ELBE
Al•bu•quer•que \'al-bə-,kər-kē, -byə-\ city central New Mexico
Al•da•bra \'al-də-brə\ island (atoll) [NW] Indian ocean [N] of Madagascar; in British Indian Ocean Territory
Al•der•ney \'ȯl-dər-nē\ island in English channel — see CHANNEL
Alep•po \ə-'lep-ō\ *or* **Alep** \ä-'lep\ *or Arabic* **Ha•lab** \hə-'lab\ *or* **Ha•leb** \-'leb\ city [N] Syria
Aleu•tian \ə-'lü-shən\ islands [SW] Alaska extending in an arc 1930 kilometers [W] from Alaska peninsula
Al•ex•an•der \,al-ig-'zan-dər, ,el-\ archipelago [SE] Alaska
Al•ex•an•dria \,al-ig-'zan-drē-ə, ,el-\ **1** city [N] Virginia **2** city [N] Egypt on Mediterranean — **Al•ex•an•dri•an** \-drē-ən\ *adj or n*
Al•ge•ria \al-'jir-ē-ə\ country [NW] Africa on Mediterranean; capital, Algiers — **Al•ge•ri•an** \-ē-ən\ *adj or n*
Al•giers \al-'jiərz\ **1** Algeria especially as one of former Barbary States **2** city, capital of Algeria — **Al•ge•rine** \,al-jə-'rēn\ *adj or n*
Al-Gizeh — see GIZA
Al•i•garh \,al-i-'gär\ city [N] India in [NW] Uttar Pradesh [N] of Agra
Al-Jīzah — see GIZA
Al Kuwait — see KUWAIT
Al•lah•abad \'al-ə-hə-,bad, -,bäd\ city [N] India in [S] Uttar Pradesh [W] of Banaras
Al•le•ghe•ny \,al-ə-'gā-nē\ mountains of Appalachian system [E] U.S. in Pennsylvania, Maryland, Virginia, & West Virginia
Al•len•town \'al-ən-,taün\ city [E] Pennsylvania
Al•ma-Ata \,al-mə-ə-'tä\ city U.S.S.R., capital of Kazakhstan
Alps \'alps\ mountain system central Europe — see MONT BLANC
Al•sace \al-'sas, -'sās, 'al-,\ *or German* **El•sass** \'el-,zäs\ *or ancient* **Al•sa•tia** \al-'sā-shē-ə, -shə\ region & former province [NE] France between Rhine river & Vosges mountains — **Al•sa•tian** \al-'sā-shən\ *adj or n*
Al•sace-Lor•raine \-lə-'rān, -lȯ-'rān\ region [N] France [W] of the Rhine including Alsace & part of Lorraine
Al•tai \'al-,tī\ mountain system central Asia between Outer Mongolia & [W] China & between Kazakhstan & Soviet Russia, Asia; highest peak Tabun Bogdo 4653 meters
Al•ta•mi•ra \,al-tə-'mir-ə\ caverns [N] Spain [WSW] of Santander
Al•to Adi•ge \,äl-tō-'äd-i-,jā\ *or* **South Ti•rol** \-tə-'rōl, -'tī-,rōl, -,tī-'; -'tir-əl\ district [N] Italy in [S] Tirol in [N] Trentino-Alto Adige region
Al•to Pa•ra•ná \,al-tō-,par-ə-'nä\ upper course of the Paraná
Ama•ga•sa•ki \,am-ə-gə-'säk-ē\ city Japan in [W] central Honshu on Osaka Bay
Am•a•ril•lo \,am-ə-'ril-ō, -'ril-ə\ city [NW] Texas
Am•a•zon \'am-ə-,zän, -zən\ *or Portuguese and Spanish* **Ama•zo•nas** \,am-ə-'zō-nəs\ river about 6275 kilometers long [N] South America flowing from Peruvian Andes into Atlantic in [N] Brazil
Am•a•zo•nia \,am-ə-'zō-nē-ə\ region [N] South America: basin of the Amazon
Amer•i•ca \ə-'mer-ə-kə\ **1** either continent (North America or South America) of western hemisphere **2** *or* **the Amer•i•cas** \-kəz\ lands of western hemisphere including North, Central, & South America & West Indies **3** UNITED STATES OF AMERICA
American Samoa *or* **Eastern Samoa** islands [SW] central Pacific; capital, Pago Pago (on Tutuila Island)
Am•man \a-'män, -'man\ city, capital of Jordan
Amnok — see YALU
Amoy \ä-'mȯi, a-, ə-\ *or* **Hsia-men** \'shä-'mən\ city [SE] China in [S] Fukien on Amoy & Ku-lang islands
Am•rit•sar \,əm-'rit-sər\ city [N] India in [NW] Punjab
Am•ster•dam \'am-stər-,dam, 'amp-\ city, official capital of the Netherlands
Amu Dar•ya \,äm-ü-'där-yə\ *or ancient* **Ox•us** \'äk-səs\ river 2575 kilometers long in central & [W] Asia flowing from the Pamirs into Aral sea
Amur \ä-'mu̇r\ *or Chinese* **Hei-lung chiang** \'hā-'lu̇ng-jē-'äng\ river 2865 kilometers long [E] Asia formed by junction of Shilka & Argun rivers flowing into the Pacific at [N] end of Tatar strait & forming part of boundary between China & Soviet Russia, Asia
An•a•heim \'an-ə-,hīm\ city [SW] California [E] of Long Beach
Aná•huac \ə-'nä-,wäk\ the central plateau of Mexico
An•a•to•lia \,an-ə-'tō-lē-ə, -'tōl-yə\ — see ASIA MINOR — **An•a•to•li•an** \-ən, -yən\ *adj or n*
An•chor•age \'ang-kə-rij, -krij\ city [S] central Alaska; largest in state
An•co•hu•ma \,ang-kə-'hü-mə, -'hyü-\ mountain peak 6388 meters [W] Bolivia; highest in Illampu massif
An•co•na \ang-'kō-nə, an-\ city central Italy, capital of the Marches
An•da•lu•sia \,an-də-'lü-zhē-ə, -zhə\ *or Spanish* **An•da•lu•cía** \,än-de-lü-'sē-ə\ region [S] Spain including Sierra Nevada & valley of the Guadalquivir — **An•da•lu•sian** \,an-də-'lü-zhən\ *adj or n*
An•da•man \'an-də-mən, -,man\ **1** islands India in Bay of Bengal [S] of Burma & [N] of Nicobar islands; in **Andaman and Nic•o•bar** \'nik-ə-,bär\ territory **2** sea arm of Bay of Bengal [S] of Burma — **An•da•man•ese** \,an-də-mə-'nēz, -'nēs\ *adj or n*
An•des \'an-dēz, -,dēz\ mountain system [W] South America extending from Panama to Tierra del Fuego — see ACONCAGUA — **An•de•an** \'an-dē-ən, an-'\ *adj* — **An•dine** \'an-,dēn, -,dīn\ *adj*
An•dhra Pra•desh \,än-drə-prə-'dāsh, -'desh\ state [S] India [N] of Tamil Nadu bordering on Bay of Bengal; capital, Hyderabad
An•dor•ra \an-'dȯr-ə, -'där-ə\ country [SW] Europe in [E] Pyrenees between France & Spain; capital, Andorra la Vella — **An•dor•ran** \-ən\ *adj or n*
An•dros **1** \'an-drəs\ island, largest of Bahamas **2** \'an-drəs, -,dräs\ island Greece in [N] Cyclades [SE] of Euboea
An•gel Falls \,än-jəl-\ waterfall 979 meters [SE] Venezuela on Auyán-tepuí Mountain

An·gers \ä^{n}-zhā\ city [W] France [ENE] of Nantes
Ang·kor \'ang-,kȯr\ ruins of ancient city [NW] Cambodia
An·gle·sey \'ang-gəl-sē\ island & former county [NW] Wales
An·glo–Egyp·tian Sudan \,ang-glō-i-,jip-shən-\ former territory [NE] Africa under joint British & Egyptian rule; since 1956 has formed republic of Sudan
An·go·la \ang-'gō-lə, an-\ *or formerly* **Portuguese West Africa** country [SW] Africa [S] of mouth of Congo river; until 1975 a dependency of Portugal; capital, Luanda — **An·go·lan** \-lən\ *adj or n*
An·gus \'ang-gəs\ former county [E] Scotland
An·hwei *or* **An·hui** \'än-'hwā, -'wā\ province [E] China [W] of Kiangsu; capital, Hofei
An·i·ak·chak Crater \,an-ē-'ak-,chak\ volcano 1347 meters [SW] Alaska on Alaska peninsula; crater 10 kilometers in diameter
An·jou \'an-,jü, ä^{n}-zhü\ region & former province [NW] France in Loire valley [SE] of Brittany; chief city Angers
An·ka·ra \'ang-kə-rə, 'äng-\ *or formerly* **An·go·ra** \ang-'gōr-ə, an-, -'gȯr-\ city, capital of Turkey in [N] central Anatolia
An·na·ba \ə-'näb-ə\ *or formerly* **Bône** \'bōn\ city [NE] Algeria
An·nam \a-'nam, ə-; 'an-,am\ region & former kingdom [E] Indochina in central Vietnam; capital, Hue
An·nap·o·lis \ə-'nap-ləs, -ə-ləs\ city, capital of Maryland
An–shan \'än-'shän\ city [NE] China in [E] central Liaoning [SSW] of Mukden
An·ta·nan·a·ri·vo \,an-tə-,nan-ə-'rē-vō\ *or formerly* **Ta·nan·a·rive** \tə-'nan-ə-,rēv\ city, capital of Madagascar
Ant·arc·ti·ca \ant-'ärk-ti-kə, 'ant-, -'ärt-i-\ *or* **Ant·arc·tic continent** \-'ärk-tik, -'ärt-ik\ body of land around the South Pole; plateau covered by great ice cap
Antarctic peninsula *or formerly* **Palm·er peninsula** \,päm-ər-, ,päl-mər-\ peninsula 1930 kilometers long [W] Antarctica [S] of [S] end of South America
An·ti·gua \an-'tē-gə\ island British West Indies in the Leewards [E] of Nevis; capital, Saint Johns
Anti–Leb·a·non \'ant-i-'leb-ə-nən, -,nän\ mountains [SW] Asia on Lebanon-Syria border — see HERMON
An·til·les \an-'til-ēz\ the West Indies excluding the Bahamas — see GREATER ANTILLES, LESSER ANTILLES — **An·til·le·an** \-'til-ē-ən\ *adj*
An·ti·och \'ant-ē-,äk\ city of ancient Syria on the Orontes; site at modern Antakya, Turkey
An·trim \'an-trəm\ county [E] Northern Ireland; includes Belfast
Antung — see TAN-TUNG
Ant·werp \'ant-wərp\ city [N] Belgium on the Scheldt
An·yang \'än-'yäng\ city [E] China in [N] Honan
An·zio \'an-zē-ō, 'än-\ *or ancient* **An·ti·um** \'an-shē-əm\ Mediterranean seaport Italy in Latium [SSE] of Rome
Ao·mo·ri \'aù-mə-rē\ city [N] Japan in [NE] Honshu on Mutsu Bay
Aorangi — see COOK
Ap·en·nines \'ap-ə-,nīnz\ mountain chain Italy extending length of the peninsula; highest point Monte Corno ([NE] of Rome) 2914 meters — **Ap·en·nine** \-,nīn\ *adj*
Apia \ə-'pē-ə\ town, capital of Western Samoa on Upolu Island
Apo, Mount \'äp-ō\ volcano Philippines in [SE] Mindanao 2594 meters; highest peak in the Philippines
Ap·pa·la·chia \,ap-ə-'lā-chə, -'lach-ə, -'lā-shə\ region [E] U.S. including Appalachian mountains from [S] central New York to central Alabama
Ap·pa·la·chian \,ap-ə-'lā-chən, -'lach-ən, -'lā-shən\ mountain system [E] North America extending from [S] Quebec to central Alabama — see MITCHELL
Ap·po·mat·tox Court House National Historical Park \,ap-ə-'mat-əks\ reservation central Virginia [E] of Lynchburg
Apu·lia \ə-'pyül-yə, -'pyü-lē-ə\ *or Italian* **Pu·glia** \'pül-yä\ *or* **Le Pu·glie** \lā-'pül-yā\ region [SE] Italy bordering on the Adriatic & Gulf of Taranto; capital, Bari — **Apu·lian** \ə-'pyül-yən, -'pyü-lē-ən\ *adj or n*
'Aqa·ba, Gulf of \'äk-ə-bə, 'ak-\ arm of Red sea [E] of Sinai peninsula
Aquid·neck Island \ə-'kwid-,nek\ *or* **Rhode Island** \'rōd\ island [SE] Rhode Island in Narragansett Bay
Aq·ui·taine \'ak-wə-,tān\ old region of [SW] France comprising later Guienne; chief city, Toulouse
Aq·ui·ta·nia \,ak-wə-'tā-nyə, -nē-ə\ a Roman division of [SW] Gaul
Ara·bia \ə-'rā-bē-ə\ peninsula of [SW] Asia including Saudi Arabia, Yemen Arab Republic, Southern Yemen, Oman, & Persian Gulf States
Ara·bi·an \ə-'rā-bē-ən\ **1** desert [E] Egypt between Red sea & the Nile **2** sea [NW] section of Indian ocean between Arabia & India
Ara·ca·ju \,ar-ə-kə-'zhü\ city [E] Brazil [NE] of Salvador
Arad \ä-'räd\ city [W] Rumania
Ar·a·fu·ra \,ar-ə-'fùr-ə\ sea between [N] Australia & [W] New Guinea
Ar·a·gon \'ar-ə-,gän, -gən\ region [NE] Spain bordering on France — **Ar·a·go·nese** \,ar-ə-gə-'nēz, -'nēs\ *adj or n*
Ar·al sea \'ar-əl\ *or Russian* **Aral·sko·ye Mo·re** \ə-,ral-skə-yə-'mȯr-ə, -yə\ *or formerly* **Lake Aral** lake U.S.S.R. in [SW] Soviet Central Asia between Kazakhstan & Uzbekistan
Ar·a·rat \'ar-ə-,rat\ *or Armenian* **Ma·sis** \mä-'sēs\ *or Turkish* **Ag·ri Da·gi** *or* **Agh·ri Dagh** \,ä-rē-dä-'ē, ,äg-rē-däg-'ē\ *or Persian* **Koh–i–nuh** \,kō-i-'nü\ mountain 5165 meters [E] Turkey near border of Iran
Ar·ca·dia \är-'kād-ē-ə\ mountain region [S] Greece in central Peloponnesus
Arch·es National Park \'är-chəz\ reservation [E] Utah
Arc·tic \'ärk-tik, 'ärt-ik\ **1** ocean [N] of Arctic circle **2** Arctic regions **3** archipelago [N] Canada constituting greater part of Franklin District, Northwest Territories
Ar·dennes \är-'den\ wooded plateau [NE] France, [W] Luxembourg, & [SE] Belgium [E] of the Meuse
Are·qui·pa \,ar-ə-'kē-pə\ city [S] Peru
Ar·gen·ti·na \,är-jən-'tē-nə\ country [S] South America between the Andes & the Atlantic [S] of the Pilcomayo; a republic; capital, Buenos Aires — **Argentine** \'är-jən-,tēn\ *adj or n* — **Ar·gen·tin·ean** *or* **Ar·gen·tin·i·an** \,är-jən-'tin-ē-ən\ *adj or n*
Ar·go·lis \'är-gə-lis\ district [S] Greece in [E] Peloponnesus
Ar·gonne \är-'gän, 'är-,\ *or* **Argonne Forest** wooded plateau [NE] France [S] of the Ardennes between Meuse & Aisne rivers
Ar·gos \'är-,gäs, -gəs\ ancient Greek city & state [S] Greece in Argolis; site at present town of Argos
Ar·gyll \är-'gīl, 'är-,\ *or* **Ar·gyll·shire** \-,shiər, -shər\ former county [W] Scotland
Ar·i·zo·na \,ar-ə-'zō-nə\ state [SW] U.S.; capital, Phoenix — **Ar·i·zo·nan** \-nən\ *or* **Ar·i·zo·nian** \-nē-ən, -nyən\ *adj or n*
Ar·kan·sas \'är-kən-,sȯ; *1 is also* är-'kan-zəs\ **1** river 2335 kilometers long [SW] central U.S. flowing [SE] into the Mississippi **2** state [S] central U.S.; capital, Little Rock — **Ar·kan·san** \är-'kan-zən\ *adj or n*
Ar·khan·gelsk \är-'kan-,gelsk\ *or* **Arch·an·gel** \'är-,kān-jəl\ city U.S.S.R. in [N] Soviet Russia, Europe, on the Northern Dvina
Ar·magh \är-'mä, 'är-,\ county [S] Northern Ireland
Ar·me·nia \är-'mē-nē-ə, -nyə\ **1** region [W] Asia in mountainous area [SE] of Black sea & [SW] of Caspian sea divided between Iran, Turkey, & U.S.S.R. **2** *or* **Ar·me·ni·an Soviet Socialist Republic** \-nē-ən, -nyən\ constituent republic of U.S.S.R. in [S] Transcaucasia; capital, Yerevan — see LESSER ARMENIA — **Ar·me·ni·an** \-nē-ən, -nyən\ *adj or n*
Arn·hem Land \'ärn-,hem, 'är-nəm\ region [N] Australia on [N] coast of Northern Territory
Ar·no \'är-nō\ river 225 kilometers long central Italy flowing through Florence into Ligurian sea
Aru·ba \ə-'rü-bə\ island Netherlands Antilles off coast of [NW] Venezuela [NW] of Curaçao; chief town, Oranjestad
Arun·a·chal Pra·desh \,är-ə-,näch-əl-prə-'dāsh, -'desh\ *or formerly* **North East Frontier Agency** territory [NE] India [N] of Assam; capital, Ziro
Asa·hi·ka·wa \,äs-ə-hē-'kä-wə\ *or* **Asa·hi·ga·wa** \-'gä-wə\ city Japan in central Hokkaido
Ashan·ti \ə-'shant-ē, -'shänt-\ *or* **Asan·te** \ə-'sänt-ē\ region central Ghana
Ashkh·a·bad \'ash-kə-,bad, -,bäd\ city U.S.S.R., capital of Turkmenistan
Asia \'ā-zhə, -shə\ continent of eastern hemisphere [N] of equator — see EURASIA
Asia Mi·nor \-'mī-nər\ *or* **An·a·to·lia** \,an-ə-'tō-lē-ə, -'tōl-yə\ peninsula in modern Turkey between Black sea on [N] & the Mediterranean on [S]
Asir \a-'siər\ province [S] Saudi Arabia on Red sea [SE] of Hejaz
As·ma·ra \az-'mär-ə, -'mar-ə\ city [N] Ethiopia, capital of Eritrea
As·sam \ə-'sam, a-; 'as-,am\ state [NE] India on edge of the Hi-

malayas [NW] of Burma; capital, Dispur — **As•sam•ese** \ˌas-ə-ˈmēz, -ˈmēs\ *adj or n*
As•syr•ia \ə-ˈsir-ē-ə\ ancient empire [W] Asia extending along the middle Tigris & over foothills to the [E]; early capital Calah, later capital Nineveh — **As•syr•i•an** \-ən\ *adj or n*
As•tra•khan \ˈas-trə-ˌkan, -kən\ city U.S.S.R. in [SE] Soviet Russia, Europe, on the Volga at head of its delta
Asun•ción \ə-ˌsün-sē-ˈōn, ä-\ city, capital of Paraguay
As•wân \a-ˈswän, ä-\ city [S] Egypt on the Nile near site of **Aswân High Dam** which forms Lake Nasser
As•yût \ˌas-ē-ˈüt, ˌäs-\ city central Egypt on the Nile
Ata•ca•ma \ˌat-ə-ˈkäm-ə\ **1** desert [N] Chile between Copiapó & Peru border **2** — see PUNA DE ATACAMA
Atchaf•a•laya \ə-ˌchaf-ə-ˈlī-ə, ˌchaf-\ river 362 kilometers long [S] Louisiana flowing [S] into Gulf of Mexico; receives waters of Red & Mississippi rivers
Ath•a•bas•ca *or* **Ath•a•bas•ka** \ˌath-ə-ˈbas-kə\ river 1231 kilometers long [NE] Alberta flowing into Lake Athabasca
Athabasca, Lake lake [W] central Canada on Alberta-Saskatchewan border
Ath•ens \ˈath-ənz\ city, capital of Greece — **Athe•nian** \ə-ˈthē-nē-ən, -nyən\ *adj or n*
At•lan•ta \ət-ˈlant-ə, at-\ city, capital of Georgia
At•lan•tic \ət-ˈlant-ik, at-\ ocean separating North America & South America from Europe & Africa
At•lan•tis \ət-ˈlant-əs, at-\ fabled island that was traditionally placed [W] of Strait of Gibraltar and that sank into sea
At•las \ˈat-ləs\ mountains [NW] Africa extending from [SW] Morocco to [N] Tunisia
At•ti•ca \ˈat-i-kə\ region [E] Greece; chief city, Athens
Auck•land \ˈo-klənd\ city [N] New Zealand on [NW] North Island
Augs•burg \ˈogz-ˌbərg, ˈaugz-ˌbu̇rg\ city West Germany in [S] Bavaria [NW] of Munich
Au•gus•ta \o-ˈgəst-ə, ə-\ city, capital of Maine
Aus•tin \ˈos-tən, ˈäs-\ city, capital of Texas
Austral — see TUBUAI
Aus•tral•asia \ˌos-trə-ˈlā-zhə, ˌäs-, -ˈlā-shə\ Australia, Tasmania, New Zealand & Melanesia — **Aus•tral•asian** \-zhən, -shən\ *adj or n*
Aus•tra•lia \o-ˈstrāl-yə, ä-, ə-\ **1** continent of eastern hemisphere [SE] of Asia **2** *or in full* **Commonwealth of Australia** dominion of British Commonwealth including continent of Australia & island of Tasmania; capital, Canberra — **Aus•tra•lian** \-yən\ *adj or n*
Australian Alps mountain range [SE] Australia in [E] Victoria & [SE] New South Wales; part of Great Dividing range
Australian Capital Territory district [SE] Australia including two areas, one containing Canberra (capital of Australia) & the other on Jervis Bay; surrounded by New South Wales
Aus•tria \ˈos-trē-ə, ˈäs-\ country central Europe; capital, Vienna — **Aus•tri•an** \-ən\ *adj or n*
Aus•tria–Hun•ga•ry \-ˈhəng-gə-rē\ dual monarchy 1867–1918 central Europe including Austria, Hungary, Czechoslovakia, Bukovina & Transylvania in Rumania, [NW] half of Yugoslavia, Galicia in Poland, & part of [NE] Italy — **Aus•tro–Hun•gar•i•an** \ˈos-trō-ˌhəng-ˈgar-ē-ən, ˈäs-, -ˈger-\ *adj or n*
Aus•tro•ne•sia \ˌos-trə-ˈnē-zhə, ˌäs-, -ˈnē-shə\ **1** islands of the [S] Pacific **2** area extending from Madagascar through Malay peninsula & archipelago to Hawaii & Easter Island — **Aus•tro•ne•sian** \-zhən, -shən\ *adj or n*
Au•vergne \ō-ˈveərn, -ˈveərn-yə, -ˈvərn\ **1** region & former province [S] central France; capital, Clermont (now Clermont-Ferrand) **2** mountains [S] central France in Massif Central; highest Puy de Sancy 1886 meters
Ave•lla•ne•da \ˌav-ə-zhə-ˈnā-də\ city [E] Argentina on Río de la Plata [E] of Buenos Aires
Avon \ˈā-vən, ˈav-ən, *in the United States also* ˈā-ˌvän\ **1** river 155 kilometers long central England rising in Northamptonshire & flowing [WSW] past Stratford-upon-Avon into the Severn **2** county [SW] England including Bristol
Ayers Rock \ˈaərz-, ˈeərz-\ outcrop central Australia in [SW] Northern Territory [SW] of Alice Springs
Ayr \ˈaər, ˈeər\ *or* **Ayr•shire** \-ˌshiər, -shər\ former county [SW] Scotland
Azer•bai•jan Soviet Socialist Republic \ˌaz-ər-ˌbī-ˈjän, ˌäz-\ constituent republic of U.S.S.R. bordering on Caspian sea; capital, Baku
Azores \ˈā-ˌzōrz, -ˌzorz, ə-ˈ\ *or* Portuguese **Aço•res** \ə-ˈsōr-ēsh\ islands [N] Atlantic belonging to Portugal & lying 1290 kilometers [W] of Portuguese coast — **Azor•e•an** *or* **Azor•i•an** \ā-ˈzor-ē-ən, ə-, -ˈzor-\ *adj or n*
Az•ov, Sea of \ˈaz-ˌof, ˈāz-, -ˌäv\ gulf of Black sea in U.S.S.R. [E] of Crimea
Baalbek — see HELIOPOLIS
Ba•bel•thu•ap \ˌbäb-əl-ˈtü-ˌäp\ island [W] Pacific; chief of Palau islands
Bab•y•lon \ˈbab-ə-lən, -ˌlän\ ancient city, capital of Babylonia; site about 80 kilometers [S] of Baghdad near the Euphrates — **Bab•y•lo•nian** \ˌbab-ə-ˈlō-nyən, -nē-ən\ *adj or n*
Bab•y•lo•nia \ˌbab-ə-ˈlō-nyə, -nē-ə\ ancient country [W] Asia in valley of lower Euphrates and Tigris rivers; capital, Babylon — **Bab•y•lo•nian** \-nyən, -nē-ən\ *adj or n*
Bac•tria \ˈbak-trē-ə\ ancient country [W] Asia between the Hindu Kush & upper Oxus in present [NE] Afghanistan — **Bac•tri•an** \-ən\ *adj or n*
Ba•den–Würt•tem•berg \ˌbäd-n-ˈwərt-əm-ˌbərg, -ˈwu̇rt-; ˈvuert-əm-ˌberk\ state West Germany [W] of Bavaria; capital, Stuttgart
Bad•lands National Monument \ˈbad-ˌlandz, -ˌlanz\ reservation [SW] South Dakota [E] of Black hills
Baf•fin \ˈbaf-ən\ island [NE] Canada in Arctic archipelago [N] of Hudson strait
Baffin Bay inlet of the Atlantic between [W] Greenland & [E] Baffin Island
Bagh•dad *or* **Bag•dad** \ˈbag-ˌdad\ city, capital of Iraq on the middle Tigris
Ba•guio \ˌbäg-ē-ˈō\ city, summer capital of the Philippines in [NW] central Luzon
Ba•ha•ma \bə-ˈhäm-ə, *by outsiders also* -ˈhā-mə\ islands in [N] Atlantic [SE] of Florida; an independent member of British Commonwealth (officially **Commonwealth of the Bahamas**); capital, Nassau — **Ba•ha•mi•an** \-ˈhā-mē-ən, -ˈhäm-ē-ən\ *or* **Ba•ha•man** \-ˈhā-mən, -ˈhäm-ən\ *adj or n*
Bahia — see SALVADOR
Bah•rain *or* **Bah•rein** \bä-ˈrān\ islands in Persian gulf off coast of Arabia; capital, Manama
Bai•kal *or* **Bay•kal** \bī-ˈkol, -ˈkäl\ lake U.S.S.R. in [S] Soviet Russia, Asia, in mountains [N] of Mongolia
Baile Atha Cliath — see DUBLIN
Ba•ja \ˈbä-hä\ BAJA CALIFORNIA
Ba•ja California \ˌbä-hä-\ peninsula [NW] Mexico [W] of Gulf of California
Baja California Nor•te \ˈnor-tē\ state [NW] Mexico [N] Baja California; capital, Mexicali
Baja California Sur \ˈsu̇r\ state [NW] Mexico in [S] Baja California; capital, La Paz
Ba•ku \bä-ˈkü\ city U.S.S.R., capital of Azerbaijan Soviet Socialist Republic on [W] coast of Caspian sea
Bakwanga — see MBUJI-MAYI
Bal•a•ton \ˈbal-ə-ˌtän, ˈbol-ə-ˌtōn\ lake [W] Hungary
Balboa Heights \bal-ˌbō-ə-\ town Panama Canal Zone; administrative center for Canal Zone
Bâle — see BASEL
Bal•e•ar•ic \ˌbal-ē-ˈar-ik\ islands [E] Spain in the [W] Mediterranean — see MAJORCA, MINORCA, IVIZA
Ba•li \ˈbäl-ē\ island Indonesia off [E] end of Java; chief town, Singaradja — **Ba•li•nese** \ˌbäl-i-ˈnēz, ˌbal-, -ˈnēs\ *adj or n*
Bal•kan \ˈbol-kən\ **1** mountains [N] Bulgaria extending from Yugoslavia border to Black sea; highest about 2380 meters **2** peninsula [SE] Europe between Adriatic & Ionian seas on the [W] & Aegean & Black seas on the [E]
Balkan States *or* **Bal•kans** \ˈbol-kənz\ countries occupying the Balkan peninsula: Yugoslavia, Rumania, Bulgaria, Albania, Greece, Turkey (in Europe)
Bal•khash *or* **Bal•kash** \bal-ˈkash, bäl-ˈkäsh\ lake U.S.S.R. in Soviet Central Asia in [SE] Kazakhstan
Bal•tic \ˈbol-tik\ sea arm of the Atlantic [N] Europe [E] of Scandinavian peninsula
Bal•ti•more \ˈbol-tə-ˌmōr, -ˌmor; ˈbol-tə-mər, ˈbol-mər\ city [N] central Maryland
Ba•lu•chi•stan \bə-ˌlü-chə-ˈstan\ arid region [S] Asia bordering on Arabian sea in [SW] Pakistan & [SE] Iran — **Ba•lu•chi** \bə-ˈlü-chē\ *n*
Ba•ma•ko \ˌbäm-ə-ˈkō\ city, capital of Mali on the Niger
Ba•na•ras *or* **Be•na•res** \bə-ˈnär-əs, -ēz\ *or* **Va•ra•na•si** \və-ˈrän-ə-sē\ city [N] India in [SE] Uttar Pradesh
Ban•dar \ˈbən-dər\ *or* **Ma•su•li•pat•nam** \ˌməs-ə-li-ˈpət-nəm\ *or* **Ma•chi•li•pat•nam** \ˌmə-shə-lē-ˈpət-nəm\ city [SE] India in [E] Andhra Pradesh

Ban•dung \'bän-,dùng\ city Indonesia in [W] Java [SE] of Jakarta

Banff \'bamf, 'bampf\ *or* **Banff•shire** \-,shiər, -shər\ former county [NE] Scotland

Banff National Park reservation [SW] Alberta on [E] slope of Rocky mountains

Ban•ga•lore \'bang-gə-,lōr, -,lór\ city [S] India [W] of Madras, capital of Karnataka

Bang•kok \'bang-,käk, bang-'\ city, capital of Thailand on Chao Phraya river

Ban•gla•desh \,bäng-glə-'desh, ,bang-, -'dāsh\ country [S] Asia [E] of India; formerly part of Pakistan; an independent republic since 1971; capital, Dacca — see EAST PAKISTAN

Ban•gui \bäⁿ-gē\ city, capital of Central African Empire

Ban•jul \'bän-,jül\ *or formerly* **Bath•urst** \'bath-,ərst, -ərst\ city, capital of Gambia

Bar•ba•dos \bär-'bād-əs, -ōz, -äs, -ōs\ island British West Indies in Lesser Antilles [E] of Windward islands; an independent dominion of British Commonwealth since 1966; capital, Bridgetown — **Bar•ba•di•an** \-'bād-ē-ən\ *adj or n*

Bar•ba•ry States \'bär-bə-rē, -brē\ the states of Morocco, Algeria, Tunisia, & Tripolitania while under Turkish flag

Bar•bu•da \bär-'büd-ə\ island British West Indies; a dependency of Antigua

Bar•ce•lo•na \,bär-sə-'lō-nə\ city [NE] Spain on the Mediterranean; chief city of Catalonia

Ba•reil•ly *or* **Ba•re•li** \bə-'rā-lē\ city [N] India in [NW] central Uttar Pradesh

Ba•rents \'bar-əns, 'bär-\ sea comprising part of Arctic ocean between Spitsbergen & Novaya Zemlya

Ba•ri \'bär-ē\ city [SE] Italy, capital of Apulia on the Adriatic

Bar•king \'bär-king\ borough of [E] Greater London, England

Bar•na•ul \,bär-nə-'ül\ city U.S.S.R. in [SW] Soviet Russia, Asia, on the Ob

Bar•net \'bär-nət\ borough of [N] Greater London, England

Ba•ro•da \bə-'rōd-ə\ city [W] India in [SE] Gujarat [SE] of Ahmadabad

Bar•qui•si•me•to \,bär-kə-sə-'māt-ō\ city [NW] Venezuela

Bar•ran•qui•lla \,bar-ən-'kē-ə, -'kē-yə\ city [N] Colombia on the Magdalena

Barren Grounds treeless plains [N] Canada [W] of Hudson Bay

Bar•row, Point \'bar-ō\ most northerly point of Alaska & of United States at about 71°25′N latitude

Ba•sel \'bäz-əl\ *or French* **Bâle** \'bäl\ city [NW] Switzerland on the Rhine

Ba•si•lan \bä-'sē-,län\ **1** island [S] Philippines **2** city on the island

Bas•il•don \'baz-əl-dən\ town [SE] England in Essex

Basque Provinces \'bask\ region [N] Spain on Bay of Biscay including Álava, Guipúzcoa, & Vizcaya provinces

Bas•ra \'bäs-rə, 'bəs-, 'bas-\ city [S] Iraq on Shatt-al-Arab

Bass \'bas\ strait separating Tasmania & continent of Australia

Bas•sein \bə-'sān\ city [S] Burma

Bas•tille \ba-'stēl\ medieval fortress, Paris; used as prison until destroyed by mobs on July 14, 1789

Basutoland — see LESOTHO

Ba•taan \bə-'tan, -'tän\ peninsula Philippines in [W] Luzon on [W] side of Manila Bay

Batavia — see JAKARTA

Bathurst — see BANJUL

Bat•on Rouge \,bat-n-'rüzh\ city, capital of Louisiana

Ba•var•ia \bə-'ver-ē-ə, -'var-\ *or German* **Bay•ern** \'bī-ərn\ state [S] West Germany bordering on Austria, Czechoslovakia, & East Germany; capital, Munich — **Ba•var•i•an** \bə-'ver-ē-ən, -'var-\ *adj or n*

Ba•ya•mon \,bī-ə-'mōn\ city [NE] central Puerto Rico

Baykal — see BAIKAL

Beard•more \'biərd-,mōr, -,mór\ glacier Antarctica descending to Ross ice shelf at about 170° [E] longitude

Beau•fort \'bō-fərt\ sea comprising part of Arctic ocean [NE] of Alaska & [NW] of Canada

Beau•mont \'bō-,mänt, bō-'\ city [SE] Texas

Bech•u•a•na•land \,bech-'wän-ə-,land, -ə-'wän-\ **1** region [S] Africa [N] of Orange river **2** — see BOTSWANA — **Bech•u•a•na** \,bech-'wän-ə, -ə-'wän-\ *adj or n*

Bed•ford•shire \'bed-fərd-,shiər, -shər\ *or* **Bedford** county [SE] England

Bedloe's — see LIBERTY

Behar — see BIHAR

Bei•rut *or* **Bay•rut** \bā-'rüt\ *or French* **Bey•routh** \bā-rüt\ *or ancient* **Be•ry•tus** \bə-'rīt-əs\ city, capital of Lebanon

Be•lém \bə-'lem\ *or* **Pa•rá** \pə-'rä\ city [N] Brazil on Pará river

Bel•fast \'bel-,fast, bel-'\ city, capital of Northern Ireland in Antrim

Belgian Congo — see ZAIRE

Bel•gium \'bel-jəm\ *or French* **Bel•gique** \bel-zhēk\ *or Flemish* **Bel•gië** \'bel-gē-ə\ country [W] Europe; capital, Brussels — **Bel•gian** \'bel-jən\ *adj or n*

Bel•grade \'bel-,grād, -,gräd, -,grad, bel-'\ *or* **Be•o•grad** \'beù-,gräd\ city, capital of Yugoslavia on the Danube

Be•lize \bə-'lēz\ *or Spanish* **Be•li•ce** \bā-'lē-sā\ **1** *or* **British Hon•du•ras** \hän-'dùr-əs, -'dyùr-\ country Central America on the Caribbean; a British colony; capital, Belmopan **2** city [E] Belize on the Caribbean

Bel•mo•pan \,bel-mō-'pan\ city, capital of Belize

Be•lo Ho•ri•zon•te \'bā-lō-,hór-ə-'zänt-ē, 'bel-ō-, -,här-\ city [E] Brazil [N] of Rio de Janeiro

Be•lo•rus•sian Soviet Socialist Republic \,bel-ō-'rəsh-ən\ *or* **Bye•lo•rus•sian Soviet Socialist Republic** \bē-,el-ō-\ constituent republic of U.S.S.R. bordering on Poland, Lithuania, & Latvia; capital, Minsk — **Belorussian** *adj or n*

Belostok — see BIALYSTOK

Beloye More — see WHITE SEA

Benares — see BANARAS

Be•ne•lux \'ben-l-,əks\ economic union comprising Belgium, Luxembourg, & the Netherlands formed 1947

Ben•gal \ben-'gól, beng-\ region [E] Indian subcontinent including delta of Ganges & Brahmaputra rivers; divided between Bangladesh & Republic of India — see EAST BENGAL, WEST BENGAL — **Ben•gal•ese** \,beng-gə-'lēz, ,ben-, -'lēs\ *adj or n*

Bengal, Bay of arm of Indian ocean between India & Burma

Ben•gha•zi *or* **Ben•ga•zi** *or* **Ben•gha•si** \ben-'gäz-ē, beng-'gaz-\ city [NE] Libya; formerly a capital of Libya

Ben•guela Current *or* **Ben•guel•la Current** \ben-'gwel-ə, 'beng-, -'gel-\ cold current of the Atlantic Ocean flowing [N] along [SW] coast of Africa

Be•nin \bə-'nin, -'nēn; 'ben-ən\ **1** *or formerly* **Da•ho•mey** \də-'hō-mē\ country [W] Africa on Gulf of Guinea; a republic; capital, Porto-Novo **2** city [SW] Nigeria — **Ben•i•nese** \bə-,nin-'ēz, -,nēn-; ,ben-i-'nēz, -'nēs\ *adj or n*

Benin, Bight of the [N] section of Gulf of Guinea

Ben Nev•is \ben-'nev-əs\ mountain 1343 meters [W] Scotland in the Grampians; highest in Great Britain

Be•no•ni \bə-'nō-nē\ city [NE] Republic of South Africa in [S] Transvaal

Ber•ga•mo \'beər-gə-,mō, 'bər-\ city [N] Italy in Lombardy [NE] of Milan

Ber•gen \'bər-gən, 'beər-\ city [SW] Norway

Be•ring \'biər-ing, 'beər-\ **1** sea arm of the [N] Pacific between Alaska & [NE] Siberia **2** strait about 90 kilometers wide between North America (Alaska) and Asia (U.S.S.R.)

Berke•ley \'bər-klē\ city [W] California on San Francisco Bay [N] of Oakland

Berk•shire \'bərk-,shiər, -shər, *for 2 British usually* 'bärk-\ **1** hills [W] Massachusetts; highest point Mount Greylock 1064 meters **2** county [S] England [W] of London

Ber•lin \bər-'lin, ,bər-\ city, former capital of Germany; since 1945 divided into East Berlin & West Berlin — **Ber•lin•er** \-'lin-ər\ *n*

Berlin, East city, capital of East Germany [ENE] of Magdeburg

Berlin, West city West Germany; an enclave lying wholly within East Germany

Ber•mu•da \bər-'myüd-ə, ,bər-\ islands [W] Atlantic [ESE] of Cape Hatteras; a British colony; capital, Hamilton — **Ber•mu•dan** \-'myüd-n\ *or* **Ber•mu•di•an** \-'myüd-ē-ən\ *adj or n*

Bern *or* **Berne** \'bərn, 'beərn\ city, capital of Switzerland — **Ber•nese** \bər-'nēz, ,bər-, -'nēs\ *adj or n*

Ber•wick \'ber-ik\ *or* **Ber•wick•shire** \-,shiər, -shər\ former county [SE] Scotland

Berytus — see BEIRUT

Bes•kids \'bes-,kidz, be-'skēdz\ mountain ranges central Europe in the [W] Carpathians including West Beskids (in Poland & Czechoslovakia [W] of Tatra mountains) & East Beskids (in [NE] Czechoslovakia)

Bes•sa•ra•bia \,bes-ə-'rā-bē-ə\ region [SE] Europe between Dniester & Prut rivers now chiefly in Moldavian Republic, U.S.S.R. — **Bes•sa•ra•bi•an** \-bē-ən\ *adj or n*

Beth•le•hem \'beth-li-,hem, -lē-həm, -lē-əm\ town of ancient Pal-

estine in Judea [SW] of Jerusalem in area occupied by Israel since 1967
Bex•ley \'bek-slē\ borough of [E] Greater London, England
Beyrouth — see BEIRUT
Bezwada — see VIJAYAWADA
Bharat — see INDIA
Bhav•na•gar \bau̇-'nəg-ər\ city [W] India in [S] Gujarat
Bho•pal \bō-'päl\ city [N] central India [NW] of Nagpur, capital of Madhya Pradesh
Bhu•tan \bü-'tan, -'tän\ country [S] Asia in the Himalayas on [NE] border of India; a protectorate of India; capital, Thimbu — **Bhu•ta•nese** \,büt-n-'ēz, -'ēs\ *adj or n*
Bi•af•ra, Bight of \bē-'af-rə, bī-, -'äf-\ the [E] section of Gulf of Guinea in [W] Africa
Bia•ly•stok \bē-'äl-i-,stȯk\ *or Russian* **Be•lo•stok** \,bel-ə-'stȯk\ city [NE] Poland
Bie•le•feld \'bē-lə-,felt\ city West Germany [E] of Münster
Big Bend National Park reservation [SW] Texas on Rio Grande
Big Thicket wilderness area [E] Texas [NE] of Houston
Bi•har *or* **Be•har** \bi-'här\ state [E] India bordering on Nepal; capital, Patna
Bi•ki•ni \bə-'kē-nē\ island (atoll) [W] Pacific in Marshall islands
Bil•bao \bil-'bä-,ō, -'bau̇, -'bā-ō\ city [N] Spain
Bil•lings \'bil-ingz\ city [S] central Montana; largest in state
Bir•ken•head \'bər-kən-,hed, ,bər-kən-'\ borough [NW] England in Merseyside
Bir•ming•ham \'bər-ming-,ham, *British usually* -ming-əm\ **1** city [N] central Alabama **2** city [W] central England in Warwickshire
Bisayas — see VISAYAN
Bis•cay, Bay of \'bis-,kā, -kē\ inlet of the Atlantic between [W] coast of France & [N] coast of Spain
Bis•marck \'biz-,märk\ **1** city, capital of North Dakota **2** archipelago [W] Pacific [N] of [E] end of New Guinea
Bis•sau \bis-'au̇\ city, capital of Guinea-Bissau
Bi•thyn•ia \bə-'thin-ē-ə\ ancient country [NW] Asia Minor bordering on Sea of Marmara and Black sea — **Bi•thyn•i•an** \-ē-ən\ *adj or n*
Black•burn \'blak-bərn, -,bərn\ borough [NW] England in Lancashire
Black Forest *or German* **Schwarz•wald** \'shfärts-,vält, 'shwȯrt-,swȯld\ forested mountain region West Germany along [E] bank of the upper Rhine
Black hills mountains [W] South Dakota & [NE] Wyoming; highest Harney Peak 2207 meters
Black•pool \'blak-,pül\ borough [NW] England in Lancashire
Black sea *or Russian* **Cher•no•ye Mo•re** \,chȯr-nə-yə-'mȯr-yə\ *or ancient* **Pon•tus Eux•i•nus** \,pän-təs-yük-'sī-nəs\ *or* **Pon•tus** \'pän-təs\ sea between Europe & Asia connected with Aegean sea through the Bosporus, Sea of Marmara, & Dardanelles
Blanc, Mont — see MONT BLANC
Blan•tyre–Lim•be \'blan-,tīr-'lim-bā\ city [S] Malawi
Bloem•fon•tein \'blüm-,fən-,tān, -,fän-\ city, judicial capital of Republic of South Africa & capital of Orange Free State
Blue Nile river 1375 kilometers long Ethiopia & Sudan flowing [NNW] into the Nile at Khartoum
Blue Ridge [E] range of the Appalachians [E] U.S. extending from [S] Pennsylvania to [N] Georgia
Bo•chum \'bō-kəm\ city West Germany in Ruhr valley
Boe•o•tia \bē-'ō-shē-ə, -shə\ district [E] central Greece [NW] of Attica; chief ancient city, Thebes — **Boe•o•tian** \-shē-ən, -shən\ *adj or n*
Bo•go•tá \,bō-gə-'tȯ, -'tä\ city, capital of Colombia
Bo•he•mia \bō-'hē-mē-ə\ region [W] Czechoslovakia; once a kingdom & later a province; chief city, Prague
Boi•se \'bȯi-sē, -zē\ city, capital of Idaho
Bokhara — see BUKHARA
Boks•burg \'bäks-,bərg\ city [NE] Republic of South Africa in [S] Transvaal
Bolerium — see LANDS END
Bo•liv•ia \bə-'liv-ē-ə\ country [W] central South America; administrative capital, La Paz; constitutional capital, Sucre — **Bo•liv•ian** \-ē-ən\ *adj or n*
Bo•lo•gna \bə-'lōn-yə, -'lōn-ə\ city [N] Italy [N] of Florence, capital of Emilia-Romagna
Bol•ton \'bōlt-n\ *or in full* **Bolton–le–Moors** \,bōlt-n-lə-'mu̇rz\ borough [NW] England in Greater Manchester
Bom•bay \bäm-'bā\ **1** former state [W] India; divided 1960 into Gujarat & Maharashtra states **2** city, capital of Maharashtra
Bône — see ANNABA
Bo•nin \'bō-nən\ *or* **Oga•sa•wa•ra** \ō-,gäs-ə-'wär-ə\ islands Japan in [W] Pacific [SE] of Honshu
Bonn \'bän, 'bȯn\ city West Germany on the Rhine [SSE] of Cologne, capital of Federal Republic of Germany
Boo•thia \'bü-thē-ə\ peninsula [N] Canada [W] of Baffin Island; its [N] tip is most northerly point on North American mainland
Bor•deaux \bȯr-'dō\ city [SW] France on the Garonne
Bor•ders \'bȯrd-ərz\ region [SE] Scotland; established 1975
Bor•neo \'bȯr-nē-,ō\ island Malay archipelago [SW] of the Philippines — see BRUNEI, KALIMANTAN, SABAH, SARAWAK
Bos•nia \'bäz-nē-ə\ region [W] Yugoslavia; [N] part of **Bosnia and Herzegovina** federated republic; capital, Sarajevo — **Bos•ni•an** \-nē-ən\ *adj or n*
Bos•po•rus \'bäs-pə-rəs, -prəs\ *or Turkish* **Ka•ra•de•niz Bo•ga•zi** \,kär-ə-də-'nēz-,bō-gä-'zē, -,bō-ä-'zē\ *or ancient* **Bospo•rus Thra•ci•us** \-'thrā-shē-əs, -shəs\ strait about 29 kilometers long between Turkey in Europe & Turkey in Asia connecting Sea of Marmara & Black sea
Bos•ton \'bȯ-stən\ city, capital of Massachusetts — **Bos•to•nian** \bȯ-'stō-nē-ən, -nyən\ *adj or n*
Bot•a•ny Bay \'bät-n-ē, 'bät-nē\ inlet of [S] Pacific [SE] Australia in New South Wales [S] of Sydney
Both•nia, Gulf of \'bäth-nē-ə\ arm of Baltic sea between Sweden & Finland
Bo•tswa•na \bät-'swän-ə\ country [S] Africa [N] of Molopo river; formerly British protectorate of Bechuanaland; now an independent republic; capital, Gaborone
Boulder Dam — see HOOVER DAM
Bourgogne — see BURGUNDY
Bourne•mouth \'bȯrn-məth, 'bȯrn-, 'bu̇rn-\ town [S] England in Dorset on English channel
Brad•ford \'brad-fərd\ city [N] England in West Yorkshire
Brah•ma•pu•tra \,bräm-ə-'pü-trə, -'pyü-\ river 2705 kilometers long [S] Asia flowing from the Himalayas in Tibet to Ganges delta in [E] Indian subcontinent
Bra•ila \brə-'ē-lə\ city [E] Rumania
Bra•sí•lia \brə-'zil-yə\ city, capital of Brazil in Federal District in [E] Goiás state
Bra•ti•sla•va \,brat-ə-'släv-ə, ,brät-\ city [S] Czechoslovakia on the Danube; chief city of Slovakia
Bratsk \'brätsk\ city U.S.S.R. in [E] central Soviet Russia, Asia, [NNE] of Irkutsk
Braunschweig — see BRUNSWICK
Bra•zil \brə-'zil\ country [E] & central South America; a federal republic; capital, Brasília — **Bra•zil•ian** \brə-'zil-yən\ *adj or n*
Brazil Current warm current of the Atlantic ocean flowing [S] along coast of Brazil
Braz•za•ville \'braz-ə-,vil, 'bräz-ə-,vēl\ city, capital of Congo Republic on [W] bank of Stanley Pool in lower Congo river
Brec•on \'brek-ən\ *or* **Breck•nock** \'brek-,näk, -nək\ *or* **Brec•on•shire** *or* **Breck•nock•shire** \-,shiər, -shər\ former county [SE] Wales
Bre•men \'brem-ən, 'brā-mən\ **1** state West Germany **2** city, its capital
Bren•ner \'bren-ər\ pass 1397 meters in the Alps between Austria & Italy
Brent \'brent\ borough of [W] Greater London, England
Bre•scia \'bresh-ə, 'brā-shə\ city [N] Italy in Lombardy [ENE] of Milan
Breslau — see WROCLAW
Brest \'brest\ **1** city [NW] France in Brittany **2** city U.S.S.R. in [SW] Belorussian Soviet Socialist Republic
Bret•on, Cape \kāp-'bret-n, kə-'bret-, -'brit-\ headland Canada; most easterly point of Cape Breton Island & of Nova Scotia
Bridge•port \'brij-,pōrt, -,pȯrt\ city [SW] Connecticut
Bridge•town \'brij-,tau̇n\ city, capital of Barbados
Brigh•ton \'brīt-n\ county borough [S] England in East Sussex on English channel
Bris•bane \'briz-bən, -,bān\ city [E] Australia, capital of Queensland
Bris•tol \'bris-tl\ **1** city [SW] England in Avon **2** channel between [S] Wales & [SW] England
Brit•ain \'brit-n\ **1** the island of Great Britain **2** UNITED KINGDOM
British Columbia province [W] Canada on Pacific coast; capital, Victoria
British Commonwealth of Nations *or* **Commonwealth of Nations** *or* **British Commonwealth** Great Britain, Northern Ireland & the British dominions, republics, & dependencies

British Guiana — see GUYANA
British Honduras — see BELIZE
British India the part of India formerly under direct British administration
British Indian Ocean Territory British colony in Indian ocean comprising Chagos archipelago & Aldabra, Farquhar, & Desroches islands
British Isles island group [W] Europe comprising Great Britain, Ireland, & adjacent islands
British Solomon Islands protectorate comprising the Solomon islands (except Bougainville, Buka, & adjacent small islands) & Santa Cruz islands; capital, Honiara
British Somaliland former British protectorate [E] Africa bordering on Gulf of Aden; capital, Hargeisa; since 1960 part of Somalia
British Virgin Islands [E] islands of Virgin islands group; a British dependency; capital, Road Town (on Tortola Island)
British West Indies islands of the West Indies belonging to the British Commonwealth & including Jamaica, Trinidad and Tobago, & the Bahama, Cayman, Windward, Leeward, & British Virgin islands
Brit•ta•ny \ˈbrit-n-ē\ *or French* **Bre•tagne** \brə-ˈtänʸ\ region & former province [NW] France [SW] of Normandy
Brno \ˈbər-nō\ city central Czechoslovakia; chief city of Moravia
Brom•ley \ˈbräm-lē\ borough of [SE] Greater London, England
Bronx \ˈbräŋs, ˈbräŋks\ *or* **The Bronx** borough of New York City on mainland [NE] of Manhattan Island
Brook•lyn \ˈbru̇k-lən\ borough of New York City at [SW] end of Long Island
Brooks Range \ˈbru̇ks\ mountains [N] Alaska
Bruges \ˈbrüzh, brüezh\ *or Flemish* **Brug•ge** \ˈbrüeg-ə\ city [NW] Belgium
Bru•nei \ˈbrü-ˌnī, -ˌnā\ sultanate [NE] Borneo; a British protectorate; capital, Brunei
Bruns•wick \ˈbrənz-wik\ *or German* **Braun•schweig** \ˈbrau̇n-ˌshwīg, -ˌshfīk\ city West Germany [W] of Berlin
Brus•sels \ˈbrəs-əlz\ city, capital of Belgium
Bryansk \brē-ˈänsk\ city U.S.S.R. in [SW] Soviet Russia, Europe, [SW] of Moscow
Bryce Canyon National Park \ˈbrīs\ reservation [S] Utah [NE] of Zion National Park
Bu•ca•ra•man•ga \ˌbü-kə-rə-ˈmäŋ-gə\ city [N] Colombia [NNE] of Bogotá
Bu•cha•rest \ˈbü-kə-ˌrest, ˈbyü-\ city, capital of Rumania
Buck•ing•ham•shire \ˈbək-iŋ-əm-ˌshiər, -shər, *in the United States also* -iŋ-ˌham-\ *or* **Buckingham** county [SE] central England
Bu•da•pest \ˈbüd-ə-ˌpest *also* ˈbyüd-, ˈbu̇d-, -ˌpesht\ city, capital of Hungary
Bue•nos Ai•res \ˌbwā-nə-ˈsaər-ēz, ˌbō-nə-, -ˈseər-, -ˈsīr-\ city, capital of Argentina on Rio de la Plata
Buf•fa•lo \ˈbəf-ə-ˌlō\ city [W] New York on Lake Erie
Bu•jum•bu•ra \ˌbü-jəm-ˈbu̇r-ə\ *or formerly* **Usum•bu•ra** \ˌü-səm-ˈbu̇r-ə\ city, capital of Burundi
Bu•ka•vu \bü-ˈkäv-ü\ city [E] Zaire
Bu•kha•ra \bü-ˈkär-ə, -ˈkar-, -ˈhär-, -ˈhar-\ *or* **Bo•kha•ra** \bō-\ city U.S.S.R. in Soviet Central Asia in [W] Uzbekistan
Bu•la•wayo \ˌbu̇l-ə-ˈwā-ō, -ˈwī-\ city [SW] Rhodesia
Bul•gar•ia \ˌbəl-ˈgar-ē-ə, bu̇l-, -ˈger-\ country [SE] Europe on Black sea; capital, Sofia
Bur•gun•dy \ˈbər-gən-dē\ *or French* **Bour•gogne** \bür-gȯnʸ\ region [E] France; a former kingdom, duchy, & province — **Bur•gun•di•an** \bər-ˈgən-dē-ən, ˌbər-\ *adj or n*
Bur•ling•ton \ˈbər-liŋ-tən\ city [NW] Vermont; largest in state
Bur•ma \ˈbər-mə\ country [SE] Asia; capital, Rangoon
Bur•sa \bu̇r-ˈsä, ˈbər-sə\ city [NW] Turkey in Asia near Sea of Marmara
Bu•run•di \bu̇-ˈrün-dē\ *or formerly* **Urun•di** \u̇-ˈrün-dē\ country [E] central Africa; a republic; capital, Bujumbura — see RUANDA-URUNDI
Bute \ˈbyüt\ **1** island [SW] Scotland in Firth of Clyde **2** *or* **Bute•shire** \-ˌshiər, -shər\ former county [SW] Scotland
Byd•goszcz \ˈbid-ˌgȯshch, -ˌgȯsh\ *or German* **Brom•berg** \ˈbräm-ˌbərg, ˈbrȯm-ˌberk\ city [NW] central Poland
Byelorussian Soviet Socialist Republic — see BELORUSSIAN SOVIET SOCIALIST REPUBLIC
Byzantium — see ISTANBUL
Caen \känⁿ\ city [NW] France
Caer•nar•von•shire \kär-ˈnär-vən-ˌshiər, -shər\ *or* **Caernarvon** former county [NW] Wales
Cae•sa•rea \ˌsē-zə-ˈrē-ə; ˌses-ə-, ˌsez-ə-\ ancient city [W] Palestine in Samaria on the Mediterranean; Roman capital of Palestine
Ca•glia•ri \ˈkäl-yə-rē\ city Italy, capital of Sardinia
Cai•ro \ˈkī-rō\ city, capital of Egypt — **Cai•rene** \kī-ˈrēn\ *adj or n*
Caith•ness \ˈkāth-nəs\ *or* **Caith•ness–shire** \-nəs-ˌshiər, -nəsh-, -shər\ former county [N] Scotland
Ca•la•bria \kə-ˈlā-brē-ə, -ˈläb-rē-\ **1** district of ancient Italy comprising area forming heel of Italian peninsula; now [S] part of Apulia **2** *or ancient* **Brut•ti•um** \ˈbru̇t-ē-əm, ˈbrət-\ region [S] Italy occupying toe of Italian peninsula; capital, Catanzaro — **Ca•la•bri•an** \kə-ˈlā-brē-ən, -ˈläb-rē-\ *adj or n*
Cal•cut•ta \kal-ˈkət-ə\ city [E] India on Hooghly river, capital of West Bengal — **Cal•cut•tan** \-ˈkət-n\ *adj or n*
Cal•e•do•nia \ˌkal-ə-ˈdō-nyə, -nē-ə\ — see SCOTLAND — **Cal•e•do•nian** \-nyən, -nē-ən\ *adj or n*
Cal•ga•ry \ˈkal-gə-rē\ city [SW] Alberta
Ca•li \ˈkäl-ē\ city [W] Colombia
Cal•i•cut \ˈkal-i-kət\ *also* **Ko•zhi•kode** \ˈkō-zhə-ˌkōd\ city [SW] India
Cal•i•for•nia \ˌkal-ə-ˈfȯr-nyə\ state [SW] U.S.; capital, Sacramento — **Cal•i•for•nian** \-nyən\ *adj or n*
California, Gulf of arm of the Pacific [NW] Mexico
California current cold current of the Pacific ocean flowing [SE] along [W] coast of North America
Ca•llao \kə-ˈyä-ō, kə-ˈyau̇\ city [W] Peru [W] of Lima
Cal•va•ry \ˈkalv-rē, -ə-rē\ *or Hebrew* **Gol•go•tha** \ˈgäl-gə-thə, gäl-ˈgäth-ə\ place outside ancient Jerusalem where Christ was crucified
Ca•ma•güey \ˌkam-ə-ˈgwā\ city [E] central Cuba
Cam•bay, Gulf of \kam-ˈbā\ inlet of Arabian sea India [N] of Bombay
Cam•ber•well \ˈkam-bər-ˌwel, -wəl\ city [SE] Australia in [S] Victoria [E] of Melbourne
Cam•bo•dia \kam-ˈbōd-ē-ə\ — see KHMER REPUBLIC — **Cam•bo•di•an** \-ē-ən\ *adj or n*
Cam•bria \ˈkam-brē-ə\ WALES — an old name
Cam•bridge \ˈkām-brij\ **1** city [E] Massachusetts [W] of Boston **2** city [E] England in Cambridgeshire
Cam•bridge•shire \ˈkām-brij-ˌshiər, -shər\ *or* **Cambridge** *or formerly* **Cambridgeshire and Isle of Ely** \ˈē-lē\ county [E] England
Cam•den \ˈkam-dən\ **1** city [SW] New Jersey **2** borough of [N] Greater London, England
Cam•er•oon *or French* **Cam•er•oun** \ˌkam-ə-ˈrün\ country [W] equatorial Africa; capital, Yaoundé — **Cam•er•oo•nian** \-ˈrü-nē-ən, -ˈrü-nyən\ *adj or n*
Cam•er•oons \ˌkam-ə-ˈrünz\ region [W] Africa on [NE] Gulf of Guinea formerly belonging to the British and French but now divided between Nigeria & Cameroon
Cam•pa•nia \kam-ˈpā-nyə, -nē-ə\ region [S] Italy bordering on Tyrrhenian sea; capital, Naples — **Cam•pa•nian** \-nyən, -nē-ən\ *adj or n*
Cam•pe•che \kam-ˈpē-chē, käm-ˈpā-chā\ state [SE] Mexico in [W] Yucatán peninsula; capital, Campeche
Cam•pi•nas \kam-ˈpē-nəs\ city [SE] Brazil [N] of São Paulo
Cam•pos \ˈkam-pəs\ city [SE] Brazil [NE] of Rio de Janeiro
Ca•naan \ˈkā-nən\ ancient region corresponding vaguely to later Palestine — **Ca•naan•ite** \ˈkā-nə-ˌnīt\ *adj or n*
Can•a•da \ˈkan-ə-də\ country [N] North America; dominion of the British Commonwealth; capital, Ottawa — **Ca•na•di•an** \kə-ˈnād-ē-ən\ *adj or n*
Canadian Shield — see LAURENTIAN HIGHLANDS
Canal Zone *or* **Panama Canal Zone** strip of territory Panama leased to U.S. for Panama canal
Ca•nary \kə-ˈneər-ē\ islands in the Atlantic off [NW] coast of Africa belonging to Spain; capital, Las Palmas
Ca•nav•er•al, Cape \kə-ˈnav-rəl, -ə-rəl\ *or 1963–1973 officially* **Cape Ken•ne•dy** \-ˈken-ə-dē\ headland [E] Florida in the Atlantic on Canaveral peninsula [E] of Indian river
Can•ber•ra \ˈkan-bə-rə, -brə, -ˌber-ə\ city, capital of Australia in Australian Capital Territory
Ca•ni•no \kə-ˈnē-nō\ village & former principality central Italy
Can•ter•bury \ˈkant-ər-ˌber-ē, ˈkant-ə-, -bə-rē, -brē\ **1** city [SE] Australia in [E] New South Wales **2** city [SE] England in Kent
Can•ton \ˈkant-n\ city [NE] Ohio
Can•ton \ˈkan-ˌtän, kan-ˈ\ *or* **Kwang•chow** \ˈgwäŋ-ˈjō\ city [SE] China, capital of Kwangtung

Can•yon•lands National Park \ˈkan-yən-ˌlandz, -ˌlanz\ reservation [SE] Utah

Cape Bret•on Island \kāp-ˌbret-n-, kə-ˌbret-, -ˌbrit-\ island [NE] Nova Scotia

Cape of Good Hope 1 — see GOOD HOPE **2** *or* **Cape Province** *or formerly* **Cape Colony** province [S] Republic of South Africa; capital, Cape Town

Ca•per•na•um \kə-ˈpər-nē-əm\ city of ancient Palestine on [NW] shore of Sea of Galilee

Cape Town *or* **Cape•town** \ˈkāp-ˌtau̇n\ *or* **Kaap•stad** \ˈkäp-ˌstät\ city Republic of South Africa, capital of Cape of Good Hope & legislative capital of Republic

Cape Verde \ˈvərd\ **1** islands in the [N] Atlantic off [W] Africa; a republic; capital, Praia; until 1975 belonged to Portugal **2** — see VERT

Cape York peninsula \ˈyȯrk\ peninsula [NE] Australia in [N] Queensland

Capitol Reef National Park reservation [S] central Utah

Cap•pa•do•cia \ˌkap-ə-ˈdō-shə, -shē-ə\ ancient country & Roman province [E] Asia Minor; capital, Caesarea Mazaca

Ca•pri \ka-ˈprē, kə-; ˈkäp-rē, ˈkap-\ island Italy [S] of Bay of Naples

Ca•ra•cas \kə-ˈrak-əs, -ˈräk-\ city, capital of Venezuela

Car•diff \ˈkärd-əf\ city, capital of Wales in South Glamorgan

Car•di•gan•shire \ˈkärd-i-gən-ˌshiər, -shər\ *or* **Cardigan** former county [W] Wales on Cardigan Bay

Ca•rib•be•an \ˌkar-ə-ˈbē-ən, kə-ˈrib-ē-ən\ sea arm of the Atlantic bounded on [N] & [E] by West Indies, on [S] by South America, & on [W] by Central America

Ca•rin•thia \kə-ˈrin-thē-ə, -ˈrint-\ **1** region central Europe in [E] Alps in [S] Austria & [NW] Yugoslavia **2** region [S] Austria; capital, Klagenfurt

Car•low \ˈkär-ˌlō\ county [SE] Ireland in Leinster

Carls•bad Caverns \ˈkärlz-ˌbad\ limestone caves [SE] New Mexico in **Carlsbad Caverns National Park**

Car•mar•then•shire \kär-ˈmär-thən-ˌshiər, kər-, kə-, -shər\ *or* **Carmarthen** former county [S] Wales

Carmel, Mount \ˈkär-məl\ mountain ridge [N] Israel; highest point about 550 meters

Car•o•li•na \ˌkar-ə-ˈlī-nə\ English colony on [E] coast of North America founded 1663 & divided 1729 into North Carolina & South Carolina (the **Carolinas**) — **Car•o•lin•i•an** \-ˈlin-e-ən\ *adj or n*

Car•o•line \ˈkar-ə-ˌlīn, -lən\ islands [W] Pacific [E] of [S] Philippines; part of Trust Territory of the Pacific Islands

Car•pa•thi•an \kär-ˈpā-thē-ən\ mountains [E] central Europe along boundary between Czechoslovakia & Poland & in [N] & central Rumania; highest Gerlachovka 2663 meters

Carpathian Ruthenia — see RUTHENIA

Car•pen•tar•ia, Gulf of \ˌkär-pən-ˈter-ē-ə, -tar-\ inlet of Arafura sea [N] of Australia

Car•son City \ˈkärs-n\ city, capital of Nevada

Car•ta•ge•na \ˌkärt-ə-ˈgā-nə, -ˈhā-\ **1** city [NW] Colombia **2** city [SE] Spain

Car•thage \ˈkär-thij\ ancient city [N] Africa [NE] of modern Tunis; capital of an empire that included at greatest extent much of [NW] Africa, [E] Spain, & Sicily — **Car•tha•gin•ian** \ˌkär-thə-ˈjin-yən, -ˈjin-ē-ən\ *adj or n*

Ca•sa•blan•ca \ˌkas-ə-ˈblang-kə, ˌkaz-\ *or Arabic* **Dar-al-Bai•da** *or* **Dar el Bei•da** \ˌdär-ˌel-bā-ˈdä\ city [W] Morocco on the Atlantic

Cas•cade Range \kas-ˈkād, ˈkas-ˈkād\ mountains [NW] U.S. in Washington, Oregon, & [N] California — see RAINIER

Cas•pi•an sea \ˈkas-pē-ən\ salt lake between Europe & Asia about 27 meters below sea level

Cas•tile \kas-ˈtēl\ *or Spanish* **Cas•ti•lla** \kä-ˈstē-lyä, -ˈstē-yä\ region & ancient kingdom central & [N] Spain

Cat•a•lo•nia \ˌkat-l-ˈō-nyə, -nē-ə\ *or Spanish* **Ca•ta•lu•ña** \ˌkät-l-ˈü-nyə\ region [NE] Spain bordering on France & the Mediterranean; chief city, Barcelona — **Cat•a•lo•nian** \-ˈō-nyən, -nē-ən\ *adj or n*

Ca•ta•nia \kə-ˈtān-yə, -ˈtän-\ city Italy in [E] Sicily at foot of Mount Etna

Ca•thay \kə-ˈthā, ka-\ CHINA — an old name

Cats•kill \ˈkat-ˌskil\ mountains in Appalachian system [SE] New York [W] of the Hudson

Cau•ca•sus \ˈkȯ-kə-səs\ **1** *or* **Cau•ca•sia** \kȯ-ˈkā-zhə, -shə\ region U.S.S.R. between Black & Caspian seas — see TRANSCAUCASIA **2** mountain system in Caucasia — see ELBRUS

Cav•an \ˈkav-ən\ county [NE] Republic of Ireland in Ulster

Cawnpore — see KANPUR

Cay•enne \kī-ˈen, kā-\ city, capital of French Guiana

Cay•man \kā-ˈman, ˈkā-, *attributively* ˈkā-mən\ islands British West Indies [NW] of Jamaica; a British colony; capital, Georgetown (on Grand Cayman Island)

Ce•bu \sā-ˈbü\ **1** island [E] central Philippines in Visayan islands **2** city on [E] coast of Cebu Island

Ce•dar Rapids \ˈsēd-ər\ city [E] Iowa

Ce•le•bes \ˈsel-ə-ˌbēz, sə-ˈlē-bēz\ *or* **Su•la•we•si** \ˌsü-lə-ˈwā-sē\ island Indonesia [E] of Borneo

Celestial Empire the former Chinese Empire

Cel•le \ˈtsel-ə, ˈsel-ə\ city West Germany [NE] of Hannover

Cel•tic \ˈkel-tik, ˈsel-\ sea inlet of the Atlantic in British Isles [SE] of Ireland, [SW] of Wales, & [W] of Cornwall

Central region central Scotland; established 1975

Central African Empire country [N] central Africa; formerly the French territory of **Uban•gi-Sha•ri** \ü-ˈbang-gē-ˈshär-ē, yü-, -ˈbang-ē-\ & later the **Central African Republic;** capital, Bangui

Central America narrow portion of North America from [S] border of Mexico to South America — **Central American** *adj or n*

Ce•ram *or* **Se•ram** \ˈsā-ˌräm\ island [E] Indonesia in central Moluccas

Cé•vennes \sā-ˈven\ mountain range [S] France [W] of the Rhone in [SE] Massif Central; highest peak Mount Mézenc 1754 meters

Cey•lon \si-ˈlän, sā-\ **1** island in Indian ocean off [S] India **2** — see SRI LANKA — **Cey•lon•ese** \ˌsā-lə-ˈnēz, ˌsē-lə-, ˌsel-ə-, -ˈnēs\ *adj or n*

Chad *or French* **Tchad** \ˈchad\ country [N] central Africa; a republic; capital, Ndjamana — **Chad•ian** \ˈchad-ē-ən\ *adj or n*

Chad, Lake shallow lake [N] central Africa at junction of boundaries of Chad, Niger, & Nigeria

Cha•gos \ˈchä-gəs\ archipelago central Indian ocean; part of British Indian Ocean Territory — see DIEGO GARCIA

Chal•cid•i•ce \kal-ˈsid-ə-sē\ peninsula [NE] Greece in [E] Macedonia

Chal•dea \kal-ˈdē-ə\ ancient region [SW] Asia on Euphrates river & Persian gulf — **Chal•de•an** \-ˈdē-ən\ *adj or n* — **Chal•dee** \ˈkal-ˌdē\ *n*

Champlain, Lake \sham-ˈplān\ lake between New York & Vermont extending [N] into Quebec

Chan•di•garh \ˈchən-dē-gər\ city [N] India [N] of Delhi in Chandigarh Territory, capital of Punjab (Punjabi Suba) & of Haryana

Changan — see SIAN

Ch'ang-chih \ˈchäng-ˈchiər\ *or* **Lu•an** \lü-ˈän\ city [E] China in [S] Shansi

Ch'ang-chou \ˈchäng-ˈjō\ *or* **Wu•tsin** \ˈwü-ˈjin\ city [E] China in [S] Kiangsu [SE] of Nanking

Ch'ang-ch'un \ˈchäng-ˈchün\ city [NE] China, capital of Kirin

Ch'ang-sha \ˈchäng-ˈshä\ city [SE] central China, capital of Hunan

Chang•teh \ˈchäng-ˈdə\ city [SE] central China in [N] Hunan

Channel 1 — see SANTA BARBARA **2** islands in English channel including Jersey, Guernsey, & Alderney & belonging to Great Britain; capital, Saint Helier

Cha•pa•la \chə-ˈpäl-ə\ lake [W] central Mexico [SE] of Guadalajara

Charles \ˈchärlz\ river 76 kilometers long [E] Massachusetts flowing into Boston harbor

Charles, Cape cape [E] Virginia [N] of entrance to Chesapeake Bay

Charles•ton \ˈchärl-stən\ city, capital of West Virginia

Char•lotte \ˈshär-lət\ city [S] North Carolina

Charlotte Ama•lie \ə-ˈmäl-yə\ city, capital of Virgin Islands of the U.S.; on Saint Thomas Island

Char•lotte•town \ˈshär-lət-ˌtau̇n\ city, capital of Prince Edward Island, Canada

Chat•ta•noo•ga \ˌchat-ə-ˈnü-gə, ˌchat-n-ˈü-\ city [SE] Tennessee

Che•bok•sa•ry \ˌcheb-ˌäk-ˈsär-ē\ city U.S.S.R. in central Soviet Russia, Europe, on the Volga [W] of Kazan

Che•kiang \ˈjəj-ē-ˈäng\ province [E] China bordering on East China sea; capital, Hangchow

Chelsea — see KENSINGTON AND CHELSEA

Che•lya•binsk \chel-ˈyä-bənsk\ city U.S.S.R. in [W] Soviet Russia, Asia, [S] of Sverdlovsk

Chemnitz — see KARL-MARX-STADT

Chen–chiang \'jəng-jē-'äng\ *also* **Chin•kiang** \'jin-jē-'äng\ city [E] China in [NW] central Kiangsu

Cheng–chou *or* **Cheng•chow** \'jəng-'jō\ *or* **Cheng•hsien** \'jəng-shē-'en\ city [NE] central China, capital of Honan

Cheng•tu \'chəng-'dü\ city [SW] central China, capital of Szechwan

Chernoye More — see BLACK SEA

Cher•so•nese \'kər-sə-ˌnēz, -ˌnēs\ any of several peninsulas (as the Gallipoli & Crimea peninsulas)

Ches•a•peake Bay \'ches-ˌpēk, -ə-ˌpēk\ inlet of the Atlantic in Virginia & Maryland

Chesh•ire \'chesh-ər, 'chesh-ˌiər\ *or* **Ches•ter** \'ches-tər\ county [W] England bordering on Wales

Chev•i•ot \'chev-ē-ət, 'chē-vē-ət\ hills along English-Scottish border

Chey•enne \shī-'an, -'en\ city, capital of Wyoming

Chia–mu–ssu — see KIAMUSZE

Chia•pas \chē-'äp-əs\ state [SE] Mexico; capital, Tuxtla Gutiérrez

Chi•ba \'chē-bə\ city [E] Japan in Honshu on Tokyo Bay [E] of Tokyo

Chi•ca•go \shə-'käg-ō, -'kȯg-\ city [NE] Illinois — **Chi•ca•go•an** \-'käg-ə-wən, -'kȯg-\ *n*

Chi•chén It•zá \chə-ˌchen-ət-'sä\ ruined Mayan city [SE] Mexico in Yucatán [ESE] of Mérida

Ch'i–ch'i–ha–erh \'chi-'chi-'hä-'eər\ city [NE] China in [W] Heilungkiang

Chihli, Gulf of — see PO HAI

Chi•hua•hua \chə-'wä-wä, shə-, -wə\ **1** state [N] Mexico bordering on U.S. **2** city, its capital

Chile \'chil-ē\ country [SW] South America; capital, Santiago — **Chil•ean** \'chil-ē-ən, chə-'lā-ən\ *adj or n*

Chi–lung \'jē-'lu̇ng\ seaport China [N] Taiwan

Chim•bo•ra•zo \ˌchim-bə-'räz-ō, ˌshim-\ mountain 6267 meters [W] central Ecuador

Chi•na \'chī-nə\ **1** country [E] Asia; capital, Peking — see TAIWAN **2** sea section of the [W] Pacific [E] & [SE] of China; divided at Taiwan strait into **East China** & **South China** seas

Chinan — see TSINAN

Chin–chou *or* **Chin•chow** \'jin-'jō\ city [NE] China in [SW] Liaoning

Chinghai — see TSINGHAI

Ching–te–chen \'jing-'də-'jən\ city [SE] China in [NE] Kiangsi

Chinkiang — see CHEN-CHIANG

Chi•os \'kī-ˌäs\ island Greece in the Aegean off [W] coast of Turkey

Chisinau — see KISHINEV

Chit•ta•gong \'chit-ə-ˌgäng, -ˌgȯng\ city [SE] Bangladesh on Bay of Bengal

Chkalov — see ORENBURG

Chong•ju \'chȯng-ˌjü\ city central South Korea

Chon•ju \'jən-ˌjü\ city [W] South Korea

Cho•sen \'chō-'sen\ KOREA — an old name

Christ•church \'krīs-ˌchərch, 'krīst-\ city New Zealand on [E] coast of South Island

Christ•mas \'kris-məs\ **1** island [E] Indian ocean [SW] of Java administered by Australia **2** island in Line islands; largest atoll in the Pacific; belongs to Great Britain

Chuan–chow \chə-'wän-'jō\ city [SE] China in Fukien on Taiwan strait

Chu•chow *or* **Chu–chou** \'chü-'jō\ city [SE] China in [E] Hunan

Chung•king *or* **Ch'ung–ch'ing** \'chu̇ng-'king\ city [SW] central China in [SE] Szechwan

Ci•li•cia \sə-'lish-ə, -'lish-ē-ə\ ancient country [SE] Asia Minor on coast [S] of Taurus mountains

Cin•cin•na•ti \ˌsin-sə-'nat-ē, -'nat-ə\ city [SW] Ohio

Cis•al•pine Gaul \sis-ˌal-ˌpīn-\ the part of Gaul lying [S] & [E] of the Alps

Ci•tlal•te•petl \sē-ˌtläl-'tā-ˌpet-l\ *or* **Pi•co de Ori•za•ba** \'pē-kō-dā-ˌȯr-ə-'zäb-ə, -ˌȯr-\ inactive volcano 5700 meters [SE] Mexico on Puebla-Veracruz border; highest point in Mexico & third highest in North America

Città del Vaticano — see VATICAN CITY

Ci•u•dad Juá•rez \ˌsē-ü-ˌthä-'hwär-əs, -ü-ˌdad-, -'wär-\ *or* **Juá•rez** \'hwär-əs, 'wär-\ city [N] Mexico in Chihuahua on Rio Grande opposite El Paso, Texas

Ciudad Trujillo — see SANTO DOMINGO

Clack•man•nan \klak-'man-ən\ *or* **Clack•man•nan•shire** \-ˌshiər, -shər\ former county central Scotland

Clare \'klaər, 'kleər\ county [W] Ireland in Munster

Cler•mont–Fer•rand \ˌkler-ˌmōⁿ-fə-'räⁿ\ city [S] central France

Cleve•land \'klēv-lənd\ **1** city [NE] Ohio **2** county [N] England [N] of North Yorkshire

Clwyd \'klüid\ county [NE] Wales; established 1974

Clyde \'klīd\ river 171 kilometers long [SW] Scotland flowing into **Firth of Clyde** (estuary)

Clydes•dale \'klīdz-ˌdāl\ valley of upper Clyde, Scotland

Cnossus — see KNOSSOS

Coa•hui•la \ˌkō-ə-'wē-lə, kwä-'wē-\ state [N] Mexico bordering on U.S.; capital, Saltillo

Coast mountains mountain range [W] British Columbia; the [N] continuation of Cascade range

Coast ranges chain of mountain ranges [W] North America extending along Pacific coast [W] of Sierra Nevada & Cascade range & through Vancouver Island into [S] Alaska to Kenai peninsula & Kodiak Island

Co•cha•bam•ba \ˌkō-chə-'bäm-bə\ city [W] central Bolivia

Co•chin China \ˌkō-chən-\ region [S] Vietnam

Cod, Cape \'käd\ peninsula [SE] Massachusetts

Coim•ba•tore \ˌkȯim-bə-'tōr, -'tȯr\ city [S] India in [W] Tamil Nadu

Col•chis \'käl-kəs\ ancient country bordering on Black sea [S] of Caucasus mountains; district now in [W] Georgia, U.S.S.R.

Co•li•ma \kə-'lē-mə\ **1** state [SW] Mexico **2** city, its capital

Co•logne \kə-'lōn\ *or German* **Köln** \'kœln\ city West Germany on the Rhine

Co•lom•bia \kə-'ləm-bē-ə\ country [NW] South America; capital, Bogotá — **Co•lom•bi•an** \-bē-ən\ *adj or n*

Co•lom•bo \kə-'ləm-bō\ city, capital of Sri Lanka

Co•lón \kə-'lōn\ city Panama on the Caribbean

Colón archipelago — see GALAPAGOS ISLANDS

Col•o•ra•do \ˌkäl-ə-'rad-ō, -'räd-\ **1** river 2335 kilometers long [SW] U.S. & [NW] Mexico flowing from [N] Colorado into Gulf of California **2** desert [SE] California **3** plateau region [SW] U.S. [W] of Rocky mountains **4** state [W] U.S.; capital, Denver — **Col•o•rad•an** \-'rad-n, -'räd-n\ *or* **Co•lo•ra•do•an** \-'rad-ə-wən, -'räd-\ *adj or n*

Colorado Springs city central Colorado

Co•lum•bia \kə-'ləm-bē-ə\ **1** river 2045 kilometers long [SW] Canada & [NW] U.S. rising in [SE] British Columbia & flowing [S] & [W] into the Pacific **2** plateau in Columbia river basin in [E] Washington, [E] Oregon, & [SW] Idaho **3** city, capital of South Carolina **4** — see UNITED STATES OF AMERICA

Co•lum•bus \kə-'ləm-bəs\ **1** city [W] Georgia **2** city, capital of Ohio

Commonwealth of Nations — see BRITISH COMMONWEALTH

Communism Peak — see GARMO PEAK

Co•mo, Lake \'kō-mō\ lake [N] Italy in Lombardy

Com•o•ro \'käm-ə-ˌrō\ islands off [SE] Africa [NW] of Madagascar; formerly a French possession; a republic (except for Mayotte Island remaining French) since 1975; capital, Moroni

Com•stock lode \ˌkäm-ˌstäk-\ gold & silver deposit at Virginia City, Nevada, discovered 1859

Con•a•kry *or* **Kon•a•kry** \'kän-ə-krē\ city, capital of Guinea

Con•cord \'käng-kərd\ **1** city, capital of New Hampshire **2** town [E] Massachusetts [NW] of Boston

Con•go \'käng-gō\ **1** *or* **Zaire** \'zīr, zä-'iər\ river 4830 kilometers long [W] equatorial Africa flowing into the Atlantic **2** — see ZAIRE **3** *or formerly* **Middle Congo** country [W] central Africa [W] of lower Congo river; capital, Brazzaville — **Con•go•lese** \ˌkäng-gə-'lēz, -'lēs\ *adj or n*

Con•nacht \'kän-ˌȯt\ province [W] Ireland

Con•nect•i•cut \kə-'net-i-kət\ **1** river 655 kilometers long [NE] U.S. flowing [S] from [N] New Hampshire into Long Island Sound **2** state [NE] U.S.; capital, Hartford

Con•stan•tine \'kän-stən-ˌtēn\ city [NE] Algeria

Constantinople — see ISTANBUL

Con•stan•tsa \kən-'stän-sə, -'stänt-\ city [SE] Rumania

Cook \'ku̇k\ **1** inlet of the Pacific [S] Alaska [W] of Kenai peninsula **2** islands [S] Pacific [SW] of Society islands belonging to New Zealand; capital, Avarua (on Rarotonga Island) **3** strait New Zealand between North Island & South Island

Cook, Mount *or formerly* **Ao•rangi** \au̇-'räng-ē\ mountain 3764 meters New Zealand in [W] central South Island in Southern Alps; highest in New Zealand

Co•pen•ha•gen \ˌkō-pən-'hā-gən, -'häg-ən\ city, capital of Denmark

Coquilhatville — see MBANDAKA

Cor•al \'kȯr-əl, 'kär-\ sea arm of the [W] Pacific [NE] of Australia
Cór•do•ba \'kȯrd-ə-bə, -ə-və\ **1** *or* **Cor•do•va** \'kȯrd-ə-və\ *or ancient* **Cor•du•ba** \'kȯrd-yə-bə, 'kȯrd-ü-bə\ city [S] Spain on the Guadalquivir **2** city [N] central Argentina
Cor•fu \kȯr-'fü; 'kȯr-,fü, -,fyü\ island [NW] Greece in Ionian islands
Cor•inth \'kȯr-ənth, 'kär-, -ənth\ **1** region of ancient Greece occupying most of Isthmus of Corinth & part of [NE] Peloponnesus **2** ancient city, its capital; site [SW] of present city of Corinth — **Co•rin•thi•an** \kə-'rin-thē-ən, -'rint-\ *adj or n*
Corinth, Gulf of inlet of Ionian sea central Greece [N] of the Peloponnesus
Corinth, Isthmus of neck of land connecting the Peloponnesus with rest of Greece
Cork \'kȯrk\ **1** county [S] Ireland in Munster **2** city [S] Ireland in County Cork
Corn•wall \'kȯrn-,wȯl, -wəl\ *or since 1974* **Cornwall and Isles of Scil•ly** \'sil-ē\ county [SW] England
Cor•o•man•del \,kȯr-ə-'man-dl, ,kär-\ coast region [SE] India on Bay of Bengal [S] of Krishna (Kistna) delta
Cor•pus Chris•ti \,kȯr-pə-'skris-tē\ city [S] Texas
Cor•reg•i•dor \kə-'reg-ə-,dȯr\ island Philippines at entrance to Manila Bay
Cor•si•ca \'kȯr-si-kə\ *or French* **Corse** \kȯrs\ island France in the Mediterranean [N] of Sardinia — **Cor•si•can** \'kȯr-si-kən\ *adj or n*
Cos•ta Bra•va \,käs-tə-'bräv-ə, ,kȯs-, ,kōs-\ coast region [NE] Spain on the Mediterranean extending [NE] from Barcelona
Costa del Sol \-del-'sȯl, -'sōl\ coast region [S] Spain on the Mediterranean extending [E] from Gibraltar
Cos•ta Ri•ca \,käs-tə-'rē-kə, ,kȯs-, ,kōs-\ country Central America between Nicaragua & Panama; a republic; capital, San José — **Cos•ta Ri•can** \-'rē-kən\ *adj or n*
Côte d'A•zur \,kōt-də-'zür\ region [SE] France on Mediterranean coast; part of the Riviera
Côte d'Ivoire — see IVORY COAST
Co•to•nou \,kōt-ə-'nü\ city [S] Benin
Cots•wold \'kät-,swōld\ hills [SW] central England in Gloucestershire
Cov•en•try \'käv-ən-trē, 'kəv-\ city central England in West Midlands
Co•zu•mel \,kō-zə-'mel\ island [SE] Mexico off [NE] coast of Quintana Roo
Cracow — see KRAKOW
Cra•io•va \krə-'yō-və\ city [S] Rumania
Cra•ter \'krāt-ər\ lake [SW] Oregon in Cascade range; main feature of **Crater Lake National Park** — see MAZAMA
Crete \'krēt\ island Greece in [E] Mediterranean; capital, Canea — **Cre•tan** \'krēt-n\ *adj or n*
Cri•mea \krī-'mē-ə, krə-\ peninsula U.S.S.R. in [S] Soviet Russia, Europe, extending into Black sea — **Cri•me•an** \krī-'mē-ən, krə-\ *adj*
Cro•atia \krō-'ā-shə, -shē-ə\ **1** region [SE] Europe in [N] Yugoslavia **2** constituent republic of Yugoslavia comprising Croatia, Slavonia, & most of Istria & the Dalmatian coast; capital, Zagreb
Croy•don \'krȯid-n\ borough of [S] Greater London, England
Cu•ba \'kyü-bə\ island in the West Indies; a republic; capital, Havana — **Cu•ban** \-bən\ *adj or n*
Cú•cu•ta \'kü-kət-ə\ city [N] Colombia
Cu•lia•cán \,kül-yə-'kän\ city [NW] Mexico, capital of Sinaloa
Cu•ma•ná \,kü-mə-'nä\ city [NE] Venezuela
Cum•ber•land \'kəm-bər-lənd\ former county [NW] England — see CUMBRIA
Cumberland plateau *or* **Cumberland mountains** mountain region [E] U.S.; part of [S] Appalachian mountains [W] of Tennessee river extending from [S] West Virginia to [NE] Alabama
Cum•bria \'kəm-brē-ə\ county [NW] England including former counties of Cumberland & Westmorland — **Cum•bri•an** \-ən\ *adj or n*
Cumbrian mountains [NW] England chiefly in Cumbria
Cu•ra•çao \'kür-ə-,sō, 'kyür-, -,saù\ island Netherlands Antilles in the [S] Caribbean; chief town, Willemstad
Cu•ri•ti•ba \,kür-ə-'tē-bə\ city [S] Brazil [SW] of São Paulo
Cush \'kəsh, 'kùsh\ ancient country [NE] Africa in upper Nile valley [S] of Egypt — **Cush•ite** \-,īt\ *n* — **Cush•it•ic** \,kəsh-'it-ik, kùsh-\ *adj*
Cut•tack \'kət-ək\ city [E] India in Orissa
Cyc•la•des \'sik-lə-,dēz\ islands Greece in [S] Aegean
Cymru — see WALES
Cy•prus \'sī-prəs\ island [E] Mediterranean [S] of Turkey; a republic of British Commonwealth; capital, Nicosia — **Cyp•ri•ot** \'sip-rē-ət, -rē-,ät\ *or* **Cyp•ri•ote** \-,ōt, -ət\ *adj or n*
Cy•re•na•ica \,sir-ə-'nā-ə-kə, ,sī-rə-\ **1** ancient region [N] Africa on coast [W] of Egypt; capital, Cyrene **2** region [E] Libya; formerly a province — **Cy•re•na•i•can** \-kən\ *adj or n*
Czecho•slo•va•kia \,chek-ə-slō-'väk-ē-ə, -'vak-\ country central Europe; a republic; capital, Prague — **Czecho•slo•vak** \-'slō-,väk, -,vak\ *adj or n* — **Czecho•slo•va•ki•an** \-slō-'väk-ē-ən, -'vak-\ *adj or n*
Cze•sto•cho•wa \,chen-stə-'kō-və\ city [S] Poland
Dac•ca \'dak-ə, 'däk-ə\ city, capital of Bangladesh
Da•cia \'dā-shə, -shē-ə\ ancient country & Roman province [SE] Europe roughly equivalent to Rumania & Bessarabia
Da•ho•mey \də-'hō-mē\ — see BENIN — **Da•ho•man** \-mən\ *or* **Da•ho•me•an** *or* **Da•ho•mey•an** \-mē-ən\ *adj or n*
Daihoku — see TAIPEI
Dai•ren \'dī-'ren\ city [NE] China in [S] Liaoning — see LÜTA
Da•kar \'dak-,är, də-'kär\ city, capital of Senegal
Da•ko•ta Territory \də-'kōt-ə\ territory 1861–89 [NW] U.S. divided 1889 into states of North Dakota & South Dakota (the **Da•ko•tas**)
Dal•las \'dal-əs, 'da-lis\ city [NE] Texas
Dal•ma•tia \dal-'mā-shə, -shē-ə\ region [W] Yugoslavia on the Adriatic — **Dal•ma•tian** \-shən\ *adj or n*
Da•mas•cus \də-'mas-kəs\ city, capital of Syria
Da•ma•vand \'dam-ə-,vand\ *or* **Dem•a•vend** \'dem-ə-,vend\ mountain 5771 meters [N] Iran [NE] of Tehran
Da Nang \dä-'näng, 'dä-\ *or formerly* **Tou•rane** \tü-'rän\ city [S] Vietnam in Annam [SE] of Hue
Dan•ube \'dan-yüb\ *or German* **Do•nau** \'dō-,naù\ river 2776 kilometers long [S] Europe flowing from [S] Germany into Black sea — **Da•nu•bi•an** \da-'nyü-bē-ən\ *adj*
Danzig — see GDANSK
Dar–al–Baida — see CASABLANCA
Dar•da•nelles \,därd-n-'elz\ *or* **Hel•les•pont** \'hel-ə-,spänt\ strait [NW] Turkey connecting Sea of Marmara & the Aegean
Dar el Beida — see CASABLANCA
Dar es Sa•laam \,där-,es-sə-'läm\ city, capital of Tanzania
Darien, Isthmus of — see PANAMA
Dar•ling \'där-ling\ river 1865 kilometers long [SE] Australia in Queensland & New South Wales flowing [SW] into the Murray
Dar•win \'där-wən\ city Australia, capital of Northern Territory
Da•vao \'däv-,aù, dä-'vaù\ city [S] Philippines in [E] Mindanao on Davao Gulf
Da•vis \'dā-vəs\ strait between [SW] Greenland & [E] Baffin Island connecting Baffin Bay & the Atlantic
Day•ton \'dāt-n\ city [SW] Ohio
Dead sea \'ded\ salt lake between Israel & Jordan; 397 meters below sea level
Dear•born \'diər-,bȯrn, -bərn\ city [SE] Michigan [SW] of Detroit
Death Valley \'deth\ arid valley [E] California & [S] Nevada containing lowest point in U.S. (86 meters below sea level); most of area included in **Death Valley National Monument**
De•bre•cen \'deb-rət-,sen\ city [E] Hungary
Dec•can \'dek-ən, -,an\ plateau region [S] India
Del•a•ware \'del-ə-,waər, -,weər, -wər\ **1** river 476 kilometers long [E] U.S. flowing [S] from [S] New York into Delaware Bay **2** state [E] U.S.; capital, Dover — **Del•a•war•ean** *or* **Del•a•war•ian** \,del-ə-'war-ē-ən, -'wer-\ *adj or n*
Delaware Bay inlet of the Atlantic between [SW] New Jersey & [E] Delaware
Del•hi \'del-ē\ **1** territory [N] India [W] of Uttar Pradesh **2** city, its capital — see NEW DELHI
De•los \'dē-,läs\ island Greece in central Cyclades — **De•lian** \'dē-lē-ən, 'dēl-yən\ *adj or n*
Del•phi \'del-,fī\ ancient town central Greece in Phocis on [S] slope of Mount Parnassus
Denali — see MCKINLEY
Den•bigh•shire \'den-bē-,shiər, -shər\ *or* **Denbigh** former county [N] Wales
Den•mark \'den-,märk\ country [N] Europe occupying most of Jutland & adjacent islands; capital, Copenhagen
Den•ver \'den-vər\ city, capital of Colorado
Der•by \'där-bē, *chiefly in the United States* 'dər-bē\ borough [N] central England in Derbyshire
Der•by•shire \'där-bē-,shiər, -shər, *United States also* 'dər-\ *or* **Derby** county [N] central England

Derry — see LONDONDERRY
Des Moines \di-'mȯin\ city, capital of Iowa
De•troit \di-'trȯit\ **1** river 50 kilometers long between SE Michigan & Ontario connecting Lakes Saint Clair & Erie **2** city SE Michigan
Dev•on \'dev-ən\ *or* **De•von•shire** \-ˌshiər, -shər\ county SW England
Dhau•la•gi•ri, Mount \ˌdau̇-lə-'giər-ē\ mountain 8172 meters W central Nepal in the Himalayas
Di•e•go Gar•cia \dē-ˌā-gō-ˌgär-'sē-ə\ island in Indian ocean; chief island of Chagos archipelago in British Indian Ocean Territory
Di•jon \dē-zhōⁿ\ city E France N of Lyons
Di•nar•ic Alps \də-ˌnar-ik-\ range of the E Alps in W Yugoslavia
Diospolis — see THEBES
District of Co•lum•bia \kə-'ləm-bē-ə\ federal district E U.S. coextensive with city of Washington
Djakarta — see JAKARTA
Djeddah — see JIDDA
Dji•bou•ti *or* **Ji•bu•ti** \jə-'büt-ē\ **1** *or formerly* **French Somaliland** *or later* **French Territory of the Afars** \'äf-ˌär, -ˌärz\ **and the Is•sas** \ē-'sä, -'säz\ republic E Africa on Gulf of Aden **2** city, its capital
Dne•pro•pe•trovsk \ˌnep-rō-pə-'trȯfsk\ city U.S.S.R. in E central Ukraine
Dnie•per \'nē-pər\ river 2255 kilometers long U.S.S.R. flowing from Valdai hills into Black sea
Dnies•ter \'nēs-tər\ river 1365 kilometers long U.S.S.R. flowing SE from the Carpathians into Black sea
Do•dec•a•nese \dō-'dek-ə-ˌnēz, 'dō-di-kə-, -ˌnēs\ islands Greece in the SE Aegean — see RHODES
Do•ha \'dō-hä\ city & port, capital of Qatar on Persian Gulf
Do•lo•mites \'dō-lə-ˌmīts, 'däl-ə-\ *or Italian* **Do•lo•mi•ti** \ˌdȯ-lə-'mēt-ē\ range of the E Alps in NE Italy
Dom•i•ni•ca \ˌdäm-ə-'nē-kə\ island British West Indies in the Leewards; capital, Roseau
Do•min•i•can Republic \də-ˌmin-i-kən-\ *or formerly* **San•to Do•min•go** \ˌsant-əd-ə-'miŋ-gō\ country West Indies in E Hispaniola; a republic; capital, Santo Domingo — **Do•min•i•can** \də-'min-i-kən\ *adj or n*
Don \'dän\ river 1930 kilometers long U.S.S.R in SW Soviet Russia, Europe, flowing into Sea of Azov
Donau — see DANUBE
Don•e•gal \ˌdän-i-'gȯl, ˌdən-\ county NW Republic of Ireland in Ulster
Do•nets basin \də-ˌnets-\ *or Russian* **Do•net•ski Bas•sein** \d[illegible]n-ˌyet-skē-bäs-'yān\ *or* **Don•bass** *or* **Don•bas** \'dän-ˌbas\ region U.S.S.R. in E Ukraine SW of Donets river
Do•netsk \də-'netsk\ city U.S.S.R. in E Ukraine in Donets basin
Dor•set \'dȯr-sət\ *or* **Dor•set•shire** \-ˌshiər, -shər\ county S England on English channel
Dort•mund \'dȯrt-ˌmu̇nt, -mənd\ city West Germany in the Ruhr
Dou•a•la *or* **Du•a•la** \du̇-'äl-ə\ city SW Cameroon
Doug•las \'dəg-ləs\ town Great Britain, capital of Isle of Man
Dou•ro \'dōr-ü, 'dȯr-\ *or Spanish* **Due•ro** \'dweər-ō\ *or ancient* **Du•ri•us** \'du̇r-ē-əs, 'dyu̇r-\ river 780 kilometers long N Spain & N Portugal flowing into the Atlantic
Do•ver \'dō-vər\ **1** city, capital of Delaware **2** borough SE England in Kent on Strait of Dover
Dover, Strait of channel between SE England & N France; the most easterly section of English channel
Down \'dau̇n\ county SE Northern Ireland
Dra•kens•berg \'dräk-ənz-ˌbərg\ mountain range E Republic of South Africa & Lesotho; highest peak Thabana Ntlenyana 3482 meters
Dres•den \'drez-dən\ city East Germany in Saxony
Dub•lin \'dəb-lən\ *or Gaelic* **Bai•le Atha Cli•ath** \blä-'klē-ə\ *or ancient* **Eb•la•na** \'eb-lə-nə\ **1** county E Ireland in Leinster **2** city, capital of Republic of Ireland in County Dublin
Dud•ley \'dəd-lē\ borough W central England in West Midlands
Duis•burg \'dü-əs-ˌbərg; 'düz-ˌbərg, 'dyüz-; *German* 'dw̅ēs-ˌbu̇rk\ city West Germany at junction of Rhine & Ruhr rivers
Du•luth \də-'lüth\ city NE Minnesota
Dum•fries \ˌdəm-'frēs\ *or* **Dum•fries•shire** \-'frēs-ˌshiər, -'frēsh-, -shər\ former county S Scotland; incorporated 1975 in **Dumfries and Gal•lo•way** \-'gal-ə-ˌwā\ region
Dun•bar•ton \ˌdən-'bärt-n\ *or* **Dun•bar•ton•shire** \-ˌshiər, -shər\ *or* **Dum•bar•ton** \ˌdəm-\ *or* **Dum•bar•ton•shire** \ˌdəm-\ former county W central Scotland
Dun•dee \ˌdən-'dē\ city E Scotland in Tayside
Dun•edin \ˌdə-'nēd-n\ city New Zealand in SE South Island
Du•que de Ca•xi•as \ˌdü-kə-də-kə-'shē-əs\ city SE Brazil NW of Rio de Janeiro
Du•ran•go \du̇-'raŋ-gō, dyu̇-\ **1** state NW central Mexico **2** city, its capital
Dur•ban \'dər-bən\ city E Republic of South Africa in E Natal
Dur•ham \'dər-əm, 'də-rəm, 'du̇r-əm\ county N England on North sea
Du•shan•be \dü-'sham-bē, dyü-, -'shäm-\ city U.S.S.R., capital of Tadzhikistan
Düs•sel•dorf \'düs-əl-ˌdȯrf, 'dyüs-, 'dæs-\ city West Germany, capital of North Rhine-Westphalia
Dutch Borneo — see KALIMANTAN
Dutch East Indies — see NETHERLANDS EAST INDIES
Dutch Guiana — see SURINAM
Dy•fed \'dəv-ed, -əd\ county SW Wales; established 1974
Dzaudzhikau — see ORDZHONIKIDZE
Ea•ling \'ē-liŋ\ borough of W Greater London, England
East An•glia \'aŋ-glē-ə\ region E England including Norfolk & Suffolk
East Bengal the part of Bengal now in Bangladesh
East China sea — see CHINA
Eas•ter \'ē-stər\ island SE Pacific 3220 kilometers W of Chilean coast; belongs to Chile
Eastern Ghats \'gȯts\ chain of low mountains SE India along coast
Eastern Samoa — see AMERICAN SAMOA
East Germany the German Democratic Republic — see GERMANY
East Indies the Malay archipelago — **East Indian** *adj or n*
East London city S Republic of South Africa in SE Cape of Good Hope province
East Lo•thi•an \'lō-t͟hē-ən\ former county SE Scotland — see LOTHIAN
East Pakistan the former E division of Pakistan comprising E portion of Bengal; now the independent republic of Bangladesh
East Prussia region N Europe on the Baltic; formerly a part of Germany; since 1945 divided between Poland & U.S.S.R.
East Ri•ding \'rīd-iŋ\ former administrative county N England in SE Yorkshire
East river strait SE New York connecting upper New York Bay & Long Island Sound & separating Manhattan Island and Long Island
East Sus•sex \-'səs-iks, *United States also* -ˌeks\ county SE England
Eblana — see DUBLIN
Ebro \'ā-brō\ river 775 kilometers long NE Spain flowing into the Mediterranean
Eca•te•pec de Mo•re•los \ā-ˌkät-ə-'pek-də-mȯ-'rāl-əs\ city central Mexico in Mexico state
Ec•ua•dor \'ek-wə-ˌdȯr\ country W South America; a republic; capital, Quito — **Ec•ua•dor•an** \ˌek-wə-'dȯr-ən, -'dōr-\ *or* **Ec•ua•dor•ean** *or* **Ec•ua•dor•ian** \-ē-ən\ *adj or n*
Ede \'ā-ˌdā\ city SW Nigeria
Ed•in•burgh \'ed-n-ˌbər-ə, -ˌbə-rə, -bə-rə, -brə\ city, capital of Scotland
Ed•mon•ton \'ed-mən-tən\ city, capital of Alberta
Edom \'ēd-əm\ *or* **Id•u•maea** *or* **Id•u•mea** \ˌij-ə-'mē-ə\ ancient country SW Asia S of Judea & Dead sea — **Edom•ite** \'ēd-ə-ˌmīt\ *n*
Egypt \'ē-jəpt\ country NE Africa & Sinai peninsula of SW Asia bordering on Mediterranean & Red seas; capital, Cairo
Eire — see IRELAND
Elam \'ē-ləm\ ancient country SW Asia at head of Persian gulf E of Babylonia; capital, Susa (Shushan) — **Elam•ite** \'ē-lə-ˌmīt\ *n*
El•ba \'el-bə\ island Italy E of N Corsica off coast of Tuscany; chief town, Portoferraio
Elbe \'el-bə, 'elb\ *or Czech* **La•be** \'lä-be\ *or ancient* **Al•bis** \'al-bəs\ river 1160 kilometers long NW Czechoslovakia & N Germany flowing NW into North sea
El•bert, Mount \'el-bərt\ mountain 4399 meters W central Colorado; highest in Colorado & the Rocky mountains
El•brus \el-'brüz\ mountain 5633 meters U.S.S.R. in NW Caucasus mountains

El•burz \el-'bu̇rz\ mountains [N] Iran — see DEMAVEND
Elis \'ē-ləs\ ancient country in [NW] Peloponnesus, Greece
Elisabethville — see LUBUMBASHI
Eliz•a•beth \i-'liz-ə-bəth\ city [NE] New Jersey on Newark Bay
Ellás — see GREECE
Elles•mere \'elz-ˌmiər\ island [N] Canada in Franklin District of Northwest Territories
Ellice — see TUVALU
El Paso \el-'pas-ō\ city [W] Texas on Rio Grande
El Sal•va•dor \el-'sal-və-ˌdȯr, -ˌsal-və-'\ country Central America bordering on the Pacific; capital, San Salvador
Elsass — see ALSACE
Ely, Isle of \'ē-lē\ district [E] England in Cambridgeshire — see CAMBRIDGE
Emi•lia-Ro•ma•gna \ā-ˌmēl-yə-rō-'män-yə\ region [N] Italy on the Adriatic [S] of the Po; capital, Bologna
En•field \'en-ˌfēld\ borough of [N] Greater London, England
En•gland \'ing-glənd *also* ing-lənd\ country [S] Great Britain; a division of United Kingdom; capital, London
English channel arm of the Atlantic between [S] England & [N] France
En•se•na•da \ˌen-sə-'näd-ə\ city [NW] Mexico in Baja California Norte
Ephra•im \'ē-frē-əm\ **1** hilly region [N] Jordan [E] of River Jordan **2** — see ISRAEL — **Ephra•im•ite** \'ē-frē-ə-ˌmīt\ *n*
Epi•rus \i-'pī-rəs\ *or Greek* **Epei•ros** \'ē-pē-ˌrȯs\ region [NW] Greece on Ionian sea
Equatorial Guinea *or formerly* **Spanish Guinea** country [W] Africa on Bight of Biafra including Río Muni & Fernando Po; a republic; capital, Malabo
Ere•bus, Mount \'er-ə-bəs\ volcano 3795 meters Antarctica on Ross Island in [SW] Ross sea
Erevan *or* **Erivan** — see YEREVAN
Er•furt \'eər-fərt, -ˌfu̇rt\ city East Germany [WSW] of Leipzig
Erie \'iər-ē\ **1** city [NW] Pennsylvania **2** canal New York between Hudson river at Albany & Lake Erie at Buffalo; built 1817–25; now superseded by New York State Barge Canal
Erie, Lake lake [E] central North America in U.S. & Canada; one of the Great Lakes
Er•in \'er-ən\ IRELAND
Er•i•trea \ˌer-ə-'trē-ə, -'trā-\ region [N] Ethiopia on Red sea; capital, Asmara
Er•na•ku•lam \er-'näk-ə-ləm\ city [SW] India in central Kerala
Er Rif *or* **Er Riff** \er-'rif\ mountain region [N] Morocco on Mediterranean coast [E] of Strait of Gibraltar
Erz•ge•bir•ge \'erts-gə-ˌbir-gə\ or **Ore mountains** mountains [E] central Germany & [NW] Czechoslovakia
Escaut — see SCHELDT
Esfahan — see ISFAHAN
Es•ki•se•hir \ˌes-ki-shə-'hiər\ city [W] central Turkey
España — see SPAIN
Española — see HISPANIOLA
Es•sen \'es-ⁿn\ city West Germany in the Ruhr
Es•sex \'es-iks\ county [SE] England on North sea
Es•to•nia \e-'stō-nē-ə, -nyə\ country [E] Europe on Baltic sea; since 1940 a constituent republic (**Estonian Republic**) of U.S.S.R.; capital, Tallinn
Ethi•o•pia \ˌē-thē-'ō-pē-ə\ **1** ancient country [NE] Africa [S] of Egypt **2** *or* **Ab•ys•sin•ia** \ˌab-ə-'sin-yə, -'sin-ē-ə\ country [E] Africa; a republic since 1975; capital, Addis Ababa
Et•na \'et-nə\ volcano 3323 meters Italy in [NE] Sicily
Etru•ria \i-'tru̇r-ē-ə\ ancient country central Italy coextensive with modern Tuscany & part of Umbria
Eu•boea \yu̇-'bē-ə\ island [E] Greece [NE] of Attica & Boeotia
Eu•phra•tes \yu̇-'frāt-ēz\ river 2735 kilometers long [SW] Asia flowing from [E] Turkey & uniting with the Tigris to form the Shatt-al-Arab
Eur•asia \yu̇-'rā-zhə, -shə\ landmass comprising Europe & Asia — **Eur•asian** \-zhən, -shən\ *adj or n*
Eu•rope \'yu̇r-əp\ continent of the eastern hemisphere between Asia & the Atlantic
Ev•ans•ville \'ev-ənz-ˌvil\ city [SW] Indiana
Ev•er•est, Mount \'ev-rəst, -ə-rəst\ mountain 8848 meters [S] Asia in the Himalayas on border between Nepal & Tibet; highest in the world
Ev•er•glades \'ev-ər-ˌglādz\ swamp region [S] Florida now partly drained; [SW] part forms **Everglades National Park**
Eyre, Lake \'aər, 'eər\ intermittent lake central Australia in [N] South Australia

Faer•oe *or* **Far•oe** \'faər-ō, 'feər-\ islands [NE] Atlantic [NW] of the Shetlands belonging to Denmark; capital, Thorshavn — **Faero•ese** \ˌfar-ə-'wēz, ˌfer-, -'wēs\ *adj or n*
Falk•land \'fȯ-klənd, 'fȯl-\ *or Spanish* **Is•las Mal•vi•nas** \ˌēz-läz-mäl-'vē-näs\ islands [SW] Atlantic [E] of [S] end of Argentina; a British colony; capital, Stanley
Far East the countries of [E] Asia & the Malay archipelago — usually considered as comprising the Asian countries bordering on the Pacific but sometimes as including also India, Sri Lanka, Bangladesh, Tibet, & Burma — **Far Eastern** *adj*
Far•go \'fär-gō\ city [E] North Dakota; largest in state
Fear, Cape \'fiər\ cape [SE] North Carolina at mouth of Cape Fear river
Federated Malay States former British protectorate (1895–1945) comprising states of Negri Sembilan, Pahang, Perak, and Selangor; now part of Federation of Malaysia
Fengtien — see MUKDEN
Fer•man•agh \fər-'man-ə\ county [SW] Northern Ireland
Fer•nan•do Po *or* **Fernando Poo** \fər-ˌnan-dō-'pō\ island Equatorial Guinea in Bight of Biafra
Fer•ra•ra \fə-'rär-ə\ city [N] Italy [NE] of Bologna
Fez \'fez\ *or* **Fès** \'fes\ city [N] central Morocco
Fife \'fīf\ *or* **Fife•shire** \-ˌshiər, -shər\ region [E] Scotland; until 1975 a county
Fi•ji \'fē-jē\ islands [SW] Pacific; a dominion of British Commonwealth; capital, Suva — **Fi•ji•an** \-jē-ən\ *adj or n*
Fin•is•terre, Cape \ˌfin-ə-'steər, -'ster-ē\ cape [NW] Spain
Fin•land \'fin-lənd\ *or Finnish* **Suo•mi** \'swȯ-mē\ *or* **Suo•men Ta•sa•val•ta** \'swȯ-mən-'tas-ə-ˌval-tə\ country [NE] Europe on gulfs of Bothnia and Finland; a republic; capital, Helsinki — **Fin•land•er** \'fin-lənd-ər\ *n*
Finland, Gulf of arm of the Baltic between Finland & Estonia
Fiume — see RIJEKA
Flan•ders \'flan-dərz\ region [W] Belgium & [N] France on North sea
Flat•tery, Cape \'flat-ə-rē\ cape [NW] Washington at entrance to Juan de Fuca strait
Flint \'flint\ city [SE] Michigan
Flint•shire \'flint-ˌshiər, -shər\ *or* **Flint** former county [NE] Wales
Flor•ence \'flȯr-əns, 'flär-\ *or Italian* **Fi•ren•ze** \fē-'rent-sā\ *or ancient* **Flo•ren•tia** \flə-'ren-chə, -chē-ə\ city central Italy, capital of Tuscany — **Flor•en•tine** \'flȯr-ən-ˌtēn, 'flär-, -ˌtīn\ *adj or n*
Flo•res \'flōr-əs, 'flȯr-\ island Indonesia in Lesser Sunda islands
Flo•ri•a•nó•po•lis \ˌflōr-ē-ə-'näp-ə-ləs, ˌflȯr-\ city [S] Brazil on an island [NE] of Pôrto Alegre
Flor•i•da \'flȯr-əd-ə, 'flär-\ state [SE] U.S.; capital, Tallahassee — **Flo•rid•i•an** \flə-'rid-ē-ən\ *or* **Flor•i•dan** \'flȯr-əd-ⁿn, 'flär-\ *adj or n*
Florida, Straits of channel between Florida Keys on [NW] & Cuba & Bahamas on [S] & [E] connecting Gulf of Mexico & the Atlantic
Florida Keys chain of islands off [S] tip of Florida
Fog•gia \'fȯ-jə, -jä\ city [SE] Italy in Apulia
Foo•chow *or* **Fu•chau** \'fü-'jō, -'chau̇\ *or formerly* **Min•how** \'min-'hō\ city [SE] China, capital of Fukien
For•a•ker, Mount \'fȯr-i-kər, 'fär-\ mountain 5304 meters [S] central Alaska in Alaska range
For•mo•sa \fȯr-'mō-sə, fər-, -zə\ — see TAIWAN — **For•mo•san** \-sən, -zən\ *adj or n*
For•ta•le•za \ˌfȯrt-ˡl-'ā-zə\ city [NE] Brazil [NW] of Recife
Fort-de-France \ˌfȯrd-ə-'fräⁿs\ city French West Indies, capital of Martinique on [W] coast
Forth \'fōrth, 'fȯrth\ river 183 kilometers long [S] central Scotland flowing [E] into North sea through **Firth of Forth** (estuary)
Fort Knox \'näks\ military reservation [N] central Kentucky [SSW] of Louisville; location of U.S. Gold Bullion Depository
Fort-Lamy — see NDJAMENA
Fort Lau•der•dale \'lȯd-ər-ˌdāl\ city [SE] Florida
Fort Wayne \'wān\ city [NE] Indiana
Fort Worth \'wərth\ city [NE] Texas
Foxe Basin \'fäks\ inlet of the Atlantic [N] Canada in [E] Franklin District [W] of Baffin Island
France \'frans\ country [W] Europe between the English channel & the Mediterranean; a republic; capital, Paris
Frank•fort \'frangk-fərt\ city, capital of Kentucky
Frank•furt \'frangk-fərt, 'frängk-ˌfu̇rt\ *or in full* **Frankfurt am**

Main \-äm-'mīn\ *or* **Frankfort on the Main** city West Germany on Main river

Frank•lin \'frang-klən\ district [N] Canada in Northwest Territories including Arctic islands & Boothia & Melville peninsulas

Fra•ser \'frā-zər, -zhər\ river 1370 kilometers long Canada in [S] central British Columbia flowing into the Pacific

Fred•er•ic•ton \'fred-rik-tən, -ə-rik-\ city, capital of New Brunswick

Free•town \'frē-,taun\ city, capital of Sierra Leone

Fre•mont \'frē-,mänt\ city [W] California

French Equatorial Africa former country [W] central Africa [N] of Congo river comprising a federation of Chad, Gabon, Middle Congo, & Ubangi-Shari territories

French Guiana country [N] South America on the Atlantic; a dependency of France; capital, Cayenne

French Guinea — see GUINEA

French Indochina — see INDOCHINA

French Morocco — see MOROCCO

French Polynesia islands in [S] Pacific belonging to France & including Society, Marquesas, Tuamotu, Gambier, & Tubuai groups; capital, Papeete

French Somaliland — see DJIBOUTI

French Sudan — see MALI

French Territory of the Afars and the Issas — see DJIBOUTI

French Togo — see TOGO

French West Indies islands of the West Indies belonging to France & including Guadeloupe, Martinique, Désirade, Les Saintes, Marie Galante, Saint Barthélemy, & part of Saint Martin

Fres•no \'frez-nō\ city [S] central California

Friendly islands — see TONGA

Fri•sian \'frizh-ən, 'frē-zhən\ islands [N] Europe in North sea including **West Frisian** islands off [N] Netherlands, **East Frisian** islands off [NW] Germany, & **North Frisian** islands off [N] Germany and [W] Denmark

Frun•ze \'frün-zə\ city U.S.S.R., capital of Kirghizia

Fuchau — see FOOCHOW

Fu•ji \'fü-jē, 'fyü-\ *or* **Fu•ji•ya•ma** \,fü-jē-'äm-ə, ,fyü-, -'yäm-\ *or* **Fu•ji–no–ya•ma** \-jē-nō-'yäm-ə\ *or* **Fu•ji•san** \-jē-'sän\ mountain 3776 meters Japan in [S] central Honshu; highest in Japan

Fu•ji•sa•wa \,fü-jē-'sä-wə\ city Japan in [SE] Honshu

Fu•kien \'fü-'kyen, -kē-'en\ province [SE] China on Formosa strait; capital, Foochow

Fu•ku•o•ka \,fü-kə-'wō-kə\ city Japan in [N] Kyushu

Fu•ku•shi•ma \,fü-kə-'shē-mə\ city Japan in [N] central Honshu [SW] of Sendai

Fu•ku•ya•ma \,fü-kə-'yäm-ə\ city Japan in [SW] Honshu

Fu•na•bashi \,fü-nə-'bäsh-ē\ city Japan in [SE] Honshu on Tokyo Bay

Fu•na•fu•ti \,fü-nə-'füt-ē, ,fyü-, -'fyüt-\ city, capital of Tuvalu

Fun•dy, Bay of \'fən-dē\ inlet of the Atlantic [SE] Canada between New Brunswick & Nova Scotia

Fu•se \'fü-,sā\ city Japan in [S] Honshu [E] of Osaka

Fu•shun \'fü-'shün\ city [NE] China [E] of Mukden

Ga•bon \ga-'bō^{n}\ country [W] equatorial Africa; capital, Libreville — **Gab•o•nese** \,gab-ə-'nēz, -'nēs\ *adj or n*

Ga•bo•rone \,gäb-ə-'rōn\ city, capital of Botswana

Gads•den Purchase \'gadz-dən\ tract of land [S] of Gila river in present Arizona & New Mexico purchased 1853 by the U.S. from Mexico

Ga•lá•pa•gos islands \gə-'läp-ə-gəs, -'lap-\ *or* **Co•lón archi•pelago** \kə-'lōn\ island group Ecuador in the Pacific 965 kilometers [W] of mainland

Ga•la•tia \gə-'lā-shə, -shē-ə\ ancient country & Roman province central Asia Minor in region centering on modern Ankara, Turkey — **Ga•la•tian** \-shən\ *adj or n*

Ga•li•cia \gə-'lish-ə, -'lish-ē-ə\ **1** region [E] central Europe now divided between Poland & Ukraine (U.S.S.R.) **2** region [NW] Spain on the Atlantic — **Ga•li•cian** \-shən\ *adj or n*

Gal•i•lee \'gal-ə-,lē\ hilly region [N] Israel — **Gal•i•le•an** \,gal-ə-'lē-ən\ *adj or n*

Galilee, Sea of *or* **Lake of Gen•nes•a•ret** \gə-'nes-ə-,ret, -rət\ *or* **Sea of Ti•be•ri•as** \tī-'bir-ē-əs\ lake [N] Israel on Syrian border traversed by Jordan river

Gal•lip•o•li \gə-'lip-ə-lē\ *or Turkish* **Ge•li•bo•lu Ya•ri•ma•da•si** \,gel-ə-bə-'lü-,yär-ə-,mäd-ə-'sē\ peninsula Turkey in Europe between the Dardanelles & Saros gulf

Gal•lo•way \'gal-ə-,wā\ district [SW] Scotland — see DUMFRIES AND GALLOWAY

Gal•way \'gȯl-,wā\ county [W] Ireland in Connacht

Gam•bia \'gam-bē-ə\ country [W] Africa; a republic; capital, Banjul — **Gam•bi•an** \-ən\ *adj or n*

Gand — see GHENT

Gan•ges \'gan-,jēz\ river 2495 kilometers long [N] India flowing from the Himalayas [SE] & [E] to unite with the Brahmaputra & empty into Bay of Bengal through a vast delta — **Gan•get•ic** \gan-'jet-ik\ *adj*

Gar•da, Lake \'gärd-ə\ lake [N] Italy [NW] of Verona

Garden Grove city [SW] California

Gar•mo Peak \'gär-mō\ *or* **Communism Peak** mountain 7495 meters Soviet Central Asia in [SE] Tadzhikistan in the Pamirs; highest in U.S.S.R.

Ga•ronne \gə-'rän, -'rōn\ river 571 kilometers long [SE] France flowing into Gironde estuary

Gary \'gaər-ē, 'geər-ē\ city [NW] Indiana on Lake Michigan

Gas•co•ny \'gas-kə-nē\ *or French* **Gas•cogne** \gá-skōn^{y}\ region and former province [SW] France

Gas•pé \gas-'pā, 'gas-,\ peninsula [SE] Quebec [E] of mouth of the Saint Lawrence — **Gas•pe•sian** \ga-'spē-zhən\ *adj or n*

Gates•head \'gāts-,hed\ borough [N] England in Tyne and Wear county

Gaul \'gȯl\ *or Latin* **Gal•lia** \'gal-ē-ə\ ancient country [W] Europe chiefly comprising region occupied by modern France & Belgium but at one time including also Po valley in [N] Italy — see CISALPINE GAUL, TRANSALPINE GAUL

Ga•za Strip \'gäz-ə, 'gaz-, 'gāz-\ district [S] Palestine on the Mediterranean; administered 1949–67 by Egypt & since 1967 by Israel; chief town, Gaza

Gdansk \gə-'dänsk, -'dansk\ *or German* **Dan•zig** \'dan-sig, 'dän-\ city [N] Poland on Gulf of Danzig

Gdyn•ia \gə-'din-ē-ə\ city [N] Poland

Gee•long \jə-'lȯng\ city [SE] Australia in [S] Victoria

Gel•sen•kir•chen \,gel-zən-'kir-kən\ city West Germany in the Ruhr [W] of Dortmund

Ge•ne•ral San Mar•tín \,hā-nā-,räl-,san-mär-'tēn\ *also* **San Mar•tín** \,san-mär-'tēn\ city [E] Argentina [NW] of Buenos Aires

Ge•ne•va \jə-'nē-və\ city [SW] Switzerland on Lake of Geneva — **Ge•ne•van** \-vən\ *adj or n*

Geneva, Lake of *or* **Lake Le•man** \'lē-mən, 'lem-ən, lə-'man\; *ancient* **Le•man•nus** \li-'man-əs\ *or* **Le•ma•nus** \li-'mān-əs\ lake on border between [SW] Switzerland & [E] France traversed by the Rhone

Gen•oa \'jen-ə-wə\ *or Italian* **Ge•no•va** \'je-nō-vä\ city [NW] Italy, capital of Liguria — **Gen•o•ese** \,jen-ə-'wēz, -'wēs\ *or* **Gen•o•vese** \-ə-'vēz, -'vēs\ *adj or n*

George•town \'jȯrj-,taun\ **1** a [W] section of Washington, District of Columbia **2** city, capital of Guyana

George Town — see PENANG

Geor•gia \'jȯr-jə\ **1** state [SE] U.S.; capital, Atlanta **2** constituent republic of U.S.S.R. on Black sea [S] of Caucasus mountains; capital, Tiflis — **Geor•gian** \'jȯr-jən\ *adj or n*

Georgia, Strait of channel Canada & U.S. between Vancouver Island & mainland [NW] of Puget Sound

Georgian Bay inlet of Lake Huron in [S] Ontario

Ger•man•town \'jər-mən-,taun\ a [NW] section of Philadelphia, Pennsylvania

Ger•ma•ny \'jərm-nē, -ə-nē\ former country central Europe bordering on North & Baltic seas; since 1949 constituting two republics: the Federal Republic of Germany (capital, Bonn) & the German Democratic Republic (capital, East Berlin)

Ger•mis•ton \'jər-mə-stən\ city [NE] Republic of South Africa in [S] Transvaal [E] of Johannesburg

Get•tys•burg National Military Park \'get-ēz-,bərg\ reservation [S] Pennsylvania near Gettysburg including site of battle 1863

Gha•na \'gän-ə, 'gan-ə\ *or formerly* **Gold Coast** country [W] Africa on Gulf of Guinea; a republic of the British Commonwealth; capital, Accra — **Gha•na•ian** \gä-'nā-ən, ga-, -yən; -'nī-ən\ *or* **Gha•ni•an** \'gän-ē-ən, 'gän-yən, 'gan-\ *adj or n*

Ghats \'gȯts\ two mountain chains [S] India — see EASTERN GHATS, WESTERN GHATS

Ghent \'gent\ *or Flemish* **Gent** \'gent\ *or French* **Gand** \gä^{n}\ city [NW] central Belgium

Gi•bral•tar \jə-'brȯl-tər\ British colony & fortress on [S] coast of Spain including Rock of Gibraltar

Gibraltar, Rock of headland on [S] coast of Spain in Gibraltar colony at [E] end of Strait of Gibraltar; highest point 426 meters — see PILLARS OF HERCULES

Gibraltar, Strait of passage between Spain & Africa connecting the Atlantic & the Mediterranean

Gi·fu \'gē-,fü\ city Japan in central Honshu

Gi·la \'hē-lə\ river 1015 kilometers long [SW] New Mexico and [S] Arizona flowing [W] into the Colorado

Gil·bert \'gil-bərt\ islands [W] Pacific [SSE] of the Marshalls; a British territory; capital, Tarawa; until 1975 formed with Ellice islands the British colony of **Gilbert and El·lice Islands** \'el-əs\

Gil·e·ad \'gil-ē-əd\ mountain region [NE] Palestine [E] of Jordan river; now in [NW] Jordan — **Gil·e·ad·ite** \-ē-ə-,dīt\ *n*

Gi·ronde \jə-'ränd, zhə-; zhē-rō^{n}d\ estuary [W] France formed by junction of Garonne & Dordogne rivers

Gi·za \'gē-zə\ *or* **Al-Gi·zeh** \al-\ *or* **Al-Jī·zah** \-'jē-zə\ city [N] Egypt on the Nile [SW] of Cairo

Gla·cier Bay \,glā-shər-\ inlet [SE] Alaska at [S] end of Saint Elias range in **Glacier Bay National Monument**

Glacier National Park 1 mountain area [NW] Montana adjoining Waterton Lakes National Park, Canada, & with it forming Waterton-Glacier International Peace Park **2** mountain area [SE] British Columbia

Glades \'glādz\ EVERGLADES

Gla·mor·gan \glə-'mȯr-gən\ *or* **Gla·mor·gan·shire** \-,shiər, ər\ former county [SE] Wales — see MID GLAMORGAN, SOUTH GLAMORGAN, WEST GLAMORGAN

Glas·gow \'glas-kō, 'glas-gō, 'glaz-gō\ city [S] central Scotland on the Clyde — **Glas·we·gian** \glas-'wē-jən\ *adj or n*

Glen·dale \'glen-,dal\ city [S] California [NE] of Los Angeles

Glouces·ter·shire \'gläs-tər-,shiər, 'glȯs-, -shər\ *or* **Gloucester** county [SW] central England

Gnossus — see KNOSSOS

Goa \'gō-ə\ district [W] India on Malabar coast belonging before 1962 to Portugal; now in **Goa, Da·man, and Diu** \də-'man . . . 'dē-ü\ territory; capital, Pangim

Go·bi \'gō-bē\ desert [E] central Asia in Mongolia & [N] China

Godt·haab \'gȯt-,hȯb, 'gät-\ town, capital of Greenland on [SW] coast

God·win Aus·ten \,gäd-wə-'nȯ-stən, -'näs-tən\ *or* K^2 \'kā-'tü\ mountain 8611 meters [N] Kashmir in Karakoram range; second highest in the world

Goi·â·nia \gȯi-'an-ē-ə\ city [SE] central Brazil [SW] of Brasília

Go·lan Heights \,gō-,län-, -lən-\ hilly region between [NE] Israel & [SW] Syria

Gol·con·da \gäl-'kän-də\ ruined city central India [W] of Hyderabad

Gold Coast 1 coast region [W] Africa on [N] shore of Gulf of Guinea [E] of Ivory Coast **2** — see GHANA

Golden Gate strait [W] California connecting San Francisco Bay and the Pacific

Golden Horn inlet of the Bosporus, Turkey in Europe; harbor of Istanbul

Golgotha — see CALVARY

Go·mel \'gō-məl, 'gȯ-\ city U.S.S.R. in [SE] Belorussian Soviet Socialist Republic

Go·mor·rah \gə-'mär-ə, -'mȯr-\ city, ancient Palestine in plain of Jordan

Good Hope, Cape of \,gu̇d-'hōp\ cape [S] Republic of South Africa in [SW] Cape Province — see CAPE OF GOOD HOPE

Go·rakh·pur \'gōr-ək-,pu̇r, 'gȯr-\ city [NE] India in [E] Uttar Pradesh [N] of Banaras

Gor·ki *or* **Gor·kiy** \'gȯr-kē\ *or formerly* **Nizh·ni Nov·go·rod** \,nizh-nē-'näv-gə-,räd\ city U.S.S.R. in central Soviet Russia, Europe, on the Volga [ENE] of Moscow

Gor·lov·ka \gȯr-'lȯf-kə, -'lȯv-\ city U.S.S.R. in [E] Ukraine in Donets basin

Go·shen \'gō-shən\ district of ancient Egypt [E] of Nile delta

Gö·te·borg \,yərt-ə-'bȯr-ē, *Swedish* ,yœ-tə-'bȯry\ *or* **Goth·en·burg** \'gäth-ən-,bərg\ city [SW] Sweden

Got·land \'gät-,land, -lənd\ island Sweden in the Baltic; capital, Visby

Göt·ting·en \'gərt-ing-ən, 'get-, 'gœt-\ city West Germany [SSW] of Brunswick

Gram·pi·an \'gram-pē-ən\ **1** hills [N] central Scotland — see NEVIS **2** region [NE] central Scotland; established 1975

Gra·na·da \grə-'näd-ə\ city [S] Spain in Andalusia

Grand Banks shoal area in the [W] Atlantic [SE] of Newfoundland

Grand Canyon gorge of Colorado river [NW] Arizona; area largely in **Grand Canyon National Park** (to the [E]) & **Grand Canyon National Monument** (to the [W])

Grand Canyon of the Snake — see HELLS CANYON

Grande, Rio — see RIO GRANDE

Grand Rapids city [SW] Michigan

Grand Te·ton National Park \'tē-,tän\ reservation [NW] Wyoming [S] of Yellowstone National Park

Grau·bün·den \grau̇-'bin-dən, -'bün-, -'bœn-\ *or French* **Grisons** \grē-zō^{n}\ canton [E] Switzerland

Gravenhage, 's — see HAGUE

Graz \'gräts\ city [S] Austria, capital of Styria

Great Australian Bight wide bay on [S] coast of Australia

Great Barrier Reef coral reef Australia off [NE] coast of Queensland

Great Basin region [W] U.S. between Sierra Nevada & Wasatch mountains including most of Nevada & parts of California, Idaho, Utah, Wyoming, and Oregon; has no drainage to ocean

Great Bear lake Canada in [N] Mackenzie District draining through Great Bear river into Mackenzie river

Great Brit·ain \'brit-n\ **1** island [W] Europe [NW] of France comprising England, Scotland, & Wales **2** UNITED KINGDOM

Great Dividing range mountain system [E] Australia & Tasmania extending [S] from Cape York peninsula — see KOSCIUSKO

Greater An·til·les \an-'til-ēz\ group of islands of the West Indies including Cuba, Hispaniola, Jamaica, & Puerto Rico — see LESSER ANTILLES

Greater London metropolitan county [SE] England comprising City of London & 32 surrounding boroughs

Greater Manchester metropolitan county [NW] England including city of Manchester

Greater Sunda — see SUNDA

Great Lakes 1 chain of five lakes (Superior, Michigan, Huron, Erie, & Ontario) central North America in U.S. & Canada **2** group of lakes [E] central Africa including Rudolf, Albert, Victoria, Tanganyika, & Nyasa

Great Plains elevated plains region [W] central U.S. & [W] Canada [E] of the Rockies; chiefly [W] of the 100th meridian extending from [W] Texas to [NE] British Columbia & [NW] Alberta

Great Rift valley \'rift\ depression [SW] Asia & [E] Africa extending with several breaks from valley of the Jordan [S] to central Mozambique

Great Salt lake [N] Utah having strongly saline waters & no outlet

Great Slave lake [NW] Canada in [S] Mackenzie District drained by Mackenzie river

Great Smoky mountains between [W] North Carolina & [E] Tennessee partly in **Great Smoky Mountains National Park;** highest Clingmans Dome 2024 meters

Greece \'grēs\ *or ancient* **Hel·las** \'hel-əs\ *or Greek* **El·lás** \e-'läs\ country [S] Europe at [S] end of Balkan peninsula; a republic; capital, Athens

Green \'grēn\ **1** mountains [E] North America in the Appalachians extending from [S] Quebec [S] through Vermont into [W] Massachusetts **2** river 1175 kilometers long [W] U.S. flowing from Wind River Range in [W] Wyoming [S] into the Colorado in [SE] Utah

Green Bay 1 inlet of [NW] Lake Michigan 193 kilometers long in [NW] Michigan & [NE] Wisconsin **2** city [NE] Wisconsin

Green·land \'grēn-lənd, -,land\ island in the [N] Atlantic off [NE] North America belonging to Denmark; capital, Godthaab

Greens·boro \'grēnz-,bər-ə, -,bə-rə\ city [N] central North Carolina

Green·wich \'grin-ij, 'gren-, -ich\ [SE] borough of Greater London, England

Green·wich Village \,gren-ich-, ,grin-, -ij-\ section of New York City in Manhattan on lower [W] side

Gre·na·da \grə-'nād-ə\ island British West Indies in [S] Windwards; capital, Saint George's

Gre·no·ble \grə-'nō-bəl, -'nȯbl\ city [SE] France

Grisons — see GRAUBÜNDEN

Gro·ning·en \'grō-ning-ən\ city [NE] Netherlands

Groz·ny \'grȯz-nē, 'gräz-\ city U.S.S.R. in [S] Soviet Russia, Europe, [N] of Caucasus mountains

Gua·da·la·ja·ra \,gwäd-ə-lə-'här-ə\ city [W] central Mexico, capital of Jalisco

Gua·dal·ca·nal \,gwäd-l-kə-'nal, ,gwäd-ə-kə-\ island [W] Pacific in the [SE] Solomons in British Solomon Islands protectorate

Gua·dal·qui·vir \,gwäd-l-'kwiv-ər, -ki-'viər\ river 602 kilometers long [S] Spain flowing into the Atlantic

Gua·da·lupe Mountains National Park \'gwäd-l-,üp\ reservation [W] Texas

Gua·de·loupe \'gwäd-l-,üp\ two islands, Basse-Terre (or Guadeloupe proper) & Grande-Terre, separated by a narrow channel in

French West Indies in central Leewards; capital, Basse-Terre (on Basse-Terre Island)
Gua•di•a•na \ˌgwäd-ē-ˈän-ə, -ˈan-\ river 829 kilometers long [S] Spain & [SE] Portugal flowing into the Atlantic
Guaíra — see SETE QUEDAS
Gua•lla•ti•ri \ˌgwä-yə-ˈtir-ē, ˌgwī-ə-\ volcano 6060 meters [N] Chile; highest volcano in world
Guam \ˈgwäm\ island [W] Pacific in [S] Marianas belonging to U.S.; capital, Agana — **Gua•ma•ni•an** \gwä-ˈmā-nē-ən\ *adj or n*
Gua•na•ba•coa \ˌgwän-ə-bə-ˈkō-ə\ city [W] Cuba
Gua•na•ba•ra Bay \ˌgwän-ə-ˈbar-ə, -ˈbär-\ inlet of the Atlantic [SE] Brazil on which city of Rio de Janeiro is situated
Gua•na•jua•to \ˌgwän-ə-ˈhwät-ō, -ˈwät-\ **1** state central Mexico **2** city, its capital
Guan•tá•na•mo Bay \gwän-ˈtän-ə-ˌmō\ inlet of the Caribbean in [SE] Cuba; site of U.S. naval station
Gua•te•ma•la \ˌgwät-ə-ˈmä-lə\ **1** country Central America; a republic **2** *or* **Guatemala City** city, its capital — **Gua•te•ma•lan** \-lən\ *adj or n*
Gua•ya•quil \ˌgwī-ə-ˈkēl, -ˈkil\ city [W] Ecuador
Guayra — see SETE QUEDAS
Guern•sey \ˈgərn-zē\ island in English channel — see CHANNEL
Guer•re•ro \gə-ˈreər-ō\ state [S] Mexico on the Pacific; capital, Chilpancingo
Gui•a•na \gē-ˈan-ə, -ˈän-ə; gī-ˈan-ə\ region [N] South America on the Atlantic bounded on [W] & [S] by Orinoco, Negro, & Amazon rivers; includes Guyana, French Guiana, Surinam, & adjacent parts of Brazil & Venezuela — **Gui•a•nan** \-ən\ *adj or n*
Guin•ea \ˈgin-ē\ **1** region [W] Africa on the Atlantic extending along coast from Gambia to Angola **2** *or formerly* **French Guinea** country [W] Africa [N] of Sierra Leone & Liberia; a republic; capital, Conakry — **Guin•ean** \ˈgin-ē-ən\ *adj or n*
Guinea, Gulf of arm of the Atlantic [W] central Africa
Guin•ea-Bis•sau \ˌgin-ē-bis-ˈaů\ *or formerly* **Portuguese Guinea** country [W] Africa; a republic since 1974; capital, Bissau
Gu•ja•rat *or* **Gu•je•rat** \ˌgü-jə-ˈrät, ˌgůj-ə-\ state [W] India [N] & [E] of Gulf of Cambay; capital, Gandhinagar
Guj•ran•wa•la \ˌgůj-rən-ˈwäl-ə, ˌgůj-\ city [NE] Pakistan
Gulf States states of U.S. bordering on Gulf of Mexico: Florida, Alabama, Mississippi, Louisiana, and Texas
Gulf Stream warm current of the Atlantic Ocean flowing from Gulf of Mexico [NE] along coast of U.S. to Nantucket Island and thence eastward
Gun•tur \gůn-ˈtůr\ city [E] India in central Andhra Pradesh
Guy•ana \gī-ˈan-ə\ *or formerly* **British Guiana** country [N] South America on the Atlantic; a republic in British Commonwealth since 1970; capital, Georgetown
Gwa•li•or \ˈgwäl-ē-ˌȯr\ city [N] central India in [NW] Andhra Pradesh [SSE] of Agra
Gwent \ˈgwent\ county [SE] Wales; established 1974
Gwyn•edd \ˈgwin-eth\ county [NW] Wales; established 1974
Habana, La — see HAVANA
Ha•chi•no•he \ˌhäch-i-ˈnō-hā\ city Japan in [N] Honshu [SE] of Aomori
Ha•chi•ō•je \ˌhäch-ē-ˈō-jē\ city Japan in [SE] central Honshu [W] of Tokyo
Hack•ney \ˈhak-nē\ borough of [N] Greater London, England
Hague, The \thə-ˈhāg\ *or Dutch* **'s Gra•ven•ha•ge** \ˌskräv-ən-ˈhäg-ə, ˌsräv-\ city [SW] Netherlands; a capital of the Netherlands
Haidarabad — see HYDERABAD
Hai•fa \ˈhī-fə\ city [NW] Israel
Hai–k'ou \ˈhī-ˈkaů, -ˈkō\ *or* **Hoi•how** \ˈhȯi-ˈhaů, ˈhī-ˈhō\ *or French* **Hoï–Hao** \ō-ē-aů\ city [SE] China on Hainan
Hai•nan \ˈhī-ˈnän\ island [SE] China in Kwangtung in South China sea
Hai•phong \ˈhī-ˈfȯŋ\ city [N] Vietnam in Tonkin
Hai•ti \ˈhāt-ē\ **1** — see HISPANIOLA **2** country West Indies in [W] Hispaniola; a republic; capital, Port-au-Prince — **Hai•tian** \ˈhā-shən\ *adj or n*
Halab *or* **Haleb** — see ALEPPO
Ha•le•a•ka•la Crater \ˌhäl-ē-ˌäk-ə-ˈlä\ crater 829 meters deep & 32 kilometers in circumference Hawaii in [E] Maui Island in **Haleakala National Park**
Hal•i•car•nas•sus \ˌhal-ə-kär-ˈnas-əs\ ancient city [SW] Asia Minor in [SW] Caria on Aegean sea
Hal•i•fax \ˈhal-ə-ˌfaks\ **1** city, capital of Nova Scotia **2** city [N] England in West Yorkshire
Hal•le \ˈhäl-ə\ city East Germany [NW] of Leipzig
Hal•ma•hera \ˌhal-mə-ˈher-ə, ˌhäl-\ island [E] Indonesia; largest of the Moluccas
Ha•ma \ˈham-ˌä\ city [W] Syria
Ha•ma•dan \ˌham-ə-ˈdan, -ˈdän\ city [W] Iran
Ha•ma•ma•tsu \ˌhäm-ə-ˈmät-sü\ city Japan in [S] Honshu
Ham•burg \ˈham-ˌbərg, ˈhäm-ˌbůrg\ city West Germany on the Elbe — **Ham•burg•er** \-ˌbər-gər, -ˌbůr-\ *n*
Ham•il•ton \ˈham-əl-tən, -əlt-n\ **1** city [S] Ontario **2** town, capital of Bermuda
Ham•mer•smith \ˈham-ər-ˌsmith\ borough of [SW] Greater London, England
Ham•mond \ˈham-ənd\ city [NW] Indiana
Hamp•shire \ˈhamp-ˌshiər, ˈham-, -shər\ **1** former county [S] England comprising present counties of Hampshire & Isle of Wight **2** county [S] England on English channel
Hamp•ton \ˈhamp-tən, ˈham-\ city [SE] Virginia
Hampton Roads channel [SE] Virginia through which James & Elizabeth rivers flow into Chesapeake Bay
Hang•chow *or* **Hang-chou** \ˈhaŋ-ˈchaů, ˈhäŋ-ˈjō\ city [E] China, capital of Chekiang
Han•kow \ˈhaŋ-ˈkaů, -ˈkō; ˈhäŋ-ˈkō\ port [E] central China — see WUHAN
Han•no•ver *or* **Han•o•ver** \ˈhan-ˌō-vər, ˈhan-ə-vər; *German* hä-ˈnō-vər\ city West Germany, capital of Lower Saxony
Ha•noi \ha-ˈnȯi, hə-, hä-\ city, capital of Vietnam in Tonkin
Han–tan \ˈhän-ˈtän\ city [NE] China in Hopeh
Han•yang \ˈhän-ˈyäŋ\ former city [E] central China — see WUHAN
Har•bin \ˈhär-bən, här-ˈbin\ *or* **Ha–erh–pin** \ˈhä-ˈer-ˈbin\ *or formerly* **Pin•kiang** \ˈbin-jē-ˈäŋ\ city [NE] China, capital of Heilungkiang
Har•in•gey \ˈhar-iŋ-ˌgā\ borough of [N] Greater London, England
Har•lem \ˈhär-ləm\ section of New York City in [N] Manhattan
Har•pers Fer•ry National Monument \ˌhär-pərz-ˈfer-ē\ historical site Maryland & West Virginia at town of Harpers Ferry, West Virginia, on the Potomac
Har•ris•burg \ˈhar-əs-ˌbərg\ city, capital of Pennsylvania
Har•row \ˈhar-ō\ borough of [NW] Greater London, England
Hart•ford \ˈhärt-fərd\ city, capital of Connecticut
Hart•le•pool \ˈhärt-lē-ˌpül\ borough [N] England in Cleveland
Ha•ry•a•na *or* **Ha•ri•a•na** \ˌhə-rē-ˈän-ə\ state [N] India formed 1966 from [S] part of state of Punjab; capital, Chandigarh
Harz \ˈhärts\ mountains central Germany between Elbe & Leine rivers
Hat•ter•as, Cape \ˈhat-ə-rəs, ˈha-trəs\ cape, North Carolina on Cape Hatteras Island in Cape Hatteras National Seashore Recreational Area
Haute–Volta — see UPPER VOLTA
Ha•vana \hə-ˈvan-ə\ *or Spanish* **La Ha•ba•na** \ˌlä-ä-ˈvän-ə, ˌlä-ˈvän-ə\ city, capital of Cuba
Hav•ant and Water•loo \ˈhav-ənt-n-ˌwȯt-ər-ˈlü, -ˌwät-\ town [S] England in Hampshire
Ha•ver•ing \ˈhāv-riŋ, -ə-riŋ\ borough of [NE] Greater London, England
Ha•waii \hə-ˈwä-ē, -ˈwī-, -ˈwȯ-, -yē\ **1** *or formerly* **Sand•wich islands** \ˌsan-ˌwich-, ˌsand-\ group of islands central Pacific belonging to U.S. **2** island, largest of the group **3** state of U.S. comprising Hawaiian islands except Midway; capital, Honolulu
Hawaii Volcanoes National Park reservation Hawaii on Hawaii Island including Mauna Loa & Kilauea
Heb•ri•des \ˈheb-rə-ˌdēz\ islands [W] Scotland in the Atlantic comprising **Outer Hebrides** (to [W]) and **Inner Hebrides** (to [E]) — see WESTERN ISLES — **Heb•ri•de•an** \ˌheb-rə-ˈdē-ən\ *adj or n*
Hei–lung chiang — see AMUR
Hei•lung•kiang \ˈhā-ˈlůŋ-jē-ˈäŋ\ province [NE] China in [N] Manchuria; capital, Harbin
He•jaz \hej-ˈaz, hij-\ province [W] Saudi Arabia on Red sea; capital, Mecca
Hel•e•na \ˈhel-ə-nə\ city, capital of Montana
He•li•op•o•lis \ˌhē-lē-ˈäp-ə-ləs\ **1** either of two cities of ancient Egypt near modern Cairo **2** city of ancient Syria; site at modern town of **Baal•bek** \ˈbā-əl-ˌbek, ˈbäl-ˌbek\ in [E] Lebanon [N] of Damascus
Hellas — see GREECE
Hellespont — see DARDANELLES
Hells Canyon \ˈhelz\ *or* **Grand Canyon of the Snake** canyon of

Snake river on Idaho-Oregon boundary
Hel•sin•ki \'hel-,sing-kē, hel-'\ *or Swedish* **Hel•sing•fors** \'hel-sing-,fȯrz\ city, capital of Finland
Helvetia — see SWITZERLAND
Heng•yang \'hang-'yäng\ city [SE] central China in [SE] Hunan
Henry, Cape \'hen-rē\ headland [E] Virginia [S] of entrance to Chesapeake Bay
Her•e•ford and Wor•ces•ter \'her-ə-fərd-n-'wu̇s-tər, *in the United States also* 'hər-fərd-\ county [W] England bordering on Wales
Her•e•ford•shire \'her-ə-fərd-,shiər, -shər, *in the United States also* 'hər-fərd-\ *or* **Hereford** former county [W] England — see HEREFORD AND WORCHESTER
Her•mon, Mount \'hər-mən\ mountain 2814 meters on Lebanon-Syria border; highest in Anti-Lebanon mountains
Her•mo•si•llo \,er-mə-'sē-ō, -yō\ city [NW] Mexico, capital of Sonora
Hert•ford•shire \'här-fərd-,shiər, *also* 'härt-, *in the United States also* 'hərt-\ *or* **Hertford** county [SE] England
Her•ze•go•vi•na \,hert-sə-gō-'vē-nə, ,hərt-\ region [W] central Yugoslavia [S] of Bosnia; now part of Bosnia and Herzegovina Federated Republic
Hesse \'hes, 'hes-ē\ *or German* **Hes•sen** \'hes-n\ state West Germany [E] of the Rhine & [N] of the Main; capital, Wiesbaden
Hi•a•le•ah \,hī-ə-'lē-ə\ city [SE] Florida
Hi•ber•nia \hī-'bər-nē-ə\ — see IRELAND — **Hi•ber•ni•an** \-ən\ *adj or n*
Hi•dal•go \hid-'al-gō\ state central Mexico; capital, Pachuca
Hi•ga•shi•ōsa•ka \hē-,gä-shē-ō-'säk-ə\ city Japan in [S] Honshu [E] of Osaka
High•land \'hī-lənd\ region [NW] Scotland; established 1975
High•lands \'hī-ləndz, -lənz\ the mountainous [N] part of Scotland lying [N] & [W] of the Lowlands
High Plains the Great Plains especially from Nebraska southward
High Tatra — see TATRA
Hil•ling•don \'hil-ing-dən\ borough of [W] Greater London, England
Hi•ma•chal Pra•desh \hi-,mäch-əl-prə-'desh, -'dāsh\ territory [NW] India comprising two areas [NW] of Uttar Pradesh — see SIMLA
Hi•ma•la•ya \,him-ə-'lā-ə; hə-'mäl-yə, -'mäl-ə-yə\ mountain system [S] Asia on border between India & Tibet & in Kashmir, Nepal, & Bhutan — see EVEREST — **Hi•ma•la•yan** \,him-ə-'lā-ən; hə-'mäl-yən, -'mäl-ə-yən\ *adj*
Hi•me•ji \hi-'mej-ē\ city Japan in [W] Honshu [WNW] of Kobe
Hin•du Kush \,hin-dü-'ku̇sh, -'kəsh\ mountain range central Asia [SW] of the Pamirs on border of Kashmir & in Afghanistan
Hin•du•stan \,hin-dü-'stan, -də-, -'stän\ **1** region [N] India [N] of the Deccan **2** the subcontinent of India **3** the Republic of India
Hip•po \'hip-ō\ ancient city [N] Africa; chief town of Numidia
Hi•ro•shi•ma \,hir-ə-'shē-mə, hə-'rō-shə-mə\ city Japan in [SW] Honshu on Inland sea
Hispalis — see SEVILLE
His•pa•nia \his-'pān-ē-ə, -'pān-yᵊ, -'pan-\ **1** the Iberian peninsula **2** — see SPAIN
His•pan•io•la \,his-pən-'yō-lə\ *or Spanish* **Es•pa•ño•la** \,es-,pän-'yō-lə\ *or formerly* **Hai•ti** \'hāt-ē\ *or* **San•to Do•min•go** \,sant-əd-ə-'ming-gō\ island West Indies in Greater Antilles divided between Haiti on [W] & Dominican Republic on [E]
Ho•bart \'hō-,bärt\ city Australia, capital of Tasmania
Ho Chi Minh City \,hō-,chē-,min-, -,shē-\ *or formerly* **Sai•gon** \sī-'gän, 'sī-,\ city [S] Vietnam
Ho•fei \'hə-'fā\ *or formerly* **Lu•chow** \'lü-'jō\ city [E] China, capital of Anhwei [W] of Nanking
Hoggar — see AHAGGAR
Hoihow *or* **Hoï-Hao** — see HAI-K'OU
Hok•kai•do \hä-'kīd-ō\ *or formerly* **Ye•zo** \'yez-ō\ island [N] Japan [N] of Honshu
Hol•land \'häl-ənd\ **1** medieval county of Holy Roman Empire bordering on North sea & comprising area now forming North & South Holland provinces of the Netherlands **2** — see NETHERLANDS — **Hol•land•er** \-ən-dər\ *n*
Holland, Parts of district & former administrative county [E] England in [SE] Lincolnshire
Hol•ly•wood \'häl-ē-,wu̇d\ **1** section of Los Angeles, California, [NW] of downtown district **2** city [SE] Florida
Hol•stein \'hōl-,stīn, -,stēn\ region [NW] Germany [S] of Jutland peninsula adjoining Schleswig — see SCHLESWIG-HOLSTEIN
Holy Land PALESTINE
Ho•nan \'hō-'nan\ province [E] central China; capital, Chengchow
Hon•du•ras \hän-'dür-əs, -'dyu̇r-\ country Central America; a republic; capital, Tegucigalpa — **Hon•du•ran** \-ən\ *or* **Hon•du•ra•ne•an** *or* **Hon•du•ra•ni•an** \,hän-dü-'rā-nē-ən, -dyü-\ *adj or n*
Hong Kong \'häng-,käng, -'käng; 'hȯng-,kȯng, -'kȯng\ British colony on coast of [SE] China including Hong Kong Island & Kowloon peninsula; capital, Victoria
Ho•no•lu•lu \,hän-l-'ü-lü, ,hōn-l-\ city, capital of Hawaii on Oahu Island
Hon•shu \'hän-shü\ *or* **Hon•do** \'hän-dō\ island Japan; largest of the four chief islands
Hood, Mount \'hu̇d\ mountain 3424 meters [NW] Oregon in Cascade range
Hoo•ghly *or* **Hu•gli** \'hü-glē\ river 193 kilometers long [E] India flowing [S] into Bay of Bengal; most westerly channel of the Ganges in its delta
Hoo•ver Dam \,hü-vər-\ *or* **Boul•der Dam** \,bōl-dər-\ dam 221 meters high in Colorado river between Arizona & Nevada — see MEAD
Ho•pei \'hō-'pā\ province [NE] China bordering on Po Hai; capital, Shihkiachwang
Ho•reb \'hōr-,eb, 'hȯr-\ *or* **Si•nai** \'sī-,nī *also* -nē-,ī\ mountain where according to the Bible the Law was given to Moses; generally thought to be in Musa on Sinai peninsula
Horn, Cape \'hȯrn\ headland [S] Chile on Horn Island in Tierra del Fuego; the most southerly point of South America at 55°59′ [S] latitude
Hos•pi•ta•let \,äs-,pit-l-'et, ,häs-\ city [NE] Spain
Hot Springs National Park reservation [SW] central Arkansas adjoining city of Hot Springs
Houns•low \'hau̇nz-,lō\ borough of [SW] Greater London, England
Hous•ton \'hyü-stən, 'yü-\ city [SE] Texas
How•rah \'hau̇-rə\ city [E] India in West Bengal on Hooghly river opposite Calcutta
Hsia-men — see AMOY
Hsiang-t'an *or* **Siang•tan** \shē-'äng-'tän\ city [SE] China [S] of Ch'ang-sha in Hunan
Hsin-hsiang *or* **Sin•siang** \'shin-shē-'äng\ city [E] China in Honan
Hsü-chou — see SÜCHOW
Huas•ca•rán \,wäs-kə-'rän\ mountain 6768 meters [W] Peru
Hu•bli-Dhar•war \,hu̇b-lē-,där-'wär\ city [SW] India in [W] Karnataka
Hud•ders•field \'həd-ərz-,fēld\ county borough [N] England in West Yorkshire [NE] of Manchester
Hud•son \'həd-sən\ **1** river 492 kilometers long [E] New York flowing [S] into New York Bay **2** bay inlet of the Atlantic in [N] Canada **3** strait [NE] Canada connecting Hudson Bay & the Atlantic
Hue \'hwā, 'wā, hü-'ā, hyü-'ā\ city central Vietnam in Annam
Hu•he•hot \'hü-hā-'hōt\ *or formerly* **Kwei•sui** \'gwā-'swā\ *or* **Ku•ku-Kho•to** \,kü-kü-'kōt-ō, -'hōt-\ city [N] China, capital of Inner Mongolia
Hull \'həl\ *or* **Kings•ton upon Hull** \'king-stən, 'kingk-\ city [N] England in Humberside
Hum•ber \'həm-bər\ estuary [E] England formed by the Ouse & the Trent & flowing into North sea
Hum•ber•side \'həm-bər-,sīd\ county [E] England; area formerly in Yorkshire
Hum•boldt \'həm-,bōlt\ glacier [NW] Greenland
Humboldt current — see PERU CURRENT
Hu•nan \'hü-'nän\ province [SE] central China; capital, Changsha
Hun•ga•ry \'həng-grē, -gə-rē\ country central Europe; capital, Budapest
Hun•ting•don \'hənt-ing-dən\ *or* **Hun•ting•don•shire** \-,shiər, -shər\ *or* **Huntingdon and Pe•ter•bor•ough** \'pēt-ər-,bər-ə, -,bə-rə, -bə-rə, -brə\ former county [E] central England; since 1974 part of Cambridgeshire
Hunt•ing•ton Beach city [SW] California
Hunts•ville \'hənts-,vil, -vəl\ city [N] Alabama
Hu•pei *or* **Hu•peh** \'hü-'pā\ province [E] central China; capital, Wuhan
Hu•ron, Lake \'hyu̇r-ən, 'yu̇r-, -,än\ lake [E] central North Ameri-

ca in U.S. & Canada; one of the Great Lakes

Hwai•nan \'hwī-'nän, 'wī-\ city [E] China in [N] central Anhwei

Hwang Ho — see YELLOW

Hy•der•abad \'hīd-rə-,bad, -ə-rə-, -,bäd\ **1** *or* **Hai•dar•abad** *same*\ city [S] central India; capital of Andhra Pradesh **2** city [SE] Pakistan on the Indus

Hy•met•tus \hī-'met-əs\ mountain ridge 1026 meters central Greece [E] & [SE] of Athens

Ia•si \'yäsh, 'yäsh-ē\ city [NE] Rumania

Iba•dan \i-'bäd-n, -'bad-\ city [SW] Nigeria

Ibe•ri•an \ī-'bir-ē-ən\ peninsula [SW] Europe occupied by Spain & Portugal

Ibi•za \ē-'vē-thə, -'bē-\ island Spain in Balearic islands [SW] of Majorca

Ice•land \'ī-slənd, -,sland\ island [SE] of Greenland between Arctic & Atlantic oceans; a republic; capital, Reykjavik — **Ice•land•er** \-slən-dər, -,slan-dər\ *n*

Ichi•ka•wa \i-'chē-,kä-wə\ city Japan in [SE] Honshu [E] of Tokyo

Ichi•no•mi•ya \,ē-chi-'nō-mē-,ä, -yä\ city Japan in [SE] Honshu [NNW] of Nagoya

Ida \'īd-ə\ **1** mountain 2498 meters Greece in central Crete **2** mountain 1771 meters [NW] Turkey in Asia [SE] of ancient Troy

Ida•ho \'īd-ə-,hō\ state [NW] U.S.; capital, Boise — **Ida•ho•an** \,īd-ə-'hō-ən\ *adj or n*

Idumaea *or* **Idumea** — see EDOM

If•ni \'if-nē\ territory [SW] Morocco on the Atlantic; formerly administered by Spain; capital, Sidi Ifni

Igua•çu *or Spanish* **Igua•zú** \,ē-gwə-'sü\ river 612 kilometers long [S] Brazil flowing [W] into the Alto Paraná; contains **Iguaçu Falls** (waterfall over 3 kilometers wide composed of numerous cataracts averaging 61 meters in height)

IJs•sel *or* **Ijs•sel** *or* **Ys•sel** \'ī-səl\ river 113 kilometers long [E] Netherlands flowing out of Rhine [N] into IJsselmeer

IJs•sel•meer \,ī-səl-'meər\ *or* **Lake Ijs•sel** \'ī-səl\ freshwater lake [N] Netherlands separated from North sea by a dike; part of former Zuider Zee (inlet of North sea)

Ika•ria \,ē-kə-'rē-ə\ *or* **Ni•ka•ria** \,nē-\ *or ancient* **Icar•ia** \ī-'ker-ē-ə, -'kar-; ik-'er-, -'ar-\ island Greece central Aegean [W] of Samos

Ilium *or* **Ilion** — see TROY

Illam•pu \ē-'äm-pü, -'yäm-\ *or* **So•ra•ta** \sə-'rät-ə\ mountain [W] Bolivia in the Andes [E] of Lake Titicaca — see ANCOHUMA

Il•li•nois \,il-ə-'nȯi *also* -'nȯiz\ state [N] central U.S.; capital, Springfield — **Il•li•nois•an** \-'nȯi-ən, -'nȯiz-\ *adj or n*

Il•lyr•ia \il-'ir-ē-ə\ ancient country [S] Europe and Balkan peninsula on the Adriatic — **Il•lyr•i•an** \-ē-ən\ *adj or n*

Ilo•ilo \,ē-lə-'wē-lō\ city central Philippines on [S] coast of Panay Island

Ilo•rin \,ē-lə-'rēn, i-'lȯr-ən\ city Nigeria [NE] of Lagos

In•chon \'in-,chän\ city South Korea on Yellow sea

In•de•pen•dence \,in-də-'pen-dəns\ city [W] Missouri [E] of Kansas City

In•dia \'in-dē-ə\ **1** peninsula region [S] Asia [S] of the Himalayas between Bay of Bengal & Arabian sea **2** *or* **Bha•rat** \'bər-ət, 'bə-rət\ country comprising major portion of the peninsula; a republic of British Commonwealth; capital, New Delhi **3** *or* **Indian Empire** before 1947 those parts of the Indian subcontinent under British rule or protection

In•di•an \'in-dē-ən\ **1** ocean [E] of Africa, [S] of Asia, [W] of Australia, & [N] of Antarctica **2** — see THAR

In•di•ana \,in-dē-'an-ə\ state [E] central U.S.; capital, Indianapolis — **In•di•an•an** \-'an-ən\ *or* **In•di•an•i•an** \-'an-ē-ən\ *adj or n*

In•di•a•nap•o•lis \,in-dē-ə-'nap-ləs, -ə-ləs\ city, capital of Indiana

Indian river lagoon 266 kilometers long [E] Florida between mainland & coastal islands

Indian Territory former territory [S] U.S. in present state of Oklahoma

In•dies \'in-dēz\ **1** EAST INDIES **2** WEST INDIES

In•do•chi•na \'in-dō-'chī-nə\ **1** peninsula [SE] Asia including Burma, Malay peninsula, Thailand, Cambodia, Laos, & Vietnam **2** *or* **French Indochina** former country [SE] Asia comprising area now forming Cambodia, Laos, & Vietnam — **In•do–Chi•nese** \-chī-'nēz, -'nēs\ *adj or n*

In•do•ne•sia \,in-də-'nē-zhə, -shə\ country [SE] Asia in Malay archipelago comprising Sumatra, Java, [S] & [E] Borneo, Celebes, [W] New Guinea, & many smaller islands; a republic; capital, Jakarta — see NETHERLANDS EAST INDIES — **In•do•ne•sian** \-zhən, -shən\ *adj or n*

In•dore \in-'dōr, -'dȯr\ city [W] central India in [W] Madhya Pradesh

In•dus \'in-dəs\ river 2900 kilometers long [S] Asia flowing from Tibet [NW] & [SSW] through Pakistan into Arabian sea

In•land \'in-,land, -lənd\ sea inlet of the Pacific in [SW] Japan between Honshu Island on [N] and Shikoku Island and Kyushu Island on [S]

Inner Hebrides — see HEBRIDES

Inner Mongolia region [N] China in [SE] Mongolia & [W] Manchuria; capital, Huhehot

Inns•bruck \'inz-,brůk, 'ins-\ city [W] Austria in Tirol

Inside Passage *or* **Inland Passage** protected shipping route between Puget Sound, Washington, & Skagway, Alaska

In•ver•ness \,in-vər-'nes\ *or* **In•ver•ness-shire** \-'nes-,shiər, -'nesh-, -shər\ former county [NW] Scotland

Io•ni•an \ī-'ō-nē-ən\ **1** sea arm of the Mediterranean between [SE] Italy & [W] Greece **2** islands [W] Greece in Ionian sea

Io•wa \'ī-ə-wə\ state [N] central U.S.; capital, Des Moines — **Io•wan** \-wən\ *adj or n*

Ipin \'ē-'pin, -'pēn\ *or formerly* **Sü•chow** \'shü-'jō, 'sü-; 'sü-'chaů\ city central China in [S] Szechwan on the Yangtze

Ipoh \'ē-pō\ city Malaysia [NNW] of Kuala Lumpur

Ips•wich \'ip-swich\ borough [SE] England in Suffolk

Iran \i-'ran, -'rän; ī-'ran\ *or formerly* **Per•sia** \'pər-zhə\ country [SW] Asia [S] of Caspian sea; a kingdom; capital, Tehran — **Irani** \i-'ran-ē, -'rän-\ *adj or n* — **Ira•nian** \i-'ran-ē-ən, -'rän-, -'rān-\ *adj or n*

Iraq \i-'räk, -'rak\ country [SW] Asia in Mesopotamia; a republic; capital, Baghdad — **Iraqi** \-'räk-ē, -'rak-\ *adj or n*

Ire•land \'īr-lənd\ **1** *or Latin* **Hi•ber•nia** \hī-'bər-nē-ə\ island [W] Europe in the Atlantic; one of the British Isles **2** *or* **Irish Republic** *or* **Ei•re** \'ar-ə, 'ar-ē, 'er-, 'ār-, 'īr-\ country occupying major portion of the island; a republic; capital, Dublin

Irian — see NEW GUINEA

Irish \'īr-ish\ sea arm of the Atlantic between Great Britain & Ireland

Ir•kutsk \iər-'kütsk, ,ər-\ city U.S.S.R. in [E] central Soviet Russia, Asia, near Lake Baikal

Ir•ra•wad•dy \,ir-ə-'wäd-ē\ river 2175 kilometers long Burma flowing [S] into Bay of Bengal

Ir•tysh \iər-'tish, ,ər-\ river 3540 kilometers long central Asia flowing [NW] & [N] from Altai mountains in Sinkiang, China, into the Ob in U.S.S.R.

Is•fa•han \,is-fə-'hän, -'han\ *or* **Es•fa•han** \,es-\ *or formerly* **Is•pa•han** \,is-pə-\ city [W] central Iran

Is•lam•abad \is-'läm-ə-,bäd, iz-'lam-ə-,bad\ city, capital of Pakistan in [NE] Pakistan

Isle of Man — see MAN

Isle Roy•ale \'īl-'rȯi-əl, -'rȯil\ island Michigan in Lake Superior in **Isle Royale National Park**

Is•ling•ton \'iz-ling-tən\ borough of [N] Greater London, England

Is•ma•ilia \,iz-mä-ə-'lē-ə\ city [NE] Egypt on Suez canal

Is•ra•el \'iz-rē-əl\ **1** ancient kingdom Palestine comprising lands occupied by the Hebrew people **2** *or* **Northern Kingdom** *or* **Ephra•im** \'ē-frē-əm\ the [N] part of the Hebrew kingdom after about 933 B.C. — see JUDAH **3** country [SW] Asia in Palestine; a republic established 1948; capital, Jerusalem — **Is•rae•li** \iz-'rā-lē\ *adj or n*

Is•tan•bul \,is-təm-'bül, -,täm-, -,tam-, -,tän-\ *or formerly* **Con•stan•ti•no•ple** \,kän-,stant-n-'ō-pəl\ *or ancient* **By•zan•tium** \bə-'zan-shəm, -shē-əm; -'zant-ē-əm\ city [NW] Turkey on the Bosporus & Sea of Marmara; former capital of Turkey

Is•tria \'is-trē-ə\ peninsula [S] central Europe extending into the [N] Adriatic; belongs to Yugoslavia except for Trieste (to Italy) — **Is•tri•an** \-trē-ən\ *adj or n*

Italian Somaliland former country [E] Africa now part of Somalia

It•a•ly \'it-l-ē\ 1 peninsula 1225 kilometers long [S] Europe extending into the Mediterranean between Adriatic & Tyrrhenian seas **2** country including the peninsula of Italy, Sicily, & Sardinia; a republic; capital, Rome

Itas•ca, Lake \ī-'tas-kə\ lake [NW] central Minnesota; source of the Mississippi

Ith•a•ca \'ith-i-kə\ island [W] Greece in Ionian islands

Iva•no•vo \i-'vän-ə-və\ city U.S.S.R. in central Soviet Russia, Europe, [WNW] of Gorki

Ivory Coast *or French* **Côte d'Ivoire** \,kōt-dēv-'wär\ country [W]

Africa on Gulf of Guinea; a republic; capital, Abidjan
Iwa•ki \i-'wäk-ē\ city Japan in [N] Honshu on coast [SE] of Fukushima
Iwo \'ē-wō\ city [SW] Nigeria [NE] of Ibadan
Iwo Ji•ma \,ē-wō-'jē-mə\ island Japan in [W] Pacific in Volcano islands about 1130 kilometers [SSE] of Tokyo
Izhevsk \'ē-,zhefsk\ city U.S.S.R. in [E] Soviet Russia, Europe, [NE] of Kazan
Iz•mir \iz-'miər\ *or formerly* **Smyr•na** \'smər-nə\ city [W] Turkey
Ja•bal•pur \'jəb-əl-,pu̇r\ *or formerly* **Jub•bul•pore** \'jəb-əl-,pōr, -,pȯr\ city central India in central Madhya Pradesh
Jack•son \'jak-sən\ city, capital of Mississippi
Jack•son•ville \'jak-sən-,vil\ city [NE] Florida
Jadotville — see LIKASI
Jaf•fa \'jaf-ə, 'yaf-ə\ *or ancient* **Jop•pa** \'jäp-ə\ former city, now part of Tel Aviv, Israel
Jai•pur \'jī-,pu̇r\ city [NW] India, capital of Rajasthan
Ja•kar•ta *or* **Dja•kar•ta** \jə-'kärt-ə\ *or formerly* **Ba•ta•via** \bə-'tā-vē-ə\ city, capital of Indonesia in [NW] Java
Ja•la•pa \hə-'läp-ə\ city [E] Mexico, capital of Veracruz
Ja•lis•co \hə-'lis-kō\ state [W] central Mexico; capital, Guadalajara
Ja•mai•ca \jə-'mā-kə\ island West Indies in Greater Antilles; a dominion of British Commonwealth; capital, Kingston — **Ja•mai•can** \-kən\ *adj or n*
James \'jāmz\ **1** river 1145 kilometers long North and South Dakota flowing [S] into the Missouri **2** river 550 kilometers long Virginia flowing [E] into Chesapeake Bay
James Bay the [S] extension of Hudson Bay between [NE] Ontario & [W] Quebec
James•town \'jām-,stau̇n\ ruined village [E] Virginia on James river; first permanent English settlement in America (1607)
Jammu and Kashmir — see KASHMIR
Jam•na•gar \jäm-'nəg-ər\ *or* **Na•va•na•gar** \,näv-ə-'nəg-ər\ city [W] India in [W] Gujarat
Jam•shed•pur \'jäm-,shed-,pu̇r\ city [E] India in [S] Bihar
Ja•pan \jə-'pan, ji-, ja-\ *or Japanese* **Nip•pon** \nip-'än\ *or* **Ni•hon** \'nē-'hȯn\ country [E] Asia comprising Honshu, Hokkaido, Kyushu, Shikoku, & other islands in the [W] Pacific; an empire; capital, Tokyo
Japan, Sea of arm of the Pacific between Japan & Asian mainland
Japan current *or Japanese* **Ku•ro•shio** \,ku̇r-ō-'shē-,ō\ warm current of the Pacific ocean flowing from [E] coast of Philippines [N] along [E] coast of Japan and thence eastward
Jas•per National Park \'jas-pər\ reservation [W] Alberta on [E] slope of Rocky mountains
Ja•va \'jäv-ə, 'jav-ə\ island Indonesia [SW] of Borneo; chief city, Jakarta — **Ja•van** \-ən\ *adj or n*
Jef•fer•son City \'jef-ər-sən\ city, capital of Missouri
Je•rez \hə-'rās\ *or in full* **Je•rez de la Fron•te•ra** \hə-'rez-də-lə-,frən-'ter-ə\ city [SW] Spain
Jer•i•cho \'jer-i-,kō\ ancient city [E] Palestine [N] of Dead sea
Jer•sey \'jər-zē\ **1** island in English channel — see CHANNEL **2** NEW JERSEY — **Jer•sey•ite** \-zē-,īt\ *n*
Jersey City city [NE] New Jersey on Hudson river
Je•ru•sa•lem \jə-'rü-sə-ləm, -sləm; -'rüz-ə-ləm, -'rüz-ləm\ city [NW] of Dead sea divided 1948–67 between Israel & Jordan; capital of Israel since 1950 & formerly of ancient kingdoms of Israel & Judah
Jhan•si \'jän-sē\ city [N] India in [SE] Uttar Pradesh [SW] of Kanpur
Jibuti — see DJIBOUTI
Jid•da \'jid-ə\ *or* **Jed•da** \'jed-ə\ *or* **Jud•dah** \'jəd-ə\ *or* **Djed•dah** \'jed-ə\ city [W] Saudi Arabia in Hejaz on Red sea; port for Mecca
João Pes•soa \,zhau̇ⁿ-pə-'sō-ə, ,zhau̇ⁿm-\ city [NE] Brazil [N] of Recife
Jodh•pur \'jäd-pər, -,pu̇r\ city [NW] India in central Rajasthan
Jo•han•nes•burg \jō-'han-əs-,bərg, -'hän-\ city [NE] Republic of South Africa in [S] Transvaal
Jo•hore Bah•ru \jə-'hōr-'bä-rü, -'hȯr-\ city Malaysia in [S] Peninsular Malaysia opposite Singapore Island
Jor•dan \'jord-n\ **1** river 320 kilometers long Israel & Jordan rising in Syria & flowing [S] from Anti-Lebanon mountains into Dead sea **2** *or formerly* **Trans•jor•dan** \trans-, tranz-, 'trans-, 'tranz-\ country [SW] Asia in [NW] Arabia; capital, Amman — **Jor•da•ni•an** \jȯr-'dā-nē-ən\ *adj or n*

Juan de Fu•ca \,hwän-də-'fyü-kə, ,wän-\ strait 160 kilometers long between Vancouver Island, British Columbia, & Olympic peninsula, Washington
Juan Fer•nán•dez \,hwän-fər-'nan-dəs, ,wän-\ group of three islands [SE] Pacific 645 kilometers [W] of Chile; belongs to Chile
Juárez — see CIUDAD JUÁREZ
Jubbulpore — see JABALPUR
Ju•dah \'jüd-ə\ ancient kingdom [S] Palestine; capital, Jerusalem — see ISRAEL
Ju•dea *or* **Ju•daea** \jü-'dē-ə, -'dā-\ ancient region Palestine constituting the [S] division (Judah) of the country under Persian, Greek, & Roman rule — **Ju•de•an** \-ən\ *adj or n*
Ju•go•sla•via \,yü-gō-'släv-ē-ə\ — see YUGOSLAVIA — **Ju•go•slav** \,yü-gō-'släv, -'slav\ *or* **Ju•go•sla•vi•an** \-'släv-ē-ən\ *adj or n*
Juiz de Fo•ra \,zhwēzh-də-'fōr-ə, -'fȯr-\ city [E] Brazil [N] of Rio de Janeiro
Jul•lun•dur \'jəl-ən-dər\ city [N] India in Punjab [SE] of Amritsar
Ju•neau \'jü-nō, jü-'\ city, capital of Alaska
Jung•frau \'yu̇ŋ-,frau̇\ mountain 4158 meters [SW] central Switzerland in Bernese Alps
Ju•ra \'ju̇r-ə\ mountain range extending along boundary between France & Switzerland [N] of Lake Geneva
Jut•land \'jət-lənd\ **1** peninsula [N] Europe extending into North sea & comprising mainland of Denmark & [N] portion of Schleswig-Holstein, West Germany **2** the mainland of Denmark
Kaapstad — see CAPE TOWN
Ka•bul \'käb-əl, kä-'bül\ city, capital of Afghanistan
Ka•di•yev•ka \kə-'dē-əf-kə, -yəf-\ city U.S.S.R. in [E] Ukraine in Donets basin
Kae•song \'kā-,sȯŋ\ city North Korea [SE] of Pyongyang
Ka•go•shi•ma \,käg-ə-'shē-mə, kä-'gō-shə-mə\ city Japan in [S] Kyushu
Kai•feng \'kī-'fəŋ\ city [E] central China in [NE] Honan
Ka Lae \kä-'lä-ā\ *or* **South Cape** *or* **South Point** most southerly point of Hawaii & of U.S.
Kal•a•ha•ri \,kal-ə-'här-ē\ desert region [S] Africa [N] of Orange river in [S] Botswana & [NW] Republic of South Africa
Kal•gan \'kal-'gan\ *or formerly* **Wan-ch'uan** \'wän-chü-'än\ city [NE] China in [NW] Hopei [NW] of Peking
Ka•li•man•tan \,kal-ə-'man-,tan, ,käl-ə-'män-,tän\ **1** BORNEO — its Indonesian name **2** the [S] & [E] portion of Borneo belonging to Indonesia; formerly (as **Dutch Borneo**) part of Netherlands East Indies
Ka•li•nin \kə-'lē-nən, -'lēn-,yēn\ city U.S.S.R. in [W] central Soviet Russia, Europe, on the Volga
Ka•li•nin•grad \kə-'lē-nən-,grad, -nyən-\ *or German* **Kö•nigs•berg** \'kā-nigz-,bərg, 'kərn-igz-, -,beərg, *German* 'kœ-niks-,berk\ city U.S.S.R. in [W] Soviet Russia, Europe, [NE] of Gdansk, Poland
Ka•lu•ga \kə-'lü-gə\ city U.S.S.R. in [W] central Soviet Russia, Europe, [WNW] of Oka
Ka•mar•ha•ti \,käm-ər-'hät-ē\ city [E] India in West Bengal [N] of Calcutta
Kam•chat•ka \kam-'chat-kə\ peninsula 1205 kilometers long U.S.S.R. in [NE] Soviet Russia, Asia, between Sea of Okhotsk & Bering sea
Ka•mensk-Ural•ski \'käm-ən-sku̇-'ral-skē\ *or formerly* **Ka•mensk** \'käm-ənsk\ city U.S.S.R. in [W] Soviet Russia, Asia, [SE] of Sverdlovsk
Kam•pa•la \käm-'päl-ə\ city, capital of Uganda
Ka•nan•ga \kə-'näŋ-gə\ *or formerly* **Lu•lua•bourg** \lü-'lü-ə-,bu̇rg, -,bu̇r\ city [S] central Zaire
Ka•na•za•wa \kə-'näz-ə-wə, ,kan-ə-'zä-wə\ city Japan in [W] Honshu [N] of Nagoya near Sea of Japan
Kan•chen•jun•ga \,kan-chən-'jəŋ-gə, -'ju̇ŋ-\ *or* **Kin•chin•jun•ga** \,kin-chən-\ mountain 8598 meters Nepal & Sikkim (India) in the Himalayas; third highest in the world
Kan•da•har \'kan-də-,här\ city [SE] Afghanistan
Ka•no \'kän-ō\ city [N] central Nigeria
Kan•pur \'kän-,pu̇r\ *or* **Cawn•pore** \'kȯn-,pōr, -,pȯr\ city [N] India in [S] Uttar Pradesh on the Ganges
Kan•sas \'kan-zəs\ state [W] central U.S.; capital, Topeka — **Kan•san** \-zən\ *adj or n*
Kansas City **1** city [NE] Kansas adjoining Kansas City, Missouri **2** city [W] Missouri
Kan•su \'kan-'sü, 'gän-\ province [NW] China; capital, Lanchow
Kao•hsiung \'kau̇-shē-'u̇ŋ, 'gau̇-\ city China in [SW] Taiwan

Kaolan — see LANCHOW
Ka•ra \'kär-ə\ sea arm of Arctic ocean off [N] coast of U.S.S.R. [E] of Novaya Zemlya
Ka•ra•chi \kə-'räch-ē\ city [S] Pakistan on Arabian sea
Karadeniz Bogazi — see BOSPORUS
Karafuto — see SAKHALIN
Ka•ra•gan•da \,kar-ə-gən-'dä\ city U.S.S.R. in central Kazakhstan
Kar•a•ko•ram *or* **Kar•a•ko•rum** \,kar-ə-'kōr-əm, -'kȯr-\ mountain system [S] central Asia in [N] Kashmir & [NW] Tibet connecting the Himalayas & the Pamirs
Ka•re•lia \kə-'rē-lē-ə, -'rēl-yə\ region [NE] Europe between Gulf of Finland & White sea; now chiefly in U.S.S.R. — **Ka•re•lian** \-'rē-lē-ən, -'rēl-yən\ *adj or n*
Karl–Marx–Stadt \kärl-'märk-,shtät, -,stät\ *or formerly* **Chem•nitz** \'kem-,nits, -nəts\ city East Germany [SE] of Leipzig
Karls•ru•he \'kärlz-,rü-ə\ city [SW] West Germany
Kar•na•ta•ka \kär-'nät-ə-kə\ *or formerly* **My•sore** \mī-'sōr, -'sȯr\ state [S] India; capital, Bangalore
Kar•roo \kə-'rü\ plateau region [W] Republic of South Africa [W] of Drakensberg mountains; divided into **Little,** or **Southern, Karroo** (in [S] Cape Province), **Great,** or **Central, Karroo** (in [S] central Cape Province), & **Northern,** or **Upper, Karroo** (in [N] Cape Province, Orange Free State, & [W] Transvaal)
Kash•gar \'kash-,gär\ city [W] China in [SW] Sinkiang
Kash•mir \'kash-,miər, 'kazh-, kash-', kazh-'\ **1** mountain region [N] Indian subcontinent [NW] of Tibet & [SW] of Sinkiang **2** *or* **Jam•mu and Kashmir** \'jəm-ü\ state comprising Kashmir & Jammu regions; claimed by India & Pakistan; capital, Srinagar; winter capital, Jammu — **Kash•miri** \kash-'miər-ē, kazh-\ *adj or n*
Kas•sel \'kas-əl, 'käs-\ city West Germany [WNW] of Erfurt
Ka•thi•a•war \,kät-ē-ə-'wär\ peninsula [W] India in Gujarat [N] of Gulf of Cambay
Kat•mai, Mount \'kat-,mī\ volcano 2047 meters [S] Alaska in Aleutian range
Kat•man•du *or* **Khat•man•du** \,kat-,man-'dü, -mən-\ city, capital of Nepal
Ka•to•wi•ce \,kät-ə-'vēt-sə\ city [S] Poland [WNW] of Krakow
Kat•te•gat \'kat-i-,gat\ arm of North sea between Sweden & [E] coast of Jutland peninsula of Denmark
Kau•ai \'kaů-,ī\ island Hawaii [NW] of Oahu
Kau•nas \'kaů-nəs, -,näs\ *or Russian* **Kov•no** \'kȯv-nō\ city U.S.S.R. in central Lithuania
Ka•wa•gu•chi \,kä-wə-'gü-chē, kä-'wäg-ů-chē\ city Japan in [E] Honshu [N] of Tokyo
Ka•wa•sa•ki \,kä-wə-'säk-ē\ city Japan in [E] Honshu [S] of Tokyo
Ka•zakh•stan *or* **Ka•zak•stan** \kə-,zak-'stan; kə-,zäk-'stän, ,kä-\ *or* **Ka•zakh Soviet Socialist Republic** \kə-,zak-, -,zäk-\ constituent republic of U.S.S.R. in Soviet Central Asia; capital, Alma-Ata
Ka•zan \kə-'zan, -'zän, -'zän-yə\ city U.S.S.R. in [E] central Soviet Russia, Europe
Kazan Retto — see VOLCANO ISLANDS
Kee•wa•tin \kē-'wāt-n\ district [N] Canada in [E] Northwest Territories [NW] of Hudson Bay
Kej•im•ku•jik National Park \,kej-mə-'kü-jik, -ə-mə-\ reservation [E] Canada in [SW] Nova Scotia
Ke•me•ro•vo \'kem-ə-rə-və, -,rō-və, -rə-,vō\ city U.S.S.R. in [S] Soviet Russia, Asia, in Kuznetsk basin
Ke•nai \'kē-,nī\ peninsula [S] Alaska [E] of Cook inlet
Ke•ni•tra \kə-'nē-trə\ *or formerly* **Port Lyau•tey** \,pȯr-lē-,ō-'tā, -'ō-,\ city [N] Morocco
Kennedy, Cape — see CANAVERAL
Ken•sing•ton and Chel•sea \'ken-zing-tən-ən-'chel-sē, 'ken-sing-\ royal borough of [W] Greater London, England
Kent \'kent\ county [SE] England — **Kent•ish** \'kent-ish\ *adj*
Ken•tucky \kən-'tək-ē\ state [E] central U.S.; capital, Frankfort — **Ken•tuck•i•an** \-ē-ən\ *adj or n*
Ken•ya \'ken-yə, 'kēn-\ **1** mountain 5194 meters central Kenya **2** country [E] Africa [S] of Ethiopia; a republic; capital, Nairobi — **Ken•yan** \-yən\ *adj or n*
Ker•a•la \'ker-ə-lə\ state [SW] India bordering on Arabian sea; capital, Trivandrum
Ker•gue•len \'kər-gə-lən, ,kər-gə-'len\ **1** archipelago [S] Indian ocean belonging to France **2** chief island of the archipelago
Ker•ry \'ker-ē\ county [SW] Ireland in Munster
Kes•te•ven, Parts of \ke-'stē-vən\ district & former administrative county [E] England in [SW] Lincolnshire
Kha•ba•rovsk \kə-'bär-əfsk\ city U.S.S.R. in [E] Soviet Russia, Asia, on the Amur
Khar•kov \'kär-,kȯf, -kȯv -kəf\ city U.S.S.R. in [NE] Ukraine
Khar•toum \kär-'tüm\ city, capital of Sudan
Kher•son \keər-'sȯn\ city U.S.S.R. in [S] Ukraine
Khmer Republic \kə-'meər-\ *or* **Cam•bo•dia** \kam-'bōd-ē-ə\ country [SE] Asia bordering on Gulf of Siam; capital, Phnom Penh
Khul•na \'kůl-nə\ city [SW] Bangladesh
Khy•ber \'kī-bər\ pass 53 kilometers long on border between Afghanistan & Pakistan [WNW] of Peshawar
Kia•mu•sze *or* **Chia–mu–ssu** \jē-'ä-'mü-'sü\ city [NE] China in [NE] Heilungkiang
Kiang•si \jē-'äng-'sē\ province [SE] China; capital, Nanchang
Kiang•su \jē-'äng-'sü\ province [E] China; capital, Nanking
Kiangtu — see YANG-CHOU
Ki•bo \'kē-bō\ mountain peak 5888 meters [NE] Tanzania; highest peak of Kilimanjaro & highest point in Africa
Kiel \'kēl\ **1** city [N] West Germany, capital of Schleswig-Holstein **2** ship canal 98 kilometers long [N] West Germany connecting Baltic & North seas
Kiel•ce \kē-'elt-sā\ city [S] Poland [S] of Warsaw
Ki•ev *or Russian* **Ki•yev** \'kē-,ef, -,ev, -əf, -,yef, -,yev, -yəf\ city U.S.S.R., capital of Ukraine
Ki•ga•li \ki-'gäl-ē\ city, capital of Rwanda
Ki•lau•ea \,kē-,laů-'ā-ə\ volcanic crater Hawaii on Hawaii Island on [E] slope of Mauna Loa in Hawaii Volcanoes National Park
Kil•dare \kil-'daər, -'deər\ county [E] Ireland in Leinster
Kil•i•man•ja•ro \,kil-ə-mən-'jär-ō, -'jar-\ mountain [NE] Tanzania; highest in Africa — see KIBO
Kil•ken•ny \kil-'ken-ē\ county [SE] Ireland in Leinster
Kil•lar•ney, Lakes of \kil-'är-nē\ three lakes [SW] Ireland in Kerry
Kim•ber•ley \'kim-bər-lē\ city Republic of South Africa in [N] Cape of Good Hope
Kin•car•dine \kin-'kärd-n\ *or* **Kin•car•dine•shire** \-,shiər, -shər\ former county [E] Scotland
Kinchinjunga — see KANCHENJUNGA
Kings Canyon National Park \'kingz-\ reservation [SE] central California in Sierra Nevada [N] of Sequoia National Park
Kings•ton \'king-stən\ city, capital of Jamaica
Kingston upon Hull — see HULL
Kingston upon Thames \'temz\ royal borough of [SW] Greater London, England
Kin•ross \kin-'rȯs\ *or* **Kin•ross–shire** \-'rȯs-,shiər, -shər, -'rȯsh-\ former county [E] central Scotland
Kin•sha•sa \kin-'shäs-ə\ *or formerly* **Lé•o•pold•ville** \'lē-ə-,pōld-,vil, 'lā-\ city, capital of Zaire
Kir•ghi•zia \kiər-'gē-zē-ə, -zhə, -zhē-ə\ *or* **Kir•giz Soviet Socialist Republic** \kiər-,gēz-\ constituent republic of U.S.S.R. in Soviet Central Asia on Sinkiang border; capital, Frunze
Ki•rin \'kē-'rin\ **1** province [NE] China in [E] Manchuria; capital, Changchun **2** city in Kirin province
Kirk•cud•bright \kər-'kü-brē\ *or* **Kirk•cud•bright•shire** \-,shiər, -shər\ former county [S] Scotland
Kir•kuk \kiər-'kük\ city [NE] Iraq
Ki•rov \'kē-,rȯf, -,rȯv, -rəf\ city U.S.S.R. in [E] Soviet Russia, Europe, [N] of Kazan
Ki•ro•vo•grad \ki-'rō-və-,grad\ city U.S.S.R. in [S] central Ukraine
Ki•san•ga•ni \,kē-sən-'gän-ē\ *or formerly* **Stan•ley•ville** \'stan-lē-,vil\ city [NE] Zaire
Ki•shi•nev \'kish-ə-,nef, -,nev\ *or Rumanian* **Chi•si•nau** \,kē-shi-'naů\ city U.S.S.R., capital of Moldavia
Ki•ta•kyu•shu \kē-'tä-kē-'ü-shü\ city Japan in [N] Kyushu
Kitch•e•ner \'kich-nər, -ə-nər\ city Canada in [SE] Ontario
Klon•dike \'klän-,dīk\ region [NW] Canada in central Yukon Territory in valley of Klondike river [E] of Dawson
Knos•sos *or* **Cnos•sus** \kə-'näs-əs, 'näs-əs\ *or* **Gnos•sus** \gə-'näs-əs, 'näs-əs\ ruined city, capital of ancient Crete near [N] coast
Knox•ville \'näks-,vil, -vəl\ city [E] Tennessee
Ko•be \'kō-bē, -,bā\ city Japan in [S] Honshu
Ko•chi \'kō-chē\ city Japan on [S] coast of Shikoku
Ko•di•ak \'kōd-ē-,ak\ island [S] Alaska [E] of Alaska peninsula
Koh–i–nuh — see ARARAT
Ko•kand \kō-'kand\ city U.S.S.R. in [E] Uzbekistan [SE] of Tashkent

Koko Nor — see TSINGHAI
Ko•la \'kō-lə\ peninsula U.S.S.R. in [NW] Soviet Russia, Europe, between Barents & White seas
Ko•lar Gold Fields \kō-'lär\ city [S] India in [SE] Karnataka [NE] of Bangalore
Kol•ha•pur \'kō-lə-,pu̇r\ city [W] India in [SW] Maharashtra [SSE] of Bombay
Köln — see COLOGNE
Ko•lom•na \kə-'lȯm-nə\ city U.S.S.R. in central Soviet Russia, Europe, [SE] of Moscow
Ko•mo•do \kə-'mōd-ō\ island Indonesia in the Lesser Sundas [W] of Flores Island
Konakry — see CONAKRY
Königsberg — see KALININGRAD
Kon•ya \kȯn-'yä\ city [SW] central Turkey
Koo•te•nay National Park \'küt-n-,ā, -n-ē\ reservation [SE] British Columbia
Ko•rea \kə-'rē-ə, *especially South* kō-\ country [E] Asia between Yellow sea & Sea of Japan; capital, Seoul; divided after World War II at 38th parallel into republics of **North Korea** (capital, Pyongyang) & **South Korea** (capital, Seoul)
Kō•ri•ya•ma \,kōr-ē-'äm-ə, ,kȯr-, -'yäm-\ city Japan in [N] central Honshu
Kos•ci•us•ko, Mount \,käz-ē-'əs-kō\ mountain 2230 meters [SE] Australia in [SE] New South Wales; highest in Great Dividing range & in Australia
Kos•tro•ma \,käs-trə-'mä\ city U.S.S.R. in [N] central Soviet Russia, Europe, on the Volga
Kovno — see KAUNAS
Kov•rov \kəv-'rȯf, -'rȯv\ city U.S.S.R. in central Soviet Russia, Europe, [E] of Moscow
Kow•loon \'kau̇-'lün\ city Hong Kong colony on Kowloon peninsula opposite Hong Kong Island
Kozhikode — see CALICUT
Krak•a•toa \,krak-ə-'tō-ə\ *or* **Krak•a•tau** \-'tau̇\ island & volcano Indonesia between Sumatra & Java
Kra•kow *or* **Cra•cow** \'kräk-,au̇, 'krak-, 'krāk-, -ō, *Polish* 'kräk-,üf\ city [S] Poland
Kra•ma•torsk \,kräm-ə-'tȯrsk\ city U.S.S.R. in [E] Ukraine
Kras•no•dar \'kras-nə-,där\ city U.S.S.R. in [S] Soviet Russia, Europe, in [N] Caucasus
Kras•no•yarsk \,kras-nə-'yärsk\ city U.S.S.R. in [W] central Soviet Russia, Asia, on the upper Yenisei
Kre•feld \'krā-,felt\ city [W] West Germany on the Rhine [WSW] of Essen
Kri•voi Rog \,kri-,vȯi-'rōg, -'rȯk\ city U.S.S.R. in [SE] central Ukraine
Kru•ger National Park \'krü-gər\ game reserve [NE] Republic of South Africa in [E] Transvaal on Mozambique border
Kru•gers•dorp \'krü-gərz-,dȯrp, 'krue̅-ərz-\ city [NE] Republic of South Africa in [S] Transvaal
K^2 — see GODWIN AUSTEN
Kua•la Lum•pur \,kwäl-ə-'lu̇m-,pu̇r, -'ləm-\ city, capital of Federation of Malaysia in Peninsular Malaysia
Kui•by•shev *or* **Kuy•by•shev** \'kwē-bə-,shef, 'kü-ē-bə-, -,shev\ city U.S.S.R. in [SE] Soviet Russia, Europe, on the Volga
Kuku–Khoto — see HUHEHOT
Ku•ma•mo•to \,küm-ə-'mōt-ō\ city Japan in [W] Kyushu
Ku•ma•si \kü-'mäs-ē, -'mas-\ city [S] central Ghana
Kun•lun *or* **Kuen•lun** *or* **Kwen•lun** \'kün-'lün\ mountain system [W] China extending [E] from the Pamirs to [SE] Tsinghai; highest peak Ulugh Muztagh 7724 meters
Kun•ming \'kün-'miŋ\ *or formerly* **Yun•nan** \yü-'nän\ *or* **Yun•nan•fu** \-'fü\ city [S] China, capital of Yunnan
Ku•ra•shi•ki \kü-'rä-shē-kē, ,ku̇r-ə-'shē-kē\ city Japan in [W] Honshu [WSW] of Okayama
Kur•di•stan \,kərd-ə-'stan, ,kərd-\ region [SW] Asia chiefly in [E] Turkey, [NW] Iran, and [N] Iraq
Ku•re \'ku̇r-ē, 'kyu̇r-ē, 'kü-rā\ city Japan in [SW] Honshu on Inland sea [SE] of Hiroshima
Kur•gan \ku̇r-'gan, -'gän\ city U.S.S.R. in [W] Soviet Russia, Asia, [SE] of Sverdlovsk
Ku•ril *or* **Ku•rile** \'kyu̇r-,ēl, kyu̇-'rēl\ islands U.S.S.R. in the Pacific between [S] Kamchatka peninsula & [NE] Hokkaido Island
Kur•nool \kər-'nül\ city [S] India in [W] Andhra Pradesh [SSW] of Hyderabad
Kuroshio — see JAPAN CURRENT
Kursk \'ku̇rsk\ city U.S.S.R. in [SW] Soviet Russia, Europe, [N] of Kharkov

Ku•tai•si \ku̇-'tī-sē\ city U.S.S.R. in [W] Georgia [WNW] of Tiflis
Ku•wait *or* **Ku•weit** \kə-'wāt\ *or* **Al Kuwait** \,al-\ **1** country [SW] Asia in Arabia at head of Persian gulf **2** city, its capital — **Ku•waiti** \-'wāt-ē\ *adj or n*
Kuybyshev — see KUIBYSHEV
Kuz•netsk basin \ku̇z-'netsk\ *or* **Kuz•bass** *or* **Kuz•bas** \'ku̇z-,bas\ basin of Tom river U.S.S.R. in [W] central Soviet Russia, Asia, extending from Tomsk to Novokuznetsk
Kwa•ja•lein \'kwäj-ə-lən, -,lān\ island (atoll) [W] Pacific in Ralik chain of Marshall islands
Kwangchow — see CANTON
Kwang•ju \'gwäŋ-,jü, 'kwäŋ-\ city [SW] South Korea
Kwang•si \'gwäŋ-'sē, 'kwäŋ-\ region & former province [S] China; capital, Nanning
Kwang•tung \'gwäŋ-'du̇ŋ, 'kwäŋ-, -'tu̇ŋ\ province [SE] China bordering on South China sea & Gulf of Tonkin; capital, Canton
Kwei•chow \'gwā-'jō, 'kwā-\ province [S] China [S] of Szechwan; capital, Kweiyang
Kwei•lin *or* **Kuei–lin** \'gwā-'lin, 'kwā-\ city [S] China in [NE] Kwangsi
Kweisui — see HUHEHOT
Kwei•yang *or* **Kuei–yang** \'gwā-'yäŋ, 'kwā-\ *or formerly* **Kwei•chu** \-'jü\ city [S] China, capital of Kweichow
Kyongsong — see SEOUL
Kyo•to \kē-'ōt-ō\ city Japan in [W] central Honshu; formerly capital of Japan
Kyu•shu \kē-'ü-shü\ island Japan [S] of [W] end of Honshu
Labe — see ELBE
Lab•ra•dor \'lab-rə-,dȯr\ **1** peninsula [E] Canada between Hudson Bay & the Atlantic divided between Quebec & Newfoundland **2** the part of the peninsula belonging to Newfoundland — **Lab•ra•dor•ean** *or* **Lab•ra•dor•ian** \,lab-rə-'dȯr-ē-ən, -'dōr-\ *adj or n*
Labrador current cold current flowing [S] from Baffin Bay through Davis strait to Newfoundland
Lac•ca•dive \'lak-ə-,dēv, -,dīv\ islands India in Arabian sea [N] of Maldive islands; part of **Laccadive, Min•i•coy, and Amin•divi Islands** \'min-i-,kȯi . . . ,əm-ən-'dē-vē\ territory
Lac•e•dae•mon \,las-ə-'dē-mən\ — see SPARTA — **Lac•e•dae•mo•nian** \,las-əd-i-'mō-nē-ən, -nyən\ *adj or n*
La•co•nia \lə-'kō-nē-ə, -nyə\ ancient country [S] Greece in [SE] Peloponnesus; capital, Sparta — **La•co•nian** \-nē-ən, -nyən\ *adj or n*
Lad•o•ga \'lad-ə-gə, 'läd-\ lake U.S.S.R. in [NW] Soviet Russia, Europe
La•gos \'lā-,gäs\ city, capital of Nigeria
La Habana — see HAVANA
La•hon•tan, Lake \lə-'hänt-n\ prehistoric lake [NW] Nevada & [NE] California
La•hore \lə-'hōr, -'hȯr\ city Pakistan in [E] Punjab province
Lake District region [NW] England in Cumbria & [NW] Lancashire containing many lakes & mountains
Lam•beth \'lam-bəth, -,beth\ borough of [S] Greater London, England
La•nai \lə-'nī\ island Hawaii [W] of Maui
Lan•ark \'lan-ərk\ *or* **Lan•ark•shire** \-,shiər, -shər\ former county [S] central Scotland; chief city, Glasgow
Lan•ca•shire \'laŋ-kə-,shiər, -shər\ *or* **Lan•cas•ter** \'laŋ-kəstər\ county [NW] England — **Lan•cas•tri•an** \laŋ-'kas-trē-ən, lan-\ *adj or n*
Lan•chow *or* **Lan–chou** \'län-'jō\ *or* **Kao•lan** \'kau̇-'län\ city [W] central China, capital of Kansu
Lands End *or* **Land's End** \'land-'zend, 'lan-\ *or ancient* **Bo•le•ri•um** \bə-'lir-ē-əm\ cape [SW] England at [SW] tip of Cornwall
Lan•gue•doc \,laŋ-gə-'däk; ,lä^{n}-gə-'dȯk, ,lä^{n}ŋ-\ region & former province [S] France on the Mediterranean [W] of Provence
Lan•sing \'lan-siŋ\ city, capital of Michigan
La•nús \lə-'nüs\ city [E] Argentina [S] of Buenos Aires
Lao–chün–miao — see YÜ-MEN
Laoighis \'lāsh, 'lēsh\ *or* **Leix** \'lāsh, 'lēsh\ *or formerly* **Queen's** \'kwēnz\ county central Ireland in Leinster
Laos \'lau̇s, 'lā-,äs, 'lā-ōs\ country [SE] Asia in Indochina [NE] of Thailand; a republic; capital, Vientiane
La Paz \lə-'paz, -'päz, -'päs\ city, administrative capital of Bolivia
Lap•land \'lap-,land, -lənd\ region [N] Europe above the arctic

circle in [N] Norway, [N] Sweden, [N] Finland, & Kola peninsula of U.S.S.R. — **Lap•land•er** \-,lan-dər, -lən-\ *n*

La Pla•ta \lə-'plät-ə\ city [E] Argentina [SE] of Buenos Aires

Las Pal•mas \lä-'späl-məs\ city Spain in the Canary islands on Grand Canary Island

La Spe•zia \lä-'spet-sē-ə\ city [NW] Italy in Liguria [SE] of Genoa

Las•sen Peak \'las-n\ volcano 3187 meters [N] California at [S] end of Cascade range in **Lassen Volcanic National Park**

Las Ve•gas \läs-'vā-gəs\ city [SE] Nevada

Lat•a•kia \,lat-ə-'kē-ə\ city [NW] Syria

Latin America **1** Spanish America and Brazil **2** all of the Americas [S] of the U.S. — **Latin-American** *adj* — **Latin American** *n*

La•tium \'lā-shē-əm, -shəm\ *or Italian* **La•zio** \'lät-sē-ō\ region central Italy on Tyrrhenian sea; capital, Rome

Lat•via \'lat-vē-ə\ country [E] Europe on Baltic sea; since 1940 a constituent republic (**Latvian Republic**) of U.S.S.R.; capital, Riga

Lau•ren•tian \lò-'ren-chən\ hills [E] Canada in [S] Quebec [N] of the Saint Lawrence on [S] edge of Laurentian Highlands

Laurentian Highlands *or* **Canadian Shield** plateau region [E] Canada & [NE] U.S. extending from Mackenzie basin [E] to Davis strait & [S] to [S] Quebec, [S] central Ontario, [NE] Minnesota, [N] Wisconsin, [NW] Michigan, and [NE] New York including the Adirondacks

La•val \lə-'val\ city [S] Quebec [NW] of Montreal

Leb•a•non \'leb-ə-nən, -,nän\ **1** *or ancient* **Lib•a•nus** \'lib-ə-nəs\ mountains Lebanon running parallel to coast; highest Dahr el Qadib 3088 meters **2** country [SW] Asia on the Mediterranean; a republic; capital, Beirut — **Leb•a•nese** \,leb-ə-'nēz, -'nēs\ *adj or n*

Leeds \'lēdz\ city [N] England in West Yorkshire

Lee•ward \'lē-wərd\ **1** islands Hawaii extending [WNW] from main islands of the group **2** islands [S] Pacific in [W] Society islands **3** islands West Indies in [N] Lesser Antilles

Le Ha•vre \lə-'hävr\ city [N] France on English channel

Leices•ter \'les-tər\ city central England in Leicestershire [ENE] of Birmingham

Leices•ter•shire \'les-tər-,shiər, -shər\ *or* **Leicester** county central England

Lein•ster \'len-stər\ province [E] Ireland

Leip•zig \'līp-sig, -sik\ city East Germany in Saxony

Lei•trim \'lē-trəm\ county [NW] Ireland in Connacht

Leix — see LAOIGHIS

Leman, Lake *or ancient* **Lemannus** *or* **Lemanus** — see GENEVA

Lemberg — see LVOV

Lem•nos \'lem-,näs, -nəs\ *or Greek* **Lím•nos** \'lēm-,nòs\ island Greece in the [N] Aegean

Le•na \'lē-nə, 'lā-\ river 4830 kilometers long U.S.S.R. in [W] Soviet Russia, Asia, flowing [NE] & [N] into Arctic ocean

Le•nin•grad \'len-ən-,grad\ *or formerly* **Saint Pe•ters•burg** \sānt-'pēt-ərz-,bərg, sənt-\ *or* **Pe•tro•grad** \'pe-trə-,grad\ city U.S.S.R. in [NW] Soviet Russia, Europe, on Gulf of Finland

Le•ón \lā-'ōn\ **1** city central Mexico in Guanajuato **2** region & ancient kingdom [NW] Spain

Léopoldville — see KINSHASA

Le Puglie — see APULIA

Les•bos \'lez-,bäs, -bəs\ *or* **Myt•i•le•ne** \,mit-l-'ē-nē\ *or Greek* **Mi•ti•lí•ni** \,mit-l-'ē-nē\ island Greece in the Aegean off [NW] coast of Asia Minor

Le•so•tho \lə-'sō-tō\ country [S] Africa surrounded by Republic of South Africa; formerly British territory of **Ba•su•to•land** \bə-'süt-ə-,land\, now an independent monarchy in British Commonwealth; capital, Maseru

Lesser An•til•les \an-'til-ēz\ islands in the West Indies including Virgin, Leeward, & Windward islands, Barbados, Trinidad, Tobago, & islands in the [S] Caribbean [N] of Venezuela — see GREATER ANTILLES

Lesser Armenia region [S] Turkey corresponding to ancient Cilicia

Lesser Sunda — see SUNDA

Le•vant \lə-'vant\ the countries bordering on the [E] Mediterranean — **Lev•an•tine** \'lev-ən-,tīn, -,tēn, lə-'van-\ *adj or n*

Lew•i•sham \'lü-ə-shəm\ borough of [SE] Greater London, England

Lew•is with Har•ris \,lü-ə-swəth-'har-əs, -swəth-\ island [NW] Scotland in Outer Hebrides

Lex•ing•ton \'lek-sing-tən\ city [N] central Kentucky

Ley•te \'lāt-ē\ island Philippines in Visayan islands [S] of Samar

Lha•sa \'läs-ə, 'las-\ city [SW] China, capital of Tibet

Liao•ning \lē-'aù-'ning\ province [NE] China in [S] Manchuria; capital, Mukden

Liao•yang \lē-'aù-'yäng\ city [NE] China in central Liaoning [NE] of Anshan

Libanus — see LEBANON

Li•be•ria \lī-'bir-ē-ə\ country [W] Africa on the Atlantic; a republic; capital, Monrovia — **Li•be•ri•an** \-ē-ən\ *adj or n*

Lib•er•ty \'lib-ərt-ē\ *or formerly* **Bed•loe's** \'bed-,lōz\ *or* **Bed•loe** \-lō\ island [SE] New York in Upper New York Bay; the Statue of Liberty is on it

Li•bre•ville \'lē-brə-,vil, -,vēl\ city, capital of Gabon

Lib•ya \'lib-ē-ə\ **1** the part of Africa [N] of the Sahara between Egypt & Gulf of Sidra — an ancient name **2** northern Africa [W] of Egypt — an ancient name **3** *or* **Libyan Arab Republic** country [N] Africa on the Mediterranean [W] of Egypt; a republic; capital, Tripoli — **Lib•y•an** \'lib-ē-ən\ *adj or n*

Libyan desert [N] Africa [W] of the Nile in Libya, Egypt, & Sudan

Li•do \'lēd-ō\ island Italy in Adriatic sea

Liech•ten•stein \'lik-tən-,stīn, -,shtīn\ country [W] Europe between Austria & Switzerland; a principality; capital, Vaduz — **Liech•ten•stein•er** \-,stī-nər, -,shtī-\ *n*

Li•ège \lē-'ezh, -'āzh\ *or Flemish* **Luik** \'līk\ city [E] Belgium

Lien-yün-chiang-shih \lē-'en-'yün-chē-'äng-'shiər\ city [E] China in Kiangsu

Lif•fey \'lif-ē\ river 80 kilometers long [E] Ireland flowing into Dublin Bay

Li•gu•ria \lə-'gyùr-ē-ə\ region [NW] Italy; capital, Genoa — **Li•gu•ri•an** \-ē-ən\ *adj or n*

Ligurian sea arm of the Mediterranean [N] of Corsica

Li•ka•si \li-'käs-ē\ *or formerly* **Ja•dot•ville** \,zhad-ō-'vēl\ city [SE] Zaire

Lille \'lēl\ city [N] France

Li•lon•gwe \li-'lòng-wā\ city, capital of Malawi

Li•ma \'lē-mə\ city, capital of Peru

Lim•burg \'lim-,bərg\ *or French* **Lim•bourg** \'lim-,bərg, la^{n}-bùr\ province [NE] Belgium

Lim•er•ick \'lim-rik, -ə-rik\ county [SW] Ireland in Munster

Límnos — see LEMNOS

Lim•po•po \lim-'pō-pō\ river 1610 kilometers long Africa flowing from Transvaal into Indian ocean in Mozambique

Lin•coln \'ling-kən\ city, capital of Nebraska

Lin•coln•shire \'ling-kən-,shiər, -shər\ *or* **Lincoln** county [E] England

Lind•sey, Parts of \'lin-zē\ district & former administrative county [E] England in [N] Lincolnshire

Line \'līn\ islands central Pacific [S] of Hawaii divided between U.S. & Great Britain

Lip•a•ri \'lip-ə-rē\ islands Italy off [NE] Sicily

Li•petsk \'lē-,petsk\ city U.S.S.R. in [S] central Soviet Russia, Europe, [N] of Voronezh

Lis•bon \'liz-bən\ *or Portuguese* **Lis•boa** \lēzh-'vō-ə\ city, capital of Portugal

Lith•u•a•nia \,lith-ə-'wā-nē-ə, ,lith-yə-, -nyə\ country [E] Europe; since 1940 a constituent republic (**Lithuanian Republic**) of U.S.S.R.; capital, Riga

Lit•tle Rock \'lit-l-,räk\ city, capital of Arkansas

Liv•er•pool \'liv-ər-,pül\ city [NW] England in Merseyside

Li•vo•nia \lə-'vō-nē-ə, -nyə\ **1** city [SE] Michigan **2** region [E] Europe on Baltic sea in Latvia & Estonia

Lju•blja•na \lē-,ü-blē-'än-ə\ city [NW] Yugoslavia in Slovenia on Sava river

Lla•no Es•ta•ca•do \'lan-ō-,es-tə-'käd-ō, 'län-\ *or* **Staked Plain** \'stākt-, 'stāk-\ plateau region [SE] New Mexico & [NW] Texas

Loanda — see LUANDA

Lodz \'lüj, 'lädz\ city central Poland [WSW] of Warsaw

Lo•fo•ten \'lō-,fōt-n\ islands [NW] Norway

Lo•gan, Mount \'lō-gən\ mountain 6050 meters [NW] Canada in Saint Elias range; highest in Canada & second highest in North America

Loire \lə-'wär\ river 1005 kilometers long central France flowing [NW] & [W] into Bay of Biscay

Lo•mas de Za•mo•ra \'lō-,mäz-də-zə-'mōr-ə, -'mòr-\ city [E] Argentina [SW] of Buenos Aires

Lom•bar•dy \'läm-,bärd-ē, -bərd-\ region [N] Italy [N] of Po river; capital, Milan

Lo•mé \lō-'mā\ city, capital of Togo

Lo•mond, Loch \'lō-mənd\ lake [S] central Scotland

Lon•don \'lən-dən\ **1** city [S] Ontario **2** city, capital of England &

of United Kingdom on the Thames; comprises **City of London** & 12 inner boroughs of Greater London — **Lon•don•er** \-də-nər\ *n*
Lon•don•der•ry \ˌlən-dən-ˈder-ē, ˈlən-dən-ˌ\ *or* **Der•ry** \ˈder-ē\ county [NW] Northern Ireland
Lon•dri•na \lō^{n}n-ˈdrē-nə, lōn-\ city [S] Brazil [W] of São Paulo
Long Beach city [SW] California [S] of Los Angeles
Long•ford \ˈlȯŋ-fərd\ county [E] central Ireland in Leinster
Long Island island 190 kilometers long [SE] New York [S] of Connecticut
Long Island Sound inlet of the Atlantic between Connecticut & Long Island, New York
Lon•gueuil \lȯŋ-ˈgāl\ city Canada in [S] Quebec [E] of Montreal
Lor•raine \lə-ˈrān, lȯ-\ region [NE] France around upper Moselle & Meuse rivers — see ALSACE-LORRAINE
Los An•ge•les \lȯ-ˈsan-jə-ləs *also* -ˈsaŋ-gə-ləs\ city [SW] California
Lo•thi•an \ˈlō-t͟hē-ən\ region [SE] Scotland [S] of Firth of Forth; established 1975; includes Edinburgh
Lou•ise, Lake \lü-ˈēz\ lake [SW] Alberta in Banff National Park
Lou•i•si•ana \lü-ˌē-zē-ˈan-ə, ˌlü-ə-zē-, ˌlü-zē-\ state [S] U.S.; capital, Baton Rouge — **Lou•i•si•an•ian** \-ˈan-ē-ən, -ˈan-yən\ *or* **Lou•i•si•an•an** \-ˈan-ən\ *adj or n*
Louisiana Purchase area [W] central U.S. between Rocky mountains & the Mississippi purchased 1803 from France
Lou•is•ville \ˈlü-i-ˌvil, -vəl\ city [N] Kentucky on the Ohio river
Lourenço Marques — see MAPUTO
Louth \ˈlau̇t͟h\ county [E] Ireland in Leinster
Low — see TUAMOTU
Low Countries region [W] Europe comprising modern Belgium, Luxembourg, & the Netherlands
Lower California — see BAJA CALIFORNIA
Lower Saxony *or German* **Nie•der•sach•sen** \ˌnēd-ər-ˈzäk-sən\ state West Germany; capital, Hannover
Low•lands \ˈlō-ləndz, -lənz, -ˌlandz, -ˌlanz\ the central & [E] part of Scotland lying between the Highlands & the Southern Uplands
Lo•yang \ˈlō-ˈyäŋ\ city [NE] central China in [N] Honan
Luan — see CH'ANG-CHIH
Lu•an•da \lü-ˈan-də\ *or* **Lo•an•da** \lō-\ city, capital of Angola
Lub•bock \ˈləb-ək\ city [NW] Texas
Lü•beck \ˈlü-ˌbek, ˈlue-\ city [N] West Germany [NE] of Hamburg
Lu•bum•ba•shi \ˌlü-büm-ˈbäsh-ē\ *or formerly* **Elis•a•beth•ville** \i-ˈliz-ə-bəth-ˌvil\ city [SE] Zaire
Lu•cerne, Lake of \lü-ˈsərn\ lake central Switzerland
Lu•chow *or* **Lu•chou** \ˈlü-ˈjō\ *or formerly* **Lu•hsien** \ˈlü-shē-ˈen\ **1** city [S] central China in [SE] Szechwan [SW] of Chungking **2** — see HOFEI
Luck•now \ˈlək-ˌnau̇\ city [N] India, capital of Uttar Pradesh
Lu•dhi•a•na \ˌlüd-ē-ˈän-ə\ city [NW] India in Punjab [SE] of Amritsar
Luik — see LIÈGE
Luluabourg — see KANANGA
Lu•sa•ka \lü-ˈsäk-ə\ city, capital of Zambia
Lüshun — see PORT ARTHUR
Lusitania — see PORTUGAL
Lü•ta \ˈlü-ˈdä\ *or* **Port Arthur–Dairen** municipality [NE] China in Liaoning including cities of Dairen & Port Arthur
Lu•ton \ˈlüt-ⁿn\ borough [SE] central England in Bedfordshire
Lux•em•bourg *or* **Lux•em•burg** \ˈlək-səm-ˌbərg, ˈlu̇k-səm-ˌbu̇rg\ **1** country [W] Europe bordered by Belgium, France, & Germany; a grand duchy **2** city, its capital — **Lux•em•bourg•er** \-ˌbər-gər, -ˌbu̇r-\ *n* — **Lux•em•bourg•ian** \ˌlək-səm-ˈbər-gē-ən, ˌlu̇k-səm-ˈbu̇r-\ *adj*
Lu•zon \lü-ˈzän\ island [N] Philippines
Lvov \lə-ˈvȯf, -ˈvȯv\ *or Polish* **Lwów** \lə-ˈvüf, -ˈvüv\ *or German* **Lem•berg** \ˈlem-ˌbərg, -ˌberg\ *or Ukrainian* **Lwiw** \lə-ˈvēf\ city U.S.S.R. in [W] Ukraine
Ly•all•pur \ˈlī-əl-ˌpu̇r\ city [NE] Pakistan [W] of Lahore
Ly•cia \ˈlish-ə, ˈlish-ē-ə\ ancient district & Roman province [SW] Asia Minor
Lyd•ia \ˈlid-ē-ə\ ancient country [W] Asia Minor on the Aegean; capital, Sardis — **Lyd•i•an** \-ē-ən\ *adj or n*
Ly•ons \lē-ˈō^{n}, ˈlī-ənz\ *or* **Lyon** \lyō^{n}\ *or ancient* **Lug•du•num** \lu̇g-ˈdü-nəm, ˌləg-\ city [SE] central France
Maas — see MEUSE
Ma•cao *or Portuguese* **Ma•cau** \mə-ˈkau̇\ **1** Portuguese territory on coast of [SE] China [W] of Hong Kong **2** city, its capital — **Mac•a•nese** \ˌmak-ə-ˈnēz, -ˈnēs\ *n*
Macassar — see UJUNG PANDANG
Mac•e•do•nia \ˌmas-ə-ˈdō-nyə, -nē-ə\ region [S] Europe in Balkan peninsula in [NE] Greece, [SE] Yugoslavia, and [SW] Bulgaria including territory of ancient kingdom of Macedonia (**Mac•e•don** \ˈmas-əd-ən, -ə-ˌdän\) — **Mac•e•do•nian** \ˌmas-ə-ˈdō-nyən, -nē-ən\ *adj or n*
Ma•ceió \ˌmas-ā-ˈō\ city [NE] Brazil
Mac•gil•li•cud•dy's Reeks \mə-ˌgil-ə-ˌkəd-ēz-ˈrēks\ mountains [SW] Ireland in Kerry; highest Carrantuohill 1041 meters
Machilipatnam — see BANDAR
Ma•chu Pic•chu \ˌmäch-ü-ˈpēk-chü\ site [SE] Peru of ancient Inca city [NW] of Cuzco
Mac•ken•zie \mə-ˈken-zē\ **1** river 1800 kilometers long [NW] Canada flowing from Great Slave Lake [NW] into Beaufort sea **2** district [NW] Canada in [W] Northwest Territories in basin of Mackenzie river
Mack•i•nac, Straits of \ˈmak-ə-ˌnȯ\ channel [N] Michigan connecting Lakes Huron & Michigan
McKinley, Mount \mə-ˈkin-lē\ *or* **De•na•li** \də-ˈnäl-ē\ mountain 6194 meters [S] central Alaska in Alaska range; highest in U.S. & North America; in **Mount McKinley National Park**
Ma•con \ˈmā-kən\ city central Georgia
Macoraba — see MECCA
Mad•a•gas•car \ˌmad-ə-ˈgas-kər\ *or formerly* **Mal•a•gasy Republic** \ˌmal-ə-ˌgas-ē\ island [W] Indian ocean off [SE] Africa; a republic; capital, Antananarivo — **Mad•a•gas•can** \ˌmad-ə-ˈgas-kən\ *adj or n*
Ma•dei•ra \mə-ˈdir-ə, -ˈder-\ **1** river 3380 kilometers long [W] Brazil flowing [NE] into the Amazon **2** islands in the [N] Atlantic [N] of the Canaries belonging to Portugal; capital, Funchal **3** island; chief of the Madeira group — **Ma•dei•ran** \-ən\ *adj or n*
Ma•dhya Pra•desh \ˌmäd-yə-prə-ˈdesh, -ˈdāsh\ state central India; capital, Bhopal
Mad•i•son \ˈmad-ə-sən\ city, capital of Wisconsin
Ma•dras \mə-ˈdras, -ˈdräs\ **1** — see TAMIL NADU **2** city [SE] India, capital of Tamil Nadu
Ma•drid \mə-ˈdrid\ city, capital of Spain
Ma•du•ra \mə-ˈdu̇r-ə\ island Indonesia [NE] of Java
Ma•du•rai \ˌmäd-ə-ˈrī\ *or* **Ma•du•ra** \ˈmaj-ə-rə\ city [S] India in [S] Tamil Nadu
Mae•ba•shi \ˌmä-yə-ˈbäsh-ē, mī-ˈbäsh-\ city Japan in central Honshu [NW] of Tokyo
Mag•de•burg \ˈmäg-də-ˌbu̇rg, ˈmag-də-ˌbərg\ city East Germany [WSW] of Berlin
Magellan, Strait of \mə-ˈjel-ən\ strait at [S] end of South America between mainland & Tierra del Fuego archipelago
Mageröy — see NORTH CAPE
Mag•gio•re, Lake \mə-ˈjōr-ē, -ˈjȯr-\ lake [N] Italy & [S] Switzerland
Mag•ni•to•gorsk \mag-ˈnēt-ə-ˌgȯrsk\ city U.S.S.R. in [W] Soviet Russia, Asia, on Ural river
Ma•hal•la el Ku•bra \mə-ˌhal-ə-el-ˈkü-brə\ city [N] Egypt in Nile delta
Ma•ha•rash•tra \ˌmä-hə-ˈräsh-trə\ state [W] India on Arabian sea; capital, Bombay
Main \ˈmīn, ˈmān\ river 490 kilometers long West Germany flowing [W] into the Rhine
Maine \ˈmān\ state [NE] U.S.; capital, Augusta
Mainz \ˈmīns\ city West Germany on the Rhine, capital of Rhineland-Palatinate
Ma•jor•ca \mə-ˈjȯr-kə, -ˈyȯr-\ *or Spanish* **Ma•llor•ca** \mə-ˈyȯr-kə\ island Spain; largest of the Balearic islands — **Ma•jor•can** \-ˈjȯr-kən, -ˈyȯr-\ *adj or n*
Ma•ka•lu \ˈmək-ə-ˌlü\ mountain 8481 meters [NE] Nepal in the Himalayas
Makasar *or* **Makassar** — see UJUNG PANDANG
Ma•ke•yev•ka \mə-ˈkā-əf-kə, -yəf-\ city U.S.S.R. in [E] Ukraine in Donets basin
Makkah — see MECCA
Mal•a•bar \ˈmal-ə-ˌbär\ coast region [SW] India on Arabian sea in Karnataka & Kerala states
Ma•la•bo \mä-ˈläb-ō\ *or formerly* **San•ta Isa•bel** \ˌsan-tə-ˈiz-ə-bel\ city, capital of Equatorial Guinea
Ma•lac•ca, Strait of \mə-ˈlak-ə, -ˈläk-\ channel between [S] Malay peninsula & island of Sumatra
Má•la•ga \ˈmal-ə-gə\ city [S] Spain in Andalusia
Ma•lang \mə-ˈläŋ\ city Indonesia in [E] Java

Ma•la•wi \mə-'lä-wē, -'lau̇-ē\ *or formerly* **Ny•asa•land** \nī-'as-ə-ˌland, nē-\ country [SE] Africa on Lake Nyasa; a former British protectorate; independent republic since 1964; capital, Lilongwe
Malawi, Lake — see NYASA
Ma•lay \mə-'lā, 'mā-lā\ **1** archipelago [SE] Asia including Sumatra, Java, Borneo, Celebes, Moluccas, & Timor; usually considered as including the Philippines & sometimes New Guinea **2** peninsula about 1100 kilometers long [SE] Asia divided between Thailand & Federation of Malaysia
Ma•laya \mə-'lā-ə, mā-\ **1** the Malay peninsula **2** *or* **Federation of Malaya** former country [SE] Asia on Malay peninsula; since 1963 part of Federation of Malaysia — see PENINSULAR MALAYSIA
Ma•lay•sia \mə-'lā-zhə, -shə, -zhē-ə, -shē-ə\ **1** the Malay archipelago **2** the Malay peninsula & Malay archipelago **3** *or* **Federation of Malaysia** country [SE] Asia, a union of Malaya, Sabah (North Borneo), Sarawak, & (until 1965) Singapore; a limited constitutional monarchy; capital, Kuala Lumpur — **Ma•lay•sian** \mə-'lā-zhən, -shən\ *adj or n*
Mal•dive \'mȯl-ˌdēv, -ˌdīv\ islands in Indian ocean [S] of the Laccadives; formerly a sultanate under British protection; since 1965 **Republic of Maldives;** capital, Male — **Mal•div•i•an** \mȯl-'div-ē-ən\ *adj or n*
Ma•le•gaon \ˌmäl-ə-'gau̇n\ city [W] India in [NW] Maharashtra [NE] of Bombay
Ma•li \'mäl-ē, 'mal-ē\ *or formerly* **French Sudan** country [W] Africa; a republic; capital, Bamako — **Ma•li•an** \-ē-ən\ *adj or n*
Malmö \'mal-ˌmər, 'mal-ˌmœ\ city [SW] Sweden
Mal•ta \'mȯl-tə\ **1** islands in the Mediterranean [S] of Sicily; a former British colony; an independent republic since 1964; capital, Valletta **2** island, chief of the group
Maluku — see MOLUCCAS
Malvinas, Islas — see FALKLAND
Mam•moth Cave \ˌmam-əth-\ limestone caverns [SW] central Kentucky in **Mammoth Cave National Park**
Man, Isle of \'man\ island British Isles in Irish sea; capital, Douglas; has own legislature & laws
Ma•na•gua \mə-'näg-wə\ city, capital of Nicaragua
Ma•na•ma \mə-'nam-ə\ city, capital of Bahrain
Ma•naus *or* **Ma•na•os** \mə-'nau̇s\ city [W] Brazil on Rio Negro 20 kilometers above its junction with the Amazon
Man•ches•ter \'man-ˌches-tər, -chə-stər\ city [NW] England in Lancashire — see GREATER MANCHESTER
Man•chu•kuo \'man-'chü-'kwō, man-'chü-ˌ\ former country (1931–45) [E] Asia in Manchuria & [E] Inner Mongolia; capital, Changchun
Man•chu•ria \man-'chu̇r-ē-ə\ *or* **Man•chow** \'män-'jō\ region [NE] China [S] of the Amur — **Man•chu•ri•an** \man-'chu̇r-ē-ən\ *adj or n*
Man•da•lay \ˌman-də-'lā\ city central Burma
Man•hat•tan \man-'hat-n, mən-\ **1** island [SE] New York in New York City **2** borough of New York City comprising chiefly Manhattan Island
Manihiki — see NORTHERN COOK
Ma•nila \mə-'nil-ə\ city Philippines in [W] Luzon
Ma•ni•pur \ˌman-ə-'pu̇r, ˌmən-\ territory [NE] India between Assam & Burma; capital, Imphal
Man•i•to•ba \ˌman-ə-'tō-bə\ province central Canada; capital, Winnipeg — **Man•i•to•ban** \-'tō-bən\ *adj or n*
Man•i•tou•lin \ˌman-ə-'tü-lən\ island 130 kilometers long [S] Ontario in Lake Huron
Mann•heim \'man-ˌhīm, 'män-\ city West Germany on the Rhine [NW] of Stuttgart
Man•za•ni•llo \ˌman-zə-'nē-ō, -yō\ city [SW] Mexico in Colima on the Pacific
Ma•pu•to \mä-'pü-tō\ *or. formerly* **Lou•ren•ço Mar•quez** \lə-ˌren-sō-ˌmär-'kes, -'märks, -'märk\ city, capital of Mozambique
Mar•a•cai•bo \ˌmar-ə-'kī-bō\ city [NW] Venezuela
Maracaibo, Lake the [S] extension of Gulf of Venezuela in [NW] Venezuela
Ma•ra•cay \ˌmär-ə-'kī\ city [N] Venezuela
Mar•a•thon \'mar-ə-ˌthän, -thən\ plain [E] Greece in Attica [NE] of Athens
March•es \'mär-chəz\ region central Italy on the Adriatic; capital, Ancona
Mar•i•ana \ˌmar-ē-'an-ə, ˌmer-\ islands [W] Pacific [N] of Caroline islands; until 1976 included (except for Guam) in Trust Territory of the Pacific Islands; voted for commonwealth relationship with U.S. June 1975
Ma•ri•a•nao \ˌmär-ē-ə-'nau̇\ city [W] Cuba [W] of Havana
Mariana Trench ocean trench [W] Pacific extending from [SE] of Guam to [NW] of Mariana islands; deepest in world
Maritime Alps section of the [W] Alps [SE] France & [NW] Italy extending [N] from Mediterranean coast
Maritime Provinces the Canadian provinces of New Brunswick, Nova Scotia, & Prince Edward Island
Mark•ham, Mount \'mär-kəm\ mountain 4351 meters Antarctica [E] of Ross Ice Shelf
Mar•ma•ra, Sea of *or* **Sea of Mar•mo•ra** \'mär-mə-rə\ *or ancient* **Pro•pon•tis** \prə-'pänt-əs\ sea [NW] Turkey connected with Black sea by the Bosporus & with Aegean sea by the Dardanelles
Marne \'märn\ river 523 kilometers long [NE] France flowing [W] into the Seine
Mar•que•sas \mär-'kā-zəz, -zəs, -səz, -səs\ islands [S] Pacific [N] of Tuamotu archipelago in French Polynesia — **Mar•que•san** \-zən, -sən\ *adj or n*
Mar•ra•kesh *or* **Mar•ra•kech** \mə-'räk-ish, ˌmar-ə-'kesh\ *or formerly* **Mo•roc•co** \mə-'räk-ō\ city central Morocco
Mar•seilles \mär-'sā, -'sälz\ *or* **Mar•seille** \mär-'sā\ *or ancient* **Mas•sil•ia** \mə-'sil-ē-ə\ city [SE] France
Mar•shall \'mär-shəl\ islands [W] Pacific [E] of the Carolines in Trust Territory of the Pacific Islands
Mar•tha's Vineyard \ˌmär-thəz-\ island [SE] Massachusetts off [SW] coast of Cape Cod [WNW] of Nantucket
Mar•ti•nique \ˌmärt-n-'ēk\ island West Indies in the Windwards; an overseas department of France; capital, Fort-de-France
Mary•land \'mer-ə-lənd\ state [E] U.S.; capital, Annapolis — **Mary•land•er** \-lən-dər, -ˌlan-\ *n*
Ma•san \'mäs-ˌän\ city South Korea [E] of Pusan
Mas•e•ru \'maz-ə-ˌrü\ city, capital of Lesotho
Mash•had \mə-'shad\ city [NE] Iran
Masis — see ARARAT
Ma•son–Dix•on line \ˌmās-n-'dik-sən-\ boundary between Maryland & Pennsylvania; was in part boundary between free & slave states
Mas•qat *or* **Mus•cat** \'məs-ˌkat, -kət\ town [E] Arabia, capital of Oman
Mas•sa•chu•setts \ˌmas-ə-'chü-səts, ˌmas-'chü-, -zəts\ state [NE] U.S.; capital, Boston
Mas•sif Cen•tral \ma-ˌsēf-ˌsen-'träl, -ˌsäⁿ-'träl\ plateau central France [W] of the Rhone-Saône valley — see AUVERGNE, CÉVENNES
Masulipatnam — see BANDAR
Mat•a•be•le•land \ˌmat-ə-'bē-lē-ˌland\ region [SW] Rhodesia; chief town, Bulawayo
Ma•to Gros•so \ˌmat-ə-'grō-sō\ plateau region [SW] Brazil in [E] central Mato Grosso state
Mat•su•do \mät-'sü-dō\ city Japan in [SE] Honshu [NE] of Tokyo
Ma•tsu•shi•ma \ˌmät-sü-'shē-mə, mät-'sü-shi-mə\ group of islets Japan off [N] Honshu [NE] of Sendai
Ma•tsu•ya•ma \ˌmät-sə-'yäm-ə\ city Japan in [W] Shikoku
Mat•ter•horn \'mat-ər-ˌhȯrn, 'mät-\ mountain 4478 meters in Pennine Alps on border between Switzerland & Italy
Maui \'mau̇-ē\ island Hawaii [NW] of Hawaii Island
Mau•na Kea \ˌmau̇-nə-'kā-ə\ extinct volcano 4205 meters Hawaii in [N] central Hawaii Island
Mau•na Loa \ˌmau̇-nə-'lō-ə\ volcano 4170 meters Hawaii in [S] central Hawaii Island in Hawaii Volcanoes National Park
Mau•re•ta•nia *or* **Mau•ri•ta•nia** \ˌmȯr-ə-'tā-nē-ə, ˌmär-, -nyə\ ancient country [NW] Africa in modern Morocco & [W] Algeria — **Mau•re•ta•ni•an** \-nē-ən, -nyən\ *adj or n*
Mauritania country [NW] Africa on the Atlantic [N] of Senegal river; a republic; capital, Nouakchott — **Mauritanian** *adj or n*
Mau•ri•tius \mȯ-'rish-əs, -'rish-ē-əs\ island in Indian ocean [E] of Madagascar; a dominion of British Commonwealth; capital, Port Louis — **Mau•ri•tian** \-'rish-ən\ *adj or n*
May, Cape \'mā\ cape [S] New Jersey at entrance to Delaware Bay
Mayo \'mā-ō\ county [NW] Ireland in Connacht
Ma•yon, Mount \mä-'yōn\ volcano 2525 meters Philippines in [SE] Luzon
Ma•za•ma, Mount \mə-'zäm-ə\ prehistoric mountain [SW] Oregon the collapse of whose summit formed Crater Lake in Crater Lake National Park
Ma•za•tlán \ˌmäz-ə-'tlän, ˌmäs-\ city [W] Mexico in Sinaloa on the Pacific

Mba•bane \ˌem-bə-ˈbän\ city, capital of Swaziland

Mban•da•ka \ˌem-ˌbän-ˈdäk-ə\ *or formerly* **Co•qui•lhat•ville** \ˌkō-kē-ˈat-ˌvil\ city W Zaire

Mbuji-Mayi \em-ˌbü-jē-ˈmī-ˌē\ *or formerly* **Ba•kwan•ga** \bə-ˈkwäng-gə\ city S Zaire

Mead, Lake \ˈmēd\ reservoir NW Arizona & SE Nevada formed by Hoover Dam in Colorado river

Meath \ˈmēth, ˈmēth\ county E Ireland in Leinster

Mec•ca \ˈmek-ə\ *or Arabic* **Mak•kah** \ˈmak-ə\ *or ancient* **Mac•o•ra•ba** \ˌmak-ə-ˈrä-bə\ city W Saudi Arabia, capital of Hejaz

Me•dan \mā-ˈdän\ city Indonesia in NE Sumatra

Me•de•llín \ˌmed-l-ˈēn, ˌmā-thə-ˈyēn\ city NW Colombia

Me•dia \ˈmēd-ē-ə\ ancient country & province of Persian Empire SW Asia in NW modern Iran

Me•di•na \mə-ˈdē-nə\ city W Saudi Arabia

Medina as-Shaab \-ˌash-ˈshäb\ city, administrative capital of People's Democratic Republic of Yemen (Southern Yemen)

Mediolanum — see MILAN

Med•i•ter•ra•nean \ˌmed-ə-tə-ˈrā-nē-ən, -nyən\ sea 3750 kilometers long between Europe & Africa connecting with the Atlantic through Strait of Gibraltar

Mee•rut \ˈmā-rət, ˈmir-ət\ city N India in NW Uttar Pradesh NE of Delhi

Me•gha•la•ya \ˌmā-gə-ˈlā-ə\ state NE India; created 1972 out of SW part of Assam; capital, Shillong

Méjico — see MEXICO

Mek•nes \mek-ˈnes\ city N Morocco

Me•kong \ˈmā-ˈkȯng, -ˈkäng\ river 4185 kilometers long SE Asia flowing from E Tibet S & SE into South China sea in S Vietnam

Mel•a•ne•sia \ˌmel-ə-ˈnē-zhə, -shə\ islands of the Pacific NE of Australia & S of Micronesia including Bismarck archipelago, the Solomons, New Hebrides, New Caledonia, & the Fijis

Mel•bourne \ˈmel-bərn\ city SE Australia, capital of Victoria

Me•los *or Greek* **Mí•los** \ˈmē-ˌläs\ island Greece in SW Cyclades — **Me•li•an** \ˈmē-lē-ən\ *adj or n*

Mel•ville \ˈmel-ˌvil\ island N Canada in NW Franklin District in Parry islands

Me•mel \ˈmā-məl\ city U.S.S.R. in W Lithuania

Mem•phis \ˈmem-fəs, ˈmemp-\ **1** city SW Tennessee **2** ancient city N Egypt S of modern Cairo

Men•do•ci•no, Cape \ˌmen-də-ˈsē-nō\ headland NW California

Menorca — see MINORCA

Mer•cia \ˈmər-shə, -shē-ə\ ancient Anglo-Saxon kingdom central England — **Mer•cian** \ˈmər-shən\ *adj or n*

Mé•ri•da \ˈmer-əd-ə\ city SE Mexico, capital of Yucatán

Mer•i•on•eth•shire \ˌmer-ē-ˈän-əth-ˌshiər, -shər\ *or* **Merioneth** former county NW Wales

Mer•sey \ˈmər-zē\ river 110 kilometers long NW England flowing NW & W into Irish sea through a large estuary

Mer•sey•side \ˈmər-zē-ˌsīd\ metropolitan county NW England; includes Liverpool

Mer•ton \ˈmərt-n\ borough of SW Greater London, England

Me•sa•bi range \mə-ˈsäb-ē\ region NE Minnesota that produces iron ore

Me•sa Verde National Park \ˌmā-sə-ˈvərd-ē, -ˈvərd\ reservation SW Colorado containing prehistoric cliff dwellings

Mes•o•po•ta•mia \ˌmes-ə-pə-ˈtā-mē-ə, -myə\ **1** region SW Asia between Euphrates & Tigris rivers **2** the entire Tigris-Euphrates valley — **Mes•o•po•ta•mian** \-mē-ən, -myən\ *adj or n*

Mes•si•na \mə-ˈsē-nə\ city Italy in NE Sicily

Messina, Strait of channel between NE Sicily & SW tip of Italian peninsula

Meuse \ˈmyüz, ˈmyərz, *French* mœz\ *or Dutch* **Maas** \ˈmäs\ *or ancient* **Mo•sa** \ˈmō-zə\ river 925 kilometers long W Europe flowing from NE France into North sea in the Netherlands

Mex•i•cali \ˌmek-si-ˈkal-ē\ city NW Mexico, capital of Baja California Norte

Mex•i•co \ˈmek-si-ˌkō\ *or Spanish* **Mé•ji•co** \ˈme-hē-kō\ **1** country S North America; a republic **2** *or* **Mexico City** city, its capital, in Federal District **3** state S central Mexico; capital, Toluca

Mexico, Gulf of inlet of the Atlantic SE North America

Mi•ami \mī-ˈam-ē, -ˈam-ə\ city SE Florida

Mich•i•gan \ˈmish-i-gən\ state N central U.S.; capital, Lansing — **Mich•i•gan•der** \ˌmish-i-ˈgan-dər\ *n* — **Mich•i•gan•ite** \ˈmish-i-gə-ˌnīt\ *n*

Michigan, Lake lake N central U.S.; one of the Great Lakes

Mi•cho•acán \ˌmē-chə-wä-ˈkän\ state SW Mexico on the Pacific; capital, Morelia

Mi•cro•ne•sia \ˌmī-krə-ˈnē-zhə, -shə\ islands of the W Pacific E of the Philippines & N of Melanesia including Caroline, Gilbert, Mariana, & Marshall groups — **Mi•cro•ne•sian** \-zhən, -shən\ *adj or n*

Middle Congo — see CONGO

Middle East the countries of SW Asia & N Africa — usually considered as including the countries extending from Libya on the W to Afghanistan on the E — **Middle Eastern** *or* **Mid•east•ern** \ˈmid-ˈē-stərn\ *adj*

Mid•dles•brough \ˈmid-lz-brə\ town N England in Cleveland; formerly a county borough in North Riding, Yorkshire

Mid•dle•sex \ˈmid-l-ˌseks\ former county SE England including NW part of present Greater London

Middle West *or* **Mid•west** \ˈmid-ˈwest\ region N central U.S. including area around Great Lakes & in upper Mississippi valley from Ohio on the E to North & South Dakota, Nebraska, & Kansas on the W — **Middle Western** *or* **Mid•west•ern** \ˈmid-ˈwes-tərn\ *adj* — **Middle Westerner** *or* **Mid•west•ern•er** \ˈmid-ˈwes-tər-nər, -tə-nər\ *n*

Mid Gla•mor•gan \ˈmid-glə-ˈmȯr-gən\ county SE Wales; established 1974

Mi•di \mē-ˈdē\ the south of France

Mid•i•an \ˈmid-ē-ən\ ancient region NW Arabia E of Gulf of Aqaba — **Mid•i•an•ite** \-ē-ə-ˌnīt\ *n*

Mid•lands \ˈmid-ləndz, -lənz\ the central counties of England — see WEST MIDLANDS

Mid•lo•thi•an \mid-ˈlō-thē-ən\ former county SE Scotland; chief city, Edinburgh

Mid•way \ˈmid-ˌwā\ islands (atoll) central Pacific in Hawaiian group 2090 kilometers WNW of Honolulu belonging to U.S.; not included in state of Hawaii

Mi•lan \mə-ˈlan, -ˈlän\ *or Italian* **Mi•la•no** \mi-ˈlän-ō\ *or ancient* **Me•di•o•la•num** \ˌmed-ē-ō-ˈlä-nəm\ city NW Italy, capital of Lombardy — **Mil•a•nese** \ˌmil-ə-ˈnēz, -ˈnēs\ *adj or n*

Milos — see MELOS

Mil•wau•kee \mil-ˈwȯ-kē\ city SE Wisconsin

Mi•nas Basin \ˌmī-nəs-\ landlocked bay central Nova Scotia; NE extension of Bay of Fundy

Min•da•nao \ˌmin-də-ˈnä-ō, -ˈnau̇\ island S Philippines

Min•do•ro \min-ˈdōr-ō, -ˈdȯr-\ island central Philippines

Minhow — see FOOCHOW

Min•ne•ap•o•lis \ˌmin-ē-ˈap-ləs, -ə-ləs\ city SE Minnesota

Min•ne•so•ta \ˌmin-ə-ˈsōt-ə\ state N central U.S.; capital, Saint Paul — **Min•ne•so•tan** \-ˈsōt-n\ *adj or n*

Mi•nor•ca \mə-ˈnȯr-kə\ *or Spanish* **Me•nor•ca** \mā-\ island Spain in Balearic islands — **Mi•nor•can** \mə-ˈnȯr-kən\ *adj or n*

Minsk \ˈminsk\ city U.S.S.R., capital of Belorussian Soviet Socialist Republic

Mi•que•lon \ˈmik-ə-ˌlän, *French* mēk-lōⁿ, mēk-ə-\ island off S coast of Newfoundland belonging to France — see SAINT PIERRE

Mis•sis•sip•pi \ˌmis-ə-ˈsip-ē, mis-ˈsip-ē\ **1** river 3975 kilometers long central U.S. flowing into Gulf of Mexico — see ITASCA **2** state S U.S.; capital, Jackson

Mis•sou•ri \mə-ˈzu̇r-ē, -ˈzu̇r-ə\ **1** river 4345 kilometers long W U.S. flowing from SW Montana to the Mississippi in E Missouri **2** state central U.S.; capital, Jefferson City — **Mis•sou•ri•an** \-ˈzu̇r-ē-ən\ *adj or n*

Mitch•ell, Mount \ˈmich-əl\ mountain 2037 meters W North Carolina in Black mountains of the Appalachians; highest in U.S. E of the Mississippi

Mitilíni — see LESBOS

Mi•ya•za•ki \mē-ˌäz-ˈäk-ē, -ˌyäz-; mē-ˈäz-ə-kē, -ˈyäz-\ city Japan in SE Kyushu

Mo•ab \ˈmō-ˌab\ region Jordan E of Dead sea; in biblical times a kingdom

Mo•bile \mō-ˈbēl,ˈmō-ˌbēl\ city SW Alabama on Mobile Bay

Moçambique — see MOZAMBIQUE

Mo•de•na \ˈmȯd-n-ə, -n-ˌä\ city N Italy SW of Venice

Moe•sia \ˈmē-shə, -shē-ə\ ancient country & Roman province S of the Danube in modern Bulgaria & SE Yugoslavia

Mog•a•di•shu \ˌmäg-ə-ˈdish-ü, -ˈdēsh-\ *or* **Mog•a•di•scio** \-ō\ city, capital of Somalia

Mo•hen•jo-Da•ro \mō-ˌhen-jō-ˈdär-ō\ prehistoric city Pakistan in Indus valley NE of modern Karachi

Mo•ja•ve *or* **Mo•ha•ve** \mə-'häv-ē\ desert [S] California [SE] of [S] end of Sierra Nevada

Mo•ji \'mō-jē\ city Japan in [N] Kyushu

Mol•da•via \mäl-'dāv-ē-ə, -vyə\ **1** region [E] Europe in [NE] Rumania & [SE] U.S.S.R. [W] of the Dniester **2** *or* **Moldavian Republic** constituent republic of U.S.S.R. in [E] Moldavia region; capital, Kishinev — **Mol•da•vian** \-vē-ən, -vyən\ *adj or n*

Mo•li•se \'mó-li-,zā\ area central Italy on the Adriatic

Mol•o•kai \,mäl-ə-'kī, ,mō-lə-\ island Hawaii [ESE] of Oahu

Molotov — see PERM

Mo•luc•cas \mə-'lək-əz\ *or* **Spice islands** \'spīs-\ *or Indonesian* **Ma•lu•ku** \mə-'lü-kü\ islands Indonesia [E] of Celebes — **Mo•luc•ca** \mə-'lək-ə\ *adj* — **Mo•luc•can** \-ən\ *adj or n*

Mom•ba•sa \mäm-'bäs-ə\ city [S] Kenya on Mombasa Island

Mo•na•co \'män-ə-,kō *also* mə-'näk-ō\ country [W] Europe on Mediterranean coast of France; a principality; capital, Monaco — **Mo•na•can** \'mä-ə-kən, mə-'näk-ən\ *adj or n* — **Mon•e•gasque** \,män-i-'gask\ *n*

Mon•a•ghan \'män-ə-hən, -,han\ county [NE] Republic of Ireland in Ulster

Mon•go•lia \män-'gōl-yə, mäng-, -'gō-lē-ə\ **1** region [E] Asia [E] of Altai mountains; includes Gobi desert **2** INNER MONGOLIA **3** MONGOLIAN PEOPLE'S REPUBLIC

Mon•go•lian People's Republic \män-,gōl-yən-, -,gōl-ē-ən-\ *or* **Outer Mongolia** country [E] Asia comprising major portion of Mongolia; capital, Ulan Bator

Mon•mouth•shire \'män-məth-,shiər, 'mən-, -shər\ *or* **Monmouth** former county [SE] Wales bordering on England

Mon•ro•via \mən-'rō-vē-ə, ,mən-\ city, capital of Liberia

Mon•tana \män-'tan-ə\ state [NW] U.S.; capital, Helena — **Mon•tan•an** \-ən\ *adj or n*

Mont Blanc \mōⁿ-'bläⁿ\ mountain 4807 meters [SE] France on Italian border; highest in the Alps

Mon•te•ne•gro \,mänt-ə-'nē-grō, -'nā-\ federated republic [S] Yugoslavia on the Adriatic; capital, Titograd — **Mon•te•ne•grin**\-grən\ *adj or n*

Mon•ter•rey \,mänt-ə-'rā\ city [NE] Mexico, capital of Nuevo León

Mon•te•vi•deo \,mänt-ə-və-'dā-ō, -'vid-ē-,ō\ city, capital of Uruguay

Mont•gom•ery \mənt-'gəm-rē, mänt-, mən-, män-, -'gäm-, -ə-rē\ city, capital of Alabama

Mont•gom•ery•shire \-,shiər, -shər\ *or* **Montgomery** former county [E] Wales

Mont•pe•lier \mänt-'pēl-yər, -'pil-\ city, capital of Vermont

Mon•tre•al \,män-trē-'ól, ,mən-\ city [S] Quebec on Montreal Island in the Saint Lawrence

Mont-Saint-Mi•chel \mōⁿ-saⁿ-mē-shel\ islet [NW] France off coast of Brittany in Gulf of Saint-Malo

Mont•ser•rat \,män-sə-'rat\ island British West Indies in the Leewards; capital, Plymouth

Mo•ra•via \mə-'rā-vē-ə\ region central Czechoslovakia; chief city, Brno

Mor•ay \'mər-ē, 'mə-rē\ *or* **Mor•ay•shire** \-,shiər, -shər\ former county [NE] Scotland

Mo•rea \mə-'rē-ə\ PELOPONNESUS — an old name — **Mo•re•an** \-'rē-ən\ *adj or n*

Mo•re•los \mə-'rā-ləs\ state [S] central Mexico; capital, Cuernavaca

Mo•roc•co \mə-'räk-ō\ **1** country [NW] Africa; a kingdom; capital, Rabat; formerly divided into **French Morocco** (capital, Rabat), **Spanish Morocco** (capital, Tetuán) & **International Zone** of Tangier **2** — see MARRAKESH — **Mo•roc•can** \-'räk-ən\ *adj or n*

Mo•rón \mə-'rón\ *or* **Seis de Sep•tiem•bre** \,sāz-də-se-'tyem-brā\ city [E] Argentina [WSW] of Buenos Aires

Mo•ro•ni \mó-'rō-nē\ city, capital of Comoro

Morris Jes•up, Cape \,mór-əs-'jes-əp, ,mär-\ headland [N] Greenland in Arctic ocean

Mosa — see MEUSE

Mos•cow \'mäs-,kaù, -kō\ *or Russian* **Mos•kva** \mäsk-'vä\ city, capital of U.S.S.R. in [W] central Soviet Russia, Europe, on Moskva river

Mo•selle \mō-'zel\ *or German* **Mo•sel** \'mō-zəl\ river 515 kilometers long [E] France & [W] Germany flowing from Vosges mountains into the Rhine at Koblenz

Moul•mein \mül-'mān, mōl-, -'mīn\ city [S] Burma at mouth of the Salween

Mount McKinley National Park — see MCKINLEY

Mount Rainier National Park — see RAINIER

Mount Rev•el•stoke National Park \'rev-əl-,stōk\ reservation [SE] British Columbia

Mo•zam•bique \,mō-zəm-'bēk\ *or Portuguese* **Mo•çam•bi•que** \,mü-səm-'bē-kə\ **1** channel [SE] Africa between Mozambique & Madagascar **2** *or formerly* **Portuguese East Africa** country [SE] Africa; formerly a dependency of Portugal; capital, Maputo

Muk•den \'mùk-dən, 'mək-; mùk-'den\ *or* **Shen•yang** \'shən-'yäng\ *or formerly* **Feng•tien** \'fəng-tē-'en\ city [NE] China in Manchuria, capital of Liaoning

Mul•tan \mùl-'tän\ city [NE] Pakistan [SW] of Lahore

Mu•nich \'myü-nik\ *or German* **Mün•chen** \'mu̇en-kən\ city West Germany, capital of Bavaria

Mun•ster \'mən-stər\ province [S] Ireland

Mün•ster \'mən-stər, 'mün-, 'myün-, 'mu̇en-\ city West Germany [NNE] of Dortmund

Mur•cia \'mər-shə, -shē-ə\ **1** region, province, & ancient kingdom [SE] Spain **2** city, its capital, [NE] of Granada — **Mur•cian** \-shən\ *adj or n*

Mur•mansk \mùr-'mansk, -'mänsk\ city U.S.S.R. in [NW] Soviet Russia, Europe, on Barents sea

Mu•ro•ran \,mùr-ə-'rän\ city Japan in [SW] Hokkaido

Mur•ray \'mər-ē, 'mə-rē\ river 1930 kilometers long [SE] Australia flowing [W] from [E] Victoria into Indian ocean in South Australia — see DARLING

Mur•rum•bidg•ee \,mər-əm-'bij-ē, ,mə-rəm-\ river 1610 kilometers long [SE] Australia in New South Wales flowing [W] into the Murray

Mu•sa, Ge•bel \,jeb-əl-'mü-sə\ mountain group [NE] Egypt in [S] Sinai peninsula; highest Gebel Katherina 2737 meters — see HOREB

Mu•sa, Je•bel \,jeb-əl-'mü-sə\ mountain 846 meters [N] Morocco opposite Rock of Gibraltar — see PILLARS OF HERCULES

Muscat — see MASQAT

Muscat and Oman — see OMAN

Mus•co•vy \mə-'skō-vē; 'məs-kə-vē, -,kō-\ **1** the principality of Moscow (founded 1295) which in 15th century came to dominate Russia **2** RUSSIA — an old name

Mu-tan-chiang \'mü-'dän-jē-'äng\ city [NE] China in [S] Heilungkiang [SE] of Harbin

Mu•zaf•far•pur \mə-'zäf-ər-,pùr\ city [NE] India in [NW] Bihar [N] of Patna

My•ce•nae \mī-'sē-nē\ ancient city [S] Greece in [NE] Peloponnesus [N] of Argos

My•sia \'mish-ə, 'mish-ē-ə\ ancient country [NW] Asia Minor bordering on the Propontis

My•sore \mī-'sōr, -'sór\ **1** — see KARNATAKA **2** city in [S] Karnataka

Myt•i•le•ne \,mit-l-'ē-nē\ **1** ancient city Greece on [E] coast of Lesbos Island; site at modern town of Mytilene **2** — see LESBOS

Nab•a•taea *or* **Nab•a•tea** \,nab-ə-'tē-ə\ ancient Arab kingdom [SE] of Palestine — **Nab•a•tae•an** *or* **Nab•a•te•an** \-'tē-ən\ *adj or n*

Na•ga•land \'näg-ə-,land\ state [E] India [N] of Manipur in Naga hills; capital, Kohima

Na•ga•no \nä-'gän-ō\ city Japan is [SE] Honshu [NW] of Tokyo

Na•ga•sa•ki \,näg-ə-'säk-ē, ,nag-ə-'sak-ē\ city Japan in [W] Kyushu

Na•goya \nə-'gói-ə, 'näg-ə-,yä\ city Japan in [S] central Honshu

Nag•pur \'näg-,pùr\ city [E] central India in [NE] Maharashtra

Na•ha \'nä-hä\ city Japan in Ryukyu islands, capital of Okinawa

Na•huel Hua•pí \nä-,wel-wä-'pē\ lake [SW] Argentina in the Andes

Nairn \'naərn, 'neərn\ *or* **Nairn•shire** \-,shiər, -shər\ former county [NE] Scotland

Nai•ro•bi \nī-'rō-bē\ city, capital of Kenya

Najd — see NEJD

Namibia — see SOUTH-WEST AFRICA

Nan•chang \'nän-'chäng\ city [SE] China, capital of Kiangsi

Nan•cy \'nan-sē, näⁿ-sē\ city [NE] France

Nan•king \'nan-'king, 'nän-\ city [E] China on the Yangtze, capital of Kiangsu

Nan•ning \'nän-'ning\ city [S] China, capital of Kwangsi [E] of Canton

Nantes \'nans\ city [NW] France

Nan•tuck•et \nan-'tək-ət\ island [SE] Massachusetts [S] of Cape Cod

Nan•tung \'nän-'tu̇ŋ\ city E China in SE Kiangsu NW of Shanghai

Na•ples \'nā-pəlz\ *or Italian* **Na•po•li** \'näp-ə-lē\ *or ancient* **Ne•ap•o•lis** \nē-'ap-ə-ləs\ city S Italy on Bay of Naples — **Ne•a•pol•i•tan** \ˌnē-ə-'päl-ət-n\ *adj or n*

Na•ra \'när-ə\ city Japan in W central Honshu E of Osaka

Na•ra•yan•ganj \nə-'rä-yən-ˌgənj\ city SE Bangladesh

Nar•ra•gan•sett Bay \ˌnar-ə-'gan-sət\ inlet of the Atlantic SE Rhode Island

Nash•ville \'nash-ˌvil, -vəl\ city, capital of Tennessee

Nas•sau \'nas-ˌȯ\ city, capital of Bahamas on New Providence Island

Na•tal \nə-'tal, -'täl\ **1** city NE Brazil **2** province E Republic of South Africa; capital, Pietermaritzburg

Nau•cal•pan de Jua•rez \nau̇-'käl-pən-də-'hwär-ˌes\ city central Mexico in Mexico state

Na•u•ru \nä-'ü-rü\ island (atoll) W Pacific W of the Gilbert islands; formerly a joint British, New Zealand, & Australian trust territory; an independent republic in British Commonwealth since 1968

Na•varre \nə-'vär\ *or Spanish* **Na•var•ra** \nə-'vär-ə\ **1** region & former kingdom N Spain & SW France in W Pyrenees **2** province N Spain W of Aragon; capital, Pamplona

Nax•os \'nak-səs, -ˌsäs\ island Greece in the Aegean; largest of the Cyclades

Na•ya•rit \ˌnī-ə-'rēt\ state W Mexico on the Pacific; capital, Tepic

Naz•a•reth \'naz-rəth, -ə-rəth\ town of ancient Palestine in central Galilee; now a city of N Israel

Ndja•me•na \en-'jäm-ə-nə\ *or formerly* **Fort–La•my** \ˌfȯr-lə-'me\ city, capital of Chad

Neagh, Lough \'nā\ lake Northern Ireland; largest in British Isles

Near East the countries of NE Africa & SW Asia — **Near Eastern** *adj*

Ne•bras•ka \nə-'bras-kə\ state central U.S.; capital, Lincoln — **Ne•bras•kan** \-kən\ *adj or n*

Neg•ev \'neg-ˌev\ *or* **Neg•eb** \-ˌeb\ desert region S Israel

Ne•gros \'nā-grōs\ island S central Philippines in Visayan islands

Neis•se \'nī-sə\ river 225 kilometers long N Europe flowing from N Czechoslovakia N into the Oder; forms part of boundary between Poland & East Germany — see ODER

Nejd \'nejd, 'nezhd\ *or* **Najd** \'najd, 'nazhd\ region central & E Saudi Arabia; capital, Riyadh

Ne•pal \nə-'pȯl, -'päl, -'pal\ country Asia on NE border of India in the Himalayas; a kingdom; capital, Katmandu — **Nep•a•lese** \ˌnep-ə-'lēz, -'lēs\ *adj or n* — **Ne•pali** \nə-'pȯl-ē, -'päl-, -'pal-\ *adj or n*

Neth•er•lands \'ne<u>th</u>-ər-lənz, -ləndz\ **1** *or Dutch* **Ne•der•land** \'näd-ər-ˌlänt\ *also* **Holland** country NW Europe on North sea; a kingdom; official capital, Amsterdam, de facto capital, The Hague **2** LOW COUNTRIES — an historical usage — **Neth•er•land** \'ne<u>th</u>-ər-lənd\ *adj* — **Neth•er•land•er** \-ˌlan-dər, -lən-\ *n* — **Neth•er•land•ish** \-dish\ *adj*

Netherlands An•til•les \an-'til-ēz\ islands of the West Indies belonging to the Netherlands: Aruba, Bonaire, Curaçao, Saba, Saint Eustatius, & S part of Saint Martin; capital, Willemstad (on Curaçao)

Netherlands East Indies *or* **Netherlands India** *or* **Dutch East Indies** former Dutch possessions in the East Indies including Indonesia

Netherlands New Guinea — see WEST IRIAN

Ne•tza•hual•có•yotl \nā-ˌtsä-wäl-'kō-ˌyōt-l\ city central Mexico in Mexico state

Ne•va \'nē-və, 'nā-\ river 65 kilometers long U.S.S.R. in NW Soviet Russia, Europe, flowing from lake Ladoga into Gulf of Finland at Leningard

Ne•vada \nə-'vad-ə, -'väd-ə\ state W U.S.; capital, Carson City — **Ne•vad•an** \-'vad-n, -'väd-n\ *or* **Ne•vad•i•an** \-'vad-ē-ən, -'väd-\ *adj or n*

Ne•vis \'nē-vəs\ island British West Indies in the Leewards — see SAINT KITTS

Nevis, Ben — see BEN NEVIS

New Am•ster•dam \'am-stər-'dam, 'amp-\ town founded 1625 on Manhattan Island by the Dutch; renamed New York 1664 by the British

New•ark \'nü-ərk, 'nü-, 'nyü-, 'nyu̇-, 'nu̇rk, 'nyu̇rk\ city NE New Jersey

New Bed•ford \'bed-fərd\ city SE Massachusetts

New Brit•ain \'brit-n\ island W Pacific, largest In Bismarck archipelago

New Bruns•wick \'brənz-wik\ province SE Canada; capital, Fredericton

New Cal•e•do•nia \ˌkal-ə-'dō-nyə, -nē-ə\ island SW Pacific SW of the New Hebrides; an overseas department of France; capital, Nouméa

New•cas•tle \'nü-ˌkas-əl, 'nyü-\ city SE Australia in E New South Wales

New•cas•tle up•on Tyne \nü-'kas-əl-ə-ˌpȯn-'tīn, nyü-, -ˌpän-, -pən-, 'nü-ˌ, 'nyü-ˌ\ city N England in Tyne and Wear

New Del•hi \-'del-ē\ city, capital of India S of city of (Old) Delhi

New England section of U.S. comprising states of Maine, New Hampshire, Vermont, Massachusetts, Rhode Island, & Connecticut — **New En•gland•er** \-'iŋ-glən-dər *also* -'iŋ-lən-\ *n*

New•found•land \'nü-fən-dlənd, 'nyü-, -lənd, -ˌdland, -ˌland; ˌnü-fən-'dland, ˌnyü-, -'land\ **1** island Canada in the Atlantic E of Gulf of Saint Lawrence **2** province E Canada comprising Newfoundland Island & Labrador; capital, Saint John's — **New•found•land•er** \-ər\ *n*

New France the possessions of France in North America before 1763

New Guin•ea \'gin-ē\ *or Indonesian* **Iri•an** \ˌir-ē-'än\ **1** island W Pacific N of E Australia divided between West Irian & Papua New Guinea **2** the NE portion of the island of New Guinea together with Bismarck archipelago, Bougainville, Buka, & adjacent small islands; now part of Papua New Guinea — **New Guin•ean** \'gin-ē-ən\ *adj or n*

New•ham \'nü-əm, 'nyü-\ borough of E Greater London, England

New Hamp•shire \'ham-shər, 'hamp-, -ˌshiər\ state NE U.S.; capital, Concord — **New Hamp•shire•man** \-mən\ *n* — **New Hamp•shir•ite** \-ˌīt\ *n*

New Ha•ven \'hā-vən\ city S Connecticut

New Heb•ri•des \'heb-rə-ˌdēz\ islands SW Pacific W of Fiji; under joint British and French administration

New Jer•sey \'jər-zē\ state E U.S.; capital, Trenton — **New Jer•sey•ite** \-ˌīt\ *n*

New Mex•i•co \'mek-si-ˌkō\ state SW U.S.; capital, Santa Fe — **New Mex•i•can** \-si-kən\ *adj or n*

New Neth•er•land \'ne<u>th</u>-ər-lənd\ former Dutch colony (1613–64) North America along Hudson & lower Delaware rivers; capital, New Amsterdam

New Or•leans \'ȯr-lē-ənz; 'ȯrl-ənz, -yənz; ȯr-'lēnz\ city SE Louisiana

New•port \'nü-ˌpōrt, 'nyü-, -ˌpȯrt\ city SE Wales

New•port News \ˌnü-ˌpōrt-'nüz, -ˌpȯrt-, -pərt-, ˌnyü...'nyüz\ city SE Virginia

New Prov•i•dence \'präv-əd-əns, -ə-ˌdens\ island NW central Bahamas; chief town, Nassau

New South Wales state SE Australia; capital, Sydney

New Spain former Spanish possessions in North America, Central America, West Indies, & the Philippines; capital, Mexico City

New Sweden former Swedish colony (1638–55) North America on W bank of Delaware river

New York \'yȯrk\ **1** state NE U.S.; capital, Albany **2** *or* **New York City** city SE New York — **New York•er** \'yȯr-kər\ *n*

New Zea•land \'zē-lənd\ country SW Pacific ESE of Australia; a dominion of British Commonwealth; capital, Wellington — **New Zea•land•er** \lən-dər\ *n*

Ni•ag•a•ra Falls \nī-'ag-rə, -ə-rə\ falls New York & Ontario in **Niagara river** (58 kilometers long flowing N from Lake Erie into Lake Ontario); divided by Goat Island into Horseshoe, or Canadian, Falls (48 meters high, 917 meters wide at crest) & American Falls (51 meters high, 323 meters wide)

Nia•mey \nē-'äm-ā, nyä-'mā\ city, capital of Niger

Ni•caea \nī-'sē-ə\ *or* **Nice** \'nīs\ ancient city W Bithynia; site at modern village of Iznik in NW Turkey — **Ni•cae•an** \nī-'sē-ən\ *adj or n* — **Ni•cene** \'nī-ˌsēn, nī-'sēn\ *adj*

Ni•ca•ra•gua \ˌnik-ə-'räg-wə\ **1** lake 160 kilometers long S Nicaragua **2** country Central America; capital, Managua — **Ni•ca•ra•guan** \-wən\ *adj or n*

Nice \'nēs\ *or ancient* **Ni•caea** \nī-'sē-ə\ city SE France

Nic•o•bar \'nik-ə-ˌbär\ islands India in Bay of Bengal S of the Andamans — see ANDAMAN

Nic•o•sia \ˌnik-ə-'sē-ə\ city, capital of Cyprus

Niedersachsen — see LOWER SAXONY

Ni•ger \'nī-jər\ **1** river 4185 kilometers long [W] Africa flowing into Gulf of Guinea **2** country [W] Africa [N] of Nigeria; a republic; capital, Niamey
Ni•ge•ria \nī-'jir-ē-ə\ country [W] Africa on Gulf of Guinea; a republic in British Commonwealth; capital, Lagos — **Ni•ge•ri•an** \-ē-ən\ *adj or n*
Nihon — see JAPAN
Nii•ga•ta \nē-'gät-ə, 'nē-gə-,tä\ city Japan in [N] Honshu on Sea of Japan
Nii•hau \'nē-,haù\ island Hawaii [WSW] of Kauai
Nikaria — see IKARIA
Ni•ko•la•yev \'nik-ə-'lī-əf\ city U.S.S.R. in [S] Ukraine
Nile \'nīl\ river 6497 kilometers long [E] Africa flowing from Lake Victoria in Uganda [N] into the Mediterranean in Egypt; in various sections called specifically **Vic•to•ria** \vik-'tōr-ē-ə, -'tòr-\, *or* **Som•er•set** \'səm-ər-sət, -,set\, **Nile** between Lake Victoria & Lake Albert, **Al•bert** \'al-bərt\ **Nile** between Lake Albert & Lake No, & **White Nile** from Lake No to Khartoum — see BLUE NILE
Nil•gi•ri \'nil-gə-rē\ hills [S] India in [W] Tamil Nadu
Nîmes \'nēm\ city [S] France [NW] of Marseilles
Nin•e•veh \'nin-ə-və\ ancient city, capital of Assyria; ruins in Iraq on the Tigris
Ning•po \'ning-'pō\ city [E] China in [N] Chekiang
Ning•sia Hui \'ning-shē-'ä-'hwē\ region [N] China; before 1954 part of former province of **Ningsia**
Nip•i•gon, Lake \'nip-ə-,gän\ lake Canada in [W] Ontario [N] of Lake Superior
Nip•pon \nip-'än\ — see JAPAN — **Nip•pon•ese** \,nip-ə-'nēz, -'nēs\ *adj or n*
Nis *or* **Nish** \'nish\ city [E] Yugoslavia in [E] Serbia
Ni•shi•no•mi•ya \,nish-ə-'nō-mē-,ä, -,yä\ city Japan in central Honshu [E] of Kobe
Ni•te•rói \,nēt-ə-'ròi\ city [SE] Brazil on Guanabara Bay opposite Rio de Janeiro
Nizhni Novgorod — see GORKI
Nizh•ni Ta•gil \,nizh-nē-tə-'gil\ city U.S.S.R. in [W] Soviet Russia, Asia, in the Urals
Nor•folk \'nòr-fək, *in the United States also* -,fòk\ **1** city [SE] Virginia **2** county [E] England on North sea
Nor•i•cum \'nòr-i-kəm, 'när-\ ancient country & Roman province [S] central Europe [S] of the Danube in modern Austria & Germany
Nor•man•dy \'nòr-mən-dē\ *or French* **Nor•man•die** \nòr-mä^n-dē\ region & former province [NW] France [NE] of Brittany; capital, Rouen
North 1 river estuary of the Hudson between [NE] New Jersey & [SE] New York **2** sea arm of the Atlantic [E] of Great Britain **3** island [N] New Zealand
North America continent of western hemisphere [NW] of South America & [N] of the equator — **North American** *adj or n*
North•amp•ton \nòrth-'am-tən, -'ham-, -'amp-, -'hamp-\ borough central England in Northamptonshire
North•amp•ton•shire \-,shiər, -shər\ *or* **Northampton** county central England
North Borneo — see SABAH
North Cape 1 headland New Zealand at [N] end of North Island **2** headland [NE] Norway on **Ma•ger•öy** \,mäg-ə-'rəi\ island
North Car•o•li•na \,kar-ə-'lī-nə\ state [E] U.S.; capital, Raleigh — **North Car•o•lin•ian** \-'lin-ē-ən, -'lin-yən\ *adj or n*
North Cas•cades National Park \kas-'kādz, 'kas-,\ reservation [N] Washington
North Da•ko•ta \də-'kōt-ə\ state [N] U.S.; capital, Bismarck — **North Da•ko•tan** \-'kōt-n\ *adj or n*
North East Frontier Agency — see ARUNACHAL PRADESH
North-East New Guinea the [NE] section of Papua New Guinea on New Guinea mainland
Northern Cook \'kùk\ *or* **Ma•ni•hi•ki** \,män-ə-'hē-kē\ islands [S] central Pacific [N] of Cook islands
Northern Ireland region [N] Ireland comprising six counties of Ulster: Antrim, Armagh, Down, Fermanagh, Londonderry, & Tyrone; a division of United Kingdom; capital, Belfast
Northern Kingdom — see ISRAEL
Northern Rhodesia — see ZAMBIA
Northern Territory territory [N] & central Australia; capital, Darwin
North Korea — see KOREA
North Rhine-Westphalia *or German* **Nord•rhein-West•fa•len** \'nòrt-,rīn-,vest-'fä-lən\ state West Germany; capital, Düsseldorf
North Ri•ding \'rī-ding\ former administrative county [N] England in [N] Yorkshire
North Slope region [N] Alaska between Brooks Range & Arctic ocean
North•um•ber•land \nòr-'thəm-bər-lənd\ county [N] England — **North•um•bri•an** \-'thəm-brē-ən\ *adj or n*
North•um•bria \nòr-'thəm-brē-ə\ ancient country Great Britain between the Humber & Firth of Forth — **North•um•bri•an** \-brē-ən\ *adj or n*
North Vietnam — see VIETNAM
Northwest Territories territory [N] Canada comprising the actic islands, the mainland [N] of 60° between Yukon Territory & Hudson Bay, & the islands in Hudson Bay — see FRANKLIN, KEEWATIN, MACKENZIE
North York•shire \'yòrk-,shiər, -shər\ county [N] England
Nor•way \'nòr-,wā\ country [N] Europe in Scandinavia; a kingdom; capital, Oslo
Nor•we•gian \nòr-'wē-jən\ sea between Atlantic & Arctic oceans [W] of Norway
Nor•wich \'nòr-wich; 'nòr-ich, 'när-\ city [E] England in Norfolk
Not•ting•ham \'nät-ing-əm, *in the United States also* -,ham\ city [N] central England in Nottinghamshire
Not•ting•ham•shire \-,shiər, -shər\ *or* **Nottingham** county [N] central England
Nouak•chott \nù-'äk-,shät\ city, capital of Mauritania
Nou•méa \nü-'mā-ə\ city, capital of New Caledonia
No•va Igua•çu \,nò-və-,ē-gwə-'sü\ city [SE] Brazil [NW] of Rio de Janeiro
No•va Sco•tia \,nō-və-'skō-shə\ province [SE] Canada; capital, Halifax — **No•va Sco•tian** \-'skō-shən\ *adj or n*
No•va•ya Zem•lya \,nō-və-yə-,zem-lē-'ä\ two islands U.S.S.R. in [NE] Soviet Russia, Europe, in Arctic ocean between Barents & Kara seas
Nov•go•rod \'näv-gə-,räd\ city U.S.S.R. in [NW] Soviet Russia, Europe
No•vi Sad \,nō-vē-'säd\ city [NE] Yugoslavia
No•vo•kuz•netsk \,nō-vō-kùz-'netsk\ city U.S.S.R. in [W] central Soviet Russia, Asia, at [S] end of Kuznetsk basin
No•vo•si•birsk \,nō-vō-sə-'biərsk\ city U.S.S.R. in [SW] Soviet Russia, Asia, on the Ob
Nu•bia \'nü-bē-ə, 'nyü-\ region [NE] Africa in Nile valley in [S] Egypt & [N] Sudan — **Nu•bi•an** \-bē-ən\ *adj or n*
Nubian desert [NE] Sudan [E] of the Nile
Nue•vo Le•ón \nù-,ā-vō-lā-'ōn\ state [N] Mexico; capital, Monterrey
Nu•ku•a•lo•fa \,nü-kə-wə-'lō-fə\ seaport, capital of Tonga
Nu•mid•ia \nù-'mid-ē-ə, nyù-\ ancient country [N] Africa [E] of Mauretania in modern Algeria; chief city, Hippo — **Nu•mid•i•an** \-ē-ən\ *adj or n*
Nu•rem•berg \'nùr-əm-,bərg, 'nyùr-\ *or German* **Nürn•berg** \'nuern-,berk\ city West Germany in [N] Bavaria
Ny•asa, Lake \nī-'as-ə, nē-\ *or* **Lake Ma•la•wi** \mə-'lä-wē, -'laù-ē\ lake [SE] Africa in Malawi, Mozambique, & Tanzania
Nyasaland — see MALAWI
Oa•hu \ə-'wä-hü\ island Hawaii; site of Honolulu
Oak•land \'ō-klənd\ city [W] California on San Francisco Bay [E] of San Francisco
Oa•xa•ca \wə-'hä-kə\ **1** state [SE] Mexico **2** city, its capital
Ob \'äb, 'òb\ river 4025 kilometers long U.S.S.R. in [W] Soviet Russia, Asia, flowing [NW] & [N] into **Gulf of Ob** (inlet of Arctic ocean)
Ober•hau•sen \'ō-bər-,haùz-n\ city West Germany in the Ruhr [WNW] of Essen
Oce•a•nia \,ō-shē-'an-ē-ə, -'ā-nē-ə\ lands of the central & [S] Pacific: Micronesia, Melanesia, Polynesia including New Zealand, & sometimes Australia & Malay archipelago — **Oce•a•ni•an** \-'an-ē-ən, -'ā-nē-\ *adj or n*
Oden•se \'ōd-n-sə, 'ü-ən-zə\ city central Denmark on Fyn Island
Oder \'ōd-ər\ *or* **Odra** \'ō-drə\ *or ancient* **Vi•ad•ua** \vī-'aj-ə-wə\ river 906 kilometers long central Europe flowing from [N] central Czechoslovakia [NW] into Baltic sea; forms part of boundary between Poland & East Germany — see NEISSE
Odes•sa \ō-'des-ə\ city U.S.S.R. in [S] Ukraine on Black sea
Of•fa•ly \'òf-ə-lē, 'äf-\ county central Ireland in Leinster
Ogasawara — see BONIN
Og•bo•mo•sho \,äg-bə-'mō-shō\ city [W] Nigeria
Ohio \ō-'hī-ō\ **1** river 1579 kilometers long [E] U.S. flowing from [W] Pennsylvania into the Mississippi **2** state [E] central U.S.;

capital, Columbus — **Ohio•an** \ō-'hī-ə-wən\ *adj or n*
Oi•ta \'ȯi-ˌtä, ō-'ēt-ə\ city Japan in [NE] Kyushu
Oka•ya•ma \ˌō-kə-'yäm-ə\ city Japan in [W] Honshu on Inland sea
Okee•cho•bee, Lake \ˌō-kē-'chō-bē\ lake [S] central Florida
Oke•fe•no•kee \ˌō-kē-fə-'nō-kē\ swamp [SE] Georgia & [NE] Florida
Okhotsk, Sea of \ō-'kätsk\ inlet of the Pacific U.S.S.R. in Soviet Russia, Asia, [W] of Kamchatka peninsula & Kuril islands
Oki•na•wa \ˌō-kə-'nä-wə, -'naü-ə\ **1** islands Japan in central Ryukyus; capital, Naha **2** island, chief of group — **Oki•na•wan** \-'nä-wən, -'naü-ən\ *adj or n*
Okla•ho•ma \ˌō-klə-'hō-mə\ state [S] U.S.; capital, Oklahoma City — **Okla•ho•man** \-mən\ *adj or n*
Oklahoma City city, capital of Oklahoma
Old•ham \'ōl-dəm\ city [NW] England in Greater Manchester
Old Point Comfort cape [SE] Virginia [N] of entrance to Hampton Roads
Ol•du•vai Gorge \'ōl-də-ˌvī\ canyon [N] Tanzania [SE] of Serengeti Plain; site of fossil beds
Olives, Mount of *or* **Ol•i•vet** \'äl-ə-ˌvet, ˌäl-ə-'\ mountain ridge [W] Jordan on [E] side of Jerusalem
Olym•pia \ə-'lim-pē-ə, ō-\ **1** city, capital of Washington **2** plain [S] Greece in [NW] Peloponnesus
Olym•pic \ə-'lim-pik, ō-\ mountains [NW] Washington on Olympic peninsula, partly in **Olympic National Park;** highest Mt. Olympus 2428 meters
Olym•pus \ə-'lim-pəs, ō-\ mountains [NE] Greece in Thessaly; home of the gods in Greek mythology
Oma•ha \'ō-mə-ˌhȯ, -ˌhä\ city [E] Nebraska
Oman \ō-'män, -'man\ *or formerly* **Mus•cat and Oman** \'məs-ˌkat, -kət\ country [SW] Asia in [SE] Arabia; a sultanate; capital, Muscat — see UNITED ARAB EMIRATES
Oman, Gulf of arm of Arabian sea between Oman & [SE] Iran
Om•dur•man \ˌäm-dər-'man, -'män\ city central Sudan on left bank of the Nile opposite Khartoum
Omi•ya \ō-'mē-ə, 'ō-mē-ˌä\ city Japan in [SE] Honshu [NW] of Tokyo
Omsk \'ȯmsk, 'ȯmpsk, 'ämsk, 'ämpsk\ city U.S.S.R. in [W] central Soviet Russia, Asia, at confluence of Irtysh & Om rivers
On•ta•ke \ōn-'täk-ē\ mountain 3063 meters Japan in central Honshu [NNW] of Nagoya
On•tar•io \än-'ter-ē-ˌō\ province [E] Canada; capital, Toronto — **On•tar•i•an** \-ē-ən\ *adj or n*
Ontario, Lake lake [E] central North America in U.S. & Canada; one of the Great Lakes
Ophir \'ō-fər\ a bibical land rich in gold; probably in Arabia
Opor•to \ō-'pȯrt-ō, -'pȯrt-\ *or Portuguese* **Pôr•to** \'pȯr-tü\ *or ancient* **Por•tus Ca•le** \ˌpōrt-əs-'kā-lē\ city [NW] Portugal
Ora•dea \ō-'räd-ē-ə\ city [NW] Rumania
Oran \ō-'rän\ city [NW] Algeria
Or•ange \'ȯr-inj, 'är-, -ənj\ river 2090 kilometers long [S] Africa flowing [W] from Drakensberg mountains into the Atlantic
Orange Free State province [E] central Republic of South Africa; capital, Bloemfontein
Or•dos \'ȯrd-əs\ in [SW] Inner Mongolia in [N] bend of Yellow river
Or•dzho•ni•kid•ze \ˌȯr-ˌjän-ə-'kid-zə\ *or formerly* **Dzau•dzhi•kau** \dzaü-'jē-ˌkaü, zaü-\ city U.S.S.R. in [SE] Soviet Russia, Europe, [N] of Tiflis
Or•e•gon \'ȯr-i-gən, 'är-, -ˌgän\ state [NW] U.S.; capital, Salem — **Or•e•go•nian** \ˌȯr-i-'gō-nē-ən, ˌär-, -nyən\ *adj or n*
Oregon Trail pioneer route to the Pacific Northwest about 3220 kilometers long from vicinity of Independence, Missouri, to Vancouver, Washington
Orel \ō-'rel, ȯr-'yȯl\ city U.S.S.R. in central Soviet Russia, Europe, [S] of Moscow
Ore mountains — see ERZGEBIRGE
Oren•burg \'ōr-ən-ˌbərg, 'ȯr-, -ˌbu̇rg\ *or formerly* **Chkalov** \chə-'käl-əf\ city U.S.S.R. in [E] Soviet Russia, Europe, on Ural river
Ori•no•co \ˌōr-ə-'nō-kō, ˌȯr-\ river 2575 kilometers long Venezuela flowing into the Atlantic
Oris•sa \ō-'ris-ə\ state [E] India; capital, Bhubaneswar
Ori•za•ba \ˌōr-ə-'zäb-ə, ˌȯr-\ city [E] Mexico in Veracruz state
Orizaba, Pico de — see CITLALTEPETL
Ork•ney \'ȯrk-nē\ islands [N] Scotland; a county
Or•lan•do \ō-'lan-dō\ city central Florida
Or•léans \ȯr-lā-äⁿ\ city [N] central France
Orsk \'ȯrsk\ city U.S.S.R. in [E] Soviet Russia, Europe, on Ural river
Osa•ka \ō-'säk-ə\ city Japan in [S] Honshu
Osh•a•wa \'äsh-ə-ˌwä\ city Canada in [SE] Ontario on lake Ontario [ENE] of Toronto
Oshog•bo \ō-'shäg-bō\ city [W] Nigeria [NE] of Lagos
Os•lo \'äz-lō, 'äs-\ city, capital of Norway
Os•sa \'äs-ə\ mountain 1978 meters [NE] Greece in [E] Thessaly near Mount Pelion
Ostra•va \'ō-strə-və\ city central Czechoslovakia in Moravia
Ota•ru \ō-'tär-ü\ city Japan in [W] Hokkaido
Otran•to, Strait of \ō-'tran-tō, 'ō-trən-ˌtō\ strait between [SE] Italy & Albania
Ot•su \'ät-ˌsü\ city Japan in [W] central Honshu [W] of Kyoto
Ot•ta•wa \'ät-ə-ˌwä, -wə, -ˌwȯ\ city, capital of Canada in [SE] Ontario on Ottawa river
Oua•ga•dou•gou \ˌwäg-ə-'dü-ˌgü\ city, capital of Upper Volta
Outer Hebrides — see HEBRIDES
Outer Mongolia — see MONGOLIAN PEOPLE'S REPUBLIC
Ovie•do \ˌō-vē-'ā-thō\ city [NW] Spain
Ox•ford \'äks-fərd\ city central England in Oxfordshire
Ox•ford•shire \'äks-fərd-ˌshiər, -shər\ *or* **Oxford** county central England
Oxus — see AMU DARYA
Ozark plateau \'ō-ˌzärk\ eroded tableland [N] Arkansas, [S] Missouri, & [NE] Oklahoma
Pa•cif•ic \pə-'sif-ik\ ocean extending from arctic circle to antarctic regions & from [W] North America & [W] South America to [E] Asia & Australia
Pacific Islands, Trust Territory of the islands in [W] Pacific under U.S. administration: the Marianas (except Guam), the Carolines, & the Marshalls — see MARIANA
Pa•dre \'päd-rē, 'pad-\ island about 160 kilometers long [S] Texas in Gulf of Mexico
Pad•u•a \'paj-ə-wə, 'pad-ə-wə\ *or Italian* **Pa•do•va** \'päd-ə-ˌvä\ *or ancient* **Pa•ta•vi•um** \pə-'tā-vē-əm\ city [N] Italy [W] of Venice
Padus — see PO
Pa•go Pa•go \ˌpäng-gō-'päng-gō, ˌpäng-ō-'pang-ō, ˌpäg-ō-'päg-ō\ town, capital of American Samoa on Tutuila Island
Pak•i•stan \ˌpak-i-'stan, ˌpäk-i-'stän\ country [S] Asia in Indian subcontinent [NW] of India; until 1971 included also an eastern division [E] of India; a republic; capital, Islamabad — see EAST PAKISTAN — **Pak•i•stani** \-'stan-ē, -'stän-ē\ *adj or n*
Pal•at•i•nate \pə-'lat-n-ət\ *or German* **Pfalz** \'pfälts, 'fälts\ either of two districts [SW] Germany once ruled by counts palatine of the Holy Roman Empire: **Rhenish Palatinate** *or* **Rhine Palatinate** *or German* **Rhein•pfalz** \'rīn-ˌpfälts, -ˌfälts\ (on the Rhine [E] of Saarland) & **Upper Palatinate** (on the Danube around Regensburg) — see RHINELAND-PALATINATE
Pa•lau \pə-'laü\ *or formerly* **Pe•lew** \pə-'lü\ islands [W] Pacific in the [W] Carolines — see BABELTHUAP
Pa•la•wan \pə-'lä-wən, -ˌwän\ island [W] Philippines between South China & Sulu seas
Pa•lem•bang \ˌpäl-əm-'bäng\ city Indonesia in [SE] Sumatra
Pa•ler•mo \pə-'lər-mō, -'leər-\ city Italy, capital of Sicily
Pal•es•tine \'pal-ə-ˌstīn, -ˌstēn\ region [SW] Asia between Syrian desert & the Mediterranean now divided between Israel & Jordan — **Pal•es•tin•ian** \ˌpal-ə-'stin-ē-ən, -'stin-yən\ *adj or n*
Pal•ma \'päl-mə\ *or* **Palma de Ma•llor•ca** \-ˌdā-mə-'yȯr-kə, -məl-\ city Spain on Majorca
Palmer peninsula — see ANTARCTIC PENINSULA
Pa•mirs \pə-'miərz\ *or* **Pa•mir** \pə-'miər\ elevated mountainous region central Asia in [E] Tadzhikistan & on borders of Sinkiang, Kashmir, & Afghanistan; many peaks over 6000 meters
Pam•li•co \'pam-li-ˌkō\ sound inlet of the Atlantic [E] North Carolina between mainland & offshore islands
Pam•plo•na \pam-'plō-nə\ city [N] Spain in Navarre
Pan•a•ma \'pan-ə-ˌmä, -ˌmȯ, ˌpan-ə-'\ **1** country [S] Central America; a republic **2** *or* **Panama City** city, its capital on the Pacific **3** canal 82 kilometers long Panama in Canal Zone connecting Atlantic & Pacific oceans — **Pan•a•ma•ni•an** \ˌpan-ə-'mā-nē-ən\ *adj or n*
Panama, Isthmus of *or formerly* **Isthmus of Dar•i•en** \-ˌdar-ē-'en\ strip of land central Panama connecting North America & South America
Panama Canal Zone — see CANAL ZONE
Pa•nay \pə-'nī\ island Philippines in Visayan islands; chief city, Iloilo

Pan•de•mo•ni•um \ˌpan-də-ˈmō-nē-əm\ the capital of Hell in John Milton's *Paradise Lost*
Panjab — see PUNJAB
Pao•ki \ˈpau̇-ˈkē\ *or* **Pao–chi** \-ˈchē\ city [N] central China in [SW] Shensi
Pao•ting \ˈbau̇-ˈding\ city [NE] China in Hopei [SW] of Peking
Pao–t'ou \ˈbau̇-ˈtō\ city [N] China in [SW] Inner Mongolia
Papal States — see STATES OF THE CHURCH
Pa•pee•te \ˌpäp-ē-ˈāt-ē; pə-ˈpāt-ē, -ˈpēt-\ city Society islands on Tahiti, capital of French Polynesia
Pap•ua, Territory of \ˈpap-yə-wə, ˈpäp-ə-wə\ former British territory comprising [SE] New Guinea & offshore islands; now part of Papua New Guinea
Papua New Guinea country combining former territories of Papua & New Guinea; formerly a United Nations trust territory administered by Australia; independent since 1975; capital, Port Moresby
Pará — see BELEM
Par•a•guay \ˈpar-ə-ˌgwī, -ˌgwā\ **1** river 2415 kilometers long central South America flowing from Brazil [S] into the Paraná in Paraguay **2** country central South America; a republic; capital, Asunción — **Par•a•guay•an** \ˌpar-ə-ˈgwī-ən, -ˈgwā-ən\ *adj or n*
Par•a•mar•i•bo \ˌpar-ə-ˈmar-ə-ˌbō\ city, capital of Surinam
Pa•ra•ná \ˌpar-ə-ˈnä\ **1** river 3285 kilometers long central South America flowing [S] from Brazil into Rio de la Plata in Argentina **2** city [NE] Argentina
Par•is \ˈpar-əs\ city, capital of France — **Pa•ri•sian** \pə-ˈrizh-ən, -ˈrēzh-\ *adj or n*
Par•ma \ˈpär-mə\ **1** city [NE] Ohio **2** city [N] Italy in Emilia-Romagna [SE] of Milan
Par•nas•sus \pär-ˈnas-əs\ massif central Greece [N] of Gulf of Corinth; highest point 2457 meters
Par•os \ˈpar-ˌäs, ˈper-\ island Greece in central Cyclades — **Par•i•an** \ˈpar-ē-ən, ˈper-\ *adj*
Par•ra•mat•ta \ˌpar-ə-ˈmat-ə\ city [SE] Australia in New South Wales [NW] of Sydney
Par•thia \ˈpär-thē-ə\ ancient country [SW] Asia in [NE] modern Iran — **Par•thi•an** \-thē-ən\ *adj or n*
Pas•a•de•na \ˌpas-ə-ˈdē-nə\ city [SW] California [E] of Glendale
Pat•a•go•nia \ˌpat-ə-ˈgō-nyə, -nē-ə\ barren region South America [S] of about 40° [S] latitude in [S] Argentina & [S] tip of Chile; sometimes considered to include Tierra del Fuego — **Pat•a•go•nian** \-nyən, -nē-ən\ *adj or n*
Patavium — see PADUA
Pat•er•son \ˈpat-ər-sən\ city [NE] New Jersey
Pat•mos \ˈpat-məs\ island Greece in the Dodecanese [SSW] of Samos
Pat•na \ˈpət-nə\ city [NE] India on the Ganges, capital of Bihar
Pat•ras \pə-ˈtras, ˈpa-trəs\ city [W] Greece in [N] Peloponnesus on Gulf of Patras
Pearl Harbor inlet Hawaii on [S] coast of Oahu [W] of Honolulu
Pee•bles \ˈpē-bəlz\ *or* **Pee•bles•shire** \ˈpē-bəl-ˌshiər, -shər\ former county [SE] Scotland
Peiraeus — see PIRAEUS
Pe•king \ˈpē-ˈking\ city, capital of China
Pelew — see PALAU
Pe•li•on \ˈpē-lē-ən\ mountain 1618 meters [NE] Greece in [E] Thessaly near Mount Ossa
Pel•o•pon•ne•sus \ˌpel-ə-pə-ˈnē-səs\ *or* **Pel•o•pon•ne•sos** \-ˈne-səs\ *or* **Pel•o•pon•nese** \ˈpel-ə-pə-ˌnēz, -ˌnēs\ peninsula forming [S] part of mainland of Greece — **Pel•o•pon•ne•sian** \ˌpel-ə-pə-ˈnē-zhən, -shən\ *adj or n*
Pe•lo•tas \pə-ˈlōt-əs\ city [S] Brazil [SW] of Pôrto Alegre
Pem•broke•shire \ˈpem-bru̇k-ˌshiər, -shər\ *or* **Pembroke** former county [SW] Wales
Pe•nang \pə-ˈnang\ *or* **Pu•lau Pi•nang** \ˌpü-ˌlau̇-pə-ˈnäng\ *or formerly* **George Town** \ˈjȯrj-ˌtau̇n\ city Federation of Malaysia on Penang Island in Peninsular Malaysia
Pen–ch'i *or* **Pen•ki** \ˈbən-ˈchē\ *or* **Pen•hsi•hu** \ˈbən–ˈshē-ˈhü\ city [NE] China in [E] central Liaoning
Peninsular Malaysia *or* **West Malaysia** territory [W] Malaysia comprising that part of Malaysia contained on Malay peninsula
Pen•nine Chain \ˈpen-ˌīn\ mountains [N] England; highest Cross Fell 893 meters
Penn•syl•va•nia \ˌpen-səl-ˈvā-nyə, -nē-ə\ state [E] U.S.; capital, Harrisburg
Pen•tel•i•cus \pen-ˈtel-i-kəs\ *or* **Pen•del•i•kon** \ˌpen-ˌdel-ē-ˈkȯn\ mountain 1109 meters [E] Greece [NE] of Athens
Pen•za \ˈpen-zə\ city U.S.S.R. in [SE] central Soviet Russia, Europe, [W] of Kuibyshev
People's Democratic Republic of Yemen — see YEMEN
Pe•o•ria \pē-ˈōr-ē-ə, -ˈȯr-\ city [N] central Illinois
Pe•rei•ra \pə-ˈreər-ə, -ˈrā-rə\ city [W] central Colombia
Per•ga•mum \ˈpər-gə-məm\ *or* **Per•ga•mus** \-məs\ ancient Greek kingdom including most of Asia Minor; at its height 263–133 B.C.; capital, Pergamum (in what is now [W] Turkey)
Perm \ˈpərm, ˈpeərm\ *or formerly* **Mo•lo•tov** \ˈmäl-ə-ˌtȯf, ˈmȯl-, ˈmōl-, -ˌtȯv\ city U.S.S.R. in [W] Soviet Russia, Europe
Pernambuco — see RECIFE
Per•pi•gnan \per-pē-nyä^{n}\ city [S] France [SE] of Toulouse
Per•sep•o•lis \pər-ˈsep-ə-ləs\ city of ancient Persia; site in [SW] Iran [NE] of Shiraz
Persia — see IRAN
Per•sian \ˈpər-zhən\ gulf arm of Arabian sea between Iran & Arabia
Persian Gulf States Kuwait, Bahrain, Qatar, & United Arab Emirates
Perth \ˈpərth\ **1** city, capital of Western Australia **2** *or* **Perth•shire** \-ˌshiər, -shər\ former county central Scotland
Pe•ru \pə-ˈrü\ country [W] South America; a republic; capital, Lima — **Pe•ru•vi•an** \pə-ˈrü-vē-ən\ *adj or n*
Peru current *or* **Hum•boldt current** \ˈhəm-ˌbōlt\ cold current of the [S] Pacific flowing [N] & [NW] along coast of [N] Chile, Peru, & Ecuador
Pe•ru•gia \pə-ˈrü-jə, -jē-ə\ city central Italy [SE] of Florence
Pes•ca•do•res \ˌpes-kə-ˈdōr-ˌēz, -ˈdȯr-, -əs\ *or Chinese* **Peng–hu** \ˈpəng-ˈhü\ islands [E] China in Taiwan strait
Pe•sha•war \pə-ˈshä-wər, -ˈshau̇-ər\ city [N] Pakistan [ESE] of Khyber pass
Pe•ter•bor•ough, Soke of \ˌsō-kəv-ˈpēt-ər-ˌbər-ə, -ˌbə-rə, -brə\ former administrative county [E] central England in Northamptonshire and later in Huntingdonshire; since 1974 part of Cambridgeshire
Pe•tra \ˈpē-trə, ˈpe-trə\ ancient city [NW] Arabia; site in [SW] Jordan
Petrograd — see LENINGRAD
Pe•tro•pav•lovsk \ˌpe-trə-ˈpav-ˌlȯfsk\ city U.S.S.R. in [N] Kazakhstan
Pe•tró•po•lis \pə-ˈträp-ə-ləs\ city [SE] Brazil [N] of Rio de Janeiro
Pe•tro•za•vodsk \ˌpe-trə-zə-ˈvätsk\ city U.S.S.R. in [NW] Soviet Russia, Europe, on Lake Onega
Pfalz — see PALATINATE
Phil•a•del•phia \ˌfil-ə-ˈdel-fyə, -fē-ə\ city [SE] Pennsylvania — **Phil•a•del•phian** \-fyən, -fē-ən\ *adj or n*
Phi•lae \ˈfī-lē\ island [S] Egypt in the Nile above Aswân; now submerged in Lake Nasser
Phil•ip•pines \ˌfil-ə-ˈpēnz, ˈfil-ə-ˌ\ *or* **Republic of the Philippines** republic, an archipelago approximately 800 kilometers off [SE] coast of Asia; capital, Quezon City — **Phil•ip•pine** \-ˈpēn, -ˌpēn\ *adj*
Phi•lis•tia \fə-ˈlis-tē-ə\ ancient country [SW] Palestine on the coast; the land of the Philistines
Phnom Penh *or* **Pnom•penh** \pə-ˈnȯm-ˈpen, ˈnȯm-, pə-ˈnäm-, ˈnäm-\ city, capital of Khmer Republic (Cambodia)
Phoe•ni•cia \fi-ˈnish-ə, -ˈnēsh-, -ē-ə\ ancient country [SW] Asia on the Mediterranean in modern Syria & Lebanon
Phoe•nix \ˈfē-niks\ city, capital of Arizona
Phry•gia \ˈfrij-ə, ˈfrij-ē-ə\ ancient country [W] central Asia Minor
Pia•cen•za \pyä-ˈchen-sə, ˌpē-ə-ˈchen-\ city [N] Italy [SE] of Milan
Pic•ar•dy \ˈpik-ərd-ē\ *or French* **Pi•car•die** \pē-kȧr-dē\ region & former province [N] France [N] of Normandy; capital, Amiens
Pico de Orizaba — see CITLALTEPETL
Pied•mont \ˈpēd-ˌmänt\ **1** plateau region [E] U.S. [E] of the Appalachians between [SE] New York & [NE] Alabama **2** *or Italian* **Pie•mon•te** \pyā-ˈmōn-tā\ region [NW] Italy [W] of Lombardy; capital, Turin — **Pied•mon•tese** \ˌpēd-mən-ˈtēz, -män-, -ˈtēs\ *adj or n*
Pierre \ˈpiər\ city, capital of South Dakota
Pie•ter•mar•itz•burg \ˌpēt-ər-ˈmar-əts-ˌbərg\ city [E] Republic of South Africa, capital of Natal
Pikes Peak \ˈpīks\ mountain 4301 meters [E] central Colorado in a range of the Rockies
Pillars of Her•cu•les \ˈhər-kyə-ˌlēz\ two promontories at [E] end of Strait of Gibraltar: Rock of Gibraltar (in Europe) & Jebel Musa (in Africa)

Pin•dus \ˈpin-dəs\ mountains [W] Greece [W] of Thessaly; highest point 2480 meters
Pinkiang — see HARBIN
Pi•rae•us *or* **Pei•rae•us** \pī-ˈrē-əs\ *or Greek* **Pi•rai•évs** \ˌpē-rē-ˈefs\ city [E] Greece on Saronic gulf; port for Athens
Pi•sa \ˈpē-zə, *Italian* ˈpē-sä\ city [W] central Italy [W] of Florence
Pit•cairn \ˈpit-ˌkaərn, -ˌkeərn\ island [S] Pacific [SE] of Tuamotu archipelago; a British colony
Pitts•burgh \ˈpits-ˌbərg\ city [SW] Pennsylvania
Pla•ta, Río de la \ˌrē-ō-ˌdel-ə-ˈplät-ə\ estuary of Paraná & Uruguay rivers between Uruguay & Argentina
Plov•div \ˈplòv-ˌdif, -ˌdiv\ city [S] Bulgaria
Plym•outh \ˈplim-əth\ city [SW] England in Devonshire
Pnompenh — see PHNOM PENH
Po \ˈpō\ *or ancient* **Pa•dus** \ˈpād-əs\ river 673 kilometers [N] Italy flowing into the Adriatic
Po Hai \ˈbō-ˈhī\ *or* **Gulf of Chih•li** \ˈchē-ˈlē, ˈjiər-ˈlē\ arm of Yellow sea [NE] China [N] of Shantung peninsula
Po•land \ˈpō-lənd\ country central Europe on Baltic sea; a republic; capital, Warsaw
Pol•y•ne•sia \ˌpäl-ə-ˈnē-zhə, -shə\ islands of the central & [S] Pacific including Hawaii, the Line, Tuvala, Phoenix, Tonga, Cook, & Samoa islands, French Polynesia, & often New Zealand
Pom•er•a•nia \ˌpäm-ə-ˈrā-nē-ə, -ˈrā-nyə\ region [N] Europe on Baltic sea; formerly in Germany, now mostly in Poland
Pom•peii \päm-ˈpā, -ˈpā-ˌē\ ancient city [S] Italy [SE] of Naples destroyed 79 A.D. by eruption of Vesuvius — **Pom•pe•ian** \-ˈpā-ən\ *adj or n*
Po•na•pe \ˈpō-nə-ˌpā\ island [W] Pacific in the [E] Carolines
Pon•ce \ˈpòn-sā\ city [S] Puerto Rico
Pon•di•cher•ry \ˌpän-də-ˈcher-ē, -ˈsher-\ territory [SE] India [SSW] of Madras; a settlement of French India before 1954
Pon•do•land \ˈpän-dō-ˌland\ territory Republic of South Africa in Transkei between Umtata river & Natal
Pon•ta Del•ga•da \ˌpänt-ə-del-ˈgäd-ə, -ˈgad-\ city Portugal in the Azores on São Miguel Island
Pont•char•train, Lake \ˈpän-chər-ˌtrān, ˌpän-chər-ˈ\ lake [SE] Louisiana [E] of the Mississippi & [N] of New Orleans
Pon•tine marshes \ˈpän-ˌtīn, -ˌtēn\ district central Italy in [SW] Latium; marshes now reclaimed
Pon•tus \ˈpänt-əs\ **1** ancient country & Roman province [NE] Asia Minor **2** *or* **Pontus Euxinus** — see BLACK SEA — **Pon•tic** \ˈpänt-ik\ *adj or n*
Poole \ˈpül\ borough [S] England in Dorset on English Channel
Poo•na \ˈpü-nə\ city [W] India in Maharashtra [ESE] of Bombay
Po•po•ca•te•petl \ˌpō-pə-ˌkat-ə-ˈpet-l\ volcano 5452 meters [SE] central Mexico in Puebla
Port Ar•thur \ˈär-thər\ *or* **Lü•shun** \ˈlü-ˈshün\ city [NE] China in [S] Liaoning — see LÜTA
Port Arthur–Dairen — see LÜTA
Port–au–Prince \ˌpōrt-ō-ˈprins, ˌpȯrt-, -ˈprans, -ˈprans\ city, capital of Haiti
Port Eliz•a•beth \əl-ˈiz-ə-bəth, i-ˈliz-\ city [S] Republic of South Africa in [SE] Cape Province
Port Har•court \ˈhär-kərt\ city [S] Nigeria
Port Jack•son \ˈjak-sən\ inlet of [S] Pacific [SE] Australia in New South Wales; harbor of Sydney
Port•land \ˈpōrt-lənd, ˈpȯrt-\ city [NW] Oregon
Port Lou•is \ˈlü-əs, ˈlü-ē, lü-ˈē\ city, capital of Mauritius
Port Lyautey — see KENITRA
Port Mores•by \ˈmōrz-bē, ˈmȯrz-\ city, capital of Papua New Guinea
Pôrto — see OPORTO
Pôr•to Ale•gre \ˌpōrt-ō-ə-ˈleg-rə, ˌpȯrt-\ city [S] Brazil
Port of Spain city [NW] Trinidad, capital of Trinidad and Tobago
Por•to–No•vo \ˌpōrt-ə-ˈnō-vō, ˌpȯrt-\ city, capital of Benin
Porto Rico — see PUERTO RICO
Port Phil•lip Bay \ˈfil-əp\ inlet of [S] Pacific [SE] Australia in Victoria; harbor of Melbourne
Port Said \sä-ˈēd, ˈsīd\ city [NE] Egypt on the Mediterranean at [N] end of Suez canal
Ports•mouth \ˈpōrt-sməth, ˈpȯrt-\ **1** city [SE] Virginia **2** city [S] England in Hampshire
Port Su•dan \sü-ˈdan, -ˈdän\ city [NE] Sudan
Por•tu•gal \ˈpōr-chi-gəl, ˈpȯr-\ *or ancient* **Lu•si•ta•nia** \ˌlü-sə-ˈtā-nē-ə, -nyə\ country [SW] Europe; a republic; capital, Lisbon
Portuguese East Africa — see MOZAMBIQUE
Portuguese Guinea — see GUINEA-BISSAU
Portuguese India former Portuguese possession on [W] coast of India including Goa, Damão, & Diu; annexed to India 1962
Portuguese West Africa — see ANGOLA
Portus Cale — see OPORTO
Po•to•mac \pə-ˈtō-mək, -mik\ river 462 kilometers long flowing from West Virginia into Chesapeake Bay & forming boundary between Maryland & Virginia
Po•wys \ˈpō-əs\ county [E] central Wales; established 1974
Poz•nan \ˈpōz-ˌnan-yə, ˈpȯz-, -ˌnän-yə, -ˌnan, -ˌnän\ city [W] central Poland
Prague \ˈpräg\ *or Czech* **Pra•ha** \ˈprä-hä\ city, capital of Czechoslovakia
Prairie Provinces the Canadian provinces of Alberta, Manitoba, & Saskatchewan
Pra•to \ˈprät-ō\ city central Italy [NW] of Florence
Pres•ton \ˈpres-tən\ borough [NW] England in Lancashire
Pre•to•ria \pri-ˈtōr-ē-ə, -ˈtȯr-\ city Republic of South Africa, capital of Transvaal & administrative capital of the Republic
Prib•i•lof \ˈprib-ə-ˌlȯf\ islands Alaska in Bering sea
Prince Al•bert National Park \ˈal-bərt\ reservation Canada in central Saskatchewan
Prince Ed•ward Island \ˌed-wərd\ island [SE] Canada in Gulf of Saint Lawrence; a province; capital, Charlottetown
Prince Ru•pert's Land \ˈrü-pərts\ historical region [N] & [W] Canada comprising drainage basin of Hudson Bay granted 1670 by King Charles II to Hudson's Bay Company
Prin•cí•pe \ˈprin-sə-pə\ island [W] Africa in Gulf of Guinea — see SÃO TOMÉ
Pro•ko•pyevsk \prə-ˈkȯp-yəfsk\ city U.S.S.R. in [W] Soviet Russia, Asia, [NW] of Novokuznetsk
Propontis — see MARMARA
Pro•vence \prə-ˈväns\ region & former province [SE] France on the Mediterranean
Prov•i•dence \ˈpräv-əd-əns, -ə-ˌdens\ city, capital of Rhode Island
Prus•sia \ˈprəsh-ə\ former kingdom &, later, state Germany; capital, Berlin — **Prus•sian** \-ən\ *adj or n*
Pu•eb•la \pü-ˈeb-lə, ˈpweb-, pyü-ˈeb-\ **1** state [SE] central Mexico **2** city, its capital
Puer•to Ri•co \ˌpōrt-ə-ˈrē-kō, ˌpȯrt-, ˌpwert-\ *or formerly* **Por•to Ri•co** \ˌpōrt-, ˌpȯrt-\ island West Indies [E] of Hispaniola; a self-governing commonwealth associated with U.S.; capital, San Juan — **Puer•to Ri•can** \-ˈrē-kən\ *adj or n*
Pu•get Sound \ˌpyü-jət-\ arm of the Pacific [W] Washington
Puglia — see APULIA
Pulau Pinang — see PENANG
Pu•na de Ata•ca•ma \ˈpü-nə-ˌdā-ˌat-ə-ˈkäm-ə, -ˌät-\ plateau region [NW] Argentina [NW] of San Miguel de Tucumán
Pun•jab *or* **Pan•jab** \ˌpən-ˈjäb, -ˈjab, ˈpən-ˌ\ **1** region [NW] Indian subcontinent in Pakistan & [NW] India in valley of the Indus **2** *or* **Pun•jabi Su•ba** \ˌpən-ˌjäb-ē-ˈsü-bə, -ˌjab-\ state [NW] India in [E] Punjab region; capital, Chandigarh — see HARYANA **3** *or formerly* **West Punjab** province [NE] Pakistan
Pu•rus \pə-ˈrüs\ river 3220 kilometers long [NW] central South America in [SE] Peru & [NW] Brazil flowing into the Amazon
Pu•san \ˈpü-ˌsän\ city South Korea on Korea strait
Pyong•yang \pē-ˈȯng-ˌyäng, pē-ˈəng-, -ˌyang\ city, capital of North Korea
Pyr•e•nees \ˈpir-ə-ˌnēz\ mountains on French-Spanish border extending from Bay of Biscay to the Mediterranean; highest Pico de Aneto (Pic de Néthou) 3404 meters
Qa•tar \ˈkät-ər, ˈgät-, ˈgət-\ country [E] Arabia on peninsula extending into Persian gulf; an independent emirate; capital, Doha
Que•bec \kwi-ˈbek, ki-\ *or French* **Qué•bec** \kā-bek\ **1** province [E] Canada **2** city, its capital, on the Saint Lawrence
Queens \ˈkwēnz\ borough of New York City on Long Island [E] of borough of Brooklyn
Queen's — see LAOIGHIS
Queens•land \ˈkwēnz-ˌland, -lənd\ state [NE] Australia; capital, Brisbane — **Queens•land•er** \-ər\ *n*
Que•moy \kwi-ˈmȯi, ki-, ˈkwē-ˌ\ island [E] China in Taiwan strait [E] of Amoy
Que•ré•ta•ro \kə-ˈret-ə-ˌrō\ **1** state central Mexico **2** city, its capital
Que•zon City \ˈkā-ˌsȯn\ city Philippines in Luzon [NE] of Manila; official capital of the Philippines
Quil•mes \ˈkēl-ˌmās, -ˌmes\ city [E] Argentina [SE] of Buenos Aires

Quin•ta•na Roo \kēn-ˌtän-ə-'rō\ state [SE] Mexico in [E] Yucatán; capital, Chetumal

Qui•to \'kē-tō\ city, capital of Ecuador

Ra•bat \rə-'bät\ city, capital of Morocco

Rad•nor•shire \'rad-nər-ˌshiər, -ˌnȯr-, -shər\ *or* **Radnor** former county [E] Wales

Ra•dom \'räd-ˌȯm\ city [E] central Poland

Rai•nier, Mount \rə-'niər, rā-\ mountain 4392 meters [W] central Washington in **Mount Rainier National Park;** highest in Cascade mountains

Rai•pur \'rī-ˌpu̇r\ city [E] India in [SE] Madhya Pradesh [E] of Nagpur

Ra•jah•mun•dry \ˌräj-ə-'mu̇n-drē\ city [E] India in [E] Andhra Pradesh

Ra•ja•sthan \'räj-ə-ˌstän\ **1** state [NW] India bordering on Pakistan; capital, Jaipur **2** RAJPUTANA

Raj•kot \'räj-ˌkōt\ city [W] India in Gujarat

Raj•pu•ta•na \ˌräj-pə-'tän-ə\ region [NW] India [S] of Punjab now largely included in Rajasthan state

Ra•leigh \'rȯ-lē, 'räl-ē\ city, capital of North Carolina

Rand — see WITWATERSRAND

Ran•goon \ran-'gün, rang-\ city, capital of Burma

Rasht \'rasht\ city [NW] Iran

Ra•ven•na \rə-'ven-ə\ city [N] Italy [NE] of Florence

Ra•wal•pin•di \ˌrä-wəl-'pin-dē, rau̇l-'pin-, rȯl-'pin-\ city [NE] Pakistan [NNW] of Lahore

Read•ing \'red-iŋ\ borough [S] England in Berkshire

Re•ci•fe \rə-'sē-fə\ *or formerly* **Per•nam•bu•co** \ˌpər-nəm-'bü-kō, -'byü-, ˌper-nəm-'bü-\ city [NE] Brazil

Red \'red\ **1** river 1638 kilometers long flowing [E] on Oklahoma-Texas boundary & into the Atchafalaya & the Mississippi in Louisiana **2** sea between Arabia & [NE] Africa

Red•bridge \'red-brij\ borough of [NE] Greater London, England

Redwood National Park reservation [NW] California

Re•gens•burg \'rā-gənz-ˌbərg, -ˌbu̇rg\ *or* **Rat•is•bon** \'rat-əs-ˌbän, -əz-\ city West Germany [NNE] of Munich

Reg•gio \'rej-ō, 'rej-ē-ˌō\ **1** *or* **Reggio di Ca•la•bria** \-ˌdē-kə-'läb-rē-ə\ city [S] Italy on Strait of Messina **2** *or* **Reggio nel-l'Emi•lia** \-ˌnel-ə-'mēl-yə\ city [N] Italy [NW] of Bologna

Re•gi•na \ri-'jī-nə\ city, capital of Saskatchewan

Reims *or* **Rheims** \'rēmz, *French* ra^{n}s\ city [NE] France

Ren•frew \'ren-ˌfrü\ *or* **Ren•frew•shire** \-ˌshiər, -shər\ former county [SW] Scotland

Rennes \'ren\ city [NW] France

Ré•union \rē-'yün-yən\ island [W] Indian ocean [E] of Madagascar; an overseas department of France; capital, Saint-Denis

Revel — see TALLINN

Rey•kja•vik \'rāk-yə-ˌvik, 'rāk-ə-ˌ, -ˌvēk\ city, capital of Iceland

Rey•no•sa \rā-'nō-sə\ city [NE] Mexico in Tamaulipas

Rheinpfalz — see PALATINATE

Rhine *or German* **Rhein** \'rīn\ *or French* **Rhin** \ra^{n}\ *or Dutch* **Rijn** \'rīn\ *or ancient* **Rhe•nus** \'rē-nəs\ river 1320 kilometers long [W] Europe flowing from [SE] Switzerland to North sea in the Netherlands — **Rhen•ish** \'ren-ish, 'rē-nish\ *adj or n*

Rhine•land \'rīn-ˌland, -lənd\ *or German* **Rhein•land** \'rīn-ˌlänt\ the part of Germany [W] of the Rhine — **Rhine•land•er** \'rīn-ˌlan-dər, -lən-\ *n*

Rhineland-Palatinate *or German* **Rhein•land-Pfalz** \-'pfälts, -'fälts\ state West Germany chiefly [W] of the Rhine; capital, Mainz

Rhode Is•land \rō-'dī-lənd\ **1** *or officially* **Rhode Island and Providence Plantations** state [NE] U.S.; capital, Providence **2** — see AQUIDNECK — **Rhode Is•land•er** \-lən-dər\ *n*

Rhodes \'rōdz\ **1** island Greece in the [SE] Aegean; chief island of the Dodecanese **2** city, its capital

Rho•de•sia \rō-'dē-zhə, -zhē-ə\ *or formerly* **Southern Rhodesia** country [S] Africa [S] of Zambezi river; a self-governing territory of the British Commonwealth; unilaterally declared itself a republic 1970; capital, Salisbury — **Rho•de•sian** \-zhən, -zhē-ən\ *adj or n*

ıon•dda \'rän-də, 'rän-thə, 'hrän-thə\ municipal borough [SE] Vales

ne *or French* **Rhône** \'rōn\ *or ancient* **Rhod•a•nus** \'räd-n-\ river 800 kilometers long Switzerland & [SE] France

•rão Prê•to \ˌrē-və-'rau̇^{n}-'prā-tü\ city [SE] Brazil [NNW] of Paulo

ond \'rich-mənd\ **1** — see STATEN ISLAND **2** city, capital of **3** *or* **Richmond upon Thames** royal borough of [SW] London, England

Rid•ing Mountain National Park \ˌrīd-iŋ-\ reservation Canada in [SW] Manitoba

Rift valley GREAT RIFT VALLEY

Ri•ga \'rē-gə\ city U.S.S.R., capital of Latvia

Ri•je•ka *or* **Ri•e•ka** \rē-'ek-ə, -'yek-\ *or* **Saint Fiu•me** \'fyü-mā, fē-'ü-\ city [NW] Yugoslavia in Croatia

Ri•mi•ni \'rim-ə-nē, 'rē-mə-\ city [N] Italy on the Adriatic

Rio \'rē-ō\ RIO DE JANEIRO

Rio de Ja•nei•ro \'rē-ō-ˌdā-zhə-'neər-ō, -ˌdē-, -də-, -jə-'neər-\ city [SE] Brazil on Guanabara Bay

Río de Oro \ˌrē-ōd-ē-'ōr-ō, -'ȯr-\ territory [NW] Africa comprising [S] zone of Western Sahara

Rio Grande \ˌrē-ō-'grand, -'grand-ē\ *or Mexican* **Río Bra•vo** \-'bräv-ō\ river 3035 kilometers long [SW] U.S. forming part of U.S.-Mexico boundary & flowing into Gulf of Mexico

Río Mu•ni \ˌrē-ō-'mü-nē\ mainland portion of Equatorial Guinea on Gulf of Guinea

Riv•er•side \'riv-ər-ˌsīd\ city [S] California

Riv•i•era \ˌriv-ē-'er-ə\ coast region [SE] France & [NW] Italy

Ri•yadh \rē-'äd, -'yäd\ city, capital of Saudi Arabia

Ro•a•noke \'rō-ə-ˌnōk, 'rō-ˌnōk\ island North Carolina [S] of entrance to Albemarle sound

Rob•son, Mount \'räb-sən\ mountain 3954 meters [W] Canada in [E] British Columbia; highest in the Canadian Rockies

Roch•es•ter \'räch-ə-stər, 'räch-ˌes-tər\ city [W] New York

Rock•ford \'räk-fərd\ city [N] Illinois

Rocky \'räk-ē\ mountains [W] North America extending [SE] from [N] Alaska to central New Mexico — see ELBERT, ROBSON

Rocky Mountain National Park reservation [N] Colorado

Romania — see RUMANIA

Rome \'rōm\ **1** *or Italian* **Ro•ma** \'rō-mä\ city, capital of Italy **2** the Roman Empire

Ron•ces•va•lles \ˌrän-səs-'vī-əs\ commune [N] Spain

Roo•de•poort-Ma•rais•burg \'rōd-ə-ˌpōrt-mə-'rā-ˌbərg, 'rō-i-ˌpōrt-, -ˌpȯrt-\ city Republic of South Africa in Transvaal

Ro•sa•rio \rō-'zär-ē-ˌō, -'sär-\ city [E] central Argentina

Ros•com•mon \rä-'skäm-ən\ county central Ireland in Connacht

Ross \'rȯs\ sea arm of [S] Pacific extending into Antarctica [E] of Victoria Land

Ross and Crom•ar•ty \'kräm-ərt-ē\ former county [N] Scotland

Ros•tock \'räs-ˌtäk, 'rȯ-ˌstȯk\ city East Germany near Baltic coast

Ros•tov \rə-'stȯf, -'stȯv\ city U.S.S.R. in [SE] Soviet Russia, Europe, on the Don

Rot•ter•dam \'rät-ər-ˌdam\ city [SW] Netherlands

Rou•baix \rü-'bā\ city [N] France [NE] of Lille

Rou•en \rü-'ä^{n}, rü-'ä^{n}\ city [N] France on the Seine

Roumania — see RUMANIA

Rox•burgh \'räks-ˌbər-ə, -ˌbə-rə, -brə\ *or* **Rox•burgh•shire** \-ˌshiər, -shər\ former county [SE] Scotland

Ru•an•da-Urun•di \ru̇-ˌän-də-u̇-'rün-dē\ former trust territory [E] central Africa bordering on Lake Tanganyika & administered by Belgium; divided 1962 into independent nations of Burundi (formerly Urundi) & Rwanda (formerly Ruanda) — see BURUNDI, RWANDA

Rub•tsovsk \'rüpt-ˌsȯfsk\ city U.S.S.R. in [SW] Soviet Russia, Asia, [SSW] of Novosibirsk

Ru•dolf, Lake \'rü-ˌdälf\ lake [N] Kenya in Great Rift valley

Ruhr \'ru̇r\ industrial district West Germany [E] of the Rhine in valley of Ruhr river

Ru•ma•nia \ru̇-'mā-nē-ə, -nyə\ *or* **Ro•ma•nia** \rō-\ *or* **Rou•ma•nia** \ru̇-\ country [SE] Europe on Black sea; capital, Bucharest

Ru•me•lia \rü-'mēl-yə, -'mē-lē-ə\ a division of the old Ottoman Empire including Albania, Macedonia, & Thrace

Run•ny•mede \'rən-ē-ˌmēd\ meadow [S] England in Surrey on [S] bank of the Thames where Magna Charta was signed 1215

Rupert's Land PRINCE RUPERT'S LAND

Ru•se \'rü-sā\ city [NE] Bulgaria

Rush•more, Mount \'rəsh-ˌmōr, -ˌmȯr\ mountain 1890 meters [W] South Dakota in Black hills [SW] of Rapid City

Rus•sia \'rəsh-ə\ **1** former empire largely coextensive with present U.S.S.R.; capital, Petrograd (Saint Petersburg) **2** UNION OF SOVIET SOCIALIST REPUBLICS

Russian Soviet Federated Socialist Republic *or* **Soviet Russia** constituent republic of U.S.S.R. in [E] Europe (**Soviet Russia, Europe**) & [N] Asia (**Soviet Russia, Asia**) bordering on Arctic & Pacific oceans & Baltic & Black seas; capital, Moscow

Ru•the•nia \rü-'thē-nyə, -nē-ə\ *or* **Car•pa•thi•an Ruthenia** \kär-'pā-thē-ən\ region U.S.S.R. in [W] Ukraine [W] of the [N] Carpathians — **Ru•the•nian** \rü-'thē-nyən, -nē-ən\ *adj or n*

Rut•land \'rət-lənd\ *or* **Rut•land•shire** \-,shiər, -shər\ former county [E] central England

Ru•wen•zo•ri \,rü-ən-'zōr-ē, -'zȯr-\ mountain group [E] central Africa between Uganda & Zaire; highest Mount Margherita (highest peak of Mount Stanley) 5019 meters

Rwan•da *or formerly* **Ru•an•da** \rü-'än-də\ country [E] central Africa, until 1962 part of Ruanda-Urundi trust territory; a republic; capital, Kigali — **Rwan•dan** \rü-'än-dən\ *adj or n*

Rya•zan \,rē-ə-'zan-yə, -'zan\ city U.S.S.R. in central Soviet Russia, Europe, [SE] of Moscow

Ry•binsk \'rib-ənsk\ *or formerly* **Shcher•ba•kov** \,shcher-bə-'kȯf, ,sher-, -'kȯv\ city U.S.S.R. in [N] central Soviet Russia, Europe, [NNE] of Moscow

Ryu•kyu \rē-'ü-kyü, -'yü-, -kü\ islands [W] Pacific extending in an arc from Kyushu, Japan, to Taiwan, China; belong to Japan — **Ryu•kyu•an** \-kyü-ən, -kü-ən\ *adj or n*

Saar \'sär, 'zär\ **1** river 135 kilometers long Europe flowing from Vosges mountains in [E] France into the Moselle in Germany **2** *or* **Saar•land** \'sär-,land, 'zär-\ district [W] Europe in valley of Saar river; a state of West Germany; capital, Saarbrücken

Sa•ba \'säb-ə\ island West Indies in Netherlands Antilles; capital, The Bottom

Sa•bah \'säb-ə\ *or formerly* **North Borneo** state Federation of Malaysia in [NE] Borneo; capital, Kota Kinabalu

Sachsen — see SAXONY

Sac•ra•men•to \,sak-rə-'ment-ō\ **1** river 615 kilometers long [N] California flowing [S] into Suisun Bay **2** city, capital of California

Sa•ga•mi \sə-'gäm-ē\ sea inlet of Pacific in central Honshu, Japan

Sag•ue•nay \'sag-ə-,nā, ,sag-ə-'\ river 200 kilometers long Canada in [S] Quebec flowing from Lake Saint John [E] into the Saint Lawrence

Sa•hara \sə-'har-ə, -'her-, -'här-\ desert region [N] Africa [N] of Sudan region extending from Atlantic coast to Red sea or, as sometimes considered, to the Nile — **Sa•har•an** \-ən\ *adj*

Sa•ha•ran•pur \sə-'här-ən-,pu̇r\ city [N] India in [NW] Uttar Pradesh [NNE] of Delhi

Saigon — see HO CHI MINH CITY

Saint Au•gus•tine \'ȯ-gə-,stēn\ city [NE] Florida

Saint Ber•nard \,sānt-bər-'närd, -bə-\ either of two mountain passes in the Alps: the **Great Saint Bernard** (2472 meters between Italy & Switzerland [E] of Mont Blanc) & the **Little Saint Bernard** (2188 meters between France & Italy [S] of Mont Blanc)

Saint Cath•a•rines \'kath-rənz, -ə-rənz\ city Canada in [SE] Ontario

Saint Clair, Lake \'klaər, 'kleər\ lake [SE] Michigan & [SE] Ontario connected by **Saint Clair river** (64 kilometers long) with Lake Huron & draining by Detroit river into Lake Erie

Saint Croix \sānt-'krȯi, sənt-\ **1** river 120 kilometers long Canada & U.S. on border between New Brunswick & Maine **2** island West Indies; largest of Virgin Islands of the U.S.

Saint Eli•as, Mount \,sānt-l-'ī-əs\ mountain 5489 meters on Alaska-Canada boundary in **Saint Elias range**

Saint Fiume — see RIJEKA

Saint George's \'jȯr-jəz\ channel British Isles between [SW] Wales & Ireland

Saint Gott•hard \sānt-'gät-ərd, -'gäth-, sənt-, ,saⁿ-gə-'tär\ **1** pass [S] central Switzerland in Saint Gotthard range of the Alps **2** tunnel 15 kilometers long near the pass

Saint He•le•na \,sānt-l-'ē-nə, ,sānt-hə-'lē-\ island [S] Atlantic; a British colony; capital, Jamestown

Saint Hel•ens \sānt-'hel-ənz, sənt-\ borough [NW] England in Merseyside [ENE] of Liverpool

Saint John \sānt-'jän, sənt-\ city Canada in New Brunswick, largest in province

Saint John's \sānt-'jänz, sənt-\ city Canada, capital of Newfoundland

Saint Kitts \'kits\ *or* **Saint Chris•to•pher** \'kris-tə-fər\ island British West Indies in the Leewards; with Nevis constitutes **Saint Kitts–Nevis** colony; capital, Basseterre (on Saint Kitts)

Saint Law•rence \sānt-'lȯr-əns, sənt-, -'lär-\ **1** river 1225 kilometers long [E] Canada in Ontario & Quebec bordering on U.S. in New York & flowing from Lake Ontario [NE] into the **Gulf of Saint Lawrence** (inlet of the Atlantic) **2** seaway Canada & U.S. in & along the Saint Lawrence between Lake Ontario & Montreal

Saint Lou•is \sānt-'lü-əs, sənt-\ city [E] Missouri on the Mississippi

Saint Lu•cia \sānt-'lü-shə, sənt-\ island British West Indies in the Windwards [S] of Martinique; capital, Castries

Saint Paul \'pȯl\ city, capital of Minnesota

Saint Pe•ters•burg \'pēt-ərz-,bərg\ **1** city [W] Florida **2** — see LENINGRAD

Saint Pierre \sānt-'piər, sənt-, -pē-'eər, *French* saⁿ-pyer\ **1** island in the Atlantic off [S] Newfoundland; with nearby island of Miquelon constitutes French territory of **Saint Pierre and Miquelon** **2** town, capital of Saint Pierre and Miquelon

Saint Thom•as \'täm-əs\ **1** island West Indies, one of Virgin Islands of the U.S.; chief town, Charlotte Amalie **2** — see SÃO TOMÉ

Saint Vin•cent \sānt-'vin-sənt, sənt-\ island British West Indies in the central Windwards; with [N] Grenadines constitutes a colony; capital, Kingstown (on Saint Vincent)

Sai•pan \sī-'pan, -'pän, 'sī-,\ island [W] Pacific in [S] central Marianas

Sa•kai \sä-'kī, 'sä-\ city Japan in [S] Honshu on Osaka Bay

Sa•kha•lin \'sak-ə-,lēn, -lən; ,sak-ə-'lēn\ *or formerly* **Sa•ghal•ien** \'sag-ə-,lēn, ,sag-ə-'\ *or Japanese* **Ka•ra•fu•to** \kə-'räf-ə-,tō\ island U.S.S.R. in [W] Pacific [N] of Hokkaido, Japan; until 1945 divided between Japan & U.S.S.R.

Sal•a•man•ca \,sal-ə-'mang-kə, ,säl-ə-'mäng-\ city [W] Spain

Sal•a•mis \'sal-ə-məs\ **1** ancient city Cyprus on [E] coast **2** island Greece in Saronic gulf off Attica

Sa•lem \'sā-ləm\ **1** city, capital of Oregon **2** city [S] India in [N] Tamil Nadu [SW] of Madras

Sa•ler•no \sə-'lər-nō, -'leər-\ city [S] Italy on Gulf of Salerno [ESE] of Naples

Sal•ford \'sȯl-fərd\ urban area [NW] England in Greater Manchester

Salis•bury \'sȯlz-,ber-ē, -bə-rē, -brē\ city, capital of Rhodesia

Sa•lon•i•ka \sə-'län-i-kə, ,sal-ə-'nē-kə\ *or* **Sal•o•ni•ki** \,sal-ə-'nē-kē\ *or* **Thes•sa•lo•ni•ca** \,thes-ə-lə-'nī-kə, -'län-i-kə\ city [N] Greece in Macedonia

Sal•op \'sal-əp\ *or* **Shrop•shire** \'shräp-,shiər, -shər\ county [W] England bordering on Wales

Sal•ta \'säl-tə\ city [NW] Argentina

Salt Lake City city, capital of Utah

Sal•va•dor \'sal-və-,dȯr, ,sal-və-'\ *or formerly* **São Salvador** \sau̇ⁿ-\ *or* **Ba•hia** \bä-'ē-ə\ city [NE] Brazil on the Atlantic — **Sal•va•dor•an** \,sal-və-'dōr-ən, -'dȯr-\ *or* **Sal•va•do•re•an** *or* **Sal•va•do•ri•an** \-ē-ən\ *adj or n*

Sal•ween \'sal-,wēn\ river 2815 kilometers long [SE] Asia flowing [S] into Gulf of Martaban in Burma

Salz•burg \'sȯlz-,bərg, 'sälz-, 'salz-, 'sȯlts-, -,bu̇rg, *German* 'zälts-,bu̇rk\ city [W] Austria

Sa•mar \'säm-,är\ island central Philippines in Visayan islands

Samarang — see SEMARANG

Sa•mar•ia \sə-'mer-ē-ə, -'mar-\ **1** district of ancient Palestine [W] of the Jordan between Galilee & Judea **2** ancient city, its capital & capital of the Northern Kingdom (Israel)

Sam•ar•kand \'sam-ər-,kand\ city U.S.S.R. in [E] Uzbekistan

Sam•ni•um \'sam-nē-əm\ ancient country [S] central Italy [SE] of Latium — **Sam•nite** \'sam-,nīt\ *adj or n*

Sa•moa \sə-'mō-ə\ islands [SW] central Pacific [N] of Tonga islands; divided at longitude 171° [W] into American, or Eastern, Samoa & Western Samoa — **Sa•mo•an** \-ən\ *adj or n*

Sa•mos \'sā-,mäs\ island Greece in the Aegean off coast of Turkey [N] of the Dodecanese — **Sa•mi•an** \-mē-ən\ *adj or n*

Sam•o•thrace \'sam-ə-,thrās\ island Greece in the [NE] Aegean

San•'a \'san-,ä, san-'ä\ city [SW] Arabia, capital of Yemen Arab Republic

San An•to•nio \,san-ən-'tō-nē-,ō\ city [S] Texas

San Ber•nar•di•no \,san-,bər-nə-'dē-nō, -nər-'dē-\ city [S] California

San Cris•tó•bal \,san-kris-'tō-bəl\ city [W] Venezuela

Sanc•ti Spi•ri•tus \,säng-tē-'spir-ə-,tüs, ,sängk-\ city [W] central Cuba

San Di•ego \,san-dē-'ā-gō\ city [SW] California

Sandwich islands — see HAWAII

San Fran•cis•co \,san-frən-'sis-kō\ city [W] California

San Isi•dro \,san-ə-'sē-drō\ city [E] Argentina [NW] of Buenos Aires

San Joa•quin \,san-wä-'kēn, -wō-\ river 563 kilometers long central California flowing [NW] into the Sacramento

San Jo•se \ˌsan-ə-ˈzā\ city [W] California [SE] of San Francisco
San Jo•sé \ˌsan-ə-ˈzā, -ō-ˈzā, -hō-ˈzā\ city, capital of Costa Rica
San Juan \san-ˈhwän, -ˈwän\ city, capital of Puerto Rico
San Lu•is Po•to•sí \ˌsän-lü-ˌē-ˌspōt-ə-ˈsē\ **1** state central Mexico **2** city, its capital
San Ma•ri•no \ˌsan-mə-ˈrē-nō\ **1** country [S] Europe on Italian peninsula [ENE] of Florence near Adriatic sea; a republic **2** town, its capital
San Martín — see GENERAL SAN MARTÍN
San Mi•guel de Tu•cu•mán \ˌsan-mig-ˌel-də-ˌtü-kə-ˈmän\ *or* **Tu•cu•mán** \ˌtü-kə-ˈmän\ city [NW] Argentina
San Sal•va•dor \san-ˈsal-və-ˌdȯr\ **1** *or formerly* **Wat•lings** \ˈwät-lingz\ island central Bahama islands **2** city, capital of El Salvador
San Se•ve•ro \ˌsan-sə-ˈver-ō\ commune [SE] Italy in Apulia [NNW] of Foggia
San•ta Ana \ˌsant-ə-ˈan-ə\ **1** city [SW] California [ESE] of Long Beach **2** city [NW] El Salvador
San•ta Bar•ba•ra \-ˈbär-brə, -bə-rə\ *or* **Channel** islands California in the Pacific off [SW] coast
San•ta Clara \-ˈklar-ə, -ˈkler-ə\ city [W] central Cuba
San•ta Cruz \-ˈkrüz\ city [E] Bolivia
San•ta Cruz de Te•ne•rife \-də-ˌten-ə-ˈrēf-ā, -ˈrēf, -ˈrif\ city Spain in [W] Canary islands on Tenerife Island
San•ta Fe \ˌsant-ə-ˈfā\ **1** city, capital of New Mexico **2** city central Argentina
Santa Fe Trail pioneer route to the Southwest 1290 kilometers long used especially 1821–80 from vicinity of Kansas City, Missouri, to Santa Fe, New Mexico
Santa Isabel — see MALABO
San•ta Mar•ta \ˌsant-ə-ˈmärt-ə\ city [N] Colombia
San•tan•der \ˌsän-ˌtän-ˈdeər, ˌsan-ˌtan-\ city [N] Spain [WNW] of Bilbao
San•ta•rém \ˌsant-ə-ˈrem\ city [N] Brazil on the Amazon
San•ti•a•go \ˌsant-ē-ˈäg-ō, ˌsänt-\ **1** city, capital of Chile **2** *or* **Santiago de los Ca•ba•lle•ros** \-də-ˌlōs-ˌkäb-ə-ˈyeər-ōs\ city [N] central Dominican Republic
Santiago de Cu•ba \-də-ˈkyü-bə\ city [SE] Cuba
San•to An•dré \ˌsan-tü-an-ˈdrā\ city [SE] Brazil [SE] of São Paulo
San•to Do•min•go \ˌsant-əd-ə-ˈming-gō\ **1** — see HISPANIOLA **2** — see DOMINICAN REPUBLIC **3** *or formerly* **Ci•u•dad Tru•ji•llo** \ˌsē-ü-ˌthä-trü-ˈhē-ō, ˌsē-ü-ˌdad-\ city, capital of Dominican Republic
San•tos \ˈsant-əs\ city [SE] Brazil
San•to To•mé de Gua•ya•na \ˌsänt-ō-tə-ˈmād-ə-gwə-ˈyän-ə\ *or* **San To•mé de Guayana** \ˌsän-tō-ˈmād-\ city [E] Venezuela
São Gon•ça•lo \ˌsaùn-gōn-ˈsal-ü, ˌsaùnng-\ city [SE] Brazil [NE] of Niteroi
São João de Me•ri•ti \saùn-ˈzhwaùn-dē-mə-ˈrē-tē\ city [SE] Brazil [NW] of Rio de Janeiro
São Lu•ís \ˌsaùn-lü-ˈēs\ city [NE] Brazil on Maranhão Island
Saône \ˈsōn\ river [E] France flowing into the Rhone
São Pau•lo \saùn-ˈpaù-lü, saunm-, -lō\ city [SE] Brazil
São Salvador — see SALVADOR
São To•mé *or* **São Tho•mé** \ˌsaùnt-ə-ˈmā, ˌsaùnnt-\ *or* **Saint Thom•as** \sānt-ˈtäm-əs\ island [W] Africa in Gulf of Guinea; with Príncipe Island, forms republic of **São Tomé and Príncipe** capital, São Tomé; until 1975 a Portuguese colony
Sap•po•ro \ˈsäp-ə-ˌrō; sə-ˈpōr-ō, -ˈpȯr-\ city Japan on [W] Hokkaido
Saragossa — see ZARAGOZA
Sa•ra•je•vo \ˈsär-ə-ye-ˌvō\ *or* **Se•ra•je•vo** \ˈser-\ city central Yugoslavia, capital of Bosnia and Herzegovina
Sa•ransk \sə-ˈränsk, -ˈransk\ city U.S.S.R. in central Soviet Russia, Europe
Sa•ra•tov \sə-ˈrät-əf\ city U.S.S.R. in [SE] Soviet Russia, Europe, on the Volga
Sa•ra•wak \sə-ˈrä-wä, -wäk, -ˌwak\ state Federation of Malaysia in [N] Borneo on South China sea; capital, Kuching
Sar•din•ia \sär-ˈdin-ē-ə, -ˈdin-yə\ island Italy in the Mediterranean [S] of Corsica; a region; capital, Cagliari — **Sar•din•ian** \-ˈdin-ē-ən, -ˈdin-yən\ *adj or n*
Sar•dis \ˈsärd-əs\ ancient city [W] Asia Minor, capital of Lydia
Sar•gas•so sea \sär-ˌgas-ō-\ area of comparatively still water in the [N] Atlantic lying chiefly between 25° & 35° [N] latitude & 40° & 70° [W] longitude
Sa•ron•ic Gulf \sə-ˌrän-ik-\ inlet of the Aegean [SE] Greece between Attica & the Peloponnesus
Sa•se•bo \ˈsäs-ə-ˌbō\ city Japan in [NW] Kyushu
Sas•katch•e•wan \sə-ˈskach-ə-wən, sa-, -ˌwän\ province [W] Canada; capital, Regina
Sas•ka•toon \ˌsas-kə-ˈtün\ city Canada in central Saskatchewan
Sas•sa•ri \ˈsäs-ə-rē\ city Italy in [NW] Sardinia
Sau•di Arabia \ˌsaùd-ē-ə-ˈrā-bē-ə, ˌsȯd-ē-, sä-ˌüd-ē-\ country [SW] Asia occupying largest part of Arabian peninsula; a kingdom; capital, Riyadh — **Saudi** *adj or n* — **Saudi Arabian** *adj or n*
Sault Sainte Ma•rie canals \ˌsü-ˌsānt-mə-ˈrē\ *or* **Soo canals** \ˌsü-\ three ship canals, two in U.S. (Michigan) & one in Canada (Ontario), at rapids in Saint Marys river connecting Lakes Superior & Huron
Sa•vaii \sə-ˈvī-ˌē\ island, largest in Western Samoa
Sa•van•nah \sə-ˈvan-ə\ city [E] Georgia
Sa•voy \sə-ˈvȯi\ *or French* **Sa•voie** \sȧ-vwȧ\ region [SE] France [SW] of Switzerland bordering on Italy — **Sa•voy•ard** \sə-ˈvȯi-ˌärd, ˌsav-ˌȯi-ˈärd; ˌsav-ˌwä-ˈyär, -ˈyärd\ *adj or n*
Sax•o•ny \ˈsak-sə-nē, ˈsak-snē\ *or German* **Sach•sen** \ˈzäk-sən\ region & former state East Germany [N] of the Erzgebirge — see LOWER SAXONY
Sca•fell Pike \ˈskȯ-ˈfel\ mountain 978 meters [NW] England in Cumbria; highest in Cumbrian mountains & in England
Scan•di•na•via \ˌskan-də-ˈnā-vē-ə, -vyə\ **1** peninsula [N] Europe occupied by Norway & Sweden **2** Denmark, Norway, Sweden, & sometimes also Iceland & Finland
Scheldt \ˈskelt\ *or* **Schel•de** \ˈskel-də\ *or French* **Es•caut** \es-kō\ *or ancient* **Scal•dis** \ˈskal-dəs\ river 435 kilometers long [W] Europe flowing from [N] France through Belgium into North sea in Netherlands
Schleswig–Hol•stein \ˈshles-wig-ˈhōl-ˌstīn, ˈsles-, -vik-ˈhōl-\ state West Germany consisting of Holstein & part of Schleswig; capital, Kiel
Schwarzwald — see BLACK FOREST
Schweiz — see SWITZERLAND
Scil•ly \ˈsil-ē\ islands [SW] England off Lands End in county of Cornwall and Isles of Scilly
Sco•tia \ˈskō-shə\ SCOTLAND — the Medieval Latin name
Scot•land \ˈskät-lənd\ *or Latin* **Cal•e•do•nia** \ˌkal-ə-ˈdō-nyə, -nē-ə\ country [N] Great Britain; a division of United Kingdom of Great Britain and Northern Ireland; capital, Edinburgh
Scran•ton \ˈskrant-n\ city [NE] Pennsylvania
Scupi — see SKOPLJE
Scyth•ia \ˈsith-ē-ə, ˈsith-\ country of the ancient Scythians comprising parts of Europe & Asia now in U.S.S.R. in regions [N] & [NE] of Black sea & [E] of Aral sea — **Scyth•i•an** \-ē-ən\ *adj or n*
Se•at•tle \sē-ˈat-l\ city [W] Washington
Seine \ˈsān, ˈsen\ river 773 kilometers long [N] France flowing [NW] into English channel
Seis de Septiembre — see MORÓN
Sek•on•di–Ta•ko•ra•di \ˌsek-ən-ˈdē-ˌtäk-ə-ˈräd-ē\ city [SW] Ghana
Sel•kirk \ˈsel-ˌkərk\ **1** range of the Rocky mountains [SE] British Columbia; highest peak, Mount Sir Donald 3390 meters **2** *or* **Sel•kirk•shire** \-ˌshiər, -shər\ former county [SE] Scotland
Se•ma•rang *or* **Sa•ma•rang** \sə-ˈmär-ˌäng\ city Indonesia in central Java
Sem•i•pa•la•tinsk \ˌsem-i-pə-ˈlä-ˌtinsk\ city U.S.S.R. in [NE] Kazakhstan
Sen•dai \sen-ˈdī, ˈsen-\ city Japan in [NE] Honshu
Sen•e•gal \ˌsen-i-ˈgȯl\ **1** river 1690 kilometers long [W] Africa flowing [W] into the Atlantic **2** country [W] Africa; a republic; capital, Dakar — **Sen•e•ga•lese** \ˌsen-i-gə-ˈlēz, -ˈlēs\ *adj or n*
Seoul \ˈsōl\ *or* **Kyong•song** \kē-ˈȯng-ˈsȯng\ city, capital of South Korea
Se•quoia National Park \si-ˈkwȯi-ə\ reservation [SE] central California; includes Mount Whitney
Serajevo — see SARAJEVO
Seram — see CERAM
Ser•bia \ˈsər-bē-ə\ federated republic [SE] Yugoslavia; capital, Belgrade
Ser•en•ge•ti Plain \ˌser-ən-ˈget-ē\ area [N] Tanzania including **Serengeti National Park**
Se•te Que•das \ˌsāt-ə-ˈkā-thəsh\ *or formerly* **Guaí•ra** *or* **Guay•ra** \gwī-ˈrä\ cataract 114 meters high in Alto Paraná on Brazil-Paraguay boundary

Se•vas•to•pol \sə-'vas-tə-ˌpōl, -ˌpȯl, -pəl; ˌsev-ə-'stō-pəl, -'stō-\ *or formerly* **Se•bas•to•pol** \-'bas-; ˌseb-ə-\ city U.S.S.R. in Soviet Russia, Europe, in [SW] Crimea
Sev•ern \'sev-ərn\ river 338 kilometers long Wales & England flowing from [E] central Wales into Bristol channel
Se•ville \sə-'vil\ *or Spanish* **Se•vi•lla** \sā-'vē-ä, -yä\ *or ancient* **His•pa•lis** \'his-pə-ləs\ city [SW] Spain
Sey•chelles \sā-'shel, -'shelz\ islands [W] Indian ocean [NE] of Madagascar; formerly a British colony; became independent 1976; capital, Victoria (on Mahé Island)
's Gravenhage — see HAGUE
Shang–ch'iu \'shäng-chē-'ü\ *or* **Shang•kiu** \'shäng-kē-'ü\ city [E] central China in Honan
Shang•hai \shang-'hī\ city [E] China in [SE] Kiangsu
Shan•non \'shan-ən\ river 386 kilometers long [W] Ireland flowing [S] & [W] into the Atlantic
Shan•si \'shän-'sē\ province [N] China bordering on Yellow river; capital, Taiyüan
Shan•tung \'shan-'təng\ **1** peninsula [E] China extending into Yellow sea **2** province [E] China including Shantung peninsula; capital, Tsinan
Shao•hing *or* **Shao•hsing** \'shau̇-'shing\ city [E] China in [N] Chekiang [SE] of Hangchow
Shao•yang \'shau̇-'yäng\ city [SE] China in central Hunan [W] of Hengyang
Shas•ta, Mount \'shas-tə\ mountain 4317 meters [N] California in Cascade range
Shatt–al–Ar•ab \ˌshat-ˌal-'ar-əb\ river 193 kilometers long [SE] Iraq formed by confluence of Euphrates & Tigris rivers & flowing [SE] into Persian gulf
Shcherbakov — see RYBINSK
She•ba \'shē-bə\ ancient country [S] Arabia
She•chem \'shē-kəm, -ˌkem\ ancient city central Palestine in Samaria; site at present city of Nablus in Jordan
Shef•field \'shef-ˌēld\ city [N] England in South Yorkshire
Shen•an•do•ah National Park \ˌshen-ən-'dō-ə, ˌshan-ə-'dō-ə\ reservation [N] Virginia in Blue Ridge mountains
Shen•si \'shen-'sē\ province [N] central China; capital, Sian
Shenyang — see MUKDEN
Sher•wood Forest \ˌshər-ˌwu̇d-\ ancient royal forest central England chiefly in Nottinghamshire
Shet•land \'shet-lənd\ **1** islands [N] Scotland [NE] of the Orkneys **2** *or* **Zet•land** \'zet-\ county comprising the Shetland islands
Shih•kia•chwang \'shiər-jē-'äj-'wäng, 'shē-jē-\ city [NE] China, capital of Hopei
Shi•ko•ku \shi-'kō-kü\ island [S] Japan [E] of Kyushu
Shi•mi•zu \shi-'mē-zü, 'shē-mi-ˌzü\ city Japan in central Honshu [NE] of Shizuoka
Shi•mo•no•se•ki \ˌshim-ə-nō-'sek-ē\ city Japan in [SW] Honshu opposite Kitakyushu
Shi•raz \shi-'räz\ city [SW] Iran
Shi•zu•o•ka \ˌshiz-ə-'wō-kə, ˌshē-zə-'ō-kə\ city Japan in central Honshu [SW] of Tokyo
Sho•la•pur \'shō-lə-ˌpu̇r\ city [W] India in [SE] Maharashtra [SE] of Bombay
Shreve•port \'shrēv-ˌpōrt, -ˌpȯrt\ city [NW] Louisiana
Shropshire — see SALOP
Shushan — see SUSA
Siam — see THAILAND
Siam, Gulf of *or* **Gulf of Thailand** arm of South China sea between Indochina & Malay peninsula
Si•an \'shē-'än\ *or* **Chang•an** \'chäng-'än\ city [E] central China, capital of Shensi
Siangtan — see HSIANG-T'AN
Si•be•ria \sī-'bir-ē-ə\ region [N] Asia in U.S.S.R. between the Urals & the Pacific roughly coextensive with Soviet Russia, Asia — **Si•be•ri•an** \-ē-ən\ *adj or n*
Sic•i•ly \'sis-ə-lē, 'sis-lē\ *or Italian* **Si•ci•lia** \sē-'chēl-yä\ island [S] Italy [SW] of toe of Italian peninsula; a region; capital, Palermo — **Si•cil•ian** \sə-'sil-yən\ *adj or n*
Si•er•ra Le•one \sē-ˌer-ə-lē-'ōn, ˌsir-ə-\ country [W] Africa on the Atlantic; a British dominion; capital, Freetown — **Si•er•ra Le•on•ean** \-'ō-nē-ən\ *adj or n*
Si•er•ra Ma•dre \sē-ˌer-ə-'mäd-rē\ mountain system Mexico including **Sierra Madre Oc•ci•den•tal** \-ˌäk-sə-ˌden-'täl\ range [W] of the central plateau, **Sierra Madre Ori•en•tal** \-ˌōr-ē-ˌen-'täl, -ˌȯr-\ range [E] of the plateau, & **Sierra del Sur** \sē-ˌer-ə-ˌdel-'su̇r\ range to the [S]
Sierra Ne•vada \-nə-'vad-ə, -'väd-\ **1** mountain range [E] California & [W] Nevada — see WHITNEY **2** mountain range [S] Spain; highest peak Mulhacén 3477 meters, highest in Spain
Sik•kim \'sik-əm, -ˌim\ region [SE] Asia on [S] slope of the Himalayas between Nepal & Bhutan; a state of Republic of India since 1975; capital, Gangtok
Si•le•sia \sī-'lē-zhə, sə-, -zhē-ə, -shə, -shē-ə\ region [E] central Europe in valley of the upper Oder bordering on Sudeten mountains; formerly chiefly in Germany now chiefly in [N] Czechoslovakia & [SW] Poland — **Si•le•sian** \-zhən, -shən\ *adj or n*
Simbirsk — see ULYANOVSK
Sim•coe, Lake \'sim-kō\ lake Canada in [SE] Ontario
Sim•fe•ro•pol \ˌsim-fə-'rō-pəl, ˌsimp-, -'rō-\ city U.S.S.R. in [S] Soviet Russia, Europe, on Crimea peninsula
Sim•la \'sim-lə\ city [N] India, capital of Himachal Pradesh
Sim•plon \'sim-ˌplän\ **1** pass between Italy & Switzerland in Lepontine Alps **2** tunnel 19.8 kilometers long near the pass
Si•nai \'sī-ˌnī\ **1** — see HOREB **2** peninsula extension of continent of Asia [NE] Egypt between Red sea & the Mediterranean
Si•na•loa \ˌsē-nə-'lō-ə, ˌsin-ə-\ state [W] Mexico on Gulf of California; capital, Culiacán
Sind \'sind\ province [S] Pakistan in lower Indus river valley; chief city Karachi
Sin•ga•pore \'sing-ə-ˌpōr, -gə-, -ˌpȯr\ **1** island off [S] end of Malay peninsula; a republic in British Commonwealth **2** city, its capital — **Sin•ga•por•ean** \ˌsing-ə-'pōr-ē-ən, -gə-, -'pȯr-\ *adj or n*
Si•ning \'shē-'ning\ city [NW] China, capital of Tsinghai
Sin•kiang \'shin-jē-'äng\ *or* **Sinkiang–Ui•ghur Region** \'wē-gər\ region & former province [W] China; capital, Urumchi
Sinsiang — see HSIN-HSIANG
Sion — see ZION
Siracusa — see SYRACUSE
Sjæl•land \'shel-ˌän\ *or* **Zea•land** \'zē-lənd\ island, largest of islands of Denmark; site of Copenhagen
Skag•ge•rak \'skag-ə-ˌrak\ arm of North sea between [S] Norway & [N] Denmark
Skop•lje \'skȯp-ˌlā, -ˌyä\ *or* **Skop•je** \-ˌyä\ *or ancient* **Scu•pi** \'skyü-ˌpī\ city [S] Yugoslavia in Macedonia
Sky•ros \'skī-rəs, -ˌräs\ *or Greek* **Skí•ros** \'skē-ˌrȯs\ island Greece in Northern Sporades [E] of Euboea
Sla•vo•nia \slə-'vō-nē-ə, -nyə\ region [N] Yugoslavia in [E] Croatia between Sava, Drava, & Danube rivers — **Sla•vo•nian** \-ne-ən, -nyən\ *adj or n*
Sli•go \'slī-gō\ county [N] Republic of Ireland in Connacht
Slo•va•kia \slō-'väk-ē-ə, -'vak-\ region [E] Czechoslovakia [E] of Moravia; chief city, Bratislava
Slo•ve•nia \slō-'vē-nē-ə, -nyə\ federated republic [NW] Yugoslavia [N] & [W] of Croatia; capital, Ljubljana — **Slo•ve•nian** \-nē-ən, -nyən\ *adj or n*
Smo•lensk \smō-'lensk\ city U.S.S.R. in [W] Soviet Russia, Europe, [WSW] of Moscow
Smyrna — see IZMIR
Snow•don \'snōd-n\ massif 1085 meters [NW] Wales; highest point in Wales
Snow•do•nia \snō-'dō-nē-ə, -nyə\ mountainous district [NW] Wales centering around Snowdon
So•chi \'sō-chē\ city U.S.S.R. in [S] Soviet Russia, Europe, on Black sea
So•ci•e•ty \sə-'sī-ət-ē\ islands [S] Pacific in French Polynesia; capital Papeete (on Tahiti)
So•co•tra *or* **So•ko•tra** \sə-'kō-trə\ island Southern Yemen in Indian ocean [E] of Gulf of Aden; capital, Tamrida
So•fia \'sō-fē-ə, 'sȯ-, sō-'\ city, capital of Bulgaria
So•ho \'sō-ˌhō\ district of central London, England, in Westminster
So•li•hull \ˌsō-li-'həl\ county borough central England in West Midlands
Sol•o•mon \'säl-ə-mən\ **1** islands [W] Pacific [E] of New Guinea divided between Papua New Guinea & British Solomon Islands **2** sea arm of Coral sea [W] of the Solomons
So•ma•lia \sō-'mäl-ē-ə, sə-, -'mäl-yə\ *or* **So•ma•li Republic** \-'mäl-ē\ country [E] Africa on Gulf of Aden & Indian ocean; a republic; capital, Mogadishu — **So•ma•li•an** \-'mäl-ē-ən, -'mäl-yən\ *adj or n*
So•ma•li•land \sō-'mäl-ē-ˌland, sə-\ region [E] Africa comprising Somalia, Djibouti, & part of [E] Ethiopia
Som•er•set \'səm-ər-ˌset, -sət\ *or* **Som•er•set•shire** \-ˌshiər, -shər\ county [SW] England

Somerset Nile — see NILE
So•no•ra \sə-'nōr-ə, -'nȯr-\ state [NW] Mexico bordering on U.S.; capital, Hermosillo
So•nor•an \sə-'nōr-ən, -'nȯr-\ *or* **Sonora** desert [SW] U.S. & [NW] Mexico in [S] Arizona, [SE] California, & [N] Sonora
Soo canals — see SAULT SAINTE MARIE CANALS
Soochow — see SU-CHOU
Sorata — see ILLAMPU
So•ro•ca•ba \ˌsōr-ə-'kab-ə, ˌsȯr-\ city [SE] Brazil [W] of São Paulo
South \'sau̇th\ island [S] New Zealand
South Africa, Republic of country [S] Africa; an independent republic; until 1961 (as **Union of South Africa**) a British dominion; administrative capital, Pretoria; legislative capital, Cape Town; judicial capital, Bloemfontein
South America continent of western hemisphere [SE] of North America & chiefly [S] of the equator — **South American** *adj or n*
South•amp•ton \sau̇th-'am-tən, -'ham-, -'amp-, -'hamp-\ city [S] England in Hampshire
South Australia state [S] Australia; capital, Adelaide — **South Australian** *adj or n*
South Bend \'bend\ city [N] Indiana
South Cape *or* **South Point** — see KA LAE
South Car•o•li•na \ˌkar-ə-'lī-nə\ state [SE] U.S.; capital, Columbia — **South Car•o•lin•i•an** \-'lin-ē-ən, -'lin-yən\ *adj or n*
South China sea — see CHINA
South Da•ko•ta \də-'kōt-ə\ state [NW] central U.S.; capital, Pierre — **South Da•ko•tan** \-'kōt-n\ *adj or n*
South•end on Sea \ˌsau̇-ˌthend-\ borough [SE] England in Essex [E] of London
Southern Alps mountain range New Zealand in [W] South Island extending almost the length of the island
Southern Rhodesia — see RHODESIA
Southern Yemen — see YEMEN
South Gla•mor•gan \glə-'mȯr-gən\ county [SE] Wales; established 1974; includes Cardiff
South Korea — see KOREA
South seas the areas of the Atlantic, Indian, & Pacific oceans in the southern hemisphere; especially, the [S] Pacific
South Shields \'shēldz, 'shēlz\ city [N] England in Tyne and Wear
South Tirol — see ALTO ADIGE
South Vietnam — see VIETNAM
South•wark \'səth-ərk, 'sau̇th-wərk\ borough of [S] London, England
South-West Africa *or* **Suid•wes-Afri•ka** \ˌsīt-ˌves-'äf-rē-kə\ *or* **Na•mib•ia** \nə-'mib-ē-ə\ territory [SW] Africa mandated 1919 to Union (now Republic) of South Africa; capital, Windhoek
South Yemen — see YEMEN
South York•shire \'yȯrk-ˌshiər, -shər\ metropolitan county [N] England
Soviet Central Asia portion of central & [SW] Asia belonging to U.S.S.R. & comprising the Kazakh, Kirgiz, Tadzhik, Turkmen, & Uzbek republics
Soviet Russia 1 — see RUSSIAN SOVIET FEDERATED SOCIALIST REPUBLIC **2** — see UNION OF SOVIET SOCIALIST REPUBLICS
Soviet Union — see UNION OF SOVIET SOCIALIST REPUBLICS
Spain \'spān\ *or Spanish* **Es•pa•ña** \ā-'spän-yä\ *or ancient* **His•pa•nia** \his-'pān-ē-ə, -'pān-yə, -'pan-\ country [SW] Europe in Iberian peninsula; a kingdom; capital, Madrid
Spanish America 1 the Spanish-speaking countries of America **2** the parts of America settled & formerly governed by the Spanish
Spanish Guinea — see EQUATORIAL GUINEA
Spanish Main \'mān\ **1** the mainland of Spanish America especially along [N] coast of South America **2** the Caribbean sea & adjacent waters especially when region was infested with pirates
Spanish Morocco — see MOROCCO
Spanish Sahara former Spanish territory [NW] Africa [SW] of Morocco comprising Río de Oro & Saguia el Hamra — see WESTERN SAHARA
Spar•ta \'spärt-ə\ *or* **Lac•e•dae•mon** \ˌlas-ə-'dē-mən\ ancient city [S] Greece in Peloponnesus, capital of Laconia
Spey•er \'shpī-ər, 'spī-; 'shpīr, 'spīr\ *or* **Spires** \'spīrz\ city West Germany on Rhine [N] of Karlsruhe
Spice islands — see MOLUCCAS
Spits•ber•gen \'spits-ˌbər-gən\ islands in Arcitc ocean [N] of Norway; chief island, West Spitsbergen — see SVALBARD
Split \'split\ *or* **Spljet** \'splʸet, splē-'et\ *or Italian* **Spa•la•to** \'späl-ə-ˌtō\ city [W] Yugoslavia in Croatia
Spo•kane \spō-'kan\ city [E] Washington
Spor•a•des \'spȯr-ə-ˌdēz, 'spär-\ two island groups Greece in the Aegean: the **Northern Sporades** (chief island, Skyros, [E] of Euboea) & **Southern Sporades** (including Samos, Icaria, & the Dodecanese, off [SW] Turkey)
Spring•field \'spring-ˌfēld\ **1** city, capital of Illinois **2** city [SW] Massachusetts **3** city [SW] Missouri
Springs \'springz\ city [NE] Republic of South Africa in [S] Transvaal
Sri Lan•ka \srē-'läng-kə, 'srē-\ *or formerly* **Cey•lon** \si-'län, sā-\ country coextensive with island of Ceylon; an independent republic in British Commonwealth; capital, Colombo
Sri•na•gar \sri-'nəg-ər\ city, summer capital of Jammu and Kashmir, in [W] Kashmir on Jhelum river
Staf•ford•shire \'staf-ərd-ˌshiər, -shər\ *or* **Stafford** county [W] central England
Staked Plain — see LLANO ESTACADO
Stalingrad — see VOLGOGRAD
Stam•ford \'stam-fərd, 'stamp-\ city [SW] Connecticut
Stan•ley \'stan-lē\ town, capital of Falkland Islands
Stanley, Mount — see RUWENZORI
Stanleyville — see KISANGANI
Stat•en Island \'stat-n\ **1** island [SE] New York [SW] of mouth of the Hudson **2** *or formerly* **Rich•mond** \'rich-mənd\ borough of New York City including Staten Island
States of the Church *or* **Papal States** temporal domain of the popes in central Italy 755–1870
Stavropol — see TOLYATTI
Stir•ling \'stər-ling\ *or* **Stir•ling•shire** \-ˌshiər, -shər\ former county central Scotland
Stock•holm \'stäk-ˌhōlm, -ˌhōm\ city, capital of Sweden
Stock•port \'stäk-ˌpōrt, -ˌpȯrt\ borough [NW] England in Greater Manchester
Stock•ton \'stäk-tən\ city central California
Stoke on Trent \ˌstō-ˌkȯn-'trent, -ˌkän-\ city central England in Staffordshire
Stone•henge \'stōn-ˌhenj, stōn-'henj\ assemblage of megaliths [S] England in Wiltshire on Salisbury Plain; erected by a prehistoric people
Stone Mountain mountain 514 meters [NW] Georgia [E] of Atlanta
Straits Settlements former British crown colony [SE] Asia on Strait of Malacca comprising Singapore Island & Penang & Malacca settlements on Malay peninsula
Stras•bourg \'sträs-ˌbu̇rg, 'sträz-, -ˌbərg\ city [NE] France
Strat•ford-upon-Avon \'strat-fərd\ borough central England in Warwickshire
Strath•clyde \strath-'klīd\ region [SW] Scotland; established 1975; includes Glasgow
Strom•bo•li \'sträm-bə-lē\ volcano 927 meters Italy in Lipari islands on Stromboli Island
Stutt•gart \'shtu̇t-ˌgärt, 'stu̇t-, 'stət-\ city West Germany, capital of Baden-Württemberg
Styr•ia \'stir-ē-ə\ region central & [SE] Austria; capital, Graz
Styx \'stiks\ chief river of Hades in Greek mythology
Su-chou *or* **Soo•chow** \'sü-'jō, -'chau̇\ *or formerly* **Wu•hsien** \'wü-shē-'en\ city [E] China in Kiangsu [W] of Shanghai
Sü•chow \'sü-'jō, 'shü-; 'sü-'chau̇\ **1** *or* **Hsü-chou** *\same* *or formerly* **Tung•shan** \'tu̇ng-'shän\ city [E] China in [NW] Kiangsu **2** — see IPIN
Su•cre \'sü-krā\ city, constitutional capital of Bolivia
Su•dan \sü-'dan, -'dän\ **1** region [N] Africa [S] of the Sahara between the Atlantic & the upper Nile **2** country [NE] Africa [S] of Egypt; a republic; capital, Khartoum — see ANGLO-EGYPTIAN SUDAN — **Su•da•nese** \ˌsüd-n-'ēz, -'ēs\ *adj or n*
Su•de•ten \sü-'dāt-n\ **1** mountains central Europe between Czechoslovakia & Poland **2** *or* **Su•de•ten•land** \sü-'dāt-n-ˌland\ region [N] Czechoslovakia in Sudeten mountains
Su•ez \sü-'ez, 'sü-ˌez\ **1** city [NE] Egypt at [S] end of Suez canal on **Gulf of Suez** (arm of Red sea) **2** canal 148 kilometers long [NE] Egypt across Isthmus of Suez
Suez, Isthmus of neck of land [NE] Egypt between Mediterranean & Red seas connecting Africa & Asia
Suf•folk \'səf-ək\ county [E] England on North sea
Suidwes-Afrika — see SOUTH-WEST AFRICA
Su•i•ta \sü-'ēt-ə\ city Japan in [S] Honshu [N] of Osaka

Sulawesi — see CELEBES
Su·lu \'sü-lü\ **1** archipelago [SW] Philippines [SW] of Mindanao — see BASILAN **2** sea [W] Philippines between Celebes & South China seas
Su·ma·tra \sü-'mä-trə\ island [W] Indonesia [S] of Malay peninsula — **Su·ma·tran** \-trən\ *adj or n*
Su·mer \'sü-mər\ the [S] division of ancient Babylonia — **Su·me·ri·an** \sü-'mer-ē-ən, -'mir-\ *adj or n*
Sun·da \'sün-də\ **1** islands Malay archipelago comprising the **Greater Sunda** islands (Sumatra, Borneo, Java, Celebes, & adjacent islands) & the **Lesser Sunda** islands (extending from Bali to Timor); with exception of [N] Borneo belongs to Indonesia **2** strait between Java & Sumatra
Sun·der·land \'sən-dər-lənd\ borough [N] England in Tyne and Wear
Suomen Tasavalta — see FINLAND
Suomi *or* **Suomen Tasavalta** — see FINLAND
Su·pe·ri·or, Lake \sü-'pir-ē-ər\ lake [E] central North America in U.S. & Canada; largest of the Great Lakes
Su·ra·ba·ja \,sür-ə-'bī-ə\ city Indonesia in [NE] Java
Su·ra·kar·ta \,sür-ə-'kärt-ə\ city Indonesia in central Java
Su·rat \'sür-ət, sə-'rat\ city [W] India in [SE] Gujarat
Su·ri·nam \'sür-ə-,nam, ,sür-ə-'näm\ *or* **Su·ri·na·me** \,sür-ə-'näm-ə\ *or formerly* **Dutch Guiana** country [N] South America between Guyana & French Guiana; a republic; until 1975 a territory of the Netherlands; capital, Paramaribo
Sur·rey \'sər-ē, 'sə-rē\ county [SE] England [SW] of London
Su·sa \'sü-zə\ *or biblical* **Shu·shan** \'shü-shən, -,shan\ ancient city, capital of Elam; ruins in [SW] Iran
Sus·sex \'səs-iks\ former county [SE] England on English channel — see EAST SUSSEX, WEST SUSSEX
Suth·er·land \'səth-ər-lənd\ *or* **Suth·er·land·shire** \-,shiər, -shər\ former county [N] Scotland
Sut·ton \'sət-n\ borough of [S] Greater London, England
Su·va \'sü-və\ city, capital of Fiji on Viti Levu Island
Sval·bard \'sfäl-,bär\ islands in Arctic ocean including Spitsbergen & Bear Island; under Norwegian administration
Sverd·lovsk \sfərd-'lófsk\ city U.S.S.R. in [W] Soviet Russia, Asia, in central Ural mountains
Swan·sea \'swän-zē\ city [SE] Wales
Swa·tow \'swä-'taù\ city [SE] China in [E] Kwangtung
Swa·zi·land \'swäz-ē-,land\ country [SE] Africa between Transvaal & Mozambique; an independent kingdom; capital, Mbabane — **Swa·zi** \'swäz-ē\ *adj or n*
Swe·den \'swēd-n\ country [N] Europe on Scandinavian peninsula bordering on Baltic sea; a kingdom; capital, Stockholm
Swit·zer·land \'swit-sər-lənd\ *or Latin* **Hel·ve·tia** \hel-'vē-shə, -shē-ə\ *or French* **Suisse** \swʸēs\ *or German* **Schweiz** \'shfīts\ *or Italian* **Sviz·ze·ra** \'zvēt-sä-rä\ country [W] Europe in the Alps; a republic; capital, Bern
Syd·ney \'sid-nē\ city [SE] Australia, capital of New South Wales
Syr·a·cuse \'sir-ə-,kyüs, -kyüz\ **1** city central New York **2** ancient city Italy in [SE] Sicily; site at modern city of **Si·ra·cu·sa** \,sē-rə-'kü-zə\
Syr·ia \'sir-ē-ə\ **1** ancient region [SW] Asia bordering on the Mediterranean **2** former French mandate (1920–44) including present Syria & Lebanon **3** country [S] of Turkey; a republic; capital, Damascus — **Syr·i·an** \'sir-ē-ən\ *adj or n*
Syrian Desert desert region [N] Saudi Arabia, [SE] Syria, [W] Iraq, & [NE] Jordan
Szcze·cin \'shchet-,sēn\ city [NW] Poland on the Oder
Sze·chwan *or* **Sze·chuan** \'sech-'wän\ province [SW] China; capital, Chengtu
Ta·bas·co \tə-'bas-kō\ state [SE] Mexico [SW] of Yucatán peninsula; capital, Villahermosa
Ta·ble Bay \,tā-bəl-\ harbor of Cape Town, Republic of South Africa
Ta·briz \tə-'brēz\ city [NW] Iran
Ta·co·ma \tə-'kō-mə\ city [W] Washington
Ta·dzhik·i·stan \tä-,jik-i-'stan, tə-, -,jēk-, -'stän\ *or* **Ta·dzhik Republic** \tä-'jik, -'jēk\ constituent republic of U.S.S.R. in Soviet Central Asia bordering on China (Sinkiang) & Afghanistan; capital, Dushanbe
Tae·gu \ta-'gü, tī-\ city South Korea [NNW] of Pusan
Tae·jon \ta-'jón, tī-\ city South Korea [NW] of Taegu
Ta·gan·rog \'tag-ən-,räg\ city U.S.S.R. in [S] Soviet Russia, Europe, [W] of Rostov
Ta·gus \'tā-gəs\ *or Spanish* **Ta·jo** \'tä-hō\ *or Portuguese* **Te·jo** \'tā-zhü\ river 911 kilometers long Spain & Portugal flowing [W] into the Atlantic
Ta·hi·ti \tə-'hēt-ē\ island [S] Pacific in French Polynesia in Society islands; chief town, Papeete — **Ta·hi·tian** \-'hē-shən\ *adj or n*
Tai·chow *or* **T'ai-chou** \'tī-'jō, -'chaù\ city [E] China in central Kiangsu [NW] of Shanghai
Tai·chung \'tī-'chüng\ city China in [W] Taiwan
Tai·nan \'tī-'nän\ city China in [SW] Taiwan
Tai·pei *or* **T'ai-pei** \'tī-'pā, -'bā\ *or formerly* **Tai·ho·ku** \'tī-'hō-,kü\ *or* **Dai·ho·ku** \'dī-'hō-,kü\ city, capital of (Nationalist) China in [N] Taiwan
Tai·wan \'tī-'wän\ *or* **For·mo·sa** \fór-'mō-sə, fər-, -zə\ **1** island China off [SE] coast; since 1949 seat of government of (Nationalist) Republic of China; capital, Taipei **2** strait between Taiwan & China mainland connecting East China & South China seas — **Tai·wan·ese** \,tī-wə-'nēz, -'nēs\ *adj or n*
T'ai-yüan \'tī-yü-'än\ *or* **Yang·ku** \'yäng-'kü\ city [N] China, capital of Shansi
Ta·ka·ma·tsu \,täk-ə-'mät-sü, tä-'käm-ət-,sü\ city Japan in [NE] Shikoku
Ta·kat·su·ki \tə-'kät-sü-kē\ city Japan in [S] Honshu [NNE] of Osaka
Ta·kla Ma·kan \,täk-lə-mə-'kän\ desert [W] China in Sinkiang in Tarim basin
Tal·la·has·see \,tal-ə-'has-ē\ city, capital of Florida
Tal·linn *or Russian* **Ta·lin** \'tal-ən, 'täl-\ *or formerly* **Re·vel** \'rā-vəl\ city U.S.S.R., capital of Estonia
Ta·mau·li·pas \,täm-,aù-'lē-pəs, təm-\ state [NE] Mexico; capital, Ciudad Victoria
Tam·bov \täm-'bóf, -'bóv\ city U.S.S.R. in central Soviet Russia, Europe, [SE] of Moscow
Tam·il Na·du \,tam-əl-'näd-ü\ *or formerly* **Ma·dras** \mə-'dras, -'dräs\ state [S] India on Bay of Bengal; capital, Madras
Tam·pa \'tam-pə\ city [W] Florida on Tampa Bay
Tam·pe·re \'tam-pə-,rā, 'täm-\ city [SW] Finland
Tam·pi·co \tam-'pē-kō\ city [E] Mexico in [S] Tamaulipas
Tananarive — see ANTANANARIVO
Tan·gan·yi·ka \,tan-gən-'yē-kə, ,tang-gən-, -gə-'nē-\ former country [E] Africa [S] of Kenya; became part of Tanzania 1964
Tanganyika, Lake lake [E] Africa between Tanzania & Zaire
Tang·shan \'täng-'shäng\ city [NE] China in [E] Hopei
Tan·ta \'tänt-ə\ city [N] Egypt in central Nile delta
Tan-tung \'dän-'düng, 'tän-'tüng\ *or* **An·tung** \'än-\ city [NE] China in [SE] Liaoning at mouth of the Yalu
Tan·za·nia \,tan-zə-'nē-ə, ,tán-\ country [E] Africa on Indian ocean; a republic formed 1964 by union of Tanganyika & Zanzibar; capital, Dar es Salaam — **Tan·za·ni·an** \-'nē-ən\ *adj or n*
Taor·mi·na \taùr-'mē-nə\ city Italy in [NE] Sicily
Ta·ran·to \'tär-ən-,tō, tə-'rant-ō\ *or ancient* **Ta·ren·tum** \tə-'rent-əm\ city [SE] Italy on Gulf of Taranto
Ta·rim \'dä-'rēm, 'tä-\ river 2010 kilometers long [W] China in Sinkiang flowing into Lop Nor (marshy depression)
Tar·shish \'tär-shish\ ancient maritime country referred to in the Bible & often identified with Tartessus
Tar·sus \'tär-səs\ ancient city of [S] Asia Minor, capital of Cilicia; now a city of [S] Turkey
Tar·tes·sus *or* **Tar·tes·sos** \tär-'tes-əs\ ancient kingdom on [SW] coast of Spain near mouth of the Guadalquivir — see TARSHISH
Tash·kent \tash-'kent\ city U.S.S.R., capital of Uzbekistan
Tas·man \'taz-mən\ sea comprising the part of the [S] Pacific between [SE] Australia & New Zealand
Tas·ma·nia \taz-'mā-nē-ə, -nyə\ *or earlier* **Van Die·men's Land** \van-'dē-mənz\ island [SE] Australia [S] of Victoria; a state; capital, Hobart — **Tas·ma·nian** \-nē-ən, -nyən\ *adj or n*
Ta·ta·ry \'tät-ə-rē\ *or* **Tar·ta·ry** \'tärt-ə-rē\ indefinite historical region in Asia & Europe extending from Sea of Japan to the Dnieper
Ta·tra \'tä-trə\ *or* **High Tatra** *or Czech* **Vy·so·ké Ta·try** \,vis-ə-,kā-'tä-trē\ mountains [E] Czechoslovakia & [S] Poland in central Carpathian mountains
Ta·tung \'dä-'tüng\ city [NE] China in [N] Shansi
Tau·rus \'tór-əs\ mountains [S] Turkey parallel to Mediterranean coast; highest 3734 meters
Tay·side \'tā-,sīd\ region [E] central Scotland; established 1975
Tbilisi — see TIFLIS

Té•tou•an \tā-twä^{n}\ *or* **Te•tuán** \te-'twän, ,tet-ə-'wän\ city [N] Morocco

Tex•as \'tek-səs, -siz\ state [S] U.S.; capital, Austin — **Tex•an** \-sən\ *adj or n*

Thai•land \'tī-,land, -lənd\ *or formerly* **Si•am** \sī-'am\ country [SE] Asia on Gulf of Siam; capital, Bangkok — **Thai•land•er** \'tī-,lan-dər, -lən-dər\ *n*

Thailand, Gulf of — see SIAM

Thames \'temz\ river 338 kilometers long [S] England flowing [E] from the Cotswolds in Gloucestershire into the North sea

Thar \'tär\ *or* **Indian** desert [E] Pakistan & [NW] Republic of India [E] of Indus river

Thebes \'thēbz\ **1** *or ancient* **The•bae** \'thē-bē\ *or later* **Di•os•po•lis** \dī-'äs-pə-ləs\ ancient city [S] Egypt, capital of Upper Egypt on the Nile on site including modern towns of Karnak & Luxor **2** ancient city [E] Greece [NNW] of Athens on site of modern village of Thivai — **The•ban** \'thē-bən\ *adj or n*

Thes•sa•lo•ni•ca \,thes-ə-lə-'nī-kə, -'län-i-kə\ — see SALONIKA — **Thes•sa•lo•nian** \-'lō-nē-ən, -'lō-nyən\ *adj or n*

Thes•sa•ly \'thes-ə-lē\ region central Greece between Pindus mountains & the Aegean — **Thes•sa•lian** \thə-'sā-lē-ən, -'sāl-yən\ *adj or n*

Thim•bu \'thim-bü\ city, capital of Bhutan

Thousand islands Canada & U.S. in the Saint Lawrence in Ontario & New York

Thrace \'thrās\ *or ancient* **Thra•cia** \'thrā-shə, -shē-ə\ region [SE] Europe in Balkan peninsula [N] of the Aegean now divided between Greece & Turkey; in ancient times extended [N] to the Danube — **Thra•cian** \'thrā-shən\ *adj or n*

Thunder Bay city Canada in [SW] Ontario

Thur•rock \'thər-ək, 'thə-rək\ district [SE] England in Essex

Ti•ber \'tī-bər\ *or Italian* **Te•ve•re** \'tā-vā-rā\ *or ancient* **Ti•ber•is** \'tī-bə-rəs\ river 360 kilometers long central Italy flowing through Rome into Tyrrhenian sea

Tiberias, Sea of — see GALILEE

Ti•bes•ti \tə-'bes-tē\ mountains [N] central Africa in central Sahara in [NW] Chad; highest 3415 meters

Ti•bet \tə-'bet\ autonomous region [SW] China on high plateau (average altitude 4875 meters) [N] of the Himalayas; capital, Lhasa

Tien Shan *or* **Tian Shan** \tē-'en-'shän, tē-'än-\ mountain system central Asia extending [NE] from Pamirs into Sinkiang; highest Pobeda Peak (in Soviet Russia, Asia) 7439 meters

Tien•tsin \tē-'en-'sin, -'ent-, 'tin-, 'tint-\ city [NE] China in Hopei

Tier•ra del Fue•go \tē-'er-ə-,del-fü-'ā-gō, -fyü-\ **1** archipelago off [S] South America [S] of Strait of Magellan **2** chief island of the group; divided between Argentina & Chile

Tif•lis \'tif-ləs, tə-'flēs\ *or* **Tbi•li•si** \tə-'bil-ə-sē, -'pil-\ city U.S.S.R., capital of Georgia

Ti•gris \'tī-grəs\ river 1850 kilometers long Turkey & Iraq flowing [SSE] & uniting with the Euphrates to form the Shatt-al-Arab

Tihwa — see URUMCHI

Ti•jua•na \,tē-ə-'wän-ə, tē-'wän-\ city [NW] Mexico on U.S. border in Baja California Norte

Til•burg \'til-,bərg\ city [S] Netherlands

Tim•buk•tu *or* **Tim•buc•too** \,tim-,bək-'tü, tim-'bək-tü\ *or* **Tom•bouc•tou** \tō^{n}-bük-tü\ town [W] Africa in Mali near Niger river

Ti•mi•soa•ra \,tē-mish-ə-'wär-ə, -mish-'wär-\ city [SW] Rumania

Ti•mor \'tē-,mȯr, tē-'\ island Indonesia [SE] of Celebes; [W] half formerly belonged to Netherlands, [E] half to Portugal

Tip•pe•rary \,tip-ə-'reər-ē\ county [S] Ireland in Munster

Ti•ra•ne *or* **Ti•ra•na** \ti-'rän-ə\ city, capital of Albania

Ti•rol *or* **Ty•rol** \tə-'rōl; 'tī-,rōl, tī-'; 'tir-əl\ *or Italian* **Ti•ro•lo** \tē-'rō-lō\ region in [E] Alps in [W] Austria & [NE] Italy — **Ti•ro•le•an** \tə-'rō-lē-ən, tī-; ,tir-ə-', ,tī-rə-'\ *or* **Tir•o•lese** \,tir-ə-'lēz, ,tī-rə-, -'lēs\ *adj or n*

Ti•ruch•chi•rap•pal•li \,tir-ə-chə-'räp-ə-lē\ *or* **Trich•i•nop•o•ly** \,trich-ə-'näp-ə-lē\ city [S] India in Tamil Nadu [NW] of Madras

Ti•ti•ca•ca, Lake \,tit-i-'käk-ə\ lake on Bolivia-Peru boundary at altitude of 3810 meters

Tlax•ca•la \tlä-'skäl-ə\ state [SE] central Mexico; capital, Tlaxcala

To•ba•go \tə-'bā-gō\ island West Indies [NE] of Trinidad in British dominion of Trinidad and Tobago

To•go \'tō-gō\ *or* **To•go•land** \-,land\ region [W] Africa on Gulf of Guinea between Benin & Ghana; until 1918 a German protectorate; then divided into two trust territories: **British Togoland** (in [W], since 1957 part of Ghana) & **French Togo** (in [E], since 1958 the **Republic of Togo**; capital, Lomé) — **To•go•land•er** \-,lan-dər\ *n* — **To•go•lese** \,tō-gō-'lēz, -'lēs\ *adj or n*

To•ku•shi•ma \,tō-kə-'shē-mə\ city Japan in [E] Shikoku

To•kyo \'tō-kē-,ō\ city, capital of Japan in [SE] Honshu on Tokyo Bay — **To•kyo•ite** \'tō-kē-,ō-,īt\ *n*

To•le•do \tə-'lēd-ō, -'lēd-ə\ **1** city [NW] Ohio **2** city central Spain [SW] of Madrid

To•lu•ca \tə-'lü-kə\ city central Mexico, capital of Mexico state

Tol•yat•ti \tól-'yät-ē\ *or formerly* **Stav•ro•pol** \stav-'rō-pəl, -'rō-\ city U.S.S.R. in [SE] Soviet Russia, Europe, [NW] of Kuibyshev

Tombouctou — see TIMBUKTU

Tomsk \'tämsk, 'tämpsk, 'tȯmsk, 'tȯmpsk\ city U.S.S.R. in [W] central Soviet Russia, Asia

Ton•ga \'täng-gə, 'täng-ə\ *or* **Friendly** islands [SW] Pacific [E] of Fiji islands; a kingdom in British Commonwealth; capital, Nukualofa — **Ton•gan** \-gən, -ən\ *adj or n*

To•pe•ka \tə-'pē-kə\ city, capital of Kansas

Tor•bay \tȯr-'bā, 'tȯr-\ town [SW] England in Devonshire

Torino — see TURIN

To•ron•to \tə-'ränt-ō, -'ränt-ə\ city, capital of Ontario

Tor•rance \'tȯr-əns, 'tär-\ city [SW] California

Tor•re•ón \,tȯr-ē-'ōn\ city [N] Mexico in [SW] Coahuila

Tor•res \'tȯr-əs\ strait between New Guinea & Cape York peninsula, Australia

Tor•tu•ga \tȯr-'tü-gə\ island Haiti off [N] coast; a resort of pirates in 17th century

To•run \'tȯr-,ün-yə, -,ün\ city [N] Poland on the Vistula

Toscana — see TUSCANY

Tot•to•ri \tə-'tȯr-ē, -'tȯr-\ city Japan in [SW] Honshu

Tou•lon \tü-lō^{n}\ city [SE] France [ESE] of Marseilles

Tou•louse \tü-'lüz\ city [S] France on the Garonne

Tou•raine \tü-'rān, -'ren\ region [NW] central France; chief city Tours

Tourane — see DA NANG

Tours \'tür\ city [NW] central France

Tow•er Hamlets \'taù-ər-, 'taùr-\ borough of [E] Greater London, England

To•ya•ma \tō-'yäm-ə\ city Japan in [W] central Honshu

To•yo•ha•shi \,tȯi-ə-'häsh-ē\ city Japan in [S] Honshu

Tra•fal•gar, Cape \trə-'fal-gər, *Spanish* ,trä-fäl-'gär\ headland [SW] Spain at [W] end of Strait of Gibraltar

Trans•al•pine Gaul \trans-,al-,pīn-, tranz-\ the part of Gaul included in modern France & Belgium

Transjordan — see JORDAN

Trans•kei \trans-'kī, 'trans-\ territory Republic of South Africa in [E] Cape Province [S] of Natal; a Bantustan; capital, Umtata

Trans•vaal \trans-'väl, tranz-\ province [NE] Republic of South Africa between Vaal & Limpopo rivers; capital, Pretoria

Tran•syl•va•nia \,trans-əl-'vā-nyə, -nē-ə\ region [W] Rumania — **Tran•syl•va•nian** \-nyən, -nē-ən\ *adj or n*

Transylvanian Alps a [S] extension of Carpathian mountains in central Rumania

Treb•i•zond \'treb-ə-,zänd\ Greek empire 1204–1461, an offshoot of Byzantine Empire; at greatest extent included Crimea, Georgia, & [N] coast of Black sea [E] of Sakarya river; capital, Trebizond (modern Trabon, in Turkey)

Tren•ton \'trent-n\ city, capital of New Jersey

Trichinopoly — see TIRUCHCHIRAPPALLI

Trier \'triər\ *or* **Treves** \'trēvz\ city West Germany on the Moselle

Tri•este \trē-'est, trē-'es-tē\ city [NE] Italy on the Adriatic

Trin•i•dad \'trin-ə-,dad\ island West Indies off [NE] coast of Venezuela; with Tobago forms (since 1962) the British dominion of **Trinidad and Tobago**; capital, Port of Spain — **Trin•i•da•di•an** \,trin-ə-'dād-ē-ən, -'dad-\ *adj or n*

Trip•o•li \'trip-ə-lē\ **1** city, capital of Libya **2** city [NW] Lebanon **3** Tripolitania when it was one of the Barbary States

Tri•pol•i•ta•nia \trip-,äl-ə-'tān-yə, ,trip-ə-lə-\ region [NW] Libya; chief city, Tripoli

Tri•pu•ra \'trip-ə-rə\ territory [E] India between Bangladesh & Assam; capital, Agartala

Tris•tan da Cu•nha \,tris-tən-də-'kü-nə\ island [S] Atlantic, chief of the Tristan da Cunha islands belonging to British colony of Saint Helena

Tri•van•drum \triv-'an-drəm\ city [S] India [NW] of Cape Comorin, capital of Kerala

Tro•as \'trō-,as\ *or* **Tro•ad** \-,ad\ territory surrounding ancient city of Troy in [NW] Mysia

Tro•bri•and \'trō-brē-,änd\ islands [SW] Pacific in Solomon sea belonging to Papua New Guinea

Troy \'trȯi\ *or* **Il•i•um** \'il-ē-əm\ *or* **Il•i•on** \'il-ē-,än, -ē-ən\ *or ancient* **Troia** \'trȯi-ə, 'trō-yə\ *or* **Tro•ja** \'trō-jə, -yə\ ancient city [NW] Asia Minor [SW] of the Dardanelles

Trucial States *or* **Trucial Oman** — see UNITED ARAB EMIRATES

Tru•ji•llo \trü-'hē-ō, -yō\ city [NW] Peru

Truk \'trək, 'trůk\ islands [W] Pacific in central Carolines; chief town, Moen (on Moen Island)

Tsaritsyn — see VOLGOGRAD

Tse•lin•o•grad \tse-'lin-ə-,grād, se-\ *or formerly* **Ak•mo•linsk** \,äk-mə-'linsk\ city U.S.S.R. in [N] central Kazakhstan

Tsi•nan *or* **Chi•nan** \'jē-'nän\ city [E] China, capital of Shantung

Tsing•hai *or* **Ching•hai** \'ching-'hī\ *or* **Ko•ko Nor** \,kō-kō-'nȯr\ province [W] China [W] of Kansu; capital, Sining

Tsing•tao \'ching-'daů, 'tsing-'taů\ city [E] China in [E] Shantung

Tsun–i *or* **Tsun•yi** \'dzü-'nē, 'zü-\ city [S] China in [N] central Kweichow

Tu•a•mo•tu \,tü-ə-'mō-tü\ *or* **Low** \'lō\ archipelago [S] Pacific in French Polynesia [E] of Society islands

Tu•buai \tüb-'wä-ē\ *or* **Aus•tral** \'ȯs-trəl, 'äs-\ islands [S] Pacific in French Polynesia [S] of Tahiti

Tuc•son \tü-'sän, 'tü-,\ city [SE] Arizona

Tucumán — see SAN MIGUEL DE TUCUMÁN

Tu•la \'tü-lə\ city U.S.S.R. in central Soviet Russia, Europe, [S] of Moscow

Tul•sa \'təl-sə\ city [NE] Oklahoma

Tung•hwa *or* **T'ung–hua** \'tůng-'hwä, -'wä\ city [NE] China in [SW] Kirin

Tungshan — see SÜCHOW

Tu•nis \'tü-nəs, 'tyü-\ **1** city, capital of Tunisia **2** Tunisia especially as one of the former Barbary States — **Tu•ni•sian** \tü-'nē-zhən, tyü-, -zhē-ən; -'nizh-ən, -ē-ən\ *adj or n*

Tu•ni•sia \tü-'nē-zhə, tyü-, -zhē-ə; -'nizh-ə, -ē-ə\ country [N] Africa on the Mediterranean [E] of Algeria; a republic; capital, Tunis — **Tu•ni•sian** \-zhən, -zhē-ən; -ən, -ē-ən\ *adj or n*

Tu•rin \'tůr-ən, 'tyůr-; tü-'rin, tyü-\ *or Italian* **To•ri•no** \tō-'rē-nō\ city [NW] Italy on the Po, capital of Piedmont

Tur•key \'tər-kē\ country [W] Asia (**Turkey in Asia**) & [SE] Europe (**Turkey in Europe**) between Mediterranean & Black seas; a republic; capital, Ankara

Turk•men•i•stan \,tərk-'men-ə-,stan\ *or* **Turk•men Republic** \,tərk-mən-\ constituent republic of U.S.S.R. in central Asia bordering on Afghanistan, Iran, & Caspian sea; capital, Ashkhabad — **Turk•me•ni•an** \,tərk-'mē-nē-ən\ *adj*

Turks and Cai•cos \,tərk-sən-'kā-kəs\ two groups of islands (Turks islands & Caicos islands) British West Indies at [SE] end of the Bahamas; a British colony

Tur•ku \'tůr-kü\ city [SW] Finland

Tus•ca•ny \'təs-kə-nē\ *or Italian* **To•sca•na** \tō-'skän-ə\ region [NW] central Italy; capital, Florence

Tu•tu•ila \,tüt-ə-'wē-lə\ island [S] Pacific, chief of American Samoa group

Tu•va•lu \tü-'väl-ü, -'vär-\ *or formerly* **El•lice** \'el-əs\ islands [W] Pacific [N] of Fiji; an independent member of British Commonwealth; capital, Funafuti — see GILBERT

Tyne and Wear \'tī-nən-'dwiər, -'wiər\ metropolitan county [N] England; includes Newcastle upon Tyne

Tyre \'tīər\ ancient city, capital of Phoenicia; now a town of [S] Lebanon — **Tyr•i•an** \'tir-ē-ən\ *adj or n*

Tyrol — see TIROL — **Tyrolean** *adj or n* — **Tyrolese** *adj or n*

Ty•rone \tir-'ōn\ county [W] central Northern Ireland

Tyr•rhe•ni•an \tə-'rē-nē-ən\ sea, part of the Mediterranean [SW] of Italy, [N] of Sicily, & [E] of Sardinia & Corsica

Tyu•men \tyü-'men\ city U.S.S.R. in [W] Soviet Russia, Asia, [ENE] of Sverdlovsk

Tzu–kung \'dzə-'gůng\ *or* **Tze•liu•tsing** \'dzə-lē-'ü-'jing\ city [S] central China in [S] Szechwan [W] of Chungking

Ubangi–Shari — see CENTRAL AFRICAN EMPIRE

Ube \'ü-bā\ city Japan in [SW] Honshu near [W] end of Inland sea

Ufa \ü-'fä\ city U.S.S.R. in [E] Soviet Russia, Europe, [NE] of Kuibyshev

Ugan•da \yü-'gan-də, -'gän-, -'gän-\ country [E] Africa [N] of Lake Victoria; a republic in British Commonwealth; capital, Kampala — **Ugan•dan** \-dən\ *adj or n*

Uj•jain \'ü-,jin\ city [NW] central India in [W] Madhya Pradesh

Ujung Pan•dang \ü-,jůng-pän-'däng\ *or formerly* **Ma•cas•sar** *or* **Ma•kas•ar** *or* **Ma•kas•sar** \mə-'kas-ər\ city Indonesia in [SW] Celebes

Ukraine \yü-'krān, 'yü-,\ constituent republic of U.S.S.R. in [E] Europe on [N] coast of Black sea

Ulan Ba•tor \,ü-,län-'bä-,tȯr\ *or formerly* **Ur•ga** \'ůr-gə\ city, capital of Mongolian People's Republic

Ulan–Ude \,ü-,län-ů-'dā\ city U.S.S.R. in [E] Soviet Russia, Asia, [E] of Lake Baikal

Ul•ster \'əl-stər\ **1** region [N] Ireland comprising Northern Ireland & [N] Republic of Ireland; a province until 1921 **2** province [N] Republic of Ireland comprising counties Donegal, Cavan, & Monaghan **3** NORTHERN IRELAND

Ul•ya•novsk *or* **Ul•ia•novsk** \ül-'yän-əfsk\ *or formerly* **Sim•birsk** \sim-'biərsk\ city U.S.S.R. in [E] central Soviet Russia, Europe, [NW] of Kuibyshev

Um•bria \'əm-brē-ə\ region central Italy in the Apennines; capital, Perugia — **Um•bri•an** \-brē-ən\ *adj or n*

Un•ga•va \,ən-'gav-ə\ **1** bay inlet of Hudson strait [NE] Canada **2** peninsula region [NE] Canada in [N] Quebec

Union of South Africa — see SOUTH AFRICA

Union of Soviet Socialist Republics *or* **Soviet Union** *or* **Soviet Russia** country [E] Europe & [N] Asia; a union of 15 constituent republics; capital, Moscow

United Arab Emir•ates \i-'mir-əts, ā-, -'miər-,āts\ *or formerly* **Tru•cial States** \'trü-shəl-\ *or* **Trucial Oman** country [E] Arabia on Persian Gulf; a republic composed of seven emirates; capital, Abu Dhabi

United Arab Republic former name (1961–71) of Arab Republic of Egypt & previously (1958–61) of union of Egypt & Syria

United Kingdom *or in full* **United Kingdom of Great Britain and Northern Ireland** country [W] Europe in British Isles comprising England, Scotland, Wales, Northern Ireland, Channel islands, & Isle of Man; capital, London

United Nations international territory; a small area in New York City in [E] central Manhattan; seat of permanent headquarters of the United Nations

United States of America *or* **United States** country North America bordering on Atlantic, Pacific, & Arctic oceans & including Hawaii; a federal republic; capital, Washington

Upper Vol•ta \'väl-tə, 'vōl-, 'vȯl-\ *or French* **Haute–Vol•ta** \ōt-vȯl-tá\ country [W] Africa [N] of Ivory Coast, Ghana, & Togo; a republic; capital, Ouagadougou — **Upper Vol•tan** \'vält-n, 'vōlt-, 'vȯlt-\ *adj or n*

Ural \'yůr-əl\ **1** mountains U.S.S.R. extending about 2575 kilometers [S] from point near Kara sea; usually considered dividing line between Europe & Asia; highest about 1830 meters **2** river 2255 kilometers long U.S.S.R. flowing from [S] end of Ural mountains into Caspian sea

Uralsk \yů-'ralsk\ city U.S.S.R. in [W] Kazakhstan

Ura•wa \ů-'rä-wə\ city Japan in central Honshu [N] of Tokyo

Uru•guay \'ůr-ə-,gwī, 'yůr-; 'yůr-ə-,gwā\ **1** river 1577 kilometers long [SE] South America rising in Brazil & flowing into Río de la Plata **2** country [SE] South America; a republic; capital, Montevideo — **Uru•guay•an** \,ůr-ə-'gwī-ən, ,yůr-; ,yůr-ə-'gwā-\ *adj or n*

Urum•chi *or* **Urum•tsi** \ü-'rům-chē, ,ůr-əm-'chē\ *or* **Ti•hwa** \'dē-'hwä, -'wä\ *or Chinese* **Wu–lu–mu–ch'i** \'wü-'lü-'mü-'chē\ city [NW] China, capital of Sinkiang

Urundi — see BURUNDI

Us•pa•lla•ta \,ü-spə-'yät-ə, -'zhät-\ mountain pass 3840 meters [S] South America in the Andes between Argentina & Chile

Ust–Ka•me•no•gorsk \'üst-kə-,mən-ə-'gȯrsk\ city U.S.S.R. in [E] Kazakhstan on Irtysh river

Usumbura — see BUJUMBURA

Utah \'yü-,tȯ, -,tä\ state [W] U.S.; capital, Salt Lake City — **Utah•an** \'yü-,tȯ-ən, -,tȯn, -,tä-ən, -,tän\ *adj or n* — **Utahn** \-,tȯ-ən, -,tȯn, -,tä-ən, -,tän\ *n*

Utrecht \'yü-,trekt\ city central Netherlands

Utsu•no•mi•ya \,üt-sə-'nō-mē-,ä, -,yä\ city Japan in central Honshu [N] of Tokyo

Ut•tar Pra•desh \,ůt-ər-prə-'desh, -'dāsh\ state [N] India bordering on Tibet & Nepal; capital, Lucknow

Uz•bek•i•stan \ůz-,bek-i-'stan, ,əz-, -'stän\ *or* **Uz•bek Soviet Socialist Republic** \'ůz-,bek, 'əz-, ůz-'\ constituent republic of U.S.S.R. in [W] central Asia between Aral sea & Afghanistan; capital Tashkent

Va•duz \vä-'düts\ town, capital of Liechtenstein
Va•len•cia \və-'len-chə, -chē-ə, -'len-sē-ə\ **1** region & ancient kingdom [E] Spain between Andalusia & Catalonia **2** city, its capital, on the Mediterranean **3** city [N] Venezuela [WSW] of Caracas
Val•la•do•lid \,val-əd-ə-'lid, -'lē\ city [NW] central Spain
Val•let•ta \və-'let-ə\ city, capital of Malta
Val•pa•rai•so \,val-pə-'rī-zō, -'rā-\ *or Spanish* **Val•pa•ra•í•so** \,väl-pä-rä-'ē-sō\ city central Chile on the Pacific [WNW] of Santiago
Van•cou•ver \van-'kü-vər\ **1** island [W] Canada in [SW] British Columbia **2** city [SW] British Columbia
Van Diemen's Land — see TASMANIA
Varanasi — see BANARAS
Vat•i•can City \,vat-i-kən-\ *or Italian* **Cit•tà del Va•ti•ca•no** \chēt-'tä-del-,vä-tē-'kä-nō\ independent papal state within commune of Rome, Italy; created 1929
Ve•ne•to \'ven-ə-,tō, 'vā-nə-\ region [NE] Italy; capital, Venice
Ven•e•zu•e•la \,ven-əz-ə-'wā-lə, -əz-'wā-, -'wē-\ country [N] South America; capital, Caracas — **Ven•e•zu•e•lan** \-lən\ *adj or n*
Ven•ice \'ven-əs\ *or Italian* **Ve•ne•zia** \və-'net-sē-ə\ city [N] Italy on islands in Lagoon of Venice — **Ve•ne•tian** \və-'nē-shən\ *adj or n*
Ve•ra•cruz \,ver-ə-'krüz, -'krüs\ state [E] Mexico; capital, Jalapa **2** city [E] Mexico in Veracruz state on Gulf of Mexico
Ver•ee•ni•ging \fə-'rā-nə-ging, -nək-əng\ city [NE] Republic of South Africa in [S] Transvaal [S] of Johannesburg
Ver•mont \vər-'mänt\ state [NE] U.S.; capital, Montpelier — **Ver•mont•er** \-ər\ *n*
Ve•ro•na \və-'rō-nə\ city [N] Italy [W] of Venice
Ver•sailles \,vər-'sī, ver-\ city [N] France; suburb [WSW] of Paris
Vert, Cape \'vərt\ *or* **Cape Verde** \'vərd\ promontory [W] Africa in Senegal; most westerly point of Africa
Ve•su•vi•us \və-'sü-vē-əs\ volcano about 1220 meters [S] Italy near Bay of Naples
Viadua — see ODER
Vi•cen•te Ló•pez \və-,sent-ə-'lō-,pez\ city [E] Argentina [N] of Buenos Aires
Vi•cen•za \vi-'chen-sə\ city [NE] Italy [W] of Venice
Vic•to•ria \vik-'tōr-ē-ə, -'tȯr-\ **1** city, capital of British Columbia on Vancouver Island **2** island [N] Canada in Arctic archipelago [S] of Melville Sound **3** state [SE] Australia; capital, Melbourne **4** city, capital of Hong Kong colony — **Vic•to•ri•an** \-ē-ən\ *adj or n*
Victoria, Lake lake [E] Africa in Tanzania, Kenya, & Uganda
Victoria Falls waterfall 107 meters high [S] Africa in the Zambezi on border between Zambia & Rhodesia
Victoria Nile — see NILE
Vi•en•na \vē-'en-ə\ *or German* **Wien** \'vēn\ *or ancient* **Vin•dob•o•na** \vin-'däb-ə-nə\ *or* **Vin•dob•na** \-'däb-nə\ city, capital of Austria on the Danube — **Vi•en•nese** \,vē-ə-'nēz, -'nēs\ *adj or n*
Vien•tiane \vyen-'tyän\ city, capital of Laos
Viet•nam *or* **Viet Nam** \vē-'et-'näm, vyet-, ,vē-ət-, vēt-, -'nam\ country [SE] Asia in Indochina; capital, Hanoi; established 1945–46 & divided 1954–75 at 17th parallel into republics of **North Vietnam** (capital, Hanoi) & **South Vietnam** (capital, Saigon)
Vi•ja•ya•wa•da \,vij-ə-yə-'wäd-ə\ *or formerly* **Bez•wa•da** \bez-'wäd-ə\ city [SE] India in [E] Andhra Pradesh
Vi•la \'vē-lə\ city, capital of New Hebrides
Vil•ni•us \'vil-nē-əs\ *or Polish* **Wil•no** \'vil-nō\ *or Russian* **Vil•na** \'vil-nə\ *or* **Vil•no** \-nō\ city U.S.S.R., capital of Lithuania
Vin•land \'vin-lənd\ a portion of the coast of North America visited and so called by Norse voyagers about 1000 A.D.; perhaps Newfoundland
Vin•ni•tsa \'vin-ət-sə\ city U.S.S.R. in [W] central Ukraine
Vin•son Massif \'vin-sən\ mountain 5139 meters [W] Antarctica in Sentinel range of Ellsworth mountains; highest in Antarctica
Vir•gin•ia \vər-'jin-yə, -'jin-ē-ə\ state [E] U.S.; capital, Richmond — **Vir•gin•ian** \-yən, -ē-ən\ *adj or n*
Virginia Beach city [SE] Virginia
Vir•gin Islands \,vər-jən-\ island group West Indies [E] of Puerto Rico — see BRITISH VIRGIN ISLANDS, VIRGIN ISLANDS OF THE UNITED STATES
Virgin Islands of the United States the [W] islands of the Virgin islands group including Saint Croix, Saint John, & Saint Thomas; capital, Charlotte Amalie (on Saint Thomas)
Vi•sa•yan \və-'sī-ən\ *or* **Bi•sa•yas** \bə-'sī-əz\ islands central Philippines including Bohol, Cebu, Leyte, Masbate, Negros, Panay, & Samar
Vis•tu•la \'vis-chə-lə, 'vish-; 'vis-tə-lə\ *or Polish* **Wis•la** \'vē-slä\ river 1015 kilometers long Poland flowing [N] from the Carpathians into Gulf of Danzig
Vi•tebsk \'vē-,tepsk, -,tebsk, və-'\ city U.S.S.R. in [NE] Belorussian Soviet Socialist Republic
Vi•ti Le•vu \,vēt-ē-'lev-ü\ island [SW] Pacific; largest of the Fiji group
Vi•to•ria \vi-'tōr-ē-ə, -'tȯr-\ city [N] Spain
Vi•tó•ria \vi-'tōr-ē-ə, -'tȯr-\ city [E] Brazil [NE] of Rio de Janeiro
Vlad•i•mir \'vlad-ə-,miər, vlə-'dē-,miər\ city U.S.S.R. in central Soviet Russia, Europe, [E] of Moscow
Vlad•i•vos•tok \,vlad-ə-və-'stäk, -'väs-,täk\ city U.S.S.R. in [SE] Soviet Russia, Asia, on Sea of Japan
Volcano islands *or* **Ka•zan Ret•to** \,käz-,än-'ret-ō\ island chain Japan in [W] Pacific [S] of Bonin islands — see IWO JIMA
Vol•ga \'väl-gə, 'vȯl-, 'vōl-\ river 3742 kilometers long U.S.S.R. in [E] Soviet Russia, Europe, flowing into Caspian sea
Vol•go•grad \'väl-gə-,grad, 'vȯl-, 'vōl-\ *or formerly* **Sta•lin•grad** \'stäl-ən-,grad, 'stal-\ *or earlier* **Tsa•ri•tsyn** \tsə-'rēt-sən, sə-\ city U.S.S.R. in [S] Soviet Russia, Europe, on the Volga
Vo•log•da \'vȯ-ləg-də\ city U.S.S.R. in [N] central Soviet Russia, Europe
Vol•ta \'väl-tə, 'vōl-, 'vȯl-\ river 160 kilometers long Ghana flowing from Lake Volta (reservoir) into Bight of Benin
Vo•ro•nezh \və-'rȯ-nish\ city U.S.S.R. in [S] central Soviet Russia, Europe
Vo•ro•shi•lov•grad \,vȯr-ə-'shē-ləf-,grad, ,vär-, -ləv-\ city U.S.S.R. in [E] Ukraine in Donets basin
Vosges \'vōzh\ mountains [NE] France on [W] side of Rhine valley; highest 1423 meters
Voy•a•geurs National Park \,vȯi-ə-'zhərz\ reservation [N] Minnesota on Rainy Lake
Vysoké Tatry — see TATRA
Wa•ka•ya•ma \,wäk-ə-'yäm-ə\ city Japan in [SW] Honshu [SW] of Osaka
Wake \'wāk\ island [N] Pacific [N] of Marshall islands; belongs to U.S.
Wa•la•chia *or* **Wal•la•chia** \wä-'lā-kē-ə\ region [S] Rumania between Transylvanian Alps & the Danube
Wales \'wālz\ *or Welsh* **Cym•ru** \'kəm-rē\ principality [SW] Great Britain; a division of United Kingdom; capital, Cardiff
Wal•la•sey \'wäl-ə-sē\ borough [NW] England in Merseyside
Wal•lis \'wäl-əs\ islands [SW] Pacific [NE] of Fiji; with Futuna islands constituting a French overseas territory (**Wallis and Futuna Islands**)
Wal•sall \'wȯl-,sȯl, -səl\ borough [W] central England in West Midlands
Wal•tham Forest \,wȯl-thəm-\ borough of [NE] Greater London, England
Wan-ch'uan — see KALGAN
Wands•worth \'wändz-wərth, 'wänz-\ borough of [SW] Greater London, England
Wan•ne-Eick•el \,vän-ə-'ī-kəl\ city West Germany in the Ruhr
Wa•ran•gal \wə-'rəng-gəl\ city [S] central India in [N] Andhra Pradesh [NE] of Hyderabad
War•ley \'wȯr-lē\ county borough [W] central England in Worcestershire
War•ren \'wȯr-ən, 'wär-\ city [SE] Michigan
War•saw \'wȯr-,sȯ\ *or Polish* **War•sza•wa** \vär-'shäv-ə\ city, capital of Poland
War•wick•shire \'wär-ik-,shiər, -shər\ *or* **Warwick** county central England
Wa•satch \'wȯ-,sach\ range of the Rockies [SE] Idaho & [N] central Utah; highest Mount Timpanogos 3660 meters (in Utah)
Wash•ing•ton \'wȯsh-ing-tən, 'wäsh-\ **1** state [NW] U.S.; capital, Olympia **2** city, capital of U.S.; coextensive with District of Columbia — **Wash•ing•to•nian** \,wȯsh-ing-'tō-nē-ən, ,wäsh-, -nyən\ *adj or n*
Washington, Mount mountain 1917 meters [N] New Hampshire; highest in White mountains
Wa•ter•bury \'wȯt-ər-,ber-ē, 'wȯt-ə-, 'wät-\ city [W] central Connecticut
Wa•ter•ford \'wȯt-ər-fərd, 'wät-\ county [S] Ireland in Munster
Wa•ter•ton Lakes National Park \'wȯt-ərt-n, 'wät-\ mountain area [W] Canada in [S] Alberta adjoining Glacier National Park,

Montana, & with it forming **Waterton–Glacier International Peace Park**
Watlings — see SAN SALVADOR
Wed•dell \wə-'del, 'wed-l\ sea arm of the [S] Atlantic [E] of Antarctic peninsula
Wei•fang \'wā-'fäŋ\ city [E] China in [E] central Shantung
Wei•mar Republic \'vī-ˌmär, 'wī-\ the German republic 1919–33
Wel•land \'wel-ənd\ canal 45 kilometers long [SE] Ontario connecting Lakes Erie & Ontario
Wel•ling•ton \'wel-ing-tən\ city, capital of New Zealand
Wen–chou \'wən-'jō\ city [E] China in [S] Chekiang
Wes•sex \'wes-iks\ ancient Anglian kingdom [S] England; capital, Winchester
West Australian Current warm current flowing [N] off [W] coast of Australia
West Bengal state [E] India; capital, Calcutta
West Brom•wich \'brəm-ij, 'bräm-, -ich\ borough [W] central England in West Midlands
Western Australia state [W] Australia; capital, Perth — **Western Australian** *adj or n*
Western Ghats \'gȯts\ chain of low mountains [SW] India
Western Isles the Outer Hebrides constituting since 1975 a regional division of [W] Scotland
Western Sahara *or formerly* **Spanish Sahara** region [NW] Africa divided 1975 between Mauritania & Morocco
Western Samoa islands Samoa [W] of 171° [W]; an independent state in British Commonwealth since 1962; capital, Apia
West Germany the Federal Republic of Germany — see GERMANY
West Gla•mor•gan \glə-'mȯr-gən\ county [S] Wales; established 1974
West Indies islands lying between [SE] North America & [N] South America & comprising the Greater Antilles, Lesser Antilles, & Bahamas — **West Indian** *adj or n*
West Iri•an \ˌir-ē-'än\ *or* **West New Guinea** *or formerly* **Netherlands New Guinea** territory of Indonesia comprising [W] half of New Guinea; capital, Djajapura
West Lo•thi•an \'lō-t͟hē-ən\ former county [SE] Scotland — see LOTHIAN
West Malaysia — see PENINSULAR MALAYSIA
West•meath \west-'mēt͟h, wes-, -'mēth\ county [E] central Ireland in Leinster
West Midlands metropolitan county [W] central England
West•min•ster \'west-ˌmin-stər, 'wes-\ *or* **City of Westminster** borough of [W] central Greater London, England
West•mor•land \'west-mər-lənd, 'wes-\ former county [NW] England
West Pakistan the former [W] division of Pakistan now coextensive with Pakistan
West•pha•lia \west-'fāl-yə, -'fā-lē-ə, wes-\ region [NW] Germany [E] of the Rhine; now part of North Rhine-Westphalia, West Germany — **West•pha•lian** \-'fāl-yən, -'fā-lē-ən\ *adj or n*
West Punjab — see PUNJAB 3
West Quod•dy Head \ˌkwäd-ē-\ cape; most easterly point of Maine & of U.S.
West Ri•ding \'rīd-ing\ former administrative county [N] England in [W] & [SW] Yorkshire
West Sus•sex \'səs-iks\ county [SE] England
West Virginia state [E] U.S.; capital, Charleston — **West Virginian** *adj or n*
West York•shire \'yȯrk-ˌshiər, -shər\ metropolitan county [NW] England
Wex•ford \'weks-fərd\ county [SE] Ireland in Leinster
White mountains [N] New Hampshire in the Appalachians — see WASHINGTON
White•horse \'hwīt-ˌhȯrs, 'wīt-\ city [NW] Canada, capital of Yukon Territory
White Nile — see NILE
White sea *or* **Be•lo•ye Mo•re** \ˌbel-ə-yə-'mȯr-yə\ sea inlet of Barents sea U.S.S.R. on [N] coast of Soviet Russia, Europe
Whit•ney, Mount \'hwit-nē, 'wit-\ mountain 4418 meters [SE] central California in Sierra Nevada in Sequoia National Park; highest in U.S. outside of Alaska
Wich•i•ta \'wich-ə-ˌtȯ\ city [S] Kansas
Wick•low \'wik-lō\ county [E] Ireland in Leinster
Wien — see VIENNA
Wies•ba•den \'vēs-ˌbäd-n, 'vis-\ city West Germany on the Rhine [W] of Frankfurt, capital of Hesse
Wight, Isle of \'wīt\ island & county [S] England in English channel
Wig•town \'wig-tən, -ˌtau̇n\ *or* **Wig•town•shire** \-ˌshiər, -shər\ former county [SW] Scotland
Wil•helms•ha•ven \ˌvil-ˌhelmz-'häf-ən, 'vil-əmz-ˌ\ city West Germany [NW] of Bremen
Wil•lem•stad \'vil-əm-ˌstät\ city, capital of Netherlands Antilles on Curaçao Island
Wil•ming•ton \'wil-ming-tən\ city [N] Delaware; largest in state
Wilno — see VILNIUS
Wilt•shire \'wilt-ˌshiər, 'wil-chər, 'wilt-shər\ county [S] England
Win•der•mere \'win-dər-ˌmiər, -də-\ lake [NW] England in Lake District
Wind•hoek \'vint-ˌhu̇k\ city, capital of South-West Africa
Wind•sor \'win-zər\ city [S] Ontario on Detroit river
Wind•ward \'win-dwərd\ islands West Indies in the [S] Lesser Antilles extending [S] from Martinique but not including Barbados, Tobago, or Trinidad
Win•ni•peg \'win-ə-ˌpeg\ city, capital of Manitoba
Winnipeg, Lake lake [S] central Manitoba
Win•ni•pe•sau•kee, Lake \ˌwin-ə-pə-'sȯ-kē\ lake central New Hampshire
Win•ston–Sa•lem \ˌwin-stən-'sā-ləm\ city [N] central North Carolina
Wis•con•sin \wis-'kän-sən\ state [N] central U.S.; capital, Madison — **Wis•con•sin•ite** \-sə-ˌnīt\ *n*
Wisla — see VISTULA
Wit•wa•ters•rand \'wit-ˌwȯt-ərz-ˌrand, -ˌwät-, -ˌränd, -ˌränt\ *or* **Rand** \'rand, 'ränd, 'ränt\ ridge of gold-bearing rock [NE] Republic of South Africa in [S] Transvaal
Wol•lon•gong \'wu̇l-ən-ˌgäng, -ˌgȯng\ city [SE] Australia in [E] New South Wales [S] of Sydney
Wol•ver•hamp•ton \'wu̇l-vər-ˌham-tən, -ˌhamp-\ borough West central England in West Midlands [NW] of Birmingham
Won•san \'wən-ˌsän\ city North Korea on [E] coast
Worces•ter \'wu̇s-tər\ city [E] central Massachusetts
Worces•ter•shire \'wu̇s-tər-ˌshiər, -tə-, -shər\ *or* **Worcester** former county [W] central England — see HEREFORD AND WORCESTER
Wran•gell, Mount \'rang-gəl\ volcano 4317 meters [S] Alaska in Wrangell range; highest volcano in U.S.
Wro•claw \'vrȯt-ˌsläf, -ˌsläv\ *or German* **Bres•lau** \'bres-ˌlau̇\ city [SW] Poland in Silesia
Wu•chang \'wü-'chäng\ former city [E] central China — see WUHAN
Wu•han \'wü-'hän\ city [S] China, capital of Hupei; formed from former separate cities of Hankow, Hanyang, & Wuchang
Wuhsien — see SU-CHOU
Wu•hu \'wü-'hü\ *or* **Wu–na–mu** \'wü-'nä-'mü\ city [E] China in [E] Anhwei
Wu–lu–mu–ch'i — see URUMCHI
Wup•per•tal \'vu̇p-ər-ˌtäl\ city West Germany in Ruhr valley [ENE] of Düsseldorf
Würt•tem•berg \'wərt-əm-ˌbərg, 'wu̇rt-; 'vuert-əm-ˌberk\ region [SW] Germany between Baden & Bavaria; chief city, Stuttgart; now part of Baden-Württemberg state of West Germany
Wu•sih *or* **Wu–hsi** \'wü-'shē\ city [E] China in [S] Kiangsu
Wutsin — see CH'ANG-CHOU
Wy•o•ming \wī-'ō-ming\ state [NW] U.S.; capital, Cheyenne — **Wy•o•ming•ite** \-ming-ˌīt\ *n*
Ya•kutsk \yə-'kütsk\ city U.S.S.R. in [E] central Soviet Russia, Asia
Ya•lu \'yäl-ü\ *or* **Am•nok** \'am-ˌnäk\ river 480 kilometers long [SE] Manchuria & North Korea flowing into Korea Bay
Ya•ma•ga•ta \'yäm-ə-gə-ˌtä, yə-'mäg-ə-\ city Japan in [N] Honshu [W] of Sendai
Yang–chou \'yäng-'jō\ *or formerly* **Kiang•tu** \jē-'äng-'dü\ city [E] China in [SW] Kiangsu
Yangku — see T'AI-YÜAN
Yang•tze \'yang-'sē; 'yangt-'sē, 'yangkt-\ *or* **Yangtze Kiang** \kē-'ang\ river 4990 kilometers long central China flowing into East China sea
Yao \'yau̇\ city Japan in [S] Honshu [E] of Osaka
Yaoun•dé \yau̇n-'dā\ city, capital of Cameroon
Yap \'yap, 'yäp\ island [W] Pacific in the [W] Carolines
Ya•ro•slavl \ˌyär-ə-'släv-əl\ city U.S.S.R. in Soviet Russia, Europe, [NE] of Moscow
Yellow 1 *or Chinese* **Hwang Ho** \'hwäng-'hō, 'wäng-\ river 4830 kilometers long [N] China flowing into Po Hai **2** sea section of

East China sea between [N] China & Korea
Yel•low•knife \'yel-ə-,nīf\ town Canada, capital of Northwest Territories
Yel•low•stone National Park \'yel-ə-,stōn\ reservation [NW] Wyoming, [E] Idaho, & [S] Montana
Ye•men \'yem-ən\ **1** *or* **Yemen Arab Republic** country [SW] Arabia bordering on Red sea; capital, San'a **2** *or* **People's Democratic Republic of Yemen** *or formerly* **Southern Yemen** *or* **South Yemen** country [S] Arabia on Gulf of Aden comprising former British protectorate of Aden; capital, Aden — **Ye•me•ni** \'yem-ə-nē\ *adj or n* — **Ye•men•ite** \-ə-,nīt\ *n*
Yen•i•sey *or* **Yen•i•sei** \,yen-ə-'sā\ river 4505 kilometers long U.S.S.R. in Soviet Russia, Asia, flowing [N] into Arctic ocean
Ye•re•van \,yer-ə-'vän\ *or* **Ere•van** *or* **Eri•van** \,yer-ə-, ,er-ə-\ city U.S.S.R., capital of Armenian Soviet Socialist Republic
Yezo — see HOKKAIDO
Yo•ho National Park \'yō-hō\ reservation [W] Canada in [SE] British Columbia on Alberta boundary
Yo•ko•ha•ma \,yō-kə-'häm-ə\ city Japan in [SE] Honshu on Tokyo Bay [S] of Tokyo
Yo•ko•su•ka \yō-'kò-sə-kə, -'kò-skə\ city Japan in [E] Honshu [W] of entrance to Tokyo Bay
Yon•kers \'yäng-kərz\ city [SE] New York [N] of New York City
York \'yȯrk\ city [N] England in North Yorkshire
York•shire \'yȯrk-,shiər, -shər\ *or* **York** former county [N] England comprising city of York & administrative counties of East Riding, North Riding, & West Riding — see CLEVELAND, HUMBERSIDE, NORTH YORKSHIRE, SOUTH YORKSHIRE, WEST YORKSHIRE
York, Cape cape [NE] Australia in Queensland at [N] tip of Cape York peninsula
Yo•sem•i•te Falls \yō-'sem-ət-ē\ waterfall [E] California in Yosemite valley in Yosemite National Park; includes two falls, the upper 436 meters & the lower 98 meters, connected by a cascade 248 meters high
Yosemite National Park reservation [E] central California in Sierra Nevada
Youngs•town \'yəng-,staun\ city [NE] Ohio
Yssel — see IJSSEL
Yu•ca•tán \,yü-kə-'tan, -'tän\ **1** peninsula [SE] Mexico & [N] Central America including Belize & [N] Guatemala **2** state [SE] Mexico; capital, Mérida
Yu•go•sla•via *or* **Ju•go•sla•via** \,yü-gō-'släv-ē-ə\ country [S] Europe on the Adriatic; a federal republic; capital, Belgrade — **Yu•go•slav** \,yü-gō-'släv, -'slav\ *or* **Yu•go•sla•vi•an** \-'släv-ē-ən\ *adj or n*
Yu•kon \'yü-,kän\ **1** river 3185 kilometers long [NW] Canada & Alaska flowing into Bering sea **2** *or* **Yukon Territory** territory [NW] Canada; capital, Whitehorse
Yü–men \'yü-'men\ *or* **Lao–chün–miao** \'lau-'chün-'myau\ city [N] central China in Kansu
Yun•nan \yü-'nän\ **1** province [SW] China bordering on Burma & Indochina; capital, Kunming **2** — see KUNMING
Yunnanfu — see KUNMING
Zab•rze \'zäb-zhā\ city [SW] Poland in Silesia
Za•ca•te•cas \,zak-ə-'tā-kəs, -'tek-əs\ **1** state [N] central Mexico **2** city; its capital
Zag•a•zig \'zag-ə-,zig\ city [N] Egypt [NNE] of Cairo
Za•greb \'zäg-,reb\ city [NW] Yugoslavia, capital of Croatia
Zaire \'zīr, zä-'iər\ **1** river in Africa — see CONGO **2** *or formerly* **Democratic Republic of the Congo** *or earlier* **Belgian Congo** country central Africa comprising most of Congo river basin [E] of lower Congo river; a republic; capital, Kinshasa
Zam•be•zi *or* **Zam•be•si** \zam-'bē-zē\ river 2655 kilometers long [SE] Africa flowing from [NW] Zambia into Mozambique channel
Zam•bia \'zam-bē-ə\ country [S] Africa [N] of the Zambezi; formerly the British protectorate of **Northern Rhodesia**; an independent republic since 1964; capital, Lusaka
Zam•bo•an•ga \,zam-bə-'wäng-gə\ city [S] Philippines in [SW] Mindanao
Zan•zi•bar \'zan-zə-,bär\ island Tanzania off [NE] Tanganyika coast; formerly a sultanate & British protectorate including also Pemba & other islands; became independent 1963; united 1964 with Tanganyika forming Tanzania
Za•po•ro•zhye \,zäp-ə-'rò-zhə\ city U.S.S.R. in [SE] Ukraine
Za•ra•go•za \,zar-ə-'gō-zə\ *or* **Sar•a•gos•sa** \,sar-ə-'gäs-ə\ city [NE] Spain in [W] Aragon
Zealand — see SJÆLLAND
Zetland — see SHETLAND
Zhda•nov \zhə-'dän-əf, 'shtän-\ city U.S.S.R. in [E] Ukraine on Sea of Azov
Zhi•to•mir \zhi-'tò-,miər\ city U.S.S.R. in [W] Ukraine
Zi•on \'zī-ən\ *or* **Si•on** \'sī-ən\ **1** the stronghold of Jerusalem conquered by David **2** a hill in Jerusalem occupied in ancient times by the Jewish Temple **3** JERUSALEM **4** ISRAEL
Zion National Park reservation [SW] Utah
Zla•to•ust \,zlät-ə-'üst\ city U.S.S.R. in [W] Soviet Russia, Asia, in the [S] Urals
Zom•ba \'zäm-bə\ city [S] Malawi
Zui•der Zee \,zīd-ər-'zā, -'zē\ former inlet of North sea [N] Netherlands now (as IJsselmeer) partly reclaimed — see IJSSELMEER
Zu•lu•land \'zü-lü-,land\ territory [E] Republic of South Africa in [NE] Natal on Indian ocean; capital, Eshowe
Zu•rich \'zu̇r-ik\ city [N] Switzerland on Lake of Zurich
Zwick•au \'tsfik-,au, 'zwik-\ city East Germany [S] of Leipzig

Handbook of Style

Punctuation

The English writing system uses punctuation marks to separate groups of words for meaning and emphasis; to convey an idea of the variations of pitch, volume, pauses, and intonations of speech; and to help avoid contextual ambiguity. English punctuation marks, together with general rules and bracketed examples of their use, follow.

Apostrophe ’

1. indicates the possessive case of nouns and indefinite pronouns — ⟨Senator Smith’s constituents⟩ ⟨the boy’s mother⟩ ⟨the boys’ mothers⟩ ⟨It is anyone’s guess how much it will cost.⟩ ⟨Rodgers and Hammerstein’s musicals⟩
2. marks omissions in contracted words — ⟨didn’t⟩ ⟨o’clock⟩
3. often forms plurals of letters, figures, and words referred to as words — ⟨You should dot your *i*’s and cross your *t*’s.⟩ ⟨His *1*’s and his *7*’s looked alike.⟩ ⟨She has trouble pronouncing her *the*’s.⟩

Brackets [ ]

1. set off extraneous data such as editorial interpolations especially within quoted material — ⟨He wrote, "I ain't [sic] going."⟩
2. function as parentheses within parentheses — ⟨Bowman Act (22 Stat., ch. 4, § [or sec.] 4, p. 50)⟩
3. set off phonetic symbols — ⟨[t] in British *duty*⟩

Colon :

1. introduces a clause or phrase that explains, illustrates, amplifies, or restates what has gone before — ⟨The sentence was poorly constructed: it lacked both unity and coherence.⟩
2. directs attention to an appositive — ⟨He had only one pleasure: eating.⟩
3. introduces a series — ⟨Three countries were represented: England, France, and Belgium.⟩
4. introduces lengthy quoted material set off from the rest of a text by indentation but not by quotation marks — ⟨I quote from the text of Chapter One:⟩
5. separates data in time-telling and data in bibliographic and biblical references — ⟨8:30 a.m.⟩ ⟨New York: Smith Publishing Co.⟩ ⟨John 4:10⟩
6. separates titles and subtitles (as of books) — ⟨*The Tragic Dynasty: A History of the Romanovs*⟩
7. follows the salutation in formal correspondence — ⟨Dear Sir:⟩ ⟨Gentlemen:⟩

Comma ,

1. separates main clauses joined by a coordinating conjunction (as *and, but, or, nor,* or *for*) and very short clauses not so joined	⟨She knew very little about him, and he volunteered nothing.⟩ ⟨I came, I saw, I conquered.⟩
2. sets off an adverbial clause (or a long phrase) that precedes the main clause	⟨When she found that her friends had deserted her, she sat down and cried.⟩
3. sets off from the rest of the sentence transitional words and expressions (as *on the contrary, on the other hand*), conjunctive adverbs (as *consequently, furthermore, however*), and expressions that introduce an illustration or example (as *namely, for example*)	⟨Your second question, on the other hand, remains open.⟩ ⟨The mystery, however, remains unsolved.⟩ ⟨She expects to travel through two countries, namely, France and England.⟩
4. separates words, phrases, or clauses in series	⟨Men, women, and children crowded into the square.⟩ ⟨It requires one to travel constantly, to have no private life, and to need no income other than living expenses on the road.—Sara Davidson⟩
NOTE: Commas separate coordinate adjectives modifying a noun.	⟨The harsh, cold wind was strong.⟩
5. sets off from the rest of the sentence parenthetic elements (as nonrestrictive modifiers and nonrestrictive appositives)	⟨Our guide, who wore a blue beret, was an experienced traveler.⟩ ⟨We visited Gettysburg, the site of a famous battle.⟩ ⟨The captain, John Jones, was an experienced mariner.⟩
6. introduces a direct quotation, terminates a direct quotation that is neither a question nor an exclamation, and encloses split quotations	⟨John said, "I am leaving."⟩ ⟨"I am leaving," John said.⟩ ⟨"I am leaving," John said with determination, "even if you want me to stay."⟩
7. sets off words in direct address, absolute phrases, and mild interjections	⟨You may go, Mary, if you wish.⟩ ⟨I fear the encounter, his temper being what it is.⟩ ⟨Ah, that's my idea of an excellent dinner.⟩
8. separates a tag question from the rest of the sentence	⟨It's a fine day, isn't it?⟩
9. indicates the omission of a word or words, and especially a word or words used earlier in the sentence	⟨Common stocks are preferred by some investors; bonds, by others.⟩
10. is used to avoid ambiguity and also to emphasize a particular phrase	⟨To Mary, Jane was someone special.⟩ ⟨The more embroidery on a dress, the higher the price.⟩
11. is used to group numbers into units of three in separating thousands, millions, etc.; however, it is generally not used in numbers of four figures, in pagination, in dates, or in street numbers	⟨Smithville, pop. 100,000⟩ *but* ⟨3600 rpm⟩ ⟨the year 1973⟩ ⟨page 1411⟩ ⟨4507 Smith Street⟩
12. punctuates an inverted name	⟨Smith, John W., Jr.⟩
13. separates a proper name from a following academic, honorary, governmental, or military title	⟨John Smith, M.D.⟩
14. sets off geographical names (as state or country from city), items in dates, and addresses from the rest of a text	⟨Shreveport, Louisiana, is the site of a large air base.⟩ ⟨On Sunday, June 23, 1940, he was wounded.⟩ ⟨Number 10 Downing Street, London, is a famous address.⟩
15. follows the salutation in informal correspondence and follows the complimentary close of a formal or informal letter	⟨Dear Mary,⟩ ⟨Affectionately,⟩ ⟨Very truly yours,⟩

Dash —

1. usually marks an abrupt change or break in the continuity of a sentence	⟨When in 1960 the stockpile was sold off—indeed, dumped as surplus—natural-rubber sales were hard hit.—Barry Commoner⟩
2. introduces a summary statement that follows a series of words or phrases	⟨Oil, steel, and wheat—these are the sinews of industrialization.⟩
3. often precedes the attribution of a quotation	⟨My foot is on my native heath . . . . —Sir Walter Scott⟩

Ellipsis ... .

1. indicates the omission of one or more words within a quoted passage ⟨The head is not more native to the heart . . . than is the throne of Denmark to thy father.—Shak.⟩

2. indicates halting speech or an unfinished sentence in dialogue ⟨"I'd like to . . . that is . . . if you don't mind . . . ." He faltered and then stopped speaking.⟩

3. indicates the omission of one or more sentences within a quoted passage or the omission of words at the end of a sentence by using four spaced dots the last of which represents the period ⟨That recovering the manuscripts would be worth almost any effort is without question . . . . The monetary value of a body of Shakespeare's manuscripts would be almost incalculable—Charlton Ogburn⟩ ⟨It will take scholars years to determine conclusively the origins, the history, and, most importantly, the significance of the finds . . . .—Robert Morse⟩

4. usually indicates omission of one or more lines of poetry when ellipsis is extended the length of the line

⟨ Thus driven
By the bright shadow of that lovely dream,
. . . .
He fled.
—P. B. Shelley⟩

Exclamation Point !

1. terminates an emphatic phrase or sentence ⟨Get out of here!⟩

2. terminates an emphatic interjection ⟨Encore!⟩

Hyphen -

1. marks separation or division at the end of a line terminating with a syllable of a word that is to be carried over to the next line ⟨mill-
stone⟩ ⟨pas-
sion⟩

2. is used between some prefix and root combinations, as
   prefix + proper name; ⟨pre-Renaissance⟩
   prefix ending with a vowel + root word beginning often with the same vowel; ⟨co-opted⟩ ⟨re-ink⟩
   stressed prefix + root word, especially when this combination is similar to a different word ⟨re-cover a sofa⟩ *but* ⟨recover from an illness⟩

3. is used in some compounds, especially those containing prepositions ⟨president-elect⟩ ⟨sister-in-law⟩ ⟨attorney-at-law⟩ ⟨good-for-nothing⟩

4. is often used between elements of a unit modifier in attributive position in order to avoid ambiguity ⟨He is a small-business man.⟩ ⟨She has gray-green eyes.⟩ ⟨He looked at her with a know-it-all expression.⟩

5. suspends the first part of a hyphened compound when used with another hyphened compound ⟨a six- or eight-cylinder engine⟩

6. is used in writing out compound numbers between 21 and 99 ⟨thirty-four⟩ ⟨one hundred twenty-eight⟩

7. is used between the numerator and the denominator in writing out fractions especially when they are used as modifiers; however, fractions used as nouns are usually styled as open compounds ⟨a two-thirds majority of the vote⟩ *but* ⟨ate two thirds of a box of candy⟩

8. serves as an arbitrary equivalent of the phrase "(up) to and including" when used between numbers and dates ⟨pages 40-98⟩ ⟨the decade 1960-69⟩

9. is used in the compounding of capitalized names ⟨the New York-Moscow flight⟩

Hyphen, Double ⸗

is used in the end-of-line division of a hyphened compound to indicate that the compound is hyphened and not closed

⟨self⸗[end of line]seeker⟩
but
⟨self-[end of line]same⟩

● The styling of compounds varies: they may be open, closed, or hyphened. When in doubt, one should consult the main vocabulary of this dictionary for the most commonly used styling.

Parentheses ( )

1. set off supplementary, parenthetic, or explanatory material when the interruption is more marked than that usually indicated by commas and when the inclusion of such material does not essentially alter the meaning of the sentence

   ⟨Three old destroyers (all now out of commission) will be scrapped.⟩
   ⟨He is hoping (as we all are) that this time he will succeed.⟩

2. enclose arabic numerals which confirm a written number in a text

   ⟨Delivery will be made in thirty (30) days.⟩

3. enclose numbers or letters in a series

   ⟨We must set forth (1) our long-term goals, (2) our immediate objectives, and (3) the means at our disposal.⟩

Period •

1. terminates sentences or sentence fragments that are neither interrogatory nor exclamatory

   ⟨Obey the law.⟩
   ⟨He obeyed the law.⟩
   ⟨He asked whether the law had been obeyed.⟩

2. follows some abbreviations and contractions

   ⟨Dr.⟩ ⟨A.D.⟩ ⟨Esq.⟩
   ⟨Jr.⟩ ⟨etc.⟩ ⟨cont.⟩

Question Mark ?

1. terminates a direct question

   ⟨Who threw the bomb?⟩
   ⟨"Who threw the bomb?" he asked.⟩
   ⟨To ask the question Who threw the bomb? is unnecessary.⟩

2. indicates the writer's ignorance or uncertainty

   ⟨Omar Khayyám, Persian poet (?–?1123)⟩

Quotation Marks, Double " "

1. enclose direct quotations in conventional usage

   ⟨He said, "I am leaving."⟩

2. enclose words or phrases borrowed from others, words used in a special way, and often slang when it is introduced into formal writing

   ⟨As the leader of a gang of "droogs," he is altogether frightening, as is this film.—Liz Smith⟩
   ⟨He called himself "emperor," but he was really just a dictator.⟩
   ⟨He was arrested for smuggling "smack."⟩

3. enclose titles of short poems, short stories, articles, lectures, chapters of books, songs, short musical compositions, and radio and TV programs
⟨Robert Frost's "Dust of Snow"⟩
⟨Pushkin's "Queen of Spades"⟩
⟨The third chapter of *Treasure Island* is entitled "The Black Spot."⟩
⟨"America the Beautiful"⟩
⟨Ravel's "Bolero"⟩
⟨NBC's "Today Show"⟩

4. are used with other punctuation marks in the following ways:

the period and the comma fall *within* the quotation marks
⟨"I am leaving," he said.⟩
⟨His camera was described as "waterproof," but "moisture-resistant" would have been a better description.⟩

the semicolon falls *outside* the quotation marks
⟨He spoke of his "little cottage in the country"; he might have called it a mansion.⟩

the dash, the question mark, and the exclamation point fall *within* the quotation marks when they refer to the quoted matter only; they fall *outside* when they refer to the whole sentence
⟨He asked, "When did you leave?"⟩
⟨What is the meaning of "the open door"?⟩
⟨The sergeant shouted, "Halt!"⟩
⟨Save us from his "mercy"!⟩

Quotation Marks, Single ‘ ’

1. enclose a quotation within a quotation in conventional usage
⟨The witness said, "I distinctly heard him say, 'Don't be late,' and then I heard the door close."⟩

2. are sometimes used in place of double quotation marks especially in British usage
⟨The witness said, 'I distinctly heard him say, "Don't be late," and then I heard the door close.'⟩

Semicolon ;

1. links main clauses not joined by coordinating conjunctions
⟨Some people have the ability to write well; others do not.⟩

2. links main clauses joined by conjunctive adverbs (as *consequently, furthermore, however*)
⟨Speeding is illegal; furthermore, it is very dangerous.⟩

3. links clauses which themselves contain commas even when such clauses are joined by coordinating conjunctions
⟨Thus our search was for people who could think in very fundamental ways, who could buttress their views with careful analysis; people who were able to hang in during deliberations with their own ideas, but who could also comfortably and effectively work within the confines of a small group.—Frank Newman⟩

Virgule /

1. separates alternatives
⟨. . . designs intended for high-heat and/or high-speed applications—F. S. Badger, Jr.⟩
⟨. . . sit hour after hour . . . and finally year after year in a catatonic/frenzied trance rewriting the Bible—William Saroyan⟩

2. separates successive divisions (as months or years) of an extended period of time
⟨the fiscal year 1972/73⟩

3. serves as a dividing line between run-in lines of poetry
⟨Say, sages, what's the charm on earth/Can turn death's dart aside?—Robert Burns⟩

4. often represents *per* in abbreviations
⟨9 ft/sec⟩ ⟨20 km/hr⟩

5. sets off phonemes and phonemic transcription
⟨/b/ as in *but*⟩

Italicization

The following are usually italicized in print and underlined in manuscript and typescript:

1. titles of books, magazines, newspapers, plays, movies, works of art, and music

   ⟨Eliot's *The Waste Land*⟩⟨*Saturday Review*⟩
   ⟨*Christian Science Monitor*⟩⟨Shakespeare's *Othello*⟩
   ⟨the movie *Gone With the Wind*⟩
   ⟨Gainsborough's *Blue Boy*⟩⟨Mozart's *Don Giovanni*⟩

2. names of ships and aircraft, and often spacecraft

   ⟨M.V. *West Star*⟩
   ⟨Lindbergh's *Spirit of St. Louis*⟩
   ⟨*Apollo 13*⟩

3. words, letters, and figures when referred to as words, letters, and figures

   ⟨The word *receive* is often misspelled.⟩
   ⟨The *g* in *align* is silent.⟩
   ⟨You should dot your *i*'s and cross your *t*'s.⟩
   ⟨The first *2* and the last *0* in the address are barely legible.⟩

4. foreign words and phrases that have not been naturalized in English

   ⟨*aere perennius*⟩
   ⟨*che sarà, sarà*⟩
   ⟨*sans peur et sans reproche*⟩
   ⟨*ich dien*⟩

5. New Latin scientific names of genera, species, subspecies, and varieties (but not groups of higher rank, as phyla, classes, or orders) in botanical and zoological names

   ⟨a thick-shelled American clam (*Mercenaria mercenaria*)⟩
   ⟨a cardinal (*Richmondena cardinalis*)⟩

6. legal citations, both in full and shortened form (''v'' for ''versus'' is set in Roman, though)

   ⟨*Jones* v. *Massachusetts*⟩
   ⟨the *Jones* case⟩⟨*Jones*⟩

Capitalization

Capitals are used for two broad purposes in English: they mark a beginning (as of a sentence) and they signal a proper noun or adjective. The following principles, each with bracketed examples, describe the most common uses of capital letters.

1. The first word of a sentence or sentence fragment is capitalized.

   ⟨The play lasted nearly three hours.⟩
   ⟨How are you feeling?⟩
   ⟨Bravo!⟩
   ⟨"Have you hand grenades?"
   "Plenty."
   "How many rounds per rifle?"
   "Plenty."
   "How many?"
   "One hundred fifty. More maybe."
   —Ernest Hemingway⟩

2. The first word of a direct quotation is capitalized.

   ⟨And God said, Let there be light.—Gen 1: 3 (AV)⟩
   ⟨He replied, "We can stay only a few minutes."⟩

3. The first word of a direct question within a sentence is capitalized.

   ⟨That question is this: Is man an ape or an angel?
   —Benjamin Disraeli⟩

4. The first word of a line of poetry is conventionally capitalized.

   ⟨The best lack all conviction, while the worst
   Are full of passionate intensity.—W. B. Yeats⟩

5. Words in titles are capitalized with the exception of internal conjunctions, prepositions, and articles.

   ⟨*The Way of the World*⟩
   ⟨*Of Mice and Men*⟩
   ⟨*Quo Vadis*⟩
   ⟨Deuteronomy⟩

6. The first word of the salutation of a letter and the first word of the complimentary close are capitalized.

   ⟨Dear Mary⟩
   ⟨My dear Mrs. Smith⟩
   ⟨Sincerely yours⟩ ⟨Yours sincerely⟩

7. The names of persons and places, of organizations and their members, of congresses and councils, and of historical periods and events are capitalized.

   ⟨Noah Webster⟩ ⟨Rome⟩ ⟨Texas⟩
   ⟨England⟩ ⟨Rotary International⟩
   ⟨Kiwanians⟩ ⟨Baptists⟩ ⟨the United Methodist Church⟩
   ⟨the Atomic Energy Commission⟩ ⟨the Yalta Conference⟩
   ⟨the Middle Ages⟩ ⟨World War II⟩

8. The names of ships, aircraft, and spacecraft are capitalized.

   ⟨M.V. *West Star*⟩
   ⟨Lindbergh's *Spirit of St. Louis*⟩
   ⟨*Apollo 13*⟩

9. Words designating peoples and languages are capitalized.

   ⟨Canadians⟩ ⟨Turks⟩
   ⟨Latin⟩ ⟨Swedish⟩
   ⟨Iroquois⟩ ⟨Ibo⟩

10. Derivatives of proper names are capitalized when used in their primary sense.

    ⟨Roman customs⟩
    ⟨Shakespearean comedies⟩
    ⟨the Edwardian era⟩
    but
    ⟨macadamize⟩
    ⟨bowdlerize⟩
    ⟨jeremiad⟩

11. Words of family relationship preceding the name of a person are capitalized.

    ⟨Uncle George⟩ ⟨Aunt Jane⟩
    ⟨Cousin Julia⟩
    ⟨Grandfather Jones⟩

12. Titles preceding the name of a person and epithets used instead of a name are capitalized.

    ⟨President Roosevelt⟩
    ⟨Professor Harris⟩
    ⟨Pope Paul⟩
    ⟨Queen Elizabeth⟩
    ⟨Old Hickory⟩ ⟨the Iron Chancellor⟩

13. The pronoun I is capitalized.

    ⟨I find ways to behave when an associate is attacked; it could be I next time.—R. T. Blackburn⟩ ⟨. . . no one but I myself had yet printed any of my work
    —Paul Bowles⟩

14. Words designating the Deity (and pronouns referring thereto) are often capitalized.

⟨The principal group that disagreed with them . . . did so only in an even greater faith—that when God chose to save the heathen He could do it by Himself.—Elmer Davis⟩
⟨Allah will not subject any believer to eternal punishment . . . because of His readiness to yield to the Prophet's intercession.—G. E. von Grunebaum⟩
⟨An anthropomorphic, vengeful Jehovah became a spiritual, benevolent Supreme Being.—A. R. Katz⟩

15. Personifications are capitalized.

⟨She dwells with Beauty—Beauty that must die;
And Joy, whose hand is ever at his lips
Bidding adieu. —John Keats⟩

16. The days of the week, the months of the year, and holidays and holy days are capitalized.

⟨Tuesday⟩ ⟨June⟩
⟨Thanksgiving⟩
⟨Independence Day⟩
⟨Easter⟩ ⟨Yom Kippur⟩

17. Names of specific courts of law are capitalized.

⟨the United States Court of Appeals for the Second Circuit⟩

18. Names of treaties are capitalized.

⟨Treaty of Versailles⟩
⟨Kellogg-Briand Pact⟩
⟨Peace of Westphalia⟩

19. Registered trademarks and service marks are capitalized.

⟨Dubonnet⟩ ⟨Orlon⟩
⟨Air Express⟩
⟨Laundromat⟩

20. Geological eras, periods, epochs, strata, and names of prehistoric divisions are capitalized.

⟨Silurian period⟩
⟨Pleistocene epoch⟩
⟨Age of Reptiles⟩
⟨Neolithic age⟩

21. Planets, constellations, asteroids, stars, and groups of stars are capitalized; however, sun, earth, and moon are not capitalized unless they are listed with other capitalized astronomical names.

⟨Venus⟩
⟨Big Dipper⟩
⟨Sirius⟩
⟨Pleiades⟩

22. Genera in binomial scientific names in zoology and botany are capitalized; names of species are not.

⟨a cabbage butterfly (*Pieris rapae*)⟩
⟨a common buttercup (*Ranunculus acris*)⟩
⟨the robin (*Turdus migratorius*)⟩
⟨the haddock (*Melanogrammus aeglefinus*)⟩

23. New Latin names of classes, families, and all groups above genera in zoology and botany are capitalized; however, their derivative adjectives and nouns are not.

⟨Gastropoda⟩ *but* ⟨gastropod⟩
⟨Thallophyta⟩ *but* ⟨thallophyte⟩

Plurals

The plurals of English words are regularly formed by the addition of the suffix *-s* or *-es* to the singular, as

⟨dog → dogs⟩
⟨race → races⟩
⟨guy → guys⟩
⟨monarch → monarchs⟩

⟨grass → grasses⟩
⟨dish → dishes⟩
⟨buzz → buzzes⟩
⟨branch → branches⟩

The plurals of words that follow other patterns, as

⟨army → armies⟩
⟨duo → duos⟩
⟨ox → oxen⟩
⟨foot → feet⟩
⟨p. → pp.⟩
⟨sheep → sheep⟩

⟨phenomenon → phenomena⟩
⟨libretto → librettos *or* libretti⟩
⟨curriculum → curricula *also* curriculums⟩
⟨alga → algae⟩
⟨corpus delicti → corpora delicti⟩
⟨sergeant major → sergeants major *or* sergeant majors⟩

are given at the appropriate vocabulary entries in the main body of the dictionary.